CHILTON'S

AIR CONDITIONING AND HEATING MANUAL

IMPORT CARS AND TRUCKS

Publisher and Editor-in-Chief Kerry A. Freeman, S.A.E

Executive Editors Dean Morgantini □ W. Calvin Settle, Jr., S.A.E

Managing Editor Nicholas L. D'Andrea

Senior Editors Eric O. Cole □ Debra Gaffney □ Jacque Gordon
Ken Grabowski, A.S.E., S.A.E. □ Mike Grady □ Kevin Maher □ Rich Rivele
Richard T. Smith □ Jim Taylor □ Ronald T. Webb

Project Managers Lawrence C. Braun, S.A.E. □ Thomas P. Browne III
Robert E. Doughten □ Joseph DeFranceso, A.S.E. □ Ben Greisler, S.A.E.
Martin J. Gunther □ Craig Nagle □ Richard Schwartz

Service Editors Jaffer A. Ahmad □ Chris Armenti □ Bradley Bower □ Robert Chabot
William C. Cottman, A.S.E. □ Leonard Davis, A.S.E. □ Michael DiFurio Jr., S.A.E. □ Robert F. Dougherty, Jr.
John J. Ferraro, A.S.E., S.A.E. □ Sam Fiorani □ Matthew E. Fredrick □ William C. Friedauer
Edward J. Giacomucci, A.S.E., S.A.E. □ Al Gibbs □ Herbert Guie □ Dawn M. Hoch □ David E. Jester
Lori Johnson □ William Kessler □ Kenneth F. Konzelman □ Neil Leonard, A.S.E. □ Robert McAnally
Raymond K. Moore □ Norman Norville □ Christine L. Nuckowski □ Eric S. Peterson, A.S.E.
Ernest H. Ralph □ Charles T. Ramsey, A.S.E. □ Roy Ripple, A.S.E. □ Don Schnell, A.S.E., S.A.E. □ Paul Shanahan
Larry E. Stiles □ Gordon L. Tobias □ Anthony Tortorici, A.S.E., S.A.E. □ Albert A. Wood, A.S.E.

Director of Manufacturing Mike D'Imperio
Assistant Manager of Manufacturing Robin S. Norman
Production Manager Andrea Steiger
Assistant Production Manager Marsha Park Herman
Production Specialists Christine Davis □ Kimberly T. Hayes □ Joseph C. McGinty □ Elizabeth E. Thompson

National Sales Manager Lawrence R. Rufo
National Administrator, Sales Mark Amentt
Eastern Regional Manager Howie Freeman
Western Regional Manager Larry W. Marshall
Mid West Regional Manager Bruce McCorkle
National Accounts Manager Kevin Mullen

OFFICERS
President, Chilton Enterprises David S. Loewith
Senior Vice President Ronald A. Hoxter

CHILTON PROFESSIONAL AUTOMOTIVE

*ONE OF THE **DIVERSIFIED PUBLISHING COMPANIES**,
A PART OF **CAPITAL CITIES/ABC, INC.***

Manufactured in USA   ©1995 Chilton Book Company • Chilton Way, Radnor, Pa. 19089
ISBN 0-8019-8694-x   1234567890 4321098765   ISSN 1082-3042

SAFETY NOTICE

Proper service and repair procedures are vital to the safe, reliable operation of all motor vehicles as well as the personal safety of those performing repairs. This manual outlines procedures for servicing and repairing vehicles using safe, effective methods. The procedures contain many NOTES, CAUTIONS and WARNINGS which should be followed along with standard safety procedures to eliminate the possibility of personal injury or improper service which could damage the vehicle or compromise its safety.

It is important to note that the repair procedures and techniques, tools and parts for servicing motor vehicles, as well as the skill and experience of the individual performing the work vary widely. It is not possible to anticipate all of the conceivable ways or conditions under which vehicles may be serviced, or to provide cautions as to all of the possible hazards that may result. Standard and accepted safety precautions and equipment should be used when handling toxic or flammable fluids, and safety glasses or other protection should be used during cutting, grinding, chiseling, or any other process that can cause material removal or projectiles.

Some procedures require the use of tools specially designed for a specific purpose. Before substituting another tool or procedure, you must be completely satisfied that neither your personal safety, nor the performance of the vehicle will be endangered.

PART NUMBERS

Part numbers listed in this reference are not recommendations by Chilton for any product by brand name. They are references that can be used with interchange manuals and aftermarket supplier catalogs to locate each brand supplier's discrete part number.

SPECIFICATIONS

ENGINE IDENTIFICATION

Year	Model	Engine Displacement Liters (cc)	Engine Series	Fuel System	No. of Cylinders	Engine Type
1993	Integra	1.7 (1678)	B17A1	PGM-FI	4	DOHC
	Integra	1.8 (1834)	B18A1	PGM-FI	4	DOHC
	Legend	3.2 (3206)	C32A1	PGM-FI	6	SOHC
	Legend Coupe	3.2 (3206)	C32A1	PGM-FI	6	SOHC
	NSX	3.0 (2977)	C30A1	PGM-FI	6	DOHC
	Vigor	2.5 (2451)	G25A1	PGM-FI	5	SOHC
1994	Integra	1.8 (1834)	B18B1	PGM-FI	4	DOHC
	Integra	1.8 (1834)	B18C1	PGM-FI	4	DOHC
	Legend	3.2 (3206)	C32A1	PGM-FI	6	SOHC
	Legend Coupe	3.2 (3206)	C32A1	PGM-FI	6	SOHC
	NSX	3.0 (2997)	C30A1	PGM-FI	6	DOHC
	Vigor	2.5 (2451)	G25A1	PGM-FI	5	SOHC
1995	Integra	1.8 (1834)	B18B1	PGM-FI	4	DOHC
	Integra	1.8 (1834)	B18C1	PGM-FI	4	DOHC
	Legend	3.2 (3206)	C32A1	PGM-FI	6	SOHC
	Legend Coupe	3.2 (3206)	C32A1	PGM-FI	6	SOHC
	NSX	3.0 (2997)	C30A1	PGM-FI	6	DOHC
	Vigor	2.5 (2451)	G25A1	PGM-FI	5	SOHC

SOHC – Single Overhead Cam
DOHC – Dual Overhead Cam
PGM-FI – Programmed Fuel Injection

REFRIGERANT CAPACITIES

Year	Model	Refrigerant (oz.)	Oil (fl. oz.)	Compressor Type
1993	Integra	32.0–34.0	2.0–3.3	Nippondenso
	Legend	32.0–34.0	3.7–4.7	Nippondenso
	Legend Coupe	32.0–34.0	3.7–4.7	Nippondenso
	NSX	32.0–34.0	2.0–3.3	Nippondenso
	Vigor	26.5–28.0	4.4–5.4	Nippondenso
1994	Integra	22.9–24.7	4.66	Nippondenso
	Legend	24.7–26.5	6.0	Nippondenso
	Legend Coupe	24.7–26.5	6.0	Nippondenso
	NSX	28.2–30.0	4.4–5.4	Nippondenso
	Vigor	26.5–28.3	4.66	Nippondenso
1995	Integra	22.9–24.7	4.66	Nippondenso
	Legend	24.7–26.5	6.0	Nippondenso
	Legend Coupe	24.7–26.5	6.0	Nippondenso
	NSX	28.2–30.0	4.4–5.4	Nippondenso
	Vigor	26.5–28.3	4.66	Nippondenso

AIR CONDITIONING BELT TENSION

Year	Model	Engine Liters	Belt Type	Specifications	
				New	Used
1993	Integra	1.8	Poly-V	0.18–0.26	0.28–0.35
	Legend	3.2	Poly-V	0.20–0.26	0.31–0.39
	Legend Coupe	3.2	Poly-V	0.20–0.26	0.31–0.39
	NSX	3.0	Poly-V	0.22–0.30	0.39–0.47
	Vigor	2.5	Poly-V	0.14–0.22	0.24–0.35
1994	Integra	1.8	Poly-V	0.20–0.26	0.30–0.37
	Legend	3.2	Poly-V	0.20–0.26	0.31–0.39
	Legend Coupe	3.2	Poly-V	0.20–0.26	0.31–0.39
	NSX	3.0	Poly-V	0.22–0.30	0.39–0.47
	Vigor	2.5	Poly-V	0.14–0.22	0.24–0.35
1995	Integra	1.8	Poly-V	0.20–0.26	0.30–0.37
	Legend	3.2	Poly-V	0.20–0.26	0.31–0.39
	Legend Coupe	3.2	Poly-V	0.20–0.26	0.31–0.39
	NSX	3.0	Poly-V	0.22–0.30	0.39–0.47
	Vigor	2.5	Poly-V	0.14–0.22	0.24–0.35

SYSTEM DESCRIPTION

General Information

Integra

Integra is equipped with either a heater only system or a manual air conditioning system. The control panel is a combination of push buttons for mode control, lever for heater/temperature control and a knob for air speed (fan) control. The air conditioning system is protected by a thermostat on the evaporator to sense temperatures and prevent freezing, a series of relays for energizing the compressor clutch, condenser cooling fan and radiator cooling fan.

Legend and Legend Coupe

These models are equipped with either a manual air conditioning system or an automatic climate control system. The manual air conditioning system is controlled and protected by a triple pressure switch, cooling fan control unit, A/C control unit and a temperature control unit. In addition, relays are used to energize the radiator and condenser fans and the blower motor. An evaporator temperature sensor cycles the compressor to prevent freezing. The manual system uses elec-trically operated air door controlled by push–button selection. The automatic climate control system uses the same controls and protection devices, plus, it uses sunlight, in–car temperature, and ambient temperature sensors to monitor and feed inputs to climate control unit to direct system operation.

NSX

NSX is equipped with an automatic climate control air conditioning system. The basic system is controlled by a triple pressure switch, cooling fan control unit, a power transistor, evaporator temperature sensor and a coolant temperature sensor. To monitor and control the automatic functions, an in–car temperature sensor, ambient temperature sensor and sunlight sensor provide input signals to the climate control unit to direct system operations.

Vigor

This model, introduced in 1992, uses a manually control air conditioning system. The manual control panel operates electrical actuators on the various air doors to provide functional operation. Relays energize the compressor clutch, blower motor, radiator fan and condenser fan circuits.

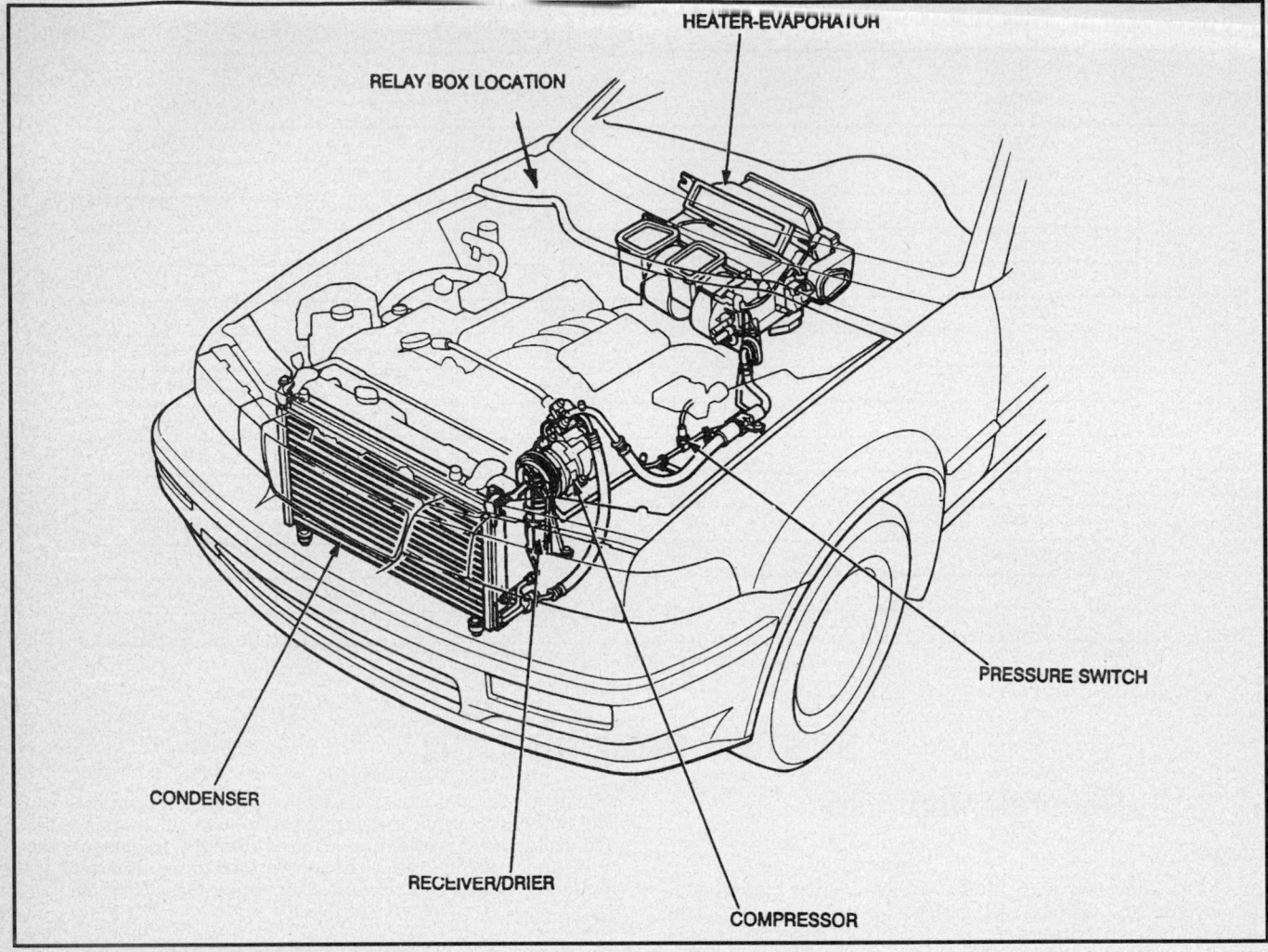

RELAY BOX LOCATION

HEATER-EVAPORATOR

PRESSURE SWITCH

CONDENSER

RECEIVER/DRIER

COMPRESSOR

Air conditioning system component layout—Vigor shown—others similar

Supplement Restraint System (SRS)

OPERATION

Before starting service procedures on components, especially under the instrument panel and near the steering column, the air bag (SRS) system must be disabled. In addition, the vehicle may be equipped with a radio anti–theft code (5 digits). Get this code from the customer before disconnecting the battery.

1. Disconnect the negative battery cable, then disconnect the positive battery cable.

2. Remove the access panel beneath the air bag on the underside of the steering wheel center housing.

3. Disconnect the connector between the air bag and the cable reel and install the short connector (red) that is provided. Install this connector on the air bag side of the connector.

4. The system is now disabled. When repairs are complete, unplug the red short connector, reconnect the air bag and cable reel connector and replace the access panel.

5. Reconnect the battery. When the word "CODE" appears, re–enter the 5–digit code in the radio, if so equipped.

6. When the ignition is turned to the II position, the SRS light on the instrument cluster should come on for about 6 seconds, then go out. If so, the system is okay.

NOTE: Do not use electrically powered test equipment on this system or related circuits. All SRS wiring is covered with a special yellow cable housing for identification.

Service Valve Locations

On Legend and Legend Coupe, the high side service valve is on the discharge line in front of the condenser and the low side valve is on the low side refrigerant line to the right of the condenser.

On NSX, the services valves are on the respective refrigerant lines near the firewall.

On Vigor, the high side service valve is on the receiver/drier and the low side service valve is on the outlet low side refrigerant line near the condenser.

System Discharging

Connect an approved refrigerant recovery/recycle system to the vehicle's air conditioning system and operate as instructed by the refrigerant recovery/recycle system manufacturer. Never vent R–12 directly to the atmosphere.

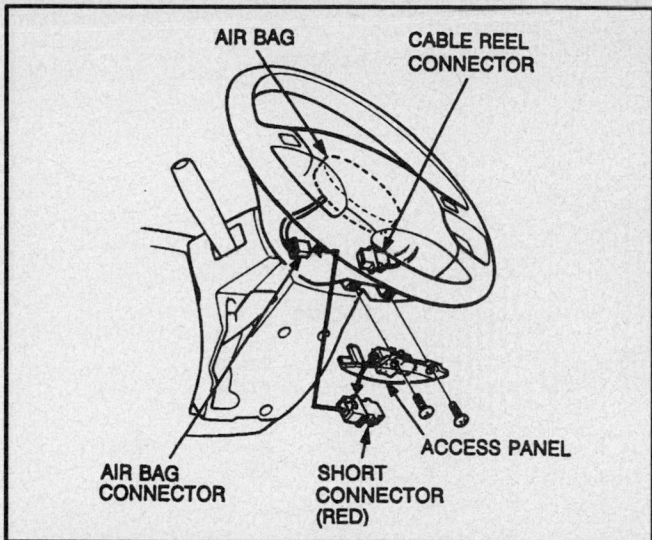

Installing short connector to disable the driver's side air bag

System Evacuating

Any time the air conditioning system has been exposed to the atmosphere, such as during a repair or installation. The system must be evacuated using a vacuum pump. If the system has been opened for several days, the receiver/drier should be replaced.

1. Connect the gauge set to the appropriate high and low side fittings and connect the center hose to the vacuum pump inlet.
2. Start the pump and open both gauge valves. Run the pump for 15 minutes. Close the valves and stop the pump. The low pressure gauge should read about 27–30 in. Hg vacuum and remain steady with the valve closed.

NOTE: If the low pressure gauge does not reach more than 27–30 in. Hg vacuum in 15 minutes, there is probably a leak in the air conditioning system. Check and repair as necessary.

3. If there are no leaks, open the valve and continue to pump for at least another 15 minutes, then close the valves, stop the pump and disconnect the center charging hose.

System Charging

Always wear eye protection and gloves while charging the air conditioning system. The air conditioning system may be charged with refrigerant by either vapor or liquid methods. If the system is overcharged, the compressor will be damaged.

1. Connect an approved charging station, recovery/recycling machine or manifold gauge set to the service valves. The red hose is normally connected to the discharge (high pressure) line, and the blue hose is connected to the suction (low pressure) line.
2. Follow the equipment manufacturer's instructions provided with the equipment and charge the system to the specified amount of refrigerant.
3. Perform a leak test.

SYSTEM COMPONENTS

Radiator

REMOVAL AND INSTALLATION

Integra

1. Air conditioning system component layout—Vigor shown; others similar.
2. Installing short connector to disable the driver's side air bag system.
3. Radiator and related components—Integra .
4. Disconnect the negative battery cable and drain the coolant from the radiator by using the drain plug located at the bottom of the radiator.
5. Remove the top and bottom radiator hoses. Remove the coolant reserve tank.
6. Disconnect the fan motor wire connection and remove the fan motor shroud retaining bolts. Remove the fan motor shroud along with the fan motor assembly.
7. If equipped, remove the automatic transaxle cooler hoses from the radiator. Plug the openings to prevent leakage.
8. Remove the radiator support bolts and bushings from the top sides of the radiator and slowly lift the radiator out of the vehicle.
9. Installation is the reverse order of the removal procedure. Refill and bleed the cooling system.

Legend, Legend Coupe, and Vigor

1. Disconnect the negative battery cable and drain the coolant from the radiator by using the drain plug located at the bottom of the radiator.
2. Remove the upper and lower radiator hoses.
3. Disconnect and plug the automatic transaxle hoses from the radiator.
4. Remove electrical connection from the thermo–sensor located in the bottom of the radiator.
5. Detach the electrical connections from the fan motor connectors.
6. Remove the radiator support bolts and bushings from the top sides of the radiator.
7. Slowly lift the radiator and fan assemblies out of the vehicle.
8. Installation is the reverse order of the removal procedure. Be sure to check the cooling system hoses for damage, leaks or deterioration and replace, if necessary. Use new a O–ring on the thermo sensor if removed. Refill and bleed the system.

NSX

1. Remove the spare tire. Properly drain the cooling system.
2. Disconnect the fan motor connector and the resistor connector.

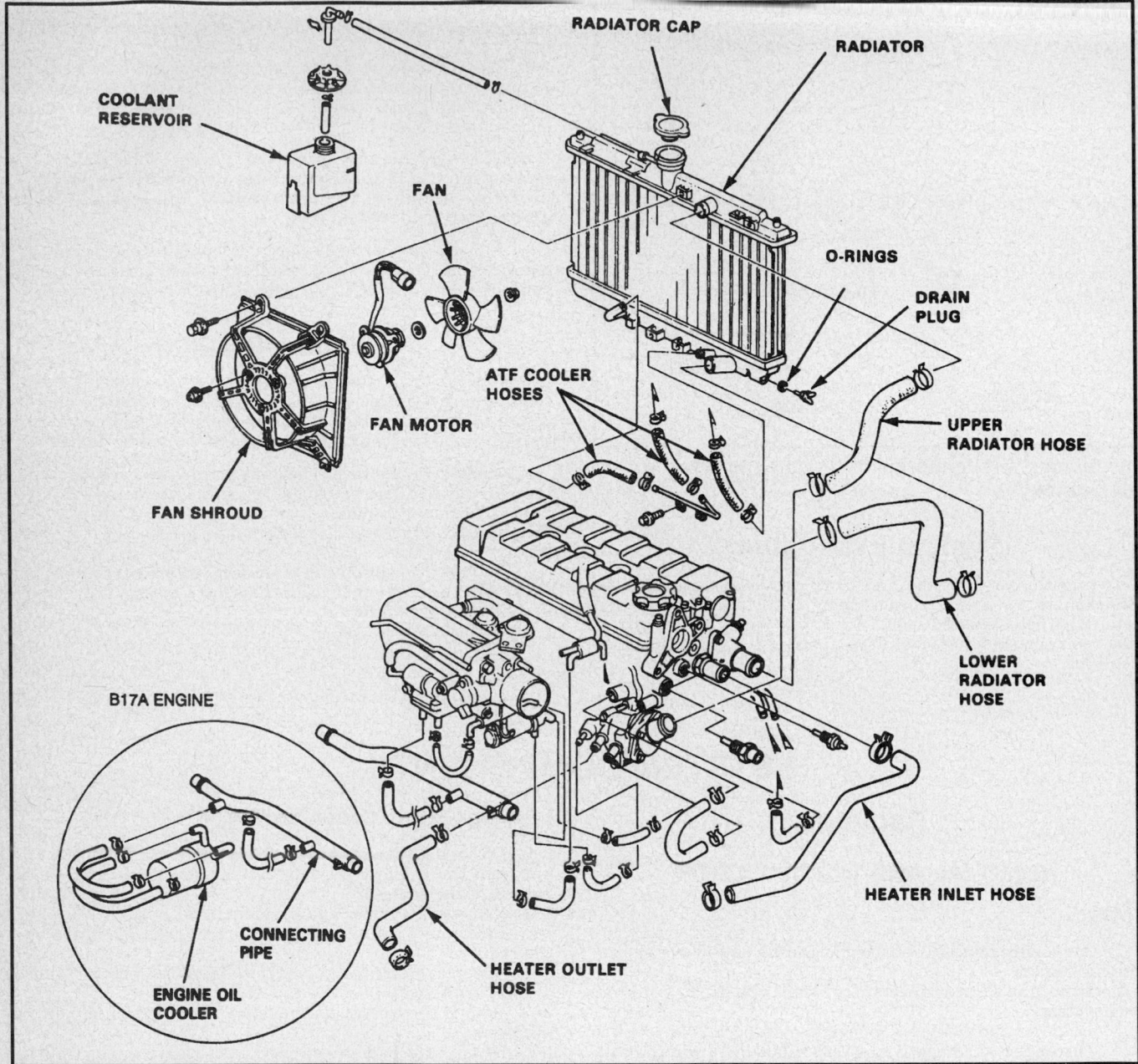

COOLANT RESERVOIR

RADIATOR CAP

RADIATOR

FAN

O-RINGS

DRAIN PLUG

FAN MOTOR

ATF COOLER HOSES

UPPER RADIATOR HOSE

FAN SHROUD

LOWER RADIATOR HOSE

B17A ENGINE

HEATER INLET HOSE

CONNECTING PIPE

ENGINE OIL COOLER

HEATER OUTLET HOSE

Radiator and related components—Integra

3. Detach the upper and lower radiator hoses from the radiator.

4. Remove the upper mounting brackets and carefully lift out the radiator with the fan motor assembly. Note position of lower mounting cushions for reinstallation.

5. Installation is the reverse of the removal procedure. Refill and bleed the system.

Electric Cooling Fan

REMOVAL AND INSTALLATION

1. Disconnect the negative battery cable.
2. Detach the electrical connectors from the fan assemblies.

3. Remove any additional components which may interfere with the fan removal.

4. Remove the fan shroud mounting bolts and carefully lift the fan assembly out of the vehicle.

5. Installation is the reverse of removal.

COOLING SYSTEM REFILLING AND BLEEDING

Except NSX

1. Start the engine for a brief period and set the heater temperature lever to obtain maximum coolant flow out of the heater core. Shut OFF the engine.

2. When the radiator is cool, remove the radiator cap and drain plug on the radiator and the drain bolt on the front of the engine block to drain the radiator.

3. Reinstall the radiator drain plug and the engine drain bolt (apply liquid gasket to the drain bolt threads) and tighten them securely.

4. Remove, drain, and reinstall the coolant reservoir. Fill the tank halfway to the MAX mark with water; then up to the MAX mark with coolant.

5. Mix the recommended anti–freeze with an equal amount of water, in a clean container.

NOTE: Use only approved anti–freeze coolant. For best corrosion protection, the coolant concentration must be maintained year–round at 50 percent minimum. Coolant concentrations less than 50 percent may not provide sufficient protection against corrosion or freezing. Coolant concentrations greater than 60 percent will impair cooling efficiency and are not recommended. Do not mix different brand anti–freeze/coolants. Do not use additional rust inhibitors or anti–rust products, they may not be compatible with the recommended coolant.

6. Loosen the air bleed bolt located in the coolant outlet. Fill the radiator to the bottom of the fill neck with the proper anti–freeze mixture. Tighten the bleed bolt as soon as the coolant flows in a steady stream without any bubbles.

7. With the radiator cap off, start the engine and run it until it reaches normal operating temperature, the coolant fan will come on twice. Then, if necessary, add more coolant to the radiator to bring the level back up to the bottom of the radiator fill neck.

8. Put the radiator cap on and run the engine. Check for leaks and repair, as necessary.

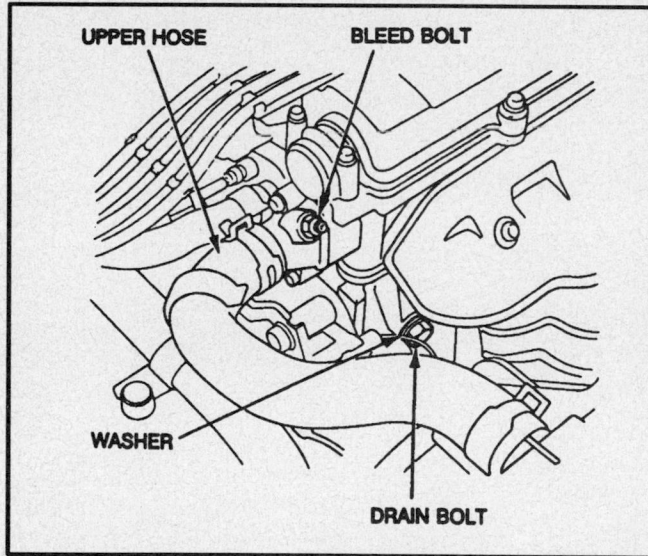

Coolant air bleed bolt—Integra

NSX

1. Turn the ignition to **ON** and slowly set the climate control temperature knob to **90**. This will allow the coolant in the heater to drain out with the rest of the system.

2. Open the hood, rear hatch and the engine cover.

3. Remove the cover protecting the water pipes and shift cables on the underside of the car.

4. Carefully loosen the coolant reserve tank cap. Loosen the drain plug at the bottom of the radiator. Remove 2 drain bolts from the water pipes. Install rubber hoses to the drain bolts at the front and rear of the engine under the cylinder bank, and loosen the drain bolts to drain the coolant.

5. Coolant will drain more quickly if all the air bleed bolts, plug and cap are opened. Be sure the coolant reserve tank has drained completely before opening the air bleed bolts.

6. Using new washers on the water pipe drain bolts, install the drain bolts and radiator drain plug.

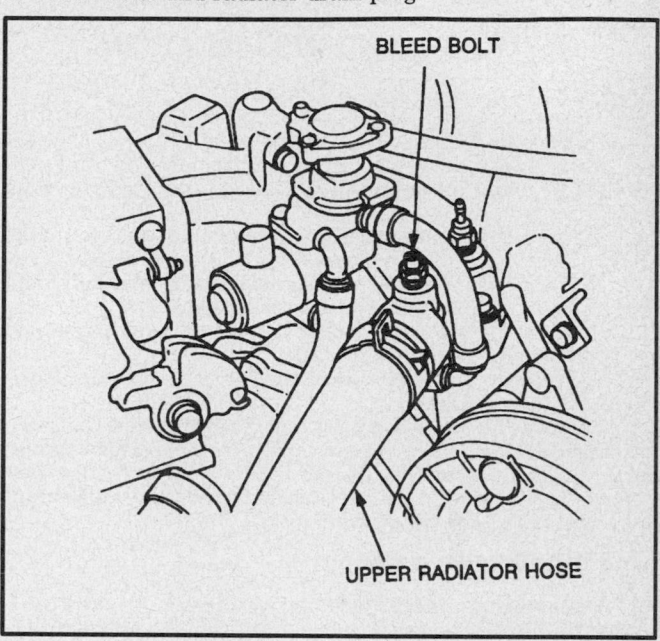

Coolant air bleed bolt—Legend and Legend Coupe

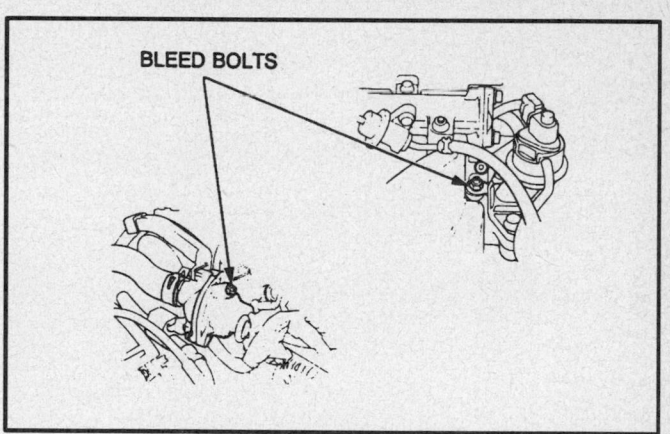

Coolant air bleed bolts—Vigor

7. Open all 4 air bleeder bolts (radiator, heater pipe, water pipe and engine thermostat cover).

8. Using approved coolant in a 50/50 mixture, fill the coolant reserve tank. Tighten the bleeders in sequence: thermostat cover bleed bolt, radiator bleed plug, heater pipe bleed cap, and water pipe bleed bolt as coolant runs out in a steady stream with no bubbles.

9. After tightening all the bleed bolts, fill the coolant tank to the MAX line. Loosen the thermostat bleed bolt to remove any remaining air.

10. When bleeding is complete, tighten the thermostat bolt and fill the coolant reserve tank to the MAX line again. Install the tank cap to the first detent.

11. Start the engine and run it to normal operating temperature (thermostat opens and radiator cooling fan runs).

12. Turn OFF the engine, check and adjust coolant to the MAX line if needed.

13. Install the coolant tank cap securely and install the car's under cover.

Condenser

REMOVAL AND INSTALLATION

Integra

1. Disconnect the negative battery cable.
2. Properly discharge the refrigerant from the air conditioning system using an approved refrigerant recovery/recycling unit.
3. Remove the radiator reservoir tank and the air intake tube.
4. Remove the radiator upper mounting brackets and remove the bolt from the suction hose bracket.
5. Remove the air conditioning hoses retaining clamp and the radiator upper mounting bracket.
6. Disconnect and cap the condenser pipe and discharge pipe from the condenser.
7. Remove the mounting bolts and remove the condenser.
8. Installation is the reverse order of the removal procedure. Evacuate and charge the system. Always use new O-rings lightly coated with refrigerant oil on any refrigerant line connection that were taken apart.

Legend and Legend Coupe

1. Disconnect the negative battery cable.
2. Properly discharge the refrigerant from the air conditioning system.
3. Remove the battery and battery tray. Remove the air intake duct.

4. Remove the throttle cable cover. Loosen the lockouts and remove the throttle cables from the holder. Disconnect the cables from the throttle drum.

NOTE: As refrigerant lines are disconnected immediately cap the openings to minimize contamination to the system.

5. Remove the bolt from the suction hose-to-pipe fitting below the battery tray location, and remove the bolt from the suction line connection near the right side of the condenser, if required.
6. Remove the receiver/drier nuts and the line attachment bolt at the front lower left of the condenser.
7. Remove the discharge line fitting bolt and the clamp bolt from the line at the lower right front of the condenser.
8. Remove the underhood relay box from the top of the fan shroud along with the top fan shroud mounting bolts.
9. Disconnect the condenser fan connector, then remove the lower mounting bolts and take out the condenser fan.
10. Remove the upper radiator mounting brackets.
11. Remove the top condenser mounting bolts and brackets, remove the nuts from the front of the upper radiator crossmember and remove the condenser.

To install:

12. Position the condenser, install the crossmember nuts, upper mounting bolts and brackets.
13. Install the condenser fan and connector. Replace the relay box.
14. Reattach the condenser lines, fittings and brackets as removed. Always use new O-rings.
15. Install the throttle cables, cover, air intake duct and the battery and tray.
16. If the condenser was replaced, add 1.0 oz. of new refrigerant oil. Evacuate, recharge and leak test the system.

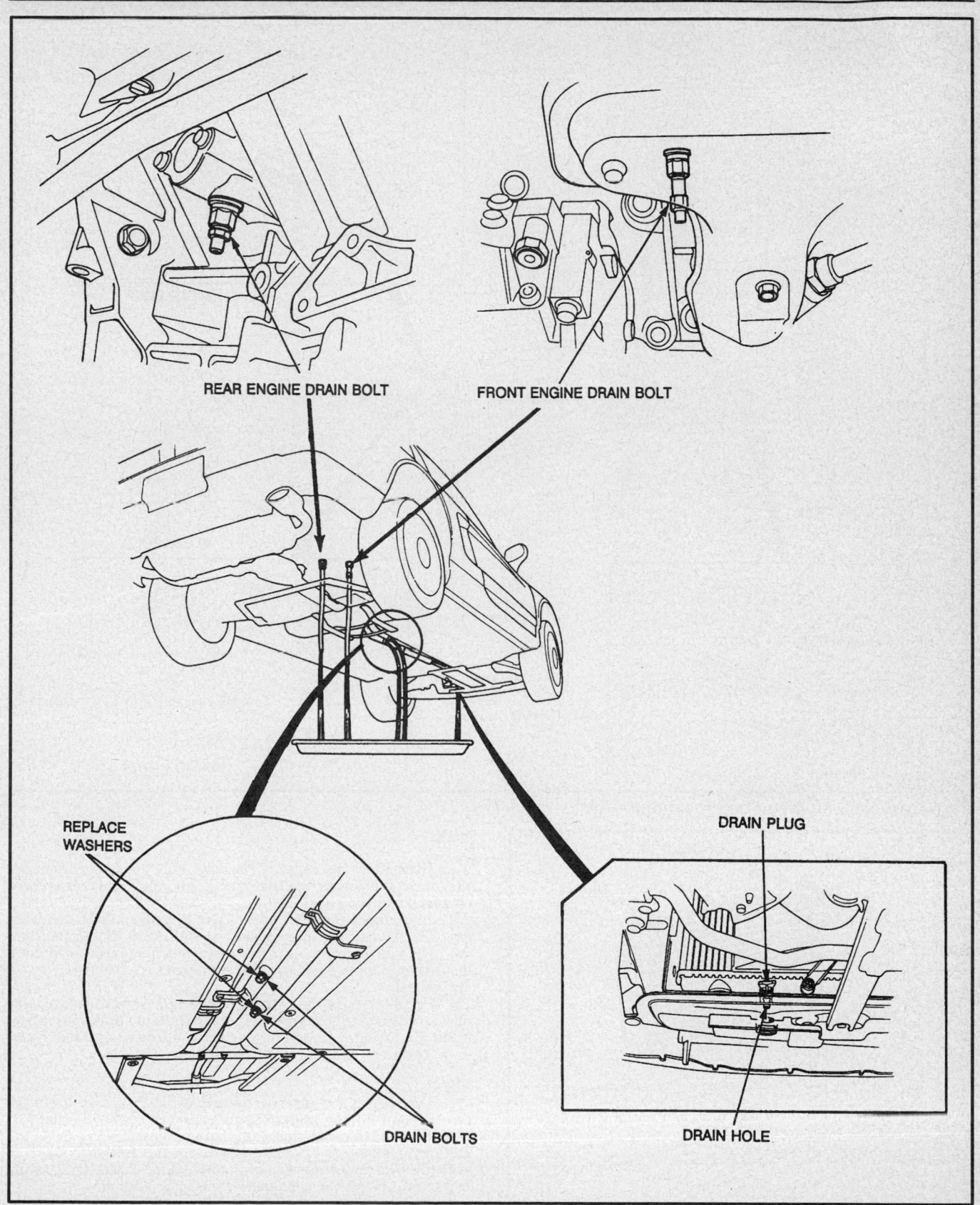

REAR ENGINE DRAIN BOLT

FRONT ENGINE DRAIN BOLT

REPLACE WASHERS

DRAIN PLUG

DRAIN BOLTS

DRAIN HOLE

Cooling system drain bolt locations—NSX

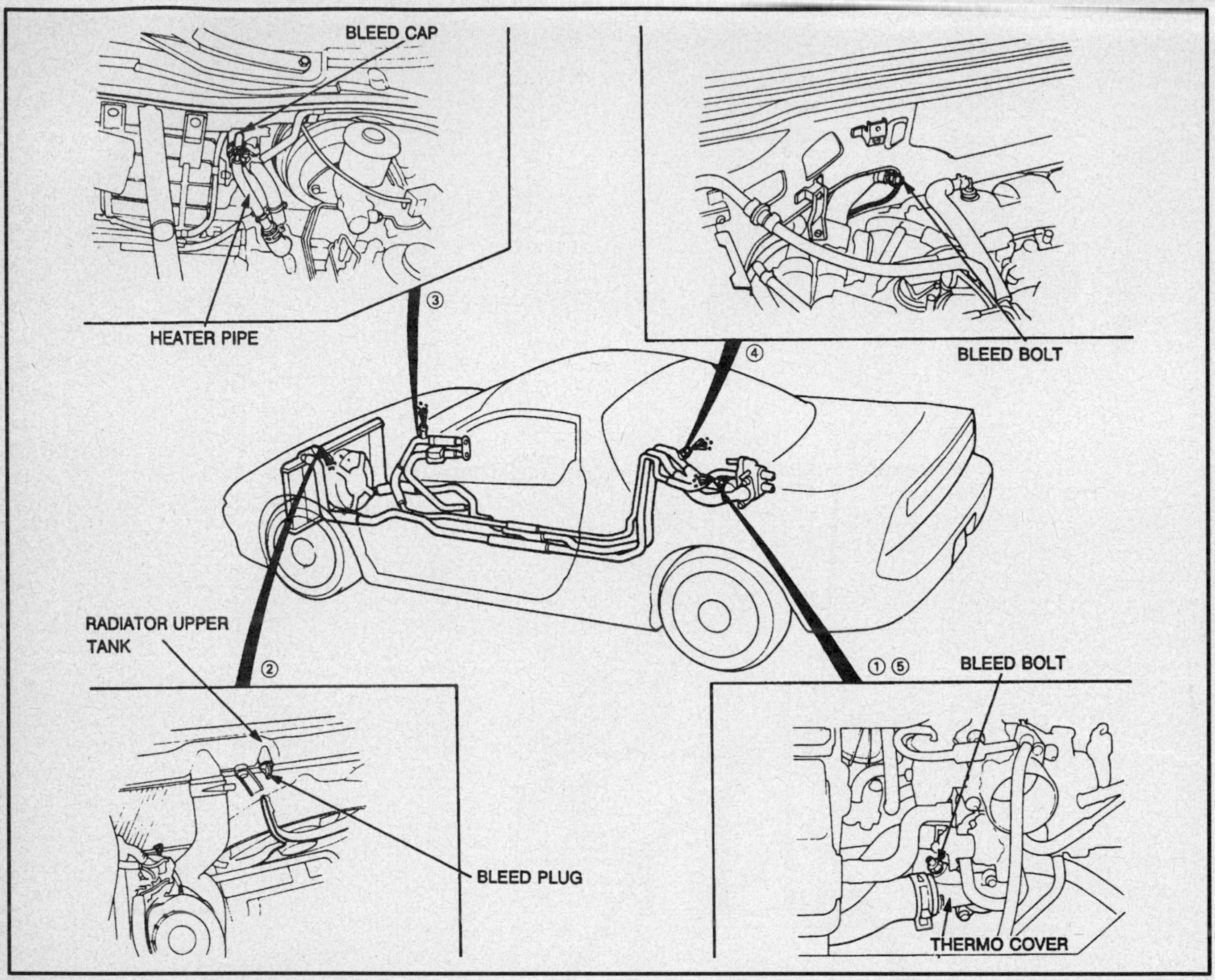

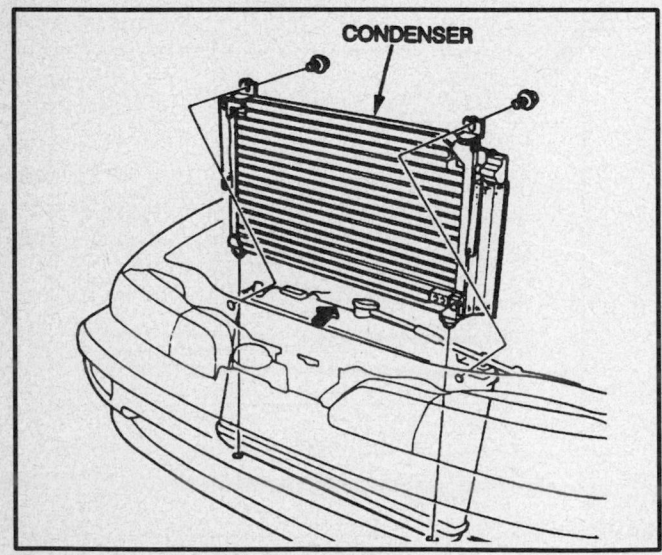

Cooling system air bleed bolt locations—NSX

Labels in diagram: BLEED CAP, HEATER PIPE, RADIATOR UPPER TANK, BLEED PLUG, BLEED BOLT, BLEED BOLT, THERMO COVER

Condenser installation—Integra

Labels in diagram: CONDENSER

NSX

1. Disconnect the negative battery cable. Properly discharge the air conditioning system using an approved refrigerant recovery/recycling system.

2. Disconnect the inlet and outlet lines from both condensers. Cap the fittings immediately to minimize contamination.

3. Detach the condenser fan motor connector, remove the 2 mounting bolts and remove the condenser.

To install:

4. Installation is the reverse of the removal procedure. Use new O–rings at all connections. Add 0.3 oz. of additional refrigerant oil during recharge for each condenser if replaced. Evacuate, recharge and leak test the system.

Vigor

1. Disconnect the negative battery cable. Properly discharge the air conditioning system using recovery type equipment.

2. Detach the radiator fan motor connector, remove the mounting bolts and lift out the radiator fan and shroud.

3. Detach the condenser connector, remove the 4 mounting bolts and lift out the condenser fan motor and shroud.

4. Remove the upper radiator bolts and brackets.

5. Disconnect the receiver/drier line and plug the openings immediately to minimize contamination. Remove the mounting bolts and take out the receiver/drier.

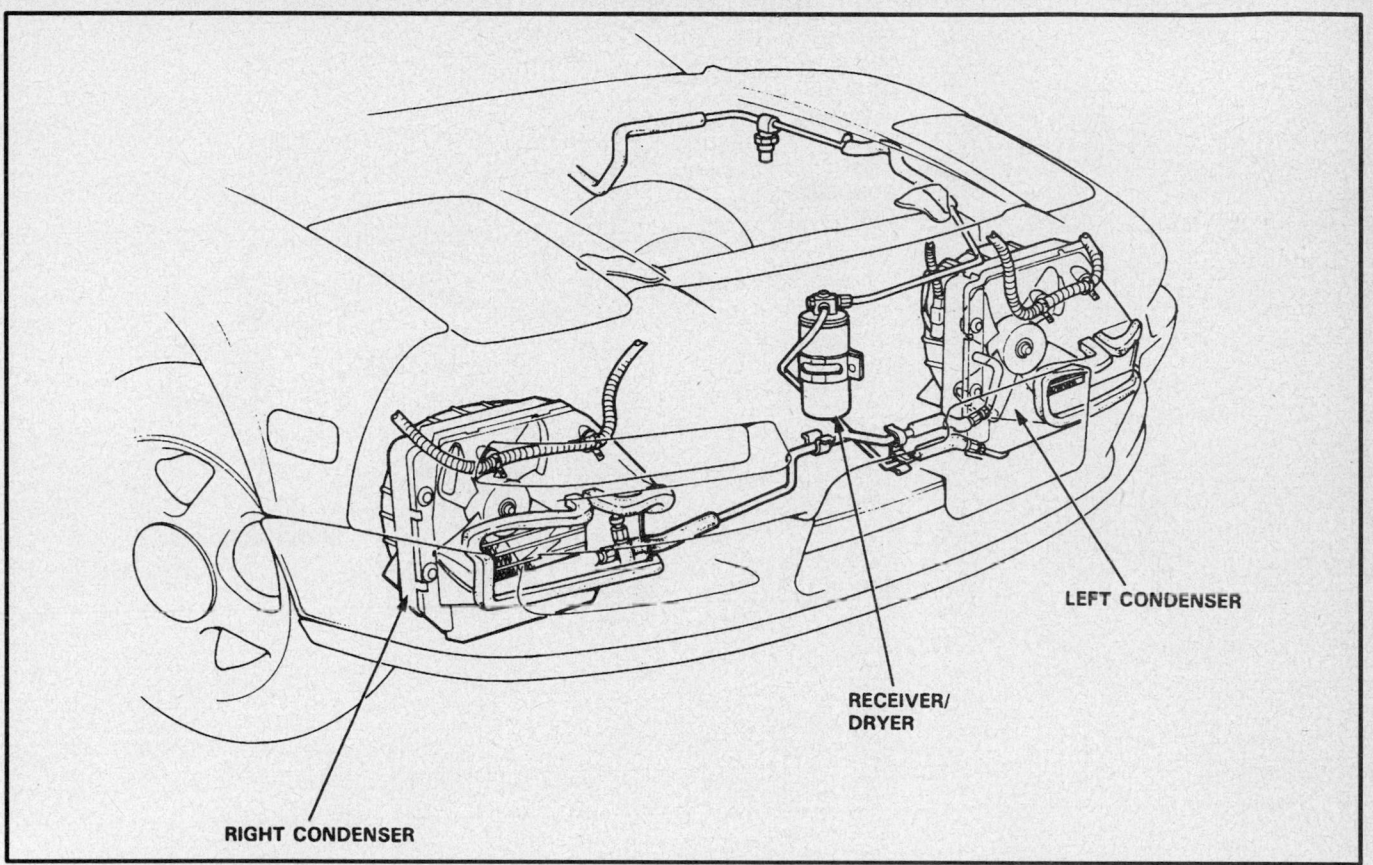

Dual condenser installation—NSX

6. Disconnect the remaining refrigerant lines from the condenser. Remove the 2 mounting bolts and lift out the condenser (avoid hitting the fins of the condenser or the radiator during removal or installation).

7. Installation is the reverse of the removal procedure. Add 0.5 oz. of refrigerant oil if condenser was replaced. Evacuate, recharge and leak test the system.

Compressor

REMOVAL AND INSTALLATION

Integra

1. If the compressor still works (even marginally), run the engine at idle speed and turn the air conditioning ON for a few minutes.

2. Properly discharge the air conditioning system using recovery type equipment. Disconnect the negative battery cable.

3. Loosen the adjusting bolt, remove 2 mounting bolts, remove the power steering pump belt, and remove the power steering pump from its mounting and position out of the way.

4. Disconnect the suction and discharge hoses from the compressor. Cap all openings immediately to minimize system contamination.

5. Disconnect the compressor connector. Remove the condenser fan connector, mounting bolts, and lift out the condenser fan and shroud.

6. Loosen the idler pulley bracket bolt. Loosen the locknut and adjusting bolt, then remove the compressor belt.

7. Remove the 4 mounting bolts and remove the compressor. Remove the compressor mounting bracket with idler pulley, if necessary.

8. Drain and measure the oil from the compressor if it is being replaced.

9. Installation is the reverse order of the removal procedure. If a new compressor was installed, from 4.66 oz., subtract the quantity of oil as drained from the old compressor. This is the amount to be drained from the replacement compressor. Evacuate, recharge and leak test the system. Always use new O-rings lightly coated with refrigerant oil.

Legend and Legend Coupe

1. If the compressor still works, run the engine at idle speed and turn the air conditioning ON for a few minutes. This returns maximum amount of refrigerant oil to the compressor.

2. Properly discharge the air conditioning system using recovery type equipment. Detach the compressor electrical connector.

3. Raise and support the vehicle safely.

4. Disconnect the suction and discharge hose from the compressor. Be sure to cap the open fittings immediately to keep dirt and moisture out of the system.

5. Loosen the idler pulley center nut and the adjusting bolt, then remove the compressor belt.

6. Support the front of the car on safety stands and remove the engine splash shield.

7. Remove the 4 compressor mounting bolts and remove the compressor. If replacing the compressor, drain and measure the oil from the compressor. Always use new O-rings lightly coated with refrigerant oil.

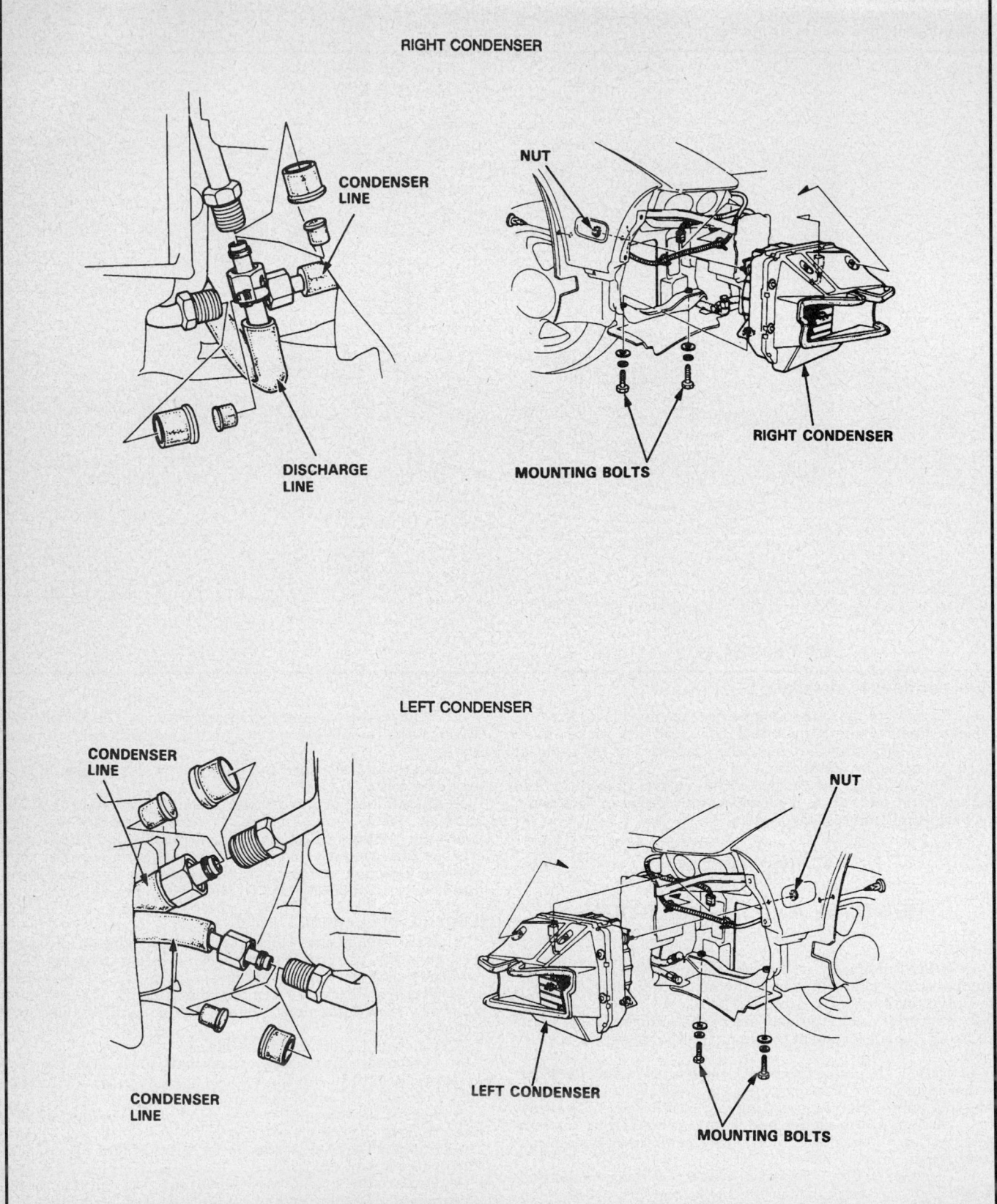

RIGHT CONDENSER

CONDENSER LINE

NUT

DISCHARGE LINE

MOUNTING BOLTS

RIGHT CONDENSER

LEFT CONDENSER

CONDENSER LINE

NUT

CONDENSER LINE

LEFT CONDENSER

MOUNTING BOLTS

Dual condenser refrigerant line connections and mounting positions—NSX Vigor

8. Installation is the reverse order of the removal procedure. If a new compressor was installed, subtract the amount of oil drained from the old compressor from 4.66 oz. The difference will be the amount of oil to be drained from the new compressor prior to installation.

9. Adjust the compressor drive belt to the proper tension. Evacuate and recharge the4 system properly.

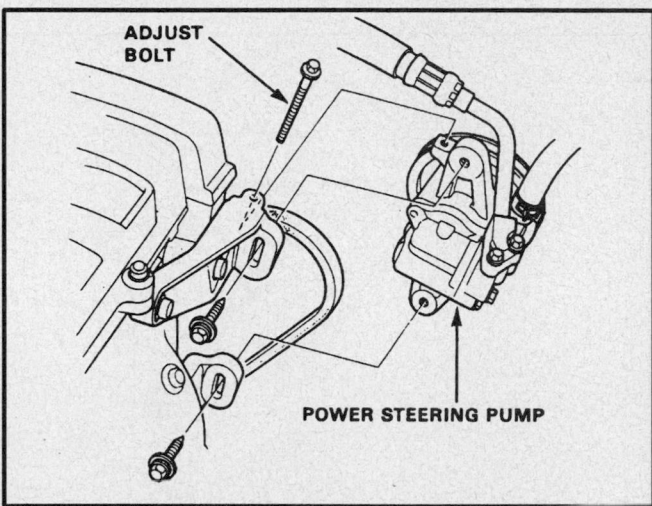

Power steering pump removal for compressor removal—Integra

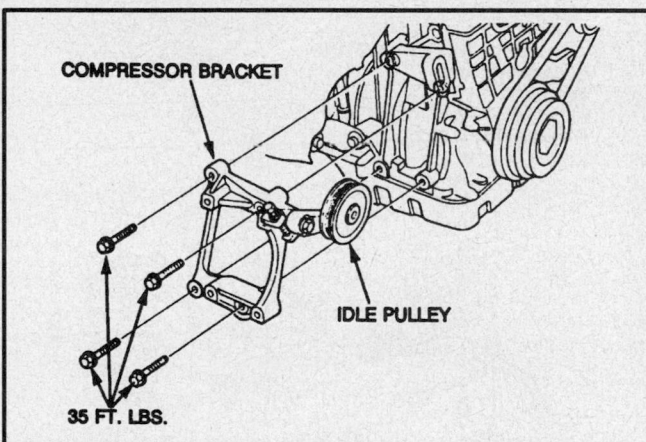

Compressor and idler pulley bracket—Integra

NSX

1. If the compressor still works, run the engine at idle for a few minutes with the air conditioning ON, then shut the engine OFF and disconnect the negative battery cable.

2. Discharge the air conditioning system using an approved refrigerant recovery/recycling unit.

3. Disconnect the electrical connector to the compressor clutch.

4. Raise the car on a hoist, making sure it's properly supported.

5. Remove the front beam to gain access to the compressor.

6. Disconnect the suction and discharge hoses from the compressor. Cap the openings immediately to prevent contamination from entering the system.

7. Loosen the idler pulley center nut and adjusting bolt, then remove the bolt from the compressor.

8. Remove the four mounting bolts which hold the compressor to the compressor bracket and remove the compressor.

9. If replacing the compressor, drain and measure the oil from the compressor. Always use new O–rings lightly coated with refrigerant oil.

10. Installation is the reverse order of the removal procedure. If a new compressor is installed, subtract the amount of oil drained from the old compressor from 4.66 oz. The difference will be the amount of oil to be drained from the new compressor prior to installation.

11. Adjust the compressor drive but to the proper tension, evacuate and recharge the system properly.

Receiver/Drier

REMOVAL AND INSTALLATION

1. Disconnect the negative battery cable.

2. Properly discharge the refrigerant from the air conditioning system.

3. Disconnect the receiver/drier air conditioning line and discharge line from the receiver/drier. Always use a back–up wrench when breaking the air conditioning line unions apart to prevent the pipes from distorting. Make sure to get the O–rings out of the fitting and to cap the lines immediately to keep moisture and dirt out of the system.

4. Remove the bolts attaching the receiver/drier to the vehicle and remove the receiver/drier.

To install:

5. Installation is the reverse order of the removal procedure. Be sure to use new O–rings that have been lightly coated with refrigerant oil whenever a system connection has been loosened or removed.

6. Evacuate the system before recharging. Check the system for leaks.

Blower Motor

REMOVAL AND INSTALLATION

Integra

— **CAUTION** —

All SRS wiring harnesses are covered with yellow outer insulation. Before disconnecting any part of the SRS wire harness, install short connections to prevent accidental discharge of the air bag system. If the SRS harness assembly should have an open circuit or damaged wiring, replace the entire affected harness.

1. Disconnect the negative battery cable.

2. Remove the passenger side lower dashboard cover.

3. Remove the glove box and the front console, if applicable.

4. Remove the right kick panel and remove the automatic should seat belt control unit (on Canadian models, remove the daytime running light relay).

5. Remove 2 bolts on the right end of the right knee holster Remove the heater to blower duct (heater only) or the evaporator to heater retaining band (air conditioning).

6. Remove the blower motor mounting bolts, disconnect the RECIRC door control cable, the electrical connections from the blower motor, and the blower motor resistor. Loosen and remove the blower motor mounting bolts and lower the blower motor.

7. Installation is the reverse of removal.

Legend and Legend Coupe

—————— CAUTION ——————

All SRS wiring harnesses are covered with yellow outer insulation. Before disconnecting any part of the SRS wire harness, install short connections to prevent accidental discharge of the air bag system. If the SRS harness assembly should have an open circuit or damaged wiring, replace the entire affected harness.

1. Disconnect the negative battery cable.
2. Remove the right side lower dashboard cover and detach the connector from the cover.
3. Remove the glove box retaining screws along with the glove box light and then remove the glove box.
4. Remove the end caps from both sides of the glove box opening. Remove the glove box frame.

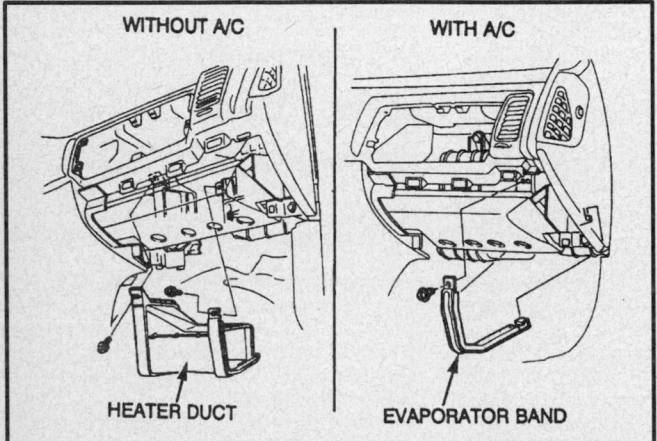

Removing the heater duct or evaporator band for blower removal—Integra

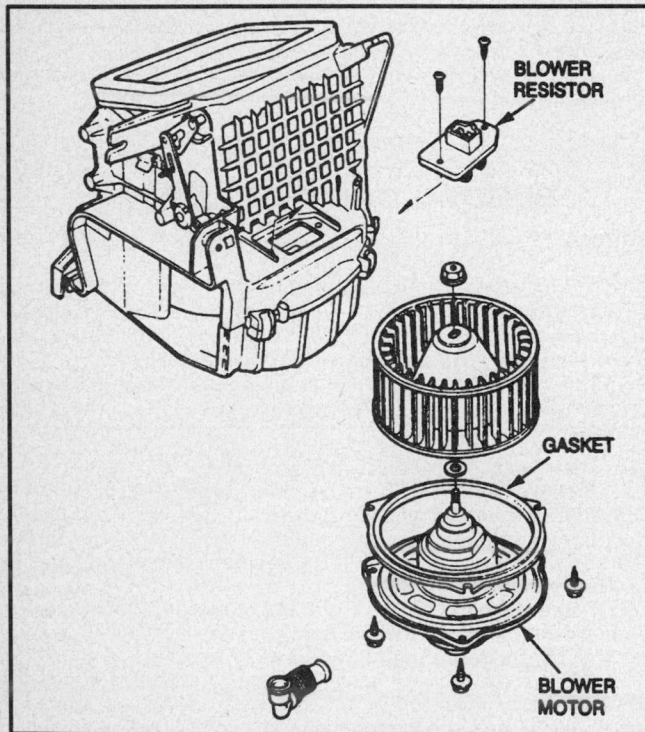

Blower motor and housing installation—Integra

5. Disconnect the wire connections from the blower motor and the automatic climate control.
6. Remove the blower retaining bolts and remove the blower motor assembly from the vehicle. Remove the blower motor from the blower motor housing.
7. Installation is the reverse order of the removal procedure.
8. Make sure when installation is complete, there is no air leakage.

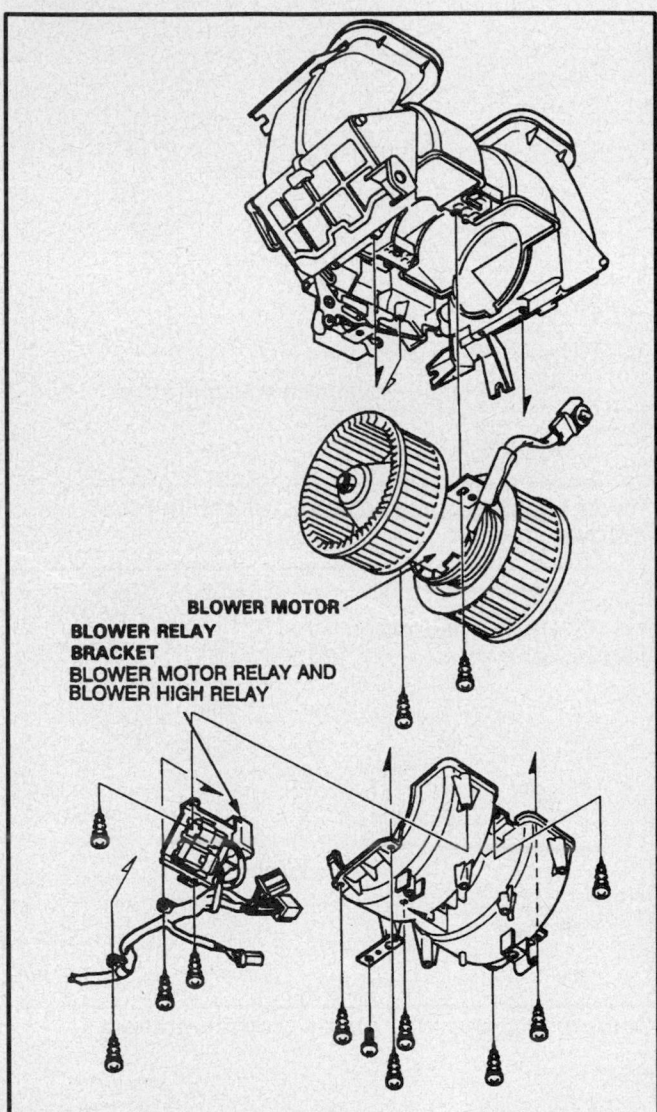

Blower motor disassembled view—Legend and Legend Coupe

NSX

1. Remove the spare tire and tire holder. Disconnect the battery cables, remove the hold–down bracket, then remove the battery.
2. Remove the under hood relay box and the water drain duct. Detach the connectors from the blower motor, power transistor and RECIRC motor.
3. Remove the blower motor mounting bolts, then remove the motor.

4. Installation is the reverse of the removal procedure. Prior to installing the spare tire, tire holder and hold down bracket, make sure the blower motor works and doe not leak air.

Vigor

1. Remove the heater–evaporator assembly

2. Remove the mounting screws, the pipe clamp and pipe cover from the heater–evaporator case.

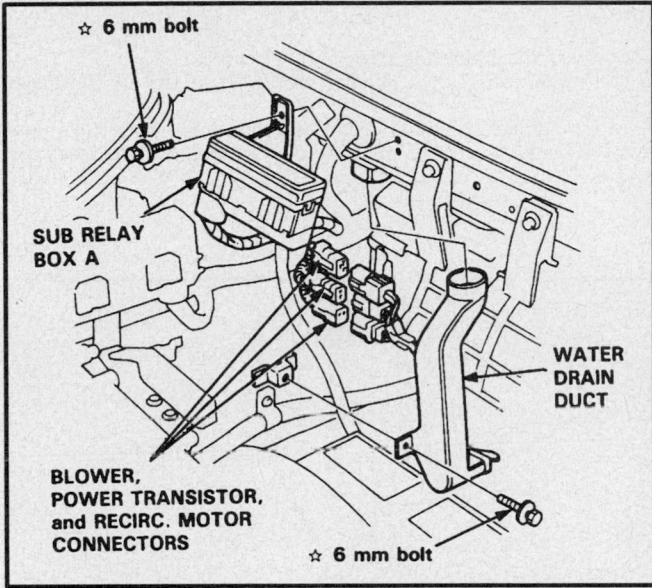

Component removal during blower motor removal—NSX

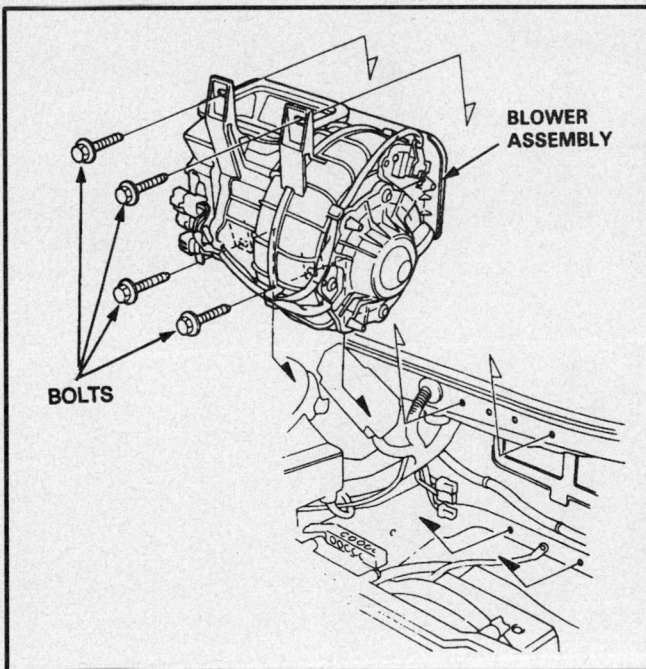

Blower assembly removal—NSX

3. Disconnect the recirculation control motor connector. Remove the RECIRC control motor.
4. Remove the left side heater duct.

5. Disconnect the blower motor connector. Remove the lower half of the heater–evaporator housing, then remove the blower motor.

6. Installation is the reverse of the removal procedure.

Heater and Evaporator

NOTE: If equipped with SRS (air bag) or an anti-theft radio, read the instructions in the front of this article before proceeding.

CAUTION

All SRS wiring harnesses are covered with yellow outer insulation. Before disconnecting any part of the SRS wire harness, install short connections to prevent accidental discharge of the air bag system. If the SRS harness assembly should have an open circuit or damaged wiring, replace the entire affected harness.

REMOVAL AND INSTALLATION

NOTE: Some models have an integral heater and evaporator assembly. Removal of either core requires removal of the entire assembly.

CAUTION

All SRS wiring harnesses are covered with yellow outer insulation. Before disconnecting any part of the SRS wire harness, install short connections to prevent accidental discharge of the air bag system. If the SRS harness assembly should have an open circuit or damaged wiring, replace the entire affected harness.

Heater Core

REMOVAL AND INSTALLATION

Integra

NOTE: If equipped with SRS (air bag) or an anti-theft radio, read the instructions before proceeding.

1. Disconnect the negative battery cable.
2. Properly drain the engine coolant.
3. Disconnect and plug the heater hoses, and remove the heater unit mounting nut at the firewall.
4. Disconnect the heater valve cable from the heater valve taking care not to damage or bend any of the fluid tubing.
5. On lever–type control systems, remove the climate control panel at this time.
6. Remove the dashboard as follows:
  - Remove the right and left dashboard lower covers.
  - Remove the front floor console.
  - Remove the driver's knee bolster.
  - Disconnect the wire harnesses and fuse box at the left side of the dashboard.
  - Lower the steering column.
  - Disconnect the ground cable at the right of the steering column.
  - Remove the heater control panel (2 knobs and bezel), pry out the hole cover and remove 7 screws holding the front trim panel around the driver's side.
  - Remove 4 screws and remove the instrument cluster, detaching the electrical and cable connections.
  - Remove the radio assembly.
  - Detach the automatic transaxle gear position switch and shift lock wire connectors from the harness connection under the ashtray area.
  - Remove the clock and both defroster bezels.

• Remove the dashboard mounting bolts and remove the dashboard.

• Remove the passenger SRS beam.

7. Remove the heater–to–blower duct or the evaporator attaching band, as equipped.

8. Detach the air mix control cable from the heater. Remove 2 mounting bolts, disconnect the wire harness from the mode control motor (push button control panel), then remove the heater assembly. The heater core can be removed at the bench.

To install:

9. Position the assembled heater to its location and secure with the 2 mounting bolts. Reattach the wiring and cable as removed.

10. Install the heater duct or evaporator band.

11. Install the dashboard in reverse of the removal procedure.

12. Install the control panel (lever type).

13. In the engine compartment, attach the heater valve cable, attach the heater hoses, and install the heater unit mounting nut.

14. Refill and bleed the cooling system. Adjust the control cables.

Evaporator Core

CAUTION

All SRS wiring harnesses are covered with yellow outer insulation. Before disconnecting any part of the SRS wire harness, install short connections to prevent accidental discharge of the air bag system. If the SRS harness assembly should have an open circuit or damaged wiring, replace the entire affected harness.

Integra

1. Disconnect the negative battery cable.

2. Properly discharge the refrigerant from the air conditioning system.

3. Disconnect the receiver and suction lines from the evaporator. Be sure to cap the open fittings immediately to keep dirt and moisture out of the system.

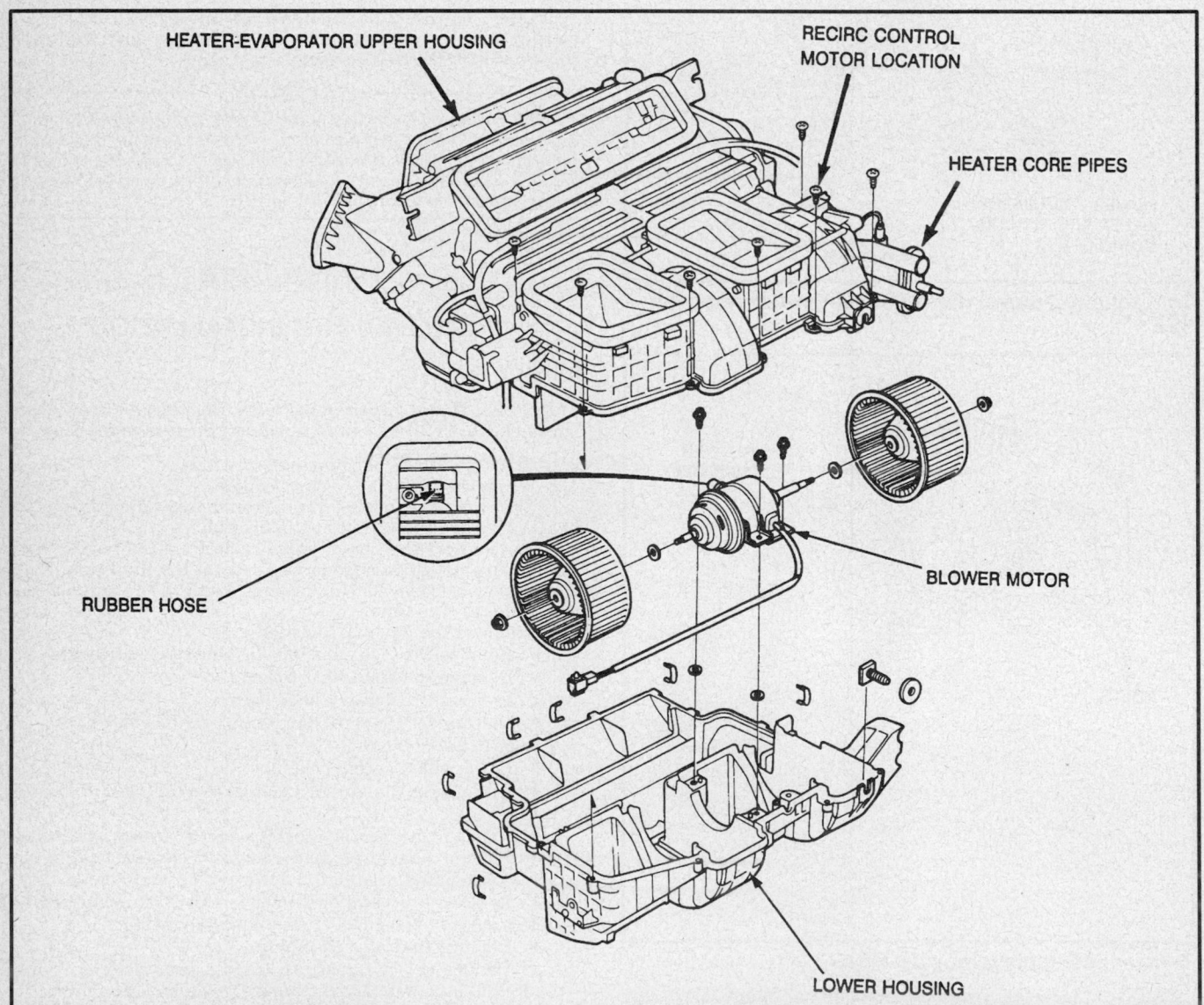

Removing the blower motor—Vigor

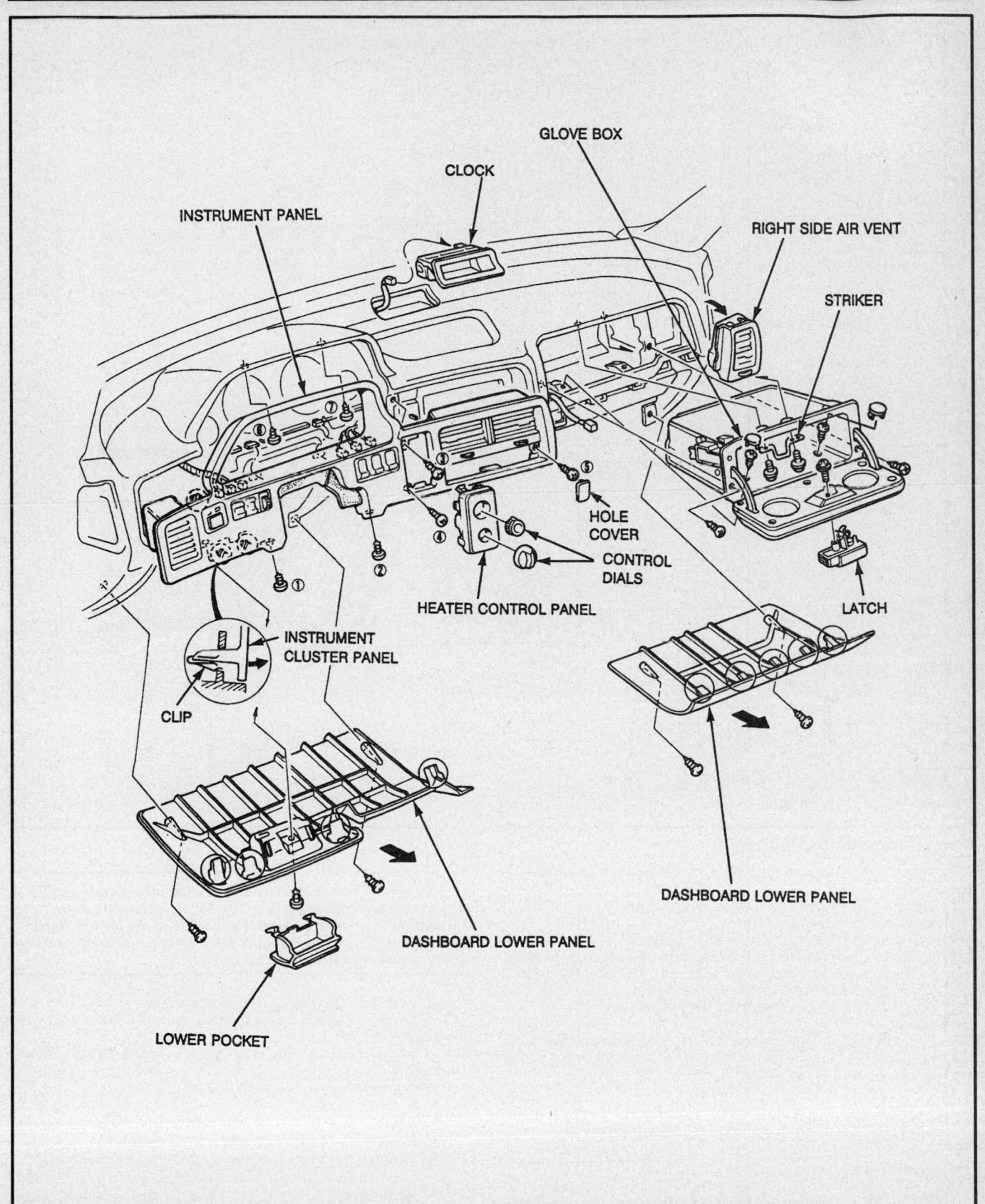

Dashboard and components for heater assembly removal–Integra

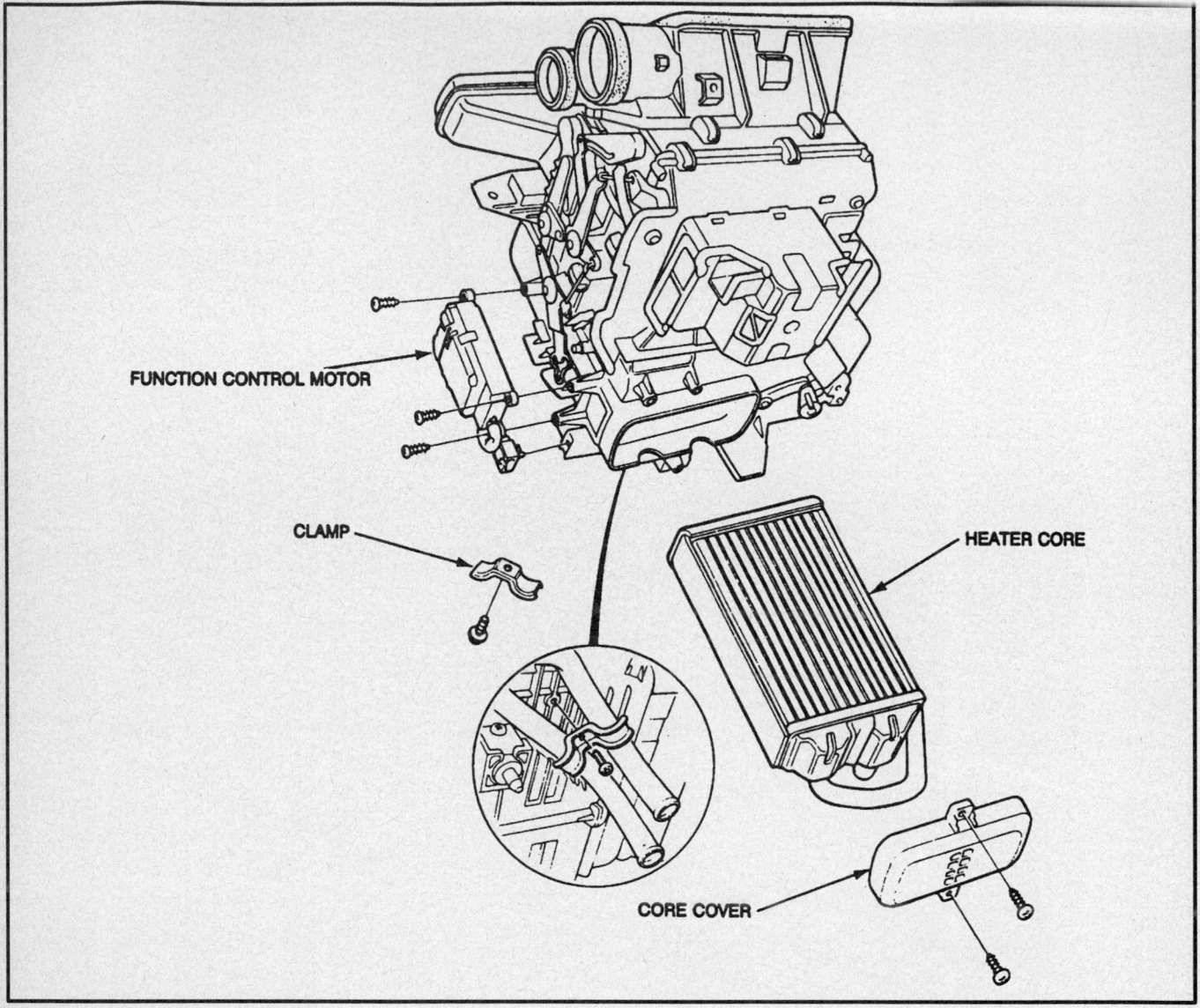

FUNCTION CONTROL MOTOR

CLAMP

HEATER CORE

CORE COVER

Heater core remova—Integra

4. Remove the passenger side and driver side lower dashboard cover.
5. Remove the glove box and the front console.
6. Remove the glove box frame.
7. Remove the passenger side knee bolster.
8. Remove the 2 screws holding the evaporator holding bands, disconnect the connector from the thermostat switch and remove the wire harness from the clamps.
9. Remove the evaporator from the vehicle.

To Install:
10. Installation is the reverse of removal. Always use new O–rings lightly coated with refrigerant oil on any connections which were loosened or removed.
11. Evacuate and charge the system.

Heater–Evaporator Assembly

Legend and Legend Coupe

NOTE: If equipped with SRS (air bag) or an anti-theft radio, read the instructions in the front of this article before proceeding.

CAUTION

All SRS wiring harnesses are covered with yellow outer insulation. Before disconnecting any part of the SRS wire harness, install short connections to prevent accidental discharge of the air bag system. If the SRS harness assembly should have an open circuit or damaged wiring, replace the entire affected harness.

---

1. Disconnect the negative battery cable.
2. Drain the engine coolant into a suitable drain pan when the engine is cool.
3. Disconnect and plug the heater hoses at the heater assembly.
4. Remove the dashboard as follows:
   - Remove the front seats.
   - Remove the center console panel and center arm rest.
   - Remove the radio assembly.
   - Remove the glove box lower panel and glove box.
   - Remove the left end plate from the glove box opening.
   - Remove the lower cover beneath the steering column and remove the kick panels.

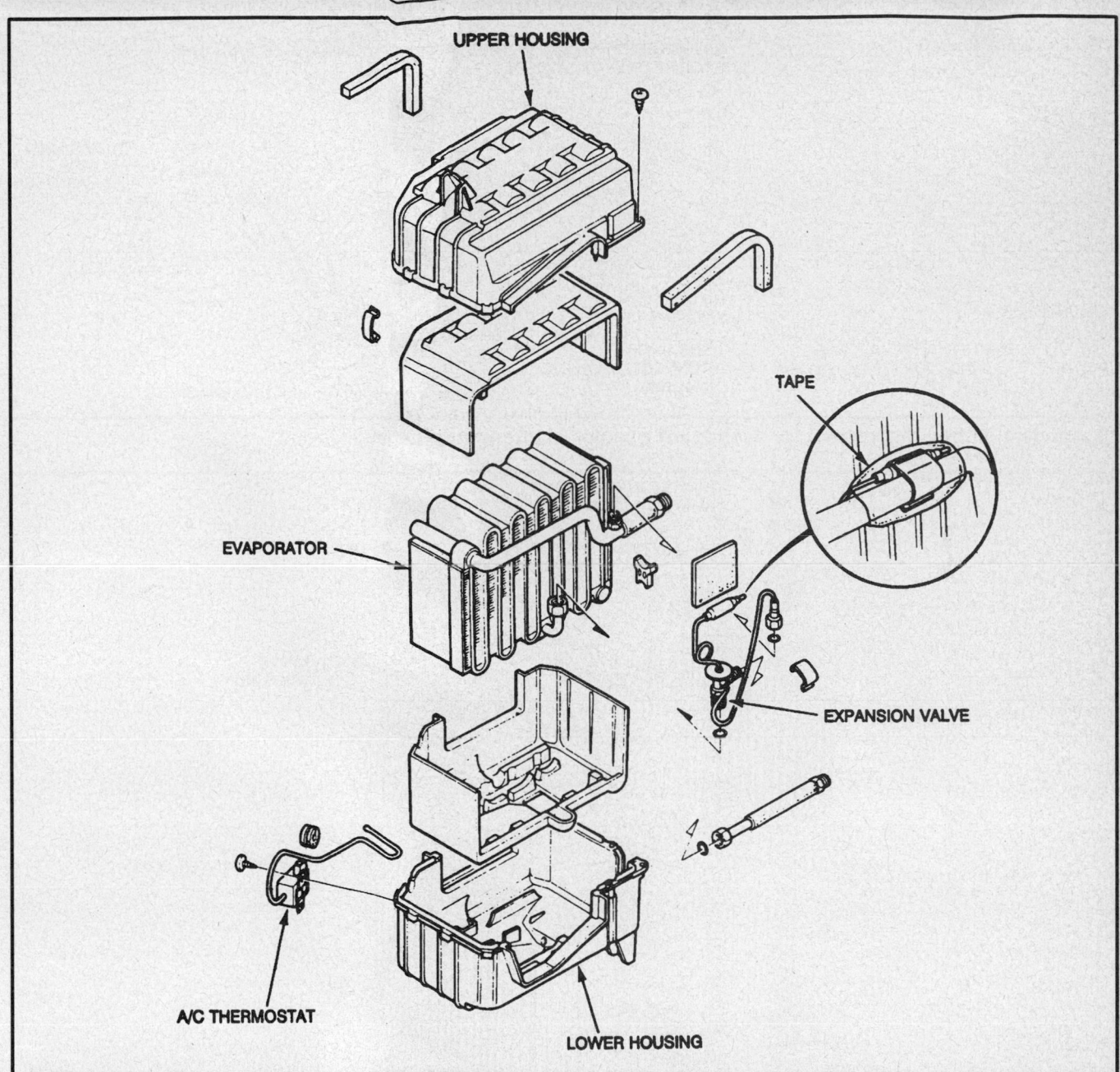

UPPER HOUSING

TAPE

EVAPORATOR

EXPANSION VALVE

A/C THERMOSTAT

LOWER HOUSING

Evaporator removal—Integra

- Lower the steering column.
- If equipped, remove the passenger's side air bag brackets, detach the connector at the air bag and install the red short connector provided, and connect the SRS short connector (07MAZ– SP00200 or equivalent) to the SRS main harness connector.
  - Detach the connectors in the glove box opening.
  - Detach the hood release cable. Remove the dashboard mounting bolts.
5. Remove the blower motor assembly.
6. Disconnect the 2 heater hoses which attach to the heater core inlet and outlet pipes on the engine side of the firewall.
7. Disconnect the heater valve cable from the heater valve.

8. Properly discharge the air conditioning system, using recovery type equipment. Remove the refrigerant lines from the firewall tube connections. Immediately cap the openings to minimize contamination of the system.
9. From the firewall, remove the nuts and the evaporator sealing plate.
10. Remove the floor duct (2 pieces), detach the connectors at the right end of the heater–evaporator unit, then remove the unit mounting nuts and bolts.
11. Disconnect the air–mix control motor wiring connector and the heater core temperature sensor connector. Remove the heater–evaporator unit.
12. Remove the cover and pipe clamps from the heater core and remove the core.

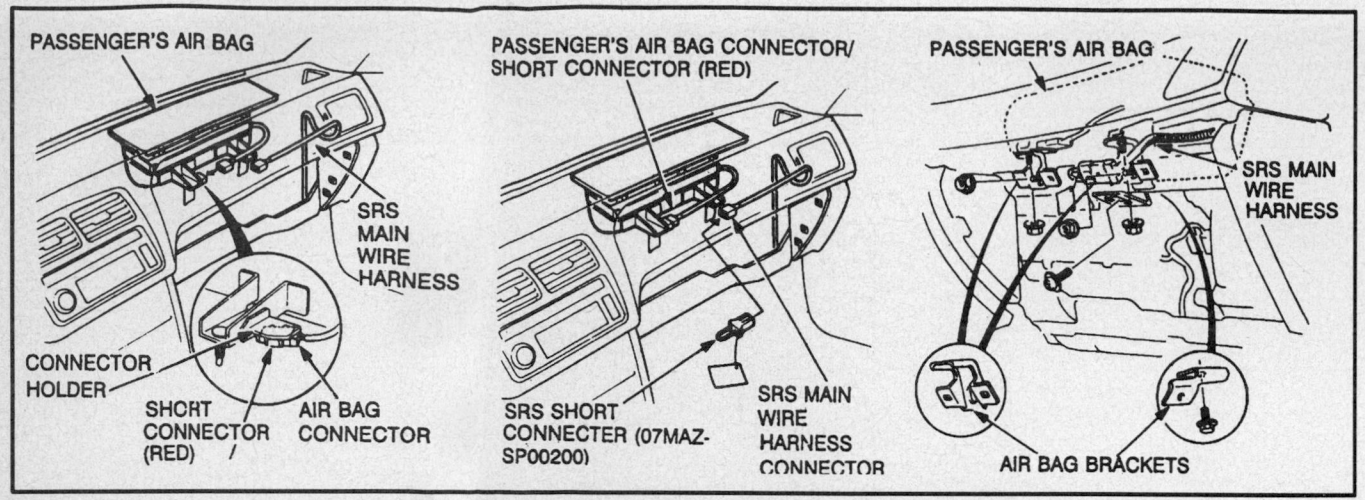

Passengers air bag disconnect for dashboard removal—Legend and Legend Coupe

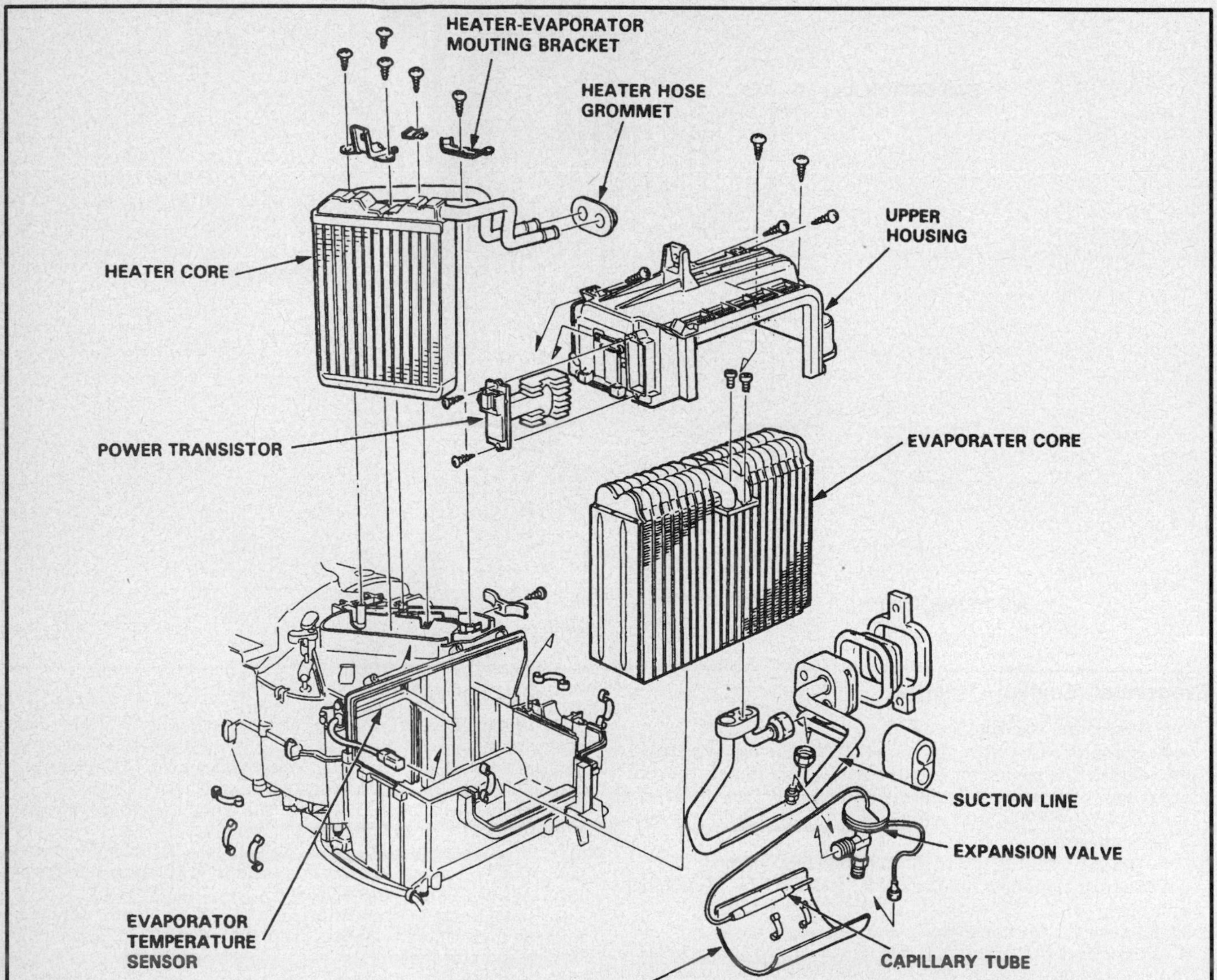

Exploded view of heater—evaporator assembly—Legend and Legend Coupe

13. Separate the housing halves, remove the expansion valve and remove the evaporator core, if necessary.

To install :

14. Installation is the reverse order of the removal procedure, except for the following:
  - Apply a suitable sealant to the grommets.
  - Do not interchange the heater hoses.
  - Before tightening the dashboard retaining bolts, be sure the dashboard is not interfering with the heater control lever or cables. Also check that no harness wires or SRS wires are pinched.
  - Loosen the bleed bolt on the engine and refill the radiator and reservoir tank with the proper coolant mixture.
  - Tighten the bleed bolt when all the trapped air has escaped from the system and the coolant begins to flow from it.
  - Connect all vacuum hoses and cables and adjust, as necessary.
  - Always use new O–rings lightly coated with refrigerant oil on any air conditioning system connections which have been loosened or disconnected.

Heater–Evaporator Assembly

NSX

NOTE: If equipped with SRS (air bag) or an anti–theft radio, read the instructions in the front of this article before proceeding.

———————CAUTION———————

All SRS wiring harnesses are covered with yellow outer insulation. Before disconnecting any part of the SRS wire harness, install short connections to prevent accidental discharge of the air bag system. If the SRS harness assembly should have an open circuit or damaged wiring, replace the entire affected harness.

1. Properly drain the cooling system. Properly discharge the air conditioning system using an approved refrigerant recovery/recycling system.
2. Remove the blower assembly.
3. Disconnect and plug the heater hoses at the firewall. Disconnect the heater valve cable from the heater valve.
4. Disconnect the refrigerant lines from their connection at the firewall. Cap all openings immediately to keep dirt and moisture from contaminating the system.
5. Remove the dashboard as follows:
  - Remove the front seats.
  - Remove the knee bolster, pad, dashboard stay and center armrest.
  - Remove the clock, center air vent and center console panel.
  - Remove the heater–A/C control panel and the radio assembly.
  - Remove the right dashboard lower panel. Remove the glove box.
  - Lower the steering column.
  - Remove the instrument cluster bezel and the instrument cluster.
  - Remove the air vents from both ends of the dashboard.
  - Remove the U–plate at the foot of the center console, rearward of the parking brake.
  - Remove the defrost outlet grille, remove the mounting bolts and lift out the dashboard. Note position of center guide pin for reinstallation.
6. Remove the heater duct.
7. Detach the connectors from the control unit and from the evaporator temperature sensor, then remove the control unit and bracket.
8. Remove the sound system speaker.
9. Detach all actuator connectors and sensor connectors from the heater–evaporator unit.
10. Remove 2 under–dash mounting bolts and remove the heater–evaporator unit through the passenger's door.
11. The unit can now be disassembled and the heater core, expansion valve, evaporator core and other components removed as needed.
12. Installation is the reverse of the removal procedure. Add 0.3 oz. of extra refrigerant oil if the evaporator core was replaced. Adjust the heater valve cable, if needed. Refill the cooling system and bleed the system completely. Failure to properly bleed the air from the cooling system could cause engine damage. Evacuate, recharge and leak test the air conditioning system.

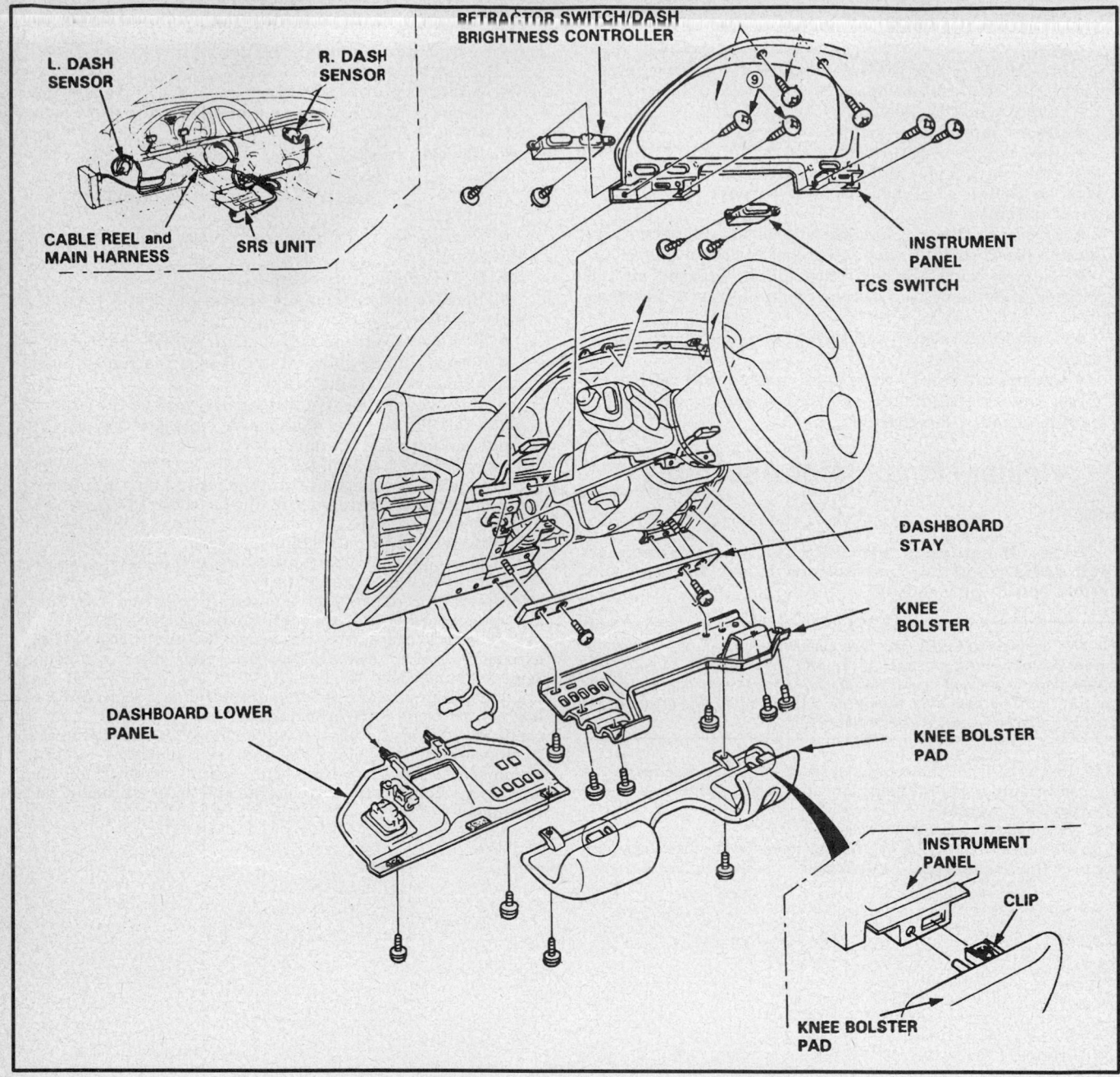

Dashboard and components for heater–evaporator assembly removal–NSX

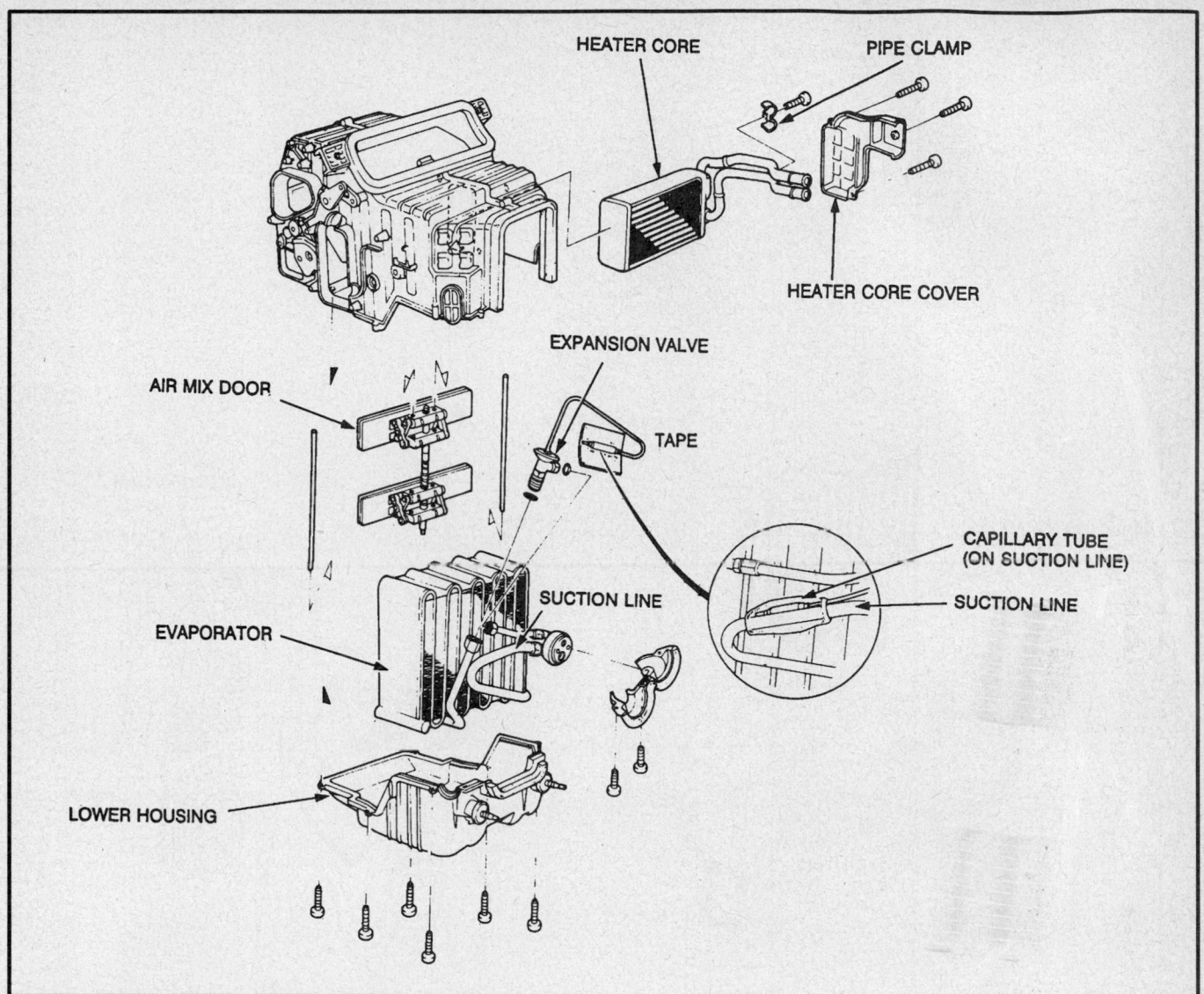

Heater−evaporator unit disassembled—NSX

Vigor

NOTE: If equipped with SRS (air bag) or an anti-theft radio, read the instructions in the front of this article before proceeding.

━━━━━━━━━━ **CAUTION** ━━━━━━━━━━

All SRS wiring harnesses are covered with yellow outer insulation. Before disconnecting any part of the SRS wire harness, install short connections to prevent accidental discharge of the air bag system. If the SRS harness assembly should have an open circuit or damaged wiring, replace the entire affected harness.

━━━━━━━━━━━━━━━━━━━━━━━━━━━━━━━

1. Remove the dashboard as follows:
   • Remove the front seats.
   • Remove the center console panel and center console.
   • Remove the lower dash board cover, knee bolster and both kick panels.
   • Lower the steering column.
   • Remove the vents from each end of the dashboard.
   • Detach the connectors at the left side of the dashboard.
   • Remove 6 bolts and remove the dashboard, noting position of the center guide pin for reinstallation.
2. Properly drain the cooling system, then properly discharge the air conditioning system using recovery type equipment.
3. Detach and plug the heater hoses at the firewall, then disconnect and cap the refrigerant lines from the connection at the firewall. Remove the heater−evaporator mounting nut to the left of the heater tubes.
4. Remove the floor air duct screws at both sides, detach the wiring from the assembly, then remove the heater−evaporator mounting bolts. Remove the assembly.
5. Installation is the reverse of the removal procedure. Apply sealer to firewall grommets. Refill and bleed the cooling system. Add 0.5 oz. of refrigerant oil if evaporator core was replaced.
6. Evacuate, recharge and leak test the system.

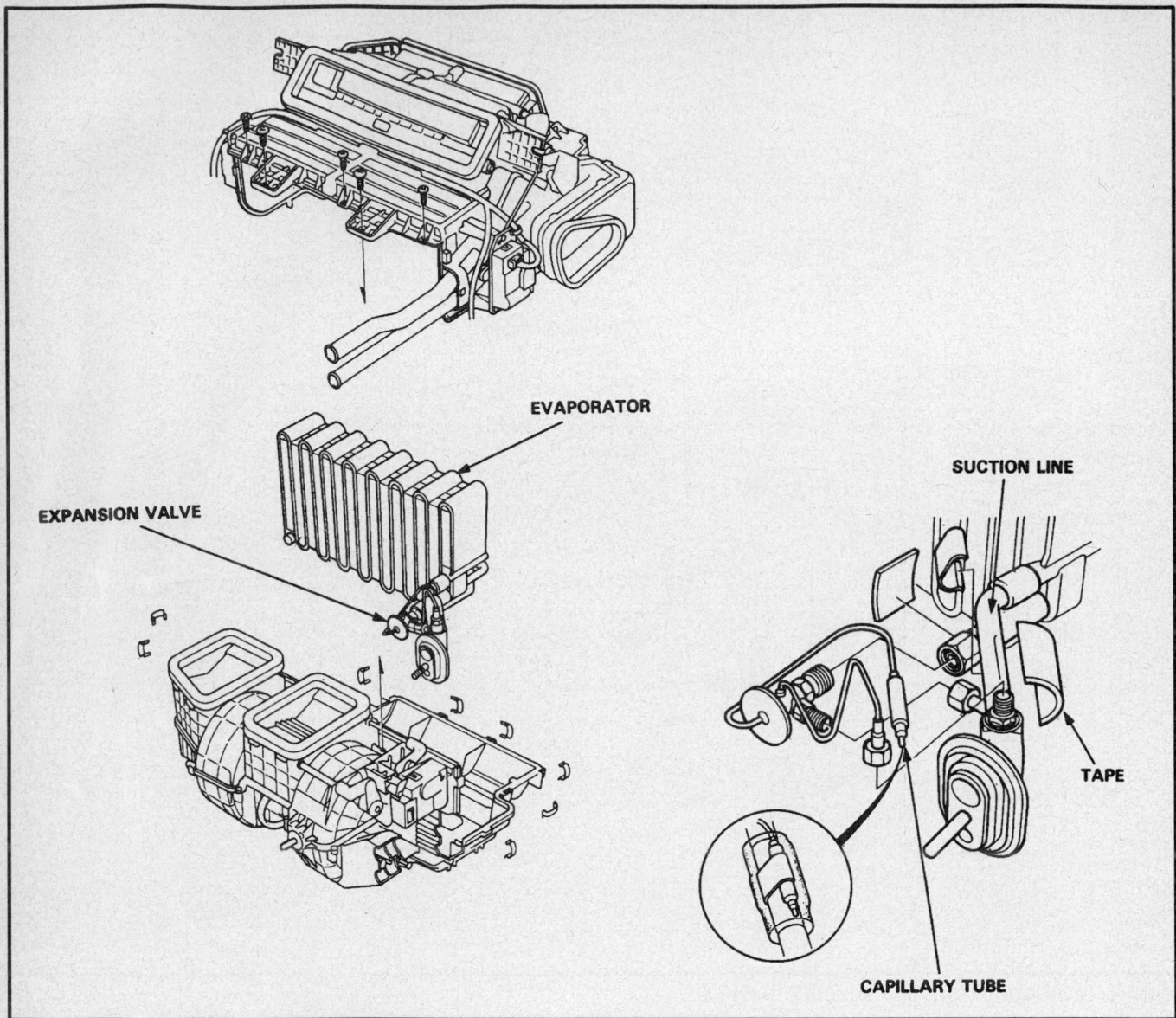

EXPANSION VALVE

EVAPORATOR

SUCTION LINE

TAPE

CAPILLARY TUBE

Evaporator core removal—Vigor

Manual Control Head

REMOVAL AND INSTALLATION

1993 Integra

1. Disconnect the negative battery cable.
2. Remove the front instrument panel trim.
3. Remove both lower dashboard covers.
4. Remove front console and the radio/cassette player.
5. Disconnect the heater valve cable, air/mix cable, and (on lever type panel), the function control cable and recirculation control cable from the heater assembly.
6. Remove the screws, pull the control panel out, detach the wire harness connectors, and remove the heater control head.

1994—95 Integra

1. Disconnect the air mix control cable from the heater unit.

2. Remove the rear window defogger switch and the hazard warning switch. The locking tabs for the hazard warning switch and the heater control panel connectors are on the bottom of each component.
3. Pull out the heater control pane and center air vent after removing the mounting screws. Disconnect the electrical connectors on the rear of the unit.
4. Installation is the reverse of the removal process. Verify proper operation of all components following reassembly.

Legend and Legend Coupe

NOTE: If equipped with SRS (air bag) or an anti-theft radio, read the instructions in the front of this article before proceeding.

1. Disconnect the negative battery cable.
2. Remove the radio assembly.
3. Remove the attaching screws and disconnect the electrical connectors from the back of the control panel.

4. Release the clips on top of the control/center air outlet assembly and remove the assembly.

5. Installation is the reverse of the removal procedure.

NSX

NOTE: If equipped with SRS (air bag) or an anti-theft radio, read the instructions in the front of this article before proceeding.

1. Remove the center console trim plate.
2. Remove the control panel retaining screws.
3. Pull the control panel outward and detach the electrical connectors. Remove the control panel assembly..
4. Installation is the reverse of the removal procedure.

Vigor

1. Remove the cap to expose the retaining screws in the bottom center of the control panel.
2. Remove the screws pull the panel outward, detach the connector and remove the control panel.
3. Installation is the reverse of the removal procedure.

Electronic Control Head

REMOVAL AND INSTALLATION

Legend Coupe

NOTE: If equipped with SRS (air bag) or an anti-theft radio, read the instructions in the front of this article before proceeding.

1. Disconnect the negative battery cable.
2. Remove the center console plate, the armrest, and remove the radio assembly.

3. Remove the 4 screws and pull out the control head.

4. Disconnect the wiring connector and remove the control head.

5. Installation is the reverse of removal.

NSX

NOTE: If equipped with SRS (air bag) or an anti-theft radio, read the instructions in the front of this article before proceeding.

1. Carefully pry the clock out of the dash and disconnect it.
2. Remove the center dash vent (2 screws), and remove the 2 screws from the top of the console panel.
3. Remove the ashtray, then remove the 2 screws behind it.
4. Remove the console storage box (lift out the bottom panel and remove 4 screws).
5. Remove the screws from the end of the console panel, pull the parking brake up, lift the panel and detach the connectors, and take the panel out.
6. Remove 4 climate control panel retaining screws, pull the panel out, detach the connectors and remove the panel.
7. Installation is the reverse of the removal procedure.

Air Mix Cable

ADJUSTMENT

Integra

1. Disconnect the heater valve cable from the heater valve arm and the clamp from the heater control arm.
2. Turn the air temperature control knob to the **MAX HEAT** position.

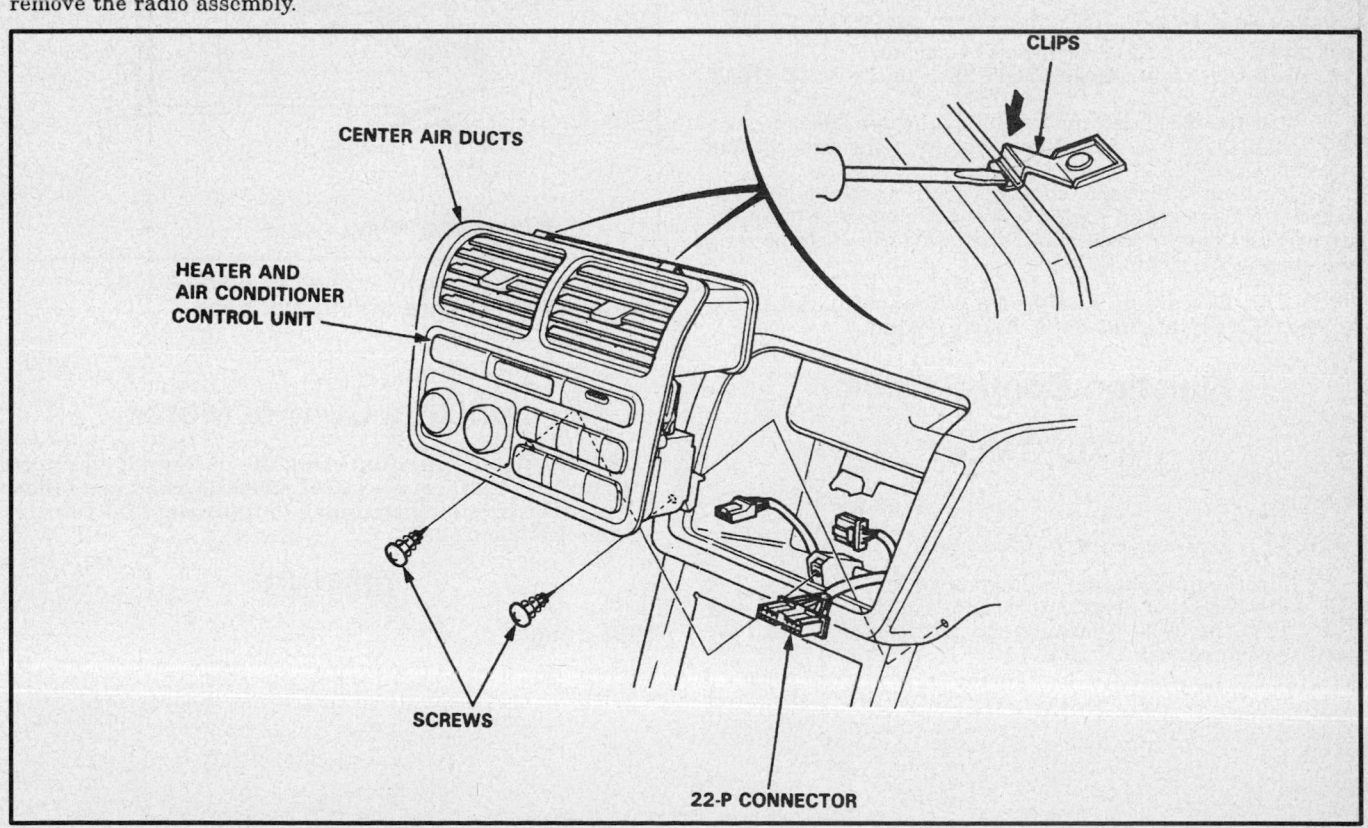

Removing the control panel—Legend and Legend Coupe

3. With the cable disconnected from the air mix door, move the air mix door shaft fully toward the front of the car and attach the end of the cable to the arm.

4. Gently slide the cable housing back from the end enough to take up the slack in the cable but not enough to make the control knob move. Snap the cable housing into the clamp.

5. After the adjustment, make sure the heater valve cable is also properly adjusted.

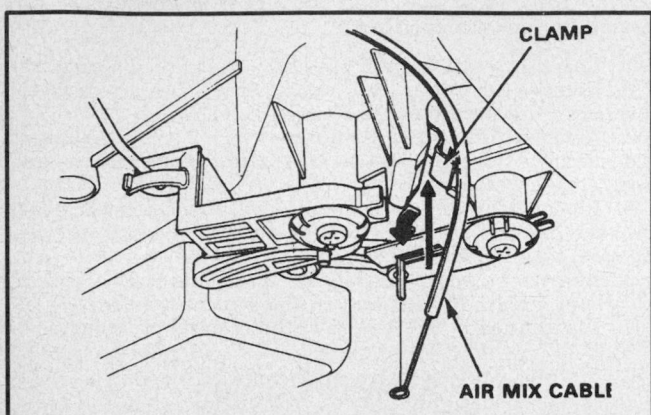

Air mix cable connection and adjustment—Integra

Heater Valve Cable

ADJUSTMENT

Integra

1. Disconnect the heater valve cable from the heater valve arm and the clamp from the heater control arm.

2. Turn the temperature control knob to the **MAX HEAT** position.

3. With the cable detached from the heater valve connection, push the valve arm fully away from the firewall and attach the cable end.

4. Gently slide the cable housing back from the end enough to take up any slack in the cable but not enough to make the temperature control knob move, then hold the cable housing and snap in the clamp.

NOTE: The air mix cable should be adjusted if the heater valve cable has been disconnected.

Function Control Cable

ADJUSTMENT

Integra

NOTE: for lever control panel only

1. Slide the function control lever to **DEF**.

2. With the cable detached from the function control door shaft, turn the cable attaching end of the lever toward the cable clip and attach the cable.

3. Gently slide the cable housing back from the end enough to remove any slack, but not enough to move the function control lever. Snap the cable into place.

Heater valve cable adjustment—Integra

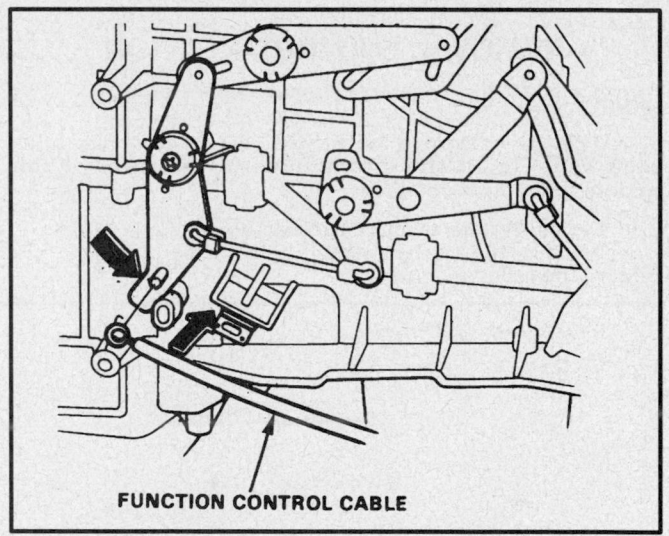

Function control cable connection and adjustments—1993 Integra with heater only

Function Control Motor

NOTE: Before disconnecting the battery, if equipped with an anti-theft code controlled radio, read and follow the procedure described under "Supplemental Restraint System Instructions".

TESTING

1993 Integra

1. Disconnect the negative battery cable.

2. Disconnect the function control motor connector.

1. Connect battery power to the No. 4 terminal of the mode control motor and connect ground to the No. 8 terminal.

2. Using a jumper wire, short the No. 8 terminal individually to the No. 1, 2, 3, 6 and 7 terminals, in that order.

   ● Each time the short circuit is made, the mode control motor should run smoothly and stop.

   NOTE: If the mode control motor does not run when shorting the first terminal, short that terminal again after shorting the other terminals.
   The mode control motor is normal if it runs when shorting the first terminal again.

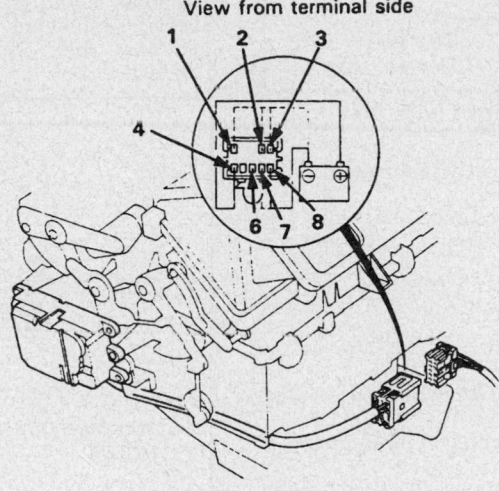

View from terminal side

3. If the mode control motor does not run in step 2, remove it, and check the mode control linkage and doors for smooth movement. If the mode control linkage and doors move smoothly, replace the mode control motor.

Function Control Motor Testing — 1994-95 Integra

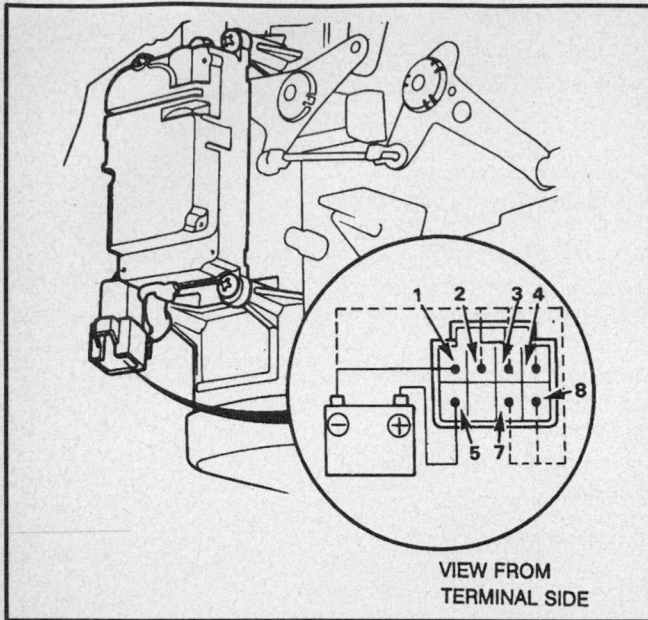

VIEW FROM
TERMINAL SIDE

Function control motor—1993 Integra with air conditioning

3. Connect battery positive power directly to terminal **5** and the battery ground to terminal **1** .

4. Using a jumper wire, connect terminal **1** alternately to terminals **2**, **3**, **4**, **7**, and **8** in that order. The motor should run each time.

1994—95 Integra

1. Disconnect the function control motor connector at the function control motor.

2. Connect battery power to terminal **4** of the mode control motor and a ground wire to terminal **8**.

3. Using a jumper wire, connect terminal **8** individually to terminals **1**, **2**, **3**, **6**, and **7** in that order.

4. Each time that a connection is made, the mode motor should run smoothly and stop.

5. If the mode control motor does not run in the previous step, remove it and check the mode control linkage and doors for smooth movement. If the mode control linkage and doors move smoothly, replace the mode control motor.

NOTE: If the mode control motor does not run when first connecting the terminals, repeat the previous steps. The mode control motor is normal if it runs when repeating the steps.

1993 Legend and Legend Coupe with Manual Air Conditioning

1. Detach the function control motor connector. Connect battery voltage to terminal **1** of the recirculation control motor connector and ground **2**.

2. The motor should run and stop at **VENT** .

3. If not, reverse the connections, the motor should run and stop at **DEF** .

4. Plug the connector back into the motor. Operate the mode switch on the panel and back–probe the connector terminals with an ohmmeter to check for continuity between terminals.

1993 Legend Coupe with automatic air conditioning

1. Using a suitable ohmmeter, measure the resistance between terminal **3** and terminal **5** on the function control motor connector. The resistance should be about 6 kilo-ohms.

2. Check the motor operation by connecting a wire from the battery (+) positive terminal to terminal **2** and the (–) ground to terminal **1** . Reverse the wires to make sure the motor will run in both directions.

NOTE: Be sure to disconnect the battery from the motor as soon as the motor starts to run. Failure to do so will damage the motor.

3. While repeating Step 2, measure the resistance between terminals **5** and **4**. The motor is normal if the resistance is about 1.2 kilo-ohms at **VENT** and 4.8 kilo-ohms at **DEF** .

4. Also check the resistance with the battery polarity reversed.

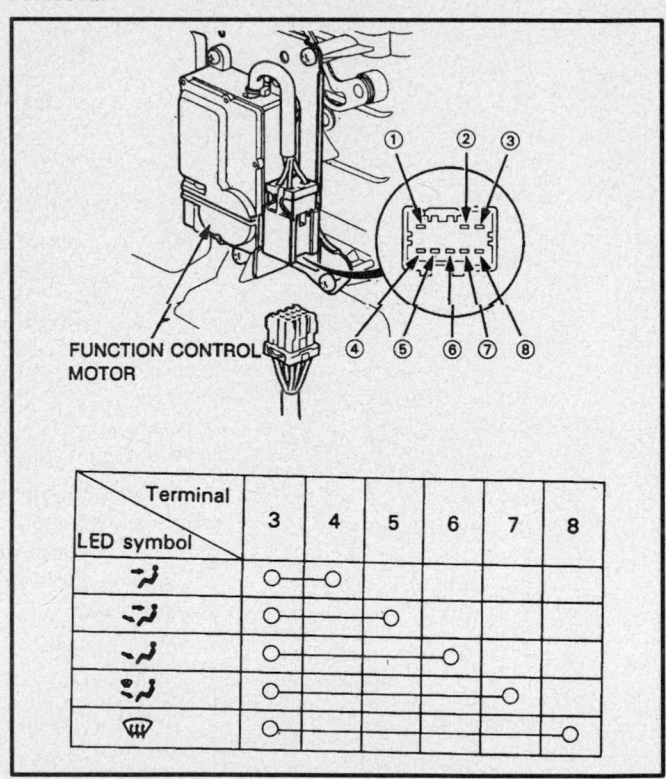

FUNCTION CONTROL MOTOR

Terminal / LED symbol	3	4	5	6	7	8
⤴	○—	—○				
⤴	○—	—○			
⤴	○—		—○		
⤴	○—			—○	
〰	○—				—○

Function control motor test—1993 Legend and Legend Coupe

1. Connect battery power to the No. 3 terminal of the mode control motor and connect ground to the No. 2 terminal.

2. Using a jumper wire, short the No. 1 terminal individually to the No. 4, No. 5, No. 6, No. 7, and No. 8 terminals, in that order.
   • Each time the short circuit is made, the mode control motor should run smoothly and stop.

   NOTE: If the mode control motor does not run when shorting the first terminal, short that terminal again after shorting the other terminals. The mode control motor is normal if it runs when shorting the first terminal again.

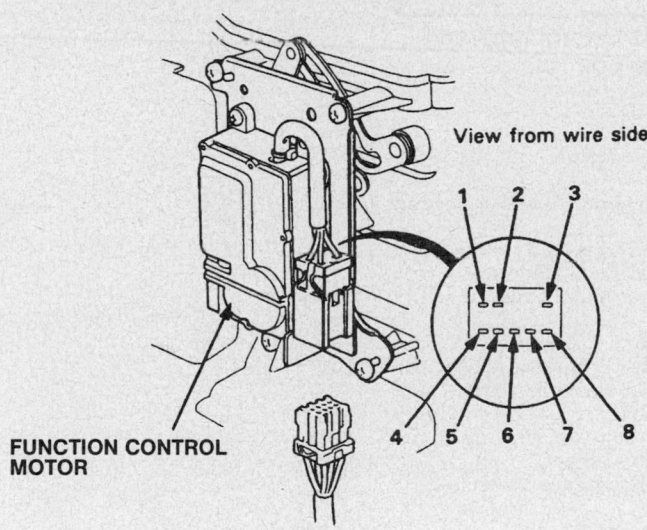

View from wire side.

FUNCTION CONTROL MOTOR

3. If the mode control motor does not run in step 2, remove it, and check the mode control linkage and doors for smooth movement. If the mode control linkage and doors move smoothly, replace the mode control motor.

Function control motor testing—1994 Legend and Legend Coupe

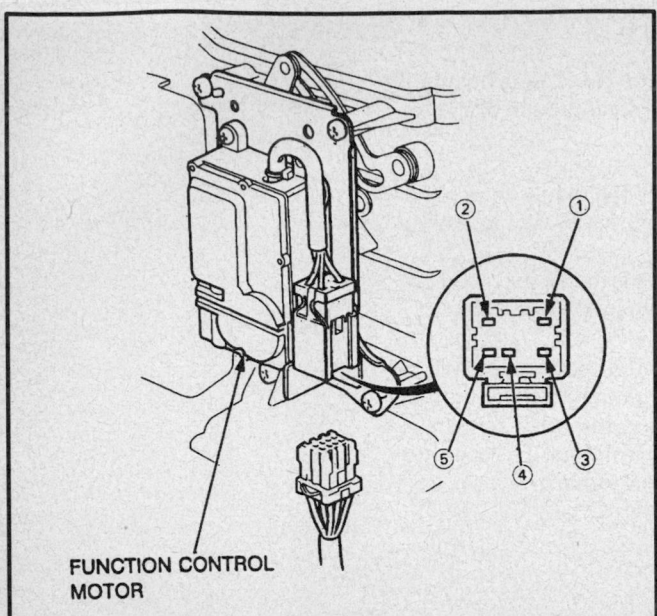

FUNCTION CONTROL MOTOR

Function control motor test—1993 Legend and Legend Coupe with automatic climate control

1994 Legend and Legend Coupe

1. Disconnect the mode control wire harness at the mode control motor.
2. Connect battery (+) power to terminal **3** and a ground wire to terminal **2**.
3. Using a jumper wire, connect the terminal **2** individually to terminals **4**, **5**, **6** and **8** in that order. Each time that a connection is made, the mode control motor should run smoothly and stop.
4. If the function control motor does not run when first making the connections to the various terminals, repeat the testing procedure. The function control motor is normal if it runs during the second testing procedure.
5. If the function control motor still does not run, check the control linkage and doors for smooth movement.
6. If the doors and linkage check OK, replace the motor.

NSX and Vigor

1. Disconnect the function control motor connector and apply battery voltage to terminal **1** of the motor and connect terminal **2** to ground. The motor should run and stop at **VENT**.

2. If this doesn't occur, reverse the connections, the motor should run and stop at **DEF** .
3. Remove the battery connections and plug the connector back in to the motor. While operating the panel controls to each mode, back–probe the connector to check for continuity of terminals as shown.

Recirculation Control Motor

TESTING

1993 Integra

1. Connect battery voltage to terminal **3** of the recirculation control motor connector and ground terminal **2**.
2. Using a jumper wire, connect terminal **2** to terminal **1** or **4**.
3. With the door at **REC** position the motor should turn with the terminals **2** and **1** connected.
4. With the recirculation door at **FRESH** position, the motor should turn with terminals **2** and **4** connected.

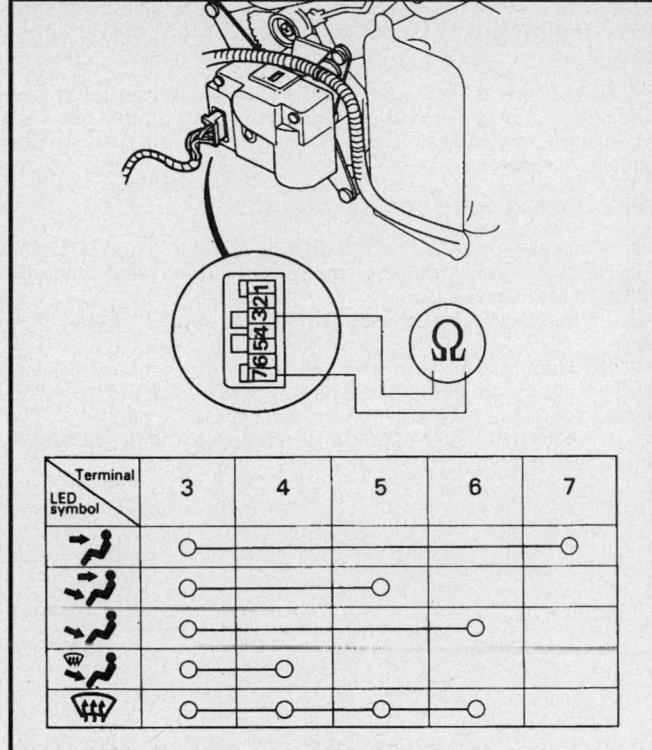

Terminal / LED symbol	3	4	5	6	7
↗ (seat)	O				O
↘↗ (seat)	O		O		
↘ (seat)	O			O	
▥ (defrost/seat)	O	O			
▥ (defrost)	O	O	O	O	

Function control motor test—NSX

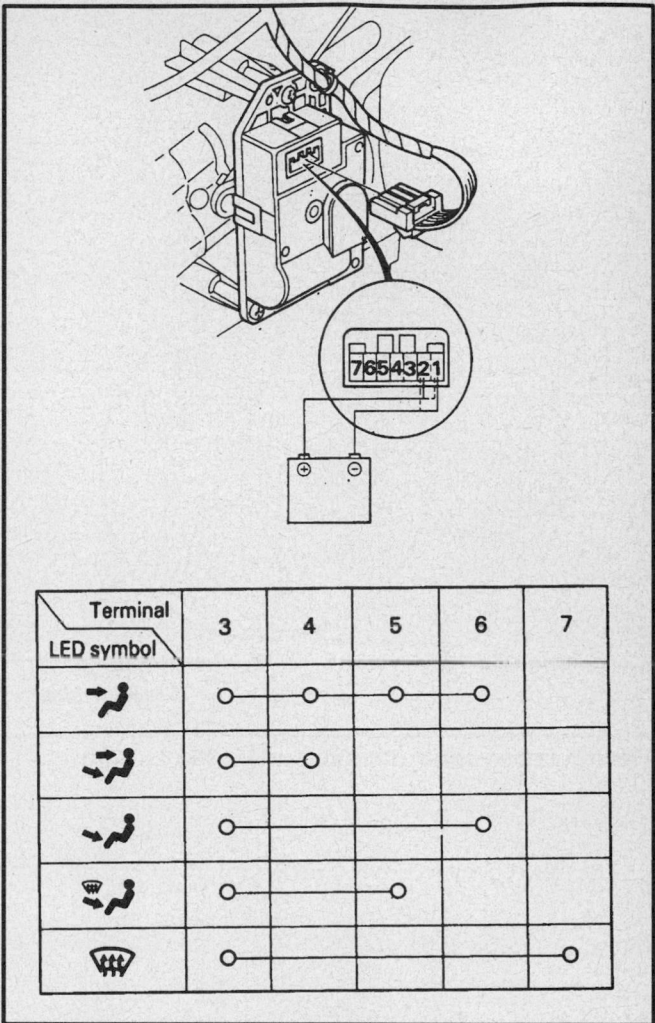

Terminal / LED symbol	3	4	5	6	7
↗	O	O	O	O	
↘↗	O	O			
↘	O			O	
▥↗	O		O		
▥	O				O

Function control motor—Vigor

5. The motor will automatically turn OFF after 1/2 turn when the jumper wire is connected.

1994–95 Integra

1. Disconnect the recirculation control motor harness connector at the recirculation control motor,

2. Connect battery power to terminal **1** of the motor and ground terminals **2** and **4** terminals. The recirculation control motor should run smoothly.

3. Disconnect the ground from terminal **2** or **4** and the motor should stop at either the **FRESH** or **RECIRCULATE** position.

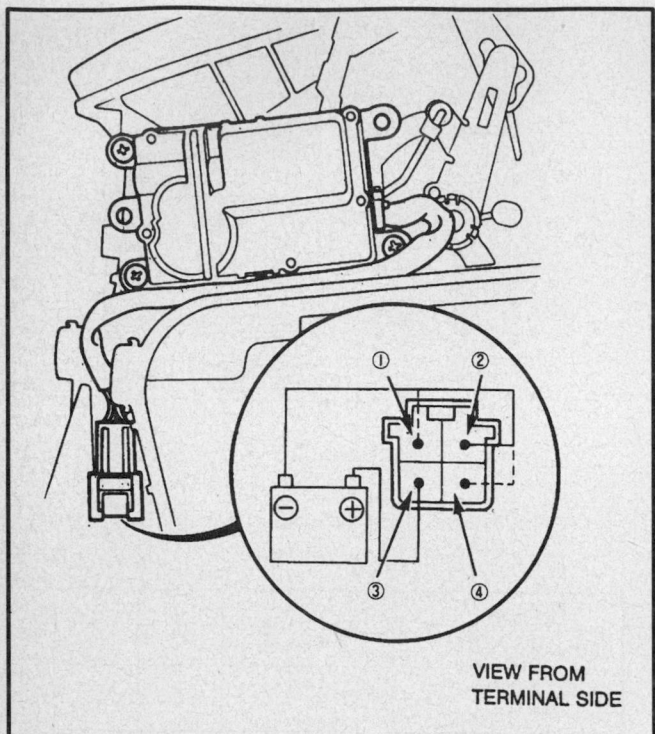

Recirculation control motor test—1993 Integra

NOTE: **Never connect the battery in the opposite direction or run the recirculation control motor for a long time.**

4. If the recirculation control motor does not run in the previous steps, remove it and check the control linkage and door for smooth movement. If the door and linkage move freely, replace the motor.

1993 Legend and Legend Coupe

1. Disconnect the connector from the recirc control motor and connect battery power to terminal **1** and ground terminal **2**. The motor should run.

2. If not, reverse the connections, the motor should now run.

3. Reconnect the connector, operate the function control while back–probing the terminals. At the **FRESH** position, there should be continuity between terminals **1** and **3**.

4. At **RECIRC** there should be continuity between terminals **1** and **4** .

1. Connect battery power to the No. 1 terminal of the recirculation control motor, and connect ground to the No. 2 and No. 4 terminals; the recirculation control motor should run smoothly.

2. Disconnect the ground from the No. 2 or No. 4 terminals; the recirculation control motor should stop at FRESH or RECIRCULATE.

   CAUTION: Never connect the battery in the opposite direction.

   NOTE: Don't cycle the recirculation control motor for a long time.

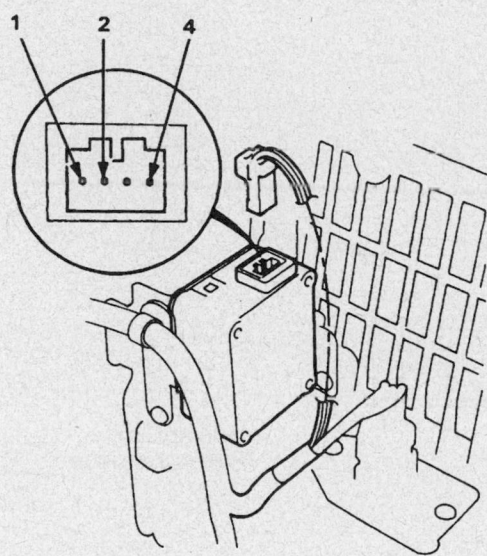

3. If the recirculation control motor does not run in step 1, remove it, and check the recirculation control linkage and door for smooth movement. If the recirculation control linkage and door move smoothly, replace the recirculation control motor.

Recirulation control motor testing—1994-95 Integra

1. Connect battery power to the No. 1 terminal of the recirculation control motor and connect ground to the No. 2 and No. 4 terminals; the recirculation control motor should run smoothly.

2. Disconnect ground from No. 2 or No. 4 terminal; the recirculation control motor should stop at FRESH or RECIRCULATE.

   CAUTION: Never connect the battery in the opposite direction, or damage will result to the recirculation control motor.

   NOTE: Don't cycle the recirculation control motor for a long time.

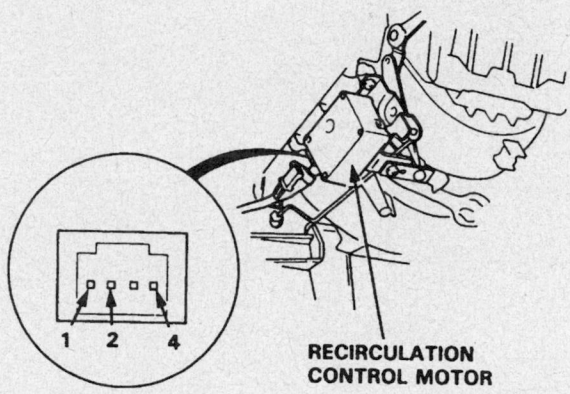

RECIRCULATION
CONTROL MOTOR

3. If the recirculation control motor does not run in step 1, remove it, and check the recirculation control linkage and doors for smooth movement. If the recirculation control linkage and doors move smoothly, replace the recirculation control motor.

Recirulation control wotor testing—1994 Legend and Legend Coupe

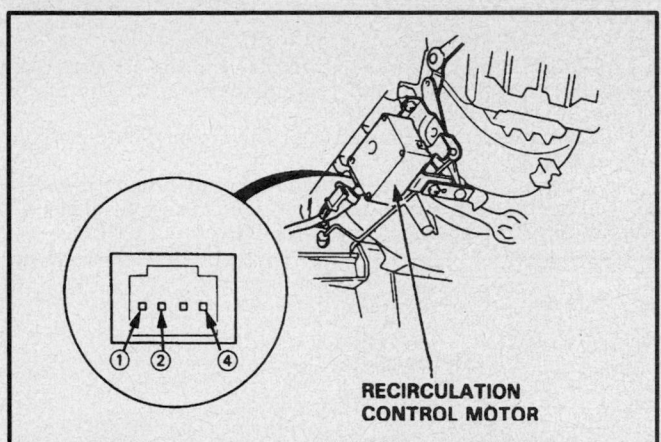

Recirculation control motor testing—1993 Legend and Legend Coupe

1994 Legend and Legend Coupe

1. Connect battery power to terminal **1** of the recirculation control motor and ground terminals **2** and **4**. The recirculation control motor should run smoothly.

2. Disconnect the ground wire from either terminal **2** or **4**. The recirculation control motor should stop at **FRESH** or **RECIRCULATE**.

3. If the recirculation motor does not run remove it and check the control linkage and doors for smooth movement. If the doors and linkage check OK, then replace the recirculation control motor.

NSX and Vigor

1. Disconnect the motor connector and connect battery voltage to terminal **1** and a ground wire to terminal **2**.

2. The motor should run. If it doesn't, reverse the connections and the motor should now run. If not, remove the motor and check the linkage and doors for binding.

3. Attach the connector and check for continuity between terminals **3** and **4** when in the **RECIRC** position and between terminals **3** and **5** when in the **FRESH** postion.

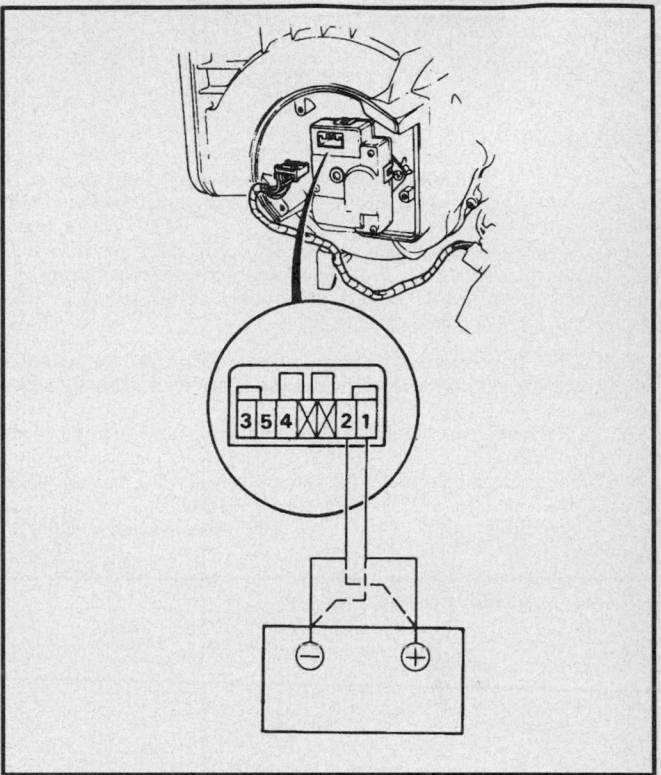

Recirculation control motor testing—NSX

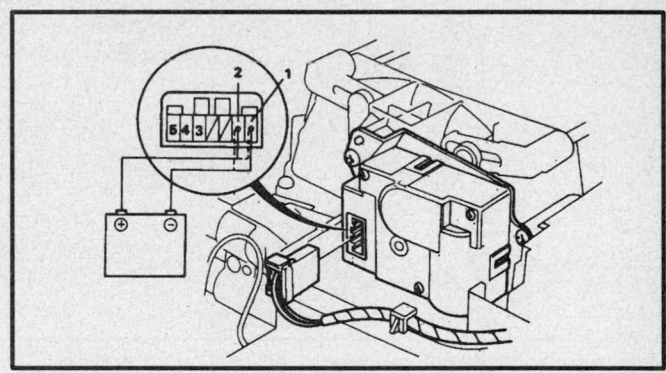

Recirculation control motor testing—Vigor

Air Mix Control Motor

TESTING

1993 Legend and Legend Coupe

1. Using a suitable ohmmeter, measure the resistance between the terminals **3** and **5**. The resistance should be about 6 kilo-ohms.

2. Check motor operation by briefly connecting positive battery power to terminal **2** of the air mix control motor and grounding terminal **1**. Reverse the connections to make sure the motor runs in both directions.

NOTE: Disconnect battery power from motor as soon as the motor starts. Failure to do so will damage the motor.

3. While repeating Step 2, measure the resistance between terminals **4** and **5**.

4. The resistance should be approximately 1.2 kilo-ohms at the **COOL** position and 4.8 kilo ohms at **HOT**.

5. Also check the resistance with the battery polarity reserved.

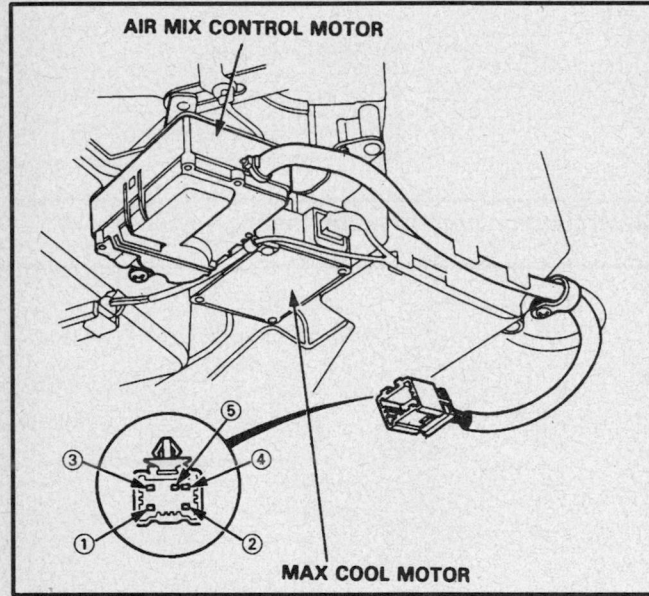

Air mix motor testing—1993 Legend and Legend Coupe

1994 Legend and Legend Coupe

1. Connect battery power to terminal **1** of the air mix control motor and ground terminal **2**. The air mix control motor should run and stop at **COOL**, If it doesn't, reverse the connections and the air mix control motor should run and stop at **HOT**.

2. Measure the resistance between terminal **3** and **5**, which should be about 6 kilo-ohms.

3. Measure the resistance between terminal **5** and **6**, which should be about 1.2 kilo-ohms at the **HOT** position and 4.8 kilo-ohms in the **COOL** position.

NSX

1. Connect battery power to terminal **1** of the air mix (temperature) control motor, and ground terminal **2**. The motor should run, then stop at **HOT**.

2. If not, reverse the connections. The motor should run and stop at **COLD**.

3. Apply 5 volts between terminals **3** and **5**, then measure the voltage between terminals **3** and **4**. It should be about 4.7 volts in the **HOT** position and about 0.3 volts in **COLD**.

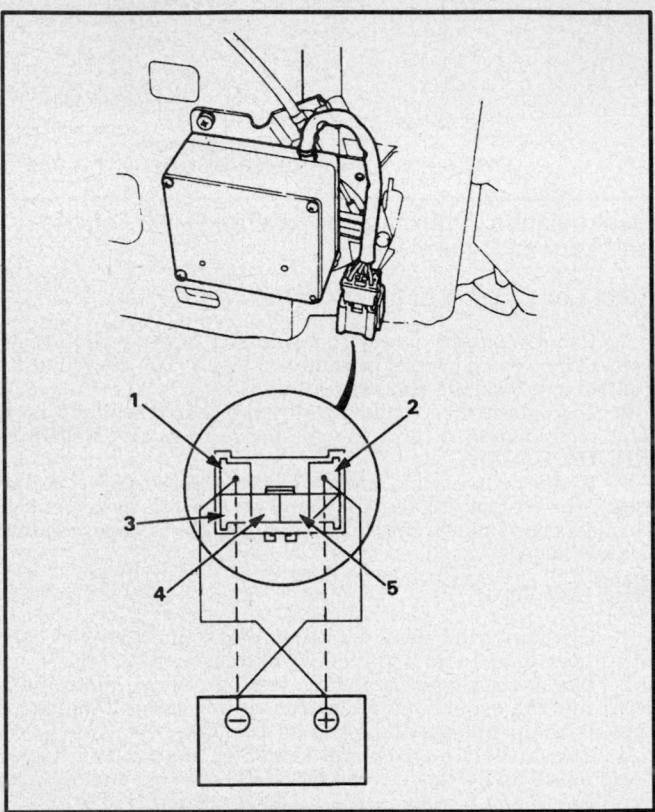

Air control motor testing—NSX

Vigor

1. Measure the resistance between terminals **3** and **5**. It should be about 10 kilo-ohms.

2. Check the motor operation by briefly applying battery voltage to terminal **2** and grounding terminal.

3. Reverse the wires to be sure the motor runs in both directions.

NOTE: Disconnect battery power from motor as soon as the motor starts. Failure to do so will damage the motor.

4. Connect battery power to terminal **2** and ground terminal **1**. Measure resistance between terminals **4** and **5**. It should be about 4.8 kilo-ohms in the **HOT** position and 1.2 kilo-ohms in the **COOL** position.

5. Check resistance with polarity reversed.

1. Connect battery power to the No. 1 terminal of the air mix control motor, and connect ground to the No. 2 terminal; the air mix control motor should run, and stop at COOL.
   If it doesn't, reverse the connections; the air mix control motor should run, and stop at HOT.

   NOTE: If the air mix control motor does not run, remove it, and check the air mix control linkage and doors for smooth movement. If the air mix control linkage and doors move smoothly, replace the air mix control motor.

2. Measure resistance between the No. 3 terminal and No. 5 terminal, it should be approx. 6 kΩ.

3. Measure resistance between the No. 5 terminal and No. 6 terminal, it should be approx. 1.2 kΩ at HOT and approx. 4.8 kΩ at COOL.

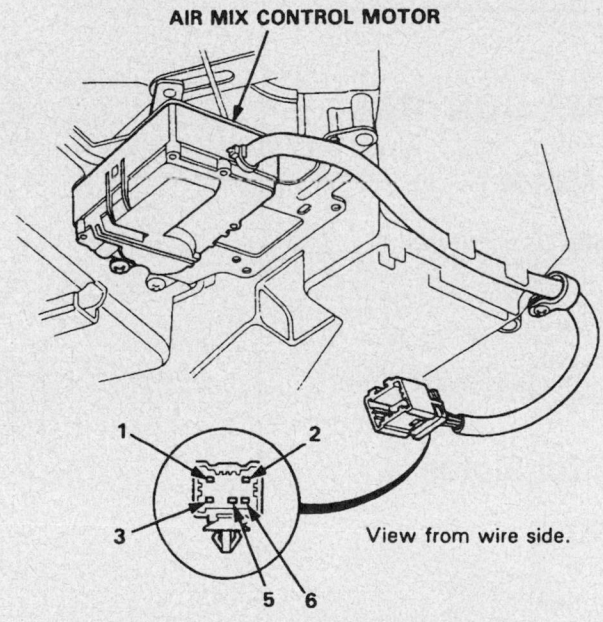

AIR MIX CONTROL MOTOR

View from wire side.

Recirulation control motor testing—1994 Legend and Legend Coupe

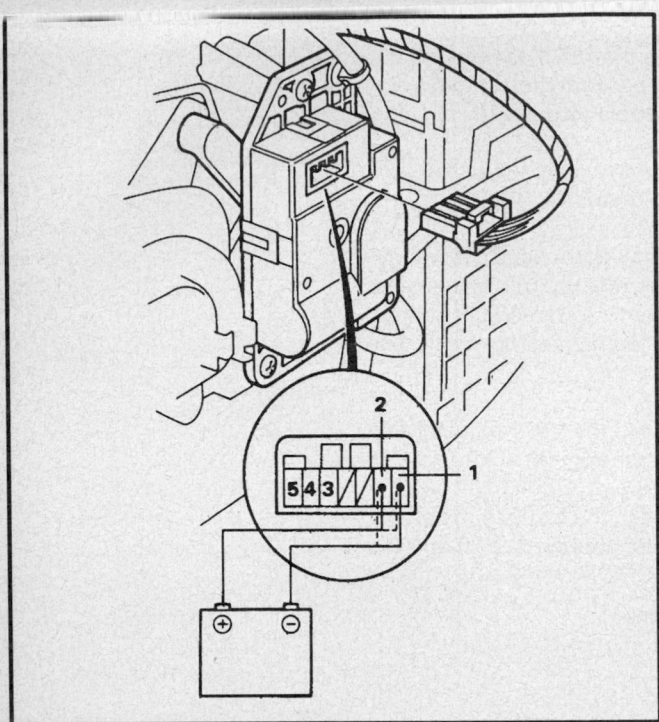

Air control motor test—Vigor

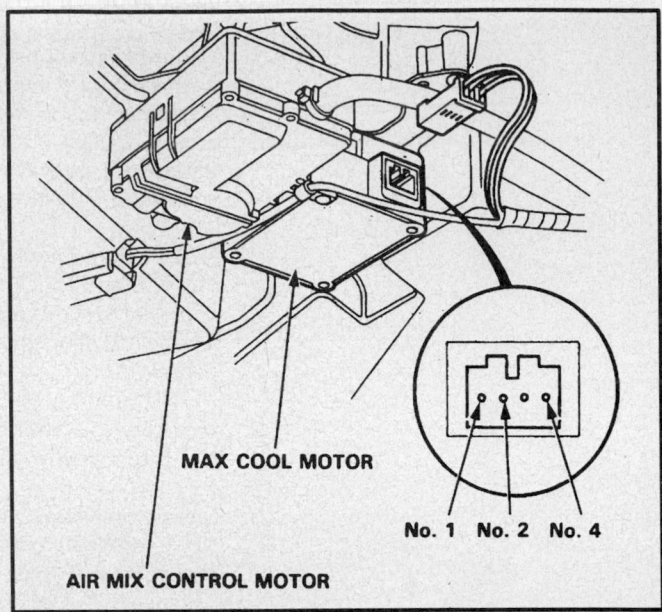

Max cool motor test—Legend and Legend Coupe with automatic climate control

AUTOMATIC CLIMATE CONTROL

MAX Cool Motor

TESTING

1993 Legend Coupe

1. Connect battery power to terminal **1** of the max cool motor and connect terminal **2** to ground.
2. The motor should run, it not, connect terminal **4**, then it should run.

Vent Door Control Motor

TESTING

NSX

1. Connect battery power to terminal **1** of the vent door control motor connector. Connect terminal **2** to ground. The motor should run and stop at **CLOSE**.
2. Measure the voltage between terminals **3** and **5** and between terminals **4** and **5**. At **OPEN** it should be about 4.7 volts. At **CLOSE** it should be about 0.3 volt.

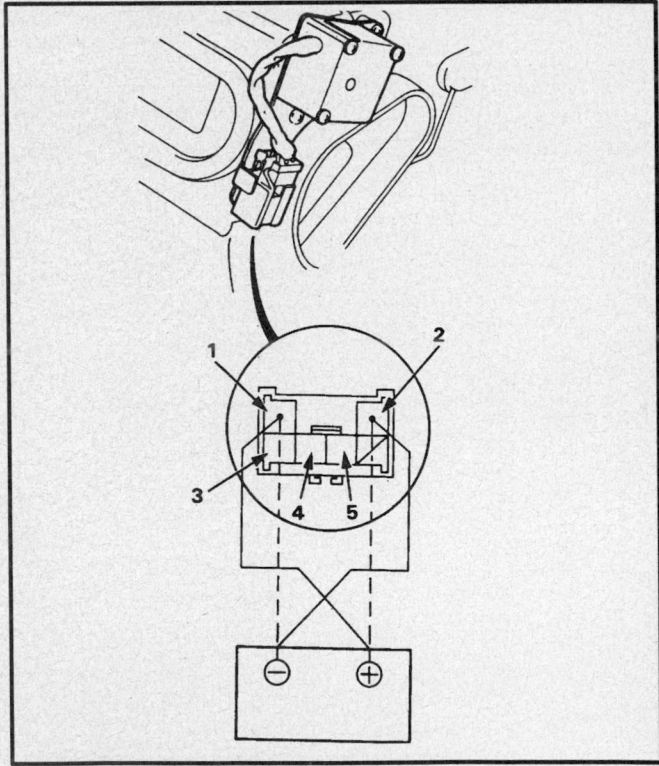

Vent door motor test—NSX

Heater Temperature Sensor

TESTING

Legend Coupe and NSX

The sensor is mounted on a clip near the air mix door motor. Using a digital multi-meter in the "20 kilo-ohm" range, compare the resistance reading between the terminals of the coolant temperature sensor at the temperatures shown. If not within specifications, replace the sensor.

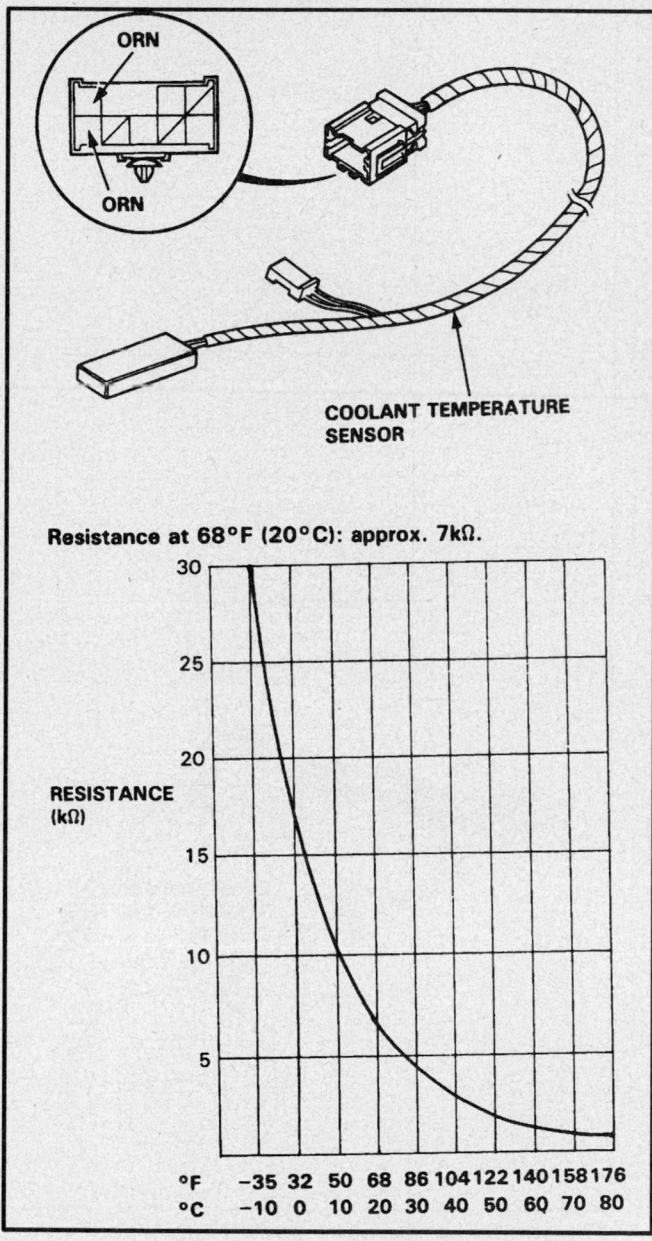

Resistance at 68°F (20°C): approx. 7kΩ.

Temperature sensor test—Legend and Legend coupe with automatic climate control

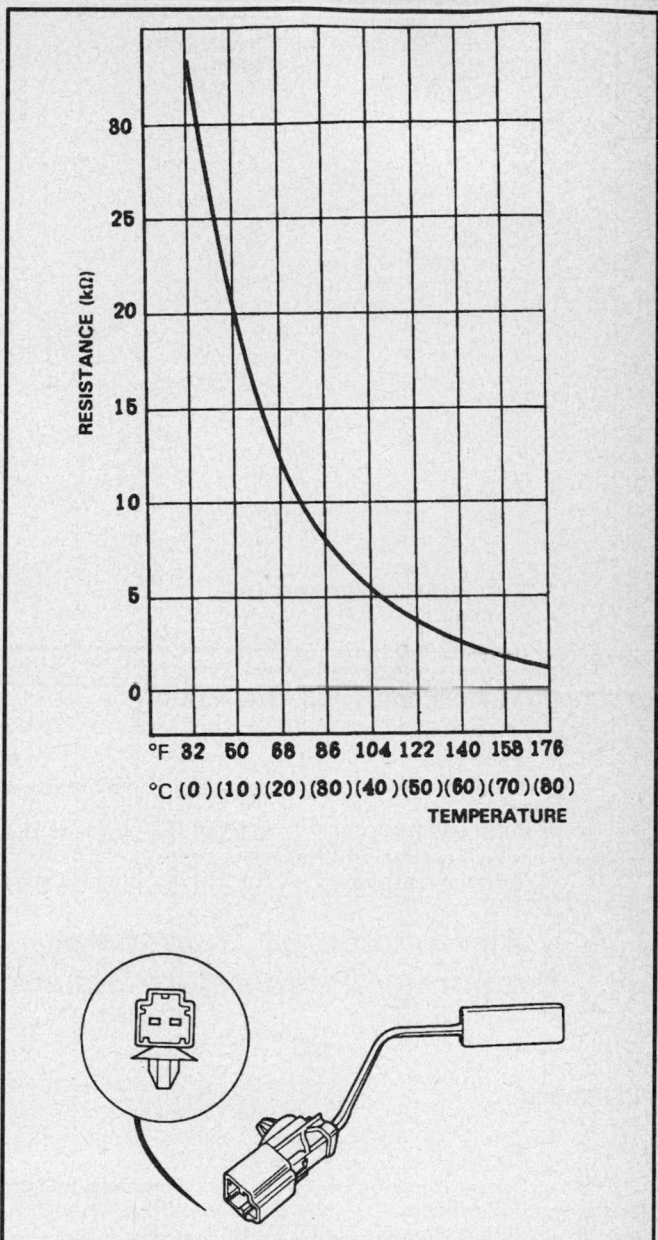

Temperature sensor test—NSX

REMOVAL AND INSTALLATION

Legend Coupe

1. Remove the glove box lower panel.
2. Disconnect the 8–pin connector of the max cool motor.
3. Remove the screw from the harness clamp, then pull the retaining clip out of the slot and remove the sensor.
4. Installation is the reverse of the removal.

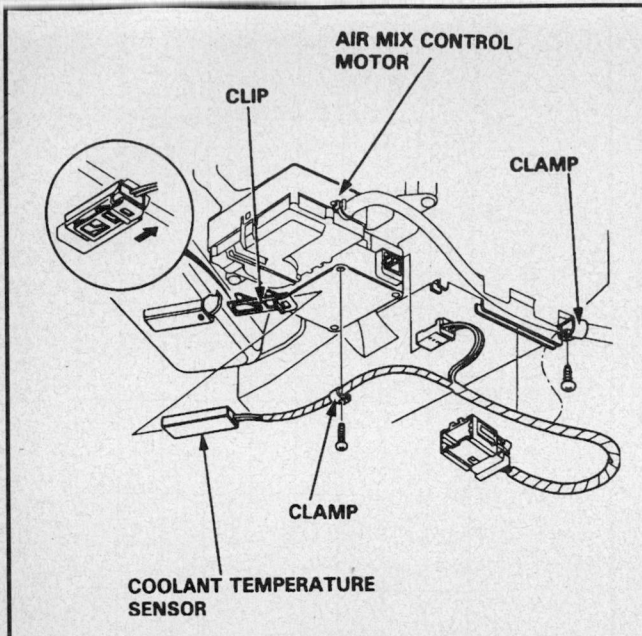

Temperature sensor removal—Legend and Legend Coupe with automatic climate control

NSX

1. Disconnect the connector from the coolant temperature sensor.
2. Remove the retaining clip holding the sensor to the side of the heater housing, and remove the sensor.
3. Installation is the reverse of the removal procedure.

Air Conditioner Thermostat/ Evaporator Temperature Sensor

TESTING

Integra

1. Attach a 12V, 3W to 18W bulb to terminals **A** and **C** while applying 12 volts to terminals **B** and **C**.
2. Check for continuity between the terminals while dipping the thermostat capillary tube into a pan filled with ice water.
3. The light should turn OFF below 37°F.
4. The light should turn ON above 39°F.
5. The cut off and cut in of the thermostat must not be gradual but sudden.
6. If the thermostat fails any part of this test, replace it with a new one.

Legend, Legend Coupe and NSX

Compare the resistance readings between the sensor terminals according to the temperature range shown on the chart. If sensor is not within the specifications, replace the sensor.

NOTE: The sensor uses a thermistor which can be damaged if high current is applied. Therefore, use only a circuit tester with an output of 1 mA or less at the 20 kilo-ohm range.

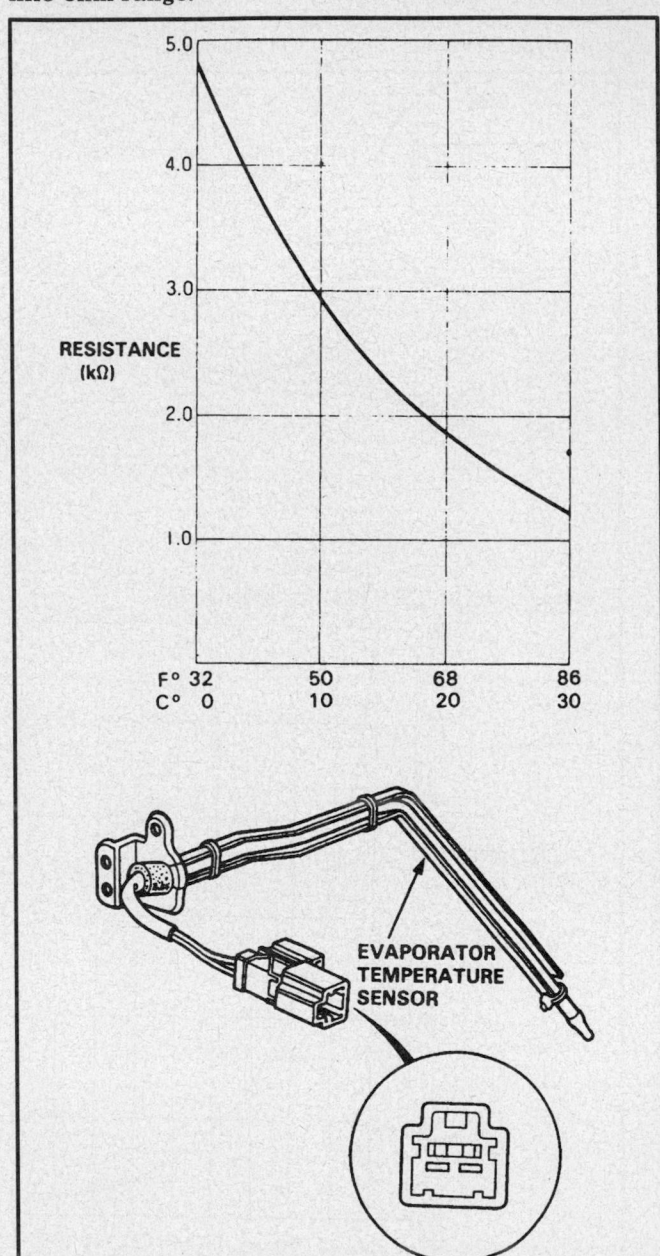

Evaporator temperature sensor test—Legend and Legend Coupe

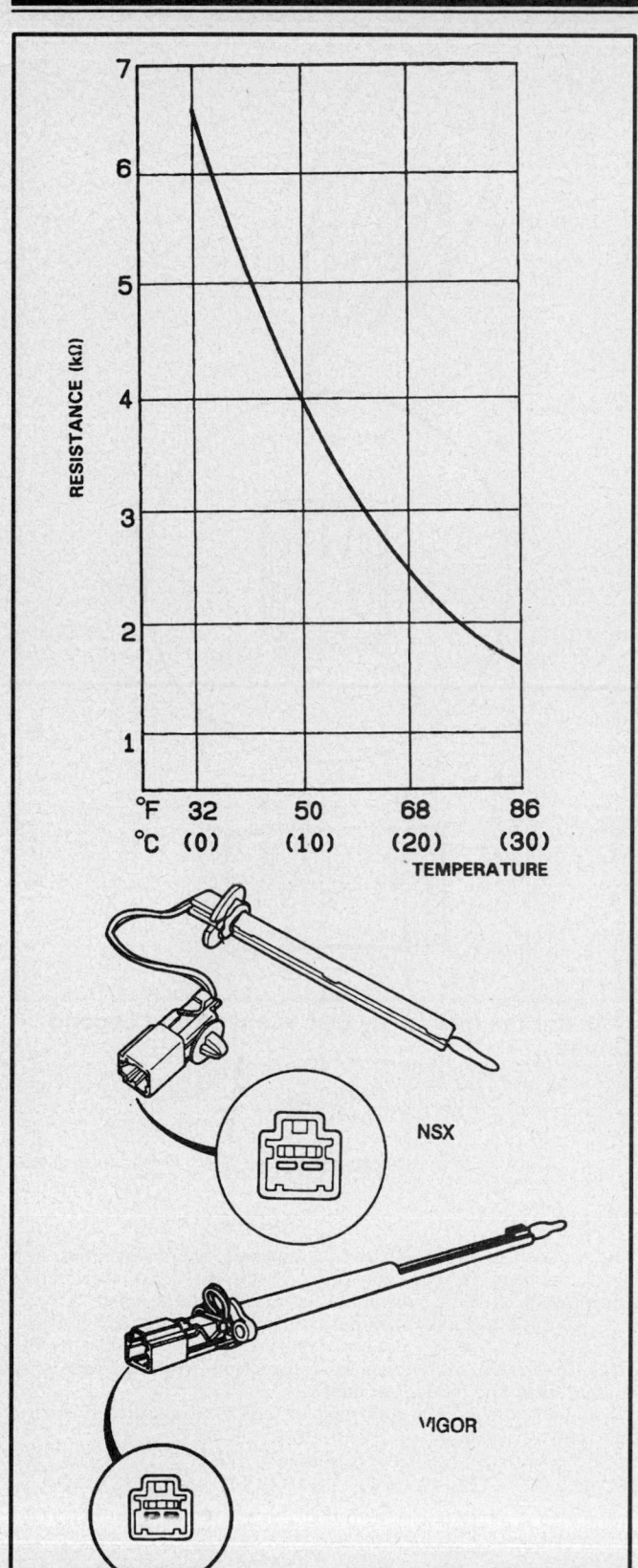

Evaporator temperature sensor test—NSX and Vigor

IN–CAR TEMPERATURE SENSOR

1994 Legend and Legend Coupe

Compare the resistance reading between terminals **1** and **2** of the in car temperature sensor with the specifications shown in the graph. Replace the sensor if it is not within specifications

NOTE: The sensor uses a thermisitor which can be damaged if high current is applied to it during the testing process. Make sure to use an ohmmeter that puts out less than 1 mA of current. (At the 20 kilo-ohm range).

Air Conditioning Relays

TESTING

All the air conditioning relays are similar and should be tested in the same way as follows:

1. Using a suitable ohmmeter, check for continuity between the contact terminals when battery voltage is applied to the coil terminals.
2. There should be no continuity across the contact point terminals when the battery is disconnected.
3. In the case of a 2 position relay, the contacts may or may not have continuity when the field is not energized.
4. If the relay fails any part of this test, replace it with a new one.

Radiator Fan Main Relay

TESTING

1. Using a suitable ohmmeter, check for continuity between terminals **A** and **C** when battery voltage is applied to terminals **D** and **E**.
2. Continuity should exist between terminals **B** and **C** when no battery voltage is applied.
3. There should be no continuity when the battery is disconnected.
4. If the relay fails any part of this test, replace it with a new one.

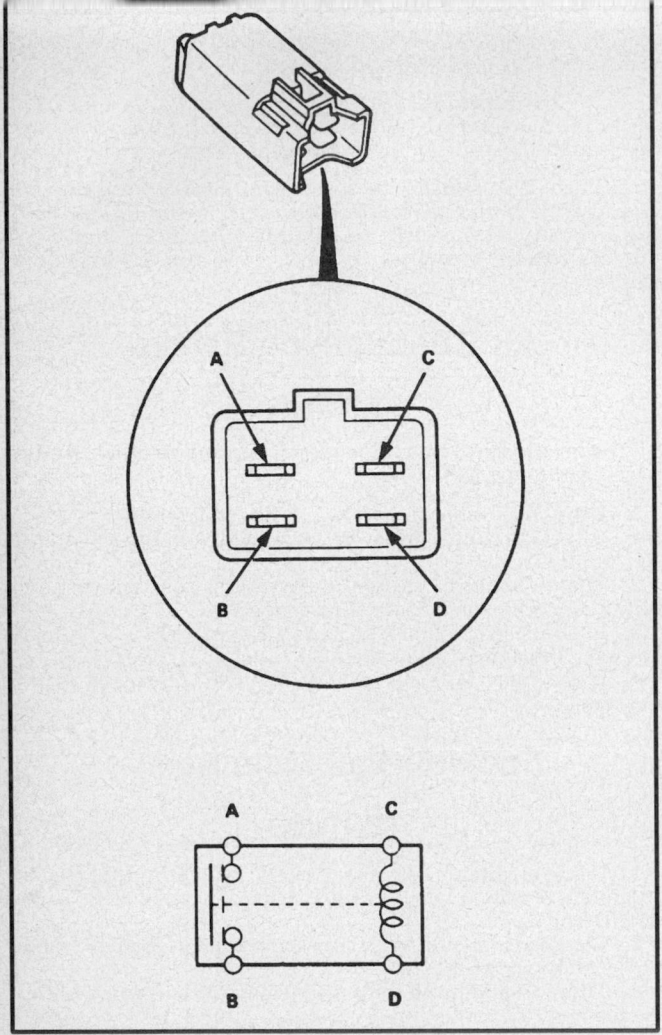

Blower, condenser and radiator fan relay test

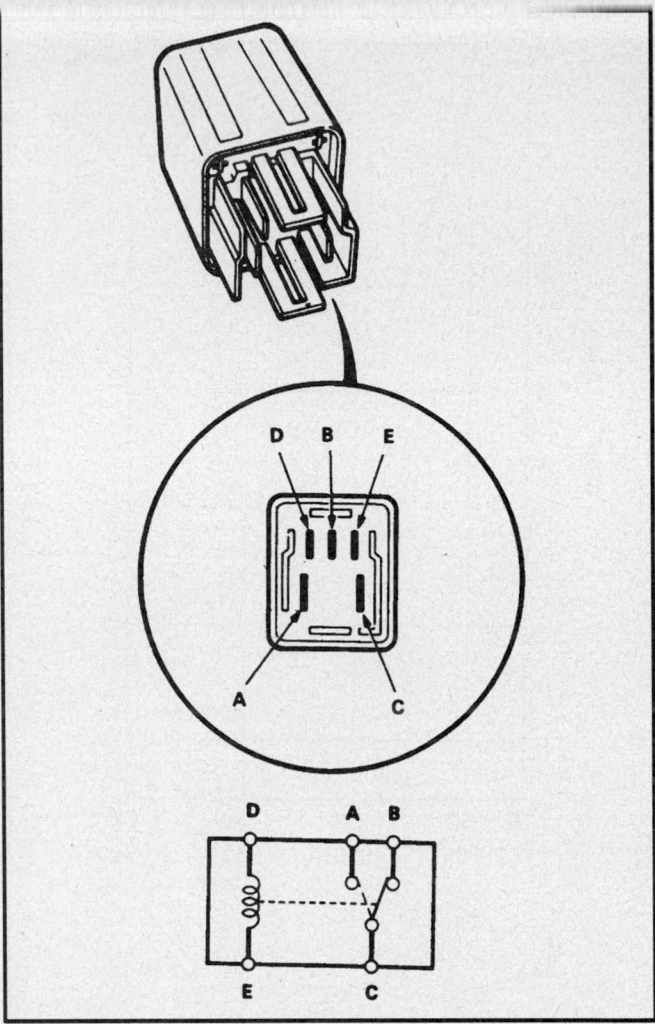

Radiator fan main relay test—Legend and Legend Coupe

Condenser Fan Relay, Compressor Clutch Relay and Radiator Fan Relay

TESTING

1. When battery power is applied to terminals **B** and **D**, there should be continuity between terminals **A** and **C**. When battery power is disconnected, there should be no continuity between terminals **A** and **C**.

2. When battery power is connected to terminals **C** and **D**, there should be continuity between terminals **A** and **B**.

3. When battery power is disconnected, there should be no continuity between terminals **A** and **B**.

Diode

TESTING

Integra

The diodes are designed to pass current in one direction and block current in the opposite direction. Only ohmmeters equipped with their own diode testers should be used.

1. Using a suitable ohmmeter, check the diodes for continuity.

2. Check for continuity in 1 direction from terminals as indicated in the diode test chart.

3. If the diode fails any part of this test, replace it with a new one.

There should be continuity between the A and C terminals when power and ground are connected to the B and D terminals.

There should be no continuity when power is disconnected.

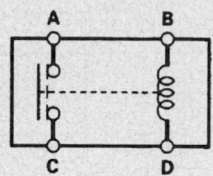

• Radiator fan relay

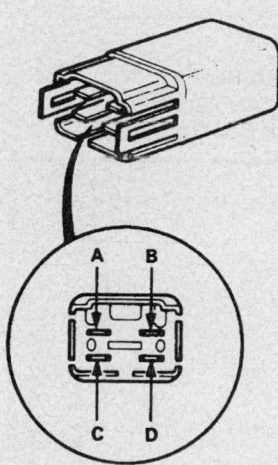

• Condenser fan relay
• Compressor clutch relay

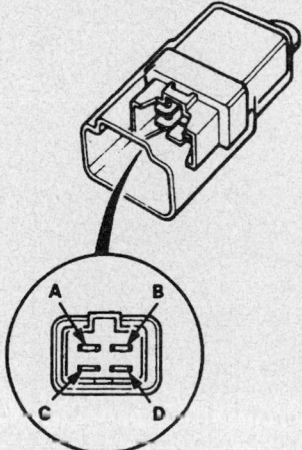

Relay testing—Integra

There should be continuity between the A and B terminals when power and ground are connected to the C and D terminals.
There should be no continuity when power is disconnected.

Power (C-D) \ Terminal	A	B
Connected	○—○	
Disconnected		

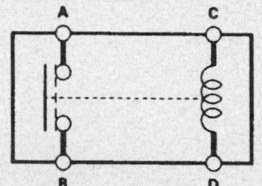

- **RADIATOR FAN RELAY**
- **CONDENSER FAN RELAY**
- **COMPRESSOR CLUTCH RELAY**

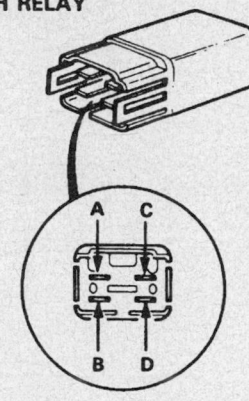

- **BLOWER MOTOR RELAY**
- **BLOWER MOTOR HIGH RELAY**

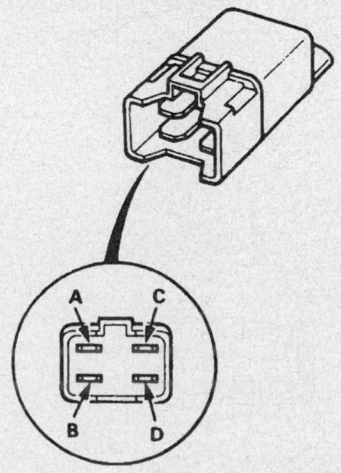

Relay testing—Legend and Legend Coupe

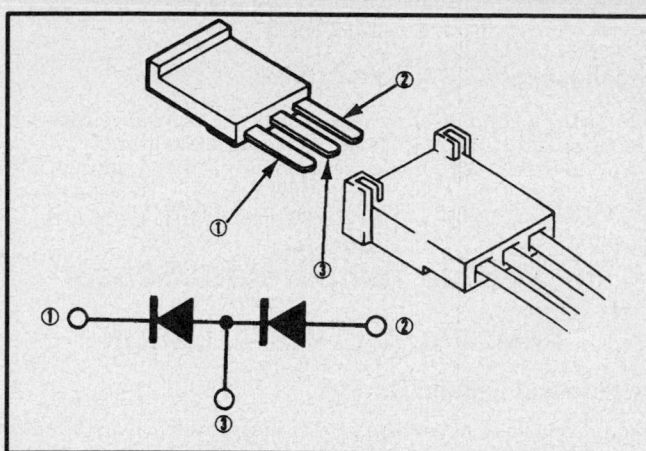

Diode test—Integra

Air Conditioning Switch

TESTING

1993 Integra

1. Test for continuity between the terminals according the table given.
2. If switch fails any part of this test, replace it.

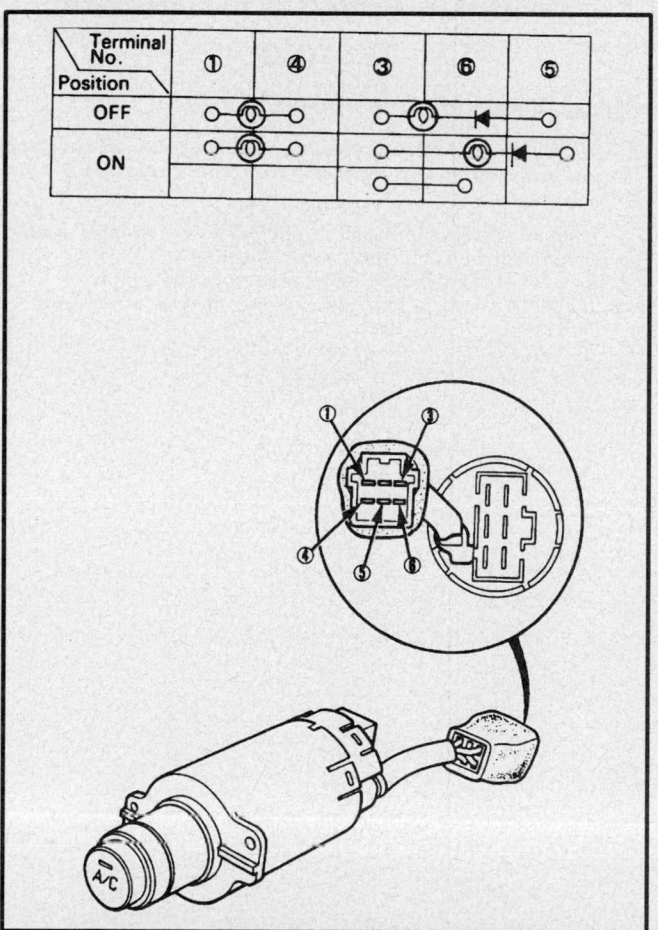

Air conditioning switch test—1993 Integra

Ambient Temperature Sensor

All the sensors used with automatic climate control systems, use a thermistor which can be damaged if a high current is applied to the sensor during testing. Therefore, use a circuit tester with measuring current of 1 mill–amp or less.

REMOVAL AND INSTALLATION

Legend, Legend Coupe and NSX

1. Disconnect the negative battery cable.
2. Remove the screw retaining the sensor to the vehicle and disconnect the wire harness.
3. Be careful not to damage the grill or front bumper during the removal or installation process.
4. Installation is the reverse of removal.

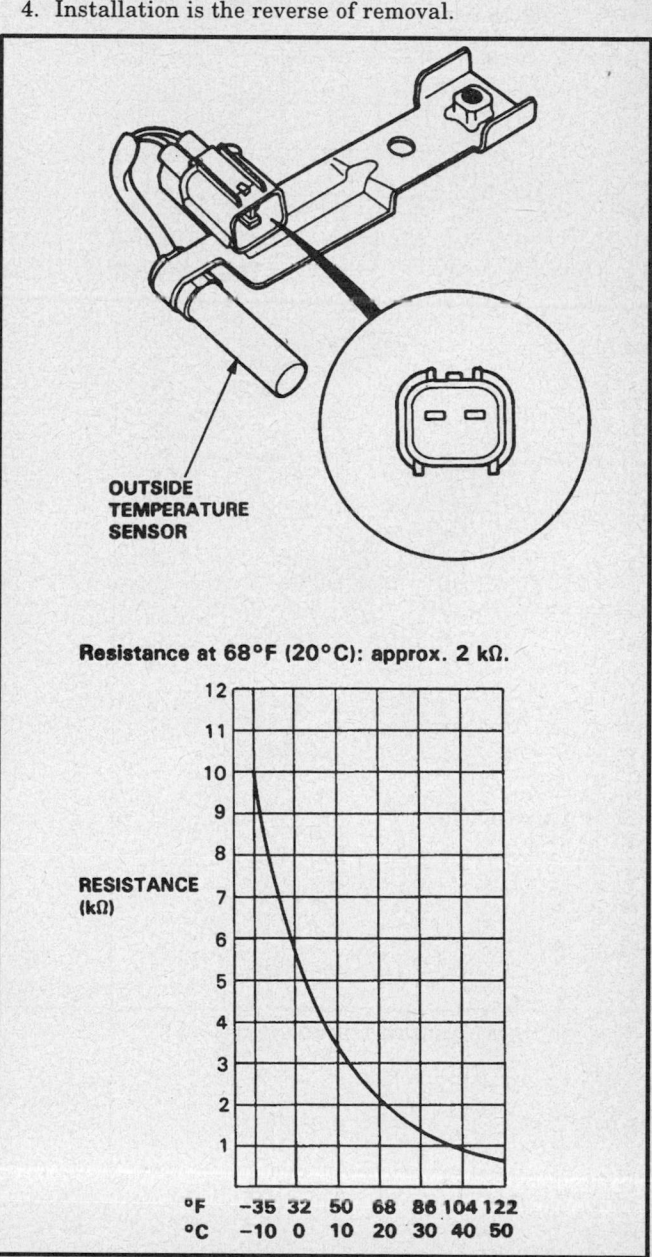

Ambient temperature sensor test—Legend and Legend Coupe

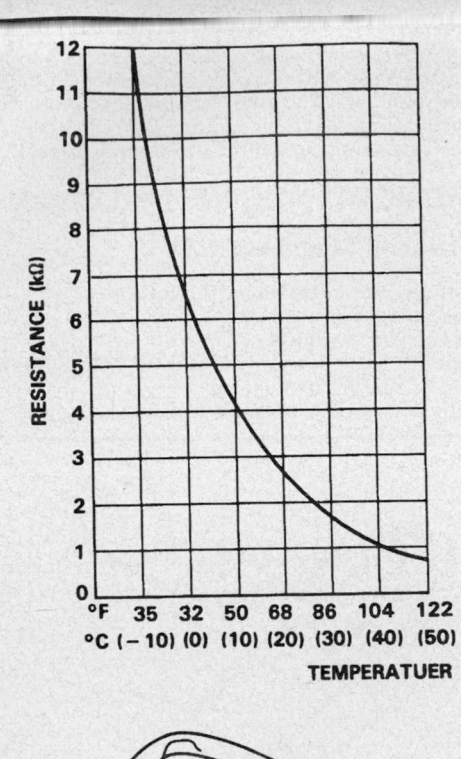

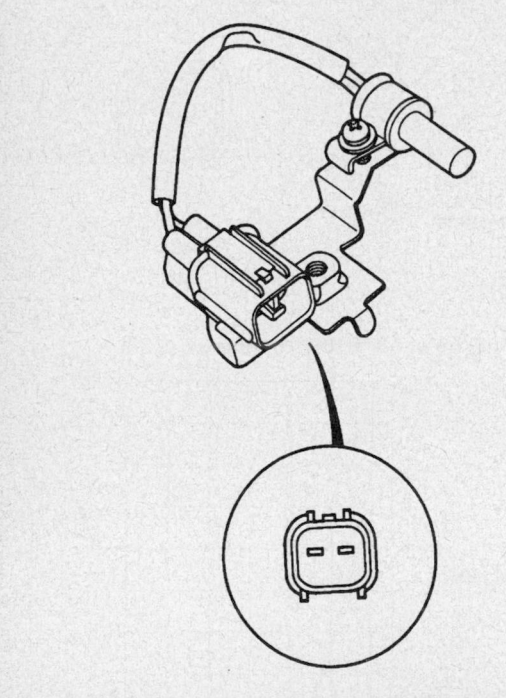

Ambient temperature sensor test—NSX

TESTING

Legend, Legend Coupe and NSX

1. Using a suitable ohmmeter, check the resistance between the terminals of the outside air temperature sensor.
2. The resistance should be as shown on the appropriate chart.
3. If the sensor fails this test, replace it with a new one.

In–Vehicle Temperature Sensor

REMOVAL AND INSTALLATION

Legend and Legend Coupe

The in–vehicle temperature sensor incorporates a small fan to draw in air past the sensor.
1. Disconnect the negative battery cable.
2. Remove the climate control unit (electronic control head).
3. Remove the front panel of the control unit, detach the sensor connector, remove the air intake tube, and release the holder claws to free the sensor.
4. Installation is the reverse of removal.

NSX

1. Remove the center console panel.
2. Remove 2 screws and remove the in–car sensor from under the side of console panel.
3. Installation is the reverse of the removal procedure.

TESTING

Legend, Legend Coupe and NSX

NOTE: It is not necessary, on Legend of Legend Coupe, to remove the sensor from the control unit for testing.

1. Using a suitable ohmmeter, check the resistance between the terminals **1** and **2** of the in–car sensor.
2. The resistance should be as shown in the graph.
3. If the sensor fails this test, replace it with a new one.

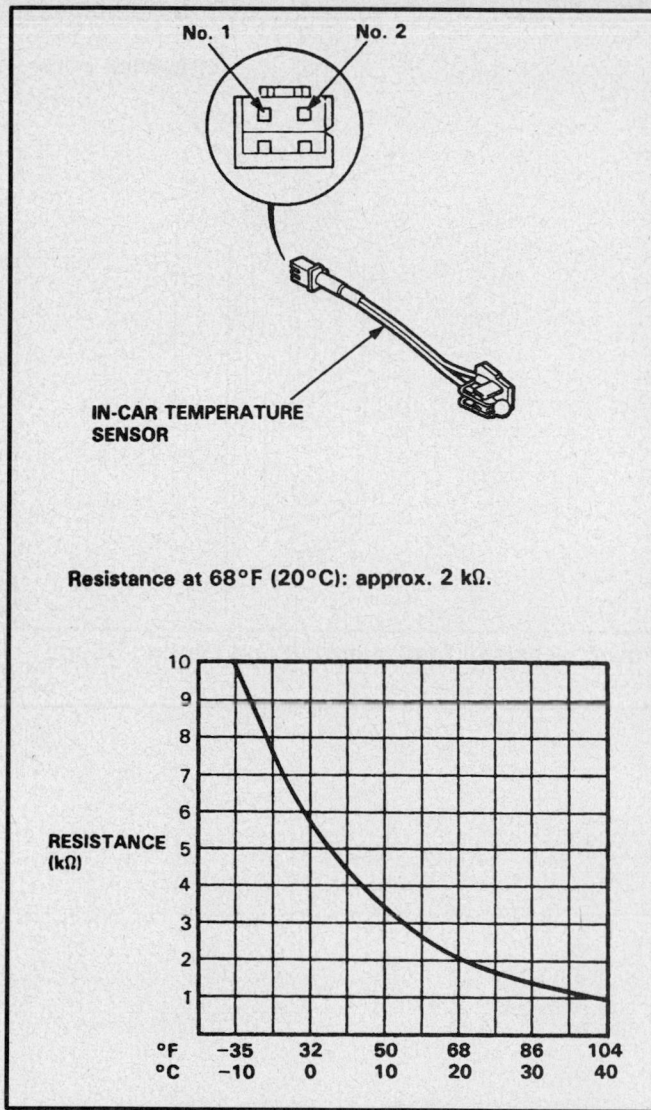

In car sensor test—Legend and Legend Coupe

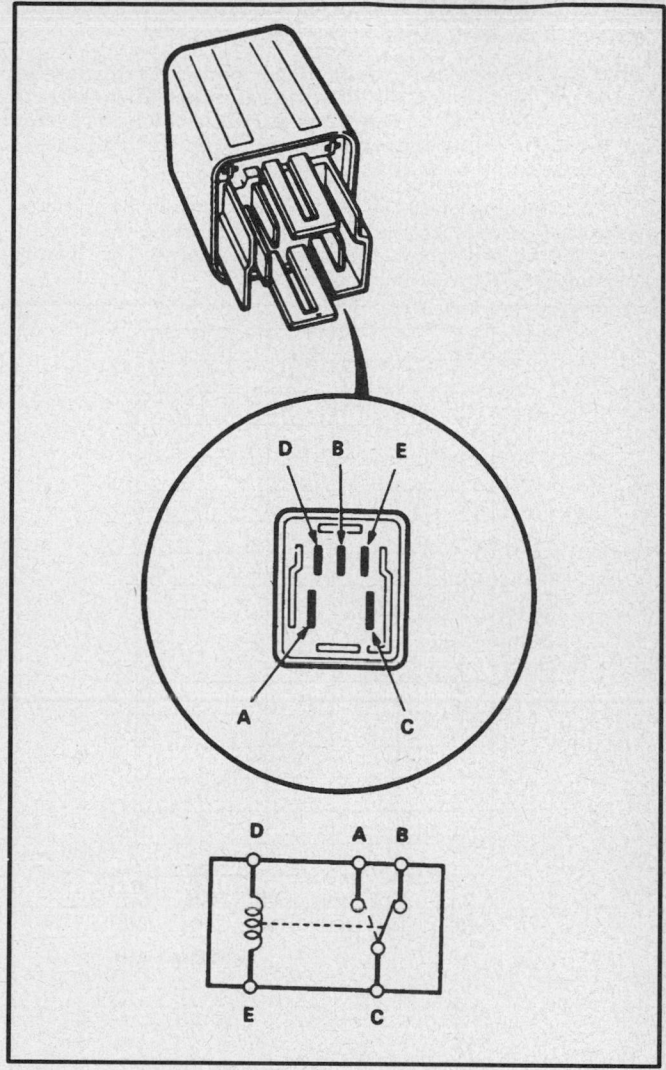

Radiator fan main relay test—Legend and Legend Coupe

2. It should be about 1.4 volts on Legend Coupe and about 0.1–0.2 volt on NSX.

3. If not within specifications, replace the sensor.

Sunlight Sensor

REMOVAL AND INSTALLATION

Legend, Legend Coupe and NSX

1. Disconnect the negative battery cable.
2. With a small prybar and protecting the dashboard, carefully pry the sensor out of the dashboard.
3. Disconnect the wire harness and remove the sensor.
4. Installation is the reverse of removal.

TESTING

Legend, Legend Coupe and NSX

1. Using an appropriate voltmeter, measure the voltage between the terminals at the sensor.

Power Transistor

TESTING

Legend and Legend Coupe

NOTE: The power transistor cannot be tested with ordinary circuit testers. If the blower does not operate properly and testing of the power transistor is needed, use only the following test for this purpose.

1. Check the blower motor and its wire harness, replace or repair, as necessary.
2. Disconnect the wire harness from the power transistor. Pull out the light green wire with the black tracer from the

connector and connect a bulb with a 1.2-3.4 watt rating. Reconnect the wire harness to the transistor.

NOTE: To avoid a loose or disconnected terminal, be careful not to damage the locking tab when disconnecting and connecting the terminal. Insulate the light green wire with the black tracer from the body until the testing is completed.

3. Turn the ignition to the **ON** position. If the blower motor now operates, the controller is faulty and must be replaced.

4. If the blower motor still does not operate, the power transistor is faulty and must be replaced.

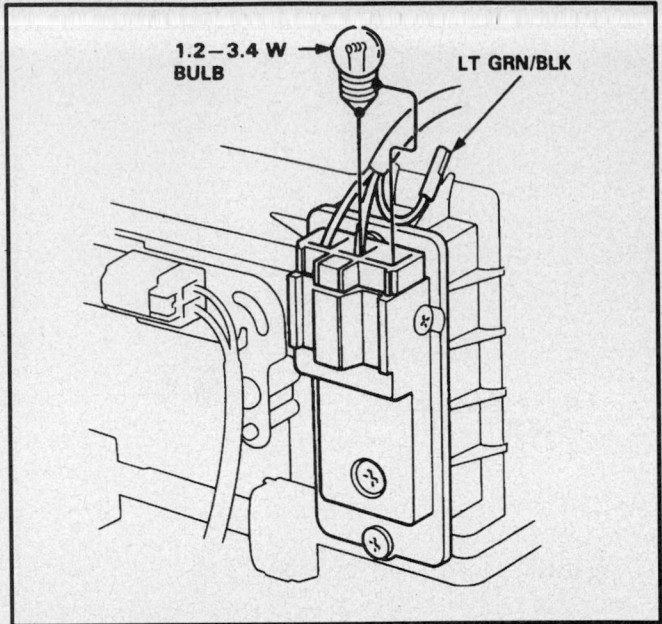

Power transistor test—Legend and Legend Coupe

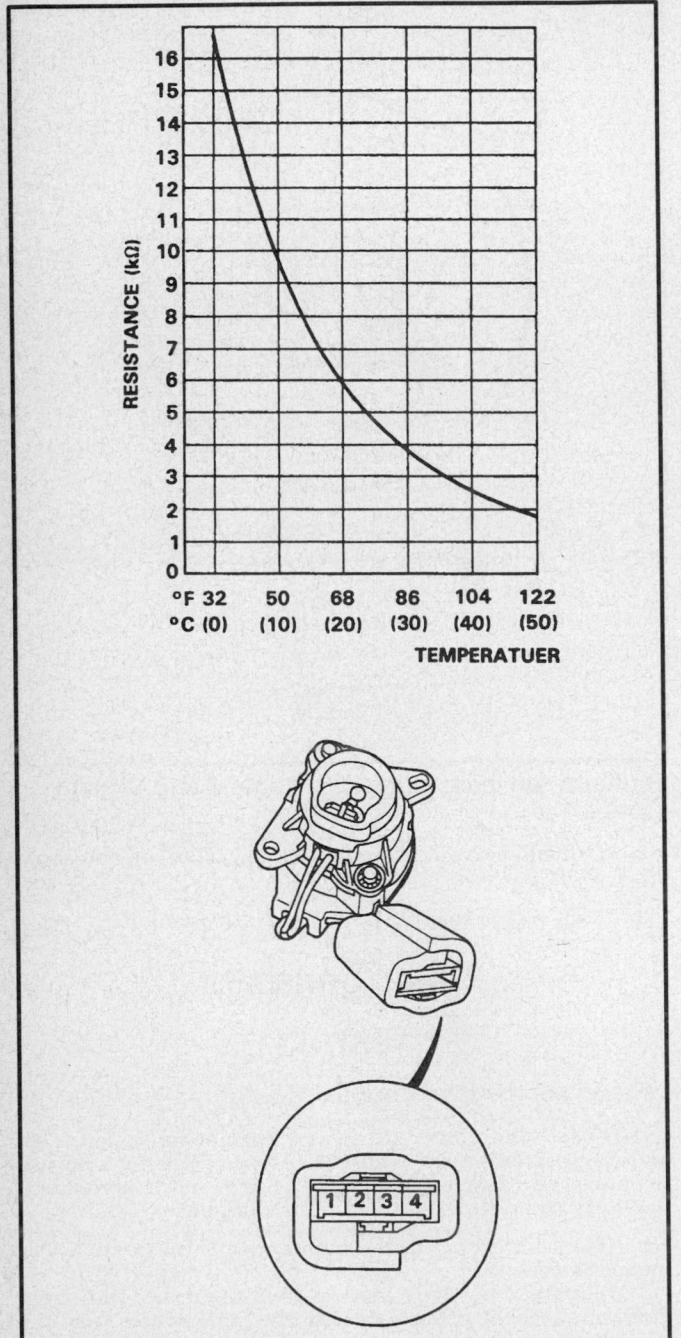

In car sensor test—NSX

The Automatic Climate Control System has a built-in self diagnosis feature. To run it, turn the ignition switch ON and turn the fan switch to the AUTO position. Set the temperature dial to 60°F (18°C), then gradually move the dial up the temperature range to 90°F (32°C). At each temperature setting, push both the AUTO and OFF buttons on the control unit at the same time. Wait for at least one minute for the system to readjust and check for problems. If any problems are found in circuits "A" through "I", the system will indicate which circuit has the problem by lighting the respective indicator light.

NOTE: The climate control unit does not memorize which self-diagnosis indicator lights come on. If you turn the ignition switch OFF, the indicator light memory will be lost.

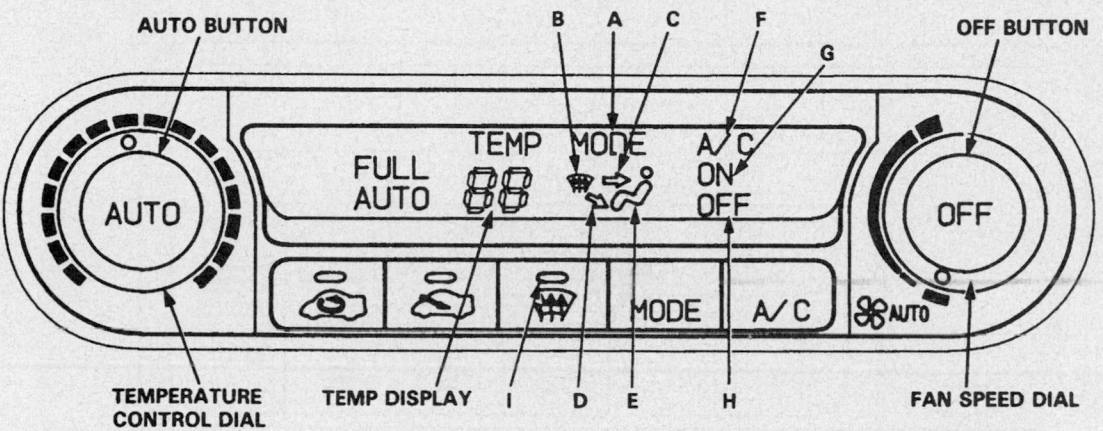

	INDICATOR	COMPONENT WITH PROBLEM	POSSIBLE CAUSE
A	MODE	IN-CAR TEMPERATURE SENSOR	Open or short circuit
B	⟨symbol⟩	OUTSIDE AIR TEMPERATURE SENSOR	Open or short circuit
C	⟨symbol⟩	SUNLIGHT SENSOR	Open or short circuit
D	⟨symbol⟩	HEATER CORE TEMPERATURE SENSOR	Open or short circuit
E	⟨symbol⟩	EVAPORATOR TEMPERATURE SENSOR	Open or short circuit
F	A/C	AIR MIX CONTROL MOTOR	Open or short circuit Air mix door stuck
G	ON (A/C)	MODE CONTROL MOTOR	Open position signal circuit Mode door stuck
H	OFF (A/C)	RECIRCULATION CONTROL MOTOR	Open position signal circuit
I	LED on defroster button	VENT DOOR CONTROL MOTOR	Open or short circuit Vent door stuck

NOTE:
● When you turn the ignition switch OFF, the self-diagnosis function will be canceled.
● After completing repair work, run once again the self-diagnosis to make sure that there are no other malfunctions.

Automatic climate control self—diagnostic test indicators—Legend and Legend Coupe

The Automatic Climate Control System has a built-in self diagnosis feature. To run it, turn the ignition switch ON. Set the temperature dial to 60°F (18°C), then gradually move the dial up the temperature range to 90°F (32°C). At each temperature setting, push both the AUTO and OFF buttons on the control unit at the same time. Wait for at least one minute for the system to readjust and check for problems. If any problems are found in circuits ''A'' through ''G'', the system will indicate which circuit has the problem by lighting the respective indicator light.

NOTE: The climate control unit does not memorize which self-diagnosis indicator lights come on. If you turn the ignition switch OFF, the indicator light memory will be lost.

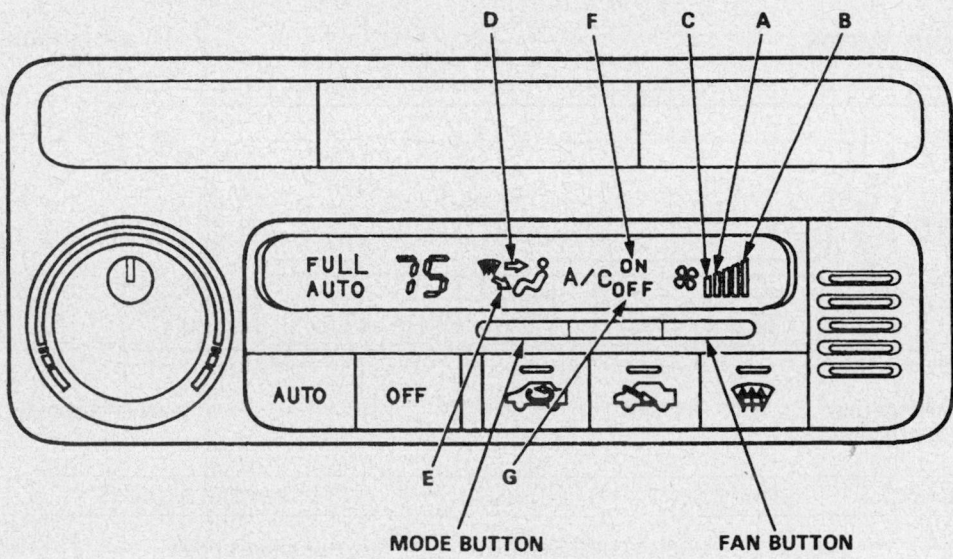

	INDICATOR	COMPONENT WITH PROBLEM	POSSIBLE CAUSE
A		IN-CAR TEMPERATURE SENSOR	Open or short circuit
B		OUTSIDE AIR TEMPERATURE SENSOR	Open or short circuit
C		SUNLIGHT SENSOR	Open or short circuit
D		HEATER CORE TEMPERATURE SENSOR	Open or short circuit
E		EVAPORATOR TEMPERATURE SENSOR	Open or short circuit
F	A/C ON	AIR MIX CONTROL MOTOR	Short GND or 5 V circuit
G	A/C OFF	MODE CONTROL MOTOR	Short GND or 5 V circuit

* The in-car temperature sensor is built into the climate control unit. If this indicator lights, replace the climate control unit.

NOTE:
● When you turn the ignition switch OFF, the self-diagnosis function will be canceled.
● After completing repair work, run once again the self-diagnosis to make sure that there are no other malfunctions.

Automatic climate control self–diagnostic test indicators—NSX

SYSTEM DIAGNOSIS

SELF−DIAGNOSTIC TEST

Legend, Legend Coupe and NSX

1. Turn ignition to **ON** and the fan setting to **AUTO**. Wait at least 1 minute on each temperature display.

2. Push **AUTO** and **OFF** button simultaneously. Any problems in the circuits will be shown by the appropriate indicator coming **ON**

3. There is no storage function in this system. If you turn the ignition switch **OFF,** the indicator light memory will be lost.

DIAGNOSTIC CHARTS

HEATER BLOWER DIAGNOSTIC CHART—1993 INTEGRA

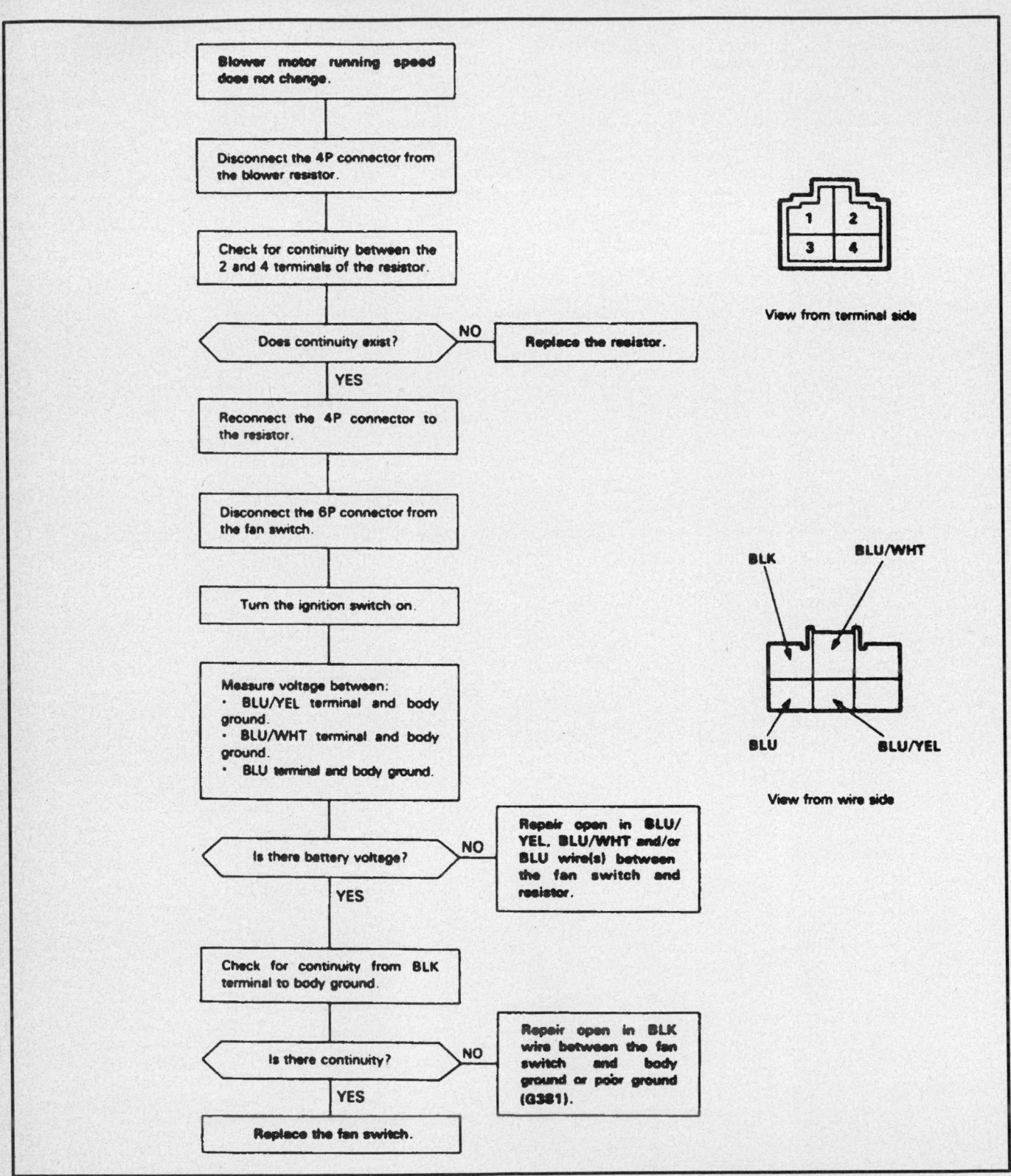

Blower motor running speed does not change.

Disconnect the 4P connector from the blower resistor.

Check for continuity between the 2 and 4 terminals of the resistor.

Does continuity exist? — **NO** → Replace the resistor.

YES

Reconnect the 4P connector to the resistor.

Disconnect the 6P connector from the fan switch.

Turn the ignition switch on.

Measure voltage between:
· BLU/YEL terminal and body ground.
· BLU/WHT terminal and body ground.
· BLU terminal and body ground.

Is there battery voltage? — **NO** → Repair open in BLU/YEL, BLU/WHT and/or BLU wire(s) between the fan switch and resistor.

YES

Check for continuity from BLK terminal to body ground.

Is there continuity? — **NO** → Repair open in BLK wire between the fan switch and body ground or poor ground (G381).

YES

Replace the fan switch.

View from terminal side

BLK   BLU/WHT

BLU   BLU/YEL

View from wire side

HEATER BLOWER DIAGNOSTIC CHART–1993 INTEGRA– CONTINUED

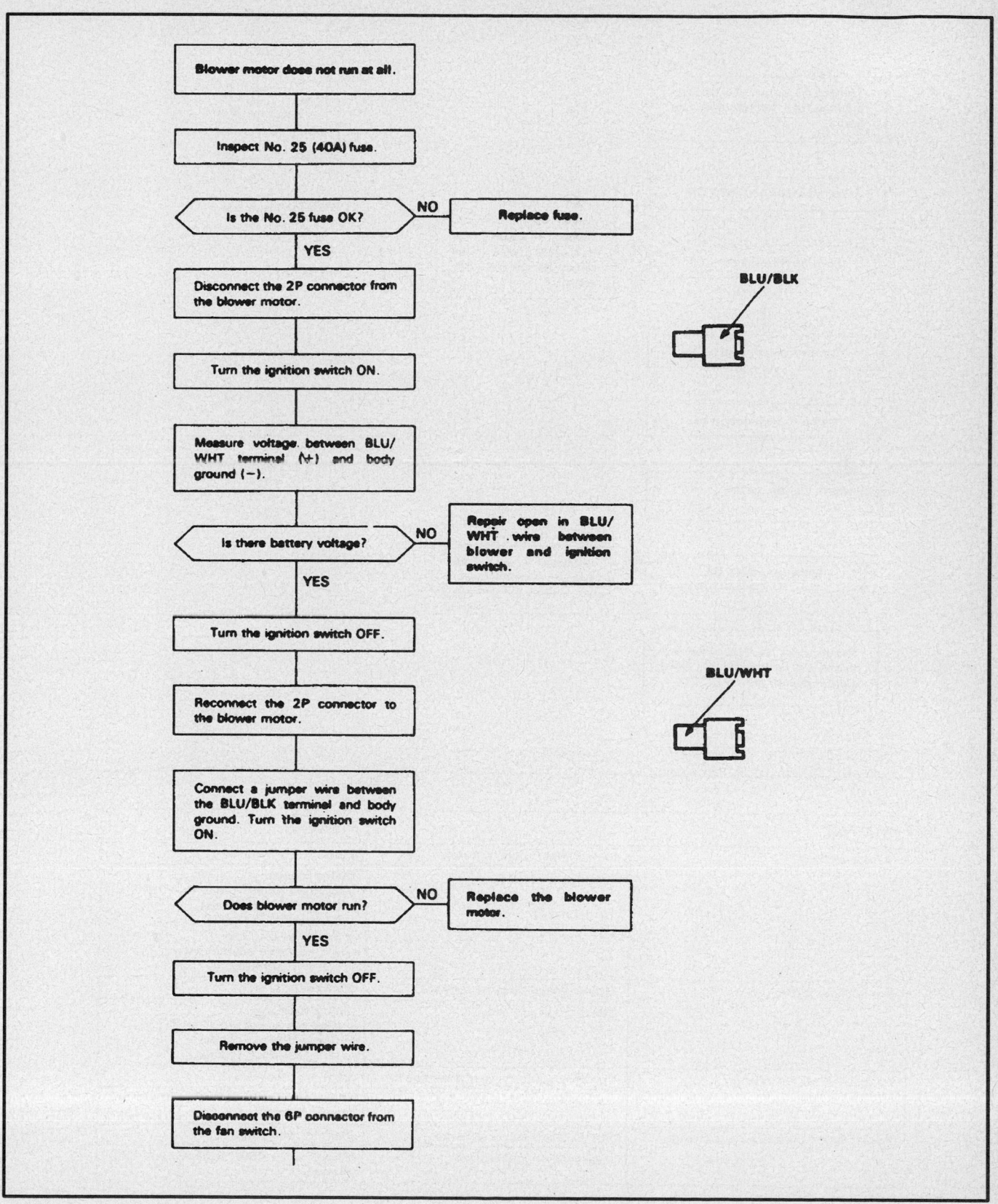

Blower motor does not run at all.

Inspect No. 25 (40A) fuse.

Is the No. 25 fuse OK? —NO→ Replace fuse.

YES

Disconnect the 2P connector from the blower motor.

BLU/BLK

Turn the ignition switch ON.

Measure voltage between BLU/WHT terminal (+) and body ground (−).

Is there battery voltage? —NO→ Repair open in BLU/WHT wire between blower and ignition switch.

YES

Turn the ignition switch OFF.

BLU/WHT

Reconnect the 2P connector to the blower motor.

Connect a jumper wire between the BLU/BLK terminal and body ground. Turn the ignition switch ON.

Does blower motor run? —NO→ Replace the blower motor.

YES

Turn the ignition switch OFF.

Remove the jumper wire.

Disconnect the 6P connector from the fan switch.

HEATER BLOWER DIAGNOSTIC CHART–1993 INTEGRA– CONTINUED

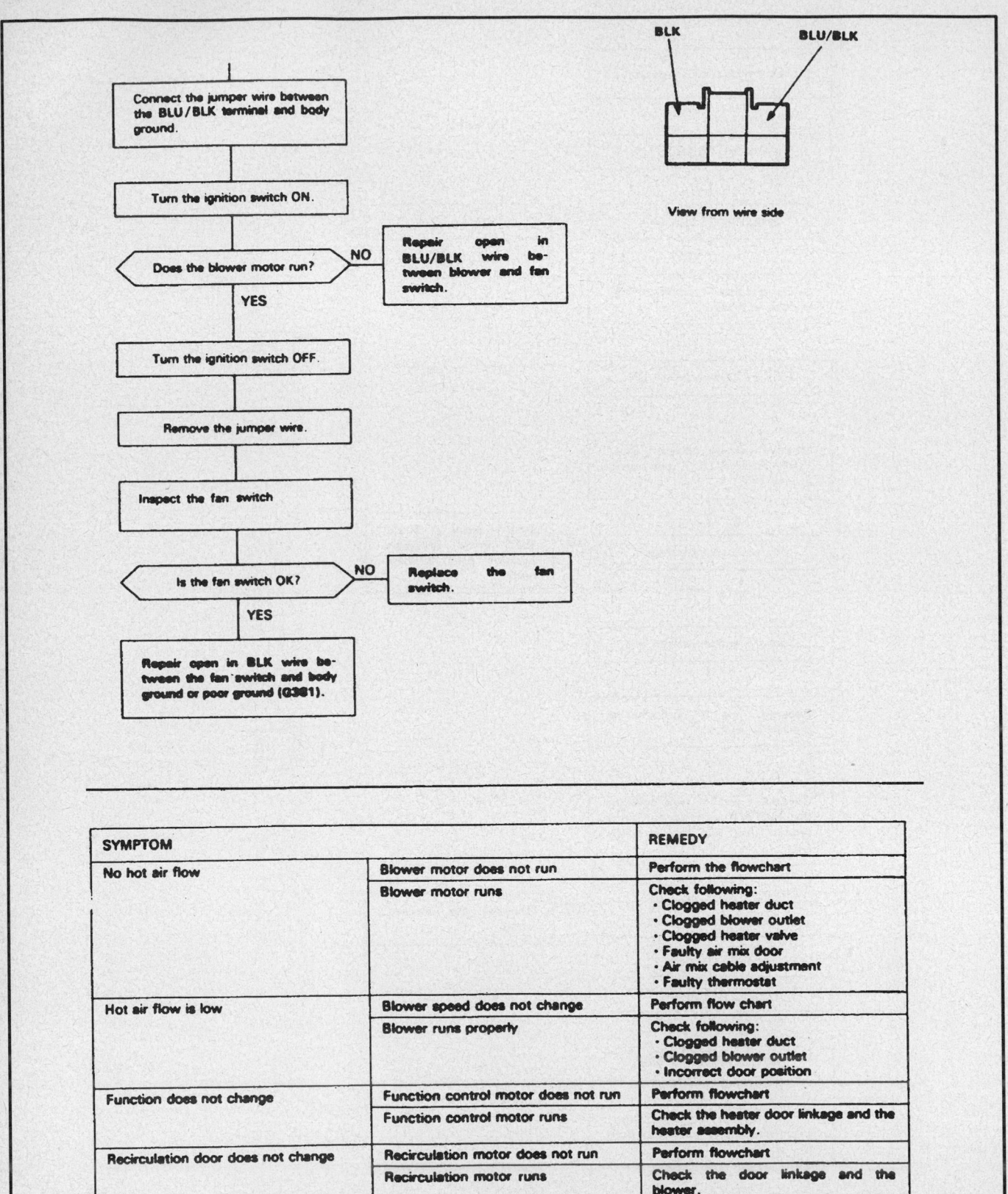

BLK   BLU/BLK

View from wire side

Connect the jumper wire between the BLU/BLK terminal and body ground.

Turn the ignition switch ON.

Does the blower motor run? — **NO** → Repair open in BLU/BLK wire between blower and fan switch.

YES

Turn the ignition switch OFF.

Remove the jumper wire.

Inspect the fan switch

Is the fan switch OK? — **NO** → Replace the fan switch.

YES

Repair open in BLK wire between the fan switch and body ground or poor ground (G381).

SYMPTOM		REMEDY
No hot air flow	Blower motor does not run	Perform the flowchart
	Blower motor runs	Check following: • Clogged heater duct • Clogged blower outlet • Clogged heater valve • Faulty air mix door • Air mix cable adjustment • Faulty thermostat
Hot air flow is low	Blower speed does not change	Perform flow chart
	Blower runs properly	Check following: • Clogged heater duct • Clogged blower outlet • Incorrect door position
Function does not change	Function control motor does not run	Perform flowchart
	Function control motor runs	Check the heater door linkage and the heater assembly.
Recirculation door does not change	Recirculation motor does not run	Perform flowchart
	Recirculation motor runs	Check the door linkage and the blower.

HEATER RECIRCULATION CONTROL COOLER DIAGNOSTIC CHART – 1993 INTEGRA

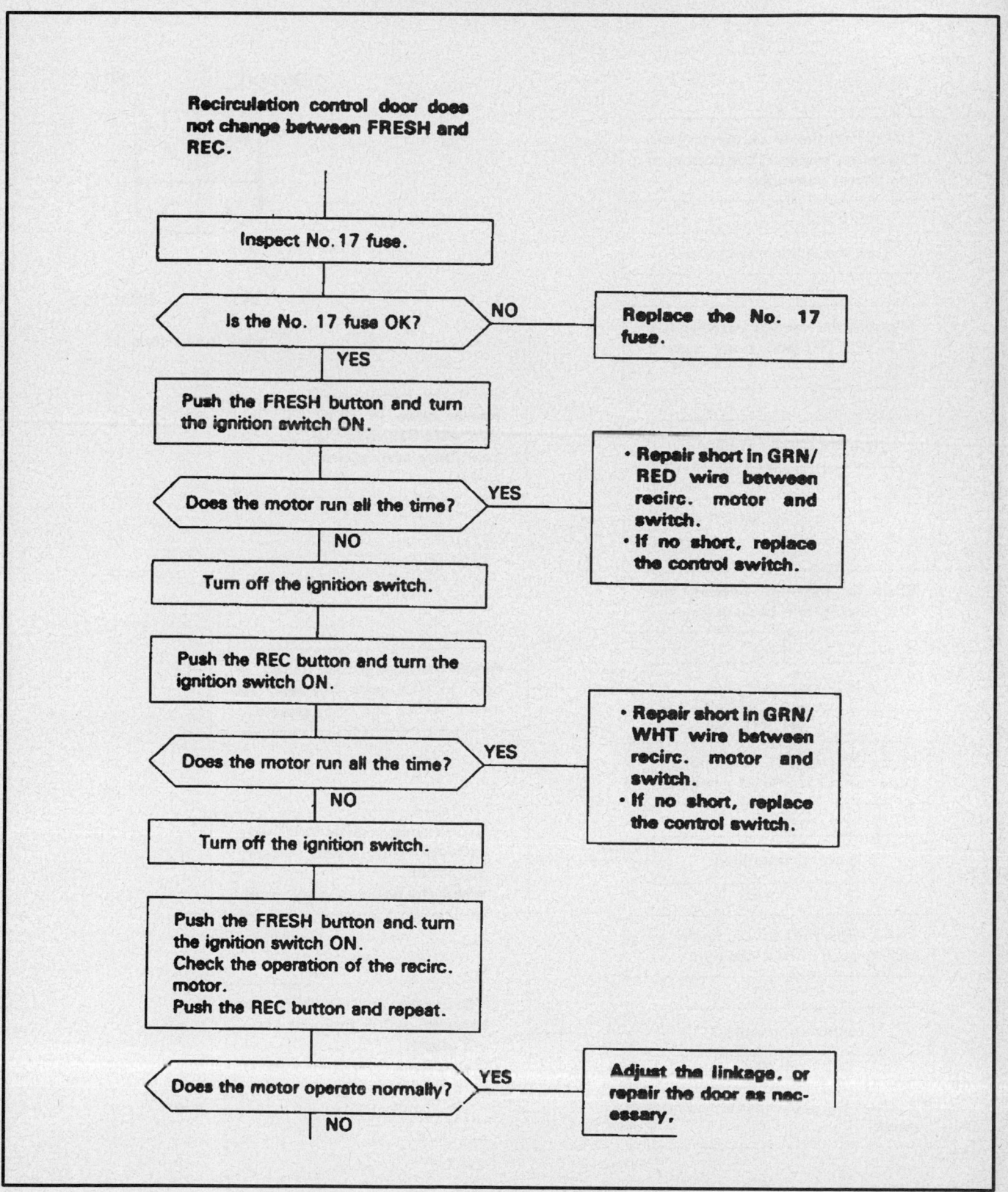

Recirculation control door does not change between FRESH and REC.

Inspect No. 17 fuse.

Is the No. 17 fuse OK? — **NO** → Replace the No. 17 fuse.

YES

Push the FRESH button and turn the ignition switch ON.

Does the motor run all the time? — **YES** → • Repair short in GRN/RED wire between recirc. motor and switch.
• If no short, replace the control switch.

NO

Turn off the ignition switch.

Push the REC button and turn the ignition switch ON.

Does the motor run all the time? — **YES** → • Repair short in GRN/WHT wire between recirc. motor and switch.
• If no short, replace the control switch.

NO

Turn off the ignition switch.

Push the FRESH button and turn the ignition switch ON.
Check the operation of the recirc. motor.
Push the REC button and repeat.

Does the motor operate normally? — **YES** → Adjust the linkage, or repair the door as necessary.

NO

HEATER RECIRCULATION CONTROL DOOR DIAGNOSTIC CHART—1993 INTEGRA—CONTINUED.

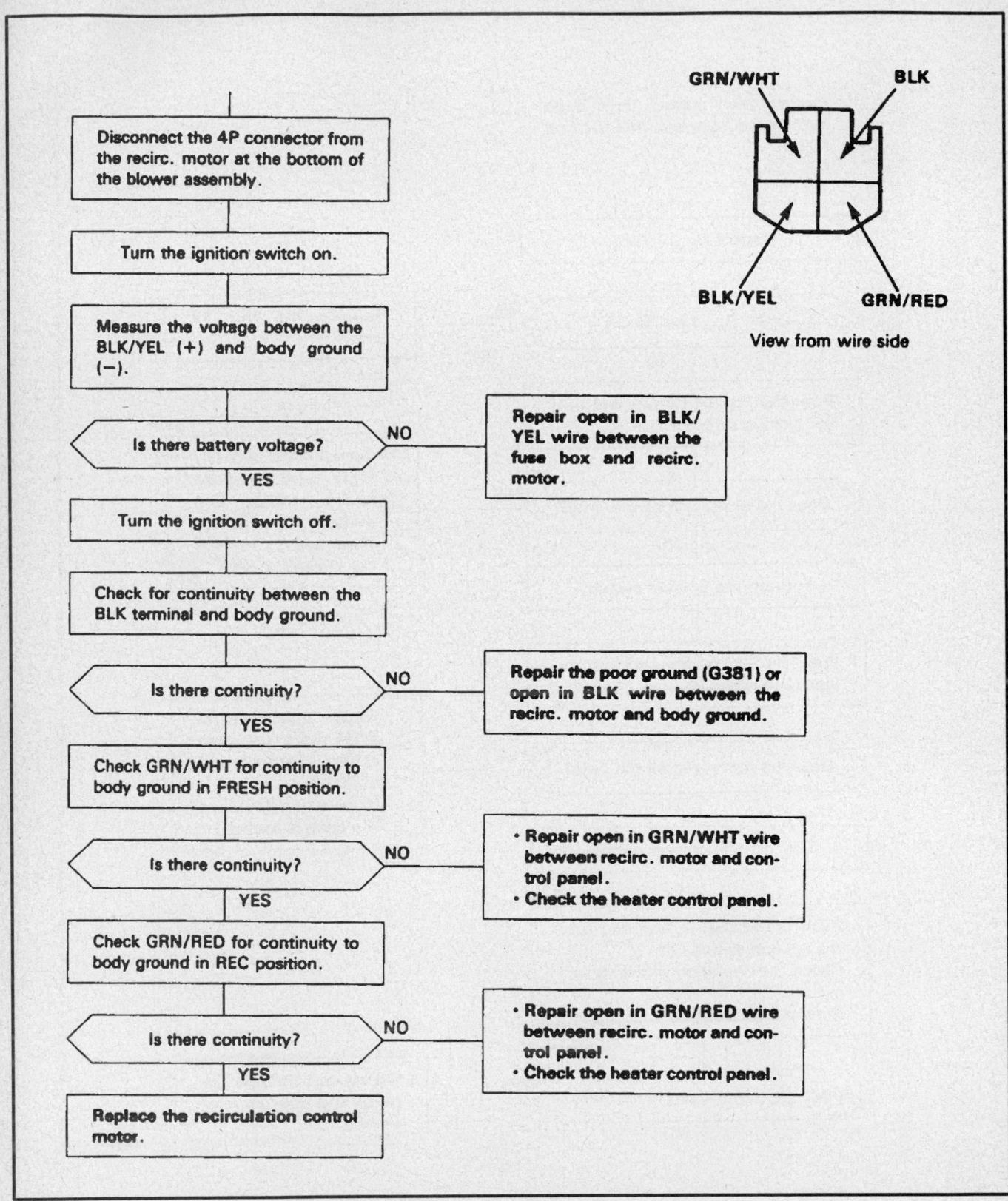

GRN/WHT   BLK

BLK/YEL   GRN/RED

View from wire side

Disconnect the 4P connector from the recirc. motor at the bottom of the blower assembly.

Turn the ignition switch on.

Measure the voltage between the BLK/YEL (+) and body ground (−).

Is there battery voltage? — NO → Repair open in BLK/YEL wire between the fuse box and recirc. motor.

YES

Turn the ignition switch off.

Check for continuity between the BLK terminal and body ground.

Is there continuity? — NO → Repair the poor ground (G381) or open in BLK wire between the recirc. motor and body ground.

YES

Check GRN/WHT for continuity to body ground in FRESH position.

Is there continuity? — NO → • Repair open in GRN/WHT wire between recirc. motor and control panel.
• Check the heater control panel.

YES

Check GRN/RED for continuity to body ground in REC position.

Is there continuity? — NO → • Repair open in GRN/RED wire between recirc. motor and control panel.
• Check the heater control panel.

YES

Replace the recirculation control motor.

HEATER FUNCTION CONTROL MOTOR DIAGNOSTIC CHART—1993 INTEGRA

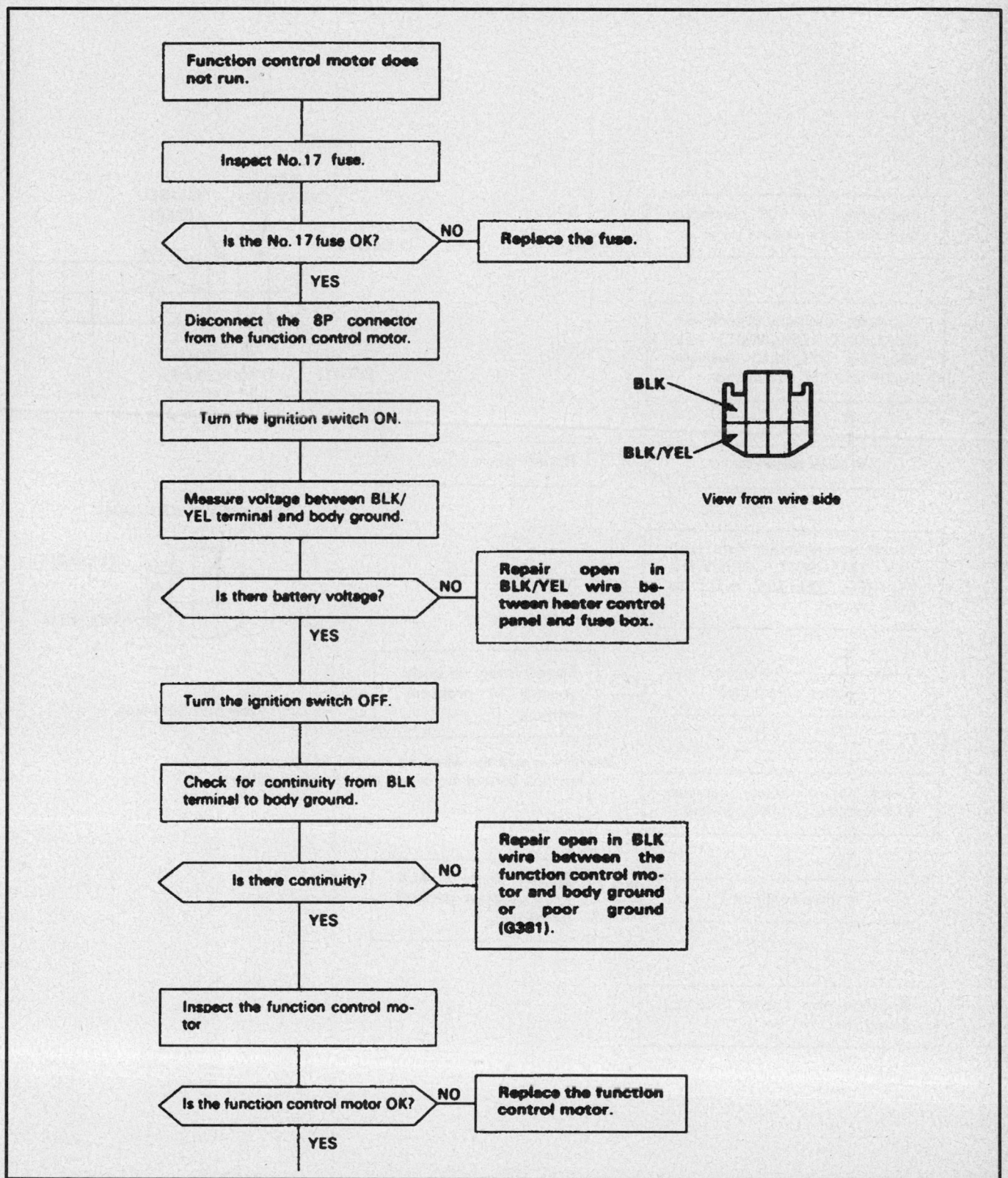

Function control motor does not run.

↓

Inspect No. 17 fuse.

↓

Is the No. 17 fuse OK? —NO→ Replace the fuse.

YES

↓

Disconnect the 8P connector from the function control motor.

↓

Turn the ignition switch ON.

BLK
BLK/YEL

View from wire side

↓

Measure voltage between BLK/YEL terminal and body ground.

↓

Is there battery voltage? —NO→ Repair open in BLK/YEL wire between heater control panel and fuse box.

YES

↓

Turn the ignition switch OFF.

↓

Check for continuity from BLK terminal to body ground.

↓

Is there continuity? —NO→ Repair open in BLK wire between the function control motor and body ground or poor ground (G381).

YES

↓

Inspect the function control motor

↓

Is the function control motor OK? —NO→ Replace the function control motor.

YES

HEATER FUNCTION CONTROL MOTOR DIAGNOSTIC CHART—1993 INTEGRA—CONTINUED.

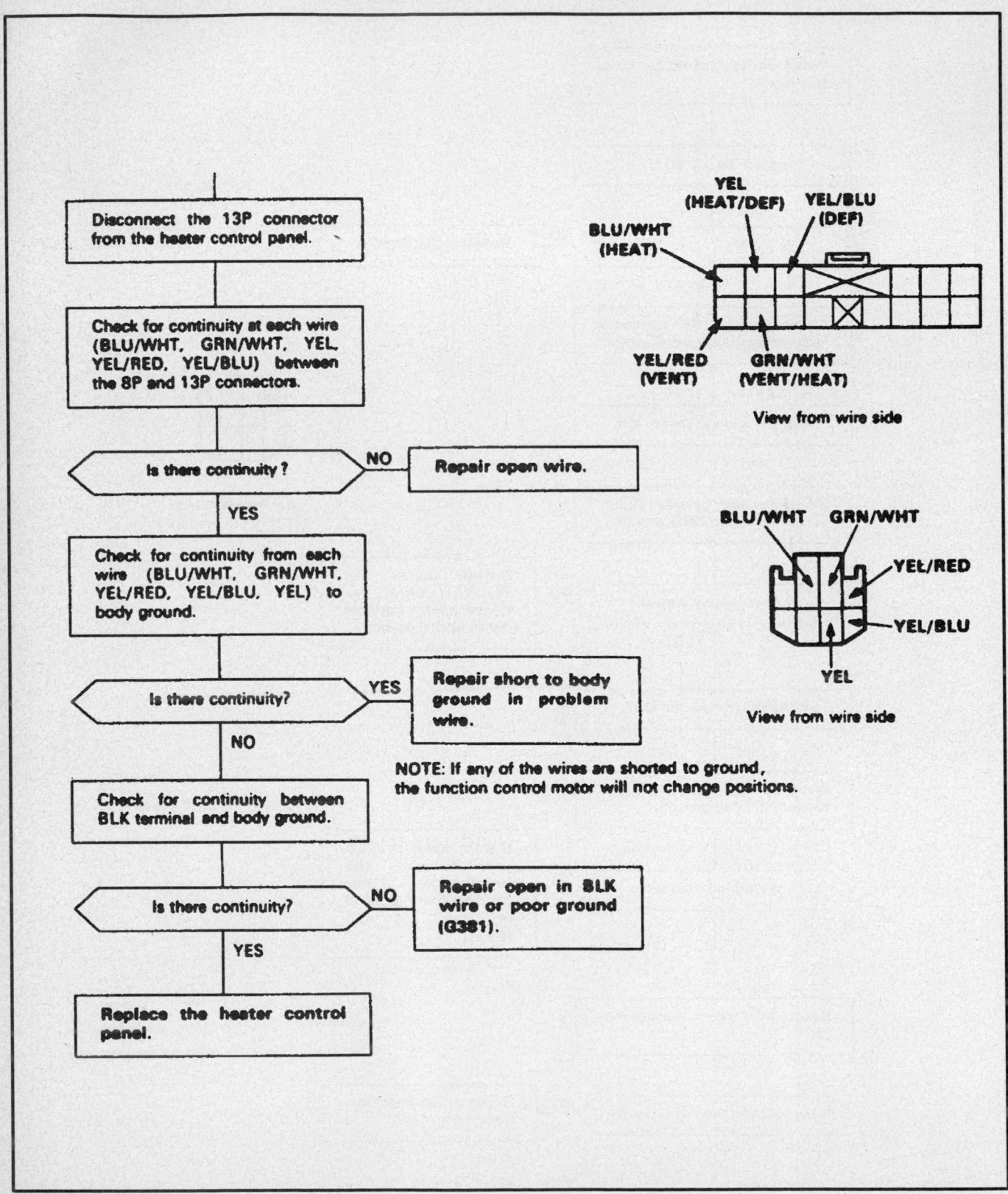

Disconnect the 13P connector from the heater control panel.

Check for continuity at each wire (BLU/WHT, GRN/WHT, YEL, YEL/RED, YEL/BLU) between the 8P and 13P connectors.

Is there continuity? → NO → Repair open wire.

YES

Check for continuity from each wire (BLU/WHT, GRN/WHT, YEL/RED, YEL/BLU, YEL) to body ground.

Is there continuity? → YES → Repair short to body ground in problem wire.

NO

Check for continuity between BLK terminal and body ground.

Is there continuity? → NO → Repair open in BLK wire or poor ground (G381).

YES

Replace the heater control panel.

YEL (HEAT/DEF)
YEL/BLU (DEF)
BLU/WHT (HEAT)
YEL/RED (VENT)
GRN/WHT (VENT/HEAT)

View from wire side

BLU/WHT   GRN/WHT
YEL/RED
YEL/BLU
YEL

View from wire side

NOTE: If any of the wires are shorted to ground, the function control motor will not change positions.

AIR CONDITIONER DIAGNOSTIC CHART—1993 INTEGRA

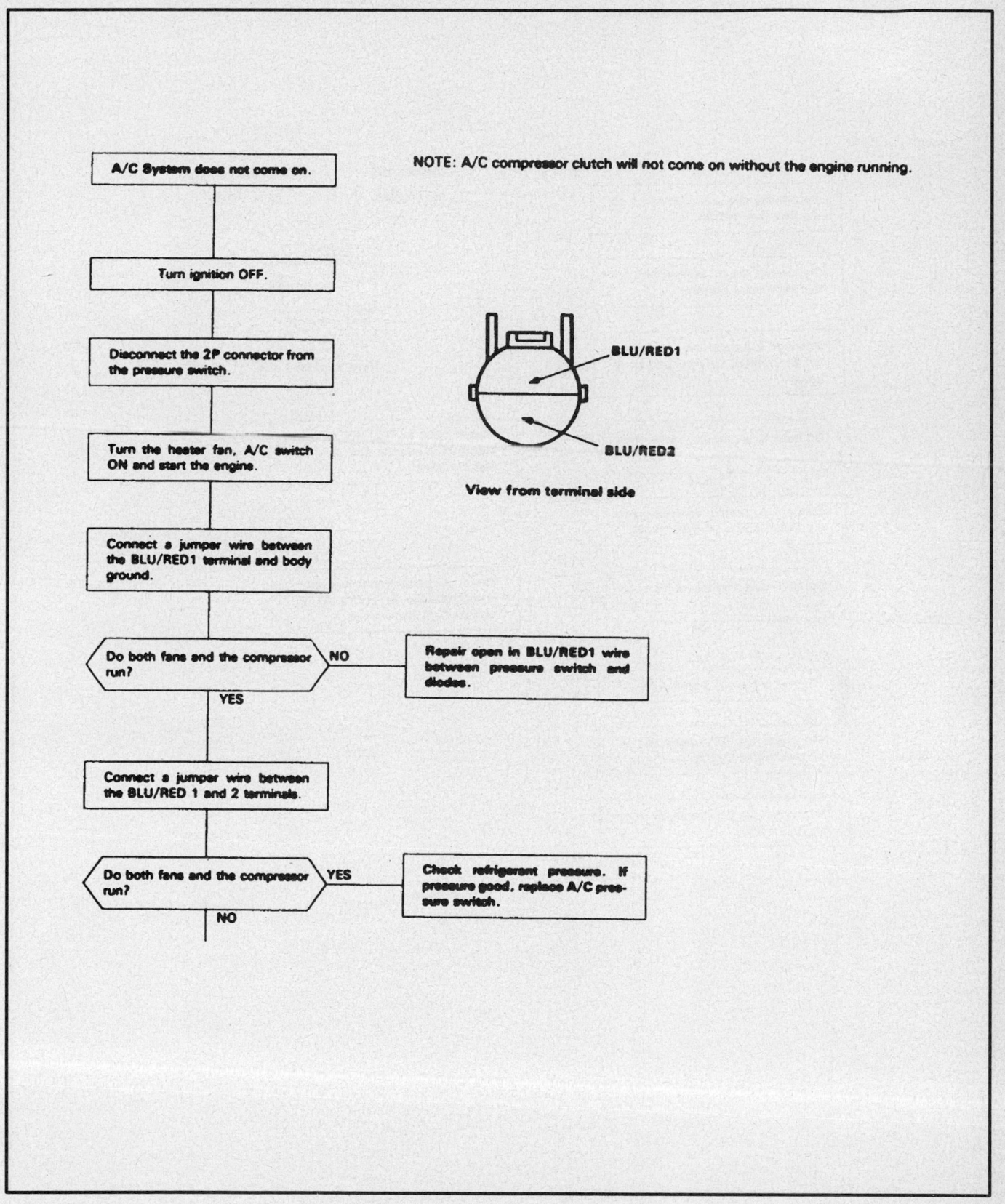

NOTE: A/C compressor clutch will not come on without the engine running.

A/C System does not come on.

Turn ignition OFF.

Disconnect the 2P connector from the pressure switch.

Turn the heater fan, A/C switch ON and start the engine.

Connect a jumper wire between the BLU/RED1 terminal and body ground.

Do both fans and the compressor run? — NO → Repair open in BLU/RED1 wire between pressure switch and diodes.

YES

Connect a jumper wire between the BLU/RED 1 and 2 terminals.

Do both fans and the compressor run? — YES → Check refrigerant pressure. If pressure good, replace A/C pressure switch.

NO

BLU/RED1

BLU/RED2

View from terminal side

AIR CONDITIONER DIAGNOSTIC CHART – 1993 INTEGRA – CONTINUED

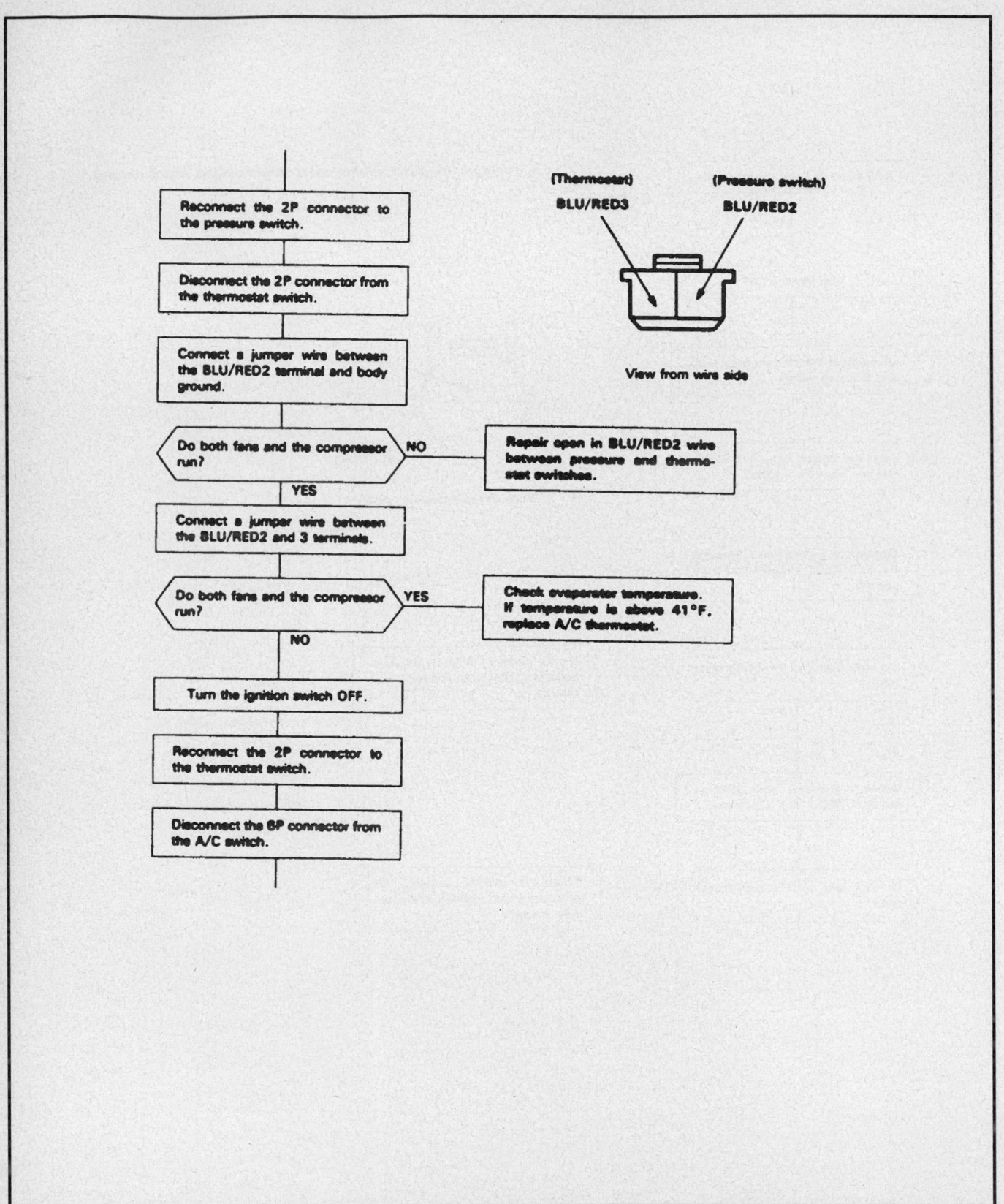

Reconnect the 2P connector to the pressure switch.

Disconnect the 2P connector from the thermostat switch.

Connect a jumper wire between the BLU/RED2 terminal and body ground.

Do both fans and the compressor run? — NO → Repair open in BLU/RED2 wire between pressure and thermostat switches.

YES

Connect a jumper wire between the BLU/RED2 and 3 terminals.

Do both fans and the compressor run? — YES → Check evaporator temperature. If temperature is above 41°F, replace A/C thermostat.

NO

Turn the ignition switch OFF.

Reconnect the 2P connector to the thermostat switch.

Disconnect the 6P connector from the A/C switch.

(Thermostat) BLU/RED3   (Pressure switch) BLU/RED2

View from wire side

AIR CONDITIONER DIAGNOSTIC CHART—1993 INTEGRA—CONTINUED

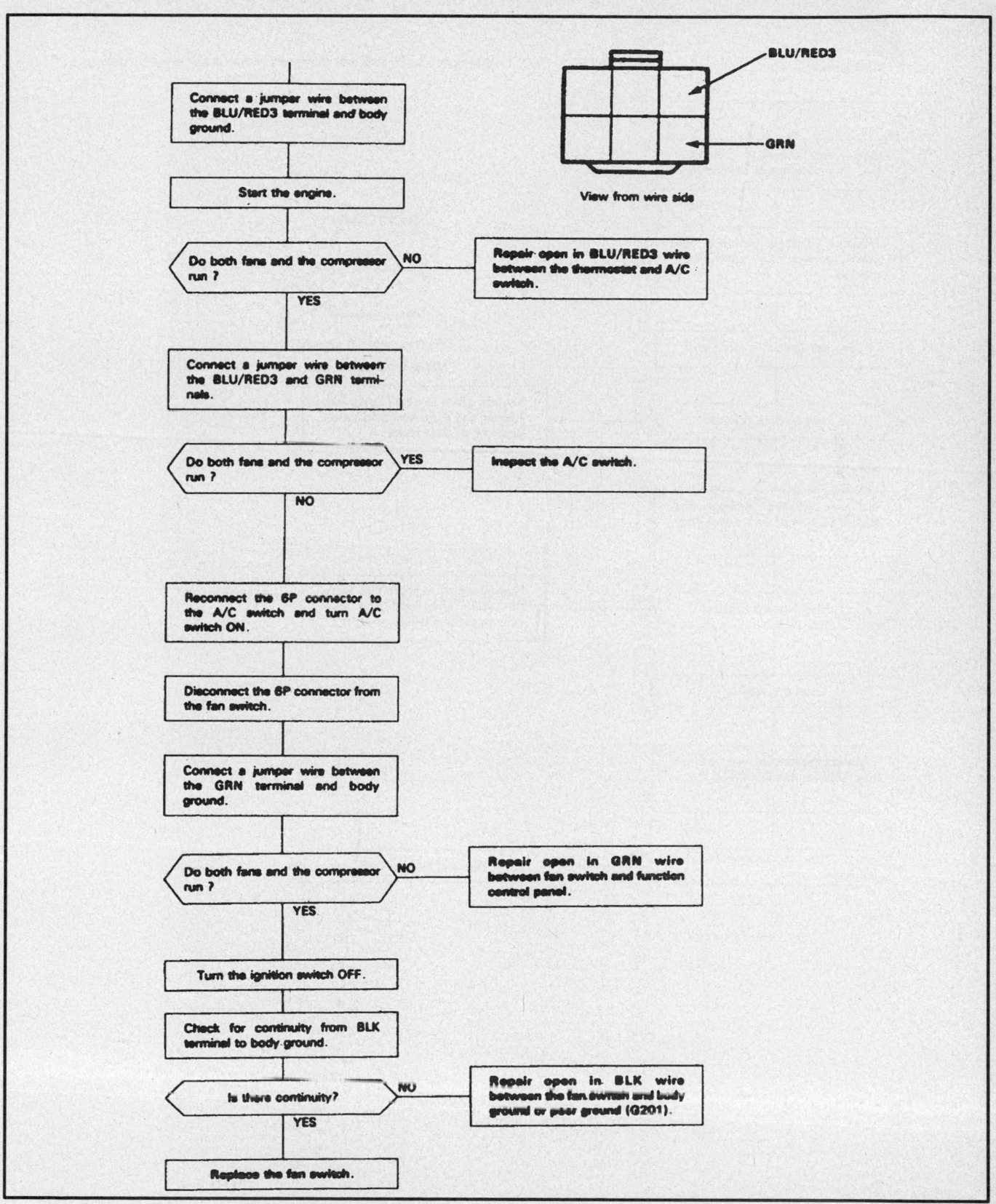

Connect a jumper wire between the BLU/RED3 terminal and body ground.

↓

Start the engine.

↓

Do both fans and the compressor run ? — NO → Repair open in BLU/RED3 wire between the thermostat and A/C switch.

YES ↓

Connect a jumper wire between the BLU/RED3 and GRN terminals.

↓

Do both fans and the compressor run ? — YES → Inspect the A/C switch.

NO ↓

Reconnect the 6P connector to the A/C switch and turn A/C switch ON.

↓

Disconnect the 6P connector from the fan switch.

↓

Connect a jumper wire between the GRN terminal and body ground.

↓

Do both fans and the compressor run ? — NO → Repair open in GRN wire between fan switch and function control panel.

YES ↓

Turn the ignition switch OFF.

↓

Check for continuity from BLK terminal to body ground.

↓

Is there continuity? — NO → Repair open in BLK wire between the fan switch and body ground or poor ground (G201).

YES ↓

Replace the fan switch.

BLU/RED3
GRN
View from wire side

AIR CONDITIONER DIAGNOSTIC CHART—1993 INTEGRA—CONTINUED

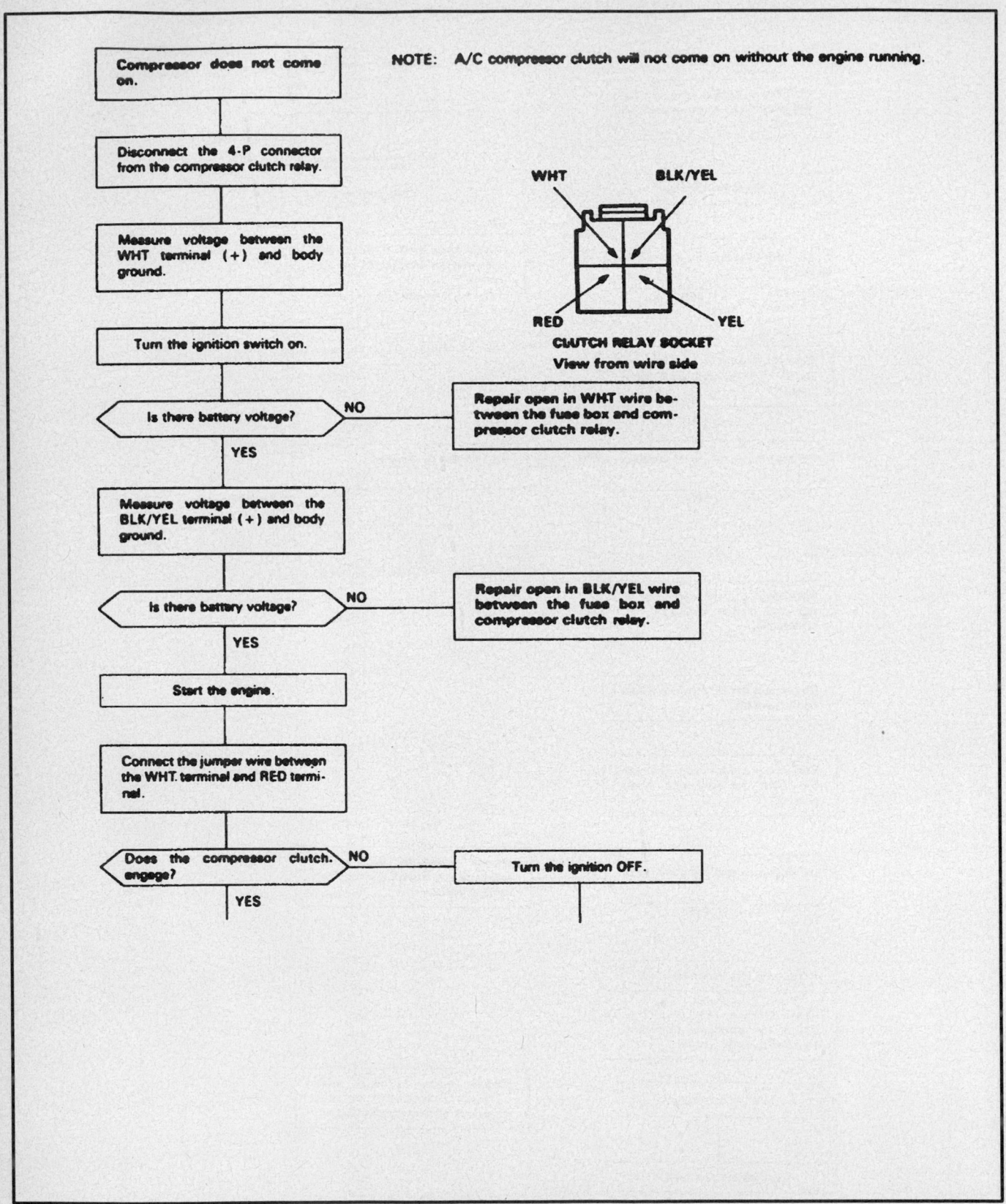

NOTE: A/C compressor clutch will not come on without the engine running.

Compressor does not come on.

Disconnect the 4-P connector from the compressor clutch relay.

Measure voltage between the WHT terminal (+) and body ground.

Turn the ignition switch on.

Is there battery voltage? — NO → Repair open in WHT wire between the fuse box and compressor clutch relay.

YES

Measure voltage between the BLK/YEL terminal (+) and body ground.

Is there battery voltage? — NO → Repair open in BLK/YEL wire between the fuse box and compressor clutch relay.

YES

Start the engine.

Connect the jumper wire between the WHT. terminal and RED terminal.

Does the compressor clutch engage? — NO → Turn the ignition OFF.

YES

WHT   BLK/YEL

RED   YEL

CLUTCH RELAY SOCKET
View from wire side

AIR CONDITIONER DIAGNOSTIC CHART–1993 INTEGRA–CONTINUED

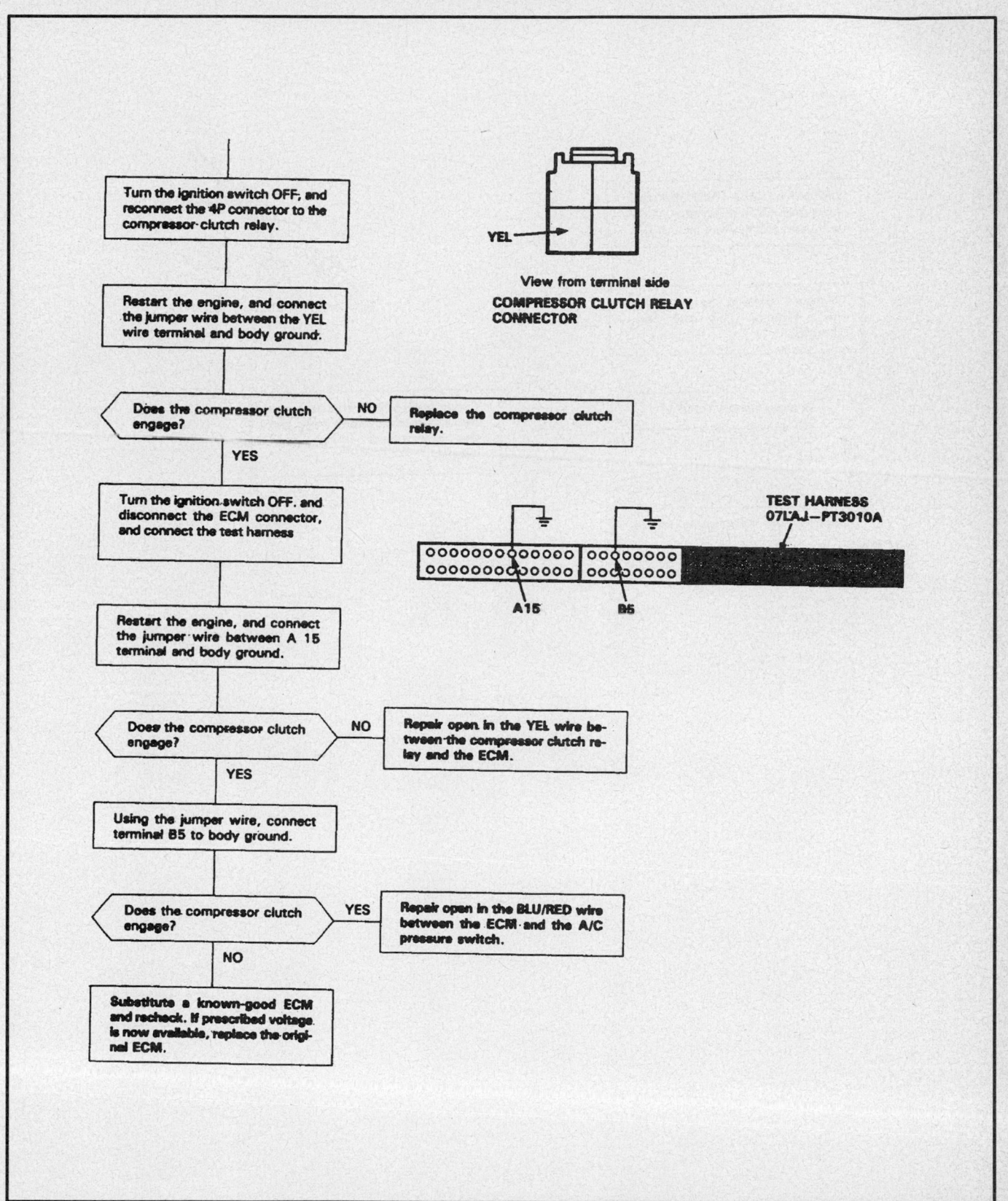

Turn the ignition switch OFF, and reconnect the 4P connector to the compressor-clutch relay.

Restart the engine, and connect the jumper wire between the YEL wire terminal and body ground.

Does the compressor clutch engage? — NO → Replace the compressor clutch relay.

YES

Turn the ignition switch OFF, and disconnect the ECM connector, and connect the test harness

Restart the engine, and connect the jumper wire between A 15 terminal and body ground.

Does the compressor clutch engage? — NO → Repair open in the YEL wire between the compressor clutch relay and the ECM.

YES

Using the jumper wire, connect terminal B5 to body ground.

Does the compressor clutch engage? — YES → Repair open in the BLU/RED wire between the ECM and the A/C pressure switch.

NO

Substitute a known-good ECM and recheck. If prescribed voltage is now available, replace the original ECM.

YEL

View from terminal side
COMPRESSOR CLUTCH RELAY CONNECTOR

TEST HARNESS 07LAJ–PT3010A

A15   B5

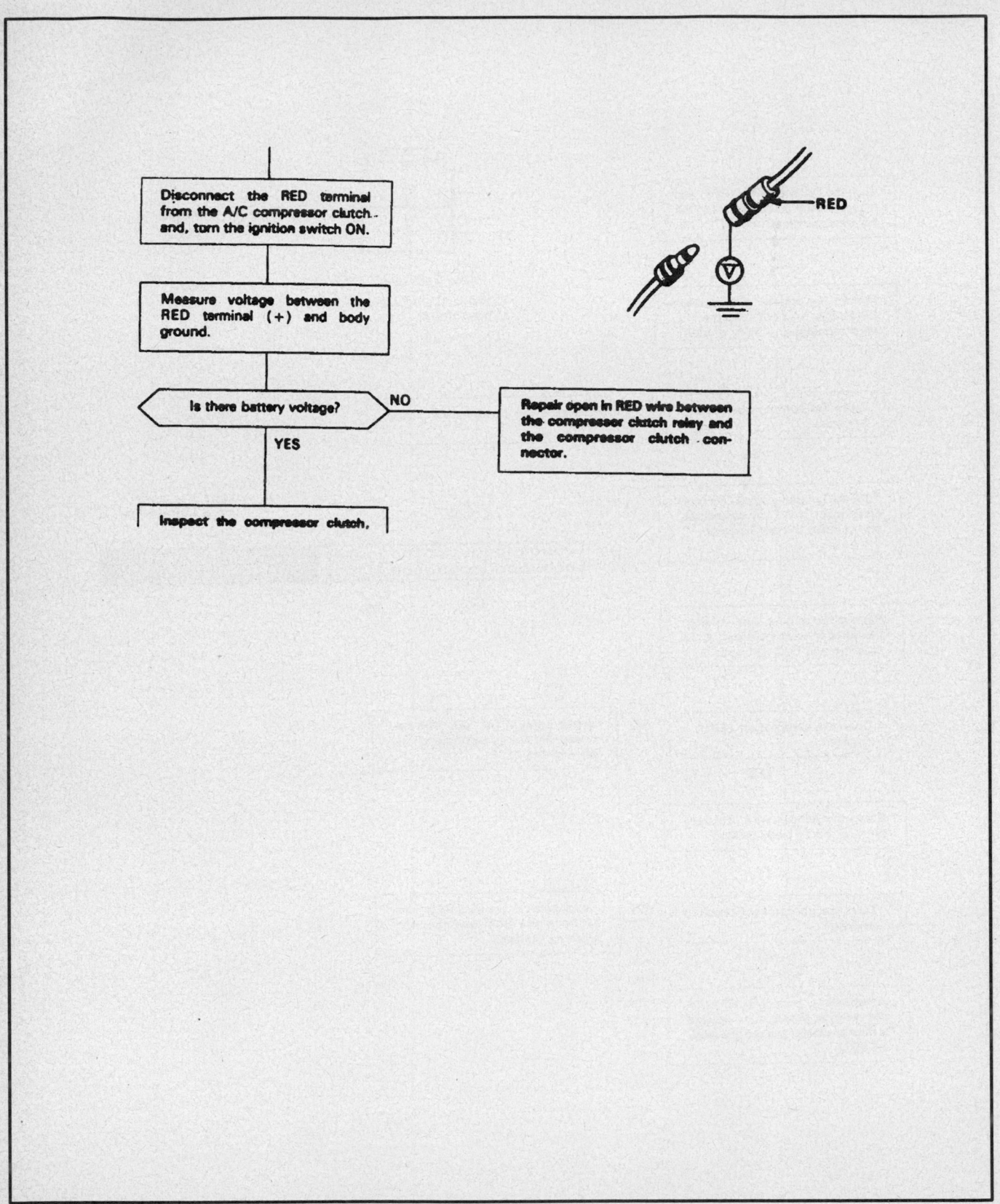

Disconnect the RED terminal from the A/C compressor clutch and, turn the ignition switch ON.

Measure voltage between the RED terminal (+) and body ground.

Is there battery voltage?

NO → Repair open in RED wire between the compressor clutch relay and the compressor clutch connector.

YES

Inspect the compressor clutch.

RED

CONDENSER FAN DIAGNOSTIC CHART—1993 INTEGRA

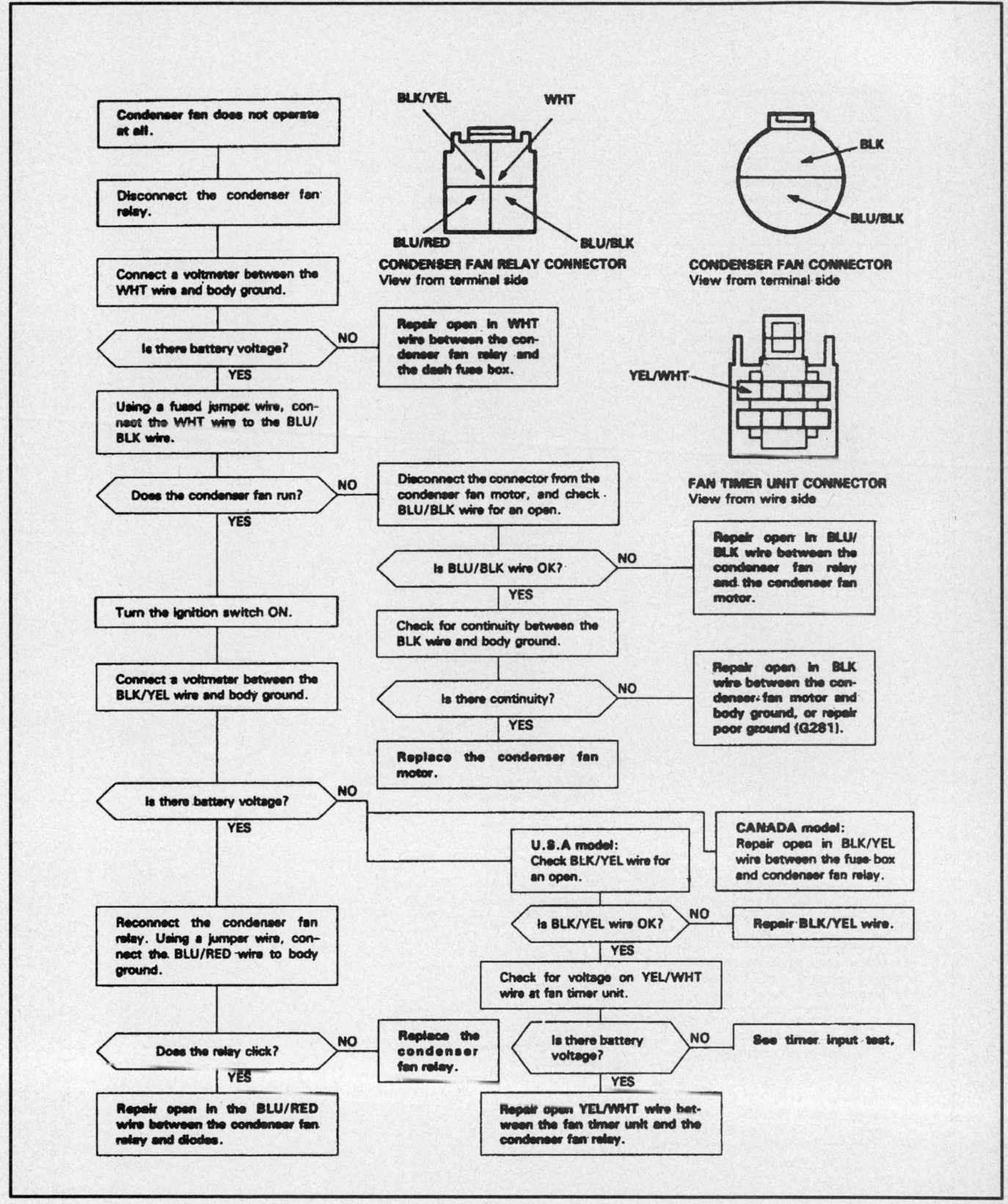

CONDENSER FAN RELAY CONNECTOR
View from terminal side

CONDENSER FAN CONNECTOR
View from terminal side

FAN TIMER UNIT CONNECTOR
View from wire side

Condenser fan does not operate at all.

Disconnect the condenser fan relay.

Connect a voltmeter between the WHT wire and body ground.

Is there battery voltage? — NO → Repair open in WHT wire between the condenser fan relay and the dash fuse box.

YES

Using a fused jumper wire, connect the WHT wire to the BLU/BLK wire.

Does the condenser fan run? — NO → Disconnect the connector from the condenser fan motor, and check BLU/BLK wire for an open.

Is BLU/BLK wire OK? — NO → Repair open in BLU/BLK wire between the condenser fan relay and the condenser fan motor.

YES

Check for continuity between the BLK wire and body ground.

Is there continuity? — NO → Repair open in BLK wire between the condenser fan motor and body ground, or repair poor ground (G281).

YES

Replace the condenser fan motor.

YES

Turn the ignition switch ON.

Connect a voltmeter between the BLK/YEL wire and body ground.

Is there battery voltage? — NO

YES

U.S.A model:
Check BLK/YEL wire for an open.

CANADA model:
Repair open in BLK/YEL wire between the fuse box and condenser fan relay.

Is BLK/YEL wire OK? — NO → Repair BLK/YEL wire.

YES

Check for voltage on YEL/WHT wire at fan timer unit.

Reconnect the condenser fan relay. Using a jumper wire, connect the BLU/RED wire to body ground.

Does the relay click? — NO → Replace the condenser fan relay.

Is there battery voltage? — NO → See timer input test.

YES

YES

Repair open in the BLU/RED wire between the condenser fan relay and diodes.

Repair open YEL/WHT wire between the fan timer unit and the condenser fan relay.

RADIATOR FAN DIAGNOSTIC CHART—1993 INTEGRA

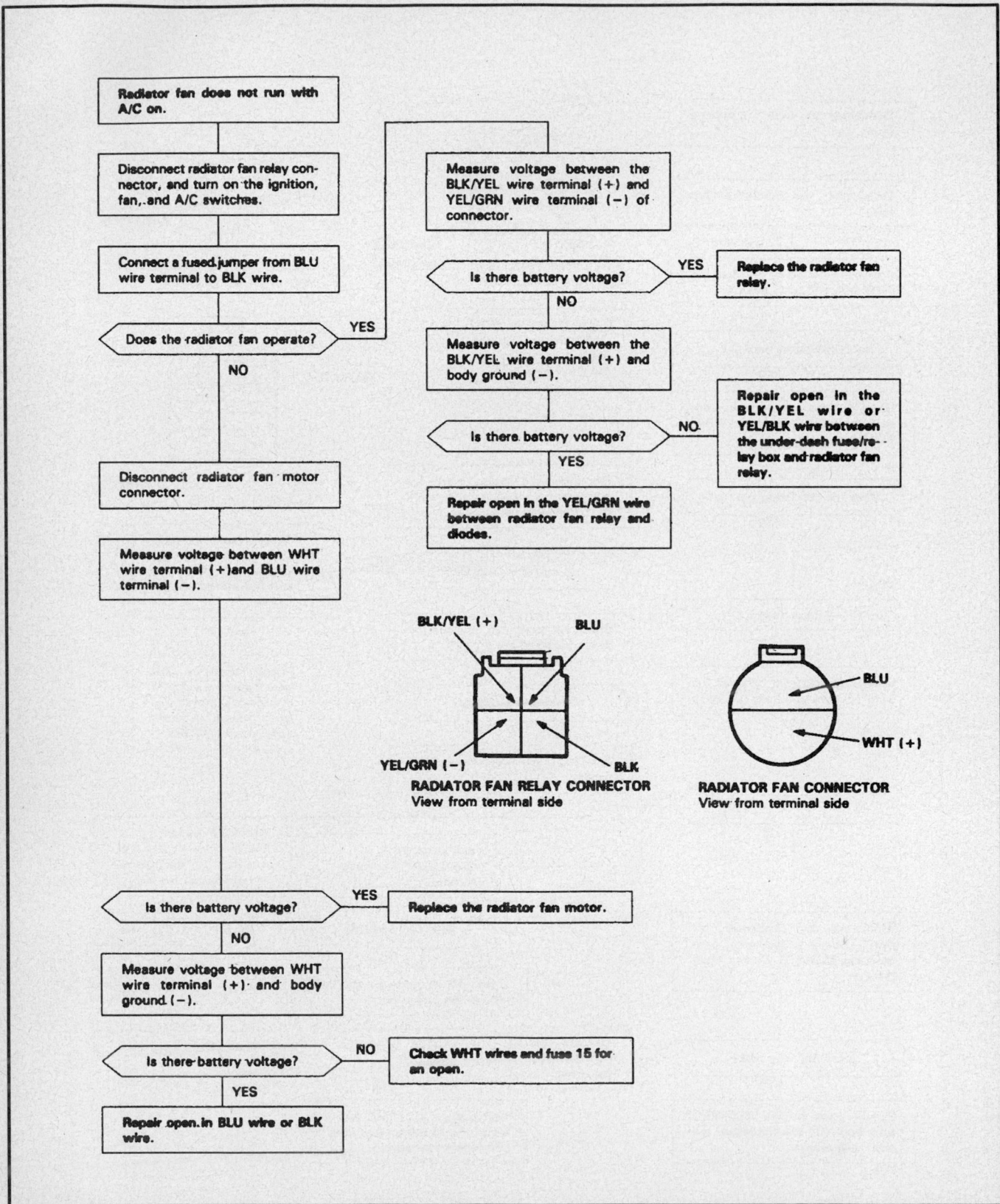

Radiator fan does not run with A/C on.

↓

Disconnect radiator fan relay connector, and turn on the ignition, fan, and A/C switches.

↓

Connect a fused jumper from BLU wire terminal to BLK wire.

↓

Does the radiator fan operate? —YES→ Measure voltage between the BLK/YEL wire terminal (+) and YEL/GRN wire terminal (−) of connector.

NO ↓

↓ (right branch)

Is there battery voltage? —YES→ Replace the radiator fan relay.

NO ↓

Measure voltage between the BLK/YEL wire terminal (+) and body ground (−).

↓

Is there battery voltage? —NO→ Repair open in the BLK/YEL wire or YEL/BLK wire between the under-dash fuse/relay box and radiator fan relay.

YES ↓

Repair open in the YEL/GRN wire between radiator fan relay and diodes.

(left branch, NO)

Disconnect radiator fan motor connector.

↓

Measure voltage between WHT wire terminal (+) and BLU wire terminal (−).

BLK/YEL (+)   BLU

YEL/GRN (−)   BLK

RADIATOR FAN RELAY CONNECTOR
View from terminal side

BLU

WHT (+)

RADIATOR FAN CONNECTOR
View from terminal side

Is there battery voltage? —YES→ Replace the radiator fan motor.

NO ↓

Measure voltage between WHT wire terminal (+) and body ground (−).

↓

Is there battery voltage? —NO→ Check WHT wires and fuse 15 for an open.

YES ↓

Repair open in BLU wire or BLK wire.

RADIATOR FAN CONTROL MODULE INPUT CHART—1993 INTEGRA

NOTE:
Perform the following tests with the radiator fan control module connected and the ignition switch ON and the A/C switch OFF.
If you find the cause of a problem, correct it before you continue.

● Located at the right side of the heater unit

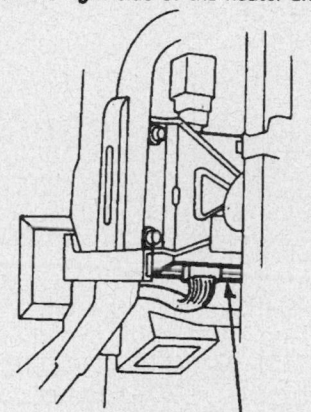

RADIATOR FAN CONTROL MODULE

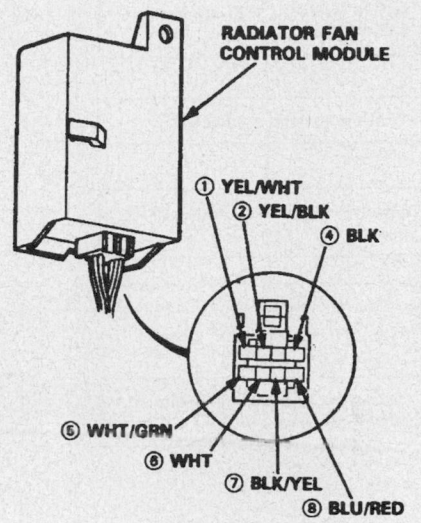

RADIATOR FAN CONTROL MODULE

① YEL/WHT
② YEL/BLK
④ BLK
⑥ WHT/GRN
⑧ WHT
⑦ BLK/YEL
⑧ BLU/RED

View from wire side

WIRE POSITION	TEST CONDITION	DESIRED RESULTS	CORRECTIVE ACTION IF DESIRED RESULTS ARE NOT OBTAINED
④ BLK	Check for voltage to body ground.	Should have less than 1 volt.	Repair open to body ground.
⑧ WHT	Check for battery voltage.	Should have battery voltage.	Check No. 20 fuse; if OK, repair open in WHT wire.
⑦ BLK/YEL	Check for battery voltage (Ignition switch—ON)		Check No. 24 fuse; if OK, repair open in BLK/YEL wire.
② YEL/BLK	Check for battery voltage (Ignition switch—ON)		Check No. 21 fuse; if OK, repair open in YEL/BLK wire.
① YEL/WHT	Check for battery voltage. (Ignition switch-ON)		Replace radiator fan control module. Before you connect the new radiator fan control module, check continuity between the YEL/WHT wire and ground, using the 20k scale on your ohmmeter. There should be no continuity. If there is continuity, the new radiator fan control module will be damaged whten you connect it.
⑧ BLU/RED	Connect to body ground. (Ignition switch ON)	Condenser fan should come on.	Check for open in the BLU/RED wire between radiator fan control module and condenser fan relay. If OK, check for open YEL/WHT and BLK/YEL [3] wires. If OK, test condenser fan relay
⑥ WHT/GRN	Check for voltage.	Approx 11V (Engine oil temperature below 108°C)	Faulty engine oil temperature switch, short to body ground, or faulty radiator fan control module.

BLOWER MOTOR DIAGNOSTIC CHART—1993 LEGEND AND LEGEND COUPE

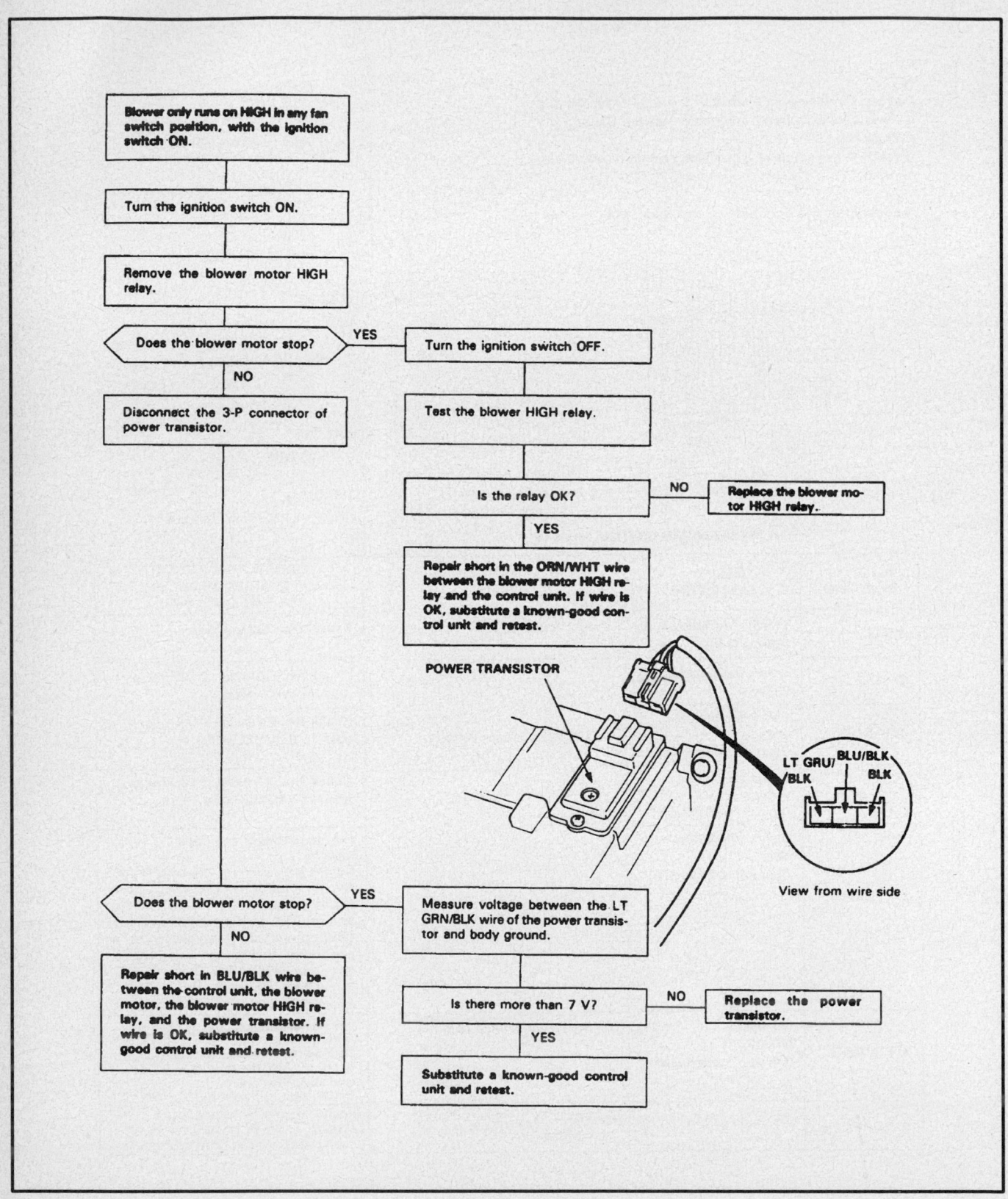

POWER TRANSISTOR

LT GRU/BLK   BLU/BLK   BLK

View from wire side

BLOWER MOTOR DIAGNOSTIC CHART–1993 LEGEND AND LEGEND COUPE–CONTINUED

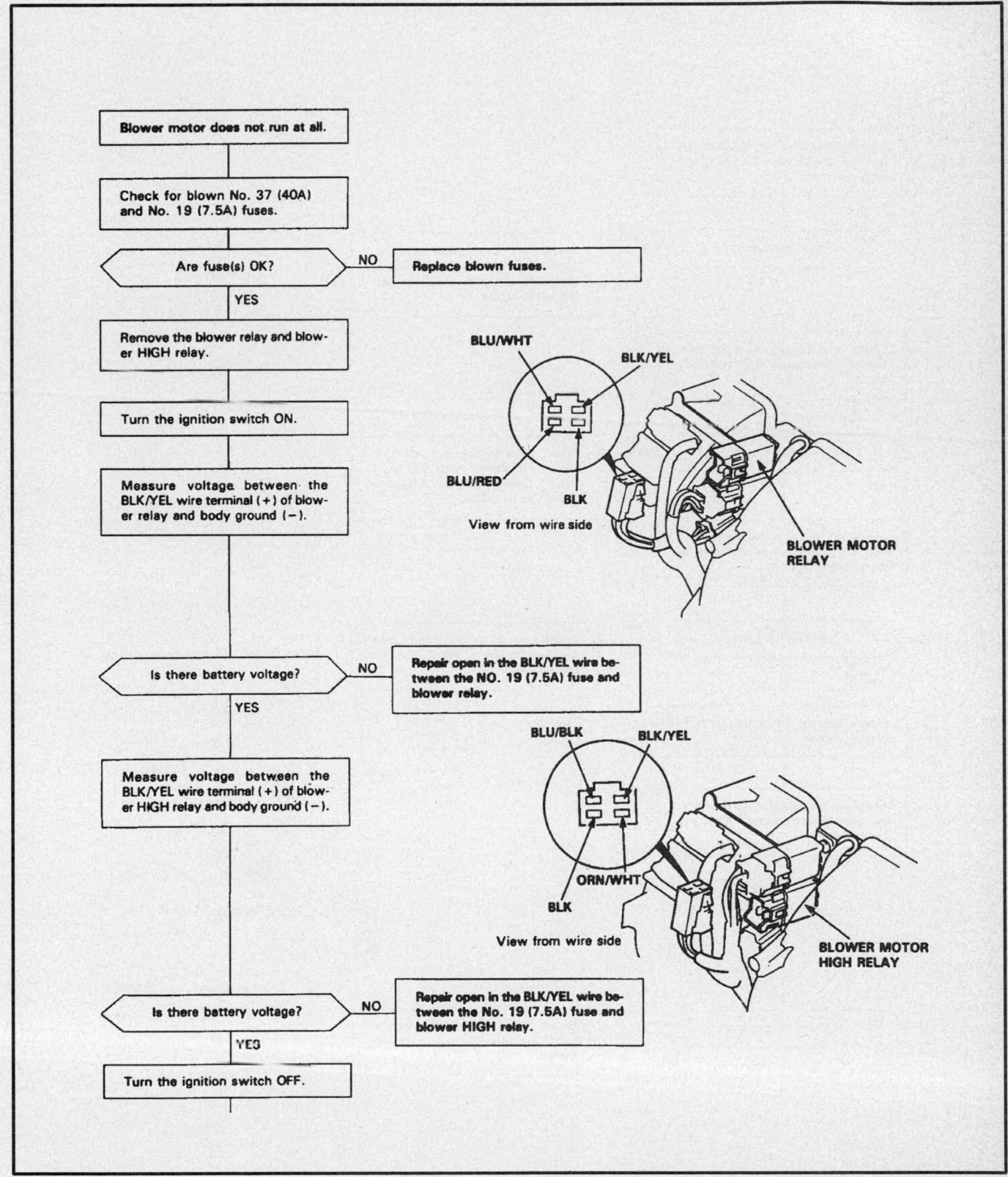

Blower motor does not run at all.

Check for blown No. 37 (40A) and No. 19 (7.5A) fuses.

Are fuse(s) OK? — NO → Replace blown fuses.

YES

Remove the blower relay and blower HIGH relay.

Turn the ignition switch ON.

Measure voltage between the BLK/YEL wire terminal (+) of blower relay and body ground (−).

BLU/WHT
BLK/YEL
BLU/RED
BLK

View from wire side

BLOWER MOTOR RELAY

Is there battery voltage? — NO → Repair open in the BLK/YEL wire between the NO. 19 (7.5A) fuse and blower relay.

YES

Measure voltage between the BLK/YEL wire terminal (+) of blower HIGH relay and body ground (−).

BLU/BLK
BLK/YEL
ORN/WHT
BLK

View from wire side

BLOWER MOTOR HIGH RELAY

Is there battery voltage? — NO → Repair open in the BLK/YEL wire between the No. 19 (7.5A) fuse and blower HIGH relay.

YES

Turn the ignition switch OFF.

BLOWER MOTOR DIAGNOSTIC CHART—1993 LEGEND AND LEGEND COUPE—CONTINUED

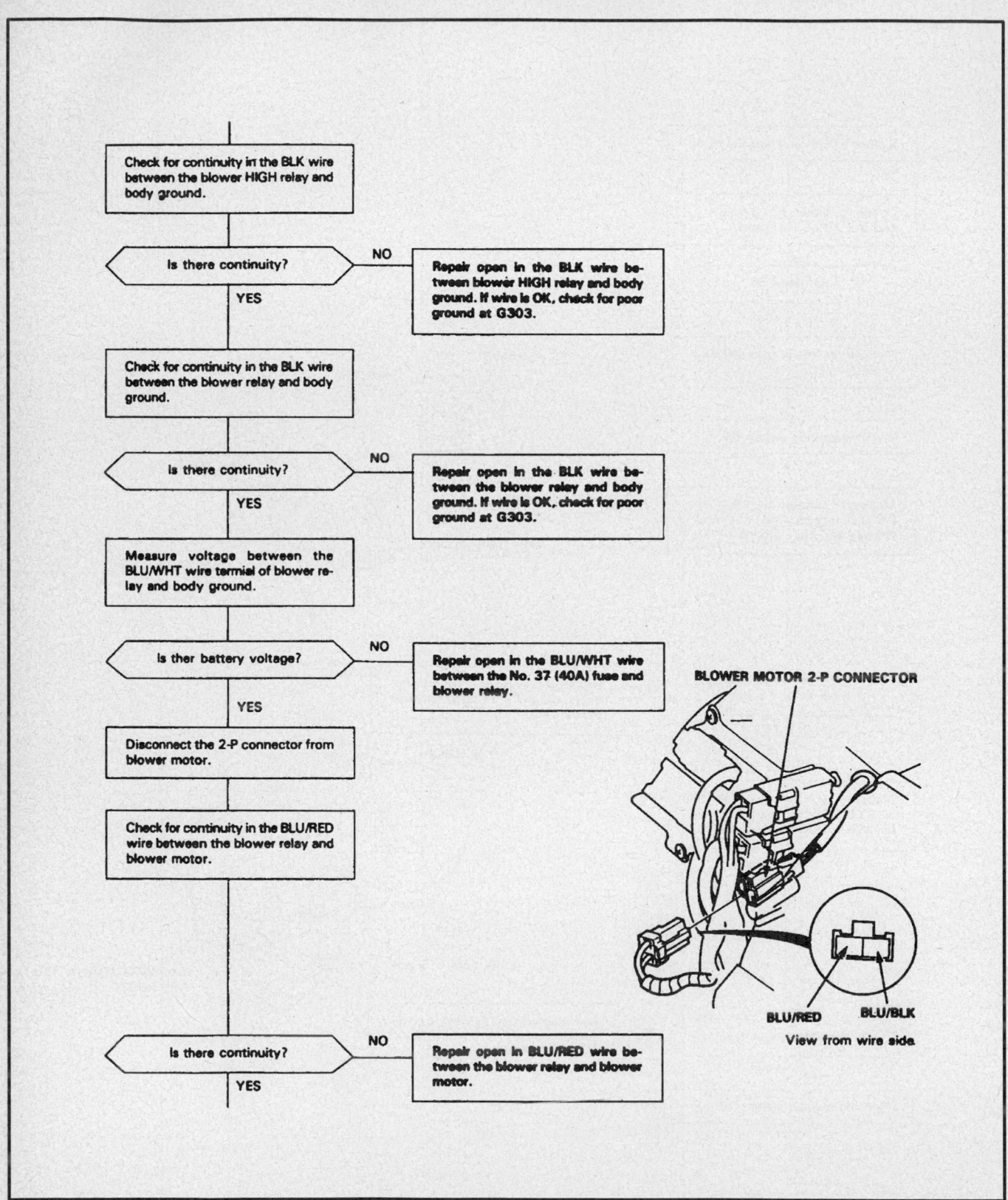

Check for continuity in the BLK wire between the blower HIGH relay and body ground.

Is there continuity? — NO → Repair open in the BLK wire between blower HIGH relay and body ground. If wire is OK, check for poor ground at G303.

YES

Check for continuity in the BLK wire between the blower relay and body ground.

Is there continuity? — NO → Repair open in the BLK wire between the blower relay and body ground. If wire is OK, check for poor ground at G303.

YES

Measure voltage between the BLU/WHT wire termial of blower relay and body ground.

Is ther battery voltage? — NO → Repair open in the BLU/WHT wire between the No. 37 (40A) fuse and blower relay.

YES

Disconnect the 2-P connector from blower motor.

Check for continuity in the BLU/RED wire between the blower relay and blower motor.

Is there continuity? — NO → Repair open in BLU/RED wire between the blower relay and blower motor.

YES

BLOWER MOTOR 2-P CONNECTOR

BLU/RED   BLU/BLK

View from wire side

BLOWER MOTOR DIAGNOSTIC CHART–1993 LEGEND AND LEGEND COUPE–CONTINUED

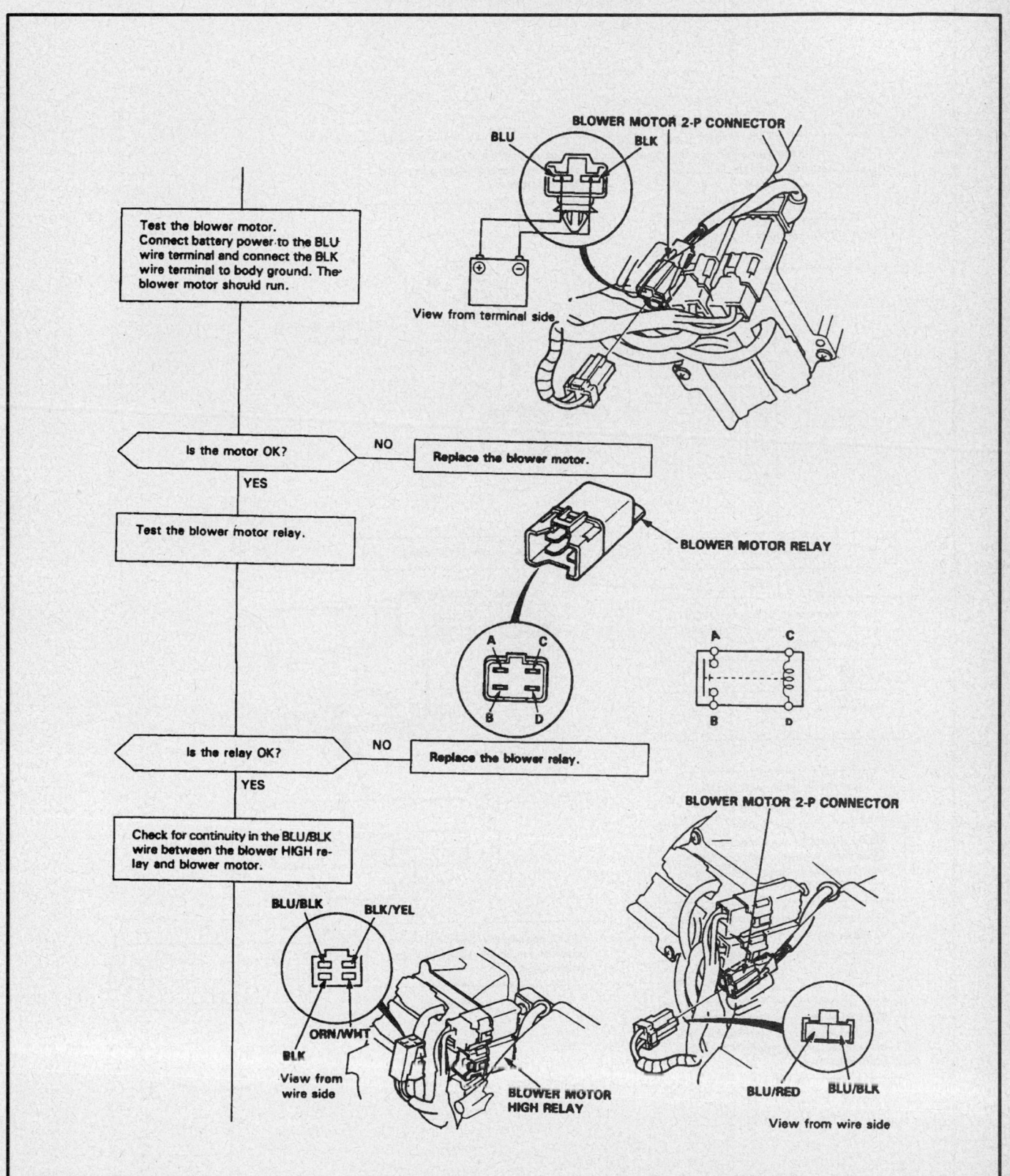

Test the blower motor.
Connect battery power to the BLU wire terminal and connect the BLK wire terminal to body ground. The blower motor should run.

BLOWER MOTOR 2-P CONNECTOR

BLU   BLK

View from terminal side

Is the motor OK? — NO → Replace the blower motor.

YES

Test the blower motor relay.

BLOWER MOTOR RELAY

A   C
B   D

Is the relay OK? — NO → Replace the blower relay.

YES

Check for continuity in the BLU/BLK wire between the blower HIGH relay and blower motor.

BLOWER MOTOR 2-P CONNECTOR

BLU/BLK   BLK/YEL

ORN/WHT

BLK

View from wire side

BLOWER MOTOR HIGH RELAY

BLU/RED   BLU/BLK

View from wire side

BLOWER MOTOR DIAGNOSTIC CHART—1993 LEGEND AND LEGEND COUPE—CONTINUED

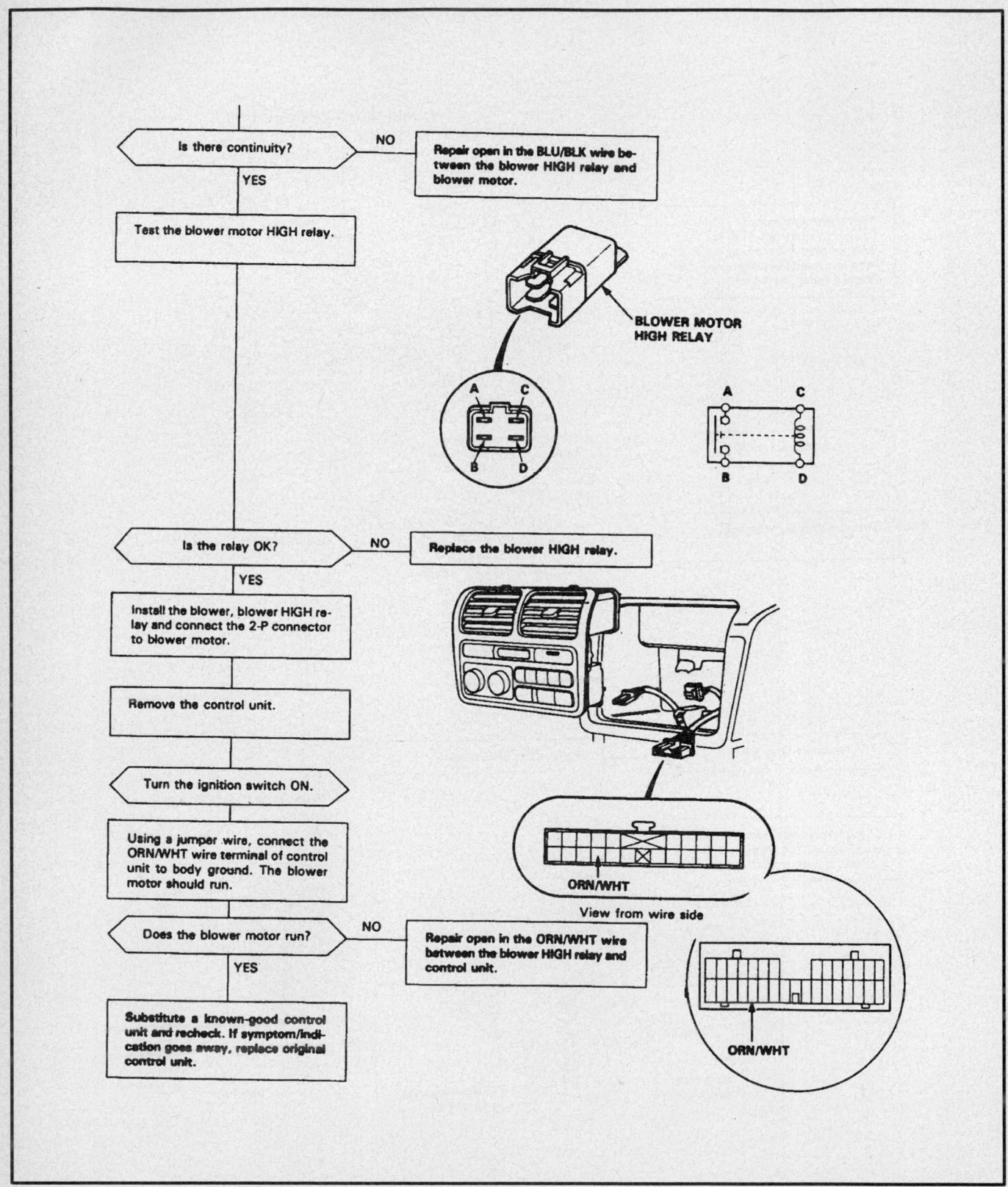

Is there continuity? — NO → Repair open in the BLU/BLK wire between the blower HIGH relay and blower motor.

YES

Test the blower motor HIGH relay.

BLOWER MOTOR HIGH RELAY

Is the relay OK? — NO → Replace the blower HIGH relay.

YES

Install the blower, blower HIGH relay and connect the 2-P connector to blower motor.

Remove the control unit.

Turn the ignition switch ON.

Using a jumper wire, connect the ORN/WHT wire terminal of control unit to body ground. The blower motor should run.

ORN/WHT

View from wire side

Does the blower motor run? — NO → Repair open in the ORN/WHT wire between the blower HIGH relay and control unit.

YES

Substitute a known-good control unit and recheck. If symptom/indication goes away, replace original control unit.

ORN/WHT

BLOWER MOTOR DIAGNOSTIC CHART—1993 LEGEND AND LEGEND COUPE—CONTINUED

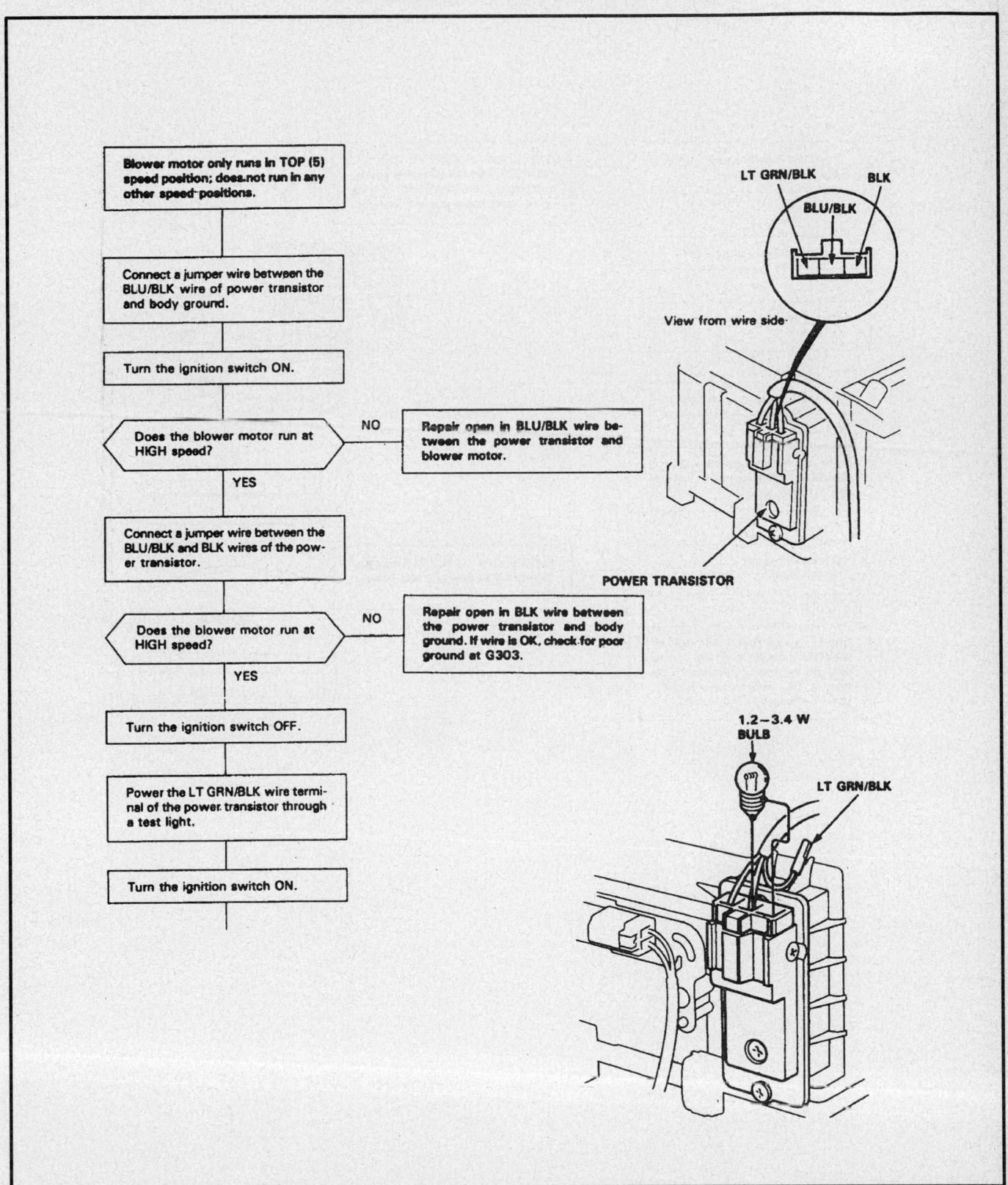

Blower motor only runs in TOP (5) speed position; does not run in any other speed positions.

Connect a jumper wire between the BLU/BLK wire of power transistor and body ground.

Turn the ignition switch ON.

Does the blower motor run at HIGH speed? — **NO** → Repair open in BLU/BLK wire between the power transistor and blower motor.

YES

Connect a jumper wire between the BLU/BLK and BLK wires of the power transistor.

Does the blower motor run at HIGH speed? — **NO** → Repair open in BLK wire between the power transistor and body ground. If wire is OK, check for poor ground at G303.

YES

Turn the ignition switch OFF.

Power the LT GRN/BLK wire terminal of the power transistor through a test light.

Turn the ignition switch ON.

LT GRN/BLK   BLK
BLU/BLK

View from wire side

POWER TRANSISTOR

1.2–3.4 W BULB

LT GRN/BLK

BLOWER MOTOR DIAGNOSTIC CHART—1993 LEGEND AND LEGEND COUPE—CONTINUED

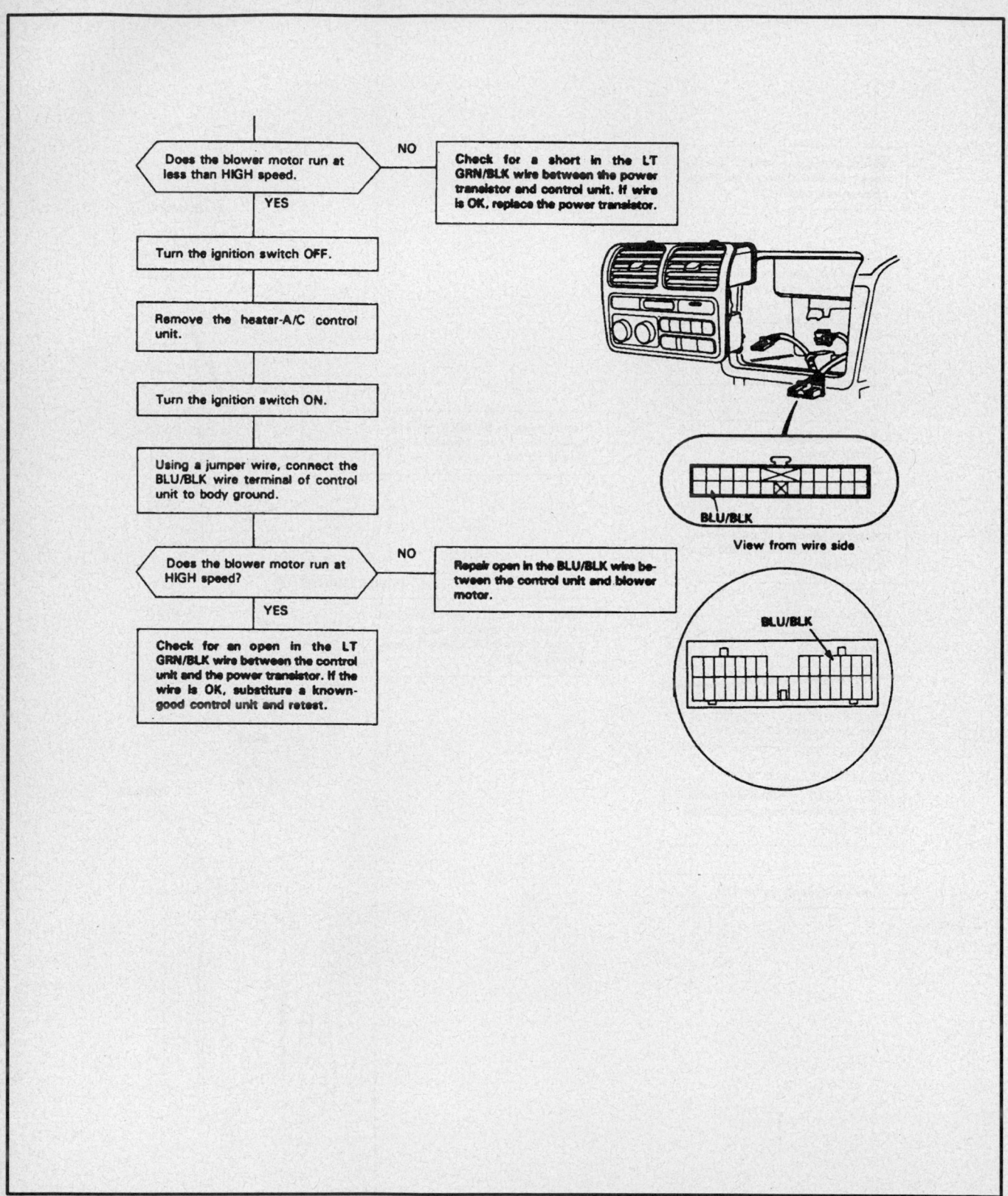

Does the blower motor run at less than HIGH speed.

NO → Check for a short in the LT GRN/BLK wire between the power transistor and control unit. If wire is OK, replace the power transistor.

YES

Turn the ignition switch OFF.

Remove the heater-A/C control unit.

Turn the ignition switch ON.

Using a jumper wire, connect the BLU/BLK wire terminal of control unit to body ground.

Does the blower motor run at HIGH speed?

NO → Repair open in the BLU/BLK wire between the control unit and blower motor.

YES

Check for an open in the LT GRN/BLK wire between the control unit and the power transistor. If the wire is OK, substitute a known-good control unit and retest.

BLU/BLK

View from wire side

BLU/BLK

AIR CONDITIONER COMPRESSOR DIAGNOSTIC CHART—1993 LEGEND AND LEGEND COUPE

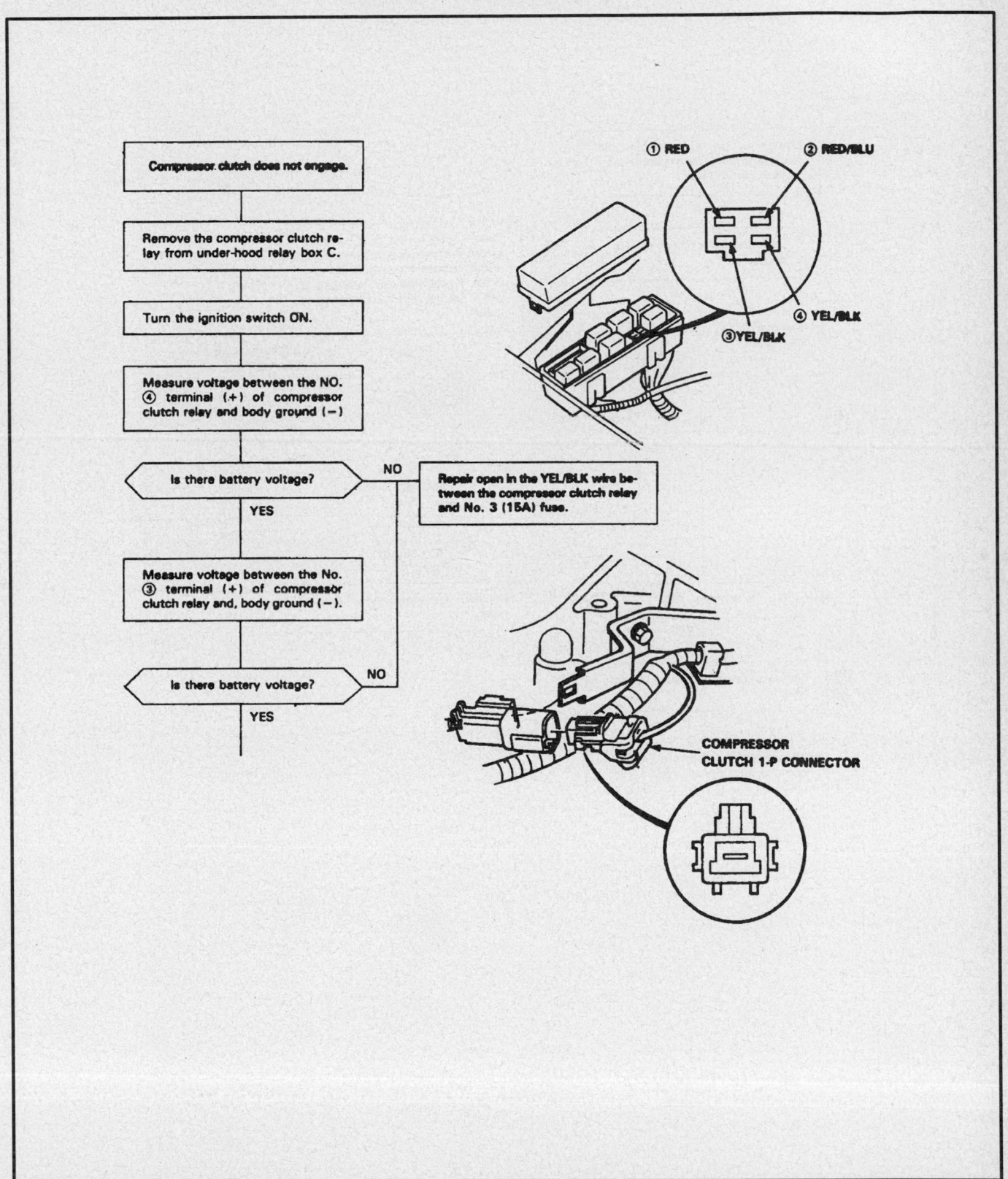

Compressor clutch does not engage.

Remove the compressor clutch relay from under-hood relay box C.

Turn the ignition switch ON.

Measure voltage between the NO. ④ terminal (+) of compressor clutch relay and body ground (−).

Is there battery voltage? — NO → Repair open in the YEL/BLK wire between the compressor clutch relay and No. 3 (15A) fuse.

YES

Measure voltage between the No. ③ terminal (+) of compressor clutch relay and, body ground (−).

Is there battery voltage? — NO

YES

① RED   ② RED/BLU
③ YEL/BLK   ④ YEL/BLK

COMPRESSOR CLUTCH 1-P CONNECTOR

AIR CONDITIONER COMPRESSOR DIAGNOSTIC CHART—1993 LEGEND AND LEGEND COUPE—CONTINUED

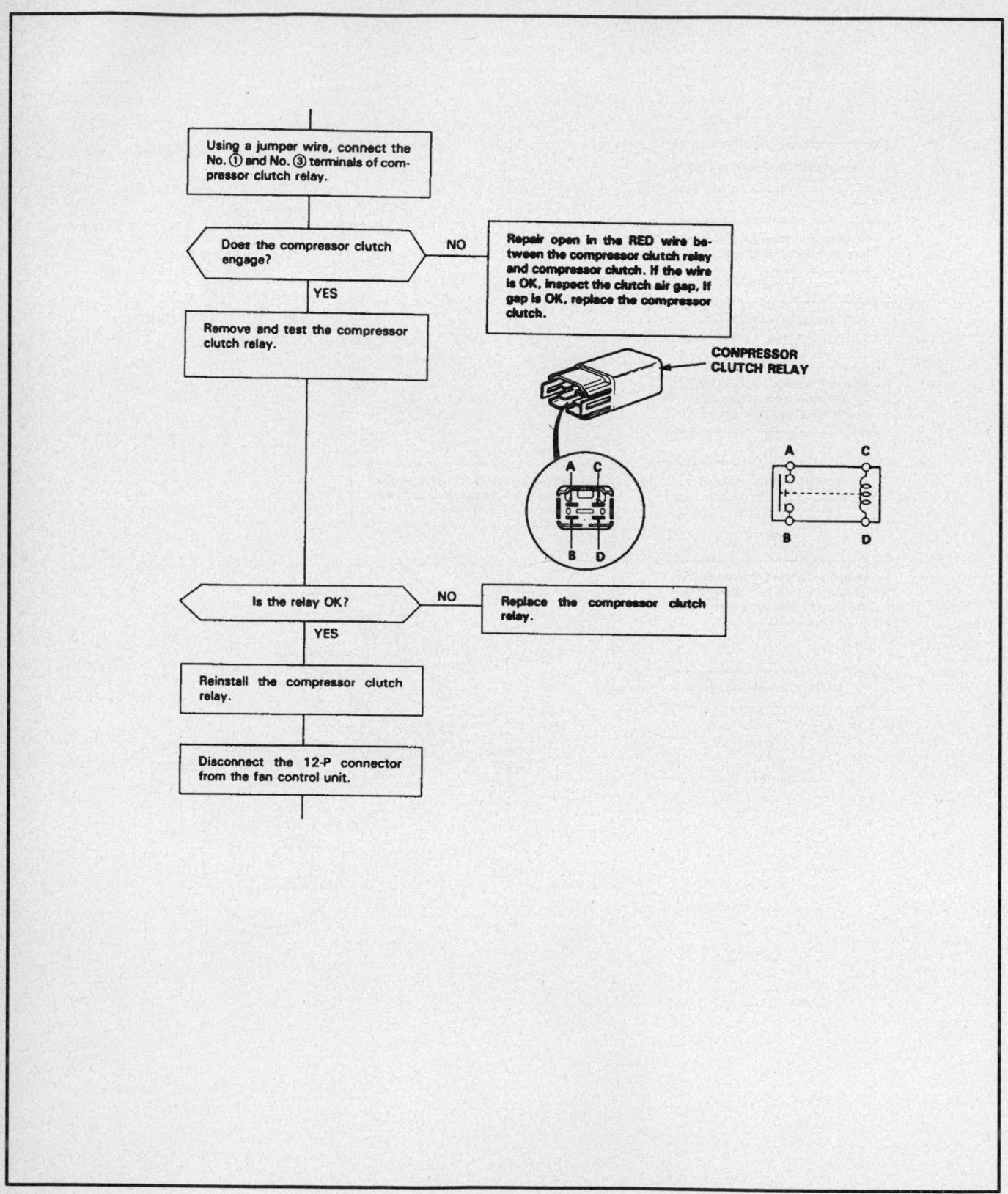

Using a jumper wire, connect the No. ① and No. ③ terminals of compressor clutch relay.

Does the compressor clutch engage? → **NO** → Repair open in the RED wire between the compressor clutch relay and compressor clutch. If the wire is OK, inspect the clutch air gap. If gap is OK, replace the compressor clutch.

YES

Remove and test the compressor clutch relay.

CONPRESSOR CLUTCH RELAY

Is the relay OK? → **NO** → Replace the compressor clutch relay.

YES

Reinstall the compressor clutch relay.

Disconnect the 12-P connector from the fan control unit.

AIR CONDITIONER COMPRESSOR DIAGNOSTIC CHART – 1993 LEGEND AND LEGEND COUPE – CONTINUED

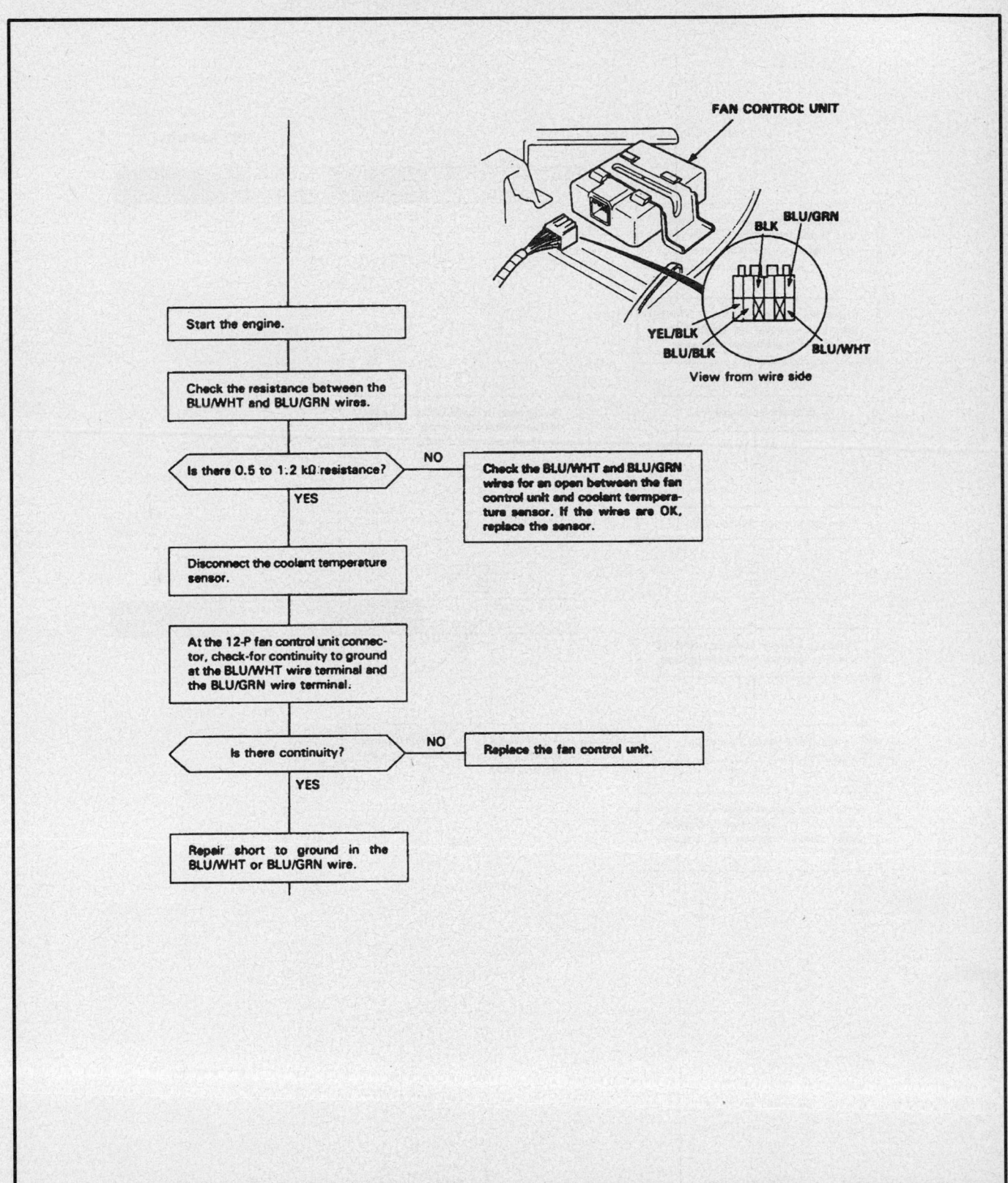

FAN CONTROL UNIT

BLK   BLU/GRN

YEL/BLK

BLU/BLK   BLU/WHT

View from wire side

Start the engine.

Check the resistance between the BLU/WHT and BLU/GRN wires.

Is there 0.5 to 1.2 kΩ resistance? —**NO**→ Check the BLU/WHT and BLU/GRN wires for an open between the fan control unit and coolant temperature sensor. If the wires are OK, replace the sensor.

YES

Disconnect the coolant temperature sensor.

At the 12-P fan control unit connector, check for continuity to ground at the BLU/WHT wire terminal and the BLU/GRN wire terminal.

Is there continuity? —**NO**→ Replace the fan control unit.

YES

Repair short to ground in the BLU/WHT or BLU/GRN wire.

AIR CONDITIONER COMPRESSOR DIAGNOSTIC CHART—1993 LEGEND AND LEGEND COUPE—CONTINUED

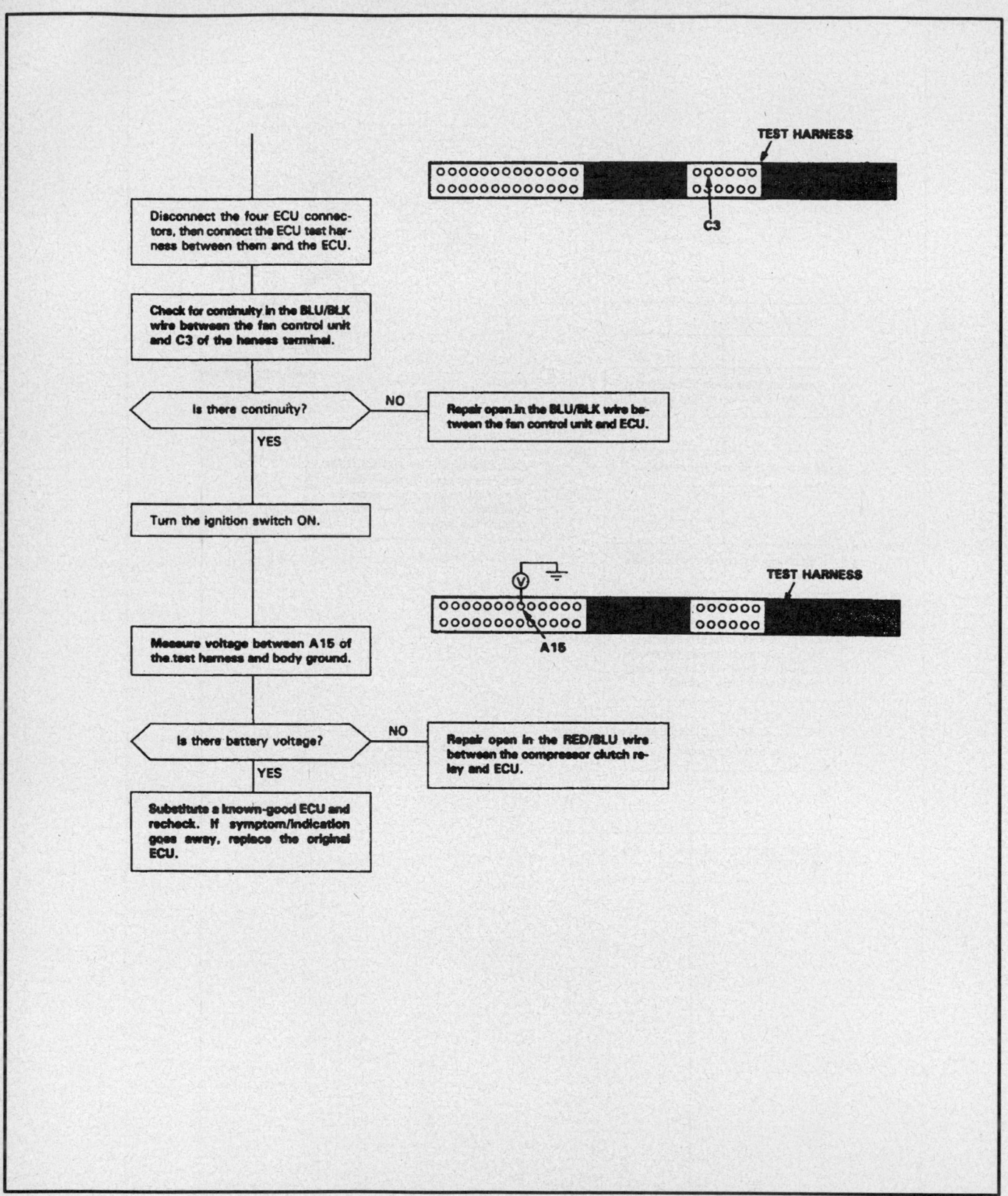

POWER CIRCUITS TO AIR CONDITIONING CONTROL UNIT DIAGNOSTIC CHART–NSX

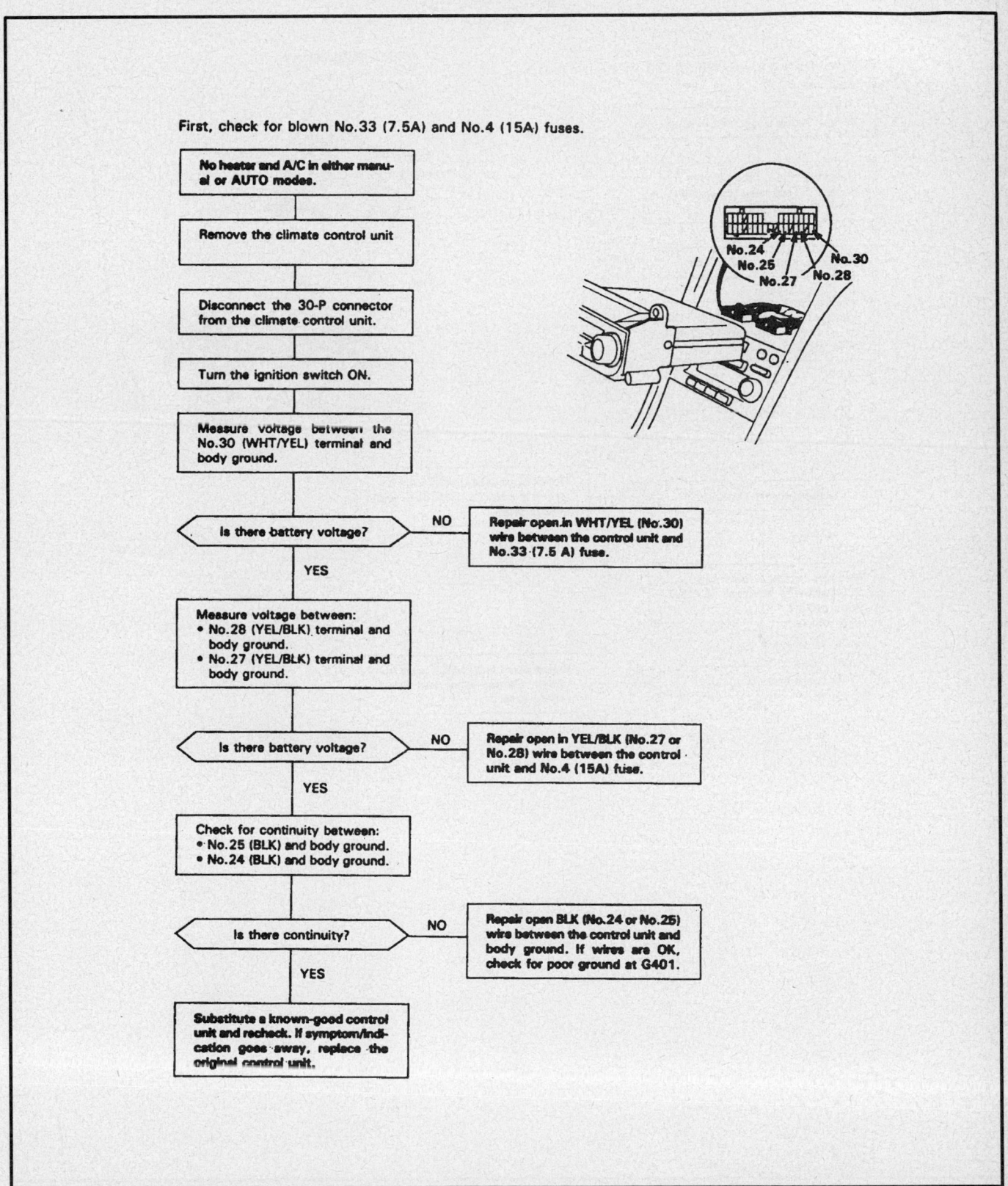

First, check for blown No.33 (7.5A) and No.4 (15A) fuses.

No heater and A/C in either manual or AUTO modes.

↓

Remove the climate control unit

↓

Disconnect the 30-P connector from the climate control unit.

↓

Turn the ignition switch ON.

↓

Measure voltage between the No.30 (WHT/YEL) terminal and body ground.

↓

Is there battery voltage? —**NO**→ Repair open in WHT/YEL (No.30) wire between the control unit and No.33 (7.5 A) fuse.

↓ **YES**

Measure voltage between:
• No.28 (YEL/BLK) terminal and body ground.
• No.27 (YEL/BLK) terminal and body ground.

↓

Is there battery voltage? —**NO**→ Repair open in YEL/BLK (No.27 or No.28) wire between the control unit and No.4 (15A) fuse.

↓ **YES**

Check for continuity between:
• No.25 (BLK) and body ground.
• No.24 (BLK) and body ground.

↓

Is there continuity? —**NO**→ Repair open BLK (No.24 or No.25) wire between the control unit and body ground. If wires are OK, check for poor ground at G401.

↓ **YES**

Substitute a known-good control unit and recheck. If symptom/indication goes away, replace the original control unit.

No.24
No.25
No.27
No.30
No.28

BLOWER MOTOR DIAGNOSTIC CHART—NSX

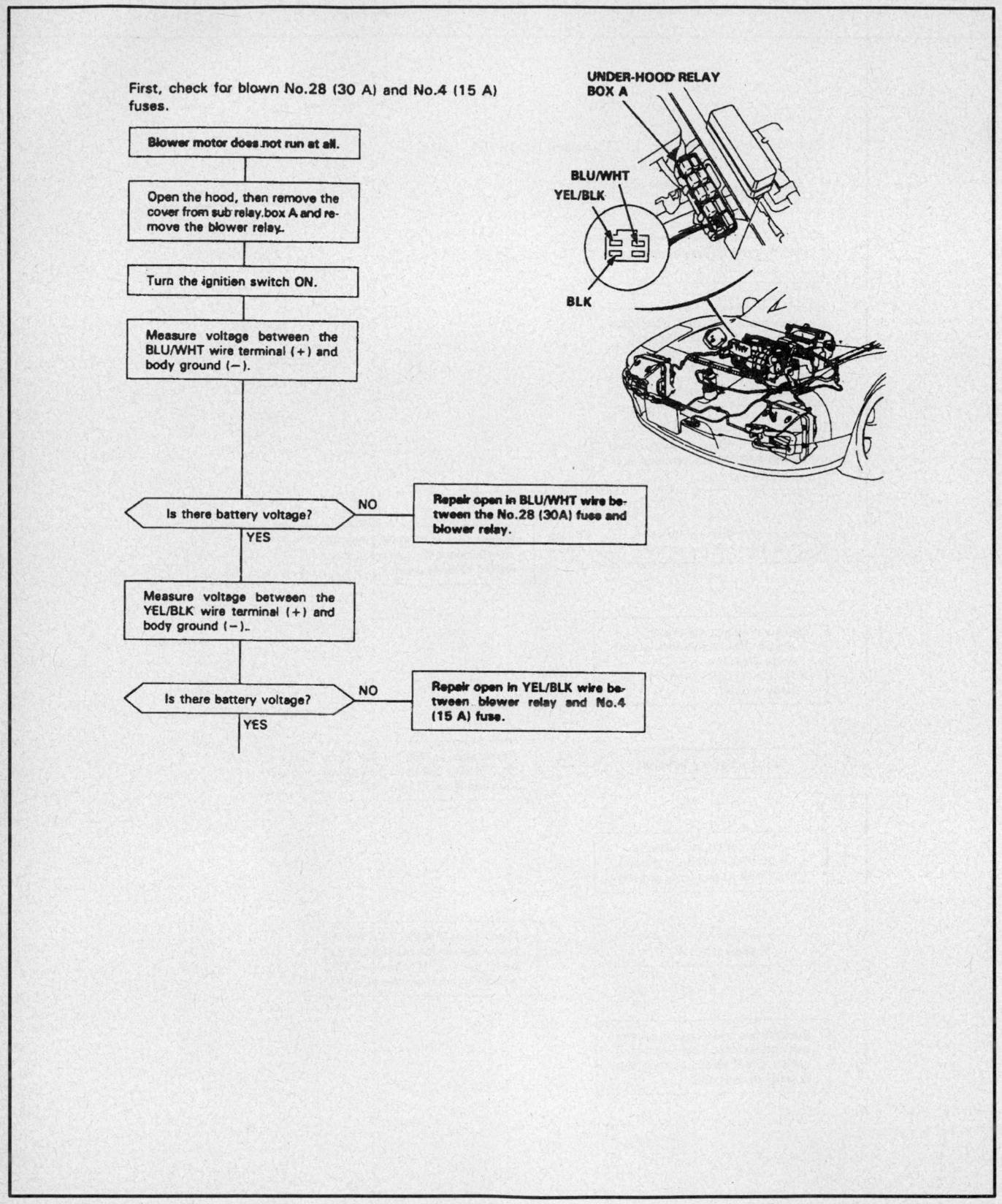

First, check for blown No.28 (30 A) and No.4 (15 A) fuses.

Blower motor does not run at all.

Open the hood, then remove the cover from sub relay box A and remove the blower relay.

Turn the ignition switch ON.

Measure voltage between the BLU/WHT wire terminal (+) and body ground (−).

Is there battery voltage? —NO→ Repair open in BLU/WHT wire between the No.28 (30A) fuse and blower relay.

YES

Measure voltage between the YEL/BLK wire terminal (+) and body ground (−).

Is there battery voltage? —NO→ Repair open in YEL/BLK wire between blower relay and No.4 (15 A) fuse.

YES

UNDER-HOOD RELAY BOX A

BLU/WHT
YEL/BLK

BLK

BLOWER MOTOR DIAGNOSTIC CHART—NSX—CONTINUED

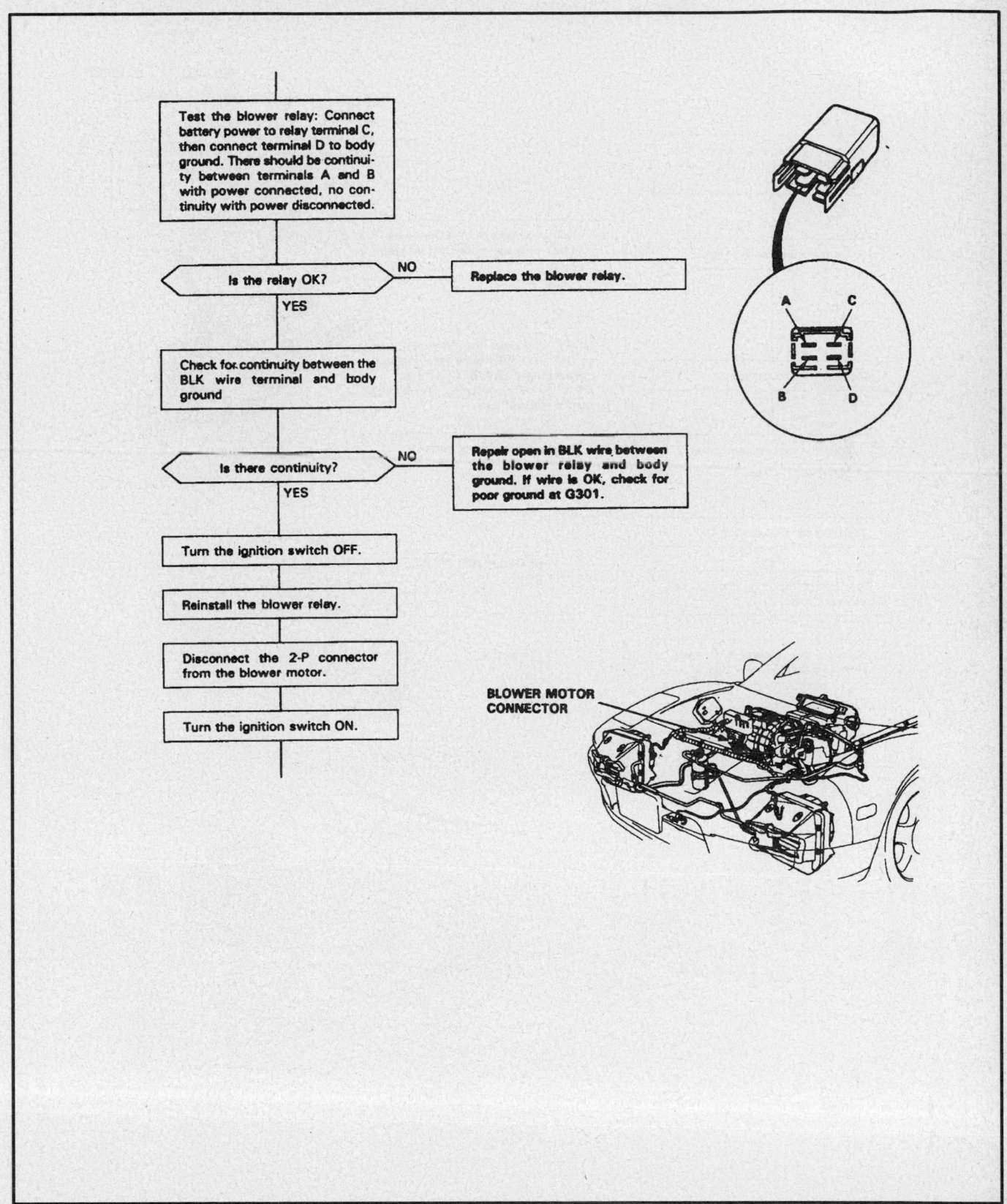

Test the blower relay: Connect battery power to relay terminal C, then connect terminal D to body ground. There should be continuity between terminals A and B with power connected, no continuity with power disconnected.

Is the relay OK? —NO→ Replace the blower relay.

YES

Check for continuity between the BLK wire terminal and body ground

Is there continuity? —NO→ Repair open in BLK wire between the blower relay and body ground. If wire is OK, check for poor ground at G301.

YES

Turn the ignition switch OFF.

Reinstall the blower relay.

Disconnect the 2-P connector from the blower motor.

Turn the ignition switch ON.

BLOWER MOTOR CONNECTOR

BLOWER MOTOR DIAGNOSTIC CHART–NSX–CONTINUED

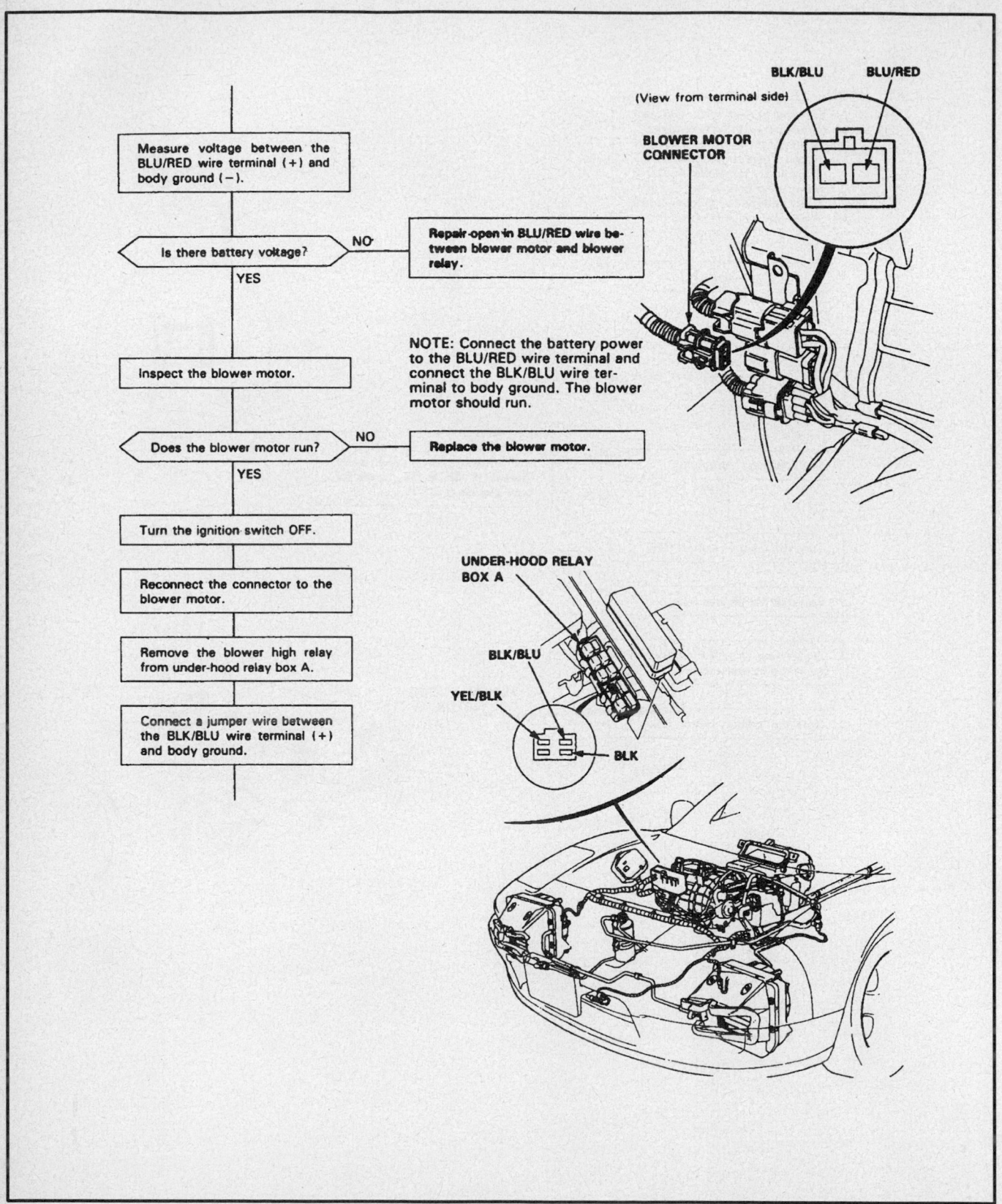

Measure voltage between the BLU/RED wire terminal (+) and body ground (−).

Is there battery voltage? — NO → Repair open in BLU/RED wire between blower motor and blower relay.

YES

(View from terminal side)

BLK/BLU   BLU/RED

BLOWER MOTOR CONNECTOR

Inspect the blower motor.

NOTE: Connect the battery power to the BLU/RED wire terminal and connect the BLK/BLU wire terminal to body ground. The blower motor should run.

Does the blower motor run? — NO → Replace the blower motor.

YES

Turn the ignition switch OFF.

Reconnect the connector to the blower motor.

UNDER-HOOD RELAY BOX A

BLK/BLU

YEL/BLK

BLK

Remove the blower high relay from under-hood relay box A.

Connect a jumper wire between the BLK/BLU wire terminal (+) and body ground.

BLOWER MOTOR DIAGNOSTIC CHART—NSX—CONTINUED

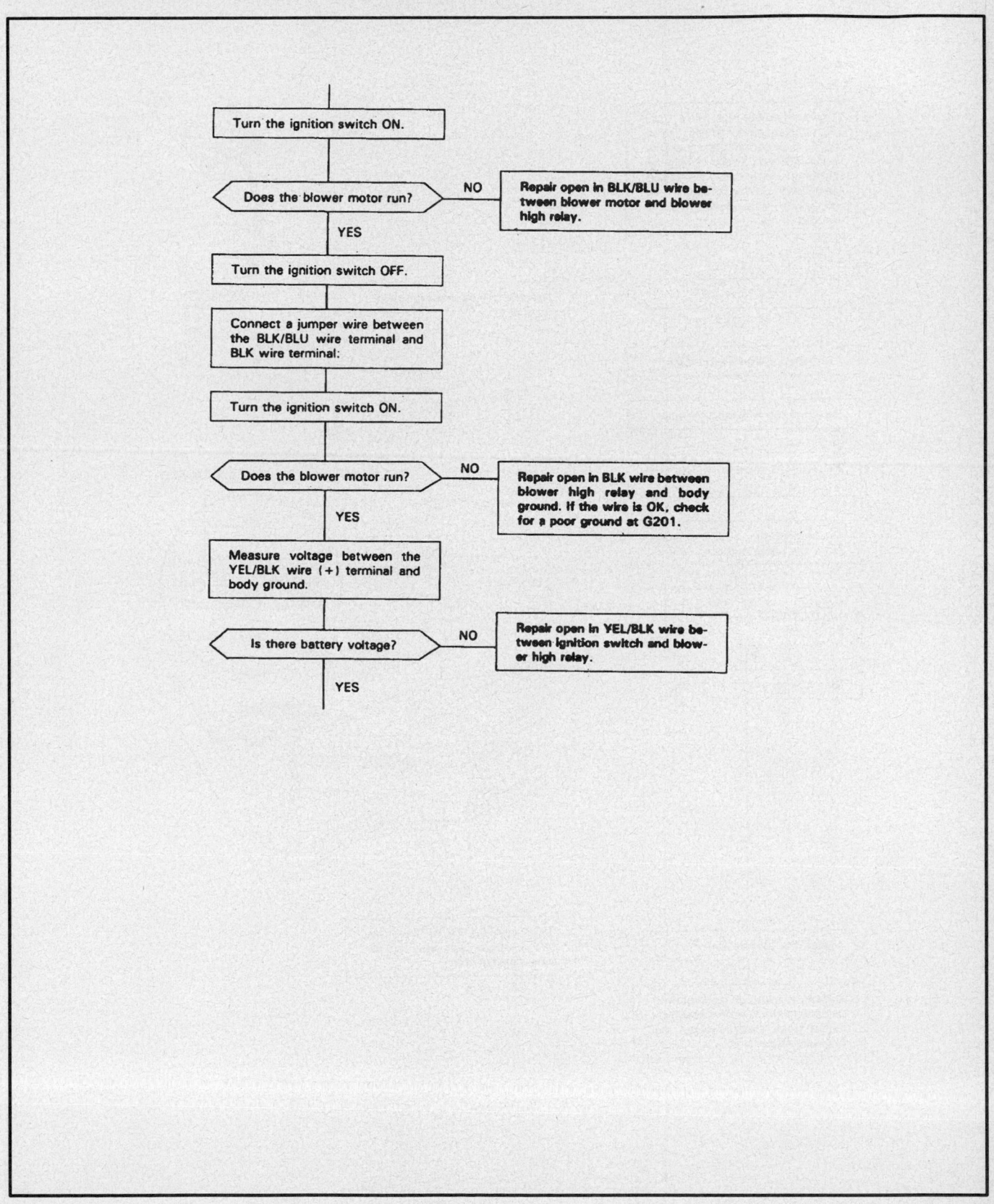

Turn the ignition switch ON.

Does the blower motor run? — **NO** → Repair open in BLK/BLU wire between blower motor and blower high relay.

YES

Turn the ignition switch OFF.

Connect a jumper wire between the BLK/BLU wire terminal and BLK wire terminal:

Turn the ignition switch ON.

Does the blower motor run? — **NO** → Repair open in BLK wire between blower high relay and body ground. If the wire is OK, check for a poor ground at G201.

YES

Measure voltage between the YEL/BLK wire (+) terminal and body ground.

Is there battery voltage? — **NO** → Repair open in YEL/BLK wire between ignition switch and blower high relay.

YES

BLOWER MOTOR DIAGNOSTIC CHART–NSX–CONTINUED

Test the blower high relay: Connect battery power to relay terminal C, then connect terminal D to body ground. There should be continuity between terminals A and B with power connected, no continuity with power disconnected.

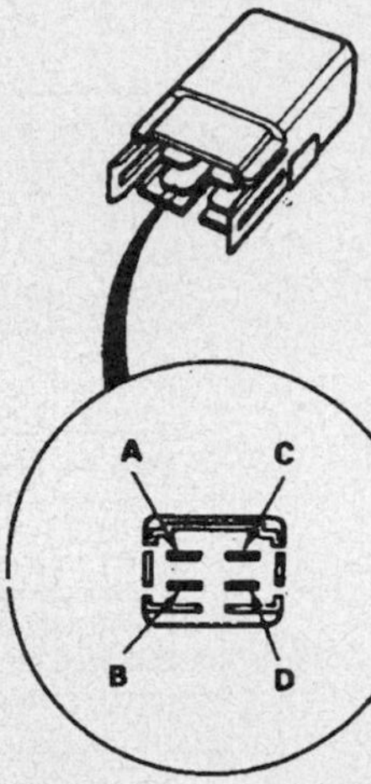

Is the relay OK? —NO→ Replace the blower high relay.

YES

Turn the ignition switch OFF.

Reinstall the blower high relay.

Remove the climate control unit.

Disconnect the 30-P connector from the climate control unit.

Connect a jumper wire between the ORN/WHT wire terminal and body ground:

Turn the ignition switch ON.

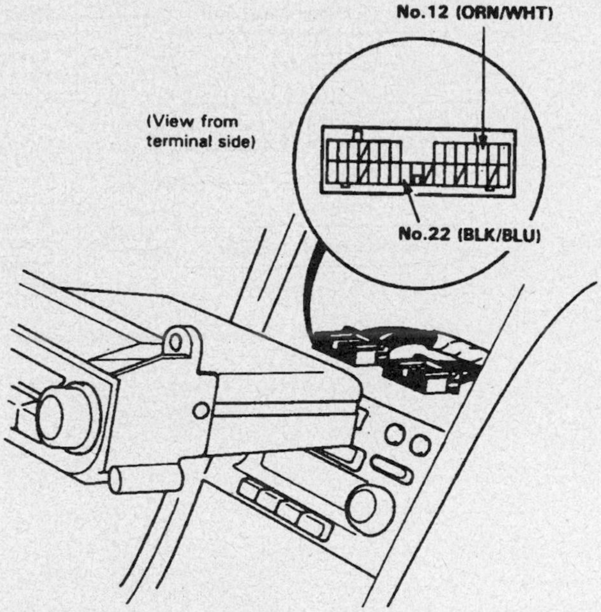

Does the blower motor run? —NO→ Repair open in ORN/WHT wire between blower high relay and climate control unit.

YES

Substitute a known-good control unit and recheck. If symptom/indication goes away, replace the original control unit.

A C

B D

No.12 (ORN/WHT)

(View from terminal side)

No.22 (BLK/BLU)

BLOWER MOTOR DIAGNOSTIC CHART—NSX—CONTINUED

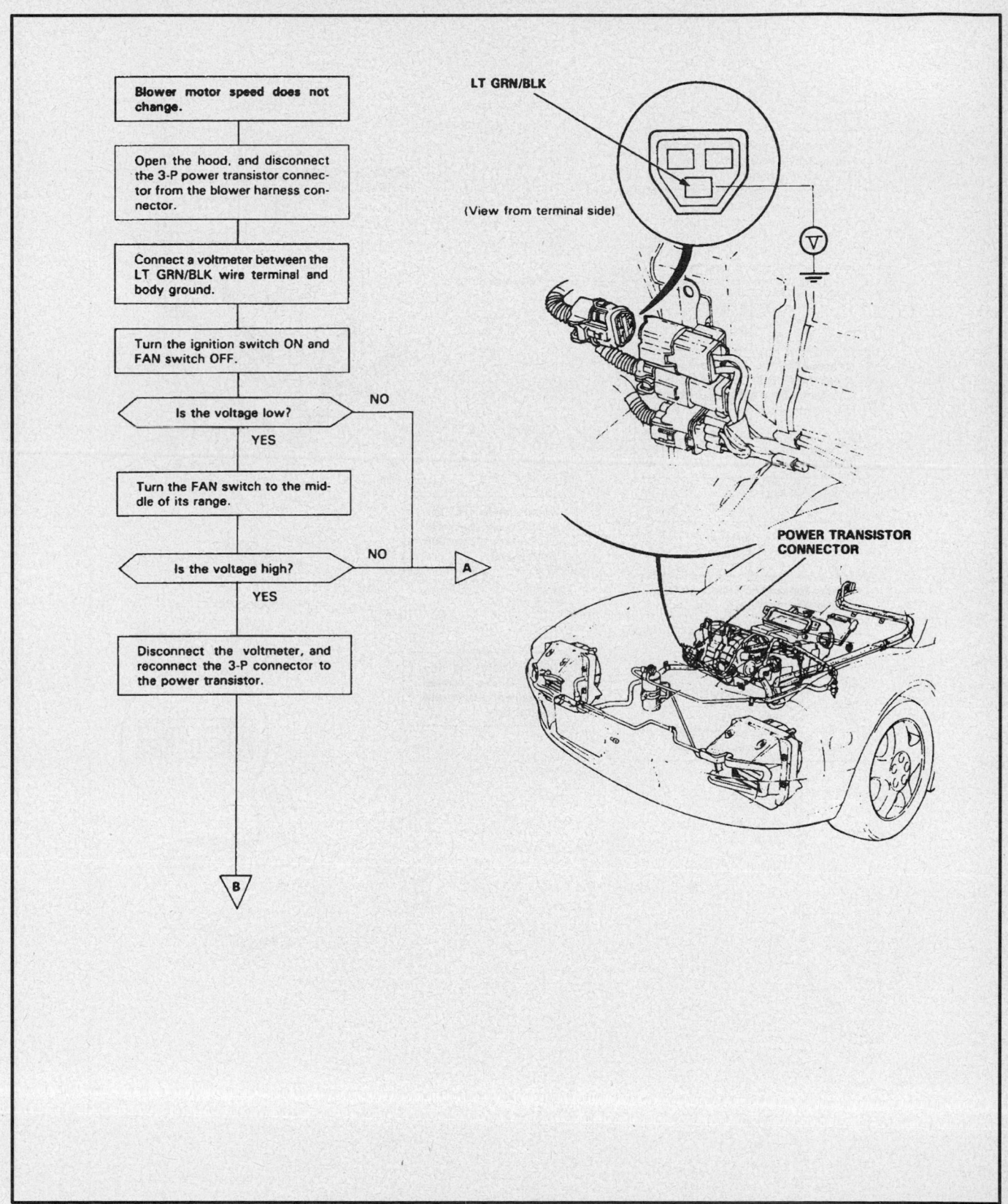

Blower motor speed does not change.

Open the hood, and disconnect the 3-P power transistor connector from the blower harness connector.

Connect a voltmeter between the LT GRN/BLK wire terminal and body ground.

Turn the ignition switch ON and FAN switch OFF.

Is the voltage low? — NO

YES

Turn the FAN switch to the middle of its range.

Is the voltage high? — NO → A

YES

Disconnect the voltmeter, and reconnect the 3-P connector to the power transistor.

B

LT GRN/BLK

(View from terminal side)

POWER TRANSISTOR CONNECTOR

BLOWER MOTOR DIAGNOSTIC CHART—NSX—CONTINUED

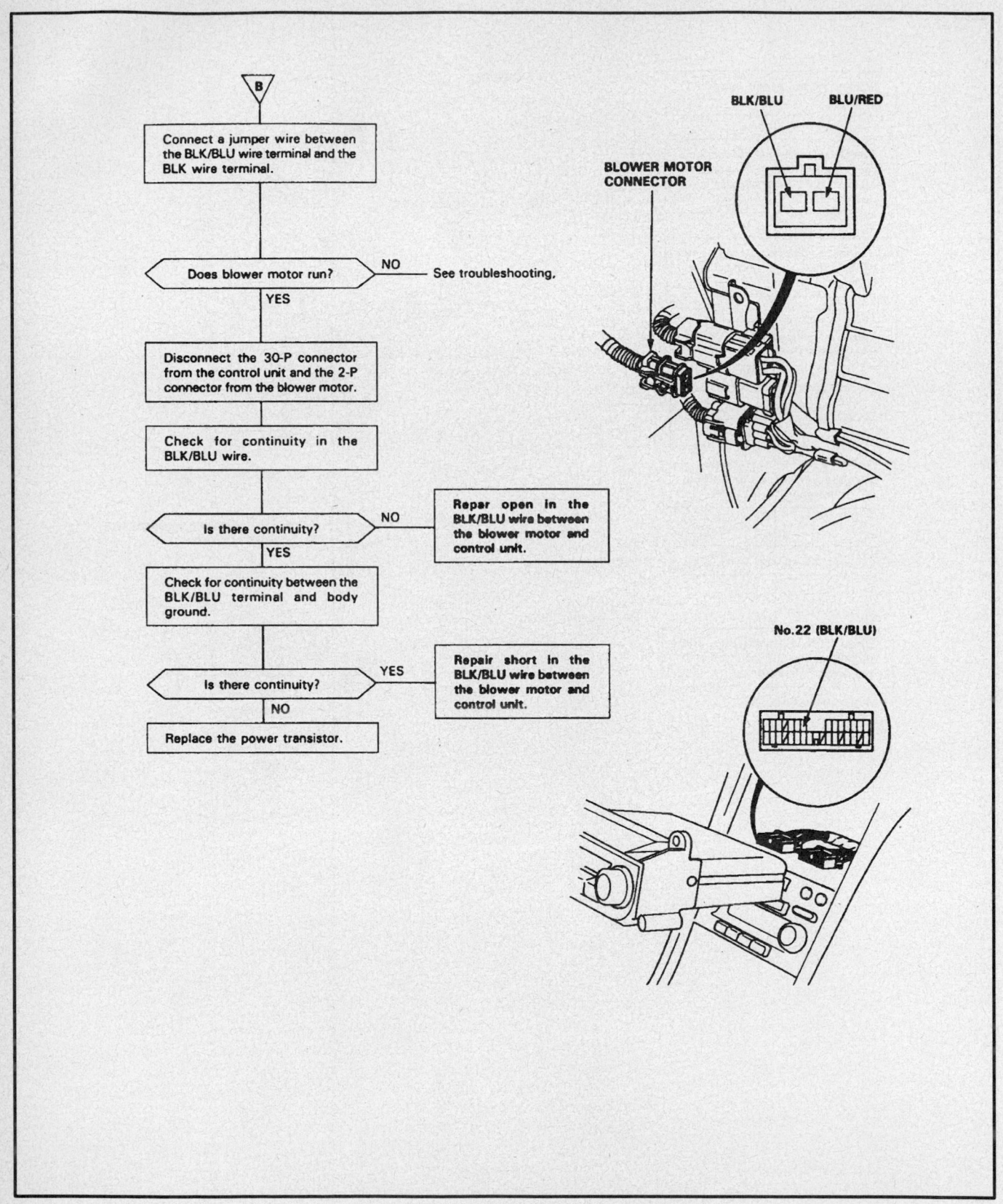

B

Connect a jumper wire between the BLK/BLU wire terminal and the BLK wire terminal.

Does blower motor run? — NO → See troubleshooting.

YES

Disconnect the 30-P connector from the control unit and the 2-P connector from the blower motor.

Check for continuity in the BLK/BLU wire.

Is there continuity? — NO → Repair open in the BLK/BLU wire between the blower motor and control unit.

YES

Check for continuity between the BLK/BLU terminal and body ground.

Is there continuity? — YES → Repair short in the BLK/BLU wire between the blower motor and control unit.

NO

Replace the power transistor.

BLK/BLU   BLU/RED

BLOWER MOTOR CONNECTOR

No.22 (BLK/BLU)

BLOWER MOTOR DIAGNOSTIC CHART—NSX—CONTINUED

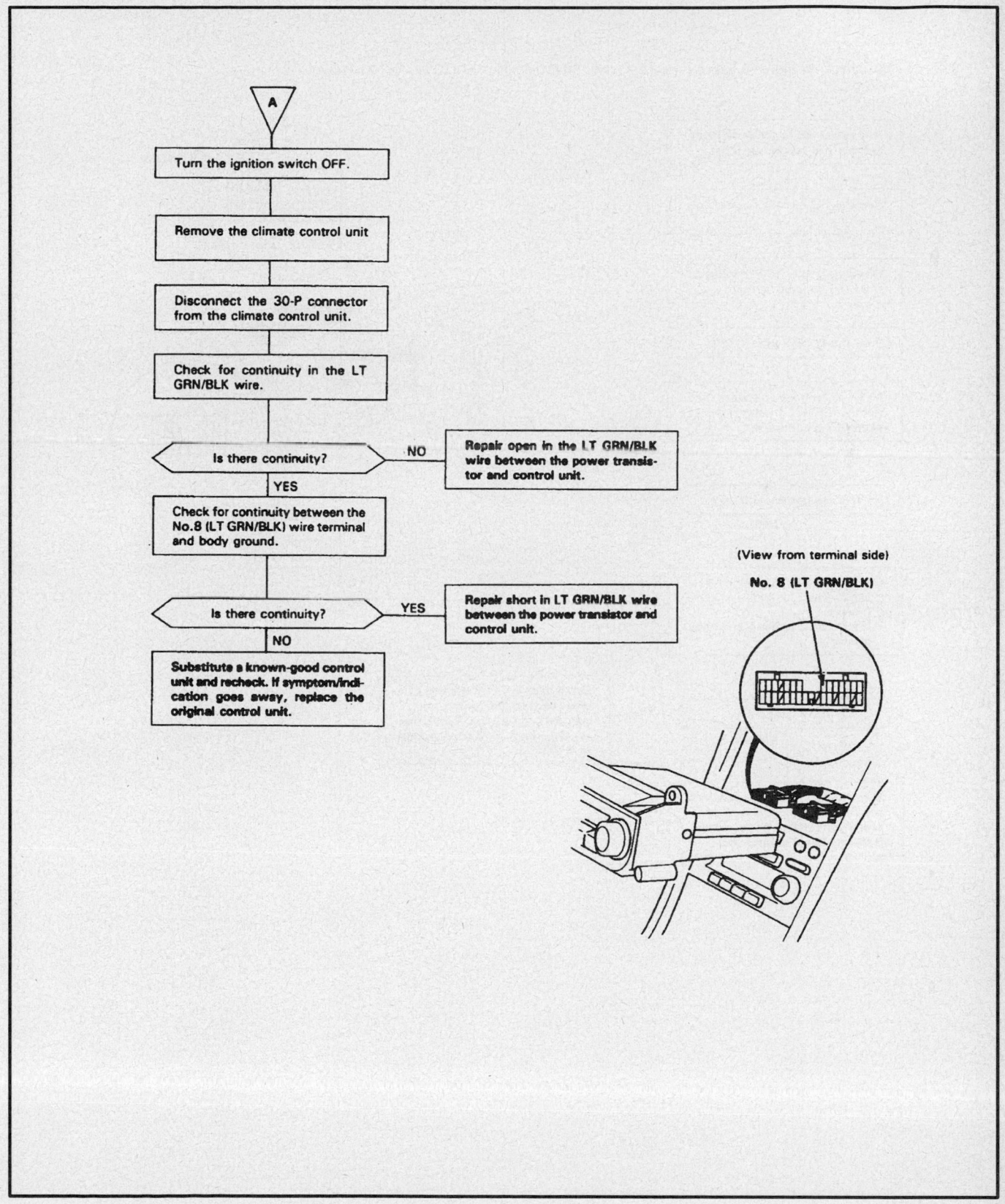

A

Turn the ignition switch OFF.

Remove the climate control unit

Disconnect the 30-P connector from the climate control unit.

Check for continuity in the LT GRN/BLK wire.

Is there continuity? — NO → Repair open in the LT GRN/BLK wire between the power transistor and control unit.

YES

Check for continuity between the No.8 (LT GRN/BLK) wire terminal and body ground.

Is there continuity? — YES → Repair short in LT GRN/BLK wire between the power transistor and control unit.

NO

Substitute a known-good control unit and recheck. If symptom/indication goes away, replace the original control unit.

(View from terminal side)

No. 8 (LT GRN/BLK)

AIR CONDITIONING SYSTEM DIAGNOSTIC CHART—NSX

First, check for blown fuses: No. 4 (15 A), No. 36 (10 A), No. 37 (10 A), No. 21 (10 A).

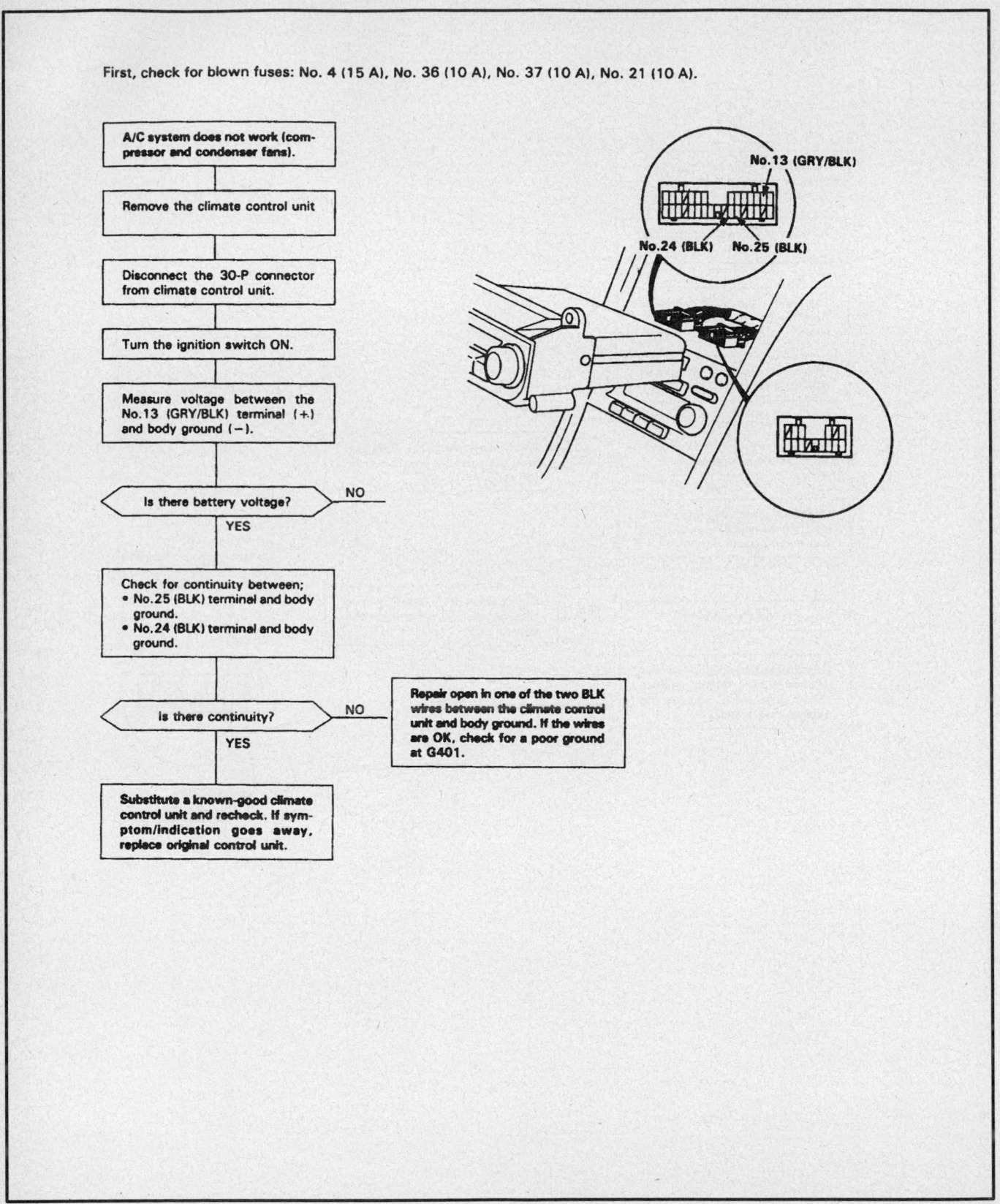

A/C system does not work (compressor and condenser fans).

Remove the climate control unit

Disconnect the 30-P connector from climate control unit.

Turn the ignition switch ON.

Measure voltage between the No.13 (GRY/BLK) terminal (+) and body ground (−).

Is there battery voltage? — NO

YES

Check for continuity between;
• No.25 (BLK) terminal and body ground.
• No.24 (BLK) terminal and body ground.

Is there continuity? — NO

Repair open in one of the two BLK wires between the climate control unit and body ground. If the wires are OK, check for a poor ground at G401.

YES

Substitute a known-good climate control unit and recheck. If symptom/indication goes away, replace original control unit.

No.13 (GRY/BLK)

No.24 (BLK)   No.25 (BLK)

AIR CONDITIONING SYSTEM DIAGNOSTIC CHART—NSX—CONTINUED

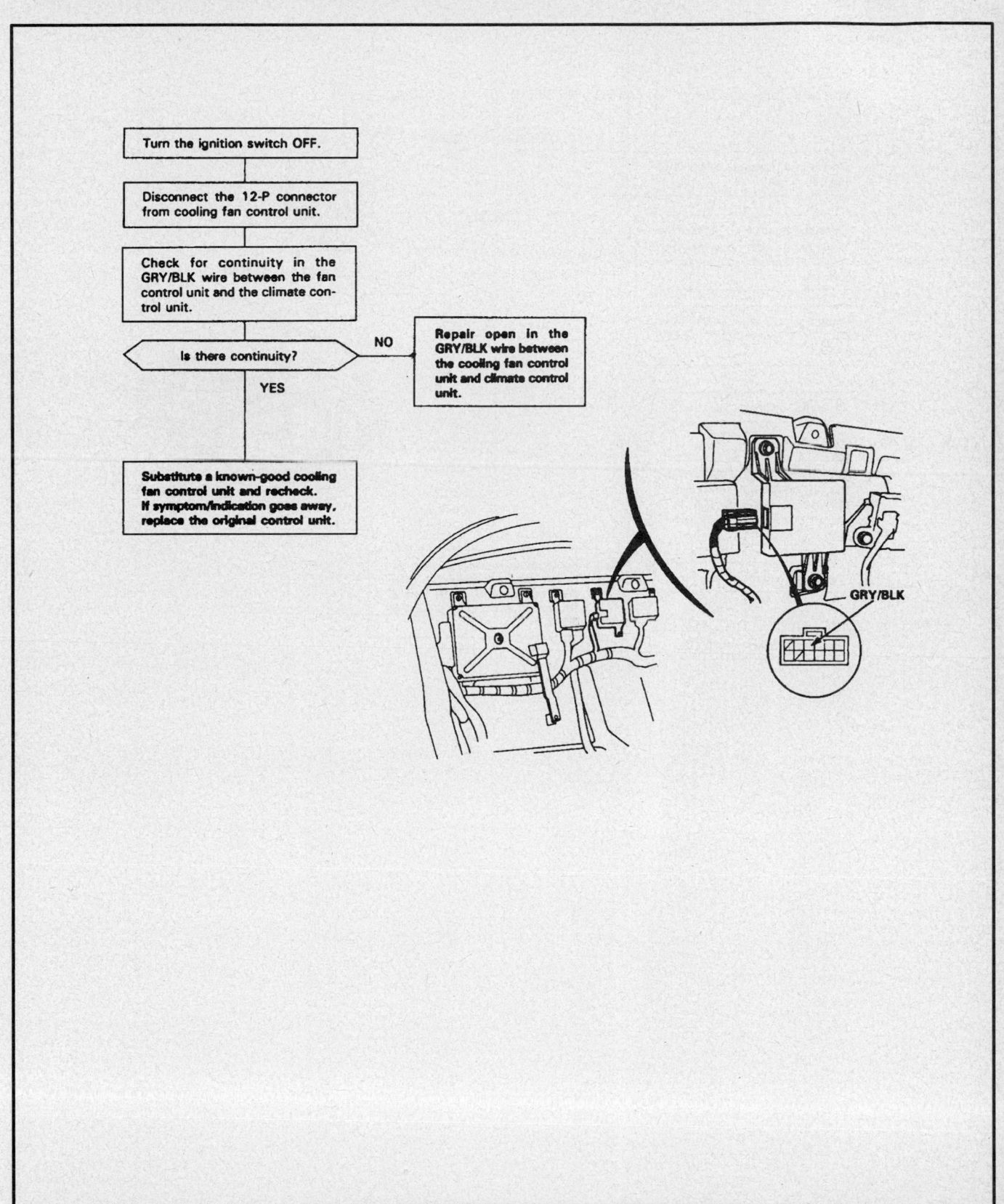

Turn the ignition switch OFF.

Disconnect the 12-P connector from cooling fan control unit.

Check for continuity in the GRY/BLK wire between the fan control unit and the climate control unit.

Is there continuity? — NO → Repair open in the GRY/BLK wire between the cooling fan control unit and climate control unit.

YES

Substitute a known-good cooling fan control unit and recheck. If symptom/indication goes away, replace the original control unit.

GRY/BLK

CONDENSER FAN DIAGNOSTIC CHART—NSX

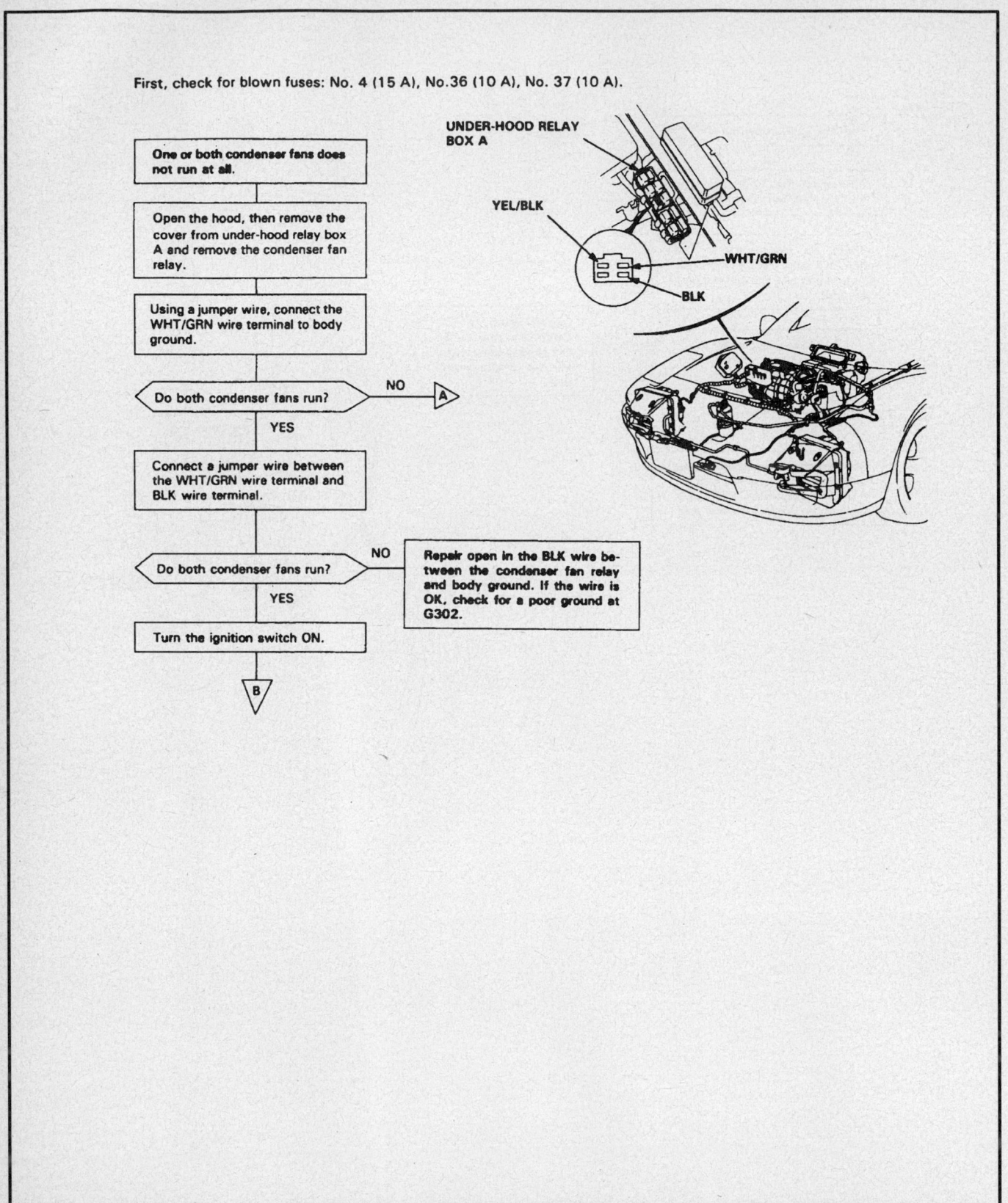

First, check for blown fuses: No. 4 (15 A), No.36 (10 A), No. 37 (10 A).

One or both condenser fans does not run at all.

Open the hood, then remove the cover from under-hood relay box A and remove the condenser fan relay.

Using a jumper wire, connect the WHT/GRN wire terminal to body ground.

Do both condenser fans run? — NO → A

YES

Connect a jumper wire between the WHT/GRN wire terminal and BLK wire terminal.

Do both condenser fans run? — NO → Repair open in the BLK wire between the condenser fan relay and body ground. If the wire is OK, check for a poor ground at G302.

YES

Turn the ignition switch ON.

B

UNDER-HOOD RELAY BOX A

YEL/BLK

WHT/GRN

BLK

CONDENSER FAN DIAGNOSTIC CHART–NSX–CONTINUED

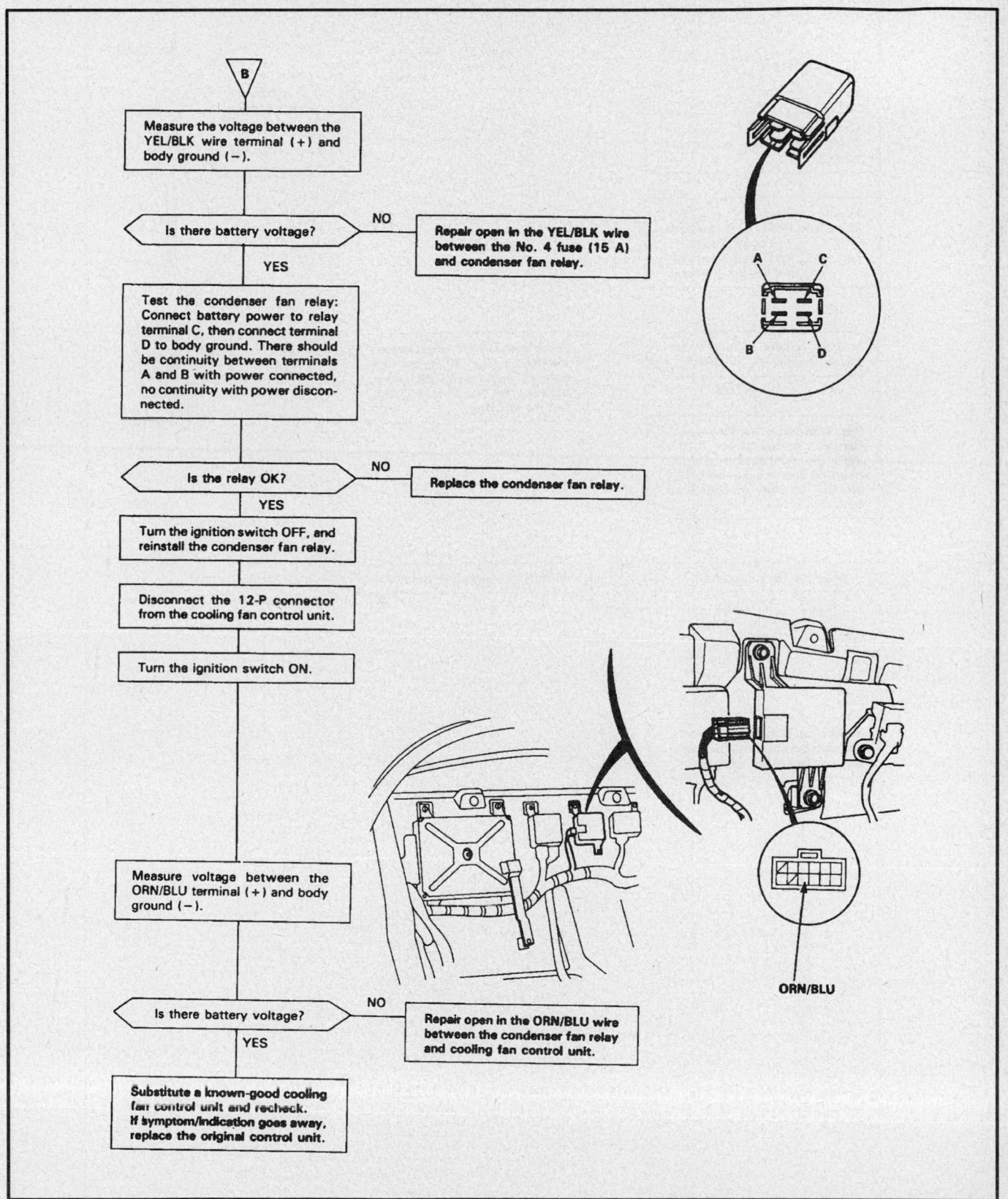

B

Measure the voltage between the YEL/BLK wire terminal (+) and body ground (−).

Is there battery voltage? — **NO** → Repair open in the YEL/BLK wire between the No. 4 fuse (15 A) and condenser fan relay.

YES

Test the condenser fan relay: Connect battery power to relay terminal C, then connect terminal D to body ground. There should be continuity between terminals A and B with power connected, no continuity with power disconnected.

Is the relay OK? — **NO** → Replace the condenser fan relay.

YES

Turn the ignition switch OFF, and reinstall the condenser fan relay.

Disconnect the 12-P connector from the cooling fan control unit.

Turn the ignition switch ON.

Measure voltage between the ORN/BLU terminal (+) and body ground (−).

Is there battery voltage? — **NO** → Repair open in the ORN/BLU wire between the condenser fan relay and cooling fan control unit.

YES

Substitute a known-good cooling fan control unit and recheck. If symptom/indication goes away, replace the original control unit.

ORN/BLU

CONDENSER FAN DIAGNOSTIC CHART—NSX—CONTINUED

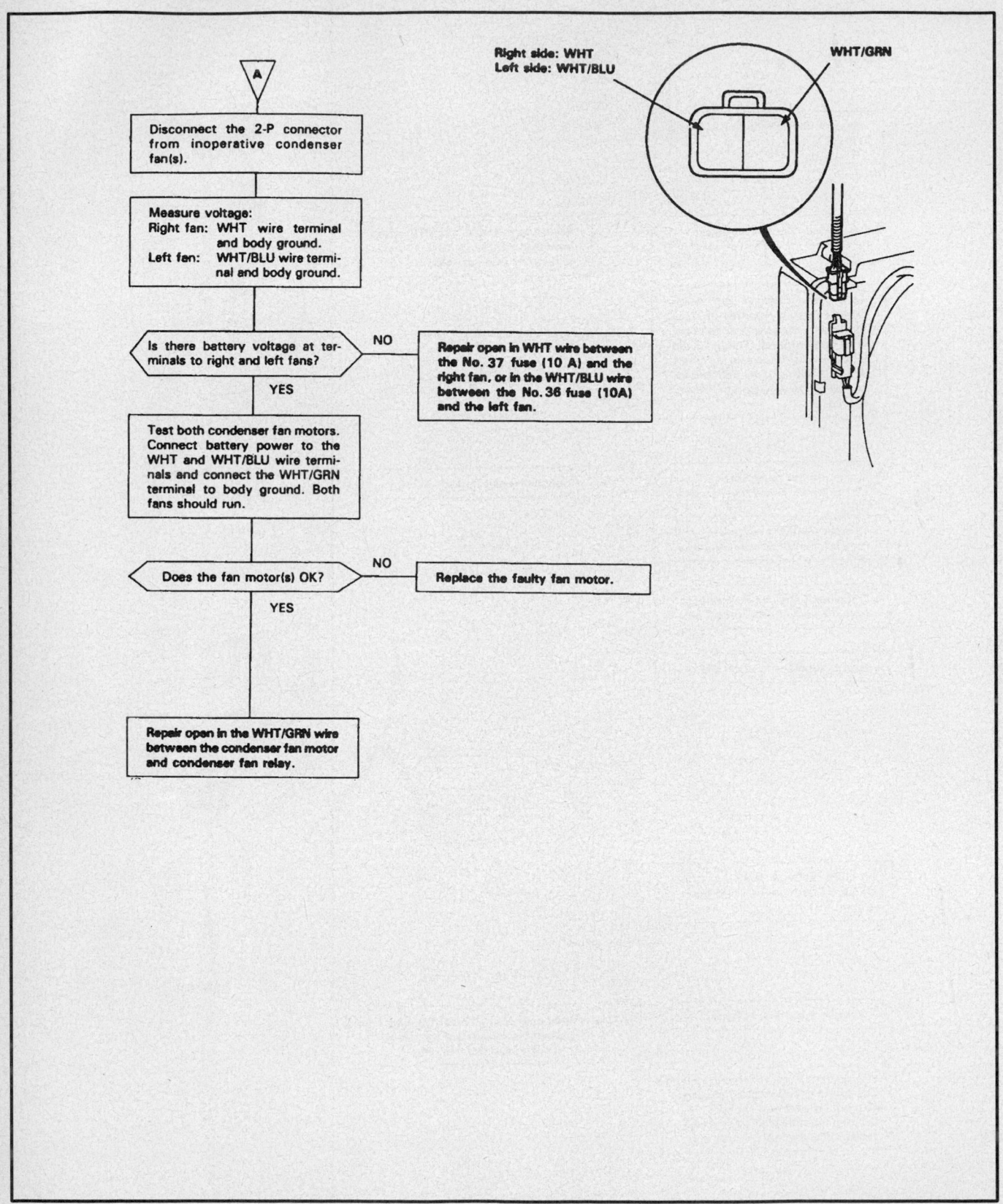

A

Disconnect the 2-P connector from inoperative condenser fan(s).

Measure voltage:
Right fan: WHT wire terminal and body ground.
Left fan: WHT/BLU wire terminal and body ground.

Is there battery voltage at terminals to right and left fans? — **NO** → Repair open in WHT wire between the No. 37 fuse (10 A) and the right fan, or in the WHT/BLU wire between the No. 36 fuse (10A) and the left fan.

YES

Test both condenser fan motors. Connect battery power to the WHT and WHT/BLU wire terminals and connect the WHT/GRN terminal to body ground. Both fans should run.

Does the fan motor(s) OK? — **NO** → Replace the faulty fan motor.

YES

Repair open in the WHT/GRN wire between the condenser fan motor and condenser fan relay.

Right side: WHT
Left side: WHT/BLU

WHT/GRN

COMPRESSOR DIAGNOSTIC CHART—NSX

First, check for blown fuses: No. 21 (10 A), No. 4 (15 A).

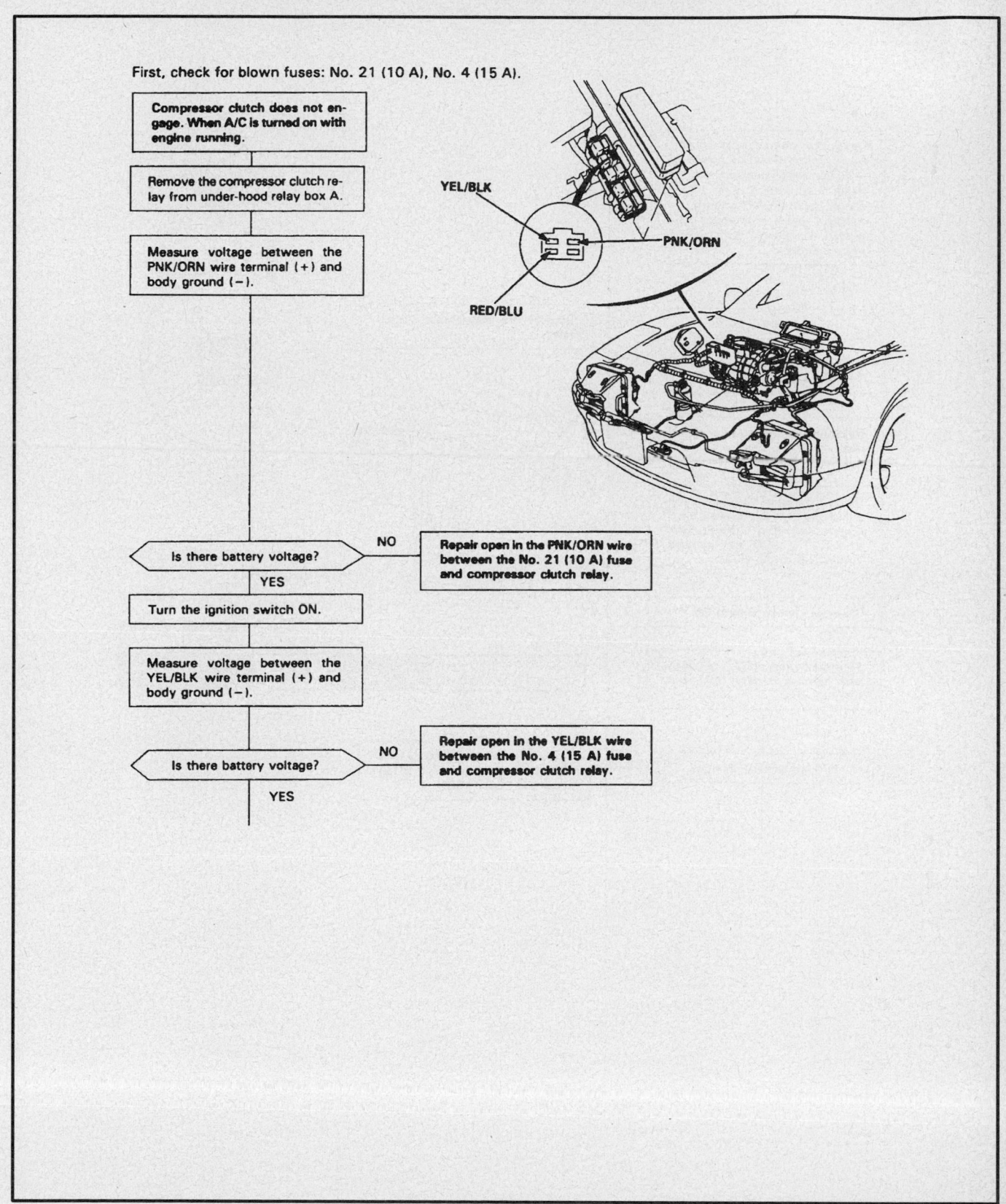

Compressor clutch does not engage. When A/C is turned on with engine running.

Remove the compressor clutch relay from under-hood relay box A.

Measure voltage between the PNK/ORN wire terminal (+) and body ground (−).

YEL/BLK

PNK/ORN

RED/BLU

Is there battery voltage? — **NO** → Repair open in the PNK/ORN wire between the No. 21 (10 A) fuse and compressor clutch relay.

YES

Turn the ignition switch ON.

Measure voltage between the YEL/BLK wire terminal (+) and body ground (−).

Is there battery voltage? — **NO** → Repair open in the YEL/BLK wire between the No. 4 (15 A) fuse and compressor clutch relay.

YES

COMPRESSOR DIAGNOSTIC CHART—NSX—CONTINUED

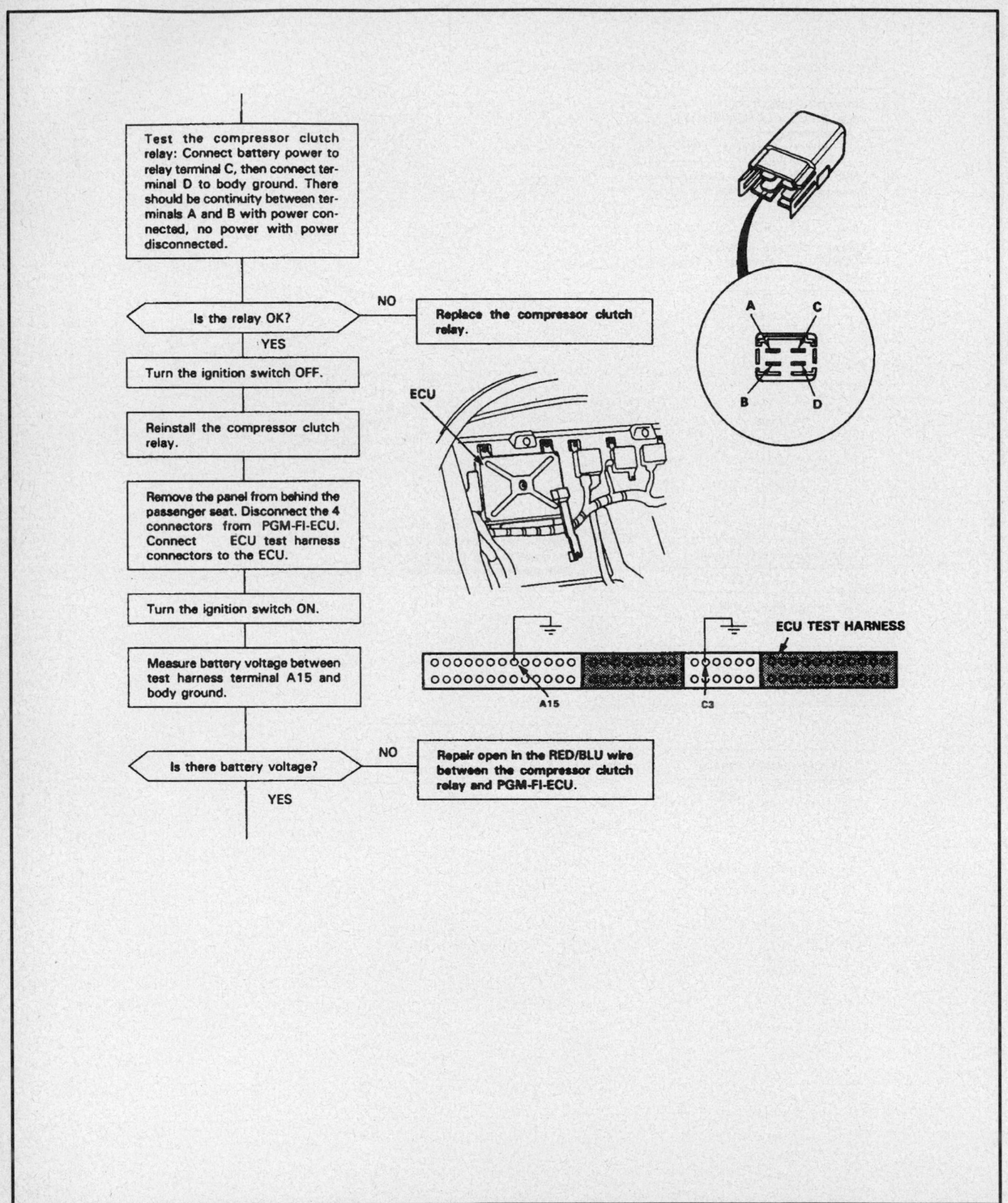

Test the compressor clutch relay: Connect battery power to relay terminal C, then connect terminal D to body ground. There should be continuity between terminals A and B with power connected, no power with power disconnected.

Is the relay OK? — NO → Replace the compressor clutch relay.

YES

Turn the ignition switch OFF.

Reinstall the compressor clutch relay.

Remove the panel from behind the passenger seat. Disconnect the 4 connectors from PGM-FI-ECU. Connect ECU test harness connectors to the ECU.

Turn the ignition switch ON.

Measure battery voltage between test harness terminal A15 and body ground.

Is there battery voltage? — NO → Repair open in the RED/BLU wire between the compressor clutch relay and PGM-FI-ECU.

YES

ECU

A   C

B   D

ECU

ECU TEST HARNESS

A15   C3

COMPRESSOR DIAGNOSTIC CHART–NSX–CONTINUED

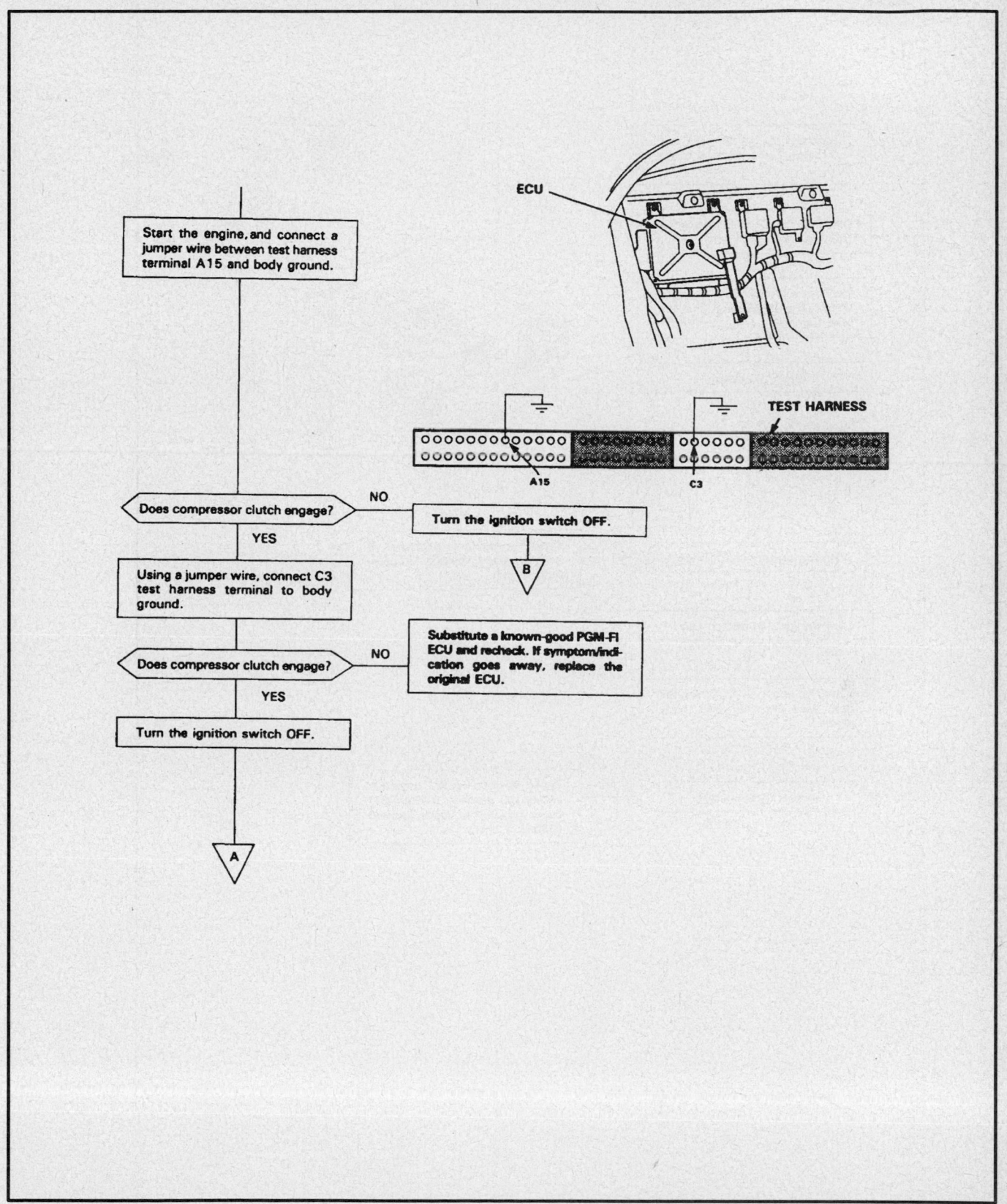

Start the engine, and connect a jumper wire between test harness terminal A15 and body ground.

Does compressor clutch engage?

NO → Turn the ignition switch OFF. → B

YES

Using a jumper wire, connect C3 test harness terminal to body ground.

Does compressor clutch engage?

NO → Substitute a known-good PGM-FI ECU and recheck. If symptom/indication goes away, replace the original ECU.

YES

Turn the ignition switch OFF.

A

ECU

TEST HARNESS

A15

C3

COMPRESSOR DIAGNOSTIC CHART—NSX—CONTINUED

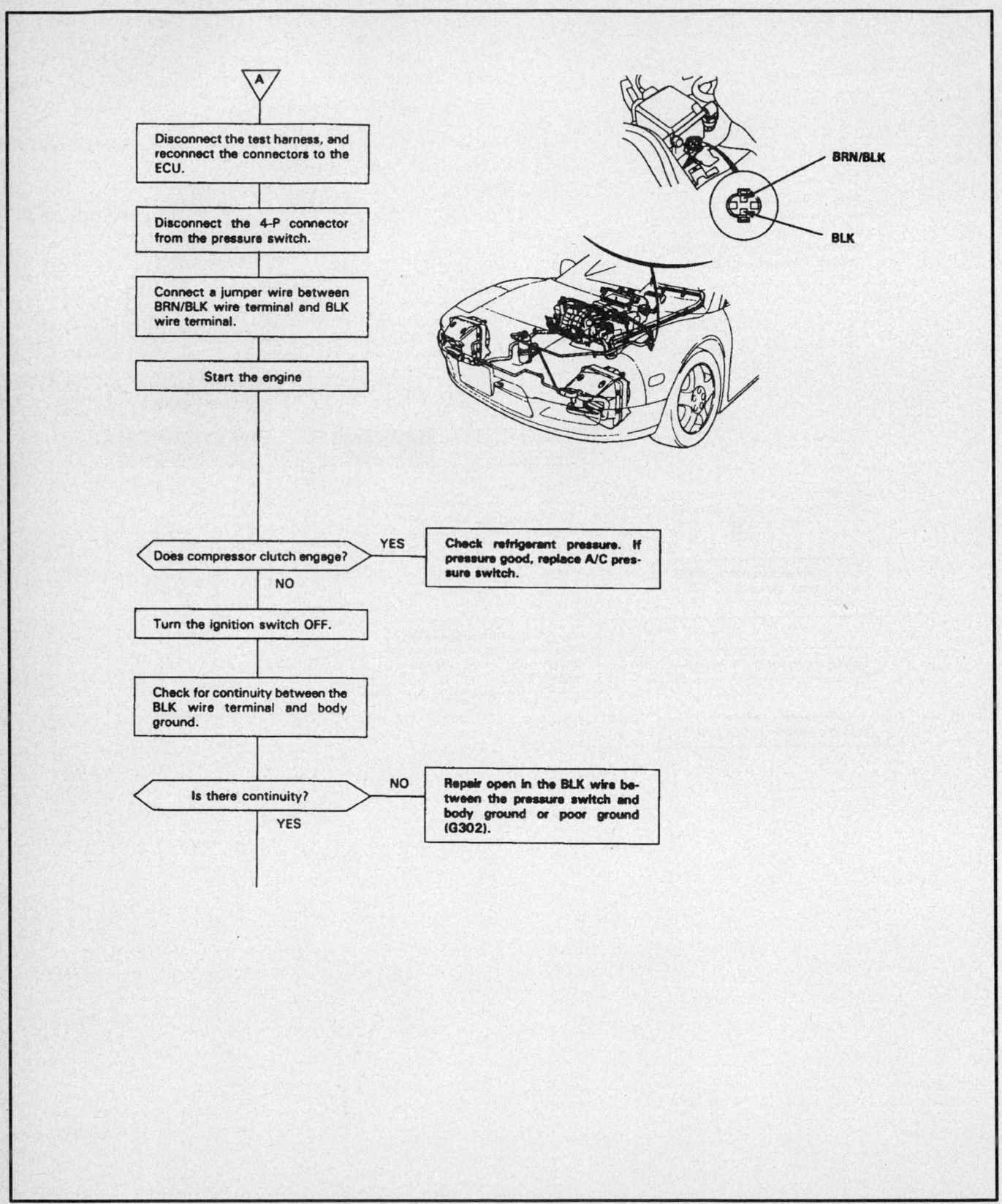

A

Disconnect the test harness, and reconnect the connectors to the ECU.

Disconnect the 4-P connector from the pressure switch.

Connect a jumper wire between BRN/BLK wire terminal and BLK wire terminal.

Start the engine

BRN/BLK

BLK

Does compressor clutch engage? — YES → Check refrigerant pressure. If pressure good, replace A/C pressure switch.

NO

Turn the ignition switch OFF.

Check for continuity between the BLK wire terminal and body ground.

Is there continuity? — NO → Repair open in the BLK wire between the pressure switch and body ground or poor ground (G302).

YES

COMPRESSOR DIAGNOSTIC CHART — NSX — CONTINUED

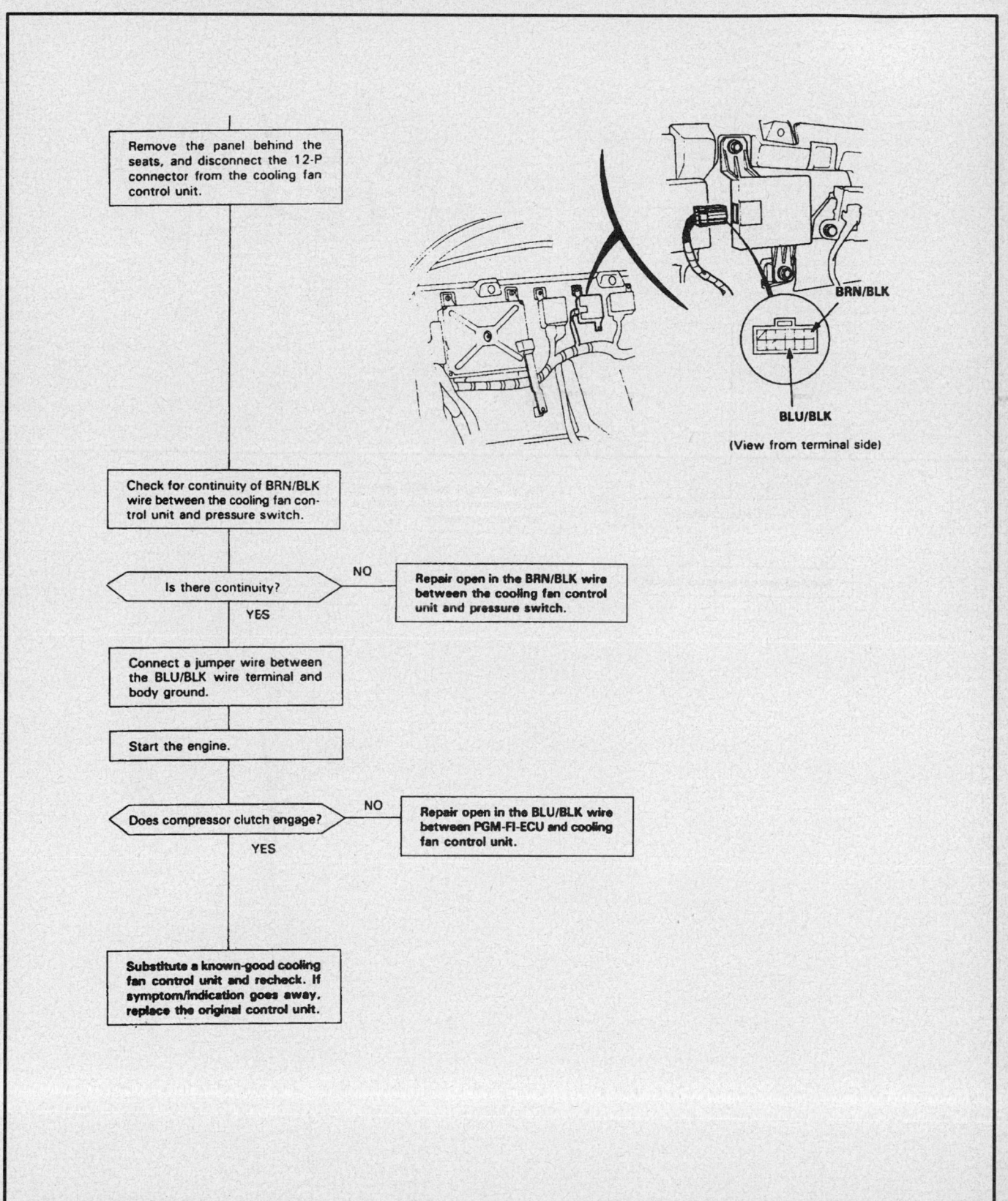

Remove the panel behind the seats, and disconnect the 12-P connector from the cooling fan control unit.

BRN/BLK

BLU/BLK

(View from terminal side)

Check for continuity of BRN/BLK wire between the cooling fan control unit and pressure switch.

Is there continuity? — NO → Repair open in the BRN/BLK wire between the cooling fan control unit and pressure switch.

YES

Connect a jumper wire between the BLU/BLK wire terminal and body ground.

Start the engine.

Does compressor clutch engage? — NO → Repair open in the BLU/BLK wire between PGM-FI-ECU and cooling fan control unit.

YES

Substitute a known-good cooling fan control unit and recheck. If symptom/indication goes away, replace the original control unit.

COMPRESSOR DIAGNOSTIC CHART—NSX—CONTINUED

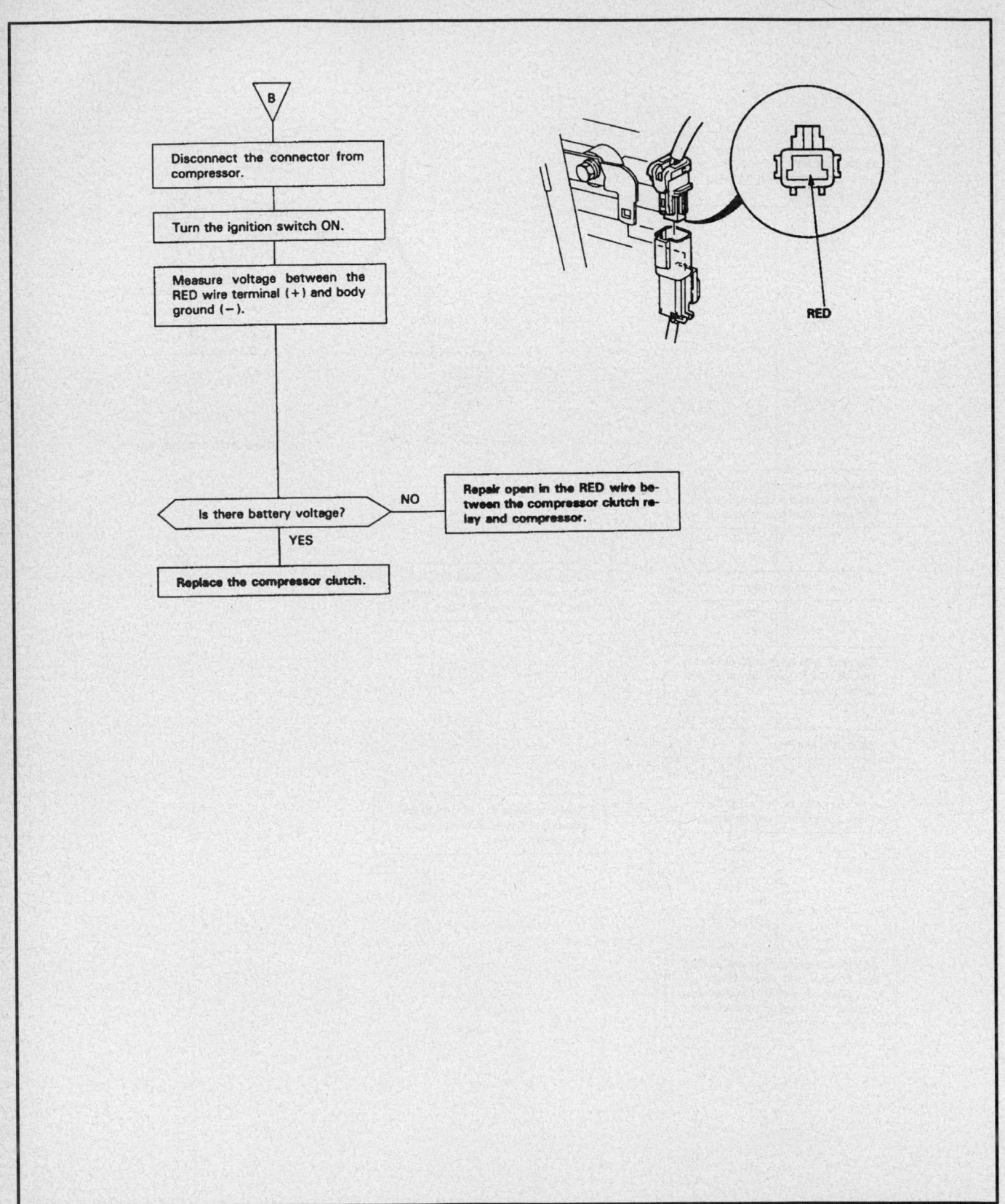

B

Disconnect the connector from compressor.

Turn the ignition switch ON.

Measure voltage between the RED wire terminal (+) and body ground (−).

Is there battery voltage? — NO → Repair open in the RED wire between the compressor clutch relay and compressor.

YES

Replace the compressor clutch.

RED

BLOWER DIAGNOSTIC CHART—VIGOR

Self-diagnosis A/C LED light indicates code 5: A problem in the blower motor circuit.
Use a digital multimeter (KS-AHM-32-003) to check it.
The speed of the blower motor is controlled by signals sent from the heater control AMP.

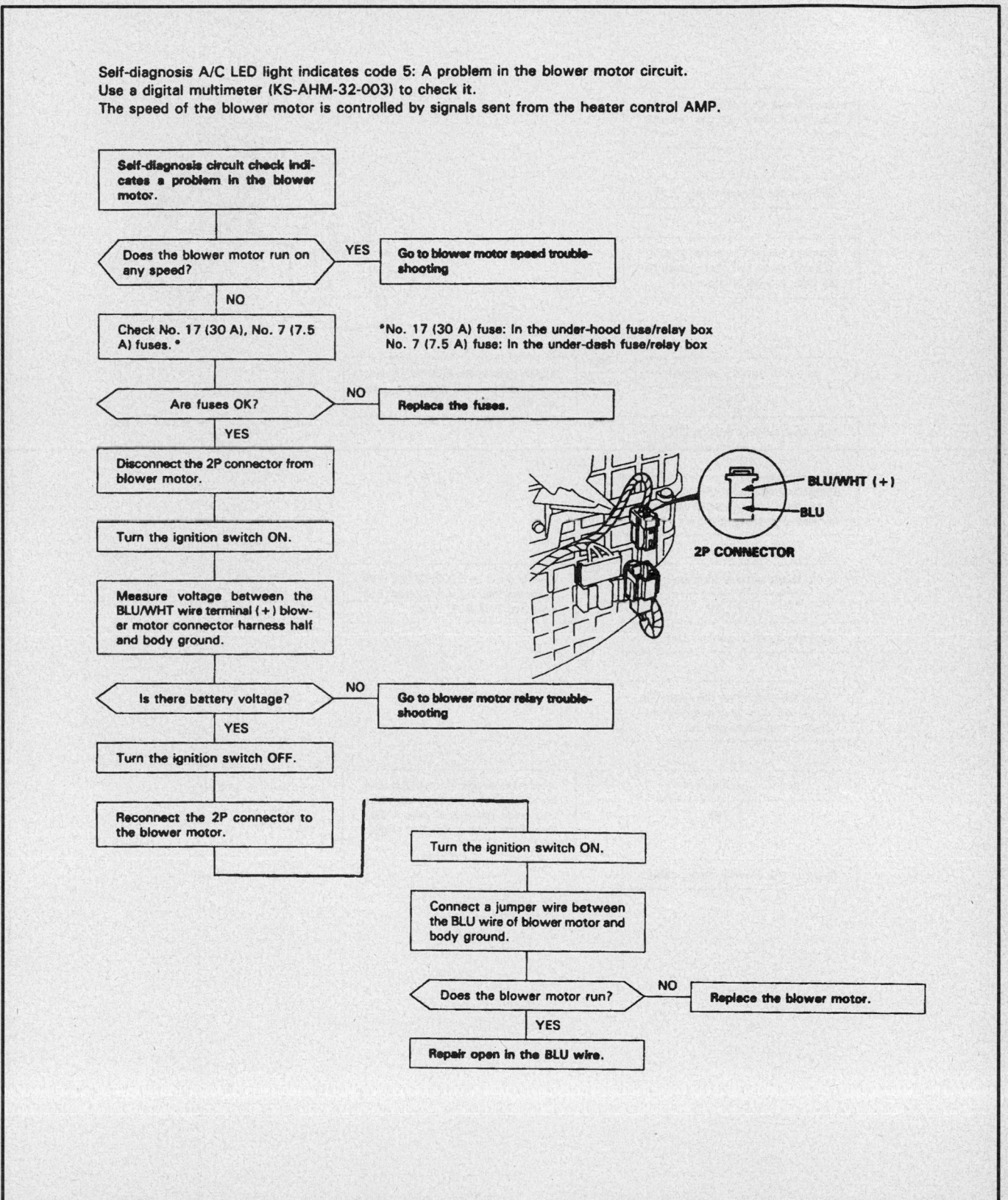

Self-diagnosis circuit check indicates a problem in the blower motor.

Does the blower motor run on any speed? — YES → Go to blower motor speed troubleshooting

NO

Check No. 17 (30 A), No. 7 (7.5 A) fuses.*

*No. 17 (30 A) fuse: In the under-hood fuse/relay box
No. 7 (7.5 A) fuse: In the under-dash fuse/relay box

Are fuses OK? — NO → Replace the fuses.

YES

Disconnect the 2P connector from blower motor.

Turn the ignition switch ON.

Measure voltage between the BLU/WHT wire terminal (+) blower motor connector harness half and body ground.

BLU/WHT (+)
BLU
2P CONNECTOR

Is there battery voltage? — NO → Go to blower motor relay troubleshooting

YES

Turn the ignition switch OFF.

Reconnect the 2P connector to the blower motor.

Turn the ignition switch ON.

Connect a jumper wire between the BLU wire of blower motor and body ground.

Does the blower motor run? — NO → Replace the blower motor.

YES

Repair open in the BLU wire.

BLOWER DIAGNOSTIC CHART–VIGOR–CONTINUED

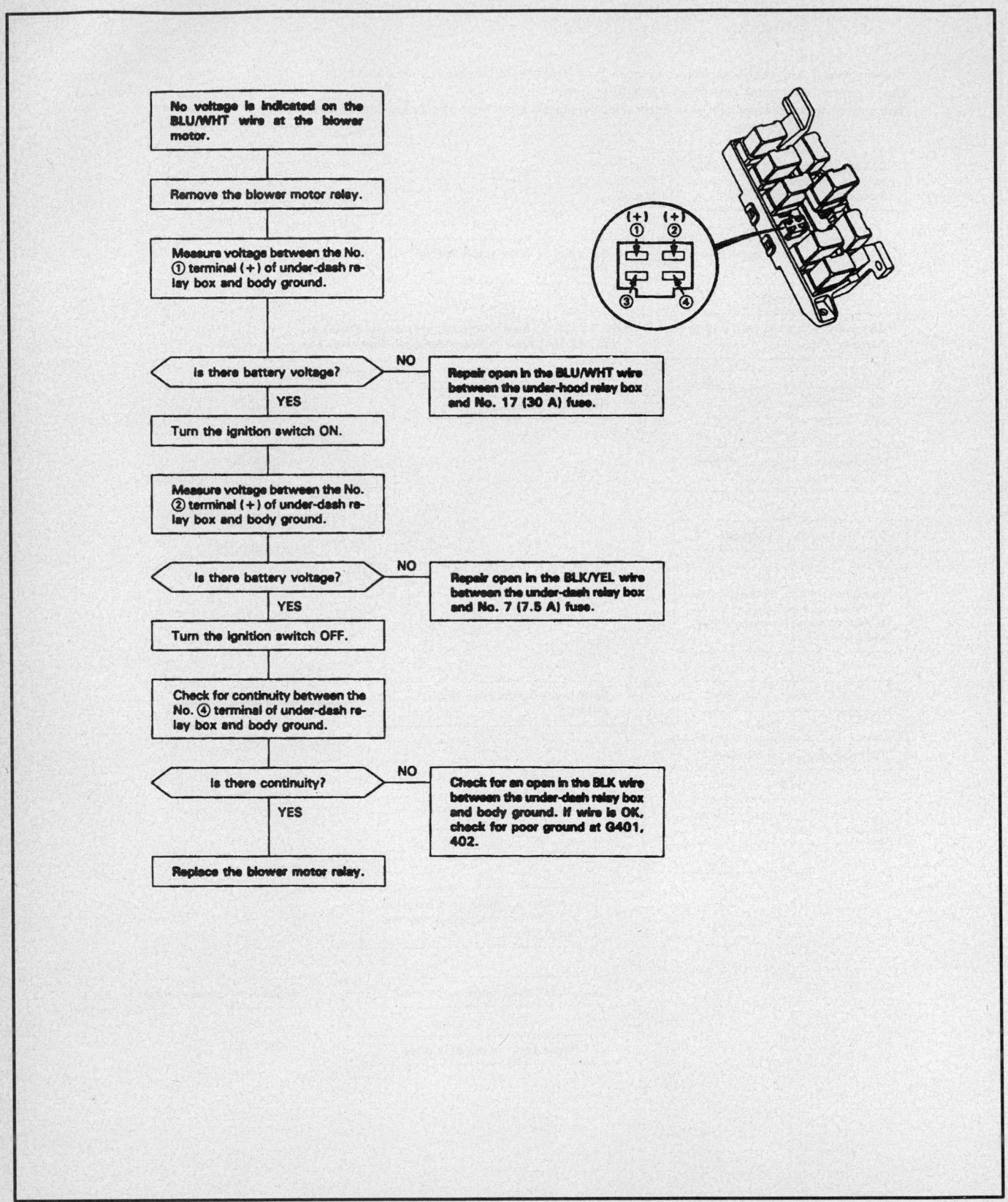

No voltage is indicated on the BLU/WHT wire at the blower motor.

Remove the blower motor relay.

Measure voltage between the No. ① terminal (+) of under-dash relay box and body ground.

Is there battery voltage? — NO → Repair open in the BLU/WHT wire between the under-hood relay box and No. 17 (30 A) fuse.

YES

Turn the ignition switch ON.

Measure voltage between the No. ② terminal (+) of under-dash relay box and body ground.

Is there battery voltage? — NO → Repair open in the BLK/YEL wire between the under-dash relay box and No. 7 (7.5 A) fuse.

YES

Turn the ignition switch OFF.

Check for continuity between the No. ④ terminal of under-dash relay box and body ground.

Is there continuity? — NO → Check for an open in the BLK wire between the under-dash relay box and body ground. If wire is OK, check for poor ground at G401, 402.

YES

Replace the blower motor relay.

BLOWER DIAGNOSTIC CHART—VIGOR—CONTINUED

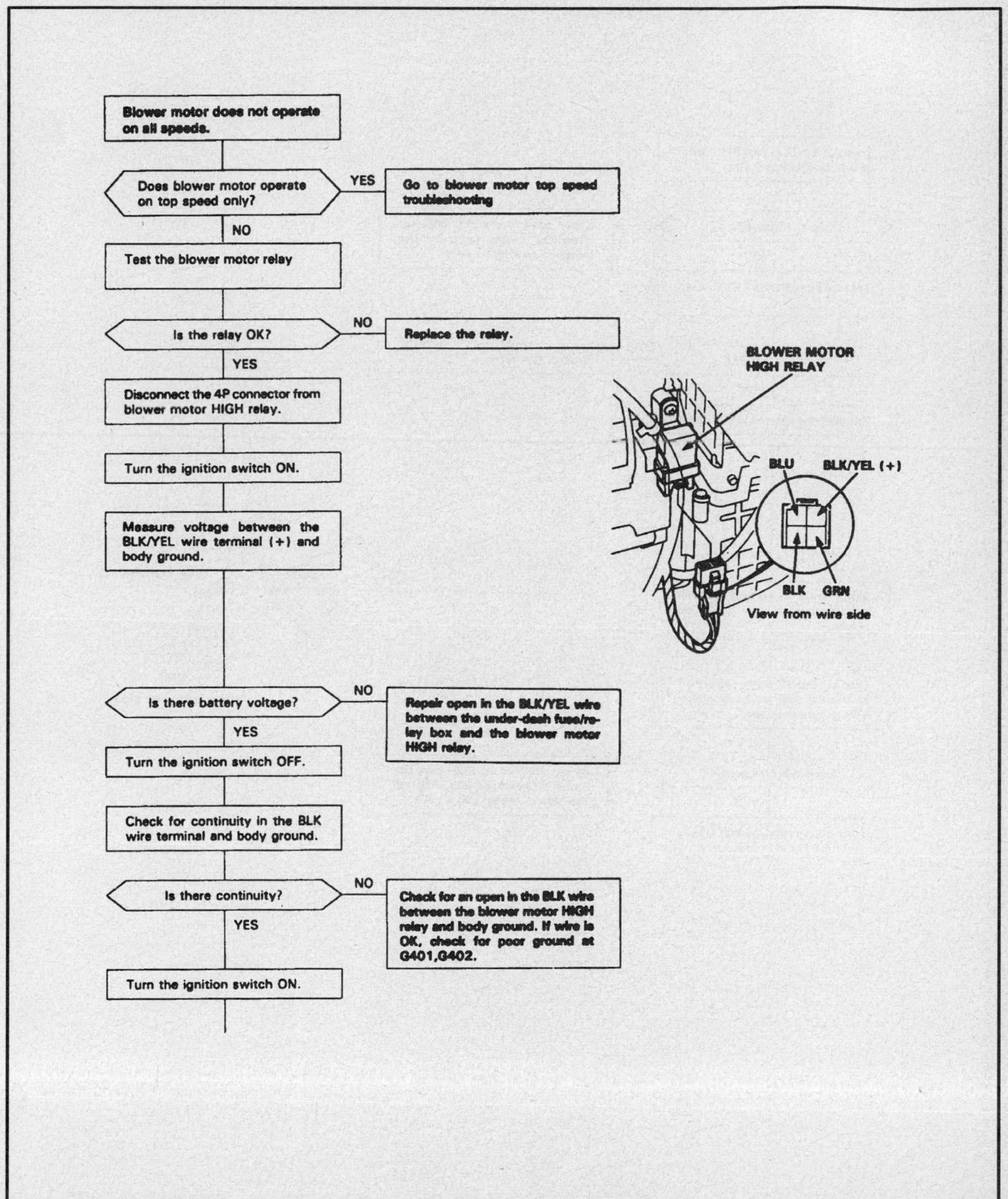

Blower motor does not operate on all speeds.

Does blower motor operate on top speed only? — YES → Go to blower motor top speed troubleshooting

NO

Test the blower motor relay

Is the relay OK? — NO → Replace the relay.

YES

Disconnect the 4P connector from blower motor HIGH relay.

Turn the ignition switch ON.

Measure voltage between the BLK/YEL wire terminal (+) and body ground.

BLOWER MOTOR HIGH RELAY

BLU   BLK/YEL (+)

BLK   GRN

View from wire side

Is there battery voltage? — NO → Repair open in the BLK/YEL wire between the under-dash fuse/relay box and the blower motor HIGH relay.

YES

Turn the ignition switch OFF.

Check for continuity in the BLK wire terminal and body ground.

Is there continuity? — NO → Check for an open in the BLK wire between the blower motor HIGH relay and body ground. If wire is OK, check for poor ground at G401, G402.

YES

Turn the ignition switch ON.

BLOWER DIAGNOSTIC CHART – VIGOR – CONTINUED

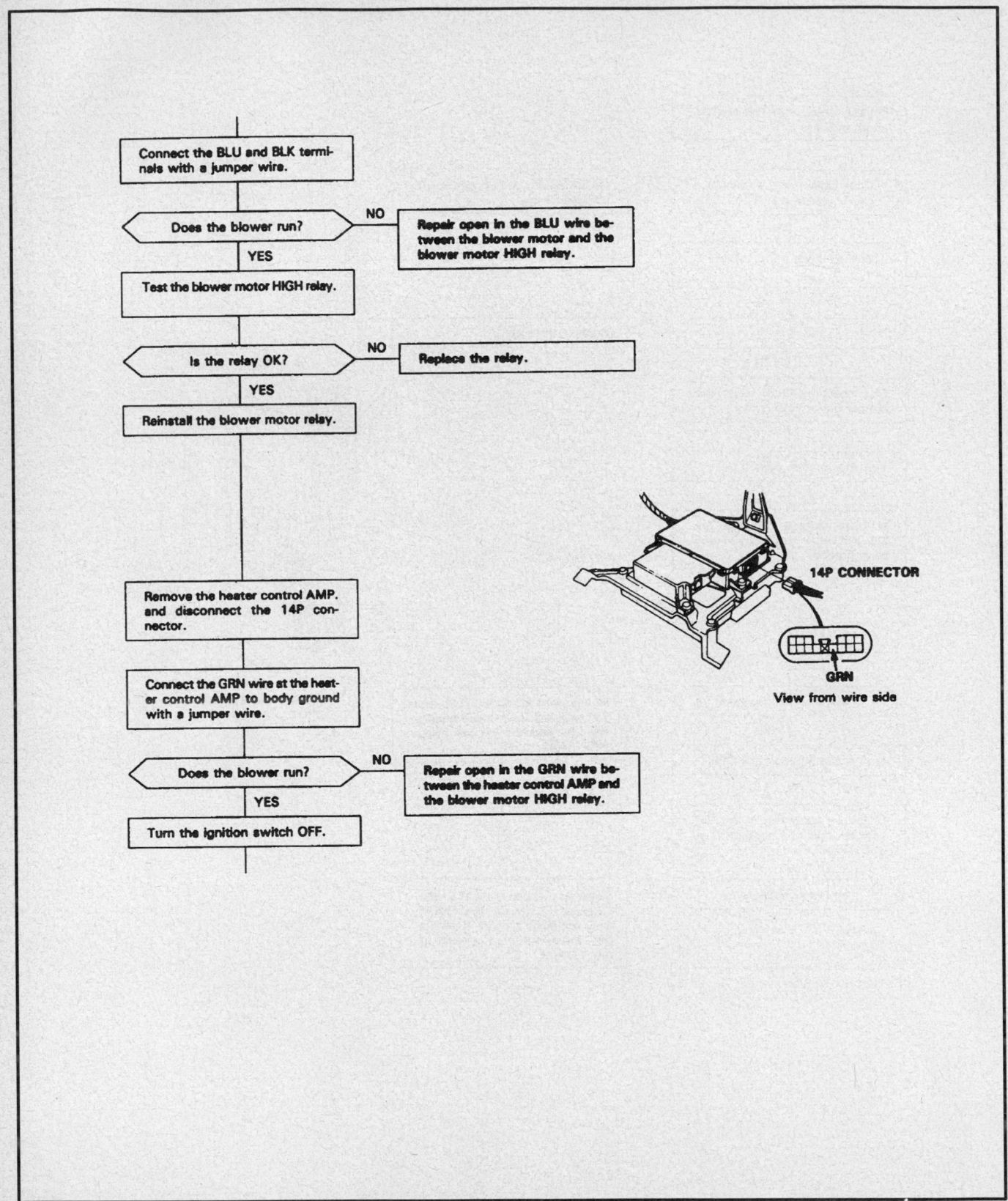

Connect the BLU and BLK terminals with a jumper wire.

Does the blower run? —NO→ Repair open in the BLU wire between the blower motor and the blower motor HIGH relay.

YES

Test the blower motor HIGH relay.

Is the relay OK? —NO→ Replace the relay.

YES

Reinstall the blower motor relay.

Remove the heater control AMP. and disconnect the 14P connector.

Connect the GRN wire at the heater control AMP to body ground with a jumper wire.

Does the blower run? —NO→ Repair open in the GRN wire between the heater control AMP and the blower motor HIGH relay.

YES

Turn the ignition switch OFF.

14P CONNECTOR

GRN

View from wire side

BLOWER DIAGNOSTIC CHART—VIGOR—CONTINUED

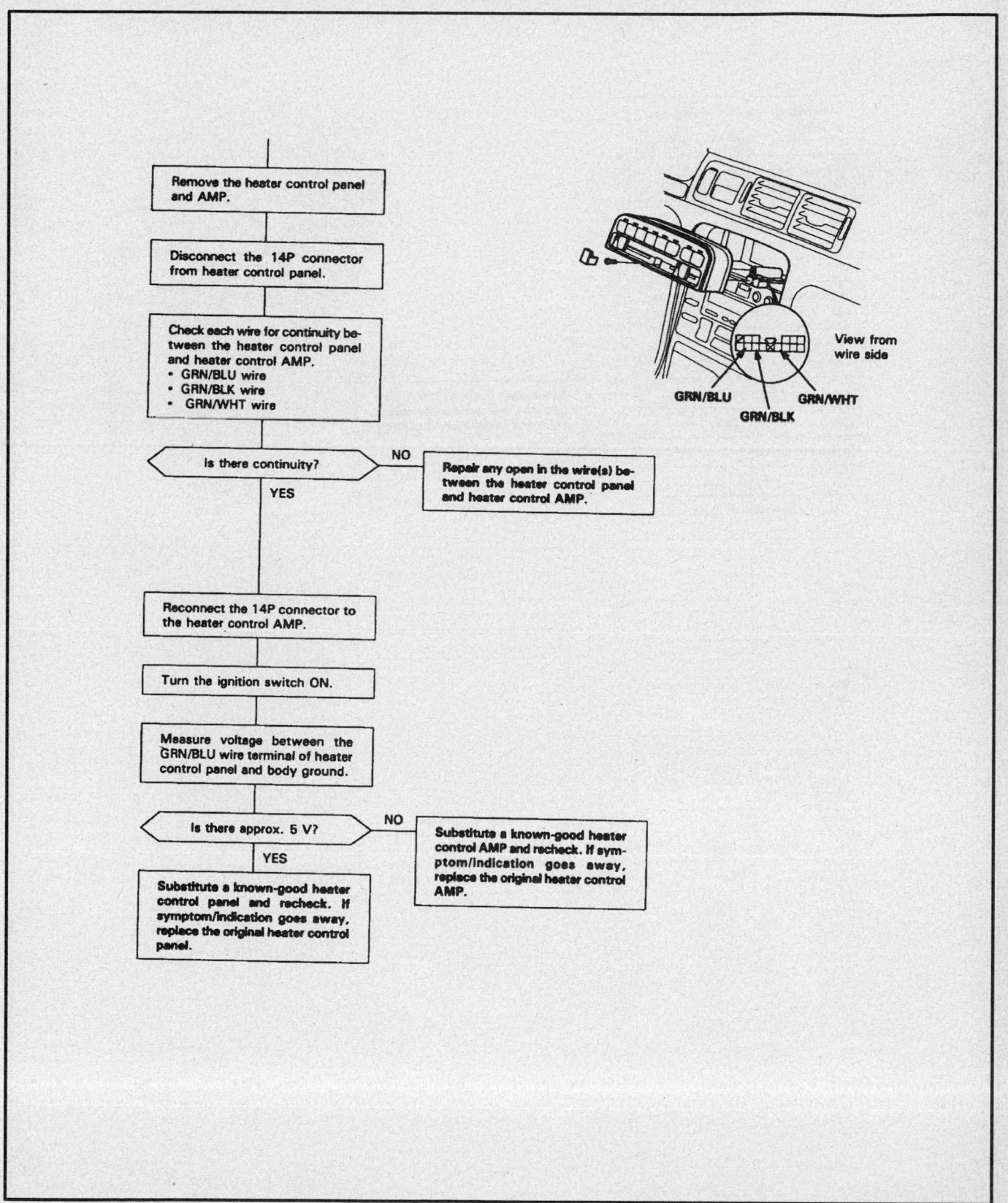

Remove the heater control panel and AMP.

Disconnect the 14P connector from heater control panel.

Check each wire for continuity between the heater control panel and heater control AMP.
- GRN/BLU wire
- GRN/BLK wire
- GRN/WHT wire

Is there continuity? —NO→ Repair any open in the wire(s) between the heater control panel and heater control AMP.

YES

View from wire side

GRN/BLU   GRN/WHT
    GRN/BLK

Reconnect the 14P connector to the heater control AMP.

Turn the ignition switch ON.

Measure voltage between the GRN/BLU wire terminal of heater control panel and body ground.

Is there approx. 5 V? —NO→ Substitute a known-good heater control AMP and recheck. If symptom/indication goes away, replace the original heater control AMP.

YES

Substitute a known-good heater control panel and recheck. If symptom/indication goes away, replace the original heater control panel.

COMPRESSOR DIAGNOSTIC CHART−VIGOR

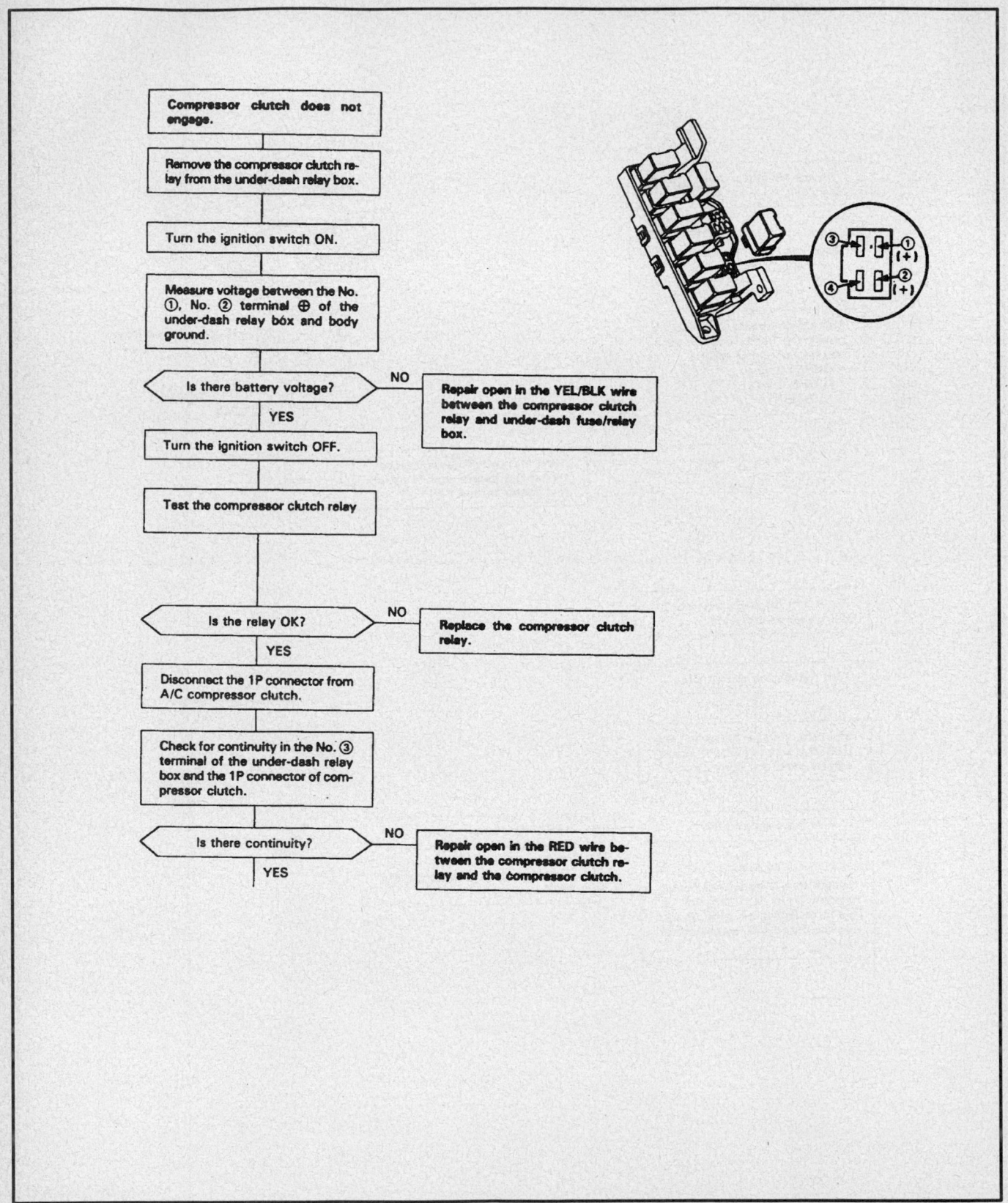

Compressor clutch does not engage.

↓

Remove the compressor clutch relay from the under-dash relay box.

↓

Turn the ignition switch ON.

↓

Measure voltage between the No. ①, No. ② terminal ⊕ of the under-dash relay box and body ground.

↓

Is there battery voltage? —**NO**→ Repair open in the YEL/BLK wire between the compressor clutch relay and under-dash fuse/relay box.

↓ **YES**

Turn the ignition switch OFF.

↓

Test the compressor clutch relay

↓

Is the relay OK? —**NO**→ Replace the compressor clutch relay.

↓ **YES**

Disconnect the 1P connector from A/C compressor clutch.

↓

Check for continuity in the No. ③ terminal of the under-dash relay box and the 1P connector of compressor clutch.

↓

Is there continuity? —**NO**→ Repair open in the RED wire between the compressor clutch relay and the compressor clutch.

↓ **YES**

COMPRESSOR DIAGNOSTIC CHART–VIGOR–CONTINUED

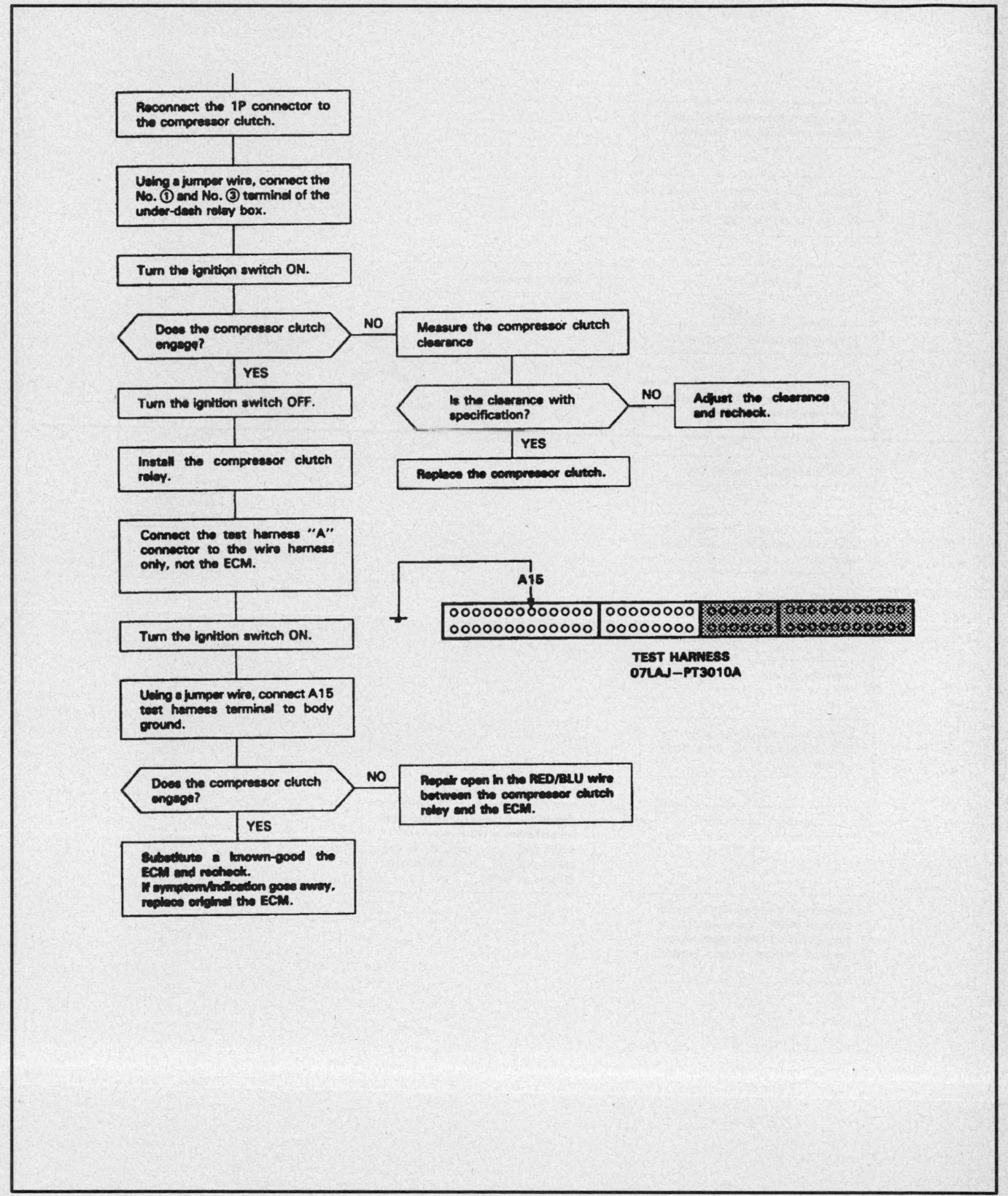

Reconnect the 1P connector to the compressor clutch.

Using a jumper wire, connect the No. ① and No. ③ terminal of the under-dash relay box.

Turn the ignition switch ON.

Does the compressor clutch engage? — NO → Measure the compressor clutch clearance

YES

Turn the ignition switch OFF.

Is the clearance with specification? — NO → Adjust the clearance and recheck.

YES

Install the compressor clutch relay.

Replace the compressor clutch.

Connect the test harness "A" connector to the wire harness only, not the ECM.

A15

Turn the ignition switch ON.

TEST HARNESS
07LAJ–PT3010A

Using a jumper wire, connect A15 test harness terminal to body ground.

Does the compressor clutch engage? — NO → Repair open in the RED/BLU wire between the compressor clutch relay and the ECM.

YES

Substitute a known-good the ECM and recheck.
If symptom/indication goes away, replace original the ECM.

AIR CONDITIONING DIAGNOSTIC CHART—VIGOR

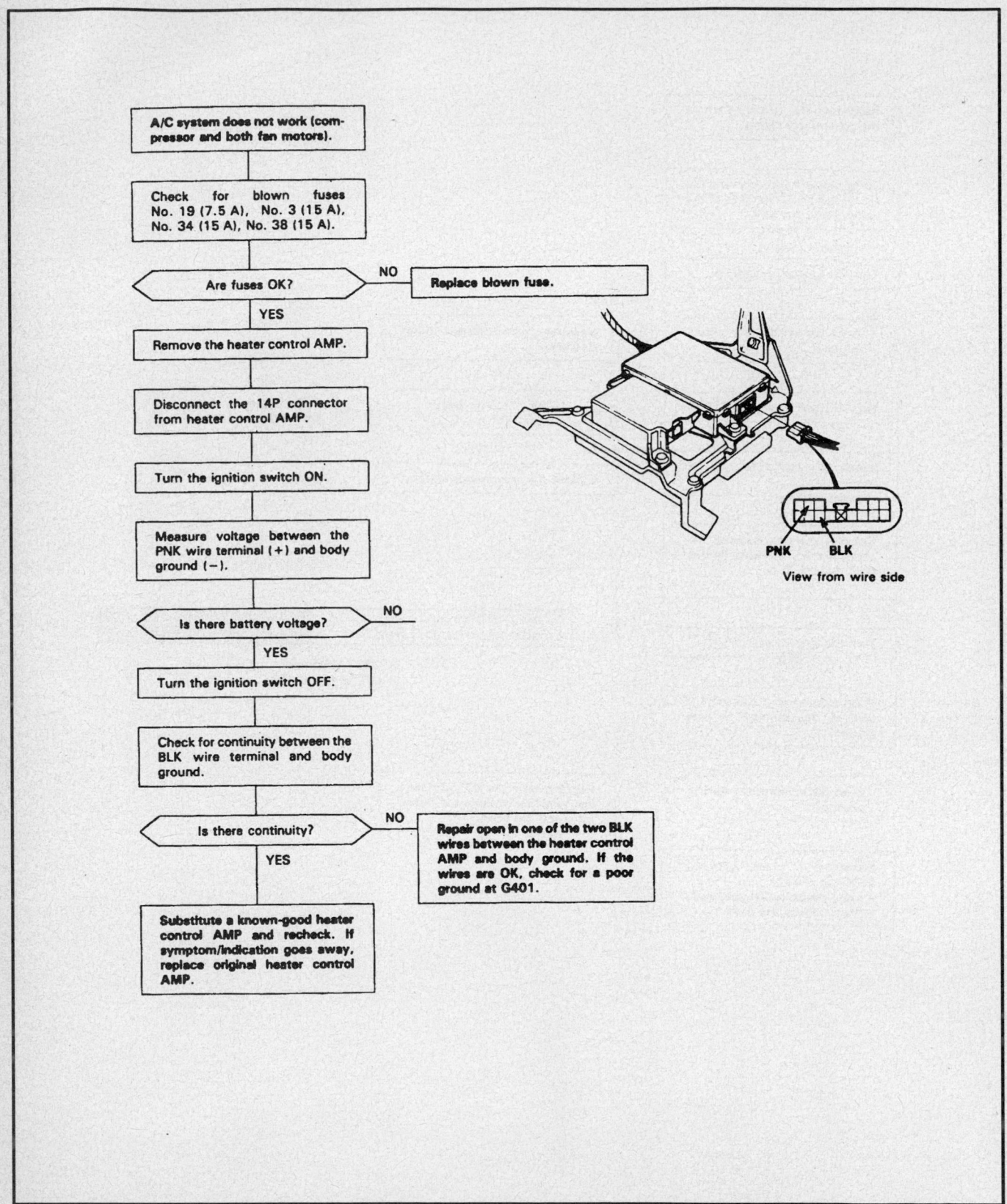

A/C system does not work (compressor and both fan motors).

Check for blown fuses No. 19 (7.5 A), No. 3 (15 A), No. 34 (15 A), No. 38 (15 A).

Are fuses OK? — NO → Replace blown fuse.

YES

Remove the heater control AMP.

Disconnect the 14P connector from heater control AMP.

Turn the ignition switch ON.

Measure voltage between the PNK wire terminal (+) and body ground (−).

Is there battery voltage? — NO

YES

Turn the ignition switch OFF.

Check for continuity between the BLK wire terminal and body ground.

Is there continuity? — NO → Repair open in one of the two BLK wires between the heater control AMP and body ground. If the wires are OK, check for a poor ground at G401.

YES

Substitute a known-good heater control AMP and recheck. If symptom/indication goes away, replace original heater control AMP.

PNK   BLK

View from wire side

AIR CONDITIONING DIAGNOSTIC CHART–VIGOR–CONTINUED

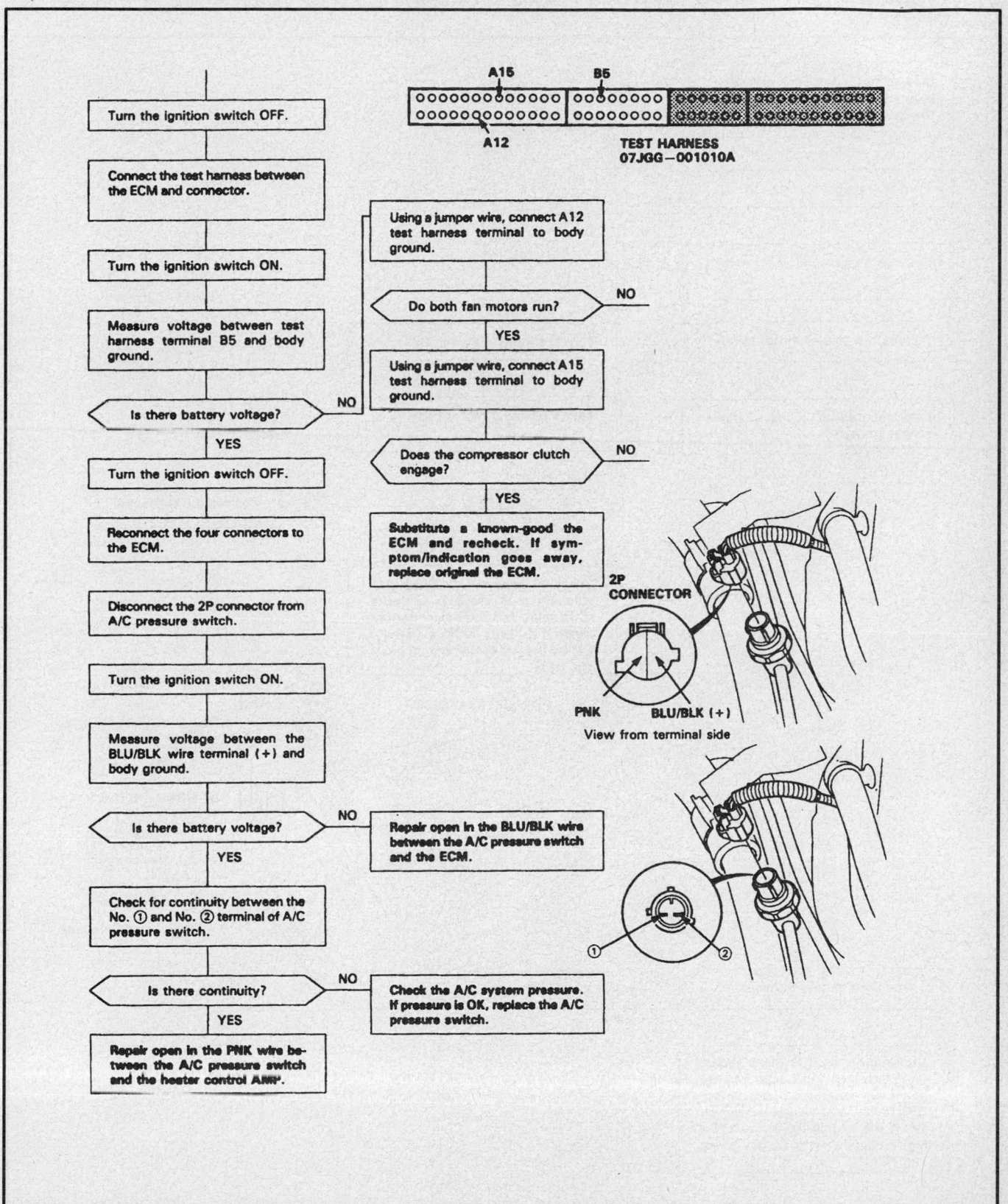

Turn the ignition switch OFF.

Connect the test harness between the ECM and connector.

Turn the ignition switch ON.

Measure voltage between test harness terminal B5 and body ground.

Is there battery voltage? — NO →

YES

Turn the ignition switch OFF.

Reconnect the four connectors to the ECM.

Disconnect the 2P connector from A/C pressure switch.

Turn the ignition switch ON.

Measure voltage between the BLU/BLK wire terminal (+) and body ground.

Is there battery voltage? — NO → Repair open in the BLU/BLK wire between the A/C pressure switch and the ECM.

YES

Check for continuity between the No. ① and No. ② terminal of A/C pressure switch.

Is there continuity? — NO → Check the A/C system pressure. If pressure is OK, replace the A/C pressure switch.

YES

Repair open in the PNK wire between the A/C pressure switch and the heater control AMP.

A15   B5

A12

**TEST HARNESS
07JGG–001010A**

Using a jumper wire, connect A12 test harness terminal to body ground.

Do both fan motors run? — NO →

YES

Using a jumper wire, connect A15 test harness terminal to body ground.

Does the compressor clutch engage? — NO →

YES

Substitute a known-good the ECM and recheck. If symptom/indication goes away, replace original the ECM.

2P CONNECTOR

PNK   BLU/BLK (+)

View from terminal side

①   ②

BLOWER MOTOR ONLY RUNS ON HIGH WITH SWITCH IN ANY POSITION DIAGNOSTIC CHART – 1994 LEGEND AND LEGEND COUPE

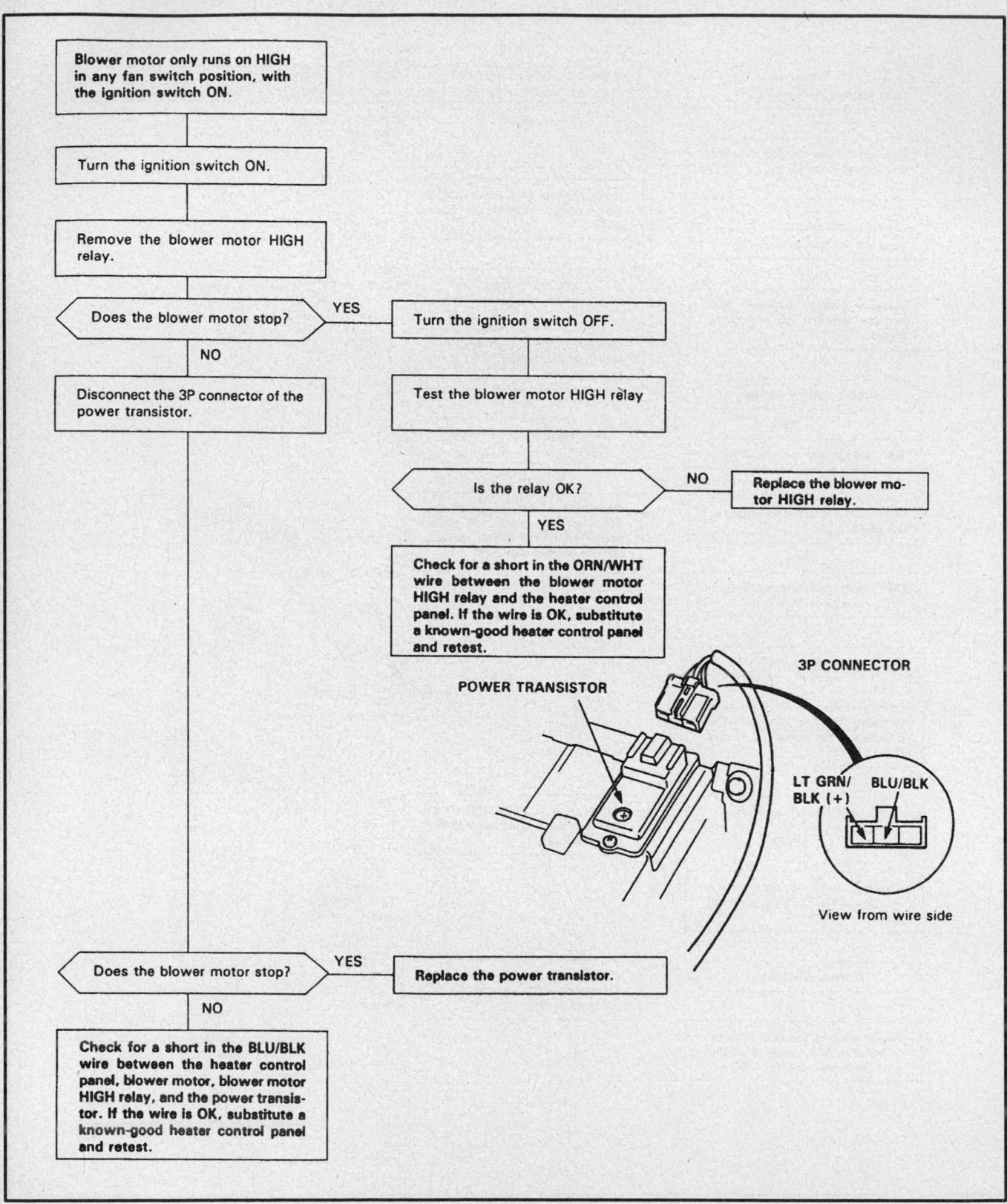

Blower motor only runs on HIGH in any fan switch position, with the ignition switch ON.

Turn the ignition switch ON.

Remove the blower motor HIGH relay.

Does the blower motor stop? — **YES** → Turn the ignition switch OFF.

NO

Disconnect the 3P connector of the power transistor.

Test the blower motor HIGH relay

Is the relay OK? — **NO** → Replace the blower motor HIGH relay.

YES

Check for a short in the ORN/WHT wire between the blower motor HIGH relay and the heater control panel. If the wire is OK, substitute a known-good heater control panel and retest.

POWER TRANSISTOR

3P CONNECTOR

LT GRN/BLK (+)   BLU/BLK

View from wire side

Does the blower motor stop? — **YES** → Replace the power transistor.

NO

Check for a short in the BLU/BLK wire between the heater control panel, blower motor, blower motor HIGH relay, and the power transistor. If the wire is OK, substitute a known-good heater control panel and retest.

BLOWER MOTOR DOES NOT RUN AT ALL DIAGNOSTIC CHART—1994 LEGEND AND LEGEND COUPE

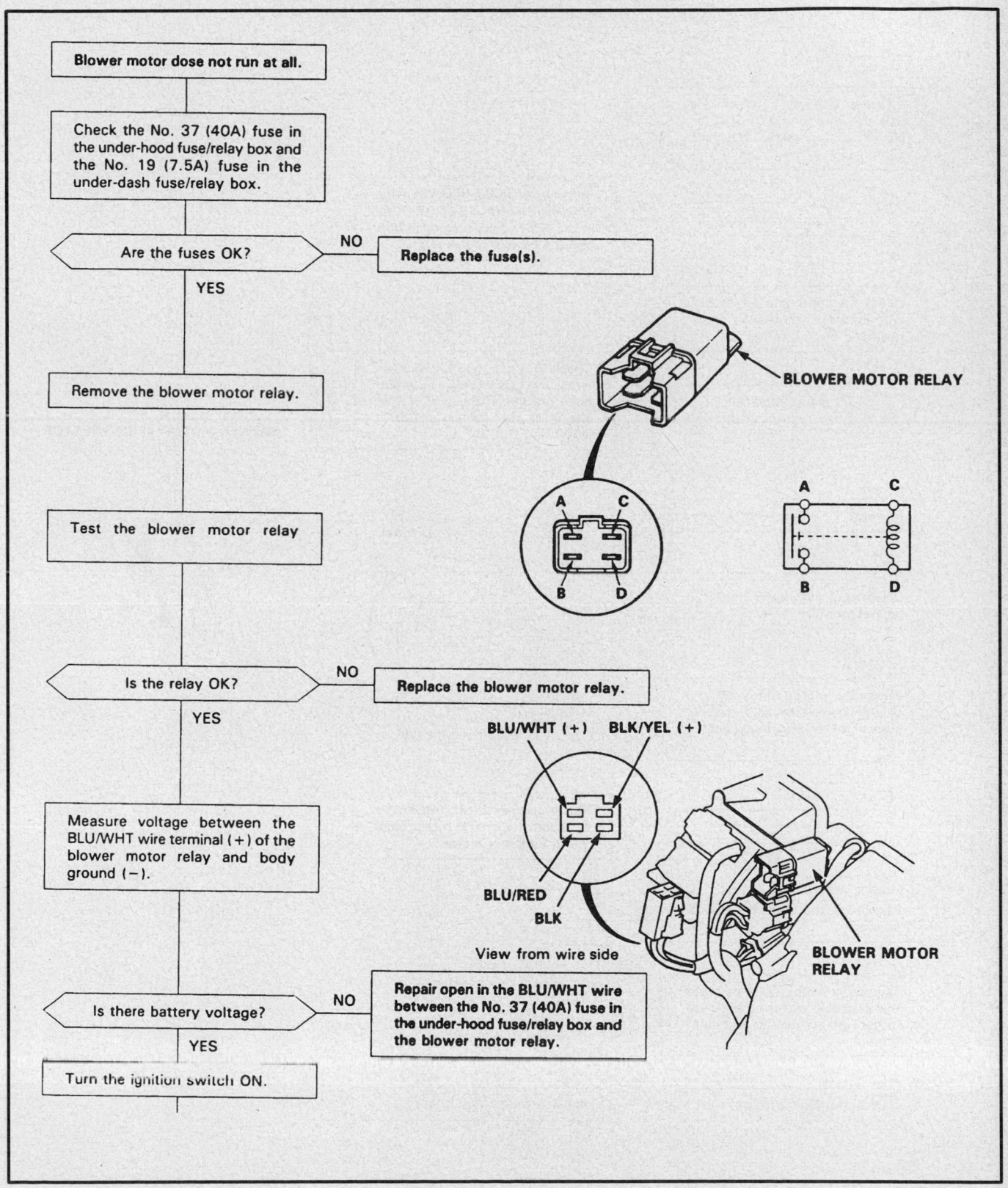

Blower motor dose not run at all.

Check the No. 37 (40A) fuse in the under-hood fuse/relay box and the No. 19 (7.5A) fuse in the under-dash fuse/relay box.

Are the fuses OK? — **NO** → Replace the fuse(s).

YES

Remove the blower motor relay.

Test the blower motor relay

BLOWER MOTOR RELAY

A   C

B   D

Is the relay OK? — **NO** → Replace the blower motor relay.

YES

BLU/WHT (+)   BLK/YEL (+)

BLU/RED

BLK

View from wire side

BLOWER MOTOR RELAY

Measure voltage between the BLU/WHT wire terminal (+) of the blower motor relay and body ground (−).

Is there battery voltage? — **NO** → Repair open in the BLU/WHT wire between the No. 37 (40A) fuse in the under-hood fuse/relay box and the blower motor relay.

YES

Turn the ignition switch ON.

BLOWER MOTOR DOES NOT RUN AT ALL DIAGNOSTIC CHART–1994 LEGEND AND LEGEND COUPE–CONTINUED

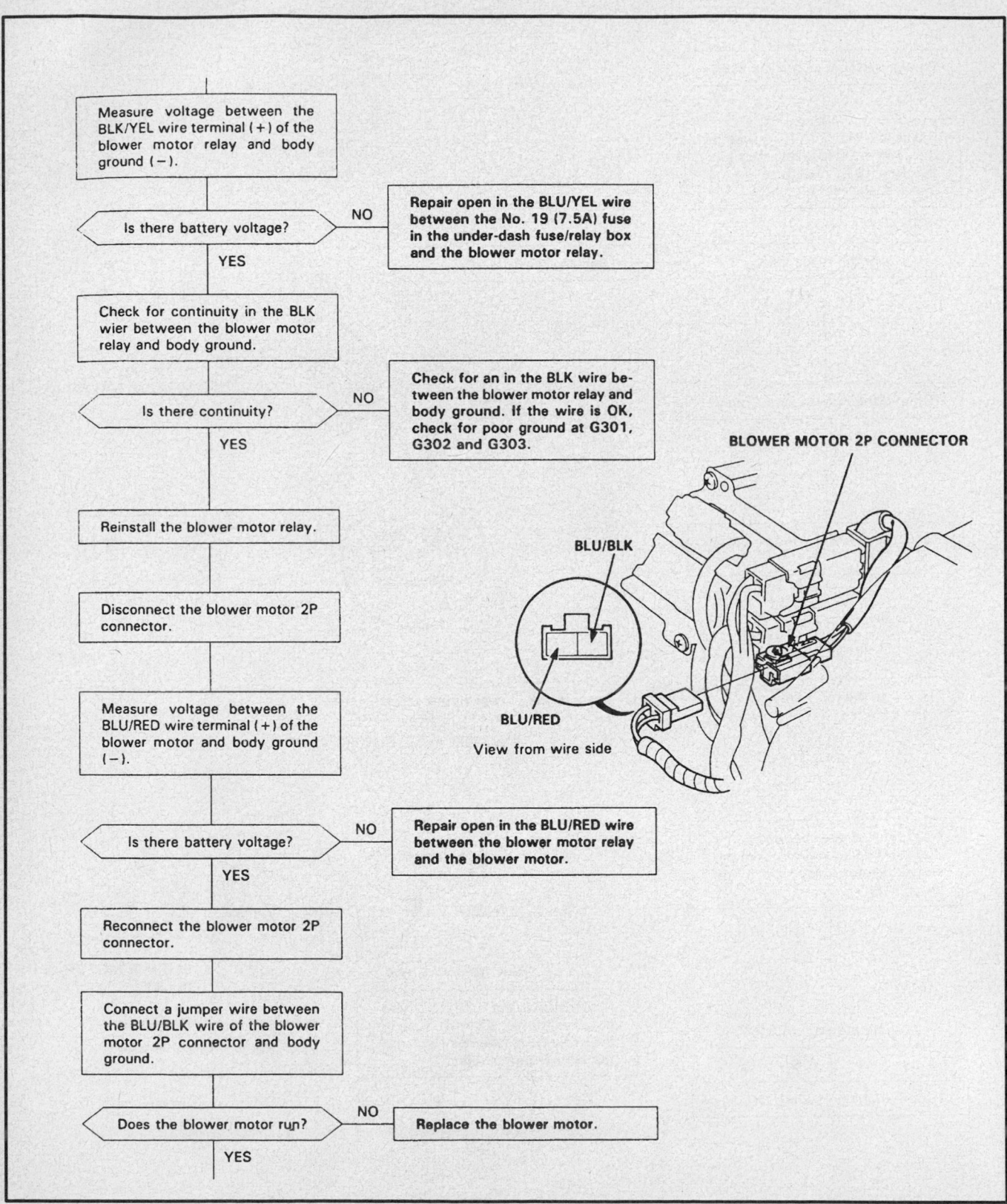

Measure voltage between the BLK/YEL wire terminal (+) of the blower motor relay and body ground (–).

Is there battery voltage? — NO — Repair open in the BLU/YEL wire between the No. 19 (7.5A) fuse in the under-dash fuse/relay box and the blower motor relay.

YES

Check for continuity in the BLK wier between the blower motor relay and body ground.

Is there continuity? — NO — Check for an in the BLK wire between the blower motor relay and body ground. If the wire is OK, check for poor ground at G301, G302 and G303.

YES

Reinstall the blower motor relay.

Disconnect the blower motor 2P connector.

Measure voltage between the BLU/RED wire terminal (+) of the blower motor and body ground (–).

Is there battery voltage? — NO — Repair open in the BLU/RED wire between the blower motor relay and the blower motor.

YES

Reconnect the blower motor 2P connector.

Connect a jumper wire between the BLU/BLK wire of the blower motor 2P connector and body ground.

Does the blower motor run? — NO — Replace the blower motor.

YES

BLOWER MOTOR 2P CONNECTOR

BLU/BLK

BLU/RED

View from wire side

BLOWER MOTOR DOES NOT RUN AT ALL DIAGNOSTIC CHART–1994 LEGEND AND LEGEND COUPE–CONTINUED

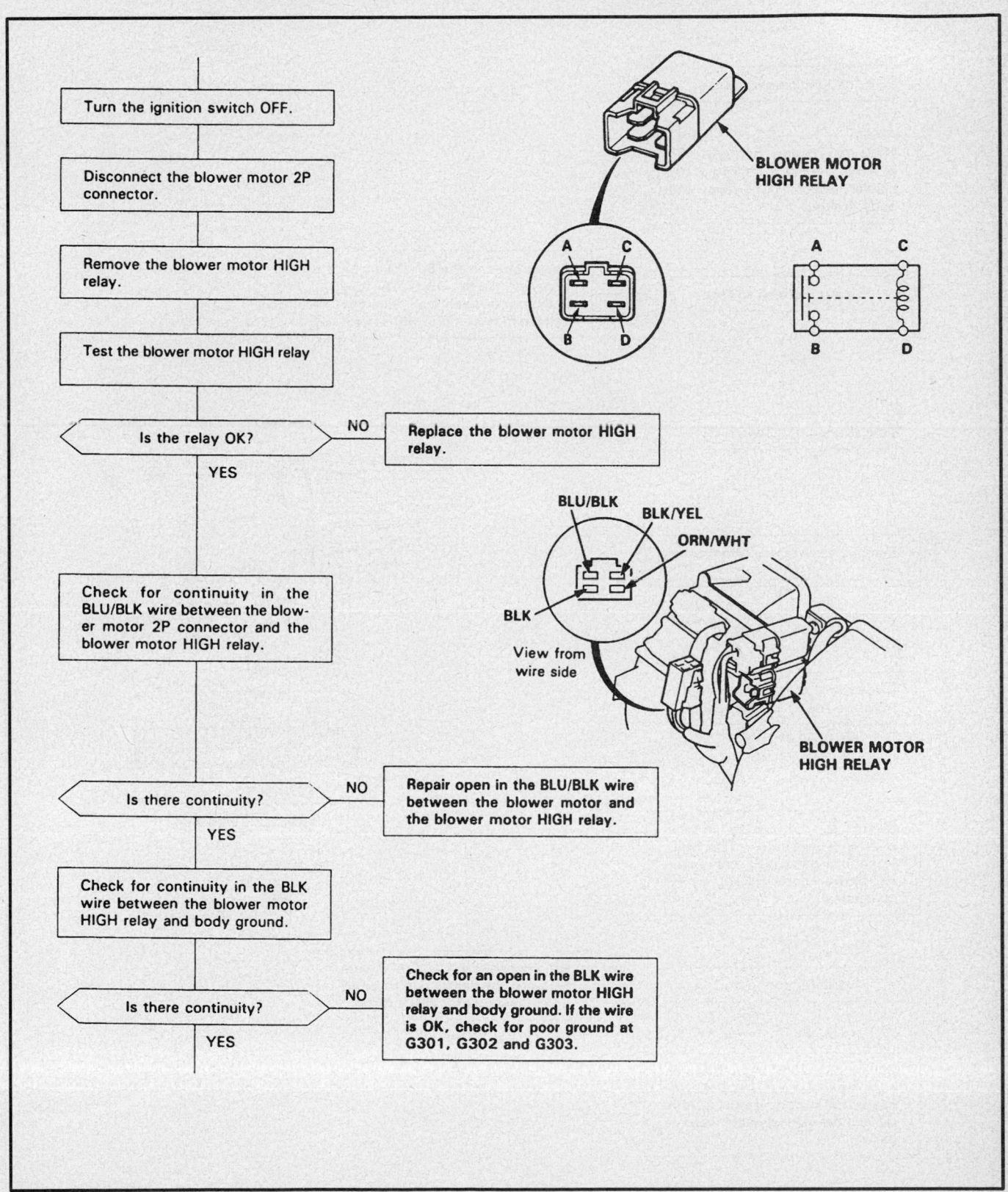

Turn the ignition switch OFF.

Disconnect the blower motor 2P connector.

Remove the blower motor HIGH relay.

Test the blower motor HIGH relay

Is the relay OK? — NO → Replace the blower motor HIGH relay.

YES

BLOWER MOTOR HIGH RELAY

A C
B D

Check for continuity in the BLU/BLK wire between the blower motor 2P connector and the blower motor HIGH relay.

BLU/BLK
BLK/YEL
ORN/WHT
BLK
View from wire side

BLOWER MOTOR HIGH RELAY

Is there continuity? — NO → Repair open in the BLU/BLK wire between the blower motor and the blower motor HIGH relay.

YES

Check for continuity in the BLK wire between the blower motor HIGH relay and body ground.

Is there continuity? — NO → Check for an open in the BLK wire between the blower motor HIGH relay and body ground. If the wire is OK, check for poor ground at G301, G302 and G303.

YES

BLOWER MOTOR DOES NOT RUN AT ALL DIAGNOSTIC CHART—1994 LEGEND AND LEGEND COUPE—CONTINUED

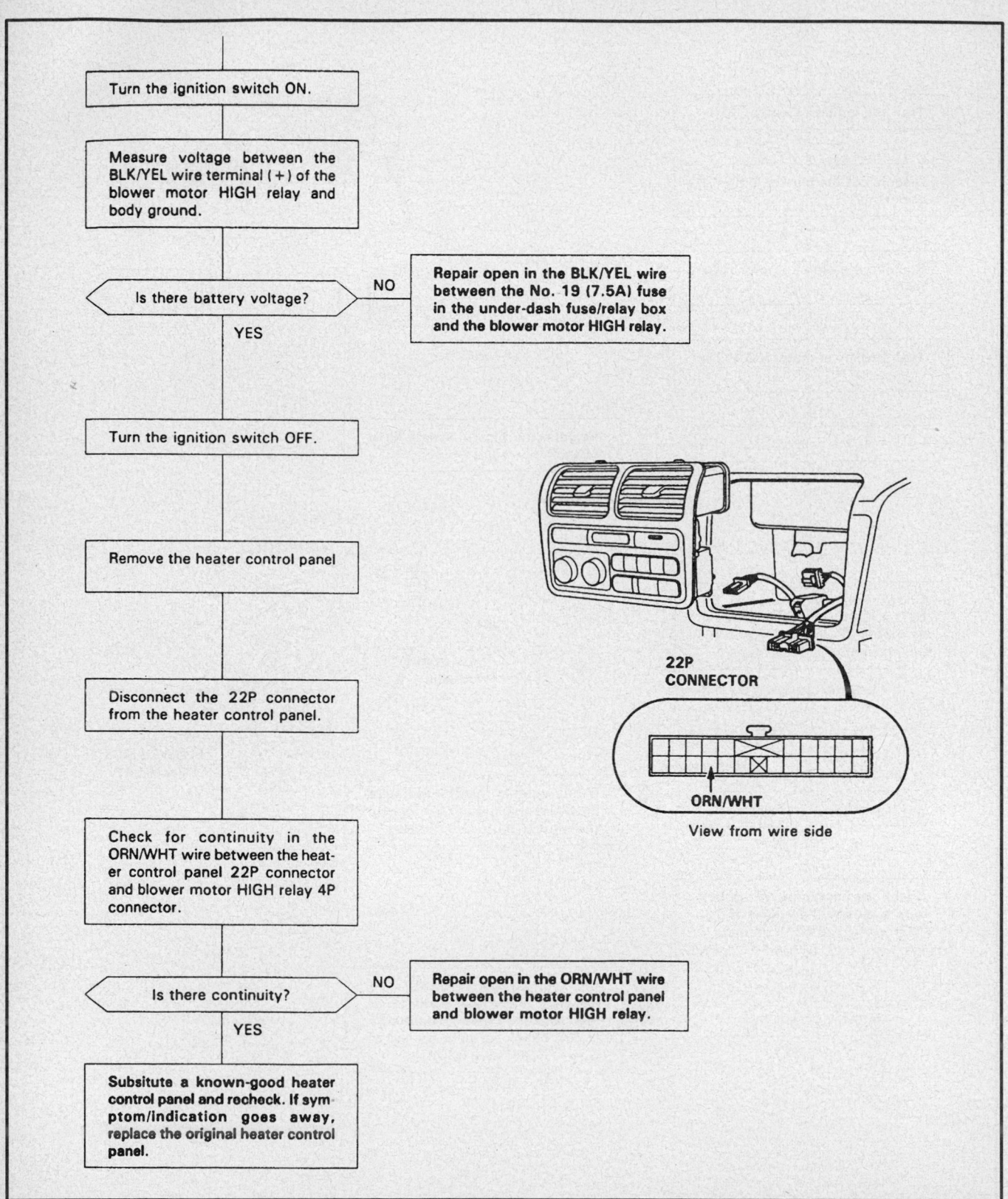

Turn the ignition switch ON.

Measure voltage between the BLK/YEL wire terminal (+) of the blower motor HIGH relay and body ground.

Is there battery voltage? → NO → Repair open in the BLK/YEL wire between the No. 19 (7.5A) fuse in the under-dash fuse/relay box and the blower motor HIGH relay.

YES

Turn the ignition switch OFF.

Remove the heater control panel

Disconnect the 22P connector from the heater control panel.

Check for continuity in the ORN/WHT wire between the heater control panel 22P connector and blower motor HIGH relay 4P connector.

Is there continuity? → NO → Repair open in the ORN/WHT wire between the heater control panel and blower motor HIGH relay.

YES

Subsitute a known-good heater control panel and recheck. If symptom/indication goes away, replace the original heater control panel.

22P CONNECTOR

ORN/WHT

View from wire side

BLOWER MOTOR ONLY RUNS IN THE HIGH SPEED POSITION–1994 LEGEND AND LEGEND COUPE

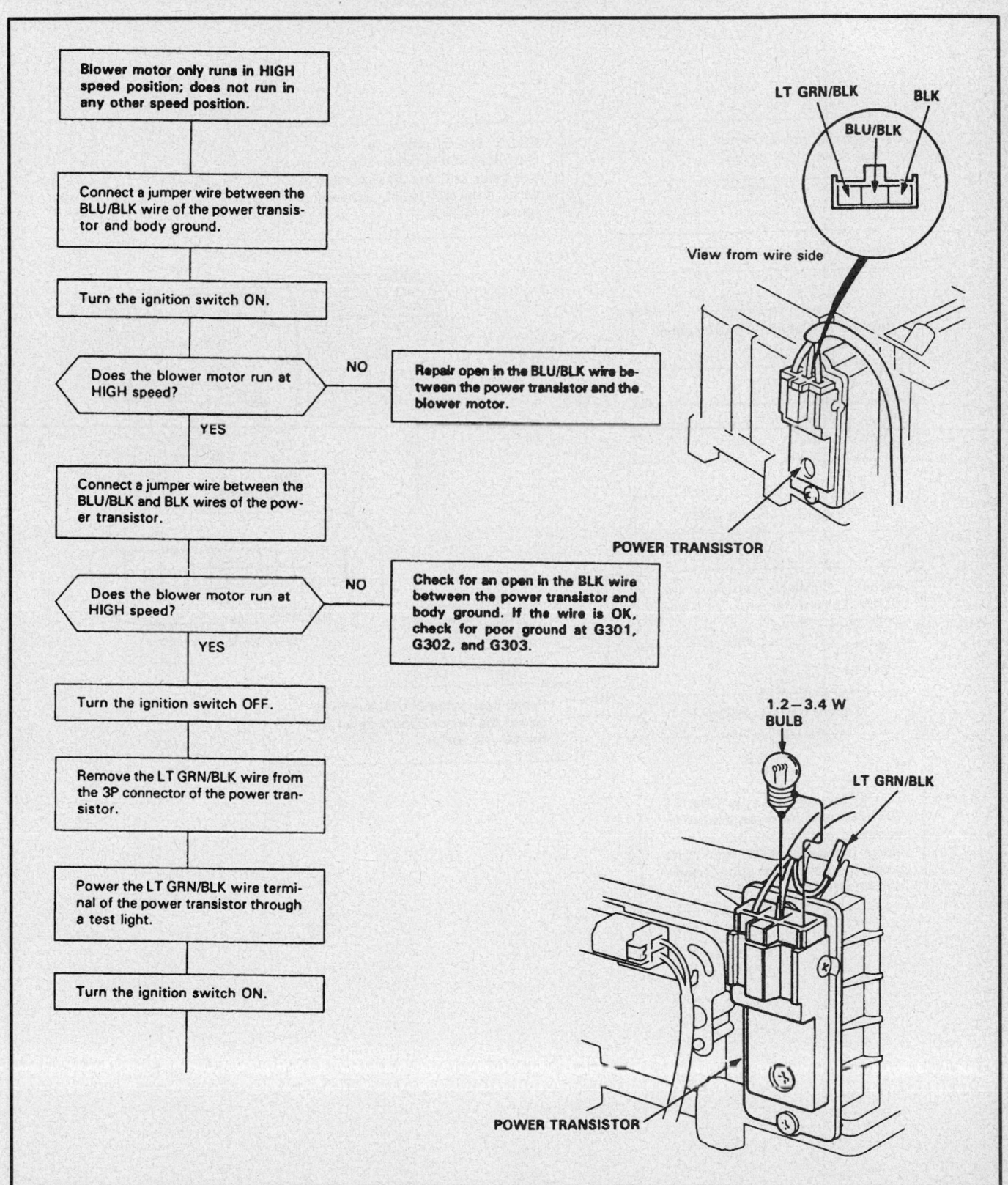

Blower motor only runs in HIGH speed position; does not run in any other speed position.

Connect a jumper wire between the BLU/BLK wire of the power transistor and body ground.

Turn the ignition switch ON.

Does the blower motor run at HIGH speed? — **NO** → Repair open in the BLU/BLK wire between the power transistor and the blower motor.

YES

Connect a jumper wire between the BLU/BLK and BLK wires of the power transistor.

Does the blower motor run at HIGH speed? — **NO** → Check for an open in the BLK wire between the power transistor and body ground. If the wire is OK, check for poor ground at G301, G302, and G303.

YES

Turn the ignition switch OFF.

Remove the LT GRN/BLK wire from the 3P connector of the power transistor.

Power the LT GRN/BLK wire terminal of the power transistor through a test light.

Turn the ignition switch ON.

LT GRN/BLK   BLK
BLU/BLK

View from wire side

POWER TRANSISTOR

1.2–3.4 W BULB

LT GRN/BLK

POWER TRANSISTOR

BLOWER MOTOR ONLY RUNS IN THE HIGH SPEED POSITION—1994 LEGEND AND LEGEND COUPE—CONTINUED

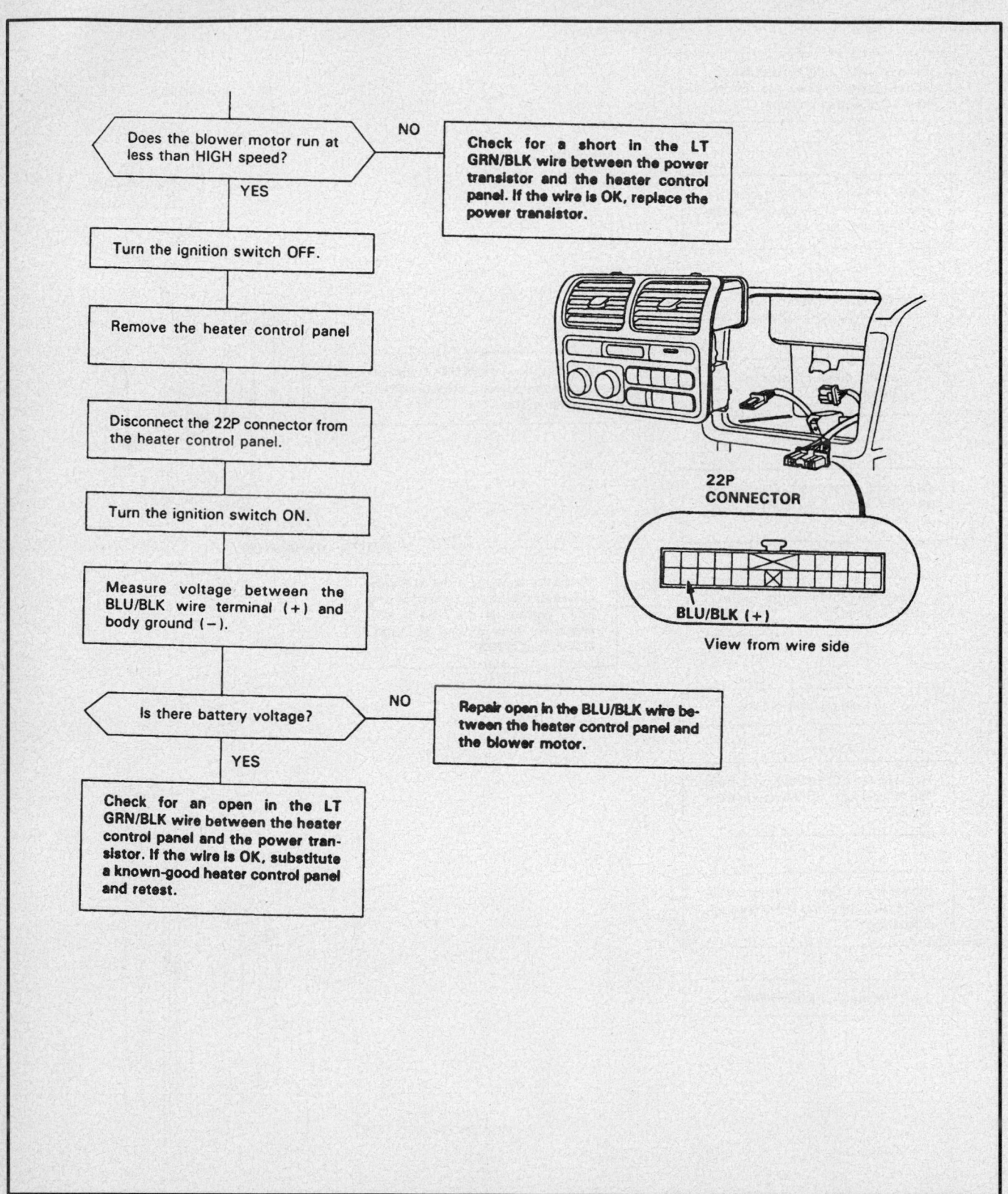

Does the blower motor run at less than HIGH speed?

NO → Check for a short in the LT GRN/BLK wire between the power transistor and the heater control panel. If the wire is OK, replace the power transistor.

YES

Turn the ignition switch OFF.

Remove the heater control panel

Disconnect the 22P connector from the heater control panel.

Turn the ignition switch ON.

Measure voltage between the BLU/BLK wire terminal (+) and body ground (−).

22P CONNECTOR

BLU/BLK (+)

View from wire side

Is there battery voltage?

NO → Repair open in the BLU/BLK wire between the heater control panel and the blower motor.

YES

Check for an open in the LT GRN/BLK wire between the heater control panel and the power transistor. If the wire is OK, substitute a known-good heater control panel and retest.

RECIRCULATION CONTROL MOTOR DIAGNOSTIC CHART—1994 LEGEND AND LEGEND COUPE

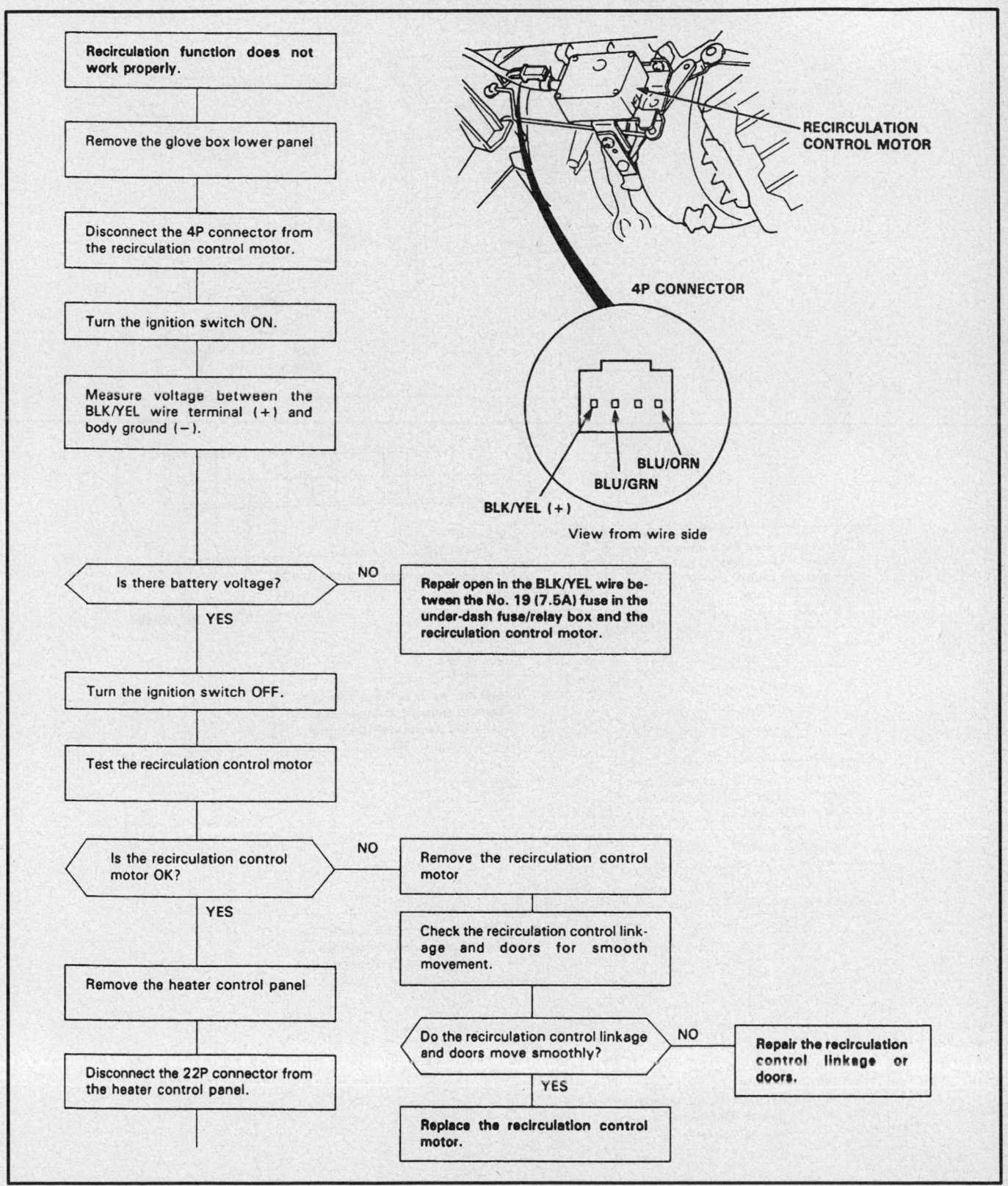

Recirculation function does not work properly.

Remove the glove box lower panel

Disconnect the 4P connector from the recirculation control motor.

Turn the ignition switch ON.

Measure voltage between the BLK/YEL wire terminal (+) and body ground (−).

RECIRCULATION CONTROL MOTOR

4P CONNECTOR

BLU/ORN
BLU/GRN
BLK/YEL (+)

View from wire side

Is there battery voltage? — NO → Repair open in the BLK/YEL wire between the No. 19 (7.5A) fuse in the under-dash fuse/relay box and the recirculation control motor.

YES

Turn the ignition switch OFF.

Test the recirculation control motor

Is the recirculation control motor OK? — NO → Remove the recirculation control motor

YES

Remove the heater control panel

Disconnect the 22P connector from the heater control panel.

Check the recirculation control linkage and doors for smooth movement.

Do the recirculation control linkage and doors move smoothly? — NO → Repair the recirculation control linkage or doors.

YES

Replace the recirculation control motor.

RECIRCULATION CONTROL MOTOR DIAGNOSTIC CHART—1994 LEGEND AND LEGEND COUPE—CONTINUED

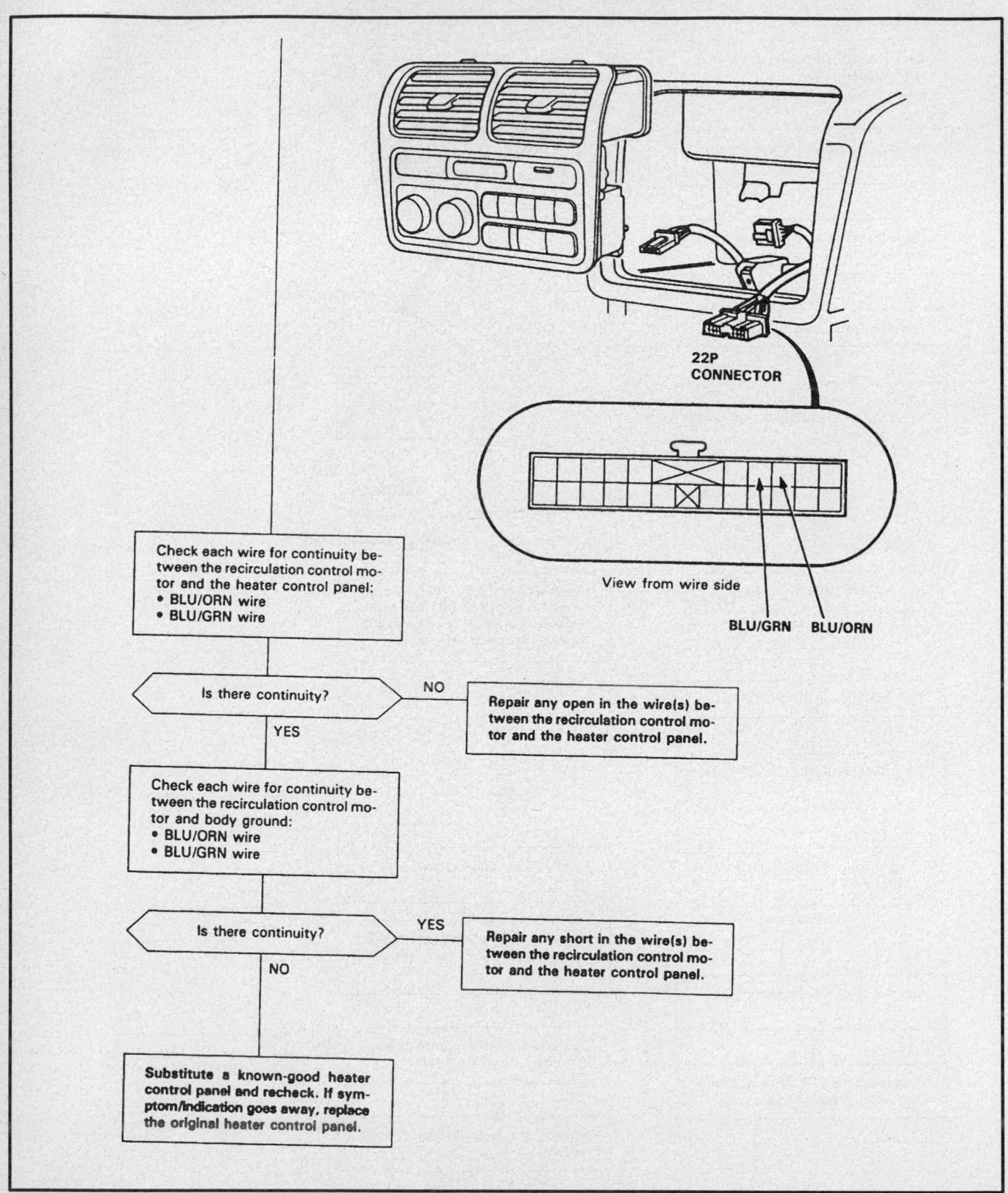

22P CONNECTOR

View from wire side

BLU/GRN   BLU/ORN

Check each wire for continuity between the recirculation control motor and the heater control panel:
• BLU/ORN wire
• BLU/GRN wire

Is there continuity? — **NO** → Repair any open in the wire(s) between the recirculation control motor and the heater control panel.

YES

Check each wire for continuity between the recirculation control motor and body ground:
• BLU/ORN wire
• BLU/GRN wire

Is there continuity? — **YES** → Repair any short in the wire(s) between the recirculation control motor and the heater control panel.

NO

Substitute a known-good heater control panel and recheck. If symptom/indication goes away, replace the original heater control panel.

MODE CONTROL MOTOR DIAGNOSTIC CHART—1994 LEGEND AND LEGEND COUPE

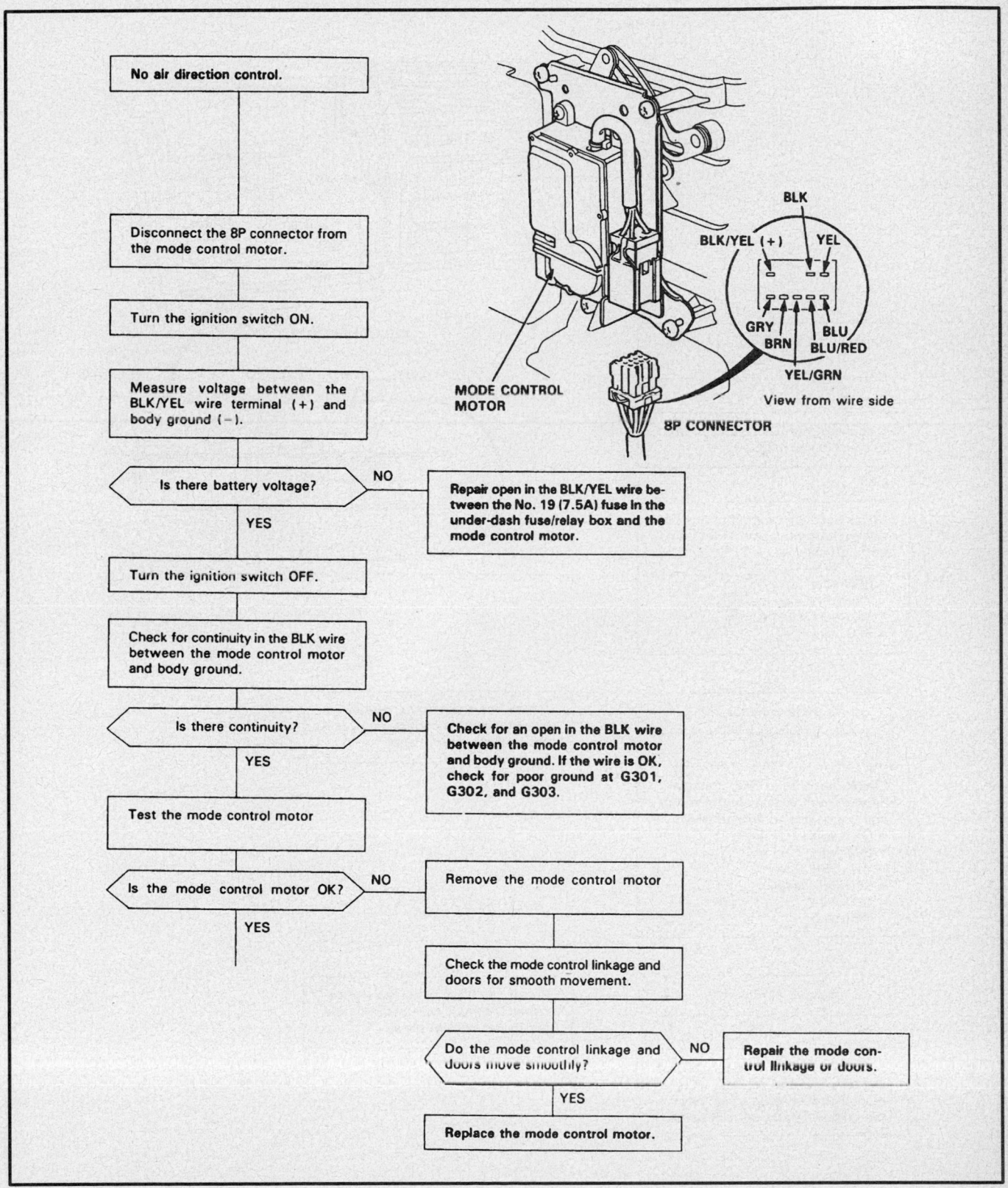

No air direction control.

↓

Disconnect the 8P connector from the mode control motor.

↓

Turn the ignition switch ON.

↓

Measure voltage between the BLK/YEL wire terminal (+) and body ground (−).

↓

Is there battery voltage? — **NO** → Repair open in the BLK/YEL wire between the No. 19 (7.5A) fuse in the under-dash fuse/relay box and the mode control motor.

YES ↓

Turn the ignition switch OFF.

↓

Check for continuity in the BLK wire between the mode control motor and body ground.

↓

Is there continuity? — **NO** → Check for an open in the BLK wire between the mode control motor and body ground. If the wire is OK, check for poor ground at G301, G302, and G303.

YES ↓

Test the mode control motor

↓

Is the mode control motor OK? — **NO** → Remove the mode control motor

YES ↓

Check the mode control linkage and doors for smooth movement.

↓

Do the mode control linkage and doors move smoothly? — **NO** → Repair the mode control linkage or doors.

YES ↓

Replace the mode control motor.

Diagram labels:
MODE CONTROL MOTOR

8P CONNECTOR

BLK

BLK/YEL (+)   YEL

GRY   BLU
BRN   BLU/RED
YEL/GRN

View from wire side

MODE CONTROL MOTOR DIAGNOSTIC CHART—1994 LEGEND AND LEGEND COUPE—CONTINUED

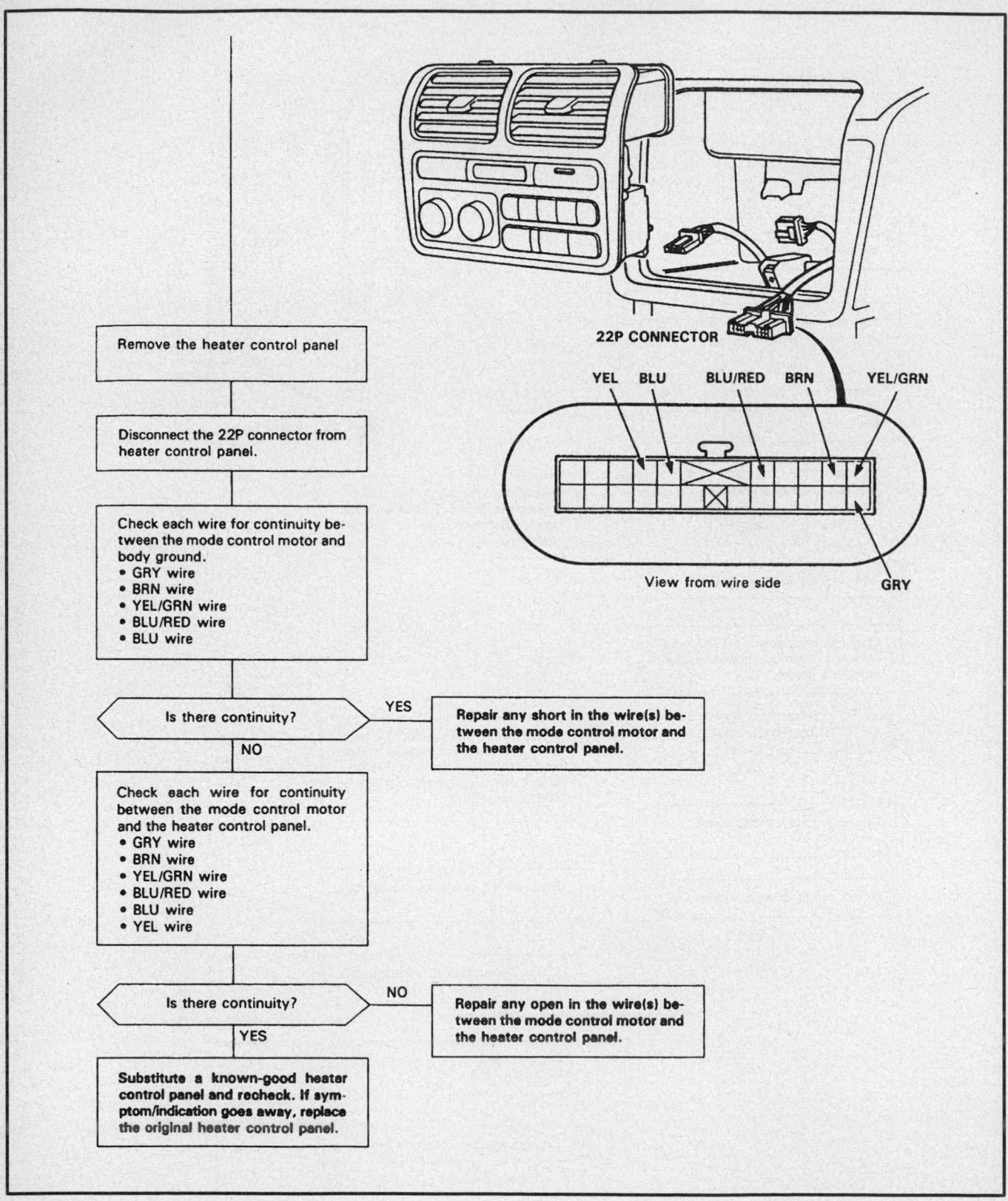

Remove the heater control panel

Disconnect the 22P connector from heater control panel.

Check each wire for continuity between the mode control motor and body ground.
• GRY wire
• BRN wire
• YEL/GRN wire
• BLU/RED wire
• BLU wire

Is there continuity? — YES → Repair any short in the wire(s) between the mode control motor and the heater control panel.

NO

Check each wire for continuity between the mode control motor and the heater control panel.
• GRY wire
• BRN wire
• YEL/GRN wire
• BLU/RED wire
• BLU wire
• YEL wire

Is there continuity? — NO → Repair any open in the wire(s) between the mode control motor and the heater control panel.

YES

Substitute a known-good heater control panel and recheck. If symptom/indication goes away, replace the original heater control panel.

22P CONNECTOR

YEL   BLU   BLU/RED   BRN   YEL/GRN

View from wire side   GRY

AIR MIX CONTROL MOTOR DIAGNOSTIC CHART–1994 LEGEND AND LEGEND COUPE

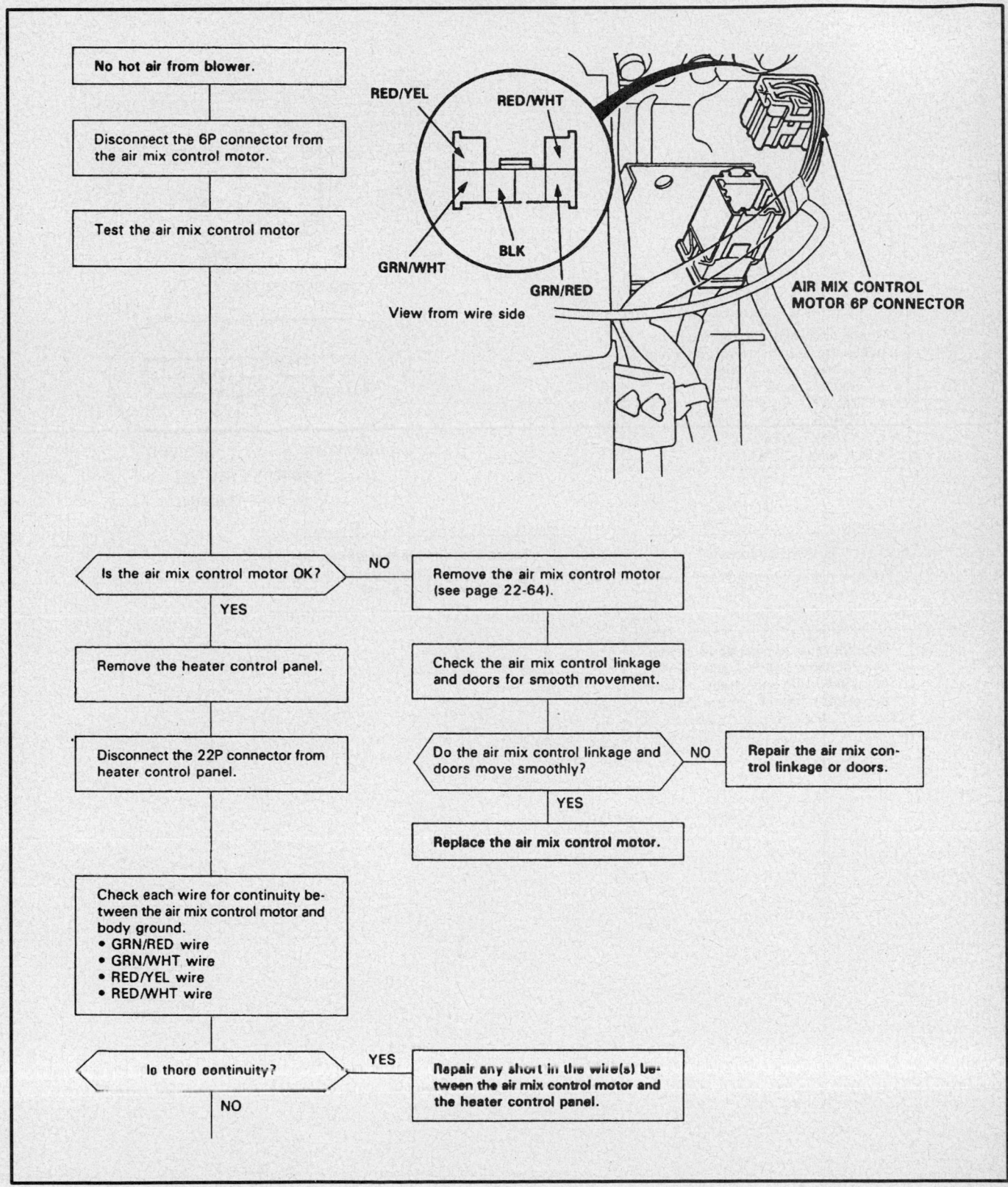

No hot air from blower.

Disconnect the 6P connector from the air mix control motor.

Test the air mix control motor

RED/YEL   RED/WHT

BLK

GRN/WHT

GRN/RED

View from wire side

AIR MIX CONTROL MOTOR 6P CONNECTOR

Is the air mix control motor OK?   —NO→ Remove the air mix control motor (see page 22-64).

YES

Remove the heater control panel.

Check the air mix control linkage and doors for smooth movement.

Disconnect the 22P connector from heater control panel.

Do the air mix control linkage and doors move smoothly?   —NO→ Repair the air mix control linkage or doors.

YES

Replace the air mix control motor.

Check each wire for continuity between the air mix control motor and body ground.
• GRN/RED wire
• GRN/WHT wire
• RED/YEL wire
• RED/WHT wire

Is there continuity?   —YES→ Repair any short in the wire(s) between the air mix control motor and the heater control panel.

NO

AIR MIX CONTROL MOTOR DIAGNOSTIC CHART–1994 LEGEND AND LEGEND COUPE–CONTINUED

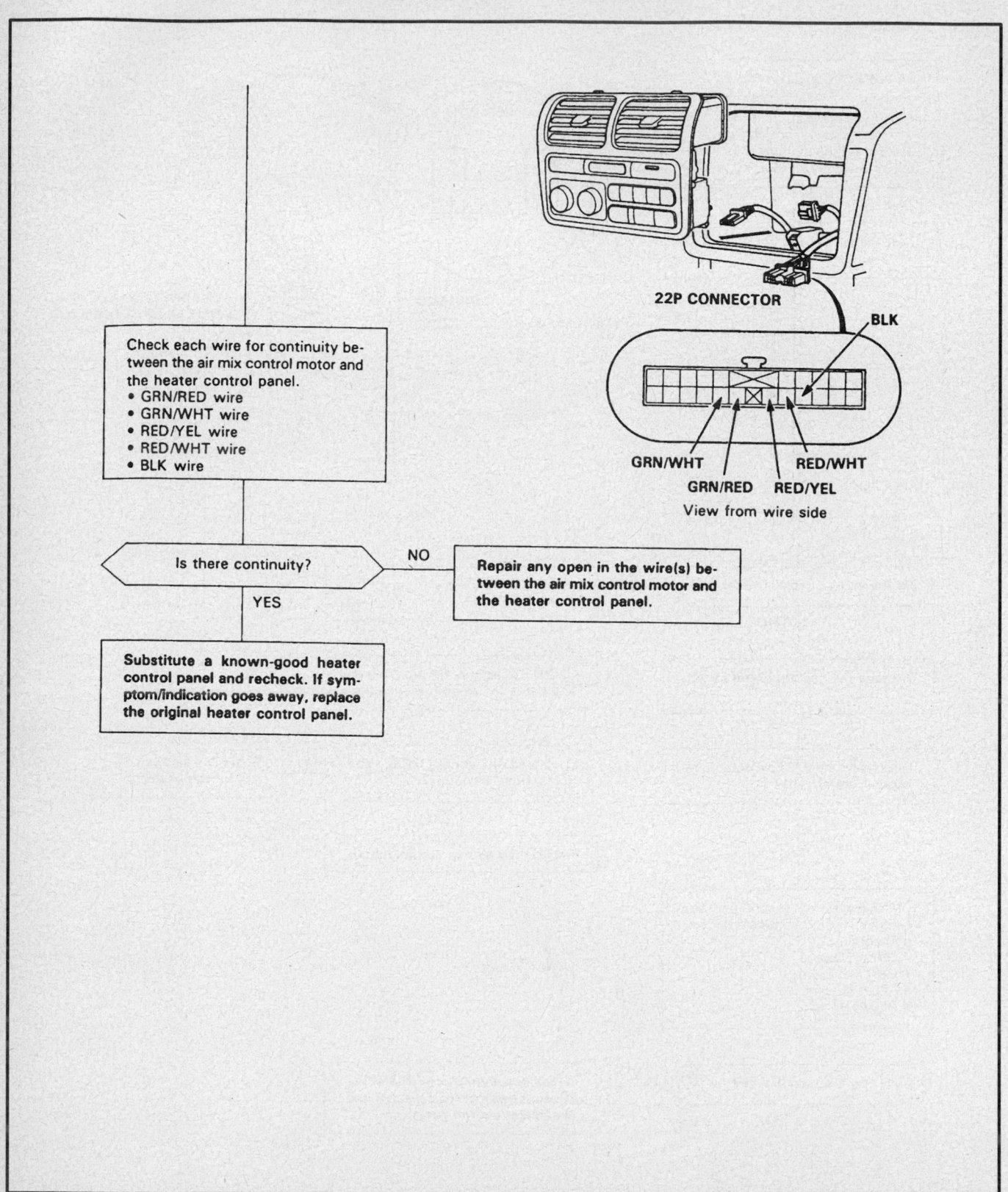

22P CONNECTOR

BLK

GRN/WHT   RED/WHT
GRN/RED   RED/YEL

View from wire side

Check each wire for continuity be-
tween the air mix control motor and
the heater control panel.
• GRN/RED wire
• GRN/WHT wire
• RED/YEL wire
• RED/WHT wire
• BLK wire

Is there continuity?   NO   Repair any open in the wire(s) be-
                                          tween the air mix control motor and
        YES   the heater control panel.

Substitute a known-good heater
control panel and recheck. If symp-
tom/indication goes away, replace
the original heater control panel.

EVAPORATOR TEMPERATURE SENSOR DIAGNOSTIC CHART—1994 LEGEND AND LEGEND COUPE

The evaporator temperature sensor is a temperature dependent resistor (thermistor). The resistance of the thermistor decreases as the evaporator outlet air temperature increases. Use a digital multimeter (KS-AHM-32-003) to check it.

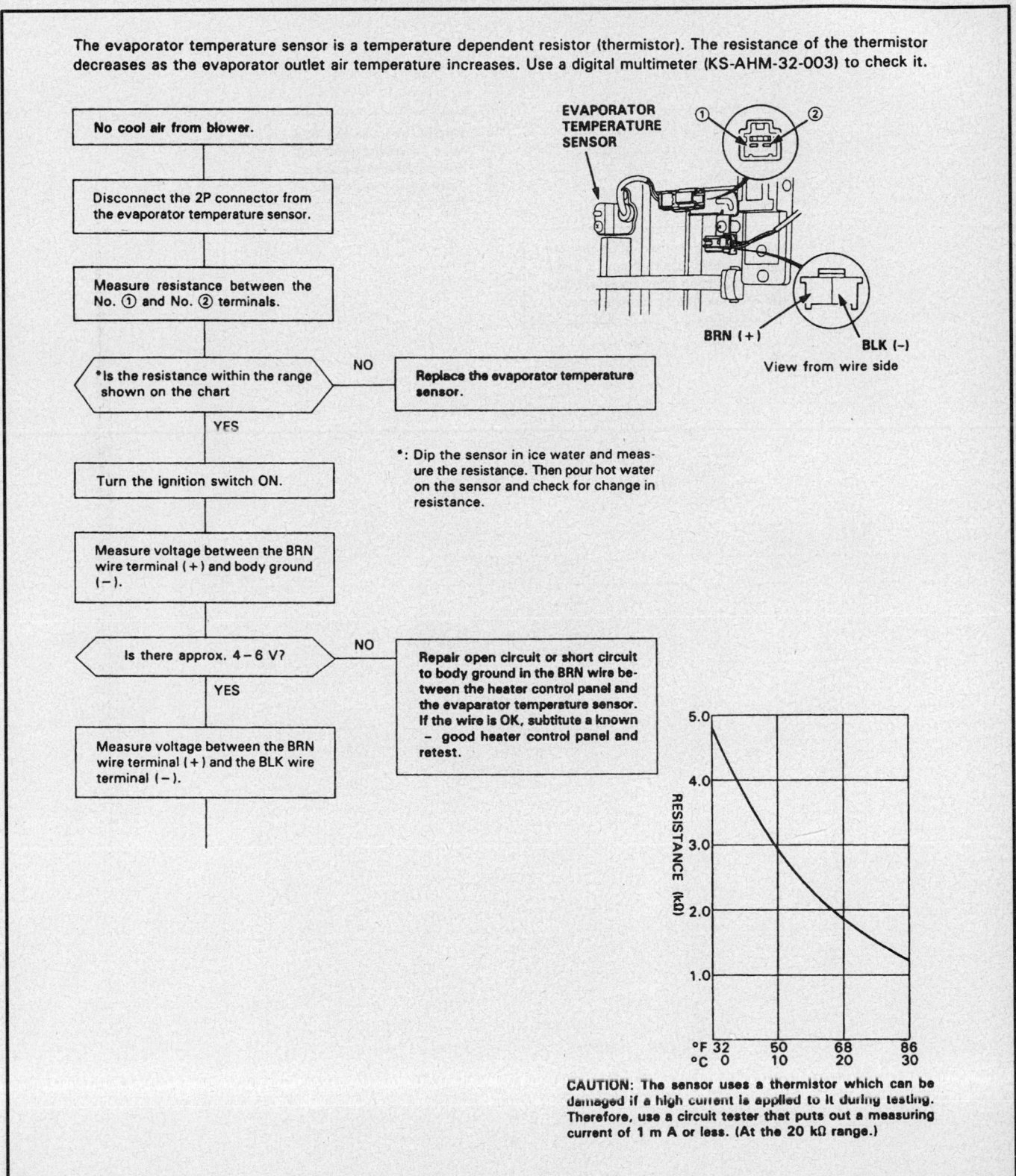

EVAPORATOR TEMPERATURE SENSOR

BRN (+)   BLK (−)

View from wire side

No cool air from blower.

Disconnect the 2P connector from the evaporator temperature sensor.

Measure resistance between the No. ① and No. ② terminals.

*Is the resistance within the range shown on the chart — **NO** → Replace the evaporator temperature sensor.

YES

*: Dip the sensor in ice water and measure the resistance. Then pour hot water on the sensor and check for change in resistance.

Turn the ignition switch ON.

Measure voltage between the BRN wire terminal (+) and body ground (−).

Is there approx. 4 – 6 V? — **NO** → Repair open circuit or short circuit to body ground in the BRN wire between the heater control panel and the evaporator temperature sensor. If the wire is OK, substitute a known – good heater control panel and retest.

YES

Measure voltage between the BRN wire terminal (+) and the BLK wire terminal (−).

RESISTANCE (kΩ)

5.0
4.0
3.0
2.0
1.0

°F 32   50   68   86
°C 0   10   20   30

CAUTION: The sensor uses a thermistor which can be damaged if a high current is applied to it during testing. Therefore, use a circuit tester that puts out a measuring current of 1 mA or less. (At the 20 kΩ range.)

EVAPORATOR TEMPERATURE SENSOR DIAGNOSTIC CHART – 1994 LEGEND AND LEGEND COUPE – CONTINUED

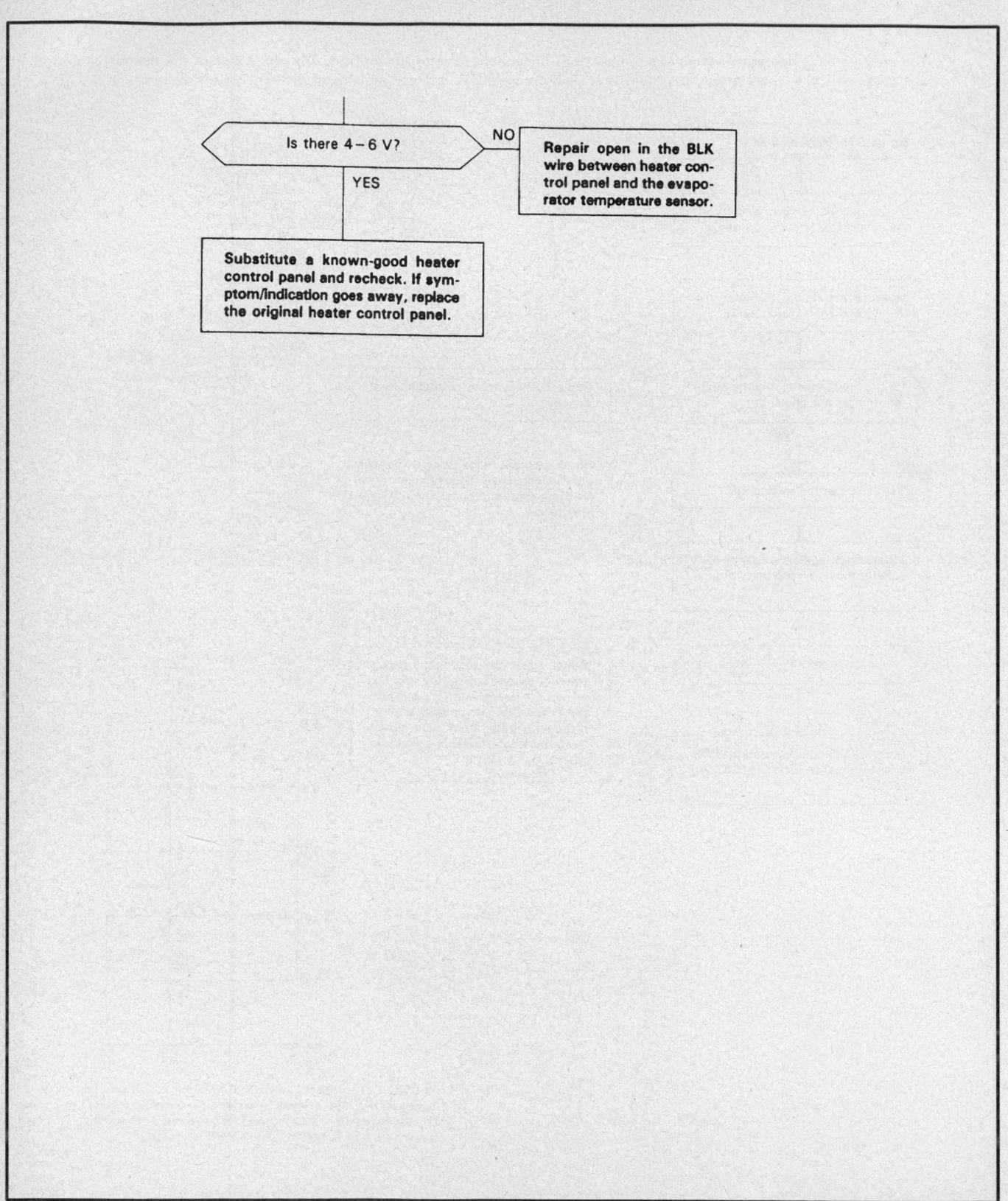

Is there 4 – 6 V?

NO → Repair open in the BLK wire between heater control panel and the evaporator temperature sensor.

YES

Substitute a known-good heater control panel and recheck. If symptom/indication goes away, replace the original heater control panel.

POWER CIRCUITS TO HEATER CONTROL PANEL DIAGNOSTIC CHART—1994 LEGEND AND LEGEND COUPE

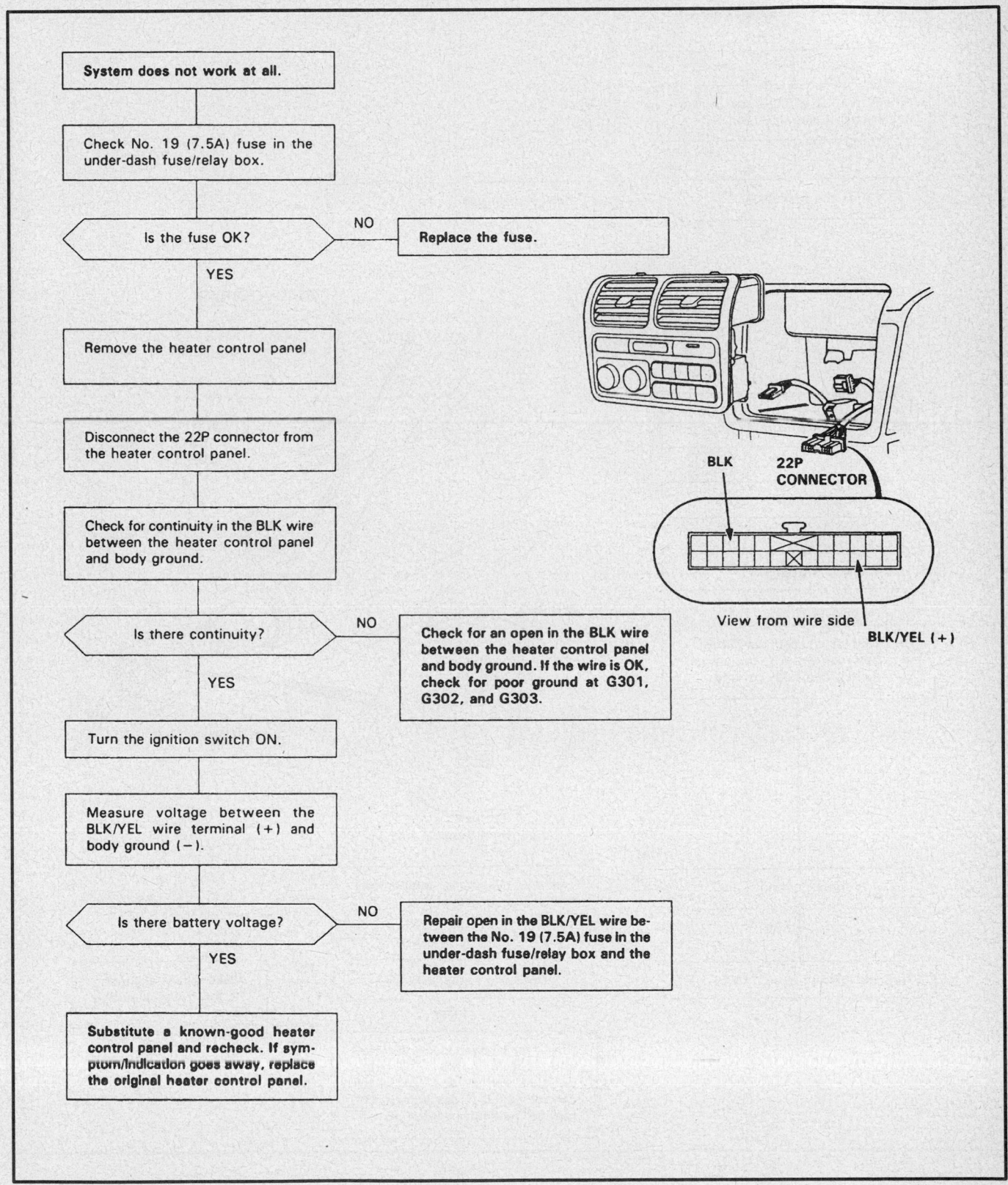

System does not work at all.

Check No. 19 (7.5A) fuse in the under-dash fuse/relay box.

Is the fuse OK? — NO → Replace the fuse.

YES

Remove the heater control panel

Disconnect the 22P connector from the heater control panel.

Check for continuity in the BLK wire between the heater control panel and body ground.

Is there continuity? — NO → Check for an open in the BLK wire between the heater control panel and body ground. If the wire is OK, check for poor ground at G301, G302, and G303.

YES

Turn the ignition switch ON.

Measure voltage between the BLK/YEL wire terminal (+) and body ground (−).

Is there battery voltage? — NO → Repair open in the BLK/YEL wire between the No. 19 (7.5A) fuse in the under-dash fuse/relay box and the heater control panel.

YES

Substitute a known-good heater control panel and recheck. If symptom/indication goes away, replace the original heater control panel.

BLK   22P CONNECTOR

View from wire side

BLK/YEL (+)

AIR CONDITIONING FLOW CHART—1994 LEGEND AND LEGEND COUPE

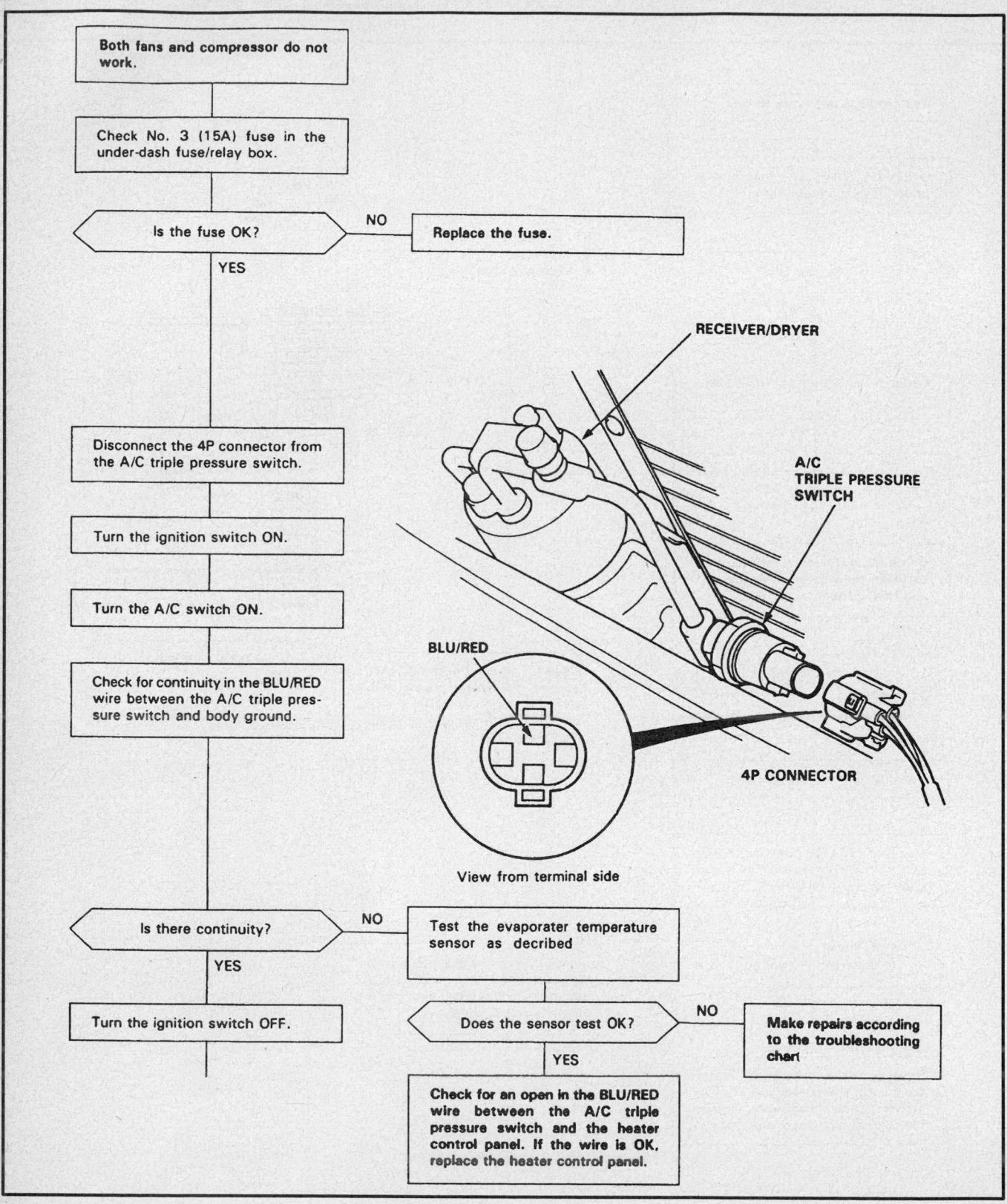

Both fans and compressor do not work.

Check No. 3 (15A) fuse in the under-dash fuse/relay box.

Is the fuse OK? — NO → Replace the fuse.

YES

Disconnect the 4P connector from the A/C triple pressure switch.

Turn the ignition switch ON.

Turn the A/C switch ON.

Check for continuity in the BLU/RED wire between the A/C triple pressure switch and body ground.

RECEIVER/DRYER

A/C TRIPLE PRESSURE SWITCH

BLU/RED

4P CONNECTOR

View from terminal side

Is there continuity? — NO → Test the evaporater temperature sensor as decribed

YES

Turn the ignition switch OFF.

Does the sensor test OK? — NO → Make repairs according to the troubleshooting chart

YES

Check for an open in the BLU/RED wire between the A/C triple pressure switch and the heater control panel. If the wire is OK, replace the heater control panel.

AIR CONDITIONING FLOW CHART – 1994 LEGEND AND LEGEND COUPE – CONTINUED

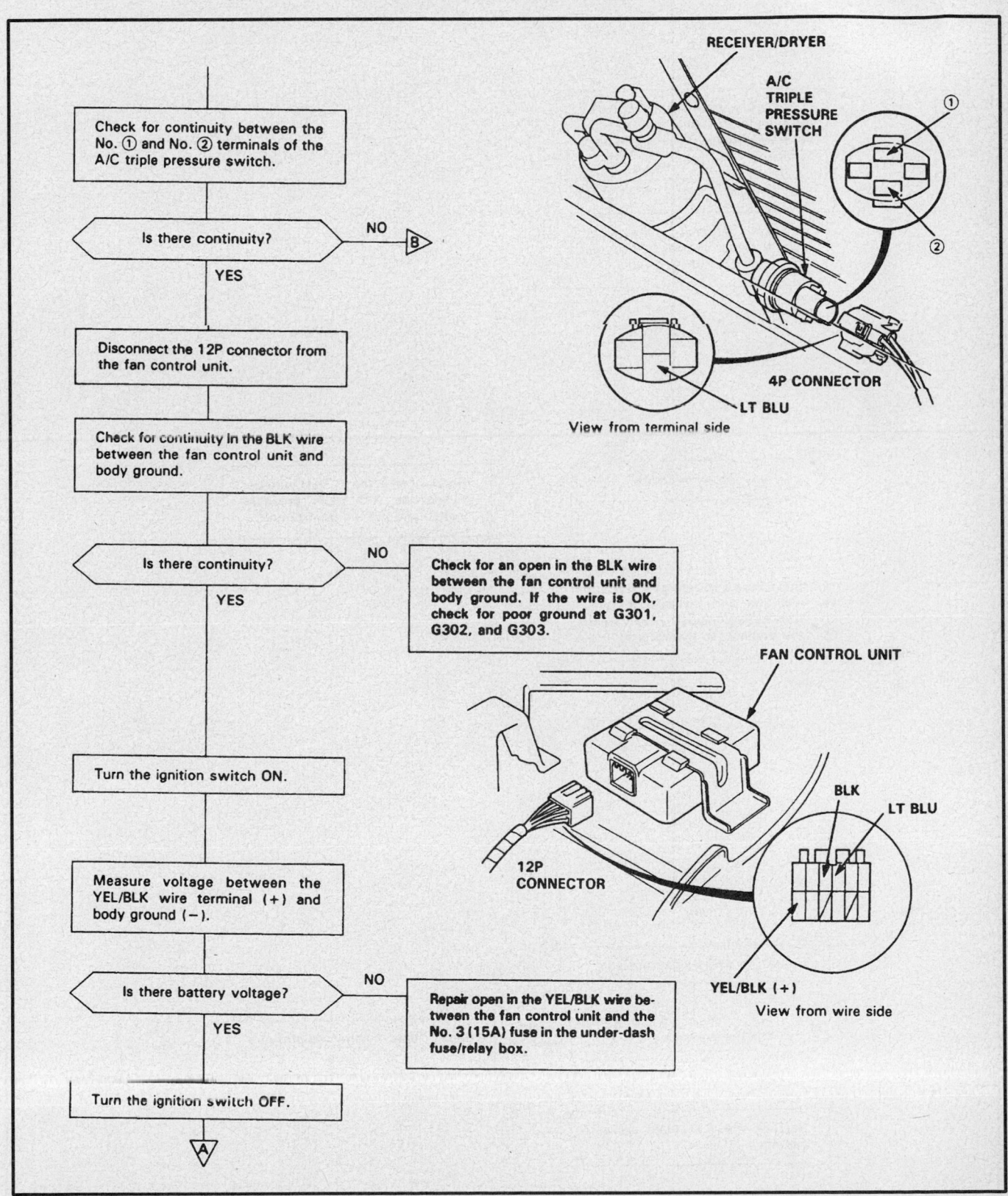

Check for continuity between the No. ① and No. ② terminals of the A/C triple pressure switch.

Is there continuity? — NO → B

YES

Disconnect the 12P connector from the fan control unit.

Check for continuity in the BLK wire between the fan control unit and body ground.

Is there continuity? — NO → Check for an open in the BLK wire between the fan control unit and body ground. If the wire is OK, check for poor ground at G301, G302, and G303.

YES

Turn the ignition switch ON.

Measure voltage between the YEL/BLK wire terminal (+) and body ground (−).

Is there battery voltage? — NO → Repair open in the YEL/BLK wire between the fan control unit and the No. 3 (15A) fuse in the under-dash fuse/relay box.

YES

Turn the ignition switch OFF.

A

RECEIVER/DRYER

A/C TRIPLE PRESSURE SWITCH

①
②

4P CONNECTOR

LT BLU

View from terminal side

FAN CONTROL UNIT

BLK

LT BLU

12P CONNECTOR

YEL/BLK (+)

View from wire side

AIR CONDITIONING FLOW CHART−1994 LEGEND AND LEGEND COUPE−CONTINUED

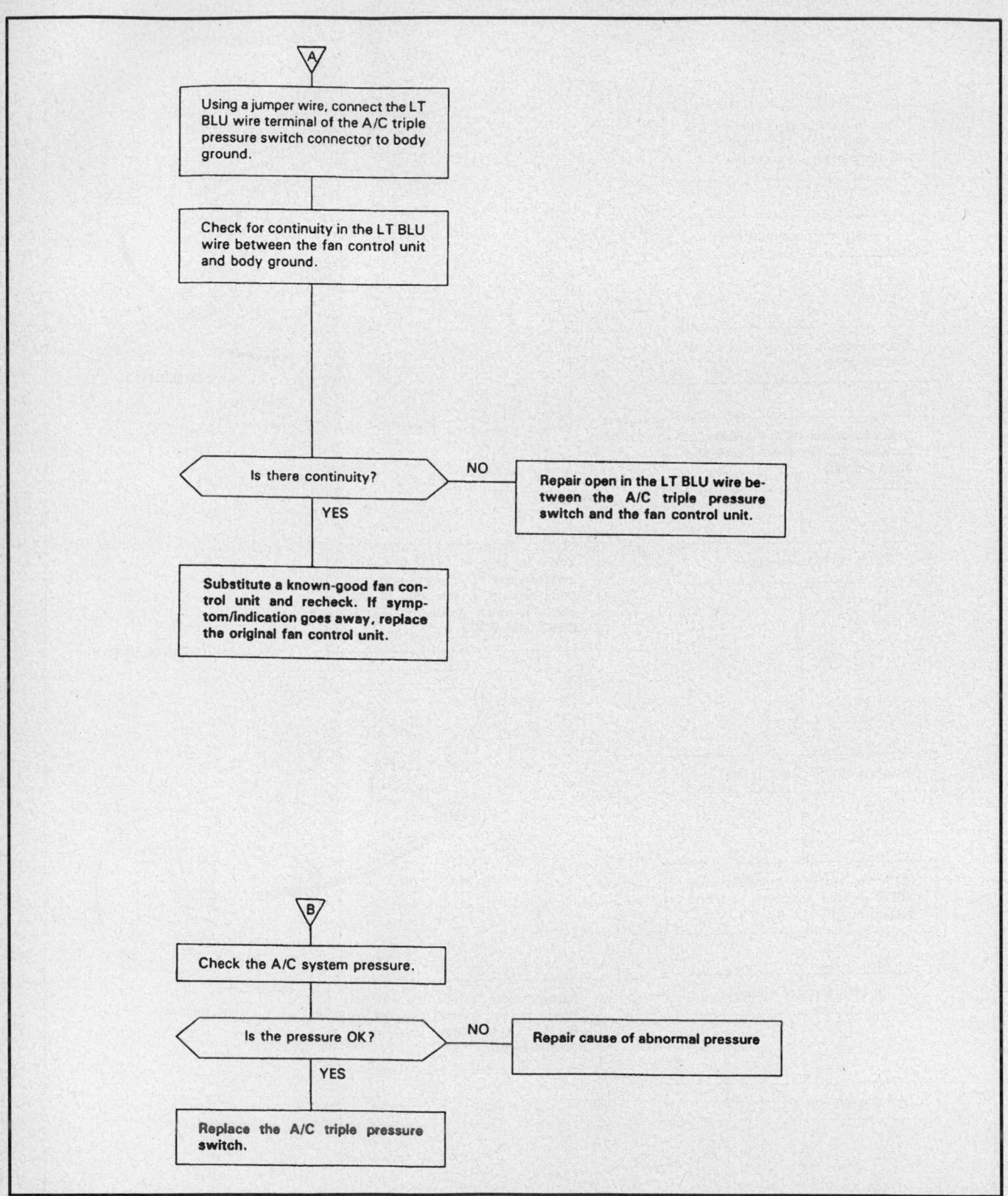

A

Using a jumper wire, connect the LT BLU wire terminal of the A/C triple pressure switch connector to body ground.

Check for continuity in the LT BLU wire between the fan control unit and body ground.

Is there continuity? — NO → Repair open in the LT BLU wire between the A/C triple pressure switch and the fan control unit.

YES

Substitute a known-good fan control unit and recheck. If symptom/indication goes away, replace the original fan control unit.

B

Check the A/C system pressure.

Is the pressure OK? — NO → Repair cause of abnormal pressure

YES

Replace the A/C triple pressure switch.

AIR CONDITIONING COMPRESSOR DIAGNOSTIC CHART—1994 LEGEND AND LEGEND COUPE

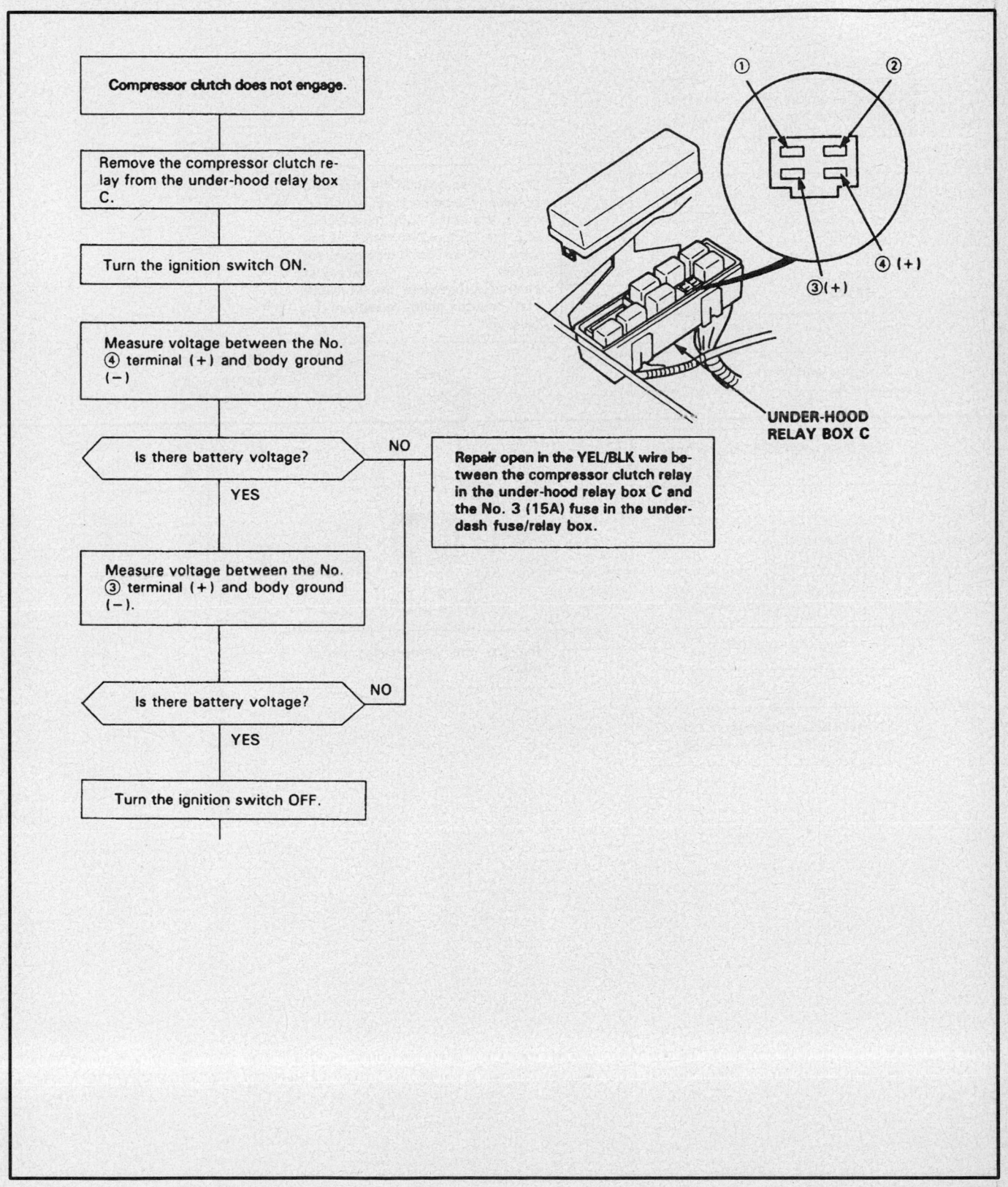

Compressor clutch does not engage.

Remove the compressor clutch relay from the under-hood relay box C.

Turn the ignition switch ON.

Measure voltage between the No. ④ terminal (+) and body ground (−)

Is there battery voltage? — NO → Repair open in the YEL/BLK wire between the compressor clutch relay in the under-hood relay box C and the No. 3 (15A) fuse in the under-dash fuse/relay box.

YES

Measure voltage between the No. ③ terminal (+) and body ground (−).

Is there battery voltage? — NO

YES

Turn the ignition switch OFF.

① ②

③(+) ④(+)

UNDER-HOOD RELAY BOX C

AIR CONDITIONING COMPRESSOR DIAGNOSTIC CHART—1994
LEGEND AND LEGEND COUPE—CONTINUED

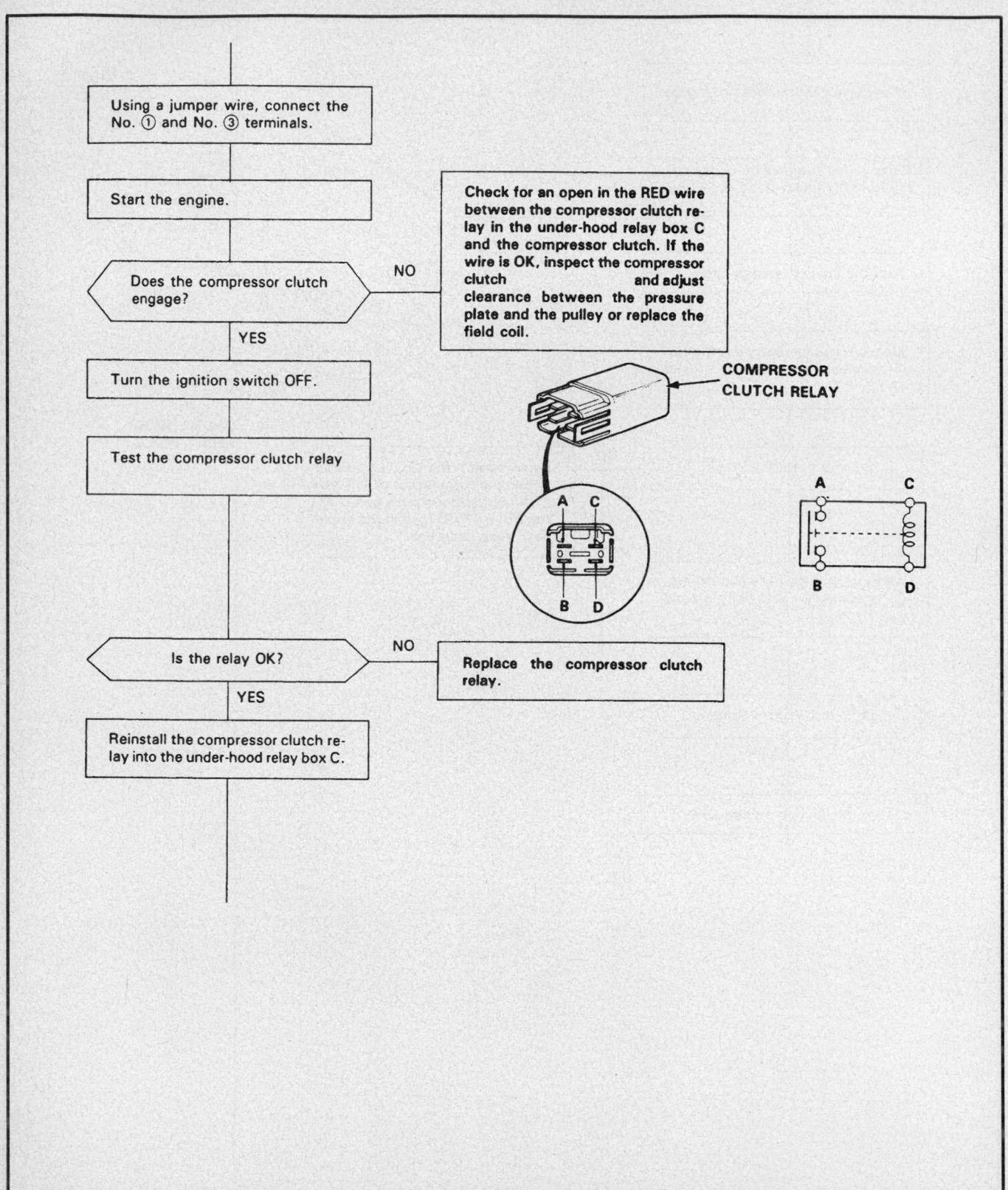

Using a jumper wire, connect the No. ① and No. ③ terminals.

Start the engine.

Does the compressor clutch engage? — NO → Check for an open in the RED wire between the compressor clutch relay in the under-hood relay box C and the compressor clutch. If the wire is OK, inspect the compressor clutch and adjust clearance between the pressure plate and the pulley or replace the field coil.

YES

Turn the ignition switch OFF.

Test the compressor clutch relay

COMPRESSOR CLUTCH RELAY

Is the relay OK? — NO → Replace the compressor clutch relay.

YES

Reinstall the compressor clutch relay into the under-hood relay box C.

AIR CONDITIONING COMPRESSOR DIAGNOSTIC CHART—1994 LEGEND AND LEGEND COUPE—CONTINUED

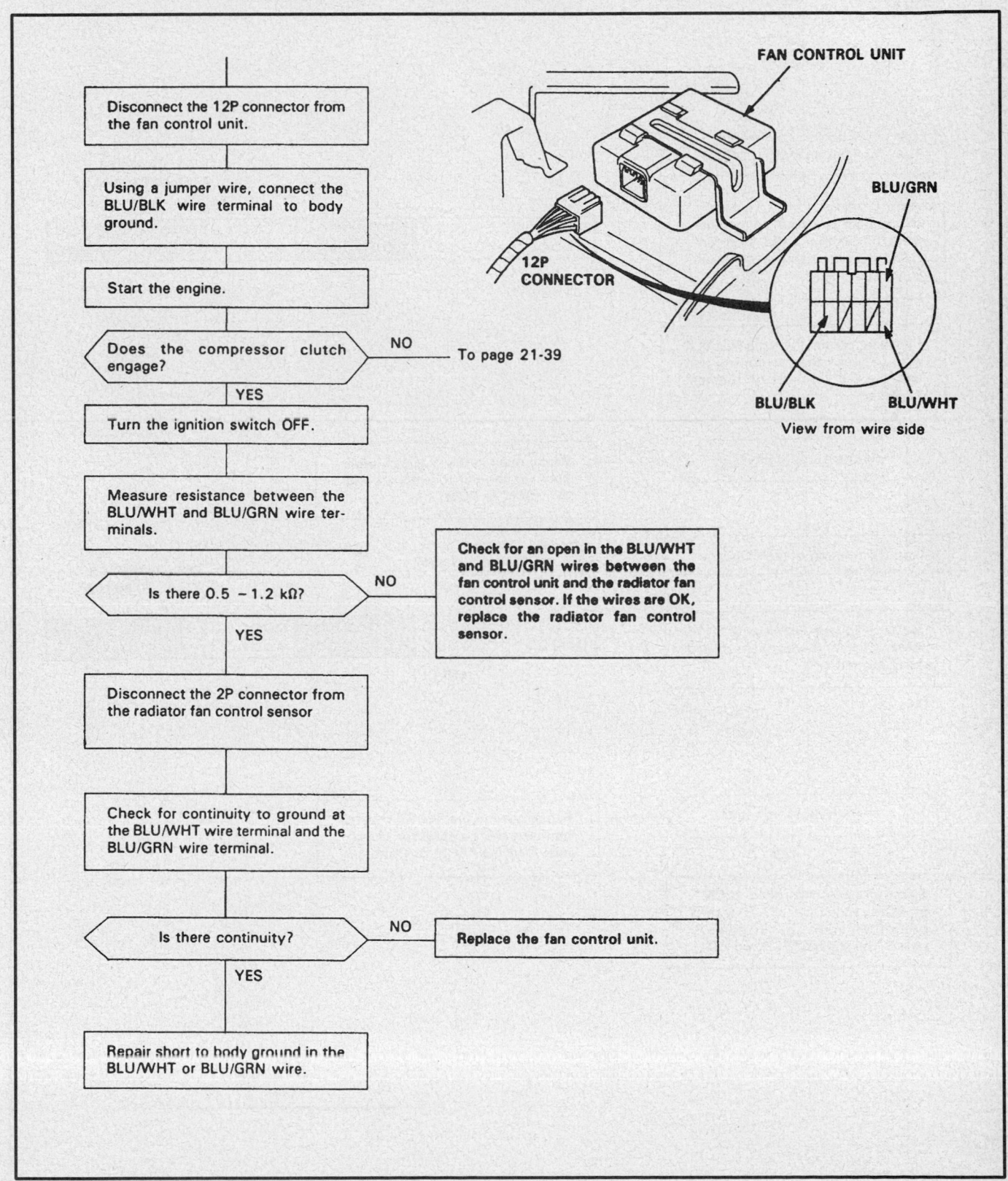

Disconnect the 12P connector from the fan control unit.

Using a jumper wire, connect the BLU/BLK wire terminal to body ground.

Start the engine.

Does the compressor clutch engage? — NO → To page 21-39

YES

Turn the ignition switch OFF.

Measure resistance between the BLU/WHT and BLU/GRN wire terminals.

Is there 0.5 – 1.2 kΩ? — NO → Check for an open in the BLU/WHT and BLU/GRN wires between the fan control unit and the radiator fan control sensor. If the wires are OK, replace the radiator fan control sensor.

YES

Disconnect the 2P connector from the radiator fan control sensor

Check for continuity to ground at the BLU/WHT wire terminal and the BLU/GRN wire terminal.

Is there continuity? — NO → Replace the fan control unit.

YES

Repair short to body ground in the BLU/WHT or BLU/GRN wire.

FAN CONTROL UNIT

12P CONNECTOR

BLU/GRN

BLU/BLK   BLU/WHT

View from wire side

AIR CONDITIONING COMPRESSOR DIAGNOSTIC CHART — 1994 LEGEND AND LEGEND COUPE — CONTINUED

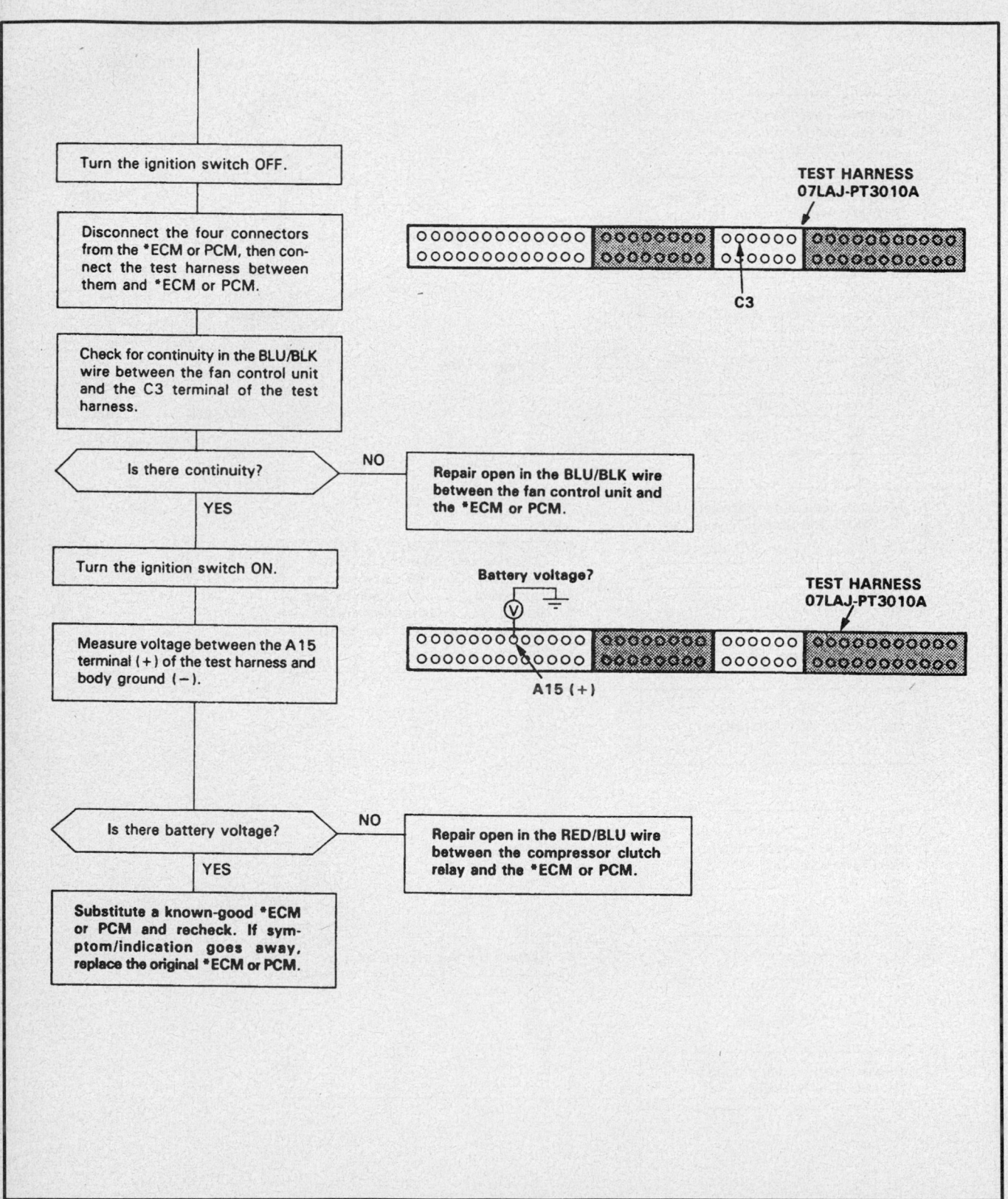

Turn the ignition switch OFF.

Disconnect the four connectors from the *ECM or PCM, then connect the test harness between them and *ECM or PCM.

TEST HARNESS 07LAJ-PT3010A

C3

Check for continuity in the BLU/BLK wire between the fan control unit and the C3 terminal of the test harness.

Is there continuity? — NO → Repair open in the BLU/BLK wire between the fan control unit and the *ECM or PCM.

YES

Turn the ignition switch ON.

Measure voltage between the A15 terminal (+) of the test harness and body ground (−).

Battery voltage?

TEST HARNESS 07LAJ-PT3010A

A15 (+)

Is there battery voltage? — NO → Repair open in the RED/BLU wire between the compressor clutch relay and the *ECM or PCM.

YES

Substitute a known-good *ECM or PCM and recheck. If symptom/indication goes away, replace the original *ECM or PCM.

BOTH FANS DIAGNOSTIC CHART—1994 LEGEND AND LEGEND COUPE

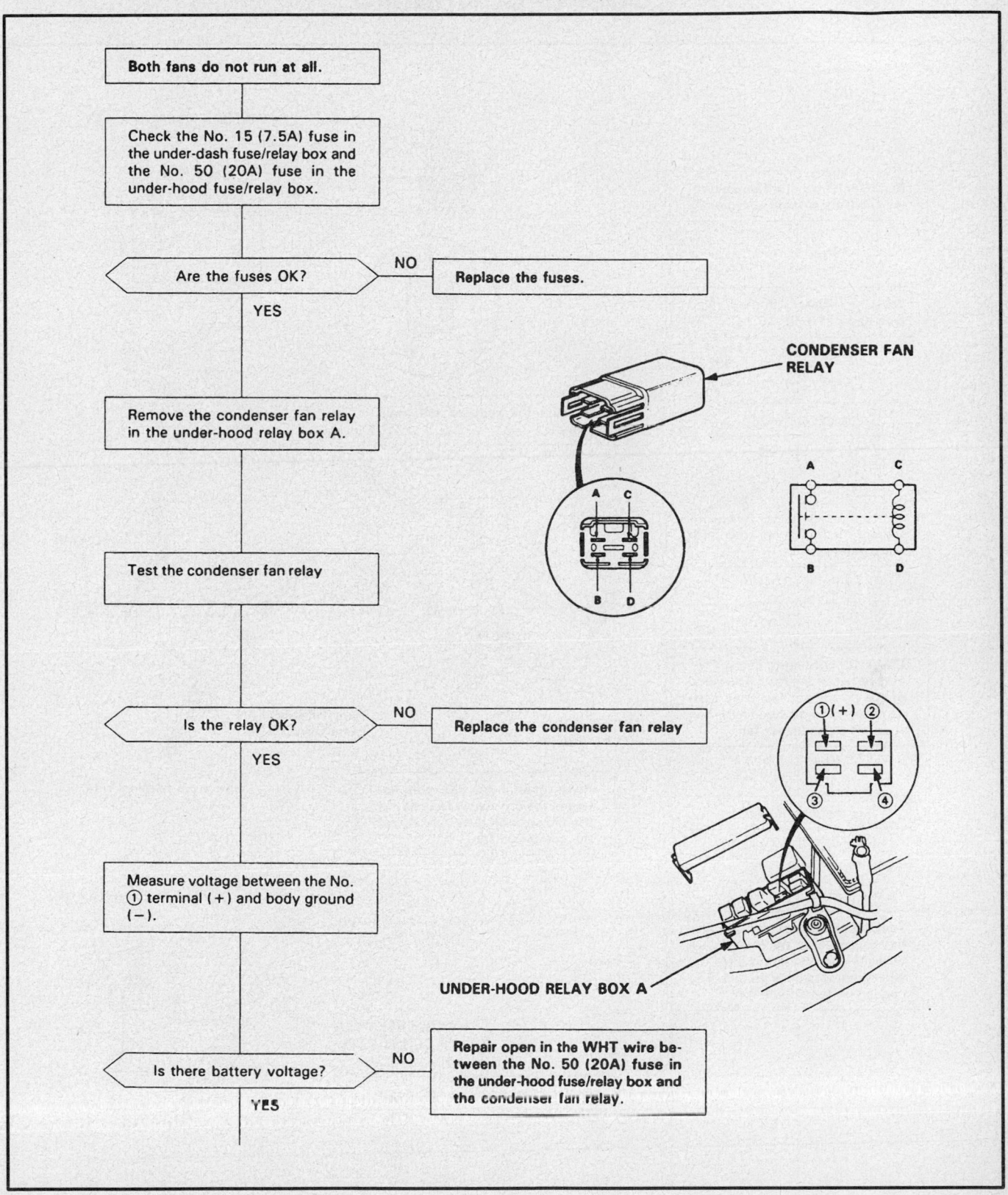

Both fans do not run at all.

Check the No. 15 (7.5A) fuse in the under-dash fuse/relay box and the No. 50 (20A) fuse in the under-hood fuse/relay box.

Are the fuses OK? — NO → Replace the fuses.

YES

CONDENSER FAN RELAY

Remove the condenser fan relay in the under-hood relay box A.

Test the condenser fan relay

Is the relay OK? — NO → Replace the condenser fan relay

YES

Measure voltage between the No. ① terminal (+) and body ground (−).

UNDER-HOOD RELAY BOX A

Is there battery voltage? — NO → Repair open in the WHT wire between the No. 50 (20A) fuse in the under-hood fuse/relay box and the condenser fan relay.

YES

BOTH FANS DIAGNOSTIC CHART—1994 LEGEND AND LEGEND COUPE—CONTINUED

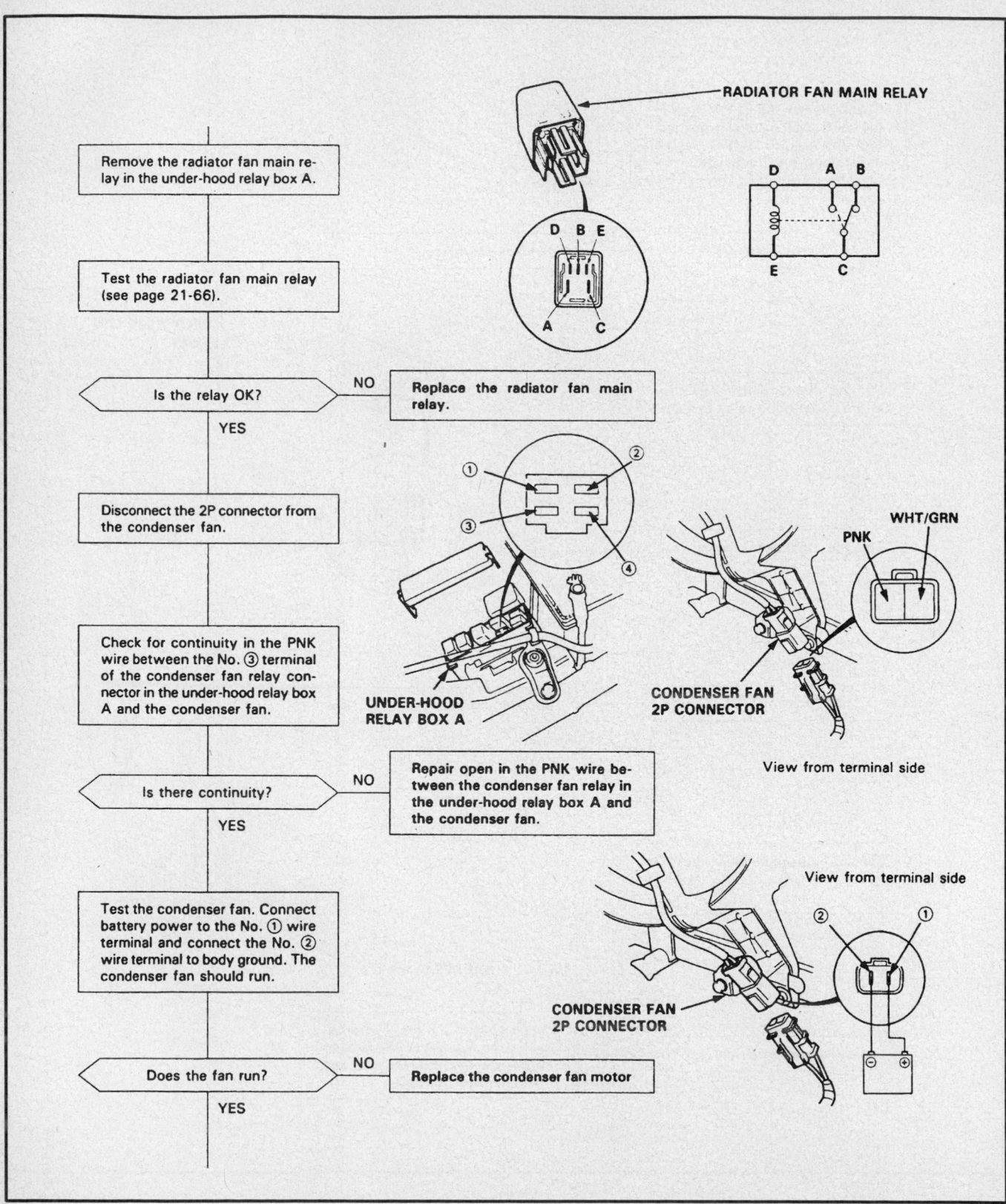

RADIATOR FAN MAIN RELAY

Remove the radiator fan main relay in the under-hood relay box A.

Test the radiator fan main relay (see page 21-66).

Is the relay OK? — NO → Replace the radiator fan main relay.

YES

Disconnect the 2P connector from the condenser fan.

Check for continuity in the PNK wire between the No. ③ terminal of the condenser fan relay connector in the under-hood relay box A and the condenser fan.

UNDER-HOOD RELAY BOX A

WHT/GRN

PNK

CONDENSER FAN 2P CONNECTOR

Is there continuity? — NO → Repair open in the PNK wire between the condenser fan relay in the under-hood relay box A and the condenser fan.

YES

View from terminal side

Test the condenser fan. Connect battery power to the No. ① wire terminal and connect the No. ② wire terminal to body ground. The condenser fan should run.

View from terminal side

CONDENSER FAN 2P CONNECTOR

Does the fan run? — NO → Replace the condenser fan motor

YES

BOTH FANS DIAGNOSTIC CHART – 1994 LEGEND AND LEGEND COUPE – CONTINUED

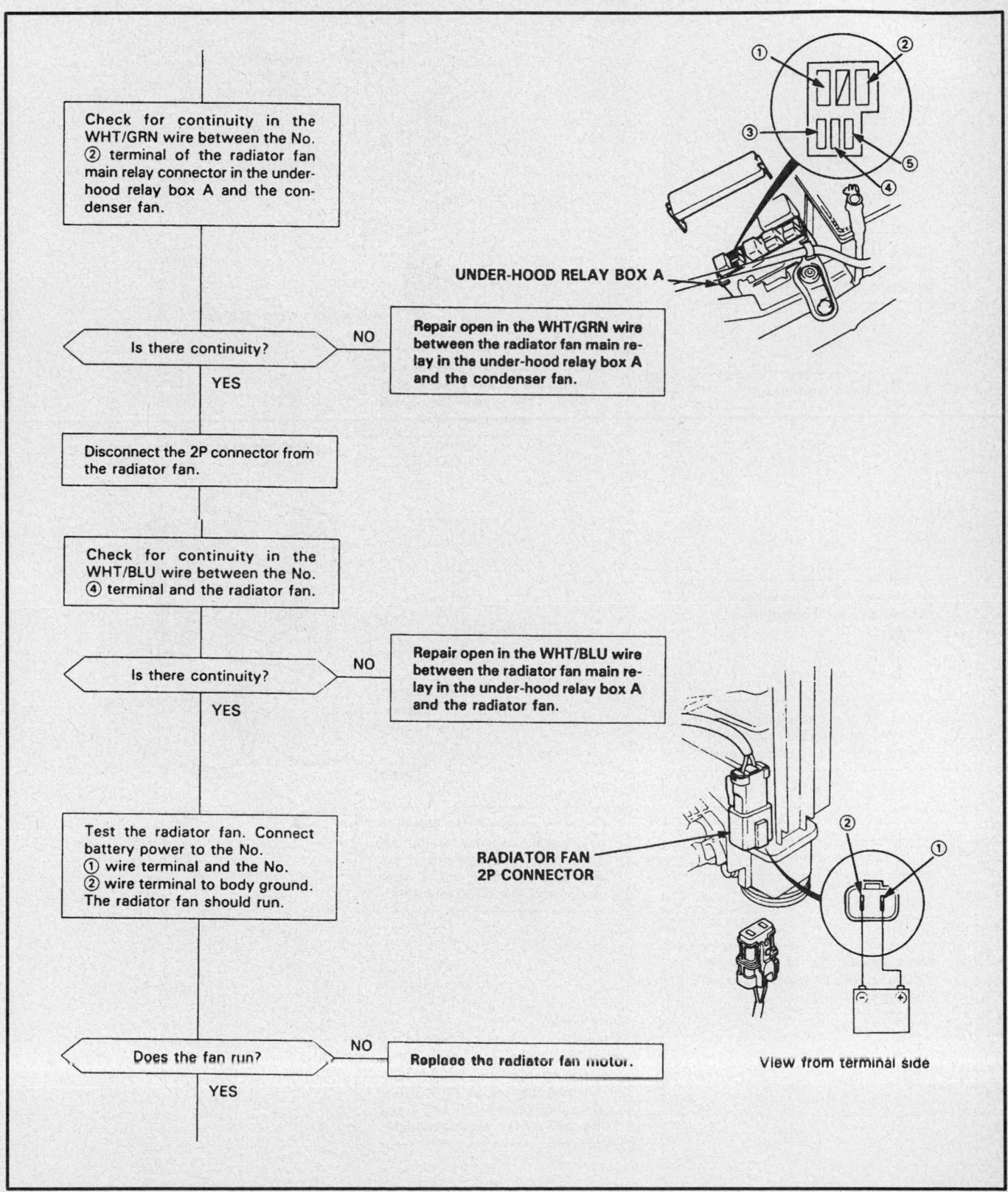

Check for continuity in the WHT/GRN wire between the No. ② terminal of the radiator fan main relay connector in the under-hood relay box A and the condenser fan.

UNDER-HOOD RELAY BOX A

Is there continuity? — NO → Repair open in the WHT/GRN wire between the radiator fan main relay in the under-hood relay box A and the condenser fan.

YES

Disconnect the 2P connector from the radiator fan.

Check for continuity in the WHT/BLU wire between the No. ④ terminal and the radiator fan.

Is there continuity? — NO → Repair open in the WHT/BLU wire between the radiator fan main relay in the under-hood relay box A and the radiator fan.

YES

RADIATOR FAN 2P CONNECTOR

Test the radiator fan. Connect battery power to the No. ① wire terminal and the No. ② wire terminal to body ground. The radiator fan should run.

Does the fan run? — NO → Replace the radiator fan motor.

YES

View from terminal side

BOTH FANS DIAGNOSTIC CHART – 1994 LEGEND AND LEGEND COUPE – CONTINUED

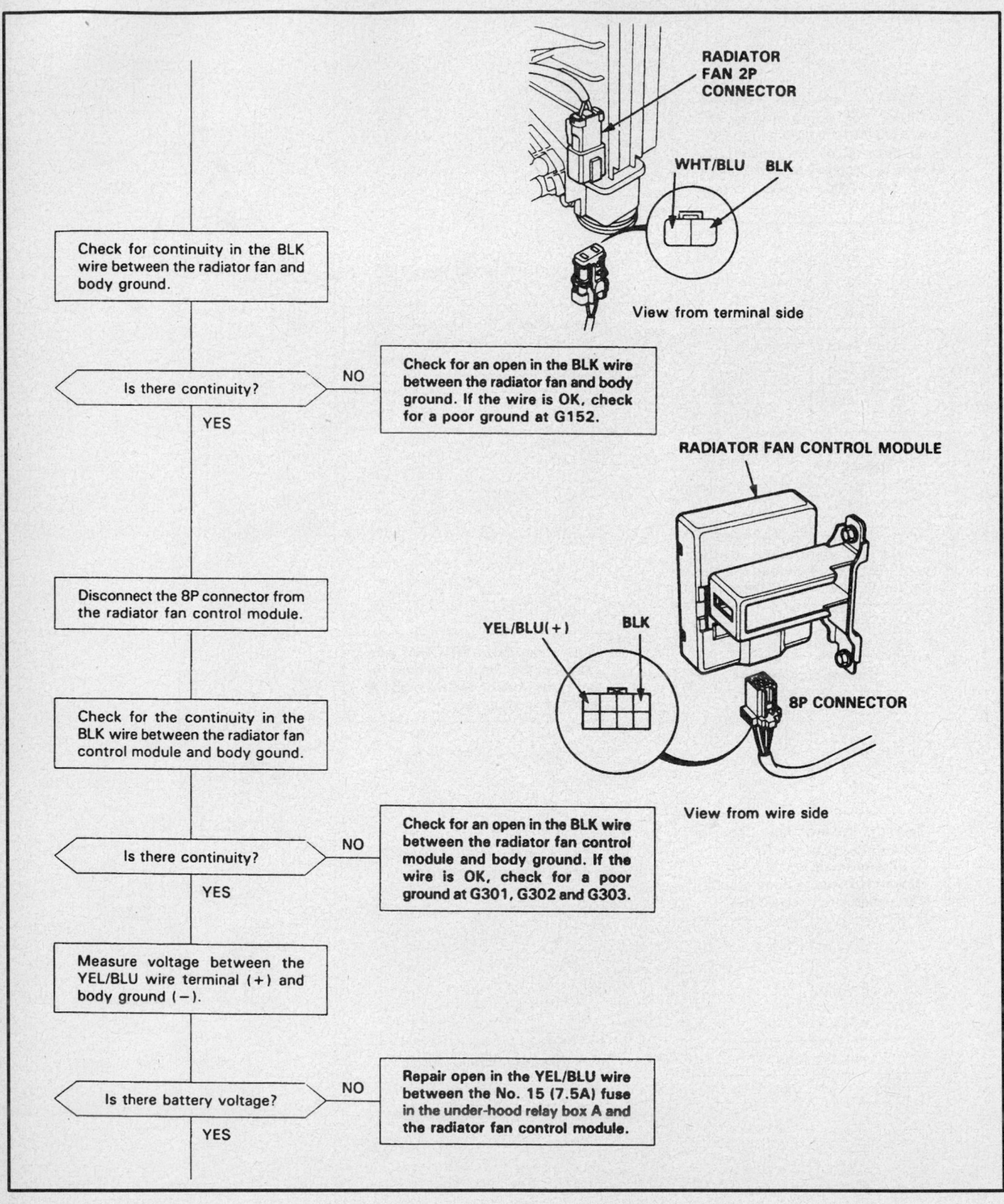

Check for continuity in the BLK wire between the radiator fan and body ground.

RADIATOR FAN 2P CONNECTOR

WHT/BLU   BLK

View from terminal side

Is there continuity?   **NO** → Check for an open in the BLK wire between the radiator fan and body ground. If the wire is OK, check for a poor ground at G152.

YES

Disconnect the 8P connector from the radiator fan control module.

RADIATOR FAN CONTROL MODULE

YEL/BLU(+)   BLK

8P CONNECTOR

Check for the continuity in the BLK wire between the radiator fan control module and body gound.

View from wire side

Is there continuity?   **NO** → Check for an open in the BLK wire between the radiator fan control module and body ground. If the wire is OK, check for a poor ground at G301, G302 and G303.

YES

Measure voltage between the YEL/BLU wire terminal (+) and body ground (−).

Is there battery voltage?   **NO** → Repair open in the YEL/BLU wire between the No. 15 (7.5A) fuse in the under-hood relay box A and the radiator fan control module.

YES

BOTH FANS DIAGNOSTIC CHART—1994 LEGEND AND LEGEND COUPE—CONTINUED

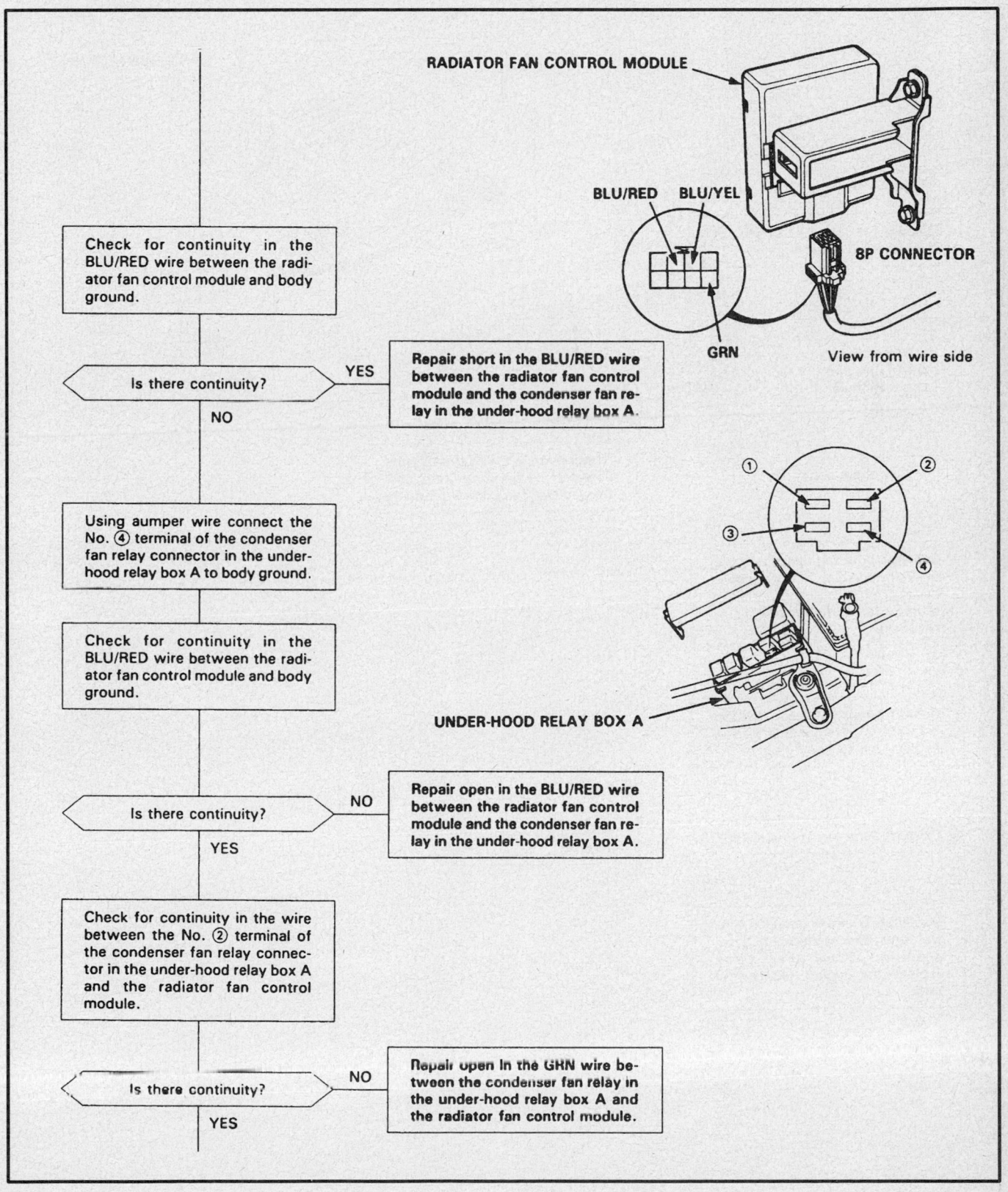

RADIATOR FAN CONTROL MODULE

BLU/RED   BLU/YEL

8P CONNECTOR

GRN

View from wire side

Check for continuity in the BLU/RED wire between the radiator fan control module and body ground.

Is there continuity? — YES → Repair short in the BLU/RED wire between the radiator fan control module and the condenser fan relay in the under-hood relay box A.

NO

Using aumper wire connect the No. ④ terminal of the condenser fan relay connector in the under-hood relay box A to body ground.

Check for continuity in the BLU/RED wire between the radiator fan control module and body ground.

UNDER-HOOD RELAY BOX A

Is there continuity? — NO → Repair open in the BLU/RED wire between the radiator fan control module and the condenser fan relay in the under-hood relay box A.

YES

Check for continuity in the wire between the No. ② terminal of the condenser fan relay connector in the under-hood relay box A and the radiator fan control module.

Is there continuity? — NO → Repair open in the GRN wire between the condenser fan relay in the under-hood relay box A and the radiator fan control module.

YES

BOTH FANS DIAGNOSTIC CHART—1994 LEGEND AND LEGEND COUPE—CONTINUED

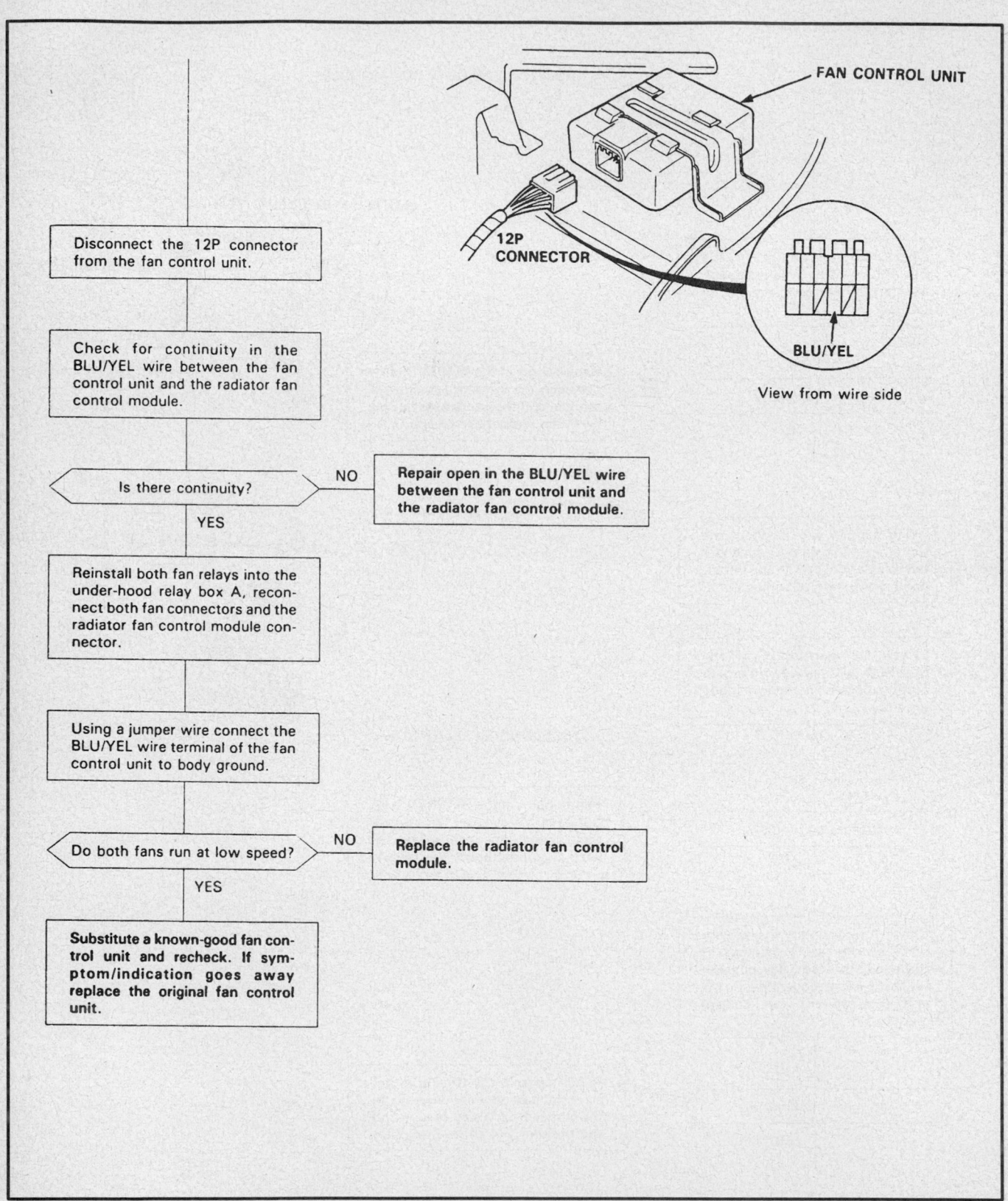

FAN CONTROL UNIT

12P CONNECTOR

BLU/YEL

View from wire side

Disconnect the 12P connector from the fan control unit.

Check for continuity in the BLU/YEL wire between the fan control unit and the radiator fan control module.

Is there continuity? — NO → Repair open in the BLU/YEL wire between the fan control unit and the radiator fan control module.

YES

Reinstall both fan relays into the under-hood relay box A, reconnect both fan connectors and the radiator fan control module connector.

Using a jumper wire connect the BLU/YEL wire terminal of the fan control unit to body ground.

Do both fans run at low speed? — NO → Replace the radiator fan control module.

YES

Substitute a known-good fan control unit and recheck. If symptom/indication goes away replace the original fan control unit.

BOTH FANS HIGH SPEED DIAGNOSTIC CHART—1994 LEGEND AND LEGEND COUPE

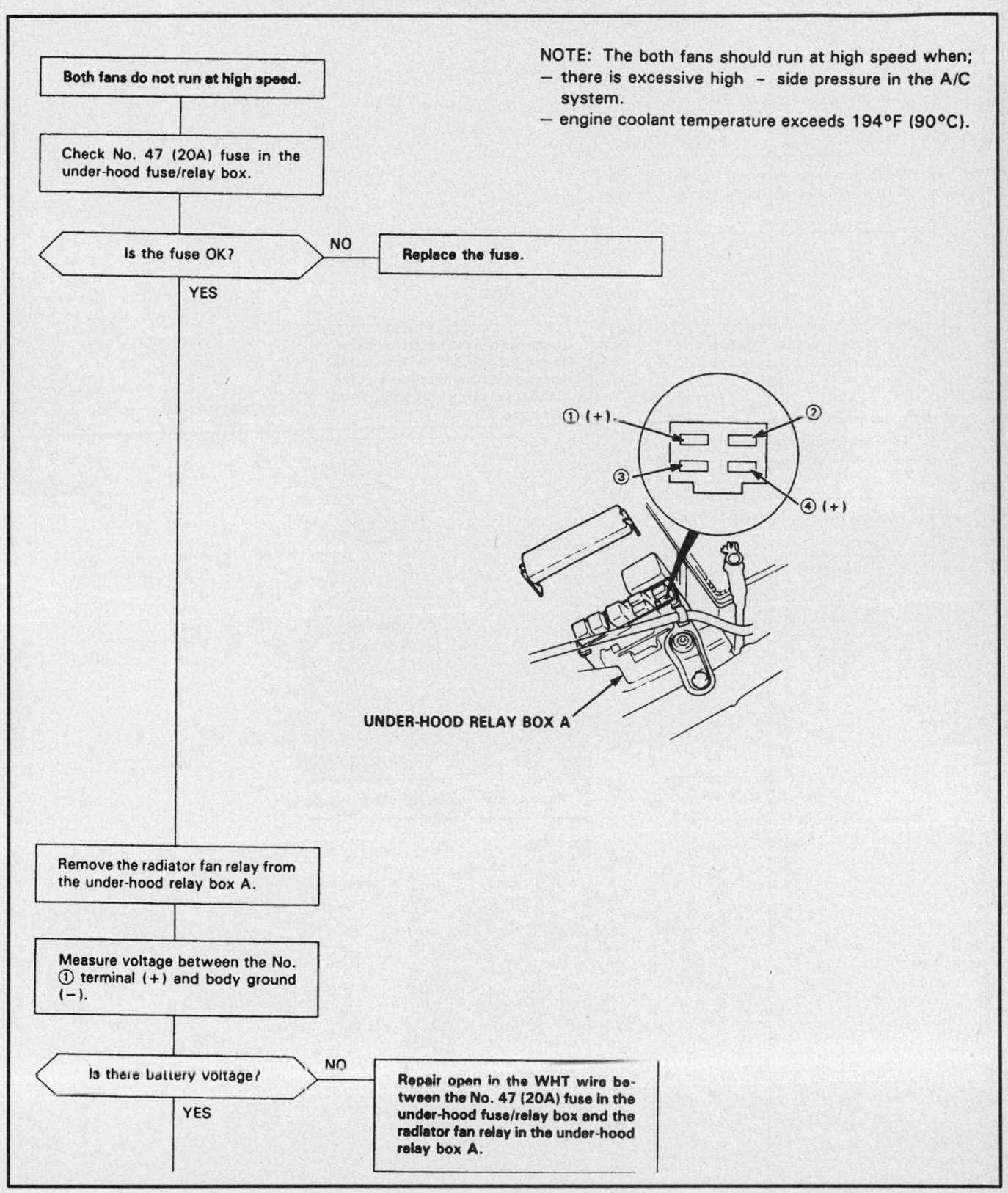

Both fans do not run at high speed.

NOTE: The both fans should run at high speed when;
— there is excessive high – side pressure in the A/C system.
— engine coolant temperature exceeds 194°F (90°C).

Check No. 47 (20A) fuse in the under-hood fuse/relay box.

Is the fuse OK? — **NO** → Replace the fuse.

YES

① (+) ②
③ ④ (+)

UNDER-HOOD RELAY BOX A

Remove the radiator fan relay from the under-hood relay box A.

Measure voltage between the No. ① terminal (+) and body ground (−).

Is there battery voltage? — **NO** → Repair open in the WHT wire between the No. 47 (20A) fuse in the under-hood fuse/relay box and the radiator fan relay in the under-hood relay box A.

YES

BOTH FANS HIGH SPEED DIAGNOSTIC CHART–1994 LEGEND AND LEGEND COUPE–CONTINUED

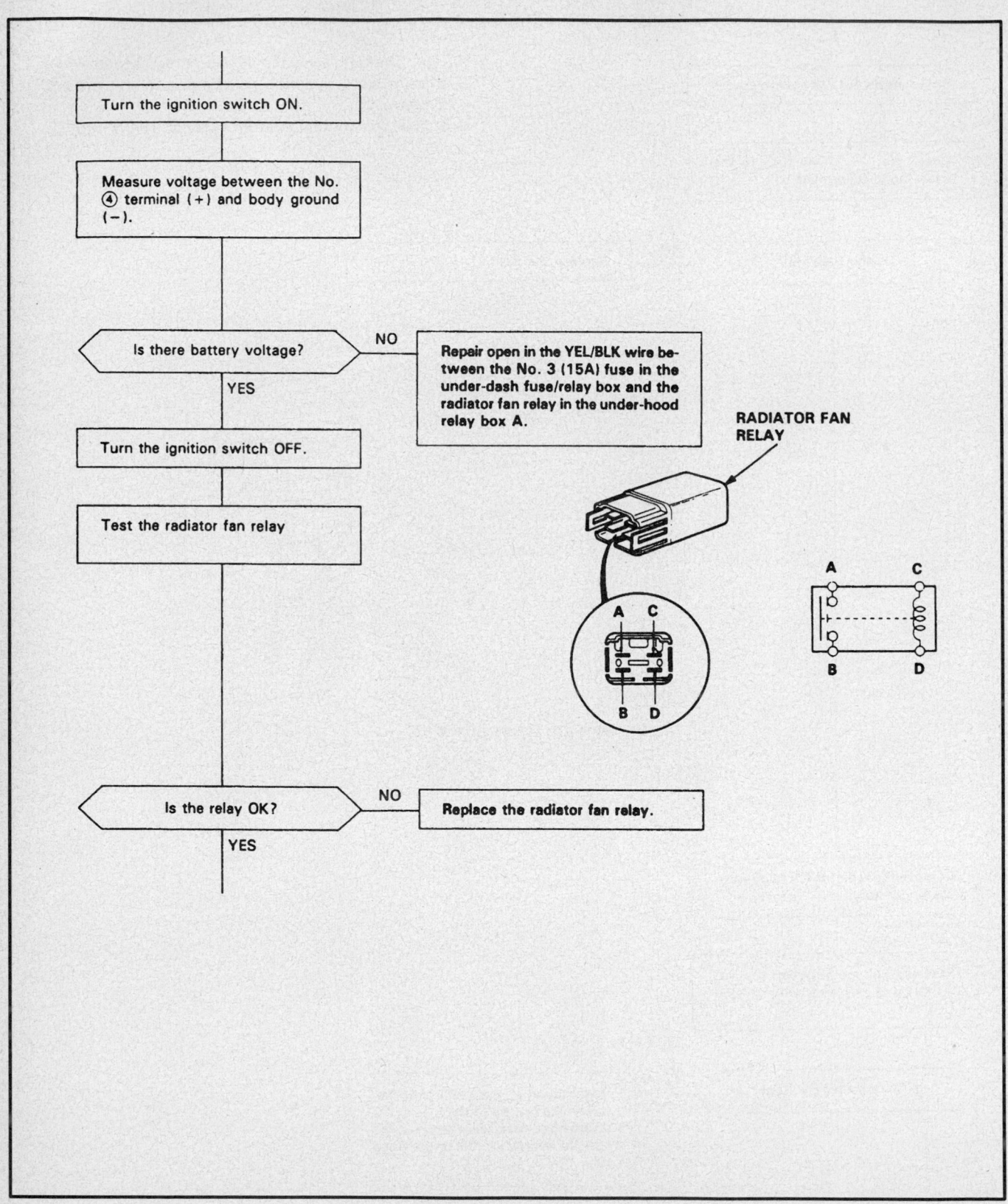

Turn the ignition switch ON.

Measure voltage between the No. ④ terminal (+) and body ground (−).

Is there battery voltage? — NO → Repair open in the YEL/BLK wire between the No. 3 (15A) fuse in the under-dash fuse/relay box and the radiator fan relay in the under-hood relay box A.

YES

Turn the ignition switch OFF.

Test the radiator fan relay

RADIATOR FAN RELAY

Is the relay OK? — NO → Replace the radiator fan relay.

YES

BOTH FANS HIGH SPEED DIAGNOSTIC CHART−1994 LEGEND AND LEGEND COUPE−CONTINUED

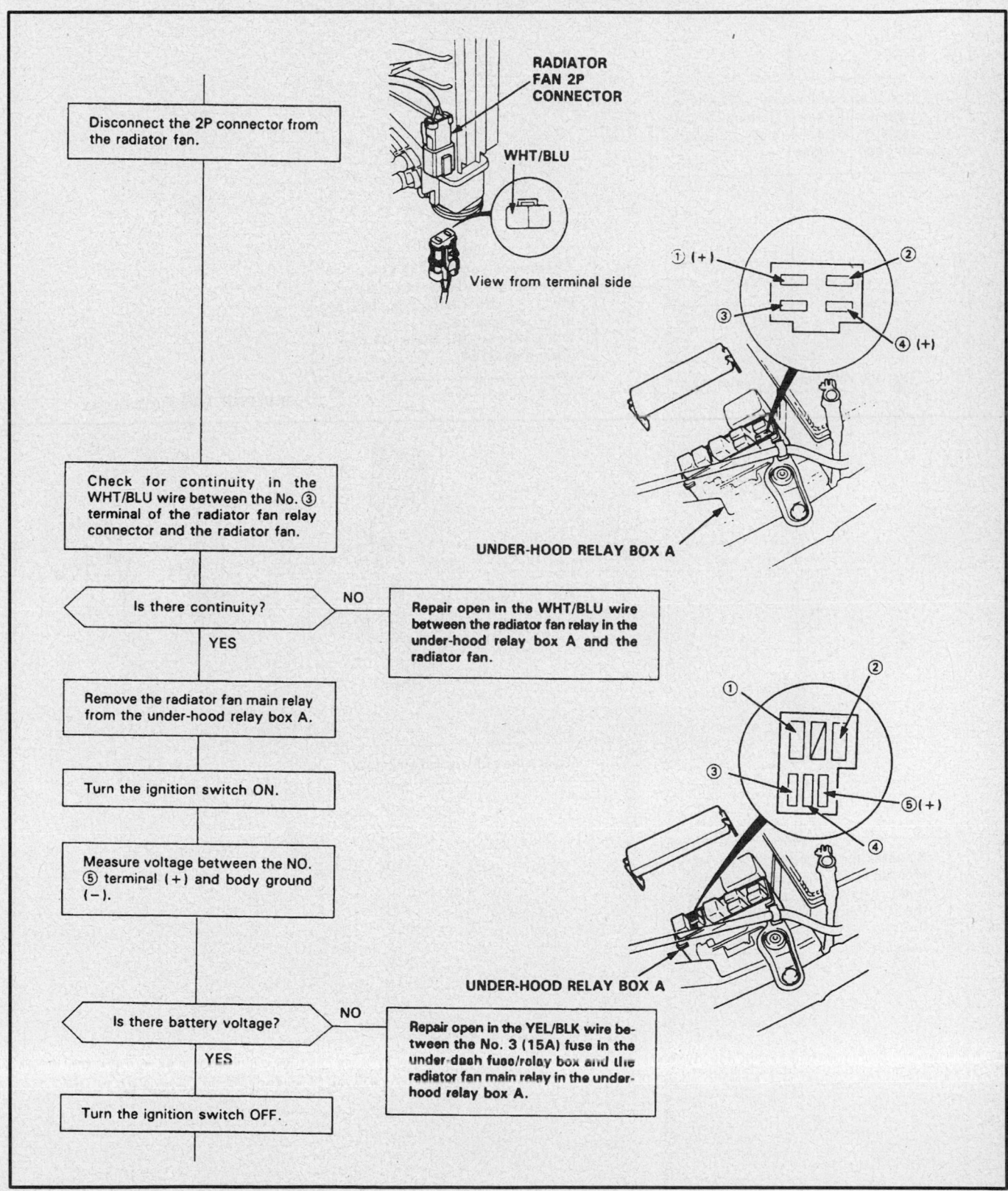

Disconnect the 2P connector from the radiator fan.

RADIATOR FAN 2P CONNECTOR

WHT/BLU

View from terminal side

① (+)   ②
③   ④ (+)

UNDER-HOOD RELAY BOX A

Check for continuity in the WHT/BLU wire between the No. ③ terminal of the radiator fan relay connector and the radiator fan.

Is there continuity?   NO → Repair open in the WHT/BLU wire between the radiator fan relay in the under-hood relay box A and the radiator fan.

YES

Remove the radiator fan main relay from the under-hood relay box A.

①   ②
③   ⑤(+)
         ④

UNDER-HOOD RELAY BOX A

Turn the ignition switch ON.

Measure voltage between the NO. ⑤ terminal (+) and body ground (−).

Is there battery voltage?   NO → Repair open in the YEL/BLK wire between the No. 3 (15A) fuse in the under-dash fuse/relay box and the radiator fan main relay in the under-hood relay box A.

YES

Turn the ignition switch OFF.

BOTH FANS HIGH SPEED DIAGNOSTIC CHART—1994 LEGEND AND LEGEND COUPE—CONTINUED

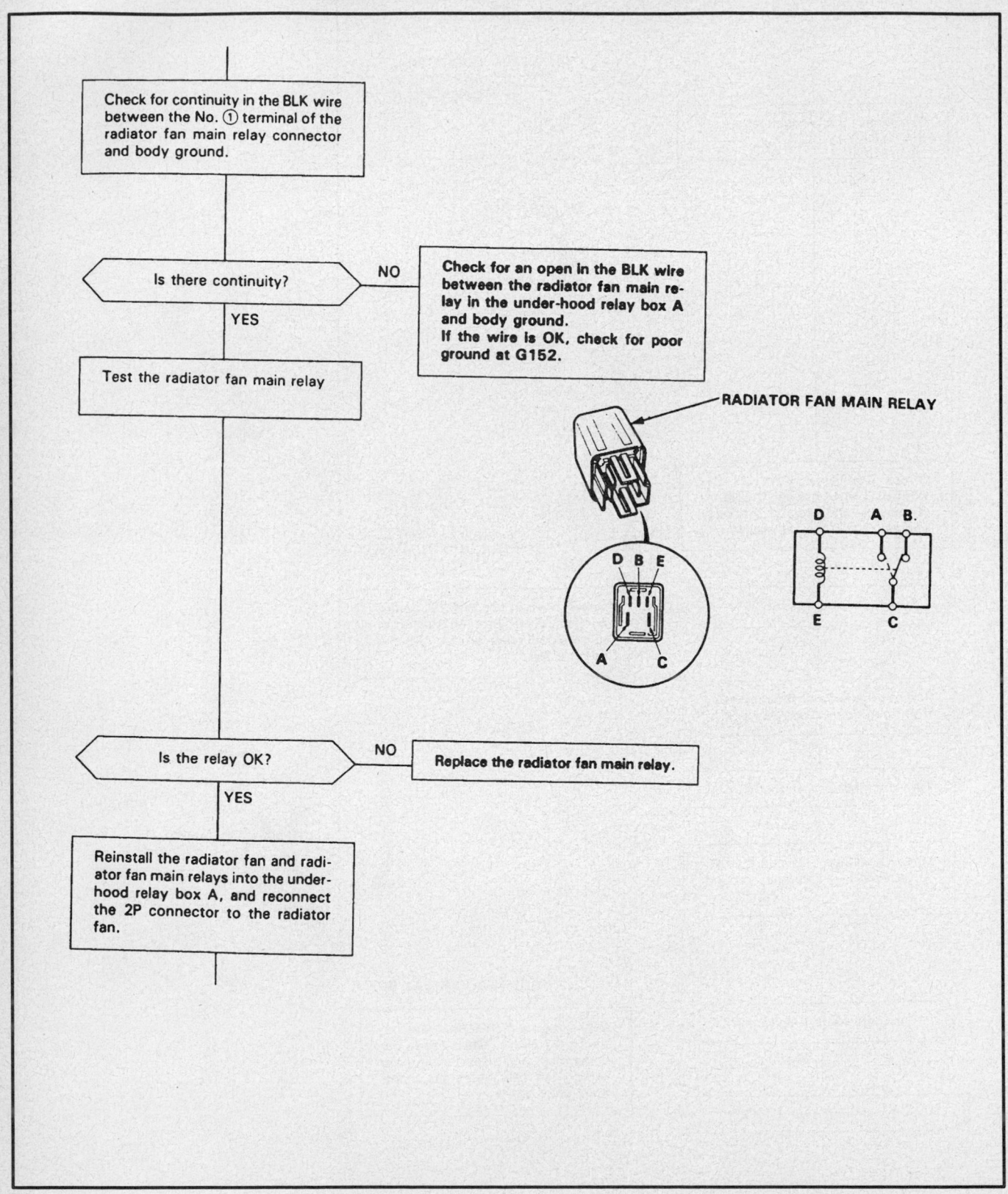

Check for continuity in the BLK wire between the No. ① terminal of the radiator fan main relay connector and body ground.

Is there continuity? —NO→ Check for an open in the BLK wire between the radiator fan main relay in the under-hood relay box A and body ground.
If the wire is OK, check for poor ground at G152.

YES

Test the radiator fan main relay

RADIATOR FAN MAIN RELAY

Is the relay OK? —NO→ Replace the radiator fan main relay.

YES

Reinstall the radiator fan and radiator fan main relays into the under-hood relay box A, and reconnect the 2P connector to the radiator fan.

BOTH FANS HIGH SPEED DIAGNOSTIC CHART–1994 LEGEND AND LEGEND COUPE–CONTINUED

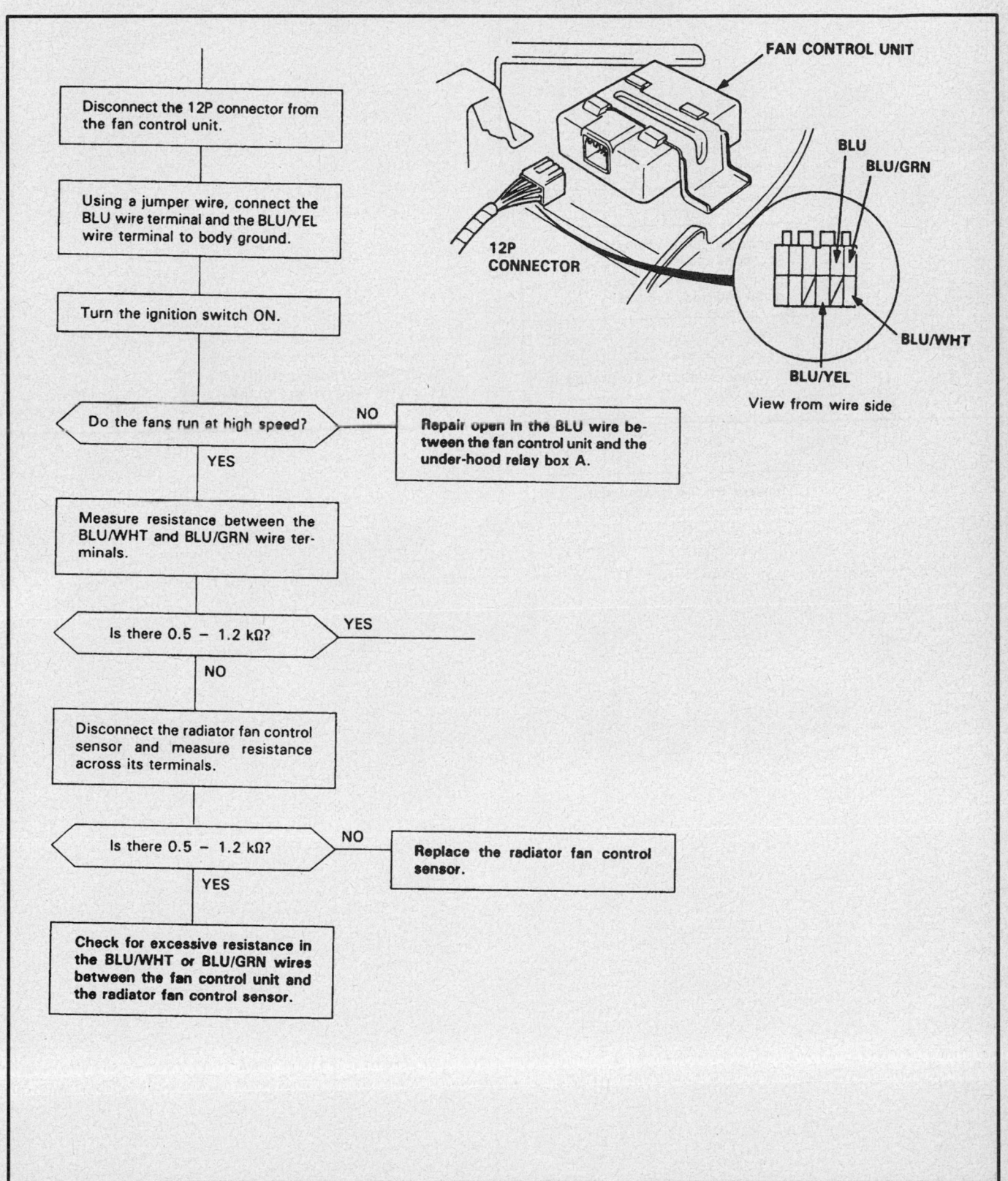

FAN CONTROL UNIT

Disconnect the 12P connector from the fan control unit.

Using a jumper wire, connect the BLU wire terminal and the BLU/YEL wire terminal to body ground.

Turn the ignition switch ON.

Do the fans run at high speed? — NO — Repair open in the BLU wire between the fan control unit and the under-hood relay box A.

YES

Measure resistance between the BLU/WHT and BLU/GRN wire terminals.

Is there 0.5 – 1.2 kΩ? — YES

NO

Disconnect the radiator fan control sensor and measure resistance across its terminals.

Is there 0.5 – 1.2 kΩ? — NO — Replace the radiator fan control sensor.

YES

Check for excessive resistance in the BLU/WHT or BLU/GRN wires between the fan control unit and the radiator fan control sensor.

12P CONNECTOR

BLU
BLU/GRN
BLU/WHT
BLU/YEL

View from wire side

BOTH FANS HIGH SPEED DIAGNOSTIC CHART—1994 LEGEND AND LEGEND COUPE—CONTINUED

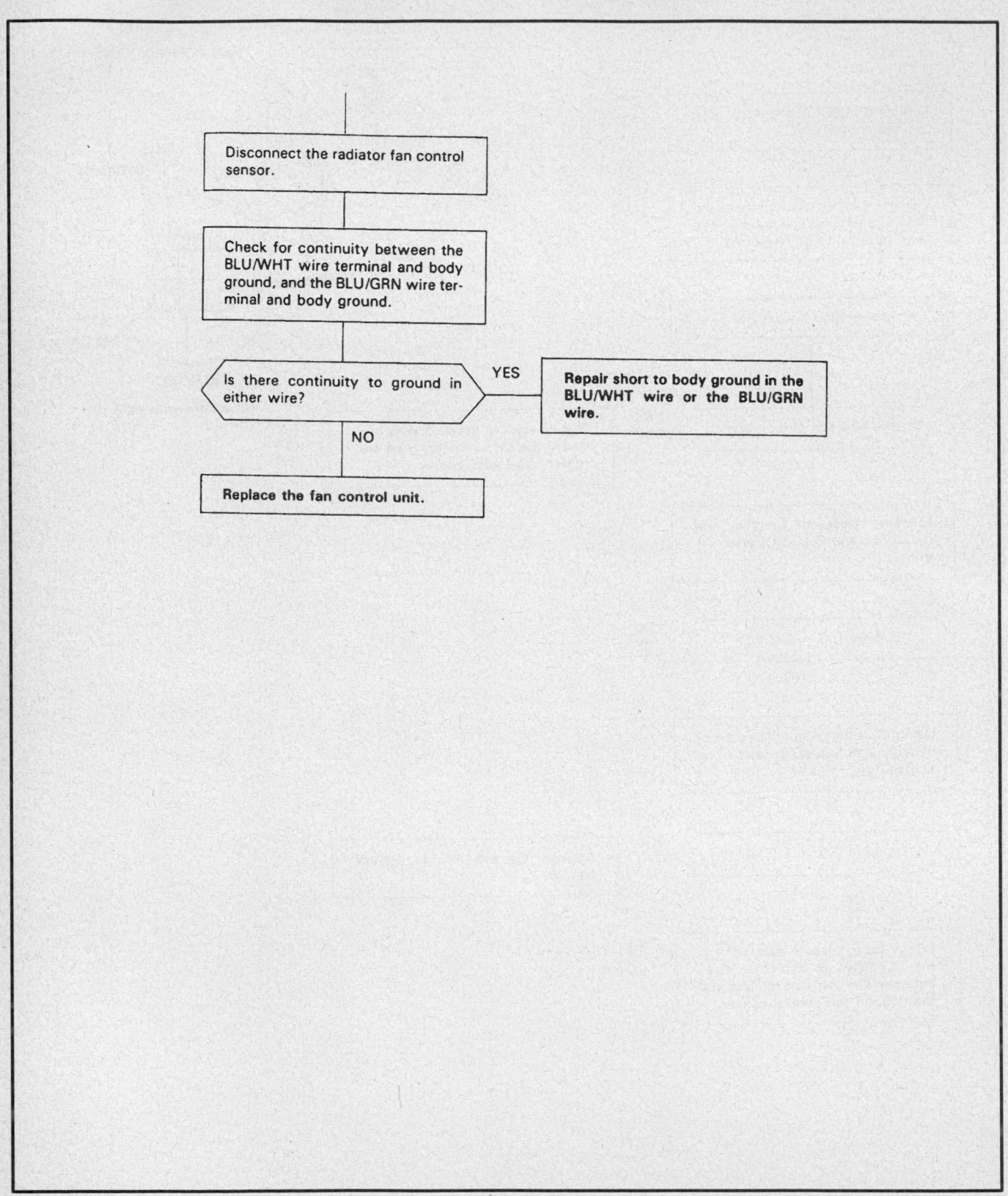

Disconnect the radiator fan control sensor.

Check for continuity between the BLU/WHT wire terminal and body ground, and the BLU/GRN wire terminal and body ground.

Is there continuity to ground in either wire?

YES → Repair short to body ground in the BLU/WHT wire or the BLU/GRN wire.

NO

Replace the fan control unit.

BOTH FANS LOW SPEED DIAGNOSTIC CHART—1994 LEGEND AND LEGEND COUPE

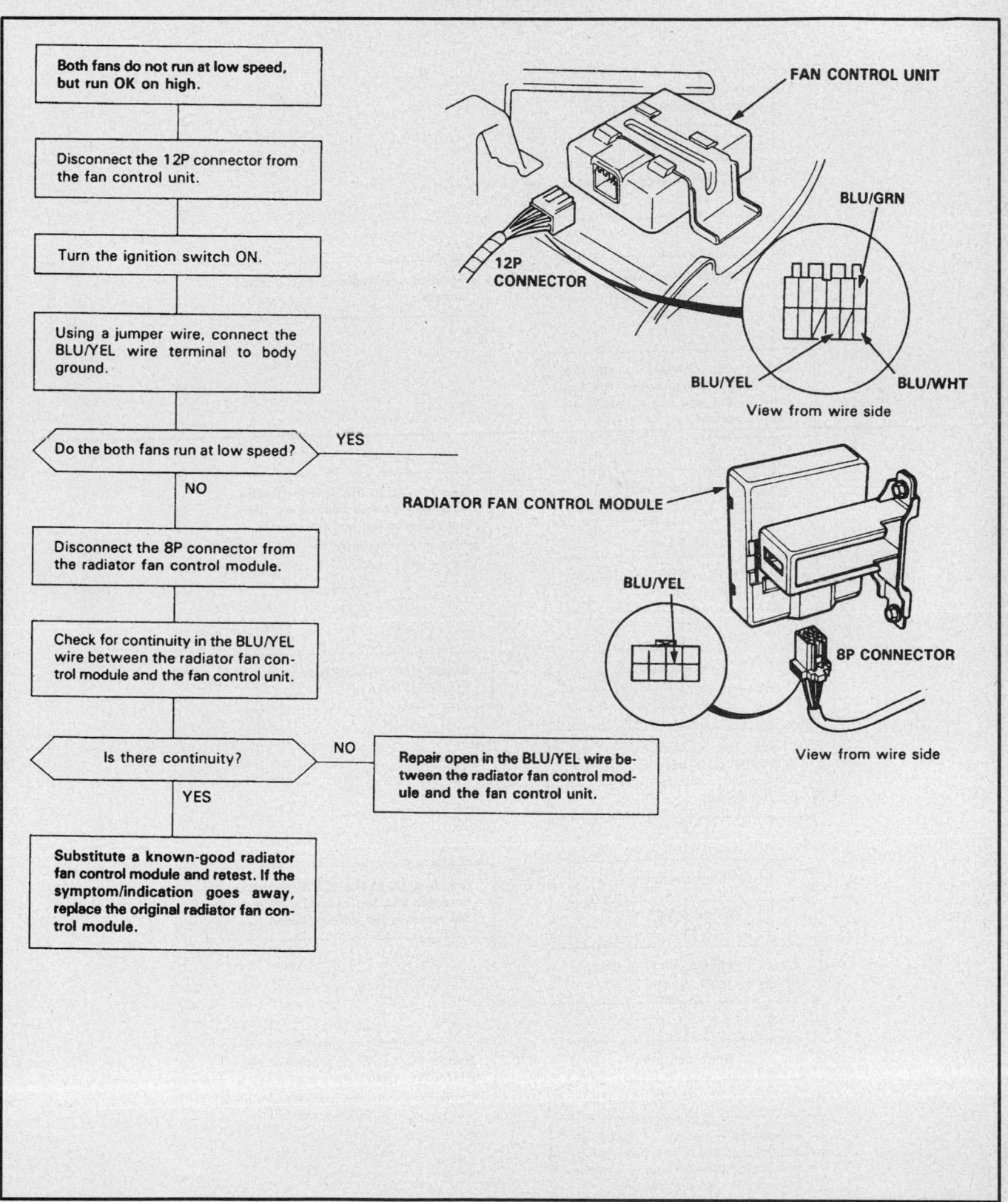

Both fans do not run at low speed, but run OK on high.

Disconnect the 12P connector from the fan control unit.

Turn the ignition switch ON.

Using a jumper wire, connect the BLU/YEL wire terminal to body ground.

Do the both fans run at low speed? — **YES**

NO

Disconnect the 8P connector from the radiator fan control module.

Check for continuity in the BLU/YEL wire between the radiator fan control module and the fan control unit.

Is there continuity? — **NO** → Repair open in the BLU/YEL wire between the radiator fan control module and the fan control unit.

YES

Substitute a known-good radiator fan control module and retest. If the symptom/indication goes away, replace the original radiator fan control module.

FAN CONTROL UNIT

12P CONNECTOR

BLU/GRN

BLU/YEL

BLU/WHT

View from wire side

RADIATOR FAN CONTROL MODULE

BLU/YEL

8P CONNECTOR

View from wire side

BOTH FANS LOW SPEED DIAGNOSTIC CHART—1994 LEGEND AND LEGEND COUPE—CONTINUED

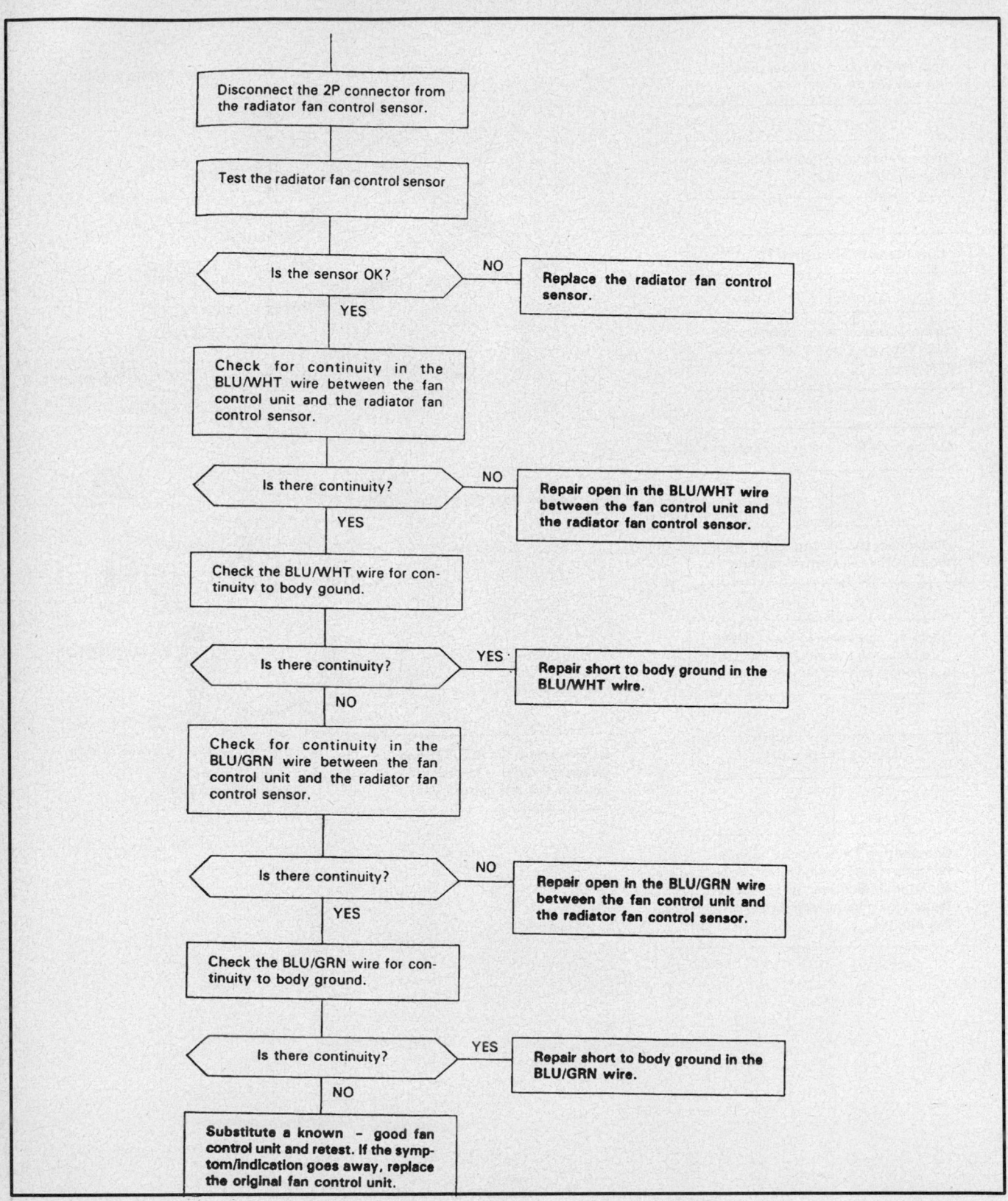

Disconnect the 2P connector from the radiator fan control sensor.

Test the radiator fan control sensor

Is the sensor OK? — NO → Replace the radiator fan control sensor.

YES

Check for continuity in the BLU/WHT wire between the fan control unit and the radiator fan control sensor.

Is there continuity? — NO → Repair open in the BLU/WHT wire between the fan control unit and the radiator fan control sensor.

YES

Check the BLU/WHT wire for continuity to body gound.

Is there continuity? — YES → Repair short to body ground in the BLU/WHT wire.

NO

Check for continuity in the BLU/GRN wire between the fan control unit and the radiator fan control sensor.

Is there continuity? — NO → Repair open in the BLU/GRN wire between the fan control unit and the radiator fan control sensor.

YES

Check the BLU/GRN wire for continuity to body ground.

Is there continuity? — YES → Repair short to body ground in the BLU/GRN wire.

NO

Substitute a known – good fan control unit and retest. If the symptom/indication goes away, replace the original fan control unit.

BLOWER MOTOR DIAGNOSTIC CHART—1994-95 INTEGRA

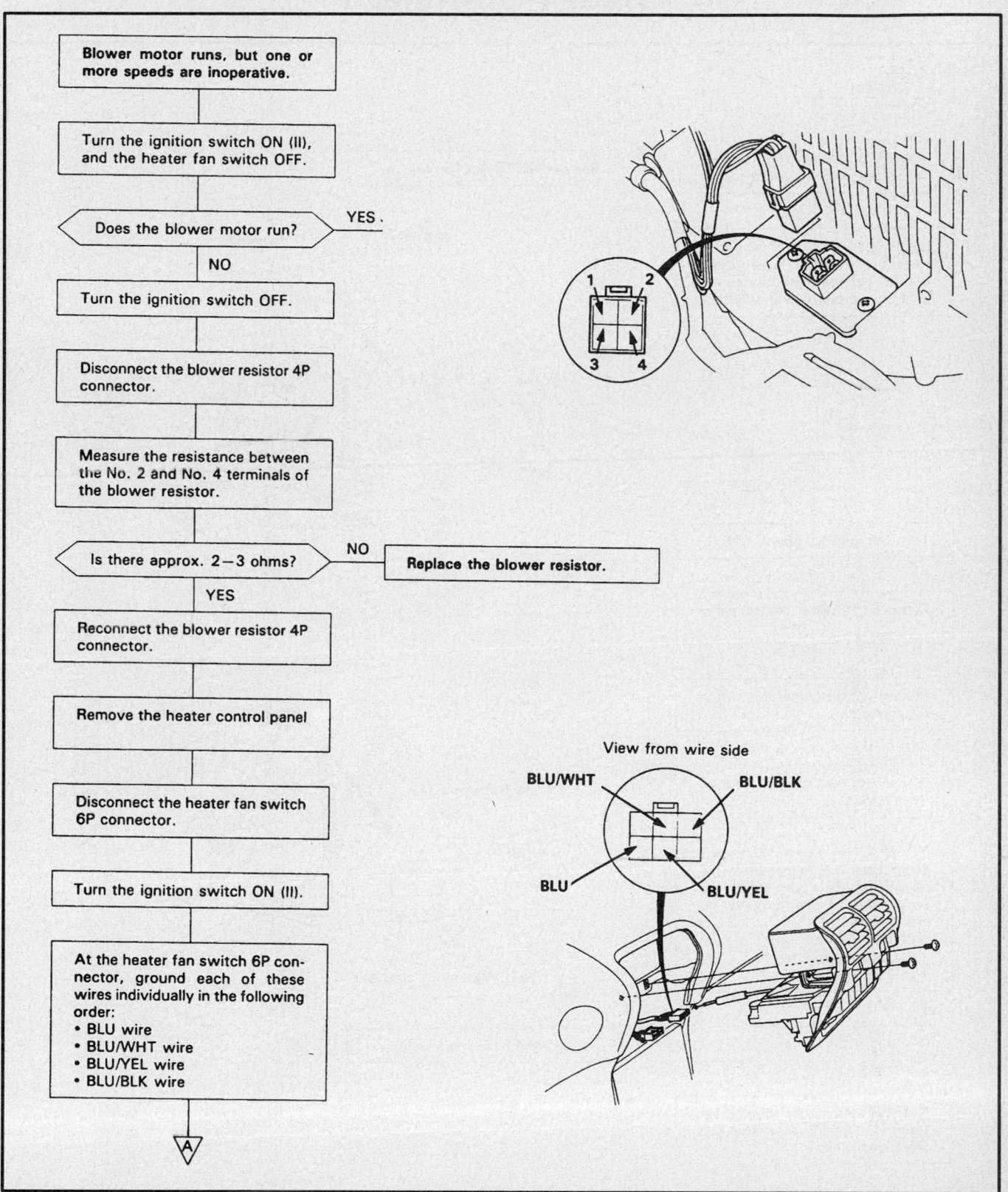

Blower motor runs, but one or more speeds are inoperative.

↓

Turn the ignition switch ON (II), and the heater fan switch OFF.

↓

Does the blower motor run? — YES

NO

↓

Turn the ignition switch OFF.

↓

Disconnect the blower resistor 4P connector.

↓

Measure the resistance between the No. 2 and No. 4 terminals of the blower resistor.

↓

Is there approx. 2—3 ohms? — NO → Replace the blower resistor.

YES

↓

Reconnect the blower resistor 4P connector.

↓

Remove the heater control panel

↓

Disconnect the heater fan switch 6P connector.

↓

Turn the ignition switch ON (II).

↓

At the heater fan switch 6P connector, ground each of these wires individually in the following order:
• BLU wire
• BLU/WHT wire
• BLU/YEL wire
• BLU/BLK wire

↓

Ⓐ

View from wire side

BLU/WHT   BLU/BLK

BLU   BLU/YEL

BLOWER MOTOR DIAGNOSTIC CHART – 1994-95 INTEGRA – CONTINUED

A

Does the blower motor run at progressively higher speeds? **YES** → Replace the heater fan switch.

NO

Repair open or cause of excessive resistance in the appropriate wire(s) between the heater fan switch and the blower resistor.

BLU/WHT   BLU/BLK

View from wire side

BLU   BLU/YEL

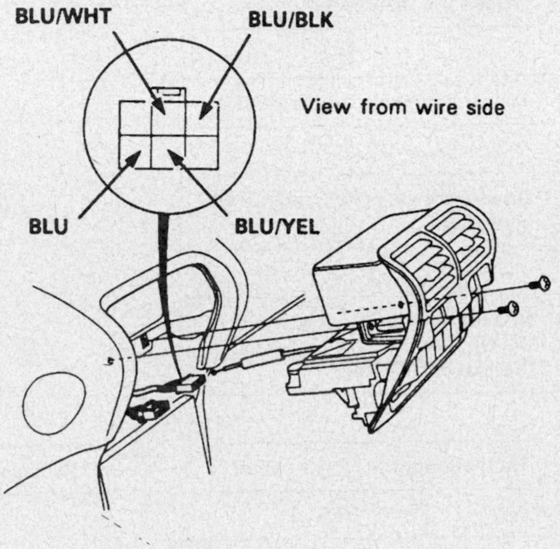

B

Turn the ignition switch OFF.

Remove the heater control panel

Disconnect the heater fan switch 6P connector.

Disconnect the blower resistor 4P connector.

Check each wire for continuity between the heater fan switch 6P connector and body ground.
• BLU wire
• BLU/WHT wire
• BLU/YEL wire
• BLU/BLK wire

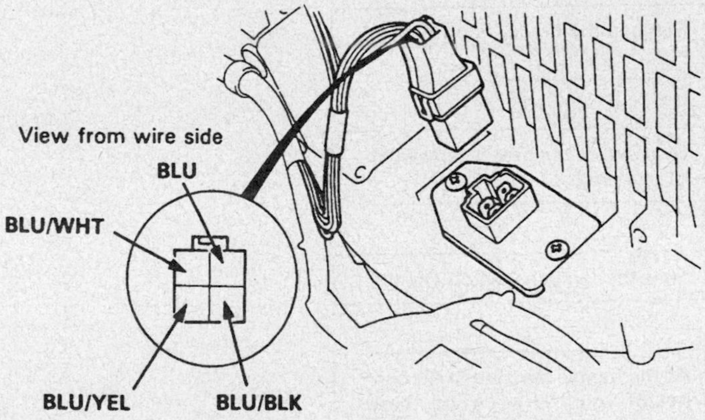

View from wire side

BLU

BLU/WHT

BLU/YEL   BLU/BLK

Is there continuity? **NO** → Replace the heater fan switch.

YES

Repair short in the wire(s) between the heater fan switch and the blower resistor.

BLOWER MOTOR DOES NOT RUN AT ALL —1994-95 INTEGRA

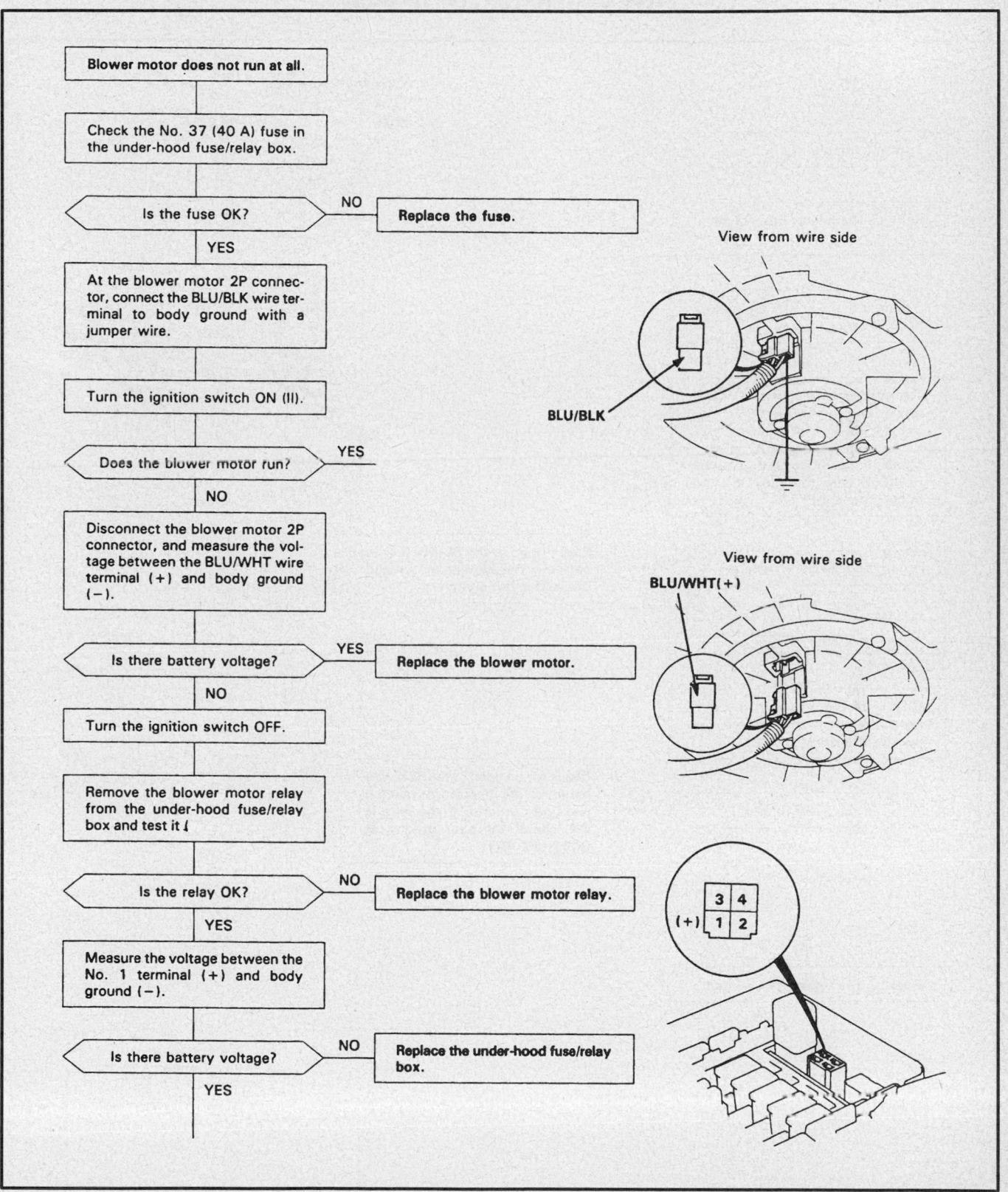

Blower motor does not run at all.

Check the No. 37 (40 A) fuse in the under-hood fuse/relay box.

Is the fuse OK? — NO → Replace the fuse.

YES

At the blower motor 2P connector, connect the BLU/BLK wire terminal to body ground with a jumper wire.

Turn the ignition switch ON (II).

Does the blower motor run? — YES

NO

Disconnect the blower motor 2P connector, and measure the voltage between the BLU/WHT wire terminal (+) and body ground (−).

Is there battery voltage? — YES → Replace the blower motor.

NO

Turn the ignition switch OFF.

Remove the blower motor relay from the under-hood fuse/relay box and test it.

Is the relay OK? — NO → Replace the blower motor relay.

YES

Measure the voltage between the No. 1 terminal (+) and body ground (−).

Is there battery voltage? — NO → Replace the under-hood fuse/relay box.

YES

View from wire side

BLU/BLK

View from wire side

BLU/WHT(+)

(+) | 3 | 4 |
    | 1 | 2 |

BLOWER MOTOR DOES NOT RUN AT ALL –1994-95 INTEGRA–CONTINUED

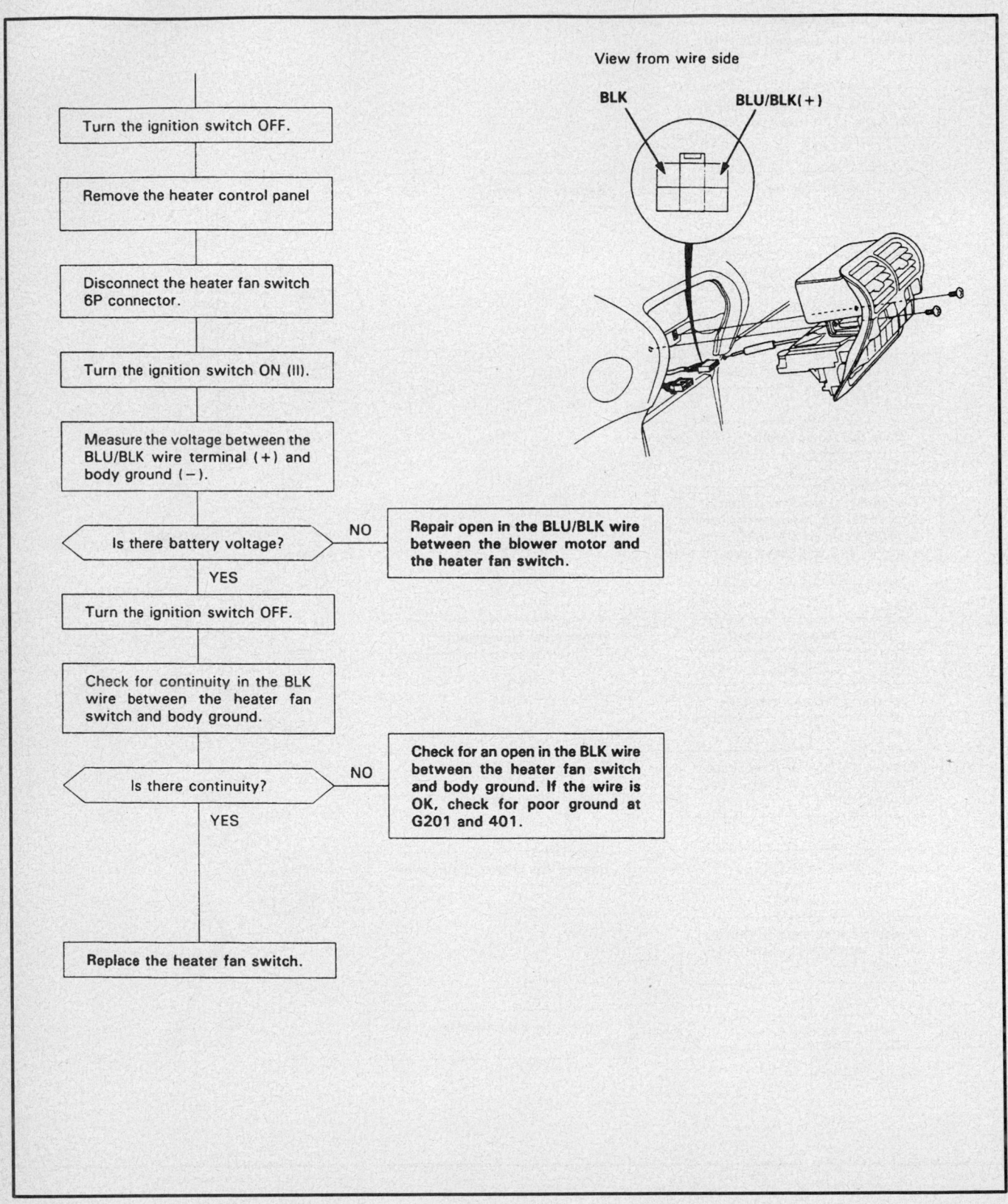

View from wire side

BLK   BLU/BLK(+)

Turn the ignition switch OFF.

Remove the heater control panel

Disconnect the heater fan switch 6P connector.

Turn the ignition switch ON (II).

Measure the voltage between the BLU/BLK wire terminal (+) and body ground (–).

Is there battery voltage? — **NO** → Repair open in the BLU/BLK wire between the blower motor and the heater fan switch.

YES

Turn the ignition switch OFF.

Check for continuity in the BLK wire between the heater fan switch and body ground.

Is there continuity? — **NO** → Check for an open in the BLK wire between the heater fan switch and body ground. If the wire is OK, check for poor ground at G201 and 401.

YES

Replace the heater fan switch.

BLOWER MOTOR DOES NOT RUN AT ALL –1994-95 INTEGRA–CONTINUED

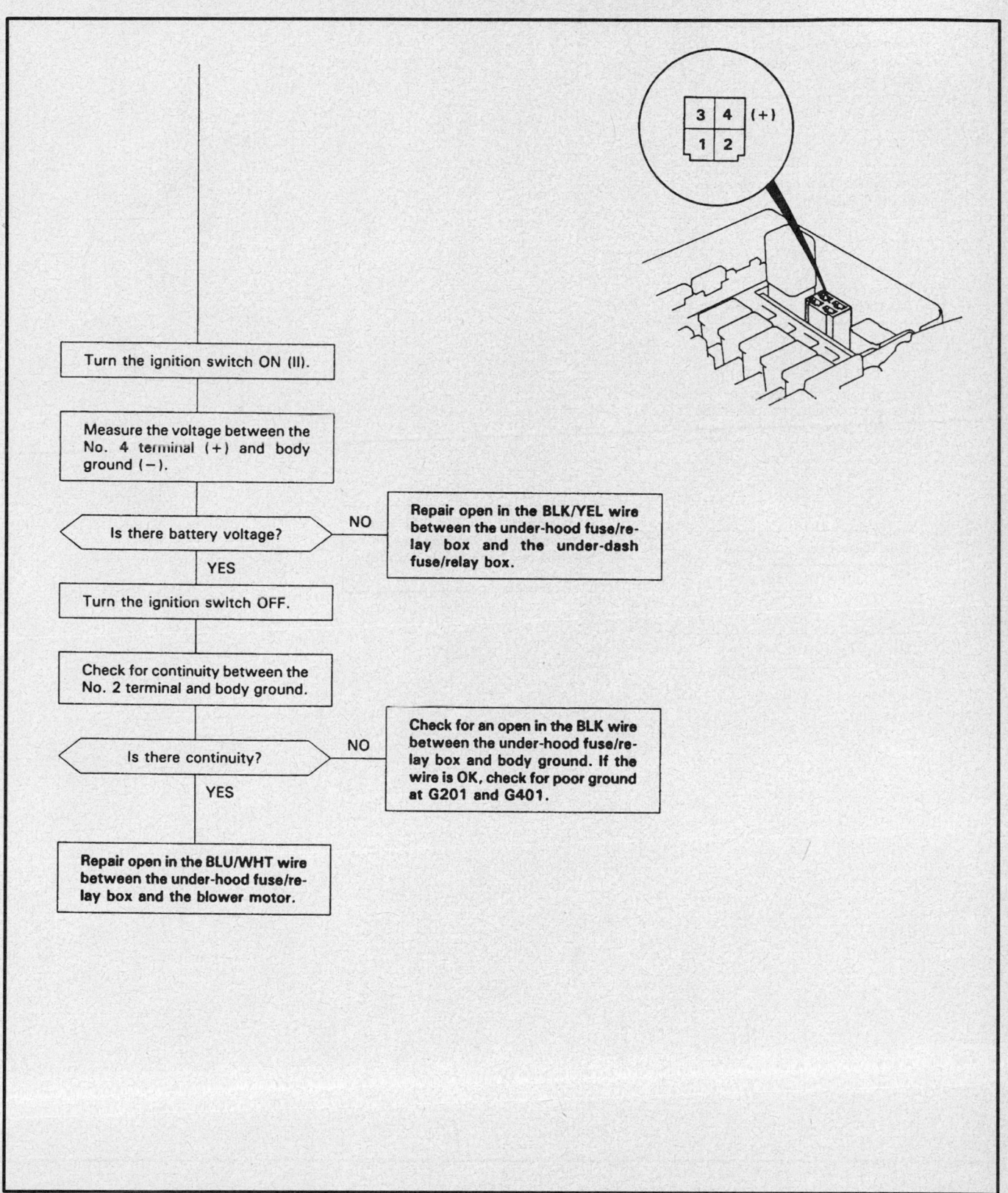

Turn the ignition switch ON (II).

Measure the voltage between the No. 4 terminal (+) and body ground (−).

Is there battery voltage? — **NO** → Repair open in the BLK/YEL wire between the under-hood fuse/relay box and the under-dash fuse/relay box.

YES

Turn the ignition switch OFF.

Check for continuity between the No. 2 terminal and body ground.

Is there continuity? — **NO** → Check for an open in the BLK wire between the under-hood fuse/relay box and body ground. If the wire is OK, check for poor ground at G201 and G401.

YES

Repair open in the BLU/WHT wire between the under-hood fuse/relay box and the blower motor.

MODE CONTROL MOTOR DIAGNOSTIC CHART—1994—95 INTEGRA

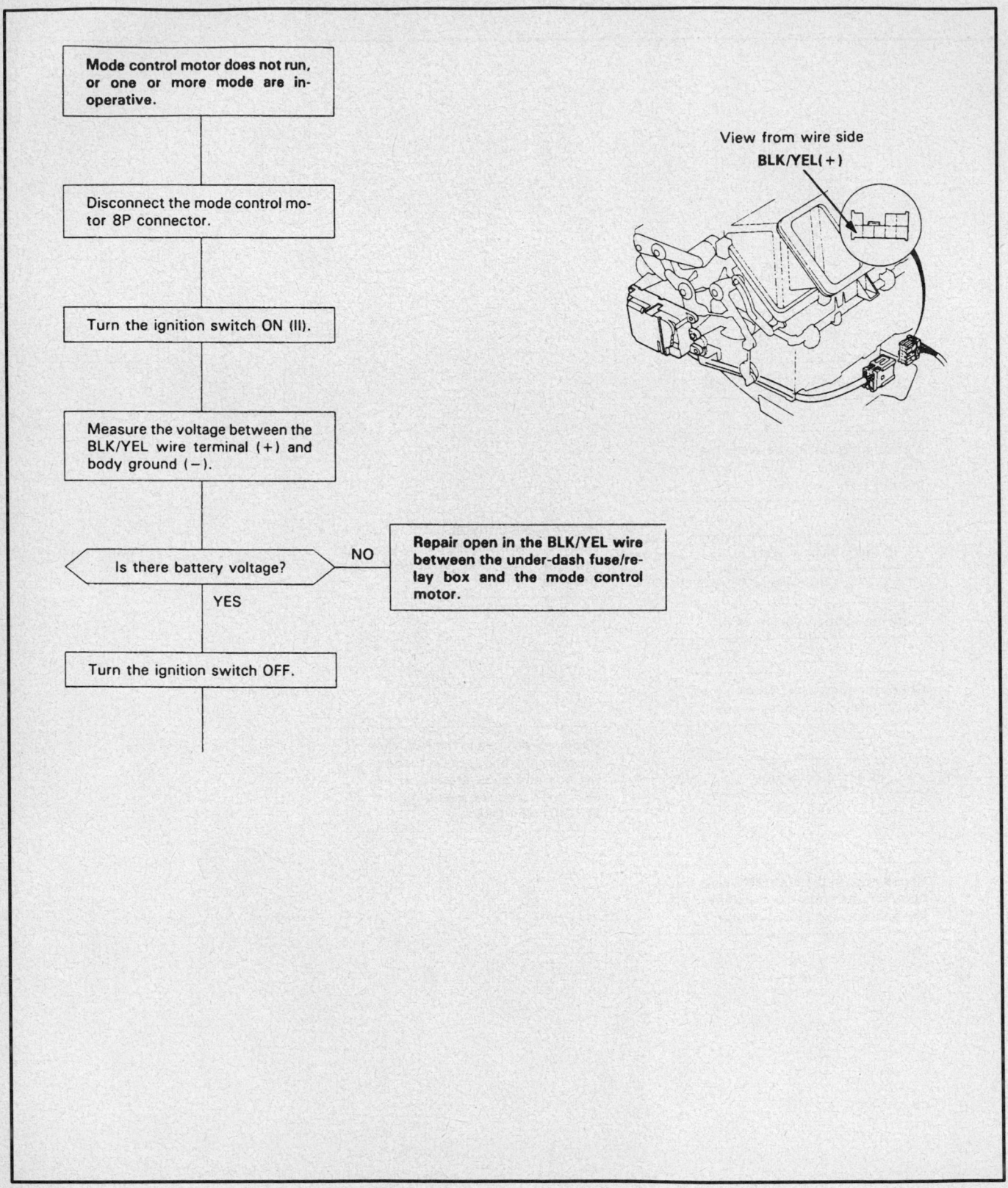

Mode control motor does not run, or one or more mode are inoperative.

Disconnect the mode control motor 8P connector.

Turn the ignition switch ON (II).

Measure the voltage between the BLK/YEL wire terminal (+) and body ground (−).

Is there battery voltage? — NO → Repair open in the BLK/YEL wire between the under-dash fuse/relay box and the mode control motor.

YES

Turn the ignition switch OFF.

View from wire side
BLK/YEL(+)

MODE CONTROL MOTOR DIAGNOSTIC CHART—1994—95 INTEGRA—CONTINUED

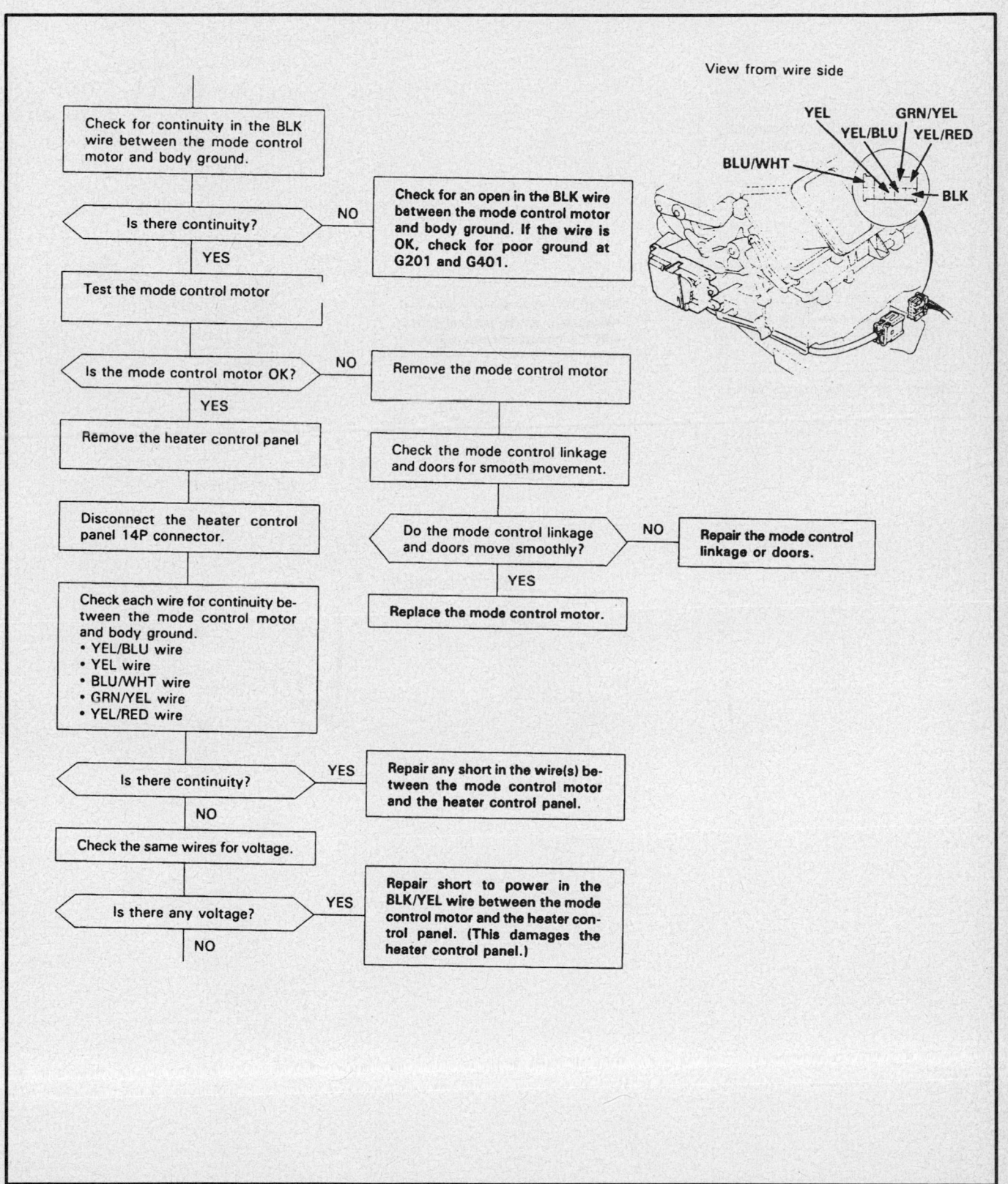

View from wire side

Check for continuity in the BLK wire between the mode control motor and body ground.

Is there continuity? — NO → Check for an open in the BLK wire between the mode control motor and body ground. If the wire is OK, check for poor ground at G201 and G401.

YES

Test the mode control motor

Is the mode control motor OK? — NO → Remove the mode control motor

YES

Remove the heater control panel

Check the mode control linkage and doors for smooth movement.

Disconnect the heater control panel 14P connector.

Do the mode control linkage and doors move smoothly? — NO → Repair the mode control linkage or doors.

YES

Check each wire for continuity between the mode control motor and body ground.
• YEL/BLU wire
• YEL wire
• BLU/WHT wire
• GRN/YEL wire
• YEL/RED wire

Replace the mode control motor.

Is there continuity? — YES → Repair any short in the wire(s) between the mode control motor and the heater control panel.

NO

Check the same wires for voltage.

Is there any voltage? — YES → Repair short to power in the BLK/YEL wire between the mode control motor and the heater control panel. (This damages the heater control panel.)

NO

MODE CONTROL MOTOR DIAGNOSTIC CHART—1994—95 INTEGRA—CONTINUED

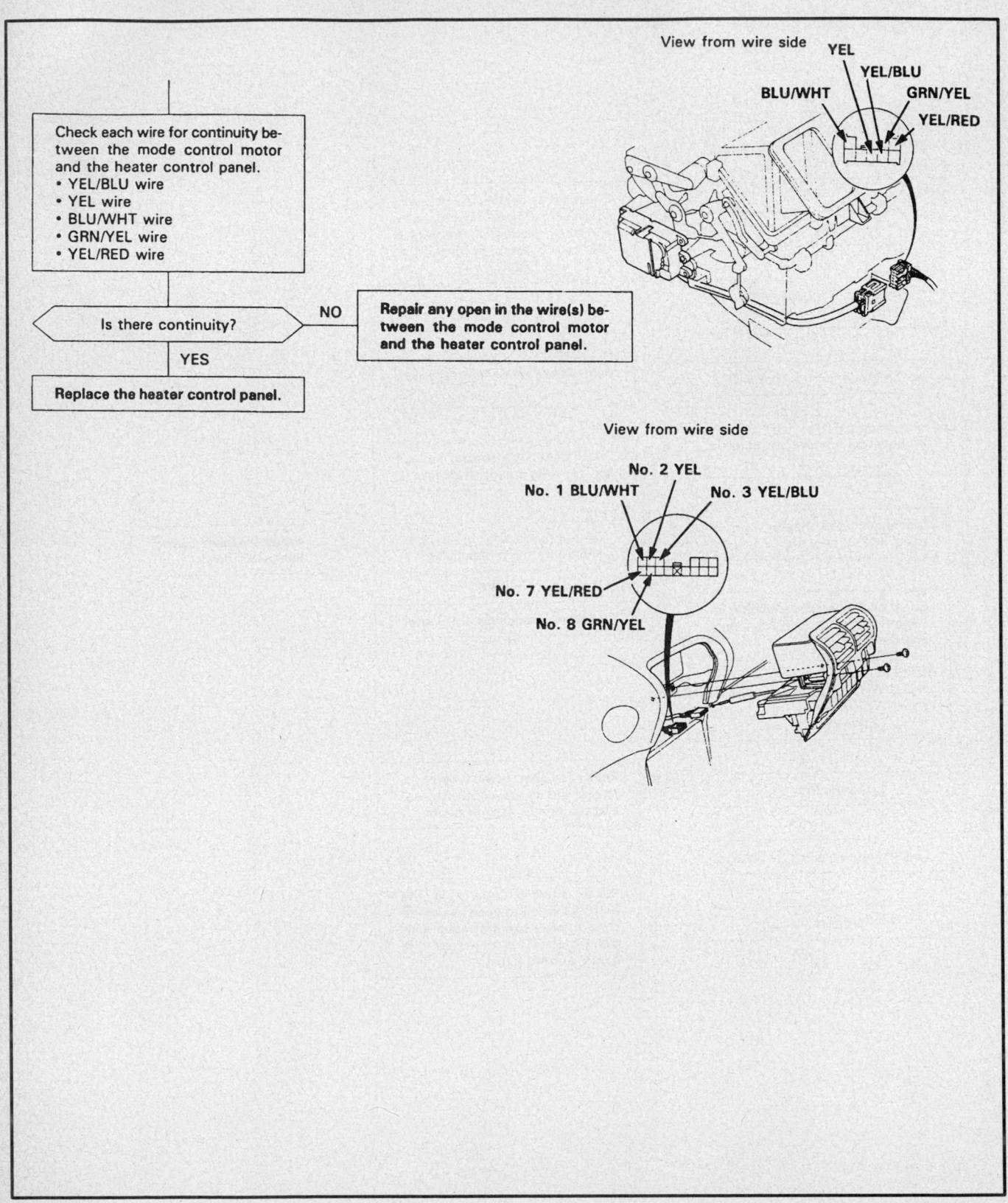

View from wire side

YEL

YEL/BLU

BLU/WHT

GRN/YEL

YEL/RED

Check each wire for continuity between the mode control motor and the heater control panel.
• YEL/BLU wire
• YEL wire
• BLU/WHT wire
• GRN/YEL wire
• YEL/RED wire

Is there continuity? —NO→ Repair any open in the wire(s) between the mode control motor and the heater control panel.

YES

Replace the heater control panel.

View from wire side

No. 2 YEL

No. 1 BLU/WHT

No. 3 YEL/BLU

No. 7 YEL/RED

No. 8 GRN/YEL

RECIRCULATION CONTROL MOTOR DIAGNOSTIC CHART—1994-95 INTEGRA

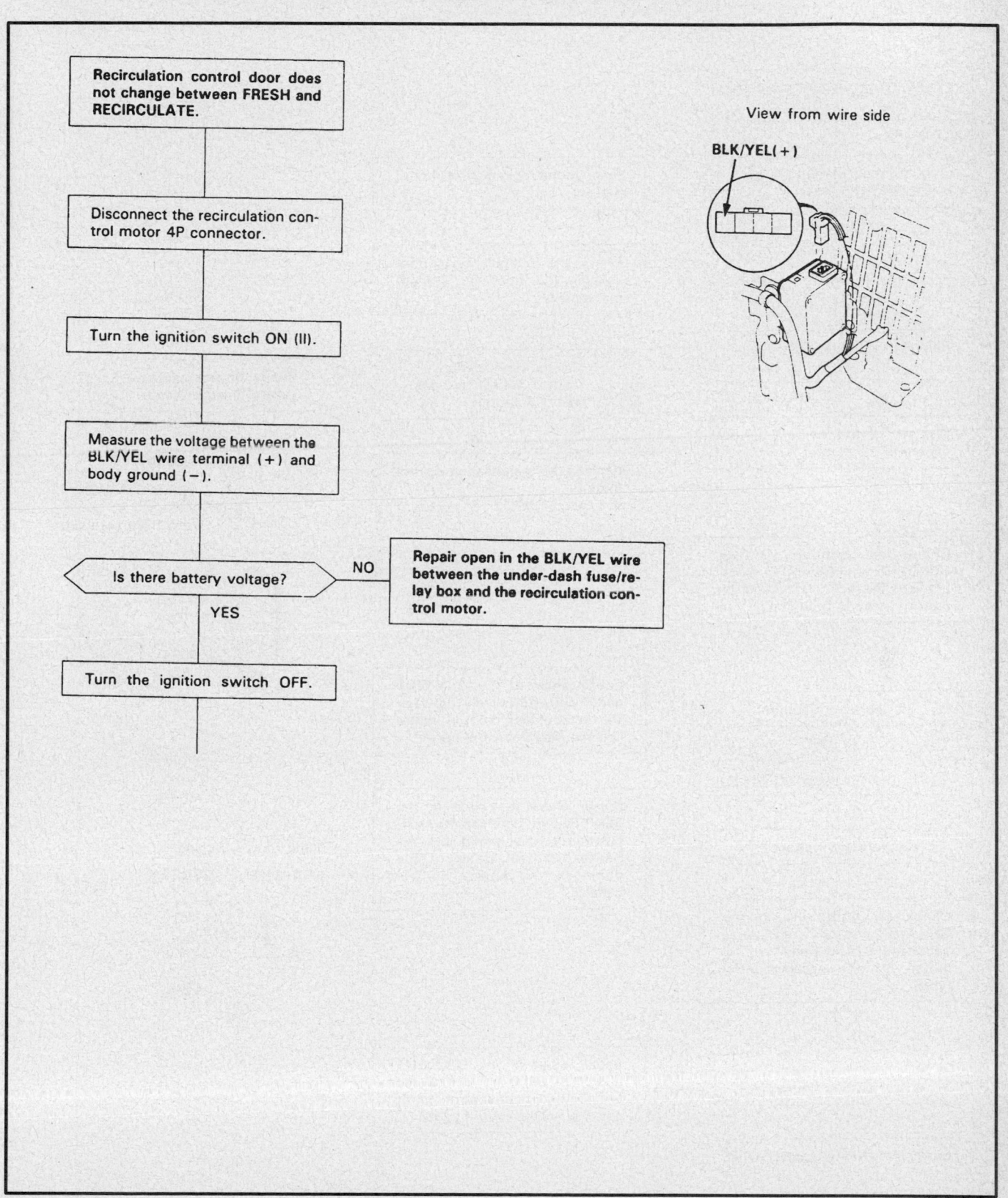

Recirculation control door does not change between FRESH and RECIRCULATE.

Disconnect the recirculation control motor 4P connector.

Turn the ignition switch ON (II).

Measure the voltage between the BLK/YEL wire terminal (+) and body ground (−).

Is there battery voltage? — NO → Repair open in the BLK/YEL wire between the under-dash fuse/relay box and the recirculation control motor.

YES

Turn the ignition switch OFF.

View from wire side

BLK/YEL(+)

RECIRCULATION CONTROL MOTOR DIAGNOSTIC CHART — 1994-95 INTEGRA

Test the recirculation control motor

Is the recirculation control motor OK? — **NO** → Remove the recirculation control motor

YES

Check the recirculation control linkage and door for smooth movement.

Do the recirculation control linkage and door move smoothly? — **NO** → Repair the recirculation control linkage or door.

YES

Replace the recirculation control motor.

Remove the heater control panel

Disconnect the heater control panel 14P connector.

No. 5 GRN/RED
No. 6 GRN/WHT
View from wire side

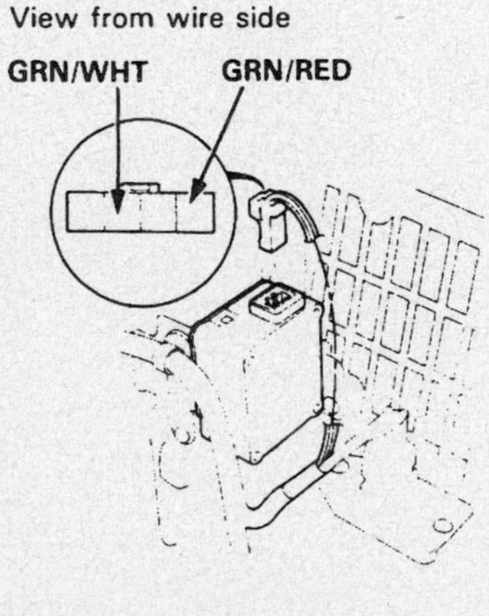

Check for continuity in the GRN/WHT and GRN/RED wires between the recirculation control motor and body ground.

Is there continuity? — **YES** → Repair short in the GRN/WHT and/or GRN/RED wire(s) between the recirculation control motor and the heater control panel.

NO

Check the same wires for voltage.

Is there any voltage? — **YES** → Repair short to power in the BLK/YEL wire between the recirculation control motor and the heater control panel. (This damages the heater control panel.)

NO

View from wire side
GRN/WHT   GRN/RED

Check for continuity in the GRN/WHT and GRN/RED wires between the recirculation control motor and the heater control panel.

Is there continuity? — **NO** → Repair open in the GRN/WHT and/or GRN/RED wire(s) between the recirculation control motor and the heater control panel.

YES

Replace the heater control panel.

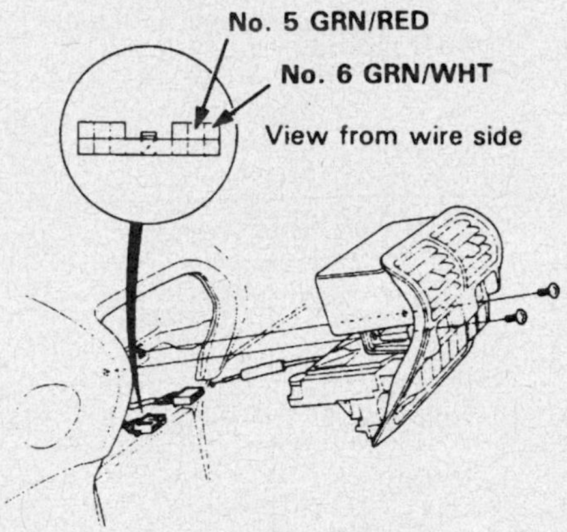

RADIATOR FAN DIAGNOSTIC CHART—1994—95 INTEGRA

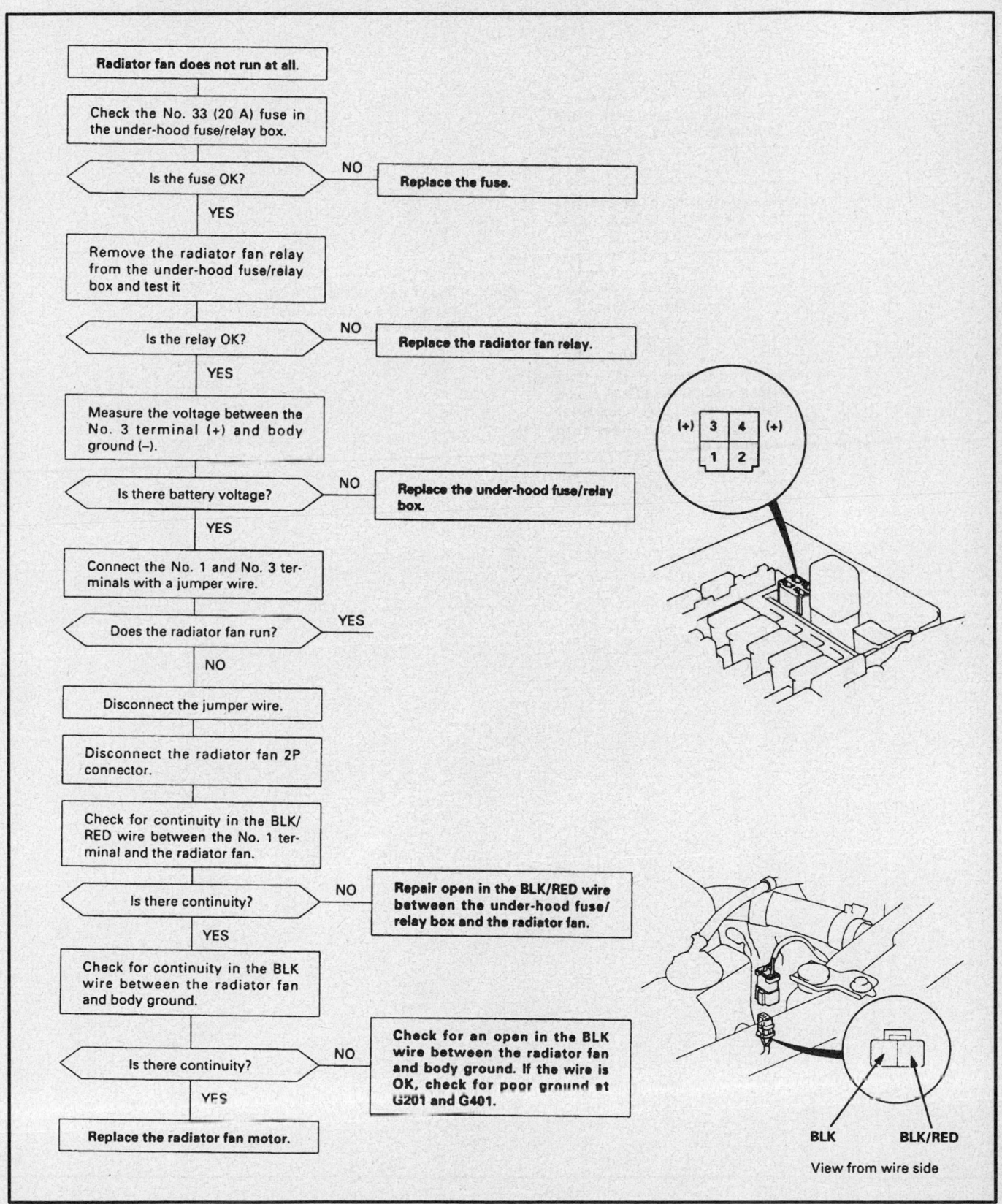

Radiator fan does not run at all.

Check the No. 33 (20 A) fuse in the under-hood fuse/relay box.

Is the fuse OK? — NO → **Replace the fuse.**

YES

Remove the radiator fan relay from the under-hood fuse/relay box and test it

Is the relay OK? — NO → **Replace the radiator fan relay.**

YES

Measure the voltage between the No. 3 terminal (+) and body ground (–).

Is there battery voltage? — NO → **Replace the under-hood fuse/relay box.**

YES

Connect the No. 1 and No. 3 terminals with a jumper wire.

Does the radiator fan run? — YES

NO

Disconnect the jumper wire.

Disconnect the radiator fan 2P connector.

Check for continuity in the BLK/RED wire between the No. 1 terminal and the radiator fan.

Is there continuity? — NO → **Repair open in the BLK/RED wire between the under-hood fuse/relay box and the radiator fan.**

YES

Check for continuity in the BLK wire between the radiator fan and body ground.

Is there continuity? — NO → **Check for an open in the BLK wire between the radiator fan and body ground. If the wire is OK, check for poor ground at G201 and G401.**

YES

Replace the radiator fan motor.

(+) 3 4 (+)
1 2

BLK   BLK/RED

View from wire side

RADIATOR FAN DIAGNOSTIC CHART—1994—95 INTEGRA—CONTINUED

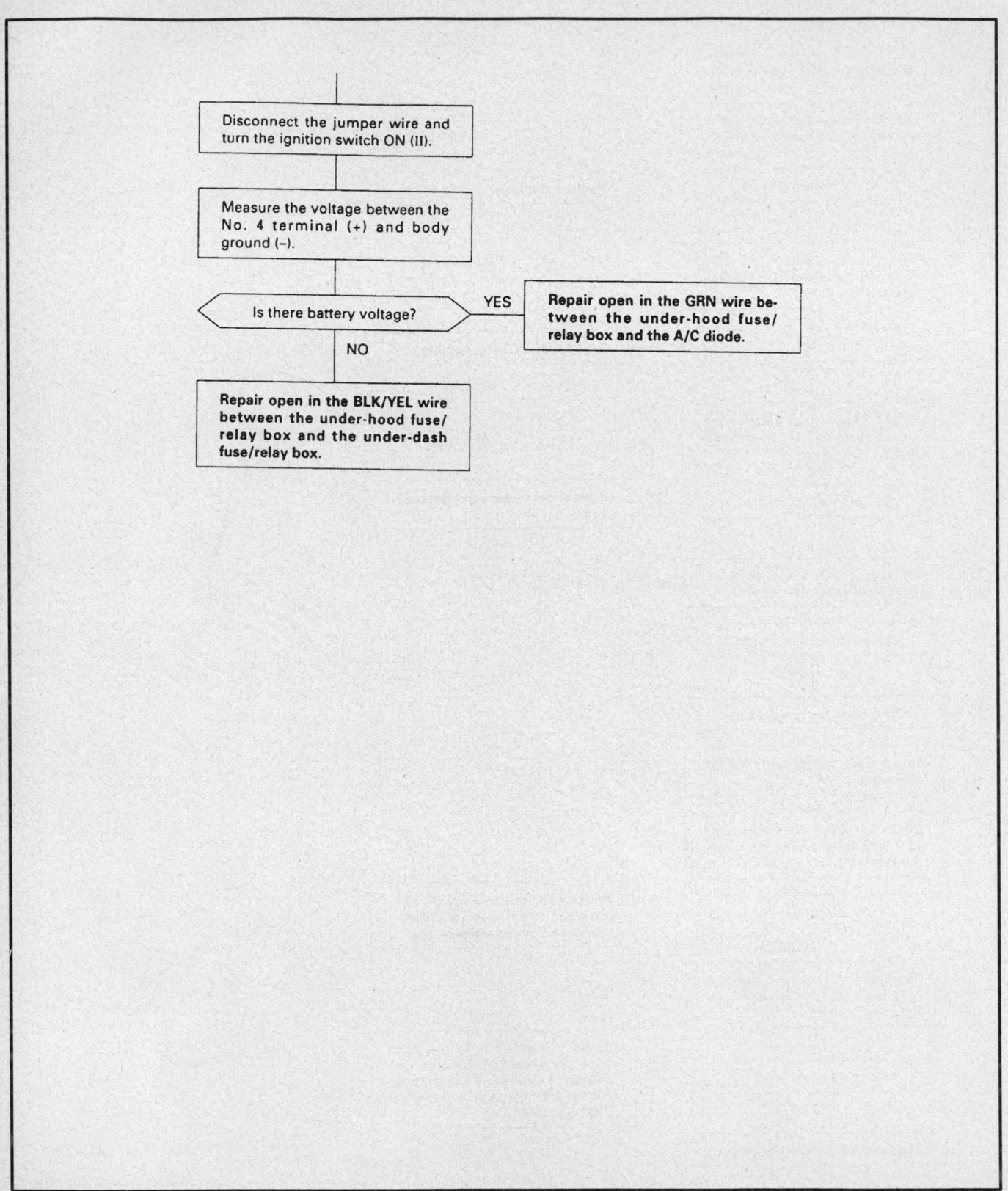

Disconnect the jumper wire and turn the ignition switch ON (II).

Measure the voltage between the No. 4 terminal (+) and body ground (−).

Is there battery voltage?

YES — Repair open in the GRN wire between the under-hood fuse/relay box and the A/C diode.

NO

Repair open in the BLK/YEL wire between the under-hood fuse/relay box and the under-dash fuse/relay box.

CONDENSER FAN DIAGNOSTIC CHART—1994—95 INTEGRA

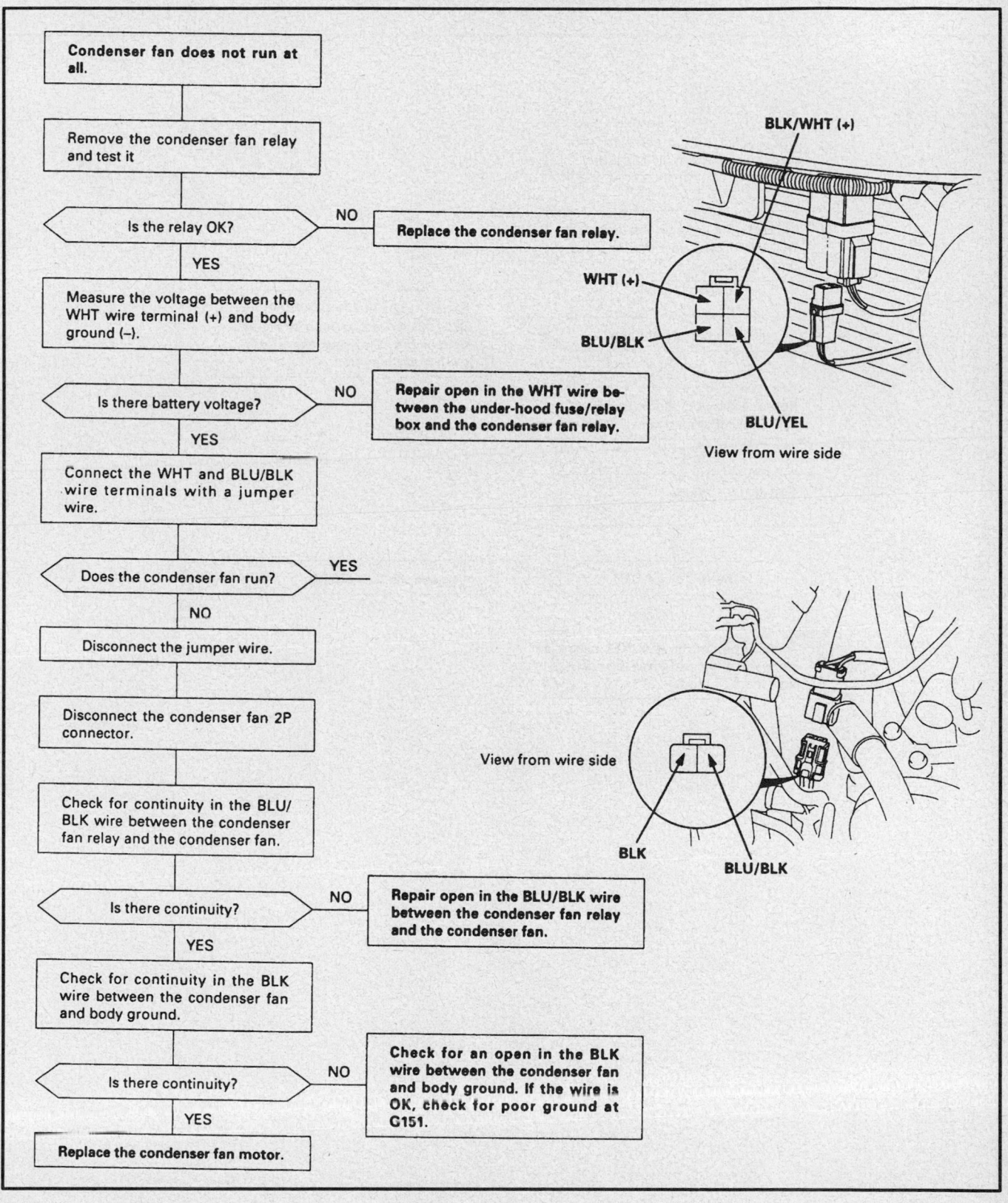

Condenser fan does not run at all.

Remove the condenser fan relay and test it

Is the relay OK? — NO → Replace the condenser fan relay.

YES

Measure the voltage between the WHT wire terminal (+) and body ground (–).

Is there battery voltage? — NO → Repair open in the WHT wire between the under-hood fuse/relay box and the condenser fan relay.

YES

Connect the WHT and BLU/BLK wire terminals with a jumper wire.

Does the condenser fan run? — YES

NO

Disconnect the jumper wire.

Disconnect the condenser fan 2P connector.

Check for continuity in the BLU/BLK wire between the condenser fan relay and the condenser fan.

Is there continuity? — NO → Repair open in the BLU/BLK wire between the condenser fan relay and the condenser fan.

YES

Check for continuity in the BLK wire between the condenser fan and body ground.

Is there continuity? — NO → Check for an open in the BLK wire between the condenser fan and body ground. If the wire is OK, check for poor ground at G151.

YES

Replace the condenser fan motor.

BLK/WHT (+)

WHT (+)

BLU/BLK

BLU/YEL

View from wire side

View from wire side

BLK

BLU/BLK

CONDENSER FAN DIAGNOSTIC CHART—1994—95 INTEGRA—CONTINUED

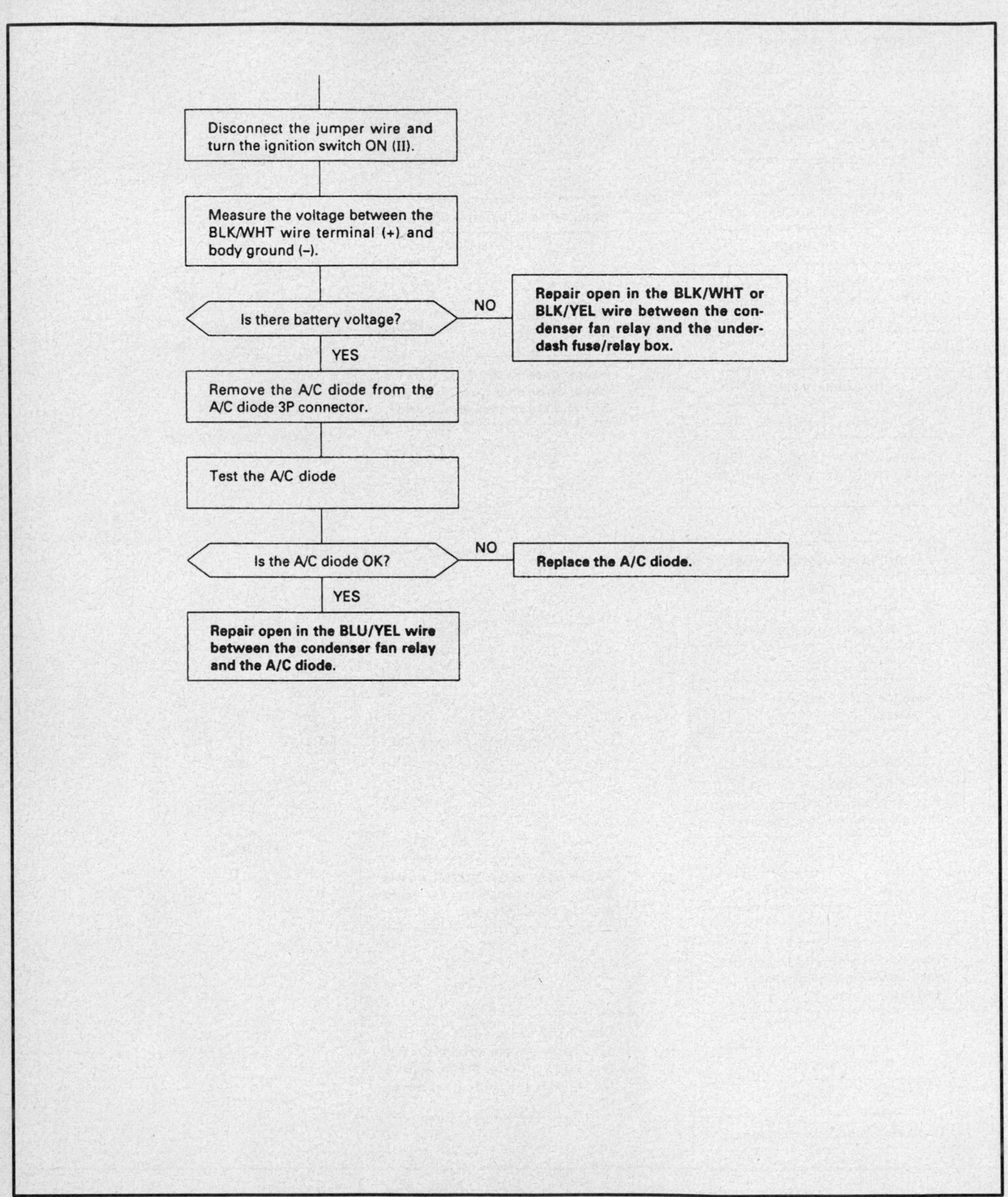

Disconnect the jumper wire and turn the ignition switch ON (II).

Measure the voltage between the BLK/WHT wire terminal (+) and body ground (−).

Is there battery voltage? — **NO** → Repair open in the BLK/WHT or BLK/YEL wire between the condenser fan relay and the under-dash fuse/relay box.

YES

Remove the A/C diode from the A/C diode 3P connector.

Test the A/C diode

Is the A/C diode OK? — **NO** → Replace the A/C diode.

YES

Repair open in the BLU/YEL wire between the condenser fan relay and the A/C diode.

CONDENSER FAN DIAGNOSTIC CHART—1994—95 INTEGRA—CONTINUED

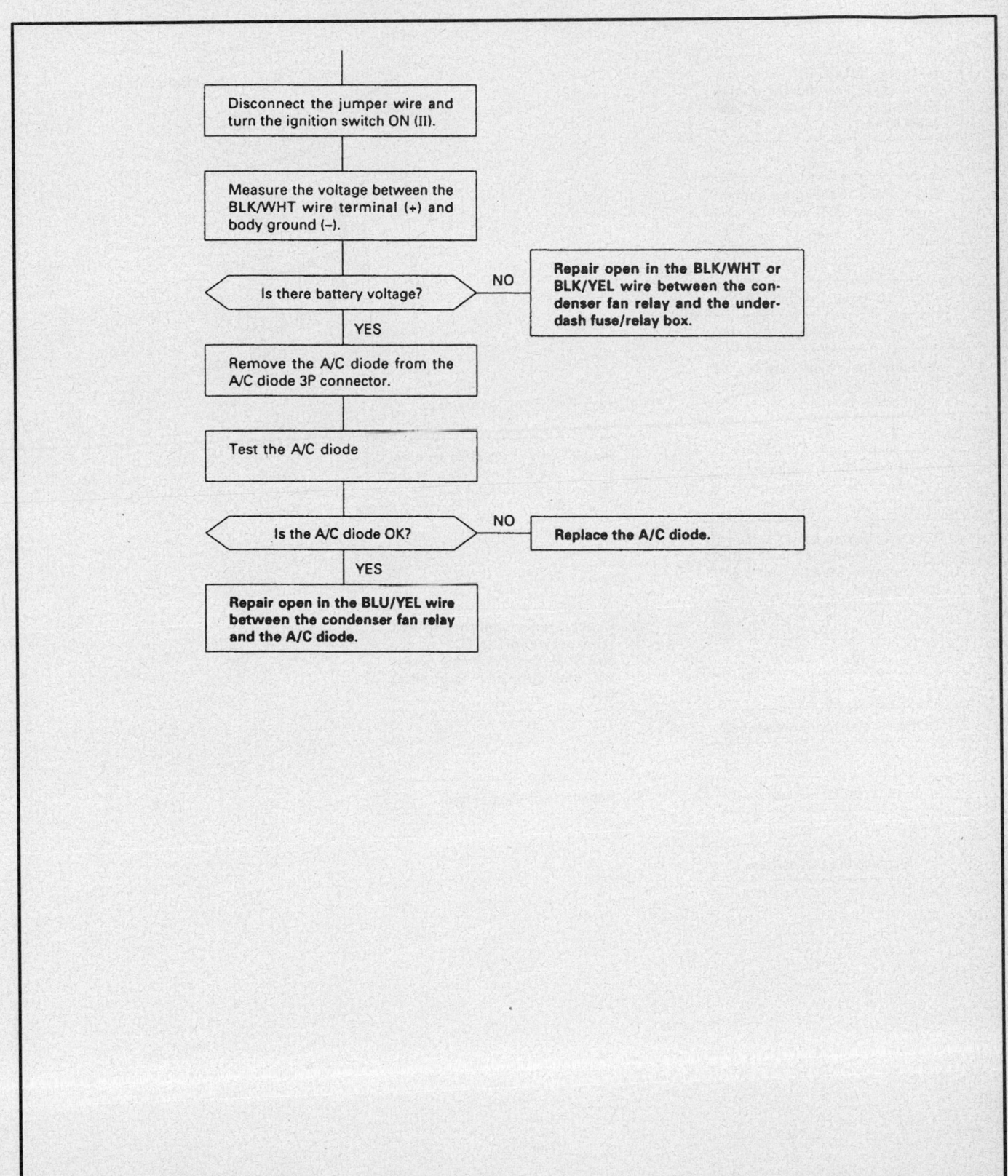

Disconnect the jumper wire and turn the ignition switch ON (II).

Measure the voltage between the BLK/WHT wire terminal (+) and body ground (–).

Is there battery voltage? — **NO** → Repair open in the BLK/WHT or BLK/YEL wire between the condenser fan relay and the under-dash fuse/relay box.

YES

Remove the A/C diode from the A/C diode 3P connector.

Test the A/C diode

Is the A/C diode OK? — **NO** → Replace the A/C diode.

YES

Repair open in the BLU/YEL wire between the condenser fan relay and the A/C diode.

ENGINE COOLANT TEMPERATURE (ECT) SWITCH DIAGNOSTIC CHART — 1994-95 INTEGRA

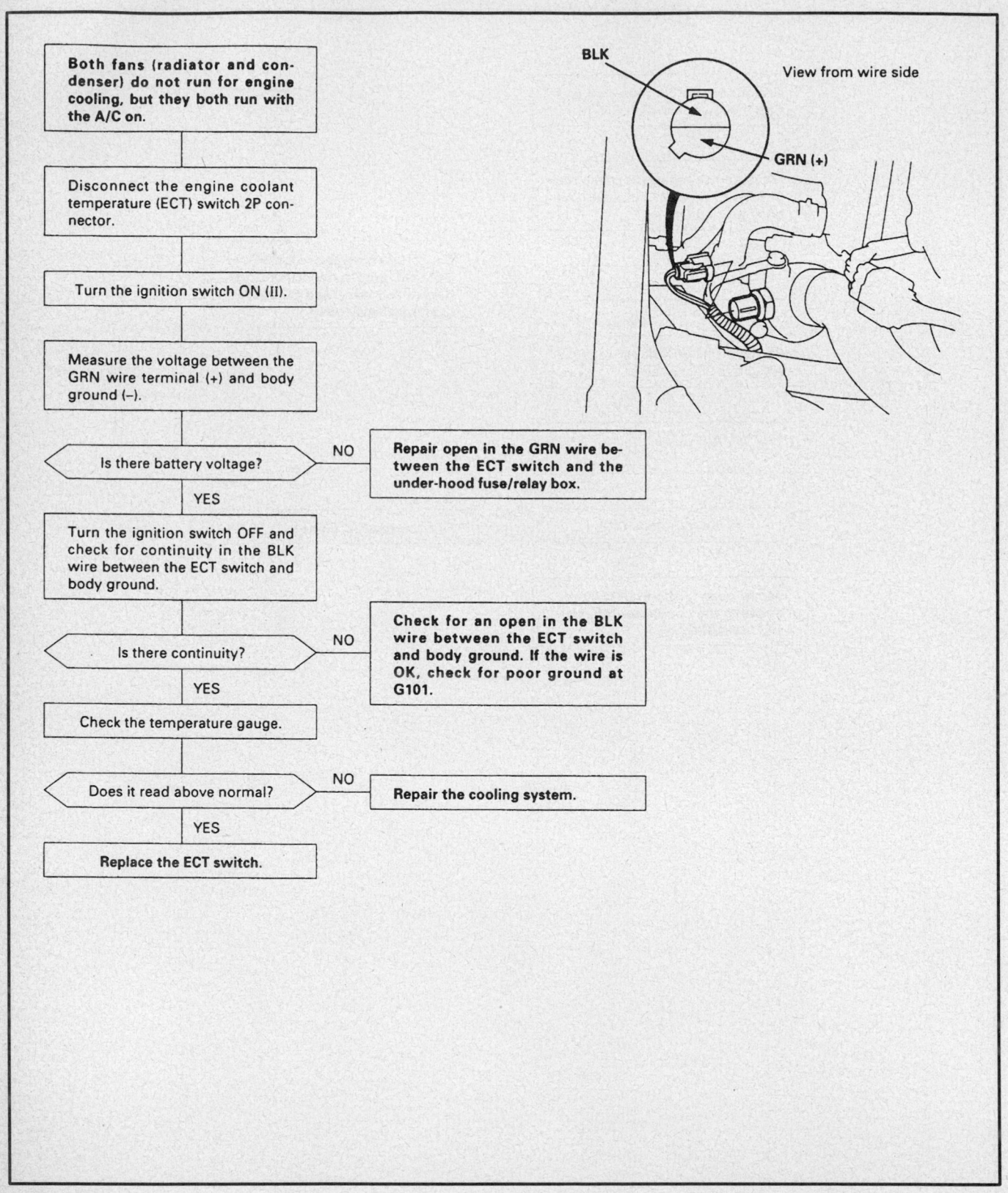

Both fans (radiator and condenser) do not run for engine cooling, but they both run with the A/C on.

↓

Disconnect the engine coolant temperature (ECT) switch 2P connector.

↓

Turn the ignition switch ON (II).

↓

Measure the voltage between the GRN wire terminal (+) and body ground (–).

↓

Is there battery voltage? — **NO** → Repair open in the GRN wire between the ECT switch and the under-hood fuse/relay box.

↓ **YES**

Turn the ignition switch OFF and check for continuity in the BLK wire between the ECT switch and body ground.

↓

Is there continuity? — **NO** → Check for an open in the BLK wire between the ECT switch and body ground. If the wire is OK, check for poor ground at G101.

↓ **YES**

Check the temperature gauge.

↓

Does it read above normal? — **NO** → Repair the cooling system.

↓ **YES**

Replace the ECT switch.

BLK

GRN (+)

View from wire side

BOTH FANS DO NOT RUN AT ALL DIAGNOSTIC CHART — 1994-95 INTEGRA

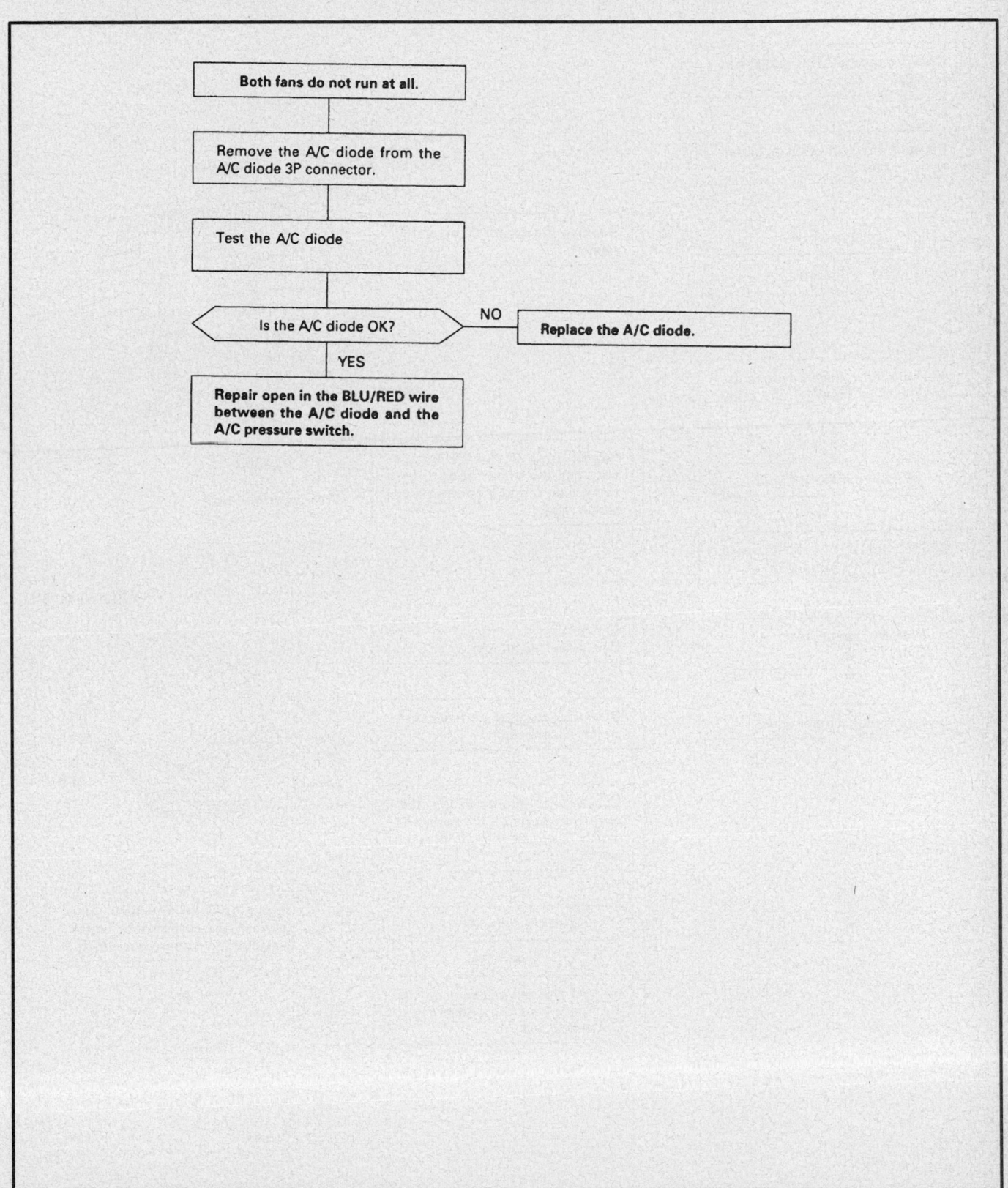

Both fans do not run at all.

Remove the A/C diode from the A/C diode 3P connector.

Test the A/C diode

Is the A/C diode OK? — NO → Replace the A/C diode.

YES

Repair open in the BLU/RED wire between the A/C diode and the A/C pressure switch.

COMPRESSOR CLUTCH DOES NOT ENGAGE DIAGNOSTIC CHART—1994—95 INTEGRA

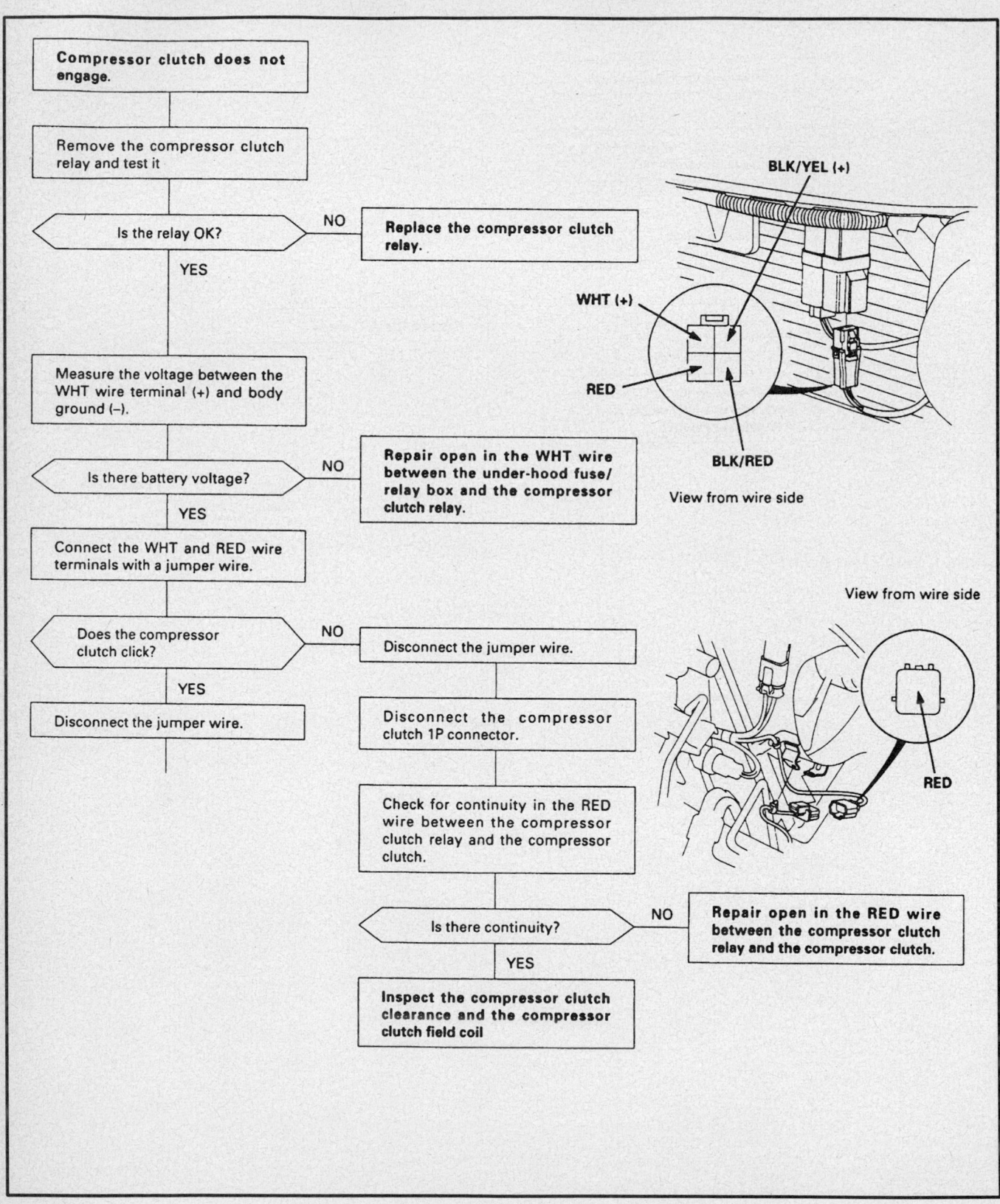

Compressor clutch does not engage.

Remove the compressor clutch relay and test it

Is the relay OK? — **NO** → Replace the compressor clutch relay.

YES

Measure the voltage between the WHT wire terminal (+) and body ground (−).

Is there battery voltage? — **NO** → Repair open in the WHT wire between the under-hood fuse/relay box and the compressor clutch relay.

YES

Connect the WHT and RED wire terminals with a jumper wire.

Does the compressor clutch click? — **NO** → Disconnect the jumper wire.

YES

Disconnect the jumper wire.

Disconnect the compressor clutch 1P connector.

Check for continuity in the RED wire between the compressor clutch relay and the compressor clutch.

Is there continuity? — **NO** → Repair open in the RED wire between the compressor clutch relay and the compressor clutch.

YES

Inspect the compressor clutch clearance and the compressor clutch field coil

BLK/YEL (+)

WHT (+)

RED

BLK/RED

View from wire side

View from wire side

RED

COMPRESSOR CLUTCH DOES NOT ENGAGE DIAGNOSTIC CHART – 1994 – 95 INTEGRA – CONTINUED

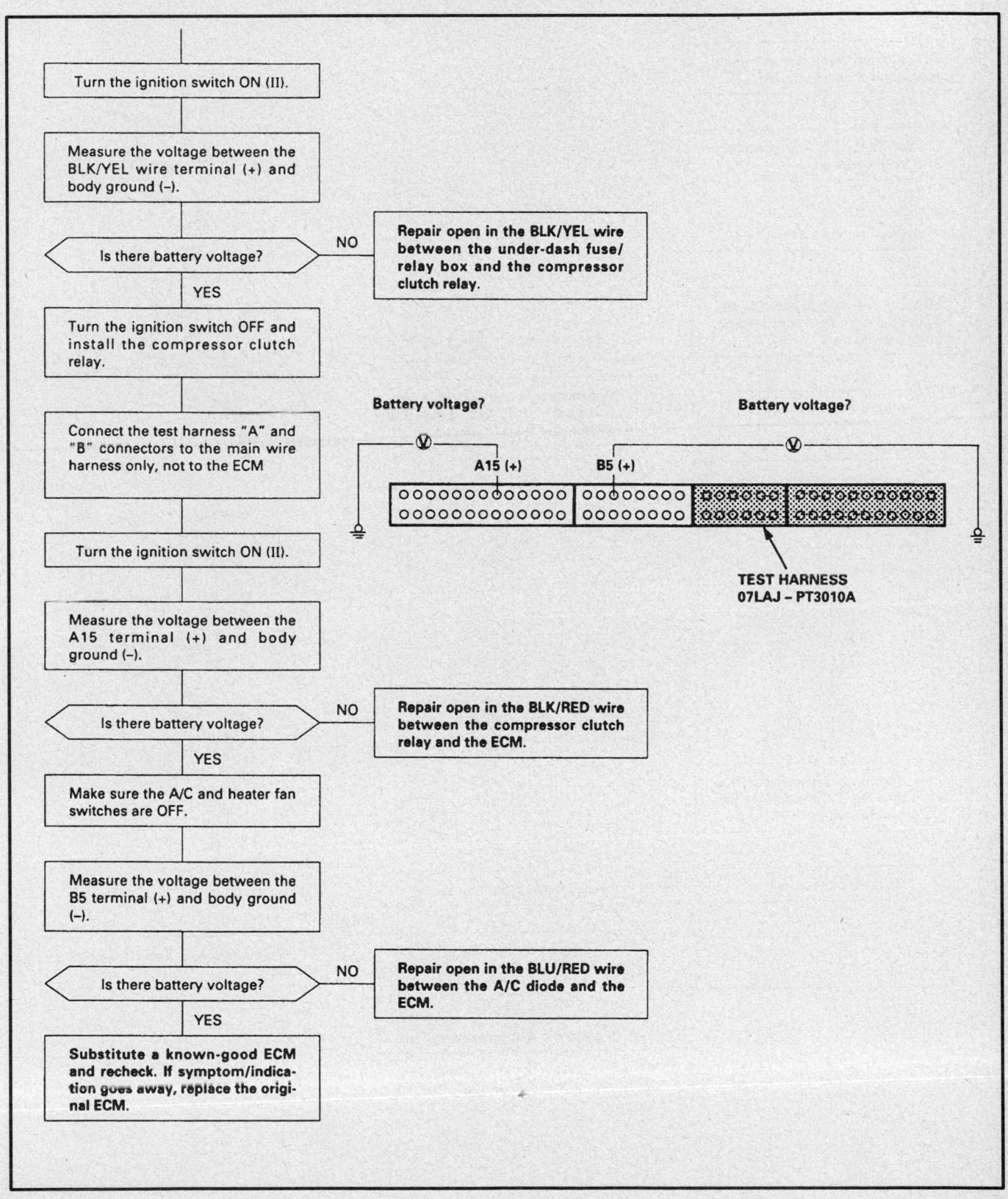

Turn the ignition switch ON (II).

Measure the voltage between the BLK/YEL wire terminal (+) and body ground (–).

Is there battery voltage? — NO → Repair open in the BLK/YEL wire between the under-dash fuse/relay box and the compressor clutch relay.

YES

Turn the ignition switch OFF and install the compressor clutch relay.

Connect the test harness "A" and "B" connectors to the main wire harness only, not to the ECM

Turn the ignition switch ON (II).

Measure the voltage between the A15 terminal (+) and body ground (–).

Is there battery voltage? — NO → Repair open in the BLK/RED wire between the compressor clutch relay and the ECM.

YES

Make sure the A/C and heater fan switches are OFF.

Measure the voltage between the B5 terminal (+) and body ground (–).

Is there battery voltage? — NO → Repair open in the BLU/RED wire between the A/C diode and the ECM.

YES

Substitute a known-good ECM and recheck. If symptom/indication goes away, replace the original ECM.

Battery voltage?   Battery voltage?

A15 (+)   B5 (+)

TEST HARNESS 07LAJ – PT3010A

AIR CONDITIONING SYSTEM DOES NOT COME ON DIAGNOSTIC CHART—1994—95 INTEGRA

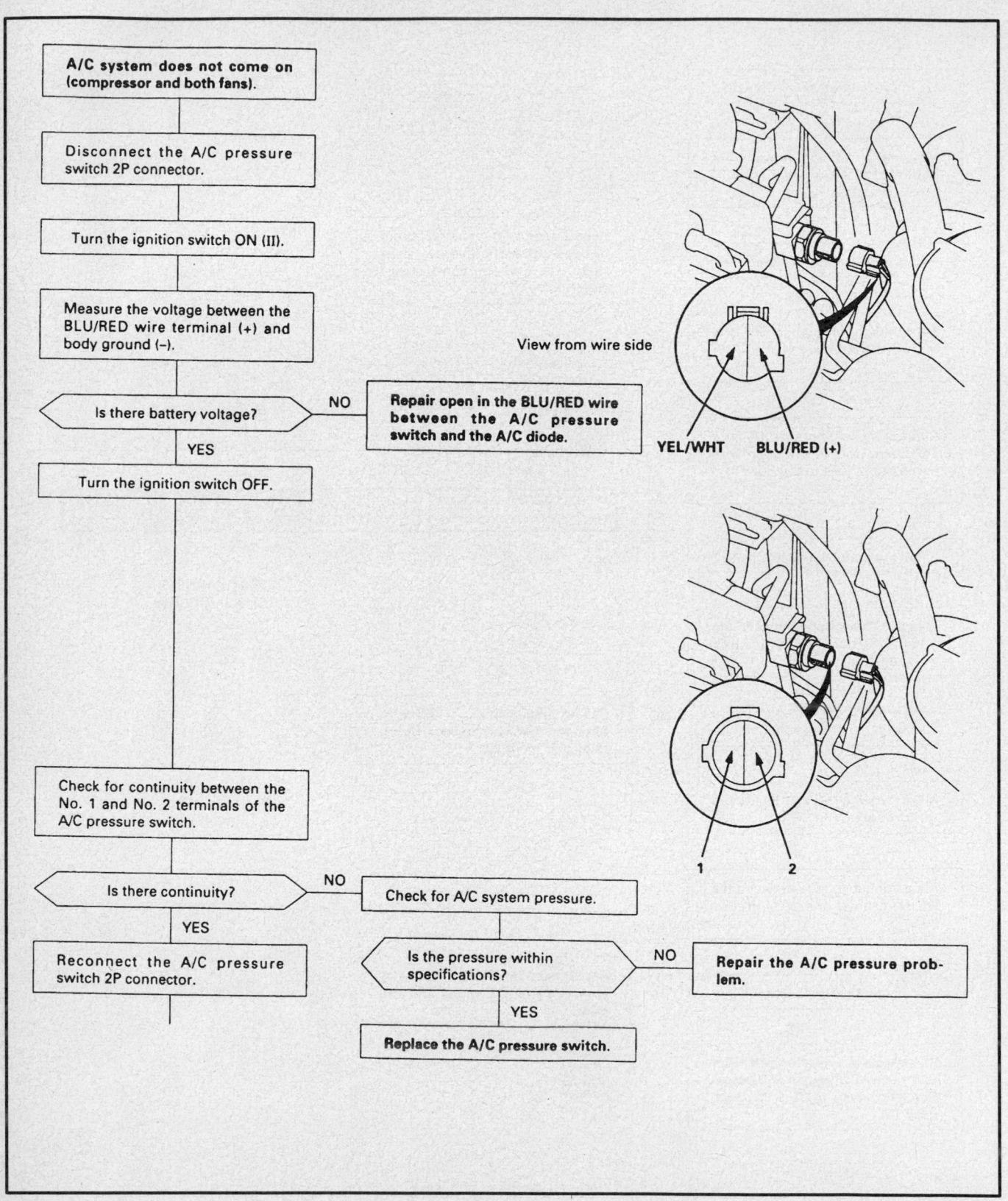

A/C system does not come on (compressor and both fans).

Disconnect the A/C pressure switch 2P connector.

Turn the ignition switch ON (II).

Measure the voltage between the BLU/RED wire terminal (+) and body ground (−).

Is there battery voltage? — **NO** → Repair open in the BLU/RED wire between the A/C pressure switch and the A/C diode.

YES

Turn the ignition switch OFF.

View from wire side

YEL/WHT   BLU/RED (+)

Check for continuity between the No. 1 and No. 2 terminals of the A/C pressure switch.

Is there continuity? — **NO** → Check for A/C system pressure.

YES

Reconnect the A/C pressure switch 2P connector.

Is the pressure within specifications? — **NO** → Repair the A/C pressure problem.

YES

Replace the A/C pressure switch.

1   2

AIR CONDITIONING SYSTEM DOES NOT COME ON DIAGNOSTIC CHART—1994—95 INTEGRA—CONTINUED

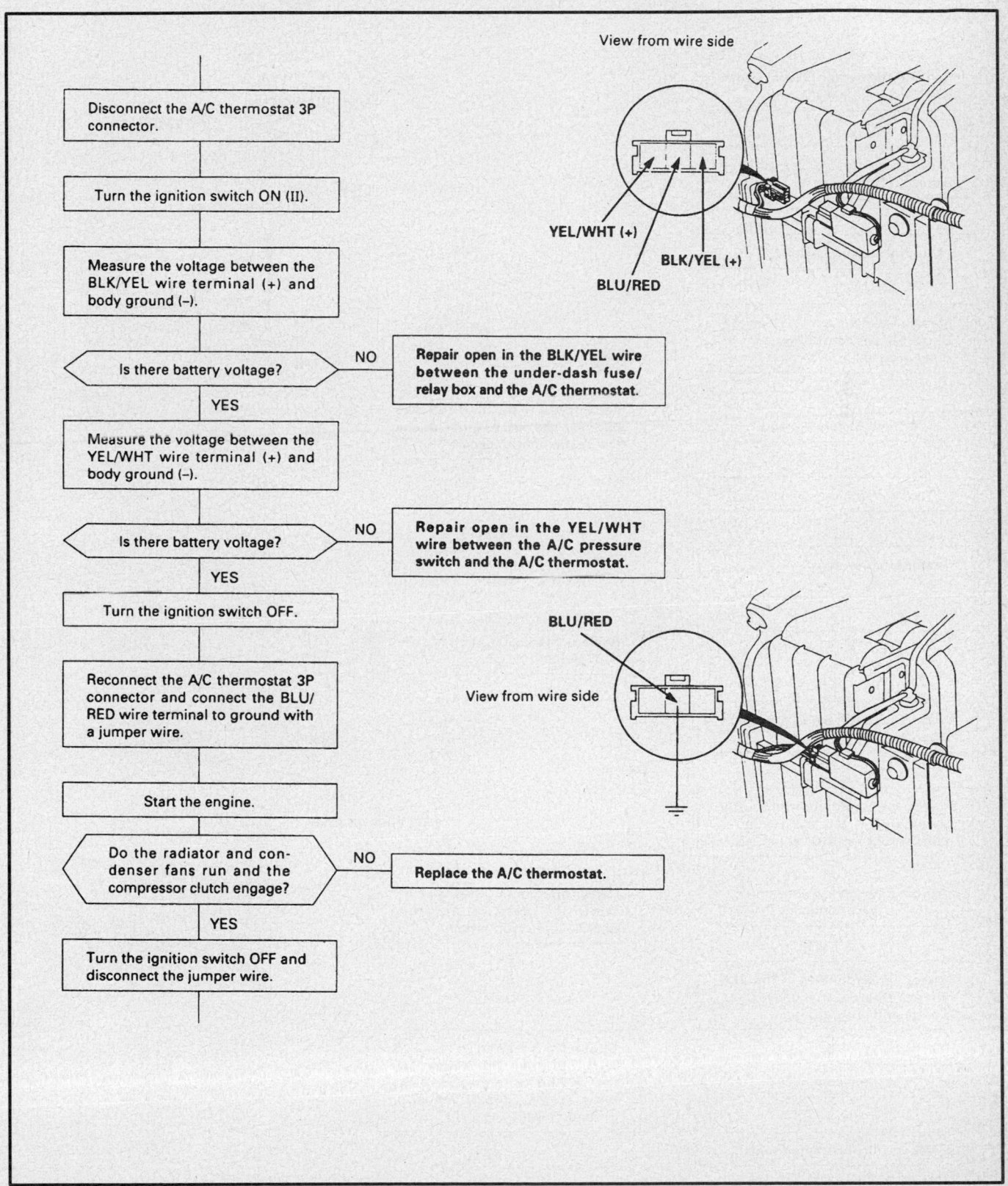

View from wire side

Disconnect the A/C thermostat 3P connector.

Turn the ignition switch ON (II).

Measure the voltage between the BLK/YEL wire terminal (+) and body ground (–).

Is there battery voltage? — NO → Repair open in the BLK/YEL wire between the under-dash fuse/relay box and the A/C thermostat.

YES

Measure the voltage between the YEL/WHT wire terminal (+) and body ground (–).

Is there battery voltage? — NO → Repair open in the YEL/WHT wire between the A/C pressure switch and the A/C thermostat.

YES

Turn the ignition switch OFF.

Reconnect the A/C thermostat 3P connector and connect the BLU/RED wire terminal to ground with a jumper wire.

Start the engine.

Do the radiator and condenser fans run and the compressor clutch engage? — NO → Replace the A/C thermostat.

YES

Turn the ignition switch OFF and disconnect the jumper wire.

YEL/WHT (+)
BLK/YEL (+)
BLU/RED

BLU/RED
View from wire side

AIR CONDITIONING SYSTEM DOES NOT COME ON DIAGNOSTIC CHART—1994—95 INTEGRA—CONTINUED

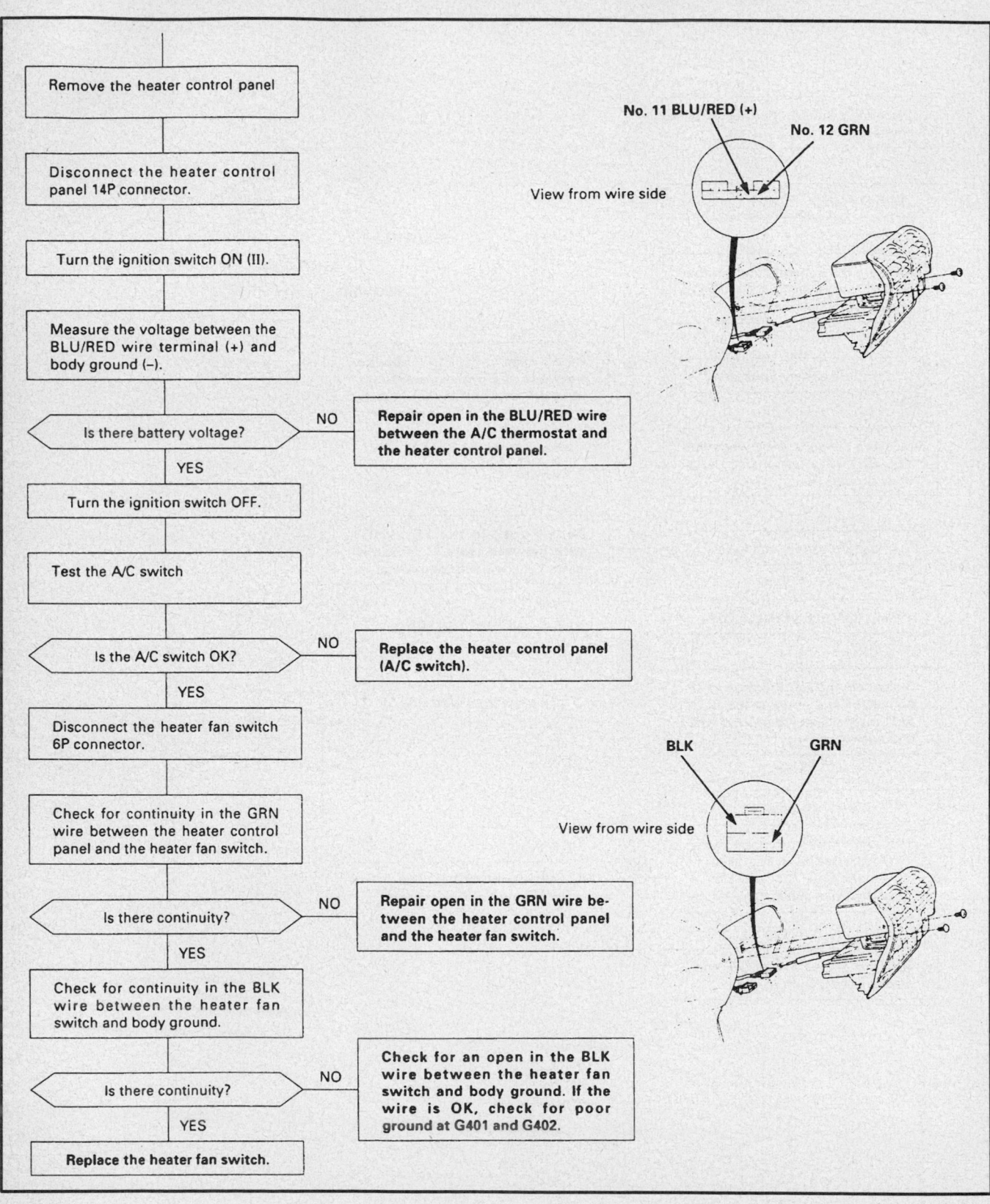

Remove the heater control panel

Disconnect the heater control panel 14P connector.

Turn the ignition switch ON (II).

Measure the voltage between the BLU/RED wire terminal (+) and body ground (–).

Is there battery voltage? — NO → **Repair open in the BLU/RED wire between the A/C thermostat and the heater control panel.**

YES

Turn the ignition switch OFF.

Test the A/C switch

Is the A/C switch OK? — NO → **Replace the heater control panel (A/C switch).**

YES

Disconnect the heater fan switch 6P connector.

Check for continuity in the GRN wire between the heater control panel and the heater fan switch.

Is there continuity? — NO → **Repair open in the GRN wire between the heater control panel and the heater fan switch.**

YES

Check for continuity in the BLK wire between the heater fan switch and body ground.

Is there continuity? — NO → **Check for an open in the BLK wire between the heater fan switch and body ground. If the wire is OK, check for poor ground at G401 and G402.**

YES

Replace the heater fan switch.

No. 11 BLU/RED (+)
No. 12 GRN
View from wire side

BLK   GRN
View from wire side

WIRING SCHEMATICS

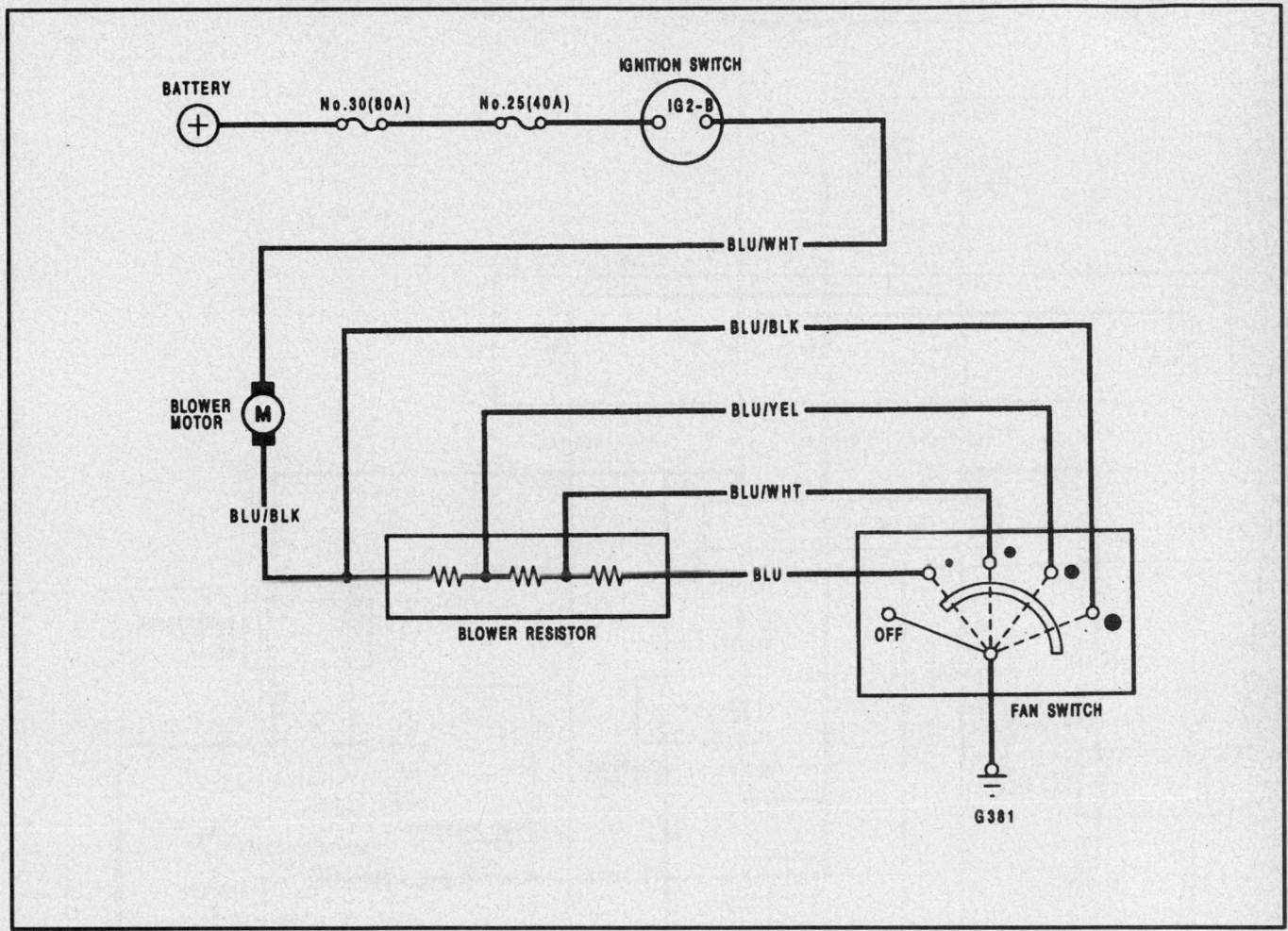

Heater only wiring schematic — Integra

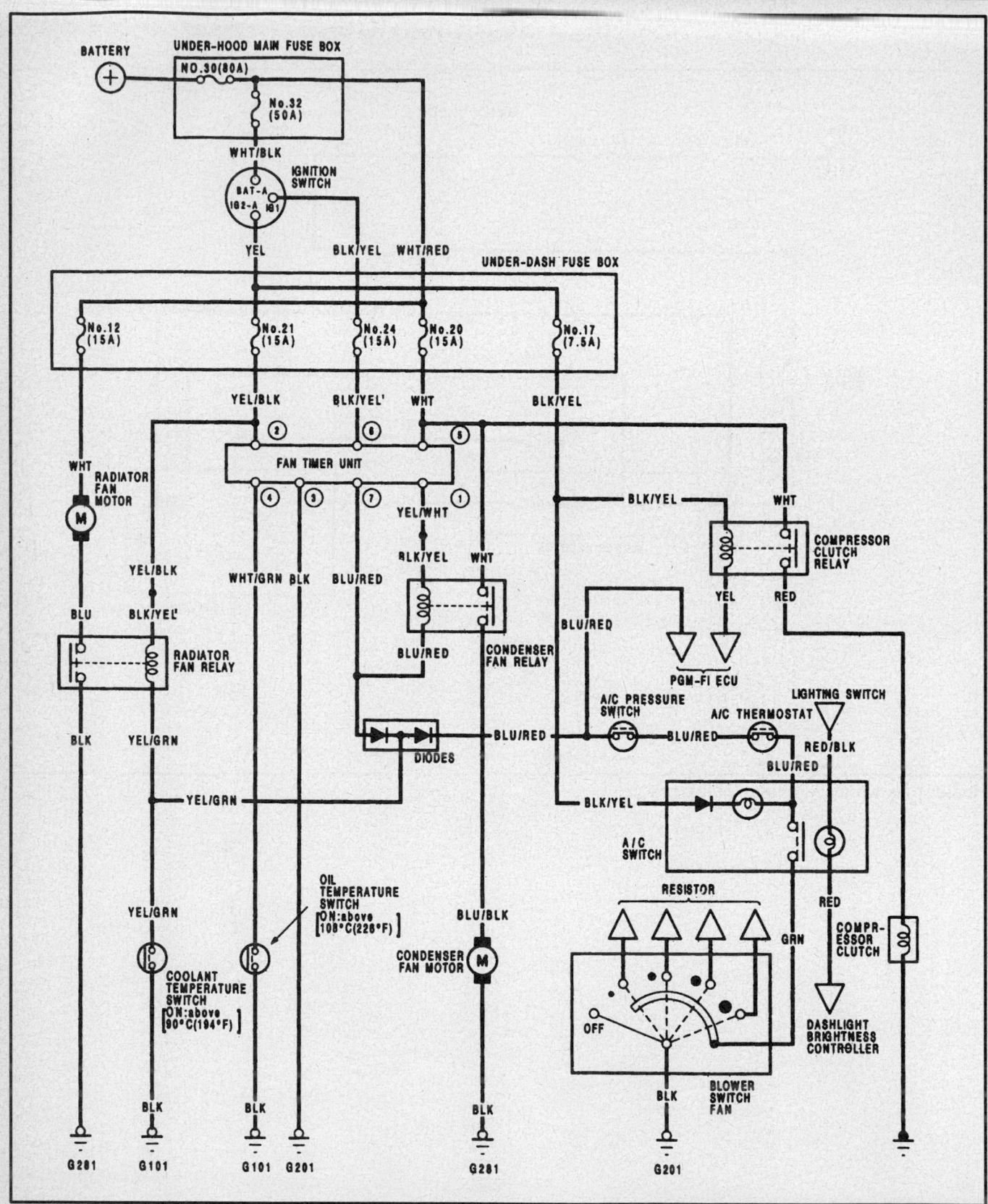

Air conditioning wiring schematic—1993 Integra (USA)

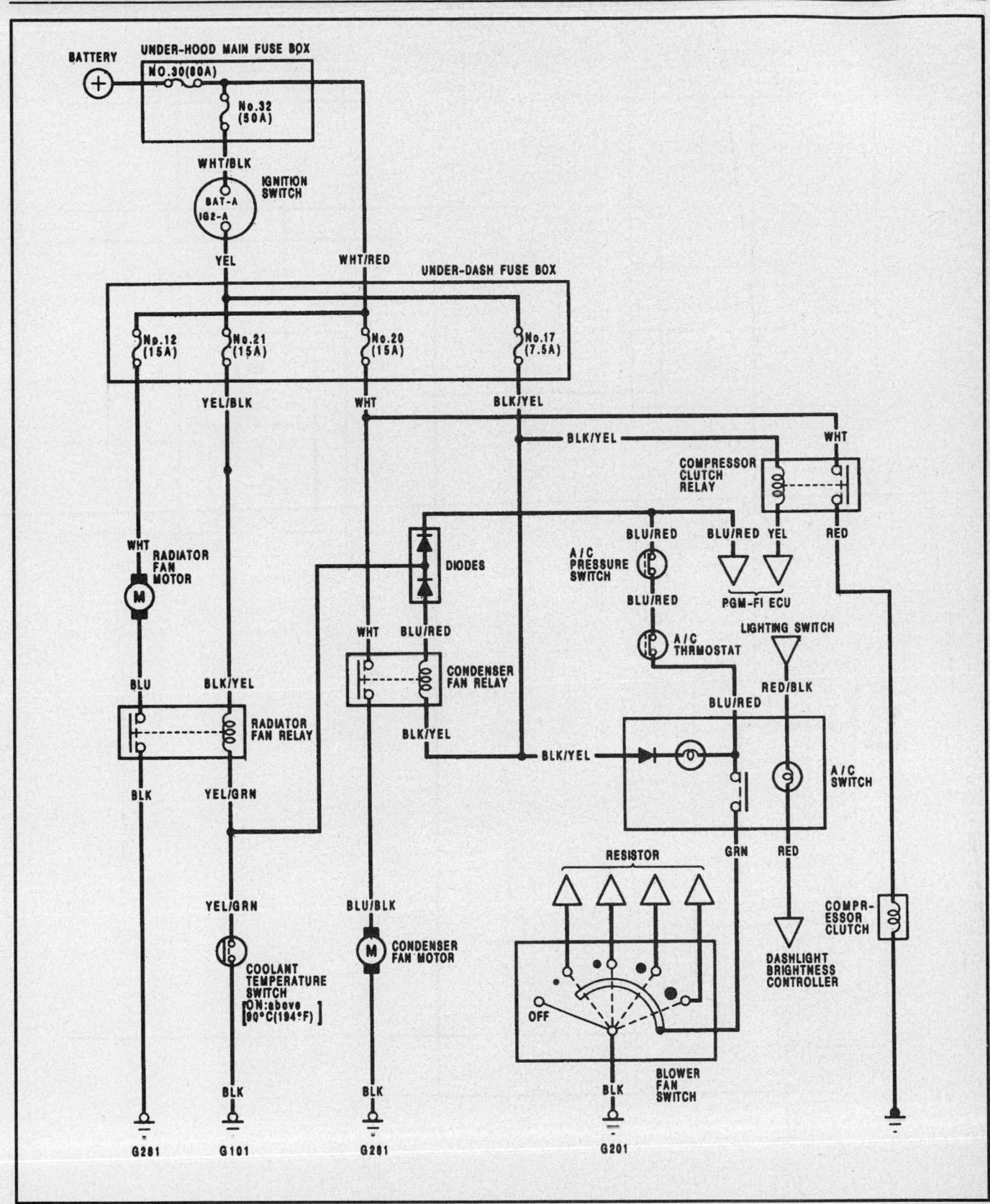

Air conditioning wiring schematic—1993 Integra (Canada)

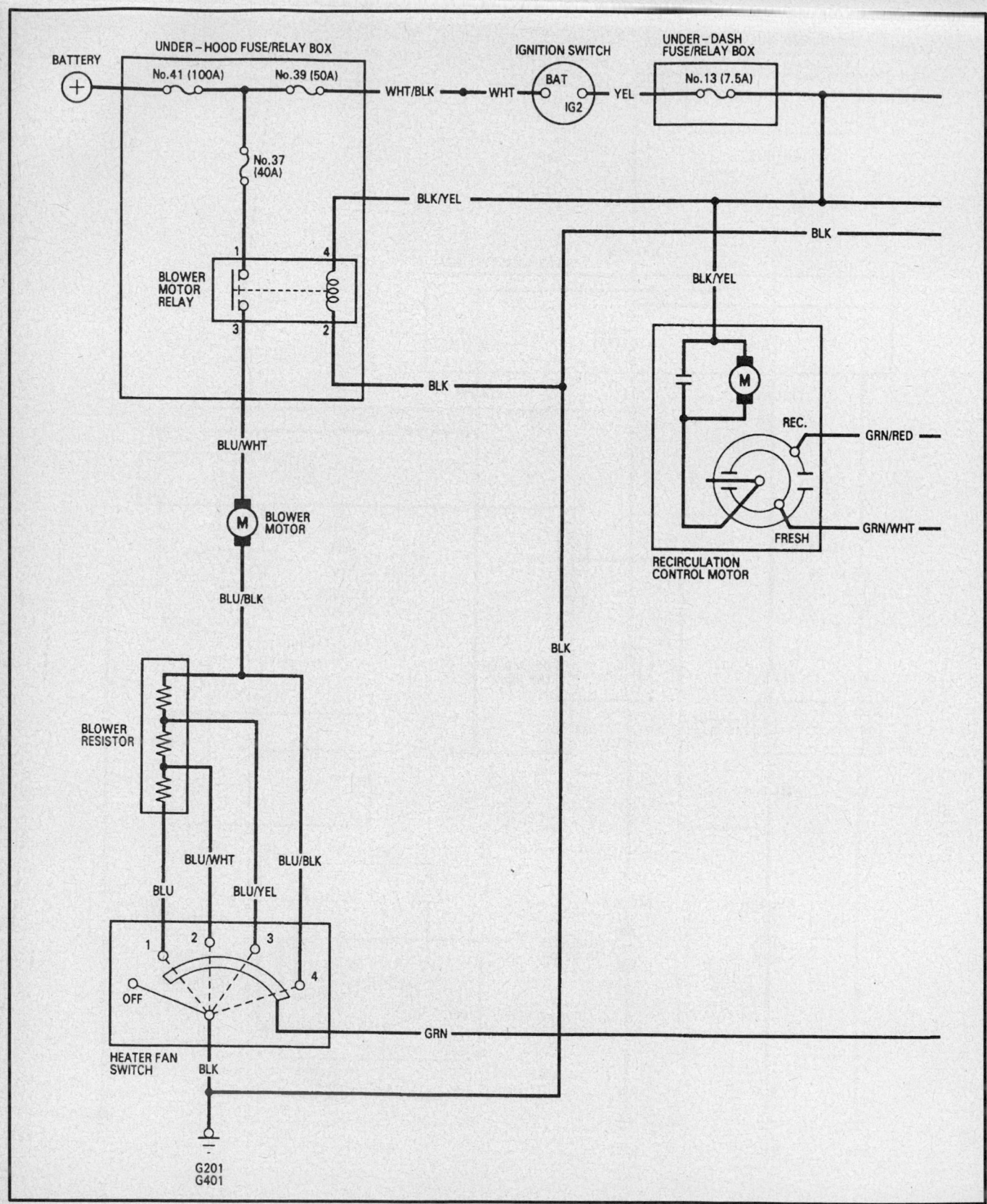

Air conditioning wiring schematic—1994—95 Integra

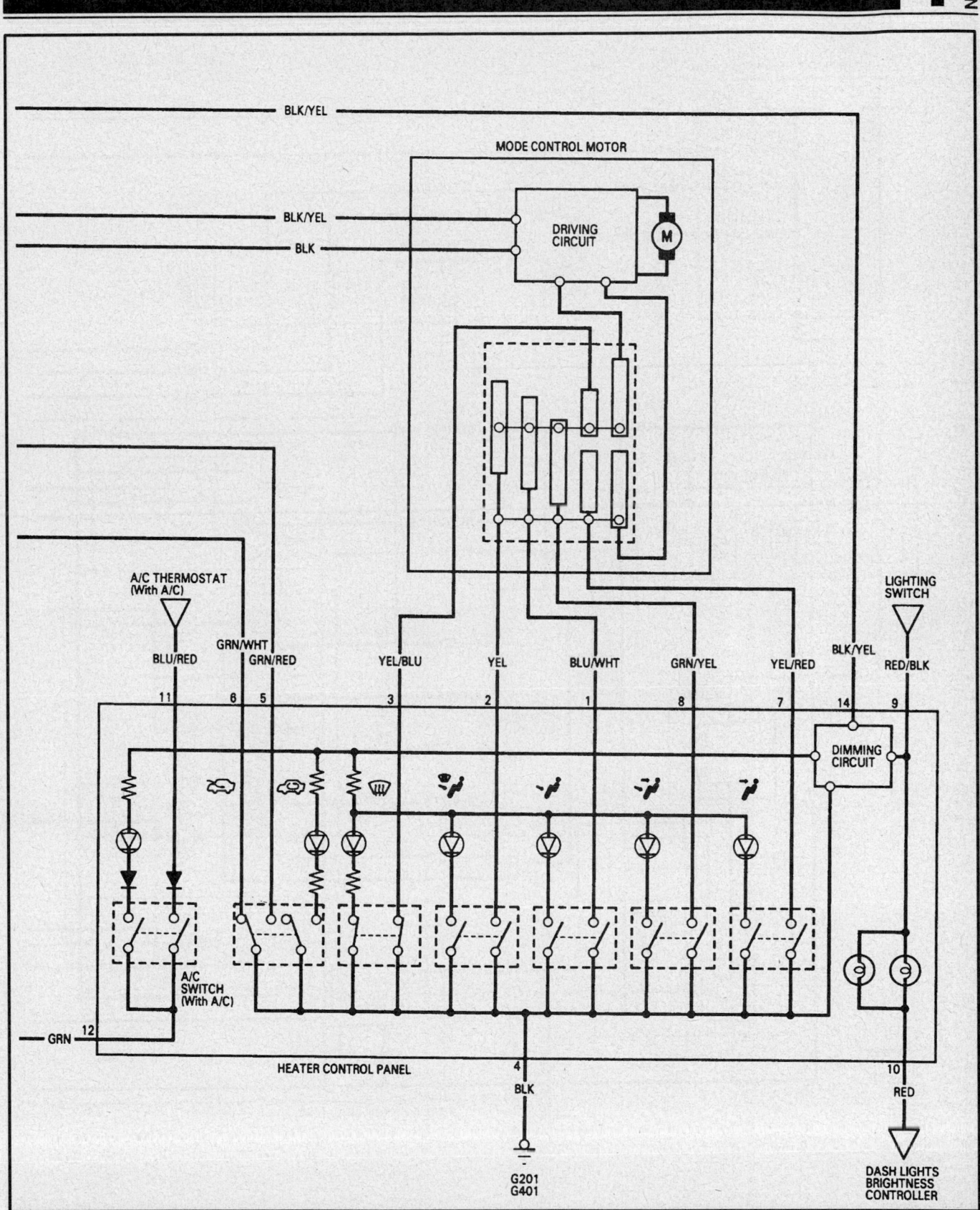

Air conditioning wiring schematic—1994–95 Integra—Cont'd

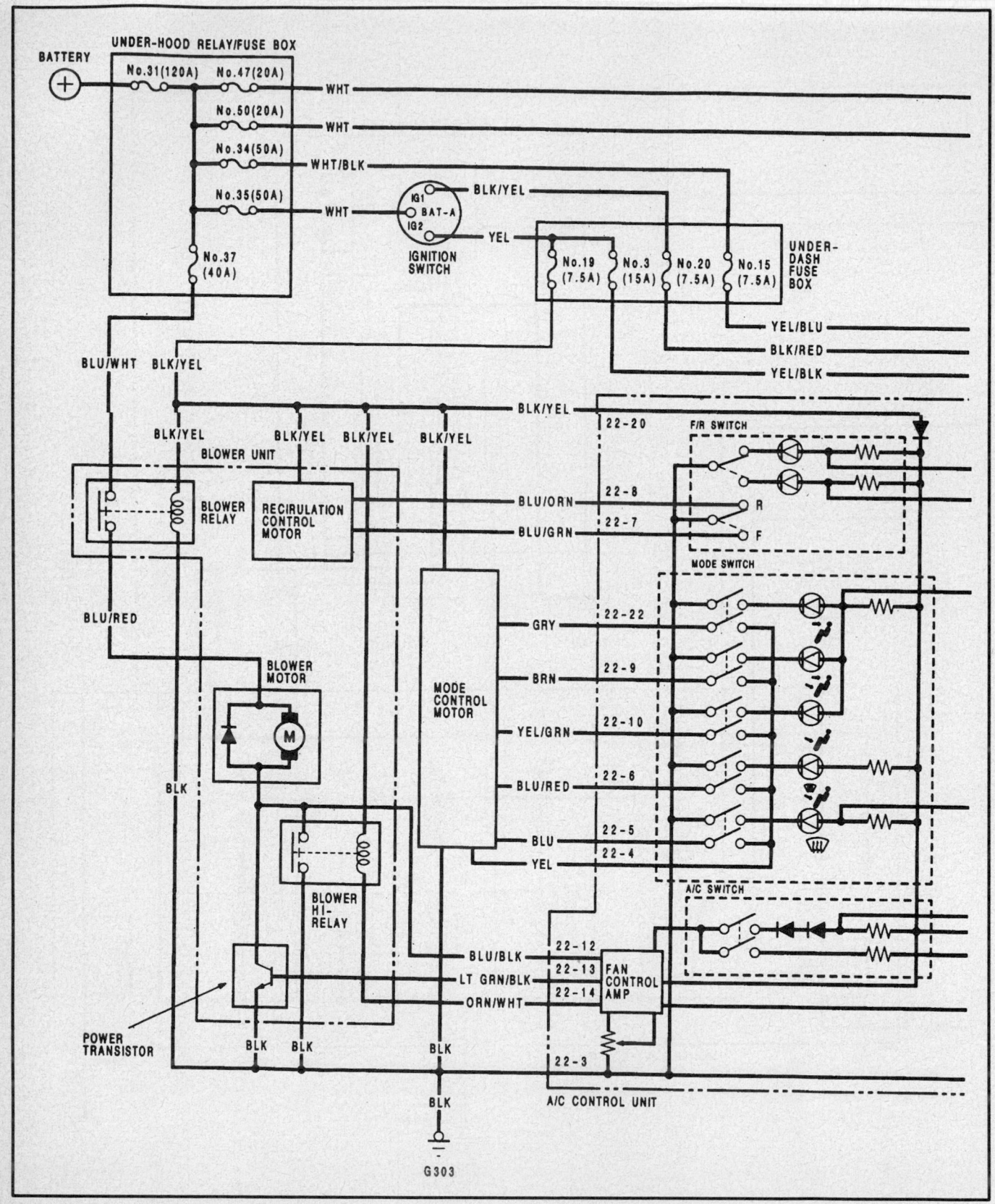

Manual air conditioning wiring schematic—1993 Legend and Legend Coupe

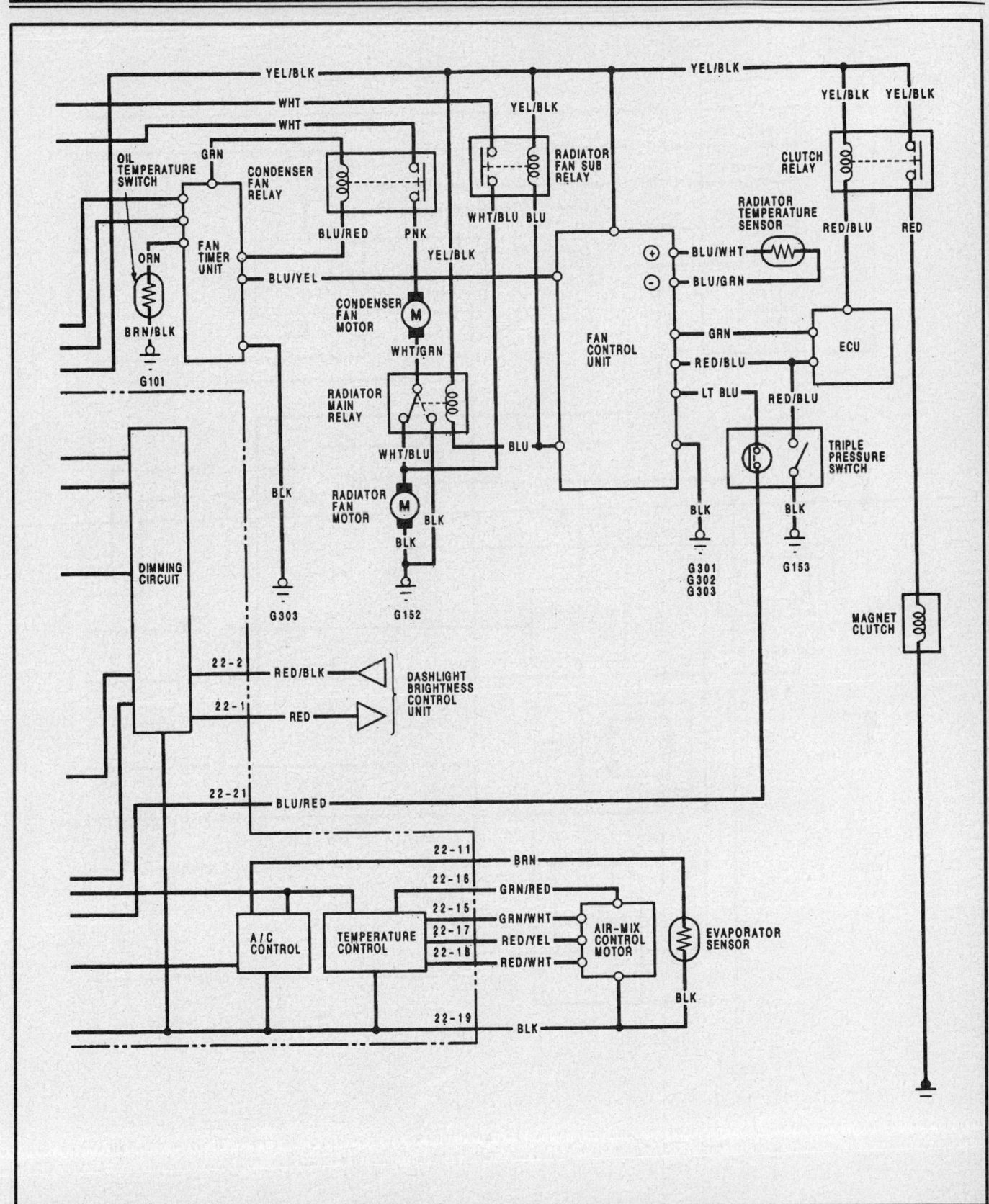

Manual air conditioning wiring schematic—1993 Legend and Legend Coupe—Cont'd

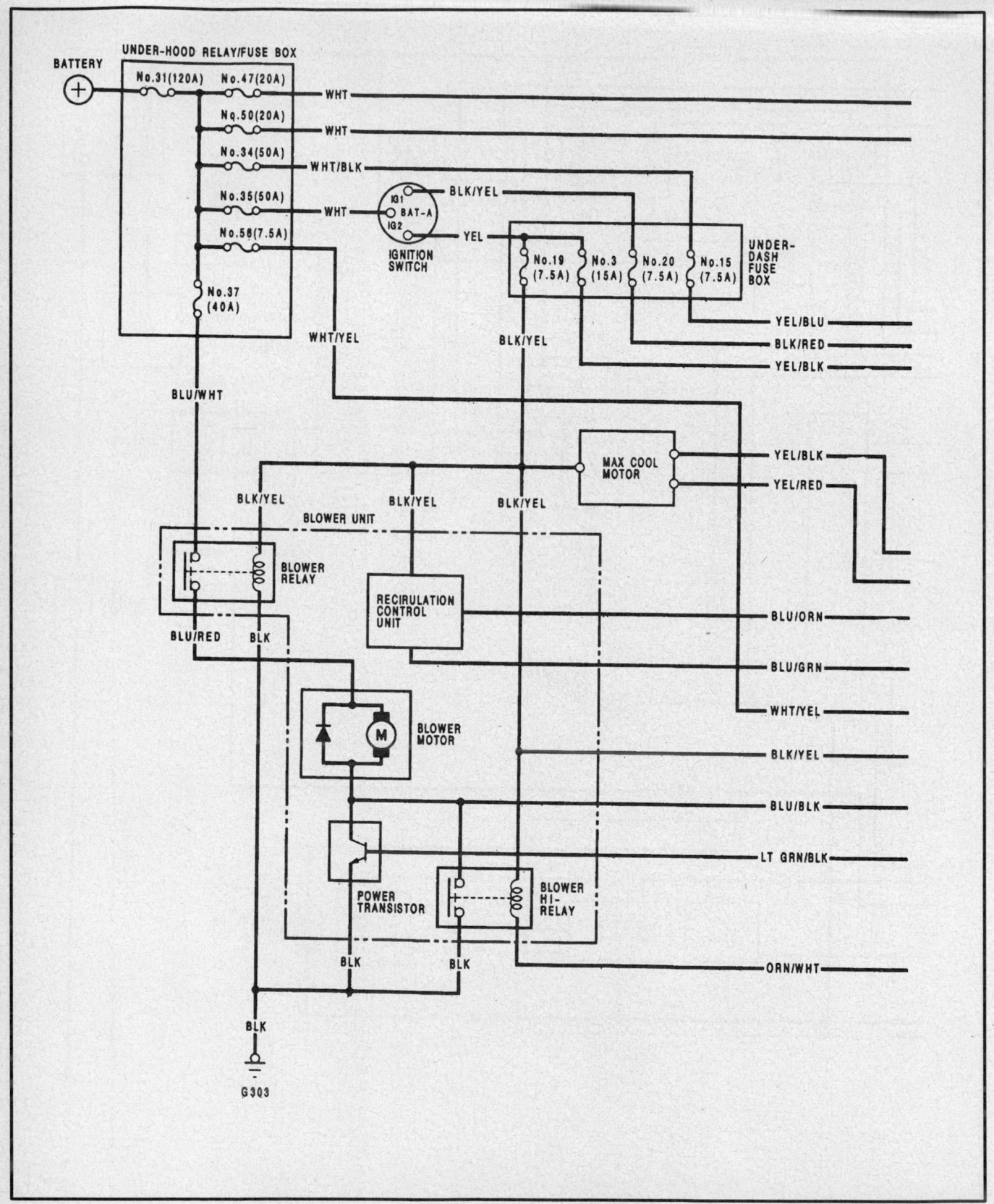

Automatic climate control wiring schematic—1993 Legend and Legend Coupe

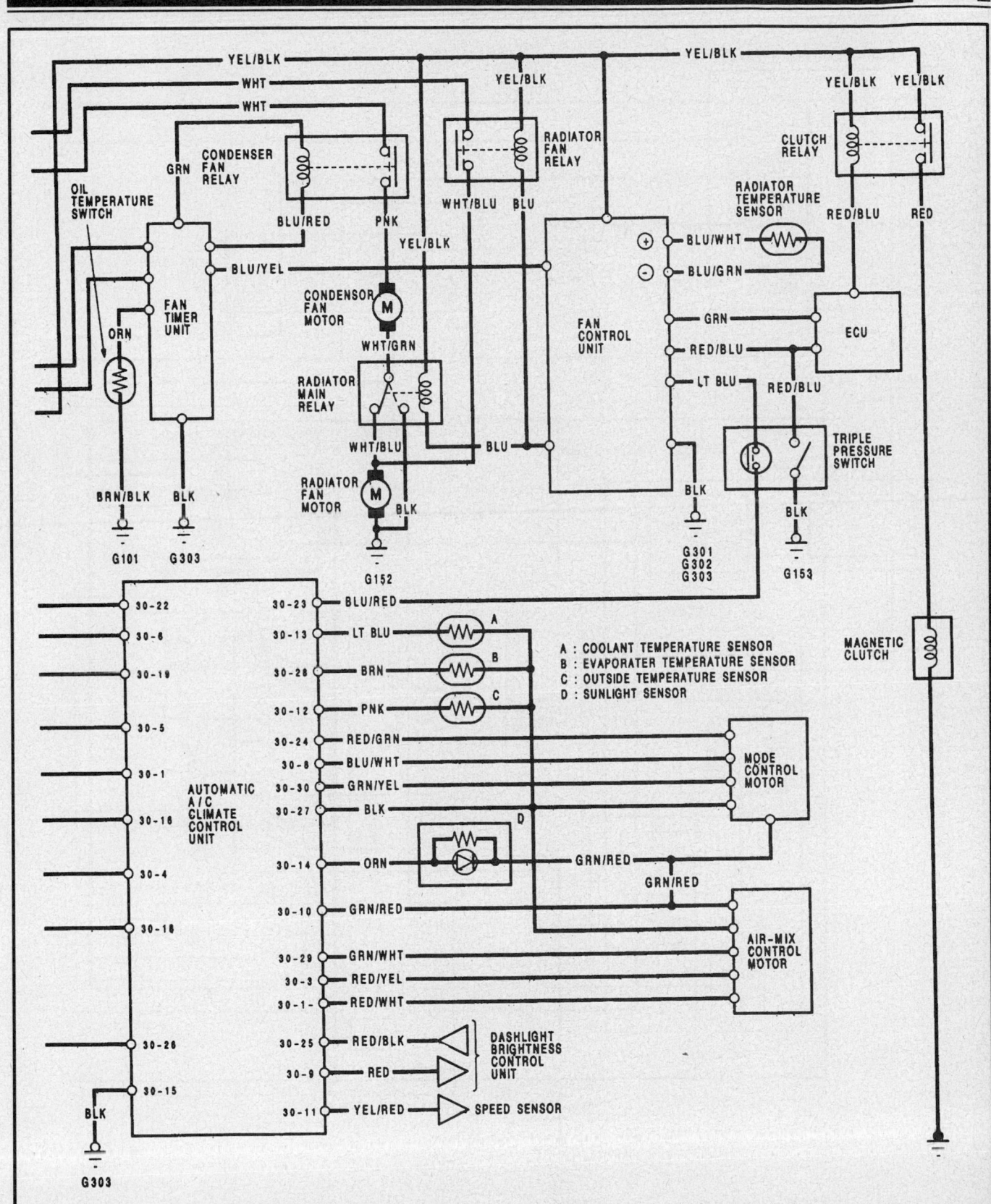

Automatic climate control wiring schematic–1993 Legend and Legend Coupe–Cont'd

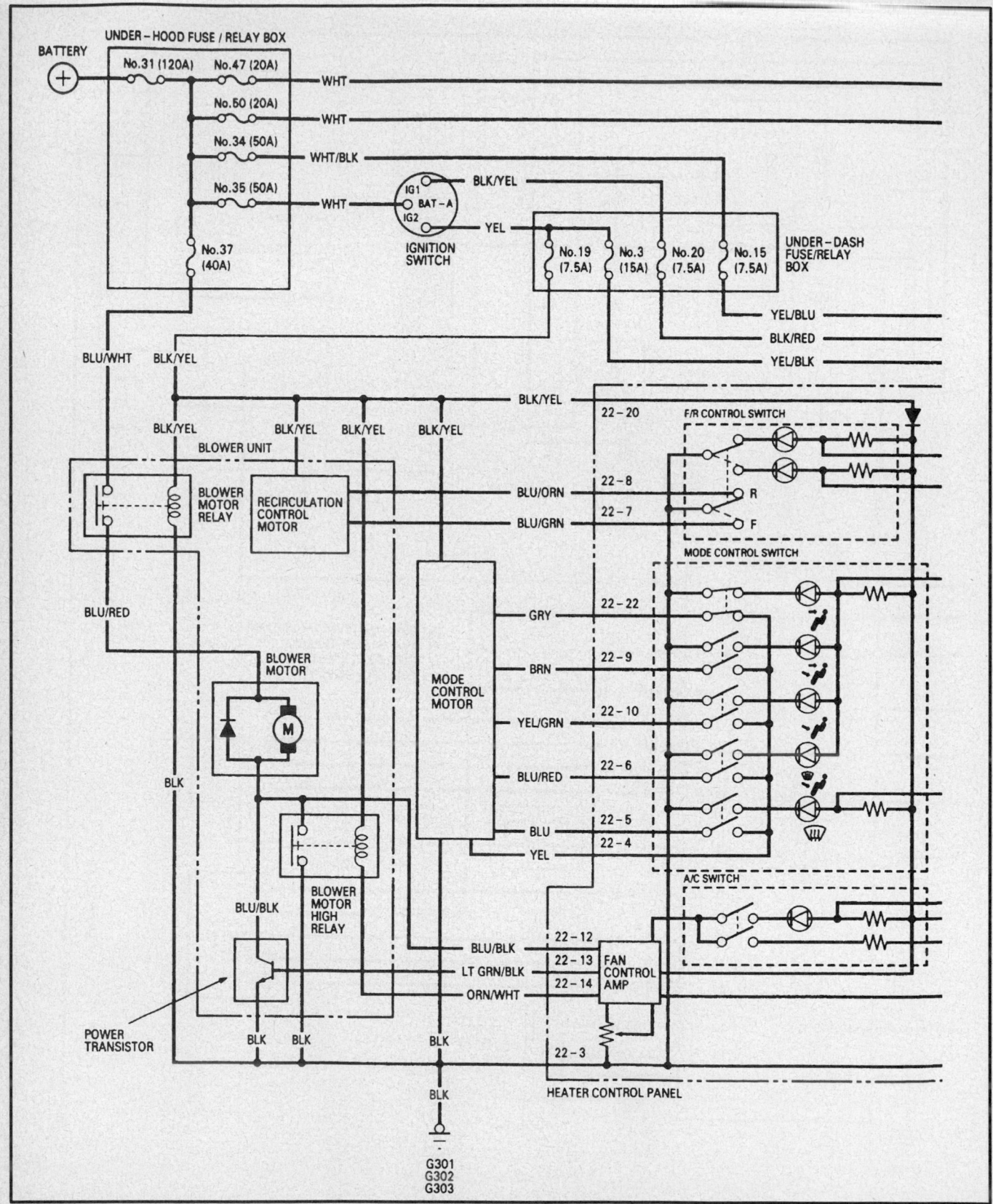

Air conditioning wiring schematic—1994 Legend and Legend Coupe

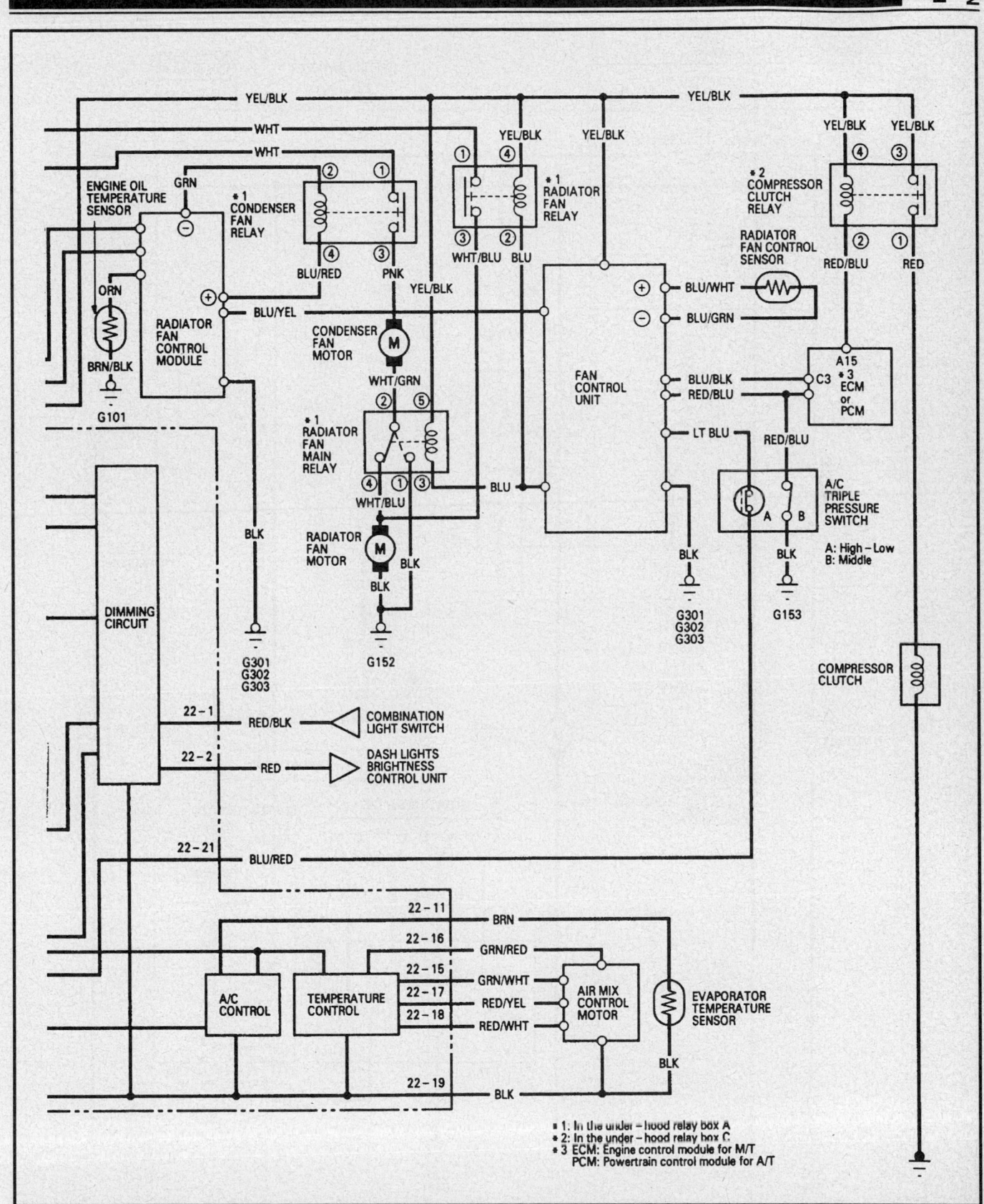

Air conditioning wiring schematic—1994 Legend and Legend Coupe—Cont'd

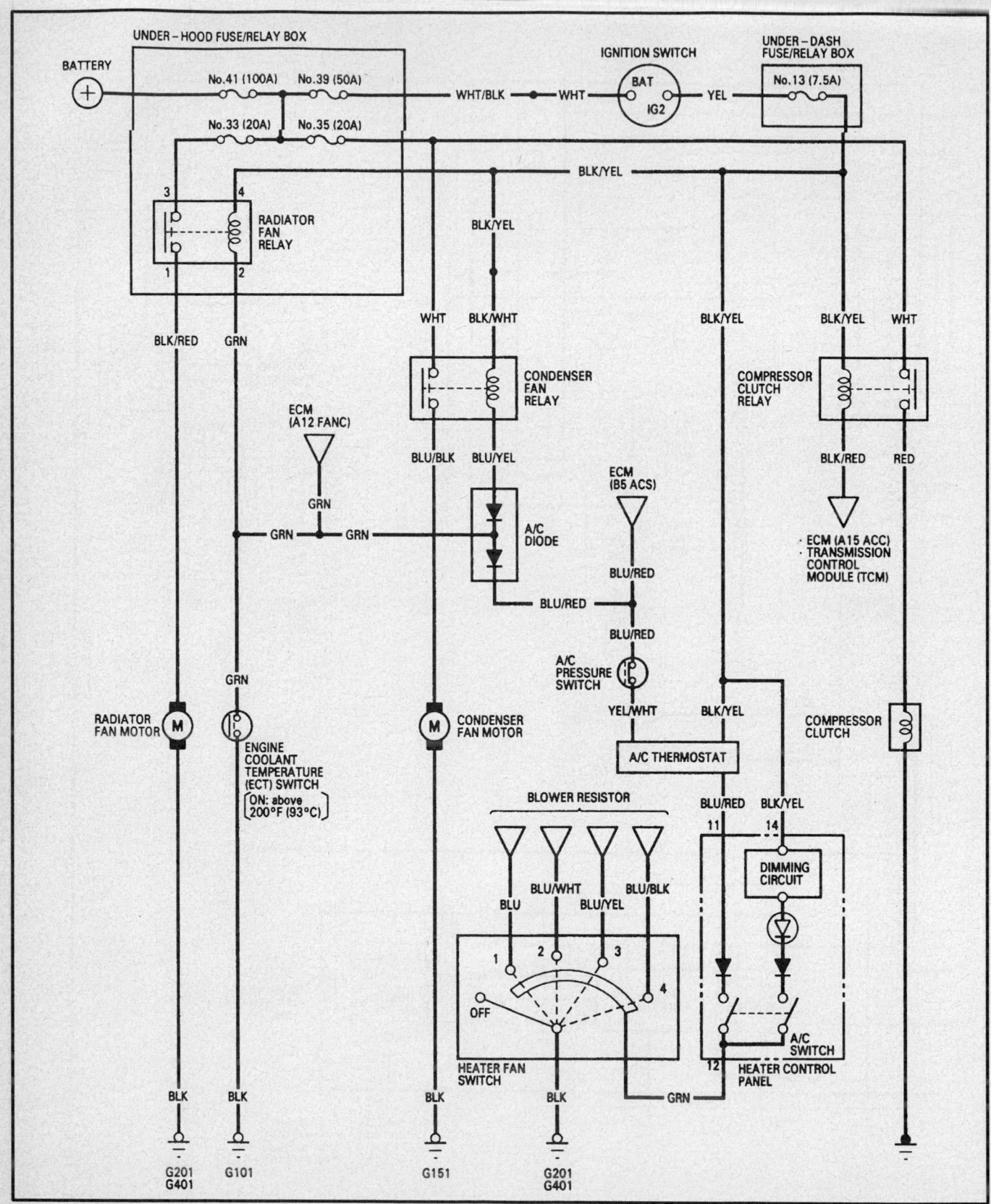

Air conditioning circuit diagram—1994–95 Integra

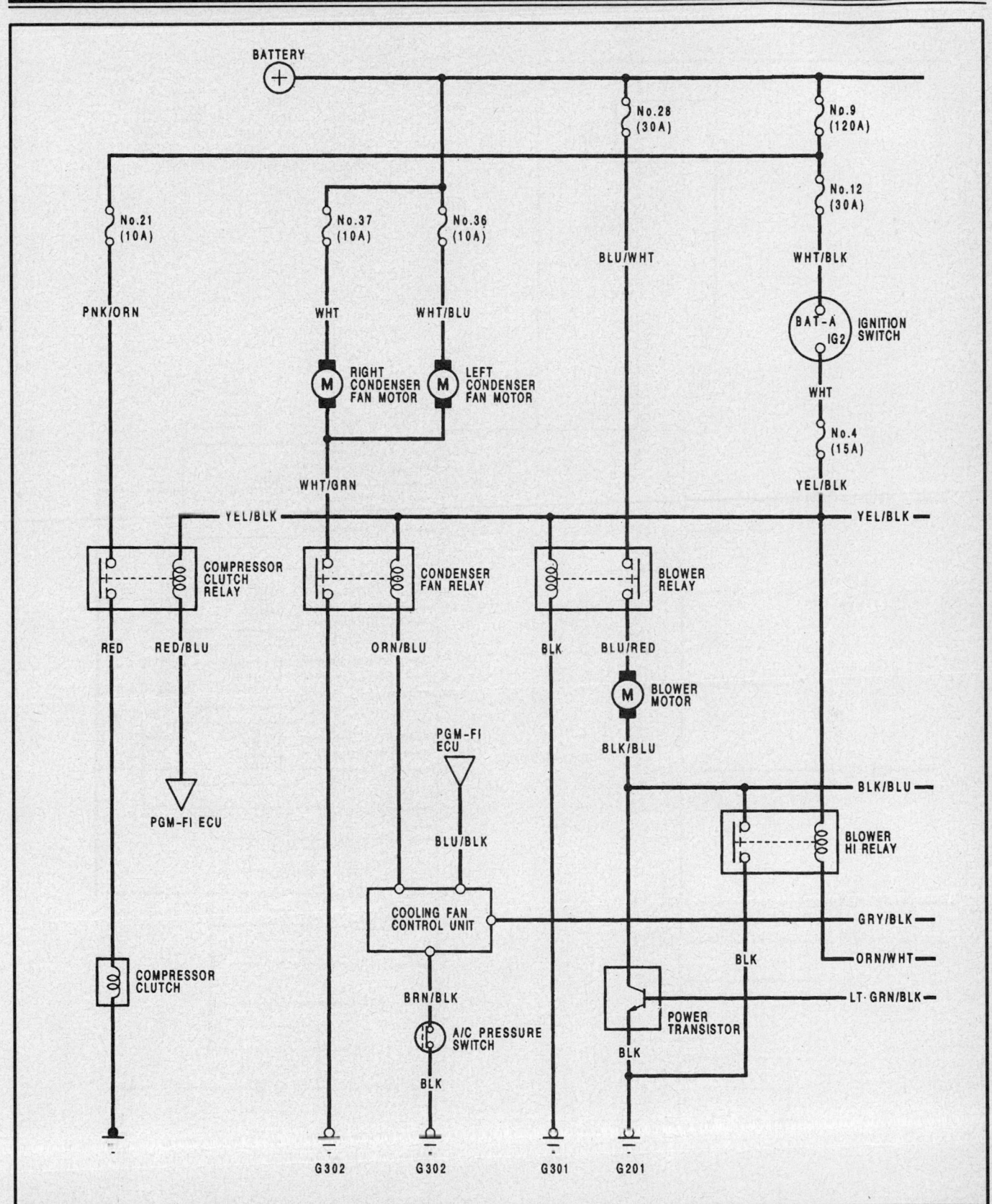

Automatic climate control wiring schematic—NSX

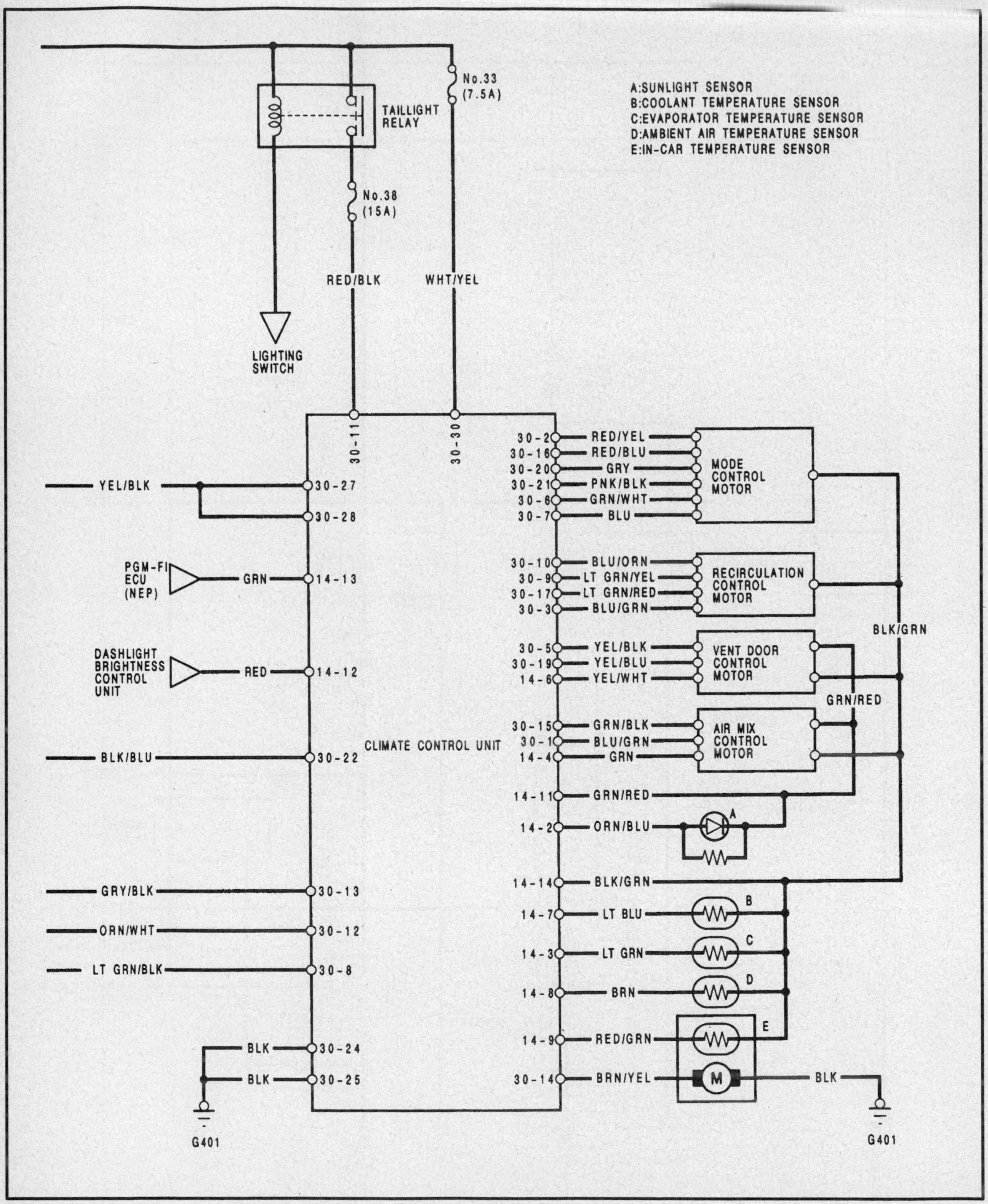

TAILLIGHT
RELAY

No.33
(7.5A)

No.38
(15A)

RED/BLK

WHT/YEL

LIGHTING
SWITCH

A:SUNLIGHT SENSOR
B:COOLANT TEMPERATURE SENSOR
C:EVAPORATOR TEMPERATURE SENSOR
D:AMBIENT AIR TEMPERATURE SENSOR
E:IN-CAR TEMPERATURE SENSOR

30-11
30-30

YEL/BLK — 30-27
30-28

PGM-FI
ECU
(NEP) — GRN — 14-13

DASHLIGHT
BRIGHTNESS
CONTROL
UNIT — RED — 14-12

CLIMATE CONTROL UNIT

BLK/BLU — 30-22

GRY/BLK — 30-13

ORN/WHT — 30-12

LT GRN/BLK — 30-8

BLK — 30-24
BLK — 30-25

G401

30-2 — RED/YEL
30-16 — RED/BLU
30-20 — GRY
30-21 — PNK/BLK
30-6 — GRN/WHT
30-7 — BLU

MODE
CONTROL
MOTOR

30-10 — BLU/ORN
30-9 — LT GRN/YEL
30-17 — LT GRN/RED
30-3 — BLU/GRN

RECIRCULATION
CONTROL
MOTOR

30-5 — YEL/BLK
30-19 — YEL/BLU
14-6 — YEL/WHT

VENT DOOR
CONTROL
MOTOR

30-15 — GRN/BLK
30-1 — BLU/GRN
14-4 — GRN

AIR MIX
CONTROL
MOTOR

14-11 — GRN/RED

14-2 — ORN/BLU — A

14-14 — BLK/GRN

14-7 — LT BLU — B

14-3 — LT GRN — C

14-8 — BRN — D

14-9 — RED/GRN — E

30-14 — BRN/YEL — M — BLK

BLK/GRN

GRN/RED

G401

Automatic climate control wiring schematic—NSX—Cont'd

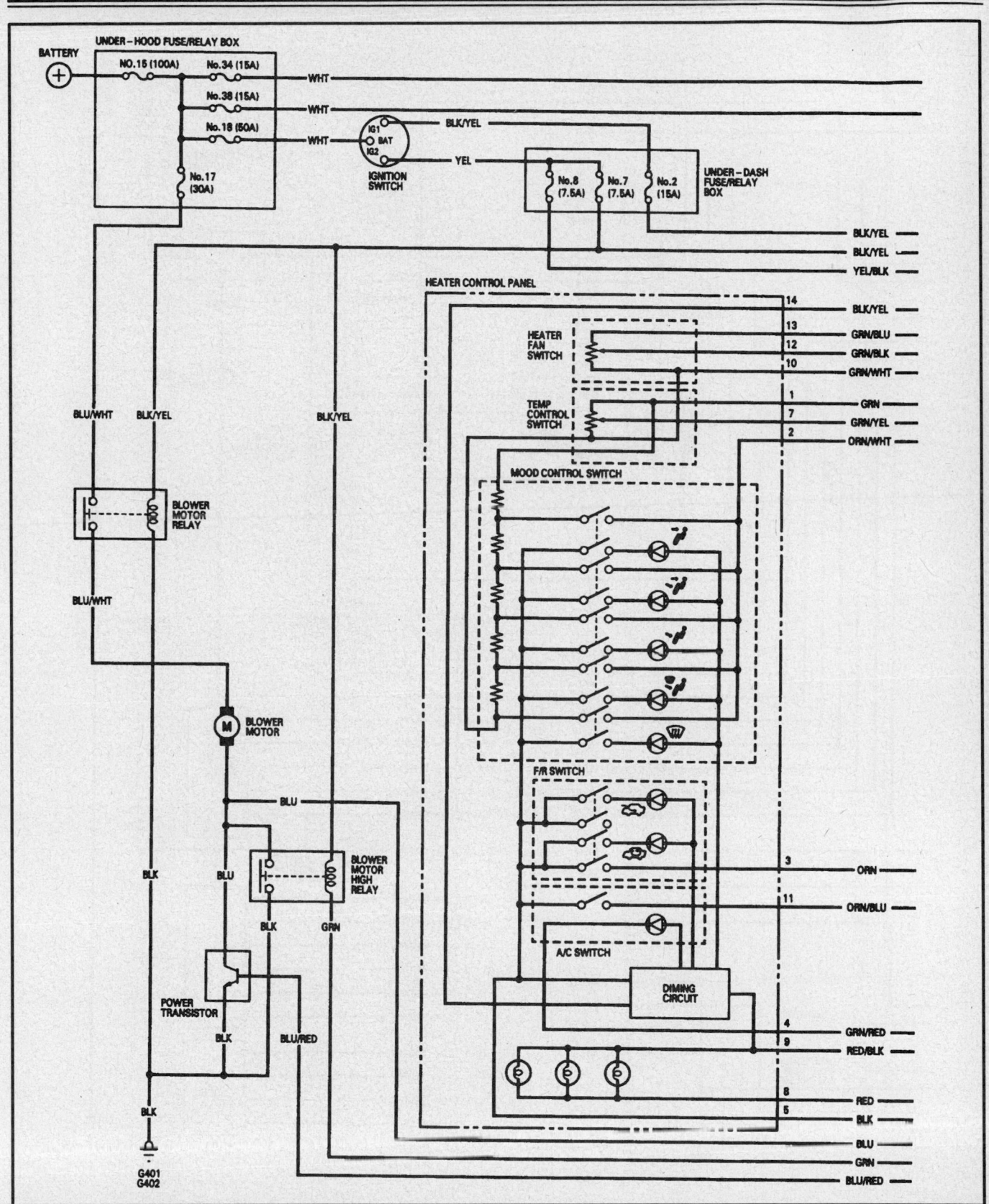

Air conditioning wiring schematic—Vigor

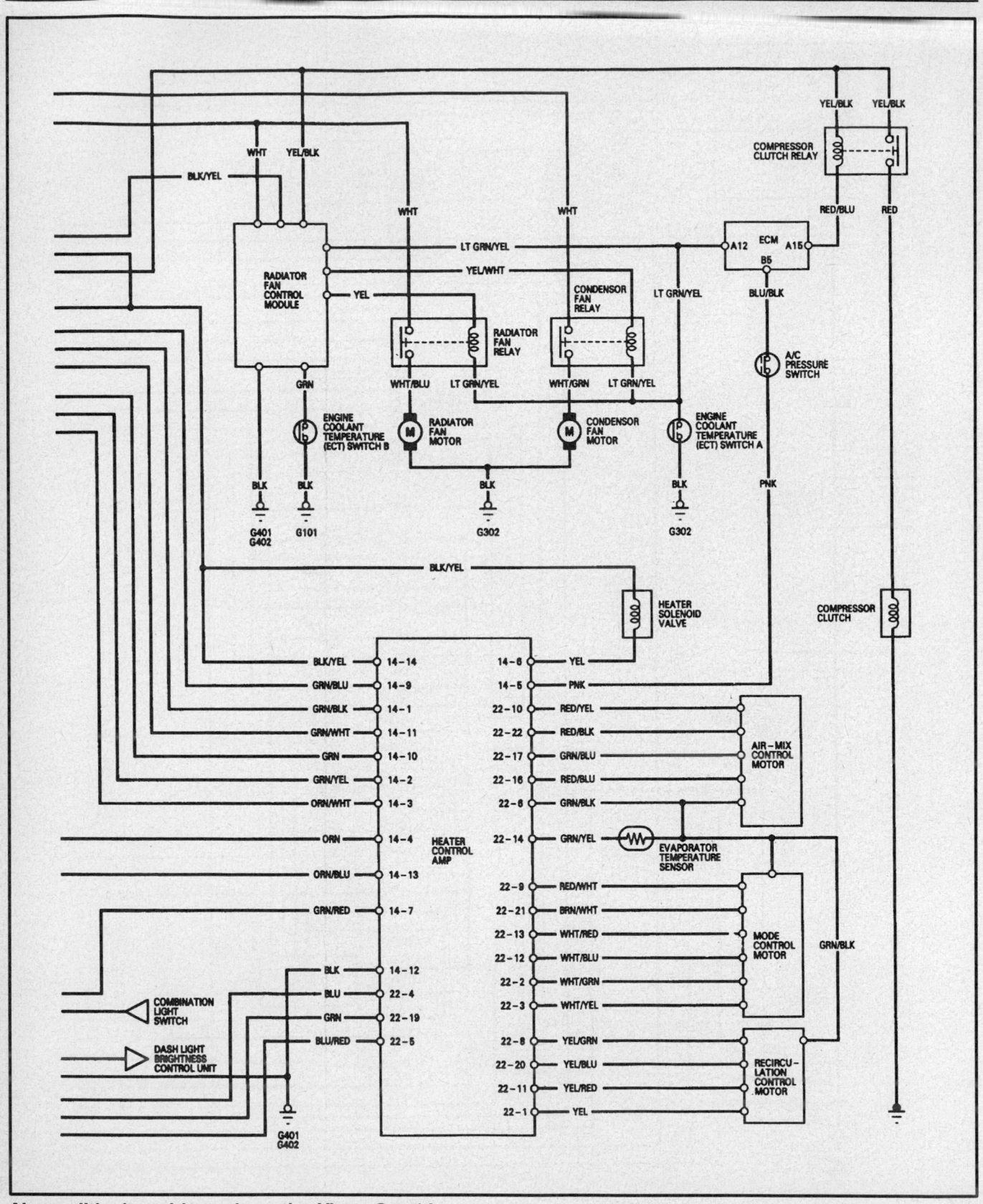

Air conditioning wiring schematic—Vigor, Cont'd

SPECIFICATIONS

ENGINE IDENTIFICATION

Year	Model	Engine Displacement Liters (cc)	Engine Series (ID/VIN)	Fuel System	No. of Cylinders	Engine Type
1993	90S	2.8 (2771)	AAH	MPI	6	OHC
	90CS	2.8 (2771)	AAH	MPI	6	OHC
	90CS Quattro	2.8 (2771)	AAH	MPI	6	OHC
	100	2.8 (2771)	AAH	MPI	6	OHC
	100S	2.8 (2771)	AAH	MPI	6	OHC
	100CS	2.8 (2771)	AAH	MPI	6	OHC
	100CS Quattro	2.8 (2771)	AAH	MPI	6	OHC
	100CS Quattro Wagon	2.8 (2771)	AAH	MPI	6	OHC
	S4 Quattro	2.2 (2226)	AAN	Motronic	5	Turbo 20V
	V8 Quattro	4.2 (4172)	ABH	Motronic	8	OHC 32V
1994	90S	2.8 (2771)	AAH	MPI	6	OHC
	90CS	2.8 (2771)	AAH	MPI	6	OHC
	90CS Quattro	2.8 (2771)	AAH	MPI	6	OHC
	100	2.8 (2771)	AAH	MPI	6	OHC
	100S	2.8 (2771)	AAH	MPI	6	OHC
	100CS	2.8 (2771)	AAH	MPI	6	OHC
	100CS Quattro	2.8 (2771)	AAH	MPI	6	OHC
	100CS Quattro Wagon	2.8 (2771)	AAH	MPI	6	OHC
	S4 Quattro	2.2 (2226)	AAN	Motronic	5	Turbo 20V
	V8 Quattro	4.2 (4172)	ABH	Motronic	8	OHC 32V
1995	90S	2.8 (2771)	AAH	MPI	6	OHC
	90CS	2.8 (2771)	AAH	MPI	6	OHC
	90CS Quattro	2.8 (2771)	AAH	MPI	6	OHC
	100	2.8 (2771)	AAH	MPI	6	OHC
	100S	2.8 (2771)	AAH	MPI	6	OHC
	100CS	2.8 (2771)	AAH	MPI	6	OHC
	100CS Quattro	2.8 (2771)	AAH	MPI	6	OHC
	100CS Quattro Wagon	2.8 (2771)	AAH	MPI	6	OHC
	S6 Quattro	2.2 (2226)	AAN	Motronic	5	Turbo 20V
	V8 Quattro	4.2 (4172)	ABH	Motronic	8	OHC 32V

MPI – Multiport Fuel Injection
OHC – Overhead Camshaft
V – Valve

REFRIGERANT CAPACITIES

Year	Model	Refrigerant (oz.)	Oil (fl. oz.)	Compressor Type
1993	90S	23.0–24.8	7.8–9.2	Zexel
	90CS	23.0–24.8	7.8–9.2	Zexel
	90CS Quattro	23.0–24.8	7.8–9.2	Zexel
	100	21.2–23.0	7.8–9.2	Zexel
	100S	21.2–23.0	7.8–9.2	Zexel
	100CS	21.2–23.0	7.8–9.2	Zexel
	100CS Quattro	21.2–23.0	7.8–9.2	Zexel
	100CS Quattro Wagon	21.2–23.0	7.8–9.2	Zexel
	S4 Quattro	21.2–23.0	7.8–9.2	Zexel
	V8 Quattro	30.0–31.8	7.8–9.2	Zexel
1994	90S	23.0–24.8	7.8–9.2	Zexel
	90CS	23.0–24.8	7.8–9.2	Zexel
	90CS Quattro	23.0–24.8	7.8–9.2	Zexel
	100	21.2–23.0	7.8–9.2	Zexel
	100S	21.2–23.0	7.8–9.2	Zexel
	100CS	21.2–23.0	7.8–9.2	Zexel
	100CS Quattro	21.2–23.0	7.8–9.2	Zexel
	100CS Quattro Wagon	21.2–23.0	7.8–9.2	Zexel
	S4 Quattro	21.2–23.0	7.8–9.2	Zexel
	V8 Quattro	30.0–31.8	7.8–9.2	Zexel
1995	90S	23.0–24.8	7.8–9.2	Zexel
	90CS	23.0–24.8	7.8–9.2	Zexel
	90CS Quattro	23.0–24.8	7.8–9.2	Zexel
	100	21.2–23.0	7.8–9.2	Zexel
	100S	21.2–23.0	7.8–9.2	Zexel
	100CS	21.2–23.0	7.8–9.2	Zexel
	100CS Quattro	21.2–23.0	7.8–9.2	Zexel
	100CS Quattro Wagon	21.2–23.0	7.8–9.2	Zexel
	S6 Quattro	21.2–23.0	7.8–9.2	Zexel
	V8 Quattro	30.0–31.8	7.8–9.2	Zexel

SYSTEM DESCRIPTION

General Information

The models utilize either automatic or manual R-134a air conditioning systems. Audi vehicles utilizing R-134a refrigerant can be identified by an R-134a identification sticker in the engine compartment and by the new style high pressure service valve. The refrigerant flow is standard, flowing from the compressor through the condenser, restrictor, evaporator, accumulator, and back to the compressor.

High and low pressure switches provide compressor cut-off in the event of extremely high or low system pressures. An additional high pressure switch is used to control high speed cooling fan operation. A pressure relief valve mounted on the variable displacement compressor is used also to protect against extreme system pressure. An inductive speed sensor is used to monitor compressor rotation speed. This information is used by the compressor clutch control module (manual systems) or the air conditioning control head (automatic systems) to calculate belt slippage as a percentage of engine speed.

Service Valve Location

The high pressure valve is mounted on the front of the condenser on all models, except for the V8. On the V8, the high pressure service valve is in the high pressure line between the condenser and the evaporator, located on the right side of the engine compartment below the intake air duct. A low pressure service valve is not utilized on Audi air conditioning systems. All refrigerant-related service operations are performed through the high pressure service valve.

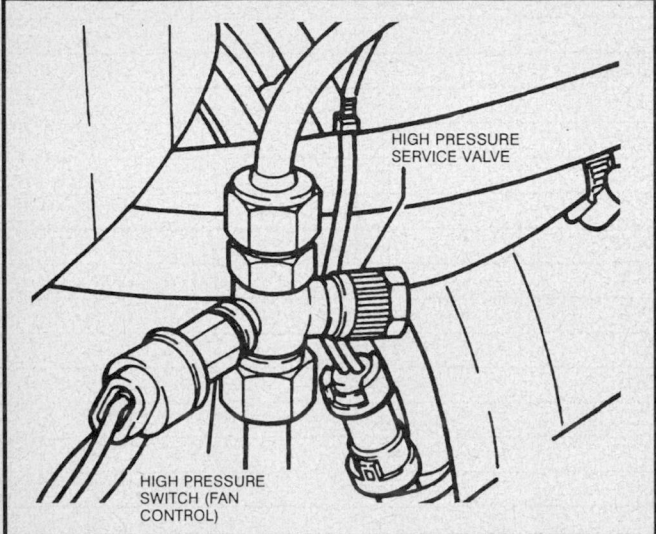

High pressure service valve—V8 Model Shown

Special Precautions

1. All refrigerant service work must be done with the proper recycling equipment. Carefully follow the manufacturer's instructions for use of that equipment. Do not allow any refrigerant to discharge to the air.
2. Any amount of water or contamination will make the system less effective. When any part of the system has been removed, plug or cap the lines to prevent moisture or contaminants from the air entering the system. When installing a new component, do not uncap the fittings until ready to attach the lines.
3. When assembling a fitting, always use a new O-ring and lightly lubricate the fitting with compressor oil. Be careful not to apply lubricant to threaded portions of connections.
4. The proper amount of oil must be maintained in the system to prevent compressor damage and to maintain system efficiency. Be sure to measure and adjust the amount of oil removed or added to the system, especially when replacing the compressor.
5. CFC-12 (R-12) refrigerant and HFC-134a (R-134a) refrigerant, and their respective lubrication oils, are not compatible, and must never be mixed in any amount. Mixing of the refrigerants or their lubrication oils may cause system failure.
6. Use only parts and equipment that are specified for use with R-134a systems.

System Discharging

1. Using the appropriate high pressure coupler, connect the refrigerant recycling equipment to the high pressure service valve according to the manufacturer's instructions. Only the high pressure hose will be connected to the air conditioning system, since a low pressure service valve is not used.

2. Open the adapter or manifold valve slowly to prevent excess oil loss. Allow the refrigerant to stop flowing before going on to the next step.

System Evacuating

1. Open the high pressure valve and run the vacuum pump for more than 5 minutes. The gauges should stabilize at 29.13-29.92 in. (740–760mm) Hg vacuum.
2. Close the valve and turn the pump OFF. Check to see that the vacuum gauge remains stable over time.
3. If the system will not hold vacuum, first check that the service equipment is properly connected and in good working order. If any connections in the vehicle system have been disturbed, make sure they have been properly reconnected. Be sure to use new lightly oiled O-rings and that the fitting is not over torqued.
4. If the system holds vacuum, open the valve and run the pump for more than 25 minutes. Close the valve, then turn the pump OFF.

System Charging

1. Always use recycling/charging station equipment. The equipment in use will determine the exact charging procedure. Carefully follow the manufacturer's instructions and add the correct amount of refrigerant and oil as noted in the specifications chart.
2. All charging is performed through the high pressure service valve. Do not run the engine or operate the air conditioning while recharging the system.
3. With the system fully charged and with the correct oil level in the compressor, manually rotate the compressor 10 rotations before starting the engine. Start the engine with the air conditioning OFF and wait for the engine idle speed to stabilize. After the idle speed has stabilized, turn the air conditioner ON and allow the compressor to run for at least 2 minutes before increasing the engine speed.
4. Stop the engine and immediately check the system for leaks using a suitable leak detector. Be sure to check at every line fitting, the service valves, the pressure switch at the receiver/drier, at the compressor shaft seals, bolt holes and clutch, and the pressure and relief valves.
5. To check the evaporator and valves inside the vehicle, insert the leak detector probe into the water drain hose for more than 10 minutes. Leaking refrigerant is heavier than air and will seek the lower exit, so always look for leaks at the lowest point.

Compressor Oil Service

The compressor is lubricated with oil that circulates with the refrigerant when the system is operating and drops out of the refrigerant when the system is stopped. Insufficient or incorrect oil will cause damage to the compressor. Too much oil will impair the system's cooling ability. When installing new parts of the system or a new compressor, the oil quantity must be adjusted.

NOTE: Systems with R-134a use a special Polyalkylene Glycol (PAG) refrigerant oil which is different from the oil used with R-12. Be sure to use the correct oil type for the specific refrigerant application.

1. If a new compressor is being installed, or if the system is discharged due to a component leak, drain the oil out of the old compressor through the drain plug and measure it. The compressor may be rotated by hand to facilitate the oil draining process.
2. Drain the fresh oil from the new compressor into a clean container and then refill the new compressor with 2.7 oz. (70 ml) of the fresh oil and replace the drain plug. This initial oil amount is necessary to ensure proper system lubrication during start up.

3. If the amount of oil drained from the compressor was greater than 2.7 oz. (70 ml), subtract 2.7 oz. (70 ml) from the total amount drained from the old compressor to find out how much additional oil to add to the system. Add the additional fresh oil amount to the evaporator or the accumulator.

4. New compressors usually come with the full amount of oil, so it is necessary to remove oil to maintain the right system level.

5. If installing another major system component, remove the component and collect the oil from it. Use compressed air to blow through the component so that all of the oil is removed. Measure the amount of oil removed from the component and add the same amount of oil to the new replacement component, plus an additional amount as follows:

- Evaporator – 0.7 oz. (20 ml)
- Condenser – 0.3 oz. (9 ml)
- Accumulator – 1.0 oz. (30 ml)
- Refrigerant line/hose – 0.3 oz. (9 ml)

6. Evacuate and recharge the air conditioning system. Be sure to rotate the compressor manually at least 10 rotations prior to system start up to prevent possible compressor damage.

7. If the recycling/recharging equipment in use provides for oil adjustment during system servicing, follow all of the equipment manufacturer's instructions.

SYSTEM COMPONENTS

NOTE: Some vehicles are equipped with air bag supplemental restraint systems. The manufacturer recommends that both the airbag voltage supply connector (located under a cover on the driver's side lower instrument panel cover) and the battery ground strap be disconnected for work on the airbag system or related systems. After disconnecting power and ground, allow at least 20 minutes for the airbag system to disarm before working on related systems.

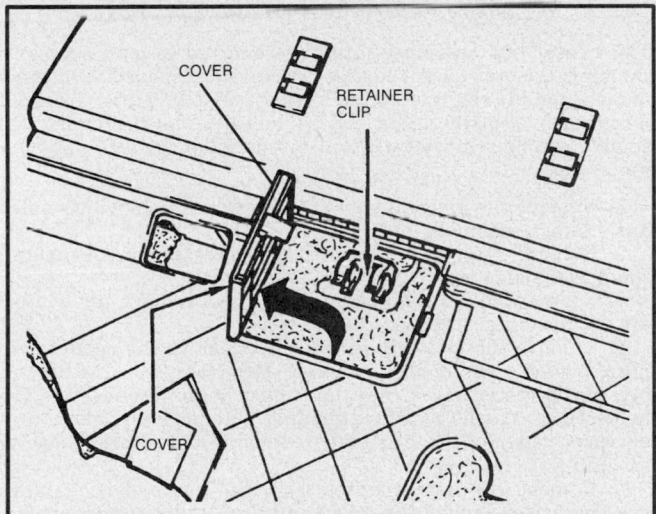

Airbag voltage supply (B+) connector location

NOTE: When removing any component of the refrigerant system, properly discharge the refrigerant into recovery equipment. Do not vent the refrigerant into the air.

Condenser

REMOVAL AND INSTALLATION

NOTE: Refer to the Refrigerant Capacities chart or the vehicle's air conditioner identification label for the correct refrigerant to use. Be sure not to intermix components, refrigerant, oil or service equipment on vehicles using different refrigerant systems.

1. Properly discharge the air conditioning system using recovery equipment.
2. Disconnect the refrigerant lines from the condenser and cap them to prevent moisture from entering the system. Disconnect any electrical connections on condenser-mounted switches.

3. Unbolt and remove the condenser. It may be necessary to remove the radiator to gain access. Drain and measure the oil from the old condenser using compressed air to blow any residual oil out of the component. Add the same amount of fresh oil, plus 0.3 oz., (9 ml) to the replacement condenser.
To install:

4. Installation is the reverse of removal. Be sure to use new O-rings.

5. Do not over torque the fittings or they will be distorted and leak. The inlet fitting should be torqued to 22.1 ft. lbs. (30 Nm). The outlet fitting should be torqued to 11.0 ft. lbs. (15 Nm).

Compressor

REMOVAL AND INSTALLATION

NOTE: Refer to the Refrigerant Capacities chart or the vehicle's air conditioner identification label for the correct refrigerant to use. Be sure not to intermix components, refrigerant, oil or service equipment on vehicles using different refrigerant systems.

1. Properly discharge the air conditioning system using recovery equipment.
2. To gain access to the air conditioning compressor on some vehicles, it may be necessary to remove the sound dampening pan and/or the cooling fan.
3. Mark the direction of travel of the ribbed belt prior to removal so that it may be reinstalled in the same direction. Remove the belt.
4. Disconnect the compressor clutch connector and the compressor speed sensor connector.
5. Remove the refrigerant line bracket, disconnect the refrigerant lines and plug them.
6. Unbolt and remove the compressor.
To install:
7. Installation is the reverse of removal. Be sure to reinstall the belt in the same direction of travel to prevent possible belt failure.
8. Do not over torque the fittings or they will be distorted and leak. The high pressure connection should be torqued to 22.1 ft. lbs. (30 Nm). The low pressure connection should be torqued to 29.5 ft. lbs. (40 Nm).

Accumulator

The manufacturer recommends accumulator and restrictor replacement whenever moisture and/or contamination have entered the air conditioning system.

REMOVAL AND INSTALLATION

NOTE: Refer to the Refrigerant Capacities chart or the vehicle's air conditioner identification label for the correct refrigerant to use. Be sure not to intermix components, refrigerant, oil or service equipment on vehicles using different refrigerant systems.

1. On all models, the accumulator is located in the low pressure side of the air conditioning system, between the evaporator and the compressor.
2. Properly discharge the air conditioning system using recovery equipment.
3. Disconnect the refrigerant lines from the accumulator and cap them to prevent moisture from entering the system.
4. Unbolt and remove the accumulator. Drain and measure the oil from the old accumulator using compressed air to blow any residual oil out of the component. Add the same amount of fresh oil, plus 1.0 oz., (30 ml) to the replacement accumulator.

To install:
5. Installation is the reverse of removal. Be sure to use new O-rings.
6. Do not over torque the fittings or they will be distorted and leak. The inlet and outlet fittings on the accumulator should be torqued to 29.5 ft. lbs. (40 Nm).

Fixed Orifice Tube (Restrictor)

NOTE: The manufacturer recommends accumulator and orifice tube replacement whenever moisture and/or contamination have entered the air conditioning system.

REMOVAL AND INSTALLATION

NOTE: Refer to the Refrigerant Capacities chart or the vehicle's air conditioner identification label for the correct refrigerant to use. Be sure not to intermix components, refrigerant, oil or service equipment on vehicles using different refrigerant systems.

1. The orifice tube is located in the evaporator inlet.
2. Properly discharge the air conditioning system using recovery equipment.
3. Remove the refrigerant line retaining bolt and loosen the refrigerant line clamp at the evaporator. Remove the refrigerant lines from the evaporator and plug or cap all open connections to prevent moisture and contamination from entering the system.
4. Use long needle-nose pliers to remove the orifice tube from the evaporator inlet. Install the new orifice tube into the evaporator inlet with the arrow pointing towards the evaporator. The restrictor should be installed into the inlet as far as it will go, and it should fit tightly.
5. Reinstall the refrigerant lines into the evaporator. Always use new O-rings on the refrigerant line fittings. The refrigerant line-to-evaporator retaining bolt should be torqued to 11.0 ft. lbs. (15 Nm).

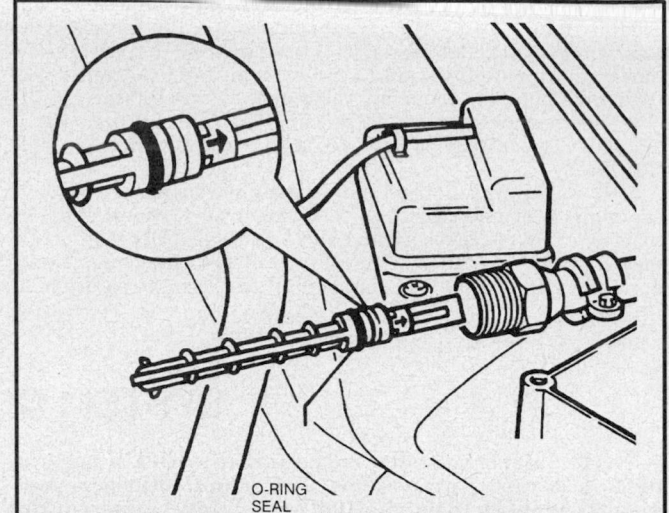

O-RING SEAL

Installing the restrictor—Fixed orifice tube

Blower Motor and Heater Core

REMOVAL AND INSTALLATION

The heater box assembly must be removed to gain access to the blower motor and/or heater core on most models. On some models the blower motor and series resistor can be accessed after removal of the glove compartment. The heater box assembly can be removed without discharging the air conditioning system.

1. Remove the plenum tray and the windshield wiper motor and linkage assembly.
2. Remove the center console, the glove compartment and the driver's side tray.
3. On manual air conditioning systems, remove the heater/air conditioning controls.
4. Remove the footwell air outlets. Remove the rubber coupling between the heater box and evaporator housing assembly, the defroster hoses, and the rubber bellows connecting the heater box and the rear heater duct. Remove any other connections between the heater box and the evaporator housing assembly.
5. Remove the heater hoses from the heater box. Remove the heater box tensioning strap and any other connections between the vehicle and the heater box assembly.
6. The manufacturer recommends the use of an engine support bridge with a claw-type puller (special tools 10-222A/1 and 2075) to loosen the heater box for removal.
7. After removal, the heater box may be disassembled to gain access to the air flaps, blower motor, and heater core.
8. Installation is the reverse of the removal procedure.

Evaporator

REMOVAL AND INSTALLATION

NOTE: Refer to the Refrigerant Capacities chart or the vehicle's air conditioner identification label for the correct refrigerant to use. Be sure not to intermix components, refrigerant, oil or service equipment on vehicles using different refrigerant systems.

The evaporator and housing cannot be disassembled and are replaced as a unit.

1. Properly discharge the air conditioning system using recovery equipment.

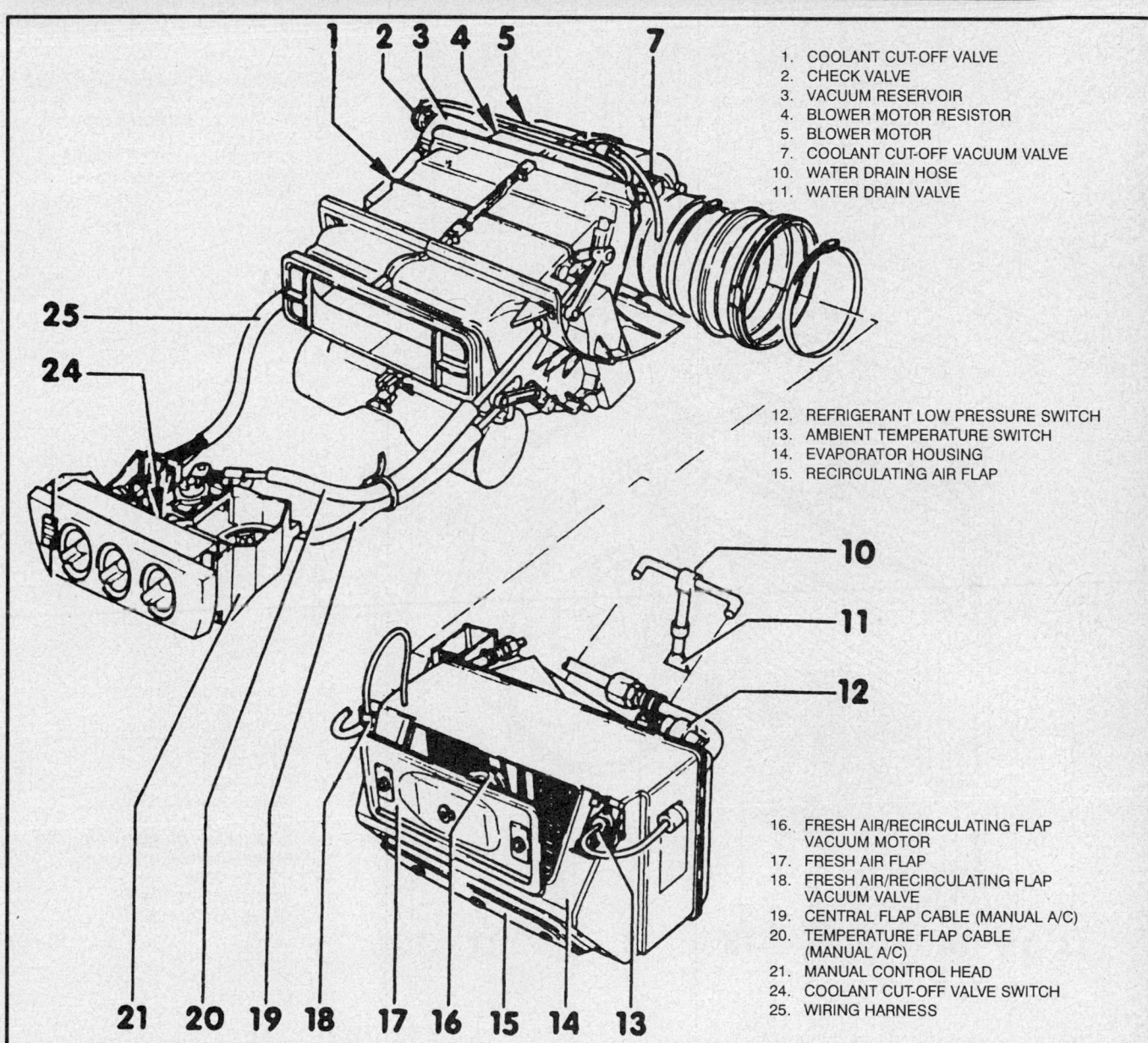

1. COOLANT CUT-OFF VALVE
2. CHECK VALVE
3. VACUUM RESERVOIR
4. BLOWER MOTOR RESISTOR
5. BLOWER MOTOR
7. COOLANT CUT-OFF VACUUM VALVE
10. WATER DRAIN HOSE
11. WATER DRAIN VALVE

12. REFRIGERANT LOW PRESSURE SWITCH
13. AMBIENT TEMPERATURE SWITCH
14. EVAPORATOR HOUSING
15. RECIRCULATING AIR FLAP

16. FRESH AIR/RECIRCULATING FLAP VACUUM MOTOR
17. FRESH AIR FLAP
18. FRESH AIR/RECIRCULATING FLAP VACUUM VALVE
19. CENTRAL FLAP CABLE (MANUAL A/C)
20. TEMPERATURE FLAP CABLE (MANUAL A/C)
21. MANUAL CONTROL HEAD
24. COOLANT CUT-OFF VALVE SWITCH
25. WIRING HARNESS

Heater box and evaporator assembly—Manual shown

2. Remove the glove compartment and the 4 bolts from the evaporator cover. Remove the plenum tray.

3. Disconnect the refrigerant lines from the evaporator. Plug or cap all open refrigerant line connections.

4. Disconnect any remaining connections from the evaporator housing and remove the evaporator housing assembly from the vehicle.

5. If the evaporator assembly is being replaced, drain and measure the oil from the old evaporator using compressed air to blow any residual oil out of the component. Add the same amount of fresh oil, plus 0.7 oz. (20 ml), to the replacement evaporator.

6. Installation is the reverse of removal. Make sure that the water drain hose and the water drain valve are routed and installed correctly and are free of kinks or other obstructions. The refrigerant line-to-evaporator retaining bolt should be torqued to 11.0 ft. lbs. (15 Nm).

Manual Control Head

REMOVAL AND INSTALLATION

1. If the vehicle has a theft protected radio, obtain the owner's security code and disconnect the negative battery cable. If equipped with an airbag system, wait 20 minutes for the system to de-energize before proceeding.

2. Remove the control knobs and the trim plate. Remove the center console.

3. Remove the four retaining screws and remove the control assembly.

4. Installation is the reverse of removal. Control cables are non-adjustable and should be replaced if they are sticking or binding.

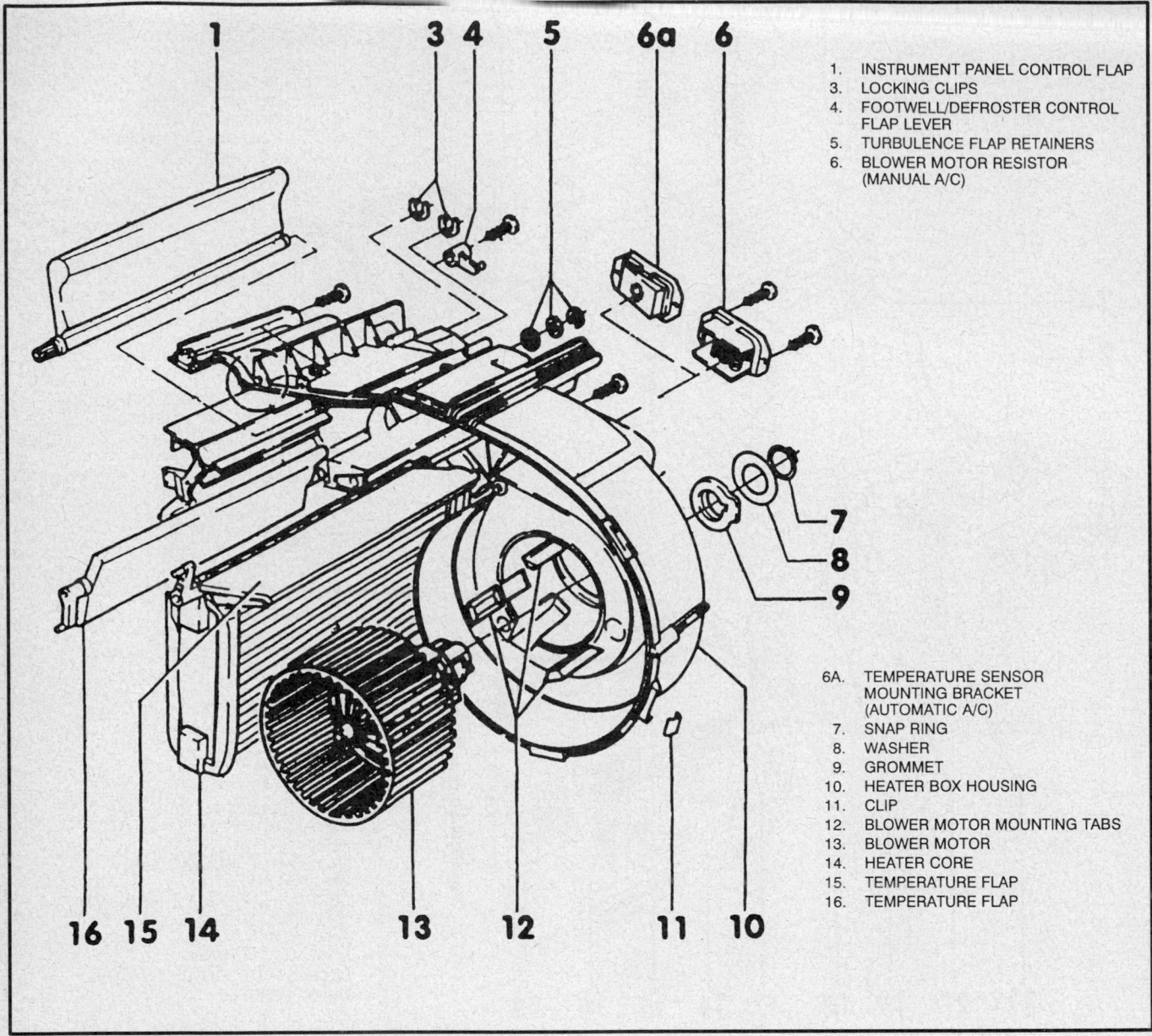

1. INSTRUMENT PANEL CONTROL FLAP
3. LOCKING CLIPS
4. FOOTWELL/DEFROSTER CONTROL FLAP LEVER
5. TURBULENCE FLAP RETAINERS
6. BLOWER MOTOR RESISTOR (MANUAL A/C)

6A. TEMPERATURE SENSOR MOUNTING BRACKET (AUTOMATIC A/C)
7. SNAP RING
8. WASHER
9. GROMMET
10. HEATER BOX HOUSING
11. CLIP
12. BLOWER MOTOR MOUNTING TABS
13. BLOWER MOTOR
14. HEATER CORE
15. TEMPERATURE FLAP
16. TEMPERATURE FLAP

Heater box assembly

Automatic Control Head

REMOVAL AND INSTALLATION

NOTE: Check the Diagnostic Trouble Code memory before removing the control head.

1. With the ignition **OFF**, carefully pry off the trim plate and remove the 2 retaining screws.
2. Remove the control head from the console.
3. Press the connector locking tabs to remove the connectors from the control head.

4. Installation is the reverse of removal.

Temperature Regulator Flap Motor

REMOVAL AND INSTALLATION

1. Remove the plenum tray and the windshield wiper assembly.
2. Remove the cover and retaining screws and remove the temperature regulator flap motor.
3. Installation is the reverse of removal. Make sure that the temperature flap moves freely before installing the motor.

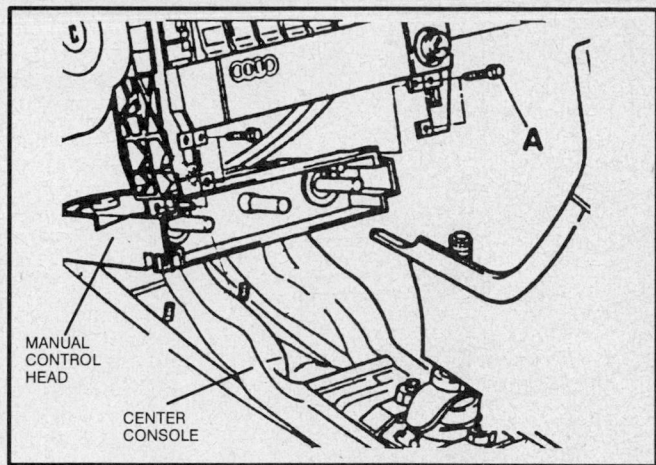

Removing the manual control head

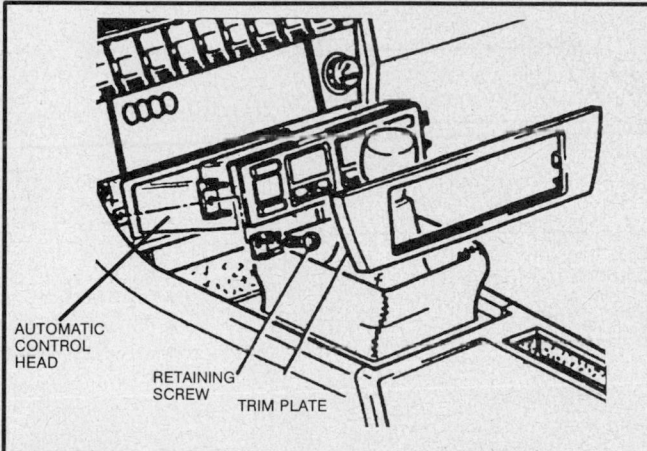

Removing the automatic control head

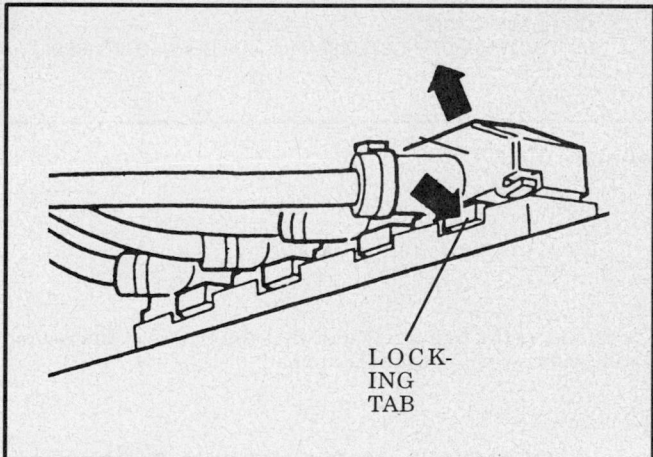

Removing the automatic control head connectors

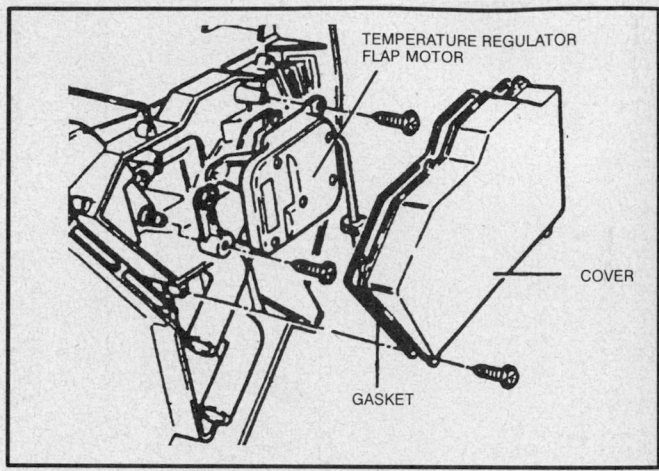

Removing the temperature regulator flap motor

Footwell/Defroster Flap Motor and Central Flap Motor

REMOVAL AND INSTALLATION

1. A support tray contains both motors. Both motors may be replaced after removal of the support tray.
2. Remove the instrument panel center console, glove compartment and driver's side tray.
3. Remove the left and right defroster hoses. Remove the 2 support tray screws on the left side of the heater box and the 2 support tray screws on the right side of the heater box.
4. Remove the red footwell/defroster flap motor connector and the blue central flap motor connector and then remove the support tray from the heater box.
5. Installation is the reverse of removal.

Coolant Cut-off Valve

TESTING

Check for vacuum and coolant leakage. Also check to make sure that the valve moves freely and closes when vacuum is applied.

REMOVAL AND INSTALLATION

Remove the plenum tray to gain access to the valve. Remove the heater hoses and the retaining screw to remove the valve.

Vacuum Reservoir and Check Valve

TESTING

1. Remove the vacuum outlet line (leading to the 2-way vacuum valves) and attach a vacuum gauge to the Reservoir outlet.
2. Start the engine and run it for 1 minute to apply vacuum to the Reservoir.
3. Stop the engine and observe the vacuum gauge. Vacuum loss must not exceed 3 in. (76.2mm) Hg. in 2 minutes.

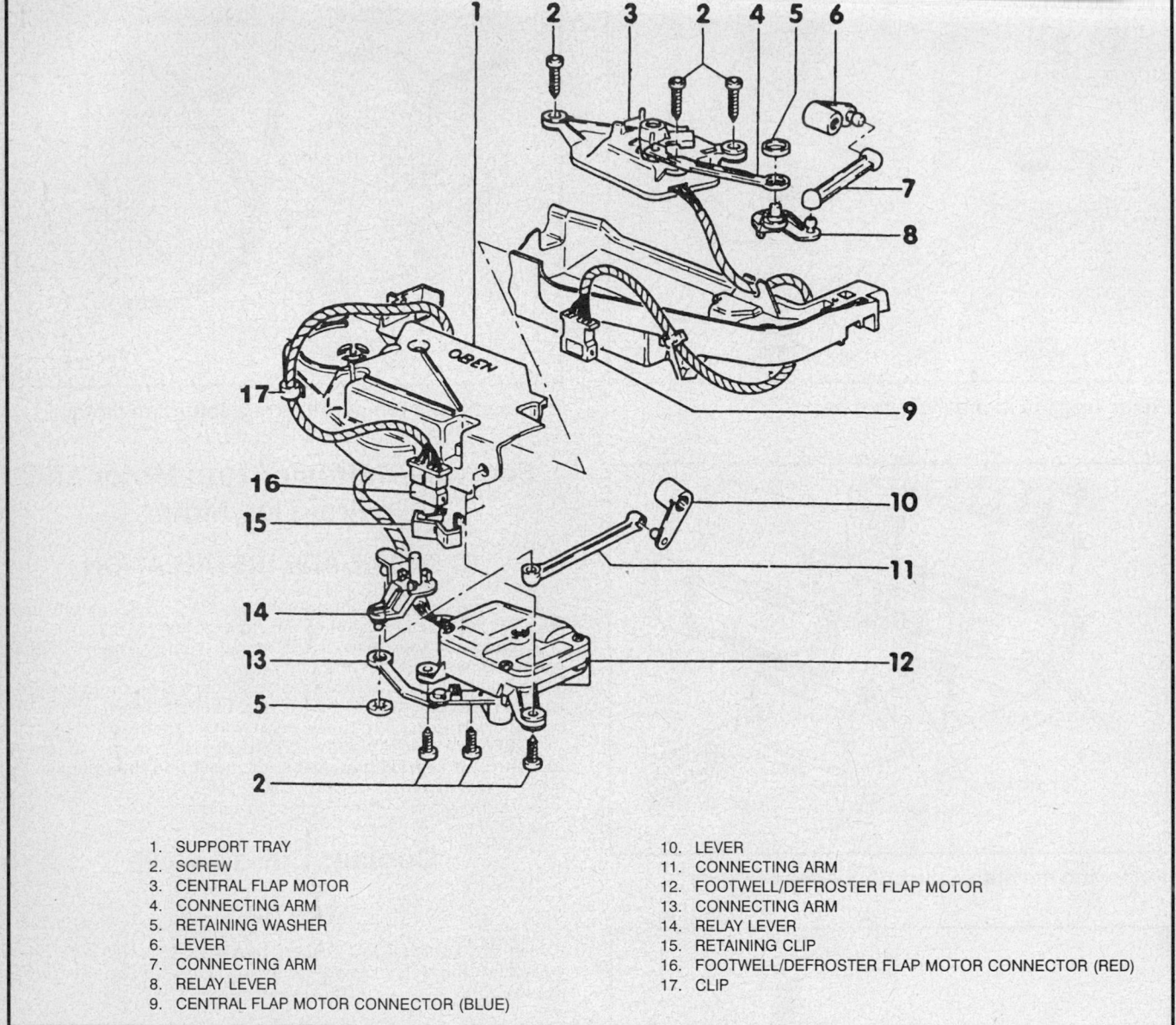

1. SUPPORT TRAY
2. SCREW
3. CENTRAL FLAP MOTOR
4. CONNECTING ARM
5. RETAINING WASHER
6. LEVER
7. CONNECTING ARM
8. RELAY LEVER
9. CENTRAL FLAP MOTOR CONNECTOR (BLUE)
10. LEVER
11. CONNECTING ARM
12. FOOTWELL/DEFROSTER FLAP MOTOR
13. CONNECTING ARM
14. RELAY LEVER
15. RETAINING CLIP
16. FOOTWELL/DEFROSTER FLAP MOTOR CONNECTOR (RED)
17. CLIP

Removing the footwell/defroster and central flap motors—Automatic A/C

REMOVAL AND INSTALLATION

Remove the plenum tray and the coolant cut-off valve to gain access. Remove the retaining screw to remove the reservoir and check valve assembly.

Fresh Air/Recirculating Flap Vacuum Motor

TESTING

Check for vacuum leaks. Also check to make sure that the motor moves the flap freely and that the flap is in the recirculating mode when vacuum is applied.

REMOVAL AND INSTALLATION

1. Remove the plenum tray and rotate the vacuum assembly 90 degrees to remove it from the mount.
2. Disconnect and secure the vacuum hose to prevent it from sliding into the evaporator housing and remove the vacuum motor.

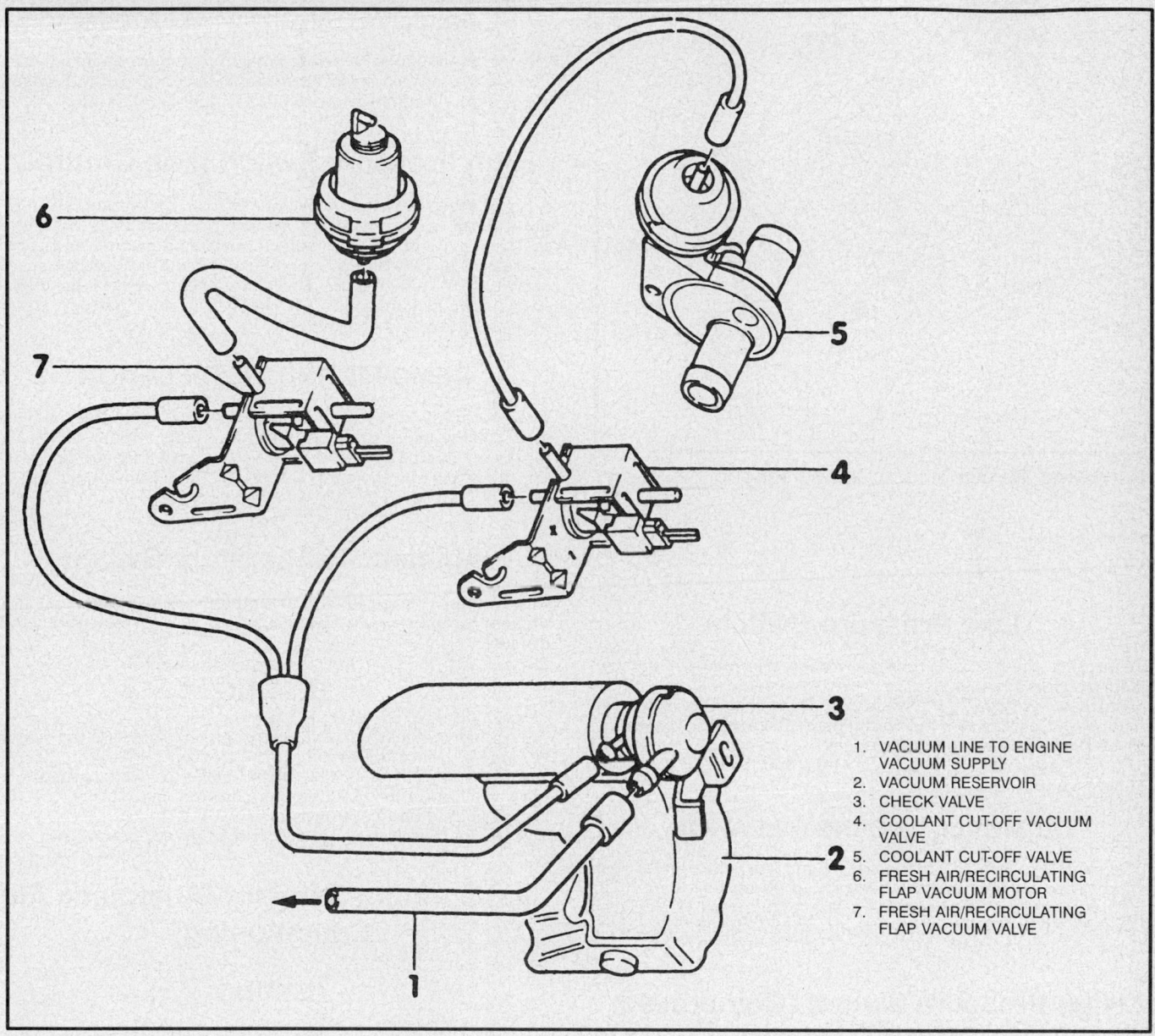

1. VACUUM LINE TO ENGINE VACUUM SUPPLY
2. VACUUM RESERVOIR
3. CHECK VALVE
4. COOLANT CUT-OFF VACUUM VALVE
5. COOLANT CUT-OFF VALVE
6. FRESH AIR/RECIRCULATING FLAP VACUUM MOTOR
7. FRESH AIR/RECIRCULATING FLAP VACUUM VALVE

Vacuum system components—Automatic A/C shown

SENSORS AND SWITCHES

Compressor Speed Sensor

TESTING

1. Turn the ignition **OFF** and disconnect the speed sensor connector.
2. Check the resistance of the sensor with an ohmmeter. Resistance between the two terminals of the sensor should be 1000–1500 ohms.

3. Check for continuity between the sensor terminals and ground. There must be no continuity.

REMOVAL AND INSTALLATION

1. Properly discharge the air conditioning system using recovery equipment.
2. Disconnect the speed sensor connector and unbolt the sensor from the compressor. Check the 4 teeth on the sensor wheel in the compressor for any sign of damage.
3. Installation is the reverse of removal. Torque the sensor mounting bolts to 44 inch lbs. (5 Nm).

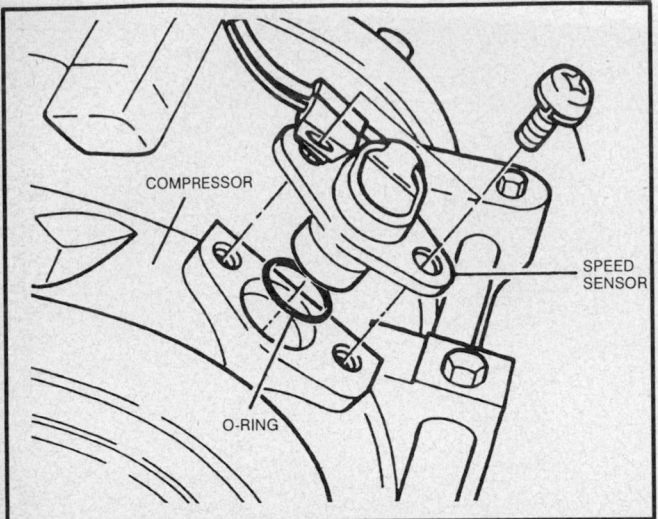

Removing the compressor speed sensor

Low Pressure Switch

To protect the air conditioning compressor against damage from refrigerant loss, the low pressure switch shuts off the compressor clutch if the low side pressure drops below a specified pressure. The switch should open (disengaging the clutch) at 21–23 psi and should close (engaging the compressor clutch) at 42–49 psi. If the switch does not operate as indicated it should be replaced.

REMOVAL AND INSTALLATION

The switch is located on the passenger side interior between the heater housing and the firewall on 90 models, and in the right plenum on other models. The switch may be replaced without discharging the refrigerant system. Torque the switch to 44 inch lbs. (5 Nm).

High Pressure Switch (Compressor Clutch Control)

A high pressure switch is used to disengage the compressor clutch in the event of extreme system pressure. The switch opens (disengaging the clutch) at 409–450 psi and closes (engaging the clutch) at 149–250 psi. If the switch does not operate as indicated it should be replaced.

REMOVAL AND INSTALLATION

The switch has a red housing and is located on the condenser. The switch may be replaced without discharging the refrigerant system. Torque the switch to 44 inch lbs. (5 Nm).

High Pressure Switch (Fan Control)

A high pressure switch is used to switch the cooling fan to second speed operation when system pressure rises beyond a specified pressure. The switch closes (turning on second speed operation) at 206–252 psi and opens (turning off second speed operation) at 170–218 psi. There must be at least 29 psi difference in the switch points. If the switch does not operate as indicated it should be replaced.

REMOVAL AND INSTALLATION

The switch has a green housing and is located on the condenser or on the right side of the engine compartment below the intake air duct. The switch may be replaced without discharging the refrigerant system. Torque the switch to 44 inch lbs. (5 Nm).

Ambient Temperature Switch

The system is equipped with an ambient temperature switch to prevent compressor clutch engagement at low ambient temperatures.

TESTING

1. Remove the switch and attach an ohmmeter to the switch terminals. Place the switch in the freezer.
2. At temperatures below 30°F (–1°C) the switch should be open (no continuity). At temperatures above 45°F (7°C) the switch should be closed (continuity).
3. If the switch does not respond as noted, replace it.

Temperature Sensors (Automatic Air Conditioning)

TESTING

1. After disconnecting the desired temperature sensor (inside temperature, outside temperature, engine coolant temperature), attach an ohmmeter between the sensor harness terminals.
2. The resistance should correspond to the temperatures given in the appropriate charts. If the resistance is not as specified in the chart, replace the sensor.

SYSTEM DIAGNOSIS

System Performance Testing

1. Vehicle must be in a well ventilated area where the engine can be safely run at 2000 rpm, and not in direct sunlight. Make sure the radiator and condenser are free from obstructions. The belt and all of the air ducts and seals must be properly installed. Also make sure that the coupling between the heater box and the evaporator housing is tight and not drawing secondary air.
2. With windows, sunroof, doors and hood closed, operate the system set for full cooling of recirculated air, blower fan on high speed. On manual systems, set the air distribution knob so that air flows from the instrument panel vents.

NOTE: Figures are provided for the sensor digital value as displayed by the automatic air conditioning control head diagnostic channel display.

RESISTANCE VALUES OF INTERIOR TEMPERATURE SENSORS

Inside temperature in °F (°C) at installation location	Diagnostic display Diagnostic channel 2 and 3	Resistance value of inside temperature sensor (ohms)
39 (4)	187	7699
43 (6)	182	6951
46 (8)	177	6308
50 (10)	171	5666
54 (12)	166	5178
57 (14)	160	4690
61 (16)	154	4259
64 (18)	148	3886
68 (20)	142	3513
72 (22)	137	3225
75 (24)	131	2938
79 (26)	125	2683
82 (28)	119	2460
86 (30)	113	2237
90 (32)	108	2062
93 (34)	103	1888
97 (36)	97	1732
100 (38)	92	1595
104 (40)	87	1459
108 (42)	83	1350
111 (44)	78	1242
115 (46)	74	1144
118 (48)	70	1058
122 (50)	65	972

RESISTANCE VALUES OF OUTSIDE TEMPERATURE SENSORS

Outside temperature in °F (°C) at installation location	Diagnostic display Diagnostic channel 4 and 5	Resistance value of outside temperature sensor (ohms)
14 (−10)	188	5836
18 (−8)	183	5097
21 (−6)	177	4558
25 (−4)	171	4088
28 (−2)	165	3588
32 (0)	159	3288
36 (2)	153	2992
39 (4)	146	2697
43 (6)	140	2439
46 (8)	134	2216
50 (10)	127	1995

RESISTANCE VALUES OF OUTSIDE TEMPERATURE SENSORS (CONT'D)

Outside temperature in °F (°C) at installation location	Diagnostic display Diagnostic channel 4 and 5	Resistance value of outside temperature sensor (ohms)
54 (12)	122	1826
57 (14)	116	1657
61 (16)	110	1508
64 (18)	104	1379
68 (20)	98	1250
72 (22)	93	1150
75 (24)	88	1050
79 (26)	83	961
82 (28)	78	883
86 (30)	73	805
90 (32)	69	744
93 (34)	65	683
97 (36)	61	628
100 (38)	57	580
104 (40)	54	532
108 (42)	50	493
111 (44)	47	455
115 (46)	44	421
118 (48)	42	390
122 (50)	39	360
126 (52)	37	335
129 (54)	34	311
133 (56)	32	289
136 (58)	30	269
140 (60)	28	249

RESISTANCE VALUES OF OUTSIDE TEMPERATURE SENSORS

Coolant temperature in °F (°C) at installation location	Diagnostic display Diagnostic channel 4 and 5	Resistance value of coolant temperature sensor (ohms)
−4 (−20)	243	14700
14 (−10)	236	9200
32 (0)	225	5600
41 (5)	219	4635
50 (10)	212	3670
59 (15)	205	3060
68 (20)	195	2450
77 (25)	187	2060
86 (30)	176	1670
95 (35)	167	1415
104 (40)	155	1160
113 (45)	145	995
122 (50)	134	830
131 (55)	124	715

RESISTANCE VALUES OF OUTSIDE TEMPERATURE SENSORS (CONT'D)

Coolant temperature in °F (°C) at installation location	Diagnostic display Diagnostic channel 4 and 5	Resistance value of coolant temperature sensor (ohms)
140 (60)	113	600
149 (65)	104	520
158 (70)	94	440
167 (75)	86	380
176 (80)	76	320
185 (85)	71	281
194 (90)	62	242
203 (95)	57	216
212 (100)	52	190
230 (110)	41	143
248 (120)	33	110
266 (130)	27	90

3 Operate the system for more than 5 minutes with the engine running at 2000 rpm, then use a thermometer to measure the air outlet temperature at the center dash vent.

4. Compare the measured temperature with the values in the outlet temperature chart. Note that the system effectiveness will decrease as the humidity increases.

SYSTEM PERFORMANCE TEMPERATURE CHART

Ambient (Outside) Temperature °F (°C)	Outlet Air Temperature °F (°C)
59 (15)	37–43 (3–6)
68 (20)	37–43 (3–6)
77 (25)	37–43 (3–6)
86 (30)	37–43 (3–6)
95 (35)	38–44 (3.5–6.5)
104 (40)	41–46 (5–8)

5. Only the high side pressure valve is used for checking system pressures. With the engine and ignition OFF, connect the high pressure hose of the refrigerant recycling/recharging unit to the high pressure service valve. Compare the pressure reading to the values in the pressure/temperature chart.

6. If the readings are lower than the specified values, the system is low on refrigerant. Repair the system as necessary and evacuate and recharge the system. If the pressure relief valve has blown, be sure to check for proper cooling fan operation and for possible kinked or restricted refrigerant lines.

7. If the system pressures correspond to the values in the chart, start the engine and set the air conditioning to maximum cooling. Verify that the compressor clutch engages and the compressor is operating. Raise the engine speed to 2000 rpm and note the pressure reading. It should increase to a maximum pressure of 290 psi.

SYSTEM PERFORMANCE PRESSURE CHART

Ambient (Outside) Temperature °F (°C)	Refrigerant Pressure in System (Engine Off) psi (bar)
59 (15)	56.5 (3.9)
68 (20)	68.2 (4.7)
77 (25)	81.2 (5.6)
86 (30)	97.2 (6.7)
95 (35)	113.1 (7.8)
104 (40)	132.0 (9.1)
113 (45)	152.3 (10.5)

Self Diagnostics

MANUAL CONTROL SYSTEM

NOTE: The manufacturer recommends the use of special scan tool VAG 1551 for on-board diagnostics and trouble code retrieval.

AUTOMATIC CONTROL SYSTEM

NOTE: The manufacturer recommends the use of special scan tool VAG 1551 for on-board diagnostics and trouble code retrieval.

In addition to the air conditioning on-board diagnosis utilizing the VAG 1551 scan tool, the digital air conditioning control head on automatic systems can also be used for diagnostic information display and does not require the use of special tools.

1. To access the diagnostic memory switch the ignition ON (or start the engine) and press and hold both the RECIRCULATION button and the upper AIR DISTRIBUTION (up arrow) button.

2. Release both buttons. The control head display should show 01c for channel one.

3. The temperature + and − buttons select the next highest or lowest channels, respectively.

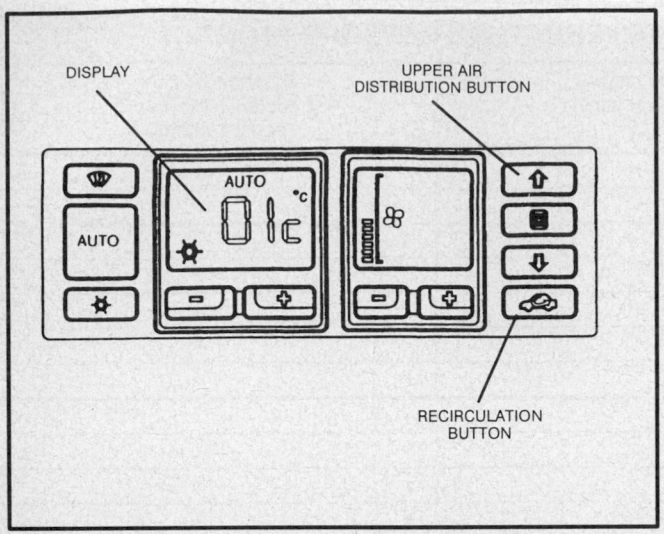

Automatic air conditioning control head

4. Select the desired diagnostic memory channel and access the channel information by pressing the **RECIRCULATION** button while the channel number is displayed on the control head.

5. Diagnostic memory channels provide information regarding specific circuits, and are not trouble codes. Diagnostic trouble codes can be accessed through memory channel **1** and referenced to the DIAGNOSTIC TROUBLE CODE CHART. After repairing failures indicated by diagnostic trouble codes, the trouble codes may be erased from the control head memory by using the VAG 1551 scan tool.

6. Diagnostic memory channel **52** provides a graphic display which will indicate conditions that cause the air conditioning compressor to be shut off. The graphic display can be decoded into its alpha-numeric code by utilizing the proper chart. Graphic segments **g1**, **g2**, and **g3** will illuminate simultaneously if system operation is normal.

7. Diagnostic memory channel **53** provides a graphic display which will indicate active electrical outputs (actuator functions). The graphic display can be decoded into its alpha-numeric code by utilizing the proper chart. Note that the decimal point does not illuminate in this channel. Graphic segments **g1, g2,** and **g3** will illuminate simultaneously if system operation is normal.

8. The diagnostic memory channel display may be exited by pressing the **AUTO** button or by switching the ignition **OFF**.

DIAGNOSTIC MEMORY CHANNEL CHART

Dianostic Channel No.	Display
1	System malfunction—displayed as a Diagnostic Trouble Code (DTC), see chart
2	Digital value of Interior Temperature Sensor, in Headliner
3	Digital value of interior Temperature Sensor, in Instrument Panel
4	Digital value of Fresh Air Intake Duct Temperature Sensor
5	Digital value of Outside Air (Ambient) Temperature Sensor
6	Digital value of Outside Air (Ambient) Temperature Sensor
7	Digital value of Ambient Temperature Sensor at Fresh Air Blower
8	Digital value of Temperature Regulator Flap Motor Potentiometer
9	Delta value of Temperature Regulator Flap
10	Non–Corrected specified value of Temperature Regulator Flap
11	Digital value of Central Flap Motor Potentiometer
12	Specified value of Central Flap
13	Digital value of Footwell/Defroster Flap Motor Potentiometer
14	Specified value of Footwell/Defroster Flap
15	Digital value of Air Flor Flap Motor Potentiometer
16	Specified value of Air Flow Flap
17	Vehicle Speed (km/h)
18	Actual Fresh Air Blower voltage (Volts)
19	Specified Fresh Air Blower voltage (Volts)
20	A/C Compressor (A/C Clutch) voltage (Volts)
21	Number of low voltage occurrences, non–transient
22	Cycle condition of A/C Refrigerant High Pressure Switch
23	Cyclings of the A/C Refrigerant High Pressure Switch
24	Cyclings of the switches, absolute non–fluctuating
25	Analog/Digital value, Kick–Down Switch
26	Analog/Digital value, Engine Coolant Temperature (ECT) Warning Light
27	Cooling value

DIAGNOSTIC MEMORY CHANNEL CHART (CONT'D)

Dianostic Channel No.	Display
28	Engine Speed (RPM)
29	A/C Compressor speed in RPM (Equals Engine Speed x 1.28)
30	Software version
31	Display check (all segments of A/C Control Head display light up)
32	Potentiometer malfunction counter, Temperature Regulator Flap
33	Potentiometer malfunction counter, Central Flap
34	Potentiometer malfunction counter, Footwell/Defroster Flap
35	Potentiometer malfunction counter, Air Flow Flap
36	Feedback value, cold end–stop, Temperature Regulator Flap Motor Potentiometer
37	Feedback value, hot end–stop, Temperature Regulator Flap Motor Potentiometer, max. stop
38	Feedback value, cold end–stop, Central Flap Motor Potentiometer
39	Feedback value, hot end–stop, Central Flap Motor Potentiometer
40	Feedback value, cold end–stop, Footwell/Defroster Flap Motor Potentiometer
41	Feedback value, hot end–stop, Footwell/Defroster Flap Motor Potentiometer
42	Feedback value, cold end–stop, Air Flow Flap Motor Potentiometer (G 113)
43	Feedback valuc, hot end–slop, Air Flow Flap Motor Potentiometer (G 113)
44	Vehicle operation cycle counter
45	Calculated interior temperature (internal software, in digits)
46	Outside (ambient) temperature, filtered, for regulation (internal software)
47	Outside (ambient) temperature, unfiltered, (internal software, in °C)
48	Outside (ambient) temperature, unfiltered (in digits)
49	Malfunction counter for specdometer (vehicle speed) signal
50	Standing time (in minutes)
51	Engine Coolant Temperature (ECT), in *C
52	Graphics channel 1 = 88.8, see chart Note When Diagnostic Channel 52 is selected, "—.–'" is displayed first. A/C compressor switch–off conditions are identified by illuminated segments of the "88.8" display.
53	Graphics channel 2 = 88.8, see chart Note When Diagnostic Channel 53 is selected, "— –'" is displayed first. A/C electrical outputs are identified by illuminated segments of the "88.8" display.
54	Control characteristics
55	Outside (ambient) temperature, in °C or °F depending on °C or °F setting on A/C control head
56	Temperature in °C, from Interior Temperature Sensor, in Headliner
57	Temperature in °C, from Interior Temperature Sensor, in Instrument Panel
58	Temperature in °C, from Fresh Air Intake Duct Temperature Sensor
59	Temperature in °C, from Outside Air (Ambient) Temperature Sensor, front
60	Temperature in °C, from Ambient Temperature Sensor At Fresh Air Blower
61	Software version (latest)

DIAGNOSTIC TROUBLE CODE CHART

Diagnostic Trouble Code (DTC)	Malfunction	Remarks
00.0	No malfunction present	
02.1	Interior Temperature Sensor, in Headliner, static open	Digital default value of 128 is programmed if sensor fails.
02.2	Interior Temperature Sensor, in Headliner, static short	See **DTC** 02.1
02.3	Interior Temperature Sensor, in Headliner, sporadic open	
02.4	Interior Temperature Sensor, in Headliner, sporadic short	
03.1	Interior Temperature Sensor, in Instrument Panel, static open	See **DTC** 02.1
03.2	Interior Temperature Sensor, in Instrument Panel, static short	See **DTC** 02.1
03.3	Interior Temperature Sensor, in Instrument Panel, sporadic open	
03.4	Interior Temperature Sensor, in Instrument Panel, sporadic short	
04.1	Fresh Air Intake Duct Temperature Sensor, static open	Value supplied by Temp. Sensor is used if sensor fails.
04.2	Fresh Air Intake Duct Temperature Sensor, static short	See **DTC** 04.1
04.3	Fresh Air Intake Duct Temperature Sensor, sporadic open	
04.4	Fresh Air Intake Duct Temperature Sensor, sporadic short	
05.1	Outside Air (Ambient) Temperature Sensor, front, static open	Value supplied by Temp. Sensor if used if sensor fails.
05.2	Outside Air (Ambient) Temperature Sensor, front, static short	See **DTC** 05.1
05.3	Outside Air (Ambient) Temperature Sensor, front, sporadic open	Digital default of 128 is programmed if Fresh Air Intake Duct and Outside Air Temperature Sensors fail.
05.4	Outside Air (Ambient) Temperature Sensor, front, sporadic short	
06.1	Engine Coolant Temperature Sensor (**ECT**), A/C, static open	Engine Coolant Temperature is calculated if sensor should fail or is not installed; diagnosis occurs only above 0°C.
06.2	Engine Coolant Temperature Sensor (**ECT**), A/C, static short	See **DTC** 06.1
06.3	Engine Coolant Temperature Sensor (**ECT**), A/C, sporadic open	
06.4	Engine Coolant Temperature Sensor (**ECT**), A/C, sporadic short	
07.1	Air Temperature Sensor At Fresh Air Blower, static open	Programmed corrective value = 0
07.2	Air Temperature Sensor At Fresh Air Blower, static short	See **DTC** 07.1
07.3	Air Temperature Sensor At Fresh Air Blower, sporadic open	
07.4	Air Temperature Sensor At Fresh Air Blower, sporadic short	
08.1	Temperature Regulator Flap Motor Potentiometer, static open	Temperature Regulator Flap Motor will no longer be controlled automatically; manual adjustment only.
08.2	Temperature Regulator Flap Motor Potentiometer, static short	See **DTC** 08.1
08.3	Temperature Regulator Flap Motor Potentiometer, sporadic open	
08.4	Temperature Regulator Flap Motor Potentiometer, sporadic short	
08.5	Temperature Regulator Flap Motor Potentiometer, static block	Motor is cycled; software attempts to eliminate block
08.6	Temperature Regulator Flap Motor Potentiometer, malfunction	
08.7	Temperature Regulator Flap Motor Potentiometer, sporadic block	

DIAGNOSTIC TROUBLE CODE CHART (CONT'D)

Diagnostic Trouble Code (DTC)	Malfunction	Remarks
11.1	Central Flap Motor Potentiometer, static open	Central Flap Motor will no longer be controlled automatically; manual adjustment only.
11.2	Central Flap Motor Potentiometer, static short	See **DTC** 11.1
11.3	Central Flap Motor Potentiometer, sporadic open	
11.4	Central Flap Motor Potentiometer, sporadic short	
11.5	Central Flap, static block	Motor is cycled; software attempts to eliminate block.
11.6	Central Flap Motor Potentiometer, malfunction	
11.7	Central Flap, sporadic block	
13.1	Footwell/Defroster Flap Motor Potentiometer, static open	Footwell/Defroster Flap Motor will no longer be controlled automatically; manual adjustment only.
13.2	Footwell/Defroster Flap Motor Potentiometer, static short	See **DTC** 13.1
13.3	Footwell/Defroster Flap Motor Potentiometer, sporadic open	
13.4	Footwell/Defroster Flap Motor Potentiometer, sporadic short	
13.5	Footwell/Defroster Flap, static block	Motor is cycled; software attempts to eliminate block.
13.6	Footwell/Defroster Flap Motor Potentiometer, failure	
13.7	Footwell/Defroster Flap, sporadic block	
15.1	Air Flow Flap Motor Potentiometer, static open	Digital value internally programmed for limp–home mode.
15.2	Air Flow Flap Motor Potentiometer, static short	See **DTC** 15.1
15.3	Air Flow Flap Motor Potentiometer, sporadic open	
15.4	Air Flow Flap Motor Potentiometer, sporadic short	
15.5	Air Flow Flap, static block	Motor is cycled; software attempts to eliminate block.
15.6	Air Flow Flap Motor Potentiometer, failure	
15.7	Air Flow Flap, sporadic block	
17.0	Vehicle Speed Signal faulty	
18.1	Fresh air blower voltage, static	
18.3	Fresh air blower voltage, sporadic	
20.1	A/C compressor voltage not OK – static	Compressor remains off until voltage is greater than 10.8 V for at least 25 seconds
20.3	A/C compressor voltage not OK – sporadic	
22.1	A/C Refrigerant High Pressure Switch, static open	Compressor remains off until switch closes.
22.3	A/C Refrigerant High Pressure Switch, sporadic open	
22.5	A/C Refrigerant High Pressure Switch, 120X open	Compressor re-engagement circuit, **VAG 1551** Scan Tool **(ST)** function
29.1	Belt slip detection "soft", static	
29.2	Belt slip detection "hard", static	
29.3	Belt slip detection "soft", sporadic	
29.4	Belt slip detection "hard", sporadic	

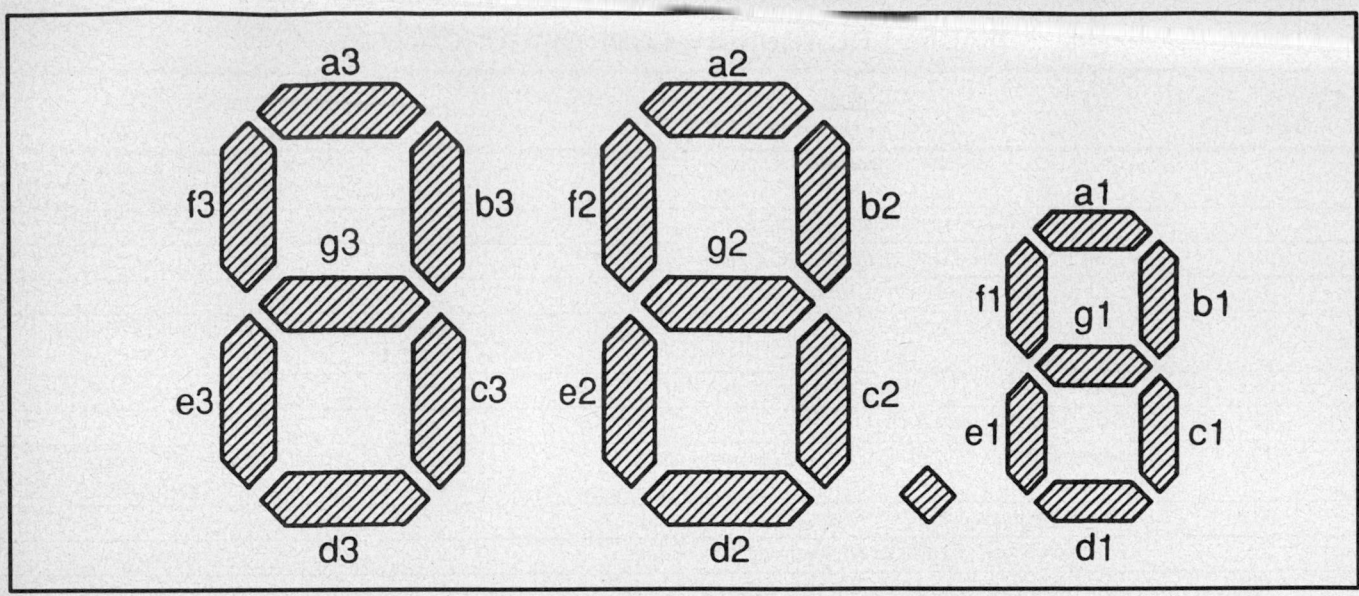

Graphics display—Diagnostic channels 52 and 53

CHANNEL 52 GRAPHICS CODES

NOTE: Decimal point visible – A/C compressor ON
       Decimal point not visible – A/C compressor OFF

Illuminated Segment	Condition
A1	Slippage of blockage, A/C Refrigerant High Pressure Switch, 120x off
B1	Engine Speed (RPM) less than 200–500
C1	—
D1	Engine Speed (RPM) greater than 6000
E1	—
F1	—
G1 ①	Normal system operation
A2	A/C manually switched off (A/C standby cancelled)
B2	Low voltage
C2	Kick–down switch (via Transmission Control Module (TCM), compressor off for 12 seconds max.)
D2	Engine Coolant Temperature (ETC) warning light switch
E2	A/C Refrigerant Low Pressure Switch
F2	A/C Refrigerant High Pressure Switch
G2 ①	Normal system operation
A3	ECON mode selected
B3	OFF selected
C3	Outside (ambient) temperature too low
D3	Engine management system (compressor will remain off for 3 – 12 seconds)
E3	High pressure occurrences more than 30 times
F3	Ambient Temperature Sensor at blower motor less than 27°F (–3°C)
G3 ①	Normal system operation

① Segments G1, G2, and G3 will illuminate simultaneously to indicate
   normal system operation.

CHANNEL 53 GRAPHICS CODES

NOTE: Decimal point does not illuminate in this channel

Illuminated Segment	Condition
A1	Fan for interior temperature sensor
B1	Fresh air/recirculation flap closed (recirculation mode)
C1	Heater valve closed
D1	Bi–directional wiring harness
E1	A/C compressor on
F1	Coolant fan first speed on
G1 ①	Normal system operation
A2	——
B2	Air flow flap open
C2	Air flow flap closed
D2	——
E2	Footwell/defrost flap in footwell position
F2	Footwell/defroster flap in defrost position
G2 ①	Normal system operation
A3	——
B3	Central flap in instrument panel outlet position
C3	Central flap in footwell outlet/defrost position
D3	——
E3	Temperature flap in cold air position
F3	Temperature flap in warm air position
G3 ①	Normal system operation

① Segments G1, G2, and G3 will illuminate simultaneously to indicate
normal system operation.

COMPONENT LAYOUTS

The following figures provide component layouts for all the main components, switches, sensors and relays on Audi models. Use these locations for service and diagnostic help.

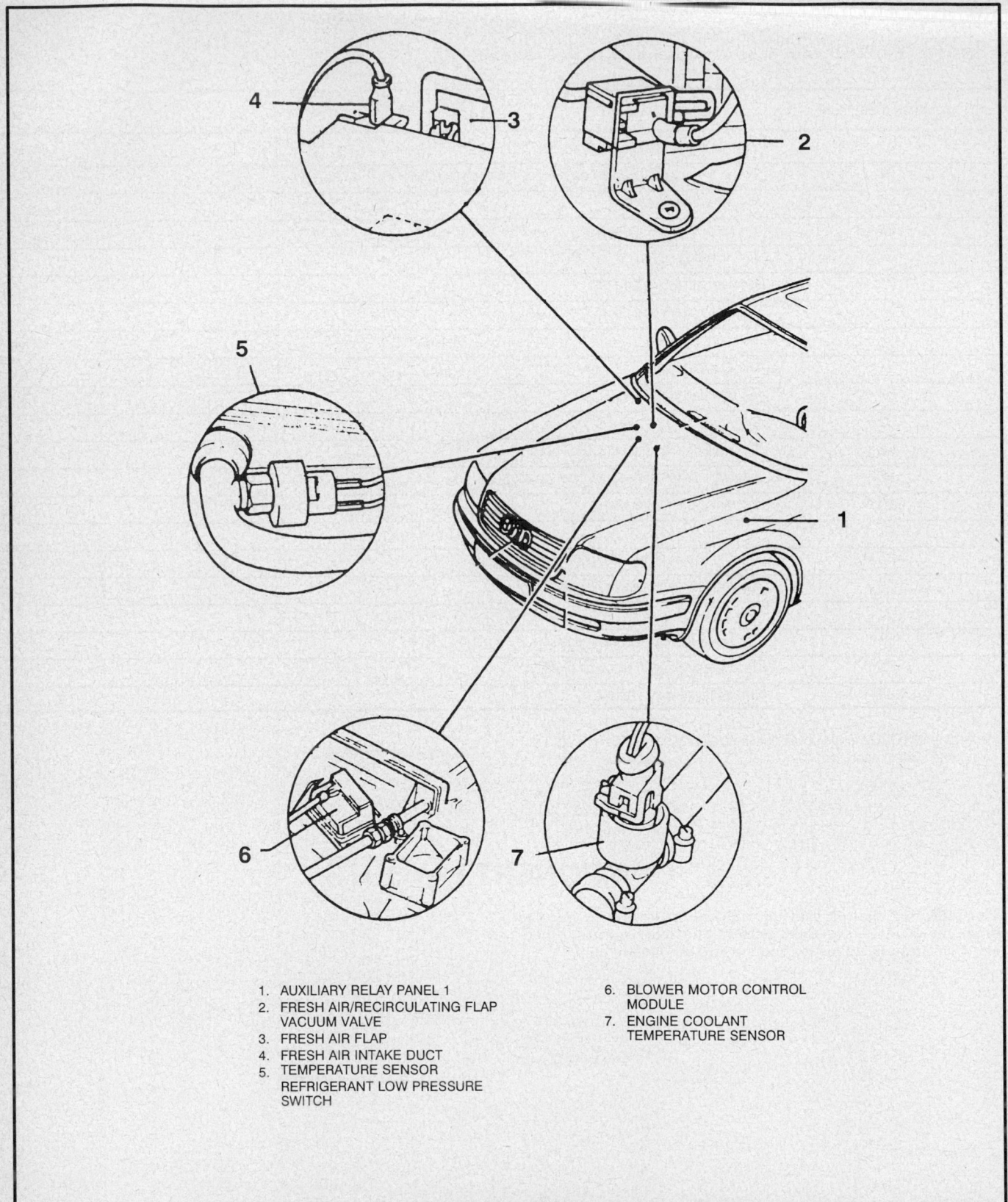

1. AUXILIARY RELAY PANEL 1
2. FRESH AIR/RECIRCULATING FLAP
   VACUUM VALVE
3. FRESH AIR FLAP
4. FRESH AIR INTAKE DUCT
5. TEMPERATURE SENSOR
   REFRIGERANT LOW PRESSURE
   SWITCH

6. BLOWER MOTOR CONTROL
   MODULE
7. ENGINE COOLANT
   TEMPERATURE SENSOR

Automatic air conditioning components—Engine compartment

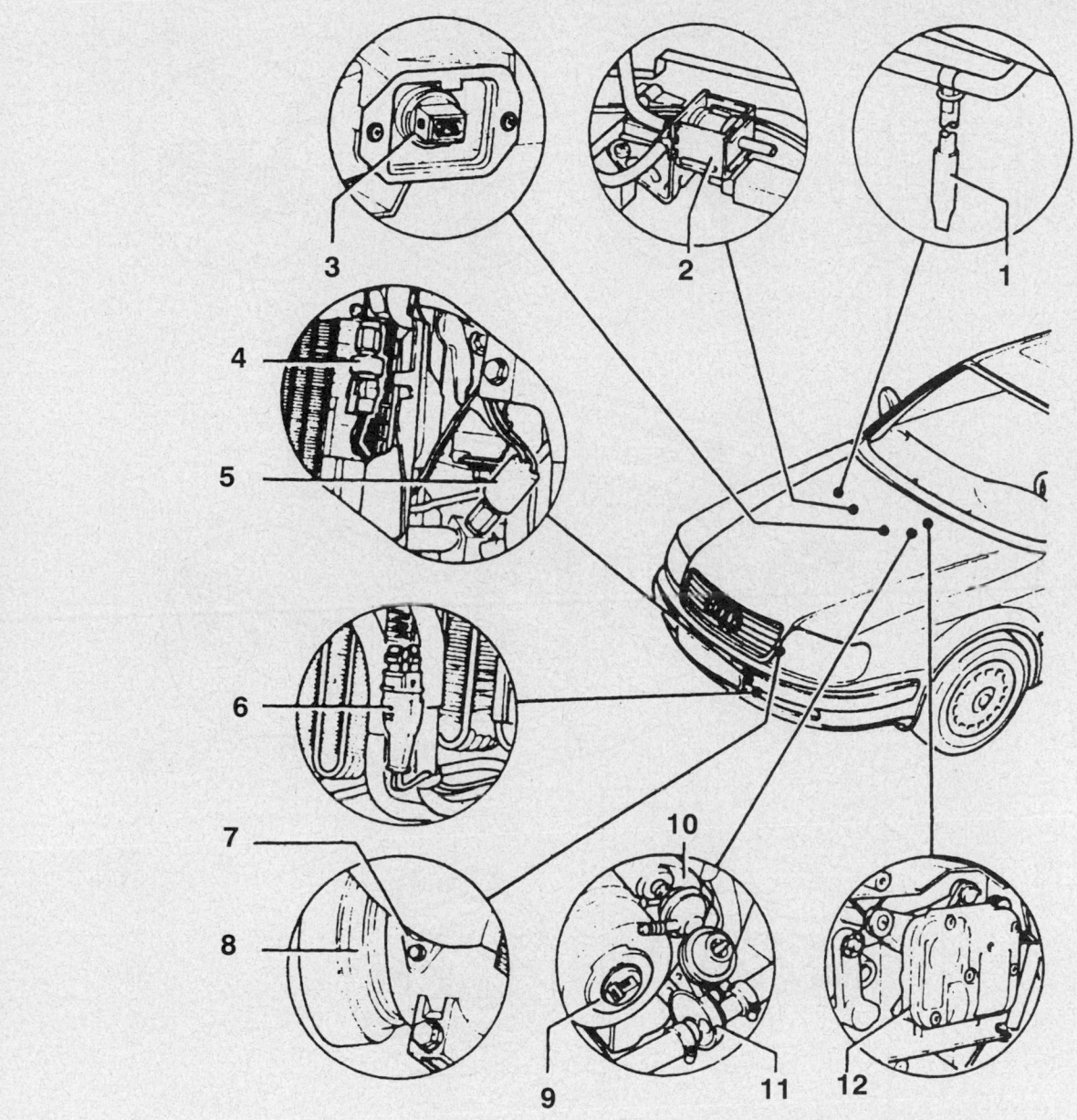

1. EVAPORATOR DRAIN HOSE AND VALVE
2. COOLANT CUT-OFF VACUUM VALVE
3. BLOWER MOTOR TEMPERATURE SENSOR
4. REFRIGERANT HIGH PRESSURE SWITCH
   (COMPRESSOR CLUTCH CONTROL)
5. REFRIGERANT HIGH PRESSURE SWITCH
   (FAN CONTROL)
6. OUTSIDE TEMPERATURE SENSOR
7. COMPRESSOR SPEED SENSOR

8. COMPRESSOR CLUTCH
9. BLOWER MOTOR
10. VACUUM CHECK VALVE AND RESERVOIR
11. COOLANT CUT-OFF VALVE
12. TEMPERATURE REGULATOR FLAP MOTOR

Automatic air conditioning components—Engine compartment Cont'd

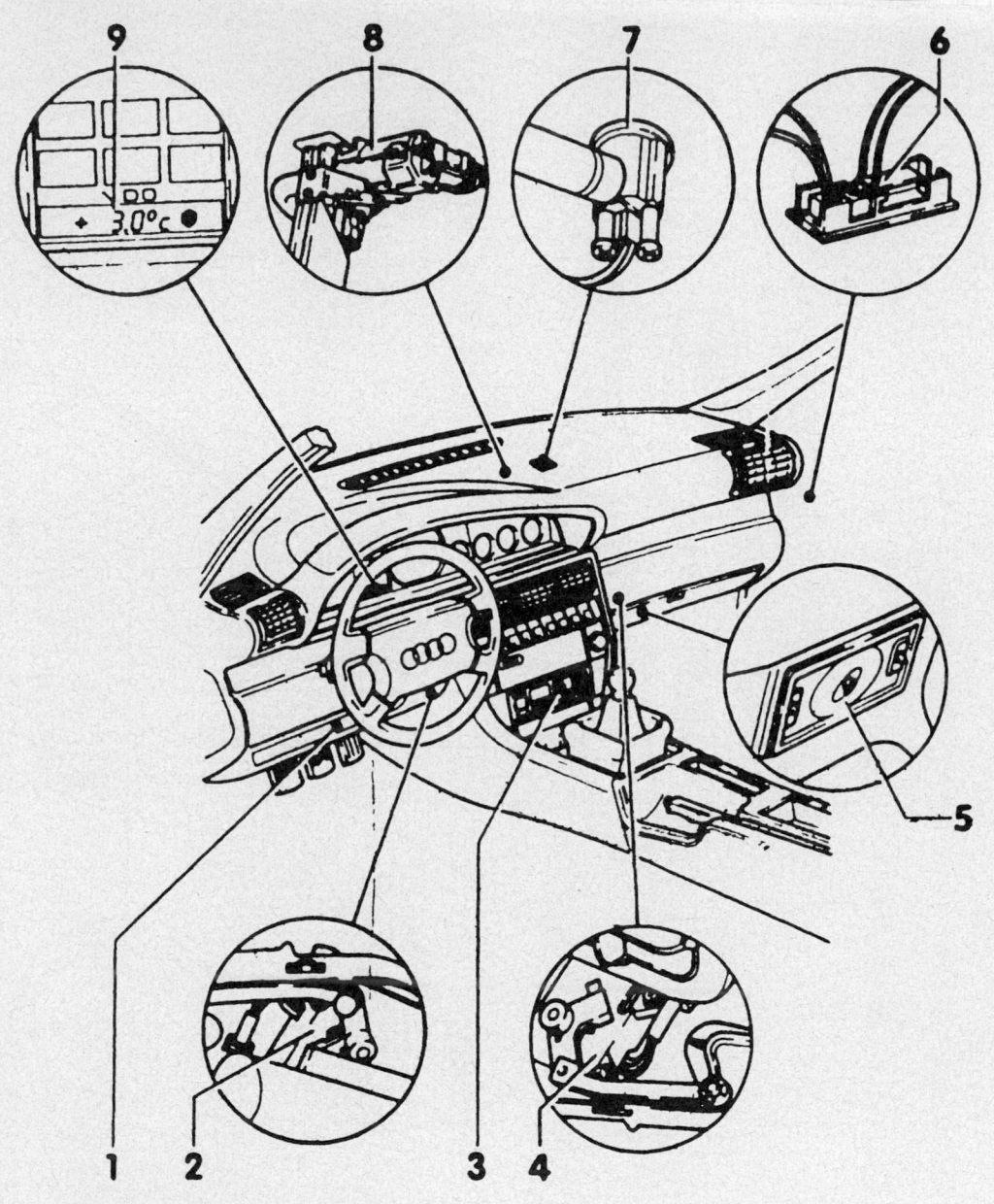

1. A/C KICKDOWN SWITCH
2. FOOTWELL/DEFROSTER FLAP MOTOR
3. A/C CONTROL HEAD
4. CENTRAL FLAP MOTOR
5. RECIRCULATING AIR FLAP
6. INTERIOR TEMPERATURE SENSOR (HEADLINER)
7. INTERIOR TEMPERATURE SENSOR (INSTRUMENT PANEL)
8. INTERIOR TEMPERATURE SENSOR FAN
9. OUTSIDE TEMPERATURE INDICATOR

Automatic air conditioning components—Passenger compartment

SPECIFICATIONS

ENGINE IDENTIFICATION

Year	Model	Engine Displacement Liters (cc)	Engine Series (ID/VIN)	Fuel System	No. of Cylinders	Engine Type
1993	318i	1.8 (1796)	M42	Motronic	4	DOHC
	318iS	1.8 (1796)	M42	Motronic	4	DOHC
	325i	2.5 (2494)	M20B25	Motronic	6	OHC
	325iS	2.5 (2494)	M20B25	Motronic	6	OHC
	525i	2.5 (2494)	M50B25L	Motronic	6	DOHC
	535i	3.5 (3430)	M30B35M	Motronic	6	OHC
	735i	3.5 (3430)	M30B35M	Motronic	6	OHC
	735iL	3.5 (3430)	M30B35M	Motronic	6	OHC
	M5	3.6 (3535)	S38Z	Motronic	6	DOHC
	750iL	5.0 (4988)	M70B50M	Motronic	12	OHC
	850i	5.0 (4988)	M70B50M	Motronic	12	OHC
	850Ci	5.0 (4988)	M70B50M	Motronic	12	OHC
1994	318i	1.8 (1796)	M42	Motronic	4	DOHC
	318iS	1.8 (1796)	M42	Motronic	4	DOHC
	325i	2.5 (2494)	M20B25	Motronic	6	OHC
	325iS	2.5 (2494)	M20B25	Motronic	6	OHC
	325iC	2.5 (2494)	N.A.	Motronic	6	DOHC
	525i	2.5 (2494)	M30B35M	Motronic	6	DOHC
	530i	3.0 (N.A.)	N.A.	Motronic	8	DOHC
	540i	4.0 (N.A.)	N.A.	Motronic	8	DOHC
	740i	4.0 (N.A.)	N.A.	Motronic	8	DOHC
	740iL	4.0 (N.A.)	N.A.	Motronic	8	DOHC
1995	318i	1.8 (1796)	M42	Motronic	4	DOHC
	318iS	1.8 (1796)	M42	Motronic	4	DOHC
	325i	2.5 (2494)	M20B25	Motronic	6	OHC
	325iS	2.5 (2494)	M20B25	Motronic	6	OHC
	325iC	2.5 (2494)	N.A.	Motronic	6	DOHC
	525i	2.5 (2494)	M30B35M	Motronic	6	DOHC
	525iT	2.5 (2494)	M30B35M	Motronic	6	DOHC
	530i	3.0 (N.A.)	N.A.	Motronic	8	DOHC
	530iT	3.0 (N.A.)	N.A.	Motronic	8	DOHC
	540i	4.0 (N.A.)	N.A.	Motronic	8	DOHC
	740i	4.0 (N.A.)	N.A.	Motronic	8	DOHC

OHC–Overhead cam
DOHC–Dual overhead cam
N.A.–Not available

REFRIGERANT CAPACITIES

Year	Model	Refrigerant (oz.)	Oil (fl. oz.)	Compressor Type
1993③	318i	33-35	6.7①	Vane type
	318iS	33-35	6.7①	Vane type
	325i	33-35	6.7①	Vane type
	325iS	33-35	6.7①	Vane type
	525i	52-54②	6.7①	Vane type
	535i	52-54②	6.7①	Vane type
	735i	52-54②	6.7①	Vane type
	735iL	52-54②	6.7①	Vane type
	M5	52-54②	6.7①	Vane type
	750iL	52-54②	6.7①	Vane type
	850i	52-54②	6.7①	Vane type
	850Ci	52-54②	6.7①	Vane type
1994	318i	33-35	6.7①	Vane type
	318iS	33-35	6.7①	Vane type
	325i	33-35	6.7①	Vane type
	325iS	33-35	6.7①	Vane type
	325IC	④	④	④
	525i	52-54②	6.7①	Vane type
	530i	④	④	④
	540i	④	④	④
	740i	④	④	④
	740iL	④	④	④
1995	318i	33-35	6.7①	Vane type
	318iS	33-35	6.7①	Vane type
	325i	33-35	6.7①	Vane type
	325iS	33-35	6.7①	Vane type
	325iC	④	④	④
	525i	52-54②	6.7①	Vane type
	525iT	④	④	④
	530i	④	④	④
	530iT	④	④	④
	540i	④	④	④
	740i	④	④	④

① With swash plate type compressor: 10.1 oz
② With 22.5 in wide condenser: 67-69 oz
③ Several models use R-134a refrigerant and corresponding oil;
   not compatible with R-12, R-12 type oil or R-12 type components
④ Information is not available

AIR CONDITIONING BELT TENSION

Year	Model	Engine Liters (cc)	Belt Type	Specifications New	Specifications Used
1993	318i	1.8 (1796)	V-belt	①	①
	318iS	1.8 (1796)	V-belt	①	①
	325i	2.5 (2494)	V-belt	①	①
	325iS	2.5 (2494)	V-belt	①	①
	525i	2.5 (2494)	V-belt	①	①
	535i	3.5 (3430)	V-belt	①	①
	735i	3.5 (3430)	Ribbed	②	②
	735iL	3.5 (3430)	Ribbed	②	②
	M5	3.6 (3535)	V-belt	①	①
	750iL	5.0 (4988)	Ribbed	②	②
	850i	5.0 (4988)	Ribbed	②	②
	850Ci	5.0 (4988)	Ribbed	②	②
1994	318i	1.8 (1796)	V-belt	④	①
	318iS	1.8 (1796)	V-belt	④	①
	325i	2.5 (2494)	V-belt	④	①
	325iS	2.5 (2494)	V-belt	④	①
	325iC	2.5 (2494)	④	④	④
	525i	2.5 (2494)	V-belt	④	①
	530i	3.0 ③	④	④	④
	540i	4.0 ③	④	④	④
	740i	4.0 ③	④	④	④
	740iL	4.0 ③	④	④	④
1995	318i	1.8 (1796)	V-belt	①	①
	318iS	1.8 (1796)	V-belt	①	①
	325i	2.5 (2494)	V-belt	①	①
	325iS	2.5 (2494)	V-belt	①	①
	325iC	2.5 (2494)	④	④	④
	525i	2.5 (2494)	V-belt	①	①
	525iT	2.5 (2494)	④	④	④
	530i	3.0 ③	④	④	④
	530iT	3.0 ③	④	④	④
	540i	4.0 ③	④	④	④
	740i	4.0 ③	④	④	④

① Use the standard deflection method to adjust. The belt should deflect no more than 1/2 inch under moderate pressure at the longest span between 2 pulleys.
② Automatic belt tensioning.
③ (cc) is not available
④ Not available

SYSTEM DESCRIPTION

General Information

The heating system on models with manually controlled systems is an air side controlled unit, where the temperature is regulated by the mixing of cold and warm air using a mixing flap. All outlets can deliver heated air using cable operated flaps. The water flow rate through the heater is regulated by an electromagnetic water valve in the water return circuit. The water valve is switched ON and OFF by the temperature control. The valve will be closed when the temperature is set to less than 68°F. The valve is normally open when no electric power is being supplied.

When air conditioning is selected, the refrigerant is injected through an expansion valve, which is located in the right side of the evaporator housing. The system uses an evaporator temperature sensor which provides signals to the solid state evaporator temperature regulator. In turn, it signals the compressor to cycle ON and OFF according to temperature needs and prevents evaporator core freezing.

The refrigerant pressure switch is also in the same circuit and monitors the high side system pressures. It will cut off the compressor if pressure falls below 22 psi, such as with refrigerant loss due to system failure or collision; it will also stop the compressor if system pressure builds above 435 psi. If the compressor clutch is de-energized, the collapsing magnetic field induces a voltage in the winding. The clutch diode provides a path to ground for the resulting current.

The control flaps are located in front of both of the blower motors and are controlled by 2 positioning motors.

As part of the air conditioning system, a 2 speed auxiliary fan is included, to aid in system cooling. The fan always runs in the first speed, when the air conditioning is switched ON. Regardless of air conditioner operation, the first speed of the auxiliary fan is switched ON when the coolant temperature is 192–199°F, (288–300°C) as determined by the coolant temperature sensor. The fan is switched OFF at a coolant temperature of 180–187°F (266–279°C).

The second speed of the auxiliary fan, regardless of air conditioner operation, is activated at a coolant temperature range of 207–214°F (315–328°C). The circuit bypasses the normal speed resistor and the fan runs at high speed. It is turned OFF at a coolant temperature of 194–201°F (291–304°C).

The system is equipped with both a high and low pressure cutoff switch, located at the receiver/drier. The high pressure switch stops the compressor when the refrigerant pressure rises above 252–363 psi and switches the compressor back on when the pressure drops below 284–320 psi. The low pressure switch stops the compressor when the refrigerant pressure drops to 24–32 psi and switches the compressor on when the pressure rises above 28–34 psi.

System Controls

All vehicles can be equipped with either a manual or automatic climate control system. The manual system is controlled by a combination of button, slide and rotary controls. The automatic system is controlled by a combination of rotary dials and push buttons.

The 5, 7 and 8-Series vehicles equipped with automatic climate control also have a separate control for the passenger compartment. This control operates independently of the main control head.

As an option, 5, 7 and 8-Series vehicles have an extra ventilation system. This system can be programmed to vent the passenger compartment when the vehicle is parked. The ventilation is controlled by a timer in conjunction with the automatic climate control system. It shares components with the climate control system in addition to it's own timer and relays. It operates the blower at low speed and controls the position of the vent flaps, all dependent on interior temperature.

Supplemental Restraint System

Air bag systems must be disabled prior to working on key components, especially around the instrument panel and steering column to avoid accidental deployment and possible injury. The driver's air bag generator and seat belt tensioner generator on the passenger's side connectors are equipped with shorting bridges. These bridges short the generator leads together when the connectors are disconnected to prevent unintentional triggering of the air bag igniter.

Only special tool 62 1260 (test lead) should be used to check the wire and loop igniter resistance.

Service Valve Location

The service valves for both the high and low pressure sides of the air conditioning system, are located in the pressure lines. They can be either at the compressor or the drier. The thinner of the 2 pressure lines is the high pressure side.

System Discharging

NOTE: Many 1993 and all 1994–95 models are charged with non-CFC R–134a. These systems use their own type of corresponding refrigerant oil. R–134a, its oil, components and service equipment must be used only on R–134a systems. Do not mix any R–12 refrigerant, oil, components or equipment with R–134a; they are not compatible and can result in system failure if mixed.

R–12 refrigerant is a chloroflourocarbon which, when mishandled, can contribute to the depletion of the ozone layer in the upper atmosphere. Ozone filters out harmful radiation from the sun. In order to protect the ozone layer, an approved R–12 Recovery/Recycling machine that meets SAE standard J1991 should be employed when discharging the system. Follow the operating instructions provided with the approved equipment exactly to properly discharge the system.

NOTE: Even though most systems now use non–CFC R–134a, these systems should not be discharged to the atmosphere. Use only approved refrigerant recovery/recycling equipment when discharging.

System Evacuating

If the air conditioning system has been opened to the atmosphere, it should be air and moisture free before being recharged with refrigerant. Moisture and air mixed with refrigerant will raise the compressor head pressure, possibly damaging the system's components and will reduce the performance of the system. Moisture will boil at normal room temperature when exposed to a vacuum. To evacuate the system of air and moisture, perform the following procedure:

1. Leak test the system and repair any leaks found.
2. Connect an approved charging station, Recovery/Recycling machine or manifold gauge set and vacuum pump to the discharge and suction ports. The red hose is normally connected to the discharge (high pressure) line and the blue hose is connected to the suction (low pressure) line.
3. Open the discharge and suction ports and start the vacuum pump. If the pump is not able to pull at least 26 in. Hg vacuum, there is a leak that must be repaired before evacuation can occur.
4. Once the system has reached at least 26 in. Hg vacuum, allow the system to evacuate for at least 15 minutes. The longer the system is evacuated, the more contaminants will be removed.

5. Close all valves and turn the pump **OFF**. If the system loses more than 2 in. Hg vacuum after 15 minutes, there is a leak that should be repaired.

System Charging

NOTE: Be sure to note whether then system uses R–12 or R–134a refrigerant and use appropriate equipment. Do not intermix components, equipment, refrigerant or oil between the 2 types of systems.

1. Connect an approved refrigerant recovery/recycling machine or manifold gauge set to the discharge and suction ports. The red hose is normally connected to the discharge (high pressure) line and the blue hose is connected to the suction (low pressure) line.
2. Follow the instructions provided with the equipment and charge the system with the specified amount of refrigerant.
3. Perform a leak test.

SYSTEM COMPONENTS

Radiator

REMOVAL AND INSTALLATION

1. Disconnect the negative battery cable. Drain the cooling system. On some engines, this requires removing the plug from the bottom radiator tank.
2. If equipped with a coolant expansion tank, remove the cap, disconnect the hose at the radiator and drain the coolant into a clean container. If equipped with a splash guard, remove it.
3. Remove the coolant hoses and disconnect the automatic transmission oil cooler lines and plug their openings as well as the openings in the cooler.
4. Disconnect any of the temperature switch wire connectors.
5. Remove the shroud from the radiator. On some vehicles, this is done by simply pressing the release tabs toward the rear of the vehicle. On others, there are metal clips that must be pulled upward and off to free the shroud from the radiator. The shroud will remain in the vehicle, resting on the fan.
6. On the 7 and 8-Series, remove the fan and shroud. Make sure to store the fan in a vertical position. The fan must be held stationary with some sort of flat blade cut to fit over the hub and drilled to fit over 2 of the studs on the front of the pulley. Then, unscrew the retaining nut at the center of the fluid drive hub turning it clockwise to remove, because it has left hand threads.
7. If equipped with the M30B35 engine, remove the fan and shroud; then, spread the retaining clip and pull the oil cooler out to the right. Remove the radiator retaining bolt(s) and lift the radiator from the vehicle.
To install:
8. The radiator is installed in the reverse order of removal.
9. Fill and bleed the cooling system.

10. Check that rubber mounts are located so as to effectively isolate the radiator from the chassis, as this will help ensure reliable radiator performance. If the vehicle uses plastic upper and lower radiator tanks and has a radiator drain plug, be careful not to over torque the plugs.
11. Torque engine oil cooler pipes to 18–21 ft. lbs. (24.4–28.5 Nm) and transmission cooler pipes to 13–15 ft. lbs. (17.6–20.3 Nm)
12. Torque the thermostatic fan hub on the 7 and 8-Series to 29–36 ft. lbs. (39.3–48.8 Nm).

COOLING SYSTEM BLEEDING

With Bleeder Screw on Thermostat Housing

Set the heat valve in the **WARM** position, start the engine and bring it to normal operating temperature. Run the engine at fast idle and open the venting screw on the thermostat housing until the coolant comes out free of air bubbles. Close the bleeder screw and refill the cooling system.

Without Bleeder Screw

Bleeder screw location—5 and 7-Series

—————— **CAUTION** ——————
Fill the cooling system, place the heater valve in the WARM position, close the pressure cap to the second (fully closed) position. Start the engine and bring to normal operating temperature. Carefully release the pressure cap to the first position and squeeze the upper and lower radiator hoses in a pumping action to allow trapped air to escape through the radiator. Recheck the coolant level and close the pressure cap to its second position.

Electric Cooling Fan

TESTING

Make sure the key is in the **OFF** position when checking the electric cooling fan. If not, the fan could turn **ON** at any time, causing serious personal injury.

1. Disconnect the negative battery cable. Unplug the fan connector.
2. Using a jumper wire, connect the female terminal of the fan connector to the negative battery terminal.

3. The fan should turn ON when the male terminal is connected to the positive battery terminal.

4. If not, the fan is defective and should be replaced.

REMOVAL AND INSTALLATION

1. Disconnect the negative battery cable.
2. Remove the bolts retaining the center front grille.
3. Remove the center grille.
4. Raise and safely support the vehicle, remove the splash shield.
5. Disconnect the cooling fan connector through the grille opening.
6. Lower the vehicle slightly and remove the fan assembly mounting bolts.
7. Lower the fan assembly from the vehicle.
8. Installation is the reverse of the removal procedure. Make sure to check the operation of the cooling fan.

Condenser

WARNING: Be sure not to intermix components, refrigerant, oil or service equipment from R–12 systems with R–134a systems.

REMOVAL AND INSTALLATION

1. Disconnect the negative battery cable.
2. Properly discharge the air conditioning system.
3. If required for access to the condenser, drain the cooling system. and remove the radiator from the vehicle.
4. If required, remove the bolts that attach the bumper and grille and remove them from the vehicle.
5. Disconnect and plug the refrigerant lines at the condenser, through the right side grille opening.
6. Disconnect the auxiliary cooling fan connector. Remove the cooling fan from the condenser.
7. Remove the condenser mounting bolts and remove the condenser upward.
To install:
8. Install the condenser in position and install the mounting bolts.

9. Install the auxiliary cooling fan.
10. Reconnect the refrigerant lines at the condenser, using O–rings.
11. Install the radiator into the vehicle. Install the grille pieces.
12. Refill the cooling system and properly recharge the air conditioning system.
13. Bleed the cooling system and reconnect the negative battery cable.

Compressor

WARNING: Be sure not to intermix components, refrigerant, oil or service equipment from R–12 systems with R–134a systems.

REMOVAL AND INSTALLATION

3-Series

1. Disconnect the negative battery cable.
2. Properly discharge the air conditioning system.
3. Disconnect the electrical lead from the compressor.
4. Disconnect and plug the refrigerant lines at the compressor to prevent contamination from entering the system..
5. Remove the upper and lower compressor mounting bolts and remove the drive belt.
6. Using dowel special sleeve puller 64 5 070 or equivalent, and the original top compressor bolt, remove the top compressor bolt sleeve enough to remove the compressor.
7. Remove the compressor from the vehicle.
To install:
8. Install the compressor in position and tighten the top compressor bolt sleeve.
9. Install the upper and lower compressor bolts. Tighten all M8 bolts to 16–17 ft. lbs. (21.7–23.0 Nm) and all M10 bolts to 31–35 ft. lbs. (42.0–47.4 Nm). Adjust the belt tension.
10. Connect the refrigerant lines to the compressor.
11. Reconnect the electrical lead to the compressor. Properly charge the air conditioning system. Check the system operation.

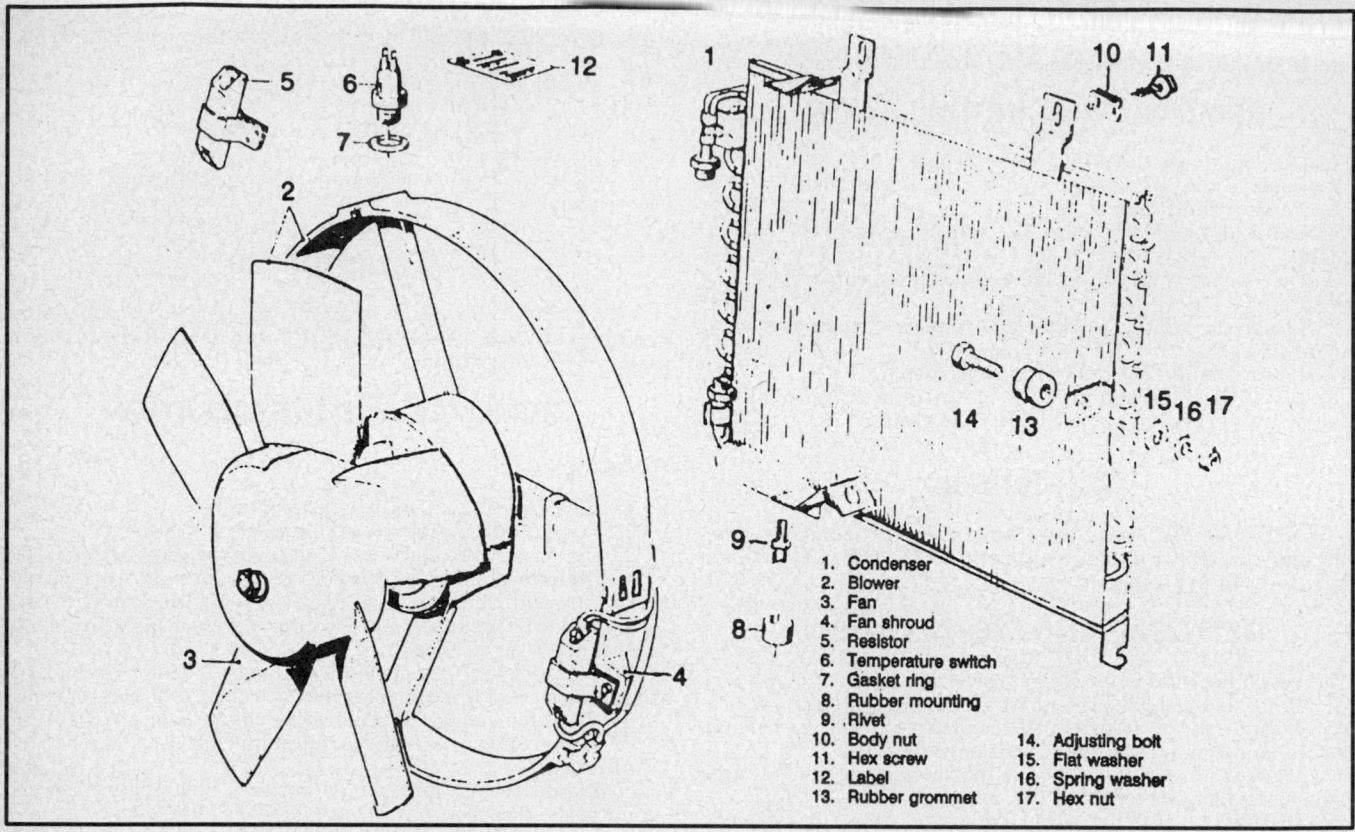

1. Condenser
2. Blower
3. Fan
4. Fan shroud
5. Resistor
6. Temperature switch
7. Gasket ring
8. Rubber mounting
9. Rivet
10. Body nut
11. Hex screw
12. Label
13. Rubber grommet
14. Adjusting bolt
15. Flat washer
16. Spring washer
17. Hex nut

Auxiliary fan components—5 and 7-Series

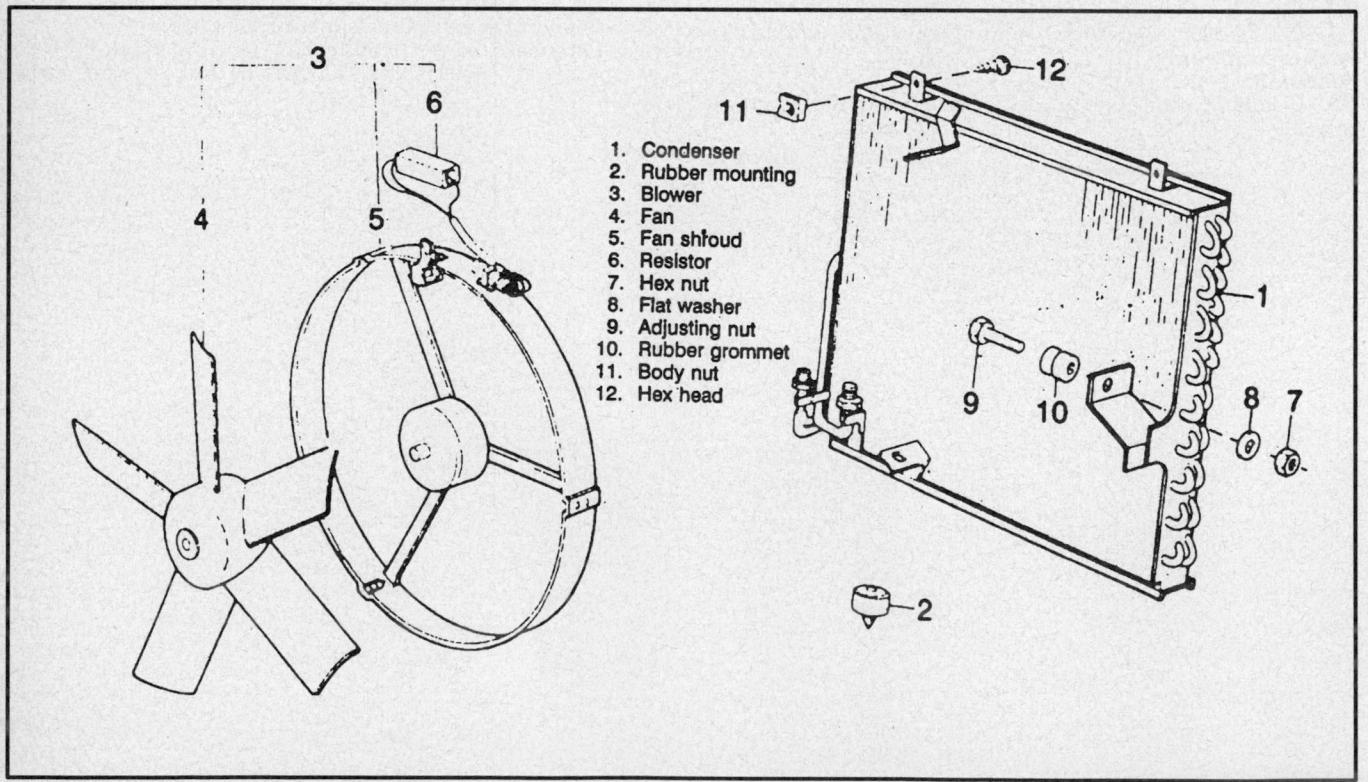

1. Condenser
2. Rubber mounting
3. Blower
4. Fan
5. Fan shroud
6. Resistor
7. Hex nut
8. Flat washer
9. Adjusting nut
10. Rubber grommet
11. Body nut
12. Hex head

Auxiliary fan components—3-Series

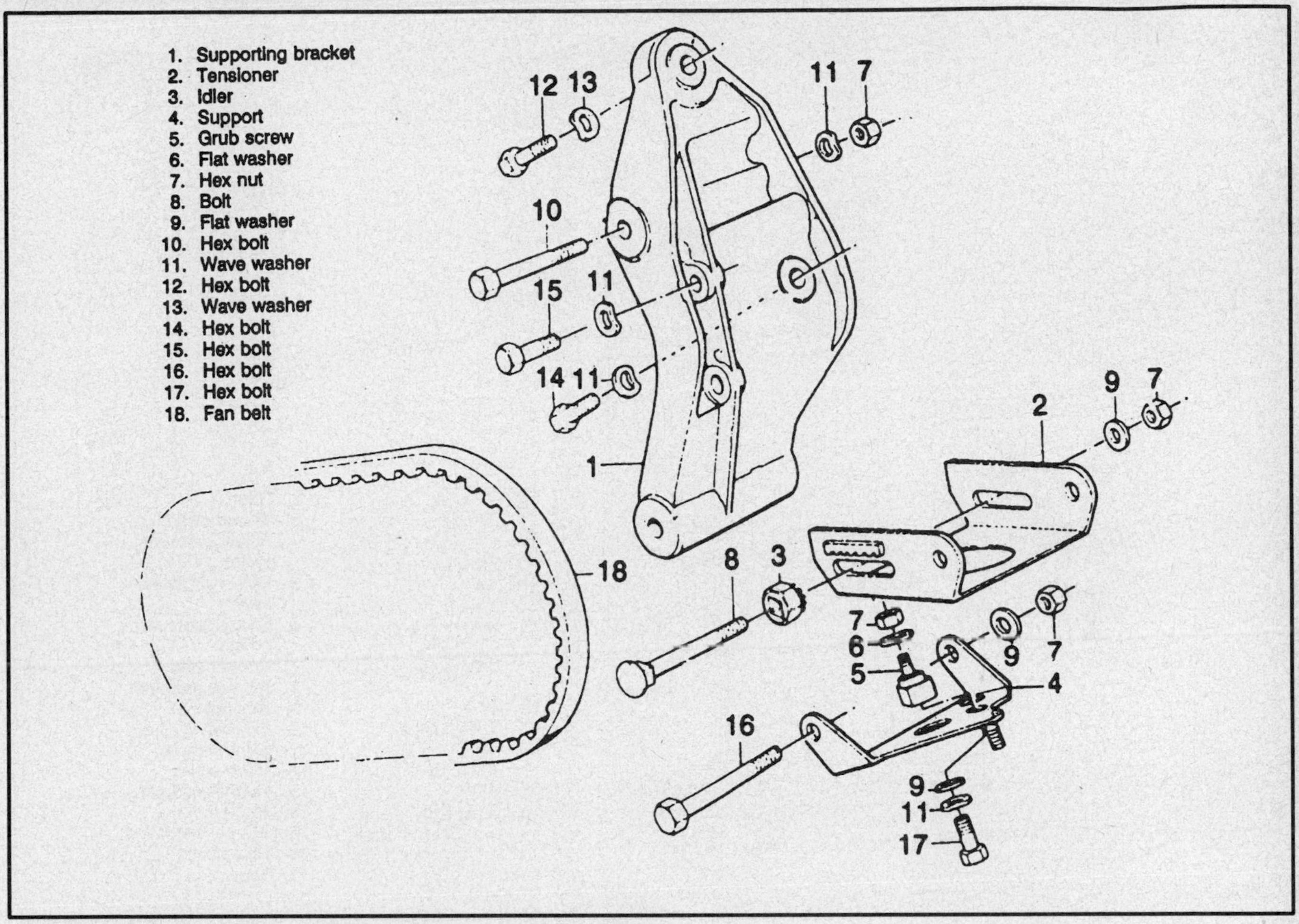

1. Supporting bracket
2. Tensioner
3. Idler
4. Support
5. Grub screw
6. Flat washer
7. Hex nut
8. Bolt
9. Flat washer
10. Hex bolt
11. Wave washer
12. Hex bolt
13. Wave washer
14. Hex bolt
15. Hex bolt
16. Hex bolt
17. Hex bolt
18. Fan belt

Air conditioning compressor mounting—5 and 7-Series

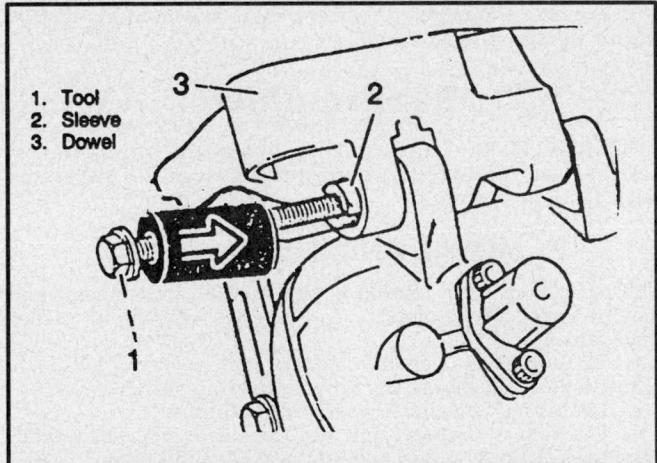

1. Tool
2. Sleeve
3. Dowel

Removing the dowel sleeve from the air conditioning compressor mounting—3-Series

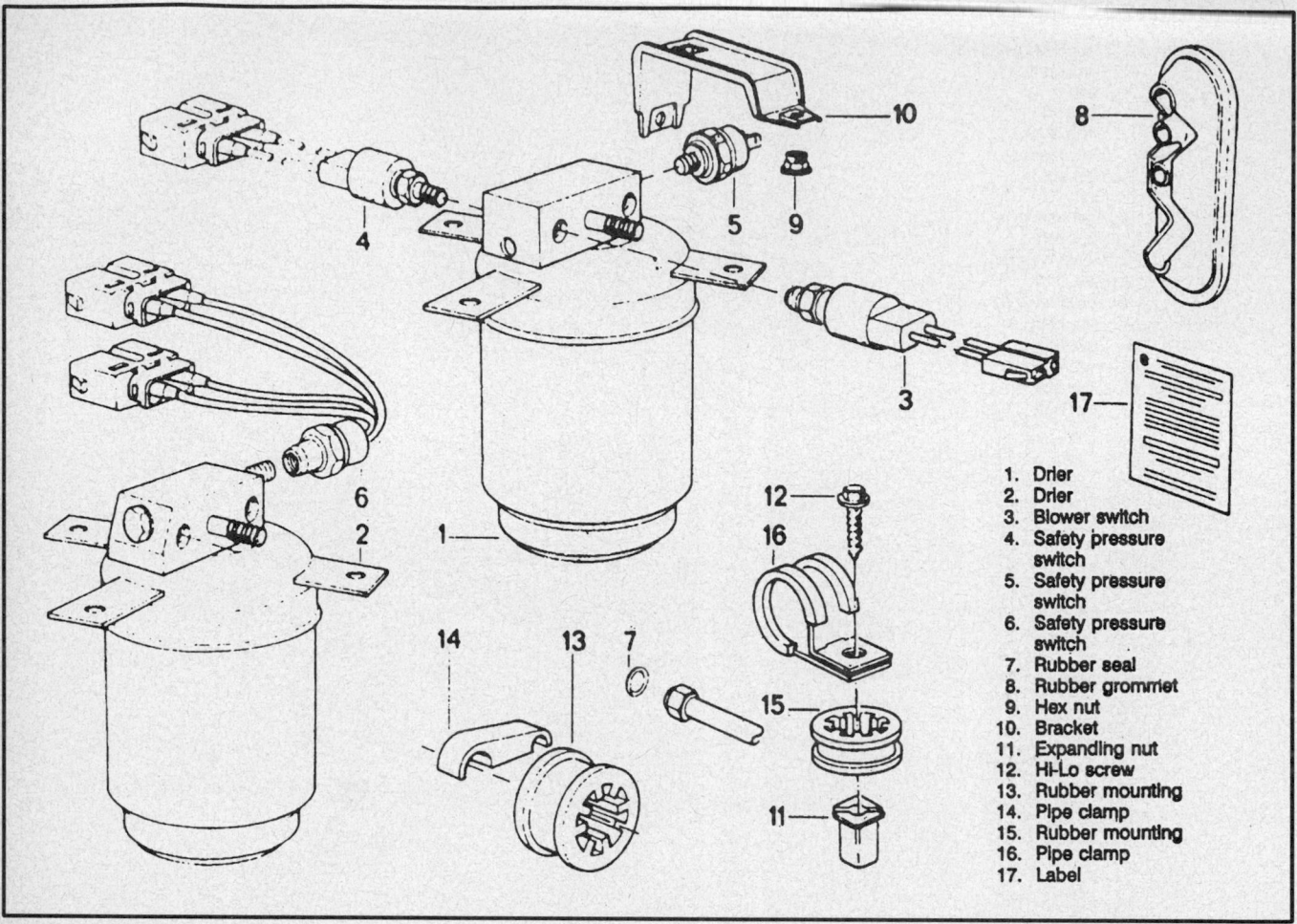

1. Drier
2. Drier
3. Blower switch
4. Safety pressure switch
5. Safety pressure switch
6. Safety pressure switch
7. Rubber seal
8. Rubber grommet
9. Hex nut
10. Bracket
11. Expanding nut
12. Hi-Lo screw
13. Rubber mounting
14. Pipe clamp
15. Rubber mounting
16. Pipe clamp
17. Label

Receiver drier components—All models

5, 7 and 8-Series

1. Disconnect the negative battery cable.
2. Properly discharge the air conditioning system.
3. Remove the air cleaner inlet hose and remove the air cleaner assembly.
4. Cut the straps retaining the compressor electrical lead and disconnect the lead.
5. Disconnect and plug the refrigerant lines at the compressor.
6. Raise and safely support the vehicle.
7. Remove the bolts retaining the splash shield and remove the splash shield.
8. Loosen the lower compressor mounting and belt tensioner bolts and remove the drive belt from the compressor pulley.
9. Remove the compressor mounting bolts, remove the compressor.

To install:
10. Install the compressor in position under the vehicle and install the retaining bolts.
11. Install the accessory drive belt and tighten the mounting bolts. Adjust the belt tensioner to the stop and tighten the tensioner bolt.
12. Tighten all M8 bolts to 16–17 ft. lbs. (21.7–23.0) and all M10 bolts to 31–35 ft. lbs. (42.0–47. 4Nm).
13. Install the splash shield and lower the vehicle.
14. Connect the refrigerant lines to the compressor.
15. Reconnect the electrical lead to the compressor. Install the air cleaner assembly.

16. Connect the negative battery cable and properly charge the air conditioning system.

Receiver/Drier

WARNING: Be sure not to intermix components, refrigerant, oil or service equipment from R–12 systems with R–134a systems.

REMOVAL AND INSTALLATION

The receiver drier is located in the engine compartment and may be under a trim panel, covered by the windshield washer fluid tank.
1. Disconnect the negative battery cable.
2. Properly discharge the air conditioning system.
3. Drain the windshield washer fluid tank.
4. Disconnect the hoses and electrical leads from the washer fluid tank. Unbolt and remove the washer fluid tank.
5. Remove the bolts retaining the plastic trim that was under the washer fluid tank. Remove the trim panel.
6. Disconnect and plug the refrigerant lines from the receiver/drier.
7. Disconnect the electrical leads from the pressure switches on the receiver/drier.
8. Remove the drier mounting bolts and remove the receiver/drier from the vehicle.

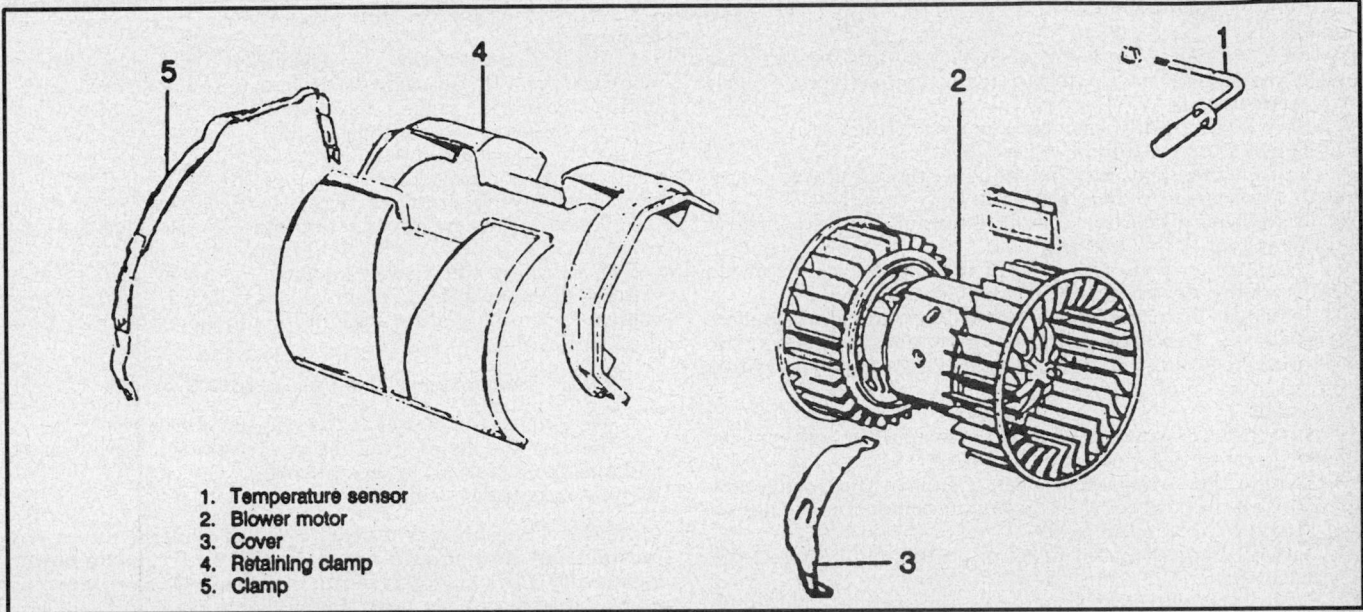

1. Temperature sensor
2. Blower motor
3. Cover
4. Retaining clamp
5. Clamp

Blower motor and upper housing cover—3-Series, others similar

To install:

9. Install the receiver/drier in position.

NOTE: If replacing the pressure switches on the drier, use a thread locking compound on the switch threads. Also check the drier for the proper quantity of oil, the correct amount is 0.35 oz.

10. Reconnect the electrical leads and the pressure lines.
11. Reinstall the trim panel over the receiver/drier assembly.
12. Install the washer fluid tank, connect the electrical lead to the washer fluid tank.
13. Connect the battery cable and properly recharge the air conditioning system.

Expansion Valve

WARNING: Be sure not to intermix components, refrigerant, oil or service equipment from R–12 systems with R–134a systems.

REMOVAL AND INSTALLATION

3-Series

The expansion valve can only be removed after removing the evaporator from the vehicle.

1. Disconnect the negative battery cable.
2. Properly discharge the air conditioning system.
3. Remove the screws retaining the center console and remove the center console. Disconnect any electrical leads.
4. Open the glove box and remove the glove box assembly retaining bolts. Remove the glove box and remove the lower left side instrument panel trim.
5. Disconnect and plug the refrigerant lines from the evaporator case.
6. Remove the evaporator case cover. Remove the foam rubber insulator and pull the evaporator from the housing.
7. Disconnect and plug the lines from the expansion valve and remove the expansion valve.

To install:

8. Install the expansion valve on the evaporator assembly, connecting the refrigerant lines.

NOTE: Before installing the evaporator into the housing, make sure the fins on the evaporator are not bent. If any fins are bent, use a fin comb or equivalent, to straighten them.

9. Install the evaporator into the housing. Install the foam cover and the plastic cover over the evaporator.
10. Connect the refrigerant lines to the evaporator.
11. Install the instrument panel trim and the glove box.
12. Install the center console, connecting any electrical leads.
13. Connect the negative battery cable. Properly recharge the air conditioning system.

5, 7 and 8-Series

The expansion valve can only be removed after removing the evaporator case.

1. Disconnect the negative battery cable.
2. Properly discharge the air conditioning system.
3. If equipped with an automatic transmission, remove the screw retaining the shift lever T–handle. On manual transmission equipped vehicles, remove the shifter knob.
4. Remove the shift lever cover and pull the window switches out of the console.
5. Remove the center console retaining screws, disconnect all electrical leads and remove the console.
6. Open the glove box and remove the glove box door assembly.
7. Remove the left and right pillar trim. Remove the left and right kick panel trim.
8. Remove the lower instrument panel trim pads. Remove the steering wheel.

—— CAUTION ——

When removing the steering wheel on airbag equipped vehicles, use extreme caution handling the air bag assembly. Store the steering wheel with the airbag assembly facing up, to avoid injury in case of accidental deployment. Replace damaged airbag assemblies. Do not try to repair or reuse deployed airbag assemblies.

9. Remove the steering column trim.
10. Remove the instrument panel pillar retaining bolts.

11. Remove the lower instrument panel retaining bolts at the kick panels.

12. Remove the instrument cluster retaining screws and remove the instrument cluster. Disconnect all instrument cluster electrical leads.

13. Remove the radio assembly and radio trim.

14. Remove the ventilation control head.

15. Remove the upper instrument panel retaining screws and pull the instrument panel away from the firewall.

16. Disconnect all electrical multi–plugs and pull the instrument panel out of the vehicle.

17. Remove the cowl cover from in the engine compartment. Disconnect the electrical leads at the blower.

18. Inside the vehicle, remove the evaporator cover. Remove the refrigerant line retaining bolt. Disconnect the refrigerant lines from the expansion valve and remove the expansion valve from the evaporator.

To install:

19. Install the expansion valve on the evaporator and connect the refrigerant lines.

20. Install the evaporator cover. Connect the refrigerant lines. Install the cowl cover in the engine compartment. Reconnect the blower electrical leads.

21. Install the instrument panel in position and connect the electrical leads.

22. Install the instrument panel retaining screws. Install the ventilation control head and the radio assembly.

23. Install the instrument cluster.

24. Install the pillar trim and the kick panel trim.

25. Install the steering column trim and the steering wheel.

26. Install the lower instrument panel trim and the glove box assembly.

27. Install the center console and the shift lever.

28. Connect the negative battery cable.

29. Properly charge the air conditioning system. Check the system operation.

Blower Motor

REMOVAL AND INSTALLATION

The blower motor assembly on all of the vehicles is accessible through the engine compartment. There is a plastic cover over the top of the motor assembly, which is located in the cowl

1. Disconnect the negative battery cable.

2. Remove the rubber hood gasket at the cowl.

3. Remove any wires that are strapped to the top of the cowl cover.

4. On 5, 7 and 8-Series vehicles, remove the coolant expansion tank from the firewall. Position it to the side, being careful not to bend the coolant return hose.

5. On 5-Series vehicles with 4 doors, remove the electrical wiring duct and air collection box. On the 5-Series 2 door model, it will be necessary to remove the fuel injection plate cover and valve cover to gain access to the blower motor cover.

6. Remove the cowl cover retaining bolts. Remove the cowl cover.

7. Disconnect the blower housing top cover. On 3-Series vehicles disconnect the 2 retaining straps. On 5, 7 and 8-Series vehicles, open the center retaining clip. Remove the cover from the vehicle.

NOTE: The cover will separate into 2 pieces.

8. Disconnect the blower motor wire connectors.

9. Release the metal retaining strap from the blower motor and pull the motor out of the housing.

10. Remove the housing gasket.

NOTE: The blower motor cages are balanced on the motor shaft and should not be removed from the motor assembly. If the motor is being replaced, it is replaced as a complete assembly with cages.

To install:

11. Install the blower motor assembly into the housing.

12. Connect the electrical leads.

NOTE: The motor can only be positioned one way in the housing. This is determined by the shape of the motor itself. Do not try to force the motor into position.

13. Latch the blower motor retaining strap into place.

14. Install the housing gasket.

15. Install the housing cover assembly, position the retaining strap(s) and secure the cover.

16. Install the cowl cover in position.

17. On 5-Series vehicles, reinstall the fuel injection plate cover and valve cover as well as the electric wiring duct and air collection box.

18. On 5, 7 and 8-Series vehicles, install the coolant expansion tank. Reposition any electrical leads along the cowl cover.

19. Reattach the rubber cowl gasket.

20. Connect the negative battery cable. Check the operation of the blower.

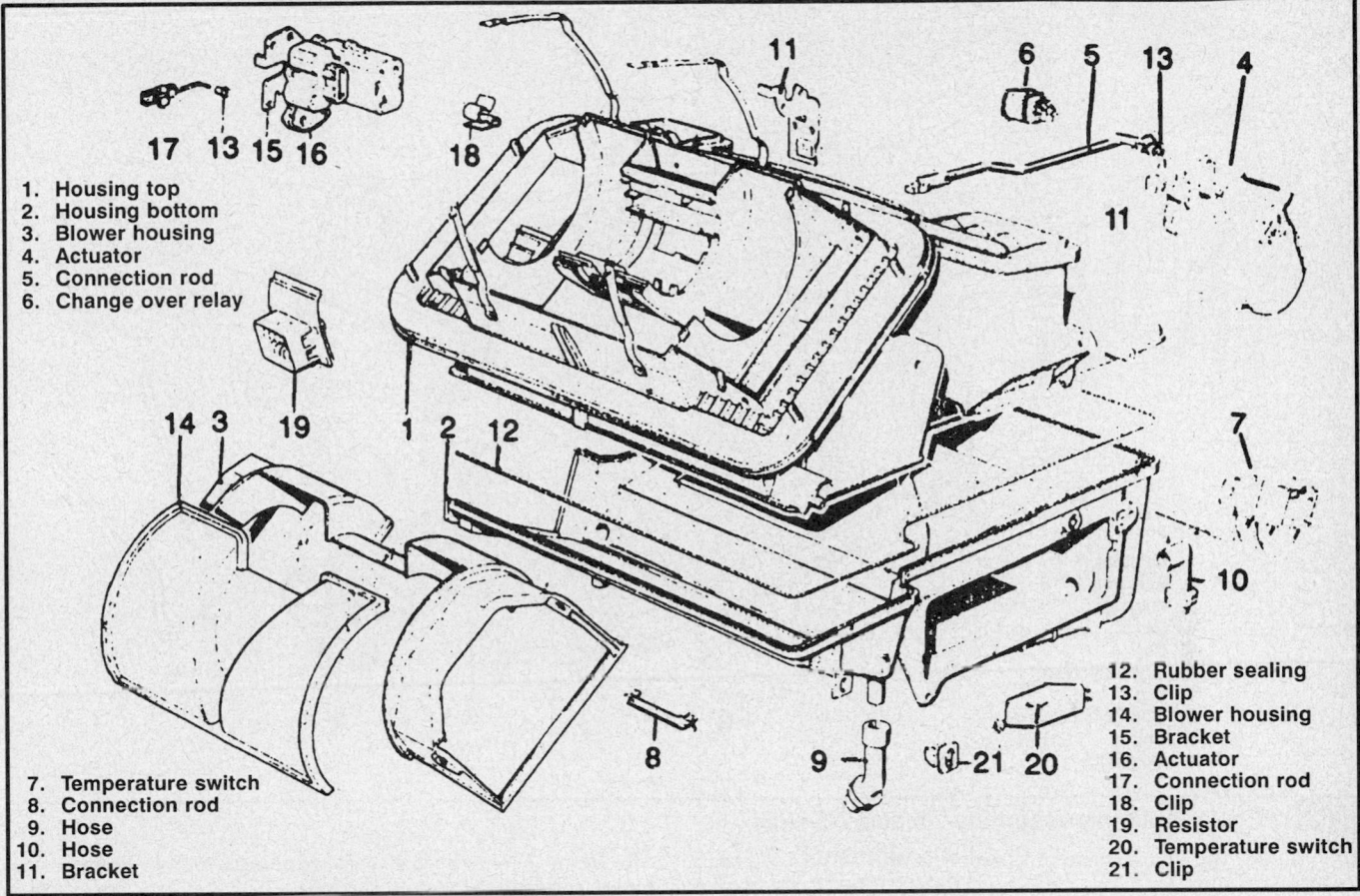

1. Housing top
2. Housing bottom
3. Blower housing
4. Actuator
5. Connection rod
6. Change over relay
7. Temperature switch
8. Connection rod
9. Hose
10. Hose
11. Bracket

12. Rubber sealing
13. Clip
14. Blower housing
15. Bracket
16. Actuator
17. Connection rod
18. Clip
19. Resistor
20. Temperature switch
21. Clip

Heater/blower housing assembly—3-Series

Heater Core

REMOVAL AND INSTALLATION

The heater case assembly must be removed to remove the heater core on all 3-Series vehicles.

3-Series

1. Disconnect the negative battery cable.
2. Drain the cooling system and properly discharge the air conditioning system.
3. If equipped with an automatic transmission, remove the screw retaining the shift lever T–handle. On manual transmission equipped vehicles, remove the shifter knob.
4. Remove the shift lever cover and pull the window switches out of the console.
5. Remove the center console retaining screws, disconnect all electrical leads and remove the console.
6. Open the glove box and remove the glove box door assembly.
7. Remove the left and right pillar trim. Remove the left and right kick panel trim.
8. Remove the lower instrument panel trim pads. Remove the steering wheel.

━━━━━━ **CAUTION** ━━━━━━

When removing the steering wheel on airbag equipped vehicles, use extreme caution handling the air bag assembly. Store the airbag with the airbag facing up, to avoid injury in case of accidental deployment. Replace damaged airbag assemblies. Do not try to repair or reuse deployed airbag assemblies.

9. Remove the steering column trim.
10. Remove the instrument panel pillar retaining bolts. Remove the lower instrument panel retaining bolts at the kick panels.
11. Remove the instrument cluster retaining screws and remove the instrument cluster. Disconnect all instrument cluster electrical leads.
12. Remove the radio assembly and radio trim.
13. Remove the ventilation control head.
14. Remove the upper instrument panel retaining screws and pull the instrument panel away from the firewall.
15. Disconnect all electrical multi–plugs and pull the instrument panel out of the vehicle.
16. Disconnect the refrigerant lines from the evaporator.
17. Remove the cowl cover from in the engine compartment. Disconnect the coolant lines from the heater core.
18. Disconnect the electrical leads from the blower.
19. Disconnect the air ducts from the heater case.
20. Remove the heater case retaining bolts from the engine compartment side and the retaining bolts from the interior side.
21. Check to make sure the flaps in the heater case are all closed.
22. Remove the case assembly from the vehicle.
23. Remove the clips retaining the case halves and remove the blower motor cover and motor.
24. Remove the heater core from the case.

To install:
25. Install the core in the case. Make sure the gasket is positioned properly.
26. Assemble the case halves and attach the blower cover, install the blower.

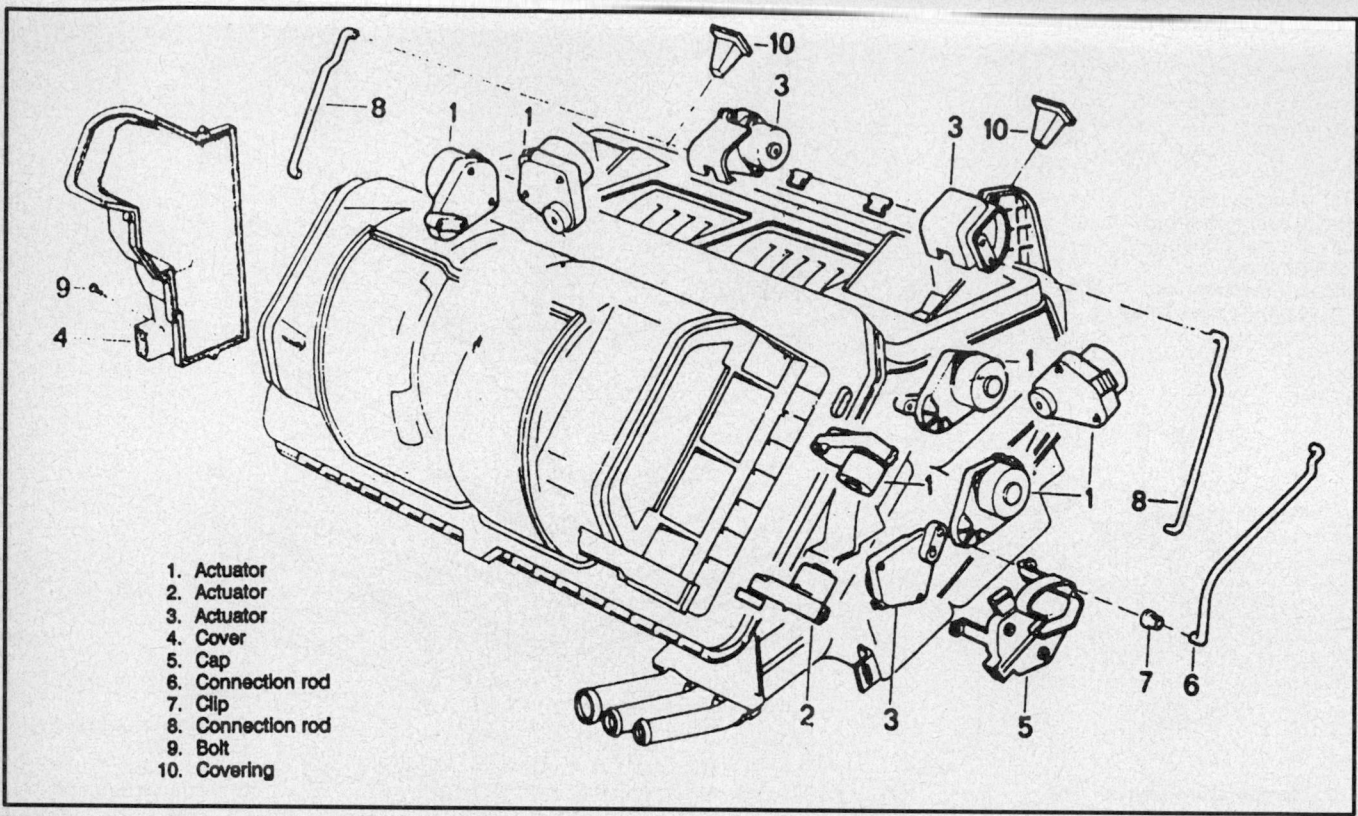

1. Actuator
2. Actuator
3. Actuator
4. Cover
5. Cap
6. Connection rod
7. Clip
8. Connection rod
9. Bolt
10. Covering

Heater/blower housing assembly—5 and 7-Series

27. Install the heater case in position in the vehicle. Re–attach the air ducts.

28. Reconnect the refrigerant lines and coolant hoses. Connect the electrical leads.

29. Reposition the instrument panel into the vehicle and connect the electrical multi–plugs. Be sure the instrument panel is properly positioned and install all retaining bolts.

30. Install the ventilation control head, the radio and the glove box assembly.

31. Install the pillar trim and the kick panel trim plates.

32. Install the lower instrument panel trim pieces.

33. Install the steering column trim and the steering wheel.

34. Install the center console and the shift lever cover. Install the shifter knob or handle.

35. Refill the cooling system and properly charge the air conditioning system.

36. Reconnect the negative battery cable. Check the operation of the heating and air conditioning system.

5, 7 and 8-Series

1. Disconnect the negative battery cable.

2. Drain the cooling system.

3. Remove the screws retaining the center console. Remove the ashtray assembly.

4. Remove the glove box door assembly.

5. Remove the right side heater case cover screws and remove the cover.

6. Remove the front vent drive motor. Disconnect the plug from the inside temperature sensor.

7. Remove the heater core cover retaining screws. Remove the cover clips and straps.

8. Remove the cover and gasket. Disconnect the coolant hoses from the heater core.

9. Remove the heater pipe–to–heater core retaining bolts. Remove the heater pipes.

10. Remove the heater core retaining bolts. Remove the heater core by tilting it to the side.

To install:

11. Install the heater core in the heater case. Install the heater core retaining bolts.

12. Install the heater pipes to the heater core. Tighten M6 bolts to 6–7 ft. lbs. (8.1–9.5 Nm) and M8 bolts to 16–17 ft. lbs. (21.7–23.0 Nm). Connect the heater hoses.

NOTE: Always use new O–rings in the heater pipes.

13. Install the heater case cover and retaining clips. Install the cover retaining screws. Make sure the cover gasket is properly positioned.

14. Install the front vent drive motor. Install the right heater case cover.

15. Connect the inside temperature sensor. Install the glove box door assembly.

16. Install the center console and the ashtray.

17. Fill the cooling system and connect the negative battery cable.

18. Check the operation of the heater.

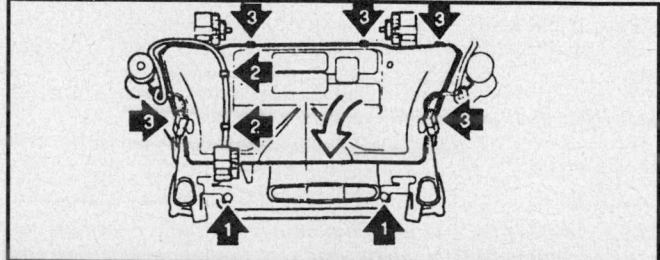

Removing heater core cover—5, 7 and 8-Series

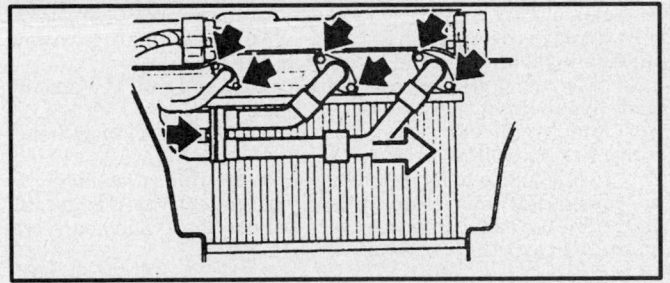

Removing heater water pipes—5, 7 and 8-Series

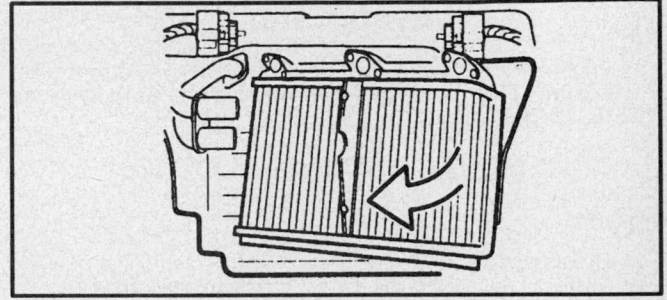

Remove the heater core by pulling it to the right—5, 7 and 8-Series

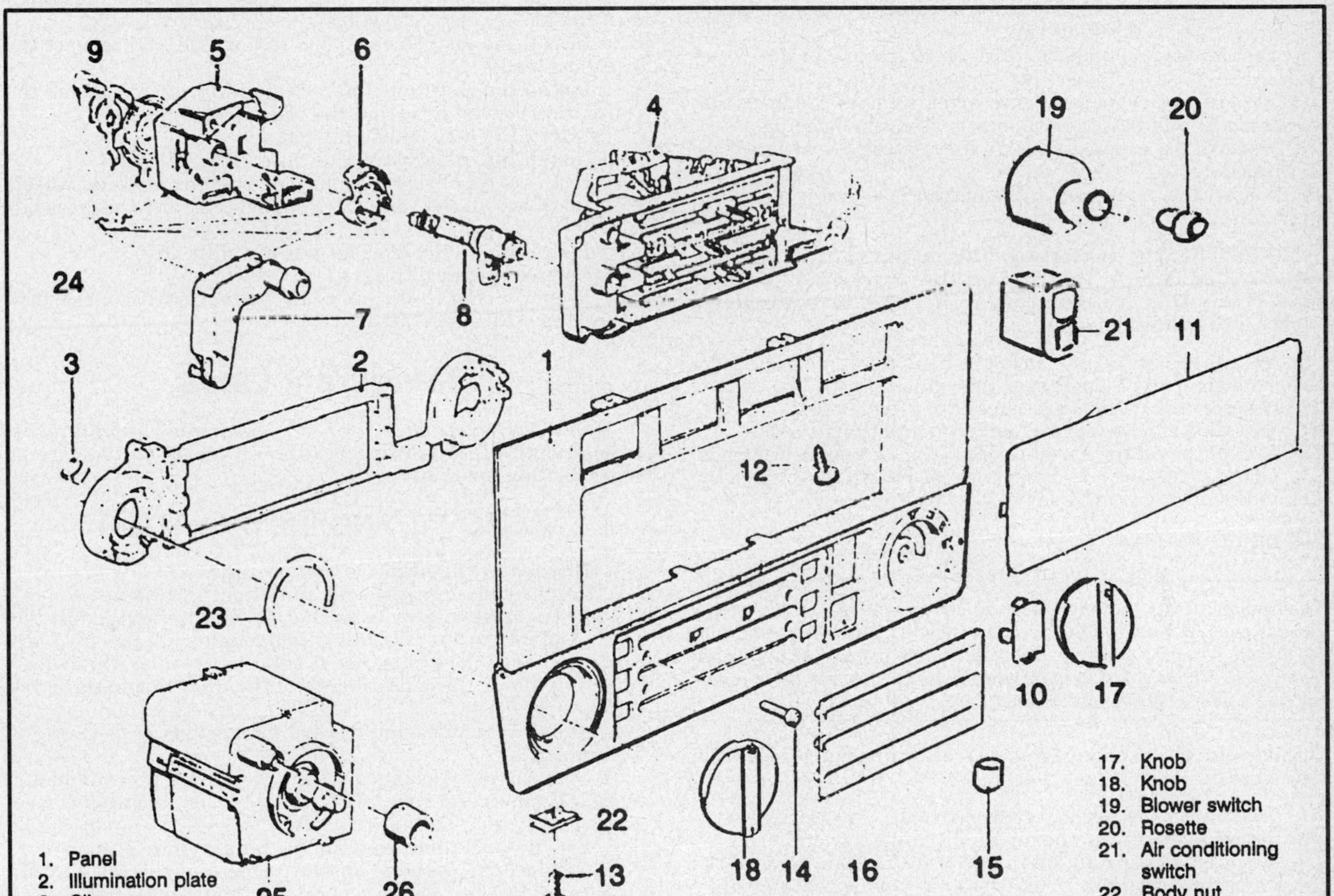

1. Panel
2. Illumination plate
3. Clip
4. Heater control
5. Supporting bracket
6. Rheostat
7. Control lever
8. Dial shaft
9. Phillips head screw
10. Plug
11. Covering
12. Screw
13. Screw
14. Screw
15. Button
16. Covering
17. Knob
18. Knob
19. Blower switch
20. Rosette
21. Air conditioning switch
22. Body nut
23. Foil
24. Temperature switch assembly
25. Control unit
26. Gasket

Exploded view of control head components—3-Series

Evaporator

WARNING: Be sure not to intermix components, refrigerant, oil or service equipment from R–12 systems with R–134a systems.

REMOVAL AND INSTALLATION

3-Series

1. Disconnect the negative battery cable.
2. Properly discharge the air conditioning system.
3. Remove the screws retaining the center console and remove the center console. Disconnect any electrical leads.
4. Open the glove box and remove the glove box assembly retaining bolts. Remove the glove box and remove the lower left side instrument panel trim.
5. Disconnect and plug the refrigerant lines from the evaporator.
6. Remove the evaporator case cover. Remove the foam rubber insulator and pull the evaporator from the housing.
7. Remove the expansion valve if replacing the evaporator.

To install:
8. Install the expansion valve on the evaporator assembly, connecting the refrigerant lines.

NOTE: Before installing the evaporator into the housing, make sure the fins on the evaporator are not bent. If any fins are bent, use a fin comb or equivalent, to straighten them.

9. Install the evaporator into the housing. Install the foam cover and the plastic cover over the evaporator.
10. Connect the refrigerant lines to the evaporator.
11. Install the instrument panel trim and the glove box.
12. Install the center console, connecting any electrical leads.
13. Connect the negative battery cable. Properly recharge the air conditioning system. Leak test.

5, 7 and 8-Series

─────────────── CAUTION ───────────────

When removing the steering wheel on airbag equipped vehicles, use extreme caution handling the air bag assembly. Store the airbag with the airbag portion facing up, to avoid injury in case of accidental deployment. Replace damaged airbag assemblies. Do not try to repair or reuse deployed airbag assemblies.

───

The evaporator can only be removed after removing the evaporator case.

1. Disconnect the negative battery cable.
2. Properly discharge the air conditioning system.
3. If equipped with an automatic transmission, remove the screw retaining the shift lever T–handle. On manual transmission equipped vehicles, remove the shifter knob.
4. Remove the shift lever cover and pull the window switches out of the console.
5. Remove the center console retaining screws, disconnect all electrical leads and remove the console.
6. Open the glove box and remove the glove box door assembly.
7. Remove the left and right pillar trim. Remove the left and right kick panel trim.
8. Remove the lower instrument panel trim pads. Remove the steering wheel.
9. Remove the steering column trim.
10. Remove the instrument panel pillar retaining bolts. Remove the lower instrument panel retaining bolts at the kick panels.
11. Remove the instrument cluster retaining screws and remove the instrument cluster. Disconnect all instrument cluster electrical leads.
12. Remove the radio assembly and radio trim.

13. Remove the ventilation control head.
14. Remove the upper instrument panel retaining screws and pull the instrument panel away from the firewall.
15. Disconnect all electrical multi–plugs and pull the instrument panel out of the vehicle.
16. Remove the cowl cover from in the engine compartment. Disconnect the electrical leads at the blower.
17. Inside the vehicle, remove the evaporator cover. Remove the refrigerant line retaining bolt. Disconnect the refrigerant lines from the expansion valve and remove the expansion valve from the evaporator.

To install:
18. Install the expansion valve on the evaporator and connect the refrigerant lines.
19. Install the evaporator cover. Connect the refrigerant lines. Install the cowl cover in the engine compartment. Reconnect the blower electrical leads.
20. Install the instrument panel in position and connect the electrical leads.
21. Install the instrument panel retaining screws. Install the ventilation control head and the radio assembly.
22. Install the instrument cluster.
23. Install the pillar trim and the kick panel trim.
24. Install the steering column trim and the steering wheel.
25. Install the lower instrument panel trim and the glove box assembly.
26. Install the center console and the shift lever.
27. Connect the negative battery cable.
28. Properly charge the air conditioning system. Leak test. Check the system operation.

Refrigerant Lines

WARNING: Be sure not to intermix components, refrigerant, oil or service equipment from R–12 systems with R–134a systems.

REMOVAL AND INSTALLATION

1. Disconnect the negative battery cable.
2. Properly discharge the air conditioning system.
3. Remove the nuts or bolts that attach the refrigerant line sealing plates to the adjoining components. If the lines are connected with flare nuts, use a back–up wrench when disassembling. Cover the exposed ends of the lines to minimize contamination.
4. Remove the lines and discard the gaskets or O–rings.

To install:
5. Coat the new gaskets or O–rings with refrigerant oil and install. Connect the refrigerant lines to the adjoining components and tighten the nuts or bolts.
6. Evacuate and recharge the air conditioning system.
7. Connect the negative battery cable and check the entire climate control system for proper operation and leaks.

Manual Control Head

REMOVAL AND INSTALLATION

3-Series

1. Disconnect the negative battery cable.
2. Remove the radio from the instrument panel.
3. Remove the switches from above the radio opening, the switches can be removed by prying them out and disconnecting the leads.
4. Remove the top 2 control panel retaining screws, through the radio opening. Remove the bottom 2 control panel retaining screws from under the panel.
5. Remove the rotary knobs from the control panel.
6. Remove the knobs from the slide controls.

7. Pull the panel outward and disconnect the electrical leads from the back. Disconnect the selector cable clamps and remove the selector cables from the control head.

8. Remove the control head from the control panel.

To install:

9. Insert the control head into the control panel.

10. Reconnect the control cables to the control head, and tighten the clamps when the cables are butted against the stop.

11. Reconnect the electrical leads to the control head.

12. Attach the control panel to the instrument panel. Install the upper and lower retaining screws.

13. Install the control knobs. Install the radio and the switches, connecting all electrical leads.

14. Connect the negative battery cable and check the operation of the system.

5-Series

1. Disconnect the negative battery cable.

2. Remove the radio assembly from the vehicle.

3. Remove the rear defogger switch, by prying it outward from the side.

4. Through the rear defogger switch opening, press the control head retaining tab.

5. With the tab pressed push the control head outward and disconnect the electrical leads.

6. Press the clip retaining the control cable and disconnect the control cable.

7. Remove the control head from the vehicle.

To install:

8. Connect the control cable to the rear of the control head. Push the cable until it is seated in the retainer.

9. Reconnect the electrical leads to the control head.

10. Push the control head into the instrument panel until it clicks into position.

11. Install the rear defogger switch. Install the radio assembly.

12. Connect the negative battery cable and check the operation of the system.

7-Series

1. Disconnect the negative battery cable.

2. Remove the rear defogger switch from the center control panel.

3. Using a small prybar, through the rear defogger switch opening, push on the lock tab and release the control head.

4. Carefully pry the control head out of the instrument panel.

5. Disconnect all electrical leads and remove the control head from the vehicle.

To install:

6. Connect the electrical leads to the control head.

7. Push the control head firmly into position in the instrument panel.

8. Install the rear defogger switch.

9. Connect the negative battery cable and check the system operation.

Manual Control Cables

REMOVAL AND INSTALLATION

3-Series

There are 4 replaceable cables used; footwell ventilation, window ventilation, temperature mixing flap and the fresh air flap. Each cable is hooked at the control headand on the heater/evaporator case.

1. Disconnect the negative battery cable.

2. Remove the lower left side instrument panel trim.

3. Remove the shift lever knob. Remove the ashtray assembly.

4. Remove the center console retaining screws and remove the center console.

5. Remove the radio assembly and the surrounding control switches from the control panel.

6. Remove the control panel retaining screws and pull the control panel forward.

7. Disconnect the control cable from the control head.

8. Disconnect the cable from its attaching point at the heater/evaporator case.

To install:

9. Reconnect the cable at the heater/evaporator case.

10. Connect the control cable to the control head. Connect the cable to the sliding arm and push the sliding arm to the far left stop. Turn the adjusting ring until it can be engaged in the opening on the cable and secure the cable in place with the clip. Install the cable retaining clamp.

11. Install the control panel in position. Install the radio assembly and the surrounding switches.

12. Install the center console and the ashtray. Install the shift lever knob.

Electronic Control Head

REMOVAL AND INSTALLATION

1. Disconnect the negative battery cable.

2. Remove the rear defogger switch from the center control panel.

3. Using a small prybar, through the rear defogger switch opening, push the lock tab and release the control head.

4. Carefully pry the control head out of the instrument panel.

5. Disconnect all electrical leads and remove the control head from the vehicle.

To install:

6. Connect the electrical leads to the control head.

7. Push the control head firmly into position in the instrument panel.

8. Install the rear defogger switch.

9. Connect the negative battery cable and check the system operation.

Automatic Climate Control Computer

REMOVAL AND INSTALLATION

5, 7 and 8-Series

The climate control computer is attached to the instrument panel, behind the ventilation control head.

1. Disconnect the negative battery cable.

2. Remove the rear defogger switch from the center control panel.

3. Using a small prybar, through the rear defogger switch opening, push the lock tab and release the control head.

4. Carefully pry the control head out of the instrument panel.

5. Reach through the control head opening and release the computer retaining clip. Pull the computer out of its mounting and release the wire connector from it.

To install:

6. Install the computer in its mounting, make sure the connector is firmly seated. Connect the electrical leads to the control head.

7. Push the control head firmly into position in the instrument panel.

8. Install the rear defogger switch.

9. Connect the negative battery cable and check the system operation.

Microfilter

REMOVAL AND INSTALLATION

5, 7 and 8-Series

The fresh air microfilter is located in the right lower side of the evaporator housing.

1. Disconnect the negative battery cable.
2. Remove the trim on the right side of the center console.
3. Open the glove box and remove the screws on the ventilation duct behind it.
4. Fold the ventilation duct down. Disconnect the blower lead from under the instrument panel.
5. Remove the screws retaining the microfilter cover and the microfilter.
6. Slide the microfilter out of the case.

To install:

7. Install the new microfilter in the case and install the retaining bolts.

8. Install the ventilation duct and retaining screws.
9. Install the center console trim.
10. Connect the negative battery cable.

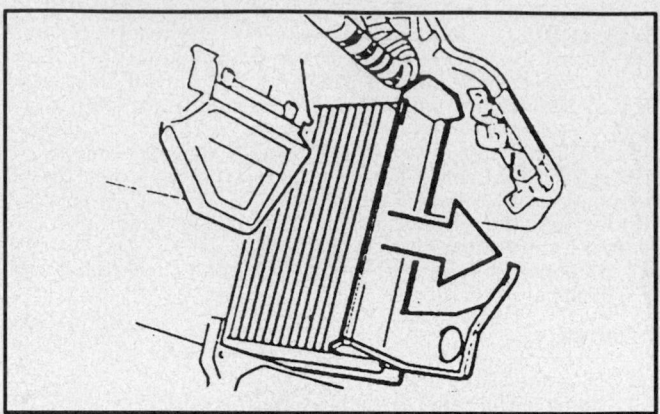

Removing the micro filter—5, 7 and 8-Series

SENSORS AND SWITCHES

Water Shut–Off Solenoid

OPERATION

3-Series

The water shut–off solenoid is located on the left side of the evaporator housing.

The water shut–off solenoid controls the flow of engine coolant through the heater core. When the solenoid is activated, coolant flow is shut off which allows maximum cooling from the air conditioning system. The solenoid is controlled by the hot water cut–off switch which is part of the air conditioning control panel TEMP control.

Battery voltage is applied through fuse 20 to the hot water cut–off switch when the ignition switch is in the **RUN** position. The hot water cut–off switch is closed when the TEMP control is rotated fully COUNTERCLOCKWISE, to the coldest position and is open when the control is rotated more than 20 degrees clockwise. When the switch is closed, battery voltage is applied through the to the Water Shut–Off solenoid and coolant flow is restricted.

WATER SHUT−OFF SOLENOID TEST: 1—3 SERIES

Measure: VOLTAGE
At: WATER SHUT-OFF SOLENOID
CONNECTOR (Disconnected)
Conditions:
- Ignition Switch: RUN
- A/C Control Panel TEMP Control:
  FULLY COUNTERCLOCKWISE

Measure Between	Correct Voltage	For Diagnosis
BU & Ground	Battery	See 1
BU & or BR	Battery	See 2

- Rotate A/C Control Panel TEMP Control to Mid-Position

Measure Between	Correct Voltage	For Diagnosis
BU & Ground	0 Volts	See 3

- If all voltages are correct, replace the Water Shut-Off Solenoid.
1. Check the BU wire and A/C In-Line Fuse for an open. If wire and Fuse are good, go to Table 2.
2. Check the BR wire for an open to ground. Check that connector C204 is properly mated.
3. Check BU wire for a wire-to-wire short to voltage. If wire is good, replace the A/C Control Panel TEMP Control.

WATER SHUT−OFF SOLENOID TEST: 2—3 SERIES

Measure: VOLTAGE
At: HOT WATER CUT-OFF SWITCH
CONNECTOR (Disconnected)
Conditions:
- Ignition Switch: RUN
- Water Shut-Off Solenoid: CONNECTED

Measure Between	Correct Voltage	For Diagnosis
GN/BR & Ground	Battery	See 1
GN/BR & BU	Battery	See 2

- If both voltages are correct, replace the A/C Control Panel TEMP Control.
1. Check the GN/BR wire for an open back to Fuse 20.
2. Check the BU wire for an open.

A: CONTROL SWITCH VOLTAGE TEST: 3-SERIES

Measure: VOLTAGE
At: CONTROL SWITCHES CONNECTOR
(Disconnected)
Conditions: • Ignition Switch: RUN
• Blower Speed Control: OFF

Measure Between	Correct Voltage	For Diagnosis
1 (GN/BR) & Ground	Battery	See 1
1 (GN/BR) & 3 (YL)	Battery	See 2 & 4
7 (GN/BR) & Ground	Battery	See 1
7 (GN/BR) & 5 (YL)	Battery	See 2 & 4
7 (GN/BR) & 6 (BR/WT)	Battery	See 3

- If all voltages are correct, do Test B.
1. Check the GN/BR wire for an open.
2. Check the YL wire for an open.
3. Check the BR/WT wire for an open.
4. If voltage is not present between the GN/BR wire and both the YL wires (terminals 3 and 5), do Test B.

B: BLOWER SPEED CONTROL TEST: 3-SERIES

Measure: VOLTAGE
AT: BLOWER SPEED CONTROL
CONNECTOR (Disconnected)
Conditions:
- Ignition Switch: RUN
- A/C Select Switch: ON (Depressed)
- Fresh/Recirculating Air Switch: FRESH (Not Depressed)

Measure Between	Correct Voltage	For Diagnosis
4 (GN/BR) & Ground	Battery	See 1
7 (YL) & Ground	Battery	See 2
• A/C Select Switch: OFF (Not Depressed)		
7 (YL) & Ground	0 Volts	See 3
4 (GN/BR) & 7 (YL)	Battery	See 4, 8, 9, & 10
4 (GN/BR) & 1 (BK)	Battery	See 5, 8, 9, & 10
4 (GN/BR) & 2 (GN)	Battery	See 6, 8, 9, & 10
4 (GN/BR) & 3 (BU)	Battery	See 7 & 10

- If all voltages are correct, replace the Blower Motor.
1. Check the GN/BR wire for an open.
2. Check the YL wire for an open between Blower Speed Control and splice S231.
3. Check the YL wire for a wire to wire short to voltage.
4. Check the YL wire for an open between splice S231 and the Blower Resistors.
5. Check the BK wire for an open.
6. Check the GN wire for an open.
7. Check the BU wire for an open.
8. If voltage is not present at the YL wire, but is present at the GN wire or BK wire, replace the Blower Resistors.
9. If voltage is not present at the YL, BK or GN wires, check for an open Blower Resistors' Safety Switch.
10. If voltage is not present at the YL, BK, GN and BU wires, do Test C.

C: BLOWER MOTOR
TEST: 3-SERIES

Measure: VOLTAGE
At: BLOWER MOTOR CONNECTOR
Conditions:
- **Ignition Switch: RUN**
- **A/C Select Switch: ON**
- **Blower Speed Control: HIGH**

Measure Between	Correct Voltage	For Diagnosis
BU & Ground	Battery	See 1
BU & BR	Battery	See 2

- If both voltages are correct, replace the Blower Motor.
1. Check the BU wire for an open. If wire is good, recheck Test B.
2. Check the BR wire to ground G200 for an open.

A: FRESH/RECIRCULATING AIR
FLAP DOOR MOTOR VOLTAGE
TEST: 3-SERIES

Measure: VOLTAGE
At: FRESH/RECIRCULATING AIR FLAP DOOR MOTOR PIGTAIL CONNECTORS
(Disconnected)
Conditions:
- **Ignition Switch: RUN**
- **Fresh/Recirculating Air Switch: RELEASED (FRESH)**

Measure Between	Correct Voltage	For Diagnosis
WT and Ground	Battery	See 1
WT and YL	Battery	See 2

- Fresh/Recirculating Air Switch: DEPRESSED (RECIRCULATING)

Measure Between	Correct Voltage	For Diagnosis
YL and Ground	Battery	See 3
YL and WT	Battery	See 3

- If all voltages are correct, replace the inoperative motor.
1. Check the WT wire for an open. If wire is good, do Test B for RH Air Relay.
2. Check the YL wire for an open. If wire is good, do Test B for LH Air Relay.
3. Do Test B for both Air Relays.

C: CONTROL SWITCHES VOLTAGE TEST: 3-SERIES

Measure: VOLTAGE
At: CONTROL SWITCHES CONNECTOR
(Disconnected)
Condition:
  • Ignition Switch: RUN

Measure Between	Correct Voltage	For Diagnosis
7 (GN/BR) & Ground	Battery	See 1
7 (GN/BR) & 8 (GN)	Battery	See 2

• If both voltages are correct, replace the Control Switches.
1. Check the GN/BR wire for an open. If wire is good, check that connector C204 is properly mated.
2. Check the GN wire for an open between the Control Switches and the LH and RH Fresh/Recirculating Air Relays.

B: FRESH/RECIRCULATING AIR RELAY VOLTAGE TEST: 3-SERIES

Measure: VOLTAGE
At: FRESH/RECIRCULATING AIR RELAY CONNECTOR (Disconnected)
Conditions:
  • Ignition Switch: RUN
  • Fresh/Recirculating Air Switch: DEPRESSED (RECIRCULATING)
  • Fresh/Recirculating Air Flap Door Motor Connectors: CONNECTED

Measure Between	Correct Voltage	For Diagnosis
87 (GN/BR) and Ground	Battery	See 1
86 (GN) and Ground	Battery	See 2
86 (GN) and 85 (BR)	Battery	See 3
86 (GN) and 87a (BR)	Battery	See 3

• If all voltages are correct, replace the suspect Fresh/Recirculating Air Relay.
1. Check the GN/BR wire for an open.
2. Check the GN wire back to the Control Switches for an open. If wire is good, do Test C.
3. Check the BR wire for an open.

A: A/C ISOLATION TEST: 1—3-SERIES

Measure: VOLTAGE
At: EVAPORATOR TEMPERATURE REGULATOR (Disconnected)
Conditions:
  • Ignition Switch: RUN (Engine need not be running)
  • A/C Selector Switch: ON (Depressed)

Measure Between	Correct Voltage	For Diagnosis
3 & Ground	Battery	See 1

• If voltage is correct, go to Table 2.
1. Go to Test E.

A: A/C ISOLATION TEST: 2—3-SERIES

Connect: FUSED JUMPER
At: EVAPORATOR TEMPERATURE
　　REGULATOR (Disconnected)
Conditions:
　• Ignition Switch: RUN
　• A/C Selector Switch: ON (Depressed)

Connect Across	Correct Result	For Diagnosis
2 & 3	Compressor Clutch Engages	See 1

• If result is correct go to Test C.
1. Go to Test B.

Blower Control Switches

OPERATION

3-Series

With the ignition switch in the **RUN** position, battery voltage is applied to the control switches and the blower speed control. If either the A/C SELECT switch or the FRESH/RECIRC switch are **ON** or the blower speed control is in the **1** position, battery voltage is applied through the blower resistor to the blower motor.

　The blower motor is a variable speed motor which runs proportional to the voltage applied to it.

B: PRESSURE SWITCH TEST: 3-SERIES

Measure: RESISTANCE
At: EVAPORATOR TEMPERATURE
　　REGULATOR CONNECTOR (Disconnected)
Conditions: • Ignition Switch: OFF
　　　　　　• Negative Battery Terminal:
　　　　　　　DISCONNECTED

Measure Between	Correct Resistance	For Diagnosis
2 & Ground	Approx 3 to 4 ohms	See 1

• If measurement is correct replace the Evaporator Temperature Regulator.
1. Check for an open Low Pressure Cut-Out Switch, High Pressure Cut-Out Switch, A/C Temperature Switch, or associated wiring　　　　　If High Pressure Cut-Out Switch is open, check refrigerant pressure to be sure it is normal before replacing the switch. If the switch and related wiring is OK, replace the Compressor Clutch.

C: EVAPORATOR TEMPERATURE REGULATOR VOLTAGE AND RESISTANCE TEST: 3-SERIES

Measure: RESISTANCE
At: EVAPORATOR TEMPERATURE REGULATOR CONNECTOR
(Disconnected)
Conditions:
- Ignition Switch: OFF
- Negative Battery Terminal: DISCONNECTED

Measure Between	Correct Resistance	For Diagnosis
1 & Ground	Approximately 3.5K to 4.5K ohms at 70°F (21°C)	See 1
4 & Ground	Less than 0.5 ohms	See 2
6 & Ground	Less than 0.5 ohms	See 2
5 & 2	Less than 0.5 ohms	See 3

- If all resistances are correct but Compressor Clutch does not operate normally, replace the Evaporator Temperature Regulator.

1. Check the BK/WT wire for an open or a short to ground   Check the BR wire for an open   If wires are good, replace the Evaporator Temperature Sensor.

2. Check the BR wire for an open

3. Check BK/YL for an open between terminal 5 and the Low Pressure Cut-Out Switch.

D: IDLE SPEED CONTROL VOLTAGE TEST: 3-SERIES

Measure: VOLTAGE
At: MOTRONIC CONTROL UNIT CONNECTOR (Connected — Universal Adapter)
Conditions:
- Ignition Switch: RUN
- A/C Control Panel: A/C ON
- Temperature Outside Car: Above 60 degrees F (16 degrees C)

Measure Between	Correct Voltage	For Diagnosis
40 (BK/GY) & Ground	Battery	See 1
41 (VI/GY) & Ground	Battery	See 2

- If the voltage is correct, repair/replace the Motronic Control Unit.

1. Check for an open in the BL/WT and BK/RD wires.

2. Check for an open in the VI/GY and BK/VI wires.

E: A/C SELECT SWITCH VOLTAGE TEST

Measure: VOLTAGE
At: CONTROL SWITCHES CONNECTOR
(Connected)
Conditions:
- Ignition Switch: RUN
- A/C Control Panel: A/C ON
- Temperature Outside Car: Above 60 degrees F (16 degrees C)

Measure Between	Correct Voltage	For Diagnosis
4 (WT) & Ground	Battery	See 1
2 (BK/VI) & Ground	Battery	See 2

- If both voltages are correct, check connections at Evaporator Temperature Regulator.
1. Check for an open in the WT and GN/BR wires.
2. Replace the A/C Select Switch.

Heater Temperature Sensor

REMOVAL AND INSTALLATION

1. Unfasten the screws on the bottom trim panel.
2. Pull the trim panel to the side out of the way.
3. Disconnect the electrical connection to the heater temperature sensor.
4. Remove the temperature sensor.
5. Installation is the reverse of the removal procedure.

Outside Temperature Sensor

REMOVAL AND INSTALLATION

1. Disconnect the negative battery cable.
2. Remove the drain hose on the expansion tank.
3. Remove the installation nuts and move the expansion tank out of the way.
4. Cut off the wire straps that hold on the wire duct cover to gain access to the wire harness.
5. Locate the 2 wires for the outside temperature sensor, cut them and remove the sensor from the vehicle.
6. Installation is the reverse of the removal process. Make sure to solder the new outside temperature sensor wires to the existing wires and use shrink wrap to insulate the connections.

FRESH/RECIRC Air Flap Motor

OPERATION

3-Series

The FRESH/RECIRC door flap motors are located on either side of the evaporator housing.

With the ignition switch in the RUN position, battery voltage is applied to terminal 7 of the control switches, the normally open contacts of the left fresh air/recirculating air relay and the normally closed contacts of the right fresh air/recirculating air relay. Depending on the switch position, the air flaps are either opened or closed and the voltage is shifted left to right at the relays as the contacts are opened and closed.

Both of the flap control motors remain energized constantly, and stall when the doors reach full travel, which holds them in position.

REMOVAL AND INSTALLATION

3-Series

1. Disconnect the negative battery cable.
2. Remove the shift lever knob.
3. Remove the ashtray and the radio assembly.
4. Remove the center console retaining screws and remove the center console.
5. Remove the ventilation control head.
6. Disconnect the air control cable.
7. Disconnect the electrical leads from the motor assembly.
8. Disconnect the motor operating rod. Remove the motor holder retaining bolts from the case and remove the holder.
9. Remove the motor from the holder.
To install:
10. Insert the motor in the holder and attach the assembly to the case.
11. Connect the operating rod to the motor and connect the electrical lead.
12. Connect the air control cable.
13. Install the ventilation control head.
14. Install the center console, ashtray and radio.
15. Install the shift lever. Connect the negative battery cable. Check the operation of the system.

Evaporator and Temperature Regulator/Sensor

OPERATION

3-Series

The evaporator temperature regulator and the evaporator temperature sensor are both located on the left side of the evaporator housing.

When the ignition switch is in the RUN position, battery voltage is applied to the air conditioning select switch. When the switch is pressed, voltage is applied to terminal 3 of the evaporator temperature regulator. The evaporator temperature regulator applies voltage from terminal 2 to the compressor clutch through the high pressure cut–out switch and the low pressure cut–out switch.

The high pressure cut–out switch will disengage the compressor clutch when the refrigerant pressure rises above 385 psi. The evaporator temperature regulator will detect the high pressure cut–out switch opening at terminal **5** and will turn **OFF** the output voltage at the compressor control terminal. The temperature regulator will not allow the compressor clutch to be turned **ON** again until circuit continuity has been restored between terminals **5** and **2**.

Whenever the compressor clutch is de–energized, the collapsing magnetic field induces a voltage in the winding. The clutch diode provides a path for the resulting current.

When the compressor clutch is turned **ON**, voltage is applied to terminal **29** of the Motronic Control Unit. The control unit uses this signal to increase the idle speed to compensate for the increased engine load from the compressor.

REMOVAL AND INSTALLATION

3-Series

The evaporator temperature sensor is located on the right side of the evaporator case.
1. Disconnect the negative battery cable.
2. Remove the lower right instrument panel trim.
3. Disconnect the electrical lead from the sensor.
4. Remove the sensor from the housing by pulling it out.
5. Install the sensor in position in the case and push it in firmly to seat it.
6. Install the right instrument panel trim. Connect the negative battery cable.

SYSTEM DIAGNOSIS

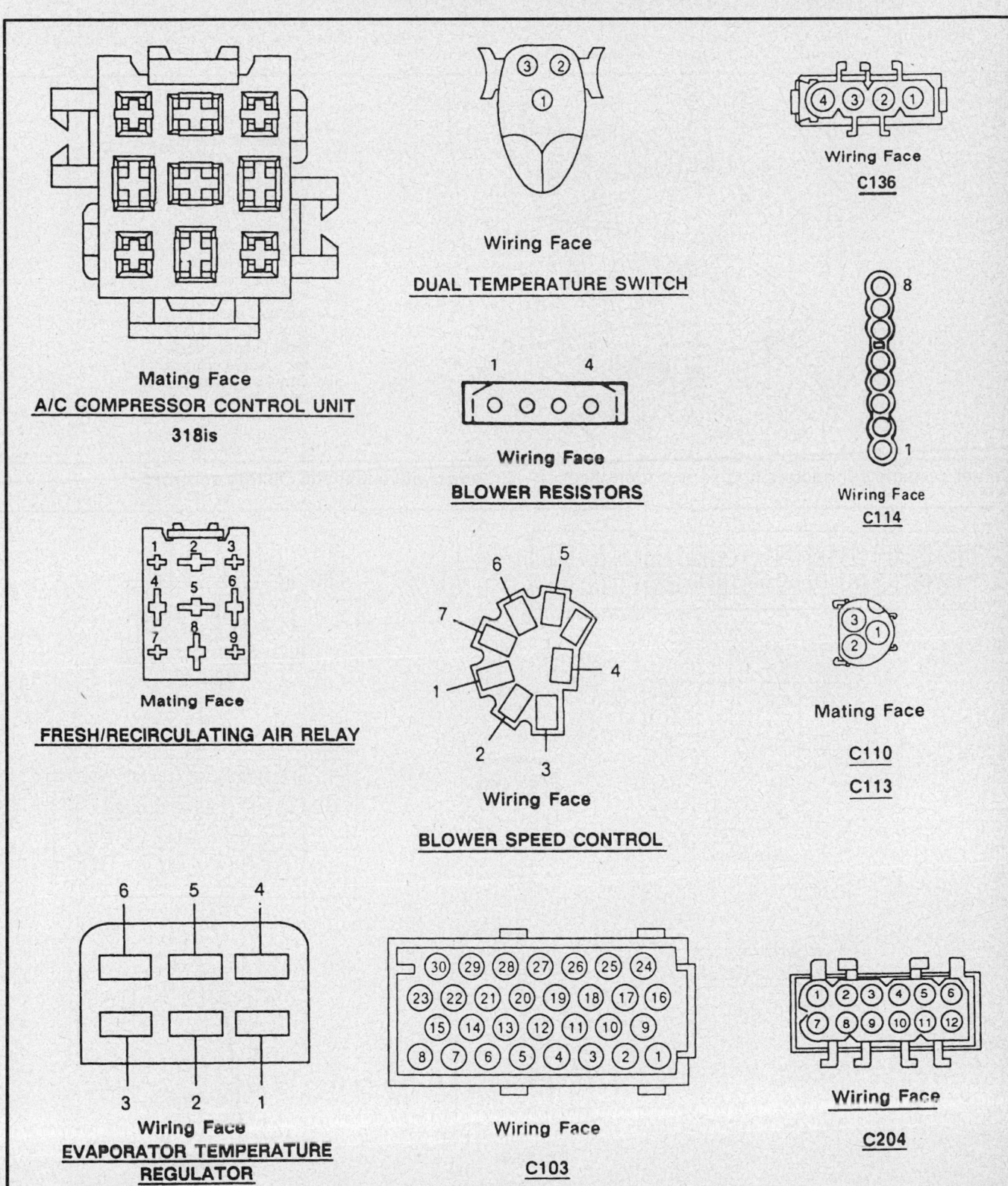

Mating Face
A/C COMPRESSOR CONTROL UNIT
318is

Wiring Face
DUAL TEMPERATURE SWITCH

Wiring Face
BLOWER RESISTORS

Wiring Face
C136

Wiring Face
C114

Mating Face
FRESH/RECIRCULATING AIR RELAY

Wiring Face
BLOWER SPEED CONTROL

Mating Face
C110
C113

Wiring Face
EVAPORATOR TEMPERATURE REGULATOR

Wiring Face
C103

Wiring Face
C204

Connector terminal locations—3-Series with manual air conditioning

Integrated Automatic Climate Control System (IHKA/IHKR)

The IHKR/IHKA climate control system is controlled by a microprocessor. The climate control computer has the ability to store defect codes in the case of system difficulty. The control unit monitors various parts of the vehicle, including the ignition system.

All stored fault codes can be read and used to determine the system problem. Codes can be read only by using the BMW Diagnostic Service Tester, or equivalent.

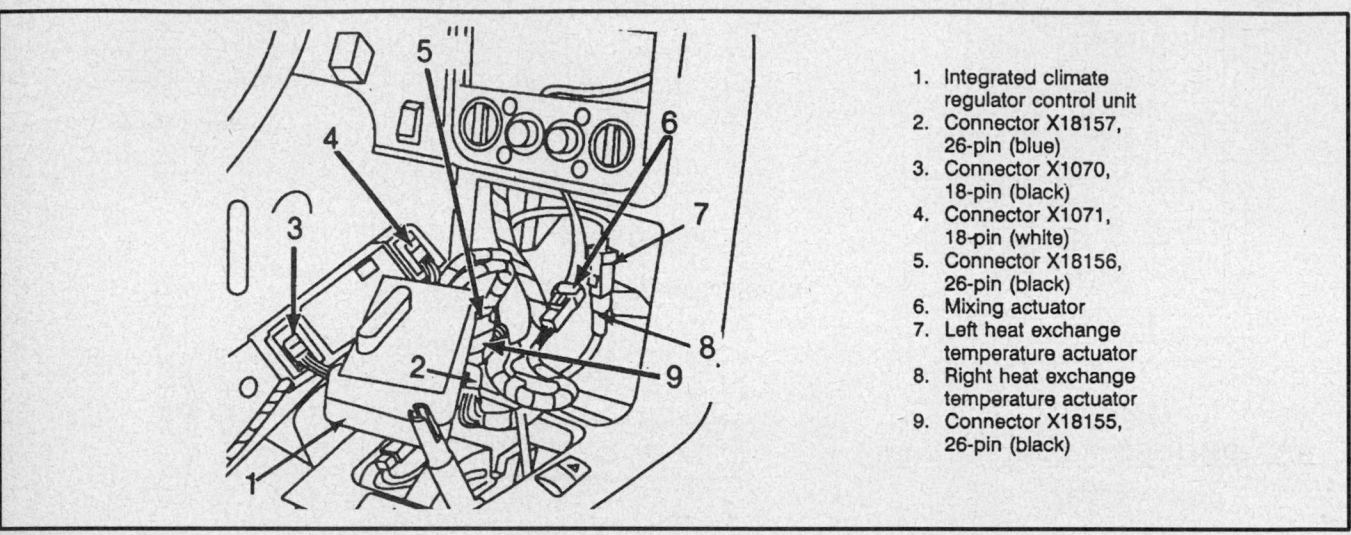

1. Integrated climate regulator control unit
2. Connector X18157, 26-pin (blue)
3. Connector X1070, 18-pin (black)
4. Connector X1071, 18-pin (white)
5. Connector X18156, 26-pin (black)
6. Mixing actuator
7. Left heat exchange temperature actuator
8. Right heat exchange temperature actuator
9. Connector X18155, 26-pin (black)

Center console connectors and sensor identification—3-Series with automatic climate control

X18154, X18155
X18156, X18157

X663, X669

X904

X87

X692

X13

X905

52, X53, X58

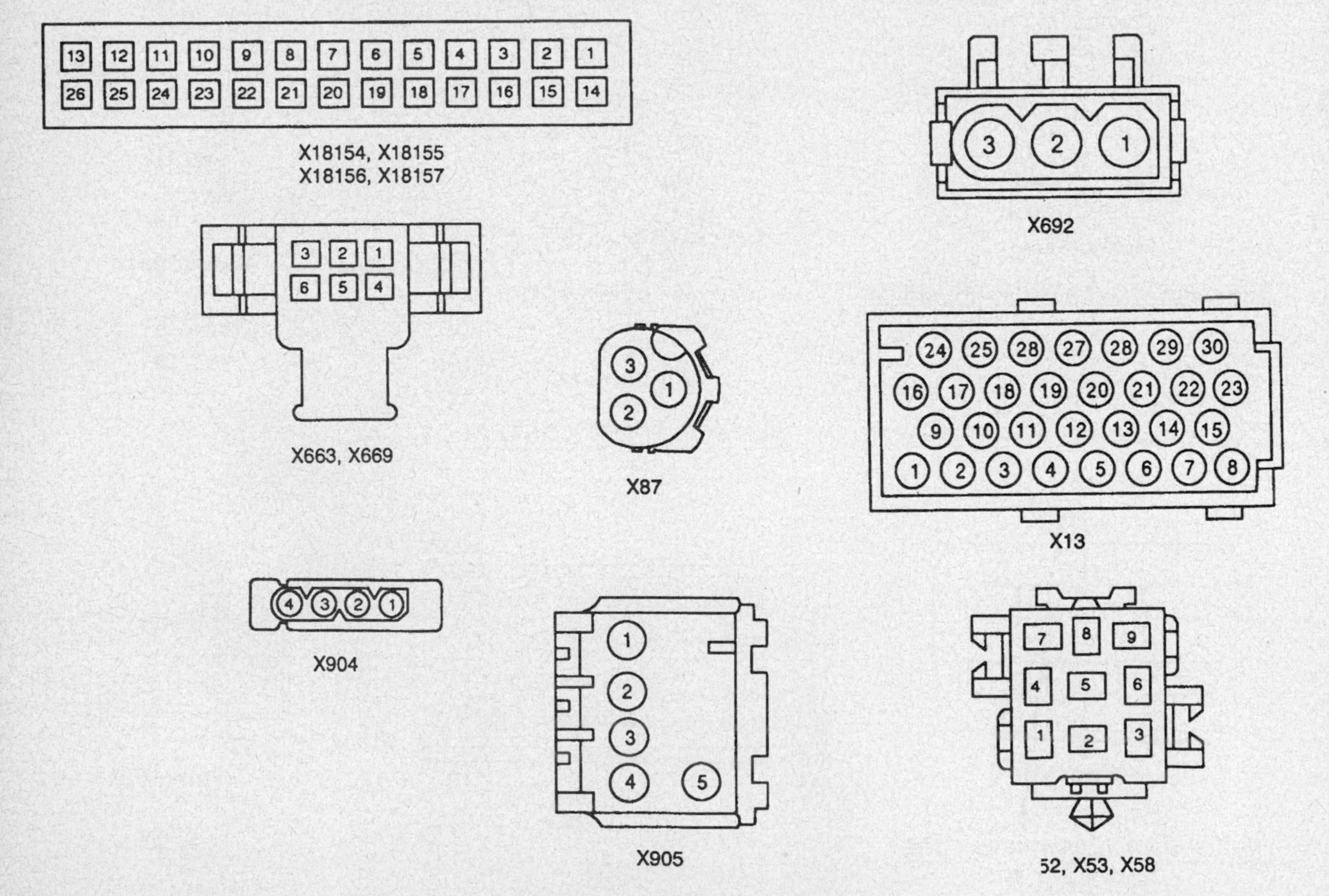

Connector terminal locations—3-Series with automatic climate control

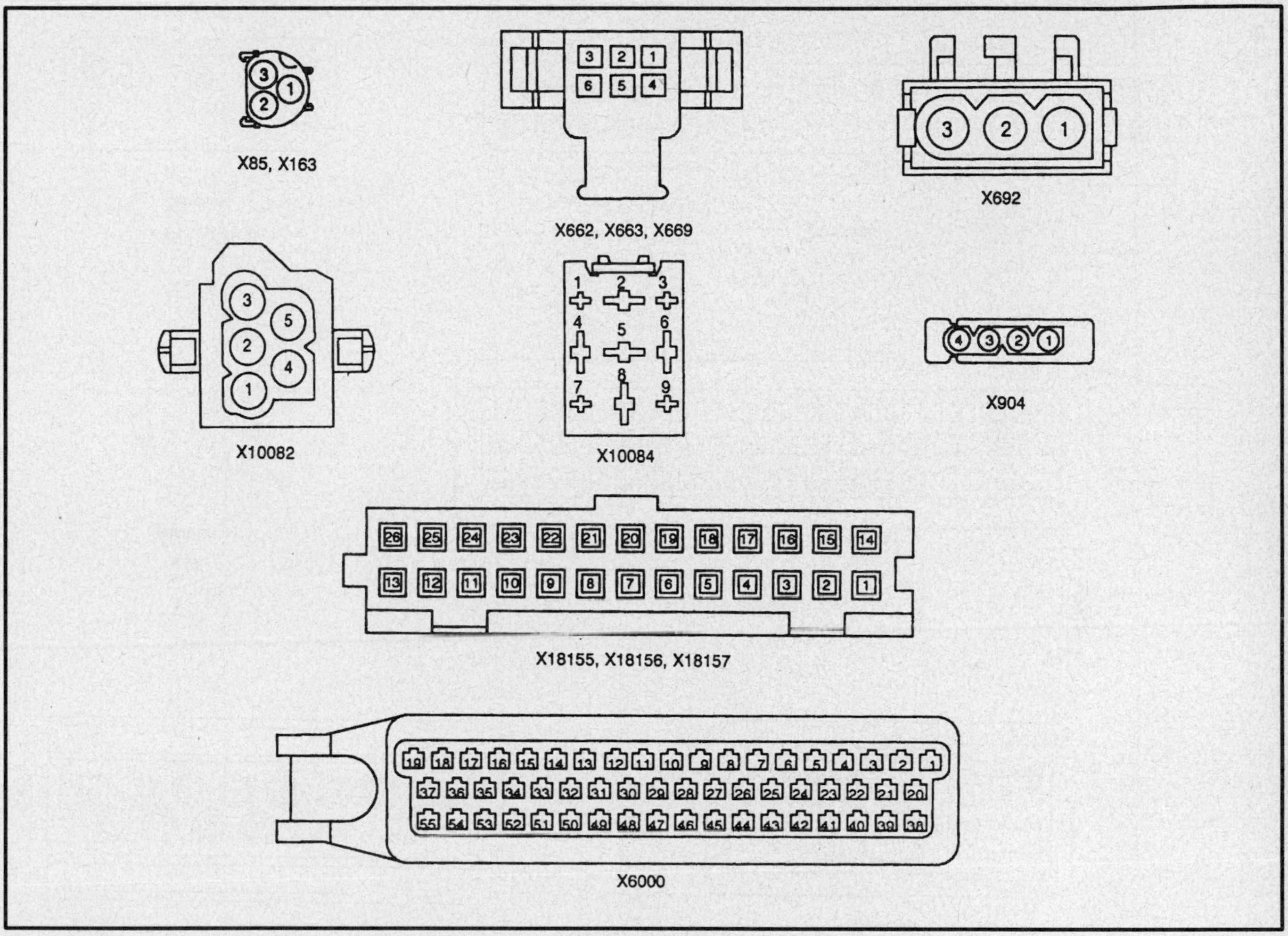

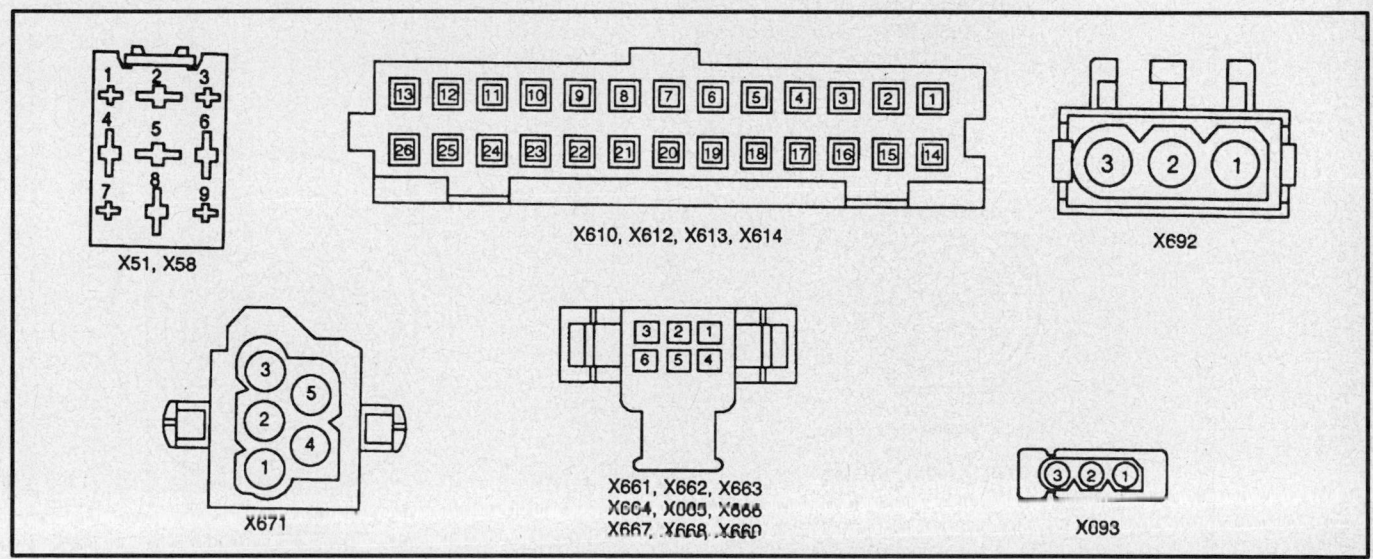

X85, X163

X662, X663, X669

X692

X10082

X10084

X904

X18155, X18156, X18157

X6000

Connector terminal locations—5-Series with automatic climate control

X51, X58

X610, X612, X613, X614

X692

X671

**X661, X662, X663
X664, X665, X666
X667, X668, X669**

X093

Connector terminal locations—7-Series with automatic climate control

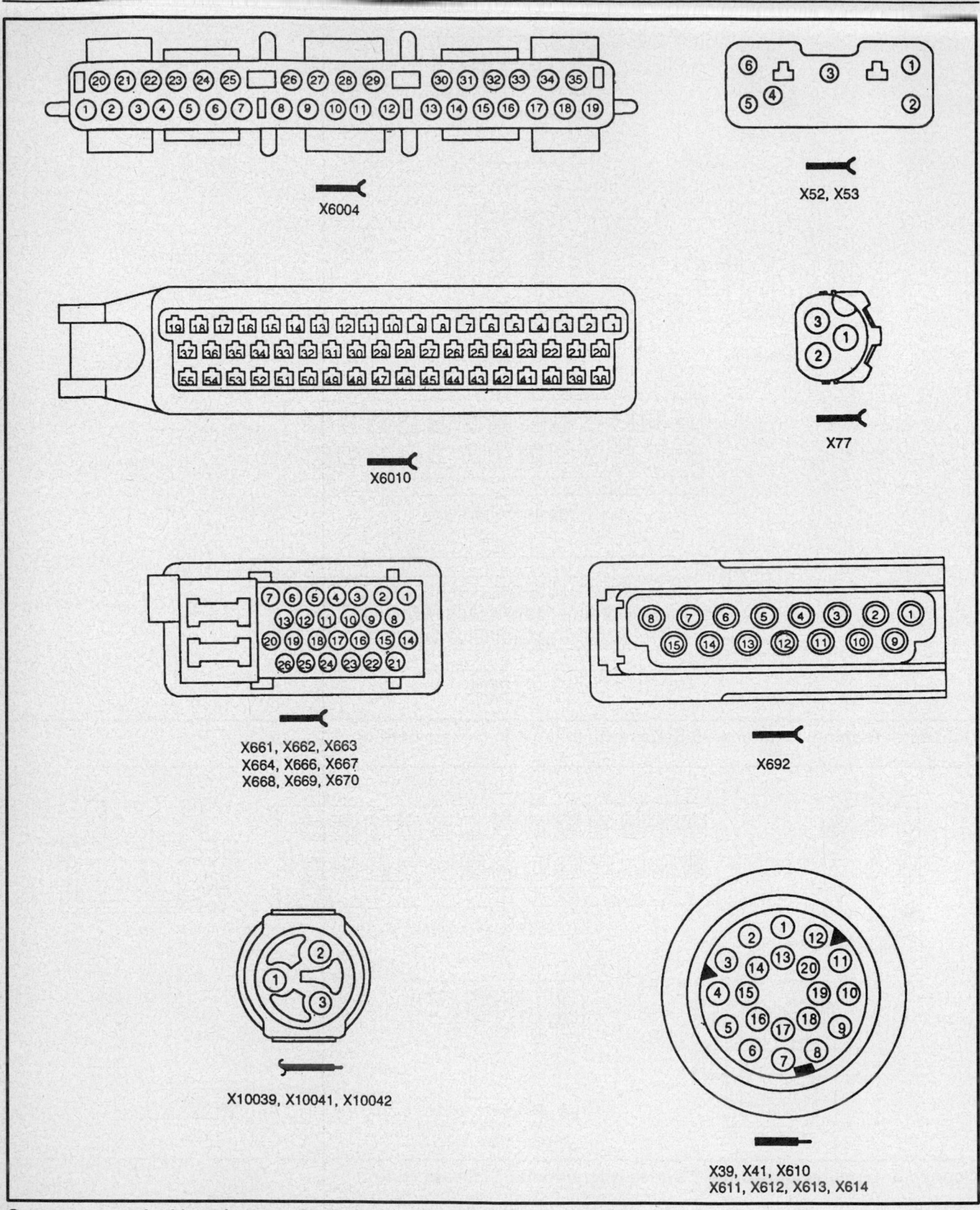

X6004

X52, X53

X6010

X77

X661, X662, X663
X664, X666, X667
X668, X669, X670

X692

X10039, X10041, X10042

X39, X41, X610
X611, X612, X613, X614

Connector terminal locations—8-Series with automatic climate control

WIRING SCHEMATICS

Connector at control unit

Abbreviation	Number	Designation
SRA	X 613	(S)Connector (R)right (A)top (26-pole blue)
SRB	X 614	(S)Connector (R)right (B)bottom (26-pole yellow)
SLA	X 610	(S)Connector (L)left (A)top (26-pole white)
SLB	X 611	(S)Connector (L)left (B)bottom (26-pole green)

Plug-type connection

Abbreviation	Number	Designation
	X 35	Connector to front section of wire harness (21-pole, black)
BSA	X 612	(B)Operating unit (S)connector (A) (26-pole, blue)
BSB	X 693	Connector plus to the water valves
BSC	X 682	Connector from operating unit (3-pole, white for independent heating / independent ventilation) to relay box
	X 671	Connector to output stage (5-pole, green)

Connector numbers, designation and abbreviations for system diagnosis—7-Series

PIN	Function	Type	Connection
1/2/14/15	Ground	E	Ground
3	Not used		
4	Set temperature value, left (potentiometer)	E	Operating unit left temperature control wheel
5	Set air volume value (potentiometer)	E	Operating unit air volume control wheel
6	Inside sensor blower (ground)	A	Operating unit
7	Outside temperature	A/E	Outside temperature sensor (solder connection)
8	Set temperature value, right (potentiometer)	E	Operating unit right temperature control wheel
9	Evaporator temperature	A/E	Evaporator sensor
10/11/23/24	Battery + for stepping motor	A	Battery + from control unit for all stepping motors
12/13/25/26	Ignition "ON" terminal 15	E	Terminal 15
16	Ground for sensors and control wheels	A	Ground from control unit for all sensors and control wheels
17	Set mixing value (potentiometer)	E	Mixing control wheel in ventilation grille
18	Heater temperature, left	A/E	Heater sensor, left
19	Starter terminal 50 (30 h)	E	Solenoid switch 30 h
20	+5 V - supply from control unit	A	All control wheels (potentiometer)
21	Inside temperature value	A/E	Operating unit inside temperature sensor
22	Heater temperature, right	A/E	Right heater sensor

Pin assignments at connector X613—5 and 7-Series control unit

PIN	Function	Type	Connection
1/2/3/4	Flap motor drive, right footwell	A	Flap motor, right footwell
5	Switch for rear window, air circulation, climate control	E	Operating unit circulation air, climate control, rear window
6	Not used		
7	Switch for independent heating, independent ventilation	E	Relay box output independent heating / independent ventilation (matrix circuit)
8	Ventilation flap switch	E	Ventilation switch
9	Speed "A" signal	E	Instrument cluster
10	Diagnosis	E	Diagnostic socket RxD
11	Switch for rear window, independent heating	E	Operating unit rear window, relay box output independent heating (matrix circuit
12	Switch for circulation air, independent ventilation	E	Operating unit, circulation air, relay box output independent ventilation (matrix circuit)
13	Switch for climate control	E	Operating unit climate control (matrix circuit)
14/15/16/17	Not used		
18/19/20/21	Mixing flap motor drive	A	Mixing flap motor
22/23/24/25/26	Not used		

Pin assignments at connector X614—5 and 7-Series control unit

PIN	Function	Type	Connection
1/2/3/4	Not used		
5	Blower output stage drive	A	Blower output stage
6	Auxiliary fan relay drive (= A/C motronic relay - DME)	A	Air conditioning system/motronic relay
7	Rear defogger relay drive	A	Rear defogger relay
8	Climate control relay drive, auxiliary fan stage 1	A	Climate control relay, auxiliary fan relay stage I
9/10/11/	Not used		
12/13/25/26	Continuous plus supply terminal 30	E	Front power distributor
14/15/16/17	Flap motor drive, circulation air	A	Circulation air flap motor
18	Function light drive A/C circulation air	A	Operating unit
19	Rear window function light drive	A	Operating unit
20	Diagnosis	A	Diagnostic connector TxD
21	Left water valve drive	A	Water valve
22	Auxiliary water pump relay drive	A	Auxiliary water pump relay K8
23	Right water valve drive	A	Water valve
24	Footwell slide control	E	Operating unit footwell slide control (potentiometer)

Pin assignments at connector X610—5 and 7-Series control unit

PIN	Function	Type	Connection
1/14/15/16	Flap motor drive, left footwell	A	Left footwell flap motor
2/3/4/5	Not used		
6/7/8/9	Fresh air flap motor drive	A	Fresh air flap motor
10/11/12/13	Not used		
17/18/19/20	Not used		
21/22/23/24	Not used		
25/26	Not used		

Pin assignments at connector X611—5 and 7-Series control unit

D 900 Defect code memory – stored defect codes:

Defect code No.	Defect location	Connector	Pin
01	Right temperature control wheel	blue	8
04	Right heater sensor	blue	22
07	Evaporator sensor	blue	9
10	Outside temperature sensor	blue	7
13	Inside temperature sensor	blue	21
16	Blower inside sensor	blue	6
22	Auxiliary fan relay (= A/C Motronic relay - DME)	white	6
25	Left temperature control wheel	blue	4
28	Left heater sensor	blue	18
31	Air volume control wheel	blue	5
32	Footwell slide control	white	24
34	Mixing control wheel	blue	16,17,20
38	Auxiliary water pump relay	white	22
40	Left water valve	white	21
44	A/C relay	white	8
46	Right water valve	white	23
48	Rear window defogger relay	white	7
52	Fresh air flap motor	green	6,7,8,9
55	Circulation air flap motor	white	14,15,16,17
61	Mixing flap motor	yellow	18,19,20,21
70	Left footwell flap motor	green	1,14,15,16
73	Right footwell flap motor	yellow	1,2,3,4

Defect code table—5-Series

PIN	Function	Type	Connection
1/2	Not used		
3	Switch for rear window, independent heating	A/E	Control unit connector X 614 pin 11
4	Switch for independent heating, independent ventilation	A	Control unit connector X 614 pin 7
5	Switch for circulation air, independent ventilation	A/E	Control unit connector X 614 pin 12
6	Switch for rear window, circulation air, climate control	A	Control unit connector X 614 pin 5
7	Rear window function light drive	E	Control unit connector X 610 pin 19
8/9/10/11/12	Not used		
13	Inside temperature value	A/E	Control unit connector X 613 pin 21
14	+5 V supply from control unit	E	Control unit connector X 613 pin 20
15	Ground for sensors and control wheels	E	Control unit connector X 613 pin 16
16	Function light drive	E	Control unit connector X 610 pin 18
17	Air volume control wheel switch Max position	E	Ignition switch terminal 15
18	Footwell slide control	A	Control unit connector X 610 pin 24
19	Operating unit lighting	E	Dimmer for instrument lighting
20	Ground for function and operating unit lighting	E	Ground
21	Set temperature value, right (potentiometer)	A	Control unit connector X 613 pin 8
22	Set temperature value, left (potentiometer)	A	Control unit connector X 613 pin 4
23	Air volume value (potentiometer)	A	Control unit connector X 613 pin 5
24	Switch for heating, climate control, circulation air	A	Control unit connector X 614 pin 13
25	Air volume control wheel switch in MAX position	A	Output stage connector X 671 pin 3
26	Inside sensor blower (ground)	E	Control unit connector X 613 pin 6

Pin assignments at connector X6—12—5 and 7-Series operating unit

Fuse	Fault when the fuse is defective
No. F09	Auxiliary water pump relay (working circuit) Compressor clutch relay - auxiliary fan stage I (working circuit)
No. F19	Blower motor does not operate (also in maximum air volume control wheel position)
No. F20	IHKR control unit (defect storage not possible)
No. F24	IHKR control unit (diagnostic procedure not possible) both water valves, inside sensor blower (IHKA) Function lighting (operating unit IHKA)
No. F25	Air conditioning system relay ON signal to DME (working circuit) Auxiliary fan relay stage 2 (working circuit)
No. F29	Compressor clutch relay - auxiliary fan relay stage 1 (control circuit) auxiliary water pump relay (control circuit) air conditioning system relay ON signal to DME (control circuit) auxiliary fan relay stage 2 (control circuit) Rear window defogger (control circuit)
No. F46	Rear defogger (working circuit)

Climate control system fuses and related fault codes—All models

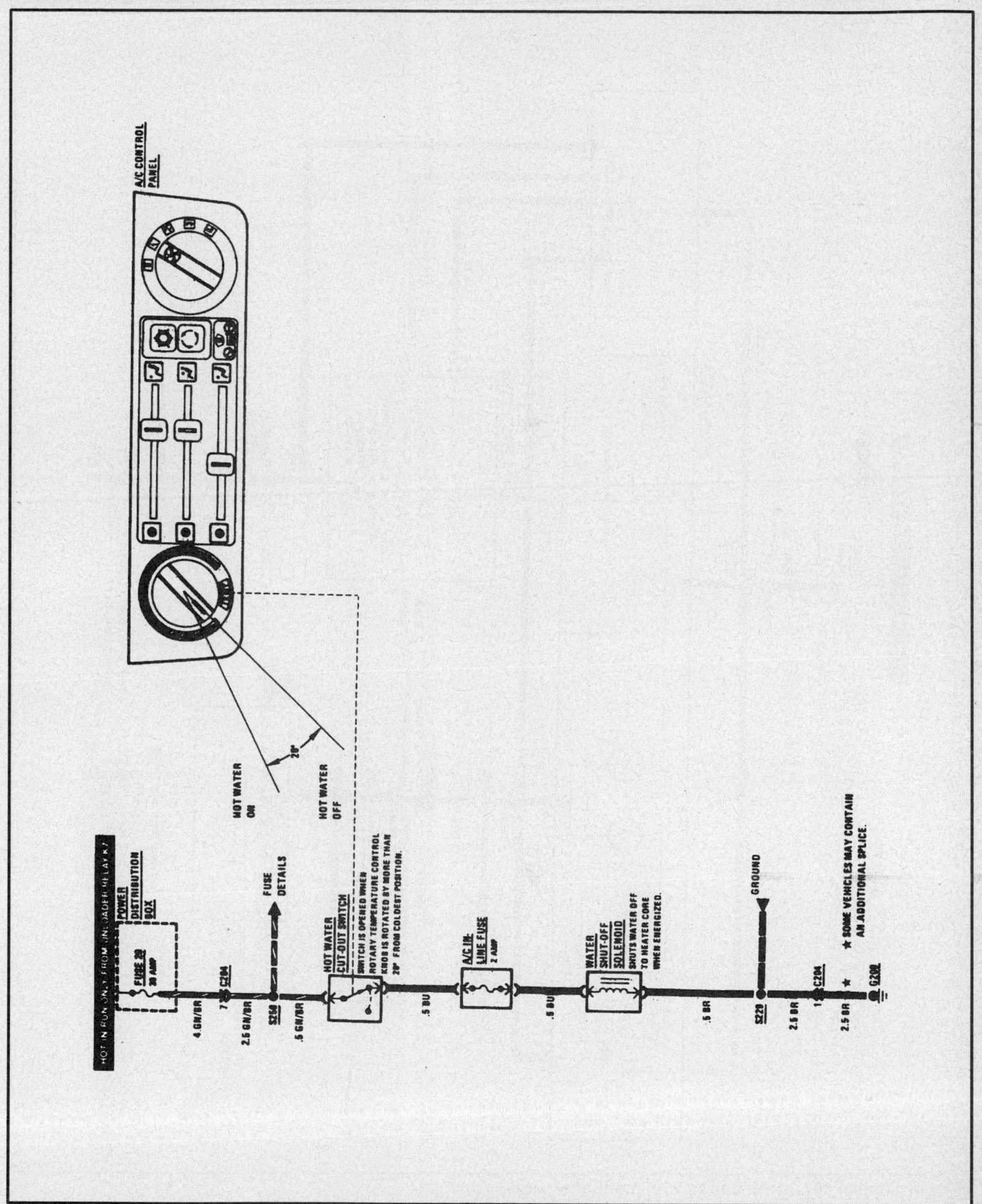

Hot water control circuit—3-Series with manual air conditioning

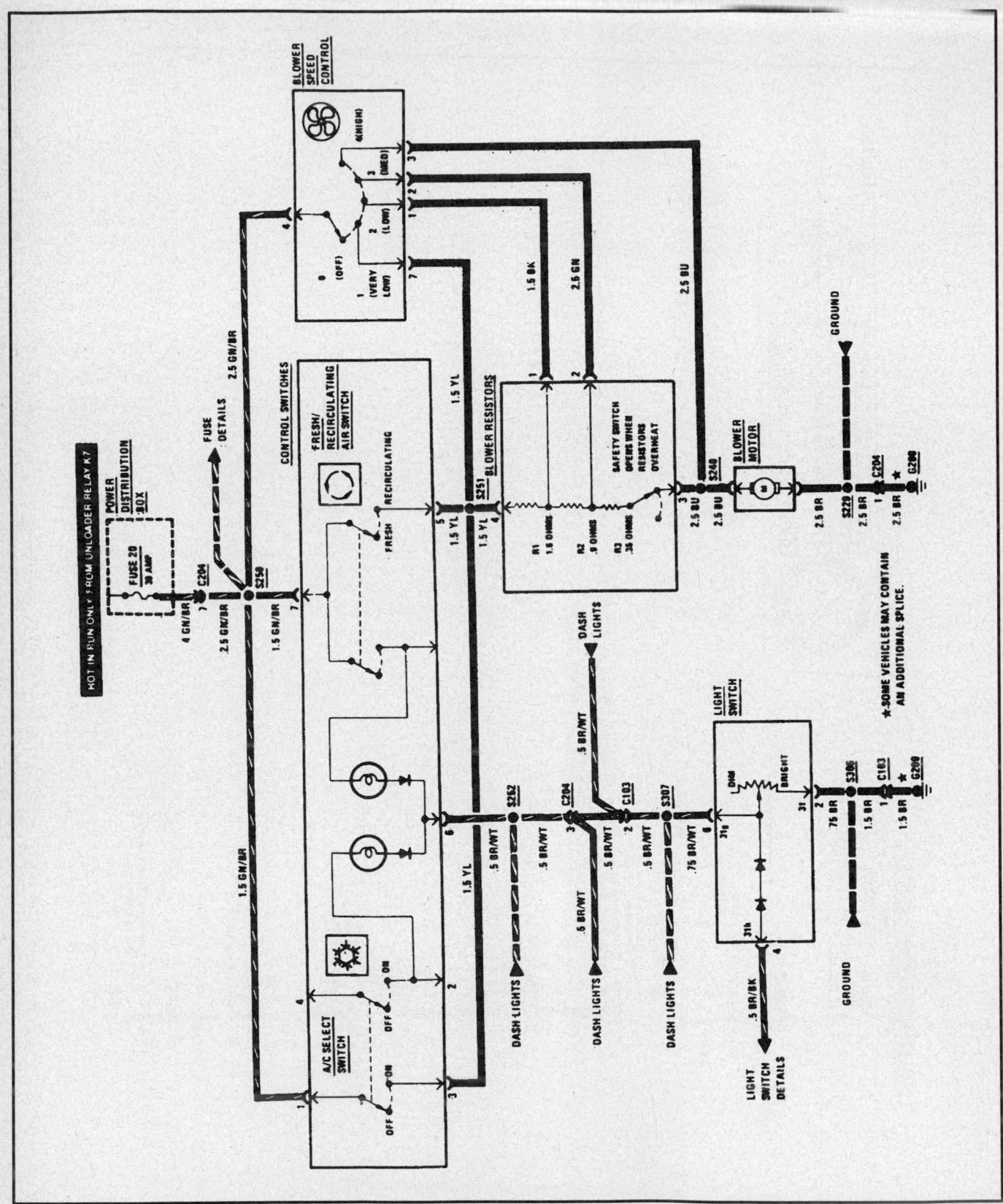

Blower control circuit—3-Series with manual air conditioning

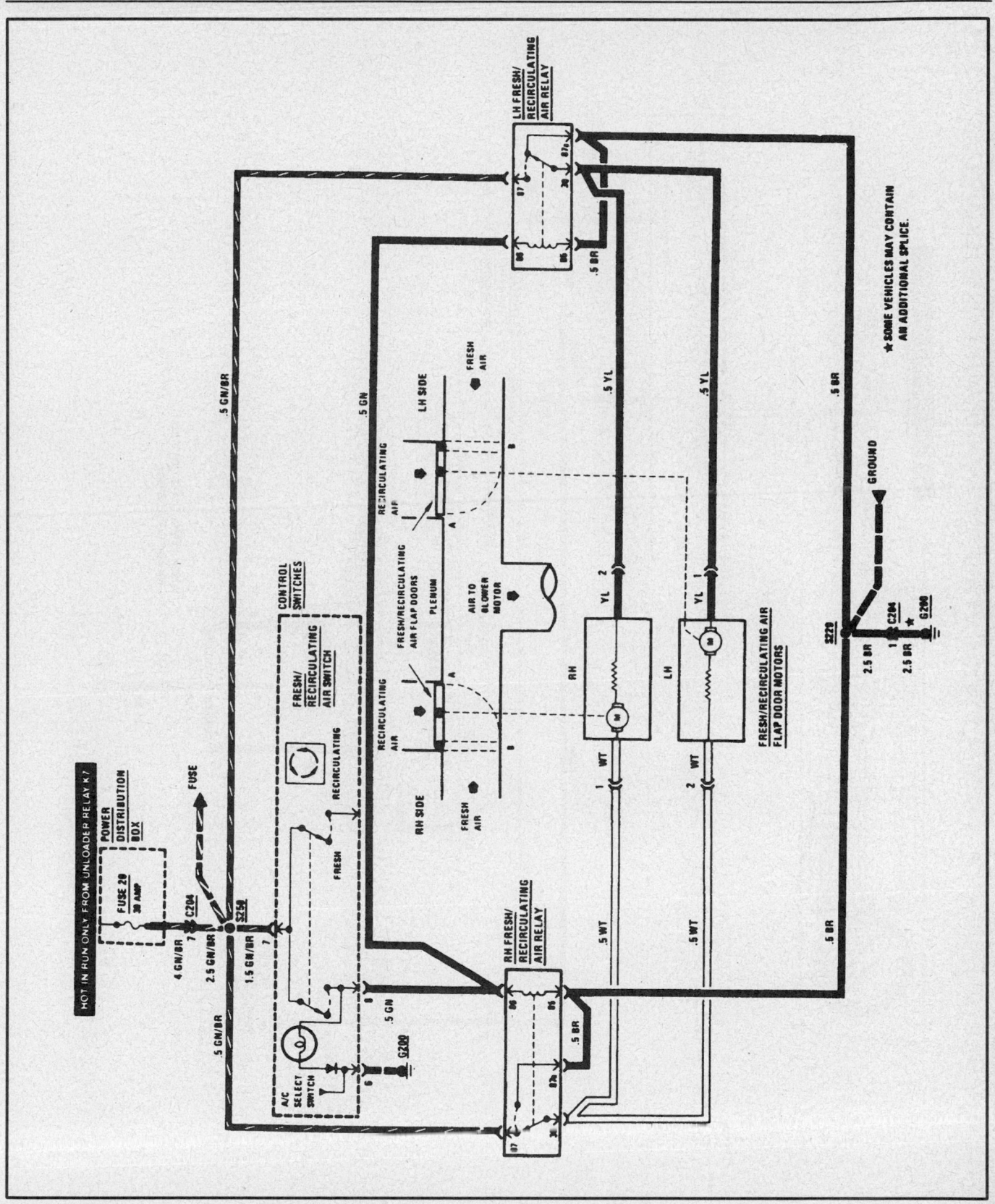

FRESH/RECIRC air control circuit-3-Series with manual air conditioning

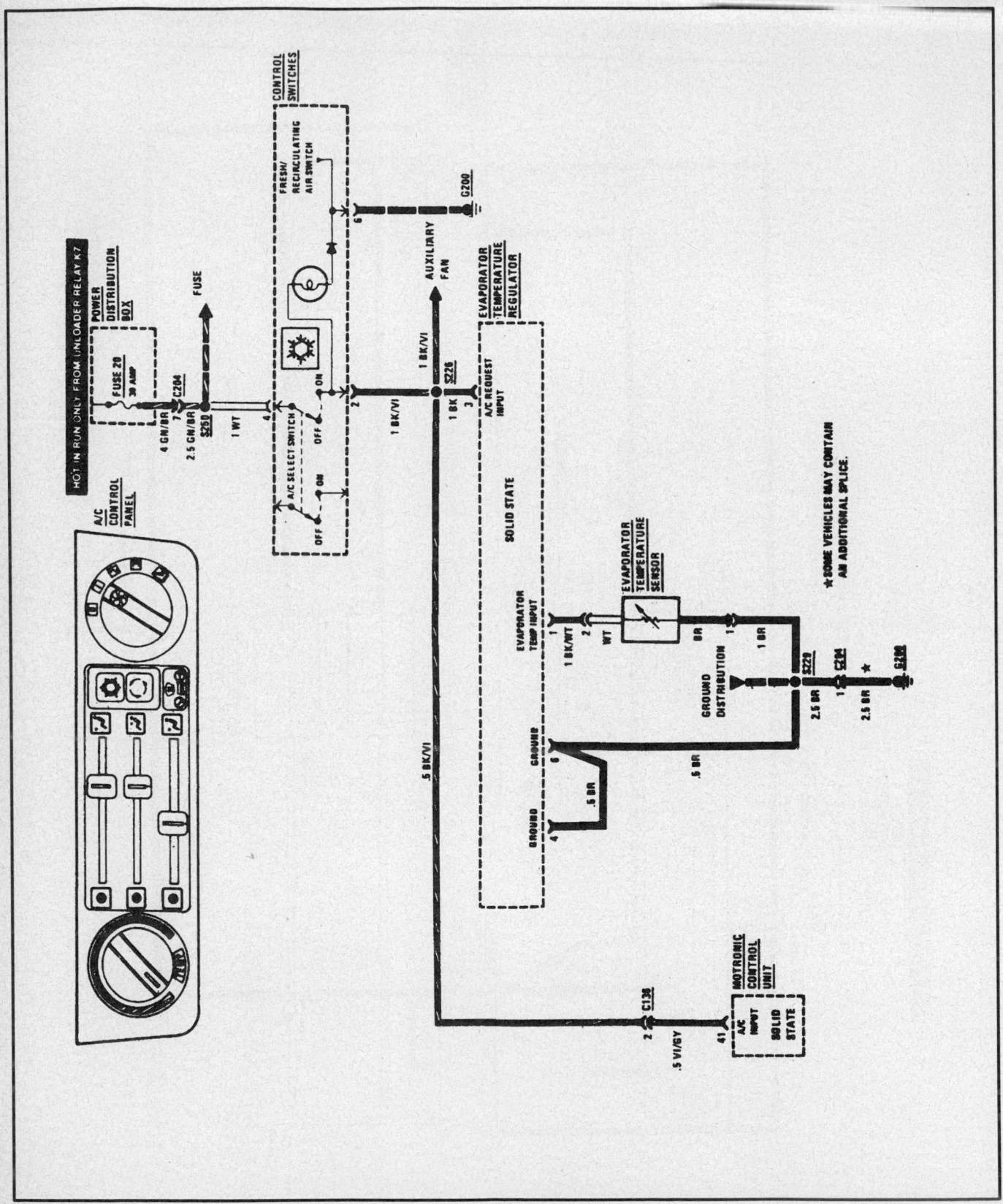

Compressor control circuit—3-Series with manual air conditioning

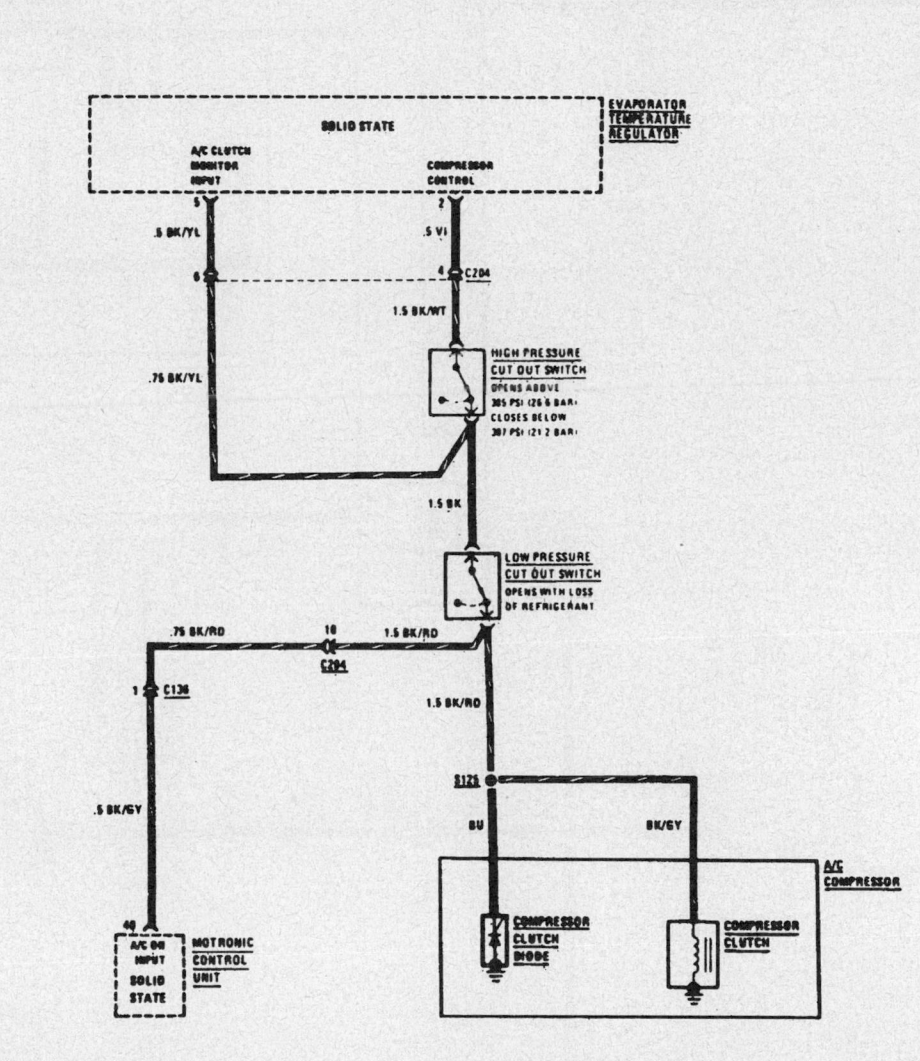

Compressor control circuit—3-Series (except 318i and 325i) with manual air conditioning

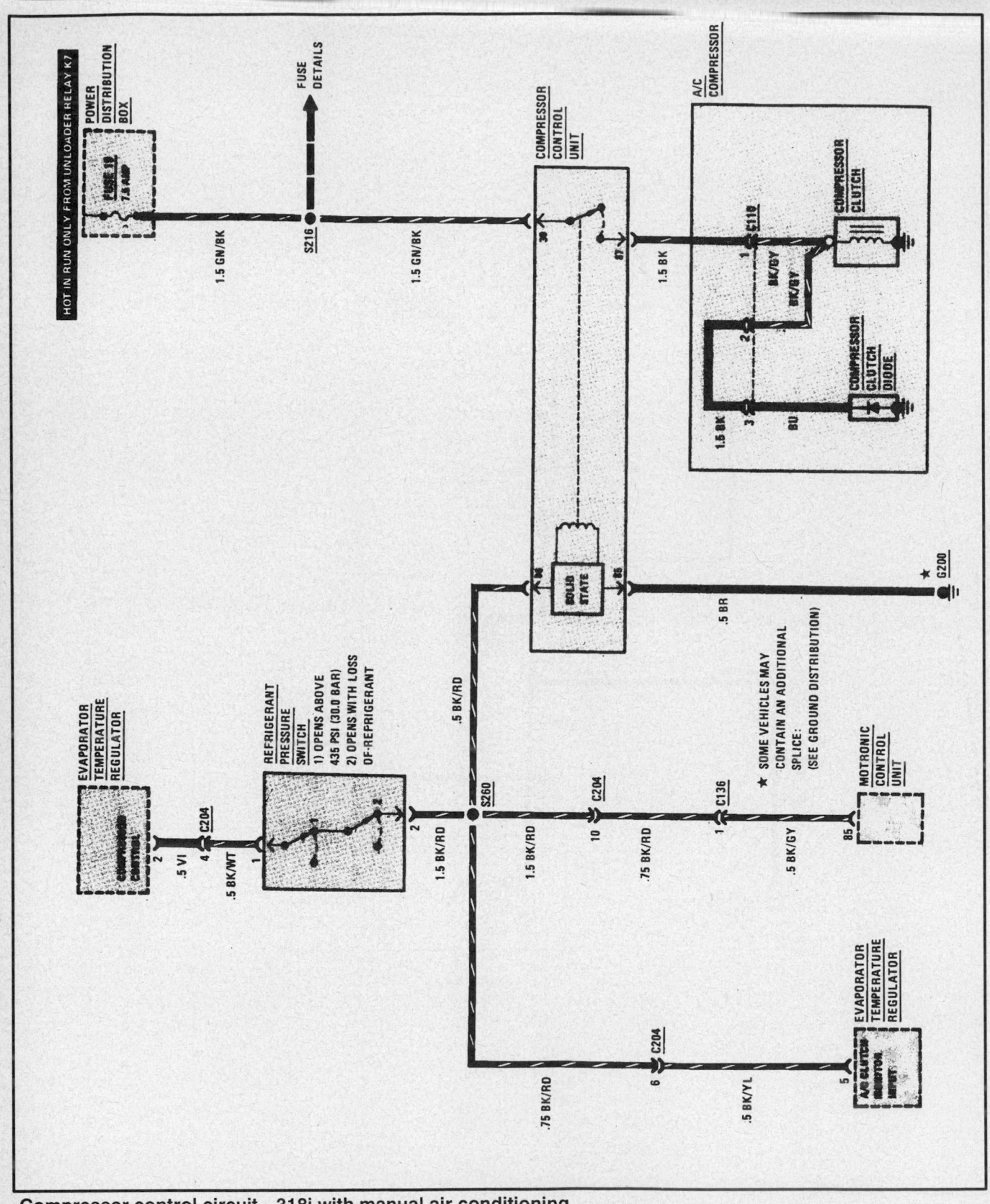

Compressor control circuit—318i with manual air conditioning

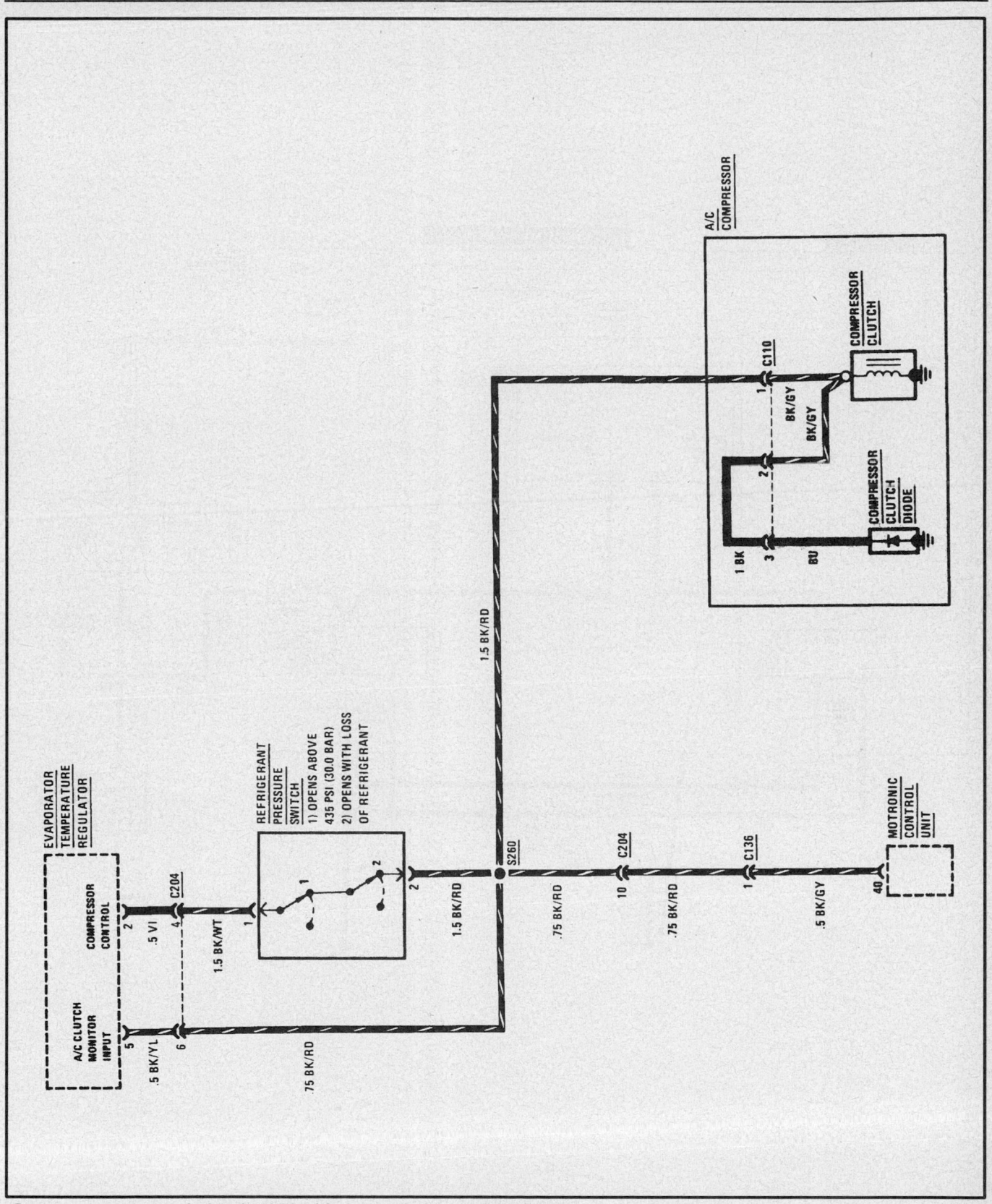

Compressor control circuit-325i with manual air conditioning

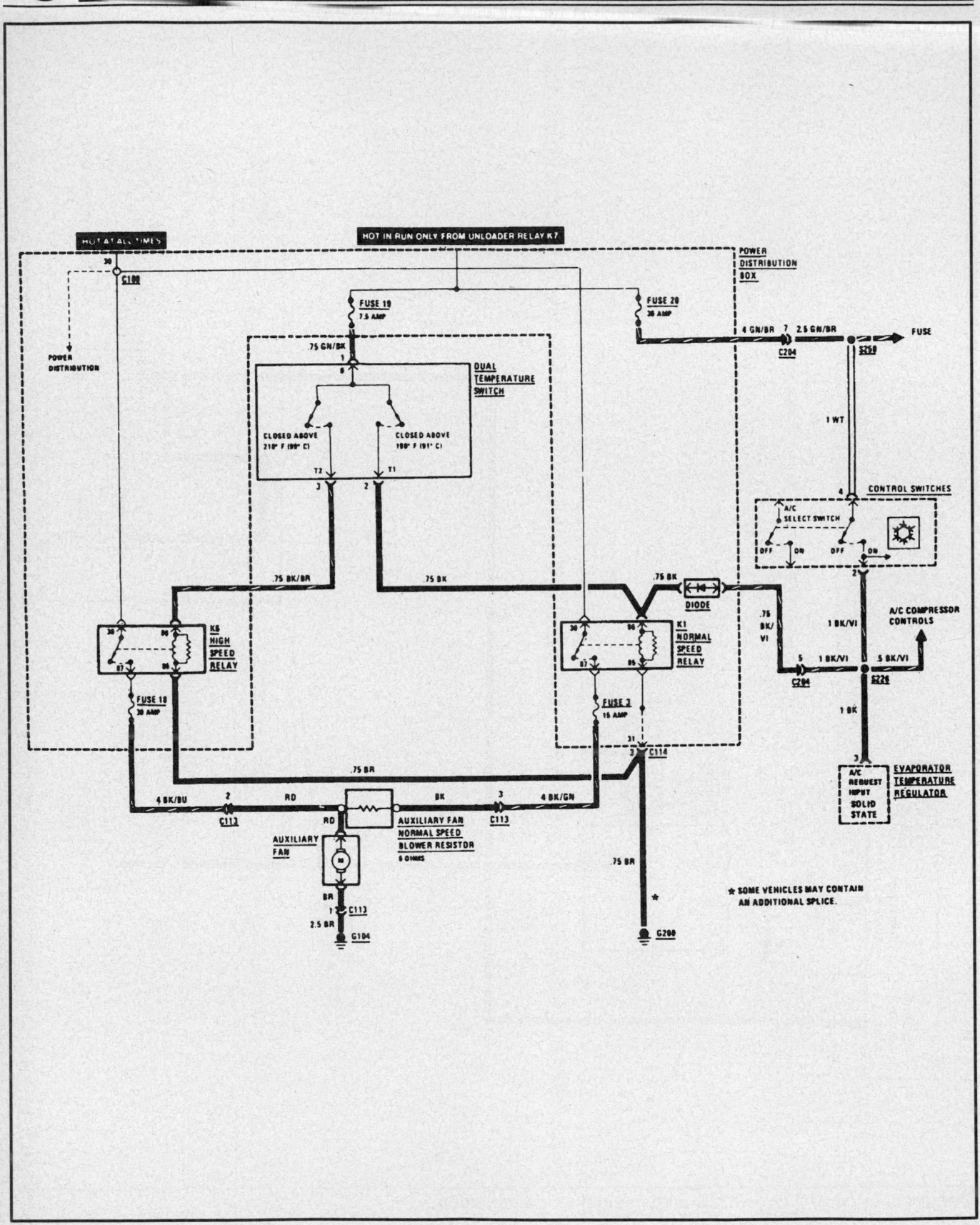

Auxiliary fan circuit—3-Series

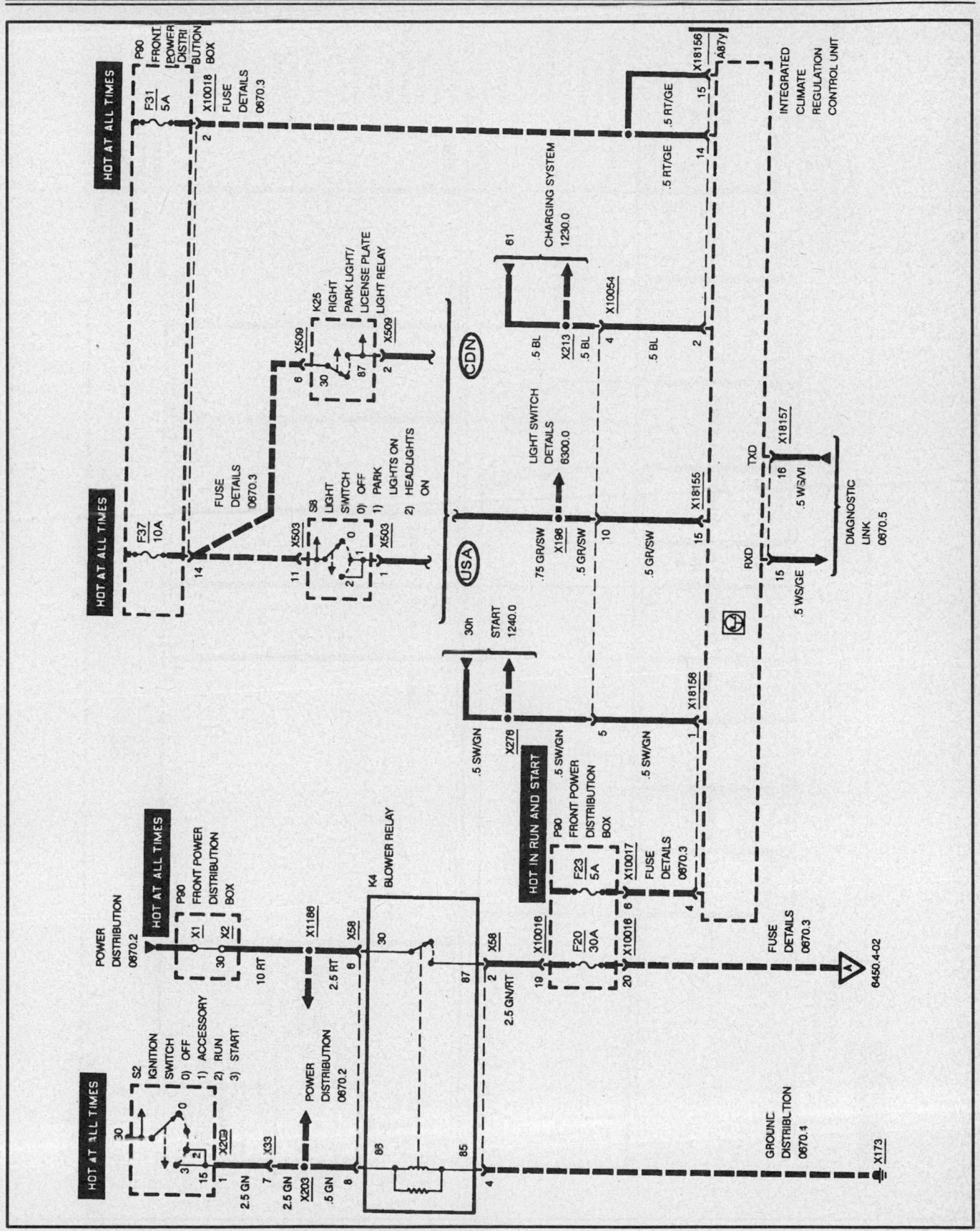

Power circuit—3-Series with automatic climate control

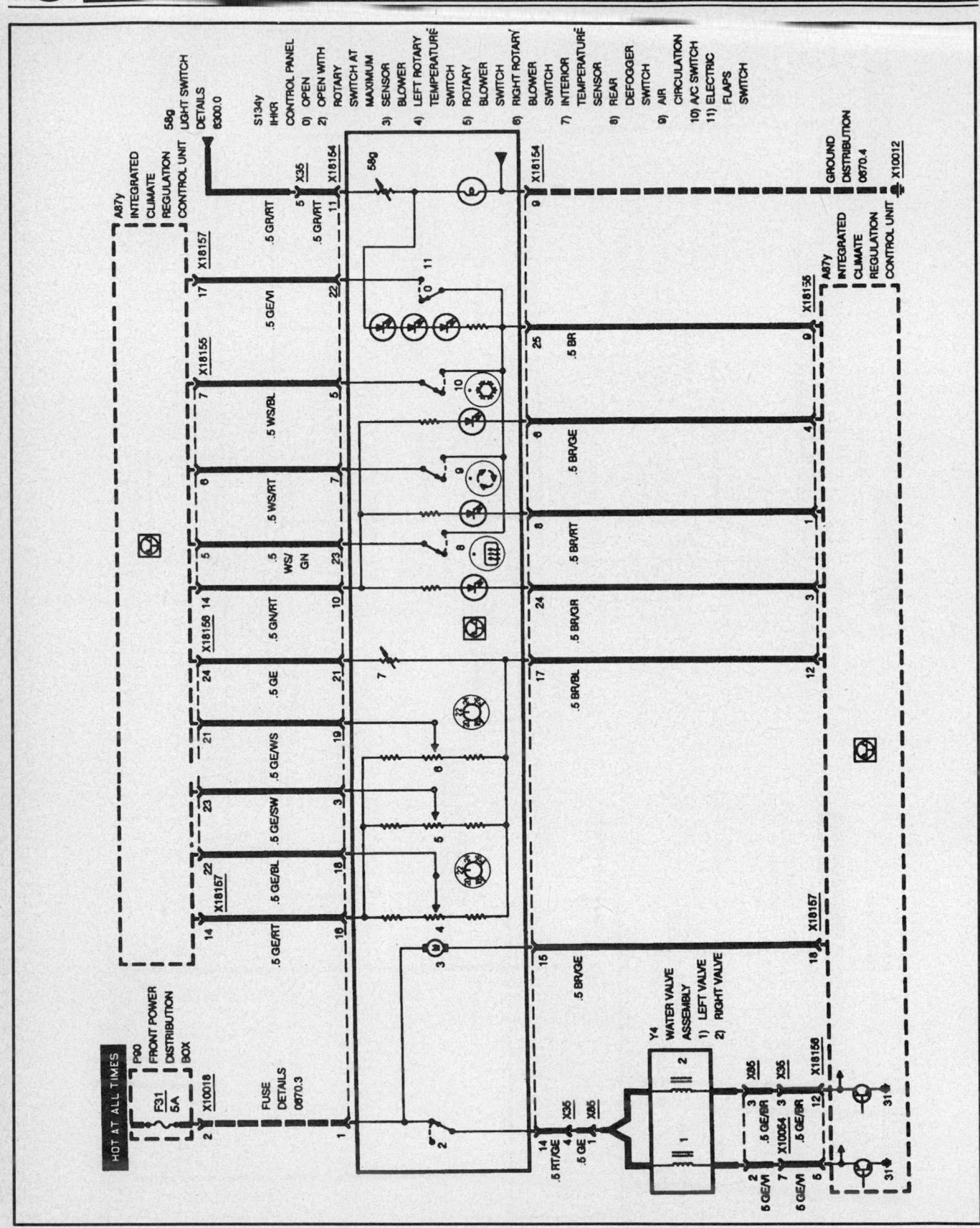

Control unit and water valve circuit—3-Series with automatic climate control

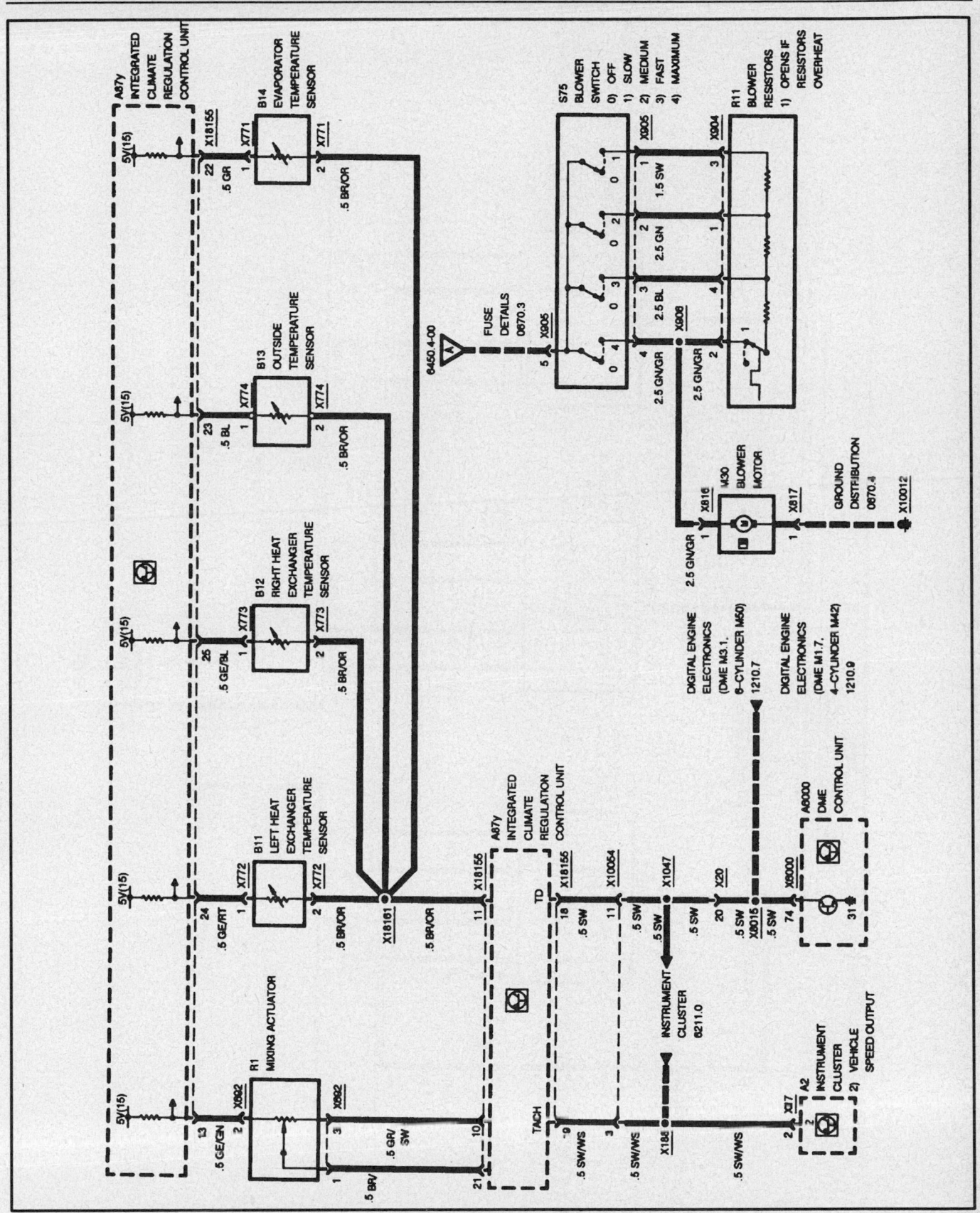

Temperature control circuit-3-Series with automatic climate control

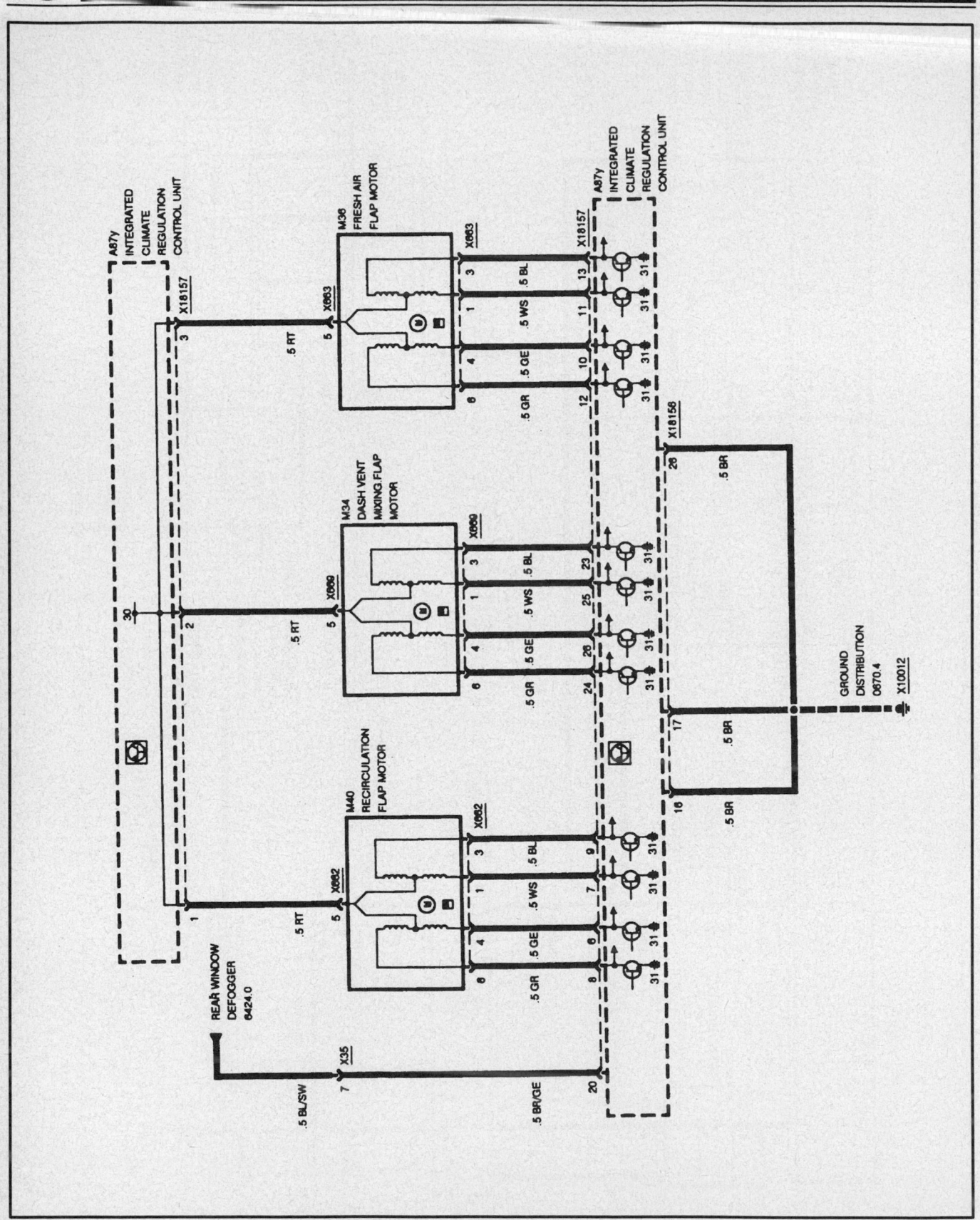

Air delivery circuit—3-Series with automatic climate control

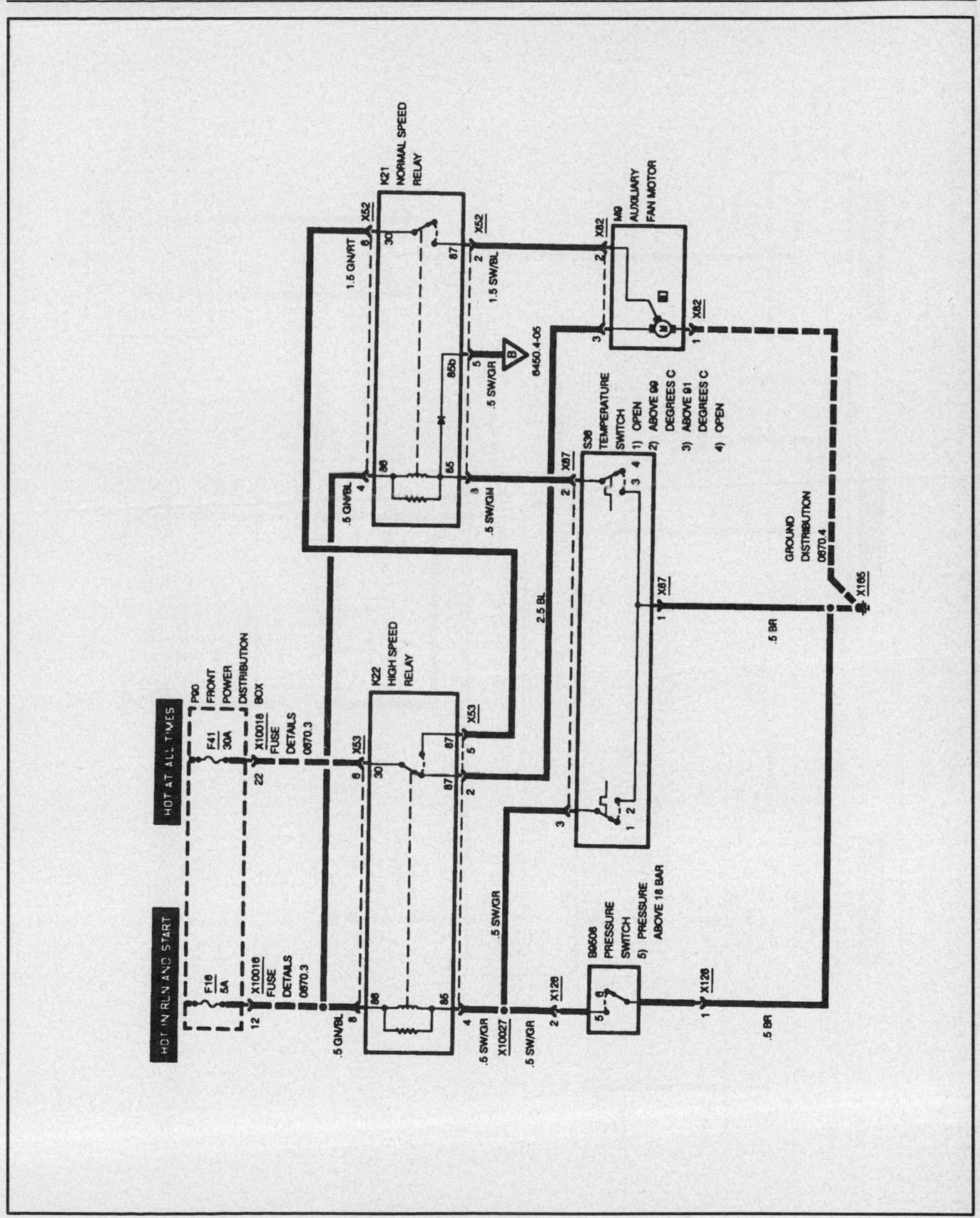

Auxiliary fan circuit—3-Series with automatic climate control

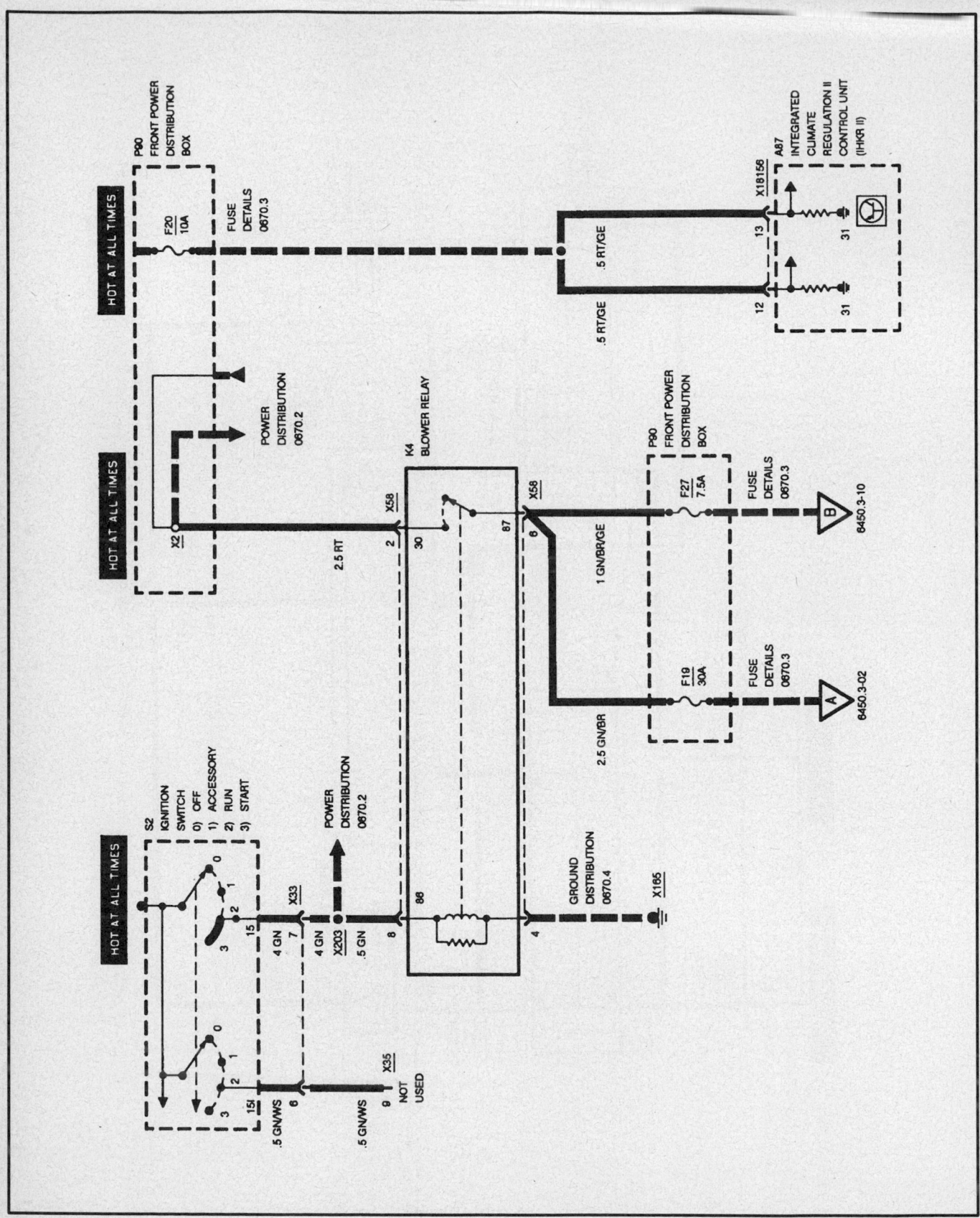

Power circuit—5-Series

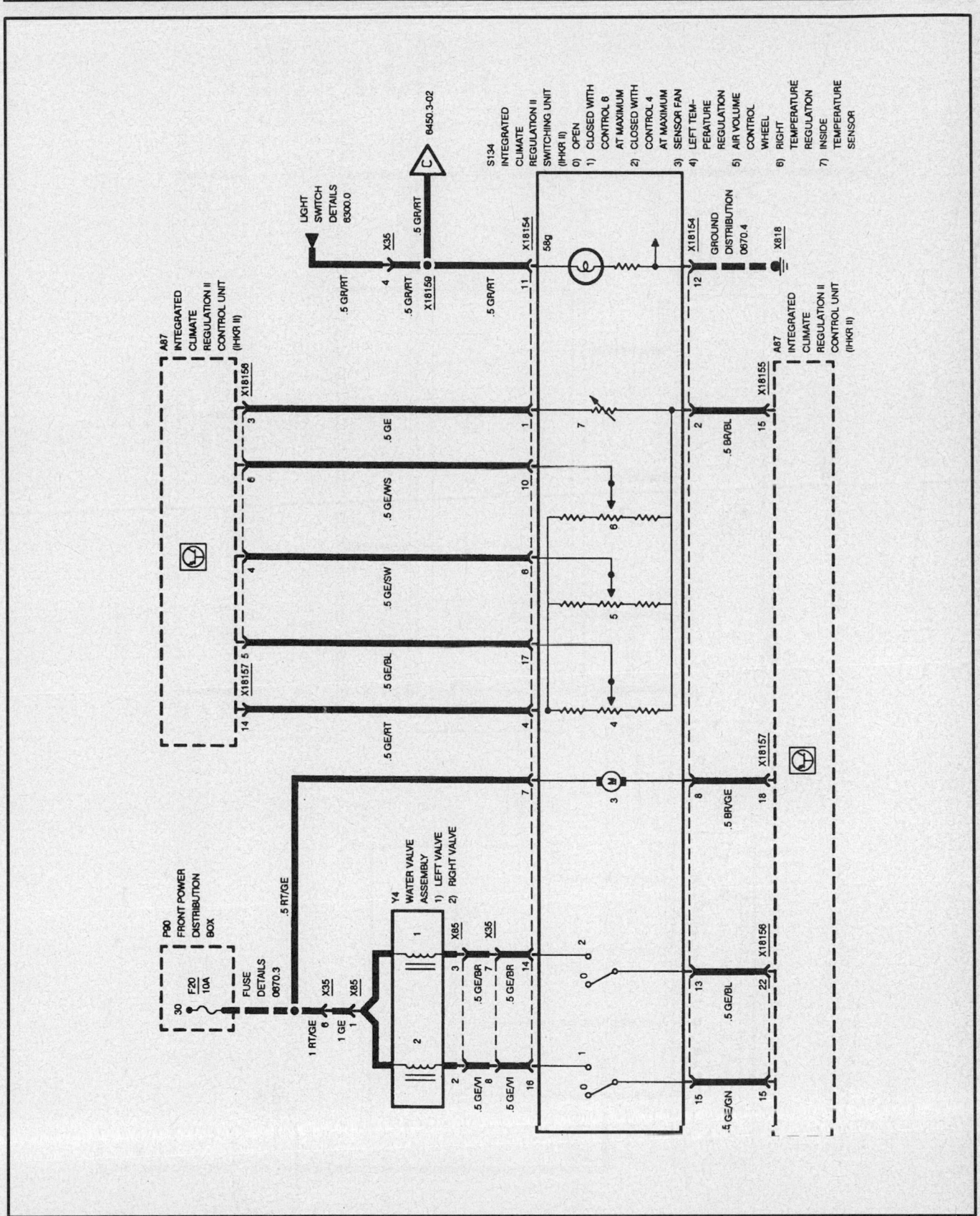

Power circuit—5-Series, cont'd

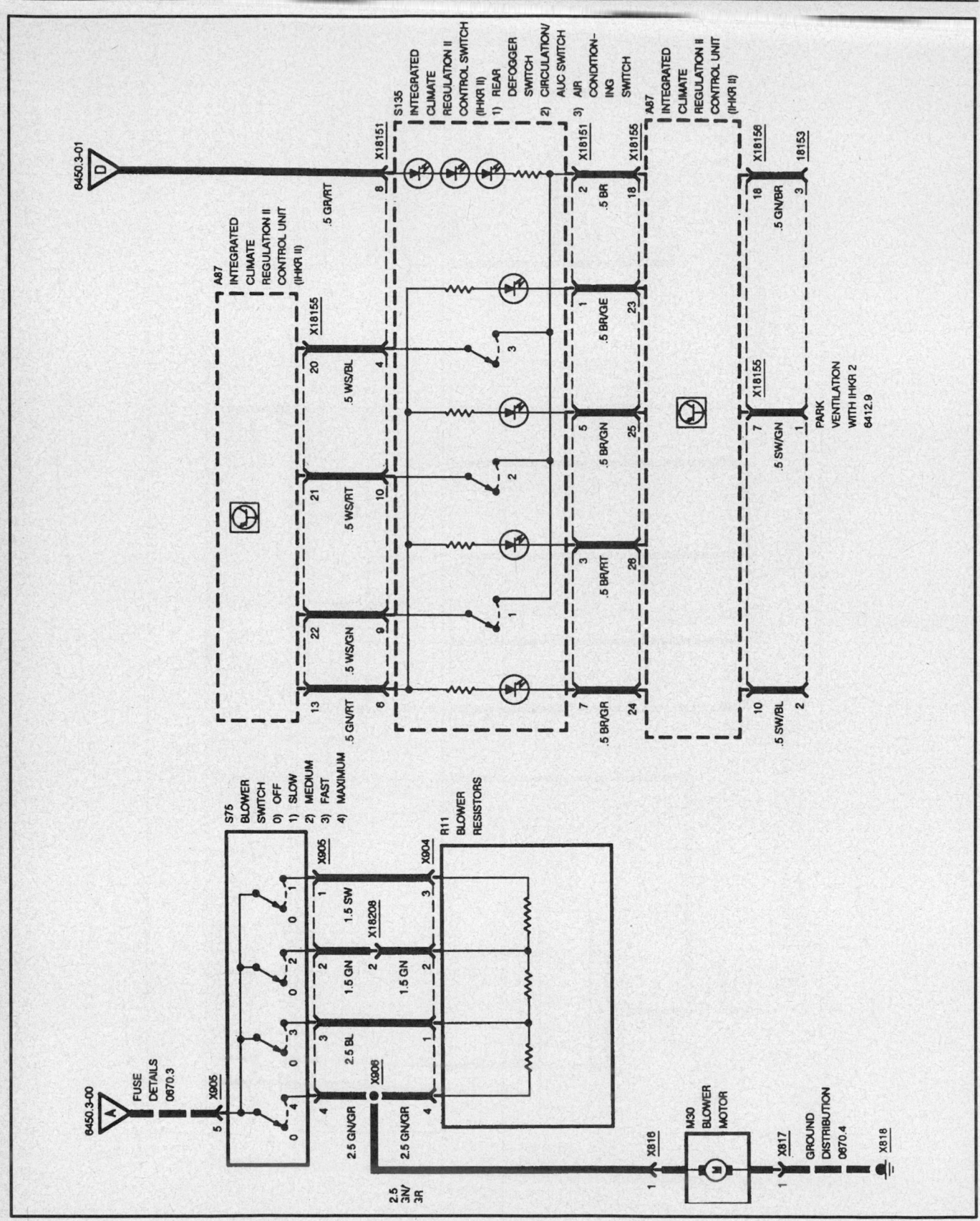

Power circuit—5-Series, cont'd

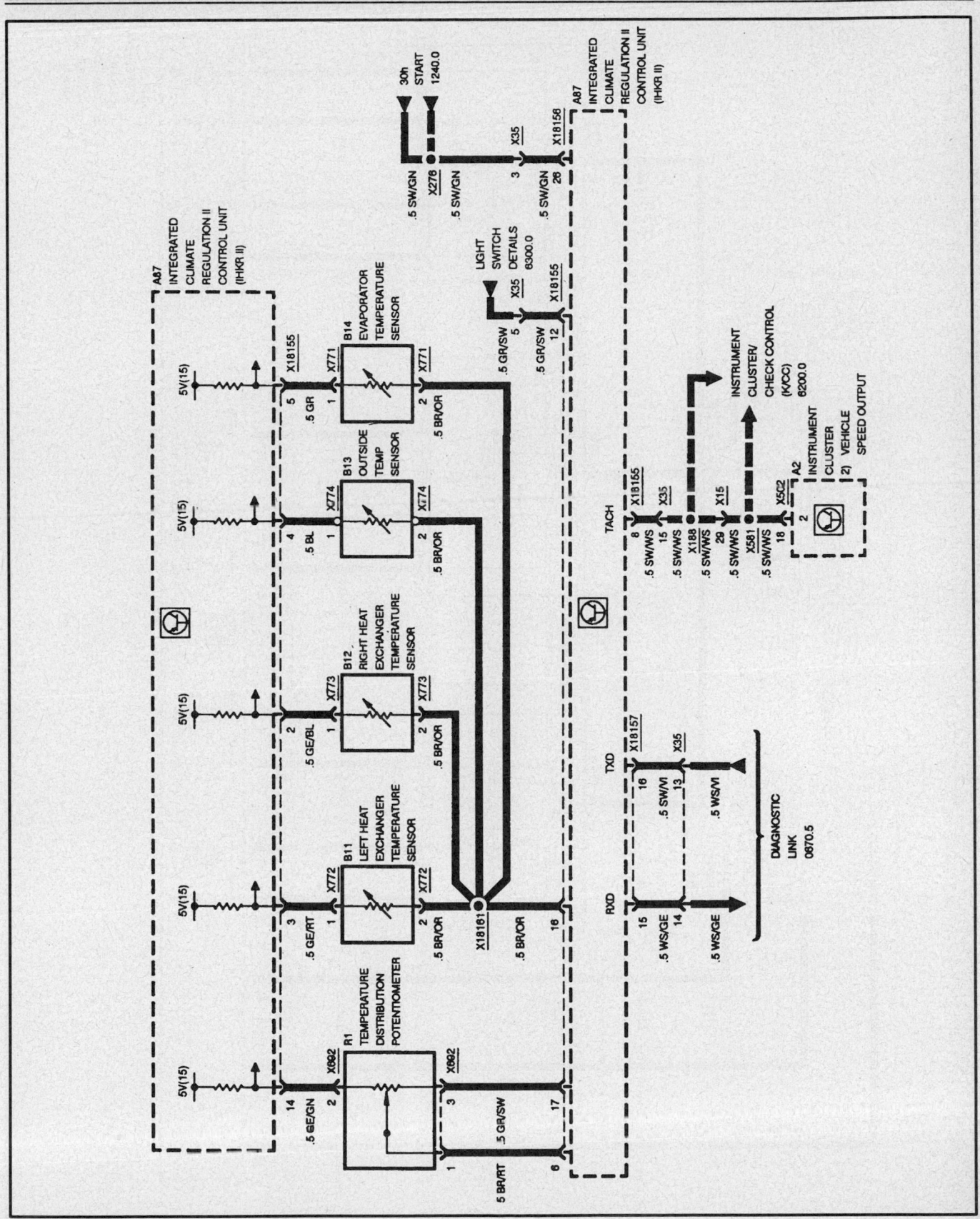

Temperature control circuit—5-Series

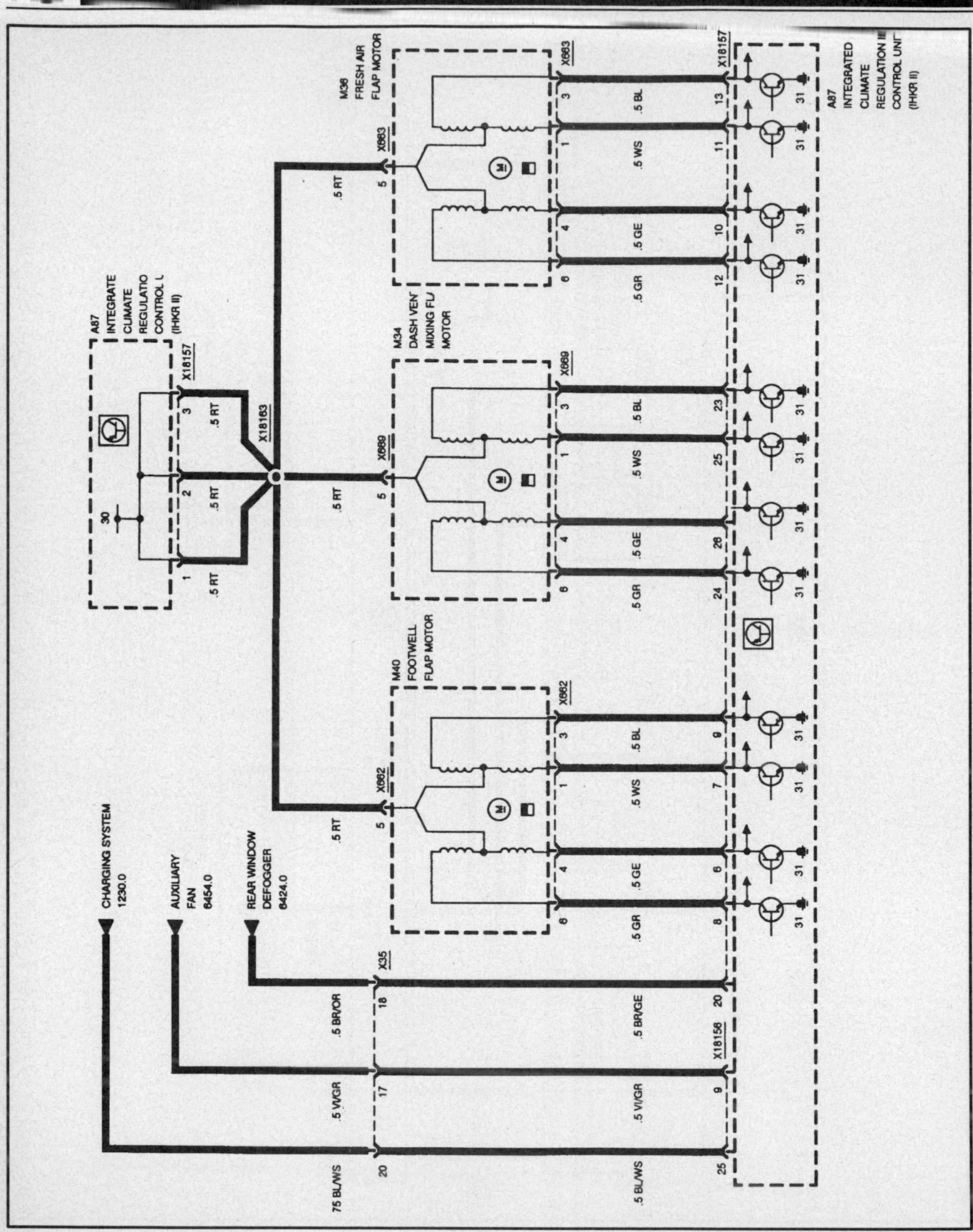

Air delivery circuit—5-Series

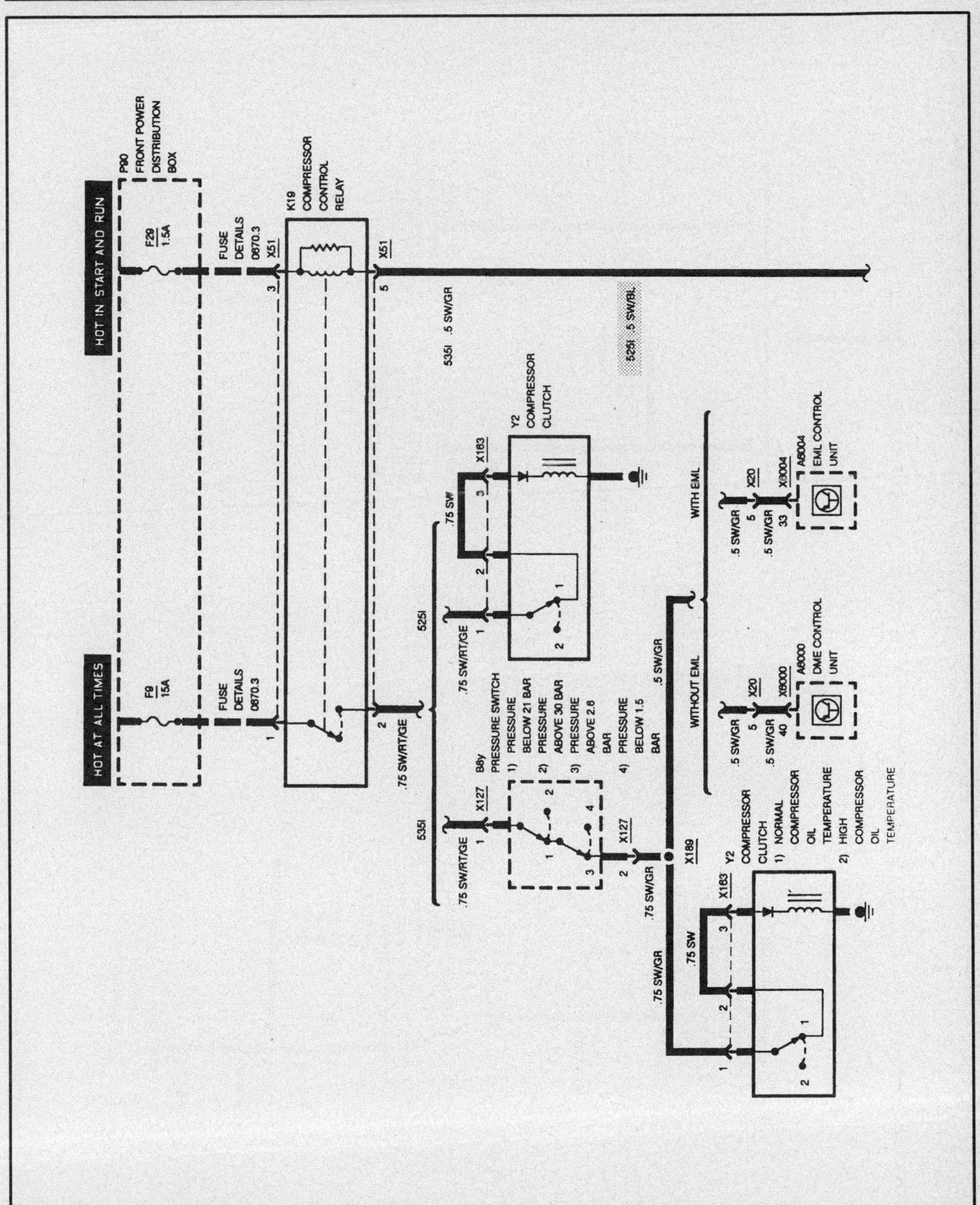

Compressor circuit—5-Series

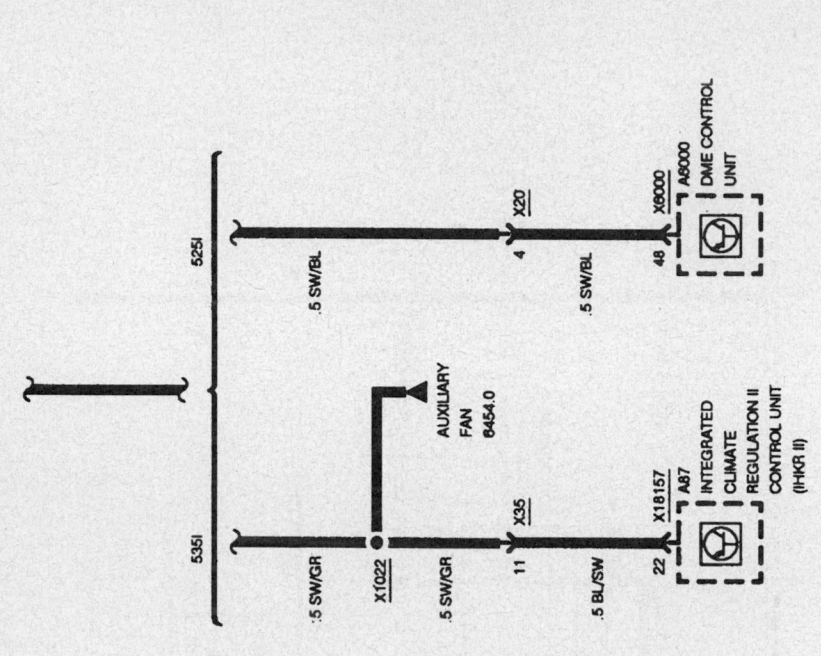

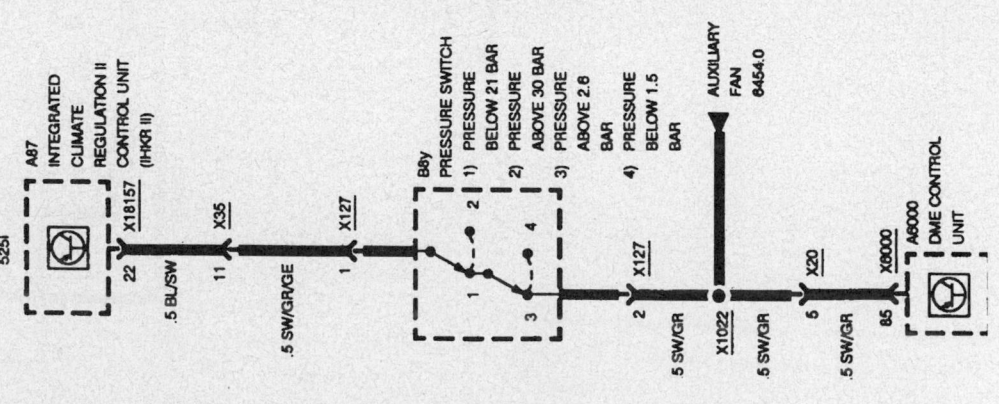

Compressor circuit—5-Series, cont'd

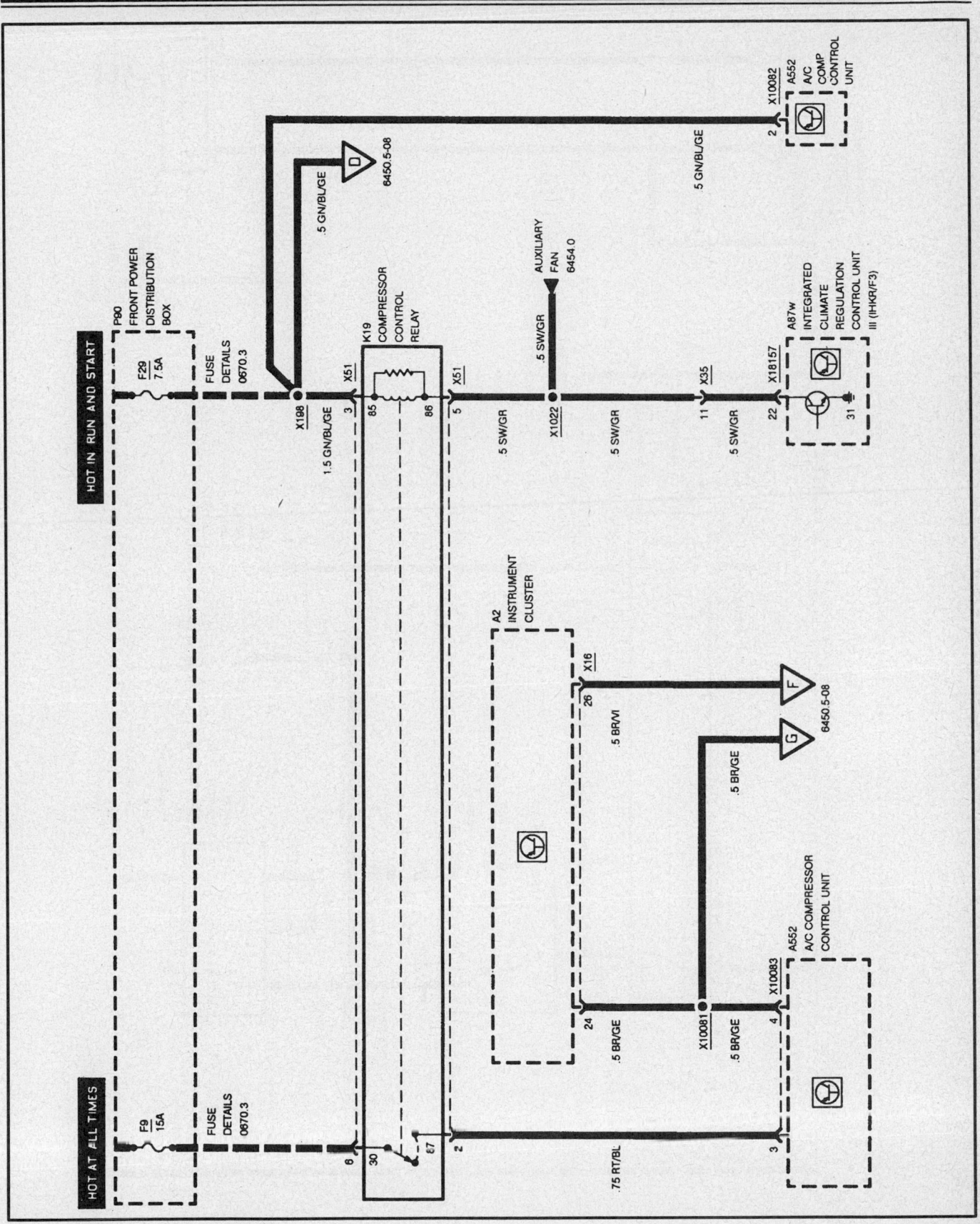

Compressor circuit—5-Series

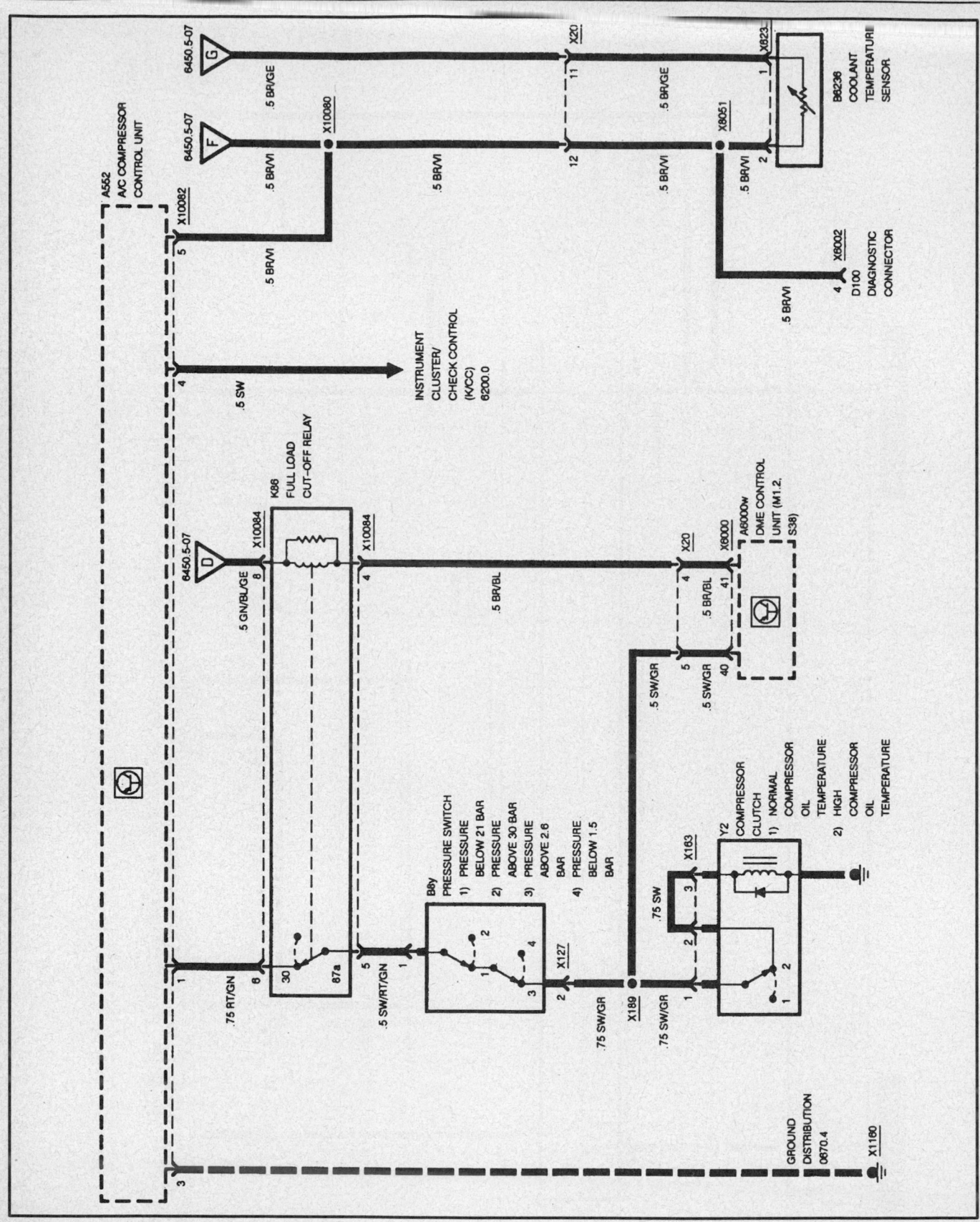

Compressor circuit—5-Series, cont'd

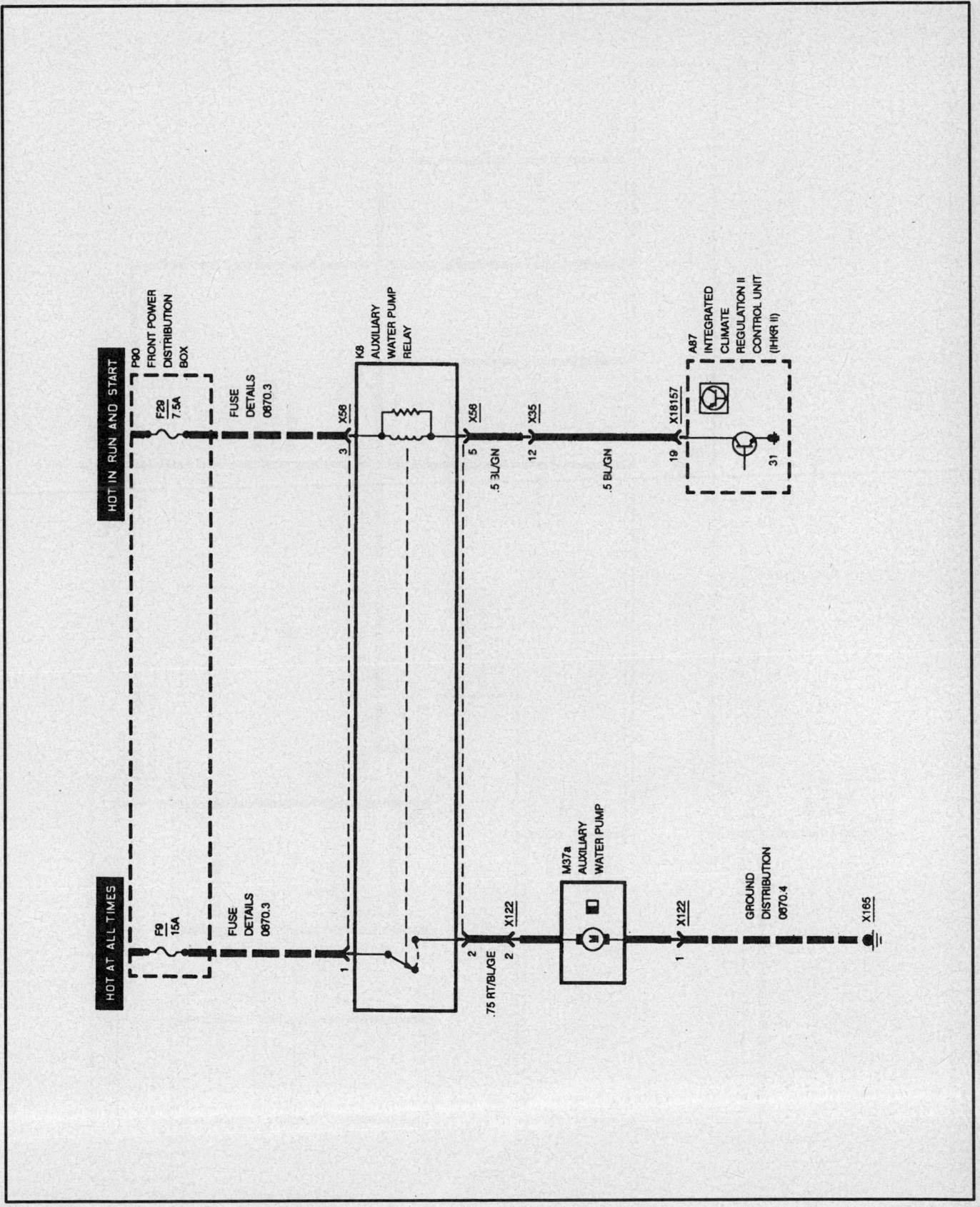

Auxiliary water pump circuit—5-Series

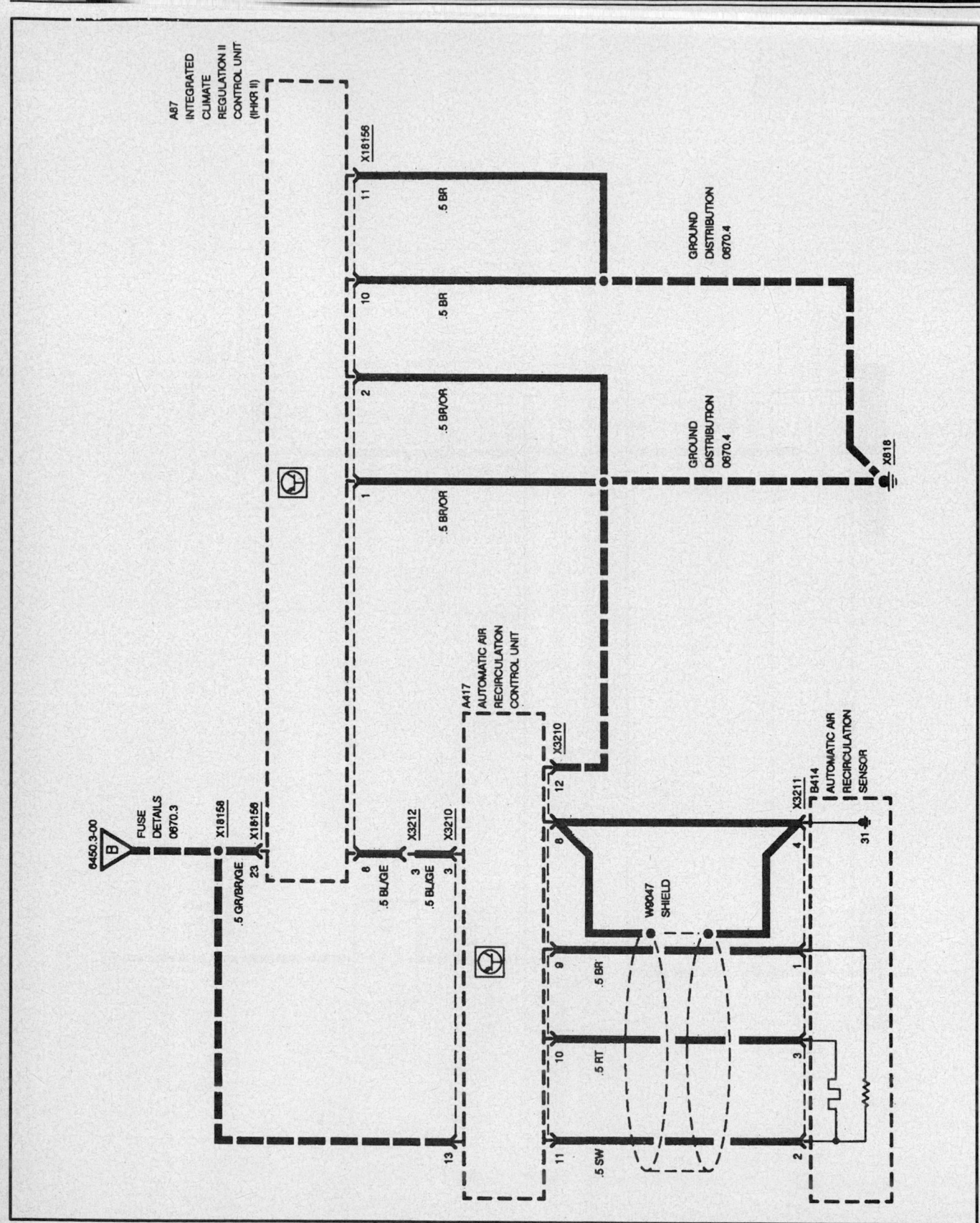

Air recirculation control circuit—5-Series

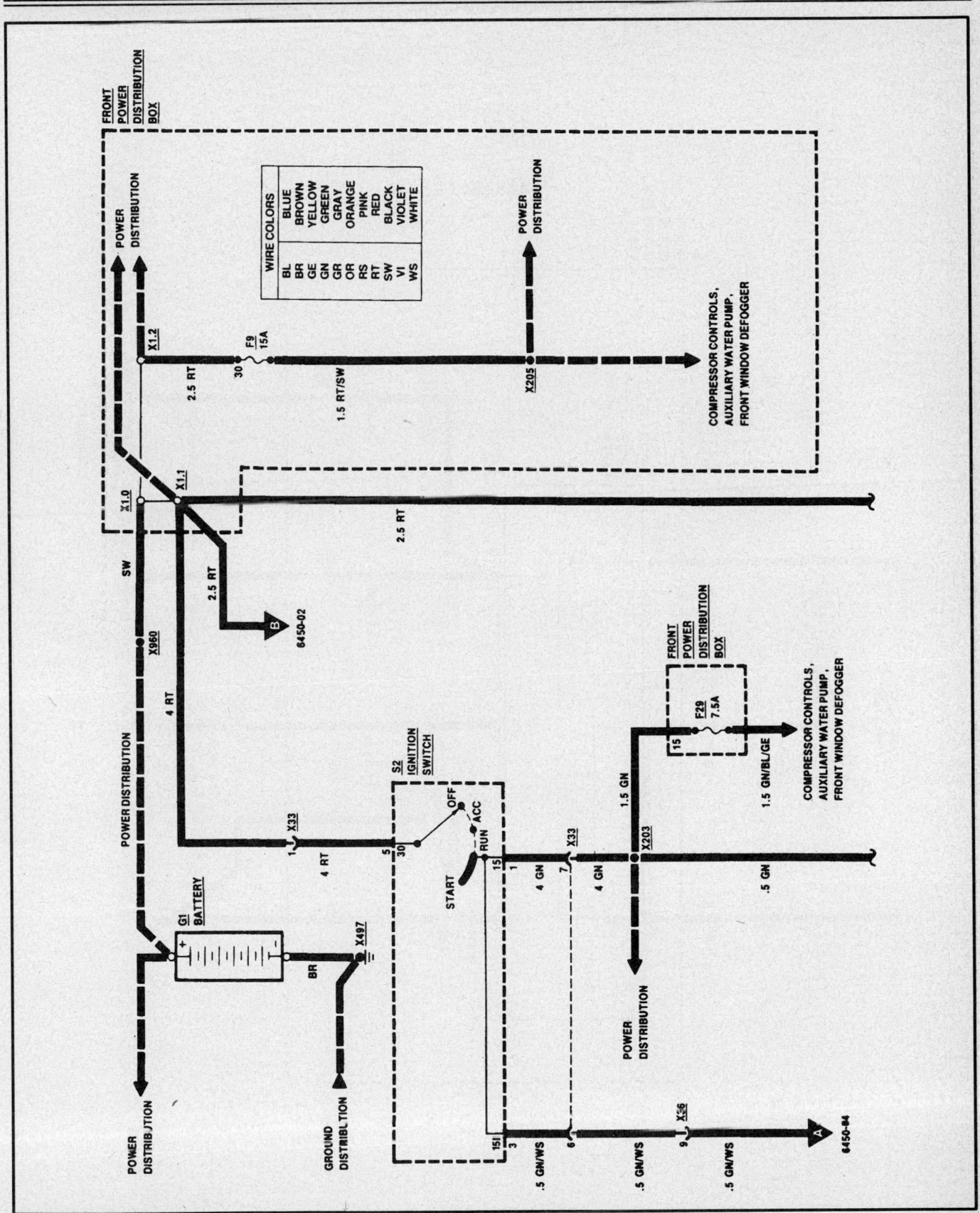

WIRE COLORS	
BL	BLUE
BR	BROWN
GE	YELLOW
GN	GREEN
GR	GRAY
OR	ORANGE
RS	PINK
RT	RED
SW	BLACK
VI	VIOLET
WS	WHITE

Power circuit—7-Series

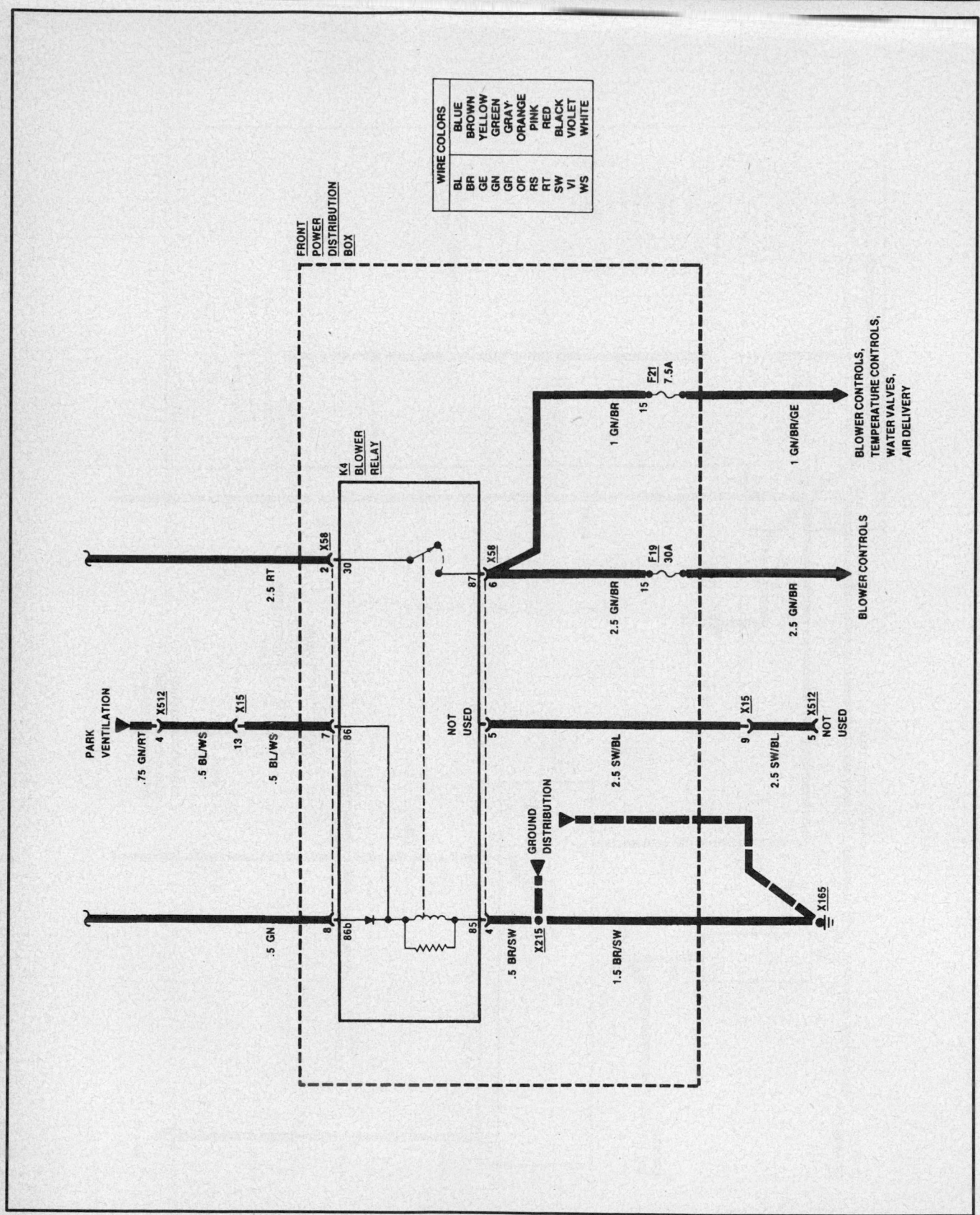

WIRE COLORS	
BL	BLUE
BR	BROWN
GE	YELLOW
GN	GREEN
GR	GRAY
OR	ORANGE
RS	PINK
RT	RED
SW	BLACK
VI	VIOLET
WS	WHITE

Power circuit—7-Series, cont'd

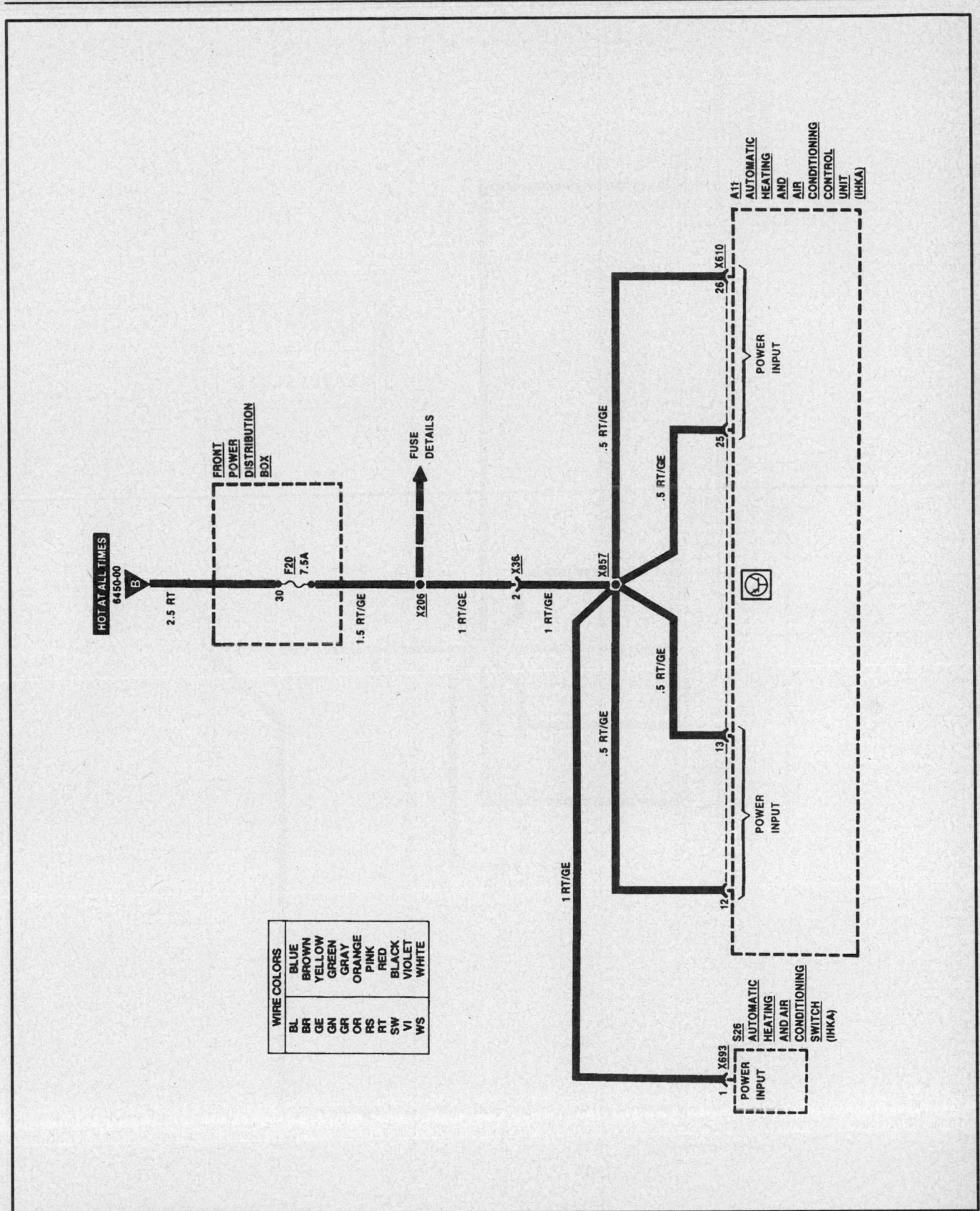

Power circuit—7-Series, cont'd

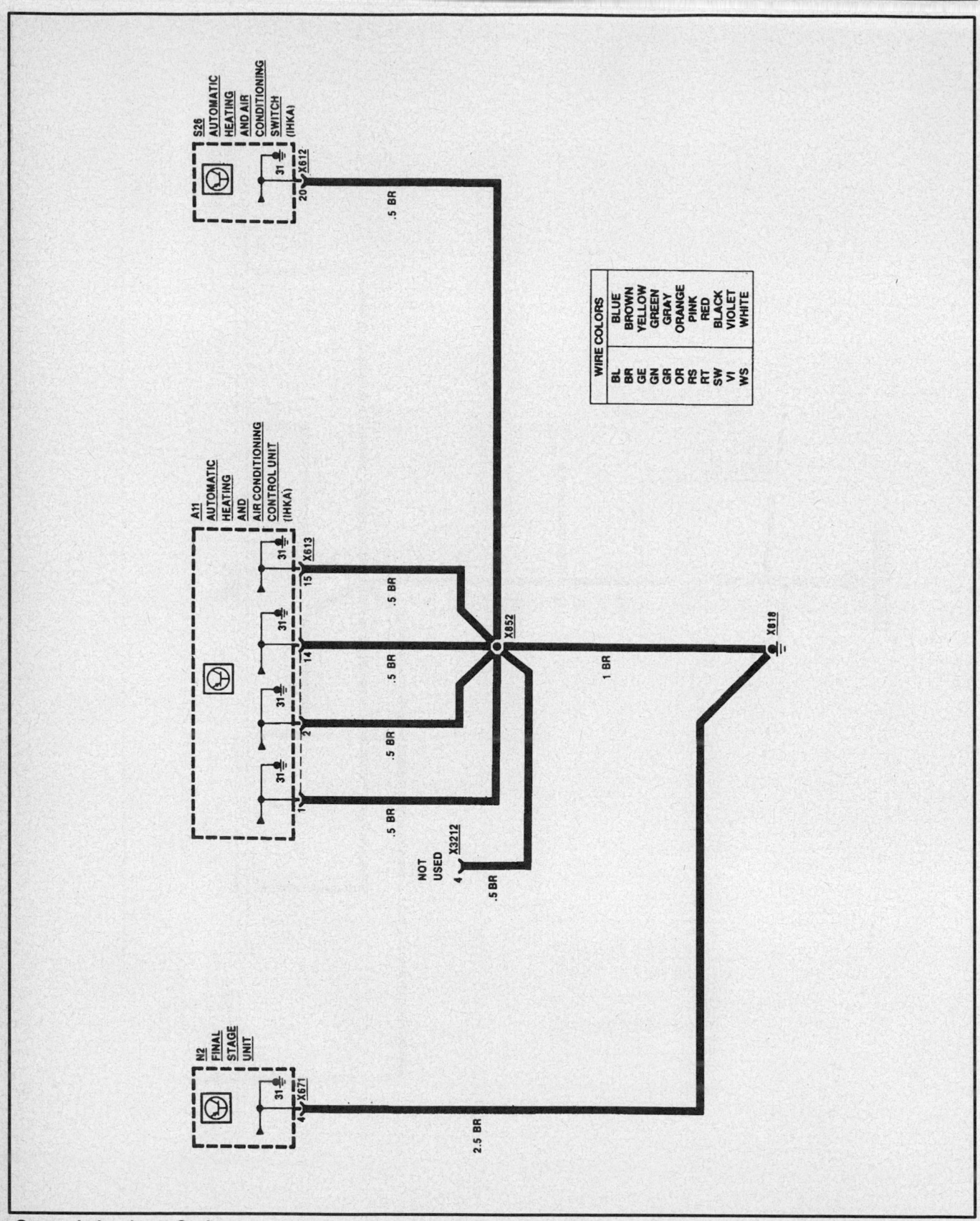

Ground circuit—7-Series

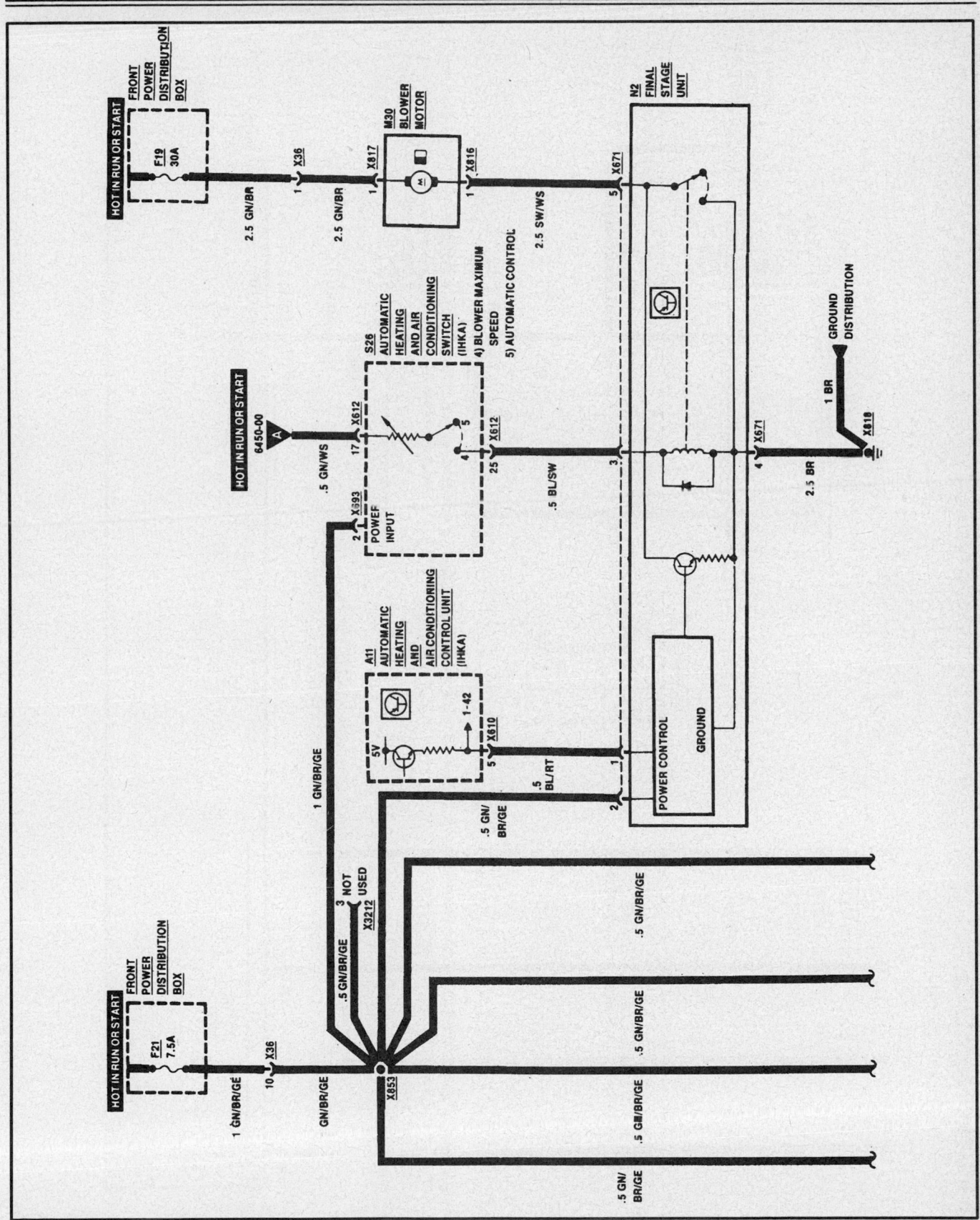

Blower control circuit—7-Series

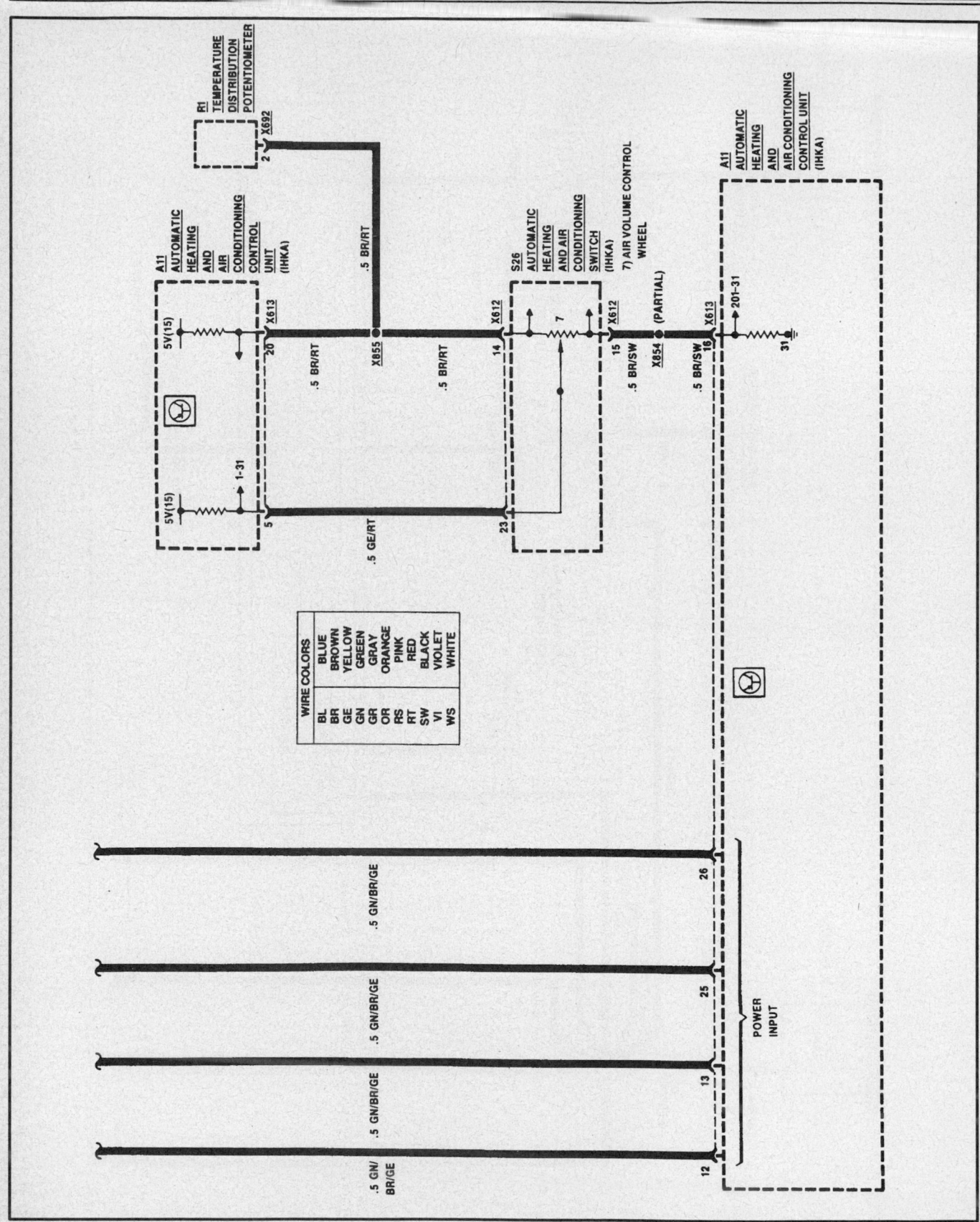

Blower control circuit—7-Series, cont'd

WIRE COLORS	
BL	BLUE
BR	BROWN
GE	YELLOW
GN	GREEN
GR	GRAY
OR	ORANGE
RS	PINK
RT	RED
SW	BLACK
VI	VIOLET
WS	WHITE

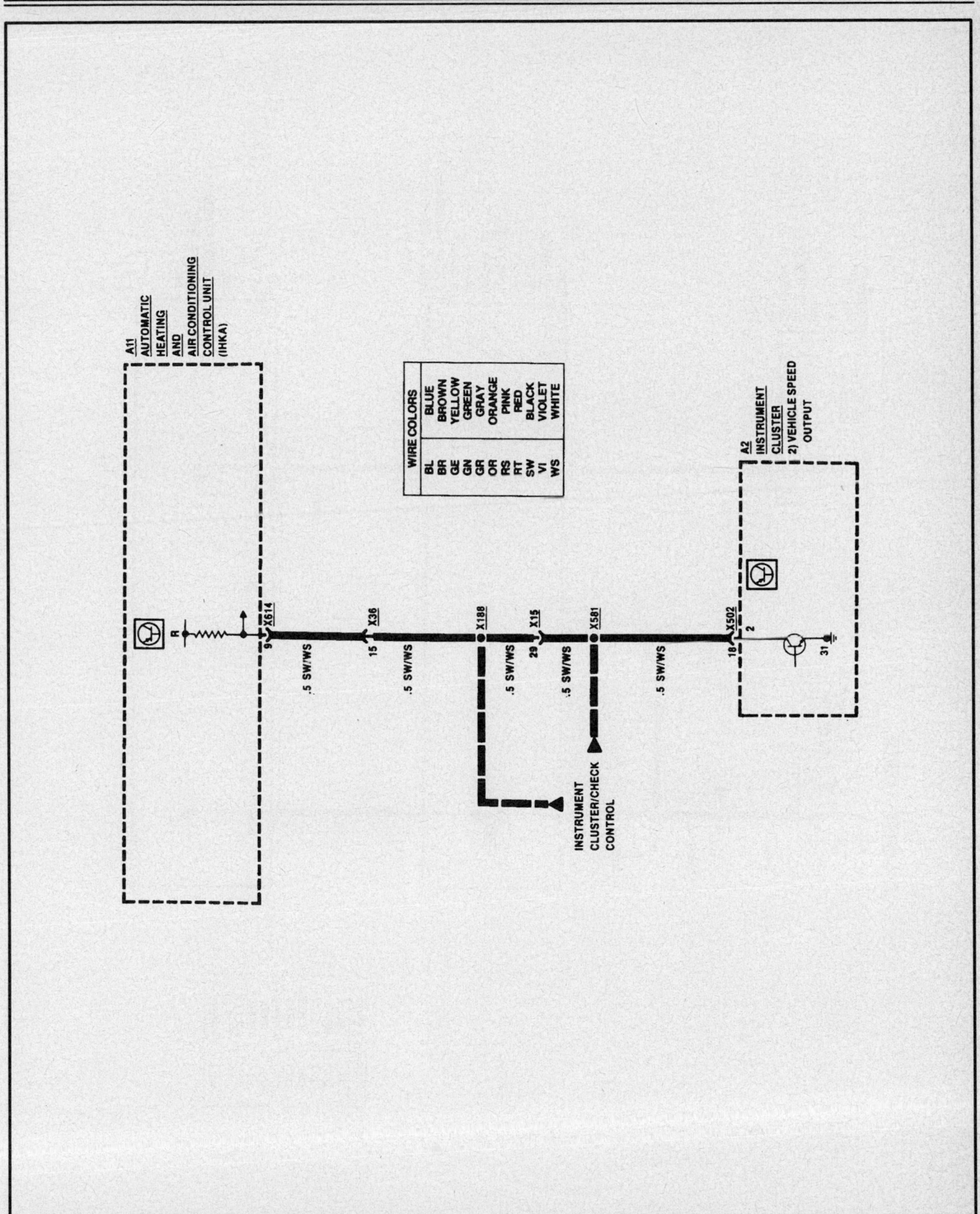

Blower control circuit—7-Series, cont'd

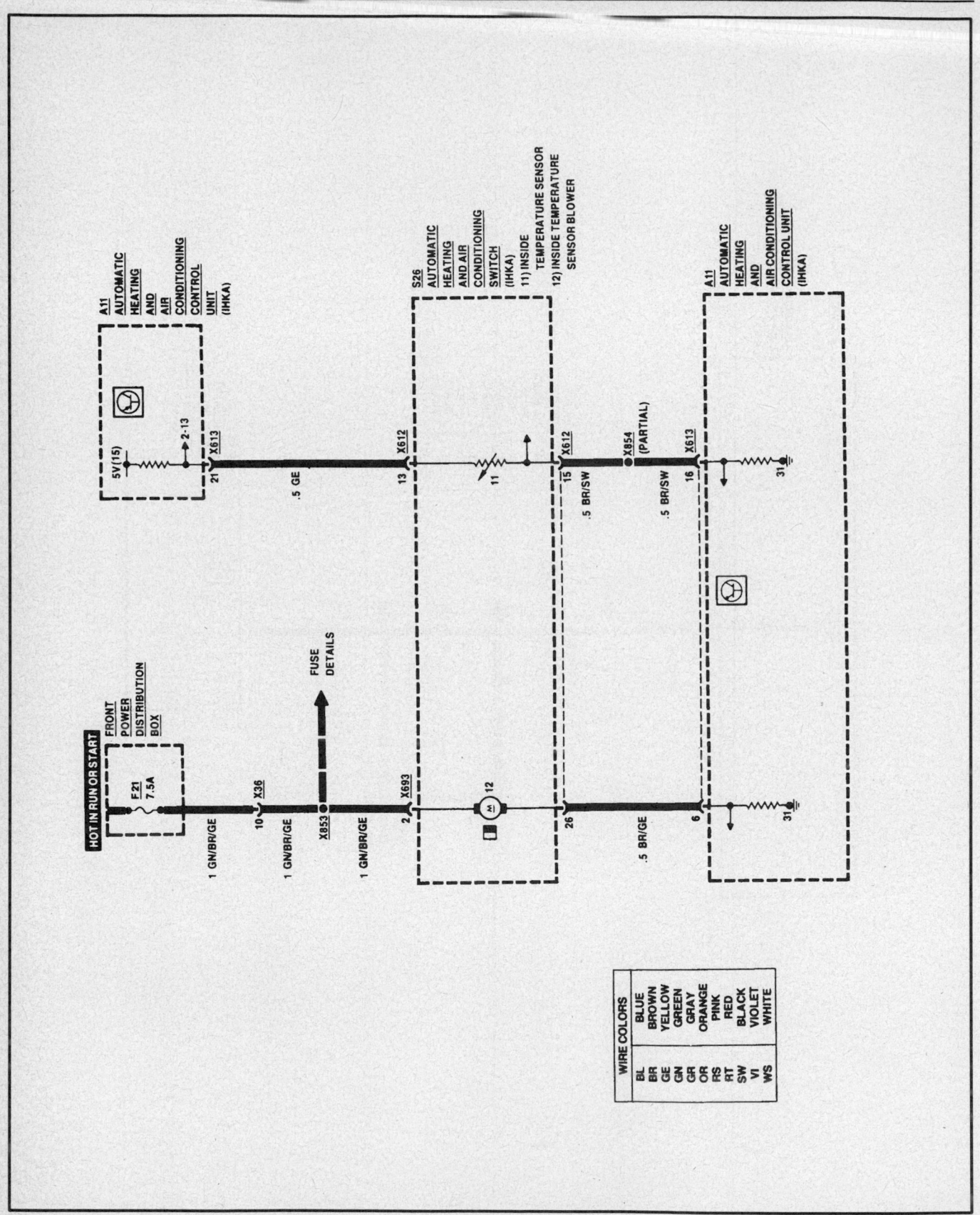

Temperature control circuit—7-Series

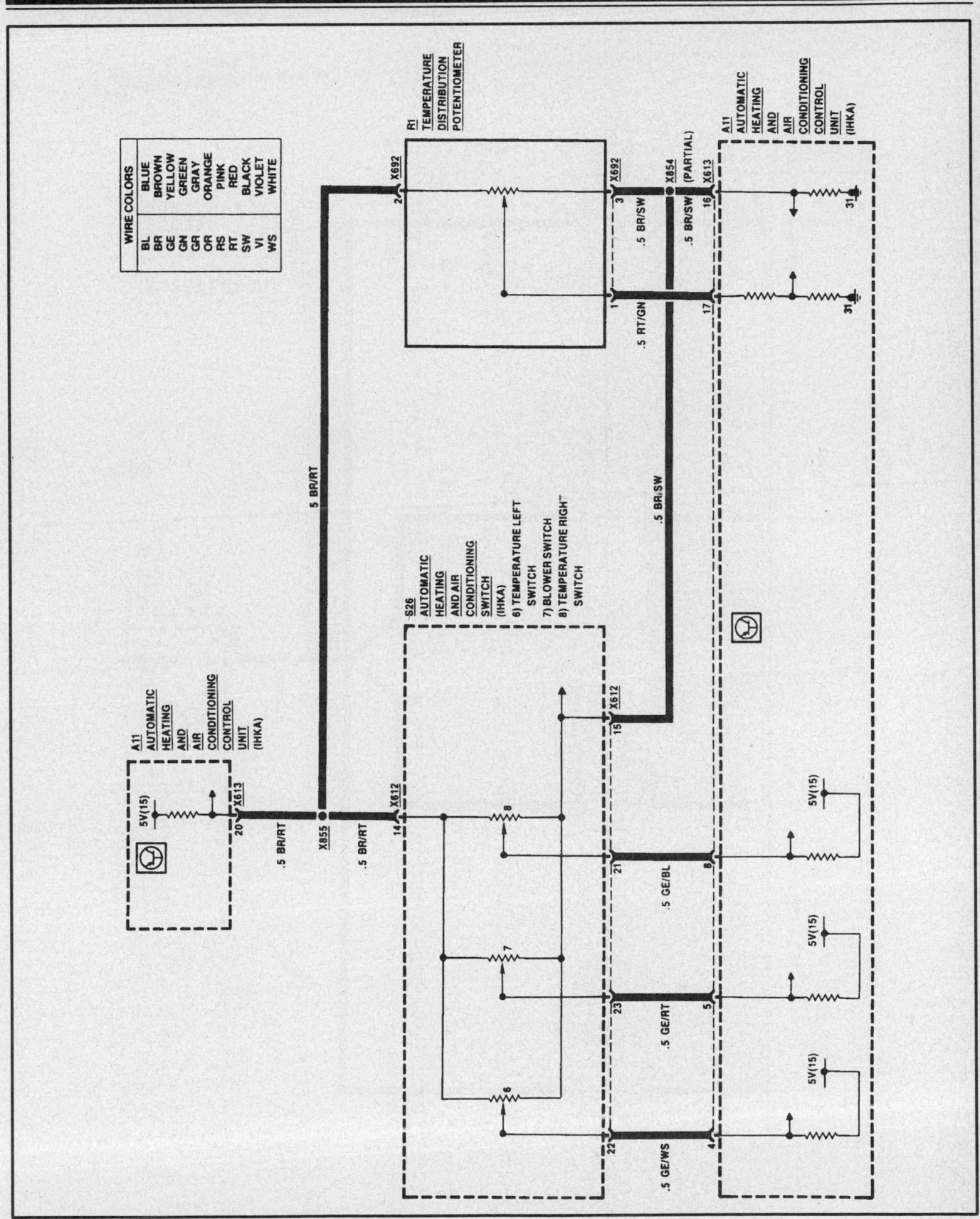

WIRE COLORS	
BL	BLUE
BR	BROWN
GE	YELLOW
GN	GREEN
GR	GRAY
OR	ORANGE
RS	PINK
RT	RED
SW	BLACK
VI	VIOLET
WS	WHITE

Temperature control circuit—7-Series, cont'd

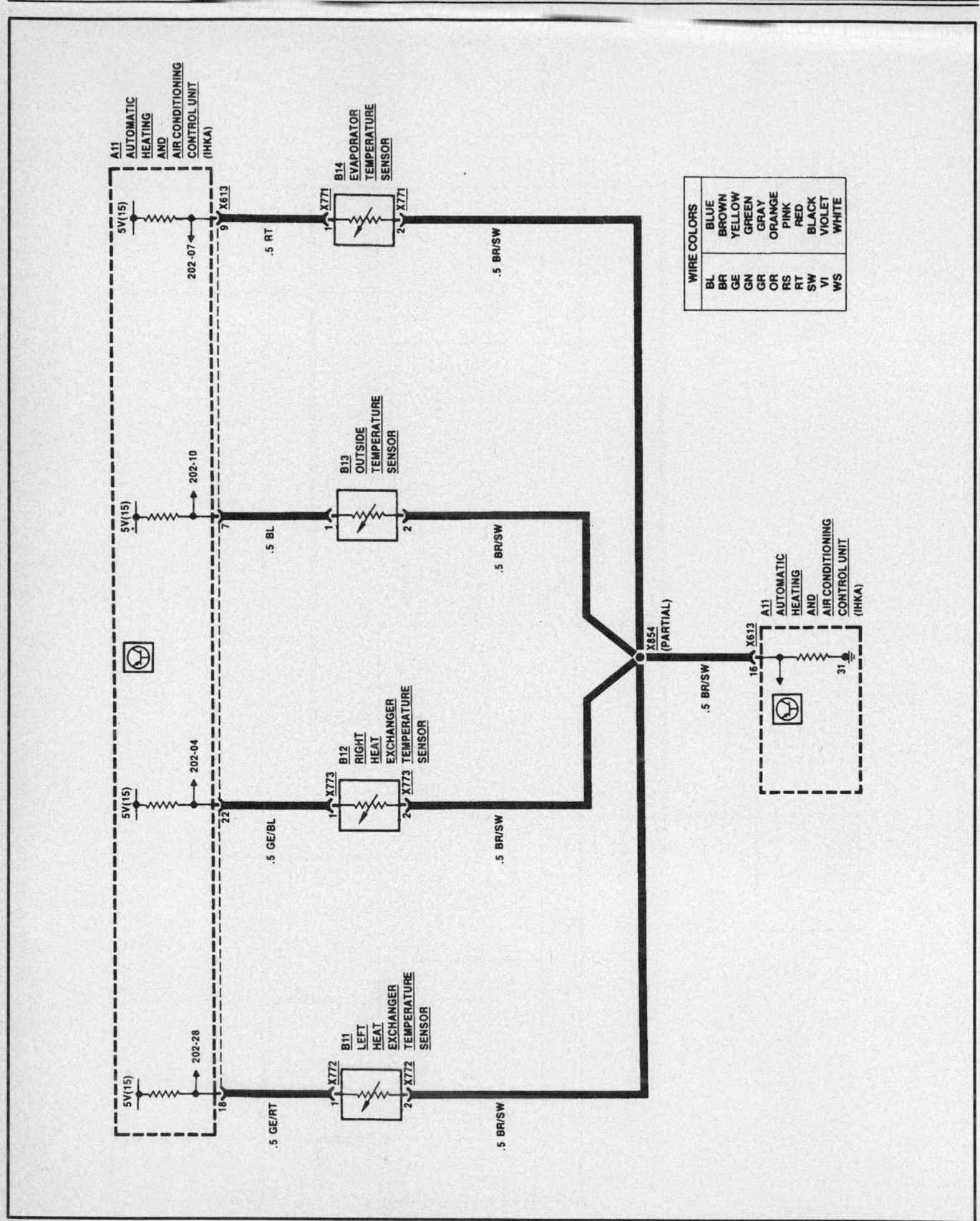

WIRE COLORS	
BL	BLUE
BR	BROWN
GE	YELLOW
GN	GREEN
GR	GRAY
OR	ORANGE
RS	PINK
RT	RED
SW	BLACK
VI	VIOLET
WS	WHITE

Temperature control circuit—7-Series, cont'd

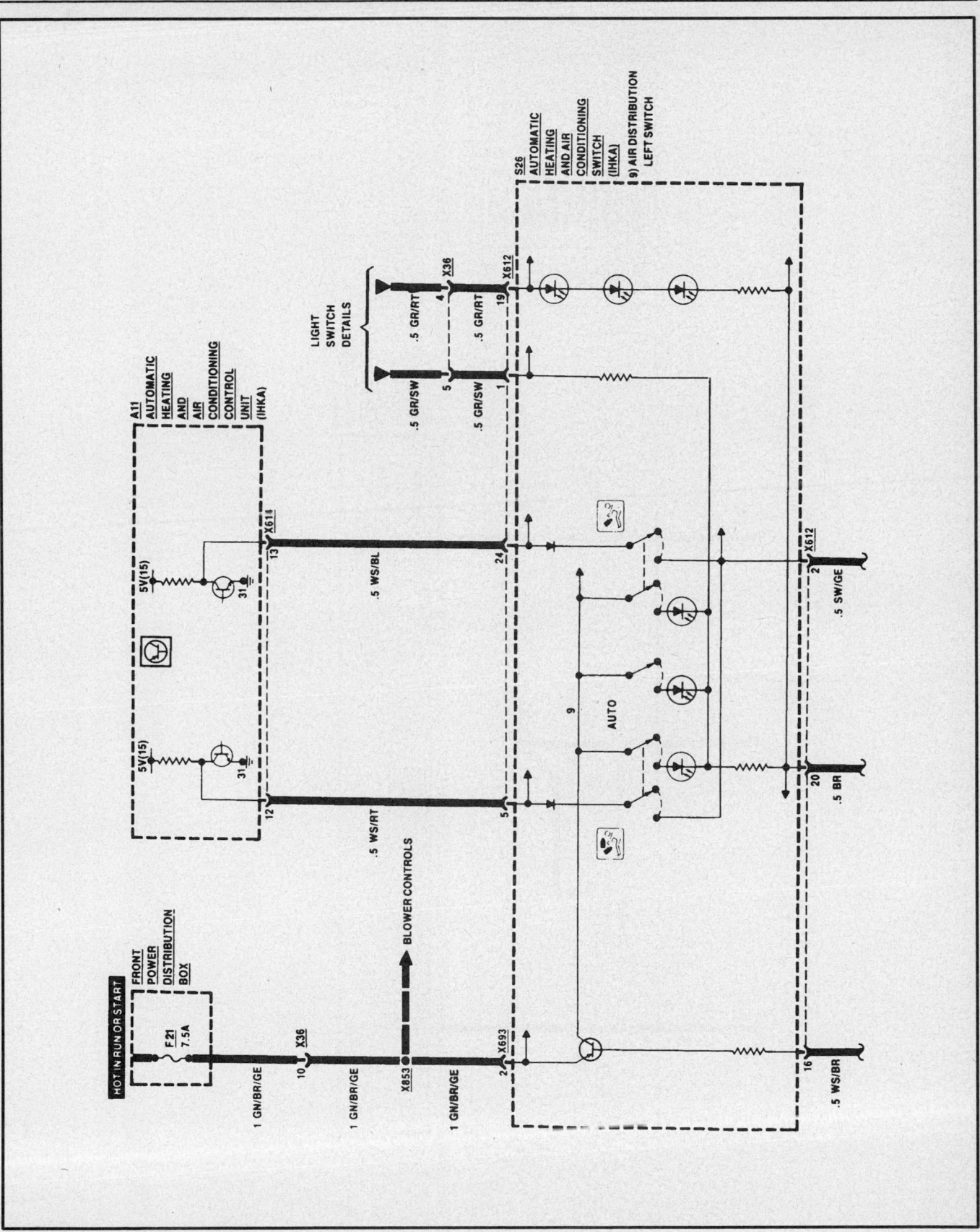

Air delivery circuit—7-Series

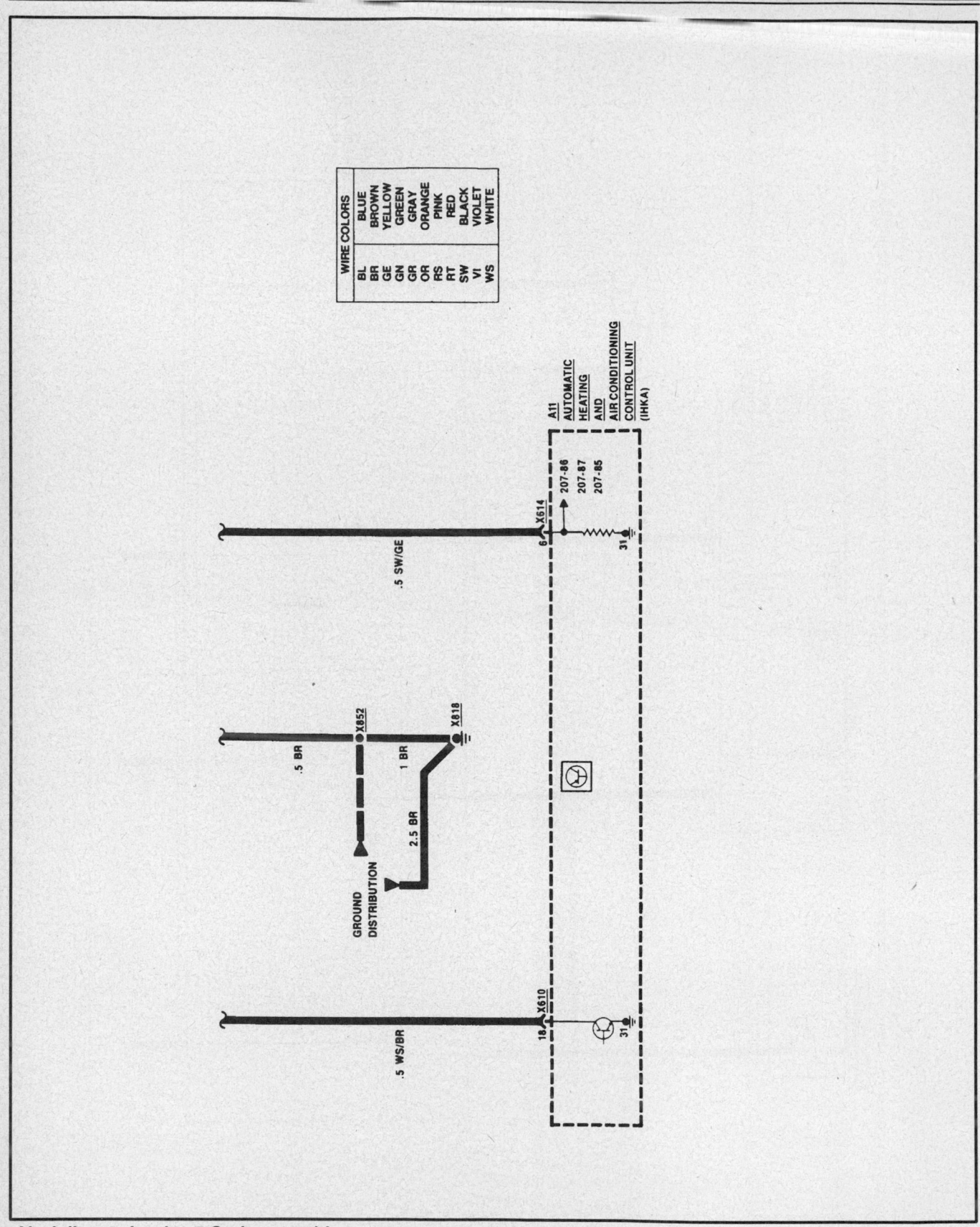

WIRE COLORS	
BL	BLUE
BR	BROWN
GE	YELLOW
GN	GREEN
GR	GRAY
OR	ORANGE
RS	PINK
RT	RED
SW	BLACK
VI	VIOLET
WS	WHITE

Air delivery circuit—7-Series, cont'd

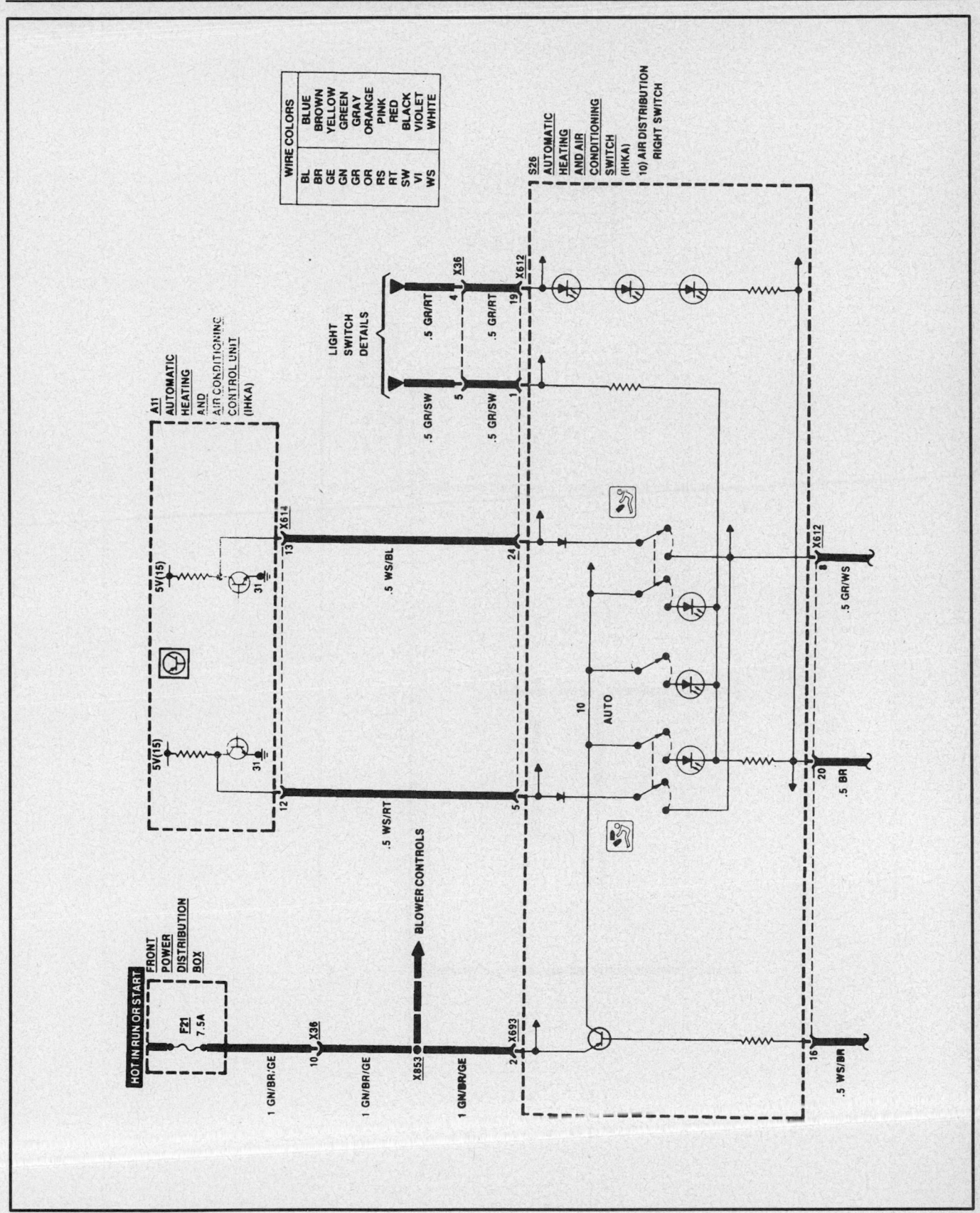

WIRE COLORS

BL	BLUE
BR	BROWN
GE	YELLOW
GN	GREEN
GR	GRAY
OR	ORANGE
RS	PINK
RT	RED
SW	BLACK
VI	VIOLET
WS	WHITE

Air delivery circuit—7-Series, cont'd

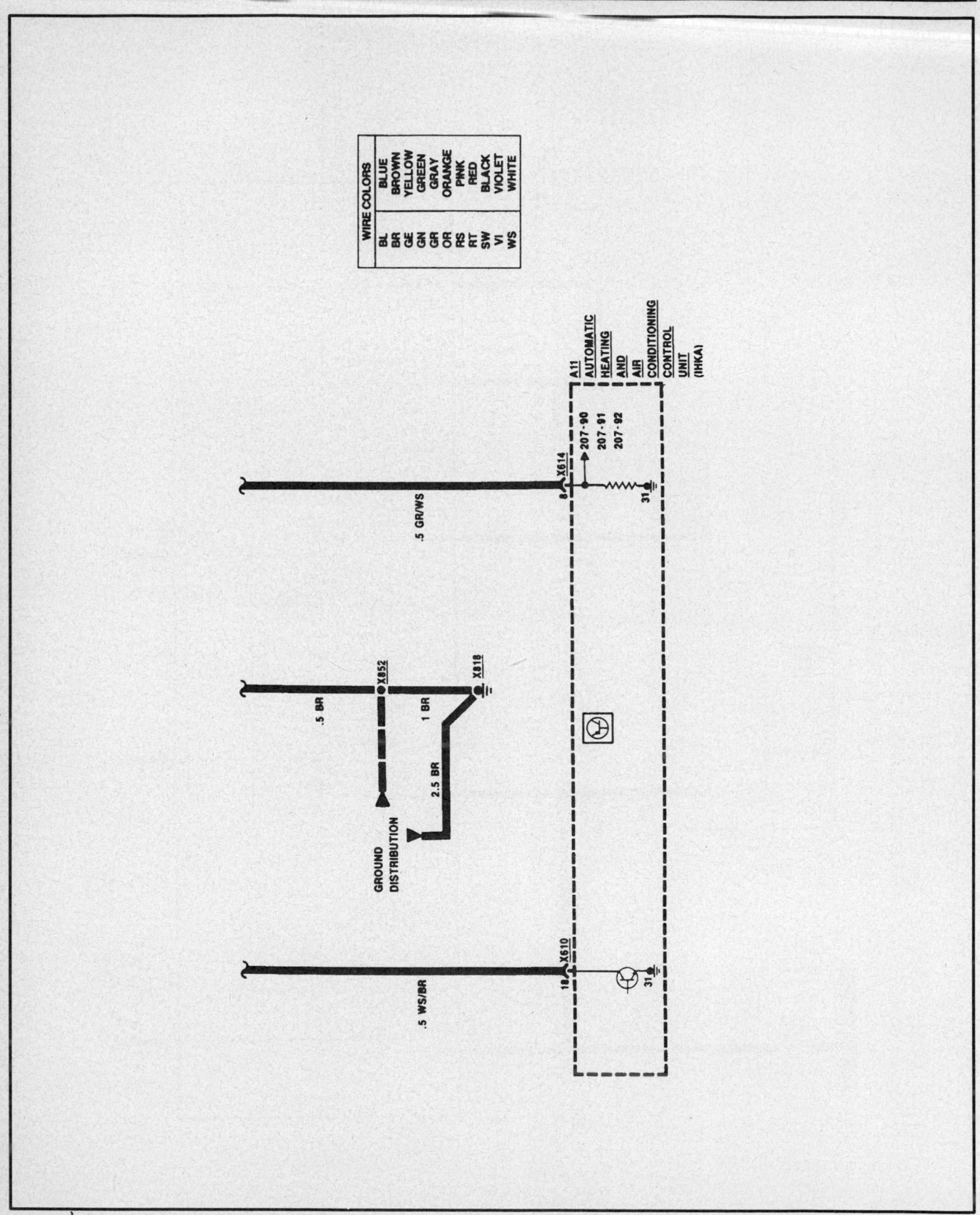

Air delivery circuit—7-Series, cont'd

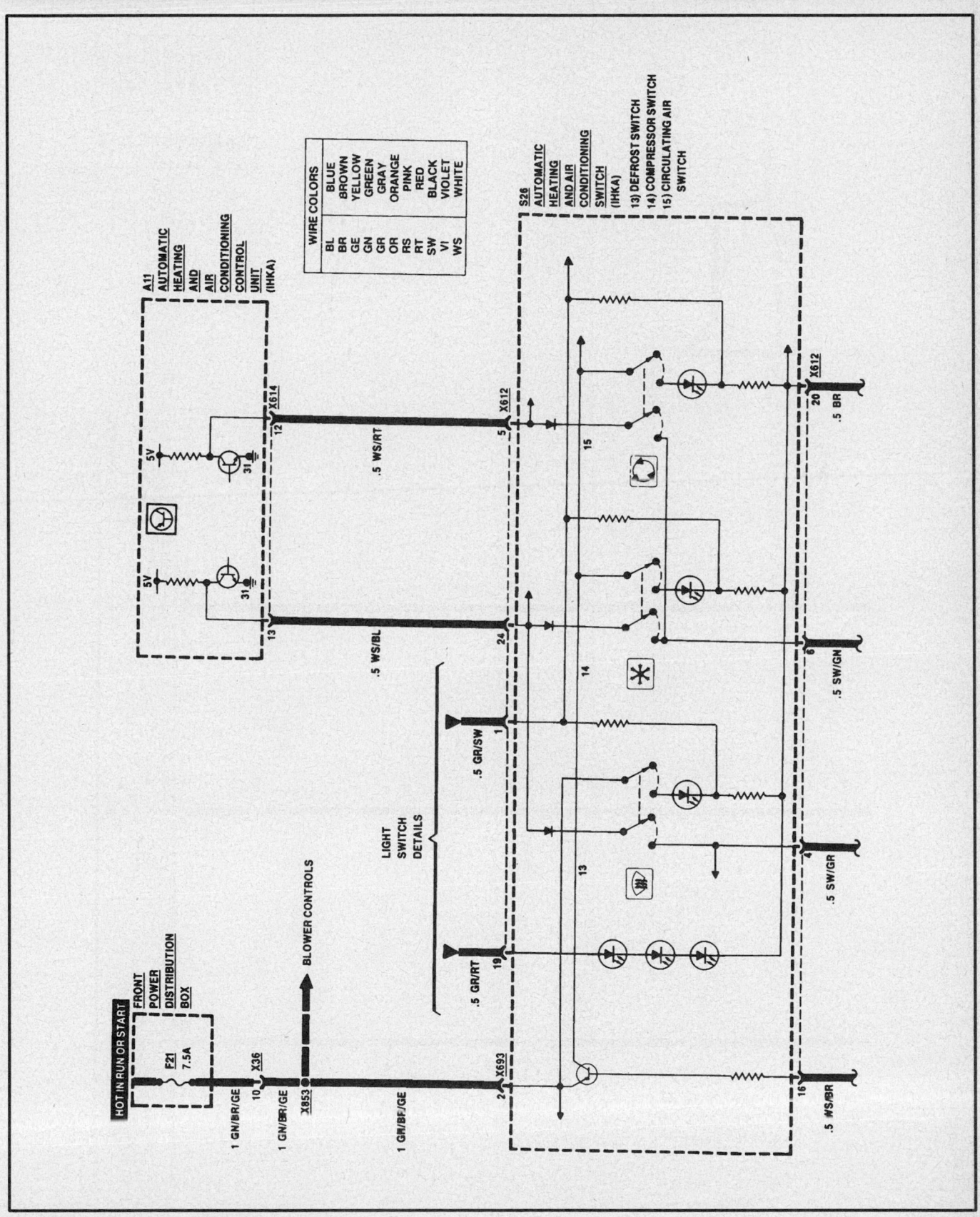

Air delivery circuit—7-Series, cont'd

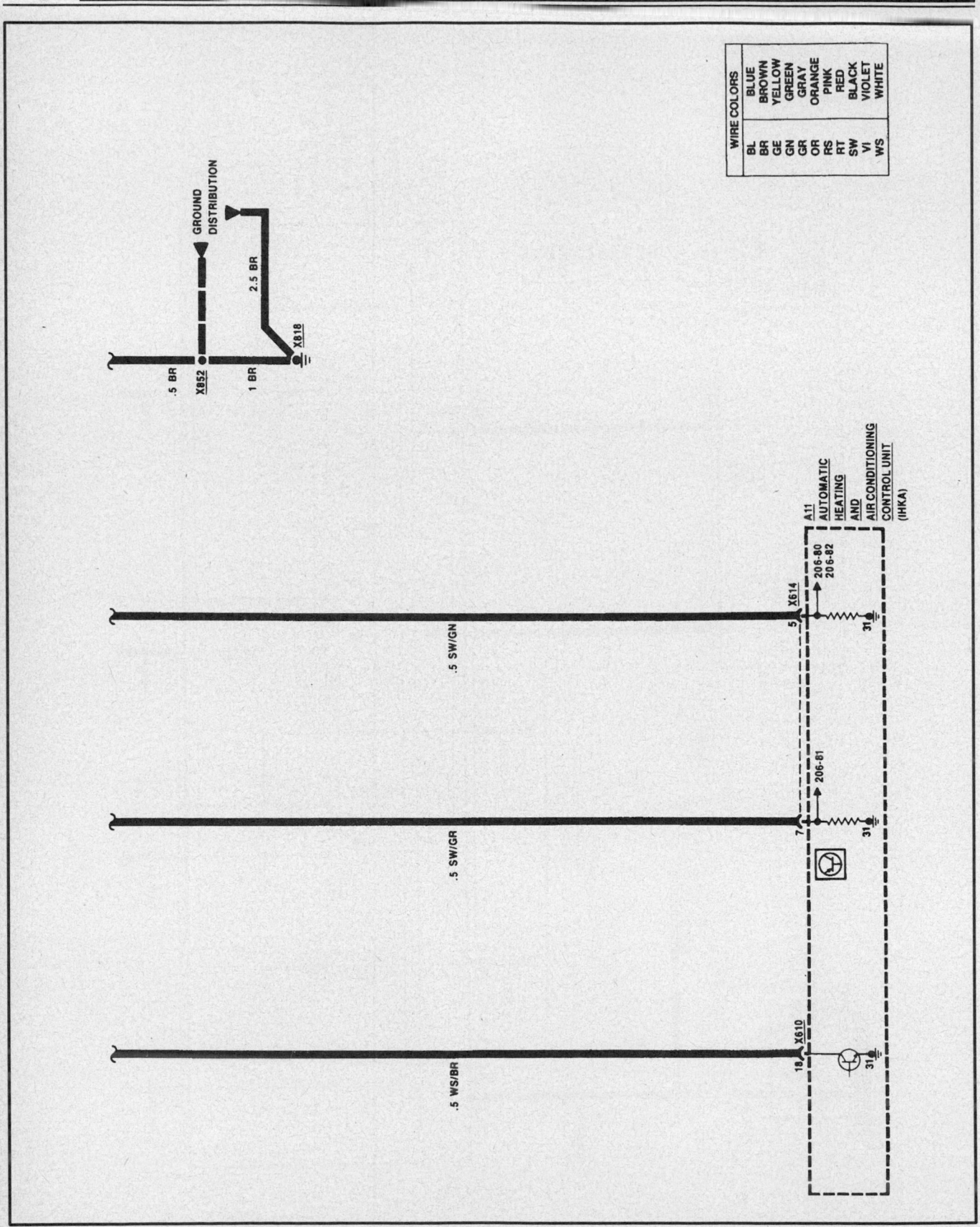

WIRE COLORS	
BL	BLUE
BR	BROWN
GE	YELLOW
GN	GREEN
GR	GRAY
OR	ORANGE
RS	PINK
RT	RED
SW	BLACK
VI	VIOLET
WS	WHITE

Air delivery circuit—7-Series, cont'd

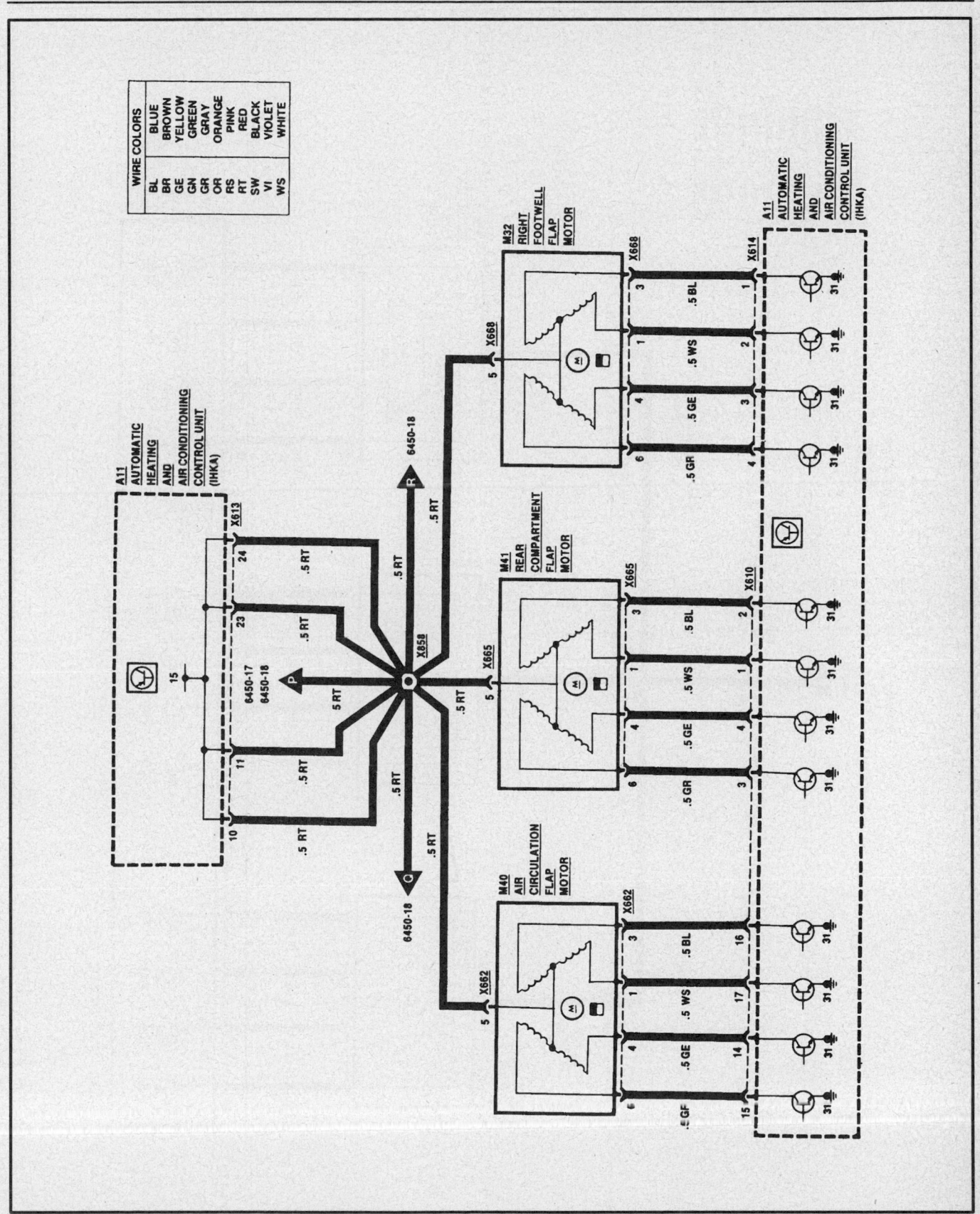

WIRE COLORS

BL	BLUE
BR	BROWN
GE	YELLOW
GN	GREEN
GR	GRAY
OR	ORANGE
RS	PINK
RT	RED
SW	BLACK
VI	VIOLET
WS	WHITE

Air delivery circuit—7-Series, cont'd

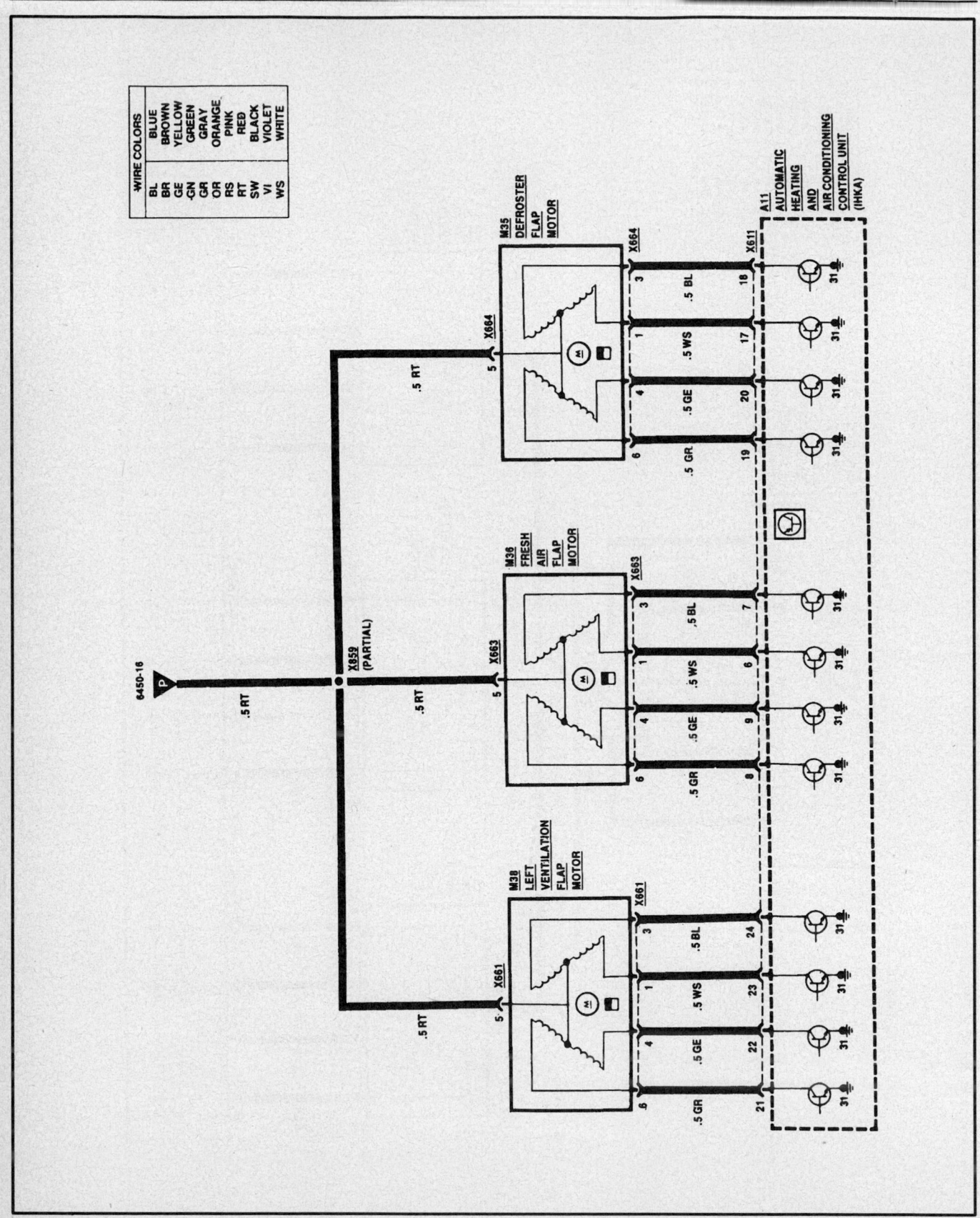

WIRE COLORS	
BL	BLUE
BR	BROWN
GE	YELLOW
GN	GREEN
GR	GRAY
OR	ORANGE
RS	PINK
RT	RED
SW	BLACK
VI	VIOLET
WS	WHITE

Air delivery circuit—7-Series, cont'd

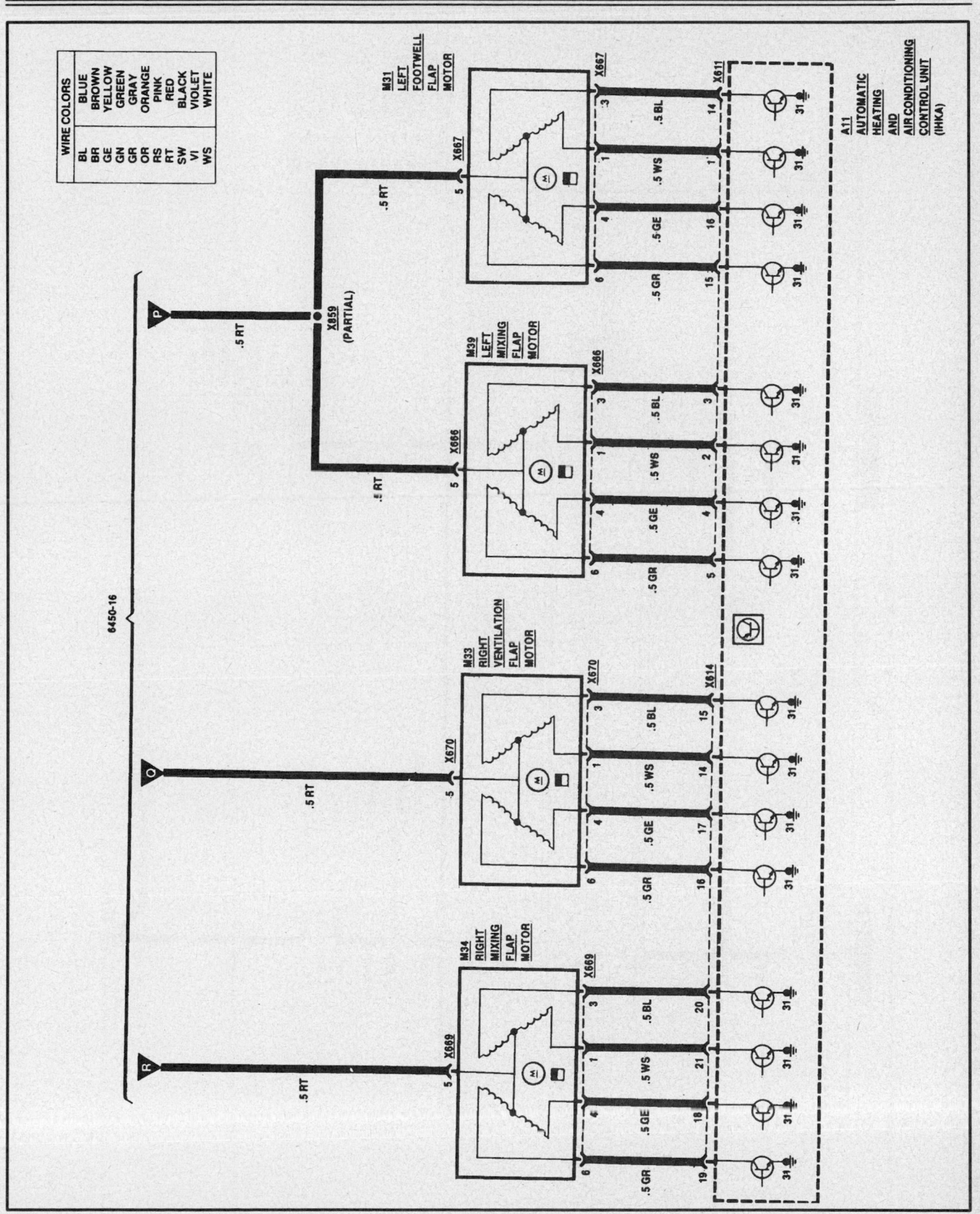

WIRE COLORS	
BL	BLUE
BR	BROWN
GE	YELLOW
GN	GREEN
GR	GRAY
OR	ORANGE
RS	PINK
RT	RED
SW	BLACK
VI	VIOLET
WS	WHITE

M31 LEFT FOOTWELL FLAP MOTOR

M39 LEFT MIXING FLAP MOTOR

M33 RIGHT VENTILATION FLAP MOTOR

M34 RIGHT MIXING FLAP MOTOR

A11 AUTOMATIC HEATING AND AIR CONDITIONING CONTROL UNIT (IHKA)

Air delivery circuit—7-Series, cont'd

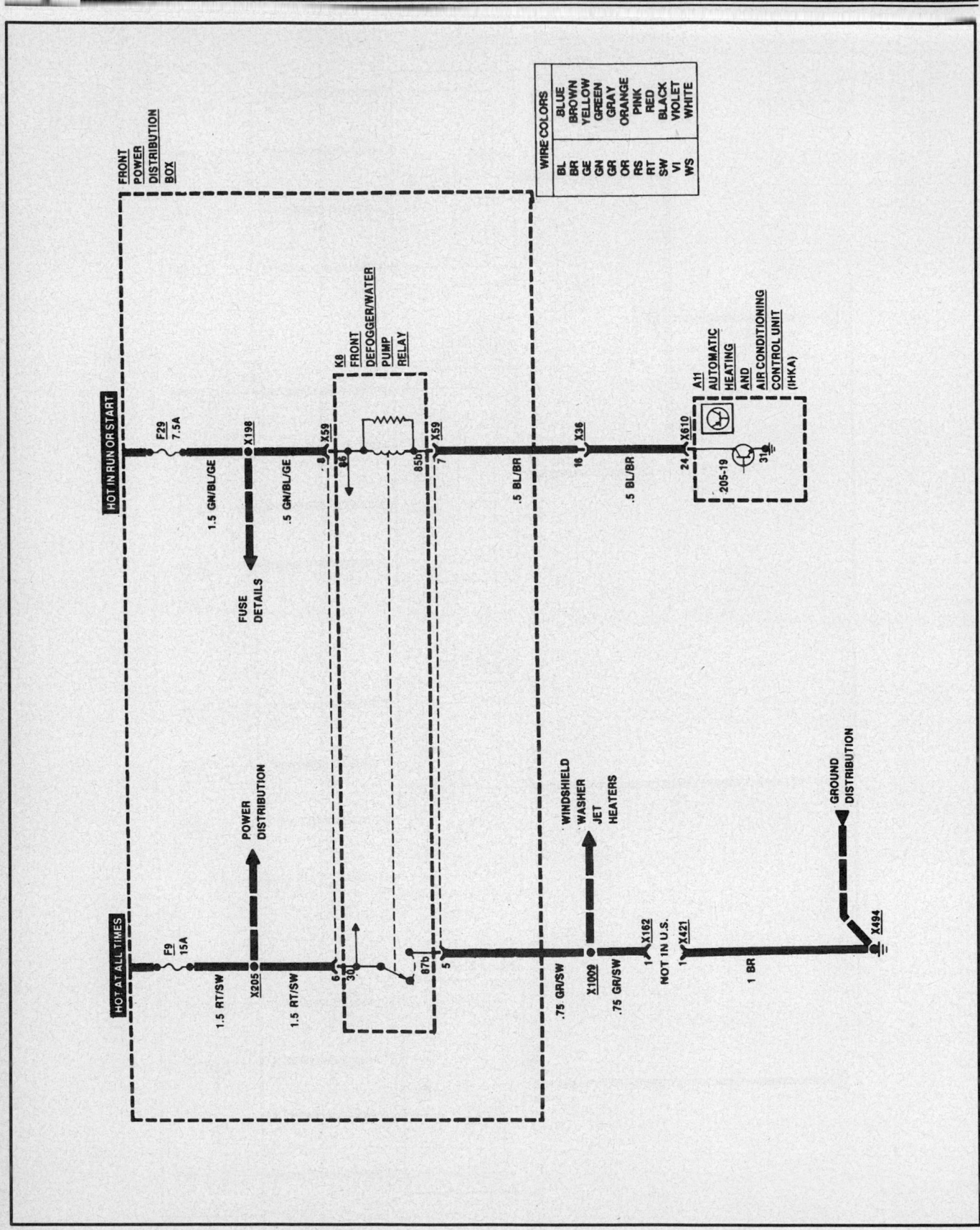

Front window defogger circuit—7-Series

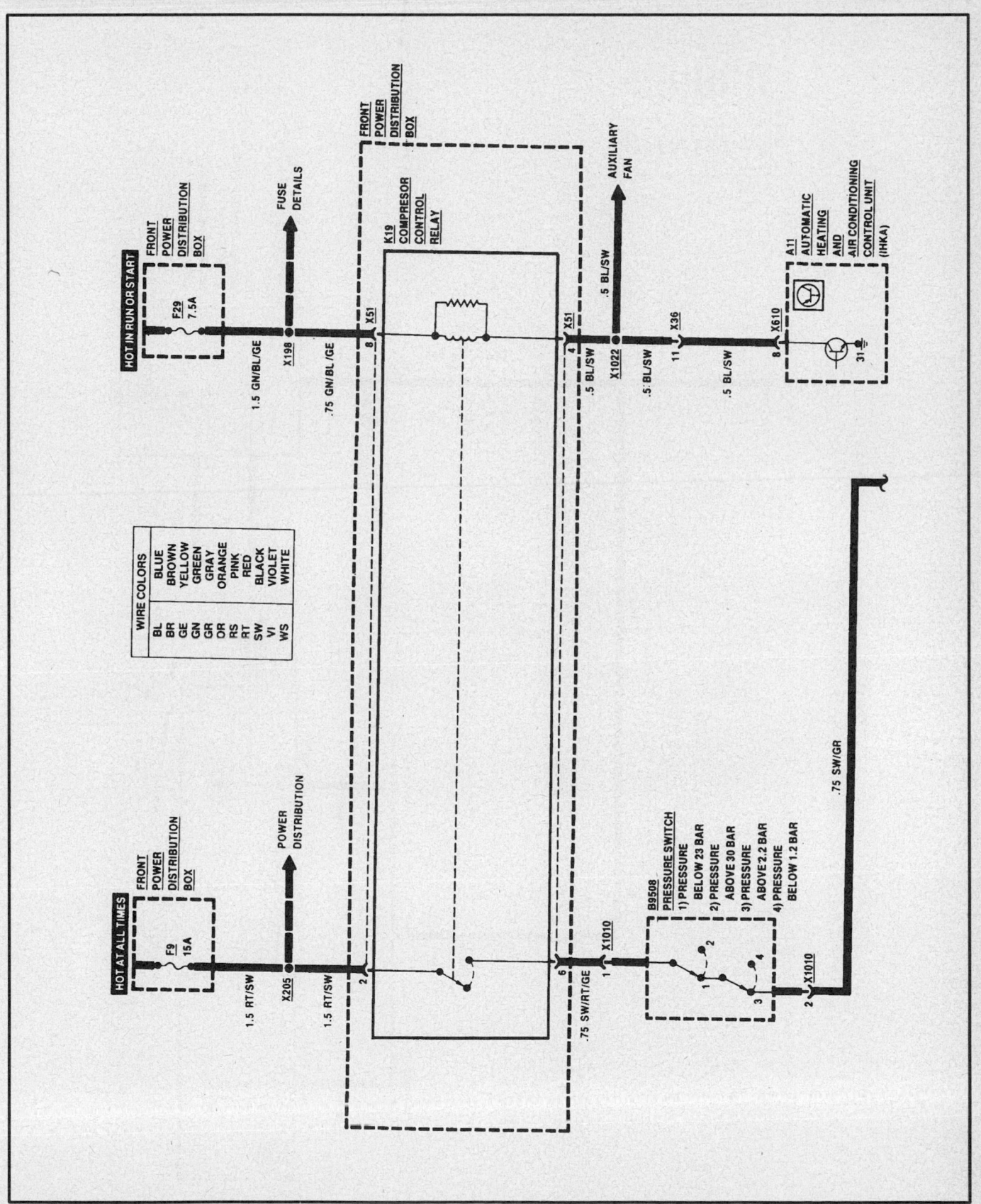

Compressor control circuit—7-Series

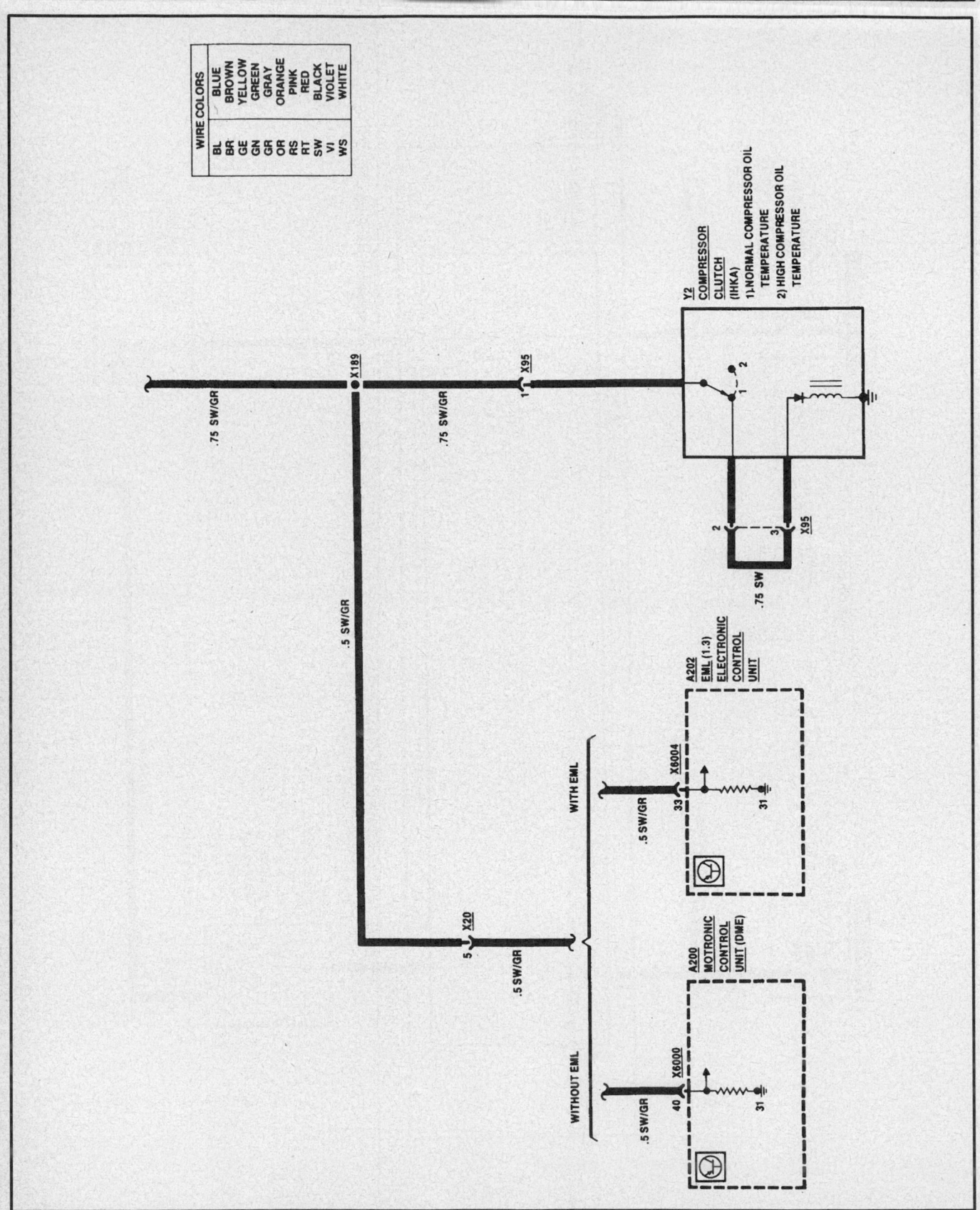

WIRE COLORS

BL	BLUE
BR	BROWN
GE	YELLOW
GN	GREEN
GR	GRAY
OR	ORANGE
RS	PINK
RT	RED
SW	BLACK
VI	VIOLET
WS	WHITE

Y2 COMPRESSOR CLUTCH (IHKA)
1) NORMAL COMPRESSOR OIL TEMPERATURE
2) HIGH COMPRESSOR OIL TEMPERATURE

A202 EML (1.3) ELECTRONIC CONTROL UNIT

WITH EML

A200 MOTRONIC CONTROL UNIT (DME)

WITHOUT EML

Compressor control circuit—7-Series, cont'd

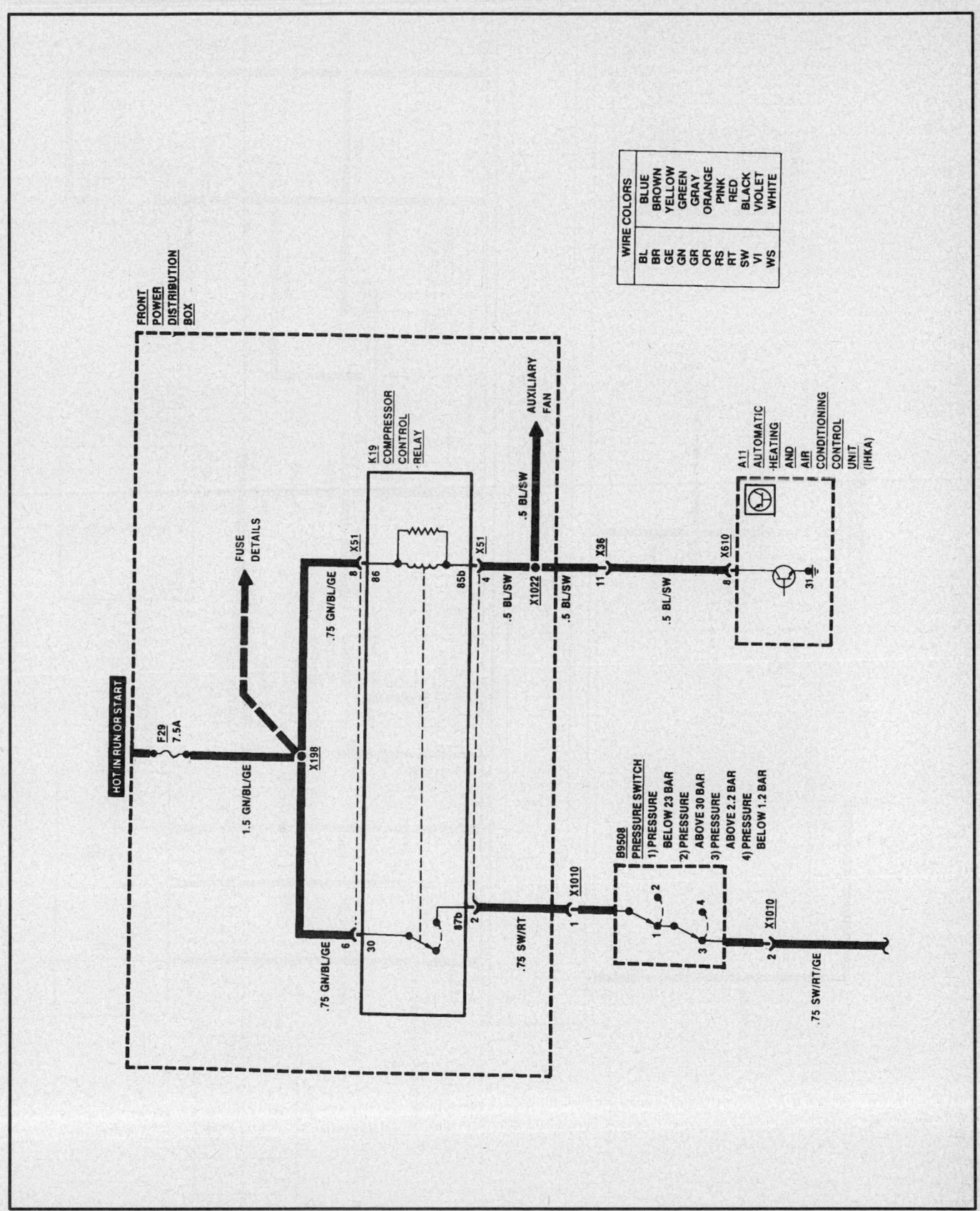

Compressor control circuit—7-Series, cont'd

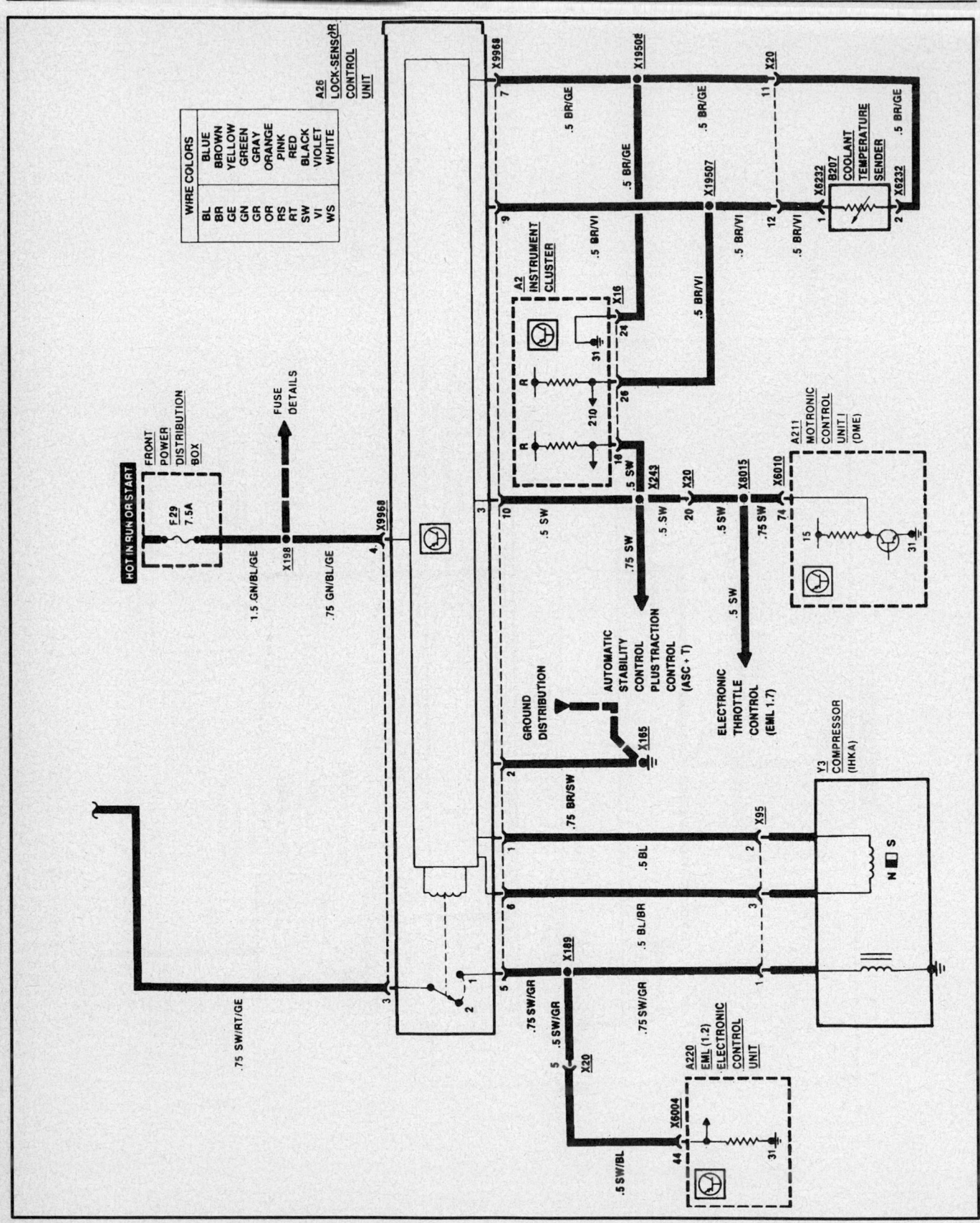

Compressor control circuit—7-Series, cont'd

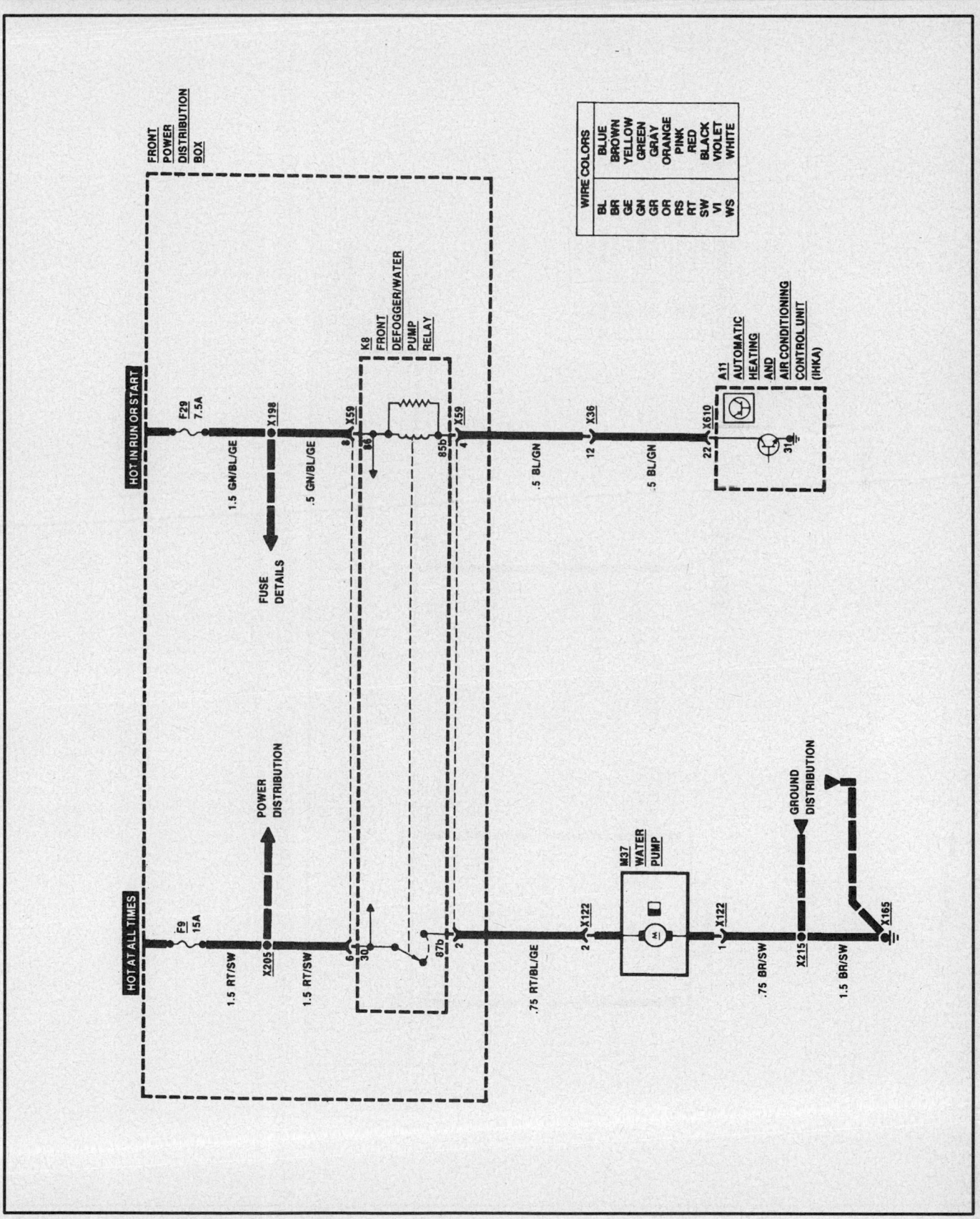

Auxiliary water pump circuit—7-Series

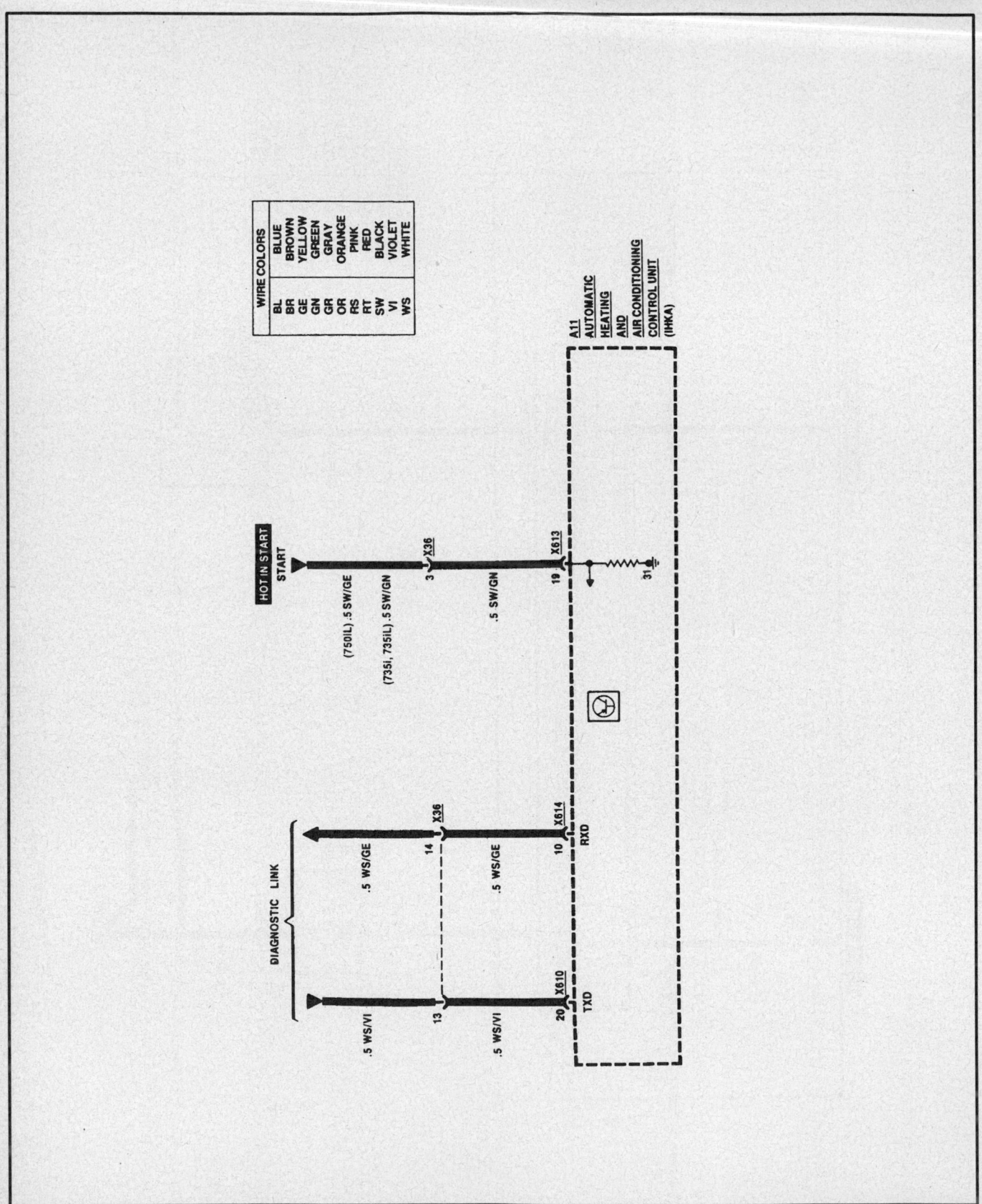

Diagnostic link and starter input circuit—7-Series

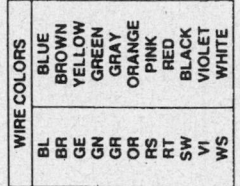

WIRE COLORS	
BL	BLUE
BR	BROWN
GE	YELLOW
GN	GREEN
GR	GRAY
OR	ORANGE
RS	PINK
RT	RED
SW	BLACK
VI	VIOLET
WS	WHITE

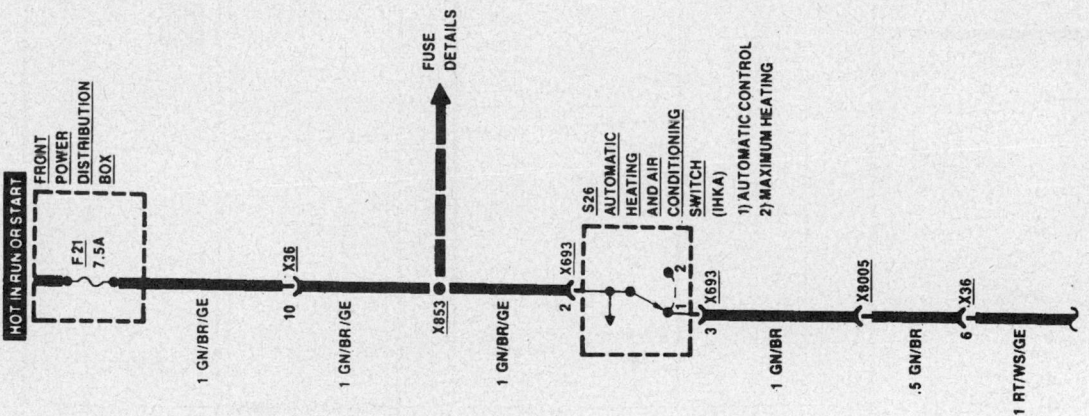

Water valve control circuit—7-Series

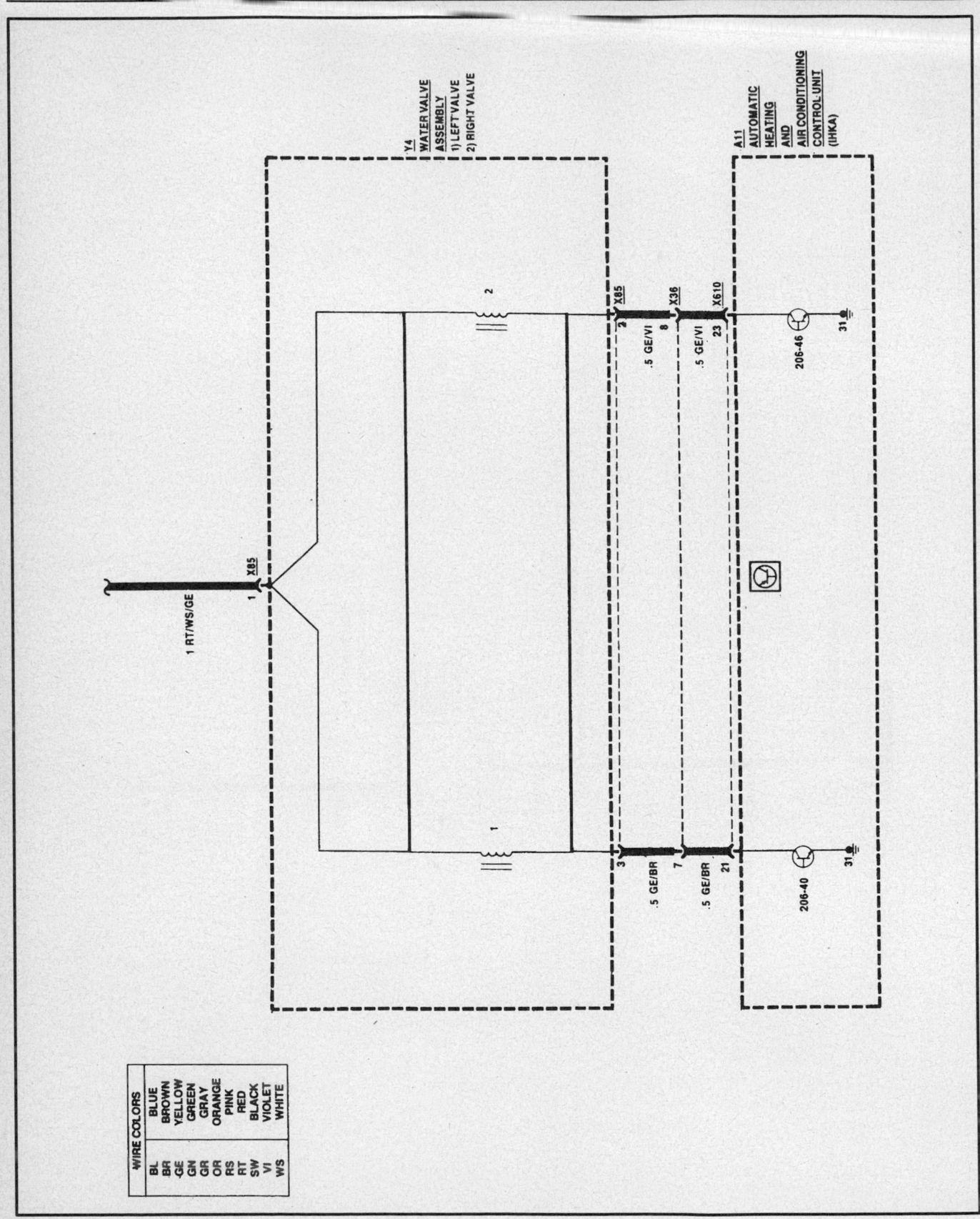

Water valve control circuit—7-Series, cont'd

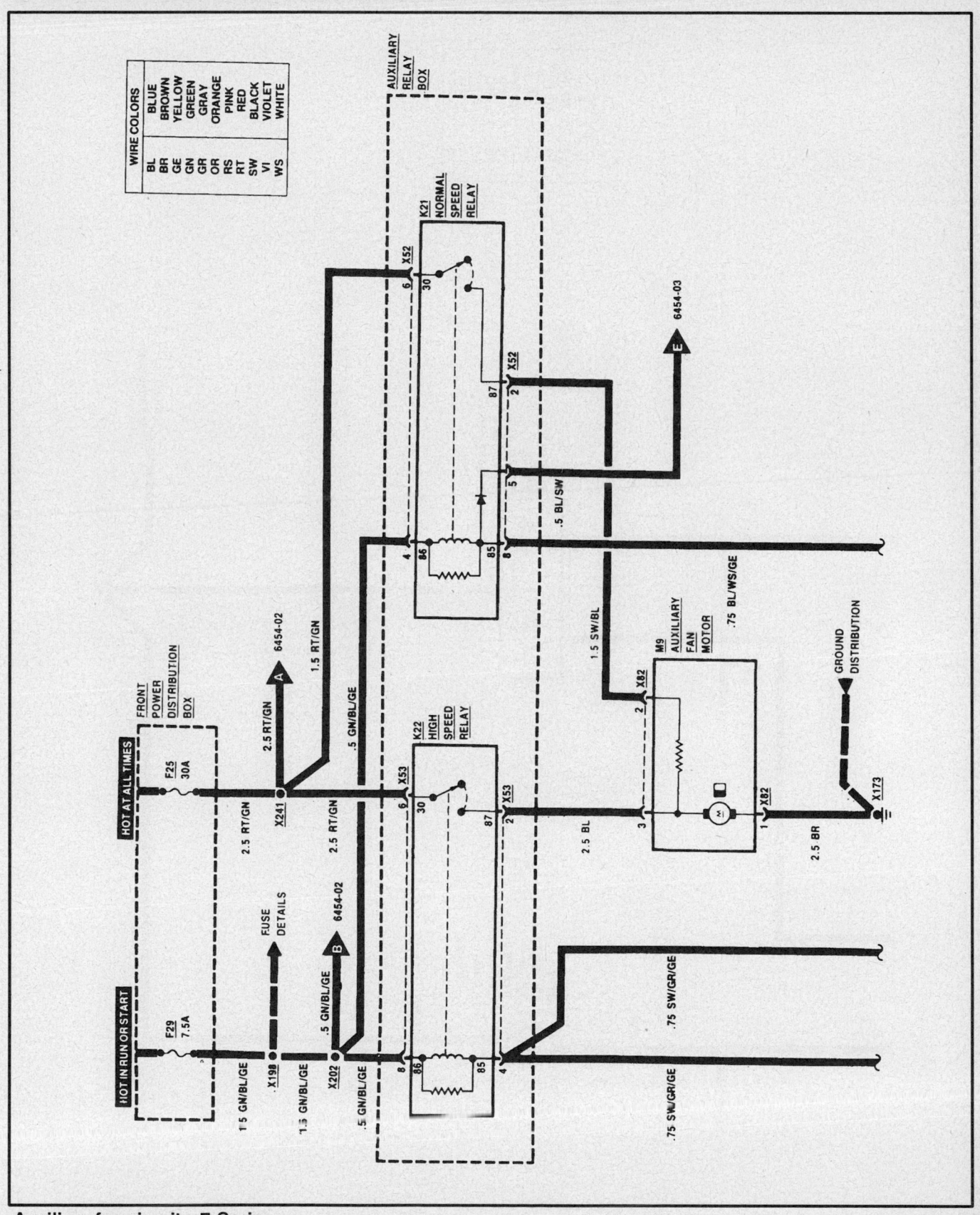

WIRE COLORS	
BL	BLUE
BR	BROWN
GE	YELLOW
GN	GREEN
GR	GRAY
OR	ORANGE
RS	PINK
RT	RED
SW	BLACK
VI	VIOLET
WS	WHITE

Auxiliary fan circuit—7-Series

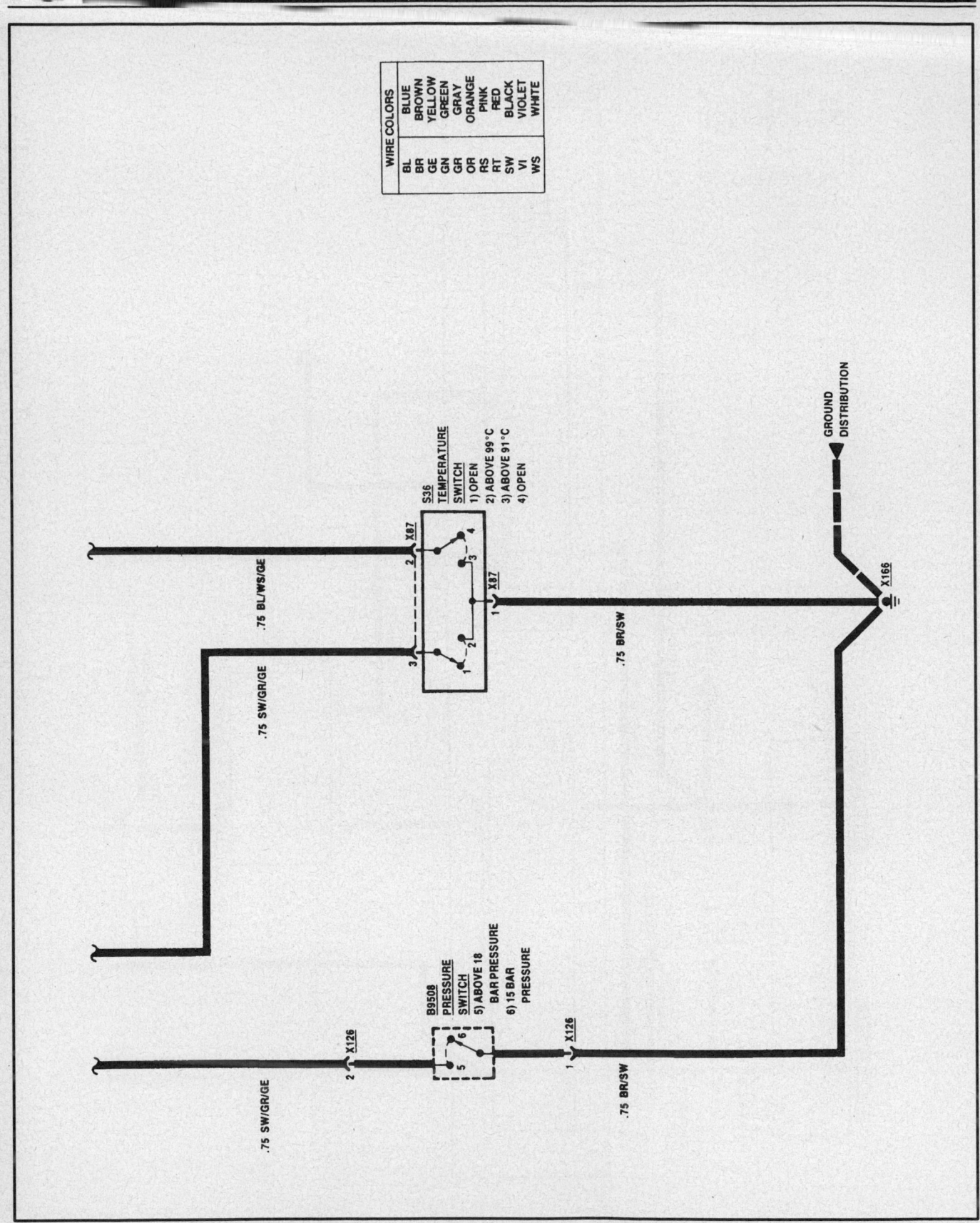

WIRE COLORS	
BL	BLUE
BR	BROWN
GE	YELLOW
GN	GREEN
GR	GRAY
OR	ORANGE
RS	PINK
RT	RED
SW	BLACK
VI	VIOLET
WS	WHITE

GROUND DISTRIBUTION

X166

S36
TEMPERATURE SWITCH
1) OPEN
2) ABOVE 99°C
3) ABOVE 91°C
4) OPEN

X87

.75 BL/WS/GE

.75 SW/GR/GE

.75 BR/SW

B9508
PRESSURE SWITCH
5) ABOVE 18 BAR PRESSURE
6) 15 BAR PRESSURE

X126

.75 SW/GR/GE

.75 BR/SW

Auxiliary fan circuit—7-Series, cont'd

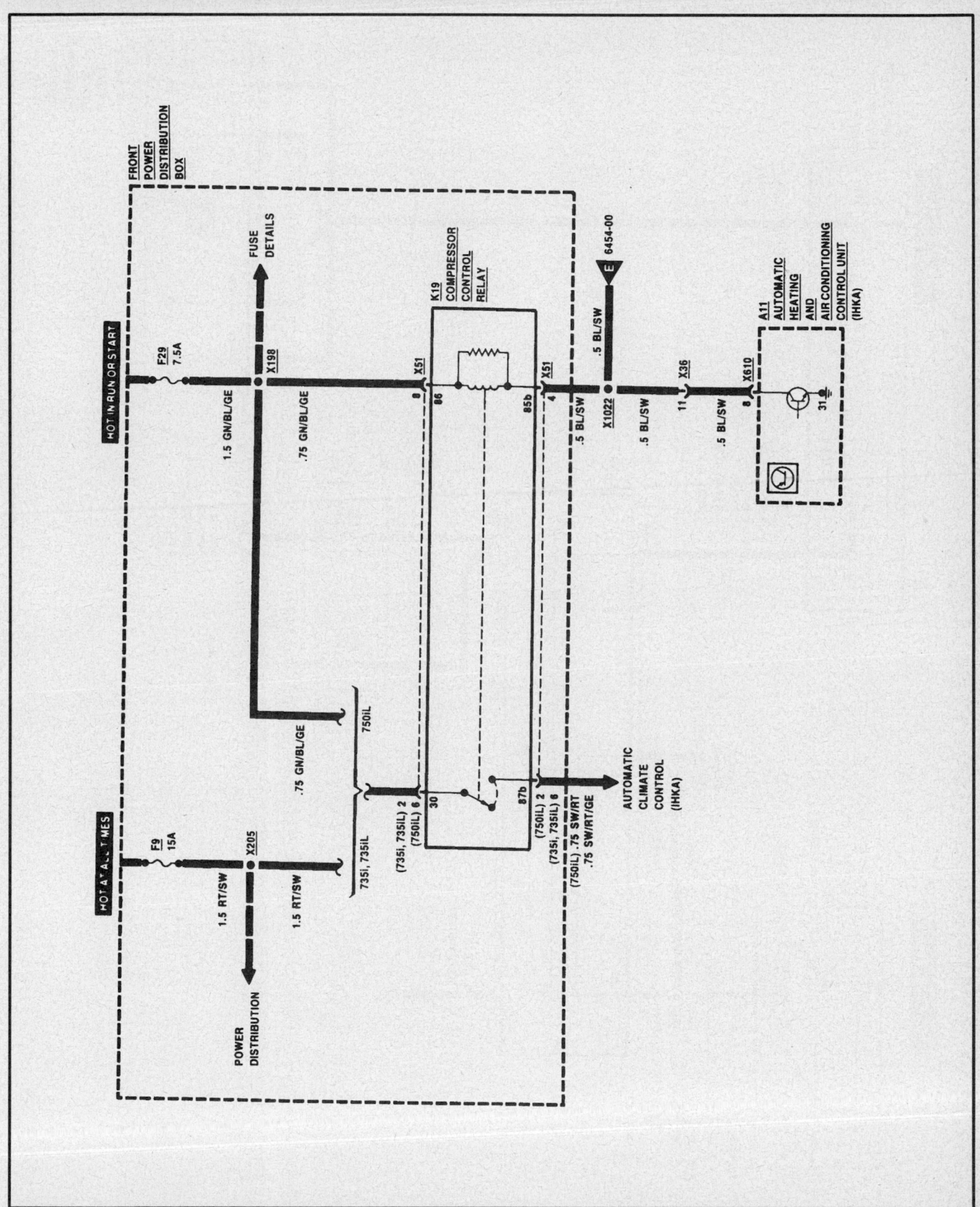

Auxiliary fan circuit—7-Series, cont'd

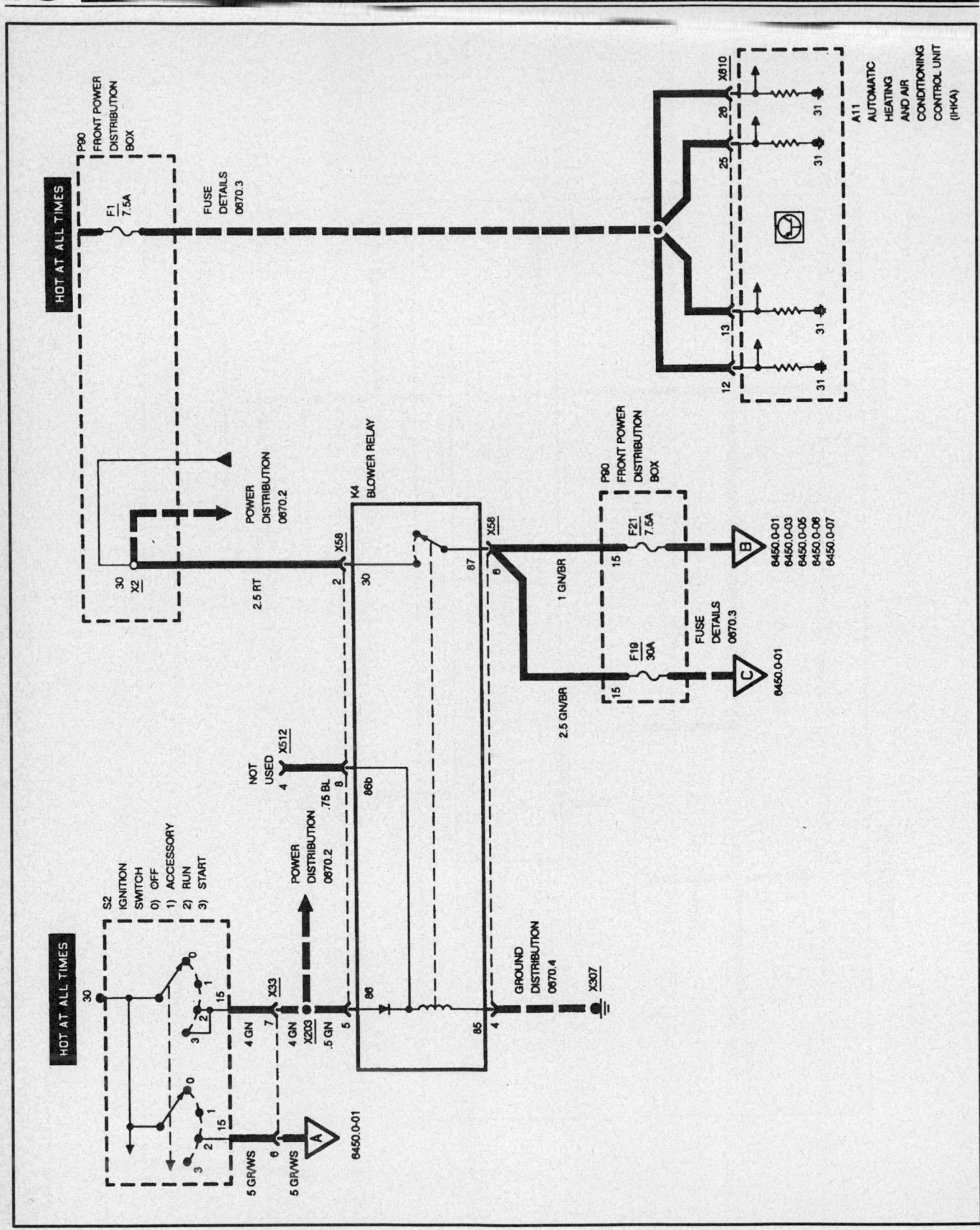

Auxiliary fan circuit—7-Series, cont'd

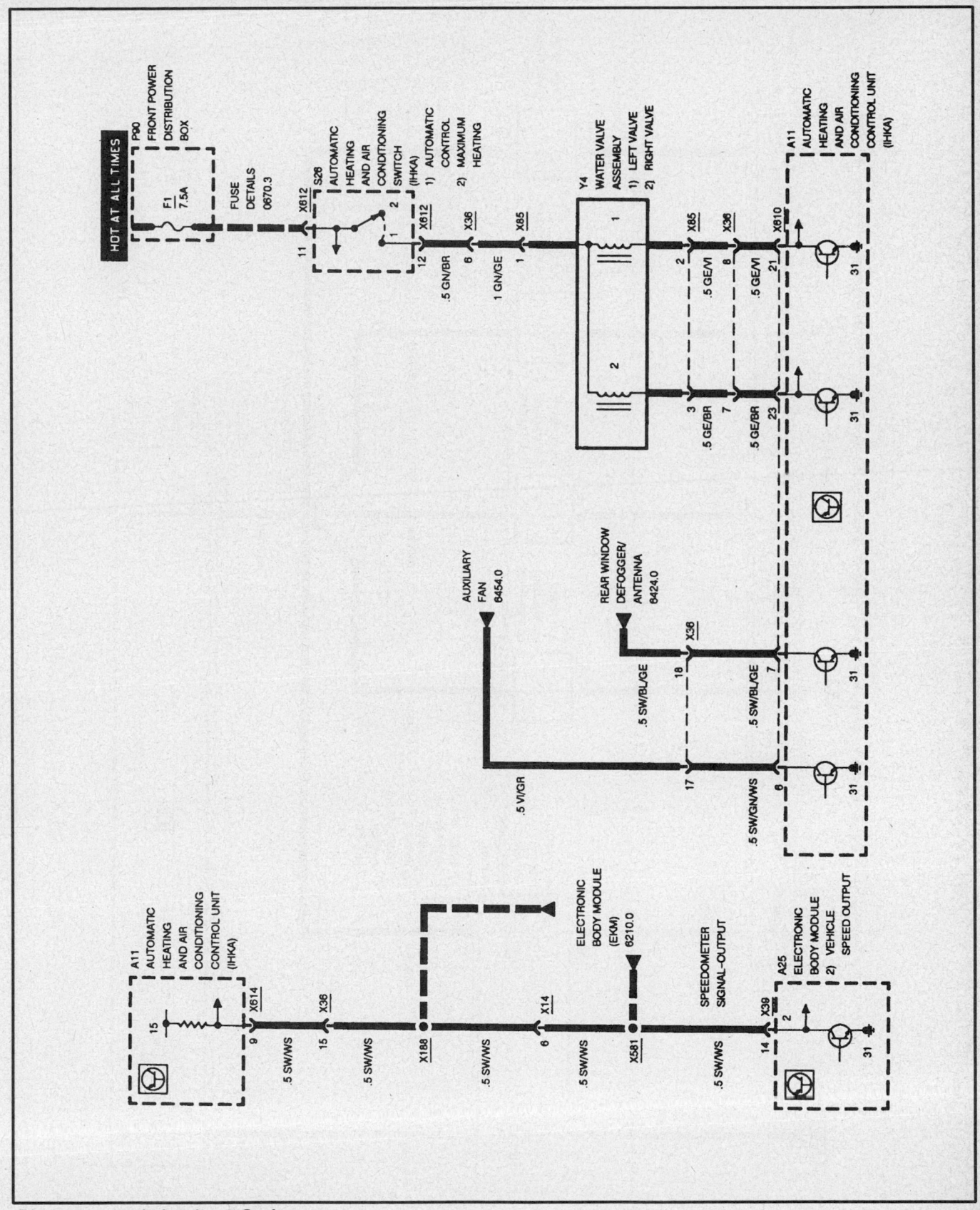

Blower control circuit—8-Series

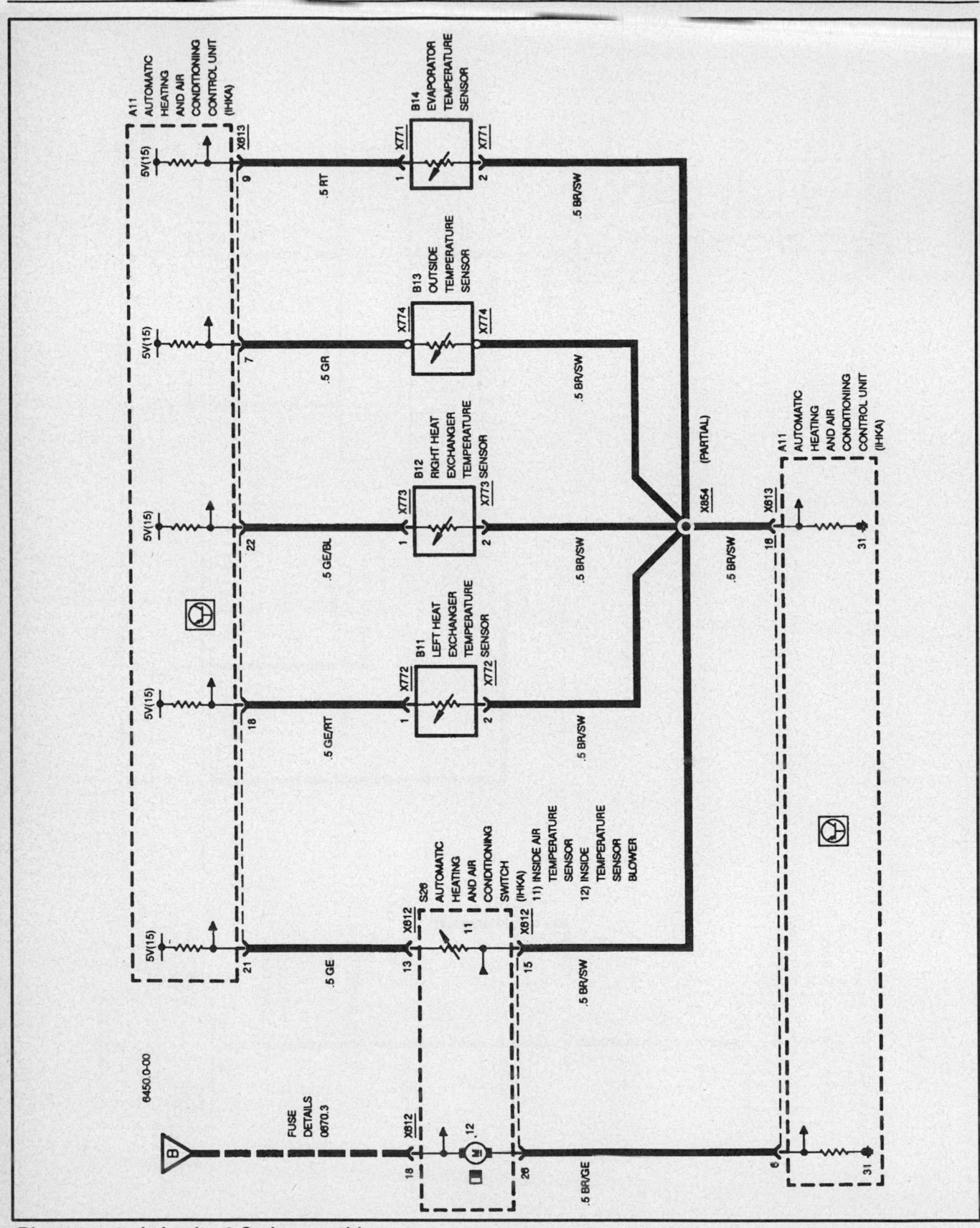

Blower control circuit—8-Series, cont'd

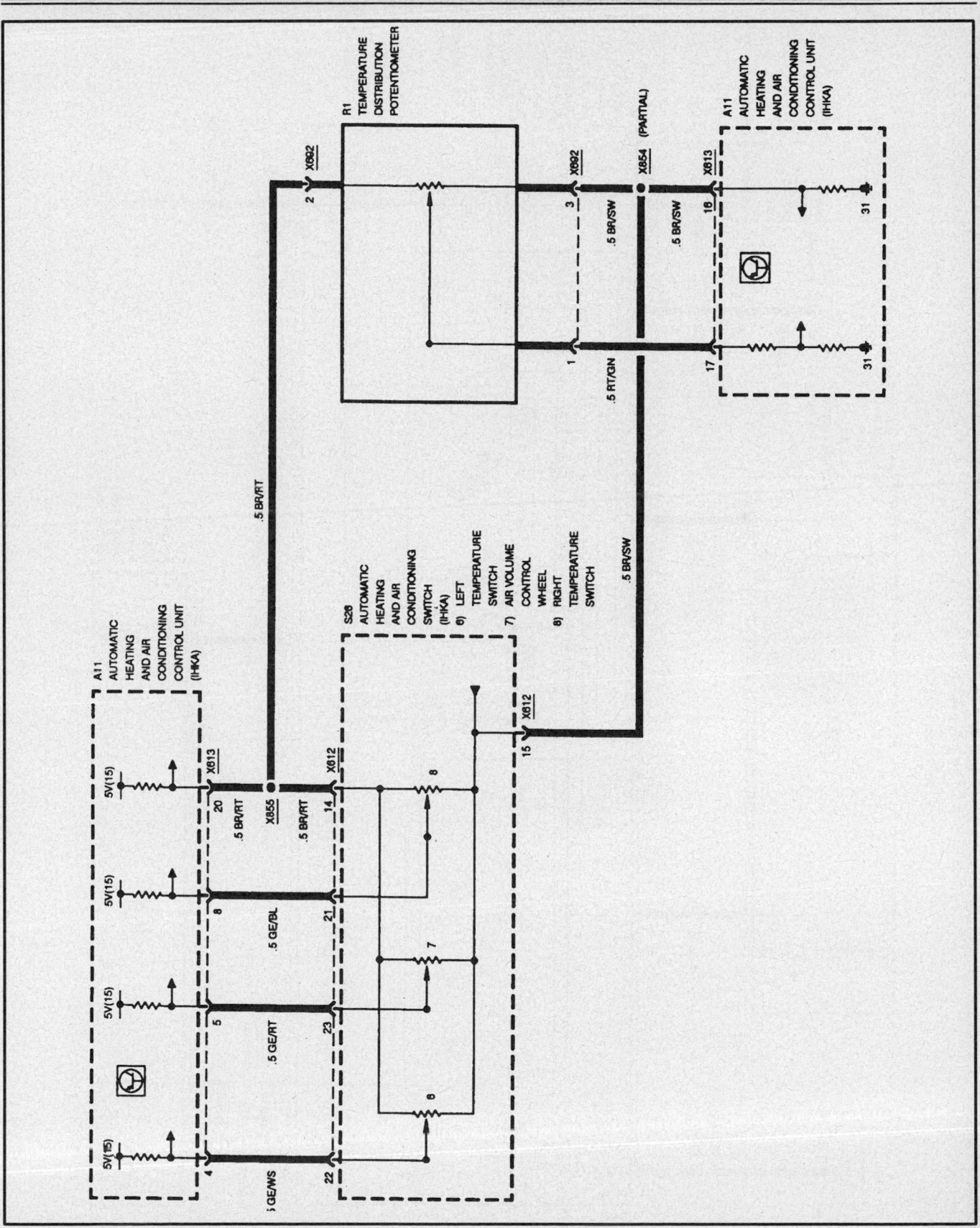

Temperature control circuit—8-Series

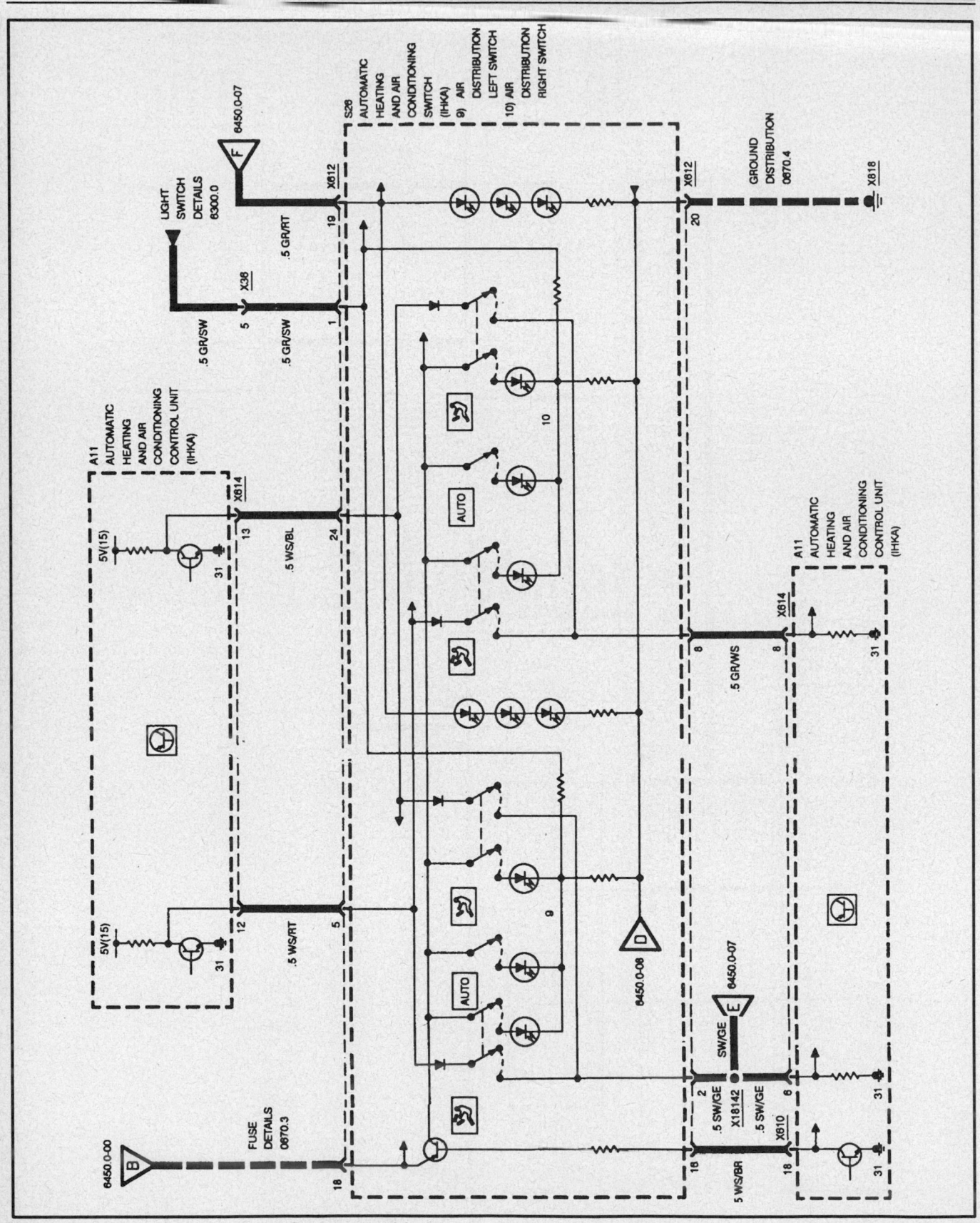

Temperature control circuit—8-Series, cont'd

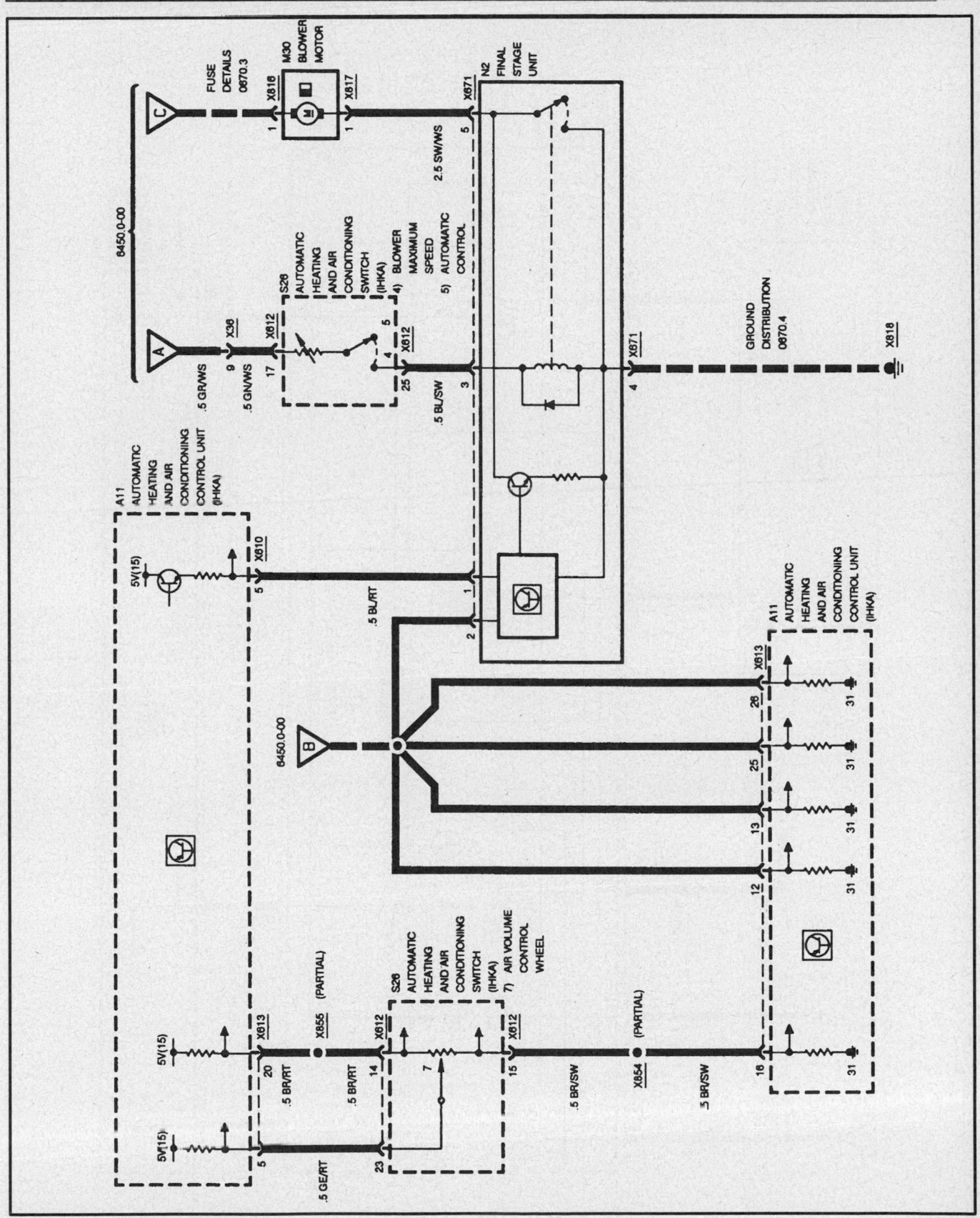

Power circuit—8-Series

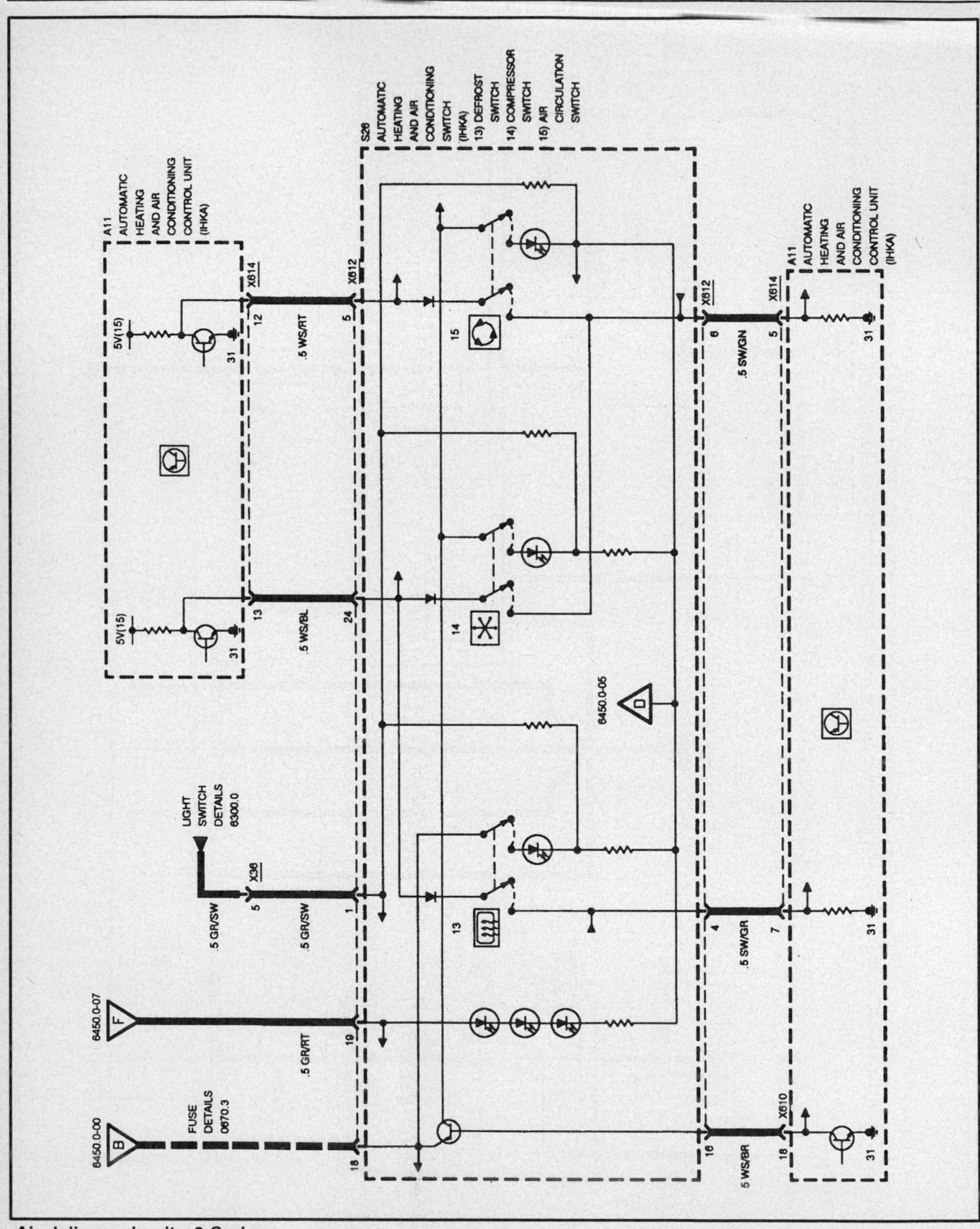

Air delivery circuit—8-Series

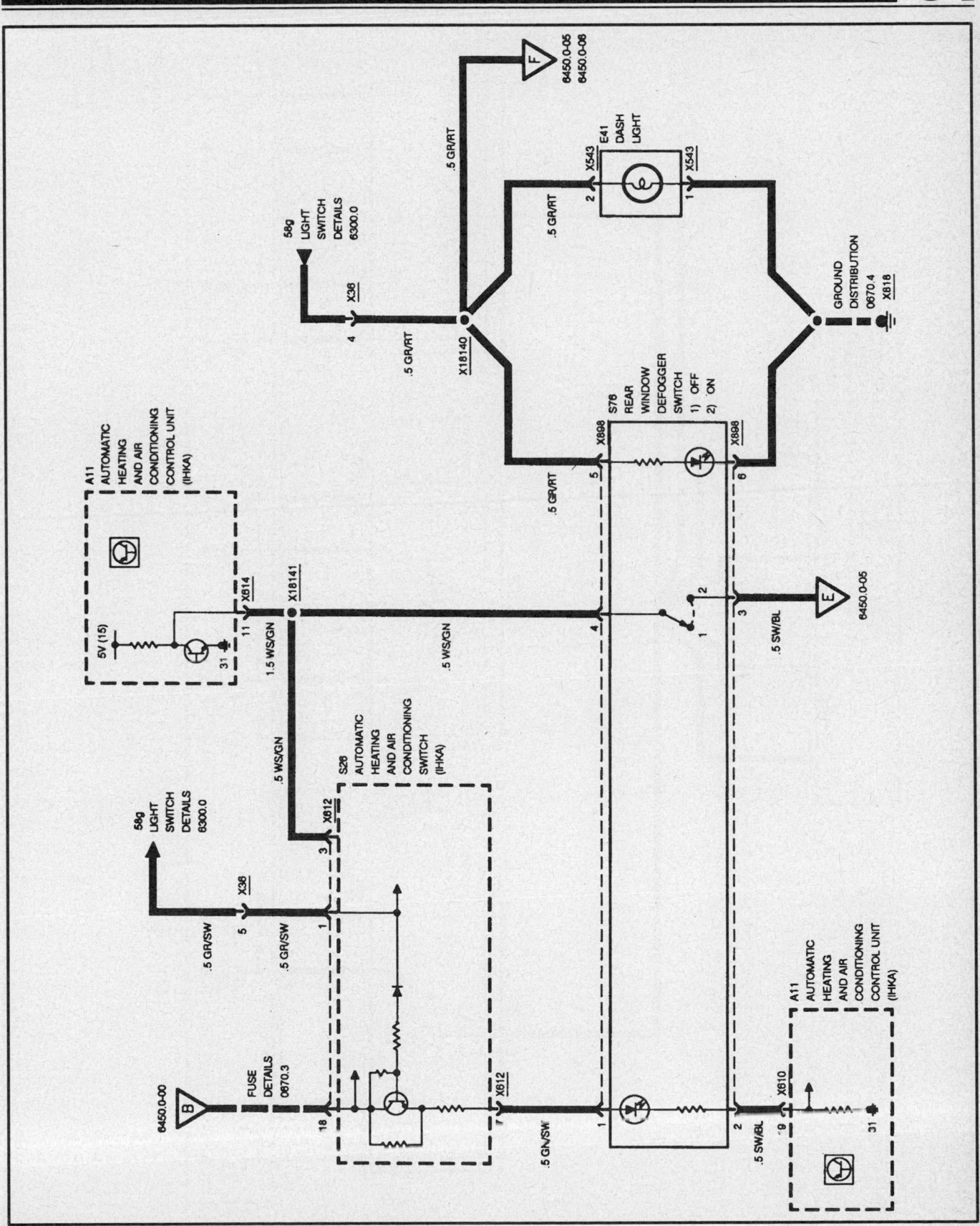

Air delivery circuit—8-Series, cont'd

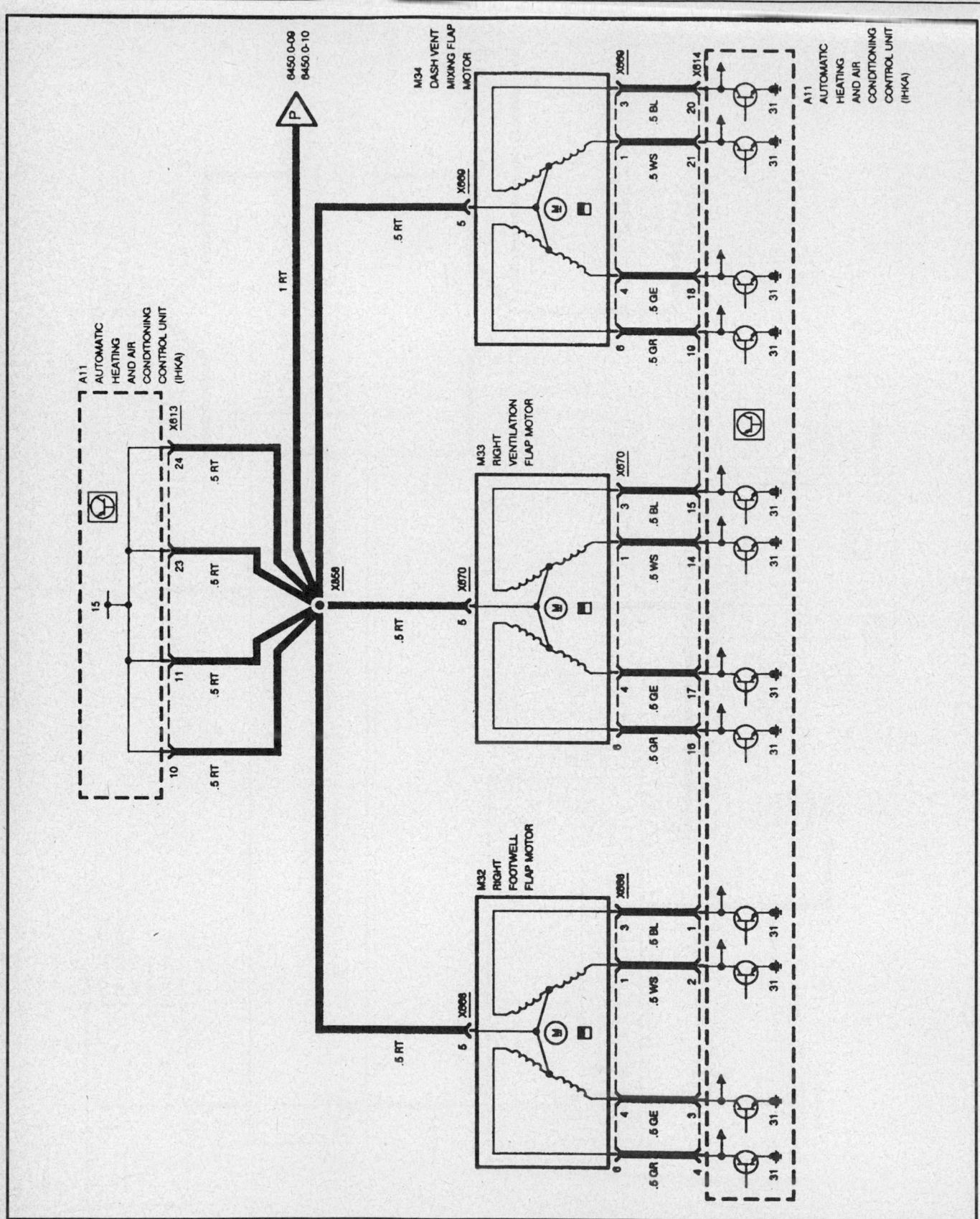

Air delivery circuit—8-Series, cont'd

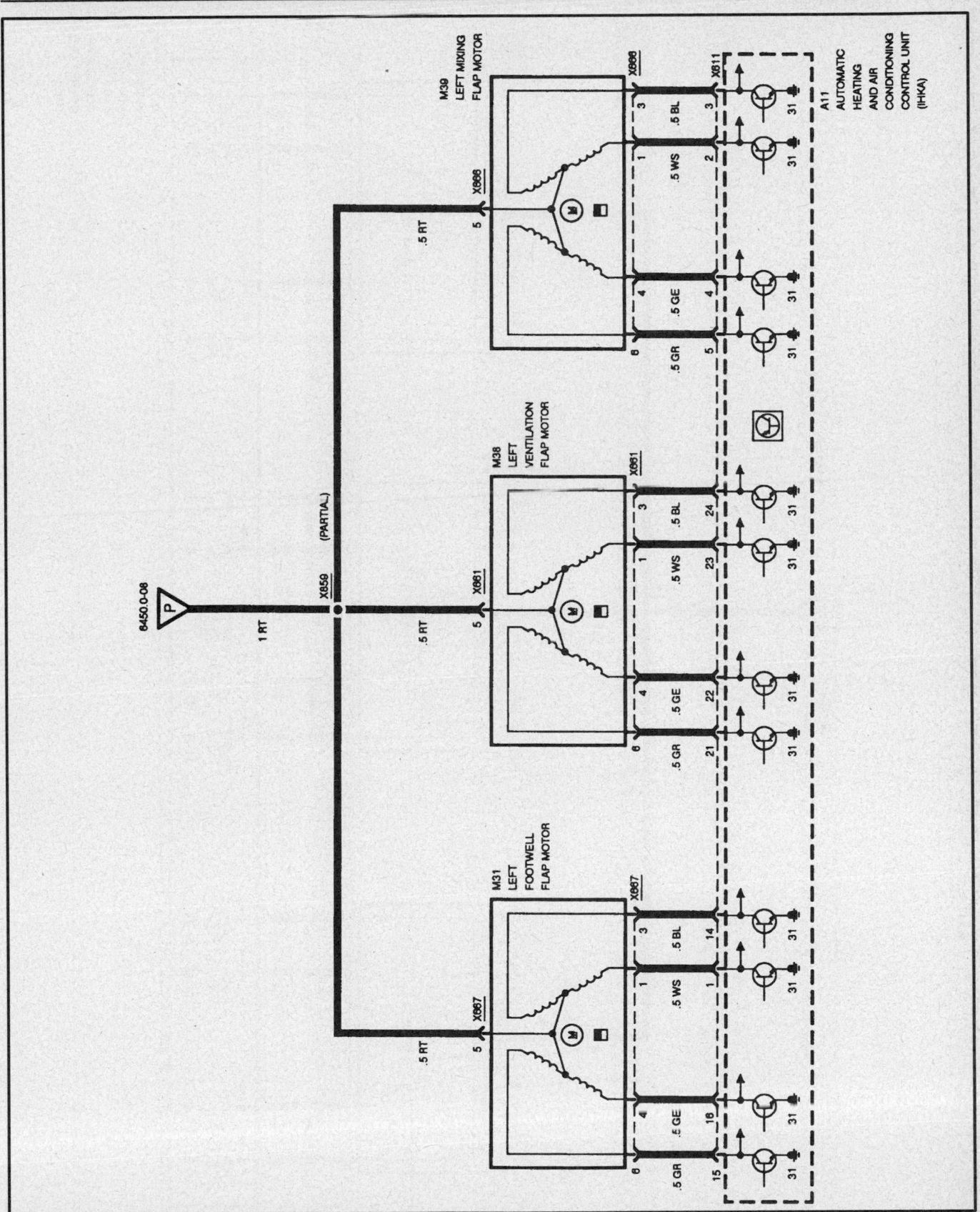

Air delivery circuit—8-Series, cont'd

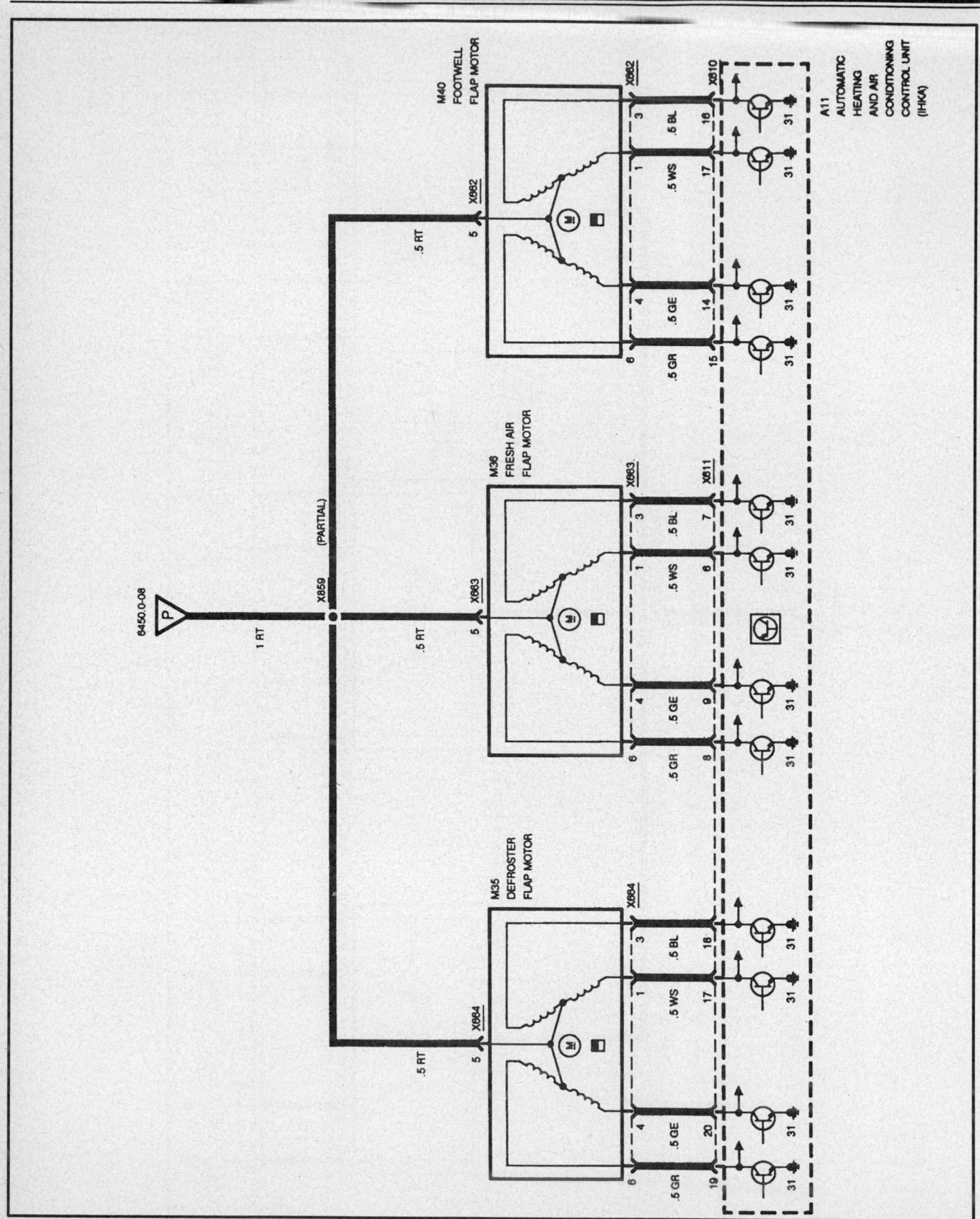

Air delivery circuit—8-Series, cont'd

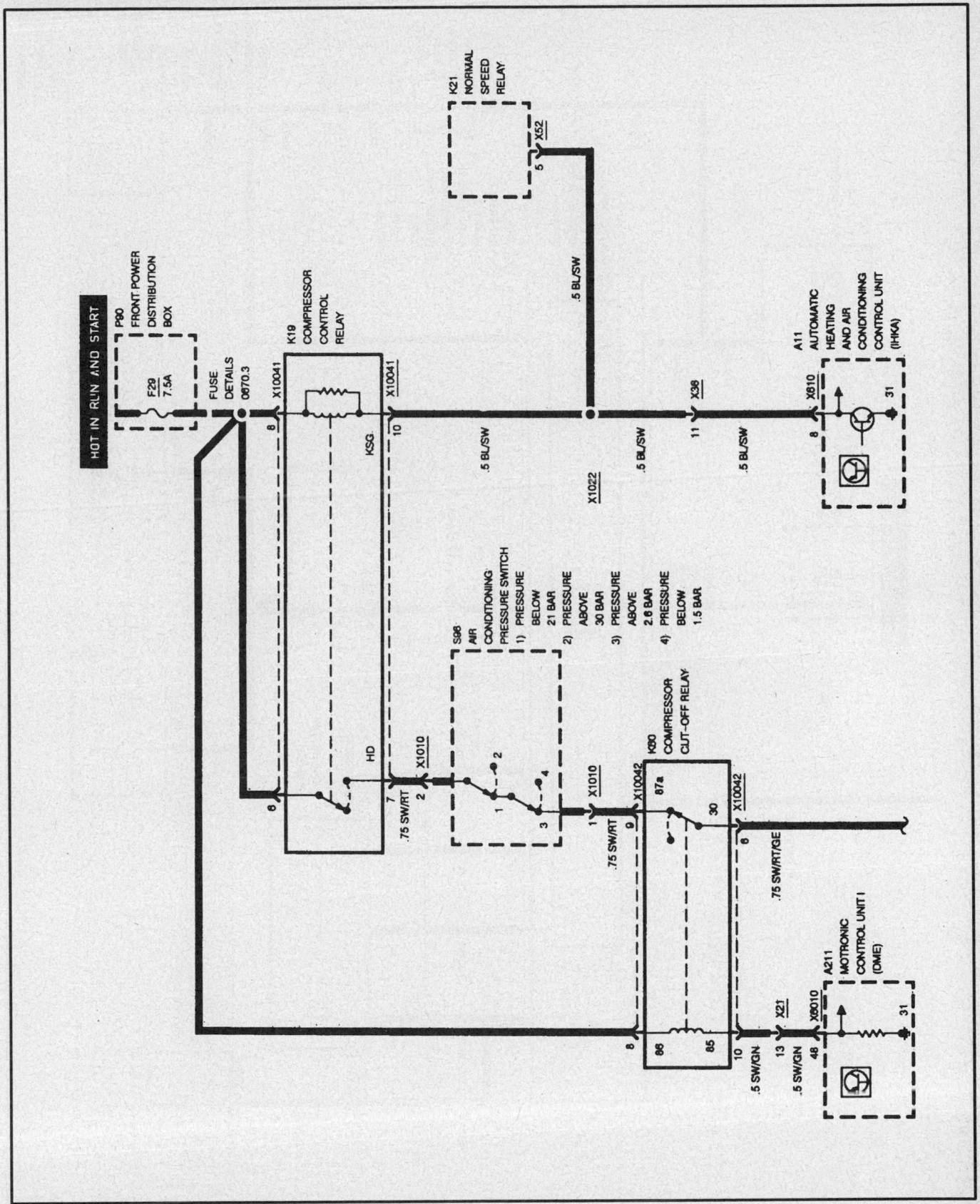

Compressor control circuit—8-Series

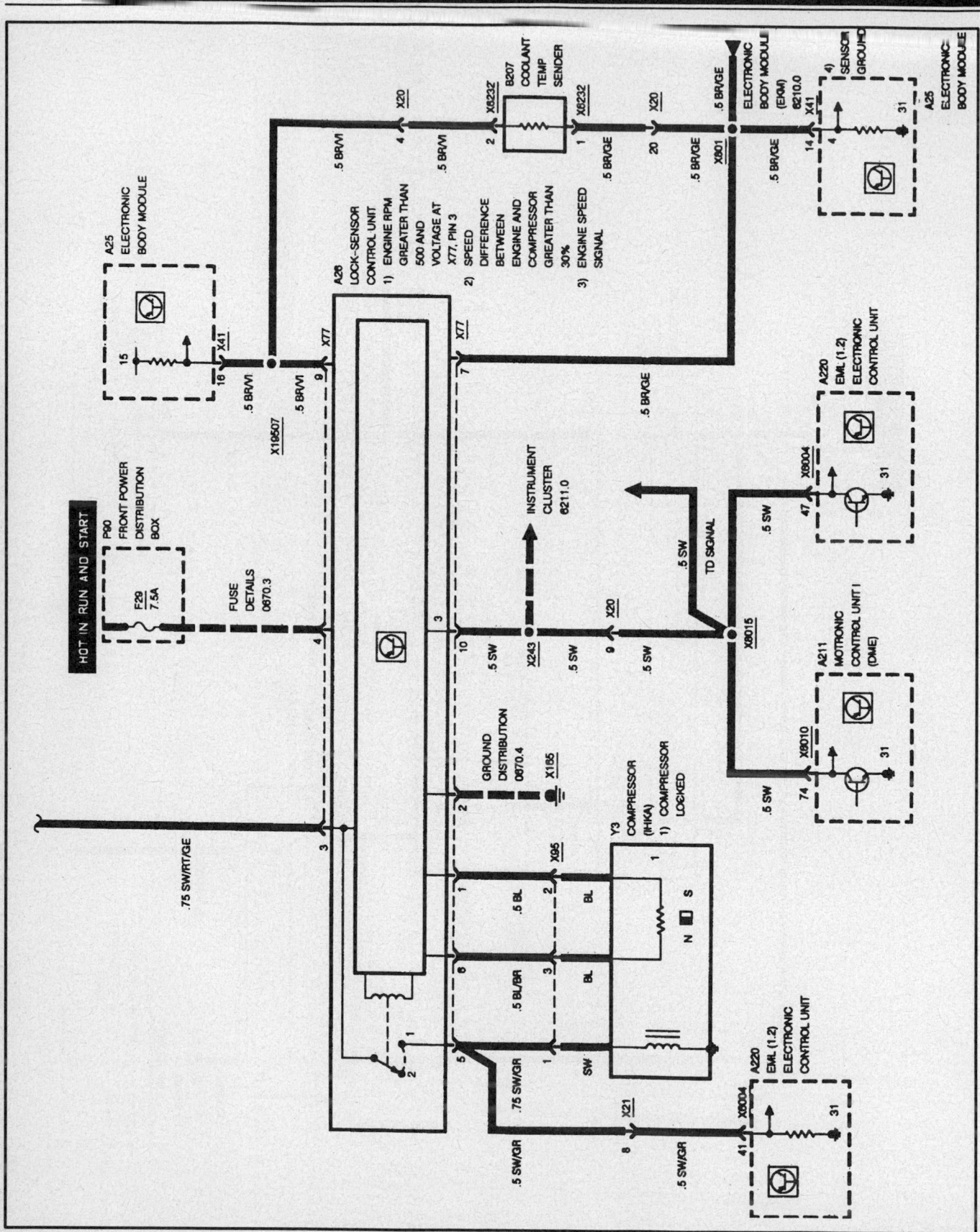

Compressor control circuit—8-Series, cont'd

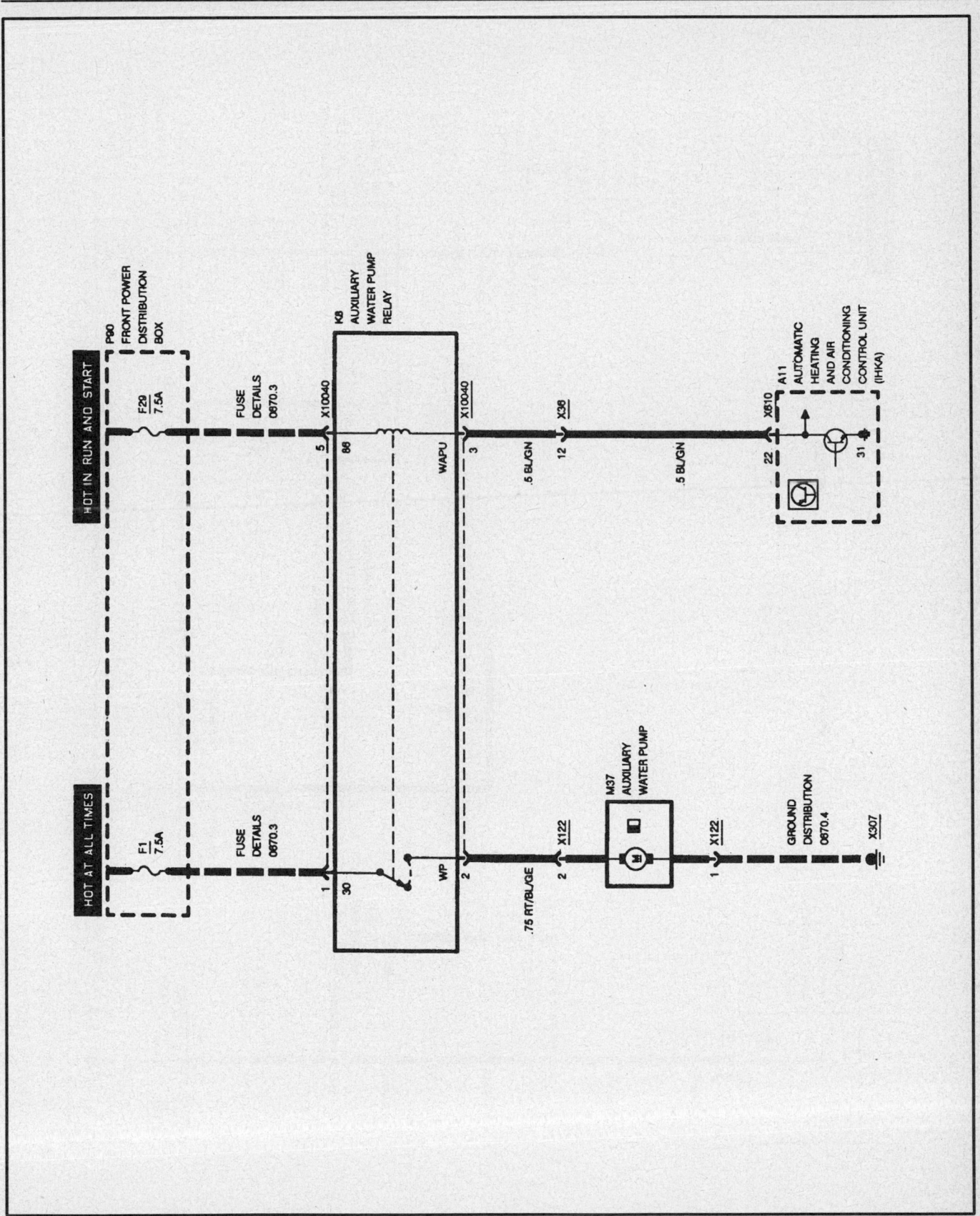

Water pump control circuit—8-Series

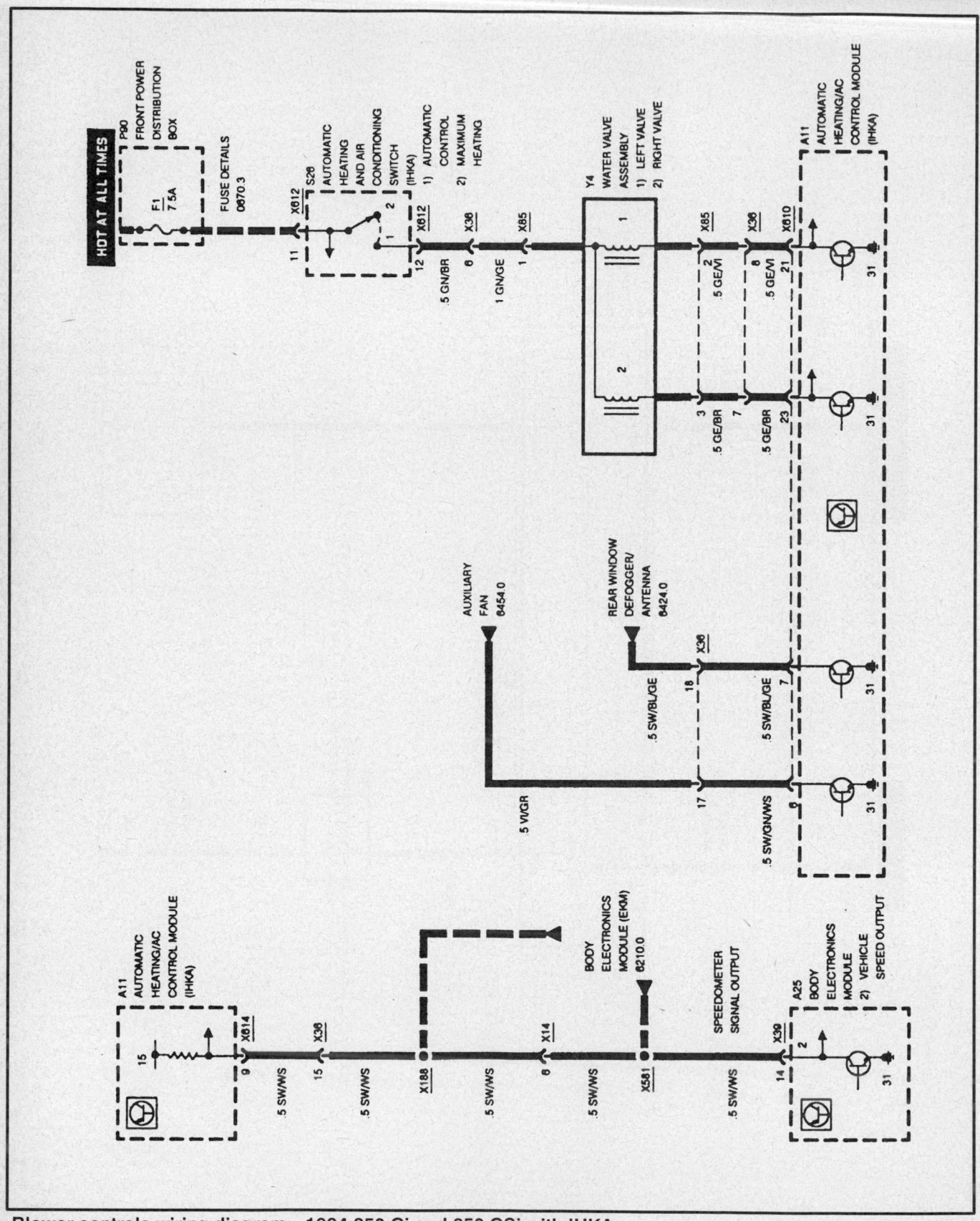

Blower controls wiring diagram—1994 850 Ci and 850 CSi with IHKA

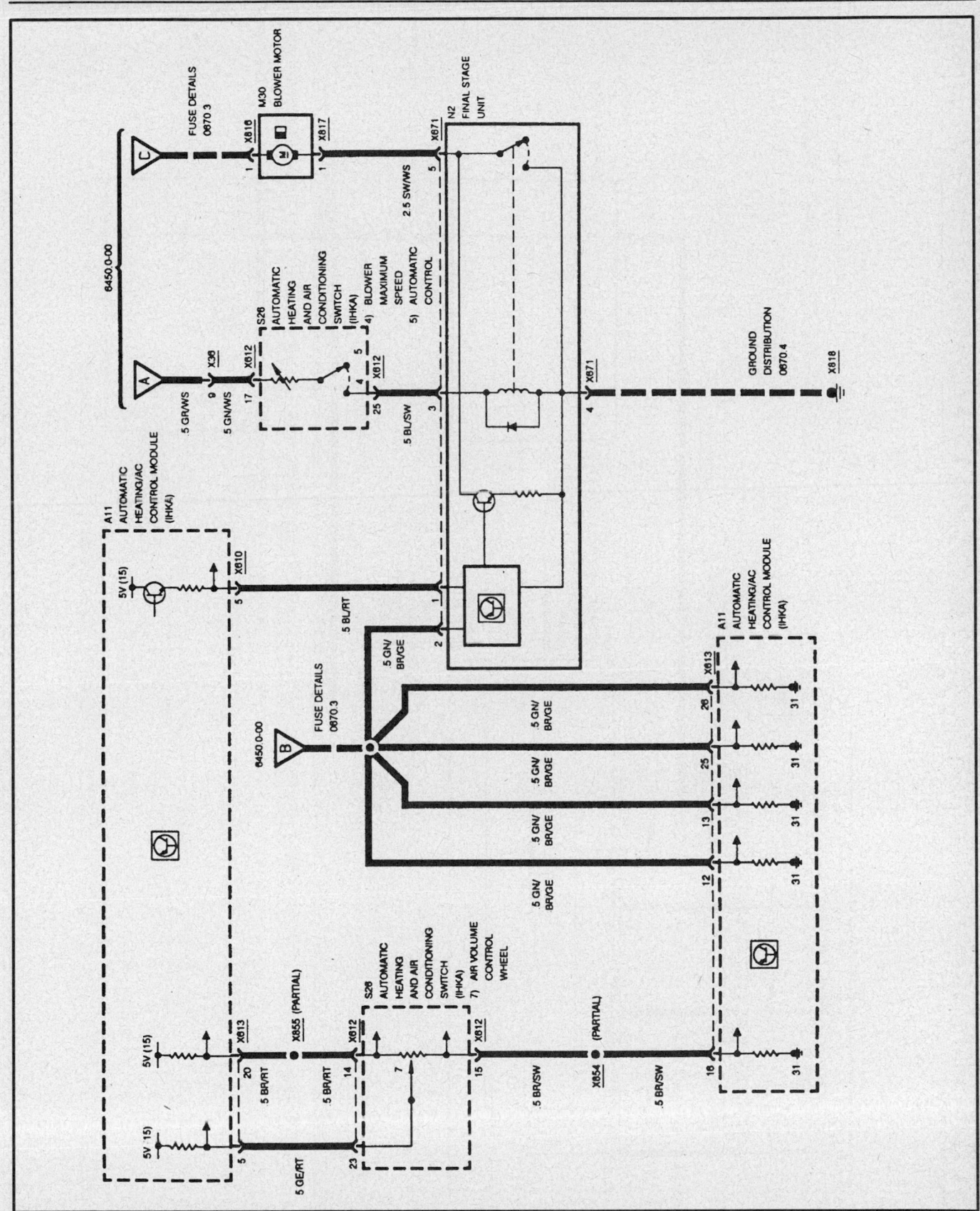

Blower controls wiring diagram—1994 850 Ci and 850 CSi with IHKA, cont'd

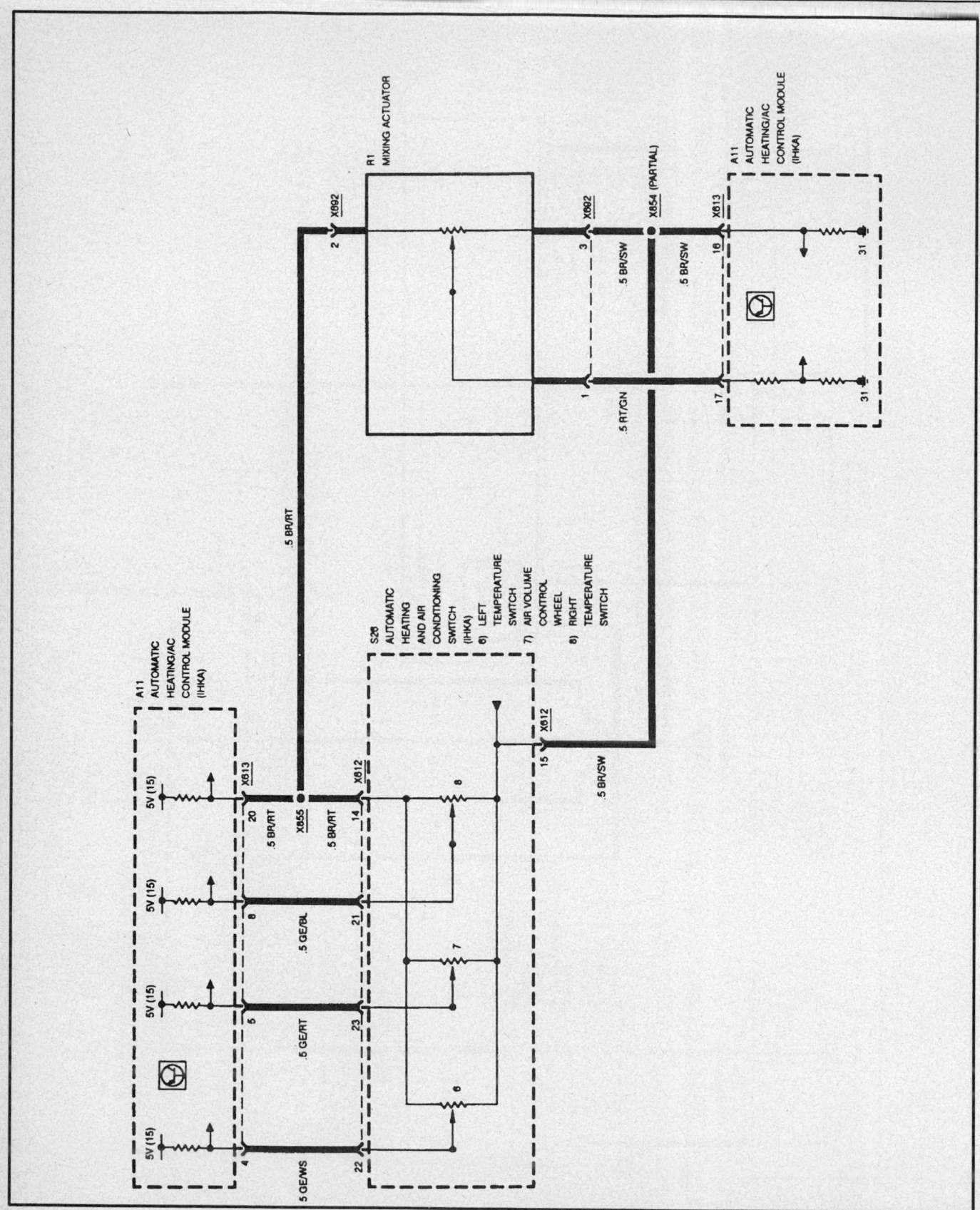

Temperature controls wiring diagram—1994 850 Ci and 850 CSi with IHKA

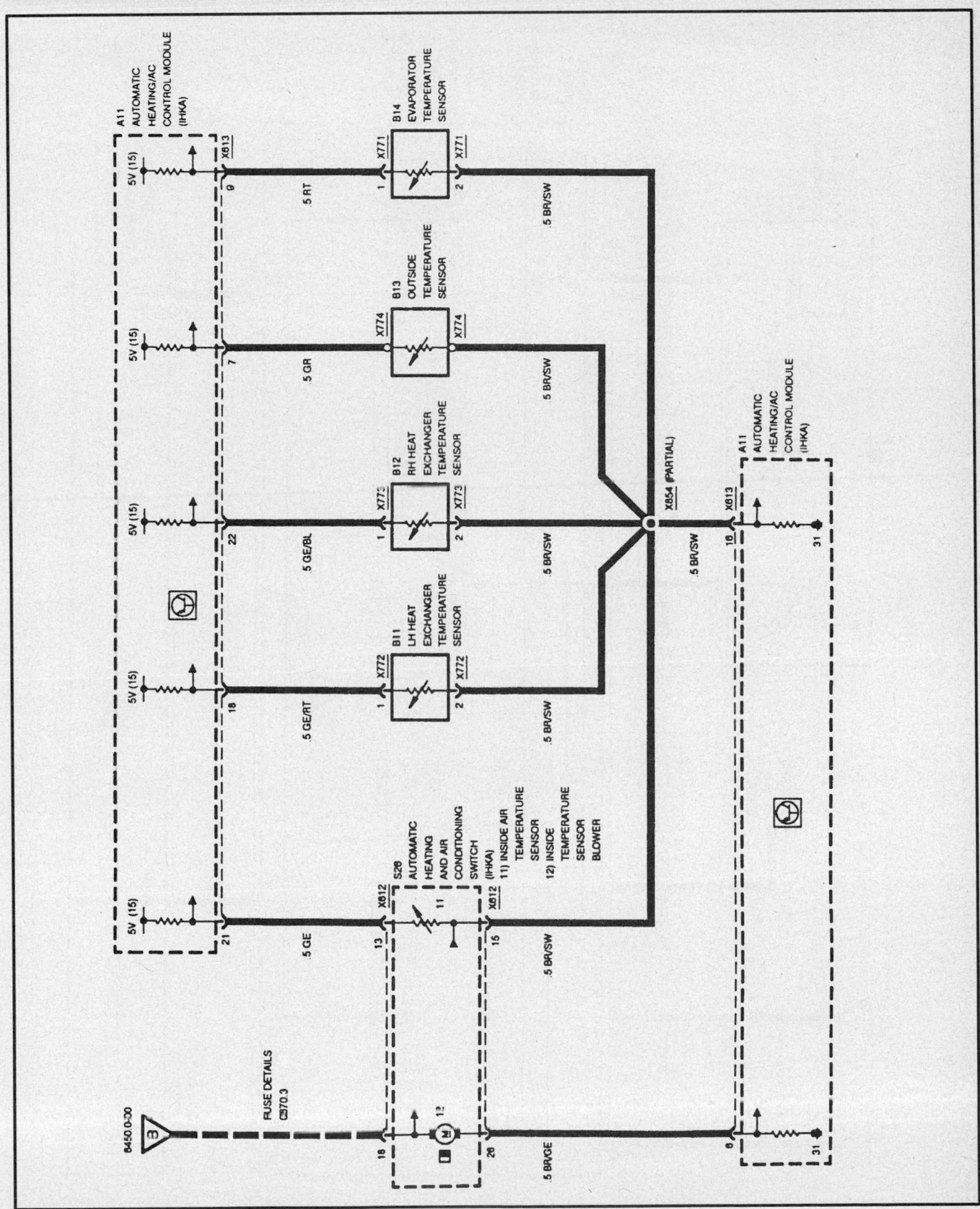

Temperature controls wiring diagram—1994 850 Ci and 850 CSi with IHKA, cont'd

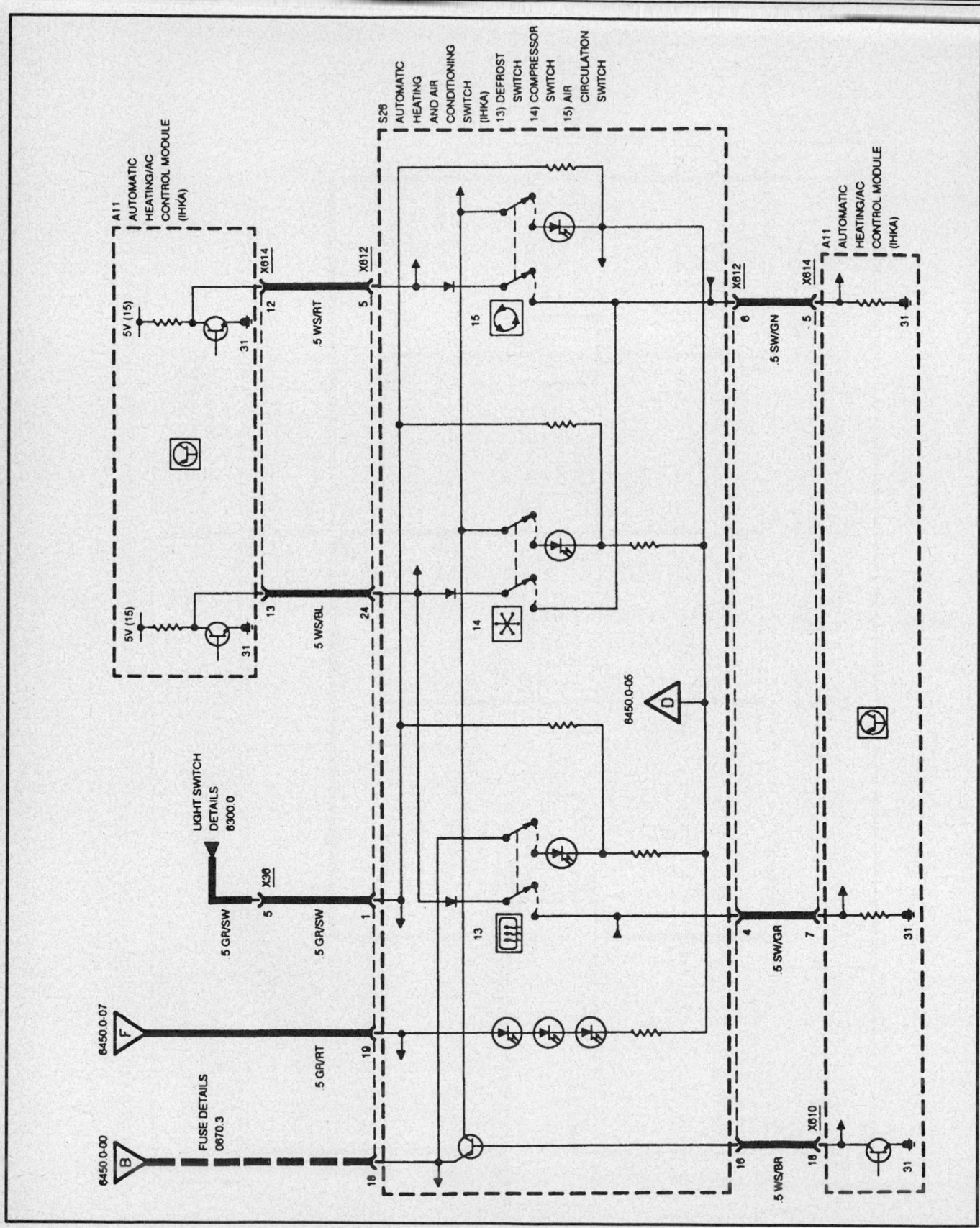

Air delivery wiring diagram—1994 850 Ci and 850 CSi with IHKA

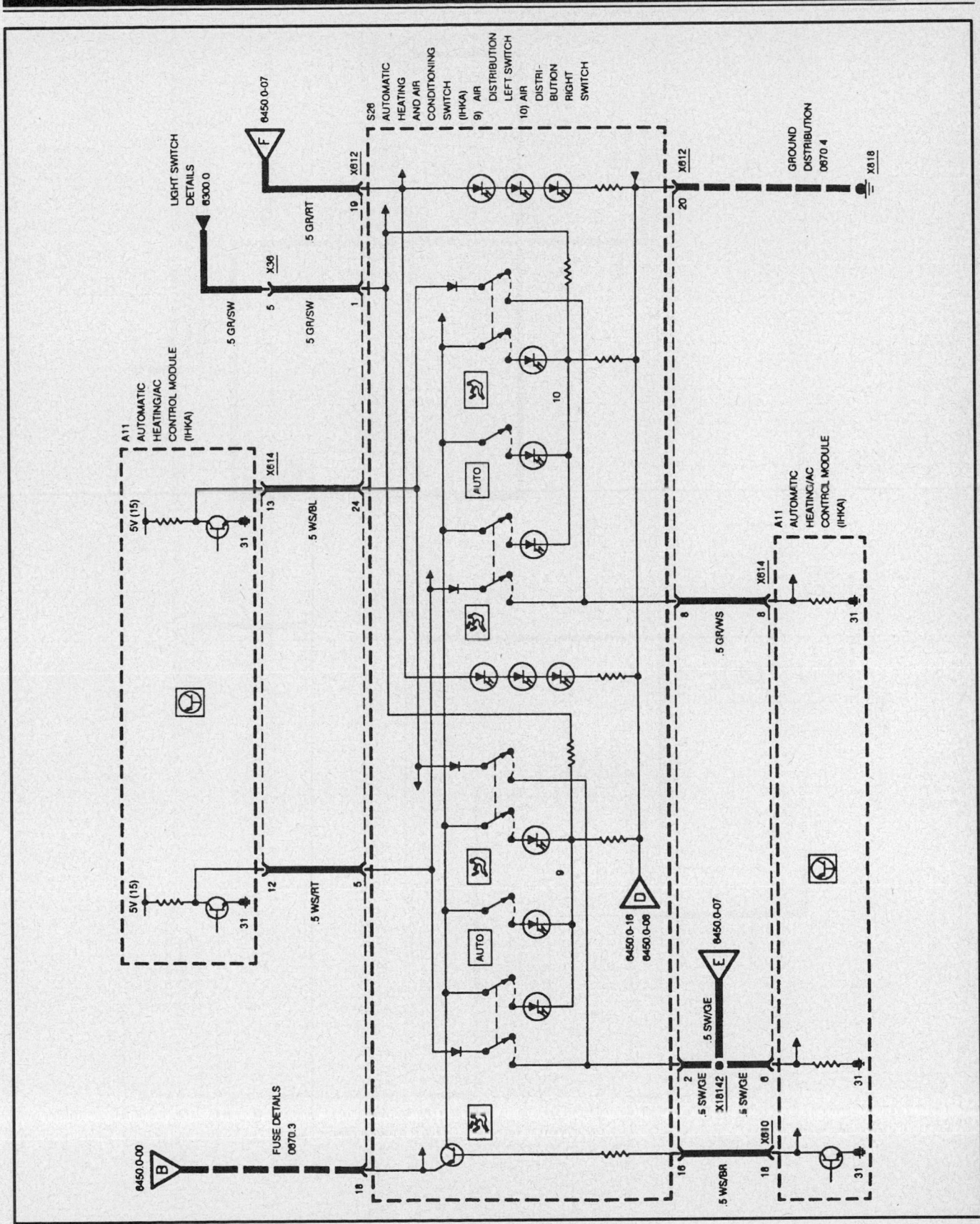

Air delivery wiring diagram—1994 850 Ci and 850 CSi with IHKA, cont'd

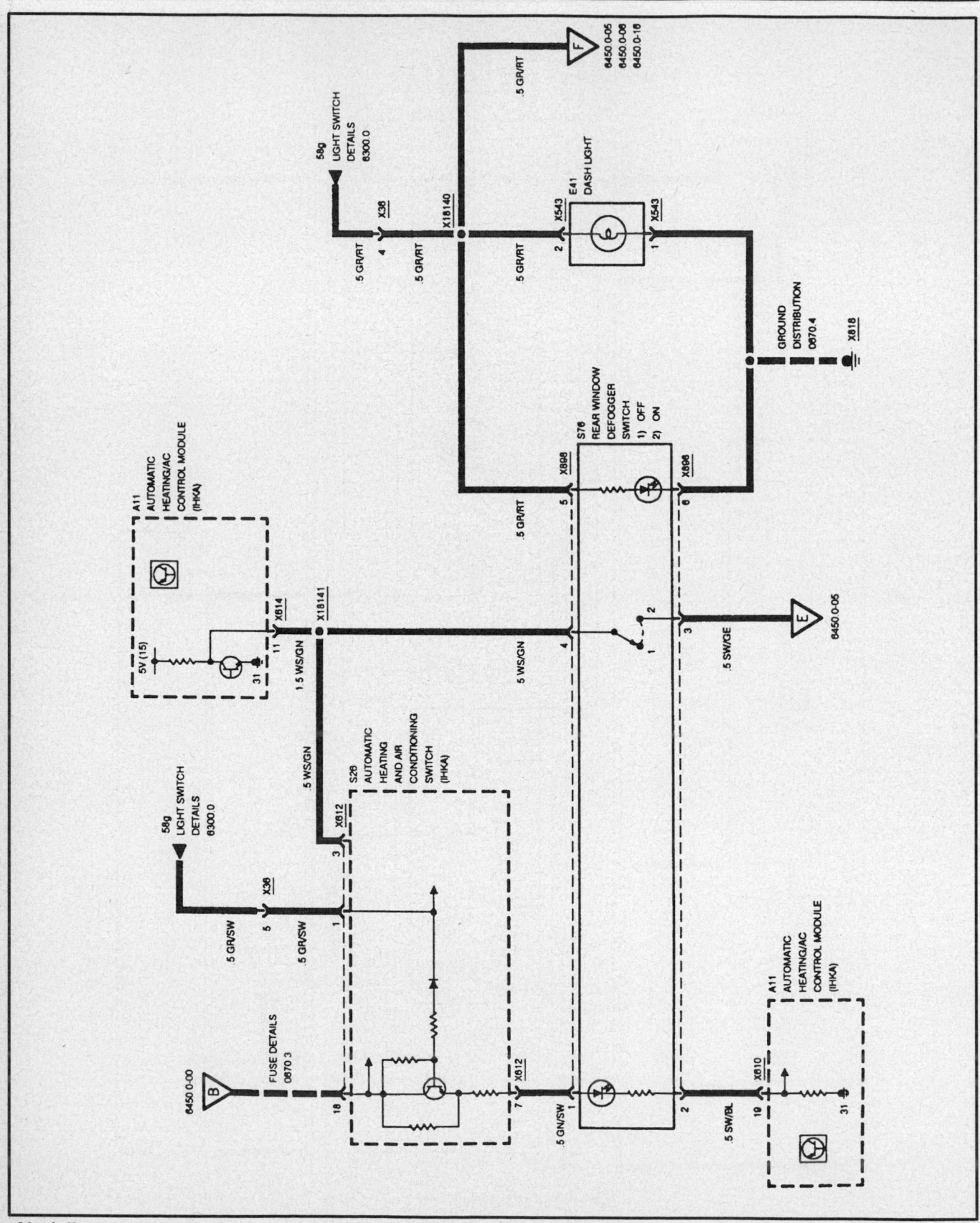

Air delivery wiring diagram—1994 850 Ci and 850 CSi with IHKA, cont'd

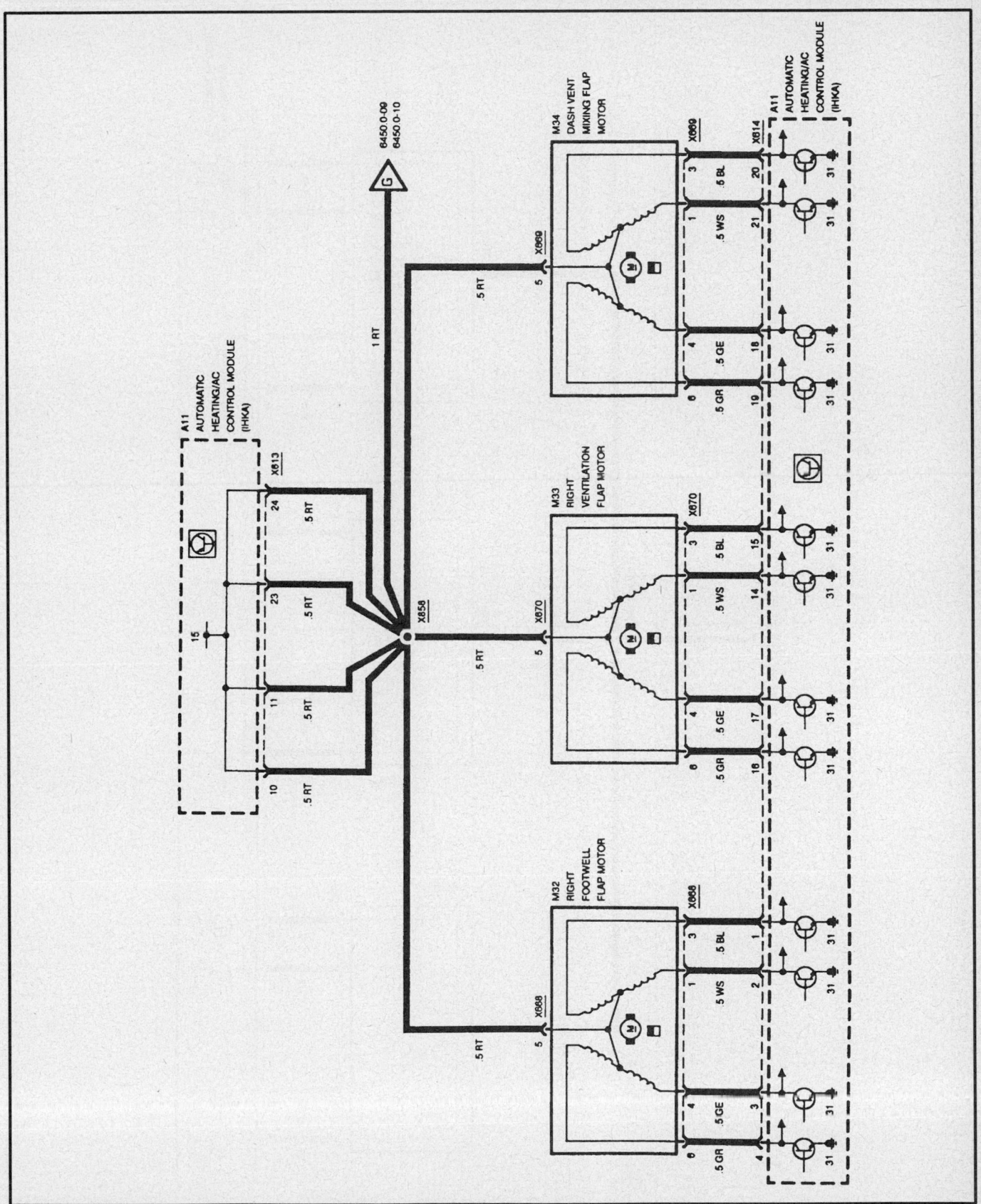

Air delivery wiring diagram—1994 850 Ci and 850 CSi with IHKA, cont'd

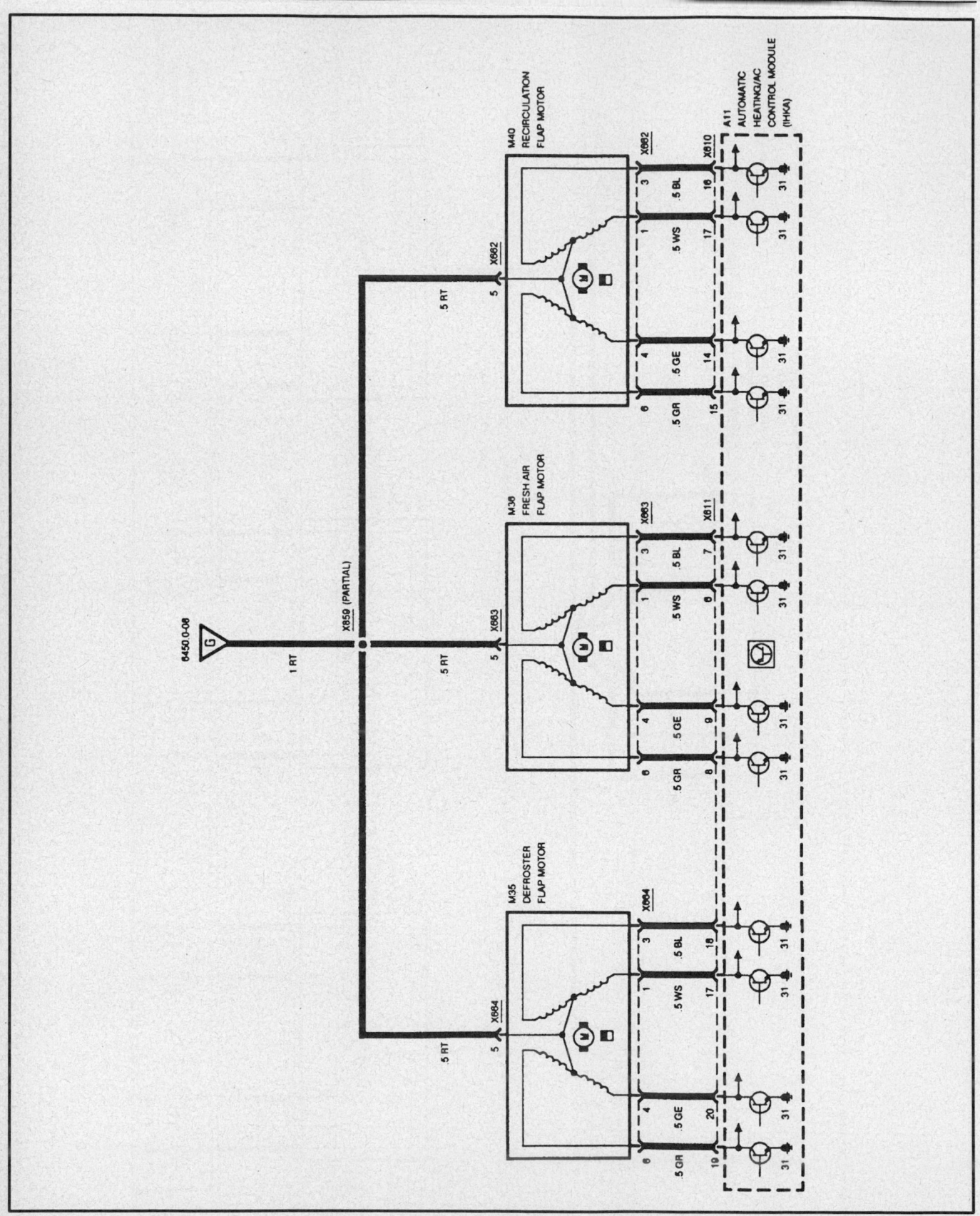

Air delivery wiring diagram—1994 850 Ci and 850 CSi with IHKA, cont'd

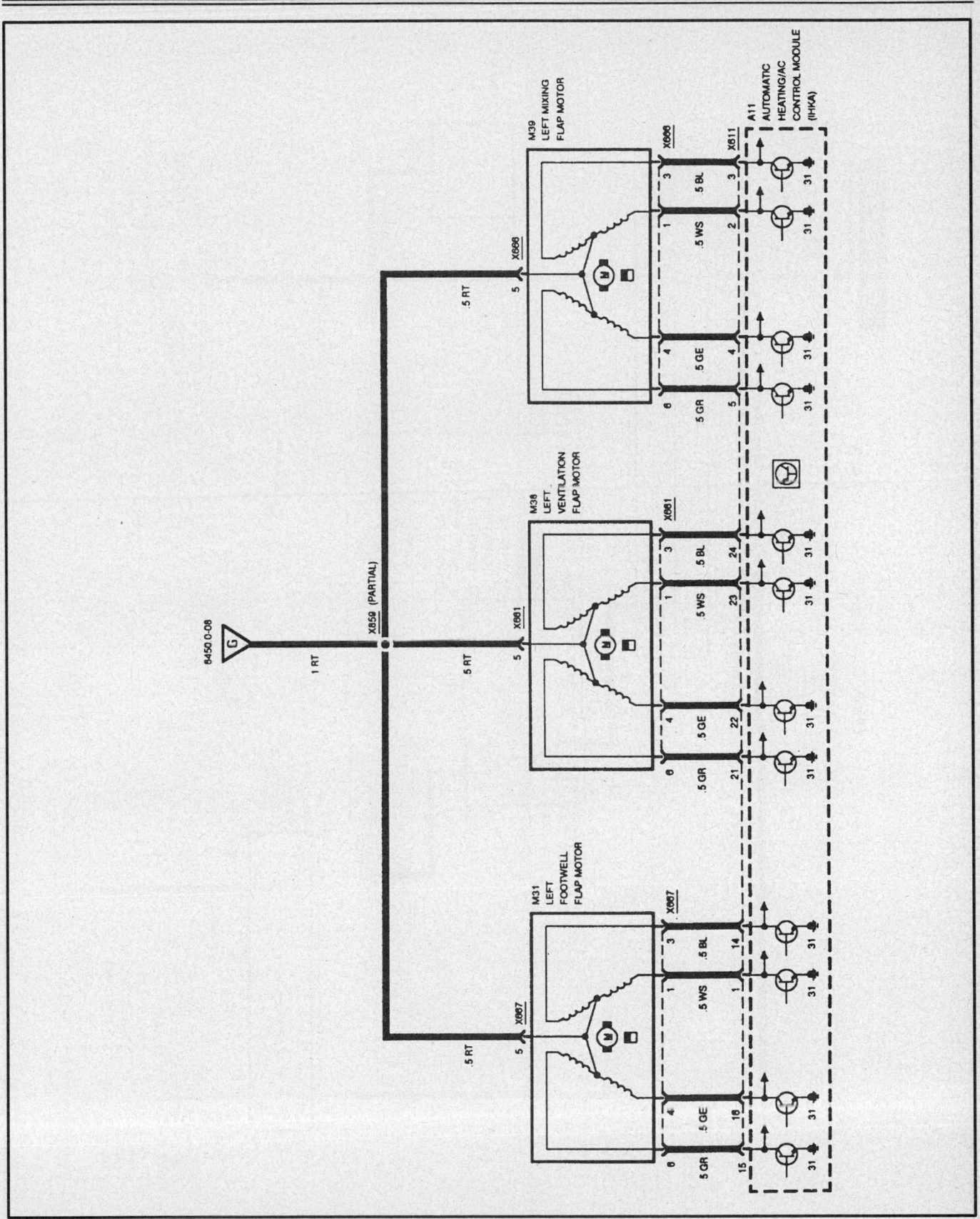

Air delivery wiring diagram—1994 850 Ci and 850 CSi with IHKA, cont'd

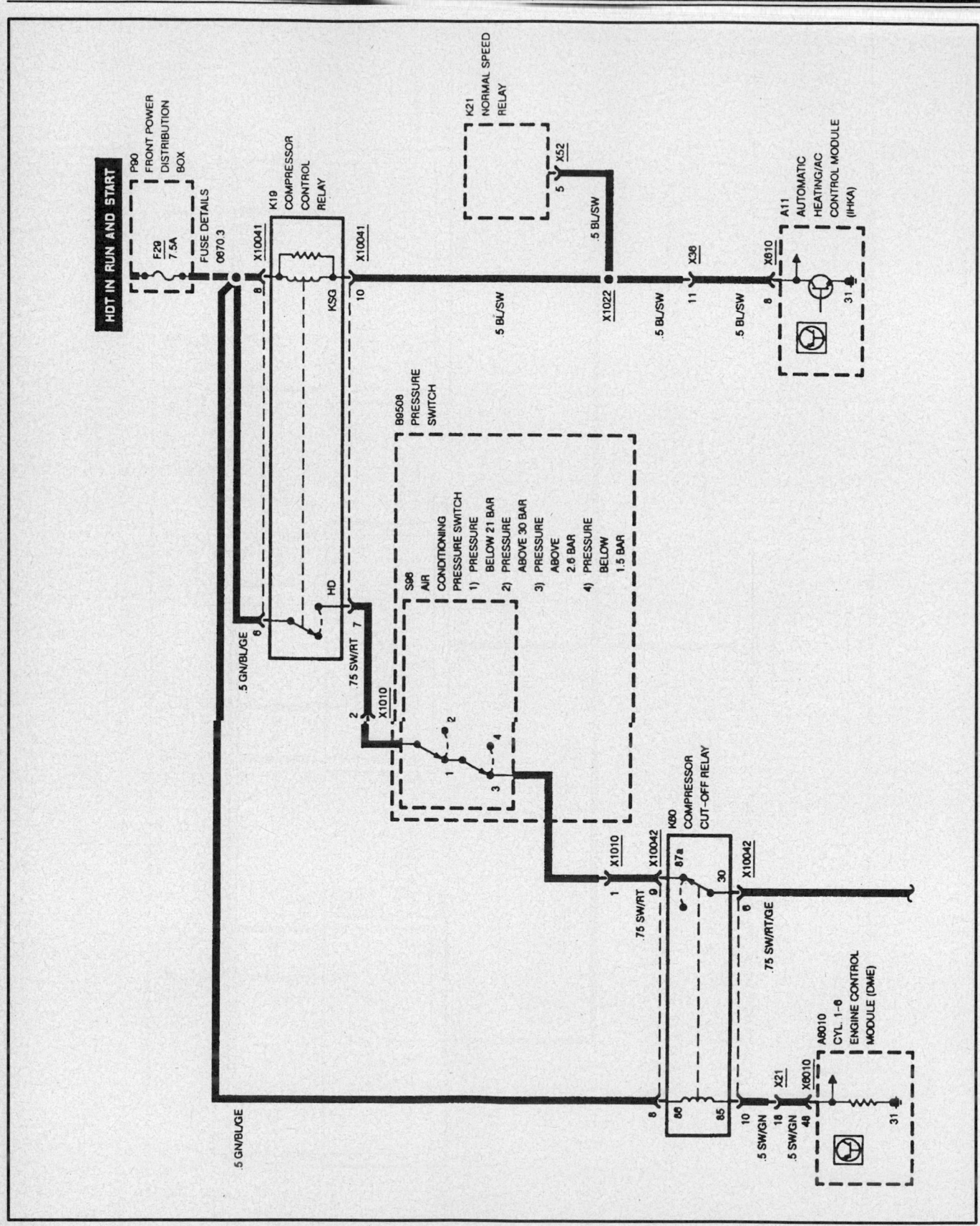

Compressor controls wiring diagram—1994 850 Ci and 850 CSi with IHKA

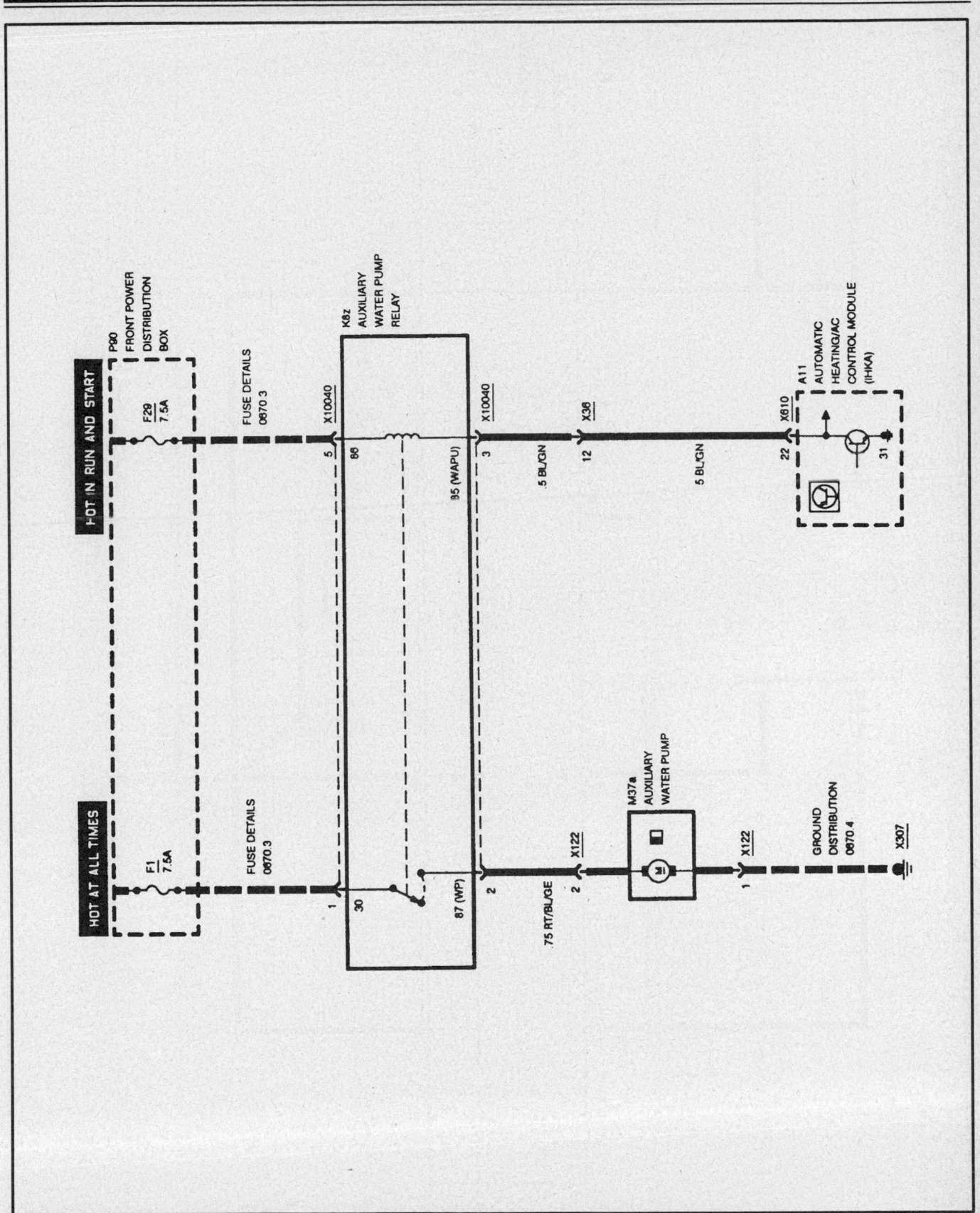

Automatic heating A/C controls wiring diagram—1994 850 Ci and 850 CSi with IHKA

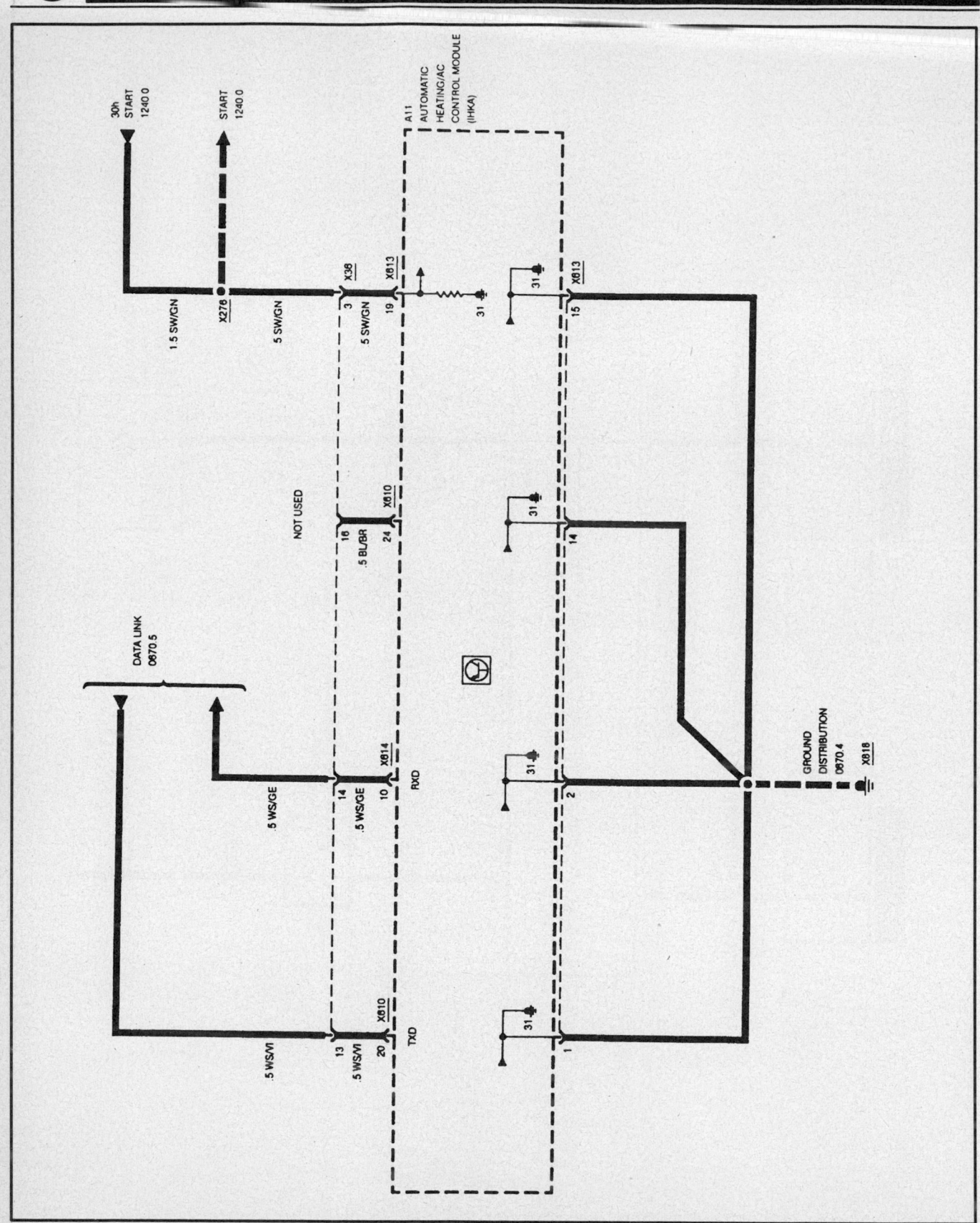

Datalink and starter input wiring diagram—1994 850 Ci and 850 CSi with IHKA

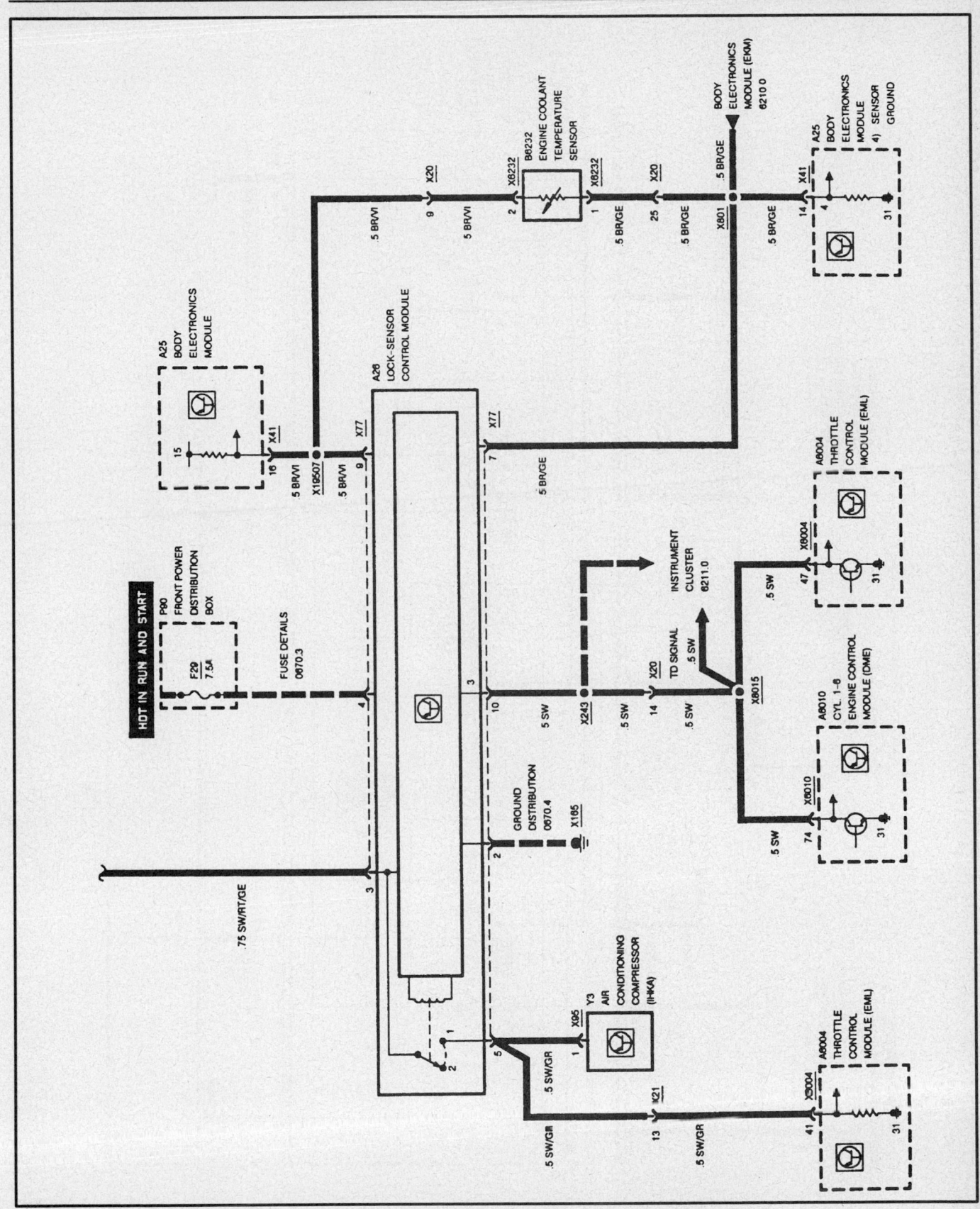

Datalink and starter input wiring diagram—1994 850 Ci and 850 CSi with IHKA, cont'd

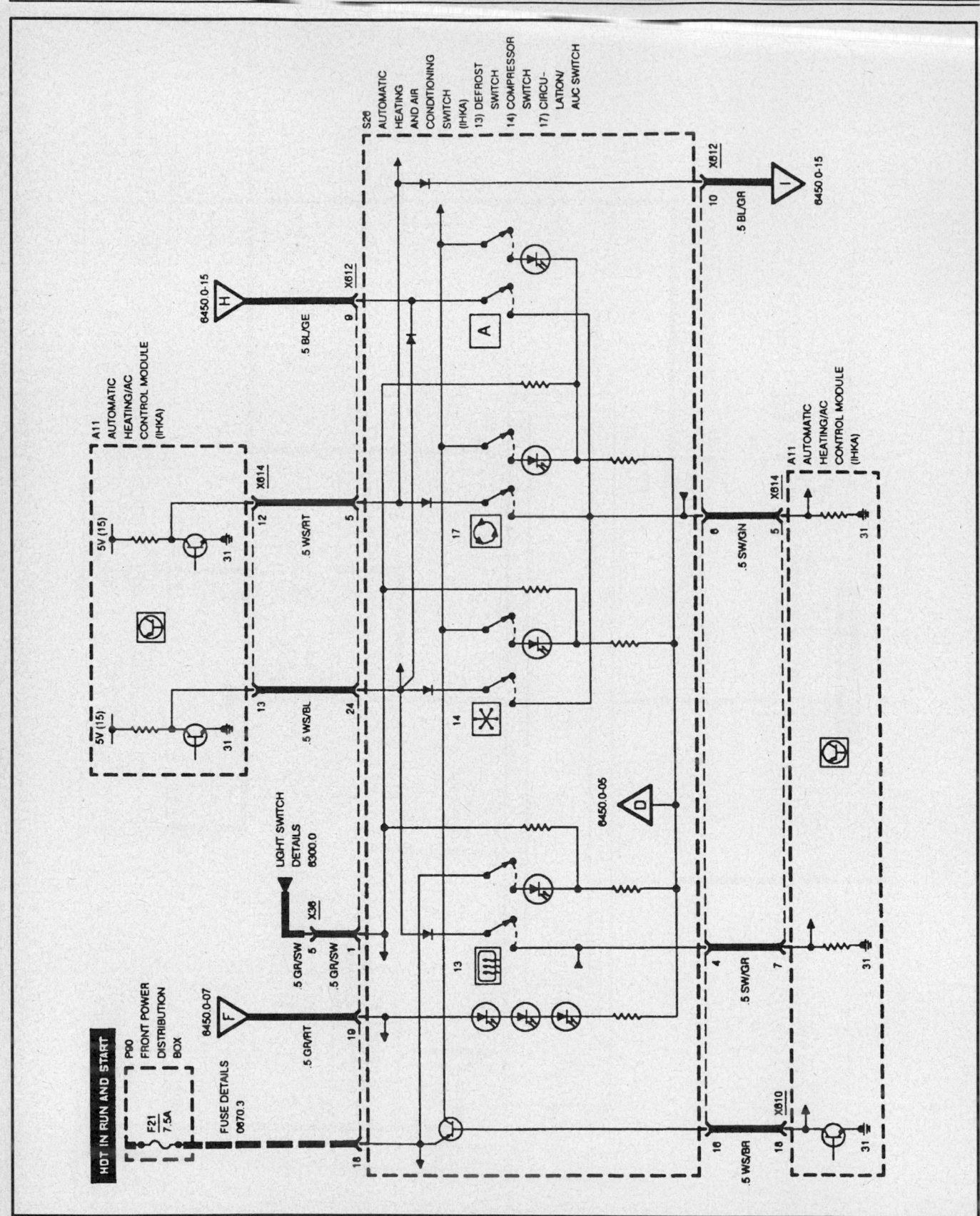

Automatic heating and A/C control module wiring diagram—1994 850 Ci and 850 CSi with IHKA

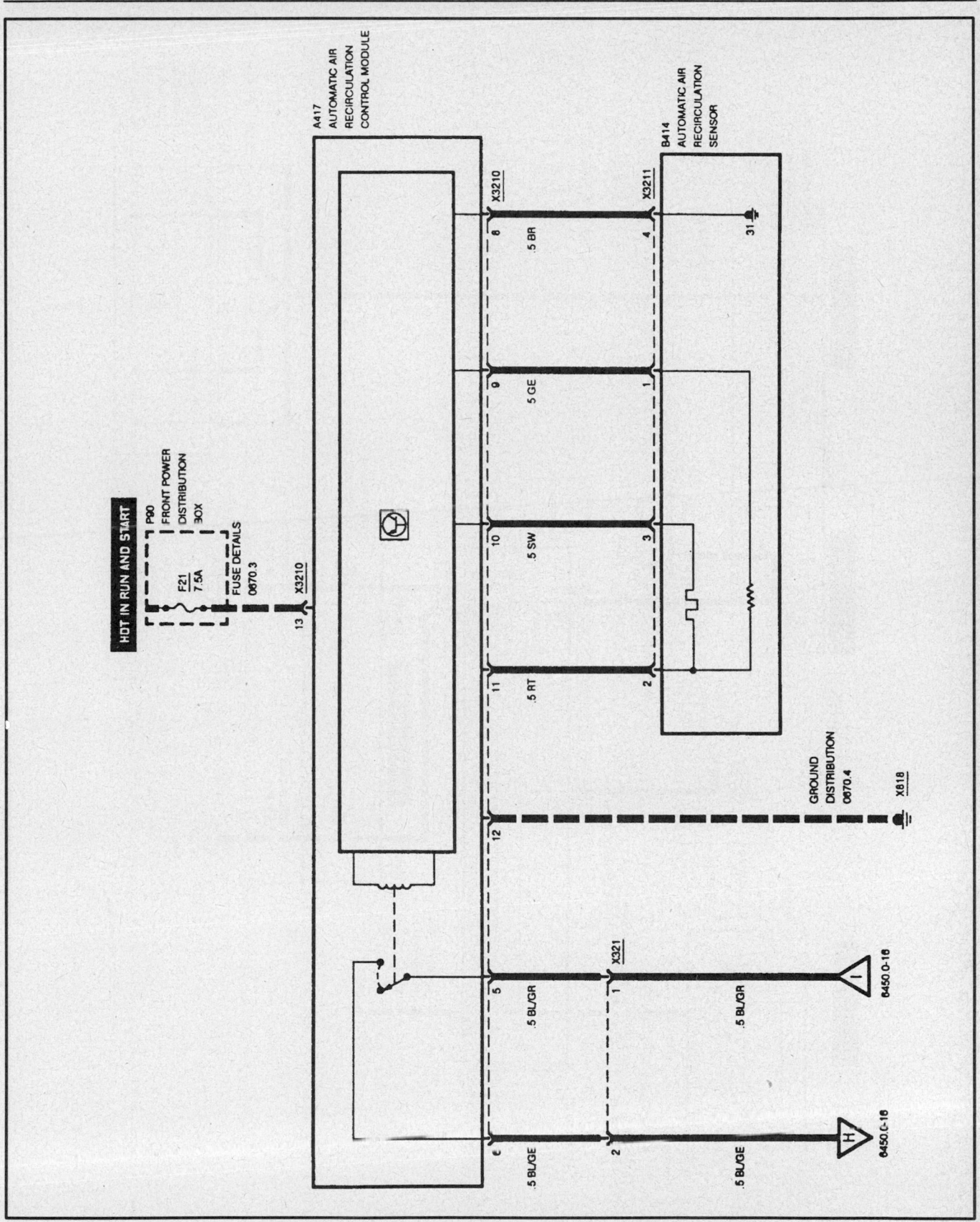

Automatic air recirculation control module wiring diagram—1994 850 Ci and 850 CSi with IHKA

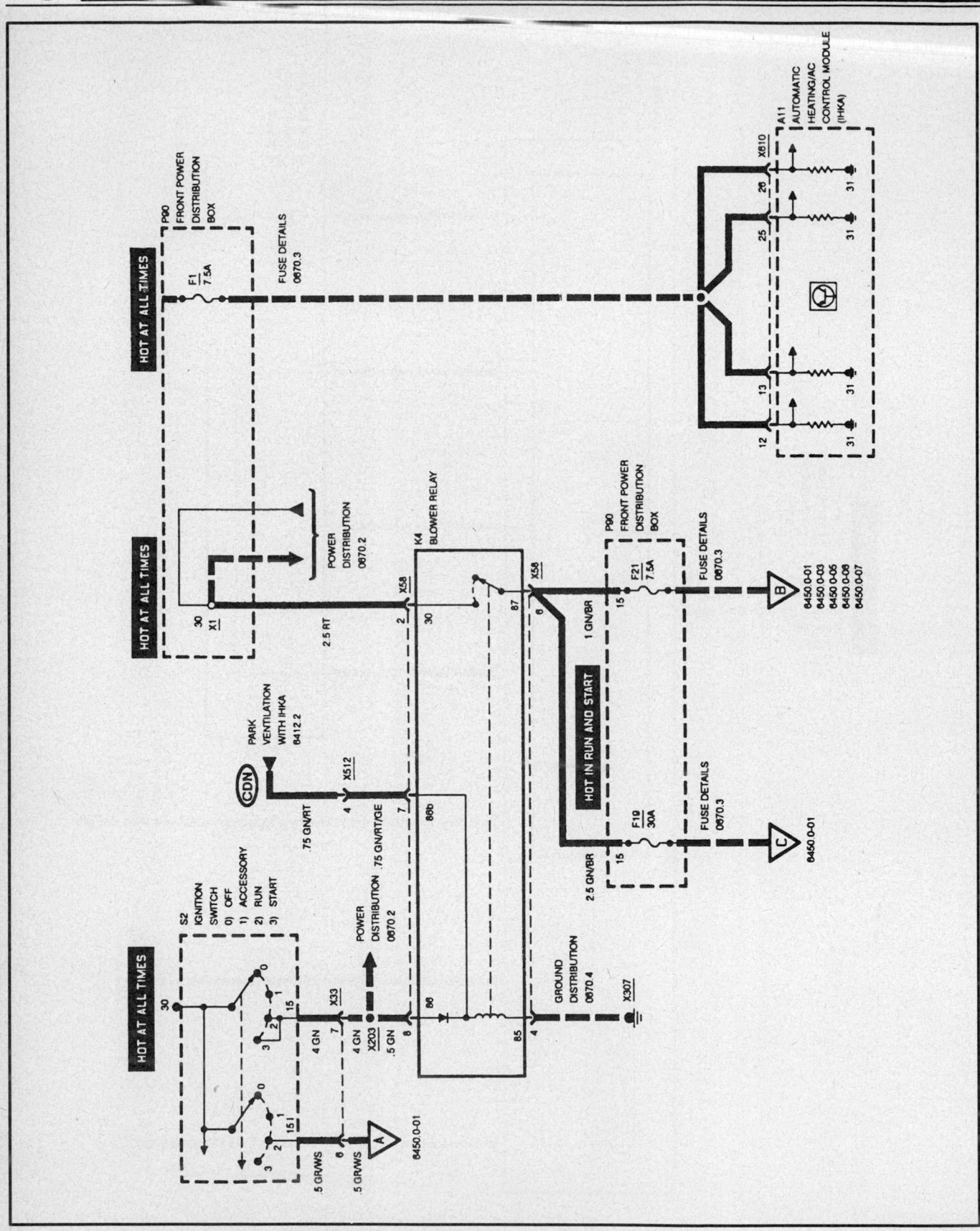

Power circuit wiring diagram—1994 850 Ci and 850 CSi with IHKA

WIRE COLORS	
BL	BLUE
BR	BROWN
GE	YELLOW
GN	GREEN
GR	GRAY
OR	ORANGE
RS	PINK
RT	RED
SW	BLACK
VI	VIOLET
WS	WHITE

Power circuit wiring diagram—1994 740i/L and 750i with IHKA

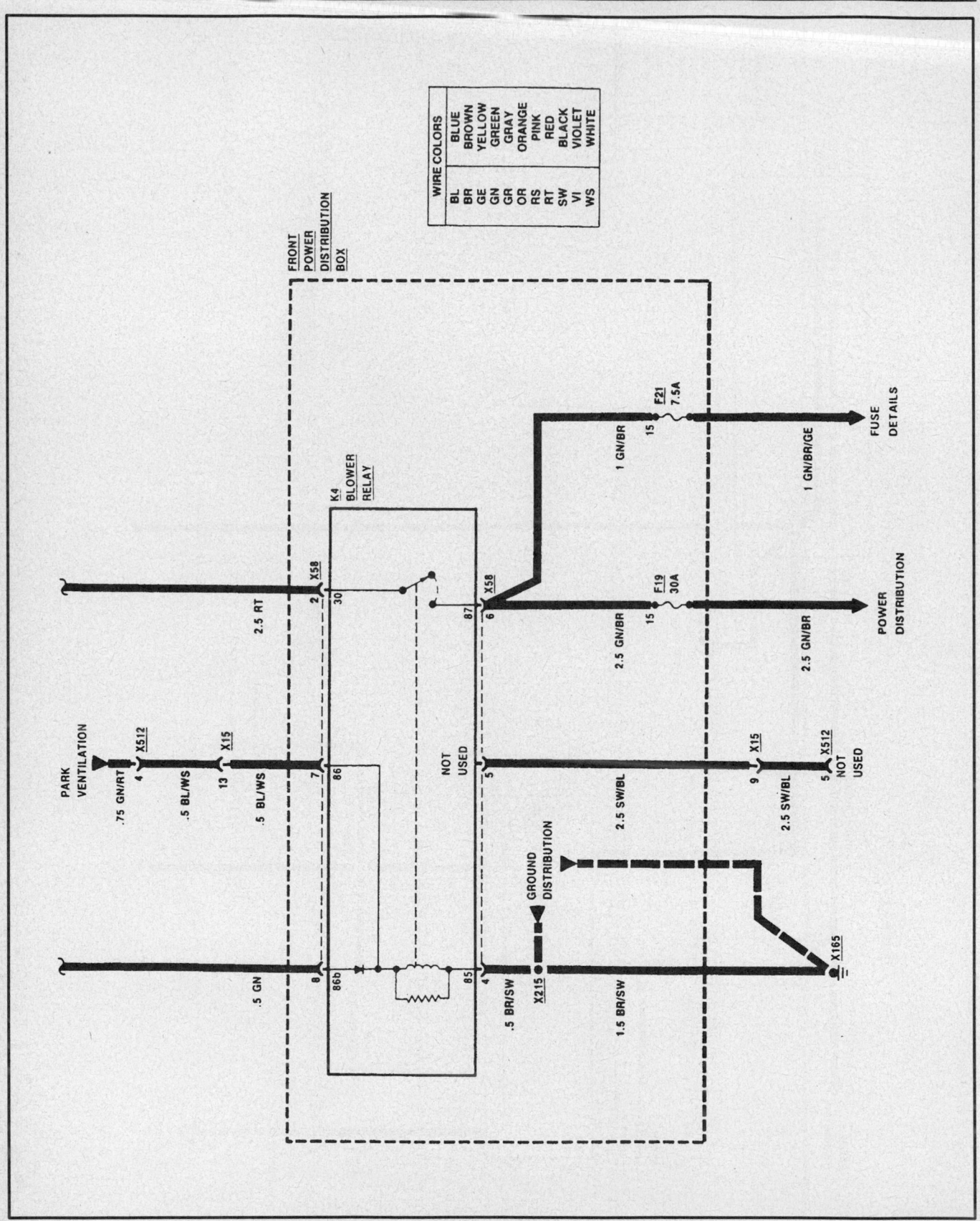

Power circuit wiring diagram—1994 740i/L and 750i with IHKA, cont'd

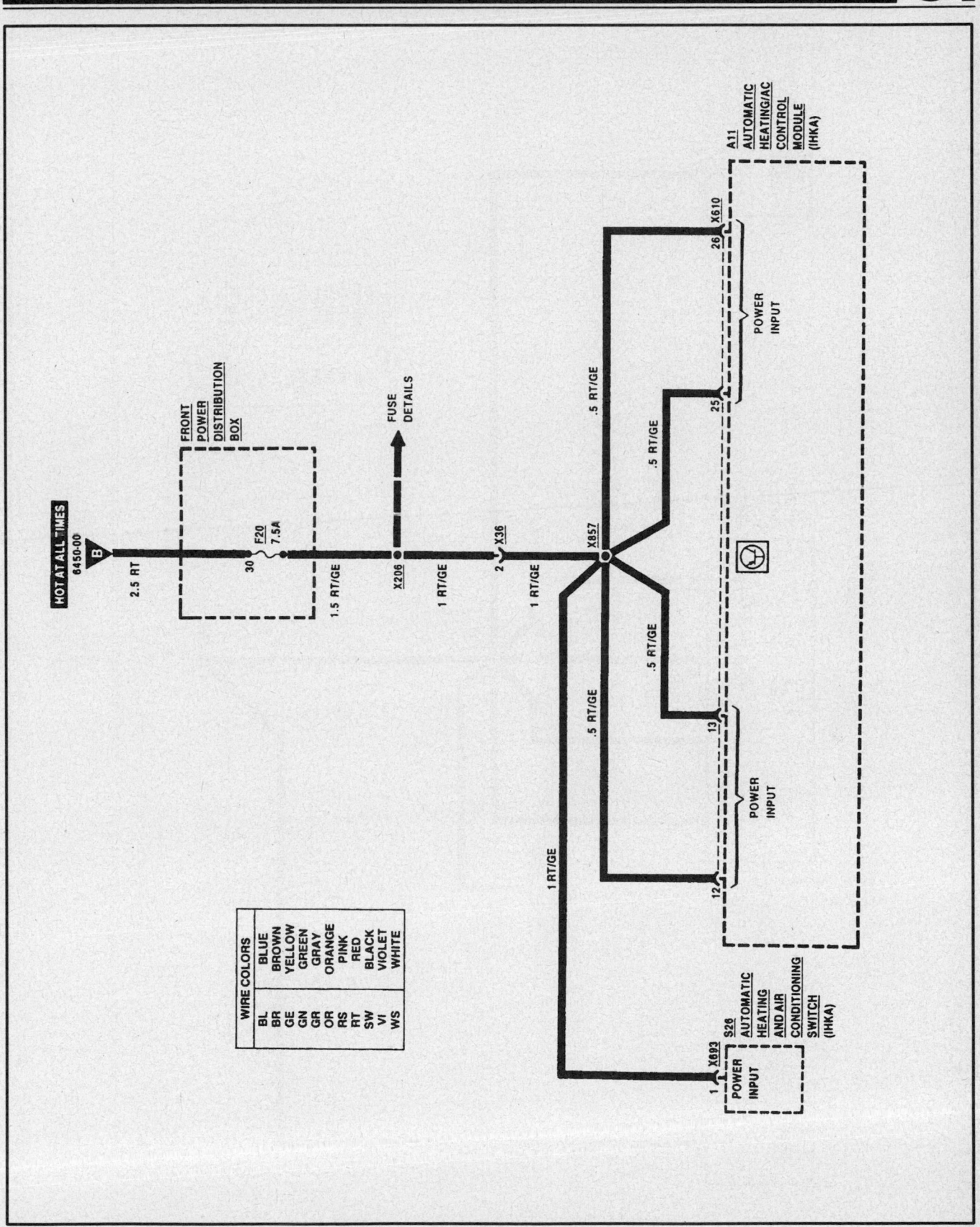

WIRE COLORS	
BL	BLUE
BR	BROWN
GE	YELLOW
GN	GREEN
GR	GRAY
OR	ORANGE
RS	PINK
RT	RED
SW	BLACK
VI	VIOLET
WS	WHITE

Power circuit wiring diagram—1994 740i/L and 750i with IHKA, cont'd

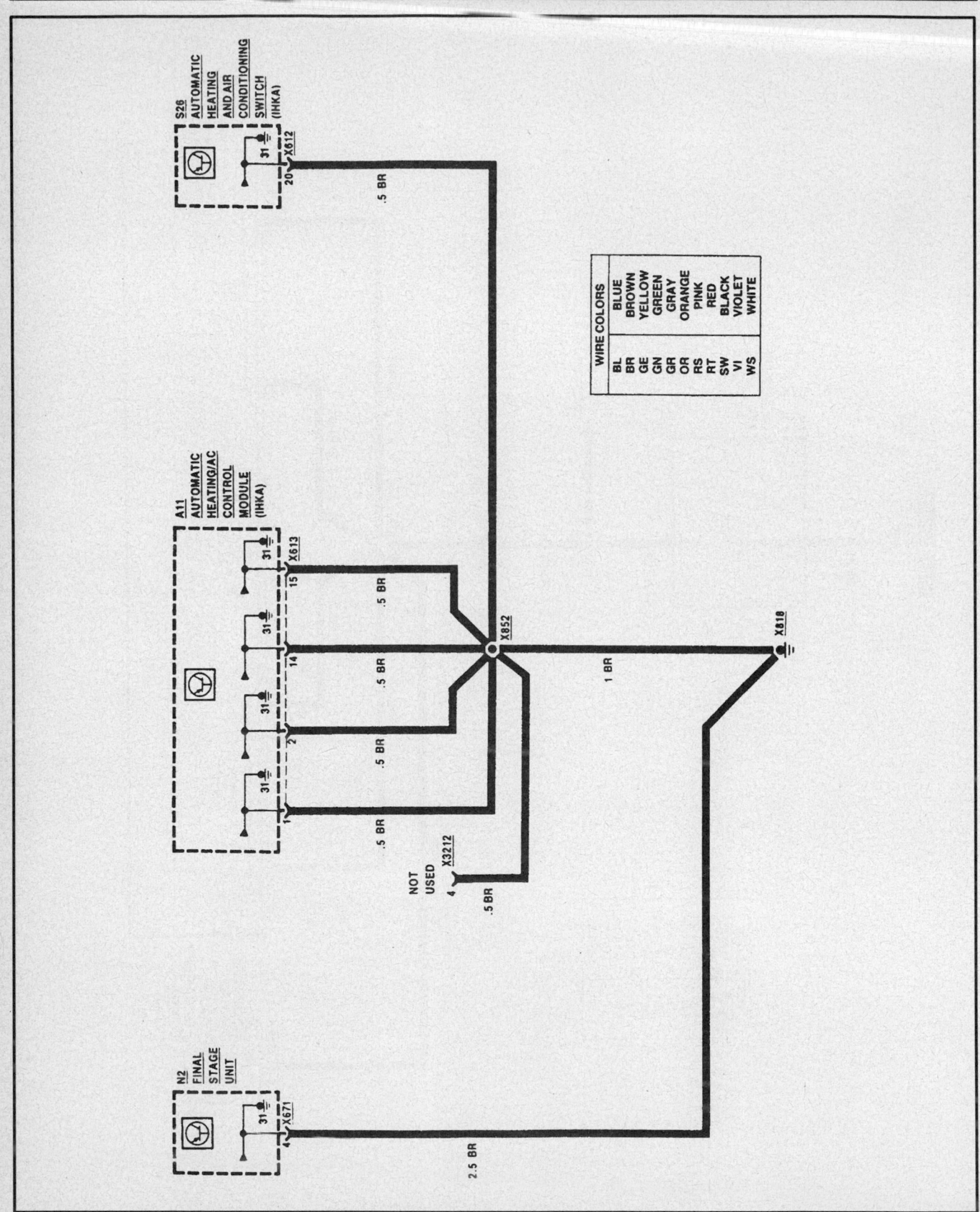

WIRE COLORS	
BL	BLUE
BR	BROWN
GE	YELLOW
GN	GREEN
GR	GRAY
OR	ORANGE
RS	PINK
RT	RED
SW	BLACK
VI	VIOLET
WS	WHITE

Ground circuit wiring diagram—1994 740i/L and 750i with IHKA

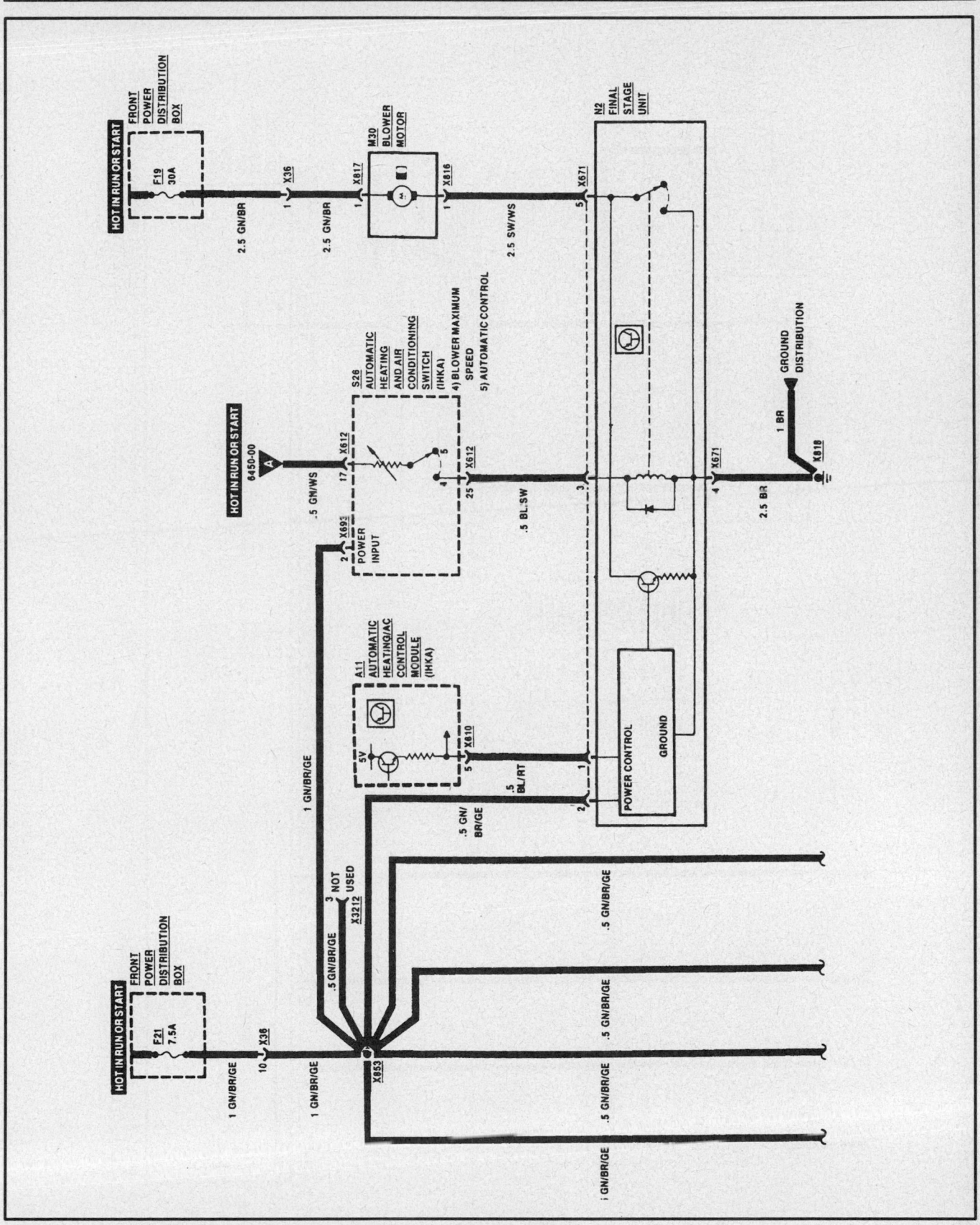

Blower control wiring diagram—1994 740i/L and 750i with IHKA

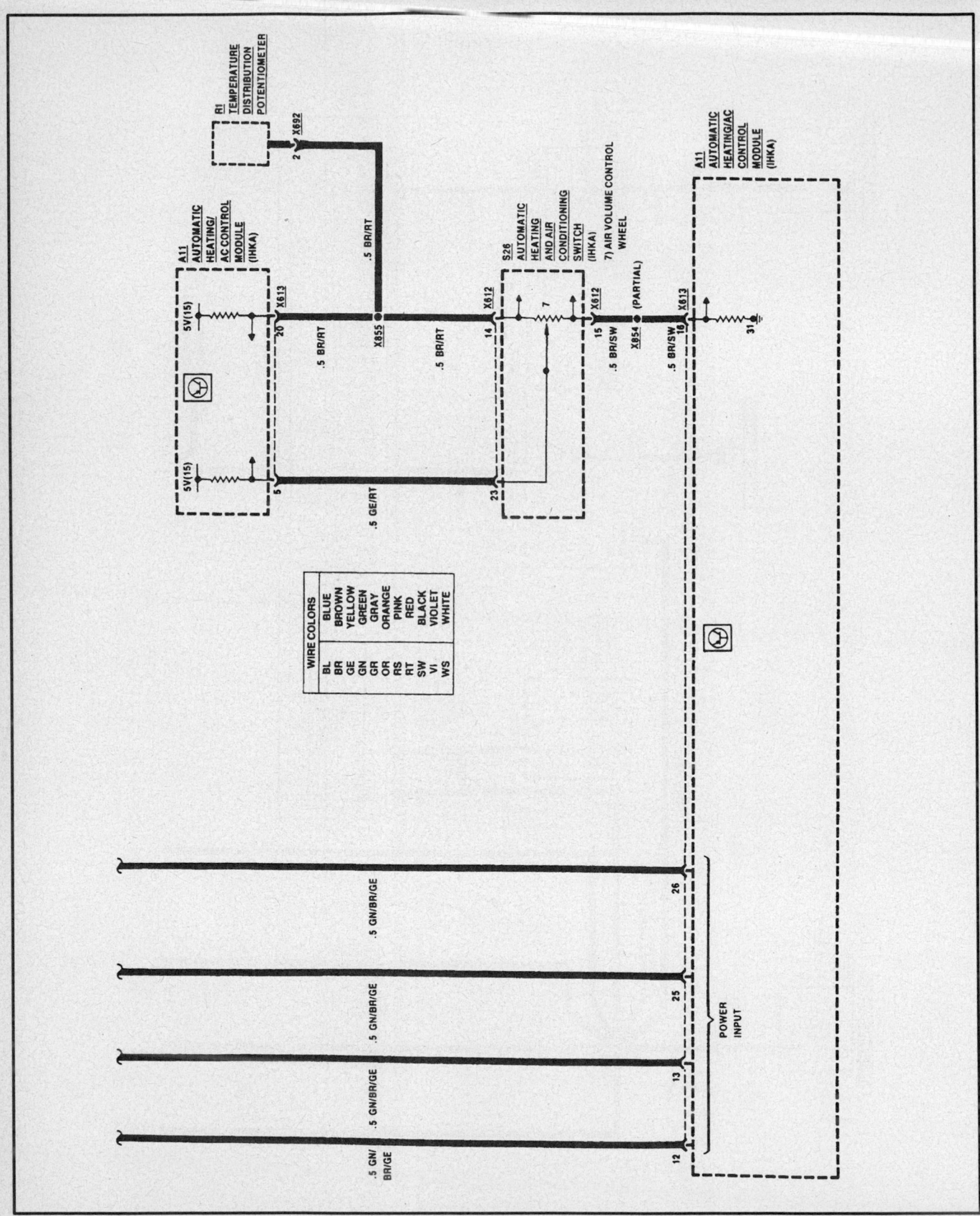

Blower control wiring diagram—1994 740i/L and 750i with IHKA, cont'd

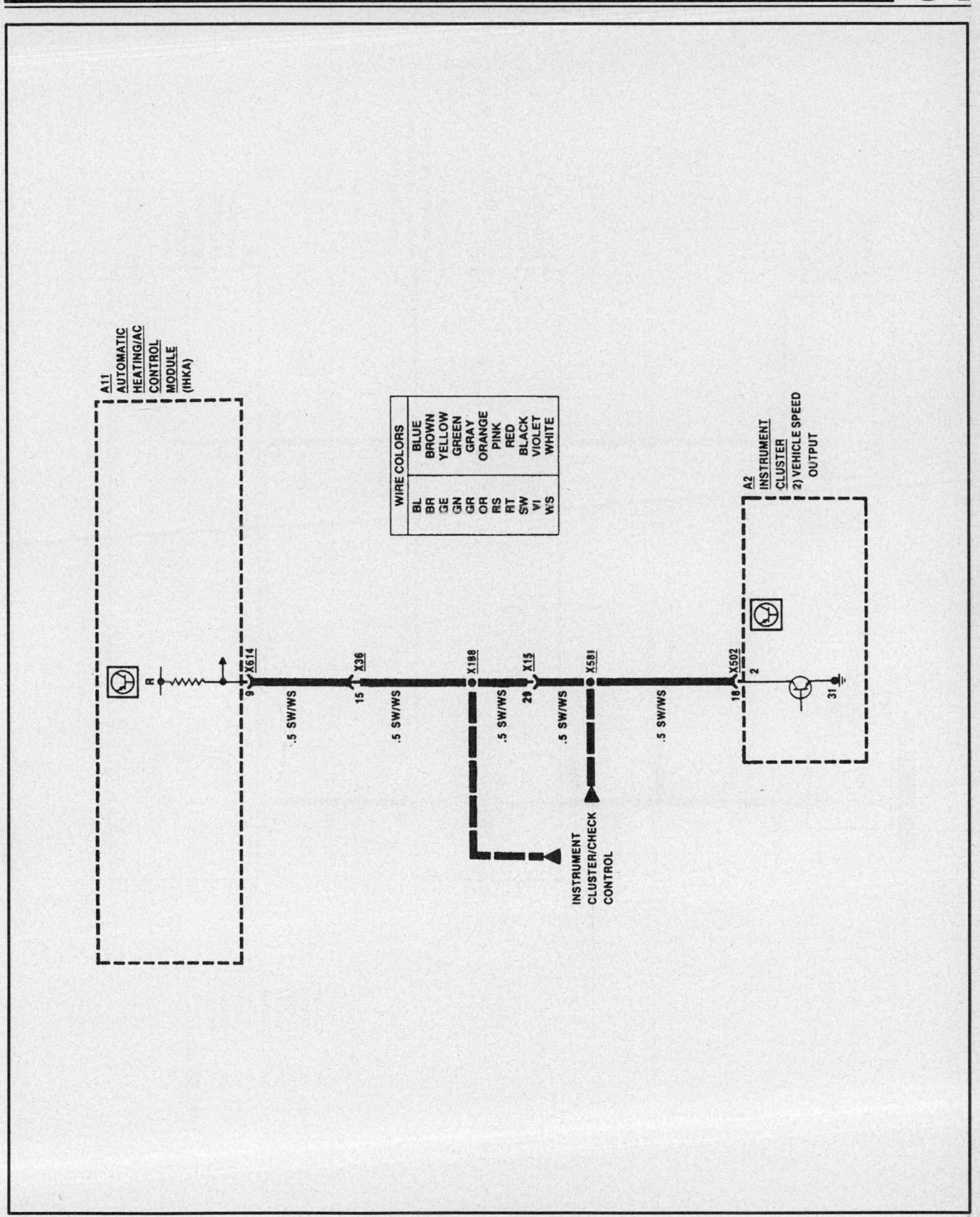

WIRE COLORS	
BL	BLUE
BR	BROWN
GE	YELLOW
GN	GREEN
GR	GRAY
OR	ORANGE
RS	PINK
RT	RED
SW	BLACK
VI	VIOLET
WS	WHITE

A11
AUTOMATIC
HEATING/AC
CONTROL
MODULE
(IHKA)

A2
INSTRUMENT
CLUSTER
2) VEHICLE SPEED
OUTPUT

INSTRUMENT
CLUSTER/CHECK
CONTROL

Blower control module wiring diagram—1994 740i/L and 750i with IHKA

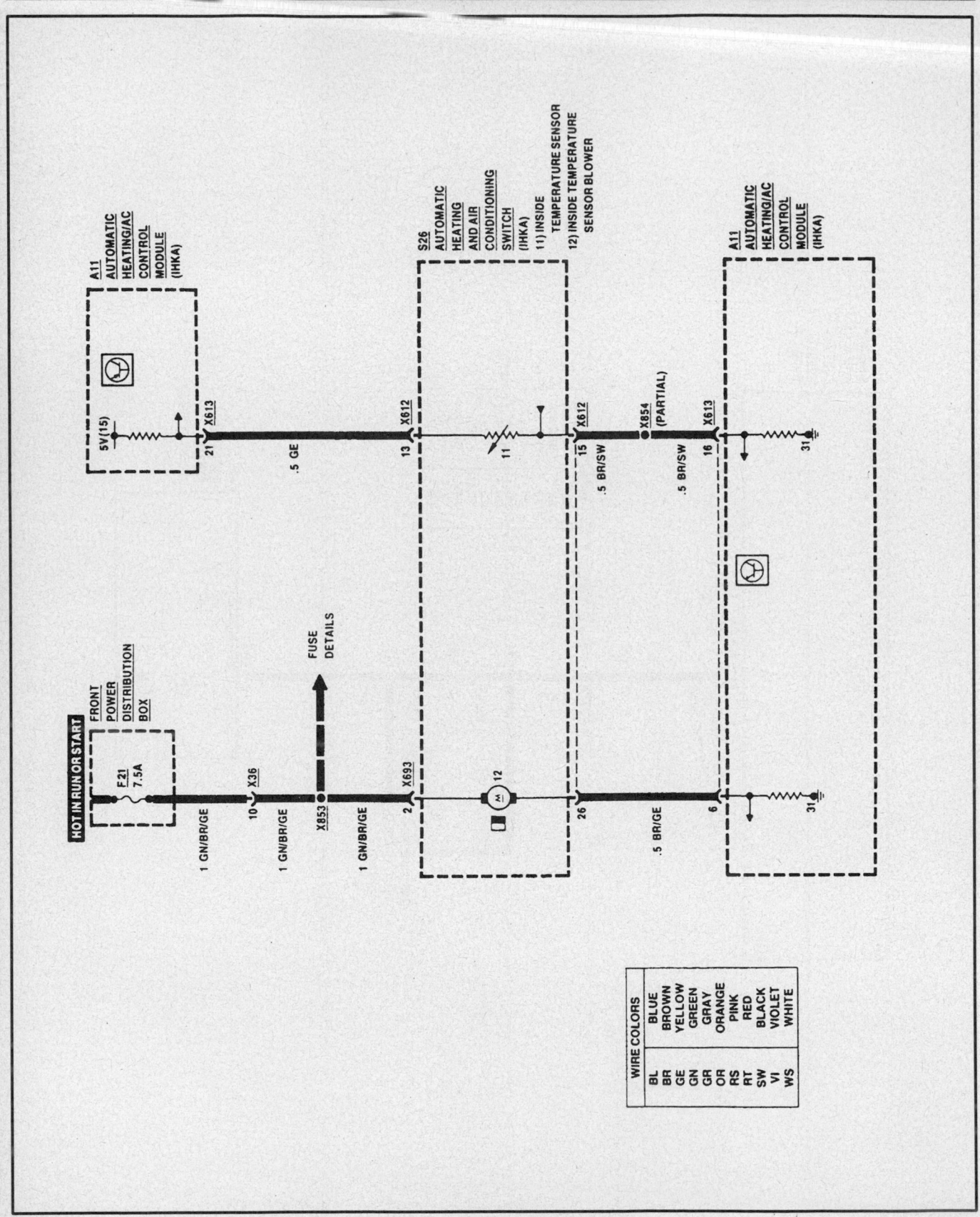

Temperature controls wiring diagram—1994 740i/L and 750i with IHKA

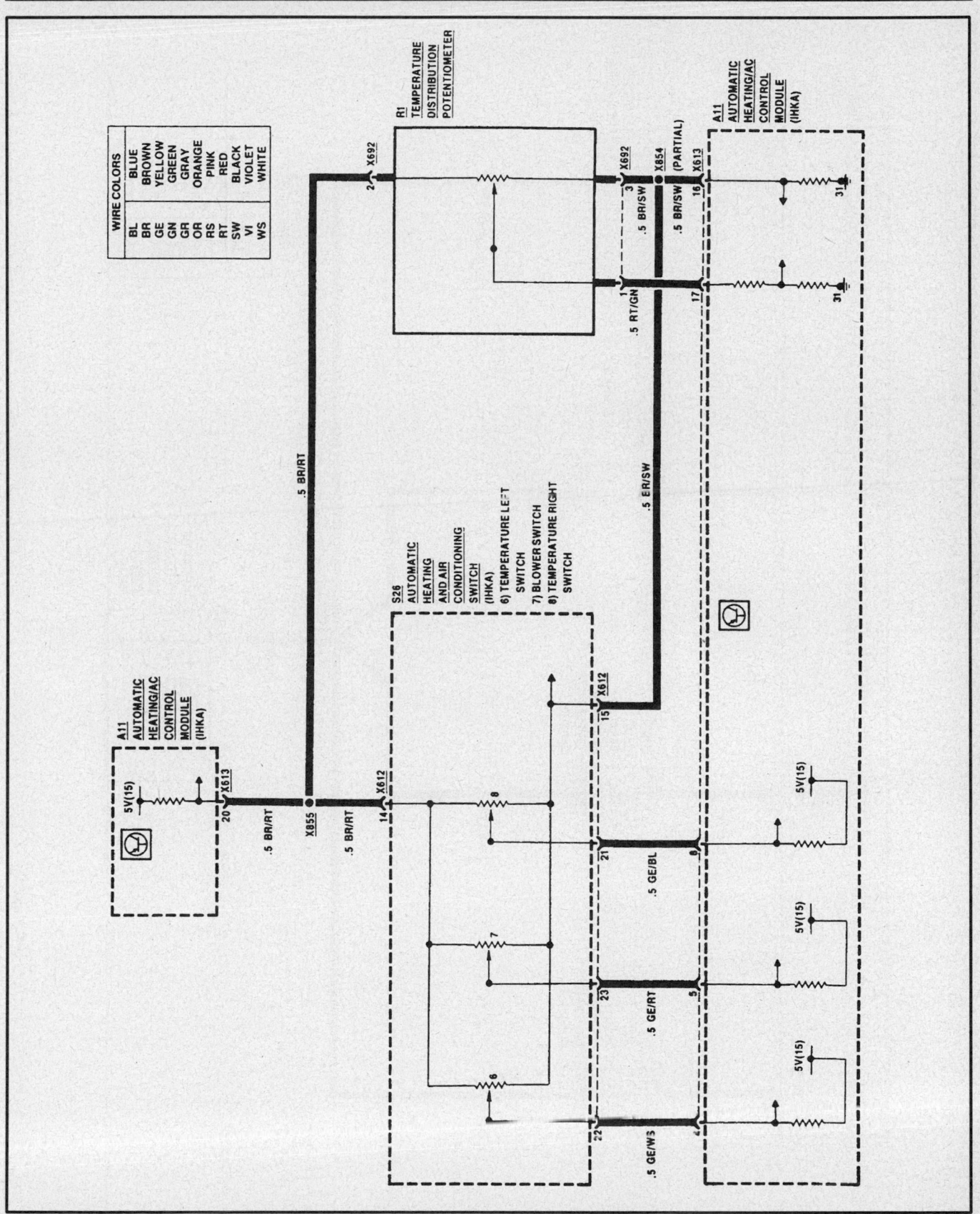

Temperature controls wiring diagram—1994 740i/L and 750i with IHKA, cont'd

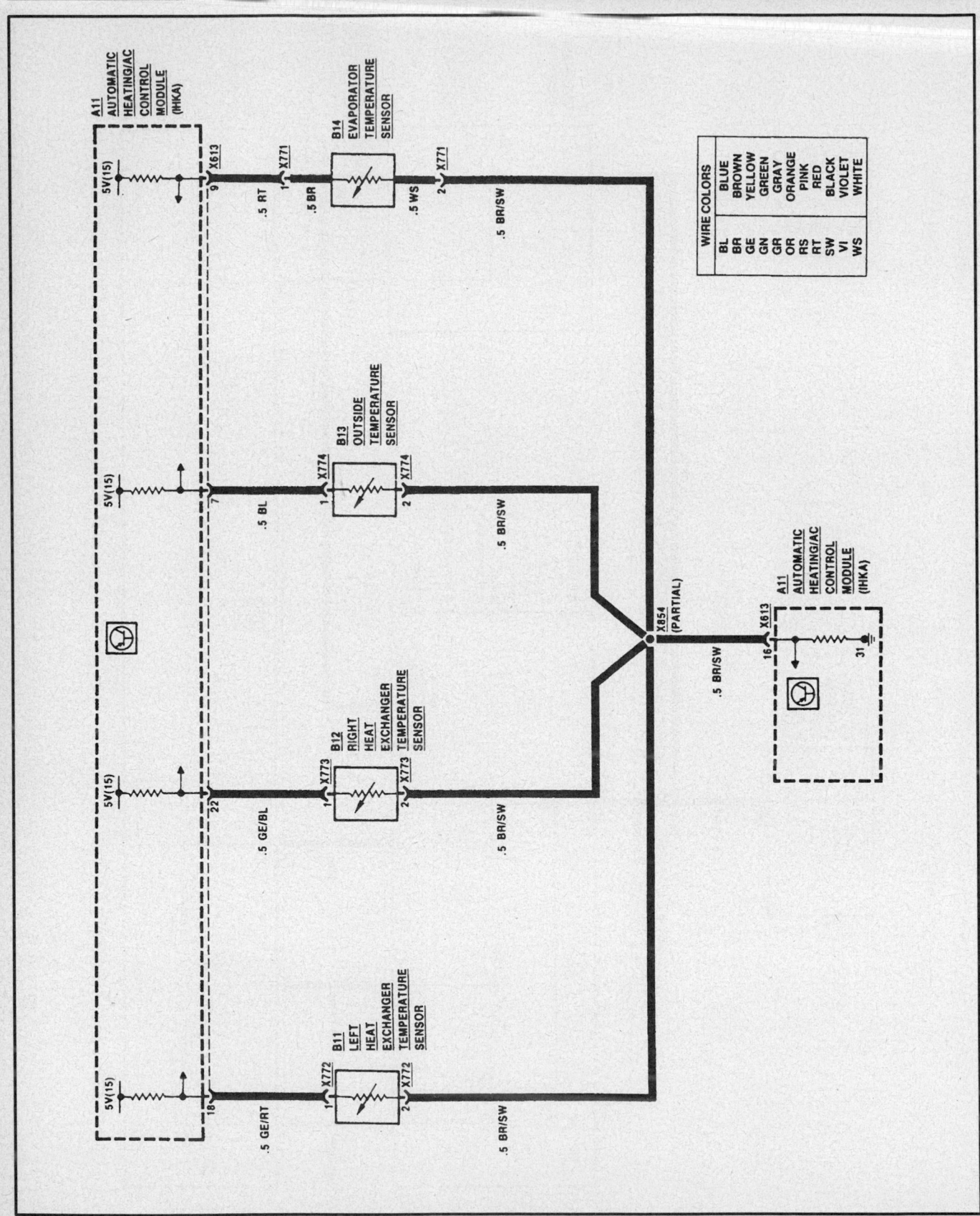

WIRE COLORS	
BL	BLUE
BR	BROWN
GE	YELLOW
GN	GREEN
GR	GRAY
OR	ORANGE
RS	PINK
RT	RED
SW	BLACK
VI	VIOLET
WS	WHITE

Temperature controls wiring diagram—1994 740i/L and 750i with IHKA, cont'd

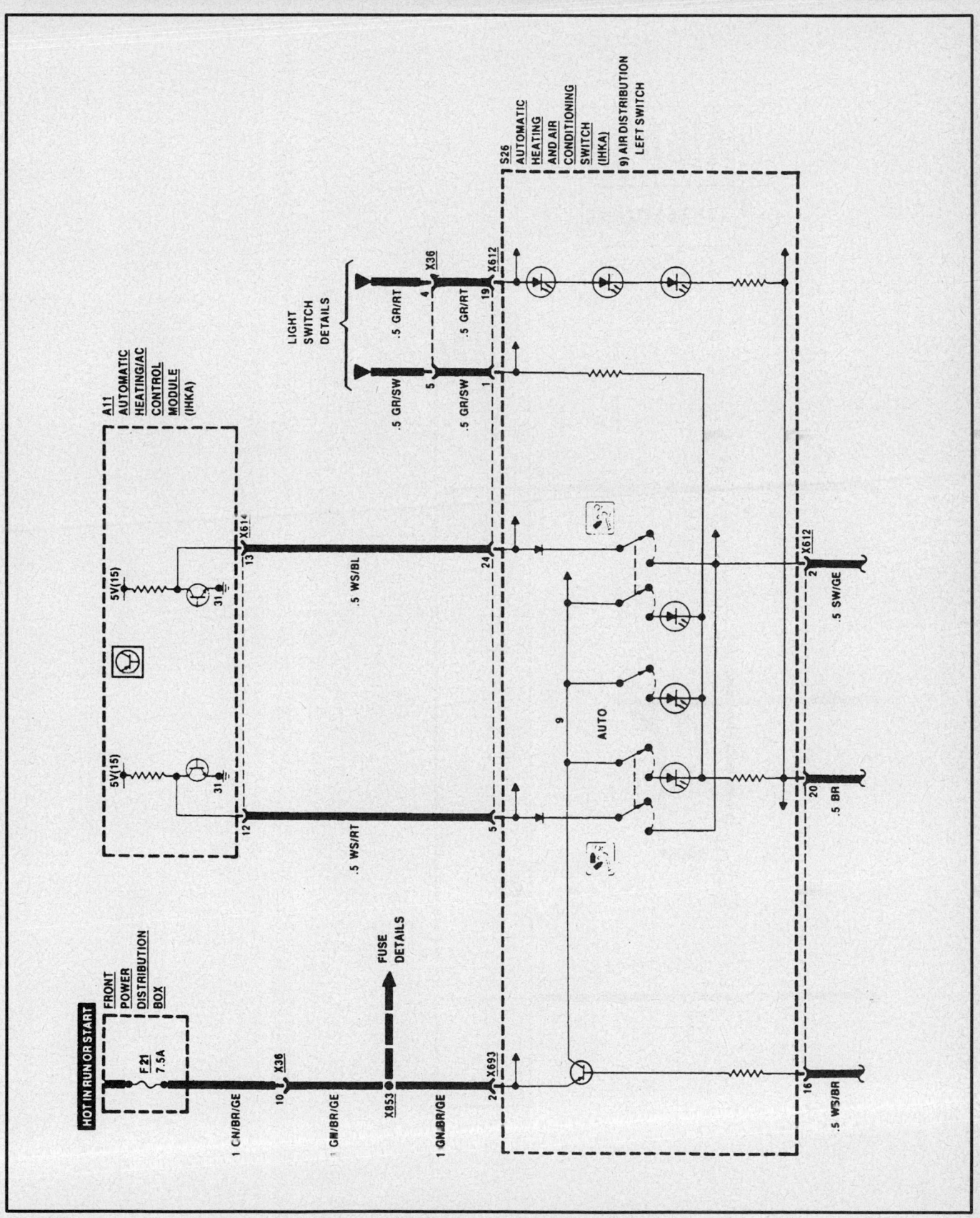

Air delivery wiring diagram, left switch—1994 740i/L and 750i with IHKA

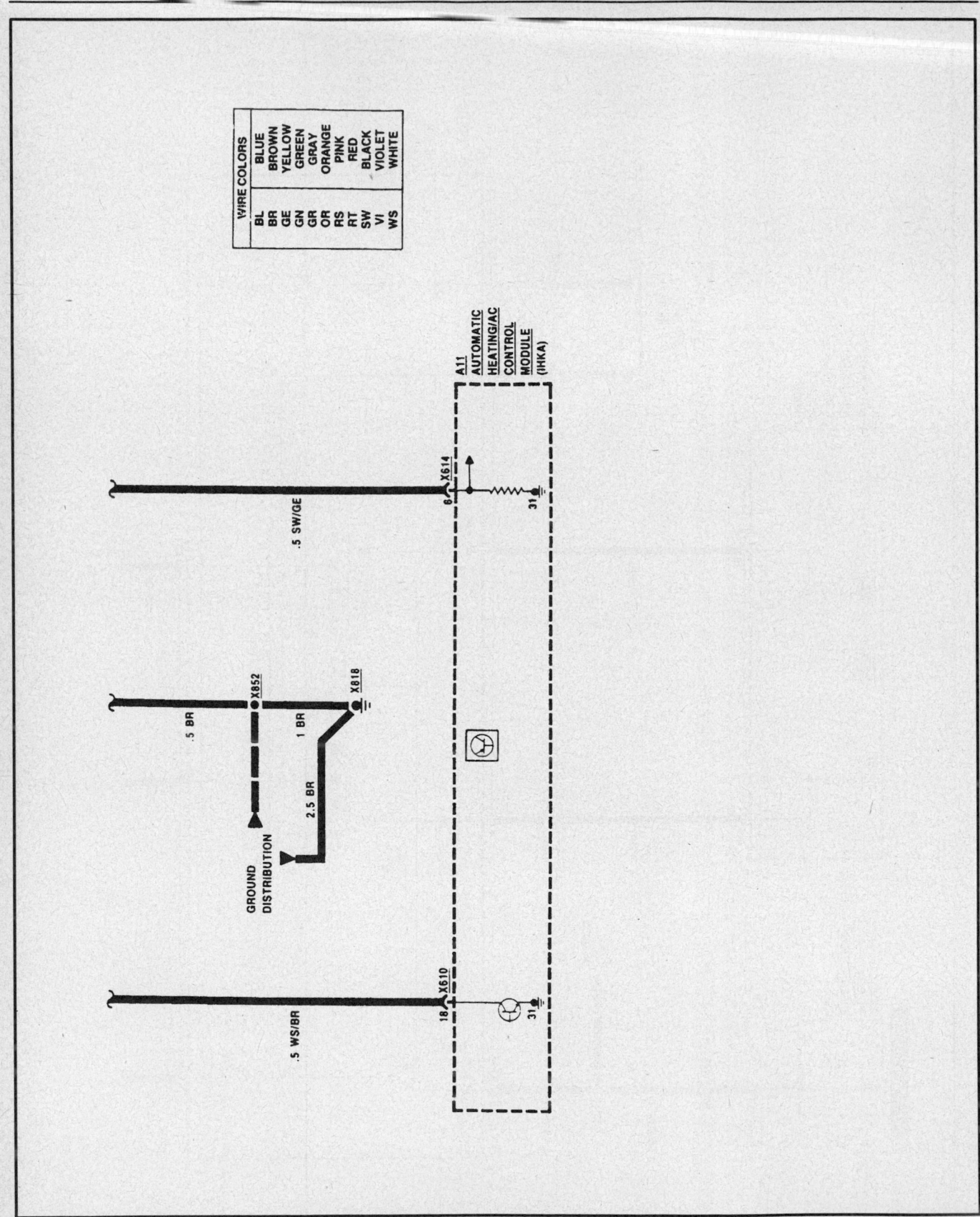

WIRE COLORS		
BL	BLUE	
BR	BROWN	
GE	YELLOW	
GN	GREEN	
GR	GRAY	
OR	ORANGE	
RS	PINK	
RT	RED	
SW	BLACK	
VI	VIOLET	
WS	WHITE	

A11
AUTOMATIC
HEATING/AC
CONTROL
MODULE
(IHKA)

.5 SW/GE

X614
6
31

.5 BR   X852   1 BR   X818

2.5 BR

GROUND
DISTRIBUTION

.5 WS/BR   X610
18
31

Air delivery wiring diagram, left switch—1994 740i/L and 750i with IHKA, cont'd

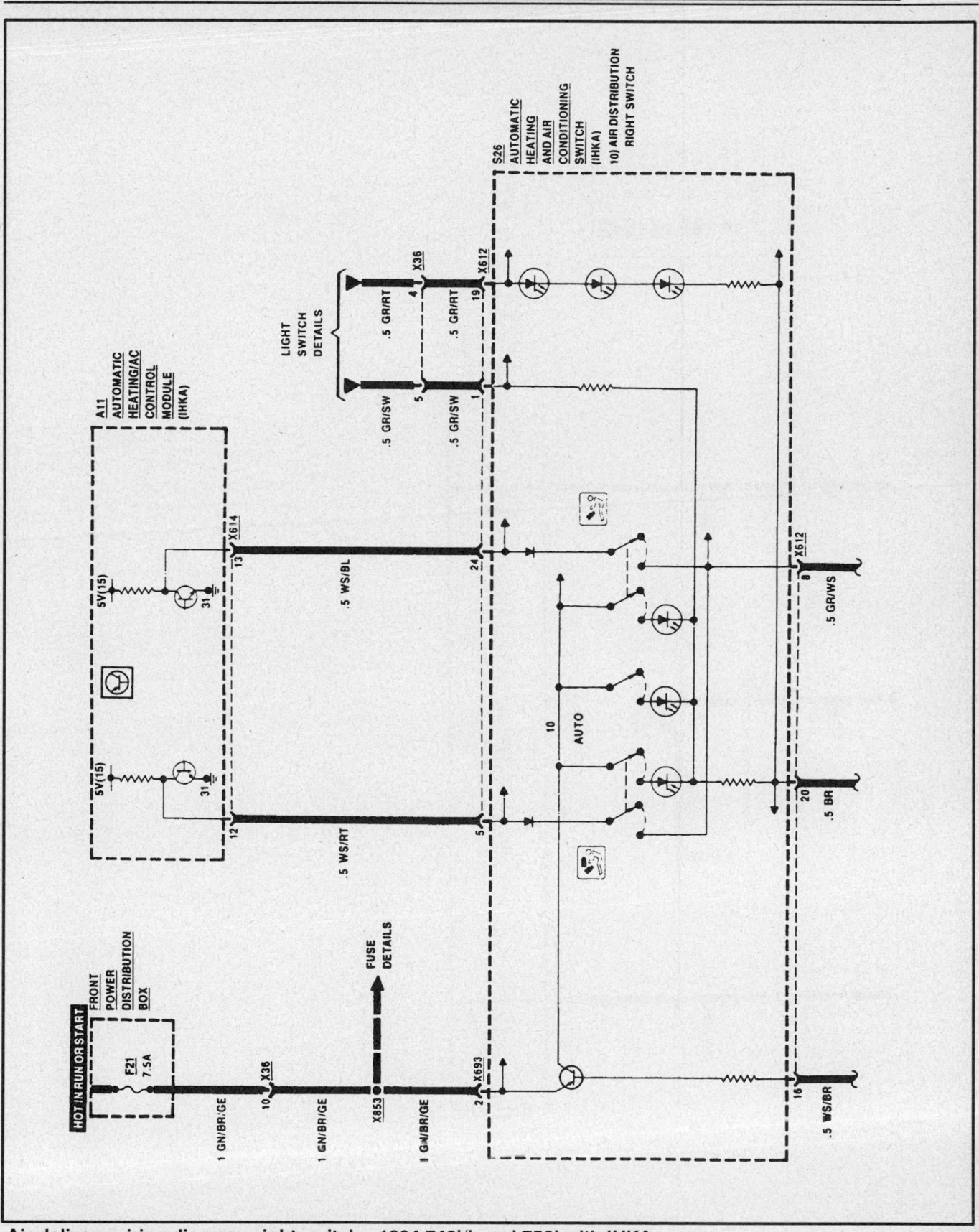

Air delivery wiring diagram, right switch—1994 740i/L and 750i with IHKA

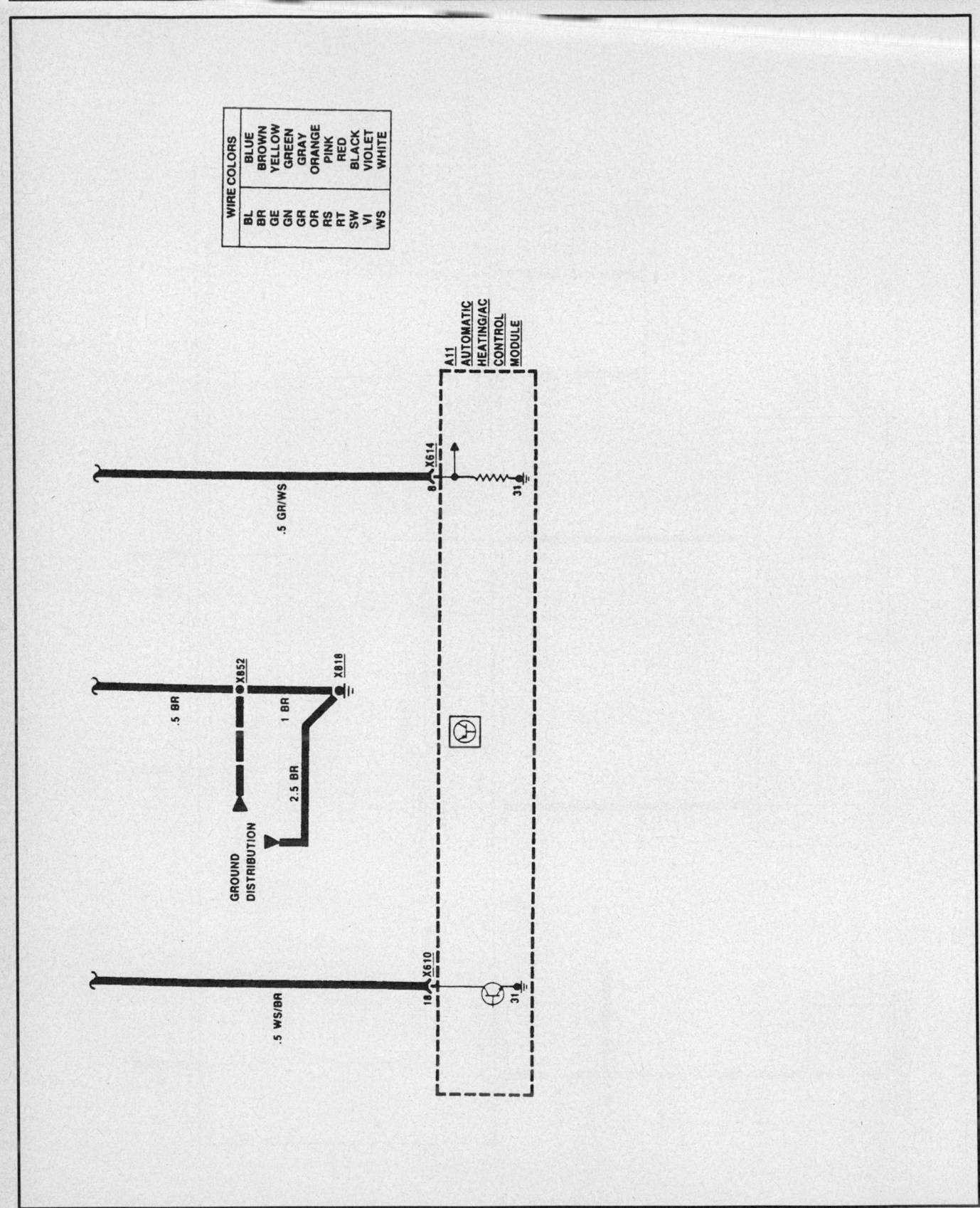

WIRE COLORS	
BL	BLUE
BR	BROWN
GE	YELLOW
GN	GREEN
GR	GRAY
OR	ORANGE
RS	PINK
RT	RED
SW	BLACK
VI	VIOLET
WS	WHITE

A11 AUTOMATIC HEATING/AC CONTROL MODULE

X614
.5 GR/WS

X652
.5 BR
1 BR
X818
2.5 BR
GROUND DISTRIBUTION

X610
.5 WS/BR

Air delivery wiring diagram, right switch—1994 740i/L and 750i with IHKA, cont'd

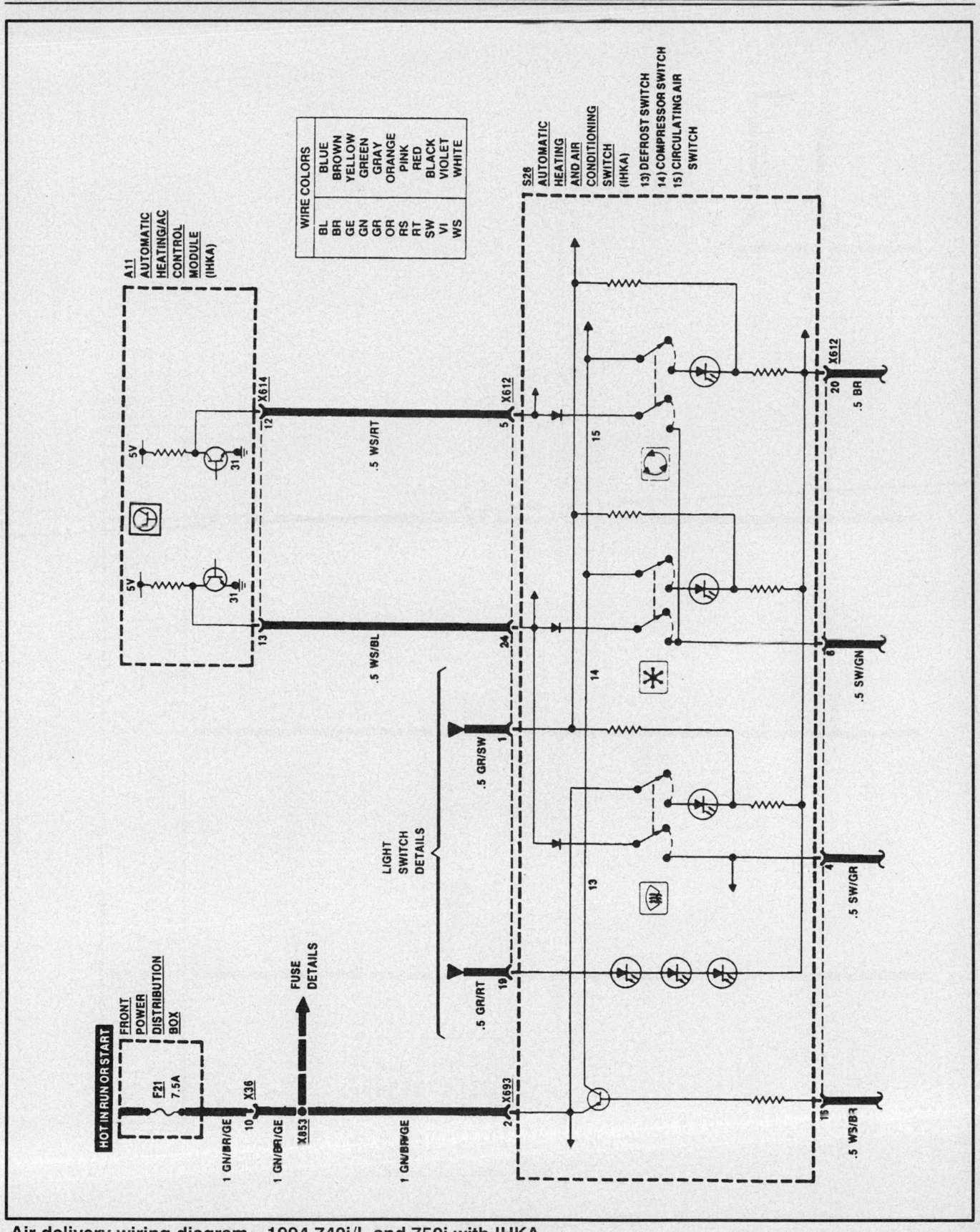

WIRE COLORS	
BL	BLUE
BR	BROWN
GE	YELLOW
GN	GREEN
GR	GRAY
OR	ORANGE
RS	PINK
RT	RED
SW	BLACK
VI	VIOLET
WS	WHITE

Air delivery wiring diagram—1994 740i/L and 750i with IHKA

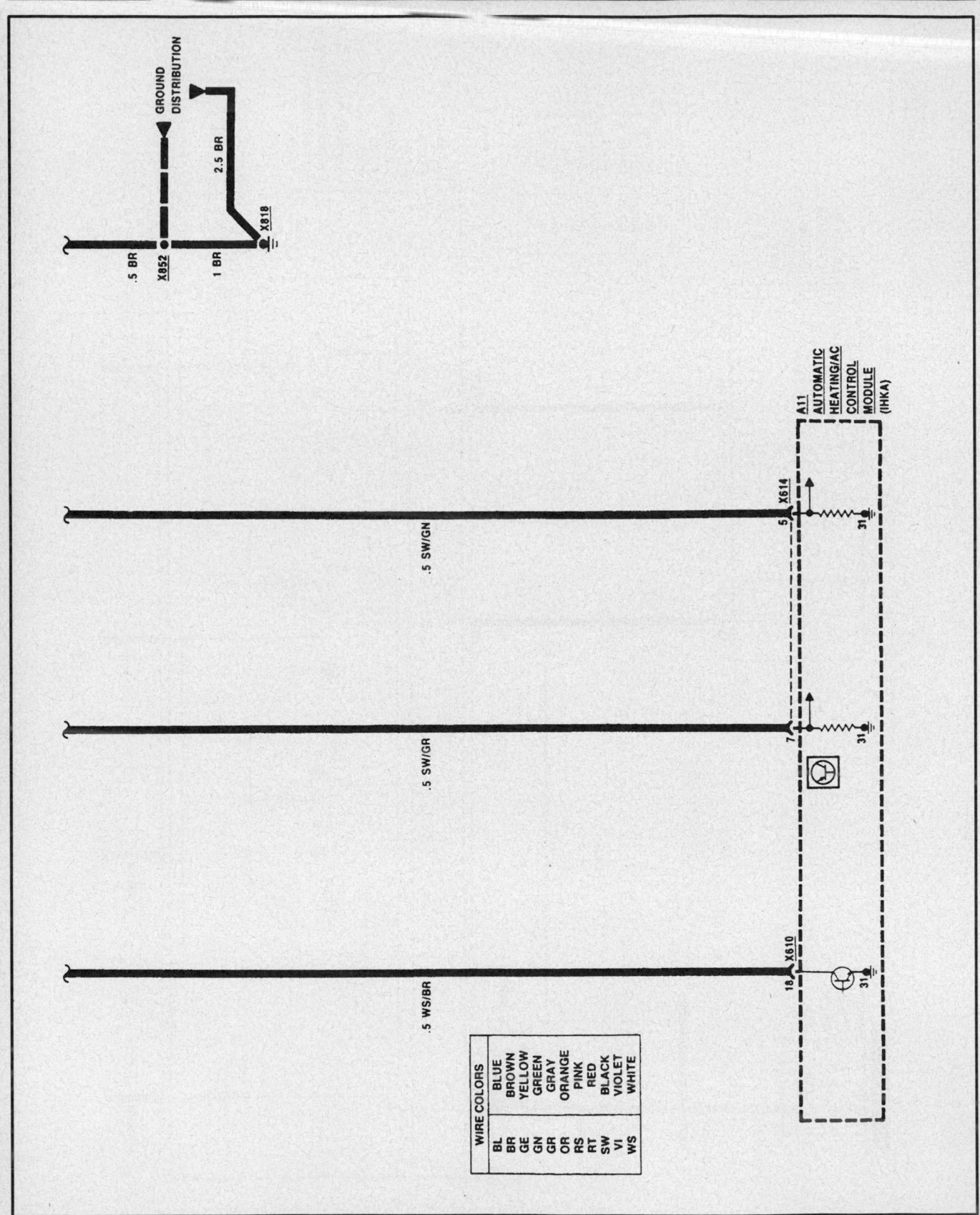

Air delivery wiring diagram—1994 740i/L and 750i with IHKA, cont'd

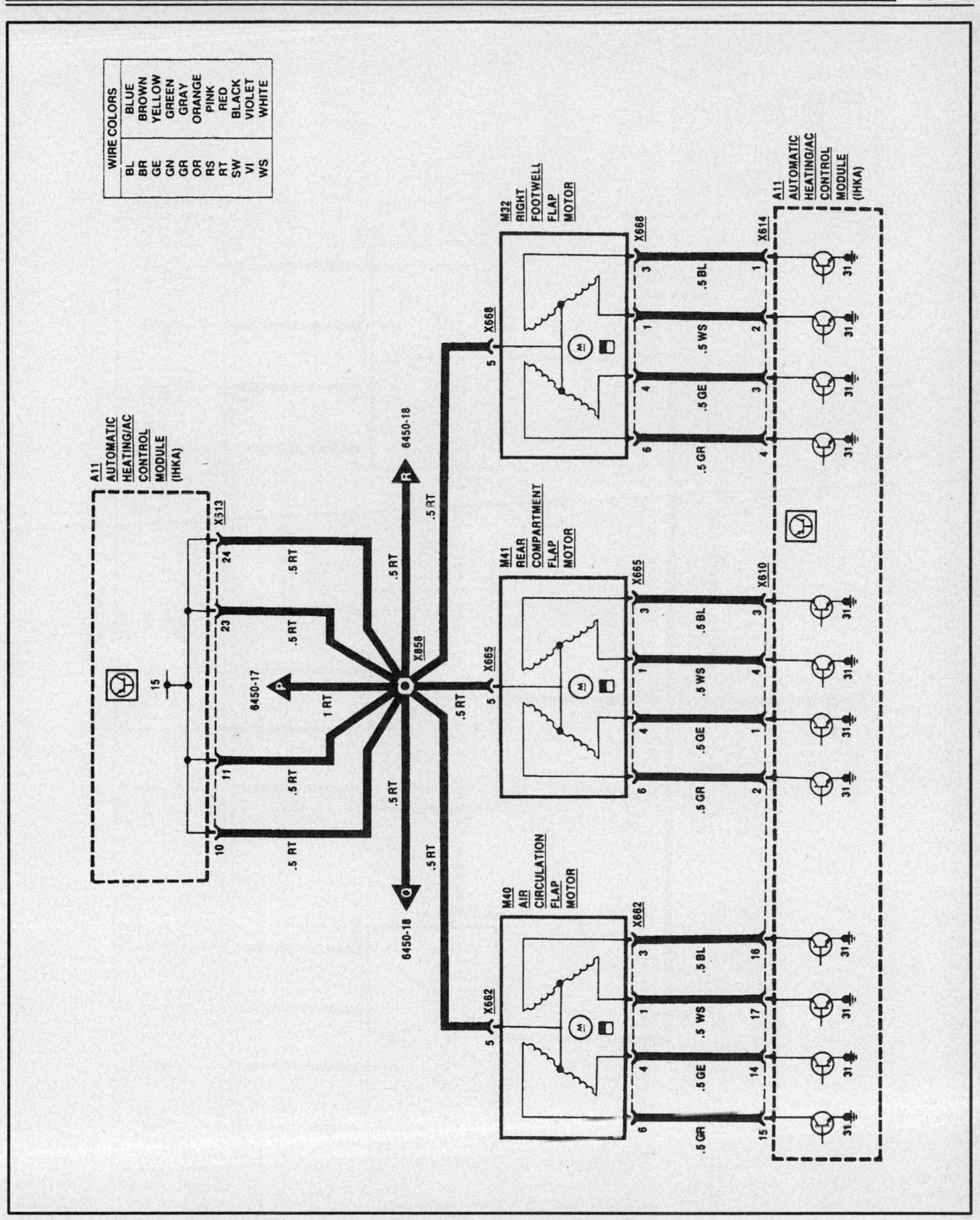

Air delivery wiring diagram, flap motors—1994 740i/L and 750i with IHKA

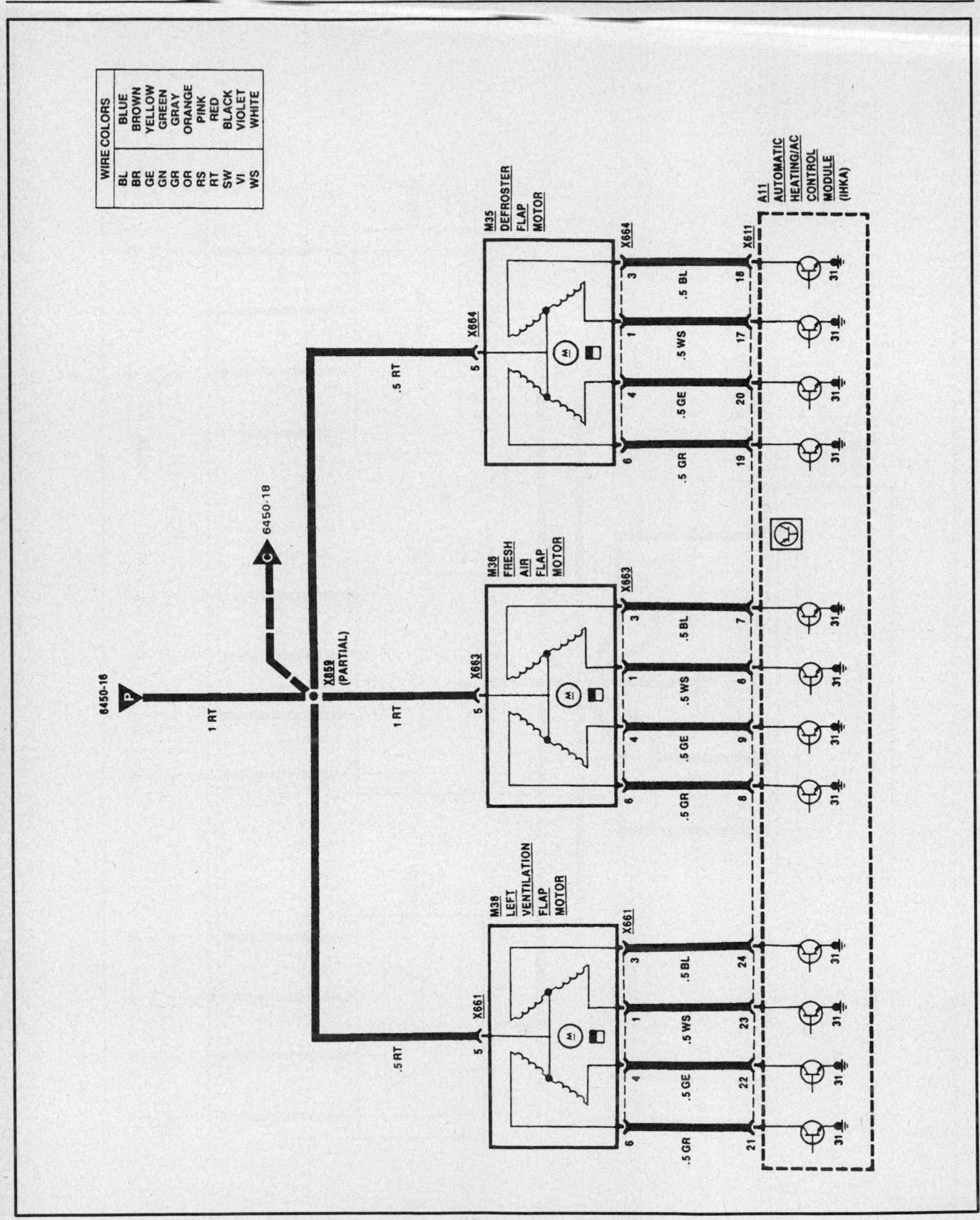

Air delivery wiring diagram, flap motors—1994 740i/L and 750i with IHKA, cont'd

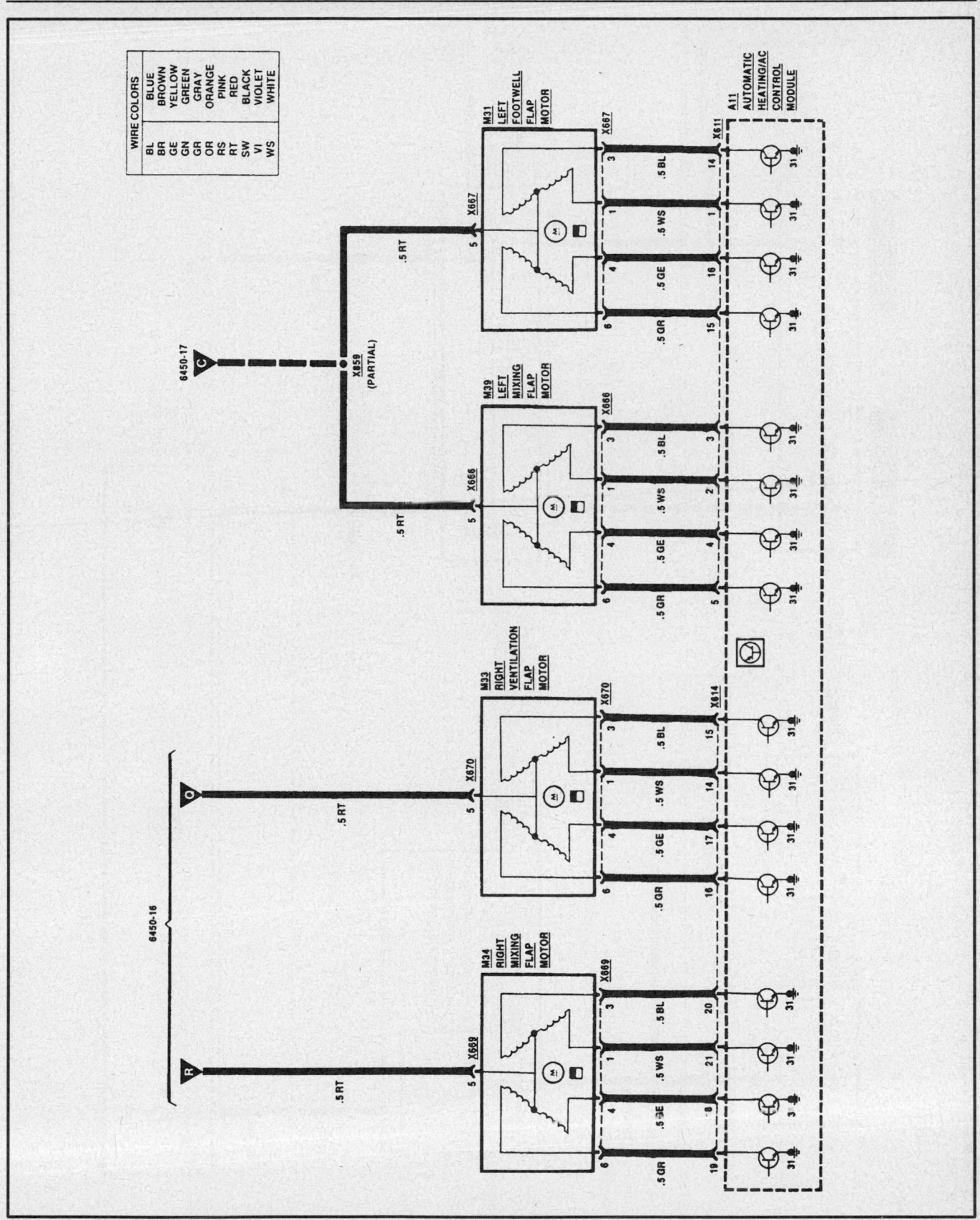

Air delivery wiring diagram, flap motors—1994 740i/L and 750i with IHKA, cont'd

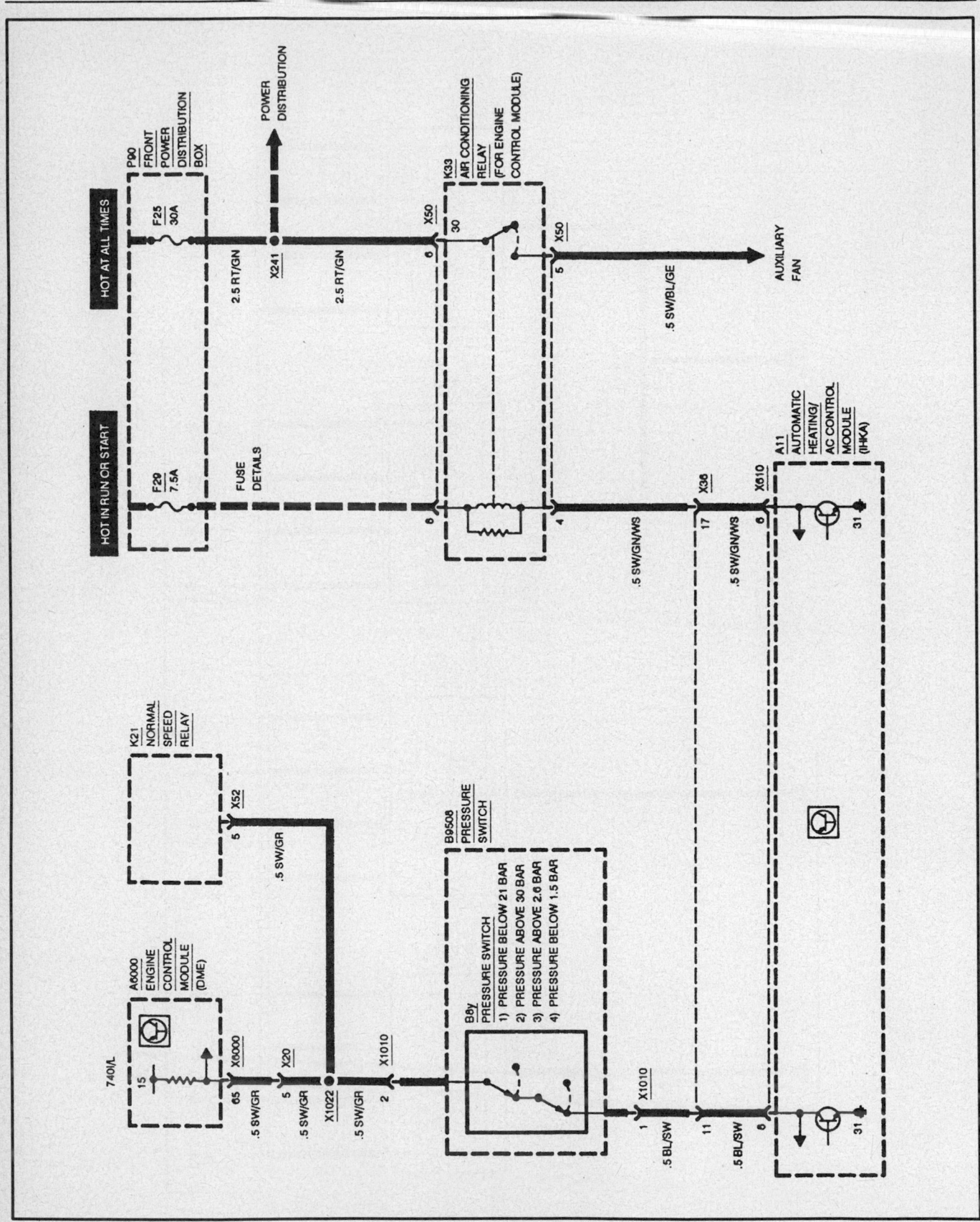

Compressor controls wiring diagram—1994 740i/L and 750i with IHKA

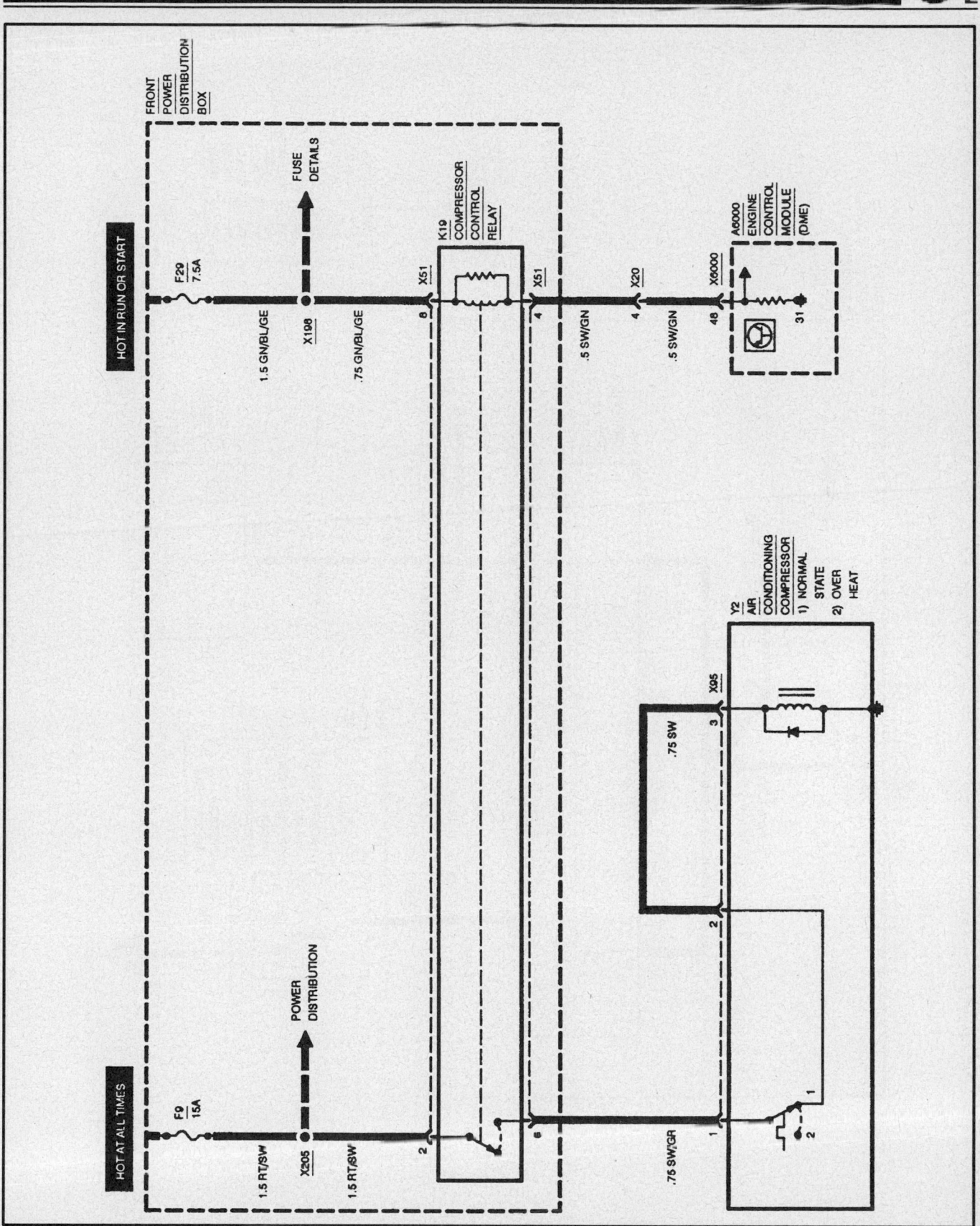

Compressor controls wiring diagram—1994 740i/L with IHKA

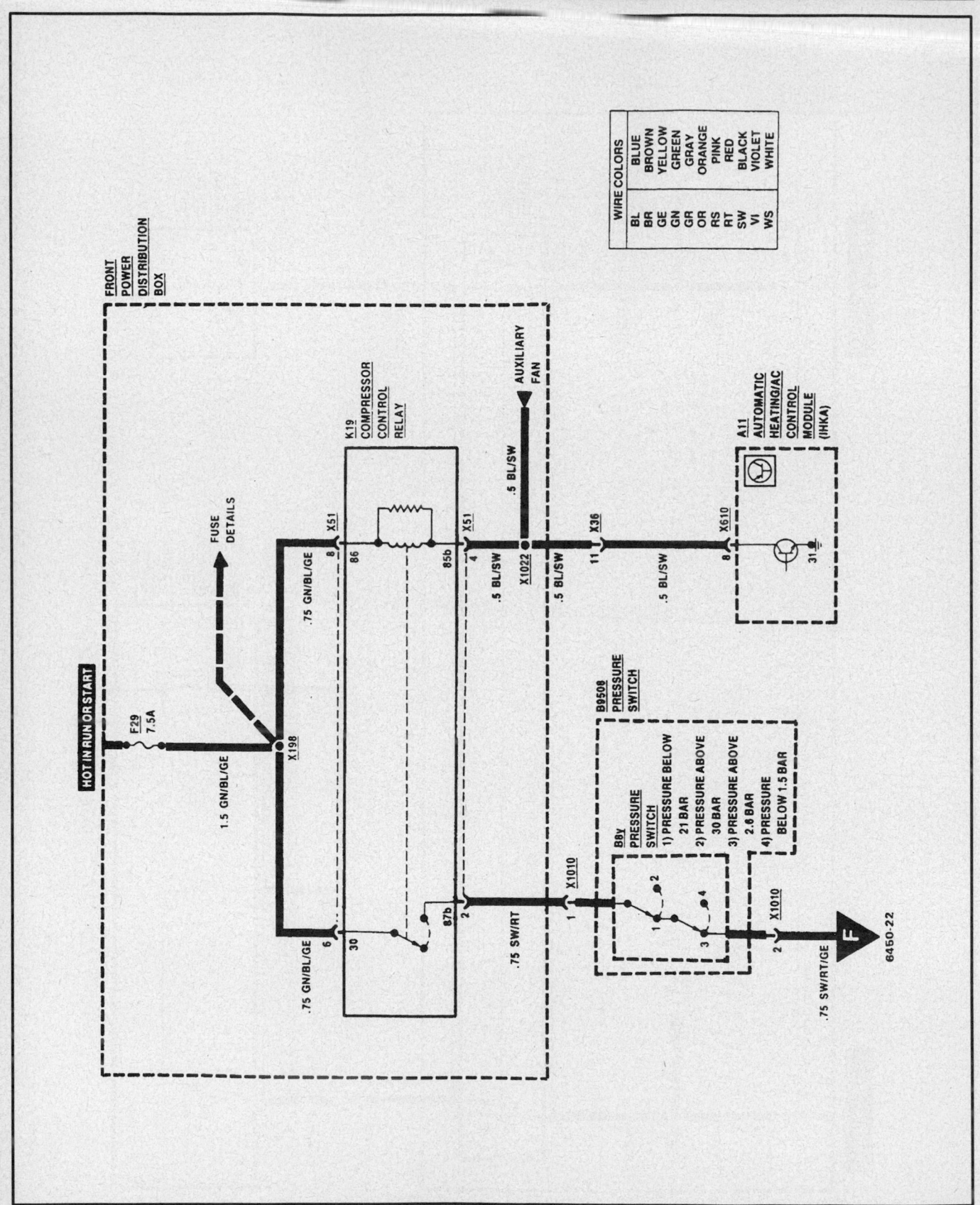

Compressor controls wiring diagram—1994 750i/L with IHKA

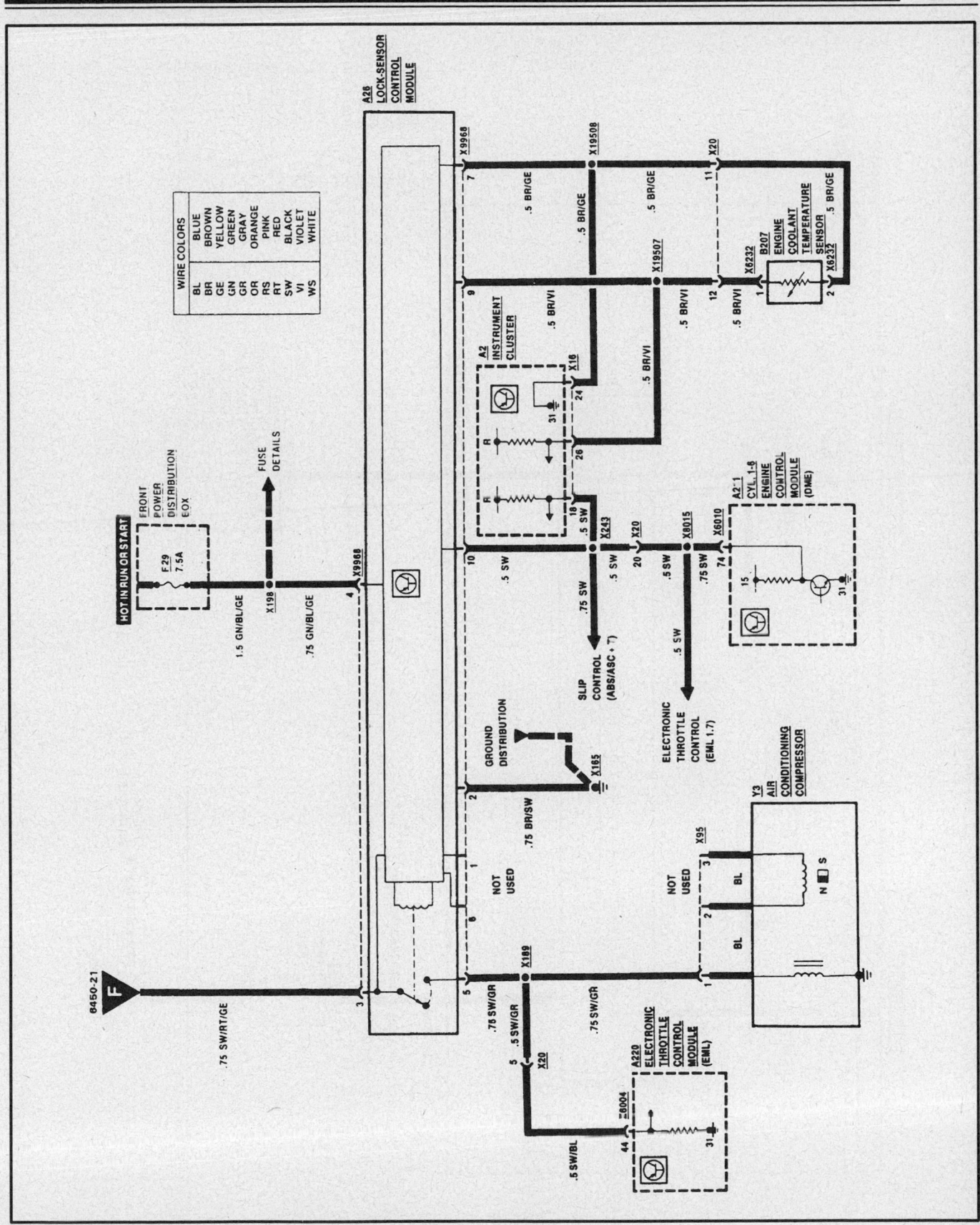

Compressor controls wiring diagram—1994 750i/L with IHKA, cont'd

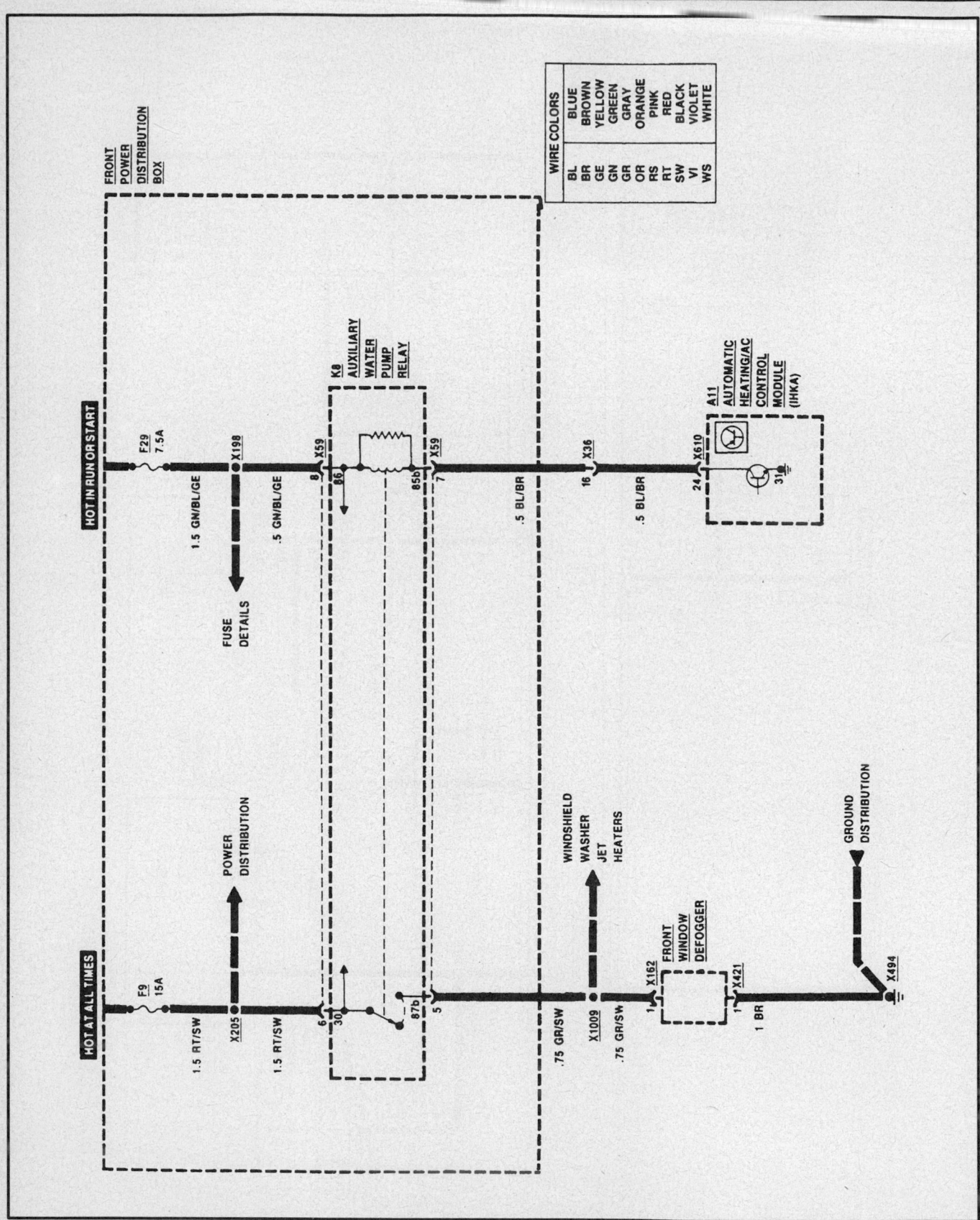

WIRE COLORS	
BL	BLUE
BR	BROWN
GE	YELLOW
GN	GREEN
GR	GRAY
OR	ORANGE
RS	PINK
RT	RED
SW	BLACK
VI	VIOLET
WS	WHITE

Front window defogger wiring diagram—1994 740i/L and 750i with IHKA

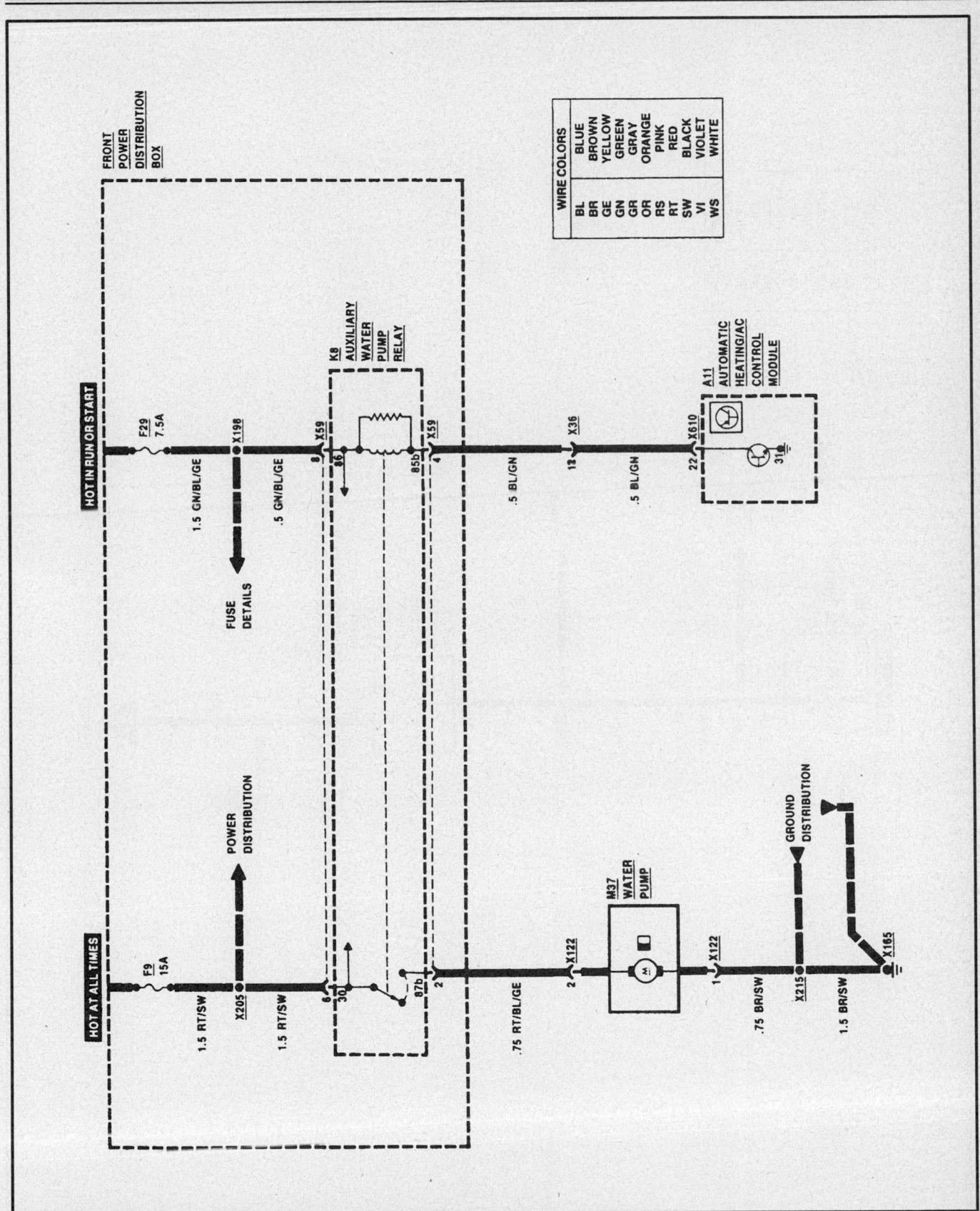

Auxiliary water pump wiring diagram—1994 740i/L and 750i with IHKA

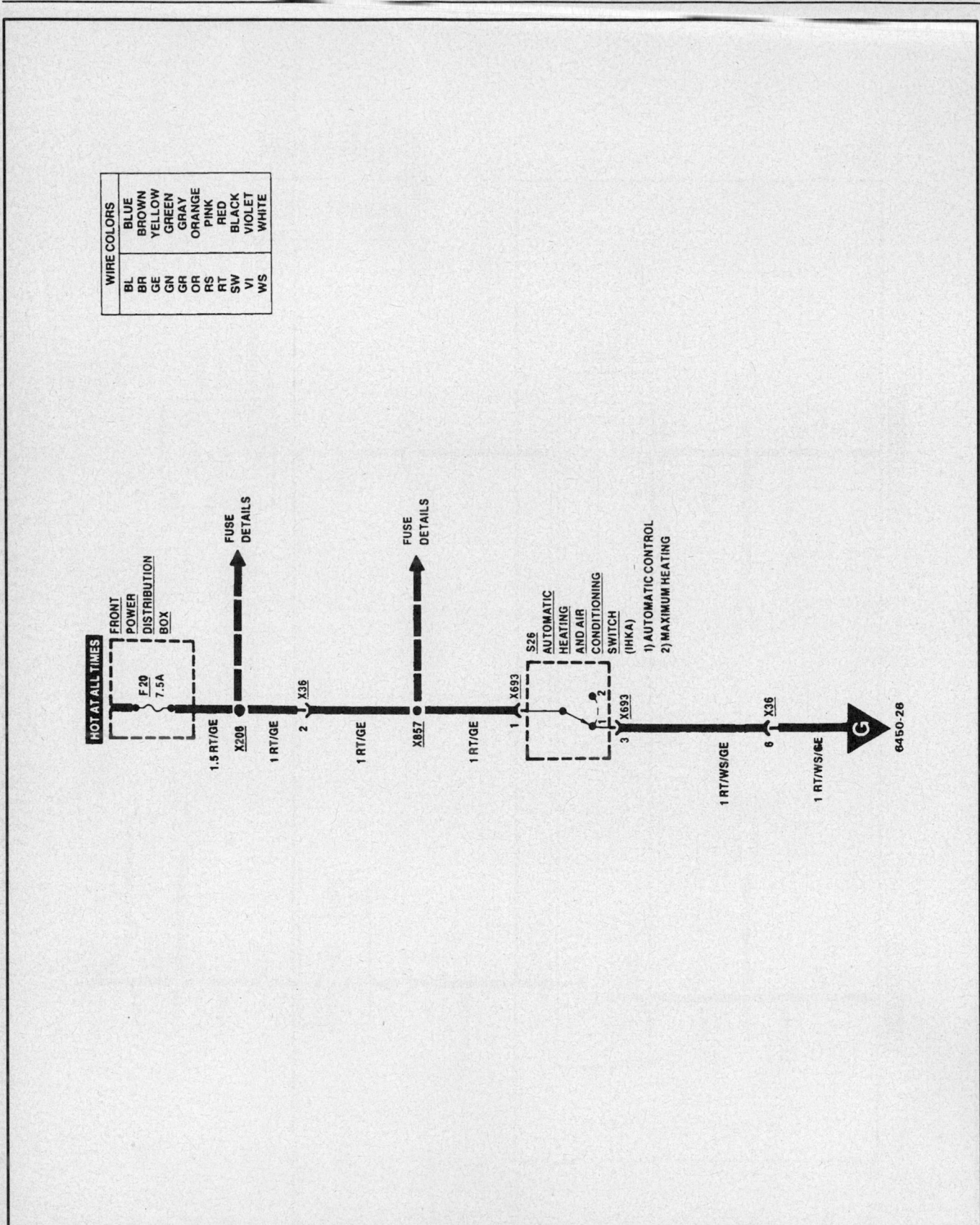

Water valves wiring diagram—1994 740i/L and 750i/L with IHKA

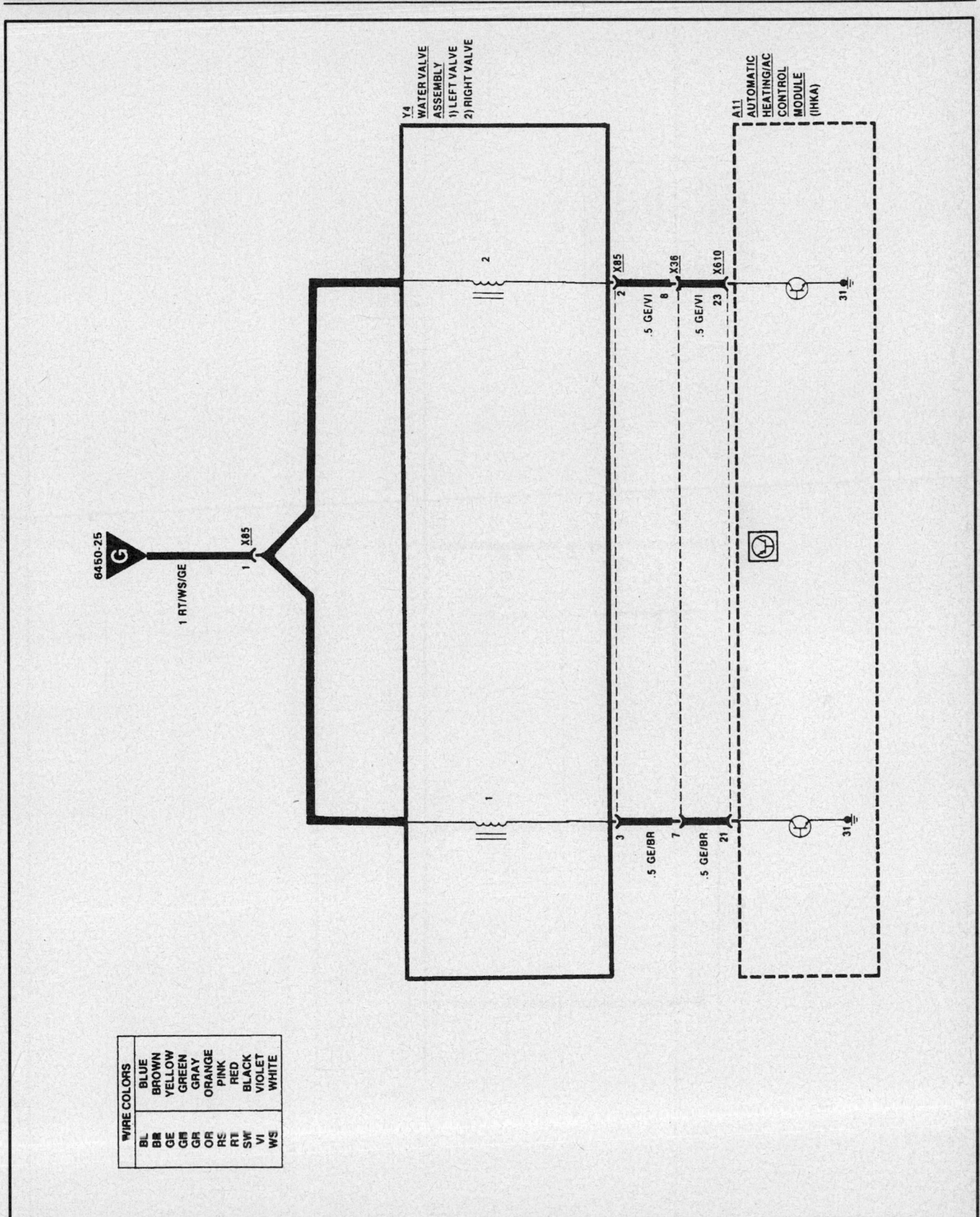

Water valves wiring diagram—1994 740i/L and 750i/L with IHKA, cont'd

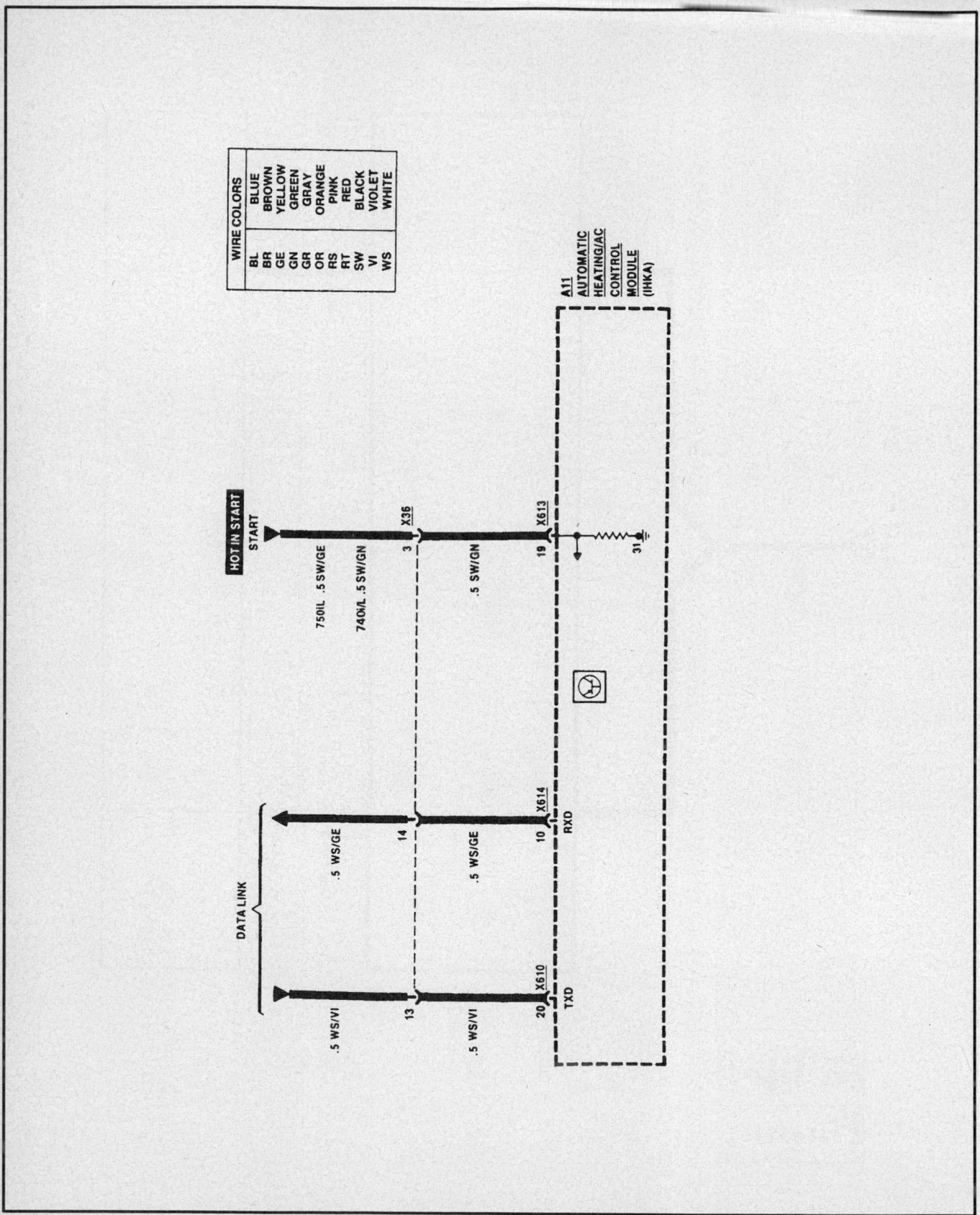

Data link and starter input wiring diagram—1994 740i/L and 750i with IHKA

SPECIFICATIONS

ENGINE IDENTIFICATION

Year	Model	Engine Displacement Liters (cc)	Engine Series (ID/VIN)	Fuel System	No. of Cylinders	Engine Type
1993	Colt	1.5 (1507)	4G15/A	MPI	4	SOHC
	Colt	1.8 (1802)	4693/C	MPI	4	SOHC
	Colt Vista	1.8 (1802)	4G93/C	MPI	4	SOHC
	Colt Vista	2.4 (2393)	4G64/G	MPI	4	SOHC
	Ram 50	2.4 (2350)	4G64/G	MPI	4	SOHC
	Ram 50	3.0 (2972)	6G72/H	MPI	6	OHC
1994	Colt	1.5 (1507)	4G15/A	MPI	4	SOHC
	Colt	1.8 (1802)	4693/C	MPI	4	SOHC
	Colt Vista	1.8 (1802)	4G93/C	MPI	4	SOHC
	Colt Vista	2.4 (2393)	4G64/G	MPI	4	SOHC
1995	Colt	1.5 (1507)	4G15/A	MPI	4	SOHC
	Colt	1.8 (1802)	4693/C	MPI	4	SOHC
	Colt Vista	1.8 (1802)	4G93/C	MPI	4	SOHC
	Colt Vista	2.4 (2393)	4G64/G	MPI	4	SOHC

MPI – Multi-Port Fuel Injection
OHC – Overhead Camshaft
SOHC – Single Overhead Camshaft

REFRIGERANT CAPACITIES

Year	Model	Refrigerant (oz.)	Refrigerant Type	Compressor Oil (fl. oz.)	Compressor Type
1993	Colt	26-30	N/A	4.4	FX105VS OR VL
	Colt Vista	30	N/A	2.7	10PA17
	Ram 50	30	R-12	4.4-5.1	FX80
1994	Colt	26-30	R-134a	4.4-5.1	N/A
	Colt Vista	26.8	R-134a	3.4-4.8	10A17C
	Colt Vista	26.8	R-134a	2.0-3.4	10A17C
1995	Colt	26-30	R-134a	4.4-5.1	N/A
	Colt Vista①	26.8	R-134a	3.4-4.8	10A17C
	Colt Vista②	26.8	R-134a	2.0-3.4	10A17C

① 1.8L engine
② 2.4L engine

AIR CONDITIONING BELT TENSION

Year	Model	Engine Displacement Liters (cc)	Belt Type	Specifications① New (lbs.)	Used (lbs.)
1993	Colt	1.5 (1507)	V-Belt	0.20-0.23	0.23-0.27
	Colt	1.8 (1802)	V-Belt	0.22-0.24	0.27–0.30
	Colt Vista	1.8 (1802)	V-Belt	0.16-0.20	0.22-0.24
	Colt Vista	2.4 (2393)	V-Belt	0.16-0.20	0.22-0.24
	Ram 50	2.4 (2350)	V-Belt	N/A	0.33-0.39
	Ram 50	3.0 (2972)	V-Belt	N/A	0.33-0.39
1994	Colt	1.5 (1507)	V-Belt	0.20-0.24	0.24-0.28
	Colt	1.8 (1802)	Serpentine	0.22-0.24	0.27–0.30
	Colt Vista	1.8 (1802)	Serpentine	0.22-0.24	0.27–0.30
	Colt Vista	2.4 (2393)	Serpentine	0.17-0.19	0.21-0.24
1995	Colt	1.5 (1507)	V-Belt	0.20-0.24	0.24-0.28
	Colt	1.8 (1802)	Serpentine	0.22-0.24	0.27–0.30
	Colt Vista	1.8 (1802)	Serpentine	0.22-0.24	0.27–0.30
	Colt Vista	2.4 (2393)	Serpentine	0.17-0.19	0.21-0.24

① Inches of deflection at center of belt using 22 lbs. force

SYSTEM DESCRIPTION

General Information

The heater unit is located in the center of the vehicle with the blower housing and blend–air system. In the blend–air system, hot air and cool air are controlled by the blend–air damper to make a fine adjustment of the temperature. The heater system is also designed as a bi–level heater in which a separator directs warm air to the windshield or to the floor and cool air through the panel outlet.

The temperature inside the vehicle is controlled by means of the temperature control lever, the position of which determines the opening of the blend–air damper and the resulting mixing ratio of cool and hot air is used to control the outlet temperature.

The air conditioning compressor coil will be energized when all of the following conditions are met:

1. The ignition switch is **ON**.
2. The air conditioner switch is depressed in either the **ECONO** or **DRY** position.
3. The blower motor switch is not in the **OFF** position.
4. The compressor refrigerant temperature switch reading is less than 194°F (90°C), if equipped.
5. The air thermo sensor is reading 38°F (3.2°C) or higher (DRY position), if equipped.
6. The dual or triple pressure switch contacts are closed. Low side refrigerant pressure must be above 32 psi. and high side refrigerant pressure must be below 370 psi.
7. The engine coolant temperature sensor is reading 226°F (108°C) or lower, if equipped.
8. The air conditioning compressor clutch relay is energized by the ECM. The ECM provides a time delay for this signal during start up and low rpm operation.

Service Valve Location

The suction (low pressure) port is located on the low pressure hose. The discharge (high pressure) port is located on the discharge line near the compressor.

System Discharging

NOTE: R–12 refrigerant is a chlorofluorocarbon which, when mishandled, can contribute to the depletion of the ozone layer in the upper atmosphere. Ozone filters out harmful radiation from the sun. In order to protect the ozone layer, an approved R–12 Recovery/Recycling machine that meets SAE standard J1991 should be employed when discharging the system. Follow the operating instructions provided with the approved equipment exactly to properly discharge the system.

R–134a refrigerant is a non–chlorofluorocarbon with different chemical characteristics than R–12. Although it is designed to be less hazardous to the ozone layer of the atmosphere, it should still be discharged only into a recycling type machine and not vented to the atmosphere. Follow equipment manufacturer's instructions for this system. Use only dedicated equipment for R–134a systems. Avoid breathing R–134a vapors, as it can cause irritation. Never pressure test or leak test R–134a service equipment with compressed air. Some mixtures of air and R–134a have been shown to be combustible, especially at higher pressures. Such a mixture may result in fire or explosion. Use appropriate cautions.

System Evacuating

If the air conditioning system has been opened to the atmosphere, it should be air and moisture free before being recharged with refrigerant. Moisture and air mixed with refrigerant will raise the compressor head pressure, possibly damage the system's components and will reduce the performance of the system. Moisture will boil at normal room temperature when exposed to a vacuum. To evacuate the system, perform the following procedure:

1. Leak test the system and repair any leaks found.
2. Connect an approved charging station, Recovery/Recycling machine or manifold gauge set and vacuum pump to the discharge and suction ports. The red hose is normally connected to the discharge (high pressure) line and the blue hose is connected to the suction (low pressure) line.
3. Open the discharge and suction ports and start the vacuum pump. Evacuate to a vacuum reading of 29.5 in. Hg (100 kPa) or higher. If the pump is not able to pull at least 29.5 in. Hg of vacuum, there is a leak that must be repaired before evacuation can occur.

4. Once the system has reached at least 29.5 in. Hg of vacuum, allow the system to evacuate for at least 10 minutes. The longer the system is evacuated, the more contaminants will be removed.
5. Close all valves and turn the pump OFF. If the system loses vacuum after 15 minutes, there is a leak that should be repaired.

System Charging

NOTE: Be sure to use dedicated equipment while charging systems using R–134a refrigerant.

1. Connect an approved charging station, Recovery/Recycling machine or manifold gauge set to the discharge and suction ports. The red hose is normally connected to the discharge (high pressure) line and the blue hose is connected to the suction (low pressure) line.
2. Follow the instructions provided with the equipment and charge the system with the specified amount of refrigerant.
3. Perform a leak test.

SYSTEM COMPONENTS

NOTE: Vehicles that are equipped with the Supplemental Inflatable Restraint or air bag system require additional service procedures. The air bag system must be disabled before performing service on or around the air bag, instrument panel components, wiring and sensors. Failure to follow safety and disabling procedures could result in accidental air bag deployment, possible personal injury and unnecessary air bag system repairs.

Radiator

REMOVAL AND INSTALLATION

1. Disconnect the negative battery cable.
2. Drain the cooling system. If necessary, remove air intake ductwork.
3. Disconnect the overflow hose. If necessary, remove the overflow reservoir.
4. Disconnect the upper and lower radiator hoses.
5. Disconnect all electrical connectors to the electric cooling fan(s) and radiator sensors, if equipped. Most of these connectors employ a waterproof connector. When disconnecting, make sure all parts of the connectors remain intact. Remove the electric cooling fan(s) or fan shroud.
6. Disconnect and plug the automatic transaxle or transmission cooler lines, if equipped.
7. Remove the upper radiator mounts and lift out the radiator assembly.
8. Reverse removal procedure to install components.
9. Refill coolant level as required.
10. Connect the negative battery cable and check for leaks.
11. Run the engine until the thermostat opens. Confirm that water is flowing by touching the radiator lower hose. Stop the engine and allow engine to cool. Recheck coolant level.

COOLING SYSTEM BLEEDING

All vehicles are equipped with a self–bleeding thermostat. Slowly fill the cooling system in the conventional manner; air will vent through the jiggle valve in the thermostat. Run the vehicle until the thermostat has opened and continue filling the radiator. Recheck the coolant level after the vehicle has cooled.

Electric Cooling Fan

TESTING

Except Ram 50

───────── **CAUTION** ─────────
Make sure the key is in the OFF position when checking the electric cooling fan. If not, the fan could turn ON at any time, causing serious personal injury.
───────────────────────────────

1. Disconnect the negative battery cable.
2. Disconnect the electrical plug from the fan motor harness.
3. Connect the appropriate terminals to the battery and make sure the fan runs smoothly, without abnormal noise or vibration.
4. Connect the negative battery cable.

REMOVAL AND INSTALLATION

Radiator Cooling Fan

1. Disconnect the negative battery cable.
2. Unplug the connector(s). Most of these connectors employ a waterproof connector. When disconnecting, make sure all parts of the connectors remain intact.
3. Remove the upper radiator hose, if necessary (partial system draining will be required).
4. Remove the mounting screws. The radiator and condenser cooling fans are separately removable.
5. Remove the fan assembly and disassemble as required.
6. Reverse removal procedure to install components.
7. Check the coolant level and refill as required.
8. Connect the negative battery cable and check the fan for proper operation.

Condenser Cooling Fan

1. Disconnect the negative battery cable.

2. Unplug the connector(s). Most of these connectors employ a waterproof connector. When disconnecting, make sure all parts of the connectors remain intact.

3. Remove the upper radiator hose, if necessary (partial cooling system draining will be required).

4. Remove the mounting screws. The radiator and condenser cooling fans are removable separately.

5. Remove the fan assembly and disassemble as required.

6. Reverse removal procedure to install components.

7. Check the coolant level and refill as required.

8. Connect the negative battery cable and check the fan for proper operation.

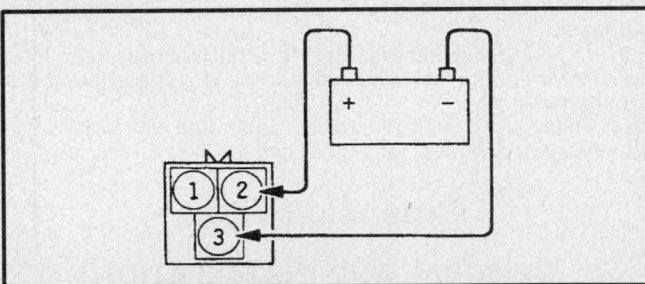

Radiator cooling fan check—Colt

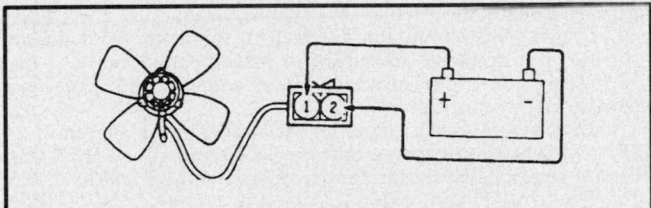

Radiator cooling fan check—Colt Vista

Condenser

REMOVAL AND INSTALLATION

Colt

1. Disconnect the negative battery cable.
2. Properly discharge the air conditioning system.
3. Remove the battery, battery tray and windshield washer reservoir.
4. Remove the upper radiator mounts to allow the radiator to be moved toward the engine. Remove both cooling fans.
5. Disconnect the refrigerant lines from the condenser. Cover the exposed ends of the lines to minimize contamination.
6. Remove the condenser mounting bolts.
7. Move the radiator toward the engine and lift the condenser from the vehicle. Inspect the lower rubber mounting insulators and replace, if necessary.

To install:

8. Lower the condenser into position and align the dowels with the lower mounting insulators. Install the bolts.
9. Using new lubricated O–rings, connect the refrigerant lines to the condenser.
10. Install the radiator mounts and cooling fans.
11. Reverse removal procedure to install components.
12. Evacuate and recharge the air conditioning system. If the condenser was replaced, add 0.5 oz. of refrigerant oil during the recharge.
13. Connect the negative battery cable and check the entire climate control system for proper operation and leaks.

Colt Vista

1. Disconnect the negative battery cable.
2. Properly discharge the air conditioning system.
3. Remove the grille assembly. The grille is held in place with 1 or 2 screws and 5 or 6 clips that may require the use of a flat–tipped tool against the tab for release.
4. Unplug the fan connector. Most of these connectors employ a waterproof connector. When disconnecting, make sure all parts of the connectors remain intact.
5. Remove the mounting screws and remove the cooling fan assembly.
6. Disconnect the refrigerant lines from the condenser. Cover the exposed ends of the lines to minimize contamination.
7. Remove the condenser mounting bolts and remove the condenser.

To install:

8. Install the condenser and mounting bolts.
9. Using new lubricated O–rings, connect the refrigerant lines to the condenser.
10. Install the cooling fan and secure with mounting screws.
11. Connect the fan connector. Connect the negative battery cable and check the fan for proper operation before assembling the remaining components. Disconnect the negative battery cable before continuing.
12. Install the grille.
13. Evacuate and recharge the air conditioning system. If the condenser was replaced, add 1.3 oz. of refrigerant oil during the recharge.
14. Connect the negative battery cable and check the entire climate control system for proper operation and leaks.

Ram 50

1. Disconnect the negative battery cable.
2. Properly discharge the air conditioning system.
3. Remove the grille assembly removing 3 screws across the top, two clips at each upper corner and five clips across the grille lower edge.
4. Using appropriate wrenches, remove the receiver/drier bracket holding receiver/drier to condenser. Remove the receiver/drier.
5. Cover the exposed ends of the refrigerant lines to minimize contamination.
6. Remove the condenser mounting bolts and remove the condenser through the grille opening.

To install:

7. Install the condenser with its mounting bolts.
8. Using new, lubricated O–rings, connect the refrigerant lines to the condenser and install receiver/drier. If installing a new receiver/drier, add 0.30 oz. of refrigerant oil during recharging.
9. Install the grille assembly.
10. Evacuate and recharge the air conditioning system. If the condenser was replaced, add 0.5 oz. of refrigerant oil during the recharge.
11. Connect the negative battery cable and check the entire climate control system for proper operation and leaks.

Compressor

REMOVAL AND INSTALLATION

Colt

1. Disconnect the negative battery cable.
2. Properly discharge the air conditioning system.
3. Remove the tensioner pulley and compressor drive belt. Disconnect the clutch coil connector.

4. Disconnect the refrigerant lines from the compressor and discard the O–rings. Cover the exposed ends of the lines to minimize contamination.

5. Remove the compressor mounting bolts and the compressor.

To install:

6. Check and adjust level of compressor oil. Install the compressor and torque the mounting bolts. Connect the clutch coil connector.

7. Using new lubricated O–rings, connect the refrigerant lines to the compressor.

8. Install the belt and tensioner pulley, if removed. Adjust the belt to specifications.

9. Evacuate and recharge the air conditioning system.

10. Connect the negative battery cable and check the entire climate control system for proper operation and leaks.

Colt Vista

1. Disconnect the negative battery cable.
2. Properly discharge the air conditioning system.
3. Remove the left side engine under cover. Loosen the tensioner adjustment bolt and remove the belt.
4. Disconnect the clutch coil connector.
5. Disconnect the refrigerant lines from the compressor and discard the O–rings. Cover the exposed ends of the lines to minimize contamination.
6. Remove the mounting bolts and remove the compressor from its mounting bracket.

To install:

7. Check and adjust level of compressor oil. Install the compressor and torque the mounting bolts. Connect the clutch coil connector.

8. Using new lubricated O–rings, connect the refrigerant lines to the compressor.

9. Install the belt and adjust to specification.

10. Install the engine under cover.

11. Evacuate and recharge the air conditioning system.

12. Connect the negative battery cable and check the entire climate control system for proper operation and leaks.

Ram 50

1. Disconnect the negative battery cable.
2. Properly discharge the air conditioning system.
3. Relieve the tension and remove the compressor drive belt from the clutch pulley. Disconnect the electrical connector from the temperature/pressure switch on the compressor.
4. Disconnect the refrigerant lines from the compressor and discard the O–rings. Cover the exposed ends of the lines and openings to the compressor to minimize contamination.
5. Remove the compressor mounting bolts, compressor and bracket.

To install:

6. Check and adjust level of compressor oil. Install the compressor mounting bracket and mounting bolts. Connect the clutch coil connector.

7. Using new, lubricated O–rings, connect the refrigerant lines to the compressor.

8. Wrap the drive belt around the pulley and adjust to specification, using tensioner bolt.

9. Evacuate and recharge the air conditioning system.

10. Connect the negative battery cable and check the entire climate control system for proper operation and leaks.

Receiver/Drier

REMOVAL AND INSTALLATION

1. Disconnect the negative battery cable.
2. Properly discharge the air conditioning system.

3. Disconnect the electrical connector from the switch on the receiver/drier, if equipped.

4. Disconnect the refrigerant lines from the receiver/drier assembly. Cover the exposed ends of the lines to minimize contamination.

5. Remove the mounting strap and the receiver/drier from its bracket. Remove the receiver/drier from the mounting strap.

To install:

6. Install the receiver/drier and mounting strap.

7. Using new lubricated O–rings. connect the refrigerant lines to the receiver/drier.

8. Connect the electrical connector to the switch, if equipped.

9. Evacuate and recharge the air conditioning system. If the receiver/drier was replaced, add 0.30 oz. of refrigerant oil during the recharge.

10. Connect the negative battery cable and check the entire climate control system for proper operation and leaks.

Expansion Valve

REMOVAL AND INSTALLATION

1. Disconnect the negative battery cable.
2. Properly discharge the air conditioning system.
3. Remove the evaporator housing and separate the upper and lower cases.
4. Remove the expansion valve from the evaporator lines.
5. Reverse removal procedure to install components.
6. Using new lubricated O-rings, connect the expansion valve to the evaporator.
7. Evacuate and recharge the air conditioning system.
8. Connect the negative battery cable and check the entire climate control system for proper operation and leaks.

Blower Motor

REMOVAL AND INSTALLATION

Colt

1. Disconnect the negative battery cable.
2. Remove the under cover below the glove box.
3. Remove the glove box, right speaker cover and the glove box cross support.
4. Remove the blower motor resistor and then the blower motor.
5. Reverse removal procedure to install components.
6. Connect the negative battery cable and check the blower motor for proper operation.

Colt Vista

1. Disconnect the negative battery cable.
2. Remove the lap heater duct.
3. Remove the glove box assembly.
4. Remove the blower resistor, the right speaker cover and the glove box frame.
5. Remove the electrical connection, the retaining screws, and lower the blower motor out of its housing.
6. Reverse removal procedure to install components.
7. Connect the negative battery cable and check the blower motor for proper operation.

Ram 50

1. Disconnect negative battery cable.
2. Remove blower motor mounting screws, lower the motor assembly and detach the blower motor wiring.

3. Reverse removal procedure to install components.
4. Connect the negative battery cable and check blower motor for proper operation.

Blower Motor Resistor

REMOVAL AND INSTALLATION

1. Disconnect the negative battery cable.
2. Remove the glove box assembly. The resistor is accessible through the glove box opening and is mounted to the blower or evaporator case.
3. Disconnect the wire harness from the resistor.
4. Remove the mounting screws and remove the resistor.
5. Reverse removal procedure to install components.
6. Connect the negative battery cable and check the blower motor for proper operation.

Heater Core

REMOVAL AND INSTALLATION

NOTE: Vehicles that are equipped with the Supplemental Inflatable Restraint or air bag system require additional service procedures. The air bag system must be disabled before performing service on or around the air bag, instrument panel components, wiring and sensors. Failure to follow safety and disabling procedures could result in accidental air bag deployment, possible personal injury and unnecessary air bag system repairs.

Colt

1. Disconnect the negative battery cable.
2. Properly drain the cooling system.
3. Remove the instrument panel as follows:
   • Remove the floor console.
   • Remove the knee panel below the steering column.
   • Remove the sun glass pocket, steering column cover and instrument cluster bezel.
   • Remove the instrument cluster, disconnecting speedometer cable and electrical connections when cluster is pulled out.
   • Remove the remote control mirror switch, rheostat or plug.
   • Remove the coin box or rear wiper switch.
   • The air outlet panel from the left side and the ashtray from the center panel.
   • Detach the air bypass cable from the lever on the heater unit. Remove the center panel bezel and air outlet assembly.
   • Remove the radio and cup holder.
   • Remove the under cover beneath the glove box, then remove the glove box and the right speaker cover (corner panel).
   • Remove the climate control panel, disconnecting electrical connectors and cables.
   • Remove both panel speakers, then take out the left and right defroster grilles.
   • Remove the hood release handle. Remove the steering column bolts and lower the column.
   • Remove the speedometer cable adapter after removing its locking pin and pulling the cable slightly rearward.

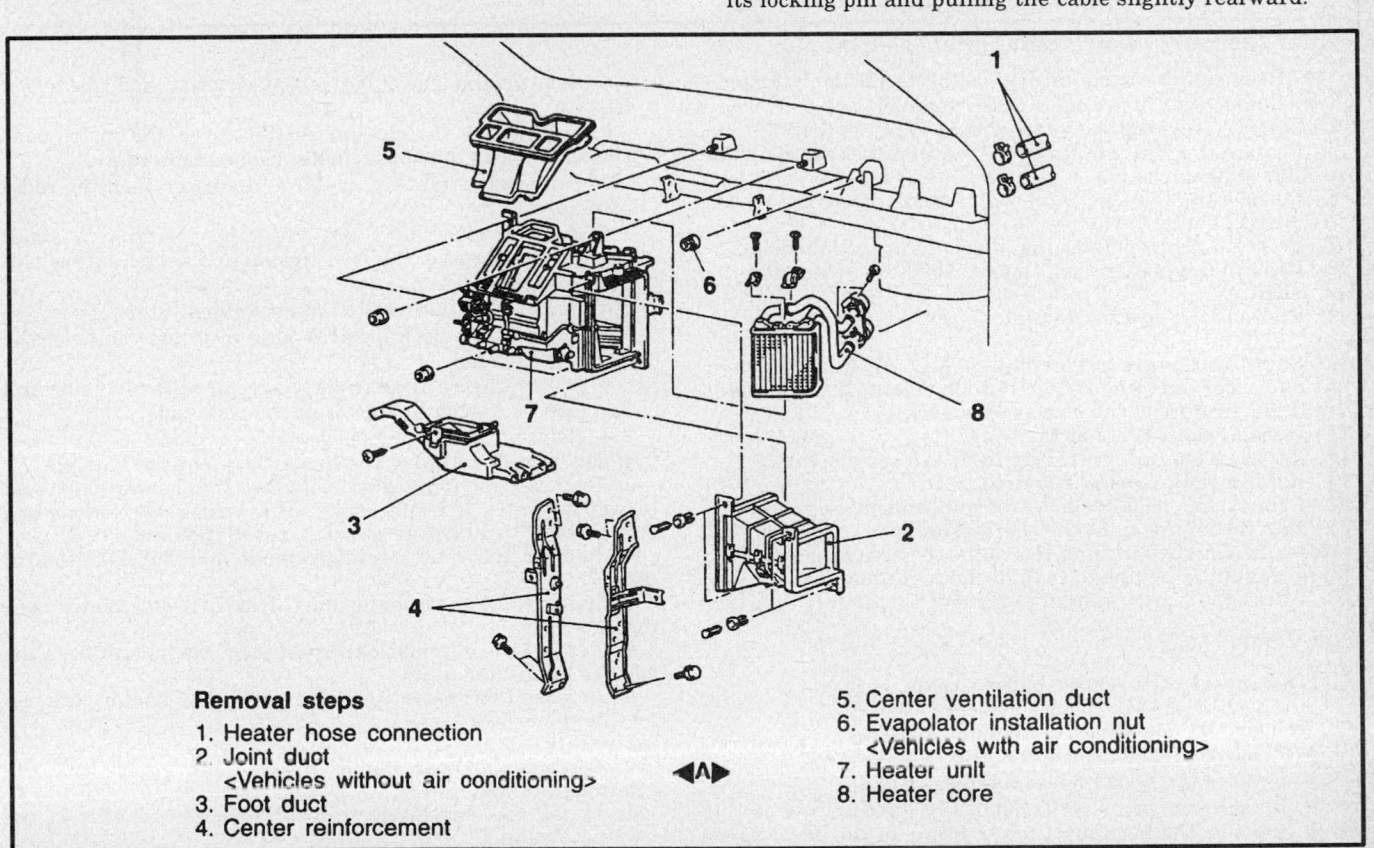

Removal steps

1. Heater hose connection
2. Joint duct
   <Vehicles without air conditioning>
3. Foot duct
4. Center reinforcement

◄A►

5. Center ventilation duct
6. Evapolator installation nut
   <Vehicles with air conditioning>
7. Heater unit
8. Heater core

Heater case and related components—Colt

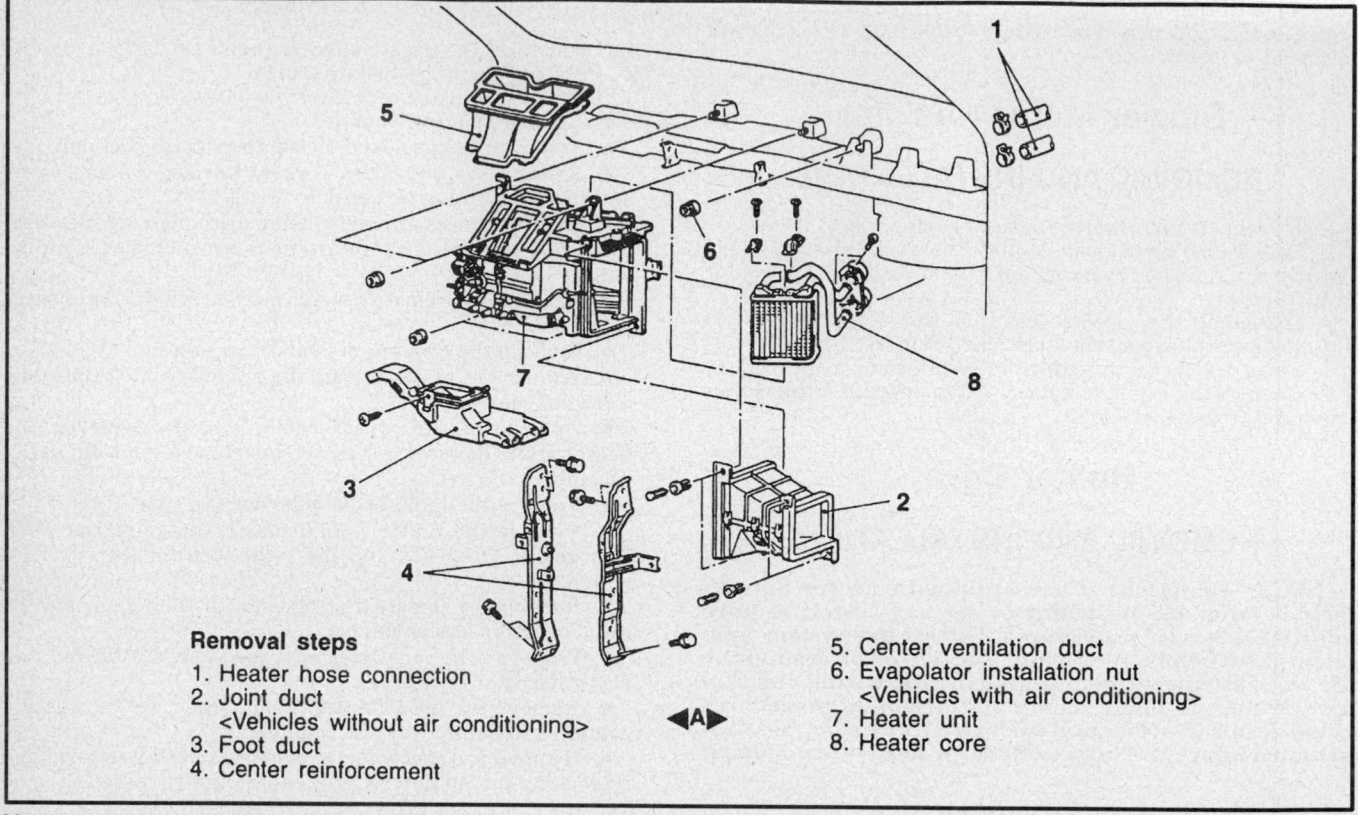

Removal steps
1. Heater hose connection
2. Joint duct
   <Vehicles without air conditioning>
3. Foot duct
4. Center reinforcement

◄A►

5. Center ventilation duct
6. Evapolator installation nut
   <Vehicles with air conditioning>
7. Heater unit
8. Heater core

Heater case and related components—Colt

- Remove the wiring harness connector at the left side.
- Remove the instrument panel assembly.
4. Remove and plug the heater hoses from the firewall.
5. Remove the joint air duct between the heater and blower assemblies (heater only).
6. Remove the foot duct, the center reinforcement and center ventilation duct.
7. Remove the evaporator installation nut (A/C models).
8. Remove the heater unit, then remove the heater core.
To install:
9. Position the heater unit in place and attach with the nuts.
10. Reinstall the evaporator nut (if A/C). Install the center vent duct, foot duct and center reinforcement. If heater only, install the air duct to the blower assembly.
11. Install heater hoses at the firewall.
12. Reverse removal procedure to install components.
13. Refill coolant level as required.
14. Connect the negative battery cable and check for leaks.
15. Run the engine until the thermostat opens. Confirm that water is flowing by touching the radiator lower hose. Stop the engine and allow engine to cool. Recheck coolant level.
16. Check the heater system for proper operation.

Colt Vista

1. Disconnect the negative battery cable.
2. Properly drain the cooling system.
3. Remove the instrument panel as follows:
- Remove the floor console.
- Remove the hood release handle.
- Remove the panel cover below the steering column.
- Remove the horizontal lower frame in the cover opening.
- Remove the floor air duct, the lap duct and the heater lap duct.

- Remove the glove box, speaker cover and glove box frame.
- Remove the instrument cluster cover, the instrument cluster (remove the speedometer cable adapter lock).
- Remove the ashtray, center panel bezel, then the radio assembly.
- Remove the center air outlet by inserting a small screwdriver through the outlet grille and detaching the clip in each upper corner.
- Remove the heater–A/C control panel.
- Remove the clock or clock plug from top center of the instrument panel.
- Detach the harness triple connector at the left side and the harness double connector at the right side.
- Remove the instrument panel.
4. Disconnect and plug the heater hoses at the firewall.
5. Remove the joint duct between the heater unit and blower assembly if heater only; otherwise, remove the plate sub–assembly and the evaporator installation nut.
6. Remove the center reinforcement and the ABS control unit.
7. Remove the rear heater duct, foot duct and center vent duct.
8. Remove the automatic transmission control unit from the front of the heater unit.
9. Remove the heater unit assembly. The heater core can now be removed.
To install:
10. Position the heater unit in place and attach with the retaining nut and bolt.
11. Install the automatic transmission control unit to the heater housing.
12. Install the center, foot and rear air ducts.

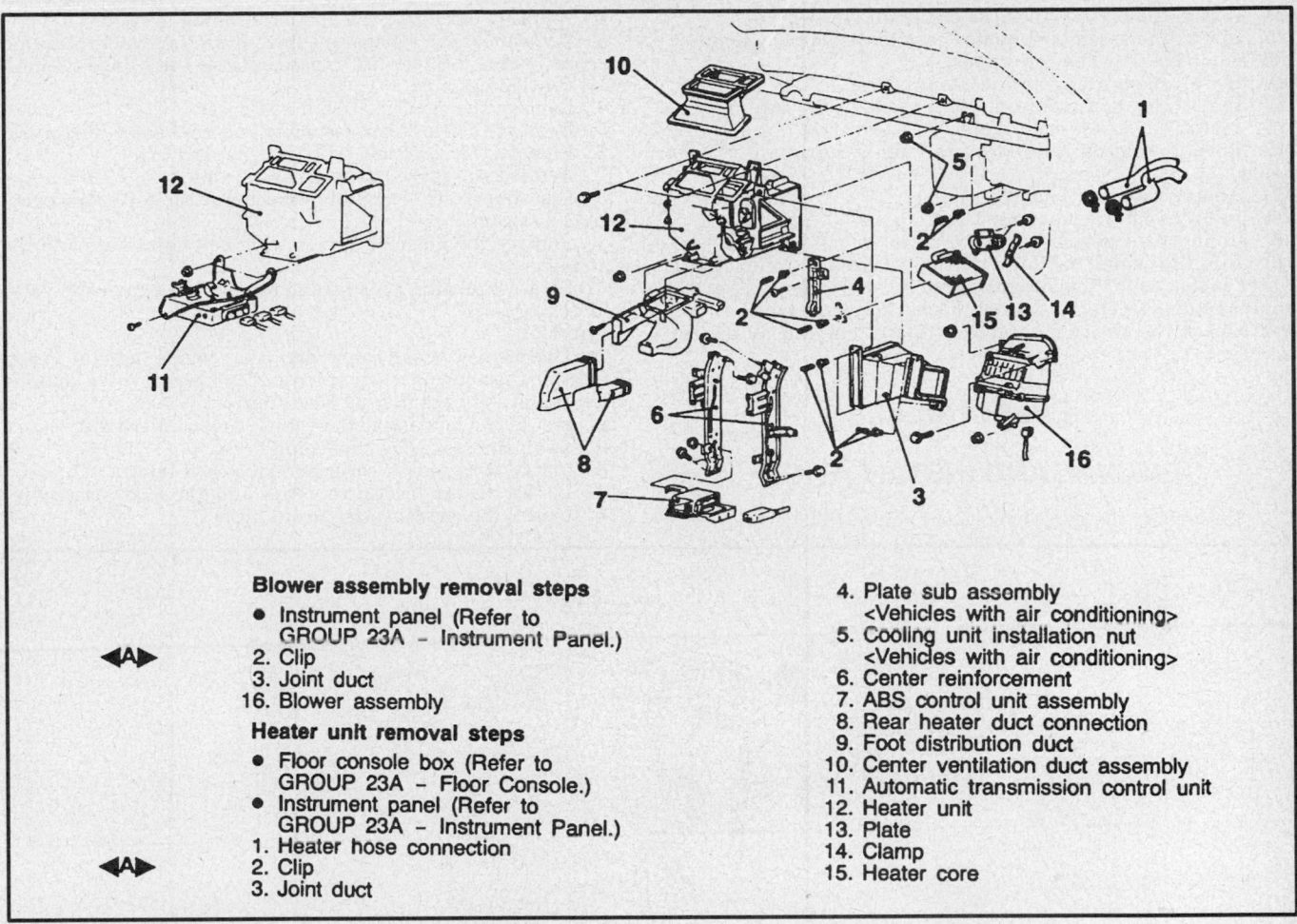

Blower assembly removal steps

- Instrument panel (Refer to GROUP 23A – Instrument Panel.)
2. Clip
3. Joint duct
16. Blower assembly

Heater unit removal steps

- Floor console box (Refer to GROUP 23A – Floor Console.)
- Instrument panel (Refer to GROUP 23A – Instrument Panel.)
1. Heater hose connection
2. Clip
3. Joint duct

4. Plate sub assembly <Vehicles with air conditioning>
5. Cooling unit installation nut <Vehicles with air conditioning>
6. Center reinforcement
7. ABS control unit assembly
8. Rear heater duct connection
9. Foot distribution duct
10. Center ventilation duct assembly
11. Automatic transmission control unit
12. Heater unit
13. Plate
14. Clamp
15. Heater core

Heater case and related components—Colt Vista

13. Install the ABS control unit, center reinforcements and install the evaporator nut and plate sub–assembly or heater joint air duct as removed.
14. Attach the heater hoses at the firewall.
15. Install the instrument panel.
16. Reverse removal procedure to install remaining components.
17. Refill coolant level as required.
18. Connect the negative battery cable and check for leaks.
19. Run the engine until the thermostat opens. Confirm that water is flowing by touching the radiator lower hose. Stop the engine and allow engine to cool. Recheck coolant level.
20. Check the heater system for proper operation.

Ram 50

1. Disconnect the negative battery cable.
2. Properly drain the cooling system.
3. Disconnect the heater hoses from the core tubes on engine side of firewall.
4. Remove the hazard flasher switch and the matching switch or cover on the other side of the column by gently prying from bottom with a trim stick.
5. Remove the instrument cluster cover and instrument cluster, disconnecting the instrument connectors during removal.
6. Remove the fuse box cover, fuse box retaining screws, and position the fuse box aside.
7. Remove the glove box assembly by detaching side retaining clips.

8. Remove the defroster ducts from each side of the heater housing assembly.
9. Label and disconnect the air, mode, and temperature control cables.
10. Remove the front speaker grilles by gently prying at spring clip area on lower left and lower right sides.
11. Remove the parcel box or clock from center of instrument panel, as equipped.
12. Remove the nut cover from the top center of the instrument panel by reaching through the clock opening, depressing the side retaining clip and pressing upward.
13. Remove the cover from lower center of the panel.
14. Remove the shifter knob and floor console assembly, if equipped.
15. Move the tilt steering column down as far as it will go.
16. Remove the instrument panel retaining nuts and bolts and carefully remove the instrument panel from the vehicle, detaching all harnesses and cables.
17. Remove the duct from the right side of the heater case.
18. Remove the defroster duct from the top center of the heater case.
19. Remove the center reinforcement braces.
20. Remove the mounting nuts and remove the heater case from the vehicle.
21. Remove the hose cover, joint hose clamp and the plate from the case.
22. Remove the heater core from the case.
To install:
23. Install the heater core to the heater case.

24. Install the plate, joint hose clamp and hose cover.
25. Install the assembled heater case to the vehicle. Connect the heater hoses to the core tubes.
26. Install the center reinforcement braces.
27. Install the defroster and center ducts to the case.
28. Install the instrument panel.
29. Reverse removal procedure to install remaining components.
30. Adjust the control cables.
31. Refill coolant level as required.
32. Connect the negative battery cable and check for leaks.
33. Run the engine until the thermostat opens. Confirm that water is flowing by touching the radiator lower hose. Stop the engine and allow engine to cool. Recheck coolant level.
34. Check the entire climate control system and all gauges for proper operation.

Evaporator

REMOVAL AND INSTALLATION

1. Disconnect the negative battery cable.

2. Properly discharge the air conditioning system.
3. Disconnect the refrigerant lines from the evaporator and discard O–rings. Cover the exposed ends of the lines to minimize contamination.
4. Remove the condensation drain hose.
5. Remove the glove box assembly and lap heater duct work.
6. Remove the cowl side trim and speaker cover.
7. Remove the glove box bezel and frame.
8. Disconnect the electrical connector at the top of the evaporator housing.
9. Remove the push clips, mounting bolts and nuts and the housing.
10. Disassemble the housing and remove the expansion valve and evaporator.

To install:
11. Thoroughly clean and dry the inside of the case. Assemble the housing, evaporator and expansion valve, making sure the gaskets are in good condition.
12. Install the housing to the vehicle and connect the connector. Install the glove box frame and bezel.
13. Install the speaker cover and side cowl trim.
14. Install the lap heater ductwork and glove box assembly.
15. Install the condensation drain hose.

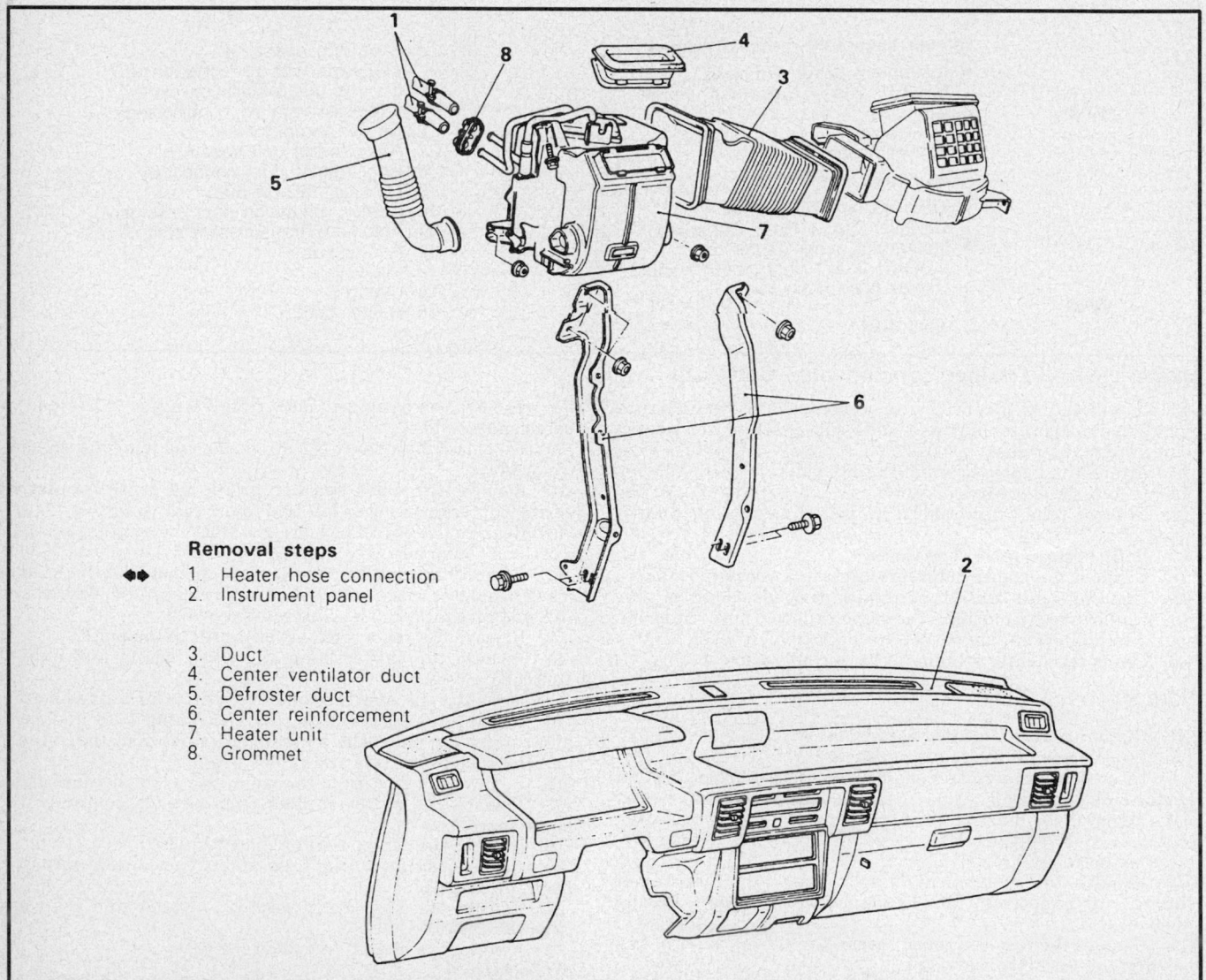

Removal steps
1. Heater hose connection
2. Instrument panel

3. Duct
4. Center ventilator duct
5. Defroster duct
6. Center reinforcement
7. Heater unit
8. Grommet

Heater case and related components—Ram 50

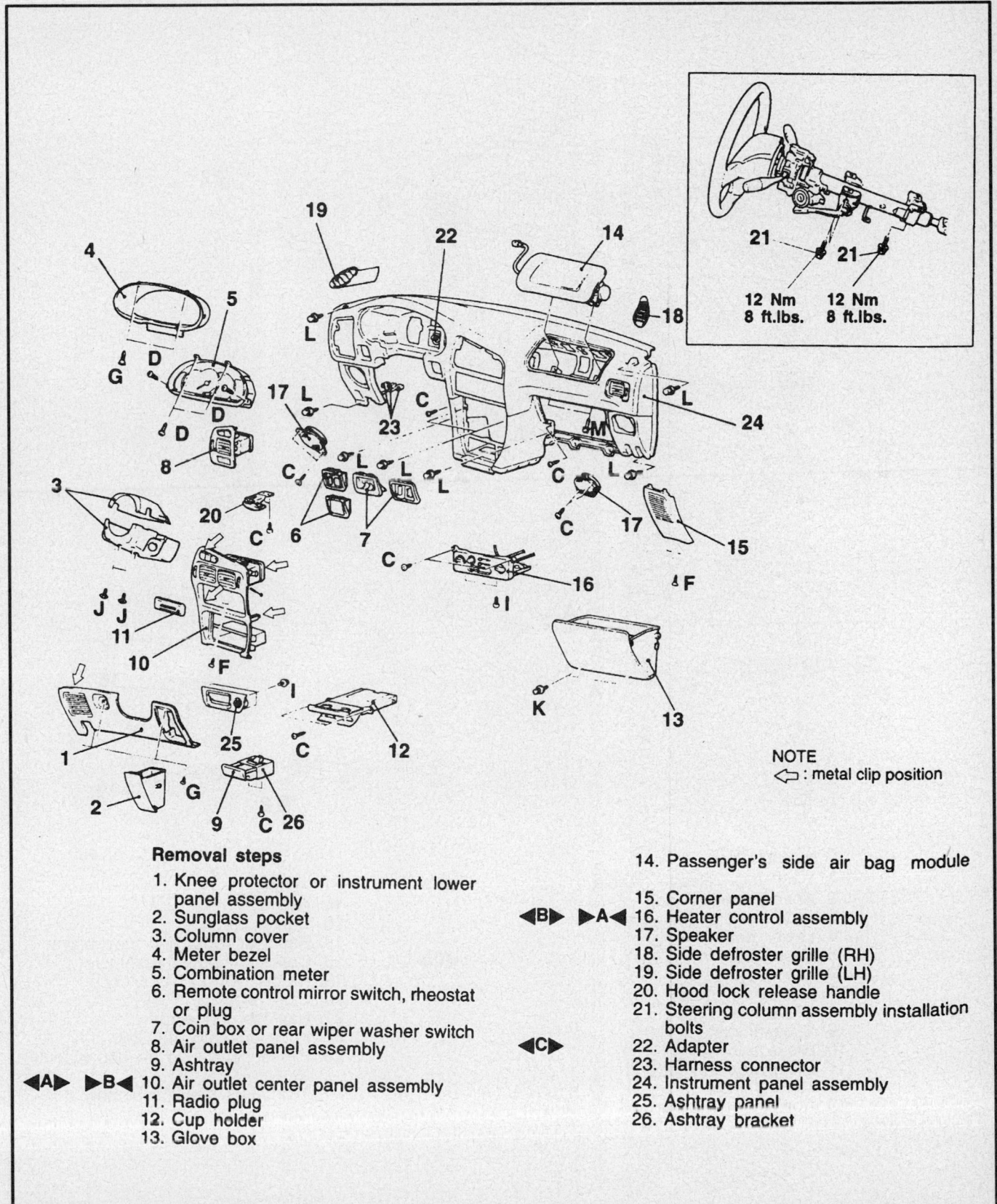

NOTE
⟵ : metal clip position

Removal steps

1. Knee protector or instrument lower panel assembly
2. Sunglass pocket
3. Column cover
4. Meter bezel
5. Combination meter
6. Remote control mirror switch, rheostat or plug
7. Coin box or rear wiper washer switch
8. Air outlet panel assembly
9. Ashtray
◀A▶ ▶B◀ 10. Air outlet center panel assembly
11. Radio plug
12. Cup holder
13. Glove box

14. Passenger's side air bag module
15. Corner panel
◀B▶ ▶A◀ 16. Heater control assembly
17. Speaker
18. Side defroster grille (RH)
19. Side defroster grille (LH)
20. Hood lock release handle
21. Steering column assembly installation bolts
22. Adapter
◀C▶ 23. Harness connector
24. Instrument panel assembly
25. Ashtray panel
26. Ashtray bracket

Instrument panel and related components—Colt

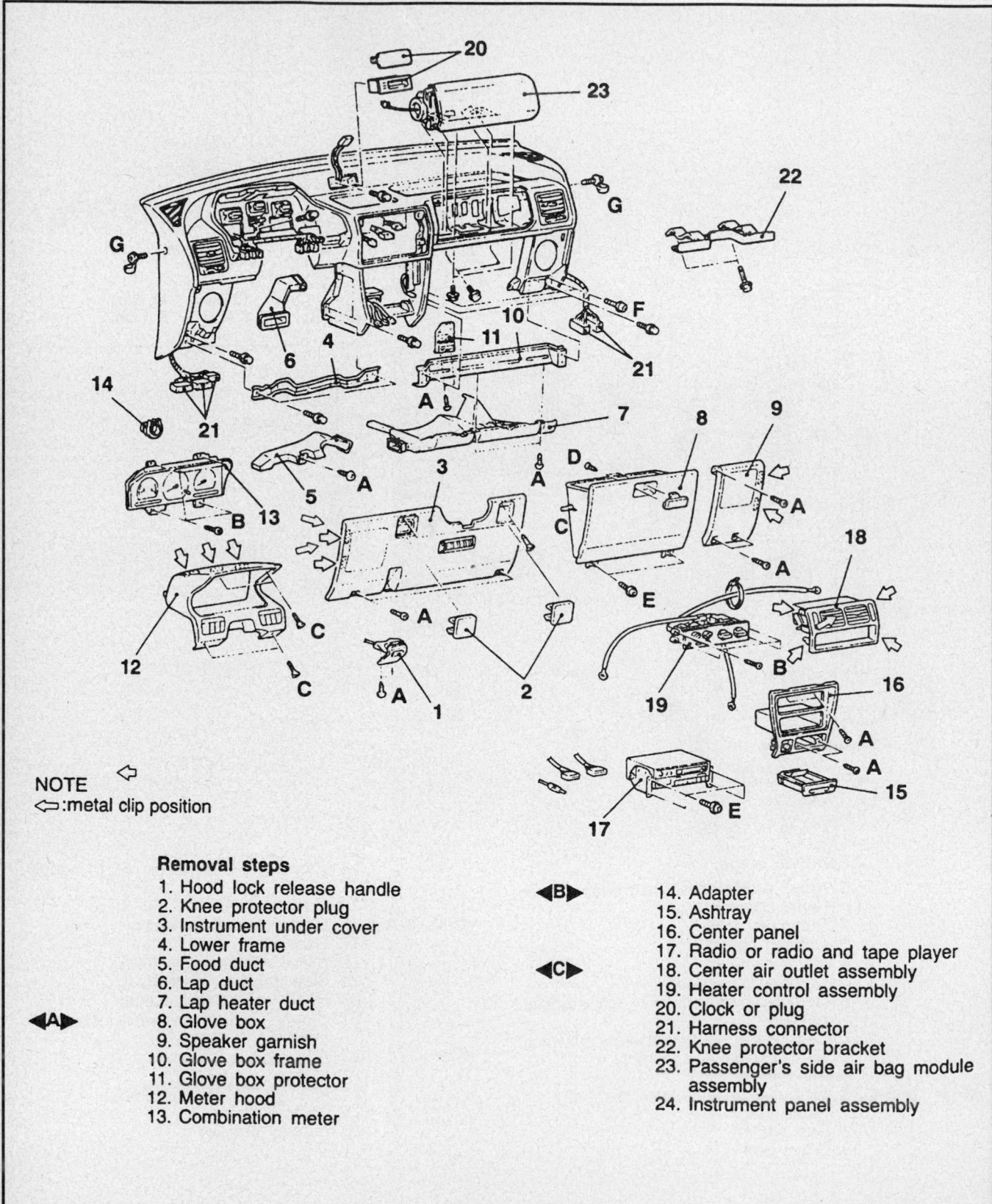

NOTE
⇦ :metal clip position

Removal steps
1. Hood lock release handle
2. Knee protector plug
3. Instrument under cover
4. Lower frame
5. Food duct
6. Lap duct
7. Lap heater duct
◄**A**► 8. Glove box
9. Speaker garnish
10. Glove box frame
11. Glove box protector
12. Meter hood
13. Combination meter

◄**B**► 14. Adapter
15. Ashtray
16. Center panel
17. Radio or radio and tape player
◄**C**► 18. Center air outlet assembly
19. Heater control assembly
20. Clock or plug
21. Harness connector
22. Knee protector bracket
23. Passenger's side air bag module assembly
24. Instrument panel assembly

Instrument panel and related components—Colt Vista

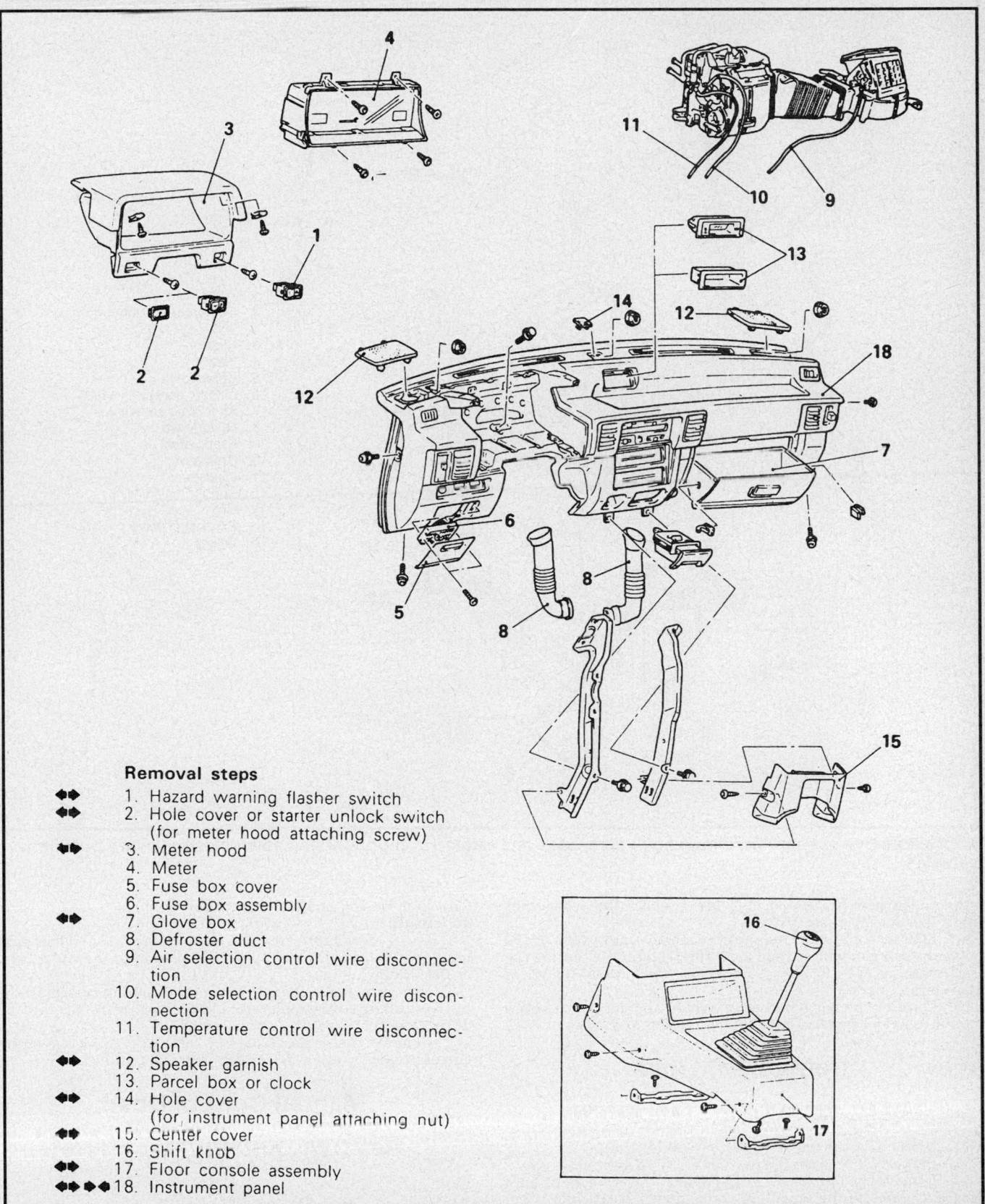

Removal steps

1. Hazard warning flasher switch
2. Hole cover or starter unlock switch
   (for meter hood attaching screw)
3. Meter hood
4. Meter
5. Fuse box cover
6. Fuse box assembly
7. Glove box
8. Defroster duct
9. Air selection control wire disconnection
10. Mode selection control wire disconnection
11. Temperature control wire disconnection
12. Speaker garnish
13. Parcel box or clock
14. Hole cover
    (for instrument panel attaching nut)
15. Center cover
16. Shift knob
17. Floor console assembly
18. Instrument panel

Instrument panel and related components—Ram 50

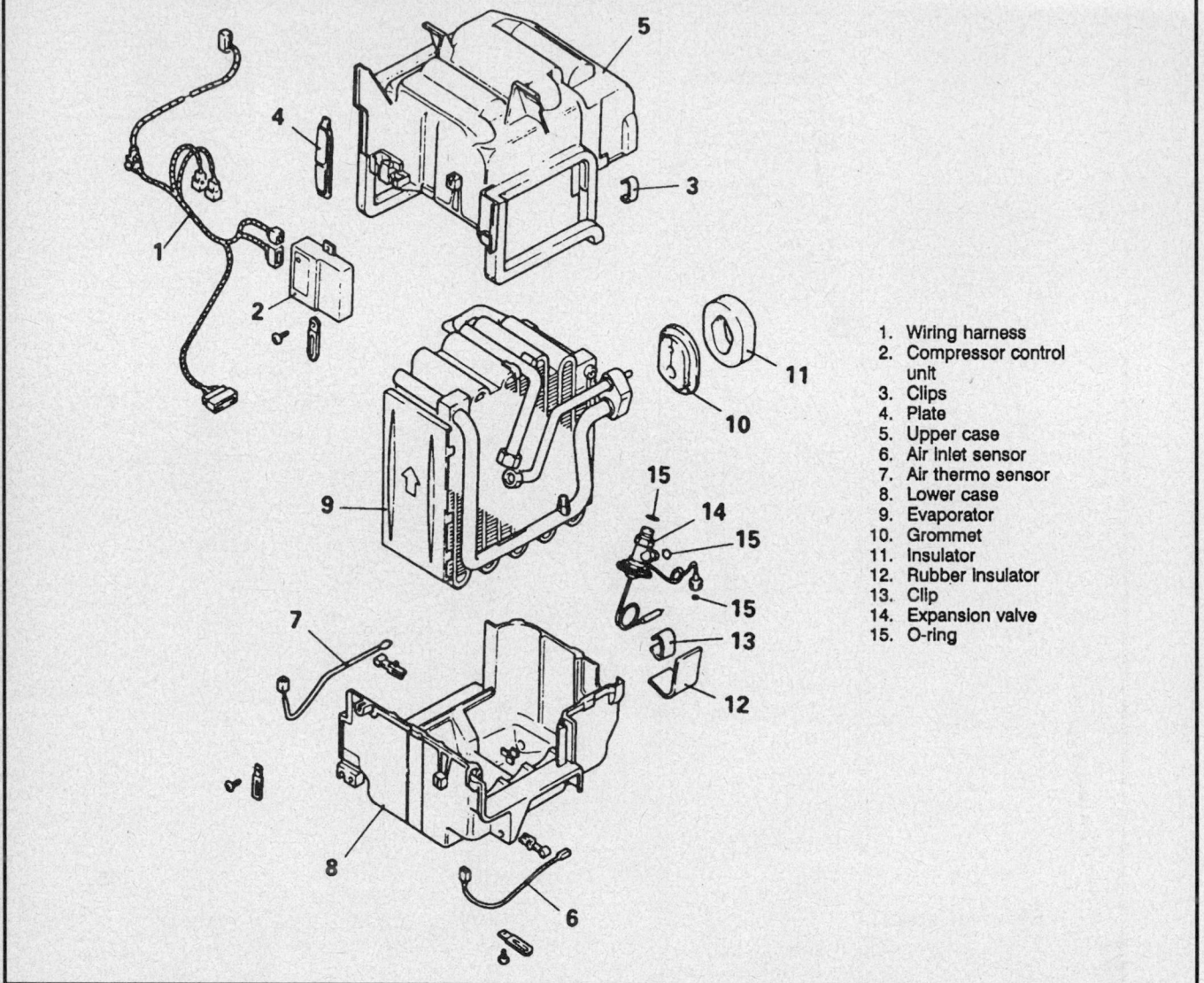

1. Wiring harness
2. Compressor control unit
3. Clips
4. Plate
5. Upper case
6. Air inlet sensor
7. Air thermo sensor
8. Lower case
9. Evaporator
10. Grommet
11. Insulator
12. Rubber insulator
13. Clip
14. Expansion valve
15. O-ring

Representative evaporator, expansion valve, case and related components—Assemblies may vary between vehicles

16. Using new lubricated O–rings, connect the refrigerant lines to the evaporator.

17. Evacuate and recharge the air conditioning system. If the evaporator was replaced, add 2 oz. of refrigerant oil during the recharge, except 1994–95 Colt Vista which uses 1.3 oz. of refrigerant oil.

18. Connect the negative battery cable and check the entire climate control system for proper operation and leaks.

Refrigerant Lines

REMOVAL AND INSTALLATION

1. Disconnect the negative battery cable.
2. Properly discharge the air conditioning system.
3. Remove the nuts or bolts that attach the refrigerant lines sealing plates to the adjoining components. If the line is not equipped with a sealing plate, separate the flare connection. Always use a back-up wrench when separating flare connections.

4. Remove the line and discard the O–rings.

To install:

5. Using new lubricated O–rings, connect the refrigerant lines to the adjoining components and tighten the nuts, bolts or flare connections.

6. Evacuate and recharge the air conditioning system. If the refrigerant line was replaced, add 0.30 oz. of refrigerant oil during the recharge.

7. Connect the negative battery cable and check the entire climate control system for proper operation and leaks.

Manual Control Head

REMOVAL AND INSTALLATION

Colt

1. Disconnect the negative battery cable.
2. Remove the knee protector panel beneath the steering column. Detach the mode selection cable from the heater unit,

then remove the center panel assembly screws and remove the panel.

3. Remove the foot duct.
4. Remove the glove box.
5. Detach the fresh/recirc cable, temperature control cable, and mode selection cable from their respective air doors.
6. Remove the control head assembly.
7. Remove the clock or plug from the bottom of the assembly.
8. Reverse removal procedure to install components.
9. Adjust the cables as required.
10. Check control head for proper operation.

Colt Vista

1. Disconnect the negative battery cable. Remove the lap heater duct beneath the glove box.
2. Remove the glove box assembly.
3. Remove the hood release handle and the knee panel under the steering column.
4. Remove the left side lap air duct.
5. Remove the ashtray, the center panel bezel, and the radio assembly.
6. Remove the clip on the lower section of the center air outlet. Then, insert a small prybar into the outlet grille and disconnect the top spring clips. Remove the air outlet assembly.
7. Detach the cables at the air doors.
8. Remove the control panel assembly, detaching electrical connectors.
9. Reverse removal procedure to install components.
10. Adjust the cables as required.
11. Check control head for proper operation.

Ram 50

1. Disconnect the negative battery cable.
2. Remove the glove box stoppers and lower the glove box. Reach inside opening and remove the air selection cable from the blower housing.
3. Remove the knobs from the control panel. Remove the center panel lower retaining screws, then use a trim stick to disengage the top edge of the panel.
4. Remove the defroster duct from under the left side of the instrument panel to gain access to the control cables on the heater housing. Label and disconnect the mode selection cable and the temperature control cable.
5. Remove the control head, disconnecting wiring from blower switch and A/C switch (if equipped).
To install:
6. Reattach switch wiring, then position and attach the control head.
7. Reconnect the temperature and mode selection cables to the control head.
8. Install the defroster duct.
9. Install the center panel, then reposition the control panel knobs.
10. Reattach the selection cable to the blower housing, then raise the glove box and install its stoppers.
11. Connect the negative battery cable.
12. Adjust the cables as required.
13. Check control head for proper operation.

Manual Control Cables

ADJUSTMENT

Colt

1. Disconnect the negative battery cable.
2. Remove the glove box, if necessary.

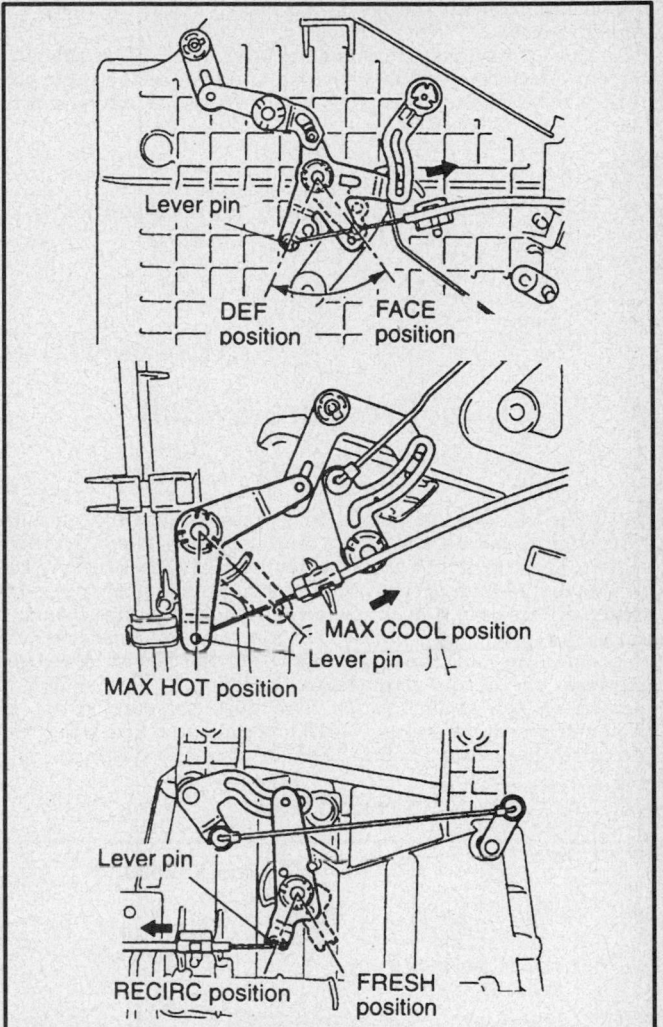

Adjusting manual control cables—Colt

3. Move the mode selection panel knob to **DEF**. Set the mode door lever (cable connection end) to the **DEF** position (push it away from the cable). Pull the outer cable cover away from the lever until the slack is gone, then clip it in place.
4. Set the temperature control knob to **MAX HOT**. Move the temperature (air mix) door lever to the **MAX HOT** position (cable attaching end pushed away from the cable). Pull the cable outer cover away from the lever until the slack is gone, then clip it in place.
5. Set the fresh/recirc selector lever to the **RECIRC** position. Move the door lever toward the cable so it is at the **RECIRC** position and attach the cable. Pull the outer cable housing to remove all slack, then clip the cable in place.

Colt Vista

1. Set the fresh/recirc control knob to **RECIRC**. Pull the top end of the air door lever toward the cable to set the lever against its stopper. Install the cable to the lever, hold the lever and pull the cable away to remove all slack. Clip the cable in place.
2. Set the mode knob to **DEF**. Move the air outlet door lever so the cable attachment moves away from the cable clip.

Attach the cable on the lever, remove all slack, then clip the cable in place.

3. Move the temperature knob to **MAX HOT**. Move the temperature door lever cable attaching end toward the cable clip until it stops. Attach the cable, remove all slack and clip it in place.

Ram 50

1. Move the mode selection lever to the **DEF** position.

2. Set the mode door lever (cable connection end) to the **DEF** position (push it away from the cable). Pull the outer cable cover away from the lever until the slack is gone, then clip it in place.

3. Pull the **VENT** damper lever completely downward and move the **VENT** damper into position. Attach the cable and clip in place

4. Pull the **FOOT/DEF** damper lever completely downward and move the **FOOT/DEF** damper into position. Attach the cable and clip into position.

SENSORS AND SWITCHES

Dual Pressure Switch

TESTING

Colt with 1.5L engine, uses a dual pressure switch. Colt with 1.8L engine and all Colt Vista models, use a triple pressure switch. These switches are a combination of a low pressure cut off switch and high pressure cut off switch. The triple pressure switch differs only that it also has a middle pressure monitoring position. The high pressure or low pressure functions will stop operation of the compressor in the event of either extreme, preventing damage to the system. The switch is located on the receiver/drier. The dual pressure switch is designed to cut off voltage to the compressor coil when the pressure either drops below 30 psi or rises above 384 psi.

TESTING

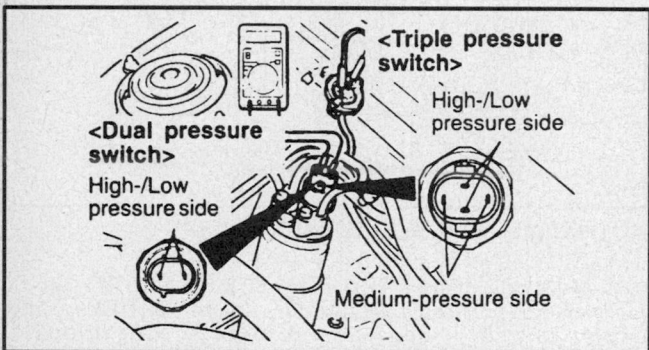

Testing dual and triple pressure switches—Colt and Colt Vista

1. Check for continuity through the switch. Under all normal conditions, the switch should be continuous.
2. If the switch is open, check for insufficient refrigerant charge or excessive pressures.
3. If neither of the above conditions exist and the switch is open, replace the switch.

REMOVAL AND INSTALLATION

1. Disconnect the negative battery cable.
2. Properly discharge the air conditioning system.
3. Remove the switch from the refrigerant line or receiver/drier.
4. Reverse removal procedure to install components.
5. Evacuate and recharge the air conditioning system.
6. Connect the negative battery cable and check the entire climate control system for proper operation and leaks.

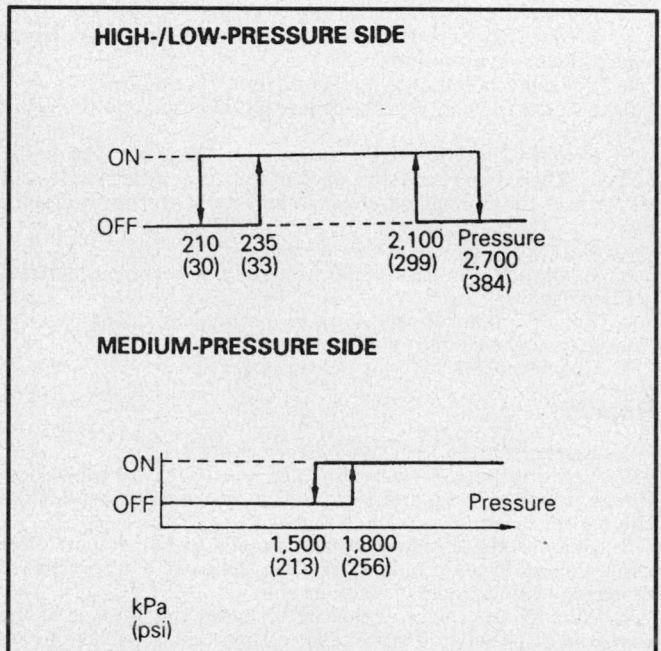

Dual and triple pressure switch operating characteristics—Colt and Colt Vista

Low Pressure Cut Off Switch

TESTING

Ram 50

On Ram 50, the low pressure cut off switch monitors the refrigerant gas pressure on the suction side of the system. The switch is connected in series with the compressor and will turn off voltage to the compressor clutch coil when the monitored pressure drops to levels that could damage the compressor. The switch is located on the receiver/drier and is a sealed unit that must be replaced if faulty.

TESTING

1. Disconnect the switch connector and use a jumper wire to jump between terminals inside the connector boot.
2. Press the A/C switch and blower switch **ON**.
3. Momentarily turn the ignition switch to **ON** (do not crank the engine). Listen for the clutch to engage.

4. If the compressor clutch does not engage, inspect the system for an open circuit.

5. If the clutch engages, connect an air conditioning manifold gauge to the system.

6. Read the low pressure gauge. The low pressure cut off switch should complete the circuit at pressures of at least 30 psi. Check the system for leaks if the pressures are too low.

7. If the pressures are nominal and the system works when the terminals are jumped, the cut off switch is faulty and should be replaced.

REMOVAL AND INSTALLATION

1. Disconnect the negative battery cable.
2. Properly discharge the air conditioning system.
3. Unplug the boot connector from the switch.
4. Using an oil pressure sending unit socket, remove the switch from the receiver/drier.

To install:

5. Seal the threads of the new switch with teflon tape.
6. Install the switch to the receiver/drier and connect the boot connector.
7. Evacuate and recharge the system. Check for leaks.
8. Check the switch for proper operation.

Refrigerant Temperature Switch

TESTING

Colt

Located on the rear of the compressor, the refrigerant temperature switch detects the temperature of the refrigerant delivered from the compressor during operation. The switch is designed to cut off the compressor when the temperature of the refrigerant exceeds 311°F (155°C), preventing overheating.

TESTING

1. Check for continuity between switch terminals at room temperature. When refrigerant temperature exceeds 311°F (155°C), the switch contacts should open and there should not be continuity.
2. If switch does not operate as above, replace the switch.

REMOVAL AND INSTALLATION

1. Disconnect the negative battery cable.
2. Properly discharge the air conditioning system.
3. Disconnect the connector.
4. Remove the mounting screws and the sensor from the compressor.
5. Reverse removal procedure to install components
6. Use a new lubricated O-ring when installing.
7. Evacuate and recharge the air conditioning system.
8. Connect the negative battery cable and check the entire climate control system for proper operation and leaks.

Engine Coolant Temperature Sensor

TESTING

Colt 1.8L and Colt Vista

The engine coolant temperature sensor converts engine coolant temperature to a voltage signal. The ECM monitors the voltage signal and energizes the compressor clutch relay. The sensor is located on or near the thermostat housing. and is part of the emission control system.

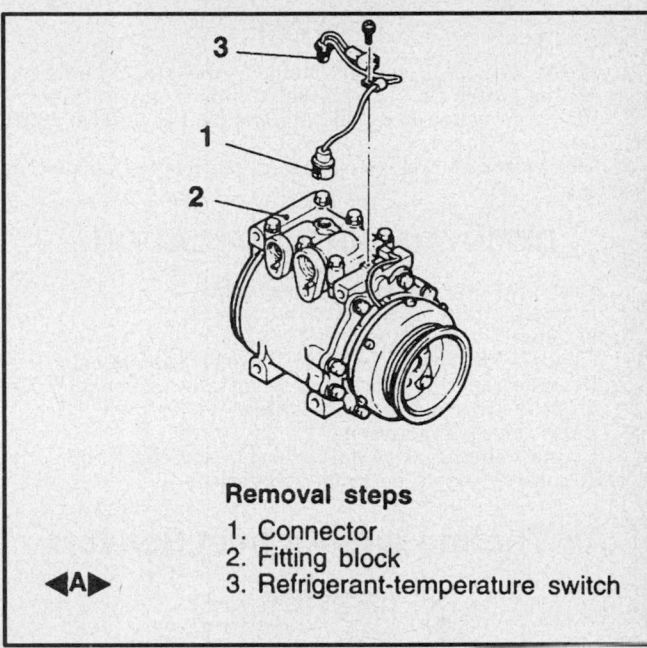

Removal steps
1. Connector
2. Fitting block
3. Refrigerant-temperature switch

◄A►

Refrigerant temperature switch—Colt

TESTING

1. Measure the voltage at the sensor terminals. Specifications are:
- 4.6 volts at –49°F (–45°C)
- 1.6 volt at 104°F (40°C)
- 0.1 volt at 284°F (140°C)

2. If sensor voltages vary by more than 10 percent from specifications, replace the sensor.

REMOVAL AND INSTALLATION

1. Disconnect the negative battery cable.
2. Partially drain out some of the coolant.
3. Unplug the connector.
4. Unscrew the switch from the thermostat housing.
5. Reverse removal procedure to install components.
6. Use sealant on the threads when installing.
7. Refill the cooling system.
8. Connect the negative battery cable and check the entire climate control system for proper operation and leaks.

Engine Coolant Temperature Switch

TESTING

Colt 1.5L and Ram 50

The engine coolant temperature switch, located on or near the thermostat housing, is connected in series with the compressor clutch relay. The switch is designed to cut off the compressor when the engine coolant temperature rises above 239°F (115°C), preventing engine overheating when the supply of cooling air is not sufficient for both the radiator and condenser.

TESTING

1. If the switch is suspect, remove the switch from the engine. The switch should be closed at room temperature.
2. Place the switch in an oil bath and heat to at least 239°F (115°C).
3. The switch should open when it reaches the above temperature.

REMOVAL AND INSTALLATION

1. Disconnect the negative battery cable.
2. Partially drain out some of the coolant.
3. Unplug the connector.
4. Unscrew the switch from the thermostat housing.
5. Reverse removal procedure to install components. Use sealant on the threads when installing.
6. Refill the cooling system.
7. Connect the negative battery cable and check the entire climate control system for proper operation.

Air Thermo and Air Inlet Sensors

TESTING

Except Ram 50

These sensors function as cycling switches. Both sensors are located inside the evaporator housing. The air inlet sensor is normally on the right side of the housing and the air thermo sensor is normally on the left side.

Colt models use only the air thermo sensor.

The air thermo sensor detects the temperature of the air in the passenger compartment and the air inlet sensor detects the temperature of the air coming into the cooling unit. The information is input to the auto compressor control unit and the information is processed, causing the compressor clutch to cycle.

TESTING

1. Disconnect the sensor connector near the evaporator case.
2. Measure the resistance across the wires of the suspect sensor.
3. On Colt, the approximate resistance specifications for the air thermo sensor at different temperatures are:
   - 32°F (0.0°C)–11.4 kilo-ohms
   - 50°F (10°C)–7.32 kilo-ohms
   - 68°F (20°C)–4.86 kilo-ohms
   - 86°F (30°C)–3.31 kilo-ohms
   - 104°F (40°C)–2.32 kilo-ohms
4. On Colt Vista, the approximate resistance specifications for the air thermo sensor at different temperatures are:
   - 32°F (0.0°C)–4.75 kilo-ohms
   - 50°F (10°C)–2.89 kilo-ohms
   - 68°F (20°C)–1.75 kilo-ohms
   - 86°F (30°C)–1.25 kilo-ohms

5. On Colt and Colt Vista, the approximate resistance specifications for the air inlet sensor at different temperatures are:
   - 32°F (0.0°C)–4.75 kilo-ohms
   - 50°F (10°C)–2.89 kilo-ohms
   - 68°F (20°C)–1.75 kilo-ohms
   - 86°F (30°C)–1.25 kilo-ohms
6. Replace the sensor if not within 10 percent of the given specifications.

REMOVAL AND INSTALLATION

1. Disconnect the negative battery cable.
2. Properly discharge the air conditioning system.
3. Remove the evaporator housing and the covers.
4. Unclip the sensor wires from the housing and remove the sensor(s).
5. Reverse removal procedure to install components.
6. Evacuate and recharge the air conditioning system.
7. Connect the negative battery cable and check the entire climate control system for proper operation and leaks.

System Relays

TESTING

Many of the systems within the air conditioning systems use relays to send current on its way and energize various components. The relays are positioned throughout the vehicles and many are interchangeable. All are conventional relays with internal contacts and a coil which pulls the contacts closed when energized.

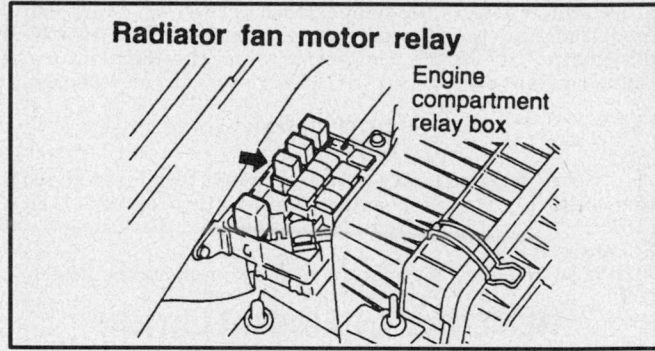

Relay block at right front of engine compartment—Colt

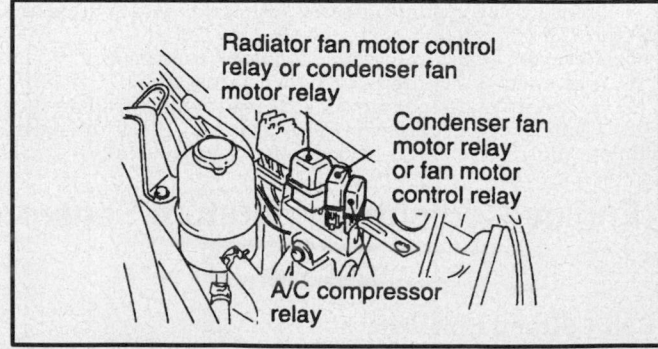

Relay cluster at left front of engine compartment—Colt

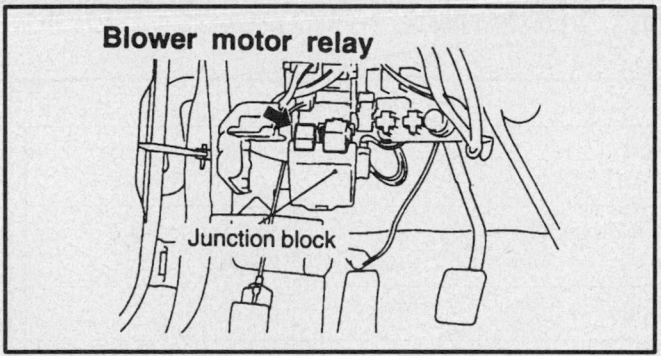

Blower motor relay—Colt

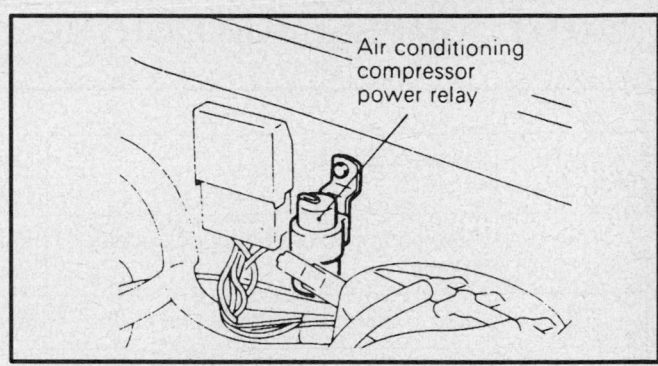

A/C compressor relay at left rear of engine compartment—Ram 50

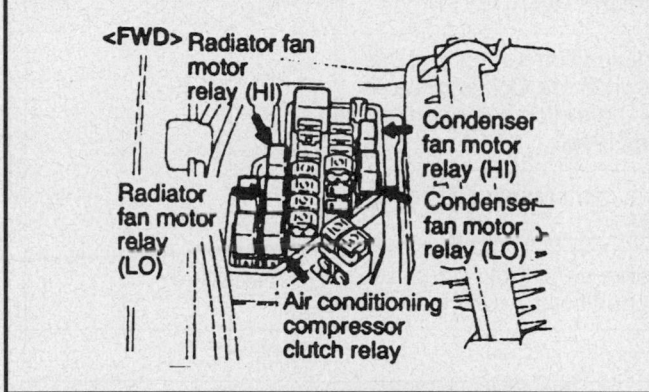

Relay block at right rear of engine compartmet—Colt Vista

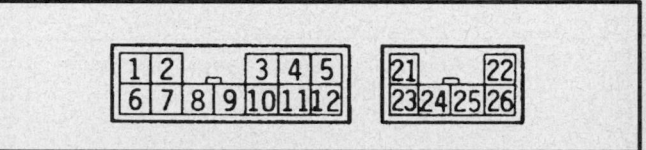

Auto compressor control unit connector terminals—Colt

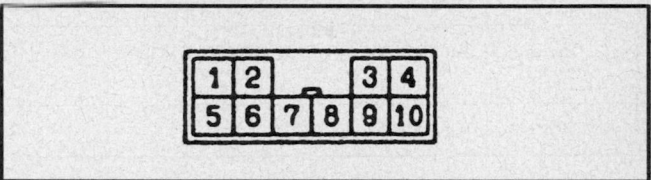

Auto compressor control unit connector terminals—Colt Vista

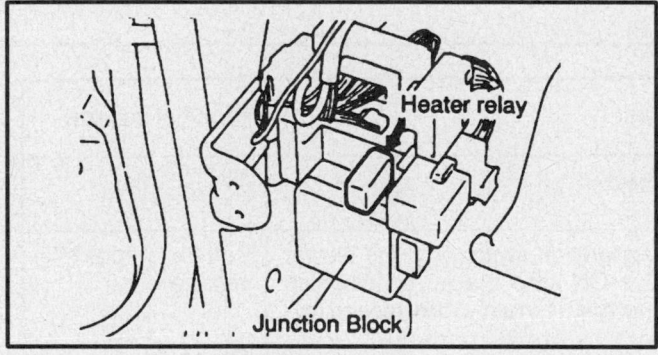

Heater relay under left side of dash—Colt Vista

AUTO COMPRESSOR CONTROL UNIT TERMINAL VOLTAGES—COLT

Terminal No.	Name of Signal	Condition	Terminal voltage
1	Auto compressor control unit power supply	Ignition switch ON	Battery positive voltage
8	Auto compressor control unit earth	At all times	0V
7	Auto compressor control unit power supply (DRY mode)	When the ignition switch and the blower switch are ON, and the air conditioning switch has been turned to the second level	Battery positive voltage
2	Auto compressor control unit power supply (ECONO mode)	When the ignition switch and the blower switch are ON, and the air conditioning switch has been turned to the first level	
6	Air conditioning compressor clutch relay	When the compressor ON conditions are satisfied	
22	Air thermo sensor power supply	The ignition switch, blower switch and air conditioning switch are all ON	Approx. 3V
26	Air thermo sensor	At all times	0V

AUTO COMPRESSOR CONTROL UNIT TERMINAL VOLTAGES—COLT VISTA

Terminal No.	Name of Signal	Condition	Terminal voltage
7	Automatic compressor control unit ground	At all time	0V
3	Automatic compressor control unit power supply (A/C mode)	When the ignition switch and the blower switch are ON, and the air conditioning switch has been turned to the second level	Battery positive voltage
5	Automatic compressor control unit power supply (ECONO mode)	When the ignition switch and the blower switch are ON, and the air conditioning switch has been turned to the first level	Battery positive voltage
1	Air conditioning compressor relay	When the compressor ON conditions are satisfied	Battery positive voltage
8	Air thermo sensor power supply	The ignition switch, blower switch and air conditioning switch are all ON	5V
10	Air thermo sensor	Sensor temperature is 25°C (77°F) [1.5 kΩ]	2.2V

AIR CONDITIONING PERFORMANCE CHART–COLT

Garage ambient temperature °C (°F)	21 (70)	26.7 (80)	32.2 (90)	37.8 (100)	43.3 (110)
Discharge air temperature °C (°F)	2.5–5.0 (36.5–41.0)	3.0–5.5 (37.4–41.9)	3.0–6.0 (37.4–42.8)	3.5–7.5 (38.3–45.5)	3.5–8.0 (38.3–46.4)
Compressor discharge pressure kPa (psi)	650–890 (92.5–126.6)	740–1,040 (105.3–147.9)	750–1,130 (106.7–160.7)	950–1,320 (135.1–187.7)	1,150–1,410 (163.6–200.5)
Compressor suction pressure kPa (psi)	140–210 (19.9–29.9)	140–210 (19.9–29.9)	140–210 (19.9–29.9)	150–220 (21.3–31.3)	150–220 (21.3–31.3)

AIR CONDITIONING PERFORMANCE CHART–COLT VISTA

Garage ambient temperature °C (°F)	20 (68)	25 (77)	35 (95)	45 (113)
Discharge air temperature °C (°F)	10.8 (51.4)	16.8 (62.2)	23.5 (74.3)	24.3 (95.7)
Compressor discharge pressure kPa (psi)	1,030 (149)	1,128 (164)	1,393 (202)	1,736 (252)
Compressor suction pressure kPa (psi)	178 (26)	184 (27)	196 (28)	210 (30)

AIR CONDITIONING PERFORMANCE CHART–RAM 50

Garage ambient temperature °C (°F)	21 (70)	26.7 (80)	32.2 (90)	37.8 (100)	43.3 (110)
Discharge air temperature °C (°F)	2.8–4.4 (37–40)	3.3–5.0 (38–41)	3.9–5.6 (39–42)	4.4–7.2 (40–45)	4.4–7.8 (40–46)
Compressor discharge pressure kPa (psi)	758–1,310 (110–190)	896–1,517 (130–220)	1,103–1,793 (160–260)	1,310–1,999 (190–290)	1,517–2,206 (220–320)
Compressor suction pressure kPa (psi)	131–165 (19–24)	138–179 (20–26)	145–186 (21–27)	152–193 (22–28)	159–200 (23–29)

A/C TROUBLESHOOTING BY SYMPTOM – COLT

No.	Trouble symptom	Problem cause	Remedy
1	Air conditioning does not operate when the ignition switch is in the ON position.	Air conditioning compressor clutch relay is defective	Replace air conditioning compressor clutch relay
		Magnetic clutch is defective	Replace the magnetic clutch
		Refrigerant leak or overfilling of refrigerant	Refill the refrigerant, repair the leak or take out some of the refrigerant
		Dual pressure switch or triple pressure switch is defective	Replace the dual pressure switch or triple pressure switch
		Air conditioning switch is defective	Replace the air conditioning switch
		Blower switch is defective	Replace the blower switch
		Air thermo sensor is defective	Replace the sensor
		Auto compressor control unit is defective	Replace the auto compressor control unit
		Refrigerant temperature switch is defective	Replace the refrigerant temperature switch
2	Interior temperature does not lower (No cold air coming out).	Refrigerant leak	Refill the refrigerant and repair the leak
		Dual pressure switch or triple pressure switch is defective	Replace the dual pressure switch or triple pressure switch
		Air thermo sensor is defective	Replace the sensor
		Refrigerant temperature switch is defective	Replace the refrigerant temperature switch
		Auto compressor control unit is defective	Replace the auto compressor control unit
3	Blower motor does not rotate.	Blower motor relay is defective	Replace the blower motor relay
		Blower motor is defective	Replace the blower motor
		Blower switch is defective	Replace the blower switch
		Resistor (for blower motor) is defective	Replace the resistor
4	Blower motor does not stop rotating.	Short circuit of the harness between the blower motor and the blower switch	Repair the harness
		Blower switch is defective	Replace the blower switch
		Blower motor relay is defective	Replace the blower motor relay
5	Condenser fan does not operate when the air conditioning is activated.	Condenser fan motor relay is defective	Replace the condenser fan motor relay
		Fan motor control relay is defective <1.8L Engine>	Replace the fan motor control relay
		Condenser fan motor is defective	Replace the condenser fan motor
		Dual pressure switch or triple pressure switch is defective	Replace the dual pressure switch or triple pressure switch
		Resistor is defective <1.8L Engine>	Replace the resistor

A/C TROUBLESHOOTING BY SYMPTOM—COLT VISTA

No.	Trouble symptom	Problem cause	Remedy
1	When the ignition switch is "ON", the air conditioning does not operate.	Air conditioning compressor clutch relay is defective	Replace air conditioning clutch compressor relay
		Magnetic clutch is defective	Replace the magnetic clutch
		Refrigerant leak or overfilling of refrigerant	Replenish the refrigerant, repair the leak or take out some of the refrigerant
		Triple pressure switch is defective	Replace the triple pressure switch
		Air conditioning switch is defective	Replace the air conditioning switch
		Blower switch is defective	Replace the blower switch
		Air thermo sensor is defective	Replace the sensor
		Automatic compressor control unit is defective	Replace the automatic compressor control unit
		Belt lock controller is defective <1.8L Engine>	Replace the belt lock controller
		Revolution pick-up sensor is defective <1.8L Engine>	Replace the revolution pick-up sensor
2	When the air conditioning is operating, temperature inside the passenger compartment doesn't decrease (No cool air)	Refrigerant leak	Replenish the refrigerant and repair the leak
		Triple pressure switch is defective	Replace the triple pressure switch
		Air thermo sensor is defective	Replace the sensor
		Automatic compressor control unit is defective	Replace the automatic compressor control unit
3	Blower motor is inoperative	Heater relay is defective	Replace the heater relay
		Blower motor is defective	Replace the blower motor
		Blower switch is defective	Replace the blower switch
		Resistor (for blower motor) is defective	Replace the resistor
4	Blower motor keeps running	Heater relay is defective	Replace heater relay
		Short circuit of the harness between the blower motor and the blower switch	Repair the harness
		Blower switch is defective	Replace the blower switch
5	When the air conditioning is operating, condenser fan does not operate.	Condenser fan motor relay is defective	Replace the condenser fan motor relay
		Condenser fan motor is defective	Replace the condenser fan motor
		Triple pressure switch is defective	Replace the triple pressure switch
		Resistor (for condenser fan motor relay LO side) is defective	Replace the resistor

A/C Control Unit/Automatic Compressor Control Unit

TESTING

The electronic control unit processes information received from various sensors and switches to control the air conditioning compressor. The unit is located behind the glove box on top or on the front side of the evaporator housing. The function of the control unit is to send current to the dual or triple pressure switch when the following conditions are met:

8. The air conditioning switch is in either the **ECONO** or **A/C** mode.
9. The refrigerant temperature switch, if equipped, is reading 311°F (155°C) or less.
10. The air thermo and air inlet sensors, if equipped are both reading at least 39°F (4°C).

TESTING

1. Disconnect the control unit connector.
2. Turn the ignition switch to the **ON** position.
3. Turn the air conditioning switch to the **ON** position.
4. Turn the temperature control lever too its **COOLEST** position.
5. Turn the blower switch to its **HIGHEST** position.
6. Follow the chart and probe the various terminals of the control unit connector under the specified conditions. This will rule out possible faulty components in the system.
7. If all checks are satisfactory, replace the control unit. If not, check the faulty system or component.

REMOVAL AND INSTALLATION

1. Disconnect the negative battery cable.
2. Remove the glove box and locate the control module.
3. Disconnect the connector to the module and remove the mounting screws.
4. Remove the module from the evaporator housing.
5. Reverse removal procedure to install components.
6. Connect the negative battery cable and check the entire climate control system for proper operation.

SYSTEM DIAGNOSIS

Air Conditioning Performance

PERFORMANCE TEST

1. Air temperature in the testing area must be at least 70°F (21°C) to ensure the accuracy of this test.
2. Connect a manifold gauge set to the system.
3. Set the controls to **RECIRC** or **MAX**, the mode lever to the **PANEL** position, temperature control level to the **COOLEST** position and the blower on its **HIGHEST** position.
4. Start the engine and adjust the idle speed to 1000 rpm with the compressor clutch engaged.
5. Allow the engine come to normal operating temperature and keep doors and windows closed.
6. Insert a thermometer in the left center panel outlet and operate the engine for 10 minutes. The clutch may cycle depending on the ambient conditions.
7. With the clutch engaged, compare the discharge air temperature to the performance chart.
8. If the values do not meet specifications, check system components for proper operation.

Air Conditioning Compressor

COMPRESSOR NOISE

Noises that develop during air conditioning operation can be misleading. A noise that sounds like serious compressor damage may only be a loose belt, mounting bolt or clutch assembly. Improper belt tension can also emit a noise that can be mistaken for more serious problems. Check and adjust all possible causes of the noise, including oil level, before replacing the compressor.

COMPRESSOR CLUTCH INOPERATIVE

1. Verify refrigerant charge by observing the sight glass located on the receiver/drier. With the engine running and the compressor clutch engaged the sight glass should be clear. If the sight glass shows bubbles or foaming , the system could be low on refrigerant. Compare the temperature of the compressor inlet and discharge lines. If there is no significant difference in temperature, the system has most of its refrigerant charge. Recharge as required.
2. Check for 12 volts at the clutch coil connection.
3. If voltage is detected, go to clutch coil testing.
4. If voltage is not detected at the clutch coil, use the appropriate wiring schematic to trace the flow of current to the compressor clutch coil. Work backwards through the system's fuses, switches, relays etc. until an open circuit is detected.
5. Inspect all suspect parts and replace as required.
6. When the repair is complete, perform a complete system performance test.

CLUTCH COIL TESTING

1. Disconnect the negative battery cable.
2. Disconnect the compressor clutch connector.
3. Apply 12 volts to the wire leading to the clutch coil. If the clutch is operating properly, an audible click will occur when the clutch is magnetically pulled into the coil. If no click is heard, inspect the coil.
4. Check the resistance across the coil lead wire and ground. The specification is 3.4–3.8 ohms at approximately 70°F (20°C).
5. If not within specifications, replace the clutch coil.

WIRING SCHEMATICS

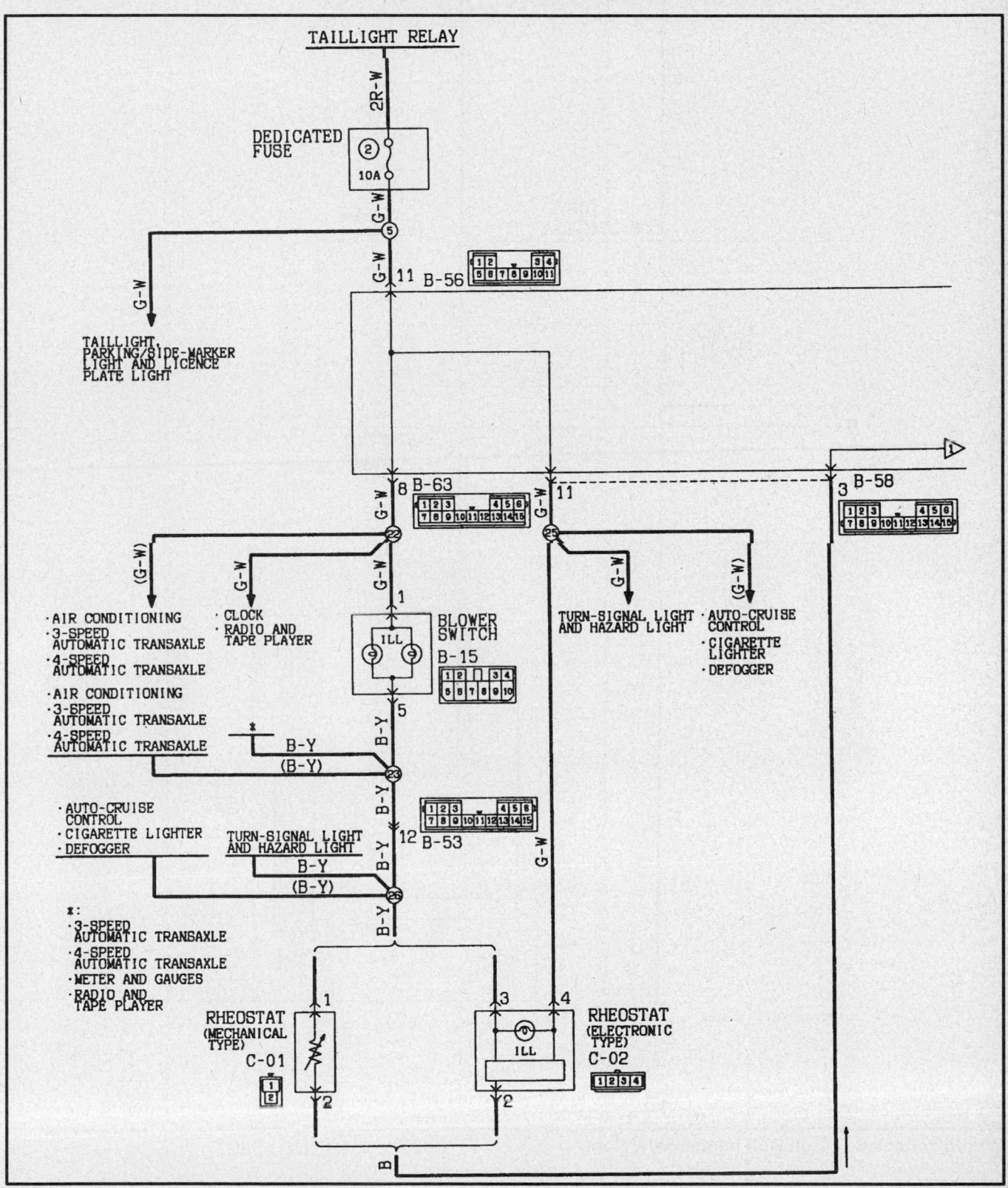

Wiring schematic—Colt with heater only

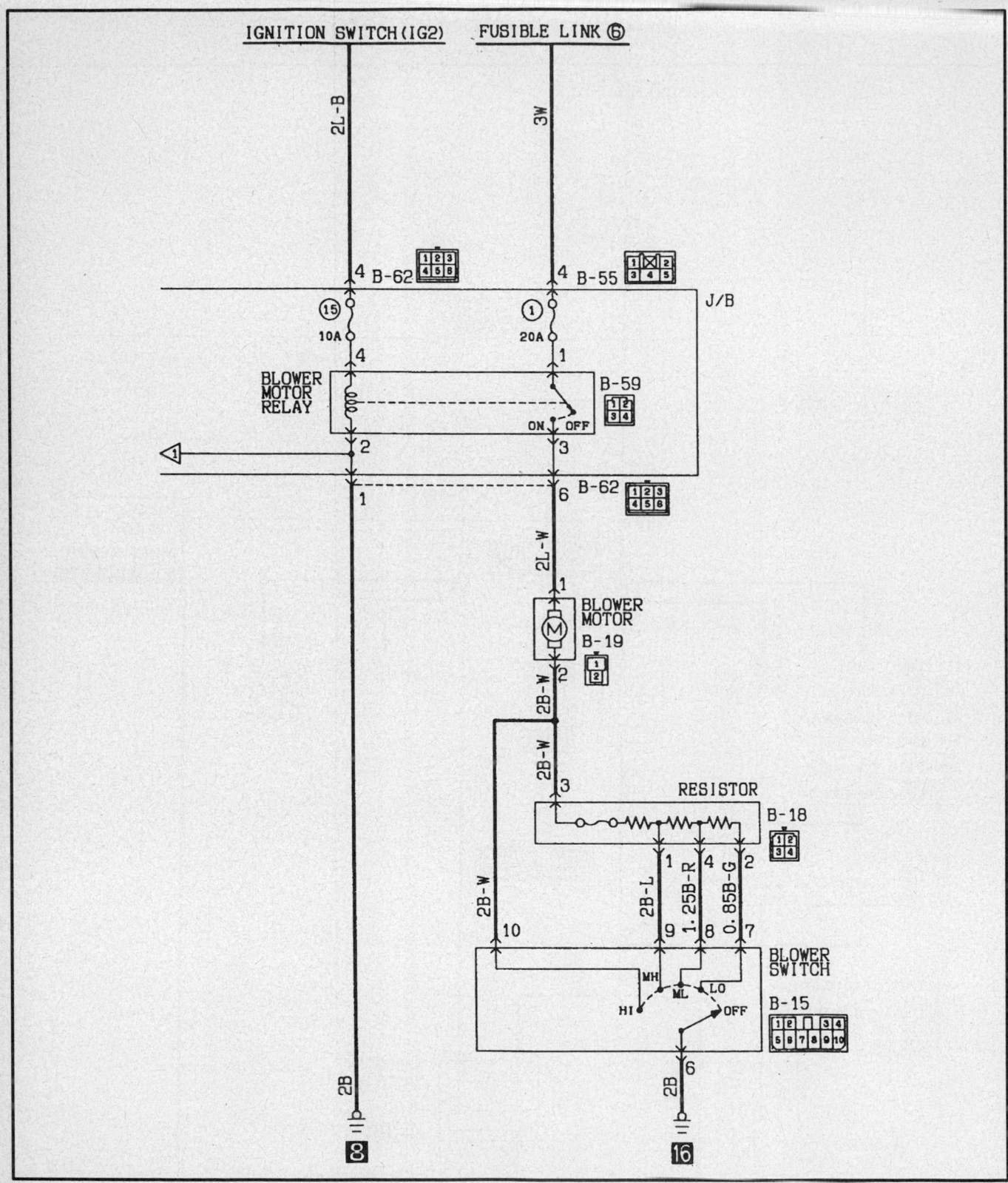

Wiring schematic—Colt with heater only, Cont.

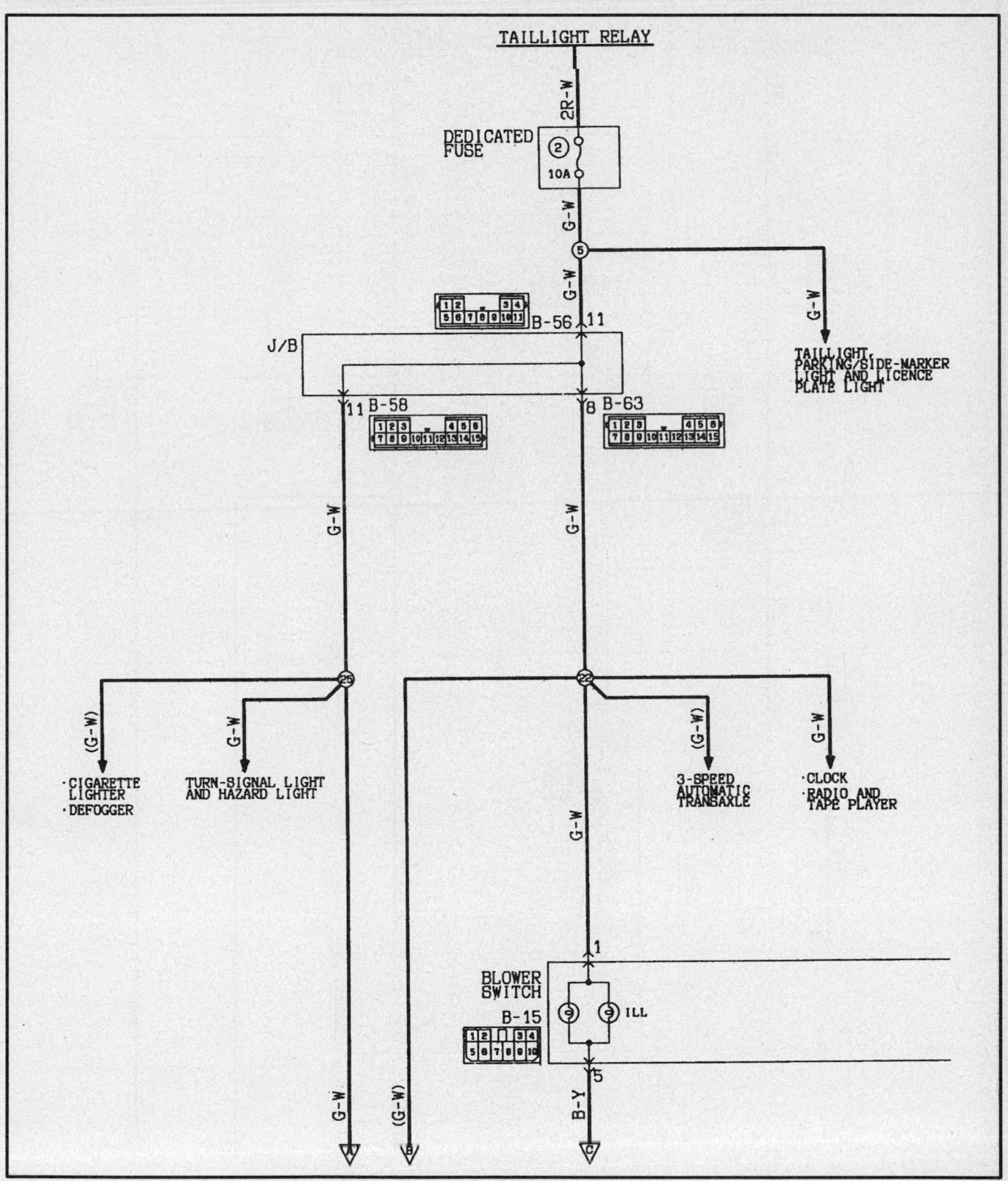

Wiring schematic—Colt with air conditioning–1.5L engine

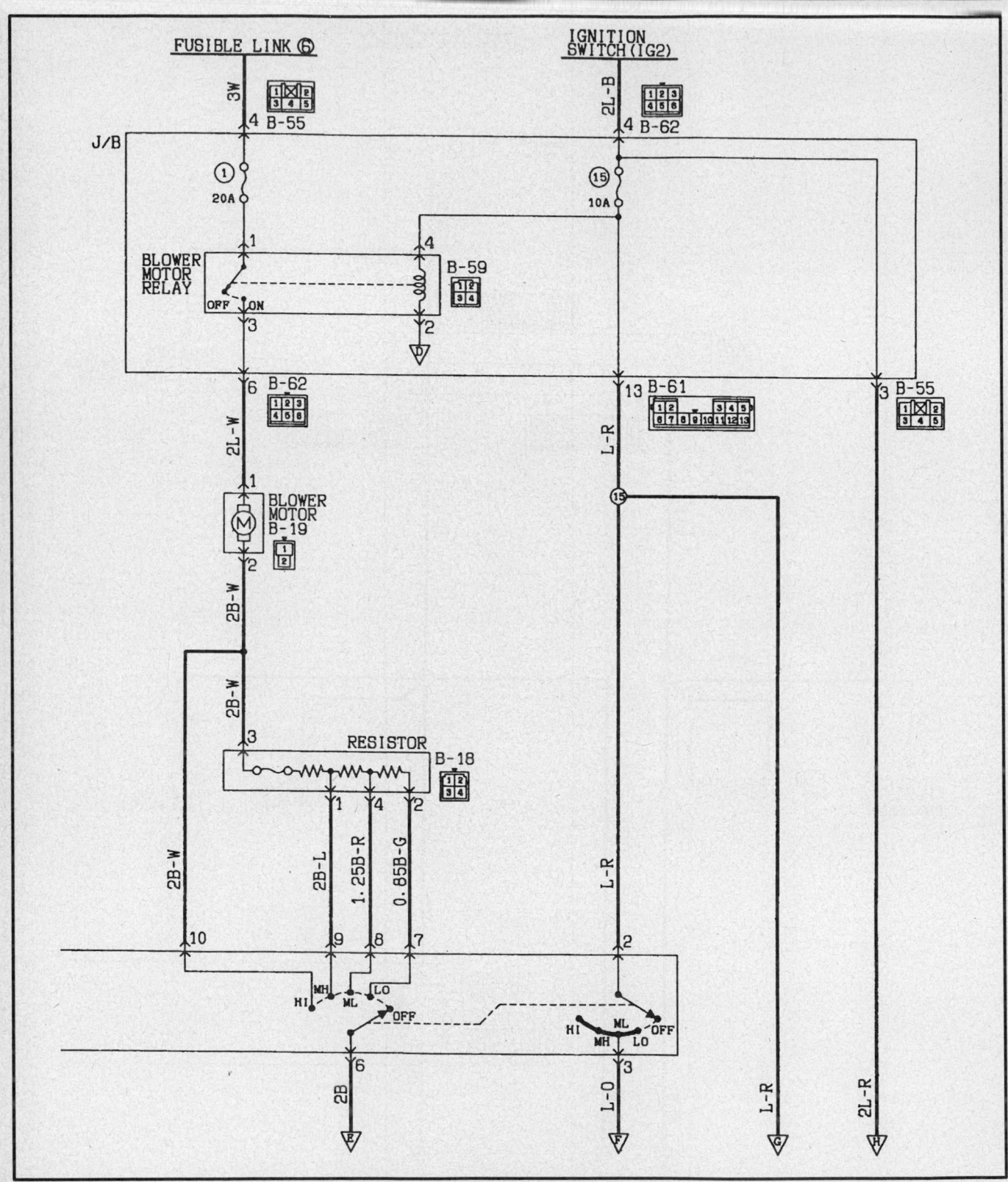

Wiring schematic—Colt with air conditioning—1.5L engine, Cont.

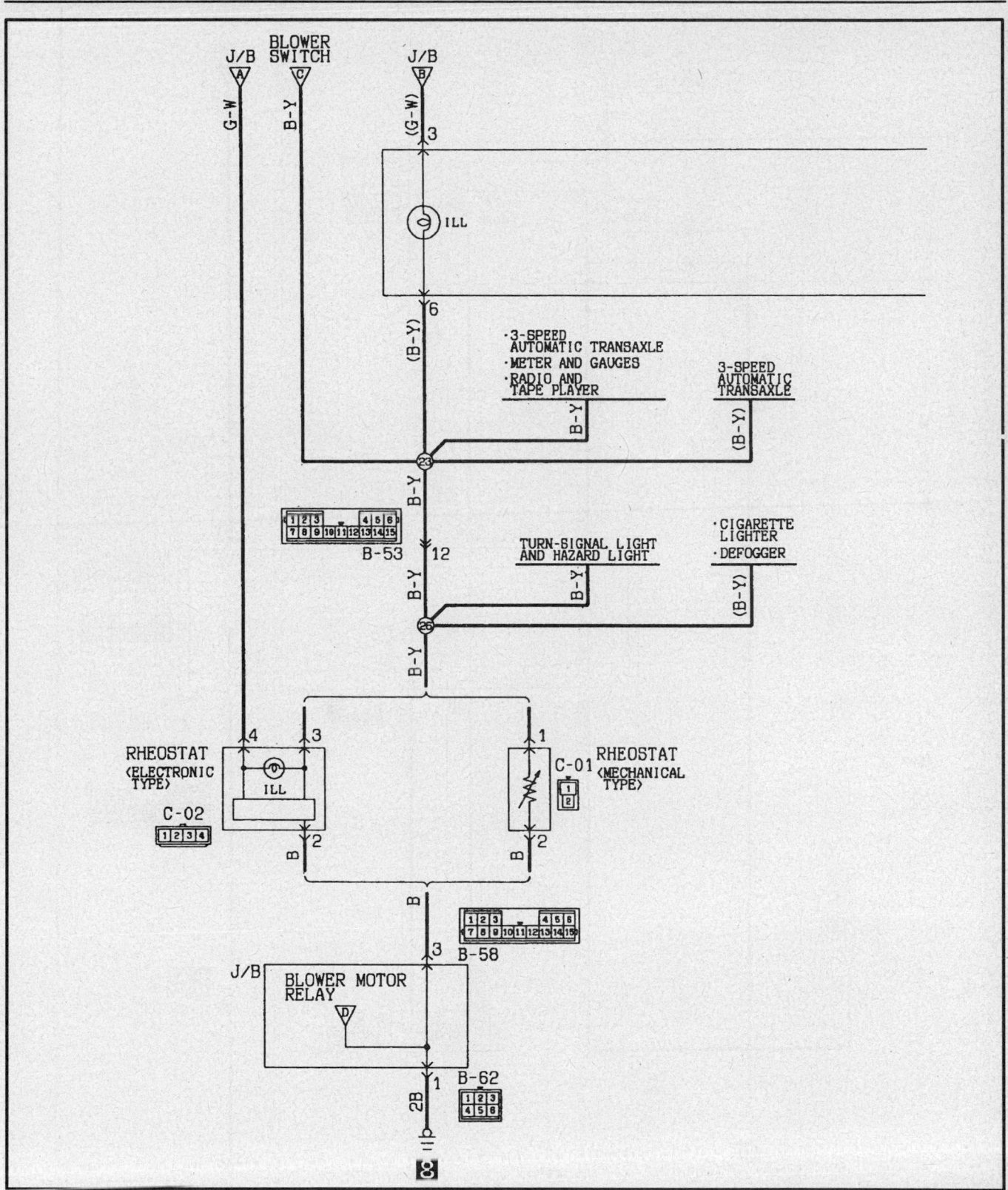

Wiring schematic—Colt with air conditioning–1.5L engine, Cont.

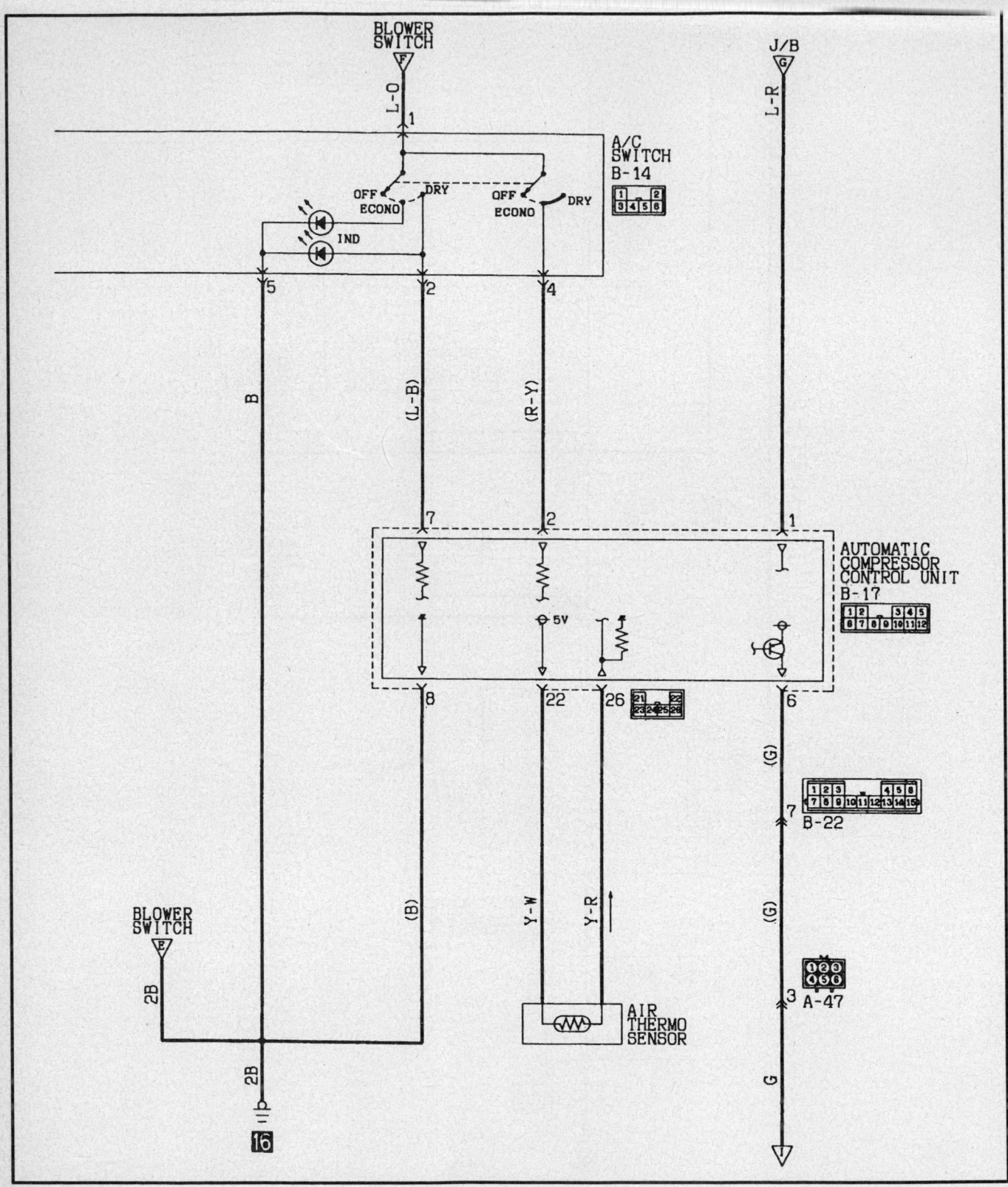

Wiring schematic—Colt with air conditioning—1.5L engine, Cont.

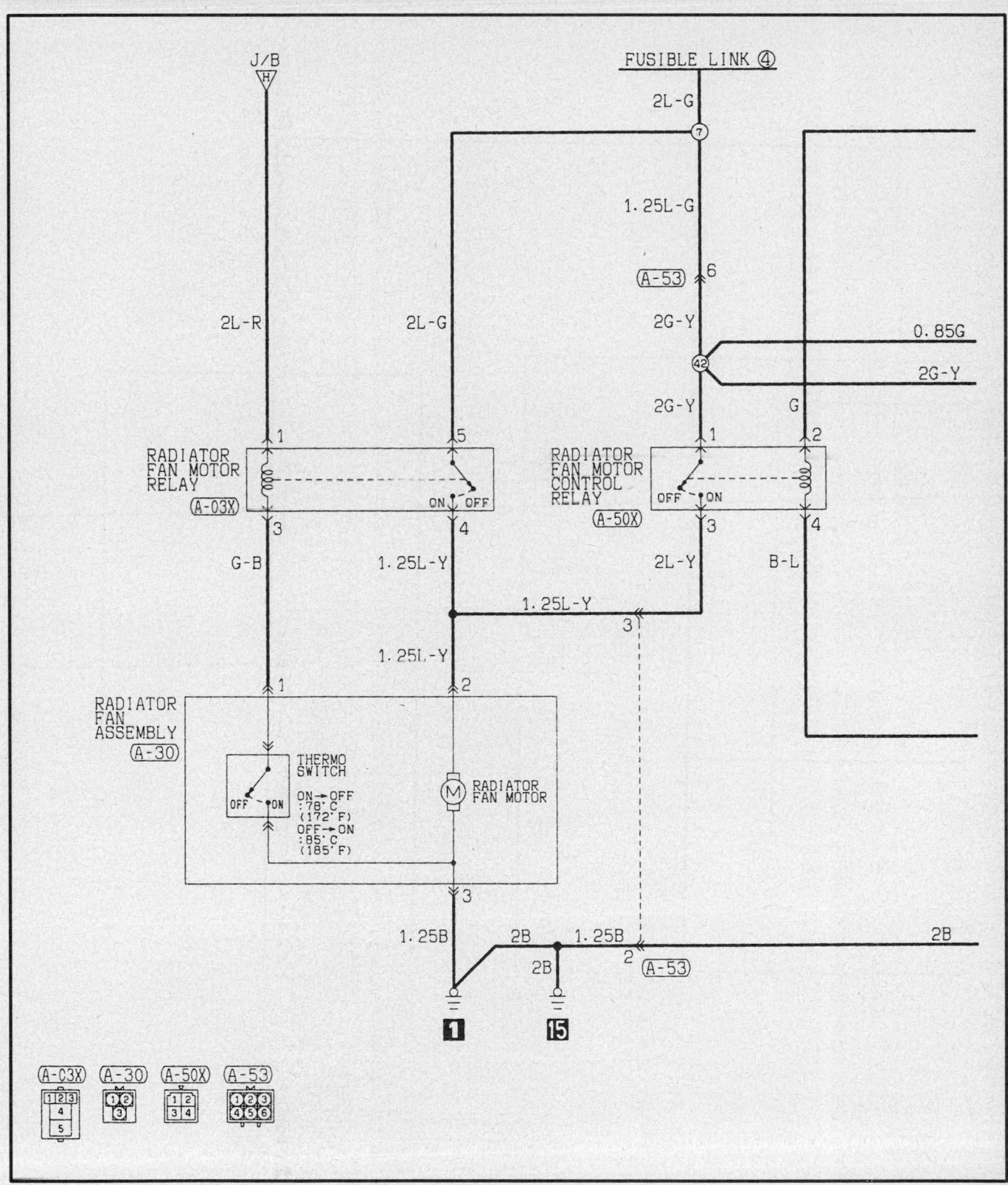

Wiring schematic—Colt with air conditioning—1.5L engine, Cont.

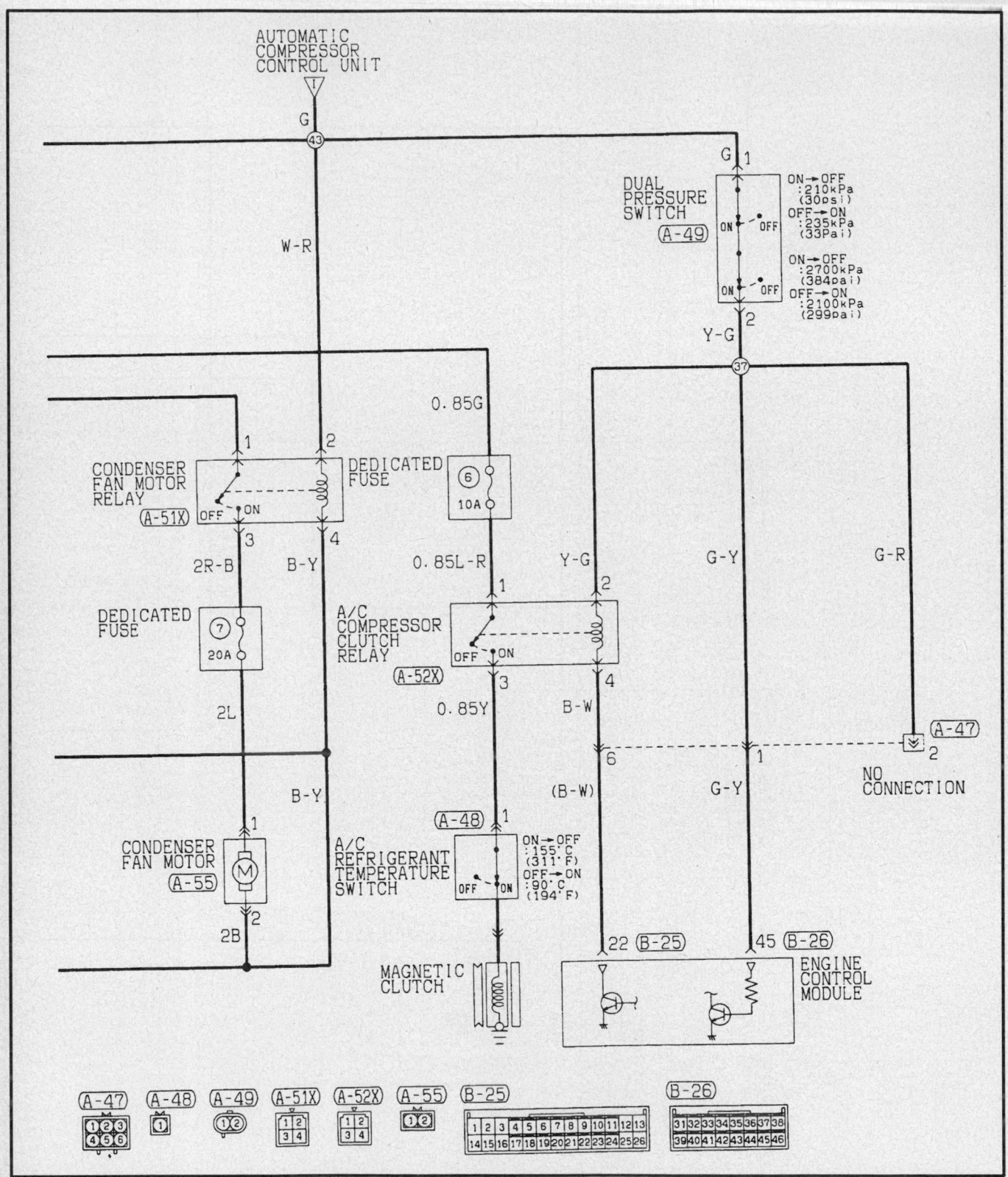

Wiring schematic—Colt with air conditioning—1.5L engine, Cont.

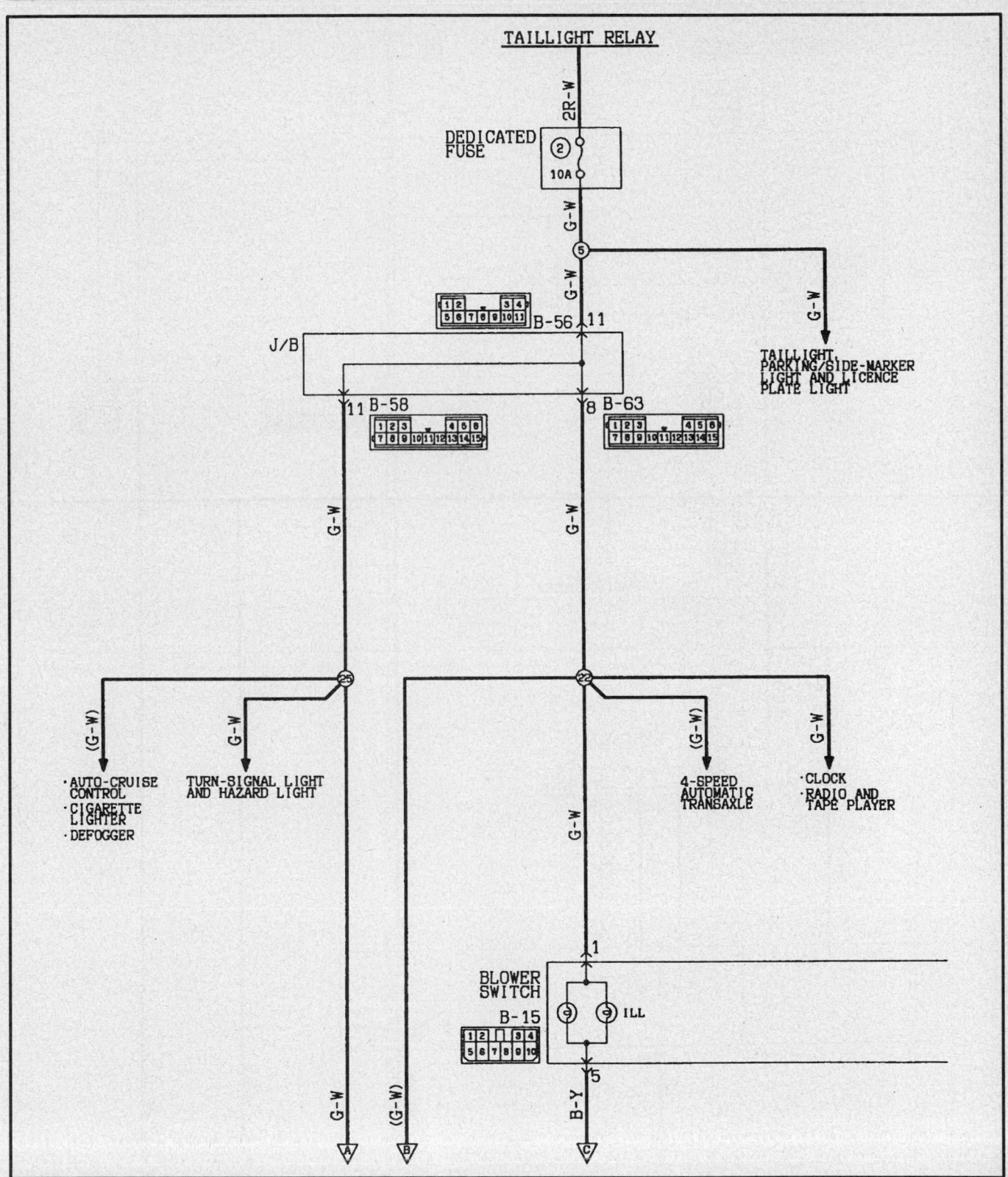

Wiring schematic—Colt with air conditioning—1.8L engine

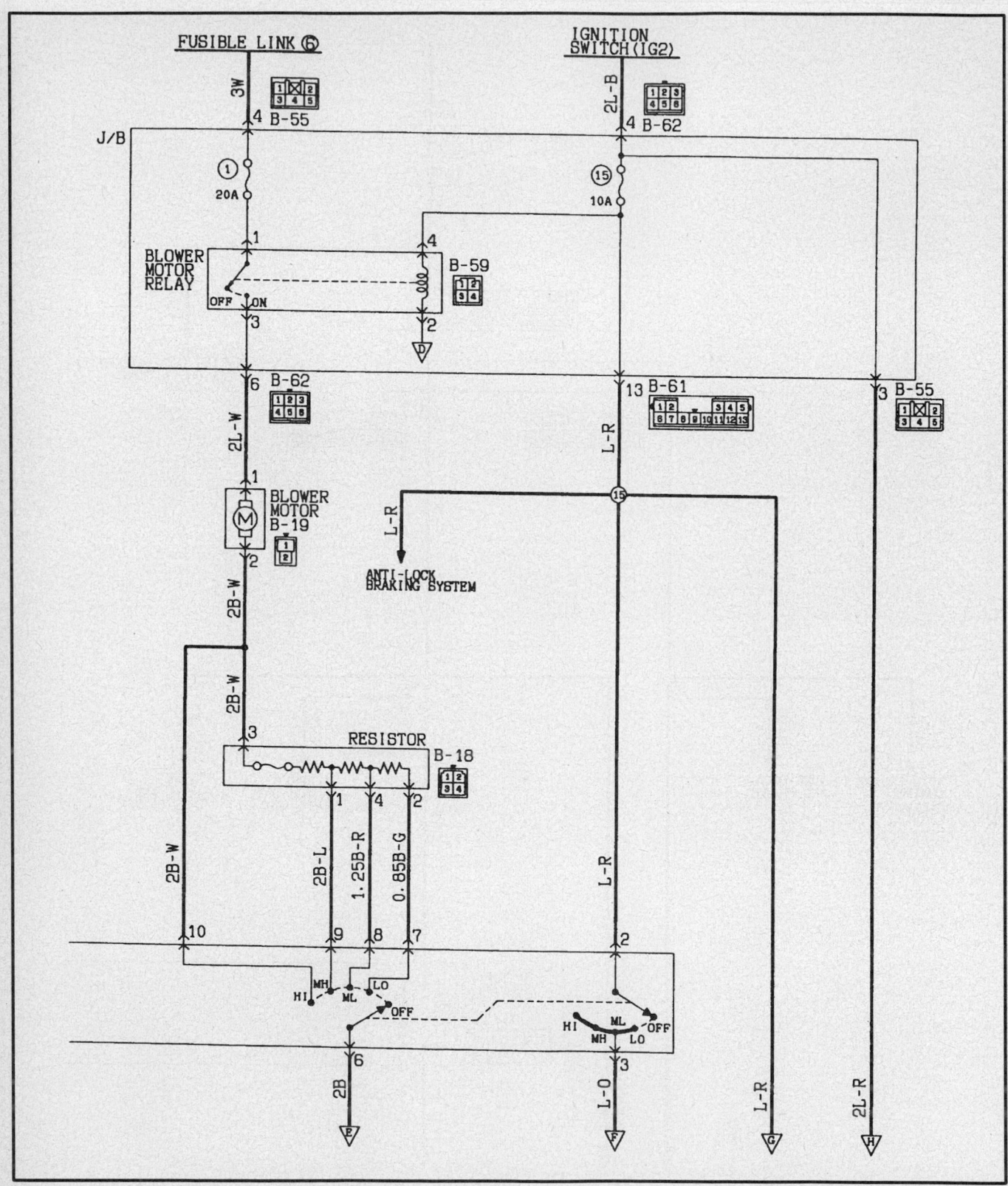

Wiring schematic—Colt with air conditioning—1.8L engine, Cont.

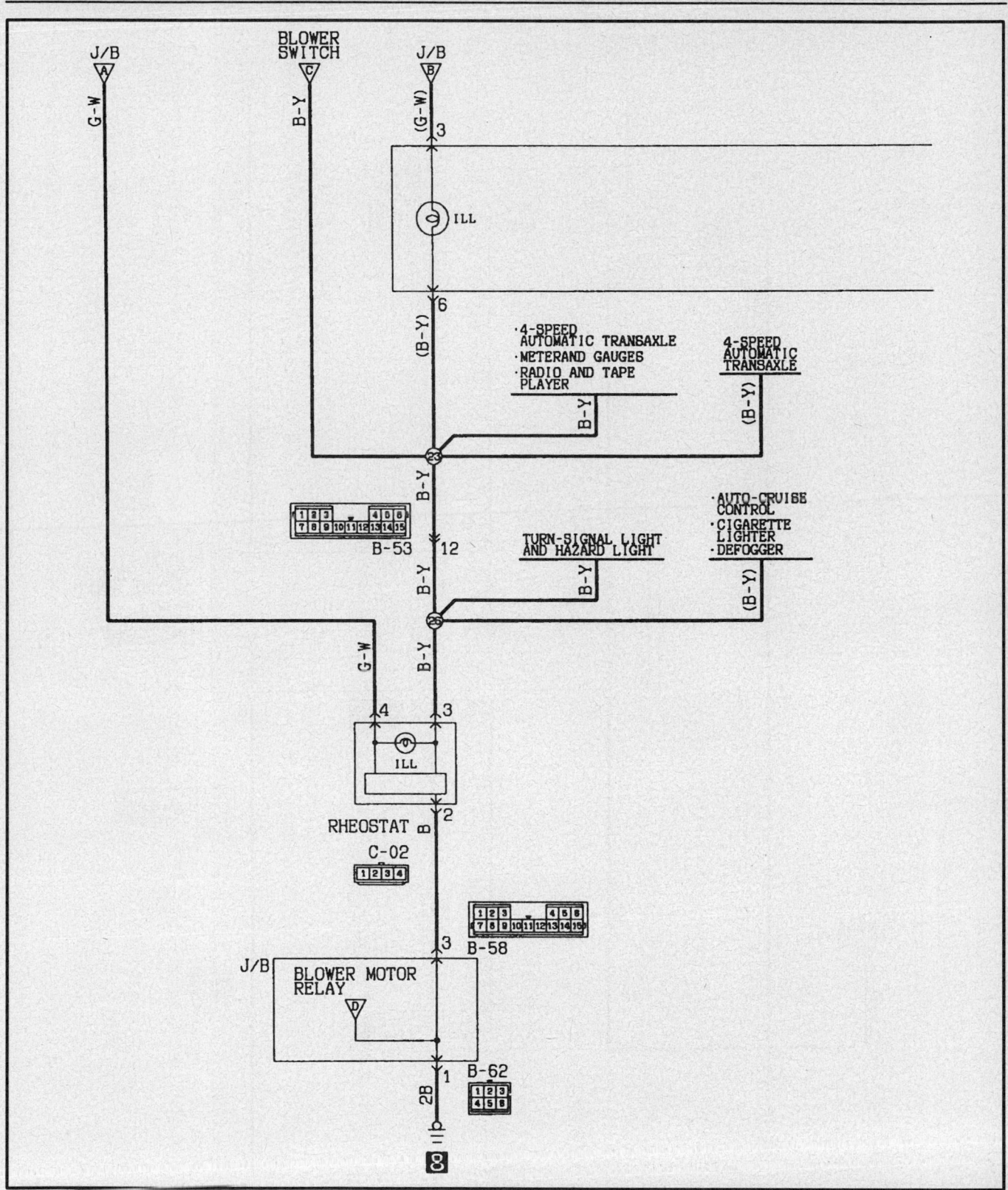

Wiring schematic—Colt with air conditioning—1.8L engine, Cont.

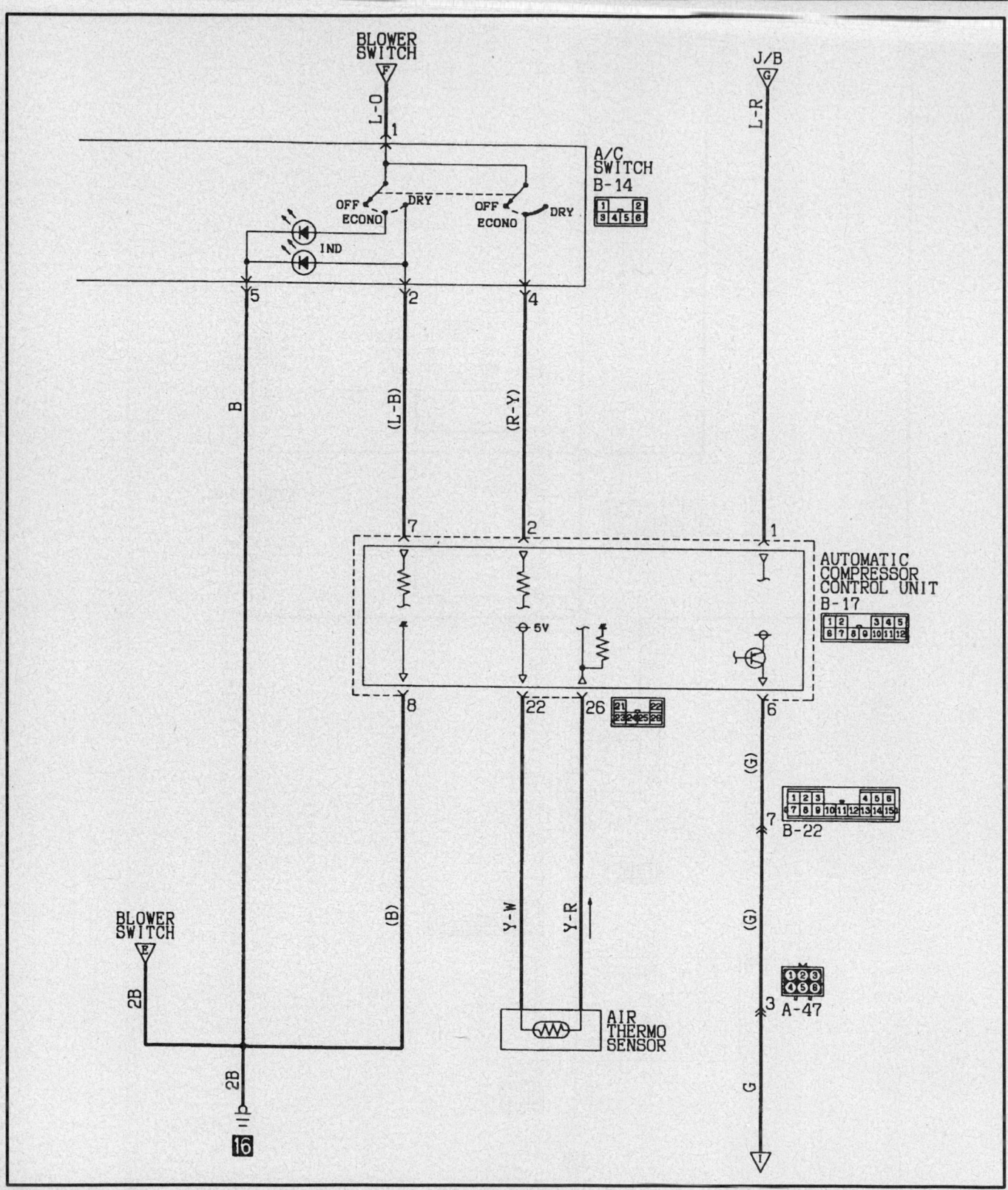

Wiring schematic—Colt with air conditioning–1.8L engine, Cont.

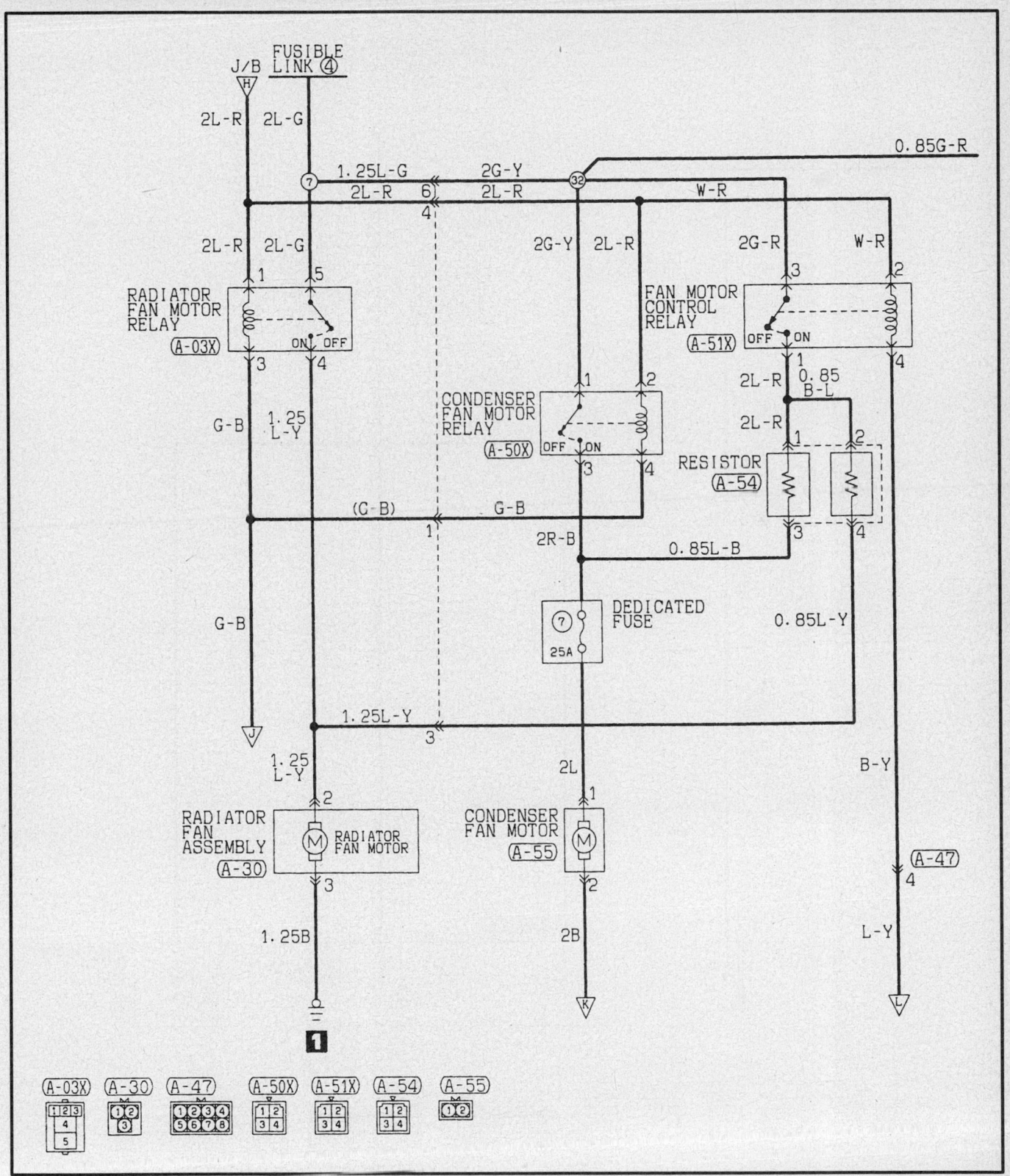

Wiring schematic—Colt with air conditioning—1.8L engine, Cont.

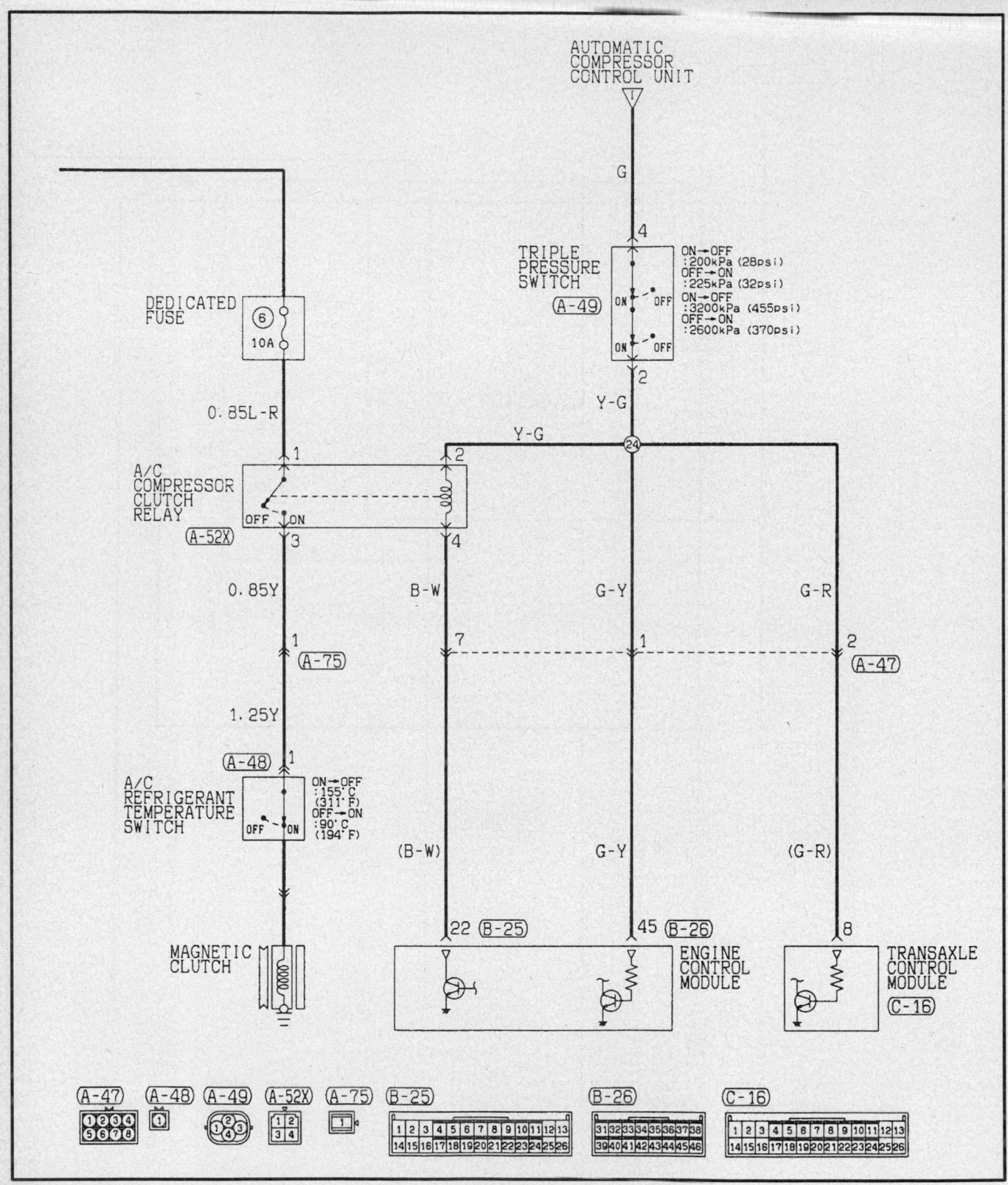

Wiring schematic—Colt with air conditioning—1.8L engine, Cont.

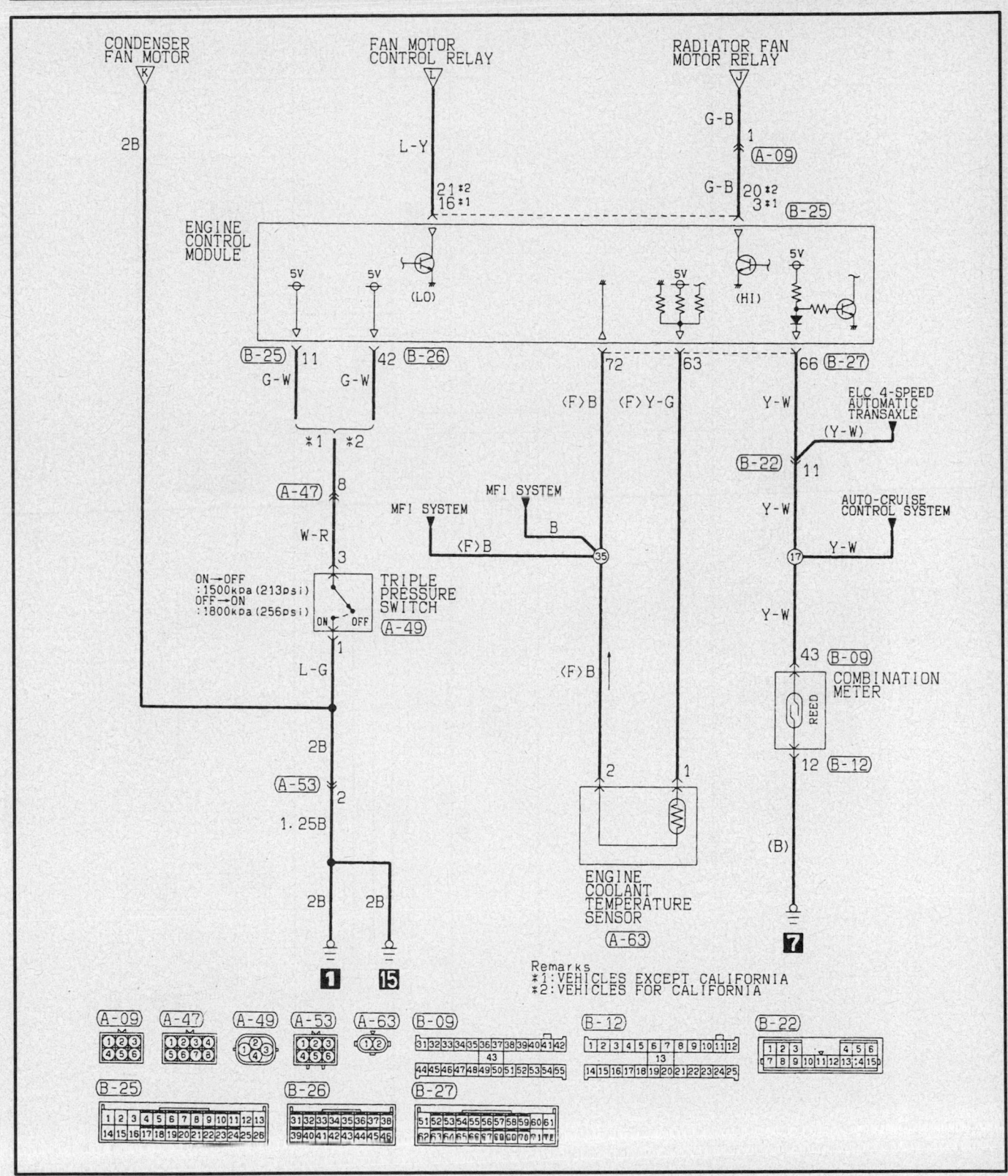

Wiring schematic—Colt with air conditioning—1.8L engine, Cont.

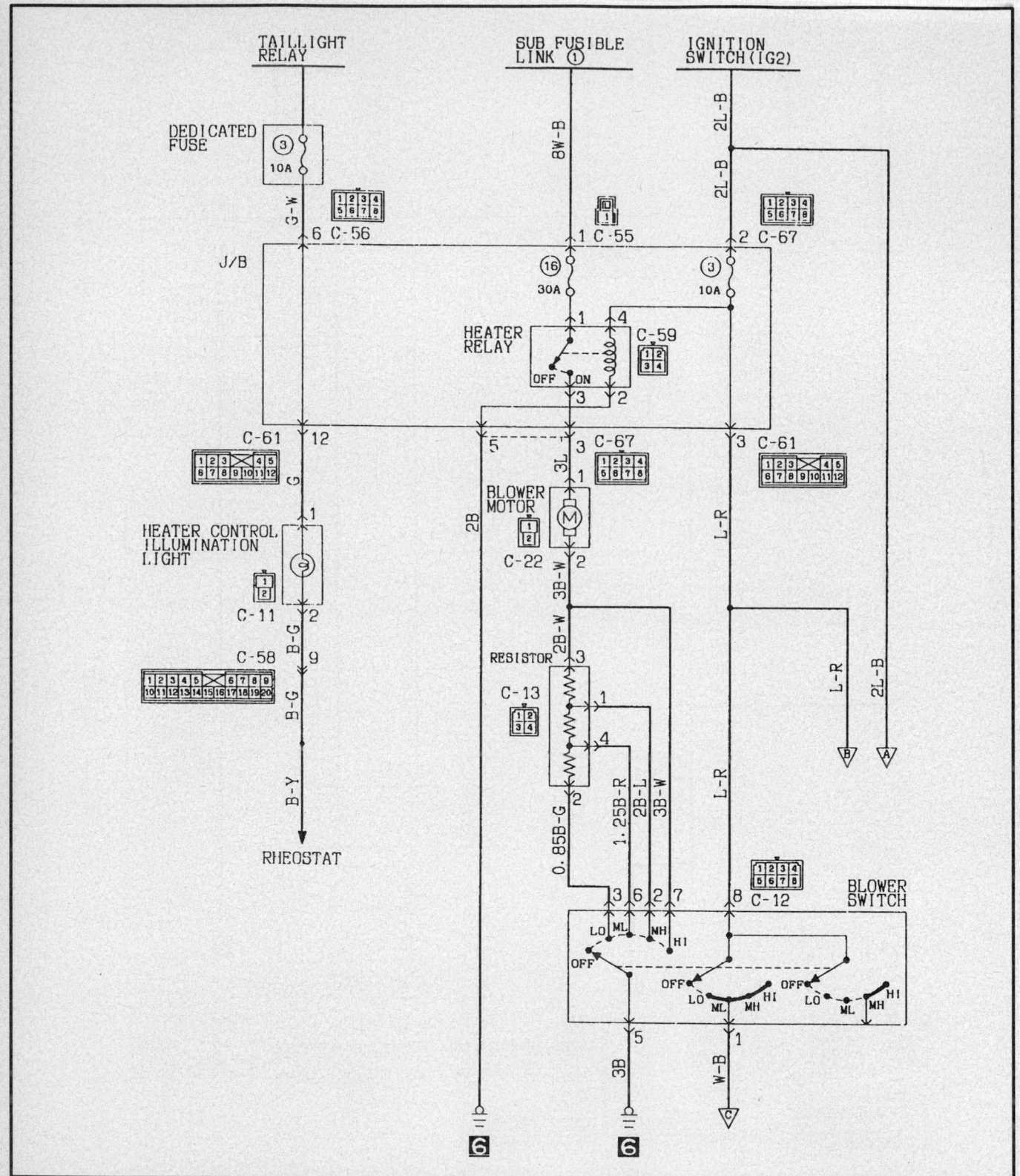

Wiring schematic—1993–94 Colt Vista with air conditioning—1.8L engine

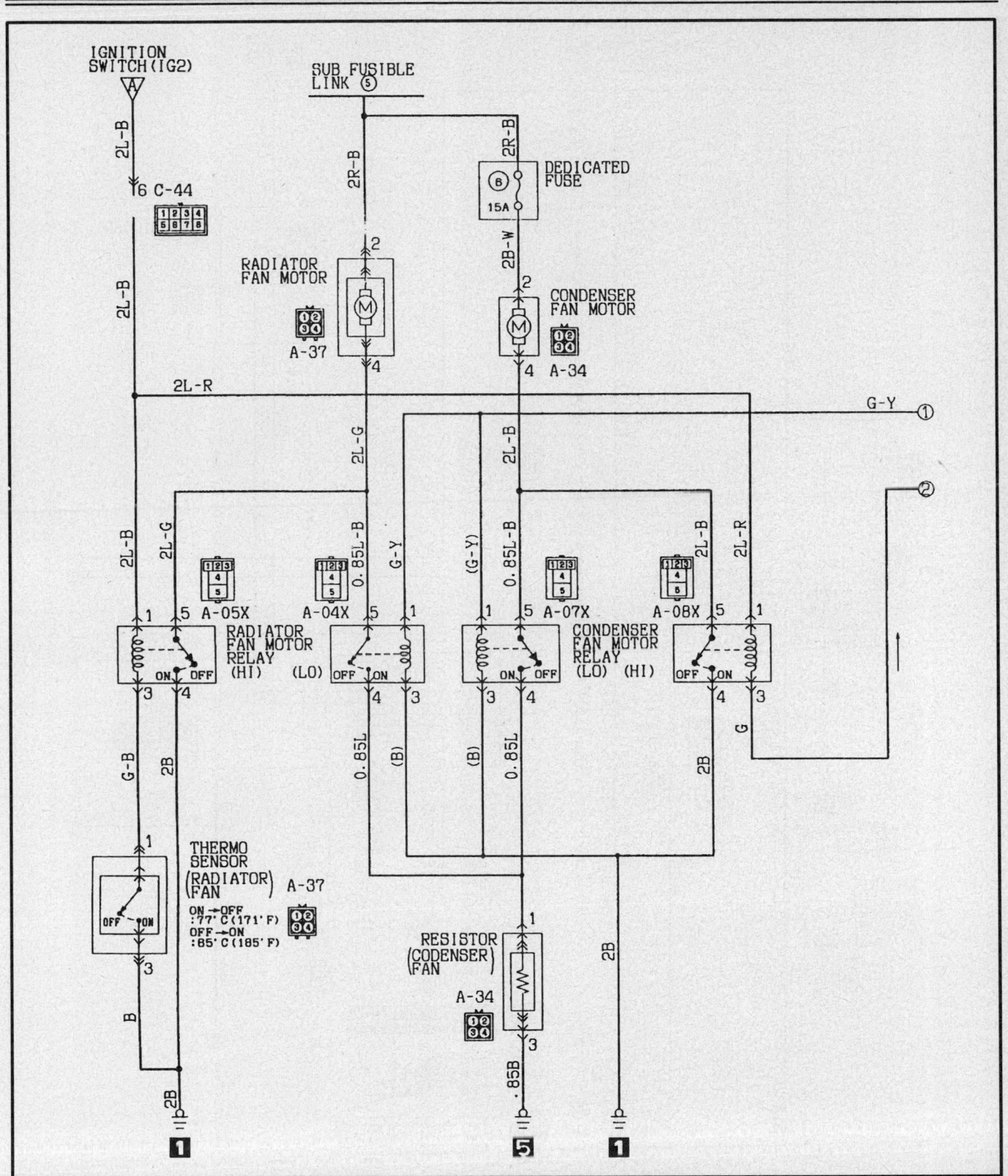

Wiring schematic—1993–94 Colt Vista with air conditioning—1.8L engine, Cont.

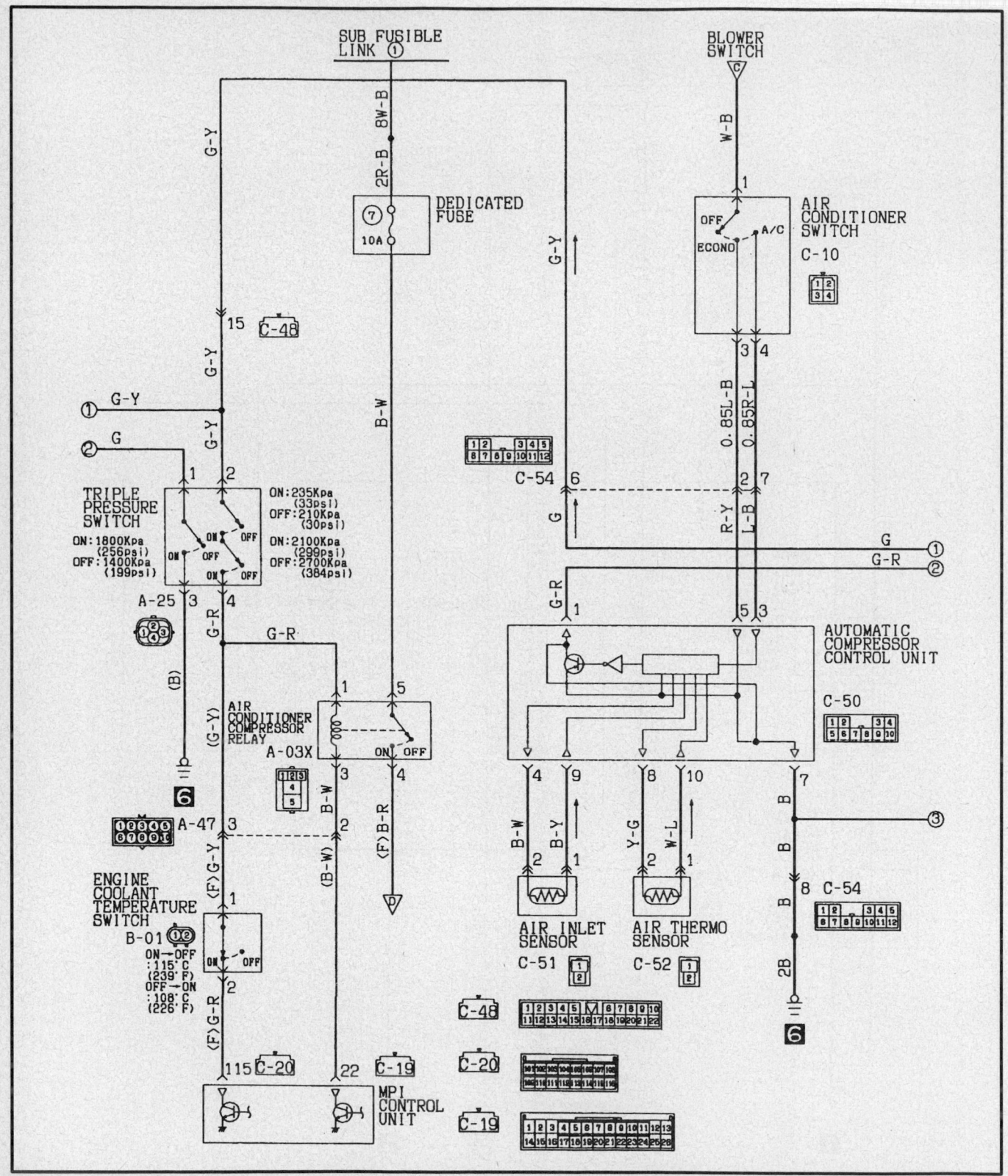

Wiring schematic—1993–94 Colt Vista with air conditioning–1.8L engine, Cont.

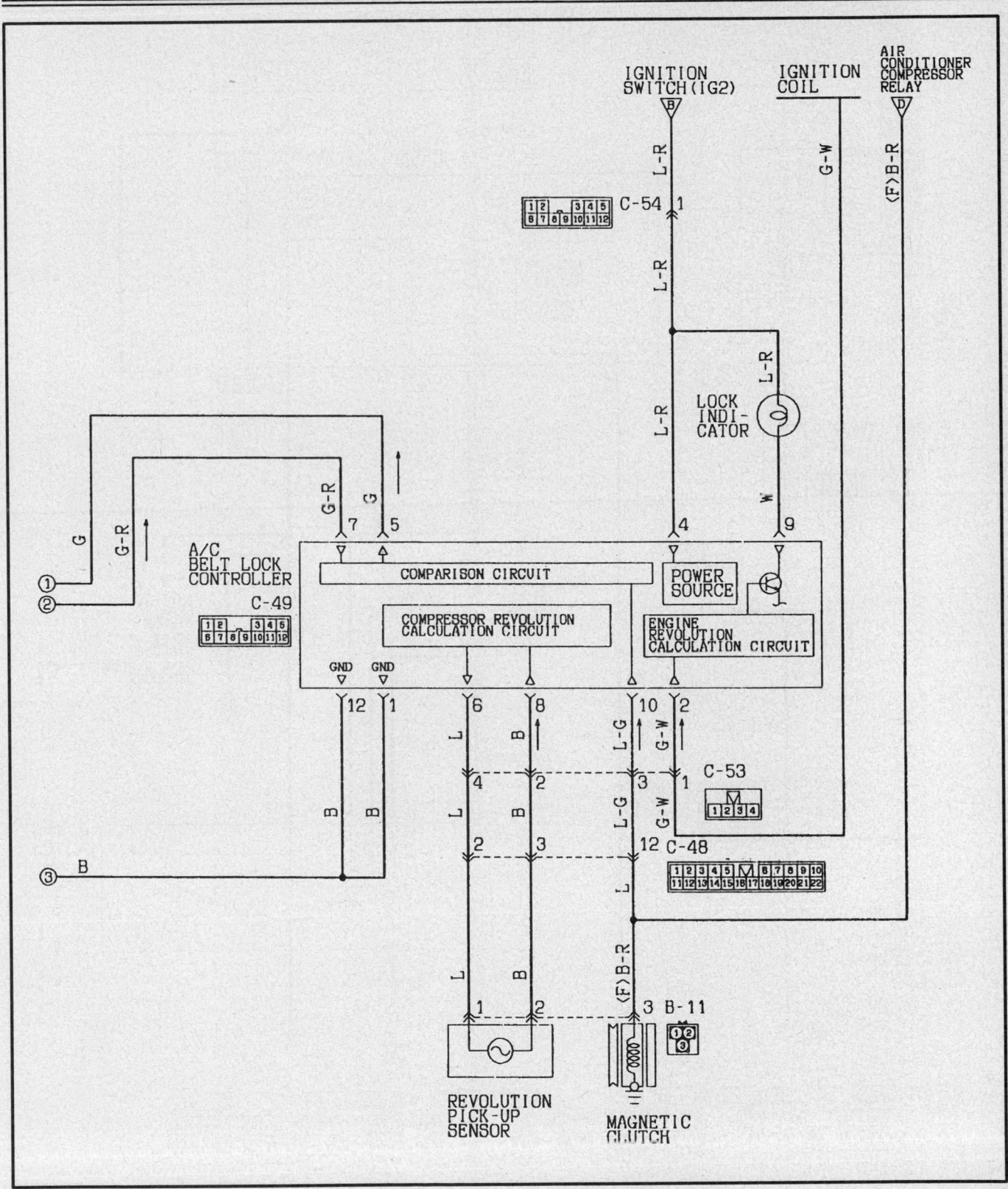

Wiring schematic—1993—94 Colt Vista with air conditioning—1.8L engine, Cont.

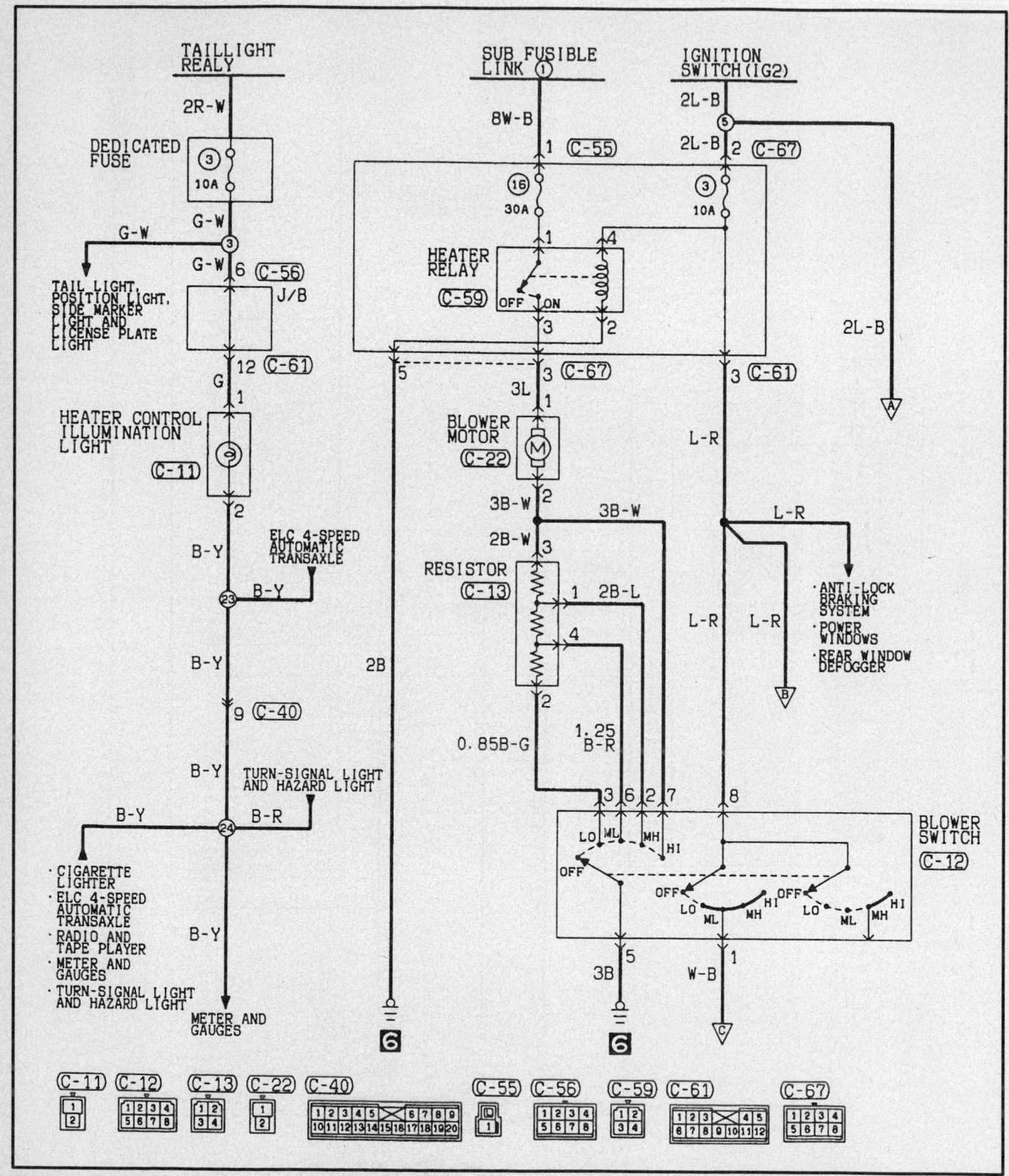

Wiring schematic—1995 Colt Vista with air conditioning—1.8L engine

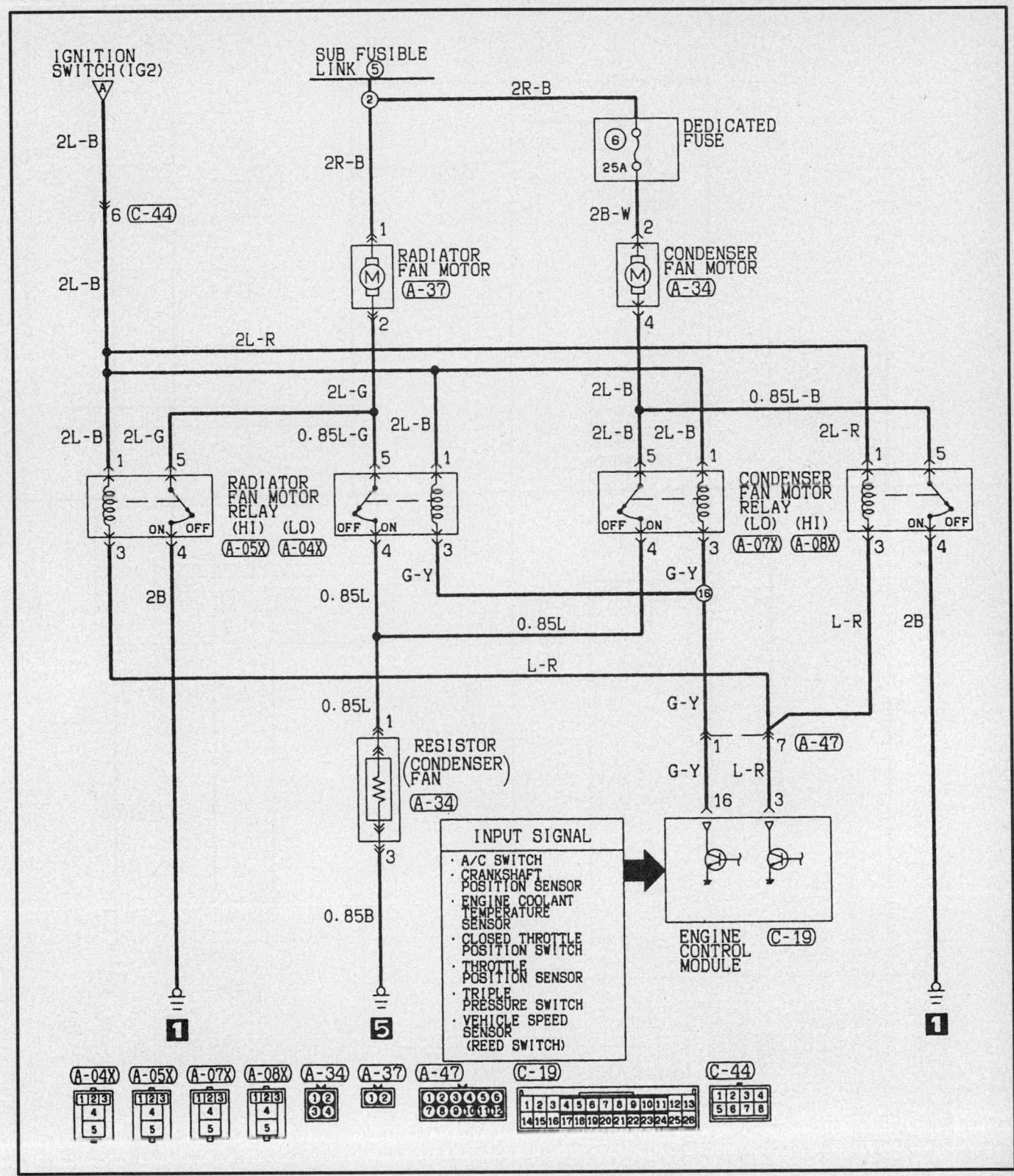

Wiring schematic—1995 Colt Vista with air conditioning—1.8L engine, Cont.

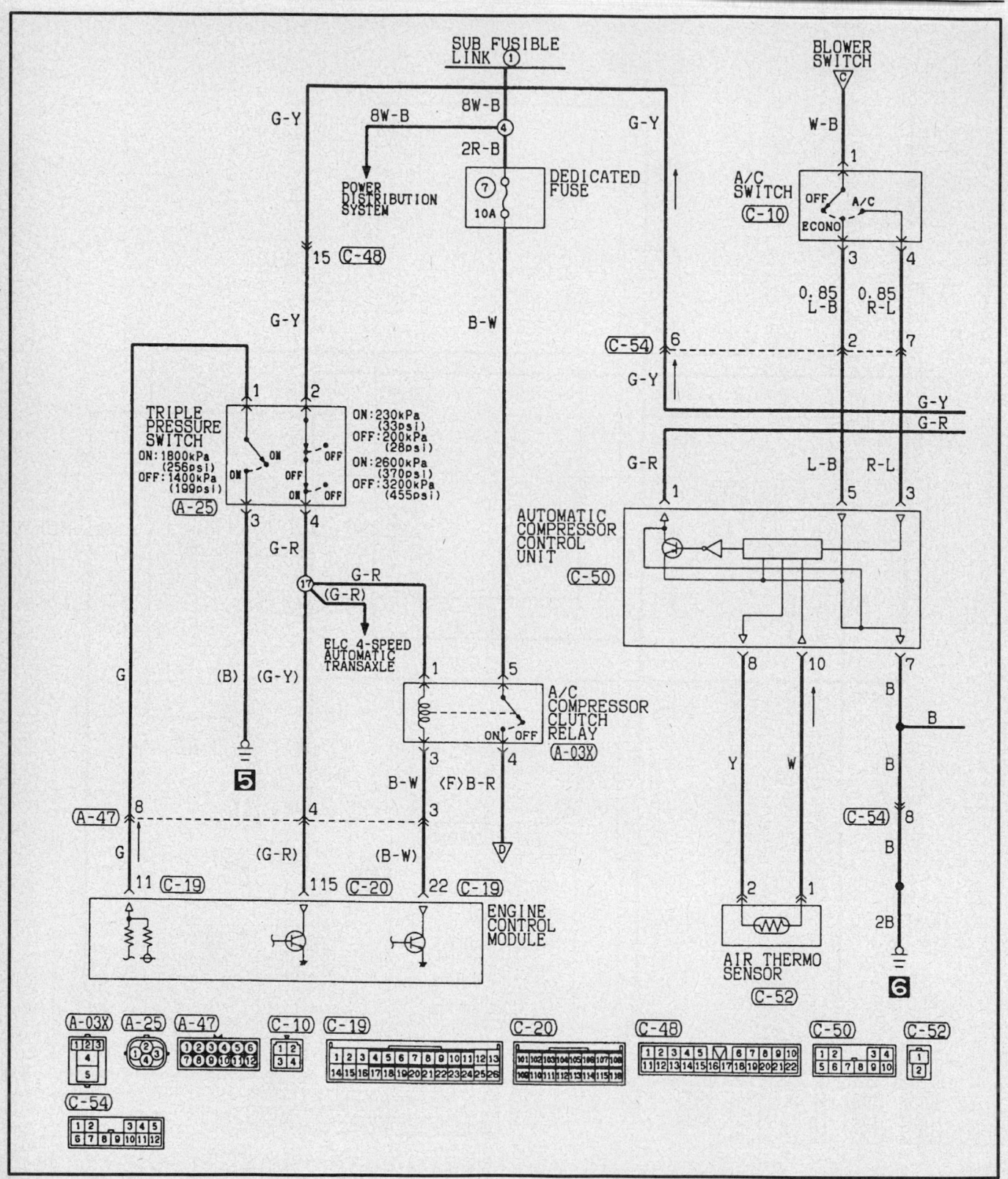

Wiring schematic—1995 Colt Vista with air conditioning–1.8L engine, Cont.

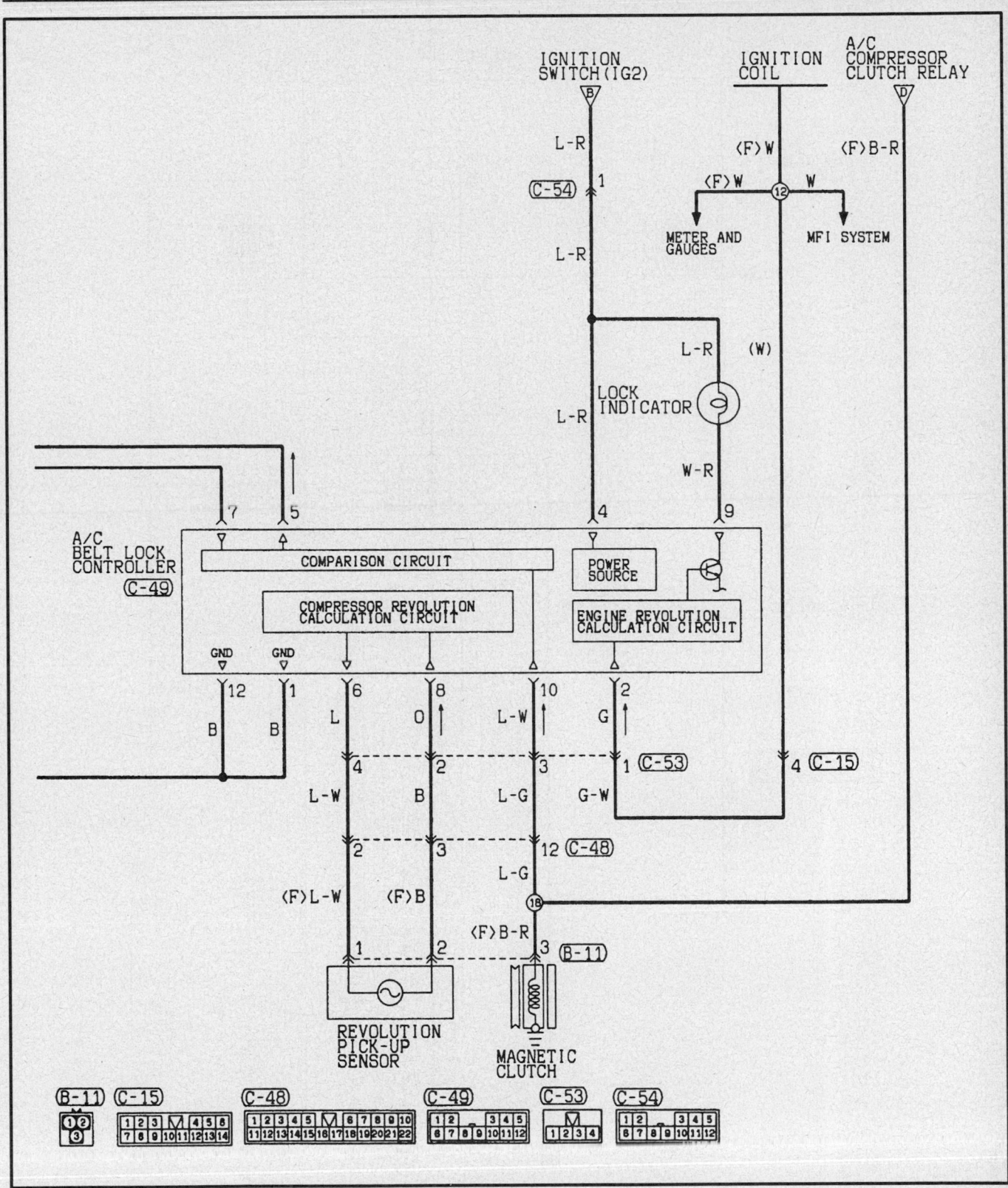

Wiring schematic—1995 Colt Vista with air conditioning—1.8L engine, Cont.

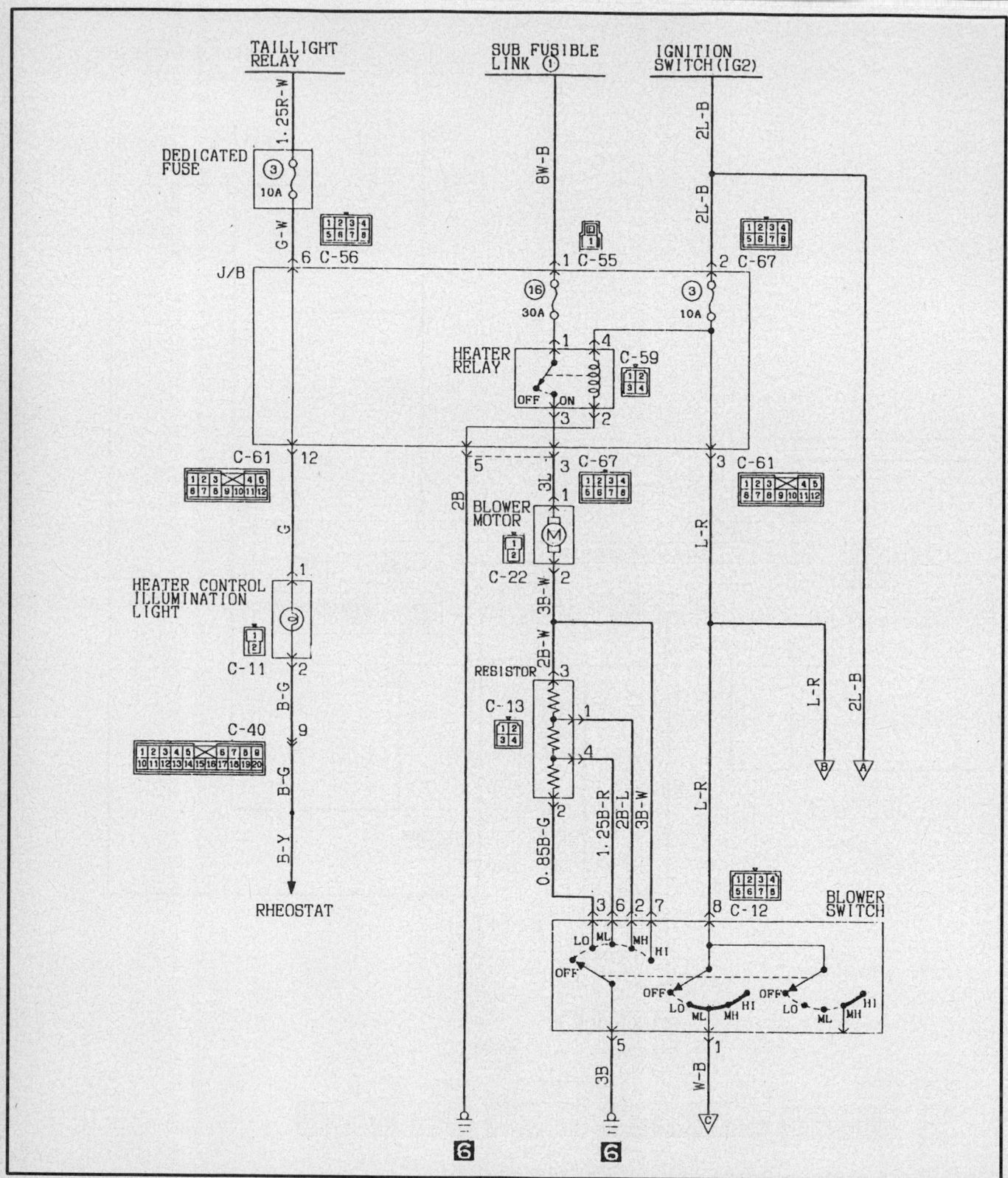

Wiring schematic—1993–94 Colt Vista with air conditioning—2.4L engine

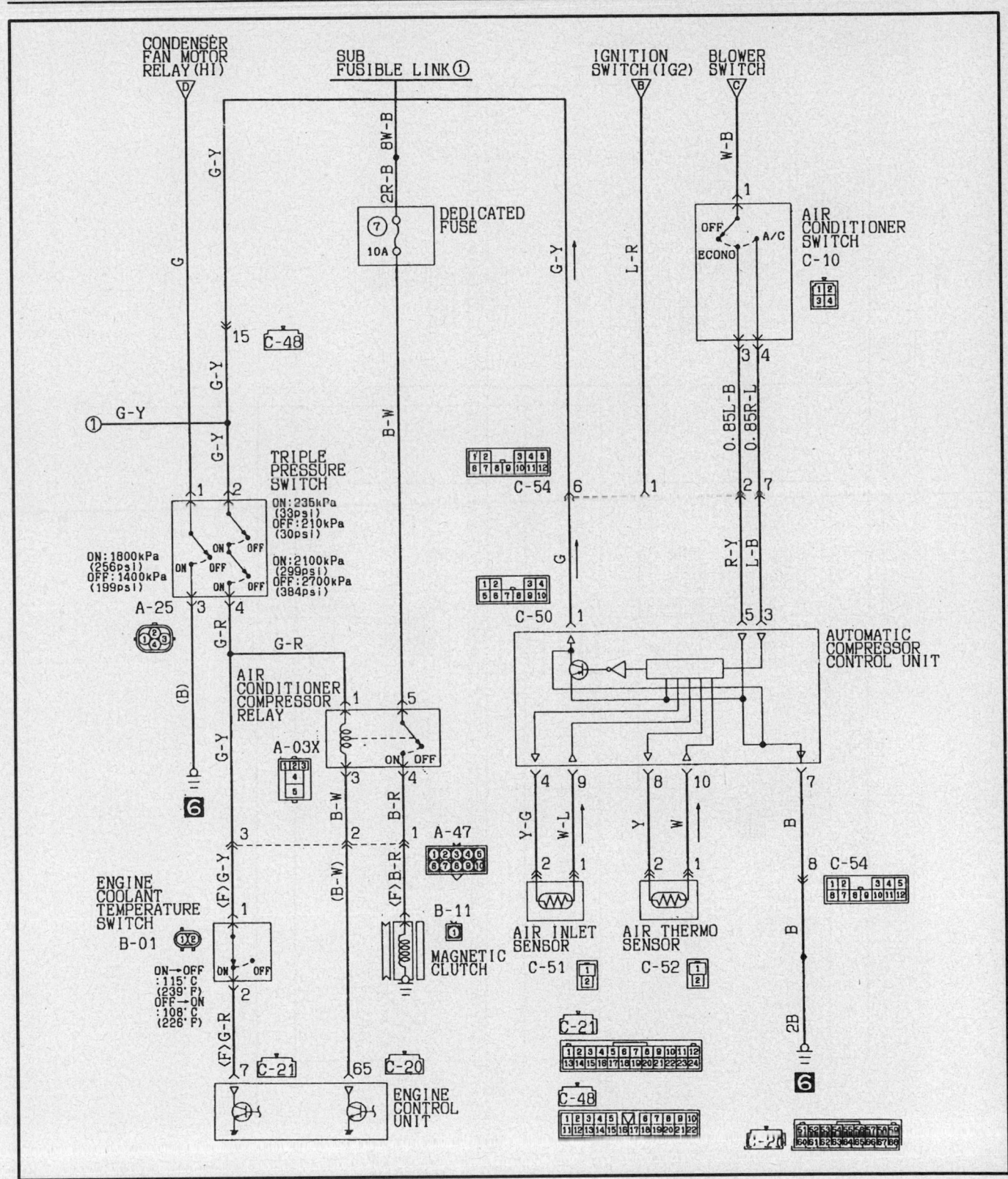

Wiring schematic—1993–94 Colt Vista with air conditioning—2.4L engine, Cont.

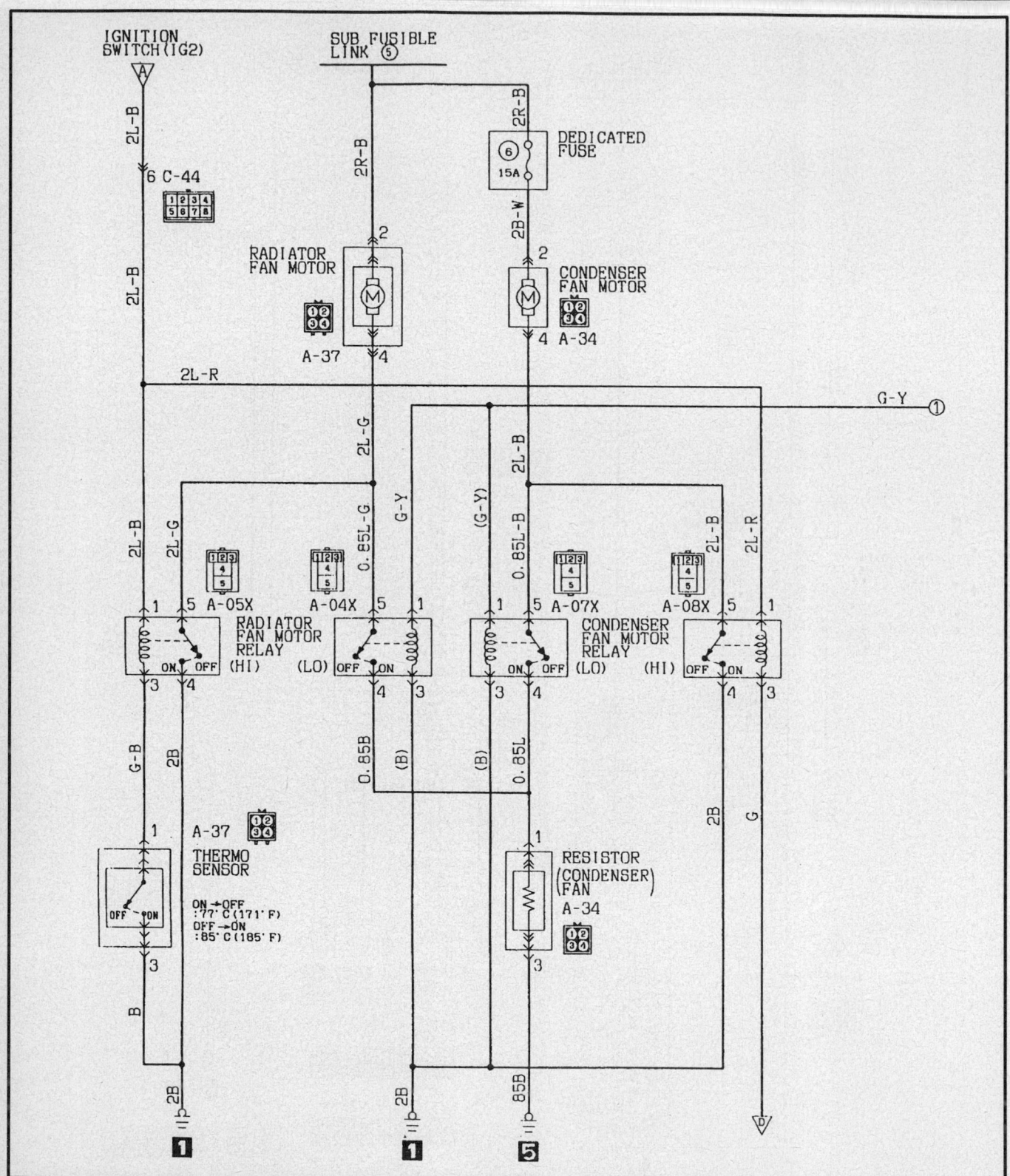

Wiring schematic—1993–94 Colt Vista with air conditioning—2.4L engine, Cont.

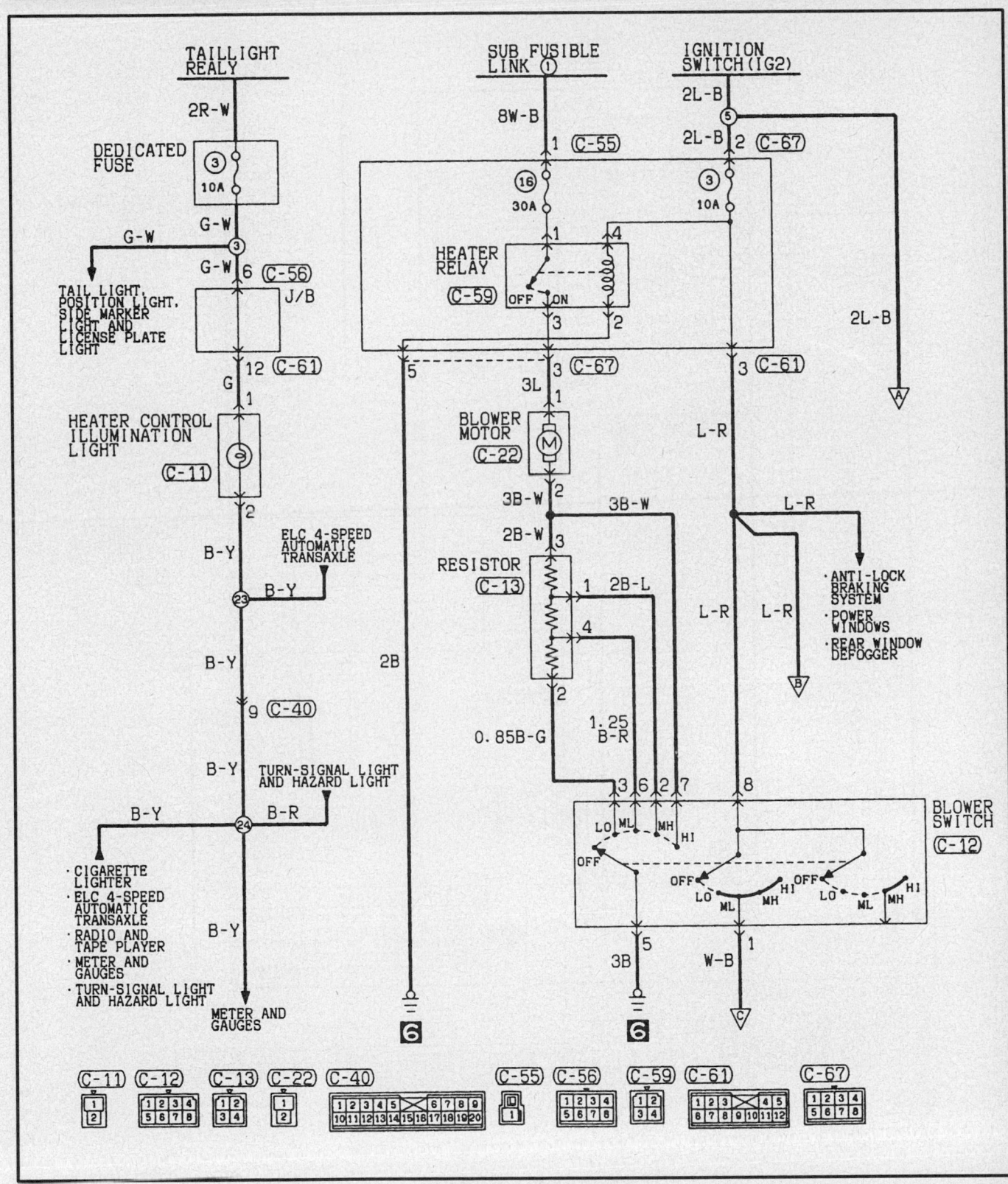

Wiring schematic—1995 Colt Vista with air conditioning—2.4L engine

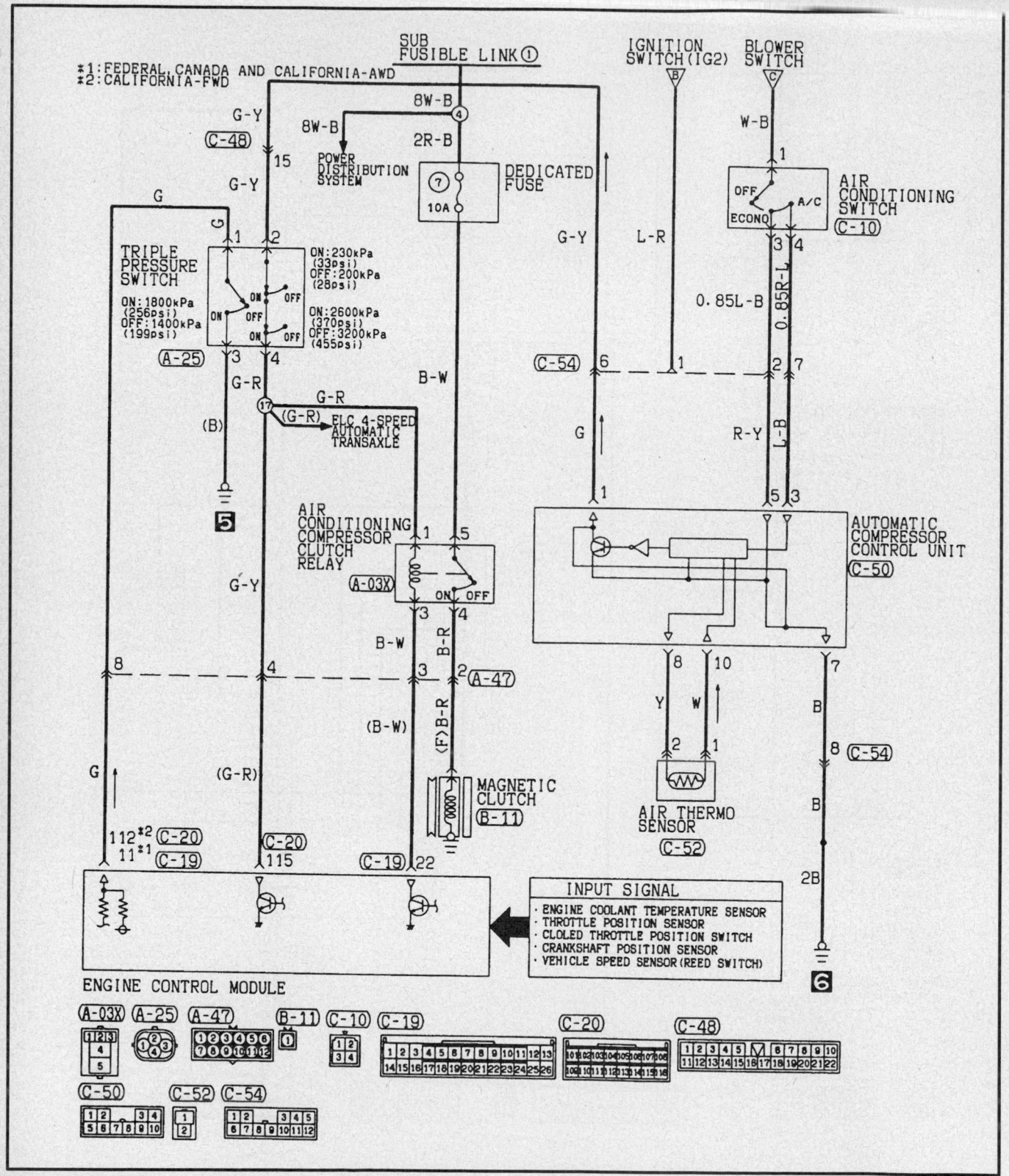

Wiring schematic—1995 Colt Vista with air conditioning—2.4L engine, Cont.

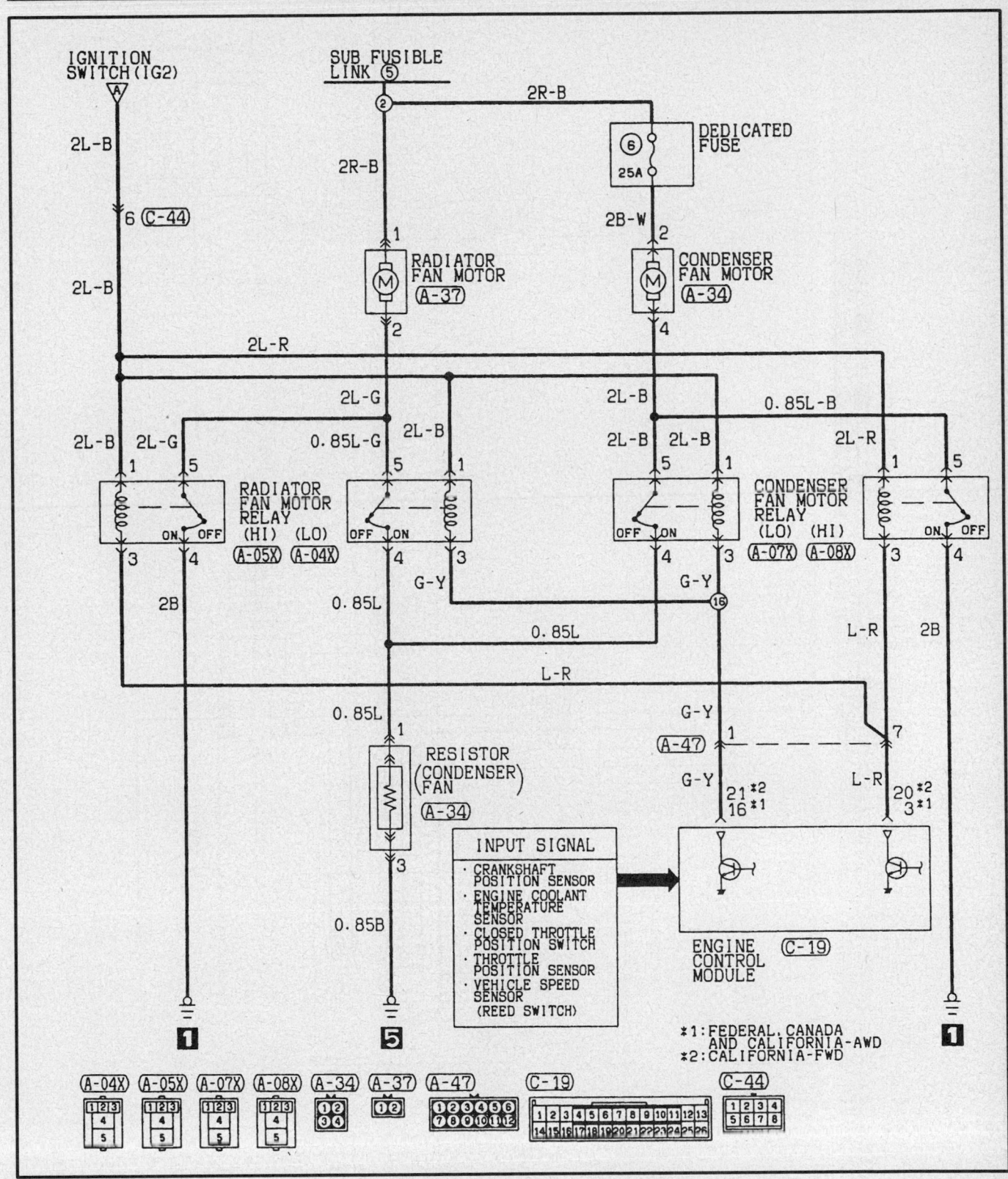

Wiring schematic—1995 Colt Vista with air conditioning—2.4L engine, Cont.

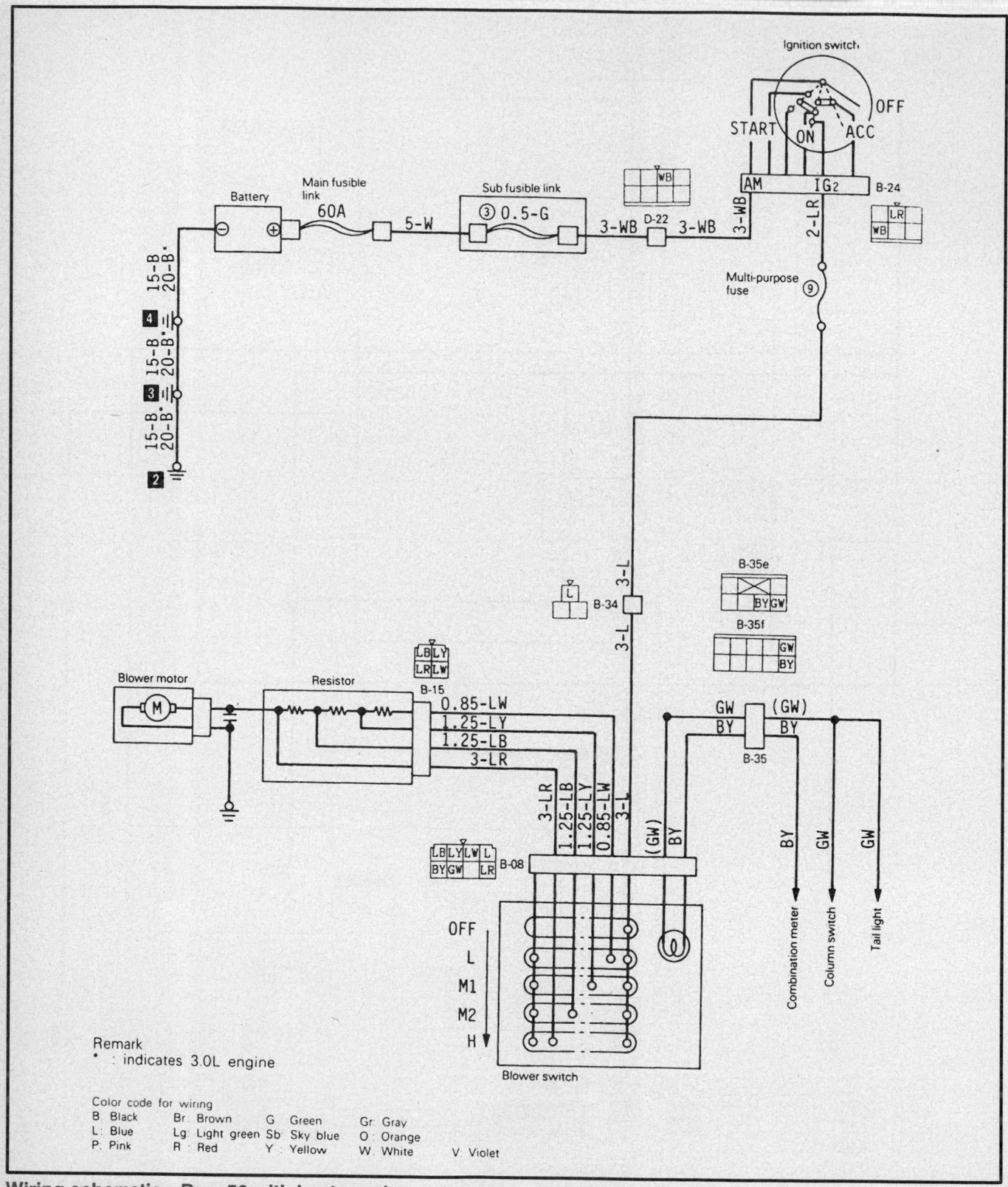

Wiring schematic—Ram 50 with heater only

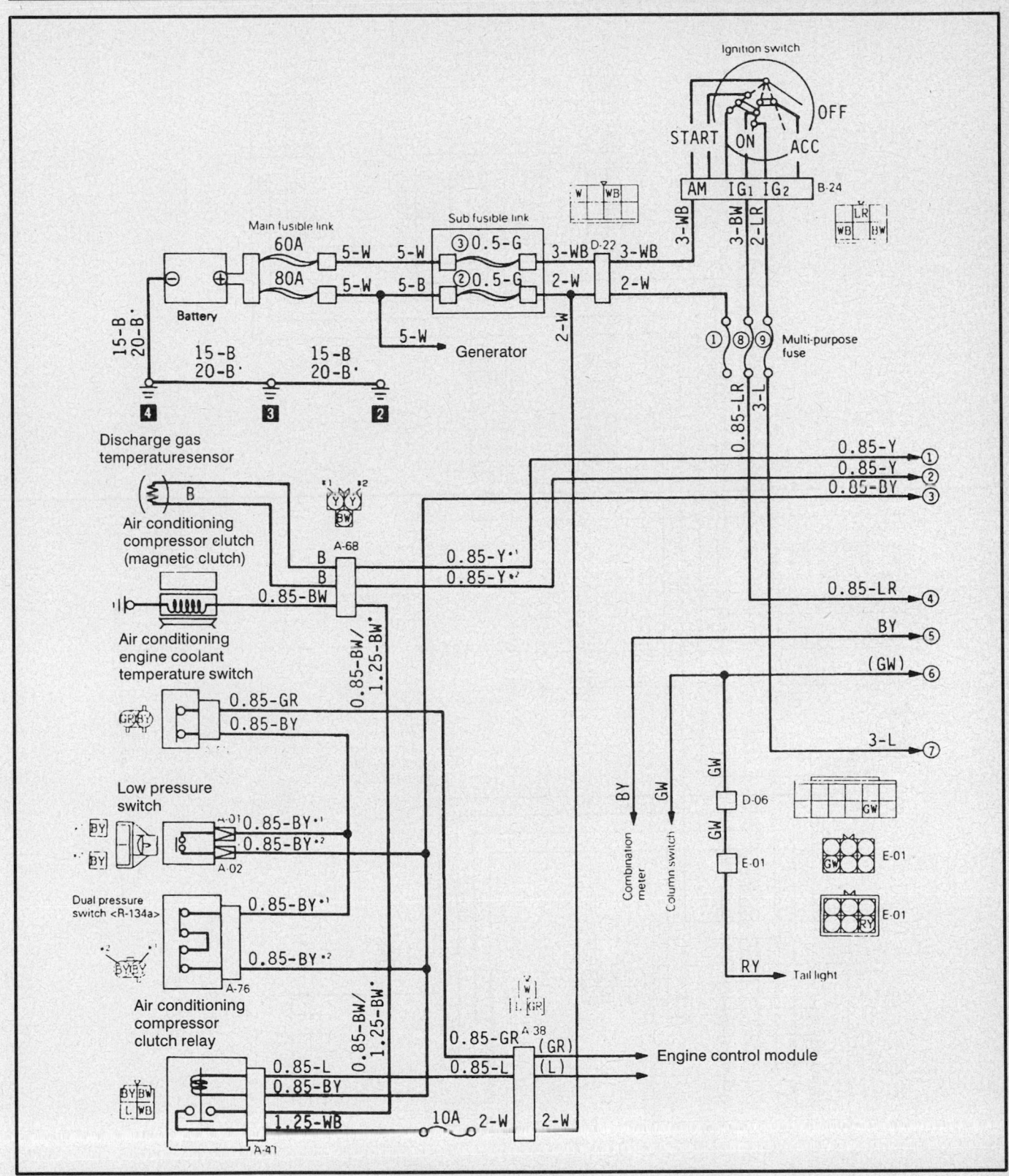

Wiring schematic—Ram 50 with air conditioning

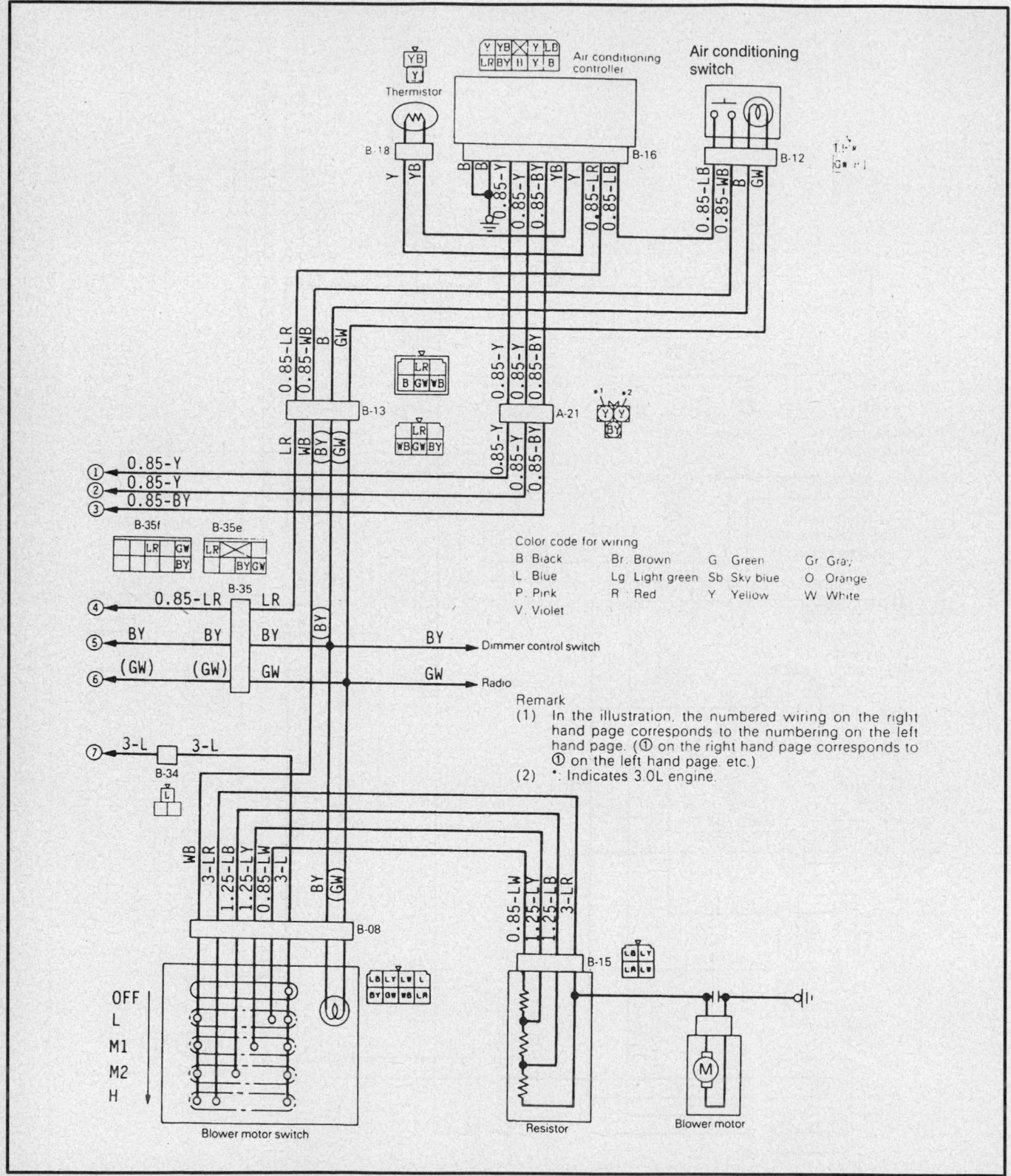

Wiring schematic—Ram 50 with air conditioning, Cont.

SPECIFICATIONS

ENGINE IDENTIFICATION

Year	Model	Engine Displacement Liters (cc)	Engine Series Identification	Fuel System	No. of Cylinders	Engine Type
1993	Civic	1.5 (1493)	D15B7	MFI	4	SOHC-16V
	Civic	1.5 (1493)	D15B8	MFI	4	SOHC-8V
	Civic	1.5 (1493)	D15Z1	MFI	4	SOHC-16V[2]
	Civic	1.6 (1590)	D16Z6	MFI	4	SOHC-16V[1]
	Accord	2.2 (2156)	F22A1	EFI	4	SOHC
	Accord	2.2 (2156)	F22A6	EFI	4	SOHC
	Prelude	2.2 (2156)	H23A1	EFI	4	DOHC
	Prelude	2.3 (2259)	H23A1	EFI	4	DOHC
	Civic del Sol	1.5 (1493)	D15B7	EFI	4	SOHC
	Civic del Sol	1.6 (1590)	D16Z6	EFI	4	SOHC
1994	Civic	1.5 (1493)	D15B7	MPI	4	SOHC-16V
	Civic	1.5 (1493)	D15B8	MPI	4	SOHC-8V
	Civic	1.5 (1493)	D15Z1	MPI	4	SOHC-16V[2]
	Civic	1.6 (1590)	D16Z6	MPI	4	SOHC-16V[1]
	Accord	2.2 (2156)	F22B1	MPI	4	SOHC
	Accord	2.2 (2156)	F22B2	MPI	4	SOHC
	Prelude	2.2 (2156)	F22A1	MPI	4	SOHC
	Prelude	2.2 (2156)	H22A1	MPI	4	DOHC
	Prelude	2.3 (2259)	H23A1	MPI	4	DOHC
	Civic del Sol	1.6 (1590)	B16A3	MPI	4	DOHC
	Civic del Sol	1.5 (1493)	D15B7	MPI	4	SOHC
	Civic del Sol	1.6 (1590)	D16Z6	MPI	4	SOHC
1995	Civic	1.5 (1493)	D15B7	MPI	4	SOHC-16V
	Civic	1.6 (1590)	D16Z6	MPI	4	SOHC-16V[1]
	Accord	2.2 (2156)	F22B1	MPI	4	SOHC-16V[1]
	Accord	2.2 (2156)	F22B2	MPI	4	SOHC
	Prelude	2.2 (2156)	F22A1	MPI	4	SOHC
	Prelude	2.2 (2156)	H22A1	MPI	4	DOHC-16V[1]
	Prelude	2.3 (2259)	H23A1	MPI	4	DOHC
	Civic del Sol	1.6 (1590)	D16Z6	MPI	4	SOHC

MFI – Multi Point Fuel Injection
EFI – Electronic Fuel Injection (manufacturer did not specify type)
SOHC – Single Overhead Cam
DOHC – Dual Overhead Cam
[1] VTEC engine
[2] VTEC-E engine

REFRIGERANT CAPACITIES

Year	Model	Refrigerant (oz.)	Oil (fl. oz.)	Compressor Type
1993	Civic	22–24	4.0–4.7	—
	Accord	28–30	3.0–4.1	Nippondenso
	Accord	28–30	4.1-4.4	Hadsys
	Prelude	26.5	4.0	Sanden
	Civic del Sol	20–30	4.0	—
1994	Civic	18.8-19.0	4.2-4.9	Sanden
	Accord	22.8-23.0	5.6-6.1	Nippondenso
	Accord	22.8-23.0	5.6-6.1	Hadsys
	Prelude	22.8-23.0	4.2-4.9	Sanden
	Civic del Sol	18.8-19.0	4.0	Sanden
1995	Civic	22–24	4.2-4.9	Sanden
	Accord	21.1-22.9	5.3	Nippondenso
	Prelude	21.1-22.9	4.0	Hadsys
	Civic del Sol	18.8-19.0	4.0	Sanden

AIR CONDITIONING BELT TENSION

Year	Model	Engine Liters (cc)	Belt Type	Specifications New	Specifications Used
1993	Civic	1.5 (1493)	Poly-V	0.28-0.35	0.35-0.43
	Civic	1.6 (1590)	Poly-V	0.28-0.35	0.35-0.43
	Accord	2.2 (2156)	Poly-V	0.33-0.43	0.39-0.49
	Prelude	2.0 (1955)	Poly-V	0.24-0.32	0.39-0.49
	Prelude	2.1 (2056)	Poly-V	0.24-0.32	0.39-0.43
1994	Civic	1.5 (1493)	Poly-V	0.20-0.28	0.26-0.41
	Civic	1.5 (1493)	Poly-V	0.20-0.28	0.26-0.41
	Accord	2.2 (2156)	Poly-V	0.20-0.28	0.31-0.41
	Prelude	2.2 (2156)	Poly-V	0.18-0.28	0.39-0.47
	Prelude	2.3 (2259)	Poly-V	0.18-0.28	0.39-0.47
	Civic del Sol	1.5 (1493)	Poly-V	0.20-0.28	0.26-0.41
	Civic del Sol	1.6 (1590)	Poly-V	0.20-0.28	0.26-0.41
1995	Civic	1.5 (1493)	Poly-V	0.20-0.28	0.26-0.41
	Civic	1.66 (1590)	Poly-V	0.20-0.28	0.26-0.41
	Accord	2.2 (2156)	Poly-V	0.20-0.28	0.31-0.41
	Prelude	2.2 (2156)	Poly-V	0.18-0.28	0.39-0.47
	Prelude	2.3 (2259)	Poly-V	0.18-0.28	0.39-0.47
	Civic del Sol	1.6 (1590)	Poly-V	0.20-0.28	0.26-0.41

SYSTEM DESCRIPTION

General Information

The heater unit is located in the center of the vehicle along the firewall. The heater system is a bi–level system designed to direct warm air through the vents to either the windshield or the floor and cool air through the panel outlet. The air conditioning system is designed to be activated in combination with a separate air conditioning switch installed in the control assembly and the fan speed switch. The system incorporates a compressor, condenser, evaporator, receiver/drier, pressure switch, expansion valve, thermo–switch, refrigerant lines and some models are equipped with an electronic control head assembly versus the standard cable operated control head.

Service Valve Location

Charging valve locations will vary from locations near the firewall line connections to fittings near the condenser. Always discharge, evacuate and recharge at the low side service fitting using the proper equipment for the vehicle and refrigerant type.

System Discharging

R–12 refrigerant is a chlorofluorocarbon, which, when mishandled, can contribute to the depletion of the ozone layer in the upper atmosphere. The ozone filters out harmful radiation from the sun. In order to protect the ozone layer, an approved R–12 recovery/recycling machine that meets SAE standard J1991 should be employed when discharging the system. Follow the operating instructions provided with the approved equipment exactly to properly discharge the system.

All 1993–95 Honda air conditioner systems use R–134a refrigerant and polyalkyleneglycol refrigerant oil, which are not compatible with R–12 refrigerant and mineral oil. Do not attempt to use R–12 servicing equipment or tools on an R–134a system as damage will result.

CAUTION

Exposure to air conditioner refrigerant and lubricant vapor or mist can irritate eyes, nose and throat. Avoid breathing the air conditioner refrigerant and lubricant vapor or mist.

System Evacuating

If the air conditioning system has been opened to the atmosphere, it should be air and moisture free before being recharged with refrigerant. Moisture and air mixed with refrigerant will raise the compressor head pressure, damage the system's components and will reduce the performance of the system. Moisture will boil at normal room temperature when exposed to a vacuum, the moisture then becomes a vapor and will be easily removed from the system by the vacuum pump.

To evacuate or rid the system of air and moisture:
1. Leak test the system and repair any leaks.
2. Connect an approved charging station, recovery/recycling machine or manifold gauge set and vacuum pump to the discharge and suction ports.
3. Open the discharge and suction ports and start the vacuum pump. If the pump is not able to pull at least 26 in. Hg vacuum, there is a leak that must be repaired before evacuation can occur.
4. Once the system has reached at least 26 in. Hg vacuum, allow the system to evacuate for 20 minutes. The longer the system is evacuated, the more contaminants will be removed.
5. Close all valves and turn the pump OFF. If the system loses more than 2 in. Hg vacuum after 15 minutes, there is a leak that should be repaired.

System Charging

1. Connect an approved charging station, recovery/recycling machine or manifold gauge set to the discharge and suction ports.
2. Follow the instructions provided with the equipment and charge the system with the specified amount of refrigerant.
3. Perform a leak test.

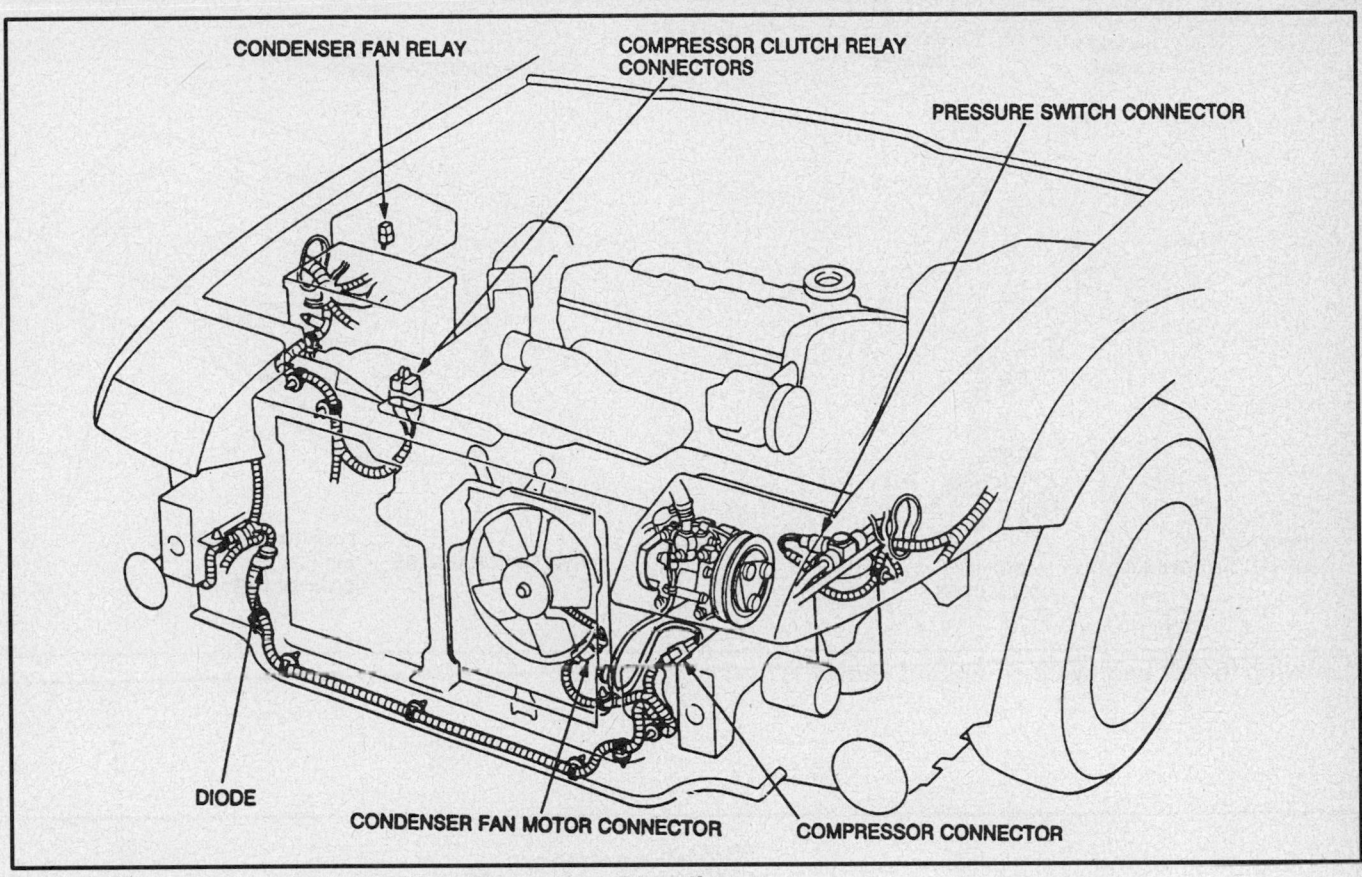

Typical air conditioning electrical components and locations

SYSTEM COMPONENTS

Supplemental Restraint System

PRECAUTIONS

If equipped with a Supplemental Restraint System (air bag), certain precautions must be taken before removing major components under the instrument panel or doing repairs. These precautions will prevent accidental deployment of the air bag.

SRS electrical wiring harnesses are covered with yellow outer insulation.

1. Check with the customer for a 5–digit radio theft protection code. GET THE CODE BEFORE DISCONNECTING THE BATTERY.
2. Disconnect the negative, then the positive battery cable.
3. Install the short connectors:
   • On the driver's side, remove the access panel from the bottom of the steering wheel and remove the short (red) connector from the panel.
   • Disconnect the connector between the driver's air bag and cable reel, then install the short (red) connector on the air bag side of the connector.
   • For the passenger's side, remove the glove box. Disconnect the connector between the air bag and the SRS main connector. Install the short (red) connector on the air bag side of the connector.

• Reverse the procedures before reconnecting the battery. When the word "CODE" appears on the radio, enter the 5–digit customer code to restore radio operations.

Radiator

REMOVAL AND INSTALLATION

1. Disconnect the negative battery cable.
2. Properly drain the cooling system.
3. Disconnect the fan motor and thermo–switch wire connector.
4. Disconnect the upper and lower radiator hoses.
5. Disconnect and plug the automatic transaxle cooling lines at the radiator, if equipped.
6. Disconnect the coolant reservoir overflow hose.
7. Remove the radiator attaching bolts and brackets.
8. Remove the radiator with the cooling fan attached.
9. Remove the cooling fan and shroud from the radiator.
To install:
10. Attach the cooling fan and shroud to the radiator and install the assembly.
11. Attach the radiator bolts and brackets.
12. Connect the coolant reservoir overflow hose.

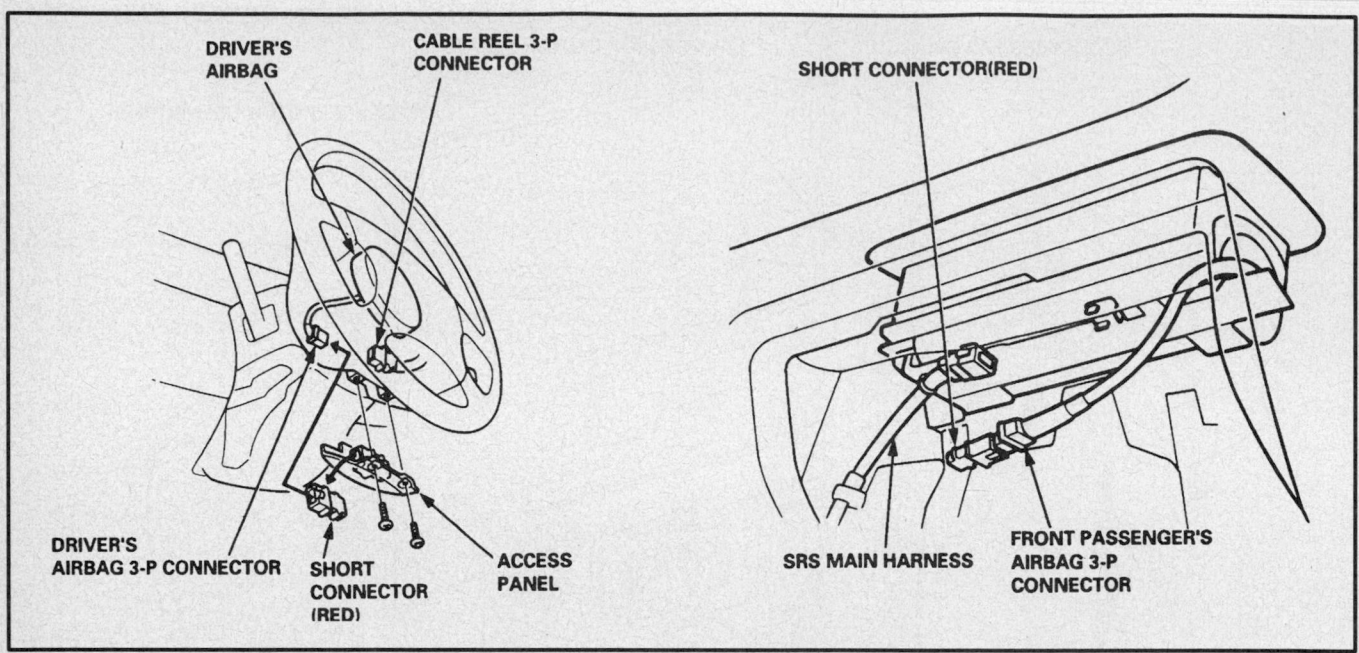

Disabling the air bag system—Accord shown

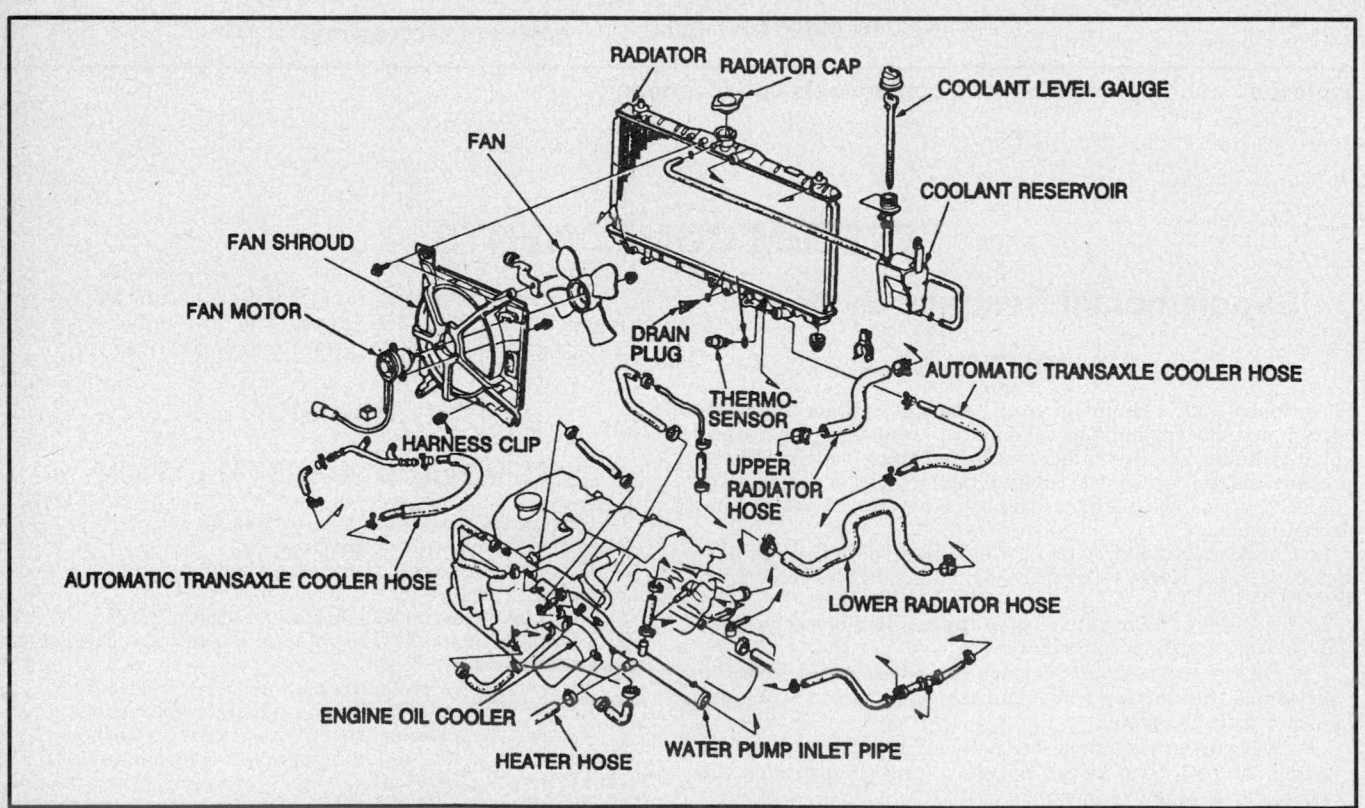

Exploded view of a typical cooling system

13. Connect the automatic transaxle cooling lines to the radiator, if equipped.
14. Connect the upper and lower radiator hoses.
15. Connect the fan motor and thermo–switch wire connector.
16. Refill the system with the proper type and quantity of coolant, check for leaks and bleed the cooling system.
17. Reconnect the negative battery cable.

COOLING SYSTEM BLEEDING

1. Loosen the air bleed bolt in the water outlet located on the top of the engine.
2. Fill the radiator to the bottom of the filler neck with the proper type and quantity of coolant.

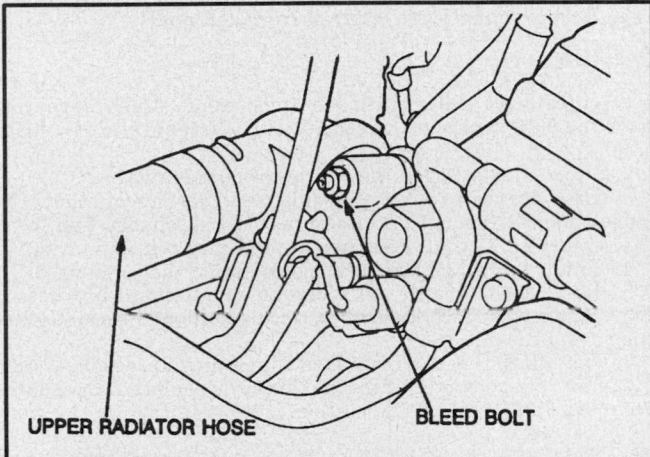

Cooling system bleed port location

3. Tighten the bleed bolt as soon as coolant flows out in a steady stream without bubbles.
4. With the radiator cap off, start and run the engine until the cooling fan cycles twice and the engine is warmed up.
5. Add coolant to bring the level up to the bottom of the radiator filler neck.
6. Install the radiator cap and check for cooling system leaks.

Condenser Fan

TESTING

1. Turn the ignition, air conditioner and blower speed switch **ON**.
2. Check for voltage at the condenser fan motor using a voltmeter.
3. There should be approximately 12 volts, if not, check the fuses, relay, wiring, ground, dual pressure switch, and, if equipped, the diode fan and control unit.
4. Turn the ignition switch **OFF**.
5. Disconnect the condenser fan wire connector.

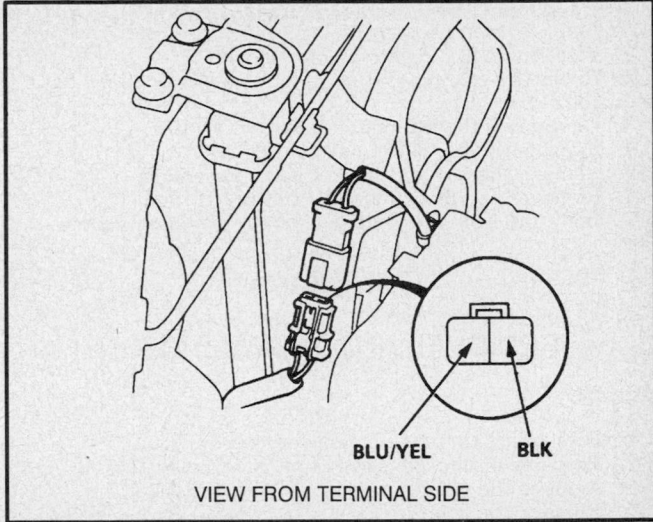

BLU/YEL   BLK
VIEW FROM TERMINAL SIDE

Condenser fan connector terminals—Prelude shown

6. Connect 12 volts to terminal **A** of the cooling fan wire connector terminal **B** of the ground terminal.
7. The cooling fan should run smoothly, if not as specified replace the fan motor.

REMOVAL AND INSTALLATION

1. Disconnect the negative battery cable.
2. Drain the cooling system and remove the upper hose, if required.
3. Disconnect the fan motor wire connector.
4. Remove the fan shroud attaching bolts.
5. Remove the fan and shroud as an assembly.
6. Remove the fan and motor from the shroud.
7. Installation is the reverse of the removal procedure.

Cooling Fan

TESTING

1. Turn the ignition switch **ON**.
2. Check for ground at the thermo–switch, when the engine reaches the proper operating temperature the switch should close and complete the ground.
3. Check the wiring, the relays, the control unit, if as specified replace the thermo–switch.
4. Turn the ignition switch **OFF**.
5. Disconnect the cooling fan wire connector.
6. Connect 12 volts to terminal **A** of the cooling fan wire connector terminal **B** of the ground terminal.
7. The cooling fan should run smoothly, if not as specified replace the cooling fan

REMOVAL AND INSTALLATION

1. Disconnect the negative battery cable.
2. Drain the cooling system and remove the upper hose, if required.
3. Disconnect the fan motor wire connector.
4. Remove the fan shroud attaching bolts.
5. Remove the fan and shroud as an assembly.
6. Remove the fan and motor from the shroud.
7. Installation is the reverse of the removal procedure.

Condenser

REMOVAL AND INSTALLATION

Accord

1. Disconnect the negative battery cable.
2. Properly discharge the air conditioning system.
3. Remove the reservoir tank, tube and bracket.
4. Remove the front grille.
5. Disconnect the fan wire connectors.
6. Remove the fan shroud attaching bolts and remove the fan assemblies.
7. Remove the upper radiator attaching bolts and brackets.
8. Disconnect and plug the condenser refrigerant lines.
9. Remove the condenser attaching bolts and remove the assembly.
10. Installation is the reverse of the removal procedure. Make sure that new O-rings that have been lightly coated with refrigerant oil are used on any connections which were taken apart.

Civic and Civic del Sol

1. Disconnect the negative battery cable.

2. Properly discharge the air conditioning system.
3. On Civic, detach the thermo switch and condenser fan connectors.
4. On Civic del Sol, detach the dual pressure switch, condenser fan and compressor clutch connectors.
5. Disconnect the refrigerant lines from the condenser. Cap all openings immediately to minimize contamination.
6. Remove the suction hose clamp and condenser bracket.
7. Carefully lift the condenser assembly, with condenser fan attached, out of the vehicle. Take care not to hit the condenser or radiator fins.
8. Installation is the reverse of the removal procedure. Add 0.6 oz. of refrigerant oil if the condenser is replaced. Evacuate, recharge and leak test the system. Make sure that new O-rings that have been lightly coated with refrigerant oil are used on any connections which were taken apart.

Prelude

1. Disconnect the negative battery cable. Make sure you have the 5 digit radio theft code prior to disconnecting the battery.
2. Properly discharge the air conditioning system.
3. Disconnect the dual pressure switch connect, then remove the condenser pipe. Disconnect the discharge line from the condenser. Cap all openings to minimize contamination.
4. Remove the A/C hose bracket on top of the condenser.
5. Remove the 4 bolts and radiator upper mount brackets.
6. Remove the 2 condenser mounting bolts and carefully lift the condenser out.
7. Installation is the reverse of the removal procedure. Add 0.4 oz. of refrigerant oil if the condenser is replaced. Evacuate, recharge and leak test the system.

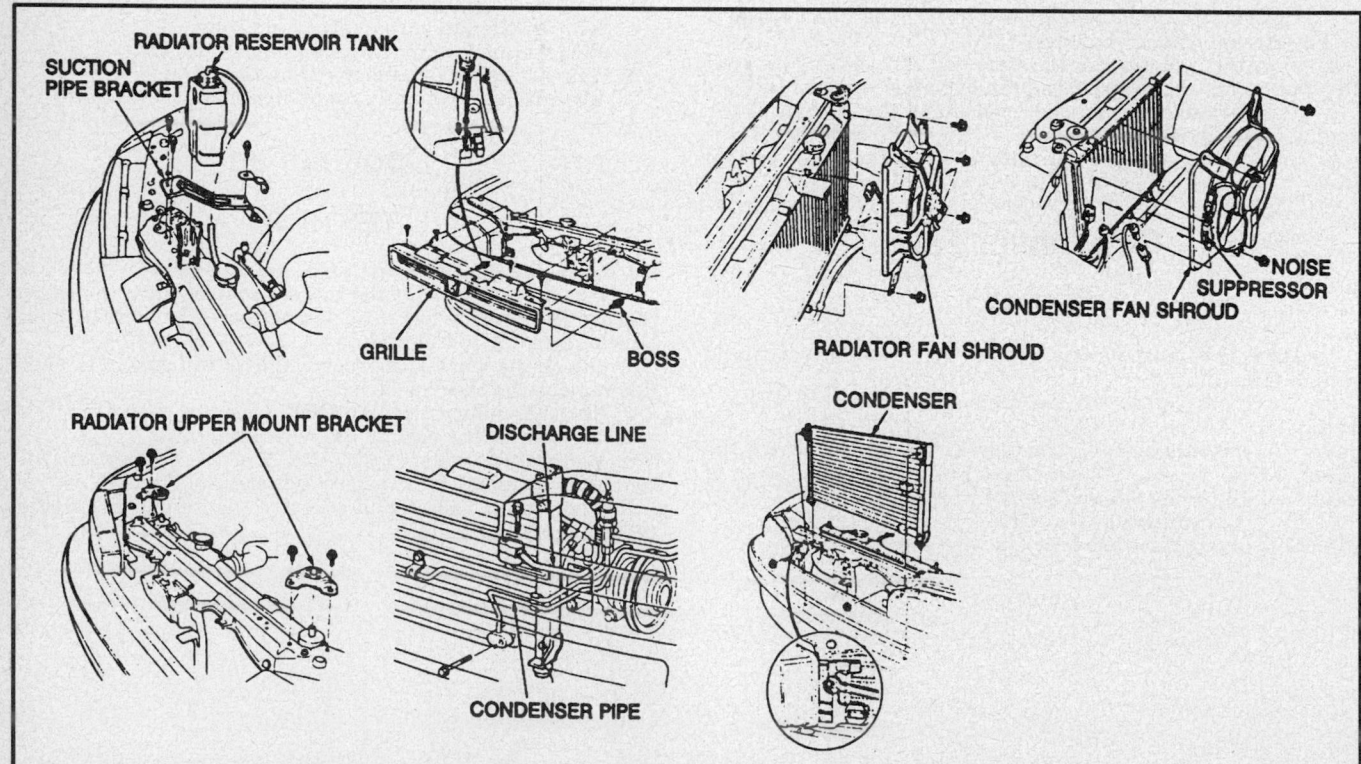

Condenser assembly removal—Accord

Compressor

REMOVAL AND INSTALLATION

Accord

NOTE: Before removing the compressor, if it can be operated, run it with the air conditioning engaged, for several minutes, then shut the engine and A/C OFF. This returns maximum oil to the compressor.

1. Disconnect the negative battery cable.
2. Properly discharge the air conditioning system slowly to minimize oil loss with the refrigerant.
3. Disconnect the magnetic clutch wire connector.
4. Loosen the power steering pump adjusting bolt and remove the belt.
5. Remove the power steering attaching bolts and remove the unit.
6. Remove the auto cruise actuator (if applicable).
7. Remove the alternator harness.

8. Remove the alternator attaching bolts.
9. Remove the alternator and the belt.
10. Disconnect and plug the compressor refrigerant lines.
11. Remove the refrigerant attaching clamps.
12. Disconnect and remove the condenser fan.
13. Remove the compressor attaching bolts and adjuster.
14. Remove the compressor belt.
15. Remove the compressor assembly.
16. Remove the compressor mounting bracket, if required. Drain and measure the oil in the compressor if it is to be replaced.
To install:
17. From 5.3 oz., subtract the amount of oil measured from the old compressor. This is the amount to drain from the replacement compressor which is supplied with a full capacity of oil.
18. Install the compressor and mounting bracket. Install and adjust the compressor belt.
19. Install and connect the condenser fan assembly.
20. Reconnect the compressor refrigerant lines.
21. Install the alternator and adjust the belt.
22. Reconnect the alternator wiring harness.

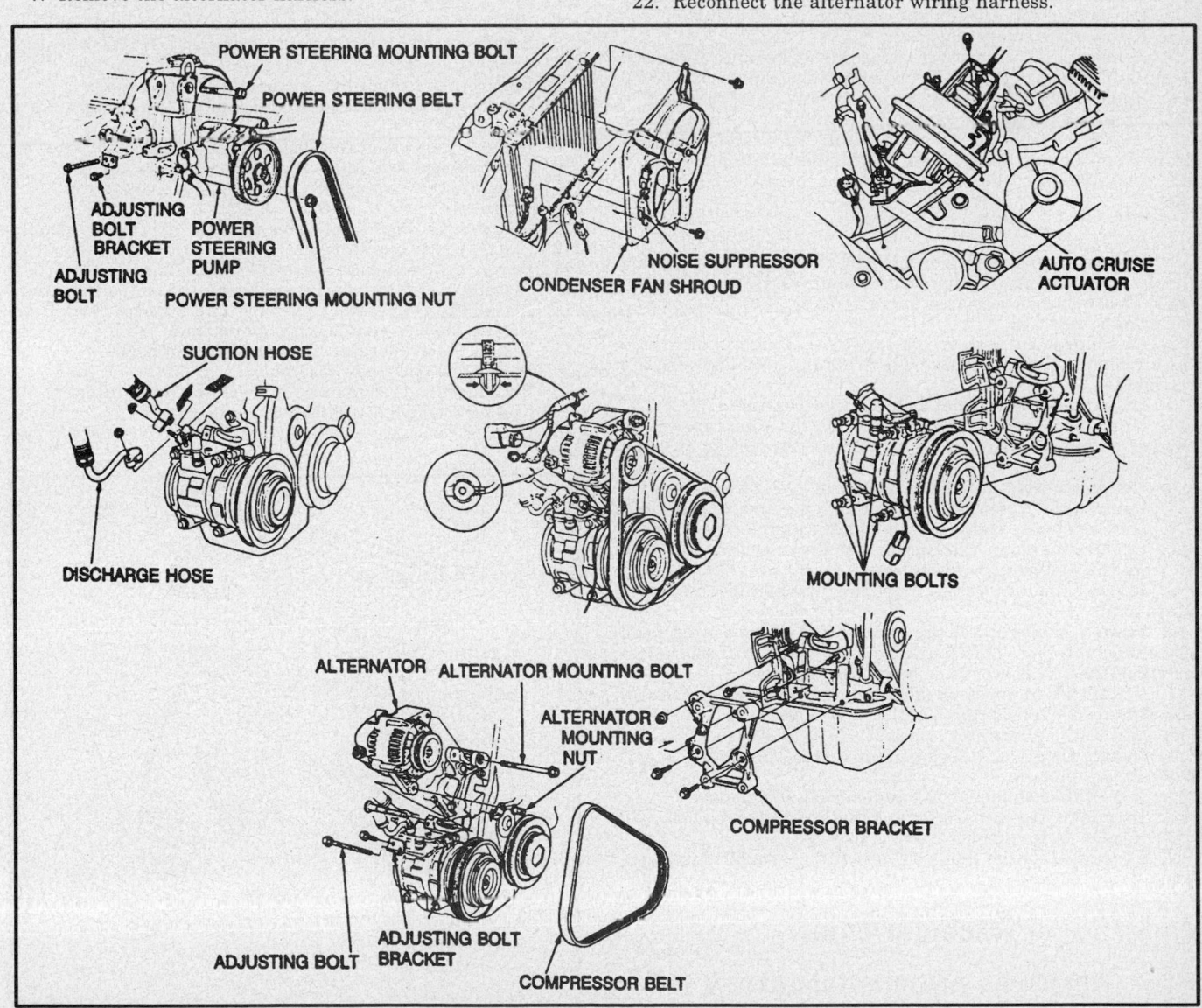

Compressor assembly removal—Accord shown, others are similar

23. Install the auto cruise actuator.
24. Install the power steering pump and adjust the belt.
25. Reconnect the compressor magnetic clutch connector.
26. Reconnect the negative battery cable.
27. Evacuate, charge and leak test the air conditioning system.

Civic and Civic del Sol

1. If the compressor is operable, run the engine at idle, with the air conditioning **ON**, for several minutes. Shut the engine **OFF**. This returns the maximum amount of oil to the compressor prior to removal.
2. Disconnect the negative battery cable. Properly discharge the air conditioning system slowly to minimize oil loss with the refrigerant.
3. Disconnect the magnetic clutch wire connector.
4. Loosen the power steering pump adjusting bolt and remove the belt (if applicable).
5. Remove the power steering attaching bolts and remove the unit.
6. Disconnect and plug the compressor refrigerant lines.
7. Loosen the compressor attaching bolts and adjuster.
8. Remove the compressor belt.
9. Remove the compressor attaching bolts and assembly. Drain and measure the oil if replacing the compressor.
10. Remove the compressor mounting bracket, if required.
11. From 4 oz. (Sanden compressor), subtract the quantity of oil as measured from the old compressor. This is the amount to drain from the new compressor prior to installation.
12. Installation is the reverse of the removal procedure.

Prelude

1. If the compressor is operable, run the engine at idle, with the air conditioning **ON**, for several minutes. Shut the engine **OFF**. This returns the maximum amount of oil to the compressor prior to removal.
2. Disconnect the negative battery cable. Properly discharge the air conditioning system slowly to minimize oil loss with the refrigerant.
3. Disconnect the magnetic clutch wire connector.
4. Disconnect the condenser fan connector, then remove the condenser fan and shroud. Now remove the power steering belt.
5. Disconnect and plug the compressor refrigerant lines.
6. Remove the compressor attaching bolts and heat shield
7. Disconnect the compressor magnetic clutch connector.
8. Remove the compressor assembly. Drain and measure the oil from the compressor if replacing it.
9. Remove the compressor mounting bracket, if required.

To install:
10. From 4 oz., subtract the quantity of oil measured from the old compressor. This is the amount to drain from the capacity of the new compressor before installation.
11. Install the compressor and mounting bracket. Reconnect the compressor refrigerant lines. Use new O-rings.
12. Install the alternator and belt.
13. Install the power steering pump and inlet hose and adjust the belt, as removed.
14. Install the condenser fan and shroud, if removed.
15. Reconnect the compressor magnetic clutch connector.
16. Reconnect the negative battery cable.
17. Evacuate, charge and leak test the air conditioning system.

Receiver/Drier

REMOVAL AND INSTALLATION

1. Disconnect the negative battery cable.
2. Properly discharge the air conditioning system.

3. Disconnect the receiver/drier pressure switch connector.
4. Disconnect and plug the receiver/drier refrigerant lines.
5. Remove the receiver/drier bracket attaching bolts.
6. Remove the receiver/drier assembly.
7. Installation is the reverse of the removal procedure. Add 0.3–0.4 oz. of oil during installation of the replacement receiver/drier.

Evaporator

REMOVAL AND INSTALLATION

NOTE: Read and follow the SRS disabling information to prevent accidental air bag deployment or injury.

Except Prelude

1. Disconnect the negative battery cable.
2. Properly discharge the air conditioning system.
3. Disconnect and plug the refrigerant lines at the evaporator.
4. Remove the glove box and support brackets.
5. Disconnect the air conditioner thermo–switch wire connector.
6. Remove the evaporator securing bolts and nuts.
7. Disconnect the drain hose and remove the evaporator assembly.
8. Remove the evaporator case attaching clips and screws.
9. Separate the case halves and remove the evaporator.
10. Separate the expansion valve from the evaporator.

To install:
11. Connect the expansion valve to the evaporator assembly.
12. Install the evaporator assembly into the case halves.
13. Secure evaporator case assembly together.
14. Install 0.7–1.0 oz. of oil if replacing the evaporator core.
15. Install the evaporator assembly and connect drain hose. Connect the thermo–switch wire connector.
16. Install the evaporator housing securing bands.
17. Install the glove box assembly.
18. Reconnect the refrigerant lines at the evaporator.
19. Connect the negative battery cable.
20. Charge, evacuate and leak test the air conditioning system.

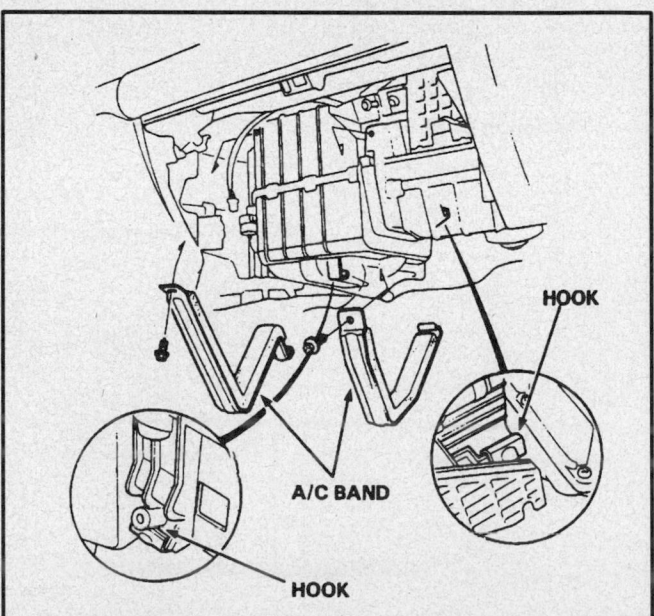

Typical evaporator assembly removal

Prelude

1. Disconnect the negative battery cable.
2. Properly discharge the air conditioning system using recovery type equipment.
3. Disconnect the refrigerant lines from the evaporator core tube and seal to prevent contamination of the system..
4. Remove the right speaker from the instrument panel. Remove the visor and the black face panel from the right front of the instrument panel.
5. Carefully detach and lift the front passenger's air bag assembly out of the dashboard. Store air bag assembly with pad surface up only.
6. Remove the air bag stay, then remove the air bag bracket.
7. Disconnect the wiring from the A/C thermostat.
8. Remove the evaporator assembly.
9. Disassemble the evaporator on the workbench.
10. Installation is the reverse of the removal procedure. Be sure to re-seal the firewall grommets to prevent air leaks. Install 0.7–1.0 oz. of refrigerant oil if the evaporator core was replaced.

Expansion Valve

REMOVAL AND INSTALLATION

1. Follow the procedures for Evaporator removal.
2. Remove the evaporator case attaching clips and screws.
3. Separate the case halves and remove the evaporator core.
4. Separate the expansion valve from the evaporator.
5. Installation is the reverse of the removal procedure.

Blower Motor

REMOVAL AND INSTALLATION

NOTE: Read and follow the SRS disabling information to prevent accidental air bag deployment or injury.

The blower motor, blower motor resistor and recirculation control motor can be removed without removing the blower unit housing.

1. Remove the glove box assembly and frame being careful to follow the procedure for deactivating the SRS air bag system.
2. Disconnect the wire connector to the blower motor.
3. Loosen the 3 screws which attach the blower motor to the bottom or the blower motor housing.
4. Lower and remove the blower motor/fan wheel assembly.
5. Installation is the reverse of the removal process.

Blower Motor Resistor

REMOVAL AND INSTALLATION

1. Disconnect the negative battery cable.
2. Remove the glove box assembly, if required.
3. Disconnect the resistor wire connector.
4. Remove the resistor attaching screws.
5. Remove the blower motor resistor.
6. Installation is the reverse of the removal procedure.

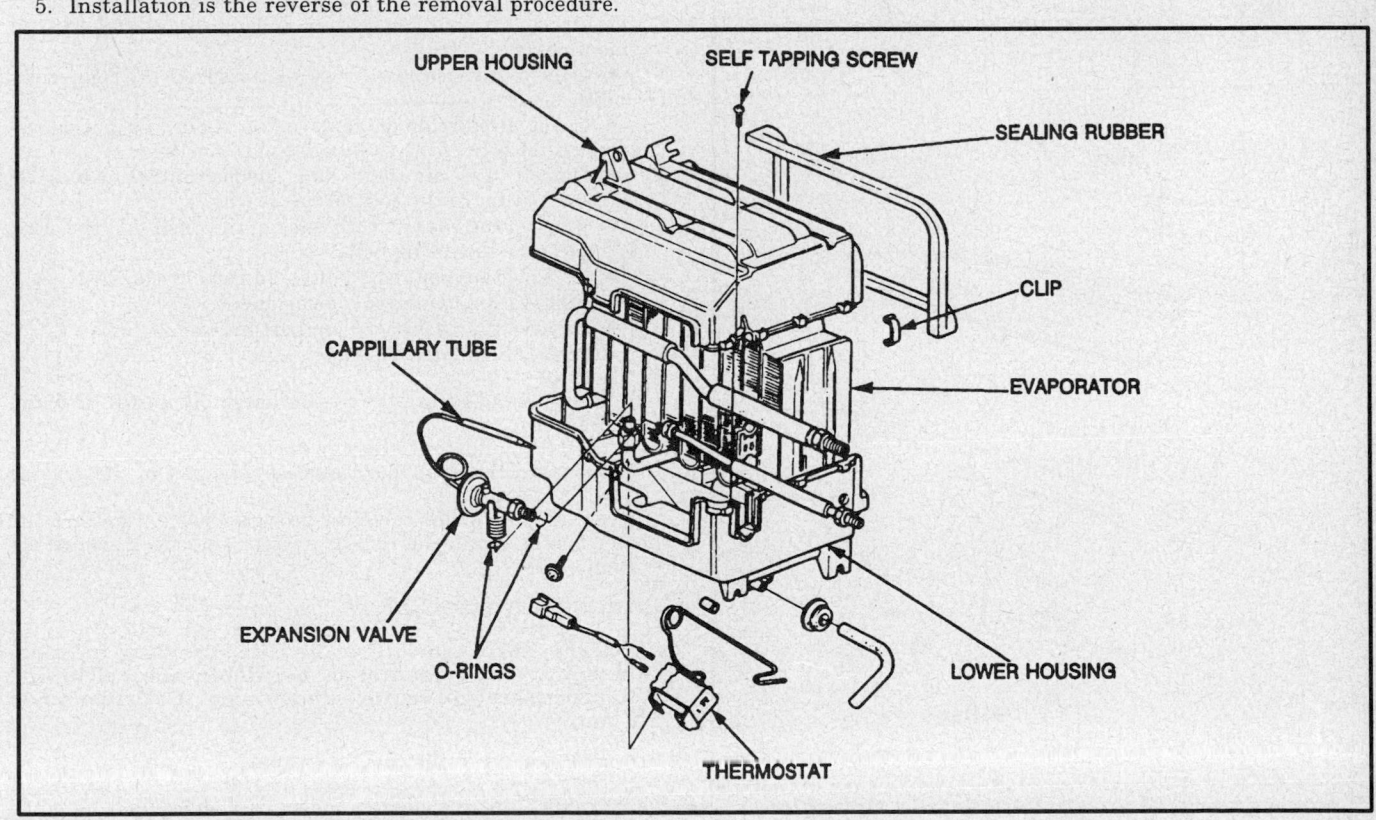

Typical exploded view of the evaporator assembly

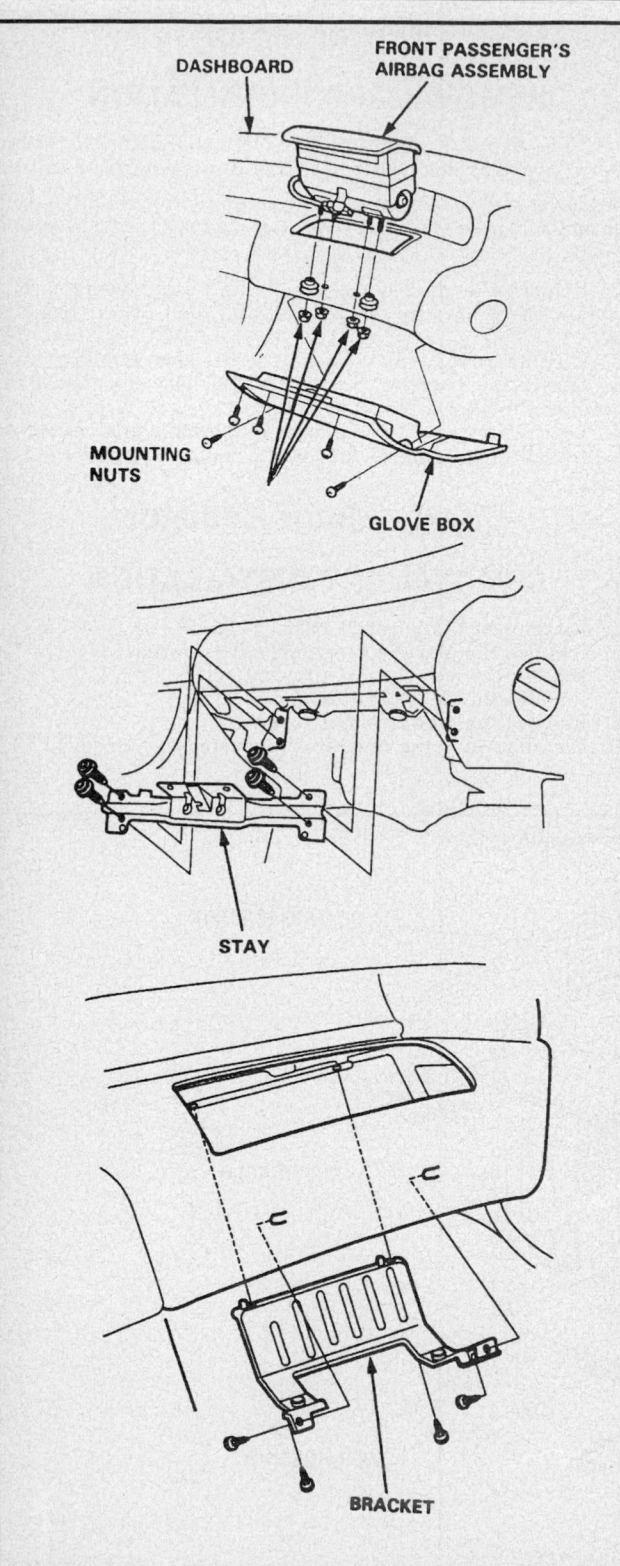

DASHBOARD

FRONT PASSENGER'S AIRBAG ASSEMBLY

MOUNTING NUTS

GLOVE BOX

STAY

BRACKET

Typical removal of the passenger side air bag assembly

Heater Core

REMOVAL AND INSTALLATION

Accord

────── CAUTION ──────

Read and follow the SRS disabling information to prevent accidental air bag deployment or injury. This procedure will require disabling of the driver's side air bag and the disabling and removal of the passenger's side air bag.

────────────────────────────

NOTE: If this vehicle's radio is equipped with a coded anti–theft device, get the customer's 5–digit code before detaching the battery, removing the circuit fuse or removing the radio.

1. Properly drain the cooling system, taking care not to drip any coolant on painted surfaces.
2. Disconnect and plug the heater hoses from the firewall tubes.
3. Detach the heater control valve from the water valve.
4. Remove the dashboard as follows:
   • Remove the front seats and the center console.
   • Remove the glove box and frame.
   • Remove the radio, pocket and the clock.
   • Remove the knee bolster and lower panel.
   • Remove the panels beneath the steering column. Detach and lower the steering column. Protect it from damage with shop towels.
   • Remove the nuts and carefully remove the passenger's side air bag lifting it straight up and out. Store with the pad side up only.
   • Detach the dashboard wire harness from the connectors and fuse box.
   • If not already done, remove the radio and pocket assembly and detach the dashboard wire harness.
   • Detach the air mix and mode control cables, if equipped. Remove the control head.
   • Remove the caps at both ends of the dash and the clock to expose the mounting bolts.
   • Remove the mounting bolts and remove the dash.
   • Remove the heater to blower duct.
   • Remove the dashboard support bracket.
5. Remove the heater assembly.

To Install:

6. Position and secure the heater assembly. Install the support bracket.
7. Install the heater to blower duct.
8. Reinstall the dashboard and components in the reverse order of removal.
9. Attach the heater cable tot he water valve. Reattach the heater hosees. Refill the cooling system and check system operation.

Civic and Civic del Sol

NOTE: Read and follow the SRS disabling information to prevent accidental air bag deployment or injury. This procedure will require disabling of the driver's side air bag.

1. Properly drain the cooling system.
2. Snap open the cable clamp and disconnect the heater valve cable from the heater valve. Disconnect and plug the heater hoses to prevent coolant leakage.
3. Remove the heater mounting nut from the engine compartment side.
4. Remove the dashboard as follows:

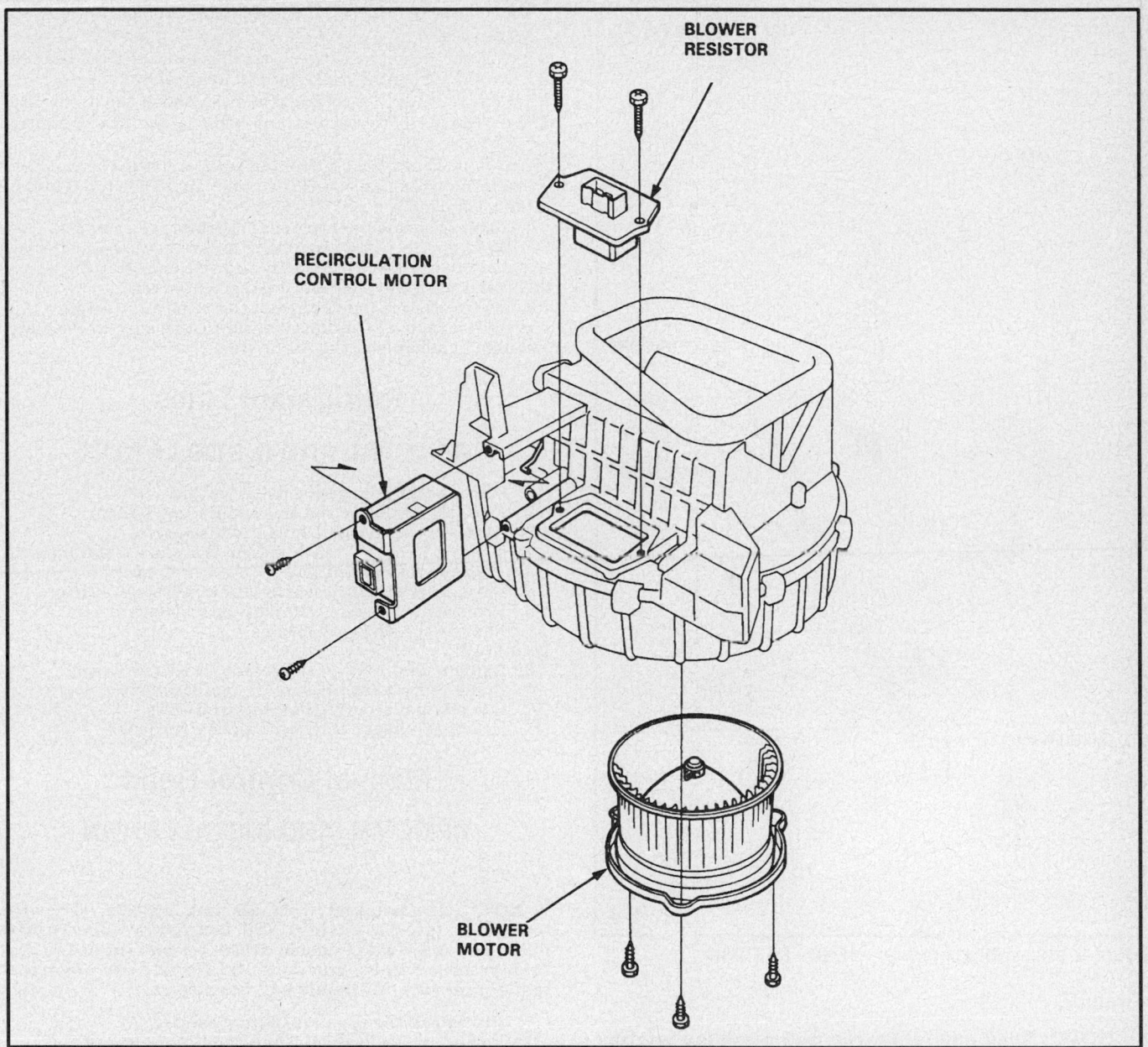

BLOWER
RESISTOR

RECIRCULATION
CONTROL MOTOR

BLOWER
MOTOR

Removal of the blower motor, blower resistor and the recirculation control motor—Prelude

- Remove the front seats.
- On Civic, remove the center lower cover in front of the center floor console.
- On Civic del Sol, remove the front and rear center consoles. Remove the radio panel and the heater control panel.
- Remove the panel cover and knee bolster (if equipped) from beneath the steering column.
- Remove the glove box.
- Detach and lower the steering column.
- Remove the side access panels, detach all wiring connectors as required, and remove the dashboard mounting bolts to remove the dashboard.
5. Remove the heater duct or evaporator .
6. Remove the steering column bracket.

7. Remove the wiring clip from the heater housing. Disconnect the wiring (and cables).
8. Remove the mounting nuts and remove the heater housing. Remove the core cover and take out the heater core, if needed.
To install:
9. Position and secure the heater housing to the dash panel. Reattach the wiring and wiring clip.
10. Install the steering column bracket. Install the heater duct or evaporator, as removed.
11. Install the dashboard and components in reverse order of removal.
12. Install the heater mounting nut in the engine compartment. Reattach the heater valve control cable. Install the heater hoses.
13. Refill the cooling system. Test the system operation.

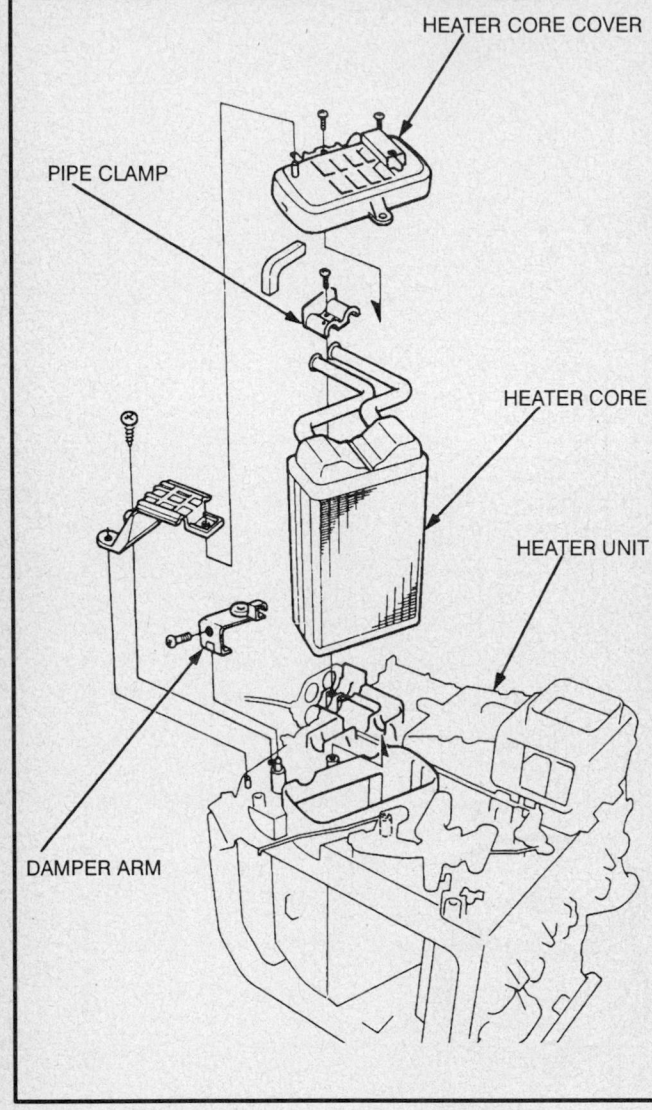

Heater assembly removal—1994–95 Civic

Prelude

NOTE: **Read and follow the SRS disabling information to prevent accidental air bag deployment or injury. This procedure will require disabling of the driver's side air bag and disabling of the passenger's side air bag.**

If this vehicle's radio is equipped with a coded anti-theft device, get the customer's 5-digit code before detaching the battery, removing the circuit fuse or removing the radio.

1. Properly drain cooling system. Detach the heater cable from the water valve. Remove and cap the heater hoses to prevent spillage of coolant on painted surfaces.
2. Remove the 2 heater nuts from the engine compartment side.
3. Remove the dashboard as follows:
   - Remove the front seats, front console and center panel.
   - Remove the glove box.
   - Remove the lower cover from beneath the steering column.
   - Remove the air conditioner duct.

- Lower the steering column to the floor (cover it for protection).
- Remove the passenger's air bag bracket from beneath the right side of the dashboard (if applicable).
- Remove the access panel on each end of the dashboard.
- Detach all connectors and remove the heater control cable.
- Remove the dash mounting bolts and remove the dashboard (note the position of the guide pin in the top center of the dash panel).

4. Remove the heater duct or evaporator, as equipped.
5. Remove the 2 mounting bolts and remove the heater assembly. Remove the pipe clamp and the defroster duct from the heater assembly and remove the heater core.
6. Installation is the reverse of the removal procedure. Adjust control cables. If equipped with A/C, be sure to evacuate, recharge and leak test the A/C system.

Refrigerant Lines

REMOVAL AND INSTALLATION

1. Disconnect the negative battery cable.
2. Properly discharge the air conditioning system.
3. Remove components as required for access.
4. Using a backup wrench loosen, disconnect and immediately plug the refrigerant line.
5. Disconnect pressure switch wire connectors, if required.
6. Remove all attaching brackets and bolts.
7. Remove the refrigerant lines.

To install:

8. Apply a light coat of refrigerant oil to new O-rings.
9. Route refrigerant lines in original locations.
10. Use original securing brackets and bolts.
11. Evacuate, charge and check system for leaks.

Manual Control Head

REMOVAL AND INSTALLATION

Accord

NOTE: **If equipped with air bag system, the wire harnesses (yellow casing) and connectors are routed nears the radio and console areas, be certain not to disturb or pinch these components. Do not use electrical test equipment on the air bag harnesses.**

1. Disconnect the negative battery cable.
2. Remove the ashtray assembly and center console.
3. Remove the instrument panel switches, coin box and air vents.
4. Remove the radio and instrument housing assembly.
5. Remove the cruise control main switch, dash dimmer control and the rear window defogger switch.
6. Disconnect the control cables at the heater assembly.
7. Remove the heater control head attaching screws and pull the unit out.
8. Disconnect the wire connectors and remove the heater control head.
9. Installation is the reverse of the removal procedure.

Civic and Civic del Sol

1. Disconnect the negative battery cable.
2. Remove the console (del Sol) or the lower center panel (Civic).
3. Remove the radio attaching screws and remove the radio assembly.
4. Disconnect the control cables at the heater unit.

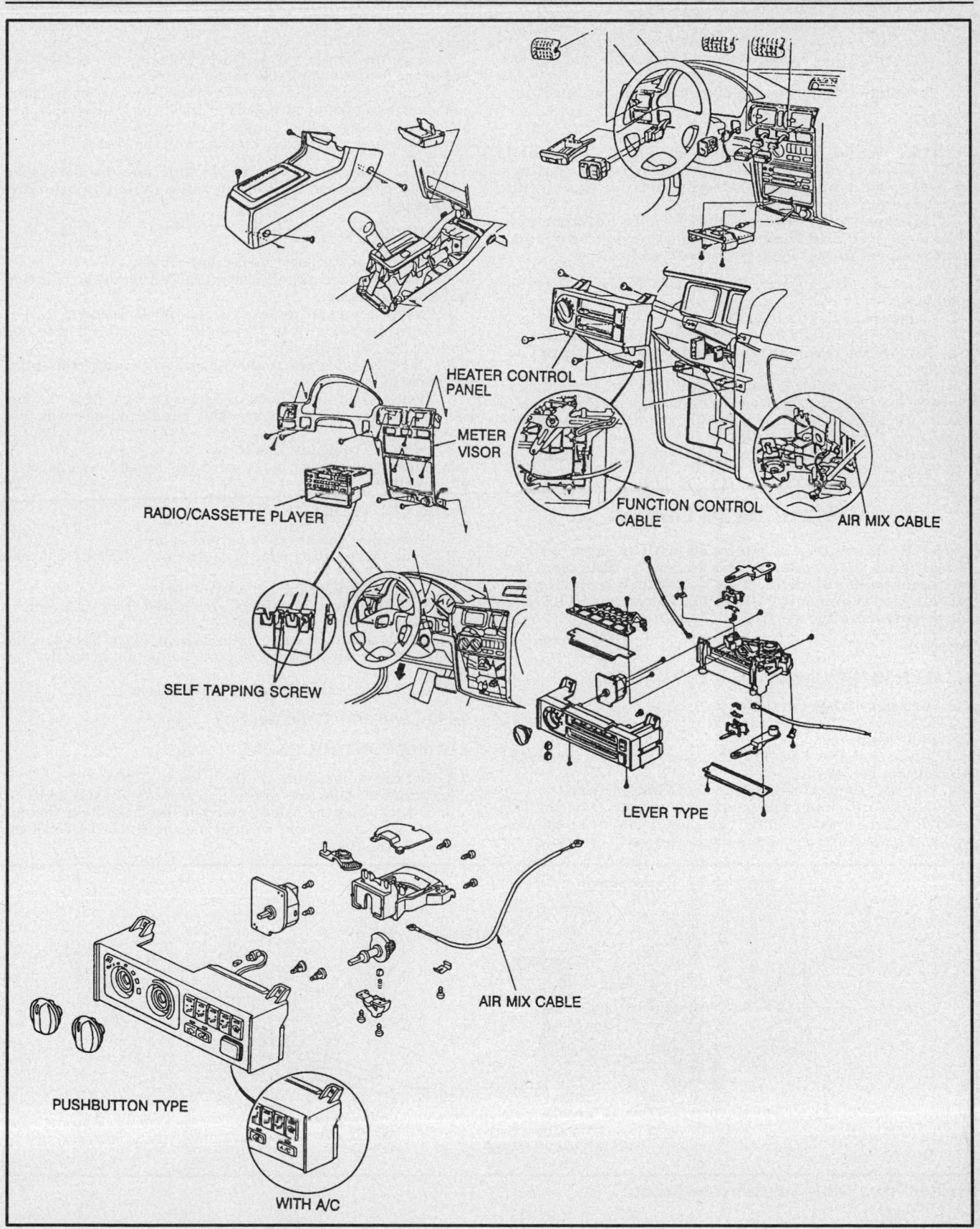

HEATER CONTROL PANEL

METER VISOR

RADIO/CASSETTE PLAYER

FUNCTION CONTROL CABLE

AIR MIX CABLE

SELF TAPPING SCREW

LEVER TYPE

AIR MIX CABLE

PUSHBUTTON TYPE

WITH A/C

Control head removal and installation—Accord

5. Remove the attaching screws at the control head and pull assembly out.

6. Disconnect the control head wire connectors and remove the unit.

7. Installation is the reverse of the removal procedure.

Prelude

NOTE: Radio may be equipped with an anti-theft code system. If so, get the 5-digit code from the customer before detaching the battery, removing the circuit fuse or removing the radio.

If equipped with SRS (air bag), be sure not to detach yellow covered SRS wiring or connectors during component removal unless system is disabled first.

1. Disconnect the negative battery cable. Remove the center console.

2. Remove the radio assembly.

3. Detach the air mix control cable from the heater unit.

4. Remove the retaining screws and take out the control assembly.

5. The control panel is removed with the center air outlet. Remove the locking tabs from the connectors, remove the 2 screws from the back of the assembly and detach the control panel from the center air outlet.

6. Installation is the reverse of the removal procedure.

7. Adjust the cables.

Control Head Cables

NOTE: If vehicle is equipped with a radio with a 5-digit anti-theft code, be sure to get the code from the customer before disconnecting the battery, removing the circuit fuse or removing the radio. The code will have to be re-entered after service is complete.

Accord

HEATER VALVE CABLE

1. Disconnect the negative battery cable.

2. Disconnect the heater valve cable from the heater valve arm and clamp.

3. Disconnect the second heater valve cable from the heater control arm and clamp.

4. Set the temperature control dial to **MAX COOL**.

5. Gently slide the cable outer housing back from the end enough to take up slack in the cable but do not make the control dial move. Hold the end of the heater valve cable housing against the stop, then snap the heater valve cable housing into the clamp.

6. Move the heater valve arm to the stop and connect the end of the heater valve cable to the heater valve arm.

7. Gently slide the heater valve cable housing back from the end enough to take up any slack in the heater valve cable, but not enough to make the temperature control dial move, then snap the heater valve cable housing into the clamp.

NOTE: The air mix control cable should always be adjusted whenever the heater valve cable has been disconnected.

AIR MIX ROD AND CABLE

1. Disconnect the negative battery cable.

2. Disconnect the air mix control cable from the air mix control arm and clamp.

3. Set the temperature lever to the **COOL** position.

4. Turn the rod arm to the engine compartment side and connect the rod to the clip.

5. Move the cable arm to the stopper and connect the end of the cable to the arm.

6. Gently slide the cable outer housing back from the end enough to take up slack in the cable but do not make the control lever move.

7. Snap the cable into the clamp.

8. After adjustment, make sure the temperature lever is properly adjusted.

MODE CONTROL CABLE

1. Disconnect the negative battery cable.

2. Slide the function control lever to the **DEFROST** position.

3. Disconnect the function control cable.

4. Turn the function control arm to the front and connect the end of the cable to the arm.

5. Gently slide the cable outer housing back from the end enough to take up slack in the cable but do not make the control lever move.

6. Connect the cable housing to the clamp.

1993 Civic and Civic del Sol

AIR MIX CONTROL CABLE

1. Set the temperature control lever to **COOL** .

2. Turn the cable arm to the stop and connect the cable.

3. Gently slide the cable outer housing back from the end enough to take up slack, without moving the lever. Snap the cable into the clamp.

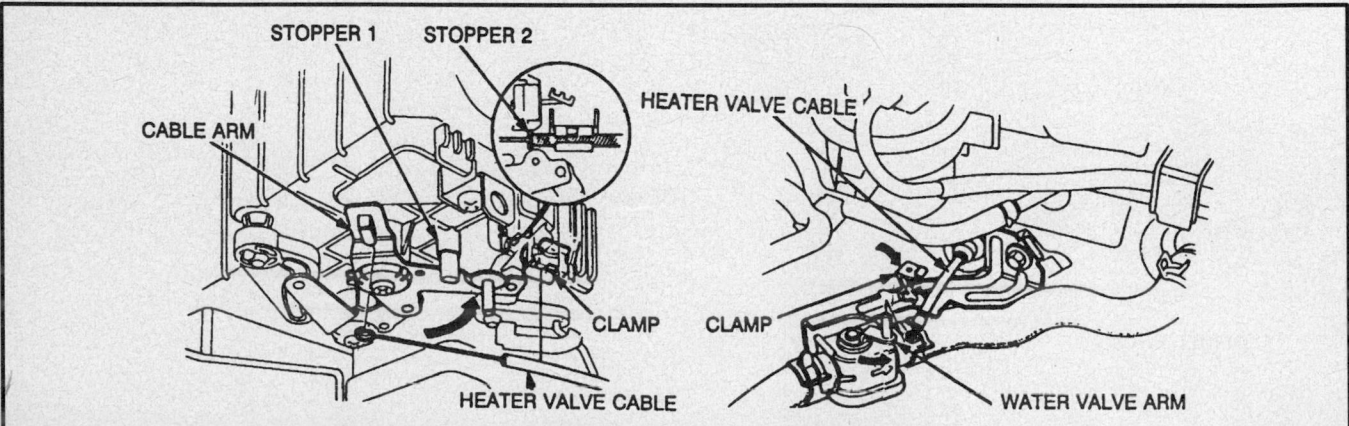

Heater valve cable adjustment—Accord

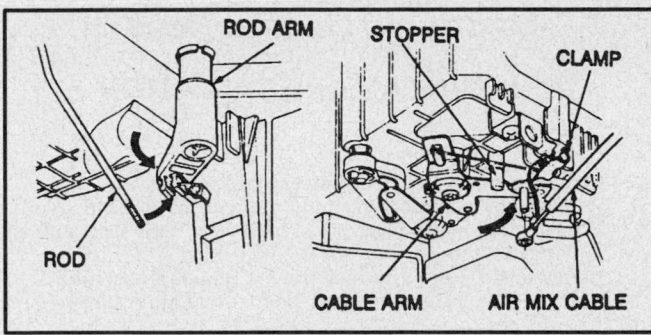

Air mix rod and cable adjustment—Accord

HEATER VALVE CONTROL CABLE

1. Disconnect the cable from the heater water valve. Set the temperature control lever to **COOL**.

2. Turn the cable arm to the stop and connect the cable. Gently slide the cable outer housing back from the end enough to take up slack, without moving the lever. Snap the cable into the clamp.

3. Turn the heater valve arm to the SHUT position and connect the cable to the arm.

4. Gently slide the cable outer housing back from the end enough to take up slack, without moving the lever. Snap the cable into the clamp.

NOTE: Mode control and recirculation control are via electric motors.

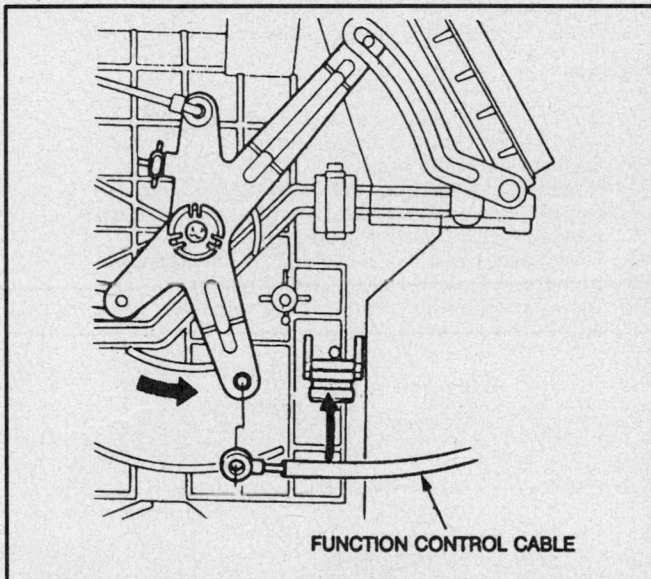

Heater function control adjustment—Accord

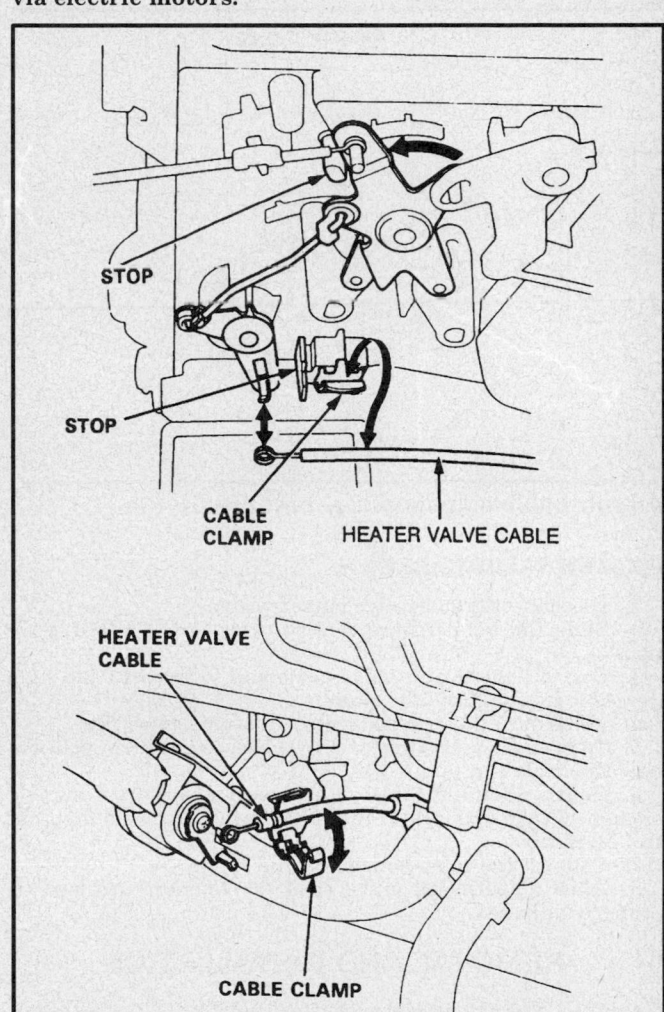

Heater valve cable adjustment — Civic and Civic del Sol

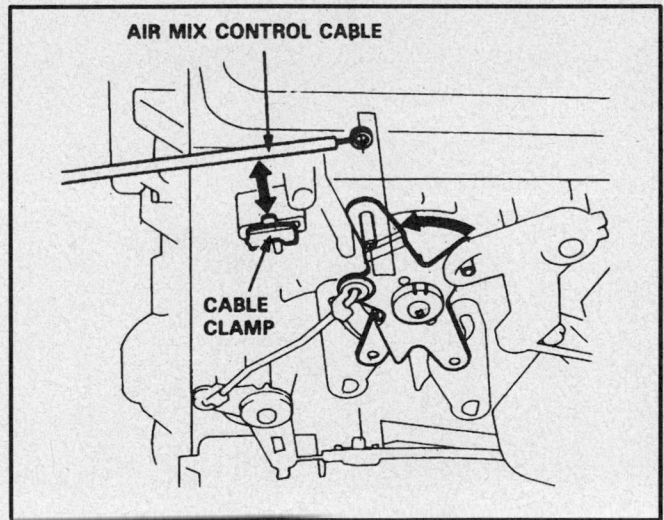

Air mix cable adjustment — Civic and Civic del Sol

Prelude

AIR MIX CABLE

1. Disconnect the negative battery cable.
2. Slide the temperature control lever to the **COOL** position.
3. Turn he function control shaft to the left and connect the end of the cable to the arm.
4. Gently slide the cable outer housing back from the end enough to take up slack in the cable but do not make the control lever move.
5. Connect the cable housing to the clamp.
6. After adjustment, make sure the temperature lever is properly adjusted.

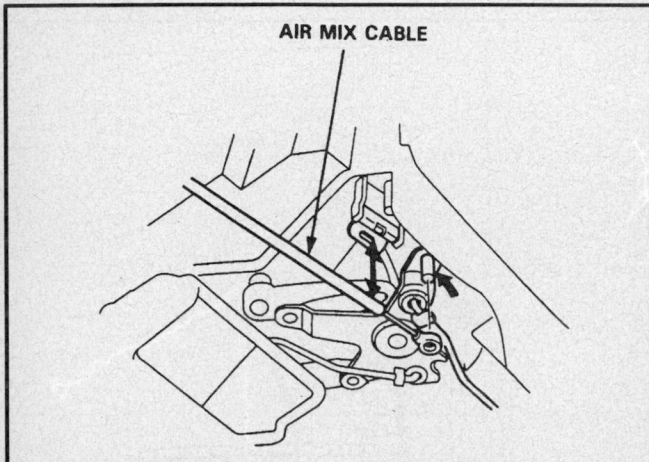

Air mix cable adjustment — Prelude

HEATER VALVE CABLE

1. Disconnect the negative battery cable.
2. Slide the temperature control lever to the **COOL** position.
3. Connect the heater valve cable end to the arm and snap the cable housing into the clamp.
4. Make sure the arm turns its full stroke smoothly.
5. Turn the heater valve arm to the closed position and connect the cable end to the arm.
6. Gently slide the cable outer housing back from the end enough to take up slack in the cable but do not make the control lever move.
7. Connect the cable housing to the clamp.
8. After adjustment, make sure the temperature lever is properly adjusted.

REMOVAL AND INSTALLATION

1. Disconnect the negative battery cable.
2. Remove the control head assembly.
3. Disconnect the control cable at the control head.
4. Remove the glove box, if required.
5. Disconnect the control cables at the heater unit.
6. Disconnect the heater control valve cable located in the engine compartment.
7. Installation is the reverse of the removal procedure.

Electronic Control Head

REMOVAL AND INSTALLATION

Accord

1. Disconnect the negative battery cable.
2. Remove the ashtray assembly and center console.
3. Remove the instrument panel switches, coin box and air vents.
4. Remove the radio and instrument housing assembly.
5. Remove the heater control head attaching screws and pull the unit out.
6. Disconnect the air mix control cable.
7. Disconnect the wire connectors and remove the heater control head.
8. Installation is the reverse of the removal procedure.

Prelude

1. Disconnect the negative battery cable.
2. Remove the center console assembly.
3. Remove the radio assembly.
4. Remove the center air vent outlet.
5. Remove the heater control head attaching screws.
6. Disconnect the control head switch wires.
7. Disconnect the air mix cable at the heater unit.
8. Remove the control head assembly.
9. Installation is the reverse of the removal procedure.

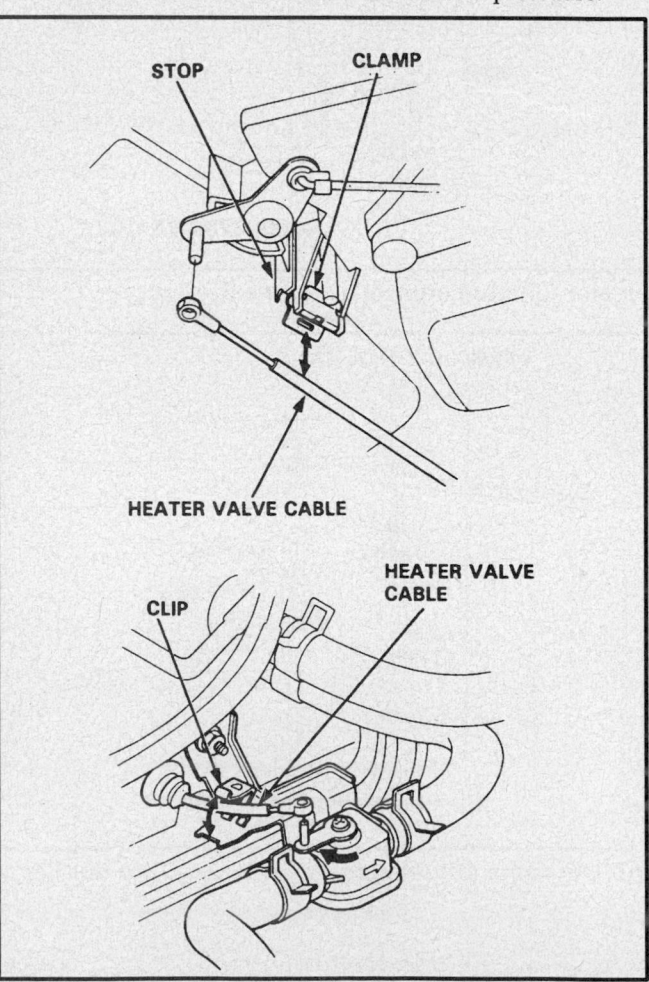

Heater valve cable adjustment — Prelude

SENSORS AND SWITCHES

Fan Switch

OPERATION

The fan switch is located with the control head and has several speeds including the OFF position. The blower motor always has approximately 12 volts and the fan switch then completes the circuit by supplying a ground through a resistor, thus varying the fan speed.

TESTING

Accord

1. Disconnect the negative battery cable.
2. Remove the fan switch and disconnect the wire connector.
3. Test for continuity as shown in the chart.
4. If not as specified, replace the fan switch.

Civic and Civic del Sol

1. Disconnect the negative battery cable.
2. Remove the fan switch and disconnect the wire connector.
3. Test for continuity as shown in the chart.
4. If not as specified, replace the fan switch.

Prelude

1. Disconnect the negative battery cable.
2. Remove the fan switch and disconnect the wire connector.
3. Test for continuity as shown in the charts.
4. If not as specified, replace the fan switch.

REMOVAL AND INSTALLATION

1. Disconnect the negative battery cable.
2. Remove the control head assembly.
3. Remove fan switch attaching screws.
4. Disconnect fan switch wire connectors.
5. Remove the fan switch.
6. Installation is the reverse of the removal procedure.

Check for continuity between the terminals according to the table below.

Terminal Position	B	A	D	E	F	G
OFF						
1	o—	—o—	—o			
2	o—	—o—	——	——	—o	
3	o—	—o—	——	——	——	—o
4	o—	—o—	——	——	——	—o

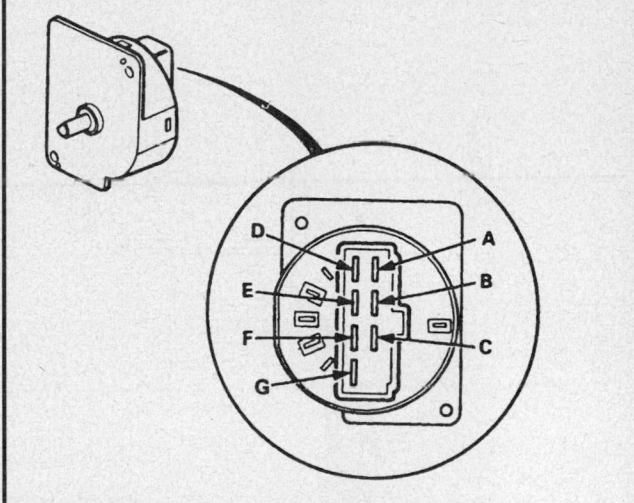

Fan switch testing — Accord

Check for continuity between the terminals according to the table below.

SWITCH CONNECTION

Terminal Position	①	②	③	④	⑤	⑥
OFF						
1	o—	—o—	—o			
2	o—	—o—	——	—o		
3	o—	—o—	——	——	—o	
4	o—	—o—	——	——	——	—o

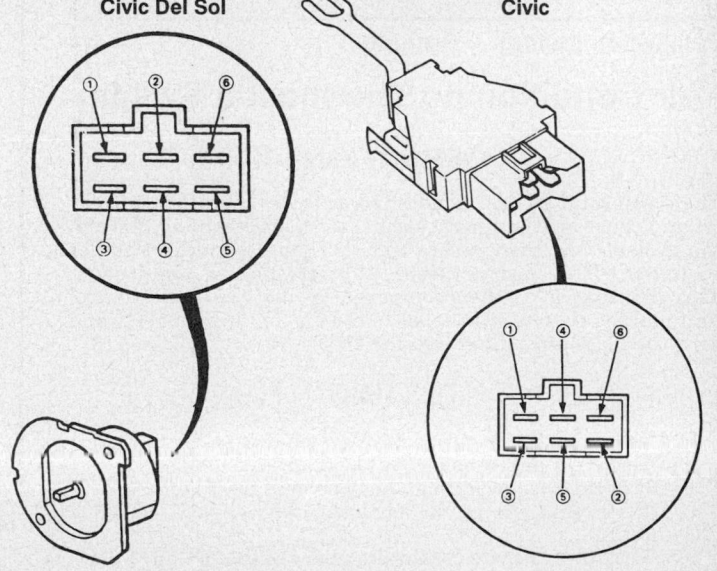

Fan switch testing — Civic and Civic del Sol

Check for continuity between the terminals according to the table below.

SWITCH CONNECTION

Position \ Terminal	1	2	3	4	5	6
OFF						
▬ A	○		○——○			
▬ B	○		○		○	
▬ C	○		○			○
▬ D	○——○——○					

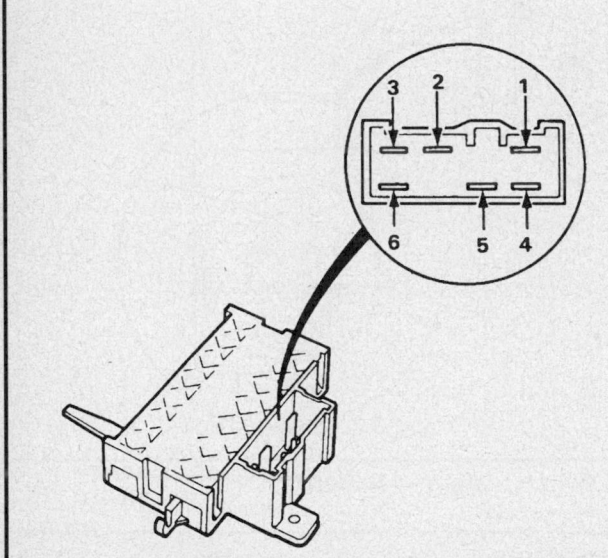

Fan switch testing — Prelude

Air Conditioning Thermostat Switch

OPERATION

The thermostat switch is mounted at the evaporator core outlet and senses the temperature of the cool air coming through the evaporator. Temperature signals then determine whether the circuit is opened or closed, thus completing the ground. This information is then compared by the electronic control unit and the results are output to the air conditioner relay and turn the magnetic clutch ON and OFF.

TESTING

1. Disconnect the negative battery cable.
2. Disconnect and remove the thermostat.
3. Place the thermostat capillary tube in ice water.
4. Check that there is no continuity below 33–35°F (0.5–1.5°C).
5. Check that there is continuity above 37–41°F (2.5–5.0°C).
6. If not within specification, replace the thermostat.

REMOVAL AND INSTALLATION

1. Disconnect the negative battery cable.
2. Properly discharge the air conditioning system.
3. Remove the evaporator assembly.
4. Separate the evaporator assembly.
5. Remove the thermostat switch.
6. Installation is the reverse of the removal procedure.

Connect battery power to the C terminal, ground the B terminal, and connect a test light between the A and B terminals.

NOTE: Use a 12 V, 3 W – 18 W test light.

Dip the A/C thermostat into a cup filled with ice water, and check the test light.

The light should go off at 36 – 39°F (2 – 4°C) or less, and should come on at 39 – 41°F (4 – 5°C) or more.

If the light doesn't come on and go off as specified, replace the A/C thermostat.

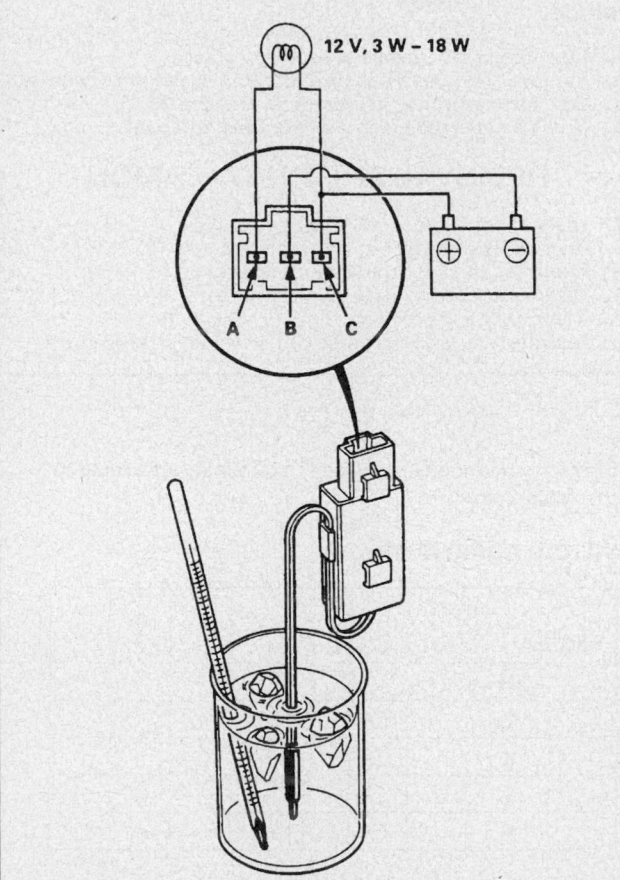

Testing of the thermostatic switch

Dual Pressure Switch

OPERATION

The dual pressure switch which turns the magnetic clutch ON or OFF as a result of irregularly high or low pressures of the refrigerant. The pressure switch is located at the receiver/drier or condenser.

TESTING

1. Disconnect the pressure switch wire connector from the receiver/drier or from the high pressure line.
2. Start the vehicle and turn the air conditioner **ON**.
3. Hook up the air conditioner gauges or charging station.
4. Check for 12 volts at the pressure switch wire connector.
5. If there is no voltage at either terminal of wire connector, check the air conditioner relay.
6. Connect a jumper wire between the 2 terminals.
7. Check to see if compressor clutch engages.
8. If the compressor magnetic clutch fails to operate check the magnetic clutch and the wiring.
9. Check for continuity through the switch using an ohmmeter.
10. At system normal operating pressures and the pressure at the high side between 28–455 psi there should be continuity voltage through the switch.

REMOVAL AND INSTALLATION

1. Disconnect the negative battery cable.
2. Properly discharge the air conditioning system.
3. If required, remove radiator grille.
4. Using 2 wrenches, remove the pressure switch.
5. Installation is the reverse of removal procedure.

Recirculate/Fresh Switch

OPERATION

The recirculate/fresh switch sends a voltage signal to the recirculation control motor which then opens the recirculate/fresh door to allow outside air to enter the vehicle or to recirculate the air that is already in the vehicle.

TESTING

Accord

1993

1. Check that there is continuity at the switch between terminals **A** and **B** with the recirculate button depressed.
2. Check that there is continuity between terminals **A** and **C** with the recirculate button not depressed.
3. If not as specified, replace the control head assembly.

1994–95

1. Check that there is continuity at the switch between terminals **2** and **3** with the recirculate button depressed.
2. Check that there is continuity between terminals **1** and **2** with the recirculate button not depressed.
3. If not as specified, replace the control head assembly.

Civic

1993

1. Check that there is continuity at the switch between terminals **B** and **C** in the **FRESH** position.
2. Check that there is continuity at the switch between terminals **A** and **C** in the **RECIRC** position.

1994–95

1. Check that there is continuity at the switch between terminals **4** and **6** in the **FRESH** position.
2. Check that there is continuity at the switch between terminals **4** and **5** in the **RECIRC** position.

Civic del Sol

1993–94

1. Check that there is continuity at the switch between terminals **1** and **3** in the **FRESH** position.
2. Check that there is continuity at the switch between terminals **2** and **3** in the **RECIRC** position.

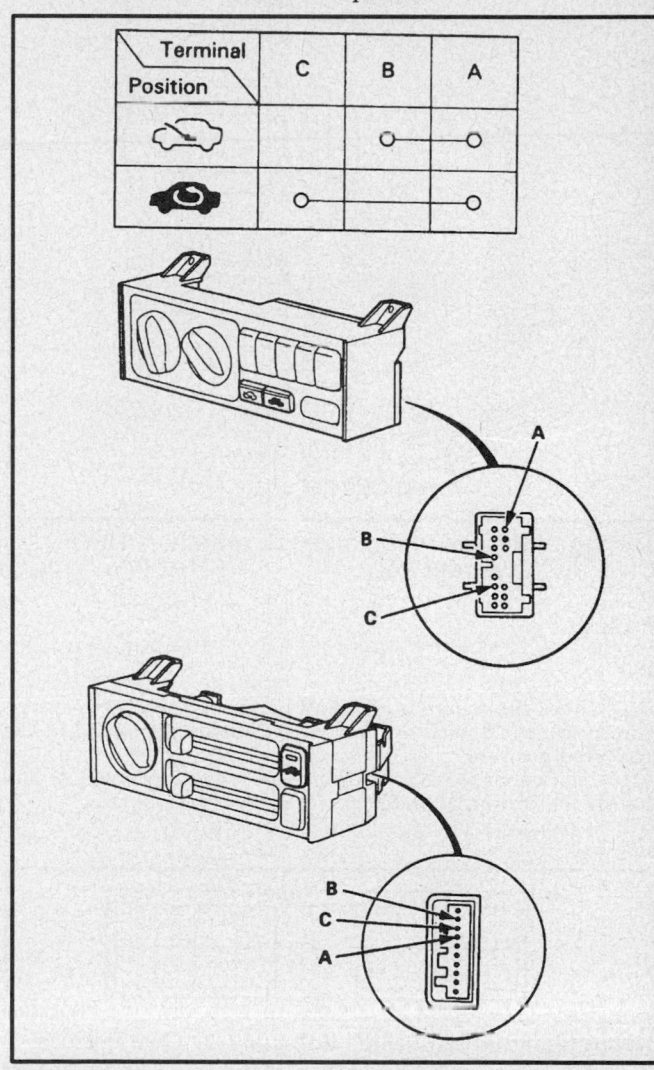

Testing of the recirculation/fresh switch — 1993 Accord

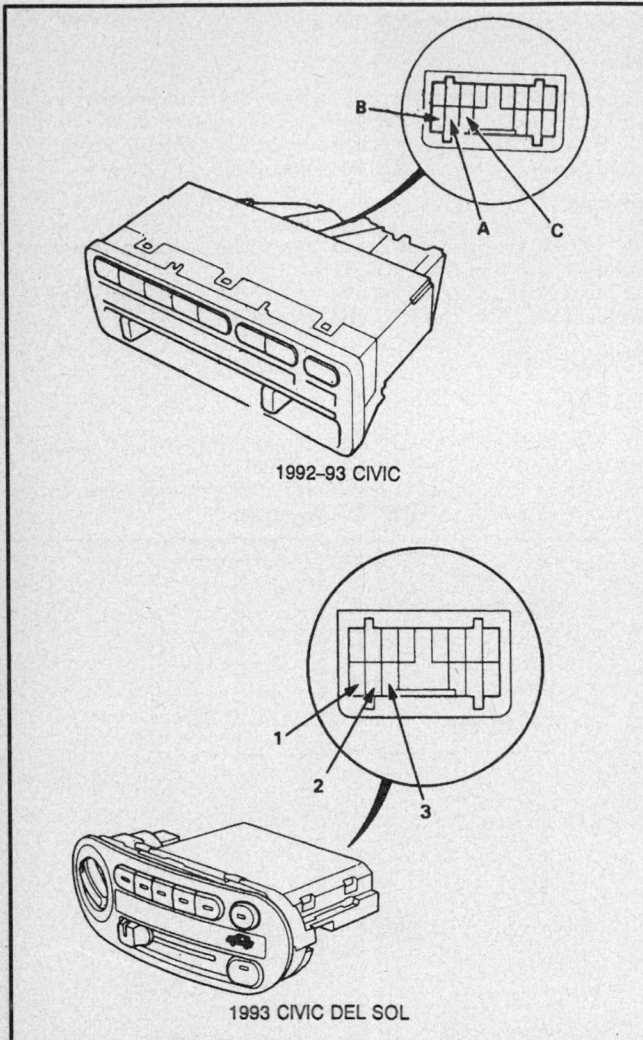

Testing of the recirculation/fresh switch — 1993 Civic and Civic del Sol

1992–93 CIVIC

1993 CIVIC DEL SOL

Prelude

1993

1. Check that there is continuity at the switch between terminals **12** and **6** with the recirculate button depressed in the activated position.
2. Check that there is continuity between terminals **11** and **6** with the recirculate button not depressed.
3. If not as specified, replace the switch.

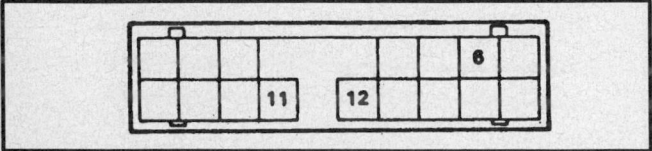

Recirculation/fresh switch terminals — 1993 Prelude

1994–95

1. Check that there is continuity at the switch between terminals **4** and **13** with the recirculate button depressed in the activated position.
2. Check that there is continuity between terminals **11** and **13** with the recirculate button not depressed.
3. If not as specified, replace the switch.

REMOVAL AND INSTALLATION

1. Disconnect the negative battery cable.
2. Remove the control head assembly.
3. Remove recirculate/fresh switch attaching screws.
4. Disconnect the switch wire connectors.
5. Remove the recirculate/fresh switch.
6. Installation is the reverse of the removal procedure.

Recirculation Control Motor

OPERATION

The recirculate/fresh switch sends a voltage signal to the recirculation control motor which then opens the recirculate/fresh door to allow outside air to enter the vehicle or to recirculate the air that is already in the vehicle.

TESTING

Accord

1993

1. Disconnect the negative battery cable.
2. Disconnect the control motor wire connector.
3. Connect a 12 volt positive lead to terminal **1** and the negative lead to terminals **2** and **3** of the control motor connector.
4. The control motor should rotate.
5. Next, disconnect the negative lead from terminals **2** or **3** and the motor should stop at the **REC** or **FRESH** position.
6. If not as specified, replace the recirculation control motor.

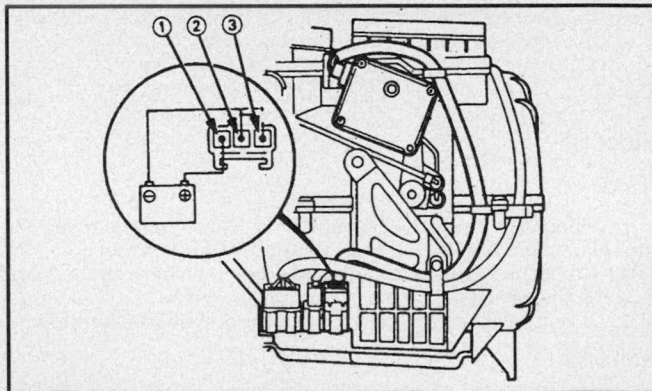

Testing of the recirculation control motor — 1993 Accord

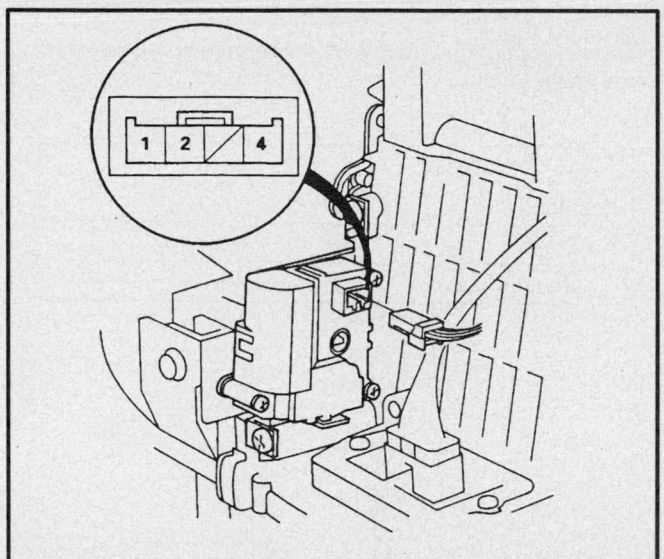

Testing of the recirculation control motor — 1994 Accord

Accord

1994–95

1. Connect battery power to the number **1** terminal and ground the number **2** and number **4** terminals.
2. The recirculation control motor should run smoothly.
3. Disconnect the number **2** or number **4** terminals from ground. The recirculation control motor should stop at **FRESH** or **REC**.

NOTE: Never connect the battery in the opposite direction or run the recirculation control motor for a long time.

4. If the recirculation control motor does not run in Step 1, remove it and check the recirculation control linkage and doors for smooth movement. If the recirculation linkage and doors move smoothly, replace the recirculation control motor.

Check for continuity between the terminals according to the table below.

Position \ Terminal	3	1	2
Fresh		o———	———o
Recirculate	o———		———o

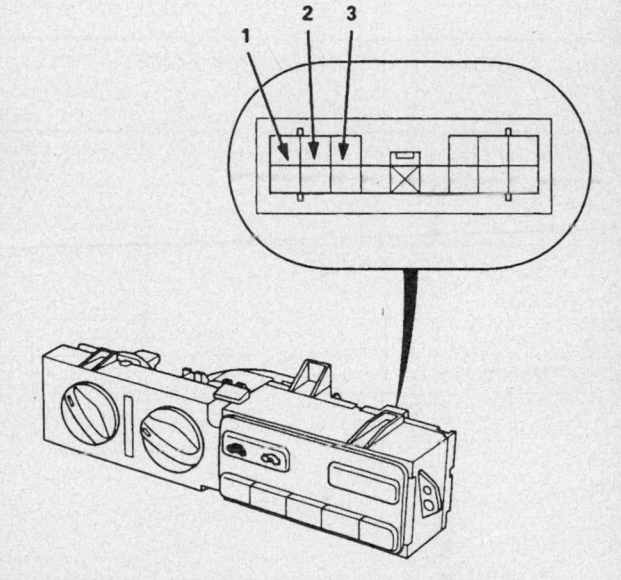

Testing of the recirculation control switch — 1994–95 Accord

Prelude

1. Disconnect the negative battery cable. Disconnect the recirculation motor connector.
2. Connect the battery power to terminal **1** of the motor connector and the ground to terminals **2** and **3**. The motor should move smoothly.
3. Disconnect the ground from terminals **2** or **3** and the motor should stop at the **FRESH** or **RECIRC** position.
4. If the motor does not run when disconnecting the ground from terminal **2** or **3**, reconnect the ground to terminals **2** and **3** and repeat step 3 above. The motor is OK if it runs at this point.

NOTE: Never connect the battery in the opposite direction or run the recirculation control motor for a long time.

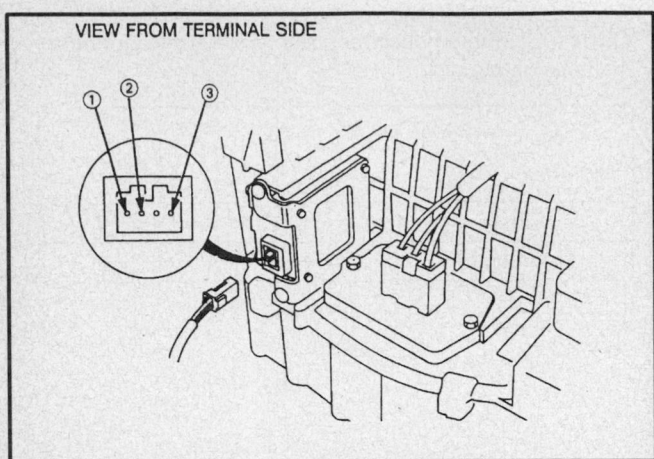

VIEW FROM TERMINAL SIDE

**Testing of the recirculation control motor —
Prelude**

Check for continuity between the terminals according to
the table below.

Position \ Terminal	2	1	3
Fresh		○——○	
Recirculate	○——————○	

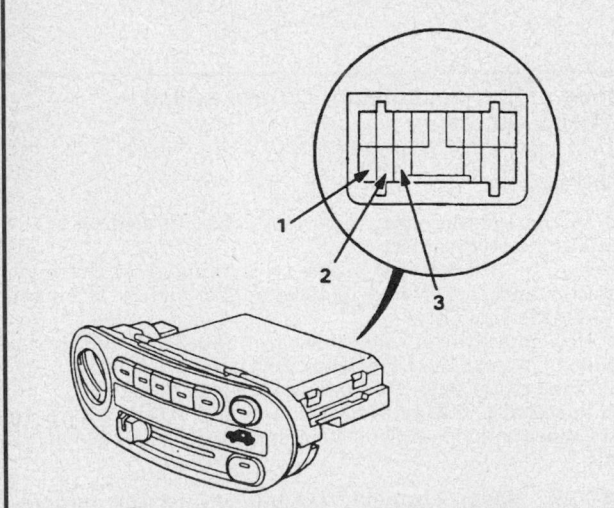

**Testing of the recirculation control switch —
1994–95 Civic del Sol**

Check for continuity between the terminals according to
the table below.

Position \ Terminal	4	6	5
Fresh	○——————○		
Recirculate	○——————————————○		○

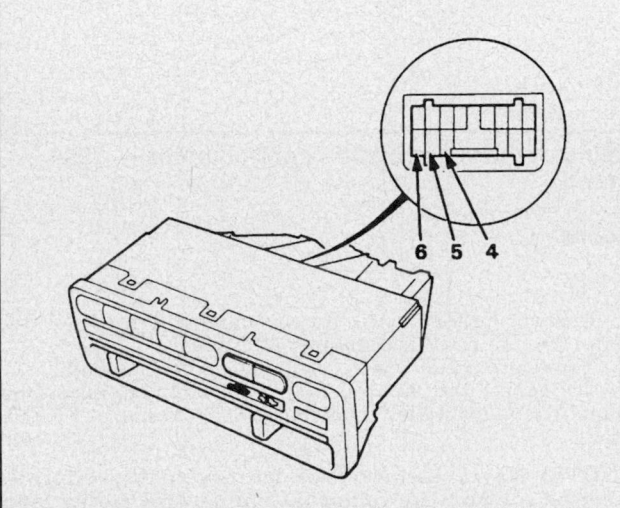

**Testing of the recirculation control switch —
1994–95 Civic**

Check for continuity between the terminals according to the table below.

Terminal Position	4	11	13
Fresh		○———	———○
Recirculate	○———		———○

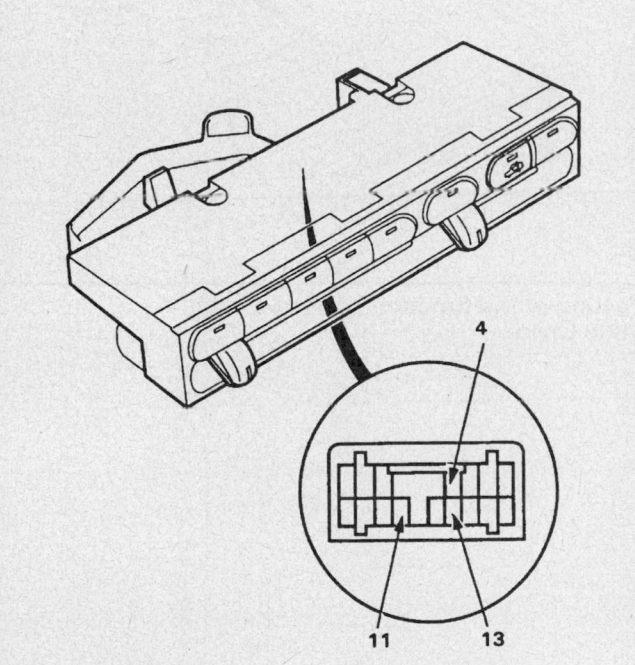

**Testing of the recirculation control switch —
1994–95 Prelude**

Function Control Switch

OPERATION

The function control switch is located at the electronic control head. The main purpose of the switch is to complete the ground circuit to the control motor, which then determines the specified air mix door to open or close.

TESTING

Accord

1. Disconnect the function switch wire connector at the electronic control head.
2. Check that there is continuity at the switch between terminals as shown in the appropriate chart.
3. If not as specified, replace the switch.

Terminal Position	1	2	3	4	5	10
↝					○———	———○
↝				○———		———○
↝			○———			———○
↝		○———				———○
▥	○———					———○

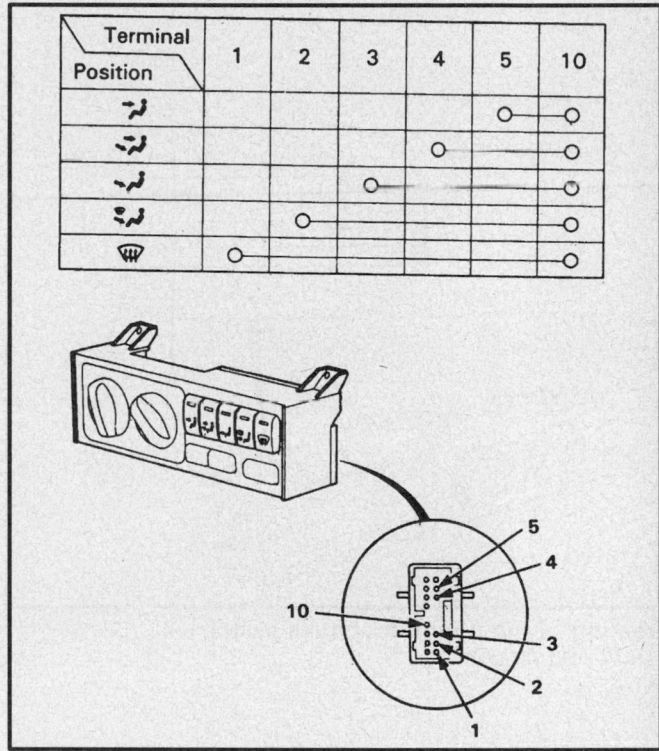

**Testing of the function control switch —
1993 Accord**

Civic and Civic del Sol

1. Disconnect the function switch wire connector at the electronic control head.
2. Check that there is continuity at the switch between terminals as shown in the applicable drawing.
3. If not as specified, replace the switch.

Check for continuity between the terminals according to the table below.

Position \ Terminal	2	14	13	12	4	5
Heat	○—○					
Heat/Def	○		○			
Def	○			○		
Vent	○				○	
Heat/Vent	○					○

Position \ Terminal	1	2	3	4	5	6
Heat	○—○					
Heat/Def	○		○			
Def	○			○		
Vent	○				○	
Heat/Vent	○					○

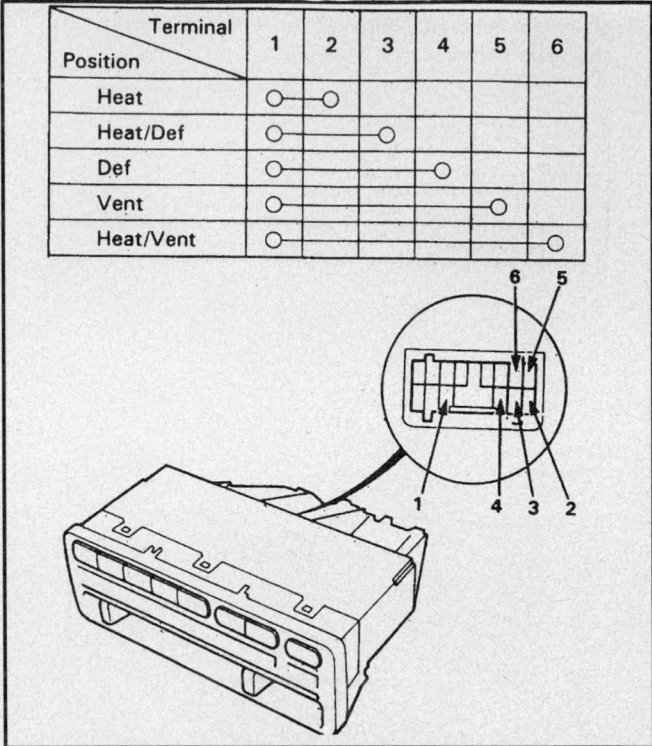

**Testing of the function control switch —
1993 Civic**

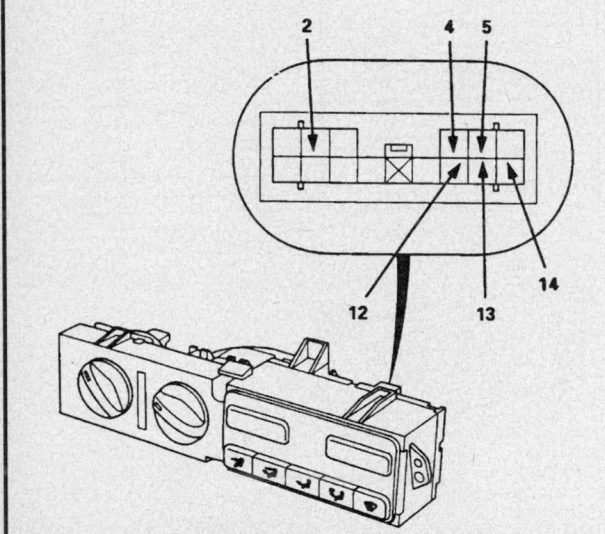

**Testing of the function control switch —
1994–95 Accord**

Check for continuity between the terminals according to the table below.

Terminal Position	4	1	2	3	7	8
Heat	O─────O					
Heat/Def	O		O			
Def	O			O		
Vent	O				O	
Heat/Vent	O					O

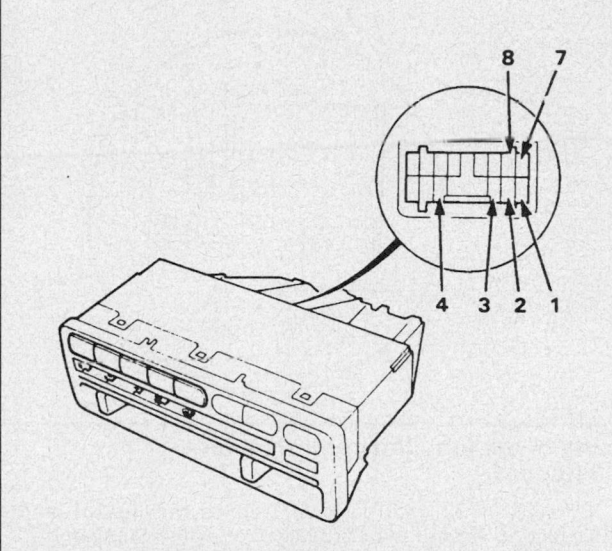

Testing of the function control switch — 1994–95 Civic

Check for continuity between the terminals according to the table below.

Terminal Position	3	6	5	4	14	13
Heat	O─────O					
Heat/Def	O		O			
Def	O			O		
Vent	O				O	
Heat/Vent	O					O

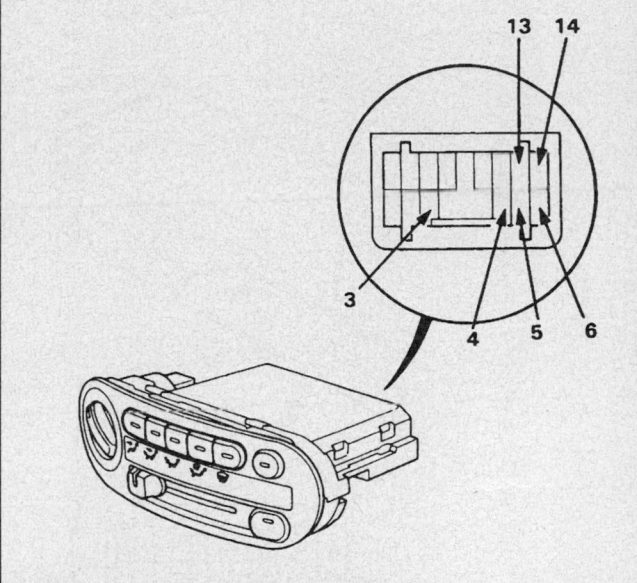

Testing of the function control switch — Civic del Sol

Prelude

1. Disconnect the function switch wire connector at the electronic control head.
2. Check that there is continuity at the switch between terminals as shown in the appropriate chart.
3. If not as specified, replace the switch.

REMOVAL AND INSTALLATION

1. Disconnect the negative battery cable.
2. Remove the electronic control head.
3. Disconnect the wire harness connectors.
4. Installation is the reverse of the removal procedure.

Check for continuity between the terminals according to the table below.

Terminal Position	13	15	14	3	7	16
Heat	○—	—○				
Heat/Def	○—	——	—○			
Def	○—	——	——	—○		
Vent	○—	——	——	——	—○	
Heat/Vent	○—	——	——	——	——	—○

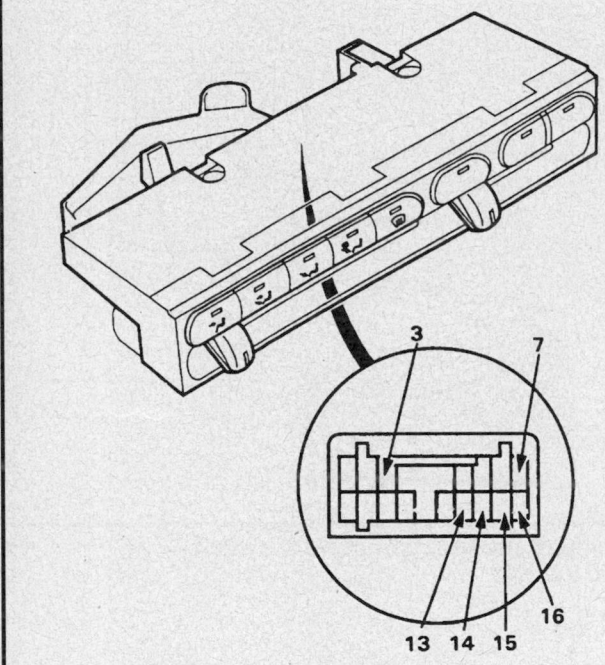

Testing of the function control switch — Prelude

Function Control Motor

OPERATION

The function control motor receives a voltage signal from the control head when each individual switch is pushed, then the control motor rotates to a predetermined position and changes the air passage ways to defrost, combination defrost and feet, feet only, face and feet or face only position.

TESTING

1993 Accord

1. Disconnect the negative battery cable.
2. Disconnect the control motor wire connector.

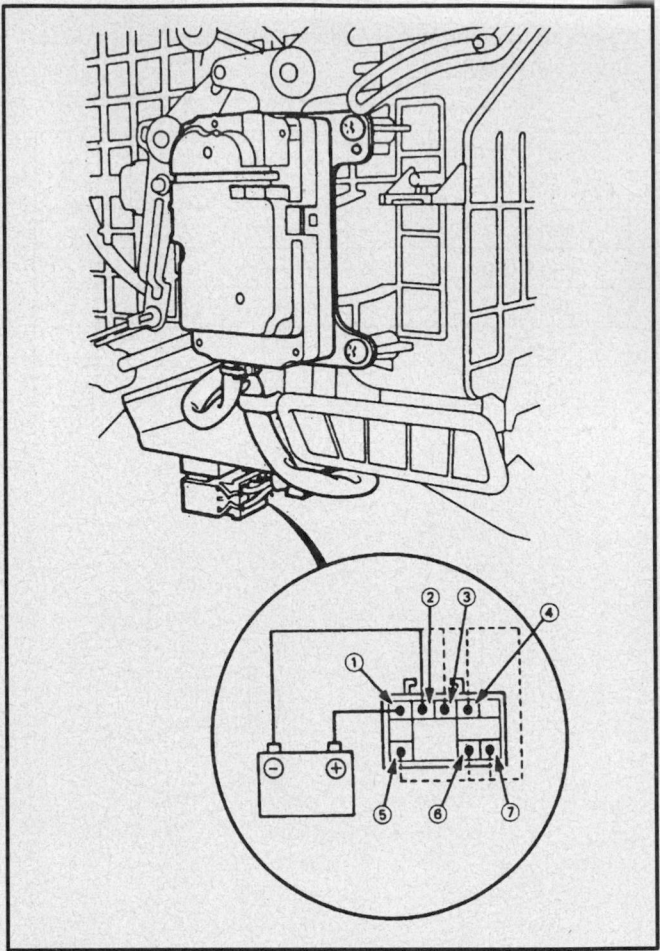

**Testing of the function control motor —
1993 Accord**

3. Connect a 12 volt positive lead to terminal **1** and a ground lead to terminal **2** of the control motor connector.
4. Using a jumper wire, connect terminal **2** to terminals **3, 4, 5, 6, 7** in that order and the motor should turn to each position.
5. If not as specified, replace the function control motor.

1994–95 Accord

1. Connect battery power to the number **1** terminal of the mode control motor and connect the number **7** terminal to ground.
2. Using a jumper wire, connect the number 7 terminal individually to the number **2, 3, 4, 5** and **6** terminals, in that order.

NOTE: Never connect the battery in the opposite direction.

3. Each time that a new connection is made, the mode control motor should run smoothly and stop.
4. If the mode control motor does not run when shorting the first terminal, short that terminal again after shorting the other terminals. The mode control motor is normal if it runs when shorting the first terminal again.
5. If the mode control motor does not run in Step 2, remove it and check the mode control linkage and doors for smooth movement. If the mode control linkage and doors move smoothly, replace the mode control motor.

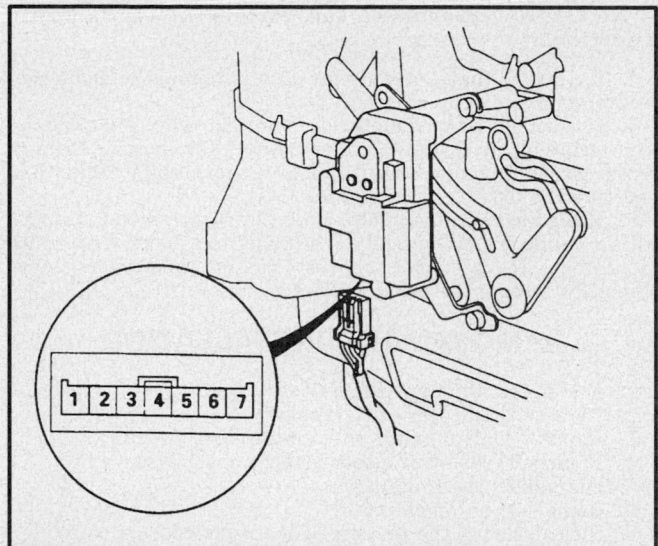

**Testing of the function control motor —
1994—95 Accord**

1993 Civic and Civic del Sol

1. Disconnect the negative battery cable.
2. Disconnect the control motor wire connector.
3. Connect a 12 volt positive lead to terminal **5** and a ground lead to terminal **1** of the control motor connector.
4. Using a jumper wire, connect terminal **1** to terminals **2, 3, 4, 7, 8** in that order and the motor should turn to each position.
5. If not as specified, replace the function control motor.

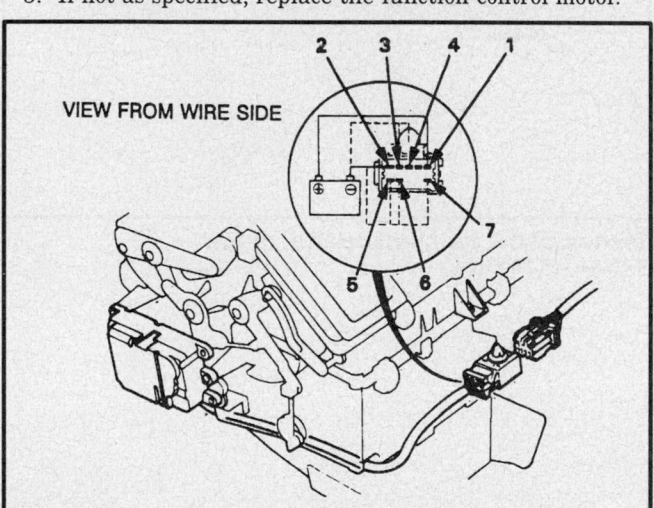

**Testing of the function control motor —
1993 Civic**

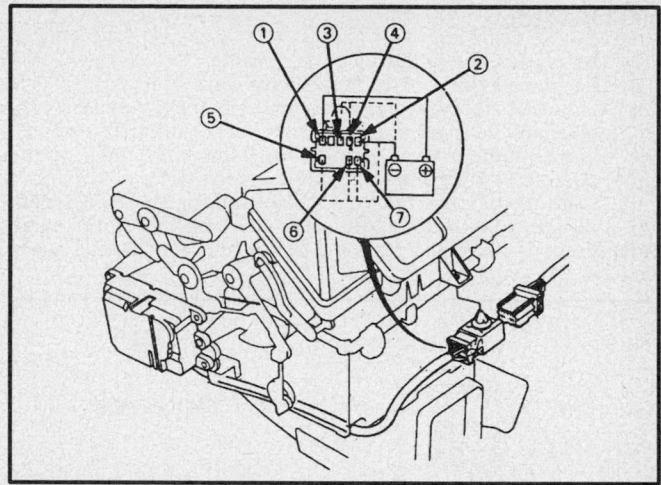

**Testing of the function control motor —
1993 Civic**

1994—95 Civic and Civic del Sol

1. Connect battery power to the number **1** terminal of the mode control motor and connect the number **2** terminal to ground.
2. Using a jumper wire, connect the number 2 terminal individually to the number **3, 4, 5, 6** and **7** terminals, in that order.

   NOTE: Never connect the battery in the opposite direction.

3. Each time that a new connection is made, the mode control motor should run smoothly and stop.
4. If the mode control motor does not run when jumping to the first terminal, short that terminal again after shorting the other terminals. The mode control motor is normal if it runs when shorting the first terminal again.
5. If the mode control motor does not run in Step 2, remove it and check the mode control linkage and doors for smooth movement. If the mode control linkage and doors move smoothly, replace the mode control motor.

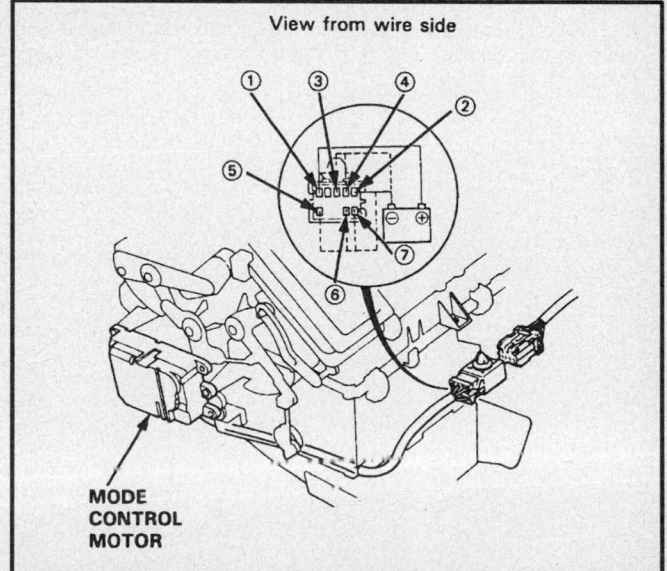

**Testing of the function control motor —
1994—95 Civic and Civic del Sol**

1993 Prelude

1. Disconnect the negative battery cable.
2. Disconnect the control motor wire connector.
3. Connect battery power to terminal **1** of the function control motor, and connect a ground wire to terminal **2**.
4. Using a jumper wire, connect the **2** terminal individually to the **3, 4, 5, 6, 7** terminals, in that order.
5. If the motor does not run when jumping the first terminal, short that terminal again after shorting the other terminals. Motor is okay if it runs when the first terminal is again shorted.

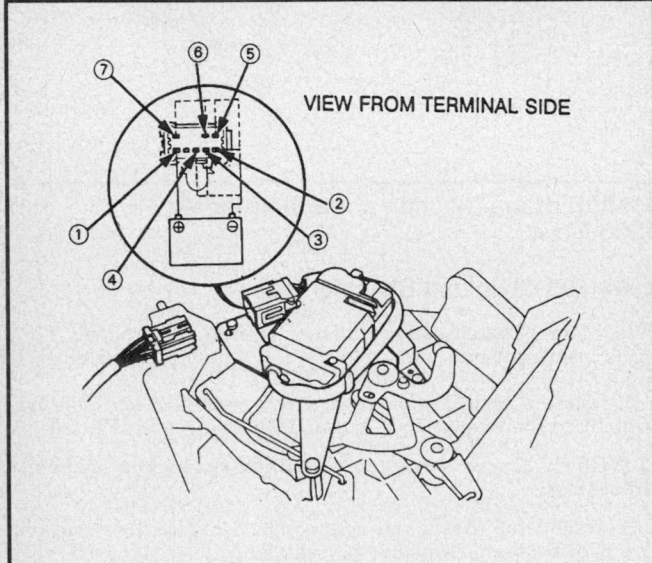

Testing of the function control motor — 1993 Prelude

1994—95 Prelude

1. Connect battery power to the number **8** terminal of the mode control motor and connect the number **4** terminal to ground.
2. Using a jumper wire, connect the number **4** terminal individually to the number **1, 2, 3, 5** and **6** terminals, in that order.

NOTE: Never connect the battery in the opposite direction.

3. Each time that a new connection is made, the mode control motor should run smoothly and stop.
4. If the mode control motor does not run when shorting the first terminal, short that terminal again after shorting the other terminals. The mode control motor is normal if it runs when shorting the first terminal again.
5. If the mode control motor does not run in Step 2, remove it and check the mode control linkage and doors for smooth movement. If the mode control linkage and doors move smoothly, replace the mode control motor.

REMOVAL AND INSTALLATION

1. Disconnect the negative battery cable.
2. Remove the heater unit, if required.
3. Remove control motor wire connectors.
4. Remove the control motor attaching screws.
5. Disconnect the linkage.
6. Remove the control motor.
7. Installation is the reverse of the removal.

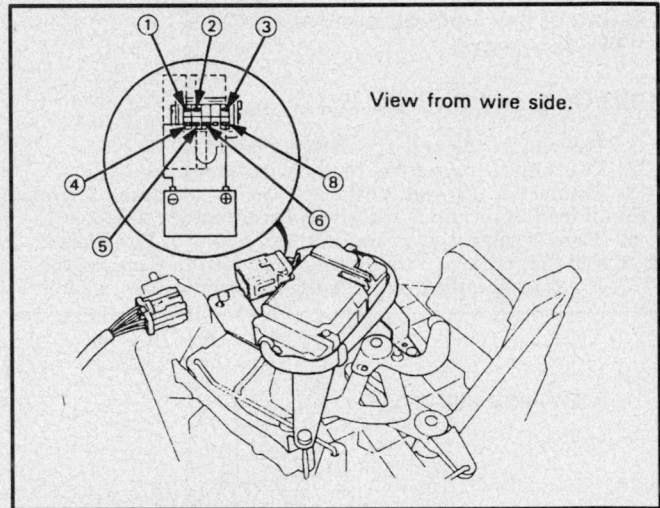

Testing of the function control motor — 1994—95 Prelude

SYSTEM DIAGNOSIS
AIR CONDITIONER COMPRESSOR DIAGNOSTIC CHART

TEST RESULTS	RELATED SYMPTOMS	PROBABLE CAUSE	REMEDY
Discharge (high) pressure abnormally high	After stopping compressor, pressure drops to about 196 kPa (28 psi) quickly, and then falls gradually	Air in system	Evacuate system; then recharge
	No bubbles in sight glass when condenser is cooled by water	Excessive refrigerant in system	Discharge refrigerant as required
	Reduced or no air flow through condenser.	• Clogged condenser or radiator fins • Condenser or radiator fan not working properly.	• Clean • Check voltage and fan rpm
	Line to condenser is excessively hot	Restricted flow of refrigerant in system	Expansion valve
Discharge pressure abnormally low	Excessive bubbles in sight glass; condenser is not hot	Insufficient refrigerant	• Charge system • Check for leak
	High and low pressures are balanced soon after stopping compressor	• Faulty compressor discharge or inlet valve • Faulty compressor seal	Replace compressor Repair
	Outlet of expansion valve is not frosted, low pressure gauge indicates vacuum	• Faulty expansion valve	Repair or Replace
Suction (low) pressure abnormally low	Excessive bubbles in sight glass; condenser is not hot Expansion valve is not frosted and low pressure line is not cold. Low pressure gauge indicates vacuum.	Insufficient refrigerant • Frozen expansion valve • Faulty expansion valve	Check for leaks. Charge as required. Replace expansion valve
	Discharge temperature is low and the air flow from vents is restricted	Frozen evaporator	Run the fan with compressor off then check the thermostat and capillary tube.
	Expansion valve frosted	Clogged expansion valve	Clean or Replace
	Receiver dryer is cool (should be warm during operation)	Clogged receiver dryer	Replace
Suction pressure abnormally high	Low pressure hose and check joint are cooler than around evaporator	• Expansion valve open too long • Loose expansion valve	Repair or Replace
	Suction pressure is lowered when condenser is cooled by water	Excessive refrigerant in system	Discharge refrigerant as necessary
	High and low pressure are balanced too equalized as soon as the compressor is stopped	• Faulty gasket • Faulty high pressure valve • Foreign particle stuck in high pressure valve	Replace compressor
Suction and discharge pressures abnormally high	Reduced air flow through condenser	• Clogged condenser or radiator fins • Condenser or radiator fan not working properly	• Clean condenser and radiator • Check voltage and fan rpm
	No bubbles in sight glass when condenser is cooled by water	Excessive refrigerant in system	Discharge refrigerant as necessary.
Suction and discharge pressure abnormally low	Low pressure hose and metal end areas are cooler than evaporator	Clogged or kinked low pressure hose parts	Repair or Replace
	Temperature around expansion valve is too low compared with that around receiver-driver.	Clogged high pressure line	Repair or Replace
Refrigerant leaks	Compressor clutch is dirty	Compressor shaft seal leaking	Replace compressor shaft seal
	Compressor bolt(s) are dirty	Leaking around bolt(s)	Replace compressor
	Compressor gasket is wet with oil	Gasket leaking	Repalce compressor

RADIATOR FAN CONTROL MODULE INPUT TESTS — 1994 PRELUDE

NOTE: Perform the following tests with the radiator fan control module connected and the ignition switch ON and the A/C switch OFF.
If you find the cause of a problem, correct it before you continue.

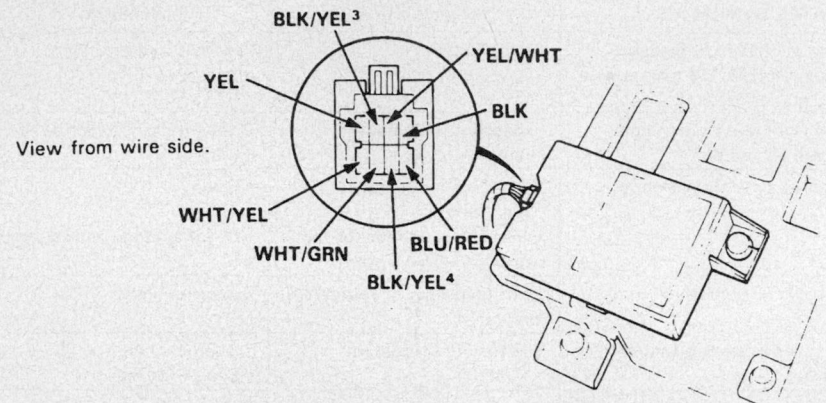

BLK/YEL[3]
YEL/WHT
YEL
BLK
View from wire side.
WHT/YEL
WHT/GRN
BLU/RED
BLK/YEL[4]

WIRE COLOR	TEST CONDITION	DESIRED RESULTS	CORRECTIVE ACTION IF DESIRED RESULTS ARE NOT OBTAINED
BLK	Check for voltage to body ground.	Should have less than one volt.	Repair open to body ground.
WHT/GRN	Check for battery voltage.	Should have battery voltage.	Check No. 45 (15 A) fuse in the under-hood fuse/relay box; if OK, repair open in the WHT/GRN wire.
BLK/YEL[4]	Check for battery voltage. (Ignition switch—ON)		Check No. 23 (15 A) fuse in the under-dash fuse/relay box; if OK, repair open in the BLK/YEL[4] wire.
BLK/YEL[3]	Check for battery voltage. (Ignition switch—ON)		Check No. 9 (15 A) fuse in the under-dash fuse/relay box; if OK, repair open in the BLK/YEL[3] wire.
YEL/WHT	Check for battery voltage. (Ignition switch—ON)		Replace radiator fan control module. Before you connect the new radiator fan control module, disconnect both fan relays. Check for continuity between the YEL/WHT (or YEL) wire and ground, using the 20 k scale on your ohmmeter. There should be no continuity. If there is continuity, the new radiator fan control module will be damaged when you connect it.
YEL	Check for battery voltage. (Ignition switch—ON)		
BLU/RED	Connect to body ground. (Ignition switch-ON)	Condenser fan and radiator fan should come on. Engine coolant temperature; below 199°F [93°C]: F22A1/H23A1 engine below 203°F [95°C]: H22A1 engine	Check for an open in the BLU/RED wire between the radiator fan control module and condenser fan relay or radiator fan relay. If OK, check for an open in the YEL/WHT wire between the radiator fan control module and condenser fan relay or the YEL wire between the radiator fan control module and radiator fan relay. If OK, test condenser fan relay or radiator fan relay.
WHT/YEL	Check for voltage.	Approx. 11 V (engine coolant temperature below 223°F [106°C])	Faulty engine coolant temperature (ECT) switch B, short to body ground or faulty radiator fan control module.

WIRING SCHEMATICS

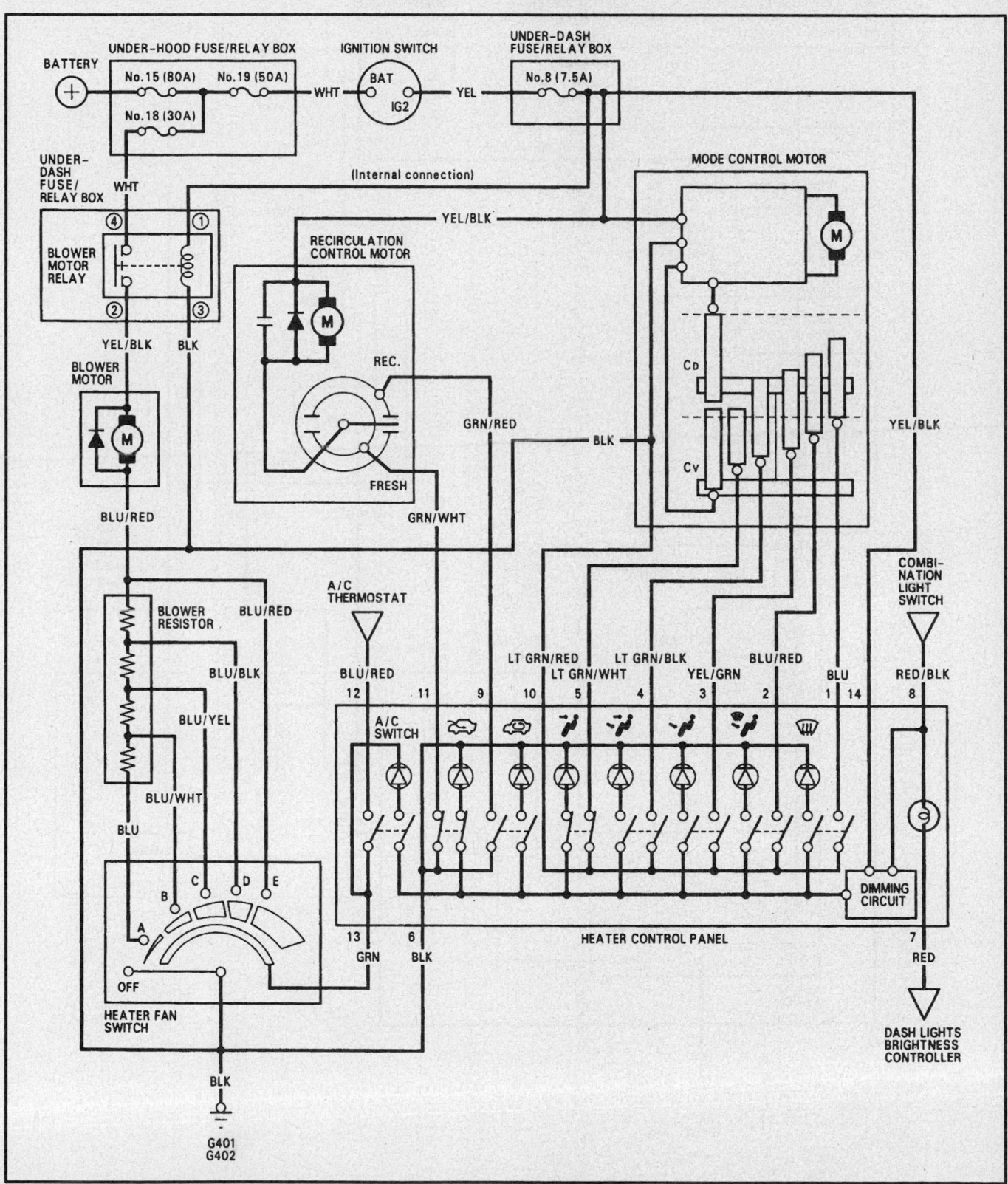

Heater electrical schematic — 1993 Accord with button type control head

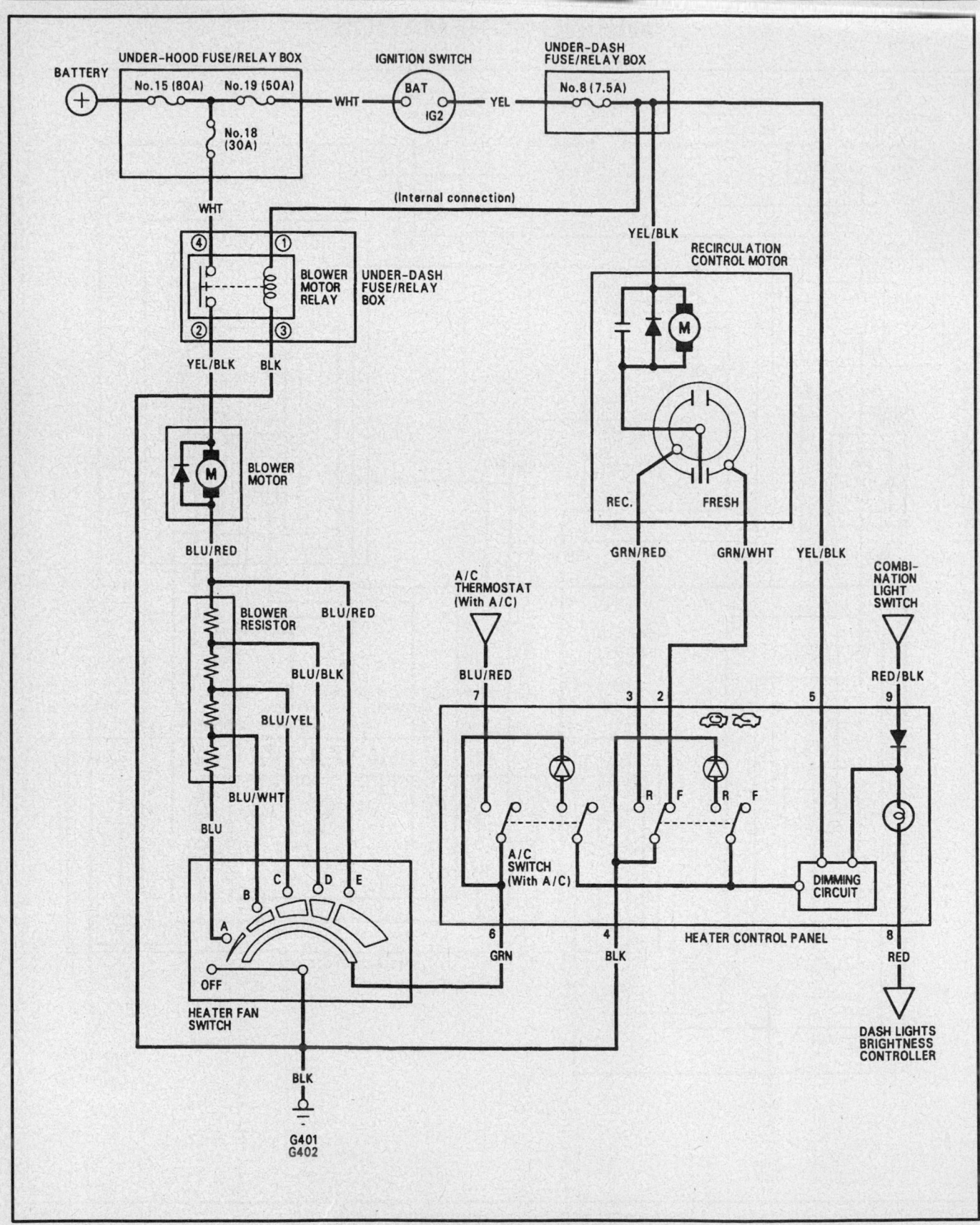

Heater electrical schematic — 1993 Accord with lever type control head

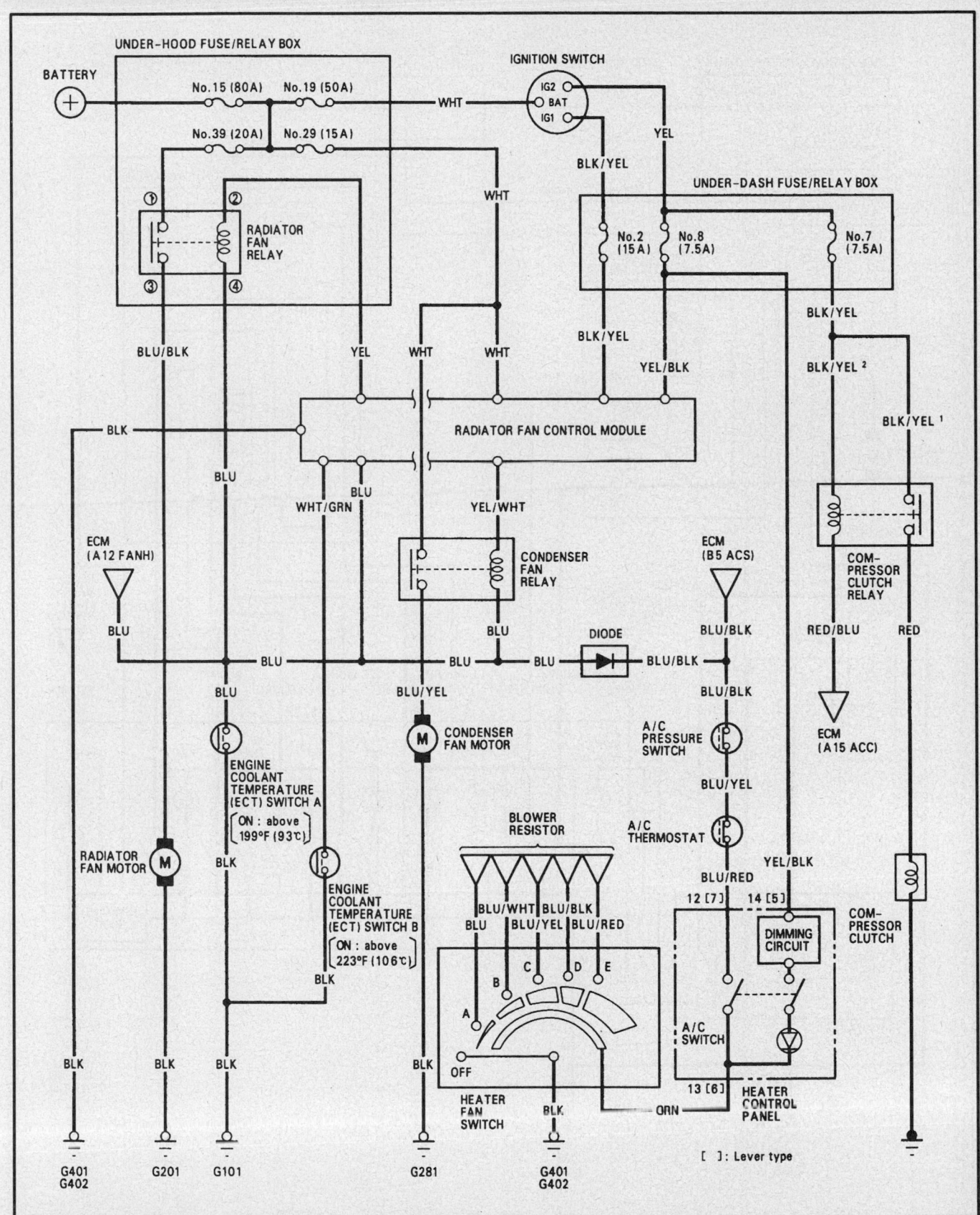

Air conditioning electrical schematic — 1993 Accord

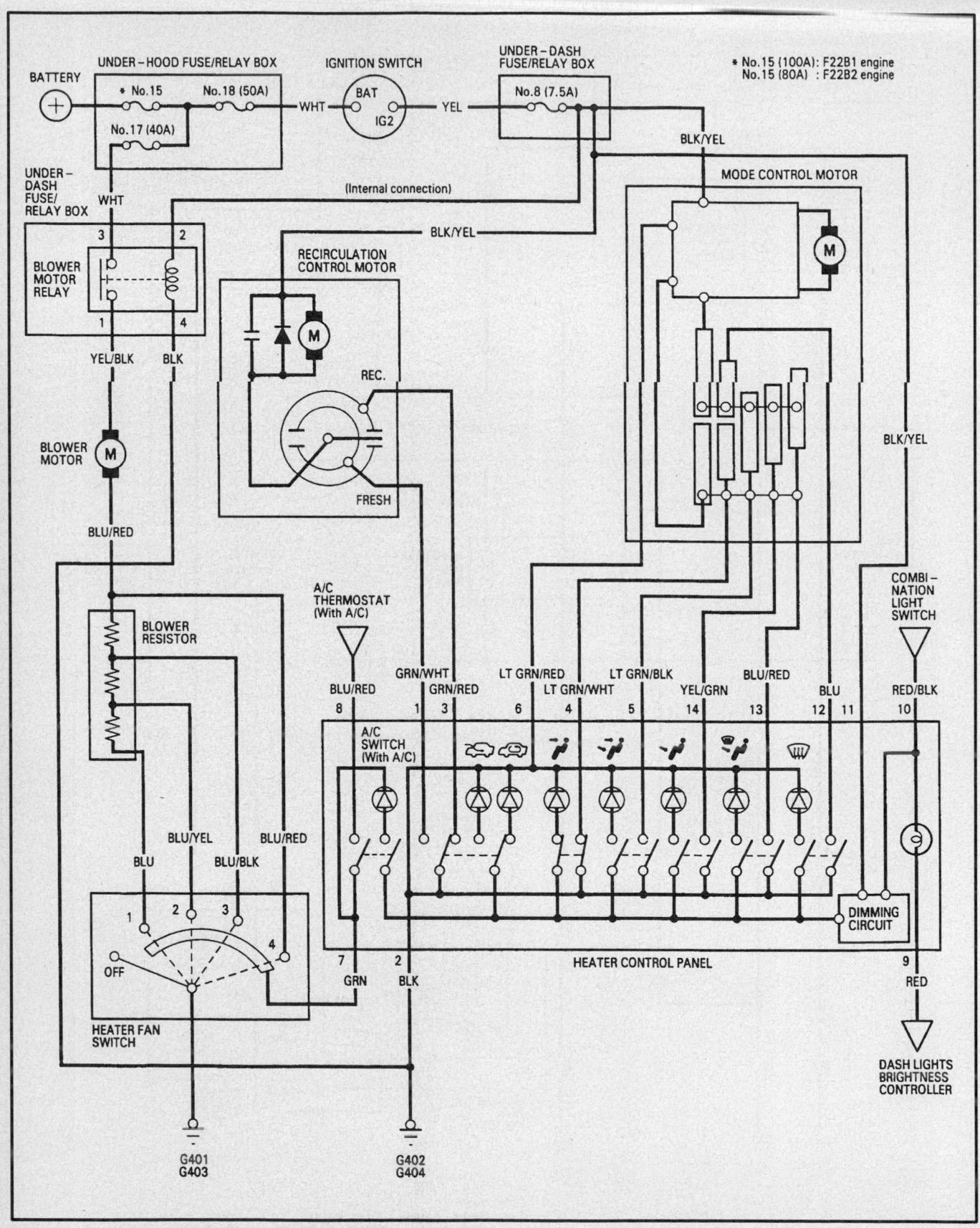

Heater electrical schematic — 1994 Accord

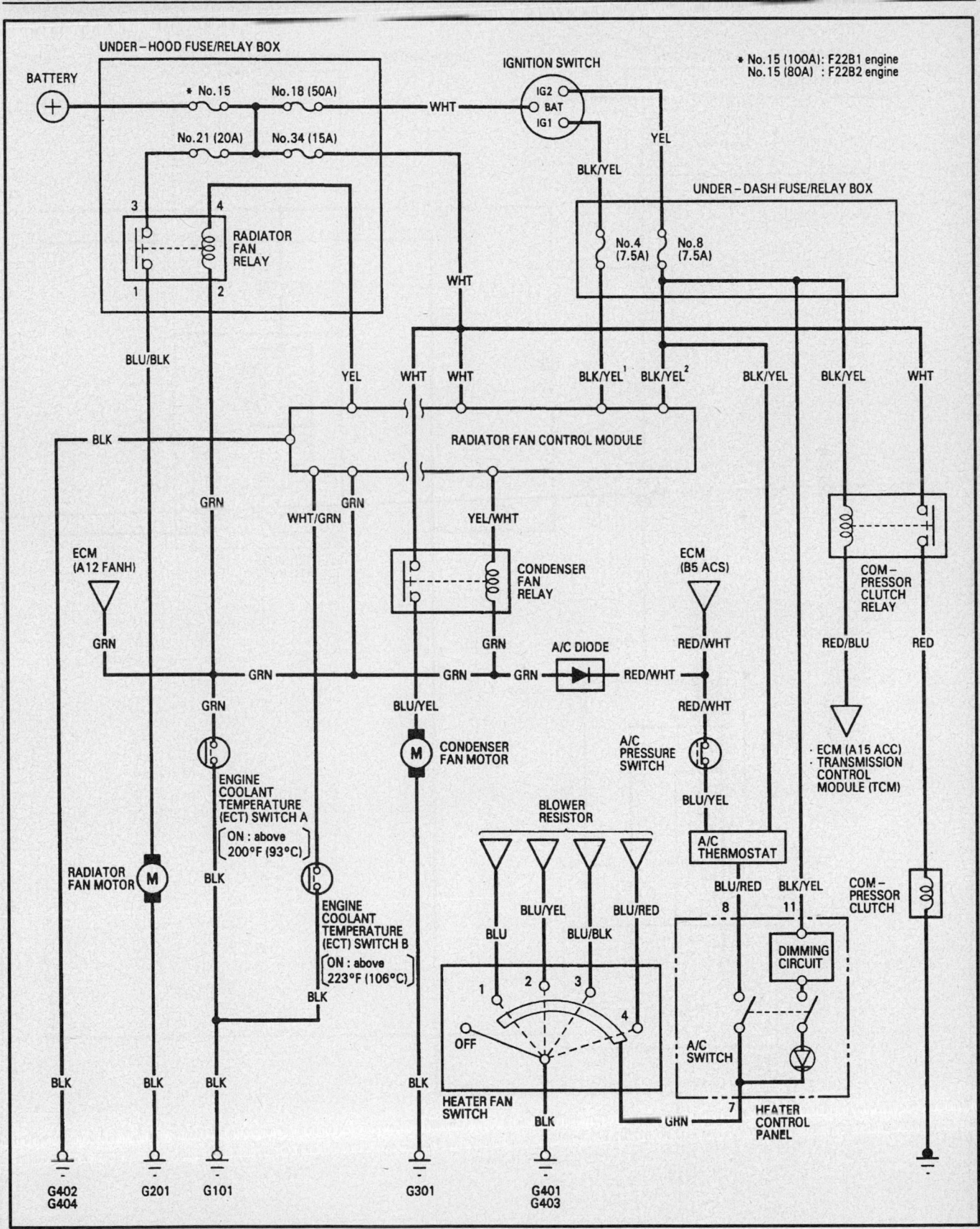

Air conditioning schematic — 1994 Accord

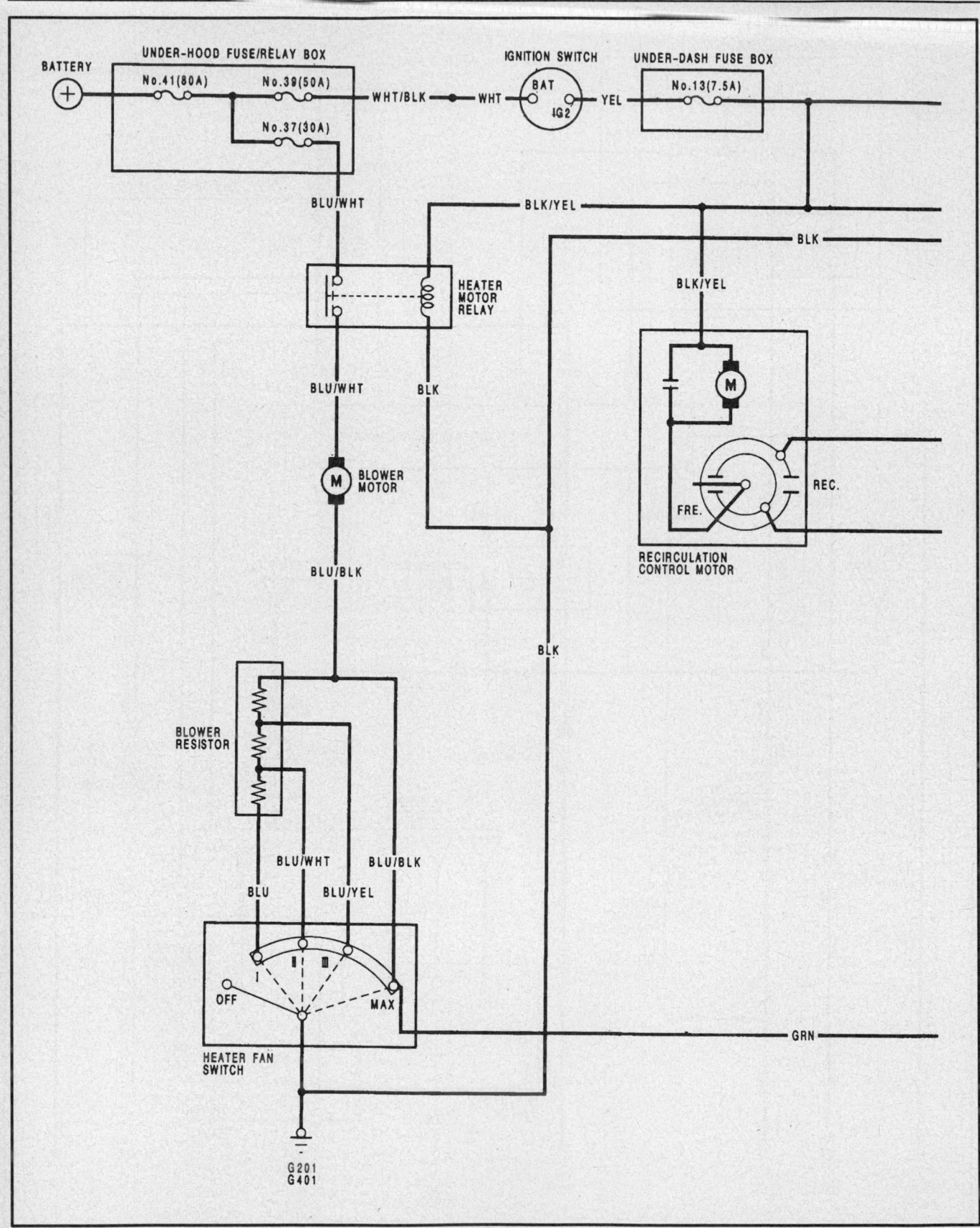

Heater electrical schematic — 1993 Civic and Civic del Sol

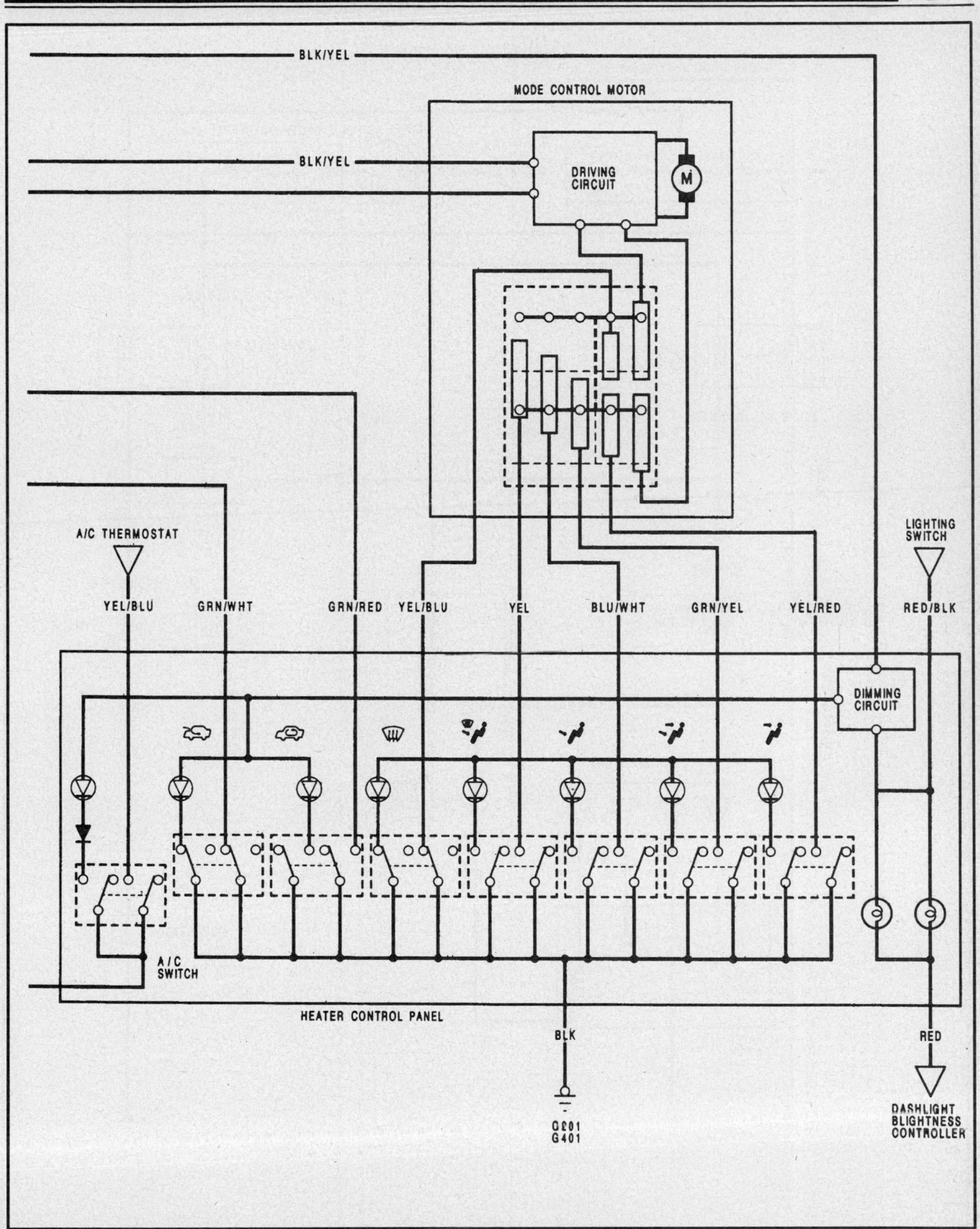

Heater electrical schematic — 1993 Civic and Civic del Sol - Continued

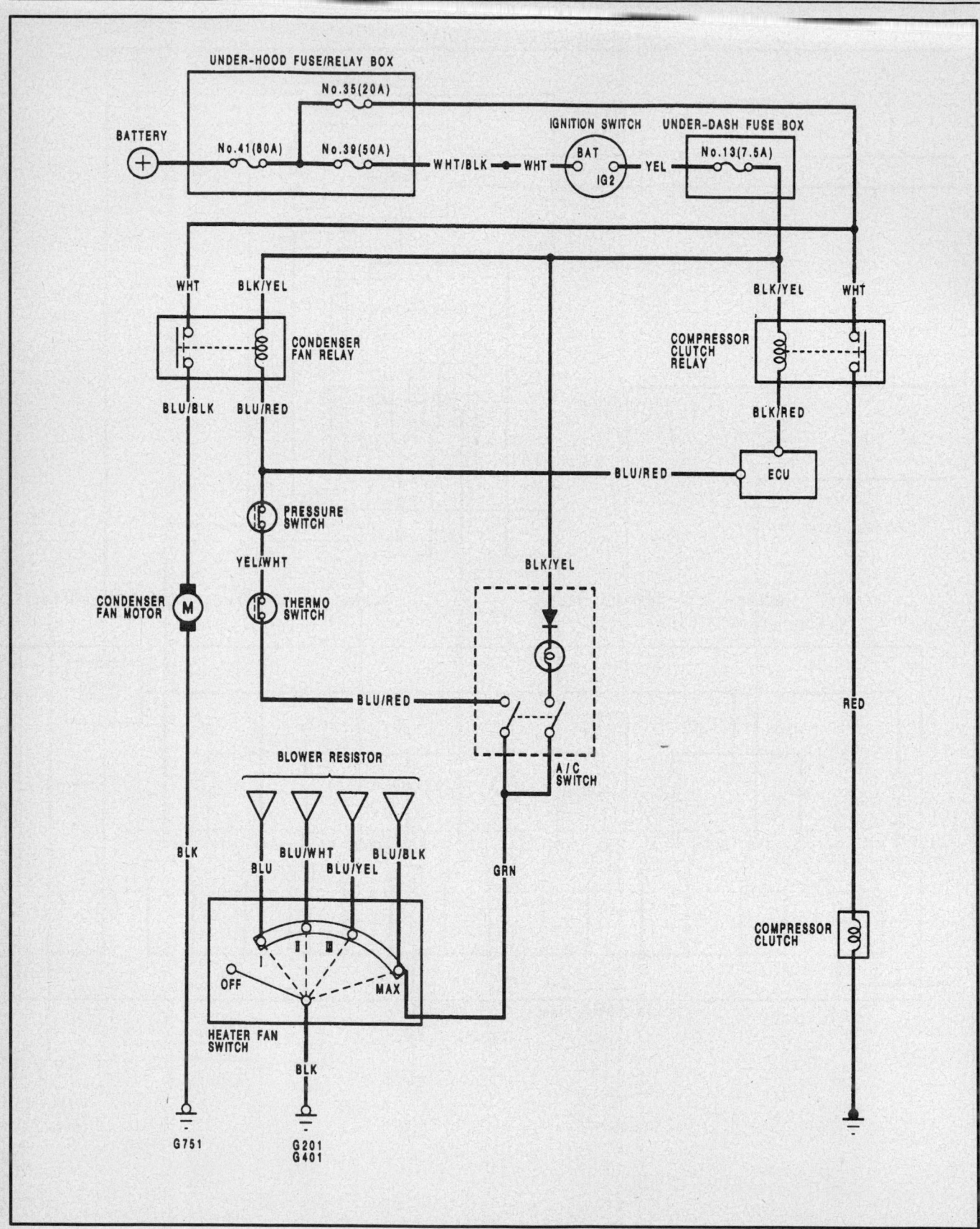

Air conditioning electrical schematic — 1993 Civic and Civic del Sol

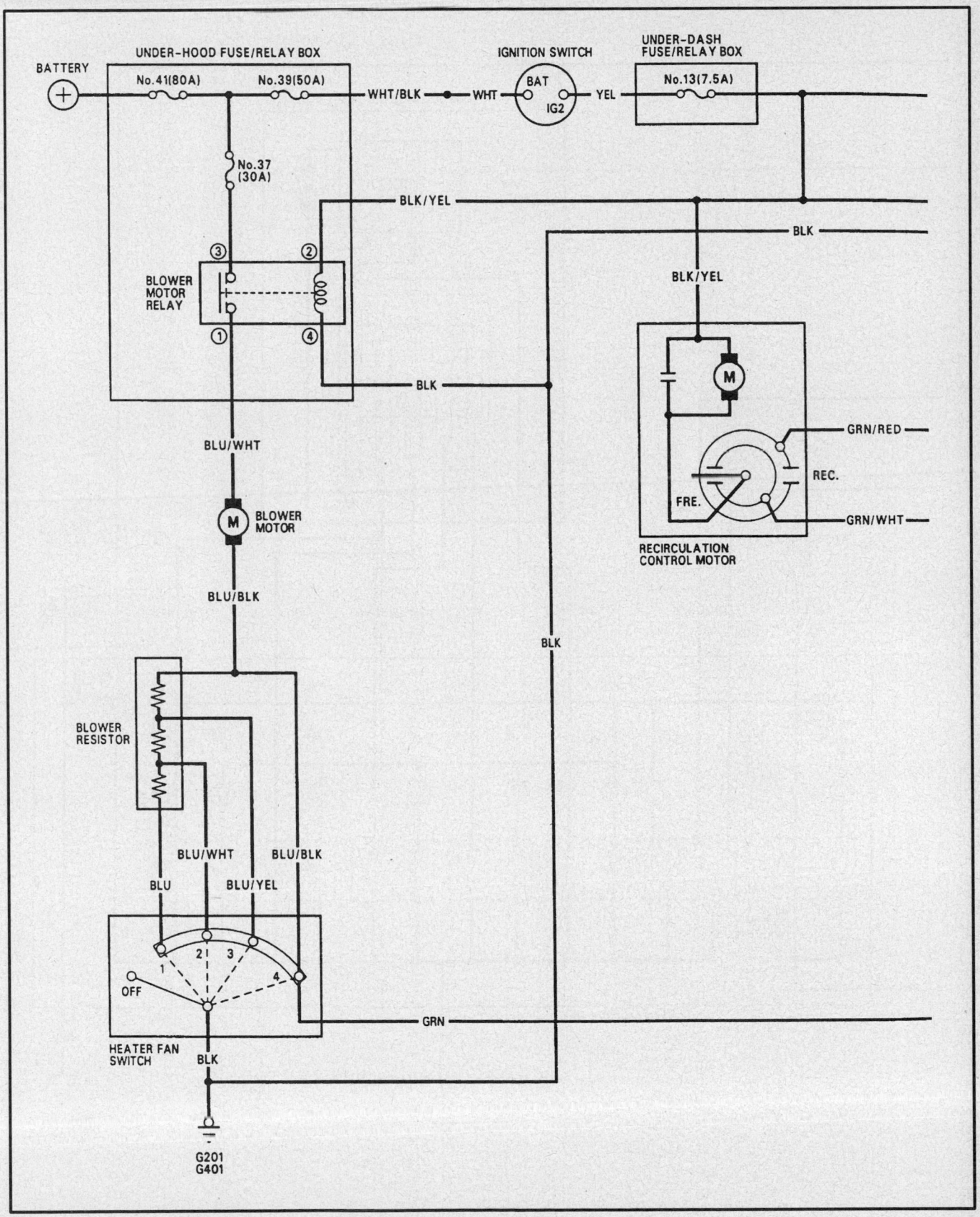

Heater electrical schematic — 1994–95 Civic and Civic del Sol

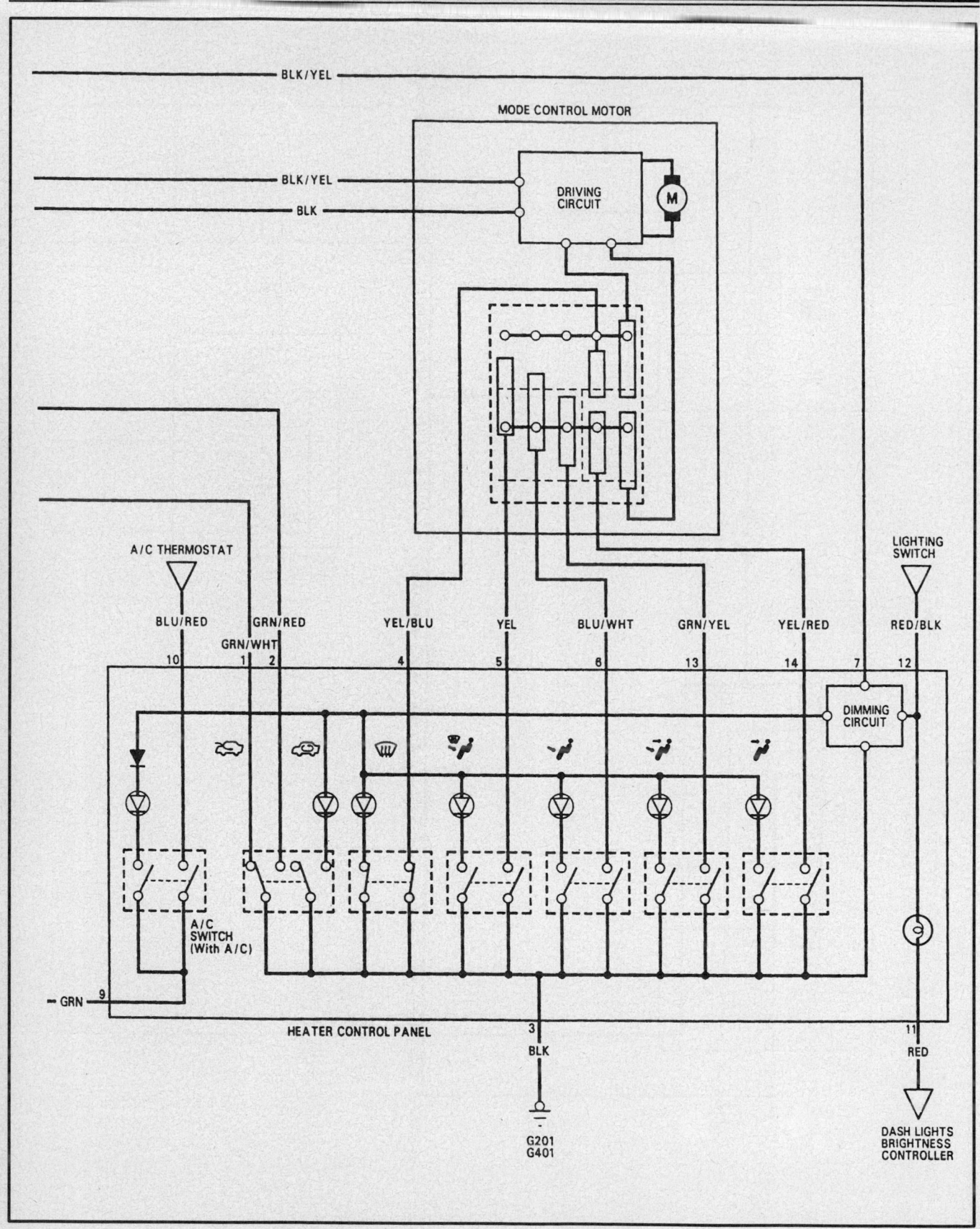

Heater electrical schematic — 1994 Civic and Civic del Sol - Continued

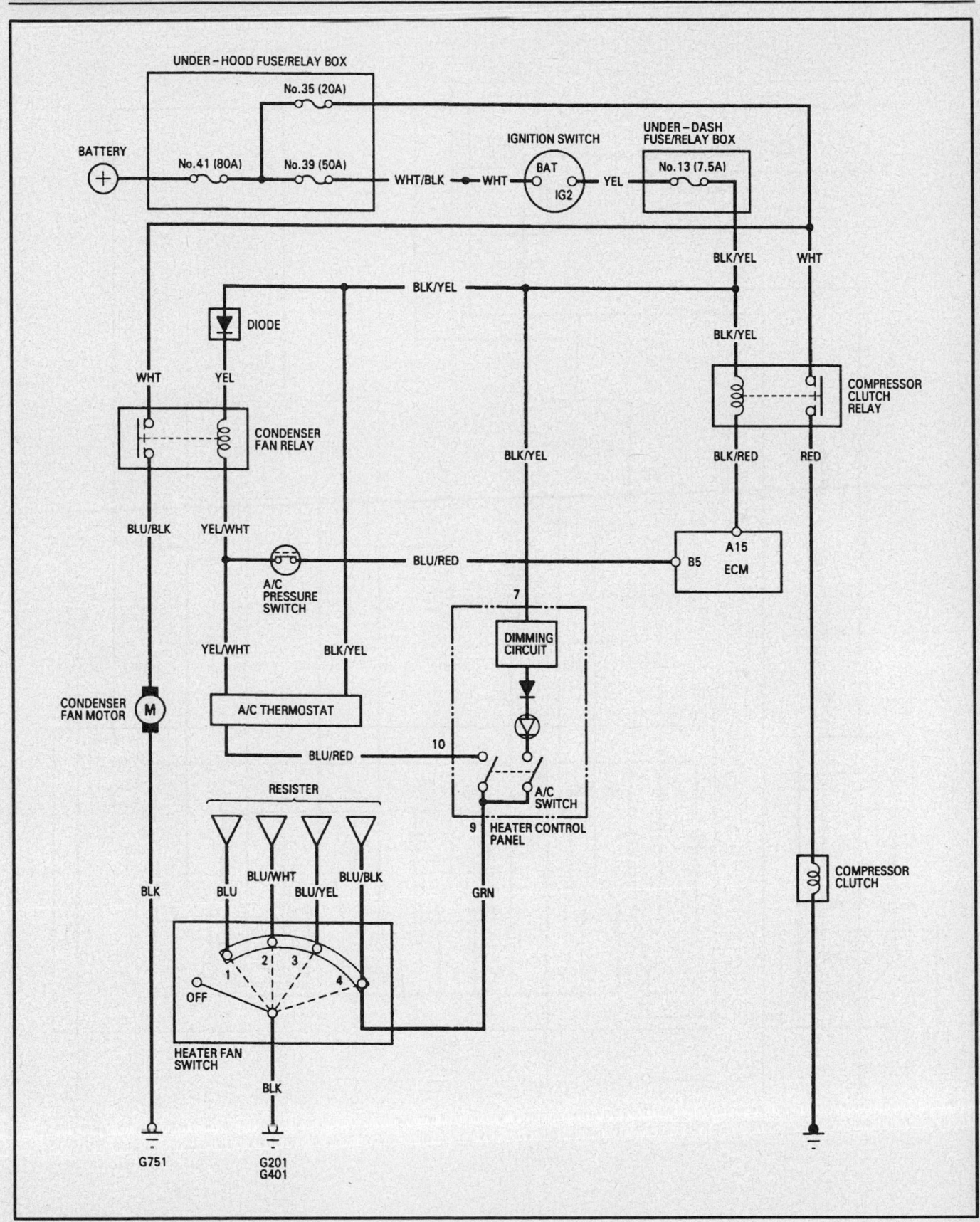

Air conditioning electrical schematic — 1994–95 Civic and Civic del Sol

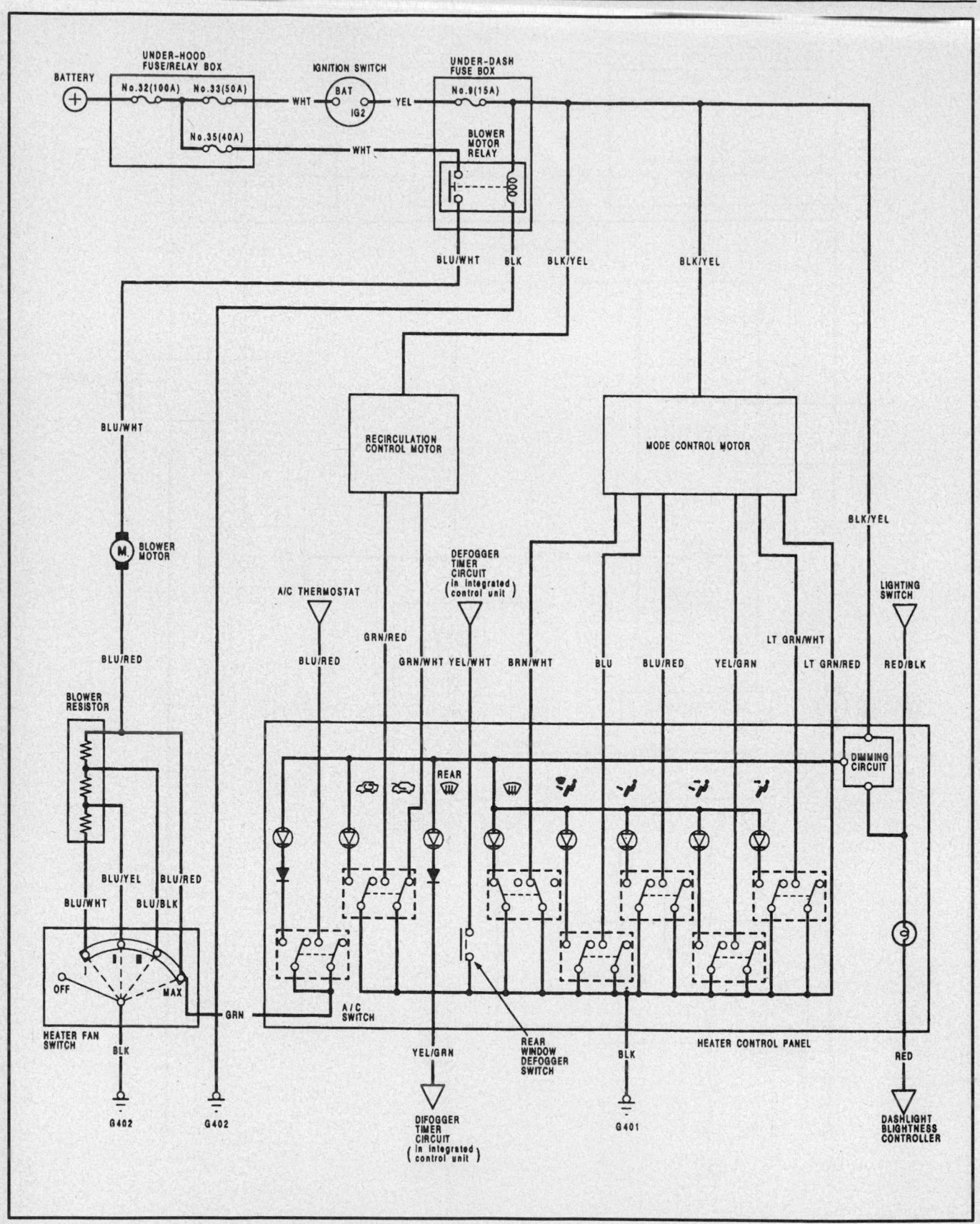

Heater electrical schematic — 1993 Prelude

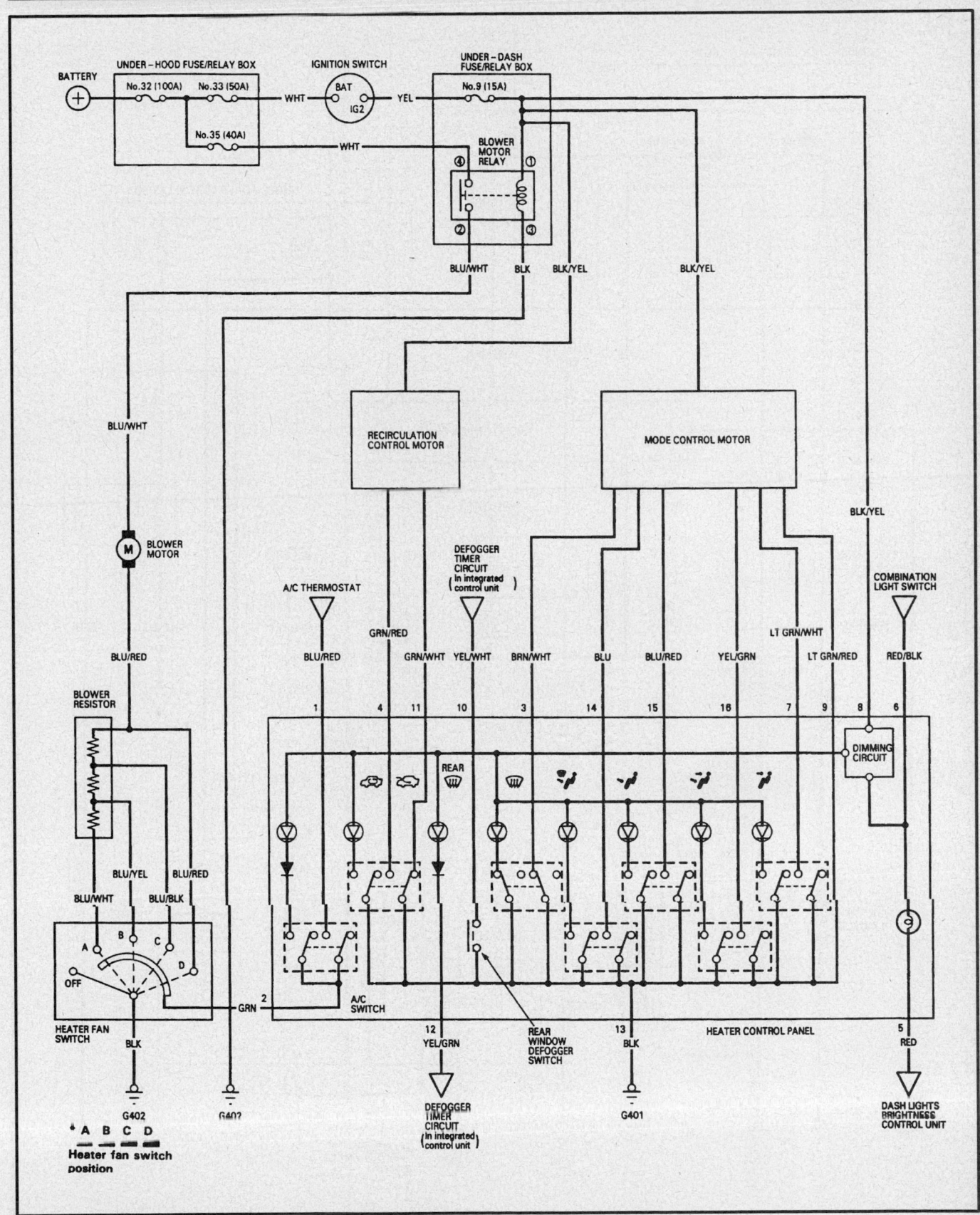

Heater electrical schematic — 1994–95 Prelude

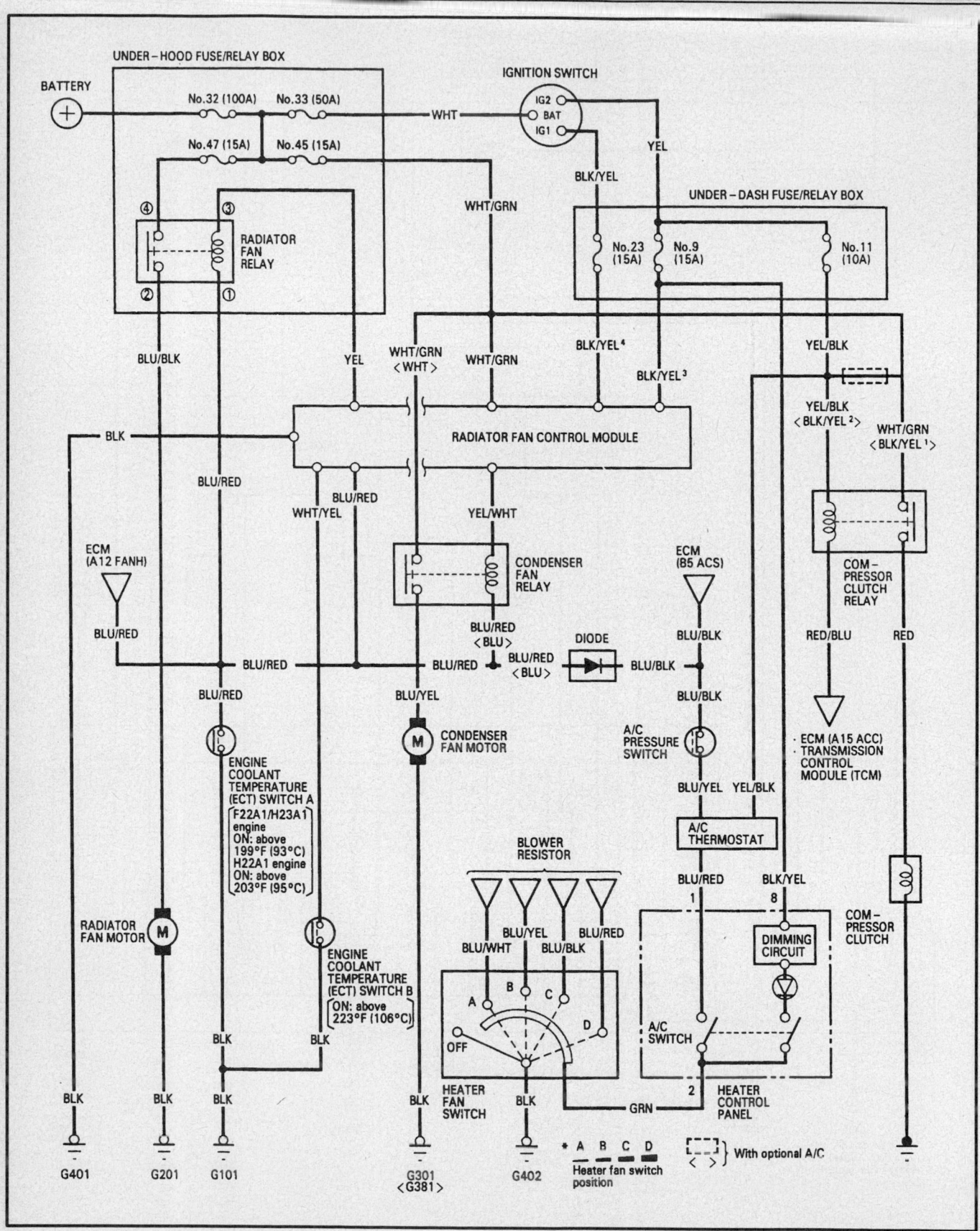

Air conditioning electrical schematic — 1994–95 Prelude

SPECIFICATIONS

ENGINE IDENTIFICATION

Year	Model	Engine Displacement Liters (cc)	Engine Series Identification	Fuel System	No. of Cylinders	Engine Type
1994	Passport	2.6	V	MPI	4	SOHC
	Passport	3.2	E	MPI	6	OHC
1995	Passport	2.6	V	MPI	4	SOHC
	Passport	3.2	E	MPI	6	OHC

REFRIGERANT CAPACITIES

Year	Model	Refrigerant (oz.)	Oil (fl. oz.)	Compressor Type
1994	Passport 2.6L Engine	22.9	5.0	—
	Passport 3.2L Engine	22.9	5.0	Nippondenso
1995	Passport 2.6L Engine	22.9	5.0	Sanden
	Passport 3.2L Engine	22.9	5.0	Nippondenso

AIR CONDITIONING BELT TENSION

Year	Model	Engine Liters (cc)	Belt Type	Specifications New	Specifications Used
1995	Passport	2.6	Serpentine	0.31-0.47	N/A
	Passport	3.2	Serpentine	0.31-0.47	N/A
1995	Passport	2.6	Serpentine	0.31-0.47	N/A
	Passport	3.2	Serpentine	0.31-0.47	N/A

SYSTEM DESCRIPTION

General Information

The heater unit is located in the center of the vehicle beneath the instrument panel. The heater system delivers fresh or recirculated air to direct warm air through the vents to either the windshield, floor or the panel outlets. The air conditioning system is designed to be activated in combination with a separate air conditioning switch installed in the control assembly and the fan speed switch. The systems, depending on model application, use a variety of devices such as relays for controlling the heater, blower, and compressor operation, and a dual pressure switch to monitor system operating pressures and stop compressor operation when extremely high or low pressure is sensed. Also used are a thermo switch, electronic thermostat, fast idle control device, special system diode and an A/C cut relay.

SERVICE VALVE LOCATION

Charging valve locations will vary, but most of the time the high or low pressure fitting will be located at the compressor, receiver/drier or along the refrigerant lines. Always discharge, evacuate and recharge at the low side service fitting.

SYSTEM DISCHARGING/EVACUATING

If the air conditioning system has been opened to the atmosphere, it should be air and moisture free before being recharged with refrigerant. Moisture and air mixed with refrigerant will raise the compressor head pressure, possibly damage the system's components and will reduce the performance of the system. Moisture will boil at normal room temperature when exposed to a vacuum, the moisture then becomes a vapor and will be easily removed by the vacuum pump.

The refrigerant must be discharged and recovered by using an approved R-134a refrigerant recovery/recycling/recharging system before removing any air conditioning system parts.

1. Connect a set of pressure gauges to the high and low pressure ports of the air conditioning system.
2. Connect the refrigerant recovery/recycling unit to the gauge assembly and recover the refrigerant following the instructions on the refrigerant recovery/recycling unit.

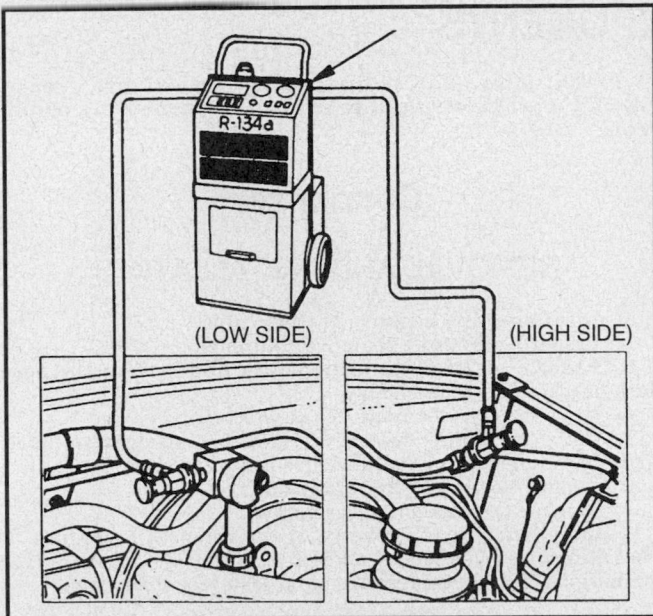

High and low side connections

3. Connect the gauge unit to a vacuum pump and evacuate the system. When the low pressure gauge indicates approximately 750 mmHg (30 inHg), continue the evacuation process for about five more minutes.

4. Close both valves on the gauge unit and shut off the vacuum pump.

5. Check to see that the vacuum readings do not change after a ten minute waiting period. If the vacuum reading decreases, it indicates that a leak exists in the air conditioning system and should be located and repaired before charging the system.

6. If the vacuum readings have held steady, the system can be recharged.

SYSTEM CHARGING

1. Connect the center hose of the gauge assembly to the R–134a weight scale. Make sure that the high and low pressure hoses are securely fastened to their respective fittings on the air conditioning system.

2. Place the refrigerant container upright on the weight scale.

3. Open the refrigerant container valve on the refrigerant can and then open the low pressure valve on the gauge set.

4. Refer to the specific instructions on the weight scale regarding the proper measurement of R–134a refrigerant being installed in the vehicle.

OIL LEVEL CHECKING

The total oil capacity is distributed with the refrigerant throughout the air conditioning system. To return the maximum amount of oil to the compressor for checking during removal and installation or replacement of the compressor, perform the following procedure, if the system has not ruptured or the compressor is functional.

NOTE: If compressor cannot be run, remove the compressor and drain the oil, adding the amounts as noted below, then reinstall the compressor (same or replacement) and make any other necessary repairs, then perform the following procedure and recheck and adjust oil accordingly.

1. Open all door and the hood. Set the A/C switch to ON. Turn the blower motor to the HIGHposition.

2. Start the engine and run the compressor for more than 20 minutes between 800–1000 rpm.

3. Stop the engine, then perform appropriate repairs. When replacing key system components, additional new refrigerant oil needs to be added to the parts being installed:
- Evaporator–1.7 oz.
- Condenser–1.0 oz.
- Receiver/drier–1.0 oz.
- Refrigerant line–0.3 oz.

4. If replacing the compressor or if low oil level is suspect, after removing the compressor, drain the oil into a calibrated container. Check the oil for any contamination.

NOTE: The new, replacement compressor is furnished with afull capacity of oil. This oil should be drained and reinstalledaccording to the adjustment level required shown below.

5. Adjust the oil level as follows:
- If amount drained is more than 3.0 oz., install the same amount as drained.
- If the amount drained is less than 3.0 oz., install 3.0 oz. of new oil.

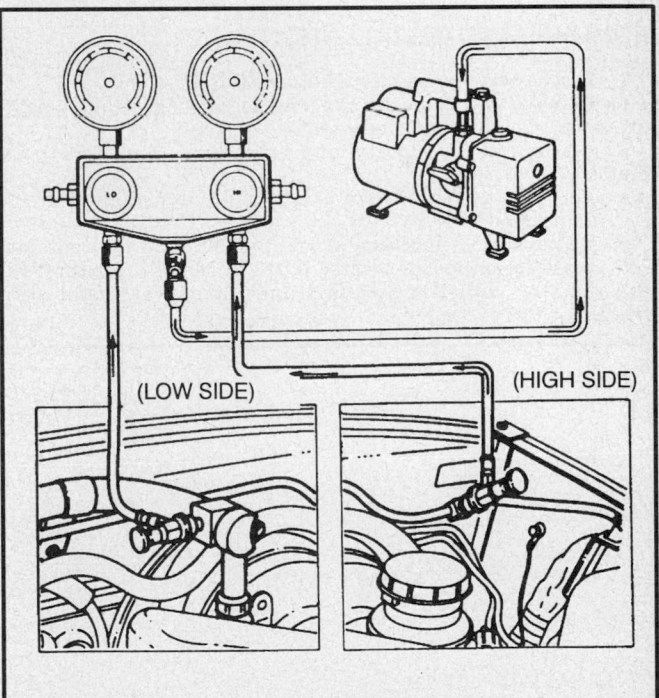

Air conditioning gage connections

SYSTEM COMPONENTS

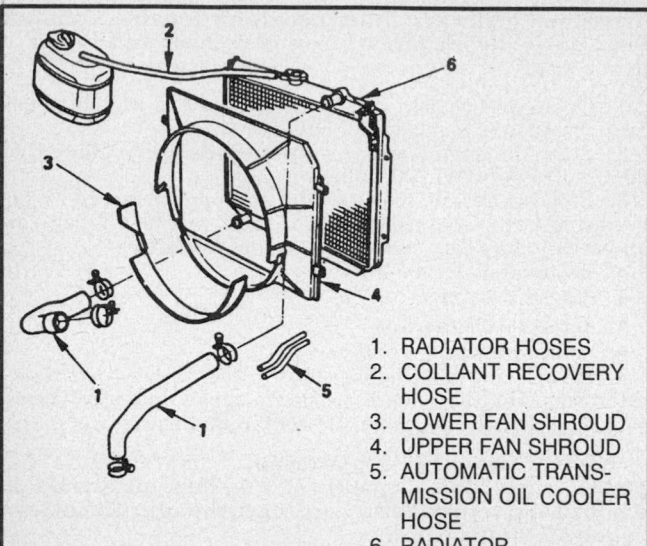

1. RADIATOR HOSES
2. COLLANT RECOVERY HOSE
3. LOWER FAN SHROUD
4. UPPER FAN SHROUD
5. AUTOMATIC TRANS-MISSION OIL COOLER HOSE
6. RADIATOR

Typical radiator assembly

RADIATOR

REMOVAL AND INSTALLATION

1. Disconnect the negative battery cable.
2. Remove the radiator cap and loosen the drain plug to drain the coolant from the system.
3. Disconnect the radiator and surge tank hoses from theradiator.
4. Remove the fan shroud and the radiator support brackets, if equipped.
5. Remove the remaining mounting bolts and the radiator.
6. Installation is the reverse of the removal procedure. Fill the radiator with the specified amount of water and anti–freeze.

NOTE: All radiators fins must be free of dirt, grease, oil and must be straight to avoid an overheating condition.

Condenser

REMOVAL AND INSTALLATION

1. Disconnect the negative battery cable.
2. Properly discharge the air conditioner.
3. Remove the radiator grille. Mark and remove the hood lock bracket or stay assembly.
4. Disconnect pressure switch connector.
5. Using a backup wrench, remove the refrigerant lines. Cap them immediately to minimize contamination.
6. Remove condenser attaching bolts.
7. Remove the condenser assembly.
8. Installation is the reverse of the removal procedure. If installing a new condenser, add 1.0 oz. of refrigerant oil during recharging. Evacuate, recharge and leak test the system.

Compressor

REMOVAL AND INSTALLATION

2.6L and 3.2L engines.

1. Disconnect the negative battery cable.
2. Properly discharge the air conditioning system.
3. Disconnect the magnetic clutch wire harness.
4. Loosen the idler pulley and remove the drive belt.
5. Remove the brace to compressor bolts.
6. Remove and immediately cap the refrigerant lines.
7. Remove the compressor bracket to engine bolts and remove the compressor.
8. Installation is the reverse of removal procedure. Measure oil level in oil compressor if installing a replacement unit.
9. Adjust oil in new unit as needed. Evacuate, recharge and leak test the system.

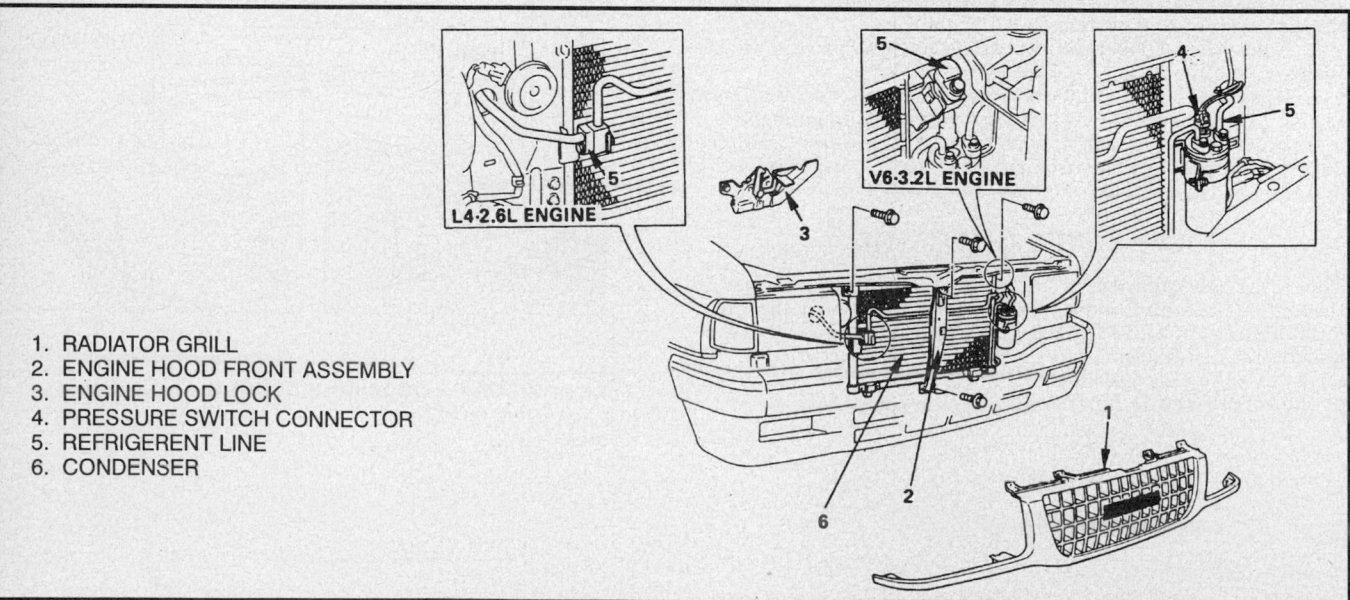

1. RADIATOR GRILL
2. ENGINE HOOD FRONT ASSEMBLY
3. ENGINE HOOD LOCK
4. PRESSURE SWITCH CONNECTOR
5. REFRIGERENT LINE
6. CONDENSER

Condensor assembly

Receiver/Drier

REMOVAL AND INSTALLATION

1. Disconnect the negative battery cable.
2. Properly discharge the air conditioning system.
3. Remove the radiator grille.

4. Remove the pressure switch wire connector.
5. Using 2 wrenches, remove the refrigerant lines. Cap all openings immediately to minimize contamination.
6. Remove the bracket attaching bolts.
7. Remove the receiver/drier.
8. Installation is the reverse of removal procedure. Add 1 oz. of new refrigerant oil to the replacement receiver/driver. Evacuate, recharge and leak test the system.

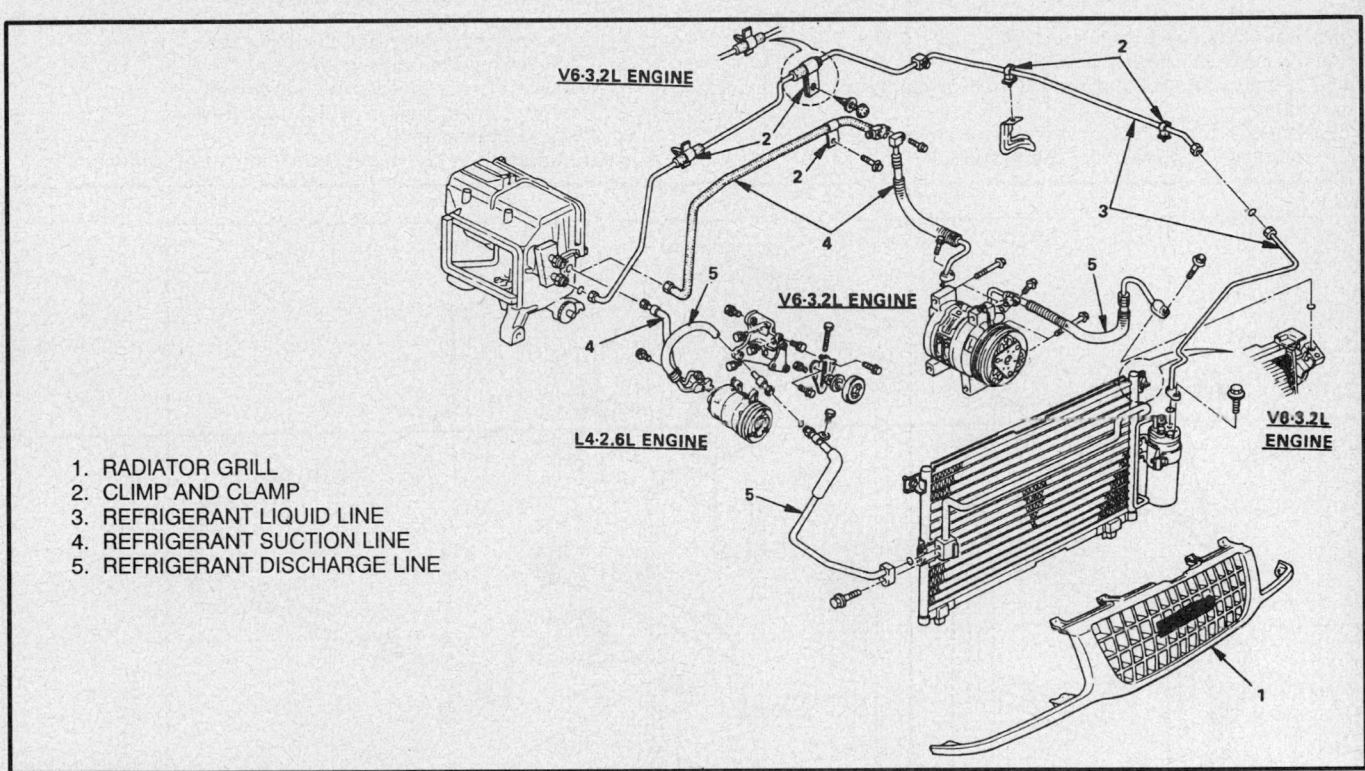

1. RADIATOR GRILL
2. CLIMP AND CLAMP
3. REFRIGERANT LIQUID LINE
4. REFRIGERANT SUCTION LINE
5. REFRIGERANT DISCHARGE LINE

Air conditioning system components

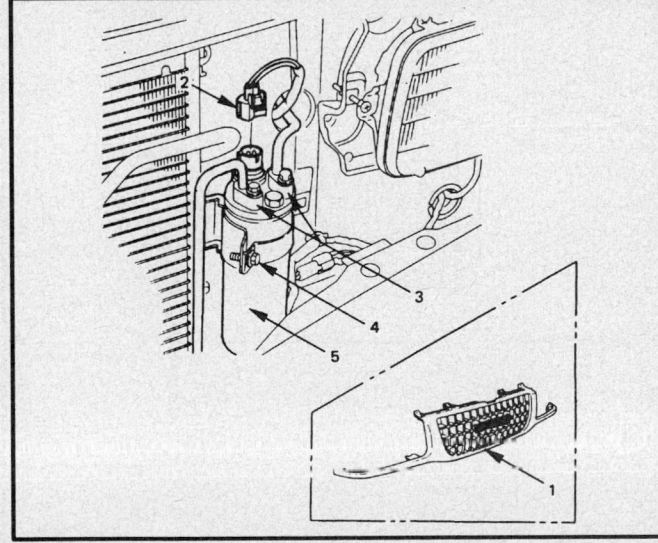

Receiver/drier with dual pressure switch — 2.6L

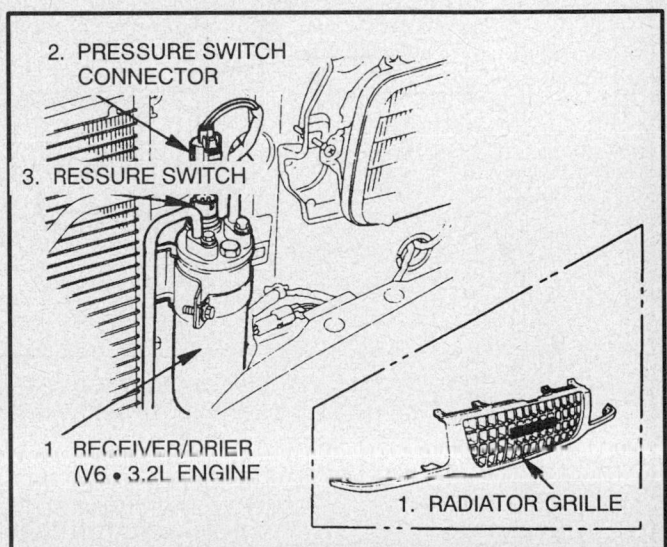

Receiver/drier with dual pressure switch — 3.2L

Expansion Valve

REMOVAL AND INSTALLATION

1. Disconnect the negative battery cable.
2. Properly discharge the air conditioning system.
3. Remove the evaporator assembly.
4. Pull the electronic thermostat from the core and remove the switch.
5. Remove the clips and screws from the evaporator case.
6. Separate the upper and lower cases.
7. Remove the evaporator core.
8. Remove the insulation, the sensor clamp and the expansion valve.
9. Installation is the reverse of removal procedure. Evacuate, recharge and leak test the system.

Blower Motor

REMOVAL AND INSTALLATION

NOTE: If removing the entire blower housing assembly, the instrument panel will have to be removed first and the air conditioning system will need to be properly discharged. The following procedure is for removing only the blower motor and wheel.

1. Disconnect the negative battery cable.
2. Remove the dash side trim panel.
3. Remove blower motor wire connector.
4. Remove blower motor attaching screws.
5. Remove blower motor.
6. Installation is the reverse of removal procedure.

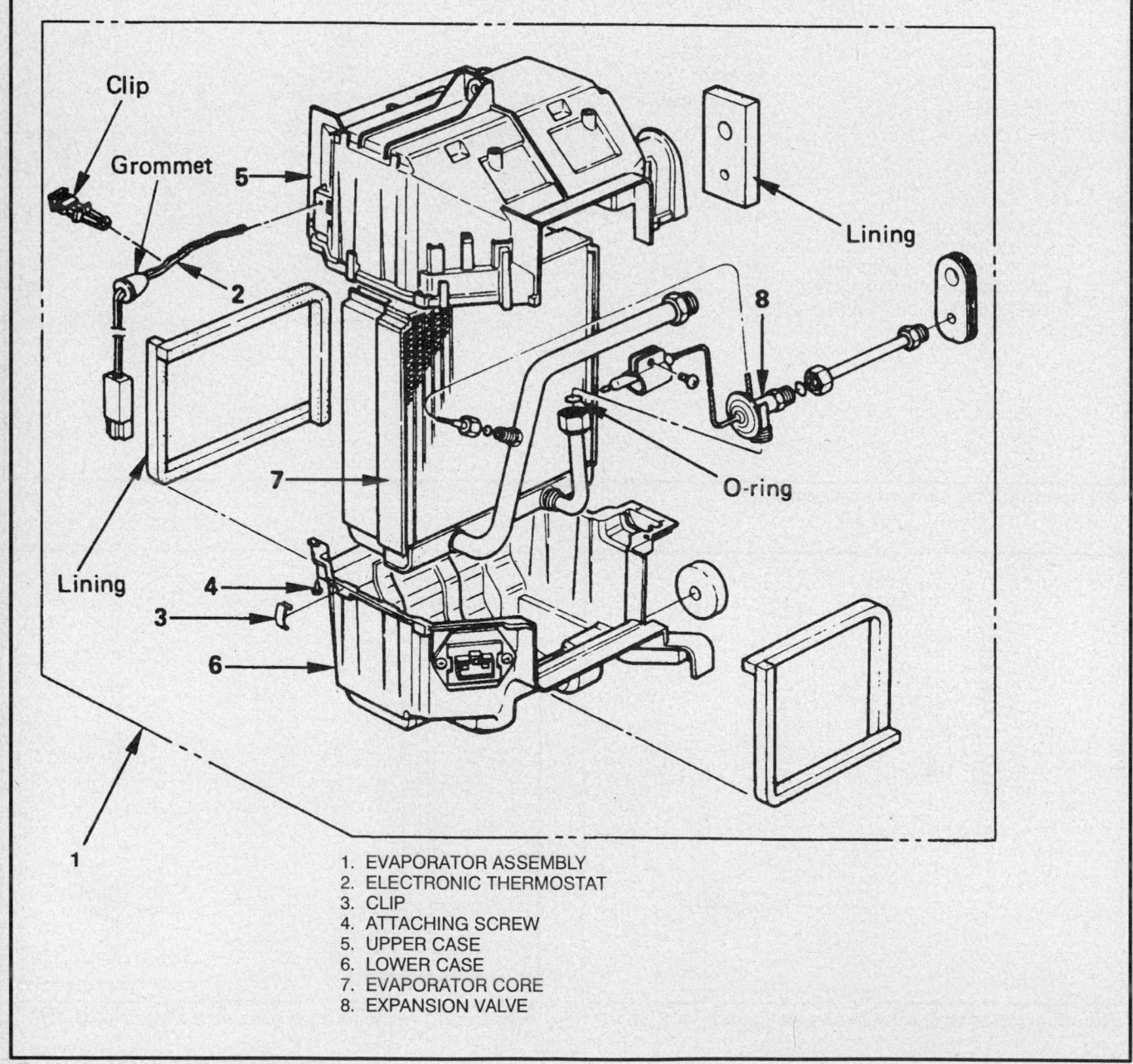

1. EVAPORATOR ASSEMBLY
2. ELECTRONIC THERMOSTAT
3. CLIP
4. ATTACHING SCREW
5. UPPER CASE
6. LOWER CASE
7. EVAPORATOR CORE
8. EXPANSION VALVE

Exploded view of the evaporator case

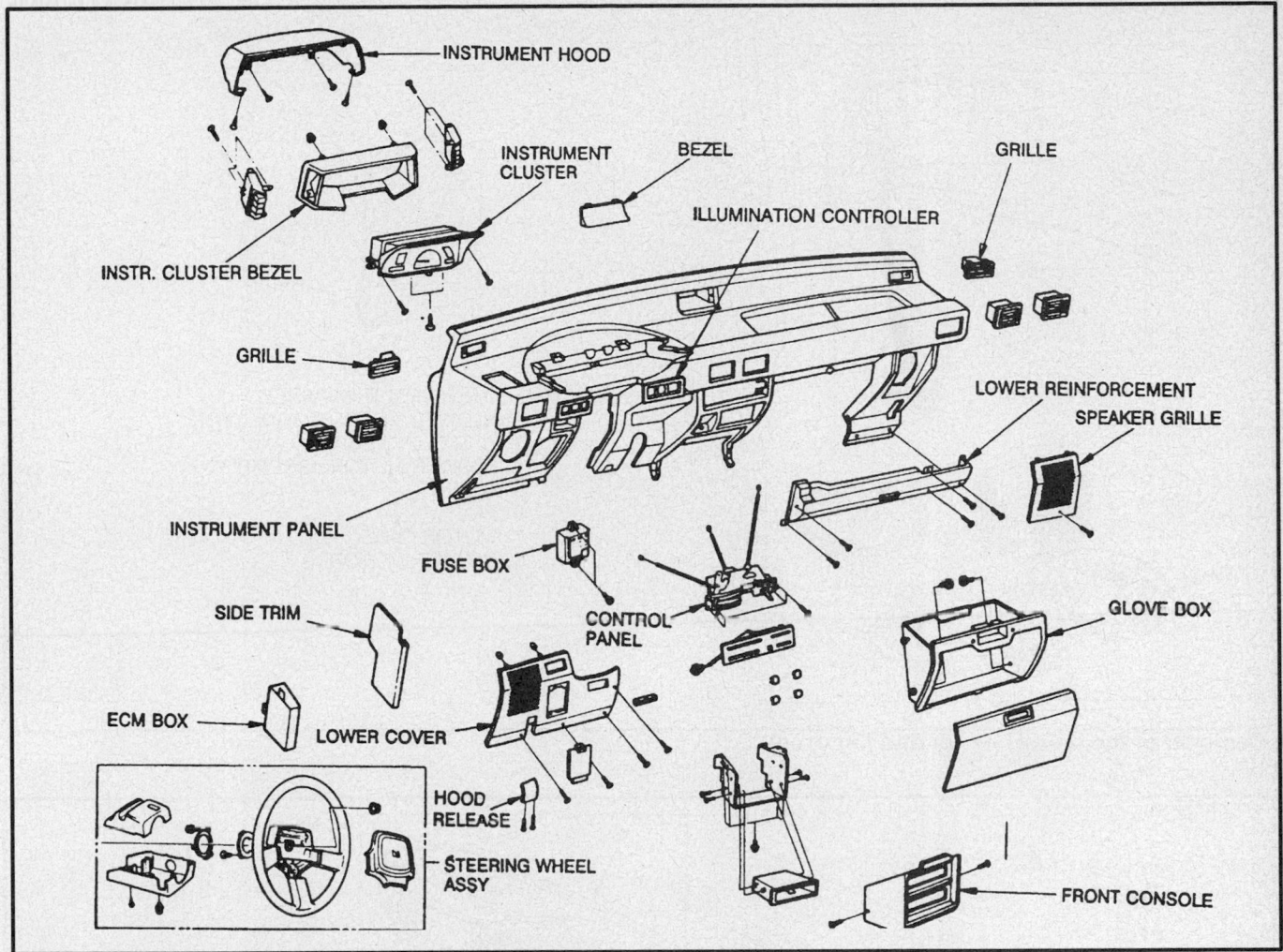

Instrument panel and related component removal

Blower Motor Resistor

REMOVAL AND INSTALLATION

The blower motor resistor will usually be located under the dash attached to the heater or evaporator housing.

1. Disconnect the battery negative terminal. Remove the glove box.
2. Disconnect the wire resistor connector and remove the mounting screw.
3. Remove the blower resistor.
4. Installation is the reverse of the removal procedure.

Heater Core

REMOVAL AND INSTALLATION

Passport

1. Disconnect the negative battery cable.
2. On A/C, properly discharge the air conditioning system and remove the evaporator lines from the fittings at the firewall.
3. Properly drain the cooling system and disconnect the heater hoses at the firewall. Plug hose ends.

4. Remove the instrument panel by removing the following components:
   • Remove the steering wheel.
   • Remove the instrument cluster bezel, then remove the instrument cluster.
   • Remove the hood release handle. Remove the lower steering column cover.
   • Remove the fuse box, the left side trim, then remove the ECM, if applicable.
   • Remove the front console and the lower reinforcement.
   • Remove the right speaker grille and the glove box.
   • Remove the knobs from the control panel, then remove the panel bezel and the control panel.
   • Remove the illumination controller (to the right of the steering column).
5. Remove the instrument panel.
6. Remove the resistor connector.
7. On heater only systems, remove the heater to blower air duct.
8. On air conditioning, remove the evaporator assembly.
9. Remove the instrument panel support.
10. Remove the heater unit attaching nuts and remove assembly.
11. Disassemble the heater unit case and remove heater core.
12. Installation is the reverse of removal procedure.

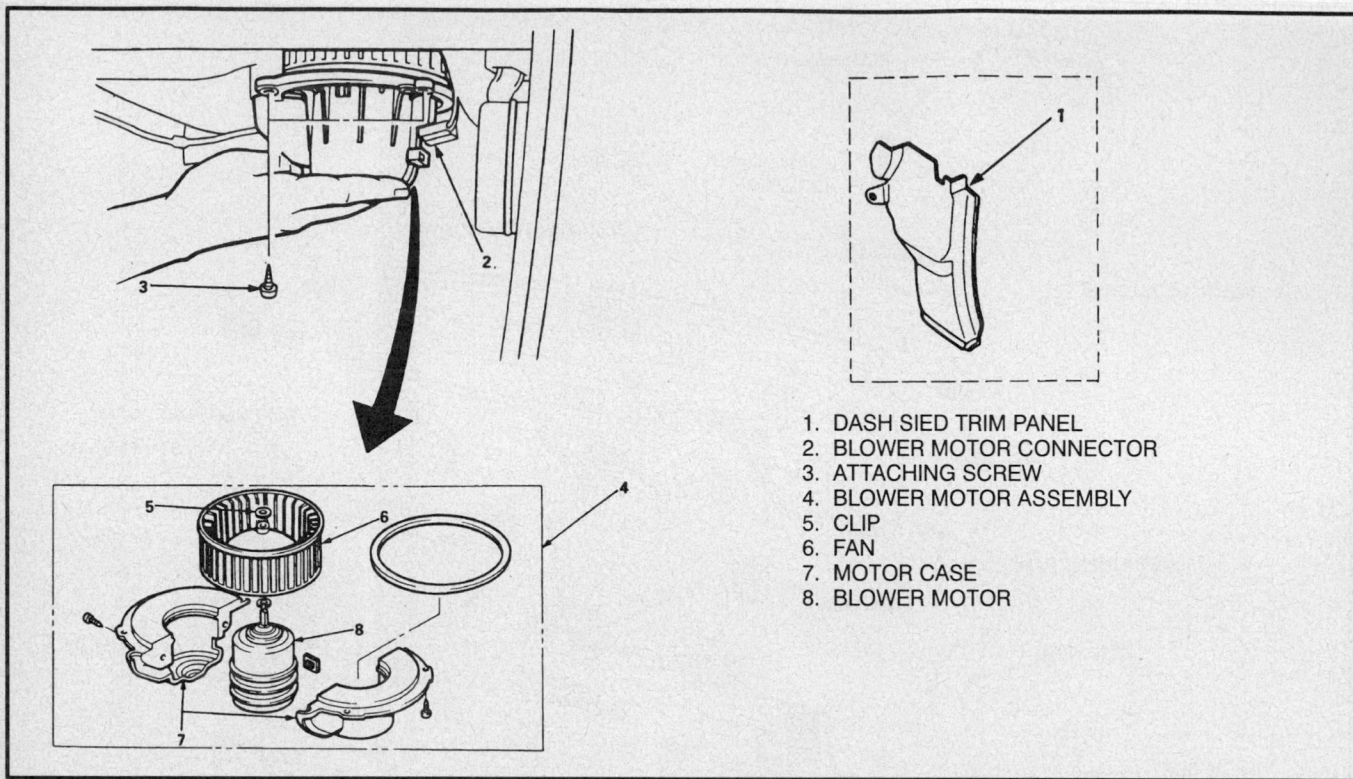

1. DASH SIED TRIM PANEL
2. BLOWER MOTOR CONNECTOR
3. ATTACHING SCREW
4. BLOWER MOTOR ASSEMBLY
5. CLIP
6. FAN
7. MOTOR CASE
8. BLOWER MOTOR

Removal of the blower motor and fanwheel

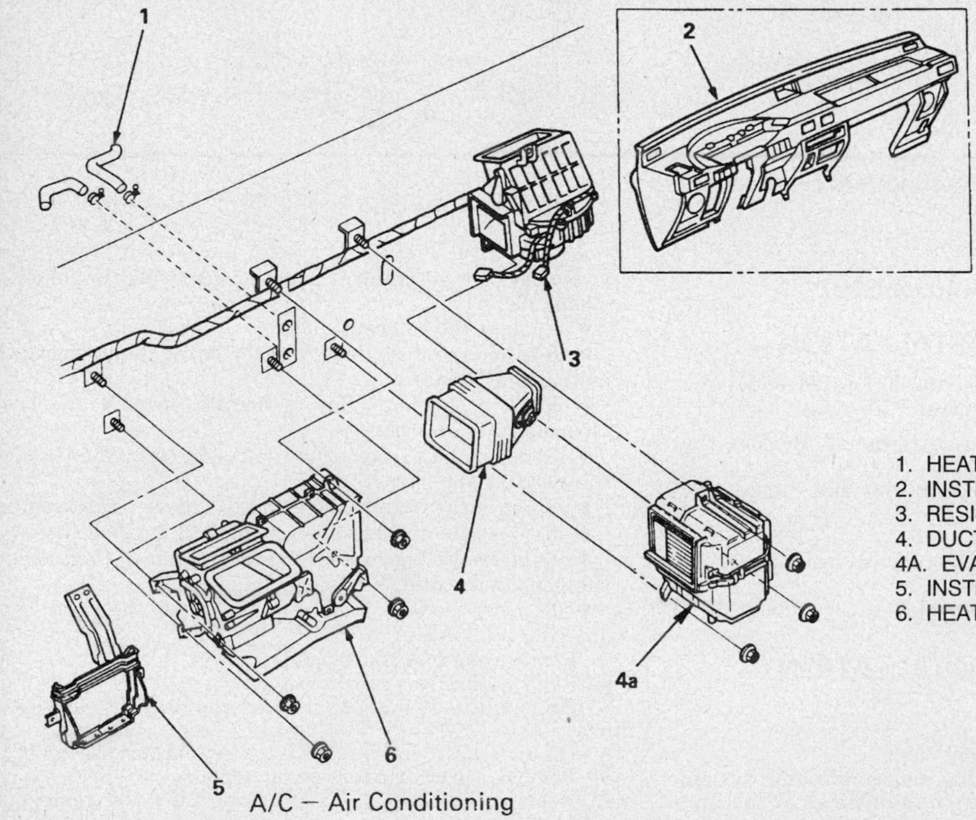

1. HEATER UNIT
2. INSTRUMENT PANEL ASSEMBLY
3. RESISTOR CONNECTOR
4. DUCT
4A. EVAPORATOR ASSEMBLY (A/C ONLY)
5. INSTRUMENT PANEL STAY
6. HEATER UNIT

A/C — Air Conditioning

Heater unit removal

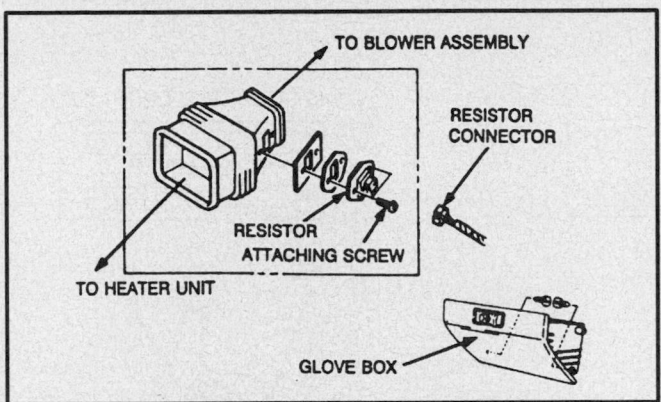

Blower motor resistor removal — Passort

Evaporator Core

REMOVAL AND INSTALLATION

Passport

1. Disconnect the negative battery cable.
2. Properly discharge the air conditioning system.

3. Disconnect the refrigerant lines from the evaporator a the firewall fittings.
4. Remove the glove box, center console, speaker cover and air duct.
5. Remove the resistor and the thermo switch connector.
6. Remove drain hose.
7. Remove the evaporator assembly.
8. Installation is the reverse of removal procedure. If evaporator core is replaced, add 1.7 oz. of new oil to the evaporator. Evacuate, recharge and leak test the system.

Refrigerant Lines

REMOVAL AND INSTALLATION

1. Disconnect the negative battery cable.
2. Properly discharge the air conditioning system.
3. If necessary, remove the grille for access to the lines at the condenser and receiver/drier.
4. Disconnect the refrigerant lines using 2 wrenches where required.
5. Remove all attaching brackets or clips.
6. Remove reservoir tanks where required.
7. Remove the refrigerant line.
8. Installation is the reverse of removal procedure.
9. Evacuate, recharge and leak check the system.

NOTE: Always route hoses in original location and use new O-rings with a thin coat of refrigerant oil.

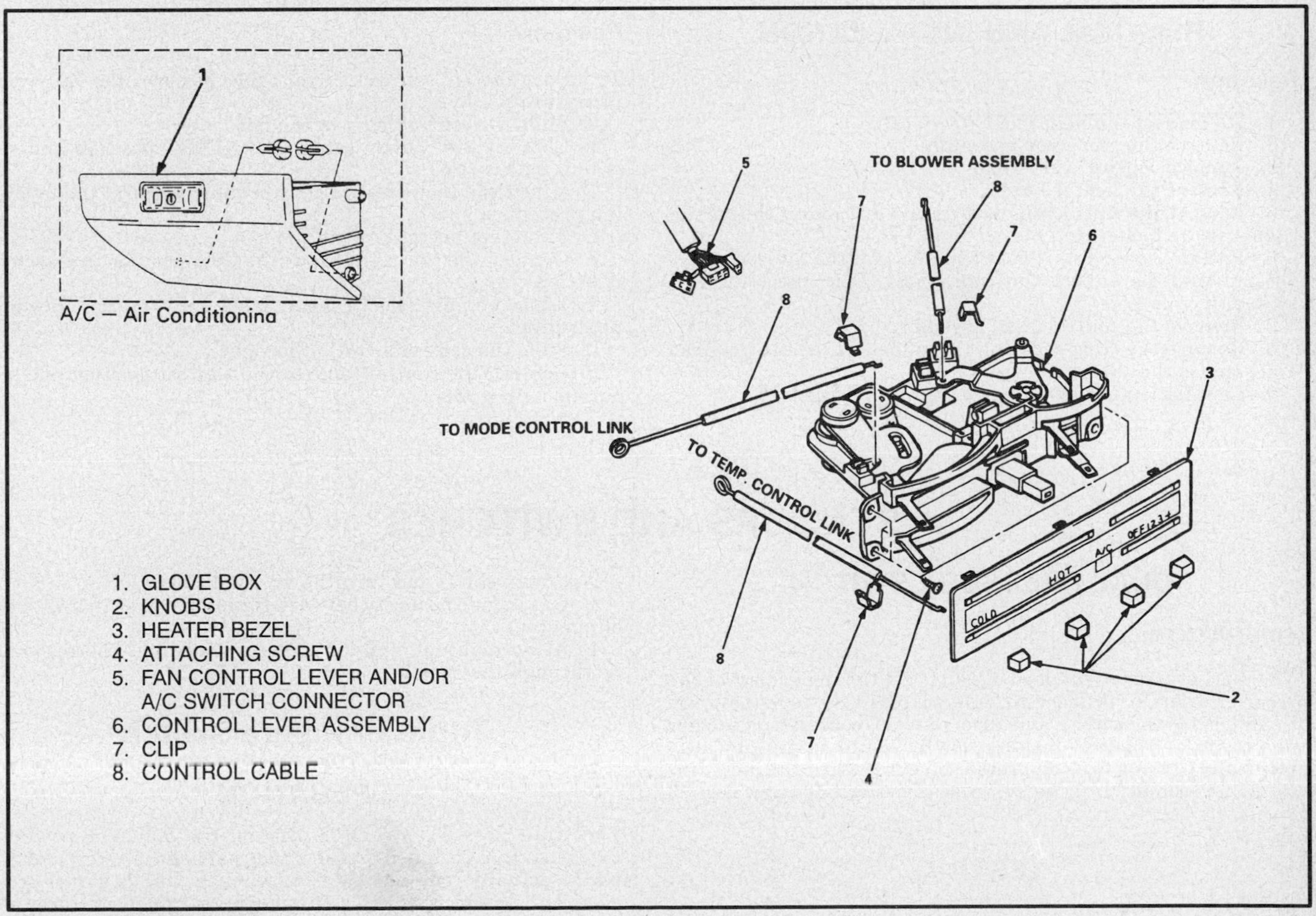

A/C — Air Conditioning

1. GLOVE BOX
2. KNOBS
3. HEATER BEZEL
4. ATTACHING SCREW
5. FAN CONTROL LEVER AND/OR A/C SWITCH CONNECTOR
6. CONTROL LEVER ASSEMBLY
7. CLIP
8. CONTROL CABLE

Manual control head

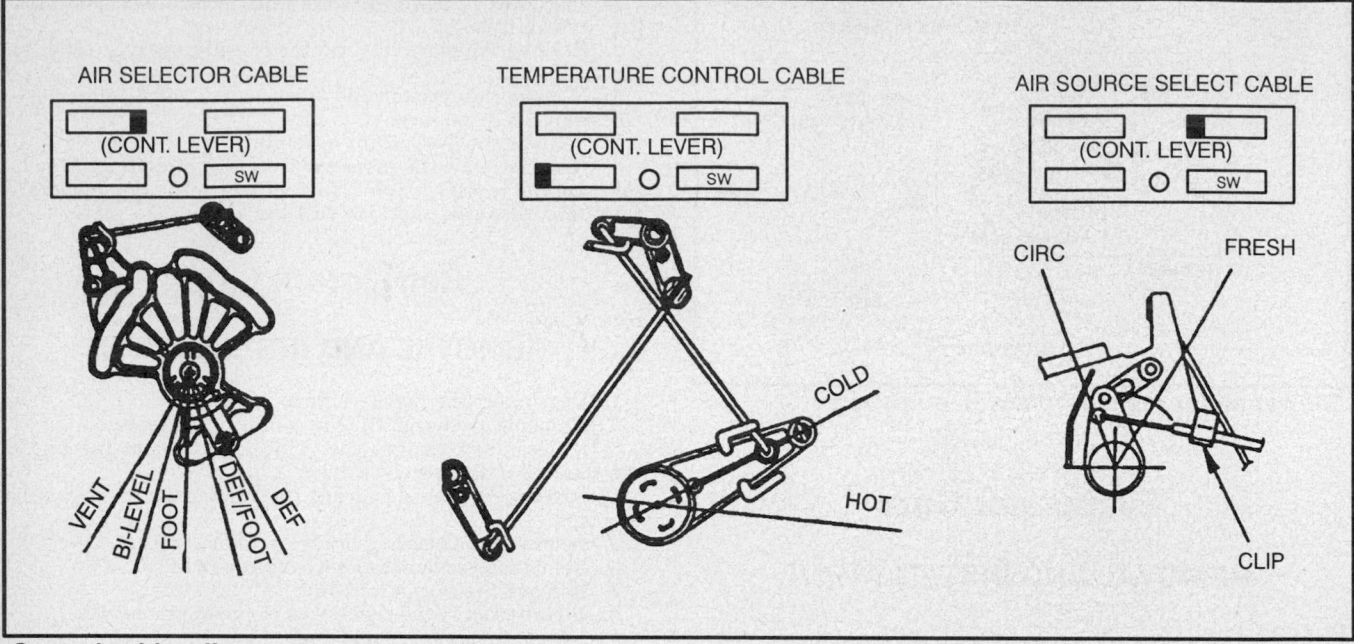

Control cable adjustment

Manual Control Head

REMOVAL AND INSTALLATION

Passport

1. Disconnect the negative battery cable.
2. Remove the glove box assembly.
3. Remove control lever knobs.
4. Remove the heater bezel.
5. Remove the 3 attaching screws and disconnect the control cables at the heater and blower unit.
6. Pull the control unit outward and pull the fan control lever out and disconnect the connectors. Disconnect the A/C switch, if equipped.
7. Remove the control head assembly.
8. Remove the clips securing the cables on the control head and remove the cables.
9. Installation is the reverse of removal procedure.

ADJUSTMENT

Passport

To adjust the air source control cable perform the following procedure:
1. Slide the control lever to the left.
2. Connect the control cable at the CIRC position and secure it with a clip.

To adjust the temperature control cable perform the following procedure:
1. Slide the control lever to the left.
2. Connect the control cable at the Cold position and secure it with a clip.

To adjust the air select control cable perform the following procedure:
1. Slide the control lever to the right.
2. Connect the control cable at the Defrost position and secure it with a clip.

SENSORS AND SWITCHES

DUAL PRESSURE SWITCH

OPERATION

The dual pressure switch is installed on the upper part of the receiver/drier, it is used to detectexcessively high pressure (high pressure switch) and also prevent compressor seizure due to the refrigerant leaking (low pressure switch), by electronically turning the compressor on or off when the pressures in the air–conditioning system rise above or fall below normal levels.

TESTING

1. Disconnect the pressure switch wire connector from the receiver/drier.

2. Start vehicle and turn the air conditioner ON.
3. Check for continuity between terminals on switch with an ohmmeter.
4. At normal high and low pressure readings there should be through the switch.

Triple pressure switch

OPERATION

The triple pressure switch is used on the 3.2L V–6 powered Passport. It is installed on the upper part of the receiver/drier and is actually comprised of two switches. One is a dual pressure switch which controls the magnetic clutch on the compressor. The second switch is a medium pressure switch that controls the condenser fan motor.

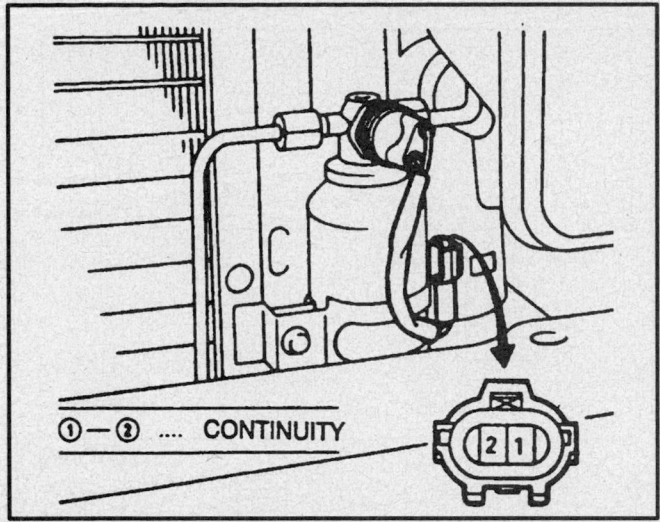
Testing of the dual pressure switch

① — ② ..... CONTINUITY

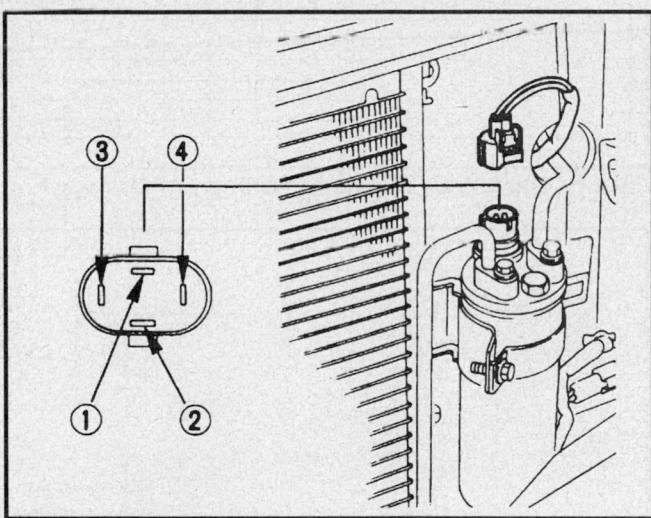
Testing of the triple pressure switch

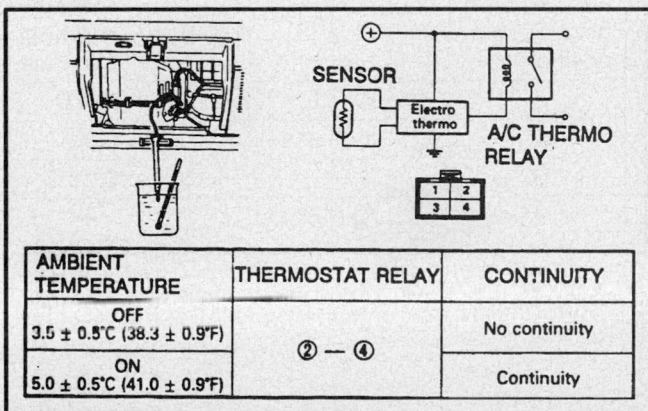

AMBIENT TEMPERATURE	THERMOSTAT RELAY	CONTINUITY
OFF 3.5 ± 0.5°C (38.3 ± 0.9°F)	② — ④	No continuity
ON 5.0 ± 0.5°C (41.0 ± 0.9°F)		Continuity

Testing the electronic thermostat

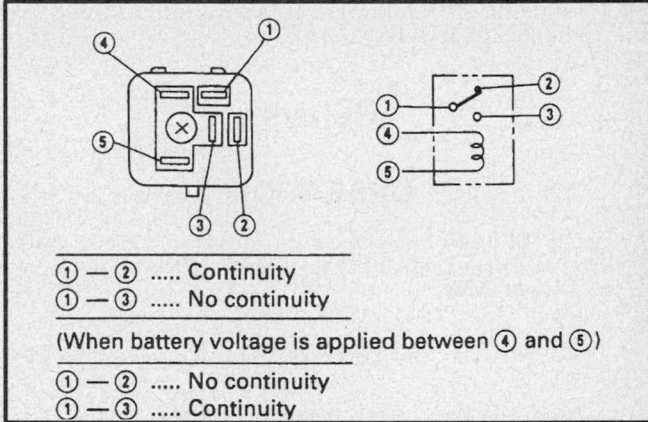

① — ② ..... Continuity
① — ③ ..... No continuity

(When battery voltage is applied between ④ and ⑤)

① — ② ..... No continuity
① — ③ ..... Continuity

Testing the heater relay

TESTING

1. Install a set of pressure gauges on the air conditioning refrigerant lines and an ohmmeter to the applicable terminals on the triple pressure switch (refer to applicable diagrams).
2. Start the vehicle and turn on the air conditioning.
3. Check the switch for continuity when the pressures are within the ranges indicated and a lack of continuity when the pressures are below or above the normal pressure range.

REMOVAL AND INSTALLATION

1. Disconnect the negative battery cable.
2. Properly discharge the air conditioning system.
3. If required, remove radiator grille.
4. Disconnect the pressure switch wire connector.
5. Use 2 wrenches to remove the pressure switch.
6. Installation is the reverse of removal procedure. Evacuate, recharge and leak test the system.

Electronic Thermostat

OPERATION

Passport

The electronic thermostat consists of the thermosensor and a thermostatic unit which function electrically to help reduce operation noise. The electronic thermosensor is mounted at the evaporator core outlet to sense cool air temperature. The thermo unit compares the results and operates the thermoswitch relay to cycle the compressor on and off to prevent evaporator freeze–up.

TESTING

Passport

1. Remove the thermosensor from the evaporator core. Start the engine.
2. Set the A/C switch to ON. Using a heated liquid source as shown, warm and cool the thermosensor to test the continuity as indicated. Check the continuity between the thermo switch relay terminals at the harness side.

REMOVAL AND INSTALLATION

1. Disconnect the negative battery cable.
2. Properly discharge the air conditioning system.
3. Remove the evaporator assembly, if required.
4. Remove the thermo sensor from the evaporator coils. Remove the electronic thermostat from the evaporator housing, if equipped.

5. Installation is the reverse of removal procedure. Evacuate, recharge and leak test the system.

Relays

OPERATION

A variety of relays are used to energize certain system switches or components, or to de–energize them as in the case of the A/C cut relay.

TESTING

1. Disconnect the battery negative terminal.
2. Disconnect the relays from the fuse and relay box.
3. Check for continuity and resistance between terminals of the relays.

REMOVAL AND INSTALLATION

Most air conditioner relays are located in one of 4 places; the left front kick panel, by the right or left fenderwell under the hood or at the evaporator housing.

FAN AND AIR CONDITIONING SWITCH

The fan switch controls blower motor speed by sending 12 volts to the resistor where it is reduced depending upon which position is selected; low, medium low, medium high, high. The air conditionerswitch is an illuminated push button switch which sends 12 volts to the air conditioner relay when depressed.

TESTING

1. Disconnect the negative battery cable.
2. Remove the control head assembly.
3. Disconnect the air conditioner and fan switch connectors.
4. Check for continuity between terminals.

19:25.5 Testing the fan and air conditioning switch

REMOVAL AND INSTALLATION

1. Disconnect the negative battery cable.
2. Remove the control head assembly.
3. Disconnect the air conditioner and fan switch connectors.
4. Installation is the reverse of the removal procedure.

Blower Resistor

OPERATION

The resistor serves to reduce or increase current reaching the blower motor, based on position of the blower switch.

TESTING

1. Disconnect the resistor connector.
2. Using an ohmmeter, check for continuity between the terminals as shown.

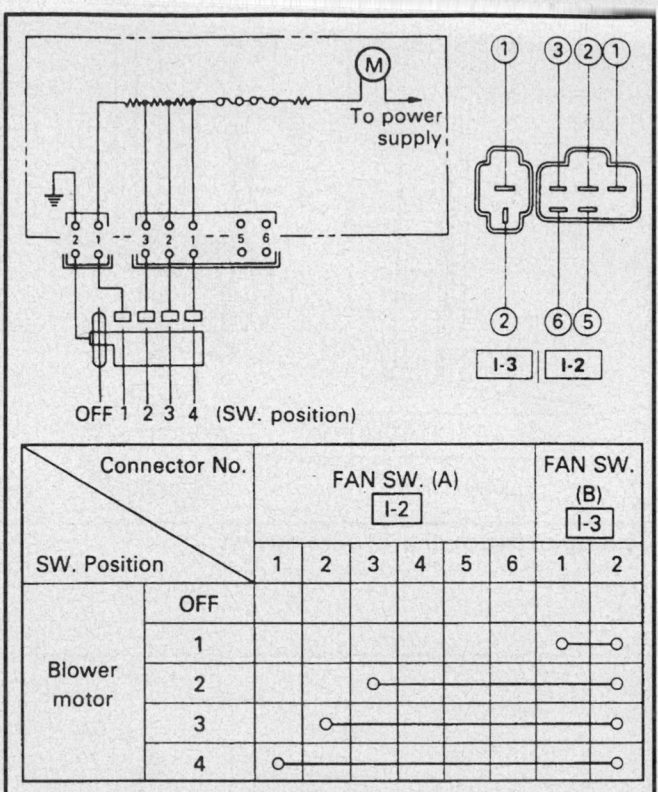

Connector No.		FAN SW. (A) I-2						FAN SW. (B) I-3	
SW. Position		1	2	3	4	5	6	1	2
Blower motor	OFF								
	1							○—○	
	2			○					○
	3		○						○
	4		○						○

Testing the fan air and conditioning switch

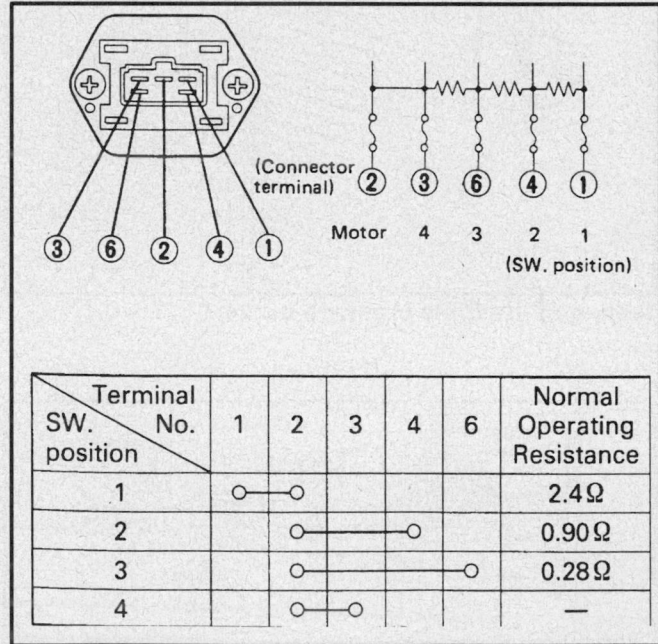

Terminal No. SW. position	1	2	3	4	6	Normal Operating Resistance
1	○—○					2.4 Ω
2		○—○				0.90 Ω
3		○—		—○		0.28 Ω
4		○—○				—

Testing the blower motor switch

SYSTEM DIAGNOSIS

CONTINUITY TESTING OF THE TRIPLE PRESSURE SWITCH

[A/C OFF]

Terminal No.	Control	Continuity
① — ②	Magnetic Clutch	Continuity
③ — ④	Condenser Fan	No Continuity

[A/C ON]

Refrigerant Pressure	Terminal No.	Continuity	Fan
Below 1079±98 kPa/156±14 psi	③ — ④	No Continuity	OFF
Above 1471±98 kpa/213±14 psi		Continuity	ON

BLOWER MOTOR DOES NOT RUN

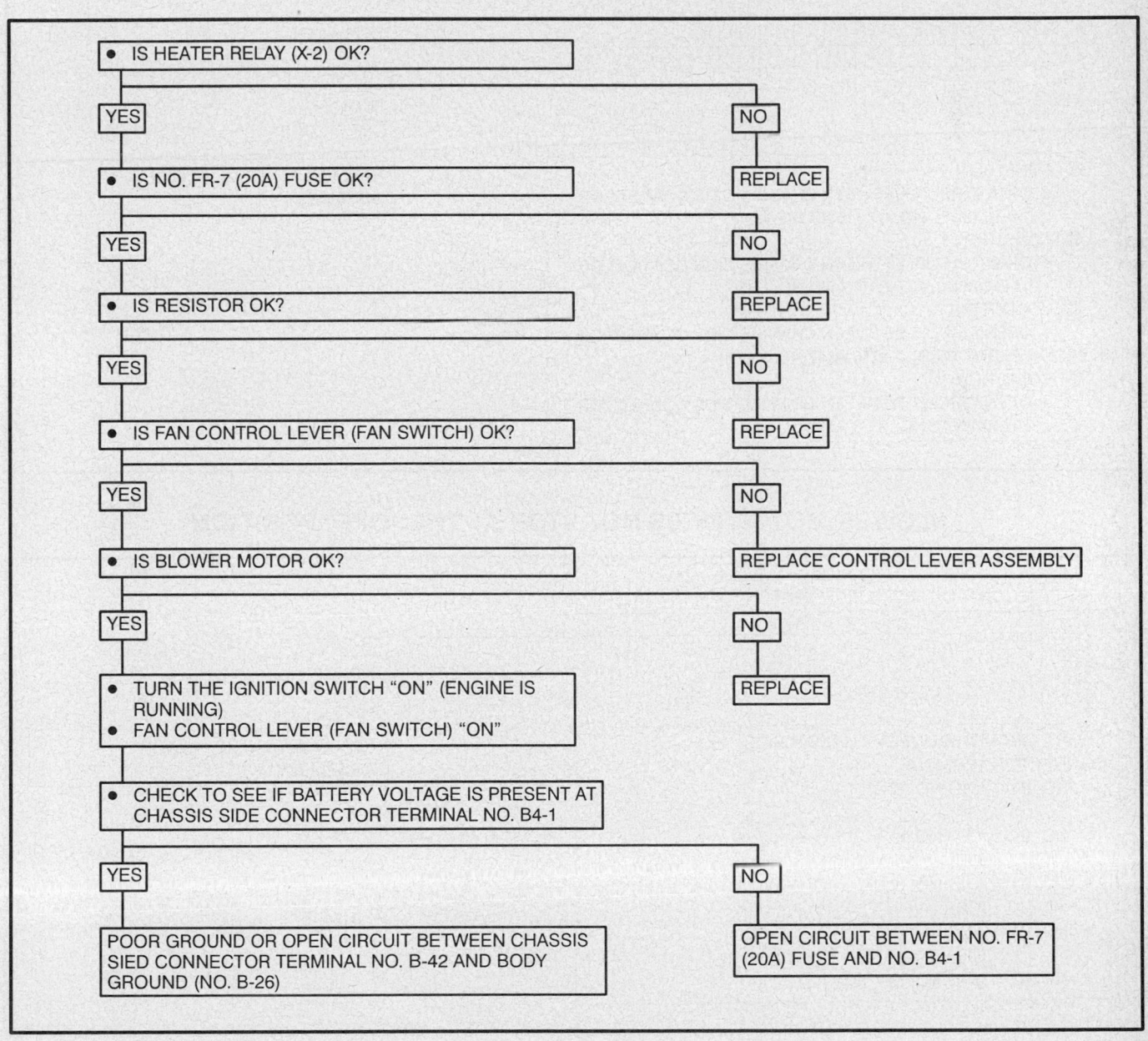

BLOWER MOTOR DOES NOT RUN IN CERTAIN POSITIONS

BLOWER MOTOR DOES
NOT RUN AT
- Ⓐ 1 : (LOW)
- Ⓑ 2 : (MEDIUM LOW) POSITION
- Ⓒ 3 : (MEDIUM HI)
- Ⓓ 4 : (HIGH)

* CHECKING IS PERFORMED ONLY WHEN IN
  THE MALFUNCTION MODE.

- IS RESISTOR OK?

YES	NO
	REPLACE

- IS FAN CONTROL LEVER (FAN SWITCH) OK?

YES	NO
	REPLACE CONTROL LEVER ASSEMBLY

- Ⓐ CONDITION:
  - OPEN CIRCUIT BETWEEN CHASSIS SIDE CONNECTOR
    TERMINAL NO. B1-1 AND NO. I3-1
- Ⓑ CONDITION:
  - OPEN CIRCUIT BETWEEN CHASSIS SIDE CONNECTOR
    TERMINAL NO. B1-4 AND NO. I2-3
- Ⓒ CONDITION:
  - OPEN CIRCUIT BETWEEN CHASSIS SIDE CONNECTOR
    TERMINAL NO. B1-6 AND NO. I2-2
- Ⓓ CONDITION:
  - OPEN CIRCUIT BETWEEN CHASSIS SIDE CONNECTOR
    TERMINAL NO. B1-3 AND NO. I2-1

BLOWER MOTOR DOES NOT STOP AT THE "OFF" POSITION

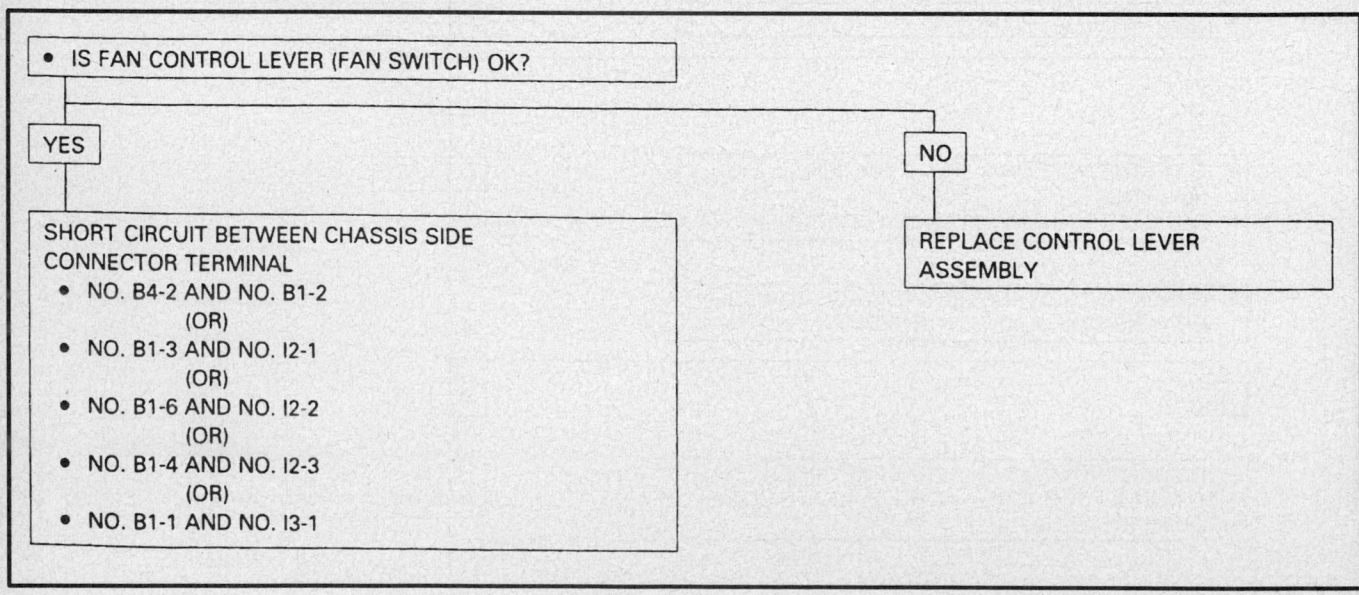

- IS FAN CONTROL LEVER (FAN SWITCH) OK?

YES	NO
	REPLACE CONTROL LEVER ASSEMBLY

SHORT CIRCUIT BETWEEN CHASSIS SIDE
CONNECTOR TERMINAL
- NO. B4-2 AND NO. B1-2
        (OR)
- NO. B1-3 AND NO. I2-1
        (OR)
- NO. B1-6 AND NO. I2-2
        (OR)
- NO. B1-4 AND NO. I2-3
        (OR)
- NO. B1-1 AND NO. I3-1

WIRING SCHEMATICS

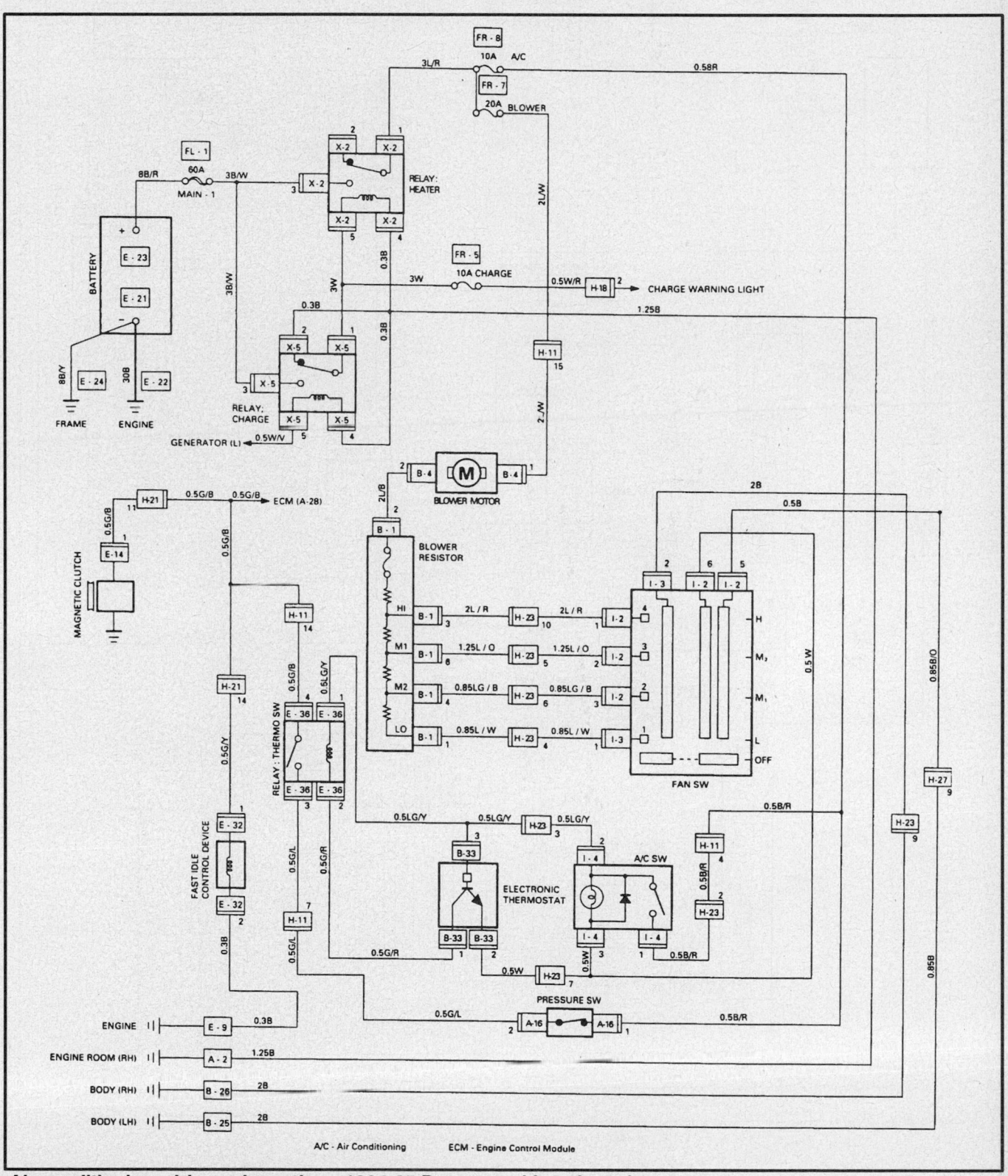

Air conditioning wiring schematic — 1994-95 Passport with 2.6L engine

A/C - Air Conditioning   ECM - Engine Control Module

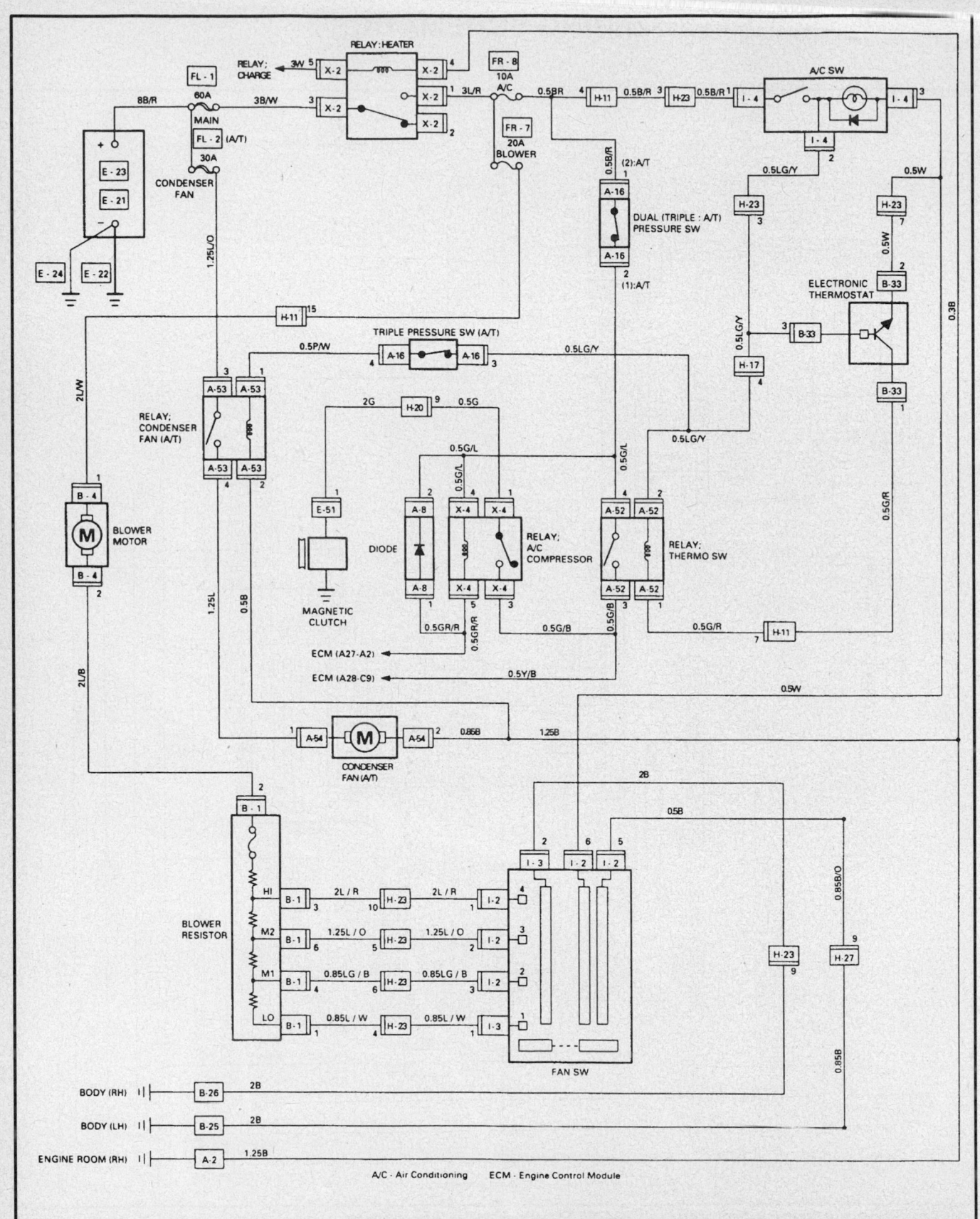

Air conditioning wiring schematic — 1994-95 passport with 3.2L engine

SPECIFICATIONS

ENGINE IDENTIFICATION

Year	Model	Engine Displacement Liters (cc)	Engine Series (ID/VIN)	Fuel System	No. of Cylinders	Engine Type
1993	Elantra	1.6 (1596)	R	MPI	4	DOHC
	Elantra	1.8 (1836)	M	MPI	4	DOHC
	Excel	1.5 (1468)	J	MPI	4	OHC
	Scoupe	1.5 (1465)	N	MPI	4	OHC
	Sonata	2.0 (1997)	P	MPI	4	DOHC
	Sonata	3.0 (2972)	T	MPI	6	OHC
1994	Elantra	1.6 (1596)	R	MPI	4	DOHC
	Elantra	1.8 (1836)	M	MPI	4	DOHC
	Excel	1.5 (1465)	J	MPI	4	OHC
	Scoupe	1.5 (1465)	E	MPI	4	OHC
	Sonata	2.0 (1997)	F	MPI	4	DOHC
	Sonata	3.0 (2972)	T	MPI	6	OHC
1995	Elantra	1.6 (1596)	R	MPI	4	DOHC
	Elantra	1.8 (1846)	M	MPI	4	DOHC
	Accent	1.5 (1495)	K	MPI	4	OHC
	Scoupe	1.5 (1495)	N	MPI	4	OHC
	Sonata	2.0 (1997)	F	MPI	4	DOHC
	Sonata	3.0 (2972)	T	MPI	6	OHC

MPI–Multi–Port Fuel Injection
OHC–Overhead Cam
DOHC–Dual Overhead Cam

REFRIGERANT CAPACITIES

Year	Model	Refrigerant (oz.)	Oil (fl. oz.)	Compressor Type
1993	Elantra	32	4.0	TRF 090
	Excel	30–32	8.1	SD–709
	Scoupe	30–32	7.6–8.1	10P15C
	Sonata	31–33	6.9–7.6	FX–15
1994	Elantra	24	8.5–9.7	FX–15
	Excel	24–25	12.6–14.0	FX–15
	Scoupe	24–25	8.5–9.7	FX–15
	Sonata	26–28	12.6–14.0	FX–15
1995	Elantra	24	8.5–9.7	FX–15
	Accent	24	12.6–14.0	FX–15
	Scoupe	24–25	8.5–9.7	FX–15
	Sonata	26–28	12.6–14.0	FX–15

AIR CONDITIONING BELT TENSION

Year	Model	Engine Liters (cc)	Belt Type	Specifications①	
				New (lbs.)	Used (lbs.)
1993	Elantra	1.6 (1596)	V–Ribbed	0.20–0.22	0.23–0.27
	Elantra	1.8 (1836)	V–Ribbed	0.20–0.21	0.23–0.28
	Excel	1.5 (1468)	V–Ribbed	0.34–0.42	0.34–0.42
	Scoupe	1.5 (1468)	V–Ribbed	0.20–0.21	0.23–0.28
	Sonata	2.0 (1997)	V–Ribbed	0.20–0.22	0.24–0.28
	Sonata	3.0 (2972)	V–Ribbed	0.18–0.22	0.18–0.22
1994	Elantra	1.6 (1596)	V–Ribbed	0.20–0.21	0.23–0.28
	Elantra	1.8 (1836)	V–Ribbed	0.20–0.21	0.23–0.28
	Excel	1.5 (1468)	V–Ribbed	0.34–0.42	0.34–0.42
	Scoupe	1.5 (1468)	V–Ribbed	0.20–0.21	0.23–0.28
	Sonata	2.0 (1997)	V–Ribbed	0.20–0.21	0.23–0.28
	Sonata	3.0 (2972)	V–Ribbed	0.20–0.21	0.23–0.28
1995	Elantra	1.6 (1596)	V–Ribbed	0.20–0.21	0.23–0.28
	Elantra	1.8 (1836)	V–Ribbed	0.20–0.21	0.23–0.28
	Accent	1.5 (1468)	V–Ribbed	0.34–0.42	0.34–0.42
	Scoupe	1.5 (1468)	V–Ribbed	0.20–0.21	0.23–0.28
	Sonata	2.0 (1997)	V–Ribbed	0.20–0.21	0.23–0.28
	Sonata	3.0 (2972)	V–Ribbed	0.20–0.21	0.23–0.28

① Inches of deflection at midpoint of the belt

SYSTEM DESCRIPTION

General Information

Two types of air conditioning systems are used. Some models use a cycling clutch orifice tube system. This system utilizes a fixed orifice tube in the condenser output line, an accumulator on the outlet side of the evaporator and a clutch cycling switch to provide on and off compressor cycling operation. In some cases, a variable displacement compressor is used which eliminates the need for the cycling switch.

The other system uses a traditional expansion valve and receiver/drier instead of the orifice tube and accumulator. This system may use an evaporator thermostat to control compressor on and off cycling.

System protection is provided by either a high pressure switch (on the accumulator) or a dual pressure switch (on the receiver/drier). These switches will interrupt compressor operation if system pressures become extreme.

Sonata models may use a semi-automatic air conditioning system which allows continuous adjustment of the preset temperature on the control panel. The in-car sensor and ambient sensor work to provide internal and external inputs to the system programmer to adjust mode, blower and cooling/heating operations to maintain the desired setting.

Service Valve Location

On most models, the high and low service valve ports are located directly at the rear of the compressor unit. On Elantra and Accent, the valves are located on their respective refrigerant lines on either side of the engine compartment.

System Discharging

—CAUTION—

The pressurized refrigerant inside the system must be discharged prior to the replacement or repair of any air conditioning system components. When discharging the system always wear protective eye wear. R134A liquid refrigerant is highly volatile. A drop on the skin of your hand could result in localized frostbite. When handling the refrigerant, be sure to wear gloves and eye protection.

1. Discharging must never be done to the open air. Always use certified, approved recovery/recycling equipment to protect the atmosphere against CFCs which can destroy the ozone layer.
2. Follow the equipment manufacturer's operating instructions to be sure proper discharging is completed.

System Evacuating

Whenever the system has been opened to the atmosphere, it is absolutely necessary that the system be evacuated to remove the air and moisture from the system. Air in the refrigerant system will cause a loss in the systems performance, a high compressor discharge pressure and oxidation of the compressor oil into gum or varnish. Moisture in the system will cause the expansion valve to malfunction.

After a new component is installed, the system should be evacuated for a minimum of 15 minutes. If an in-service component was opened for repair, evacuate the system for 30 minutes.

1. Connect the manifold gauge set to the compressor or refrigerant lines and a long test hose from the gauge set manifold center connection to a vacuum pump. This should be done with the engine not running.
2. Close both manifold gauge set valves.
3. Start the vacuum pump and then open the high and low manifold pressure valves.
4. After 10 minutes, check that the low pressure gauge reads more than 37.7 in. Hg of vacuum. If the pressure rises or a vacuum cannot be obtained, there is a leak in the system. If a leak is suspected, stop the pump, charge the system with a 1 lb. can of refrigerant and check for leaks with a suitable leak detector. Repair any leaks in the system and discharge and evacuate the system.
5. If no leaks are found, continue operation of the vacuum pump.
6. Open both manifold valves to obtain as close to a vacuum of 37.7 in. Hg as possible. After the low pressure gauge reads approximately 37.7 in. Hg, continue evacuating the system for 15 min., 30 min. for in-service repairs.
7. After the system has been evacuated for 15 or 30 minutes, close both manifold gauge valves and stop the vacuum pump.
8. Disconnect the hose from the vacuum pump and charge the system.

System Charging

1. Use only certified and approved recovery/recycling equipment for recharging (charging station). Use of this equipment allows the reuse of the captured refrigerant and provides added assurance of proper refrigerant levels.
2. Follow the equipment manufacturer's instructions for recharging.

Compressor and Component Oil Adjustments

Whenever components are replaced or if the system has had a major leak, such as due to collision damage to the system, after the specific repairs have been made to eliminate leaks and when components are replaced, the oil level must be adjusted.

SD-709 and 10P15C Compressors

1. If possible, run the air conditioning system and maximum cooling and high blower speed for about 20–30 minutes in order to return as much system oil to the compressor as possible.
2. Stop the engine, discharge the refrigerant and remove the compressor.

NOTE: It is easier to drain more oil from the compressor while it is still warm.

3. Drain the compressor oil through the refrigerant line connections into a clean, calibrated container and note the quantity drained.
4. If the amount drained was less than 2.1 oz., there may be a leak in the system, allowing refrigerant and oil to escape. Leak test the system, make necessary repairs, then continue with oil level adjustment.
5. If the amount drained was between 2.1–2.3 oz., add 2.3 oz. of new oil to the compressor.
6. If the amount drained was more than 2.3 oz., add the same amount as drained.

NOTE: This procedure should also be used if installing a new compressor. Drain the oil from the new compressor and install the amount needed according to the above procedure. Always use new oil of the specified type for this compressor.

FX-15 Compressor

1. If possible, run the air conditioning system and maximum cooling and high blower speed for about 20–30 minutes in order to return as much system oil to the compressor as possible.
2. Stop the engine, discharge the refrigerant and remove the compressor.

NOTE: It is easier to drain more oil from the compressor while it is still warm.

3. Drain the compressor oil through the refrigerant line connections into a clean, calibrated container and note the quantity drained.
4. If the amount drained was between 3.0–5.0 oz. of oil, add the same amount of oil to the compressor.
5. If the amount of oil drained was more than 5.0 oz., add 5.0 oz. of oil to the compressor.
6. If the amount of oil drained was less than 3.0 oz., add 3.0 oz. of oil to the compressor.

NOTE: This procedure should also be used if installing a new compressor. Drain the oil from the new compressor and install the amount needed according to the above procedure. Always use new oil of the specified type for this compressor.

Component Oil Replacement

When replacing system components, be sure to add the following amount of new oil to the parts during replacement.

Accent
Evaporator Core, add 1.3 oz. of oil.
Condenser, add 1.0 oz. of oil.
Receiver/Drier, add 1.0 oz. of oil.

Excel
Evaporator core, add 3.0 oz. of oil.
Condenser, add 1.0 oz. of oil.
Accumulator, add 1.0 oz. of oil.

Elantra
Evaporator core, add 1.6 oz. of oil.
Condenser, add 1.0 oz. of oil.
Receiver/Drier, add 0.3 oz. of oil.

Scoupe (Receiver/Drier with expansion valve)
Evaporator core, add 1.4–1.7 oz. of oil.
Condenser, add 1.4–1.7 oz. of oil.
Receiver/Drier, add 0.3 oz. of oil.

Sonata with 10P15C compressor
Evaporator core, add 3.0 oz. of oil.
Condenser, add 1.0 oz. of oil.
Accumulator, add 1.0 oz. of oil.

Sonata with FX-15 compressor
Evaporator core, add 1.6 oz. of oil.
Condenser, add 1.0 oz. of oil.
Accumulator, drain and add same amount, plus 2.0 oz. of oil.

Spring-Lock Coupling Procedures

Several connections will be joined with a spring-lock (garter) coupling which requires a special tool (09977-33600 or equivalent) for removal.

1. Properly discharge the system using recovery/recycling equipment.

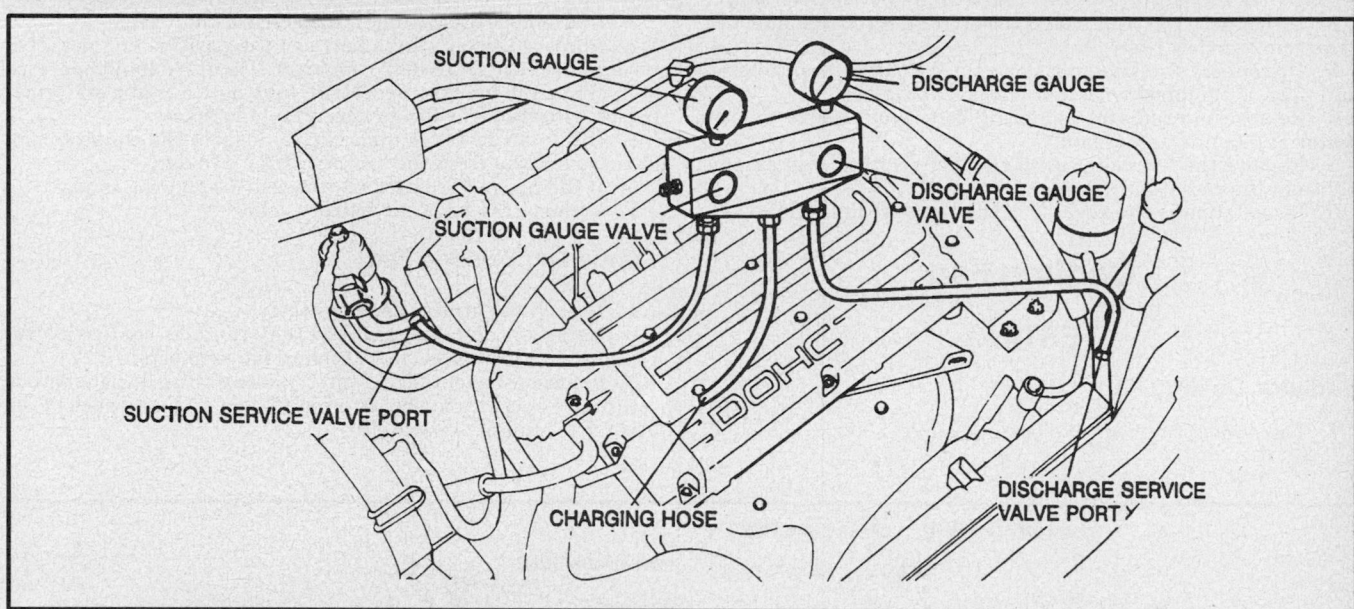

Service valve connections—Elantra; Accent is similar

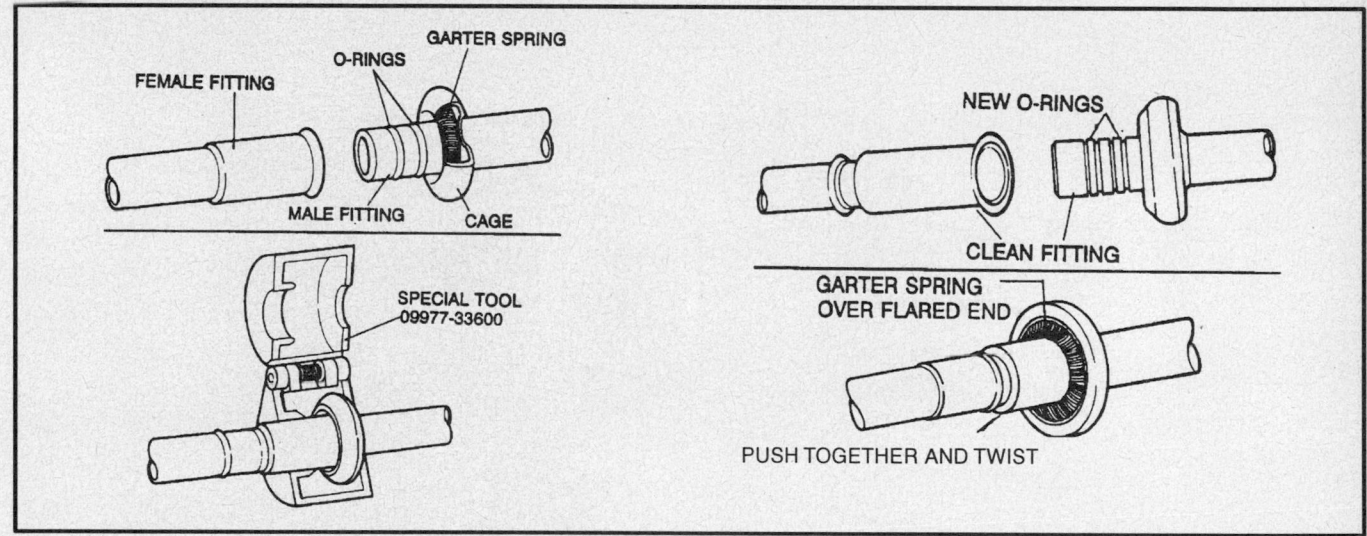

PUSH TOGETHER AND TWIST

Spring lock coupling and connector procedure.

2. Install the special tool on the coupling and push the tool into the spring-lock cage to release the female fitting from the garter spring.

3. Pull the male and female fittings apart and remove the tool.

4. Check for a missing or damaged garter spring. If necessary to remove the spring, use only a small hooked wire to grab the spring and pull it out.

5. After cleaning the fittings, install new O-rings lubricated with new refrigerant oil.

6. Connect the fittings by pushing together with a twisting motion.

7. Visually check that the garter spring is over the flared end of the female fitting.

SYSTEM COMPONENTS

Radiator

REMOVAL AND INSTALLATION

1. Disconnect the negative battery cable.

2. Disconnect the fan motor and thermo sensor (if equipped) connection.

3. Set the heater control to the **HOT** position.

4. Remove the radiator drain plug and drain the radiator coolant.

5. Disconnect the upper and lower radiator hoses and the reservoir overflow hose.

6. Disconnect the transmission cooler lines at the radiator and plug, if equipped with automatic transaxle.

7. Remove the radiator mounting bolts and remove the radiator and fan as an assembly.

8. Remove the fan motor mounting bolts and the fan assembly from the radiator.

9. Installation is the reverse of the removal procedure.

Cooling Fan

TESTING

Radiator Cooling Fan

1. Disconnect the negative battery cable.

2. Disconnect the cooling fan electrical connector.

3. Apply a 12 volt source between the positive and negative terminals of the fan motor connector. The fan should operate.

4. While the fan is in operation, take notice to any abnormal noises, vibrations or fan-to-shroud interference.

5. If the fan motor is inoperative, inspect the connector an harness leading from the fan motor, for damage.

6. If the fan motor checks good, test the thermo sensor.

7. Connect the negative battery cable.

Condenser Cooling Fan

1. Detach the cooling fan connector.

2. Using an ohmmeter, check that there is continuity between the 2 terminals of the cooling fan connector.

3. Sonata connector is a 3-pin connector. Check that there is continuity between the black (ground) terminal and each of the other 2 terminals separately.

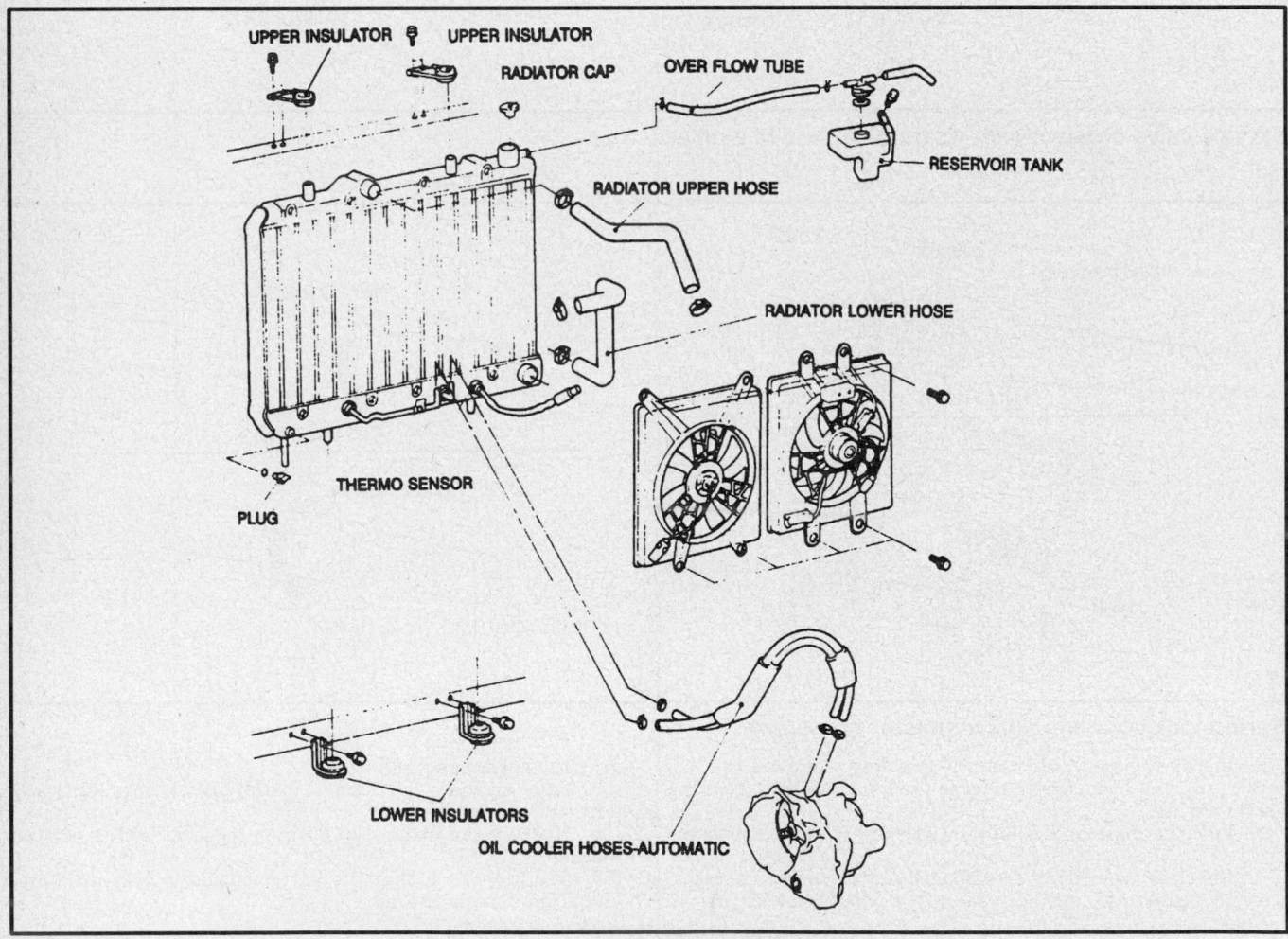

Exploded view of the radiator and related components—Excel and Scoupe

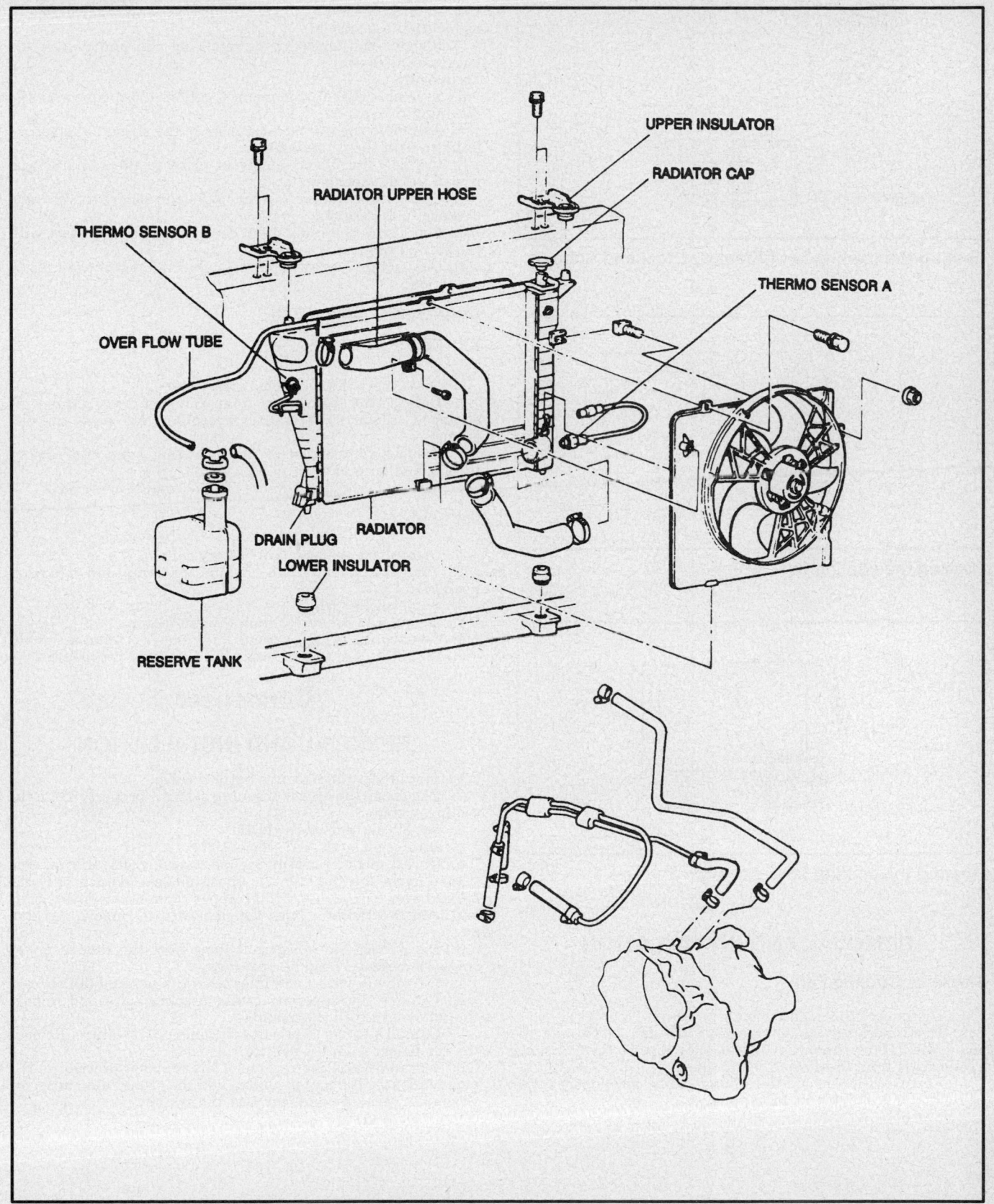

Exploded view of the radiator and related components — Sonota

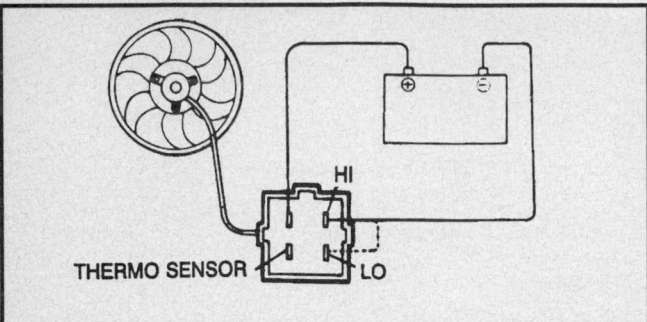

Testing the cooling fan—Elantra, Excel and Scoupe

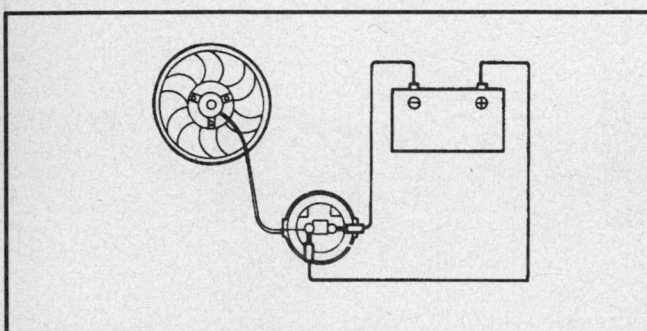

Testing the cooling fan—Sonata

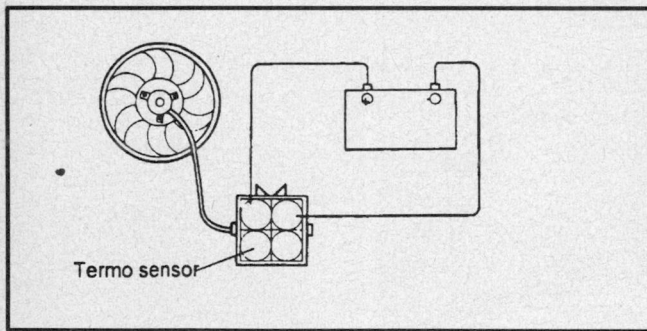

Testing the cooling fan—Accent

REMOVAL AND INSTALLATION

Radiator Cooling Fan

1. Disconnect the negative battery cable.
2. Disconnect the connectors from the fan motor and remove the harness from the shroud. Also remove the transaxle cooler lines from the shroud, if equipped.
3. Remove the shroud-to-radiator bolts and remove the shroud and fan motor as an assembly.

4. Remove the fan motor-to-shroud bolts and remove the fan motor from the shroud.
5. Remove the fan-to-motor retaining clip and detach the fan from the motor.

To install:

6. Assemble the fan and motor together and secure with the retaining clip.
7. Assemble the fan motor assembly the shroud and secure in place with the retaining nuts.
8. Position the fan assembly in place to the radiator and install the mounting bolts.
9. Connect the fan motor connectors and secure the harness in place to the shroud.
10. Make sure the cooling fan does not come in contact with the shroud when it is installed.
11. Connect the negative battery cable and test the fan motor operation.

Condenser Cooling Fan

EXCEPT SONATA

1. Disconnect the negative battery cable.
2. Detach the connector from the fan and shroud. If equipped, remove the transaxle cooling line from the fan shroud.
3. Remove the condenser fan mounting bolts and remove the fan and shroud.
4. Installation is the reverse of the removal procedure.

SONATA

1. Disconnect the negative battery cable.
2. Remove the left front combination lamp and left front headlamp.
3. Remove the grille.
4. Detach the connector from the fan motor.
5. Remove the mounting bolts and remove the fan assembly.
6. Installation is the reverse of the removal procedure.

Condenser

REMOVAL AND INSTALLATION

1. Disconnect the negative battery cable.
2. Discharge the air conditioning system. Properly drain the cooling system.
3. On Excel, remove the grille.
4. On Accent with ABS, remove the air duct.
5. On all models, except Scoupe with a receiver/drier system, remove the radiator. On these models, detach only the top radiator hose, remove the 4 upper radiator mounting bolts and lean the radiator back for clearance to remove the condenser.
6. Disconnect the refrigerant lines from the condenser fittings. Immediately cap all openings.
7. Detach all wiring and lines from the fan and fan shroud.
8. Remove the upper mounting bracket bolts and remove the condenser with the mounts.
9. Cap all fittings to prevent the entry of moisture. Remove the condenser from the vehicle.
10. Installation is the reverse of the removal procedure. If a new condenser is being installed, add the proper amount of oil. Evacuate, recharge and leak test the system.

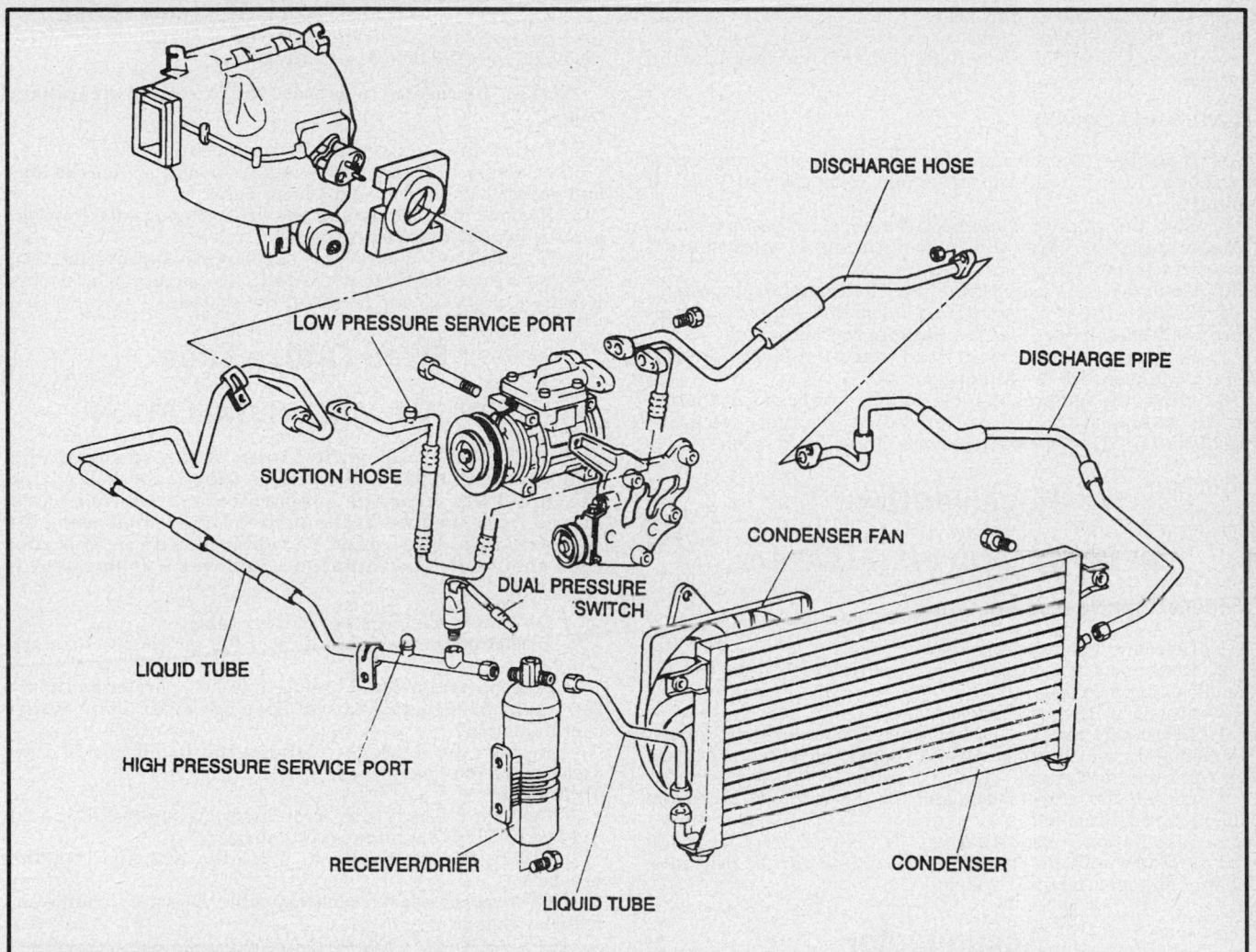

System component layout—1993 Scoupe

Compressor

REMOVAL AND INSTALLATION

Excel

1. If possible, run the air conditioning system at high blower and maximum cooling for at least 10 minutes, then stop the engine.
2. Disconnect the negative battery cable and discharge the air conditioning system.
3. Remove the distributor assembly.
4. Loosen the tension pulley and remove the drive belt.
5. Remove the electrical harness from the magnetic clutch.
6. Remove the high and low pressure refrigerant lines. Immediately cap all openings to minimize system contamination.
7. Remove the compressor. Drain and measure the compressor oil.
8. Installation is the reverse of the removal procedure. Adjust the compressor oil as necessary. Evacuate, recharge and leak test the system.

Accent and Scoupe

1. If possible, run the engine at idle and the air conditioning system at high blower and maximum cooling for at least 10 minutes, then stop the engine.
2. Disconnect the negative battery cable. Detach the magnetic clutch wire from the compressor.
3. Properly discharge the air conditioning system using recycling/recovery equipment.
4. Raise and properly support the vehicle.
5. Detach the suction hose fitting, then remove the suction hose and discharge hose from the compressor. Immediately cap all openings to minimize system contamination.
6. Loosen the adjusting bolt and lock nut, then remove the compressor belt.
7. Remove the 3 compressor mounting bolts and lay the compressor on the driveshaft.
8. Remove the compressor mounting bracket with the idler pulley, then remove the compressor from the vehicle.
9. Drain and measure the oil from the compressor.
To install:
10. Adjust the compressor oil level
11. Position the compressor, install the mounting bracket, then attach the compressor to the mounting bracket.
12. Install the compressor drive belt and adjust as needed.

13. Attach the refrigerant hoses to the compressor and reattach the suction hose fittings.

14. Lower the vehicle. Evacuate, recharge and leak test the system.

Elantra and Sonata

1. If possible, run the engine at idle and the air conditioning system at high blower and maximum cooling for at least 10 minutes.

2. Stop the engine, disconnect the negative battery cable, then properly discharge the air conditioning system using recovery/recycling equipment.

3. Disconnect the magnetic clutch wire from the compressor.

4. Remove the refrigerant lines from the compressor. Immediately cap all openings to minimize contamination.

5. Remove the drive belt, then remove the compressor. Drain and measure the compressor oil.

6. Adjust the compressor oil level. Then perform installation in the reverse of the removal procedure. Evacuate, recharge and leak test the system. Adjust the drive belt tension.

Receiver/Drier

REMOVAL AND INSTALLATION

Accent, Elantra and Scoupe

1. Disconnect the negative battery cable.

2. Disconnect the pressure switch lead wire from the air conditioning harness.

3. Discharge the air conditioning system.

4. Disconnect the 2 liquid line tubes from the receiver/drier. Immediately cap the open fittings to keep moisture out of the air conditioning system.

5. Loosen the bracket bolt and lift the receiver/drier from the mounting bracket.

6. Installation is the reverse of the removal procedure. Add 0.3 oz. of new oil when replacing the receiver/drier. Evacuate, charge and leak test the system.

Accumulator

REMOVAL AND INSTALLATION

1. Disconnect the negative battery cable.

2. Disconnect the pressure switch connector from the accumulator.

3. Properly discharge the air conditioning system.

4. Disconnect the 2 liquid line tubes from the accumulator. Immediately cap the open fittings to keep moisture out of the air conditioning system.

5. Loosen the bracket bolt and lift the accumulator from the mounting bracket.

6. Installation is the reverse of the removal procedure. Add the proper amount of oil to the accumulator if it is being replaced.

Expansion Valve

REMOVAL AND INSTALLATION

Accent, Elantra and Scoupe

NOTE: In order to remove the expansion valve, the cooling unit must be removed and disassembled.

1. After the cooling unit (evaporator assembly) is removed, the housing can be disassembled.

2. Remove the seal from the cases.

3. Remove the 7 clips holding the case halves together.

4. Remove the pipe mounting screw and remove the upper case half with the thermostat attached.

NOTE: Be careful to protect the thermostat capillary tube.

5. Detach the capillary tube from the outlet fitting.

6. Disconnect the liquid tube and suction tube from the inlet and outlet fittings of the expansion valve.

7. Remove the packing and the heat sensing tube from the suction tube. Remove the expansion valve.

8. Installation is the reverse of the removal procedure. Use new O-rings at all fittings. Install the evaporator assembly. Evacuate, recharge and leak test the system.

Fixed Orifice Tube

REMOVAL AND INSTALLATION

NOTE: The fixed orifice tube in a non-adjustable, non-serviceable part. The orifice tube is located within the liquid line near the evaporator and can not be removed from the line. If the orifice tube is defective, the complete liquid line must be replaced. The fixed orifice tube should also be replaced whenever a compressor is replaced.

1. Disconnect the negative battery cable.

2. Discharge the refrigerant from the air conditioning system.

3. Disconnect the liquid line from the evaporator and at the condenser. Immediately cap all openings to minimize system contamination.

4. Remove the brackets retaining the liquid line in place and remove the line.

To install:

5. Coat the O-rings with compressor oil and install the liquid line to the evaporator and condenser.

6. Secure the liquid line in place the with the retaining brackets.

7. Connect the negative battery cable. Evacuate, charge and test the system.

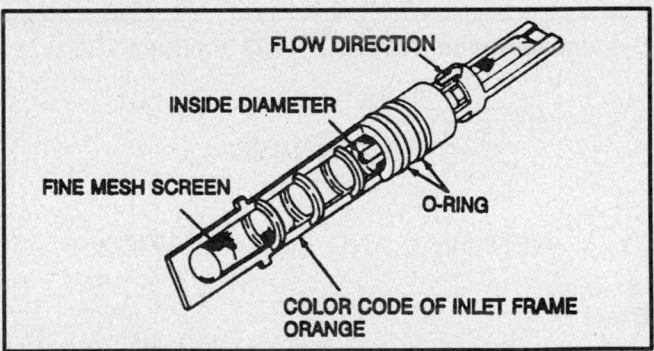

Cross—sectional view of the fixed orifice tube

Blower Motor

REMOVAL AND INSTALLATION

1. Disconnect the negative battery cable.

2. Remove the instrument under cover and the glove box.

3. On Elantra, loosen the 3 evaporator mounting bolts.

4. On Accent, remove the main crash pad assembly.

5. Disconnect the resistor and blower motor wire connector.

6. Remove the attaching screws and remove the blower assembly from the blower case.

7. Pull the blower unit out and disconnect the RECIRC/FRESH vacuum connector.

To install:

8. Position the blower motor onto the blower case and install the attaching screws.

9. Connect the RECIRC/FRESH vacuum connector.

10. Connect the resistor and blower motor wire connector.

11. Tighten the evaporator mounting bolts (Elantra). Install the glove box and instrument panel undercover.

12. Connect the negative battery cable.

13. Check the blower for proper operation.

Blower Motor Resistor

REMOVAL AND INSTALLATION

1. Disconnect the negative battery cable.

2. Remove the glove box unit.

3. Disconnect the resistor wire connector from the resistor.

4. Remove the heater unit.

5. Remove the resistor retaining screws and remove the resistor from the heater case.

To install:

6. Position the resistor assembly in the heater case opening and install the retaining screws.

NOTE: When installing a replacement resistor, the new resistor must be the equivalent and specified applicable to the blower unit. Do not apply sealer to the resistor board mounting surface.

7. Connect the resistor harness connector to the resistor.

8. Install the glove box unit. Connect the negative battery cable.

9. Check the blower for proper operation.

Heater Core

REMOVAL AND INSTALLATION

Accent

1. Disconnect the negative battery cable and wait 90 seconds for the SRS memory battery to drain.

2. Drain the coolant from the radiator.

3. Remove the coolant inlet and outlet hoses with the vacuum hose from the heater unit.

4. Discharge refrigerant from the air conditioning system.

5. Remove the suction and discharge hoses from the evaporator.

6. Remove the steering wheel and multi-function switch assembly.

7. Remove the front and rear console assemblies.

8. Remove the lower crash pad.

9. Remove the center facia panel and disconnect the connectors and vacuum connector from the heater control assembly.

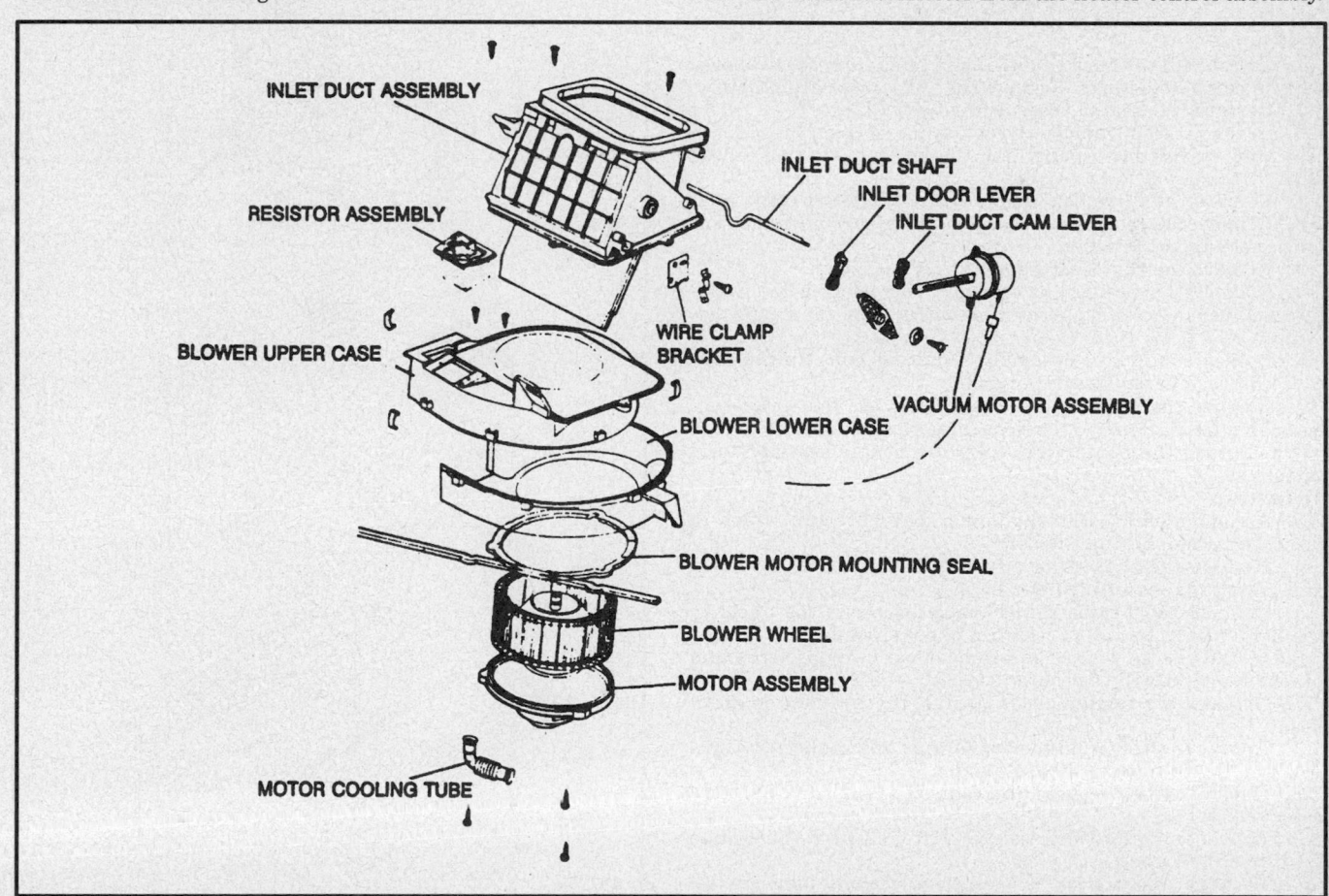

Exploded view of the blower motor assembly—Accent

10. Remove the heater control assembly and the audio system.

11. Remove the glove box.

12. Remove the 4 mounting bolts from the passenger air bag mounting bracket, if equipped.

13. Remove the main crash pad assembly.

14. Disconnect the cables from the heater unit and the thermostatic switch connector from the evaporator unit.

15. Disconnect any remaining connectors.

16. Remove the main crash pad assembly.

17. Remove the 3 evaporator mounting bolts (or nuts).

18. Remove the evaporator unit.

19. Remove the 3 mounting bolts from the heater unit.

20. Remove the heater unit.

To install:

21. Installation is the reverse of the removal process.

22. Be sure to use new O-rings on the liquid and suction lines and coat them lightly with compressor oil.

23. Refill the cooling system and reconnect the negative battery cable.

24. Evacuate, charge and test the air conditioning system for proper operation.

25. Recheck and top off the radiator coolant level as required.

Excel and Scoupe

1. Disconnect the negative battery cable.

2. Set the temperature control to the **HOT** position.

3. Drain the cooling system. Discharge the air conditioning system.

4. Disconnect the suction and liquid lines from the evaporator and cap all openings. Remove the evaporator drain hose.

5. Remove the heater hoses at the firewall.

6. In the interior, remove the center panel trim, the console assembly, cluster facia panel and the lower crash pad center trim.

7. Remove the glove box assembly and the lower crash pad.

8. Remove the control panel assembly, then remove the center panel support bracket.

9. Remove the rear heating joint duct assembly.

10. Remove the evaporator assembly mounting bolts. Separate and remove the evaporator assembly from the heater assembly.

11. Loosen the heater assembly mounting bolts on the firewall and remove the heater assembly.

12. Remove the heater cover and disconnect the water control valve links. Remove the hose, pipe clamps and the heater valve. Detach the heater core from the heater assembly and remove it.

To install:

13. Assemble and install the heater assembly and attach to firewall with mounting the bolts.

14. Position the evaporator assembly to the heater assembly and install the mounting bolts.

15. Connect the heater control cable. Connect the ducts to the heater unit. Install the control panel assembly.

16. Install the glove box, instrument panel trim pieces and brackets and install the center console.

17. Connect the heater hoses. Install the evaporator drain hose.

18. Apply compressor oil to new O-rings and connect the suction and liquid lines to the evaporator.

19. Fill the cooling system and connect the negative battery cable.

20. Evacuate, charge and test the system. Check the system for proper operation.

21. Recheck and top off the radiator coolant level, as required.

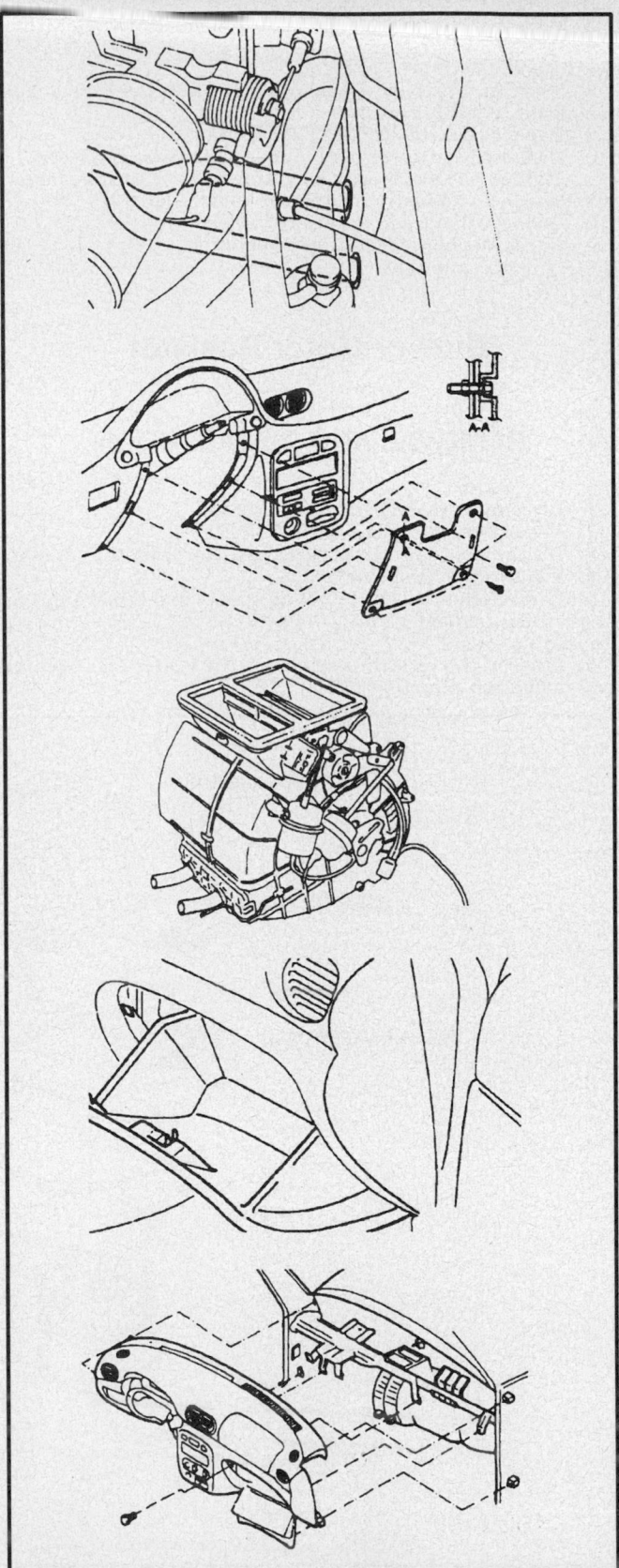

Access to the heater core—Accent

Elantra and Sonata

1. Disconnect the negative battery cable.
2. Drain the cooling system. Properly discharge the air conditioning system using recovery/recycling equipment.
3. Remove the heater hoses and the evaporator drain hose.
4. Remove the evaporator suction and liquid tubes. Immediately cap the openings to minimize contamination of the system.
5. Remove the front and rear console assembly and remove both side covers.
6. Remove the glove box, center pad cover, the center crash pad and the cassette assembly.
7. Remove the lower crash pad. Remove the console mounting bracket and the center support bracket.
8. Disconnect the rear heater ducts from the heater unit.
9. Remove the control assembly.
10. Remove the blower speed control actuator connector and the blend door actuator connector, if equipped with semi-automatic temperature control.
11. Remove the 4 retaining bolts and remove the heater assembly.

To install:

12. Install the heater assembly and attach to dash panel with mounting the bolts.
13. Install the heater control assembly. Connect the ducts to the heater unit.
14. Install the console mounting bracket and the center support bracket.
15. Install the lower crash pad and both side covers.
16. Install the front and rear console assembly.
17. Connect the evaporator tubes, heater hoses and drain hose.
18. Fill the cooling system and connect the negative battery cable.
19. Check the system for proper operation.

Evaporator

REMOVAL AND INSTALLATION

Accent

1. Disconnect the negative battery cable.
2. Discharge the refrigerant.
3. Disconnect the liquid and suction lines from the evaporator.
4. Remove the water drain hose from the evaporator.
5. Remove the grommet cover from the dash panel (2 screws).
6. Remove the three glove box assembly bolts.
7. Disconnect the thermostatic switch connector.
8. Remove the three evaporator mounting bolts.
9. Remove the evaporator unit.

To Install:

10. Installation is the reverse of removal.
11. If the evaporator unit is to be replaced with a new unit, add 40cc of compressor oil to the compressor.
12. Evacuate, charge and test the system.

Excel and Scoupe

1. Disconnect the negative battery cable.
2. Discharge the refrigerant from the air conditioning system.
3. Disconnect the refrigerant lines from the fittings at the evaporator core tubes. Immediately cap the openings.
4. Remove the evaporator drain hose.
5. Remove the inlet and outlet pipe grommets.
6. Remove the console assembly (except Elantra).
7. Remove the glove box assembly.
8. Remove the lower crash pad and the lower crash pad center panel. Remove the ashtray, radio, digital clock and the rheostat, as needed.

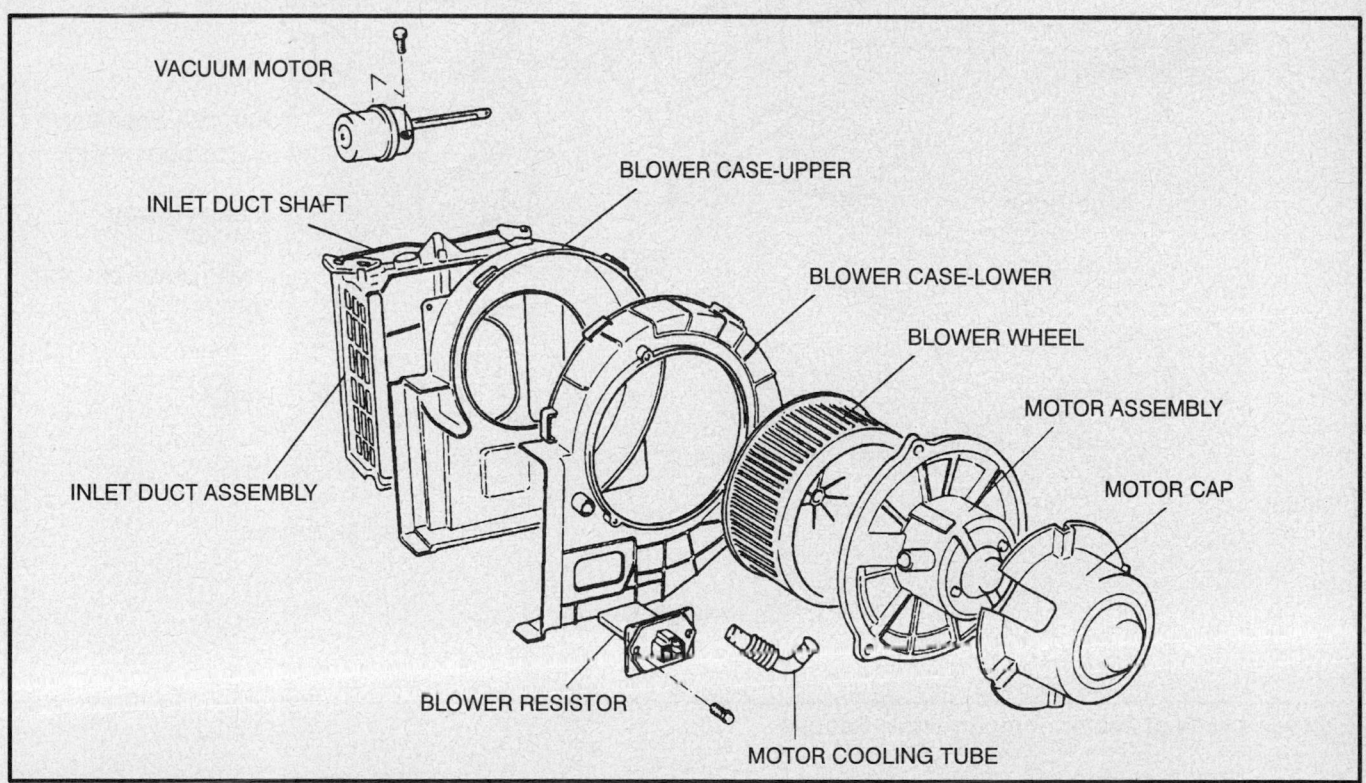

Exploded view of blower unit—Accent

9. On some models, it may be necessary to remove the control panel assembly. Remove the blower motor assembly mounting bolts and remove the blower assembly.

10. Remove the evaporator assembly mounting bolts. Detach any electrical or vacuum connectors from the housing. Remove the evaporator assembly from the heater assembly. Disassemble the unit and remove the evaporator core.

To install:

11. If a new evaporator core is installed, be sure to add the appropriate amount of new refrigerant oil to the unit.

12. Position the evaporator assembly in place to the heater assembly and install the mounting bolts.

13. Install the blower assembly mounting bolts.

14. Install the crash pads, panels, trim, control panel and other components as removed.

15. Install the console assembly, if removed. Install the glove box assembly.

16. Coat the O-rings with compressor oil, install the grommet over the evaporator lines and connect the lines to the evaporator.

17. Evacuate, charge and test the system. Connect the negative battery cable.

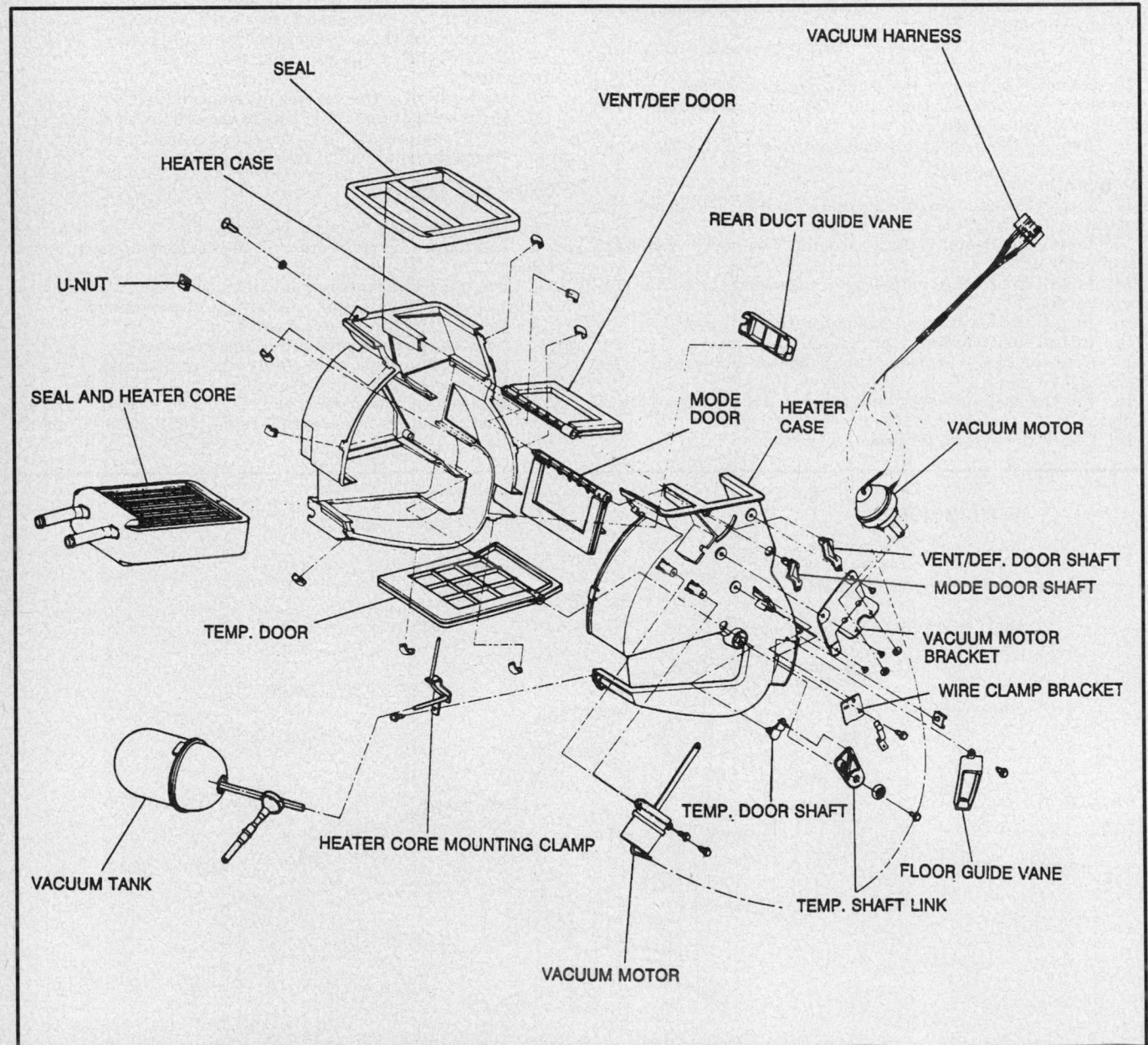

Exploded view of heater components—Scoupe

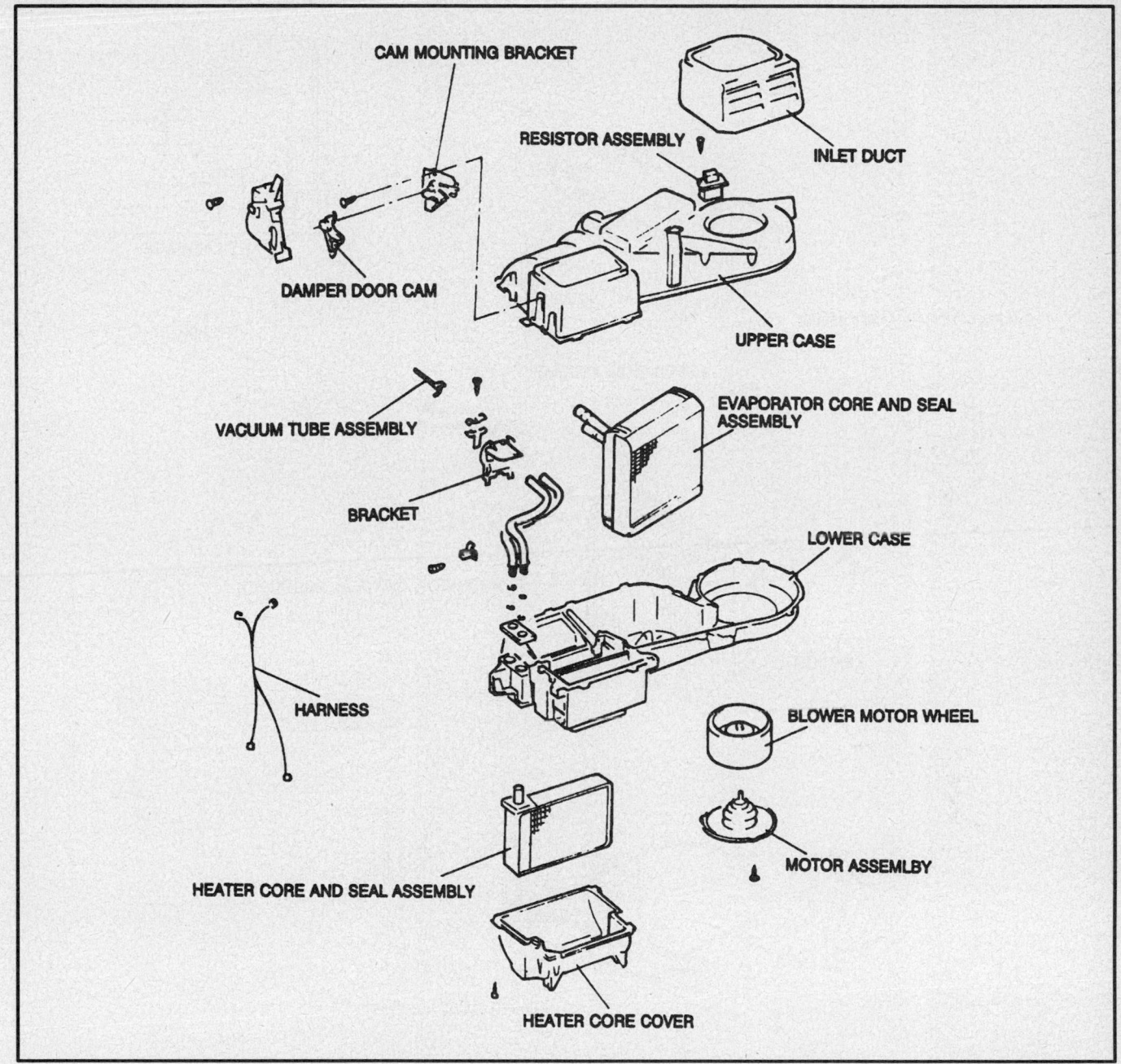

CAM MOUNTING BRACKET

RESISTOR ASSEMBLY

INLET DUCT

DAMPER DOOR CAM

UPPER CASE

VACUUM TUBE ASSEMBLY

EVAPORATOR CORE AND SEAL ASSEMBLY

BRACKET

LOWER CASE

HARNESS

BLOWER MOTOR WHEEL

MOTOR ASSEMLBY

HEATER CORE AND SEAL ASSEMBLY

HEATER CORE COVER

Exploded view of the heater assembly—Sonota

Sonata

1. Disconnect the negative battery cable and discharge the air conditioning system.

2. Disconnect the low pressure suction hose from the cooling unit outlet fitting. Cap the fitting.

3. Disconnect the liquid line pipe from the cooling unit inlet fitting. Cap the fitting

4. Remove the inlet and outlet pipe grommets.

5. Remove the instrument panel undercover and glove box.

6. Remove the connector to the control switch, connector to the power supply and the connector to the magnetic clutch of the compressor.

7. Remove the drain hose and disconnect the piping in the engine compartment.

8. Disconnect the electrical harness from the cooling unit housing.

9. Remove the lower bolt and 2 upper bracket nuts and remove the cooling unit from the vehicle.

10. Remove the clip securing the inlet and outlet pipes.

11. Remove the upper and lower case half retaining clamps.

12. Remove the lower case cover.

13. Remove the 2 screws that hold the thermostat to the cooling housing.

14. Remove the thermostat and remove the screws that secure the capillary tube from inside the cooling unit fins.

15. Lift the evaporator coil (cooling unit) assembly from the lower cooling unit case to remove it. Be sure to hold the lower cooling unit case firmly when removing the evaporator coil (cooling unit) assembly.

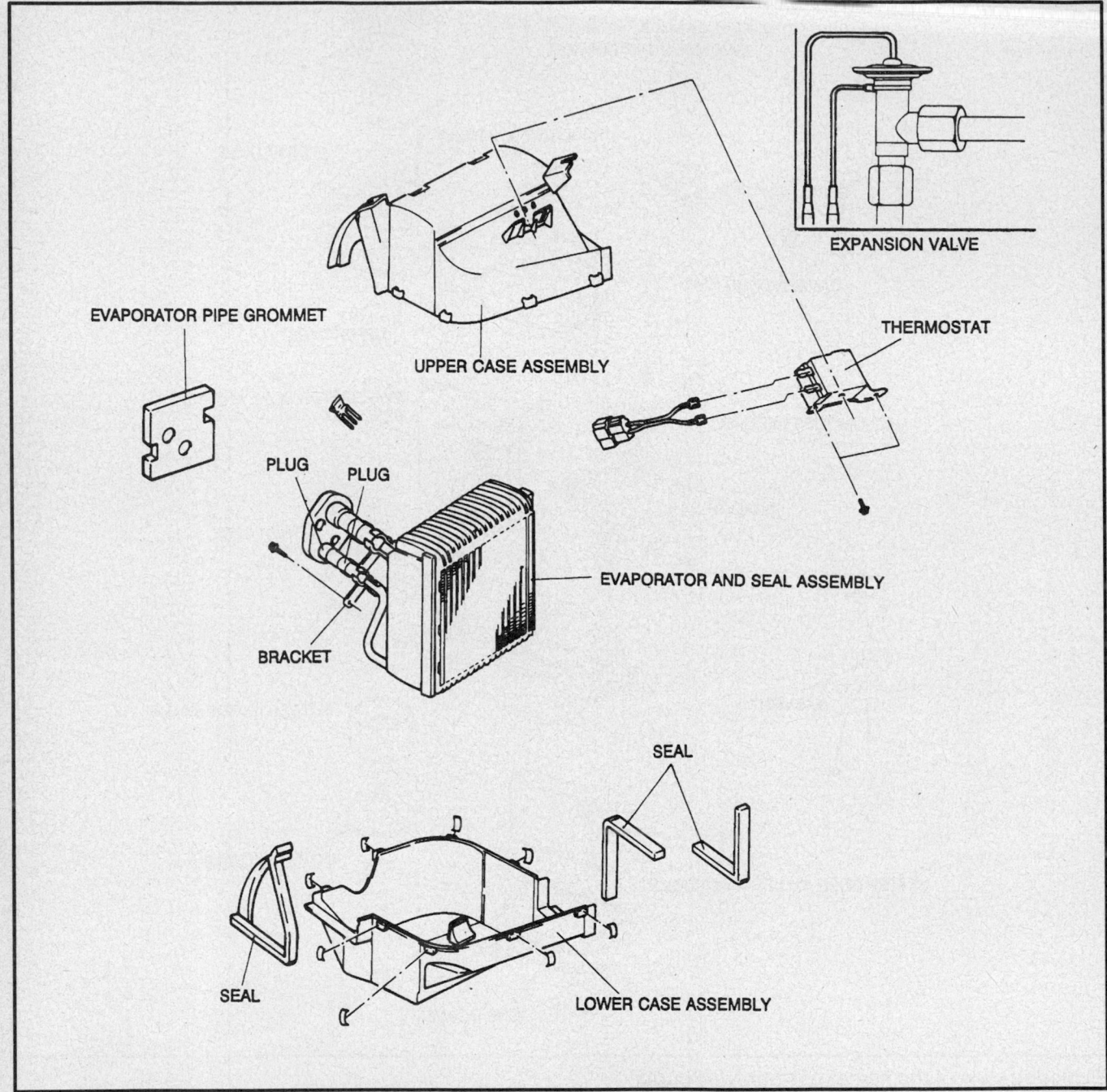

EXPANSION VALVE

EVAPORATOR PIPE GROMMET

UPPER CASE ASSEMBLY

THERMOSTAT

PLUG   PLUG

EVAPORATOR AND SEAL ASSEMBLY

BRACKET

SEAL

SEAL   LOWER CASE ASSEMBLY

Exploded view of the evaporator assembly—Elantra and Scoupe with expansion valve

To install:
16. If a new evaporator core was installed, add 3.0 oz. of clean compressor oil. Install the evaporator into the lower case.
17. Install the thermostat.

NOTE: When installing the thermostat, insert the capillary tube end to a depth of 2.0 in. and 1.6 in. from the third core fin on the left side of the evaporator.

18. Install the lower case cover.
19. Connect the upper and lower case halves and lock the clips.
20. Install the inlet and outlet pipe retaining clip.

21. Position the cooling unit onto its mounting with the lower bolt and 2 upper nuts. Adjust the position of the cooling unit so the inlet and outlet connections are aligned with the heater and blower unit connections.
22. Install the drain hose.
23. Connect the air conditioning wire harness.
24. Install the inlet and outlet pipe grommets.
25. Install the glove box and lower cover.
26. Connect the suction hose to the cooling unit inlet fitting.
27. Connect the discharge hose to the cooling unit outlet fitting.
28. Evacuate, charge and test the system. Connect the negative battery cable.

Refrigerant Lines

REMOVAL AND INSTALLATION

1. Depending on application, when disconnecting or connecting refrigerant lines, always use 2 wrenches or use the spring-lock coupling procedure.

2. Use protective plugs and plug each open line, to prevent contamination and moisture from entering the lines and related components.

3. Clean contaminated O-rings during installation. Never use compressed air. Use only new O-rings during installation.

4. Coat the new O-ring with compressor oil prior to installation.

5. Install the O-ring against the shoulder to ensure proper seating.

6. On union nut couplings, when connecting 2 lines together, insert the tube section into the union and tighten the retaining nut by hand. Then, tighten the nut to 29–33 ft. lbs. (39–44 Nm). Otherwise, use the spring-lock coupling procedure.

Manual Control Head

REMOVAL AND INSTALLATION

Accent

1. Disconnect the battery ground cable.
2. Pull out the ashtray and remove the 2 screws.

3. Disconnect the air mix control cable on the heater unit.

4. Using a flat tip screwdriver, pry loose 2 clips, pull out the center facia panel and disconnect the connectors.

5. Remove the 4 mounting bolts of the heater control assembly from behind the center facia panel and then remove the center facia panel.

6. Disconnect connectors from the heater control assembly.

7. Disconnect the vacuum connector.

8. Remove the heater control assembly.

9. Installation is the reverse of disassembly.

Elantra and Excel

1. Disconnect the negative battery cable.

2. Pull out the ashtray and remove the lower crash pad center facia panel.

3. Remove the cluster facia panel.

4. Remove the heater control switch retaining screws and pull the control switch away from the dash.

5. Disconnect the electrical and vacuum connections at the switch.

6. Disconnect the heater control cables and remove the control switch.

To install:

7. Insert the control switch into the dash cavity. Connect the control cables to the control levers.

8. Plug the electrical and vacuum connectors into the control switch.

9. Secure the control switch to the dash with the retainings crews and adjust the cables accordingly.

10. Install the center and lower crash panels. Connect the negative battery cable and test the switch operation.

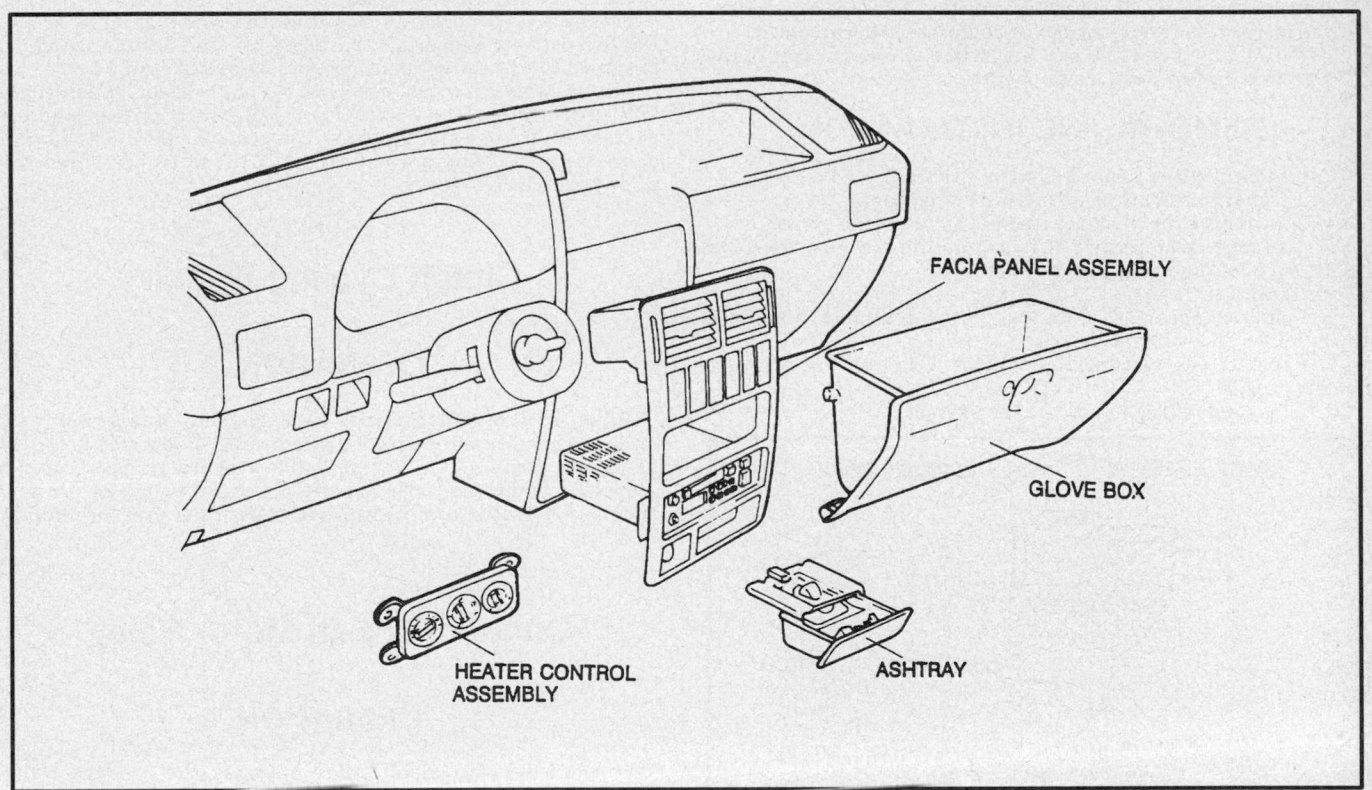

FACIA PANEL ASSEMBLY

GLOVE BOX

HEATER CONTROL ASSEMBLY

ASHTRAY

Component removal for control assembly removal—Excel and Scoupe shown, others are similar

Scoupe

1. Disconnect the negative battery cable.
2. Remove the transmission gearshift knob. Pry loose 2 clips and remove the front console cover (detach the cigarette lighter wiring).
3. Pull out the ashtray and remove 2 screws. Pry loose 4 clips and detach the connectors.
4. Remove the center facia panel.
5. Pry out and detach the clock assembly. Remove the rheostat switch.
6. Remove the cluster facia panel (6 screws).
7. Remove 4 bolts, pull out the control panel assembly and detach the connectors, air mix control cable and the vacuum connector.

8. Installation is the reverse of the removal procedure. Adjust the cable, if needed.

Manual Control Cables

ADJUSTMENT

1. Slide the temperature control lever to **HOT**.
2. Turn the air mix door shaft arm to the left and connect the end of the cable to the arm.
3. Gently slide the cable outer housing back from the end to take up any slack (without moving the temperature control lever), then snap the cable housing into the clamp.
4. Check the lever, cable and door for proper operation.

SENSORS AND SWITCHES

Dual Pressure Switch

OPERATION

The dual pressure switch is a sensing device in the high pressure side of the system, located on the receiver/drier. It will stop compressor operation if high side system pressure drops below approximately 28 psi or rises above 455 psi. On Accent, the pressures are below 28 psi or above 470 psi.

This protection device stops compressor operation under these circumstances which usually mean there has been a loss of refrigerant, severe blockage or compressor break down.

Between 30 psi and 299 psi, the switch allows current to the compressor circuit for normal operation.

REMOVAL AND INSTALLATION

1. Disconnect the negative battery cable.
2. Discharge the air conditioning refrigerant.
3. Disconnect the electrical connector from the switch.
4. Unscrew the pressure switch from the receiver/drier and plug the opening immediately.
To install:
5. Apply compressor oil on the O-ring seal and thread the switch into the receiver/drier.
6. Connect the electrical connector. Connect the negative battery cable.
7. Evacuate, charge and test the system.

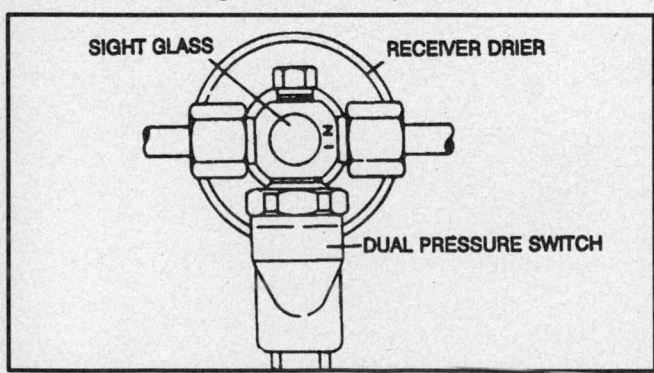

View of the dual pressure switch and receiver/drier

High Pressure Switch

OPERATION

This switch is used on 1994 Sonata's with cycling clutch orifice tube systems. These systems also use a cycling clutch switch to control normal on and off cycling of the compressor and to help maintain system pressures. The high pressure switch is located in the high pressure line.

Scoupe uses a normally closed switch which is on at or below 355 psi and open or off above 383 psi. The Scoupe switch is designed to protect against high pressure build-up.

Sonata uses a switch which is normally open. When high side pressure exceeds 233–247 psi, the switch closes, sending current to ground and stopping compressor operation. It will open again, allowing normal current flow, when pressures are at or below 183–198 psi.

Clutch Cycling Switch

OPERATION

Used on cycling clutch orifice tube systems, this switch will cycle the compressor on and off, according to low side pressures at the accumulator. It prevents evaporator freeze-up by stopping compressor operation at pressures below 24 psi and then will turn the compressor back **ON** when pressure builds to 47 psi.

Condenser Fan Motor Relay

OPERATION

The condenser fan motor relay operates the condenser fan when the condenser pressure exceeds a predetermined value. The condenser fan relay is located in the right side engine compartment relay box or separately near the battery.

TESTING

Elantra

1. Disconnect the negative battery cable and remove the condenser fan relay from the relay box.
2. When 12 volts is applied to terminals **1** and **3**, there should be continuity between terminals **2** and **4**.
3. When power is not supplied to terminals **1** and **3**, there should be no continuity between terminals **2** and **4**.

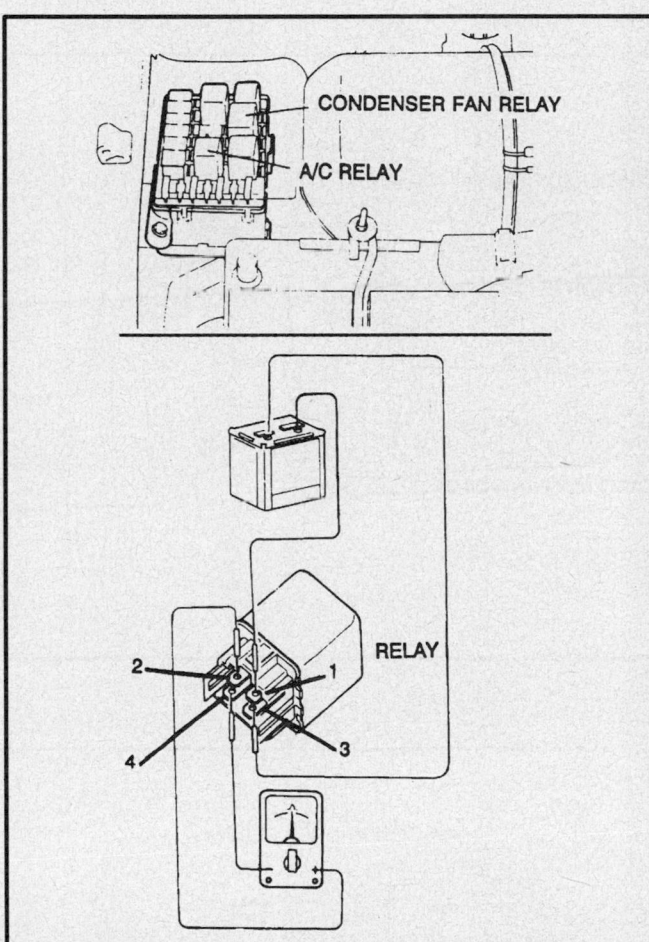

Testing the condenser fan and air conditioning relays—Elantra

Excel and Sonata

1. Using an ohmmeter, check that there is no continuity between terminals **L** and **B**.
2. Apply 12 volts across terminals **S1** and **S2**, then check for continuity between terminals **L** and **B**.
3. If continuity does not exist, replace the relay.

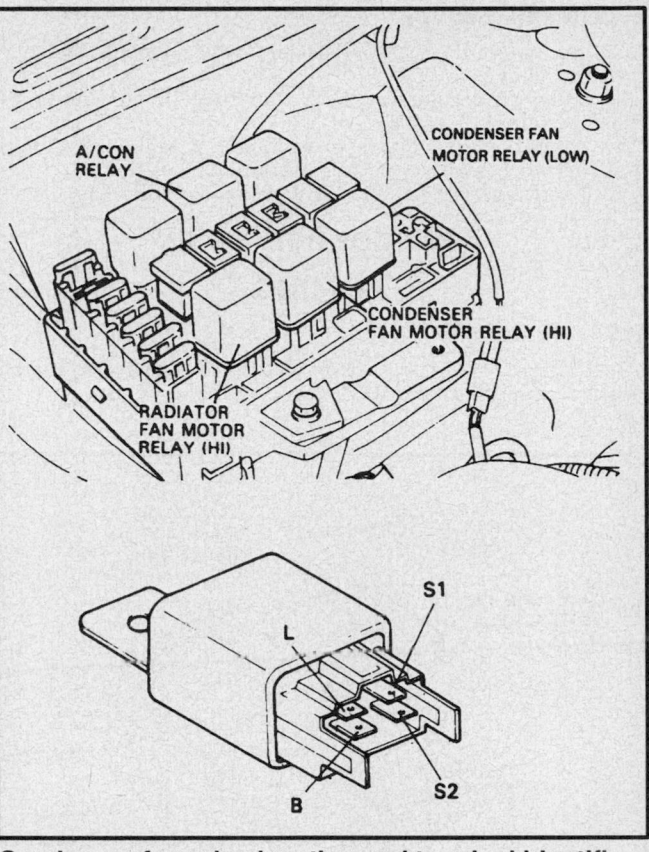

Condenser fan relay location and terminal identification—Sonata

Accent and Scoupe

1. Using an ohmmeter, check that there is constant continuity between terminals **1** and **2**.
2. Apply battery voltage to terminals **1** and **2**; there should now be continuity between terminals **2** and **3**.
3. If continuity is not as indicated, replace the relay (also check the relay connections and wiring).

Air Conditioning Relay

The air conditioning relay sends current to activate the compressor when the A/C switch is **ON** and other system conditions are normal.

TESTING

Elantra

1. Disconnect the negative battery cable and remove the condenser fan relay from the relay box.
2. When 12 volts is applied to terminals **1** and **3**, there should be continuity between terminals **2** and **4**.
3. When power is not supplied to terminals **1** and **3**, there should be no continuity between terminals **2** and **4**.

Excel and Sonata

1. Using an ohmmeter, check that there is no continuity between terminals **L** and **B**.
2. Apply 12 volts across terminals **S1** and **S2**, then check for continuity between terminals **L** and **B**.
3. If continuity does not exist, replace the relay. Also check the relay connections and wiring.

Accent and Scoupe

1. Disconnect the negative battery cable. Remove the relay from the relay box.
2. Using an ohmmeter, check that there is continuity between terminals **1** and **3**.
3. Apply battery voltage to terminals **1** and **3** and check that there is continuity between terminals **2 and 4**.
4. If continuity is not as specified, replace the relay.

Radiator Fan Relay

TESTING

1994—95 Sonata

1. Using an ohmmeter, check that there is no continuity between terminals **L** and **B** .

2. Apply 12 volts across terminals **S1** and **S2**, then check for continuity between terminals **L** and **B**.
3. If continuity is not as indicated, replace the relay (also check the relay connections and wiring).

1994—95 Elantra

1. Using an ohmmeter, verify that there is continuity between terminals **1** and **3**.
2. Apply 12 volts to terminals **1** and **3** and verify that there is continuity between terminals **2** and **4**.
3. If continuity is not as indicated, replace the relay (also check the relay connections and wiring).

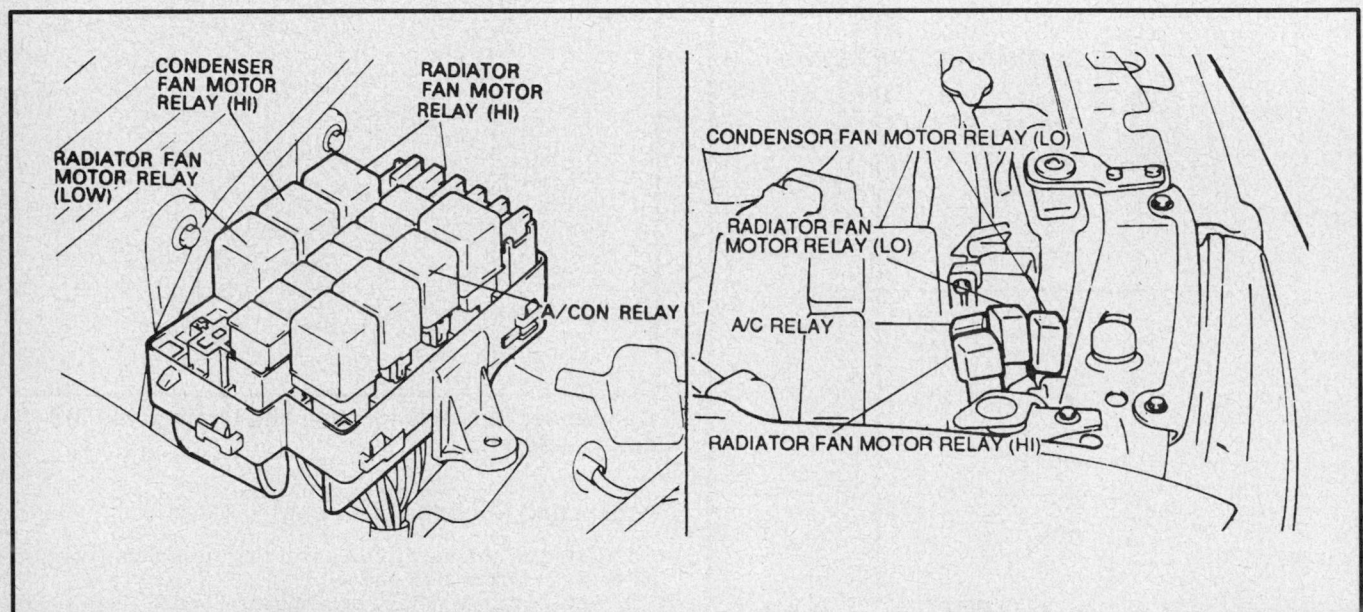

Air conditioning relay locations—1993 Sonata

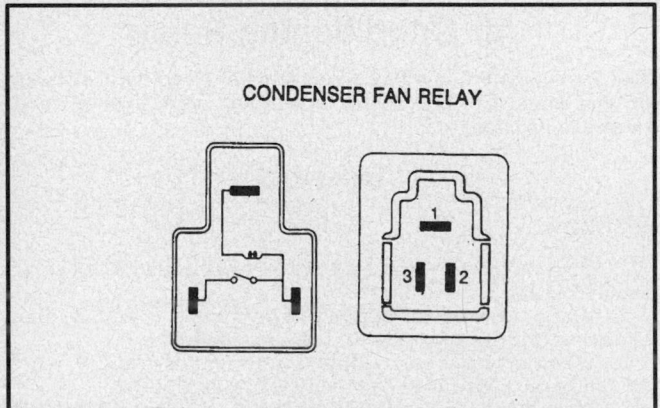

Condenser fan relay identification—1993 Scoupe

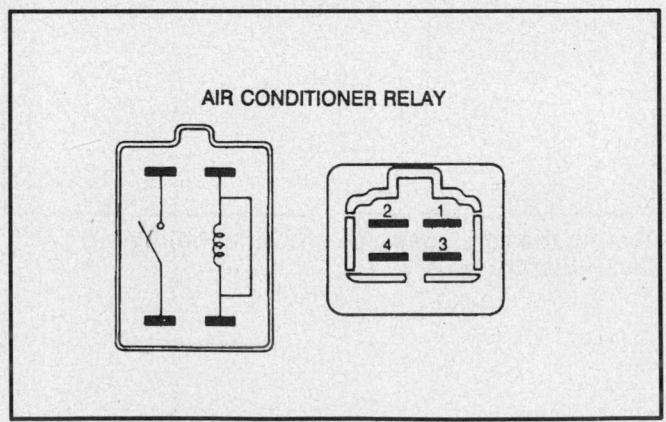

Air conditioner relay terminal identification — Typical

Blower Fan Relay

1995 Accent, 1994–95 Elantra and 1994–1995 Scoupe

1. Using an ohmmeter, verify that there is constant continuity between terminals **1** and **3**.
2. Apply 12 volts to terminals **1** and **3** and verify that there is continuity between terminals **2** and **4**.
3. If the continuity is not as indicated, replace the relay (also check the relay connections and wiring).

Blower Motor Resistor

TESTING

1. Check the resistance of the blower motor resistor by checking the resistance at the indicated terminals.

Accent
Between terminals **3** and **4** should be 2.9 ohms
Between terminals **3** and **2** should be 1.2 ohms
Between terminals **3** and **1** should be 0.4 ohms

Except Accent
Between terminals **1** and **2** should be 2.4 ohms
Between terminals **2** and **4** should be 1.2 ohms
Between terminals **2** and **6** should be 0.4 ohms

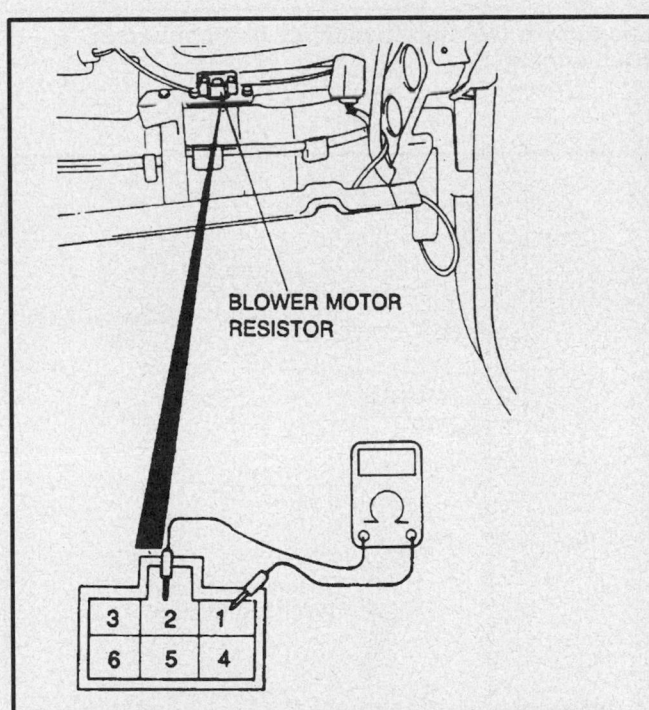

BLOWER MOTOR RESISTOR

3 2 1
6 5 4

Testing the blower motor resistor.

REMOVAL AND INSTALLATION

1. Disconnect the negative battery cable.
2. Remove the glove box assembly.

3. Disconnect the wiring harness connector from the resistor assembly.
4. Remove the resistor-to-heater case retaining screws and remove the resistor from the case.
To install:
5. Attach the wiring harness connector to the resistor. Install the glove box assembly.
6. Connect the negative battery cable and test the resistor operation.

In-Car Sensor (Semi-Automatic A/C)

The sensor is located under the instrument panel and is accessible behind the glove box. The sensor provides an input signal on actual in-car temperature.

TESTING

1. Disconnect the sensor connector.
2. Using an ohmmeter, measure the resistance between the terminals.
3. At 77°F (25°C), resistance should be 30 kilo-ohms.

REMOVAL AND INSTALLATION

1. Disconnect the negative battery cable.
2. Remove the glove box and remove the lower crash pad.
3. Detach the connector from the in-car sensor.
4. Remove the sensor (2 screws).
5. Installation is the reverse of the removal procedure.

Ambient Sensor (Semi-Automatic A/C)

This sensor is located behind the grille in the front of the condenser. It provides an input signal on actual outside air temperature.

TESTING

1. Using an ohmmeter, measure the resistance between the sensor terminals.
2. At 68°F (20°C), resistance should be 37 kilo-ohms.

REMOVAL AND INSTALLATION

1. Disconnect the negative battery cable.
2. Remove the grille
3. Detach the connector from the sensor.
4. Remove the sensor.
5. Installation is the remove of the removal procedure.

Thermostatic Switch (Thermistor)

TESTING

1995 Accent

1. Remove the glove box assembly.
2. Turn the blower and air conditioning switches **ON**.
3. Start the engine.
4. With the thermostatic switch in the coupled state, install a voltmeter between terminals **2** and **3** and check for a change in voltage between the terminals according to the temperature of the evaporator surface.

Operating temp	Thermo switch operation	Terminal voltage (2 and 3)	Remarks
1.5±1.0°C (34.7±1.8°F)	OFF	0 V	Compressor clutch should be disengaged
4.3±1.0°C (39.7±1.8°F)	ON	12 V	Compressor clutch should be engaged

* Thermostatic switch circuit

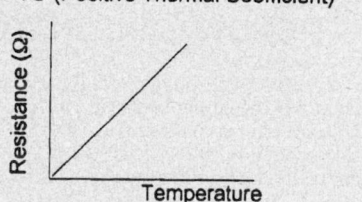

Thermistor

* Type : PTC (Positive Thermal Coefficient)

Operation

1. When the resistance (the temperature of the evaporator) in the thermistor increases :
   →TR1"ON"→TR2"ON"→Thermostatic switch"ON".

2. When the resistance (the temperature of the evaporator) in the thermistor decreases :
   →TR1"OFF"→TR2"OFF"→Thermostatic switch "OFF"

Testing of the thermostatic switch — 1995 Accent

Operating temp	Thermo Switch	Voltage (② and ③)	Remarks
1.5 ± 1.0°C (34.7 ± 1.8°F)	OFF	0V	Compressor clutch should be engaged,
4.3 ± 1.0°C (39.7 ± 1.8°F)	ON	12V	Compressor clutch should be disengaged

Testing specifications for the thermostatic switch–1995 Elantra

5. If conditions are not satisfied, remove the evaporator unit and replace the thermostatic switch.

1995 Elantra

1. Remove the glove box and lower crash pad (if necessary).

2. Turn the blower and air conditioning switches on.
3. Start the engine.
4. With the thermostatic switch connector in the coupled state, install a voltmeter between terminals 2 and 3 (-) and check for a change in voltage according to the temperature of the evaporator surface.
5. If conditions are not satisfied, remove the evaporator unit and replace the thermostatic switch.

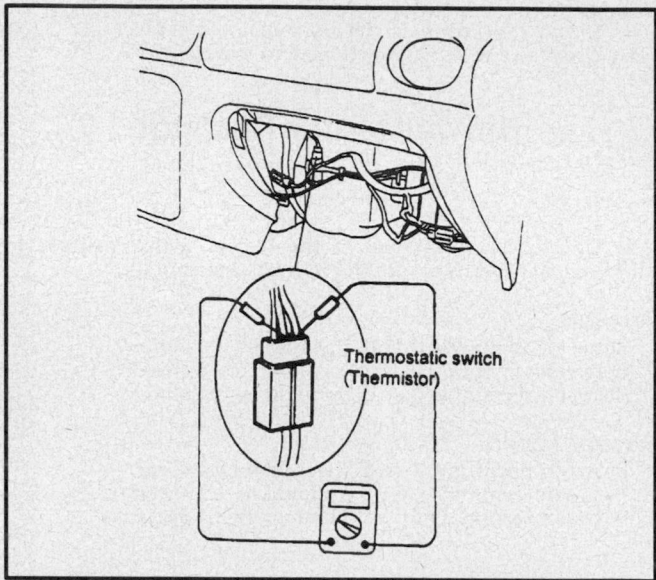

Location of the thermostatic switch connector — 1995 Accent

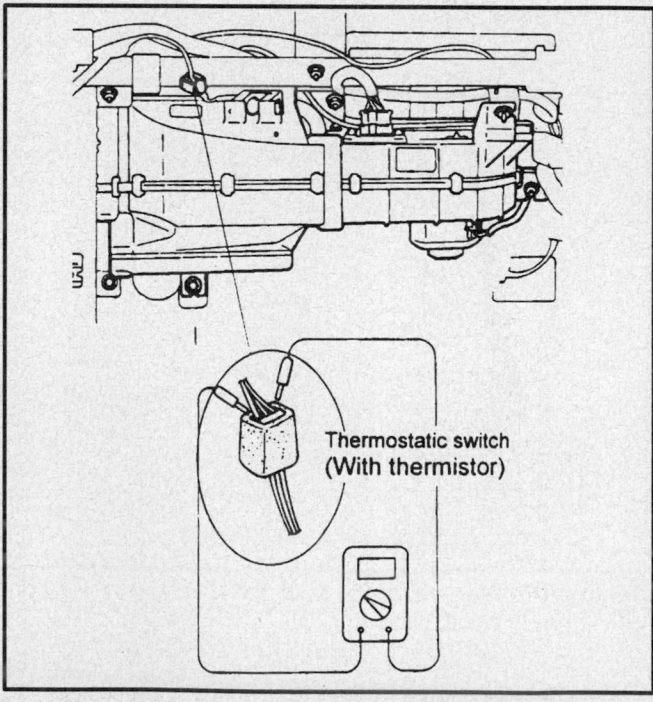

Location of the thermostatic switch connector — 1995 Elantra

SYSTEM DIAGNOSIS

System Performance Evaluation

RECORDING OPERATING CONDITIONS

1. Attach a manifold gauge set to the system.
2. Clock and record the compressor on time in seconds and the compressor off time in seconds.
3. Insert a thermometer in the center air outlet to measure output temperature.
4. Record the ambient temperature.
5. Using the appropriate charts, compare test results.
6. Draw a vertical line for the recorded ambient temperature and draw a horizontal line for each of the other test readings as appropriate to each chart.

7. If the point where the lines intersect is within the band, the system is operating normally.
8. If the lines cross outside the acceptable band, the problem should be pinpointed using the "System Pressure and Clutch Cycle Timing Chart."

TEST CONDITIONS

1. Run the engine at 1500 rpm for 10 minutes.
2. Operate the air conditioning system on maximum cooling and high blower.
3. Ambient temperature range should be 70–80°F (21–26°C).

INSUFFICIENT OR NO COOLING—FIXED ORIFICE TUBE CYCLING SYSTEM

TEST STEP		RESULT	ACTION TO TAKE
A1	**VERIFY THE CONDITION**		
	Check system operation	System cooling properly	INSTRUCT vehicle owner on proper use of the system
		System not cooling Properly	GO to A2
A2	**CHECK A/C COMPRESSOR CLUTCH**		
	Does the A/C compressor clutch engage?	Yes	GO to A3
		No	
A3	**CHECK OPERATION OF COOLING FAN**		
	Check that the cooling fan runs when the A/C compressor clutch is engaged	Yes	GO to A4
		No	Check for cooling fan electric circuit
A4	**COMPONENT CHECK**		
	o Under-hood check of the following: Loose, missing or damaged compressor drive belt. Loose or disconnected A/C clutch or clutch cycling pressure switch connectors. Disconnected resistor assembly. Loose vacuum lines or misadjusted control cables o Inside vehicle check for: Blown fuse or improper blower motor operation. Vacuum motors/temperature door movement-full travel. Electrical and vacuum connections.	OK but still not cooling	GO to A6
		Not OK	REPAIR AND GO to A5
A5	**CHECK SYSTEM**		
	Check system operation	OK	Condition Corrected GO to A1
		Not OK	GO to A6

INSUFFICIENT OR NO COOLING—FIXED ORIFICE TUBE CYCLING SYSTEM—CONT.

TEST STEP		RESULT	ACTION TO TAKE
A8	**CHECK SYSTEM PRESSURES**		
	Compare readings with normal system pressure ranges.	Clutch cycles within limits. System pressure within limits	System OK GO to A1
		Compressor runs continuously (normal operation in ambient temperature above 27°C (80°F.) depending on humidity conditions).	
		Compressor cycles high or low ON above 359 kPa (52 psi) OFF below 144 kPa (21 psi).	REPLACE clutch cycling pressure switch. Do not discharge system Switch timing has Schrader valve CHECK system OK.GO to A1 NOT OK.GO to A9
A9	**CHECK SYSTEM**		
	Check system for leaks	Leak found	REPAIR, discharge, evacuate and charge system. System OK GO to A1
		No Leak found	Low refrigerant charge or moisture in system. Discharge, evacuate and charge system. System OK
A10	**CHECK CLUTCH CYCLING**		
	Disconnect blower motor wire and check for clutch cycling off at 144 kPa (21 psi) (suction pressure)	Clutch cycles OFF at 144—179 kPa (21—26 psi)	Connect blower motor wire. System OK GO to A1
		Pressure falls below 144 kPa (21 psi)	REPLACE clutch cycling pressure switch. Do not discharge system. Switch fitting has Schrader valve. System OK.GO to A1

CYCLING CLUTCH ORIFICE TUBE PERFORMANCE EVALUATION CHARTS

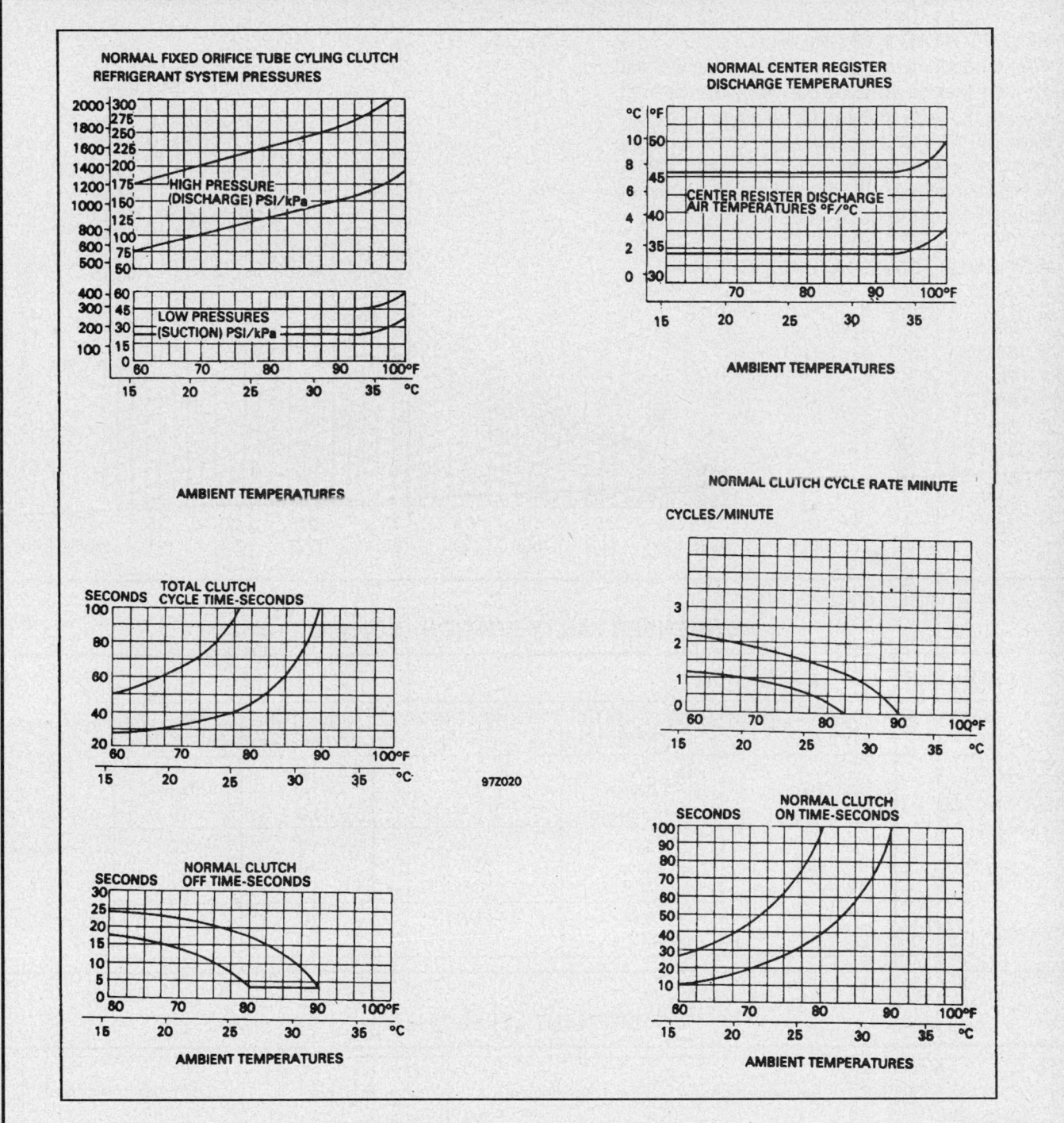

97Z020

WET BULB TEMPERATURE CHART

HOW TO READ THE GRAPH :

After measuring the temperatures of the wet and dry-bulb thermometers at the evaporator air inlet, relative humidity (%) can be obtained.

Example : Dry-and wet-bulb temperatures at the evaporator air inlet are 25°C (77°F) and 19.5°C (67°F) respectively, the point of intersection of the dotted lines in the graph is 60%.

WET-BULB TEMPERATURE [°C(°F)]

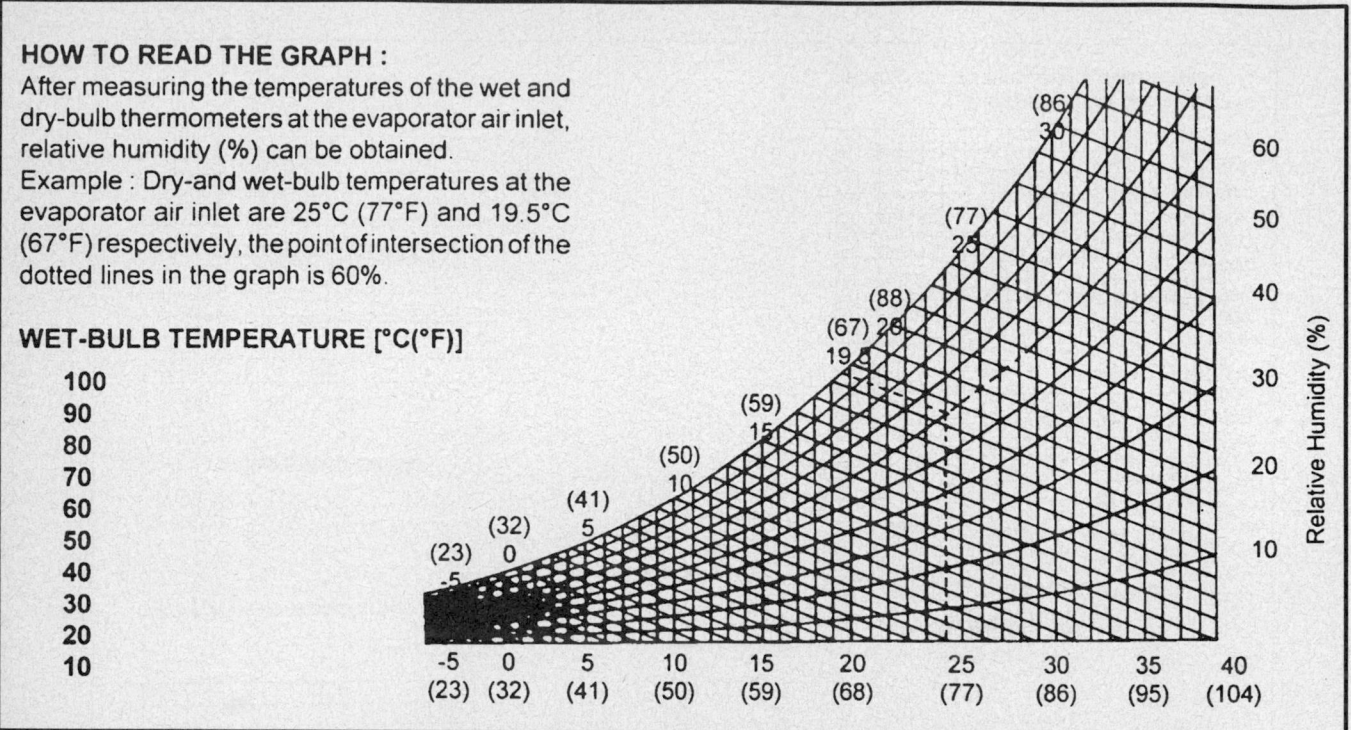

CONDENSER FAN OPERATION – SONATA

CONDENSER FAN OPERATION

AIR-COND SWITCH	PRESSURE SWITCH (II)	THERMO SWITCH (90°C)	THERMO SENSOR (II) (105°C)	RADIATOR FAN MOTOR	CONDENSER FAN MOTOR
ON	ON	ON	ON	HI	HI
		ON	OFF	HI	HI
		OFF	OFF	LO	HI
	OFF	ON	ON	HI	LO
		ON	OFF	HI	LO
		OFF	OFF	LO	LO
OFF	-	ON	ON	HI	LO
		ON	OFF	LO	LO

REFRIGERANT LEVEL CHECK

Amount of refrigerant / Check item	Almost refrigerant	Insufficient	Suitable	Too much refrigerant
Temperature of high pressure and low pressures lines	Almost no difference between high pressure and low pressure side temperature	High pressure side is warm and low pressure side is fairly cold	High pressure side is hot and low pressure side is cold	High pressure side is abnormally hot
Repair	Stop compressor and conduct an overall check	Check for gas leakage, repair as required, replenish and charge system		Discharge refrigerant from sevice valve of low pressure side

SYSTEM PRESSURE AND CLUTCH RECYCLING TIME CHART

High (Discharge) pressure	Low (suction) pressure	Clutch cycle time			Component-Causes
		Rate	ON	OFF	
High	High		Continuous run		Condenser-Inadequate Airflow
High	Normal to high				Engine overheating
Normal to High	Normal				Air in system refrigerant overcharge(a) Humidity or ambient temp very high(b)
Normal	High				Fixed orifice tube-Missing. O-rings Leaking/Missing
Normal	High	Slow	Long	Long	Clutch cycling switch-High Cut-in
Normal	Normal	Slow or no cycle	Long or continuous	Normal or no cycle	Moisture in refrigerant system. Excessive refrigerant oil.
		Fast	Short	Short	Clutch cycling switch- Low Cut-in or High Cut-Out
Normal	Low	Slow	Long	Long	Clutch cycling switch- Low Cut-Out
Normal to low	High		Continuous run		Compressor-Low Performance
Normal to low	Normal to high				A/C suction line-Partially Restricted or Plugged(c)
Normal to low	Normal	Fast	Short	Normal	Evaporator-Low Airflow
			Short to very short	Normal to long	Condenser, fixed orifice tube, or A/C liquid line-Partially Restricted or Plugged
			Short to very short	Short to very short	Low refrigerant charge
			Short to very short	Long	Evaporator core-Partially Restricted or Plugged
Normal to low	Low		Continuous run		A/C suction line-Partially Restricted or Plugged.(d). Clutch cycling switch-Sticking Closed

NOTE
Normal system conditional requirements must be maintained to properly evaluate refrigerant system pressures. Refer to charts applicable to system being tested.

SYSTEM PRESSURE AND CLUTCH RECYCLING TIME CHART–CONT.

High (Discharge) pressure	Low (Suction) pressure	Clutch cycle time			Component-Causes
		Rate	ON	OFF	
Low	Normal	Very fast	Very short	Very short	Clutch cycling switch-Cycling Range Too Close
Erratic operation or compressor not running		—	—	—	Clutch cycling switch-Dirty Contacts or Sticking Open. Poor connection at A/C clutch connector or clutch cycling switch connector. A/C electrical circuit erratic-See A/C Electrical Cicuit Wiring Diagram
Additional possible causes associated with inadequate compressor operation					
o Compressor clutch slipping. o Loose drive belt o Clutch coil open-Shorted or loose mounting o Control assembly switch-Dirty contacts or sticking open o Clutch wiring circuit-High resistance. Open or blown fuse					
Additional possible causes associated with a damaged compressor					
o Clutch cycling switch-Sticking closed or compressor clutch seized o Suction accumulator drier-Refrigerant oil bleed hole plugged o Refrigerant leaks					

1) Compressor may make noise on initial start-up. This condition can be caused by excessive liquid refrigerant.
2) Compressor clutch may not cycle in ambient temperatures above 80°F depending on humidity.
3) Low pressure reading will be normal to high if the pressure readings are taken at the accumulator and if the restriction is down stream of the service access valve.
4) Low pressure reading will be low if pressure readings are taken near the compressor and the restriction is upstream of the service access valve.

WIRING SCHEMATICS

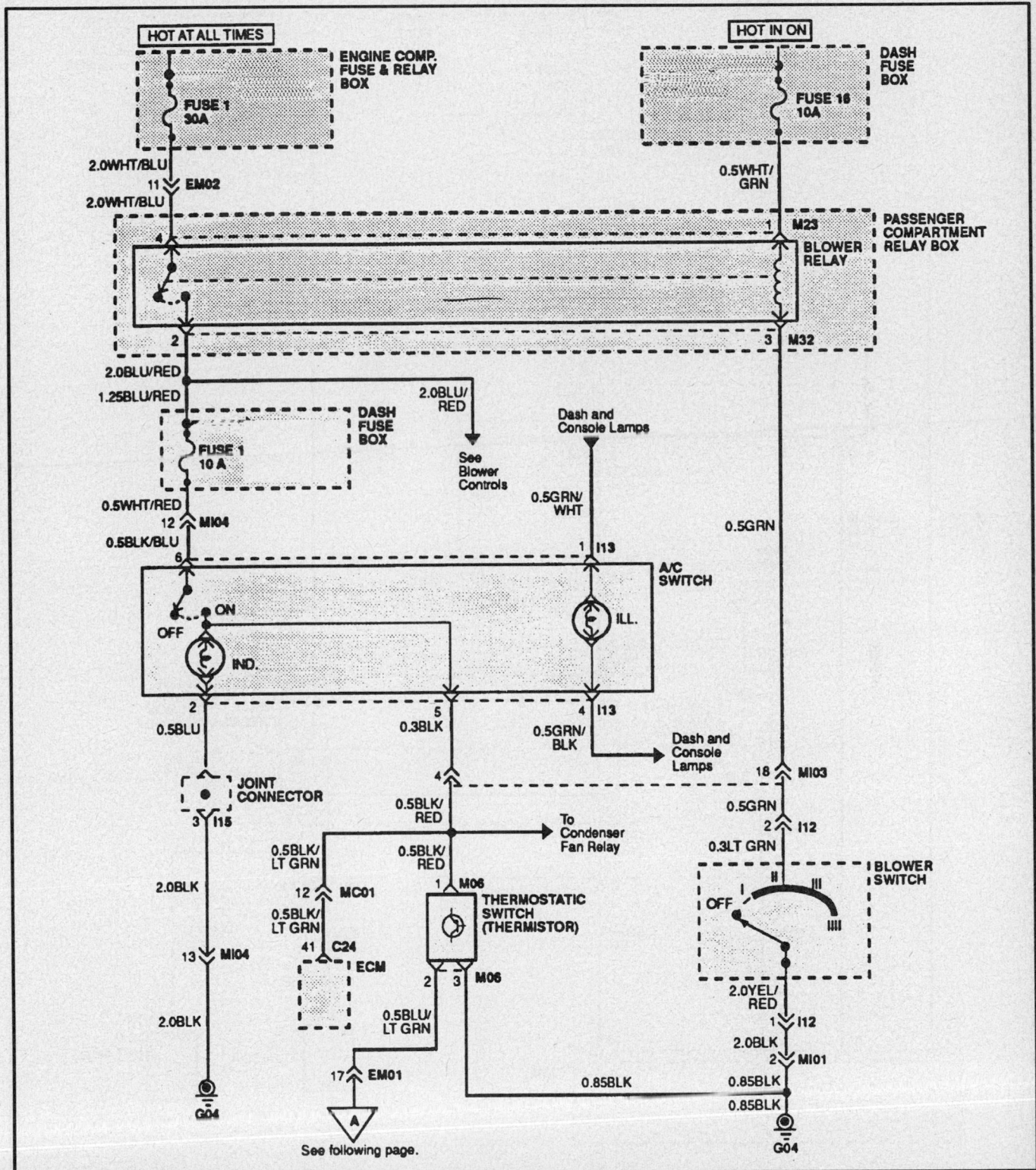

Air conditioning compressor control wiring schematic—1995 Accent

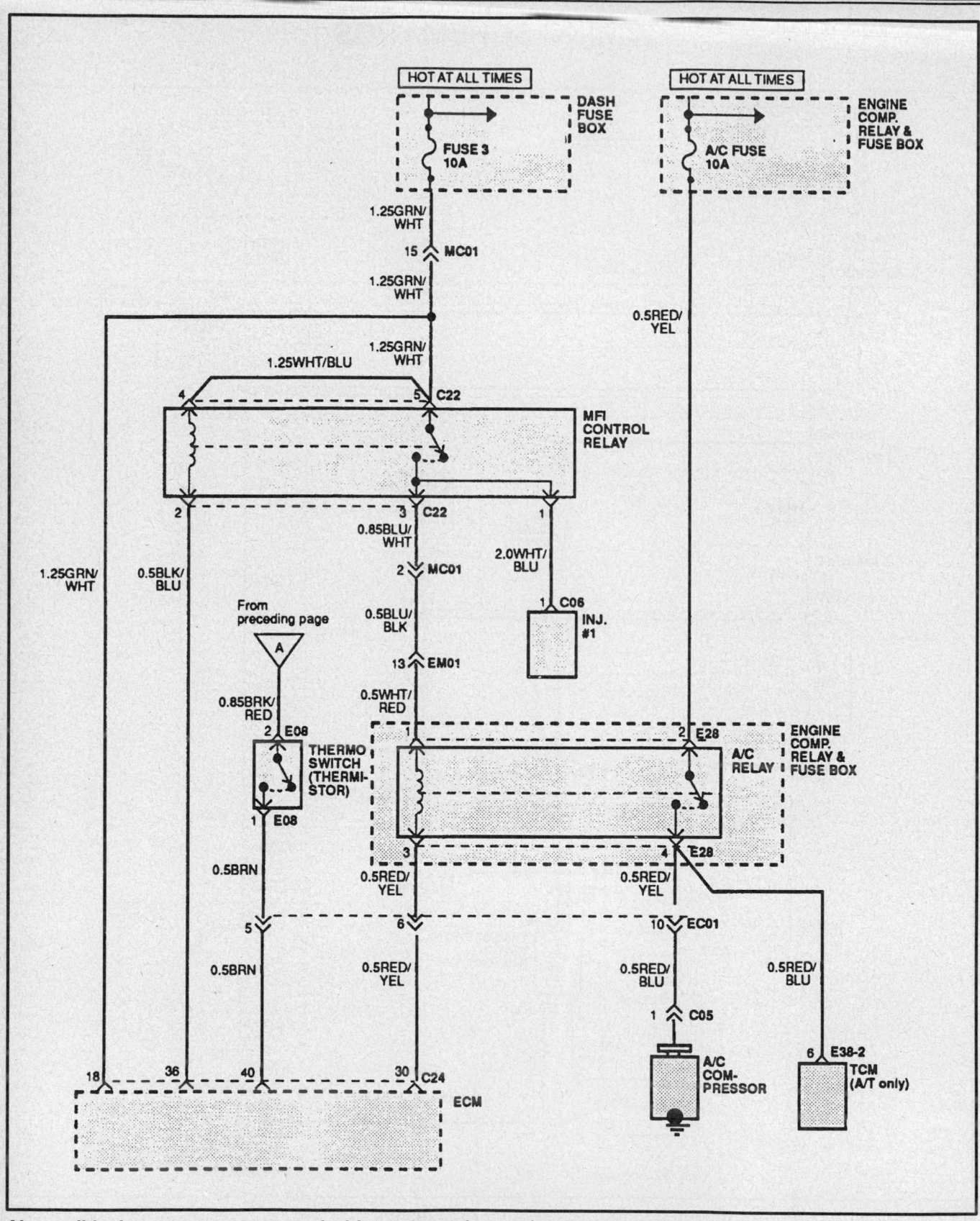

Air conditioning compressor control wiring schematic — 1995 Accent continued

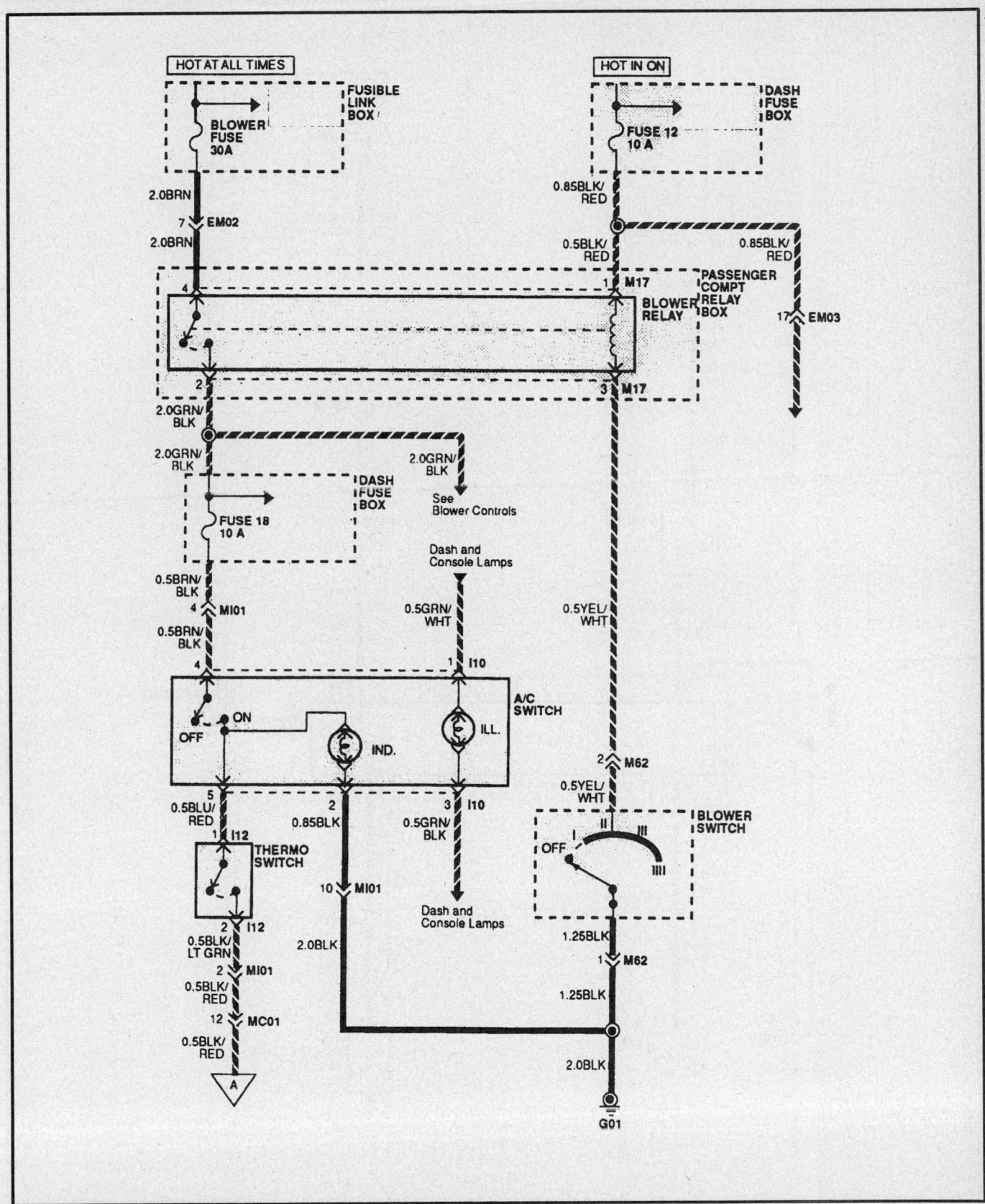

Air conditioning system wiring schematic—1993 Elantra

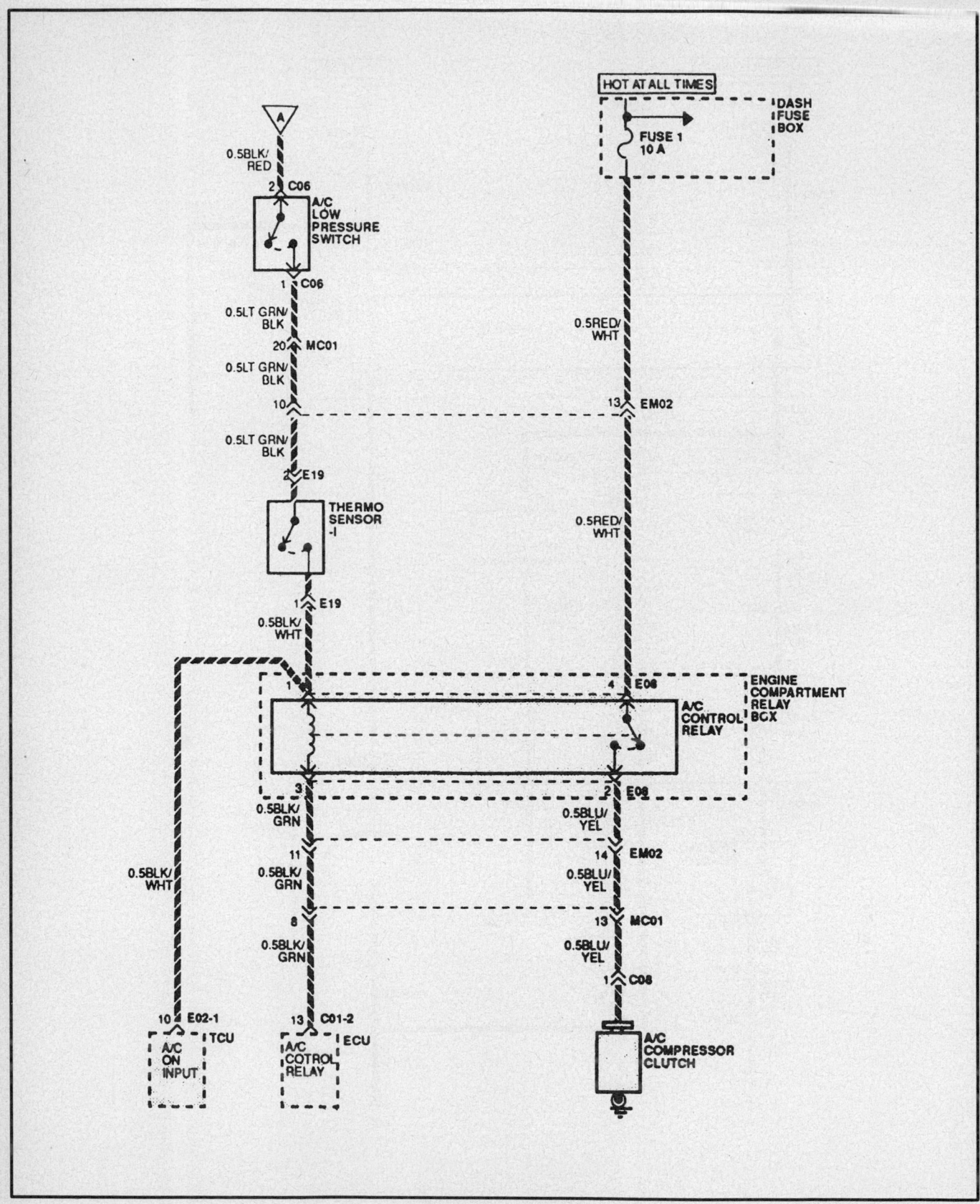

Air conditioning system wiring schematic—1993 Elantra continued

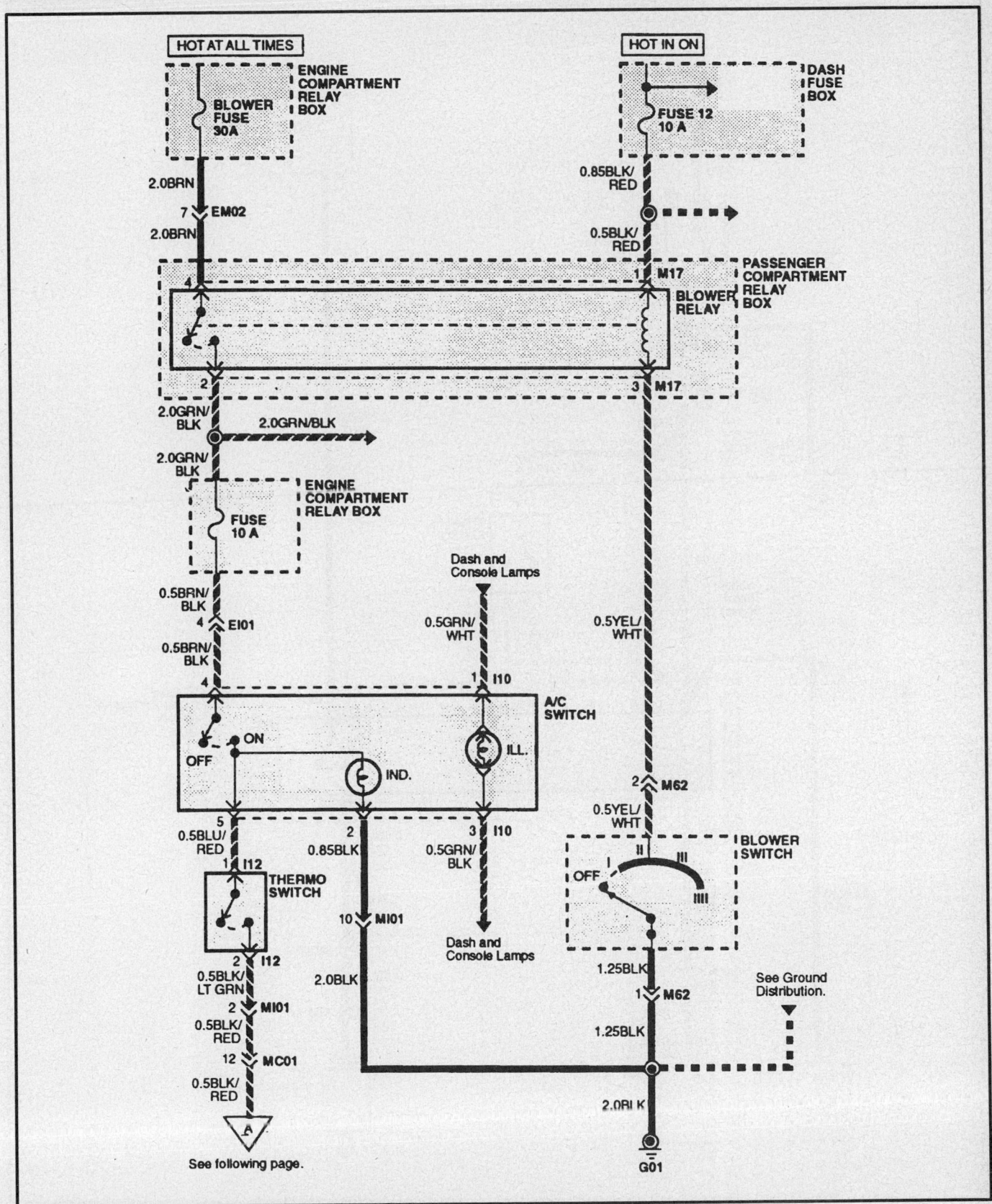

Air conditioning compressor control wiring schematic — 1994 Elantra

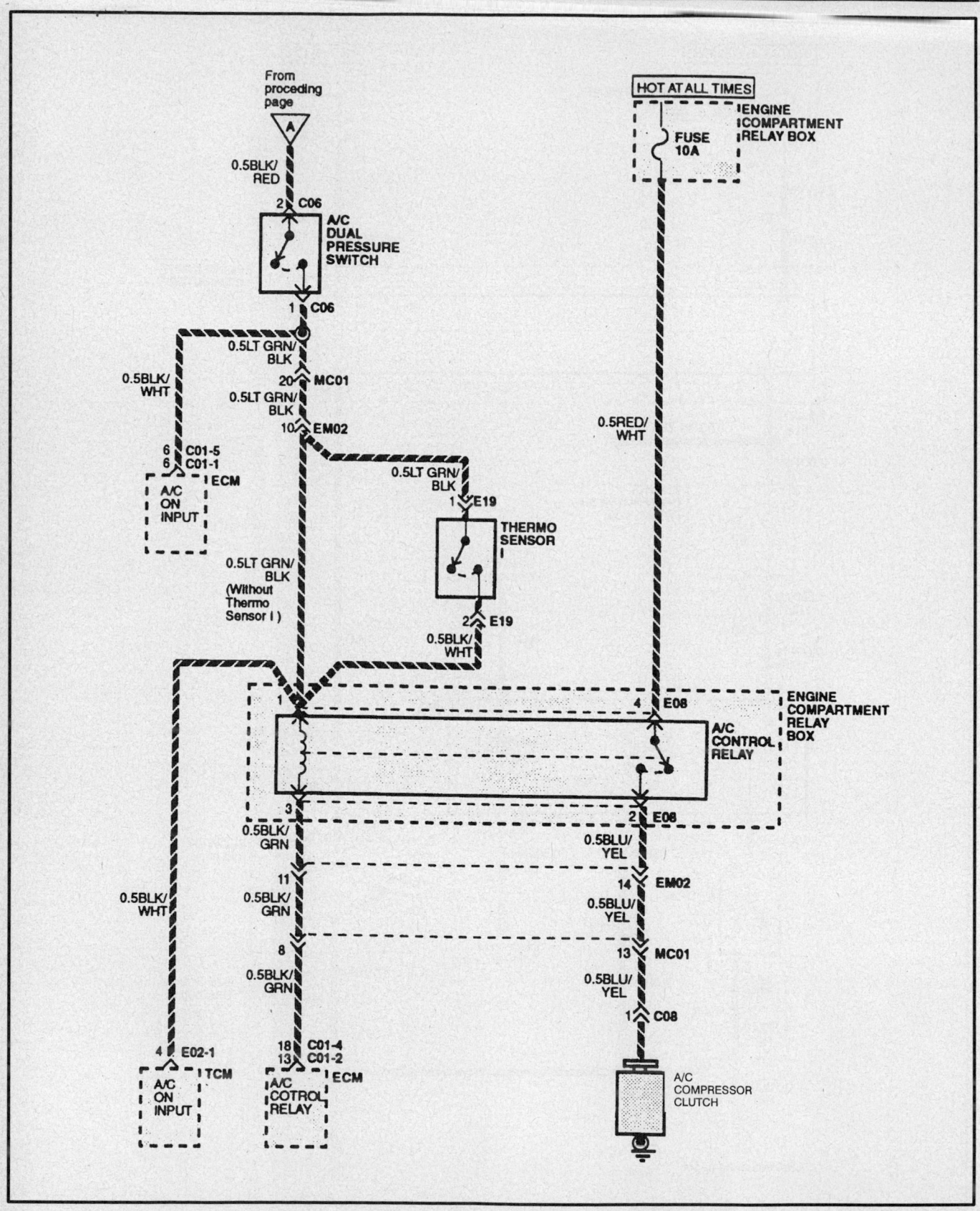

Air conditioning compressor control wiring schematic — 1994 Elantra continued

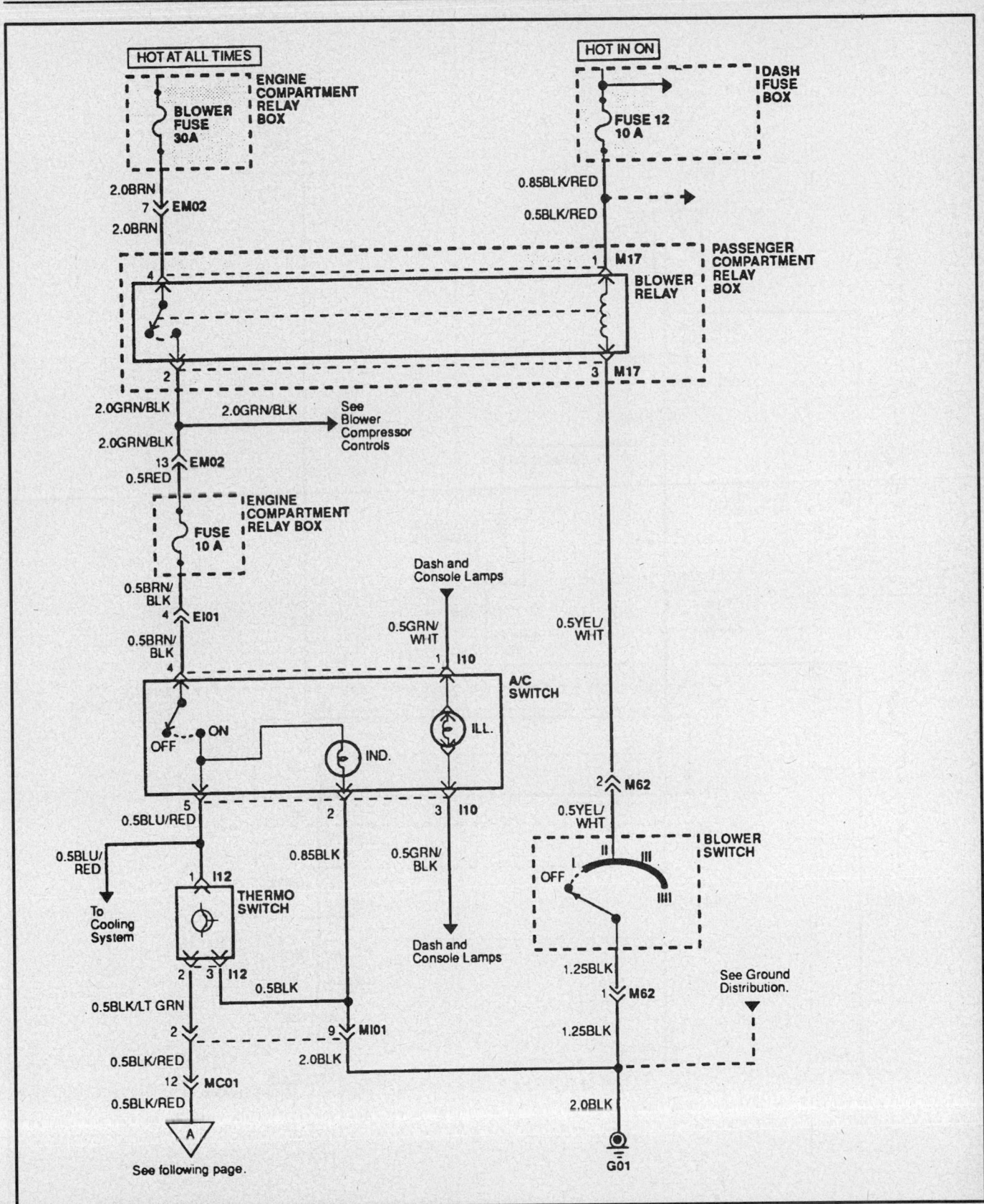

Air conditioning system wiring schematic—1995 Elantra

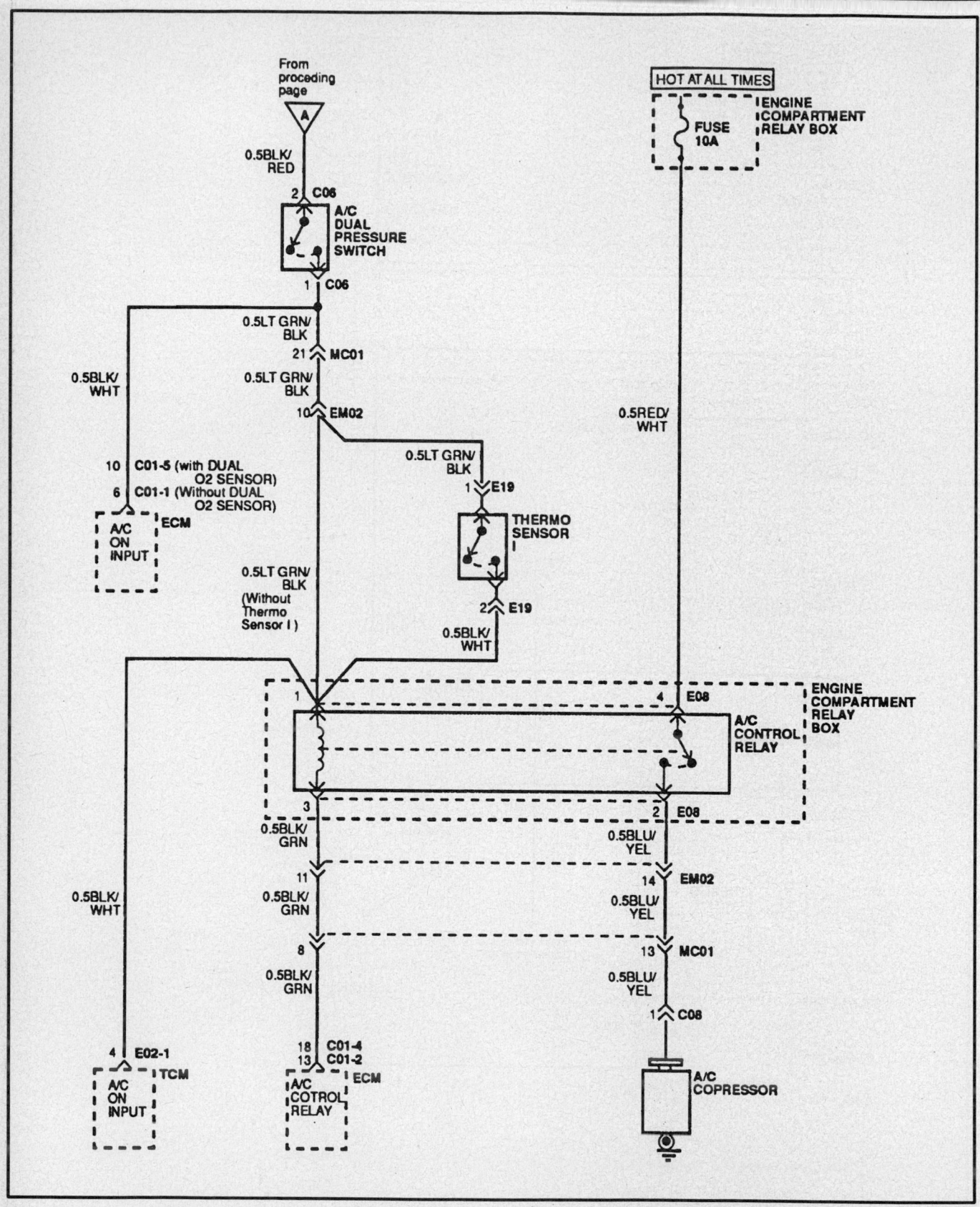

Air conditioning compressor control wiring schematic —1995 Elantra continued

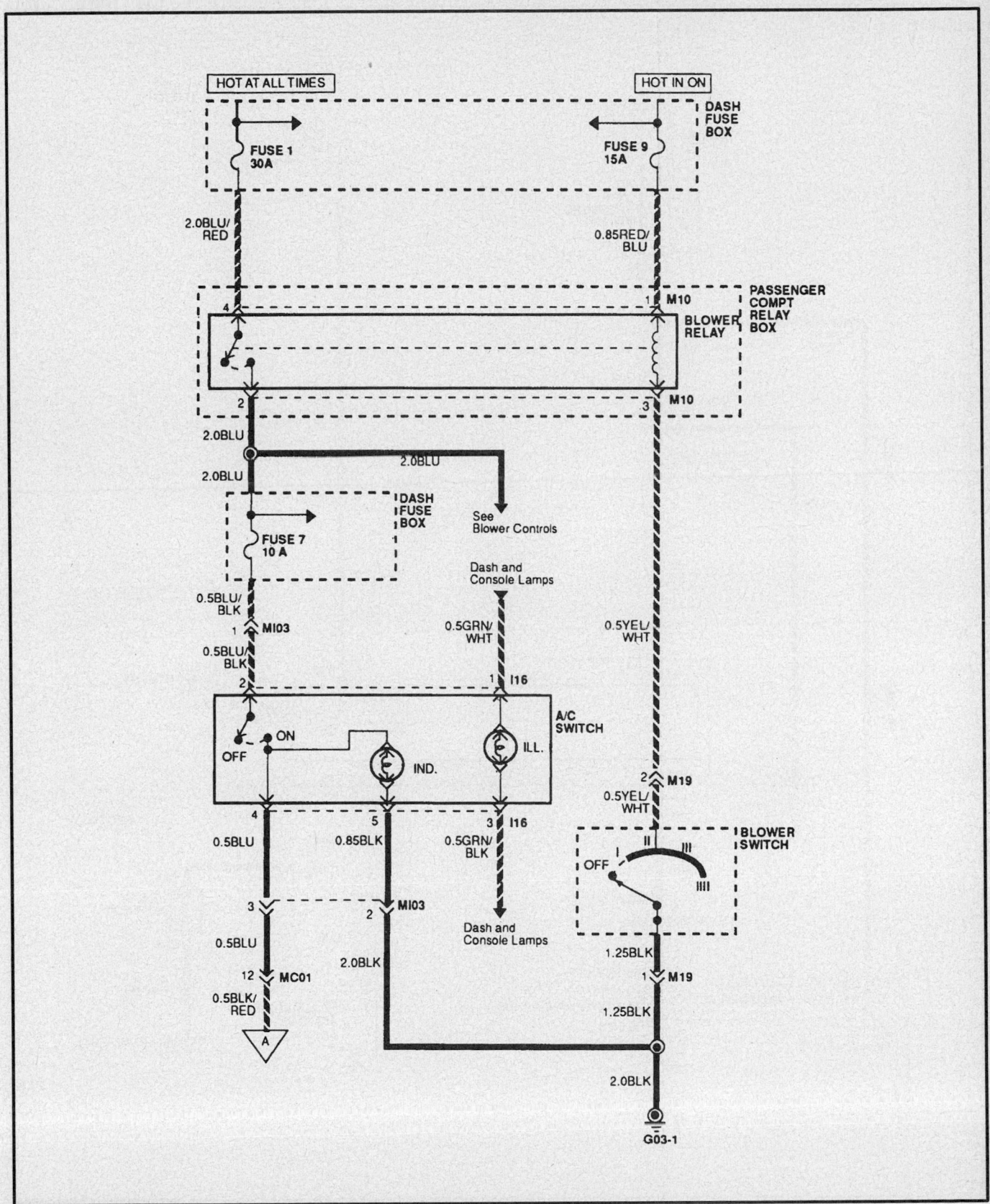

HOT AT ALL TIMES

HOT IN ON

DASH FUSE BOX

FUSE 1
30A

FUSE 9
15A

2.0BLU/RED

0.85RED/BLU

PASSENGER COMPT RELAY BOX

4 M10 1

BLOWER RELAY

2 M10 3

2.0BLU

2.0BLU

2.0BLU

DASH FUSE BOX

FUSE 7
10 A

See Blower Controls

0.5BLU/BLK

Dash and Console Lamps

1 MI03

0.5GRN/WHT

0.5YEL/WHT

0.5BLU/BLK

2 1 I16

A/C SWITCH

ON

OFF

IND.

ILL.

2 M19

0.5YEL/WHT

4 5 3 I16

BLOWER SWITCH

0.5BLU

0.85BLK

0.5GRN/BLK

OFF

3

2 MI03

Dash and Console Lamps

0.5BLU

2.0BLK

1.25BLK

1 M19

12 MC01

0.5BLK/RED

1.25BLK

A

2.0BLK

G03-1

Air conditioning compressor control wiring schematic—1993 Excel

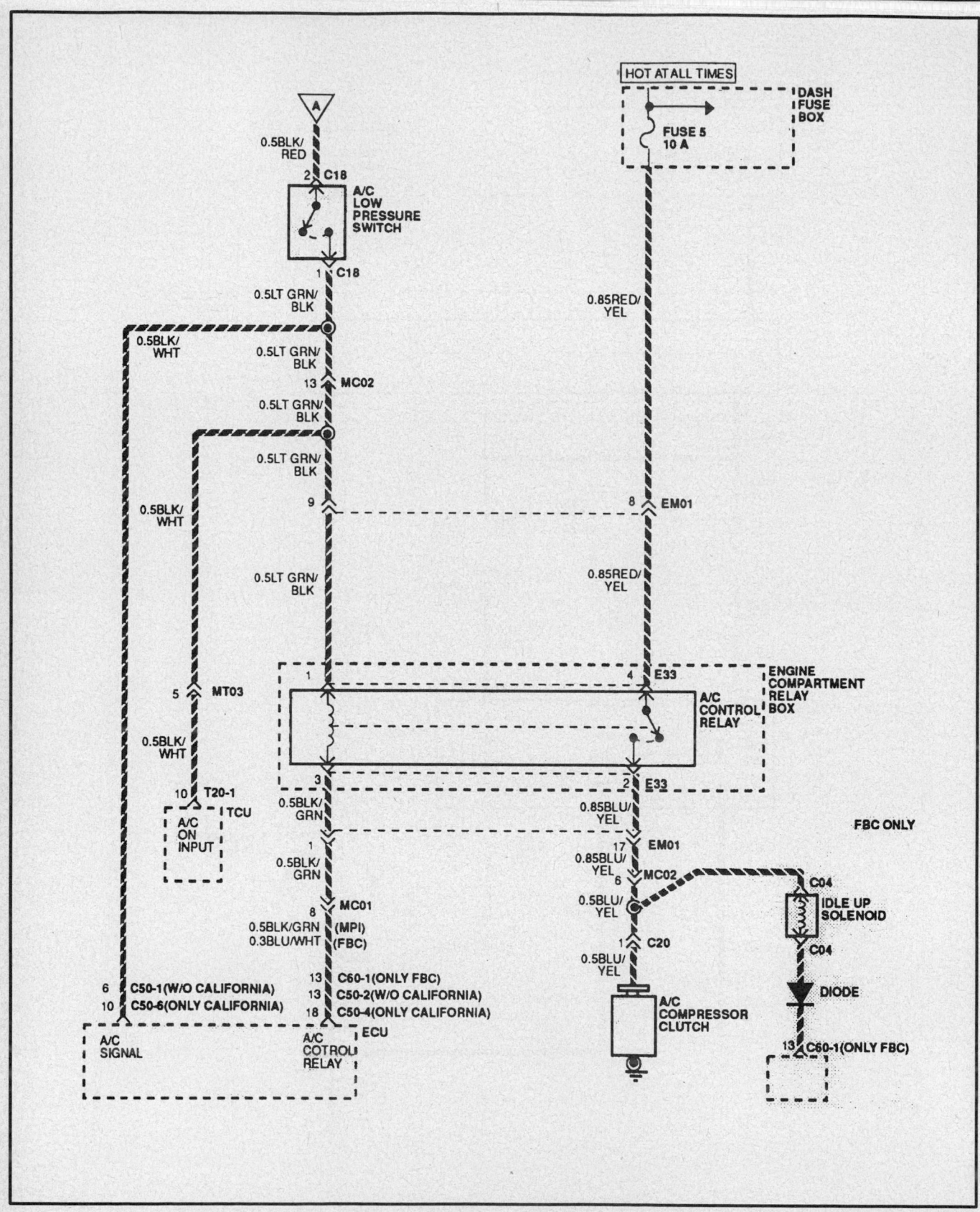

Air conditioning compressor control wiring schematic — 1993 Excel Continued

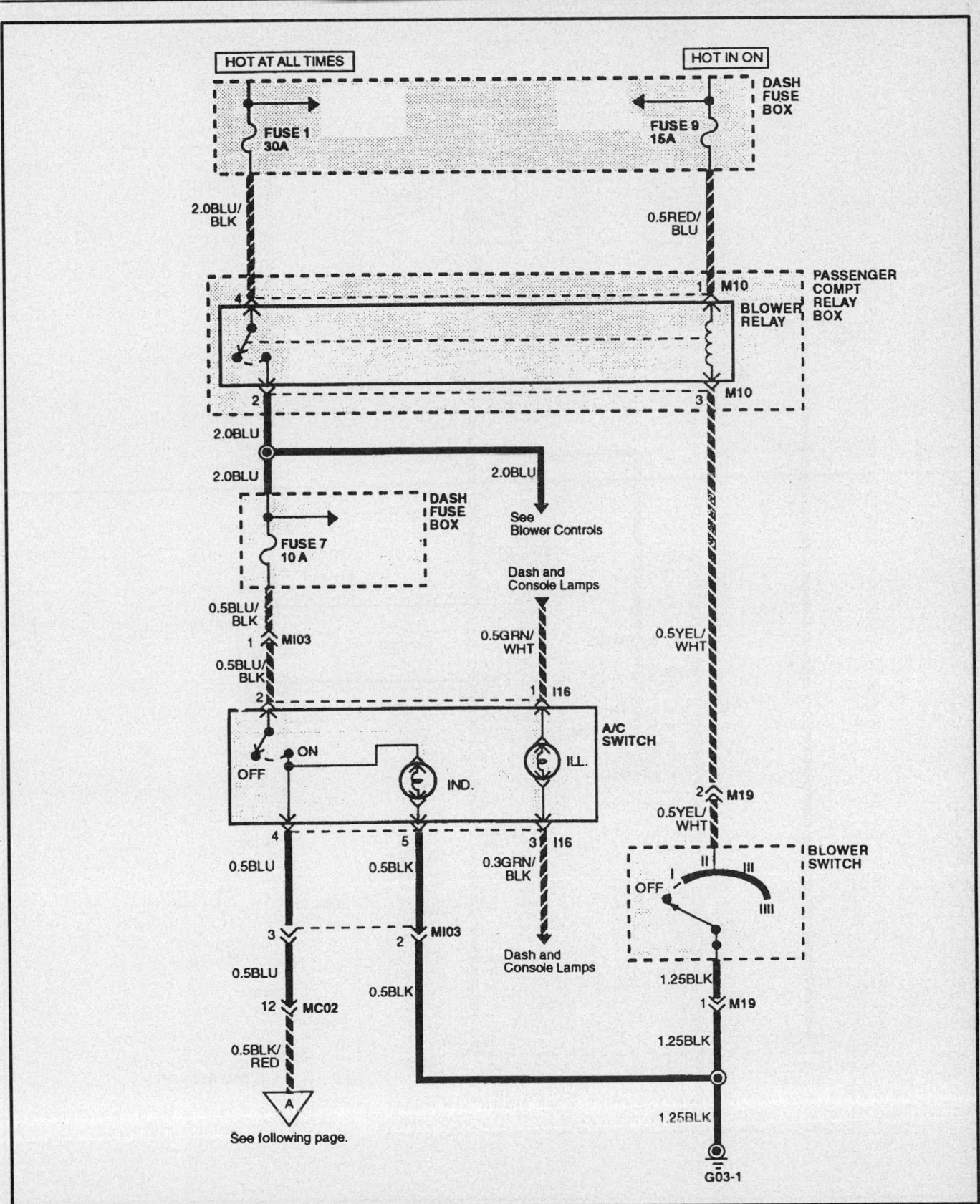

Air conditioning compressor control wiring schematic—1994 Excel

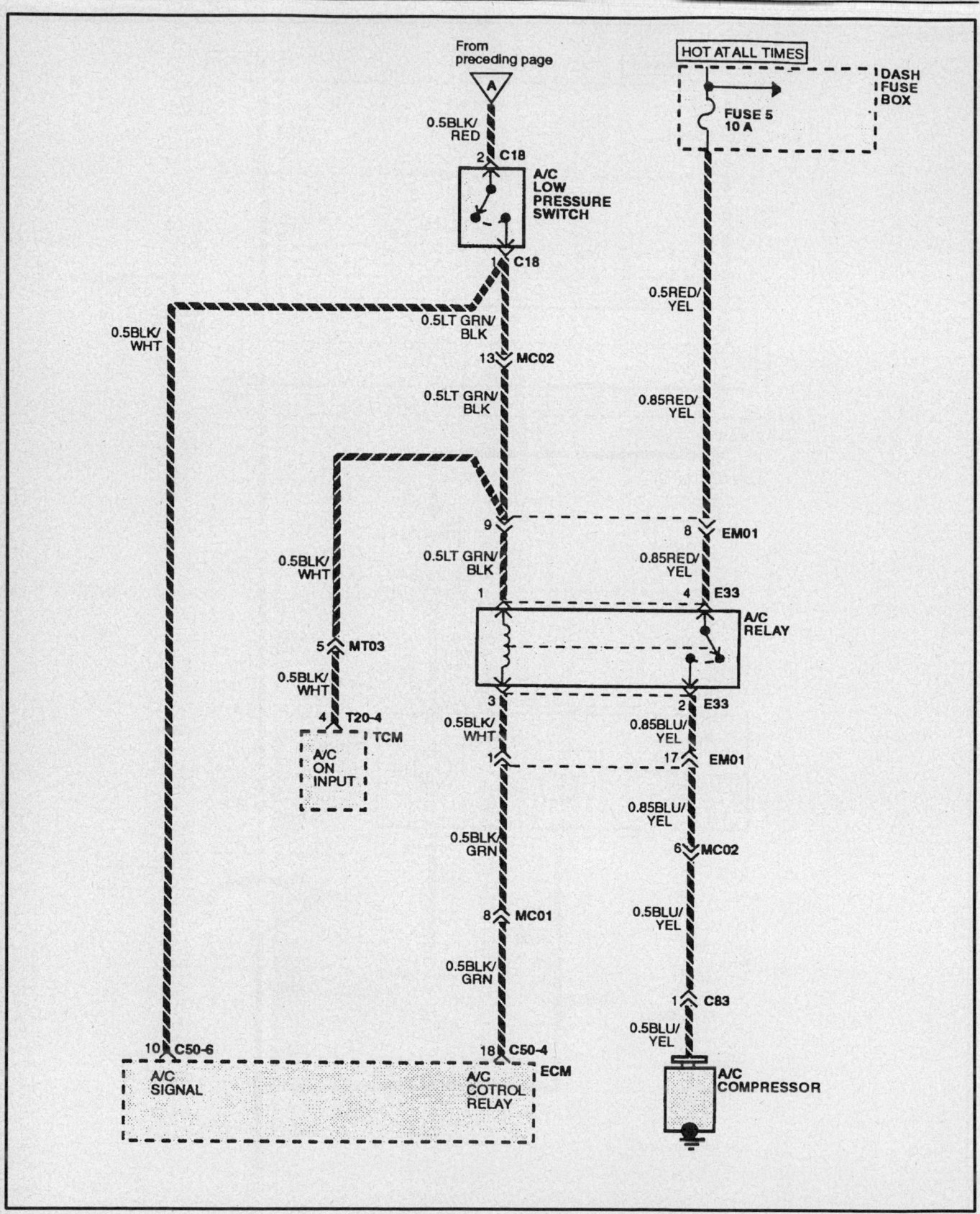

Air conditioning compressor control wiring schematic — 1994 Excel continued

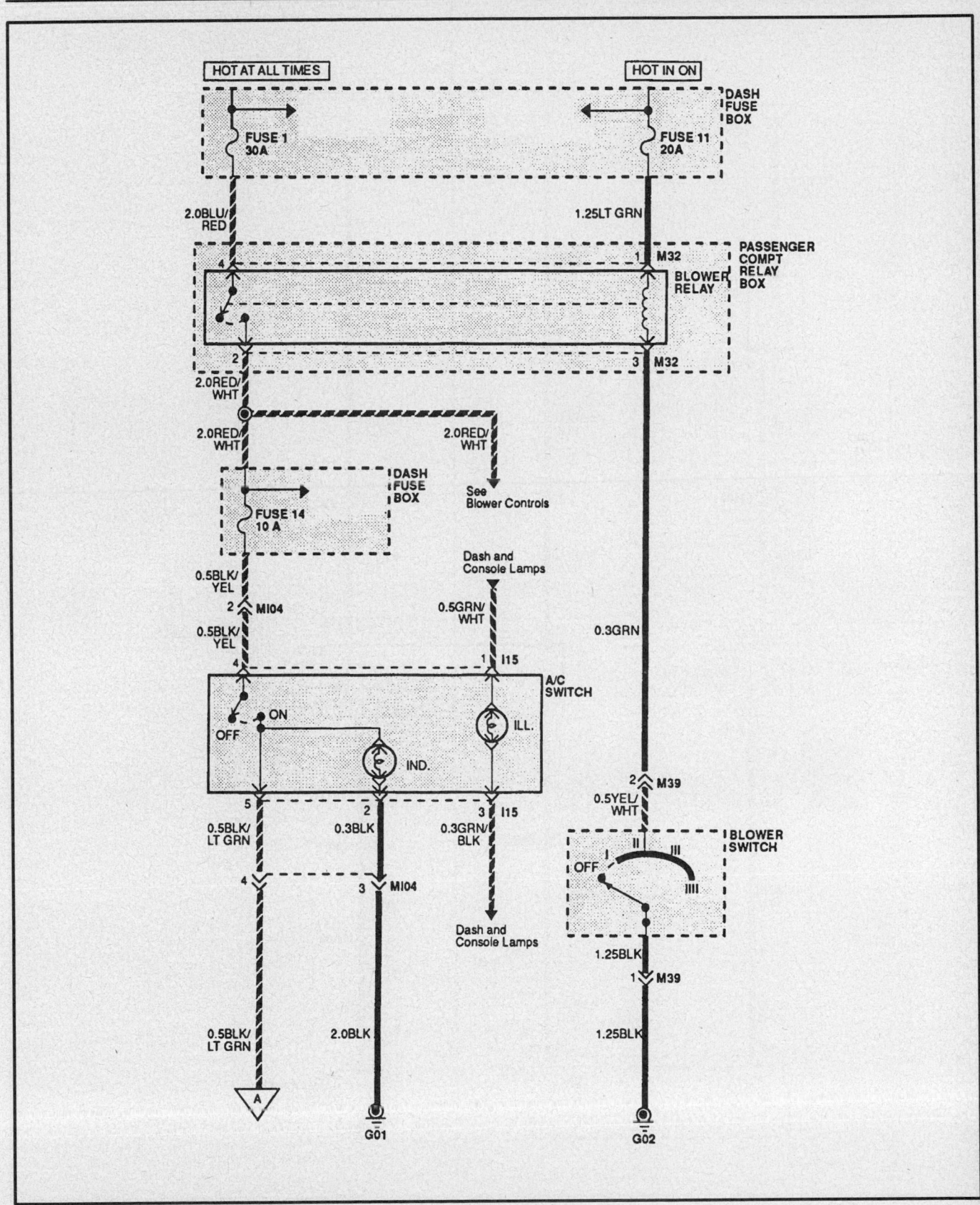

Air conditioning compressor control wiring schematic—1994 Scoupe

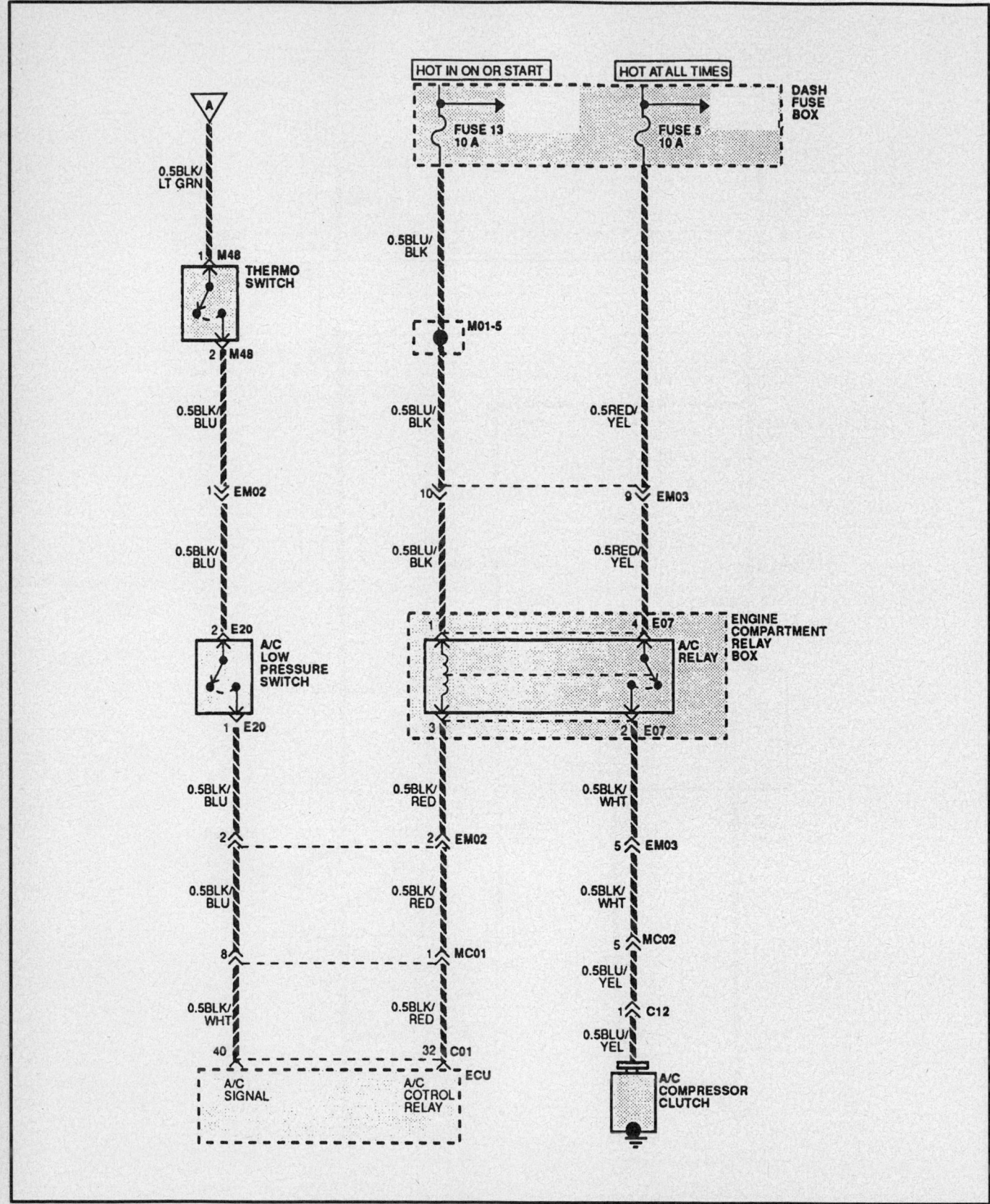

Air conditioning compressor control wiring schematic—1994 Scoupe continued

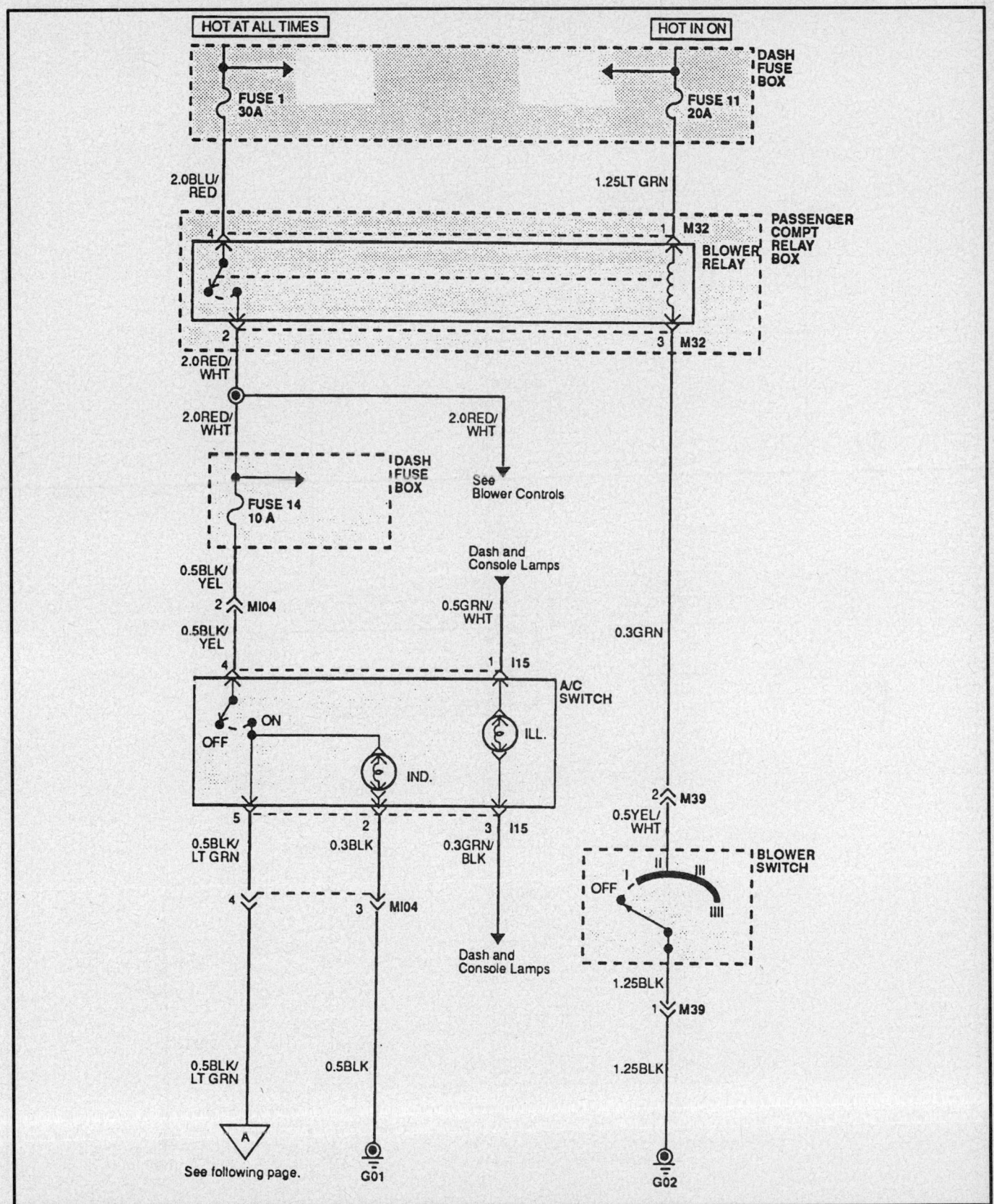

Air conditioning compressor control wiring schematic—1995 Scoupe

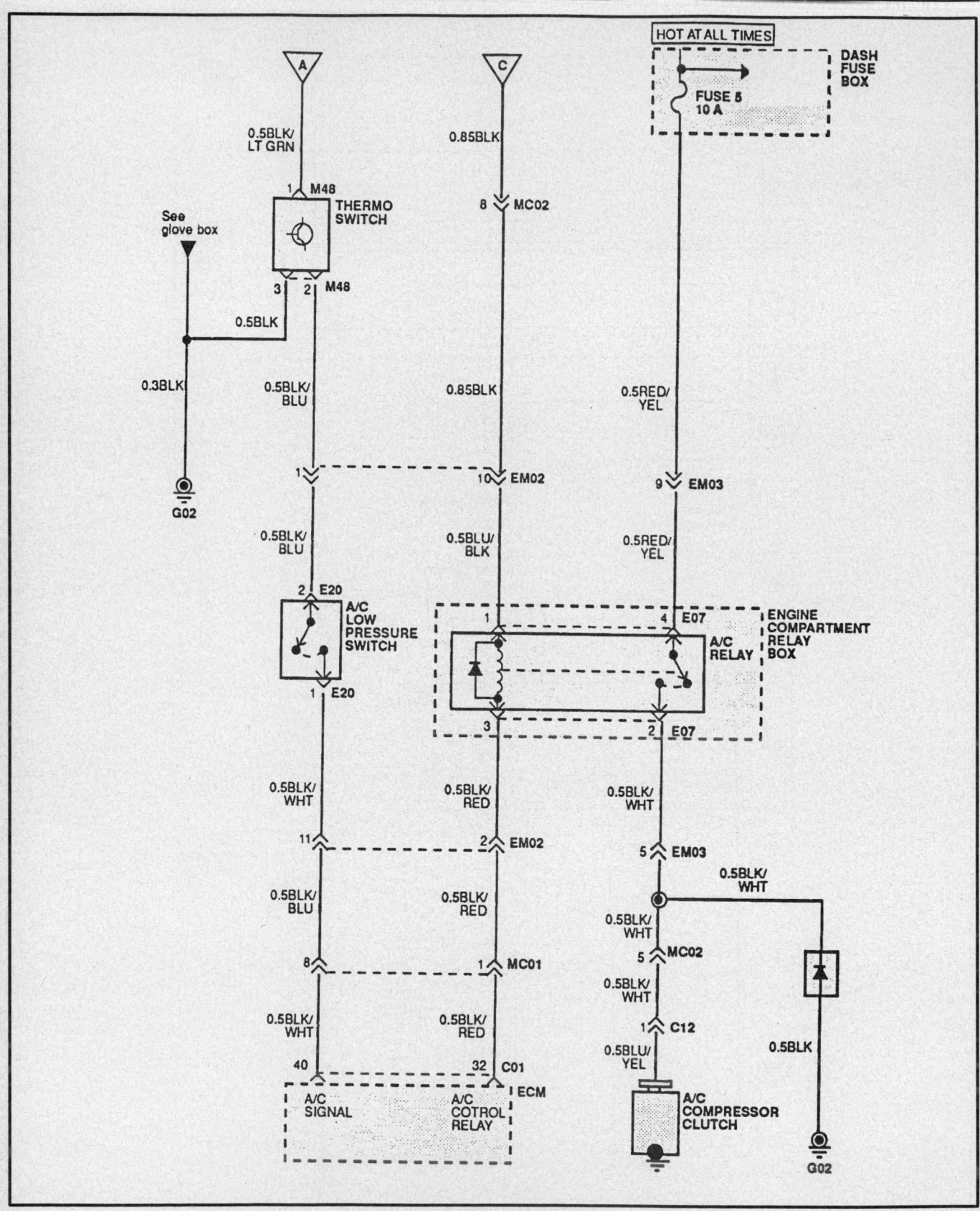

Air conditioning compressor control wiring schematic—1995 Scoupe continued

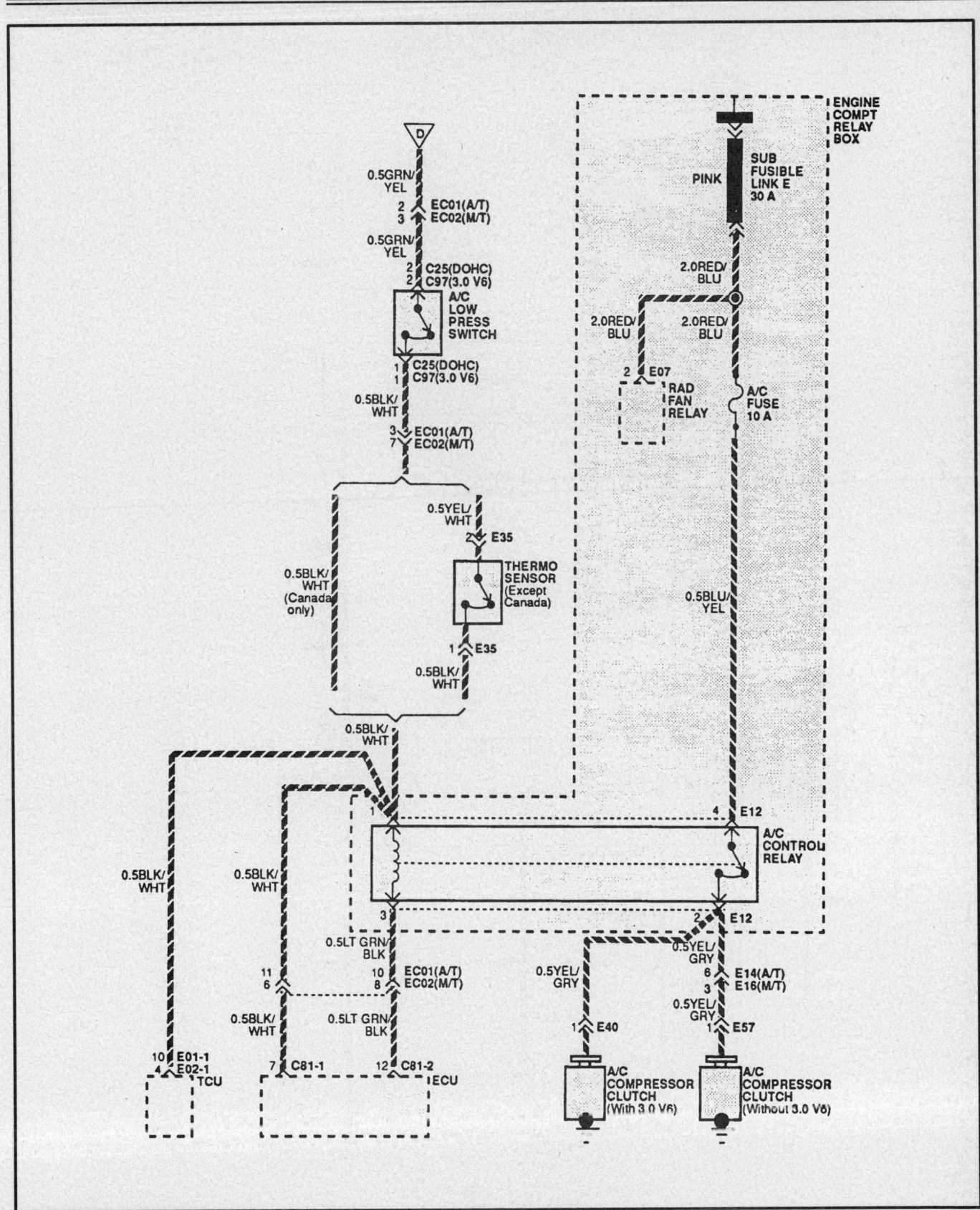

Air conditioning compressor control wiring schematic—1993 Sonata

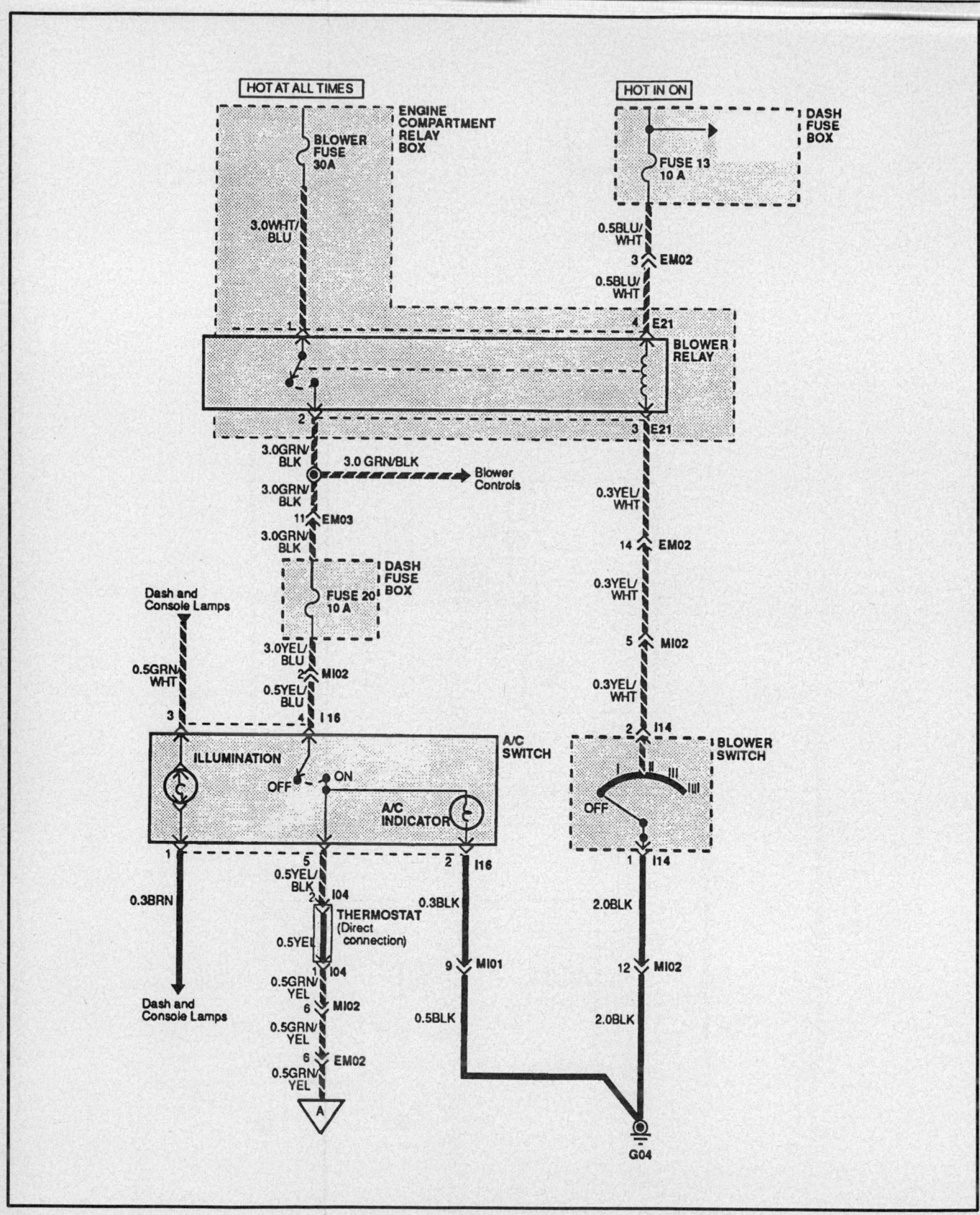

Air conditioning compressor control wiring schematic—1993 Sonata continued

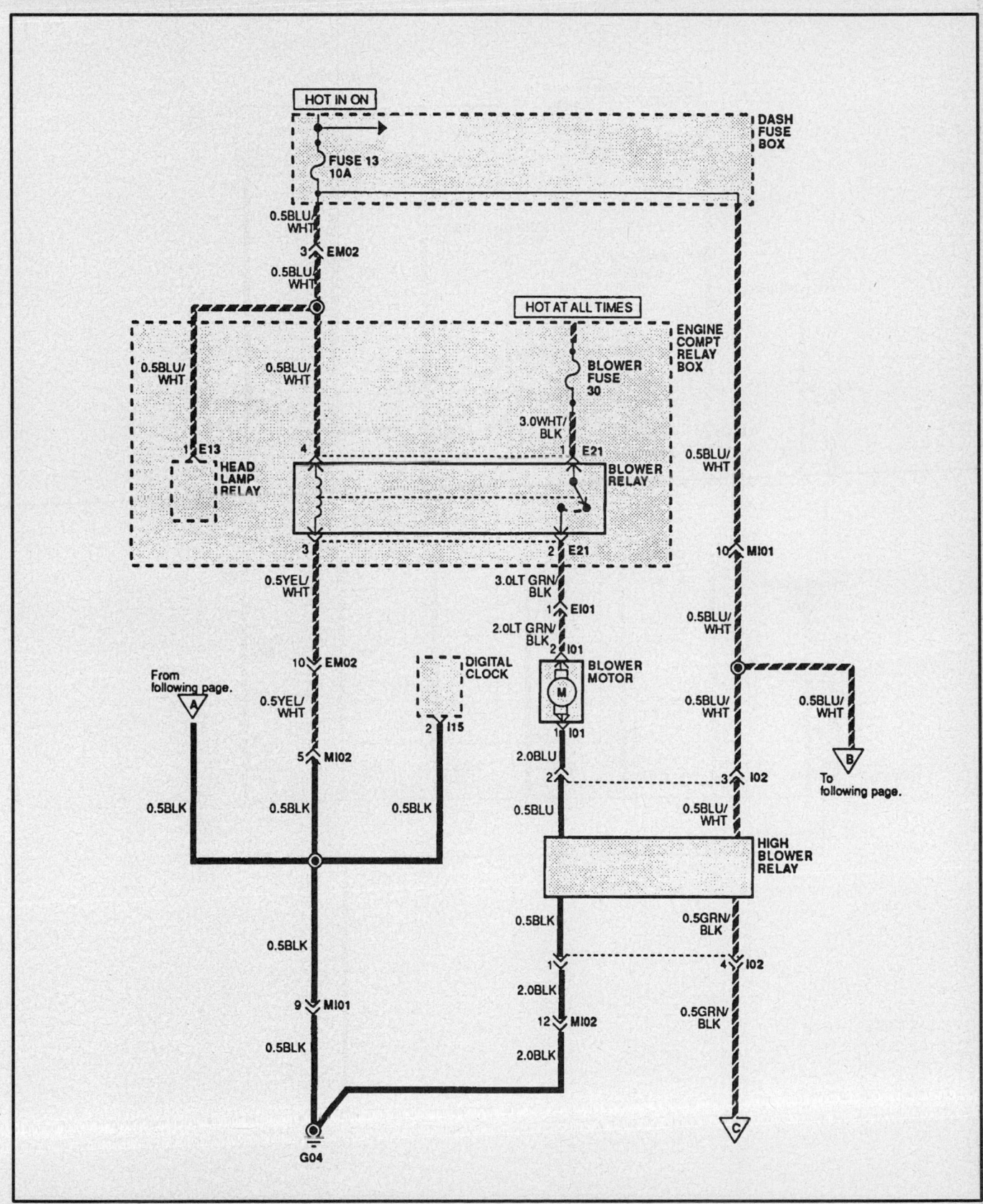

Semi-automatic air conditioning compressor control wiring schematic—1993 Sonata continued

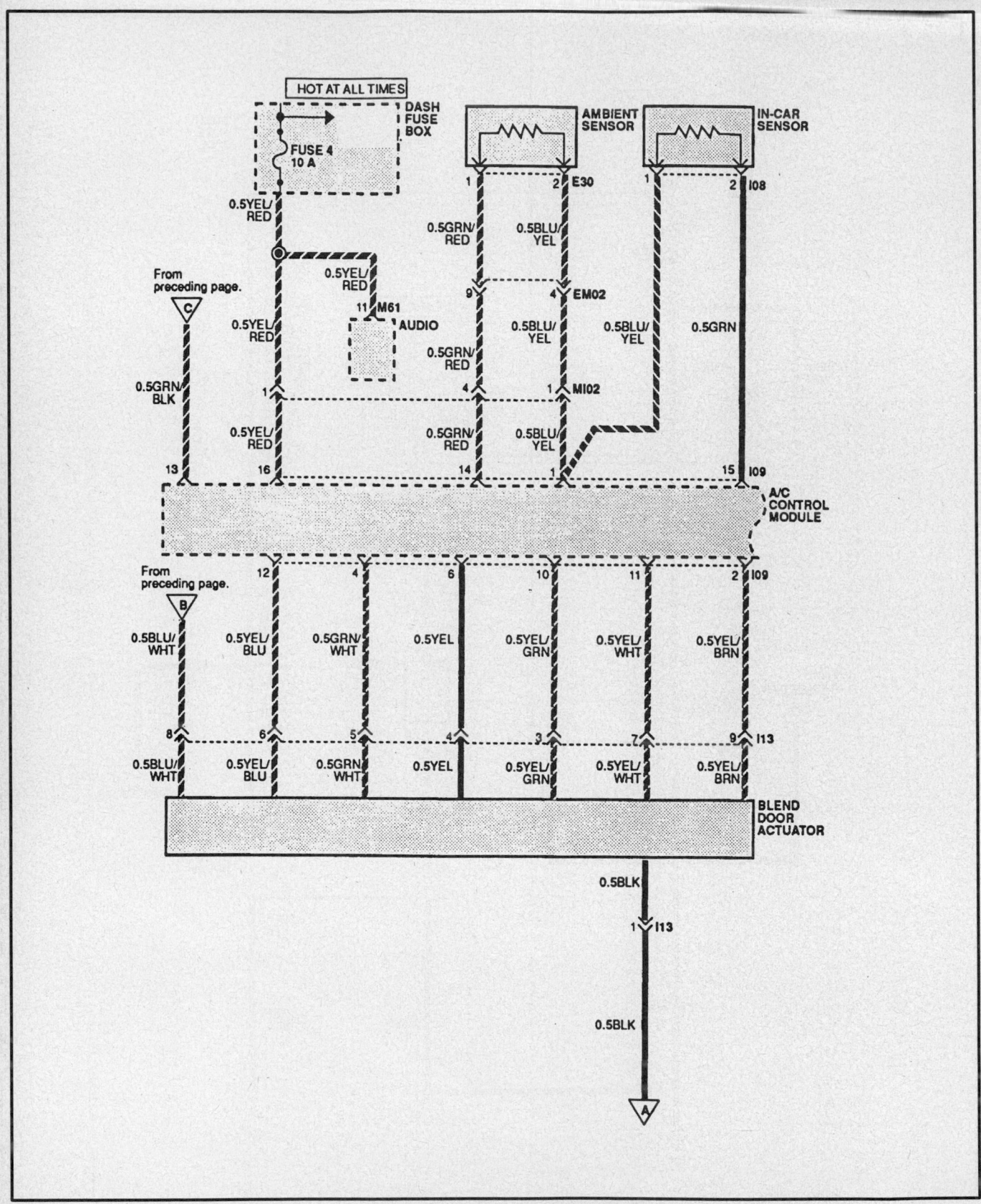

Semi-automatic air conditioning compressor control wiring schematic—1993 Sonata continued

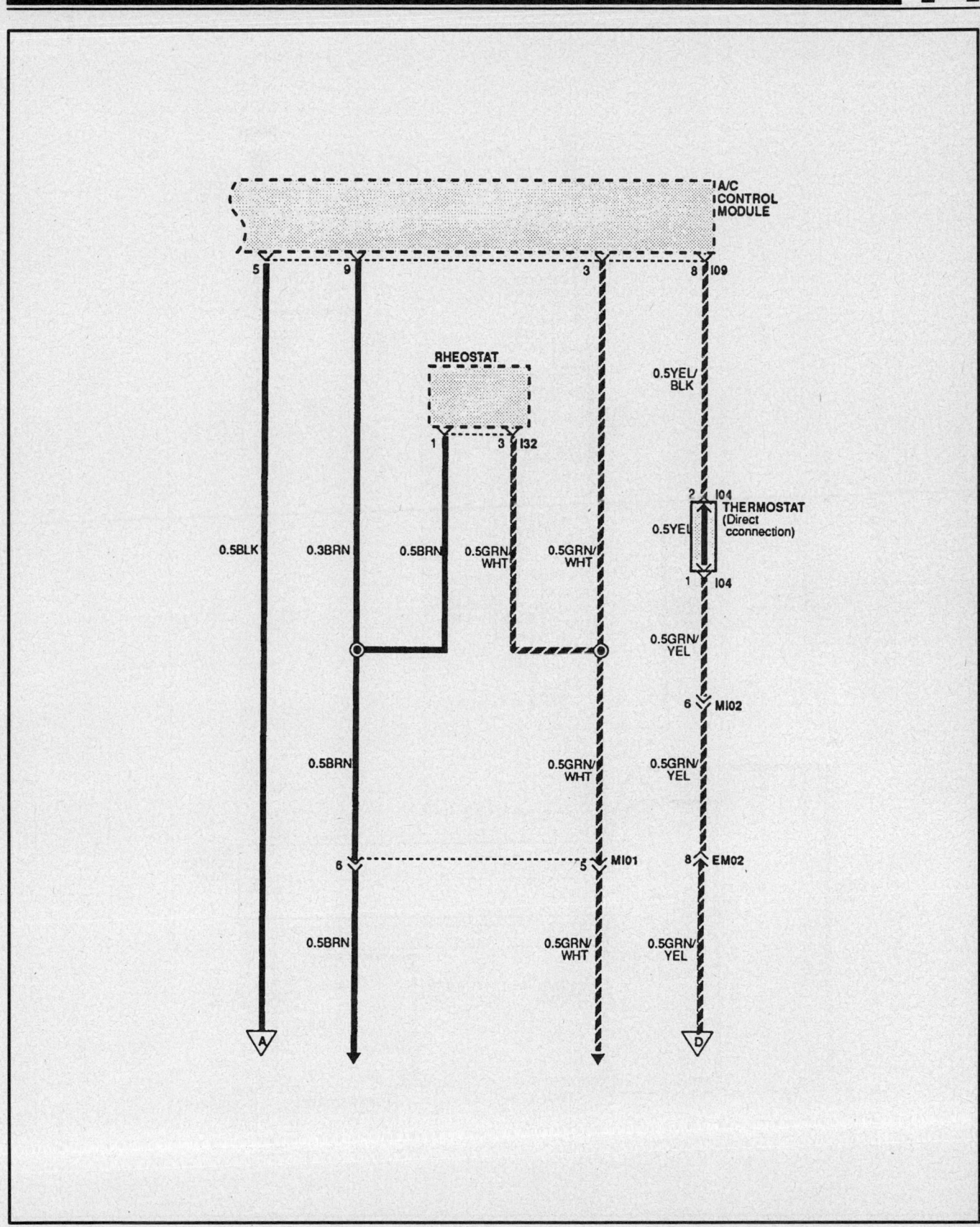

Semi-automatic air conditioning compressor control wiring schematic—1993 Sonata continued

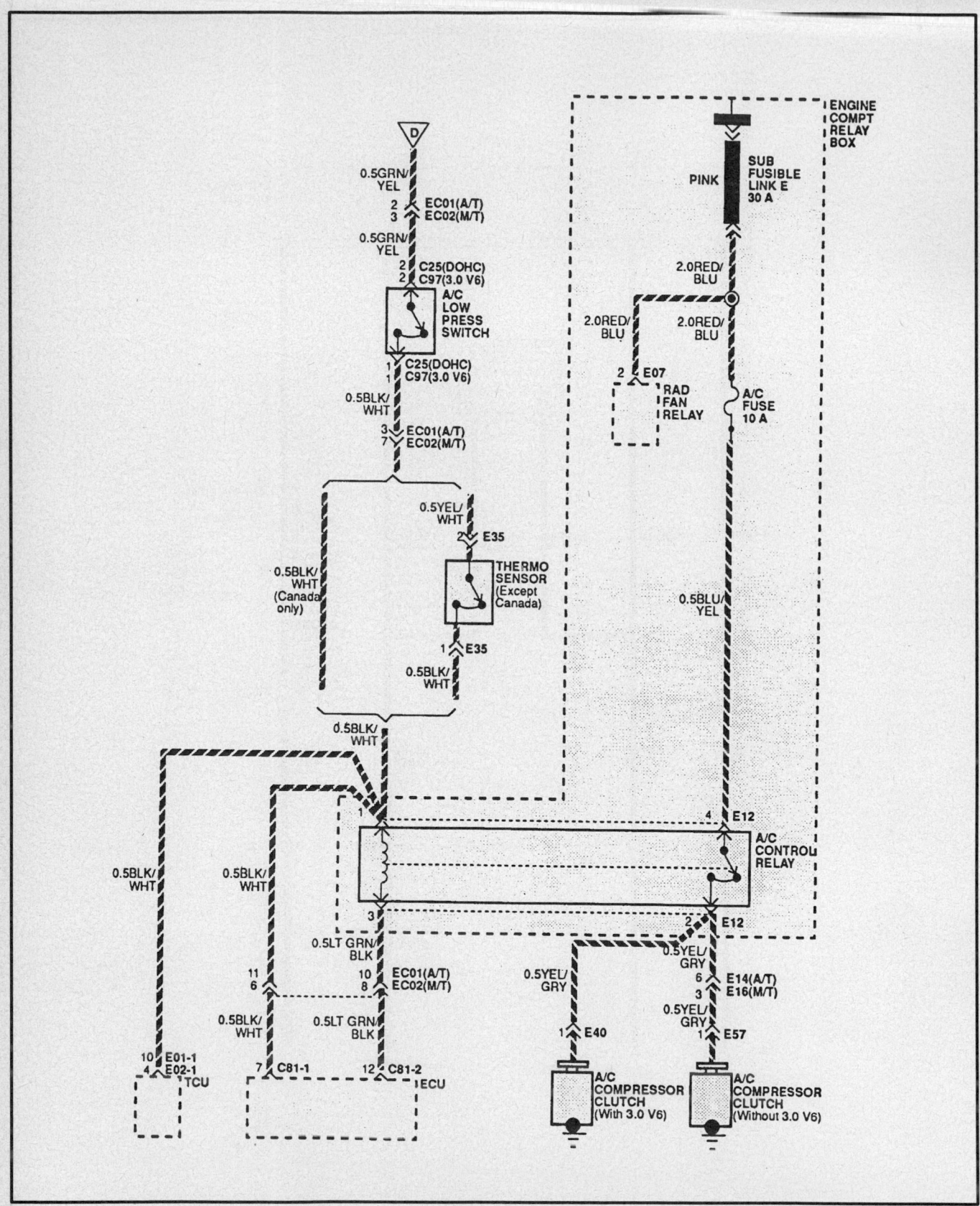

Semi-automatic air conditioning compressor control wiring schematic—1993 Sonata continued

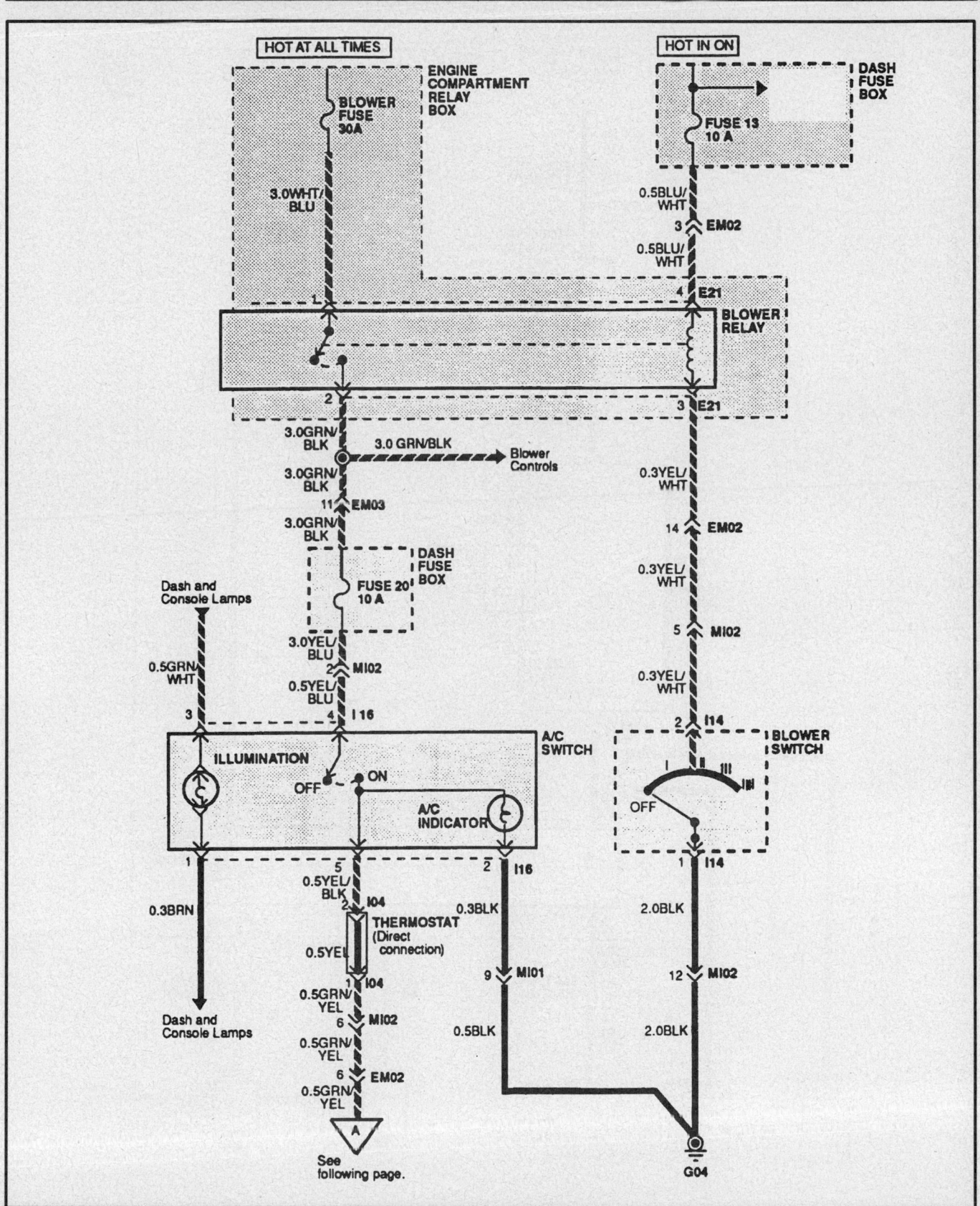

Air conditioning compressor control wiring schematic—1994 Sonata

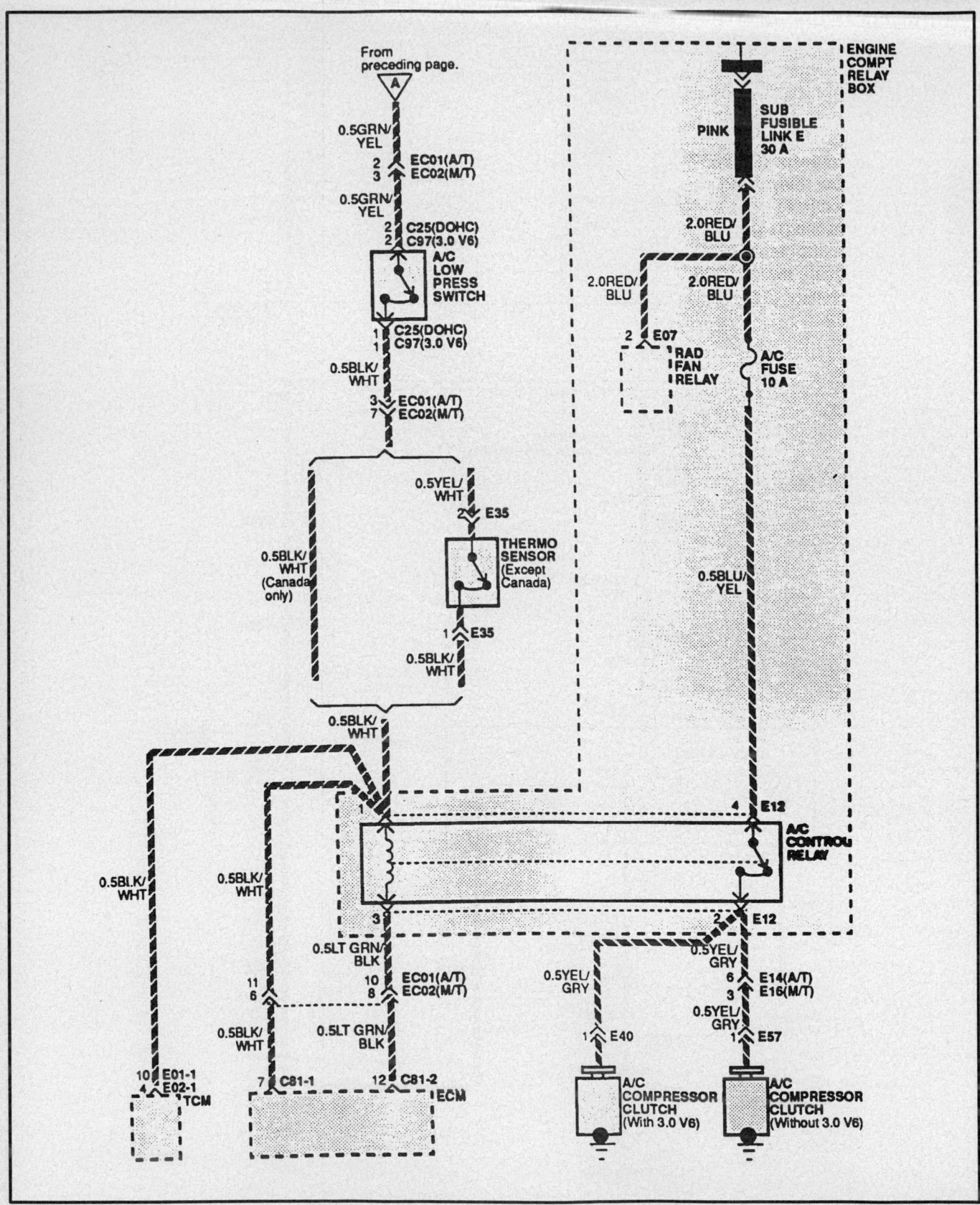

Air conditioning compressor control wiring schematic—1994 Sonata continued

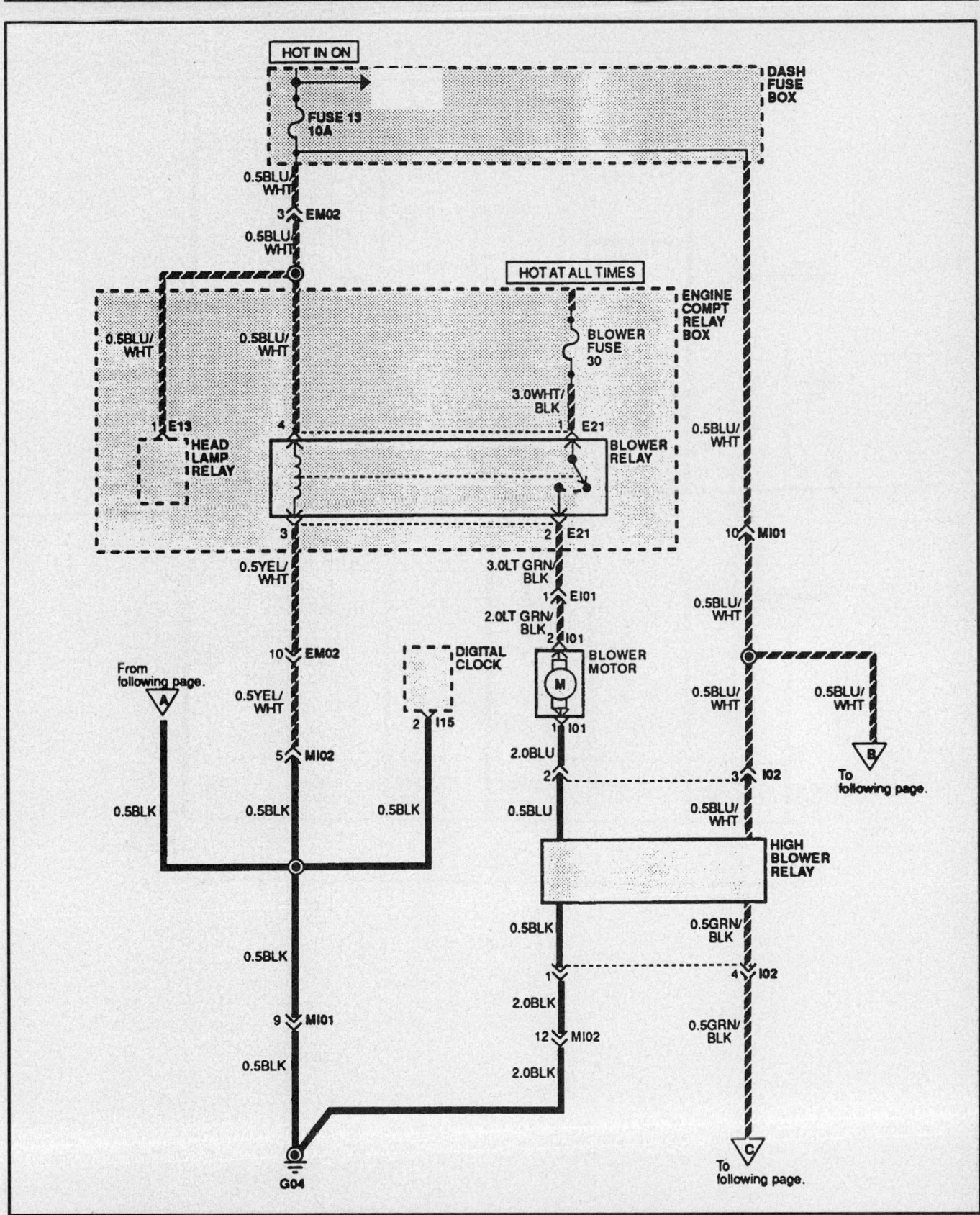

Semi-automatic air conditioning compressor control wiring schematic—1994 Sonata

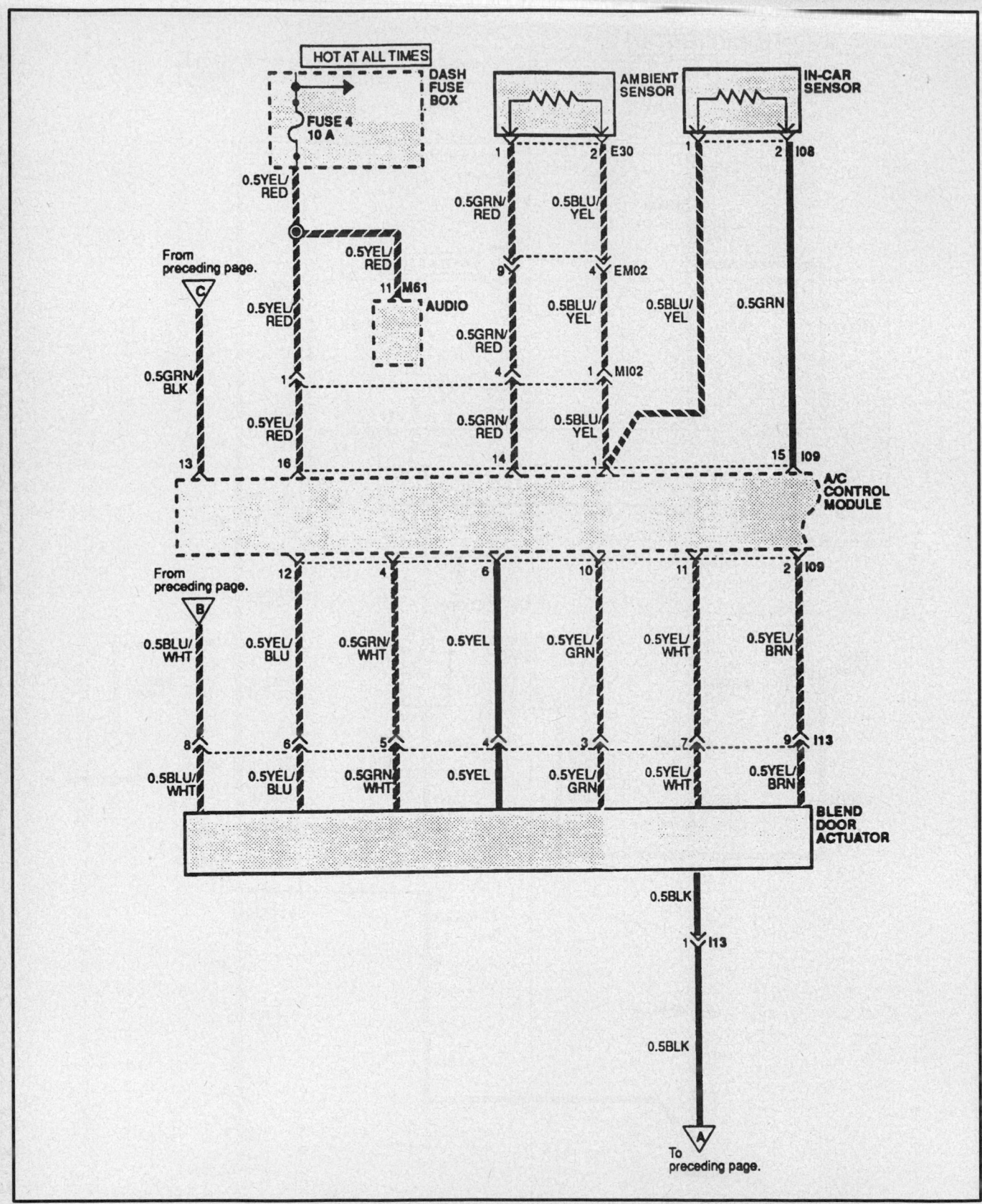

Semi-automatic air conditioning compressor control wiring schematic—1994 Sonata continued

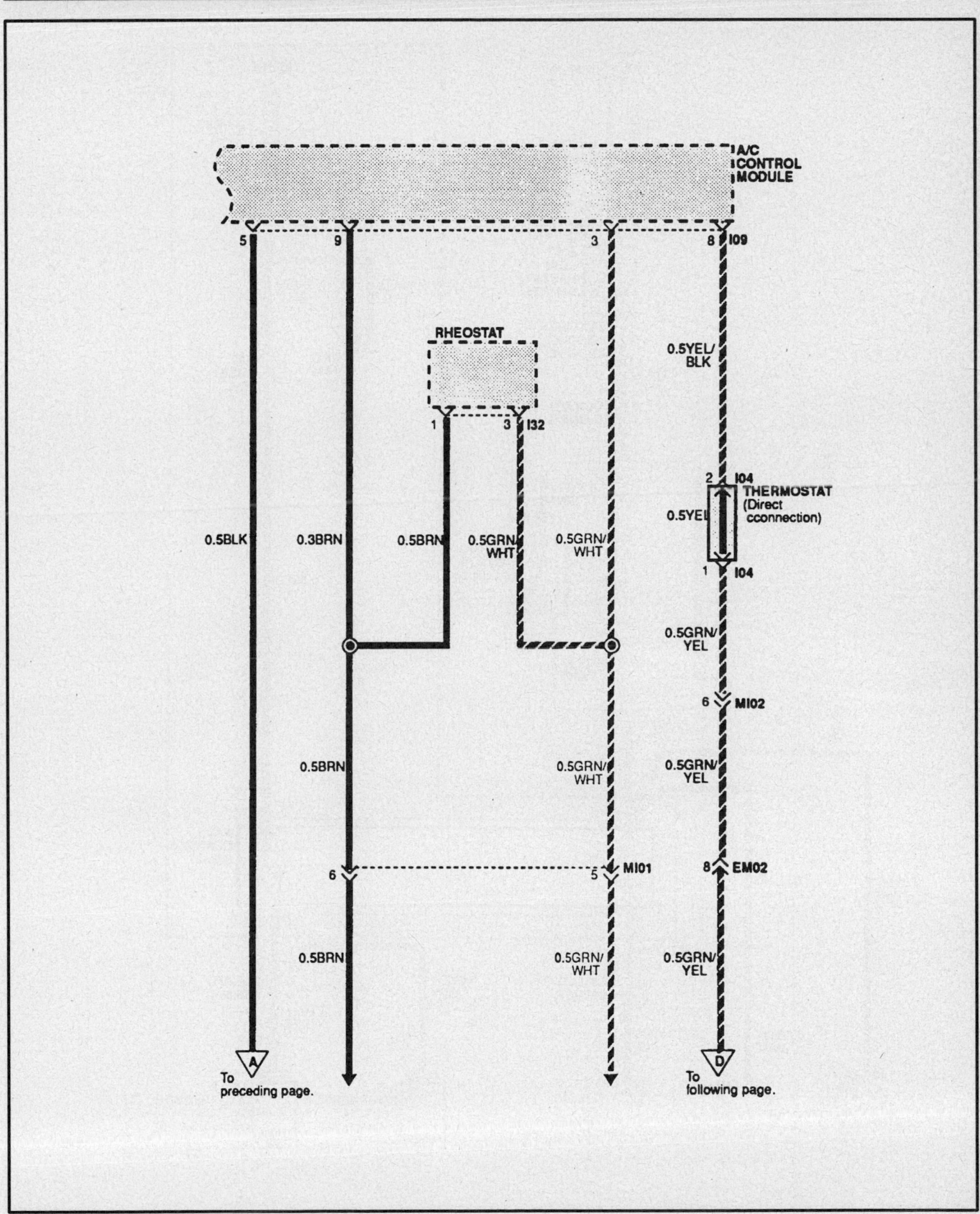

Semi automatic air conditioning compressor control wiring schematic—1994 Sonata continued

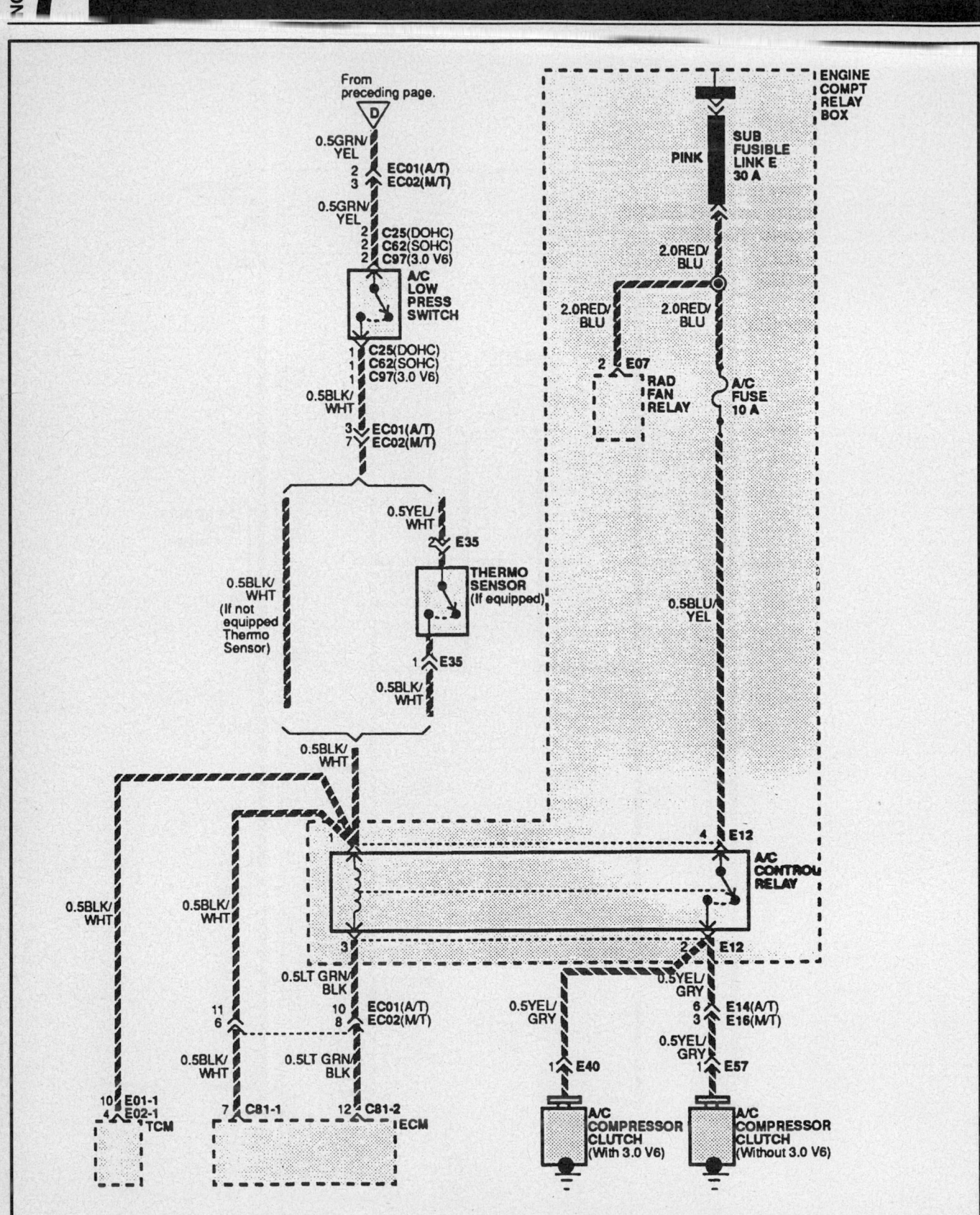

Semi-automatic air conditioning compressor control wiring schematic—1994 Sonata continued

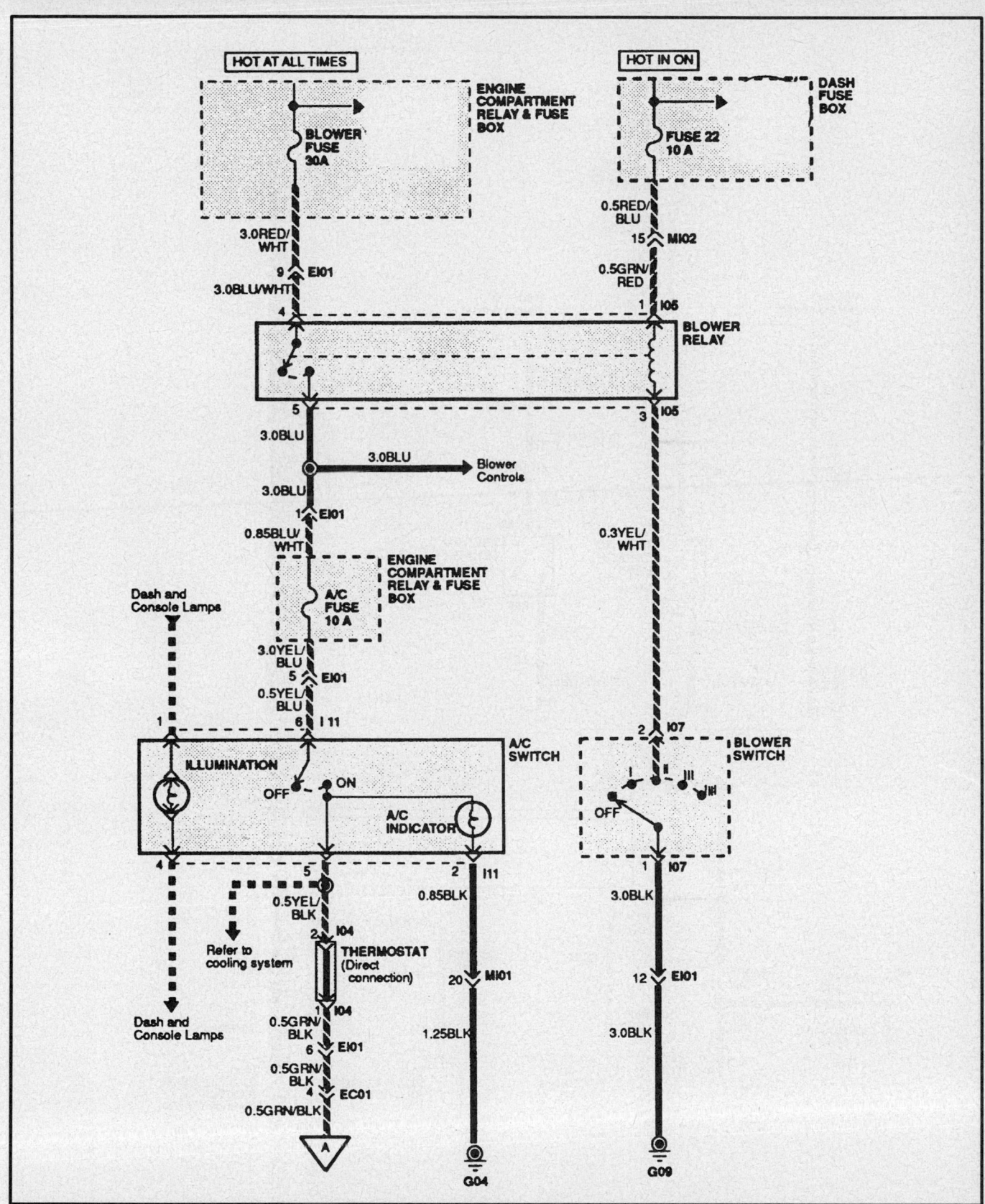

Air conditioning compressor control wiring schematic—1995 Sonata

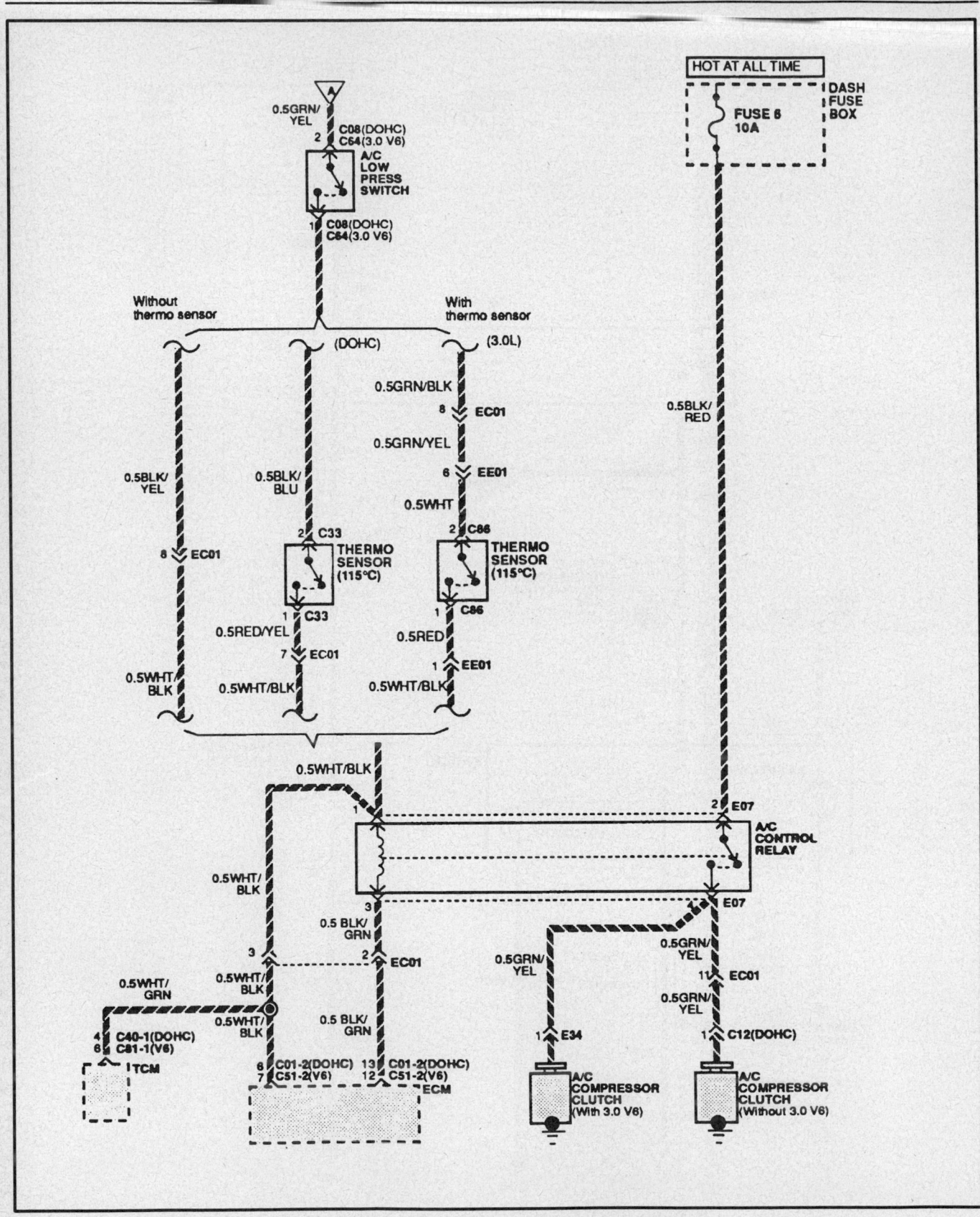

Air conditioning compressor control wiring schematic—1995 Sonata continued

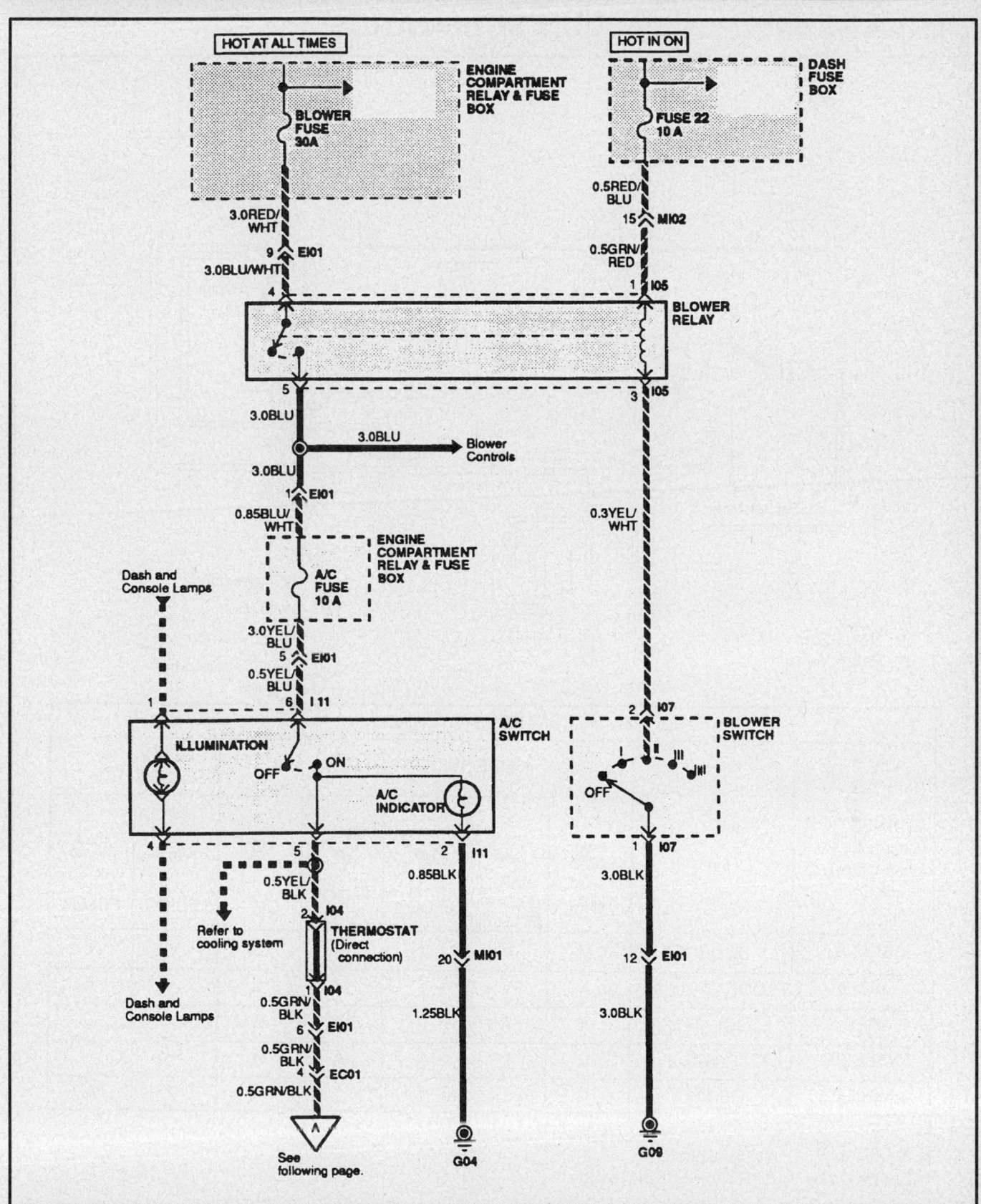

Air conditioning compressor control wiring schematic—1995 Sonata continued

VACUUM SCHEMATICS

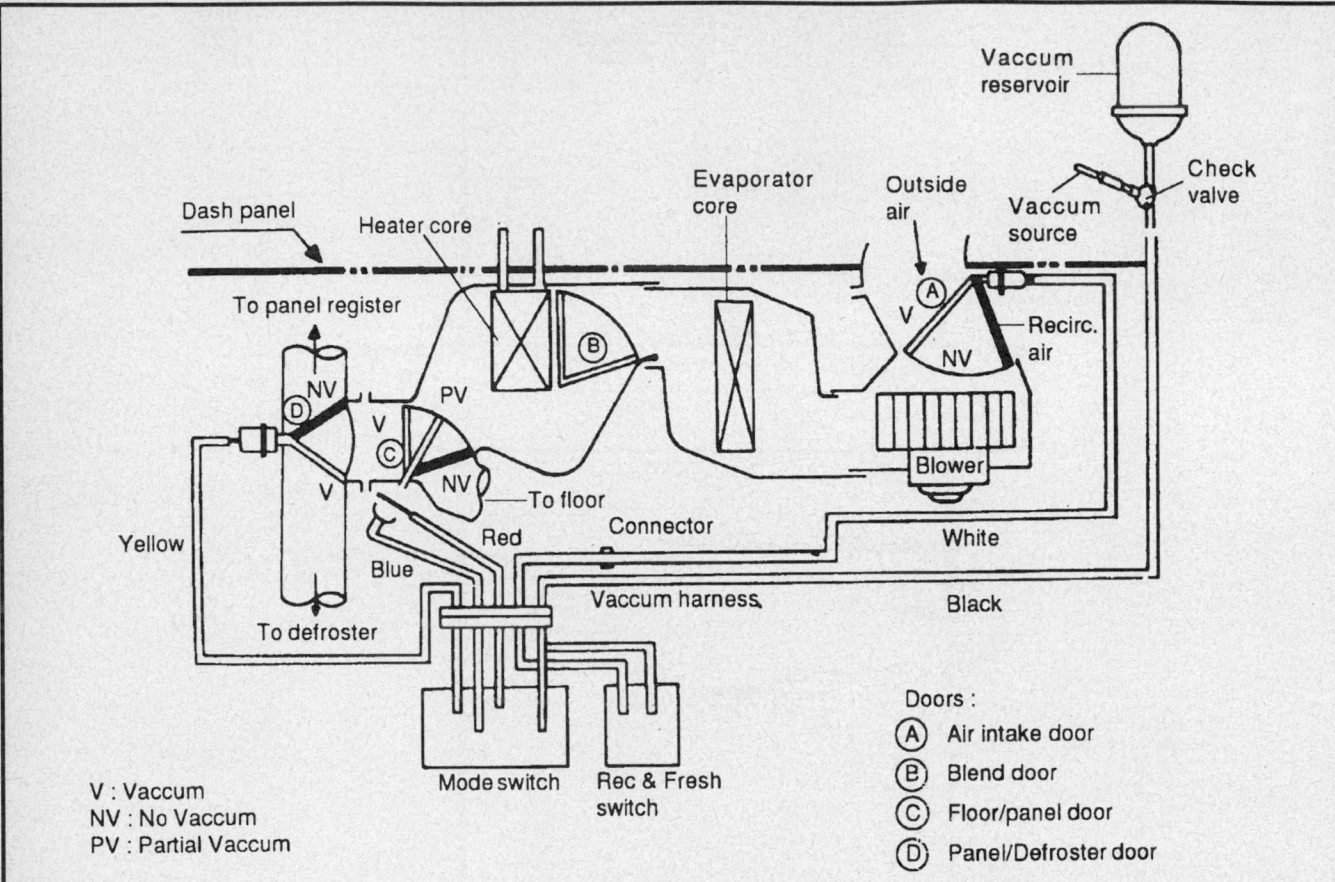

V : Vaccum
NV : No Vaccum
PV : Partial Vaccum

Doors :
(A) Air intake door
(B) Blend door
(C) Floor/panel door
(D) Panel/Defroster door

CONNECTION (Vacuum Hose Color)	FUNCTION	MODE SWITCH BUTTON					FRESH/ REC-BUTTON	
		PANEL	PANEL FLOOR (BI-LEVEL)	FLOOR	FLOOR DEF	DEF.	RECIRC.	FRESH
BLACK	SOURCE	V	V	V	V	V	V	V
BLUE	FLOOR (PARTIAL)	A	V	V	V	A	-	-
RED	FLOOR (FULL)	A	A	V	A	A	-	-
YELLOW	PANEL	V	V	A	A	A	-	-
WHITE	RECIRC	*	*	*	*		V	A

V=Vacuum   A=Atmosphere
*=Controlled by "RECIRC" or "FRESH" button.

Vacuum schematic — 1994-95 Scoupe and 1995 Accent

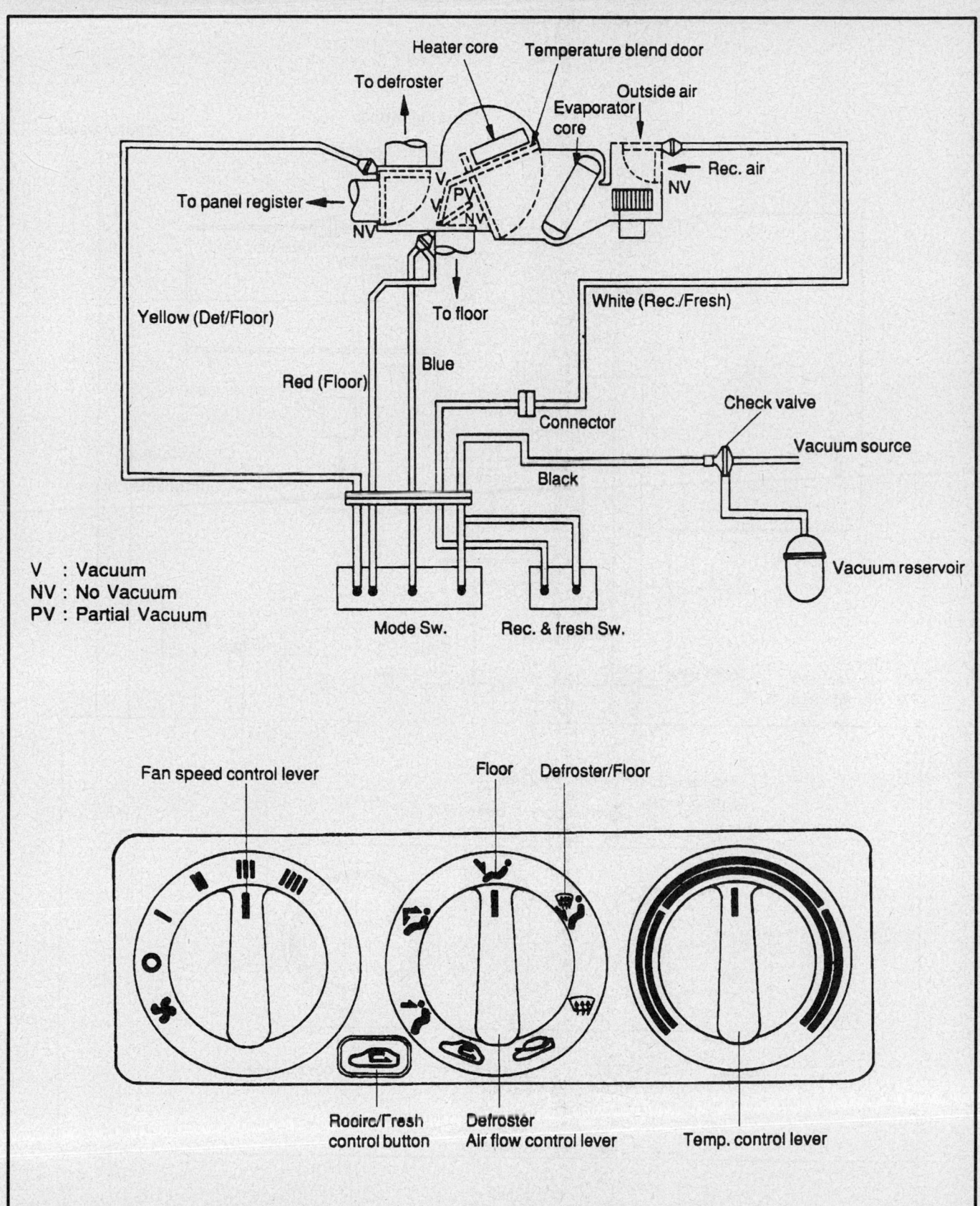

Vacuum schematic — 1994-95 Elantra

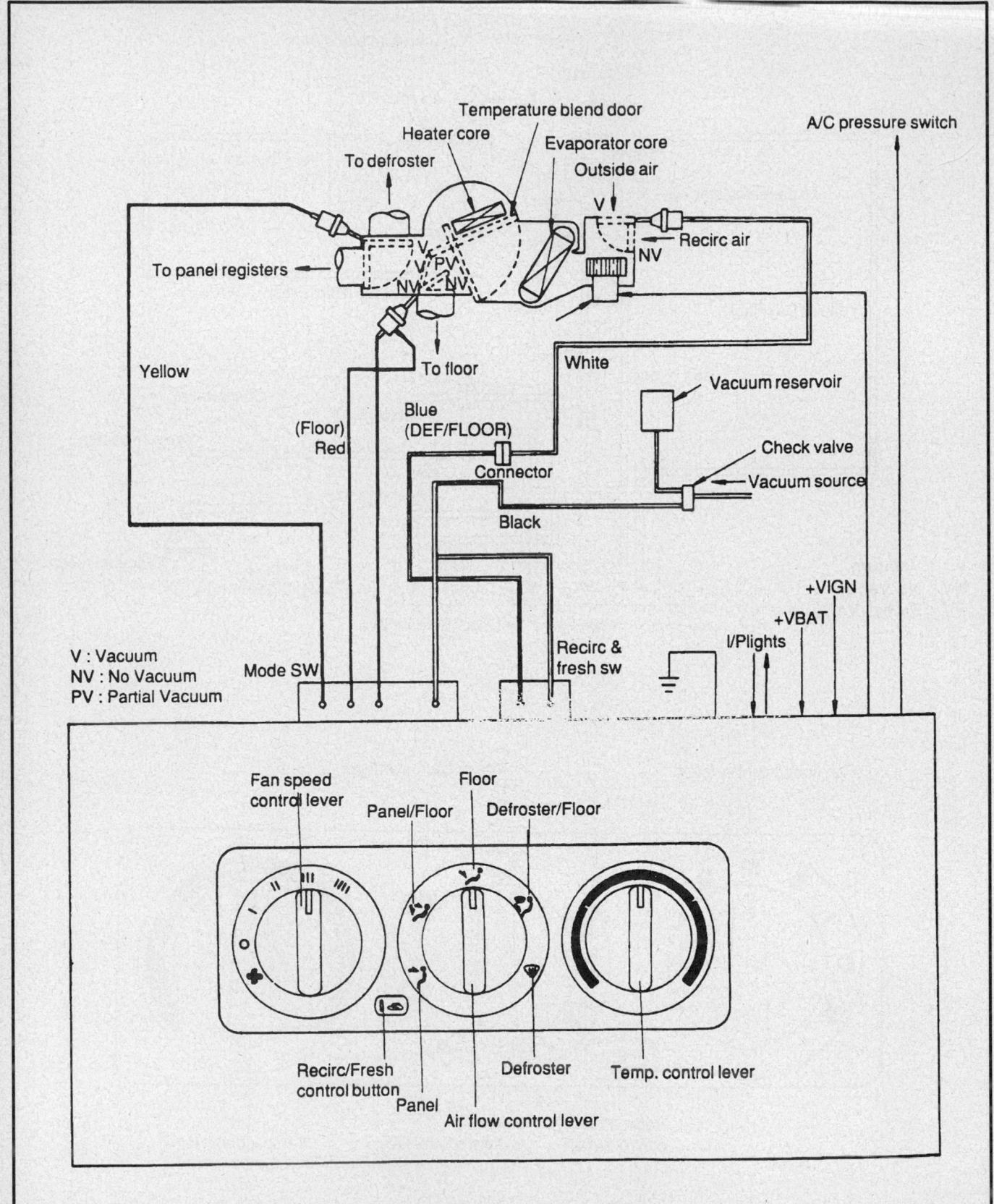

Vacuum schematic — 1994 Excel

SPECIFICATIONS

ENGINE IDENTIFICATION

Year	Model	Engine Displacement Liters (cc)	Engine Series Identification	Fuel System	No. of Cylinders	Engine Type
1993	Q45	4.5 (4494)	VH45DE(N)	MPFI	8	DOHC
	G20	2.0 (1998)	SR20DE(C)	MPFI	4	DOHC
	J30	3.0 (2960)	VG30DE(A)	MPFI	6	DOHC
1994	Q45	4.5 (4494)	VH45DE(N)	MPI	8	DOHC
	G20	2.0 (1998)	SR20DE(C)	MPI	4	DOHC
	J30	3.0 (2960)	VG30DE(A)	MPI	6	DOHC
1995	Q45	N/A	N/A	N/A	N/A	N/A
	G20	N/A	N/A	N/A	N/A	N/A
	J30	3.0 (2960)	VG30DE(Y)	MPI	6	DOHC

N/A – Not Available

REFRIGERANT CAPACITIES

Year	Model	Refrigerant (oz.)	Oil (fl. oz.)	Compressor Type
1993	G20	24.7-28.1	6.8	NVR140S
	Q45	38.9-42.5	8.0	V-5
	J30①	24.6-26.4①	8.5①	V-6①
1994	Q45①	26.7-29.1	6.8	V-6
	G20①	24.7-28.2	6.8	DW-14C
	J30①	24.7-28.2	8.5	V-6
1995	Q45①	N/A	N/A	N/A
	G20①	N/A	N/A	N/A
	J30①	24.7-28.2	8.5	V-6

① Uses refrigerant 134A and equipment
  oil not compatible with R12.
N/A – Not Available

AIR CONDITIONING BELT TENSION

Year	Model	Engine Liters (cc)	Belt Type	Specifications New (lbs)	Specifications Used (lbs)
1993	G20	2.0 (1998)	Poly-V	0.26-0.30	0.28-0.31
	Q45	4.5 (4494)	Poly-V	0.30-0.33	0.34-0.37
	J30	3.0 (2960)	Poly-V	0.30-0.33	0.34-0.37
1994	G20	2.0 (1998)	Poly V	0.28-0.31	0.31-0.35
	Q45	4.5 (4494)	Poly V	0.29-0.33	0.33-0.37
	J30	3.0 (2960)	Poly V	0.29-0.33	0.33-0.37
1995	G20	N/A	N/A	N/A	N/A
	Q45	N/A	N/A	N/A	N/A
	J30	3.0 (2960)	Poly V	0.29-0.33	0.33-0.37

N/A – Not Available

SYSTEM DESCRIPTION

General Information

On models using a manually operated air conditioning system, controls are with push–button mode operations and lever–controlled temperature setting. Fan speed is controlled by either a knob type function switch or a lever selector switch. The system uses typical blend–air type heater and air conditioning components and air distribution. All air doors, except the temperature blend door, are driven by electric motors with linkage connections to the doors.

On automatic air conditioning systems, the temperature lever is replaced by an "increase" or "decrease" temperature button which then shows the selected temperature on the control panel LED display. Self diagnostic readouts are available through the control panel display. The automatic system uses the same basis air conditioning and heating components as the manual system.

Both systems use a series of switches, sensors and relays to monitor and control component functions:

• A dual pressure switch guards against extremely high or low system pressures.

• An A/C relay energizes the compressor when the A/C switch is depressed.

• A compressor thermal protector (manual system only) cuts off compressor operation at high system temperatures.

• A thermocontrol amplifier and thermistor (manual A/C only) monitors temperatures of the evaporator.

• A fast idle control device (FICD) to maintain engine idle when A/C is engaged.

• A blower relay to energize the blower motor when the blower switch is set to any **ON** position.

• Radiator and condenser fan relays to control cooling fan operations based on engine temperatures.

• An ambient temperature sensor, sun load sensor, in–vehicle sensor, and intake air sensor (auto A/C systems only) to sense various temperature conditions to control heating or cooling operations automatically.

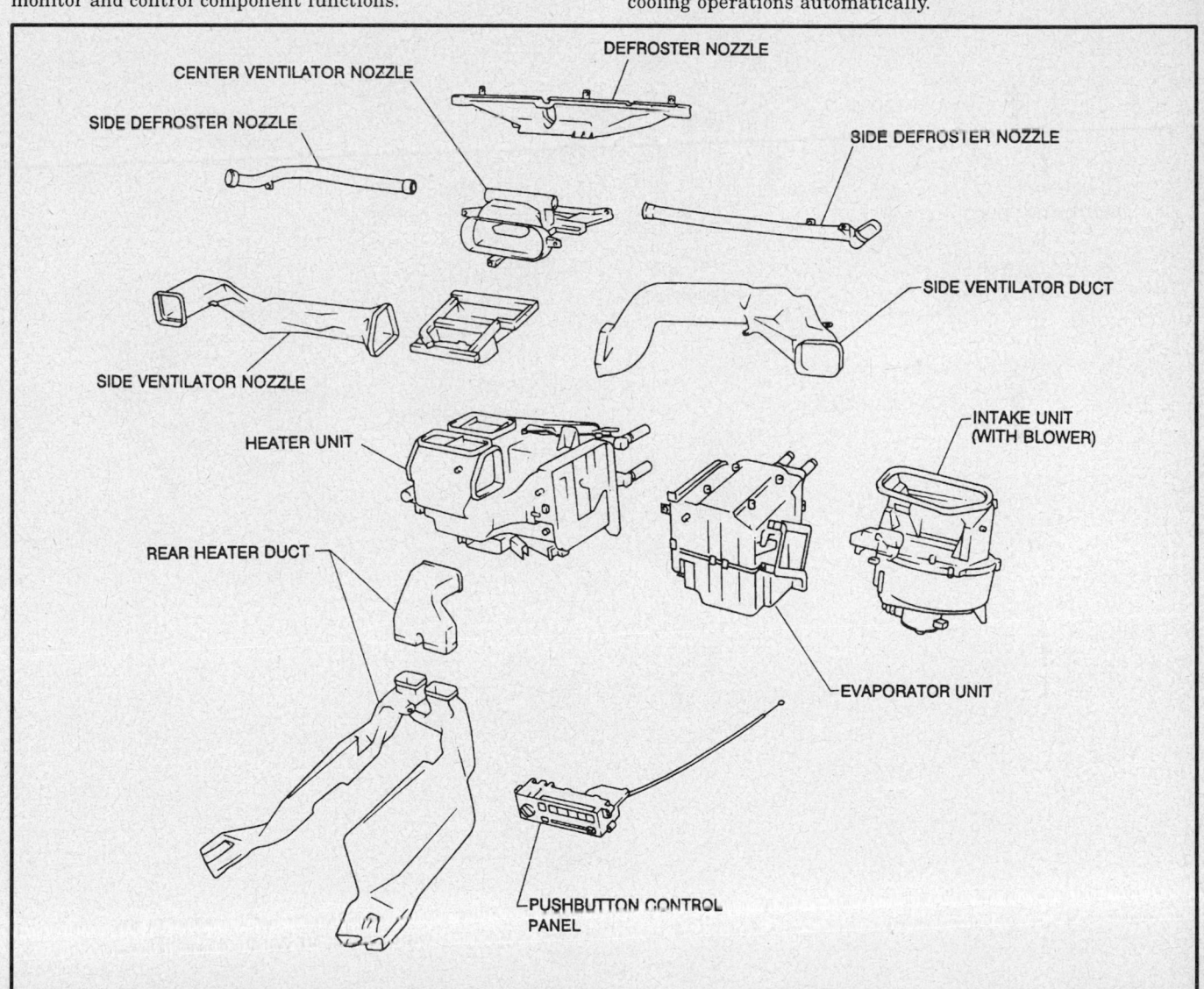

Heater–air conditioning system component layout – G20

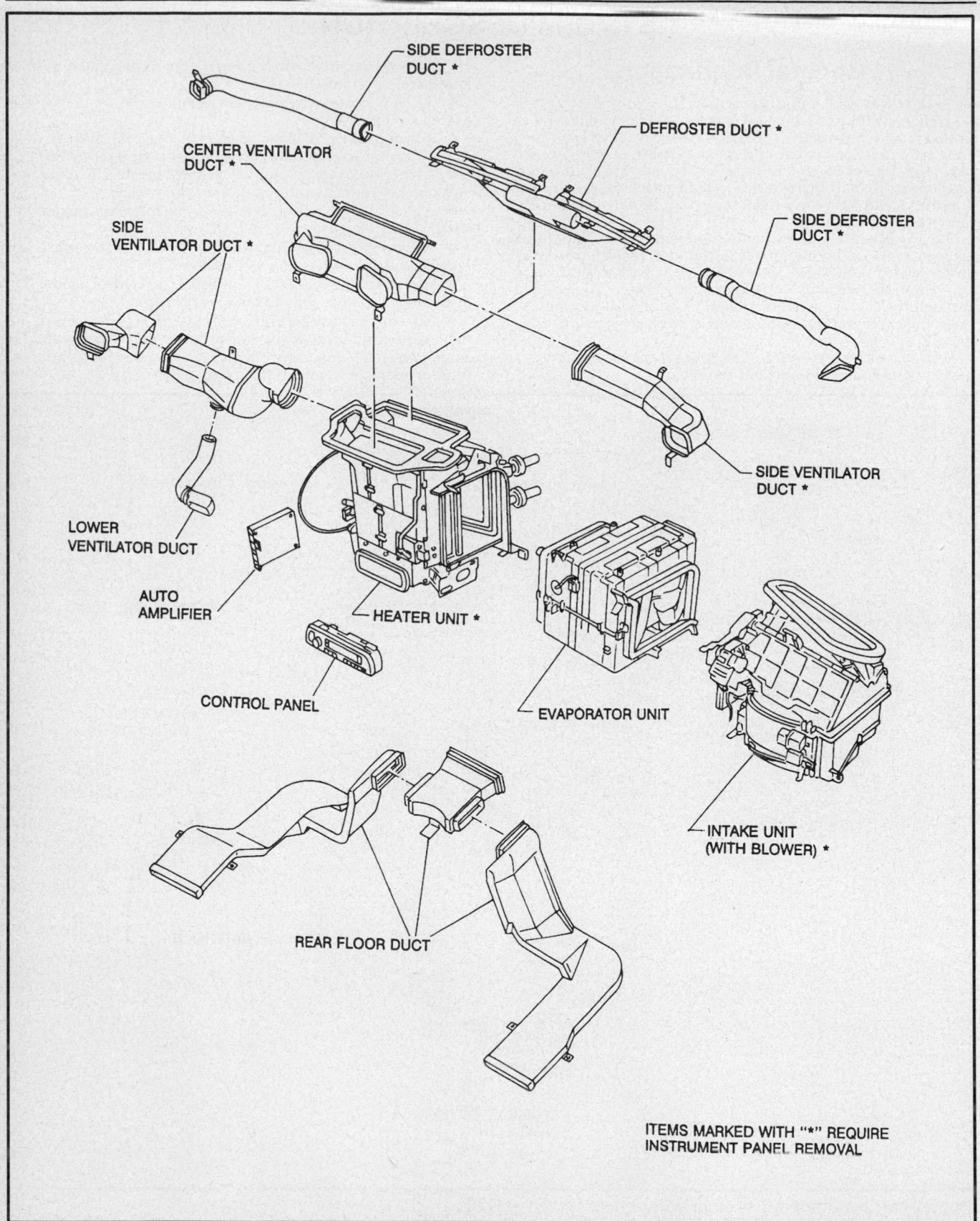

SIDE DEFROSTER DUCT *

CENTER VENTILATOR DUCT *

DEFROSTER DUCT *

SIDE VENTILATOR DUCT *

SIDE DEFROSTER DUCT *

SIDE VENTILATOR DUCT *

LOWER VENTILATOR DUCT

AUTO AMPLIFIER

HEATER UNIT *

CONTROL PANEL

EVAPORATOR UNIT

INTAKE UNIT (WITH BLOWER) *

REAR FLOOR DUCT

ITEMS MARKED WITH "*" REQUIRE INSTRUMENT PANEL REMOVAL

Heater−air conditioning system component layout − J30

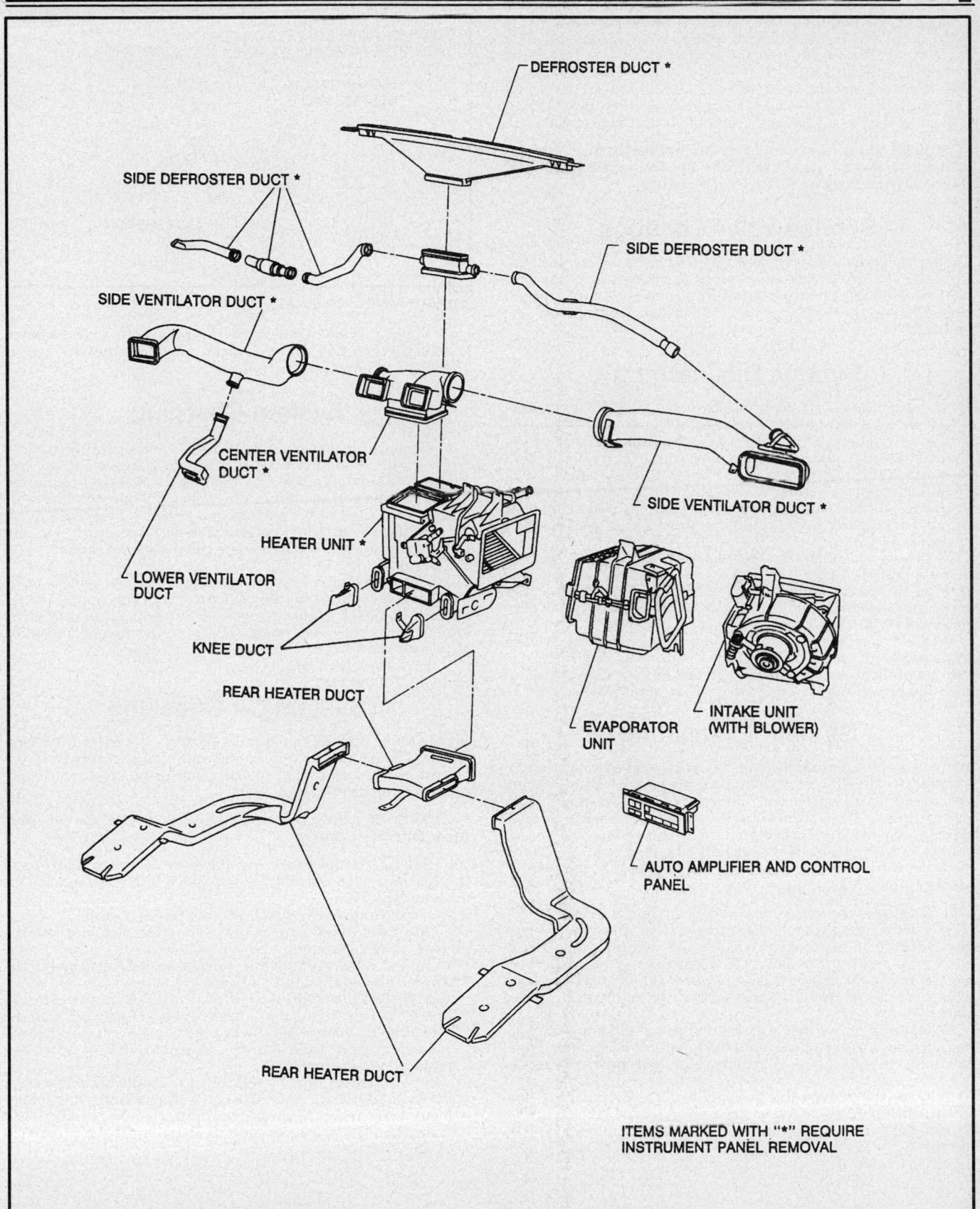

DEFROSTER DUCT *

SIDE DEFROSTER DUCT *

SIDE DEFROSTER DUCT *

SIDE VENTILATOR DUCT *

CENTER VENTILATOR DUCT *

SIDE VENTILATOR DUCT *

HEATER UNIT *

LOWER VENTILATOR DUCT

KNEE DUCT

EVAPORATOR UNIT

INTAKE UNIT (WITH BLOWER)

REAR HEATER DUCT

AUTO AMPLIFIER AND CONTROL PANEL

REAR HEATER DUCT

ITEMS MARKED WITH "*" REQUIRE INSTRUMENT PANEL REMOVAL

Heater−air conditioning system component layout − Q45

A RECIRC button allows outside air to be cut off and interior air recirculated for maximum cooling or when outside air is not desired. The switch does not work when DEF or F/D (floor/defrost) is selected.

R–134a refrigerant is used in 1993 J30 and all 1994 and 1995 models. It is a non–CFC refrigerant and requires its own dedicated service equipment, components and refrigeration oil.

NOTE: Do not mix directly or indirectly any amount of R–12 or R–12 type oil with the R–134a system. Component malfunction or failure may result.

Service Valve Location

The suction valve is located on the low pressure line near the firewall. The discharge service valve is located near the firewall on the high pressure outlet line from the evaporator on the G20 or on the discharge line near the condenser on the J30 and Q45.

System Discharging

R–12 refrigerant is a chlorofluorocarbon which, when mishandled, can contribute to the depletion of the ozone layer in the upper atmosphere. Ozone filters out harmful radiation from the sun. Inorder to protect the ozone layer, an approved R–12 Recovery/Recycling machine that meets SAE standard J1991 should be employed when discharging the system. Follow the operating instructions provided with the approved equipment exactly to properly discharge the system. Never vent R–12 to the atmosphere.

R–134a, a non–chlorofluorocarbon (non–CFC) is used in 1993 J30 and 1994–95 G20, J30 and Q45 systems. It also requires the use of special recovery/recycling equipment. This equipment must be dedicated to R–134a, as the system is not compatible with R–12.

Different size service valve fittings may be used on R–134a systems to eliminate the possibility of intermixing R–12 service equipment on an R–134a system. Follow the equipment manufacturer's instructions for R–134a applications.

System Evacuating

If the air conditioning system has been opened to the atmosphere, it should be air and moisture free before being recharged with refrigerant. Moisture and air mixed with refrigerant will raise the compressor head pressure, possibly damage the system's components and will reduce the performance of the system. Moisture will boil at normal room temperature when exposed to a vacuum. To evacuate the system, perform the following procedure:

1. Leak test the system and repair any leaks found.
2. Connect an approved charging station, Recovery/Recycling machine or manifold gauge set and vacuum pump to the discharge and suction ports. The red hose is normally connected to the discharge (high pressure) service valve and the blue hose is connected to the suction (low pressure) service valve.
3. Open the discharge and suction ports and start the vacuum pump. If the pump is not able to pull at least 26 in. Hg of vacuum, there is a leak that must be repaired before evacuation can occur.
4. Once the system has reached at least 26 in. Hg of vacuum, allow the system to evacuate for at least 10 minutes. The longer the system is evacuated, the more contaminants will be removed.

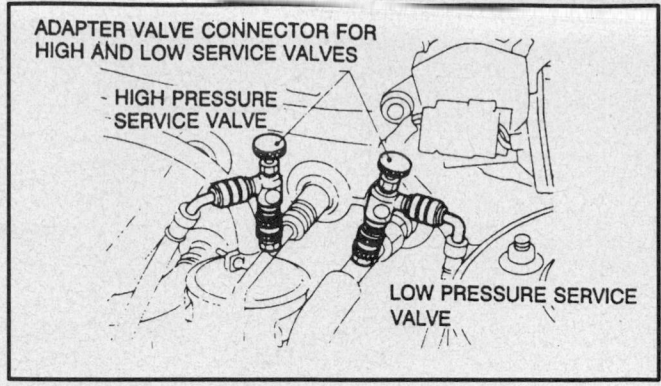

Service valve locations – G20

5. Close all valves and turn the pump off. If the system loses more than 2 in. Hg of vacuum after 15 minutes, there is a leak that should be repaired.

System Charging

1. Connect an approved R–12 or R–134a charging station, Recovery/Recycling machine or manifold gauge set to the discharge and suction ports. The red hose is normally connected to the discharge (high pressure) service valve and the blue hose is connected to the suction (low pressure) service valve.
2. Follow the instructions provided with the equipment and charge the system with the specified amount and type of refrigerant.
3. Note the manifold gauge readings. Normal system operating pressures are 199–256 psi for the high side and 21–43 psi for the low side. Systems using R–134a readingswill be slightly lower). Also check the system sight glass for proper indication of refrigerant charge.
4. Perform a leak test.

System Oil Checking

If possible to operate the system, perform the following procedure to ensure the maximum amount of oil is returned to the compressor before removing the compressor or other components for repair or replacement:

NOTE: If excessive oil leakage is noted, do not perform this procedure.

1. Set A/C temperature control lever to full **COLD**, push the A/C switch to **ON**, set the fan speed to **HIGH** and the air mode to **RECIR**.
2. Operate the engine at 1200 rpm for 10 minutes.
3. After the compressor is removed, drain and measure the amount of oil remaining.
4. Adjust the amount of new refrigerant oil furnished in the replacement compressor as follows:
   a. NVR140S compressor: If oil drained from the old compressor is less than 3.0 oz., drain 3.0 oz. of new oil from the replacement compressor. If the oil drained from the old compressor is more than 3.0 oz., drain only 0.7 oz. from the replacement compressor.
   b. V–5 compressor: If oil drained from the old compressor is less than 3.2 oz., drain 0.7 oz. of new oil from the replacement compressor. If oil drained from the old compressor is more than 3.2 oz., drain only 5.1oz. from the replacement compressor.

c. V–6 compressor: Check quantity of oil recovered with recycling equipment. Add that amount to the measured amount of oil drained from the old compressor. Drain the oil from the new compressor and measure out a quantity equal to the recovered amount and old compressor amount, plus 0.2 oz. of new oil should then be put into new compressor.

5. When replacing components on G20, J30, and Q45 systems, add new oil as follows:
- 2.5 oz. if replacing the evaporator
- 2.5 oz. if replacing the condenser
- 0.2 oz. if replacing the accumulator
- 1.0 oz. if repairing a large leak

Air Bag Information

All Supplemental Restraint System ("air bag") wiring harnesses and connectors are covered with yellow outer insulation. Do not use electrical test equipment on any circuit related to the air bag system.

If vehicle is equipped with an air bag, before servicing any component which may required removal of key instrument panel components or may jar the air bag system, be sure the air bag is disabled.

1. Turn the ignition switch to **OFF** position. Disconnect the negative battery cable.
2. Wait 10 minutes before attempting component removal inside the vehicle, as the air bag can still be deployed for this period of time.
3. After the appropriate component installation or repairs are completed, reconnect the negative battery cable. Turn the ignition switch to the **ON** or **START** position. Note the "Air Bag" indicator light, it should be on for about 7 seconds, meaning the system is properly operational.

SYSTEM COMPONENTS

Radiator

REMOVAL AND INSTALLATION

G20

1. Disconnect the negative battery cable.

NOTE: If equipped with an air bag, wait 10 minutes before starting component removal to ensure air bag is fully disabled.

2. Properly drain the cooling system.
3. Remove the upper radiator hose.
4. If equipped with automatic transmission, remove and plug the oil cooler hoses.
5. Disconnect the electrical fan connector.
6. Remove the lower radiator hose.
7. Remove the fan shroud and fan assembly.
8. Remove the reservoir tank. Remove 2 upper radiator mounting screws and lift the radiator out of the 2 lower mounting rubber insulators.
9. To install, reverse the removal procedure.

J30, Q45

1. Disconnect the negative battery cable. Remove the engine under cover.

NOTE: If equipped with an air bag, wait 10 minutes before starting component removal to ensure air bag is fully disabled.

2. Properly drain the cooling system.
3. Disconnect the upper and lower radiator hoses.
4. Remove the automatic transmission cooling hoses, if equipped. Plug hoses and openings to prevent leakage.
5. Remove the lower radiator shroud.
6. Remove the intake air duct.
7. Disconnect the reservoir hose from the radiator.
8. Remove the radiator mounting bolts, disconnect electrical connections for the thermoswitch on the bottom of the radiator, and lift out the radiator.
9. Installation is the reverse of the removal procedure.

COOLING SYSTEM BLEEDING

G20 (J30, Q45 Automatic Bleed)

1. Set the temperature lever to maximum heat position. Remove the radiator cap, air relief plug, and the air bleeder cap.
2. Fill the radiator and reservoir tank with coolant (fill the reservoir to the MAX line). Install the air relief plug when coolant begins to spill from the air relief opening.
3. Reinstall the air bleeder cap. Install a temporary radiator cap, with a steel wire placed as shown, to divert all air and coolant into the reservoir tank.
4. Warm the engine to normal operating temperature. Run the engine up to 2500 rpm for 10 seconds and return to idle. Repeat 2 or 3 more times.
5. Stop the engine and let it cool (use an auxiliary fan if needed to speed cooling time).
6. Remove the temporary radiator cap. If coolant level is down, add more up to the radiator filler neck and to the MAX reservoir line. Repeat steps 4 through 6 two to three more times to be sure coolant level is stabilized and air is out of the system.
7. Install the proper radiator cap. Warm the engine and check for proper coolant flow (listen at the heater water valve as temperature lever is moved to several heat positions). Run the engine to high rpm as needed to maximize coolant flow.
8. If noise is heard at the water valve, air remains in the system and must be bled as follows:
   a. Cool the engine down and remove the air bleeder cap on the heater inlet hose.
   b. Attach a transparent hose to the bleeder pipe and put the other end into the coolant of the reservoir tank.
   c. Install the temporary radiator cap. Be sure all hose connections are tight.
   d. Start the engine and watch for bubbles in the reservoir coolant. Move the temperature lever to maximum **COOL** to push coolant through the transparent hose.
   e. Run engine up to 2300 rpm until bubble disappear.
   f. Move the temperature lever to maximum **HOT** position and listen again at the water valve. If noise remains, repeat the process.
   g. Once bleeding is complete, stop the engine and let it cool. Carefully remove the transparent hose and temporary radiator cap. Install the bleeder cap and the proper radiator cap.

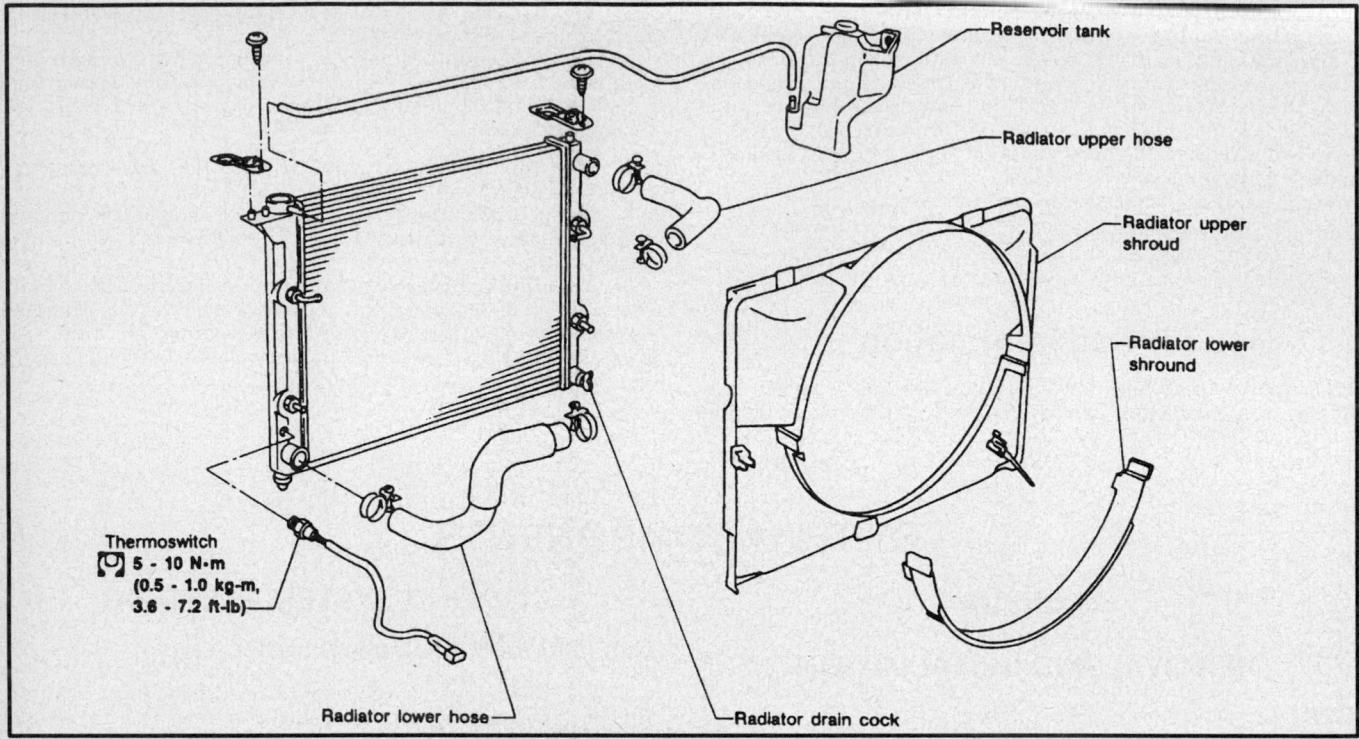

Exploded view of radiator components — Q45

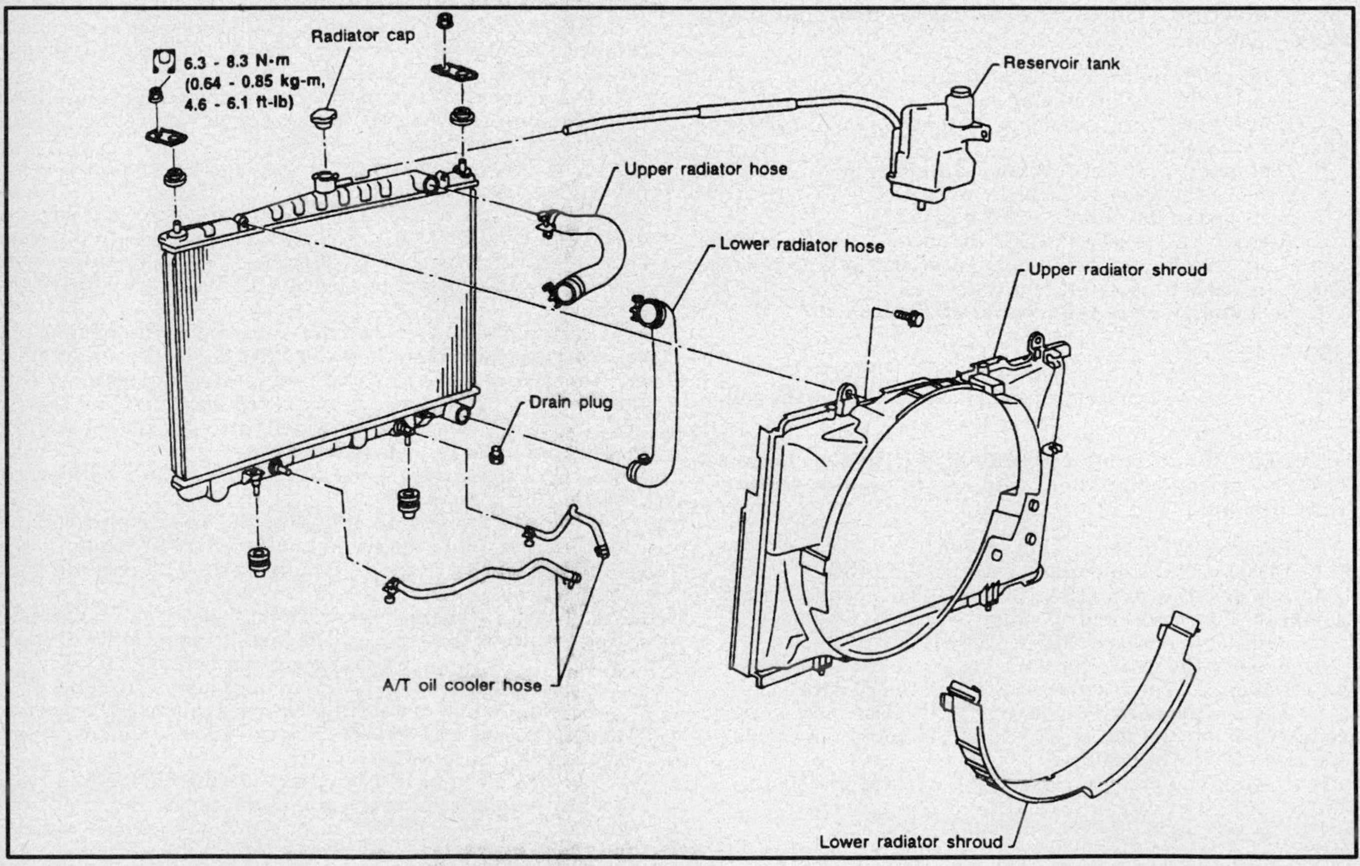

Exploded view of radiator components — J30

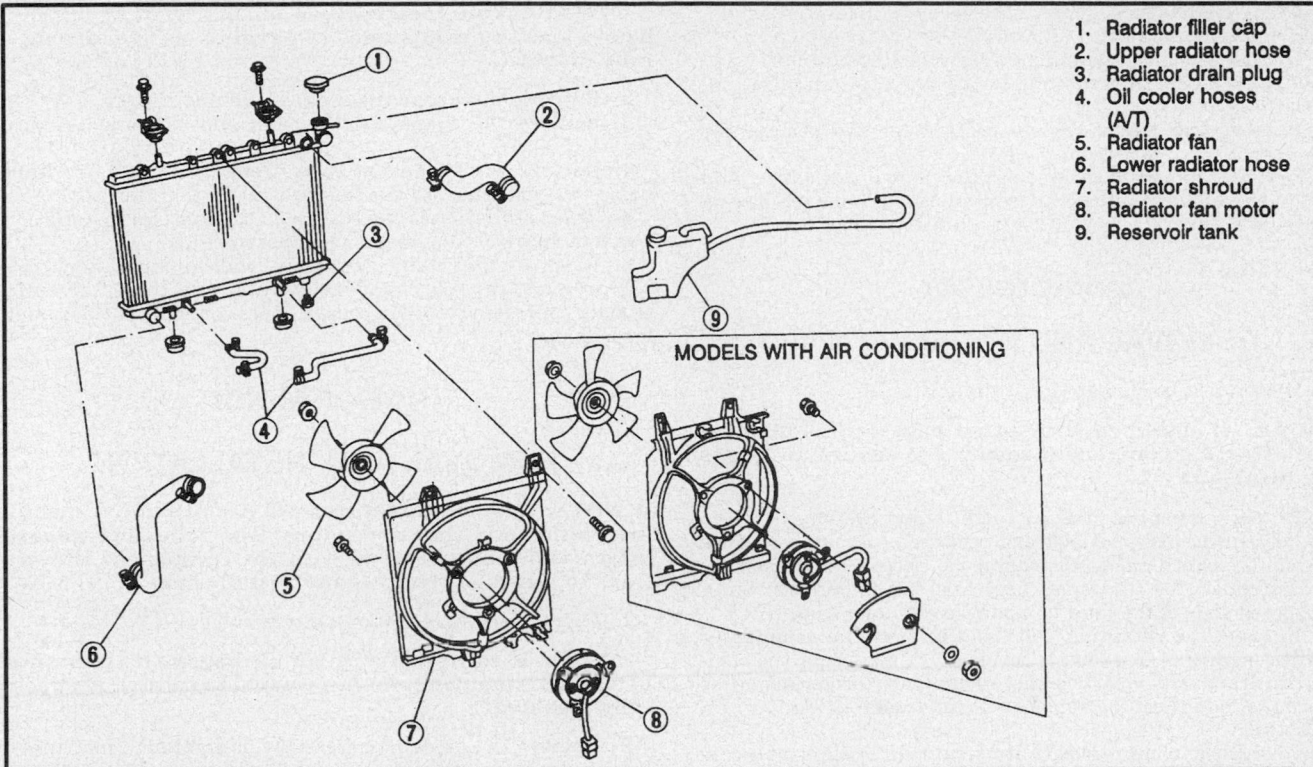

1. Radiator filler cap
2. Upper radiator hose
3. Radiator drain plug
4. Oil cooler hoses (A/T)
5. Radiator fan
6. Lower radiator hose
7. Radiator shroud
8. Radiator fan motor
9. Reservoir tank

MODELS WITH AIR CONDITIONING

Exploded view of radiator components – G20

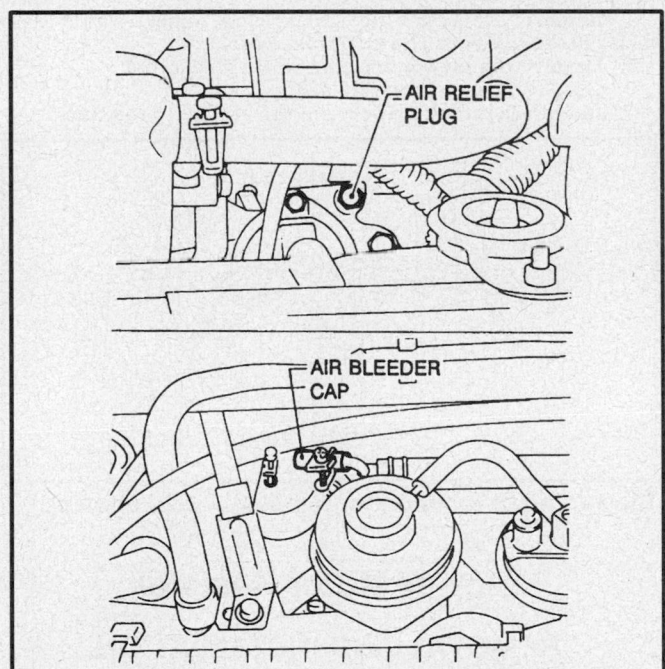

AIR RELIEF PLUG

AIR BLEEDER CAP

Location of air relief plug and air bleeder cap for cooling system bleeding – G20 shown

Cooling Fan

REMOVAL AND INSTALLATION

G20

1. Disconnect the negative battery cable.

NOTE: If equipped with an air bag, wait 10 minutes before starting component removal to ensure air bag is fully disabled.

2. Disconnect electric fan connector.
3. Remove fan and shroud mounting bolts and carefully lift fan and shroud assembly out of the vehicle.
4. Installation is the reverse of the removal procedure.

Condenser

REMOVAL AND INSTALLATION

NOTE: The manufacturer did not provide a specific instruction for this procedure. The following general information may be used with the component illustrations to assist in removal and installation.

1. Disconnect the negative battery cable.

NOTE: If equipped with an air bag, wait 10 minutes before starting component removal to ensure air bag is fully disabled.

2. Properly discharge the air conditioning system.
3. Remove the grille assembly or radiator, as necessary, to gain access to the condenser mounting screws and for removal access.
4. Remove the bracket holding the receiver/drier.

5. Using 2 wrenches, remove the receiver drier and adjoining refrigerant lines.

6. Disconnect any remaining refrigerant lines from the condenser. Cover the exposed ends of the lines to minimize contamination.

7. Remove the condenser mounting bolts and remove the condenser.

8. Installation is the reverse of the removal procedure. Add 1.0–1.7 oz. of new refrigerant oil to the condenser during installation. Install 2.5 oz. of oil if condenser is new.

Compressor

REMOVAL AND INSTALLATION

1. Disconnect the negative battery cable.

NOTE: If equipped with an air bag, wait 10 minutes before starting component removal to ensure air bag is fully disabled.

2. Properly discharge the air conditioning system.

3. Loosen the tensioner bolt and remove the compressor drive belt from the clutch pulley. Disconnect the electrical connector.

4. Disconnect the refrigerant lines from the compressor. Cover the exposed ends of the lines to minimize contamination.

5. Remove the retaining bolts and remove the compressor from its mounting bracket. If servicing or replacing the compressor, drain and measure the amount of refrigerant oil so the same amount can be replaced during installation.

To install:

6. Install the compressor to its mounting bracket and connect the connector.

7. Using new lubricated O-rings, connect the refrigerant lines to the compressor. Torque the retaining bolts to 1.2 ft. lbs. (12 Nm).

8. Wrap the drive belt around the pulley and adjust to specification.

9. Evacuate and recharge the air conditioning system. If the compressor was overhauled or replaced, be sure to adjust oil level during recharge.

10. Connect the negative battery cable and check the entire climate control system for proper operation and leaks.

Receiver/Drier

REMOVAL AND INSTALLATION

1. Disconnect the negative battery cable.
2. Properly discharge the air conditioning system.
3. Disconnect the refrigerant lines from the receiver/drier assembly. Cover the exposed ends of the lines to minimize contamination.
4. Remove the retaining clamp, the receiver/drier mounting bolts and remove the receiver/drier from the vehicle.
5. The installation is the reverse of the removal procedure.
6. Evacuate and recharge the air conditioning system. If the receiver/drier was replaced, add 0.5–0.8 oz. of refrigerant oil during the recharge.
7. Connect the negative battery cable and check the entire climate control system for proper operation and leaks.

Expansion Valve

REMOVAL AND INSTALLATION

1. Disconnect the negative battery cable.

NOTE: If equipped with an air bag, wait 10 minutes before starting component removal to ensure air bag is fully disabled.

2. Properly discharge the air conditioning system.
3. Remove the evaporator housing and separate the case halves.
4. Remove the expansion valve from the evaporator lines, using two wrenches on the flare nut fittings of the valve.
5. The installation is the reverse of the removal installation. Use new lubricated O-rings when assembling.
6. Evacuate and recharge the air conditioning system.
7. Connect the negative battery cable and check the entire climate control system for proper operation. Check the system for leaks.

Blower Motor

REMOVAL AND INSTALLATION

NOTE: The manufacturer did not provide a specific instruction for this procedure. The following general information may be used with the component illustrations to assist in removal and installation.

1. Disconnect the negative battery cable.

NOTE: If equipped with an air bag, wait 10 minutes before starting component removal to ensure air bag is fully disabled.

2. Remove the glove box assembly or right side instrument panel trim as needed for access to the blower motor.
3. Detach the cooling tube and the electrical connector from the blower motor.
4. Remove the retaining screws and remove the blower motor assembly from the air intake unit.
5. Remove the blower resistor block, if required.
6. Disassemble on a workbench.
7. Installation is the reverse of the removal procedure.

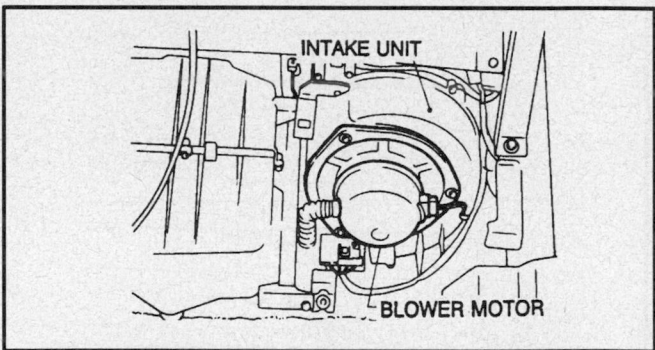

Blower motor location for removal — G20 shown

Blower Motor Resistor

REMOVAL AND INSTALLATION

1. Disconnect the negative battery cable.
2. Remove the blower motor assembly, if necessary.
3. Disconnect the wire harness from the resistor.
4. Remove the mounting screws and remove the resistor.
5. The installation is the reverse of the removal procedure.
6. Connect the negative battery cable and check for proper operation.

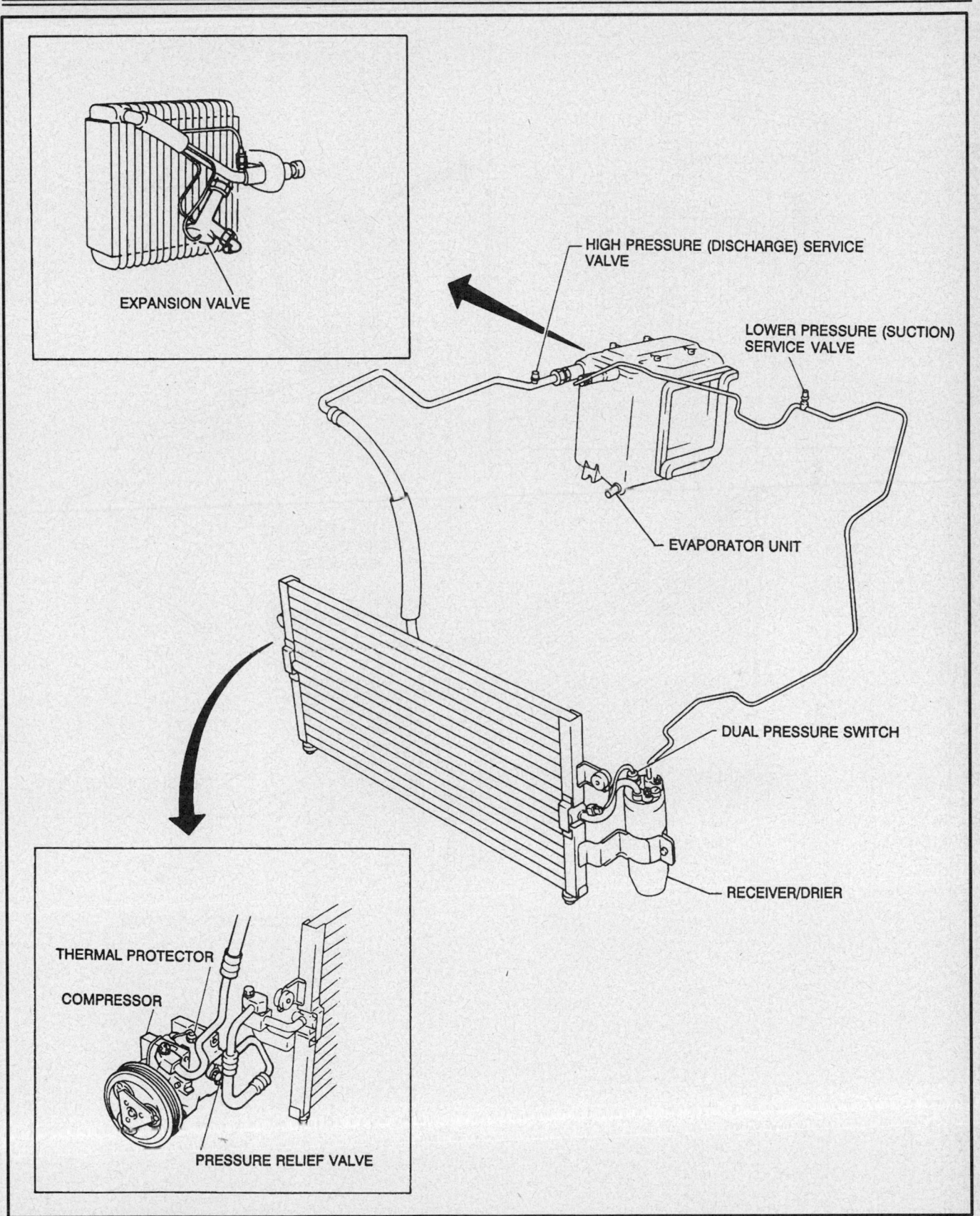

EXPANSION VALVE

HIGH PRESSURE (DISCHARGE) SERVICE VALVE

LOWER PRESSURE (SUCTION) SERVICE VALVE

EVAPORATOR UNIT

DUAL PRESSURE SWITCH

RECEIVER/DRIER

THERMAL PROTECTOR

COMPRESSOR

PRESSURE RELIEF VALVE

Refrigerant line routing — G20

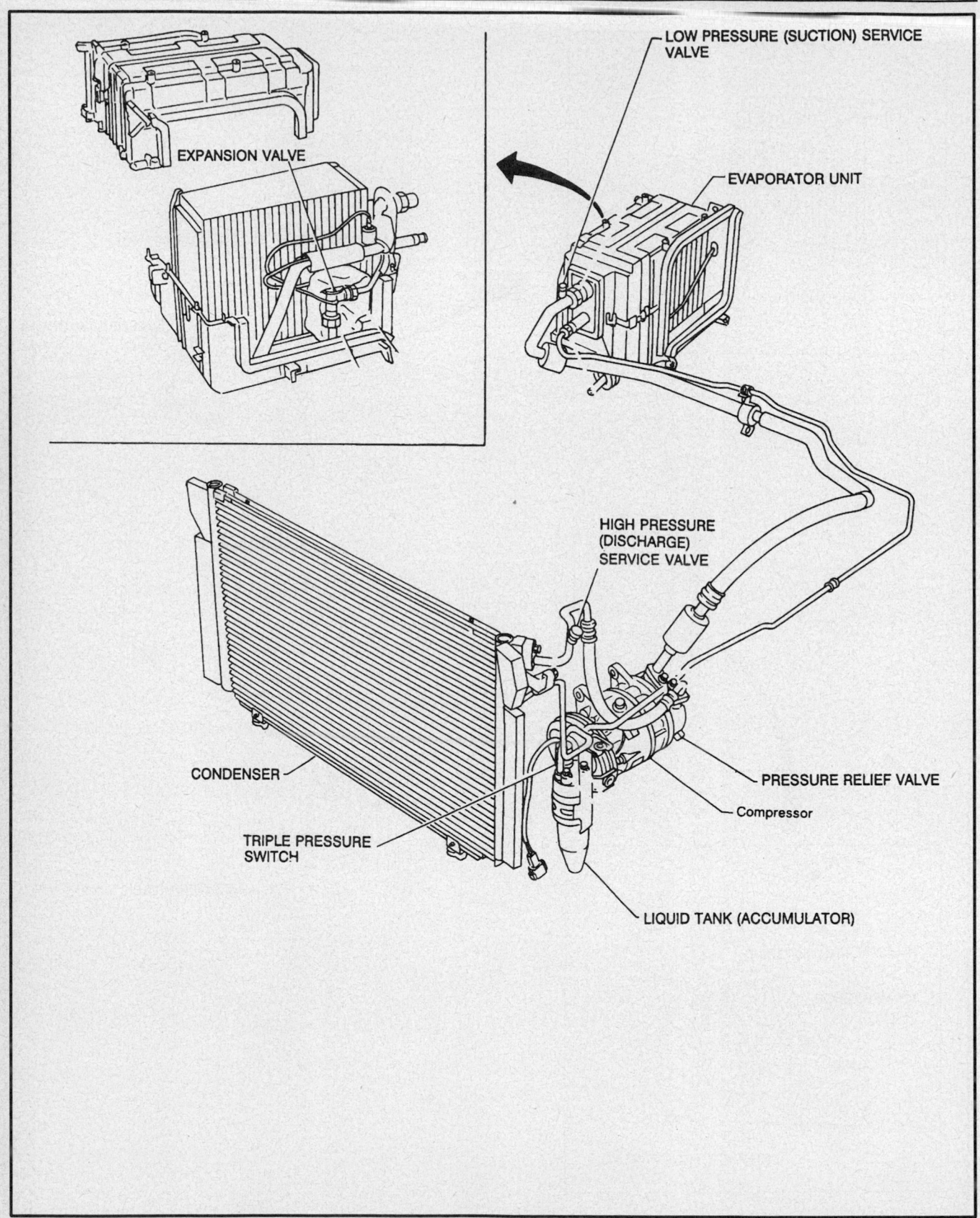

EXPANSION VALVE

LOW PRESSURE (SUCTION) SERVICE VALVE

EVAPORATOR UNIT

HIGH PRESSURE (DISCHARGE) SERVICE VALVE

CONDENSER

TRIPLE PRESSURE SWITCH

PRESSURE RELIEF VALVE

Compressor

LIQUID TANK (ACCUMULATOR)

Refrigerant line routing – J30

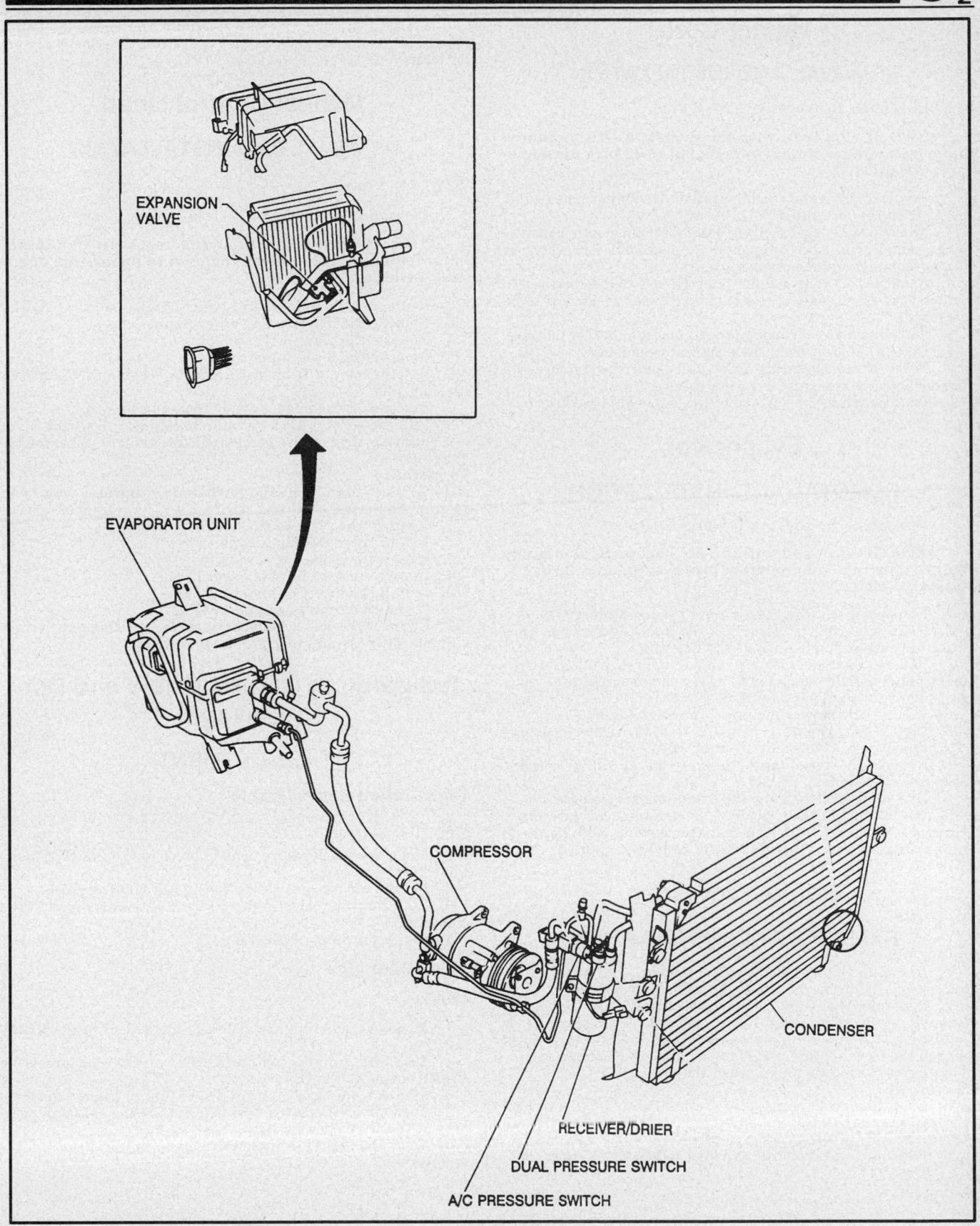

EXPANSION VALVE

EVAPORATOR UNIT

COMPRESSOR

CONDENSER

RECEIVER/DRIER

DUAL PRESSURE SWITCH

A/C PRESSURE SWITCH

Refrigerant line routing – Q45

Heater Core

REMOVAL AND INSTALLATION

1. Disconnect the negative battery cable.

NOTE: **If equipped with an air bag, wait 10 minutes before starting component removal to ensure air bag is fully disabled.**

2. Properly drain the cooling system. Disconnect the heater hoses from the core tubes.
3. Remove the center console assembly and/or other instrument panel trim and components as needed for access to heater housing and for removal clearance.
4. Remove the rear heater duct (it may be necessary to remove the front seats if the entire rear heater duct is to be removed).
5. Disconnect any electric connections from heater housing.
6. Detach the unit from the evaporator housing.
7. Remove the mounting nuts and bolts and remove the heater housing assembly from the vehicle.
8. Installation is the reverse of the removal procedure.

Evaporator

REMOVAL AND INSTALLATION

1. Disconnect the negative battery cable.

NOTE: **If equipped with an air bag, wait 10 minutes before starting component removal to ensure air bag is fully disabled.**

2. Properly discharge the air conditioning system.
3. Use 2 wrenches to disconnect the liquid and suction lines from the evaporator fittings at the firewall.
4. Remove the glove box assembly and/or any other instrument panel trim or components as needed to access the evaporator housing and for removal clearance.
5. Remove the blower motor/air intake assembly.
6. Detach the evaporator housing from the heater housing.
7. Remove the condensation drain hose.
8. Remove the retaining bolts and remove the evaporator case from the vehicle.
9. Disassemble evaporator case and remove evaporator.
10. Installation is the reverse of the removal procedure. Evacuate, recharge and leak test the system. Add 2.5 oz. of new refrigerant oil if the evaporator core was replaced.

Refrigerant Lines

REMOVAL AND INSTALLATION

1. Disconnect the negative battery cable.
2. Properly discharge the air conditioning system.
3. Separate the flare connection. Always use a backup wrench when separating flare connections. If the line is equipped with a sealing plate, remove the nuts or bolts that attach the lines sealing plates to the adjoining components.
4. Remove the line and discard the O-rings.
To install:
5. Coat the new O-rings refrigerant oil and install. Connect the refrigerant lines to the adjoining components and tighten the nuts, bolts or flare connections.
6. Evacuate and recharge the air conditioning system.

7. Connect the negative battery cable and check the entire climate control system for proper operation. Check the system for leaks.

Manual Control Head

REMOVAL AND INSTALLATION

G20

1. Disconnect the negative battery cable.

NOTE: **If equipped with an air bag, wait 10 minutes before starting component removal to ensure air bag is fully disabled.**

2. Remove the center control panel bezel.
3. Remove the driver's side lower panel.
4. Remove the glove box assembly.
5. Remove the 8 retaining screws.
6. Disconnect the temperature control cable at the heater housing side.
7. Disconnect the push-button harness connector.
8. Pull the control head out and disconnect all wiring.
9. Remove the control head from the vehicle. Disassemble as required.
To install:
10. Connect the wiring and push-button harness connector. Install the control head and secure with the retaining screws.
11. Connect the cable to the heater housing.
12. Install the retaining screws.
13. Install the glove box assembly.
14. Install the driver's side lower panel.
15. Install the driver's side lower panel.
16. Install the center control panel bezel.
17. Connect the negative battery cable and check the entire climate control system for proper operation.

Temperature Control Cable and Door Linkage

ADJUSTMENT

Temperature Control Cable

G20

1. Move the temperature control lever to the full **HOT** position.
2. Set the air mix door lever in the full **HOT** position.
3. Pull the outer cable in the director of the arrow, and then clamp it.
4. Check for proper operation.

Mode Door Link

G20

1. Move the side link and hold the mode door in the **VENT** position.
2. Turn the ignition switch to **ACC** or **ON** and press the VENT button to the **ON** position.
3. Attach mode door motor rod side link to the rod holder.
4. Turn the DEF switch **ON**. Check that the side link operates at the fully open position.
5. Turn the VENT switch **ON** again to check for proper operation.

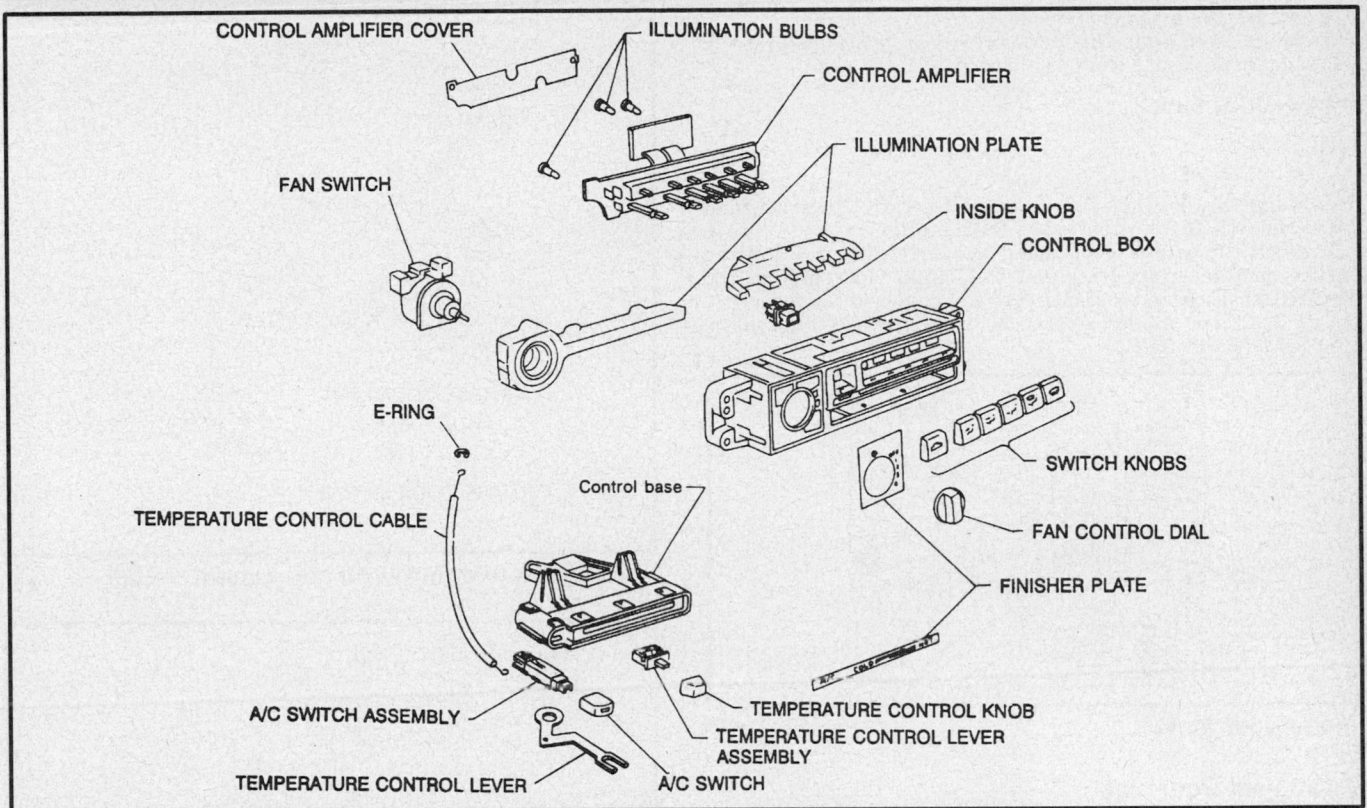

Disassembled view of the manual control head – G20

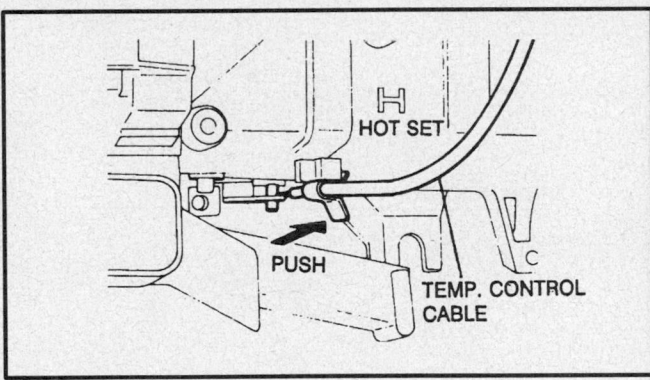

Temperature control cable adjustment

Mode Door

1994–95 J30, 1994 Q45

1. Install the mode door motor on heater unit and connect to the wire harness.
2. Set up code 41 in self diagnosis Step 4.
3. Move the side link by hand and hold the mode door in the vent mode.
4. Attach mode door motor rod to the side link rod holder.
5. Check that the mode door operates properly when changing codes from 41 through 46.

Air Mix Door

1994–95 J30, 1994 Q45

1. Install the air mix door motor on the heater unit and connect it to the wire harness.

2. Set up code 41 in self diagnosis Step 4.
3. On J30:
   a. Set the air mix door to the full cool position.
   b. Pull rod A toward the drivers side of the vehicle (full cold) and secure it to the rod holder.
   c. Set the air mix door to the full hot position.
   d. Push rod B toward the passenger side of the vehicle (full hot) and secure it to the rod holder.
4. On Q45:
   e. Move the air mix door lever by hand and hold it at full cold.
   f. Attach the air mix door lever to the rod holder.
5. On all models, make sure that the air mix door operates properly when the codes are changed from 41 through 46.

Water valve cable adjustment

1994–95 J30

1. Set up code 41 in self diagnosis Step 4.
2. Set the air mix door to full cool.
3. Pull the inner cable of the water valve control cable back and attach it to the link on the water valve. Clamp the outer cable to the housing.
4. Make sure that the cable moves freely with a clearance of .08–.12 in. (2–3mm) when the air door is set to full hot using either the air mix door control or by setting code 46 in step 4 of the self diagnosis.

Max. cold door

1994–95 J30

1. Install the max cold door motor on the heater unit and connect it to the wire harness.
2. Set up code 41 in self diagnosis Step 4.
3. Move the max cold door link by hand and hold it in the closed position.

4. Attach the max cold door lever to the rod holder.

5. Make sure that the max cold door operates properly when changing codes from 41 through 46.

Intake Door Link

G20

1. Turn the ignition switch to **ACC** or **ON** position, and press the RECIRC button to the **OFF** position.

2. With the intake door motor properly installed and the intake door lever in place, set the intake door link in the **FRESH** position and fasten rod to the holder of the lever.

3. Check for proper operation with RECIRC button is pressed **ON** and **OFF**.

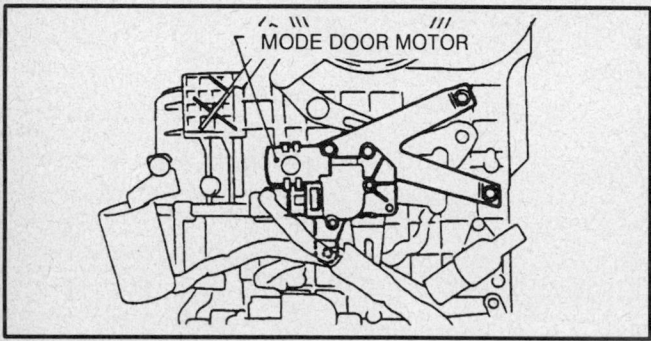

Mode door motor

Fresh Vent Door Link

G20

1. With the door motor harness connector properly attached, turn the ignition switch to the **ACC** position.

2. Turn the FRESH VENT switch to **OFF**.

3. Pull the shaft toward the link and pull the link outer casing toward the shaft, attach the link and clamp it in place.

4. Check for proper operation.

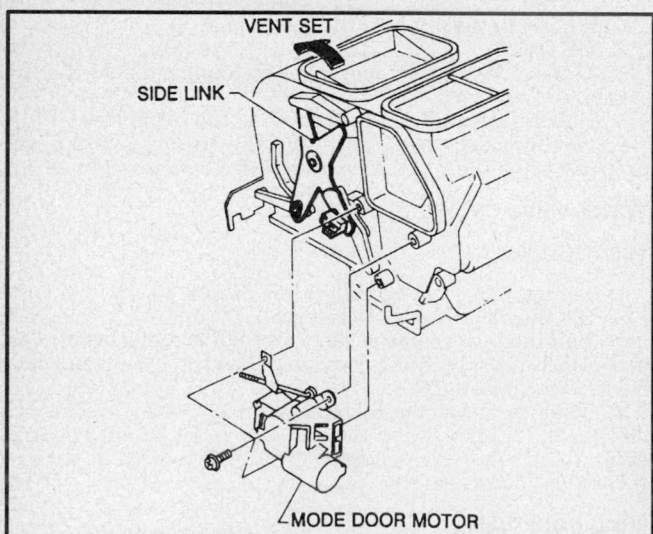

Vent door control rod adjustment – G20

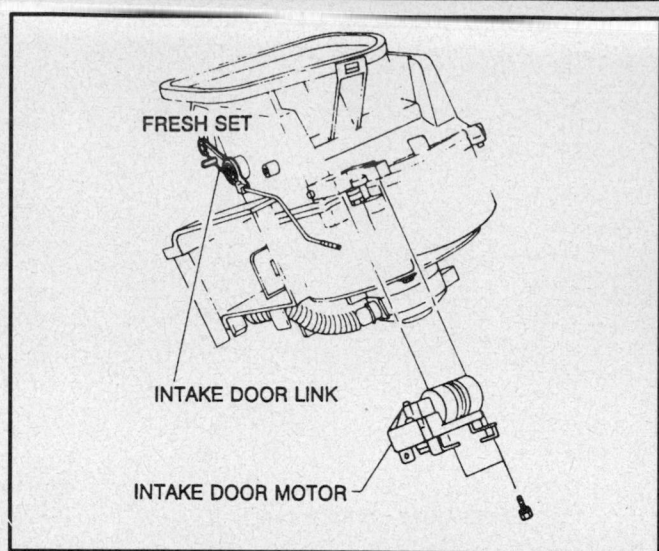

Fresh air door control rod adjustment – G20

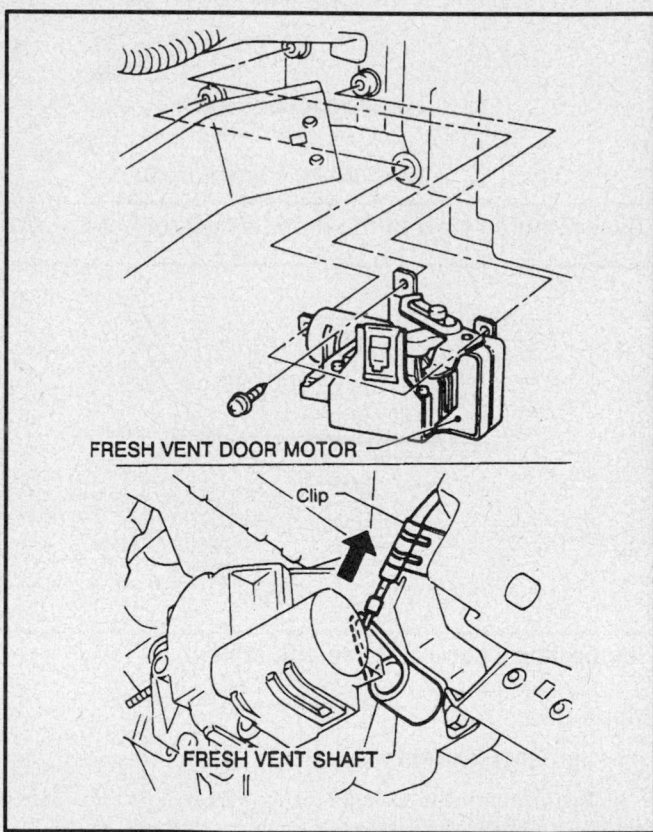

Fresh vent control rod adjustment – G20

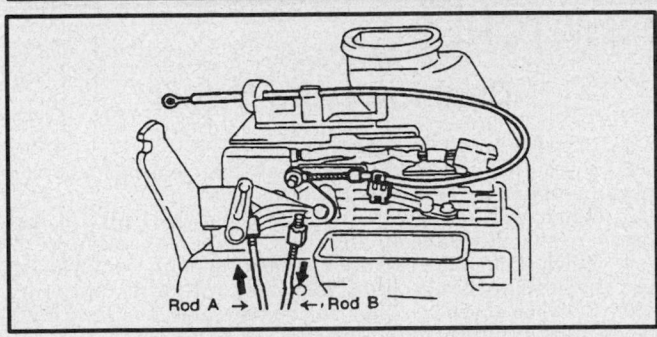

A and B water valve rods

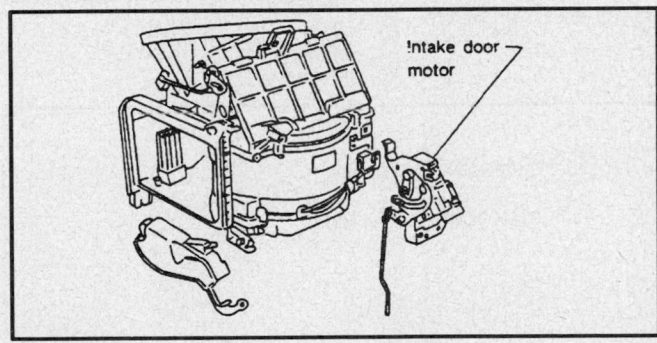

Air mix door motor

Intake door motor

	VENT	B/L1	B/L2	F/D1	F/D2	DEF
	41	42	43	44	45	46

Mode door codes

	FULL/COOL	FULL/COOL	FULL/HOT	FULL/HOT	FULL/HOT	FULL/HOT
	41	42	43	44	45	46

Air mix door codes — 1994 J30, 1994 Q45

	REC	20% FRE	20% FRE	80% FRE	FRESH	FRESH
	41	42	43	44	45	46

Intake door codes

Max. cold door motor

Max. cold door motor

41	42	43	44	45	46
Shut	Open		Shut		

Control linkage adjustment codes

8–17

SENSORS AND SWITCHES

NOTE: Refer to the appropriate wiring schematic for pin/terminal locations referenced in the following tests.

Thermo Control Amplifier

TESTING

G20

1. Run the engine and operate the A/C system.
2. Connect a voltmeter between terminal 59 and a body ground.
3. With panel outlet air at approximately 38°F (3°C), the thermo control amplifier should be **OFF** (12 volts). Above about 40°F (5°C), the thermo control amplifier should be **ON** (0 volts).
4. Using a suitable voltmeter, check the power supply circuit for the thermo control amplifier with the ignition switch ON.
5. Disconnect the thermo control amplifier harness connector. Connect the voltmeter from the harness side.
6. Measure the voltage across terminal 34 and body ground. There should be approximately 12 volts.
7. With the ignition switch **ON**, the A/C switch **ON** and the blower **ON** and the harness disconnected as above, attach an ohmmeter to harness side terminal 13 and the body ground.
8. There should be continuity.
9. If voltage or ohm readings were not as specified, check ground connections and condition of connector and wiring. If okay, replace thermo control amplifier.

NOTE: If the thermo control amplifier or the thermistor require removal, this can be done without removing the evaporator assembly or discharging the system.

Dual Pressure Switch

1. Install a manifold gauge set.
2. Disconnect the dual pressure switch connector and connect an ohmmeter to the switch terminals.
3. When high side pressure is less than 26–31 psi, the dual pressure switch will be off and there will be no continuity.
4. When high side pressure increases to more than 270–341 psi, the switch will also be off and there will be no continuity.
5. Between these readings on the high side, the switch will be on and continuity will exist.
6. If switch does not respond within the limits, check the wiring connections in the circuit. If okay, replace the dual pressure switch.

Triple Pressure Switch

1. Install a manifold gauge set
2. Disconnect the triple pressure switch connector and connect an ohmmeter to the switch terminals.
3. When the high side decreases to 22–29 psi or increases to 356–412 psi, the pressure switch will be off and there will be no continuity.
4. When the high side pressure increases to 23–33 psi or decreases to 270–327 psi, the pressure switch will be on and there will be continuity.
5. Between these readings on the high side, the switch will be on and continuity will exist.
6. If the switch does not respond within limits, replace the triple pressure switch.

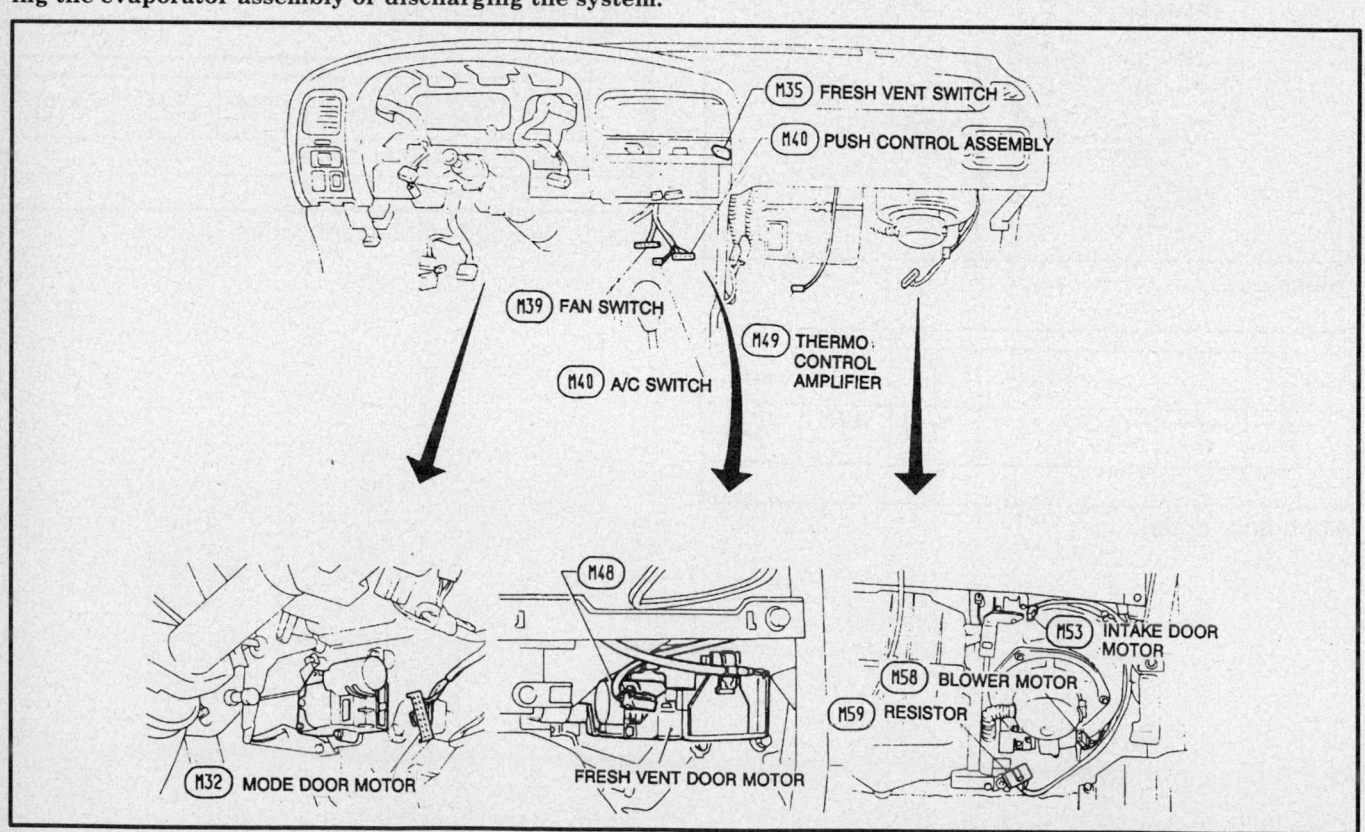

Passenger compartment component locations – G20

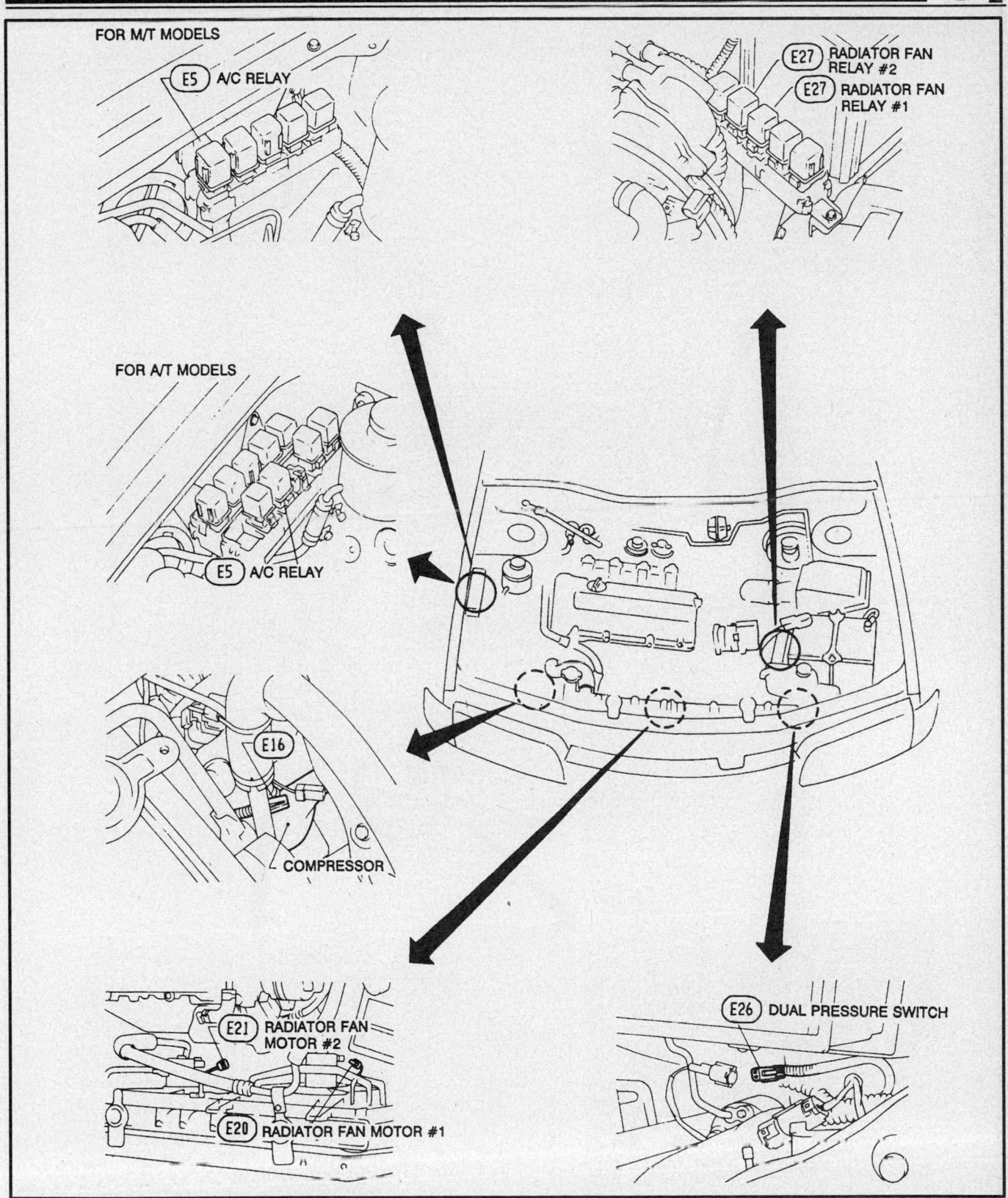

FOR M/T MODELS

E5 A/C RELAY

E27 RADIATOR FAN RELAY #2
E27 RADIATOR FAN RELAY #1

FOR A/T MODELS

E5 A/C RELAY

E16

COMPRESSOR

E21 RADIATOR FAN MOTOR #2
E20 RADIATOR FAN MOTOR #1

E26 DUAL PRESSURE SWITCH

Underhood component locations – G20

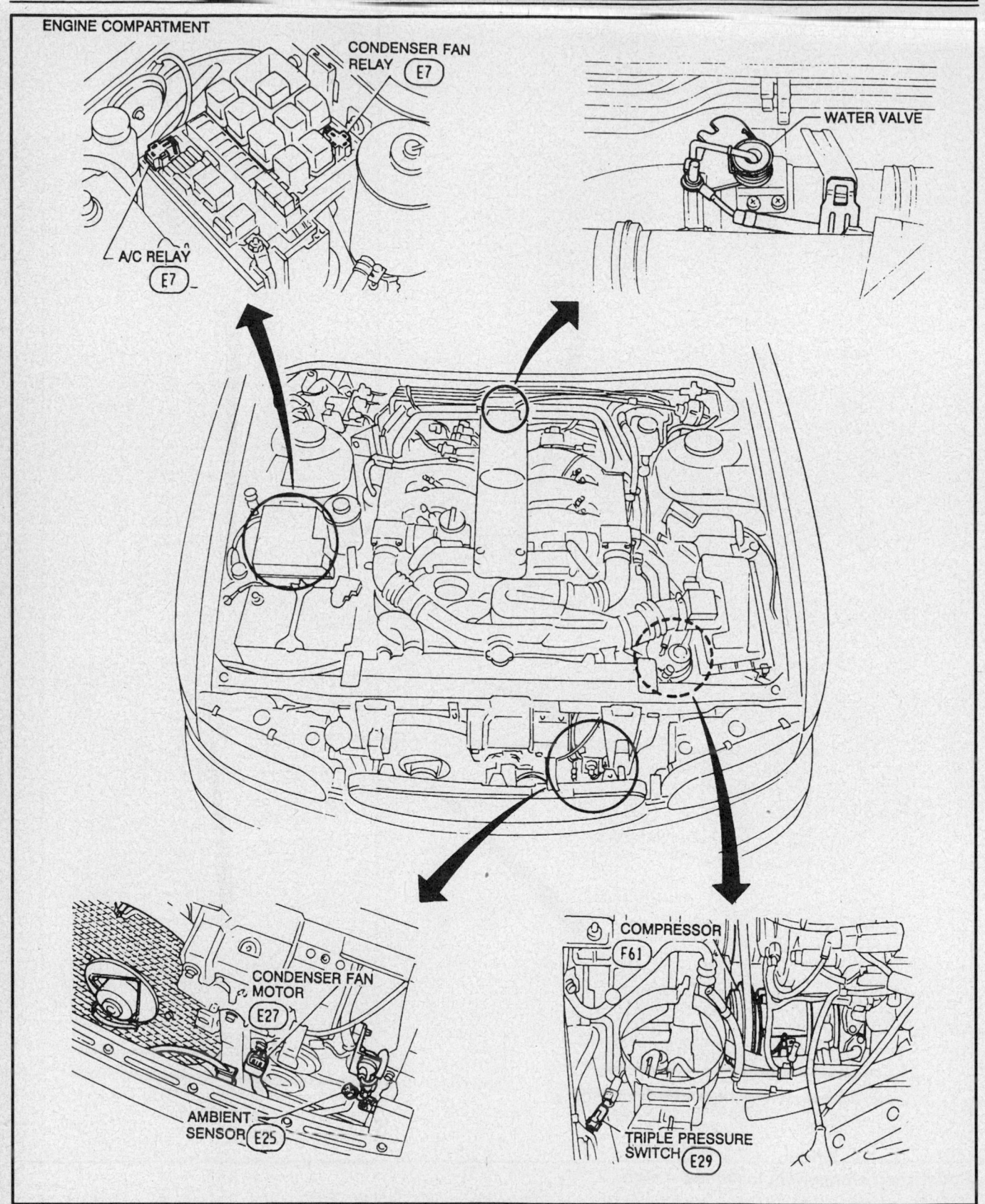

ENGINE COMPARTMENT

CONDENSER FAN RELAY E7

A/C RELAY E7

WATER VALVE

CONDENSER FAN MOTOR E27

AMBIENT SENSOR E25

COMPRESSOR F61

TRIPLE PRESSURE SWITCH E29

Automatic A/C system engine compartment component locations – J30

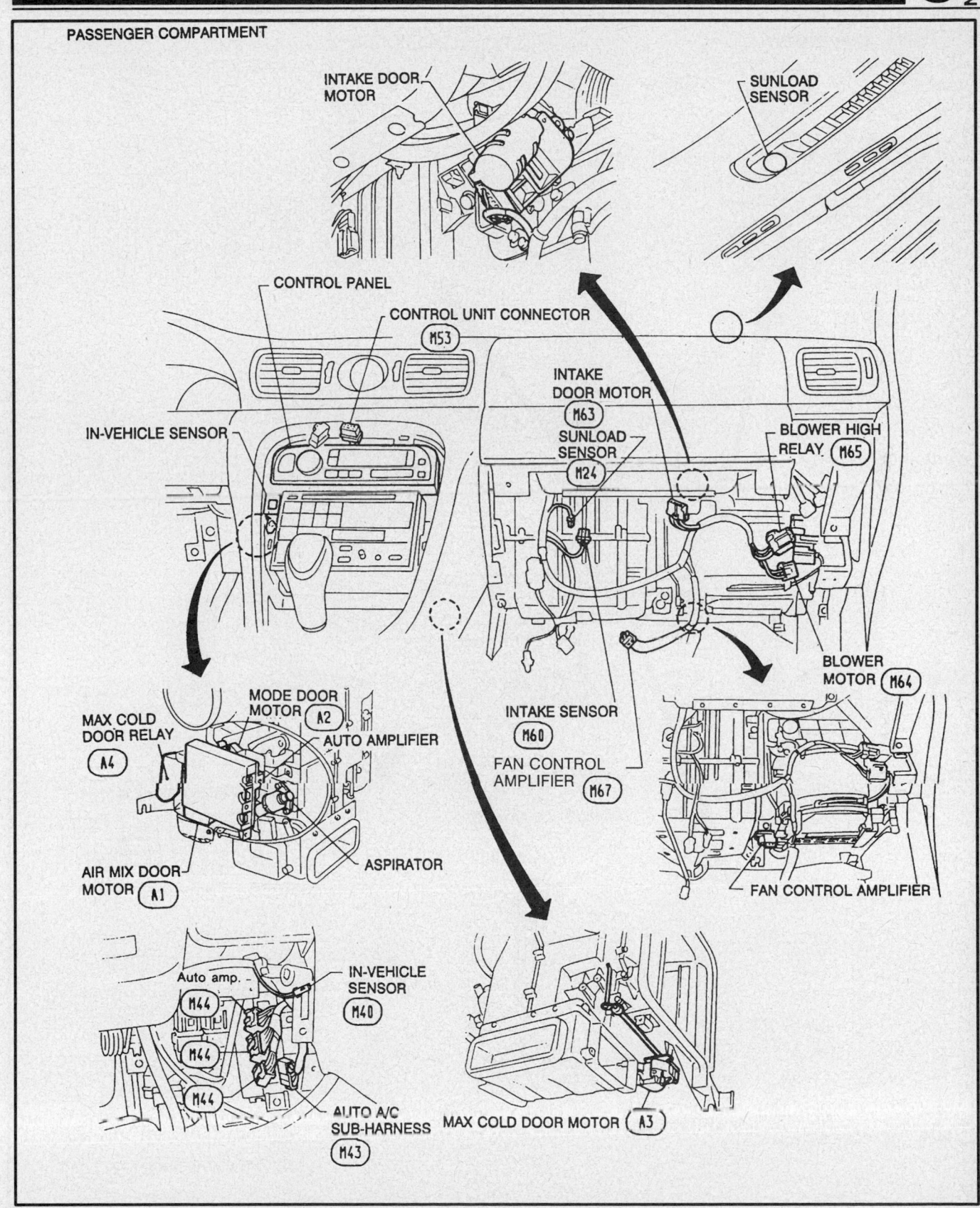

PASSENGER COMPARTMENT

INTAKE DOOR MOTOR

SUNLOAD SENSOR

CONTROL PANEL

CONTROL UNIT CONNECTOR (M53)

INTAKE DOOR MOTOR (M63)

SUNLOAD SENSOR (M24)

BLOWER HIGH RELAY (M65)

IN-VEHICLE SENSOR

MAX COLD DOOR RELAY (A4)

MODE DOOR MOTOR (A2)

AUTO AMPLIFIER

INTAKE SENSOR (M60)

FAN CONTROL AMPLIFIER (M67)

BLOWER MOTOR (M64)

AIR MIX DOOR MOTOR (A1)

ASPIRATOR

FAN CONTROL AMPLIFIER

Auto amp.

M44

M44

M44

IN-VEHICLE SENSOR (M40)

AUTO A/C SUB-HARNESS (M43)

MAX COLD DOOR MOTOR (A3)

Automatic A/C system passenger compartment component locations – J30

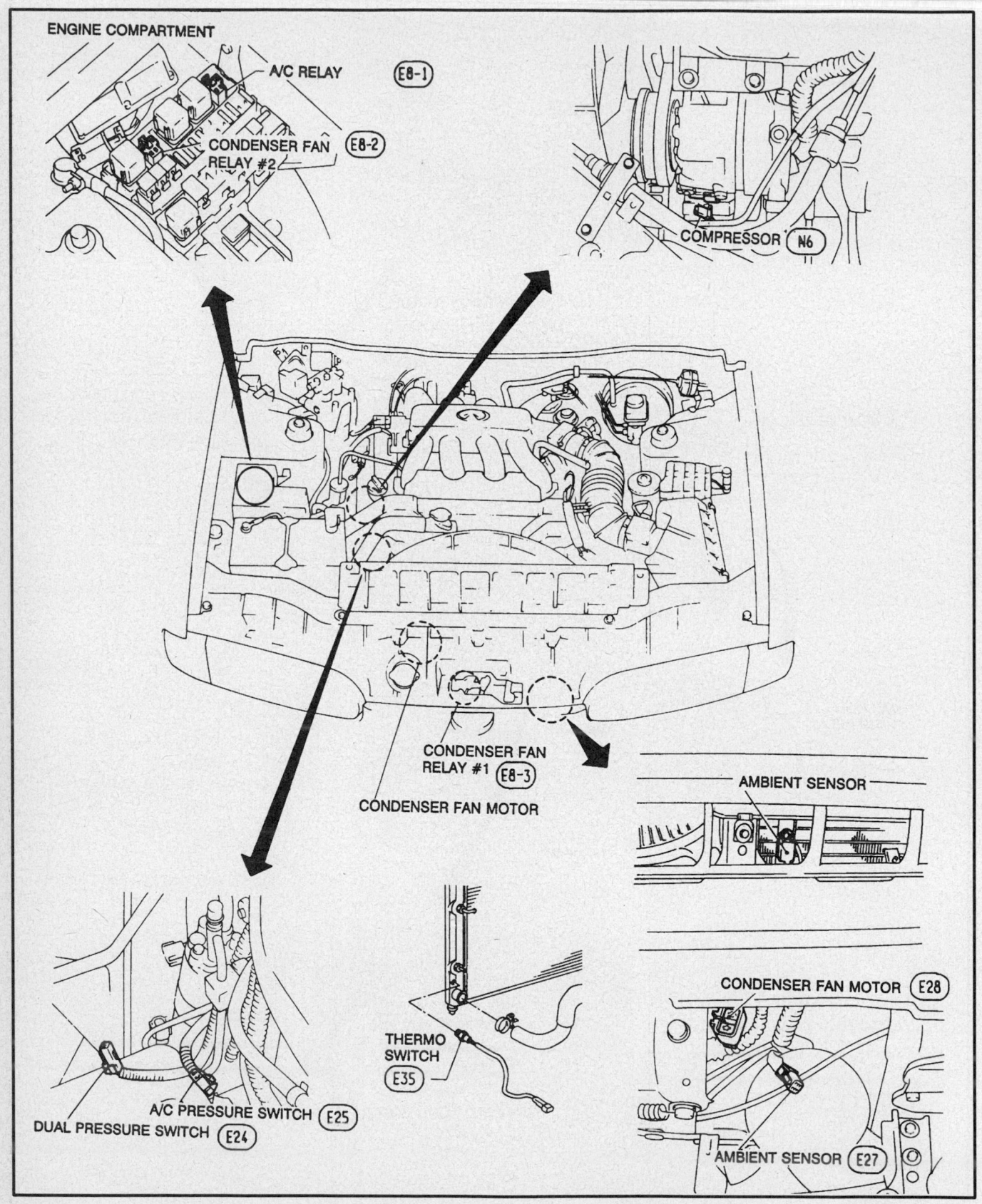

ENGINE COMPARTMENT

A/C RELAY E8-1

CONDENSER FAN RELAY #2 E8-2

COMPRESSOR N6

CONDENSER FAN RELAY #1 E8-3

CONDENSER FAN MOTOR

AMBIENT SENSOR

CONDENSER FAN MOTOR E28

THERMO SWITCH E35

A/C PRESSURE SWITCH E25

DUAL PRESSURE SWITCH E24

AMBIENT SENSOR E27

Automatic A/C system engine compartment component locations – Q45

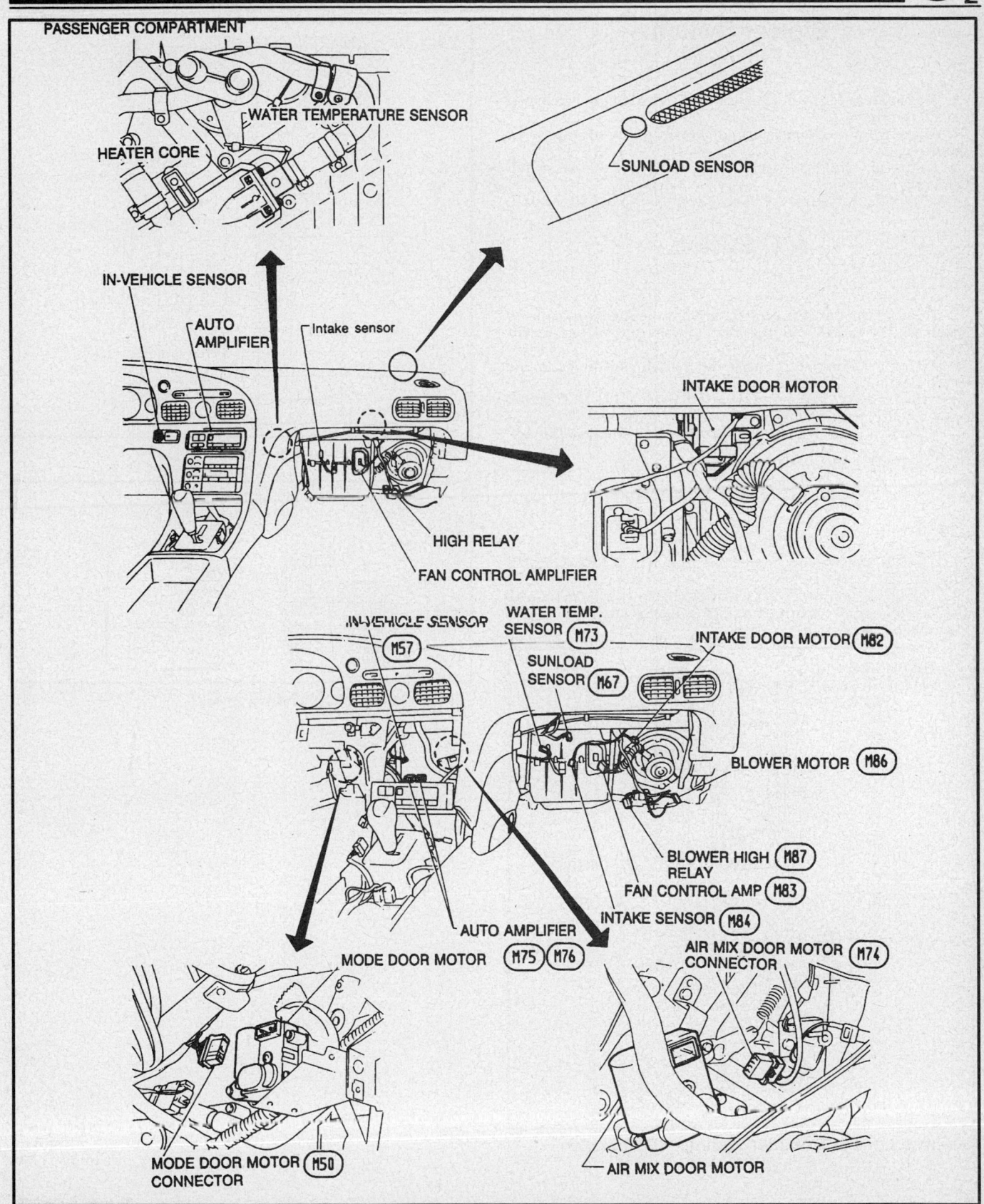

PASSENGER COMPARTMENT

WATER TEMPERATURE SENSOR

HEATER CORE

SUNLOAD SENSOR

IN-VEHICLE SENSOR

AUTO AMPLIFIER

Intake sensor

INTAKE DOOR MOTOR

HIGH RELAY

FAN CONTROL AMPLIFIER

IN-VEHICLE SENSOR (M57)

WATER TEMP. SENSOR (M73)

INTAKE DOOR MOTOR (M82)

SUNLOAD SENSOR (M67)

BLOWER MOTOR (M86)

BLOWER HIGH RELAY (M87)

FAN CONTROL AMP (M83)

INTAKE SENSOR (M84)

AUTO AMPLIFIER (M75) (M76)

AIR MIX DOOR MOTOR (M74) CONNECTOR

MODE DOOR MOTOR

MODE DOOR MOTOR (M50) CONNECTOR

AIR MIX DOOR MOTOR

Automatic A/C system passenger compartment component locations – Q45

Blower Switch

G20

1. Gain access to the back side of the control panel (removal may be required).
2. Disconnect the harness connector from the blower speed switch.
3. Using an ohmmeter, check for continuity at the switch terminals as shown.
4. If switch continuity is not as specified, replace the switch.

A/C Switch

G20

1. Remove the harness connector from the A/C switch (leave switch in the panel and the rest of the control panel connected).
2. Using an ohmmeter, check the switch continuity at the switch terminals 12 and 1.
3. When the A/C switch is **ON** or **OFF** while the DEF button is **ON** or **OFF**, there should always be continuity.
4. If switch does not respond as indicated, replace the A/C switch.

Fresh Vent Switch

G20

1. Detach the wiring connector from the FRESH VENT switch.
2. Using an ohmmeter attached to the switch terminals as shown, check that continuity exists at each switch position. If not, replace the switch.

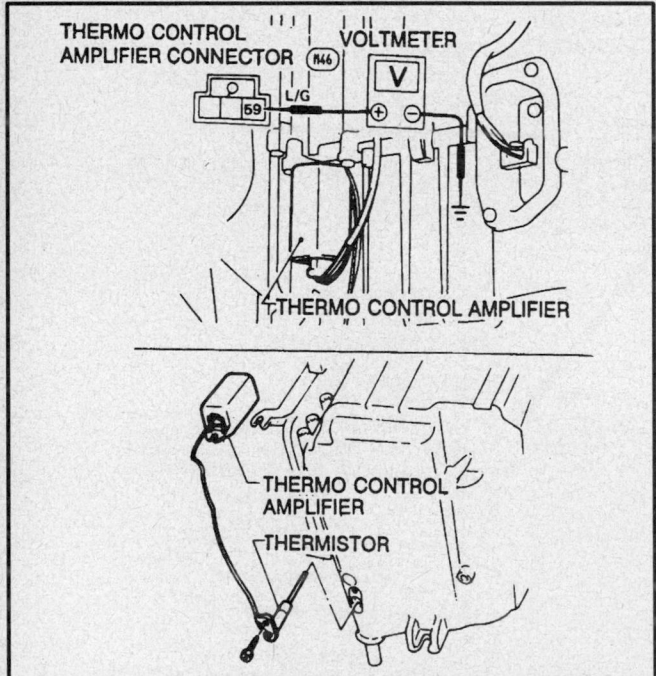

Thermo control amplifier testing – G20 shown

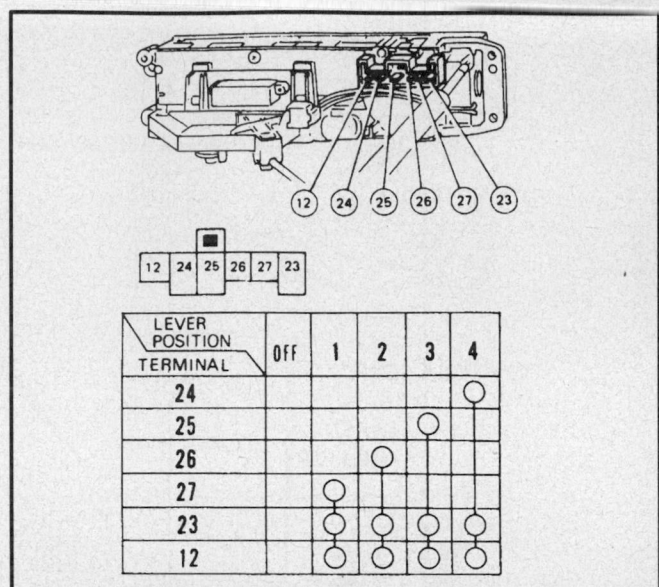

LEVER POSITION TERMINAL	OFF	1	2	3	4
24					○
25				○	
26			○		
27		○		○	○
23		○	○	○	○
12		○	○	○	○

Blower switch testing – G20

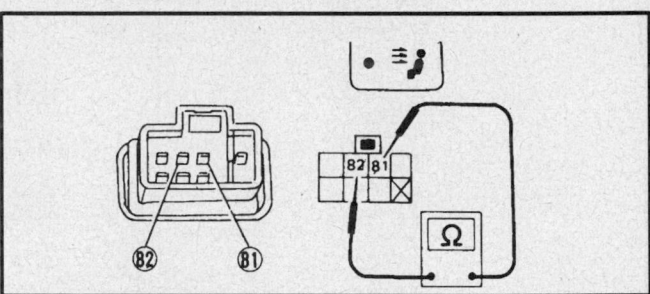

Fresh vent switch testing – G20

SYSTEM DIAGNOSIS

Air Conditioning Performance Check

TEST CONDITIONS

The vehicle should be in a shaded, well-ventilated place. Install a manifold gauge set. The doors closed, driver's window open, the hood open, TEMPERATURE lever at maximum COLD, MODE switch at VENT, RECIRC switch ON, blower switch at HIGH speed and engine at 1500 rpm.

Run engine at indicated speed for more than 10 minutes before checking results. Compare results, based on temperatures and humidity to the "Performance Check Test Readings" chart.

AIR CONDITIONING PERFORMANCE CHECK TEST READINGS

Recirculating-to-discharge air temperature table

Inside air (Recirculating air) at blower assembly inlet		Discharge air temperature at center ventilator °C (°F)
Relative humidity %	Air temperature °C (°F)	
40–60	20 (68)	2.5–4.6 (37–40)
	25 (77)	6.3–9.0 (43–48)
	30 (86)	10.8–13.9 (51–57)
	35 (95)	16.5–20.6 (62–69)
	40 (104)	22.5–27.5 (73–82)
60–80	20 (68)	4.6–7.3 (40–45)
	25 (77)	9.0–12.0 (48–54)
	30 (86)	13.9–17.7 (57–64)
	35 (95)	20.6–25.6 (69–78)
	40 (104)	27.5–34.0 (82–93)

Ambient air temperature-to-compressor pressure table

Ambient air		High-pressure (Discharge side) kPa (kg/cm², psi)	Low-pressure (Suction side) kPa (kg/cm², psi)
Relative humidity %	Air temperature °C (°F)		
40–80	20 (68)	686–1,020 (7.0–10.4, 100–148)	59–127 (0.6–1.3, 9–18)
	25 (77)	883–1,226 (9.0–12.5, 128–178)	78–147 (0.8–1.5, 11–21)
	30 (86)	1,118–1,451 (11.4–14.8, 162–210)	98–177 (1.0–1.8, 14–26)
	35 (95)	1,373–1,736 (14.0–17.7, 199–252)	127–226 (1.3–2.3, 18–33)
	40 (104)	1,657–2,020 (16.9–20.6, 240–293)	196–314 (2.0–3.2, 28–46)

AIR CONDITIONING PERFORMANCE CHECK TEST READINGS — R-134a SYSTEMS

Recirculating-to-discharge air temperature table

Inside air (Recirculating air) at blower assembly inlet		Discharge air temperature at center ventilator °C (°F)
Relative humidity %	Air temperature °C (°F)	
50–60	20 (68)	1.7–2.5 (35–37)
	25 (77)	4.3–5.3 (40–42)
	30 (86)	8.4–10.2 (47–50)
	35 (95)	13.0–15.3 (55–60)
60–70	20 (68)	2.5–3.7 (37–39)
	25 (77)	5.3–7.0 (42–45)
	30 (86)	10.2–12.0 (50–54)
	35 (95)	15.3–18.5 (60–65)

ACTUATORS TEST PATTERN CHART

Code No.	Mode Door	Intake Door	Air Mix Door	Blower Motor	Compressor
41	Vent	Recirc	Full Cold	4–5V	On
42	B/L	Recirc	Full Cold	9–11V	On
43	B/L	20% Fresh	Full Hot	7–9V	On
44	D/F 1	Fresh	Full Hot	7–9V	Off
45	D/F 2	Fresh	Full Hot	7–9V	Off
46	Def	Fresh	Full Hot	10–12 V	On

DIAGNOSTIC PROCEDURES

1993–94 G20

The manufacturer uses a series of symbols throughout its diagnostic procedures. Key symbols to be noted are whether the test connections to be used as viewed from either the Terminal Side (T.S.) or from the Harness Side (H.S.).

Also indicated is whether the harness is Disconnected or Connected to the appropriate switch or sensor connector during the diagnostic test.

Additionally, connectors are referenced to the main wiring schematic by a number within an oval. These indicators are on the diagnostic procedures and also on the main wiring schematic.

Blower Inoperative

1. Disconnect blower harness connector and, with key **ON**, check for 12 volts between terminal **30** and ground. If no voltage, check fuse.
2. If okay, turn key **OFF** and check for continuity between connector terminal **24** and ground. If okay, replace blower motor (after checking motor operation separately).
3. If no continuity, reconnect blower motor harness, turn key **ON** and check for 12 volts between blower resistor connector terminal **24** and ground. If okay, disconnect the resistor and check it separately. If no good, replace the resistor.
4. If voltage did not exist in Step 3, disconnect the blower motor and resistor harness connectors. With the key **OFF** and checking from the harness side, check for continuity between terminals **24** on both connectors. If continuity does not exist, repair circuit wiring or replace the connector.

5. Check for 12 volts, with the key in **ACC** and harness connected, between each terminal of the fan switch connector and ground. Also check for continuity between each fan switch connector and resistor connector (same terminals). If not okay, repair wiring, replace connector or replace the fan switch.
6. With key **OFF** and connector disconnected, check circuit continuity between terminal **23** of the fan switch and terminal **92** on the blower relay connector.

Sensors and abnormalities codes

Code No.	Sensor	Open circuit	Short circuit
21	Ambient sensor	Less than −41.9°C (−43°F)	Greater than 100°C (212°F)
22	In-vehicle sensor	Less than −41.9°C (−43°F)	Greater than 100°C (212°F)
23	Water temperature sensor	Less than −25.6°C (−14°F)	Greater than 150°C (302°F)
24	Intake sensor	Less than −41.9°C (−43°F)	Greater than 100°C (212°F)
25	Sunload sensor*2	Less than 0.0152 mA	Greater than 0.545 mA
26	P.B.R.*1	Greater than 50%	Less than 30%
27	Thermal transmitter	Greater than 11.5V	Less than 2.2V

Amblent air temperature-to-compressor pressure table

Ambient air		High-pressure (Discharge side) kPa (kg/cm², psi)	Low-pressure (Suction side) kPa (kg/cm², psi)
Relative humidity %	Air temperature °C (°F)		
50–70	20 (68)	843–1,030 (8.6–10.5, 122–149)	147–177 (1.5–1.8, 21–26)
	25 (77)	1,040–1,275 (10.6–13.0, 151–185)	147–186 (1.5–1.9, 21–27)
	30 (86)	1,255–1,540 (12.8–15.7, 182–223)	157–196 (1.6–2.0, 23–28)
	35 (95)	1,500–1,824 (15.3–18.6, 218–264)	167–216 (1.7–2.2, 24–31)
	40 (104)	1,746–2,128 (17.8–21.7, 253–309)	196–265 (2.0–2.7, 28–38)

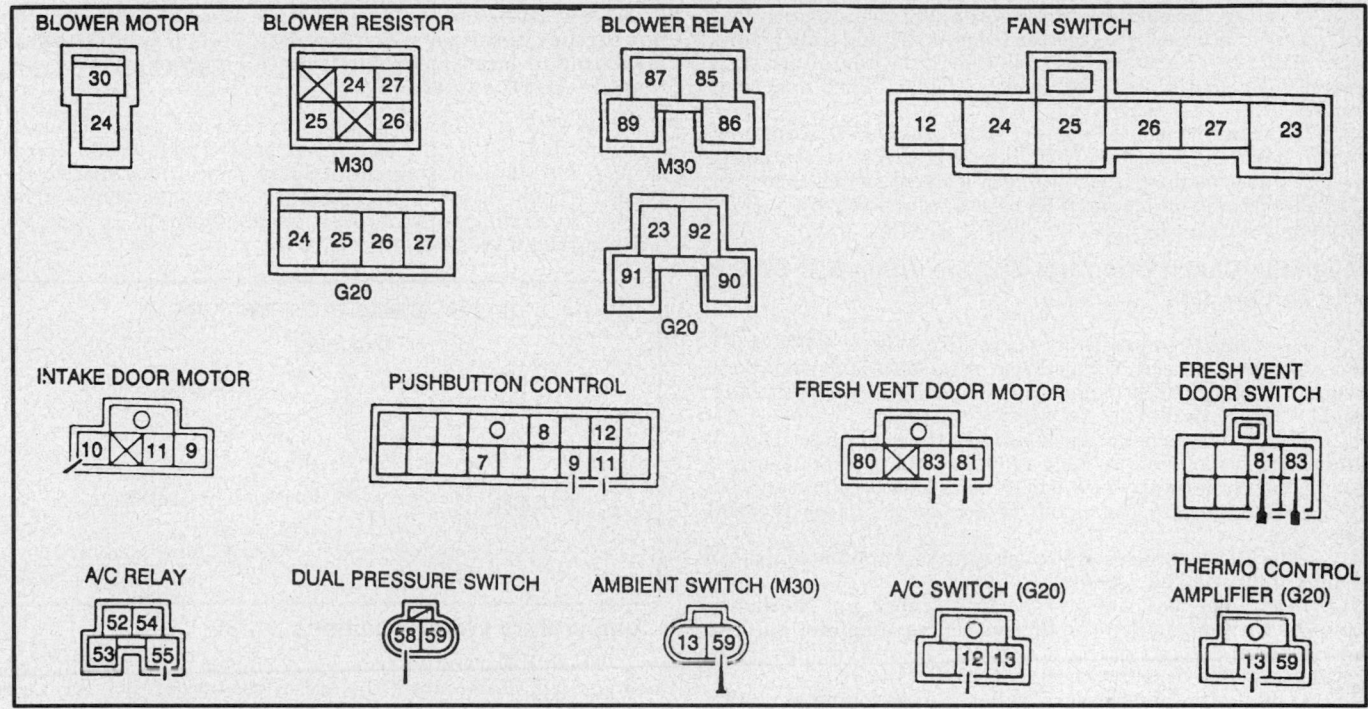

Component harness connector terminal identification

7. If okay, check for 12 volts between terminal **90** and body ground. If there is no voltage, check fuse block.

8. Check circuit continuity between blower relay harness terminal **23**, **91** and body ground. If not okay, replace blower relay.

Air Outlet Does Not Change

1. Check mode door motor position switch by turning VENT switch **ON** and ignition switch **ON**. Then, turn off ignition and disconnect control panel push–button connector. Check separately for continuity between terminals **1** through **3** and body ground. Depress each mode switch as continuity checks are made as follows:

- VENT: terminal **1** or **2** and body ground.
- B/L: terminal **2** or **3** and body ground.
- FOOT: terminal **3** or **4** and body ground.
- F/D: terminal **4** or **5** and body ground.
- DEF: terminal **5** or **6** and body ground.

2. If continuity is okay, check door control side link for operation and proper attachment.

3. If continuity was not okay, disconnect the mode door motor connector. With the key **ON**, check for continuity between terminal **22** and body ground.

4. If continuity was okay, check continuity between each terminal (**1** through **8**) on the push–button control unit connector and the corresponding terminal on the mode door motor connector.

5. Reconnect the push–button connector and the mode door motor harness connector, turn the key to **ACC** and check for 12 volts between terminals 7 and 8 of both connectors. If this checks okay, replace the mode door motor. If not, replace the control amplifier built into the push–button control panel.

Intake Door Does Not Change

1. Disconnect the intake door motor harness connector. With key in **ACC**, check for 12 volts between terminal **10** and body ground. If no voltage, check fuse.

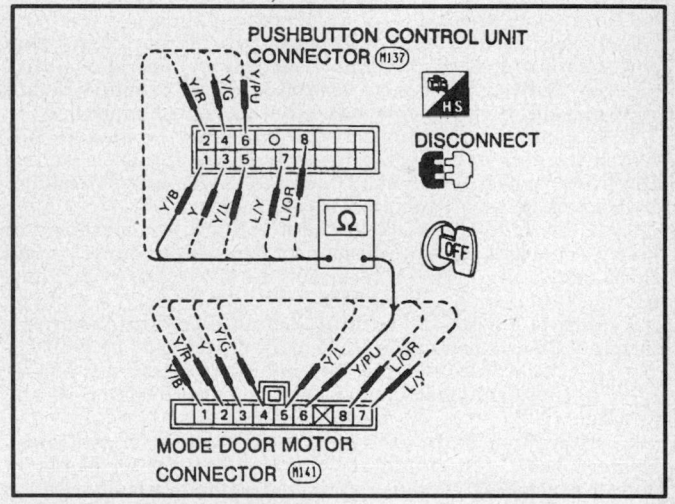

Air outlet circuit testing

2. If okay, turn key **OFF** and REC button **ON**, check for continuity between terminal **9** and body ground. Then turn REC button **OFF** and check for continuity between terminal **11** and body ground. If okay, replace the intake door motor.

3. If continuity was not okay, disconnect the push–button control connector. With key **OFF**, check continuity between push–button control unit terminals **9** and **11** and their corresponding terminals on the intake door motor connector. If okay, replace the control amplifier built into the push–button control unit.

Fresh Vent Door Does Not Change

1. Disconnect the fresh vent door motor connector. With key in **ACC**, check for 12 volts between door motor connector terminal **80** and body ground. If no voltage, check fuse box.

2. If voltage was okay, turn key **OFF** and check for continuity between door motor connector terminal **81** and body ground with FRESH VENT switch **ON**. Check for continuity with switch **OFF** at terminal **80**. If okay, replace fresh vent door motor.

3. If continuity check was not okay, disconnect fresh vent switch harness connector. With key **OFF**, check for continuity between door motor connector and fresh vent switch connector terminal **81** and on terminal **83** of each connector. If not okay, replace fresh vent switch.

Magnetic Clutch Does Not Engage When A/C Switch and Fan are ON

1. Disconnect compressor harness wire. With key **ON**, check for voltage between compressor wire terminal and body ground. If okay, check magnetic clutch coil (if this is not okay, replace magnetic clutch).

2. If voltage was not okay disconnect thermal protector wire and check for 12 volts to body ground. If okay, check thermal protector for continuity between its connector terminal and the compressor harness connector. If not okay, replace thermal protector.

3. Check for 8–9 volts at thermo control amplifier connector terminal **59** and body ground.

4. If voltage was not as specified, check for continuity between terminals **59** of the thermo control amplifier harness and the dual or triple pressure switch harness. If dual or triple pressure switch does not check out, replace it.

5. If dual or triple pressure switch is functioning normally, check circuit continuity between ECCS (ECM) control unit harness terminal **41** and dual pressure switch harness terminal **58**. If okay, check ECCS (ECM) control unit.

6. If voltage in Step 3 was okay and thermo control amp power supply is okay, disconnect the thermo control amplifier harness connector and check for continuity at terminal **13** and body ground. If okay, replace the thermo control amplifier.

7. If continuity to ground was not okay, disconnect A/C switch harness and check continuity between thermo control amplifier harness terminal **13** and A/C switch harness terminal **1**. If not okay, repair harness or connector.

8. If continuity was okay, check A/C switch operation. If faulty, replace it. If okay, disconnect fan switch connector and check continuity between terminals **12** of the A/C switch harness and the fan switch harness.

9. If okay, check for continuity between fan switch harness terminal **23** and body ground. If okay, switch may be faulty.

10. If continuity in Step 9 was not okay, disconnect blower relay harness and check for 12 volts between terminal **90** and ground.

11. If terminal **90** to ground was okay, check for continuity between body ground and blower relay harness terminals **91** and **92** separately. If okay, reconnect the fan switch harness. If not okay, repair circuit or connector.

12. Check for 12 volts between blower relay harness terminal **23** and body ground. If okay, blower relay may be faulty.

13. If voltage was not okay, disconnect fan switch connector and check continuity between terminals **23** of the fan switch harness and the blower relay harness. If not okay, repair circuit or harness.

Automatic A/C Systems Diagnosis

ENTERING AUTOMATIC A/C SYSTEMS SELF–DIAGNOSIS

1. Start the engine. On Q45, press the panel **OFF** switch for at least 5 seconds. On J30, press the panel **VENT** button and hold it for at least 5 seconds. For all models, this switch must be pressed within 10 seconds of starting the engine.

NOTE: Refer to the appropriate charts in this article for further detail on specifics tests. Self–diagnostics can be exited at any time by turning the engine off or pressing the AUTO switch.

2. On Q45, shifting from one diagnostic step to another is accomplished with the **UP** (Hot) or **DOWN** (Cold) arrow switch. On J30, shifting the display for various diagnostic steps is done with the Temperature Switch as shown. The switch to auxiliary mechanism (when required) is done by pressing the **FAN** switch.

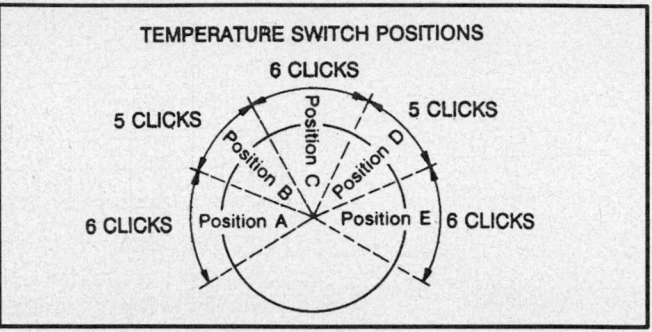

Temperature switch positions — J30

3. The L.E.D.s and system segments will be checked in step one and will illuminate if the are in good order. If L.E.D.s do not light up, the OFF switch is malfunctioning or the fluorescent tube is bad.

4. Use the UP or DOWN arrows to check each system segment. If arrow switches do not move to next segment check, the switch may be faulty.

5. On Q45, press the **UP** switch to display 2. On J30, select position **B** on the temperature switch. This checks all sensors. If sensors are okay, the display will then show 20. If the sensor circuit is open or short, the display code will correspond to conditions as shown in Faulty Sensor Circuit Chart.

6. On Q45, press the **UP** arrow again to display check 3. On J30, select temperature switch position **C**. If all mode door motor position switch are okay, display will read 30. If not, fault code will be as follows:

- 31: Vent
- 32: Bi–Level
- 33: Bi–Level (Q45) or Foot/Def 1 (J30)
- 34: Foot–Defrost 1 (Q45) or Foot/Def 2 (J30)
- 35: Foot–defrost 2 (Q45) or Def (J30)
- 36: Defrost (Q45) or Fresh (J30)
- 37: 80% Fresh (J30 only)
- 38: 20% Fresh (J30 only)
- 39: Recirc (J30 only)

7. Press the UP arrow again (Q45) or set position **D** on the temperature switch and a display of 41 through 46 will be displayed, depending on actuators and related conditions. Actual results must be made by visual checks, listening for noise or feeling air outlets for air flow. See Actuators Test Pattern chart in this article.

8. On Q45, press the **UP** arrow again to display 5. On J30, select position **E** on the temperature switch. As the **DEFROST** button is pressed, the temperature detected by the ambient sensor, in–vehicle sensor and intake sensor will be shown on the display.

9. On J30, by selecting position **E** on the temperature switch, then pressing the **RECIRC** switch, a 52 display means the signal direction is okay. A 52 with a fan symbol means a communications error from the control unit to the auto amplifier is detected. If symbol blinks, the communications error is from auto amp to the control unit.

10. Turn the ignition switch **OFF** or press the **AUTO** button to end the diagnostics.

11. Press the **FAN** switch to check the temperature setting trimmer. The trimmer compensates for differences between the temperature setting and the actual temperature felt by the driver or passenger. Press the **UP** arrow or **DOWN** arrow as desired. Each time the arrow switch is pressed, the temperature will change 0.5 degrees.

NOTE: When the battery cable is disconnected the trimmer operation is canceled and the temperature differential returns to "0".

MAIN POWER SUPPLY AND GROUND CIRCUIT CHECK

1. Check the power supply circuit for the auto amplifier with the ignition switch **ON**. Disconnect the connector from the auto amplifier and working from the harness side, check for 12 volts between terminals **1**, **2**, and **5** and the body ground for Q45 and **1**, **2**, and **11** for J30 and the body ground.

2. Turn the ignition switch **OFF** and check for continuity (using an ohmmeter) between terminal **11** and the body ground for the Q45. There should be continuity. For the J30, check for continuity (using an ohmmeter) between terminals **5** and **42** and the body ground. There should be continuity.

IN–VEHICLE SENSOR TEST

After disconnecting the in–vehicle sensor harness, measure resistance between the terminals as shown and compare results to the In-Vehicle Resistance Test Chart.

AMBIENT SENSOR TEST

After disconnecting the ambient sensor harness, measure resistance between the terminals shown at the sensor side of the harness. Compare results to the Ambient Sensor Resistance Test Chart.

SUNLOAD SENSOR TEST

With the vehicle parked in direct sunlight, disconnect the auto amplifier harness and measure the voltage, from the harness side, between terminals of sunload sensor as shown.

INTAKE SENSOR TEST

The intake sensor is located on the evaporator and converts the temperature of the air passing through the evaporator into a resistance value which becomes an input signal to the auto amplifier. After detaching the intake sensor harness connector, measure resistance between the terminals as shown, from the

sensor terminal side of the harness. Compare results to the "Intake Sensor Resistance Test Chart."

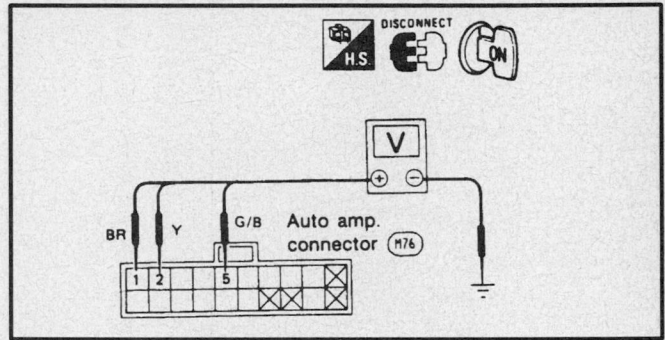

Main power supply circuit check – Q45

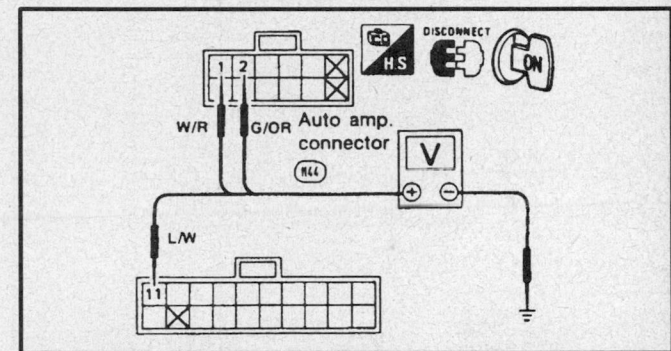

Main power supply circuit check – J30

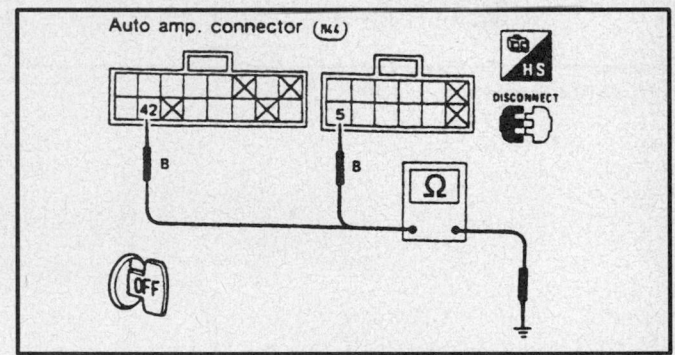

Main power supply ground circuit check – Q45

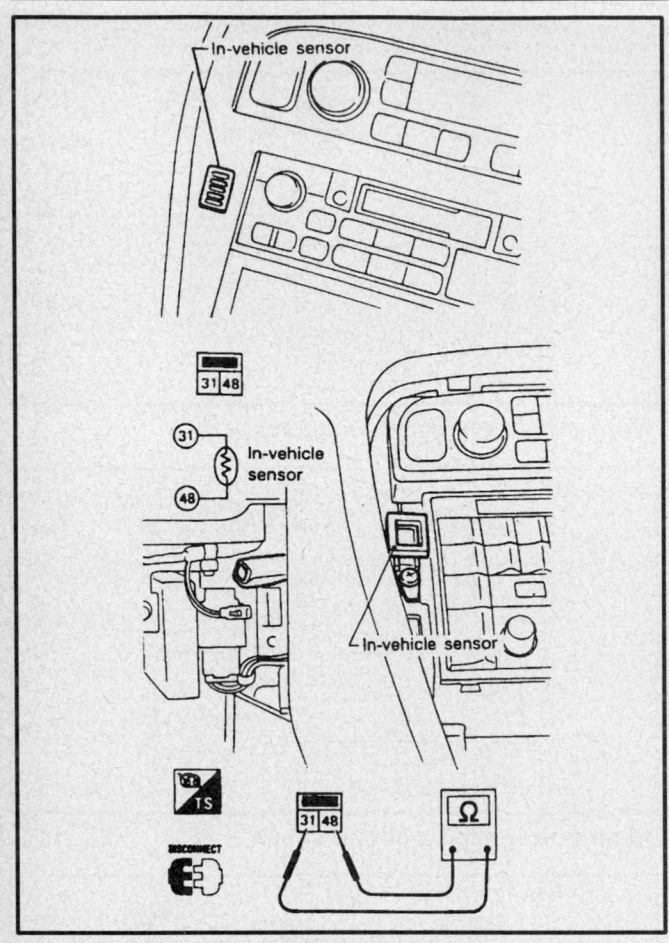

In vehicle sensor – J30

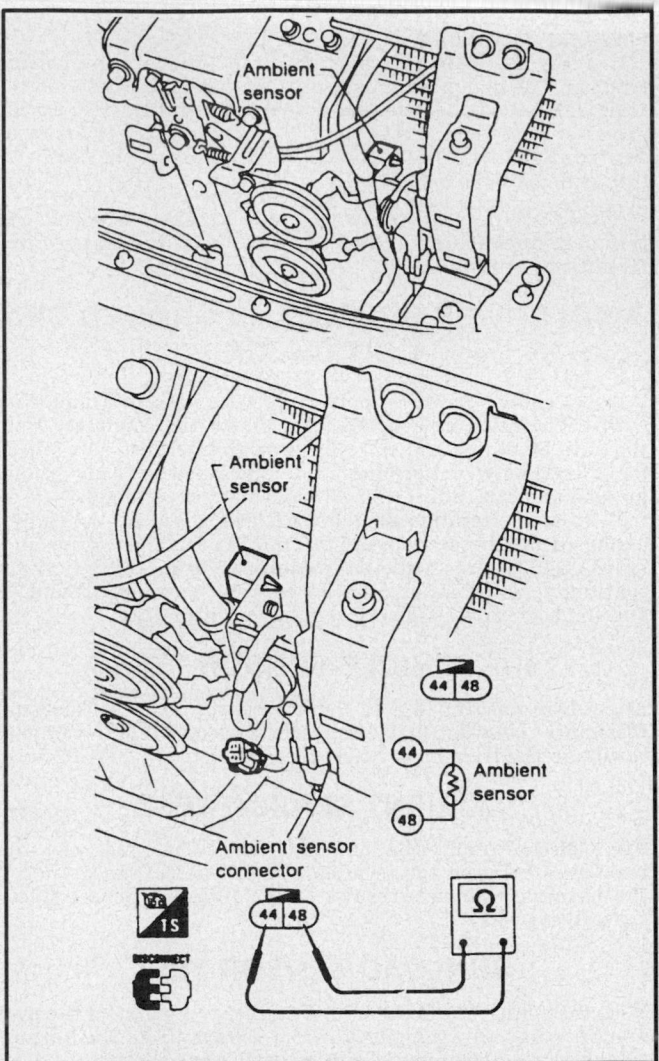

Ambient sensor – J30

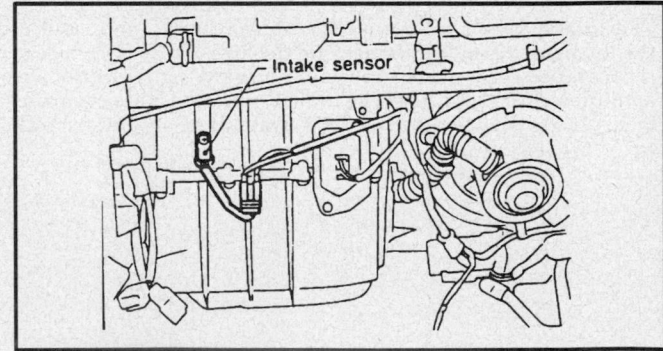

Intake sensor – Q45

INTAKE SENSOR RESISTANCE TEST CHART

Temperature °F (°C)	J30	Q45
32 (0)	6.00	6.19
41 (5)	4.80	4.95
50 (10)	3.87	3.99
59 (15)	3.14	3.24
68 (20)	2.57	2.65
77 (25)	2.12	2.19
86 (30)	1.76	1.81
95 (35)	1.47	1.51

AMBIENT SENSOR RESISTANCE TEST CHART

Temperature °F (°C)	J30	Q45
32 (0)	6.19	6.19
41 (5)	4.95	4.95
50 (10)	3.99	3.99
59 (15)	3.24	3.24
68 (20)	2.65	2.65
77 (25)	2.19	2.19
86 (30)	1.81	1.81
95 (35)	1.51	1.51

IN-VEHICLE RESISTANCE TEST CHART

Temperature °F (°C)	J30	Q45
32 (0)	6.19	6.41
41 (5)	4.95	5.17
50 (10)	3.99	4.21
59 (15)	3.24	3.46
68 (20)	2.65	2.87
77 (25)	2.19	2.41
86 (30)	1.81	2.03
95 (35)	1.51	1.73

G20 AUTO. A/C SYSTEMS DIAGNOSTIC PROCEDURE 1

TROUBLE DIAGNOSES

	INCIDENT	Flow chart No.
1	Fan fails to rotate.	1
2	Fan does not rotate at 1-speed.	2
3	Fan does not rotate at 2-speed.	3
4	Fan does not rotate at 3-speed.	4
5	Fan does not rotate at 4-speed.	5

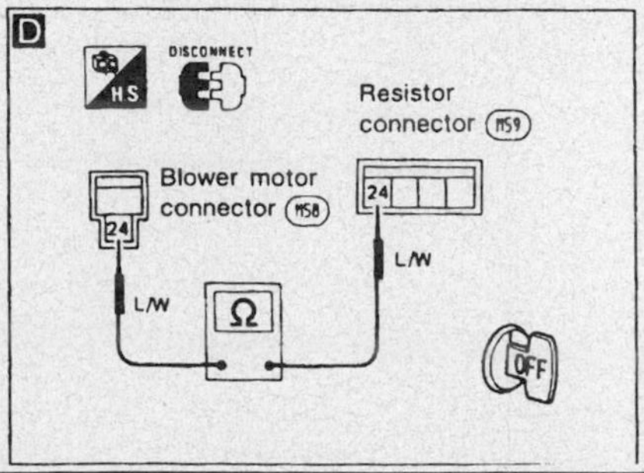

Diagnostic Procedure 1

SYMPTOM: Blower motor does not rotate.

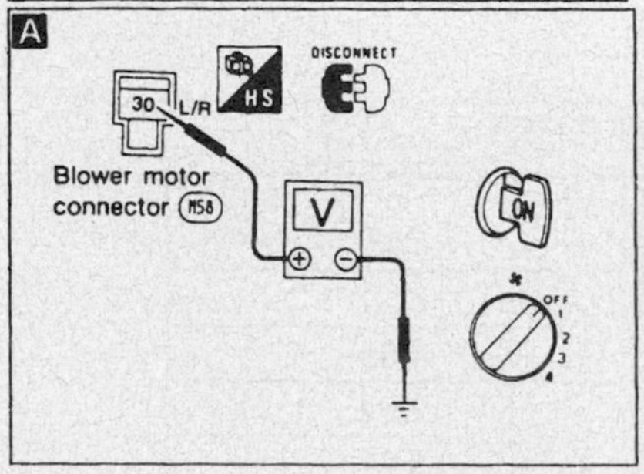

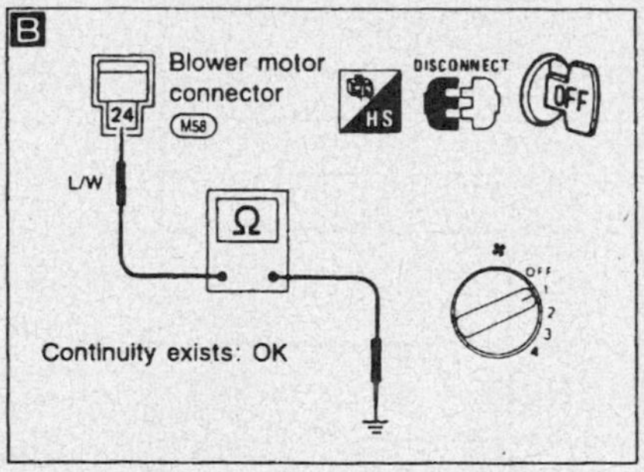

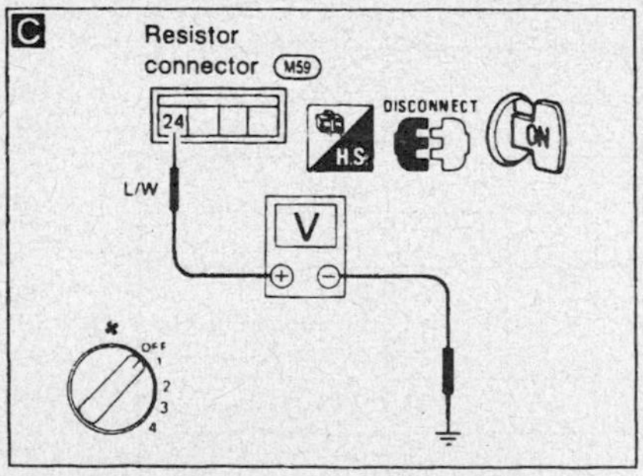

● **Perform PRELIMINARY CHECK 2 before referring to the following flow chart.**

Check if blower motor rotates properly at each fan speed.
Conduct checks as per flow chart at left.

5 → Ⓔ
4 → Ⓓ
3 → Ⓒ
2 → Ⓑ

(Go to next page.)

A

1

CHECK POWER SUPPLY FOR BLOWER MOTOR.
Disconnect blower motor harness connector.
Do approx. 12 volts exist between blower motor harness terminal No. ㉚ and body ground?

→ No → Check 15A fuses at fuse block.

↓ Yes

B

Check circuit continuity between blower motor harness terminal No. ㉔ and body ground.

→ NG → Reconnect blower motor harness connector.

↓ OK

CHECK BLOWER MOTOR.

↓ NG

Replace blower motor.

C

CHECK BLOWER MOTOR CIRCUIT BETWEEN BLOWER MOTOR AND RESISTOR.
Do approx. 12 volts exist between resistor harness terminal No. ㉔ and body ground?

→ No → Disconnect blower motor and resistor harness connectors.

↓ Yes

Ⓐ
(Go to next page.)

D Note

Check circuit continuity between blower motor harness terminal No. ㉔ and resistor harness terminal No. ㉔

Note:
If the result is NG after checking circuit continuity, repair harness or connector.

A

Blower motor connector (M58)

30 L/R

B

Blower motor connector (M58)

24

L/W

Continuity exists: OK

C

Resistor connector (M59)

24

L/W

D

Resistor connector (M59)

Blower motor connector (M58)

24

24

L/W

L/W

8–32

G20 AUTO. A/C SYSTEMS DIAGNOSTIC PROCEDURE 1 – CONT.

TROUBLE DIAGNOSES
Diagnostic Procedure 1 (Cont'd)

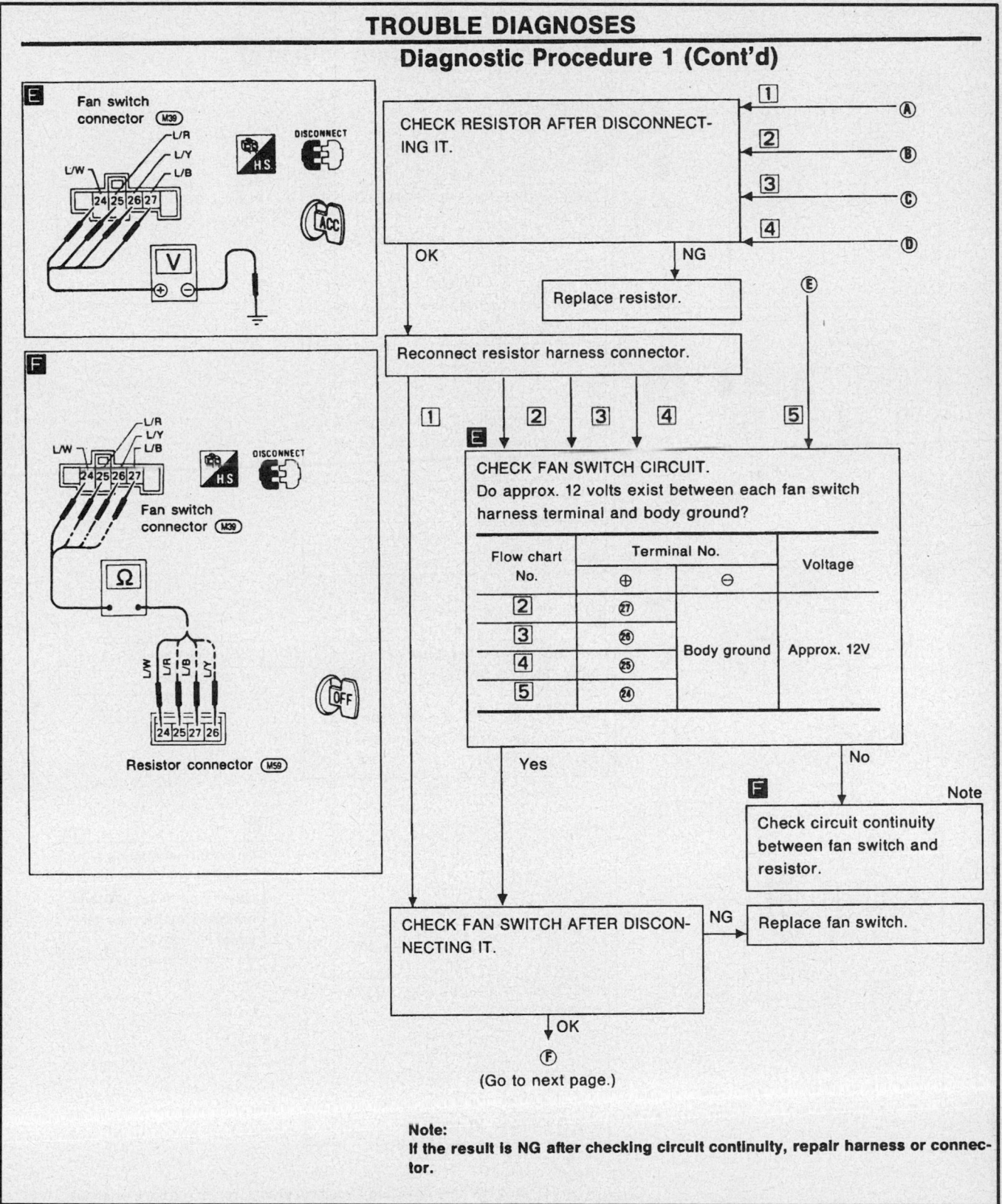

G20 AUTO. A/C SYSTEMS DIAGNOSTIC PROCEDURE 1 – CONT.

TROUBLE DIAGNOSES
Diagnostic Procedure 1 (Cont'd)

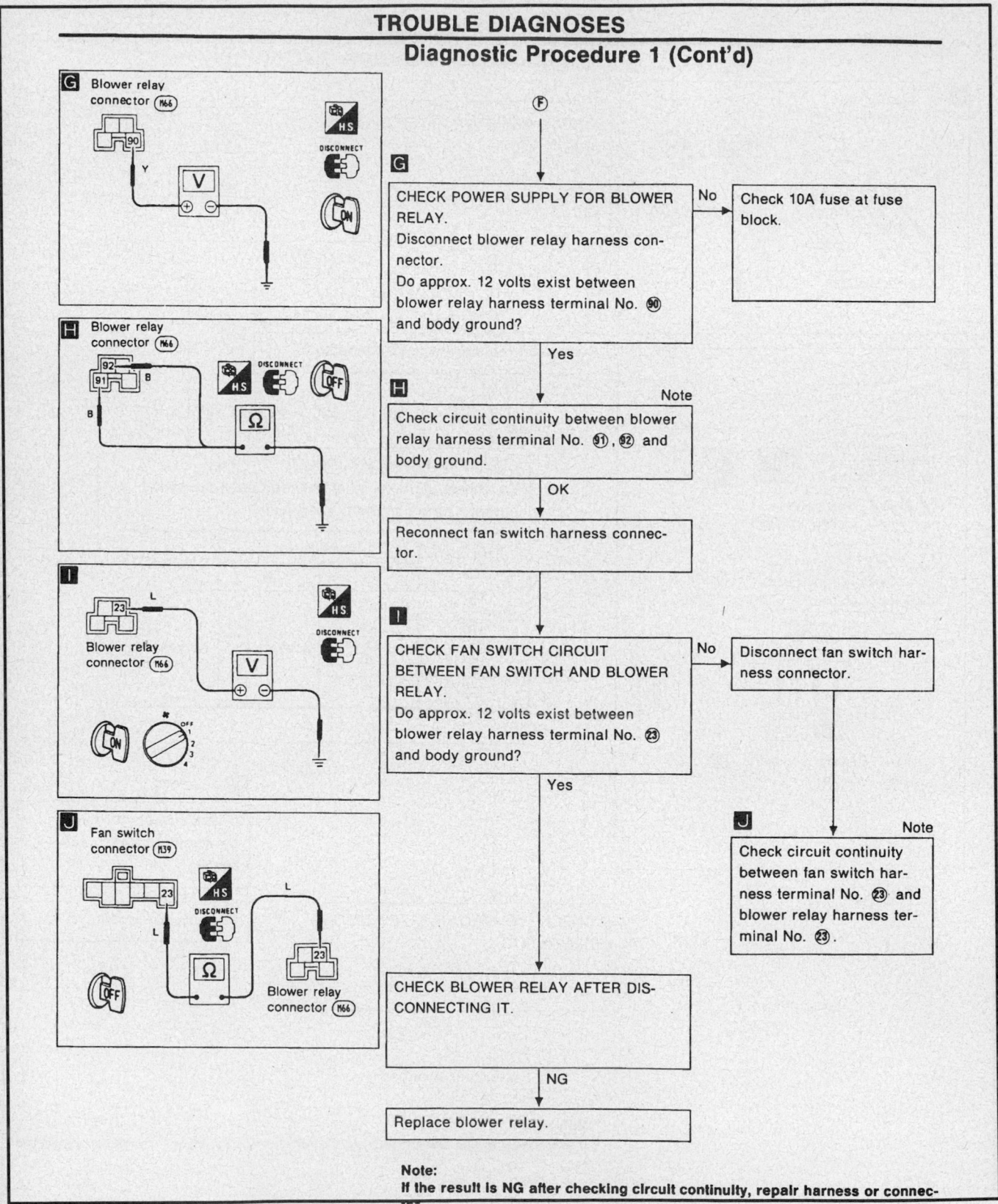

G CHECK POWER SUPPLY FOR BLOWER RELAY.
Disconnect blower relay harness connector.
Do approx. 12 volts exist between blower relay harness terminal No. (90) and body ground?

→ No → Check 10A fuse at fuse block.

↓ Yes

H Note
Check circuit continuity between blower relay harness terminal No. (91), (92) and body ground.

↓ OK

Reconnect fan switch harness connector.

I CHECK FAN SWITCH CIRCUIT BETWEEN FAN SWITCH AND BLOWER RELAY.
Do approx. 12 volts exist between blower relay harness terminal No. (23) and body ground?

→ No → Disconnect fan switch harness connector.

↓ Yes

J Note
Check circuit continuity between fan switch harness terminal No. (23) and blower relay harness terminal No. (23).

CHECK BLOWER RELAY AFTER DISCONNECTING IT.

↓ NG

Replace blower relay.

Note:
If the result is NG after checking circuit continuity, repair harness or connec-

G20 AUTO. A/C SYSTEMS DIAGNOSTIC PROCEDURE 2

TROUBLE DIAGNOSES

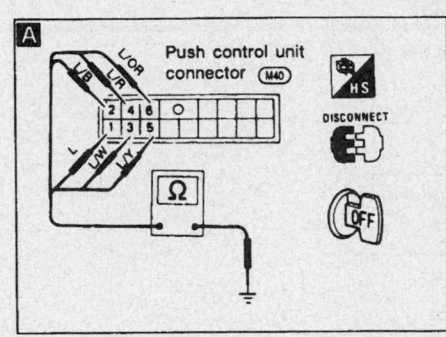

A Push control unit connector (M40)

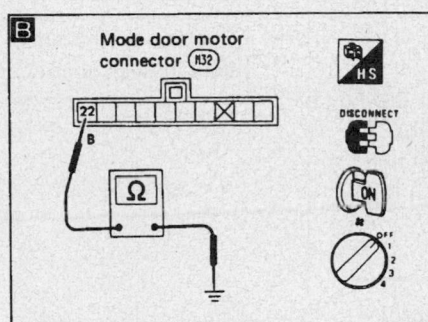

B Mode door motor connector (M32)

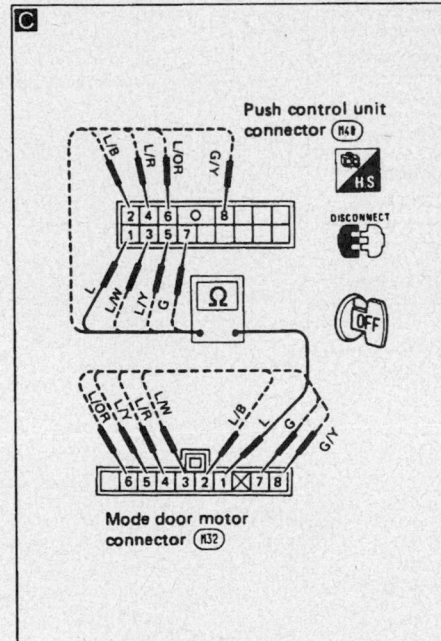

C Push control unit connector (M40)

Mode door motor connector (M32)

Diagnostic Procedure 2

SYMPTOM: Air outlet does not change.

● Perform PRELIMINARY CHECK 4, Main Power Supply and Ground Circuit Check before referring to flow chart below.

A

CHECK MODE DOOR MOTOR POSITION SWITCH.
1. Turn VENT switch ON with ignition switch at ACC position.
2. Turn ignition switch OFF. Disconnect push control unit connector.
3. Check for continuity between terminal ① or ② of push control unit harness connector and body ground.
4. Using above procedures, check for continuity in any other mode, as indicated in chart.

Mode switch	Terminal No.		Continuity
	⊕	⊖	
VENT	① or ②		
B/L	② or ③		
FOOT	③ or ④	Body ground	Yes
F/D	④ or ⑤		
DEF	⑤ or ⑥		

↓ OK

CHECK SIDE LINK.

→ NG → Disconnect mode door motor harness connector.

↓

B Note

CHECK BODY GROUND CIRCUIT FOR MODE DOOR MOTOR.
Does continuity exist between mode door motor harness terminal No. ㉒ and body ground?

↓ Yes

C Note

Check circuit continuity between each terminal on push control unit and on mode door motor.

Terminal No.		Continuity
⊕	⊖	
Push control unit	Mode door motor	
①	①	
②	②	
③	③	
④	④	Yes
⑤	⑤	
⑥	⑥	
⑦	⑦	
⑧	⑧	

↓ OK

Ⓐ

(Go to next page.)

Note:
If the result is NG after checking circuit continuity, repair harness or connector.

G20 AUTO. A/C SYSTEMS DIAGNOSTIC PROCEDURE 2 – CONT.

TROUBLE DIAGNOSES
Diagnostic Procedure 2 (Cont'd)

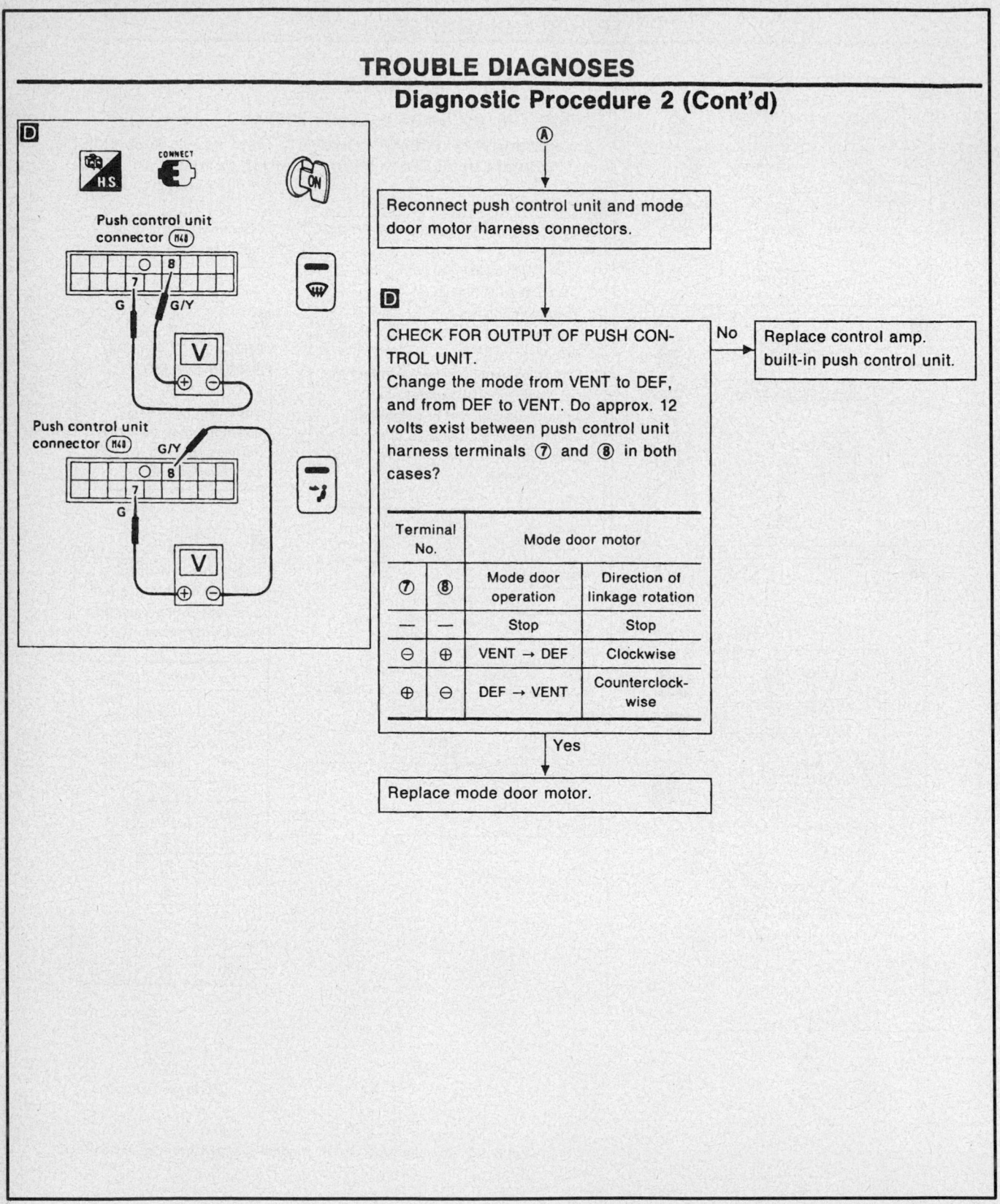

Ⓐ

Reconnect push control unit and mode door motor harness connectors.

Ⓓ

CHECK FOR OUTPUT OF PUSH CONTROL UNIT.
Change the mode from VENT to DEF, and from DEF to VENT. Do approx. 12 volts exist between push control unit harness terminals ⑦ and ⑧ in both cases?

No → Replace control amp. built-in push control unit.

Terminal No.		Mode door motor	
⑦	⑧	Mode door operation	Direction of linkage rotation
—	—	Stop	Stop
⊖	⊕	VENT → DEF	Clockwise
⊕	⊖	DEF → VENT	Counterclockwise

Yes

Replace mode door motor.

G20 AUTO. A/C SYSTEMS DIAGNOSTIC PROCEDURE 3

TROUBLE DIAGNOSES

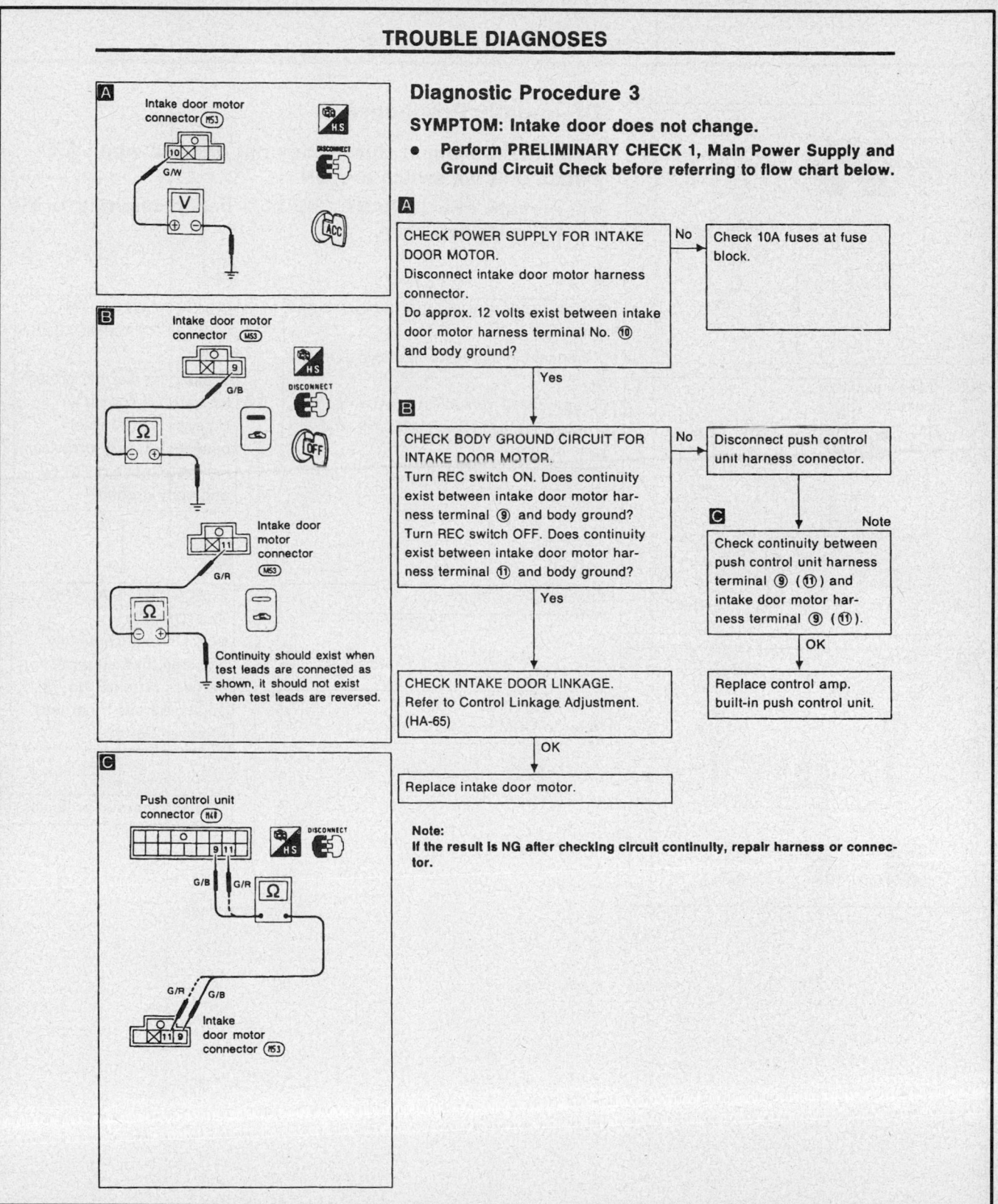

Diagnostic Procedure 3

SYMPTOM: Intake door does not change.

- **Perform PRELIMINARY CHECK 1, Main Power Supply and Ground Circuit Check before referring to flow chart below.**

A

| CHECK POWER SUPPLY FOR INTAKE DOOR MOTOR.
 Disconnect intake door motor harness connector.
 Do approx. 12 volts exist between intake door motor harness terminal No. ⑩ and body ground? | No → | Check 10A fuses at fuse block. |

Yes ↓

B

| CHECK BODY GROUND CIRCUIT FOR INTAKE DOOR MOTOR.
 Turn REC switch ON. Does continuity exist between intake door motor harness terminal ⑨ and body ground?
 Turn REC switch OFF. Does continuity exist between intake door motor harness terminal ⑪ and body ground? | No → | Disconnect push control unit harness connector. |

C   Note

| Check continuity between push control unit harness terminal ⑨ (⑪) and intake door motor harness terminal ⑨ (⑪). |

OK ↓

| Replace control amp. built-in push control unit. |

Yes ↓

| CHECK INTAKE DOOR LINKAGE.
 Refer to Control Linkage Adjustment. (HA-65) |

OK ↓

| Replace intake door motor. |

Note:
If the result is NG after checking circuit continuity, repair harness or connector.

G20 AUTO. A/C SYSTEMS DIAGNOSTIC PROCEDURE 4

TROUBLE DIAGNOSES

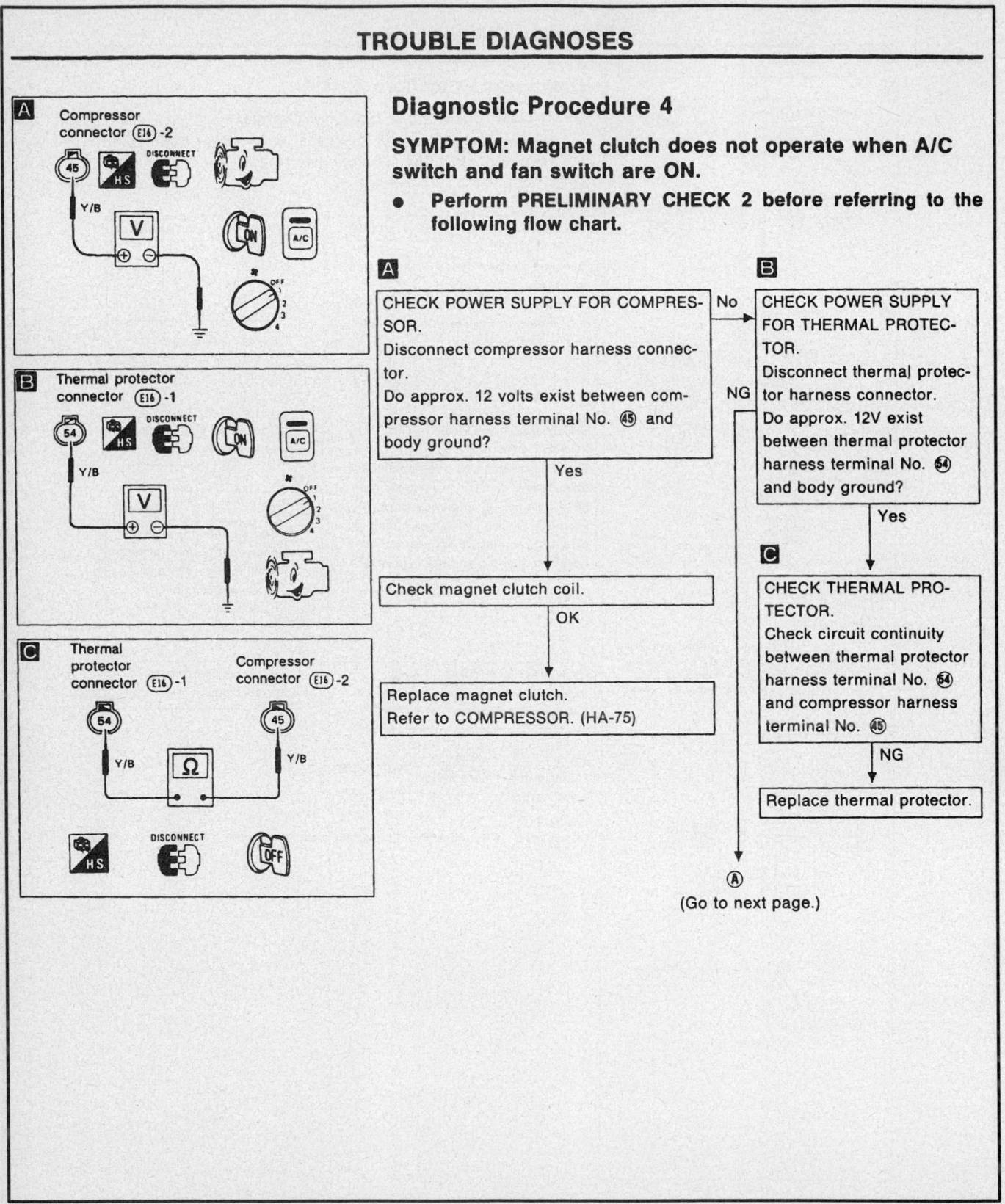

Diagnostic Procedure 4

SYMPTOM: Magnet clutch does not operate when A/C switch and fan switch are ON.

● **Perform PRELIMINARY CHECK 2 before referring to the following flow chart.**

A

CHECK POWER SUPPLY FOR COMPRESSOR.
Disconnect compressor harness connector.
Do approx. 12 volts exist between compressor harness terminal No. ㊺ and body ground?

No →

B

CHECK POWER SUPPLY FOR THERMAL PROTECTOR.
Disconnect thermal protector harness connector.
Do approx. 12V exist between thermal protector harness terminal No. ㊹ and body ground?

Yes ↓

Check magnet clutch coil.

OK ↓

Replace magnet clutch.
Refer to COMPRESSOR. (HA-75)

NG →

Yes ↓

C

CHECK THERMAL PROTECTOR.
Check circuit continuity between thermal protector harness terminal No. ㊹ and compressor harness terminal No. ㊺

NG ↓

Replace thermal protector.

Ⓐ
(Go to next page.)

8-38

G20 AUTO. A/C SYSTEMS DIAGNOSTIC PROCEDURE 4 — CONT.

TROUBLE DIAGNOSES

Diagnostic Procedure 4 (Cont'd)

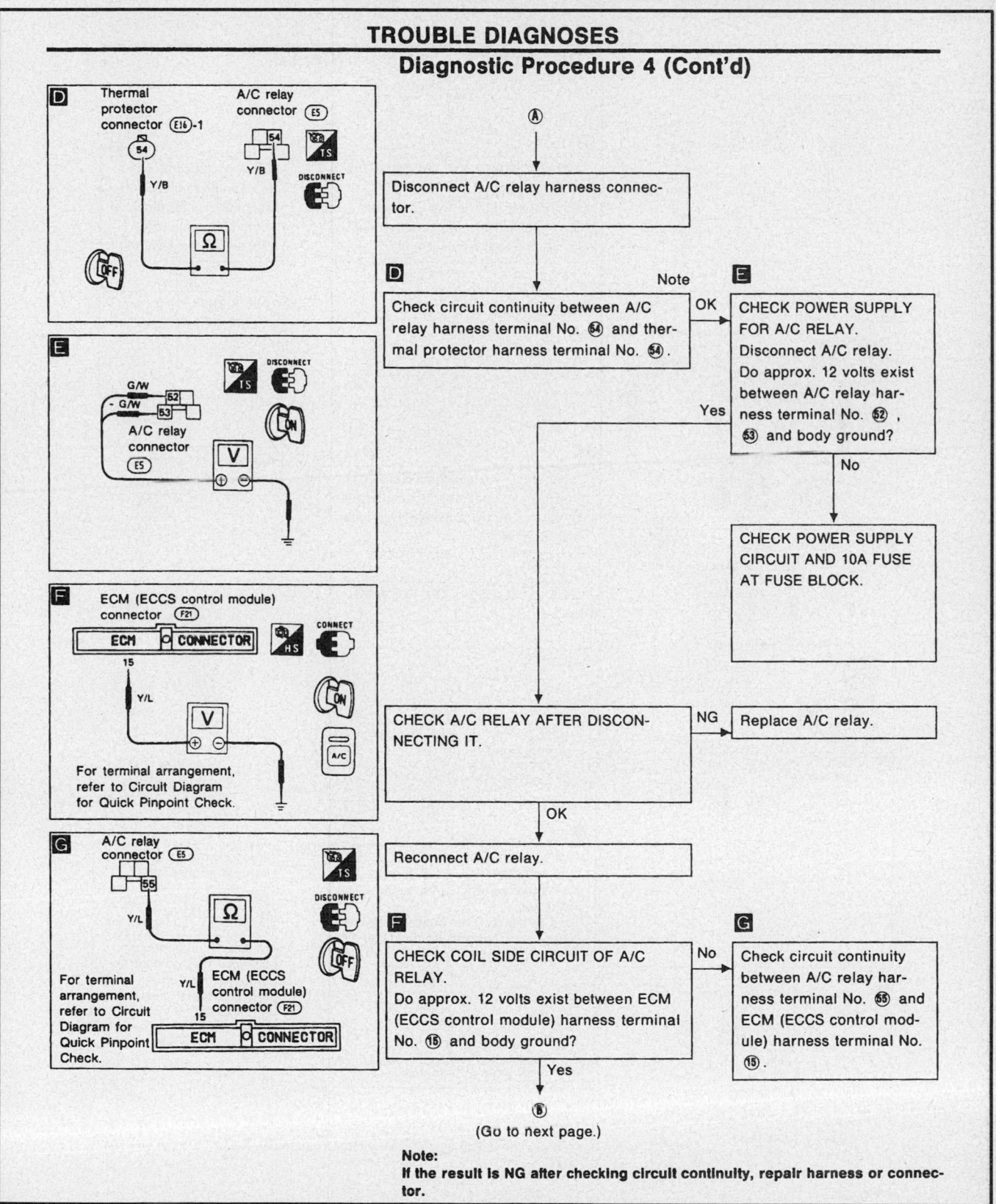

Note:
If the result is NG after checking circuit continuity, repair harness or connector.

G20 AUTO. A/C SYSTEMS DIAGNOSTIC PROCEDURE 4 - CONT.

TROUBLE DIAGNOSES
Diagnostic Procedure 4 (Cont'd)

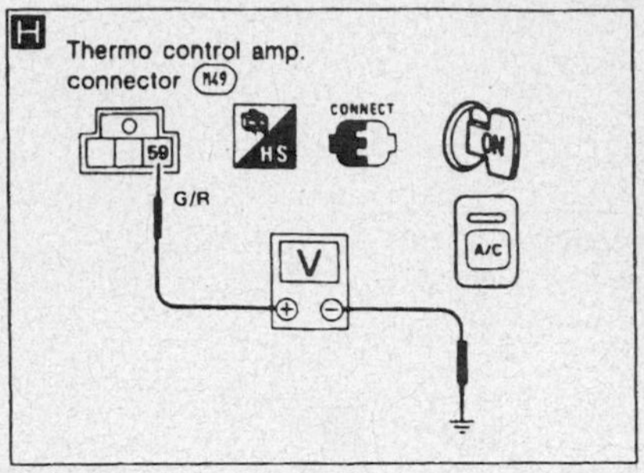

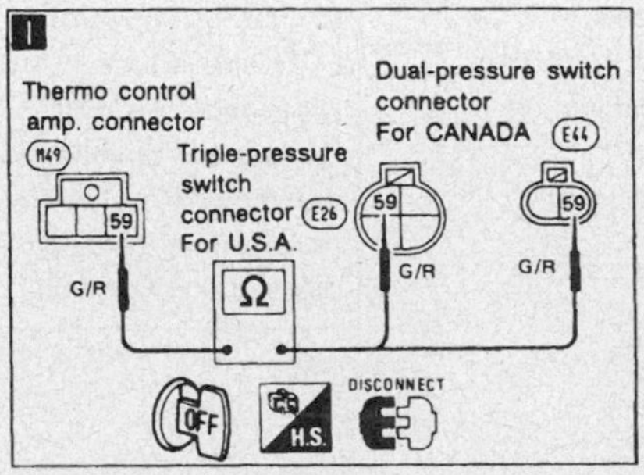

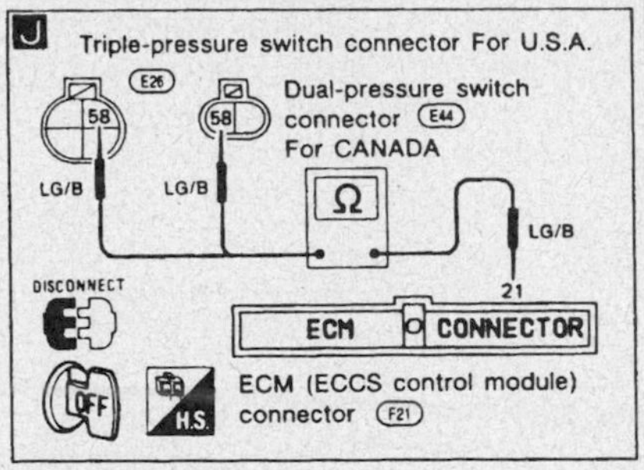

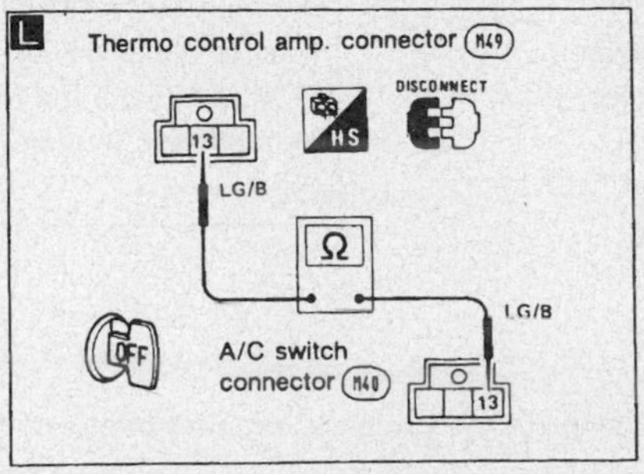

H Thermo control amp. connector (M49)

CONNECT
HS
ON
A/C

59
G/R
V
⊕ ⊖

I

Thermo control amp. connector (M49)

Triple-pressure switch connector (E26) For U.S.A.

Dual-pressure switch connector For CANADA (E44)

59

59 59

G/R G/R G/R

Ω

OFF HS DISCONNECT

J Triple-pressure switch connector For U.S.A.

(E26)

58

Dual-pressure switch connector (E44) For CANADA

58

LG/B LG/B

Ω

LG/B

DISCONNECT

21

OFF HS ECM (ECCS control module) connector (F21)

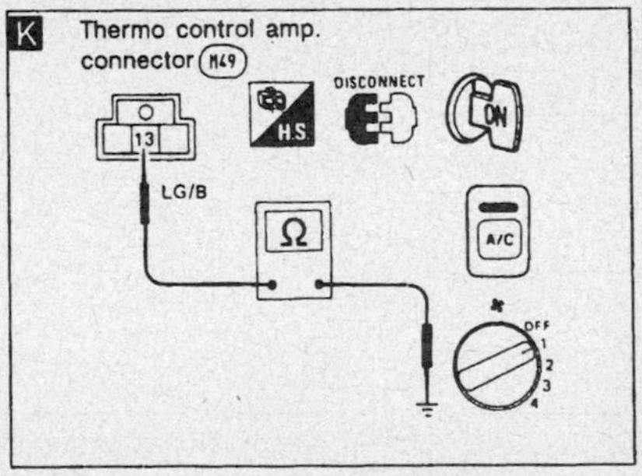

ECM CONNECTOR

K Thermo control amp. connector (M49)

HS DISCONNECT ON

13 A/C

LG/B

Ω

OFF
1
2
3
4

L Thermo control amp. connector (M49)

HS DISCONNECT

13

LG/B

Ω

LG/B

OFF A/C switch connector (M40)

13

B

H CHECK VOLTAGE FOR THERMO CONTROL AMP.
Do more than 8 volts exist between thermo control amp. harness terminal No. 59 and body ground?

→ No → **I** Note
Check circuit continuity between thermo control amp. harness terminal 59 and triple or dual-pressure switch terminal 59.

↓ OK

CHECK TRIPLE OR DUAL-PRESSURE SWITCH.

OK →

↓ NG

Replace triple or dual-pressure switch.

↓ Yes

C

J Note
Check circuit continuity between ECM (ECCS control module) harness terminal 21 and dual/triple pressure switch harness terminal 58.

↓ OK

CHECK ECM (ECCS CONTROL MODULE).

C

CHECK POWER SUPPLY FOR THERMO CONTROL AMP.

↓ OK

K CHECK BODY GROUND CIRCUIT FOR THERMO CONTROL AMP.
Disconnect thermo control amp. harness connector.
Does continuity exist between thermo control amp. harness terminal No. 13 and body ground?

→ No → Disconnect A/C switch harness connector.

↓

L Note
Check circuit continuity between thermo control amp. harness terminal 13 and A/C switch harness terminal 13.

↓ OK

D

↓ Yes

Replace thermo control amp.

Note:
If the result is NG after checking circuit continuity, repair harness or connector.

G20 AUTO. A/C SYSTEMS DIAGNOSTIC PROCEDURE 4 – CONT.

TROUBLE DIAGNOSES
Diagnostic Procedure 4 (Cont'd)

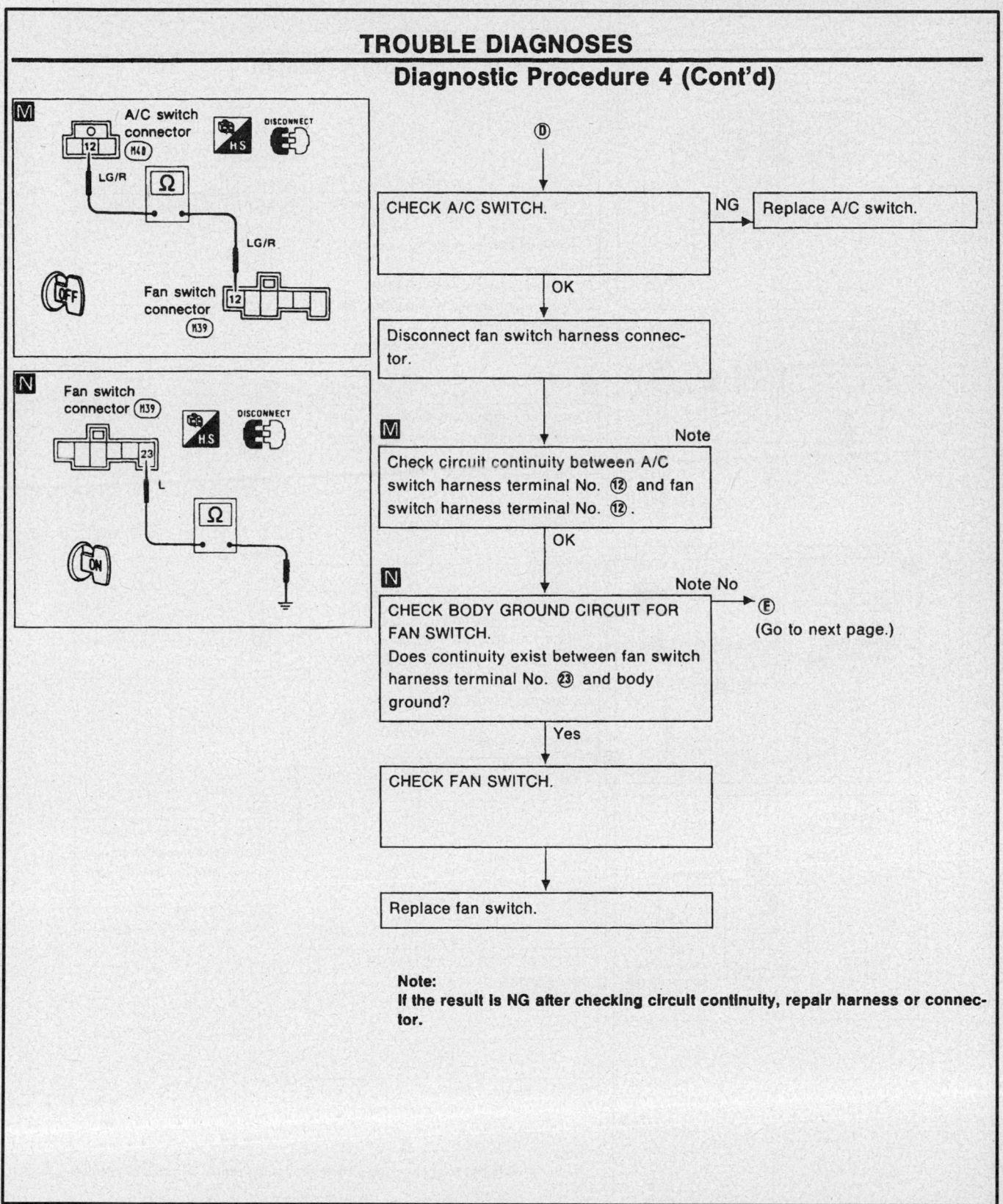

Ⓓ

CHECK A/C SWITCH. ──NG──▶ Replace A/C switch.

│OK

Disconnect fan switch harness connector.

Ⓜ ─────────────────── Note

Check circuit continuity between A/C switch harness terminal No. ⑫ and fan switch harness terminal No. ⑫.

│OK

Ⓝ ─────────────── Note No

CHECK BODY GROUND CIRCUIT FOR FAN SWITCH. ──▶ Ⓔ
Does continuity exist between fan switch harness terminal No. ㉓ and body ground? (Go to next page.)

│Yes

CHECK FAN SWITCH.

│

Replace fan switch.

Note:
If the result is NG after checking circuit continuity, repair harness or connector.

G20 AUTO. A/C SYSTEMS DIAGNOSTIC PROCEDURE 4 – CONT.

TROUBLE DIAGNOSES
Diagnostic Procedure 4 (Cont'd)

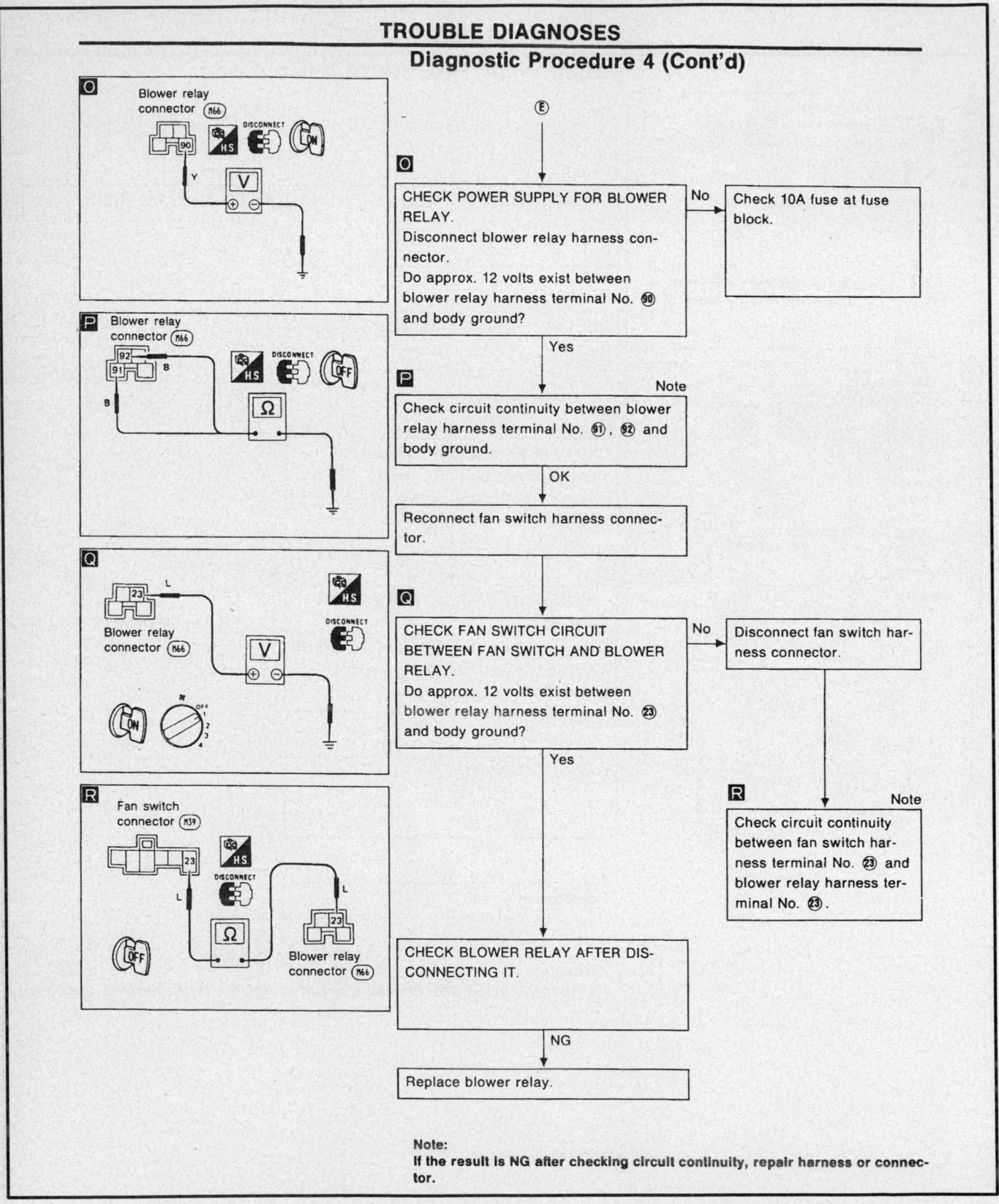

(E)

O

CHECK POWER SUPPLY FOR BLOWER RELAY.
Disconnect blower relay harness connector.
Do approx. 12 volts exist between blower relay harness terminal No. ⑨⓪ and body ground? → **No** → Check 10A fuse at fuse block.

Yes

P   Note

Check circuit continuity between blower relay harness terminal No. ⑨①, ⑨② and body ground.

OK

Reconnect fan switch harness connector.

Q

CHECK FAN SWITCH CIRCUIT BETWEEN FAN SWITCH AND BLOWER RELAY.
Do approx. 12 volts exist between blower relay harness terminal No. ㉓ and body ground? → **No** → Disconnect fan switch harness connector.

Yes

R   Note

Check circuit continuity between fan switch harness terminal No. ㉓ and blower relay harness terminal No. ㉓.

CHECK BLOWER RELAY AFTER DISCONNECTING IT.

NG

Replace blower relay.

Note:
If the result is NG after checking circuit continuity, repair harness or connector.

G20 AUTO. A/C SYSTEMS DIAGNOSTIC PROCEDURE 5

TROUBLE DIAGNOSES

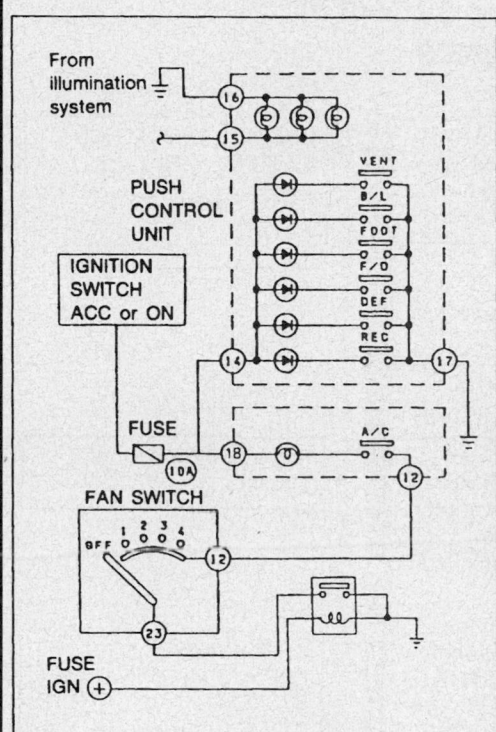

From illumination system

PUSH CONTROL UNIT

IGNITION SWITCH ACC or ON

FUSE
10A

FAN SWITCH
OFF 1 2 3 4

FUSE IGN

Diagnostic Procedure 5

SYMPTOM: Illumination or indicators of push control unit do not come on.

● **Perform Main Power Supply and Ground Circuit Check before referring to the following flow chart.**

> Turn ignition switch and lighting switch ON.

> CHECK ILLUMINATION AND INDICATORS.
> ● Turn A/C, REC and fan switches ON.
> ● Push VENT, B/L, FOOT, F/D and DEF switches in order.
> ● Check for incidents and follow the repairing methods as shown:

ILL. Push control unit	INCIDENTS							"How to repair"
	VENT	B/L	FOOT	F/D	DEF	REC	A/C	
×	○	○	○	○	○	○	—	Go to DIAGNOSTIC PROCEDURE 5-1.
—	○	○	○	○	○	○	×	Go to DIAGNOSTIC PROCEDURE 5-2.
—	×	×	×	×	×	×	—	Go to DIAGNOSTIC PROCEDURE 5-3.
—	∧						—	Replace control amp. built-in push control unit.

○: Illumination or indicator comes on.
×: Illumination or indicator does not come on.
△: Some indicators for VENT, B/L, FOOT, F/D, DEF or REC come on.

G20 AUTO. A/C SYSTEMS DIAGNOSTIC PROCEDURE 5 — CONT.

TROUBLE DIAGNOSES

Diagnostic Procedure 5 (Cont'd)
DIAGNOSTIC PROCEDURE 5-1

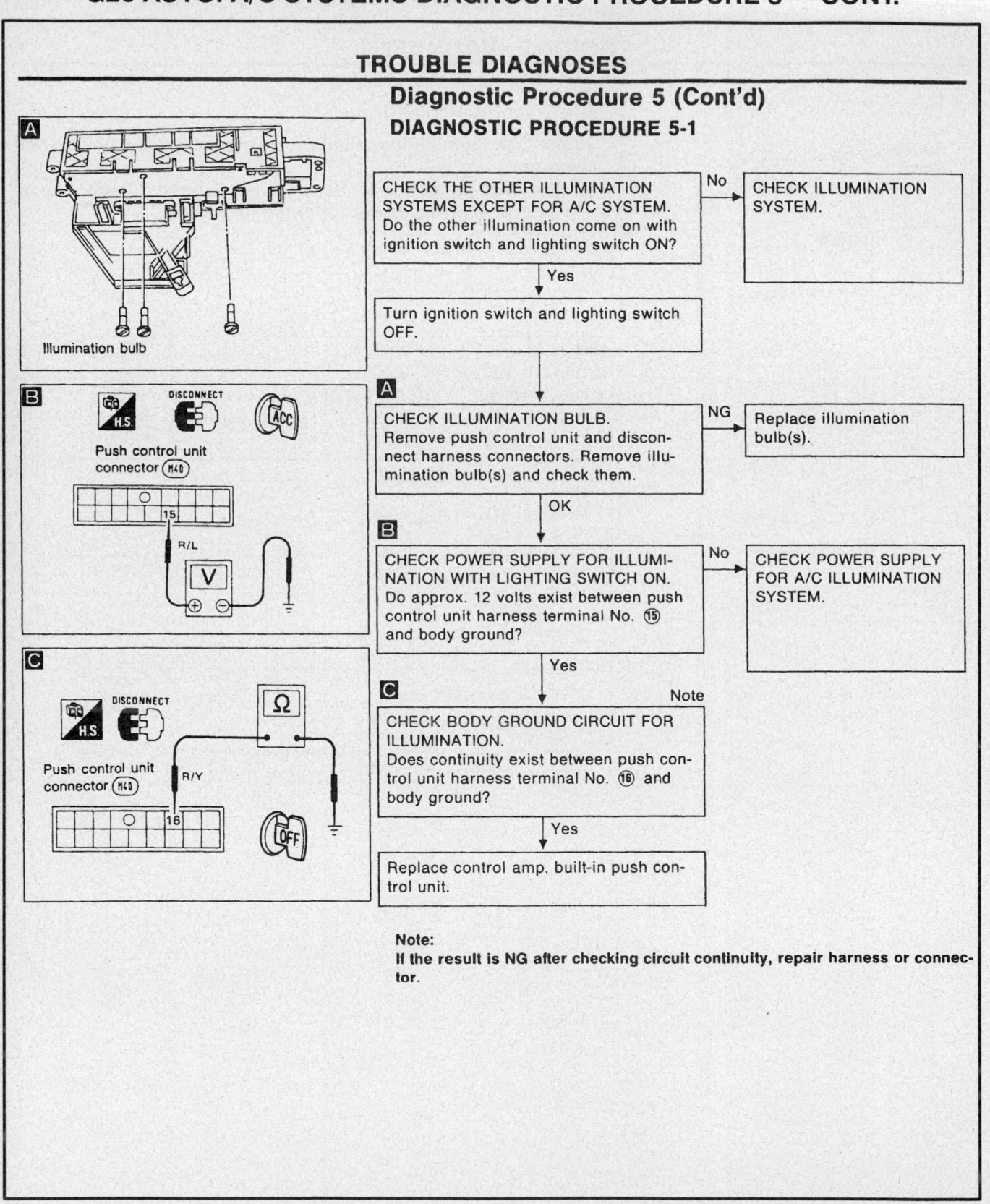

A Illumination bulb

B Push control unit connector (M40)
15
R/L

C Push control unit connector (M40)
R/Y   16

CHECK THE OTHER ILLUMINATION SYSTEMS EXCEPT FOR A/C SYSTEM. Do the other illumination come on with ignition switch and lighting switch ON? → No → CHECK ILLUMINATION SYSTEM.

↓ Yes

Turn ignition switch and lighting switch OFF.

↓

A CHECK ILLUMINATION BULB. Remove push control unit and disconnect harness connectors. Remove illumination bulb(s) and check them. → NG → Replace illumination bulb(s).

↓ OK

B CHECK POWER SUPPLY FOR ILLUMINATION WITH LIGHTING SWITCH ON. Do approx. 12 volts exist between push control unit harness terminal No. ⑮ and body ground? → No → CHECK POWER SUPPLY FOR A/C ILLUMINATION SYSTEM.

↓ Yes

C   Note
CHECK BODY GROUND CIRCUIT FOR ILLUMINATION. Does continuity exist between push control unit harness terminal No. ⑯ and body ground?

↓ Yes

Replace control amp. built-in push control unit.

Note:
If the result is NG after checking circuit continuity, repair harness or connector.

G20 AUTO. A/C SYSTEMS DIAGNOSTIC PROCEDURE 5 − CONT.

TROUBLE DIAGNOSES

Diagnostic Procedure 5 (Cont'd)
DIAGNOSTIC PROCEDURE 5-2

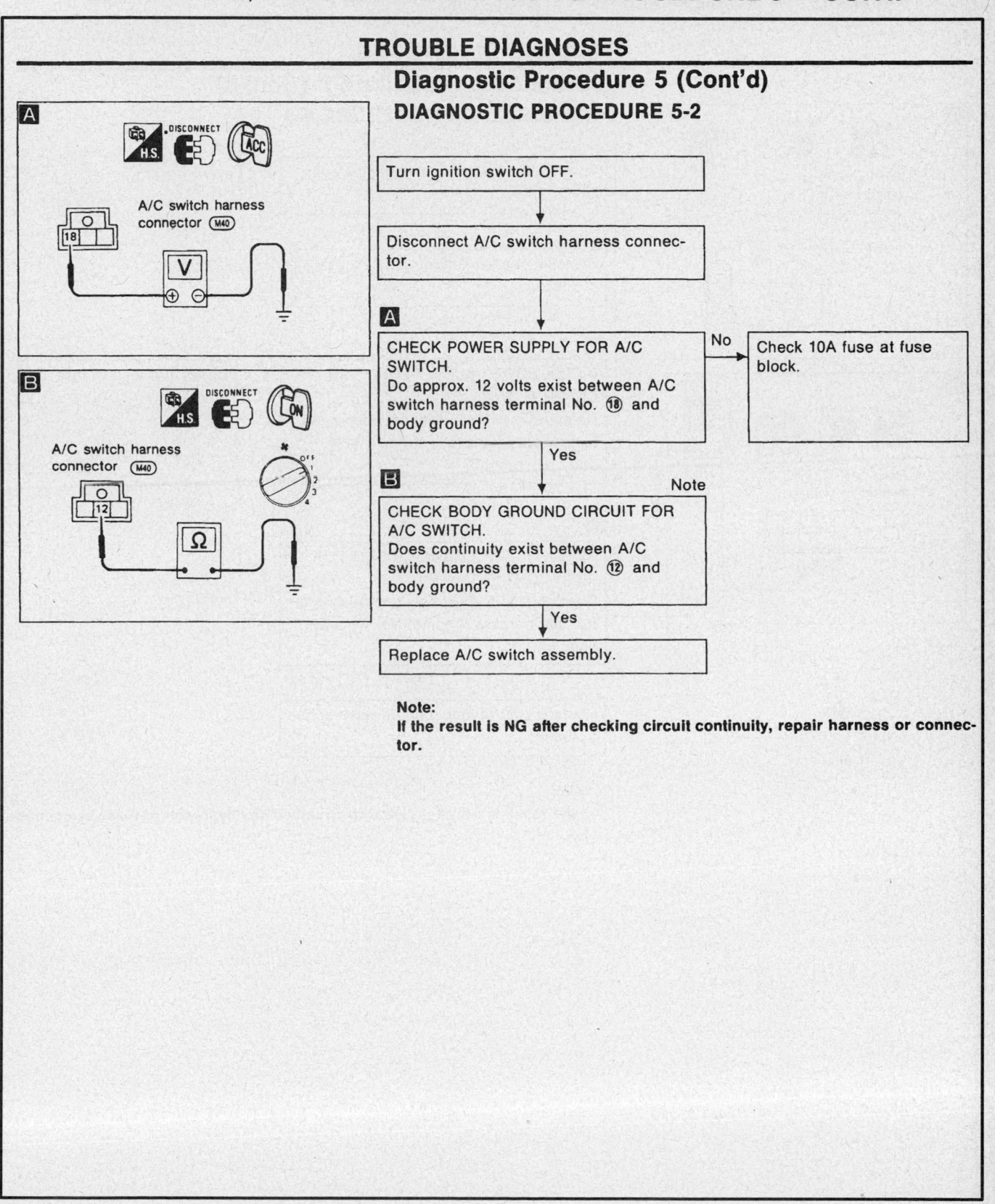

A

A/C switch harness connector (M40)

B

A/C switch harness connector (M40)

Turn ignition switch OFF.

↓

Disconnect A/C switch harness connector.

↓

A
CHECK POWER SUPPLY FOR A/C SWITCH.
Do approx. 12 volts exist between A/C switch harness terminal No. ⑱ and body ground?

→ No → Check 10A fuse at fuse block.

↓ Yes

B   Note
CHECK BODY GROUND CIRCUIT FOR A/C SWITCH.
Does continuity exist between A/C switch harness terminal No. ⑫ and body ground?

↓ Yes

Replace A/C switch assembly.

Note:
If the result is NG after checking circuit continuity, repair harness or connector.

G20 AUTO. A/C SYSTEMS DIAGNOSTIC PROCEDURE 5 – CONT.

TROUBLE DIAGNOSES

Diagnostic Procedure 5 (Cont'd)
DIAGNOSTIC PROCEDURE 5-3

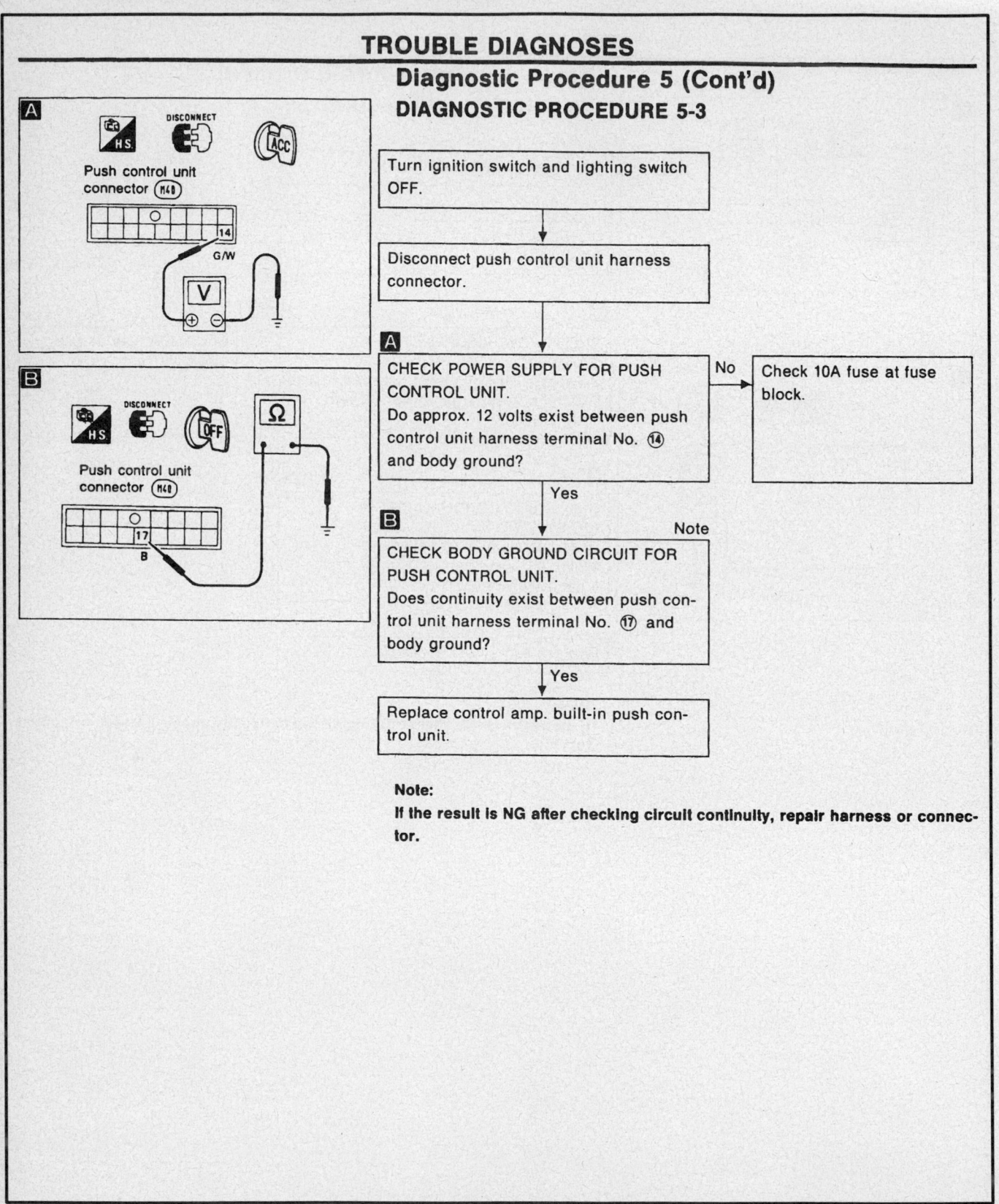

A

Push control unit connector (M48)

G/W

B

Push control unit connector (M48)

B

Turn ignition switch and lighting switch OFF.

↓

Disconnect push control unit harness connector.

↓

A CHECK POWER SUPPLY FOR PUSH CONTROL UNIT.
Do approx. 12 volts exist between push control unit harness terminal No. ⑭ and body ground?

No → Check 10A fuse at fuse block.

Yes ↓

B CHECK BODY GROUND CIRCUIT FOR PUSH CONTROL UNIT.
Does continuity exist between push control unit harness terminal No. ⑰ and body ground?

Note

Yes ↓

Replace control amp. built-in push control unit.

Note:
If the result is NG after checking circuit continuity, repair harness or connector.

1993 J30 AUTO. A/C SYSTEMS DIAGNOSTIC PROCEDURES 1 AND 2

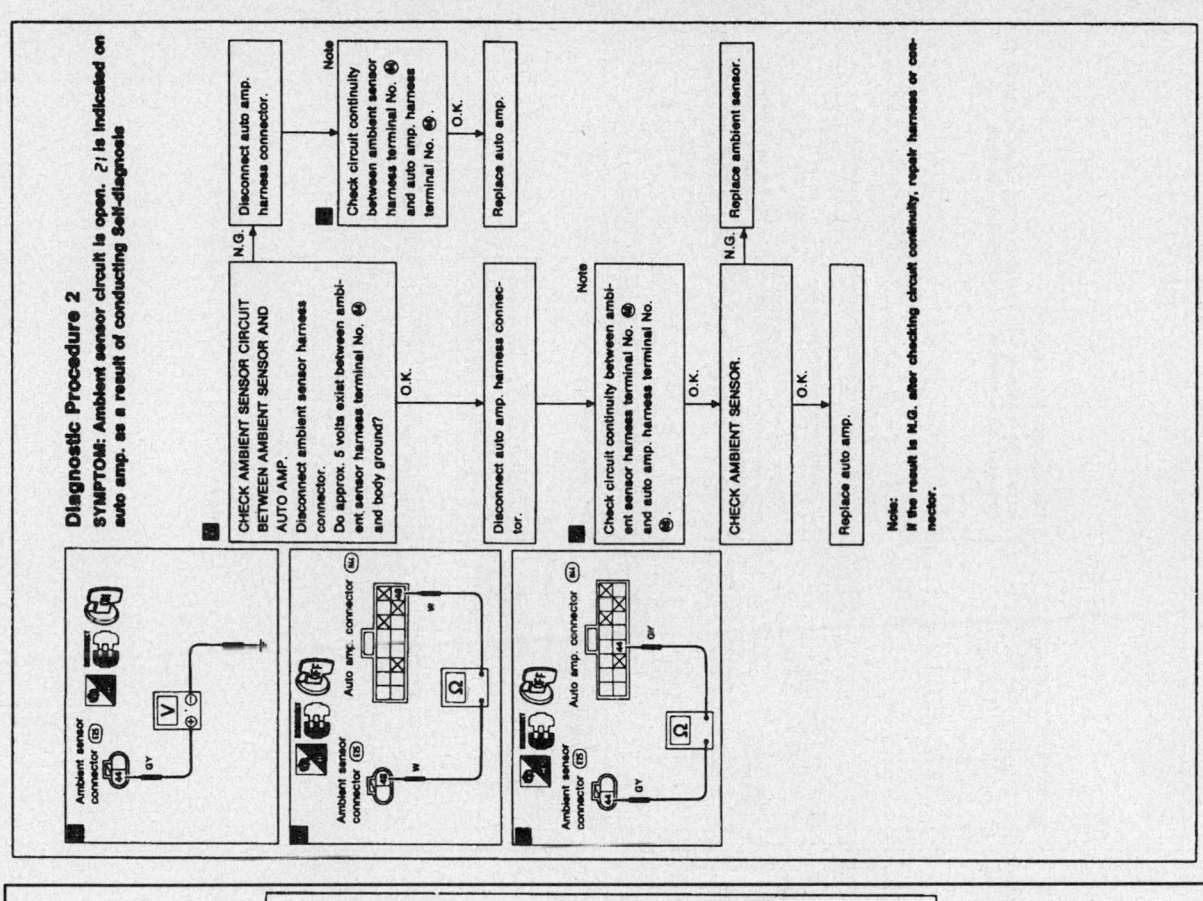

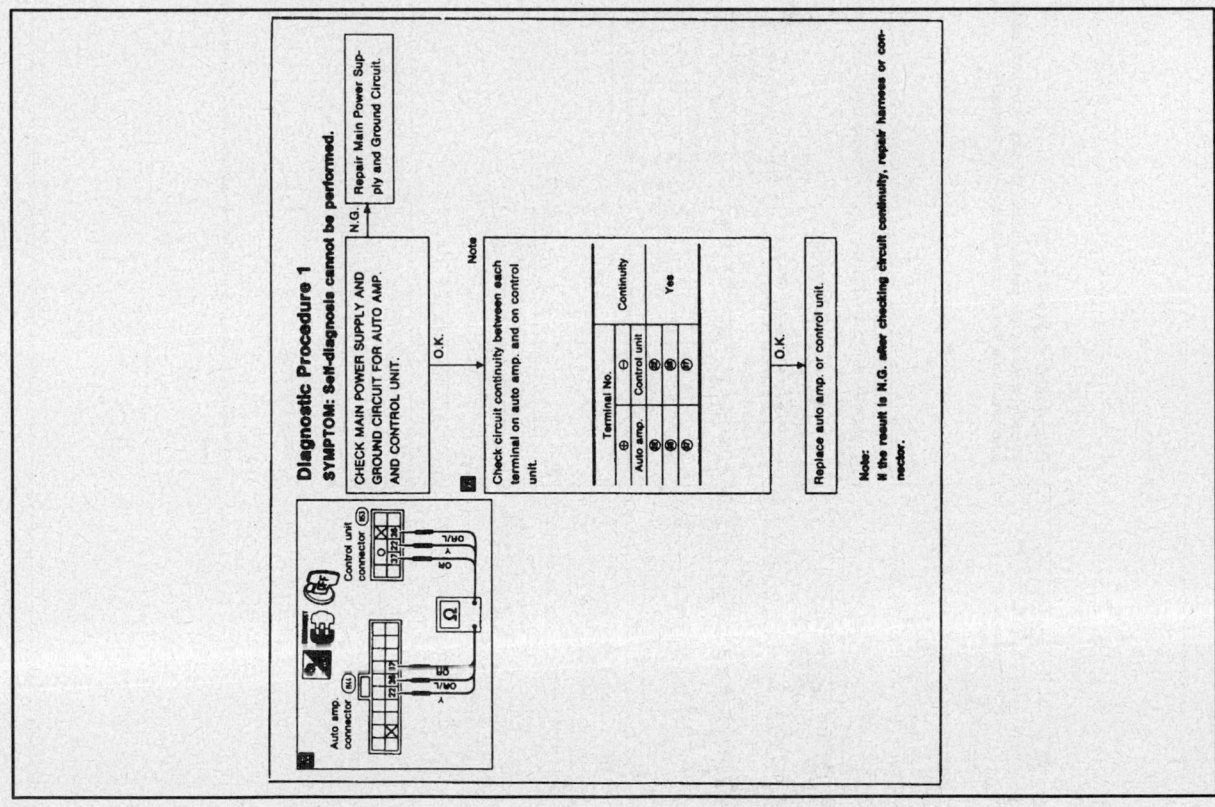

1993 J30 AUTO. A/C SYSTEMS DIAGNOSTIC PROCEDURES 3 AND 4

Diagnostic Procedure

SYMPTOM: Intake sensor circuit is open. 24 is indicated on auto amp. as a result of conducting Self-diagnosis.

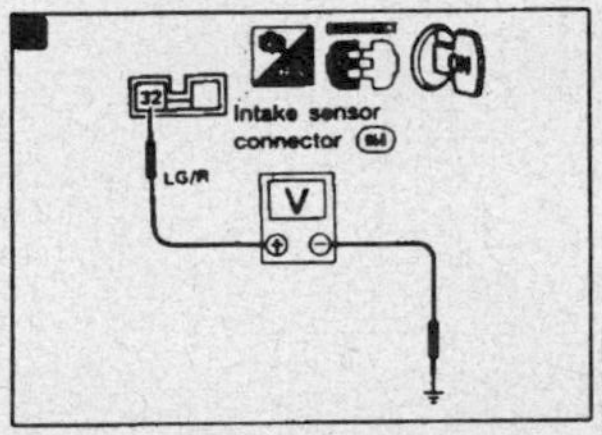

CHECK INTAKE SENSOR CIRCUIT BETWEEN INTAKE SENSOR AND AUTO AMP.
Disconnect intake sensor harness connector.
Do approx. 5 volts exist between intake sensor harness terminal No. 28 and body ground?

N.G. →
Disconnect auto amp. harness connector.
Check circuit continuity between intake harness terminal No. 28 and auto amp. harness terminal No. 68.
O.K. → Replace auto amp.

O.K. ↓

Disconnect auto amp. harness connector.
Check circuit continuity between intake sensor harness terminal No. 68 and auto amp. harness terminal No. 28.
CHECK INTAKE SENSOR.

N.G. → Replace intake sensor.

O.K. ↓

Replace auto amp.

Note:
If the result is N.G. after checking circuit continuity, repair harness or connector.

Diagnostic Procedure 3

SYMPTOM: In-vehicle sensor circuit is open. 22 is indicated on auto amp. as a result of conducting Self-diagnosis.

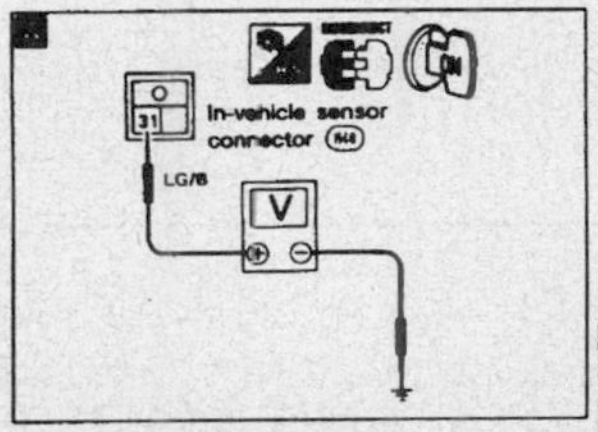

CHECK IN-VEHICLE SENSOR CIRCUIT BETWEEN IN-VEHICLE SENSOR AND AUTO AMP.
Disconnect in-vehicle sensor harness connector.
Do approx. 5 volts exist between in-vehicle sensor harness terminal No. 31 and body ground?

N.G. →
Disconnect auto amp. harness connector.
Check circuit continuity between in-vehicle sensor harness terminal No. 31 and auto amp. harness terminal No. 67.
O.K. → Replace auto amp.

O.K. ↓

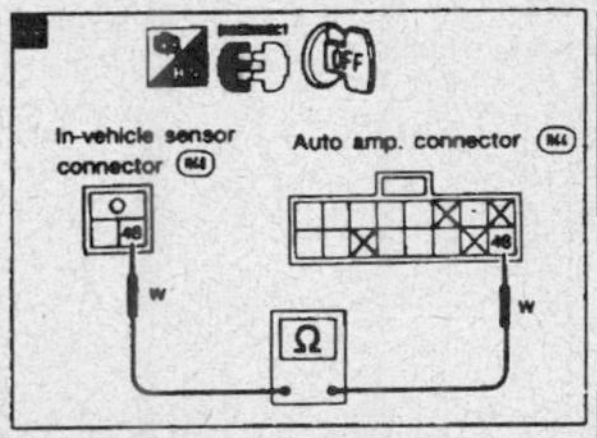

Disconnect auto amp. harness connector.
Check circuit continuity between in-vehicle sensor harness terminal No. and auto amp. harness terminal No. 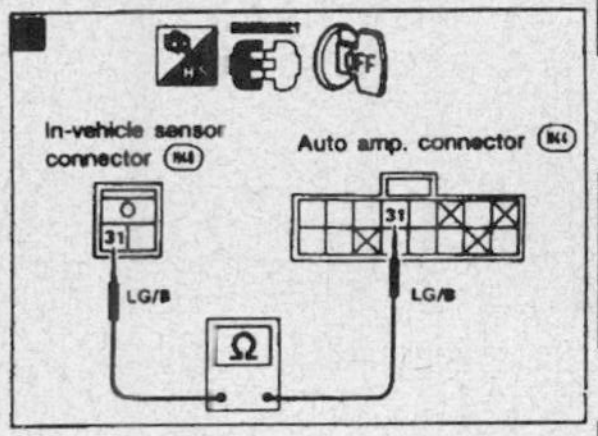
CHECK IN-VEHICLE SENSOR.

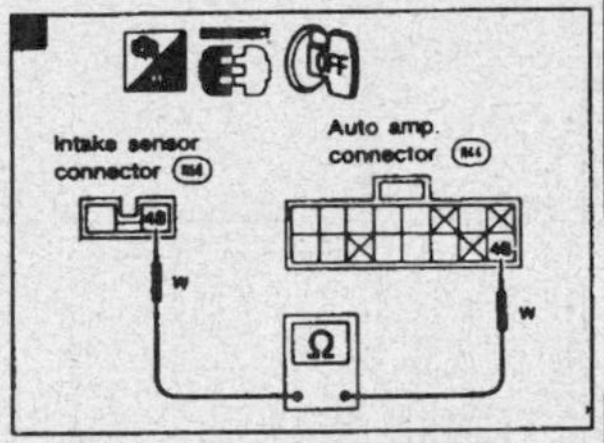

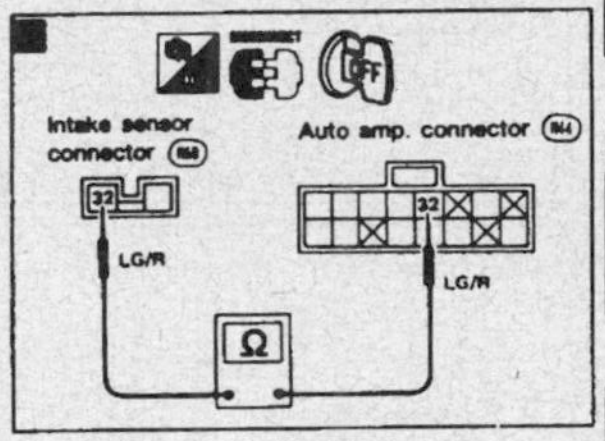

N.G. → Replace in-vehicle sensor.

O.K. ↓

Replace auto amp.

Note:
If the result is N.G. after checking circuit continuity, repair harness or connector.

1993 J30 AUTO. A/C SYSTEMS DIAGNOSTIC PROCEDURES 5 AND 6

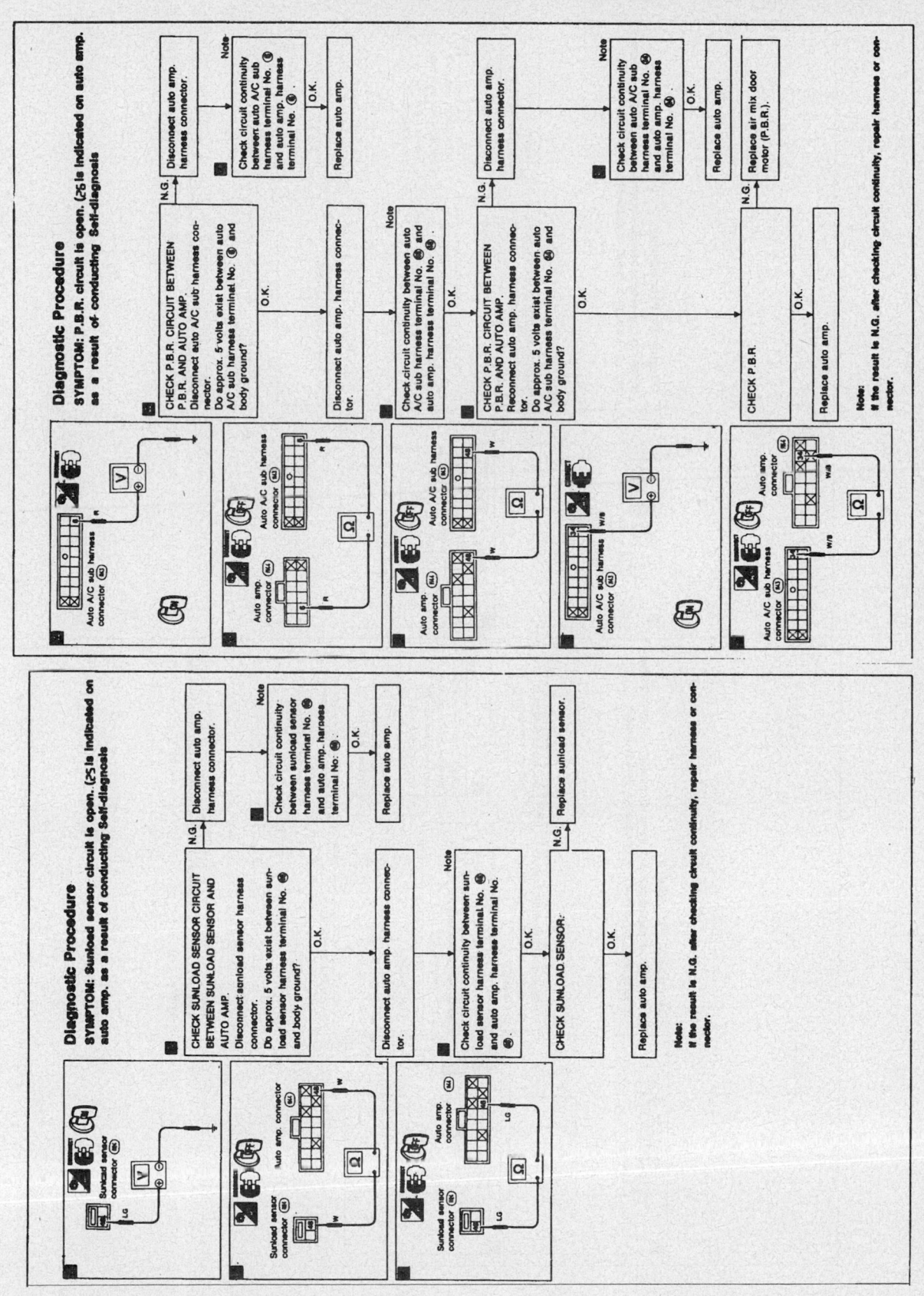

1993 J30 AUTO. A/C SYSTEMS DIAGNOSTIC PROCEDURES 7 AND 8

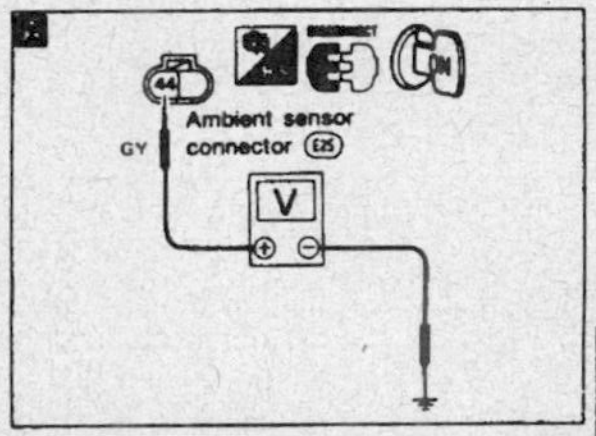

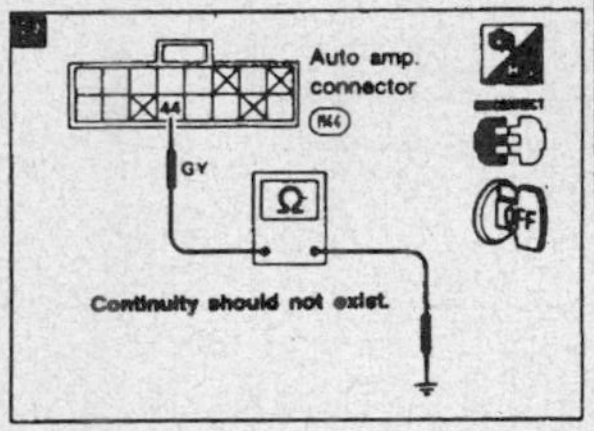

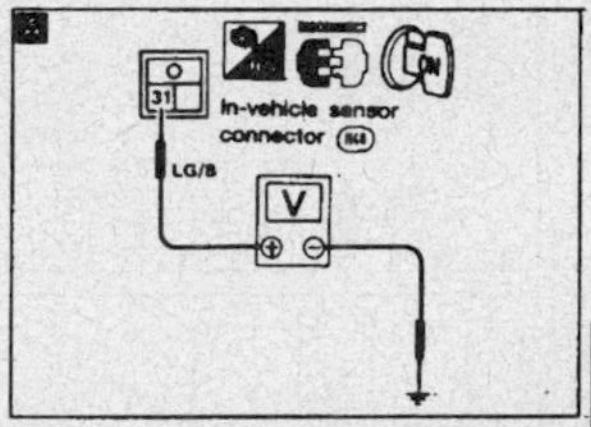

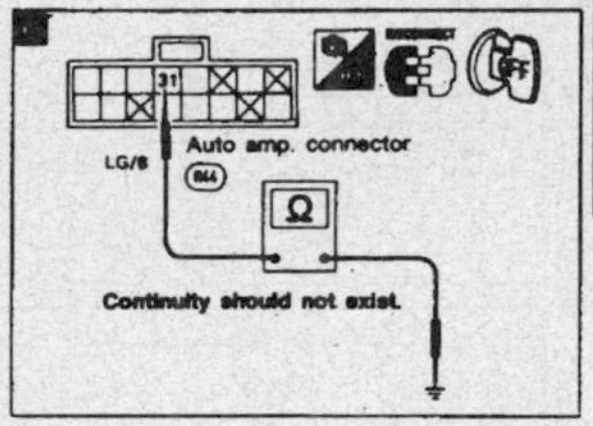

Diagnostic Procedure

SYMPTOM: In-vehicle sensor circuit is shorted. -22 is indicated on auto amp. as a result of conducting Self-diagnosis.

CHECK IN-VEHICLE SENSOR CIRCUIT BETWEEN IN-VEHICLE SENSOR AND AUTO AMP.
Disconnect in-vehicle sensor harness connector.
Do approx. 5 volts exist between in-vehicle sensor harness terminal No. ㉗ and body ground?

→ N.G. → Disconnect auto amp. harness connector.
→ Note
Check circuit continuity between auto amp. harness terminal No. ㉘ and body ground.
→ O.K. → Replace auto amp.
→ N.G. → Replace in-vehicle sensor.

→ O.K. → CHECK IN-VEHICLE SENSOR.
→ O.K. → Replace auto amp.

Note:
If the result is N.G. after checking circuit continuity, repair harness or connector.

Diagnostic Procedure

SYMPTOM: Ambient sensor circuit is shorted. -21 is indicated on auto amp. as a result of conducting Self-diagnosis.

CHECK AMBIENT SENSOR CIRCUIT BETWEEN AMBIENT SENSOR AND AUTO AMP.
Disconnect ambient sensor harness connector.
Do approx. 5 volts exist between ambient sensor harness terminal No. ㊸ and body ground?

→ N.G. → Disconnect auto amp. harness connector.
→ Note
Check circuit continuity between auto amp. harness terminal No. ㊹ and body ground.
→ O.K. → Replace auto amp.
→ N.G. → Replace ambient sensor.

→ O.K. → CHECK AMBIENT SENSOR.
→ O.K. → Replace auto amp.

Note:
If the result is N.G. after checking circuit continuity, repair harness or connector.

1993 J30 AUTO. A/C SYSTEMS DIAGNOSTIC PROCEDURES 9 AND 10

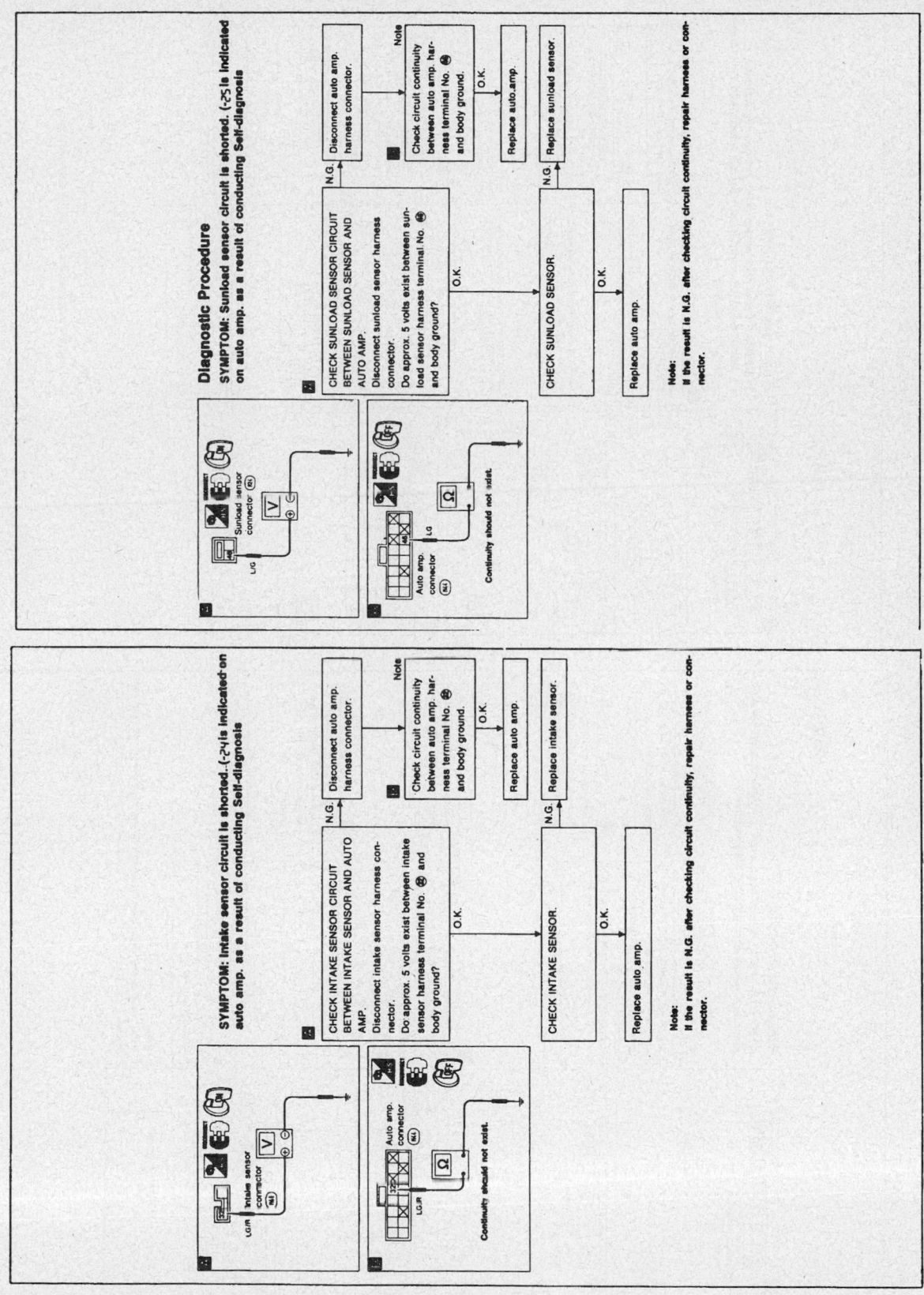

1993 J30 AUTO. A/C SYSTEMS DIAGNOSTIC PROCEDURES 11 AND 12

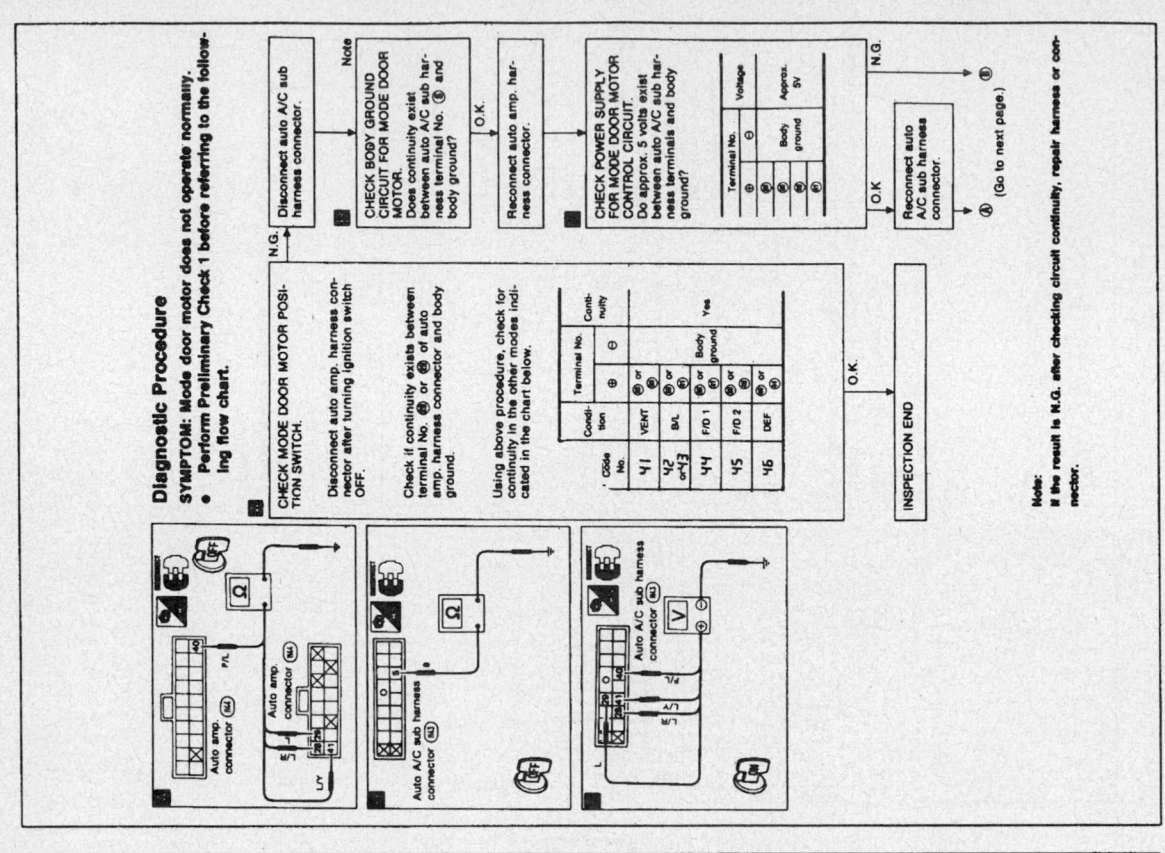

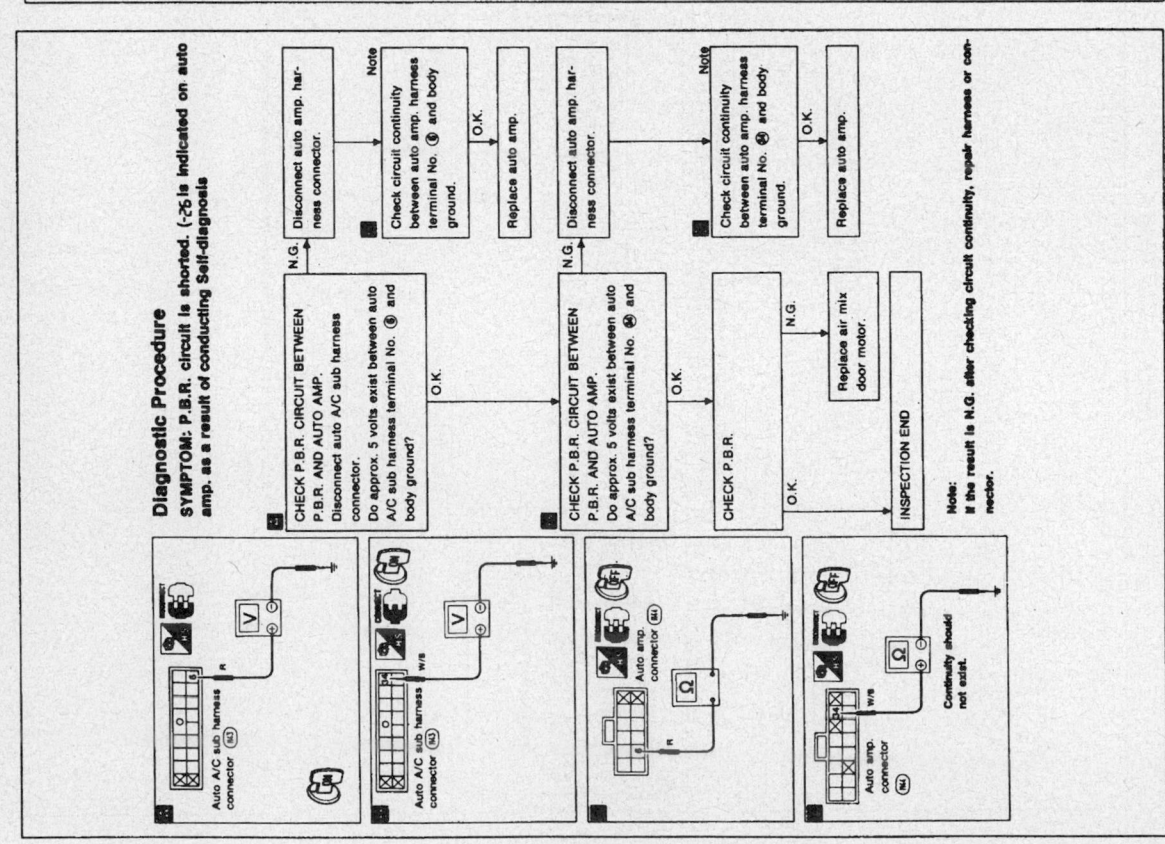

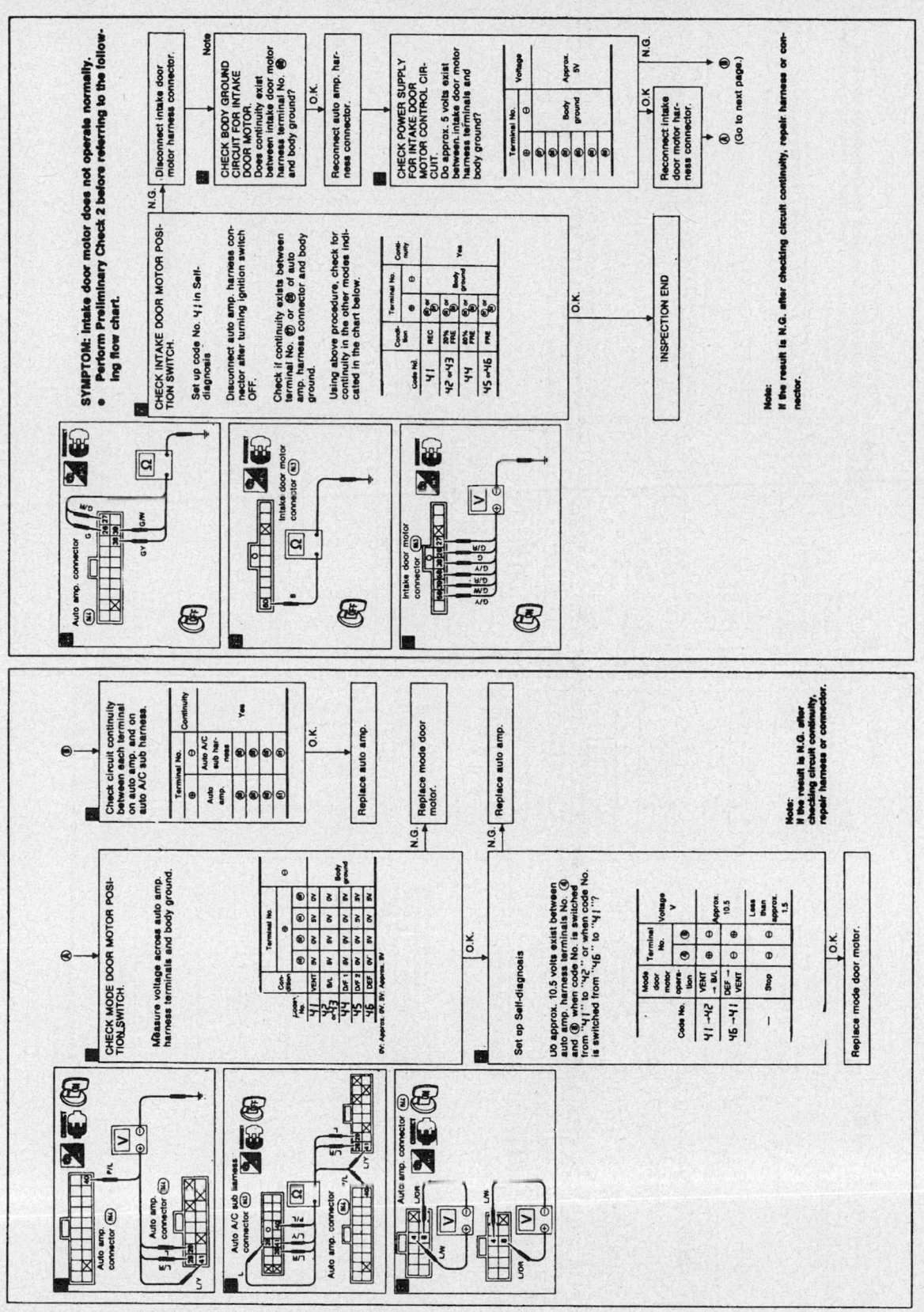

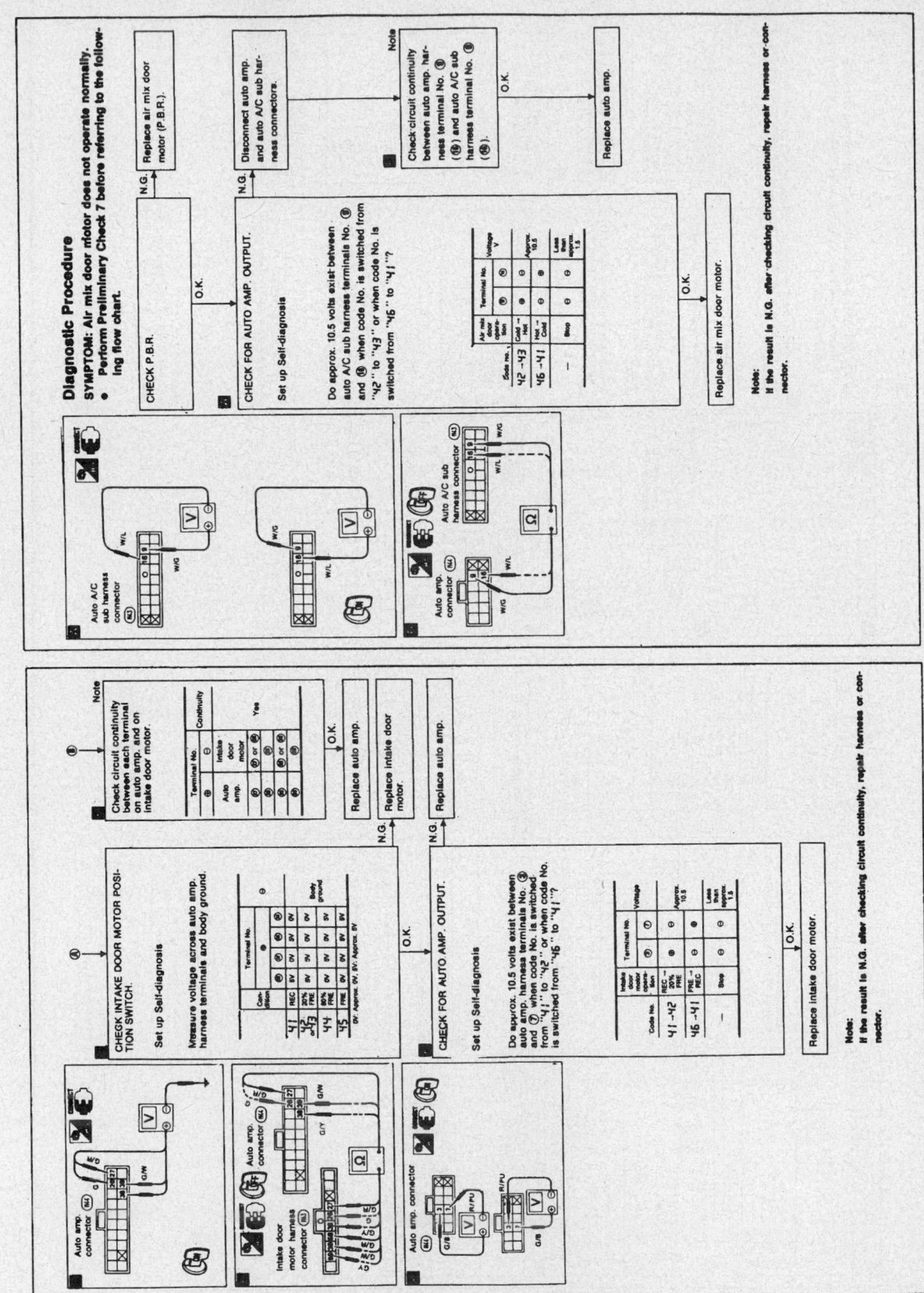

1993 J30 AUTO. A/C SYSTEMS DIAGNOSTIC PROCEDURE 15

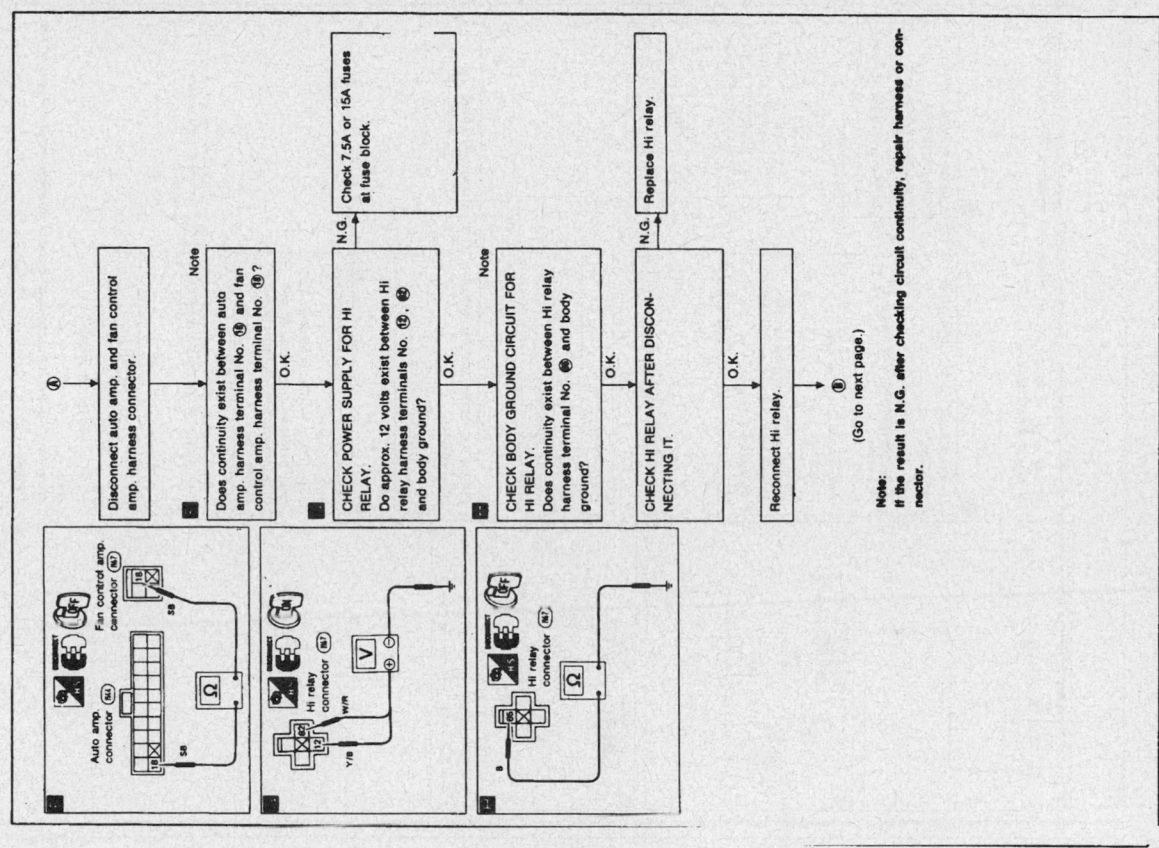

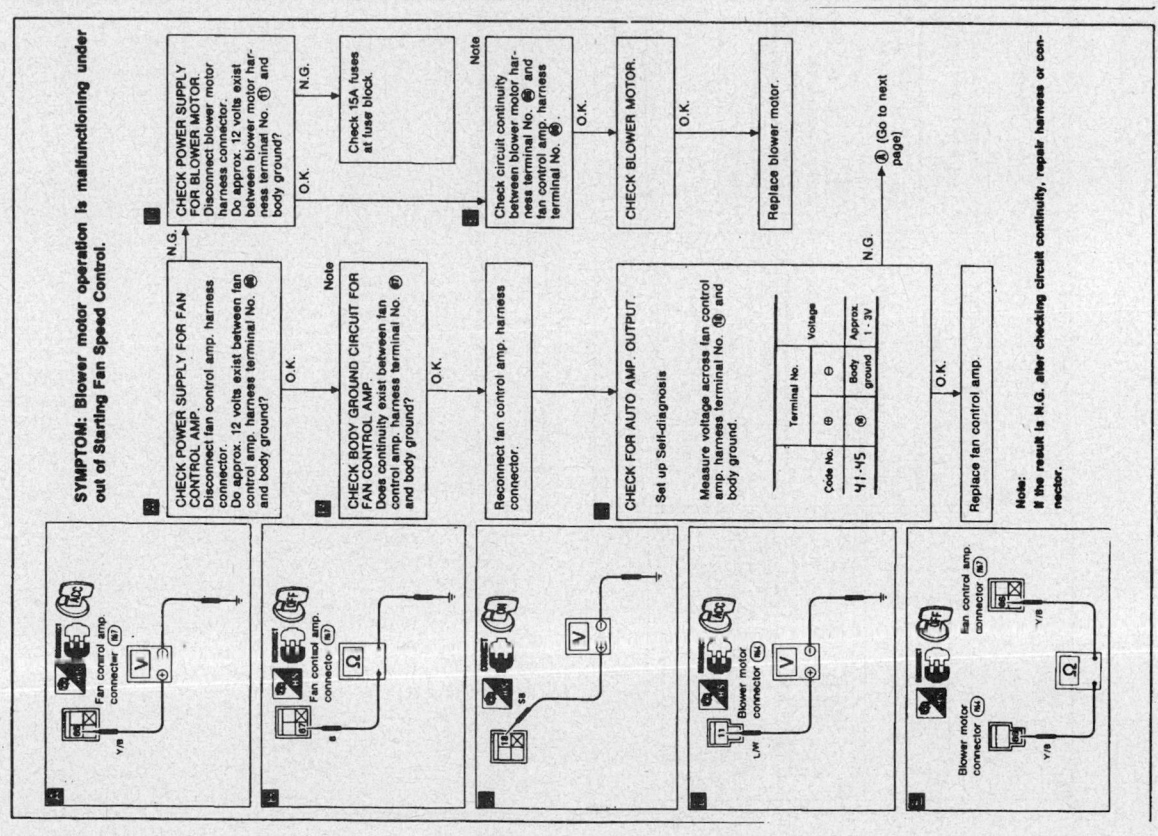

1993 J30 AUTO. A/C SYSTEMS DIAGNOSTIC PROCEDURES 15, CONT'D. AND 16

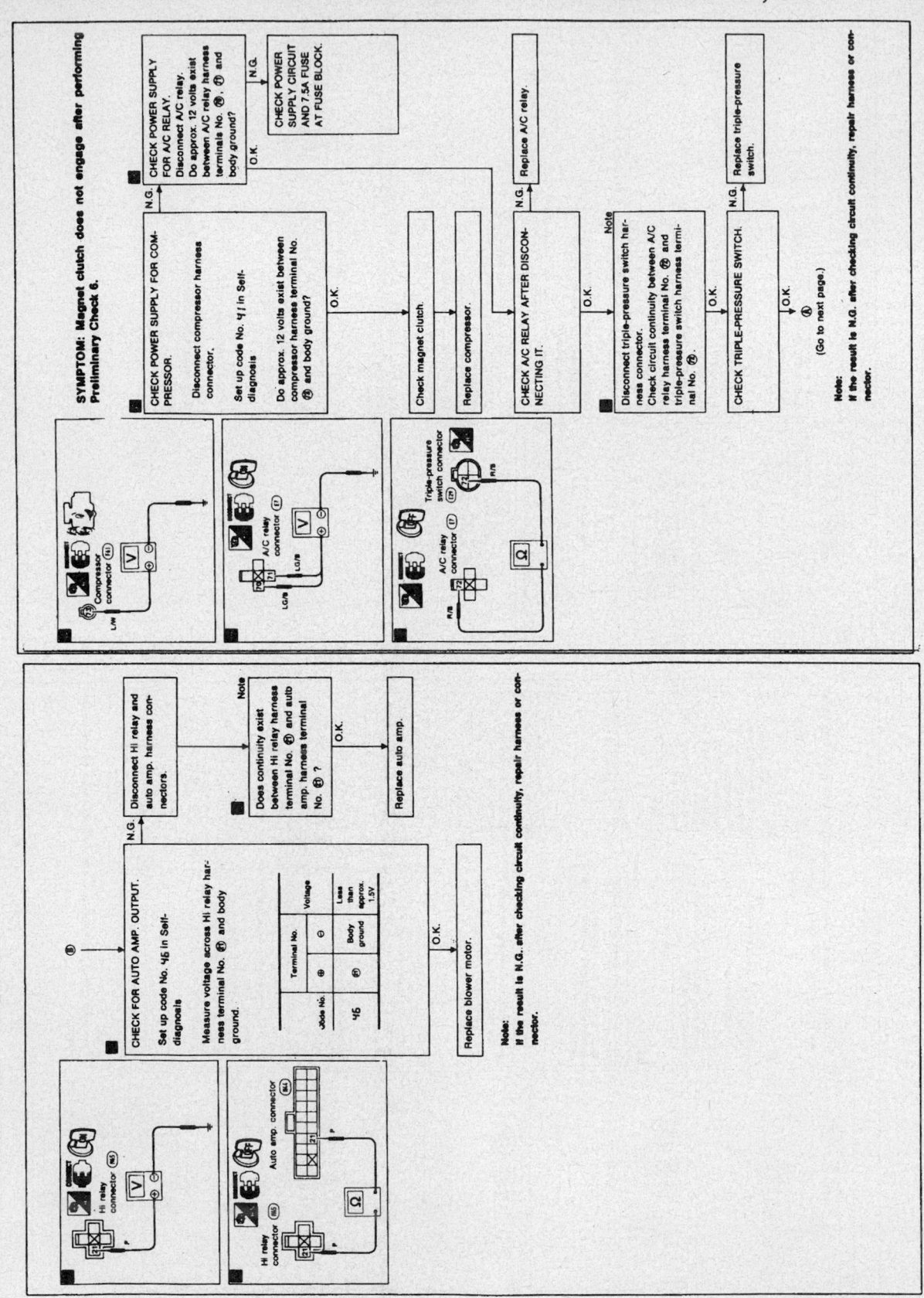

1993 J30 AUTO. A/C SYSTEMS DIAGNOSTIC PROCEDURE 16, CONT'D.

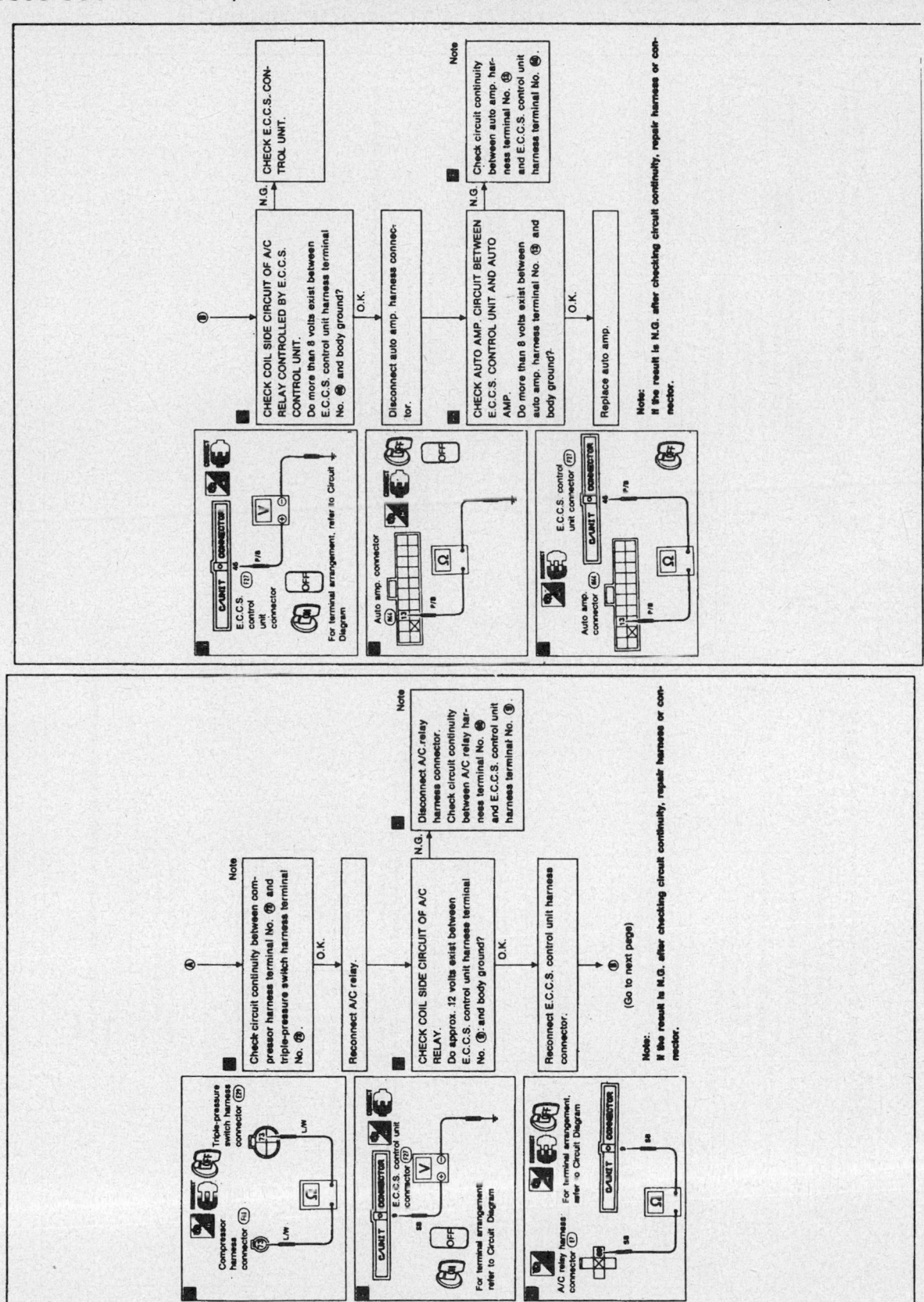

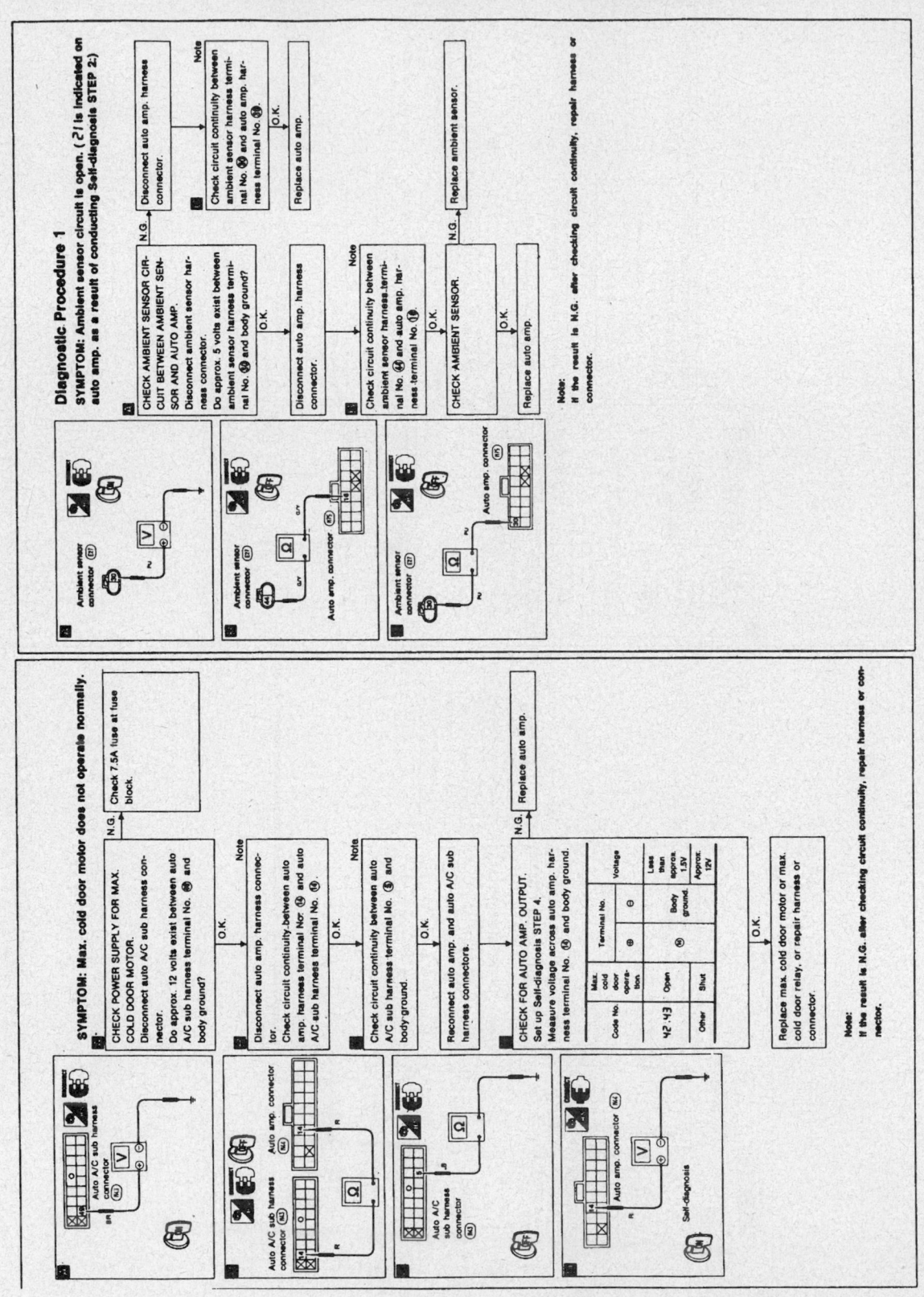

1993 J30 AUTO. A/C SYSTEMS DIAGNOSTIC PROCEDURE 1 AND Q45 AUTO. A/C SYSTEMS DIAGNOSTIC PROCEDURE 1

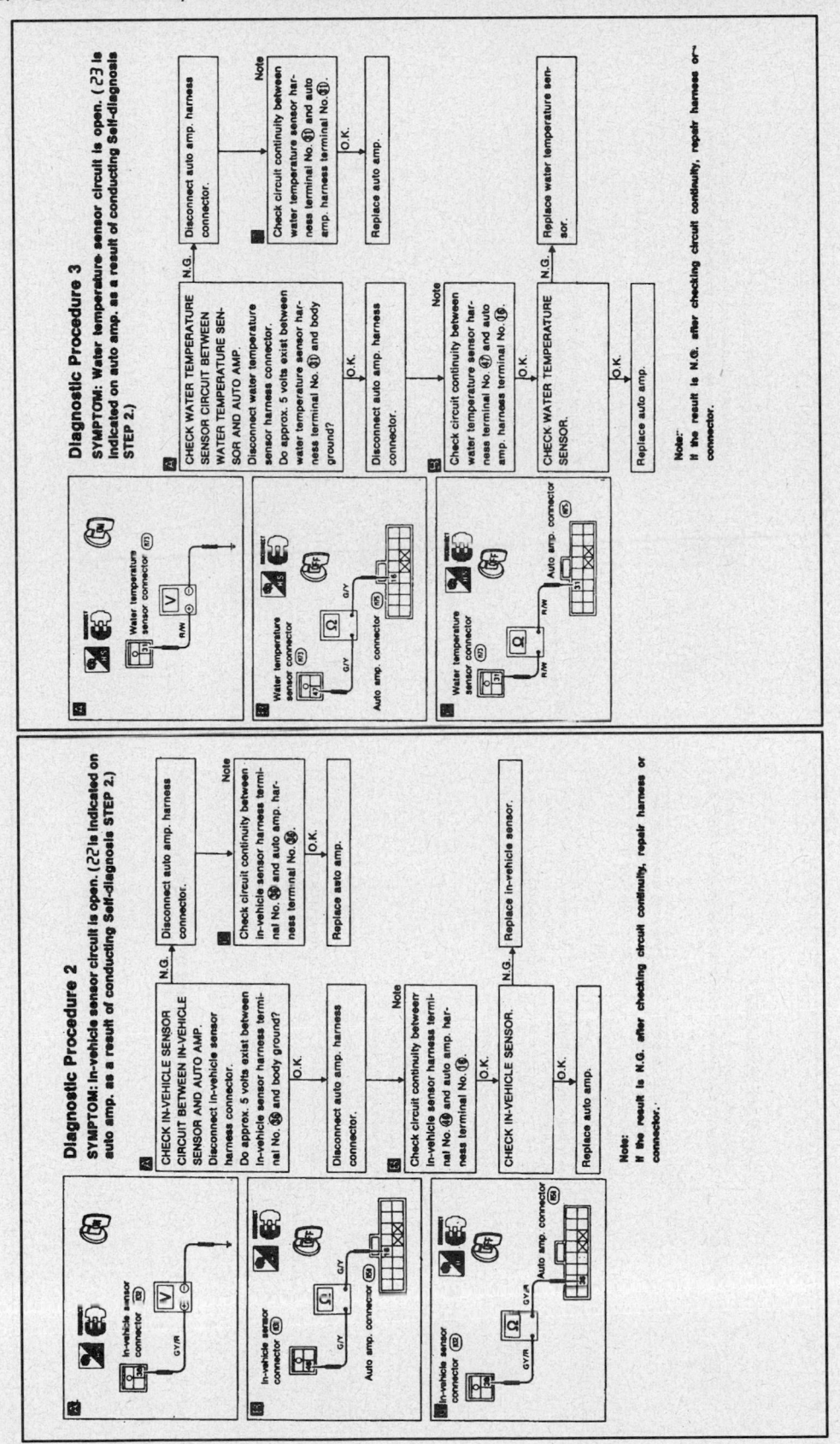

SECTION 8

INFINITI
G20 • J30 • Q45

1993 Q45 AUTO. A/C SYSTEMS DIAGNOSTIC PROCEDURES 4 AND 5

Diagnostic Procedure 5

SYMPTOM: Sunload sensor circuit is open. (25 is indicated on auto amp. as a result of conducting Self-diagnosis STEP 2.)

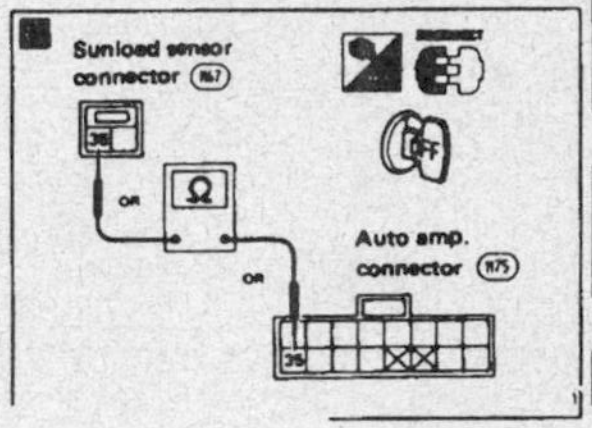

A — CHECK SUNLOAD SENSOR CIRCUIT BETWEEN SUNLOAD SENSOR AND AUTO AMP.
Disconnect sunload sensor harness connector.
Do approx. 5 volts exist between sunload sensor harness terminal No. 59 and body ground?

N.G. → Disconnect auto amp. harness connector.

Note
Check circuit continuity between sunload sensor harness terminal No. 59 and auto amp. harness terminal No. 35.

O.K. → Replace auto amp.

O.K. ↓

B — Disconnect auto amp. harness connector.

Note
Check circuit continuity between sunload sensor harness terminal No. 59 and auto amp. harness terminal No. 16.

O.K. ↓

CHECK SUNLOAD SENSOR.

N.G. → Replace sunload sensor.

O.K. → Replace auto amp.

Note:
If the result is N.G. after checking circuit continuity, repair harness or connector.

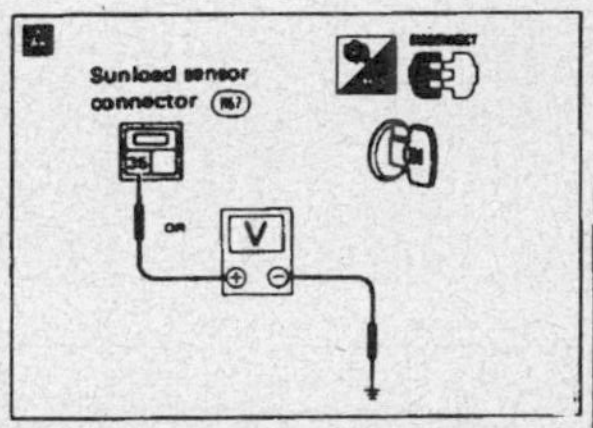

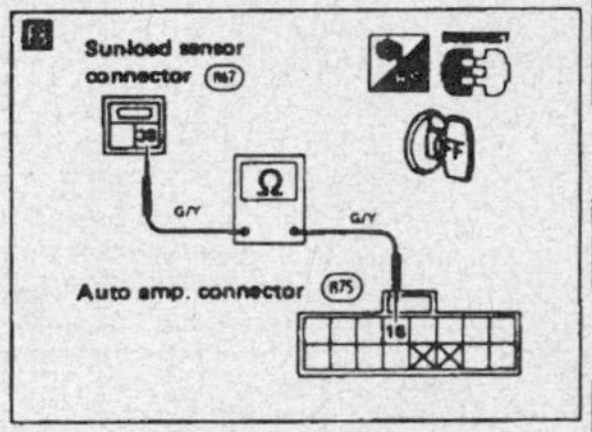

Sunload sensor connector (M6)

Auto amp. connector (M5)

Diagnostic Procedure 4

SYMPTOM: Intake sensor circuit is open. (24 is indicated on auto amp. as a result of conducting Self-diagnosis STEP 2.)

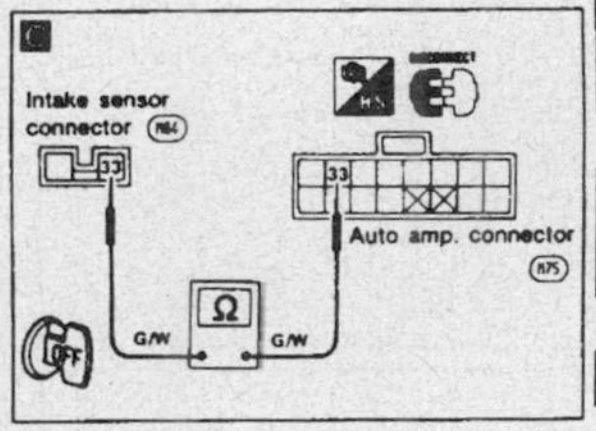

A — CHECK INTAKE SENSOR CIRCUIT BETWEEN INTAKE SENSOR AND AUTO AMP.
Disconnect intake sensor harness connector.
Do approx. 5 volts exist between intake sensor harness terminal No. 33 and body ground?

N.G. → Disconnect auto amp. harness connector.

Note
Check circuit continuity between intake sensor harness terminal No. 33 and auto amp. harness terminal No. 35.

O.K. → Replace auto amp.

O.K. ↓

B — Disconnect auto amp. harness connector.

Note
Check circuit continuity between intake sensor harness terminal No. 37 and auto amp. harness terminal No. 16.

O.K. ↓

CHECK INTAKE SENSOR.

N.G. → Replace intake sensor.

O.K. → Replace auto amp.

Note:
If the result is N.G. after checking circuit continuity, repair harness or connector.

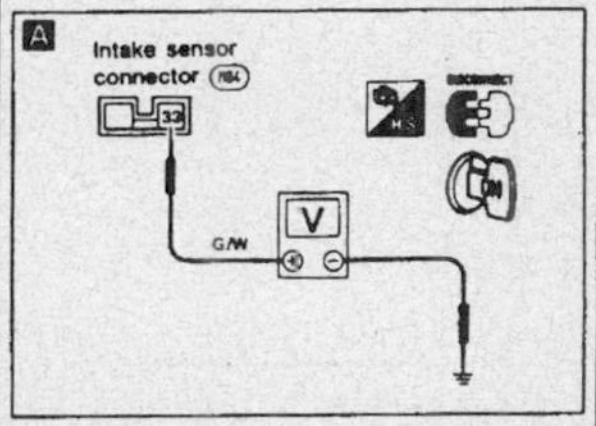

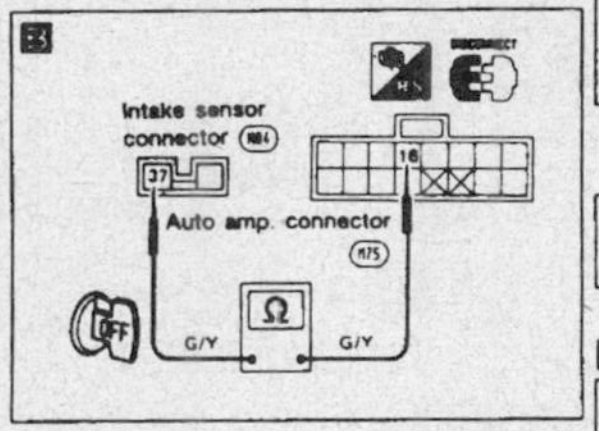

Intake sensor connector (M6)

Auto amp. connector (M5)

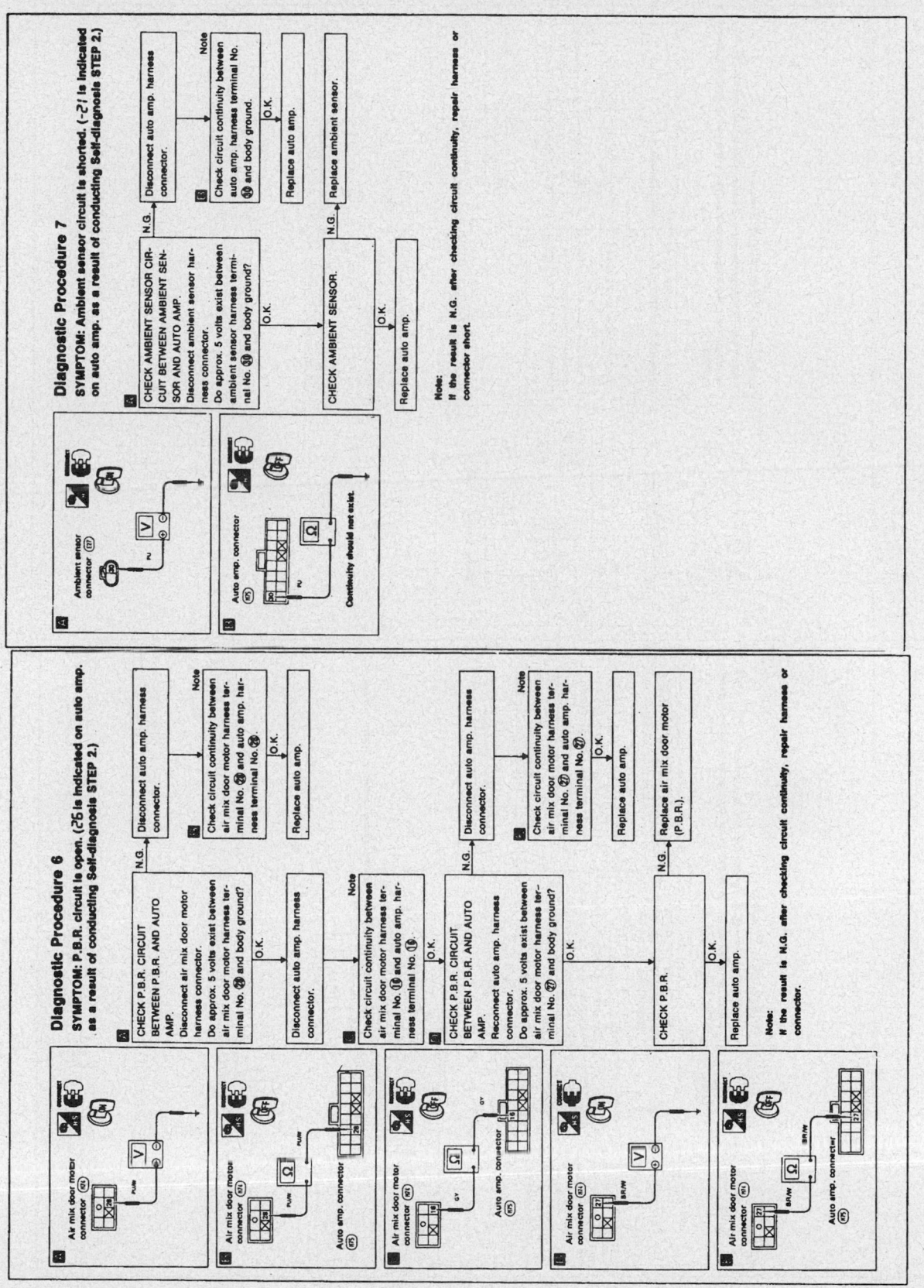

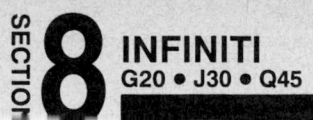

1993 Q45 AUTO. A/C SYSTEMS DIAGNOSTIC PROCEDURES 8 AND 9

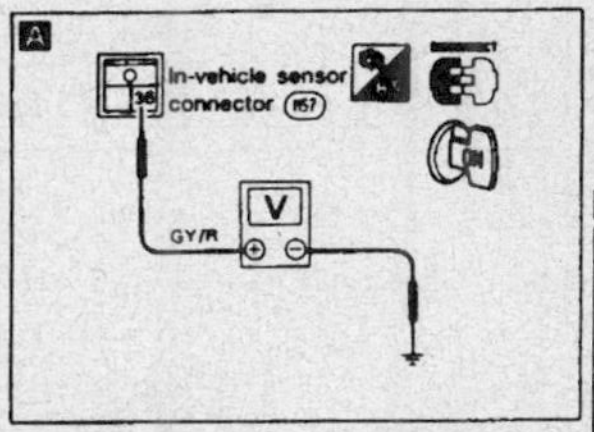

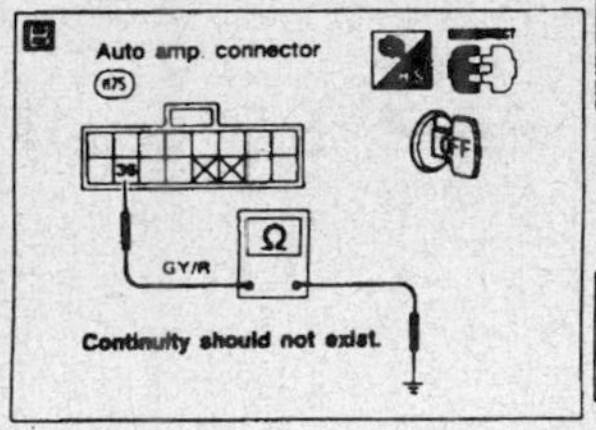

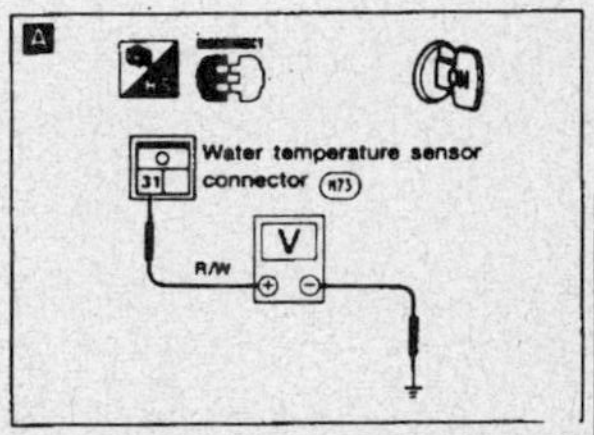

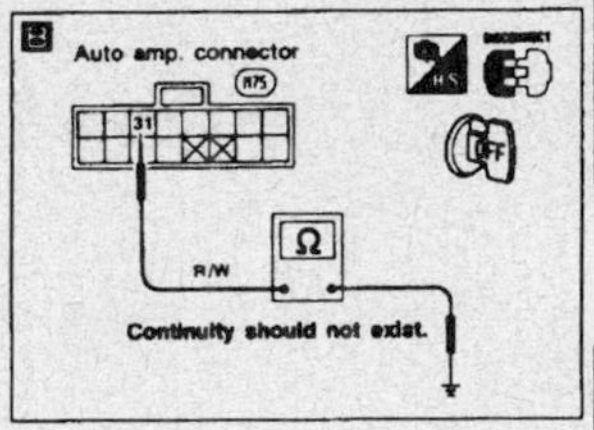

Diagnostic Procedure 9

SYMPTOM: Water temperature sensor circuit is shorted. (-23 is indicated on auto amp. as a result of conducting Self-diagnosis STEP 2.)

A CHECK WATER TEMPERATURE SENSOR CIRCUIT BETWEEN WATER TEMPERATURE SENSOR AND AUTO AMP.
Disconnect water temperature sensor harness connector.
Do approx. 5 volts exist between water temperature sensor harness terminal No. 31 and body ground?

→ N.G. → Disconnect auto amp. harness connector.

B Check circuit continuity between auto amp. harness terminal No. 31 and body ground.

→ O.K. → Replace auto amp.

Note

→ O.K. (from A) → CHECK WATER TEMPERATURE SENSOR.

→ O.K. → Replace auto amp.

→ N.G. → Replace water temperature sensor.

Note:
If the result is N.G. after checking circuit continuity, repair harness or connector short.

Water temperature sensor connector (M7)

R/W

Auto amp. connector (M5)

R/W

Continuity should not exist.

Diagnostic Procedure 8

SYMPTOM: In-vehicle sensor circuit is shorted. (-22 is indicated on auto amp. as a result of conducting Self-diagnosis STEP 2.)

A CHECK IN-VEHICLE SENSOR CIRCUIT BETWEEN IN-VEHICLE SENSOR AND AUTO AMP.
Disconnect in-vehicle sensor harness connector.
Do approx. 5 volts exist between in-vehicle sensor harness terminal No. 36 and body ground?

→ N.G. → Disconnect auto amp. harness connector.

B Check circuit continuity between auto amp. harness terminal No. 36 and body ground.

→ O.K. → Replace auto amp.

Note

→ O.K. (from A) → CHECK IN-VEHICLE SENSOR.

→ O.K. → Replace auto amp.

→ N.G. → Replace in-vehicle sensor.

Note:
If the result is N.G. after checking circuit continuity, repair harness or connector short.

In-vehicle sensor connector (M8)

G/YR

Auto amp. connector (M5)

G/YR

Continuity should not exist.

1993 Q45 AUTO. A/C SYSTEMS DIAGNOSTIC PROCEDURES 10 AND 11

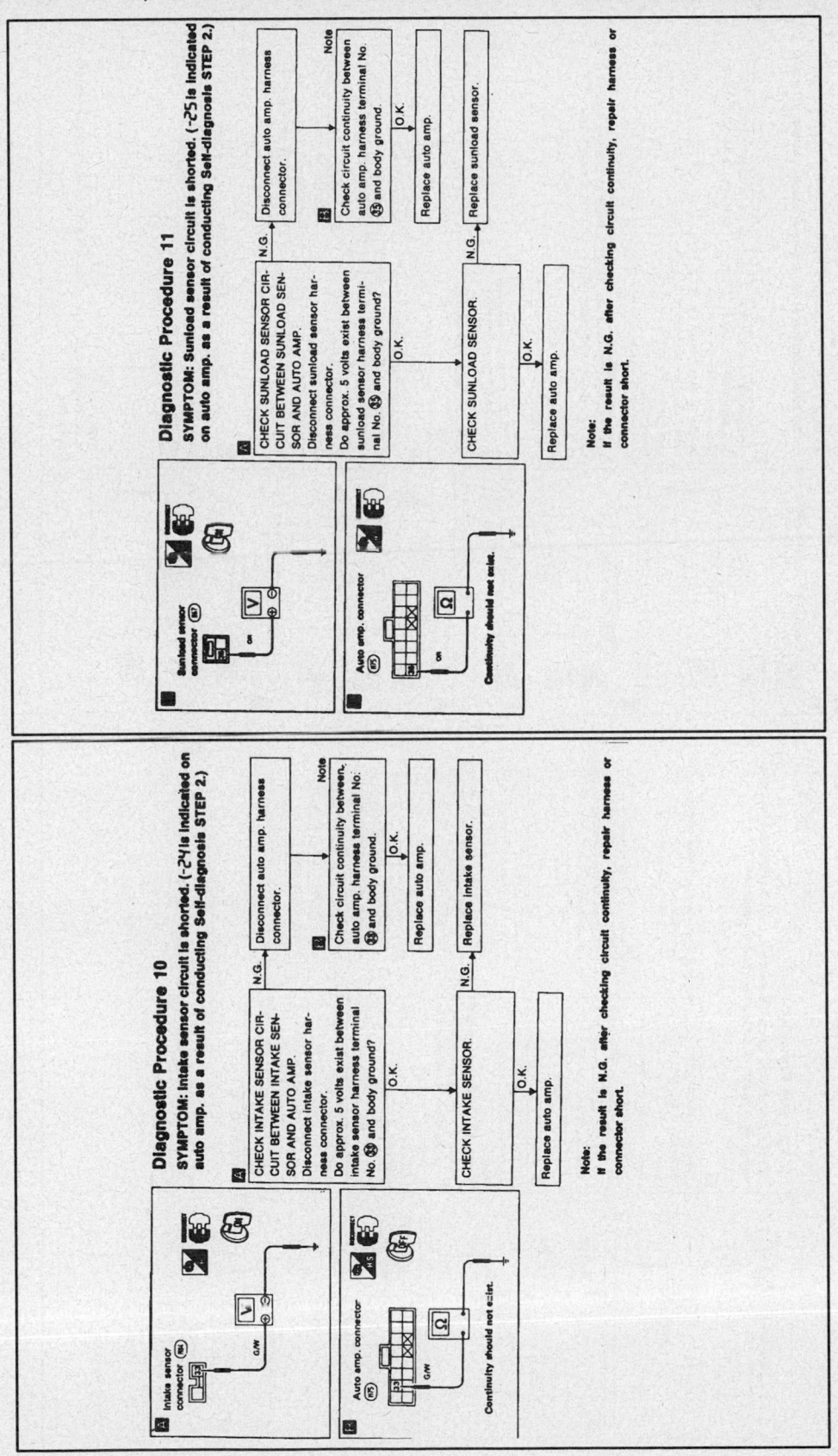

1993 Q45 AUTO. A/C SYSTEMS DIAGNOSTIC PROCEDURES 12 AND 13

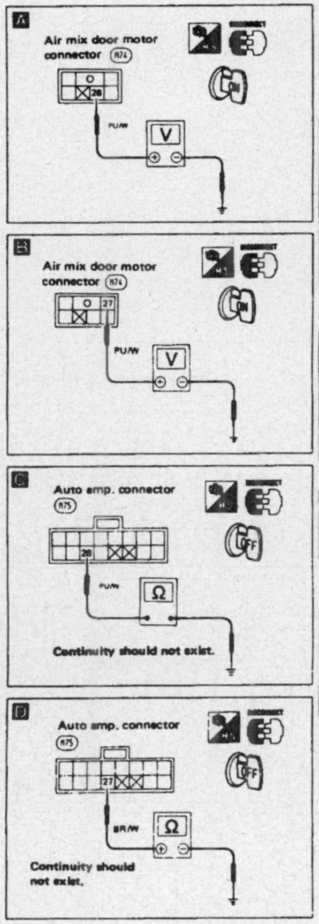

Diagnostic Procedure 13

SYMPTOM: Condenser fan motor does not operate normally.

A CHECK POWER SUPPLY FOR CONDENSER FAN RELAY.
Disconnect condenser fan relay.
Do approx. 12 volts exist between condenser fan relay harness terminal No. ⑥, ⑥ and body ground?

N.G. → CHECK POWER SUPPLY CIRCUIT AND 10A FUSE AT FUSE BLOCK

O.K. → **B** CHECK CONDENSER FAN RELAY AFTER DISCONNECTING IT.

N.G. → Replace condenser fan relay.

O.K. → Reconnect condenser fan relay harness connector and disconnect thermoswitch harness connector.

C CHECK COIL SIDE CIRCUIT OF CONDENSER FAN RELAY.
Do approx. 12 volts exist between thermoswitch harness terminal No. ⑥ and body ground?

N.G. → Disconnect condenser fan relay harness connector.
Note
C Check circuit continuity between condenser fan relay harness terminal No. ⑥ and thermoswitch harness terminal No. ⑥.

O.K. → **D** Check circuit continuity between thermoswitch harness terminal No. ⑥ and body ground?

O.K. → **A**

Note:
If the result is N.G. after checking circuit continuity, repair harness or connector.

Condenser fan relay connector

Thermoswitch connector

Condenser fan relay connector

Thermoswitch connector

Diagnostic Procedure 12

SYMPTOM: P.B.R. circuit is shorted. (−25 is indicated on auto amp. as a result of conducting Self-diagnosis STEP 2.)

A CHECK P.B.R. CIRCUIT BETWEEN P.B.R. AND AUTO AMP.
Disconnect air mix door motor harness connector.
Do approx. 5 volts exist between air mix door motor harness terminal No. ㉖ and body ground?

N.G. → Disconnect auto amp. harness connector.
Note
C Check circuit continuity between auto amp. harness terminal No. ㉖ and body ground.

O.K. → Replace auto amp.

O.K. → **B** CHECK P.B.R. CIRCUIT BETWEEN P.B.R. AND AUTO AMP.
Do approx. 5 volts exist between air mix door motor harness terminal No. ㉗ and body ground?

N.G. → Disconnect auto amp. harness connector.
Note
D Check circuit continuity between auto amp. harness terminal No. ㉗ and body ground.

O.K. → Replace auto amp.

O.K. → **B** CHECK P.B.R.

O.K. → N.G. → Replace air mix door motor.

O.K. → INSPECTION END

Note:
If the result is N.G. after checking circuit continuity, repair harness or connector short.

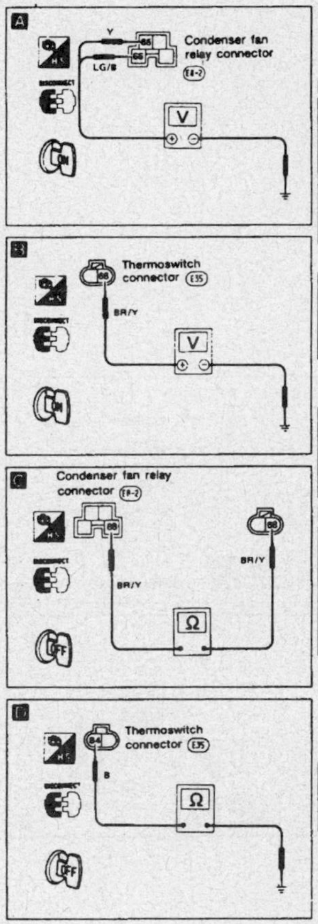

Air mix door motor connector

Air mix door motor connector

Auto amp. connector
Continuity should not exist.

Auto amp. connector
Continuity should not exist.

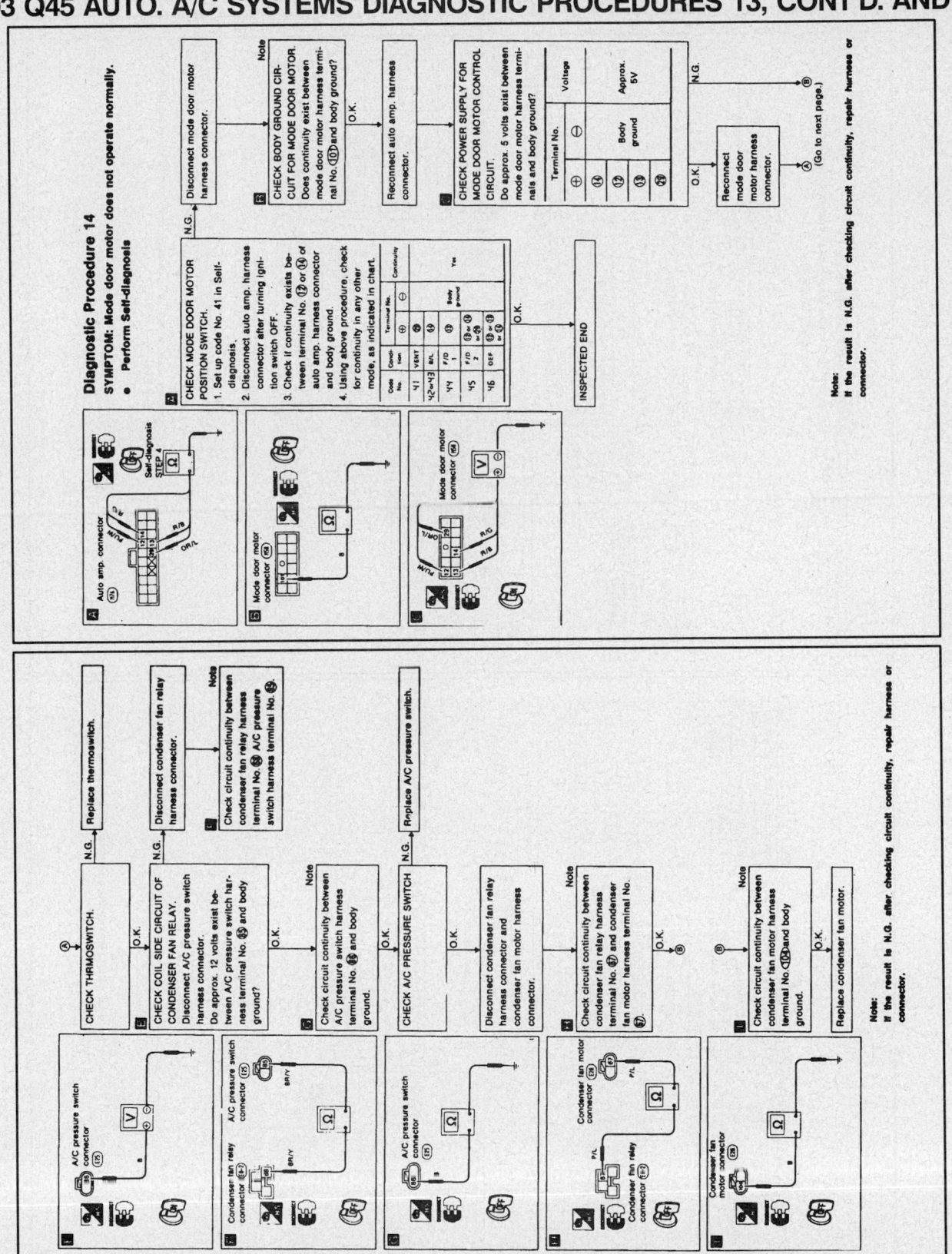

1993 Q45 AUTO. A/C SYSTEMS DIAGNOSTIC PROCEDURES 14, CONT'D. AND 15

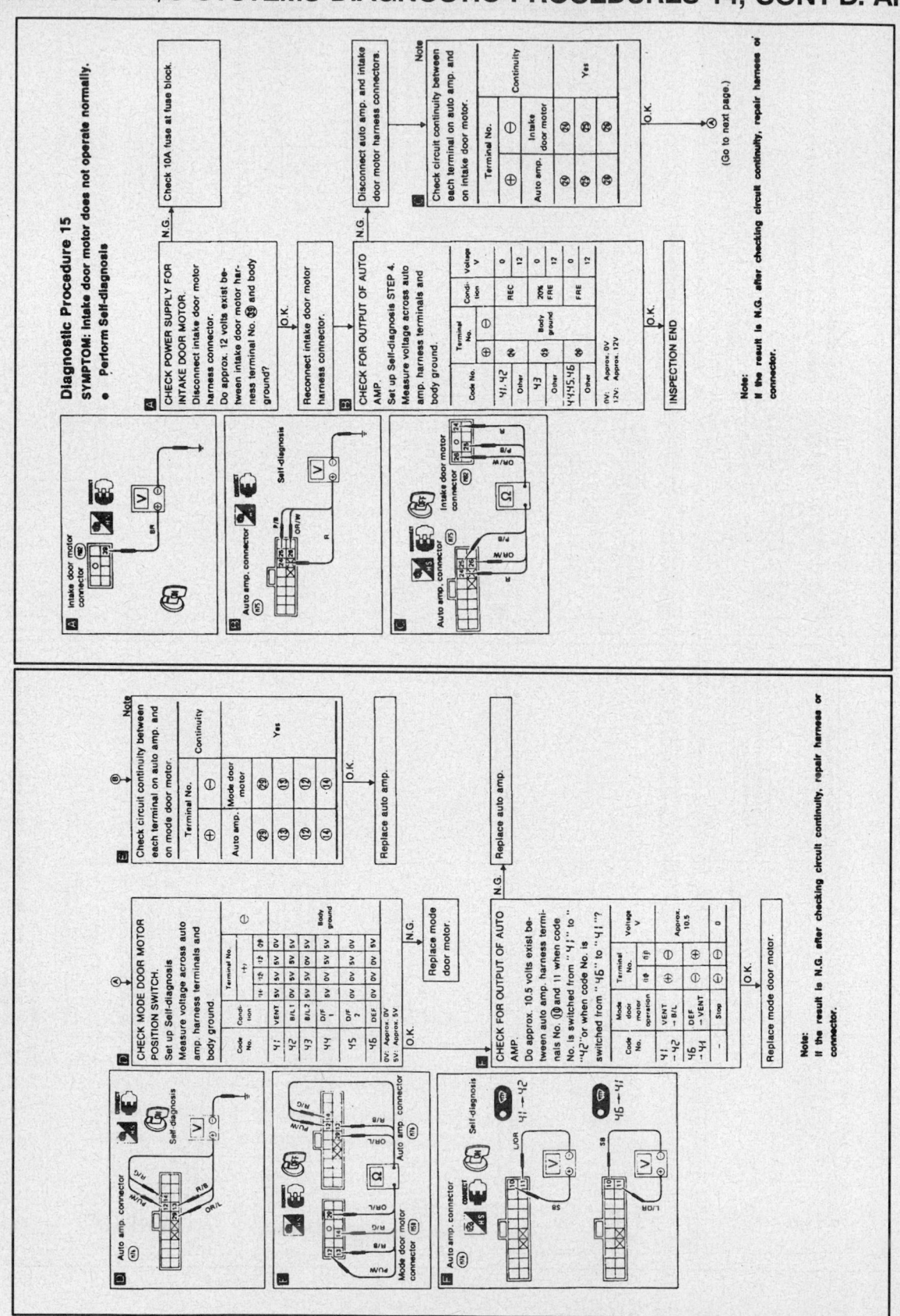

1993 Q45 AUTO. A/C SYSTEMS DIAGNOSTIC PROCEDURES 15, CONT'D. AND 16

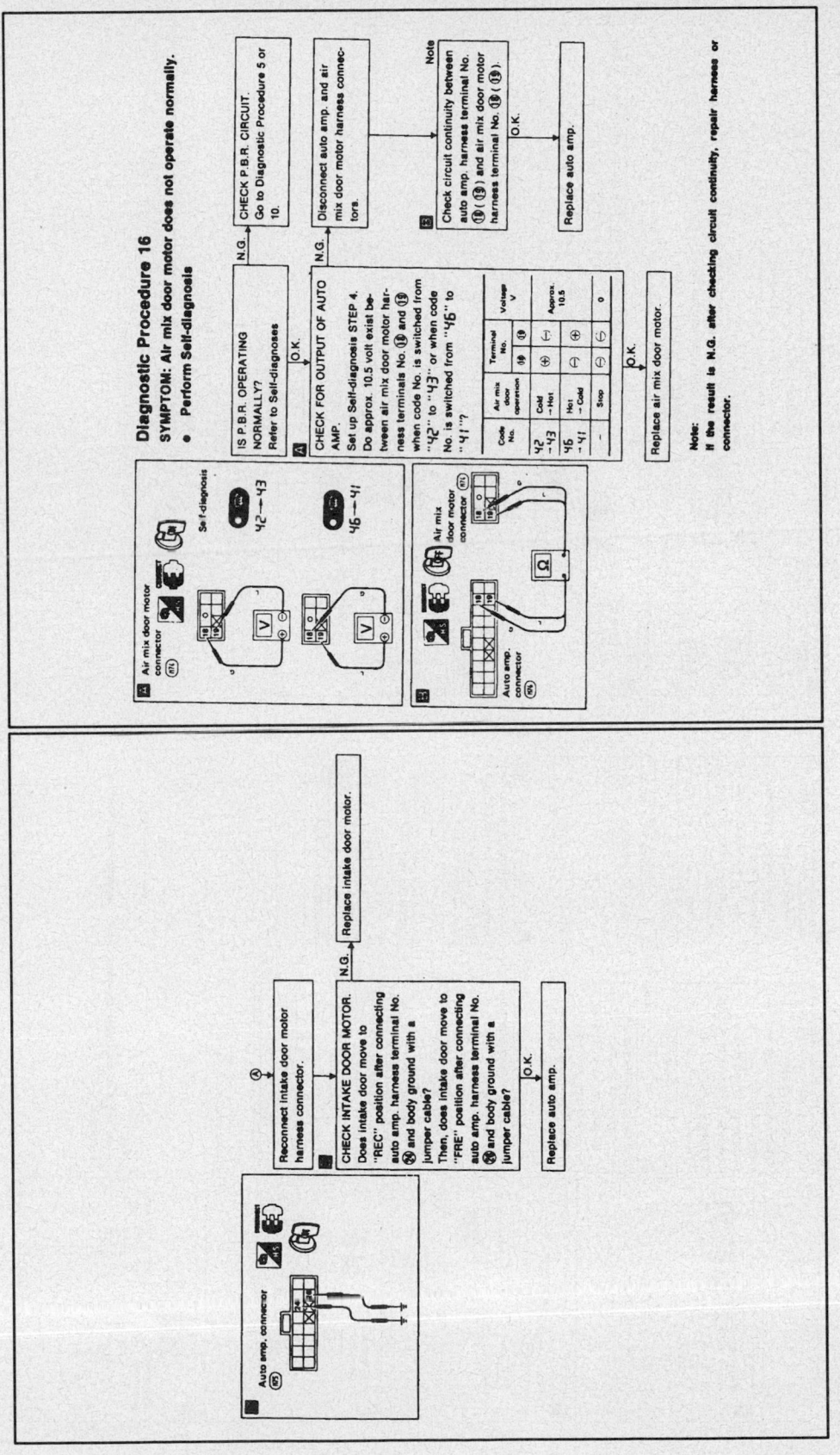

1993 Q45 AUTO. A/C SYSTEMS DIAGNOSTIC PROCEDURE 17

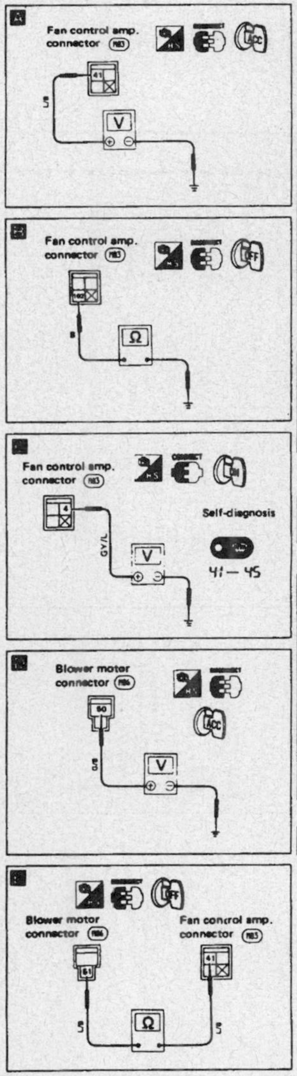

(Top section — continued, A)

Disconnect auto amp. and fan control amp. harness connector.

F — Does continuity exist between auto amp. harness terminal No. 4 and fan control amp. harness terminal No. 4? Note

CHECK POWER SUPPLY FOR HI RELAY. Do approx. 12 volts exist between Hi relay harness terminals No. 4, 5 and body ground?
— N.G. → Check 10A or 15A fuses at fuse block.
— O.K.

CHECK BODY GROUND CIRCUIT FOR HI RELAY. Does continuity exist between Hi relay harness terminal No. 103 and body ground? Note
— O.K.

CHECK HI RELAY AFTER DISCONNECTING IT.
— N.G. → Replace Hi relay.
— O.K.

Reconnect Hi relay.

(Go to next page.) B

Note:
If the result is N.G. after checking circuit continuity, repair harness or connector.

Diagnostic Procedure 17

SYMPTOM: Blower motor operation is malfunctioning under out of Starting Fan Speed Control.

- Perform Preliminary Check 5 before referring to the following flow chart.

A — CHECK POWER SUPPLY FOR FAN CONTROL AMP. Disconnect fan control amp. harness connector. Do approx. 12 volts exist between fan control amp. harness terminal No. 41 and body ground?
— N.G. → C — CHECK POWER SUPPLY FOR BLOWER MOTOR. Disconnect blower motor harness connector. Do approx. 12 volts exist between blower motor harness terminal No. 50 and body ground?
— N.G. → Check 15A fuses at fuse block.
— O.K.

B — CHECK BODY GROUND CIRCUIT FOR FAN CONTROL AMP. Does continuity exist between fan control amp. harness terminal No. 102 and body ground? Note
— O.K.

E — Check circuit continuity between blower motor harness terminal No. 51 and fan control amp. harness terminal No. 41? Note
— O.K. → CHECK BLOWER MOTOR.
— N.G. → Replace blower motor.

D — Reconnect fan control amp. harness connector.

CHECK FOR OUTPUT OF AUTO AMP. Set up Self-diagnosis STEP 4. Measure voltage across fan control amp. harness terminal No. 4 and body ground.

Code No.	Terminal No.		Voltage
41 - 45	+ ①	Body ground ⊖	Approx. 1 - 3V

— O.K. → Replace fan control amp.

(Go to next page.) A

Note:
If the result is N.G. after checking circuit continuity, repair harness or connector.

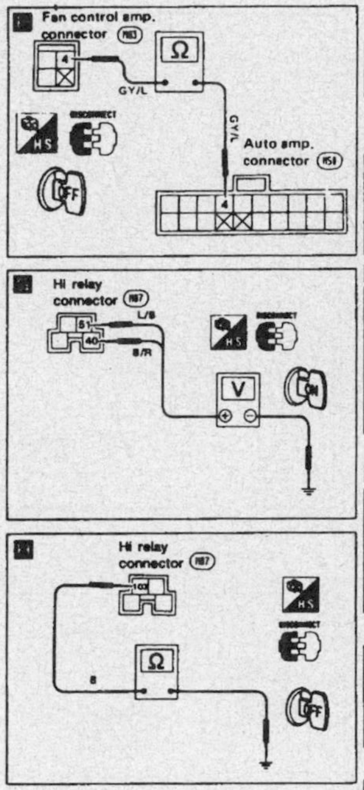

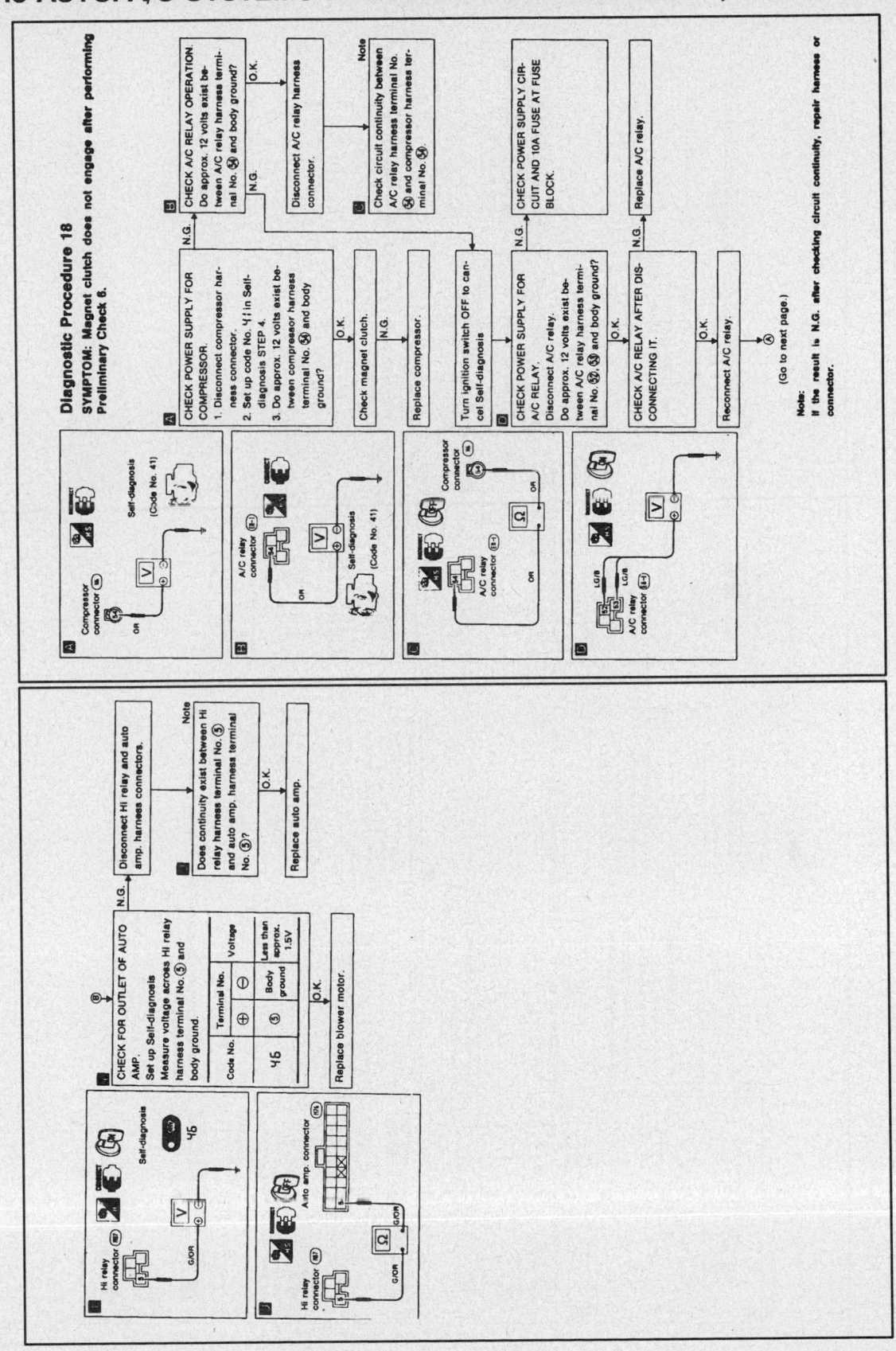

1993 Q45 AUTO. A/C SYSTEMS DIAGNOSTIC PROCEDURE 18, CONT'D.

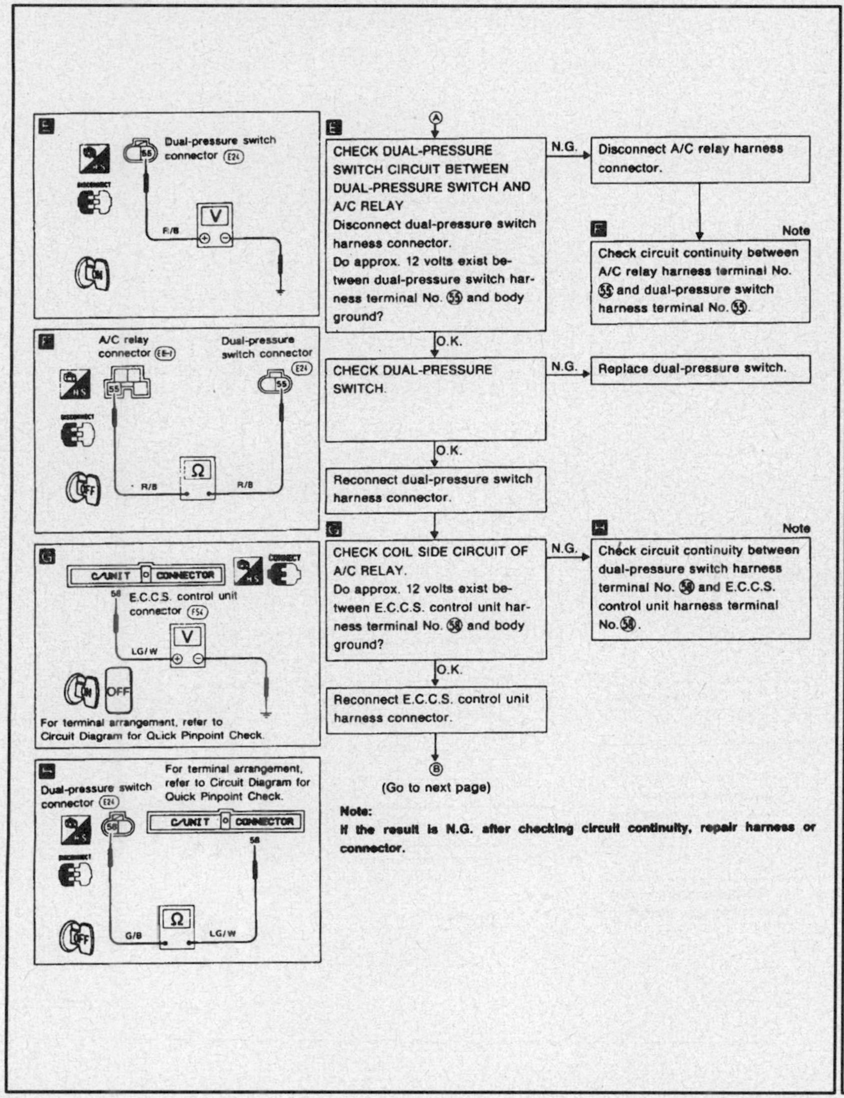

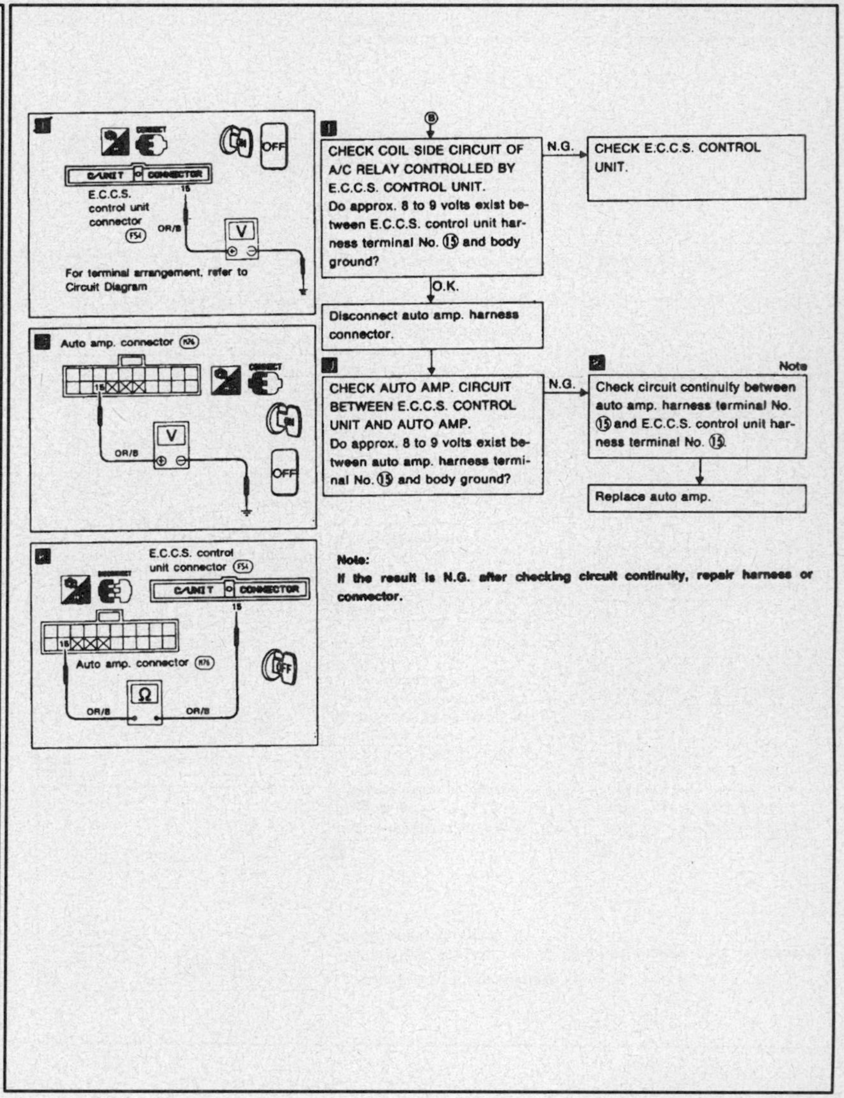

1994 Q45 AUTO. A/C SYSTEMS DIAGNOSTIC PROCEDURE 1

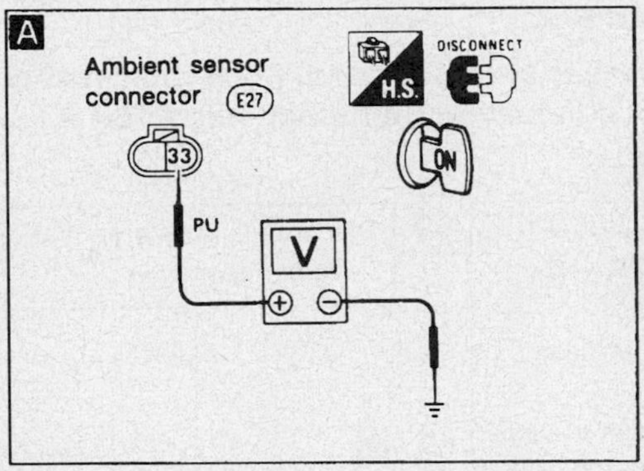

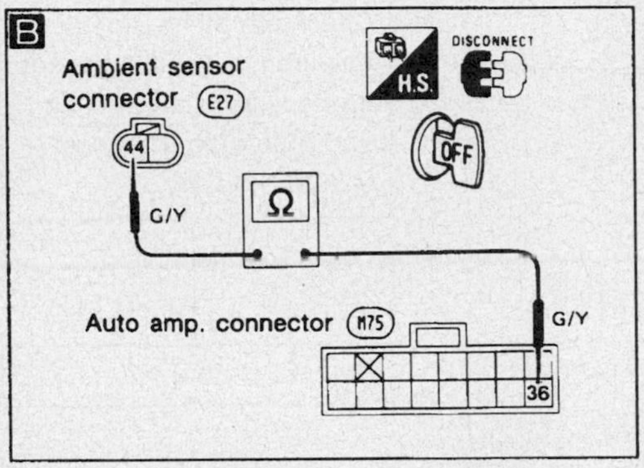

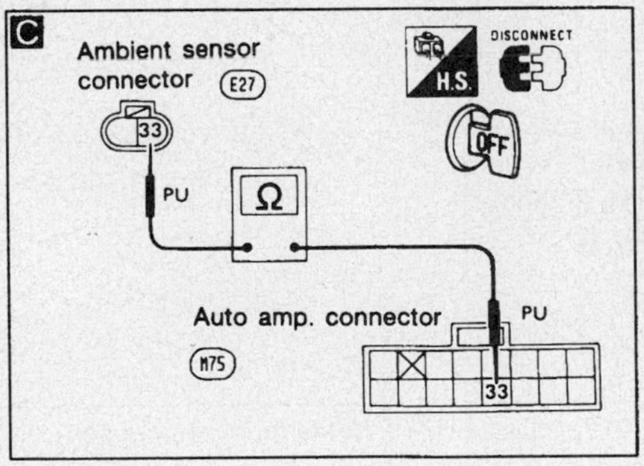

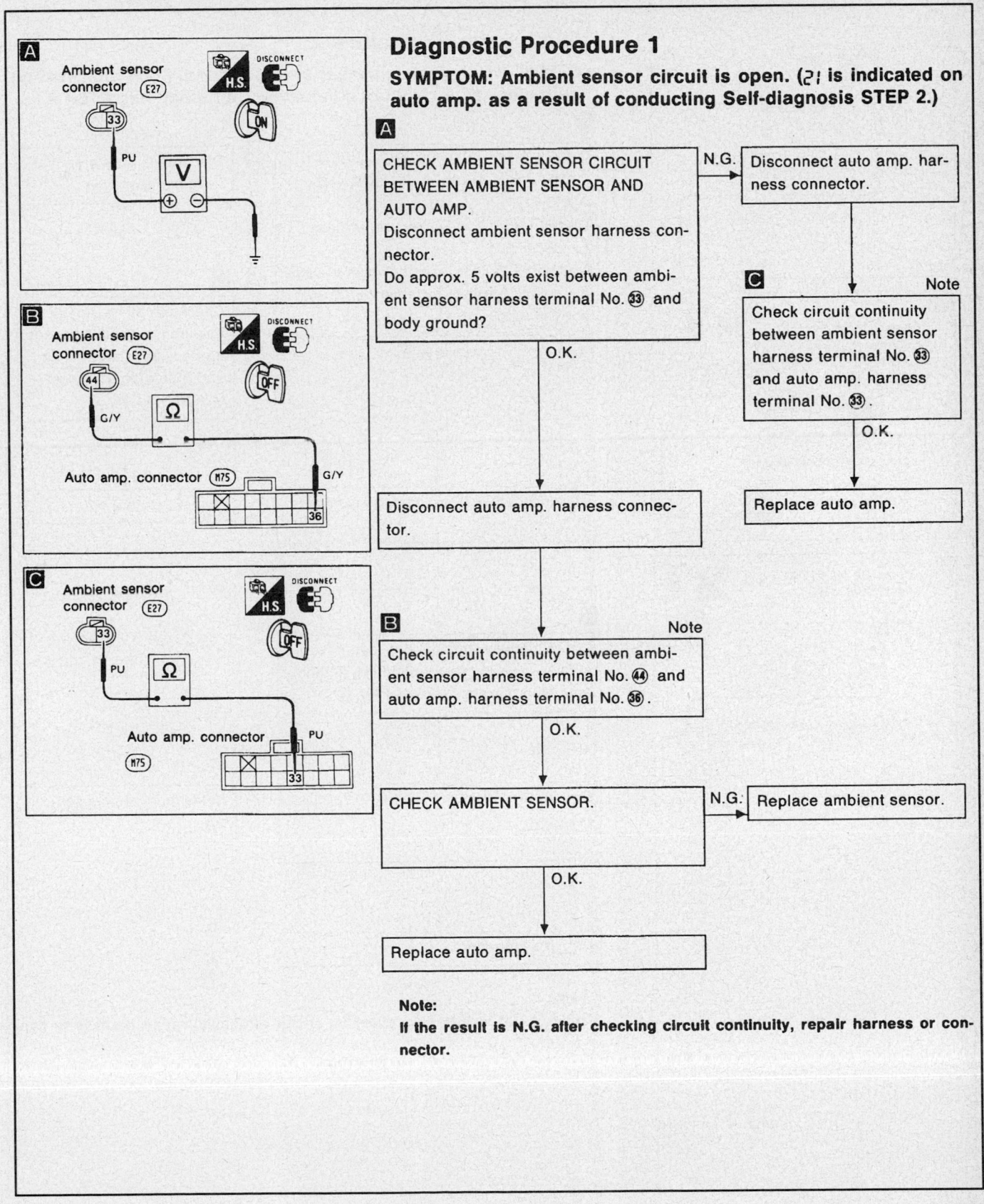

Diagnostic Procedure 1

SYMPTOM: Ambient sensor circuit is open. (21 is indicated on auto amp. as a result of conducting Self-diagnosis STEP 2.)

A

CHECK AMBIENT SENSOR CIRCUIT BETWEEN AMBIENT SENSOR AND AUTO AMP.
Disconnect ambient sensor harness connector.
Do approx. 5 volts exist between ambient sensor harness terminal No. ㉝ and body ground?

- N.G. → Disconnect auto amp. harness connector.
  ↓
  C Note
  Check circuit continuity between ambient sensor harness terminal No. ㉝ and auto amp. harness terminal No. ㉝.
  ↓ O.K.
  Replace auto amp.

- O.K. ↓

Disconnect auto amp. harness connector.

↓

B Note

Check circuit continuity between ambient sensor harness terminal No. ㊹ and auto amp. harness terminal No. ㊱.

↓ O.K.

CHECK AMBIENT SENSOR.

- N.G. → Replace ambient sensor.
- O.K. ↓

Replace auto amp.

Note:
If the result is N.G. after checking circuit continuity, repair harness or connector.

1994 Q45 AUTO. A/C SYSTEMS DIAGNOSTIC PROCEDURE 2

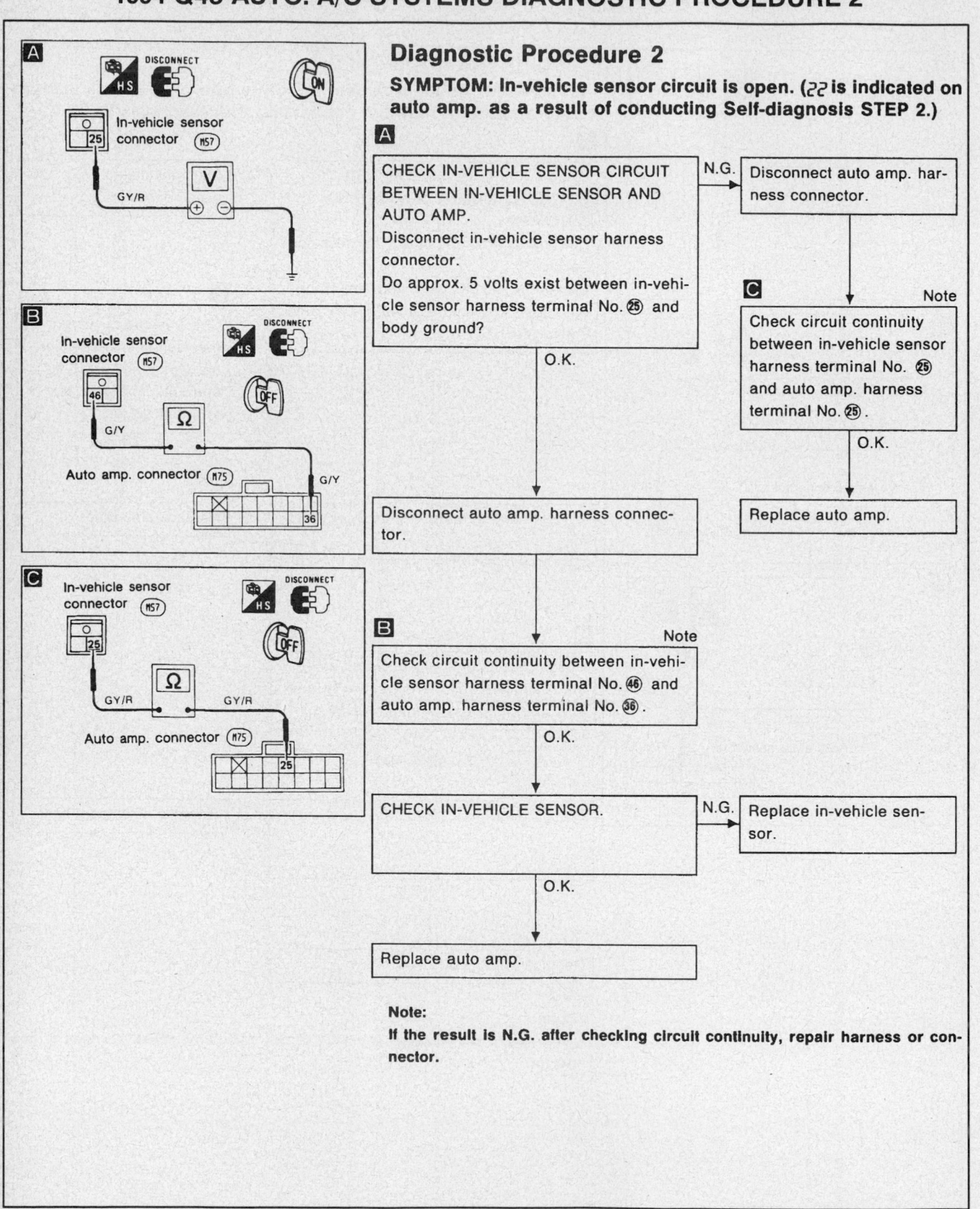

Diagnostic Procedure 2

SYMPTOM: In-vehicle sensor circuit is open. (22 is indicated on auto amp. as a result of conducting Self-diagnosis STEP 2.)

A

CHECK IN-VEHICLE SENSOR CIRCUIT BETWEEN IN-VEHICLE SENSOR AND AUTO AMP.
Disconnect in-vehicle sensor harness connector.
Do approx. 5 volts exist between in-vehicle sensor harness terminal No. ㉕ and body ground?

→ N.G. → Disconnect auto amp. harness connector.

C Note
Check circuit continuity between in-vehicle sensor harness terminal No. ㉕ and auto amp. harness terminal No. ㉕.

O.K. →

Replace auto amp.

O.K. ↓

Disconnect auto amp. harness connector.

B Note

Check circuit continuity between in-vehicle sensor harness terminal No. ㊺ and auto amp. harness terminal No. ㊱.

O.K. ↓

CHECK IN-VEHICLE SENSOR.   → N.G. → Replace in-vehicle sensor.

O.K. ↓

Replace auto amp.

Note:
If the result is N.G. after checking circuit continuity, repair harness or connector.

1994 Q45 AUTO. A/C SYSTEMS DIAGNOSTIC PROCEDURE 3

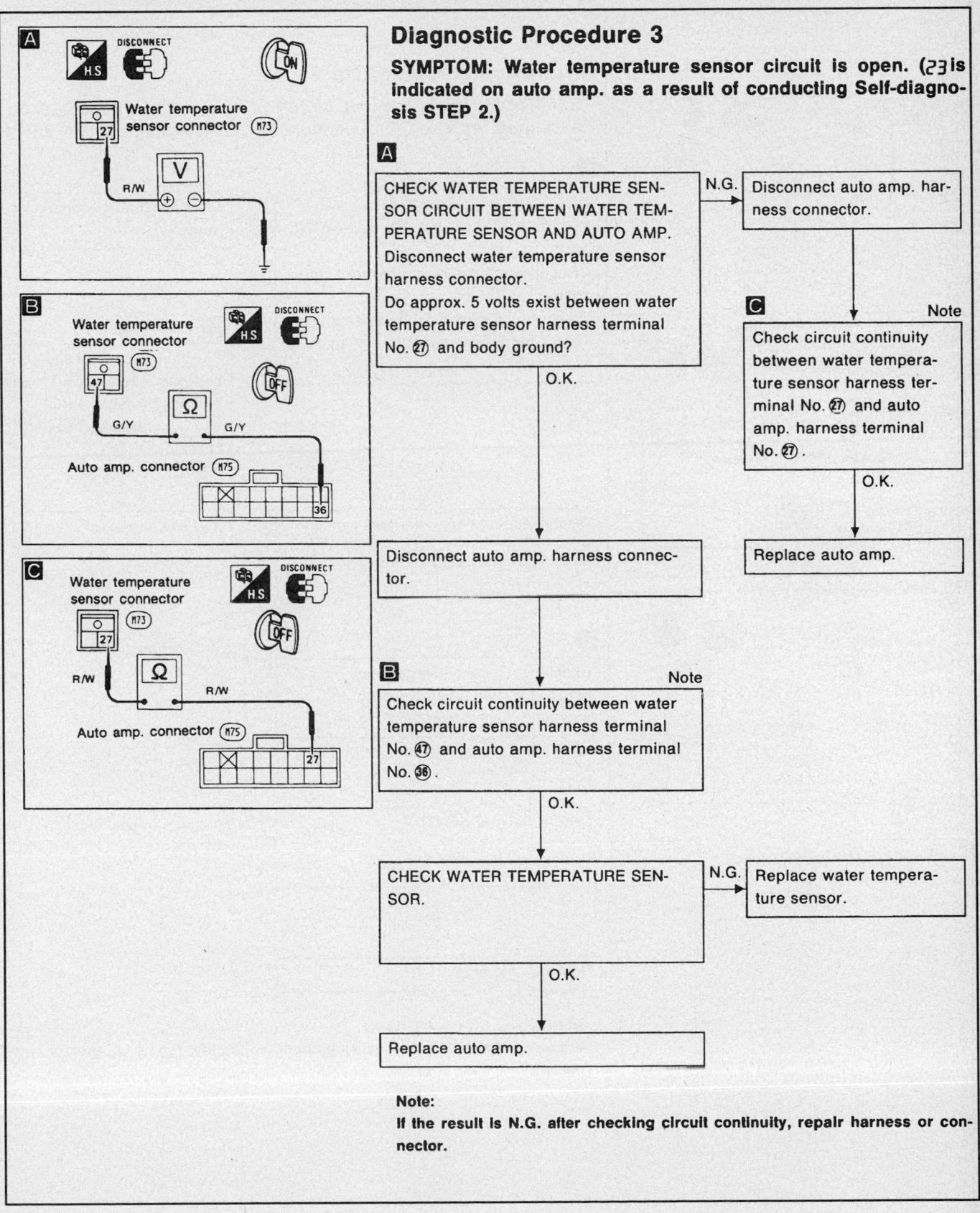

Diagnostic Procedure 3

SYMPTOM: Water temperature sensor circuit is open. (23 is indicated on auto amp. as a result of conducting Self-diagnosis STEP 2.)

A

CHECK WATER TEMPERATURE SENSOR CIRCUIT BETWEEN WATER TEMPERATURE SENSOR AND AUTO AMP.
Disconnect water temperature sensor harness connector.
Do approx. 5 volts exist between water temperature sensor harness terminal No. ㉗ and body ground?

→ N.G. → Disconnect auto amp. harness connector.

↓ O.K.

Disconnect auto amp. harness connector.

C Note
Check circuit continuity between water temperature sensor harness terminal No. ㉗ and auto amp. harness terminal No. ㉗.

↓ O.K.

Replace auto amp.

B Note
Check circuit continuity between water temperature sensor harness terminal No. ㊼ and auto amp. harness terminal No. ㊱.

↓ O.K.

CHECK WATER TEMPERATURE SENSOR.

→ N.G. → Replace water temperature sensor.

↓ O.K.

Replace auto amp.

Note:
If the result is N.G. after checking circuit continuity, repair harness or connector.

1994 Q45 AUTO. A/C SYSTEMS DIAGNOSTIC PROCEDURE 4

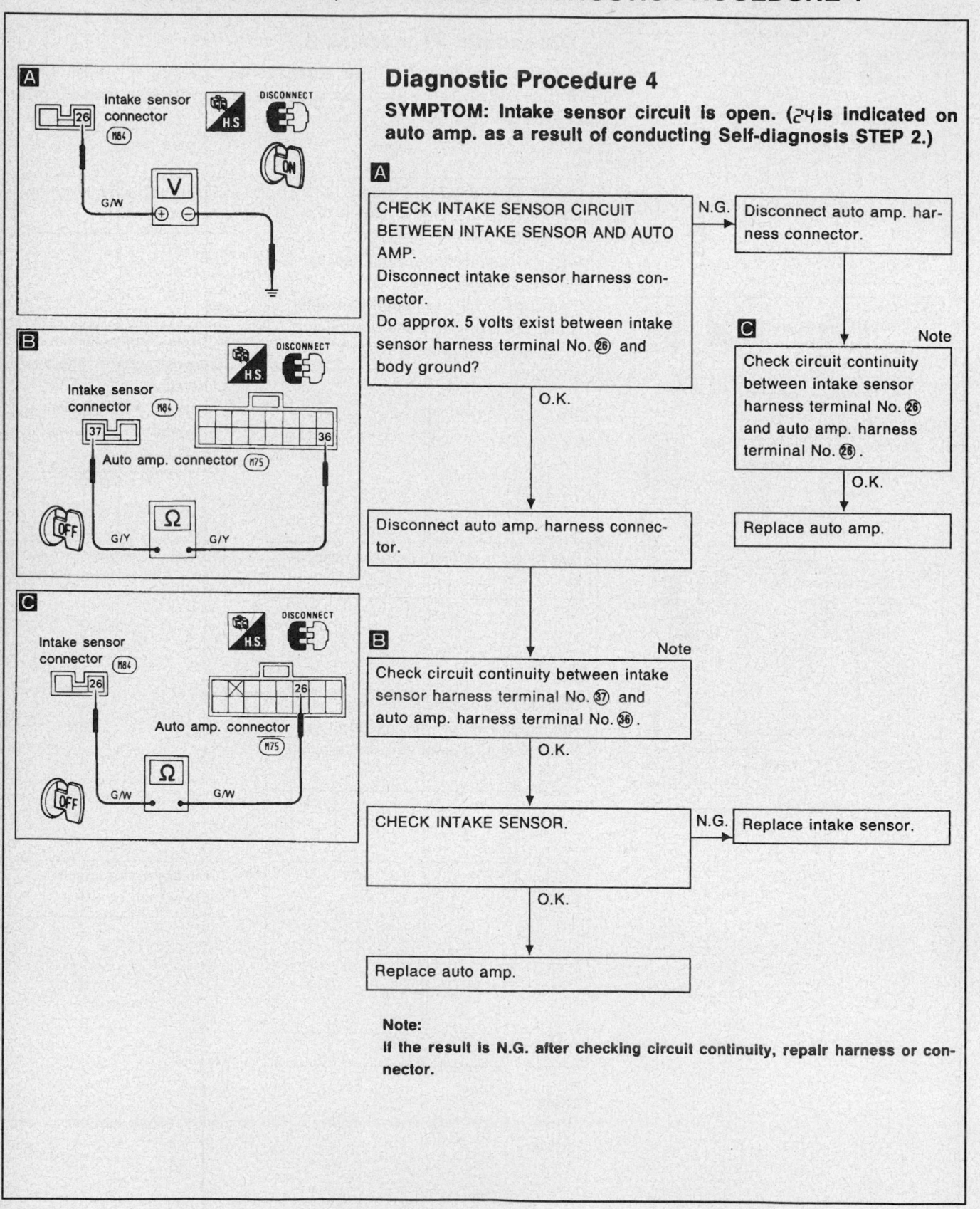

Diagnostic Procedure 4

SYMPTOM: Intake sensor circuit is open. (24 is indicated on auto amp. as a result of conducting Self-diagnosis STEP 2.)

A

| CHECK INTAKE SENSOR CIRCUIT BETWEEN INTAKE SENSOR AND AUTO AMP. Disconnect intake sensor harness connector. Do approx. 5 volts exist between intake sensor harness terminal No. 26 and body ground? | →N.G. | Disconnect auto amp. harness connector. |

↓O.K.

C   Note

| | Check circuit continuity between intake sensor harness terminal No. 26 and auto amp. harness terminal No. 26. |

↓O.K.

| Disconnect auto amp. harness connector. | | Replace auto amp. |

B   Note

| Check circuit continuity between intake sensor harness terminal No. 37 and auto amp. harness terminal No. 36. |

↓O.K.

| CHECK INTAKE SENSOR. | →N.G. | Replace intake sensor. |

↓O.K.

| Replace auto amp. |

Note:

If the result is N.G. after checking circuit continuity, repair harness or connector.

1994 Q45 AUTO. A/C SYSTEMS DIAGNOSTIC PROCEDURE 5

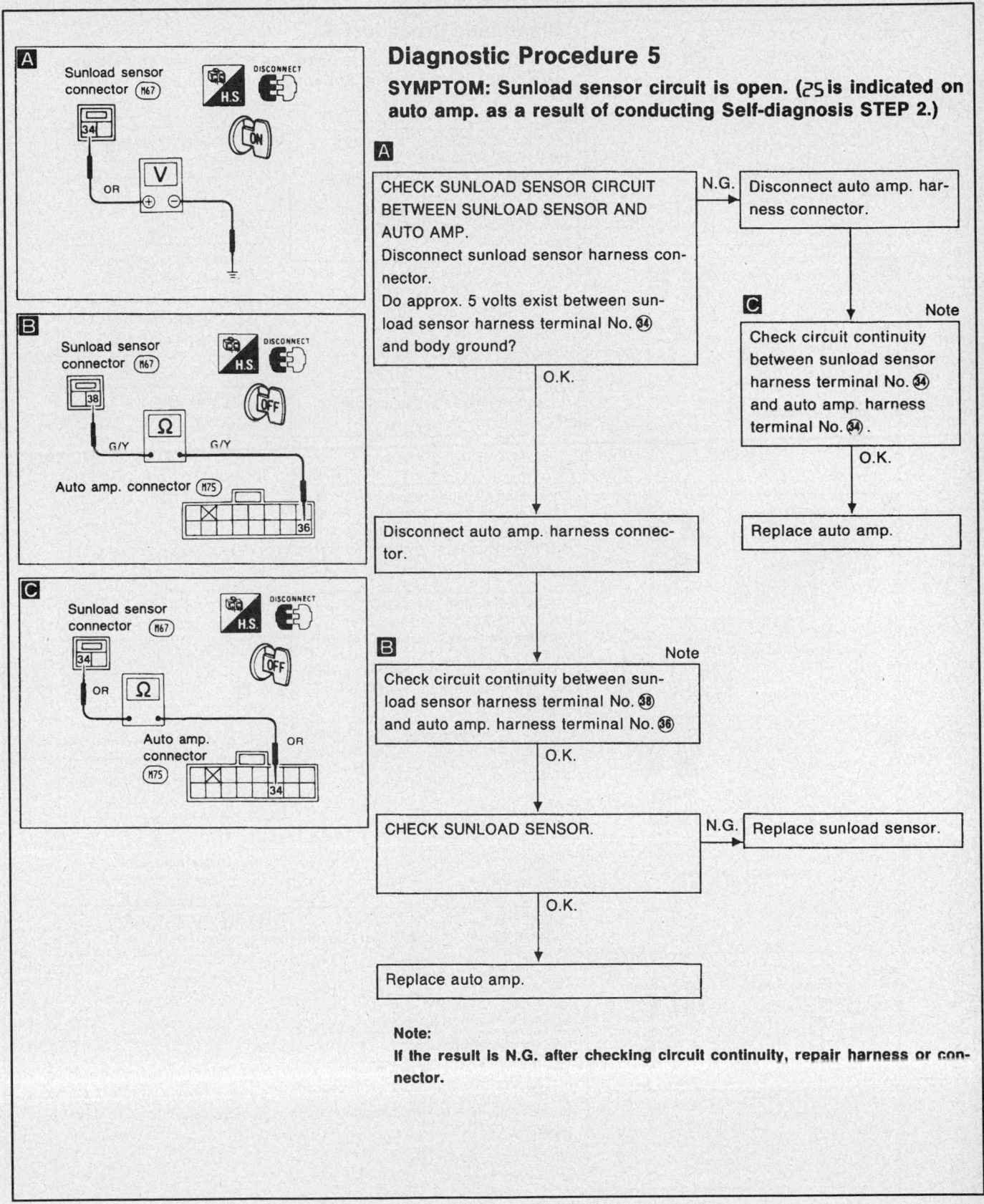

A Sunload sensor connector (M67)

B Sunload sensor connector (M67)
Auto amp. connector (M75)

C Sunload sensor connector (M67)
Auto amp. connector (M75)

Diagnostic Procedure 5

SYMPTOM: Sunload sensor circuit is open. (25 is indicated on auto amp. as a result of conducting Self-diagnosis STEP 2.)

A
CHECK SUNLOAD SENSOR CIRCUIT BETWEEN SUNLOAD SENSOR AND AUTO AMP.
Disconnect sunload sensor harness connector.
Do approx. 5 volts exist between sunload sensor harness terminal No. ㉞ and body ground?

→ N.G. → Disconnect auto amp. harness connector.

→ O.K.

C Note
Check circuit continuity between sunload sensor harness terminal No. ㉞ and auto amp. harness terminal No. ㉞.

→ O.K.

Replace auto amp.

Disconnect auto amp. harness connector.

B Note
Check circuit continuity between sunload sensor harness terminal No. ㉘ and auto amp. harness terminal No. ㊱

→ O.K.

CHECK SUNLOAD SENSOR.   → N.G. → Replace sunload sensor.

→ O.K.

Replace auto amp.

Note:
If the result is N.G. after checking circuit continuity, repair harness or connector.

1994 Q45 AUTO. A/C SYSTEMS DIAGNOSTIC PROCEDURE 6

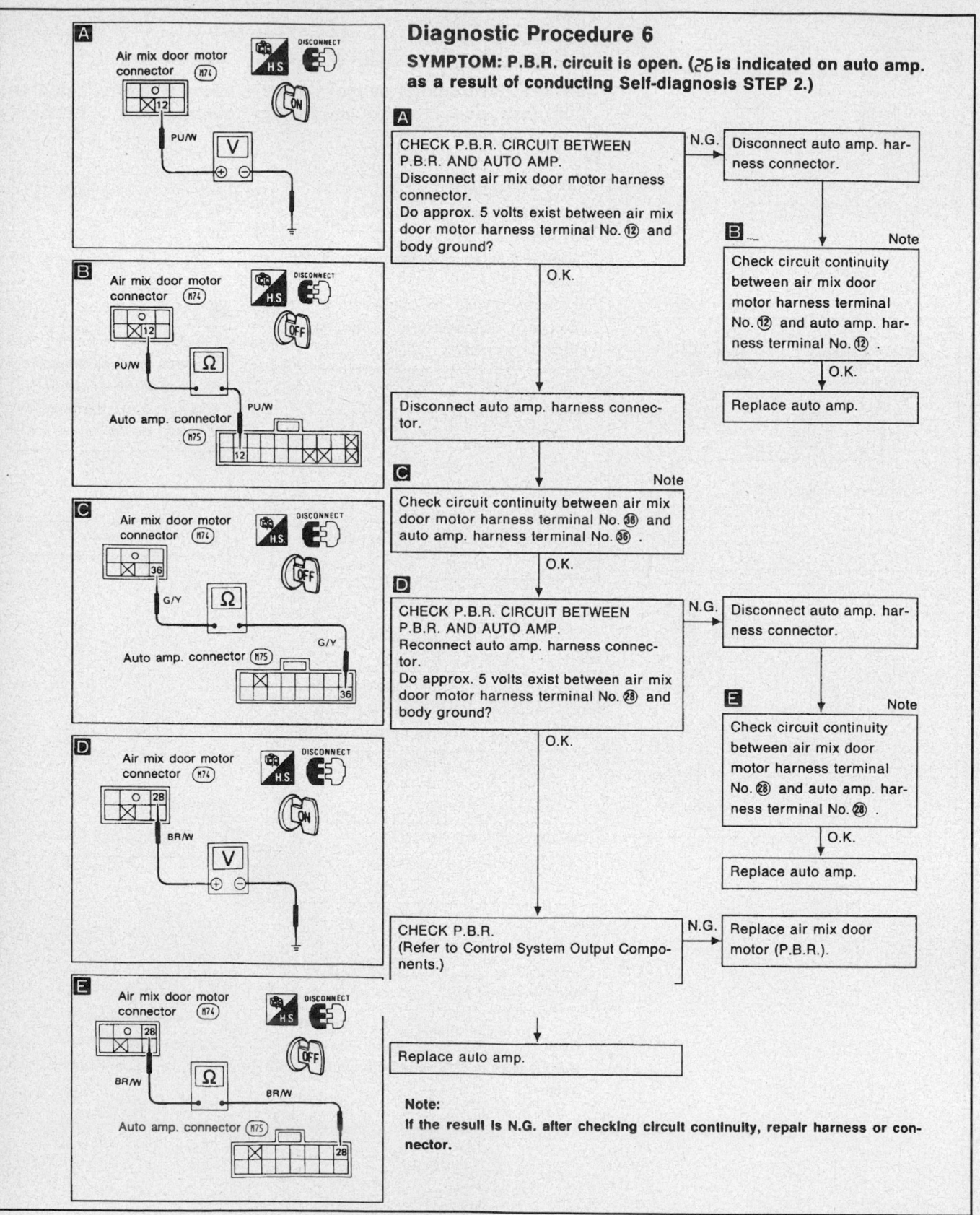

Diagnostic Procedure 6

SYMPTOM: P.B.R. circuit is open. (25 is indicated on auto amp. as a result of conducting Self-diagnosis STEP 2.)

A Air mix door motor connector (M74)

PU/W

A
CHECK P.B.R. CIRCUIT BETWEEN P.B.R. AND AUTO AMP.
Disconnect air mix door motor harness connector.
Do approx. 5 volts exist between air mix door motor harness terminal No. ⑫ and body ground?
→ N.G. → Disconnect auto amp. harness connector.

↓ O.K.

B Note
Check circuit continuity between air mix door motor harness terminal No. ⑫ and auto amp. harness terminal No. ⑫ .

↓ O.K.

Replace auto amp.

B Air mix door motor connector (M74)
PU/W
Auto amp. connector (M75)
PU/W

Disconnect auto amp. harness connector.

↓

C Note
Check circuit continuity between air mix door motor harness terminal No. ㊱ and auto amp. harness terminal No. ㊱ .

↓ O.K.

C Air mix door motor connector (M74)
G/Y
Auto amp. connector (M75)
G/Y

D
CHECK P.B.R. CIRCUIT BETWEEN P.B.R. AND AUTO AMP.
Reconnect auto amp. harness connector.
Do approx. 5 volts exist between air mix door motor harness terminal No. ㉘ and body ground?
→ N.G. → Disconnect auto amp. harness connector.

↓ O.K.

E Note
Check circuit continuity between air mix door motor harness terminal No. ㉘ and auto amp. harness terminal No. ㉘ .

↓ O.K.

Replace auto amp.

D Air mix door motor connector (M74)
BR/W

CHECK P.B.R.
(Refer to Control System Output Components.)
→ N.G. → Replace air mix door motor (P.B.R.).

↓

Replace auto amp.

E Air mix door motor connector (M74)
BR/W
Auto amp. connector (M75)
BR/W

Note:
If the result is N.G. after checking circuit continuity, repair harness or connector.

1994 Q45 AUTO. A/C SYSTEMS DIAGNOSTIC PROCEDURE 7

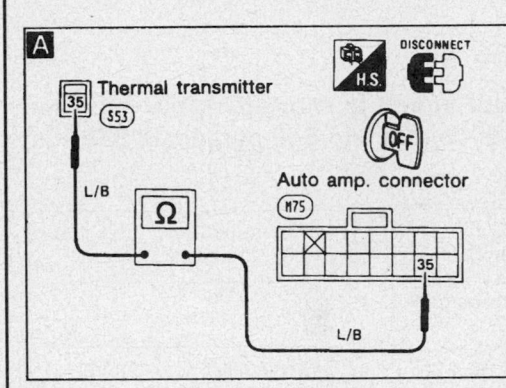

Diagnostic Procedure 7

SYMPTOM: Thermal transmitter circuit is open. (27 is indicated on auto amp. as a result of conducting Self-diagnosis STEP 2.)

A   Note

CHECK THERMAL TRANSMITTER CIRCUIT BETWEEN THERMAL TRANSMITTER AND AUTO AMP.
Disconnect thermal transmitter harness connector and auto amp. harness connector.
Check circuit continuity between thermal transmitter harness terminal No. ㉟ and auto amp. harness terminal No. ㉟ .

↓ O.K.

CHECK THERMAL TRANSMITTER.
Refer to EL section.

↓ O.K.

Replace auto amp.

Note:

If the result is N.G. after checking circuit continuity, repair harness or connector.

1994 Q45 AUTO. A/C SYSTEMS DIAGNOSTIC PROCEDURES 8 AND 9

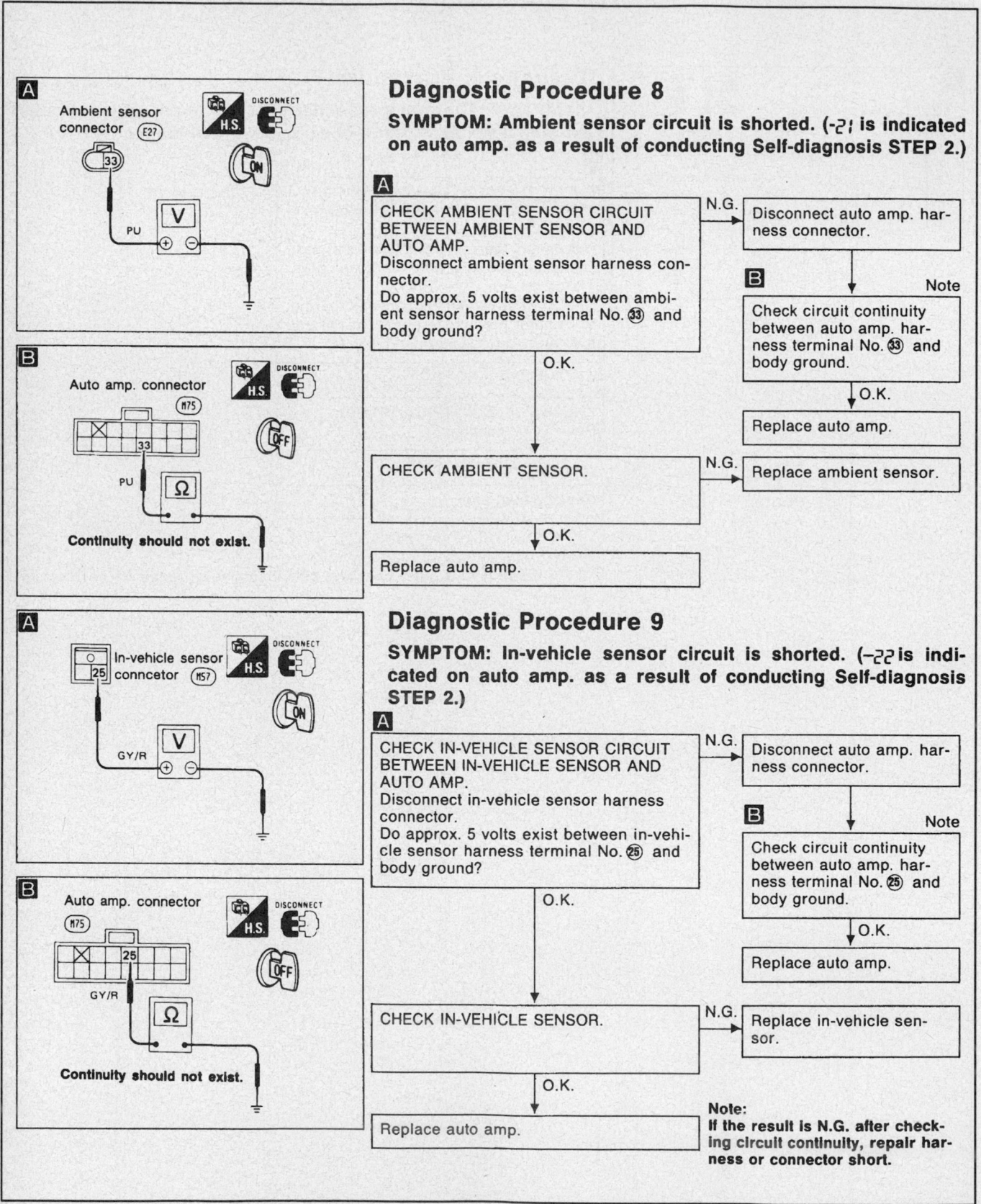

A Ambient sensor connector (E27)

33

PU

V
(+) (-)

B Auto amp. connector (M75)

33

PU

Ω

Continuity should not exist.

A In-vehicle sensor conncetor (M57)

25

GY/R

V
(+) (-)

B Auto amp. connector (M75)

25

GY/R

Ω

Continuity should not exist.

Diagnostic Procedure 8

SYMPTOM: Ambient sensor circuit is shorted. (-21 is indicated on auto amp. as a result of conducting Self-diagnosis STEP 2.)

A CHECK AMBIENT SENSOR CIRCUIT BETWEEN AMBIENT SENSOR AND AUTO AMP.
Disconnect ambient sensor harness connector.
Do approx. 5 volts exist between ambient sensor harness terminal No. 33 and body ground?

N.G. → Disconnect auto amp. harness connector.

B Note
Check circuit continuity between auto amp. harness terminal No. 33 and body ground.

O.K. ↓

Replace auto amp.

O.K. ↓

CHECK AMBIENT SENSOR. — N.G. → Replace ambient sensor.

O.K. ↓

Replace auto amp.

Diagnostic Procedure 9

SYMPTOM: In-vehicle sensor circuit is shorted. (—22 is indicated on auto amp. as a result of conducting Self-diagnosis STEP 2.)

A CHECK IN-VEHICLE SENSOR CIRCUIT BETWEEN IN-VEHICLE SENSOR AND AUTO AMP.
Disconnect in-vehicle sensor harness connector.
Do approx. 5 volts exist between in-vehicle sensor harness terminal No. 25 and body ground?

N.G. → Disconnect auto amp. harness connector.

B Note
Check circuit continuity between auto amp. harness terminal No. 25 and body ground.

O.K. ↓

Replace auto amp.

O.K. ↓

CHECK IN-VEHICLE SENSOR. — N.G. → Replace in-vehicle sensor.

O.K. ↓

Replace auto amp.

Note:
If the result is N.G. after checking circuit continuity, repair harness or connector short.

1994 Q45 AUTO. A/C SYSTEMS DIAGNOSTIC PROCEDURES 10 AND 11

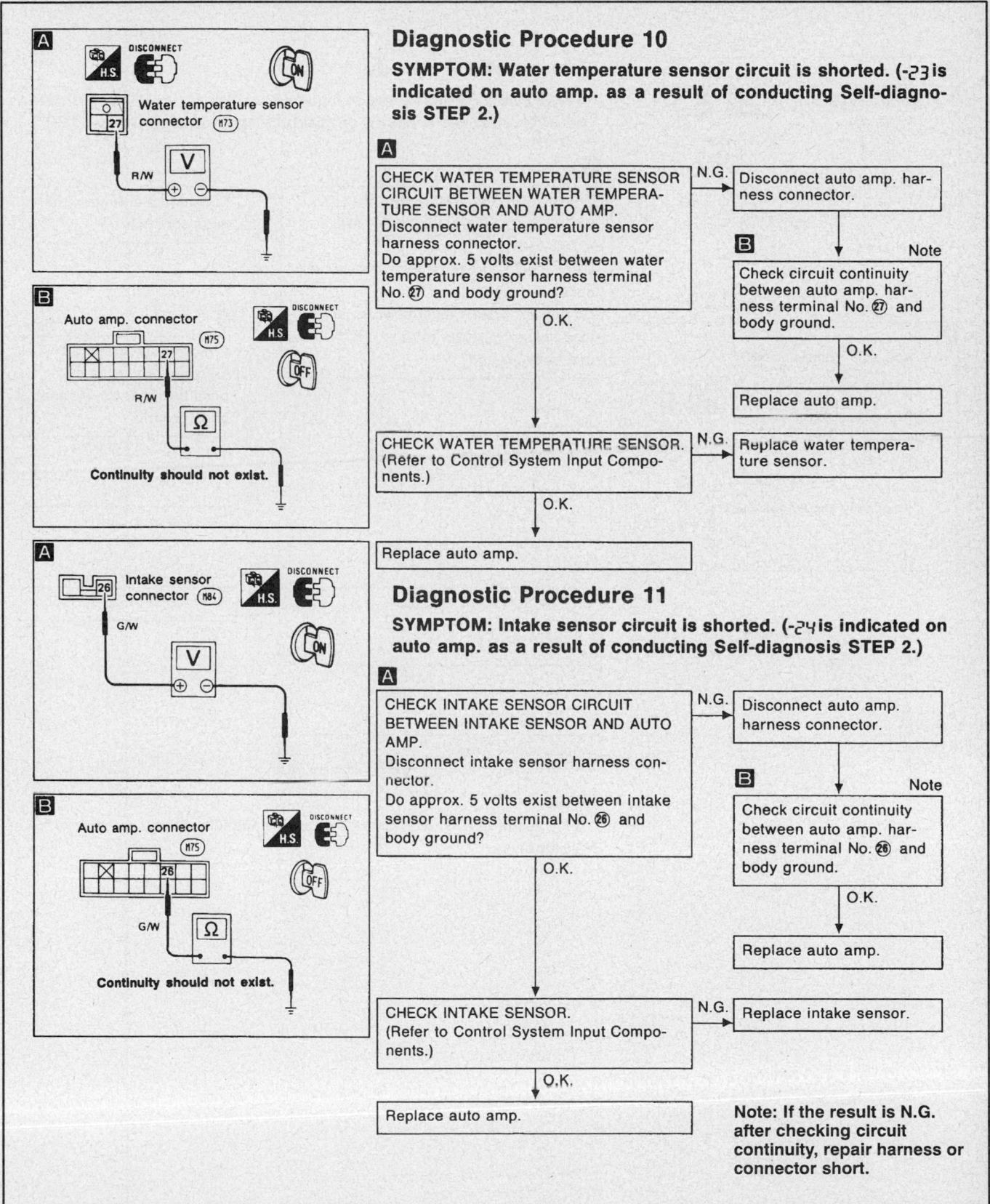

Diagnostic Procedure 10

SYMPTOM: Water temperature sensor circuit is shorted. (-23 is indicated on auto amp. as a result of conducting Self-diagnosis STEP 2.)

A

CHECK WATER TEMPERATURE SENSOR CIRCUIT BETWEEN WATER TEMPERATURE SENSOR AND AUTO AMP.
Disconnect water temperature sensor harness connector.
Do approx. 5 volts exist between water temperature sensor harness terminal No. ㉗ and body ground?

→ N.G. → Disconnect auto amp. harness connector.

B Note

Check circuit continuity between auto amp. harness terminal No. ㉗ and body ground.

→ O.K. → Replace auto amp.

↓ O.K.

CHECK WATER TEMPERATURE SENSOR.
(Refer to Control System Input Components.)

→ N.G. → Replace water temperature sensor.

↓ O.K.

Replace auto amp.

Diagnostic Procedure 11

SYMPTOM: Intake sensor circuit is shorted. (-24 is indicated on auto amp. as a result of conducting Self-diagnosis STEP 2.)

A

CHECK INTAKE SENSOR CIRCUIT BETWEEN INTAKE SENSOR AND AUTO AMP.
Disconnect intake sensor harness connector.
Do approx. 5 volts exist between intake sensor harness terminal No. ㉖ and body ground?

→ N.G. → Disconnect auto amp. harness connector.

B Note

Check circuit continuity between auto amp. harness terminal No. ㉖ and body ground.

→ O.K. → Replace auto amp.

↓ O.K.

CHECK INTAKE SENSOR.
(Refer to Control System Input Components.)

→ N.G. → Replace intake sensor.

↓ O.K.

Replace auto amp.

Note: If the result is N.G. after checking circuit continuity, repair harness or connector short.

1994 Q45 AUTO. A/C SYSTEMS DIAGNOSTIC PROCEDURE 12

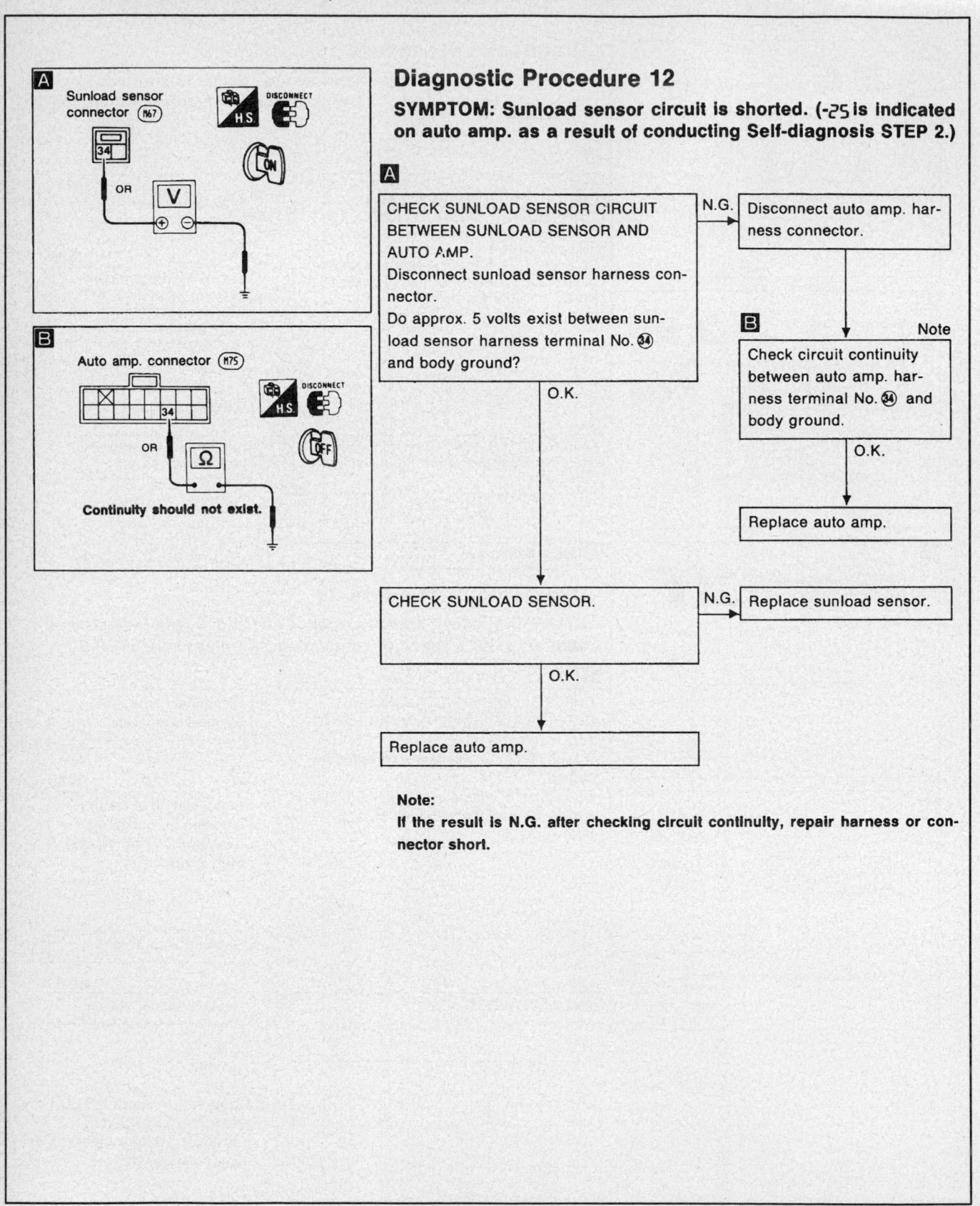

A

Sunload sensor connector (N67)

DISCONNECT
H.S.

ON

V
(+) (−)

OR

B

Auto amp. connector (M75)

34

DISCONNECT
H.S.

OFF

Ω

OR

Continuity should not exist.

Diagnostic Procedure 12

SYMPTOM: Sunload sensor circuit is shorted. (-25 is indicated on auto amp. as a result of conducting Self-diagnosis STEP 2.)

A

| CHECK SUNLOAD SENSOR CIRCUIT BETWEEN SUNLOAD SENSOR AND AUTO AMP.
Disconnect sunload sensor harness connector.
Do approx. 5 volts exist between sunload sensor harness terminal No. ㉞ and body ground? | → N.G. → | Disconnect auto amp. harness connector. |

O.K. ↓

B   Note

| Check circuit continuity between auto amp. harness terminal No. ㉞ and body ground. |

O.K. ↓

| Replace auto amp. |

| CHECK SUNLOAD SENSOR. | → N.G. → | Replace sunload sensor. |

O.K. ↓

| Replace auto amp. |

Note:
If the result is N.G. after checking circuit continuity, repair harness or connector short.

1994 Q45 AUTO. A/C SYSTEMS DIAGNOSTIC PROCEDURE 13

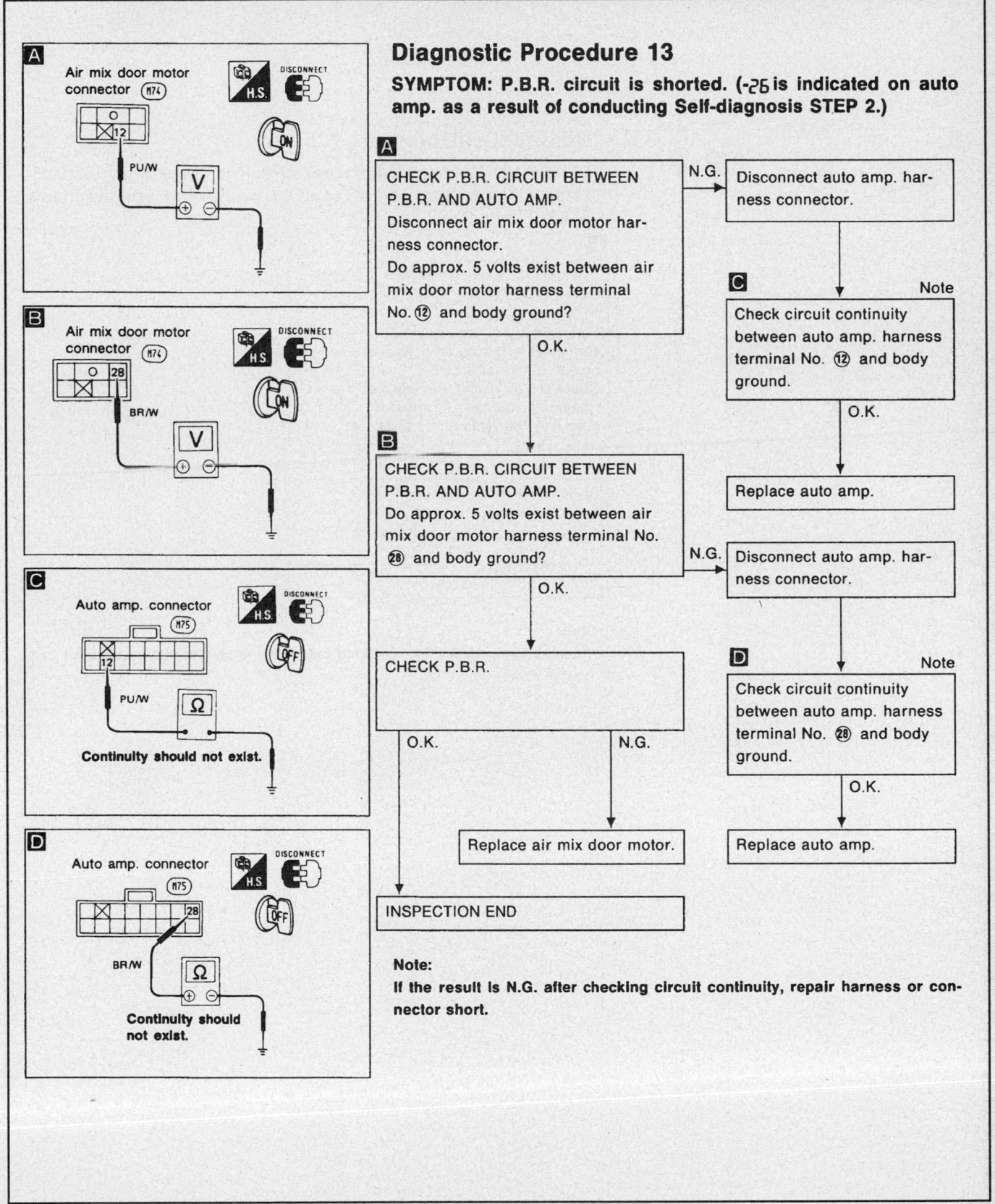

Diagnostic Procedure 13

SYMPTOM: P.B.R. circuit is shorted. (-26 is indicated on auto amp. as a result of conducting Self-diagnosis STEP 2.)

A

CHECK P.B.R. CIRCUIT BETWEEN P.B.R. AND AUTO AMP.
Disconnect air mix door motor harness connector.
Do approx. 5 volts exist between air mix door motor harness terminal No. ⑫ and body ground?

N.G. → Disconnect auto amp. harness connector.

O.K. ↓

B

CHECK P.B.R. CIRCUIT BETWEEN P.B.R. AND AUTO AMP.
Do approx. 5 volts exist between air mix door motor harness terminal No. ㉘ and body ground?

O.K. ↓

N.G. → Disconnect auto amp. harness connector.

CHECK P.B.R.

O.K.   N.G.

C   Note

Check circuit continuity between auto amp. harness terminal No. ⑫ and body ground.

O.K. ↓

Replace auto amp.

D   Note

Check circuit continuity between auto amp. harness terminal No. ㉘ and body ground.

O.K. ↓

Replace auto amp.

Replace air mix door motor.

INSPECTION END

Note:
If the result is N.G. after checking circuit continuity, repair harness or connector short.

Left panels:

A Air mix door motor connector (M74) — 12 — PU/W — V

B Air mix door motor connector (M74) — 28 — BR/W — V

C Auto amp. connector (M75) — 12 — PU/W — Ω — **Continuity should not exist.**

D Auto amp. connector (M75) — 28 — BR/W — Ω — **Continuity should not exist.**

1994 Q45 AUTO. A/C SYSTEMS DIAGNOSTIC PROCEDURE 14

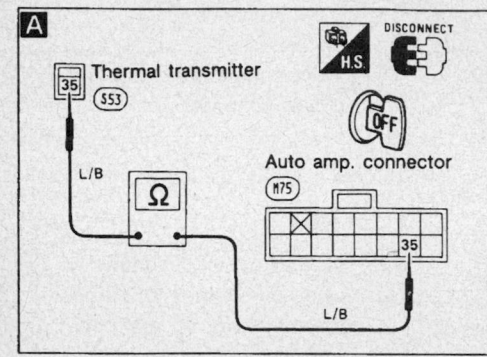

Diagnostic Procedure 14

SYMPTOM: Thermal transmitter circuit is shorted. (-27 is indicated on auto amp. as a result of conducting Self-diagnosis STEP 2.)

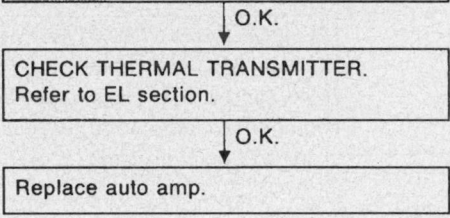
Note

CHECK THERMAL TRANSMITTER CIRCUIT BETWEEN THERMAL TRANSMITTER AND AUTO AMP.
Disconnect thermal transmitter harness connector and auto amp. harness connector.
Check circuit continuity between thermal transmitter harness terminal No. ㉟ and auto amp. harness terminal No. ㉟.

↓ O.K.

CHECK THERMAL TRANSMITTER.
Refer to EL section.

↓ O.K.

Replace auto amp.

Note:
If the result is N.G. after checking circuit continuity, repair harness or connector short.

1994 Q45 AUTO. A/C SYSTEMS DIAGNOSTIC PROCEDURE 15

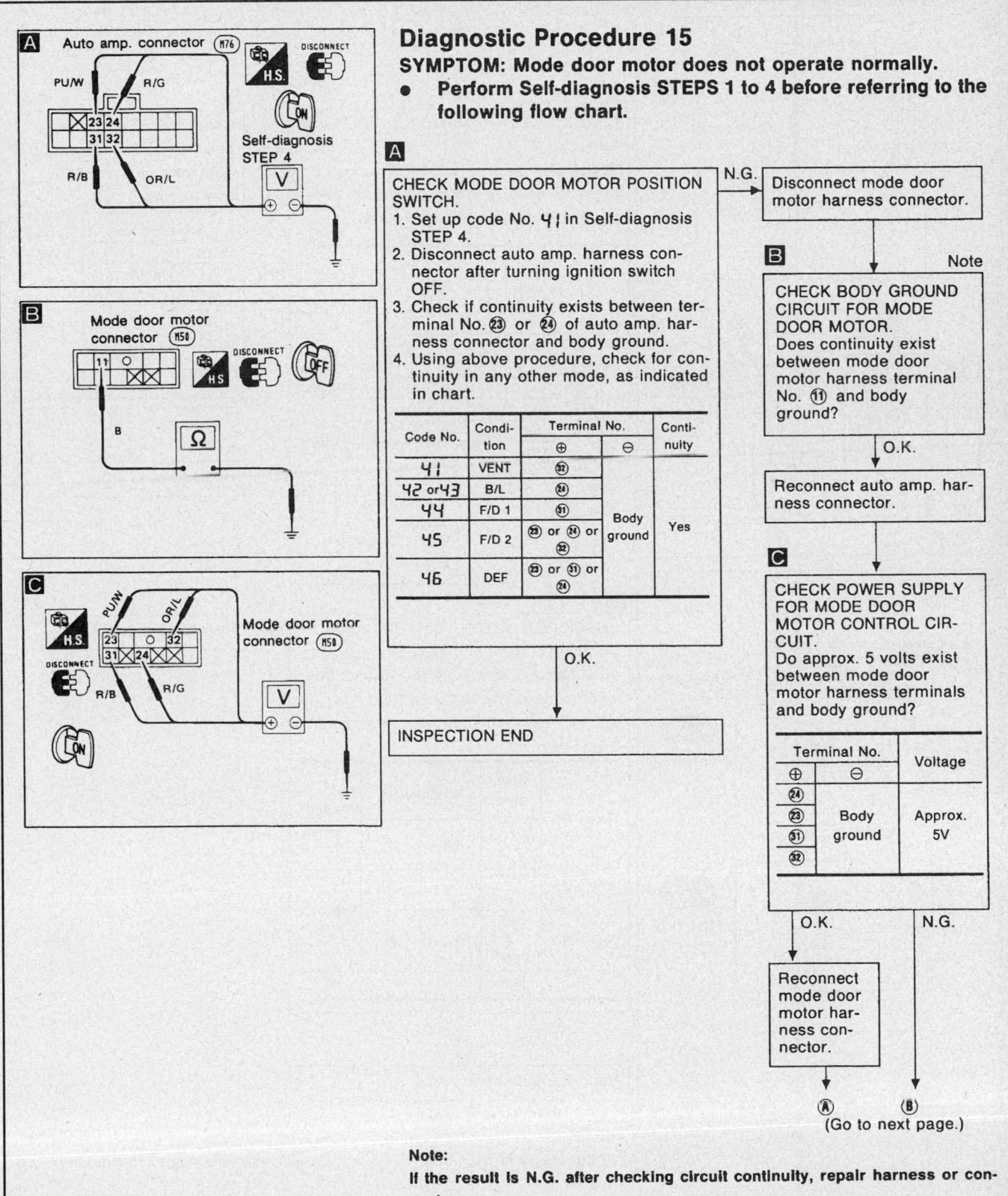

A Auto amp. connector (M76)

PU/W   R/G

23 24
31 32

R/B   OR/L

Self-diagnosis
STEP 4

B Mode door motor
connector (M50)

11

B

C Mode door motor
connector (M50)

PU/W   OR/L

23   32
31 24

R/B   R/G

Diagnostic Procedure 15

SYMPTOM: Mode door motor does not operate normally.

● **Perform Self-diagnosis STEPS 1 to 4 before referring to the following flow chart.**

A

CHECK MODE DOOR MOTOR POSITION SWITCH.
1. Set up code No. 41 in Self-diagnosis STEP 4.
2. Disconnect auto amp. harness connector after turning ignition switch OFF.
3. Check if continuity exists between terminal No. ㉓ or ㉔ of auto amp. harness connector and body ground.
4. Using above procedure, check for continuity in any other mode, as indicated in chart.

Code No.	Condition	Terminal No. ⊕	Terminal No. ⊖	Continuity
41	VENT	㉜		
42 or 43	B/L	㉔		
44	F/D 1	㉛	Body ground	Yes
45	F/D 2	㉓ or ㉔ or ㉜		
46	DEF	㉓ or ㉛ or ㉔		

O.K. → INSPECTION END

A N.G. → Disconnect mode door motor harness connector.

B Note

CHECK BODY GROUND CIRCUIT FOR MODE DOOR MOTOR.
Does continuity exist between mode door motor harness terminal No. ⑪ and body ground?

O.K. ↓

Reconnect auto amp. harness connector.

C

CHECK POWER SUPPLY FOR MODE DOOR MOTOR CONTROL CIRCUIT.
Do approx. 5 volts exist between mode door motor harness terminals and body ground?

Terminal No. ⊕	Terminal No. ⊖	Voltage
㉔		
㉓	Body ground	Approx. 5V
㉛		
㉜		

O.K. ↓   N.G. ↓

Reconnect mode door motor harness connector.

Ⓐ   Ⓑ
(Go to next page.)

Note:
If the result is N.G. after checking circuit continuity, repair harness or connector.

1994 Q45 AUTO. A/C SYSTEMS DIAGNOSTIC PROCEDURE 15 — CONT'D.

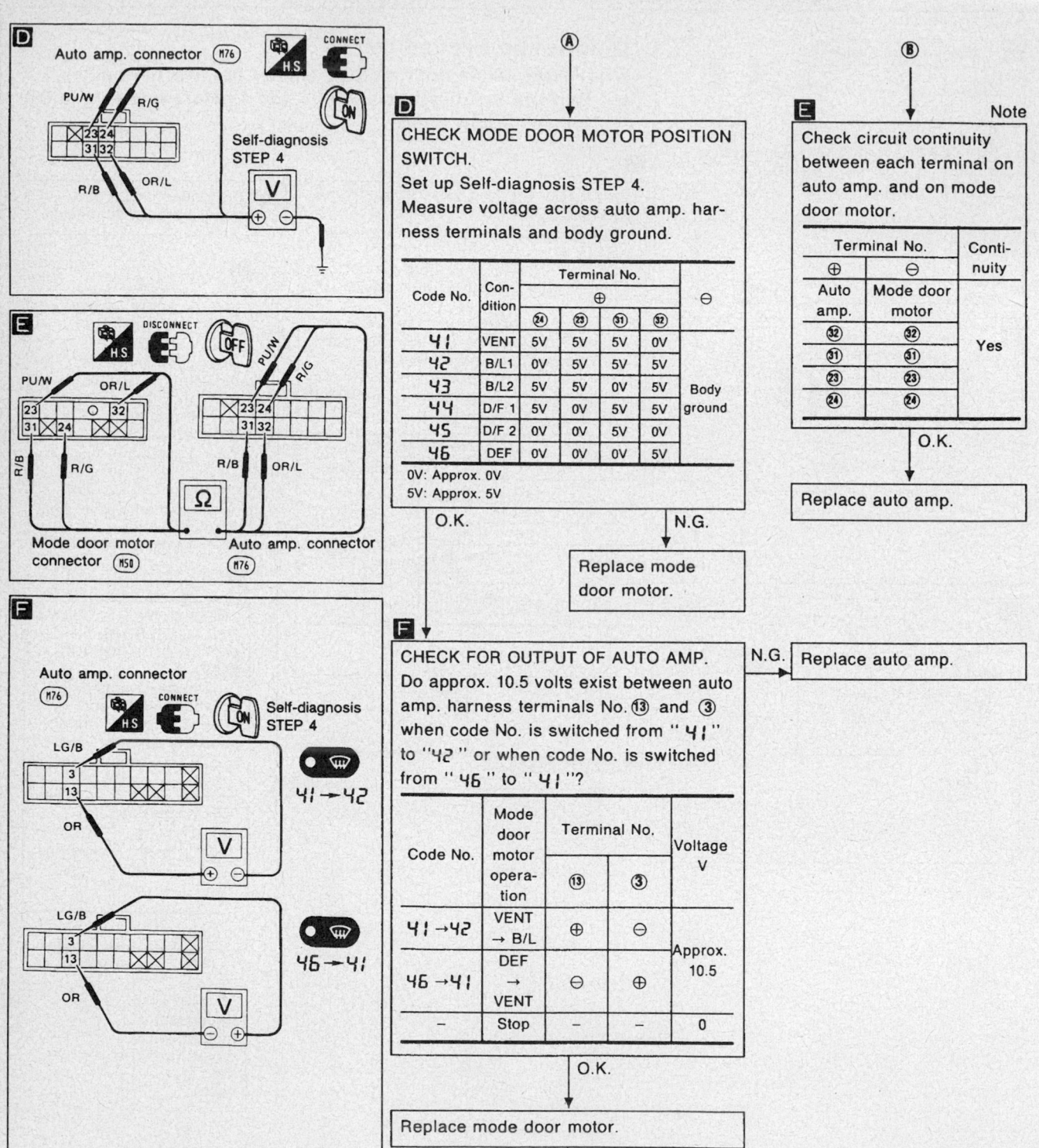

D

Auto amp. connector M76

Self-diagnosis STEP 4

E

Mode door motor connector M50   Auto amp. connector M76

F

Auto amp. connector M76

Self-diagnosis STEP 4

41 → 42

46 → 41

D

CHECK MODE DOOR MOTOR POSITION SWITCH.
Set up Self-diagnosis STEP 4.
Measure voltage across auto amp. harness terminals and body ground.

Code No.	Con-dition	Terminal No. ⊕				⊖
		㉔	㉓	㉛	㉜	
41	VENT	5V	5V	5V	0V	
42	B/L1	0V	5V	5V	5V	
43	B/L2	5V	5V	0V	5V	Body ground
44	D/F 1	5V	0V	5V	5V	
45	D/F 2	0V	0V	5V	0V	
46	DEF	0V	0V	0V	5V	

0V: Approx. 0V
5V: Approx. 5V

O.K. → (F)   N.G. →

Replace mode door motor.

F

CHECK FOR OUTPUT OF AUTO AMP.
Do approx. 10.5 volts exist between auto amp. harness terminals No. ⑬ and ③ when code No. is switched from " 41 " to " 42 " or when code No. is switched from " 46 " to " 41 "?

Code No.	Mode door motor opera-tion	Terminal No. ⑬	③	Voltage V
41 → 42	VENT → B/L	⊕	⊖	
46 → 41	DEF → VENT	⊖	⊕	Approx. 10.5
–	Stop	–	–	0

N.G. → Replace auto amp.

O.K. ↓

Replace mode door motor.

E

Check circuit continuity between each terminal on auto amp. and on mode door motor.

Terminal No. ⊕ Auto amp.	⊖ Mode door motor	Conti-nuity
㉜	㉜	
㉛	㉛	Yes
㉓	㉓	
㉔	㉔	

O.K. ↓

Replace auto amp.

Note:
If the result is N.G. after checking circuit continuity, repair harness or connector.

1994 Q45 AUTO. A/C SYSTEMS DIAGNOSTIC PROCEDURE 16

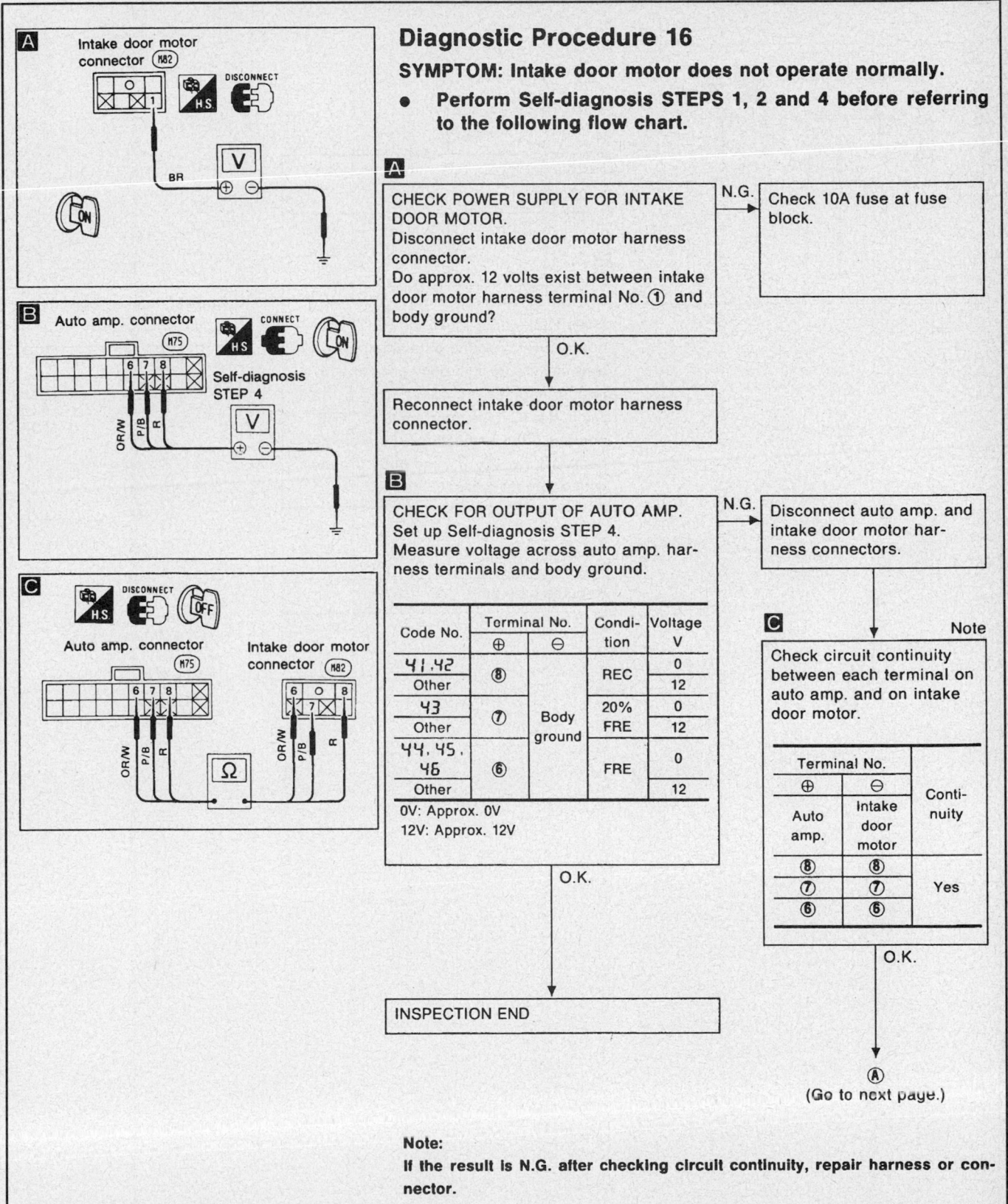

Diagnostic Procedure 16

SYMPTOM: Intake door motor does not operate normally.

- Perform Self-diagnosis STEPS 1, 2 and 4 before referring to the following flow chart.

A

CHECK POWER SUPPLY FOR INTAKE DOOR MOTOR.
Disconnect intake door motor harness connector.
Do approx. 12 volts exist between intake door motor harness terminal No. ① and body ground?

N.G. → Check 10A fuse at fuse block.

O.K.

Reconnect intake door motor harness connector.

B

CHECK FOR OUTPUT OF AUTO AMP.
Set up Self-diagnosis STEP 4.
Measure voltage across auto amp. harness terminals and body ground.

N.G. → Disconnect auto amp. and intake door motor harness connectors.

Code No.	Terminal No. ⊕	Terminal No. ⊖	Condition	Voltage V
41.42	⑧	Body ground	REC	0
Other				12
43	⑦		20% FRE	0
Other				12
44.45. 46	⑥		FRE	0
Other				12

0V: Approx. 0V
12V: Approx. 12V

C   Note

Check circuit continuity between each terminal on auto amp. and on intake door motor.

Terminal No. Auto amp. ⊕	Terminal No. Intake door motor ⊖	Continuity
⑧	⑧	Yes
⑦	⑦	
⑥	⑥	

O.K.

O.K.

INSPECTION END

Ⓐ
(Go to next page.)

Note:
If the result is N.G. after checking circuit continuity, repair harness or connector.

1994 Q45 AUTO. A/C SYSTEMS DIAGNOSTIC PROCEDURE 16 – CONT'D.

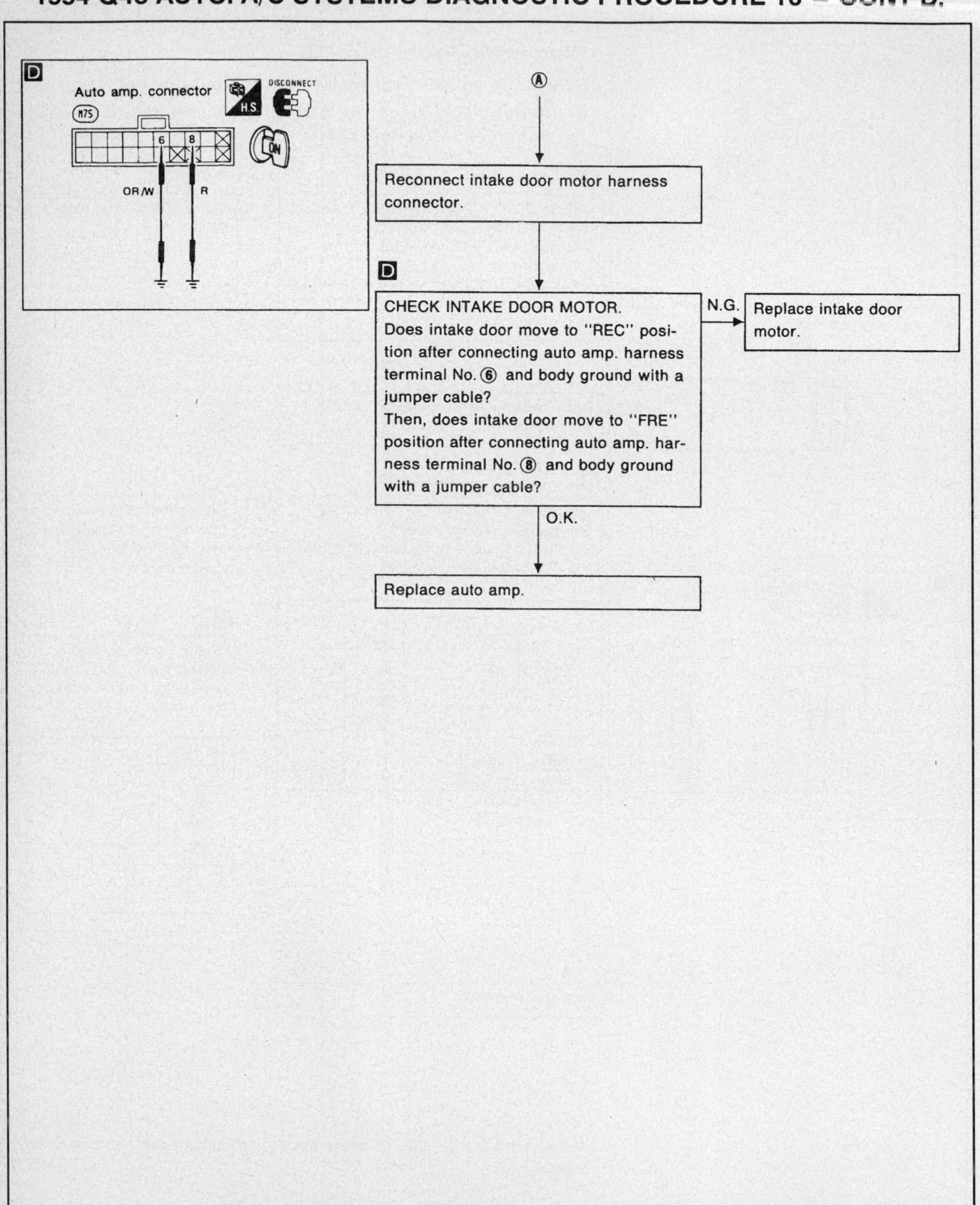

D Auto amp. connector
(M75)

6 8

OR/W   R

Ⓐ

Reconnect intake door motor harness connector.

D CHECK INTAKE DOOR MOTOR.
Does intake door move to "REC" position after connecting auto amp. harness terminal No. ⑥ and body ground with a jumper cable?
Then, does intake door move to "FRE" position after connecting auto amp. harness terminal No. ⑧ and body ground with a jumper cable?

N.G. → Replace intake door motor.

O.K.

Replace auto amp.

1994 Q45 AUTO. A/C SYSTEMS DIAGNOSTIC PROCEDURE 17

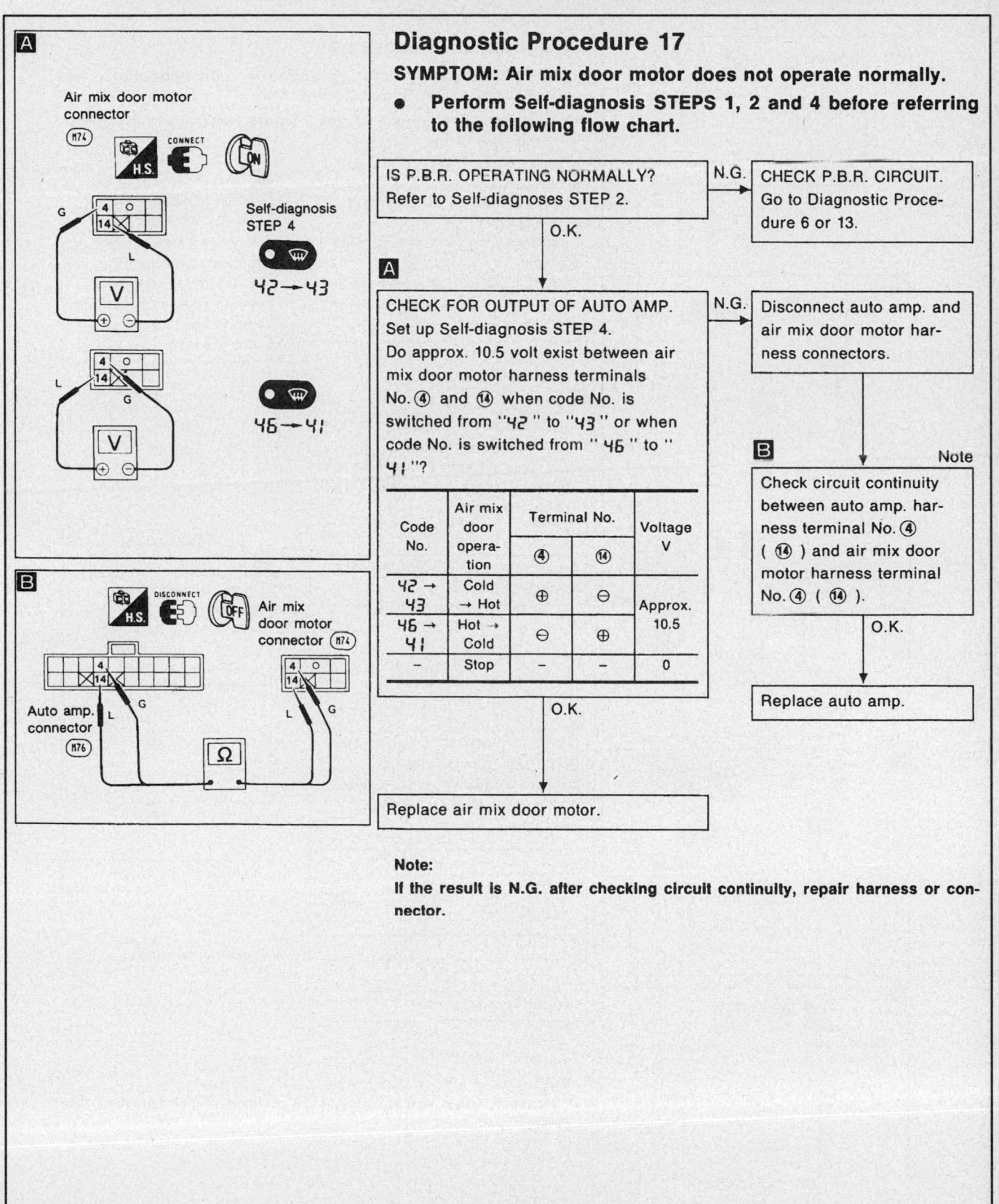

Diagnostic Procedure 17

SYMPTOM: Air mix door motor does not operate normally.

- **Perform Self-diagnosis STEPS 1, 2 and 4 before referring to the following flow chart.**

A — Air mix door motor connector (M74)

Self-diagnosis STEP 4

42 → 43

46 → 41

B — Air mix door motor connector (M74)

Auto amp. connector (M76)

IS P.B.R. OPERATING NORMALLY?
Refer to Self-diagnoses STEP 2.

→ N.G. → CHECK P.B.R. CIRCUIT.
Go to Diagnostic Procedure 6 or 13.

↓ O.K.

A

CHECK FOR OUTPUT OF AUTO AMP.
Set up Self-diagnosis STEP 4.
Do approx. 10.5 volt exist between air mix door motor harness terminals No. ④ and ⑭ when code No. is switched from "42" to "43" or when code No. is switched from "46" to "41"?

→ N.G. → Disconnect auto amp. and air mix door motor harness connectors.

Code No.	Air mix door opera-tion	Terminal No. ④	Terminal No. ⑭	Voltage V
42 → 43	Cold → Hot	⊕	⊖	Approx. 10.5
46 → 41	Hot → Cold	⊖	⊕	
–	Stop	–	–	0

↓ O.K.

B — Note

Check circuit continuity between auto amp. harness terminal No. ④ (⑭) and air mix door motor harness terminal No. ④ (⑭).

↓ O.K.

Replace auto amp.

Replace air mix door motor.

Note:
If the result is N.G. after checking circuit continuity, repair harness or connector.

1994 Q45 AUTO. A/C SYSTEMS DIAGNOSTIC PROCEDURE 18

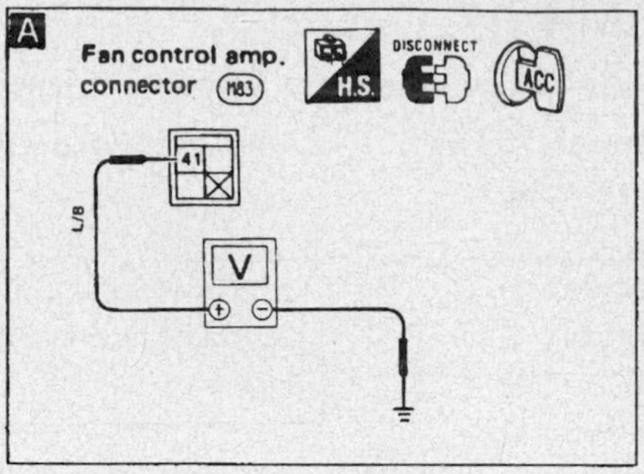

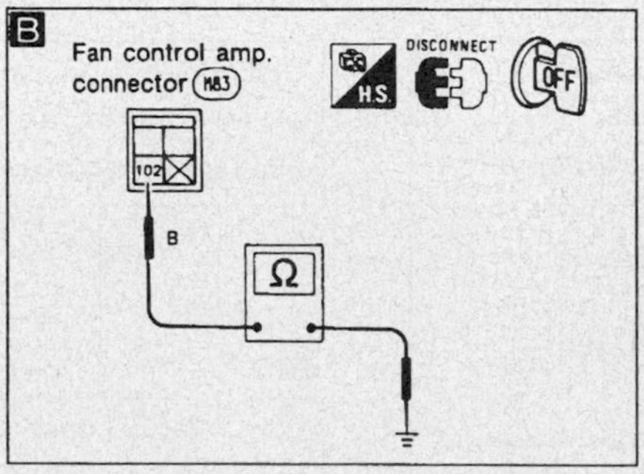

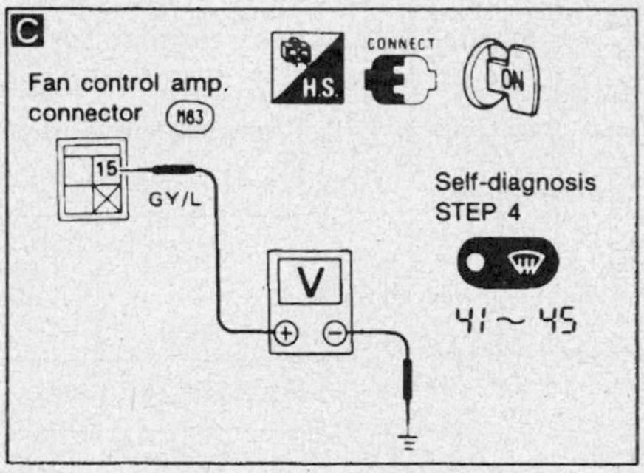

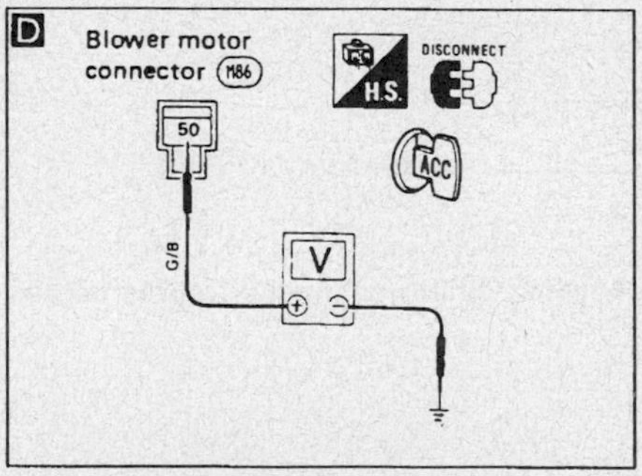

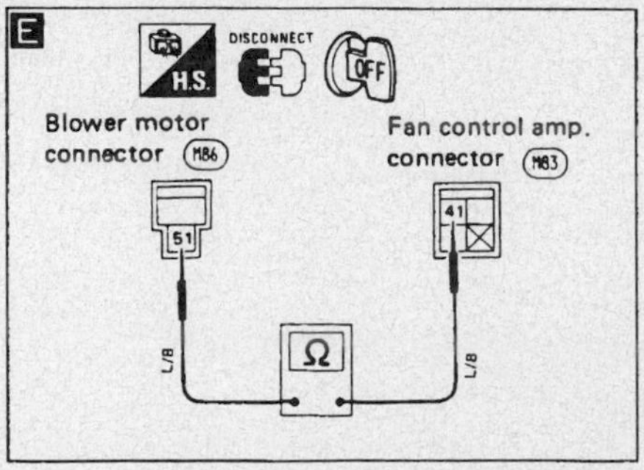

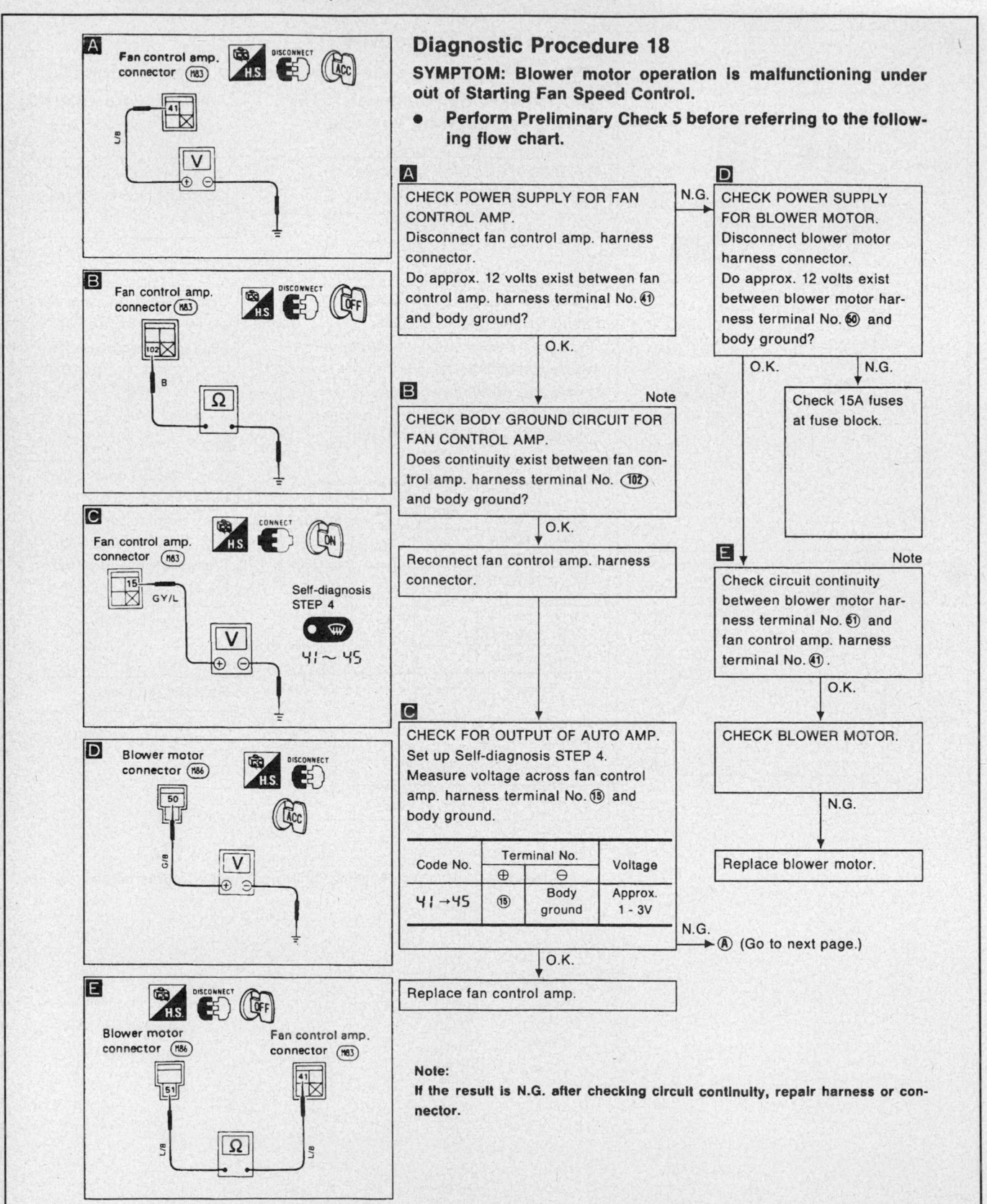

Diagnostic Procedure 18

SYMPTOM: Blower motor operation is malfunctioning under out of Starting Fan Speed Control.

- **Perform Preliminary Check 5 before referring to the following flow chart.**

A CHECK POWER SUPPLY FOR FAN CONTROL AMP.
Disconnect fan control amp. harness connector.
Do approx. 12 volts exist between fan control amp. harness terminal No. ㊶ and body ground?

- N.G. → D
- O.K. ↓

B (Note) CHECK BODY GROUND CIRCUIT FOR FAN CONTROL AMP.
Does continuity exist between fan control amp. harness terminal No. (102) and body ground?

- O.K. ↓

Reconnect fan control amp. harness connector.

↓

C CHECK FOR OUTPUT OF AUTO AMP.
Set up Self-diagnosis STEP 4.
Measure voltage across fan control amp. harness terminal No. ⑮ and body ground.

Code No.	Terminal No. ⊕	Terminal No. ⊖	Voltage
41 → 45	⑮	Body ground	Approx. 1 - 3V

- N.G. → Ⓐ (Go to next page.)
- O.K. ↓

Replace fan control amp.

D CHECK POWER SUPPLY FOR BLOWER MOTOR.
Disconnect blower motor harness connector.
Do approx. 12 volts exist between blower motor harness terminal No. ㊿ and body ground?

- N.G. → Check 15A fuses at fuse block.
- O.K. → E

E (Note) Check circuit continuity between blower motor harness terminal No. ㊿51 and fan control amp. harness terminal No. ㊶.

- O.K. ↓

CHECK BLOWER MOTOR.

- N.G. ↓

Replace blower motor.

Note:
If the result is N.G. after checking circuit continuity, repair harness or connector.

1994 Q45 AUTO. A/C SYSTEMS DIAGNOSTIC PROCEDURE 18 — CONT'D.

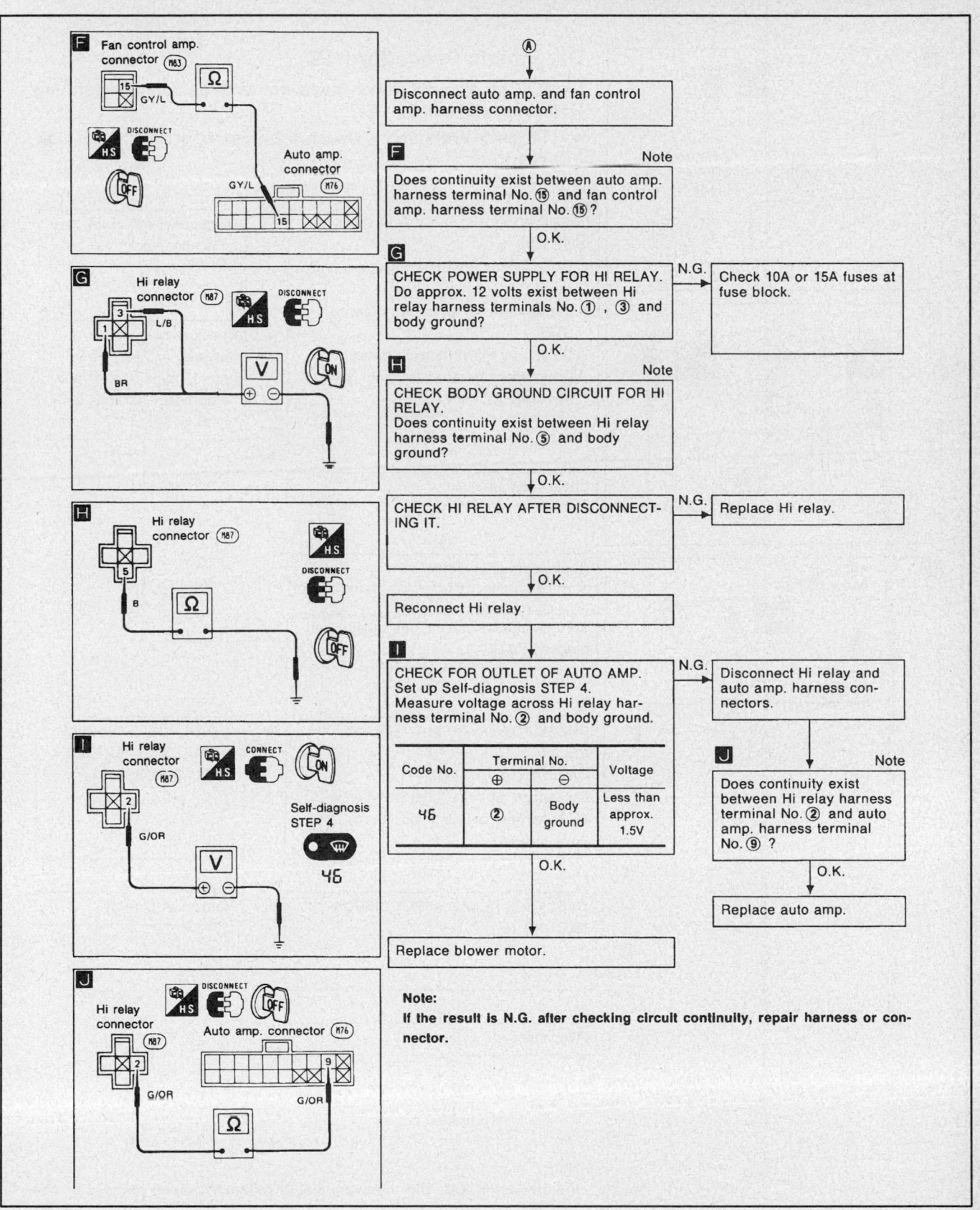

Ⓐ

Disconnect auto amp. and fan control amp. harness connector.

F   Note

Does continuity exist between auto amp. harness terminal No. ⑮ and fan control amp. harness terminal No. ⑮ ?

↓ O.K.

G

CHECK POWER SUPPLY FOR HI RELAY. Do approx. 12 volts exist between Hi relay harness terminals No. ① , ③ and body ground?   N.G. → Check 10A or 15A fuses at fuse block.

↓ O.K.

H   Note

CHECK BODY GROUND CIRCUIT FOR HI RELAY. Does continuity exist between Hi relay harness terminal No. ⑤ and body ground?

↓ O.K.

CHECK HI RELAY AFTER DISCONNECTING IT.   N.G. → Replace Hi relay.

↓ O.K.

Reconnect Hi relay.

I

CHECK FOR OUTLET OF AUTO AMP. Set up Self-diagnosis STEP 4. Measure voltage across Hi relay harness terminal No. ② and body ground.   N.G. → Disconnect Hi relay and auto amp. harness connectors.

Code No.	Terminal No. ⊕	Terminal No. ⊖	Voltage
46	②	Body ground	Less than approx. 1.5V

↓ O.K.

Replace blower motor.

J   Note

Does continuity exist between Hi relay harness terminal No. ② and auto amp. harness terminal No. ⑨ ?

↓ O.K.

Replace auto amp.

Note:
If the result is N.G. after checking circuit continuity, repair harness or connector.

1994 Q45 AUTO. A/C SYSTEMS DIAGNOSTIC PROCEDURE 19

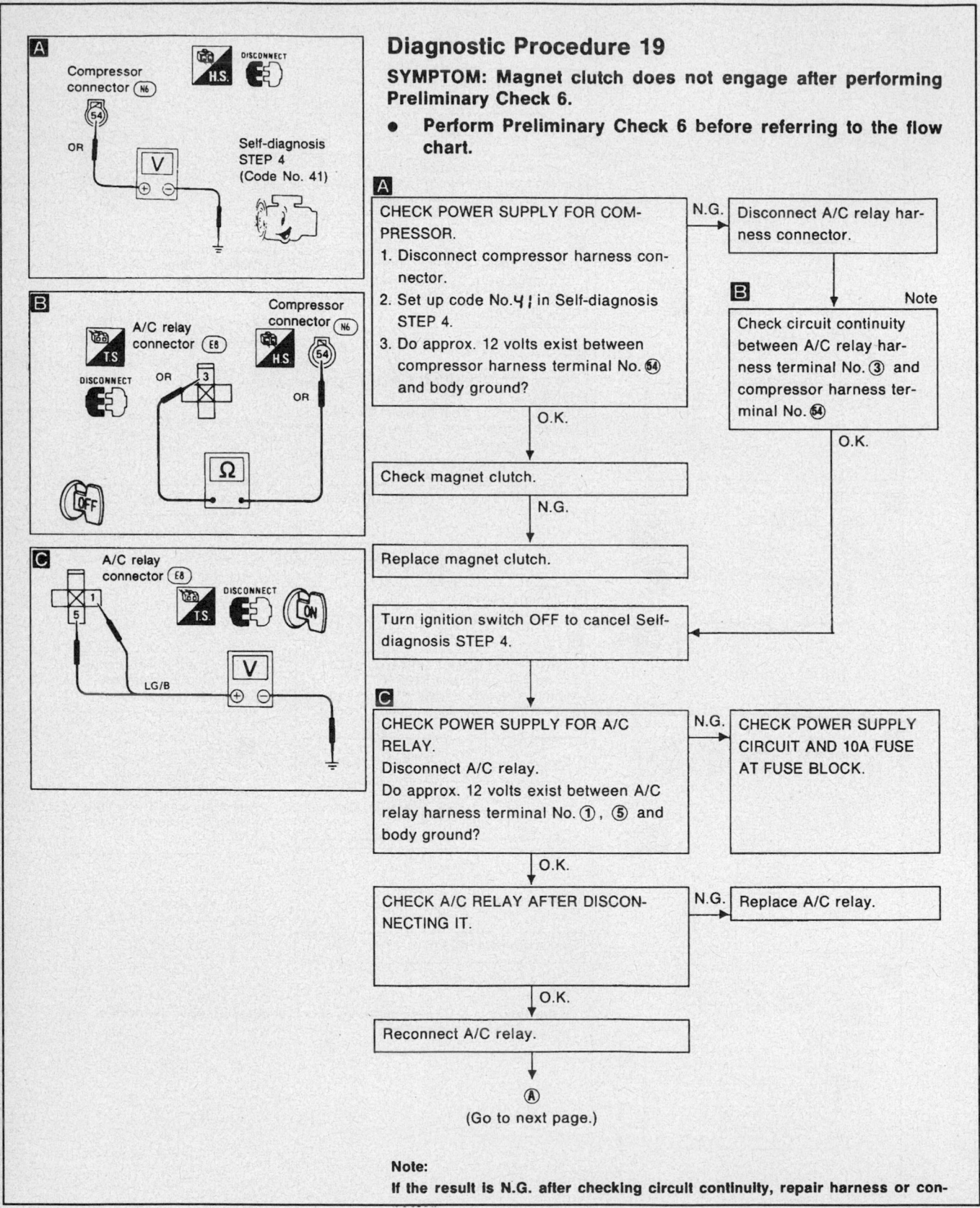

Diagnostic Procedure 19

SYMPTOM: Magnet clutch does not engage after performing Preliminary Check 6.

● **Perform Preliminary Check 6 before referring to the flow chart.**

A
CHECK POWER SUPPLY FOR COMPRESSOR.
1. Disconnect compressor harness connector.
2. Set up code No. 41 in Self-diagnosis STEP 4.
3. Do approx. 12 volts exist between compressor harness terminal No. 54 and body ground?

→ N.G. → Disconnect A/C relay harness connector.

B   Note
Check circuit continuity between A/C relay harness terminal No. 3 and compressor harness terminal No. 54.

↓ O.K.

Check magnet clutch.

↓ N.G.

Replace magnet clutch.

Turn ignition switch OFF to cancel Self-diagnosis STEP 4. ← O.K.

C
CHECK POWER SUPPLY FOR A/C RELAY.
Disconnect A/C relay.
Do approx. 12 volts exist between A/C relay harness terminal No. 1, 5 and body ground?

→ N.G. → CHECK POWER SUPPLY CIRCUIT AND 10A FUSE AT FUSE BLOCK.

↓ O.K.

CHECK A/C RELAY AFTER DISCONNECTING IT.

→ N.G. → Replace A/C relay.

↓ O.K.

Reconnect A/C relay.

↓

Ⓐ
(Go to next page.)

Note:
If the result is N.G. after checking circuit continuity, repair harness or con-

1994 Q45 AUTO. A/C SYSTEMS DIAGNOSTIC PROCEDURE 19 — CONT'D.

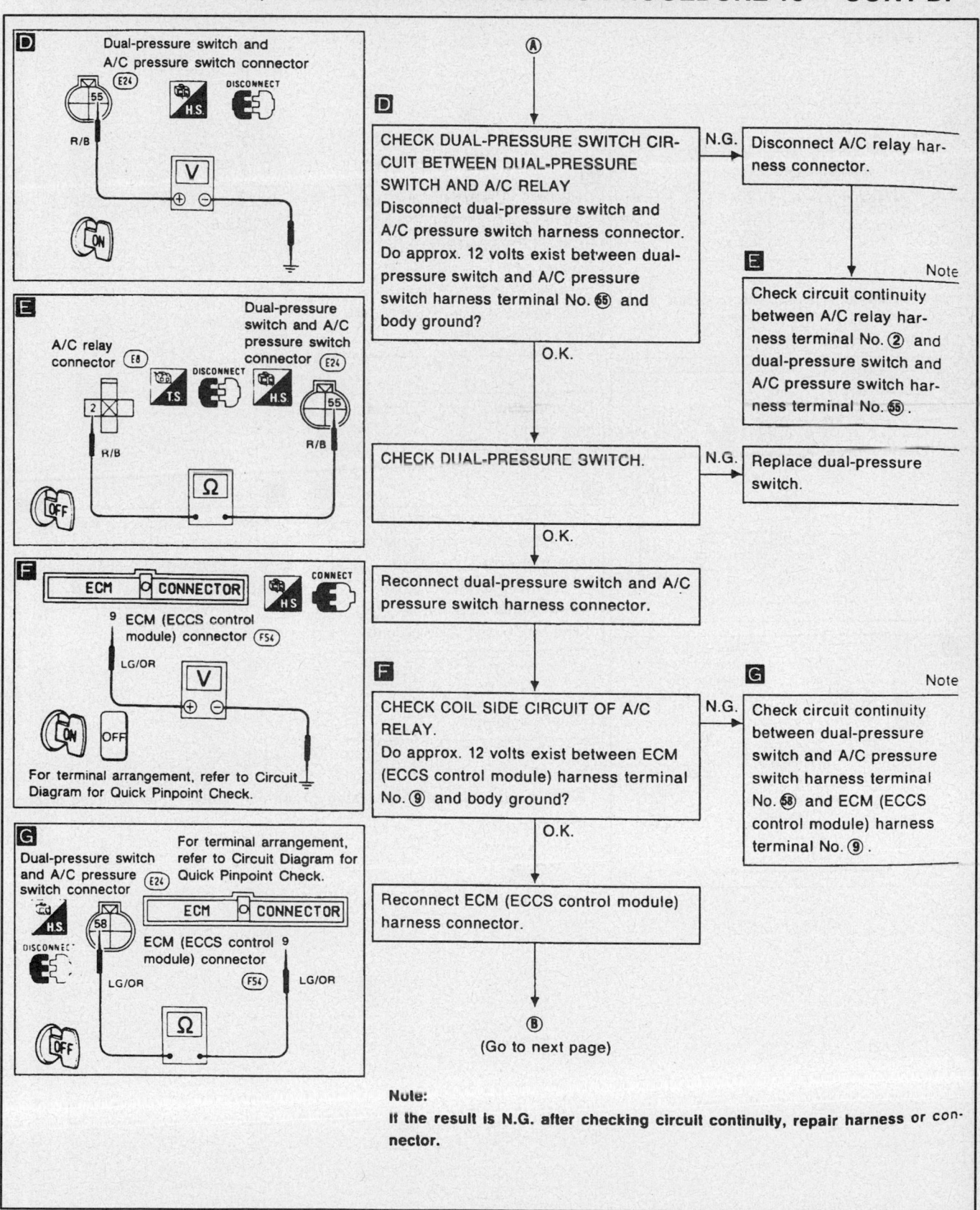

D Dual-pressure switch and A/C pressure switch connector

E A/C relay connector — Dual-pressure switch and A/C pressure switch connector

F ECM CONNECTOR — 9 ECM (ECCS control module) connector (F54) LG/OR

For terminal arrangement, refer to Circuit Diagram for Quick Pinpoint Check.

G Dual-pressure switch and A/C pressure switch connector (E24) — For terminal arrangement, refer to Circuit Diagram for Quick Pinpoint Check. — ECM CONNECTOR — ECM (ECCS control module) 9 connector (F54)

(A)

D CHECK DUAL-PRESSURE SWITCH CIRCUIT BETWEEN DUAL-PRESSURE SWITCH AND A/C RELAY
Disconnect dual-pressure switch and A/C pressure switch harness connector.
Do approx. 12 volts exist between dual-pressure switch and A/C pressure switch harness terminal No. 55 and body ground?

→ N.G. → Disconnect A/C relay harness connector.

↓ O.K.

E Note
Check circuit continuity between A/C relay harness terminal No. 2 and dual-pressure switch and A/C pressure switch harness terminal No. 55.

CHECK DUAL-PRESSURE SWITCH.
→ N.G. → Replace dual-pressure switch.

↓ O.K.

Reconnect dual-pressure switch and A/C pressure switch harness connector.

F CHECK COIL SIDE CIRCUIT OF A/C RELAY.
Do approx. 12 volts exist between ECM (ECCS control module) harness terminal No. 9 and body ground?

→ N.G. →

G Note
Check circuit continuity between dual-pressure switch and A/C pressure switch harness terminal No. 58 and ECM (ECCS control module) harness terminal No. 9.

↓ O.K.

Reconnect ECM (ECCS control module) harness connector.

↓

(B)
(Go to next page)

Note:
If the result is N.G. after checking circuit continuity, repair harness or connector.

1994 Q45 AUTO. A/C SYSTEMS DIAGNOSTIC PROCEDURE 19 — CONT'D.

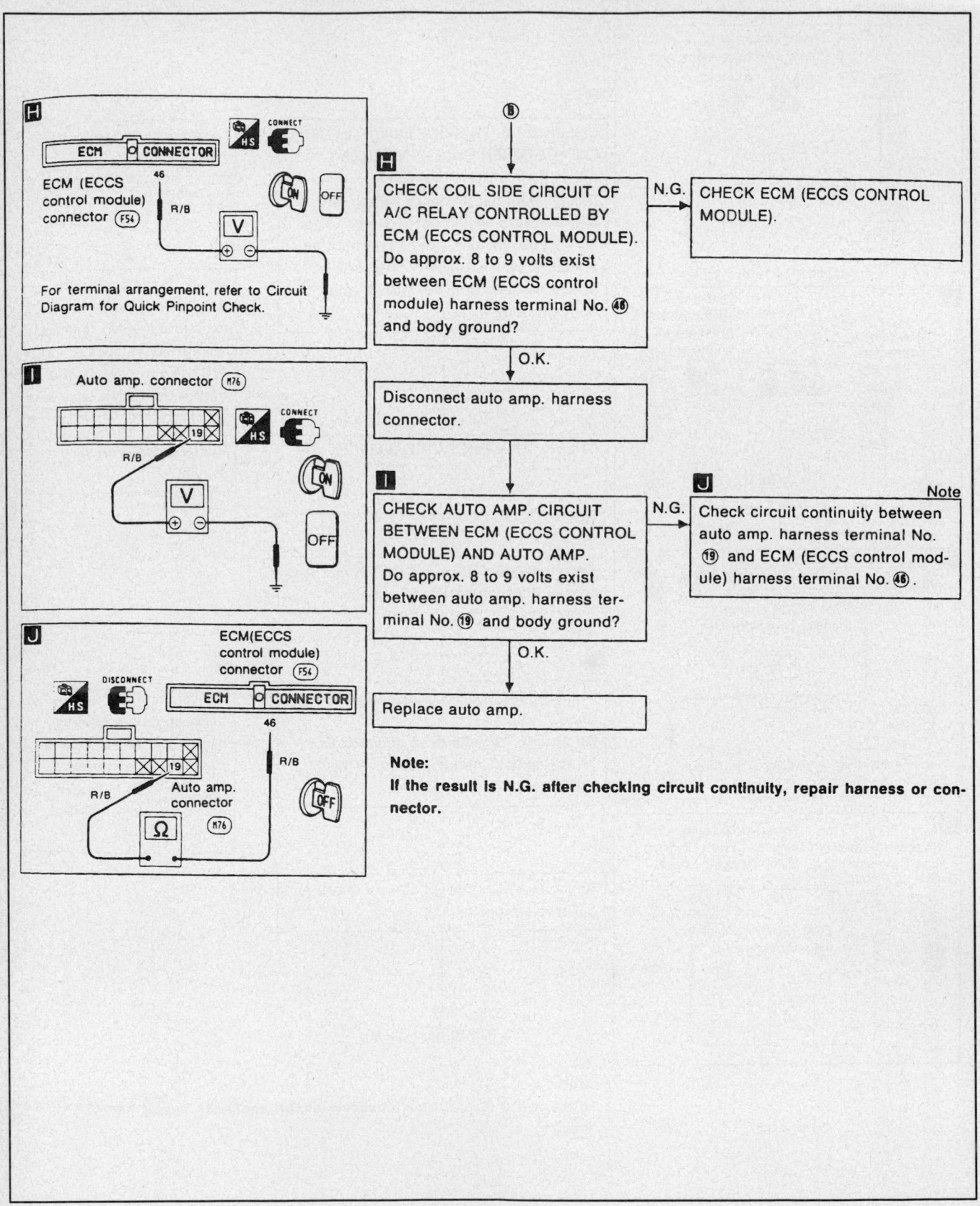

H

ECM (ECCS control module) connector (F54)

For terminal arrangement, refer to Circuit Diagram for Quick Pinpoint Check.

I

Auto amp. connector (M76)

J

ECM(ECCS control module) connector (F54)

Auto amp. connector (M76)

H

CHECK COIL SIDE CIRCUIT OF A/C RELAY CONTROLLED BY ECM (ECCS CONTROL MODULE). Do approx. 8 to 9 volts exist between ECM (ECCS control module) harness terminal No. 46 and body ground?

→ N.G. → CHECK ECM (ECCS CONTROL MODULE).

↓ O.K.

Disconnect auto amp. harness connector.

I

CHECK AUTO AMP. CIRCUIT BETWEEN ECM (ECCS CONTROL MODULE) AND AUTO AMP. Do approx. 8 to 9 volts exist between auto amp. harness terminal No. 19 and body ground?

→ N.G. → **J** Note

Check circuit continuity between auto amp. harness terminal No. 19 and ECM (ECCS control module) harness terminal No. 46.

↓ O.K.

Replace auto amp.

Note:
If the result is N.G. after checking circuit continuity, repair harness or connector.

WIRING SCHEMATICS

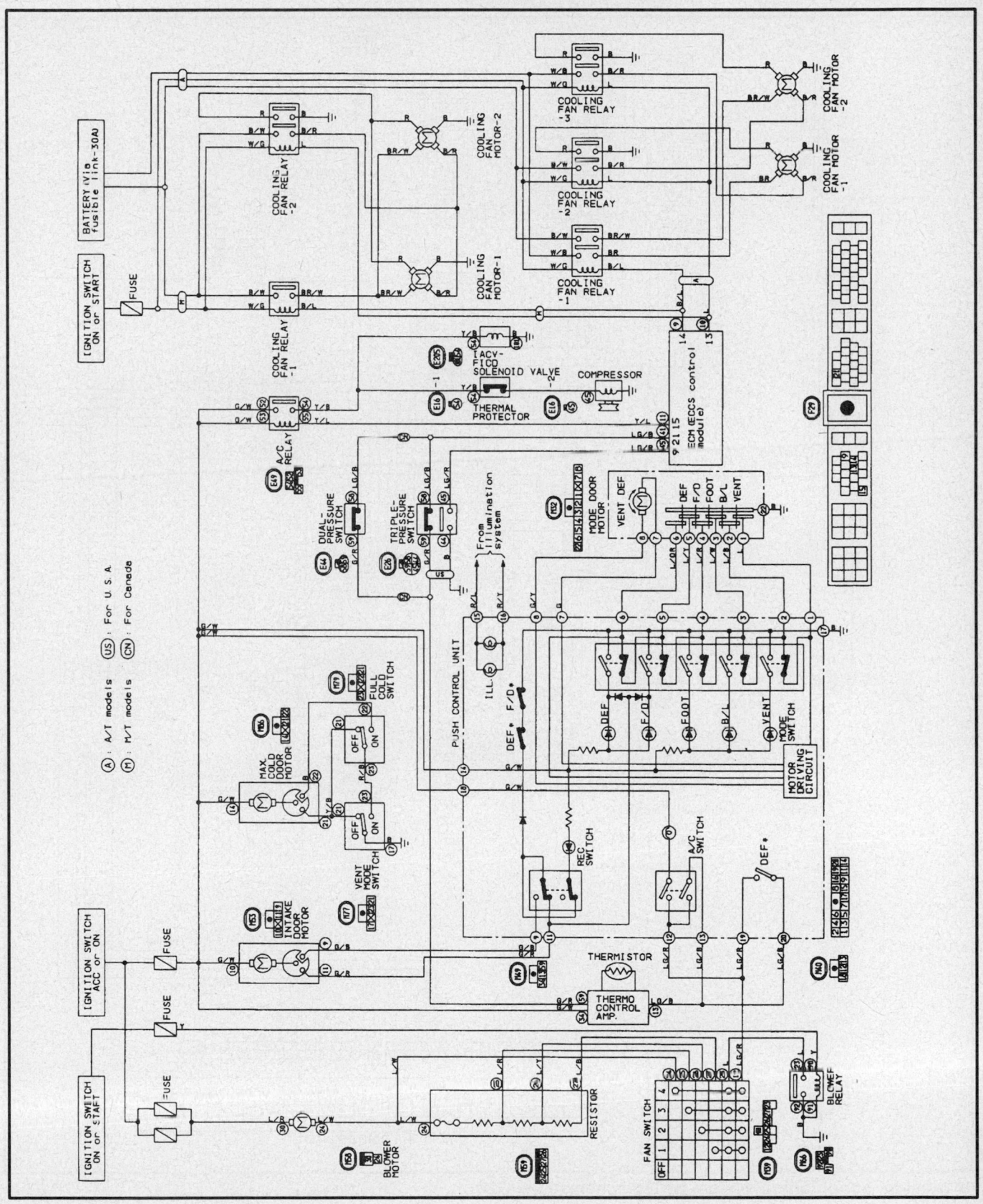

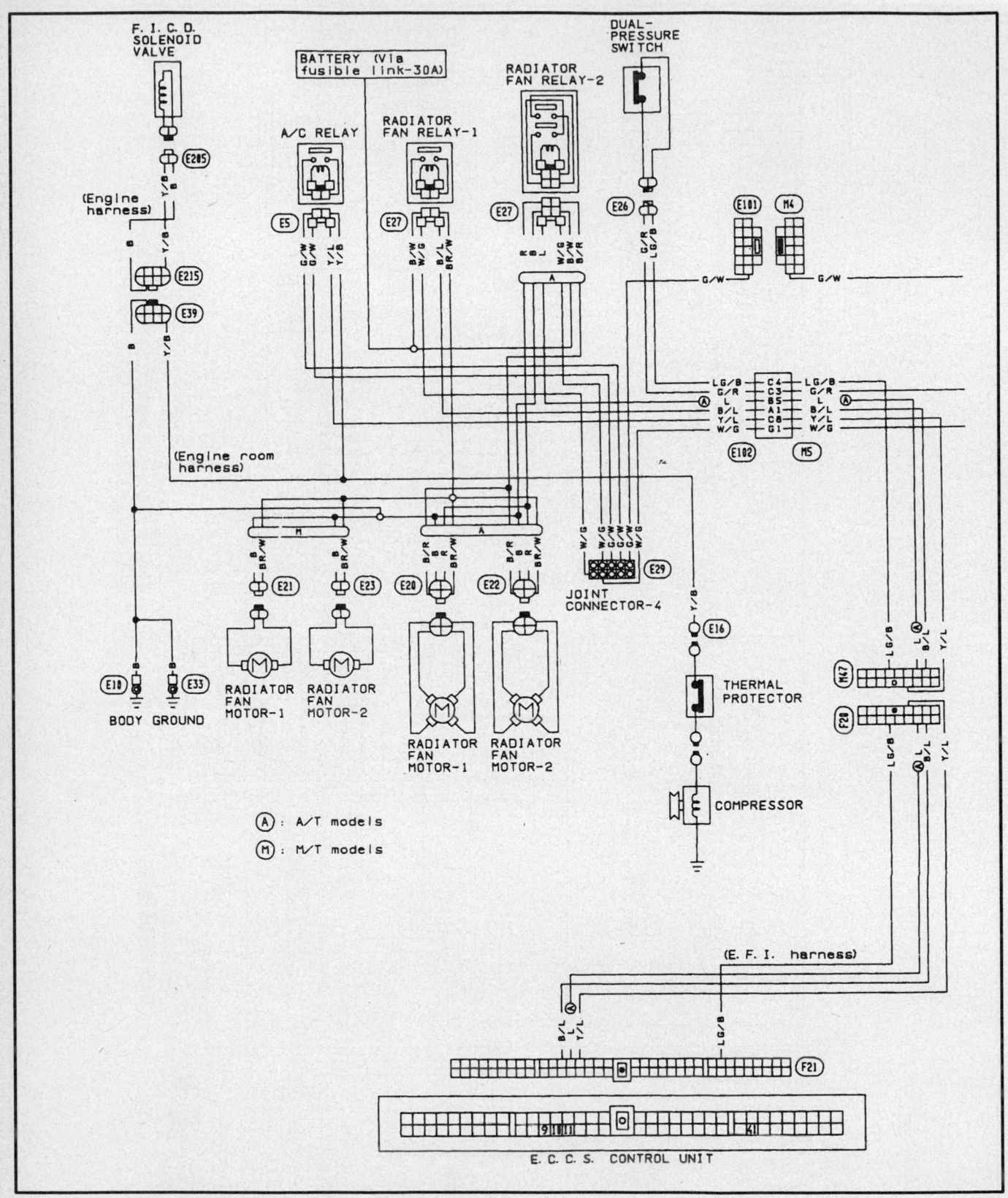

Manual air conditioning system wiring schematic — G20

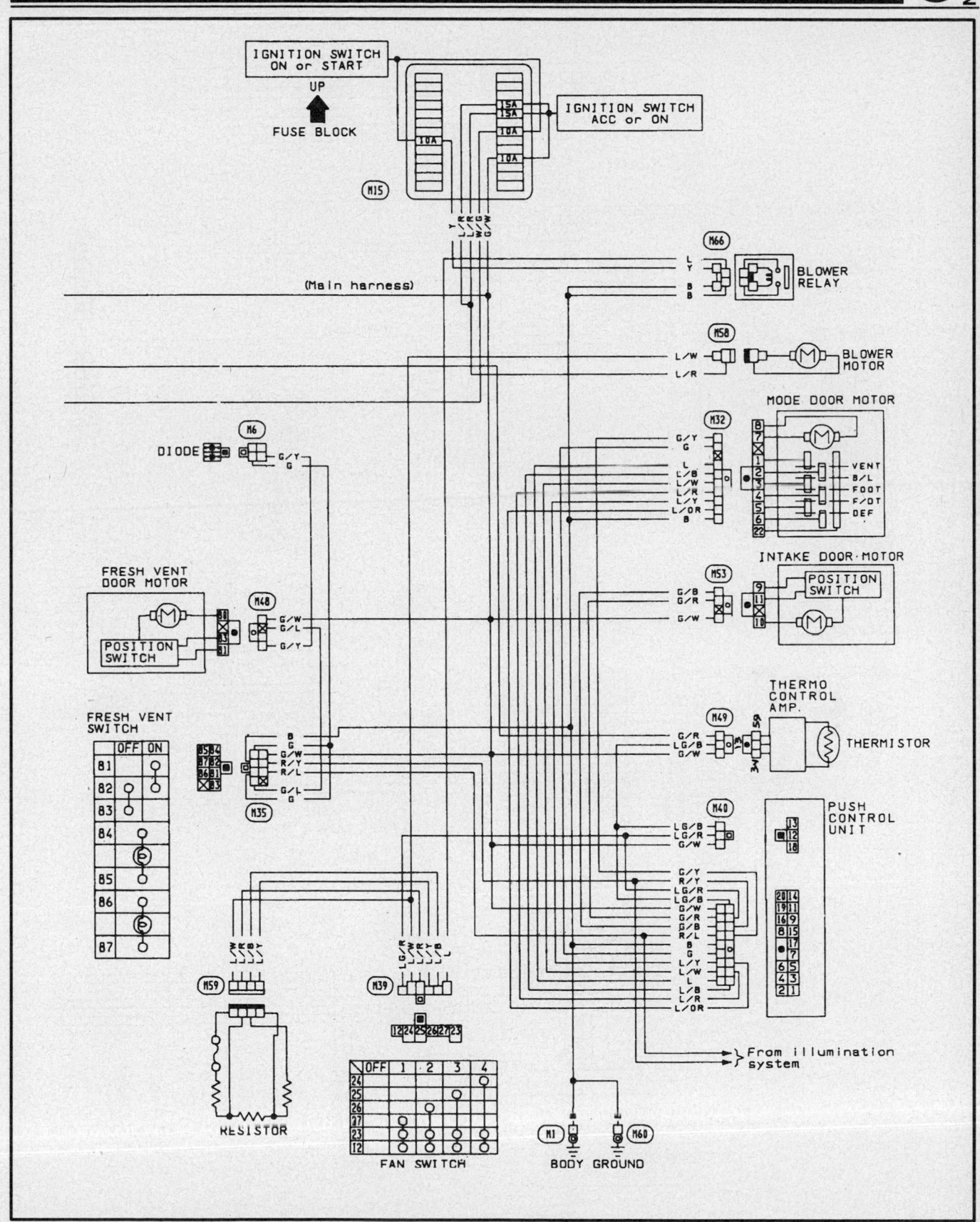

Manual air conditioning system wiring schematic — G20, Cont'd.

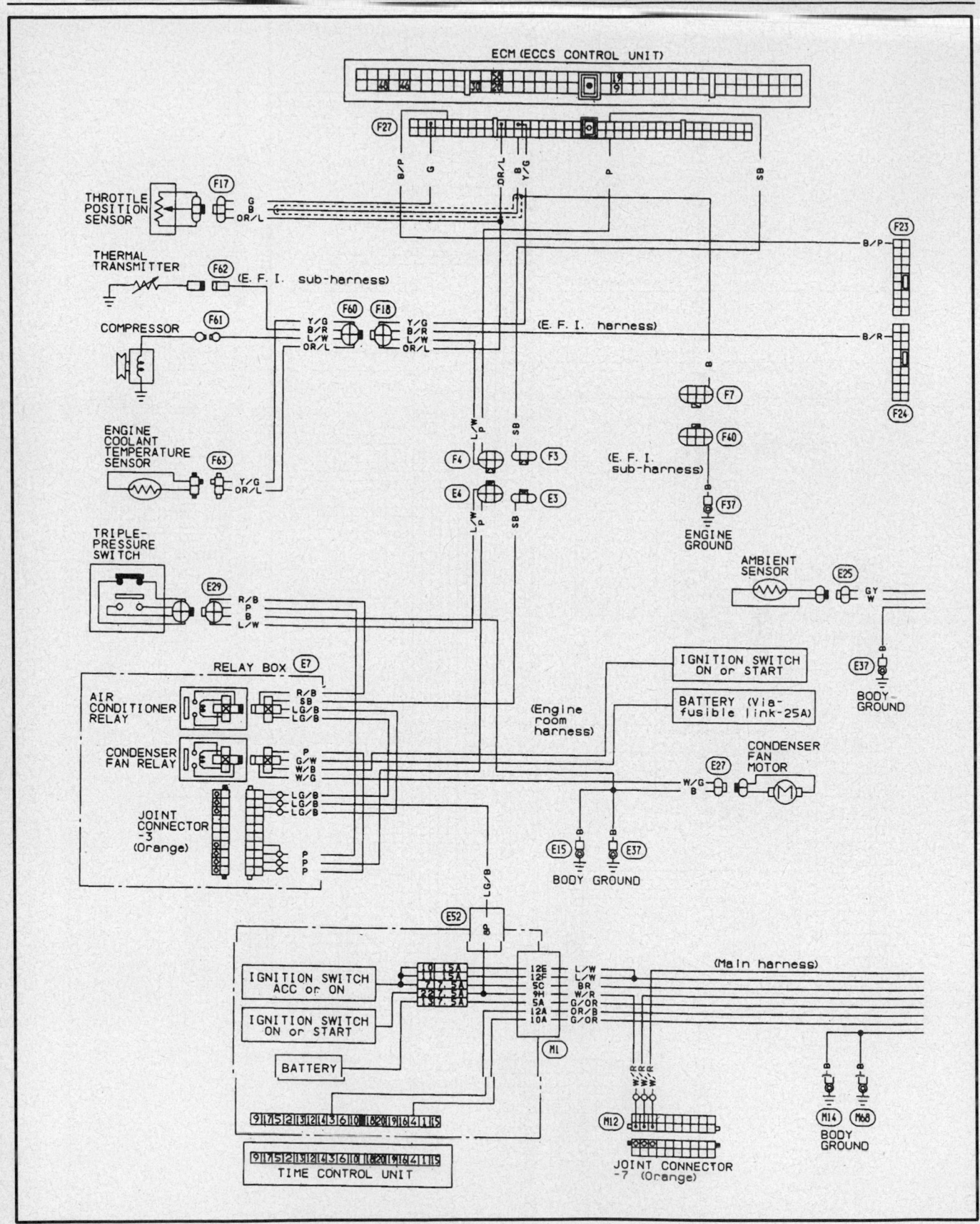

Automatic air conditioning system wiring schematic – J30

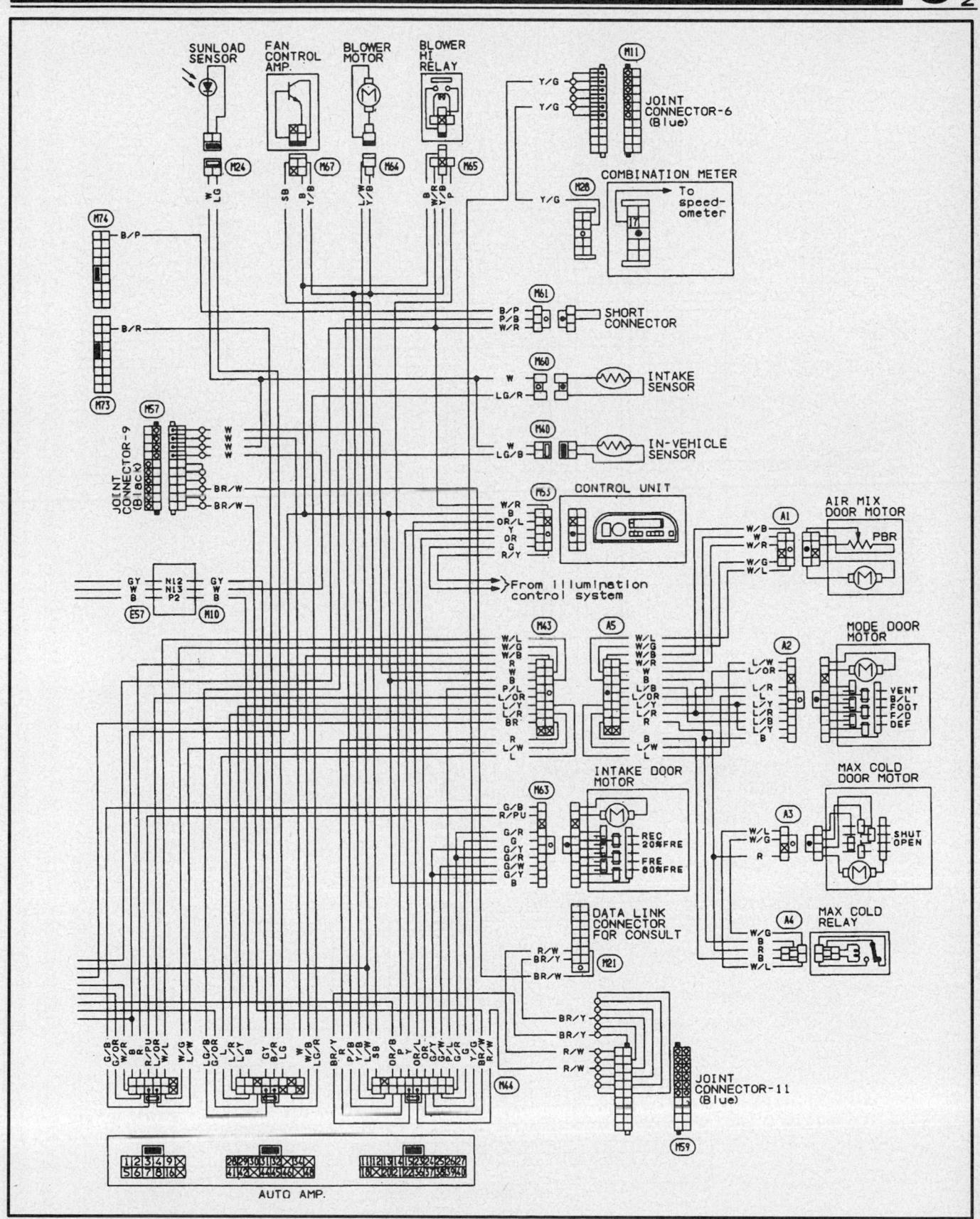

Automatic air conditioning system wiring schematic — J30, Cont'd.

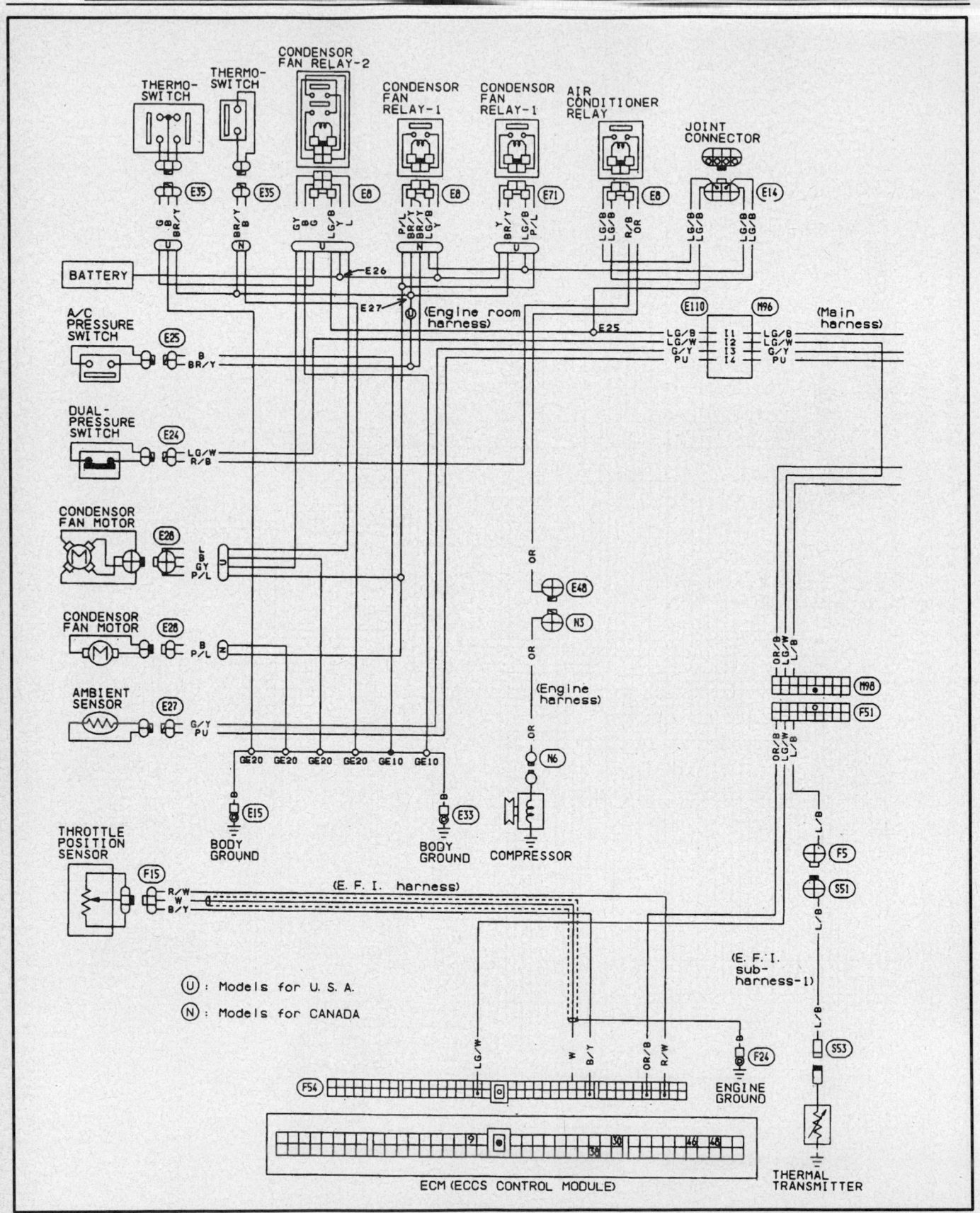

Automatic air conditioning system wiring schematic – 1993 Q45

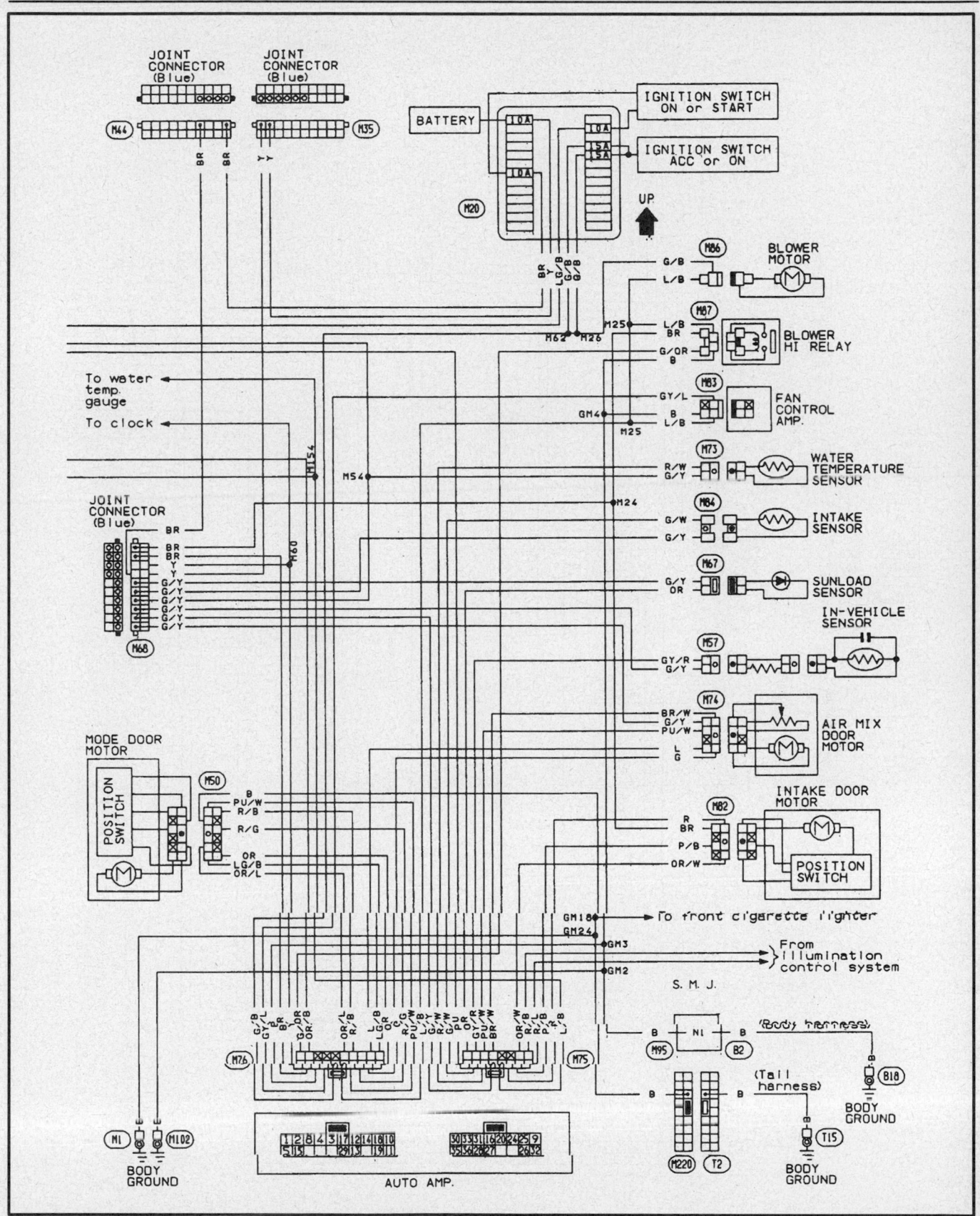

Automatic air conditioning system wiring schematic – 1993 Q45, Cont'd.

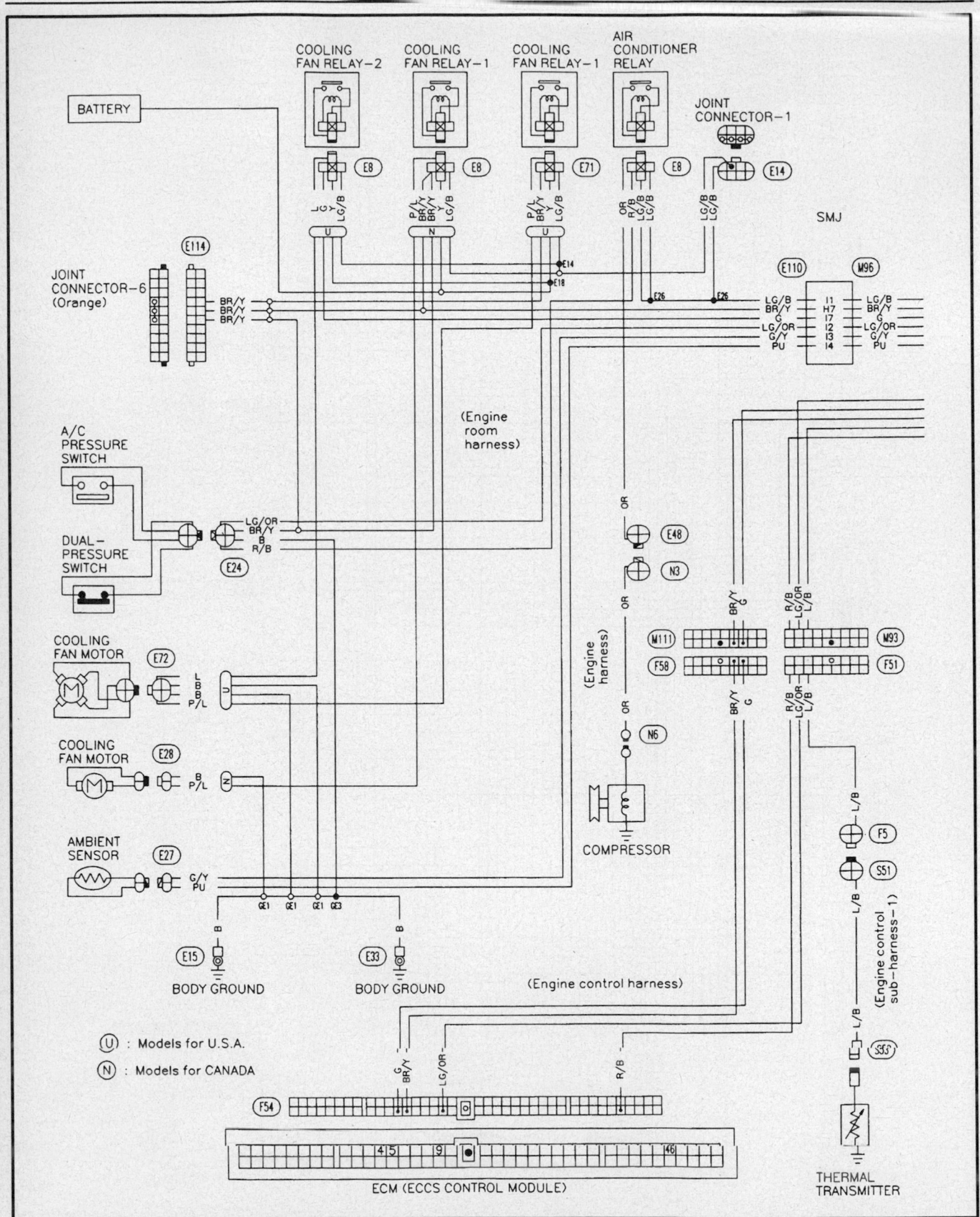

Automatic air conditioning system wiring schematic – 1994 Q45

SPECIFICATIONS

ENGINE IDENTIFICATION

Year	Model	Engine Displacement Liters (cc)	Engine series (ID/VIN)	Fuel System	No. of Cylinders	Engine Type
1993	Amigo	2.3 (2254)	4ZD1(L)	2-bbl	4	SOHC
	Pick-Up	2.3 (2254)	4ZD1(L)	2-bbl	4	SOHC
	Amigo	2.6 (2559)	4ZE1(E)	PFI	4	SOHC
	Pick-Up	2.6 (2559)	4ZE1(E)	PFI	4	SOHC
	Pick-Up	3.1 (3137)	CPC(Z)	TBI	6	OHV
	Rodeo	2.6 (2559)	4ZE1(E)	PFI	4	SOHC
	Rodeo	3.2 (3165)	6VD1(V)	MFI	6	SOHC
	Stylus	1.6 (1588)	4XE1(6)	EFI	4	DOHC
	Stylus	1.8 (1809)	4XF1(8)	EFI	4	DOHC
	Trooper	3.2 (3165)	6VD1(V)	MFI	6	SOHC
	Trooper	3.2 (3165)	6VD1(W)	MFI	6	SOHC
1994	Amigo	2.6 (2559)	4ZE1(E)	PFI	4	SOHC
	Pick-Up	2.3 (2254)	4ZD1(L)	PFI	4	SOHC
	Pick-Up	2.6 (2559)	4ZE1(E)	PFI	4	SOHC
	Pick-Up	3.1 (3137)	CPC(Z)	TFI	6	OHV
	Rodeo	2.6 (2559)	4ZE1(E)	PFI	4	SOHC
	Rodeo	3.2 (3165)	6VD1(V)	MFI	6	SOHC
	Trooper	3.2 (3165)	6VD1(V)	MFI	6	SOHC
	Trooper	3.2 (3165)	6VD1(W)	MFI	6	SOHC

EFI – Electronic Fuel Injection
MFI – Multi–Fuel Injection
PFI – Port Fuel Injection
TBI – Throttle Body Injection

OHV – Overhead Valves
DOHC – Dual Overhead Cam
SOHC – Single Overhead Cam

REFRIGERANT CAPACITIES

Year	Model	Refrigerant (oz.)	Oil (fl. oz.)	Compressor Type
1993	Amigo	26.4	5.0	DKS-13CH
	Pick-Up	26.4	5.0	DKS-13CH
	Pick-Up①	26.4	6.0	R-4
	Rodeo	35.2	5.0	DKS-175
	Rodeo	N/A	N/A	N/A
	Stylus	21.1	5.0	D-220WX
	Trooper	29.9	5.0	DKU-14D
1994	Amigo	22.9	7.5-8.5	DKS-13CH
	Amigo	22.9	7.5-8.5	R-4
	Pick-Up	22.9	7.5-8.5	DKS-13CH
	Pick-Up	22.9	7.5-8.5	R-4
	Rodeo	22.9	5.0	DKS-17CH
	Rodeo	22.9	5.0	DKU-14D
	Trooper	26.4	5.0	DKU-14D

① 3.1L Engine

AIR CONDITIONING BELT TENSION

Year	Model	Engine Displacement	Belt Type	Specifications New	Used
1993	Amigo	2.3 (2254)	V-Belt	0.4 (10 mm)	0.4 (10 mm)
	Amigo	2.6 (2559)	V-Belt	0.4 (10 mm)	0.4 (10 mm)
	Pick-Up	2.3 (2254)	V-Belt	0.4 (10 mm)	0.4 (10 mm)
	Pick-Up	2.6 (2559)	V-Belt	0.4 (10 mm)	0.4 (10 mm)
	Pick-Up	3.1 (3137)	Serpentine	②	②
	Rodeo	2.6 (2559)	V-Belt	0.4 (10 mm)	0.4 (10 mm)
	Rodeo	3.2 (3165)	V-Belt	0.4 (10 mm)	0.4 (10 mm)
	Stylus	1.6 (1588)	V-Belt	130-160①	130-160①
	Stylus	1.8 (1809)	Serpentine	②	②
	Trooper	3.2 (3165)	V-Belt	0.4 (10 mm)	0.4 (10 mm)
1994	Amigo	2.6 (2559)	V-Belt	0.4 (10 mm)	0.4 (10 mm)
	Pick-Up	2.3 (2254)	V-Belt	0.4 (10 mm)	0.4 (10 mm)
	Pick-Up	2.6 (2559)	V-Belt	0.4 (10 mm)	0.4 (10 mm)
	Pick-Up	3.1 (3137)	Serpentine	0.4 (10 mm)	0.4 (10 mm)
	Rodeo	2.6 (2559)	V-Belt	0.4 (10 mm)	0.4 (10 mm)
	Rodeo	3.2 (3165)	Serpentine	0.4 (10 mm)	0.4 (10 mm)
	Trooper	3.2 (3165)	Serpentine	0.4 (10 mm)	0.4 (10 mm)

① Lbs. of tension using belt tension gauge.
② Self adjusting tensioner.

SYSTEM DESCRIPTION

General Information

The heater unit is located in the center of the vehicle beneath the instrument panel. The heater system delivers fresh or recirculated air to direct warm air through the vents to either the windshield, floor or the panel outlets. The air conditioning system is designed to be activated in combination with a separate air conditioning switch installed in the control assembly and the fan speed switch. The systems, depending on model application, use a variety of devices such as relays for controlling the heater, blower, and compressor operation, and a dual or triple pressure switch to monitor system operating pressures and stop compressor operation when extremely high or low pressure is sensed. Also used are a thermo switch, electronic thermostat, fast idle control device, special system diode and an A/C cut relay.

Trooper may also use a rear heater assembly located beneath the rear seat. Other Trooper models use rear heat distribution duct system to deliver heated air to the rear passenger compartment.

NOTE: If equipped with a Supplement Inflatable Restraint (SIR) system, be sure to set the ignition switch to the LOCK position and remove, tape and secure the negative battery cable to prevent any contact with the negative battery terminal. Also, do not use any electrically powered or vehicle battery powered test equipment on the vehicle.

Service Valve Location

Charging valve locations will vary, but most of the time the high or low pressure fitting will be located at the compressor, receiver/drier or along the refrigerant lines. Always discharge, evacuate and recharge at the low side service fitting.

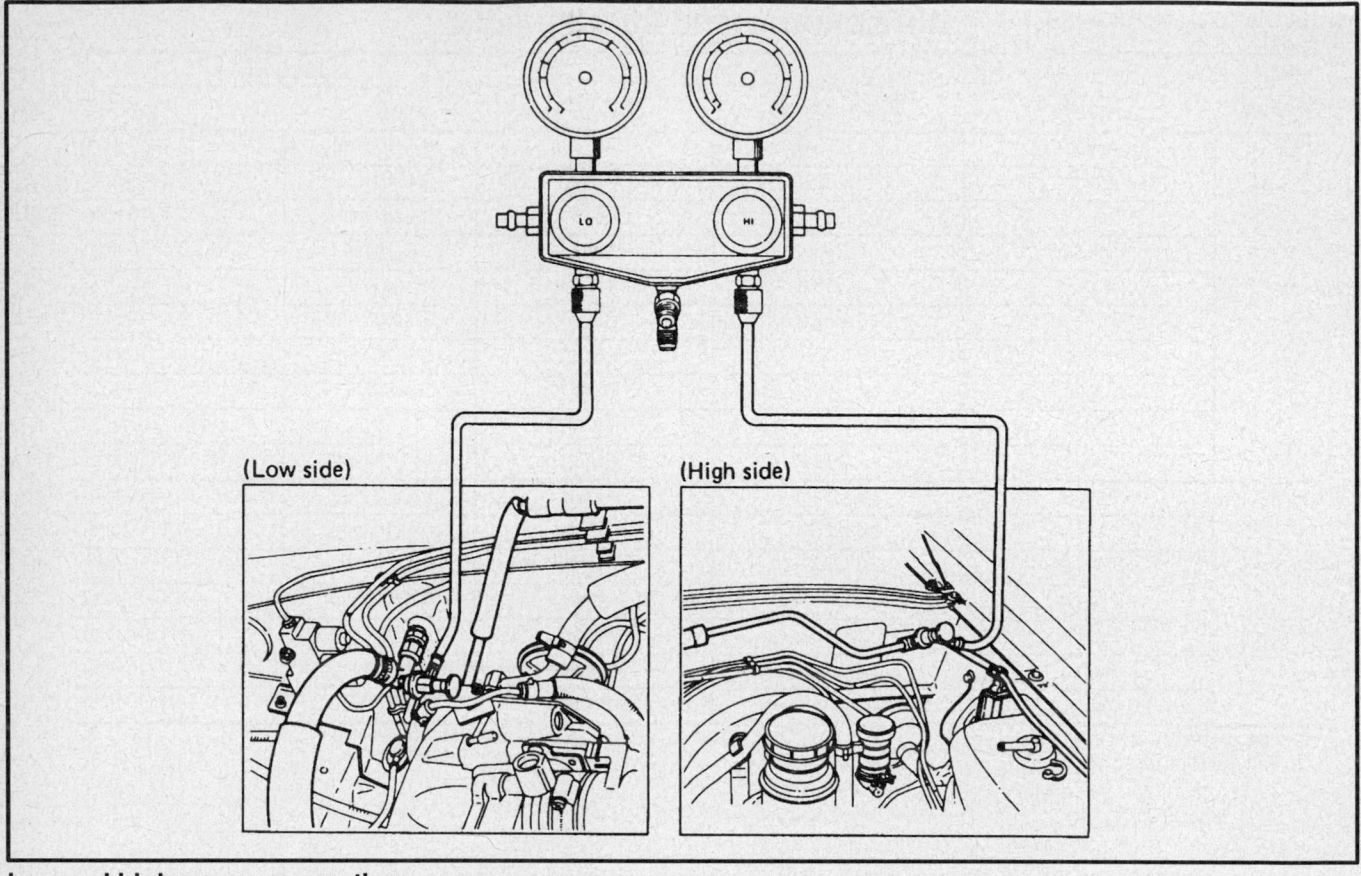

Low and high gauge connections

System Discharging

R-12 refrigerant is a chloroflourocarbon which, when mishandled, can contribute to the depletion of the ozone layer in the upper atmosphere. Ozone filters out harmful radiation from the sun. In order to protect the ozone layer, an approved R-12 Recovery/Recycling machine that meets SAE standard J1991 should be employed when discharging the system. Follow the operating instructions provided with the approved equipment exactly to properly discharge the system.

Vehicles that use R-134a refrigerant in the air conditioning system have a caution plate fixed to the rear wall of the engine compartment. Components designed solely for use with R-134a are also marked to distinguish them from components designed solely for R-12.

R-12 and R-134a systems require different types of lubricating oil. Components, refrigerant, oil and charging/evacuation equipment must never be interchanged between system types.

System Evacuating

If the air conditioning system has been opened to the atmosphere, it should be air and moisture free before being recharged with refrigerant. Moisture and air mixed with refrigerant will raise the compressor head pressure, possibly damage the system's components and will reduce the performance of the system. Moisture will boil at normal room temperature when exposed to a vacuum, the moisture then becomes a vapor and will be easily removed by the vacuum pump.

1. Leak test the system and repair any leaks found.

2. Connect an approved charging station, Recovery/Recycling machine or manifold gauge set and vacuum pump to the discharge and suction ports, following the instructions for the particular units in use.

3. Open the discharge and suction ports and start the vacuum pump. If the pump is not able to pull at least 26 in. Hg vacuum, there is a leak that must be repaired before evacuation can occur.

4. Once the system has reached at least 26 in. Hg vacuum, allow the system to evacuate for at least 10 minutes. The longer the system is evacuated, the more contaminants will be removed.

5. Close all valves and turn the pump OFF. If the system loses more than 2 in. Hg vacuum after 15 minutes, there is a leak that should be repaired.

System Charging

1. Connect an approved charging station, Recovery/Recycling machine or manifold gauge set to the discharge and suction ports. Follow the manufacturer's instructions for the correct hookup and use of the equipment.

2. Charge the system with the specified amount of refrigerant.

3. Perform a leak test.

Oil Level Checking

The total oil capacity is distributed with the refrigerant throughout the air conditioning system. To return the maximum amount of oil to the compressor for checking during removal and installation or replacement of the compressor, perform the following procedure, if the system has not ruptured or the compressor is functional.

NOTE: If compressor cannot be run, remove the compressor and drain the oil, adding the amounts as noted below, then reinstall the compressor (same or replacement) and make any other necessary repairs, then perform the following procedure and recheck and adjust oil accordingly.

1. Open all door and the hood.
2. Set the A/C switch to **ON**. Turn the blower motor to the **HIGH** position.
3. Start the engine and run the compressor for more than 20 minutes between 800–1000 rpm.
4. Stop the engine, then perform appropriate repairs. When replacing key system components, additional new refrigerant oil needs to be added to the parts being installed:
- Evaporator–1.7 oz.
- Condenser–1.0 oz.
- Receiver/drier–1.0 oz.
- Refrigerant line–0.3 oz.

5. If replacing the compressor or if low oil level is suspect, after removing the compressor, drain the oil into a calibrated container. Check the oil for any contamination.

NOTE: The new, replacement compressor is furnished with a full capacity of oil. This oil should be drained and reinstalled according to the adjustment level required.

6. Adjust the oil level on all except the R–4 compressor as follows:
- If amount drained is more than 3.0 oz., install the same amount as drained.
- If the amount drained is less than 3.0 oz., install 3.0 oz. of new oil.

7. On R–4 compressors, adjust the oil level as follows:
- If amount drained is more than 1.0 oz., install the same amount as drained.
- In amount drained is less than 1.0 oz., install 2.0 oz. of new oil.

8. If oil drained has chips or other foreign material or looks red, flush the system, replace the receiver/drier and add a full capacity amount of oil to the compressor:
- On all except R–4 compressors, install 5.0 oz.
- On R–4 compressors, install 6.0 oz.

SYSTEM COMPONENTS

Radiator

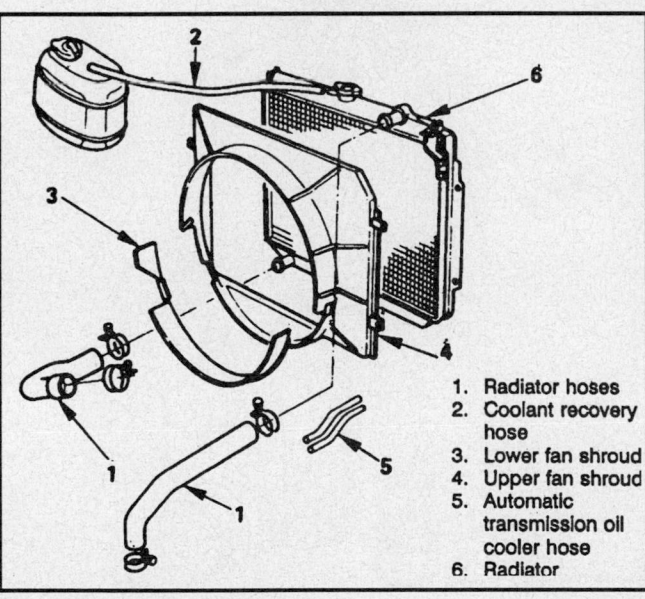

1. Radiator hoses
2. Coolant recovery hose
3. Lower fan shroud
4. Upper fan shroud
5. Automatic transmission oil cooler hose
6. Radiator

Typical radiator assembly

REMOVAL AND INSTALLATION

Except Stylus

1. Disconnect the negative battery cable.
2. Remove the radiator cap and loosen the drain plug to drain the coolant from the system.
3. Disconnect the radiator and surge tank hoses from the radiator.

4. Disconnect the cooling fan and thermo switch connectors, if equipped.
5. Remove the fan shroud and the radiator support brackets, if equipped.
6. Remove the remaining mounting bolts and the radiator.
7. Installation is the reverse of the removal procedure. Fill the radiator with the specified amount of water and anti–freeze.

Stylus

1. Disconnect the negative battery cable.
2. Remove the radiator cap and loosen the drain plug to drain the coolant from the system.
3. Disconnect the radiator and surge tank hoses.
4. Disconnect the fan motor and thermo switch connectors.
5. Disconnect the transaxle cooler hoses, if equipped.
6. Remove the upper end panel.
7. Remove the radiator assembly and cooling fan as an assembly.
8. Installation is the reverse of the removal procedure. Fill the radiator with enough water and anti–freeze.

NOTE: All radiator fins must be free of dirt, grease, oil and must be straight to provide for optimum cooling of the engine coolant mixture.

Radiator Cooling Fan

TESTING

Stylus

1. Disconnect the electrical connector at the cooling fan motor.
2. Connect battery voltage to the fan terminals to see that it operates smoothly.
3. Using an ammeter, check that current draw is 5.8–7.4 amps.

REMOVAL AND INSTALLATION

Stylus

1. Disconnect the negative battery cable. Properly drain the cooling system.
2. Remove the upper radiator hose.
3. Disconnect the fan motor connector.
4. Remove the cooling fan mounting bolts and remove the cooling fan and shroud assembly.
5. Installation is the reverse of the removal procedure.

Compressor

REMOVAL AND INSTALLATION

2.3L and 2.6L Engines

1. Disconnect the negative battery cable.
2. Properly discharge the air conditioning system.
3. Remove power steering pump and brackets.
4. Disconnect magnetic clutch wire connector.
5. Loosen the center nut of the compressor idler pulley and then loosen the tension adjustment bolt and remove the belt.
6. Remove and immediately cap the compressor refrigerant lines.
7. Remove compressor attaching bolts.

8. Remove bolts attaching brackets to compressor and remove compressor.
9. Installation is the reverse of removal procedure. Measure oil level in oil compressor if installing a replacement unit. Adjust oil in new unit as needed. Evacuate, recharge and leak test the system.

2.8L, 3.1L and 3.2L Engines

1. Disconnect the negative battery cable.
2. Properly discharge the air conditioning system.
3. Disconnect the magnetic clutch wire harness.
4. Remove the fan shroud on the 3.2L Rodeo.
5. Remove the cooling fan on the 3.2L Trooper.
6. Loosen the idler pulley and remove the drive belt.
7. Remove and immediately cap the refrigerant lines.
8. On models with the 3.1L engine, remove the compressor and mounting bracket as an assembly. On others, remove the compressor mounting bolts and remove the compressor from the vehicle.
9. Remove the brace to compressor bolts.
10. If equipped, remove the compressor dynamic damper.
11. Remove and immediately cap the refrigerant lines.
12. Remove the compressor bracket to engine bolts and remove the compressor.
13. Installation is the reverse of removal procedure. Measure oil level in oil compressor if installing a replacement unit. Adjust oil in new unit as needed. Evacuate, recharge and leak test the system.

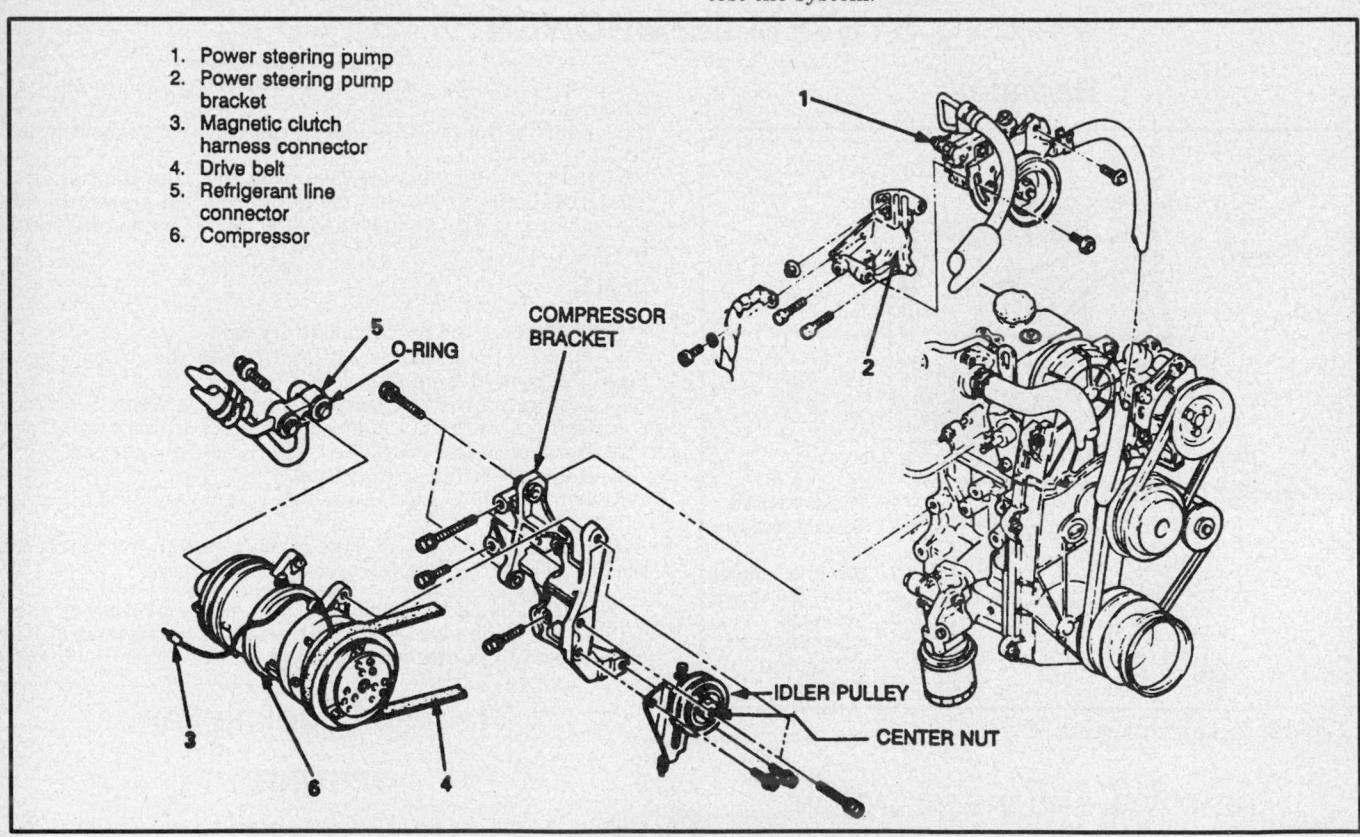

1. Power steering pump
2. Power steering pump bracket
3. Magnetic clutch harness connector
4. Drive belt
5. Refrigerant line connector
6. Compressor

Compressor and related components—Pick-Up and Rodeo with 2.3L and 2.6L engines

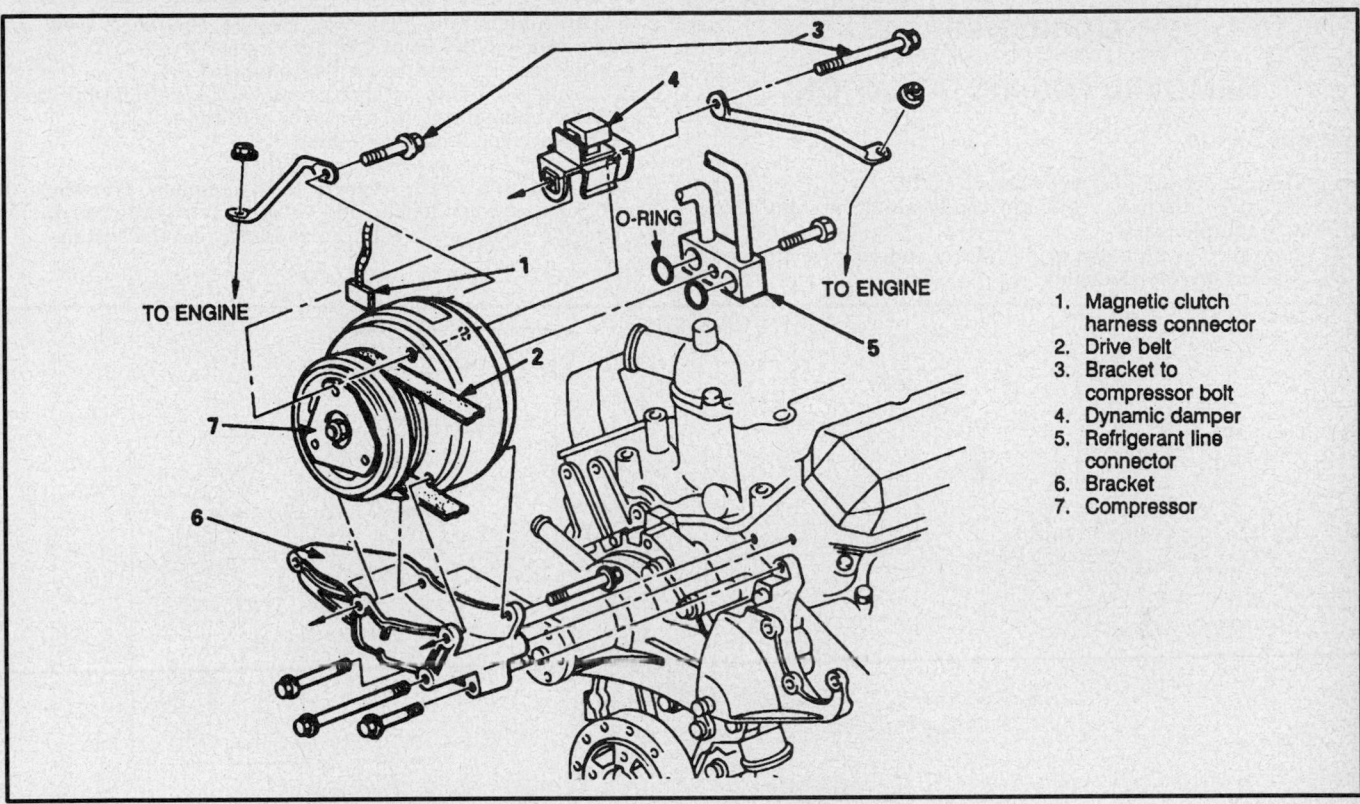

1. Magnetic clutch harness connector
2. Drive belt
3. Bracket to compressor bolt
4. Dynamic damper
5. Refrigerant line connector
6. Bracket
7. Compressor

Compressor and related components—3.1L engine

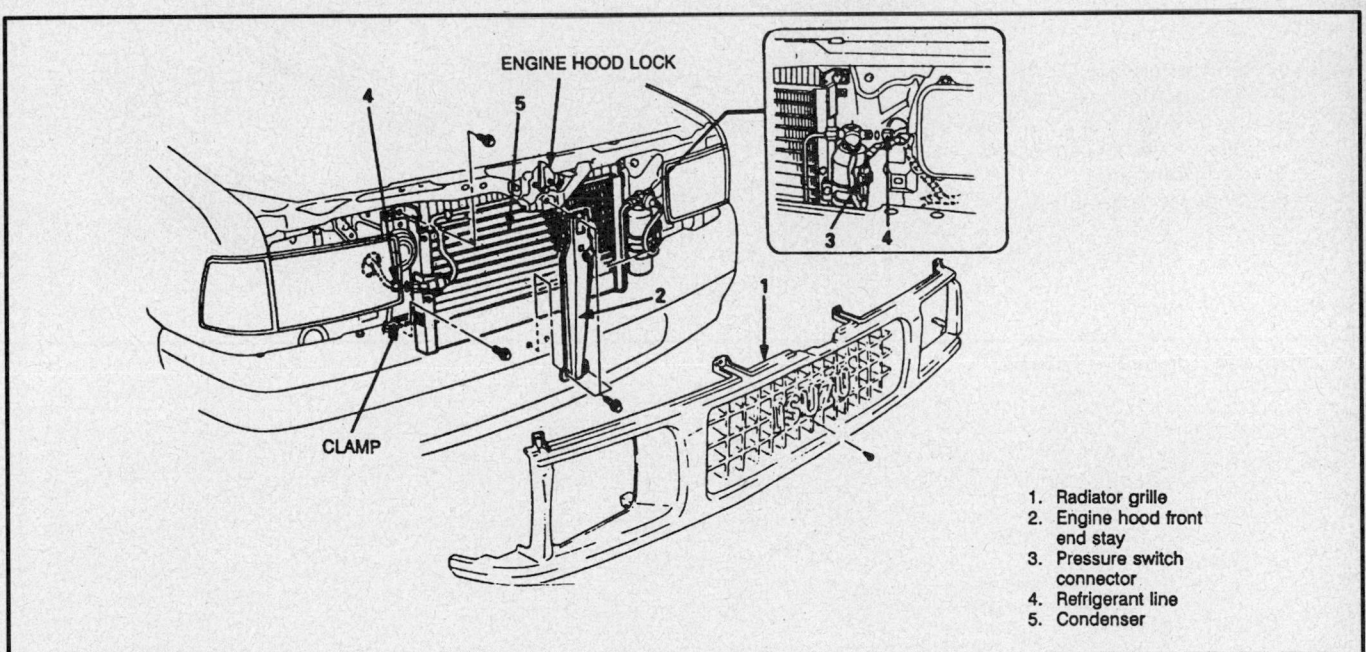

1. Radiator grille
2. Engine hood front end stay
3. Pressure switch connector
4. Refrigerant line
5. Condenser

Condenser assembly—Amigo, Pick-Up and Rodeo

Condenser

REMOVAL AND INSTALLATION

Except Stylus

1. Disconnect the negative battery cable.
2. Properly discharge the air conditioning system using recovery equipment.
3. Remove the radiator grille. Mark and remove the hood lock bracket or stay assembly.

4. On Amigo and Pick–Up, remove the hood lock. On Trooper, remove the front bumper
5. Disconnect pressure switch connector.
6. Using a backup wrench, remove the refrigerant lines. Cap them immediately to minimize contamination.
7. Remove condenser attaching bolts.
8. Remove the condenser assembly.
9. Installation is the reverse of the removal procedure. If installing a new condenser, add 1.0 oz. of refrigerant oil during recharging. Evacuate, recharge and leak test the system.

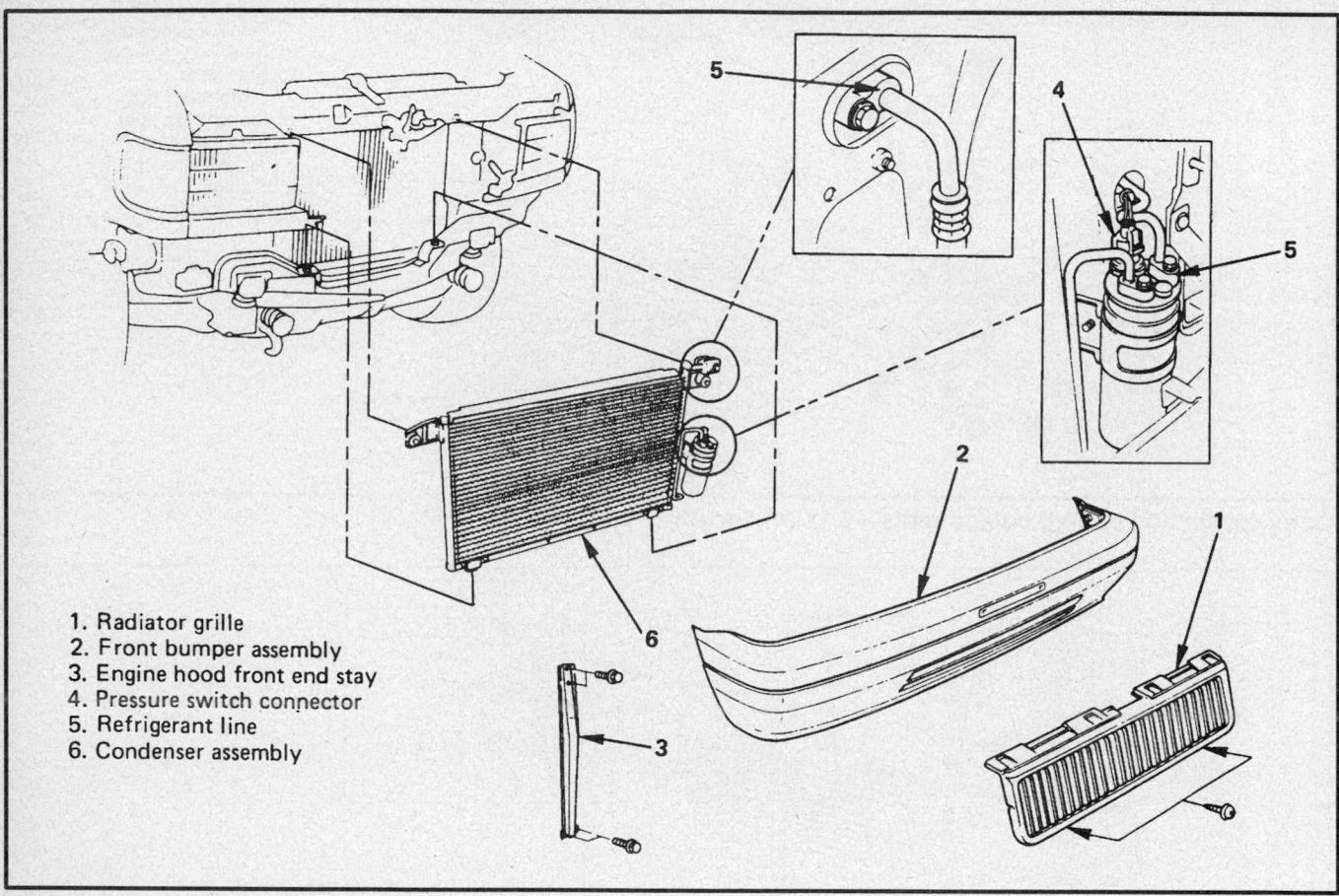

1. Radiator grille
2. Front bumper assembly
3. Engine hood front end stay
4. Pressure switch connector
5. Refrigerant line
6. Condenser assembly

Condenser removal—Trooper

Stylus

1. Disconnect the negative battery cable.
2. Properly discharge the air conditioning system.
3. Remove the front upper end panel.
4. If equipped with a turbocharger, remove radiator fan and the hood lock assembly.
5. Disconnect triple pressure switch and condenser fan connectors.
6. Remove refrigerant line connector.

   NOTE: Always use 2 wrenches when removing or installing refrigerant lines.

7. Remove refrigerant outlet line.
8. Move the radiator back and remove the condenser.
9. Installation is the reverse of the removal procedure. Use new O–rings and apply a light coat of oil to them. If a new condenser is installed, add 1.0 oz. of refrigerant oil to the condenser. Evacuate, recharge and leak test the system.

Condenser cooling fan

TESTING

Stylus

1. Disconnect the condenser fan connector.
2. Connect the battery positive cable to the No. **1** terminal of the fan and the negative cable to the No. **3** terminal.
3. The fan should operate smoothly.

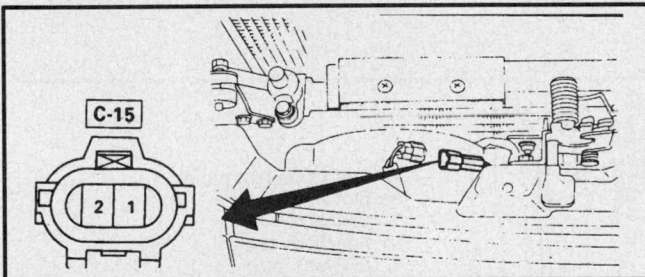

Testing the condenser cooling fan—Stylus

REMOVAL AND INSTALLATION

Stylus

1. Disconnect the negative battery cable. Properly drain the cooling system.
2. Remove the upper radiator hose.
3. Disconnect the fan motor connector.
4. Remove the cooling fan mounting bolts and remove the cooling fan and shroud assembly.
5. Installation is the reverse of the removal procedure

Receiver/Drier

REMOVAL AND INSTALLATION

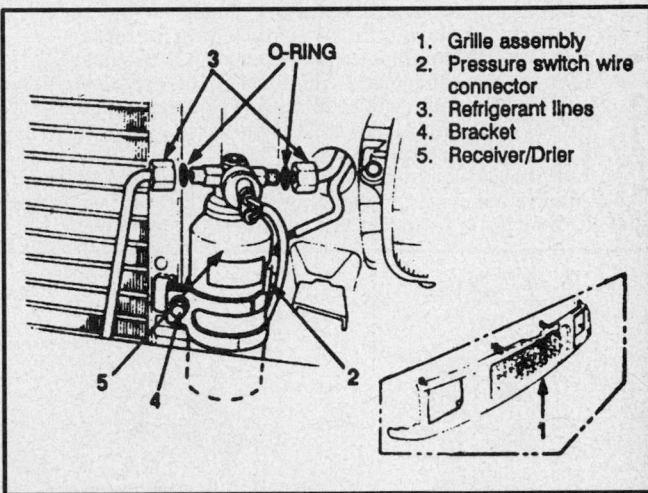

1. Grille assembly
2. Pressure switch wire connector
3. Refrigerant lines
4. Bracket
5. Receiver/Drier

Typical receiver drier assembly—Rodeo shown.

1. Disconnect the negative battery cable.
2. Properly discharge the air conditioning system.
3. If required, remove the radiator grille.
4. Remove the pressure switch wire connector.
5. Using 2 wrenches, remove the refrigerant lines. Cap all openings immediately to minimize contamination.
6. Remove the bracket attaching bolts.
7. Remove the receiver/drier.
8. Installation is the reverse of removal procedure. Add 1 oz. of new refrigerant oil to the replacement receiver/driver. Evacuate, recharge and leak test the system.

Expansion Valve

REMOVAL AND INSTALLATION

Except Stylus

1. Disconnect the negative battery cable.
2. Properly discharge the air conditioning system.
3. Remove the evaporator assembly.
4. Pull the thermo switch sensor from the core and remove the switch.
5. Remove the clips and screws from the evaporator case.
6. Separate the upper and lower cases.
7. Remove the evaporator core.
8. Remove the insulation, the sensor clamp and the expansion valve.

9. Installation is the reverse of removal procedure. Evacuate, recharge and leak test the system.

Stylus

1. Disconnect the negative battery cable.
2. Properly discharge the air conditioning system.
3. Remove the expansion valve clamp near the firewall.
4. Remove the refrigerant line nuts at the expansion valve. Cap the lines immediately to minimize contamination.
5. Remove the clip at the expansion valve.
6. Remove the expansion valve.
7. Installation in the reverse of the removal procedure.
8. Always use new O-rings applying a thin coat of refrigerant oil. Evacuate, recharge and leak test the system.

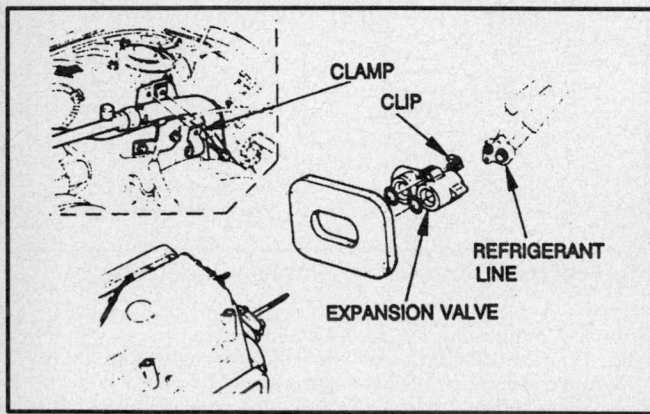

Expansion valve removal—Stylus

Blower Motor

REMOVAL AND INSTALLATION

NOTE: If removing the entire blower housing assembly, the instrument panel will have to be removed first. The following procedure is for removing only the blower motor and wheel.

1. Disconnect the negative battery cable.
2. Remove the dash side trim panel.
3. Remove blower motor wire connector.
4. Remove blower motor attaching screws.
5. Remove blower motor.
6. Installation is the reverse of removal procedure.

Blower Motor Resistor

REMOVAL AND INSTALLATION

The blower motor resistor will usually be located under the dash attached to the heater air duct, in the case of a vehicle without air conditioning or in the evaporator housing for vehicles equipped with air conditioning.

1. Disconnect the battery negative terminal. Remove the glove box.
2. Disconnect the wire resistor connector and remove the mounting screw.
3. Remove the blower resistor.
4. Installation is the reverse of the removal procedure.

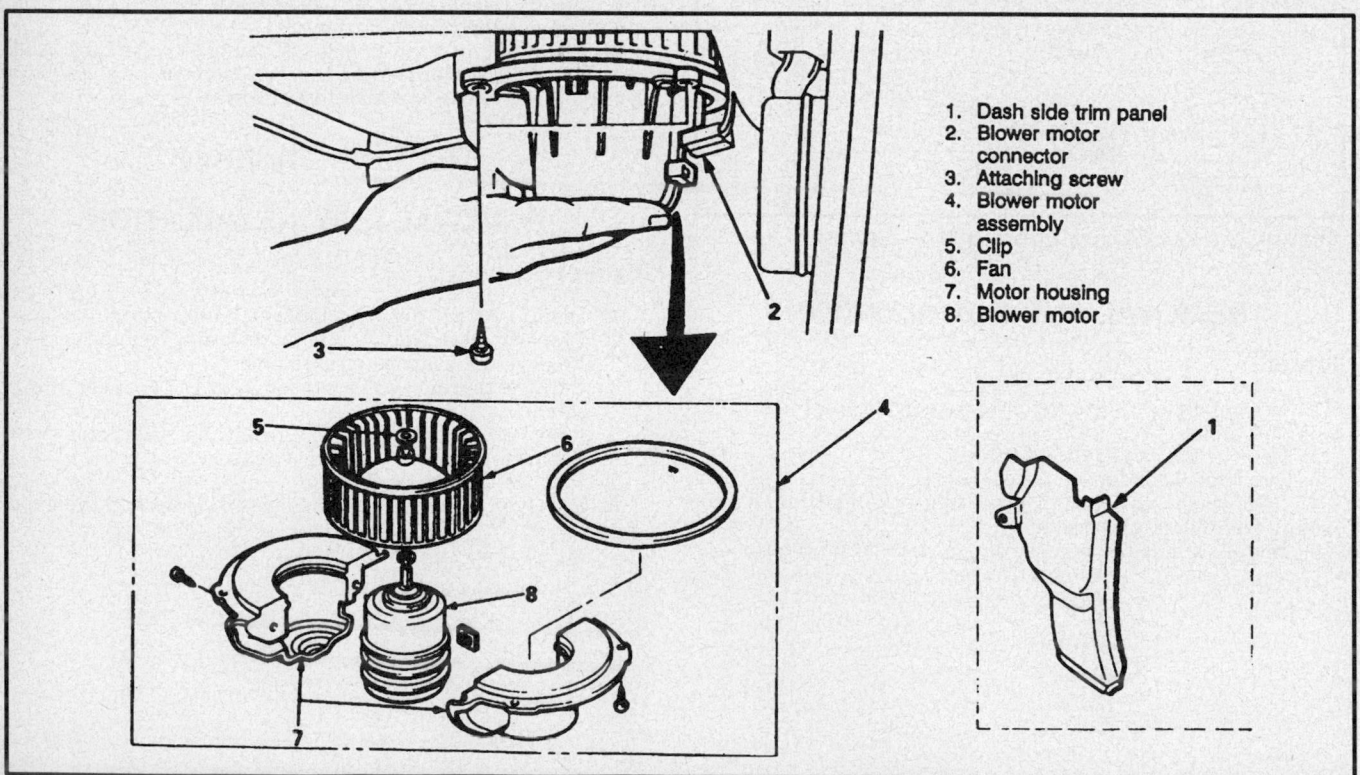

1. Dash side trim panel
2. Blower motor connector
3. Attaching screw
4. Blower motor assembly
5. Clip
6. Fan
7. Motor housing
8. Blower motor

Typical blower motor assembly

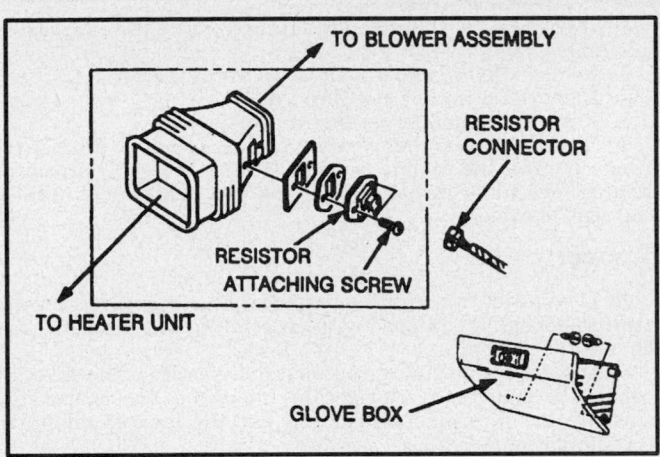

Typical blower motor resistor—non air conditioned vehicles

Heater Core

REMOVAL AND INSTALLATION

Amigo, Pick-Up and Rodeo

1. Disconnect the negative battery cable.

2. On A/C, properly discharge the air conditioning system and remove the evaporator lines from the fittings at the firewall.

3. Properly drain the cooling system and disconnect the heater hoses at the firewall. Plug hose ends.

4. Remove the instrument panel by removing the following components:
   • Remove the steering wheel.
   • Remove the instrument cluster bezel, then remove the instrument cluster.
   • Remove the hood release handle. Remove the lower steering column cover.
   • Remove the fuse box, the left side trim, then remove the ECM.
   • Remove the front console and the lower reinforcement.
   • Remove the right speaker grille and the glove box.
   • Remove the knobs from the control panel, then remove the panel bezel and the control panel.
   • Remove the illumination controller (to the right of the steering column).
   • Remove the instrument panel.

5. Remove the resistor connector.

6. On heater only systems, remove the heater to blower air duct.

7. On air conditioning, remove the evaporator assembly.

8. Remove the instrument panel support.

9. Remove the heater unit attaching nuts and remove assembly.

10. Disassemble the heater unit case and remove heater core.

11. Installation is the reverse of removal procedure.

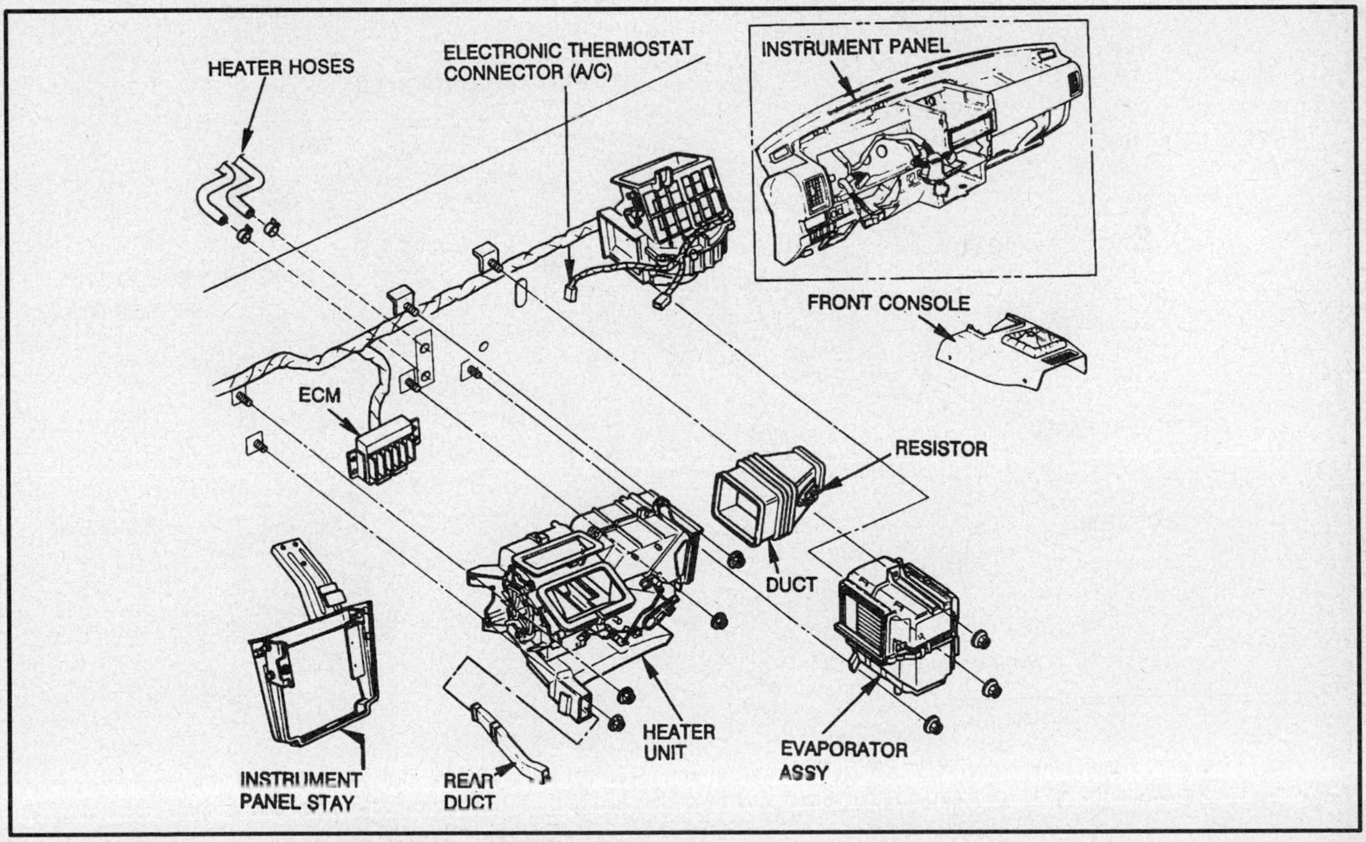

Heater unit removal—Amigo, Pick-Up, Rodeo and Trooper

Stylus

1. Disconnect the negative battery cable. Properly drain the cooling system. If equipped with air conditioning, properly evacuate the refrigerant system using recovery equipment.
2. Remove the heater hoses at the firewall connections. Plug the hoses to minimize leakage of remaining coolant.
3. Remove the instrument panel assembly as follows:
   • Pull the switch bezel out and disconnect the switch connectors.
   • Pull the cigarette lighter bezel out and disconnect the electrical connector, then remove the bezel.
   • Disconnect the hood release handle.
   • Remove the knee pad assembly.
   • Remove the 2 hinge pins from inside the glove box and remove the glove box.
   • Remove the front console bracket.
   • Remove the instrument cluster hood and the instrument cluster.
   • Remove the front hole covers and the front cover.
   • Remove the instrument panel assembly.
4. Remove the resistor from the air duct or the evaporator housing.

5. If equipped with air conditioning, remove the evaporator assembly.
6. Remove the mix and mode actuator connector.
7. Remove the center ventilator duct.
8. Remove the heater assembly.
9. Installation is the reverse of the removal procedure. Properly refill the cooling system. If equipped with air conditioning, evacuate, recharge and leak test the system. Adjust the control cables.

Trooper

1. Disconnect the negative battery cable. Properly drain the cooling system. If equipped with air conditioning, properly discharge the system.
2. Disconnect and plug the heater hoses from the firewall tubes. Disconnect the refrigerant lines from the evaporator tubes at the firewall. Immediately cap the lines to minimize contamination.
3. Remove the instrument panel as follows:
   • Remove the steering column cowl.
   • Remove the instrument panel trim from the front left side of the panel.

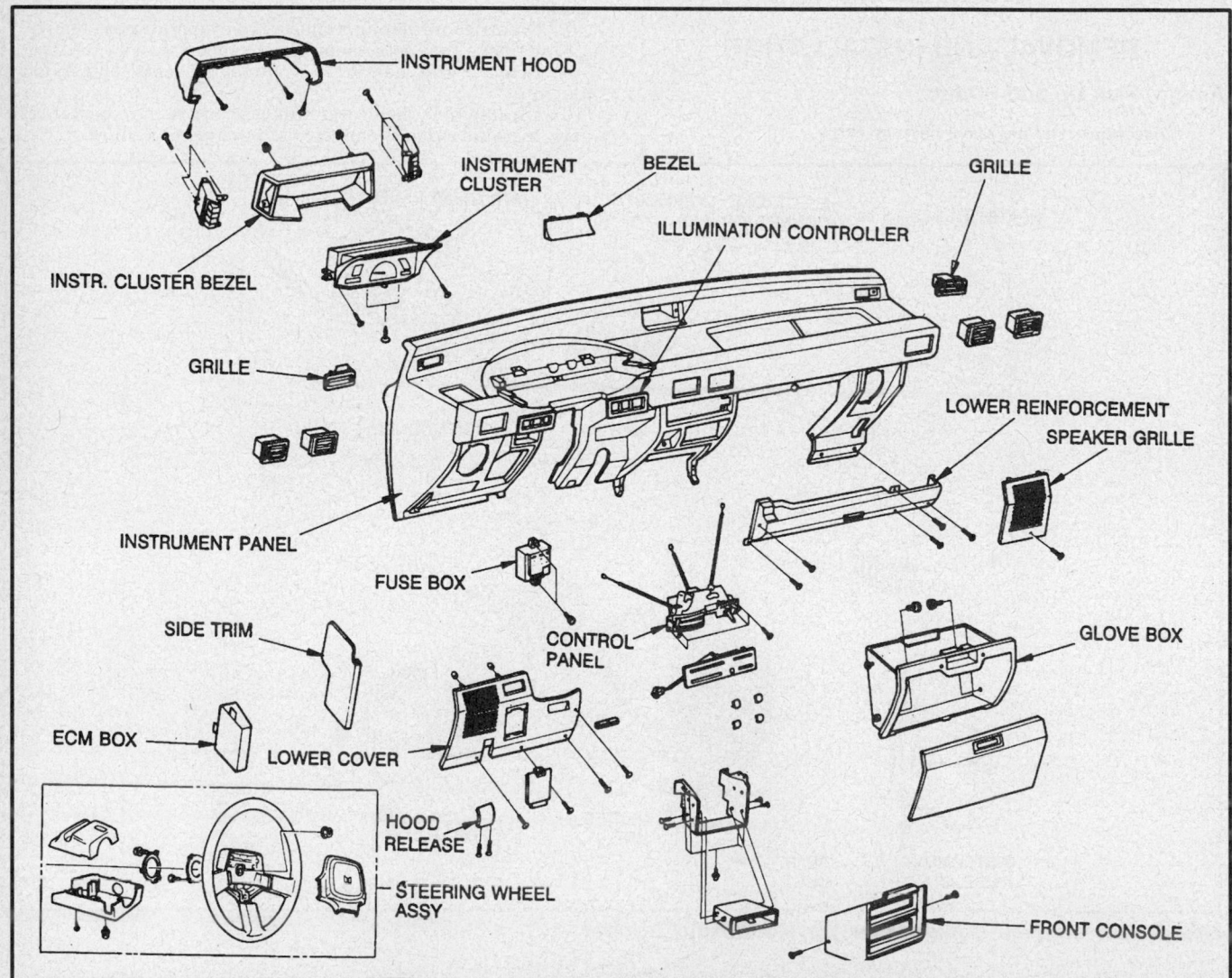

Instrument panel and related component removal—Amigo, Pick-Up and Rodeo

- Remove the instrument cluster assembly.
- Remove the ECM cover and the instrument panel hood.
- Remove the steering lower cover.
- Remove the fuse box from its mounting.
- Remove the hood release handle.
- Remove the glove box assembly.
- Remove the climate control panel assembly.
- Remove the radio.
- Remove the right speaker cover, both side defroster grilles and both dash side trim panels.
- Remove the ashtray, then remove the instrument panel.

4. Remove the resistor connector at the blower housing. Remove the air duct (heater only) or the evaporator housing (A/C).

5. Do not disconnect, but remove the ECM from its mounting.

6. Remove the instrument panel support, the front console and the rear heater duct.

7. Remove The heater assembly, then disassemble to remove the heater core on the bench.

8. Install in the reverse of the removal procedure. Refill cooling system. Evacuate, recharge and leak test air conditioning system, if equipped.

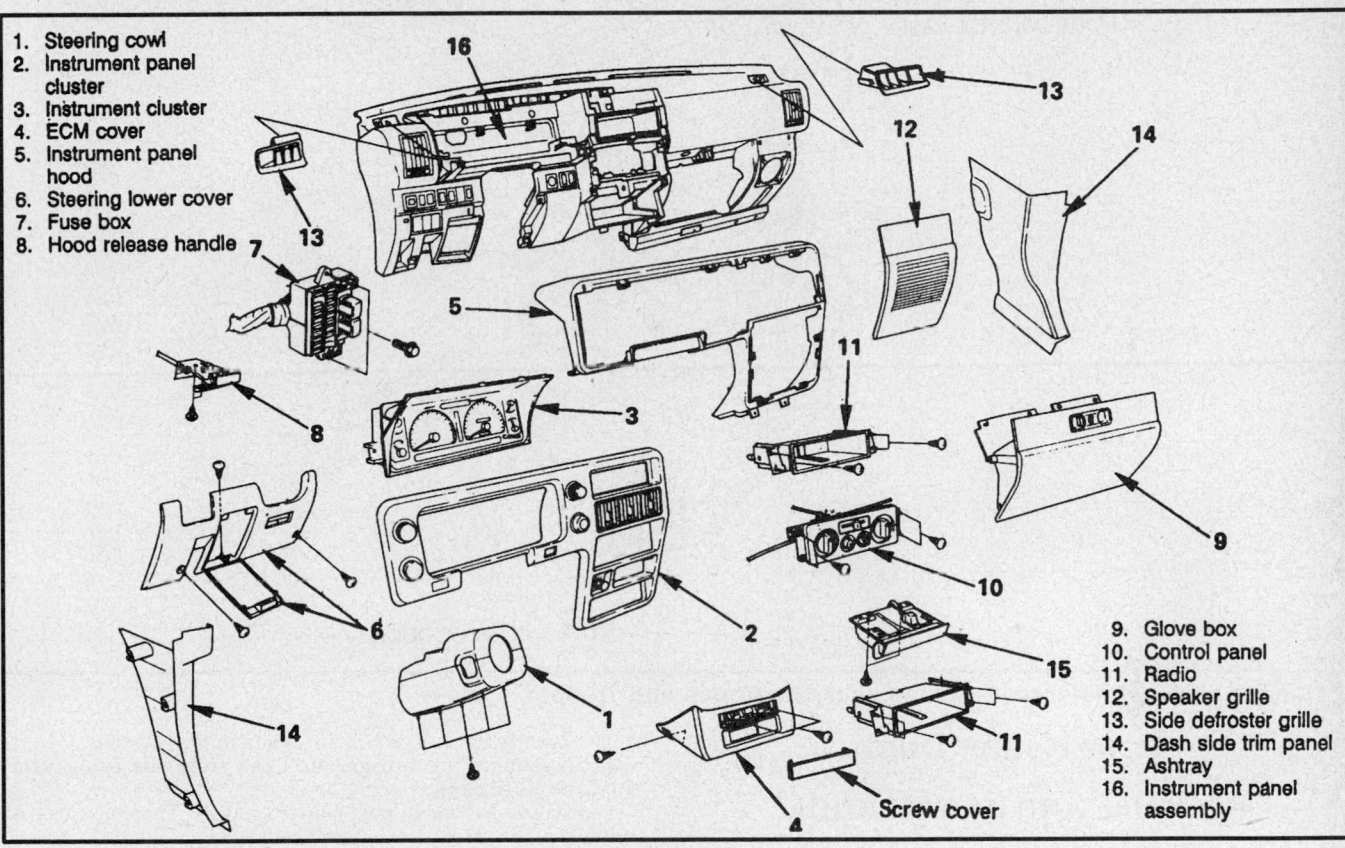

1. Steering cowl
2. Instrument panel cluster
3. Instrument cluster
4. ECM cover
5. Instrument panel hood
6. Steering lower cover
7. Fuse box
8. Hood release handle

9. Glove box
10. Control panel
11. Radio
12. Speaker grille
13. Side defroster grille
14. Dash side trim panel
15. Ashtray
16. Instrument panel assembly

Screw cover

Instrument panel and related component removal—Trooper

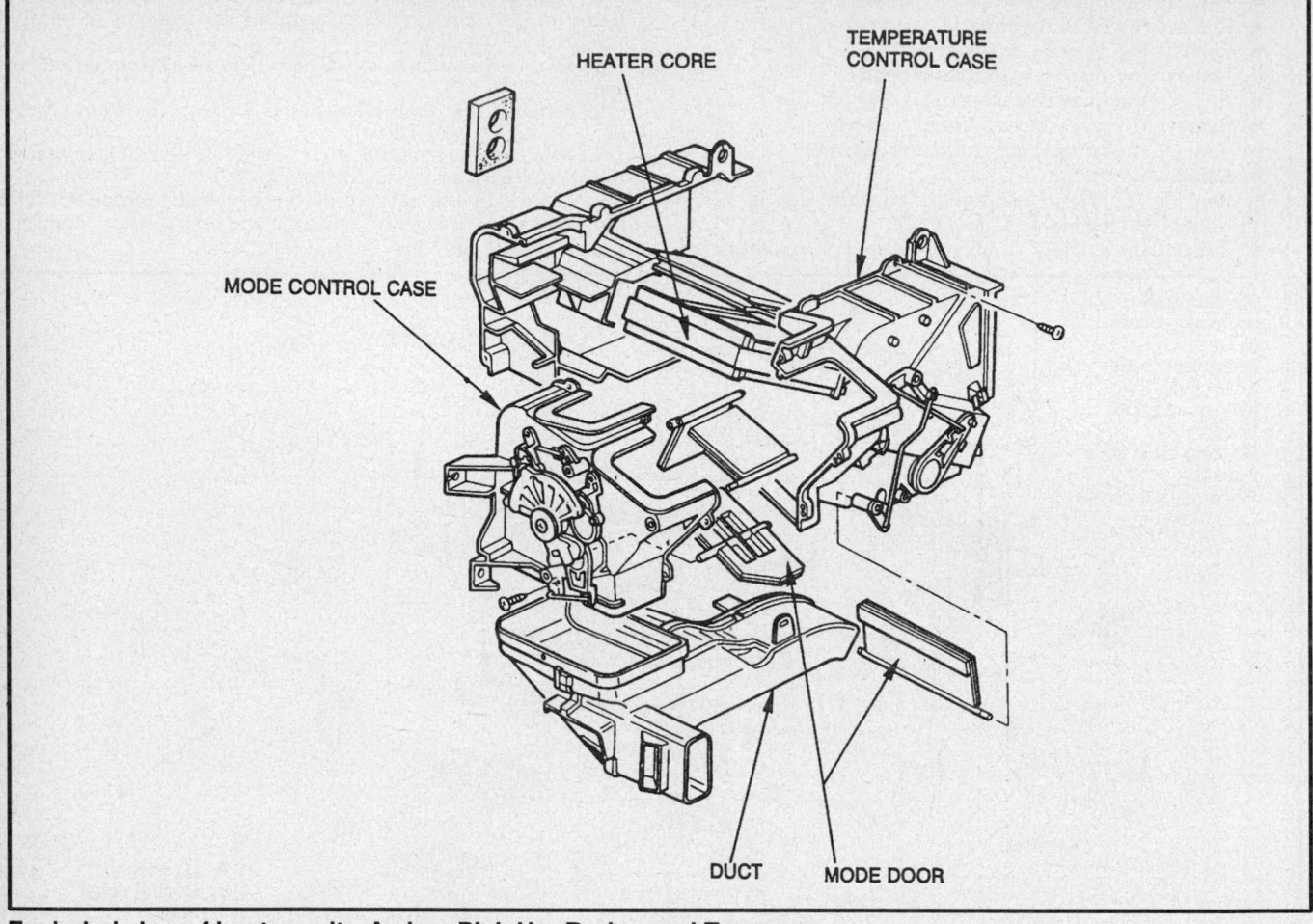

Exploded view of heater unit—Amigo, Pick-Up, Rodeo and Trooper

Rear Heater Duct

REMOVAL AND INSTALLATION

Trooper

1. Disconnect the negative battery cable.
2. Remove the shift knob, the front console and the rear console.
3. Remove the rear heater duct.
4. Installation is the reverse of the removal procedure.

Evaporator Core

REMOVAL AND INSTALLATION

Amigo, Pick-Up and Rodeo

1. Disconnect the negative battery cable.

2. Properly discharge the air conditioning system.
3. Disconnect the refrigerant lines from the evaporator a the firewall fittings.
4. Remove the glove box, center console, speaker cover and air duct.
5. Remove the resistor and the thermo switch connector.
6. Remove the diode connector, if equipped.
7. Remove drain hose.
8. Remove the evaporator assembly.
9. Installation is the reverse of removal procedure. If evaporator core is replaced, add 1.7 oz. of new oil to the evaporator. Evacuate, recharge and leak test the system

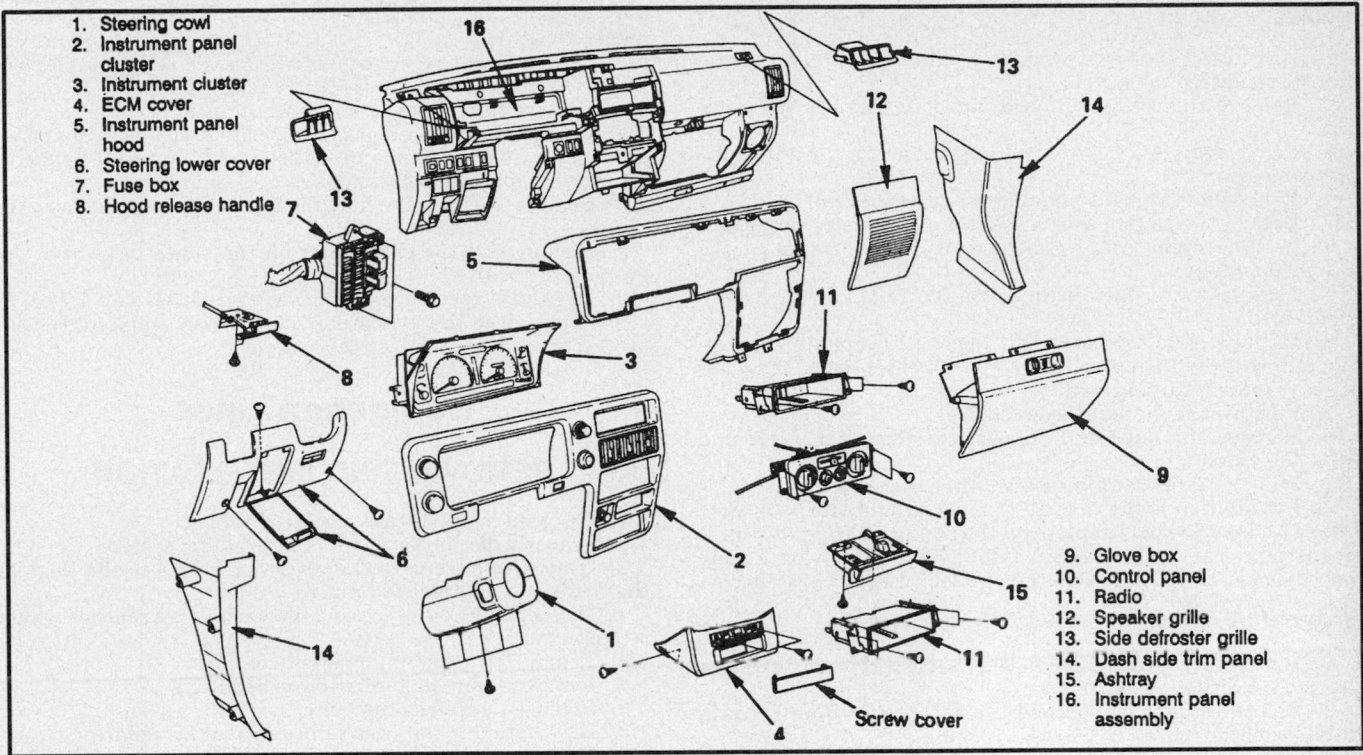

1. Steering cowl
2. Instrument panel cluster
3. Instrument cluster
4. ECM cover
5. Instrument panel hood
6. Steering lower cover
7. Fuse box
8. Hood release handle

9. Glove box
10. Control panel
11. Radio
12. Speaker grille
13. Side defroster grille
14. Dash side trim panel
15. Ashtray
16. Instrument panel assembly

Screw cover

Typical evaporator and related component removal

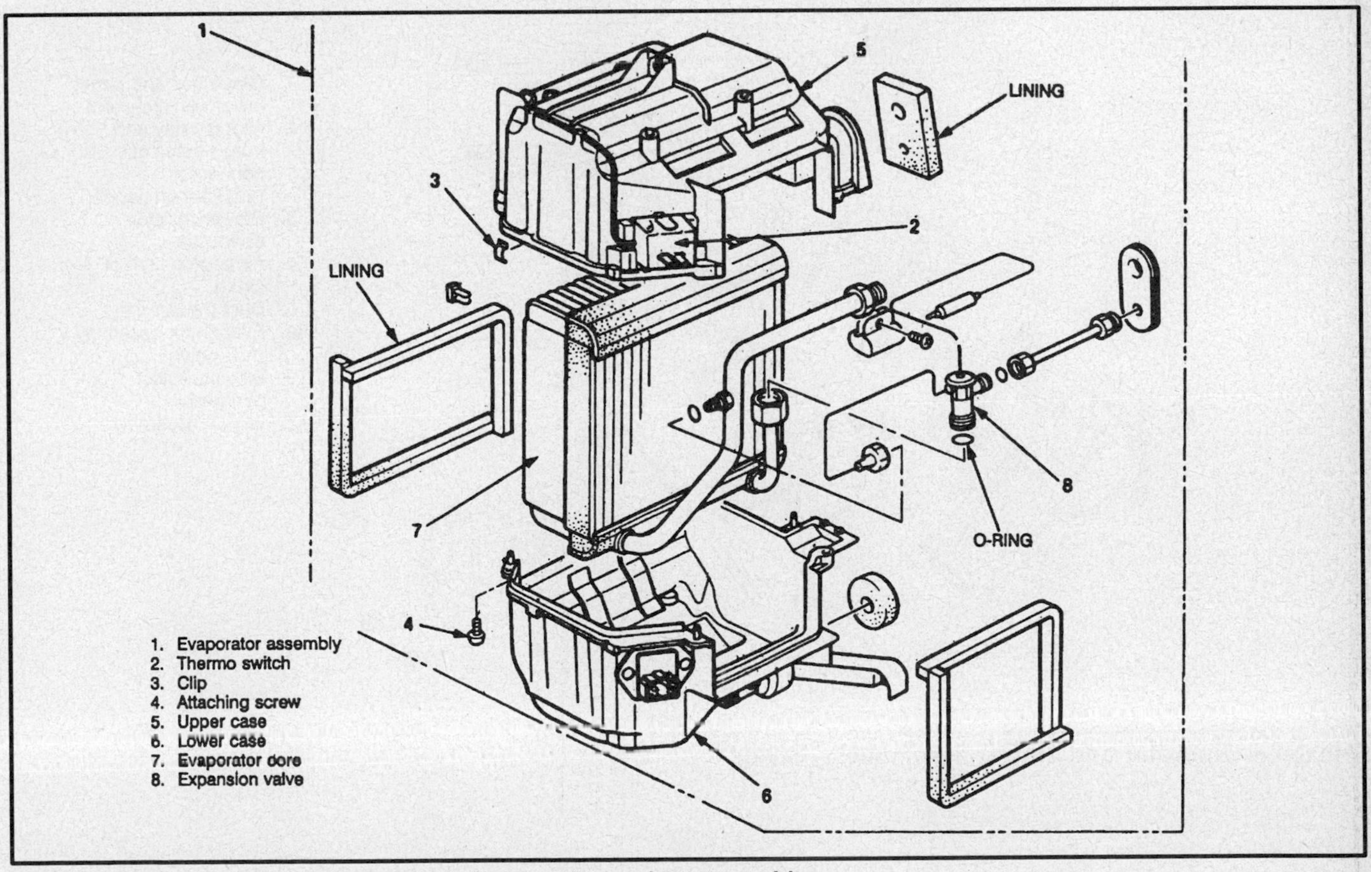

LINING

LINING

O-RING

1. Evaporator assembly
2. Thermo switch
3. Clip
4. Attaching screw
5. Upper case
6. Lower case
7. Evaporator core
8. Expansion valve

Typical thermo switch, evaporator and expansion valve assembly

Stylus

1. Disconnect the negative battery cable. Properly discharge the air conditioning system.
2. Remove the condensation drain hose. Remove the glove box.
3. Remove the A/C cut control unit connector for automatic transmission.
4. Remove instrument panel lower reinforcement.
5. Detach the electro thermo sensor and resistor connector.
6. In the engine compartment, remove the clamp at the expansion valve.
7. Loosen the refrigerant line attaching nuts at the expansion valve.
8. In the engine compartment, remove 1 evaporator retaining nut; then, in the passenger compartment, remove the other 2 evaporator retaining nuts.
9. Remove the evaporator assembly.
10. Remove the clips and screws from the evaporator and split the cases.
11. Pull the evaporator core from the lower case.
12. Installation is the reverse of removal procedure.
13. Use new O–rings applying a thin coat of refrigerant oil. If evaporator core was replaced, add 1.7 oz. of new oil during installation. Evacuate, recharge and leak test the system.

Trooper

1. Disconnect the negative battery cable. Properly discharge the air conditioning system.
2. Remove the glove box and the ECM cover from beneath the glove box.
3. Remove the right speaker cover.
4. Remove the instrument panel lower horizontal reinforcement.
5. Detach electrical connections from the resistor and electronic thermostat at the evaporator housing.
6. Remove the condensation drain hose.
7. Using back–up wrenches, properly disconnect the refrigerant lines from the evaporator tubes at the firewall. Immediately cap all openings to minimize contamination.
8. Remove the 3 nuts holding the evaporator housing in place.
9. Disassemble the evaporator on the bench to remove the evaporator core.
10. To install, reverse the removal procedure. Add 1.7 oz. of refrigerant oil to the evaporator if core was replaced. Evacuate, recharge and leak test the system.

Refrigerant Lines

REMOVAL AND INSTALLATION

1. Disconnect the negative battery cable.
2. Properly discharge the air conditioning system.
3. If necessary, remove the grille for access to the lines at the condenser and receiver/drier.
4. Disconnect the refrigerant lines using 2 wrenches where required.
5. Remove all attaching brackets or clips.
6. Remove reservoir tanks where required.
7. Remove the refrigerant line.
8. Installation is the reverse of removal procedure.
9. Evacuate, recharge and leak check the system.

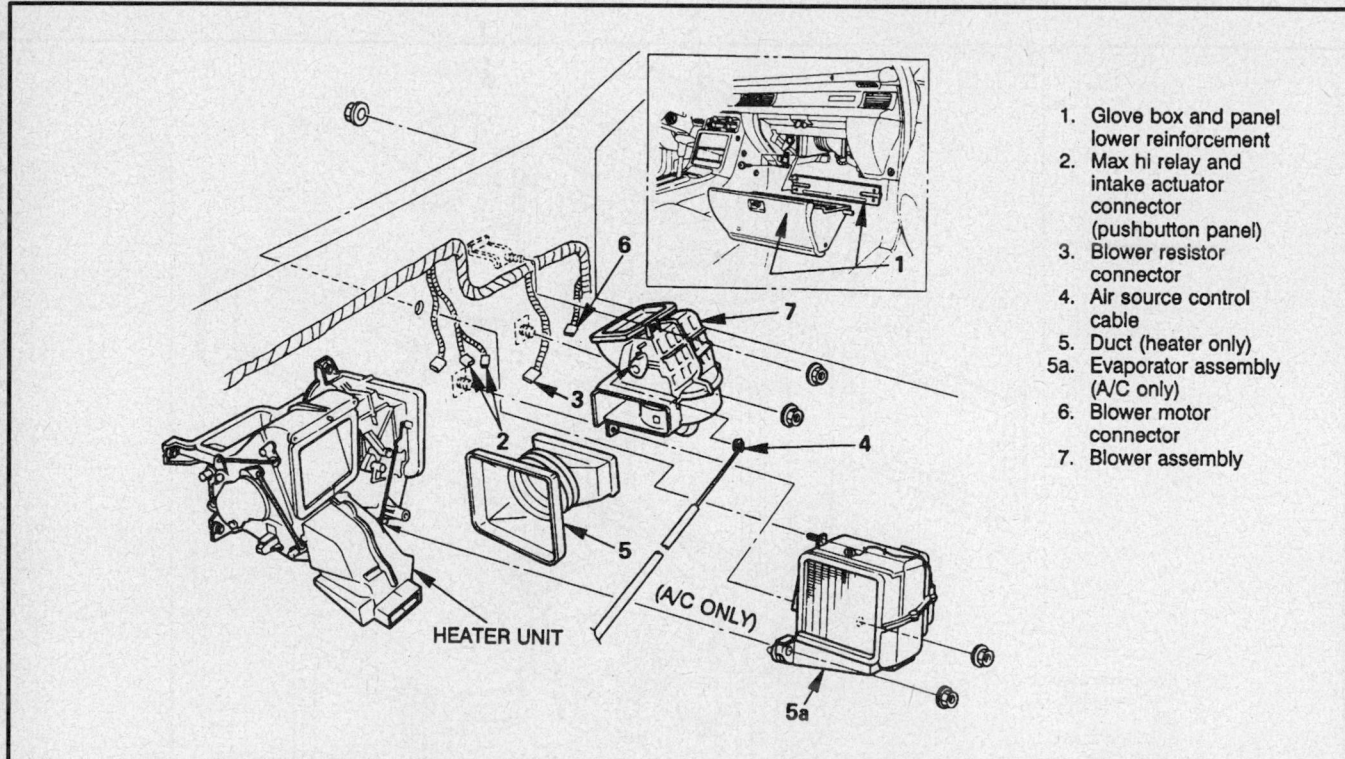

1. Glove box and panel lower reinforcement
2. Max hi relay and intake actuator connector (pushbutton panel)
3. Blower resistor connector
4. Air source control cable
5. Duct (heater only)
5a. Evaporator assembly (A/C only)
6. Blower motor connector
7. Blower assembly

HEATER UNIT

(A/C ONLY)

Heater, evaporator and blower assemblies—Stylus

NOTE: Always route hoses in original location and use new O–rings with a thin coat of refrigerant oil.

Manual Control Head

REMOVAL AND INSTALLATION

Amigo, Pick-Up, Rodeo and Trooper

1. Disconnect the negative battery cable.
2. Remove the glove box assembly.
3. Remove control lever knobs.
4. Remove the heater bezel.
5. On Trooper, remove the steering column cowl and the front instrument panel trim from around the center control console and steering column area.
6. Remove the 3 attaching screws and disconnect the control cables at the heater and blower unit.

7. Pull the control unit outward and pull the fan control lever out and disconnect the connectors. Disconnect the A/C switch, if equipped.
8. Remove the control head assembly.
9. Remove the clips securing the cables on the control head and remove the cables.
10. Installation is the reverse of removal procedure.

Stylus

1. Disconnect the battery negative cable.
2. Remove the glove box.
3. Remove the front console and knobs.
4. Disconnect the control cables at the heater unit and blower assembly.
5. Remove control attaching screws and pull unit out.
6. Disconnect fan control lever and/or air conditioner switch connector.
7. Remove control assembly.
8. Installation is the reverse of removal procedure.

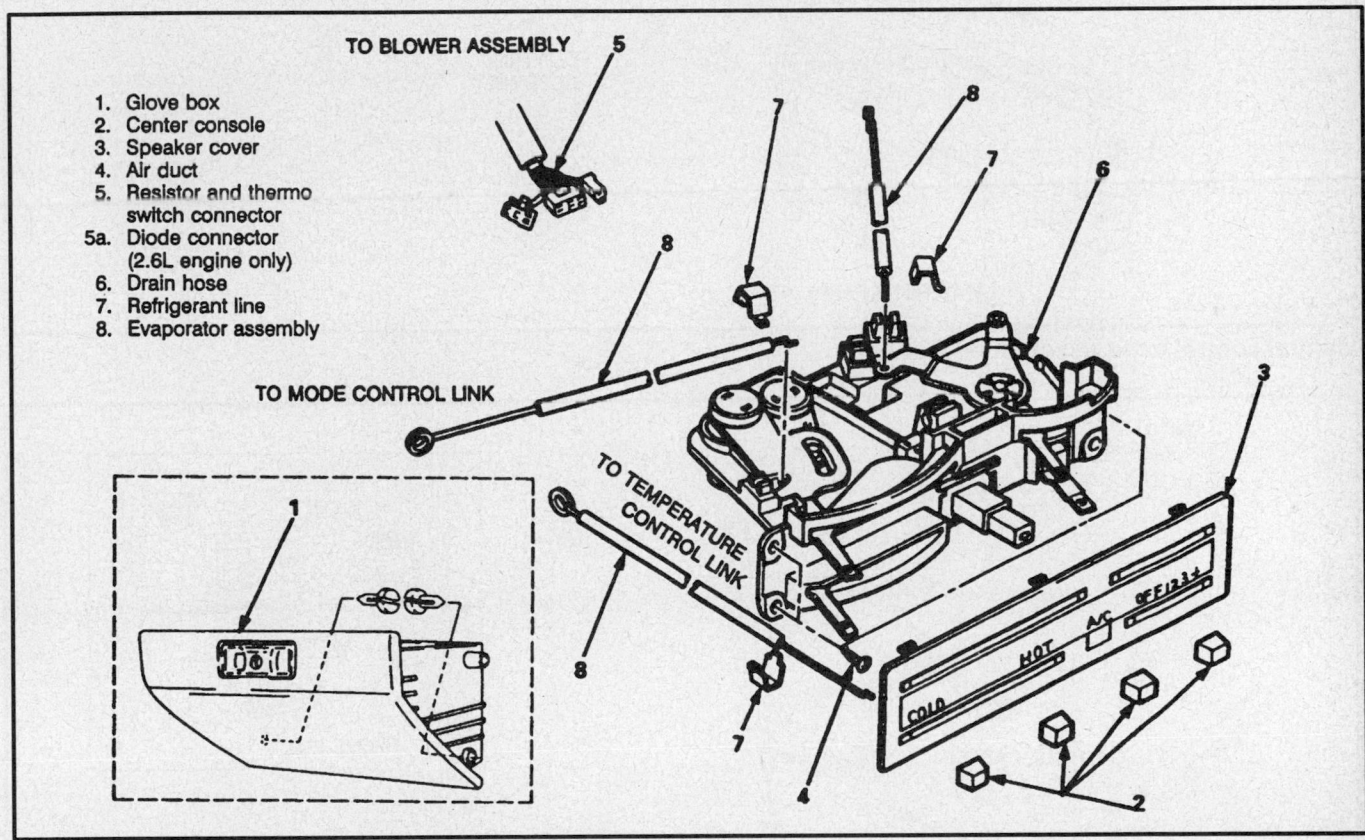

1. Glove box
2. Center console
3. Speaker cover
4. Air duct
5. Resistor and thermo switch connector
5a. Diode connector (2.6L engine only)
6. Drain hose
7. Refrigerant line
8. Evaporator assembly

Manual control head—Amigo, Pick-Up and Rodeo

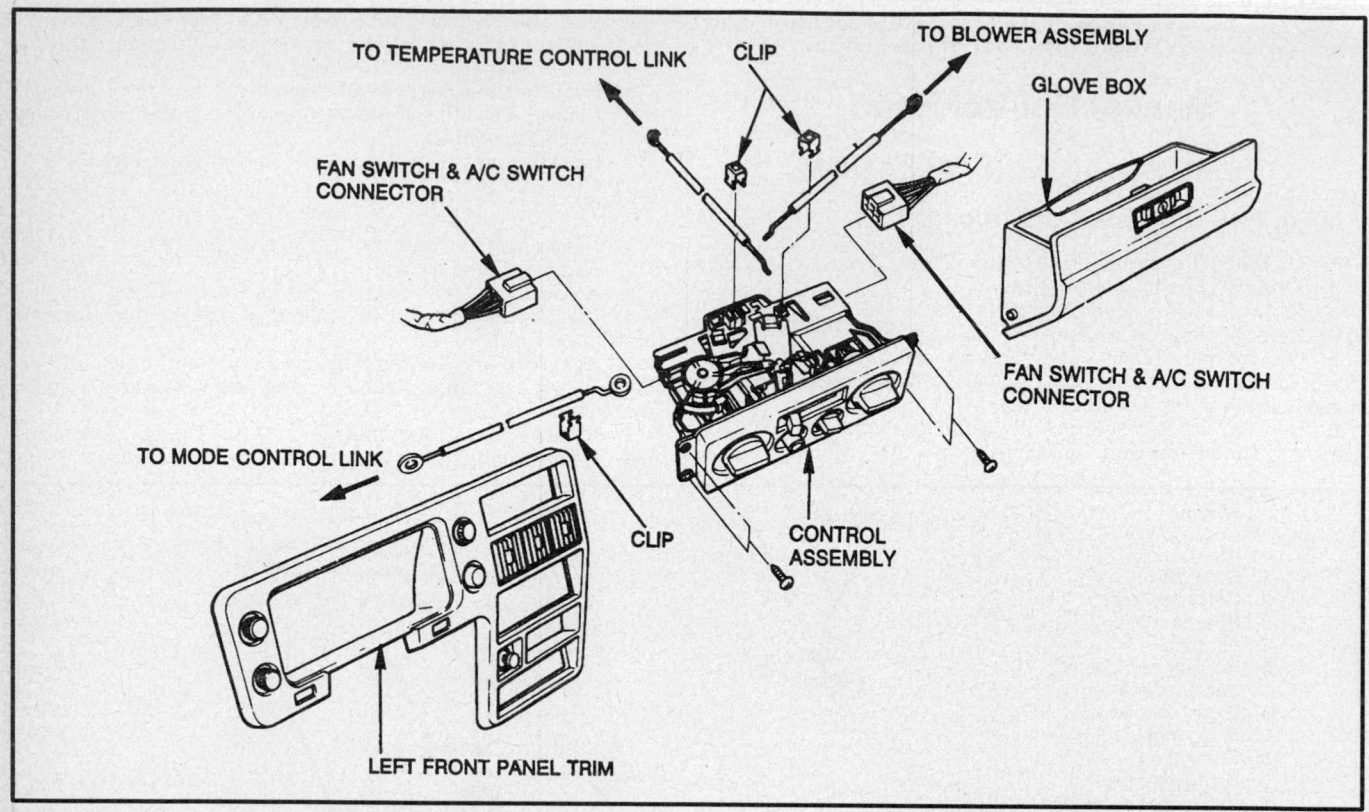

Manual control head assembly—Trooper

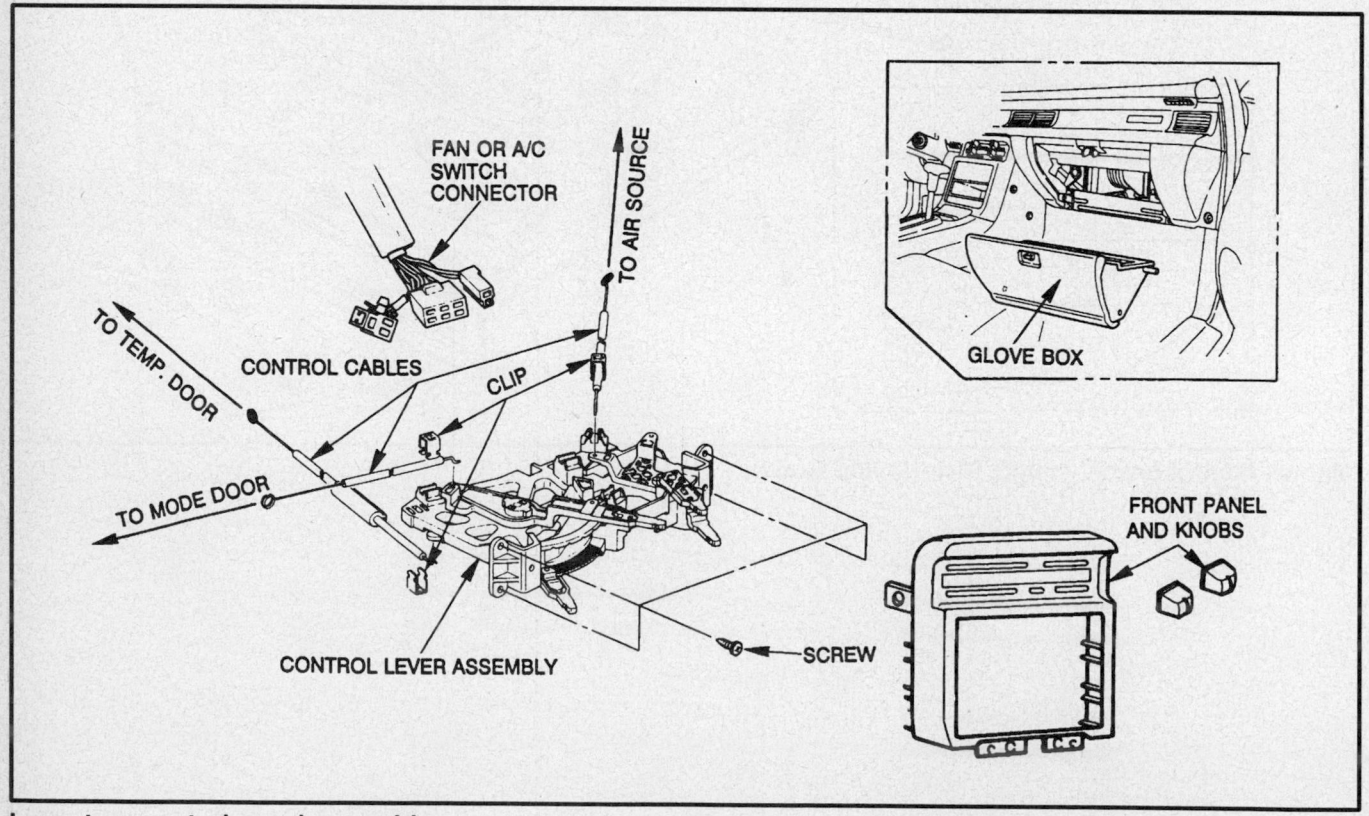

Lever type control panel assembly

Electronic Control Head

REMOVAL AND INSTALLATION

Stylus

1. Disconnect the negative battery cable.
2. Remove the ashtray.
3. Remove the front console panel.
4. Remove the attaching screws from the control assembly and remove the control head.
5. Installation is the reverse of removal procedure.

CONTROL CABLE ADJUSTMENT

Amigo, Pick-Up, Rodeo and Trooper

1. To adjust the air source control cable perform the following procedure:
   • Slide the control lever to the left.
   • Connect the control cable at the **CIRC** position and secure it with a clip.

2. To adjust the temperature control cable perform the following procedure:
   • Slide the control lever to the left.
   • Connect the control cable at the **COLD** position and secure it with a clip.
3. To adjust the air select control cable. Slide the control lever to the right.
4. Connect the control cable at the **DEFROST** position and secure it with a clip.

Stylus

1. Adjust the air source control cable, slide the select lever to the left, set the door lever to **CIRC** position and connect the control cable at the circulate position with the clip.
2. Adjust the temperature control cable, slide the select lever to the left, set the door lever to **COLD** position and connect the control cable at the cold position with the clip.
3. Adjust the air select control cable, slide the select lever to the right, set the door lever to **DEF** position and connect the control cable at the defrost position with the clip.
4. Check operation of unit.

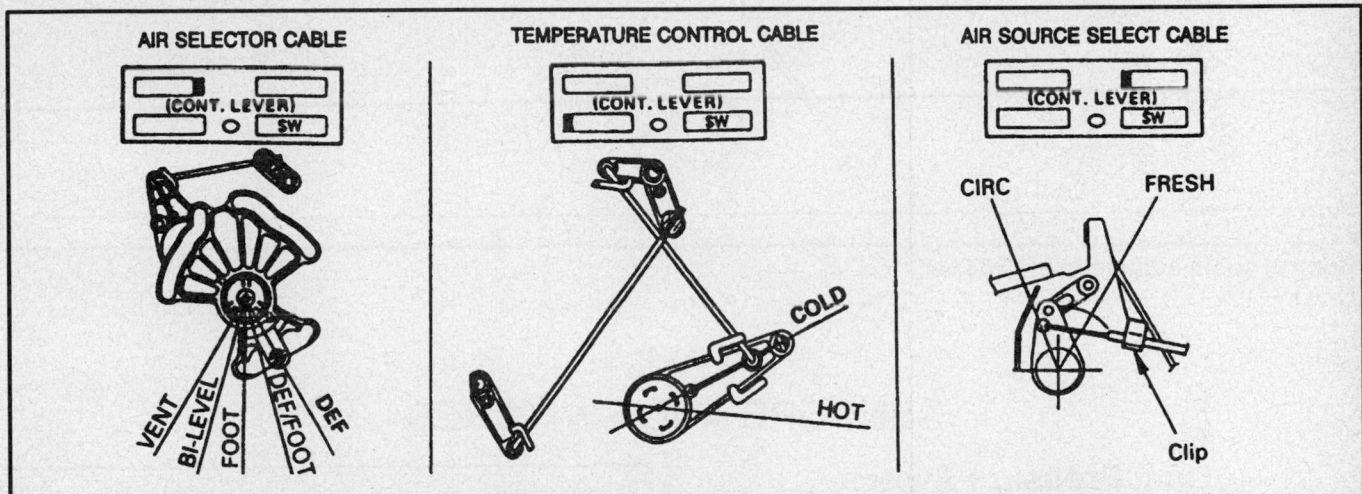

Control cable adjustment—Amigo, Pick-Up and Rodeo

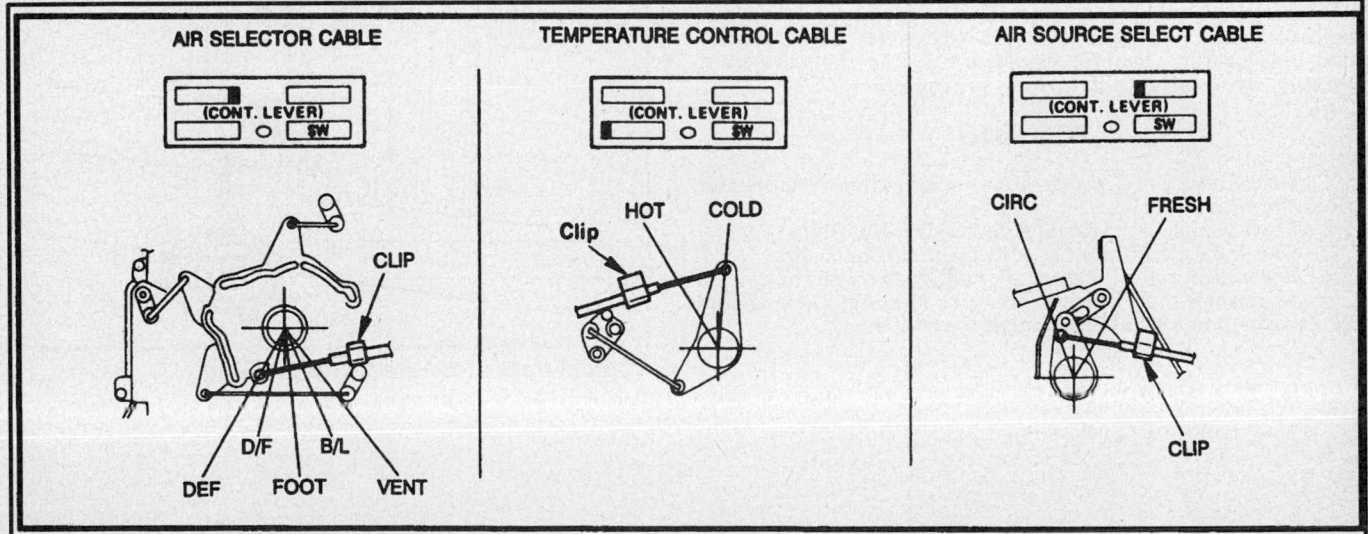

Control cable adjustment—Stylus

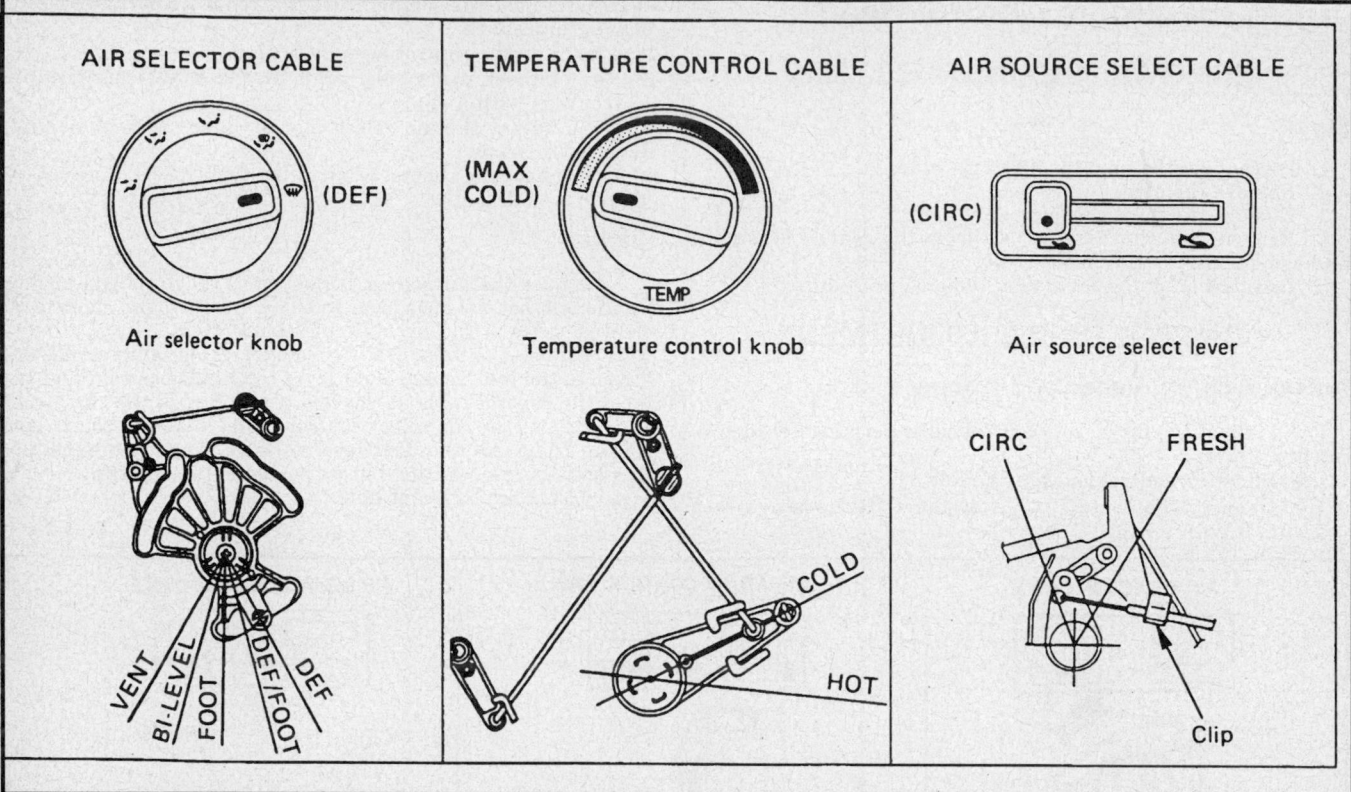

Control cable adjustment—Trooper

SENSORS AND SWITCHES

Dual Pressure Switch

OPERATION

The dual pressure switch is installed on the upper part of the receiver/drier, it is used to detect excessively high pressure and also prevent compressor seizure due to the refrigerant leaking by electronically turning the compressor ON or OFF.

TESTING

1. Disconnect the 2 prong pressure switch wire connector from the receiver/drier.
2. Start vehicle and turn the air conditioner **ON**.
3. Check for continuity between terminals on switch.
4. Reconnect wire and check for voltage through the switch.
5. At normal high and low pressure readings there should be 12 volts and continuity through the switch.

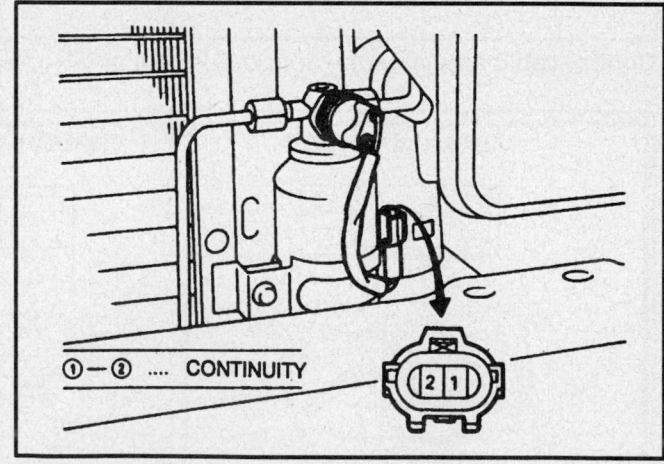

Typical dual pressure switch testing

REMOVAL AND INSTALLATION

1. Disconnect the negative battery cable.
2. Properly discharge the air conditioning system.
3. If required, remove radiator grille.
4. Disconnect the pressure switch wire connector.
5. Use 2 wrenches to remove the pressure switch.
6. Installation is the reverse of removal procedure. Evacuate, recharge and leak test the system.

Triple Pressure Switch

OPERATION

The triple pressure switch incorporates a medium pressure switch, a high pressure switch and a low pressure switch to cycle ON and OFF the condenser fan according to system pressure on the high side and is mounted in the receiver/drier.

TESTING

1. Disconnect the 4 prong triple pressure switch connector from the receiver/dryer.
2. Check for continuity between the terminals of the triple pressure switch side connector.
3. Whether the condenser fan is turned ON or OFF is determined by continuity across terminals 3 and 4. Continuity is established when the air conditioner is turned ON and the refrigerant pressure reaches 21.3–14.2 psi.

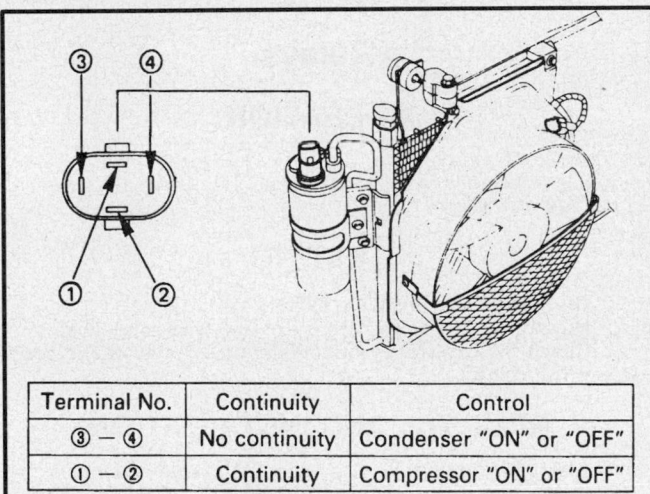

Terminal No.	Continuity	Control
③ — ④	No continuity	Condenser "ON" or "OFF"
① — ②	Continuity	Compressor "ON" or "OFF"

Typical triple switch testing

REMOVAL AND INSTALLATION

1. Disconnect the negative battery cable.
2. Properly discharge the air conditioning system.
3. Remove radiator support bracket, if necessary.
4. Remove refrigerant high pressure connection above condenser.
5. Disconnect pressure switch wire connector.
6. Using 2 wrenches, turn the triple pressure switch counterclockwise and remove.
7. Installation is the reverse of removal procedure.

Thermo Sensor and Electronic Thermostat

OPERATION

Amigo, Pick-Up and Trooper

1. Remove the thermo sensor from the evaporator core. Start the engine.
2. Set the A/C switch to **ON**. Using a heated liquid source as shown, warm and cool the thermo sensor to test the continuity as indicated. Check the continuity between the thermo switch relay terminals at the harness side.

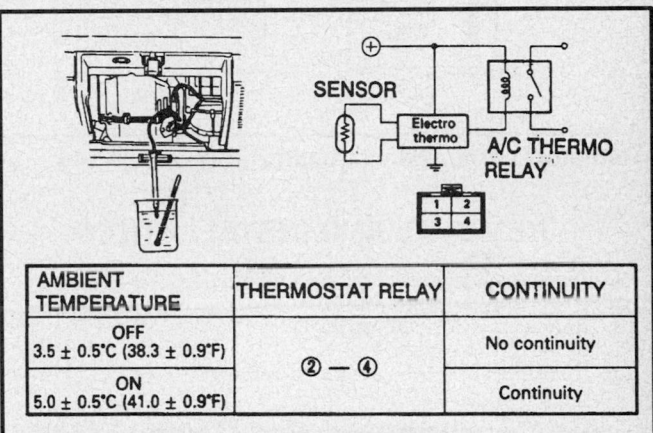

AMBIENT TEMPERATURE	THERMOSTAT RELAY	CONTINUITY
OFF 3.5 ± 0.5°C (38.3 ± 0.9°F)	② — ④	No continuity
ON 5.0 ± 0.5°C (41.0 ± 0.9°F)		Continuity

Electronic thermostat testing—Amigo, Pick-Up and Trooper

REMOVAL AND INSTALLATION

1. Disconnect the negative battery cable.
2. Properly discharge the air conditioning system.
3. Remove the evaporator assembly, if required.
4. Remove the thermo sensor from the evaporator coils. Remove the electronic thermostat from the evaporator housing, if equipped.
5. Installation is the reverse of removal procedure. Evacuate, recharge and leak test the system.

Thermo Switch

OPERATION

The coolant system uses a thermo switch to turn on the coolant fan when the coolant temperature reaches between 180°–190°F and higher.

TESTING

Stylus

1. Disconnect negative battery terminal.
2. Drain the cooling system.
3. Remove the sensor.

4. Set the sensor portion in the water and increase the temperature.

5. Check that there is continuity when the water temperature is between 180°–190°F or higher.

6. Next reduce the water temperature and check that there is no continuity between 167°–178°F or lower.

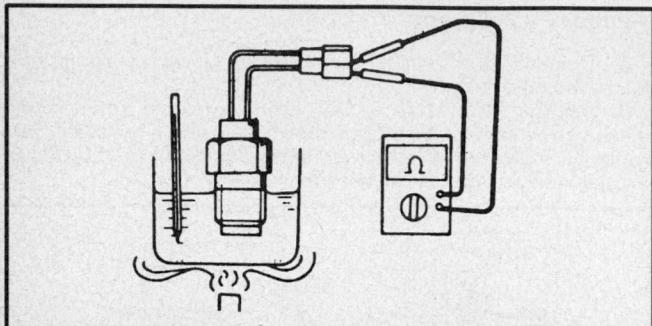

Radiator thermo switch testing—Stylus

REMOVAL AND INSTALLATION

1. Disconnect negative battery terminal.
2. Drain the cooling system.
3. Remove sensor connecting wire.
4. Remove the sensor.
5. Installation is the reverse of removal.

Air Conditioning Cut Control Unit

On Stylus equipped with automatic transaxle, an air conditioning cut control unit is used. The unit is located on the instrument panel lower reinforcement behind the glove box. The control unit senses the engine water temperature and the signal of the meter reed switch during operation of the air conditioner. Then, in order to prevent abnormal rise of engine water temperature and to maintain cooling efficiency at high engine water temperature, it commands the ECM to turn ON and OFF the compressor.

TESTING

Stylus

When the engine coolant temperature is above 220°F and the vehicle speed is below 20 mph the air conditioner compressor will be ON. At this temperature with speeds above 20 mph the compressor will cycle in 15 second intervals.

REMOVAL AND INSTALLATION

1. Disconnect the negative battery.
2. Remove the glove box assembly.
3. Remove the instrument panel lower reinforcement.
4. Remove the control unit wire connector.
5. Unbolt and remove the control unit.
6. Installation is the reverse of the removal.

Diode

TESTING

Stylus

1. Disconnect the diode from the fuse and relay box near the left fenderwell.
2. Set the circuit tester to the resistance range and check the continuity.

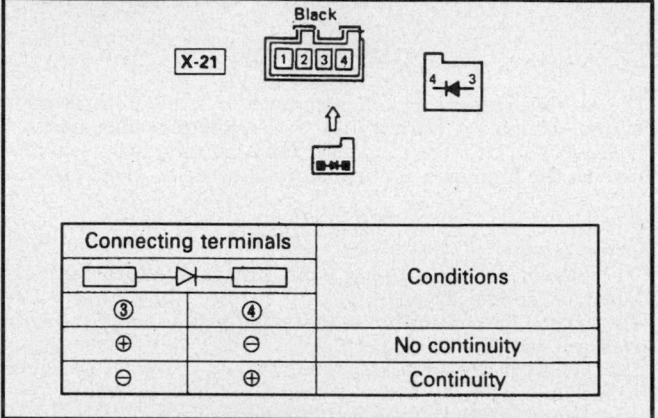

Connecting terminals		Conditions
③	④	
⊕	⊖	No continuity
⊖	⊕	Continuity

Testing the diode—Stylus

Relays

OPERATION

A variety of relays are used to energize certain system switches or components, or to de–energize them as in the case of the A/C cut relay.

TESTING

1. Disconnect the negative battery terminal.
2. Disconnect the relays from the fuse and relay box.
3. Check for continuity and resistance between the terminals of the relays.

REMOVAL AND INSTALLATION

Most air conditioner relays are located in one of 4 places; the left format kick panel, by the left or right fenderwell under the hood or at the evaporator housing.

Fan and Air Conditioning Switch

The fan switch controls blower motor speed by sending 12 volts to the resistor where it is reduced depending upon which position is selected; low, medium low, medium high, high. The air conditioner switch is an illuminated push button switch which sends 12 volts to the air conditioner relay when depressed.

TESTING

1. Disconnect the negative battery cable.
2. Remove the control head assembly.
3. Disconnect the air conditioner and fan switch connectors.
4. Check for continuity between terminals.

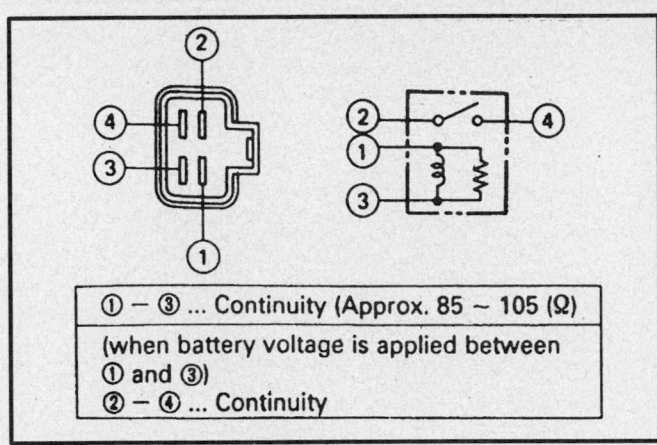

① – ③ ... Continuity (Approx. 85 ~ 105 (Ω))

(when battery voltage is applied between ① and ③)

② – ④ ... Continuity

Testing the condenser, compressor and thermo switch relay—Stylus

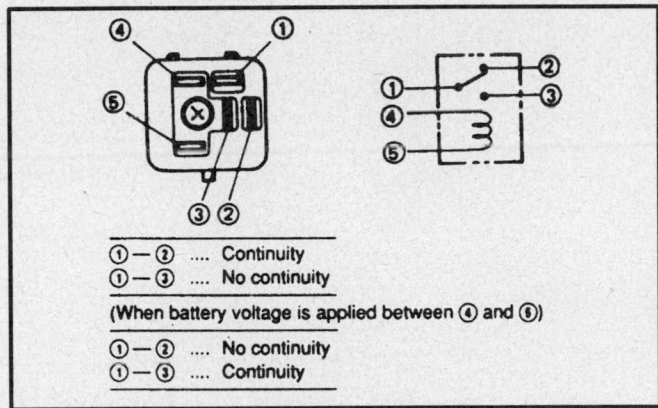

① – ② .... Continuity

① – ③ .... No continuity

(When battery voltage is applied between ④ and ⑤)

① – ② .... No continuity

① – ③ .... Continuity

Air conditioner cut relay, thermo switch relay and heater relay testing

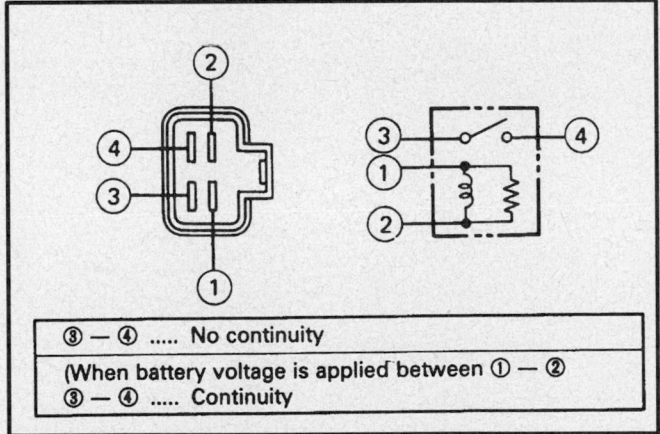

③ – ④ ..... No continuity

(When battery voltage is applied between ① — ②)

③ – ④ ..... Continuity

Compressor relay, thermo switch relay and blower relay testing—Amigo, Pick-Up and Trooper

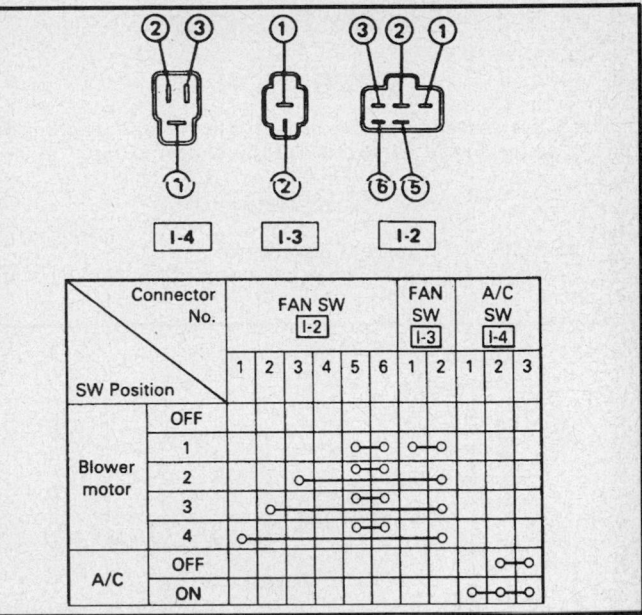

Connector No.	FAN SW I-2						FAN SW I-3		A/C SW I-4		
SW Position	1	2	3	4	5	6	1	2	1	2	3
Blower motor OFF											
1					o—o	o—o					
2			o—o			o—o					
3		o—o				o—o					
4	o—o					o—o					
A/C OFF									o—o		
A/C ON									o—o—o		

Fan switch and A/C switch testing—Amigo and Pick-up

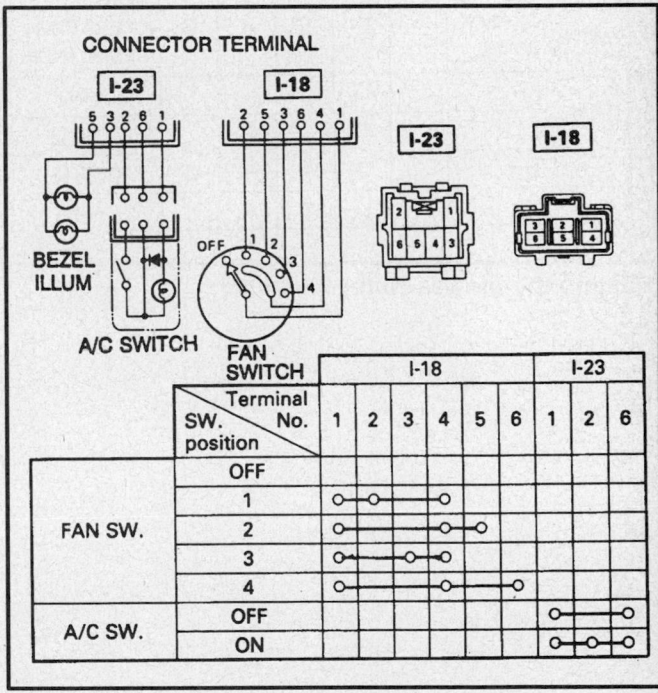

CONNECTOR TERMINAL

FAN SWITCH Terminal No. SW. position	I-18						I-23		
	1	2	3	4	5	6	1	2	6
FAN SW. OFF									
1	o—o				o—o				
2	o—o	o—o							
3	o—o		o—o						
4	o—o			o—o					
A/C SW. OFF							o—o		o—o
A/C SW. ON							o—o—o		

Fan switch and A/C switch testing—Trooper

Blower Resistor

OPERATION

The resistor serves to reduce or increase current reaching the blower motor, based on position of the blower switch.

TESTING

1. Disconnect the resistor connector.
2. Using an ohmmeter, check for continuity between the terminals.

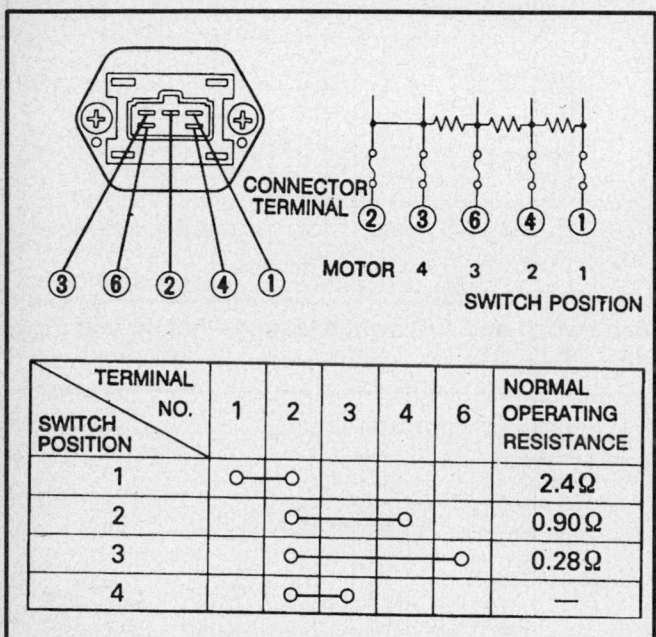

SWITCH POSITION	TERMINAL NO. 1	2	3	4	6	NORMAL OPERATING RESISTANCE
1	o—o					2.4 Ω
2		o——o				0.90 Ω
3		o—————o				0.28 Ω
4		o—o				—

Testing the blower motor resistor

SYSTEM DIAGNOSIS
AIR CONDITIONING DIAGNOSTIC CHART

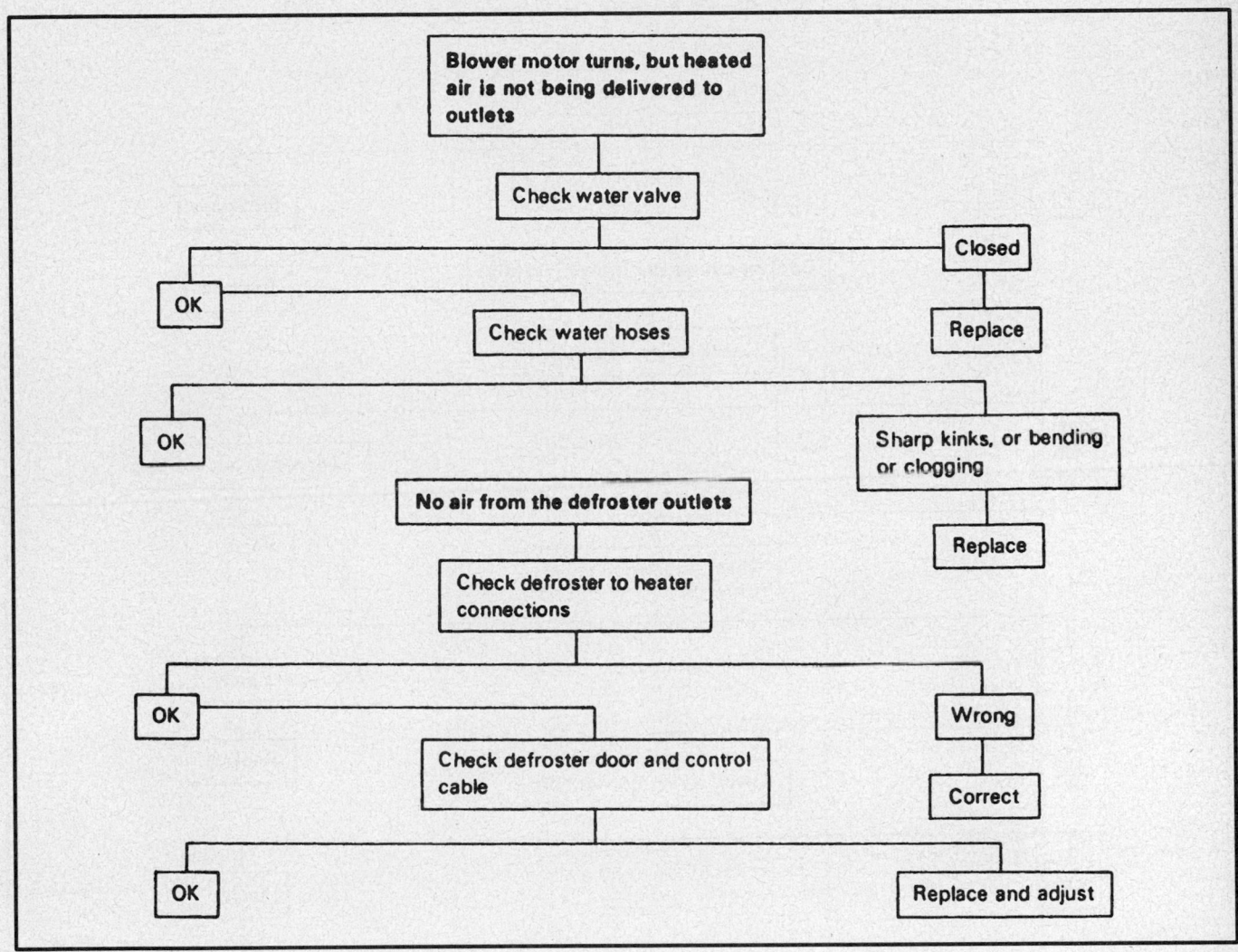

AIR CONDITIONING DIAGNOSTIC CHART, CONTINUED

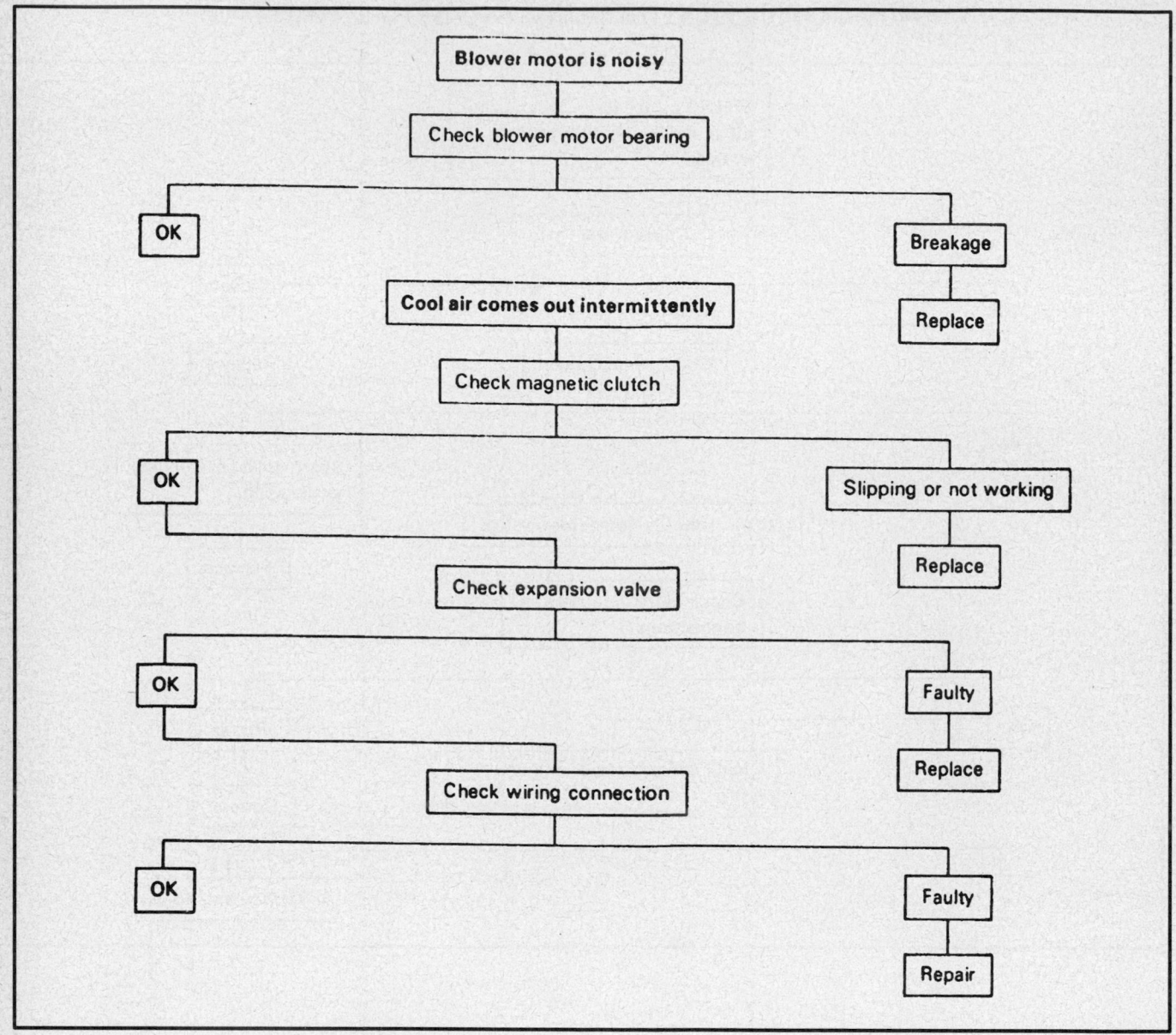

AIR CONDITIONING DIAGNOSTIC CHART, CONTINUED

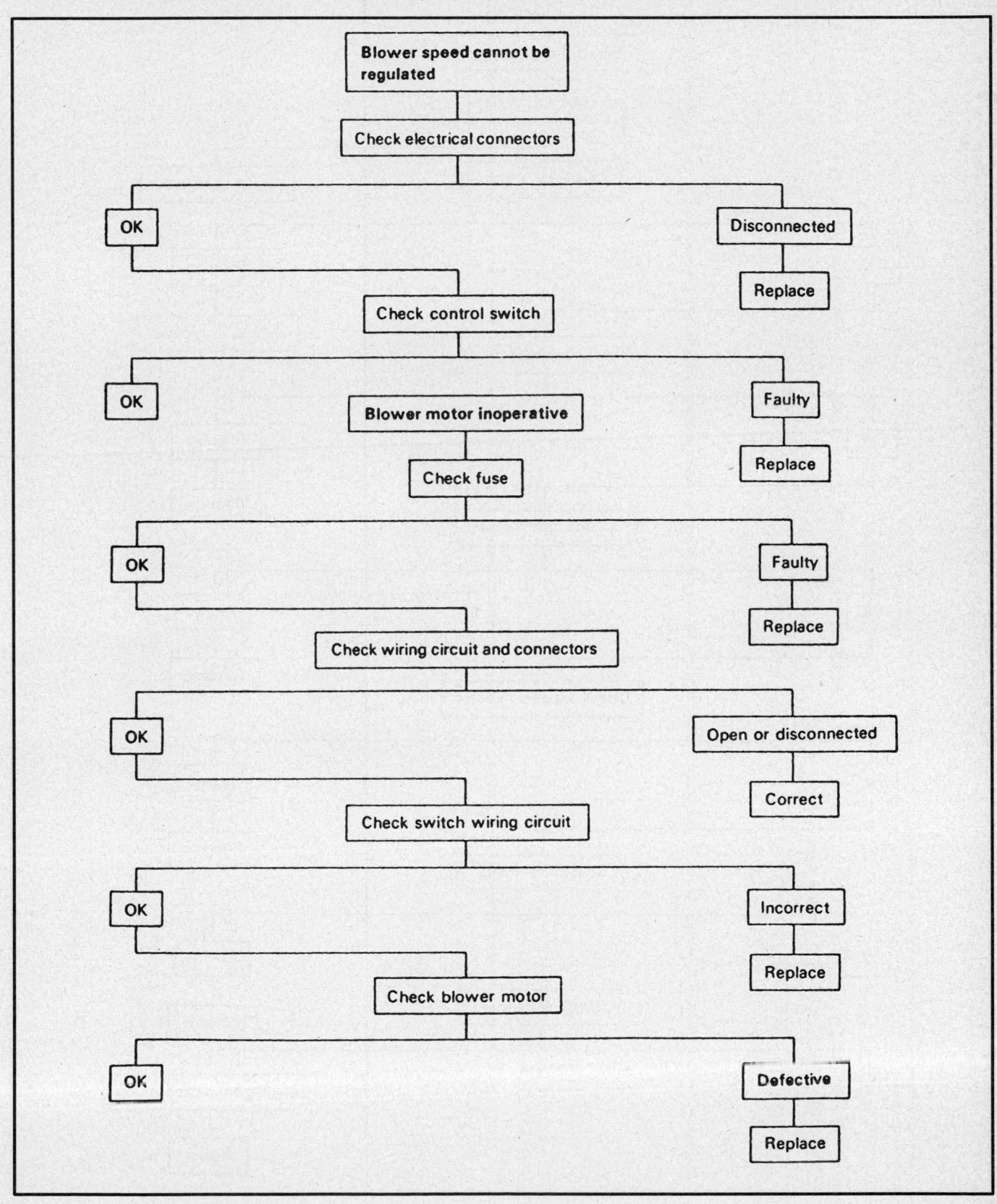

Blower speed cannot be regulated

Check electrical connectors

OK — Disconnected — Replace

Check control switch

OK — Faulty — Replace

Blower motor inoperative

Check fuse

OK — Faulty — Replace

Check wiring circuit and connectors

OK — Open or disconnected — Correct

Check switch wiring circuit

OK — Incorrect — Replace

Check blower motor

OK — Defective — Replace

AIR CONDITIONING DIAGNOSTIC CHART, CONTINUED

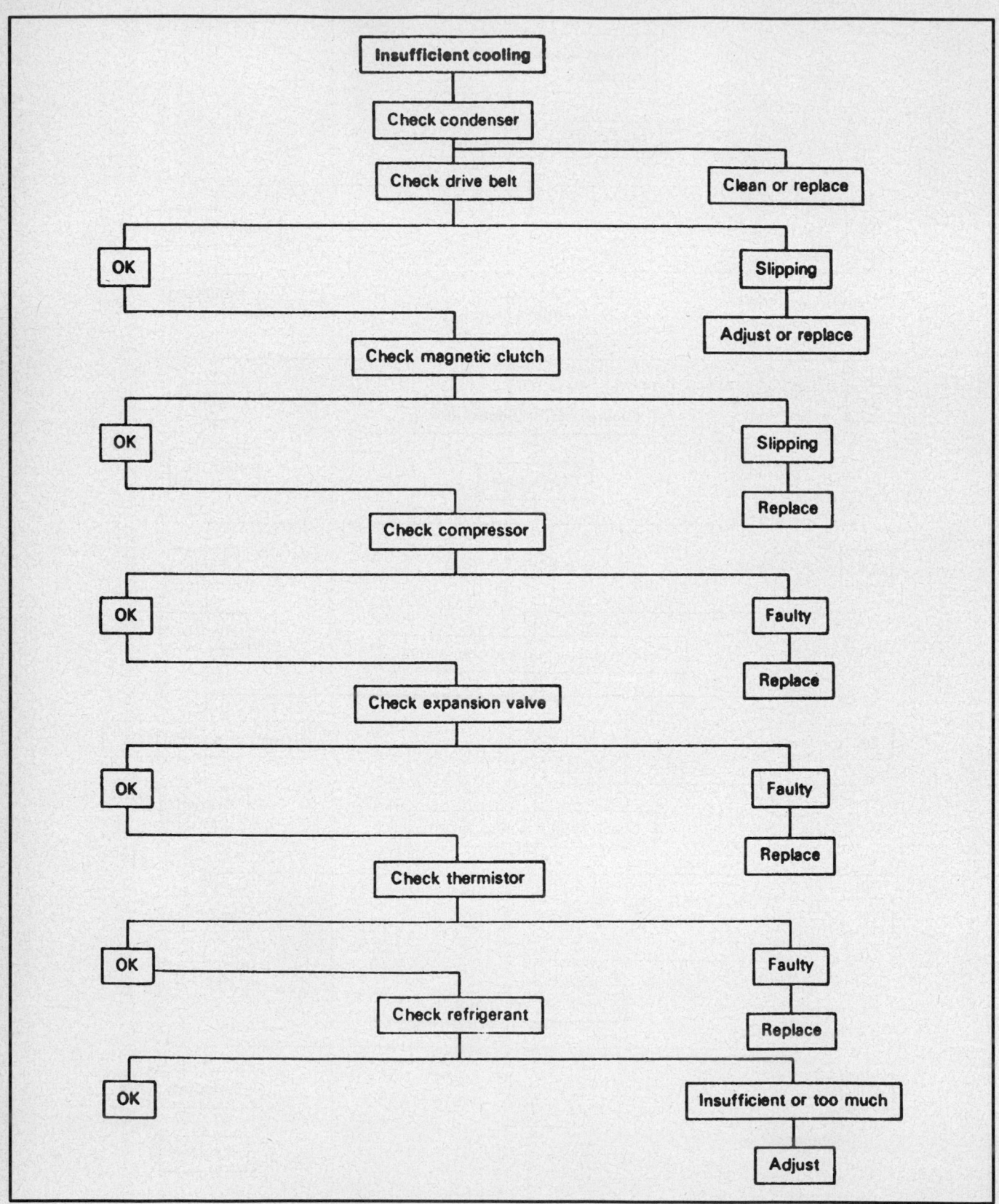

WIRING SCHEMATICS

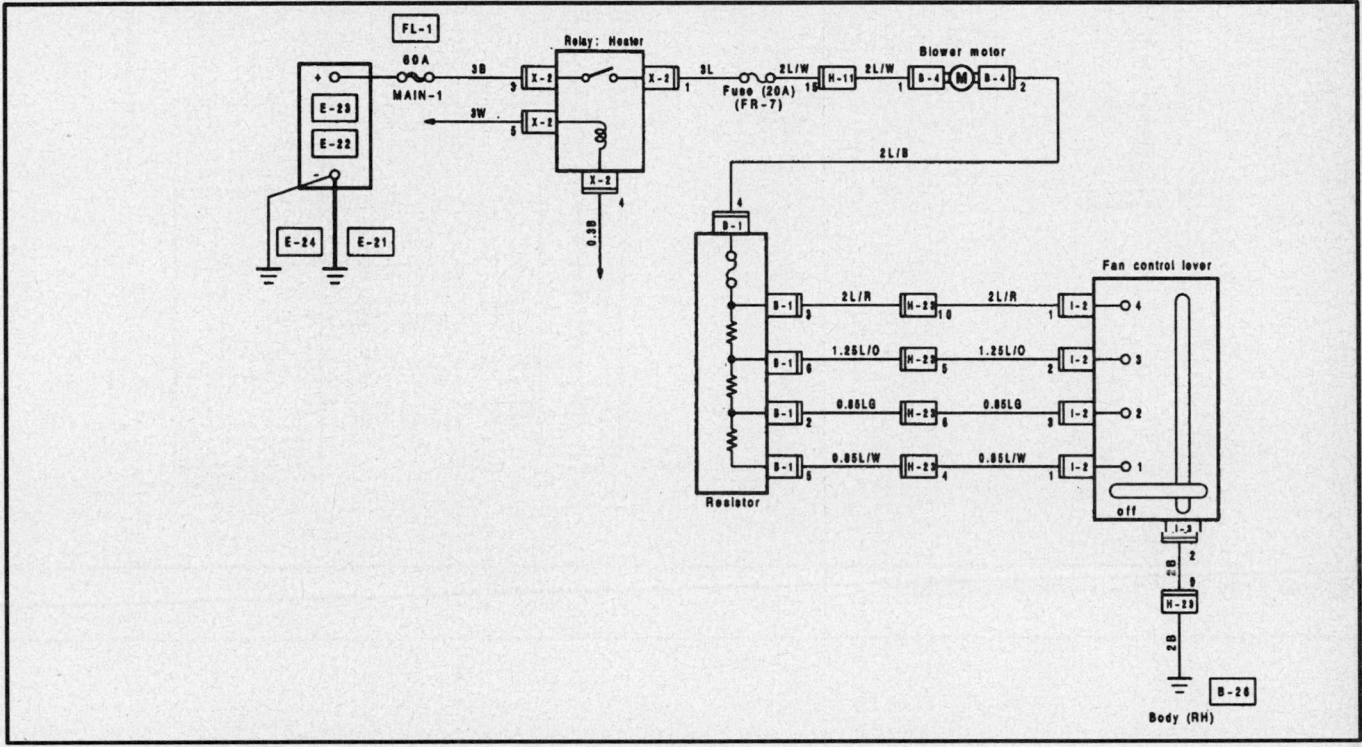

Heater only wiring schematic—Amigo and Pick-Up with 2.3L and 2.6L engines

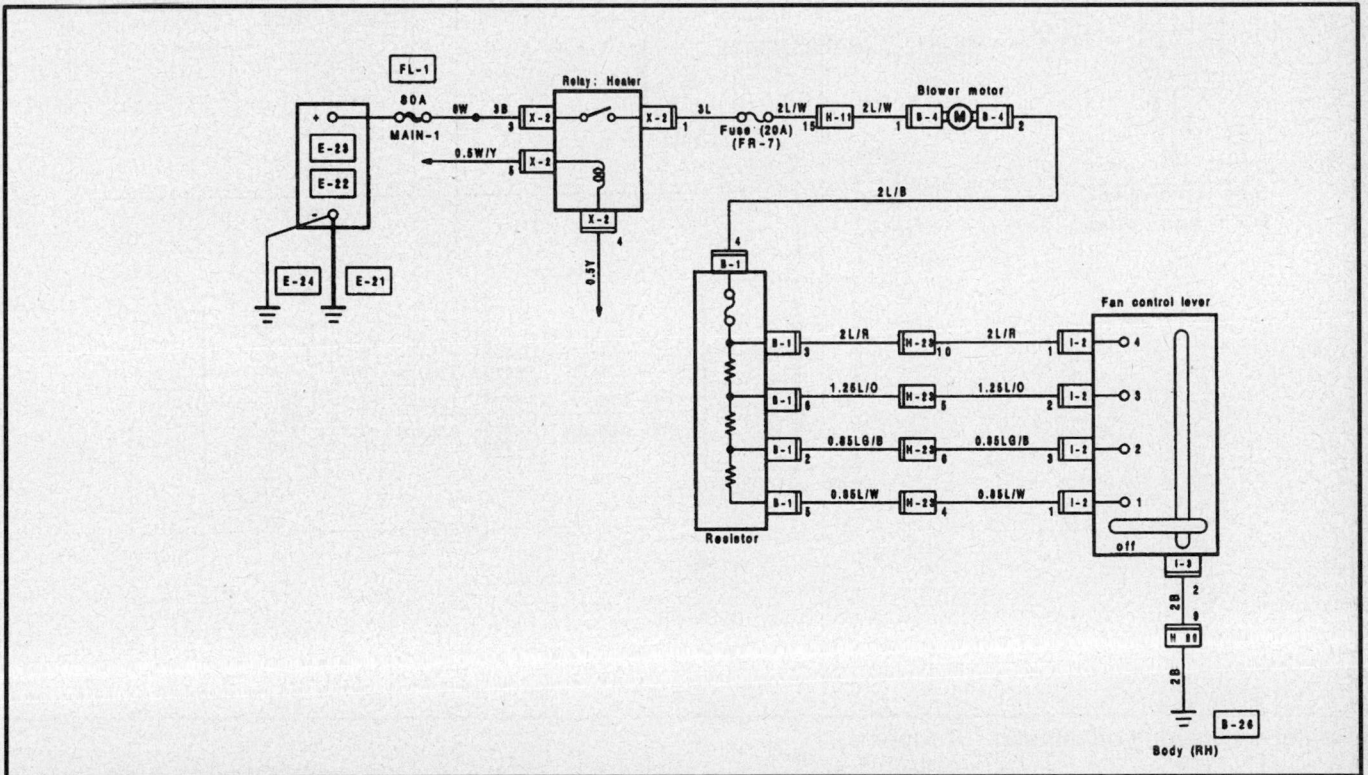

Heater only wiring schematic—Amigo, Pick-Up and Rodeo with 3.1L engines

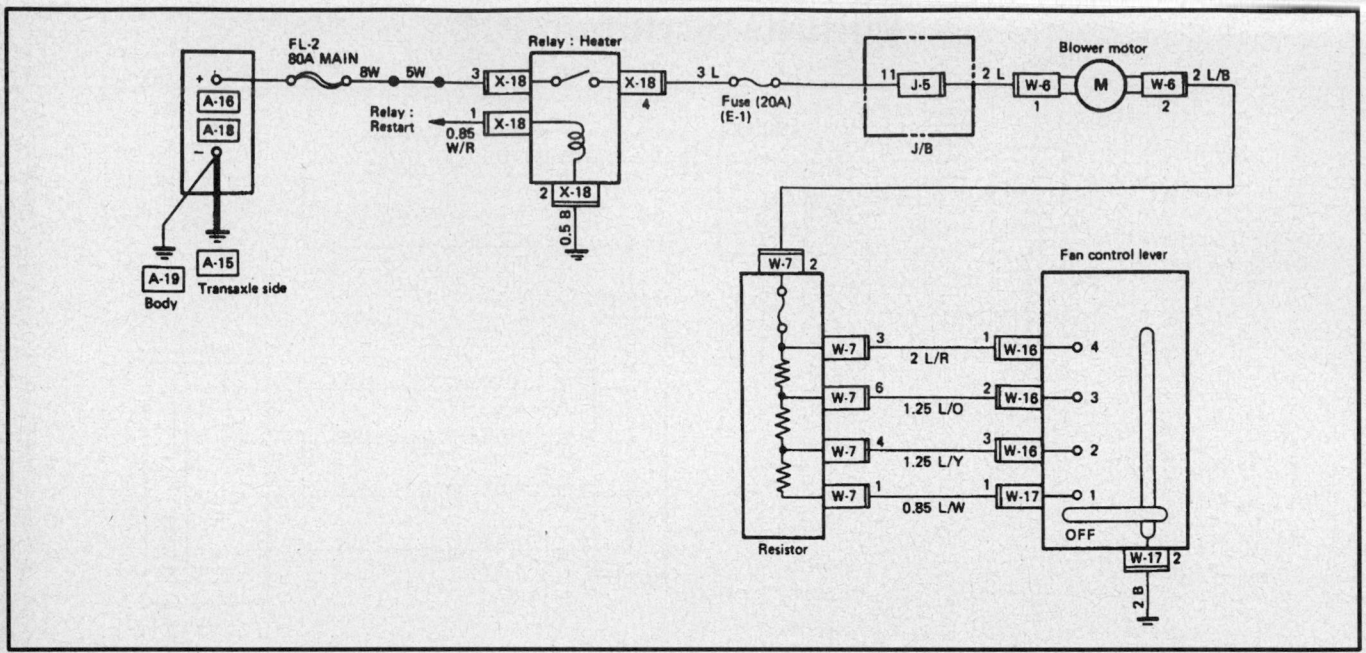

Heater only wiring schematic—Stylus

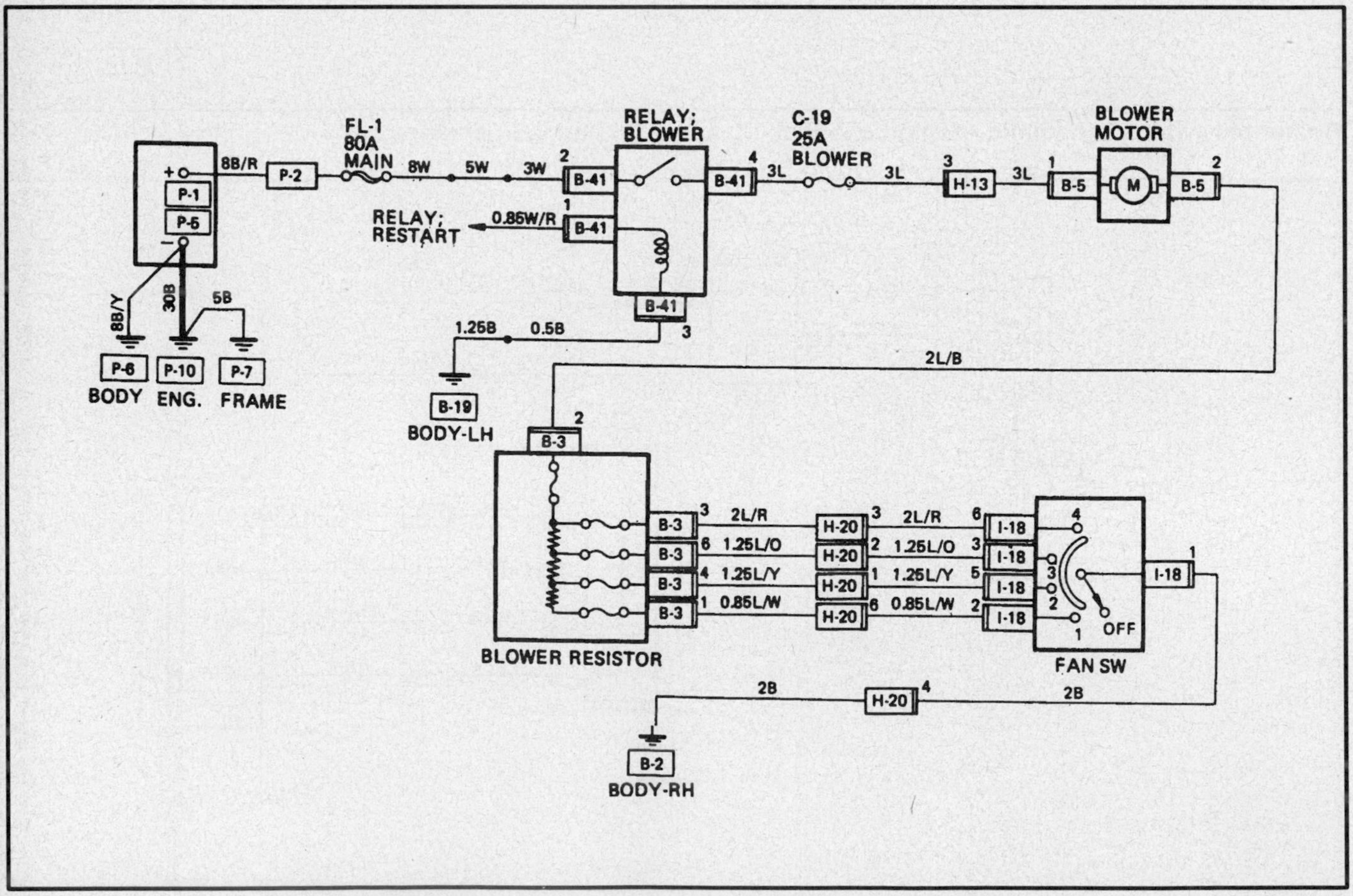

Heater only wiring schematic—Trooper

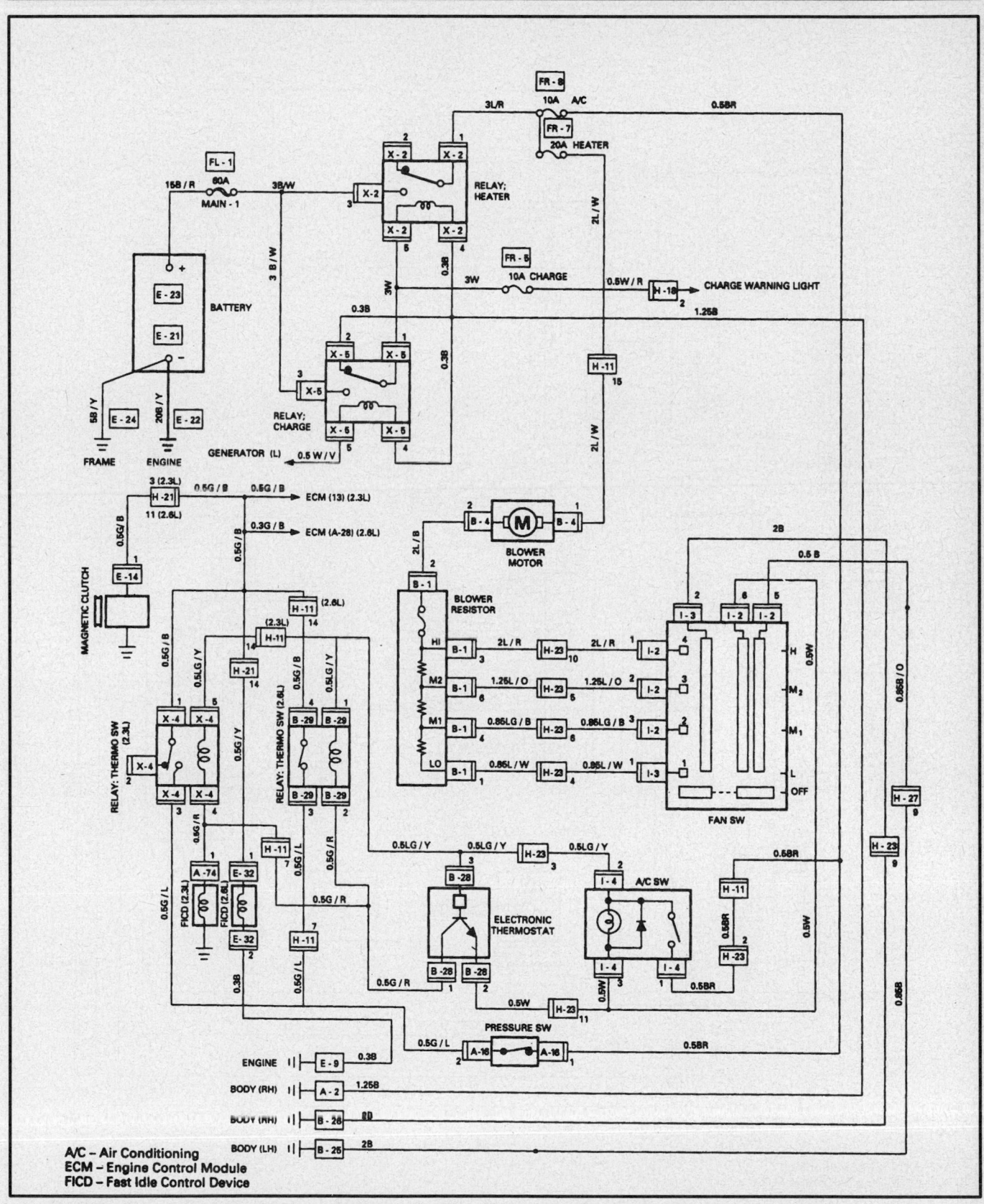

Air conditioning wiring schematic—1993 Amigo, Pick-Up and Rodeo with 2.3L and 2.6L engines

A/C – Air Conditioning
ECM – Engine Control Module
FICD – Fast Idle Control Device

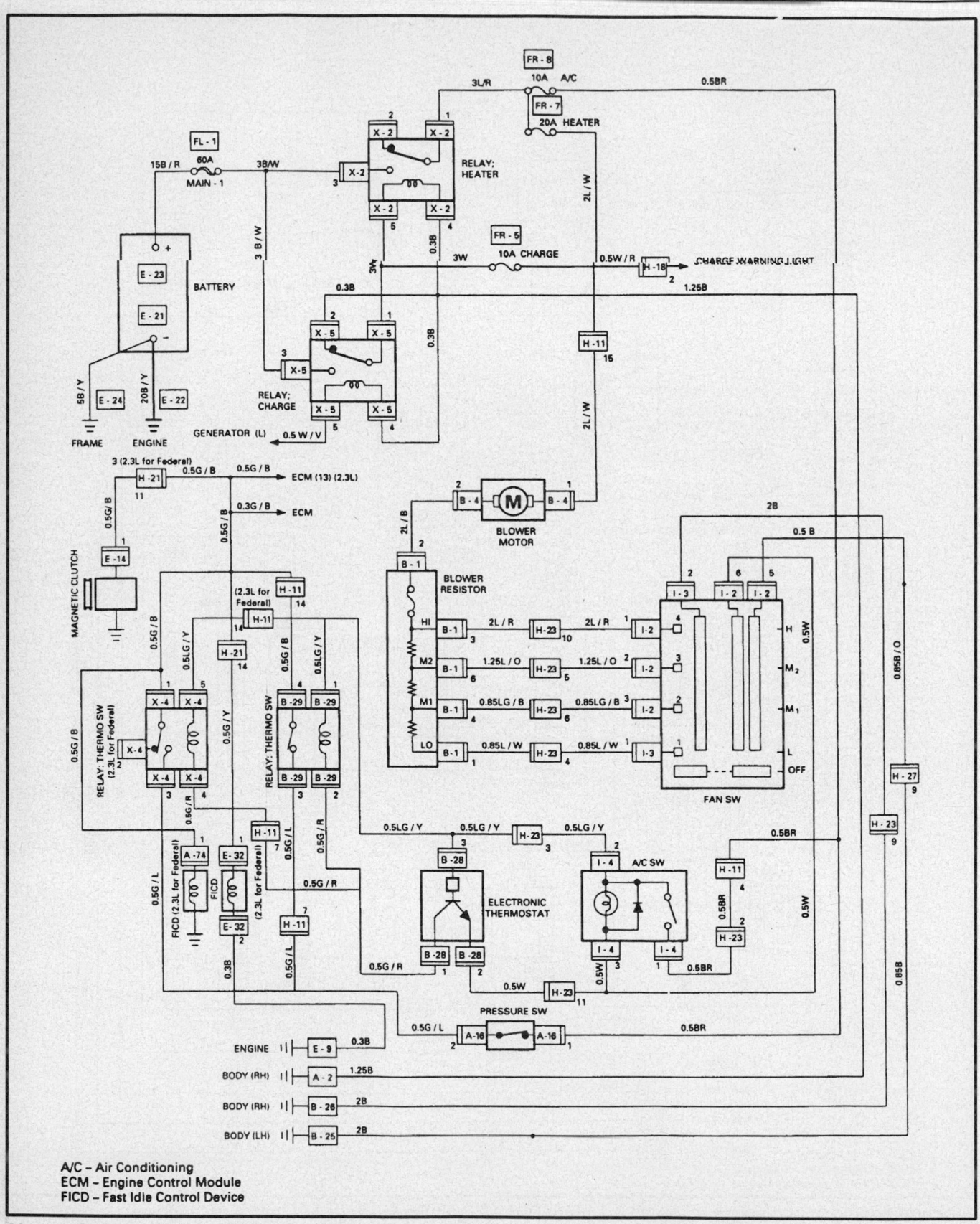

A/C – Air Conditioning
ECM – Engine Control Module
FICD – Fast Idle Control Device

Air conditioning wiring schematic—1994 Amigo and Pick-up with 2.3L and 2.6L engines

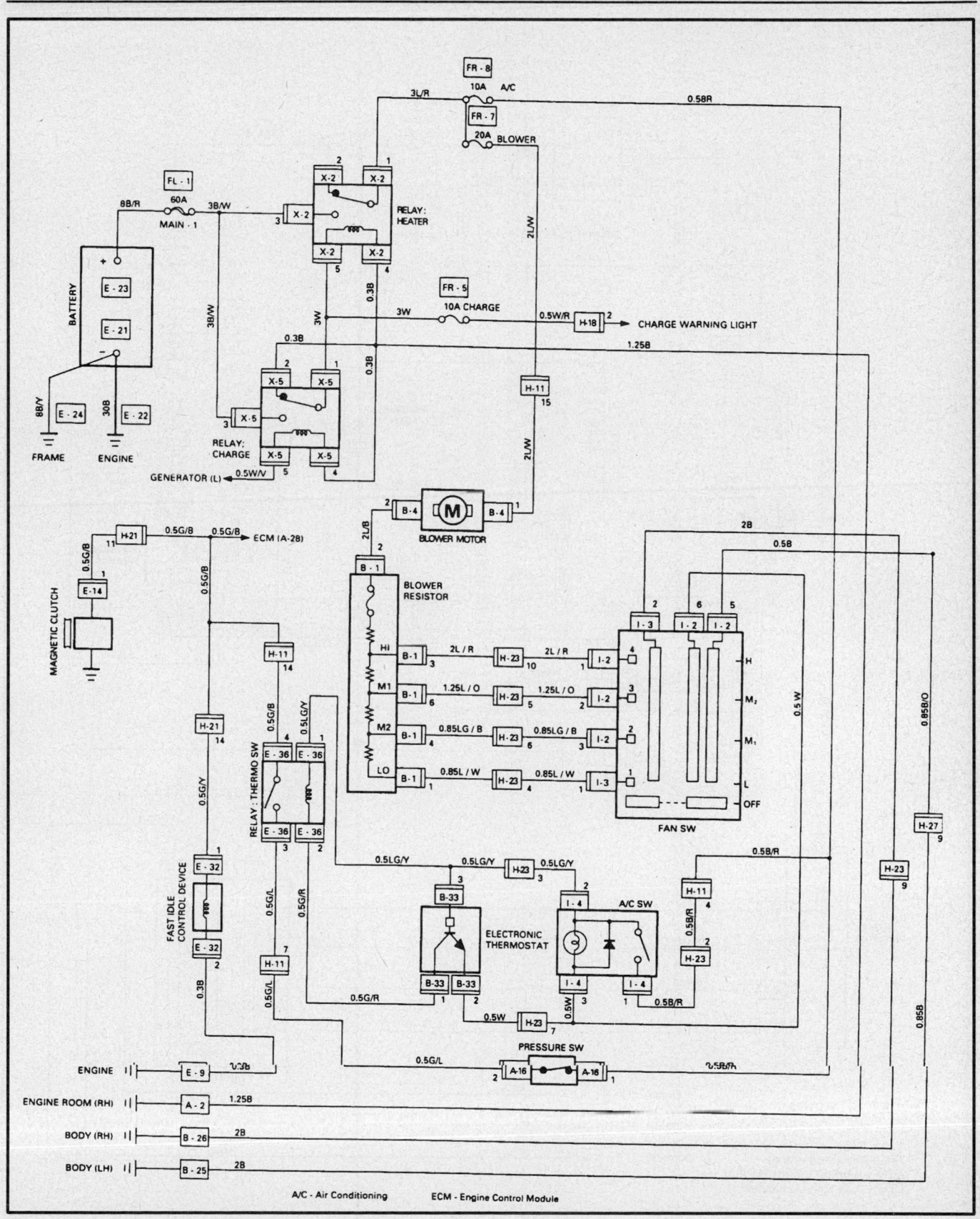

Air conditioning wiring schematic—1994 Rodeo with 2.6L engine

A/C - Air Conditioning   ECM - Engine Control Module

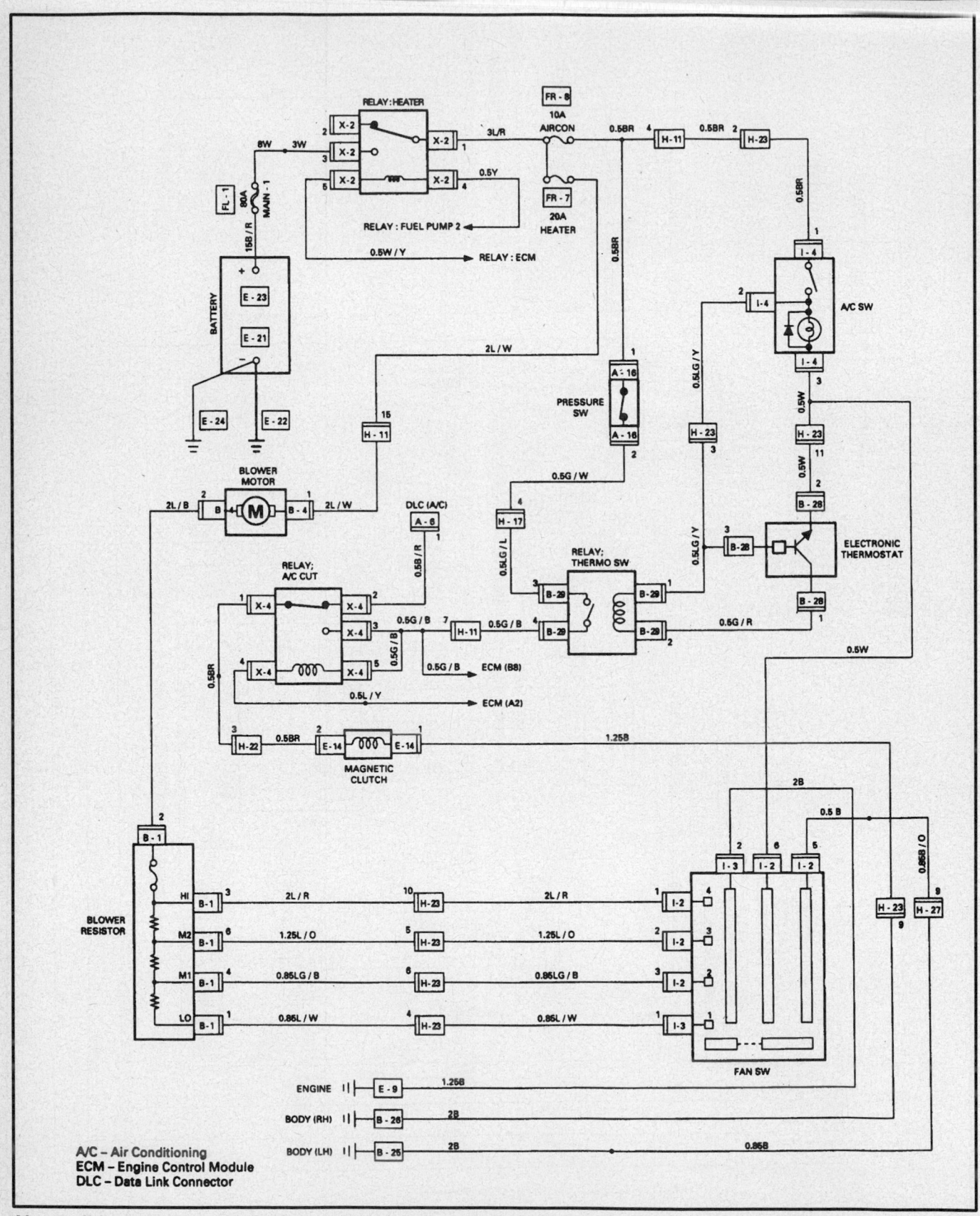

Air conditioning wiring schematic—1993-94 Amigo, Pick-Up and 1993 Rodeo with 3.1L engine

A/C – Air Conditioning
ECM – Engine Control Module
DLC – Data Link Connector

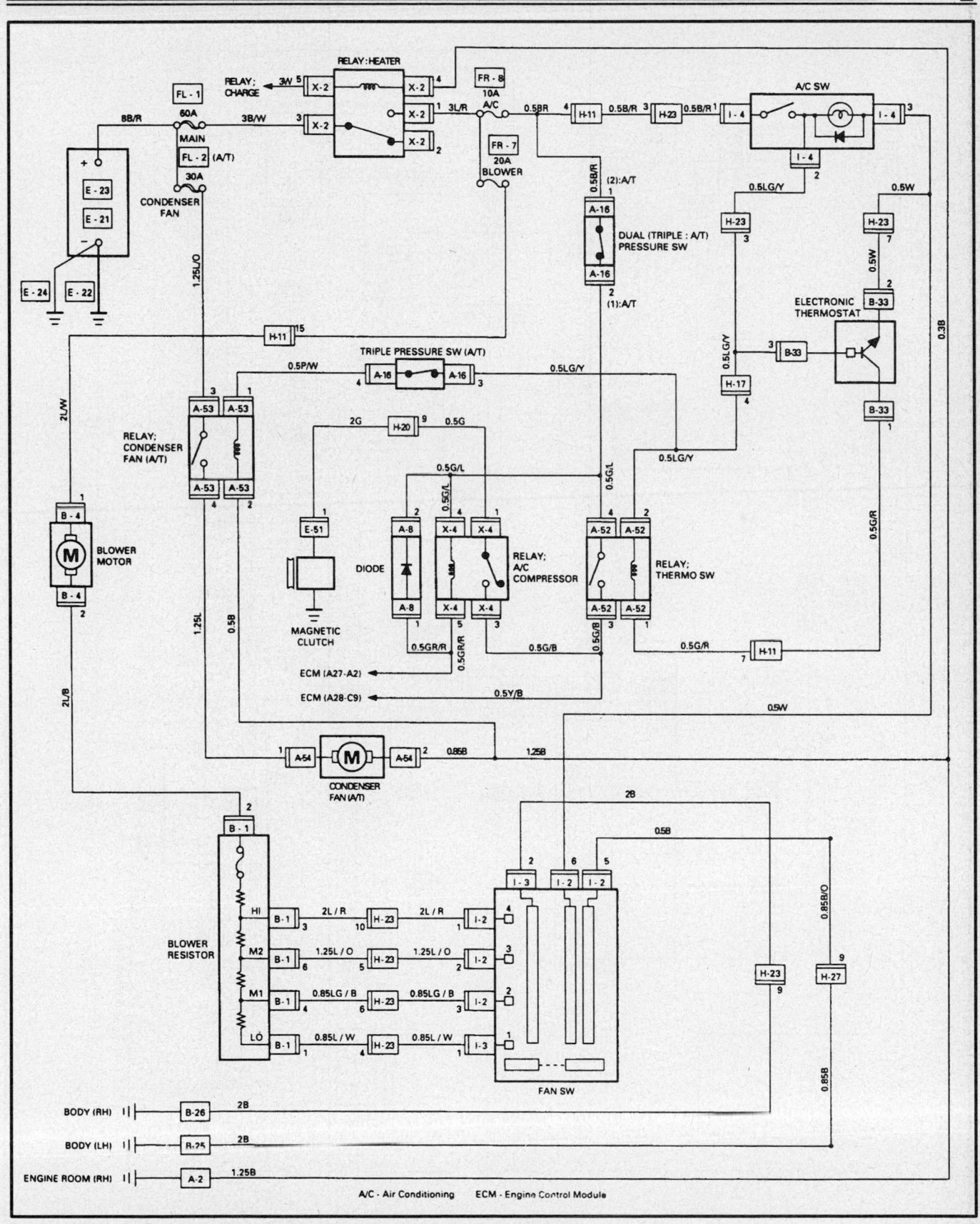

Air conditioning wiring schematic—1994 Rodeo with 3.2L engine

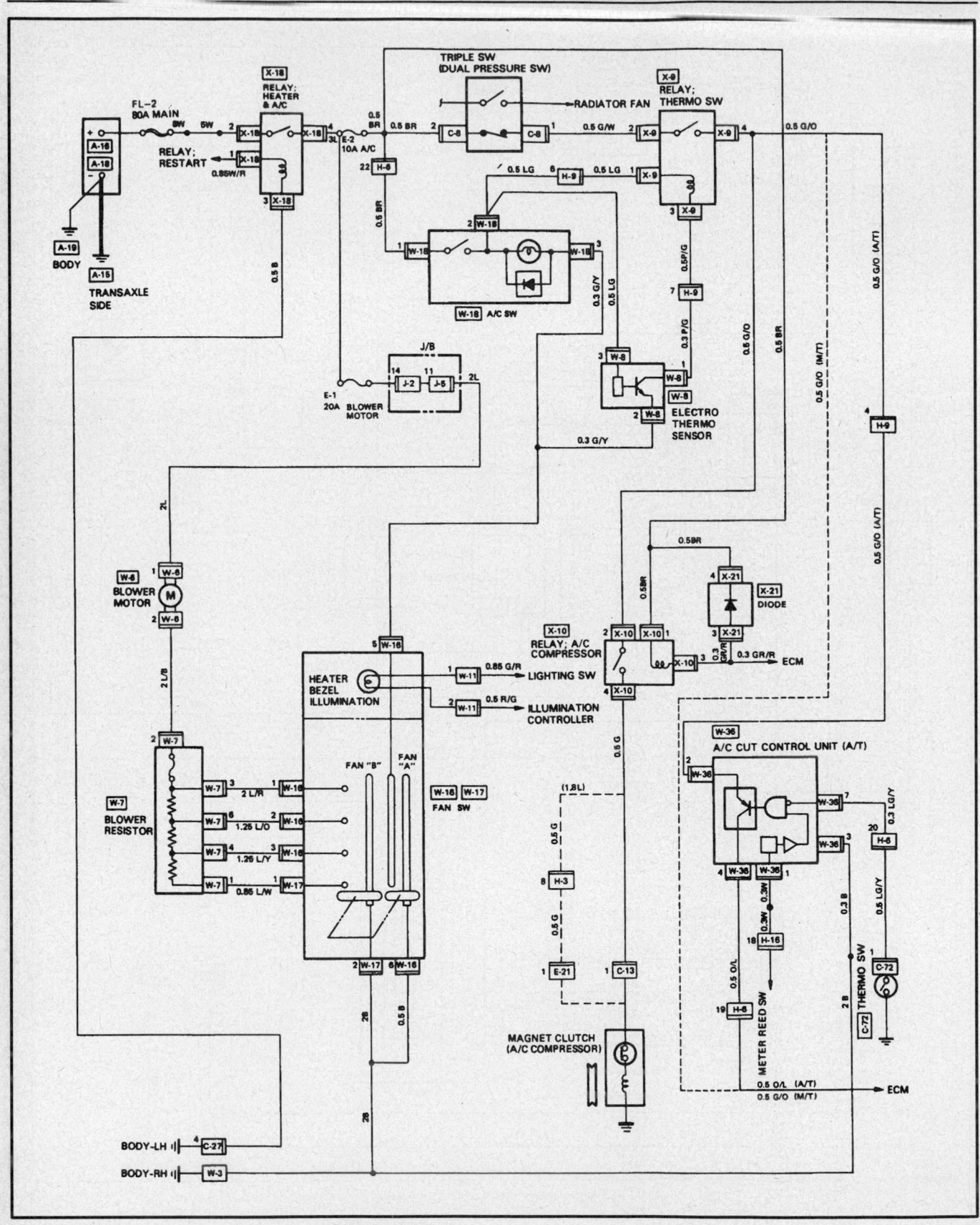

Air conditioning wiring schematic—1993 Stylus

SPECIFICATIONS

SYSTEM DESCRIPTION

SYSTEM COMPONENTS

RELAYS, SENSORS AND SWITCHES

SYSTEM DIAGNOSIS

SPECIFICATIONS

ENGINE IDENTIFICATION

Year	Model	Engine Displacement Liters (cc)	Engine Series (ID/VIN)	Fuel System	No. of Cylinders	Engine Type
1993	XJS	4.0 (3980)	AJ16	EFI	6	DOHC
	XJ6	4.0 (3980)	AJ16	EFI	6	DOHC
1994	XJS	4.0 (3980)	AJ16	EFI	6	DOHC
	XJS	6.0 (5993)	V12	EFI	12	DOHC
	XJ6	4.0 (3980)	AJ16	EFI	6	DOHC
	XJ12	6.0 (5993)	V12	EFI	12	DOHC
1995	XJR	4.0 (3980)	AJ16	EFI	6	DOHC
	XJS	4.0 (3980)	AJ16	EFI	6	DOHC
	XJS	6.0 (5993)	V12	EFI	12	DOHC
	XJ6	4.0 (3980)	AJ16	EFI	6	DOHC
	XJ12	6.0 (5993)	V12	EFI	12	DOHC

DOHC – Dual Overhead Cam
EFI – Electronic Fuel Injection

REFRIGERANT CAPACITIES

Year	Model	Refrigerant (oz.)	Oil (fl. oz.)	Compressor Type
1993	XJS	40	4.6	SANDEN SD–709 7 CYL.
	XJ6	40	4.5	SANDEN SD–7H15 7 CYL.
1994	XJS	40	4.6	SANDEN SD–709 7–CYL.
	XJS	40	4.7	HARRISON (GM) 6 CYL.
	XJ6	40	1.1–1.3	①
	XJ12	40	1.1–1.3	①
1995	XJR	40	N.A.	①
	XJS	40	4.6	SANDEN SD–709 7 CYL.
	XJS	40	4.7	HARRISON (GM) 6–CYL.
	XJ6	40	1.1–1.3	①
	XJ12	40	1.1–1.3	①

① Information Not Available

AIR CONDITIONING BELT TENSION CHART

Year	Model	Engine Liters (cc)	Belt Type	Specifications New	Specifications Used
1993	XJS	4.0 (3980)	SERPENTINE	0.17in. (4.4mm)	N.A.
	XJ6	4.0 (3980)	SERPENTINE	0.22in. (5.6mm)	N.A.
1994	XJS	4.0 (3980)	SERPENTINE	0.17in. (4.4mm)	N.A.
	XJS	6.0 (5993)	SERPENTINE	②	②
	XJ6	4.0 (3980)	SERPENTINE	0.22in. (5.6mm)	N.A.
	XJ12	6.0 (5993)	SERPENTINE	②	②

AIR CONDITIONING BELT TENSION CHART

Year	Model	Engine Liters (cc)	Belt Type	Specifications	
				New	Used
1995	XJR	4.0 (3980)	①	①	①
	XJS	4.0 (3980)	SERPENTINE	0.17in. (4.4mm)	N.A.
	XJS	6.0 (5993)	SERPENTINE	②	②
	XJ6	4.0 (3980)	SERPENTINE	0.22in. (5.6mm)	N.A.
	XJ12	6.0 (5993)	SERPENTINE	②	②

N.A. Not Adjustable
① Information Not Available

② Burroughs Method: New belt is 790N, rotate engine 3 times (minimum) and reset at 790N. In service if tension falls below 270N, reset at 630N.

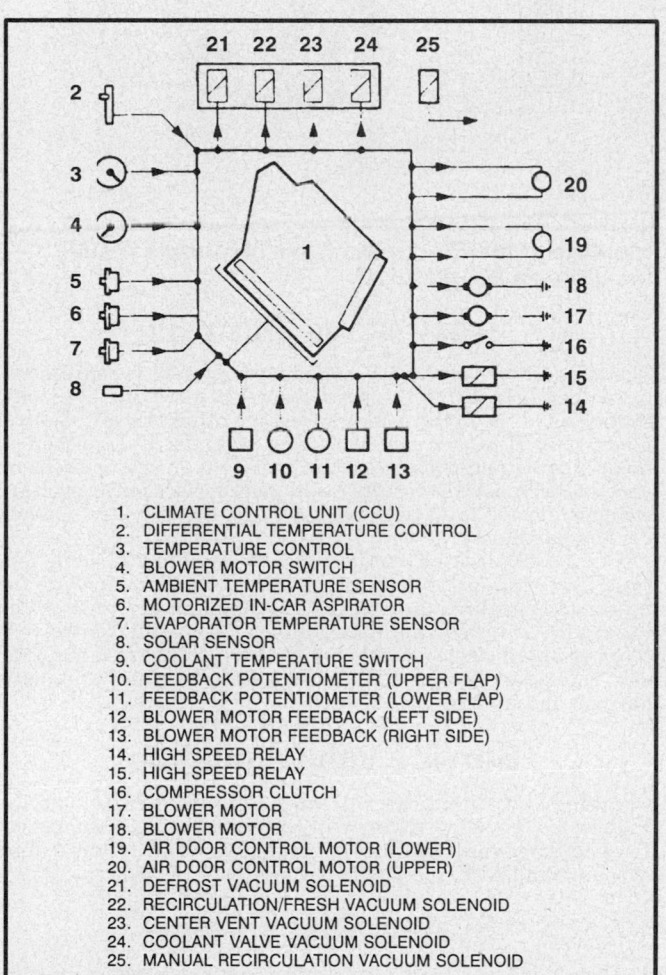

1. CLIMATE CONTROL UNIT (CCU)
2. DIFFERENTIAL TEMPERATURE CONTROL
3. TEMPERATURE CONTROL
4. BLOWER MOTOR SWITCH
5. AMBIENT TEMPERATURE SENSOR
6. MOTORIZED IN-CAR ASPIRATOR
7. EVAPORATOR TEMPERATURE SENSOR
8. SOLAR SENSOR
9. COOLANT TEMPERATURE SWITCH
10. FEEDBACK POTENTIOMETER (UPPER FLAP)
11. FEEDBACK POTENTIOMETER (LOWER FLAP)
12. BLOWER MOTOR FEEDBACK (LEFT SIDE)
13. BLOWER MOTOR FEEDBACK (RIGHT SIDE)
14. HIGH SPEED RELAY
15. HIGH SPEED RELAY
16. COMPRESSOR CLUTCH
17. BLOWER MOTOR
18. BLOWER MOTOR
19. AIR DOOR CONTROL MOTOR (LOWER)
20. AIR DOOR CONTROL MOTOR (UPPER)
21. DEFROST VACUUM SOLENOID
22. RECIRCULATION/FRESH VACUUM SOLENOID
23. CENTER VENT VACUUM SOLENOID
24. COOLANT VALVE VACUUM SOLENOID
25. MANUAL RECIRCULATION VACUUM SOLENOID

Identifying the Climate Control Unit (CCU) Components – 1993 XJ6

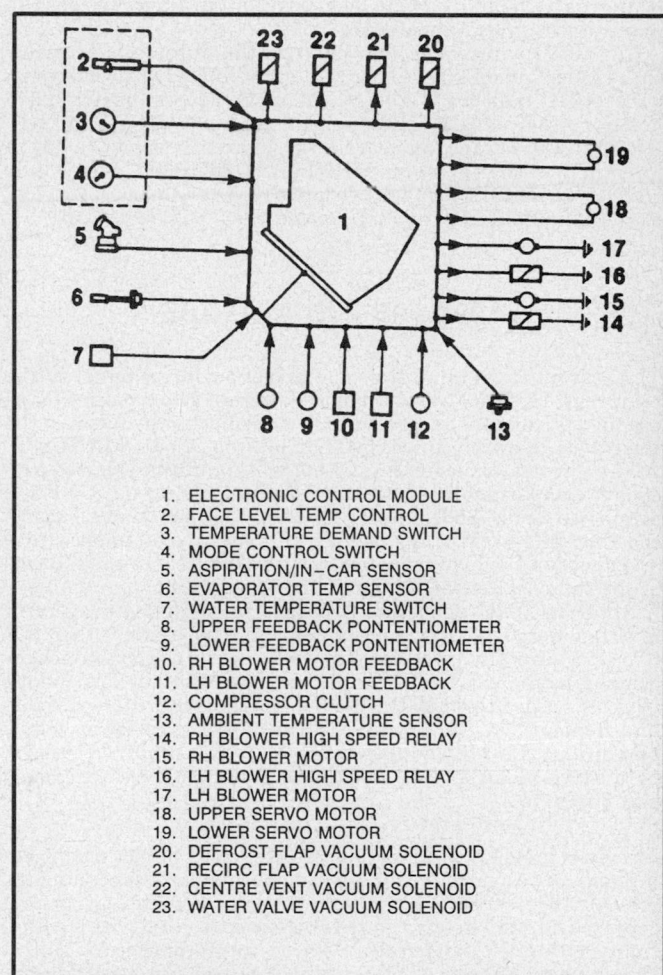

1. ELECTRONIC CONTROL MODULE
2. FACE LEVEL TEMP CONTROL
3. TEMPERATURE DEMAND SWITCH
4. MODE CONTROL SWITCH
5. ASPIRATION/IN-CAR SENSOR
6. EVAPORATOR TEMP SENSOR
7. WATER TEMPERATURE SWITCH
8. UPPER FEEDBACK PONTENTIOMETER
9. LOWER FEEDBACK PONTENTIOMETER
10. RH BLOWER MOTOR FEEDBACK
11. LH BLOWER MOTOR FEEDBACK
12. COMPRESSOR CLUTCH
13. AMBIENT TEMPERATURE SENSOR
14. RH BLOWER HIGH SPEED RELAY
15. RH BLOWER MOTOR
16. LH BLOWER HIGH SPEED RELAY
17. LH BLOWER MOTOR
18. UPPER SERVO MOTOR
19. LOWER SERVO MOTOR
20. DEFROST FLAP VACUUM SOLENOID
21. RECIRC FLAP VACUUM SOLENOID
22. CENTRE VENT VACUUM SOLENOID
23. WATER VALVE VACUUM SOLENOID

Identifying the Climate Control Unit (CCU) components – 1994–95 XJ6

SYSTEM DESCRIPTION

General Information

1993 XJS AND XJ6

AUTOMATIC TEMPERATURE CONTROL SYSTEM

The automatic temperature control system uses in–car temperature sensors. The sensors compare vehicle interior temperature to temperature set on the control panel. These comparisons provide electrical signals to the Climate Control Unit (CCU). The CCU sends an electrical signal to the servomotor and blower relays mounted on the heater box. This signal changes the heater box air door position and blower speed to maintain interior temperature.

The temperature selection knob on the automatic temperature control panel allows selection of the temperature between 65°F (18°C) and 85°F (29°C). The mode control switch has 5 positions: **OFF**, **LOW**, **MEDIUM** (normal position), **HIGH** and **DEFROST**. The blower fan operates at a variable speed on any of the other settings except in **HIGH** and **DEFROST** positions. A slide lever controls air temperature delivered through face level vents without affecting automatic temperature setting.

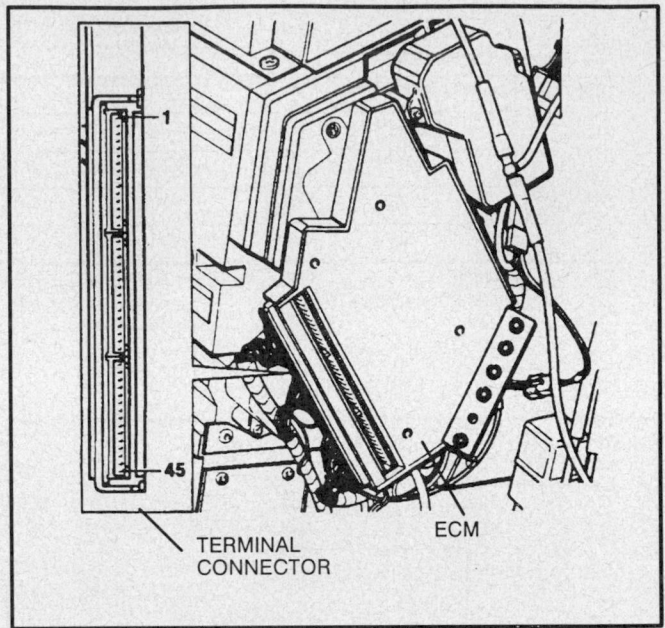

Identifying the Electronic Control Module (ECM) location—XJ6 and XJ12

1994–95 XJR AND XJS

The system is operated from the driver's control panel by the temperature, face level and mode switches. The 2 main operating modes, manual and automatic, are selected by pushing the temperature switch in (**AUTO**) or pulling it out (**MANUAL**). In the automatic mode, the system will maintain selected passenger compartment temperature over a wide range of climatic conditions from 66.2–84.4°F (19–29°C). In the manual mode, the control system is overridden and the in–car temperature and speed of the blower motors respond directly to the settings of the temperature and mode control switches.

Air from 2 blower motors is passed through the evaporator matrix where it is dried and cooled. The cooled air is then distributed directly into the air vents within the passenger compartment, or is heated or blended with hot air. The quantity of air passed through the heater matrix is infinitely variable and depends on the position of the upper and lower rotary blend flaps. Each blend flap is driven to the required position by a servo motor and its position is monitored by a feedback potentiometer.

The Electronic Control Module (ECM) drives the air conditioning unit in response to signals from the driver's control panel, temperature sensors and feedback potentiometers. A signal representing the in–car temperature is compared with a signal representing the temperature set on the temperature control switch. Any difference between the 2 causes the air conditioning unit to direct a flow of air into the car that is hot, cold or a blend of both.

Manual Mode: In this mode the system is overridden and the temperature demand switch controls the position of the blend flaps and the speed of the blower motors. Although the blower motors are disabled by signal from the water temperature switch when engine coolant temperature is below 86°F (30°C).

Automatic Mode: In the automatic mode, manually selected temperature is replaced by the error drive signal, that is the difference between the selected temperature and the in–car temperature offset by the ambient temperature.

1994–95 XJ6 AND XJ12

The temperature of the passenger compartment is continuously compared with the temperature selected on the electronic control head. A digital microprocessor within the A/C Control Module (A/CCM) receives the data signals. Comparison of these signals and those from the system temperature sensors and feedback devices results in the appropriate output voltage changes needed to vary the blend of air flow into the passenger compartment.

The A/CCM located on the right side of the A/C unit, controls the functions of the system. These functions include the in–car temperature control, the in–car humidity control and the air flow/volume and distribution. The climate control system peripherals communicate with the A/CCM via 3 main device categories comprising of the manual inputs, automatic outputs and inputs.

Service Valve Location

Charging valve locations will vary, but most of the time the high or low pressure fitting will be located at the compressor, receiver/drier or along the refrigerant lines. Always discharge, evacuate and recharge at the low side service fitting.

System Discharging

R–12 refrigerant is a chloroflourocarbon which, when mishandled, can contribute to the depletion of the ozone layer in the upper atmosphere. Ozone filters out harmful radiation from the sun. In order to protect the ozone layer, an approved R–12 Recovery/Recycling machine that meets SAE standard J1991 should be employed when discharging the system. Follow the operating instructions provided with the approved equipment exactly to properly discharge the system.

System Evacuating

If the air conditioning system has been opened to the atmosphere, it should be air and moisture free before being recharged with refrigerant. Moisture and air mixed with refrigerant will raise the compressor head pressure, possibly damage the system's components and will reduce the performance of the system. Moisture will boil at normal room temperature when exposed to a vacuum, the moisture then becomes a vapor and will be easily removed by the vacuum pump.

To evacuate, or rid the system of air and moisture:

1. Leak test the system and repair any leaks found.

2. Connect an approved charging station, Recovery/Recycling machine or manifold gauge set and vacuum pump to the discharge and suction ports. The red hose is normally connected to the discharge (high pressure) line, and the blue hose is connected to the suction (low pressure) line.

3. Open the discharge and suction ports and start the vacuum pump. If the pump is not able to pull at least 26 in. Hg vacuum, there is a leak that must be repaired before evacuation can occur.

4. Once the system has reached at least 26 in. Hg vacuum, allow the system to evacuate for at least 10 minutes. The longer the system is evacuated, the more contaminants will be removed.

5. Close all valves and turn the pump OFF. If the system loses more than 2 in. Hg vacuum after 15 minutes, there is a leak that should be repaired.

System Charging

1. Connect an approved charging station, Recovery/Recycling machine or manifold gauge set to the discharge and suction ports. The red hose is normally connected to the discharge (high pressure) line, and the blue hose is connected to the suction (low pressure) line.

2. Follow the instructions provided with the equipment and charge the system with the specified amount of refrigerant.

3. Perform a leak test.

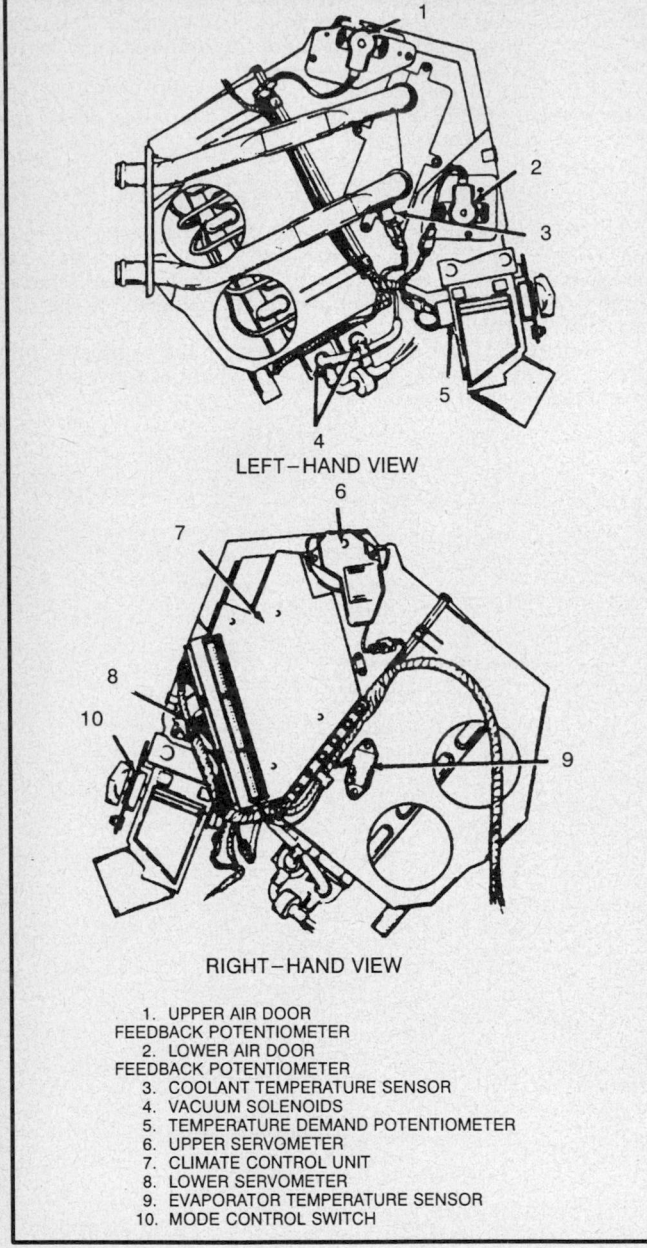

Automatic A/C system components—Typical, 1993 XJS shown

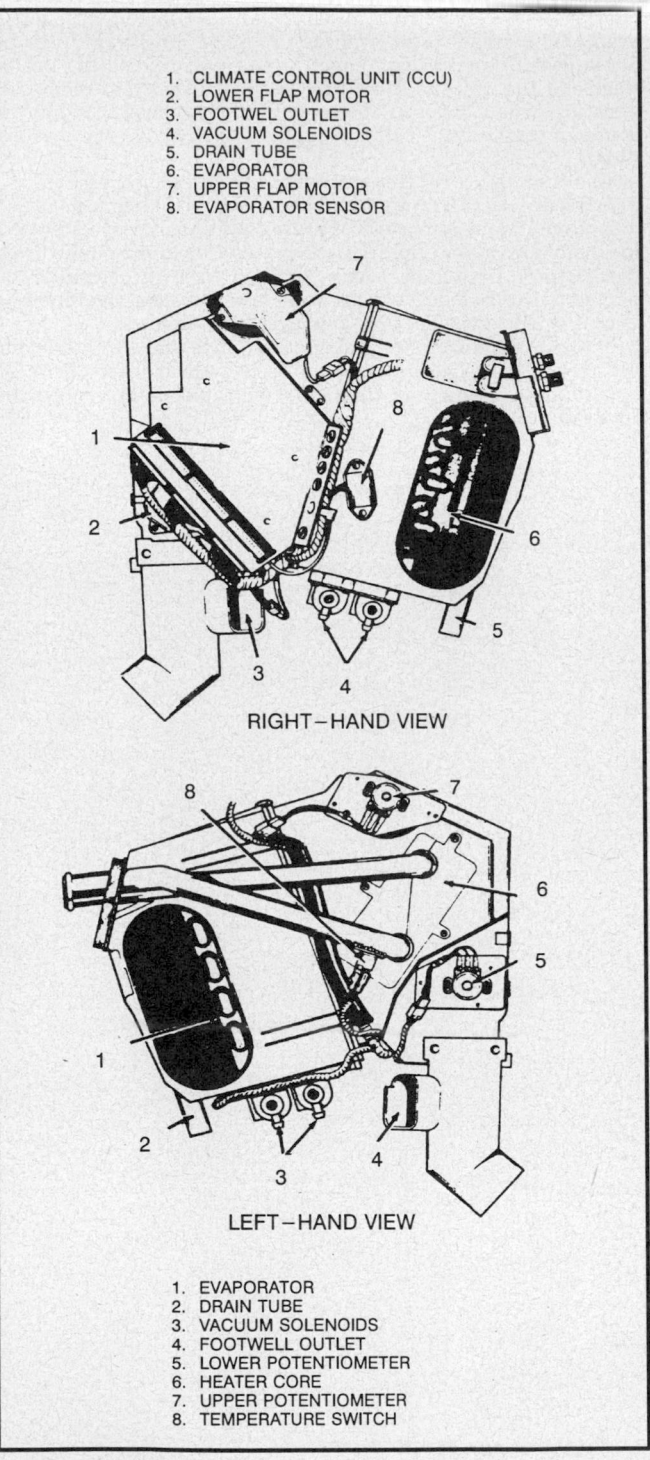

1. CLIMATE CONTROL UNIT (CCU)
2. LOWER FLAP MOTOR
3. FOOTWEL OUTLET
4. VACUUM SOLENOIDS
5. DRAIN TUBE
6. EVAPORATOR
7. UPPER FLAP MOTOR
8. EVAPORATOR SENSOR

RIGHT—HAND VIEW

LEFT—HAND VIEW

1. EVAPORATOR
2. DRAIN TUBE
3. VACUUM SOLENOIDS
4. FOOTWELL OUTLET
5. LOWER POTENTIOMETER
6. HEATER CORE
7. UPPER POTENTIOMETER
8. TEMPERATURE SWITCH

Automatic A/C system components—Typical, 1993 XJ6 shown

LEFT—HAND VIEW

RIGHT—HAND VIEW

1. UPPER AIR DOOR
   FEEDBACK POTENTIOMETER
2. LOWER AIR DOOR
   FEEDBACK POTENTIOMETER
3. COOLANT TEMPERATURE SENSOR
4. VACUUM SOLENOIDS
5. TEMPERATURE DEMAND POTENTIOMETER
6. UPPER SERVOMETER
7. CLIMATE CONTROL UNIT
8. LOWER SERVOMETER
9. EVAPORATOR TEMPERATURE SENSOR
10. MODE CONTROL SWITCH

SYSTEM COMPONENTS

CAUTION

Some vehicles are equipped with the Supplemental Inflatable Restraint or air bag system. The air bag system must be disabled by disconnect the battery negative terminal and the air bag module connector, located near the steering wheel, before performing service on or around the air bag, instrument panel components, wiring and sensors. Failure to follow safety and disabling procedures could result in accidental air bag deployment, possible personal injury and unnecessary air bag system repairs.

Radiator

REMOVAL AND INSTALLATION

4.0L Engine

1. Disconnect the negative battery terminal.
2. Properly drain and recover the coolant.
3. Remove the radiator hoses and coolant reserve tank hose from the radiator.
4. Disconnect the bleed hose pipe retaining nuts and displace the pipe from the top rail.
5. Release the ratchet strap and disconnect the thermostatic switch multi–plug connector.
6. Remove the receiver/drier unit mounting bracket to top rail securing nuts. Displace the unit from the top rail.
7. Disconnect and remove the top rail to body outer securing bolts, reposition the ground straps.
8. Disconnect and remove the radiator–to–top rail securing nuts. Remove the rubber mounting bushings.
9. Disconnect and remove the top rail from the vehicle.
10. On automatic transmission vehicles, place a suitable drain container in position beneath the transmission oil cooler pipes.
11. Disconnect the oil cooler pipe union nuts and disconnect the pipes from the radiator, and drain the oil.
12. Discard sealing rings from the pipes and plug openings.
13. Remove the radiator from its lower mounting and carefully lift and remove from vehicle.
To install:
14. Lower the radiator into position. Position and reattach the radiator as removed.
15. Connect the automatic transmission oil cooler pipes.
16. Connect the radiator hoses and coolant reserve tank hose.
17. Fill the system with coolant.
18. Connect the negative battery, run the vehicle until the thermostat opens, fill the radiator completely and check the automatic transmission fluid level.
19. Once the vehicle has cooled, recheck the coolant level.

6.0L Engine

1. Disconnect the negative battery terminal.
2. Properly drain and recover the coolant.
3. Remove the radiator hoses and coolant reserve tank hose from the radiator.
4. Disconnect and remove the automatic transmission cooling hoses.
5. From beneath the vehicle, disconnect and remove the fan cowl lower securing nuts.
6. From above the vehicle, disconnect the relay connector from the top panel mounting bracket.
7. Disconnect and remove the fan cowl to the radiator top panel securing nuts. Disconnect the ground cables.
8. Disconnect and remove the receiver/drier from the top panel.
9. Disconnect and detach the condenser to the top panel securing nuts.

10. Disconnect and remove the top panel–to–body securing bolts.
11. Cut the harness–to–panel ratchet straps, remove the panel and carefully lay on top of the engine.
12. Position suitable container to catch possible residue, and remove the transmission cooler pipes from the right side of the radiator.
13. Disconnect the radiator from the lower mountings and remove from the vehicle.
To install:
14. Lower the radiator into position and reattach as removed.
15. Connect the automatic transmission cooler lines.
16. Connect the radiator hoses and coolant reserve tank hose.
17. Fill the system with coolant.
18. Connect the negative battery cable, run the vehicle until the thermostat opens, fill the radiator completely and check the automatic transmission fluid level.
19. Once the vehicle has cooled, recheck the coolant level.

Cooling Fan

TESTING

NOTE: This test also checks the function of the air conditioning system and cooling fan override relay.

1. Ensure that the right side air conditioning switch is set to **OFF**.
2. Disconnect the connectors from the thermostatic switch at the front of the water pump.
3. Switch **ON** the ignition.
4. Reconnect the thermostatic switch connector. DO NOT rotate the engine.
5. SHORT together the sockets in the connectors. The relay should operate, and fan should start.
6. Remove the SHORT, switch **OFF** the ignition and reconnect the thermostatic switch connector.
7. Switch **ON** the ignition. DO NOT rotate the engine.
8. Set the left side air conditioning control to 65°F (18°C).
9. Set right side control to **MEDIUM**. The air conditioning relay should operate, the fan should start and the compressor clutch should engage.
10. Switch **OFF** the ignition and set the right side air conditioning system control to **OFF**.

REMOVAL AND INSTALLATION

1. Disconnect the negative battery terminal.
2. Remove the left side air cleaner cover and element.
3. Through the blades of the fan, access the fan mounting frame nuts.
4. Remove the nuts, washers and spacers securing the motor mounting frame.
5. Remove the fan and motor assembly.
6. Installation is the reverse of the removal procedure.

Condenser

REMOVAL AND INSTALLATION

1. Disconnect the negative battery terminal.
2. Properly discharge the A/C system using the approved refrigerant recovery/recycling equipment.
3. Disconnect the A/C lines from the receiver/drier and condenser.
4. Remove and discard the O-rings.
5. Plug condenser and line openings.
6. Move headlight wiring harness and hood rubber buffer to one side.

7. Remove the top brace and the engine fan shroud bolts.

8. Remove the fan shroud.

9. Remove the condenser bolts and A/C line clips.

10. Move the receiver/drier and the mounting bracket clear of the radiator.

11. Carefully push the radiator toward the engine, and lift the condenser from the brackets.

12. Installation is the reverse of the removal procedures. Evacuate and recharge the A/C system.

Compressor

REMOVAL AND INSTALLATION

1. Disconnect the negative battery terminal.

2. Discharge the A/C system using approved refrigerant recovery/recycling equipment.

3. Remove the compressor thermal fuse.

4. Remove the link air-to-compressor bolts.

5. Loosen the pivot bolt, and remove the belt.

6. Remove the bolts securing the freon cooler and clamp the plate to the compressor.

7. Remove the bolt securing the compressor discharge and the suction lines.

8. Disconnect the discharge and suction lines.

9. Plug the compressor and the line openings.

10. Remove the remaining compressor bolts.

11. Remove the compressor.

12. Installation is the reverse of the removal procedure. Ensure NEW O-rings are in place when installing the discharge and suction lines. Ensure proper refrigerant oil level. Evacuate and recharge A/C system.

Receiver/Drier

REMOVAL AND INSTALLATION

1. Disconnect the negative battery terminal.

2. Discharge the A/C system using approved refrigerant recovery/recycling equipment.

3. Disconnect the refrigerant lines from the receiver/drier, and plug the openings.

4. Remove the receiver/drier bolts.

5. Remove the receiver/drier.

6. Installation is the reverse of the removal procedure. Ensure NEW O-rings are in place when installing the discharge and suction lines. Ensure proper refrigerant oil level. Evacuate and recharge the A/C system.

Evaporator

REMOVAL AND INSTALLATION

XJR and XJS

1. Disconnect the negative battery terminal.

2. Discharge the A/C system using approved refrigerant recovery/recycling equipment.

3. Drain the engine coolant system.

4. Remove fascia board:

- Loosen steering wheel adjuster and pull steering wheel to its full extent.
- Remove the setting column lower shroud and plate.
- Remove the steering column upper shroud.
- Remove the steering column pinch bolt and remove the steering wheel.
- Remove the fascia side trims. and driver's dash liner.
- the light rheostat wires, trip cable (if equipped), and remove the dash liner.

- Remove the light switch know.
- Remove the trim panel around the instrument cluster, ignition switch and light switch.
- Disconnect the fiber optics harness and the speedometer cable (if equipped).
- Disconnect the harness connectors to the instrument panel.
- Remove the instrument panel.
- Remove the passenger side dash liner and the glove box.

5. Remove the A/C unit assembly.

6. Remove the heater pip guide plate.

7. Remove the evaporator sensor from the evaporator.

8. Remove the solenoid mounting plate.

9. Remove the electrical connectors and vacuum hoses as needed.

10. Separate the A/C unit casing and remove the evaporator from the unit.

11. Remove the expansion valve guide plate from the evaporator.

12. Installation is the reverse of the removal procedure. Replace the receiver/drier when replacing the evaporator. Check for proper refrigerant oil level. Evacuate and recharge the A/C system.

XJ6 and XJ12

1. Discharge the A/C system using approved refrigerant recovery/recycling equipment.

2. Drain the engine coolant system.

3. Remove the right and left dash liners.

4. Remove the left and right dash end panels.

5. Remove the steering wheel.

6. Remove the instrument module and control panel.

7. Remove the glove box door.

8. Remove the center dash panel and vent grille.

9. Remove the center console trim, ashtray, radio, rear vent outlet and glove box.

10. Remove the center console.

11. Disconnect the battery terminals and remove the battery.

12. Disconnect the evaporator line from the expansion valve.

13. Remove and discard O-rings. Plug the refrigerant line openings.

14. Disconnect heater hoses at the firewall.

15. Remove the sponge collars from the heater pipes, and retain for installation.

16. From the engine compartment side, remove the heater assembly-to-firewall nuts.

17. Loosen the Climate Control Unit (CCU) upper screw.

18. Remove the lower screw and remove the unit.

19. Remove the defrost flexible ducting. Remove the left and right blower motor flexible ducting.

20. Disconnect the electrical connections at the main wiring harness, left and right blower motors and the in-car sensor.

21. Note the position of the vacuum hoses, and disconnect from the vacuum solenoids and vacuum actuators.

22. Remove the heater unit-to-dash bolts.

23. Carefully move the assembly, and disconnect the evaporator drain tubes from the floor pan tunnel.

24. Carefully remove the assembly from the vehicle.

25. Installation is the reverse of the removal procedure. Replace the receiver/drier when replacing the evaporator. Install NEW O-rings. Ensure proper refrigerant oil level, and recharge the A/C system.

Expansion valve

REMOVAL AND INSTALLATION

1. Disconnect the negative battery terminal.

2. Discharge the A/C system using approved refrigerant recovery/recycling equipment.

3. Loosen the capillary tube clamp screws.

4. Disconnect the A/C hoses at the expansion valve, and plug the openings.

5. Support the expansion valve to avoid pressure on the evaporator.

6. Remove the expansion valve by carefully unscrewing the union nut and pulling the capillary tube from the clamps.

7. Installation is the reverse of the removal procedure. Ensure the proper refrigerant oil lever, and recharge the A/C system.

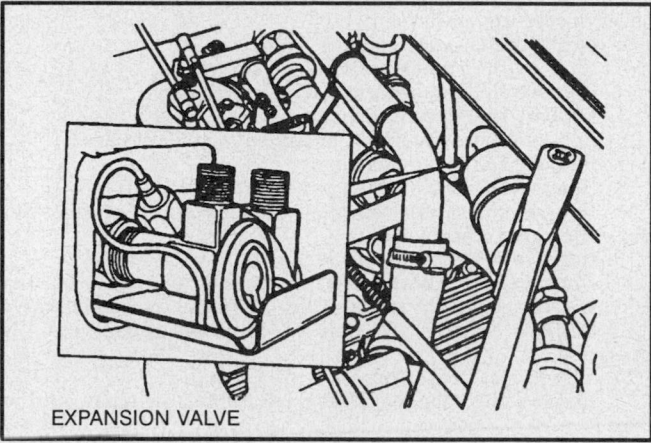

EXPANSION VALVE

Locating the expansion valve—XJS

Blower Motor

REMOVAL AND INSTALLATION

XJR and XJS

LEFT SIDE

1. Disconnect the negative battery terminal.

2. Remove the left side footwell trim pan, dash liner and console side cover.

3. Remove bulb failure unit from component panel.

4. Remove the component panel–to–blower assembly nuts, and move the panel aside.

5. Disconnect the blower motor harness connector.

6. Disconnect the flexible ducting at blower housing.

7. Disconnect the ambient temperature sensor.

8. Remove footwell vent control nuts and remove the control

9. Disconnect vacuum hose at the actuator.

10. Manually open the recirculation flap and wedge in the open position with a block of wood.

11. Remove the blower assembly bolts and nuts. Remove the blower assembly.

12. Installation is the reverse of the removal procedure.

RIGHT SIDE

1. Disconnect the negative battery terminal.

2. Remove the right side footwell trim pad, dash liner, console trim pad and glove box.

3. Remove the component panel–to–blower housing nuts, and remove the panel.

4. Disconnect the blower wire harness connector.

5. Remove the in–car sensor pipe from flexible ducting.

6. Disconnect the flexible ducting from the blower housing.

7. Disconnect the vacuum hose at the actuator.

8. Manually open the recirculation flap and wedge in the open position with block of wood.

9. Remove the blower assembly bolts and nuts.

10. Remove the blower assembly.

11. Installation is the reverse of the removal procedure.

XJ6 and XJ12

LEFT SIDE

1. Disconnect the negative battery terminal.

2. Remove the left side dash liner.

3. Remove the CCU lower screw.

4. Disconnect ground wire, and remove the spacers.

5. Loosen the CCU upper screw, and move the CCU aside.

6. Remove the screws and the CCU bracket

7. Disconnect the flexible ducting at the blower motor housing.

8. Remove blower motor housing bolts.

9. Remove the in–car sensor pipe from the flexible ducting.

10. Disconnect the electrical connector at the blower motor.

11. Disconnect the vacuum hose at the vacuum actuator.

12. Remove the blower motor housing.

13. Disconnect the ambient temperature sensor.

14. Remove the rubber gasket from the housing, and remove blower motor.

15. Installation is the reverse of the removal procedure.

RIGHT SIDE

1. Disconnect the negative battery terminal.

2. Remove right side dash liner and glove box door.

3. Remove the CCU lower screw.

4. Disconnect the ground wire and remove the spacers.

5. Loosen the CCU upper screw, and move the CCU aside.

6. Remove screws and the CCU bracket.

7. Disconnect the flexible ducting at the blower motor housing.

8. Remove the blower motor housing bolts.

9. Remove the in–car sensor pipe from the flexible ducting.

10. Disconnect the electrical connector at the blower motor.

11. Disconnect the vacuum hose at vacuum actuator.

12. Remove the blower motor housing.

13. Disconnect the ambient temperature sensor.

14. Remove the rubber gasket from the housing, and remove the blower motor.

15. Installation is the reverse of the removal procedure.

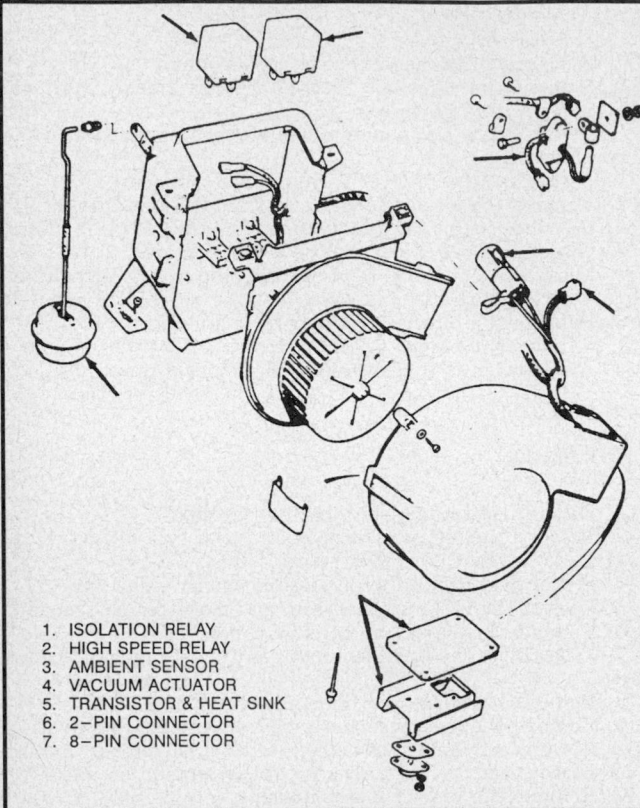

1. ISOLATION RELAY
2. HIGH SPEED RELAY
3. AMBIENT SENSOR
4. VACUUM ACTUATOR
5. TRANSISTOR & HEAT SINK
6. 2–PIN CONNECTOR
7. 8–PIN CONNECTOR

Right blower motor exploded view—XJR and XJS

Blower Motor Resistor

REMOVAL AND INSTALLATION

1. Disconnect the negative battery terminal.
2. Remove the left side dash liner.
3. Note the position of the wire connectors on the resistor, and disconnect the wiring.
4. Remove the retaining screws and remove the resistor.
5. Installation is the reverse of the removal procedure.

Heater Core

REMOVAL AND INSTALLATION

XJR and XJS

1. Disconnect the negative battery terminal.
2. Drain the engine cooling system.
3. Remove the left side console casing and dash liner.
4. Remove the glove box.
5. Remove the heater box cover screws.
6. Remove the rear heater box panel and move the front panel and foam seal out of the way for access.
7. Disconnect the heater pipe from the heater box.
8. Remove and the discard gasket.
9. Disconnect the wire from the coolant temperature switch.

10. Remove the foam pad from pipes and remove the vacuum hoses out of the way.
11. Remove the front heater panel.
12. Disconnect the heater hoses from the heater core and remove heater core.
13. Installation is the reverse of the removal procedure.

XJ6 and XJ12

1. Discharge the A/C system using approved refrigerant recovery/recycling equipment.
2. Drain the engine coolant system.
3. Remove the right and left dash liners.
4. Remove the left and right dash end panels.
5. Remove the steering wheel.
6. Remove the instrument module and control panel.
7. Remove the glove box door.
8. Remove the center dash panel and vent grille.
9. Remove the center console trim, ashtray, radio, rear vent outlet and glove box.
10. Remove the center console.
11. Disconnect the battery terminals and remove the battery.
12. Disconnect the evaporator line from the expansion valve.
13. Remove and discard O-rings. Plug the refrigerant line openings.
14. Disconnect heater hoses at the firewall.
15. Remove the sponge collars from the heater pipes, and retain for installation.
16. From the engine compartment side, remove the heater assembly–to–firewall nuts.
17. Loosen the Climate Control Unit (CCU) upper screw.
18. Remove the lower screw and remove the unit.
19. Remove the defrost flexible ducting. Remove the left and right blower motor flexible ducting.
20. Disconnect the electrical connections at the main wiring harness, left and right blower motors and the in–car sensor.
21. Note the position of the vacuum hoses, and disconnect from the vacuum solenoids and vacuum actuators.
22. Remove the heater unit–to–dash bolts.
23. Carefully move the assembly, and disconnect the evaporator drain tubes from the floor pan tunnel.
24. Carefully remove the assembly from the vehicle.
25. Installation is the reverse of the removal procedure. Replace the receiver/drier when replacing the evaporator. Install NEW O-rings. Ensure proper refrigerant oil level, and recharge the A/C system.

Refrigerant Lines

REMOVAL AND INSTALLATION

NOTE: If equipped with an air bag or anti–theft coded radio, read "Air Bag and Radio Service Precautions" before proceeding.

1. Disconnect the battery negative terminal.
2. Properly discharge the air conditioning system.
3. Remove chassis, engine or body parts, if required.
4. Using a backup wrench, loosen, disconnect and immediately plug the refrigerant line.
5. Disconnect wire connectors, if required.
6. Remove all attaching brackets and bolts.
7. Remove the refrigerant lines.
To install:
8. Installation is the reverse of the removal procedure.
9. Apply a light coat of refrigerant oil to new O-rings.
10. Route refrigerant lines in original locations.
11. Use original securing brackets and bolts.
12. Evacuate, charge and check system for leaks.

Electronic Control Head

TESTING

XJR and XJS

Remove the electronic control head. Perform all voltage test using Digital Volt–Ohmmeter (DVOM) with a minimum 10-megohm input impedance, using the appropriate Electronic Control Head Pin Assignment chart.

1993 XJ6

Remove the electronic control head. Perform all voltage test using Digital Volt–Ohmmeter (DVOM) with a minimum 10-megohm input impedance, using the appropriate Electronic Control Head Pin Assignment chart.

1994–95 XJ6 and XJ12

1. Remove the center panel.
2. Using a voltmeter, measure the voltage at each terminal, using the appropriate Electronic Control Head Terminal Voltage Chart.

REMOVAL AND INSTALLATION

XJR and XJS

1. Disconnect the negative battery terminal.
2. Remove the right dash liner.
3. Remove the console side casing.
4. Disconnect the CCU harness connector.
5. Remove the CCU screws, and remove the CCU.
6. Installation is the reverse of the removal procedure.

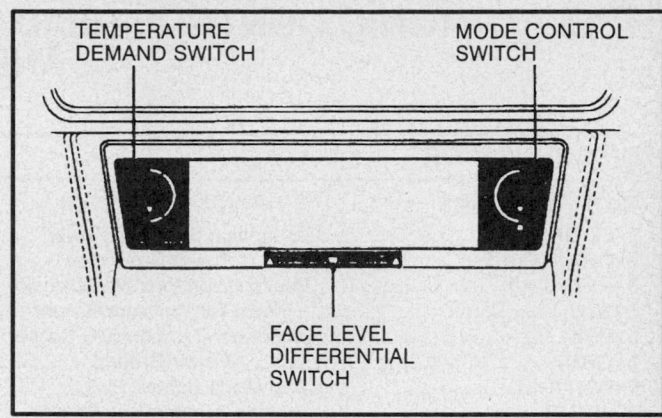

Electronic Control Head—XJS, XJR is similar

XJ6 and XJ12

1. Disconnect the negative battery terminal.
2. Remove the center console ashtray.
3. Remove the center console trim plate.
4. Remove the screws and remove the radio console.
5. Loosen the control panel top and side screws.
6. Pull Control panel outward, disconnect the connector as the control module is removed.
7. Installation is the reverse of the removal procedure.

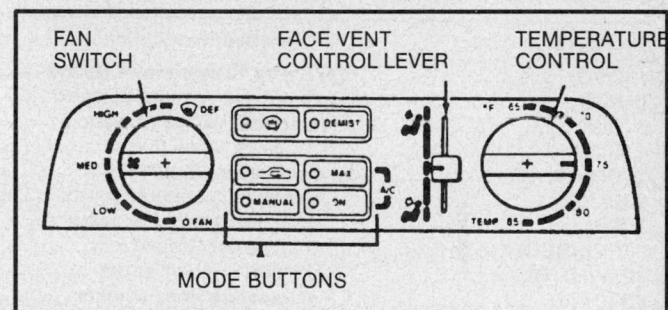

Electronic Control Head—XJ6 and XJ12

ELECTRONIC CONTROL HEAD PIN ASSIGNMENT CHART – XJR AND XJS

TOP CONNECTOR

Pin No. (Wire Color)	Function/Description	Signal Type Or Voltage Value
1 (LT GRN)	Ignition Switched Power	13.5-14.2 Volts (On); Zero Volts (Off)
2 (GRN/RED)	Power Ground	Ground Circuit
3 (RED/BLU)	Recirculation Vacuum Solenoid	12 Volts (On); Zero Volts (Off)
4 (BLU)	Inside Temperature Sensor	2.73 Volts At 0°C (On); Zero Volts (Off)
5 (PNK)	Evaporator Temperature Sensor	2.73 Volts At 0°C (On); Zero Volts (Off)
6 (GRN)	Power Ground	Ground Circuit
9 (WHT/RED)	Mode Control Switch	Zero Volts (On); 4 Volts (Off)
10 (GRN)	Inside Temperature Sensor	Ground Circuit
11 (ORG/RED)	Defrost Temperature Solenoid	12 Volts
12 (GRY/BLU)	Defrost Solenoid Mode Switch	12 Volts (On); 4 Volts (Off)
13 (PNK/BLK)	Mode Switch/LOW	Zero Volts (On); 4 Volts (Off)
14 (GRY/BLK)	Mode Switch/"M"	Zero Volts (On); 4 Volts (Off)
15 (RED/BLK)	Mode Switch/HIGH	Zero Volts (On); 4 Volts (Off)

¹ – Pin assignments not listed are not used.

CENTER CONNECTOR

Pin No. (Wire Color)	Function/Description	Signal Type Or Voltage Value
1 (ORG)	High Speed Blower Motor Relays	12 Volts (On); Zero Volts (Off)
2 (RED)	Coolant Valve Vacuum Solenoid	12 Volts (Closed); Zero Volts (Open)
3 (BLK)	Center Vent Vacuum Solenoid	12 Volts (Open); Zero Volts (Closed)
4 (BLU)	Manual Mode Switch	Zero Volts (On); 4 Volts (Off)
5 (GRN/WHT)	Compressor Clutch Relay	12 Volts (On); Zero Volts (Off)
6 (BLK)	Coolant Temperature Switch	5 Volts (More Than 40°C); Zero Volts (Less Than 40°C)
7 (PPL)	Left Blower Motor Feedback	5 Volts (Low); 2 Volts (Medium); 1 Volt (High)
9 (PPL/RED)	Power Ground	Ground Circuit
12 (WHT/BLK)	Mode Switch/Defrost	Zero Volts (On); 4 Volts (Off)
13 (ORG)	Temperature Potentiometer	2.89 Volts (Cool); Zero Volts (Warm)
14 (RED)	Lower Feedback Potentiometer	0.1 Volt (Full Cold); 1.2 Volts (Full Hot); 2.9 Volts (Defrost)
15 (YEL)	Upper Feedback Potentiometer	0.2 Volt (Full Cold); 1.9 Volts (Full Hot); 1.9 Volts (Defrost)

¹ – Pin assignments not listed are not used.

BOTTOM CONNECTOR

Pin No. (Wire Color)	Function/Description	Signal Type Or Voltage Value
1 (BLU)	Left Blower Motor Power Transistor	1.2 Volts (Low); 1 Volt (High)
2 (PNK)	Right Blower Motor Power Transistor	1.2 Volts (Low); 1 Volt (High)
3 (PNK/BLU)	Right Blower Motor Feedback	5 Volts (Low); 2 Volts (Medium); 1 Volt (High)
4 (YEL/RED)	Ambient Temperature Sensor	2.93 Volts At 0°C (On); Zero Volts (Off)
5 (BRN)	Temperature Demand Potentiometer	Zero Volts (Full Cool); 2.89 Volts (Full Hot)
7 (PPL/RED)	Lower Servo	7 Volts (On); Zero Volts (Off)
8 (GRN/RED)	Power Ground	Ground Circuit
10 (GRY/BLK)	Upper Servo	7 Volts (On); Zero Volts (Off)
11 (WHT/BLK)	Lower Servo	7 Volts (On); Zero Volts (Off)
12 (YEL/RED)	Upper Servo	7 Volts (On); Zero Volts (Off)
13 (GRY)	Sensor Reference Voltage	5 Volts (On); Zero Volts (Off)
14 (ORG/BLK)	Mode Control Switch	12 Volts (On); Zero Volts (Off)
15 (YEL/GRN)	Power Ground	Ground Circuit

¹ – Pin assignments not listed are not used.

ELECTRONIC CONTROL HEAD PIN ASSIGNMENT CHART—1993 XJ6

TOP CONNECTOR

Pin No. (Wire Color)	Function/Description	Signal Type Or Voltage Value
1 (LT GRN-ORG)	Ignition Switched Power	12 Volts (On); Zero Volts (Off)
2 (BLK-PNK)	Power Ground	Ground Circuit
3 (RED-BLU)	Recirculation Flap Solenoid	12 Volts (On); Zero Volts (Off)
4 (BLU)	In-Car Temperature Sensor	2.73 Volts At 0°C (On); Zero Volts (Off)
5 (PNK)	Evaporator Temperature Sensor	2.73 Volts At 0°C (On); 2.93 Volts At 20°C (Off)
6 (BLK-PNK)	Power Ground	Ground Circuit
8 (YEL-LT GRN)	DEMIST Input From Control Panel	Zero Volts (On); 4 Volts (Off)
9 (WHT-RED)	ON Input From Control Panel	12 Volts (On-All Speeds); Zero Volts (Off)
10 (GRN)	In-Car Temp. Sensor Ground	Ground Circuit
11 (ORG-RED)	Defrost Flap Solenoid	12 Volts (On); Zero Volts (Off)
12 (WHT-BLK)	Defrost Flap Solenoid	12 Volts (On); Zero Volts (Off)
13 (ORG-GRN)	LOW Input From Control Panel	Zero Volts (Off); 4 Volts (On)
14 (GRY-BLK)	MED Input From Control Panel	Zero Volts (Off); 4 Volts (On)
15 (RED-BLK)	HIGH Input From Control Panel	Zero Volts (Off); 4 Volts (On)

¹ – Pin assignments not listed are not used.

CENTER CONNECTOR

Pin No. (Wire Color)	Function/Description	Signal Type Or Voltage Value
1 (ORG)	High Speed Relays	12 Volts (On); Zero Volts (Off)
2 (RED-GRY)	Coolant Valve Solenoid	Zero Volts (Off); 12 Volts (On)
3 (GRY-GRN)	Center Vent Solenoid	12 Volts (Vent Open); Zero Volts (Vent Closed)
4 (YEL-BLK)	MANUAL/AUTO Input From Control Panel	Ground (MAN); 4 Volts (AUTO)
5 (GRN-BRN)	A/C Compressor Clutch Relay	12 Volts (On); Zero Volts (Off)
6 (BLK-PNK)	Coolant Temperature Switch	5 Volts (Greater Than 40°C); Zero Volts (Less Than 40°C)
7 (PPL)	Left Blower Speed Feedback	8 Volts (Low); 5 Volts (Med.); Zero Volt (High/Defrost)
8 (RED-ORG)	ECON Input From Control Panel	4 Volts (On); Zero Volts (Off)
9 (BLU)	MAX Input From Control Panel	Zero Volts (On); 4 Volts (Off)
11 (PPL-RED)	ON/NORMAL Input From Control Panel	Zero Volts (On); 4 Volts (Off)
12 (WHT-BLK)	DEF Input From Control Panel	Zero Volts (On); 4 Volts (Low/Med./High)
13 (ORG-WHT)	FACE TEMP Input From Control Panel	2.9 Volts (Cool); .03 Volts (Cool)
14 (RED)	Lower Flap Feedback Potentiometer	0.1 Volt (Full Cold); 1.1 Volts (Full Hot); 2.9 Volts (Defrost)
15 (YEL)	Upper Flap Feedback Potentiometer	0.1 Volt (Full Cold); 1.9 Volts (High/Defrost)

¹ – Pin assignments not listed are not used.

BOTTOM CONNECTOR

Pin No. (Wire Color)	Function/Description	Signal Type Or Voltage Value
1 (BLU)	Left Blower Motor Transistor (MAN)	1.27 Volts (Low); 1.46 Volts (Med); 0.9 Volt (High/Defrost)
2 (PNK)	Right Blower Motor Transistor (MAN)	1.27 Volts (Low); 1.46 Volts (Med); 0.9 Volt (High/Defrost)
3 (PNK-BLK)	Right Blower Feedback (MAN)	8 Volts (Low); 5 Volts (Med); One Volt (High/Defrost)
4 (YEL-RED)	Ambient Temperature Sensor	2.93 Volts At 20°C (On); Zero Volts (Off)
5 (BRN-GRN)	Temperature Demand Input From Control Panel	.06 Volt (Full Cold); 2.9 Volts (Full Hot)
6 (PPL)	Solar Load Sensor	2.88 Volts (Max. Light); .02 Volt (Dark)
7 (WHT-BLK)	Lower Servo Drive	7 Volts (On); Zero Volts (Off)
8 (BLK-PNK)	Power Ground	Ground Circuit
10 (YEL-BLU)	Upper Servo Drive	7 Volts (On); Zero Volts (Off)
11 (PPL-RED)	Lower Servo Drive	7 Volts (On); Zero Volts (Off)
12 (GRY-BLK)	Upper Servo Drive	7 Volts (On); Zero Volts (Off)
13 (GRY)	Voltage Supply To Sensors	5 Volts
14 (ORG-BLK)	Main Recirc. Input From Control Panel	12 Volts (On); Zero Volts (Off)
15 (BLK-PNK)	Power Ground	Ground Circuit

¹ – Pin assignments not listed are not used.

ELECTRONIC CONTROL HEAD TERMINAL VOLTAGE CHART—1994–95 XJ6 AND XJ12

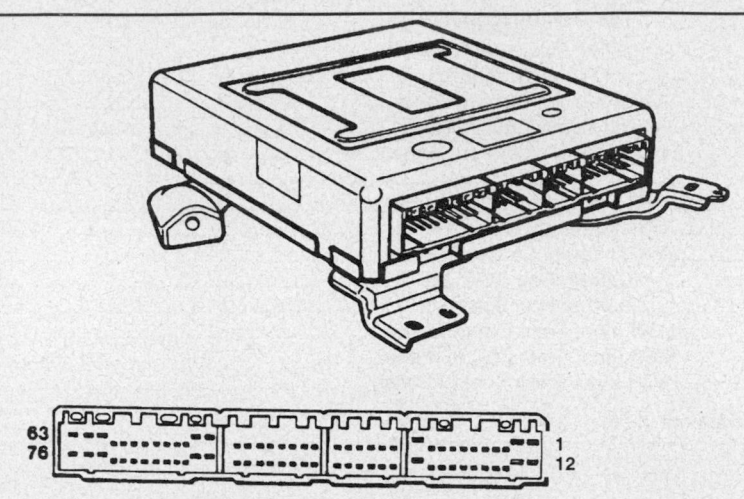

A/C CM Pin No.	Input / Output	Function	Specification
1 (22–way)	Input	Ignition positive supply	
2 (22–way)	Input	Battery isolate supply	Activated when IGN ON and for 30 seconds after IGN OFF
3 (22–way)	Input	Auxiliary ground	Auxiliary switch closed to ground
4 (22–way)	Output	Auxiliary positive to control panel	
5 (22–way)	Input	Battery supply	
6 (22–way)	Input	Engine speed input	Open collector, 3 pulses per rev.
7 (22–way)	Input	Electrical load drive inhibit	Active low signal from EMS
8 (22–way)	Output	Sensor +5V	
9 (22–way)	Output	Clutch request	Open collector R = 1KΩ, connected to IGN, activated high
10 (22–way)	Input	Diagnostic L–Line	
11 (22–way)	Input	Water pump motor current	Current detection resistance 7mΩ
12 (22–way)	Output	Ignition (+VE) to control panel	
13 (22–way)		System Ground	
14 (22–way)	Output	Ground to control panel	
15 (22–way)	Output	Air con isolation relay	Activated when IGN ON and for 30 seconds after IGN OFF
16 (22–way)	Input	Vehicle speed input	
17 (22–way)	Input	Pressure switch	Ground for normal pressure. IGN+ for abnormal pressure
18 (22–way)	Output	Aspirator motor (In-car sensor)	0.05A at 12V, activated high during ON mode only
19 (22–way)	Input	Sensor ground	
20 (22–way)		Logic ground for diagnostic lines	
21 (22–way)	Output	Diagnostic K–Line	

ELECTRONIC CONTROL HEAD TERMINAL VOLTAGE CHART—1994—95 XJ6 AND XJ12, CONTINUED

A/C CM Pin No.	Input / Output	Function	Specification
22 (22-way)	Output	Water pump ground	
23 (12-way)	Output	Screen request to EMS	Open collector R = 57Ω, connected to IGN, activated low
24 (12-way)	Output	CLOCK signal to control panel	Open collector R = 1KΩ, connected to IGN, activated high
25 (12-way)	Output	DATA OUT signal to control panel	Open collector R = 1KΩ, connected to IGN, activated high
26 (12-way)	Input	Compressor lock signal	
27 (12-way)	Input	Ambient air temperature sensor	Voltage / temperature values
28 (12-way)	Input	Heater Matrix temperature sensor	Voltage / temperature values
29 (12-way)	Input	DATA IN signal from control panel	
30 (12-way)	Output	START signal to control panel	Open collector R = 1KΩ, connected to IGN, activated high
31 (12-way)	Not used		
32 (12-way)	Input	Compressor lock select	AJ16 – Ground (lock sensor not fitted) V12 – Ign. voltage (lock sensor fitted)
33 (12-way)	Input	In–car temperature sensor	Voltage / temperature values
34 (12-way)	Input	Evaporator sensor	Voltage / temperature values
35 (16-way)	Input	Solar sensor	Voltage / temperature values
36 (16-way)	Input	Centre vent servo motor feedback potentiometer	Resistance 6KΩ. ±10% 0% closed – 1V, 100% open – 4V
37 (16-way)	Input	RH air intake servo motor feedback potentiometer F / R	Resistance 6KΩ ±10%. 0% closed – 1V, 100% open – 4V
38 (16-way)	Not used		
39 (16-way)	Input	Cool air bypass servo motor feedback potentiometer	Resistance 6KΩ. ±10%. 0% closed – 1V, 100% open – 4V
40 (16-way)	Input	Coolant temperature signal	Pulse width modulated signal
41 (16-way)	Input	RH blower motor voltage feedback	
42 (16-way)	Output	RH blower motor drive signal	0V to 3V max.
43 (16-way)	Input	Differential potentiometer	Resistance 10KΩ. ±10%. Min. 1V, Max. 4V
44 (16-way)	Input	Defrost servo motor feedback potentiometer	Resistance 6KΩ. ±10%. 0% closed – 1V, 100% open – 4V
45 (16-way)	Input	LH air intake servo motor feedback potentiometer – F / R	Resistance 6KΩ. ±10%. 0% closed – 1V, 100% open – 4V
46 (16-way)	Not used		
47 (16-way)	Input	Foot servo motor feedback potentiometer	Resistance 6KΩ. ±10%. 0% closed – 1V, 100% open – 4V
48 (16-way)	Not used		
49 (16-way)	Input	LH blower motor voltage feedback	
50 (16-way)	Output	LH blower motor drive signal	0V to 3V max.
51 (26-way)	Input	Compressor ON signal	Battery voltage when compressor ON
52 (26-way)	Output	Water valve	1 amp at 12 volts
53 (26-way)	Output	RH Blower motor relay	Load 105Ω at 12V IGN, activated low
54 (26-way)	Output	Heated front screen relays	Load 36Ω at 12V IGN, activated low
55 (26-way)	Output	Heated Door Mirror relay	Load 105Ω at 12V IGN, activated low

ELECTRONIC CONTROL HEAD TERMINAL VOLTAGE CHART—1994–95
XJ6 AND XJ12, CONTINUED

A/C CM Pin No.	Input / Output	Function	Specification
56 (26–way)	Output	Defrost servo motor (+VE)	Battery voltage when operated
57 (26–way)	Output	Centre vent servo motor (+VE)	Battery voltage when operated
58 (26–way)	Output	LH air intake servo motor F / R (+VE)	Battery voltage when operated
59 (26–way)	Output	RH air intake servo motor F / R (+VE)	Battery voltage when operated
60 (26–way)	Not used		
61 (26–way)	Not used		
62 (26–way)	Output	Foot servo motor (+VE)	Battery voltage when operated
63 (26–way)	Output	Cool air bypass servo motor (+VE)	Battery voltage when operated
64 (26–way)	Output	RH High speed relay	Load 105Ω at 12V IGN, activated low
65 (26–way)	Output	LH High speed relay	Load 105Ω at 12V IGN, activated low
66 (26–way)	Output	LH Blower motor relay	Load 105Ω at 12V IGN, activated low
67 (26–way)	Output	Water pump motor relay	Load 105Ω at 12V IGN, activated low
68 (26–way)	Output	Heated rear window relay	Load 72Ω at 12V IGN, activated low
69 (26–way)	Output	Defrost servo motor (–VE)	Battery voltage when operated
70 (26–way)	Output	Centre vent servo motor (–VE)	Battery voltage when operated
71 (26–way)	Output	LH air intake servo motor F / R (–VE)	Battery voltage when operated
72 (26–way)	Output	RH air intake servo motor F / R (–VE)	Battery voltage when operated
73 (26–way)	Not used		
74 (26–way)	Not used		
75 (26–way)	Output	Foot servo motor (–VE)	Battery voltage when operated
76 (26–way)	Output	Cool air bypass servo motor (–VE)	Battery voltage when operated

RELAYS, SENSORS AND SWITCHES

Relay

OPERATION

There are several types of relays within the air conditioning system. There is the A/C compressor clutch relay, 2 blower motor high–speed relay (right and left side), 2 blower motor relays (right and left side), and circulation pump relays.

The A/C compressor clutch is engaged or disengaged through the compressor clutch relay. The A/C compressor clutch is energized by battery voltage when the compressor clutch relay is closed (energized) by voltage signal from the CCU center connector pin No. **5** (**GREEN/WHITE** wire).

When the mode switch is set to HIGH, the high–speed relays are energized from the CCU center connector pin No. **1** (**ORANGE** wire), opening a path to ground, allowing full battery voltage to be applied to the motor. High–speed relays are located in the blower motor assemblies.

The circulation pump relay is an output of the A/C CM. Matrix temperature is controlled by a valve which opens to raise the temperature (admit engine coolant) and closes to reduce it (recirculates coolant within the circuit). The circulation pump relay operates on a 6 second duty cycle during which it may be open for whatever period to control the system as it dictates coolant flow.

TESTING

A/C Clutch Relay

1. Disconnect the negative battery terminal.
2. Disconnect the relay wire connector.
3. Check for continuity between the terminals of the relay.
4. There should be no continuity between the terminal combinations.
5. If not as specified, replace the relay.

Blower Motor Relays and Blower Motor High–Speed Relay

1. Remove the appropriate relay and check that there is no continuity between the terminals.
2. Apply battery voltage to pin No. **1** and ground.
3. Ensure continuity is between pins No. **3** and **5** when the relay is operated.
4. Ensure that the relay coil impedance of 75–135 ohms is across pin No. **1** and **2**.
5. Ensure the correct seating of the relay base. Examine the pins for damage or deformity.
6. Check continuity of the wiring from fuse F12 (located in the right heelboard fuse box) to the relay pin No. **1** and from relay pin No. **2** to the A/C CM pin No. **53** (26–way connector).
7. Check for continuity of the wiring from the fuse F11 (located in the right heelboard fuse box) to the relay pin No. **3**, from relay pin No. **5** to the motor pin No. **5**, from the motor pin No. **13** to the A/CCM pin No. **41** (16–way connector), from the motor pin No. **8** to ground and from the motor pin No. **10** to the A/C CM pin No. **42** (16–way connector).
8. If not as specified, replace the relay.

Circulation Pump Relay

1. Disconnect the negative battery terminal.
2. Disconnect the relay wire connector.
3. Using a continuity tester, check that resistance between the terminals is between 60–80 ohms.
4. Apply 12 volts across the terminals. Check that there is continuity between the terminals.
5. If not as specified, replace the relay.

REMOVAL AND INSTALLATION

1. Disconnect the negative battery terminal.
2. Remove the drier and/or the side dash liner.
3. Disconnect the vacuum hose from the blower motor assembly.
4. Fit a dummy hose to the vacuum servo, and apply vacuum to open the lower door.
5. Seal off the vacuum.
6. Disconnect the lower door connecting rod clips, and disconnect the rods from the lower door.
7. Open the door for access, and remove the relay from the blower assembly.
8. Installation is the reverse of the removal procedure.

Sensors

OPERATION

XJS and XJ6

The system has 4 temperature sensors which feed information to the CCU for system control. An ambient temperature sensor, mounted in the right blower air duct, informs the CCU of incoming air temperature. An in–car temperature sensor, mounted in the center–dash vent duct of the XJS and mounted in the right lower A/C duct of the XJ6, informs the CCU of the passenger compartment interior temperature. An evaporator temperature sensor informs the CCU of the evaporator fin temperature. A solar sensor, mounted in the top center of the dash panel (XJ6), informs the CCU of direct sunlight entering the passenger compartment.

TESTING

XJS and XJ6

Ambient Temperature Sensor and In–Car Temperature Sensor

1. Disconnect the negative battery terminal.
2. Disconnect the sensor wiring connector.
3. Measure the resistance between the 2 terminals.
4. If the sensors resistance is not 2.9–3.1 kilo–ohms at 77°F (25°C), replace the sensor.

Evaporator Temperature Sensor

1. Using an ohmmeter, check continuity across the sensor terminals.
2. Continuity should exist until evaporator temperature is less than 36°F (2°C).
3. Ensure the electrical power is supplied to the thermostat through Yellow/Brown wire.
4. If the electrical power is not present with the engine running and the system on, check the in–line 10-amp fuse and wire harness.
5. If the fuse remains okay, fault is in the compressor clutch.
6. If the fuse blows with the compressor clutch disconnected, replace the sensor.

Solar Sensor

1. Disconnect the negative battery terminal.
2. Disconnect the sensor wire connector.
3. Measure the resistance between the terminals, with the positive lean on terminal **1** and ground on terminal **2**. There should be 10 kilo–ohms – infinity.
4. Measure the resistance between the terminals, with the positive lead on terminal **2** and ground on terminal **1**. There should be 0–199 ohms.

5. Set the tester at the 3 milli–amp range.

6. Hold an incandescent light of 60W, 5.9 inches from the sensor.

7. If less than 0.2 milli–amp, replace the sensor.

8. If a trouble code was indicated during the self–diagnosis, check for an open circuit. If okay, replace the sensor.

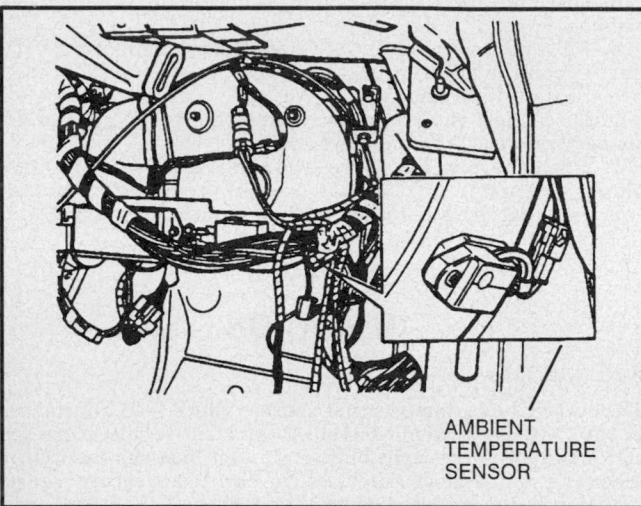

Ambient temperature sensor location—XJS

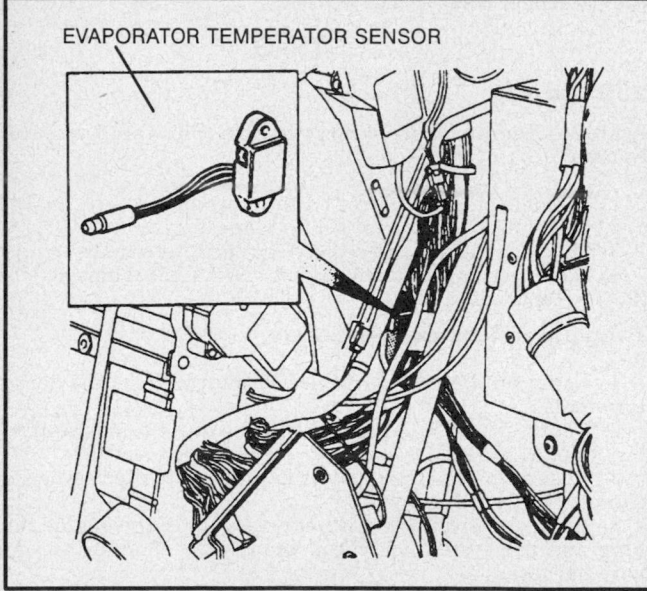

Evaporator temperature sensor location—XJS

REMOVAL AND INSTALLATION

1. Disconnect the negative battery terminal.

2. Locate the sensor and disconnect the wire connector.

3. It may be necessary on some sensors to gently pry from the top of the instrument panel to remove the sensor.

4. Remove the attaching bolt and remove the sensor.

5. Installation is the reverse of the removal procedure.

Switches

OPERATION

Switches used to control the air conditioning system are : refrigerant pressure switch, coolant temperature switch, temperature demand switch, and an upper and lower and feedback potentiometer (switch).

The refrigerant pressure switch is located under the hood on the high side line. The contacts of the switches open when abnormal pressures are sensed. This action inhibits the compressor clutch driver. A coolant temperature switch is fitted to the lower side of the heater core inlet. The switch contacts are open to prevent the blower motors from operating until the coolant temperature in the heater core reached 86°F (30°C). The coolant temperature switch is overridden when cold air is demanded.

The in–car temperatures are selected by the temperature demand switch. The temperature demand switch is coupled to a 2000–ohm potentiometer, which is supplied with 5 volts from the CCU bottom connector Pin No. **13** (**GRAY** wire). Rotation of the switch is restricted mechanically to 180 degrees of travel. The in–car temperature may be selected manually by pulling out the control knob and rotating.

The upper feedback potentiometer (switch) determines position of the upper blend door and sends this information to the CCU. The CCU then commands the upper door servomotor to move the door to a new position and maintain temperature of the air at the dashboard, center, screen and the side demist vents. The switch receives 5 volts from the CCU bottom connector pin No. **13** (**GRAY** wire) and return its signal on the CCU control connector pin No. **15** (**YELLOW/GREEN** wire). The lower feedback potentiometer (switch) determines the position of the lower blend door and signals this information to the CCU. The CCU then commands the lower servomotor to move the door to a new position to maintain air temperature. The switch receives 5 volts from the CCU bottom connector pin No. **13** (**GRAY** wire) and returns its signal on the CCU center connector pin No. **14** (**ORANGE/BLACK** wire).

TESTING

Refrigerant Pressure Switch

1. Test the refrigerant pressure switch and harness continuity between pin No. **17** (22–way connector) and the pin No. **13** (22–way connector of the A/C control module).

2. If there is no continuity, replace the A/C control module, and test continuity of the switch between the BLACK 2–way connector pin No. **2** and ground (pin No. **1**).

3. The switch circuit should now be closed. If the switch circuit opened, suspect a faulty switch or an incorrect gas charge.

4. If the switch operates correctly, inspect the switch harness for an open or short to ground. Correct as necessary.

5. Using a voltmeter, measure the voltage at each terminal, using the appropriate Electronic Control Head Terminal Voltage Chart. If not as specified, replace the pressure switch.

Coolant Temperature Switch, Temperature Demand Switch, and Upper and Lower Feedback Potentiometer (Switch)

1. Remove the appropriate switch.

2. Using a voltmeter, measure the voltage at each terminal, using the appropriate Electronic Control Head Terminal Voltage Chart. If not as specified, replace the appropriate switch.

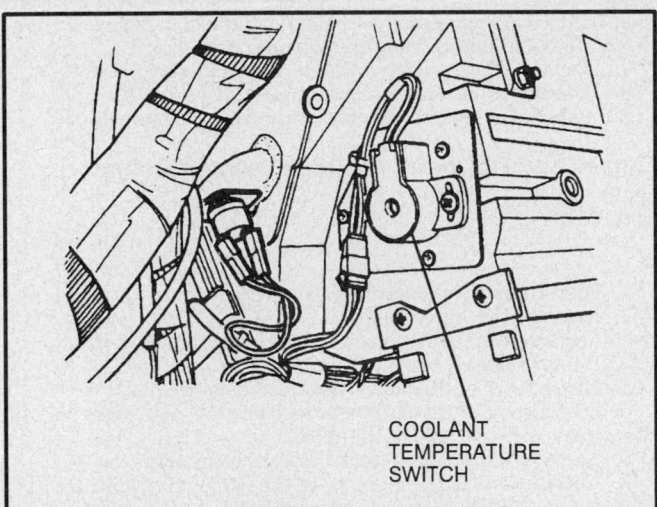

Coolant Temperature Switch—XJS

REMOVAL AND INSTALLATION

1. Disconnect the negative battery terminal.
2. Properly discharge the air conditioning system.
3. If necessary, remove the radiator grille.
4. Disconnect the pressure switch wire connector.
5. Using 2 wrenches, remove the pressure switch.
6. Installation is the reverse of the removal procedure.

Thermo—Switch

OPERATION

The thermo–switch is mounted at the evaporator core outlet and senses the temperature of the cool air coming through the evaporator. Temperature signals are then input to the thermo unit. This information is then compared by the thermo unit. Results are output to operate the air conditioner relay and turn the magnetic clutch ON and OFF.

TESTING

1. Disconnect the negative battery terminal.
2. Remove the thermo–switch.
3. Place the thermo–switch in ice water.
4. Check continuity through the switch.
5. There should be no continuity through the switch when it reaches 32°F (0°C).
6. If not as specified, replace the thermo–switch.

REMOVAL AND INSTALLATION

1. Disconnect the negative battery terminal.
2. Properly discharge the air conditioning system.
3. Remove the cooling unit.
4. Disassemble the cooling unit.
5. Remove the thermo–switch.
6. Installation is the reverse of the removal procedure.

Actuators

OPERATION

XJS and XJ6

When the mode switch on the control head panel is depressed, an output signal corresponding to the depressed switch is issued to the actuator. The actuator, which then shifts to the selected position, performs opening and closing of the mode door and stops in the specified position.

The system uses 5 solenoid–controlled vacuum actuators to control air delivery: 1 defrost/demist, 1 dash–center vent, 1 heater coolant valve, and 2 recirculation mode. Each solenoid vacuum circuit is color coded. The defrost solenoid vacuum circuit is identified by Green vacuum hoses. The recirculation circuit uses Blue vacuum hoses. the heater coolant valve vacuum circuit uses Red vacuum hoses, and the center vent circuit uses Black vacuum hoses.

TESTING

Heater Coolant Valve Actuator, Recirculation Actuator, Center Vent Actuator, Defrost Actuator, Center and Defrost Air Door Vacuum Actuator

XJS and XJ6

1. Disconnect the negative battery terminal.
2. Locate and disconnect the selector actuator wire connector.
3. Apply 12 volts, the positive lead to one terminal and ground the other.
4. The motor should rotate the to the specified position.
5. If not as specified, replace the appropriate solenoid vacuum actuator.

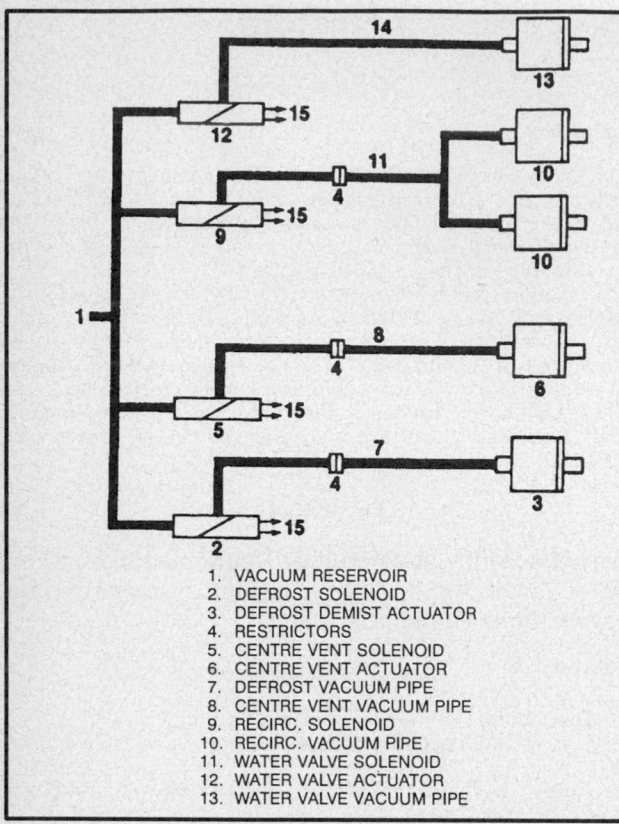

1. VACUUM RESERVOIR
2. DEFROST SOLENOID
3. DEFROST DEMIST ACTUATOR
4. RESTRICTORS
5. CENTRE VENT SOLENOID
6. CENTRE VENT ACTUATOR
7. DEFROST VACUUM PIPE
8. CENTRE VENT VACUUM PIPE
9. RECIRC. SOLENOID
10. RECIRC. VACUUM PIPE
11. WATER VALVE SOLENOID
12. WATER VALVE ACTUATOR
13. WATER VALVE VACUUM PIPE

Vacuum actuator control system—XJS

REMOVAL AND INSTALLATION

Heater Coolant Valve Actuator

XJS and XJ6

1. Disconnect the negative battery terminal.
2. Drain engine coolant.
3. Disconnect the vacuum hose, and move the air vent to one side.
4. Remove the coolant valve–to–firewall bolts.
5. Pull valve out to access coolant hoses.
6. Disconnect the coolant hoses, and remove the coolant valve.
7. Installation is the reverse of the removal procedure.

Recirculation Actuator, Center Vent Actuator, Defrost Actuator

XJS and XJ6

1. Disconnect the negative battery terminal.
2. Remove the console side trim.
3. Remove the footwell duct screws, and remove the duct assembly.
4. Remove the solenoid actuator bracket bolts and move the plate for access.
5. Disconnect the **White** vacuum hose from the vacuum "T".

6. Mark the vacuum hoses for installation reference, and disconnect the hoses from the solenoid actuator.
7. Disconnect the solenoid actuator harness connector.
8. Remove the solenoid actuator from the plate.
9. Installation is the reverse of the removal procedure.

Center and Defroster Air Door Vacuum Actuator

1993 XJ6

1. Disconnect the negative battery terminal.
2. Remove the glove box.
3. Remove the dash center vent trim and vent grille.
4. Remove the upper dash panel.
5. Disconnect and remove the solar sensor.
6. Disconnect the vacuum hose from the actuator, and lift the center air door out of the dash.
7. Remove clips, and remove the vacuum actuator.
8. Installation is the reverse of the removal procedure.

1994–95 XJ6

1. Disconnect the negative battery terminal.
2. Remove the fascia board.
3. Disconnect the Green actuator vacuum hose.
4. Slacken the actuator to connection rod lock bolt.
5. Remove the screws securing the actuator.
6. Remove the actuator.
7. Installation is the reverse of the removal procedure.

Servomotor

XJS and XJ6

1. Disconnect the negative battery terminal.
2. Remove the right console cover.
3. Remove the 4 screws, and remove the right footwell vent.
4. Note the air door operation rod position, and disconnect at the servomotor.
5. Mark the vacuum hoses for installation reference, and remove the hoses.
6. Disconnect the electrical connector at the servomotor.
7. Remove the servomotor cap nut and servomotor.
8. Installation is the reverse of the removal procedure.

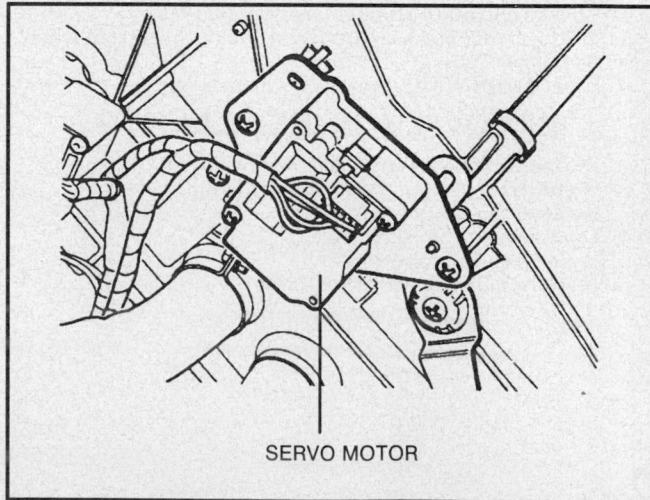

SERVO MOTOR

Servomotor location—XJ6 and XJ12

SYSTEM DIAGNOSIS

Automatic Air Conditioning

SELF−DIAGNOSTIC FUNCTION

XJ6 and XJ12

The control head has a self−diagnosis feature, and is capable of displaying and deleting stored fault codes. The automatic air conditioning system is an integrated system, therefore it is recommended that the Portable Diagnostic Unit (PDU) is used for fault diagnosis. The fault codes displayed with the control panel self−diagnosis feature are not as comprehensive as those of the PDU. The PDU will display the relevant fault code, fault code description and information of the system peripherals at the time the fault occurred.

Fault Code Extraction and Deletion Procedure

System error information is stored in the A/CCM up to a maximum of 5 faults. Should a fault occur, there will be an audible beep and the message Er will be displayed on the control panel LCM display for about 5 seconds after ignition is turned ON. This will happen only once in any ignition switch cycle. The error source may be accessed by the following procedure:

- Switch OFF the ignition.
- Press and hold the **AUTO** and **FRESH/RECIRC** buttons simultaneously, and switch ON the ignition.
- All the control panel LED's and all LCD segments will flash ON and OFF. Any function LED indicator which does not flash ON/OFF suggest a fault condition within that area of the panel or, with the LED.
- Any LCD element which fails to flash ON/OFF indicates a fault within the panel or display element.
- Press **AUTO**.
- Press **FACE** to scroll through a maximum of 5 fault codes.

NOTE: If 0 is displayed, there are no stored fault codes. Wait 30 seconds to allow system self-test.

- The control panel display will flash repeatedly indicating a list of 2 digit numbers.
- If, when a code is displayed, an accompanying beep is emitted. The indicated fault is current and therefore still present within the system. A code displayed without an ac-companying beep indicates a fault had previously occurred but is not within the system.

NOTE: Displayed error codes are NOT compatible with the Jaguar Diagnostic Equipment (JDE).
It is advisable to check all areas indicated with cleared fault codes. Such faults may re−occur if intermittent problems are present in the system.

- To delete stored and cleared fault codes, simultaneously press HRW and FACE switches.
- After investigating and correcting all stored faults, press the **PUSH OFF** button to restore normal operation with default panel settings (example: AUTO at (75.2°F 24°C)).

Panel Communcations Check

The panel communications check verifies the inputs and outputs from the control panel to the A/CCM. To exit the panel communications check mode, press the system **ON** button.

Actuator Self−check

The system self−test procedure drives all the actuator motors, to check their operation. If an actuator is operating incorrectly or operating outside of its limits then a fault code will be present. Before commencing with the actuator check procedure, ensure the vehicle is operating under normal conditions. The actuator check procedure is as follows:

- Switch OFF the ignition.
- Press and hold the **AUTO** and **FRESH/RECIRC** buttons simultaneously, and run the engine.
- All control panel LED's and all LCD segments will flash ON and OFF. Any function LED indicator which does not flash ON/OFF suggests a fault condition within that area of the panel or, with the LED.
- Any LCD element which fails to flash ON/OFF indicates a fault within the display element or panel.
- Press **AUTO**.
- Press **FRESH/RECIRC** button to begin the actuator check mode.
- Use FACE to cycle through the actuator mode conditions Codes 20 to 27.
- Press the **PUSH OFF** button to restore normal operation with default panel settings (example: AUTO at 75.2°F (24°C)).

AUTOMATIC A/C FAULT CODE CHART—XJ6 AND XJ12

Fault Code	Item	Description
0	Normal Operation	No fault codes present, wait 30 seconds for system self–check.
11	Motorized In–car Aspirator	Open / short circuit. Panel fault codes are not stored for blown aspirator failure.
12	Ambient Temperature Sensor	Open / short circuits.
13	Evaporator Temperature Sensor	Open / short circuits.
14	Engine Coolant Temperature Input	Instrument pack output.
15	Heater Matrix Temperature Sensor	Open / short circuits.
21	Solar Sensor	Open / short circuits.
22	Compressor Lock Signal	Open / short circuits. Low gas charge, low compressor oil, loose belt.
23	Refrigerant Pressure Switch	Open / short circuits. Low gas charge*
24	Differential Potentiometer.	Open / short circuits
31	LH Fresh / Recirc. Potentiometer	Open / short circuit in pot. feed. In certain circumstances, the motor can over–travel and log further faults. Cycling the ignition two or three times can cure this.
32	RH Fresh / Recirc. Potentiometer	
33	Cool Air Bypass Potentiometer	
34	Defrost Potentiometer	
35	Centre Vent Potentiometer	
36	Foot Potentiometer	
41	LH Fresh / Recirc. Motor	Check for short / open circuits in motor drive lines. Motor flap sticking / jammed.
42	RH Fresh / Recirc. Motor	
43	Cool Air Bypass Motor	
44	Defrost Motor	
45	Centre Vent Motor	
46	Foot Motor	

Associated Faults

Other symptoms that may exist without storing fault codes:

No heat	Airlock in system. Water pump inoperative. Water valve stuck closed. Faulty engine coolant thermostat.
One vent failing to open / close	Broken linkage.
Poor airflow	Blower motors – incorrect operation.

AUTOMATIC A/C PANEL COMMUNICATIONS CHECK CHART—XJ6 AND XJ12

Action	Result
Simultaneously hold FACE and FAN and switch the ignition ON	Control panel inputs for clock, start, data, ignition +ve and auxiliary +ve are simultaneously examined and cause indicator LED's to illuminate on satisfactory line test.

Item	Check LED	Condition
Ignition	Defrost	IGN input at 12V, check LED is illuminated
Auxiliary	Face	AUX input at 12V, check LED is illuminated
Clock	Feet / face	Clock input normal, check LED is illuminated
Start input	Foot	Start input normal, check LED is illuminated
Data out	Screen / foot	Data out input normal, check LED is illuminated
Dimmer override	Recirc.	Dimmer override input ON, check LED is illuminated

AUTOMATIC A/C ACTUATOR CHECK CHART—XJ6 AND XJ12

Code	Blower Level	Outlet				Fresh / Recirc.	Com-pressor	Water valve	Water pump
		Centre vent	Foot	Defrost	Cool air by–pass				
20	0	open	closed	closed	closed	fresh	OFF	closed	OFF
21	1	open	closed	closed	closed	fresh	OFF	closed	ON
22	10	open	closed	closed	open	half open	A/C ON	closed	ON
23	17	bleed	half open	closed	half open	half open	A/C ON	6s pulse*	ON
24	17	bleed	half open	closed	closed	recirc.	A/C ON	6s pulse*	ON
25	23	closed	open	bleed	closed	recirc.	A/C ON	open	ON
26	23	closed	half open	half open	closed	recirc.	A/C ON	open	ON
27	31	closed	closed	open	closed	open	A/C ON	open	ON

Note: * The water valve operates on a 6 second pulse, ie 3 seconds ON, 3 seconds OFF.

WIRING SCHEMATICS

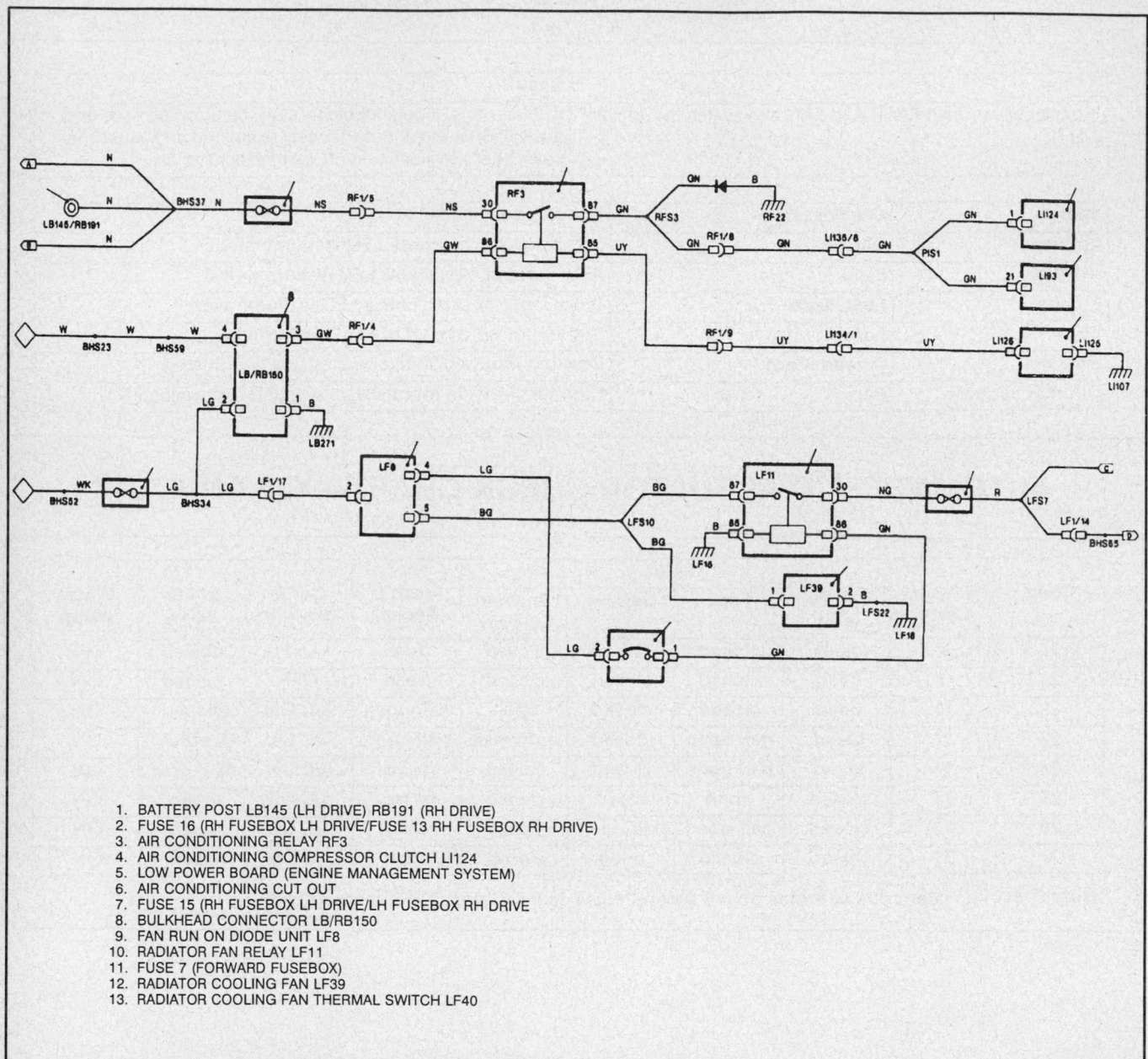

1. BATTERY POST LB145 (LH DRIVE) RB191 (RH DRIVE)
2. FUSE 16 (RH FUSEBOX LH DRIVE/FUSE 13 RH FUSEBOX RH DRIVE)
3. AIR CONDITIONING RELAY RF3
4. AIR CONDITIONING COMPRESSOR CLUTCH LI124
5. LOW POWER BOARD (ENGINE MANAGEMENT SYSTEM)
6. AIR CONDITIONING CUT OUT
7. FUSE 15 (RH FUSEBOX LH DRIVE/LH FUSEBOX RH DRIVE
8. BULKHEAD CONNECTOR LB/RB150
9. FAN RUN ON DIODE UNIT LF8
10. RADIATOR FAN RELAY LF11
11. FUSE 7 (FORWARD FUSEBOX)
12. RADIATOR COOLING FAN LF39
13. RADIATOR COOLING FAN THERMAL SWITCH LF40

Automatic A/C system electrical schematic—XJS

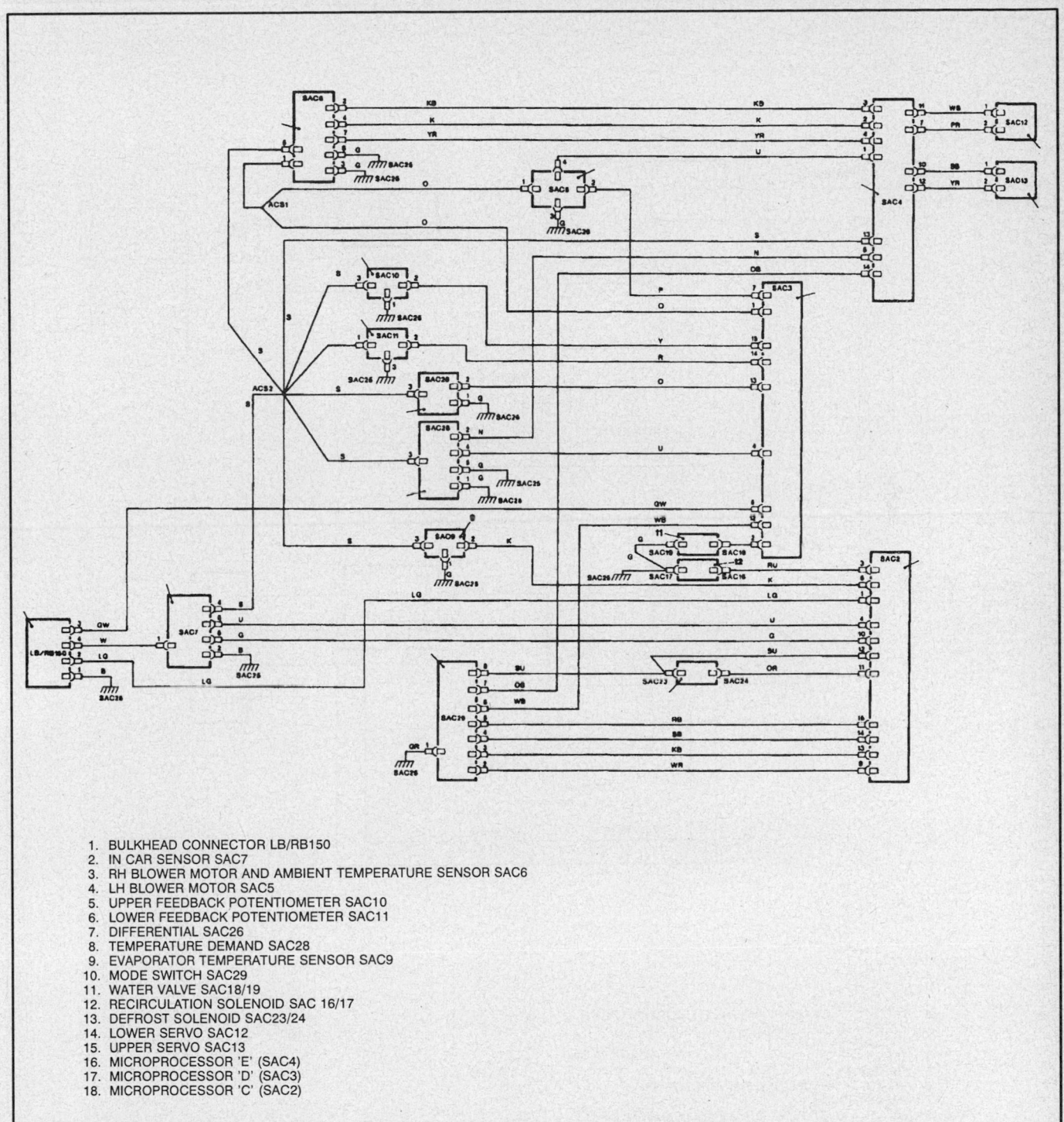

1. BULKHEAD CONNECTOR LB/RB150
2. IN CAR SENSOR SAC7
3. RH BLOWER MOTOR AND AMBIENT TEMPERATURE SENSOR SAC6
4. LH BLOWER MOTOR SAC5
5. UPPER FEEDBACK POTENTIOMETER SAC10
6. LOWER FEEDBACK POTENTIOMETER SAC11
7. DIFFERENTIAL SAC26
8. TEMPERATURE DEMAND SAC28
9. EVAPORATOR TEMPERATURE SENSOR SAC9
10. MODE SWITCH SAC29
11. WATER VALVE SAC18/19
12. RECIRCULATION SOLENOID SAC 16/17
13. DEFROST SOLENOID SAC23/24
14. LOWER SERVO SAC12
15. UPPER SERVO SAC13
16. MICROPROCESSOR 'E' (SAC4)
17. MICROPROCESSOR 'D' (SAC3)
18. MICROPROCESSOR 'C' (SAC2)

Automatic A/C system electrical schematic—XJS, Cont'd

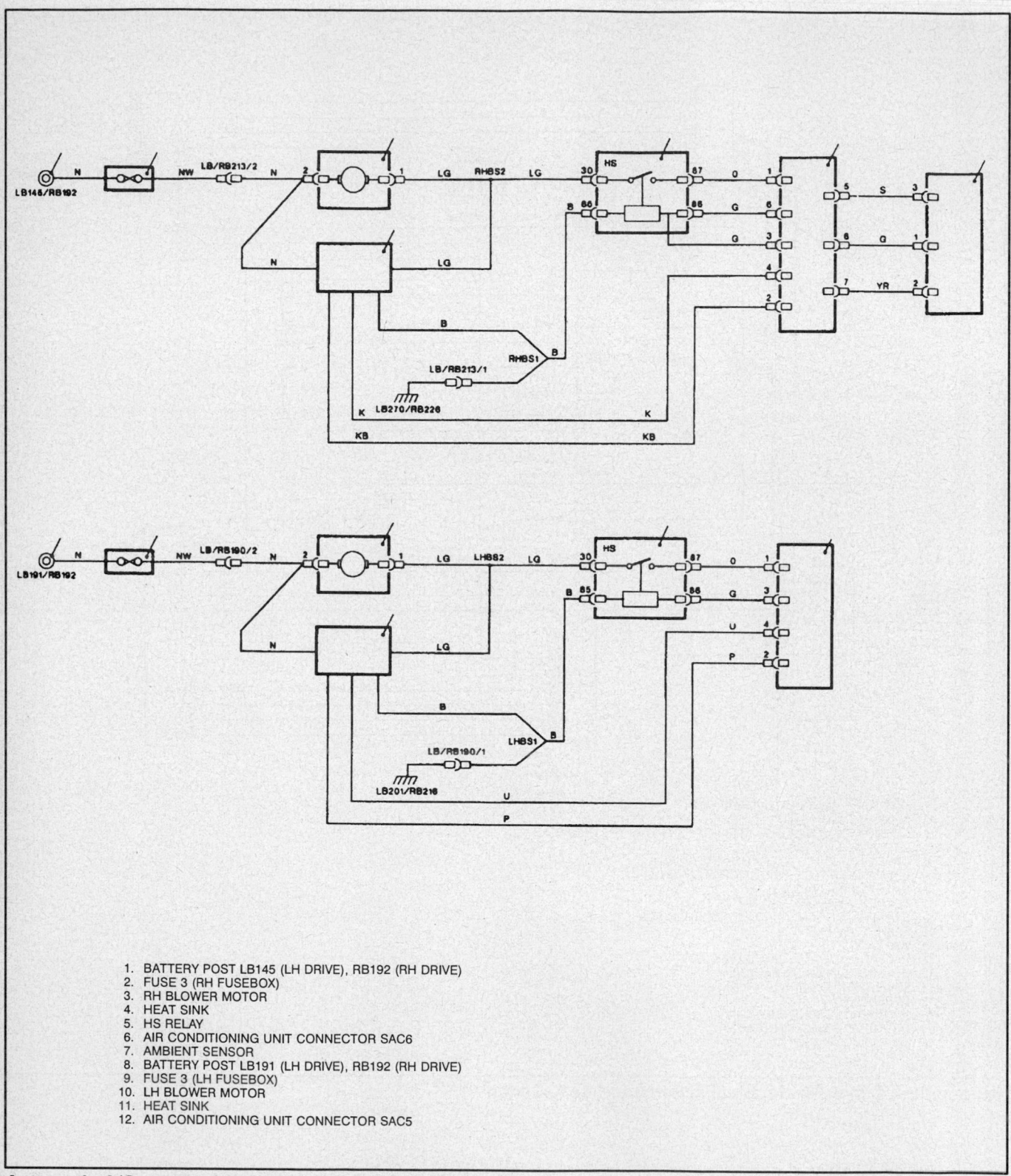

1. BATTERY POST LB145 (LH DRIVE), RB192 (RH DRIVE)
2. FUSE 3 (RH FUSEBOX)
3. RH BLOWER MOTOR
4. HEAT SINK
5. HS RELAY
6. AIR CONDITIONING UNIT CONNECTOR SAC6
7. AMBIENT SENSOR
8. BATTERY POST LB191 (LH DRIVE), RB192 (RH DRIVE)
9. FUSE 3 (LH FUSEBOX)
10. LH BLOWER MOTOR
11. HEAT SINK
12. AIR CONDITIONING UNIT CONNECTOR SAC5

Automatic A/C system electrical schematic—XJS, Cont'd

SPECIFICATIONS

ENGINE IDENTIFICATION

Year	Model	Engine Displacement Liters (cc)	Engine Series (ID/VIN)	Fuel System	No. of Cylinders	Engine Type
1993	ES 300	3.0 (2959)	3VZ–FE	EFI	6	DOHC
	SC 300	3.0 (2997)	2JZ–GE	EFI	6	DOHC
	LS 400	4.0 (3969)	1UZ–FE	EFI	8	DOHC
	SC 400	4.0 (3969)	1UZ–FE	EFI	8	DOHC
1994	ES 300	3.0 (2952)	1MZ–FE	EFI	6	DOHC
	GS 300	3.0 (2997)	2JZ–GE	EFI	6	DOHC
	SC 300	3.0 (2997)	2JZ–GE	EFI	6	DOHC
	LS 400	4.0 (3969)	1UZ–FE	EFI	8	DOHC
	SC 400	4.0 (3969)	1UZ–FE	EFI	8	DOHC
1995	ES 300	3.0 (2952)	1MZ–FE	EFI	6	DOHC
	GS 300	3.0 (2997)	2JZ–GE	EFI	6	DOHC
	SC 300	3.0 (2997)	2JZ–GE	EFI	6	DOHC
	LS 400	4.0 (3969)	1UZ–FE	EFI	8	DOHC
	SC 400	4.0 (3969)	1UZ–FE	EFI	8	DOHC

EFI–Electronic Fuel Injection
DOHC–Dual Overhead Cam

REFRIGERANT CAPACITIES

Year	Model	Refrigerant (oz.)	Oil (fl. oz.)	Compressor Type
1993	ES 300	32–35	NA	Nippondenso
	SC 300	32–35	NA	Nippondenso
	LS 400	36.8	6.8–7.4	Nippondenso
	SC 400	32–35	NA	Nippondenso
1994	ES 300	28–32	NA	Nippondenso
	GS 300	28–32	NA	Nippondenso
	SC 300	28–32	NA	Nippondenso
	LS 400	33.6	NA	Nippondenso
	SC 400	32–35	NA	Nippondenso
1995	ES 300	28–32	NA	Nippondenso
	GS 300	28–32	NA	Nippondenso
	SC 300	28–32	NA	Nippondenso
	LS 400	29–31	NA	Nippondenso
	SC 400	28–32	NA	Nippondenso

NA–Not Available

AIR CONDITIONING BELT TENSION

Year	Model	Engine Liters (cc)	Belt Type	Specifications New (lbs.)	Used (lbs.)
1993	ES 300	3.0 (2959)	V–Ribbed	140–190①	65–110①
	SC 300	3.0 (2997)	V–Ribbed	②	②
	LS 400	4.0 (3969)	V–Ribbed	②	②
	SC 400	4.0 (3969)	V–Ribbed	②	②
1994	ES 300	3.0 (2952)	V–Ribbed	139–191①	66–110①
	GS 300	3.0 (2997)	V–Ribbed	②	②
	SC 300	3.0 (2997)	V–Ribbed	②	②
	LS 400	4.0 (3969)	V–Ribbed	②	②
	SC 400	4.0 (3969)	V–Ribbed	②	②
1995	ES 300	3.0 (2952)	V–Ribbed	165①	88①
	GS 300	3.0 (2997)	V–Ribbed	②	②
	SC 300	3.0 (2997)	V–Ribbed	②	②
	LS 400	4.0 (3969)	V–Ribbed	②	②
	SC 400	4.0 (3969)	V–Ribbed	②	②

① Lbs. using belt tension gauge
② Automatic tensioner

SYSTEM DESCRIPTION

General Information

The climate control system on Lexus vehicles use a series of electronic and standard air conditioning components to control system operation and maintain selected settings. There are valves, sensors and switches to regulate both cooling and heating functions.

To control the temperature and airflow inside the vehicle, a control assembly operated by the driver controls the blower motor and the doors that direct the airflow through the various ducts leading to the floor, dash registers and defroster nozzles. Some models are equipped with automatic temperature control. The driver sets the preferred temperature and the climate control system automatically regulates the mixture of cool and warm air, as well as blower speed, to maintain the desired temperature.

The 1993 LS 400 and all 1994–95 models, use R–134a a non–CFC refrigerant and a special ND–Oil 8 lubricant. The R–134a, oil, components, and service equipment cannot be intermixed with R–12 systems. Component failure or system malfunction will occur.

Supplemental Restraint System

Lexus models are equipped with a supplemental restraint (airbag) system. On some models a passenger's side airbag is also included. Work relating to removal of key components in or around any of the airbag system sensors, connectors or components must be done only AFTER the airbag system has been de-energized.

To do so, turn the ignition to LOCK, disconnect the negative battery cable and wait for 90 seconds while the system, its sensors and computer de-energize.

Failure to properly de-energize the system can result in deployment of the airbag and result in physical injury or costly replacement of the airbag components. Do not use electrically powered test equipment on or around the airbag circuits.

Service Valve Location

The high pressure service valve is located in the liquid line between the condenser and the evaporator. The low pressure service valve is located in the suction line between the evaporator and the compressor.

NOTE: R–12 refrigerant is a chlorofluorocarbon (CFC), which is believed to cause harm by depleting the ozone layer that helps to protect the earth from the ultraviolet rays of the sun. Therefore, use a recovery machine as well as charging hose stop valves to prevent the release of refrigerant to the atmosphere.

―――――――― CAUTION ――――――――
Although R–134a is a non–CFC refrigerant, it should not be vented to the open air. Always use approved recovery and recycling equipment for discharging and recharging.

1. Connect a manifold gauge set as follows:
   • Close both hand valves of the manifold gauge set.
   • Remove the caps from the service valves on the refrigerant lines.
   • Connect the manifold gauge high pressure hose to the high pressure service valve.
   • Connect the manifold gauge low pressure hose to the low pressure service valve.

• Tighten the hose nuts by hand.

NOTE: Do not apply refrigerant oil to the seat of the connection. To prevent releasing refrigerant, use charging hoses with a stop valve when installing the manifold gauge set to the service valves on the refrigerant lines. If using a stop valve, close the valve prior to connecting the hoses to the service valves.

2. Connect the center manifold gauge hose to a recovery machine.
3. Operate the recovery machine.
4. Open both high and low pressure hand valves of the manifold gauge set.

NOTE: When operating the recovery machine, always follow the directions given in the instruction manual for the machine. After recovery, the amount of refrigerant oil removed must be measured and the same amount added into the system when recharging.

5. Stop the recovery machine when discharging has been completed.
6. Remove the manifold gauge set and replace the service valve caps.

System Evacuating

NOTE: Before charging the system with refrigerant, be sure to completely evacuate the system.

1. Properly connect a manifold gauge set to the service valves.
2. Discharge the refrigerant from the system according to the proper procedure but leave the high and low pressure manifold gauge hoses connected to the service valves.
3. Connect the center hose of the manifold gauge set to a vacuum pump.
4. Open both the high and low pressure hand valves and run the vacuum pump.

NOTE: If opening the low pressure hand valve pulls the high pressure gauge into the vacuum range, there is no blockage in the system.

5. After 10 minutes or more, check that the low pressure gauge indicates 29.53 in. Hg or more of vacuum.

NOTE: If the reading is not 29.53 in. Hg or more of vacuum, close both the high and low hand valves of the manifold gauge set and stop the vacuum pump. Then, check the system for leaks and repair, as necessary.

6. Close both the high and low hand valves and stop the vacuum pump.
7. Leave the system in this condition for 5 minutes or longer and check that there is no change in the gauge indicator.

System Charging

Use only approved recharging/recycling service equipment. The use of small cans is not recommended as adequate control of refrigerant charge is less manageable with small cans. Always follow equipment manufacturers instructions for recharging the system.

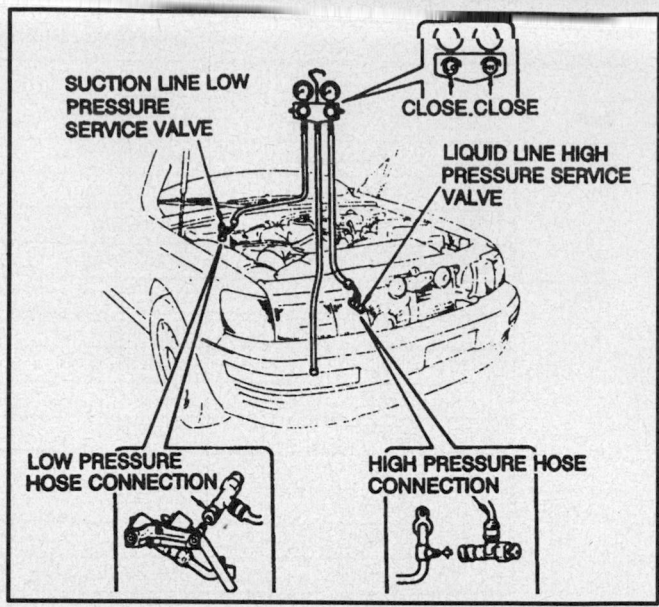

Manifold gauge set to service valve connections—1993 LS 400

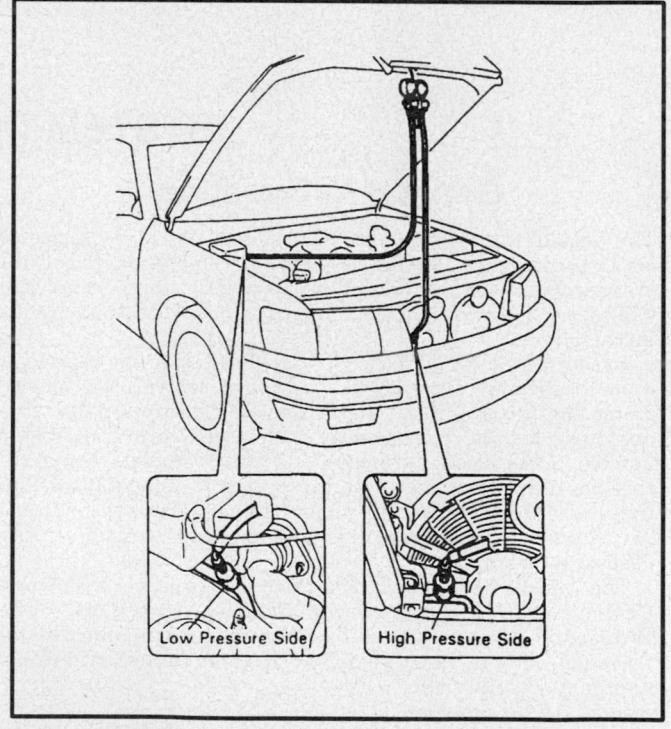

Manifold gauge set to service valve connections—1994 LS 400

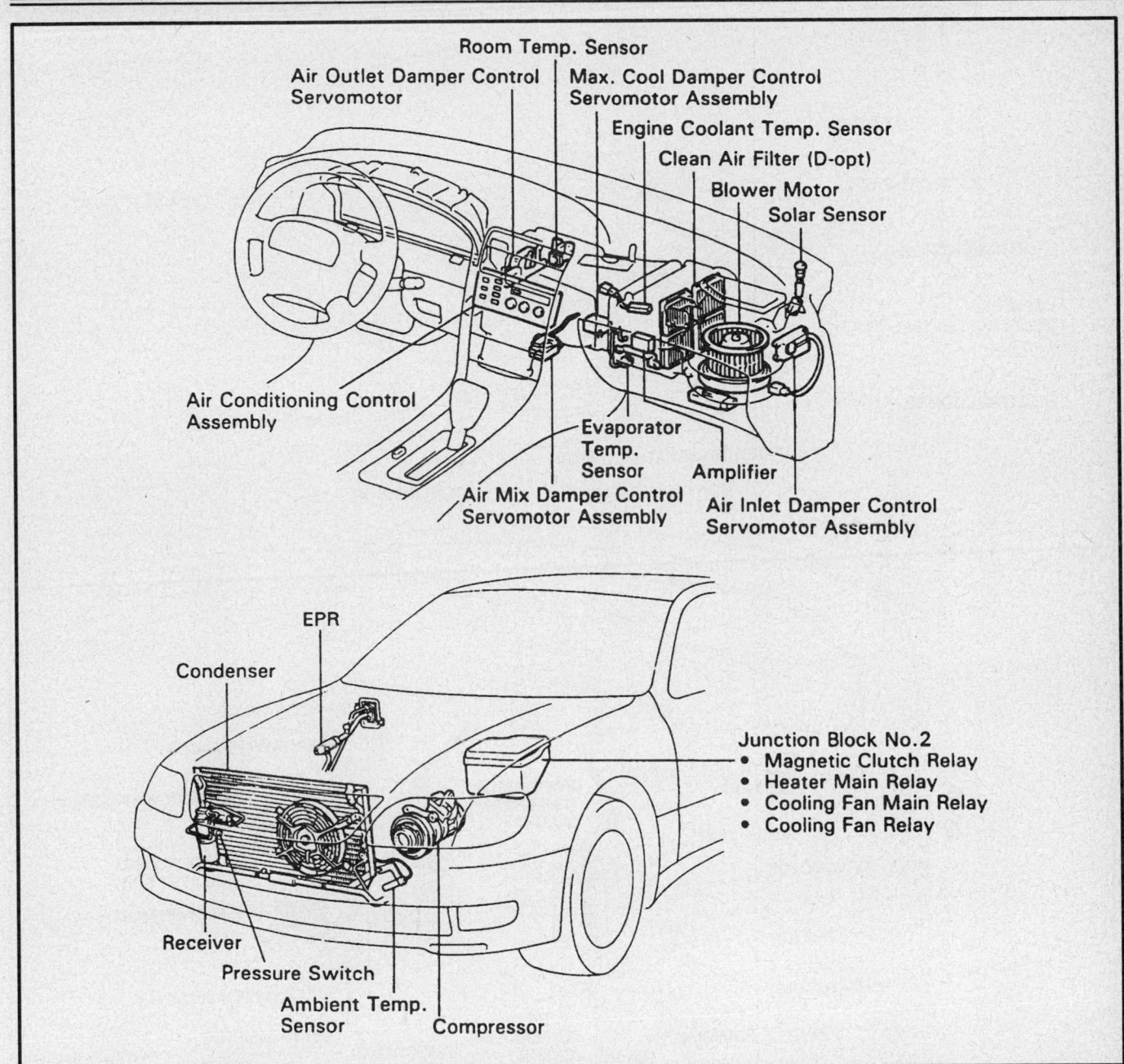

Air conditioning and heating system components—GS 300

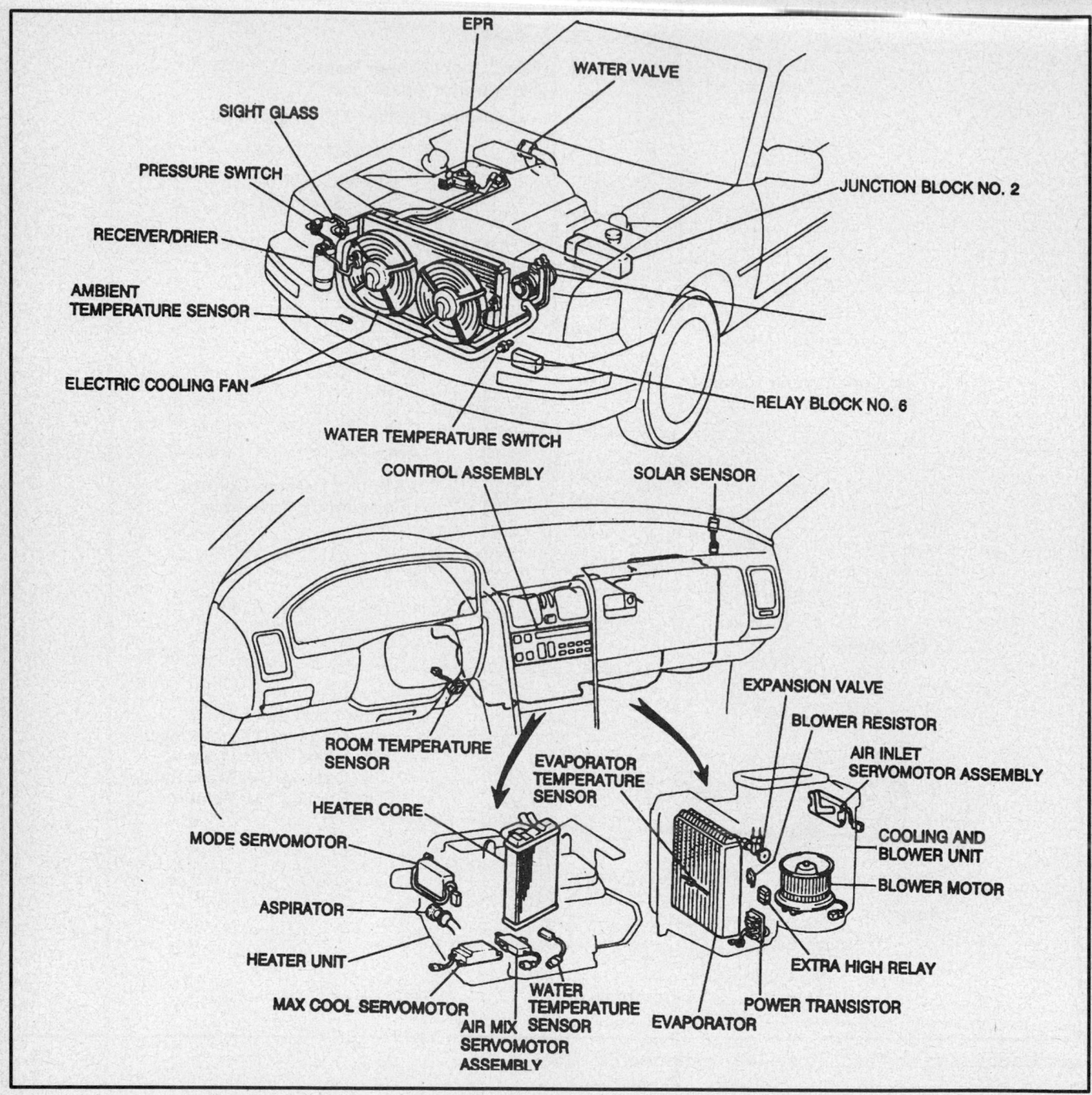

EPR

WATER VALVE

SIGHT GLASS

PRESSURE SWITCH

RECEIVER/DRIER

AMBIENT
TEMPERATURE SENSOR

ELECTRIC COOLING FAN

WATER TEMPERATURE SWITCH

JUNCTION BLOCK NO. 2

RELAY BLOCK NO. 6

CONTROL ASSEMBLY

SOLAR SENSOR

ROOM TEMPERATURE
SENSOR

EVAPORATOR
TEMPERATURE
SENSOR

EXPANSION VALVE

BLOWER RESISTOR

AIR INLET
SERVOMOTOR ASSEMBLY

COOLING AND
BLOWER UNIT

BLOWER MOTOR

HEATER CORE

MODE SERVOMOTOR

ASPIRATOR

HEATER UNIT

MAX COOL SERVOMOTOR

AIR MIX
SERVOMOTOR
ASSEMBLY

WATER
TEMPERATURE
SENSOR

EVAPORATOR

EXTRA HIGH RELAY

POWER TRANSISTOR

Air conditioning and heating system components—1993-94 LS 400

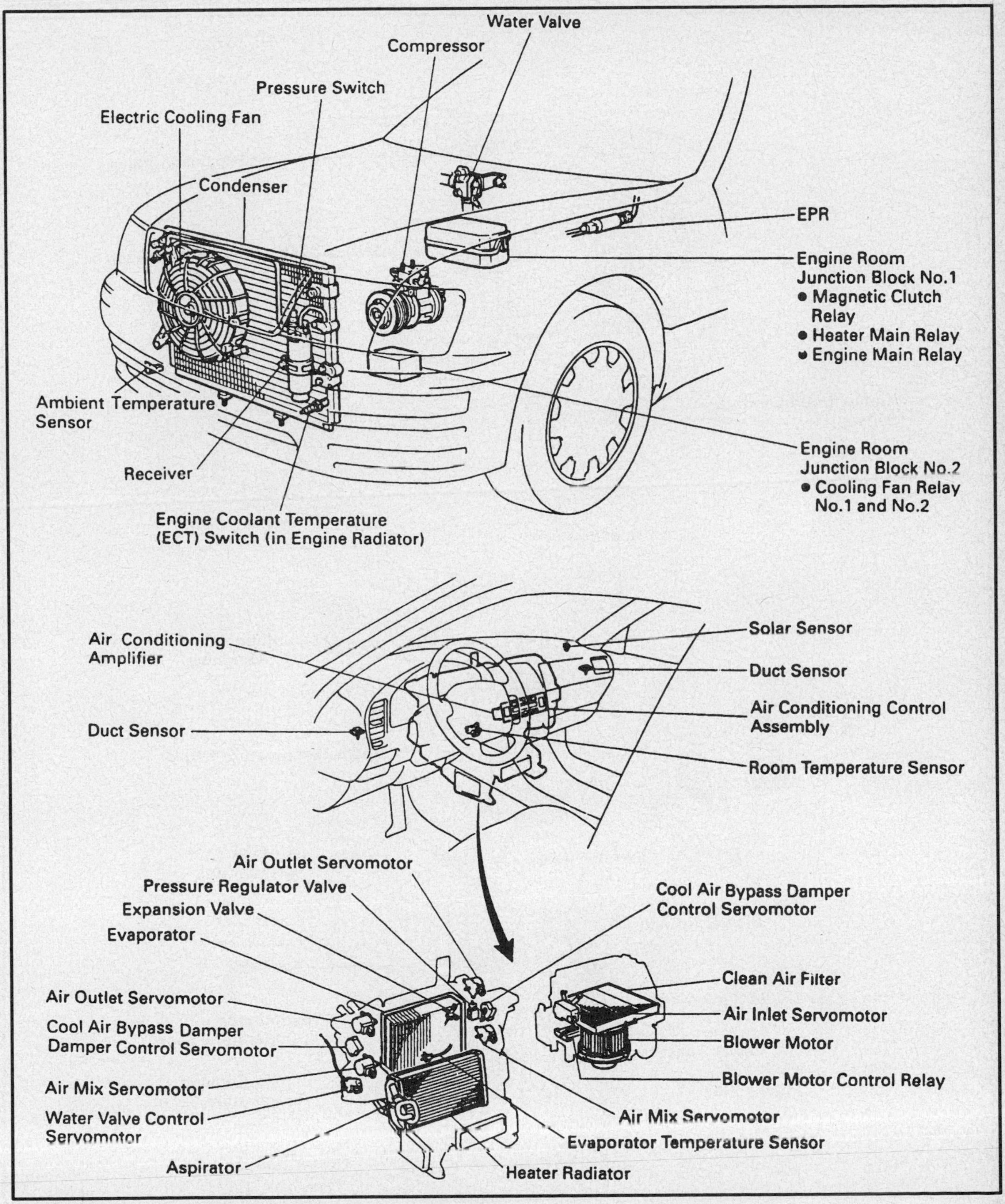

Water Valve

Compressor

Pressure Switch

Electric Cooling Fan

Condenser

EPR

Engine Room
Junction Block No.1
• Magnetic Clutch
Relay
• Heater Main Relay
• Engine Main Relay

Ambient Temperature
Sensor

Receiver

Engine Room
Junction Block No.2
• Cooling Fan Relay
No.1 and No.2

Engine Coolant Temperature
(ECT) Switch (in Engine Radiator)

Air Conditioning
Amplifier

Solar Sensor

Duct Sensor

Air Conditioning Control
Assembly

Duct Sensor

Room Temperature Sensor

Air Outlet Servomotor

Pressure Regulator Valve

Expansion Valve

Evaporator

Cool Air Bypass Damper
Control Servomotor

Air Outlet Servomotor

Cool Air Bypass Damper
Damper Control Servomotor

Air Mix Servomotor

Water Valve Control
Servomotor

Aspirator

Clean Air Filter

Air Inlet Servomotor

Blower Motor

Blower Motor Control Relay

Air Mix Servomotor

Evaporator Temperature Sensor

Heater Radiator

Air conditioning and heating system components—1995 LS 400

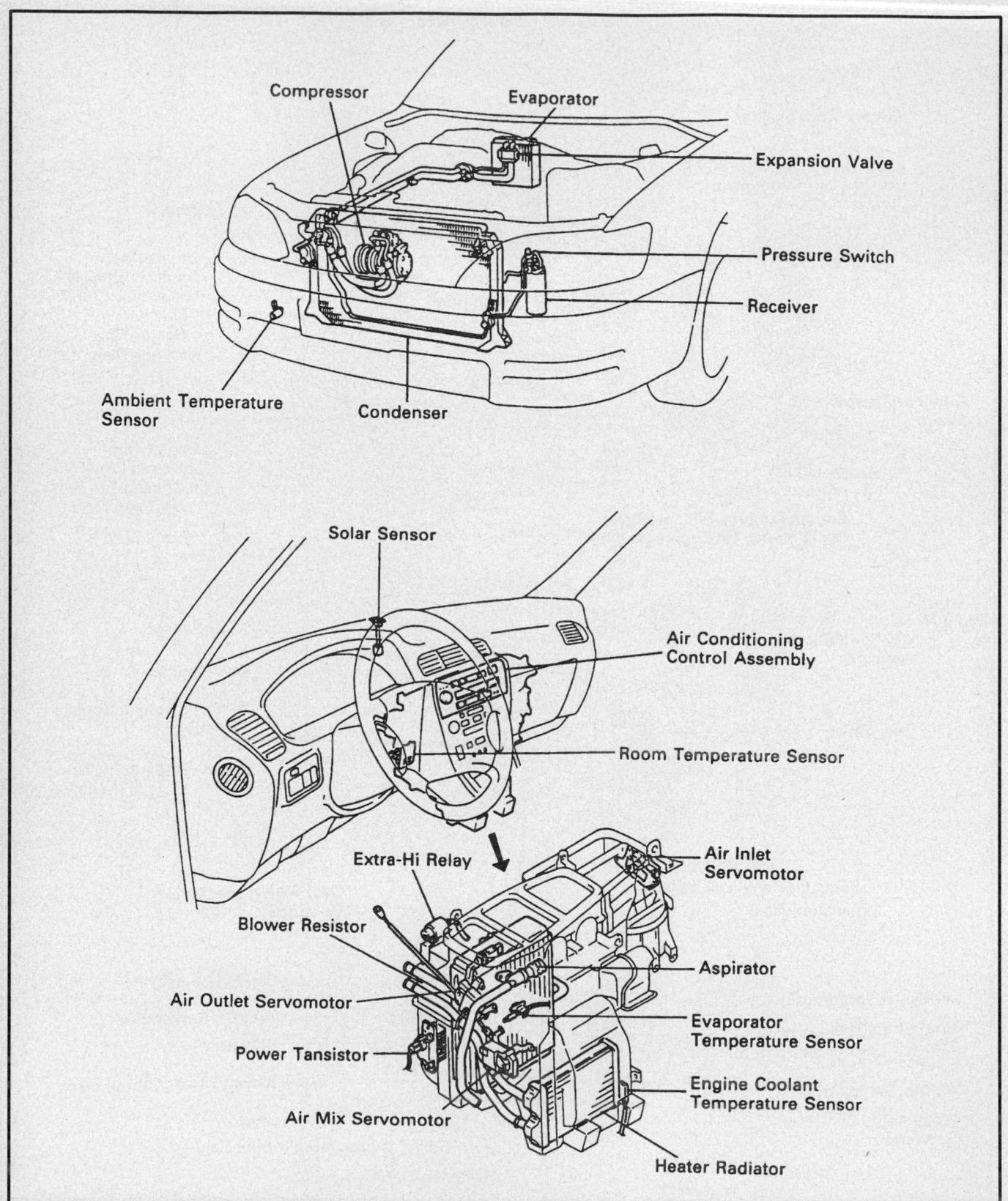

Air conditioning and heating system components—1994-95 ES 300

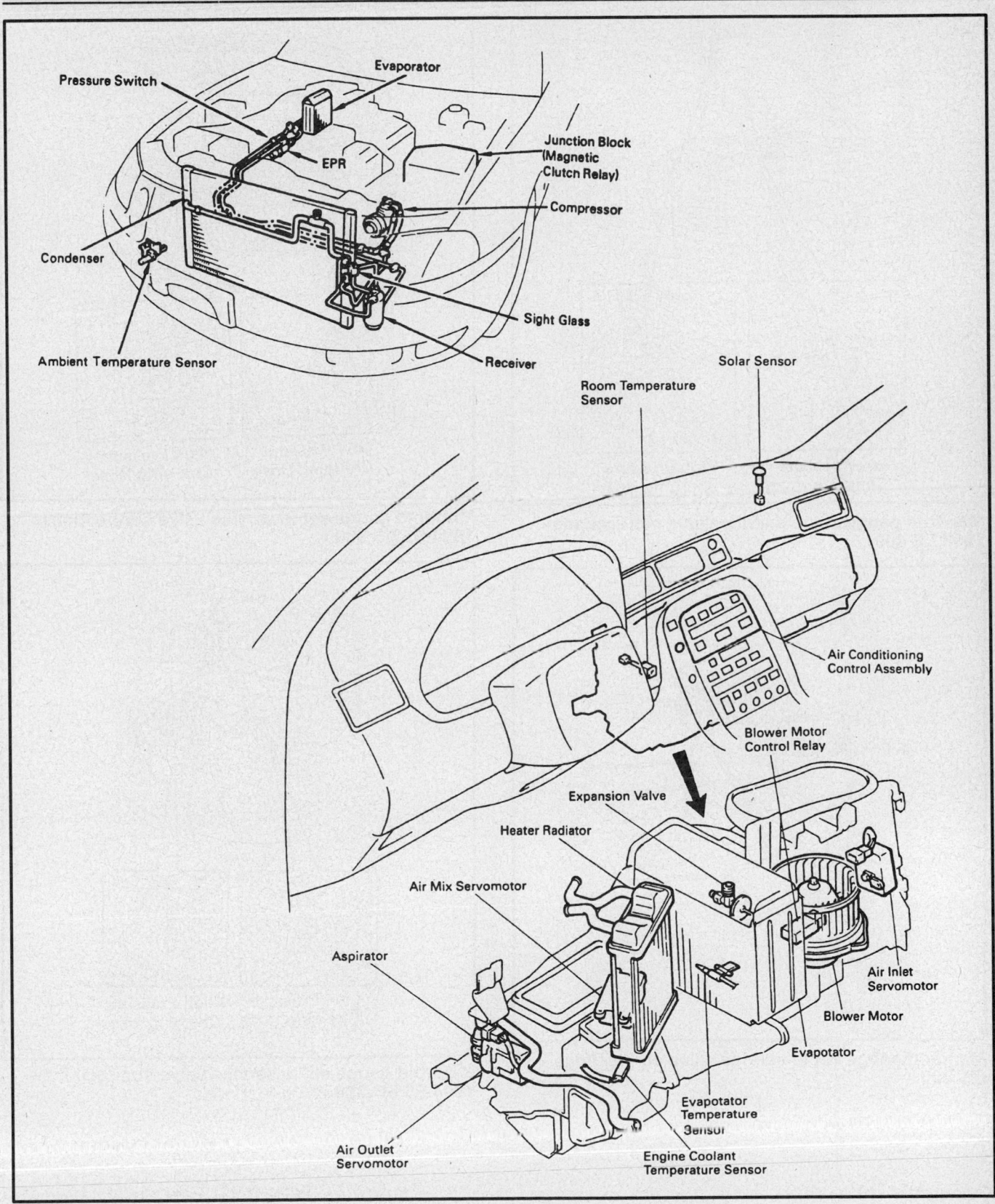

Air conditioning and heating system components—1994-95 SC 300 and SC 400

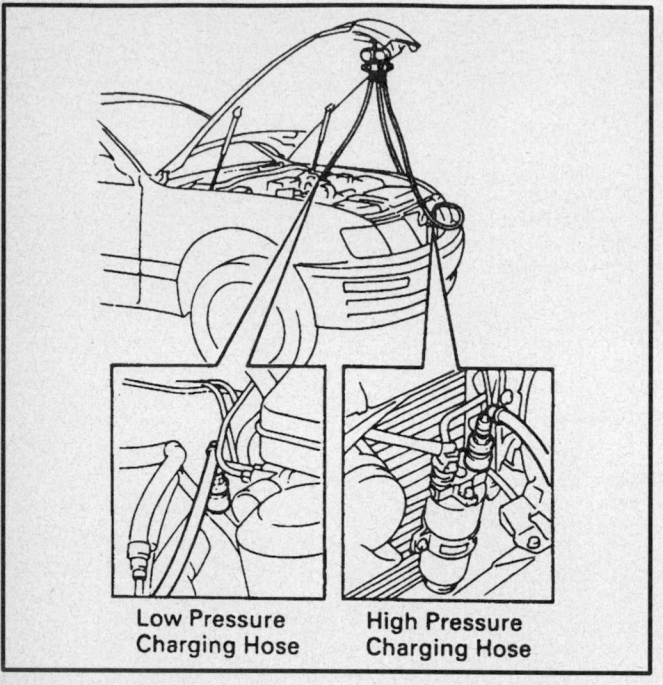

Low Pressure Charging Hose   High Pressure Charging Hose

Manifold gauge set to service valve connections—1995 LS 400

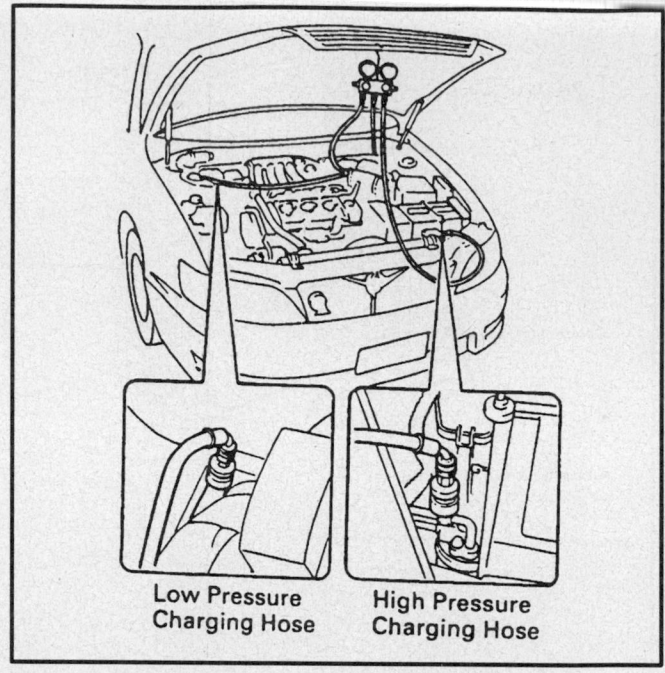

Low Pressure Charging Hose   High Pressure Charging Hose

Manifold gauge set to service valve connections—1994-95 ES 300

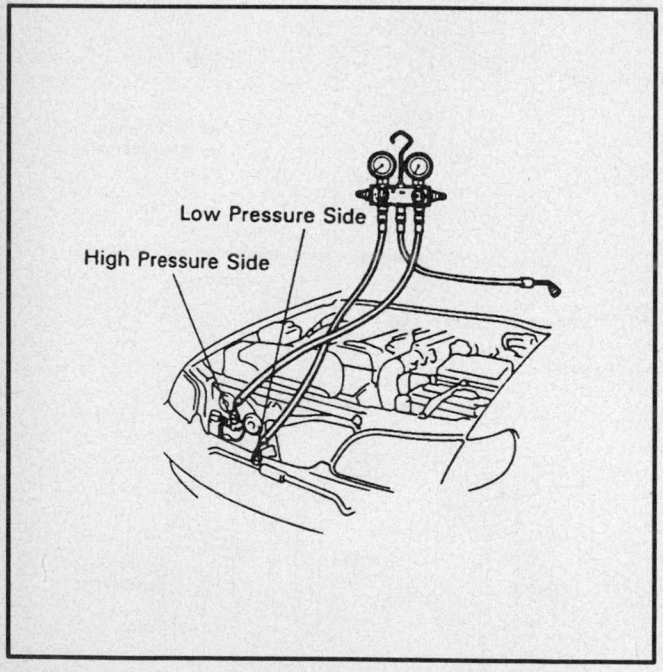

Low Pressure Side

High Pressure Side

Manifold gauge set to service valve connections—GS 300

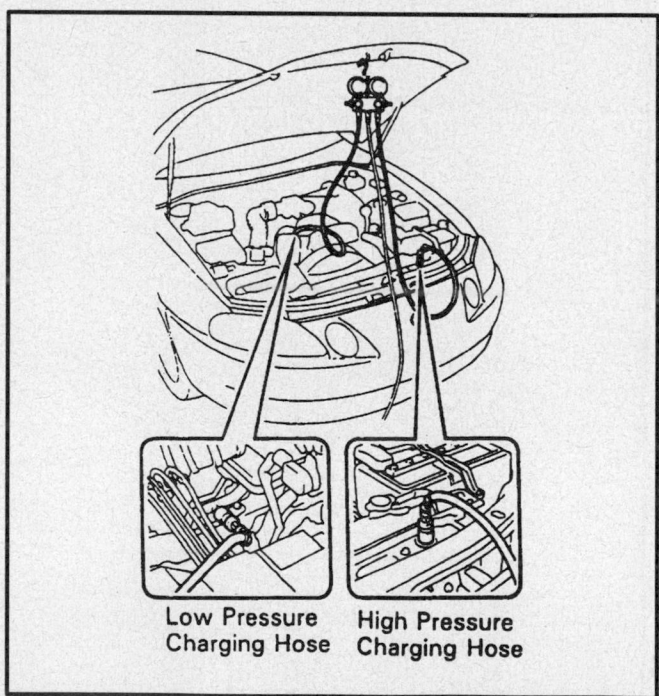

Low Pressure Charging Hose   High Pressure Charging Hose

Manifold gauge set to service valve connections—1994-95 SC 300

SYSTEM COMPONENTS

Radiator

REMOVAL AND INSTALLATION

GS 300

1. Disconnect the negative battery cable, wait 90 seconds before starting work while airbag system becomes de-energized. Properly drain the cooling system.
2. Remove the engine under cover.
3. Remove the air cleaner duct and the No. 2 fan shroud.
4. Disconnect the radiator reservoir hose.
5. Disconnect the radiator hoses.
6. Disconnect the cooling fan connectors.
7. If equipped with automatic transaxle, disconnect the oil cooler hoses.
8. Remove the 2 bolts and the radiator supports, then remove the radiator and electric cooling fans.
9. Remove the electric cooling fans from the radiator.

To install:
10. Install the electric cooling fans to the radiator.
11. Place the radiator in position and install the 2 supports and mounting bolts. After installation, check that the rubber cushions of the supports are not depressed.
12. If equipped with automatic transaxle, connect the oil cooler hoses.
13. Connect the cooling fan connectors and the radiator hoses. Connect the radiator reservoir hose.
14. Install the engine under cover.
15. Install the No. 2 fan shroud and the air cleaner duct.
16. Install the battery and connect the battery cables.
17. Fill the cooling system, start the engine and check for coolant leaks.
18. If equipped with automatic transaxle, check the transaxle fluid level.

ES 300 and SC 300

1. Disconnect the negative battery cable, wait 90 seconds before starting work while airbag system becomes de-energized. Properly drain the cooling system. On SC 300, remove the battery and the battery tray.
2. Remove the cruise control actuator wire from the clamp. Remove the union bolt and gasket and disconnect the pressure hose from the hydraulic motor.
3. Remove the upper radiator hose and the coolant reservoir hose.
4. On ES 300 and SC 400, disconnect the hydraulic motor return hose.
5. Raise and properly support the vehicle. Remove the engine under cover.
6. Disconnect the lower radiator hose and the oil cooler hoses. On SC 400, disconnect the cooling fan inlet pipe from the fan shroud.
7. On SC 300, remove the No. 2 fan shroud. On SC 400, remove the coolant reservoir tank and the water temperature sensor connector.
8. Remove 2 bolts and upper supports and lift out the radiator with the fan assembly.
9. Installation is the reverse of the removal procedure. Use a new gasket when connecting the pressure hose at the hydraulic motor (ES 300). Refill the cooling system and check for leaks.

LS 400

1. Turn the ignition to **LOCK**, disconnect the negative battery cable, and wait at least 90 seconds before beginning work while airbag system becomes de-energized.
2. On 1995 model, remove the oil pan protector.

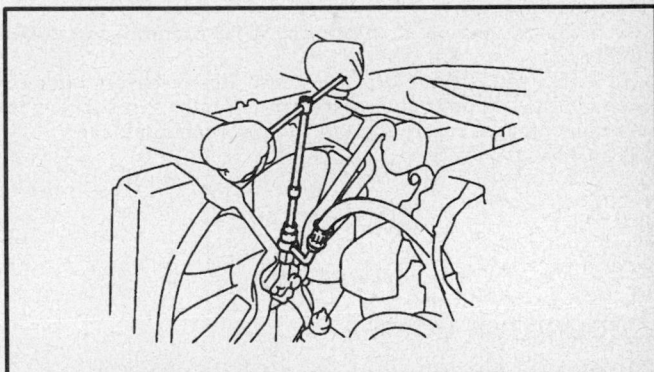

Removing high pressure line from hydraulic fan motor—ES 300 and SC 400

3. On all models, remove the engine under cover.
4. Properly drain the cooling system.
5. Remove the battery clamp cover.
6. Remove the air cleaner cover and hose. On 1995 model, remove the air cleaner inlet.
7. Disconnect the upper and lower radiator hoses, the coolant reservoir hose and the 2 oil cooler hoses.
8. Remove the No. 2 fan shroud (2 clips).
9. Disconnect the fan and ECT switch connectors, remove the upper radiator supports and lift out the radiator assembly.
10. Installation is the reverse of the removal procedure. Refill the system and check for leaks before installing the engine under cover.

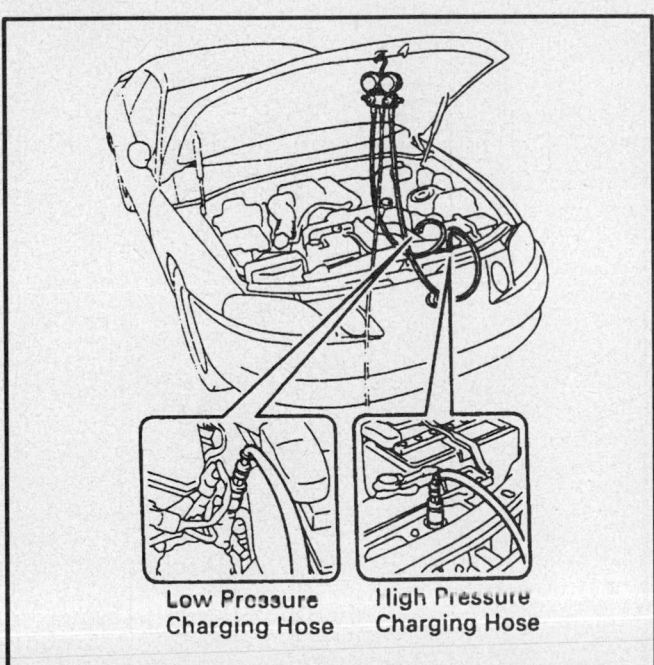

Low Pressure Charging Hose | High Pressure Charging Hose

Manifold gauge set to service valve connections— 1994-95 SC 400

COOLING SYSTEM BLEEDING

The following procedures should be used to ensure a complete refill after the cooling system has been completely drained.

ES 300, GS 300 and SC 300

1. Make sure the drain cocks on the engine and radiator are closed.
2. Slowly fill the reservoir, then the radiator with 50/50 mix of coolant and water.
3. Start the engine and check for leaks. When engine comes to normal operating temperature, refill the system as needed.

LS 400 and SC 400

1. Remove the reservoir tank cap and the filler plug from the water inlet housing.
2. Make sure the drain cocks on the engine and radiator are both closed.
3. Turn the ignition switch and the air conditioning blower motor **ON**. Using the air conditioning temperature control button, raise the temperature setting to the highest temperature. Make sure the lever of the water valve is in the open position.
4. Slowly add coolant to the water inlet housing until it is full. Use an ethylene–glycol and water mixture containing more than 50 percent but less than 70 percent ethylene–glycol.
5. Install a new gasket and tighten the plug of the water inlet housing.
6. Slowly add coolant to the reservoir tank.

NOTE: The coolant level in the reservoir tank will drop after a while. Keep adding coolant until the coolant level no longer drops.

7. Start the engine and let it idle for at least 10 minutes.
8. While the engine is idling, add coolant up to the reservoir tank inlet to just below the overflow pipe. Securely tighten the reservoir tank cap.
9. Stop the engine after running it for 5 minutes at 2000 – 3000 rpm.
10. After the coolant drops, remove the reservoir tank cap and add coolant up to the reservoir tank inlet to just below the overflow pipe. Securely tighten the reservoir tank cap.
11. Check for leaks.

Cooling Fan

TESTING

COOLING FAN MOTORS

1. Connect a battery and ammeter to the cooling fan connector.
2. Check that the fan rotates smoothly and watch the ammeter.
3. On GS 300, the reading should be 6.0–7.4 amps on the No. 1 and the No. 2 fan motors.
4. On 1994 LS 400, the reading should be 4.2–4.4 amps on the No. 1 and the No. 2 fan motors.

ES 300 and SC 400

HYDRAULIC COOLING FAN SYSTEM BLEEDING

1. Check and adjust the level of the fluid; add ATF Dexron® II as needed.
2. Jumper terminals **E1** and **OP1** of the check connector. Start the engine with pressing the accelerator.
3. Let the engine run for several seconds until the foaming or bubbling stops in the hydraulic reservoir tank. Top off the fluid as needed.

COOLING FAN ECU CIRCUIT

1. Remove the glove box, the lower trim panel and the under panel to remove the ECU.
2. Disconnect the cooling fan ECU.
3. Using a volt/ohmmeter, check the terminals on the wiring harness side connector as shown in the appropriate chart.

REMOVAL AND INSTALLATION

ES 300, SC 300 and SC 400

1. Turn ignition to **LOCK**. Disconnect the negative battery cable and wait at least 90 seconds while airbag system de–energizes.
2. Drain the cooling system, remove the cruise control actuator cover, and disconnect the hydraulic pressure hose. Discard the gasket.

NOTE: Prepare to catch leaking hydraulic fluid as hose is loosened.

3. Disconnect the upper radiator hose, remove the coolant reservoir hose and disconnect the hydraulic motor return hose.
4. Remove 6 bolts and take out the hydraulic cooling fan assembly. The motor can be removed at the bench.
5. Installation is the reverse of the removal procedure. Use a new gasket at the hose connections. Bleed the cooling system and the hydraulic fan fluid system.

GS 300

1. Turn ignition to **LOCK**. Disconnect the negative battery cable and wait at least 90 seconds while airbag system de–energizes. Drain the cooling system.
2. Remove the engine under cover and the air cleaner duct.
3. Disconnect the upper radiator hose, the cooling fan connector and the ECT switch wire from the wire clamp.
4. Remove the cooling fan.

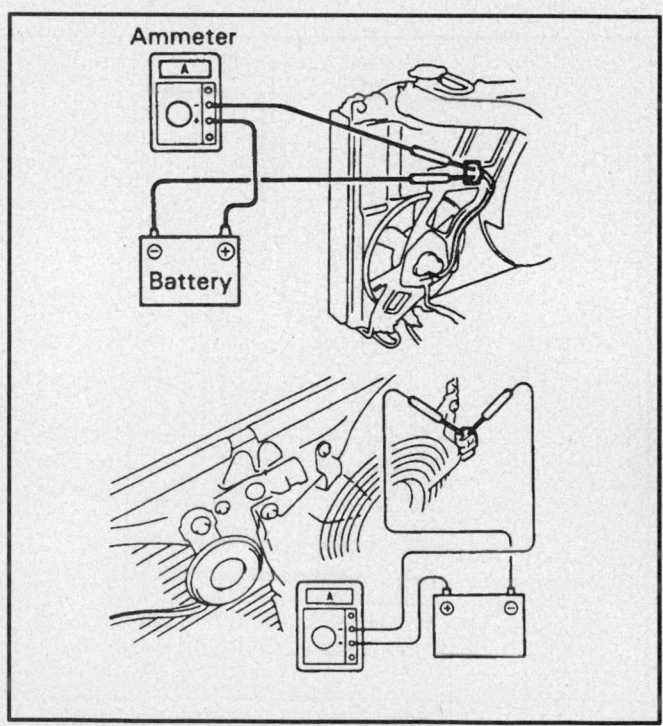

Cooling fan motor testing–GS 300

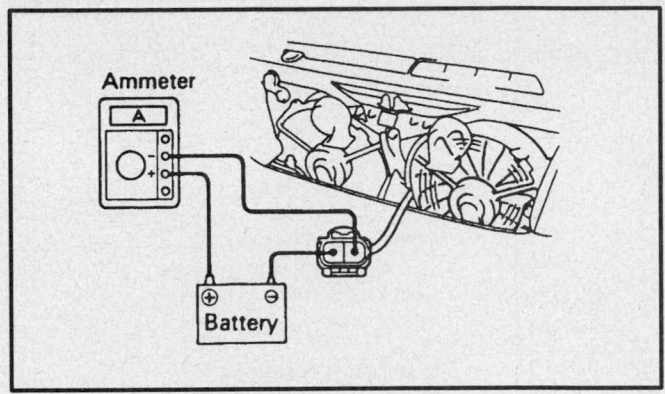

Cooling fan motor testing—LS 400

5. Installation is the reverse of the removal procedure.

LS 400

1. With the ignition at **LOCK**, disconnect the negative battery cable and wait 90 seconds for airbag system to de-energize.
2. Remove the engine under cover, ground effect, side clearance lights, headlight and fog light assembly, and the upper bumper retainer strip (beneath the grille).
3. Detach the A/C ambient temperature switch connector.
4. Remove the front bumper, bumper reinforcement and the right side horn.
5. Remove the hood lock support and the cooling fans.
6. Installation is the reverse of the removal procedure.

ELECTRONICALLY CONTROLLED HYDRAULIC COOLING FAN ECU CHECK SPECIFICATIONS—ES 300 AND 1993 SC 400

Check for	Tester connection	Condition	Specified value
Voltage	1 – Ground	Ignition switch ON	Battery voltage
Resistance	2 – 3	Solenoid valve at cold (25°C (77°F))	7.6 ~ 8.0 Ω
Continuity	4 – Ground		Continuity
Continuity	5 – Ground	Throttle valve open	No continuity
		Throttle valve closed	Continuity
Continuity	8 – Ground	A/C pressure SW connector disconnected	No continuity
		A/C pressure SW connector connected	Continuity
Resistance	9 – 10	Coolant temperature at 80°C (176°F)	1.48 – 1.58 kΩ

ELECTRONICALLY CONTROLLED HYDRAULIC COOLING FAN ECU CHECK SPECIFICATIONS—1994-95 SC 400

Check for	Tester connection	Condition	Specified value
Voltage	1 – Ground	Ignition switch ON	Battery voltage
Resistance	2 – 3	Solenoid valve at cold (20°C (68°F))	7.5 – 8.5 Ω
Continuity	4 – Ground	———	Continuity
Continuity	5 – Ground	Throttle valve open	No continity
		Throttle valve closed	Continuity
Resistance	9 – 10	Coolant temp. at 80°C (176°F)	1.48 – 1.58 kΩ

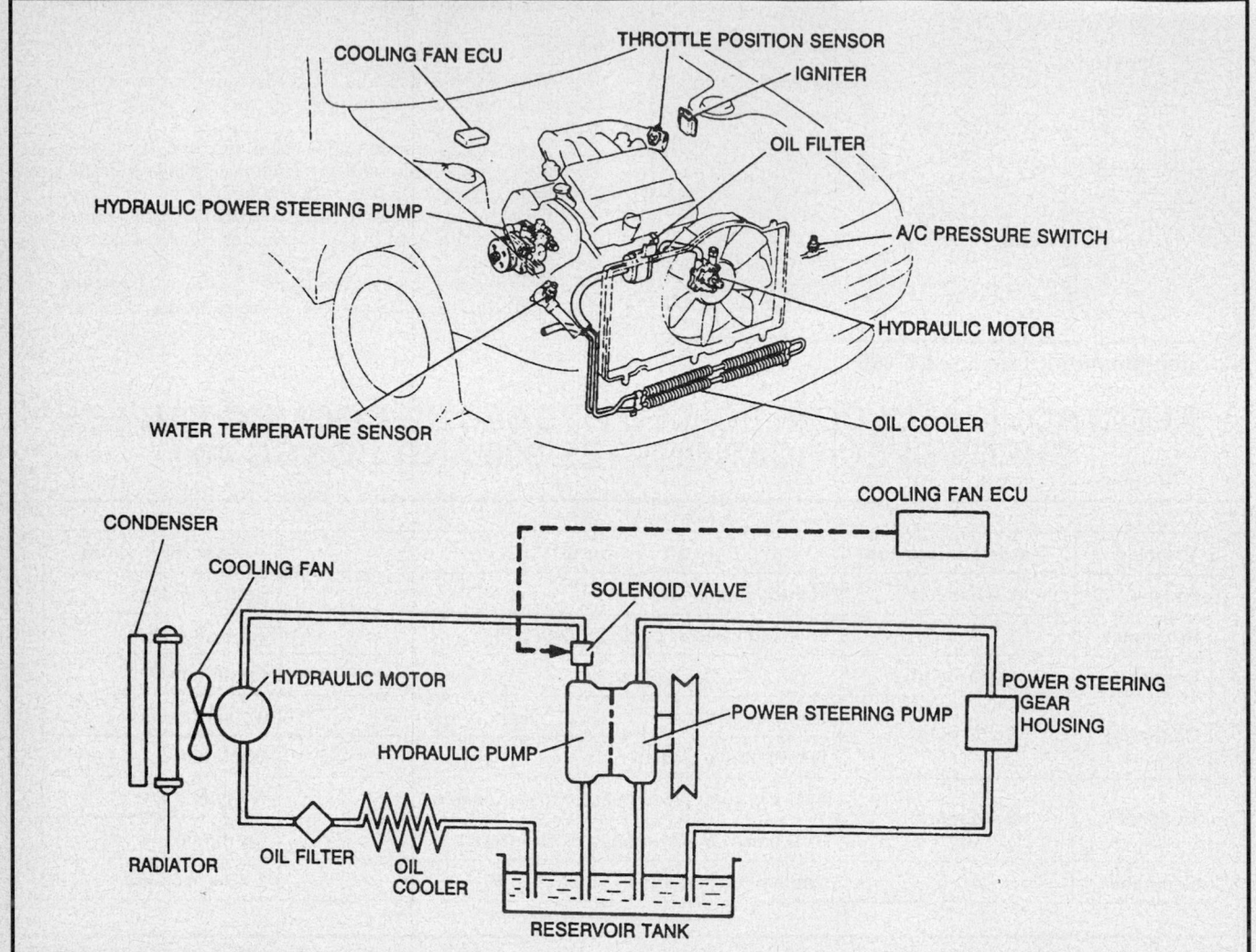

Electronically controlled hydraulic cooling fan system components—ES 300

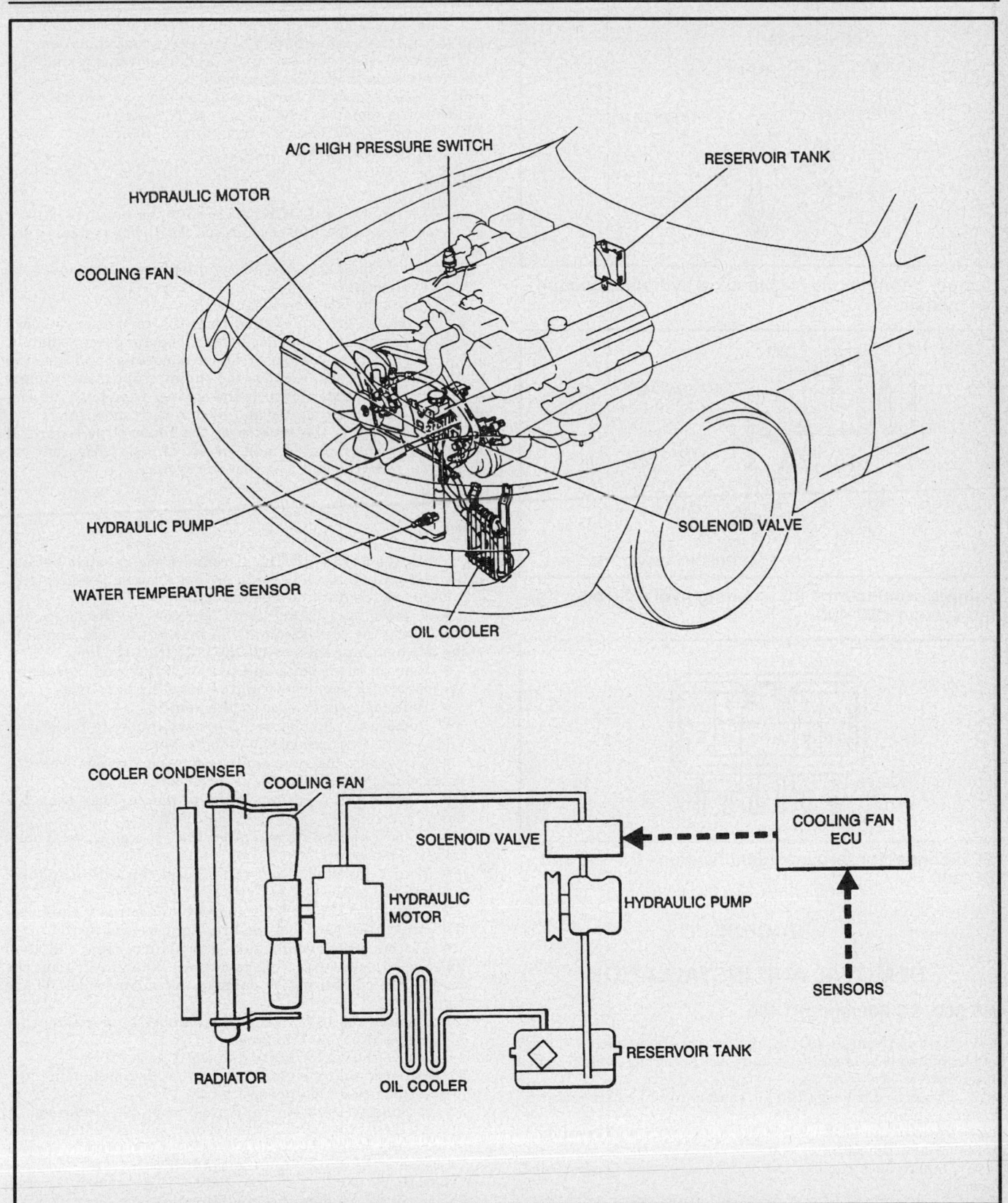

A/C HIGH PRESSURE SWITCH

RESERVOIR TANK

HYDRAULIC MOTOR

COOLING FAN

HYDRAULIC PUMP

SOLENOID VALVE

WATER TEMPERATURE SENSOR

OIL COOLER

COOLER CONDENSER

COOLING FAN

SOLENOID VALVE

COOLING FAN ECU

HYDRAULIC MOTOR

HYDRAULIC PUMP

RADIATOR

OIL COOLER

RESERVOIR TANK

SENSORS

Electronically controlled hydraulic cooling fan system components—SC 400

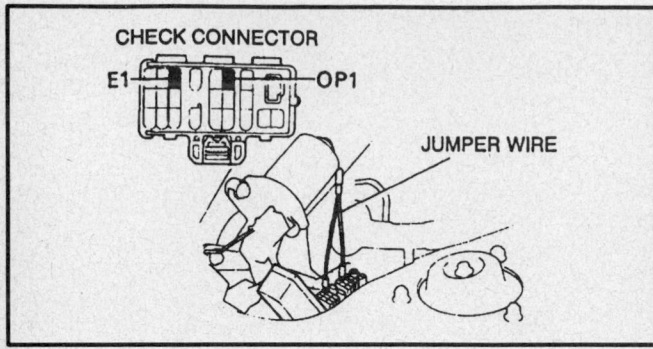

Jumper connections for bleeding hydraulic cooling fan system – ES 300

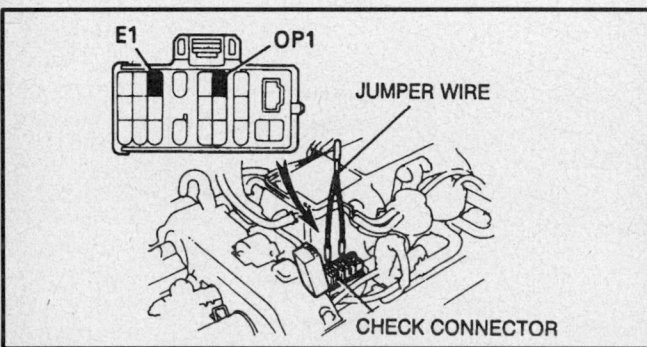

Jumper connections for bleeding hydraulic cooling fan system – SC 400

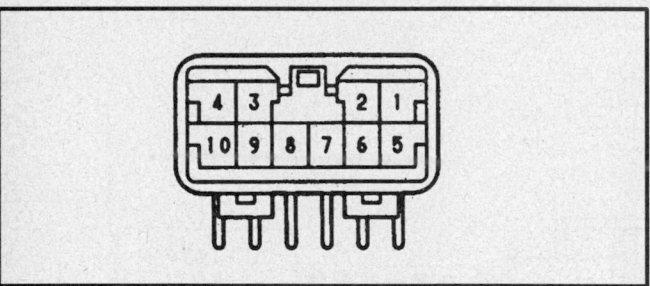

ECU connector terminal identification – ES 300 and SC 400

Condenser

REMOVAL AND INSTALLATION

ES 300, SC 300 and SC 400

1. With ignition at **LOCK**, disconnect the negative battery cable and wait at least 90 seconds for the airbag system to de-energize.
2. Properly discharge the air conditioning system using recovery equipment.
3. Remove the battery. Remove the upper radiator/condenser cover and the radiator bolt.
4. On ES 300, remove the left front engine compartment bracket.
5. On SC 300 and SC 400, remove the under cover and air flow cover.
6. On ES 300, remove the cooling fan and upper support.

7. Disconnect the refrigerant lines from the condenser and cap the openings immediately to minimize contamination.
8. Remove the retaining nuts or bolts, lean the radiator backward and remove the condenser.
9. Installation is the reverse of the removal procedure. If condenser is replaced, add 1.2–1.4 oz. (ES 300) or 1.4–1.7 oz. (SC 300 and SC 400) of new refrigerant oil. Evacuate, recharge and leak test the system.

GS 300

1. With ignition at **LOCK**, disconnect the negative battery cable and wait at least 90 seconds for the airbag system to de-energize.
2. Properly discharge the air conditioning system using recovery equipment.
3. Remove the No. 2 air cleaner hose.
4. Disconnect the liquid tube from the condenser. Remove the receiver from the condenser. Cap all openings immediately.
5. Disconnect the condenser upper mountings and turn the mountings downward. Remove the radiator upper mountings.
6. Push the radiator towards the engine. Then push the condenser towards the radiator and lift out the condenser.
7. Installation is the reverse of the removal procedure. If the condenser is replaced, add 1.4 oz. of new refrigerant oil. Evacuate, recharge and leak test the system.

LS 400

1993–94

1. With the key at **LOCK**, disconnect the negative battery cable and wait 90 seconds while air bag system de-energizes.
2. Remove the front bumper as follows:
   - Remove the parking lights by removing the screw, disconnecting the connection at the rear of the light and pulling the light out. Disconnect the bulb from the light.
   - Remove the 3 bolts and nut retaining each headlight. Disconnect the connectors and remove the headlights.
   - Raise and safely support the vehicle.
   - Remove the 8 bolts and 5 screws retaining the engine under cover and remove the under cover.
   - Disconnect the tube and remove the 7 screws from the lower wind guide. Remove the lower wind guide.
   - Remove the 6 screws and the fender liner from the bumper.
   - Remove the 2 nuts and a retainer, as well as the 2 bolts from the bumper.
   - Loosen the clips, then remove the clip with a suitable tool and the upper bumper retainer.
   - Disconnect the bulbs from the bumper and if equipped, disconnect the hose from the headlight washer nozzle.
   - Disconnect the connection at the bumper rear end, then pull the bumper forward to remove it. When pulling out the bumper, be careful not to damage the serrated part of the side bolts.
   - Remove the 10 bolts and the bumper reinforcement.
3. Remove the 2 electric fans.
4. Remove the center brace and the 2 horns.
5. Discharge the refrigerant from the air conditioning system according to the proper procedure.
6. Disconnect the refrigerant lines from the condenser. To prevent the entrance of moisture or dirt, caps should be placed on the openings immediately.
7. Remove the 2 nuts and the condenser.
To install:
8. Install the condenser with the 2 nuts.
9. Connect the refrigerant lines. Tighten the suction line to 24 ft. lbs. (32 Nm) and the discharge and liquid lines to 7 ft.

lbs. (10 Nm). Do not remove the caps until the lines are installed.

NOTE: If the condenser was replaced, add 1.4–1.7 oz. (40–50 cc) of clean refrigerant oil to the new condenser to maintain the required total system oil charge.

On 1993 LS 400, the system is charged with R–134a. Be sure to use the appropriate refrigerant, refrigerant oil, component and service equipment so R–12 or its oil are not mixed with this system.

10. Connect the negative battery cable. Evacuate and charge the air conditioning system according to the proper procedure. Observe all safety precautions.

11. Using a leak tester, check for refrigerant leaks.

12. Disconnect the negative battery cable. Again, wait for at least 90 seconds while the airbag system de–energizes.

13. Install the 2 horns and the center brace.

14. Install the 2 electric fans.

15. Install the front bumper. by reversing the removal procedure. Observe the following points:

   • When installing the bumper on the body, be careful not to damage the serrated part of the side bolts.

   • When installing the stay, place the retainer in the hole, then push in the head of the clip and install it.

• After installing the headlight, adjust the light aiming.

1995

1. With the key at **LOCK**, disconnect the negative battery cable and wait 90 seconds while air bag system de–energizes.

2. Properly discharge the air conditioning system using recovery equipment.

3. Remove the air cleaner hose and the radiator upper mountings.

4. Disconnect the liquid tube from the condenser. Remove the bolt and receiver with the receiver holder. Cap the openings immediately to keep moisture out of the system.

5. Remove the hood lock support and disconnect the cooling fan electrical connector. Remove the cooling fan.

6. Disconnect the discharge tube from the condenser. Cap the open fittings immediately to keep moisture out of the system.

7. Push the radiator towards the engine. Remove the condenser bolts and push the condenser towards the radiator and pull the condenser out.

8. Installation is the reverse of the removal procedure. If the condenser is replaced, add 1.4 oz. of new refrigerant oil. Evacuate, recharge and leak test the system.

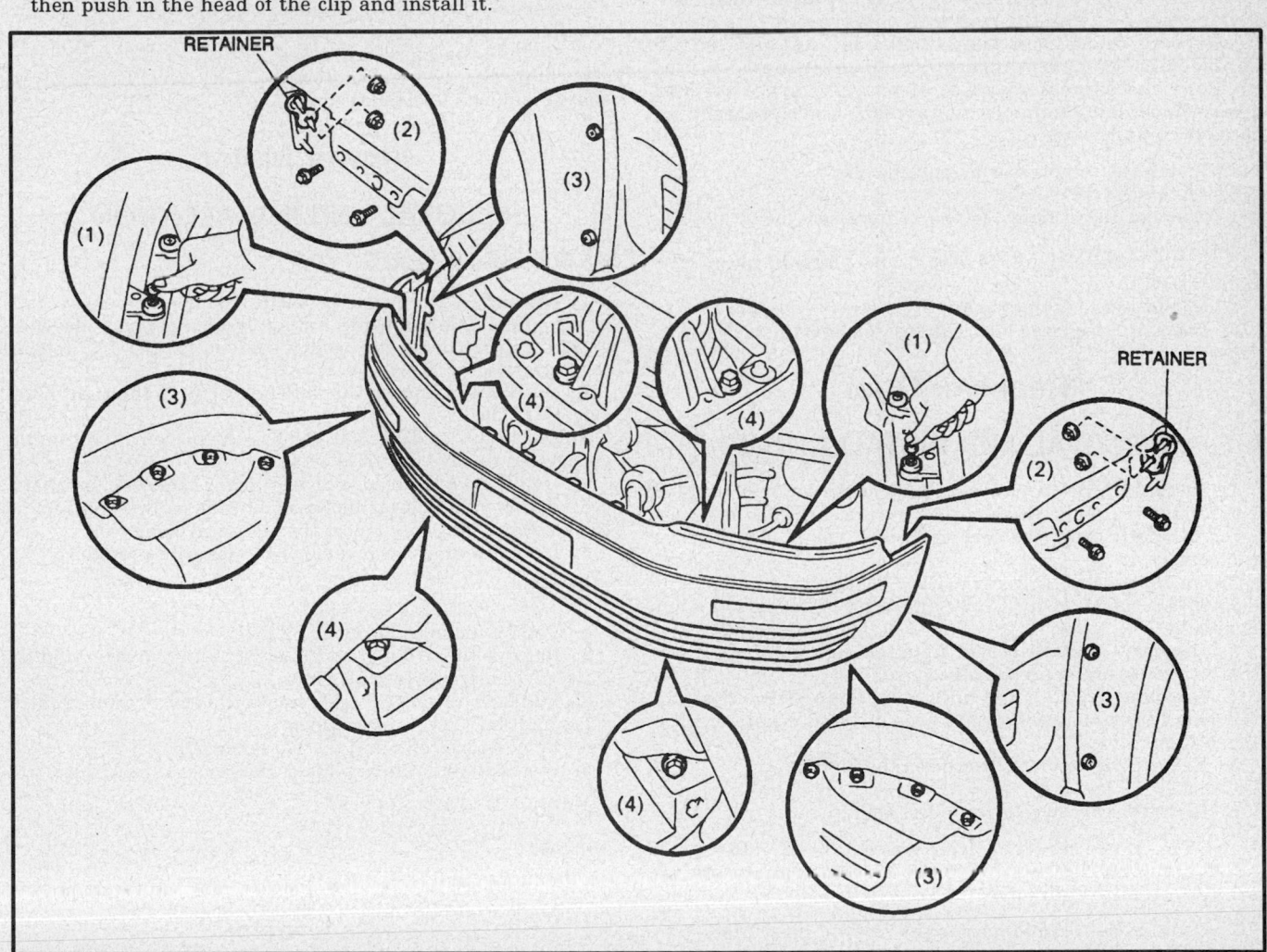

Front bumper removal for radiator and/or condenser removal–LS 400

Compressor

REMOVAL AND INSTALLATION

ES 300

1. Run the engine at idle speed with the air conditioning **ON** for 10 minutes.
2. Stop the engine.
3. Disconnect the battery cables, wait 90 seconds for the airbag system to de–energize, then remove the battery.
4. Remove the cooling fan.
5. Disconnect the connector from the magnetic clutch, temperature switch and revolution detecting sensor.
6. Discharge the refrigerant from the air conditioning system according to the proper procedure.
7. Disconnect the 2 hoses from the compressor service valves. Cap the open fittings immediately to keep moisture and dust out of the system.
8. Loosen or remove the drive belt, remove the compressor mounting bolts, and remove the compressor.

To install:

NOTE: If the compressor is being replaced, drain the refrigerant oil from the removed compressor into a calibrated container. Then drain the refrigerant oil from the replacement compressor into a clean calibrated container. Pour the same amount of clean refrigerant oil into the replacement compressor, as was drained from the removed compressor.

9. Install the compressor mounting bolts.
10. Install the drive belt.
11. Connect the 2 hoses to the compressor, using new O–rings.
12. Connect the clutch lead wire to the wiring harness.
13. Install the cooling fan and battery.
14. Connect the battery cables.
15. Evacuate, recharge and leak test the system.

Receiver/Drier

REMOVAL AND INSTALLATION

1. Disconnect the negative battery cable, wait 90 seconds before starting work while airbag system becomes de–energized. Properly drain the cooling system. On SC 300, remove the battery.
2. On 1993–94 LS 400, remove the headlight from the right side of the vehicle. On SC 300 and SC 400, remove the left headlight.
3. Discharge the refrigerant from the air conditioning system according to the proper procedure.
4. Disconnect the 2 liquid lines from the receiver/drier. Cap the open fittings immediately to keep dirt and moisture out of the system.
5. Remove the receiver/drier from the holder.

To install:

6. Install the receiver/drier in the holder.

NOTE: If the receiver/drier was replaced, add 0.4–0.7 oz. of clean refrigerant oil to the system to maintain total system oil requirements.

7. Connect the 2 liquid lines to the receiver/drier. Tighten to 48 inch lbs. (5.4 Nm). Do not remove the caps until the lines are connected.

8. Connect the negative battery cable. Evacuate and charge the air conditioning system according to the proper procedure. Observe all safety precautions.
9. Use a leak tester to check for refrigerant leaks.
10. On LS 400, SC 300 and SC 400, install the headlight.

Expansion Valve

REMOVAL AND INSTALLATION

NOTE: Expansion valve removal requires evaporator/cooling and blower unit removal.

1. Disconnect the negative battery cable and wait at least 90 seconds for the airbag system to de–energize.
2. Discharge the refrigerant from the air conditioning system according to the proper procedure.
3. Disconnect the suction and liquid lines from the evaporator housing. Cap the open fittings immediately to keep dirt and moisture out of the system.
4. Remove the evaporator assembly.
5. Disconnect the liquid line from the inlet fitting of the expansion valve.
6. Remove the packing and heat sensing tube from the suction line of the evaporator.
7. Remove the expansion valve.
8. To install, reverse the removal procedure. Evacuate, recharge and leak test the system.

Blower Motor

REMOVAL AND INSTALLATION

ES 300, SC 300 and SC 400

1. Disconnect the negative battery cable, wait 90 seconds before starting work while airbag system becomes de–energized. Properly drain the cooling system. On SC 300, remove the battery.
2. On ES 300, remove the under cover from the right lower side of the dash.
3. On SC 300 and SC 400, remove the glove box, lift up the carpet and remove the ECU cover.
4. On all models, remove blower motor connector bracket.
5. Remove the blower motor mounting screws and remove the blower motor. Disconnect the electrical connector.
6. Installation is the reverse of the removal procedure.

GS 300

1. Set the air inlet mode on **FRESH**.
2. Remove the instrument panel No. 2 under cover and the front passenger's door scuff plate.
3. Pull back the carpet and remove the blower motor control relay and the blower motor cover.
4. Remove 3 screws and the blower motor.
5. Installation is the reverse of the removal procedure.

LS 400

1993–94

1. Disconnect the negative battery cable and wait at least 90 seconds while the airbag system de–energizes.
2. Set the air inlet mode on **FRESH**.
3. Remove the clips and remove the under cover from the lower right side of the dash.

4. Disconnect the connectors, remove the 2 screws and remove the connector bracket from the evaporator–blower unit.

5. Remove 9 retaining clips and the front passenger's door scuff plate.

6. Pull back the cowl side portion of the floor carpet.

7. Disconnect the shaft from the control lever, remove the 2 screws and remove the blower lower case.

8. Disconnect the electrical connector, remove the 3 screws and the blower motor.

To install:

9. Install the blower motor with the 3 screws and connect the electrical connector.

10. Install the blower lower case with the 2 screws. Install the blower lower case control lever on the shaft by turning it counterclockwise.

11. Reposition the carpet and install the front passenger's door scuff plate.

12. Install the connector bracket to the evaporator–blower unit with the 2 screws. Connect the connectors.

13. Install the instrument panel under cover.

14. Connect the negative battery cable.

1995

1. Disconnect the negative battery cable and wait for 90 seconds while the airbag system de–energizes.

2. Remove the No. 2 undercover and the glove compartment door finish plate.

3. Disconnect the airbag connector and remove the glove compartment.

4. Disconnect the blower motor connector and remove the blower motor.

5. Installation is the reverse of the removal procedure.

Blower Motor Resistor

REMOVAL AND INSTALLATION

1993 ES 300, 1993–94 SC 300 and SC 400

1. Disconnect the negative battery cable and wait for 90 seconds while the airbag system de–energizes.

2. Remove the glove box.

3. Detach the connector and remove the resistor.

4. Installation is the reverse of the removal procedure.

1994–95 ES 300

1. Disconnect the negative battery cable and wait for 90 seconds while the airbag system de–energizes. Properly discharge the refrigerant from the system using recovery equipment.

2. Remove the air conditioning unit.

3. Remove 2 screws and the resistor.

4. Installation is the reverse of the removal procedure.

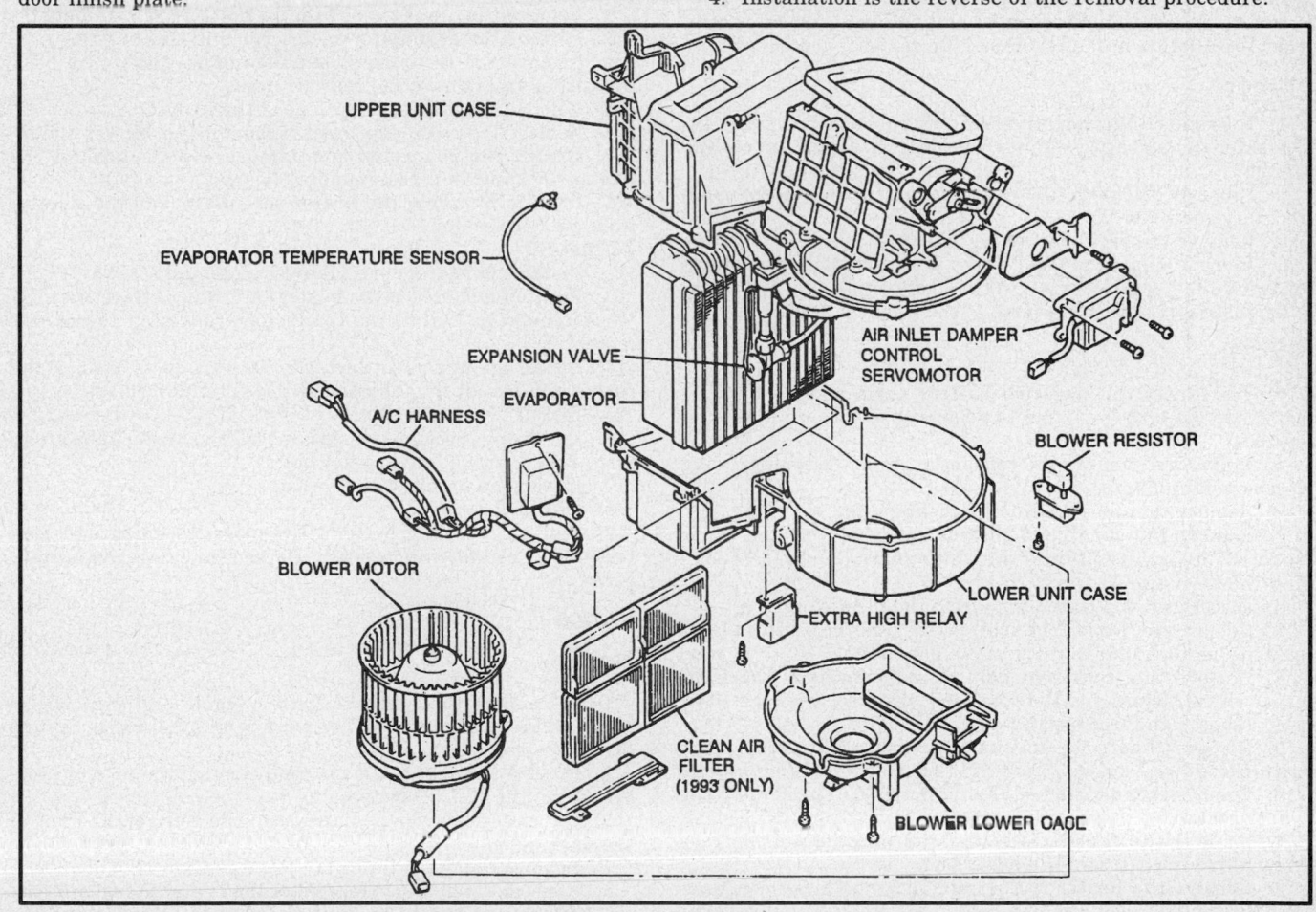

Cooling and blower housing operations–LS 400

1993–94 LS 400

1. Disconnect the negative battery cable and wait 90 seconds before performing any other work while the airbag system de-energizes.
2. Remove the clips and remove the under cover from the lower right side of the dash.
3. Disconnect the connectors, remove the 2 screws and remove the connector bracket from the evaporator–blower unit.
4. Disconnect the connector, remove the 2 screws and remove the resistor from the evaporator–blower unit.
5. Installation is the reverse of the removal procedure.

Heater Core

REMOVAL AND INSTALLATION

ES 300

1993

1. Disconnect the negative battery cable and wait 90 seconds before doing any further work while airbag system de-energizes.
2. Properly drain the cooling system.
3. Remove the heater case side cover. Remove 3 screws and 3 clamps holding the heater core in place.
4. Disconnect the heater pipes and pull out the heater core.
5. Installation is the reverse of the removal procedure.

1994–95

1. Disconnect the negative battery cable and wait 90 seconds for the airbag system to de-energize. Drain the cooling system.
2. Properly discharge the refrigerant from the system using recovery equipment.
3. Remove the air conditioning unit.
4. Remove clips and the heater protector. Remove clamps and pull the heater core out of the heater case.
5. Installation is the reverse of the removal procedure.

GS 300

1. Disconnect the negative battery cable and wait 90 seconds for the airbag system to de-energize. Drain the cooling system.
2. Properly discharge the refrigerant from the system using recovery equipment.
3. Remove the air conditioning cooling unit.
4. Remove the clamp and the control cable from the water valve. Remove the bolts and the water valve. Remove the bolts and the EGR pipe.
5. Disconnect the water hose from the heater unit.
6. Remove the front door scuff plates, rear door scuff plates and the center pillar lower garnish panels.
7. Remove the front seat belt shoulder anchors, the front seat belt retractors and the front seat track covers.
8. Remove the front seats.
9. Remove the roof side inner garnishes, the front pillar garnishes, the steering wheel and the steering column covers.
10. Remove the instrument cluster finish panel and the No. 1 under cover.
11. Remove the finish plate, the end pad the outside rear view mirror switch and the lower pad.
12. Remove the heater to register duct No. 2, the combination switch, the combination meter and the front passenger airbag assembly.
13. Remove register No. 3. Disconnect the connectors and remove the ash tray and the radio with the air conditioner control assembly.

14. Remove the shift lever knob. Disconnect the connectors and remove the upper console panel and the console box register.
15. Remove the console box, the console box mounting bracket and the console box duct.
16. Remove the side defroster nozzles, the air heater guide and the instrument panel.
17. Remove the heater to register duct No. 3, the steering column assembly, the lower mounting brackets, the instrument panel braces and the instrument panel reinforcement.
18. Remove the heater unit. Remove the pipe clamps and pull out the heater core from the heater unit.
19. Installation is the revers of the removal procedure.

SC 300 and SC 400

NOTE: Removal of the heater core requires removal of the entire heater–A/C assembly.

1. Disconnect the negative battery cable and wait 90 seconds before doing any further work while the airbag system de-energizes.
2. Properly discharge the air conditioning system using recovery equipment. Properly drain the cooling system, detach and plug the heater hoses.
3. Remove the engine.
4. Remove the heater water valve, then remove the insulator grommet around the heater core tubes.
5. Remove the brake tubes bracket bolts from dash panel.
6. Remove the evaporator as described in this article.
7. Remove the instrument panel reinforcement, pull back the carpet and remove the rear air ducts.
8. Remove the upper air duct near the heater.
9. Remove the connector bracket from under blower motor.
10. Detach the connector and remove 6 bolts holding the heater–A/C unit in place. Remove the unit.
11. Remove 2 screws, the heater core plate, and the clamps, then pull the heater core out.
To install:
12. Install the heater core, clamps, plate and screws.
13. Position and attach the heater–A/C unit. Attach the electrical connector. Install the connector bracket on the blower motor.
14. Install the upper air duct, the rear air ducts, replace the carpet and install the instrument panel reinforcement.
15. Install the evaporator.
16. In the engine compartment, install the heater tube grommet and the brake line bracket bolts.
17. Install the heater water valve.
18. Install the engine.
19. Refill the cooling system. Evacuate, recharge and leak test the air conditioning system. Connect the negative battery cable.

LS 400

1993–94

1. Disconnect the negative battery cable and wait 90 seconds before doing any further work while the airbag system de-energizes.
2. Properly discharge the air conditioning system and properly drain the cooling system.
3. Disconnect and immediately cap the refrigerant lines at the dash panel.
4. Remove the drain hose clamp at the front side member.
5. Remove the heater–to–register ducts and the mirror control ECU.
6. Remove the connector bracket under the blower motor. Detach the wiring from the cooling and blower housing.

7. Remove the 4 nuts and 2 screws to take out the cooling and blower assembly.

8. Remove the water valve. Disconnect and plug the heater hoses. Remove the heater hose firewall grommet.

9. Remove the instrument panel safety pad as follows:
- Remove the steering wheel and column covers.
- Remove the center console.
- Remove the left panel under cover. Remove the hood release lever.
- Remove the key cylinder pad.
- Remove the lower left knee pad.
- Remove the parking brake lever.
- Remove the outer mirror switch assembly.
- Remove the instrument cluster trim and the instrument cluster.
- Remove the air outlet grille from the top center of the panel control console (insert a small screwdriver between the grille slots to free the 3 top and 2 lower retaining clips).
- Remove the radio and the A/C control assembly.
- Remove the lower right under cover.
- On 1993, pry out the glove box finish plate, remove 2 screws and detach the passenger airbag wiring connector.
- Remove the glove box assembly.
- On 1993, remove the passenger airbag door assembly (3 bolts lower; 2 clips upper).
- Remove the right lower knee pad.
- Remove the ABS ECU.
- Remove the heater–to–register air ducts in the center and right side.
- Detach the junction block at the left side, remove 3 clips at the floor carpet and remove 4 screws at the combination switch.
- Detach the center connector through the glove box opening, remove the bolt and bond cable, detach 3 clips at the carpet.
- Remove 9 bolts and 1 nut and remove the instrument panel safety pad.

10. Remove the rear air ducts and the heater ducts.

11. Remove 4 nuts and remove the heater unit.

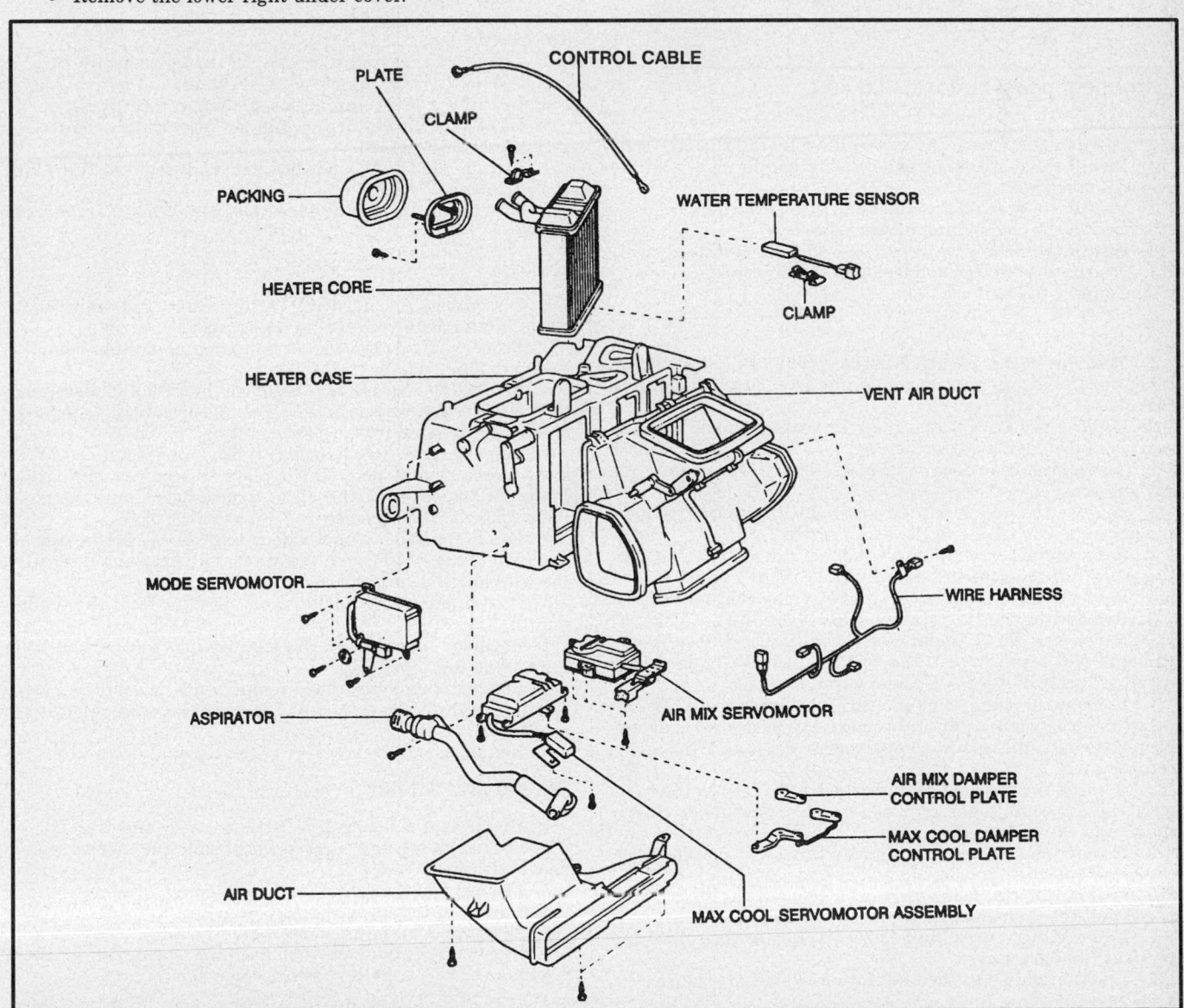

Heater unit exploded view—1993-94 LS 400

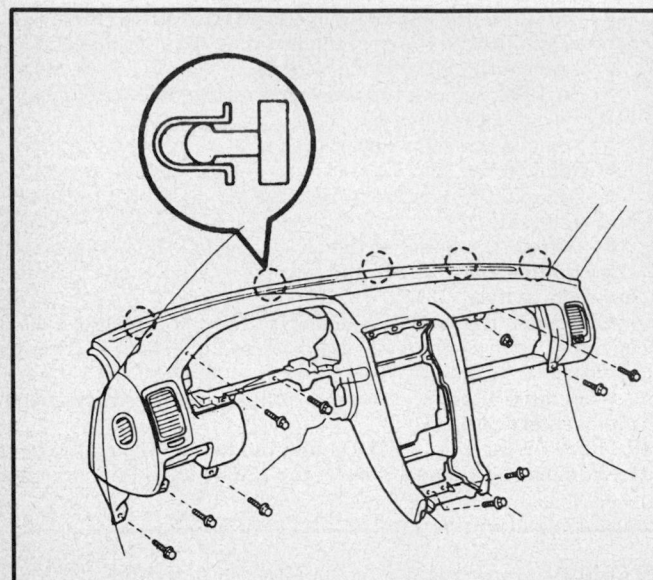

Instrument panel removal—LS 400

To install:

12. Position and attach the heater unit. Install the air ducts.

13. Install the instrument panel safety pad in reverse of the removal procedure.

14. Install the firewall grommet and attach the heater hoses.

15. Install the cooling and blower assembly.

16. Install the heater water valve. Refill the cooling system.

17. Evacuate, recharge and leak test the air conditioning system. Connect the battery.

1995

1. Disconnect the negative battery cable and wait 90 seconds for the airbag system to de-energize. Drain the engine coolant.

2. Remove the front seats, the rear seat cushions, the rear seat belts lower side bolts, the rear seat back, the front door scuff plates, the rear door scuff plates and the rear seat side garnishes.

3. Remove the high mounted stop light, the speaker grilles, the package tray trim and the assist grips.

4. Remove the personal lights, the roof side inner garnishes, the center pillar garnishes and the front pillar garnishes.

5. Remove the steering wheel and steering column covers.

6. Remove the parking brake release lever, the hood lock release lever, the No. 1 under cover, the finish plate, the end pad, the No. 1 safety pad, the coin box, the No. 2 heater to register duct and the No. 2 under cover.

7. Remove the glove compartment door finish plate. Disconnect the airbag connector and remove the passenger side airbag assembly, the glove compartment door and the glove compartment.

8. Remove the steering column, the No. 2 register, the radio with the air conditioner control assembly, the upper cluster finish and the combination meter.

9. Remove the cluster finish panel, the lower console cover, the lower console box, the cup holder and the console box.

10. Disconnect the connectors and remove the instrument panel and the instrument panel reinforcement and braces.

11. Remove the screws, disconnect the heater core pipes and pull out the heater core.

12. Installation is the reverse of the removal procedure.

Evaporator

REMOVAL AND INSTALLATION

ES 300

1. Disconnect the negative battery cable and wait 90 seconds before doing any further work while the airbag system de-energizes.

2. Remove the glove compartment, then the ECU and bracket.

3. Remove the electrical connector bracket at the blower housing.

4. Remove the connectors, 3 screws, 1 nut and then the blower unit from the vehicle.

5. Disconnect and immediately cap the refrigerant lines from the evaporator tubes.

6. Remove the evaporator cover (2 bolts for the tubes and 8 screws for the cover).

7. Remove the evaporator core. If necessary, the expansion valve can now be removed.

To install:

8. Install the evaporator core (if a replacement core is installed, add 1.6 oz. of new refrigerant oil).

9. Install the cover and attach the refrigerant lines.

10. Install the blower motor unit and reattach the connectors and connector bracket.

11. Install the ECU and bracket and replace the glove compartment.

12. Evacuate, recharge and leak test the system. Connect the battery.

GS 300

1. Disconnect the negative battery cable and wait 90 seconds for the airbag system to de-energize.

2. Properly discharge the air conditioning system using recovery equipment.

3. Remove the equalizer tubes from the EPR and disconnect the liquid tube and suction tube. Cap the open fittings immediately to keep moisture out of the system.

4. Remove the instrument panel No. 2 under cover and the glove compartment door finish plate. Disconnect the airbag connector and remove the glove compartment and the glove compartment reinforcement.

5. Remove the passenger's door scuff plate, the heater air duct guide, the ECM cover, the air conditioning amplifier with the wire harness and the cooling unit.

6. If equipped, remove the clean air filter from the cooling unit.

7. Remove the grommet. Cut the packings and remove from the cooling unit openings.

8. Remove the evaporator temperature sensor connector clamp. Separate the upper and lower cases and remove the evaporator.

9. Installation is the reverse of the removal procedure.

SC 300 and SC 400

1. Disconnect the negative battery cable and wait 90 seconds before doing any further work while the airbag system de-energizes.

2. Properly discharge the air conditioning system.

3. Detach and remove the ABS actuator.

4. Disconnect and immediately cap the refrigerant lines.

5. Remove the equalizer tube from the evaporator pressure regulator (EPR). Cap the openings immediately.

6. Remove the glove box and side air duct.

7. Detach the connectors and remove the power steering relay box, cooling fan computer and TRC computer.

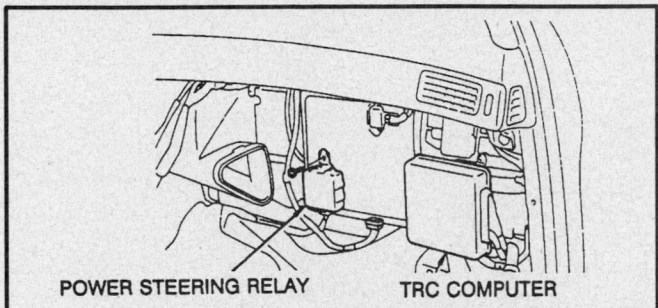

POWER STEERING RELAY   TRC COMPUTER

Power steering and TRC computer locations under instrument panel—SC 300 and SC 400

8. Pull the carpet down and remove the computer cover.

9. Remove the evaporator cover and the foot air duct.

10. Remove 6 bolts, remove the lower case and remove the evaporator core. The expansion can now be removed if needed.

To install:

11. Install the evaporator core. If replacing the core, add 1.4–1.7 oz. of new refrigerant oil.

12. Install the floor duct, evaporator cover, computer cover and replace the carpet.

13. Install and connect the TRC, power steering and cooling fan computers.

14. Install the side air duct and then the glove box.

15. Connect the EPR line and both refrigerant lines, using new O–rings.

16. Evacuate, recharge and leak test the system. Connect the battery.

LS 400

1. Disconnect the negative battery cable and wait 90 seconds before doing any further work while the airbag system de–energizes.

2. Discharge the refrigerant from the air conditioning system according to the proper procedure.

3. Remove the cruise control actuator.

4. Remove the bolt and remove both tubes from the evaporator pressure regulator.

5. Remove the 2 bolts and both the liquid and suction lines.

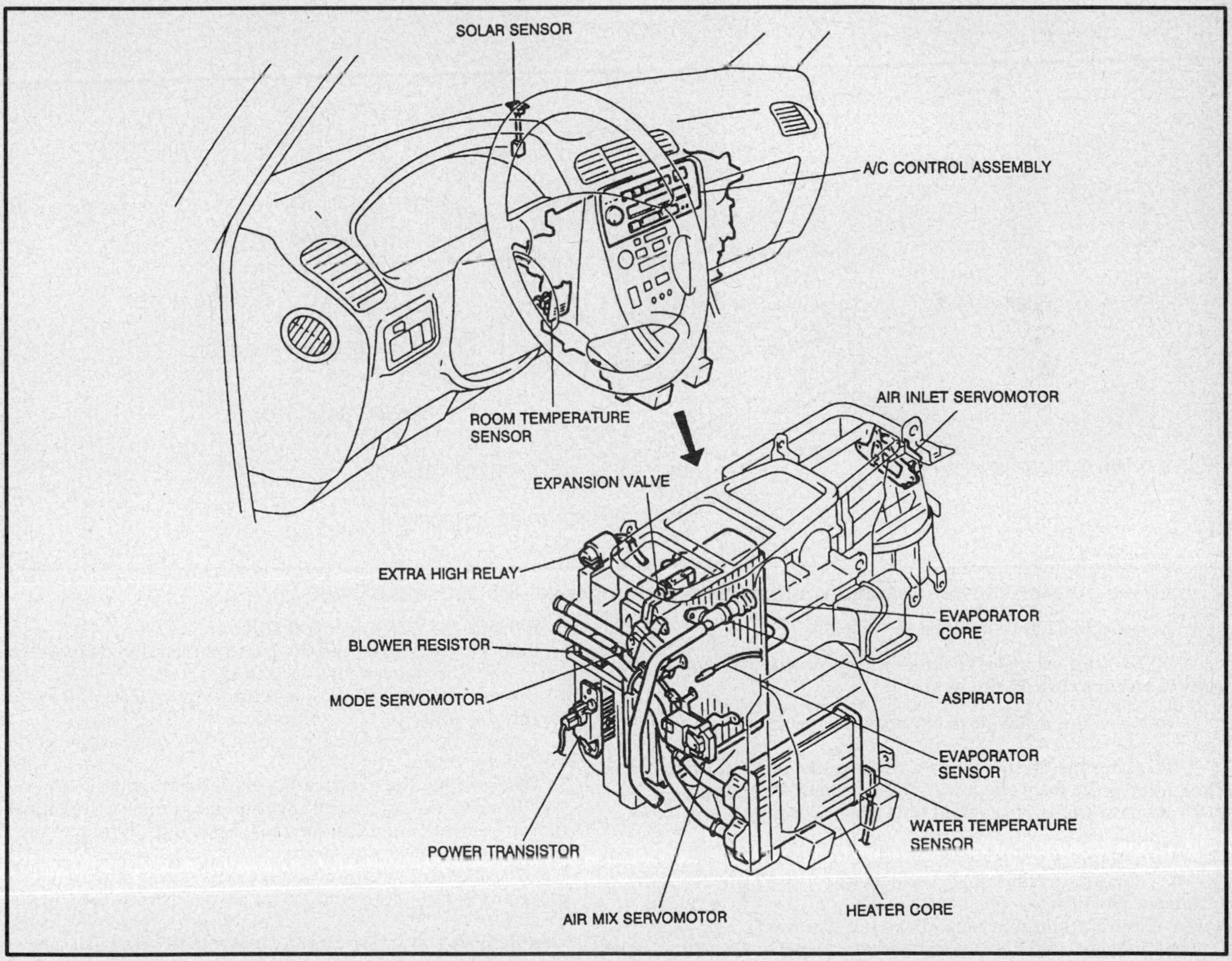

SOLAR SENSOR

A/C CONTROL ASSEMBLY

ROOM TEMPERATURE SENSOR

AIR INLET SERVOMOTOR

EXPANSION VALVE

EXTRA HIGH RELAY

EVAPORATOR CORE

BLOWER RESISTOR

ASPIRATOR

MODE SERVOMOTOR

EVAPORATOR SENSOR

WATER TEMPERATURE SENSOR

POWER TRANSISTOR

AIR MIX SERVOMOTOR

HEATER CORE

Air conditioning housing and system components—ES 300

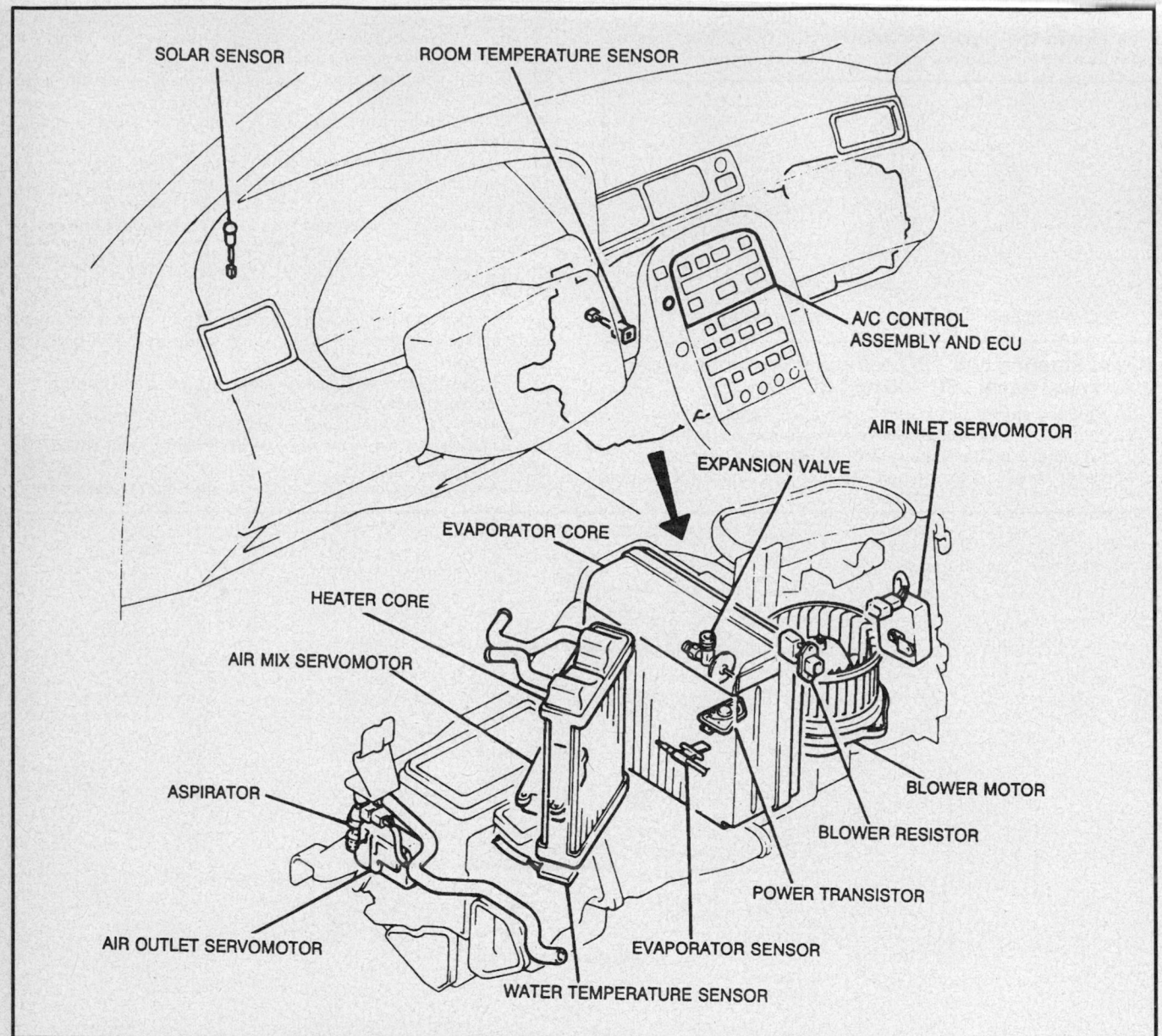

SOLAR SENSOR

ROOM TEMPERATURE SENSOR

A/C CONTROL ASSEMBLY AND ECU

AIR INLET SERVOMOTOR

EXPANSION VALVE

EVAPORATOR CORE

HEATER CORE

AIR MIX SERVOMOTOR

ASPIRATOR

BLOWER MOTOR

BLOWER RESISTOR

POWER TRANSISTOR

AIR OUTLET SERVOMOTOR

EVAPORATOR SENSOR

WATER TEMPERATURE SENSOR

Heater, evaporator, blower assembly and system components—SC 300 and SC 400

6. Remove the 2 nuts and the cover plate.

NOTE: Cap all open fittings immediately to keep dirt and moisture out of the system.

7. Remove the drain hose clamp from the front side member.

8. Working inside the vehicle, remove the clips and remove the under cover from the lower right corner of the dash.

9. Remove the glove compartment as follows:
   • Remove the glove compartment panel.
   • Disconnect the left side check arm from the door.
   • Using a suitable tool, push in the top of the clip and remove the 5 clips.
   • Insert a suitable plate between the upper side of the compartment and the safety pad, to protect the pad. Pry against the plate to pry out the compartment and remove it.
   • Disconnect the electrical connector.

10. Remove the heater ducts, side air ducts and registers.

11. Remove the mirror control ECU.

12. Remove the 2 bolts and the bracket from the evaporator-blower unit. Disconnect the connectors.

13. Disconnect the vehicle side wire harness from the evaporator-blower unit.

14. Remove the 4 nuts and 2 screws, then remove the evaporator-blower unit.

15. Disassemble the evaporator-blower unit as follows:
   • Remove the screw and cover and disconnect the connector for the air inlet servomotor assembly. Remove the 3 screws and remove the servomotor assembly.
   • Remove the screw and remove the power transistor. Remove the screw and remove the plate. Disconnect the connector.
   • Remove the screw and the extra high relay. Disconnect the connector.
   • Disconnect the connector, remove the 2 screws and the blower resistor.

- Remove the air conditioning wire harness. Remove the 8 screws and separate the upper and lower case.

16. Pull out the evaporator sensor from the evaporator fins. Remove the 2 bolts and separate the evaporator and the expansion valve.

To install:

17. Install the expansion valve to the evaporator and tighten the bolts to 48 inch lbs. (5.4 Nm). Position the evaporator sensor.

18. Assemble the evaporator–blower unit as follows:
- Install the evaporator in the lower case and install the upper case. Install the screws.
- Attach the air conditioning wire harness.
- Install the blower resistor, extra high relay, power transistor and the air inlet servomotor assembly. Connect the electrical connectors.

NOTE: If the evaporator core was replaced, add 1.4–1.7 oz. of clean refrigerant oil to the system to maintain the total system oil requirements.

19. Install the evaporator–blower unit and secure with the nuts and screws.

20. Connect the vehicle side wire harness to the evaporator–blower unit. Install the connector bracket.

21. Install the mirror control ECU and connect the electrical connector.

22. Install the air ducts as removed.

23. Install the glove compartment.

24. Install the drain hose clamp to the front side member and install the cover plate.

25. Connect the liquid and suction lines. Tighten the bolts to 7 ft. lbs. (10 Nm).

26. Connect the equalizer tube to the evaporator pressure regulator. Tighten the bolt to 7 ft. lbs. (10 Nm).

27. Install the cruise control actuator.

28. Connect the negative battery cable. Evacuate and charge the system according to the proper procedure. Observe all safety precautions.

29. Check for refrigerant leaks and for proper operation.

Refrigerant Lines

REMOVAL AND INSTALLATION

1. Disconnect the negative battery cable and wait 90 seconds before doing any further work while the airbag system de–energizes.

2. Discharge the refrigerant from the air conditioning system according to the proper procedure.

3. Disconnect the refrigerant line to be replaced at the connection fittings. Cap the open connections on the vehicle to prevent the entrance of dirt and moisture.

4. Remove the refrigerant line.

To install:

5. Route the new refrigerant line into place with the protective end caps installed.

6. Remove the protective caps and connect the line to the connection fittings. Tighten to the proper torque specification.

7. Connect the negative battery cable. Evacuate and charge the system according to the proper procedure. Observe all safety precautions.

8. Inspect for refrigerant leaks and for proper system operation.

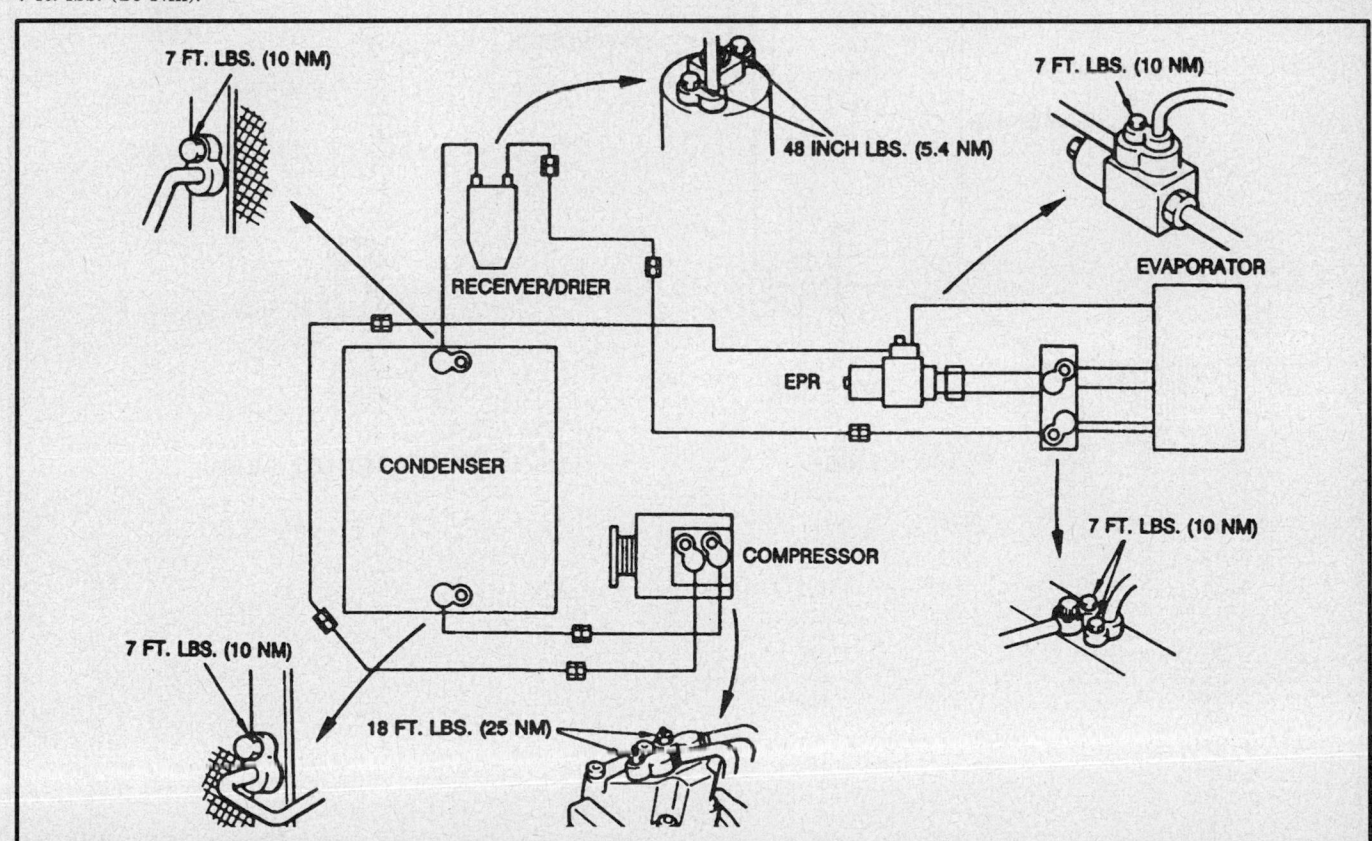

Refrigerant line connection torque specifications – LS 400

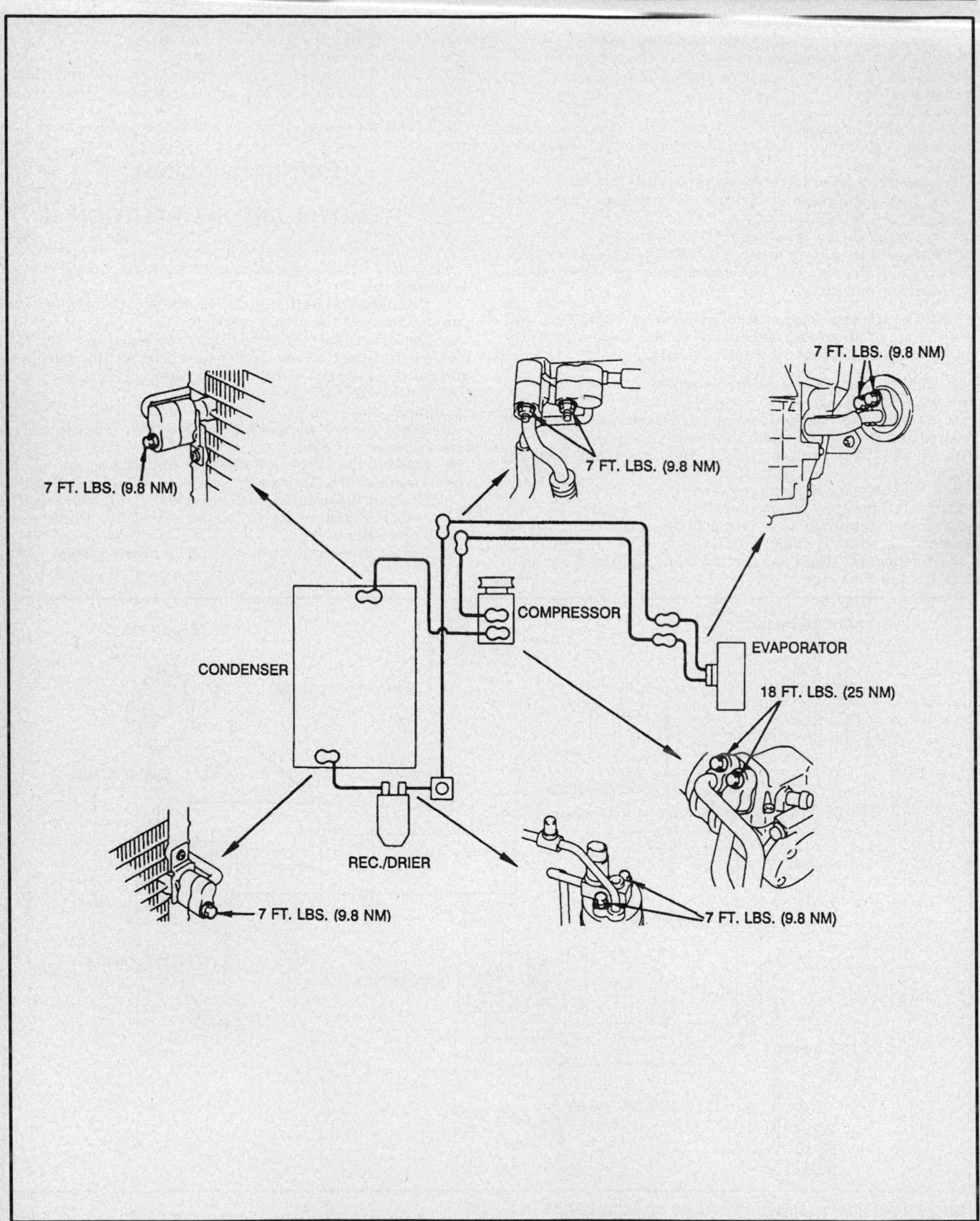

Refrigerant line connection torque specifications—ES 300

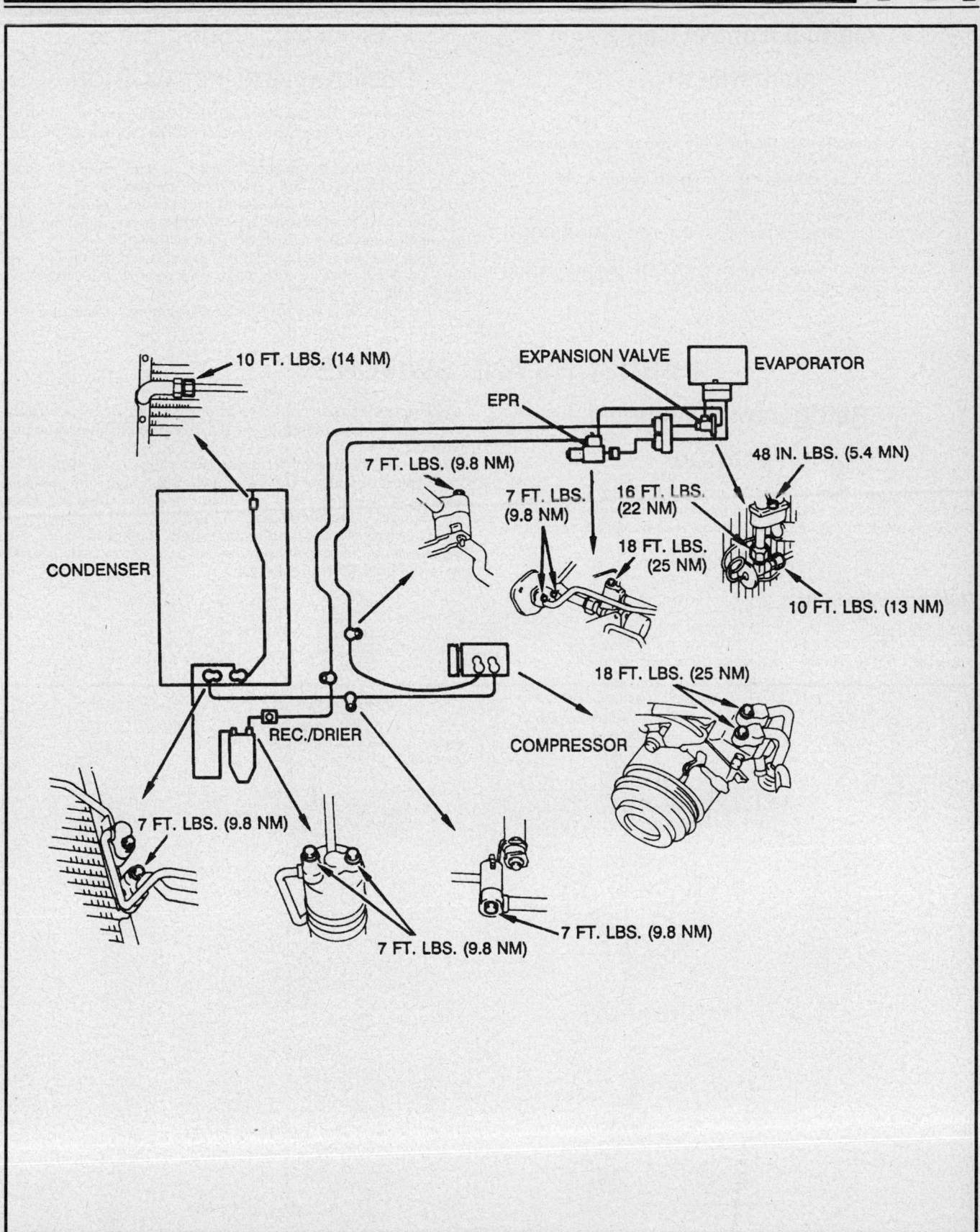

10 FT. LBS. (14 NM)

EXPANSION VALVE

EVAPORATOR

EPR

CONDENSER

7 FT. LBS. (9.8 NM)

7 FT. LBS. (9.8 NM)

16 FT. LBS. (22 NM)

48 IN. LBS. (5.4 MN)

18 FT. LBS. (25 NM)

10 FT. LBS. (13 NM)

REC./DRIER

18 FT. LBS. (25 NM)

COMPRESSOR

7 FT. LBS. (9.8 NM)

7 FT. LBS. (9.8 NM)

7 FT. LBS. (9.8 NM)

Refrigerant line connection torque specifications—SC 300 and SC 400

Manual Control Cable

ADJUSTMENT

LS 400

The manual control cable connects the air mix servomotor and the water valve.

1. Disconnect the control cable from the water valve.
2. Turn the ignition switch **ON**.
3. Turn the blower switch **ON**.
4. Set the temperature control switch on the **MAX COOL** position.
5. Set the water valve lever on the **COOL** position, install the control cable and lock the clamp.

Electronic Control Head

REMOVAL AND INSTALLATION

1. Disconnect the negative battery cable and wait 90 seconds before doing any other work while the airbag system de-energizes.
2. Remove the center control console trim plate to expose the radio and A/C control panel retaining screws.
3. If necessary, remove the center instrument panel register.
4. Remove the mounting screws and remove the radio with the control assembly. Disconnect the connectors.
5. Remove the screws, open the brackets on the outside, release the connection of the claws and remove the control assembly from the radio.
6. Installation is the reverse of the removal procedure.

SENSORS AND SWITCHES

Refrigerant Switches

OPERATION

Refrigerant switches are located in the refrigerant lines. Their function is to sense refrigerant pressure and signal the compressor clutch to engage and disengage at the proper times.

TESTING

Dual Pressure Switch

1993 Models

1. On LS 400, remove the right headlight for access.

2. Disconnect the connector from the dual pressure switch.
3. Install a manifold gauge set according to the proper procedure.
4. Use an ohmmeter to check that there is continuity between the terminals of the switch when the high side pressure is between 30 psi and 384 psi. Below or above these readings, there should be no continuity.
5. If switch did not read as indicated, replace it.
6. Remove the manifold gauge set and connect the connector to the dual pressure switch.

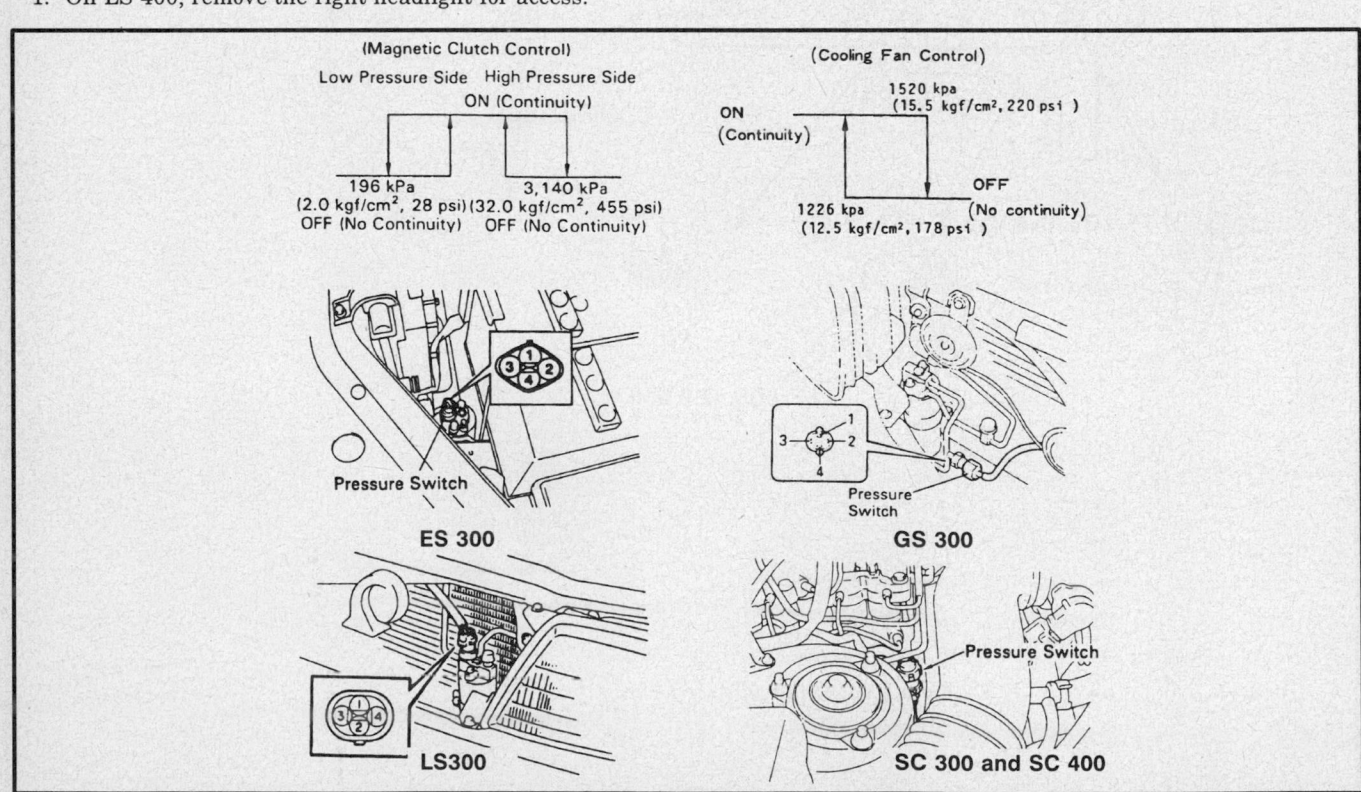

Pressure switch testing—1994-95 Models except 1994 LS 400

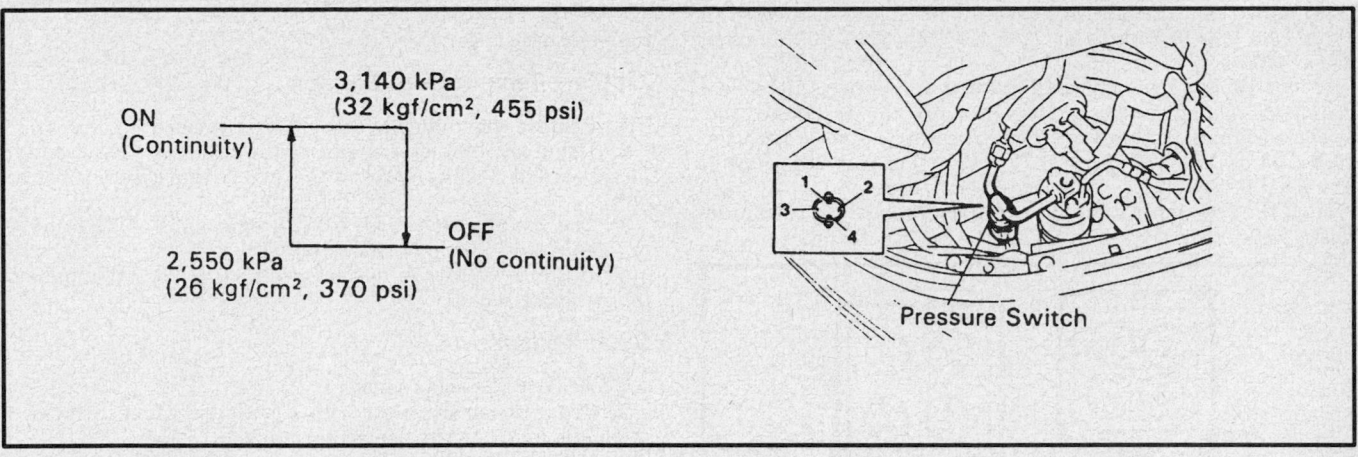

ON
(Continuity)

3,140 kPa
(32 kgf/cm², 455 psi)

2,550 kPa
(26 kgf/cm², 370 psi)

OFF
(No continuity)

1 2
3 4

Pressure Switch

Pressure switch testing—1994 LS 400

Pressure Switch

1994 LS 400

1. Disconnect the connector from the pressure switch.
2. Install a manifold gauge set according to the proper procedure.
3. Run the engine at approximately 2000 rpm.
4. When the air conditioning switch is **OFF**, use an ohmmeter to check that there is continuity between the terminals and that the high side pressure is 370 psi or lower.
5. When the air conditioning switch and blower switches are **ON**, check that there is no continuity between terminals and the high pressure is 455 psi or higher.

Except 1994 LS 400

1. Disconnect the connector from the pressure switch.
2. Install a manifold gauge set according to the proper procedure.
3. Run the engine at approximately 2000 rpm.
4. Check the magnetic clutch control continuity by connecting the positive lead of the ohmmeter to terminal **4** and the negative lead to terminal **1**. Check the continuity between the terminals when the refrigerant pressure changes as shown.
5. Check the cooling fan control continuity by connecting the positive lead of the ohmmeter to terminal **2** and the negative lead to terminal **3**. Check the continuity between the terminals when the refrigerant pressure changes as shown.
6. If pressure switch operation is not as specified, replace the pressure switch.

Engine Coolant Temperature Switch

1995 LS 400

1. Remove the engine coolant temperature switch.
2. Place the switch in cold water. While varying the temperature of the water, check the continuity between the switch terminals.
3. Check that there is no continuity when the temperature is above 199°F (93°C) and that there is continuity when the temperature is below 181°F (83°C).
4. If the switch operation is not as specified, replace the engine coolant temperature switch.

REMOVAL AND INSTALLATION

Pressure Switch

1. Disconnect the negative battery cable and wait 90 seconds for the airbag system to de-energize.

2. Discharge the refrigerant from the air conditioning system according to the proper procedure.
3. On LS 400, remove the right side headlight.
4. Disconnect the electrical connector and remove the switch.

To install:

5. Install the pressure switch and tighten to 7 ft. lbs. (10 Nm).

NOTE: Be careful not to deform the refrigerant line during switch installation.

6. Connect the connector.
7. Install the headlight, if removed.
8. Evacuate and charge the system according to the proper procedure. Observe all safety precautions.
9. Check for refrigerant leaks and proper system operation.

Engine Coolant Temperature Switch

1995 LS 400

1. Disconnect the negative battery cable and wait 90 seconds for the airbag system to de-energize. Drain the engine coolant.
2. Remove the fan shroud and the engine coolant temperature switch.
3. Installation is the reverse of the removal procedure. Tighten the switch to 5.5 ft. lbs. (7.4 Nm).

Sensors

OPERATION

Sensors are used in the air conditioning system mostly to provide temperature information. The sensors are especially important in supplying input to the automatic temperature control systems.

TESTING

Revolution Detecting (RPM) Sensor

ES 300, SC 300 and SC 400

1. On ES 300, disconnect the sensor connector. Using an ohmmeter, measure the resistance (between terminals **1** and **2**) at the harness side of the connector. It should be 65–125 ohms at 68°F (20°C) or 90–150 ohms at 212°F (100°C).
2. On 1993 SC 300 and SC 400, disconnect the sensor connector. Using an ohmmeter, measure the resistance (between

terminals **1** and **2**) at the harness side of the connector. It should be 530–650 ohms at 77°F (25°C) or 670–890 ohms at 212°F (100°C).

3. On 1994–95 SC 300 and SC 400, disconnect the sensor connector. Using an ohmmeter, measure the resistance (between terminals **1** and **2**) at the harness side of the connector. It should be 170–220 ohms at 77°F (25°C) or 210–290 ohms at 212°F (100°C).

4. If the resistance is not as specified, replace the revolution detecting sensor.

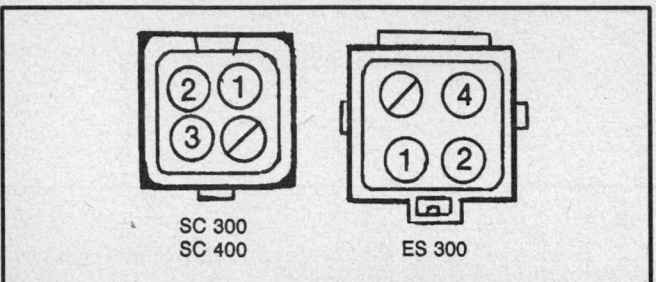

SC 300
SC 400

ES 300

RPM sensor connector terminal identification

Evaporator Temperature Sensor

1. Remove the sensor.
2. Place the thermistor in cold water. While varying the temperature of the water, measure the resistance at the connector and at the same time, measure the temperature of the water with a thermometer.
3. For ES 300, SC 300 and SC 400, the readings should be 4.6–5.1 kilo–ohms at 32°F (0°C) and 2.1–2.6 kilo–ohms at 59°F (15°C).
4. For GS 300 and LS 400, the readings should be 4.5–5.2 kilo–ohms at 32°F (0°C) and 2.0–2.7 kilo–ohms at 59°F (15°C).
5. If the resistance is not as specified, replace the sensor.

EVAPORATOR TEMPERATURE SENSOR RESISTANCE CHART

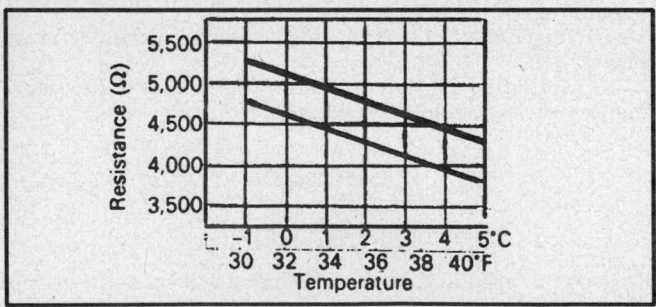

Room Temperature Sensor

1. Remove the room temperature sensor.
2. Using an ohmmeter, measure the resistance between terminals **1** and **2** while varying the temperature with a hot air gun.
3. For ES 300, SC 300 and SC 400, the readings should be 1.6–1.8 kilo–ohms at 77°F (25°C) or 0.5–0.7 kilo–ohms at 122°F (50°C).
4. For GS 300 and LS 400, the readings should be 1.65–1.75 kilo–ohms at 77°F (25°C) or 0.55–0.65 kilo–ohms at 122°F (50°C).

5. If the resistance is not as specified, replace the room temperature sensor.

Ambient Temperature Sensor

1. Remove the ambient temperature sensor.
2. Using an ohmmeter, measure the resistance between terminals **1** and **2** while varying the temperature with a hot air gun.
3. The reading should be 1.6–1.8 kilo–ohms at 77°F (25°C) or 0.5–0.7 kilo–ohms at 122°F (50°C).
4. If the resistance is not as specified, replace the ambient temperature sensor.

Solar Sensor

1. Remove the solar sensor.
2. Cover the solar sensor with a cloth and connect the leads of an ohmmeter to the sensor terminals.
3. Remove the cloth from the solar sensor and subject the sensor to an electric light. Measure the resistance. The reading should be approximately 4 kilo–ohms. When the light is moved away from the sensor, the resistance should increase.
4. If the resistance is not as specified, replace the sensor.

Duct Sensor

1995 LS 400

1. Remove the duct sensor.
2. Using an ohmmeter, measure the resistance between terminals **1** and **2** while varying the temperature with a hot air gun.
3. The reading should be 4.8–5.2 kilo–ohms at 32°F (0°C) or 1.6–2.0 kilo–ohms at 122°F (50°C).
4. If the resistance is not as specified, replace the sensor.

Engine Coolant Temperature Sensor

Except 1995 LS 400

1. Remove the engine coolant temperature sensor.
2. Place the sensor in cold water. While varying the temperature of the water, measure the resistance at terminals **1** and **2** (ES 300) or terminals **1** and **3** (other models) and at the same time, measure the temperature of the water with a thermometer.
3. For ES 300, the readings should be 50 kilo–ohms or less at 32°F (0°C), 2.5–2.7 kilo–ohms at 104°F (40°C) and 2.0 kilo–ohms or more at 212°F (100°C).
4. For other models, the readings should be 16.5–17.5 kilo–ohms at 32°F (0°C), 2.4–2.8 kilo–ohms at 104°F (40°C) and 0.7–1.0 kilo–ohms at 158°F (70°C).
5. If the resistance is not as specified, replace the sensor.

REMOVAL AND INSTALLATION

Revolution Detecting Sensor

ES 300, SC 300 and SC 400

1. Disconnect the negative battery cable and wait 90 seconds before doing any further work while the airbag system de–energizes.
2. Properly discharge the air conditioning system.
3. If necessary for access, remove the compressor.
4. Remove the RPM sensor.
5. Installation is the reverse of the removal procedure. Use new O–rings at the appropriate fittings. Evacuate, recharge and leak test.

Evaporator Temperature Sensor

1. Disconnect the negative battery cable and wait 90 seconds before doing any other work while the airbag system de-energizes.
2. Discharge the refrigerant from the air conditioning system according to the proper procedure.
3. Remove the evaporator assembly from the vehicle.
4. Remove the evaporator temperature sensor.
5. Installation is the reverse of the removal procedure. Evacuate and charge the system according to the proper procedure. Observe all safety precautions.

Room Temperature Sensor

SC 300, SC 400 and LS 400

1. Disconnect the negative battery cable and wait 90 seconds before doing any other work while the airbag system de-energizes.
2. Working inside the vehicle, remove the 3 screws from the cover under the lower left side of the instrument panel. Use a suitable prying tool to remove the cover. Disconnect the valve from the cover.
3. Remove the 2 screws and the hood release lever. Disconnect the release cable from the lever.
4. Using a suitable prying tool, remove the key cylinder pad.
5. Remove the 6 bolts and the lower pad from under the steering column. Remove the sensor from the lower pad.
6. Installation is the reverse of the removal procedure.

ES 300

1. Disconnect the negative battery cable and wait 90 seconds before doing any other work while the airbag system de-energizes.
2. Remove the panel insert at the lower left front of the instrument panel.
3. Detach the connector and remove the room temperature sensor.
4. Installation is the reverse of the removal procedure.

GS 300

1. Disconnect the negative battery cable and wait 90 seconds before doing any other work while the airbag system de-energizes.
2. Remove the instrument panel as described in the evaporator removal and installation.
3. Remove the room temperature sensor from the instrument panel.
4. Installation is the reverse of the removal procedure.

Ambient Temperature Sensor

1. Disconnect the negative battery cable and wait 90 seconds before doing any other work while the airbag system de-energizes.
2. On SC 300 and SC 400, remove the engine under cover.
3. On all models, remove the clip and the sensor from the bumper reinforcement or from behind the grille. Disconnect the connector.
4. Installation is the reverse of the removal procedure.

Solar Sensor

1. Disconnect the negative battery cable and wait 90 seconds before doing any other work while the airbag system de-energizes.

2. Use a suitable tool to pry loose the clips and remove the passenger's side defroster nozzle garnish if required to remove the sensor.
3. Remove the solar sensor and disconnect the connector.
4. Installation is the reverse of the removal procedure.

Engine Coolant Temperature Sensor

1. Disconnect the negative battery cable and wait 90 seconds before doing any other work while the airbag system de-energizes.
2. Discharge the refrigerant from the air conditioning system according to the proper procedure.
3. Drain the cooling system into a suitable container.
4. Remove the heater unit (GS 330, LS 400) or the A/C unit (ES 300, SC 300 and SC 400).
5. Remove the water temperature sensor from the heater unit by taking off the clamp and disconnect the connector.
6. Installation is the reverse of the removal procedure. Fill the cooling system to the proper level and evacuate and charge the refrigerant system according to the proper procedure.

Duct Temperature Sensors

1. Disconnect the negative battery cable and wait 90 seconds before doing any other work while the airbag system de-energizes.
2. Remove the instrument panel as described in the evaporator removal and installation.
3. Remove the driver's sensor from the No. 3 heater to register duct and/or the passenger's sensor from the No. 1 heater to register duct.
4. Installation is the reverse of the removal procedure.

Servomotors and Stepmotors

OPERATION

Servomotors and stepmotors are electric motors that operate the air doors in the heater and evaporator units. The air doors control airflow as follows: mixing hot and cool air to attain the desired temperature, mixing outside and recirculated air and controlling the direction of air flow, directing airflow to the instrument panel registers, floor ducts or defroster nozzles.

TESTING

Air Inlet Servomotor

1994–95 ES 300 and GS 300

1. Remove the air inlet control servomotor.
2. Connect the positive battery voltage lead to terminal 2 and the negative lead to terminal 1. Check that the lever moves smoothly to the **REC** position.
3. Connect the positive battery voltage lead to terminal 1 and the negative lead to terminal 2. Check that the lever moves smoothly to the **FRS** position.
4. If the servomotor operation is not as specified, replace the air inlet servomotor.

1994–95 LS 400

1. Remove the air inlet control servomotor.
2. Connect the positive battery voltage lead to terminal 5 and the negative lead to terminal 4. Check that the lever moves smoothly to the **REC** position.

3. Connect the positive battery voltage lead to terminal **4** and the negative lead to terminal **5**. Check that the lever moves smoothly to the **FRS** position.

4. If the servomotor operation is not as specified, replace the air inlet servomotor.

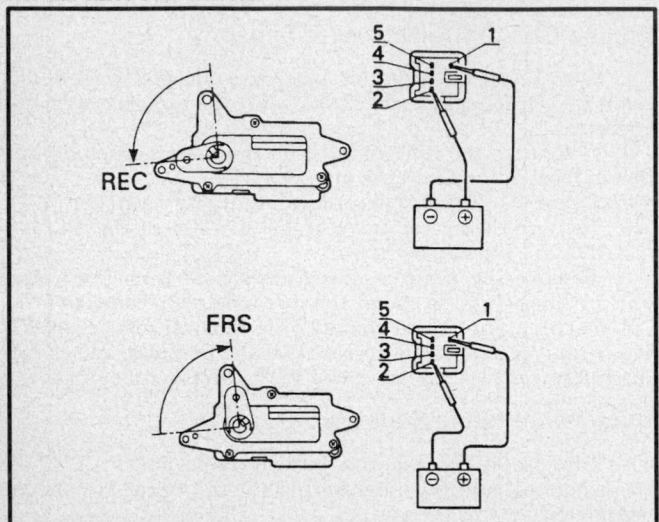

Air inlet control servomotor testing—1994–95 ES 300

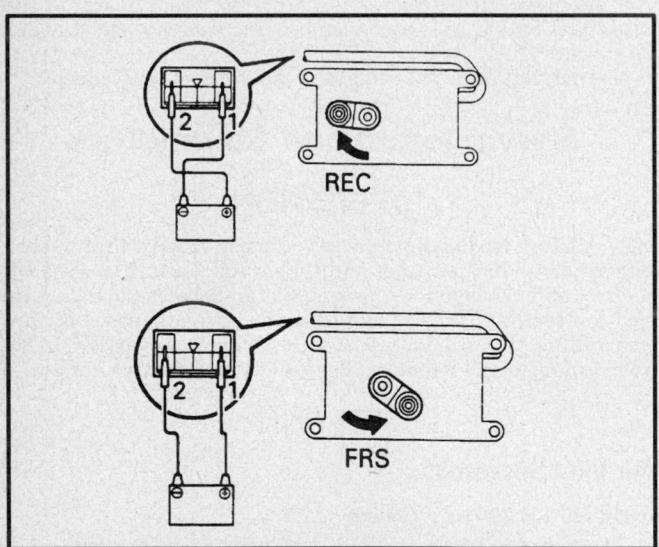

Air inlet control servomotor testing—1994–95 GS 300

1994–95 SC 300 and SC 400

1. Remove the air inlet control servomotor.

2. Connect the positive battery voltage lead to terminal **6** and the negative lead to terminal **2**. Check that the lever moves smoothly to the **REC** position.

3. Connect the positive battery voltage lead to terminal **2** and the negative lead to terminal **6**. Check that the lever moves smoothly to the **FRS** position.

4. If the servomotor operation is not as specified, replace the air inlet servomotor.

Air Mix Servomotor

1994–95 ES 300 and GS 300

1. Remove the air mix control servomotor.

2. Connect the positive battery voltage lead to terminal **1** and the negative lead to terminal **2**. Check that the lever moves smoothly to the **COOL** position.

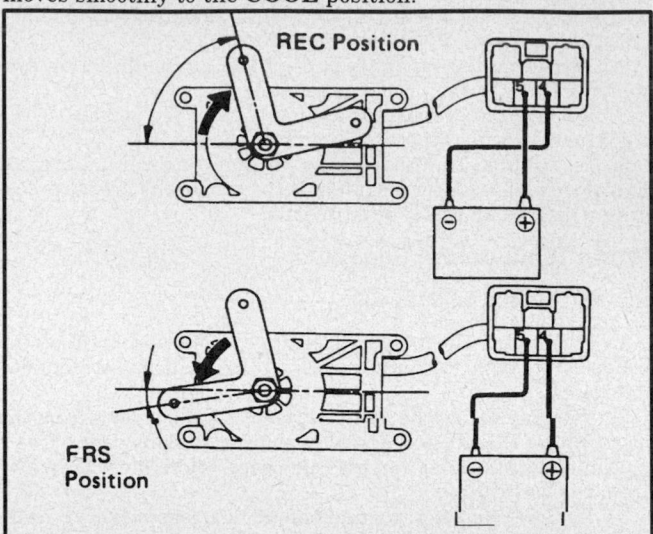

Air inlet control servomotor testing—1994 LS 400

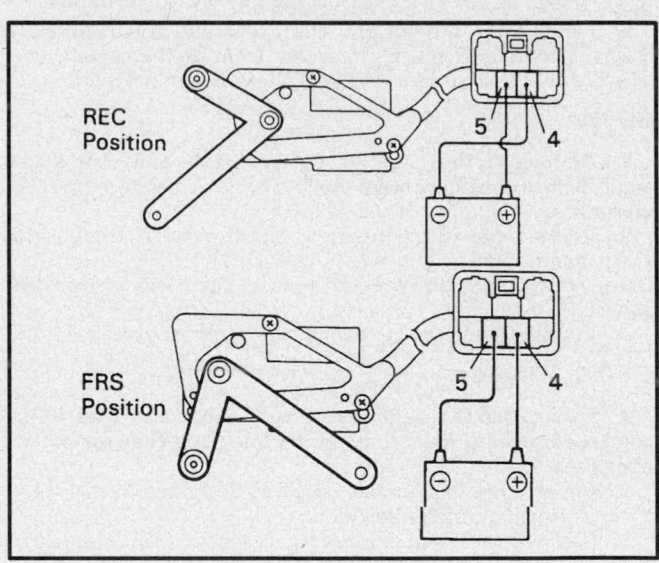

Air inlet control servomotor testing—1995 LS 400

3. Connect the positive battery voltage lead to terminal **2** and the negative lead to terminal **1**. Check that the lever moves smoothly to the **HOT** position.

4. If the servomotor operation is not as specified, replace the air mix servomotor.

1994 LS 400

1. Remove the air mix control servomotor.

2. Connect the positive battery voltage lead to terminal **6** and the negative lead to terminal **2**. Check that the lever moves smoothly to the **COOL** position.

3. Connect the positive battery voltage lead to terminal **2** and the negative lead to terminal **6**. Check that the lever moves smoothly to the **HOT** position.

4. If the servomotor operation is not as specified, replace the air mix servomotor.

1994 SC 300 and SC 400

1. Remove the air mix control servomotor.
2. Connect the positive battery voltage lead to terminal 4 and the negative lead to terminal 5. Check that the lever moves smoothly to the **COOL** position.

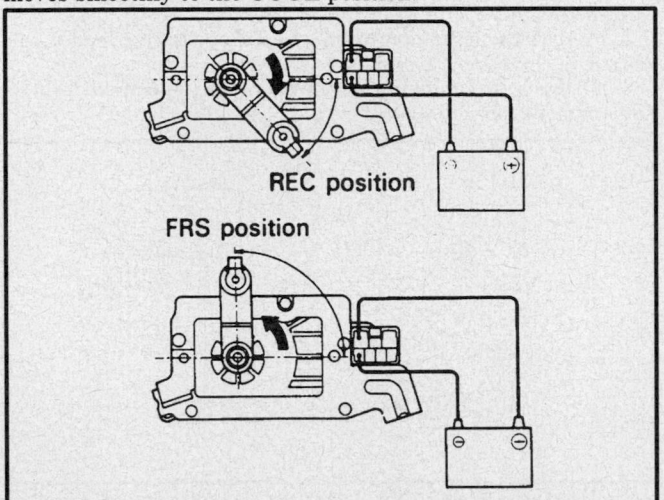

Air inlet control servomotor testing—1994 SC 300, SC 400

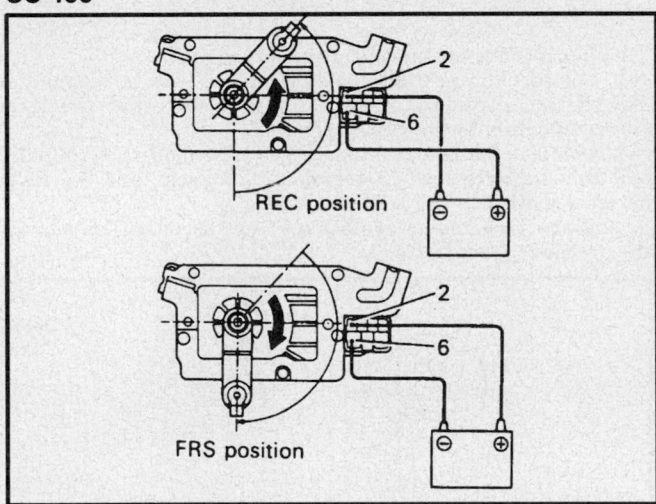

Air inlet control servomotor testing—1995 SC 300, SC 400

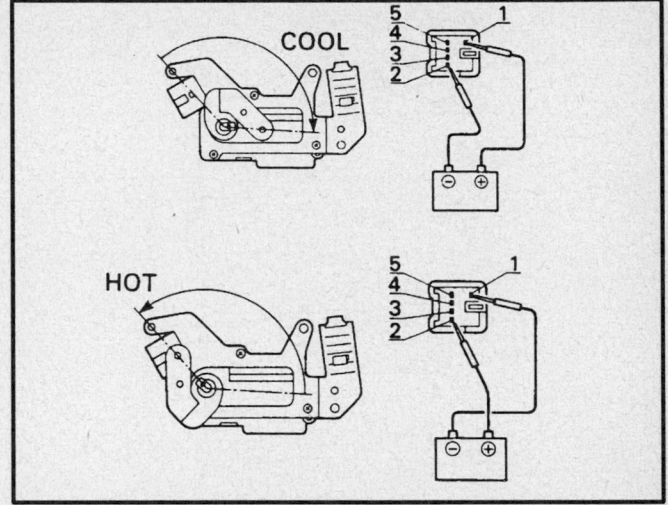

Air mix control servomotor testing—1995-95 ES 300

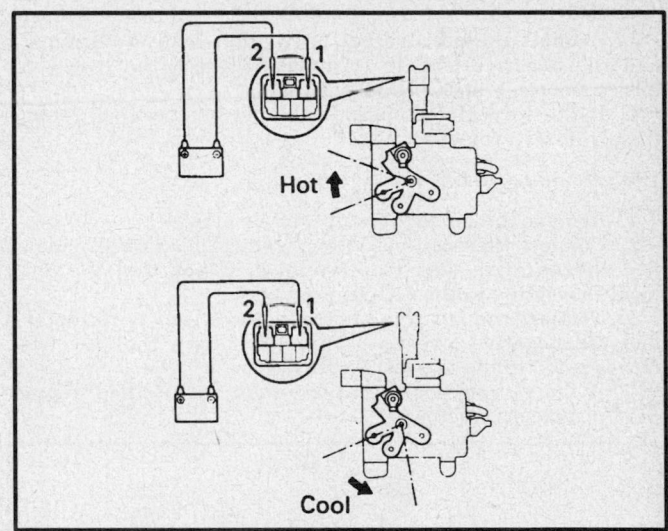

Air mix control servomotor testing—1995-95 GS 300

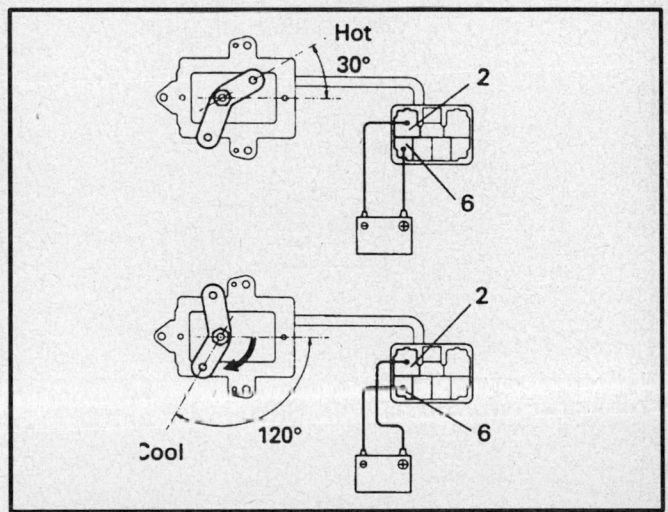

Air mix control servomotor testing—1994 LS 400

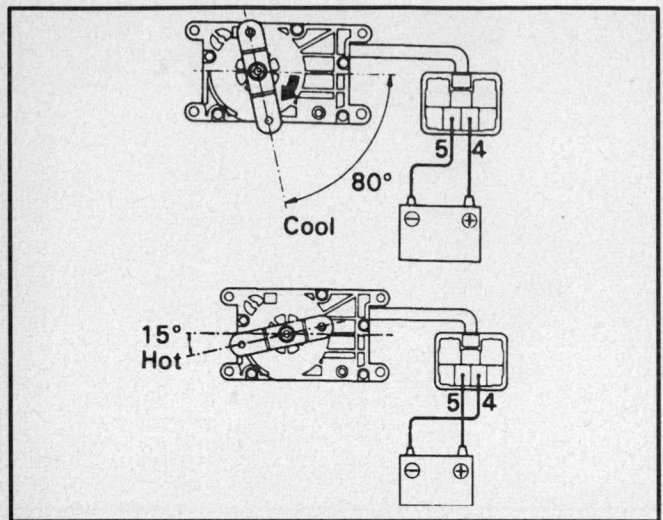

Air mix control servomotor testing—1994 SC 300, SC 400

3. Connect the positive battery voltage lead to terminal **5** and the negative lead to terminal **4**. Check that the lever moves smoothly to the **HOT** position.

4. If the servomotor operation is not as specified, replace the air mix servomotor.

1995 SC 300 and SC 400

1. Remove the air mix control servomotor.

2. Connect the positive battery voltage lead to terminal **5** and the negative lead to terminal **4**. Check that the lever moves smoothly to the **COOL** position.

3. Connect the positive battery voltage lead to terminal **4** and the negative lead to terminal **5**. Check that the lever moves smoothly to the **HOT** position.

4. If the servomotor operation is not as specified, replace the air mix servomotor.

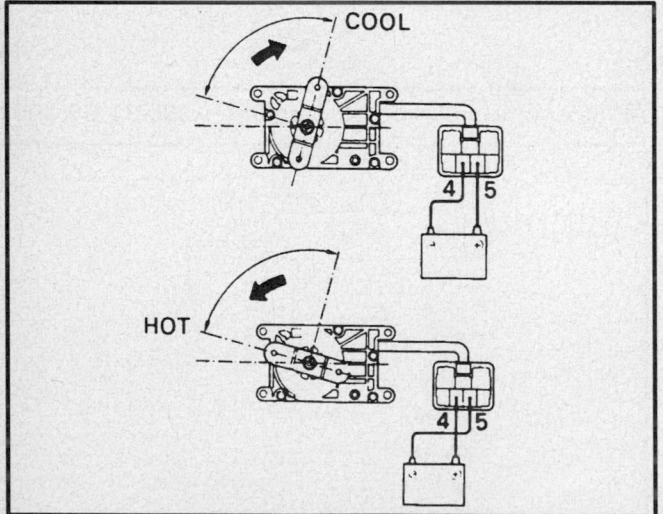

Air mix control servomotor testing—1995 SC 300, SC 400

Air Mode Servomotor

1994–95 ES 300

1. Remove the air mode control servomotor.

2. Connect the positive battery voltage lead to terminal **2** and the negative lead to terminal **1**.

3. Check the lever operation when the negative lead is connected to the other terminals as shown.

4. If the servomotor operation is not as specified, replace the air mode servomotor.

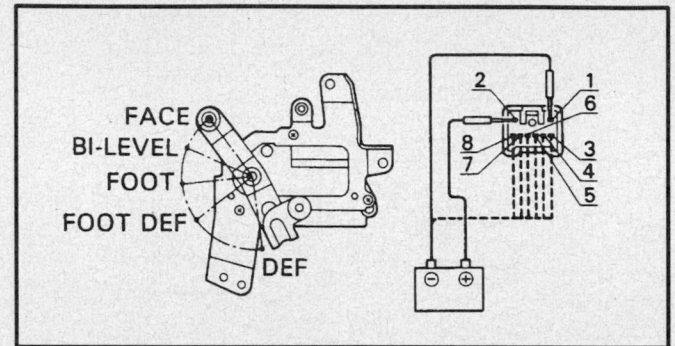

Air mode control servomotor testing—1994-95 ES 300

GS 300

1. Remove the air mode control servomotor.

2. Connect the positive battery voltage lead to terminal **1** and the negative lead to terminal **2**. Check that the lever moves smoothly to the **FACE** position.

3. Connect the positive battery voltage lead to terminal **2** and the negative lead to terminal **1**. Check that the lever moves smoothly to the **DEF** position.

4. If the servomotor operation is not as specified, replace the air mode servomotor.

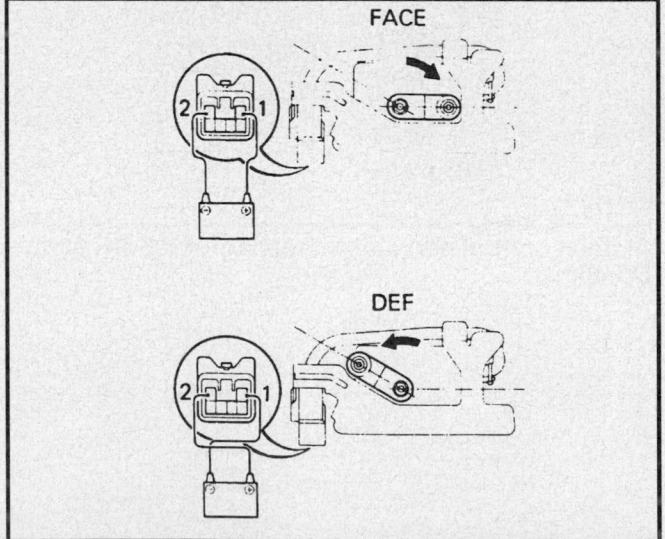

Air mode control servomotor testing—GS 300

1994 LS 400

1. Remove the air mode control servomotor.
2. Connect the positive battery voltage lead to terminal **6** and the negative lead to terminal **7**.
3. Check the lever operation when the negative lead is connected to the other terminals as shown.
4. If the servomotor operation is not as specified, replace the air mode servomotor.

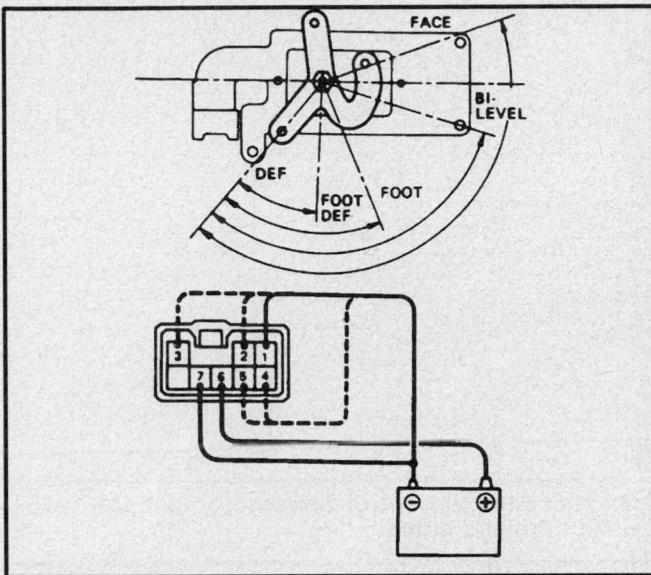

Air mode control servomotor testing—1994 LS 400

1994–95 SC 300 and SC 400

1. Remove the air mode control servomotor.
2. Connect the positive battery voltage lead to terminal **4** and the negative lead to terminal **5**. Check that the lever moves smoothly to the **FACE** position.
3. Connect the positive battery voltage lead to terminal **5** and the negative lead to terminal **4**. Check that the lever moves smoothly to the **DEF** position.
4. If the servomotor operation is not as specified, replace the air mode servomotor.

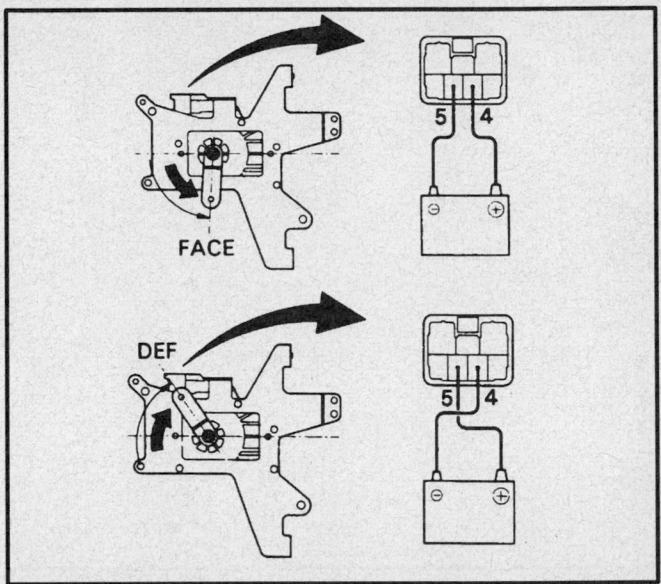

Air mode control servomotor testing—1994 SC 300, SC 400

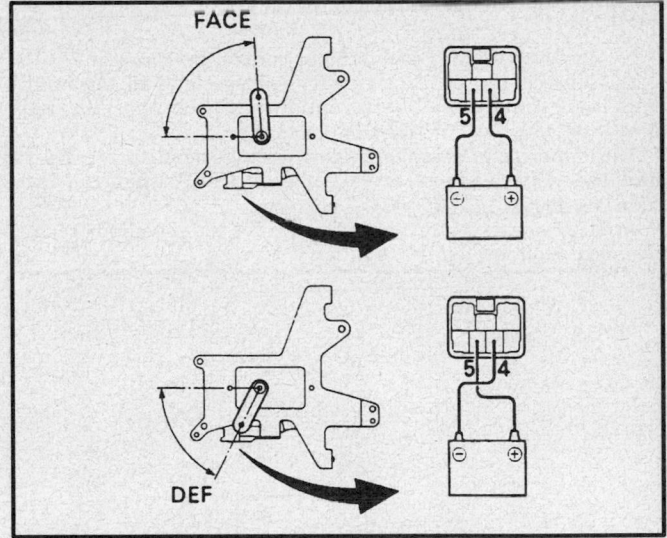

Air mode control servomotor testing—1995 SC 300, SC 400

Max Cool Damper Servomotor

GS 300

1. Remove the max cool damper control servomotor.
2. Connect the positive battery voltage lead to terminal **1** and the negative lead to terminal **2**. Check that the lever moves smoothly to the **OPEN** position.
3. Connect the positive battery voltage lead to terminal **1** and the negative lead to terminal **4**. Check that the lever moves smoothly to the **SHUT** position.
4. If the servomotor operation is not as specified, replace the max cool damper servomotor.

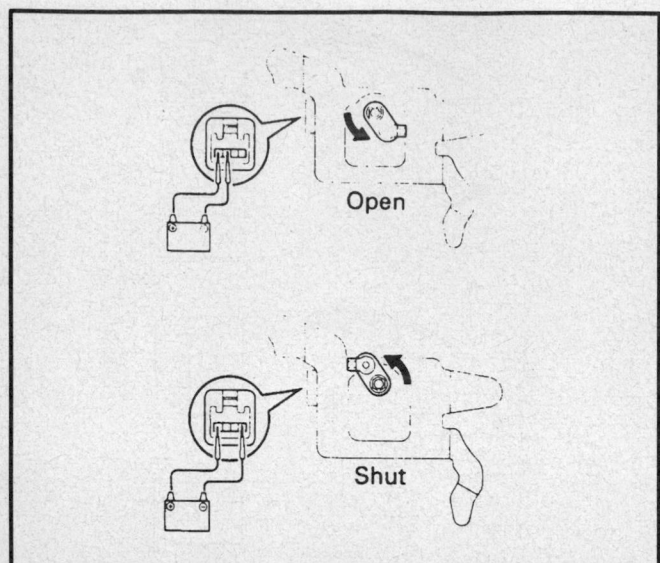

Max cool damper control servomotor testing—GS 300

1994 LS 400

1. Remove the max cool damper control servomotor.
2. Connect the positive battery voltage lead to terminal **1** and the negative lead to terminal **2**. Check that the lever moves smoothly to the **OPEN** position.
3. Connect the positive battery voltage lead to terminal **2** and the negative lead to terminal **1**. Check that the lever moves smoothly to the **SHUT** position.
4. If the servomotor operation is not as specified, replace the max cool damper servomotor.

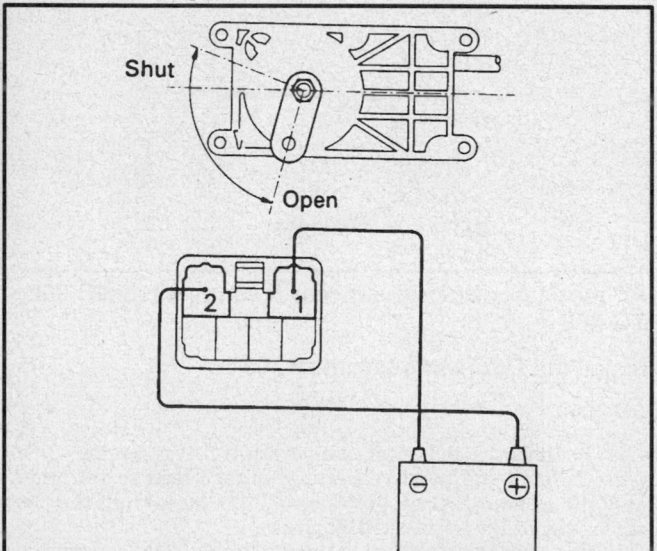

Max cool damper control servomotor testing—1994 LS 400

1995 LS 400

1. Remove the max cool damper control servomotor.
2. Connect the positive battery voltage lead to terminal **4** and the negative lead to terminal **5**. Check that the lever moves smoothly to the **OPEN** position.

3. Connect the positive battery voltage lead to terminal **5** and the negative lead to terminal **4**. Check that the lever moves smoothly to the **SHUT** position.
4. If the servomotor operation is not as specified, replace the max cool damper servomotor.

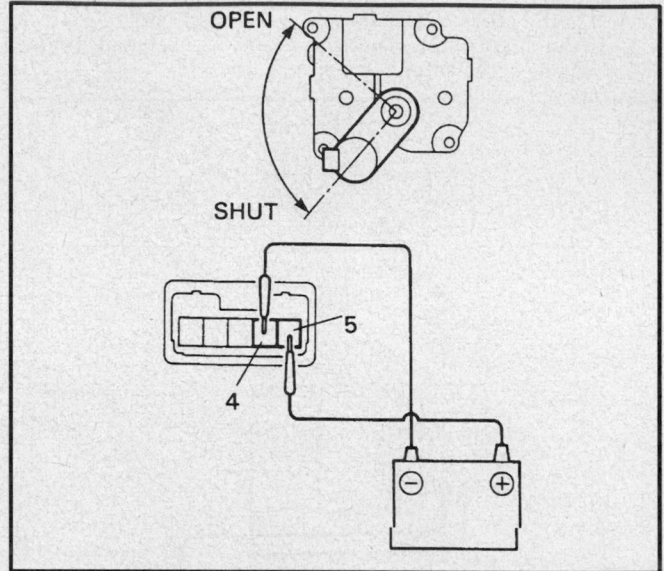

Max cool damper control servomotor testing—1995 LS 400 (driver's side)

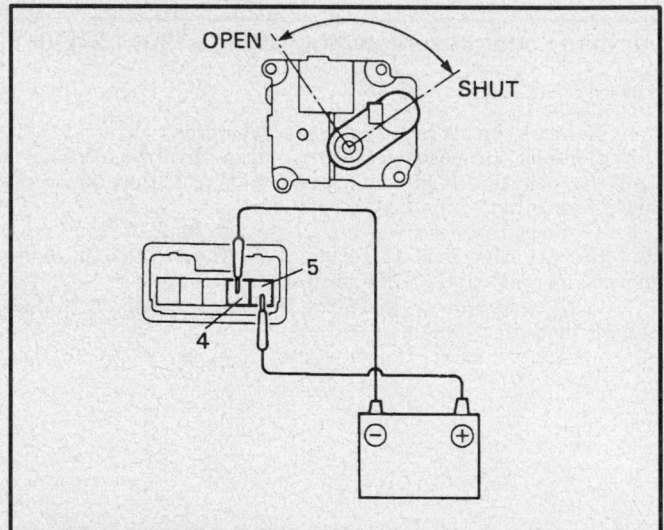

Max cool damper control servomotor testing—1995 LS 400 (passenger's side)

Water Valve Control Servomotor

1995 LS 400

1. Remove the water valve control servomotor.
2. Connect the positive battery voltage lead to terminal **1** and the negative lead to terminal **2**. Check that the lever moves smoothly to the **OPEN** position.
3. Connect the positive battery voltage lead to terminal **1** and the negative lead to terminal **3**. Check that the lever moves smoothly to the **SHUT** position.
4. If the servomotor operation is not as specified, replace the water valve control servomotor.

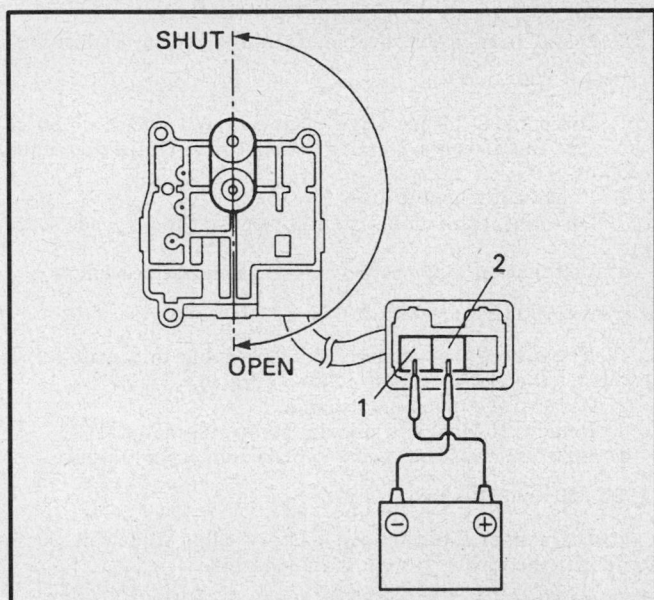

Water valve control servomotor testing – 1995 LS 400

Air Mix Control And Air Mode Control Stepmotor

1995 LS 400

1. Remove the control stepmotor.
2. Measure the resistance between terminals **3** or **4** and the other terminal as shown. the resistance should be 16.0–18.0 ohms.
3. If the resistance is not as specified, replace the stepmotor.

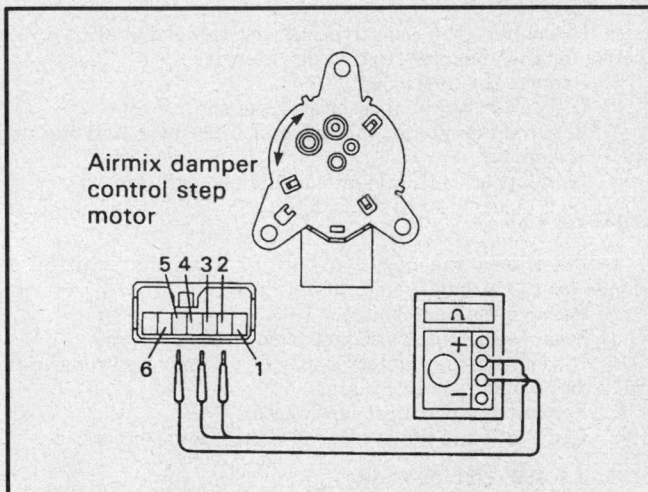

Stepmotor testing – 1995 LS 400 (driver and passenger sides)

REMOVAL AND INSTALLATION

Air Inlet Servomotor

1994–95 ES 300

1. Disconnect the negative battery cable and wait 90 seconds for the airbag system to de-energize.
2. Remove the under cover No. 2, the instrument lower panel and the glove compartment finish plate.
3. Disconnect the passenger airbag system connector.
4. Remove the glove compartment door and the glove compartment.
5. Remove the relay block No. 6, the heater to register No. 4, the ECU and ECU bracket.
6. Disconnect the connector and remove the servomotor.
7. Installation is the reverse of the removal procedure.

1994 GS 300

1. Disconnect the negative battery cable and wait 90 seconds for the airbag system to de-energize.
2. Remove the heater unit.
3. Remove the air inlet servomotor from the heater unit.
4. Installation is the reverse of the removal procedure.

1995 GS 300

1. Disconnect the negative battery cable and wait 90 seconds for the airbag system to de-energize.
2. Remove the cooling unit.
3. Remove the blower unit.
4. Remove the air inlet servomotor from the blower unit.
5. Installation is the reverse of the removal procedure.

1994 LS 400

1. Disconnect the negative battery cable and wait 90 seconds for the airbag system to de-energize.
2. Remove the cooling and blower unit.
3. Remove the air inlet servomotor from the cooling and blower unit.
4. Installation is the reverse of the removal procedure.

1995 LS 400

1. Disconnect the negative battery cable and wait 90 seconds for the airbag system to de-energize.
2. Remove the blower unit.
3. Remove the air inlet stepmotor from the blower unit.
4. Installation is the reverse of the removal procedure.

1994–95 SC 300 and SC 400

1. Disconnect the negative battery cable and wait 90 seconds for the airbag system to de-energize.
2. Remove the air conditioning unit.
3. Remove the air inlet servomotor from the blower unit.
4. Installation is the reverse of the removal procedure.

Air Mix Servomotor

1994–95 ES 300

1. Disconnect the negative battery cable and wait 90 seconds for the airbag system to de-energize.

2. Remove the safety pad No. 2 and the heater to register No. 2 duct.

3. Disconnect the control cable and remove the air mix servomotor.

4. Installation is the reverse of the removal procedure.

1994–95 GS 300

1. Disconnect the negative battery cable and wait 90 seconds for the airbag system to de–energize. Drain the engine coolant.

2. Remove the heater unit.

3. Remove the clamps, the water valve control cable and disconnect the shaft.

4. Remove the air mix servomotor.

5. Installation is the reverse of the removal procedure.

1994 LS 400

1. Disconnect the negative battery cable and wait 90 seconds for the airbag system to de–energize. Drain the engine coolant.

2. Remove the heater unit.

3. Remove the No. 1 air duct. Disconnect the connector and remove the max cool damper control servomotor.

4. Disconnect the connector, remove the clip and the air mix damper control plate

5. Remove the air mix servomotor.

6. Installation is the reverse of the removal procedure.

1995 LS 400 (Driver's Side)

1. Disconnect the negative battery cable and wait 90 seconds for the airbag system to de-energize.

2. Remove the No. 1 under cover.

3. Remove the drivers side air mix stepmotor.

4. Installation is the reverse of the removal procedure.

1995 LS 400 (Passenger's Side)

1. Disconnect the negative battery cable and wait 90 seconds for the airbag system to de-energize.

2. Remove the blower unit.

3. Remove the passenger's side air mix stepmotor.

4. Installation is the reverse of the removal procedure.

1994–95 SC 300 and SC 400

1. Disconnect the negative battery cable and wait 90 seconds for the airbag system to de-energize.

2. Disconnect the connector and remove the air mix servomotor.

3. Installation is the reverse of the removal procedure.

Air Mode Servomotor

1994–95 ES 300

1. Disconnect the negative battery cable and wait 90 seconds for the airbag system to de-energize.

2. Remove the safety pad No. 2 and the heater to register No. 2 duct.

3. Disconnect the connector, remove the clip and the air mode servomotor..

4. Installation is the reverse of the removal procedure.

1994–95 GS 300

1. Disconnect the negative battery cable and wait 90 seconds for the airbag system to de-energize.

2. Remove the instrument panel the instrument panel brace and the instrument panel reinforcement.

3. Remove the heater to register No. 3 duct, the wire harnes, the wiper relay and the PPS ECU relay.

4. Remove the air mode air mode servomotor.

5. Installation is the reverse of the removal procedure.

1994 LS 400

1. Disconnect the negative battery cable and wait 90 seconds for the airbag system to de–energize. Drain the engine coolant.

2. Remove the heater unit.

3. Disconnect the connector and remove the air mode servomotor.

4. Installation is the reverse of the removal procedure.

1995 LS 400 (Driver's Side)

1. Disconnect the negative battery cable and wait 90 seconds for the airbag system to de-energize.

2. Remove the instrument panel.

3. Remove the driver's side air mode stepmotor.

4. Installation is the reverse of the removal procedure.

1995 LS 400 (Passenger's Side)

1. Disconnect the negative battery cable and wait 90 seconds for the airbag system to de-energize.

2. Remove the blower unit.

3. Remove the passenger's side air mode stepmotor.

4. Installation is the reverse of the removal procedure.

1995 SC 300 and SC 400

1. Disconnect the negative battery cable and wait 90 seconds for the airbag system to de-energize.

2. Remove the instrument panel and the instrument panel reinforcement.

3. Disconnect the connector and remove the air mode servomotor.

4. Installation is the reverse of the removal procedure.

Max Cool Servomotor

GS 300

1. Disconnect the negative battery cable and wait 90 seconds for the airbag system to de–energize.

2. Remove the heater unit.

3. Disconnect the connector and the shaft.

4. Remove the clamp, the air mix link cover and the max cool servomotor.

5. Installation is the reverse of the removal procedure.

1994 LS 400

1. Disconnect the negative battery cable and wait 90 seconds for the airbag system to de–energize.

2. Remove the heater unit.

3. Remove the No. 1 air duct from the heater unit.

4. Disconnect the connector, pry out 2 clips and remove the max cool damper control plates.

5. Remove the max cool servomotor.

6. Installation is the reverse of the removal procedure.

1995 LS 400 (Driver's Side)

1. Disconnect the negative battery cable and wait 90 seconds for the airbag system to de–energize.

2. Remove the instrument panel.

3. Remove the driver's side max cool stepmotor.

4. Installation is the reverse of the removal procedure.

1995 LS 400 (Passenger's Side)

1. Disconnect the negative battery cable and wait 90 seconds for the airbag system to de–energize.

2. Remove the blower unit.
3. Remove the passenger's side max cool stepmotor.
4. Installation is the reverse of the removal procedure.

Water Valve Servomotor

1995 LS 400

1. Disconnect the negative battery cable and wait 90 seconds for the airbag system to de–energize.
2. Remove the instrument panel.
3. Disconnect the control cable and the connector.
4. Remove the water valve servomotor.
5. Installation is the reverse of the removal procedure.

System Relays

OPERATION

Many of the systems within the air conditioning systems use relays to energize various components. All are conventional relays with internal contacts and a coil which pulls the contacts closed when energized. All models use a main relay, a heater relay and a magnetic clutch relay as well as several cooling fan relays. ES 300 and 1993–94 LS 400 vehicles are equipped with an extra high relay in the blower motor circuit.

On ES 300, the heater relay is located behind the right kick panel (relay box No. 4). In the same box is the 40 amp heater fuse. The magnetic clutch relay is in the relay box in the left side of the engine compartment (relay box No 5); it is the second inboard relay. The extra high relay is located on the left side of the evaporator housing, behind the center console.

On GS 300, all the relays are located in junction block No. 2 in the driver's side of the engine compartment.

On SC 300, the heater relay and the magnetic clutch relay are located in the relay block on the left side of the engine compartment.

On LS 400, all relays except the extra high relay are located in junction blocks in the driver's side of the engine compartment. The extra high relay is located in the evaporator–blower assembly behind the glove box.

TESTING

Magnetic Clutch Relay

ES 300, SC 300 and SC 400

1. Remove the magnetic clutch relay.
2. Check for continuity between terminals **1** and **2**.
3. Check for no continuity between terminals **3** and **5**.
4. Connect battery voltage between terminals **1** and **2** and check for continuity between terminals **3** and **5**.
5. If continuity or operation is not as specified, replace the magnetic clutch relay.

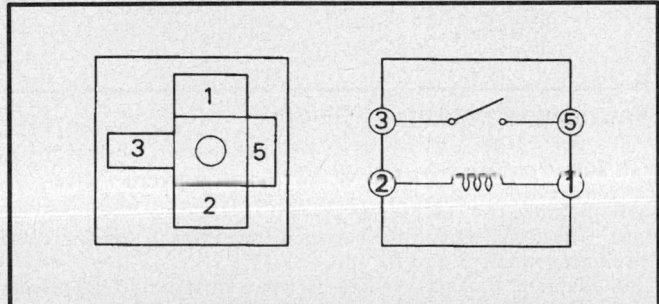

Magnetic clutch relay—ES 300, SC 300, SC 400

GS 300

1. Remove the magnetic clutch relay.
2. Check for continuity between terminals **3** and **4**.
3. Check for no continuity between terminals **1** and **2**.
4. Connect battery voltage between terminals **3** and **4** and check for continuity between terminals **1** and **2**.
5. If continuity or operation is not as specified, replace the magnetic clutch relay.

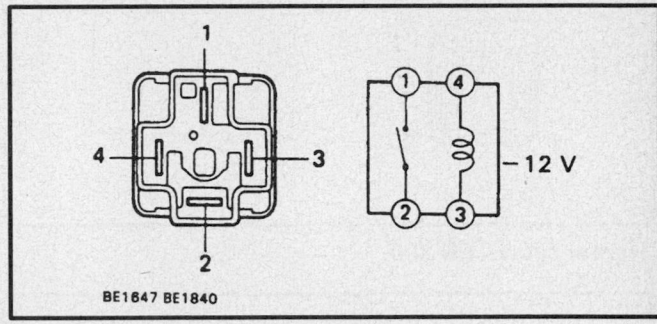

BE1647 BE1840

Magnetic clutch relay—GS 300

LS 400

1. Remove the magnetic clutch relay.
2. Check for continuity between terminals **1** and **3**.
3. Check for no continuity between terminals **2** and **4**.
4. Connect battery voltage between terminals **1** and **3** and check for continuity between terminals **2** and **4**.
5. If continuity or operation is not as specified, replace the magnetic clutch relay.

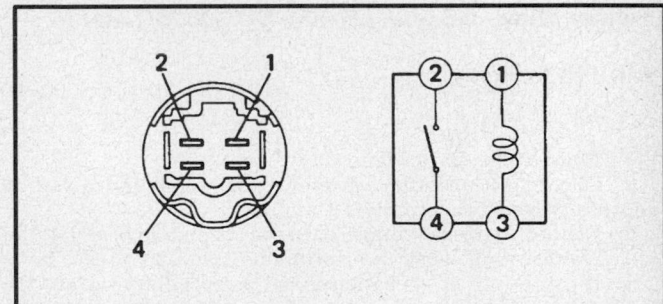

Magnetic clutch relay—LS 400

Heater Relay

ES 300

1. Remove the heater relay.
2. Check for continuity between terminals **2** and **4** and between terminals **3** and **5**.
3. Check for no continuity between terminals **1** and **4**.
4. Connect battery voltage between terminals **3** and **5** and check for no continuity between terminals **2** and **4** and for continuity between terminals **1** and **2**.
5. If continuity or operation is not as specified, replace the heater relay.

GS 300, LS 400, SC 300 and SC 400

1. Remove the heater relay.
2. Check for continuity between terminals **1** and **3** and between terminals **2** and **4**.
3. Check for no continuity between terminals **4** and **5**.

4. Connect battery voltage between terminals **1** and **3** and check for no continuity between terminals **2** and **4** and for continuity between terminals **4** and **5**.

5. If continuity or operation is not as specified, replace the heater relay.

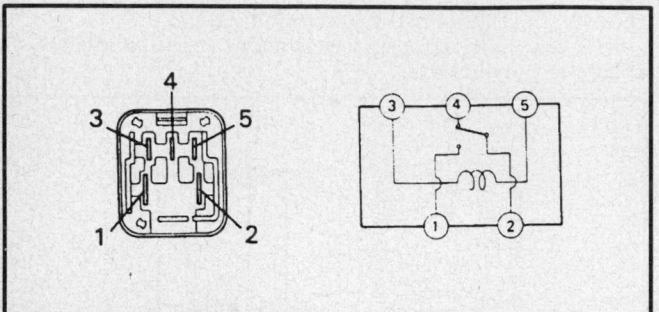

Heater relay—ES 300

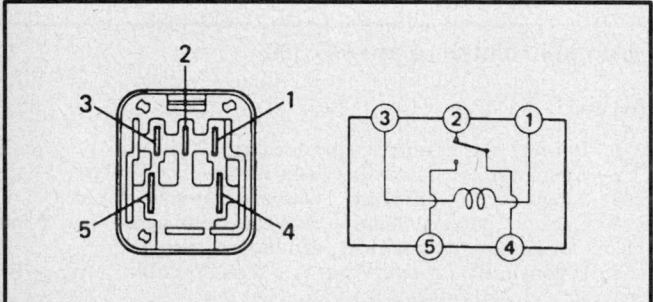

Heater relay—GS 300, LS 400, SC 300, SC 400

Extra High Relay

ES 300

1. Remove the extra high relay.
2. Check for continuity between terminals **3** and **4** and no continuity between terminals **1** and **2**.
3. Connect battery voltage between terminals **3** and **4** and check for continuity between terminals **1** and **2**.
4. If continuity or operation is not as specified, replace the extra high relay.

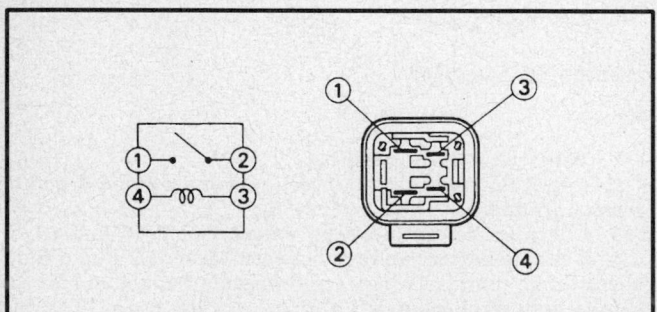

Extra high relay—ES 300

LS 400

1. Remove the extra high relay.
2. Check for continuity between terminals **2** and **3** and no continuity between terminals **5** and **1**.
3. Connect battery voltage between terminals **2** and **3** and check for continuity between terminals **5** and **1**.

4. If continuity or operation is not as specified, replace the extra high relay.

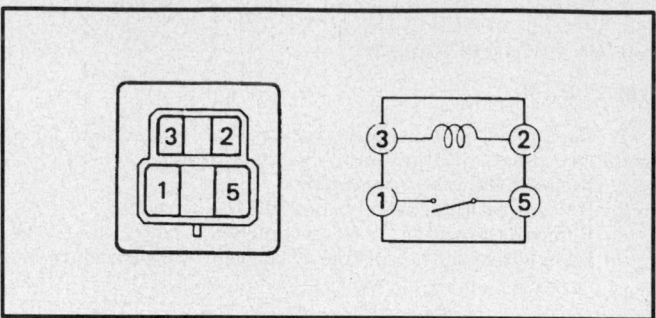

Extra high relay—LS 400

Cooling Fan Relays

GS 300 (Fan Main Relay)

1. Remove the fan main relay.
2. Check for continuity between terminals **3** and **5** and between terminals **2** and **4**. Check for no continuity between terminals **1** and **4**.
3. Connect battery voltage between terminals **3** and **5** and check for continuity between terminals **1** and **2** and no continuity between terminals **2** and **4**.
4. If continuity or operation is not as specified, replace the fan main relay.

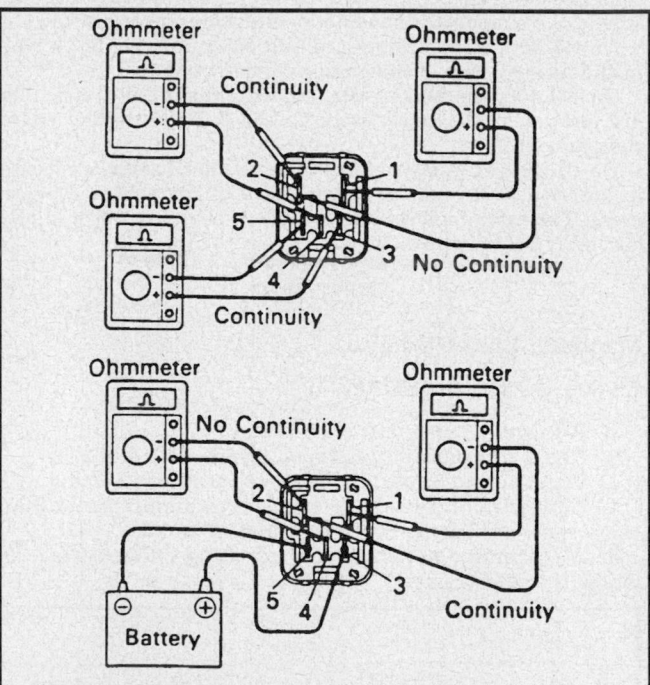

Fan main relay testing—GS 300

GS 300 (Cooling Fan Relay)

1. Remove the cooling fan relay.
2. Check for continuity between terminals **1** and **2** and between terminals **3** and **4**.
3. Connect battery voltage between terminals **1** and **2** and check for no continuity between terminals **3** and **4**.

4. If continuity or operation is not as specified, replace the cooling fan relay.

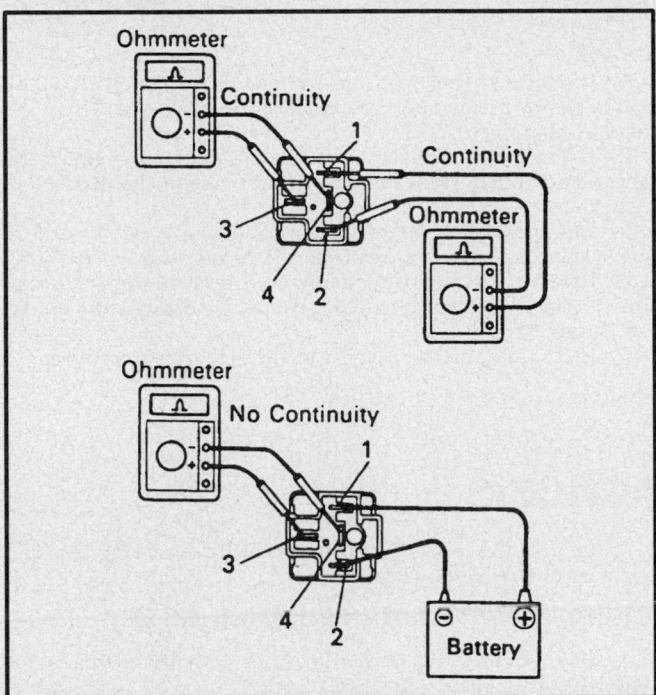

Cooling fan relay testing—GS 300

LS 400 (Cooling Fan Relays No. 1 and No. 2)

1. Remove the cooling fan relay.
2. Check for continuity between terminals 1 and 2 and between terminals 3 and 4.
3. Connect battery voltage between terminals 1 and 2 and check for no continuity between terminals 3 and 4.
4. If continuity or operation is not as specified, replace the cooling fan relay.

LS 400 (Cooling Fan Relay No. 3)

1. Remove the cooling fan relay No. 3.
2. Check for continuity between terminals 3 and 5 and between terminals 2 and 4. Check for no continuity between terminals 1 and 2.
3. Connect battery voltage between terminals 3 and 5 and check for continuity between terminals 1 and 2 and no continuity between terminals 2 and 4.
4. If continuity or operation is not as specified, replace the cooling fan relay No. 3.

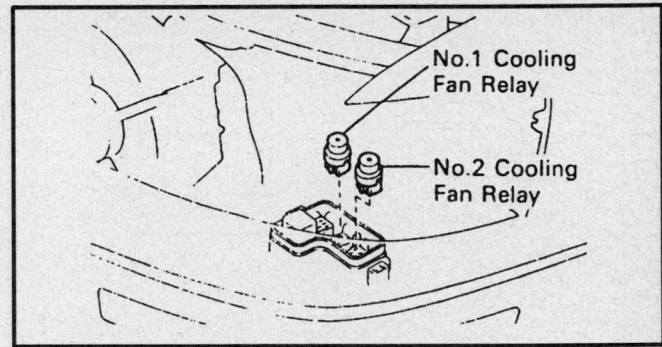

Cooling fan relay location—1994 LS 400

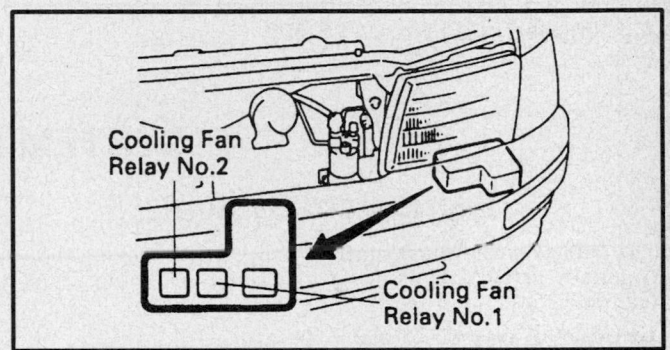

Cooling fan relay location—1995 LS 400

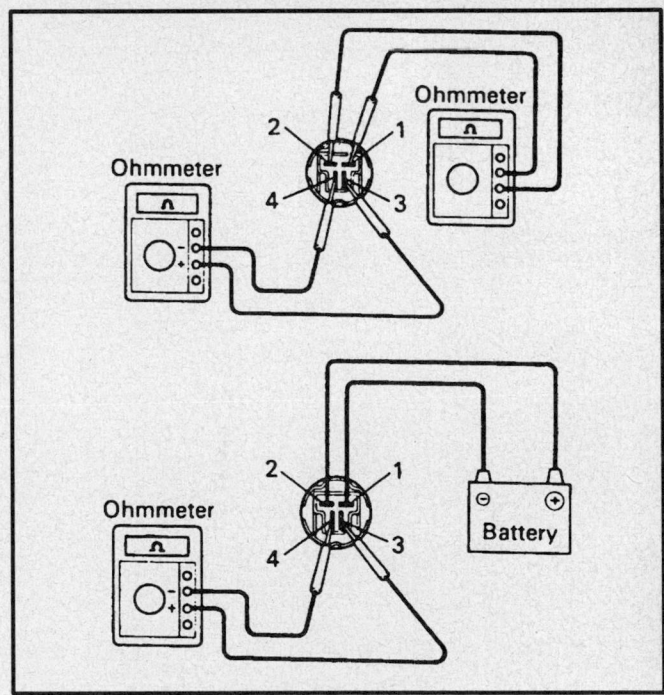

Cooling fan relays No. 1 and No. 2—LS 400

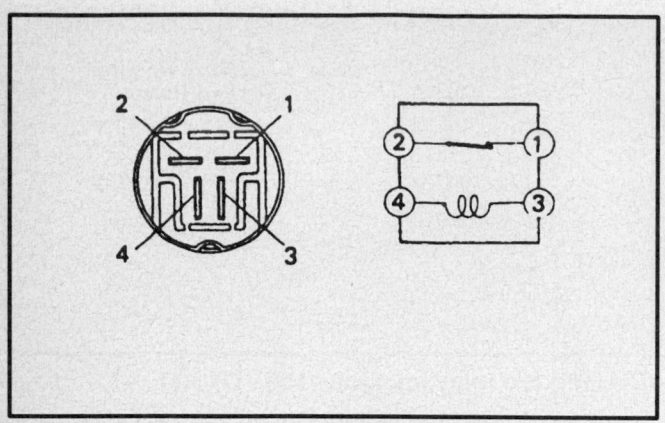

Cooling fan relay No. 3–LS 400

REMOVAL AND INSTALLATION

Extra High Relay

LS 400

1. Disconnect the negative battery cable and wait 90 seconds before performing any other work while the airbag system de–energizes.

2. Using a suitable tool, remove the clips and remove the lower cover panel from the passenger's side of the instrument panel.

3. Disconnect the connectors, remove the 2 screws and remove the connector bracket from the evaporator–blower unit.

4. Remove the mounting screw and remove the extra high relay from the evaporator–blower unit. Disconnect the electrical connector.

5. Installation is the reverse of the removal procedure.

SYSTEM DIAGNOSIS

Refrigerant System

The following conditions must be met before checking the refrigerant system for volume and checking for cooling using a manifold gauge set:

REFRIGERANT VOLUME

1. Run the engine at approximately 2000 rpm.

2. Operate the air conditioning at maximum cooling for a few minutes.

3. Inspect the amount of refrigerant by observing the sight glass on the receiver/drier.

CHECKING WITH A MANIFOLD GAUGE SET

1. The temperature at the air inlet with the switch set at **RECIRC** is 86–95°F (30–35°C).

2. Run the engine at 2000 rpm.

3. Set the blower fan speed switch at high speed.

4. Set the temperature control switch at **MAX COOL**.

NOTE: Manifold gauge indications may vary slightly due to ambient temperature conditions.

REFRIGERANT VOLUME DIAGNOSIS

Item	Symptom	Amount of refrigerant	Remedy
1	Bubbles present in sight glass	Insufficient*	(1) Check for gas leakage with gas leak tester and repair if necessary (2) Add refrigerant until bubbles disappear
2	No bubbles present in sight glass	None, sufficient or too much	Refer to items 3 and 4
3	No temperature difference between compressor inlet and outlet	Empty or nearly empty	(1) Check for gas leakage with gas leak tester and repair if necessary (2) Add refrigerant until bubbles disappear
4	Temperature between compressor inlet and outlet is noticeably different	Proper or too much	Refer to items 5 and 6
5	Immediately after air conditioner is turned off, refrigerant in sight glass stays clear	Too much	(1) Recover refrigerant (2) Evacuate air and charge proper amount of purified refrigerant
6	When air conditioner is turned off, refrigerant foams and then stay clear	Proper	

REFRIGERANT SYSTEM DIAGNOSIS USING A MANIFOLD GAUGE SET

No	Gauge reading kg/cm² (psi, kPa)	Condition	Probable cause	Remedy
1	LO: 1.5 – 2.0 (21 – 28, 147 – 196) HI: 14.5 – 15.0 (206 – 213, 1,422 – 1,471) 	Normal cooling	Normally functioning system	
2	During operation, pressure at low pressure side sometimes becomes a vacuum and sometimes normal 	Periodically cools and then fails to cool	Moisture present in refrigeration system	(1) Replace receiver (2) Remove moisture in system through repeatedly evacuating air

REFRIGERANT SYSTEM DIAGNOSIS USING A MANIFOLD GAUGE SET, CONT'D

No	Gauge reading kg/cm² (psi, kPa)	Condition	Probable cause	Remedy
3	Pressure low at both low and high pressure sides	• Insufficient cooling • Bubbles seen in sight glass	Insufficient refrigerant	(1) Check for gas leakage with gas leak tester and repair if necessary (2) Add refrigerant until bubbles disappear
		• Insufficient cooling • Frost on tubes from receiver to unit	Refrigerant flow obstructed by dirt in receiver	Replace receiver
4	Pressure too high at both low and high pressure sides	Insufficient cooling	Insufficient cooling of condenser	(1) Clean condenser (2) Check fan motor operation
5			Refrigerant overcharged	(1) Check amount of refrigerant If refrigerant is overcharged (2) Recover refrigerant (3) Evacuate air and charge proper amount of purified refrigerant
6			Air present in system	(1) Replace receiver (2) Check compressor oil to see if dirty (3) Remove air in system through repeatedly evacuating air

REFRIGERANT SYSTEM DIAGNOSIS USING A MANIFOLD GAUGE SET, CONT'D

No.	Gauge reading kg/cm² (psi, kPa)	Condition	Probable cause	Remedy
7		• Insufficient cooling • Frost or Large amount of dew on piping at low pressure side	Expansion valve improperly mounted, heat sensing tube defective (Opens too wide)	(1) Check heat sensing tube installation condition If (1) is normal (2) Check expansion valve and replace If defective
3	Pressure low at both low and high pressure sides 	• Insufficient cooling • Bubbles seen in sight glass	Insufficient refrigerant	(1) Check for gas leakage with gas leak tester and repair if necessary (2) Add refrigerant until bubbles disappear
		• Insufficient cooling • Frost on tubes from receiver to unit	Refrigerant flow obstructed by dirt in receiver	Replace receiver
4	Pressure too high at both low and high pressure sides 	Insufficient cooling	Insufficient cooling of condenser	(1) Clean condenser (2) Check fan motor operation
5			Refrigerant overcharged	(1) Check amount of refrigerant If refrigerant is overcharged (2) Recover refrigerant (3) Evacuate air and charge proper amount of purified refrigerant
6			Air present in system	(1) Replace receiver (2) Check compressor oil to see if dirty (3) Remove air in system through repeatedly evacuating air
7		• Insufficient cooling • Frost or Large amount of dew on piping at low pressure side	Expansion valve improperly mounted, heat sensing tube defective (Opens too wide)	(1) Check heat sensing tube installation condition If (1) is normal (2) Check expansion valve and replace if defective

REFRIGERANT SYSTEM DIAGNOSIS USING A MANIFOLD GAUGE SET, CONT'D

No.	Gauge reading kg/cm² (psi, kPa)	Condition	Probable cause	Remedy
8	Vacuum indicated at low pressure side, very low pressure indicated at high pressure	• Does not cool(Cools from time to time in some cases) • Frost or dew seen on piping before and after receiver or expansion valve	Refrigerant does not circulate	(1)Check heat sensing tube for gas leakage and replace expansion valve if defective If (1) is normal (2) Clean out dirt in expansion valve by blowing with air If not able to remove dirt, replace expansion valve (3) replace receiver
	Pressure too high at low pressure side, pressure too low at high pressure side	Does not cool	Insufficient compression	Repair or replace compressor

AUTOMATIC TEMPERATURE CONTROL TROUBLESHOOTING PROCEDURE

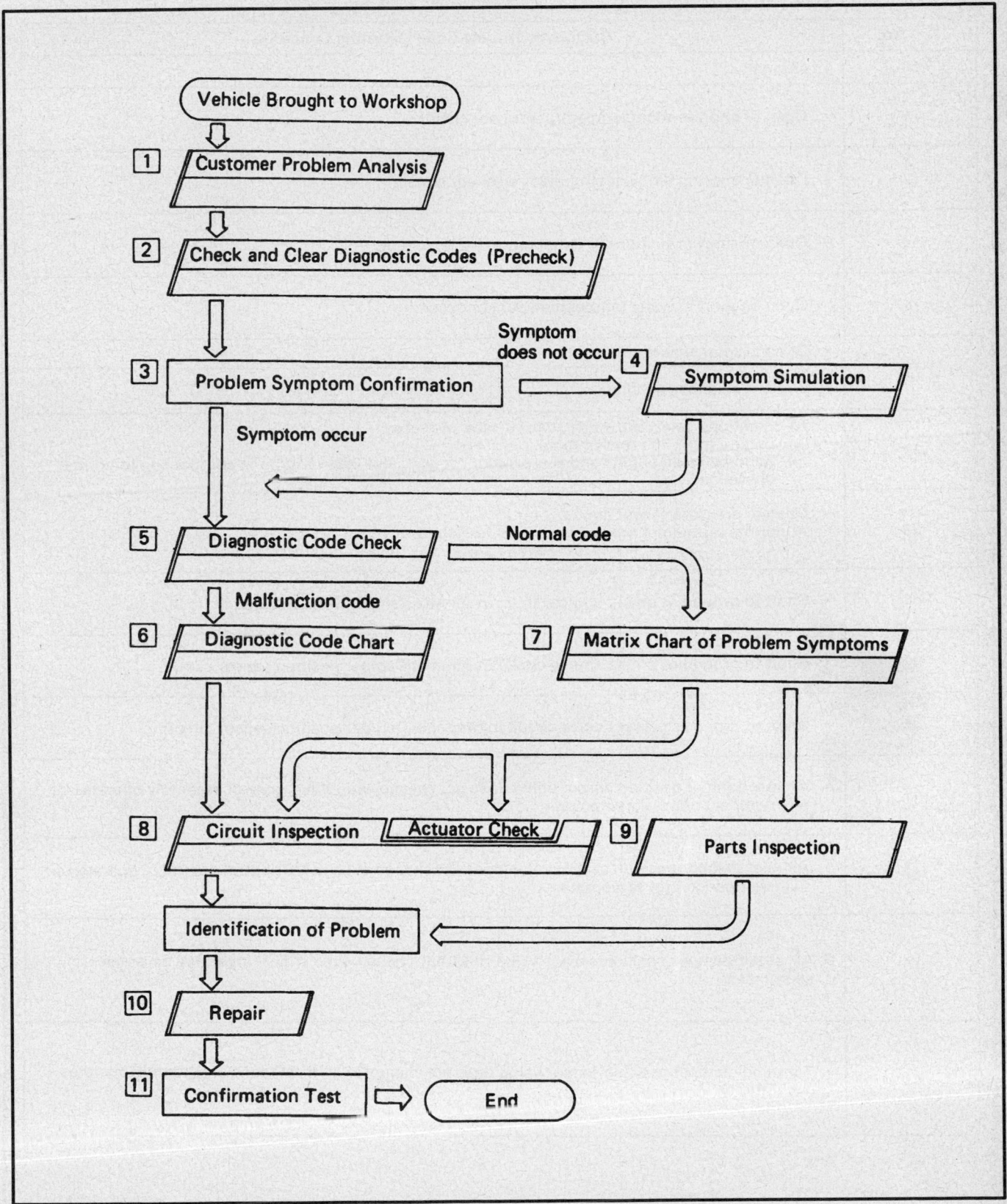

Vehicle Brought to Workshop

1 Customer Problem Analysis

2 Check and Clear Diagnostic Codes (Precheck)

3 Problem Symptom Confirmation

Symptom does not occur

4 Symptom Simulation

Symptom occur

5 Diagnostic Code Check

Normal code

Malfunction code

6 Diagnostic Code Chart

7 Matrix Chart of Problem Symptoms

8 Circuit Inspection Actuator Check

9 Parts Inspection

Identification of Problem

10 Repair

11 Confirmation Test End

DIAGNOSTIC TROUBLE CODE EXPLANATION CHART

TDC No.	Diagnostic Trouble Code Detecting Condition
00	• Normal
11	• Open or short in room temperature sensor circuit.
12	• Open or short in ambient temperature sensor circuit.
13	• Open or short in evaporator temperature sensor circuit.
14	• Open or short in water temperature sensor circuit.
21	• Open in solar sensor circuit. • Short in solar sensor circuit.
22	• All conditions below are detected for 3 secs. or more. (a) Engine rpm : 450 rpm or more. (b) Ratio between engine and compressor rpm deviates 20% or more in comparison to normal operation.
23	• Open in pressure sensor circuit. • Abnormal refrigerant pressure below 196 kPa (2.0 kgf/cm², 28 psi) over 3,140 kPa (32.0 kgf/cm², 455 psi)
31	• Short to ground or power source circuit in Air Mix Damper position sensor circuit.
32	• Short to ground or power source circuit in Air Inlet Damper position sensor circuit.
34	• Short to groud or power source circuit in Max cool Damper position sensor circuit.
41	• Air mix damper position sensor value does not change even if A/C control assembly operates air mix damper control servomotor.
42	• Air inlet damper position sensor value does not change even if A/C control assembly operates air inlet damper control servomotor.
43	• Air outlet damper position sensor value does not change even if ECU operates air outlet servomotor.
44	• Max cool damper position sensor value does not change even if A/C control assembly operates servomotor.

AUTOMATIC TEMPERATURE CONTROL TROUBLESHOOTING MATRIX CHART

Table 1

Group	Symptom	Volume of refrigerant	Drive belt tension	Inspect refrigeration system with manifold gauge set	Backup power source circuit	IG power source circuit	Acc power source circuit	Heater main relay circuit	Blower motor circuit	Power transistor circuit	Ex-Hi relay circuit	Air mix damper position sensor circuit	Air inlet damper position sensor circuit	Air mix servomotor circuit	Air inlet servomotor circuit	Mode servomotor circuit	Max. cool servomotor circuit	Room temp. sensor circuit
Air Flow Control	No blower operation					1	2	3	4									
Air Flow Control	No blower control					1		4	5	2	3							
Air Flow Control	Insufficient air flow									1								
Temperature Control	No cool air comes out	1	2	3								7		8				9
Temperature Control	No warm air comes out											2		3				4
Temperature Control	Output air is warmer or colder than the set temperature or response is slow	1	2	3								11	13	12	14			7
Temperature Control	No temperature control (only Max. cool or Max. warm)											3		4				1
	No air inlet control												1		2			
	No air flow mode control															1	2	
	Engine idle up does not occur, or is continuous																	
	Diagnostic code not recorded. Set mode is cleared when IG switch is turned off.				1													

Table 2

Group	Symptom	Ambient temp. sensor circuit	Evaporator temp. sensor circuit	Water temp. sensor circuit	Solar sensor circuit	Compressor lock sensor circuit	Compressor circuit	Pressure switch circuit	Igniter circuit	ECU (A/C control assy)	Cooling fan system	Water valve	Condenser	Receiver	Evaporator	Radiator (in heater unit)	Expansion valve
Air Flow Control	No blower operation			5						6							
Air Flow Control	No blower control			6						7							
Air Flow Control	Insufficient air flow																
Temperature Control	No cool air comes out	10				6	4	5	11	12							
Temperature Control	No warm air comes out	5	6							7		1					
Temperature Control	Output air is warmer or colder than the set temperature or response is slow	8	9	10	6					20	4	5	15	16	17	18	19
Temperature Control	No temperature control (only Max. cool or Max. warm)	2								5							
	No air inlet control									3							
	No air flow mode control									3							
	Engine idle up does not occur, or is continuous								1	2							
	Diagnostic code not recorded. Set mode is cleared when IG switch is turned off.									2							

Automatic Temperature Control

DIAGNOSTIC CODE PROCEDURE

Indicator Check

1. On all models except ES 300, turn the ignition switch **ON** while pressing the air conditioner control **AUTO** switch and **REC** switch simultaneously.

2. On ES 300, turn the ignition switch **ON** while pressing the AUTO button and the **DOWN** arrow button simultaneously.

3. Check that all the indicators light up and go off at 1 second intervals 4 times in succession.

4. Make sure the buzzer sounds when the indicators light up in Step 2.

5. After the indicator check is ended, the diagnostic code check begins automatically. Press the **OFF** switch when desiring to cancel the check mode.

Diagnostic Code Check – Sensor Check

1. Perform an indicator check. After the indicator check is completed, the system enters the diagnostic code check mode automatically.

2. Read the code displayed on the panel. The codes are output at the temperature display. If a slower display is desired, press the **UP** switch (LS 400), the **LEFT** arrow (ES 300 and GS 300), or the **FRESH** switch (SC 300 and SC 400) and change it to step operation. Each time the appropriate button is pushed, the display changes by 1 step.

3. Note the following points during the diagnostic code check:

• If the buzzer sounds when a code is being read, it means the trouble indicated by that code continues to occur. If the buzzer does not sound when a code is being read, it means the trouble indicated by that code occurred earlier.

• If the ambient temperature is −22°F (−30°C) or lower, a malfunction code may be output even though the system is normal.

• Codes are displayed in order from the smallest code numbers to the largest.

• If the diagnostic code check is being performed in a dark place, Code 21, solar sensor circuit abnormal, could be displayed. In this case, perform the diagnostic code check again while shining a light on the solar sensor. If Code 21 is still displayed, there could be trouble in the solar sensor circuit.

Clearing Diagnostic Codes

1. On LS 400, SC 300 and SC 400, pull out the DOME fuse in junction block No. 2, located in the engine compartment on the driver's side, for 10 seconds or longer to clear the memory of diagnostic codes. On ES 300 and GS 300, use the same process, but pull out the ECU–B fuse in junction block No. 1.

2. After reinserting the fuse, check that the normal code is output.

Actuator Check

1. After entering the sensor check mode, press the **REC** switch.

2. Since each damper, motor and relay automatically operates at 1 second intervals beginning in order from 20 in the temperature display, check the temperature and air flow visually and by hand.

3. If a slower display is desired, press the switch as indicated in the procedure above and change it to step operation. Each time the switch is now pressed, the display changes by 1 step.

4. Note the following points during the actuator check:

• The buzzer sounds when the display code changes.

• Codes are displayed in order from the smaller to the larger numbers.

• To cancel the check mode, press the **OFF** switch.

AUTOMATIC TEMPERATURE CONTROL ECU TERMINAL CHART—
1993 ES 300

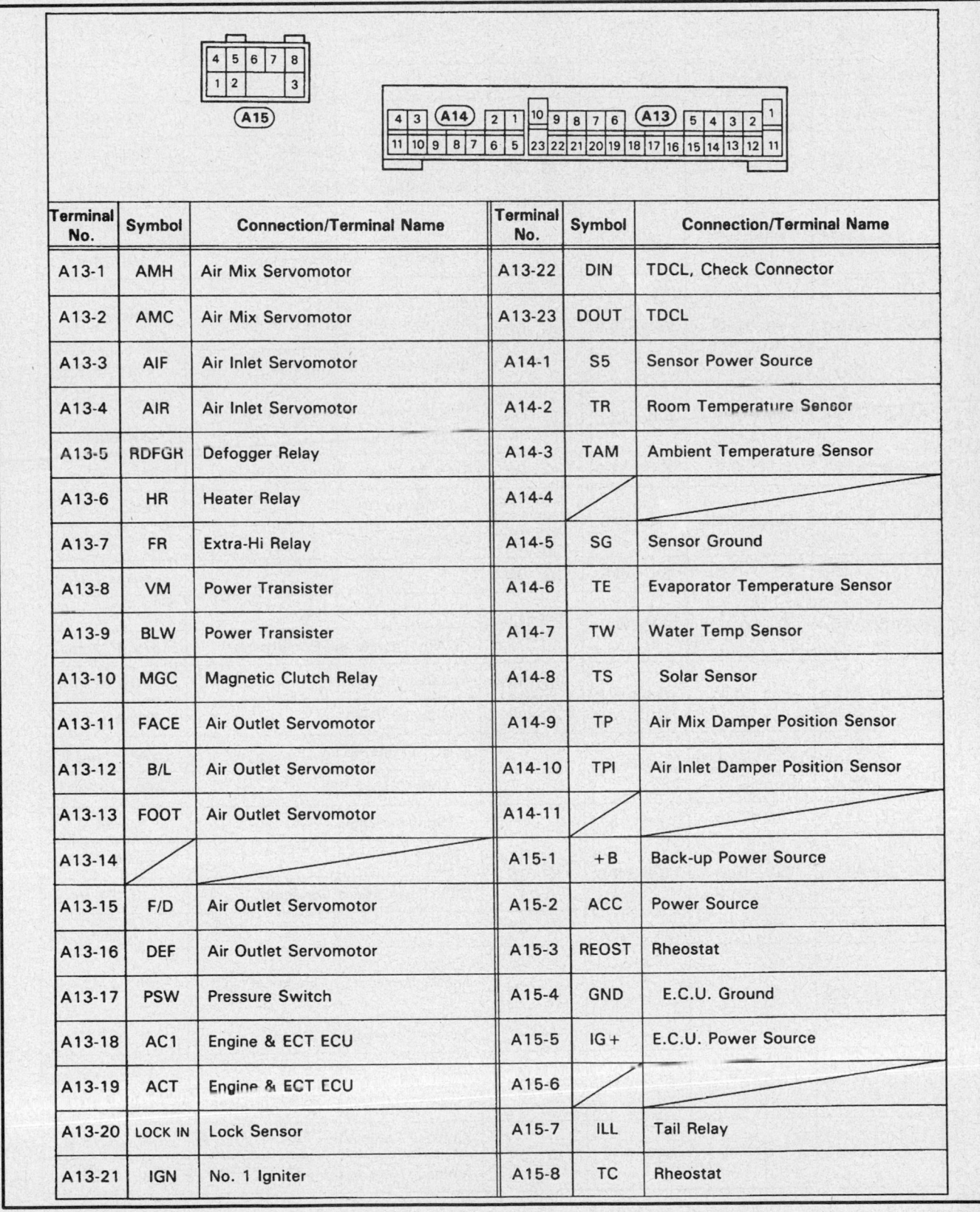

Terminal No.	Symbol	Connection/Terminal Name	Terminal No.	Symbol	Connection/Terminal Name
A13-1	AMH	Air Mix Servomotor	A13-22	DIN	TDCL, Check Connector
A13-2	AMC	Air Mix Servomotor	A13-23	DOUT	TDCL
A13-3	AIF	Air Inlet Servomotor	A14-1	S5	Sensor Power Source
A13-4	AIR	Air Inlet Servomotor	A14-2	TR	Room Temperature Sensor
A13-5	RDFGR	Defogger Relay	A14-3	TAM	Ambient Temperature Sensor
A13-6	HR	Heater Relay	A14-4		
A13-7	FR	Extra-Hi Relay	A14-5	SG	Sensor Ground
A13-8	VM	Power Transister	A14-6	TE	Evaporator Temperature Sensor
A13-9	BLW	Power Transister	A14-7	TW	Water Temp Sensor
A13-10	MGC	Magnetic Clutch Relay	A14-8	TS	Solar Sensor
A13-11	FACE	Air Outlet Servomotor	A14-9	TP	Air Mix Damper Position Sensor
A13-12	B/L	Air Outlet Servomotor	A14-10	TPI	Air Inlet Damper Position Sensor
A13-13	FOOT	Air Outlet Servomotor	A14-11		
A13-14			A15-1	+B	Back-up Power Source
A13-15	F/D	Air Outlet Servomotor	A15-2	ACC	Power Source
A13-16	DEF	Air Outlet Servomotor	A15-3	REOST	Rheostat
A13-17	PSW	Pressure Switch	A15-4	GND	E.C.U. Ground
A13-18	AC1	Engine & ECT ECU	A15-5	IG+	E.C.U. Power Source
A13-19	ACT	Engine & ECT ECU	A15-6		
A13-20	LOCK IN	Lock Sensor	A15-7	ILL	Tail Relay
A13-21	IGN	No. 1 Igniter	A15-8	TC	Rheostat

ECU TERMINAL STANDARD VALUE TEST CHART
1993 ES 300

Terminals	Symbols	Wiring Color	Condition		Standard Value
A13-1↔A13-2	AMH↔AMC	O↔P	IG OFF		13~19 Ω
A13-3↔A13-4	AIF↔AIR	RL↔R	IG OFF		13~19 Ω
A13-5↔A15-4	RDFGR↔GND	L-O↔W-B	IG ON	Rear Defogger Switch ON	Below 1 V
				Rear Defogger Switch OFF	10~14 V
A13-6↔A15-4	HR↔GND	L-W↔W-B	IG ON	Turn the Blower Motor	Below 1 V
				Do Not Turn the Blower Motor	10~14 V
A13-7↔A15-4	FR↔GND	W-G↔W-B	IG ON	Blower Level Hi or Set Temp: Max Hot or Max Cool	Below 1 V
				Blower Level OFF~Medium	10~14 V
A13-8↔A15-4	VM↔GND	B-W↔W-B	IG ON	Push Blower Switch to Change the Blower Speed from 1 to 5	Speed ① 9.6 V / Speed ⑤ below 1.5 V
A13-9↔A15-4	BLW↔GND	Y-W↔W-B	IG ON	Turn the Blower Motor	Below 1.5 V
A13-10↔A15-4	MGC↔GND	L-Y↔W-B	Start the Engine and Push Auto Switch	A/C Switch ON	Below 1 V
				A/C Switch OFF	10~14 V
A13-17↔A15-4	PSW↔GND	R-L↔W-B	IG ON		Below 1 V
A13-18↔A15-4	AC1↔GND	B-Y↔W-B	Start the Engine	Operate the Compressor	Below 1 V
				Do Not Operate the Compressor	1 V or More
A13-19↔A15-4	ACT↔GND	LG-R↔W-B	Start the Engine (Idling)	A/C Switch ON	10~14 V
				A/C Switch OFF	Below 1.5 V
A13-20↔A15-4	LOCK IN ↔GND	W-L↔W-B	IG OFF	at 20 °C (68 °F)	540 ~ 950 Ω
				at 100 °C (212 °F)	690 ~ 1230 Ω
A13-21↔A15-4	IGN↔GND	B↔W-B		Start the Engine	10~14 V
A13-22↔A15-4	DIN↔GND	LG-R↔W-B	IG ON	Connect Tc and E₁ of DCL2 or DCL1	Below 1 V
				Other Than Above Condition	10~14 V
A14-1↔A14-5	S5↔SG	L↔W-R	IG ON		4~6 V
A14-1↔A14-8	S5↔TS	L-W	IG ON	Sensor Subjected to Electrical Light	Below 4 V
				Sensor Covered by a Cloth	4~4.5 V
A14-2↔A14-5	TR↔SG	G-Y↔W-R	IG ON	Cabin Temperature: 25 °C (77 °F)	1.8~2.2 V
				Cabin Temperature: 40 °C (104 °F)	1.2~1.6 V
A14-3↔A14-5	TAM↔SG	B-R↔W-R	IG ON	Ambient Temperature: 25 °C (77 °F)	1.35~1.75 V
				Ambient Temperature: 40 °C (104 °F)	0.85~1.25 V

ECU TERMINAL STANDARD VALUE TEST CHART— 1993 ES 300, CONT'D

Terminals	Symbols	Wiring Color	Condition		Standard Value
A14-5↔Body Ground	SG↔Body Grounds	W-R↔Body Ground	Always		1 Ω or less
A14-6↔A14-5	TE↔SG	L-W↔W-R	IG ON	Evaporator Temp.: 0 °C (32 °F)	2.0~2.4 V
				Evaporator Temp.: 15 °C (77 °F)	1.4~1.8 V
A14-7↔A14-5	TW↔SG	Y-B↔W-R	IG ON	Engine Coolant Temp.: 0 °C (32 °F)	2.8~3.2 V
				Engine Coolant Temp.: 40 °C (104 °F)	1.8~2.2 V
				Engine Coolant Temp.: 70 °C (158 °F)	0.9~1.3 V
A14-8↔A14-5	TS↔SG	W↔W-R	IG ON	Sensor Subjected to Electrical Light	1 V or more
				Sensor Covered by Cloth	Below 1 V
A14-9↔A14-5	TP↔SG	B-Y↔W-R	IG ON	Set Temp.: Max Cool	3.5~4.5 V
				Set Temp.: Max Hot	0.5~1.8 V
A14-10↔A14-5	TPI↔SG	L-Y↔W-R	IG ON	Push Recircu Switch	3.5~4.5 V
				Push Fresh Switch	0.5~1.8 V
A15-1↔A15-4	B+↔GND	L-Y↔W-B	IG OFF		10~14 V
A15-2↔A15-4	ACC↔GND	L-R↔W-B	Turn Ignition Switch ACC		10~14 V
A15-4↔Body Ground	GND↔Body Ground	W-B↔Body Ground	Always		1 Ω or less
A15-5↔A15-4	IG+↔GND	R-L↔W-B	IG ON		10~14 V
A15-3↔A15-4	REOST↔GND	B↔W-B	Light Control Switch :Tail Position	Rheostat Volume:Most Upward	Below 1 V
				Rheostat Volume: Most Downward	10~14 V
A15-7↔A15-4	ILL↔GND	G↔W-B	Turn the Light Control Switch to Tail Position		10~14 V
A15-8↔A15-4	TC↔GND	R-L↔W-B	Light Control Switch :Tail Position	Pheostat Volume: Most Upward	Below 1 V
				Rheostat Volume: Most Downward	10~14 V

AUTOMATIC TEMPERATURE CONTROL ECU TERMINAL CHART– 1994-95 ES 300

Terminal No.	Symbol	Connection/Terminal Name	Terminal No.	Symbol	Connection/Terminal Name
A11-1	AMH	Air Mix Control Servomotor	A11-22	DIN	DCL2, DCL1
A11-2	AMC	Air Mix Control Servomotor	A11-23	DOUT	DCL2
A11-3	AIF	Air Inlet Control Servomotor	A10-1	S5	Sensor Power Source
A11-4	AIR	Air Inlet Control Servomotor	A10-2	TR	Room Temperature Sensor
A11-5	RDFGR	Defogger Relay	A10-3	TAM	Ambient Temperature Sensor
A11-6	HR	Heater Relay	A10-4	TEL IN	Telephone Transceiver
A11-7	FR	Extra-Hi Relay	A10-5	SG	Sensor Ground
A11-8	VM	Power Transister	A10-6	TE	Evaporator Temperature Sensor
A11-9	BLW	Power Transister	A10-7	TW	Engine Coolant Temp. Sensor
A11-10	MGC	Magnetic Clutch Relay	A10-8	TS	Solar Sensor
A11-11	FACE	Air Outlet Control Servomotor	A10-9	TP	Air Mix Damper Position Sensor
A11-12	B/L	Air Outlet Control Servomotor	A10-10	TPI	Air Inlet Damper Position Sensor
A11-13	FOOT	Air Outlet Control Servomotor	A10-11	SPEED	Speed Meter
A11-14			A12-1	+B	Back-up Power Source
A11-15	F/D	Air Outlet Control Servomotor	A12-2	ACC	Power Source
A11-16	DEF	Air Outlet Control Servomotor	A12-3	REOST	Rheostat
A11-17	PSW	Pressure Switch	A12-4	GND	E.C.U. Ground
A11-18	AC1	ECM	A12-5	IG	E.C.U. Power Source
A11-19	ACT	ECM	A12-6		
A11-20	LOCK IN	Lock Sensor	A12-7	ILL+	Tail Relay
A11-21	IGN	No. 1 Igniter	A12-8	TC	Rheostat

ECU TERMINAL STANDARD VALUE TEST CHART—1994-95 ES 300

Terminals	Symbols	Wiring Color	Condition		Standard Value
A11-1↔A11-2	AMH↔AMC	O↔P	IG OFF		13~19 Ω
A11-3↔A11-4	AIF↔AIR	RL↔R	IG OFF		13~19 Ω
A11-5↔A12-4	RDFGR↔GND	L-O↔W-B	IG ON	Rear Defogger Switch ON	Below 1 V
				Rear Defogger Switch OFF	10~14 V
A11-6↔A12-4	HR↔GND	L-W↔W-B	IG ON	Turn the Blower Motor	Below 1 V
				Do Not Turn the Blower Motor	10~14 V
A11-7↔A12-4	FR↔GND	W-G↔W-B	IG ON	Blower Level Hi or Set Temp: Max Hot or Max Cool	Below 1 V
				Blower Level OFF~Medium	10~14 V
A11-8↔A12-4	VM↔GND	B-W↔W-B	IG ON	Push Blower Switch to Change the Blower Speed from 1 to 5	Speed ① 9.6 V / Speed ⑤ below 1.5 V
A11-9↔A12-4	BLW↔GND	Y-W↔W-B	IG ON	Turn the Blower Motor	Below 1.5 V
A11-10↔A12-4	MGC↔GND	L-Y↔W-B	Start the Engine and Push Auto Switch	A/C Switch ON	Below 1 V
				A/C Switch OFF	10~14 V
A11-17↔A12-4	PSW↔GND	R-L↔W-B	IG ON		Below 1 V
A11-18↔A12-4	AC1↔GND	B-Y↔W-B	Start the Engine	A/C Switch ON	Below 1 V
				A/C Switch OFF	1 V or More
A11-19↔A12-4	ACT↔GND	LG-R↔W-B	Start the Engine (Idling)	Operate the Compressor	10~14 V
				Do Not Operate the Compressor	Below 1.5 V
A11-20↔A12-4	LOCK IN ↔GND	W-L↔W-B	IG OFF	at 20 °C (68 °F)	65~125 Ω
A11-21↔A12-4	IGN↔GND	B↔W-B		Start the Engine	10~14 V
A11-22↔A12-4	DIN↔GND	LG-R↔W-B	IG ON	Connect Tc and E₁ of DCL2 or DCL1	Below 1 V
				Other Than Above Condition	10~14 V
A10-1↔A10-5	S5↔SG	L↔W-R	IG ON		4~6 V
A10-1↔A10-8	S5↔TS	L-W	IG ON	Sensor Subjected to Electrical Light	Below 4 V
				Sensor Covered by a Cloth	4~4.5 V
A10-2↔A10-5	TR↔SG	G-Y↔W-R	IG ON	Cabin Temperature: 25 °C (77 °F)	1.8~2.2 V
				Cabin Temperature: 40 °C (104 °F)	1.2~1.6 V
A10-3↔A10-5	TAM↔SG	B-R↔W-R	IG ON	Ambient Temperature: 25 °C (77 °F)	1.35~1.75 V
				Ambient Temperature: 40 °C (104 °F)	0.85~1.25 V

ECU TERMINAL STANDARD VALUE TEST CHART—1994-95 ES 300, CONT'D

Terminals	Symbols	Wiring Color	Condition		Standard Value
A10-5 ↔ Body Ground	SG ↔ Body Grounds	W-R ↔ Body Ground	Always		1 Ω or less
A10-6 ↔ A10-5	TE ↔ SG	L-W ↔ W-R	IG ON	Evaporator Temp.: 0 °C (32 °F)	2.0 ~ 2.4 V
				Evaporator Temp.: 15 °C (59 °F)	1.4 ~ 1.8 V
A10-7 ↔ A10-5	TW ↔ SG	Y-B ↔ W-R	IG ON	Engine Coolant Temp.: 0 °C (32 °F)	2.8 ~ 3.2 V
				Engine Coolant Temp.: 40 °C (104 °F)	1.8 ~ 2.2 V
				Engine Coolant Temp.: 70 °C (158 °F)	0.9 ~ 1.3 V
A10-8 ↔ A10-5	TS ↔ SG	W ↔ W-R	IG ON	Sensor Subjected to Electrical Light	1 V or more
				Sensor Covered by Cloth	Below 1 V
A10-9 ↔ A10-5	TP ↔ SG	B-Y ↔ W-R	IG ON	Set Temp.: Max Cool	3.5 ~ 4.5 V
				Set Temp.: Max Hot	0.5 ~ 1.8 V
A10-10 ↔ A10-5	TPI ↔ SG	L-Y ↔ W-R	IG ON	Push Recircu Switch	3.5 ~ 4.5 V
				Push Fresh Switch	0.5 ~ 1.8 V
A12-1 ↔ A12-4	B + ↔ GND	L-Y ↔ W-B	IG OFF		10 ~ 14 V
A12-2 ↔ A12-4	ACC ↔ GND	L-R ↔ W-B	Turn Ignition Switch ACC		10 ~ 14 V
A12-4 ↔ Body Ground	GND ↔ Body Ground	W-B ↔ Body Ground	Always		1 Ω or less
A12-5 ↔ A12-4	IG + ↔ GND	R-L ↔ W-B	IG ON		10 ~ 14 V
A12-3 ↔ A12-4	REOST ↔ GND	B ↔ W-B	Light Control Switch :Tail Position	Rheostat Volume:Most Upward	Below 1 V
				Rheostat Volume: Most Downward	10 ~ 14 V
A12-7 ↔ A12-4	ILL ↔ GND	G ↔ W-B	Turn the Light Control Switch to Tail Position		10 ~ 14 V
A12-8 ↔ A12-4	TC ↔ GND	R-L ↔ W-B	Light Control Switch :Tail Position	Rheostat Volume: Most Upward	10 ~ 14 V
				Rheostat Volume: Most Downward	Below 1 V

AUTOMATIC TEMPERATURE CONTROL ECU TERMINAL CHART – GS 300

Terminal No.	Symbol	Connection/Terminal Name	Terminal No.	Symbol	Connection/Terminal Name
A8-1	AMH	Air Mix Damper Control Servomotor	A9-1	S5	Sensor Power Source
A8-2	AMC	Air Mix Damper Control Servomotor	A9-2	TR	Room Temp. Sensor
A8-3	AIF	Air Inlet Damper Control Servomotor	A9-3	TAM	Ambient Temp. Sensor
A8-4	AIR	Air Inlet Damper Control Servomotor	A9-5	SG	Sensor Ground
A8-5	RDFGR	Defogger Relay	A9-6	TE	Evaporator Temp. Sensor
A8-6	AOD	Air Outlet Damper Control Servomotor	A9-7	TW	Engine Coolant Temp. Sensor
A8-7	AOF	Air Outlet Damper Control Servomotor	A9-8	TS	Solar Sensor
A8-9	BLW	Blower Motor Control	A9-9	TP	Air Mix Damper Position Sensor
A8-10	MGC	A/C Lock Amplifier	A9-10	TPI	Air Inlet Damper Position Sensor
A8-12	CBLS	Max Cool Damper Control Servomotor	A9-11	TPO	Air Outlet Damper Position Sensor
A8-13	CBLO	Max Cool Damper Control Servomotor	A10-1	+B	Back-up Power Source
A8-16	HR	Heater Main Relay	A10-2	ACC	ACC Power Source
A8-17	PSW	Pressure Switch	A10-5	GND	A/C Control Assembly Ground
A8-18	TEL IN	Telephone Transceiver	A10-6	IG	IG Power Source
A8-19	SPEED	Combination Meter	A10-8	ILL+	Illumination Power Source
A8-20	LOCK IN	A/C Lock Amplifier	A10-9	REOST	Rheostat
A8-21	VER1	A/C Control Assembly Ground (CANADA)			
A8-22	DIN	DLC1 DLC2			
A8-23	DOUT	DLC2			

ECU TERMINAL STANDARD VALUE TEST CHART—GS 300

Terminals	Symbols	Wiring Color	Condition			Standard Value
A8-1↔A10-5	AMH↔GND	P↔W-B	IG ON	Set temp.: Max Hot		10 ~ 14 V
				Set temp.: Max Cool		Below 1 V
A8-2↔A10-5	AMC↔GND	P-B↔W-B	IG ON	Set temp.: Max Cool		10 ~ 14 V
				Set temp.: Max Hot		Below 1 V
A8-3↔A10-5	AIF↔GND	R-L↔W-B	IG ON	Push FRS switch		Below 1 V
				Push REC switch		10 ~ 14 V
A8-4↔A10-5	AIR↔GND	R-W↔W-B	IG ON	Push FRS switch		10 ~ 14 V
				Push REC switch		Below 1 V
A8-5↔A10-5	RDFGR↔GND	G-B↔W-B	IG ON	Rear defogger switch ON		Below 1 V
				Rear defogger switch OFF		10 ~ 14 V
A8-6↔A10-5	AOD↔GND	BR-W↔W-B	IG ON	Air outlet: FACE		Below 1 V
				Air outlet: FDEF		10 ~ 14 V
A8-7↔A10-5	AOF↔GND	Y-G↔W-B	IG ON	Air outlet: FACE		10 ~ 14 V
				Air outlet: FDEF		Below 1 V
A8-9↔A10-5	BLW↔GND	P-L↔W-B	IG ON	Turn the blower motor		1~3 V
A8-10↔A10-5	MGC↔GND	L-B↔W-B	Start the engine and push AUTO SW	A/C Switch ON		10 ~ 14 V
				A/C Switch OFF		Below 1 V
A8-12↔A10-5	CBLS↔GND	Y↔W-B	IG ON	Set temp.: Max Cool Air outlet: FACE		10 ~ 14 V
				Set temp.: Max Cool Air outlet: Ex. FACE		Below 1 V
A8-13↔A10-5	CBLO↔GND	L-R↔W-B	IG ON	Set temp.: Max Cool Air outlet: FACE		10 ~ 14 V
				Set temp.: Max Cool Air outlet: Ex. FACE		Below 1 V
A8-16↔A10-5	HR↔GND	L-Y↔W-B	IG ON	Turn the blower motor		Below 1 V
				Don't turn the blower motor		10 ~ 14 V
A8-17↔A10-5	PSW↔GND	L↔W-B	IG ON			Below 1 V
A8-20↔A10-5	LOCK IN↔GND	Y-R↔W-B	Start the engine and push AUTO SW	A/C Switch ON		10 ~ 14 V
A8-22↔A10-5	DIN↔GND	Y-L↔W-B	IG ON	Connect Te and E1 of DLC1,DLC2		Below 1 V
				Other than above condition		Below 5 V
A9-1↔A9-5	S5↔SG	R-Y↔B-W	IG ON			4.5 ~ 5.5 V
A9-2↔A9-5	TR↔SG	G↔B-W	IG ON	Cabin temp.: 25°C (77° F)		1.8 ~ 2.2 V
				Cabin temp.: 40°C (104° F)		1.2 ~ 1.6 V
A9-3↔A9-5	TAM↔SG	B↔B-W	IG ON	Ambient temp.: 25°C (77° F)		1.35 ~ 1.75 V
				Ambient temp.: 40°C (104° F)		0.85 ~ 1.25 V
A9-6↔A9-5	TE↔SG	B-L↔B-W	IG ON	Evaporator temp.: 0°C (32° F)		2.0 ~ 2.4 V
				Evaporator temp.: 15°C (59° F)		1.4 ~ 1.8 V
A9-7↔A9-5	TW↔SG	G-R↔B-W	IG ON	Water temp.: 0°C (32° F)		2.8 ~ 3.2 V
				Water temp.: 40°C (104° F)		1.8 ~ 2.2 V
				Water temp.: 70°C (158° F)		1.3 ~ 1.5 V
A9-8↔A9-5	TS↔SG	G-B↔B-W	IG ON	Sensor subjected to electric light		0.8 ~ 4.3 V
				Sensor covered by a cloth		Below 0.8 V

ECU TERMINAL STANDARD VALUE TEST CHART—GS 300, CONT'D

Terminals	Symbols	Wiring Color	Condition		Standard Value
A9-9↔A9-5	TP↔SG	L-O↔B-W	IG ON	Set temp.: Max Cool	3.5 ~ 4.5 V
				Set temp.: Max Hot	0.5 ~ 1.5 V
A9-10↔A9-5	TPI↔SG	R-B↔B-W	IG ON	Push REC switch	3.5 ~ 4.5 V
				Push FRS switch	0.5 ~ 1.5 V
A9-11↔A9-5	TPO↔SG	Y-B↔B-W	IG ON	Air outlet: FACE	3.5 ~ 4.5 V
				Push Front DEF SW	0.5 ~ 1.5 V
A10-1↔A10-5	+B↔GND	W-R↔W-B	Always		10 ~ 14 V
A10-2↔A10-5	ACC↔GND	P-L↔W-B	Turn ignition switch ACC		10 ~ 14 V
A10-5↔Body Ground	GND↔Body Ground	W-B↔Body Ground	Always		Below 1 Ω
A10-6↔A10-5	IG↔GND	B-Y↔W-B	Turn ignition switch IG		10 ~ 14 V
A10-8↔A10-5	ILL+↔GND	LG↔W-B	Turn the light control switch to TAIL position		10 ~ 14 V
A10-9↔A10-5	REOST↔GND	W-G↔W-B	IG ON and turn head light control SW to TAIL position. Turn rheostat position from most right to most left position		Most Right 0 ~ 1 V ↓ Most Left 10 ~ 14 V

AUTOMATIC TEMPERATURE CONTROL ECU TERMINAL CHART—
1993 SC 300 AND SC 400

Terminal No.	Symbol	Connection/Terminal Name	Terminal No.	Symbol	Connection/Terminal Name
A14-1	+B	Back-up Power Source	A13-1	IGN	No. 1 Igniter
A14-2	MH	Air Mix Servomotor	A13-2	A/C IN	Compressor
A14-3	MC	Air Mix Servomotor	A13-3	LCK I	Lock Sensor
A14-4	MFRS	Air Inlet Servomotor	A13-4	SAUTO	Temperature and Automatic Control Switch
A14-5	MREC	Air Inlet Servomotor	A13-5	LP	Pressure Switch
A14-6	IG+	ECU Power Source	A13-6	DIN	TDCL, Check Connector
A14-7	E	ECU Ground	A13-7	TR	Room Temp. Sensor
A14-8	MFACE	Air Outlet Servomotor	A13-8	TAM	Ambient Temp. Sensor
A14-9	MDEF	Air Outlet Servomotor	A13-9	TE	Evaporator Temp. Sensor
A14-10	—	——————	A13-10	TW	Water Temp. Sensor
A14-11	—	——————	A13-11	TS	Solar Sensor
A14-12	—	——————	A13-12	SET1	Temperature and Automatic Control Switch
A14-13	—	——————	A13-13	SET2	Temperature and Automatic Control Switch
A14-14	—	——————	A13-14	SET3	Temperature and Automatic Control Switch
A14-15	ACC	Power Source	A13-15	SET4	Temperature and Automatic Control Switch
A12-1	—	——————	A13-16	SET5	Temperature and Automatic Control Switch
A12-2	REOST	Rheostat	A13-17	DOUT	TDCL
A12-3	WV	Water Valve VSV	A13-18	S5	Sensor Power Source
A12-4	MGC	Engine & ECT ECU	A13-19	—	——————
A12-5	TC	Rheostat	A13-20	SG	Sensor Ground
A12-6	TAIL	Taillight Relay	A13-21	—	——————
A12-7	LV	Power Transistor	A13-22	TP	Air Mix Damper Position Sensor
A12-8	BLR	Power Transistor	A13-23	TPI	Air Inlet Damper Position Sensor
A12-9	HR	Heater Relay	A13-24	—	——————
A12-10	RDFGR	Defogger Relay	A13-25	TPM	Air Outlet Damper Position Sensor
A12-11	FAN	Cooling Fan ECU (SC 400 ONLY)			

ECU TERMINAL STANDARD VALUE TEST CHART—
1993 SC 300 AND SC 400

Terminals	Symbols	Wiring Color	Condition		Standard Value
A14-1↔A14-7	B↔E	R↔W-B	IG OFF		10 ~ 14 V
A14-2↔A14-3	MH↔MC	V↔R-Y	IG OFF		13 ~ 19 Ω
A14-4↔A14-5	MFRS↔MREC	G↔G-R	IG OFF		13 ~ 19 Ω
A14-6↔A14-7	IG+↔E	R-L↔W-B	IG ON		10 ~ 14 V
A14-7↔Body Ground	E↔Body Ground	W-B↔Body Ground	Always		Below 1 Ω
A14-8↔A14-9	FACE↔DEF	W↔Y-L	IG OFF		13 ~ 19 Ω
A14-15↔A14-7	ACC↔E	L-R↔W-B	Turn ignition switch ACC		10 ~ 14 V
A12-2↔A14-7	REOST↔E	W-G↔W-B	IG ON and turn headlight control SW to TAIL position. Turn Rheostat volume from most right to left position.		Most Right : 0 ~ 1 V ↓ Most Left : 10 ~ 14 V
A12-3↔A14-7	WV↔E	B-Y↔W-B	Start the engine	Temp. Control Switch: MAX COLD	10 ~ 14 V
				Temp. Control Switch: MAX HOT	Below 1 V
A12-4↔A14-7	MGC↔E	L-R↔W-B	Start the engine and push AUTO SW	A/C switch ON	Below 1 V
				A/C switch OFF	10 ~ 14 V
A12-5↔A14-7	TC↔E	L↔W-B	IG ON H.L.C. SW : TAIL position	Rheostat Volume : Most Right	Below 1 V
				Rheostat Volume : Turn Left	10 ~ 14 V
A12-6↔A14-7	TAIL↔E	G↔W-B	Turn the light control switch to TAIL position		10 ~ 14 V
A12-7↔A14-7	LV↔E	Y↔W-B	IG ON	Push blower SW to change the blower speed from 1 to 10.	Speed 1: 10 ~ 14 V ↓ Speed 10: Below 2 V
A12-8↔A14-7	BLR↔E	B-R↔W-B	IG ON	Turn the blower motor	Below 1.5 V
A12-9↔A14-7	HR↔E	L-W↔W-B	IG ON	Turn the blower motor	Below 1 V
				Don't turn the blower motor	10 ~ 14 V
A12-10↔A14-7	RDFGR↔E	R-Y↔W-B	IG ON	Rear defogger switch ON	Below 1 V
				Rear defogger switch OFF	10 ~ 14 V
A12-11↔A14-7	FAN↔E	R-G↔W-B	IG ON and AUTO SW ON	A/C SW ON and MAX COLD	10 ~ 14 V
				A/C SW OFF	Below 1 V
A13-1↔A14-7	IGN↔E	B↔W-B	Start the engine		10 ~ 14 V

ECU TERMINAL STANDARD VALUE TEST CHART—
1993 SC 300 AND SC 400, CONT'D

Terminals	Symbols	Wiring Color	Condition		Standard Value
A13-2↔A14-7	A/C IN↔E	L-Y↔W-B	Operate the compressor		10 ~ 14 V
			Not operate the compressor		Below 1 V
A13-3↔A14-7	LOCK IN↔E	G-Y↔W-B	IG OFF	at 25°C (77°F)	530 ~ 650 Ω
				at 100°C (212°F)	670 ~ 890 Ω
A13-4↔A14-7	SAUTO↔E	V-W↔W-B	IG ON	AUTO switch ON	Below 1 V
				AUTO switch OFF	10 ~ 14 V
A13-5↔A14-7	LP↔E	L-B↔W-B	IG ON		Below 1 V
A13-6↔A14-7	DIN↔E	P-B↔W-B	IG ON	Connect Tc and E1 of TDCL, Check connector	Below 1 V
				Other than above condition	10 ~ 14 V
A13-7↔A13-20	TR↔SG	Y-L↔BR	IG ON	Cabin temp.: 25°C (77°F)	1.8 ~ 2.2 V
				Cabin temp.: 40°C (104°F)	1.2 ~ 1.6 V
A13-8↔A13-20	TAM↔SG	P↔BR	IG ON	Ambient Temp.: 25°C (77°F)	1.35 ~ 1.75 V
				Ambient Temp.: 40°C (104°F)	0.85 ~ 1.25 V
A13-9↔A13-20	TE↔SG	L-Y↔BR	IG ON	Evaporator ambient temp.: 0°C (32°F)	2.0 ~ 2.4 V
				Evaporator ambient temp.: 15°C (59°F)	1.4 ~ 1.8 V
A13-10↔A13-20	TW↔SG	LG-R↔BR	IG ON	Water temp.: 0°C (32°F)	2.8 ~ 3.2 V
				Water temp.: 40°C (104°F)	1.8 ~ 2.2 V
				Water temp.: 70°C (158°F)	0.9 ~ 1.3 V
A13-11↔A13-20	TS↔SG	Y-G↔BR	IG ON	Sensor subjected to electric light	1 V or more
				Sensor covered by a cloth	Below 1 V
A13-12↔A13-20	SET1↔SG	V-R↔BR	IG ON	Turn temp. control SW from most left to right position	Change 5 V and 0 V 11 times (15 times)*
A13-13↔A13-20	SET2↔SG	G-O↔BR			Change 5 V and 0 V 5 times (8 times)*
A13-14↔A13-20	SET3↔SG	Y↔BR			Change 5 V and 0 V 2 times (4 times)*
A13-15↔A13-20	SET4↔SG	B-R↔BR			Change 5 V and 0 V 2 times
A13-16↔A13-20	SET5↔SG	B-Y↔BR			Change 5 V and 0 V Once

ECU TERMINAL STANDARD VALUE TEST CHART — 1993 SC 300 AND SC 400, CONT'D

Terminals	Symbols	Wiring Color	Condition		Standard Value
A13-18↔A13-20	S5↔SG	BR-W↔BR	IG ON		A ~ 6 V
A13-20↔Body Ground	SG↔Body Ground	BR↔Body Ground	Always		Below 1 Ω
A13-22↔A13-20	TP↔SG	G-W↔BR	IG ON	Set temp.: Max Cool	3.5 ~ 4.5 V
				Set temp.: Max Hot	0.5 ~ 1.8 V
A13-23↔A13-20	TP1↔SG	GR↔BR	IG ON	Push REC switch	3.5 ~ 4.5 V
				Push FRS switch	0.5 ~ 1.8 V
A13-25↔A13-20	TPM↔SG	Y-R↔BR	IG ON	Air outlet : FACE	3.5 ~ 4.5 V
				Push Front DEF SW	0.5 ~ 1.8 V

AUTOMATIC TEMPERATURE CONTROL ECU TERMINAL CHART—
1994-95 SC 300 AND SC 400

BE6351

Terminal No.	Symbol	Connection/Terminal Name	Terminal No.	Symbol	Connection/Terminal Name
A10-1	B+	Back-up Power Source	A12-1	IGN	No. 1 Igniter
A10-2	MH	Air Mix Servomotor	A12-2	A/C IN	Compressor
A10-3	MC	Air Mix Servomotor	A12-3	LCK I	Lock Sensor
A10-4	MFRS	Air Inlet Servomotor	A12-4	SAUTO	Temperature and Automatic Control Switch
A10-5	MREC	Air Inlet Servomotor	A12-5	LP	Pressure Switch
A10-6	IG+	ECU Power Source	A12-6	DIN	DLC2, DLC1
A10-7	E	ECU Ground	A12-7	TR	Room Temp. Sensor
A10-8	MFACE	Air Outlet Servomotor	A12-8	TAM	Ambient Temp. Sensor
A10-9	MDEF	Air Outlet Servomotor	A12-9	TE	Evaporator Temp. Sensor
A10-10	—	————	A12-10	TW	Engine Coolant Temp. Sensor
A10-11	—	————	A12-11	TS	Solar Sensor
A10-12	—	————	A12-12	SET1	Temperature and Automatic Control Switch
A10-13	—	————	A12-13	SET2	Temperature and Automatic Control Switch
A10-14	—	————	A12-14	SET3	Temperature and Automatic Control Switch
A10-15	ACC	Power Source	A12-15	SET4	Temperature and Automatic Control Switch
A11-1	AMOUT	Comb. Meter	A12-16	SET5	Temperature and Automatic Control Switch
A11-2	REOST	Rheostat	A12-17	DOUT	DLC2
A11-3	WV	Water Valve VSV	A12-18	S5	Sensor Power Source
A11-4	MGC	ECM	A12-19	—	————
A11-5	TC	Rheostat	A12-20	SG	Sensor Ground
A11-6	TAIL	Taillight Relay	A12-21	—	————
A11-7	LV	Power Transistor	A12-22	TP	Air Mix Damper Position Sensor
A11-8	BLR	Power Transistor	A12-23	TPI	Air Inlet Damper Position Sensor
A11-9	HR	Heater Relay	A12-24	SPEED	Comb. Meter
A11-10	RDFGR	Defogger Relay	A12-25	TPM	Air Outlet Damper Position Sensor
A11-11	FAN	Cooling Fan ECU (SC400 Only)			

ECU TERMINAL STANDARD VALUE TEST CHART—
1994-95 SC 300 AND SC 400

Terminals	Symbols	Wiring Color	Condition			Standard Value
A10-1 ⟷ A10-7	B⟶E	R⟶W-B	IG OFF			10 ~ 14 V
A10-2 ⟷ A10-3	MH⟶MC	V⟶R-Y	IG OFF			13 ~ 19 Ω
A10-4 ⟷ A10-5	MFRS⟶MREC	G⟶G-R	IG OFF			13 ~ 19 Ω
A10-6 ⟷ A10-7	IG+⟶E	R-L⟶W-B	IG ON			10 ~ 14 V
A10-7 ⟷ Body Ground	E⟶Body Ground	W-B⟶Body Ground	Always			Below 1 Ω
A10-8 ⟷ A10-9	FACE⟶DEF	W⟶Y-L	IG OFF			13 ~ 19 Ω
A10-15 ⟷ A10-7	ACC⟶E	L-R⟶W-B	Turn ignition switch ACC			10 ~ 14 V
A11-2 ⟷ A10-7	REOST⟶E	W-G⟶W-B	IG ON and turn headlight control SW to TAIL position. Turn Rheostat volume from most right to left position.			Most Right : 0 ~ 1 V ↓ Most Left : 10 ~ 14 V
A11-3 ⟷ A10-7	WV⟶E	B-Y⟶W-B	Start the engine	Temp. Control Switch: MAX COLD		10 ~ 14 V
				Temp. Control Switch: MAX HOT		Below 1 V
A11-4 ⟷ A10-7	MGC⟶E	L-R⟶W-B	Start the engine and push AUTO SW	A/C switch ON		Below 1 V
				A/C switch OFF		10 ~ 14 V
A11-5 ⟷ A10-7	TC⟶E	L⟶W-B	IG ON H.L.C. SW : TAIL position	Rheostat Volume : Most Right		Below 1 V
				Rheostat Volume : Turn Left		10 ~ 14 V
A11-6 ⟷ A10-7	TAIL⟶E	G⟶W-B	Turn the light control switch to TAIL position			10 ~ 14 V
A11-7 ⟷ A10-7	LV⟶E	Y⟶W-B	IG ON	Push blower SW to change the blower speed from 1 to 10.		Speed 1: 10 ~ 14 V ↓ Speed 10: Below 2 V
A11-8 ⟷ A10-7	BLR⟶E	B-R⟶W-B	IG ON	Turn the blower motor		Below 1.5 V
A11-9 ⟷ A10-7	HR⟶E	L-W⟶W-B	IG ON	Turn the blower motor		Below 1 V
				Don't turn the blower motor		10 ~ 14 V
A11-10 ⟷ A10-7	RDFGR⟶E	R-Y⟶W-B	IG ON	Rear defogger switch ON		Below 1 V
				Rear defogger switch OFF		10 ~ 14 V
A11-11 ⟷ A10-7 (SC400 Only)	FAN⟶E	R-G⟶W-B	IG ON and AUTO SW ON	A/C SW ON and MAX COLD		10 ~ 14 V
				A/C SW OFF		Below 1 V
A12-1 ⟷ A10-7	IGN⟶E	B⟶W-B	Start the engine			10 ~ 14 V

ECU TERMINAL STANDARD VALUE TEST CHART–
1994-95 SC 300 AND SC 400, CONT'D

Terminals	Symbols	Wiring Color	Condition		Standard Value
A12-2 ⟷ A10-7	A/C IN⟷ E	L-Y⟷W-B	Operate the compressor		10 ~ 14 V
			Not operate the compressor		Below 1 V
A12-3 ⟷ A10-7	LOCK IN ⟷E	G-Y⟷W-B	IG OFF	at 25°C (77°F)	530 ~ 650 Ω
				at 100°C (212°F)	670 ~ 890 Ω
A12-4 ⟷ A10-7	SAUTO⟷E	V-W⟷W-B	IG ON	AUTO switch ON	Below 1 V
				AUTO switch OFF	10 ~ 14 V
A12-5 ⟷ A10-7	LP⟷E	L-B⟷W-B	IG ON		Below 1 V
A12-6 ⟷ A10-7	DIN⟷E	P-B⟷W-B	IG ON	Connect Tc and E1 of DLC2, DLC1	Below 1 V
				Other than above condition	10 ~ 14 V
A12-7 ⟷ A12-20	TR⟷SG	Y-L⟷BR	IG ON	Cabin temp.: 25°C (77°F)	1.8 ~ 2.2 V
				Cabin temp.: 40°C (104°F)	1.2 ~ 1.6 V
A12-8 ⟷ A12-20	TAM⟷SG	P⟷BR	IG ON	Ambient Temp.: 25°C (77°F)	1.35 ~ 1.75 V
				Ambient Temp.: 40°C (104°F)	0.85 ~ 1.25 V
A12-9 ⟷ A12-20	TE⟷SG	L-Y⟷BR	IG ON	Evaporator ambient temp. : 0°C (32°F)	2.0 ~ 2.4 V
				Evaporator ambient temp. : 15°C (59°F)	1.4 ~ 1.8 V
A12-10 ⟷ A12-20	TW⟷SG	LG-R⟷BR	IG ON	Engine coolant temp.: 0°C (32°F)	2.8 ~ 3.2 V
				Engine coolant temp.: 40°C (104°F)	1.8 ~ 2.2 V
				Engine coolant temp.: 70°C (158°F)	0.9 ~ 1.3 V
A12-11 ⟷ A12-20	TS⟷SG	Y-G⟷BR	IG ON	Sensor subjected to electric light	1 V or more
				Sensor covered by a cloth	Below 1 V
A12-12 ⟷ A12-20	SET1⟷SG	V-R⟷BR	IG ON	Turn temp. control SW from most left to right position	Change 5 V and 0 V 11 times (15 times)*
A12-13 ⟷ A12-20	SET2⟷SG	G-O⟷BR			Change 5 V and 0 V 5 times (8 times)*
A12-14 ⟷ A12-20	SET3⟷SG	Y⟷BR			Change 5 V and 0 V 2 times (4 times)*
A12-15 ⟷ A12-20	SET4⟷SG	B-R⟷BR			Change 5 V and 0 V 2 times
A12-16 ⟷ A12-20	SET5⟷SG	B-Y⟷BR			Change 5 V and 0 V Once

ECU TERMINAL STANDARD VALUE TEST CHART—
1994-95 SC 300 AND SC 400, CONT'D

Terminals	Symbols	Wiring Color	Condition		Standard Value
A12-18 ⟷ A12-20	S5↔SG	BR-W↔BR	IG ON		4 ~ 6 V
A12-20 ⟷ Body Ground	SG↔Body Ground	BR↔Body Ground	Always		Below 1 Ω
A12-22 ⟷ A12-20	TP↔SG	G-W↔BR	IG ON	Set temp.: Max Cool	3.5 ~ 4.5 V
				Set temp.: Max Hot	0.5 ~ 1.8 V
A12-23 ⟷ A12-20	TP1↔SG	GR↔BR	IG ON	Push REC switch	3.5 ~ 4.5 V
				Push FRS switch	0.5 ~ 1.8 V
A12-25 ⟷ A12-20	TPM↔SG	Y-R↔BR	IG ON	Air outlet : FACE	3.5 ~ 4.5 V
				Push Front DEF SW	0.5 ~ 1.8 V

AUTOMATIC TEMPERATURE CONTROL ECU TERMINAL CHART— 1993-94 LS 400

(A-14)

14	13	12	11	10	9	8	7	/	5	4	3	2	1
28	27	26	25	24	/	/	21	20	19	18	17	16	15
/	/	/	/	/	/	/	/	33		32	31	30	/

(A-15)

8	7	6	5	/	4	3	2	1
/	/	/	14	13	/	/	/	9
/	/	/	22	/	/	/	19	18

Terminal No.	Symbol	Connection/Terminal Name	Terminal No.	Symbol	Connection/Terminal Name
A14-1	FOOT	Air Vent Mode Damper Control Servomotor	A14-26	AMC	Air Mix Damper Control Servomotor
A14-2	F/D	Air Vent Mode Damper Control Servomotor	A14-27	AIR	Air Inlet Damper Control Servomotor
A14-3	DEF	Air Vent Mode Damper Control Servomotor	A14-28	ABO	Max Cool Damper Control Servomotor
A14-4	DIN	DLC1 DLC2	A14-30	IGN	No. 1 Igniter
A14-5	DOUT	DLC2	A14-31	SPEED	Combination Meter
A14-7	GND	A/C Control Assembly Ground	A14-32	RDFGR	Defogger Relay
A14-8	+B	Back-up Power Source	A14-33	HR	Heater Main Relay
A14-9	ACC	ACC Power Source	A15-1	TR	Room Temp. Sensor
A14-10	IG	IG Power Source	A15-2	TAM	Ambient Temp. Sensor
A14-11	BLW	Power Transistor	A15-3	TE	Evaporator Temp. Sensor
A14-12	AMH	Air Mix Damper Control Servomotor	A15-4	TW	Water Temp. Sensor
A14-13	AIF	Air Inlet Damper Control Servomotor	A15-5	TS	Solar Sensor
A14-14	ABS	Max Cool Damper Control Servomotor	A15-6	TP	Air Mix Damper Position Sesnor
A14-15	FACE	Air Vent Mode Damper Control Servomotor	A15-7	TPI	Air Inlet Damper Position Sensor
A14-16	B/L	Air Vent Mode Damper Control Servomotor	A15-8	TPB	Max Cool Damper Position Sensor
A14-17	TEL IN	Telephone & Speaker Relay	A15-9	S5	Sensor Power Source
A14-18	A/C IN	Compressor	A15-13	SG	Sensor Ground
A14-19	PSW	Pressure Switch	A15-14	REOST	Rheostat
A14-20	FR	Ex–Hi Relay	A15-18	ILL+	Illumination Power Source
A14-21	AM OUT	Combination Meter	A15-19	TC	Light Control Rheostat Volume
A14-24	MGC	ECM	A15-22	LOCK IN	Compressor Lock Sensor
A14-25	VM	Power Transistor			

ECU TERMINAL STANDARD VALUE TEST CHART— 1993-94 LS 400

Terminals	Symbols	Wiring Color	Condition		Standard Value
A14-1 ↔ A14-7	FOOT ↔ GND	LG-R ↔ W-B	FOOT switch ON		Below 1 V
			FOOT switch OFF		10 ~ 14 V
A14-2 ↔ A14-7	F/D ↔ GND	B-W ↔ W-B	F/D switch ON		Beloow 1 V
			F/D switch OFF		10 ~ 14 V
A14-3 ↔ A14-7	DEF ↔ GND	Y-B ↔ W-B	Front DEF switch ON		Below 1 V
			Front DEF switch OFF		10 ~ 14 V
A14-4 ↔ A14-7	DIN ↔ GND	P-G ↔ W-B	IG ON	Connect Tc and E1 of DLC1, DLC2	Below 1 V
				Other than above condition	10 ~ 14 V
A14-7 ↔ Body Ground	GND ↔ Body Ground	W-B ↔ Body Ground	Always		Below 1 Ω
A14-8 ↔ A14-7	+B ↔ GND	R ↔ W-B	Always		10 ~ 14V
A14-9 ↔ A14-7	ACC ↔ GND	GR ↔ W-B	Turnignition switch ACC		10 ~ 14 V
A14-10 ↔ A14-7	IG ↔ GND	R-Y ↔ W-B	Turn ignition switch IG		10 ~ 14 V
A14-11 ↔ A14-7	BLW ↔ GND	G-B ↔ W-B	IG ON Turn the blower motor		1 ~ 2 V
A14-12 ↔ A14-26	AMH ↔ AMC	V-R ↔ Y-R	IG OFF		13 ~ 19 Ω
A14-13 ↔ A14-27	AIF ↔ AIR	P ↔ Y	IG OFF		13 ~ 19 Ω
A14-14 ↔ A14-28	ABS ↔ ABO	L-R ↔ Y-L	IG OFF		13 ~ 19 Ω
A14-15 ↔ A14-7	FACE ↔ GND	BR-W ↔ W-B	FACE switch ON		Below 1 V
			FACE switch OFF		10 ~ 14 V
A14-16 ↔ A14-7	B/L ↔ GND	G-R ↔ W-B	B/L switch ON		Below 1 V
			B/L switch OFF		10 ~ 14V
A14-18 ↔ A14-7	A/C IN ↔ GND	B-W ↔ W-B	Operate the compressor		10 ~ 14 V
			Not operate the compressor		Below 1 V
A14-19 ↔ A14-7	PSW ↔ GND	L-B ↔ W-B	IG ON		Below 1 V
A14-20 ↔ A14-7	FR ↔ GND	G-O ↔ W-B	IG ON	Turn the blower motor HI	Below 1 V
				Turn the blowe motor except HI	10 ~ 14 V
A14-24 ↔ A14-7	MGL ↔ GND	B ↔ W-B	Start the engine and push AUTO SW	A/C switch ON	Below 1 V
				A/C switch OFF	10 ~ 14 V
A14-25 ↔ A14-7	VM ↔ GND	L-B ↔ W-B	IG ON	Push blower SW +0 change the blower speed	LO → HI Above 8.4 V→Below 2V
A14-30 ↔ A14-7	IGN ↔ GND	B ↔ W-B	Start the engine		PULSE
A14-32 ↔ A14-7	RDFGR ↔ GND	R-B ↔ W-B	IG ON	Rear defogger switch ON	Below 1 V
				Rear defogger switch OFF	10 ~ 14 V
A14-33 ↔ A14-7	HR ↔ GND	L-Y ↔ W-B	IG ON	Turn the blower motor	Below 1 V
				Don't turn the blower motor	10 ~ 14 V
A15-1 ↔ A15-13	TR ↔ SG	Y-L ↔ Y-G	IG ON	Cabin temp: 25°C (77°F)	1.8 ~ 2.2 V
				Cabin temp: 40°C (104°F)	1.2 ~ 1.6 V
A15-2 ↔ A15-13	TAM ↔ SG	L-W ↔ Y-G	IG ON	Ambient temp: 25°C (77°F)	1.35 ~ 1.75 V
				Ambient temp: 40°C (104°F)	0.85 ~ 1.25 V

ECU TERMINAL STANDARD VALUE TEST CHART– 1993-94 LS 400, CONT'D

Terminals	Symbols	Wiring Color	Condition		Standard Value
A15-3 ↔ A15-13	TE↔SG	Y-R↔Y-G	IG ON	Evaporator ambient temp.: 0°C (32°F)	2.0 ~ 2.4 V
				Evaporator ambient temp.: 15°(59°F)	1.4 ~ 1.8 V
A15-4↔A15-13	TW↔SG	V↔Y-G	IG ON	Water temp.: 0°C (32°F)	2.8 ~ 3.2 V
				Water temp.: 40°C (104°F)	1.8 ~ 2.2 V
				Water temp.: 70°C (158°F)	0.9 ~ 1.3 V
A15-5↔A15-13	TS↔SG	G-B↔Y-G	IG ON	Sensor subjected to electric light	0.8 ~ 4.3 V
				Sensor covered by a cloth	Below 0.8 V
A15-6↔A15-13	TP↔SG	Y↔Y-G	IG ON	Set temp.: Max Cool	3.5 ~ 4.5V
				Set temp.: Max Hot	0.5 ~ 1.8 V
A15-7↔A15-13	TPΓ↔SG	L-R↔Y-G	IG ON	Push REC switch	3.5 ~ 4.5 V
				Push REC switch	0.5 ~ 1.8 V
A15-8↔A15-13	TPB↔SG	W-L↔Y-G	IG ON	Set temp.: Max Cool	3.5 ~ 4.5 V
				Set temp.: Max Hot	0.5 ~ 1.8 V
A15-9↔A15-13	S5↔SG	L↔Y-G	IG ON		4.5 ~ 5.5 V
A15-14↔A14-7	REOST↔GND	W-G↔W-B	IG ON and turn head light control SW to Tail position Turn Rheostat volume from most right to left position		Most . 0 ~ 1 V Right . ↓ Most . Left . 10 ~ 14 V
A15-18↔A14-7	ILL+↔GND	G↔W-B	Turn the light control switch to TAIL position		10 ~ 14 V
A14-15↔A14-7	TC↔GND	B-R↔W-B	IG ON and turn head light control switch to TAIL position	Rheostat . Most Volume . Right	Below 1 V
				Rheostat . Turn Volume . Left	10 ~ 14 V
A15-22↔A14-7	LOCK IN ↔GND	W-G↔W-B	IG OFF	at 25°C (77°F)	1050 ~ 570 Ω
				at 100°C (212°F)	1440 ~ 720 Ω
A14-7↔Body Ground	GND↔Body Ground	W-G↔Body Ground	Always		Below 1 Ω
A15-13↔Body Ground	SG↔Body Ground	Y-G↔Body Ground	Always		Below 1 Ω

ECU TERMINAL STANDARD VALUE TEST CHART—1995 LS 400

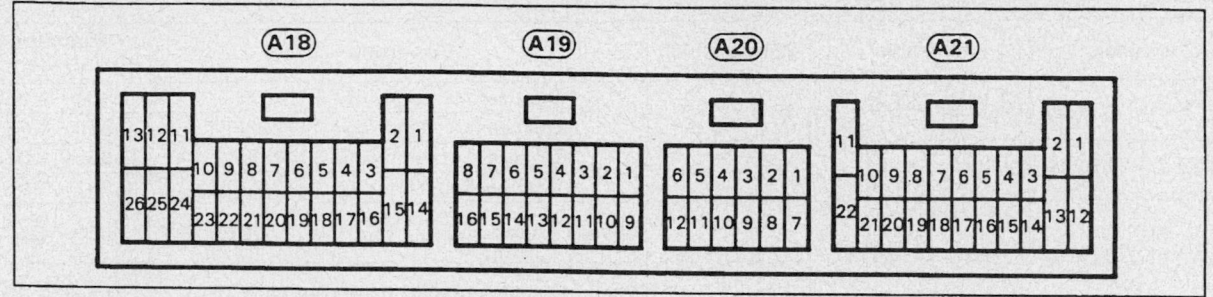

Terminal	Symbols	Wiring Color	Condition		Standard Value
A18-1 → A21-11	PSW → GND	L-B → W-B	IG ON		Below 1 V
A18-2 → A21-11	RDFGR → GND	R-B → W-B	IG ON	Rear defogger switch ON	Below 1 V
				Rear defogger switch OFF	10 ~ 14 V
A18-10 → A21-11	WVO → GND	R-G → W-B	Change display code 22 to display code 23 While moving the W/V servomotor		Below 1 V
A18-11 → A21-11	AIF → GND	BR-R → W-B	Display code 20		10 ~ 14 V
A18-12 → A21-11	ABODr → GND	B-W → W-B	Change display code 29 to display code 20 While moving the A/B servomotor		10 ~14 V
A18-13 → A21-11	ABOPa → GND	LG → W-B	Change display code 29 to display code 20 While moving the A/B servomotor		10 ~14 V
A18-14 → A21-11	MGC → GND	B-R → W-B	Display code 22		Below 1 V
A18-15 → A21-11	DOUT → GND	GR-G → W-B	DIN ≦ 1 V		PULSE
A18-16 → A21-11	DIN → GND	P-G → W-B	IG ON	Connect Tc and E1 of DLC1, DLC2	Below 1 V
				Other than above condition	10 ~ 14 V
A18-17 → A21-11	RLW → GND	LG-R → W-B	Display code 21		PULSE
A18-18 → A21-11	HR → GND	L-Y → W-B	Display code 21		Below 1 V
A18-23 → A21-11	WVS → GND	G-W → W-B	Change display code 29 to display code 20 While moving the W/V servomotor		Below 1 V
A18-24 → A21-11	AIR → GND	P-B → W-B	Display code 23		10 ~ 14 V
A18-25 → A21-11	ABSDr → GND	L-R → W-B	Change display code 22 to display code 23 While moving the A/B servomotor		10 ~ 14 V
A18-26 → A21-11	ABSPa → GND	V-Y → W-B	Change display code 22 to display code 23 While moving the A/B servomotor		10 ~ 14 V
A19-1 → A19-16	S5 → SG	W-R → Y-G	IG ON		4.5 ~ 5.5 V
A19-2 → A19-16	TR → SG	L → Y-G	IG ON	Cabin temp: 25°C (77°F)	1.8 ~ 2.2 V
				Cabin temp: 40°C (104°F)	1.2 ~ 1.6 V
A19-3 → A19-16	TAM → SG	L-W → Y-G	IG ON	Ambient temp: 25°C (77°F)	1.35 ~ 1.75 V
				Cabin temp: 40°C (104°F)	0.85 ~ 1.25 V
A19-4 → A19-16	TE → SG	Y-R → Y-G	IG ON	Evaporator ambient temp: 0°C (32°F)	2.0 ~ 2.4 V
				Evaporator ambient temp: 15°C (59°F)	1.4 ~ 1.8 V
A19-6 → A19-16	TSDr → SG	W → Y-G	IG ON	Solar sensor subjected to electric light	0.8 ~ 4.3 V
				Solar sensor covered by a cloth	Below 0.8 V
A19-7 → A19-16	TSPa → SG	GR → Y-G	IG ON	Solar sensor subjected to electric light	0.8 ~ 4.3 V
				Solar sensor covered by a cloth	Below 0.8 V
A19-8 → A19-16	TPI → SG	R-W → Y-G	Display code 20		0.5 ~ 1.8 V
			Display code 23		3.5 ~ 4.5 V

ECU TERMINAL STANDARD VALUE TEST CHART—1995 LS 400, CONT'D

Terminals	Symbols	Wiring Color	Condition		Standard Value
A19-9 ↔ A19-16	TFACEDr ↔ SG	GR-R ↔ Y-G	IG ON	Duct sensor temp: 25°C (77°F)	1.95 ~ 2.05 V
				Duct sensor temp: 50°C (122°F)	0.95 ~ 1.15 V
A19-10 ↔ A19-16	TFACEPa ↔ SG	GR-L ↔ Y-G	IG ON	Duct sensor temp: 25°C (77°F)	1.95 ~ 2.05 V
				Duct sensor temp: 50°C (122°F)	0.95 ~ 1.15 V
A19-11 ↔ A19-16	TPBDr ↔ SG	V-G ↔ Y-G	Change display code 29 to display code 20		3.5 ~ 4.5 V
			Change display code 22 to display code 23		0.5 ~ 1.8 V
A19-12 ↔ A19-16	TPBPa ↔ SG	R-B ↔ Y-G	Change display code 29 to display code 20		3.5 ~ 4.5 V
			Change display code 22 to display code 23		0.5 ~ 1.8 V
A19-16 ↔ Body Ground	SG ↔ Body Ground	Y-G ↔ Body Ground	Always		Below 1 Ω
A20-1 ↔ A21-11	IGN ↔ GND	B-Y ↔ W-B	Start the engine		PULSE
A20-2 ↔ A21-11	REOST ↔ GND	W-G ↔ W-B	IG ON and turn head light control SW to TAIL position Turn Rheostat volume from most right to left position		Below 1 V ↓ 10 ~ 14 V
A20-3 ↔ A21-11	TELIN ↔ GND	O ↔ W-B	Hand free Telephone ON		Below 1.5 V
A20-4 ↔ A21-11	SPD ↔ GND	V-W ↔ W-B	The vehicle move		PULSE
A20-5 ↔ A21-11	AMOUT ↔ GND	L ↔ W-B	IG ON		PULSE
A20-6 ↔ A21-11	TW ↔ GND	V ↔ W-B	IG ON		PULSE
A20-7 ↔ A21-11	ILL+ ↔ GND	G ↔ W-B	Turn the light control switch to TAIL position		10 ~ 14 V
A20-8 ↔ A21-11	TC ↔ GND	B-R ↔ W-B	IG ON and turn head light control switch to TAIL position	Turn rheostat to most right	Below 1 V
				Turn rheostat to most left	10 ~ 14 V
A20-9 ↔ A21-11	A/C IN ↔ GND	B-W ↔ W-B	Operate the compressor		10 ~ 14 V
			Not operate the compressor		Below 1 V
A20-11 ↔ A19-16	LOCK ↔ SG	W-G ↔ Y-G	A/C switch ON		PULSE
A21-1 ↔ A21-11	+B ↔ GND	W-R ↔ W-B	Always		10 ~ 14 V
A21-2 ↔ A21-11	IG ↔ GND	R-L ↔ W-B	Turn ignition switch ON		10 ~ 14 V
A21-3 ↔ A21-11	AMDr1 ↔ GND	V-R ↔ W-B	Change display code 29 to display code 20 While moving the A/M step motor		PULSE
A21-4 ↔ A21-11	AMDr2 ↔ GND	O ↔ W-B	Change display code 29 to display code 20 While moving the A/M step motor		PULSE
A21-5 ↔ A21-11	AMDr3 ↔ GND	P-L ↔ W-B	Change display code 29 to display code 20 While moving the A/M step motor		PULSE
A21-6 ↔ A21-11	AMDr4 ↔ GND	Y-B ↔ W-B	Change display code 29 to display code 20 While moving the A/M step motor		PULSE

ECU TERMINAL STANDARD VALUE TEST CHART—1995 LS 400, CONT'D

Terminals	Symbols	Wiring Color	Condition	Standard Value
A21-7 ↔ A21-11	AMPa1 ↔ GND	GR-G ↔ W-B	Change display code 29 to display code 20 While moving the A/M step motor	PULSE
A21-8 ↔ A21-11	AMPa2 ↔ GND	LG-B ↔ W-B	Change display code 29 to display code 20 While moving the A/M step motor	PULSE
A21-9 ↔ A21-11	AMPa3 ↔ GND	BR-W ↔ W-B	Change display code 29 to display code 20 While moving the A/M step motor	PULSE
A21-10 ↔ A21-11	AMPa4 ↔ GND	G-Y ↔ W-B	Change display code 29 to display code 20 While moving the A/M step motor	PULSE
A21-11 ↔ Body Ground	GND ↔ Body Ground	W-B ↔ Body Ground	Always	Below 1 Ω
A21-12 ↔ A21-11	ACC ↔ GND	P-L ↔ W-B	Turn ignition switch ACC	10 ~ 14 V
A21-13 ↔ A21-11	ST ↔ GND	B ↔ W-B	Start the engine	6 ~ 14 V
A21-14 ↔ A21-11	AODr1 ↔ GND	Y ↔ W-B	Change display code 29 to display code 20	PULSE
A21-15 ↔ A21-11	AODr2 ↔ GND	B-Y ↔ W-B	Change display code 29 to display code 20	PULSE
A21-16 ↔ A21-11	AODr3 ↔ GND	R-B ↔ W-B	Change display code 29 to display code 20	PULSE
A21-17 ↔ A21-11	AODr4 ↔ GND	P-G ↔ W-B	Change display code 29 to display code 20	PULSE
A21-18 ↔ A21-11	AOPa1 ↔ GND	G-O ↔ W-B	Change display code 29 to display code 20	PULSE
A21-19 ↔ A21-11	AOPa2 ↔ GND	L-B ↔ W-B	Change display code 29 to display code 20	PULSE
A21-20 ↔ A21-11	AOPa3 ↔ GND	G-R ↔ W-B	Change display code 29 to display code 20	PULSE
A21-21 ↔ A21-11	AOPa4 ↔ GND	P ↔ W-B	Change display code 29 to display code 20	PULSE

WIRING SCHEMATICS

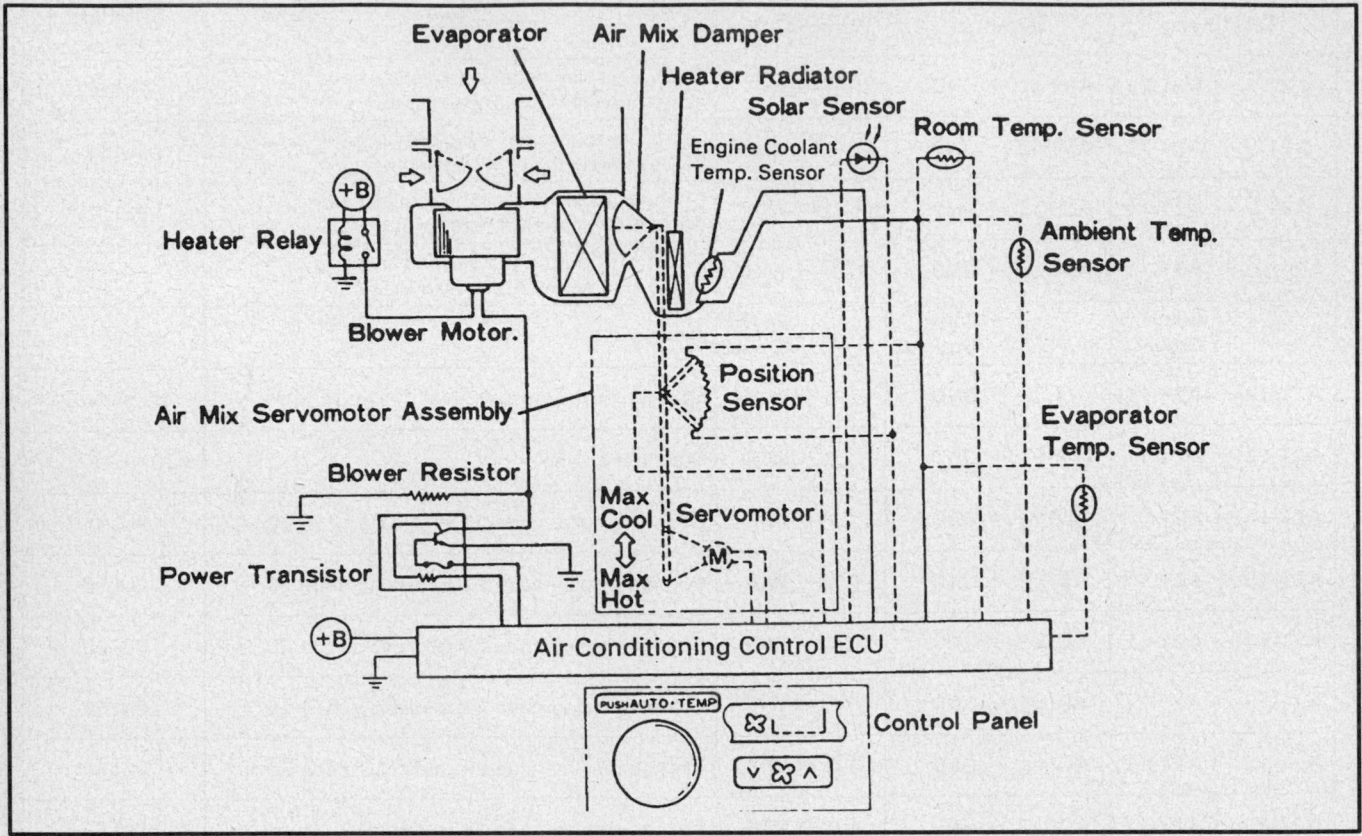

Wiring schematic for blower fan speed control system—all models

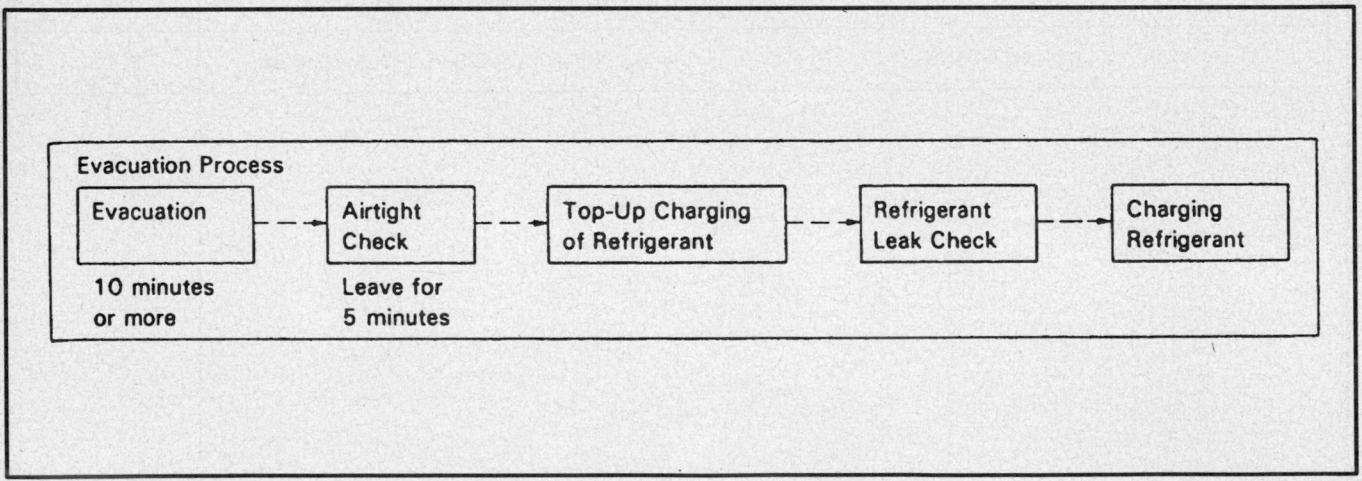

Refrigerant evacuation process—all models

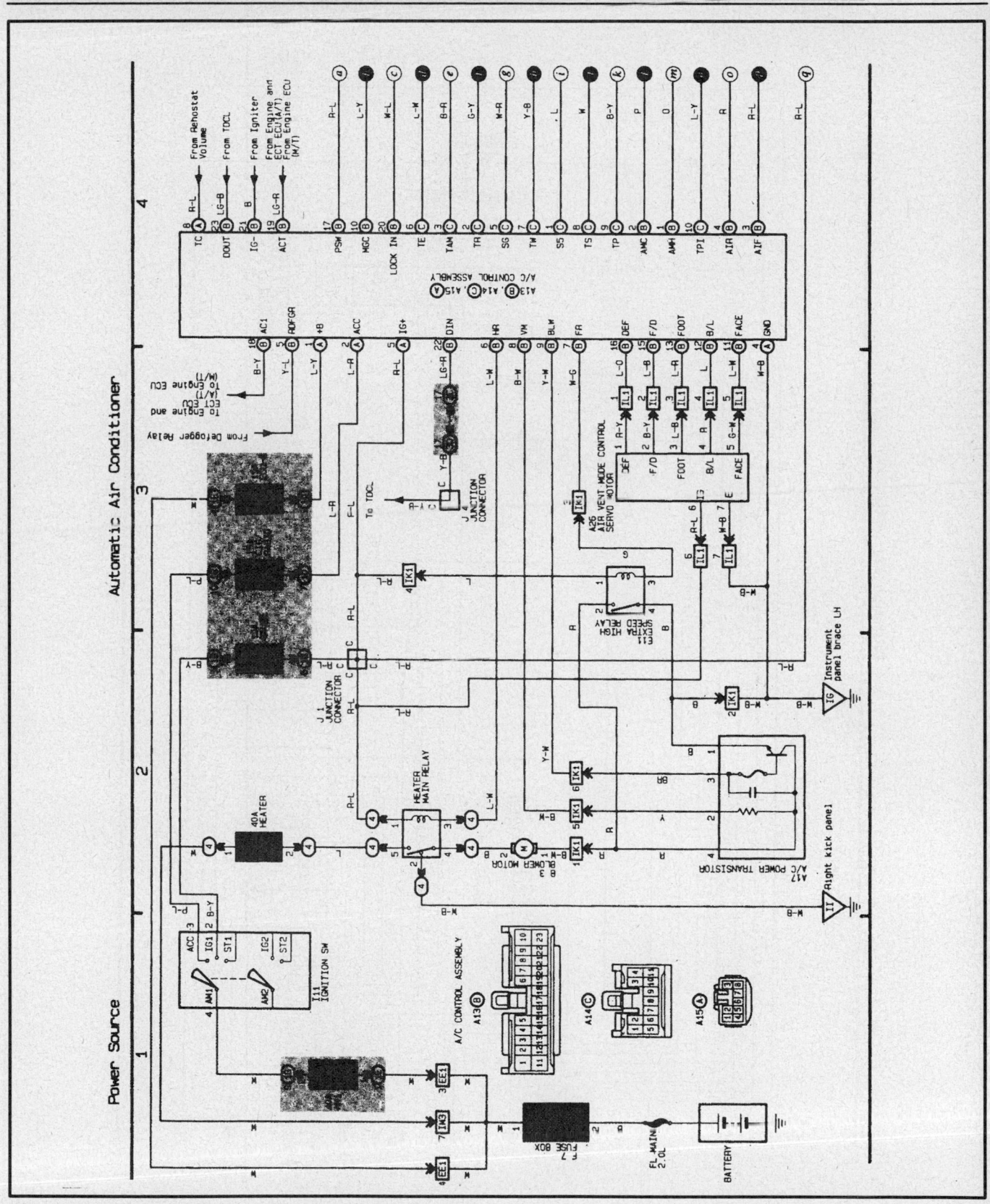

Automatic climate control wiring schematic—ES 300

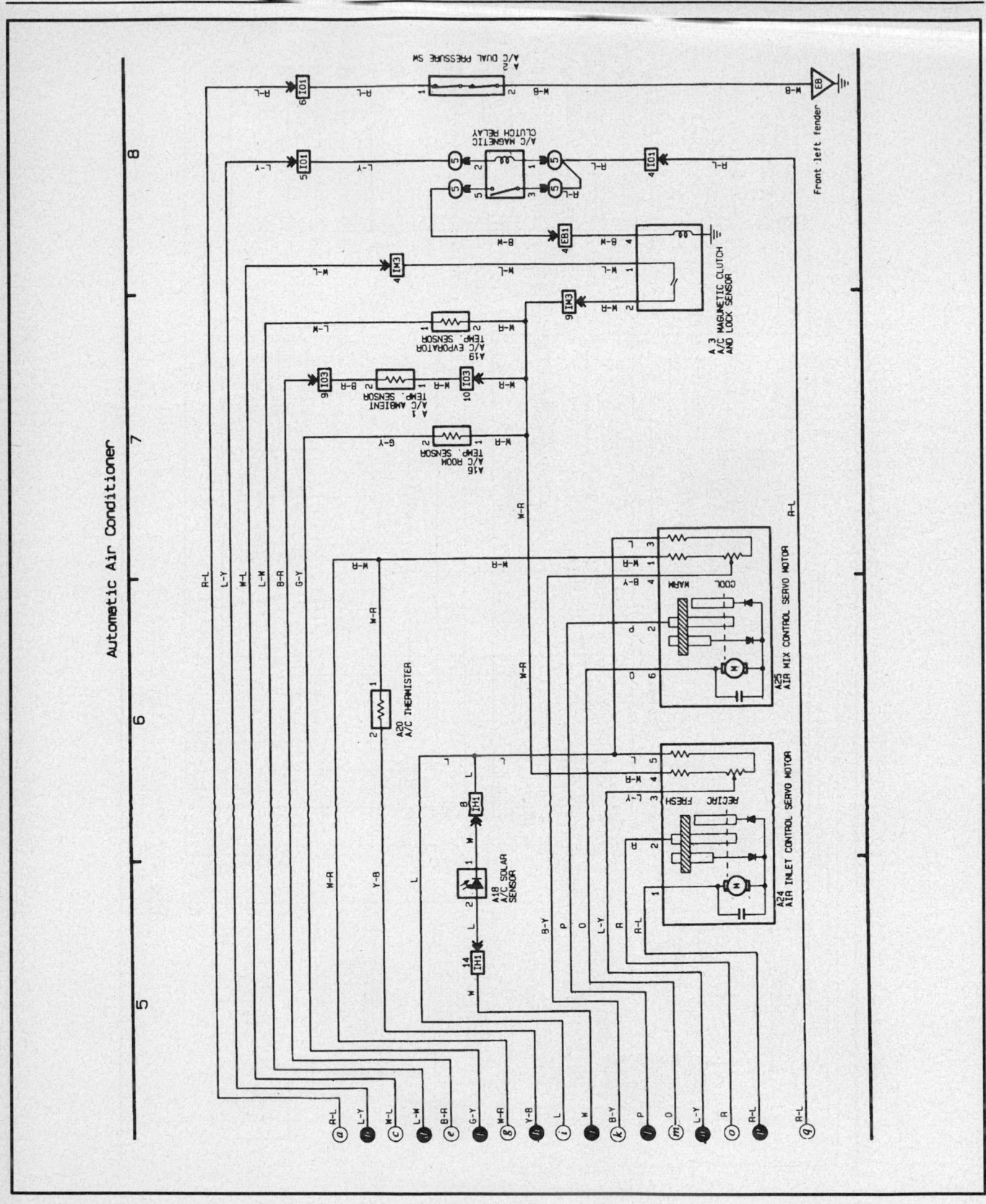

Automatic climate control wiring schematic—ES 300, Cont'd

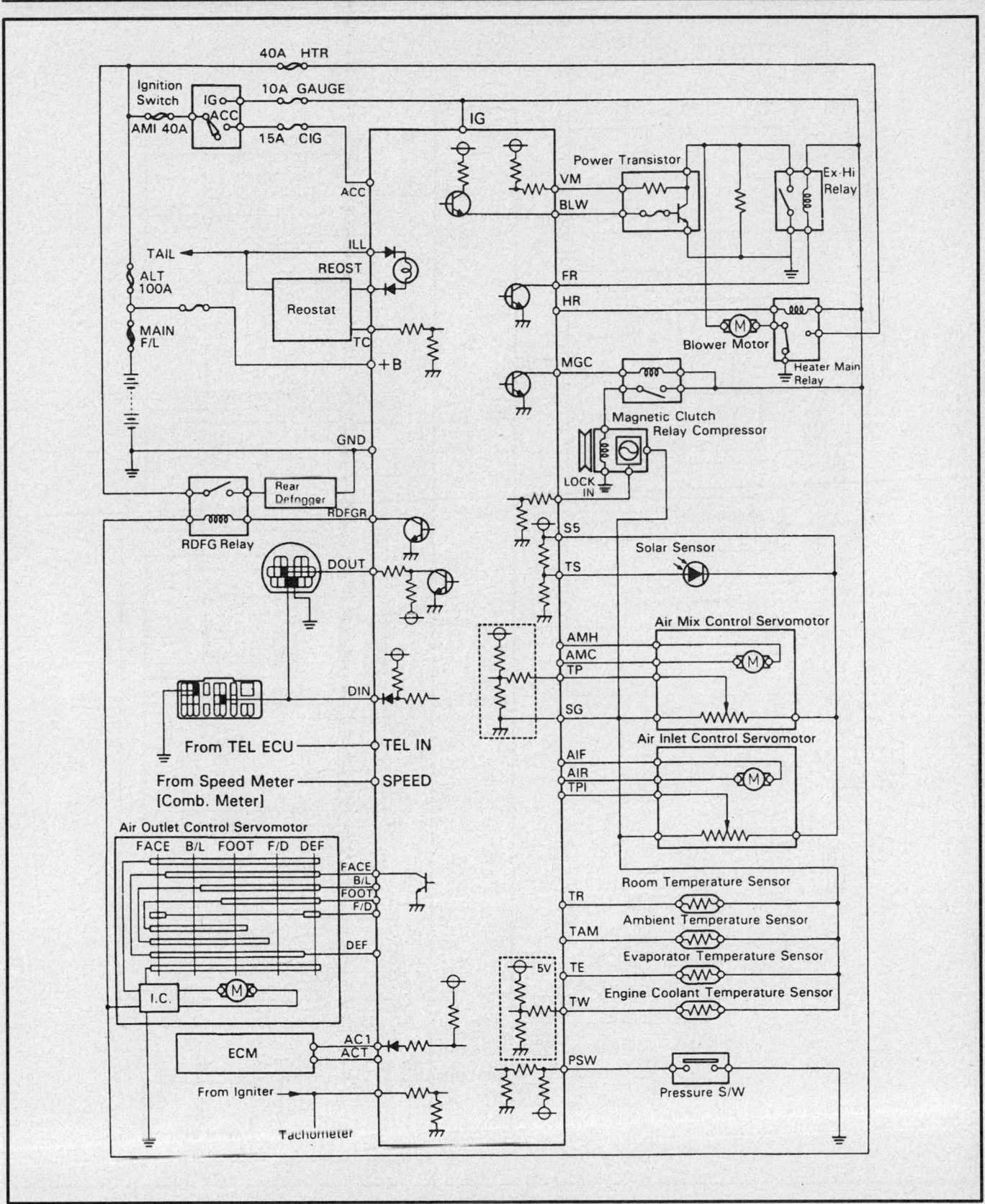

Automatic climate control wiring schematic—1994-95 ES 300

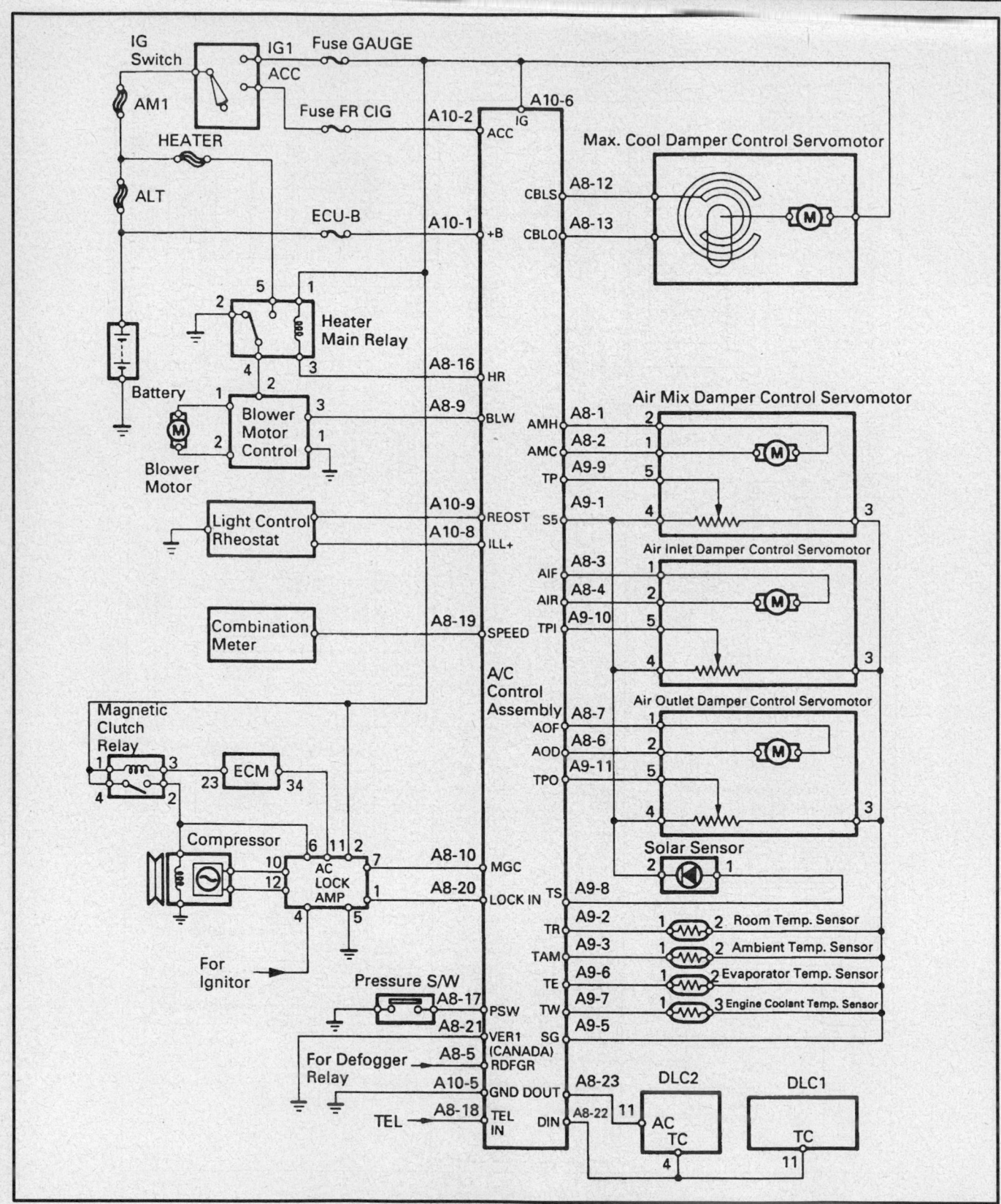

Automatic climate control wiring schematic—1994-95 ES 300, Cont'd

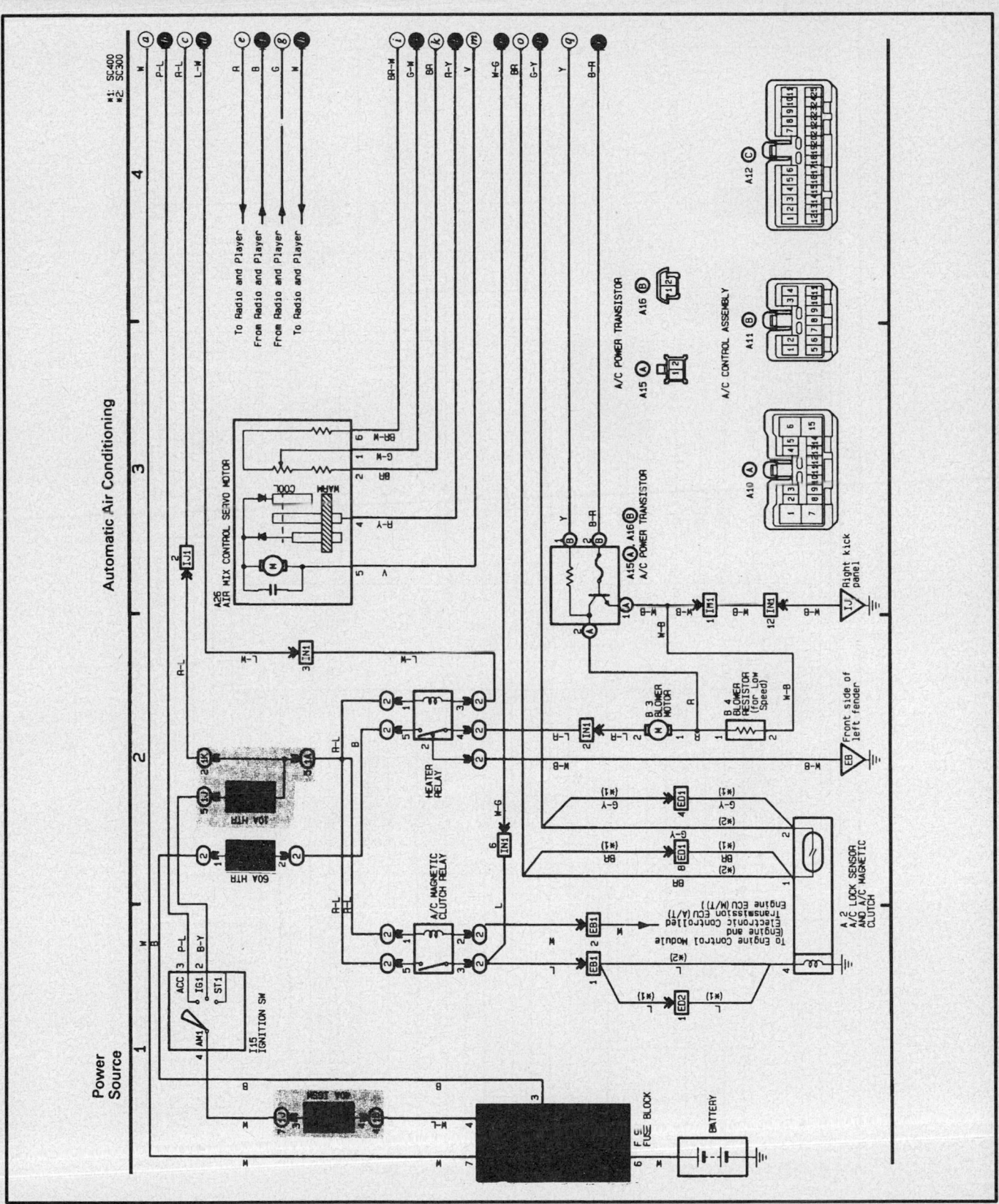

Automatic climate control wiring schematic—1993 SC 300 and SC 400

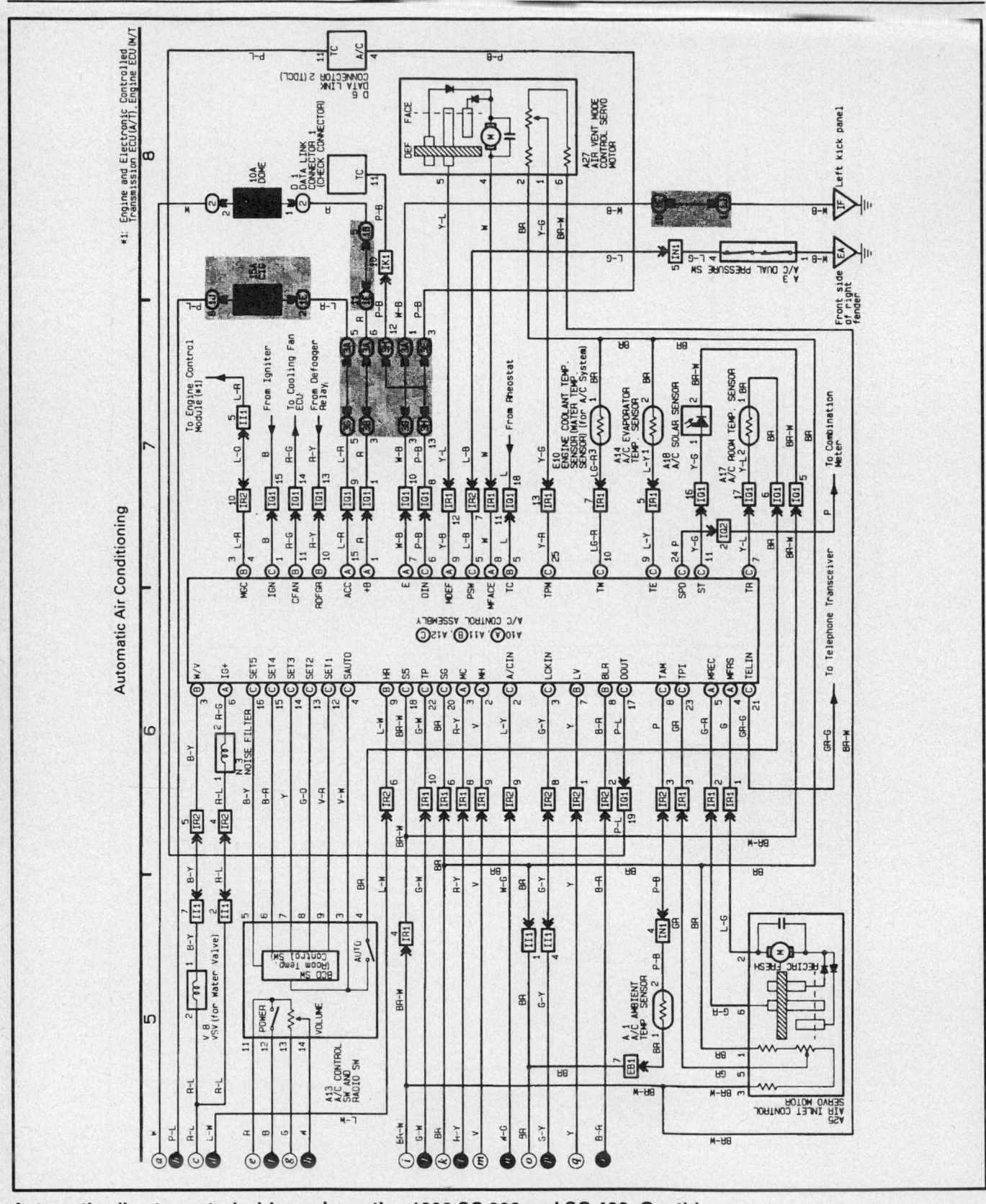

Automatic climate control wiring schematic—1993 SC 300 and SC 400, Cont'd

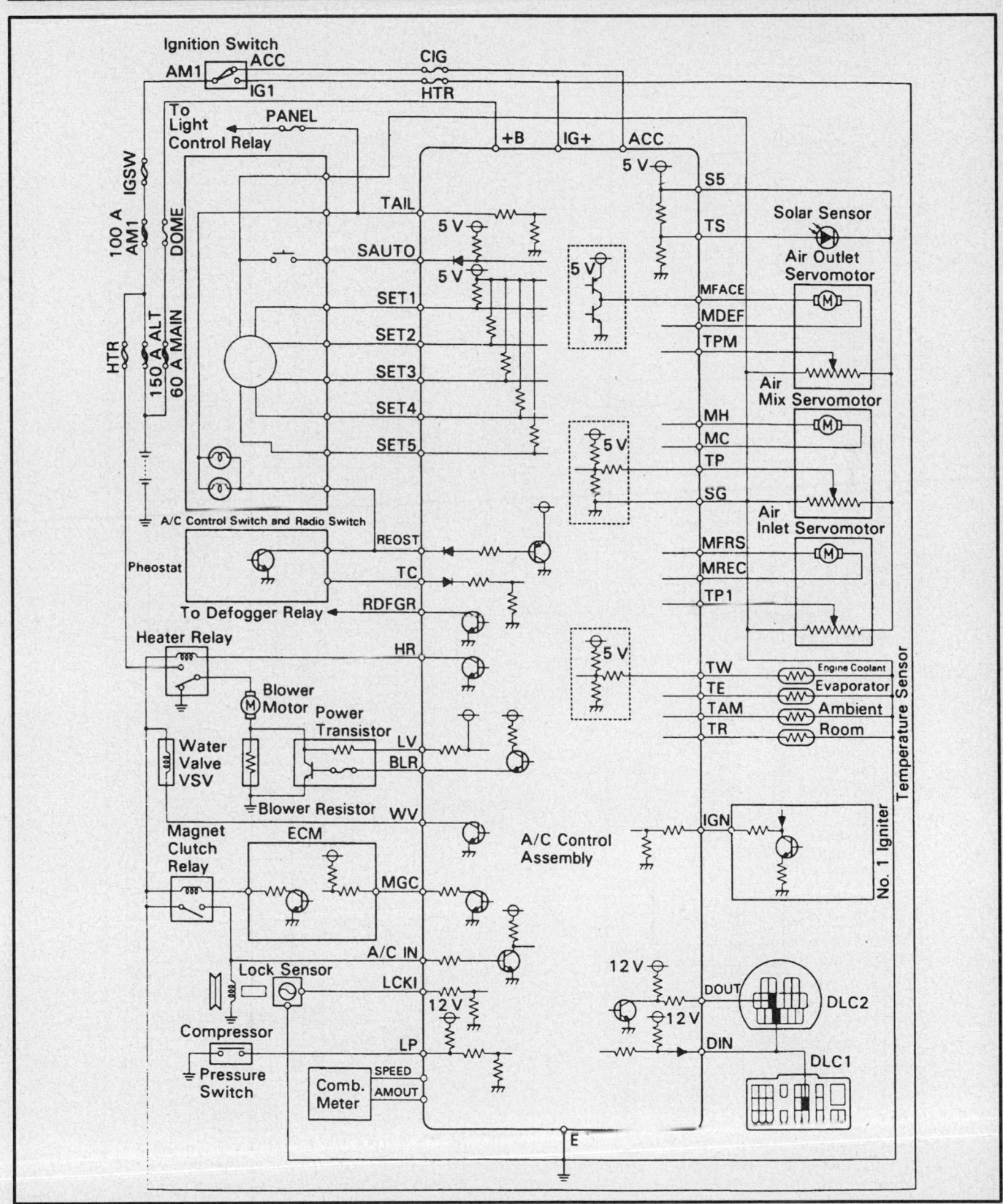

Automatic climate control wiring schematic—1994 SC 300

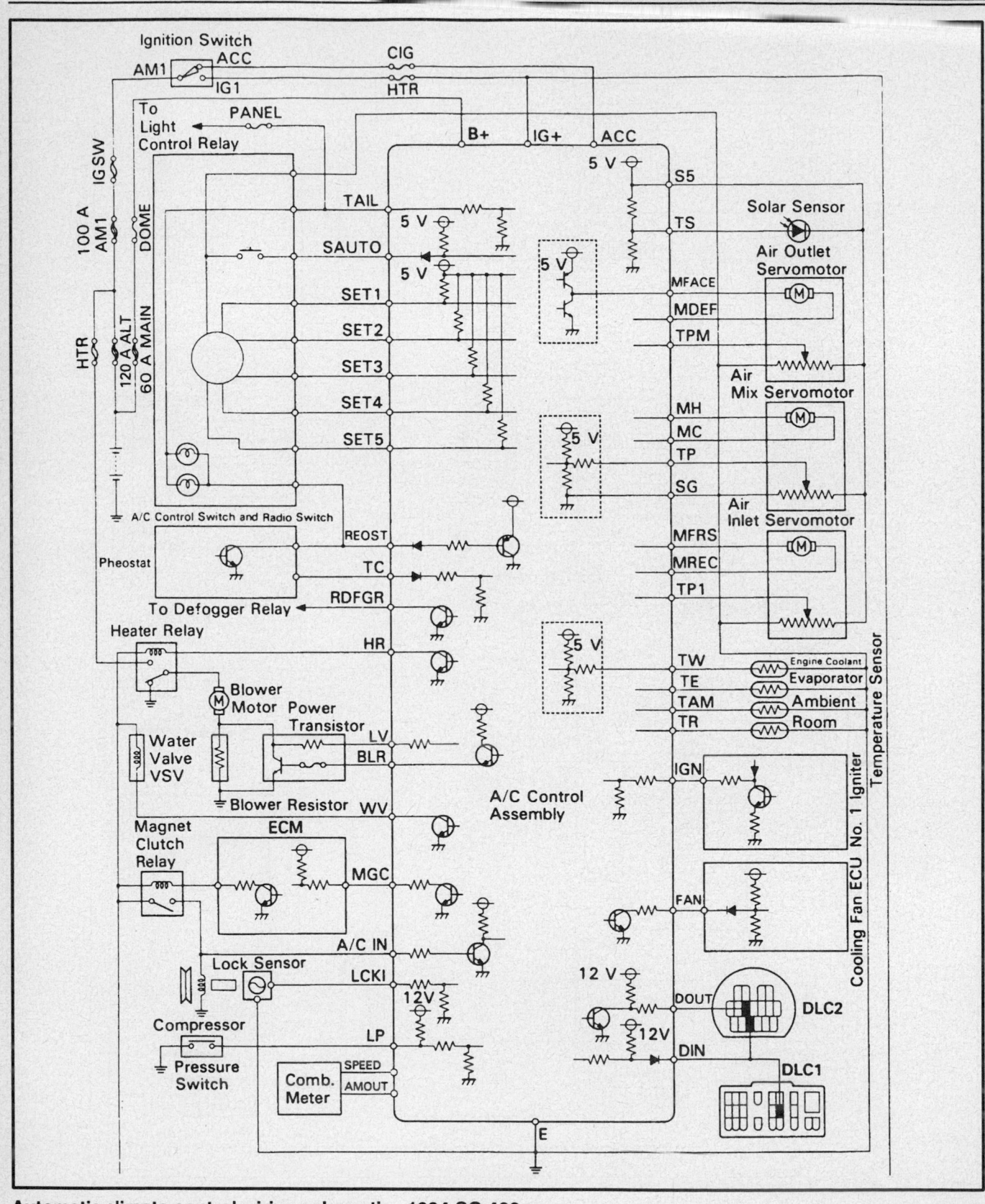

Automatic climate control wiring schematic—1994 SC 400

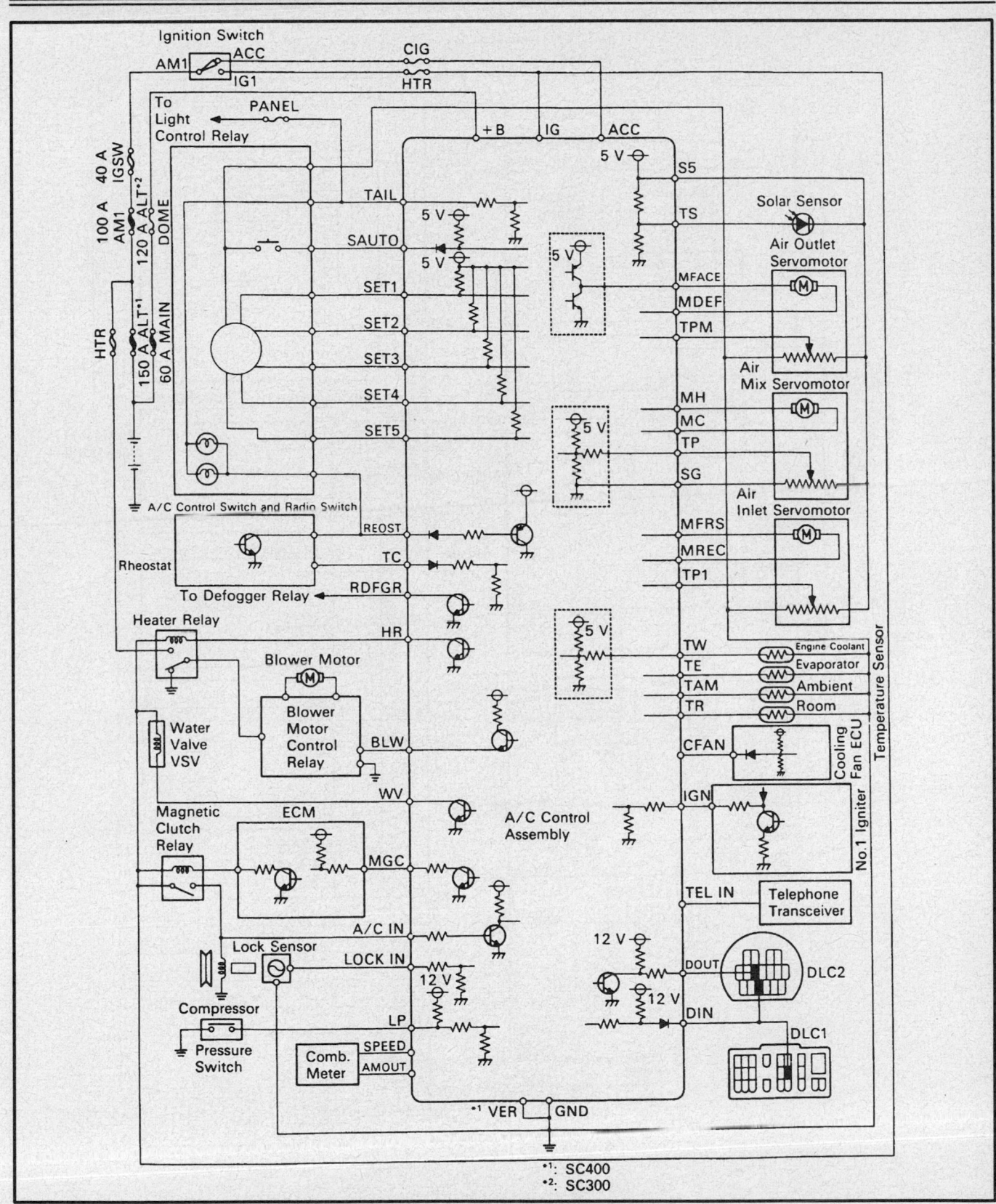

Automatic climate control wiring schematic—1995 SC 300 and SC 400

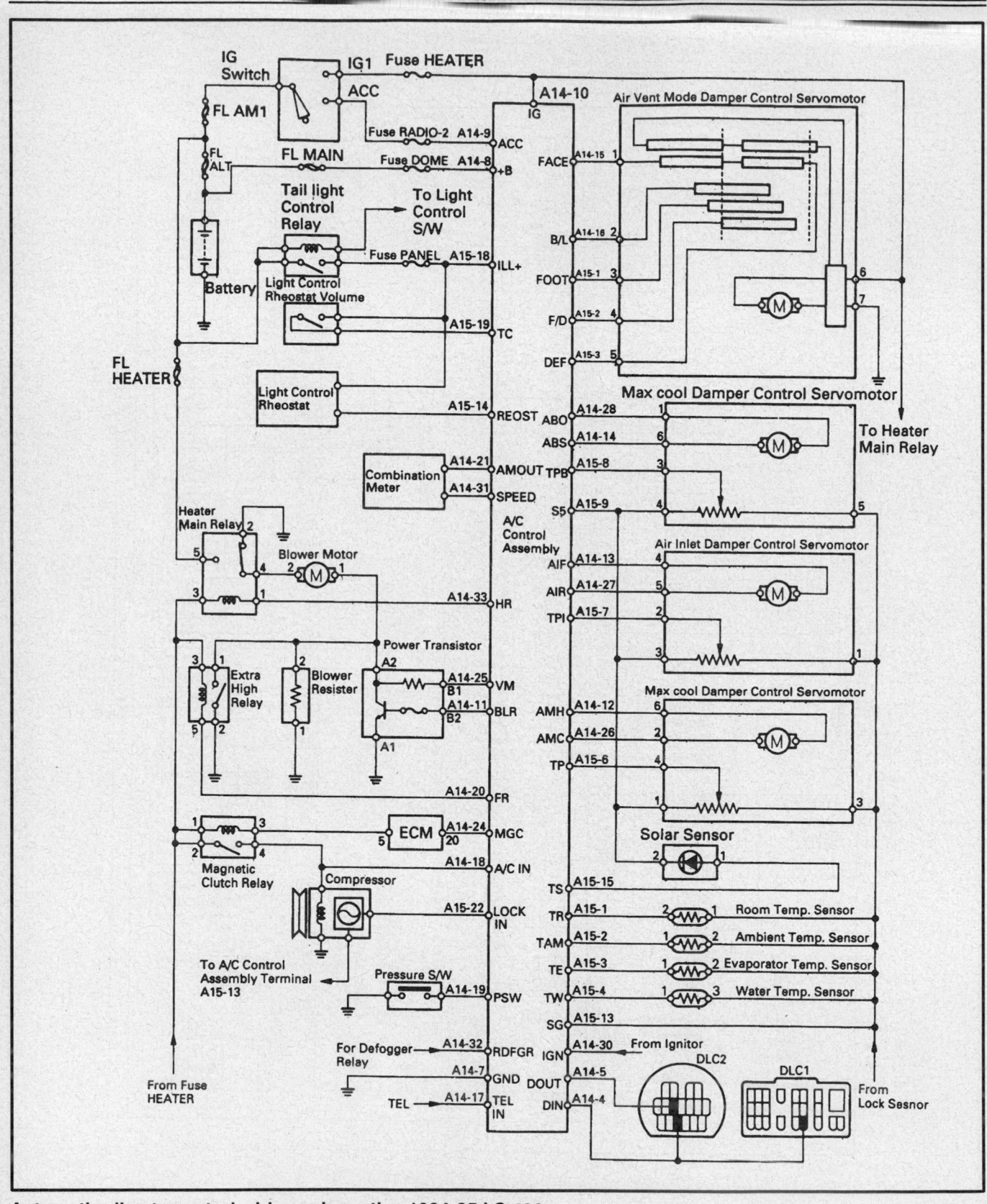

Automatic climate control wiring schematic—1994-95 LS 400

SPECIFICATIONS

ENGINE IDENTIFICATION

Year	Model	Engine Displacement Liters (cc)	Engine Series	Fuel System	No. of Cylinders	Engine Type
1993	323	1.6 (1597)	B6E	EFI	4	SOHC
	Protege	1.8 (1839)	BPE	EFI	4	SOHC-16V
	Protege	1.8 (1839)	BPD	EFI	4	DOHC-16V
	626	2.0 (1991)	FS	EFI	4	DOHC-16V
	MX-6	2.0 (1991)	FS	EFI	4	DOHC-16V
	626	2.5 (2496)	KL	EFI	6	DOHC-24V
	MX-6	2.5 (2496)	KL	EFI	6	DOHC-24V
	929	3.0 (2954)	JE	EFI	6	DOHC
	MX-3	1.6 (1597)	B6E	EFI	4	SOHC-16V
	MX-3	1.8 (1845)	K8D	EFI	6	DOHC-24V
	Miata	1.6 (1597)	B6ZE	EFI	4	DOHC
	RX-7	1.3 (1308)	13B	EFI	–	Rotary-Turbo
1994	323	1.6 (1597)	B6E	EFI	4	SOHC
	Protege	1.8 (1839)	BPE	EFI	4	SOHC-16V
	Protege	1.8 (1839)	BPD	EFI	4	DOHC-16V
	626	2.0 (1991)	FS	EFI	4	DOHC-16V
	MX-6	2.0 (1991)	FS	EFI	4	DOHC-16V
	626	2.5 (2496)	KL	EFI	6	DOHC-24V
	MX-6	2.5 (2496)	KL	EFI	6	DOHC-24V
	929	3.0 (2954)	JE	EFI	6	DOHC
	MX-3	1.6 (1597)	B6E	EFI	4	SOHC-16V
	MX-3	1.8 (1845)	K8D	EFI	6	DOHC-24V
	Miata	1.8 (1840)	BP	EFI	4	DOHC
	RX-7	1.3 (1308)	13B	EFI	–	Rotary-Turbo
1995	323	1.6 (1597)	B6E	EFI	4	SOHC
	Protege	1.8 (1839)	BPE	EFI	4	SOHC-16V
	Protege	1.8 (1839)	BPD	EFI	4	DOHC-16V
	626	2.0 (1991)	FS	EFI	4	DOHC-16V
	MX-6	2.0 (1991)	FS	EFI	4	DOHC-16V
	626	2.5 (2496)	KL	EFI	6	DOHC-24V
	MX-6	2.5 (2496)	KL	EFI	6	DOHC-24V
	929	3.0 (2954)	JE	EFI	6	DOHC
	MX-3	1.6 (1597)	B6E	EFI	4	SOHC-16V
	MX-3	1.8 (1845)	K8D	EFI	6	DOHC-24V
	Millenia	2.3 (2299)	KJ	EFI	6	DOHC
	Millenia	2.5 (2496)	KL	EFI	6	DOHC
	Miata	1.8 (1840)	BP	EFI	4	DOHC
	RX-7	1.3 (1308)	13B	EFI	–	Rotary-Turbo

EFI – Electronic Fuel Injection
DOHC – Dual Overhead Cam
SOHC – Single Overhead Cam

REFRIGERANT CAPACITIES

Year	Model	Refrigerant (oz.)	Oil (fl. oz.)	Compressor Type
1993	323	28.2	3.9–4.5	NA
	Protege	28.2	3.9–4.5	NA
	626	31.8	4.4	NA
	MX-6	31.8	4.4	NA
	929	28.2	4.7	NA
	Miata	28.2	①	NA
	RX-7	21.2	3.7–6.1	Nippondenso
	MX-3	NA	NA	NA
1994	323	28.2	3.9–4.5	NA
	Protege	28.2	3.9–4.5	NA
	626	31.8	4.4	NA
	MX-6	31.8	4.4	NA
	929	28.2	4.7	NA
	Miata	28.2	①	NA
	RX-7	15.9–19.4	4.4–5.7	Nippondenso
	MX-3	NA	NA	NA
1995	323	28.2	3.9–4.5	NA
	Protege	28.2	3.9–4.5	NA
	626	31.8	4.4	NA
	MX-6	31.8	4.4	NA
	Millenia 2.3L	28.2	①	NA
	Millenia 2.5L	NA	NA	NA
	Miata	28.2	①	NA
	RX-7	15.9–19.4	4.4–5.7	Nippondenso
	MX-3	NA	NA	NA

NA – Not Available
① Total oil amount not specified by manufacturer. When draining compressor oil, replace with same amount as drained, plus 0.65 oz.

AIR CONDITIONING BELT TENSION

Year	Model	Engine Liters (cc)	Belt Type	New (lbs.)	Used (lbs.)
1993	323	1.6 (1597)	V-Belt	0.31–0.35	0.35–0.39
	Protege	1.8 (1839)	V-Belt	0.31–0.35	0.35–0.39
	626	2.0 (1991)	V-Belt	0.27–0.35	0.31–0.39
	MX-6	2.0 (1991)	V-Belt	0.27–0.35	0.31–0.39
	929	3.0 (2954)	V-Belt	0.48–0.51	0.51–0.55
	MX-3	1.6 (1597)	V-Belt	0.31–0.35	0.35–0.39
	MX-3	1.8 (1845)	V-Belt	0.31–0.35	0.35–0.39
	Miata	1.6 (1597)	V-Belt	0.31–0.35	0.35–0.39
	RX-7	1.3 (1308)	V-Belt	0.24–0.31	0.31–0.35
	MX-6	2.5 (2496)	V-Belt	0.22–0.25	0.26–0.29
	626	2.5 (2496)	V-Belt	0.22–0.25	0.26–0.29

AIR CONDITIONING BELT TENSION

Year	Model	Engine Liters (cc)	Belt Type	Specifications New (lbs.)	Used (lbs.)
1994	323	1.6 (1597)	V-Belt	0.31–0.35	0.35–0.39
	Protege	1.8 (1839)	V-Belt	0.31–0.35	0.35–0.39
	626	2.0 (1991)	V-Belt	0.30–0.35	0.32–0.37
	MX-6	2.0 (1991)	V-Belt	0.30–0.35	0.32–0.37
	929	3.0 (2954)	V-Belt	0.23–0.25	0.26–0.30
	MX-3	1.6 (1597)	V-Belt	0.31–0.35	0.35–0.39
	MX-3	1.8 (1845)	V-Belt	0.31–0.35	0.35–0.39
	Miata	1.8 (1840)	V-Belt	0.31–0.35	0.35–0.39
	RX-7	1.3 (1308)	V-Belt	0.24–0.31	0.31–0.35
	MX-6	2.5 (2496)	V-Belt	0.22–0.25	0.26–0.29
	626	2.5 (2496)	V-Belt	0.22–0.25	0.26–0.29
1995	323	1.6 (1597)	V-Belt	0.31–0.35	0.35–0.39
	Protege	1.8 (1839)	V-Belt	0.31–0.35	0.35–0.39
	626	2.0 (1991)	V-Belt	0.30–0.35	0.32–0.37
	MX-6	2.0 (1991)	V-Belt	0.30–0.35	0.32–0.37
	929	3.0 (2954)	V-Belt	0.23–0.25	0.26–0.30
	MX-3	1.6 (1597)	V-Belt	0.31–0.35	0.35–0.39
	MX-3	1.8 (1845)	V-Belt	0.31–0.35	0.35–0.39
	Millenia	2.3 (2299)	V-Belt	0.22–0.25	0.26–0.29
	Millenia	2.5 (2496)	V-Belt	0.22–0.25	0.26–0.29
	RX-7	1.3 (1308)	V-Belt	0.24–0.31	0.31–0.35
	MX-6	2.5 (2496)	V-Belt	0.22–0.25	0.26–0.29
	626	2.5 (2496)	V-Belt	0.22–0.25	0.26–0.29

SYSTEM DESCRIPTION

General Information

The heater unit is located in the center of the vehicle along the firewall. The heater system is a bi–level system designed to direct warm air through the vents to either the windshield or the floor and cool air through the panel outlet. The air conditioning system is designed to be activated in combination with a separate air conditioning switch installed in the control assembly and the fan speed switch. The system incorporates a compressor, condenser, evaporator, receiver/drier, pressure switch, expansion valve, thermo–switch, refrigerant lines and some models are equipped with an electronic control head assembly versus the standard cable operated control head. The 929 model utilizes a self diagnostic program built into the control head assembly.

The Millennia heating and air conditioning system also incorporates a solar ventilation system. The solar ventilation system has a solar ventilation switch, temperature switch, fan, solar cell and a Solar Ventilation Control Unit (SVCU).

Service Valve Location

Charging valve locations will vary, but most of the time the high or low pressure fitting will be located at the compressor, receiver/drier or along the refrigerant lines. Always discharge, evacuate and recharge at the low side service fitting.

System Discharging

R–12 refrigerant is a chloroflourocarbon which, when mishandled, can contribute to the depletion of the ozone layer in the upper atmosphere. Ozone filters out harmful radiation from the sun. In order to protect the ozone layer, an approved R–12 Recovery/Recycling machine that meets SAE standard J1991 should be employed when discharging the system. Follow the operating instructions provided with the approved equipment exactly to properly discharge the system.

System Evacuating

If the air conditioning system has been opened to the atmosphere, it should be air and moisture free before being recharged with refrigerant. Moisture and air mixed with refrigerant will raise the compressor head pressure, possibly damage the system's components and will reduce the performance of the system. Moisture will boil at normal room temperature when exposed to a vacuum, the moisture then becomes a vapor and will be easily removed by the vacuum pump.

To evacuate or rid the system of air and moisture:

1. Leak test the system and repair any leaks found.

2. Connect an approved charging station, Recovery/Recycling machine or manifold gauge set and vacuum pump to the discharge and suction ports. The red hose is normally connected to the discharge (high pressure) line, and the blue hose is connected to the suction (low pressure) line.

3. Open the discharge and suction ports and start the vacuum pump. If the pump is not able to pull at least 26 in. Hg vacuum, there is a leak that must be repaired before evacuation can occur.

4. Once the system has reached at least 26 in. Hg vacuum, allow the system to evacuate for at least 10 minutes. The longer the system is evacuated, the more contaminants will be removed.

5. Close all valves and turn the pump OFF. If the system loses more than 2 in. Hg vacuum after 15 minutes, there is a leak that should be repaired.

System Charging

1. Connect an approved charging station, Recovery/Recycling machine or manifold gauge set to the discharge and suction ports. The red hose is normally connected to the discharge (high pressure) line, and the blue hose is connected to the suction (low pressure) line.

2. Follow the instructions provided with the equipment and charge the system with the specified amount of refrigerant.

3. Perform a leak test.

Air Bag and Radio Service Precautions

1. Before disconnecting the negative battery cable for any service operation, equipped with a coded anti–theft radio,

obtain the code number and deactivate the anti–theft function first.

2. Before disconnecting or removing any air bag system components, first disconnect the negative battery cable, then disconnect the orange and blue clockspring connectors located under the lower steering column cover.

3. Do not repair any open, short, pinched or frayed wiring in the air bag circuit. Replace the wiring harness.

4. Do not use an ohmmeter to check the air bag module, or it could trigger the module to deploy the air bag.

5. When carrying a live air bag module, hold the trim cover side away from you and always store it on the bench with the trim cover up.

6. Always wear gloves and safety glasses when working around the air bag system or components. The system contains caustic substances (sodium hydroxide) which can be harmful.

7. Whenever the steering wheel is removed, before reinstalling it, adjust the clock spring connector as follows:
   ● Set the front wheels straight ahead.
   ● Turn the clockspring connector clockwise until it stops (do not force it).
   ● Return the connector 2 3/4 turns counterclockwise.
   ● Align the marks of the clock spring connector and the outer housing.

8. To disconnect the double–lock type connector, press the orange knob and detach the orange connector, then press the blue knob and detach the blue connector. Reconnect in the reverse order.

9. After service, verify system operation by noting that the air bag warning lamp comes ON when the ignition switch is turned ON, then goes OFF after about 6 seconds.

10. Check that the horn sounds. If not, remove the air bag module and check the connections of the module and horn switch connectors.

11. Reactivate the anti–theft code in the radio system.

SYSTEM COMPONENTS

----------CAUTION----------

Some vehicles are equipped with the Supplemental Inflatable Restraint or air bag system. The air bag system must be disabled by disconnecting the battery negative terminal and the orange–blue connector located near steering wheel before performing service on or around the air bag, instrument panel components, wiring and sensors. Failure to follow safety and disabling procedures could result in accidental air bag deployment, possible personal injury and unnecessary air bag system repairs.

NOTE: Some vehicles also have an anti–theft code radio. Before disconnecting the negative battery cable on these models, get the code from the customer and decode the radio first.

Radiator

REMOVAL AND INSTALLATION

Except RX–7

1. Disconnect the negative terminal at the battery.
2. Drain the cooling system.
3. Disconnect the coolant reservoir hose.
4. Remove the fresh air duct or resonance chamber, as equipped. On Miata and Millenia, remove the under cover.
5. Remove the upper and lower radiator hoses.
6. Disconnect electric fan and thermo–switch wire connector, if equipped.

7. Remove electric fan or clutch fan and cowling assembly.
8. Disconnect and plug automatic transmission cooler lines, if equipped.
9. Remove radiator mounting brackets and bolts.
10. Remove radiator assembly with electric fan(s), if equipped.

To install:
11. Install the radiator assembly.
12. Install the radiator mounting brackets and bolts.
13. Connect and automatic transmission cooler lines, if equipped.
14. Install the electric or clutch fan and cowling assembly.
15. Install the upper and lower radiator hoses.
16. Install the fresh air duct or resonance chamber. On Miata and Millenia, install the under cover.
17. Connect the coolant reservoir hose.
18. Refill radiator with specified type and quantity of coolant.
19. Check the automatic transmission fluid level, if equipped.
20. Check cooling system for leaks.
21. Reconnect the negative battery terminal.

RX–7

1. Disconnect the negative battery cable. Raise and support the vehicle on safety stands.
2. Properly drain the cooling system.
3. Remove the fresh air intake duct and the air cleaner assembly.
4. Remove the battery and battery carrier.
5. Remove the upper radiator hose, remove the relay box and detach the cooling fan connector.

6. Remove the engine under cover, then remove the stabilizer and bracket.

7. Remove the lower radiator hose, air separation hose and the oil cooler hose (if A/T).

8. Remove 4 retaining bolts, position and secure the condenser slightly away from the radiator, then remove the radiator and cooling fan assembly.

9. Installation is the reverse of the removal procedure.

Cooling Fan

TESTING

1993 323, Miata, 1993 Protege and MX-3

SINGLE SPEED FAN

1. Attach a jumper wire across the fan test (**TFA**) terminal and the ground (**GND**) terminal of the diagnosis connector.

2. Turn the ignition switch **ON** and verify that the fan operates; if the fan does not operate, inspect the cooling fan system components and the wiring harness.

3. Remove the radiator filler cap and place a thermometer in the filler neck.

4. Start the engine.

5. Verify that the fan operates when the coolant temperature reaches 207°F (97°C), if not, check the water thermo-switch.

6. Disconnect the fan motor connector.

7. Connect the battery and an ammeter to the fan motor connector.

8. Verify that current is 5.3–6.5 amps on Miata and approximately 6.6 amps on 323, Protege and MX-3 (SOHC), or 11.0 amps on MX-3 (DOHC with M/T).

9. If current is not within specification or the fan does not turn smoothly, replace the fan motor.

1994–95 323 and Protege

SINGLE SPEED FAN

1. Verify that the battery is fully charged (12.4 volts).

2. Disconnect the cooling fan connector.

3. Connect the battery (–) negative terminal to terminal **A**, and an ammeter to the battery (+) positive terminal, and to terminal **B** of the connector.

4. Verify that current is 2.6–4.2 amps on the Z5 engine or 5.6–7.6 amps on the BP engine.

5. If not as specified, replace the cooling fan motor.

1993 323 and 1993–95 MX-3 With Automatic Transmission

TWO SPEED FAN

1. Attach a jumper wire across the fan test (**TFA**) terminal and the ground (**GND**) terminal of the diagnosis connector.

2. Turn the ignition switch **ON** and verify that the fan operates; if the fan does not operate, inspect the cooling fan system components and the wiring harness.

3. Remove the radiator filler cap and place a thermometer in the filler neck.

4. Start the engine.

5. Verify that the fan operates when the coolant temperature reaches 207–212°F (97–100°C), if not, check the water thermo-switch.

6. Disconnect the fan motor connector.

7. Connect the battery and an ammeter to the fan motor connectors for low speed testing.

8. Verify that the fan motor operates smoothly and the current is 8.8–9.7 amps for 323 or 12.0 amps for MX-3.

9. Connect the battery and an ammeter to the fan motor connection for high speed testing.

10. Verify that the fan motor operates smoothly and the current is 13.3–14.6 amps for 323 or 16.8 amps for MX-3.

11. If fan motor test results are not as specified, replace the fan motor.

626 and MX-6

SINGLE–SPEED FANS

1. Ground terminal **10** of the data link connector and open the throttle slightly.

2. Turn the ignition switch **ON** and verify that the fan is operating.

3. If the fan does not operate, inspect the cooling fan system components and harness.

4. Remove the radiator filler cap and place a thermometer in the filler neck.

5. Start the engine.

6. Verify that the fan operates when the coolant temperature reaches 207°F (97°C), if not, check the water thermo-switch.

NOTE: If equipped with automatic transmission, the above procedure cannot be used to test the high speed fan operation. The high speed operation requires 226°F (108°C) or above.

7. Disconnect the fan motor connector.

8. Connect the battery and an ammeter to the fan motor connector.

9. If current is not within specification or the fan does not turn smoothly, replace the fan motor.

TWO–SPEED FAN (1993 MODELS WITH A/T)

1. Ground terminal **10** of the data link connector and open the throttle slightly.

2. Turn the ignition switch **ON** and verify that the fan is operating.

3. If the fan does not operate, inspect the cooling fan system components and harness.

4. Remove the radiator filler cap and place a thermometer in the filler neck.

5. Start the engine.

6. Verify that the fan operates when the coolant temperature reaches 207°F (97°C), if not, check the water thermo-switch.

7. Disconnect the fan motor connector.

8. Connect the battery and an ammeter to the fan motor connector.

9. If current is not within 8.0–14.0 amps for low speed operation or within 11.5–17.5 amps for high speed operation, or if the fan does not turn smoothly, replace the fan motor.

Millenia

SINGLE SPEED FAN (KL ENGINE)

1. Verify that the battery is fully charged (12.4 volts).

2. Disconnect the coolant fan connector.

3. Connect battery voltage and an ammeter to the coolant fan motor connector.

4. Verify that the coolant fan motor operates smoothly at the standard current draw (8.5–14.5 amps).

5. If not as specified, replace the coolant fan motor.

TWO SPEED FAN

1. Verify that the battery is fully charged (12.4 volts).

2. Disconnect the coolant fan connector.

3. Connect battery voltage and an ammeter to the coolant fan motor connector for LOW–SPEED inspection.

4. Verify that the coolant fan motor operates smoothly at the standard current draw (9–15 amps).

5. Connect battery positive voltage and an ammeter to the coolant fan motor connector for HIGH–SPEED operation.

6. Verify that the coolant fan motor operates smoothly at the standard current draw (12.3–18.3 amps).

7. If not as specified, replace the coolant fan motor.

RX–7

1. Disconnect the electric cooling fan connector.

2. Apply 12 volts to one side of fan motor connector and ground the other side of connector.

3. If the fan motor does not operate smoothly, replace the unit.

4. If the fan motor does operate smoothly, turn the ignition switch **ON**.

5. Measure the voltage between the terminals of the wire connector.

6. If equipped with a 3–speed fan, connect battery voltage and an ammeter to the 4–pin connector as shown to verify low speed operation. Amperage should read 5.8–11.8 amps.

7. Move the ammeter connection and include a switch as shown for checking medium speed operation. Amperage should be 6.5–12.5 amps.

8. Move the ammeter connection as shown for high speed operation checking. Amperage should be 10.6–16.6 amps.

9. In all cases motor should turn smoothly. If it does not, or if amperage is not as specified, replace the fan motor.

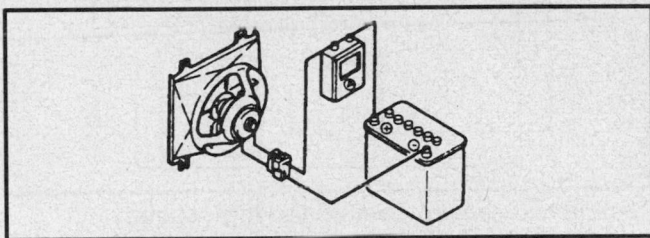

Typical radiator fan testing procedure

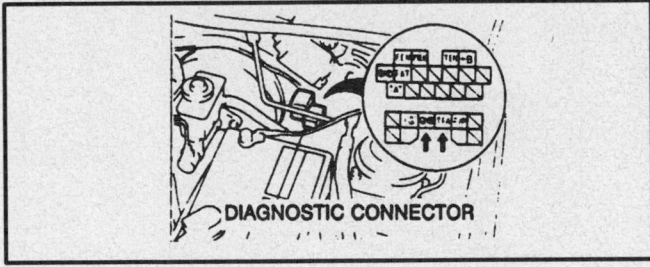

Cooling fan test terminal — 1993 323, 1994–95 MX–3, and 1993 Protege

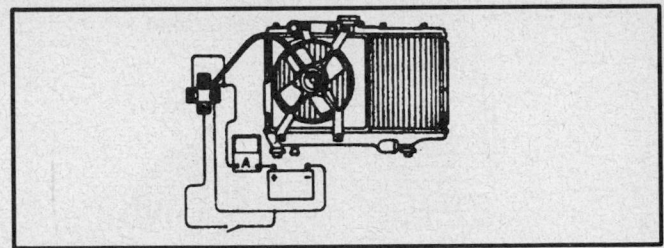

Testing two–speed cooling fan high operation — 1993 323 and Protege only

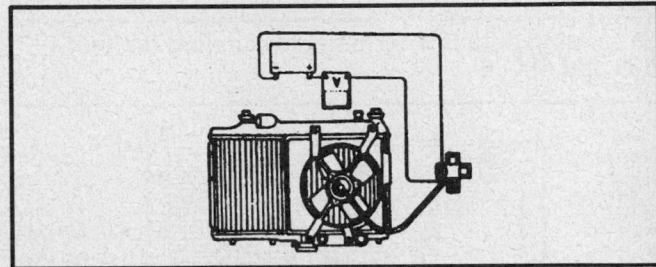

Testing two–speed cooling fan low operation — 1993 323, Miata and Protege

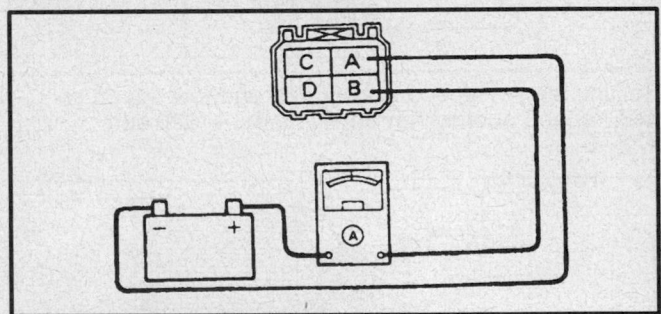

Testing cooling fan operation — 1994–95 323 and Protege

Grounding data link terminal for cooling fan test — 626 and MX-6

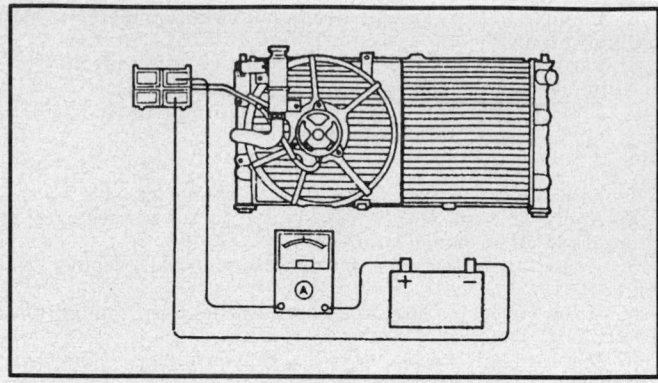

Testing two-speed cooling fan low speed operation — MX-3

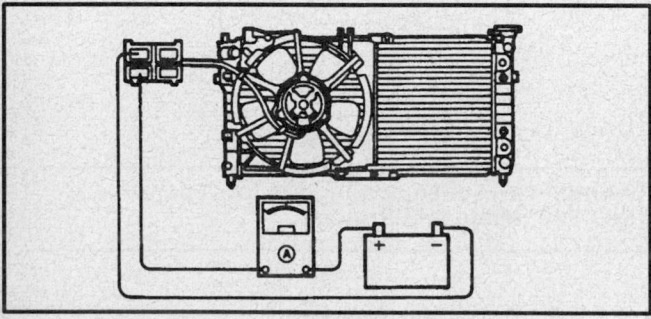

Testing single-speed cooling fan and low speed on two-speed cooling fan applications — 626 and MX-6

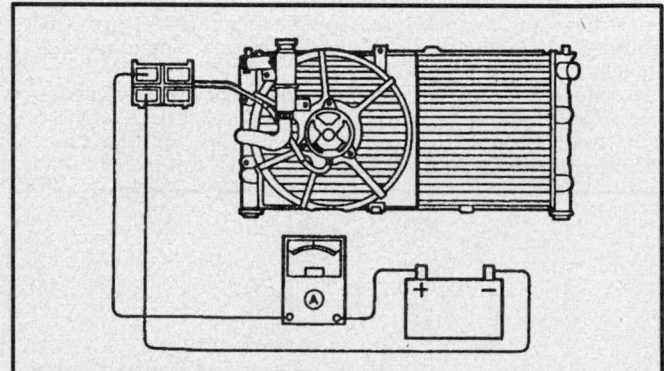

Testing two-speed cooling fan high speed operation — MX-3

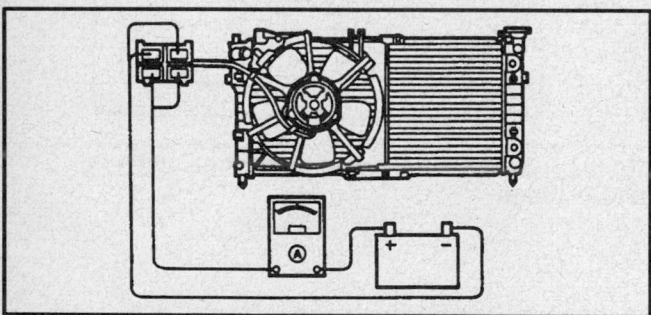

Testing two-speed cooling fan high speed operation — 626 and MX-6

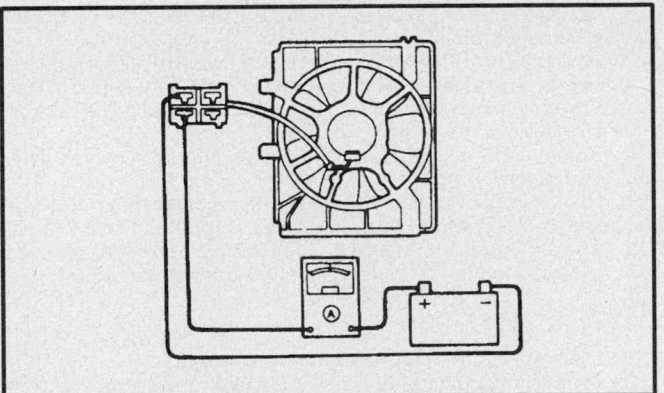

Testing single–speed cooling fan — Millenia

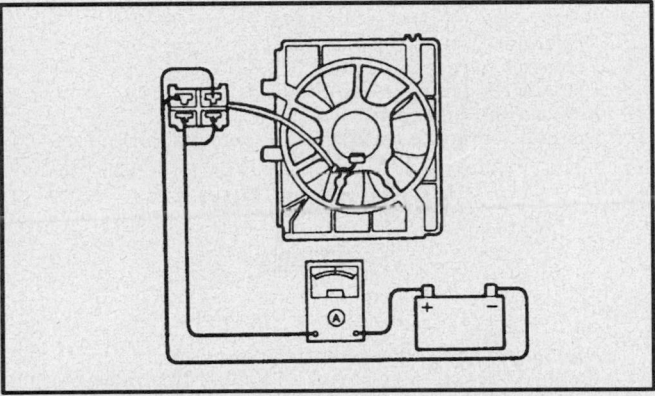

Testing two–speed cooling fan low and high — Millenia

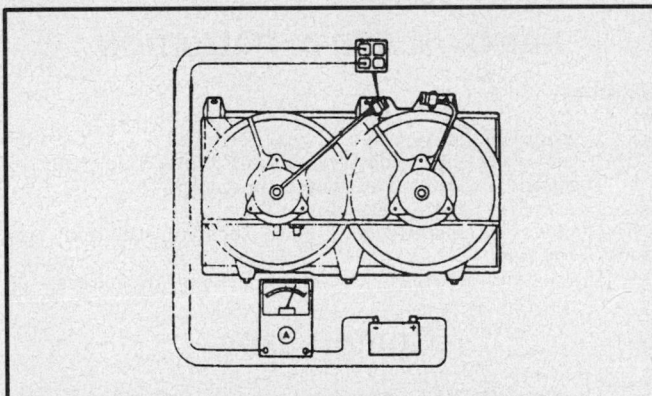

Testing three–speed cooling fan low speed operation — RX-7

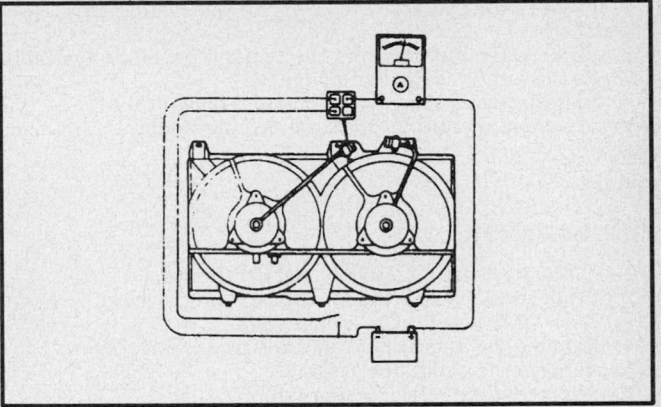

Testing three–speed cooling fan medium speed operation — RX-7

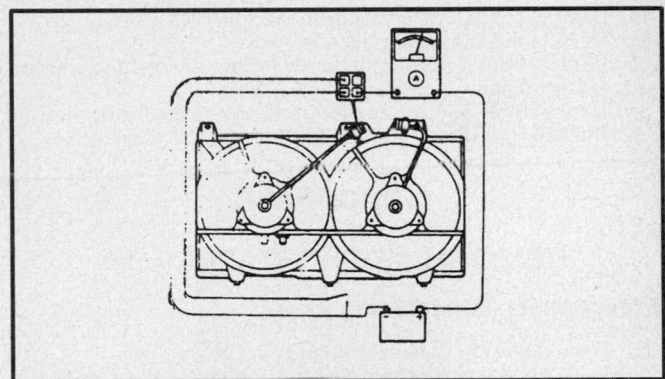

Testing three–speed cooling fan high speed operation — RX-7

REMOVAL AND INSTALLATION

Except Millenia and RX-7

1. Disconnect the negative terminal at the battery.
2. Remove the fresh air duct, if equipped.
3. Drain the radiator coolant.
4. Remove the upper radiator hose.
5. Disconnect thermo–switch wire connector, if equipped.
6. Remove electric fan and cowling assembly.
7. Remove electric fan motor from assembly.
8. Installation is the reverse of the removal procedure.

Millenia

1. Disconnect the negative battery terminal.
2. Remove the radiator grille on the 2.3L engine.
3. Remove the radiator reservoir.
4. Disconnect the coolant fan motor connector.

5. Remove the radiator cowling with the cooling fan assembly attached.
6. Remove the nut securing the coolant fan blade assembly.
7. Remove the coolant fan motor.
8. Installation is the reverse of the removal procedure. Use sealant when installing the nut on the coolant fan blade assembly.

RX−7

SINGLE FAN MODELS

1. Disconnect the negative battery terminal.
2. Properly discharge the air conditioning system.
3. Remove the coolant reservoir tank.
4. Remove the plastic clips and the upper duct covers.
5. Remove the hood lock assembly.
6. Remove the electric cooling fan.
7. Installation is the reverse of the removal procedure.

DUAL FAN MODELS

1. Disconnect the negative battery cable.
2. Detach the fan motor wiring.
3. Remove the 2 upper bolts and remove the fan shroud with fan attached.
4. Disassemble the fan blades and motors as required.
5. Installation is the reverse of the removal procedure.

Condenser

REMOVAL AND INSTALLATION

Except Miata, Millenia and RX−7

1. Disconnect the negative battery terminal.
2. Properly discharge the air conditioning system.
3. Raise front of vehicle, if necessary. Remove the front grille. On 626 and MX−6, remove the lower cover.
4. Remove the air seal cover and air duct, if equipped.
5. Disconnect the refrigerant lines at condenser. Plug the openings immediately to minimize air, moisture and dirt contamination.
6. Remove the receiver/drier, if required.
7. Remove the radiator support brackets.
8. Cover radiator fins with cardboard to avoid damage.
9. Lift radiator and push toward front of engine, if required.
10. Remove condenser mounting bolts.
11. Remove the condenser.
12. Installation is the reverse of removal.

Miata

1. Disconnect the negative battery terminal.
2. Properly discharge the air conditioning system.
3. Raise and support the vehicle safely.
4. Remove the splash shield and air guide.
5. Disconnect and plug the refrigerant lines at receiver/drier and condenser.
6. Unbolt condenser assembly.
7. Remove receiver/drier and condenser as an assembly.
8. Unbolt receiver/drier and remove it from condenser.
9. Installation is the reverse of the removal procedure.

Millenia

1. Disconnect the negative battery terminal.
2. Properly discharge the air conditioning system.
3. Raise the front of the vehicle.
4. Remove the radiator grille, mud guard, splash shield and hood seal.
5. Remove the ambient temperature sensor attached above the front bumper.

6. Disconnect the ambient temperature sensor connector and harness clamp.
7. Remove the radiator brackets and coolant reservoir.
8. Insert a protector (such as cardboard) between the condenser and the radiator. Lean the radiator toward the engine.
9. Disconnect the cooler pipe No. 1.
10. Remove the assembled cooler pipe No. 2, receiver drier and condenser.
11. Disassemble the cooler pipe No. 2, receiver drier and condenser. DO NOT allow compressor oil to spill.
12. Plug all open fittings to keep moisture out of the system.
13. Installation is the reverse of the removal procedure.

RX−7

1. Disconnect the negative battery terminal.
2. Properly discharge the air conditioning system.
3. Remove the coolant reservoir tank.
4. Remove the plastic clips and the upper duct covers.
5. Remove the hood lock assembly.
6. Remove the electric cooling fan.
7. Disconnect the refrigerant lines.
8. Remove the receiver/drier.
9. Remove condenser mounting bolts.
10. Remove the condenser.
11. Installation is the reverse of the removal procedure.

Ventilation Fan

TESTING

Millenia

1. Disconnect the negative battery terminal.
2. Remove the trunk end trim and left trunk side trim.
3. Disconnect the fan connectors.
4. Connect battery positive voltage to terminal **A** and ground terminal **B**. Verify the fan operates.
5. If not as specified, replace the ventilation fan.

REMOVAL AND INSTALLATION

Millenia

1. Disconnect the negative battery terminal.
2. Remove the trunk end trim and left trunk side trim.
3. Disconnect the fan and switch connectors.
4. Disconnect the harness clip.
5. Remove the screws and bolts securing the fan, and remove the fan.
6. Installation is the reverse of the removal procedure.

Compressor

REMOVAL AND INSTALLATION

1. Run the engine for about 10 minutes with the air conditioning on at **MAXIMUM** cooling and **HIGH** blower.
2. Disconnect the negative battery terminal. Properly discharge the air conditioning system.
3. On RX−7, remove the battery and battery box. On other models, it may be necessary to remove the air guides (Miata), intake air duct and air cleaner (929), lower cover (323, Protege, 626, MX−6, and Miata), and splash shield (Millenia).
4. Disconnect the magnetic clutch wire connector.
5. Loosen the locknut and adjusting bolts and remove the compressor belt.
6. Disconnect and plug refrigerant lines from compressor.

7. Remove compressor mounting bolts and remove compressor. Drain and measure the oil.

NOTE: On some models the compressor will come out through the bottom of the engine compartment.

8. Installation is the reverse of the removal procedure. Add new oil to the compressor during installation; the same amount as drained during removal or at least 2.0 oz.

Receiver/Drier

REMOVAL AND INSTALLATION

Except Miata and RX-7

1. Disconnect the negative battery terminal.
2. Properly discharge the air conditioning system.
3. Remove the radiator grille.
4. Disconnect the refrigerant lines at the receiver/drier. Immediately cap all openings to prevent contamination.
5. Disconnect the pressure switch wire connector, if equipped.
6. Remove attaching bolts at receiver/drier.
7. Remove the receiver/drier.
8. Installation is the reverse of removal.

Miata

1. Disconnect the negative battery terminal.
2. Properly discharge the air conditioning system.
3. Raise and support the vehicle safely.
4. Remove the splash shield and air guide.
5. Disconnect and plug the refrigerant lines at receiver/drier and condenser.
6. Unbolt condenser assembly.
7. Remove receiver/drier and condenser as an assembly.
8. Unbolt receiver/drier and remove from condenser.
9. Installation is the reverse of the removal procedure.

RX-7

1. Disconnect the negative battery terminal.
2. Properly discharge the air conditioning system.
3. Remove the coolant reservoir tank.
4. Remove the plastic clips and the upper duct covers.
5. Disconnect the refrigerant lines.
6. Remove the receiver/drier.
7. Installation is the reverse of the removal procedure.

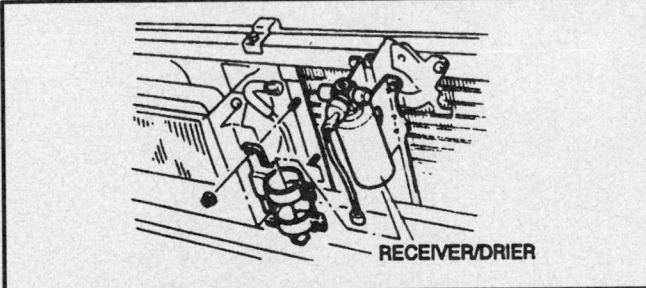

RECEIVER/DRIER

Typical receiver/drier removal

Evaporator

NOTE: If equipped with an air bag or anti-theft coded radio, read "Air Bag and Radio Service Precautions" before proceeding.

REMOVAL AND INSTALLATION

1. Disconnect the negative battery terminal.
2. Properly discharge the air conditioning system.
3. Disconnect and plug the refrigerant lines at the evaporator.
4. Remove the grommets at the expansion valve, if equipped.
5. Remove the glove box, lower panel and panel stay, as required for access.
6. Remove the air flow ducts if interfering.
7. On Millenia disconnect the **ORANGE** and **BLUE** connectors, and remove passenger side air bag module.
8. Remove the evaporator unit drain hose.
9. Remove the seal plates from both sides of the evaporator unit.
10. Disconnect the air conditioning wiring harness at the evaporator.
11. Remove the attaching bolts at the evaporator and remove the unit.
12. Installation is the reverse of the removal procedure.

Expansion Valve

NOTE: If equipped with an air bag or anti-theft coded radio, read "Air Bag and Radio Service Precautions" before proceeding.

REMOVAL AND INSTALLATION

1. Disconnect the negative battery terminal.
2. Properly discharge the air conditioning system.
3. Disconnect and immediately plug the refrigerant lines at the evaporator.
4. Remove the grommets at the expansion valve, if equipped.
5. Remove the glove box, lower panel, and panel stay as required.
6. Remove the air flow ducts, if interfering.
7. Remove the evaporator unit.
8. Remove evaporator clamps.
9. Disassemble the unit.
10. Remove the thermo-switch.
11. Remove the capillary tube from the outlet pipe.
12. Remove the expansion valve.
13. Installation is the reverse of the removal procedure.

Blower Motor

NOTE: If equipped with an air bag or anti-theft coded radio, read "Air Bag and Radio Service Precautions" before proceeding.

REMOVAL AND INSTALLATION

1. Disconnect the negative battery terminal.
2. Remove the glove box and lower panel, if required.
3. Disconnect the blower motor wire connector.
4. Remove the attaching screws and remove the blower motor.
5. Installation is the reverse of the removal procedure.

Blower Motor Resistor

NOTE: If equipped with an air bag or anti-theft coded radio, read "Air Bag and Radio Service Precautions" before proceeding.

REMOVAL AND INSTALLATION

1. Disconnect the negative battery terminal.
2. Remove the glove box and lower panel, if required.
3. Disconnect the blower motor resistor wire connector.
4. Remove the attaching screw and remove the resistor.
5. Installation is the reverse of the removal procedure.

Heater Core

NOTE: If equipped with an air bag or anti-theft coded radio, read "Air Bag and Radio Service Precautions" before proceeding.

REMOVAL AND INSTALLATION

1. Disconnect the negative battery terminal.
2. Drain the engine coolant.
3. Disconnect heater core hoses.
4. Remove transmission selector lever or knob. Remove center console.
5. Remove the steering wheel. Remove the upper and lower steering column covers. Remove the combination switch.
6. Remove the instrument meter hood. Remove the instrument cluster assembly.
7. Disconnect the speedometer cable.
8. Remove the heater ducts. Remove the instrument hosing lower panels. Remove the glove box assembly.
9. Remove the heater control switch and cables. Remove header and side trim, if required. Remove the center cap, the side covers and the center bracket bolts on the instrument panel.

10. Remove the steering shaft bolts. Disconnect any necessary wire harness connectors. Remove the instrument panel.
11. Remove the seal plate.
12. Remove the attaching nuts.
13. Remove the heater unit.
14. Remove the attaching clips on heater unit and separate assembly.
15. Remove heater core.

To install:

16. Install heater core.
17. Reattach heater case halves with clips.
18. Install the heater unit. Install the seal plates.
19. Install the instrument panel. Connect the wire harness connectors.
20. Install the steering shaft bolts. Install the center cap, the side covers and the center bracket bolts on the instrument panel.
21. Install header and side trim, if removed. Install the heater control switch and cables.
22. Install the glove box assembly. Install the instrument hosing lower panels. Install the heater ducts.
23. Reconnect speedometer cable. Install the instrument cluster and meter hood assembly.
24. Install the upper and lower steering column covers. Install the steering wheel.
25. Install the center console and the shift lever or knob.
26. Reconnect heater core hoses.
27. Reconnect the negative battery terminal.
28. Refill cooling system with proper quantity and type of antifreeze.
29. Check system for leaks.

1. Rear console
2. Upper plate
3. Front console
4. Glove compartment
5. Side cover
6. Side cover
7. Box
8. Ashtray
9. Center panel
10. Heater control assembly
11. Steering wheel ornament
12. Steering wheel
13. Column cover
14. Switch panel
15. Cap
16. Meter hood
17. Duct
18. Duct and undercover
19. Undercover
20. Duct
21. Meter assembly
22. Instrument panel

Typical instrument panel and center console assembly — 1993 626 and MX-6 shown

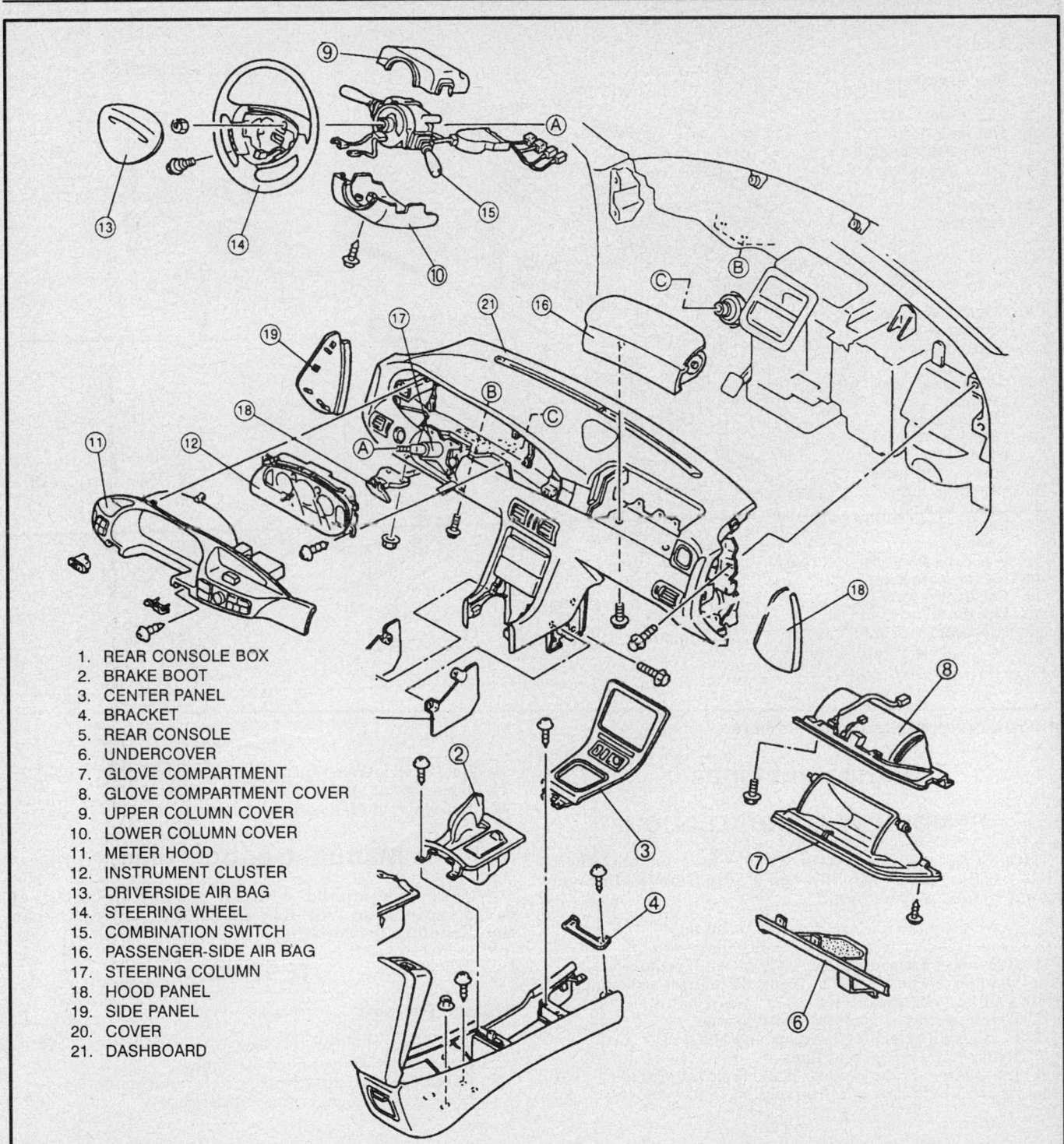

1. REAR CONSOLE BOX
2. BRAKE BOOT
3. CENTER PANEL
4. BRACKET
5. REAR CONSOLE
6. UNDERCOVER
7. GLOVE COMPARTMENT
8. GLOVE COMPARTMENT COVER
9. UPPER COLUMN COVER
10. LOWER COLUMN COVER
11. METER HOOD
12. INSTRUMENT CLUSTER
13. DRIVERSIDE AIR BAG
14. STEERING WHEEL
15. COMBINATION SWITCH
16. PASSENGER-SIDE AIR BAG
17. STEERING COLUMN
18. HOOD PANEL
19. SIDE PANEL
20. COVER
21. DASHBOARD

Instrument panel removal — Millenia

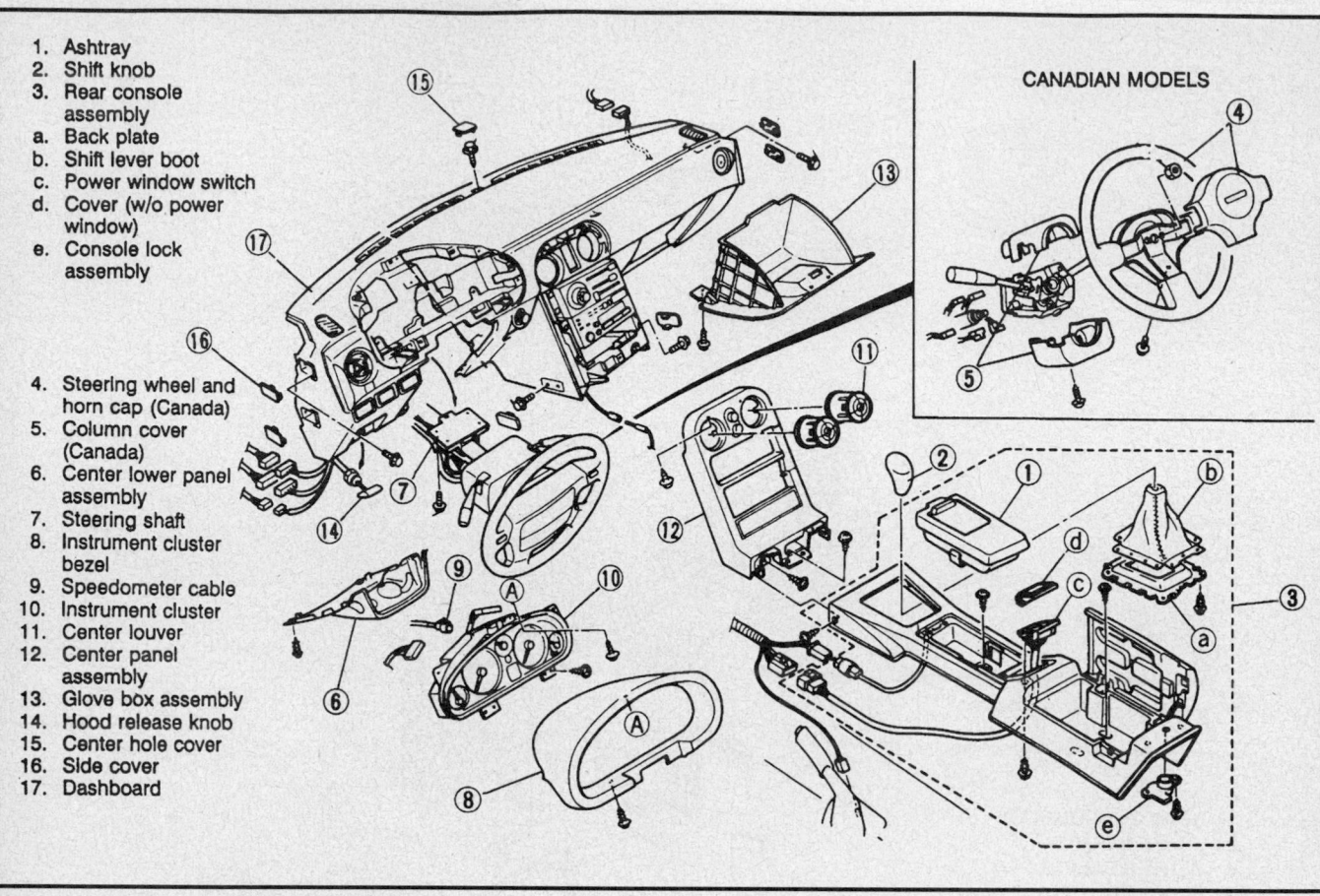

1. Ashtray
2. Shift knob
3. Rear console assembly
   a. Back plate
   b. Shift lever boot
   c. Power window switch
   d. Cover (w/o power window)
   e. Console lock assembly
4. Steering wheel and horn cap (Canada)
5. Column cover (Canada)
6. Center lower panel assembly
7. Steering shaft
8. Instrument cluster bezel
9. Speedometer cable
10. Instrument cluster
11. Center louver
12. Center panel assembly
13. Glove box assembly
14. Hood release knob
15. Center hole cover
16. Side cover
17. Dashboard

CANADIAN MODELS

Instrument panel removal — Miata

Refrigerant Lines

REMOVAL AND INSTALLATION

NOTE: If equipped with an air bag or anti-theft coded radio, read "Air Bag and Radio Service Precautions" before proceeding.

1. Disconnect the battery negative terminal.
2. Properly discharge the air conditioning system.
3. Remove chassis, engine or body parts, if required.
4. Using a backup wrench loosen disconnect and immediately plug the refrigerant line.
5. Disconnect wire connectors, if required.
6. Remove all attaching brackets and bolts.
7. Remove the refrigerant lines.
8. Installation is the reverse of the removal procedure.
9. Apply a light coat of refrigerant oil to new O-rings.

10. Route refrigerant lines in original locations.
11. Use original securing brackets and bolts.
12. Evacuate, charge and check system for leaks.

Manual Control Head

NOTE: If equipped with an air bag or anti-theft coded radio, read "Air Bag and Radio Service Precautions" before proceeding.

TESTING

323 and Protege

1. Disconnect the negative battery terminal.
2. Remove the control head assembly.
3. Check each circuit as indicated for continuity.
4. If not as specified, replace as necessary.

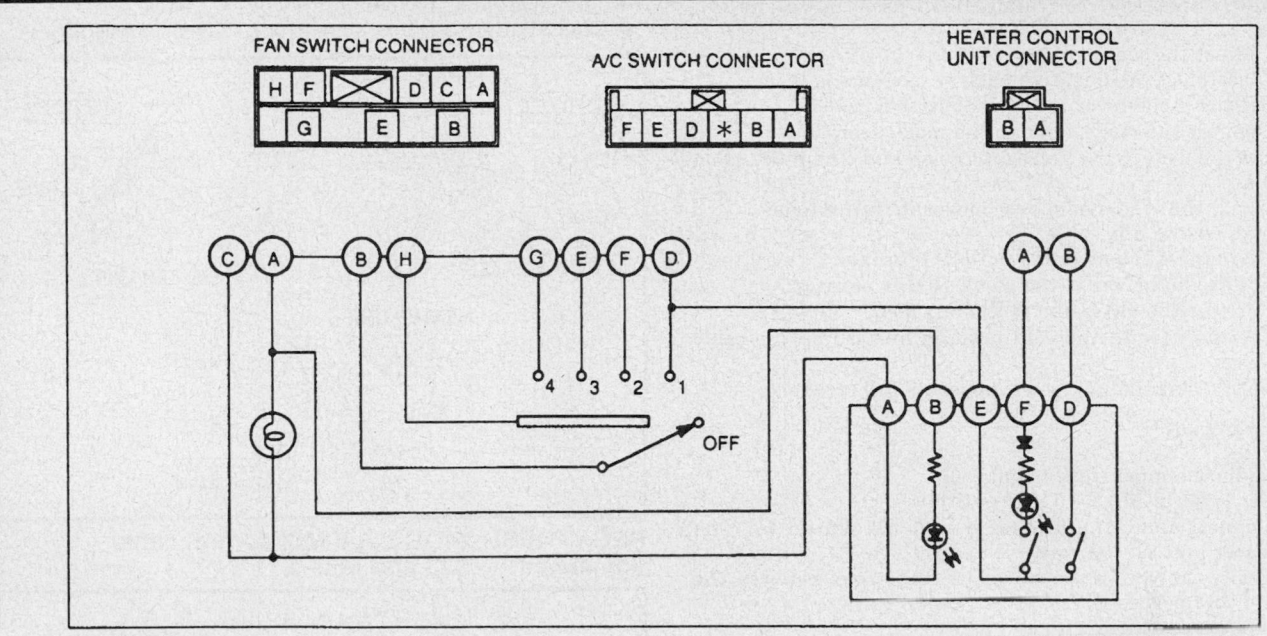

○——○ : Continuity

Terminal Switch position	Fan switch								A/C switch					Heater control unit	
	A	B	C	D	E	F	G	H	A	B	D	E	F	A	B
Constant	○—		—○						○—	—○	○			○—	—○
			○—	—○							○—	—○	—○		
OFF															
1		○—	—○												
2		○—				○—		—○							
3		○—		—○				—○							
4		○—					○—	—○							

Testing manual control head terminals — 323 and Protege

REMOVAL AND INSTALLATION

323 and Protege

1. Disconnect the negative battery terminal.
2. Remove heater control bezel and screws.
3. Remove heater control assembly.
4. Disconnect the mode, mix and recirculate–fresh cable.
5. Installation is the reverse of the removal procedure.

626 and MX–6

1. Disconnect the negative battery terminal.
2. Remove the ashtray and radio box.
3. Remove the screws and disconnect the cigarette lighter connector, then remove the center panel.
4. Disconnect the temperature, airflow and recirculate–fresh mode unit cable.
5. Remove the control unit screws and remove assembly.
6. Installation is the reverse of the removal procedure.

MX–3

1. Disconnect the negative battery terminal.
2. Remove the side panel, lower panel, rear console, console panel, front console and the meter hood.
3. Remove the mix wire from the mix door link.
4. Remove the screws securing the manual control head.
5. Installation is the reverse of the removal procedure.

Miata

1. Disconnect the negative battery terminal.
2. Remove shift lever knob and center console.
3. Remove outlet vents.
4. Remove switch panel attaching screws and remove assembly.
5. Remove heater switch attaching screws.
6. Remove switch assembly and disconnect heater control cables.
7. Installation is the reverse of the removal procedure.

Manual Control Cables

ADJUSTMENT

323, MX–3 and Protege

1. To adjust recirculate–fresh cable:
   • Disconnect negative battery terminal.
   • Set the recirculate–fresh lever to the **FRESH** position.
   • Connect the recirculate–fresh cable to the recirculate–fresh door.
   • Set the door to the fresh position and clamp the cable into place.

● Verify that the recirculate–fresh lever moves its full stroke.

2. To adjust the mode cable:
   ● Disconnect the negative battery terminal.
   ● Set the mode lever to the **DEFROST** position.
   ● Connect the mode cable to the mode door.
   ● Set the door to the defrost position and clamp the cable into place.
   ● Verify that the mode lever moves its full stroke.

3. To adjust the mix cable:
   ● Disconnect the negative battery terminal.
   ● Set the mix lever to the **MAX COLD** position.
   ● Connect the mix cable to the mix door.
   ● Set the door to the cold position and clamp the cable into place.
   ● Verify that the mix lever moves its full stroke.

626 and MX-6

1. To adjust temperature blend cable:
   ● Set lever at **MAX-COLD** position.
   ● Connect and clamp the cable with the shutter lever on the heater unit all the way to the right side.
   ● Verify that the lever moves its full stroke between the hot and cold positions.

2. To adjust the airflow mode cable:
   ● Set the mode control lever to the **DEFROST** position.
   ● Connect and clamp the cable with the shutter lever on the heater unit at its closest point.
   ● Verify that the lever moves its full stroke between the defrost and vent positions.

3. To adjust the recirculate–fresh cable:
   ● Set the selector lever to the **RECIRCULATE** position.
   ● Connect and clamp the cable with the shutter lever on the blower unit at its closest point.
   ● Verify that the lever moves its full stroke between the recirculate and fresh positions.

Miata

1. To adjust temperature blend cable:
   ● Set lever at **MAX-HOT** position.
   ● Connect and clamp the cable with the shutter lever on the heater unit all the way to the right side.
   ● Verify that the lever moves its full stroke between the hot and cold positions.

2. To adjust the airflow mode cable:
   ● Set the mode control lever to the **VENT** position.
   ● Connect and clamp the cable with the shutter lever on the heater unit at its closest point.
   ● Verify that the lever moves its full stroke between the defrost and vent positions.

3. To adjust the recirculate–fresh cable.
   ● Set the selector lever to the **FRESH** position.
   ● Connect and clamp the cable with the shutter lever on the blower unit at its closest point.
   ● Verify that the lever moves its full stroke between the recirculate and fresh positions.

REMOVAL AND INSTALLATION

323, MX-3 and Protege

1. Disconnect the negative battery terminal.
2. Remove the instrument housing side and lower panels.
3. Remove the instrument panel meter hood.
4. Remove the glove box assembly.
5. Disconnect the mode, mix and recirculate–fresh cable.
6. Remove heater control bezel and screws.
7. Remove heater control assembly.

8. Remove cable attaching screws and cables.
9. Installation is the reverse of the removal procedure.

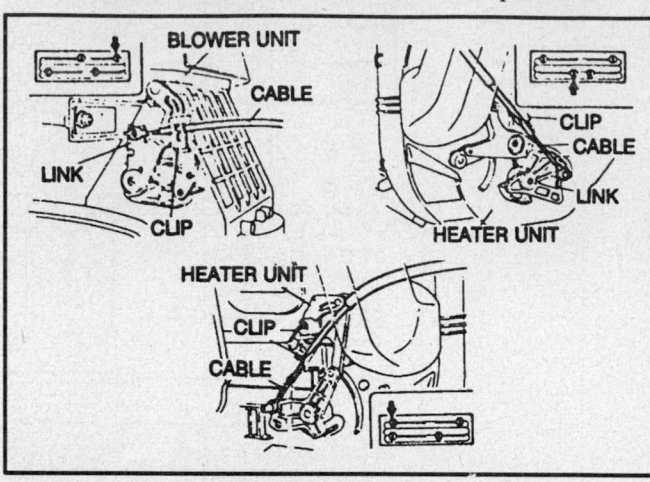

REC–FRESH, MODE and MIX control cable adjustment — 323 and MX-3

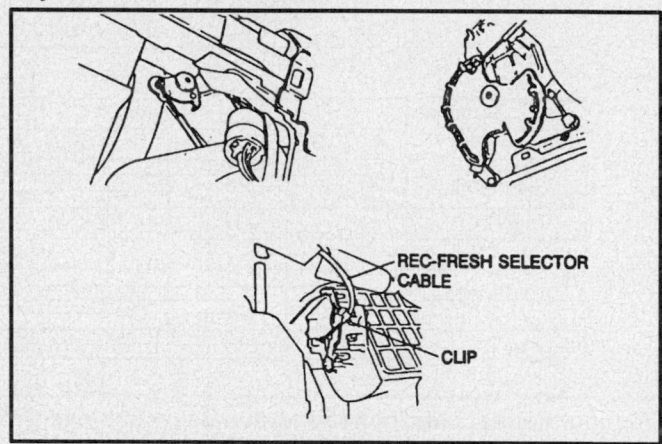

Temperature, Airflow and REC–FRESH cable adjustment — 1993 626 and MX-6

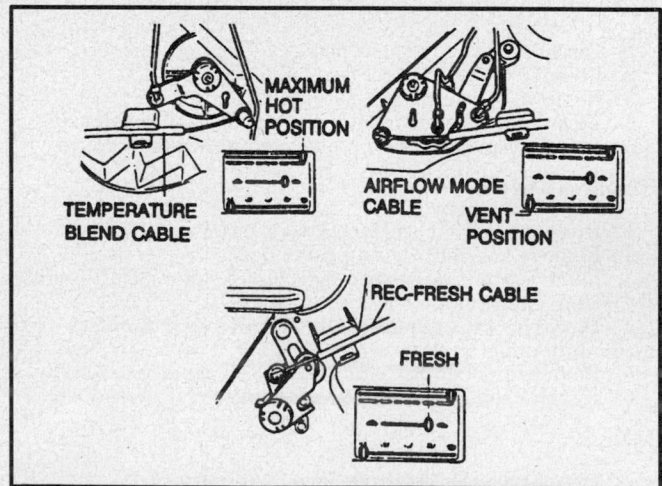

Temperature, Airflow and REC–FRESH blend cable adjustment — Miata

626 and MX-6

1. Disconnect the negative battery terminal.
2. Remove the glove box and undercover assembly.
3. Disconnect the temperature and recirculate–fresh heater unit cable.
4. Remove the duct and undercover on driver's side.
5. Disconnect the airflow mode cable.
6. Remove the ashtray and radio box.
7. Remove the screws and disconnect the cigarette lighter connector, the remove the center panel.
8. Remove the temperature control screws and remove assembly.
9. Disconnect the control cables and remove the cables.
10. Installation is the reverse of the removal procedure.

Miata

1. Disconnect the negative battery terminal.
2. Remove shift lever knob and center console.
3. Remove outlet vents.
4. Remove switch panel attaching screws and remove assembly.
5. Remove heater switch attaching screws.
6. Remove switch assembly and disconnect heater control cables.
7. Remove glove box assembly to gain access to heater unit control cables.
8. Disconnect and remove control cables.
9. Installation is the reverse of the removal procedure.

Electronic Control Head

TESTING

323 and Protege

1. Disconnect the negative battery terminal.
2. Remove the control head assembly.
3. Supply 12 volts to terminal **F** and ground terminal **J**.
4. Checking REC switch:
   - Connect a 1 kilo–ohm resister between terminals **C** and **F**.
   - Turn the REC switch **ON**, and measure the voltage between terminals **C** and **J**.
   - In the **ON** position the REC switch should be 1 volt or less.
   - In the **OFF** position the REC switch should be 12 volts or more.

- If not as specified, replace the electronic control head.
5. Checking the FRESH switch:
   - Connect a 1 kilo–ohm resistor between the terminals **A** and **F**.
   - Turn the FRESH switch **ON**, and measure the voltage between terminals **A** and **J**.
   - In the **ON** position the FRESH switch should be 1 volt or less.
   - In the **OFF** position the FRESH switch should be 12 volts or more.
   - If not as specified, replace the electronic control head.
6. Checking the MODE switch:
   - Connect a 1 kilo–ohm resistor between the terminals **J** and **L**.
   - Connect a jumper wire between terminals **J** (or the negative battery terminal) and **R**.
   - There should be 12 volts between terminals **J** and **L**.
   - If not as specified, replace the electronic control head.
   - Connect a 1 kilo–ohm resistor between the terminals **J** and **N**.
   - Connect a jumper wire between terminals **J** (or the negative battery terminal) and **P**.
   - There should be 12 volts between terminals **J** and **N**.
   - If not as specified, replace the electronic control head.
   - Connect a 1 kilo–ohm resistor between the terminals **J** and **N**.
   - Connect a jumper wire between terminals **J** (or the negative battery terminal) and **P**.
   - There should be 1 volt or less between the terminals **J** and **L**.
   - If not as specified, replace the electronic control head.
   - Connect a 1 kilo–ohm resistor between the terminals **J** and **N**.
   - Connect a jumper wire between terminals **J** (or the negative battery terminal) and **R**.
   - There should be 1 volt or less between the terminals **J** and **N**.
   - Check for continuity between the terminals as indicated while pressing the MODE switches.
   - If not as specified, replace the electronic control head.

626 and MX-6

1. Remove the center panel.
2. Using a voltmeter, measure the voltage at each terminal, using the appropriate Terminal Voltage Chart.

ELECTRONIC CONTROL HEAD TERMINAL VOLTAGE REFERENCE CHART — 1993−94 626 AND MX−6

Connector	Terminal	Wire	Connected to	Test condition	Correct voltage (V)
Connector A (10 pins)	A	G/W	Mix Actuator	Any	About 5
	B	BR		Any	0
	C	G/B		Temperature lever moved hot to cold (Mix actuator operating hot to cold)	0
	D	G		Temperature lever in hot position	5
				Temperature lever in cold position	0
	F	G/Y		Temperature lever moved cold to hot (Mix actuator operating cold to hot)	0
	H	Y/B	Airflow mode actuator	VENT switch ON (Airflow mode actuator operating DEF to VENT)	B+
	I	Y/G		DEF switch ON (Airflow mode actuator operating VENT to DEF)	B+
	J	B	Body ground	Any	0
	K	—	—	—	—
	L	L	Ignition switch	Ignition switch ON	B+
Connector B (14 pins)	A	W	Airflow mode actuator	DEF switch ON (Airflow mode actuator operating VENT to DEF)	0
	B	GY	Panel lamp control switch	—	—
	C	W/B	Airflow mode actuator	VENT switch ON (Airflow mode actuator operating DEF to VENT)	About 10
	D	O	TNS relay	Light switch ON	B+
	E	R	A/C amplifier	Blower switch OFF	B+
	F	L/W		A/C switch and blower switch ON	0
	H	G/L	Intake actuator	Fresh switch ON	B+
	I	L		Recirculation switch ON	B+
	K	Y/W	Airflow mode actuator	DEF switch ON	0
	L	Y		HEAT/DEF switch ON	0
	M	W/L		HEAT switch ON	0
	N	W/Y		VENT switch ON	0
	O	W/G		BI-LEVEL switch ON	0
	P	B/R	Swing louver	Ignition switch ON	B+
				Swing louver ON	Approx. 1
Connector C (6 pins)	A	L/R	Resistor assembly	Blower switch in 3rd position	0
	B	L/W	Resistor assembly blower motor	Blower switch in 3rd or 4th position	0
	C	L	Resistor assembly	Blower switch in 2nd position	0
	D	L/B	ECU	Blower switch in 4th position	0
	E	L/Y	Resistor assembly A/C amplifier	Blower switch in 1st position	0
	F	B	Body ground	Any	0

ELECTRONIC CONTROL HEAD TERMINAL VOLTAGE REFERENCE CHART — 1995 626 AND MX-6

B+: Battery positive voltage

Connector	Terminal	Wire	Connection	Test condition	Voltage (V)
Connector A (10 pin)	1A	(G/W)	Air mix actuator	Any	Approx. 6
	1B	(BR)		Any	0
	1C	(P)		Temperature lever moved from hot to cold (Air mix actuator operating at MAX COLD)	B+
	1D	(G)		Temperature lever in hot position	5
				Temperature lever in cold position	Approx. 1
	1F	(G/Y)		Temperature lever moved from cold to hot (Air mix actuator operating at MAX HOT)	B+
	1H	(Y/B)	Airflow mode actuator	VENT switch on (only while airflow mode actuator is operating from DEF to VENT)	B+
	1I	(Y/G)		DEF switch on (only while airflow mode actuator is operating from VENT to DEF)	B+
	1J	(B)	GND	Any	0
	1K	—	—	—	—
	1L	(L)	Ignition switch	Ignition switch at ON	B+
Connector B (14 pin)	2A	(W)	Airflow mode actuator	DEF switch on (only while airflow mode actuator is operating from VENT to DEF)	0
	2B	(GY)	Panel light control switch	Light switch on and panel light control switch at maximum illumination	0
				Light switch on and panel light control switch at minimum illumination	Approx. 10
	2C	(W/B)	Airflow mode actuator	VENT switch on (only while airflow mode actuator is operating fromDEF to VENT)	B+
	2D	(O)	TNS relay	Light switch on	B+
	2E	(R)	A/C amplifier	Fan switch off	B+
	2F	(L/W)		A/C switch and fan switch on	0
	2H	(G/L)	Air intake actuator	Fresh switch on*	B+
	2J	(L)		Recirculation switch on*	B+
	2K	(Y/W)	Airflow mode actuator	DEF switch on	0
	2L	(Y)		HEAT/DEF switch on	0
	2M	(W/L)		HEAT switch on	0
	2N	(W/Y)		VENT switch on	0
	2O	(W/G)		BI-LEVEL switch on	0
	2P	(B/R)	Swing louver	Ignition switch at ON	B+
				Swing switch on	Approx. 1
Connector C (6 pin)	A	Y/B	Resistor	Fan switch in 3rd position	0
	B	L/W	Resistor, blower motor	Fan switch in 4th position	0
	C	L	Resistor	Fan switch in 2nd position	0
	D	L/B	PCM	Fan switch in 3rd or 4th position	0
	E	L/Y	Resistor, A/C amplifier	Fan switch in 1st position	0
	F	B	GND	Any	0

* It will take a while to get the normal voltage.

929

1. Remove the electronic control head.
2. With a voltmeter, measure the voltage at each terminal using the appropriate A/C Amplifier Terminal Voltage Reference Chart.
3. If not as specified, replace the A/C amplifier and/or the electronic control head.

Millenia

1. Disconnect the negative battery terminal.
2. Disconnect the A/C amplifier connector.
3. Disconnect the heater control unit.
4. Check for continuity between the switch terminals.
5. Verify that there is continuity between all the terminals and between the terminals J and L of the heater control unit connector.
6. If there is no continuity, replace the electronic control head.
7. Apply battery positive voltage to terminal N and ground to terminals E, H, I, G, K and verify that the indicators turn ON.
8. If not as specified, replace the electronic control head.

1993 RX-7

1. Disconnect the negative battery terminal.
2. Remove the control head assembly.
3. Supply 12 volts to terminal l and ground terminal h, except during continuity tests.
4. Checking temperature control circuit.
   - Set the temperature control lever to the midway position.
   - Connect a jumper wire between terminals D and E.
   - Check that there is 12 volts between terminals F and G.
   - If not as specified, replace the control assembly.
   - Disconnect the jumper wire.
   - Connect a jumper wire between terminals C and D.
   - Check that there is 12 volts between terminals G and F.
   - If not as specified, replace the control assembly.
5. Continuity tests:
   - Check for continuity between terminal h and N with the VENT switch pushed ON.
   - Check for continuity between terminal h and M with the B/L switch pushed ON.
   - Check for continuity between terminal h and L with the HEAT switch pushed ON.
   - Check for continuity between terminal h and K with the H/D switch pushed ON.
   - Check for continuity between terminal h and J with the DEF switch pushed ON.
   - If any terminals do not have continuity, replace the control head assembly.
6. Checking indicator lamps:
   - Check for illumination of the indicator lamp as each switch is pushed.
   - If any lamp fails to illuminate, replace the control head assembly.
   - Connect a jumper wire between terminals l and j, and verify that the indicator lamps dim.
   - If they do not, replace the control head assembly.
7. Checking mode control circuit:
   - Connect a jumper wire between terminals h and O.
   - Measure the voltage between terminals P and Q.
   - There should be approximately 12 volts between terminals P and Q.
   - If not as specified, replace the control head assembly.
   - Disconnect the jumper wire.
   - Connect a jumper wire between terminals h and H.

   - Measure the voltage between terminals Q and P.
   - There should be approximately 12 volts between terminals Q and P.
   - If not as specified, replace the control head assembly.
8. Checking unit illumination lamp:
   - Connect a jumper wire between terminals b and l.
   - Check for illumination of the unit illumination lamps.
   - If there is no illumination of either lamp, replace the control head assembly.
9. Checking heater relay output:
   - Connect a test light between terminal l and the 5-pin connector terminal d.
   - Turn the blower switch ON.
   - If the test light does not light, check the fan amp.
   - If the fan amp is good, replace the control head assembly.
10. Checking the air conditioner indicator lamp:
    - Connect a test light between terminals l and f.
    - Turn the blower switch ON.
    - If the test light does not light, check the fan amp.
    - If the fan amp is good, replace the control head assembly.
11. Checking the EX–HI relay output:
    - Connect a test light between terminals l and terminal b of the 5 pin connector.
    - Set the blower switch to maximum.
    - If the test light does not light, check the fan amp.
    - If the fan amp is good, replace the control head assembly.
12. Checking power transistor output:
    - Measure the voltage at terminal a while turning the blower switch.
    - Verify that the voltage with the switch at maximum position is more than the voltage at OFF position.
    - If not, check the fan amp.
    - If the fan amp is good, replace the control head assembly.
13. Checking REC/FRESH select switch:
    - Check for continuity between terminals h and with the FRESH switch depressed.
    - Check for continuity between terminals h and k with the REC switch depressed.
    - Both tests should have continuity, if not as specified replace the control head assembly.
14. Checking REC/FRESH indicator lamp:
    - Depress the FRESH switch, indicator lamp should be OFF.
    - Depress REC switch, indicator lamp should be ON.
    - If not as specified, replace the control head assembly.
15. Checking REC/FRESH motor circuit:
    - Connect a jumper wire between terminals c and h.
    - Measure the voltage between terminals h and d.
    - There should be approximately 12 volts between terminals h and d.
    - If not as specified, replace the control head assembly.
16. Checking the air conditioner switch:
    - Check for continuity between terminal e and the 5-pin connector terminal e.
    - With the air conditioner switch ON, there should be continuity.
    - With the air conditioner switch OFF, there should be no continuity.
    - If not as specified, replace the control head assembly.
17. Checking air conditioner indicator lamp:
    - Connect a jumper wire between terminals h and e.
    - Check that the indicator lamp is ON when the air conditioner switch is ON.
    - Check that the indicator lamp is OFF when the air conditioner switch is OFF.

- If not as specified, replace the control head assembly.

Switch \ Terminal	J	T	S	Q	O	M
VENT	○—————○					
BI-LEVEL	○————————————○					
HEAT	○————————————————————○					
HEAT/DEF	○					
DEFROSTER	○————————————————————————————————○					

○—○ : Continuity

Testing electronic control head continuity — 323 and Protege

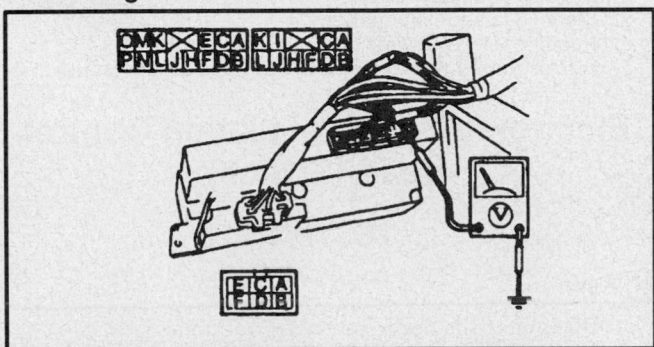

Electronic control head terminal identification — 1993–94 626 and MX–6

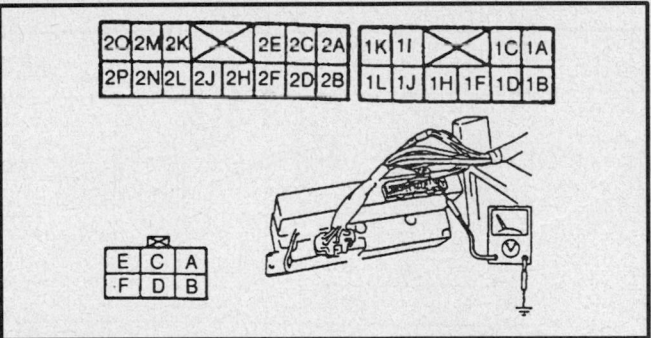

Electronic control head terminal identification — 1995 626 and MX–6

REMOVAL AND INSTALLATION

323 and Protege

1. Disconnect the negative battery terminal.
2. Remove the control head bezel and screws.
3. Remove the control head assembly.
4. Disconnect the mode, mix and recirculate–fresh cables.
5. Installation is the reverse of the removal procedure.

626 and MX–6

1. Disconnect the negative battery terminal.
2. Remove the ashtray and radio box.
3. Remove the screws and disconnect the cigarette lighter connector, then remove the center panel.
4. Remove the control unit screws and remove assembly.
5. Disconnect the control unit wire harness.
6. Installation is the reverse of the removal procedure.

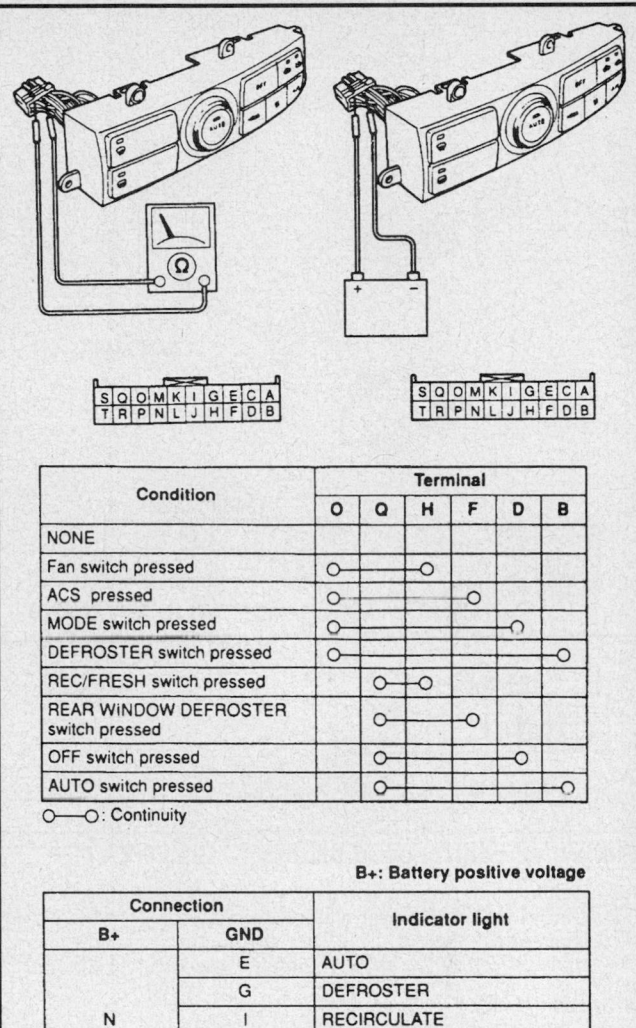

Condition	Terminal					
	O	Q	H	F	D	B
NONE						
Fan switch pressed	○—————————○					
ACS pressed	○———————————————○					
MODE switch pressed	○———————————————————————————○					
DEFROSTER switch pressed	○———————————————————————————————————○					
REC/FRESH switch pressed		○———○				
REAR WINDOW DEFROSTER switch pressed		○———————————○				
OFF switch pressed		○———————————————————○				
AUTO switch pressed		○———————————————————————————————○				

○—○ : Continuity

B+: Battery positive voltage

Connection		Indicator light
B+	GND	
N	E	AUTO
	G	DEFROSTER
	I	RECIRCULATE
	K	REAR WINDOW DEFROSTER
	M	FRESH

Electronic control head terminal identification and testing — Millenia

929

1. Disconnect the negative battery terminal.
2. Remove the steering wheel and column covers.
3. Remove the instrument panel screws and pull the switch panel outward.
4. Disconnect the instrument panel wire connectors.
5. Remove the instrument panel.
6. Remove the heater control head panel screws and pull switch assembly outward.
7. Disconnect control head wire harness and remove assembly.
8. Installation is the reverse of the removal procedure.

Millenia (except Solar)

1. Disconnect the negative battery terminal.
2. Remove the column cover and meter hood.

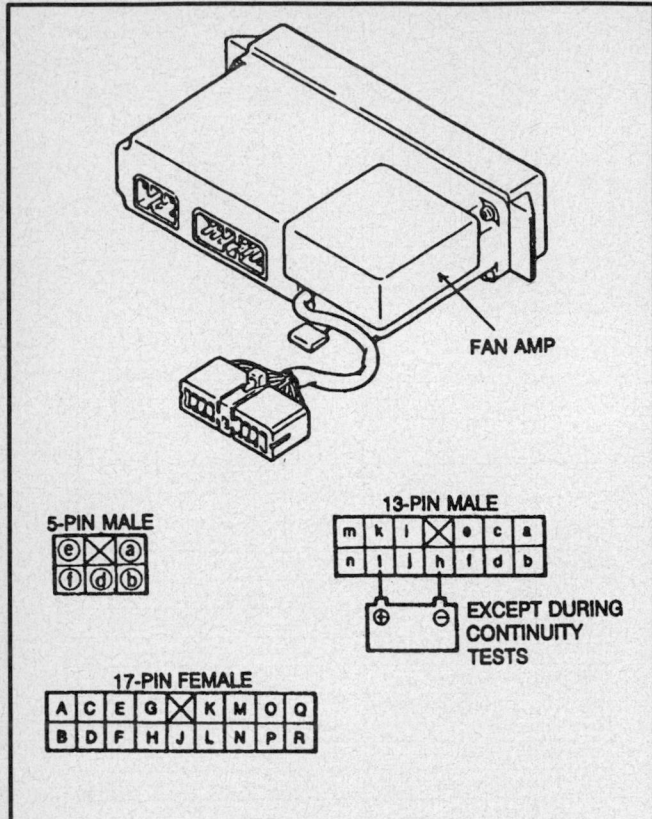

FAN AMP

5-PIN MALE

13-PIN MALE

EXCEPT DURING
CONTINUITY
TESTS

17-PIN FEMALE

Electronic control head testing — 1993 RX-7

3. Remove the hazard warning switch.
4. Disconnect the heater control unit.
5. Disconnect the A/C amplifier connector.
6. Installation is the reverse of the removal procedure.

Millenia (Solar)

1. Disconnect the negative battery terminal.
2. Remove crews securing the center panel, console box and the brake boot panel.
3. Disconnector the connector, and remove the control head (switch).
4. Installation is the reverse of the removal procedure.

1993 RX-7

1. Disconnect the negative battery terminal.
2. Remove the center louver and ashtray.
3. Remove the center panel attaching screws.
4. Disconnect the cigarette lighter connector.
5. Remove the center panel.
6. Remove the heater control attaching screws.

7. Remove the dash panel center cap and bolt.
8. Turn the dash panel 30 degrees toward the front of vehicle and remove the dash panel.
9. Disconnect the control head assembly connector and remove it from the clip.
10. Tie a string to the harness connector so the harness can be pulled through the dash during installation.
11. Disconnect the control head connector and remove the assembly.
12. Installation is the reverse of the removal procedure.

1994—95 RX-7

1. Disconnect the negative battery cable.
2. Remove the meter hood.
3. Remove the console panel.
4. Remove the electronic control head.
5. Installation is the reverse of the removal procedure.

Electronic Solar Ventilation Control Head (Switch)

TESTING

Millenia

1. Disconnect the negative battery terminal.
2. Remove the electronic solar ventilation control head (switch).
3. Check for continuity between the terminals.
4. If not as specified, replace the switch.

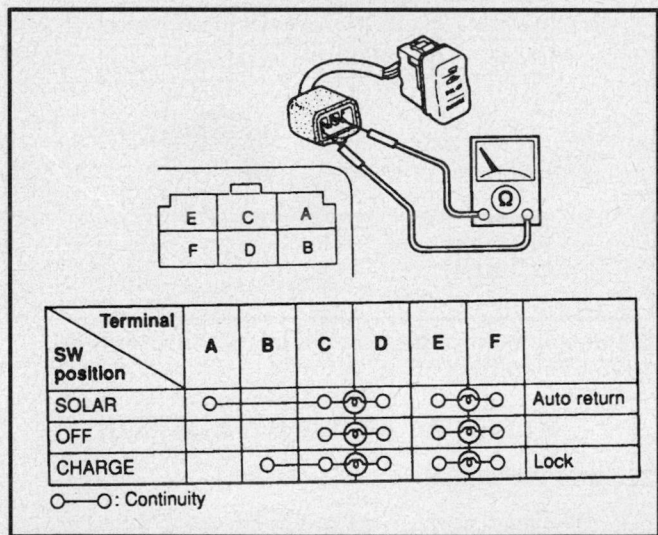

Terminal SW position	A	B	C	D	E	F	
SOLAR	o—		o—(T)—o		o—(T)—o		Auto return
OFF			o—(T)—o		o—(T)—o		
CHARGE		o—	—o—(T)—o		o—(T)—o		Lock

O——O : Continuity

Electronic solar ventilation control head (switch) testing — Millenia

SENSORS, SWITCHES AND RELAYS

Pressure Switches

OPERATION

There are 2 styles of pressure switches being used, the first pressure switch, which switches the magnetic clutch ON or OFF as a result of irregularly high or low pressures of the refrigerant. The second pressure switch is used on vehicles with automatic transmission to cycle ON and OFF the condenser fan according to system pressure. Both pressure switches are located on the high side.

TESTING

1. Disconnect the pressure switch wire connector from the receiver/drier or from the high pressure line.
2. Start vehicle and turn the air conditioner **ON**.
3. Hook up the air conditioner gauges or charging station.
4. Check for 12 volts at pressure switch wire connector.
5. If there is no voltage at either terminal of wire connector, check air conditioner relay.
6. Connect a jumper wire between the 2 terminals.
7. Check to see if compressor clutch engages or if condenser fan operates, on vehicles with automatic transmission.
8. If condenser fan and compressor magnetic clutch fail to operate check the unit and the wiring to the unit.
9. Check for continuity through the switch, at normal operating pressures there will be continuity through the switch.

REMOVAL AND INSTALLATION

NOTE: If equipped with an anti-theft coded radio, read "Air Bag and Radio Service Precautions" before disconnecting the negative battery cable.

Except RX-7

1. Disconnect the negative battery cable.
2. Properly discharge the air conditioning system.
3. If required, remove radiator grille.
4. Disconnect the pressure switch wire connector.
5. Using 2 wrenches, remove the pressure switch.
6. Installation is the reverse of removal procedure, and using a new O-ring..

RX-7

1. Disconnect the negative battery cable.
2. Properly discharge the air conditioning system.
3. Remove the coolant reservoir tank and upper duct cover.
4. Disconnect the pressure switch wire connector.
5. Using 2 wrenches, remove the pressure switch.
6. Installation is the reverse of removal procedure.

Thermo–Switch

OPERATION

The electro thermo-sensor is mounted at the evaporator core outlet and senses the temperature of the cool air coming through the evaporator. Temperature signals are then input to the thermo unit. This information is then compared by the thermo unit and the results are output to operate the air conditioner relay and turn the magnetic clutch ON and OFF.

TESTING

323, MX-3, Miata and Protege

1. Disconnect negative battery terminal.
2. Remove the thermo-switch.
3. Place thermo-switch in ice water.
4. Check continuity through the switch.
5. There should be no continuity through the switch when it reaches 32°F (0°C).

626 and MX-6

1. Disconnect the negative battery terminal.
2. Remove the coolant unit.
3. Remove the thermo-switch from the cooling unit.
4. Immerse the sensor part of the thermo-switch in a container of ice water.
5. Check for continuity between terminals **A** and **B**.
6. At below 32°F (0°C) there should be no continuity.
7. At above 36°F (2°C) there should be continuity.
8. If not as specified, replace thermo-switch.

1993 RX-7

1. Disconnect negative battery terminal.
2. Remove the thermo-switch.
3. Place thermo-switch in ice water.
4. Check continuity through the switch.
5. There should be no continuity through the switch when it reaches 32.9–36.5°F (0.5–2.5°C), if equipped with a Nippon Denso compressor or 32–35.6°F (0–3°C), if equipped with a Sanden compressor.

1994–95 RX-7

1. Disconnect the negative battery terminal.
2. Disconnect the thermo-switch connector.
3. Check for continuity between terminals **A** and **B** and terminals **C** and **D**.
4. If not as specified, replace the thermo-switch.

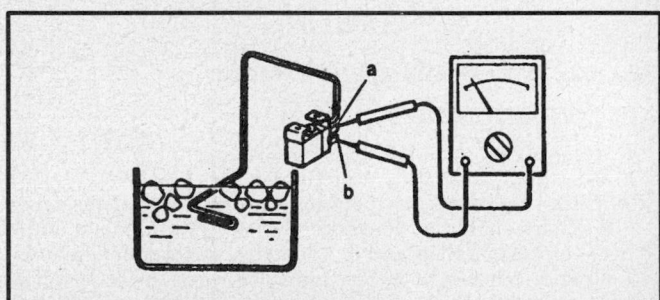

Typical thermo–switch testing

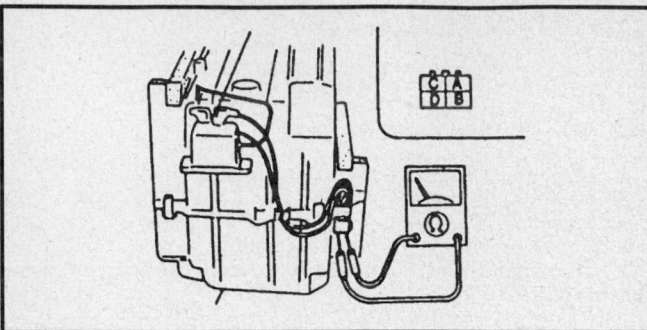

Thermo—switch testing — 1994–95 RX–7

REMOVAL AND INSTALLATION

NOTE: If equipped with an air bag or anti-theft coded radio, read "Air Bag and Radio Service Precautions" before proceeding.

1. Disconnect the negative battery terminal.
2. Remove the glove box and undercover.
3. Properly discharge the air conditioning system. Remove the cooling unit.
4. Disassemble the cooling unit.
5. Remove the thermo–switch.
6. Installation is the reverse of the removal procedure.

Relays

OPERATION

Battery and load location may require that a switch be placed some distance from either component. This means a longer wire and a higher voltage drop. The installation of a relay between the battery and the load reduces the voltage drop. Because the switch controls the relay, this means amperage through the switch can be reduced.

TESTING

323, 626, MX–6, Miata, and Protege

AIR CONDITIONING RELAY

1. Connect the negative battery terminal.
2. Disconnect the relay wire connector.
3. Check for continuity between the terminals of the relay:
   • There should be continuity between terminals **a** and **b**, between terminals **a** and **d**, and between terminals **e** and **c**.
   • There should be no continuity between the other terminal combinations.
4. If not as specified, replace the relay.
5. Apply 12 volts to terminal **d** and ground terminal **a**.
6. Check for continuity between terminals **c** and **e**.
7. If not as specified, replace the relay.

CONDENSER FAN RELAY

1. Disconnect the negative battery terminal.
2. Disconnect the relay wire connector.
3. Check that there is continuity between the terminals **a** and **b** of the relay, but not between terminals **c** and **d**.
4. If not as specified, replace the relay.
5. Apply 12 volts to terminal **a** and ground terminal **b**. There should be continuity between terminals **c** and **d**.
6. If not as specified, replace the relay.

BLOWER MOTOR RELAY

1. Disconnect the negative battery terminal.
2. Disconnect the relay connector.
3. Check that there is continuity between terminals **A** and **F**, and terminals **F** and **B**.
4. If not as specified, replace the relay.

929

AIR CONDITIONING RELAY

1. Remove the relay and check that there is no continuity between terminals **a** and **c**. Also be sure there is continuity between terminals **b** and **d**.
2. Apply battery voltage to terminals **b** and **d**. There should now be continuity between terminals **a** and **c**.
3. If not as specified, replace the relay.

1993 MAX–HI RELAY AND HEATER RELAY

1. Remove the relay and check that there is no continuity between terminals **a** and **b**. Also be sure there is continuity between terminals **c** and **d**.
2. Apply battery voltage to terminals **c** and **d**. There should now be continuity between terminals **a** and **b**.
3. If not as specified, replace the relay.

1994–95 MAX–HI RELAY AND HEATER RELAY

1. Remove the relay, and check that there is no continuity between terminals **D** and **E**.
2. Apply battery voltage to terminal **A** and ground terminal **C**, and check for continuity between terminals **D** and **E**.

Millenia

AIR CONDITIONING RELAY, CONDENSER FAN RELAY NO. 1 AND NO. 2

1. Disconnect the negative battery terminal.
2. Locate and remove the relay.
3. There should be no continuity between terminals **C** and **D** of the relay connector.
4. Connect battery (+) positive voltage to terminal **A** and ground to terminal **B** of the relay connector.
5. There should be continuity between terminals **C** and **D**.
6. If not as specified, replace the relay.

BLOWER RELAY AND MAX–HI RELAY

1. Disconnect the negative battery terminal.
2. Locate and remove the relay.
3. There should be no continuity between terminals **B** and **F** of the relay connector.
4. Connect battery (+) positive voltage to terminal **A** and ground to terminal **E** of the relay connector.
5. There should be continuity between terminals **B** and **F**.
6. If not as specified, replace relay.

RX–7

AIR CONDITIONING MAIN RELAY

1. Disconnect the negative battery terminal.
2. Disconnect the relay wire connector.
3. Check for continuity between the terminals of the relay.
4. If not as specified, replace the relay.
5. Apply 12 volts to terminal **b** and ground terminal **a**.
6. Check for continuity between terminals **c** and **d**.
7. If not as specified, replace the relay.

REMOVAL AND INSTALLATION

1. Disconnect negative battery terminal.
2. Locate relay and disconnect wire connector.
3. If required, remove attaching bolt and remove relay.
4. Installation is the reverse of the removal procedure.

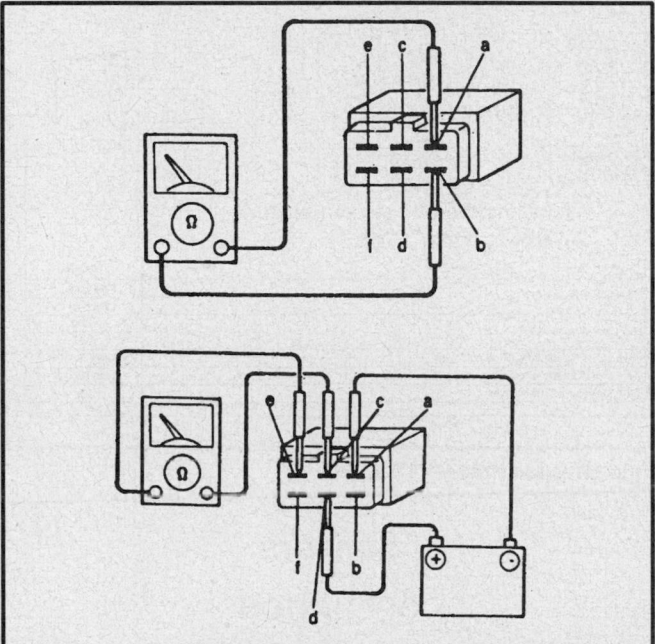

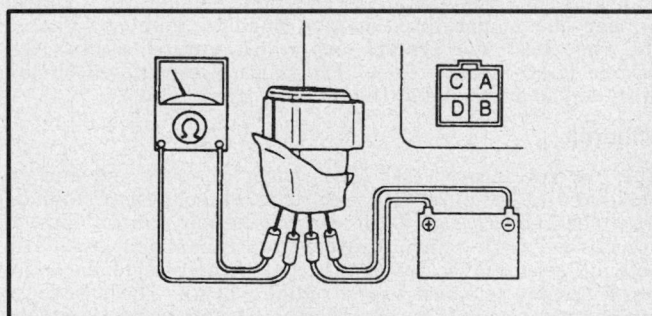

Testing air conditioning relay — 323, Protege and Miata

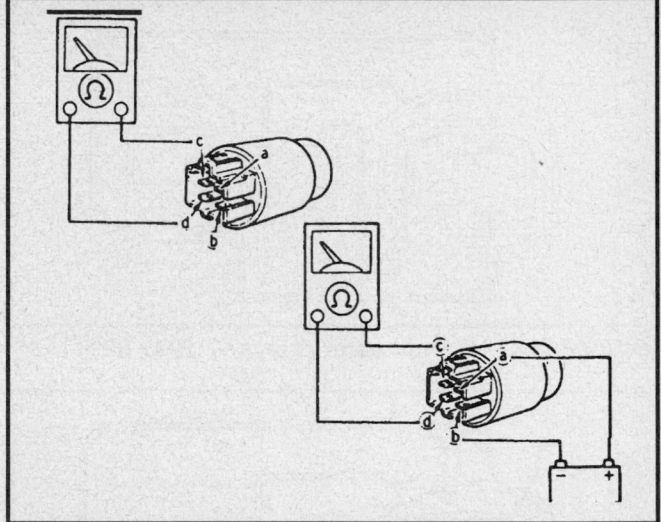

Testing condenser fan relay — 323, Protege and Miata

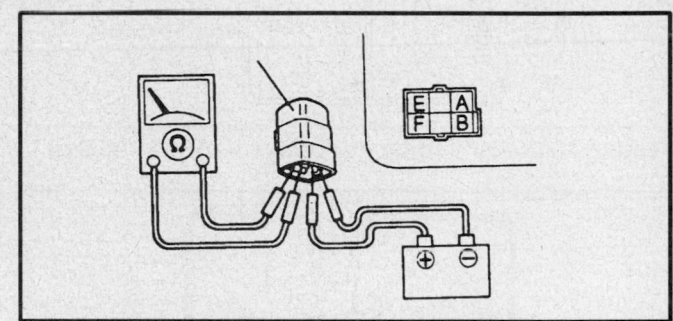

Testing air conditioning relay, Blower relay and MAX–HI relay — Millenia

Testing air conditioning relay, condenser fan relay No. 2 and No. 3 — Millenia

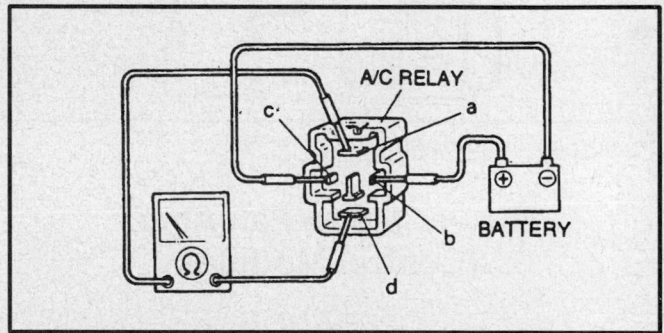

Testing air conditioning relay — 1993 929

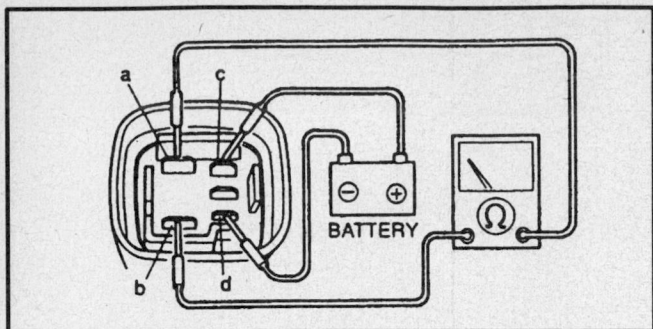

Testing MAX−HI and heater relays — 1993 929

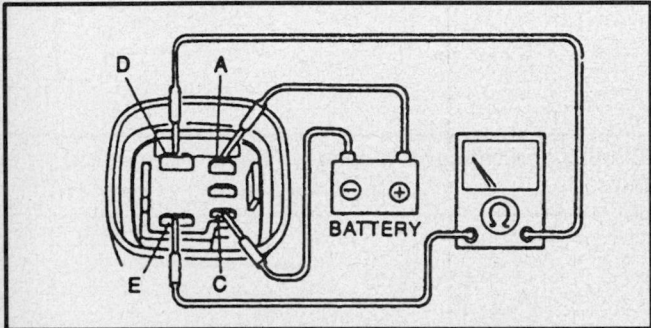

Testing MAX−HI and heater relays — 1994−95 929

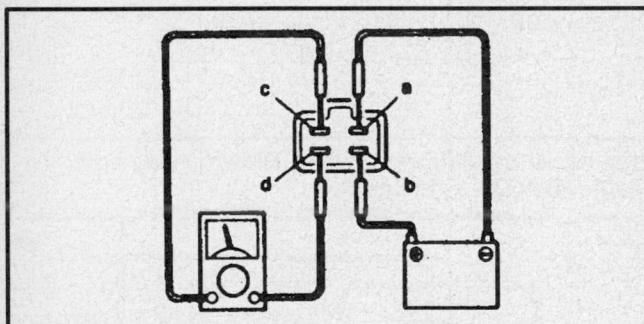

Testing air conditioning relay — RX−7

Blower Motor Fan Amp (Control Module)

OPERATION

1993 RX−7

The blower motor fan amp or control module is located on the electronic control head assembly. The main function of the fan amp is to electronically regulate voltage signals to the blower motor.

TESTING

1993 RX−7

Checking the fan amp:

1. Turn the ignition switch **ON**.
2. Turn the air conditioner switch **ON**.

3. Measure the voltage at the terminal wires of the fan amp.

4. If not as specified, replace the fan amp.

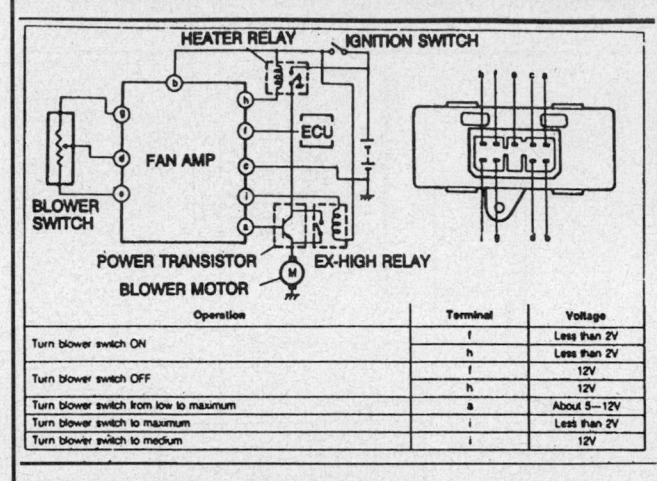

Operation	Terminal	Voltage
Turn blower switch ON	f	Less than 2V
	h	Less than 2V
Turn blower switch OFF	f	12V
	h	12V
Turn blower switch from low to maximum	a	About 5−12V
Turn blower switch to maximum	i	Less than 2V
Turn blower switch to medium	i	12V

Fan amp testing — 1993 RX−7

Sensors

OPERATION

929 with Automatic A/C

The 929 incorporates a passenger compartment, ambient air, duct and sun sensor into the electronic temperature control system. The temperature sensitive conductor inputs a signal to the air conditioner control unit which in turn adjusts the vehicle inside comfort zone. The sensors are located on the dash, at the ducts and at the receiver/drier.

Millenia

The Millenia incorporates a passenger compartment and an ambient air system into the electronic control system. Signals from the sensors signal the air conditioner control unit to adjust the vehicle temperature inside compartment area. The ambient sensor is located at the front of the vehicle above the front bumper attached to the radiator brace. The passenger compartment temperature sensor is located under the right side of the dash next to the blower motor inside the sensor cover. The solar radiation sensor is located on the upper right side of the dash above the airbag module.

TESTING

929 with Automatic A/C

PASSENGER COMPARTMENT SENSOR, AMBIENT AIR SENSOR AND EVAPORATOR/DUCT SENSOR

1. Disconnect the negative battery terminal.
2. Disconnect the sensor wire connector.
3. Measure the resistance between the 2 terminals.
4. If the sensors resistance is not 2.9−3.1 Kilo-ohms at 77°F (25°C), replace the sensor.

SUN SENSOR

1. Disconnect the negative battery terminal.
2. Disconnect the sensors wire connector.

3. Measure the resistance between the terminals, with the positive lead on terminal **1** and ground on terminal **2** there should be 10 kilo-ohms–infinity .

4. Measure the resistance between the terminals, with the positive lead on terminal **2** and ground on terminal **1** there should be 0–199 ohms.

5. Set the tester at the 3 milli–amp range.

6. Hold an incandescent lamp of 60W, 5.9 inches from the sensor.

7. Measure the current.

8. If less than 0.2 milli–amp, replace the sensor.

9. If a Code **02** was indicated during self–diagnosis, check for open/short circuit. If okay, replace the sensor.

SOLAR RADIATION SENSOR

1. Disconect the negative battery terminal.

2. Remove the solar radiation sensor.

3. Shine an incandescent light (60W) on the sensor from a distance of approximately 3.9 in. (10cm).

4. Connect a positive lead to terminal **A** and negative lead to terminal **B** of the sensor connector.

5. If the output voltage is not above 0.45 volts, replace the sensor.

Millenia with Automatic A/C

AMBIENT AIR TEMPERATURE SENSOR

1. Disconnect the negative battery terminal.

2. Disconnect the sensor wire connector.

3. Measure the temperature around the ambient temperature sensor.

4. Measure the resistance between terminals **A** and **B** of the sensor. Resistance should be 13 kilo–ohms at 122°F (50°C).

5. If not as specified, replace the sensor.

PASSENGER COMPARTMENT TEMPERATURE SENSOR

1. Disconnect the negative battery terminal.

2. Disconnect the sensor wire connector.

3. Remove the sensor.

4. Measure the resistance between terminals **A** and **B** of the sensor. Resistance should be 7 kilo–ohms at 122°F (50°C).

5. If not as specified, replace the sensor.

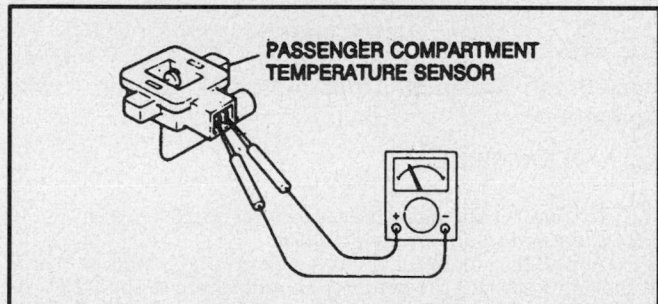

Passenger compartment temperature sensor testing — 929

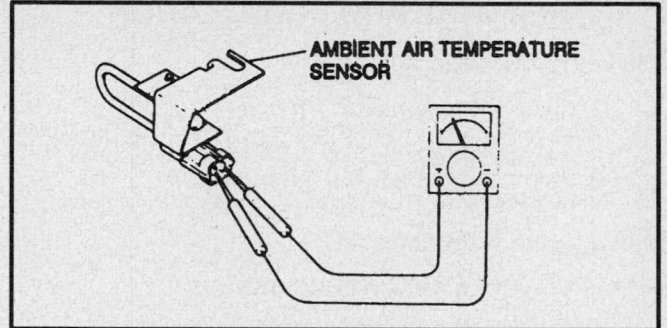

Ambient air temperature sensor testing — 929

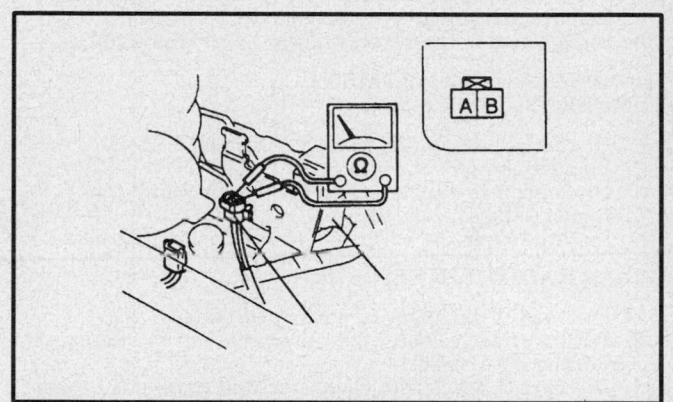

Ambient air temperature sensor — Millenia

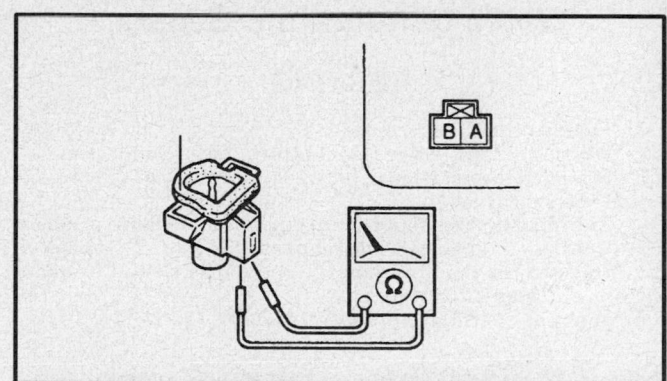

Passenger compartment temperature sensor — Millenia

REMOVAL AND INSTALLATION

929 with Automatic A/C

1. Disconnect negative battery terminal.
2. Locate sensor and disconnect wire connector. The sensor can be gently pried from the top of the instrument panel.
3. Remove attaching bolt and remove sensor.
4. Installation is the reverse of the removal procedure.

Millenia with Automatic A/C

AMBIENT AIR TEMPERATURE SENSOR

1. Disconnect the negative battery terminal.
2. Remove the radiator grille.
3. Locate the sensor and disconnect the wire connector.
4. Remove attaching bolt, and remove the sensor.
5. Installation is the reverse of the removal procedure.

PASSENGER COMPARTMENT TEMPERATURE SENSOR

1. Disconnect the negative battery terminal.
2. Remove the sensor cover.
3. Disconnect the air hose and the sensor connector.
4. Remove the sensor.
5. Installation is the reverse of the removal procedure.

SOLAR RADIATION SENSOR

1. Disconnect the negative battery terminal.
2. With a protected screwdriver, pry the solar radiation sensor from the dashboard.
3. Disconnect the sensor connector, and remove the sensor
4. Installation is the reverse of the removal procedure.

Water Temperature Sensor

TESTING

1. Remove the center console.
2. Disconnect the water temperature sensor connector
3. Measure the resistance between terminals of the connector on the sensor side.
4. The resistance should be about 5.0 kilo–ohms at about 110°F (43°C) or about 13 kilo–ohms at 60°F (2°C), except on the Millenia. On the Millenia, the resistance should be about 35 kilo–ohms at 122°F (50°C).
5. If not as specified, replace the sensor.

Ambient Temperature Switch (Solar Type)

TESTING

Millenia

1. Disconnect the negative battery terminal.
2. Remove the trunk end trim and the trunk left side trim.
3. Disconnect the switch connector.
4. Check for continuity between terminals **A** and **B** of the switch.
5. If at less than 36°F (2°C) there is continuity, replace the switch.
6. If at more than 67°F (19.5°C) there is no continuity, replace the switch.

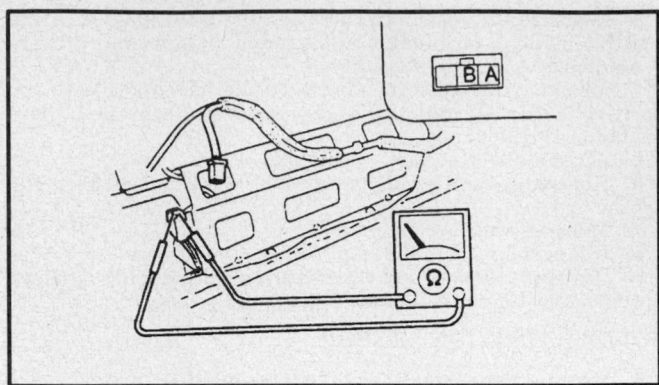

Ambient temperature switch (solar type) testing — Millenia

REMOVAL AND INSTALLATION

Millenia

1. Disconnect the negative battery terminal.
2. Remove the trunk end trim, left trunk side trim and the rear under cover.
3. Disconnect the switch connector.
4. Dis–engage the grommet from the switch connector.
5. Remove the screw attaching the switch, and remove the switch.
6. Installation is the reverse of the removal procedure.

Actuators

OPERATION

When the mode switch on the control head panel is depressed, an output signal corresponding to the depressed switch is issued to the mode actuator. The mode actuator, which then shifts to the selected position, performs opening and closing of the mode door and stops in the specified position.

TESTING

Rec–Fresh Selector Door Actuator or Air Intake Actuator

323 AND PROTEGE

1. Disconnect the negative battery terminal.
2. Remove the air intake actuator.
3. Apply 12 volts to terminal **A** and ground terminal **G** or **K** of the actuator, and the actuator should rotate to the **REC** and **FRESH** positions.
4. If not as specified, replace the actuator.

1993 626 AND MX–6

1. Disconnect the negative battery terminal.
2. Remove the glove box and the undercover.
3. Disconnect the **REC–FRESH** selector door actuator wire connector.
4. Apply 12 volts, the positive lead to terminal **e** and ground terminal **f** and the motor should rotate to the **REC** position.

5. Apply 12 volts, the positive lead to terminal **f** and ground terminal **e**. The motor should rotate to the **FRESH** position.

6. If not as specified, replace the actuator.

1994–95 626 AND MX–6

1. Disconnect the negative battery terminal.
2. Disconnect the air intake actuator connector.
3. Connect battery positive voltage to terminal **A** and ground terminal **B**, and the actuator should rotate to **REC** position.
4. Connect battery positive voltage to terminal **A** and ground terminal **C**, and the actuator should rotate to **FRESH** position.
5. If not as specified, replace the actuator.

MX–3

1. Disconnect the negative battery terminal.
2. Disconnect the air intake actuator connector.
3. Apply 12 volts, with the positive lead connected to terminal **D** and ground terminal **C**, and the actuator should rotate to the **FRESH** position.
4. Apply 12 volts, with the positive lead connected to terminal **D** and ground terminal **A**, and the actuator should rotate to the **REC** position.
5. If not as specified, replace the actuator.

929

1. Locate the intake (fresh/recirc) actuator on the side of the blower housing. If necessary, remove the glove box and surrounding components for access.
2. Detach the intake actuator connector and apply positive battery voltage to terminal **a** and negative battery voltage to terminal **f**.
3. When the intake door is in the **FRESH** position, there should be continuity between terminals **e** and **d** and between terminals **d** and **c**.
4. When the intake door is in the **RECIR** position, there should be continuity between terminals **e** and **b** and between terminals **b** and **c**.
5. When the intake door is at 1/3 **FRESH** position, there should be continuity between terminals **e** and **b** and between terminals **b** and **d**.
6. If continuity is as specified, but operation is not normal, check the harness wiring for continuity.

MILLENIA

1. Disconnect the negative battery terminal.
2. Remove the air intake actuator.
3. Connect battery positive voltage to terminal **J** and ground to terminal **I**, and the actuator should rotate to 1/3 **FRESH** and to **RECIRULATE** positions.
4. Connect battery positive voltage to terminal **I** and ground to terminal **J**, and the actuator should rotate to 1/3 **FRESH** and to **FRESH** positions.
5. If not as specified, replace the actuator.

1993 RX–7

1. Disconnect the negative battery terminal.
2. Remove the blower unit.
3. Disconnect the **REC–FRESH** door select actuator wire connector.

4. Apply 12 volts, the positive lead to terminal **b** and ground terminal **a** and the motor should rotate.
5. If not as specified, replace the actuator.

1994–95 RX–7

1. Disconnect the negative battery terminal.
2. Remove the blower unit, if necessary for access.
3. Disconnect the air intake actuator connector.
4. Apply battery positive voltage to terminal **A** and connect terminal **B** or **C** to ground. Check air intake actuator operation.
5. If not as specified, replace the air intake actuator.

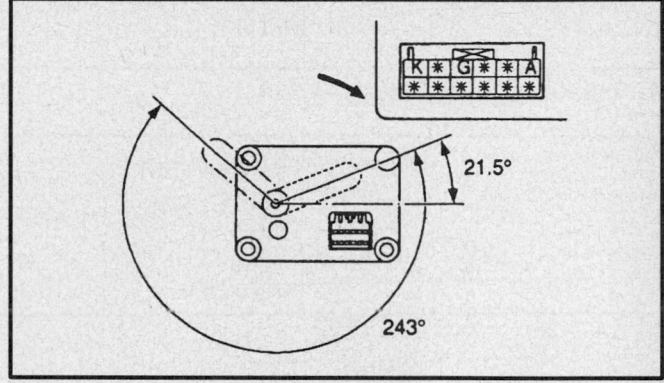

REC–FRESH actuator door testing — 323 and Protege

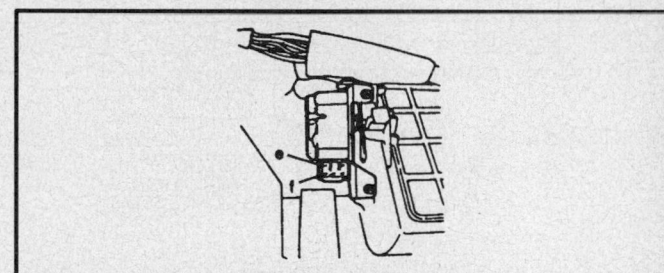

REC – FRESH actuator door testing — 1993 626 and MX–6

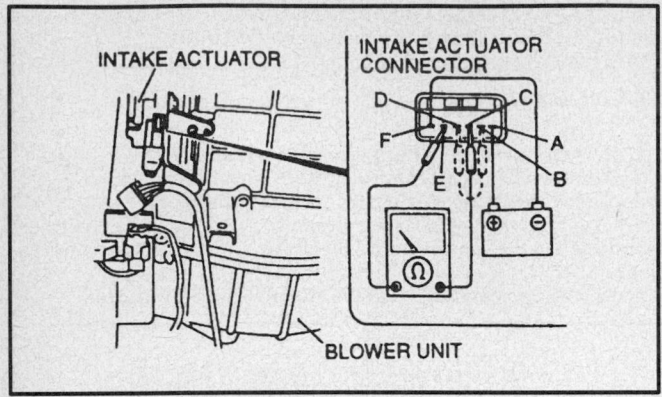

Air intake actuator testing — 929

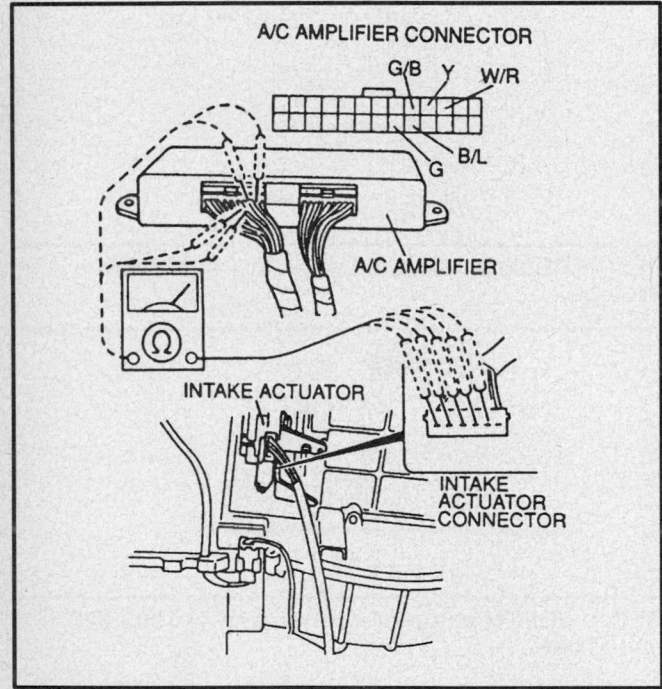

Air intake actuator wiring continuity testing — 929

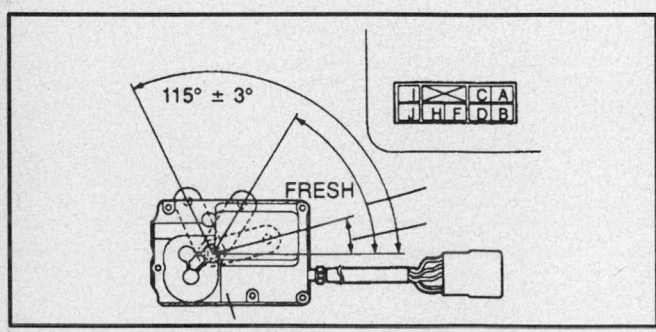

Air intake actuator testing — Millenia

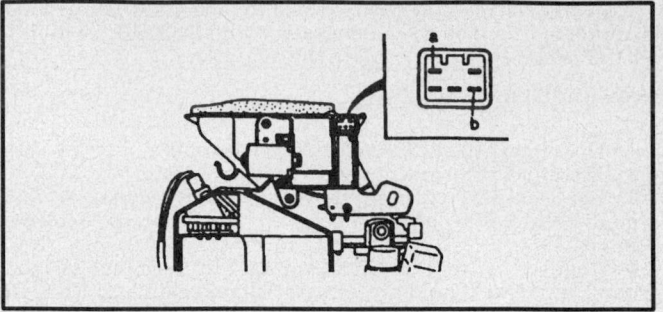

REC—FRESH actuator door testing — 1993 RX-7

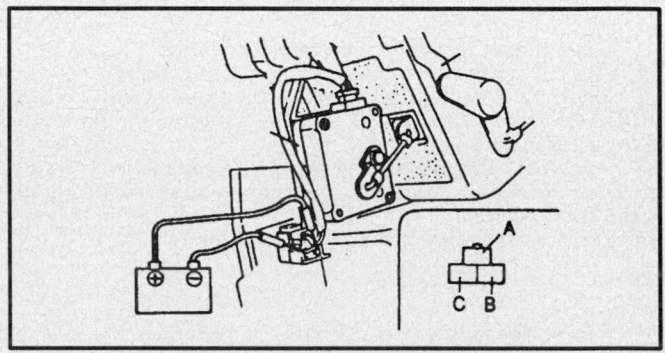

Air intake actuator testing — 1994-95 RX-7

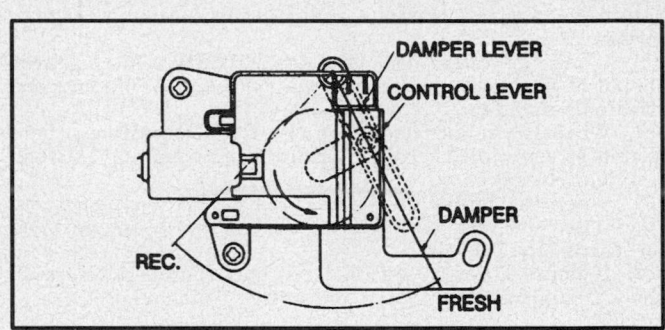

REC—FRESH actuator door action — 1993 RX-7

Airflow Mode Door Actuator

626 AND MX-6

1. Disconnect the airflow mode actuator connector.
2. Connect battery voltage to terminals **i** and **j** and the actuator should move from **VENT** to **DEFROST** position.
3. When battery connections are reversed, the motor should move in the opposite direction.
4. If not as specified, check the connections, wiring and ground circuit. If these are okay, replace the airflow mode actuator.

929

1. Remove the instrument panel.

2. Apply battery voltage to terminals **f** and **e**, with positive cable on terminal **f**. The actuator should move counterclockwise as the door moves from **DEFROST** to **VENT** position.

3. Reverse the battery leads and the door should move in the opposite direction.

MX–3

1. Disconnect the negative battery terminal.
2. Remove the coolant unit.
3. Disconnect the airflow mode door actuator connector.
4. Apply 12 volts, with the positive lead connected to terminal **L** and ground terminal **J**, and the actuator should rotate to the **DEF** position.
5. Apply 12 volts, with the positive lead connected to terminal **J** and ground terminal **L**, and the actuator should rotate to **VENT** position.
6. If not as specified, replace actuator.

MILLENIA

1. Disconnect the negative battery terminal.
2. Disconnect the actuator wire connector, and remove the actuator.
3. Connect battery positive voltage to terminal **G** and ground to terminal **H**, and the actuator should rotate to the **DEFROSTER** position.
4. Connect battery positive voltage to terminal **H** and ground to terminal **G**, and the actuator should rotate to the **VENT** position.
5. If not as specified, replace the actuator.

1993 RX–7

1. Disconnect the negative battery terminal.
2. Remove the instrument panel.
3. Disconnect the actuator wire connector.
4. Apply 12 volts, the positive lead to terminal **P** and ground terminal **Q** and the motor should rotate to the **DEF** position.
5. Apply 12 volts, the positive lead to terminal **Q** and ground terminal **P** and the motor should rotate to the **VENT** position.
6. If not as specified, replace the actuator.

1994–95 RX–7

1. Disconnect the negative battery terminal
2. Remove the instrument panel.
3. Disconnect the actuator wire connector.
4. Apply battery positive voltage to terminal **J** and connect terminal **K** to ground. Verify that the airflow mode door actuator operates **VENT** to **DEF** positions.
5. Check for continuity between the terminals of the actuator.
6. If not as specified, replace the airflow mode door actuator.

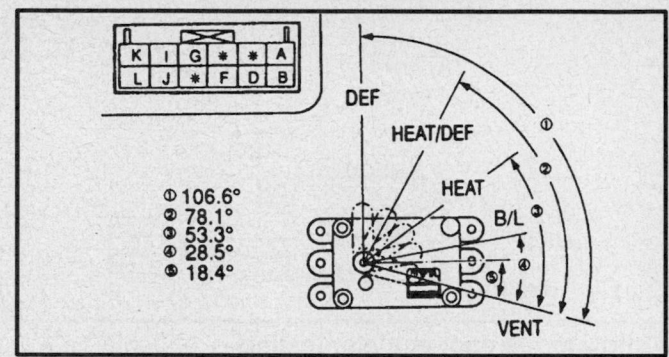

Airflow mode control door actuator testing — 323 and Protege

Terminal / Mode	K	I	G	D	F	J	L
VENT			O—	—O	O—	—O	—O
BI–LEVEL	O—	—O			O—	—O	—O
HEAT	O—	—O			O—	—O	—O
HEAT/DEF	O—	—O	O—	—O		O—	—O
DEFROSTER	O—	—O	O—	—O	—O		

O——O: Continuity

Airflow mode control door actuator continuity testing — 323 and Protege

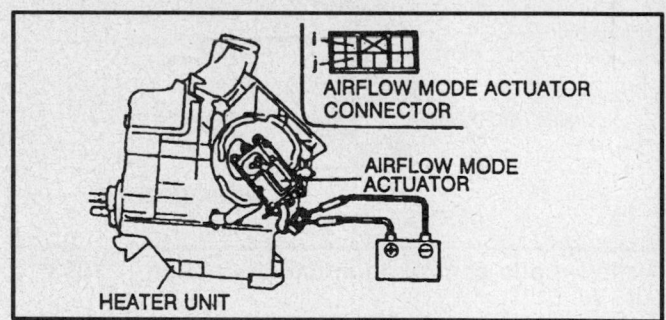

Airflow mode door actuator testing — 626 and MX–6

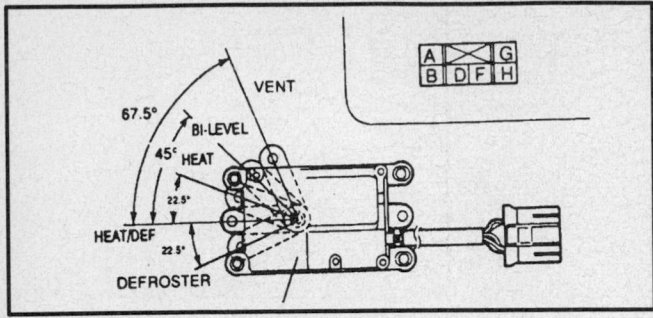

Airflow mode door actuator testing — Millenia

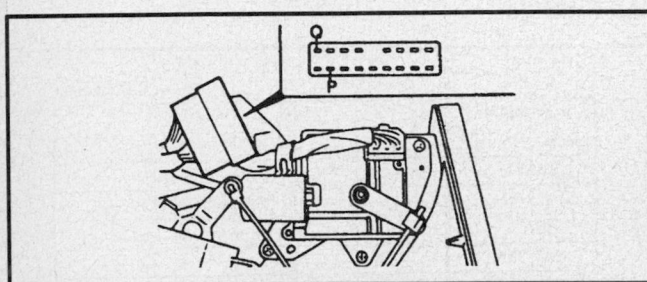

Airflow mode control door actuator testing — 1993 RX–7

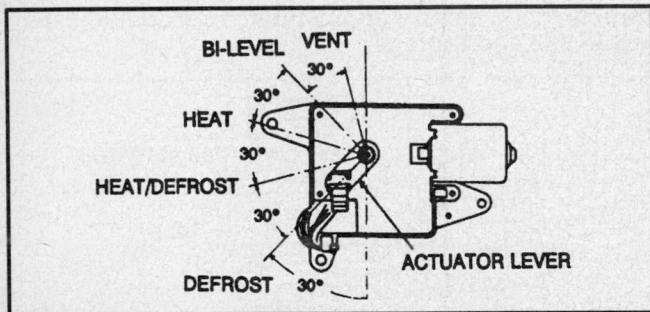

Airflow mode control door actuator action — 1993 RX–7

Temperature Control Door Actuator or Air Mix Actuator

323 AND PROTEGE

1. Disconnect the negative battery terminal.
2. Remove the airflow mode door actuator.
3. Apply 12 volts to terminal **B** or **A** and ground terminal **A** or **B** of the actuator, and the actuator should rotate to **DEF** and **VENT**.
4. Check for continuity between the terminals of the actuator as specified.
5. If not as specified, replace the actuator.

626 AND MX–6

1. With the mix actuator (on the side of the heater unit) disconnected, connect battery positive voltage to terminal **g** and the battery ground to the connector terminal **h**.

2. Measure resistance between terminals **a** and **b**. At full **COLD** position, the resistance should be 0.8 kilo–ohms.
3. Reverse the battery connections on terminals **h** and **g** and measure resistance between terminals **b** and **d**. The resistance should be 5.5 kilo–ohms when the door is at full **HEAT** position (actuator moves clockwise).

929

1. Remove the instrument panel to access the temperature (mix) actuator located on the lower right side of the heater housing.
2. If the rear air duct is interfering, remove it, remove it.
3. With the mix actuator disconnected, connect battery positive voltage to terminal **h** and the battery ground to the connector terminal **g**. The door should move from **HOT** to **COLD** position (actuator moves counterclockwise).
4. Measure resistance between terminals **a** and **b**. At **FULL COLD** position, the resistance should be 1.0 kilo–ohms.
5. Reverse the battery connections on terminals **h** and **g** and measure resistance between terminals **b** and **d**. The resistance should be 5.5 kilo–ohms at **FULL COLD** position.

MILLENIA

1. Disconnect the negative battery terminal.
2. Disconnect the actuator.
3. Remove the actuator.
4. Connect battery positive voltage to terminal **F** and ground to terminal **E**, and the actuator should rotate to the **COLD** position.
5. Connect battery positive voltage to terminal **E** and ground to terminal **F**, and the actuator should rotate to the **HOT** position.
6. If not as specified, replace the actuator.

1993 RX–7

1. Disconnect the negative battery terminal.
2. Remove the instrument panel.
3. Disconnect the actuator wire connector.
4. Apply 12 volts, the positive lead to terminal **d** and ground terminal **e** and the motor should rotate to the **HOT** position.
5. Apply 12 volts, the positive lead to terminal **e** and ground terminal **d** and the motor should rotate to the **COLD** position.
6. If not as specified, replace the actuator.

1994–95 RX–7

1. Disconnect the negative battery terminal.
2. Remove the instrument panel.
3. Disconnect the actuator wire connector.
4. Connect battery positive voltage between terminals **G** and **H**. Verify that the air mix actuator door operates, and the resistance of the potentiometer is as specified.
5. If not as specified, replace the air mix door actuator.

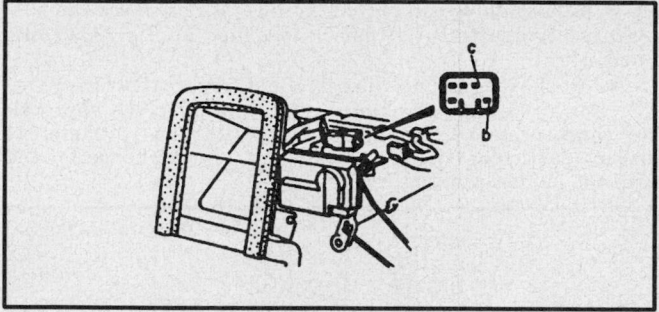

Temperature blend door actuator testing — 626 and MX-6

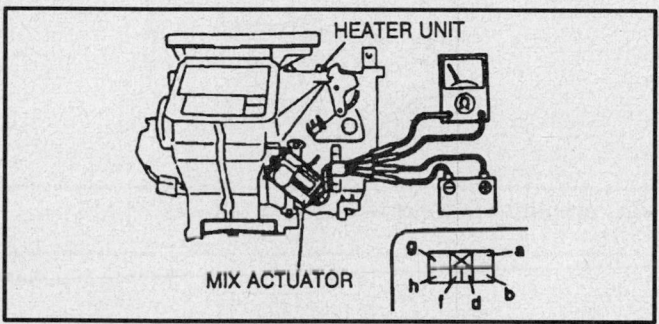

Temperature blend (mix) actuator testing — 1993 626 and MX-6

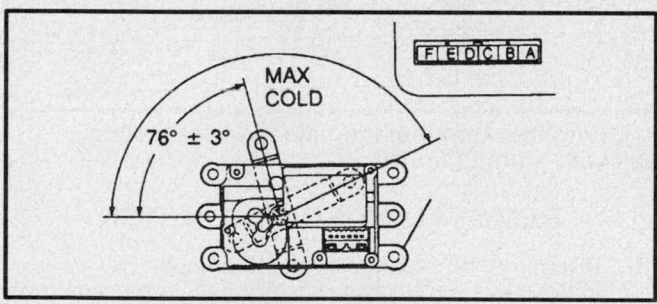

Air mix actuator testing — Millenia

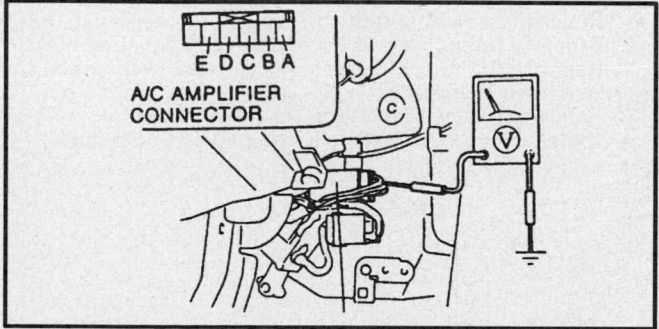

Temperature blend door actuator testing — 1993 RX-7

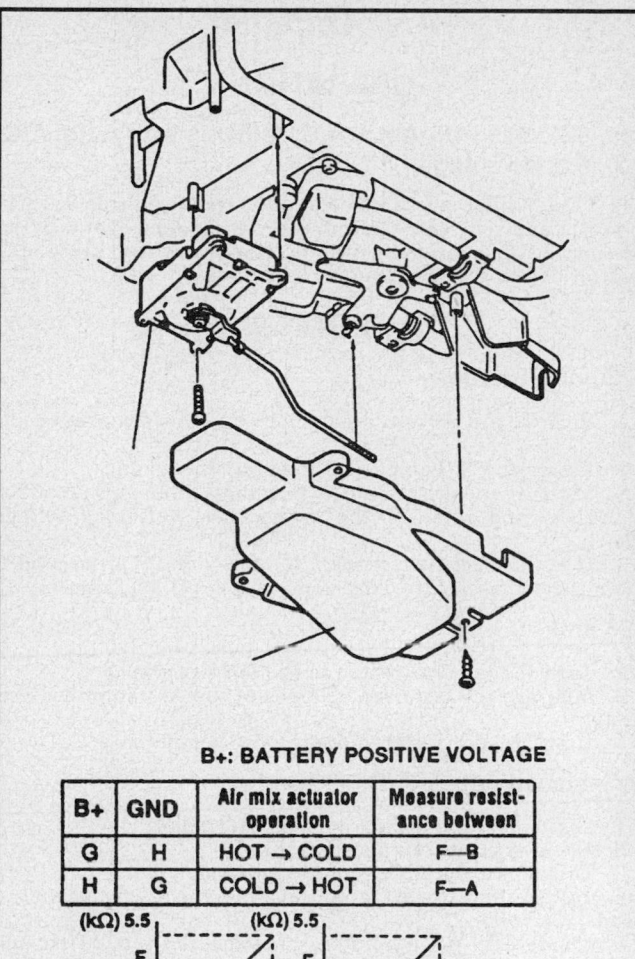

B+: BATTERY POSITIVE VOLTAGE

B+	GND	Air mix actuator operation	Measure resistance between
G	H	HOT → COLD	F—B
H	G	COLD → HOT	F—A

Air mix actuator testing — 1994–95 RX-7

REMOVAL AND INSTALLATION

1. Disconnect negative battery terminal.
2. Locate the actuator.
3. Remove the instrument panel, heater unit, rear console, or glove box and cover, if required.
4. Disconnect the actuator wire connector.
5. Remove actuator attaching screws.
6. Remove the actuator.
7. Installation is the reverse of the removal procedure.

A/C Amplifier

OPERATION

323, 626, 929 with Auto. A/C, Millenia with Auto. A/C, MX−6 and Protege

The A/C amplifier is located behind the center console and acts to accept and send signals from the various components of the automatic air conditioning system. It is the central processing unit for defining proper system operation.

TESTING

323 and Protege

1. Remove the glove compartment and glove compartment cover.
2. Locate the A/C amplifier, and start the engine.
3. Measure the voltage at the terminals of the A/C amplifier connector, and refer to the appropriate Terminal Voltage Chart.
4. If not as specified, inspect the appropriate areas, and if the inspected areas are okay, replace the A/C amplifier.

626 and MX−6

1. Turn the ignition switch to the **ON** position.
2. Measure the terminal voltages of the A/C amplifier connector.
3. If not as specified, replace the A/C amplifier.

Millenia with Auto. A/C

1. Disconnect the negative battery terminal.
2. Remove the electronic control head.
3. Disconnect the A/C amplifier connector.
4. Disassemble the A/C amplifier from the electronic control head.
5. Connect the A/C amplifier connectors (26–pin, 23–pin and 20–pin) and information display connector.
6. Start engine.
7. Measure the voltage at the terminals of the A/C amplifier connector, and refer to the appropriate Terminal Voltage Chart.
8. If not as specified, replace the A/C amplifier.

929 with Auto. A/C

POWER SYSTEM INSPECTION

1. Remove the center console and the switch panel, and access the back of the A/C amplifier.
2. Turn the ignition switch **ON** and measure the voltage at the indicated wiring terminals and take specified action:
   • **LG/R**: should read battery voltage; if not, check 15A A/C fuse and/or repair the wiring.

• **L/R**: should read battery voltage; if not, check the passenger compartment ("room") 15A fuse and/or repair the wiring.
   • **B**: should read no voltage; if not, repair the wiring.
3. For a complete check of the A/C amplifier, the appropriate chart provided should be used with the voltmeter to inspect particular circuits. These test should be performed with the engine running.

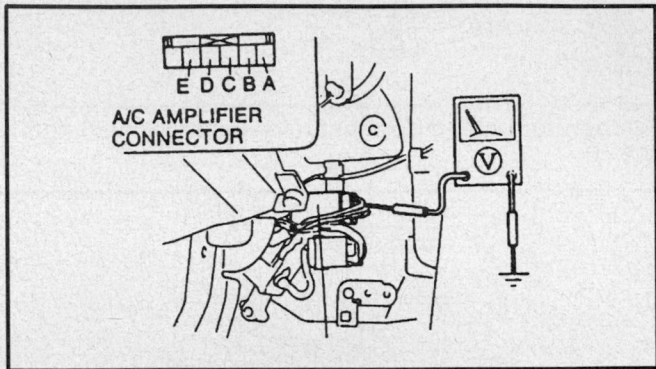

A/C amplifier testing — 626 and MX−6

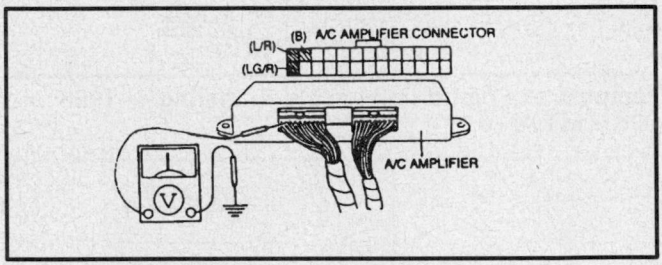

A/C amplifier terminal identification for testing — 929 with automatic A/C

REMOVAL AND INSTALLATION

1. Disconnect the negative battery terminal.
2. Remove the glove compartment, under cover, side cover and sidewall.
3. Disconnect the A/C amplifier.
4. Properly discharge the air conditioning system.
5. Remove the cooling unit.
6. Seperate the upper and lower case of the cooling unit.
7. Remove the thermosensor probe, and disconnect the thermo–switch connector.
8. Remove the A/C amplifier from the cooling unit.
9. Installation is the reverse of the removal procedure.

A/C AMPLIFIER TERMINAL VOLTAGE REFERENCE CHART — 323 AND PROTEGE

B+: Battery positive voltage

```
F E D C B A
```

Terminal	Signal name	Connection	Test condition	Voltage (V)	Inspection area
A	IG2	A/C 10 A fuse	Ignition switch at ON	B+	• Continuity [Fuse—A/C amplifier: A/C 10 A—A]
			Ignition switch at LOCK, ACC, START	0	• A/C 10 A fuse
B	A/C signal	Refrigerant pressure switch	Magnetic clutch on	0.6	• Continuity [PCM—Refrigerant pressure switch: 1K—B, Refrigerant pressure switch—A/C amplifier: A—B] • Terminal voltage of A/C amplifier (C) • Refrigerant pressure switch
			Magnetic clutch off	B+	• PCM
C	A/C switch signal	• A/C switch (wire type) • Heater control unit (logic type)	A/C switch off	B+	Terminal voltage of A/C amplifier (A)
			A/C switch on and fan switch at 1st position	0	(Wire type) • Continuity [A/C amplifier—A/C switch: C—D, Fan switch (B)—GND] • A/C switch • Fan switch
					(Llogic type) • Continuity [A/C amplifier-Heater control unit: C—B, Heater control unit—Fan switch: D—D, Fan switch (B)—Ground] • Heater control unit • Fan switch
D	—	—	—	—	—
E	—	—	—	—	—
F	—	—	—	—	—

A/C AMPLIFIER TERMINAL VOLTAGE REFERENCE CHART
— MILLENIA (1 OF 7)

```
1Y 1W 1U 1S 1Q 1O 1M 1K 1I 1G 1E 1C 1A    2U 2S 2Q 2O 2M 2K 2I 2G 2E 2C 2A    3S 3Q 3O 3M 3K 3I 3G 3E 3C 3A
1Z 1X 1V 1T 1R 1P 1N 1L 1J 1H 1F 1D 1B    2V 2T 2R 2P 2N 2L 2J 2H 2F 2D 2B    3T 3R 3P 3N 3L 3J 3H 3F 3D 3B
```

Terminal	Signal name	Connected	Test condition	Voltage (V)	Inspection area
1A	Potentiometer power source	• Air mix actuator • Airflow mode actuator • Solar radiation sensor	Ignition switch at ACC	5	• Short circuit (A/C amplifier — Air mix actuator: [W] — [Y/R] wire, A/C amplifier — Solar radiation sensor: [W] wire, A/C amplifier — Airflow mode actuator: [W] wire) • Air mix actuator • Airflow mode actuator • Terminal voltage of A/C amplifier connector (1C, 1Z, 2S)
			Ignition switch at OFF	0	
1B	Serial communication	Information display	—	—	Refer to "Serial communication system inspection"
1C	Ground	Ground	Any	0	Continuity (A/C amplifier — Ground: [W/B] — [L/Y] wire)
1D	Battery	• ROOM 15 A fuse • Information display	Any	B+	• Short circuit (ROOM 15 A fuse — A/C amplifier, Information display: [L/R] wire) • Continuity (ROOM 15 A fuse — A/C amplifier: [L/R] wire) • ROOM 15 A fuse
1E	Vehicle speed signal	Speedometer	Raise front wheels and rotate front wheels by hand	Meter needle make a rotate move between 0 V and 5 V	• Continuity or short circuit (Speedometer — A/C amplifier; [G/R] wire) • Speedometer
1F	—	—	—	—	—
1G	TNS signal	• Panel light control switch • Information display	Light switch on and panel light control switch at max. illumination	0.4	• Short circuit (A/C amplifier — Panel light control switch, Information display: [W/V] wire) • Continuity (A/C amplifier — Panel light control switch: [W/V] wire) • Panel light control switch • Heater control unit • Terminal voltage of A/C amplifier connector (2A) • Terminal voltage of information display connector (3C)
			Light switch on and panel light control switch at min. illumination	11.5	
			Light switch off	0	
1H	—	—	—	—	—

A/C AMPLIFIER TERMINAL VOLTAGE REFERENCE CHART — MILLENIA (2 OF 7)

Terminal	Signal name	Connected	Test condition	Voltage (V)	Inspection area
1I	Serial communication	Information display	—	—	Refer to "Serial communication system inspection"
1J	Electrical load idle-up signal	ECM	Fan speed 1st/2nd	B+	• Terminal voltage of A/C amplifier connector (3H, 3O) • Continuity or short circuit (ECM — A/C amplifier: [V] wire) • ECM
			Fan speed 3rd/4th	0	
1K	Blower relay control signal	Blower relay	Fan switch on	0.2	• Continuity or short circuit (Blower relay — A/C amplifier: [B/Y] wire, BLOWER 15 A fuse — Blower relay: [R/W] wire) • Blower relay
			Fan switch off	B+	• Terminal voltage of A/C amplifier connector (3H) • BLOWER 15 A fuse
1L	Recirculate signal	Air intake actuator	RECIRCULATE or operating	0	Terminal voltage of A/C amplifier connector (1R)
			FRESH or 1/3 FRESH	5	
1M	1/3 FRESH signal	Air intake actuator	1/3 FRESH or operating	0	Terminal voltage of A/C amplifier connector (1R)
			FRESH or RECIRCULATE	5	
1N	Fresh signal	Air intake actuator	RECIRCULATE or 1/3 FRESH	5	Terminal voltage of A/C amplifier connector (1R)
			FRESH or operating	0	
1O	Fan speed control signal	Power transistor	Fan switch off	0	• Continuity (A/C amplifier — Power transistor: [L/R] wire, A/C amplifier — Power transistor, MAX–HI relay, Blower motor: [L/W] wire, Blower relay — Blower motor: [L/R] — [L] — [L/R] wire, HEATER 40 A fuse — Blower relay : [L] wire, Power transistor, MAX–HI relay — Ground: [B] wire) • Short circuit (A/C amplifier — Power transistor: [L/R] wire, A/C amplifier — Power transistor, MAX–HI relay, Blower motor: [L/W] wire, Blower relay — Blower motor: [L/R] — [L] — [L/R] wire, HEATER 40 A fuse — Blower relay: [L] wire) • Power transistor • Blower motor • HEATER 40 A fuse • Terminal voltage of A/C amplifier connector (1K, 2U)
			Fan switch at 1st position	1.3	
			Fan switch at 2nd position	1.4	
			Fan switch at 3rd position	1.6	
			Fan switch at 4th position	0.6	
1P	—	—	—	—	—
1Q	Blower motor feedback signal	• Power transistor • MAX–HI relay • Blower motor	Fan switch off	6.1	Terminal voltage of A/C amplifier connector (1O)
			Fan switch at 1st position	9.5	
			Fan switch at 2nd position	6.1	
			Fan switch at 3rd position	3.2	
			Fan switch at 4th position	0.2	

A/C AMPLIFIER TERMINAL VOLTAGE REFERENCE CHART — MILLENIA (3 OF 7)

Terminal	Signal name	Connected	Test condition	Voltage (V)	Inspection area
1R	Common power source	Air intake actuator	Moving to RECIRCULATE	0	• Continuity or short circuit (A/C amplifier — air intake actuator: [L/O], [L/Y], [L/R] — [R], [L], [W/L] — [LG/R], [LG/R] — [LG/B], [BR] wire) • Air intake actuator • Terminal voltage of A/C amplifier connector (3H)
			Moving to FRESH & stopped	5	
1S	Motor drive signal	Airflow mode actuator	Moving to VENT	B+	Terminal voltage of A/C amplifier connector (2N)
			Moving to DEFROSTER	0.6	
			30 seconds after stopped	0	
1T	Common power source	Air intake actuator	Moving to FRESH	0	Terminal voltage of A/C amplifier connector (1R)
			Moving to RECIRCULATE & stopped	5	
1U	Motor drive signal	Airflow mode actuator	Moving to VENT	0.6	Terminal voltage of A/C amplifier connector (2N)
			Moving to DEFROSTER	B+	
			30 seconds after stopped	0	
1V	Motor drive signal	Air mix actuator	Moving to HOT	B+	Terminal voltage of A/C amplifier connector (2K)
			Moving to COLD	0.6	
			30 seconds after stopped	0	
1W	Motor drive signal	Air intake actuator	Stopped	0.6	Terminal voltage of A/C amplifier connector (1R)
			Moving to RECIRCULATE	B+	
			Moving to FRESH	0.8	
1X	Motor drive signal	Air mix actuator	Moving to HOT	0.6	Terminal voltage of A/C amplifier connector (2K)
			Moving to COLD	B+	
			30 seconds after stopped	0	
1Y	Motor drive signal	Air intake actuator	Stopped	0.6	Terminal voltage of A/C amplifier connector (1R)
			Moving to RECIRCULATE	0.8	
			Moving to FRESH	B+	
1Z	ACC	• Information display • RADIO 10 A fuse	Ignition switch at ACC	B+	• Continuity (RADIO 10 A fuse — A/C amplifier: [P/G] wire) • Short circuit (RADIO 10 A fuse — A/C amplifier, information display: [P/G] wire) • RADIO 10 A fuse
			Ignition switch at OFF	0	
2A	TNS signal	TNS relay	Light switch on	B+	• Continuity or short circuit (TNS relay — A/C amplifier: [R] wire) • TNS relay
			Light switch off	0	
2B	—	—	—	—	—

A/C AMPLIFIER TERMINAL VOLTAGE REFERENCE CHART
— MILLENIA (4 OF 7)

Terminal	Signal name	Connected	Test condition	Voltage (V)	Inspection area
2C	Ground	• Airflow mode actuator • Air mix actuator • Ambient temperature sensor • Passenger compartment temperature sensor • Water temperature sensor • Solar radiation sensor • Evaporator temperature sensor	Any	0	Terminal voltage of A/C amplifier connector (1C)
2D	On-board diagnosis signal	Data link connector TAC terminal	Ignition switch at ACC	11.6	• Short circuit (A/C amplifier — Data link connector; [BR/W] — [BR/Y] wire) • Terminal voltage of A/C amplifier connector (1Z)
			Ignition switch at OFF	0	
2E	Ambient temperature switch signal	Information display	AMB switch hold on	0	• Continuity (A/C amplifier — Information display: [W/B], [G] wires) • Short circuit (A/C amplifier — Information display: [W/B] wire) • Terminal voltage of A/C amplifier connector (1C, 1Z, 2S) • Information display
			AMB switch off	3.6	
2F	—	—	—	—	—
2G	Serial communication	Information display	—	—	Refer to "Serial communication system inspection"
2H	On-board diagnosis signal	Data link connector FAC terminal	• Connect the **SST** (NGS) • Block the light to solar radiation sensor		• Continuity or short circuit (A/C amplifier — Data link connector: [O/B] — [BR/W] wire) • **SST** (NGS) • Terminal voltage of A/C amplifier connector (1C, 1Z, 2S)
2I	A/C signal	Refrigerant pressure switch	Magnetic clutch on	3.1—3.7 or below 1.5	• Continuity or short circuit (A/C amplifier — Refrigerant pressure switch ; [G/B] wire, Refrigerant pressure switch — ECM; [G] wire) • Terminal voltage of A/C amplifier connector (1C, 1Z, 2S) • Refrigerant pressure switch • ECM
			Magnetic clutch off	5	
2J	Serial communication	Information display	—	—	Refer to "Serial communication system inspection"
2K	Potentiometer signal	Air mix actuator	Set temperature at 18.0 °C {65 °F}	0.7	• Continuity (Air mix actuator — A/C amplifier: [G/B], [G/Y], [G], [Y/R] — [W], [G/Ω] wires) • Short circuit (Air mix actuator — A/C amplifier: [G/B], [G/Y], [G] wires) • Terminal voltage of A/C amplifier connector (1A, 3R, 3S, 3T)
			Set temperature at 32.0 °C {90 °F}	4.3	

A/C AMPLIFIER TERMINAL VOLTAGE REFERENCE CHART
— MILLENIA (5 OF 7)

Terminal	Signal name	Connected	Test condition	Voltage (V)	Inspection area
2L	—	—	—	—	—
2M	Evaporator temperature sensor input signal	Evaporator temperature sensor	Depends on temperature surrounding sensor		• Continuity (A/C amplifier — Evaporator temperature sensor; [R/W], [G/O] wire) • Short circuit (A/C amplifier — Evaporator temperature sensor; [R/W] wire) • Evaporator temperature sensor • Terminal voltage of A/C amplifier connector (1C, 1Z, 2S)
2N	Potentiometer signal	Airflow mode actuator	VENT	4.3	• Continuity (Airflow mode actuator — A/C amplifier: [L], [LG/B], [P], [W], [G/O] wires) • Short circuit (Airflow mode actuator — A/C amplifier: [L], [LG/B], [P] wires) • Terminal voltage of A/C amplifier connector (1A, 3B, 3D, 3O)
			DEFROSTER	0.7	
2O	Ambient temperature sensor input signal	Ambient temperature sensor	Depends on temperature surrounding sensor		• Continuity (A/C amplifier — Ambient temperature sensor: [R/G], [G/O] wires) • Short circuit (A/C amplifier — Ambient temperature sensor: [R/G] wire) • Ambient temperature sensor • Terminal voltage of A/C amplifier connector (1C, 1Z, 2S)
2P	Solar radiation sensor input signal	Solar radiation sensor	Incandescent-light (60 W) shining on solar radiation sensor from distance of approx. 10 cm {3.9 in}	1.7	• Continuity or short circuit (A/C amplifier — Solar radiation sensor; [R/Y], [W] wires) • Terminal voltage of A/C amplifier connector (1A) • Solar radiation sensor
			Light to solar radiation sensor blocked	0.2	
2Q	Passenger compartment temperature sensor input signal	Passenger compartment temperature sensor	Depends on temperature surrounding sensor		• Continuity (A/C amplifier — Passenger compartment temperature sensor; [W/V], [G/O] wires) • Short circuit (A/C amplifier — Passenger compartment temperature sensor; [W/V] wire) • Passenger compartment temperature sensor • Terminal voltage of A/C amplifier connector (1C, 1Z, 2S)
2R	Water temperature sensor input signal	Water temperature sensor	Depends on temperature surrounding sensor		• Continuity (A/C amplifier — Water temperature sensor; [R/B] — [R], [G/O] wires) • Short circuit (A/C amplifier — Water temperature sensor; [R/B] — [R] wire) • Water temperature sensor • Terminal voltage of A/C amplifier connector (1C, 1Z, 2S)

A/C AMPLIFIER TERMINAL VOLTAGE REFERENCE CHART — MILLENIA (6 OF 7)

Terminal	Signal name	Connected	Test condition	Voltage (V)	Inspection area
2S	IG2	• A/C 10 A fuse • Information display	Ignition switch at ON	B+	• Short circuit (A/C 10 A fuse — A/C amplifier: [V] wire, A/C 10A fuse — MAX-HI relay: [V] — [B/W] wire) • Continuity (A/C 10 A fuse — A/C amplifier: [V] wire) • A/C 10 A fuse
			Ignition switch at OFF	0	
2T	REAR WINDOW DEFROSTER relay control signal	REAR WINDOW DEFROSTER relay	REAR WINDOW DEFROSTER switch on	0.2	• Continuity or short circuit (REAR WINDOW DEFROSTER relay — A/C amplifier: [P] wire) • REAR WINDOW DEFROSTER relay • Terminal voltage of A/C amplifier connector (3F)
			REAR WINDOW DEFROSTER switch off	B+	
2U	MAX-HI relay operation signal	MAX-HI relay	Fan switch at 4th position	0.2	• Continuity or short circuit (MAX-HI relay — A/C amplifier: [O] — [L] wire) • MAX-HI relay • Terminal voltage of A/C amplifier connector (3H)
			Fan switch at any position except 4th	B+	
2V	Ground	Information display	Any	0	Terminal voltage of A/C amplifier connector (1C)
3A	Serial communication	Heater control unit	—	—	Refer to "Serial communication system inspection"
3B	DEFROSTER switch and AUTO switch signal	Heater control unit	DEFROSTER switch or AUTO switch hold on	2.3	• Heater control unit • Terminal voltage of A/C amplifier connector (1C, 1Z, 2S)
			DEFROSTER switch and AUTO switch off	0	
3C	Serial communication	Heater control unit	—	—	Refer to "Serial communication system inspection"
3D	MODE switch and OFF switch signal	Heater control unit	MODE switch or OFF switch hold on	2.3	• Heater control unit • Terminal voltage of A/C amplifier connector (1C, 1Z, 2S)
			MODE switch and OFF switch off	0	
3E	AUTO indicator light illumination signal	Heater control unit	AUTO indicator light on	0.1	• Heater control unit • Terminal voltage of A/C amplifier connector (1C, 1Z, 2S)
			AUTO indicator light off	11.6	
3F	REAR WINDOW DEFROSTER switch and ACS signal	Heater control unit	REAR WINDOW DEFROSTER switch or ACS hold on	2.3	• Heater control unit • Terminal voltage of A/C amplifier connector (1C, 1Z, 2S)
			REAR WINDOW DEFROSTER switch and ACS off	0	
3G	DEFROSTER indicator light illumination signal	Heater control unit	DEFROSTER indicator light on	0.1	• Heater control unit • Terminal voltage of A/C amplifier connector (1C, 1Z, 2S)
			DEFROSTER indicator light off	11.0	
3H	REC/FRESH switch and fan switch signal	Heater control unit	REC/FRESH switch or fan switch hold on	2.3	• Heater control unit • Terminal voltage of A/C amplifier connector (1C, 1Z, 2S)
			REC/FRESH switch and fan switch off	0	

A/C AMPLIFIER TERMINAL VOLTAGE REFERENCE CHART
— MILLENIA (7 OF 7)

Terminal	Signal name	Connected	Test condition	Voltage (V)	Inspection area
3I	REC indicator light illumination signal	Heater control unit	REC indicator light on	0.1	• Heater control unit
			REC indicator light off	11.6	• Terminal voltage of A/C amplifier connector (1C, 1Z, 2S)
3J	TNS signal	Heater control unit	Light switch on	B+	• Heater control unit
			Light switch off	0	• Terminal voltage of A/C amplifier connector (2A)
3K	REAR WINDOW DEFROSTER indicator light illumination signal	Heater control unit	REAR WINDOW DEFROSTER indicator light on	0.1	• Heater control unit
			REAR WINDOW DEFROSTER indicator light off	11.6	• Terminal voltage of A/C amplifier connector (1C, 1Z, 2S)
3L	Panel light control switch signal	Heater control unit	Light switch on and panel light control switch at max. illumination	0.5	Terminal voltage of A/C amplifier connector (1G)
			Light switch on and panel light control switch at min. illumination	11.5	
			Light switch off	0	
3M	FRESH indicator light illumination signal	Heater control unit	FRESH indicator light on	0.1	• Heater control unit
			FRESH indicator light off	11.6	• Terminal voltage of A/C amplifier connector (1C, 1Z, 2S)
3N	Indicator light power source	Heater control unit	Light switch off	B+	• Heater control unit
			Light switch on	1.9	• Terminal voltage of A/C amplifier connector (1C, 1Z, 2S)
3O	Fan switch, MODE switch, ACS and DEFROSTER switch signal	Heater control unit	Fan switch, MODE switch, ACS, or DEFROSTER switch hold on	2.3	• Heater control unit
			Fan switch, MODE switch, ACS, and DEFROSTER switch off	4.7	• Terminal voltage of A/C amplifier connector (1C, 1Z, 2S)
3P	—	—	—	—	—
3Q	REC/FRESH switch, REAR WINDOW DEFROSTER switch, OFF switch, and AUTO switch signal	Heater control unit	REC/FRESH switch, REAR WINDOW DEFROSTER switch, OFF switch, or AUTO switch hold on	2.3	• Heater control unit
			REC/FRESH switch, REAR WINDOW DEFROSTER switch, OFF switch, and AUTO switch off	4.7	• Terminal voltage of A/C amplifier connector (1C, 1Z, 2S)
3R	TEMP circuit	Heater control unit	Ignition switch at ACC	5	• Heater control unit
			Ignition switch at OFF	0	• Terminal voltage of A/C amplifier connector (1C, 1Z, 2S)
3S	ACC	Heater control unit	Ignition switch at ACC	B+	• Heater control unit
			Ignition switch at OFF	0	• Terminal voltage of A/C amplifier connector (1Z)
3T	Ground	Heater control unit	Any	0	Terminal voltage of A/C amplifier connector (1C)

INTAKE ACTUATOR – A/C AMPLIFIER WIRING CONTINUITY CHART
— 1993 929

B+: Battery positive voltage

Connector	Terminal	Wire	Connected to	Condition	Voltage (V)	For inspection of
22-pin	a	O/B	Power transistor	Blower speed 1st/2nd/3rd/4th	1.3/1.4/1.6/1.3	A/C amplifier Power transistor
	b	L/W	Blower motor	Blower speed OFF/1st/2nd/3rd/4th	5/8.5/5.5/3/0.4	A/C amplifier Blower fan Heater relay
	c	R/L	Max-hi relay	Blower speed 4th/OTHERS	0/B+	A/C amplifier Max-hi relay
	d	P/B	Heater relay	Off switch ON/OFF	B+/0	A/C amplifier Heater relay
	e	R/W	Heater control unit	Ignition switch ON/OFF	4/0	A/C amplifier Heater control unit
	f	BR/Y	Heater control unit	Ignition switch ON/OFF	4/0	A/C amplifier Heater control unit
	g	L	Heater control unit	Ignition switch ON/OFF	3/0	A/C amplifier Heater control unit
	h	G/Y	Heater control unit	Ignition switch ON/OFF	3/0	A/C amplifier Heater control unit
	i	G/O	Heater control unit	Ignition switch ON/OFF	3/0	A/C amplifier Heater control unit
	j	W	Heater control unit	Ignition switch ON/OFF	4/0	A/C amplifier Heater control unit
	l	GY/R	Self-Diagnostic Checker	Ignition switch ON/OFF	B+/0	A/C amplifier
	m	L/B	Wiper motor	Wiper switch ON/OFF	B+/0	A/C amplifier Wiper motor
	o	P	ACS (Passenger Compartment Temperature)	—	—	A/C amplifier ACS (Passenger Compartment Temperature)
	p	R	Ground	Constant	0	A/C amplifier
	q	P/B	Heater control unit	Ignition switch ON/OFF	5/0	A/C amplifier Heater control unit
	r	B/R	Airflow mode actuator Mix actuator	Ignition switch ON/OFF	5/0	A/C amplifier Airflow mode actuator Mix actuator
	s	L/O	Sensor ground	Any	0	A/C amplifier
	t	B/W	ACS (Water Temperature)	—	—	A/C amplifier ACS (Water Temperature)
	u	L/Y	ACS (Ambient Temperature)	—	—	A/C amplifier ACS (Ambient Temperature)
	v	W/L	Airflow mode actuator	Mode switch VENT/BI-LEVEL/ HEAT/HEAT-DEF/DEF	4.3/3.5/2.5/1.5/0.6	A/C amplifier Airflow mode actuator

A/C AMPLIFIER TERMINAL VOLTAGE REFERENCE CHART — 626 AND MX−6

B+: Battery positive voltage

Terminal	Wire	Connection	Test condition	Voltage (V)
A	(L)	Ignition switch	Ignition switch at ON	B+
			Ignition switch at OFF	0
B	(L/B)	PCM	A/C compressor on	0
			A/C compressor off	B+
C	(L/W)	Heater control unit	A/C switch and fan switch on	0
			A/C switch and fan switch off	B+
D	(R)	Heater control unit	Fan switch off	B+
			Fan switch on	0
E	(L/Y)	Fan switch Resistor	Fan switch on	B+
			Fan switch off	0

A/C AMPLIFIER TERMINAL VOLTAGE REFERENCE CHART — 1993 929

B+: Battery positive voltage

Connector	Terminal	Wire	Connected to	Condition	Voltage (V)	For inspection of
26-pin	a	G/R	Mix actuator	Temperature switch 32°C (90°F) →18°C (64°F)	4.4 → 0.6	A/C amplifier Mix actuator
	b	Y/B	ACS (Evaporator)	A/C switch A/C / A/C ECON	2.2↔2.5/2.1↔1.6	A/C amplifier ACS (Evaporator)
	c	B/O	ECU (A/C relay)	COMPRESSOR ON/OFF	1.4—3.4/5	A/C amplifier ECU
	d	GY	ACS (Solar Radiation)	—	—	A/C amplifier ACS (Solar radiation)
	e	W/R	Intake actuator	Ignition switch ON/OFF	5/0	A/C amplifier Intake actuator
	f	Y/R	Self-Diagnosis Checker	Ignition switch ON/OFF	B+/0	A/C amplifier
	g	Y	Intake actuator motor	Intake actuator ON/OFF	B+/0	A/C amplifier Intake actuator
	h	L/B	Rear-vent switch	Rear-vent switch ON/OFF	0/B+	A/C amplifier Rear-vent switch
	i	G/B	Intake actuator	Intake actuator 1/3 FRESH/OTHERS	0/B+	A/C amplifier Intake actuator
	j	B/L	Intake actuator	Intake actuator REC/FRESH	0/5	A/C amplifier Intake actuator
	k	BR	Heater control unit	Ignition switch ON/OFF	3.5/0	A/C amplifier Heater control unit
	l	G	Intake actuator	Intake actuator FRESH/REC	0/5	A/C amplifier Intake actuator
	m	G/Y	Rear-vent amplifier	Rear-vent switch 2, 3/OFF, 1	7.5/0	A/C amplifier Rear ventilation amplifier
	n	BR/W	Rear-vent switch	IG switch ON/OFF	3.5/0	A/C amplifier Rear-vent switch
	p	G/R	Rear-vent amplifier	Rear-vent switch 1, 3/OFF, 2	7.5/0	A/C amplifier Rear-vent amplifier
	q	B/Y	Mix actuator	Mix actuator • COLD → HOT • OFF: MAX HOT/OTHERS	B+ B+/0	A/C amplifier Mix actuator
	r	GY	Mix actuator	Mix actuator • HOT → COLD • OFF: MAX COLD/OTHERS	B+ B+/0	A/C amplifier Mix actuator
	s	Y/R	Airflow mode actuator	Mode actuator • DEF → VENT • OFF: VENT/OTHERS	B+ B+/0	A/C amplifier Airflow mode actuator
	t	G/W	Airflow mode actuator	Mode actuator • VENT → DEF • OFF: DEF/OTHERS	B+ 0/B+	A/C amplifier Airflow mode actuator
	u	G/O	Rear-vent amplifier	REAR switch (heater control assembly) ON/OFF	0/B+	A/C amplifier Heater control unit Rear-vent amplifier
	v	Y	ECU (idle-up)	Compressor • Blower speed high • Blower speed low	0 9	A/C amplifier ECU
	w	B	Ground	Constant	0	A/C amplifier
	x	R	Swing motor	Swing switch ON/OFF	0/B+	A/C amplifier Swing motor
	y	L/R	Battery	Constant	B+	A/C amplifier Fuse
	z	LG/R	Ignition switch	Ignition switch ON/OFF	B+/0	A/C amplifier Fuse

A/C AMPLIFIER TERMINAL VOLTAGE REFERENCE CHART
— 1993 929 CONT'D

B+: Battery positive voltage

Connector	Terminal	Wire	Connected to	Condition	Voltage (V)	For inspection of
26-pin	2A	G/R	Air mix actuator	Temperature setting dial 32°C {90°F} →18°C {65°F}	4.4→0.6	A/C amplifier Air mix actuator
	2B	Y/B	Evaporator temperature sensor	A/C switch A/C / A/C ECON	2.2↔2.5/2.1↔1.6	A/C amplifier Evaporator temperature sensor
	2C	B/O	PCM	A/C compressor ON/OFF	1.4—3.4/5	A/C amplifier PCM
	2D	GY	Solar radiation sensor	—	—	A/C amplifier Solar radiation sensor
	2E	W/R	Air intake actuator	Ignition switch ON/OFF	5/0	A/C amplifier Air intake actuator
	2F	Y/R	Data link connector	Ignition switch ON/OFF	B+/0	A/C amplifier
	2G	Y	Air intake actuator motor	Air intake actuator ON/OFF	B+/0	A/C amplifier Air intake actuator
	2I	G/B	Air intake actuator	Air intake actuator 1/3 FRESH/other	0/B+	A/C amplifier Air intake actuator
	2J	B/L	Air intake actuator	Air intake actuator REC/FRESH	0/B+	A/C amplifier Air intake actuator
	2K	BR	Heater control unit	Ignition switch ON/OFF	3.5/0	A/C amplifier Heater control unit
	2L	G	Air intake actuator	Air intake actuator FRESH/REC	0/5	A/C amplifier Air intake actuator
	2N	BR/W	Heater control unit	Ignition switch ON/OFF	3.5/0	A/C amplifier Heater control unit
	2Q	B/Y	Air mix actuator	Air mix actuator • COLD→HOT • OFF: MAX HOT/other	B+ B+/0	A/C amplifier Air mix actuator
	2R	GY	Air mix actuator	Air mix actuator • HOT→COLD • OFF: MAX COLD/other	B+ B+/0	A/C amplifier Air mix actuator
	2S	Y/R	Airflow mode actuator	Airflow mode actuator • Defrost→VENT • OFF: VENT/other	B+ B+/0	A/C amplifier Air mix actuator
	2T	G/W	Airflow mode actuator	Airflow mode actuator • VENT→Defrost • OFF: DEF/other	B+ 0/B+	A/C amplifier Airflow mode actuator
	2V	Y	PCM	A/C compressor • Fan switch in 4th • Fan switch in 1st to 3rd	0 9	A/C amplifier PCM
	2W	B	Ground	Constant	0	A/C amplifier
	2Y	L/R	Battery	Constant	B+	A/C amplifier Fuse
	2Z	LG/R	Ignition switch	Ignition switch ON/OFF	B+/0	A/C amplifier Fuse

A/C AMPLIFIER TERMINAL VOLTAGE REFERENCE CHART
— 1994–95 929

B+: Battery positive voltage

Connector	Terminal	Wire	Connected to	Condition	Voltage (V)	For inspection of
22-pin	1A	O/B	Power transistor	Blower speed 1st/2nd/3rd/4th	1.3/1.4/1.6/1.3	A/C amplifier Power transistor
	1B	L/W	Blower motor	Blower speed OFF/1st/2nd/3rd/4th	5/8.5/5.5/3/0.4	A/C amplifier Blower motor A/C off relay
	1C	R/L	MAX-HI relay	Blower speed 4th/other	0/B+	A/C amplifier MAX-HI relay
	1D	P/B	A/C off relay	Off switch ON/OFF	B+/0	A/C amplifier A/C off relay
	1E	R/W	Heater control unit	Ignition switch ON/OFF	4/0	A/C amplifier Heater control unit
	1F	BR/Y	Heater control unit	Ignition switch ON/OFF	4/0	A/C amplifier Heater control unit
	1G	L	Heater control unit	Ignition switch ON/OFF	3/0	A/C ampligier Heater control unit
	1H	G/Y	Heater control unit	Ignition switch ON/OFF	3/0	A/C amplifier Heater control unit
	1I	G/O	Heater control unit	Ignition switch ON/OFF	3/0	A/C amplifier Heater control unit
	1J	W	Heater control unit	Ignition swtich ON/OFF	4/0	A/C amplifier Heater control unit
	1L	GY/R	Data link connector	Ignition switch ON/OFF	B+/0	A/C amplifier
	1O	P	Passenger compartment temperature sensor	—	—	A/C amplifier Passenger compartment temperature sensor
	1P	R	Body ground	Constant	0	A/C amplifier
	1Q	P/B	Heater control unit	Ignition switch ON/OFF	5/0	A/C amplifier Heater control unit
	1R	B/R	Heater control unit Air mix actuator	Ignition switch ON/OFF	5/0	A/C amplifier Airflow mode actuator Air mix actuator
	1S	L/O	Sensor ground	Constant	0	A/C amplifier
	1T	B/W	Water temperature sensor	—	—	A/C amplifier Water temperature sensor
	1U	L/Y	Ambient temperature sensor	—	—	A/C amplifier Water temperature sensor
	1V	W/L	Airflow mode actuator	Mode switch VENT, BI-LEVEL, HEAT HEAT/DEF, DEFROSTER	4.3/3.5/2.5/1.5/0.6	A/C amplifier Airflow mode actuator

A/C AMPLIFIER TERMINAL VOLTAGE REFERENCE CHART
— 1994–95 929, CONT'D

B+: Battery positive voltage

Connector	Terminal	Wire	Connected to	Condition	Voltage (V)	For inspection of
26-pin	2A	G/R	Air mix actuator	Temperature setting dial 32°C {90°F} →18°C {65°F}	4.4→0.6	A/C amplifier Air mix actuator
	2B	Y/B	Evaporator temperature sensor	A/C switch A/C / A/C ECON	2.2↔2.5/2.1↔1.6	A/C amplifier Evaporator temperature sensor
	2C	B/O	PCM	A/C compressor ON/OFF	1.4—3.4/5	A/C amplifier PCM
	2D	GY	Solar radiation sensor	—	—	A/C amplifier Solar radiation sensor
	2E	W/R	Air intake actuator	Ignition switch ON/OFF	5/0	A/C amplifier Air intake actuator
	2F	Y/R	Data link connector	Ignition switch ON/OFF	B+/0	A/C amplifier
	2G	Y	Air intake actuator motor	Air intake actuator ON/OFF	B+/0	A/C amplifier Air intake actuator
	2I	G/B	Air intake actuator	Air intake actuator 1/3 FRESH/other	0/B+	A/C amplifier Air intake actuator
	2J	B/L	Air intake actuator	Air intake actuator REC/FRESH	0/B+	A/C amplifier Air intake actuator
	2K	BR	Heater control unit	Ignition switch ON/OFF	3.5/0	A/C amplifier Heater control unit
	2L	G	Air intake actuator	Air intake actuator FRESH/REC	0/5	A/C amplifier Air intake actuator
	2N	BR/W	Heater control unit	Ignition switch ON/OFF	3.5/0	A/C amplifier Heater control unit
	2Q	B/Y	Air mix actuator	Air mix actuator • COLD→HOT • OFF: MAX HOT/other	B+ B+/0	A/C amplifier Air mix actuator
	2R	GY	Air mix actuator	Air mix actuator • HOT→COLD • OFF: MAX COLD/other	B+ B+/0	A/C amplifier Air mix actuator
	2S	Y/R	Airflow mode actuator	Airflow mode actuator • Defrost→VENT • OFF: VENT/other	B+ B+/0	A/C amplifier Air mix actuator
	2T	G/W	Airflow mode actuator	Airflow mode actuator • VENT→Defrost • OFF: DEF/other	B+ 0/B+	A/C amplifier Airflow mode actuator
	2V	Y	PCM	A/C compressor • Fan switch in 4th • Fan switch in 1st to 3rd	0 9	A/C amplifier PCM
	2W	B	Ground	Constant	0	A/C amplifier
	2Y	L/R	Battery	Constant	B+	A/C amplifier Fuse
	2Z	LG/R	Ignition switch	Ignition switch ON/OFF	B+/0	A/C amplifier Fuse

Solar Cell Assembly

TESTING

Millenia

1. Open the sunroof, and remove the lower panel cover.
2. Disconnect the solar cell connector.
3. Set 10 110 watt fluorescent lights 34.3 in. (870mm) directly above the solar cell assembly.
4. Position a reflector (white board) over the fluorescent lights.
5. Turn ON the fluorescent lights.
6. Verify the brightness directly on the solar cell is more than 8000:1 ratio.

   NOTE: Set the difference between the center of the solar battery and that of the fluorescent lights below 19.7 in. (500mm).

7. Measure the voltage at terminal **A** of the solar cell connector.
8. If the voltage is less than 6 volts, replace the glass panel.

Solar Ventilation Control Unit (SVCU)

TESTING

Millenia

1. Measure the voltages at the terminal wires of the SVCU connector.
2. If not as specified, per the appropriate Terminal Voltage Chart, replace the SVCU.

3. Disconnect the SVCU connector and check for continuity between the SVCU and the main wiring harness terminals.
4. If there is continuity at terminal **A**, replace the SVCU.
5. If at less than 36–53°F (2–12°C), there is continuity at terminal **F**, replace the SVCU.
6. If at more than 51–67°F (10.5–19.5°C), there is continuity at terminal **E**, replace the SVCU.

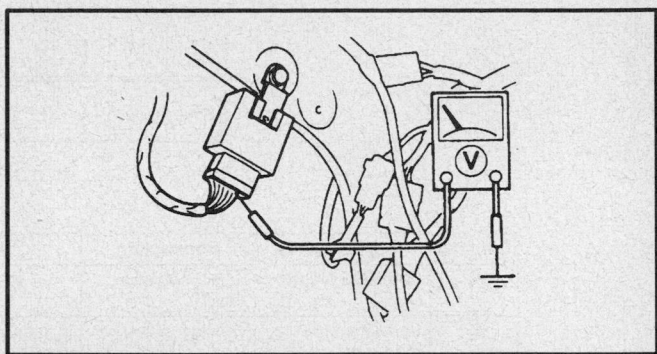

Solar ventilation control unit (SVCU) testing — Millenia

REMOVAL AND INSTALLATION

Millenia

1. Disconnect the negative battery terminal
2. Remove the trunk end trim and the left trunk side trim.
3. Disconnect the SVCU connector.
4. Remove the bolt securing the SVCU and the SVCU.
5. Installation is the reverse of the removal procedure.

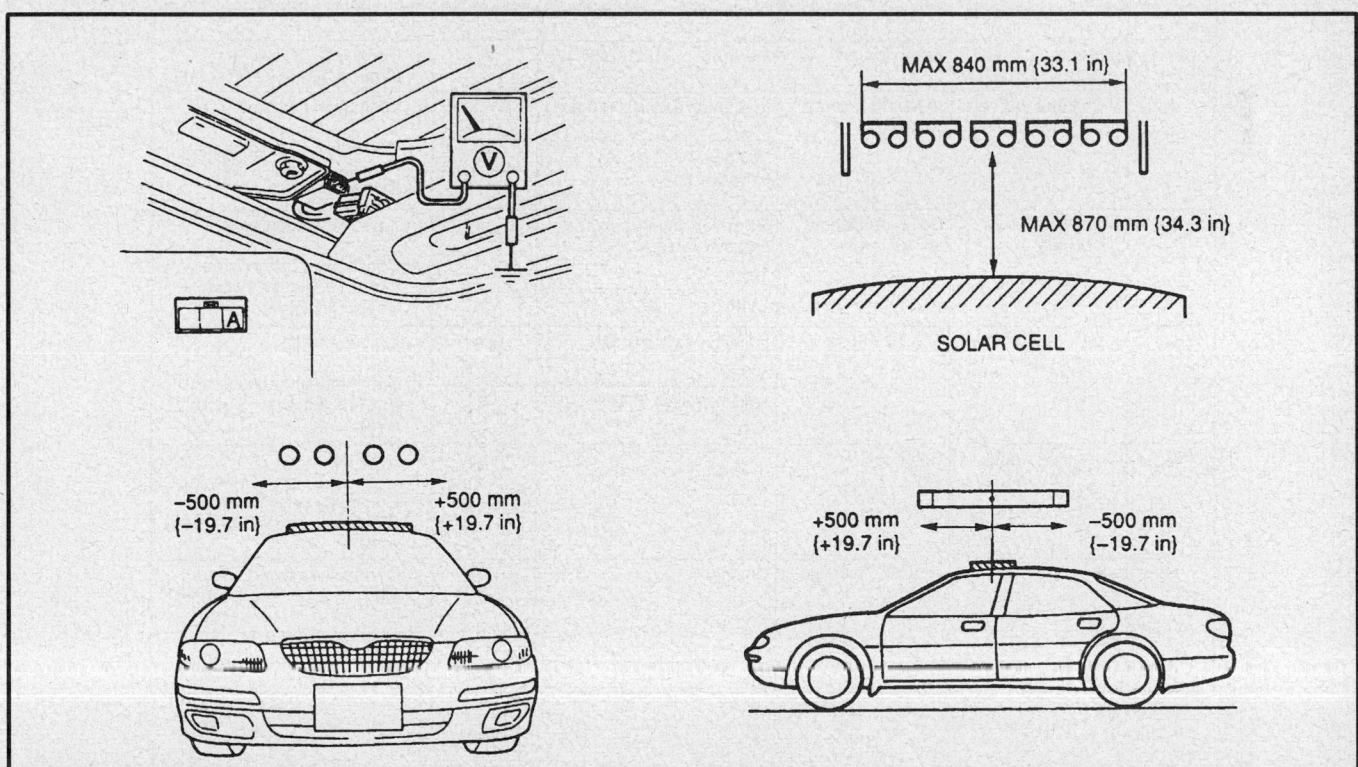

MAX 840 mm {33.1 in}

MAX 870 mm {34.3 in}

SOLAR CELL

−500 mm {−19.7 in}   +500 mm {+19.7 in}

+500 mm {+19.7 in}   −500 mm {−19.7 in}

Solar cell testing — Millenia

SOLAR VENTILATION CONTROL UNIT (SVCU) TERMINAL REFERENCE CHART — MILLENIA

O	M	K	⊠		E	C	A
P	N	L	J	H	F	D	B

Vsc: Solar cell voltage   B+: Battery positive voltage

Terminal	Signal name	Connection	Test condition	Voltage (V)	Inspection area
A	CHARGE mode signal	Solar ventilation switch	—	—	—
B	Ventilation fan No.1 drive signal	Ventilation fan No.1	In manual exhaust mode	9—11	• Ventilation fan No.1
			Ventilation fan No.1 stopped	0	• Continuity or short circuit (Ventilation fan — SVCU: [BR] wire)
C	Key reminder switch signal	Key reminder switch	Key removed (Key reminder switch off)	0	• Key reminder switch
			Key inserted (key reminder switch on)	B+	• Continuity or short circuit (Key reminder switch — SVCU: [L/B] wire)
D	Solar ventilation indicator signal	Solar ventilation switch (Indicator light)	Indicator light at on	9—11	• Continuity or short circuit (Solar ventilation switch — SVCU: [P/G] wire)
			Indicator light at off	0	
E	Ambient temperature switch signal	Ambient temperature switch	—	—	—
F	—	—	—	—	—
H	Ground	Body ground	Constant	0	• Continuity (SVCU — Ground: [B] — [B/W] wire)
J	Ventilation fan No.2 drive signal	Ventilation fan No.2	In manual exhaust mode	9—11	• Ventilation fan No.2
			Ventilation fan No.2 stopped	0	• Continuity or short circuit (Ventilation fan — SVCU: [W/L] wire)
K	Manual exhaust mode signal	Solar ventilation switch	Solar ventilation switch pressed (Manual exhaust side)	0	• Solar ventilation switch
			Other	5	• Continuity or short circuit (Solar ventilation switch — SVCU: [W/R] wire)
L	IG2	A/C 10 A fuse	Ignition switch at ON	B+	• Ignition switch
			Ignition switch at OFF	0	• Continuity or short circuit (A/C 10 A fuse — SVCU: [G] wire)
M	Solar cell signal	Solar cell	—	Vsc	• Solar cell
					• Continuity or short circuit (Solar cell — SVCU: [BR/W] wire)
N	+B	ROOM 15 A fuse	Constant	B+	• Continuity or short circuit (ROOM 15 A fuse — SVCU: [L/R] wire)
O	—	—	—	—	—
P	—	—	—	—	—

SYSTEM DIAGNOSIS

Automatic Air Conditioning

SELF–DIAGNOSTIC FUNCTION

929

These models require the use of a special diagnostic scan tool attached to the data link connector. By utilizing the scan tool, the system can provide "Present Failure Indication" (current problems detected and stored as service codes), "Past Failure Indication" (past problems and intermittents detected and stored as service code), and output device operation check. Basic charts for performing these test are included in this article.

SETTING UP DIAGNOSTIC CONDITION

Millenia

1. Set up the diagnostic conditions as follows:
- Warm the engine to normal operating temperature, then turn engine **OFF**.
- Connect the NGS set (49 T088 0A0) to the date link connector and battery.
- Set the cable for 17–pin (49 T088 003) to **AUX 1**.
- Select VEHICLE AND ENGINE SELECTION on the hand–held control unit (49 T088 001) display, and then select the vehicle model, engine type and model year.
- Select DIAGNOSTIC DATA LINK on the hand–held control unit display.
- Select A/C–AIR CONDITIONER MODULE on the hand–held control unit display.
- Select DIAGNOSTIC TEST MODE on the hand–held control unit display.
- Start the on–board diagnosis function as indicated on the hand–held control unit display.

NOTE: If the solar radiation sensor is not lit, a failure will be indicated.

- Start the PRESENT DIAGNOSTIC TEST MODE, PAST DIAGNOSTIC TEST MODE, or OUTPUT DEVICE Operation CHECK MODE.
- If past failures are indicated, carry out ERASING PAST FAILURE MEMORY after correcting all failed systems.
2. Follow the Operation FLOW CHART.

929

1. Set up the diagnostic conditions as follows:
- Warm the engine to normal operating temperature, then turn the engine **OFF**.
- Place a 60W bulb about 4 inches from the solar sensor.
- Install the special system selector tool (49 B019 9A0 or equivalent).
- Set the dial to position **4**.
- Set the test switch to **SELF TEST**.
- Connect the special diagnostic scan tool (49 H018 9AT or equivalent) to the system selector tool and ground the other scan tool lead.

- Set the select switch to position **A**.
- Turn the ignition switch to **ON**. Verify that the scan tool flashes 88 for about 5 seconds on the display screen.
2. Follow the "Self Diagnostic Flow Chart".

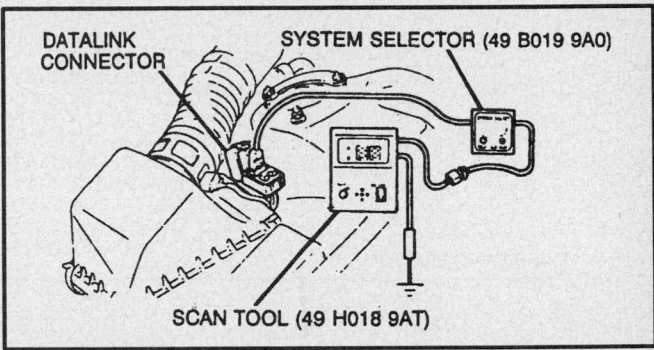

Scan tool and system selector tool hook–up for self–diagnosis — 1993 939

OUTPUT DEVICE OPERATION CHECK

Millenia

1. When the AUTO switch is depressed with the system in PRESENT DIAGNOSTIC TEST MODE, the A/C amplifier changes to OUTPUT DEVICE Operation CHECK MODE.
2. In this mode, all output devices, indicator lights, and the information display operate individually according to a designated pattern, as indicated.
3. Each step is changed by pressing the REC/FRESH switch.
4. If the AUTO switch is pressed again, the on–board diagnostic function will return to PRESENT DIAGNOSTIC TEST MODE.

929

1. If the AUTO switch is pressed while the system is in the present failure indication mode, the A/C amplifier changes to output device operation check mode.
2. In this mode, either each press of the REC or FRESH switch, all output devices are made to operate individually according to the pattern shown in the appropriate "Output Device Operation Check Chart".
3. If a device does not operate as shown in the chart, check the "System Input/Output Diagnostic Flow Chart".

ELIMINATION OF PAST FAILURE MEMORY

Millenia and 929

1. Start the self–diagnostic function and set it to the past failure indication mode.
2. Press the AUTO and REC switches at the same time and verify that service Code **01** is momentarily indicated on the display.
3. Now verify that **00** is shown.

OPERATION FLOW CHART — MILLENIA

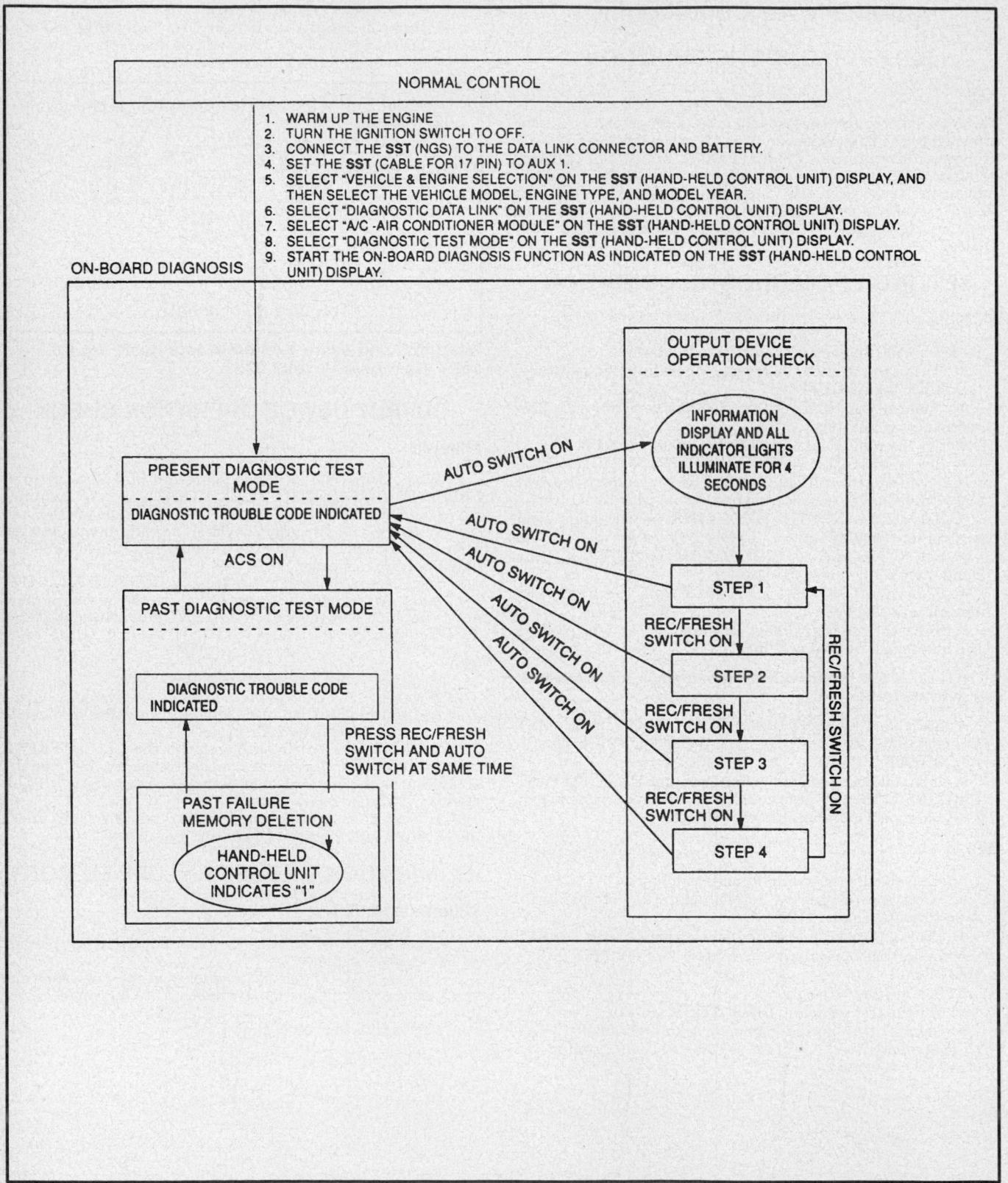

NORMAL CONTROL

1. WARM UP THE ENGINE
2. TURN THE IGNITION SWITCH TO OFF.
3. CONNECT THE **SST** (NGS) TO THE DATA LINK CONNECTOR AND BATTERY.
4. SET THE **SST** (CABLE FOR 17 PIN) TO AUX 1.
5. SELECT "VEHICLE & ENGINE SELECTION" ON THE **SST** (HAND-HELD CONTROL UNIT) DISPLAY, AND THEN SELECT THE VEHICLE MODEL, ENGINE TYPE, AND MODEL YEAR.
6. SELECT "DIAGNOSTIC DATA LINK" ON THE **SST** (HAND-HELD CONTROL UNIT) DISPLAY.
7. SELECT "A/C -AIR CONDITIONER MODULE" ON THE **SST** (HAND-HELD CONTROL UNIT) DISPLAY.
8. SELECT "DIAGNOSTIC TEST MODE" ON THE **SST** (HAND-HELD CONTROL UNIT) DISPLAY.
9. START THE ON-BOARD DIAGNOSIS FUNCTION AS INDICATED ON THE **SST** (HAND-HELD CONTROL UNIT) DISPLAY.

ON-BOARD DIAGNOSIS

OUTPUT DEVICE OPERATION CHECK

PRESENT DIAGNOSTIC TEST MODE
DIAGNOSTIC TROUBLE CODE INDICATED

AUTO SWITCH ON

INFORMATION DISPLAY AND ALL INDICATOR LIGHTS ILLUMINATE FOR 4 SECONDS

ACS ON

PAST DIAGNOSTIC TEST MODE

AUTO SWITCH ON
AUTO SWITCH ON
AUTO SWITCH ON
AUTO SWITCH ON

STEP 1
REC/FRESH SWITCH ON
STEP 2
REC/FRESH SWITCH ON
STEP 3
REC/FRESH SWITCH ON
STEP 4

REC/FRESH SWITCH ON

DIAGNOSTIC TROUBLE CODE INDICATED

PRESS REC/FRESH SWITCH AND AUTO SWITCH AT SAME TIME

PAST FAILURE MEMORY DELETION

HAND-HELD CONTROL UNIT INDICATES "1"

OUTPUT DEVICE OPERATION — MILLENIA

Step	Operating device	Operating conditions	Other device conditions
1	Blower motor speed	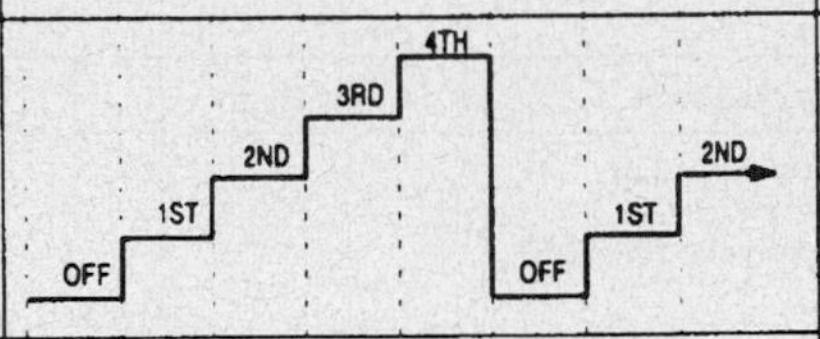 (graph) OFF, 1ST, 2ND, 3RD, 4TH, OFF, 1ST, 2ND	• Air mix actuator operation ...50% • Airflow mode actuator operation ...VENT • Air intake actuator operation...FRESH • A/C compressor operation ...ON • Condenser fan operation ... ON • A/C compressor idle-up operation ... ON
	Electrical load idle-up signal	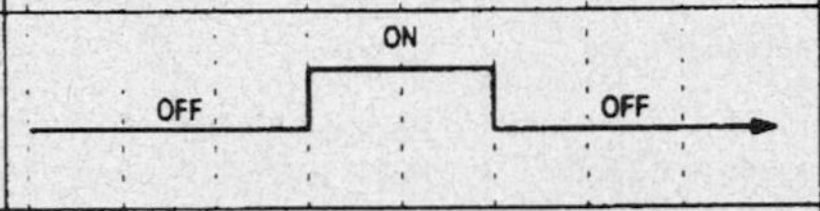 (graph) OFF, ON, OFF	
2	Air mix actuator operation (100%=MAX HOT, 0%=MAX COLD)	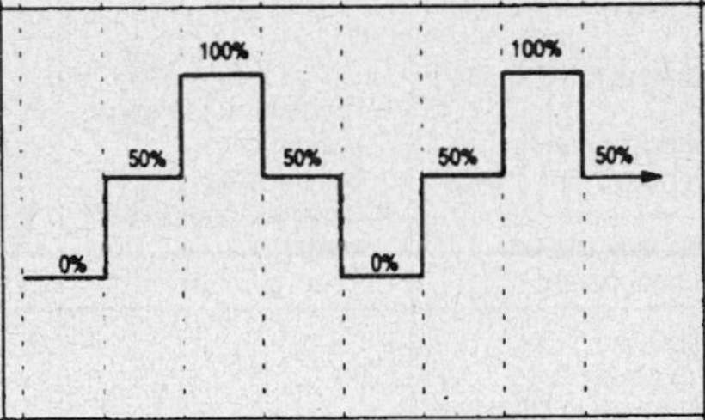 (graph) 0%, 50%, 100%, 50%, 0%, 50%, 100%, 50%	• Blower motor speed ... 2ND • Electrical load idle-up signal ...OFF • Airflow mode actuator operation ... VENT • Air intake actuator operation ...FRESH • A/C compressor operation ...ON • Condenser fan operation ... ON • A/C compressor idle-up operation ... ON
3	Airflow mode actuator operation	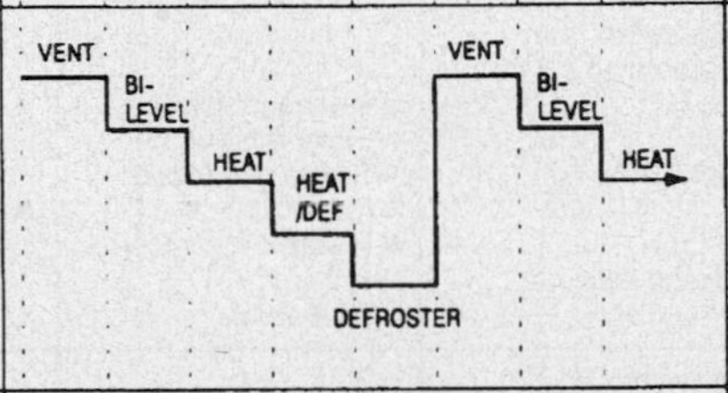 (graph) VENT, BI-LEVEL, HEAT, HEAT/DEF, DEFROSTER, VENT, BI-LEVEL, HEAT	• Blower motor speed...2ND • Electrical load idle-up signal ...OFF • Air mix actuator operation ...50% • Air intake actuator operation...FRESH • A/C compressor operation ...ON • Condenser fan operation ... ON • A/C compressor idle-up operation ... ON
4	Air intake actuator operation	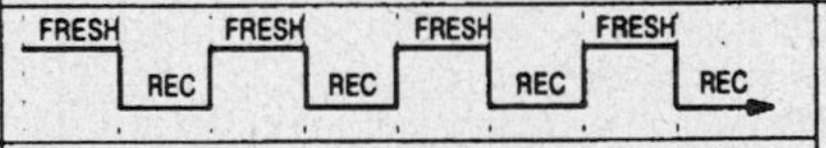 (graph) FRESH, REC, FRESH, REC, FRESH, REC, FRESH, REC	• Blower motor speed ... 2ND • Electrical load idle-up signal ...OFF • Air mix actuator operation ...0% • Airflow mode actuator operation ...VENT
	A/C compressor operation A/C compressor idle-up operation	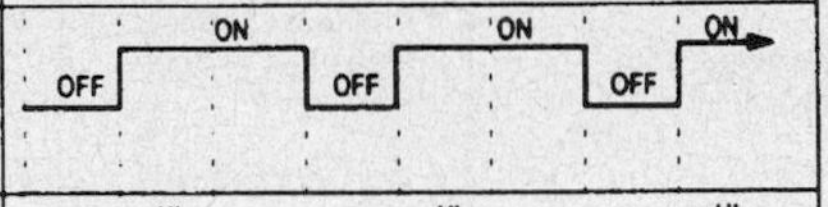 (graph) OFF, ON, OFF, ON, OFF, ON	
	Condenser fan operation	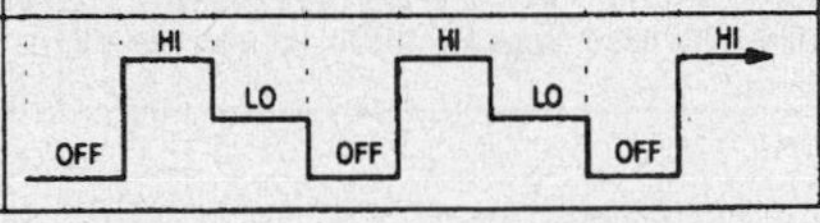 (graph) OFF, HI, LO, OFF, HI, LO, OFF, HI	

Operating conditions time axis: Start, 4, 8, 12, 16, 20, 24, 28 [SECOND]

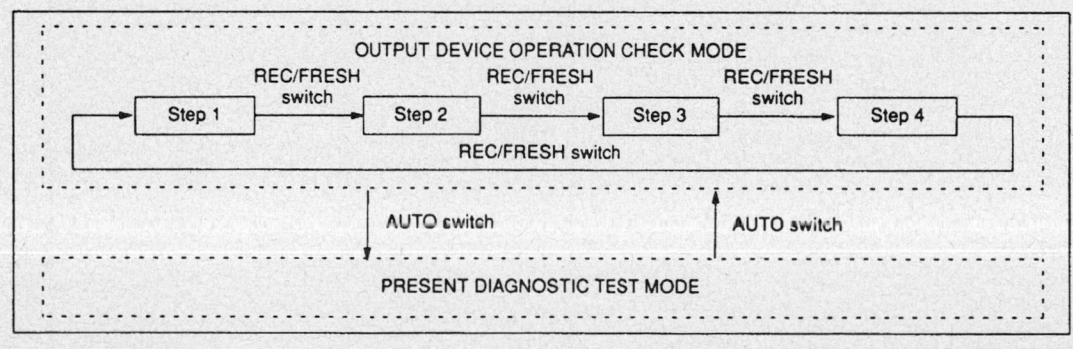

OUTPUT DEVICE OPERATION CHECK MODE

Step 1 → REC/FRESH switch → Step 2 → REC/FRESH switch → Step 3 → REC/FRESH switch → Step 4

REC/FRESH switch

AUTO switch ↓   ↑ AUTO switch

PRESENT DIAGNOSTIC TEST MODE

AUTO. A/C SYMPTOM DIAGNOSTIC CHART — 929

UNDERSTANDING TROUBLE SYMPTOMS

The precise understanding of observed conditions is the key to troubleshooting.

Symptom	Verify condition	Analysis	Action
Airflow temperature ● Outlet air not cool ● Outlet air not warm	1. Turn ignition switch ON 2. Turn AUTO switch ON 3. Set temperature to 18—32°C {64—90°F} (1) Airflow temperature does not change (2) Airflow changes along with change of airflow temperature 4. Set temperature to 18°C {64°F} (3) Idle-up control operates; compressor does not (4) Compressor and idle-up control do not operate	● Incorrect mix actuator control ● Incorrect blower motor control ● Problem in refrigerant system or compressor ● Incorrect compressor control	● Check control system by using self-diagnosis function ● Check control system by using self-diagnosis function ● Check control and refrigerant systems ● Check control system by using self-diagnosis function
Airflow output ● No air output ● Airflow output insufficient	1. Turn ignition switch ON 2. Turn AUTO switch ON 3. Set MODE switch to VENT 4. Shift blower switch from manual 1st through 4th in order (1) Blower motor does not operate (2) Airflow volume does not change	● Incorrect blower motor control ● Problem in blower motor ● Problem in airflow system ● Air leakage	● Check control system by using self-diagnosis function ● Check airflow system by using self-diagnosis function
Airflow mode ● Incorrect airflow outlet ● Airflow outlet not changed	Turn ignition switch ON 2. Turn AUTO switch ON 3. Set airflow outlet by using MODE switch. (1) No airflow output from designated outlet (2) Airflow outlet does not change	● Problem in airflow mode link or door ● Incorrect airflow mode actuator control	● Check control system by using self-diagnosis function ● Check control system by using self-diagnosis function

AUTO. A/C SYMPTOM DIAGNOSTIC CHART, — 929 CONT'D

Symptom	Verify Condition	Analysis	Action
Intake air ● Intake air not changed	1. Turn ignition switch ON 2. Turn AUTO switch ON 3. Change intake air mode by pressing REC and FRESH switches (1) Intake door will not change	● Incorrect intake actuator control	● Check control system by using self-diagnosis function
Compressor operation ● A/C mode not changed ● Compressor not operated	1. Turn ignition switch ON 2. Turn AUTO switch ON 3. Change A/C mode by pressing A/C switch (1) A/C mode does not change (2) Idle-up control operates; compressor does not operate (3) Idle-up and compressor do not operate	● Incorrect compressor control ● Problem in refrigerant system or compressor ● Incorrect compressor control	● Check control system by using self-diagnosis function ● Check refrigerant system and control system ● Check control system by using self-diagnosis function
Compressor noise	1. Turn ignition switch ON 2. Turn AUTO switch ON 3. Set temperature to 18°C (64°F) (1) When compressor is operating, drive belt squeaks (2) When compressor is operating, grinding noise is heard (3) When compressor stops, compressor squeaks (4) Compressor repeats ON and OFF generating vane noise	● Improper adjustment of drive belt ● Problem in refrigerant system (refrigerant or compressor oil leakage) ● Problem in compressor ● Problem in compressor control	● Check drive belt adjustment ● Inspect refrigerant system ● Inspect refrigerant system ● Inspect control system by using self-diagnosis function

SELF–DIAGNOSTIC PROGRAM CHART

SELF-DIAGNOSIS FUNCTION
Outline
The A/C amplifier is programmed with a self-diagnosis function to locate and indicate malfunctions in the heating and air conditioning systems. If called upon to make a complete system check, the A/C amplifier operates as described below.
The three steps of the check are:
1. Present failure indication................. Present failures are detected and indicated as service codes.
2. Past failure indication .... Past failures (intermittent problems) are detected and indicated as service codes.
3. Output device operation check .... All output devices are made to operate individually according to a designated pattern.

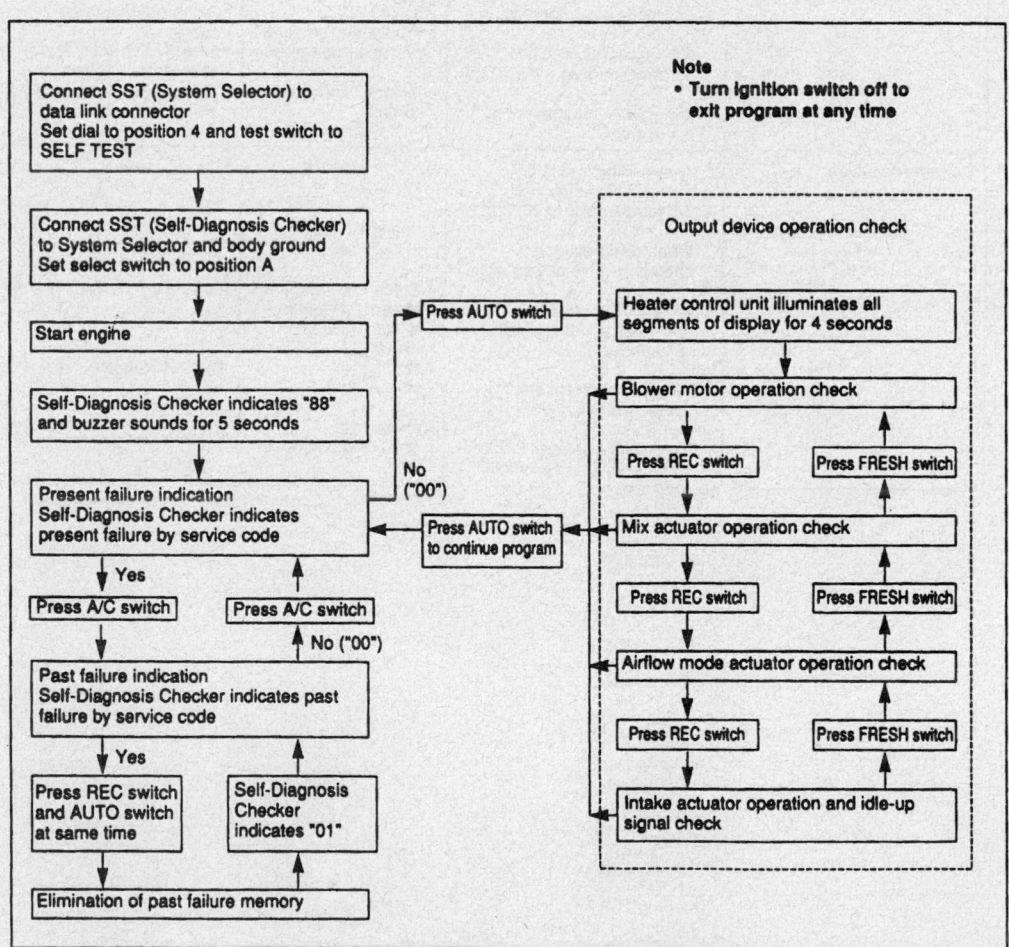

SELF–DIAGNOSTIC PROGRAM CHART, CONT'D

Workflow
To activate the self-diagnosis function, the SSTs (Self-Diagnosis Checker and System Selector [at position 4]) must be connected to the data link connector with the ignition switch ON, or the engine running. To run the A/C amplifier through the self-diagnosis program, press the switches as shown below.

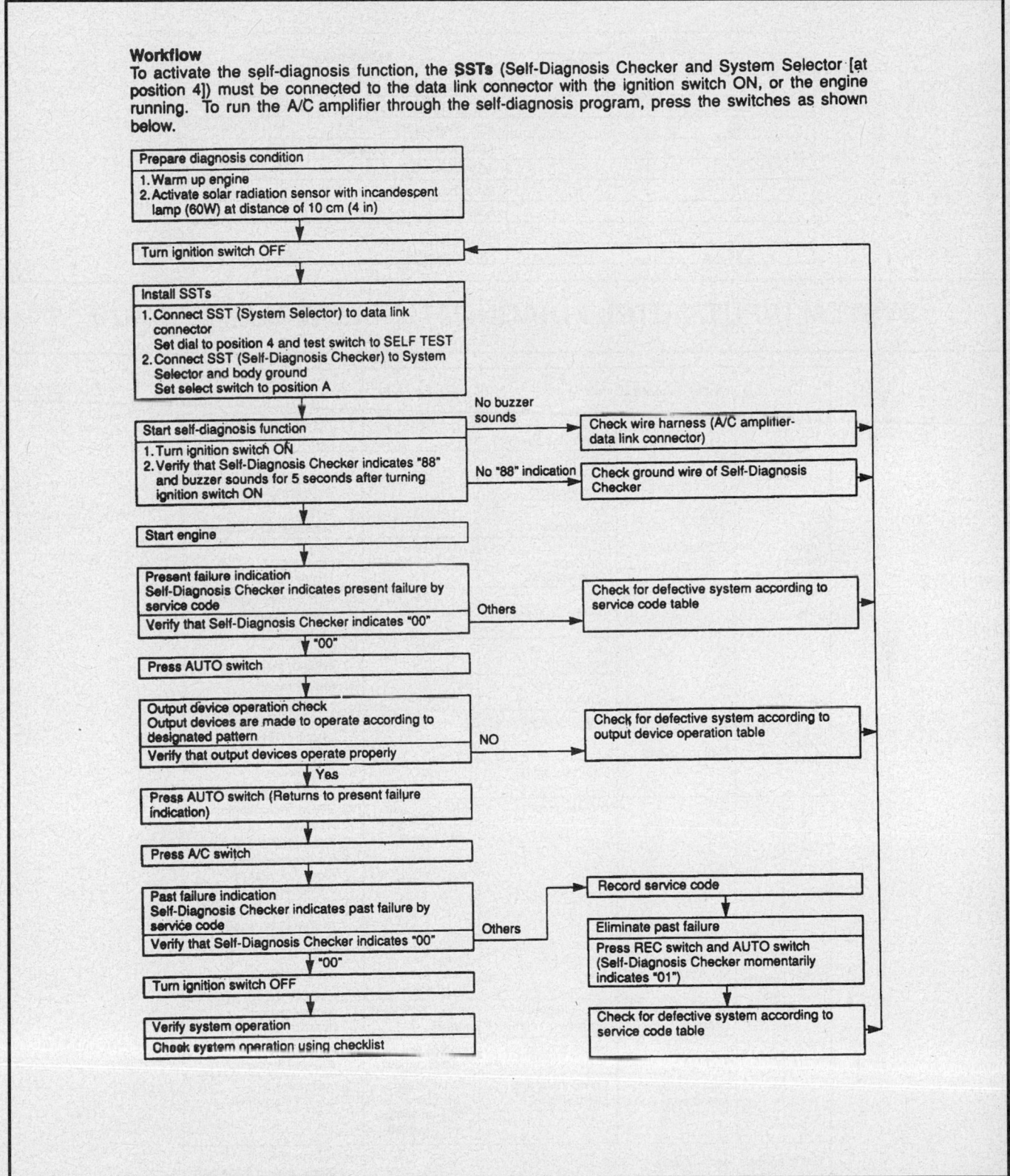

SELF—DIAGNOSTIC PROGRAM CHART, CONT'D

Service code		Failure device
Present failure	Past failure	
02	—	ACS (Solar Radiation)
06	07	ACS (Passenger Compartment Temperature)
10	11	ACS (Evaporator)
12	13	ACS (Ambient Temperature)
14	15	ACS (Water Temperature)
18	19	Mix actuator
21	22	Airflow mode actuator
47	—	Idle-up signal
46	—	A/C relay signal

SYSTEM INPUT/OUTPUT DIAGNOSTIC FLOW CHART — 929

Input / Output device			Service code	Flowchart
Input device	Present failure / Past failure	ACS (Solar Radiation)	02	1. ACS (Solar Radiation) inspection
		ACS (Passenger Compartment Temperature)	06 07	2. ACS (Passenger compartment Temperature) inspection
		ACS (Evaporator)	10 11	3. ACS (Evaporator) inspection
		ACS (Ambient Temperature)	12 13	4. ACS (Ambient Temperature) inspection
		ACS (Water Temperature)	14 15	5. ACS (Water Temperature) inspection
		Mix actuator	18 19	6. Mix actuator inspection
		Airflow mode actuator	21 22	7. Airflow mode actuator inspection
Output device	Present failure	Idle-up signal	47	8. Idle-up signal control inspection
		A/C relay signal	46	9. Compressor control inspection
Output device	Output device operation check	Blower motor	• No air output • Airflow output insufficient	10. Blower motor control inspection (does not work at all)
				11. Blower motor inspection (does not work in 4th speed)
				12. Blower motor inspection (works in 4th speed only)
		Mix actuator	Output air temperature not changed	6. Mix actuator inspection
		Airflow mode actuator	• Incorrect airflow outlet	7. Airflow mode actuator inspection
	Intake actuator and idle-up signal	Intake actuator	• Intake air not changed	13. Air intake actuator inspection
		Compressor and idle-up signal	• Compressor not operated • Idle-up control not operated	9. Compressor control inspection
Self-diagnosis function does not start up				14. A/C amplifier power system inspection

OUTPUT DEVICE OPERATION CHECK CHART — 929

Output Device Operation Check

If the AUTO switch is pressed while the system is in the present failure indication mode, the A/C amplifier changes to output device operation check mode.

In this mode, with each press of the REC or FRESH switch, all output devices are made to operate individually according to a designated pattern, as shown below. If an output device does not operate as shown in the following table, check the system by referring to the flowchart shown on the next page.

Output device operation check

Step	Operating device	Operating conditions								Other device conditions
		START	4	8	12	16	20	24	28	
1	Blower fan	OFF (SPEED)	1ST	2ND	3RD	4TH	OFF		1ST	Mix actuator ....50% Airflow mode ...VENT Compressor ....ON
2	Mix actuator	0% (MOVEMENT)	50%	100%		50%	0%	50%	100%	Blower motor .....2ND Airflow mode ...VENT Compressor ....ON
3	Airflow mode actuator	VENT (MODE)	BI-LEVEL	HEAT	HEAT/DEF	DEF	VENT	BI-LEVEL		Blower motor .....2ND Mix actuator ......50% Intake actuator ...FRESH Compressor ....ON
4	Intake actuator and idle-up signal	FRESH (MODE) OFF	REC ON	FRESH	REC	FRESH OFF	REC	FRESH ON	REC	Blower motor .....2ND Mix actuator ....0% Airflow mode ...VENT

Note
- Operating device conditions are indicated on the display of the heater control unit.
- Each step is changed by pressing the REC or FRESH switches.

Output device operation check

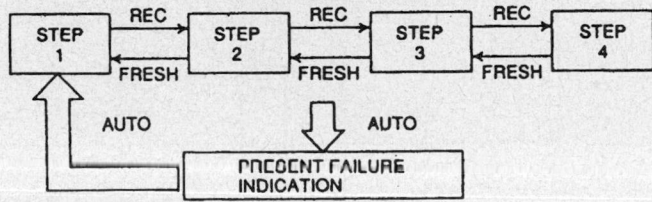

WIRING SCHEMATICS

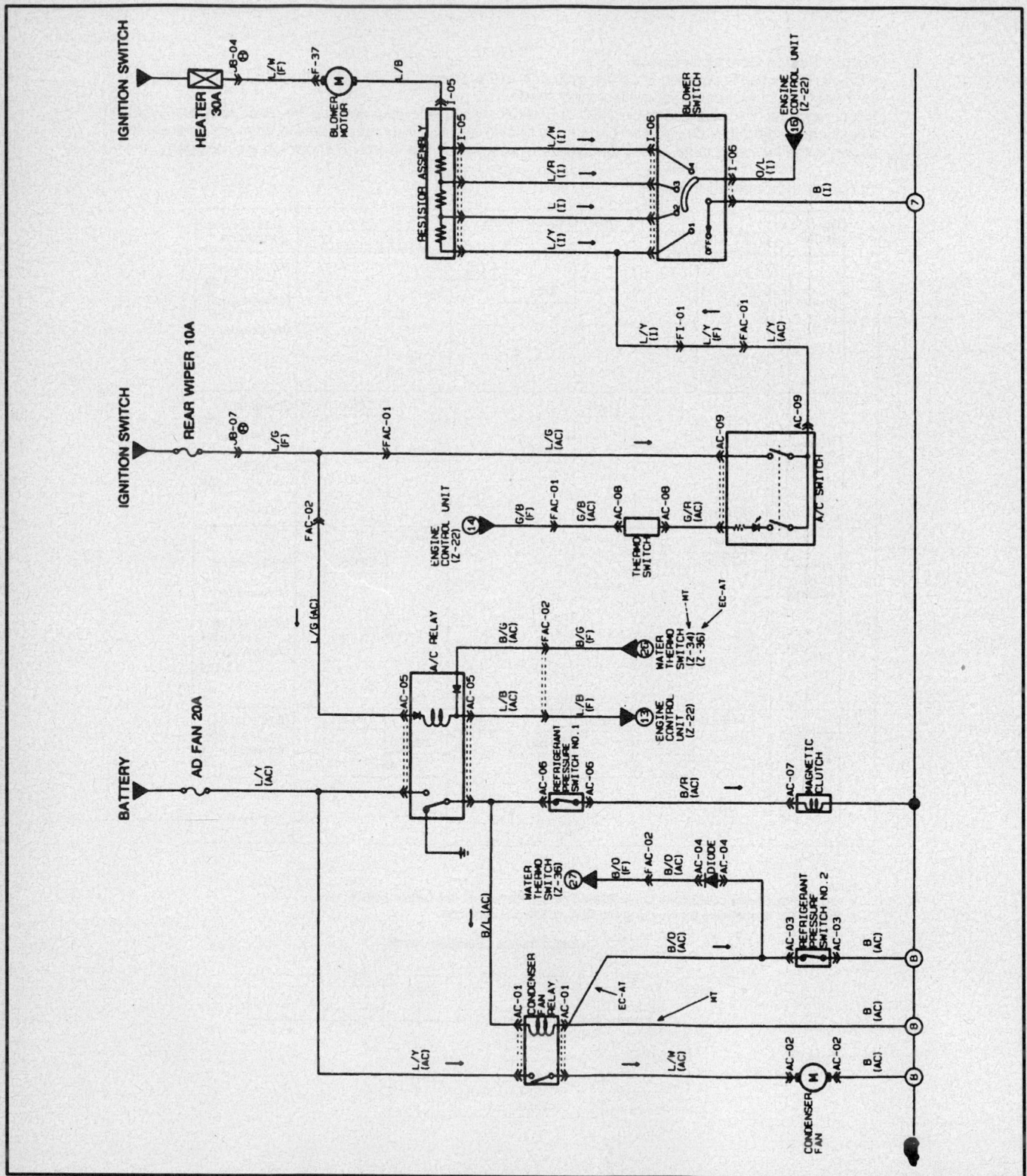

Air conditioning system electrical schematic — 1993 323 and Protege

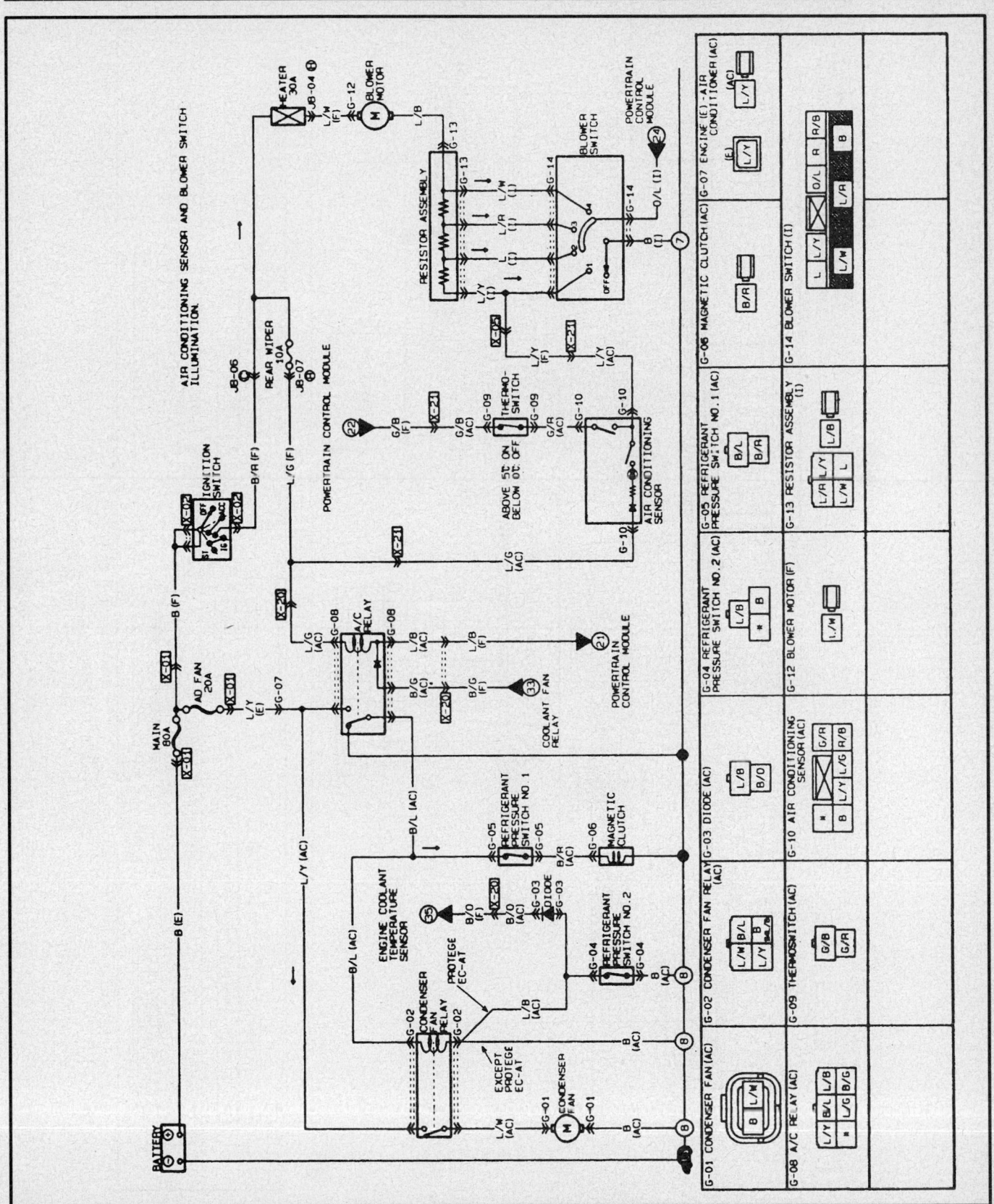

Air conditioning system electrical schematic — 1994 323 and Protege

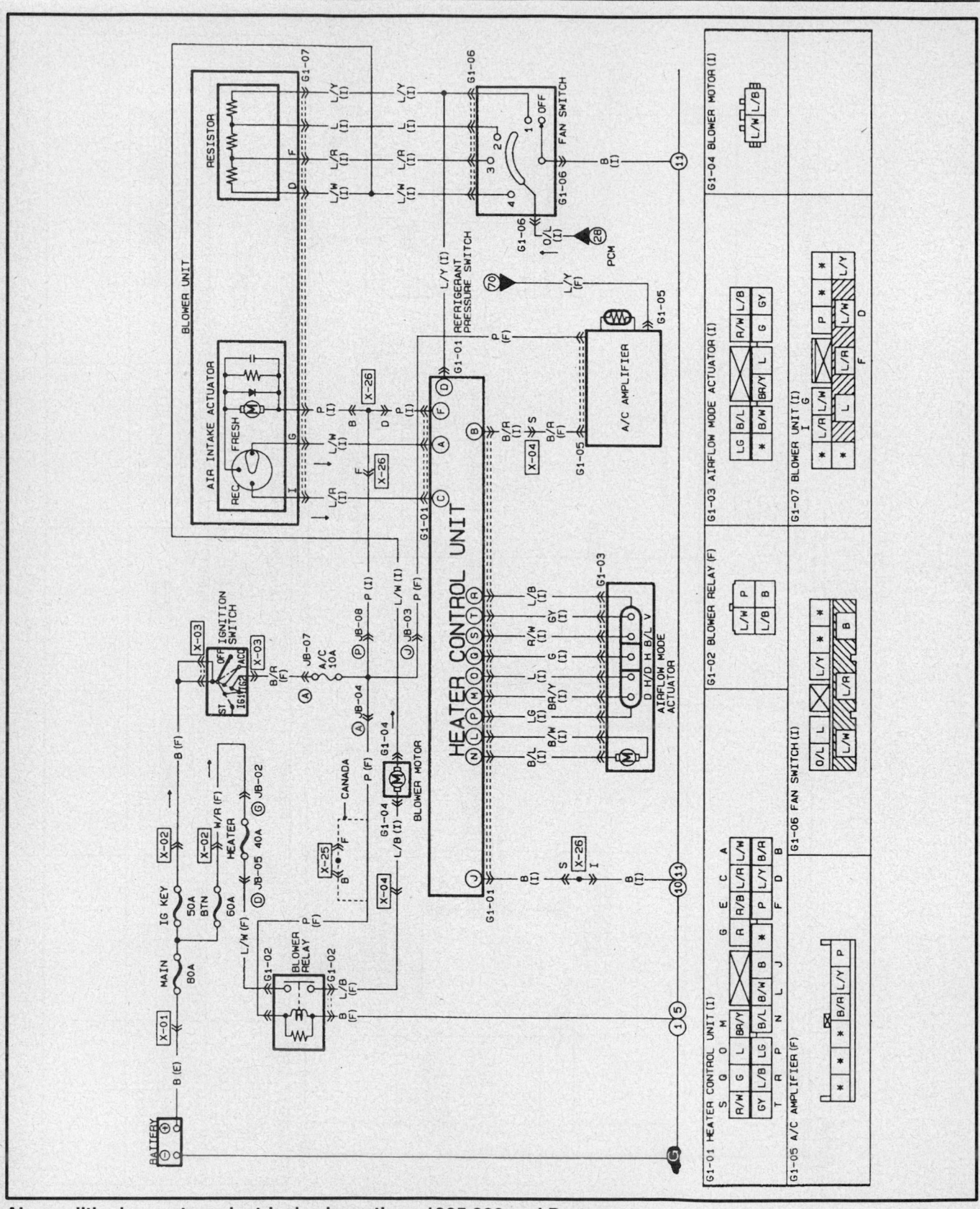

Air conditioning system electrical schematic — 1995 323 and Protege

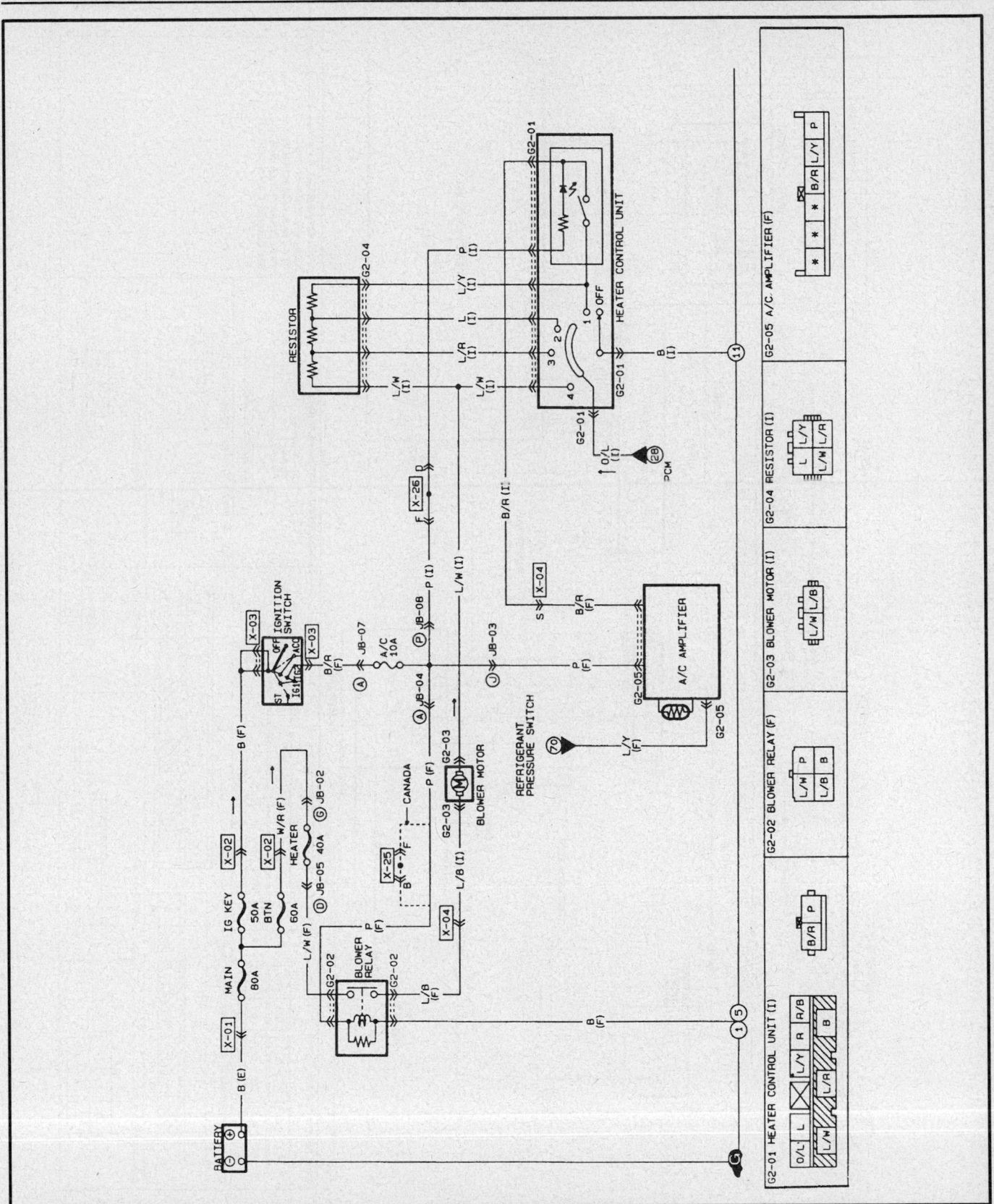

Air conditioning system electrical schematic — 1995 323 and Protege, Cont'd

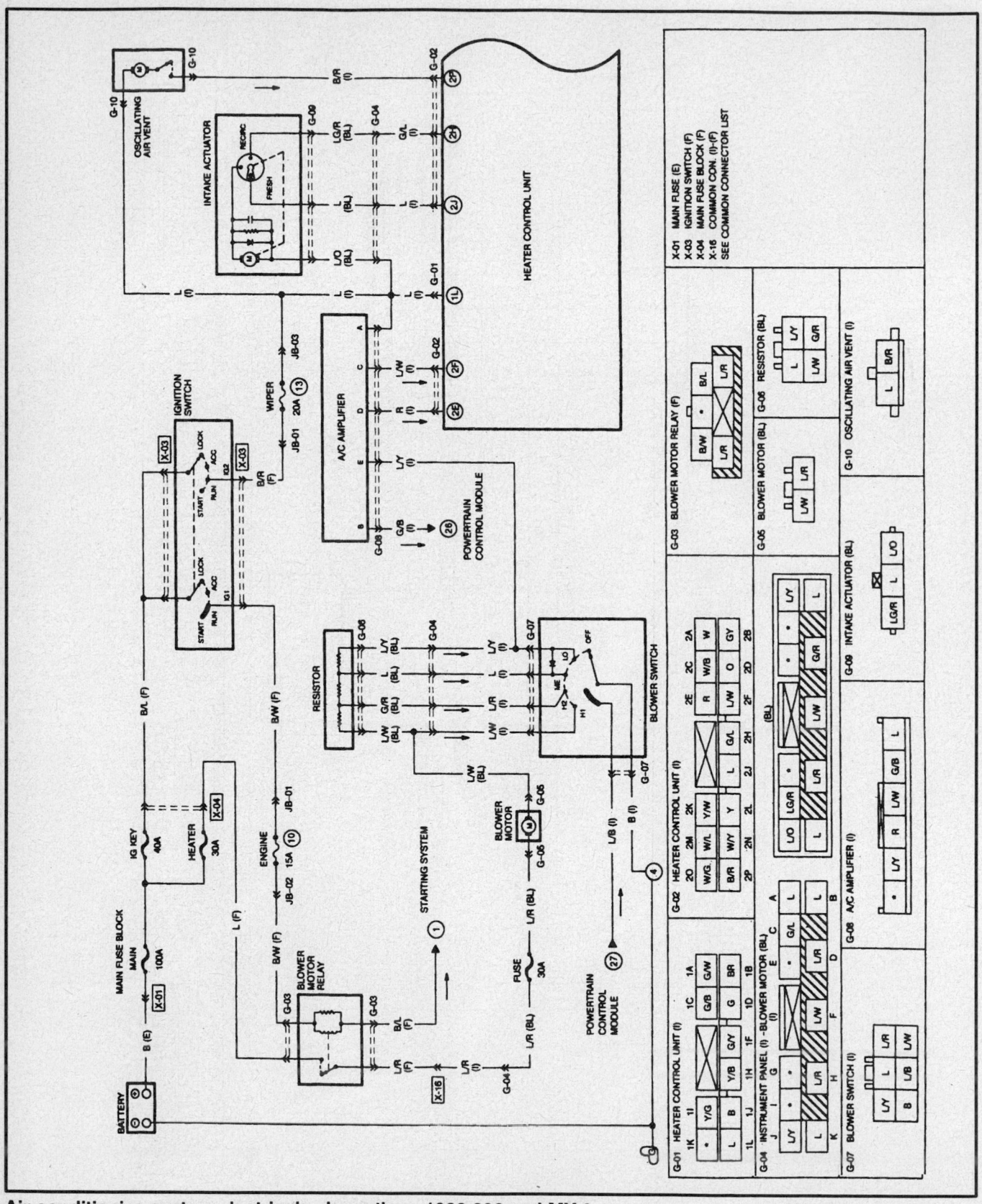

Air conditioning system electrical schematic — 1993 626 and MX-6

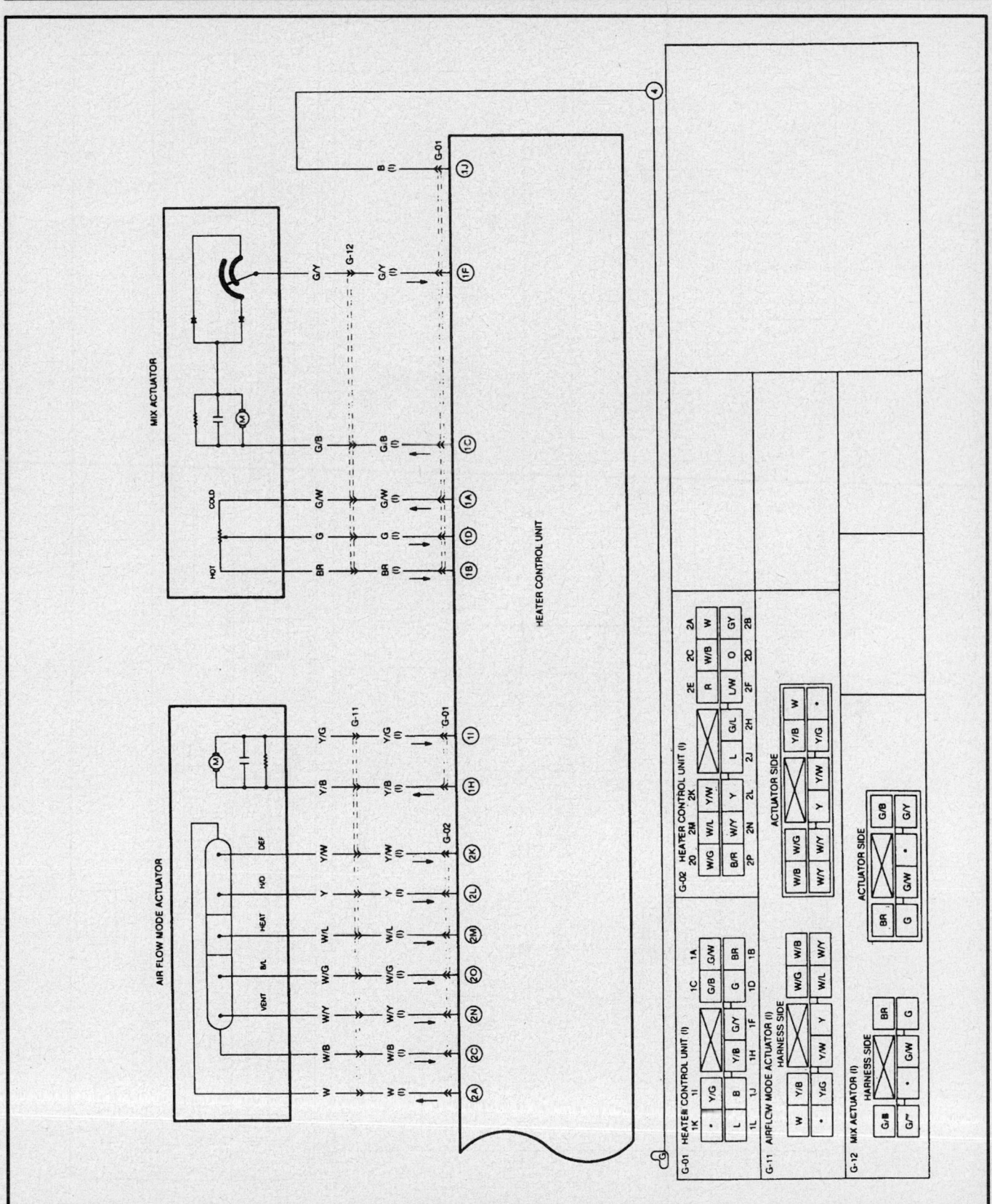

Air conditioning system electrical schematic — 1993 626 and MX-6, Cont'd

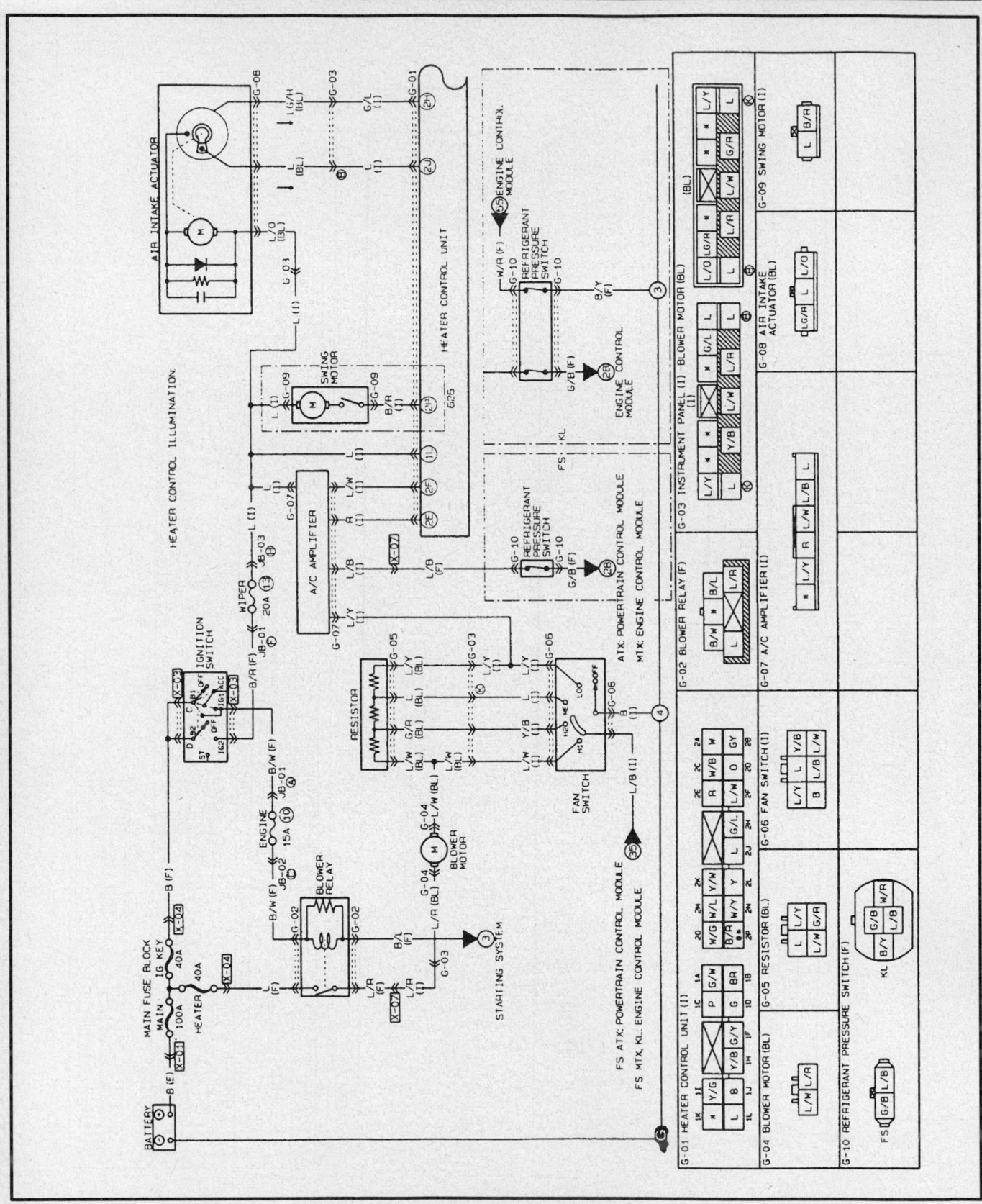

Air conditioning system electrical schematic — 1994-95 626 and MX-6

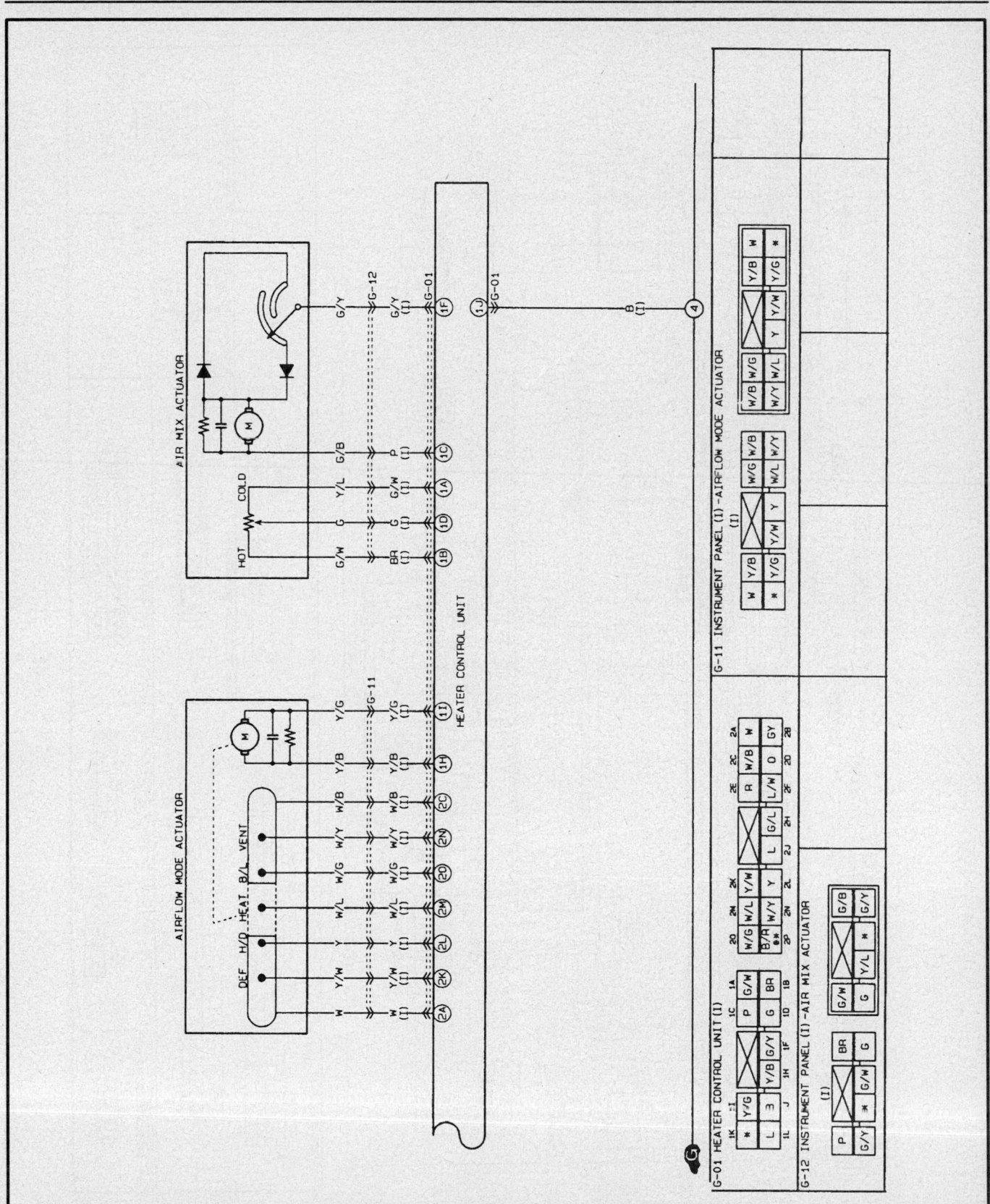

Air conditioning system electrical schematic — 1994–95 626 and MX-6, Cont'd

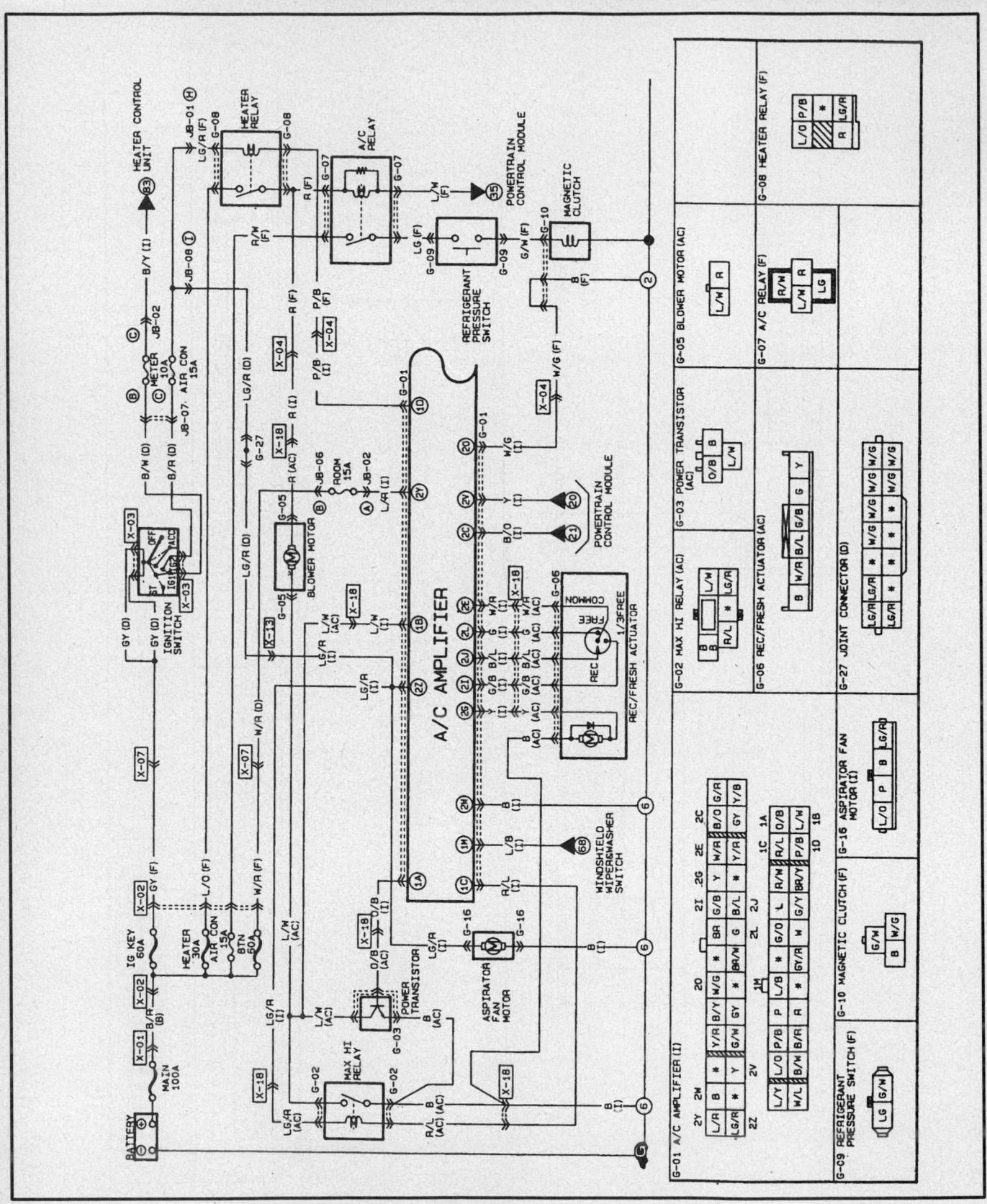

Air conditioning system electrical schematic — 1993 929

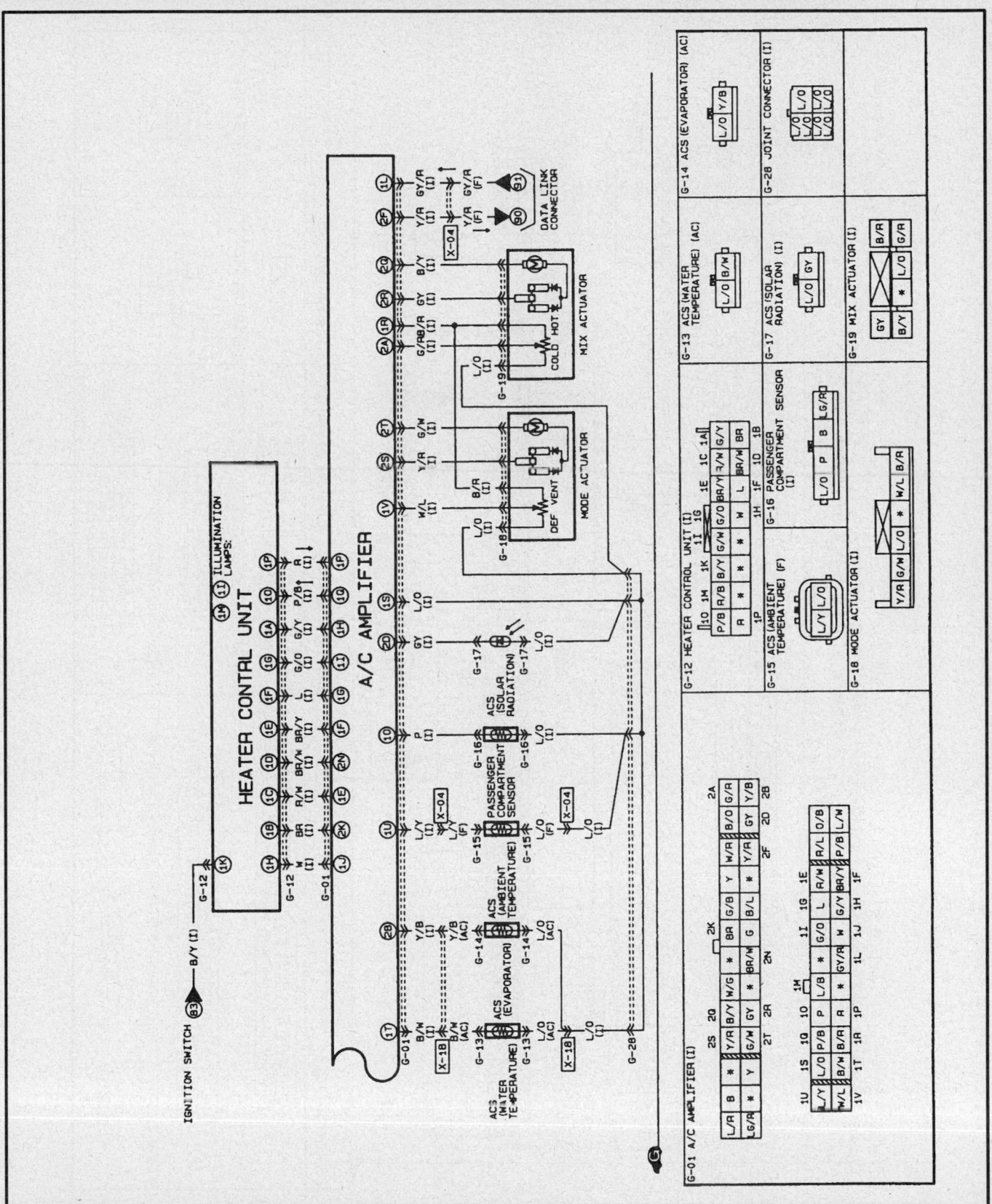

Air conditioning system electrical schematic — 1993 929, Cont'd

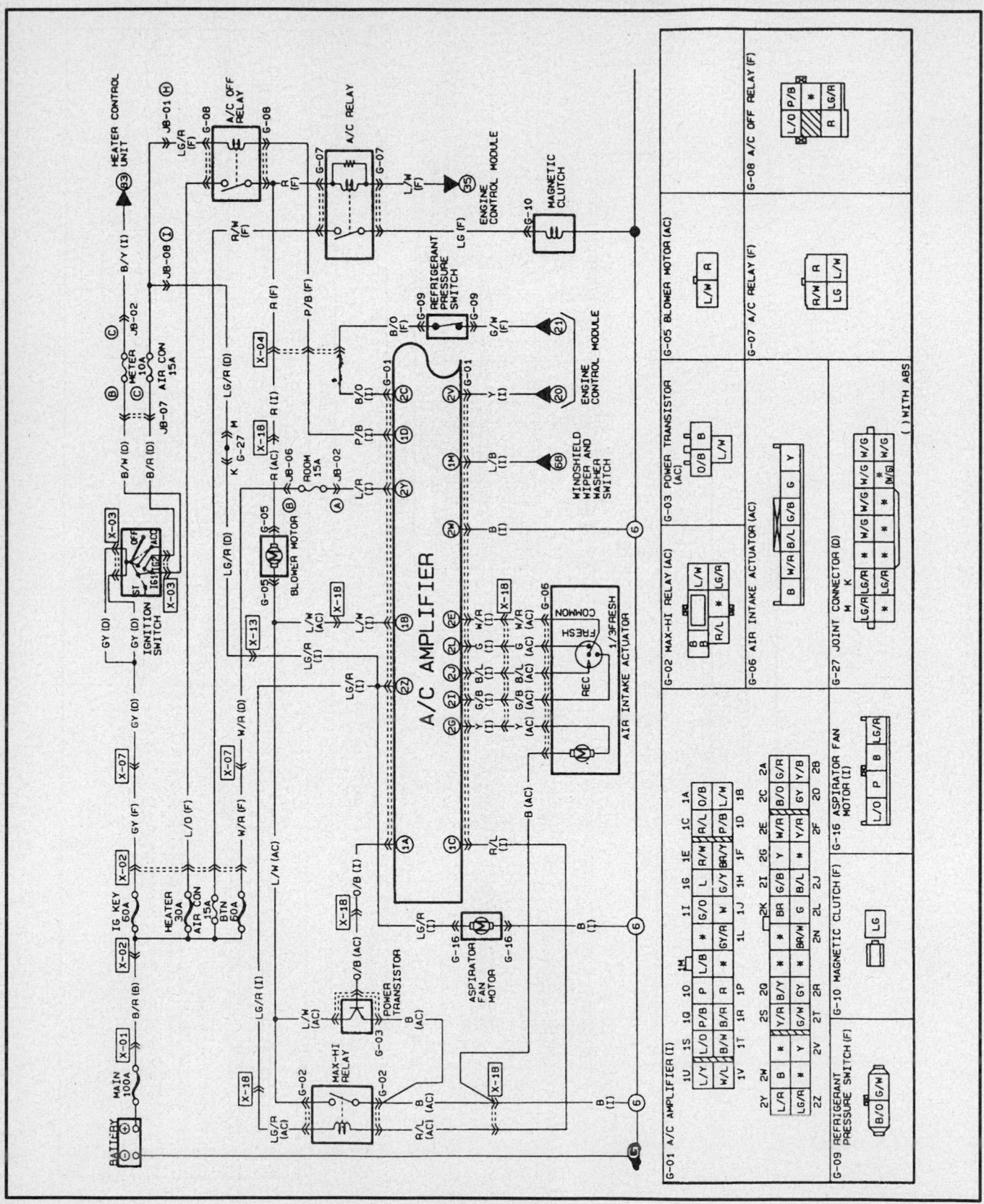

Air conditioning system electrical schematic — 1994–95 929

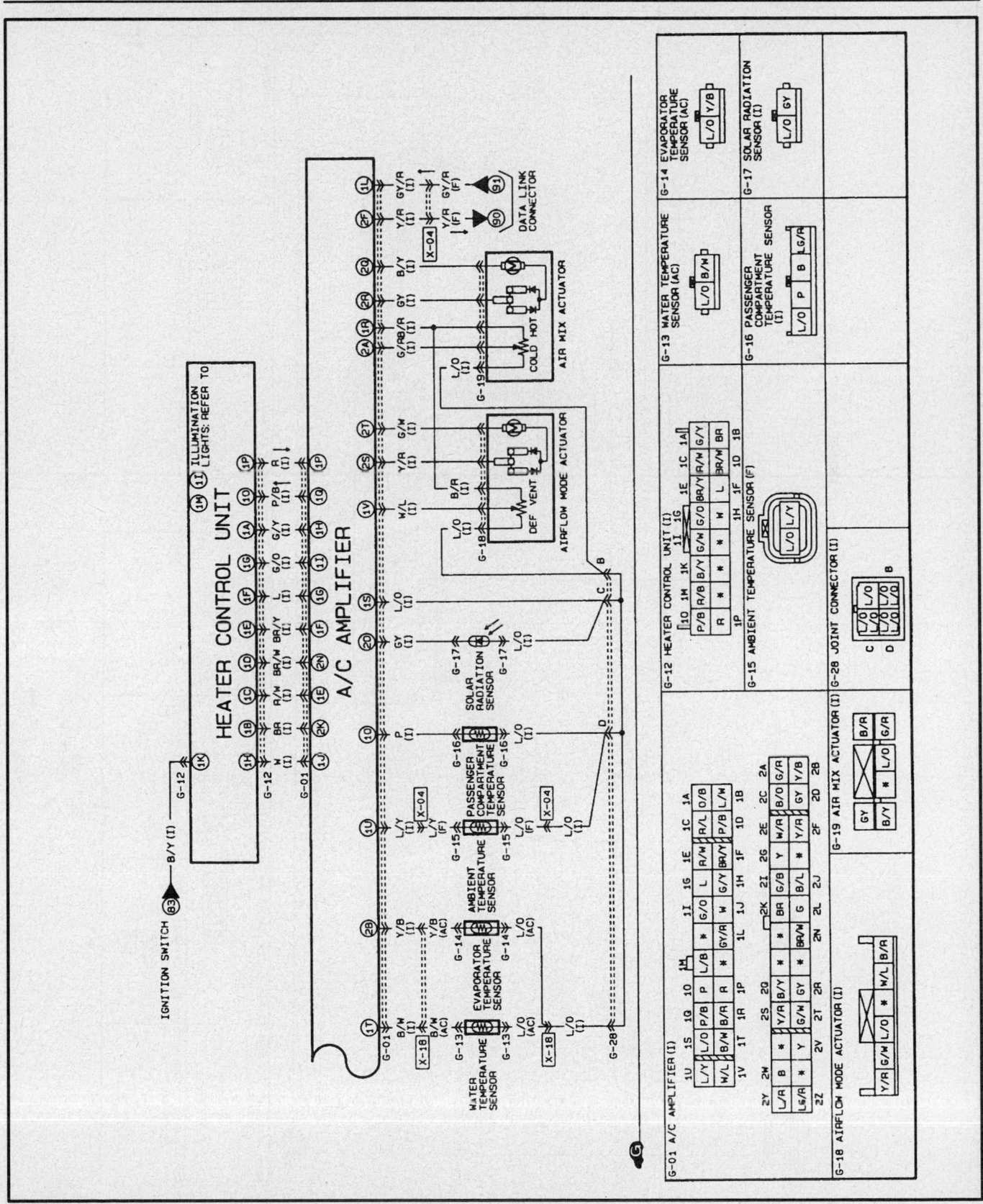

Air conditioning system electrical schematic — 1994–95 929, Cont'd

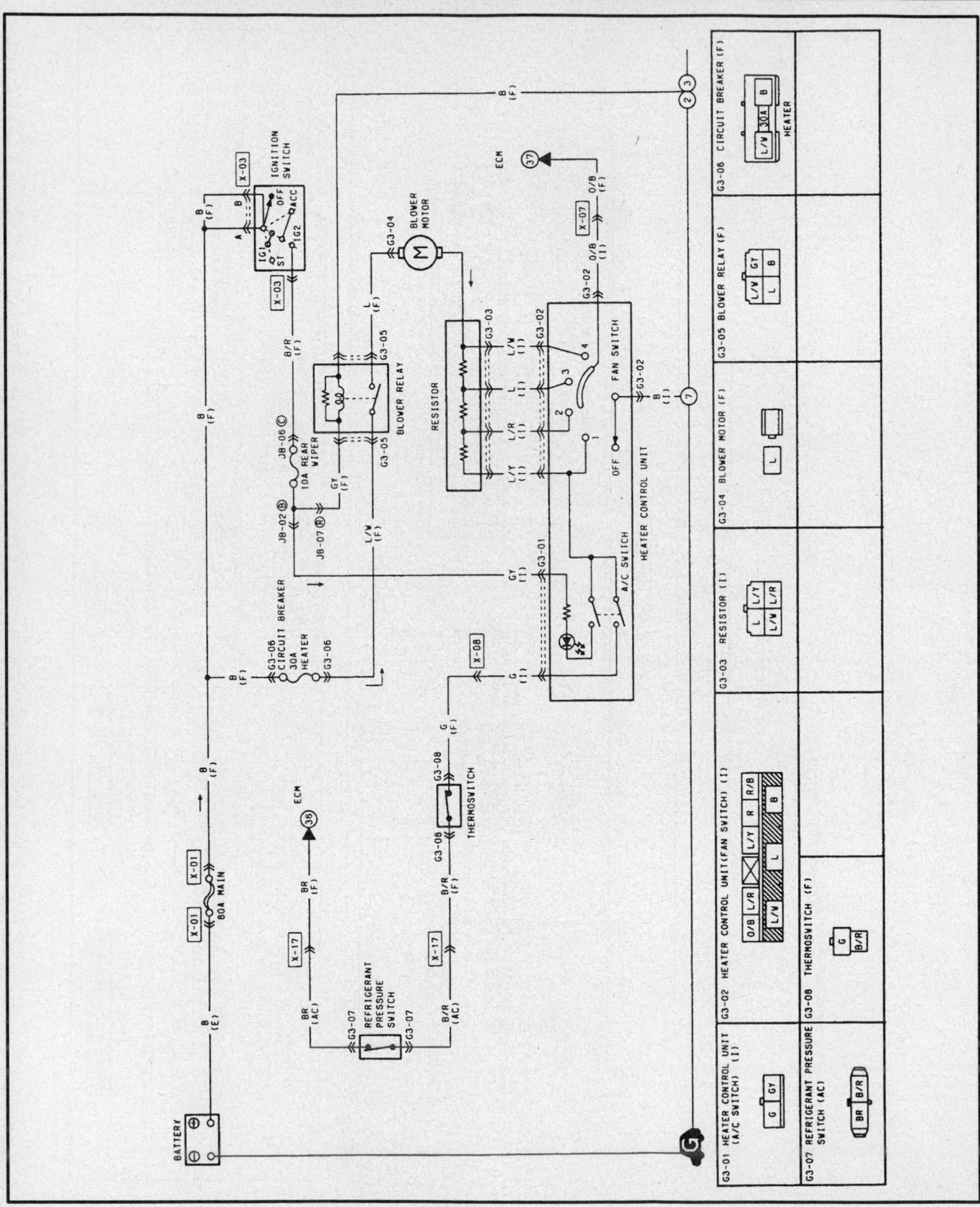

Air conditioning system electrical schematic — MX-3

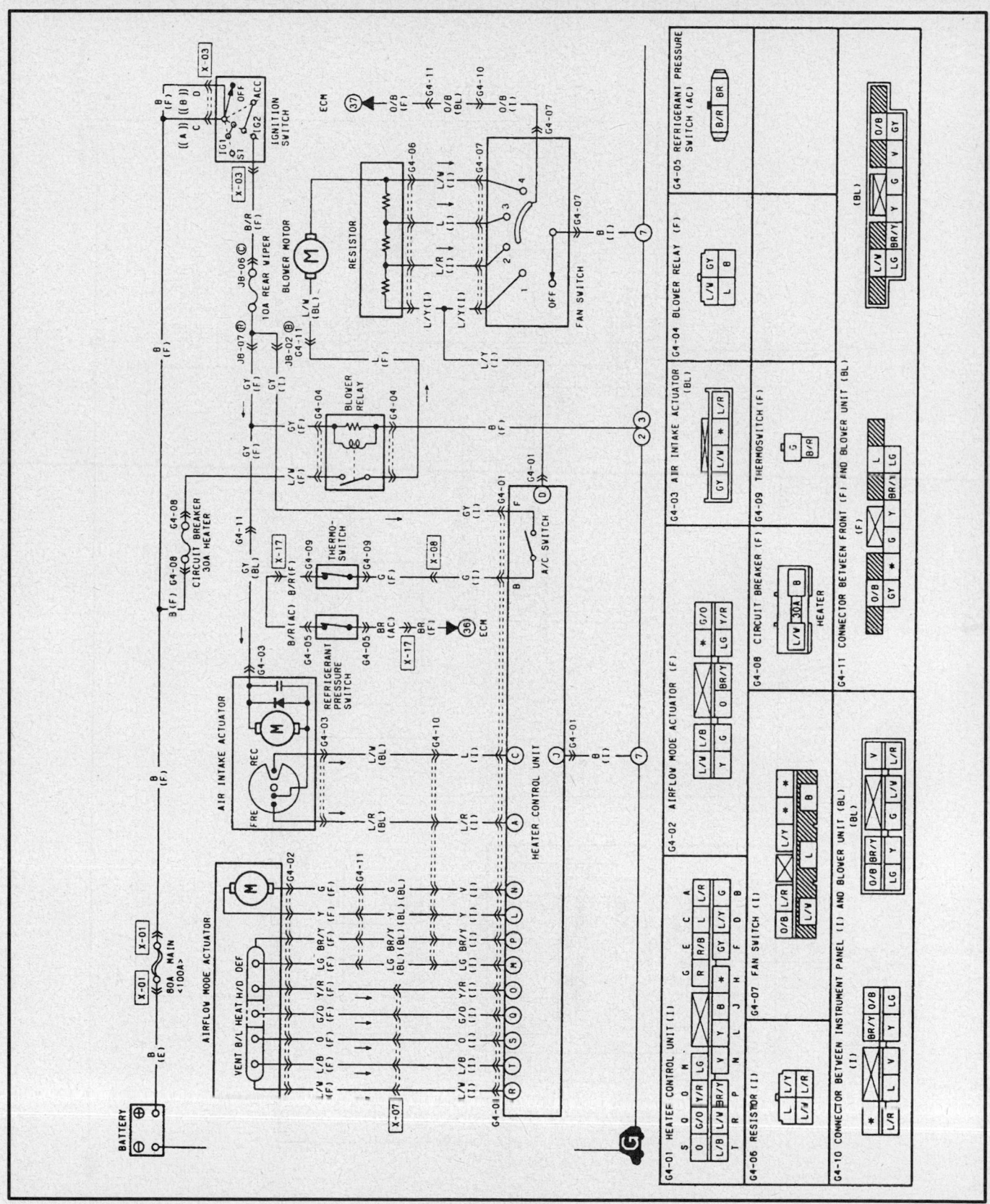

Air conditioning system electrical schematic — MX-3, Cont'd

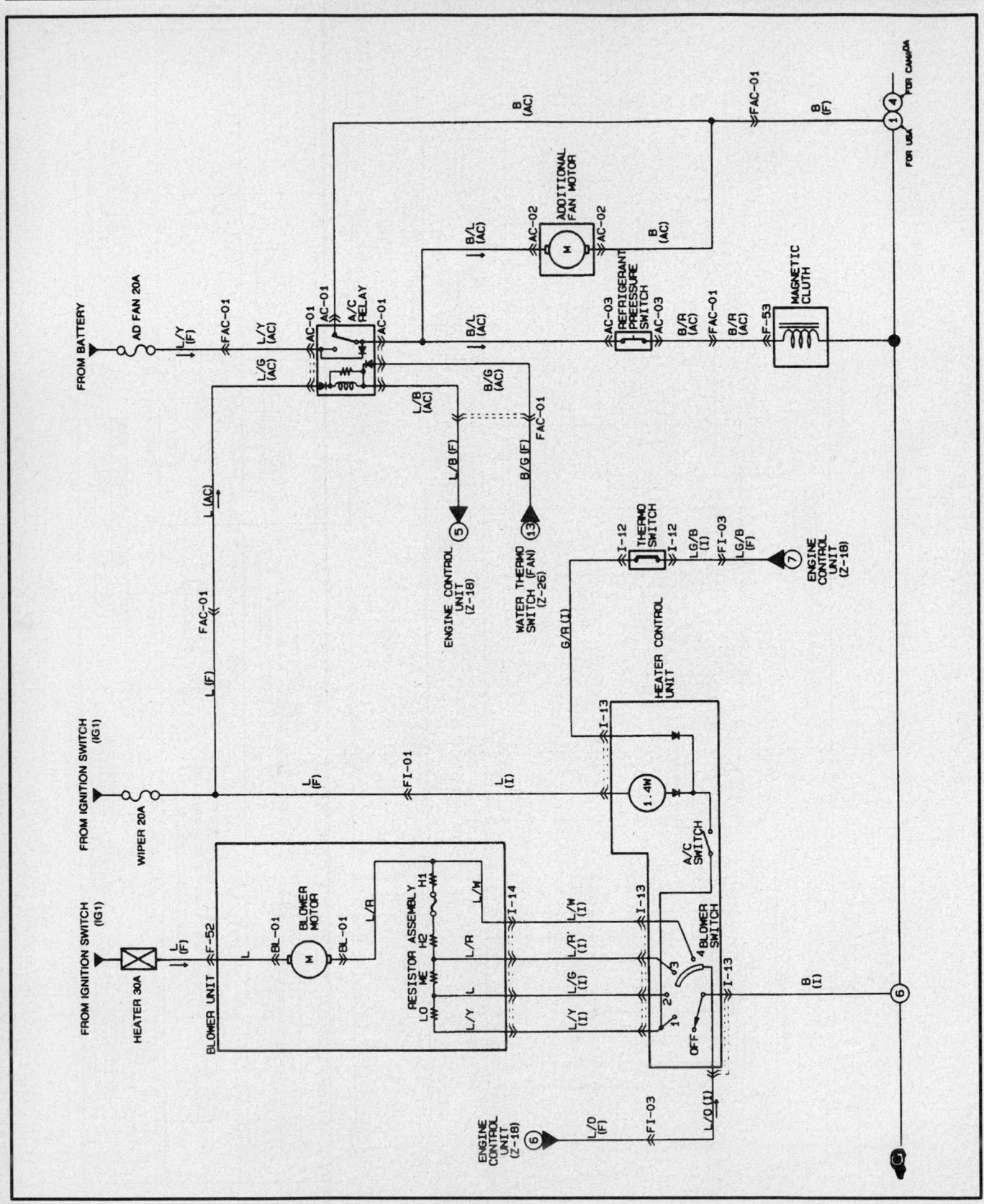

Air conditioning system electrical schematic — 1993 Miata

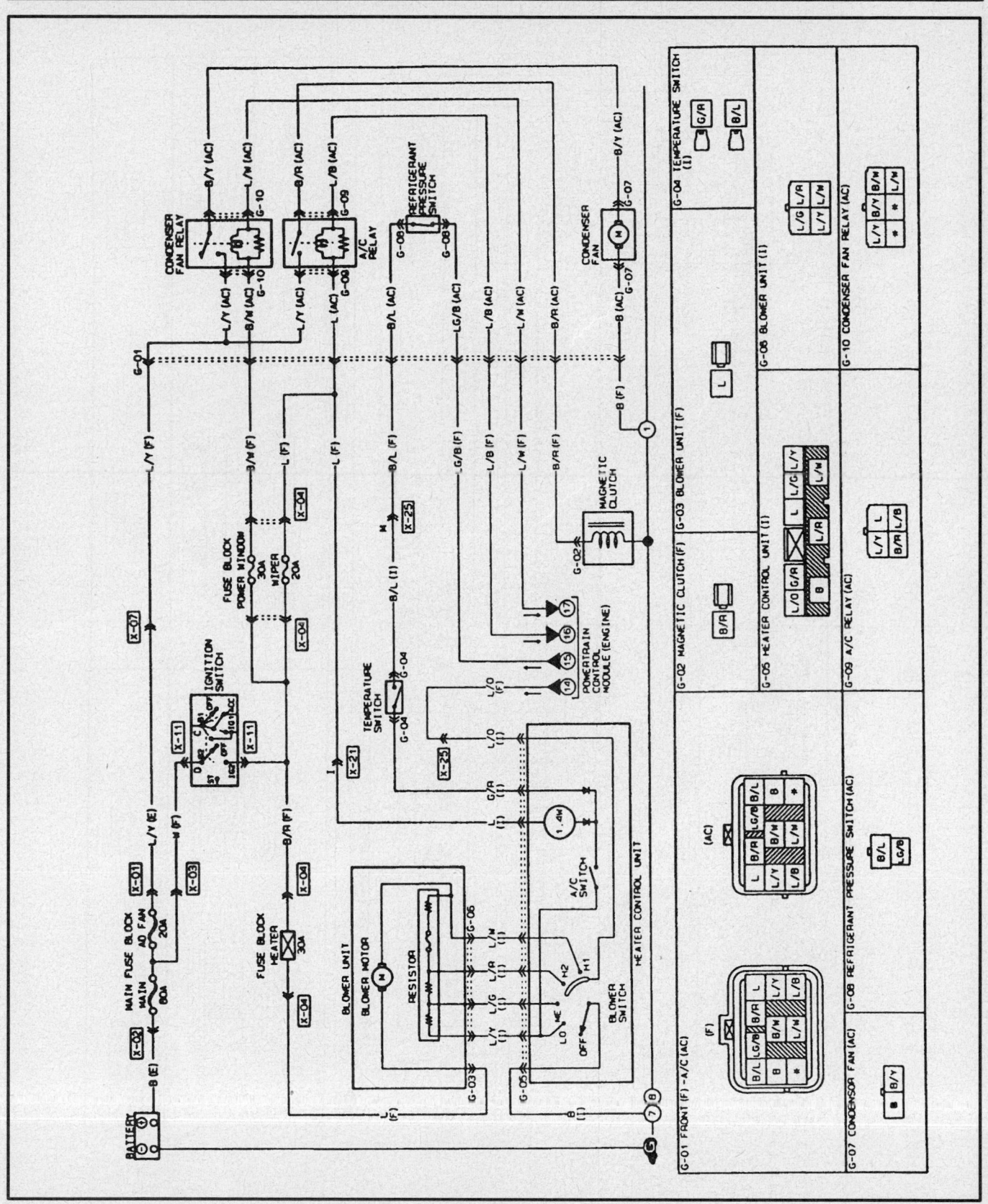

Air conditioning system electrical schematic — 1994 Miata

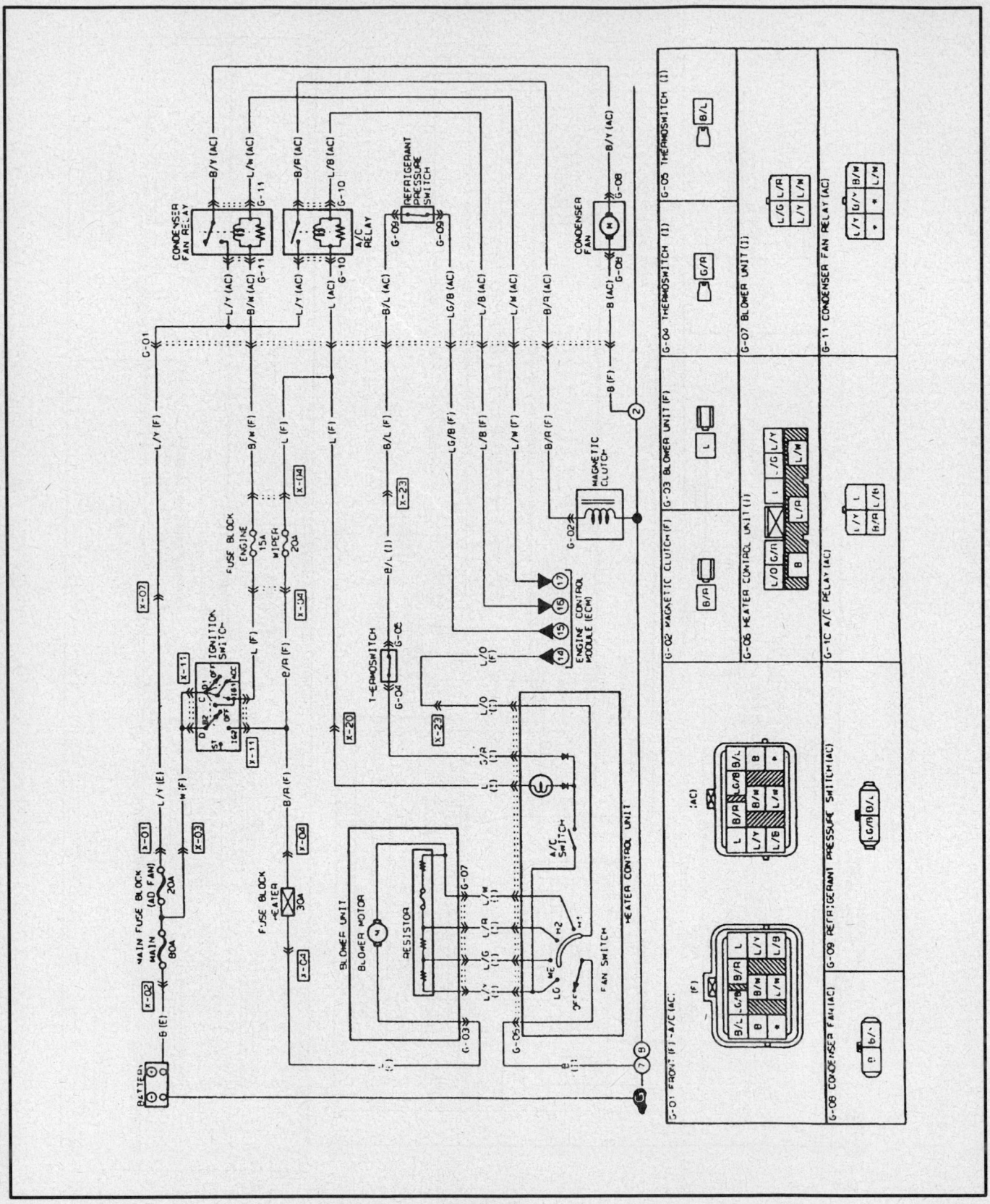

Air conditioning system electrical schematic — 1995 Miata

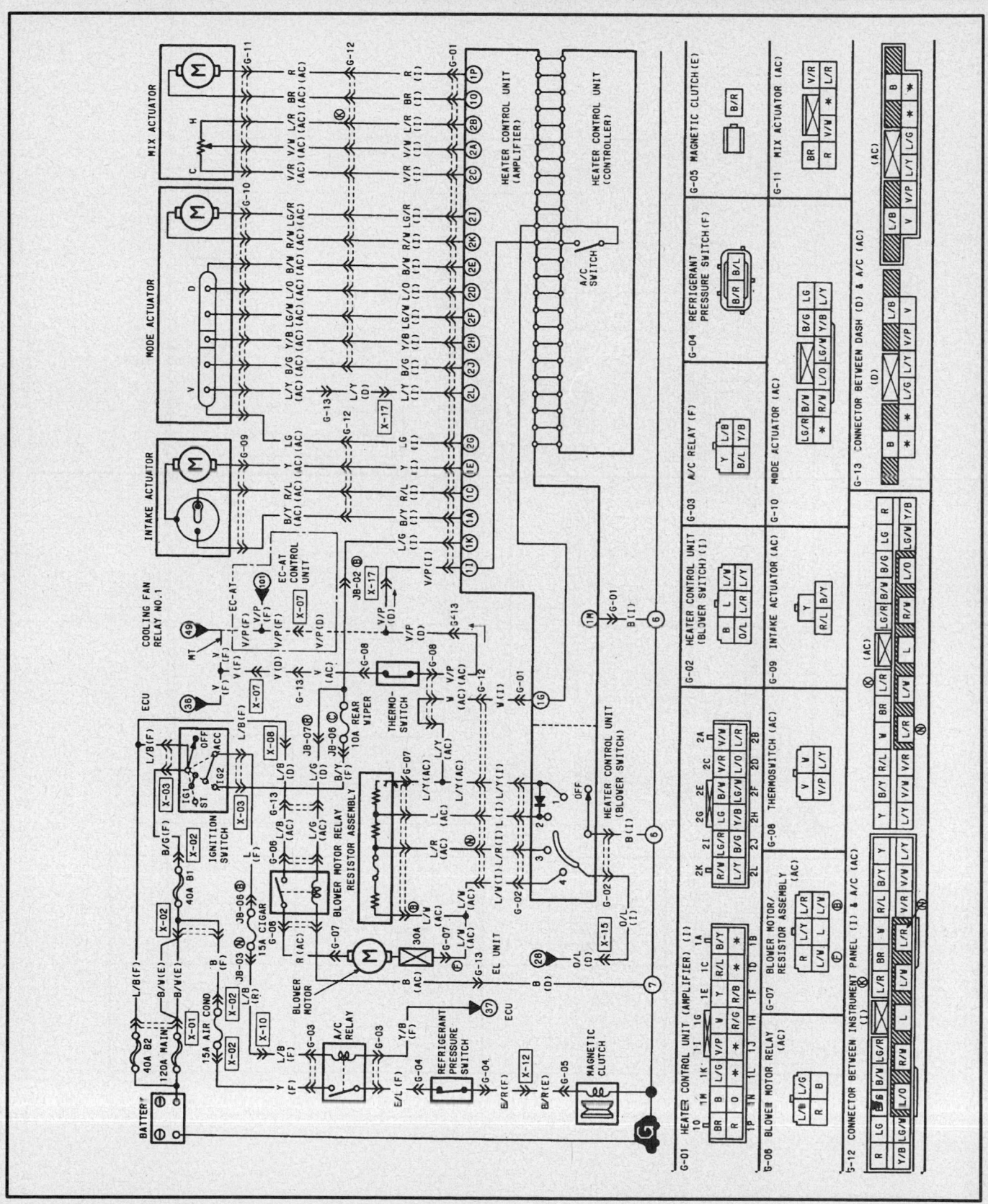

Air conditioning system electrical schematic — 1993 RX-7

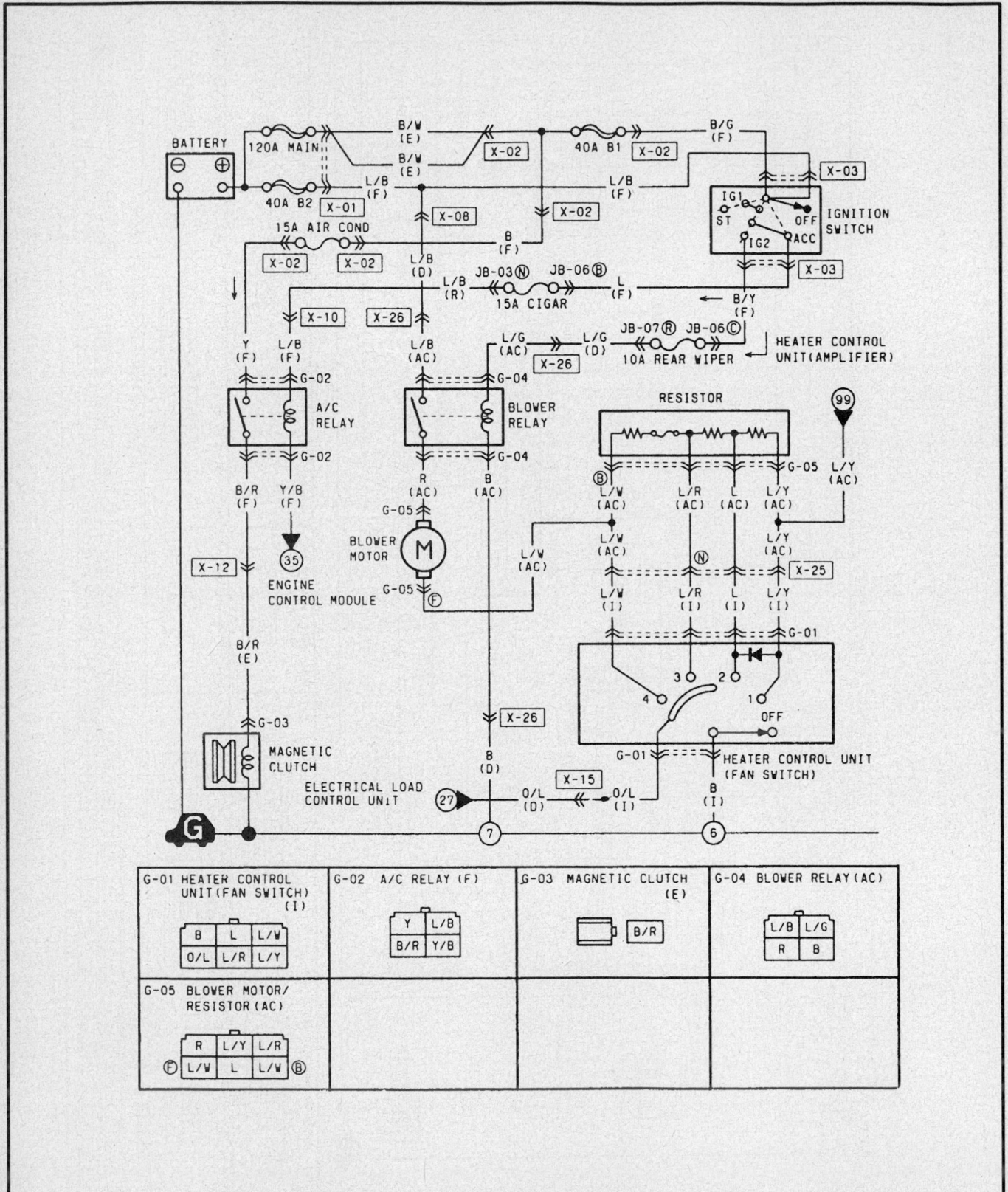

Air conditioning system electrical schematic — 1994–95 RX-7, Cont'd

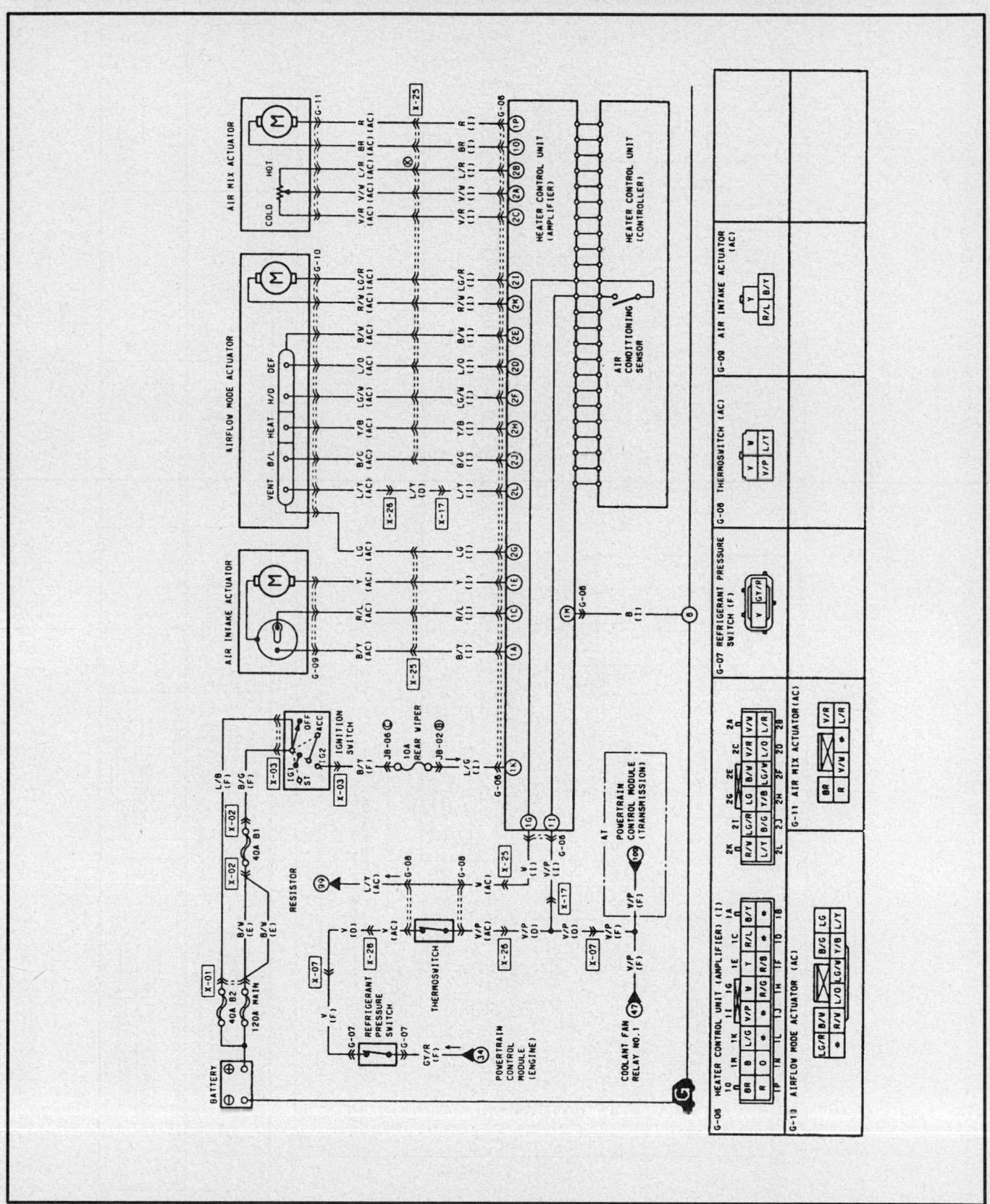

Air conditioning system electrical schematic — 1994–95 RX-7, Cont'd

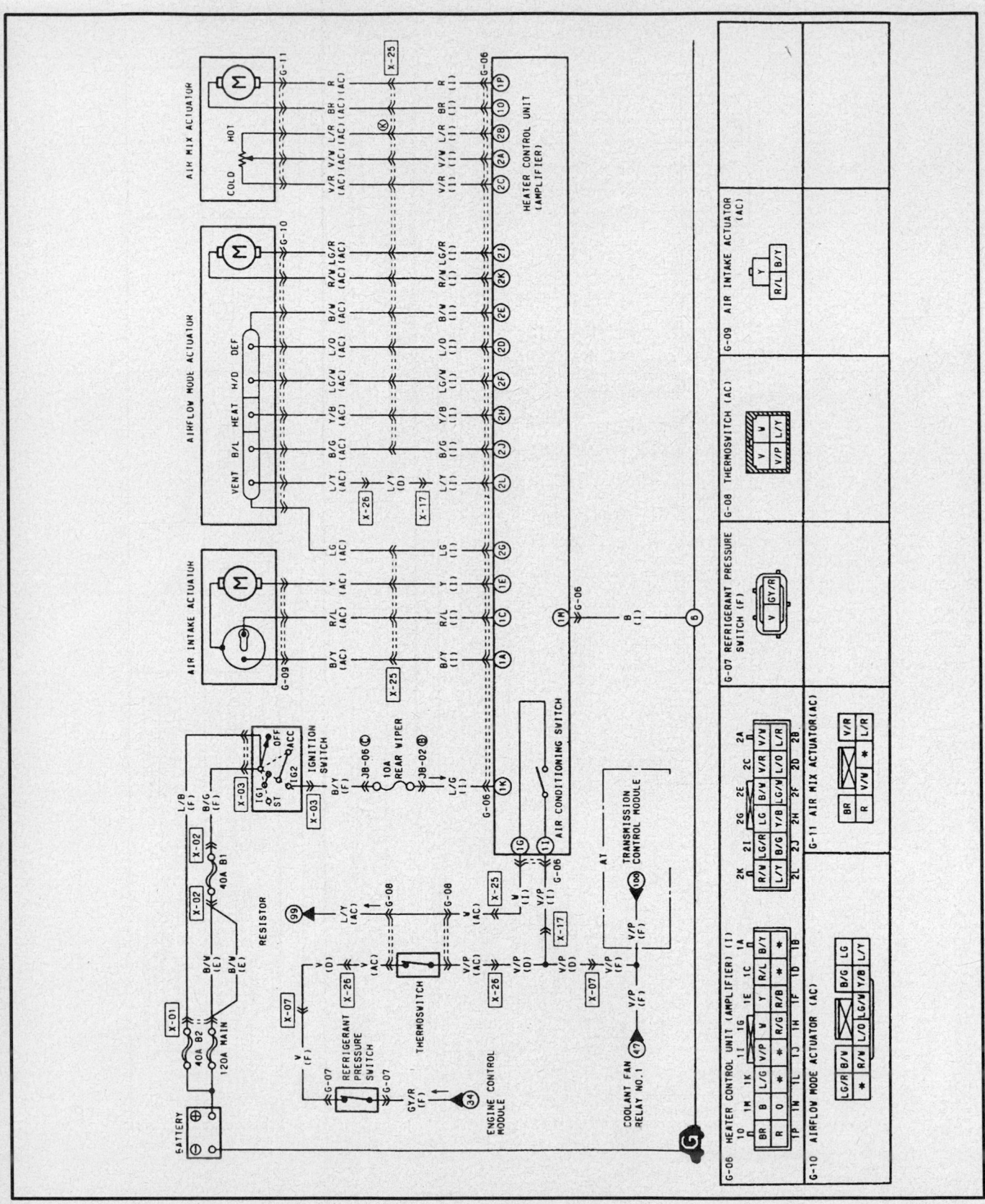

Air conditioning system electrical schematic — 1994–95 RX-7, Cont'd

ENGINE IDENTIFICATION

Year	Model	Engine Displacement Liters (cc)	Engine Series (ID/VIN)	Fuel System	No. of Cylinders	Engine Type
1993	B2200	2.2 (2184)	F2	EFI①	4	OHC
	B2600i	2.6 (2606)	G6	EFI	4	OHC
	MPV	2.6 (2606)	G6	EFI	4	OHC
	MPV	3.0 (2954)	JE	EFI	6	OHC
	Navajo	4.0 (4016)	②	EFI	6	OHV
1994	B2300	2.3 (2299)	③	EFI	4	OHC
	B3000	3.0 (2968)	④	EFI	6	OHC
	B4000	4.0 (4000)	②	EFI	6	OHV
	MPV	2.6 (2600)	G6	EFI	4	OHC
	MPV	3.0 (2954)	JE	EFI	6	OHC
	Navajo	4.0 (4000)	②	EFI	6	OHV
1995	B2300	2.3 (2299)	③	EFI	4	OHC
	B3000	3.0 (2968)	④	EFI	6	OHC
	B4000	4.0 (4000)	②	EFI	6	OHV
	MPV	2.6 (2606)	G6	EFI	4	OHC
	MPV	3.0 (2954)	JE	EFI	6	OHC
	Navajo	4.0 (4000)	②	EFI	6	OHV

EFI —Electronic Fuel Injection
OHC—Overhead Cam
OHV—Overhead Valve
① 2.2L also equipped with 2-barrel feedback carburetor.
② Engine type not specified. VIN code is "X".
③ Engine type not specified. VIN code is "U".
④ Engine type not specified. VIN code is "A".

REFRIGERANT CAPACITIES

Year	Model	Refrigerant (oz.)	Oil (fl. oz.)	Compressor Type
1993	B2200	28.2	8.2	①
	B2600i	28.2	8.2	①
	MPV-front A/C only	37-42 ②	4.9-6.1	①
	MPV-front & rear A/C	51-58 ②	4.9-6.1	①
	Navajo	28.0	7.0	FX-15
1994	B2300	28.2	8.2	Sanden
	B3000	28.2	8.2	Sanden
	B4000	28.2	8.2	Sanden
	MPV-front A/C only	37.07	3.38-3.89	Nippondenso
	MPV-front & rear A/C	44.13	3.38-3.89	Nippondenso
	Navajo	28.0	7.0	FX-15
1995	B2300	28.2	8.2	Sanden
	B3000	28.2	8.2	Sanden
	B4000	28.2	8.2	Sanden
	MPV-front A/C only	31.8	6.76-7.26	Nippondenso
	MPV-front & rear A/C	35.3	6.76-7.26	Nippondenso

REFRIGERANT CAPACITIES

Year	Model	Refrigerant (oz.)	Oil (fl. oz.)	Compressor Type
	Navajo	28.0	7.0	FX-15

① Compressor type not specified
② Check refrigerant charge against normal operating pressures:
Low side: 21-43 psi
High side: 171-235 psi.

AIR CONDITIONING BELT TENSION

Year	Model	Engine Liters (cc)	Belt Type	Specifications	
				New (lbs.)①	Used (lbs.)①
1993	B2200	2.2 (2184)	V-Belt	0.39-0.47	0.47-0.55
	B2600i	2.6 (2606)	V-Belt	0.33-0.39	0.39-0.45
	MPV	2.6 (2606)	V-Belt	0.16-0.18	0.18-0.22
	MPV	3.0 (2954)	V-Belt	0.33-0.39	0.39-0.45
	Navajo	4.0 (4016)	Serpentine	108-132②	108-132②
1994	B2300	2.3 (2299)	V-Belt	4°-25°③	4°-25°③
	B3000	3.0 (2968)	V-Belt	4°-19°③	4°-19°③
	B4000	4.0 (4000)	V-Belt	108-132②	108-132②
	MPV	2.6 (2606)	V-Belt	0.34-0.39	0.40-0.45
	MPV	3.0 (2954)	V-Belt	0.16-0.17	0.18-0.21
	Navajo	4.0 (4000)	V-Belt	108-132②	108-132②
1995	B2300	2.3 (2299)	V-Belt	4°-25°③	4°-25°③
	B3000	3.0 (2968)	V-Belt	4°-19°③	4°-19°③
	B4000	4.0 (4000)	V-Belt	108-132②	108-132②
	MPV	2.6 (2606)	V-Belt	0.34-0.39	0.40-0.45
	MPV	3.0 (2954)	V-Belt	0.16-0.17	0.18-0.21
	Navajo	4.0 (4000)	V-Belt	108-132②	108-132②

① Inches of deflection measured at midpoint of belt with 22 lbs. pressure.
② Lbs. measured using tension gauge. For checking only, if below minimum, adjuster needs to be reset.
③ Automatic tensioner with built-in pointer and gauge indicator. Replace belt when pointer is not within range limits.

SYSTEM DESCRIPTION

General Information

The heater unit is located in the center of the vehicle along the firewall. The heater system is a bi–level system designed to direct warm air through the vents to either the windshield or the floor and cool air through the panel outlet. The air conditioning system is designed to be activated in combination with a separate air conditioning switch installed in the control assembly and the fan speed switch. The system incorporates a compressor, condenser, evaporator, receiver/drier or accumulator, pressure switch, expansion valve or fixed orifice tube, thermo switch or clutch cycling switch, refrigerant lines and some models are equipped with an electronic control head assembly versus the standard cable operated control head.

The MPV model offers an auxiliary rear heater unit which is mounted under the driver's seat, the unit incorporates a heater core, blower motor and water valve. The MPV also offers an auxiliary air conditioning unit which is located at the left rear compartment of the vehicle, the unit incorporates an evaporator, blower motor, expansion valve and thermo switch.

The Navajo uses an electronic engine control system which monitors and regulates the air conditioning system by working through the wide open throttle relay disengaging the air conditioning clutch under the following conditions, immediately after start–up, for a brief period during wide open throttle, if engine coolant temperature approaches an overheating condition and when engine rpm is approaching a stall speed. In addition, the electronic engine control senses the output clutch cycling pressure switch and momentarily delays clutch engagement until the engine rpm is raised to an acceptable rate.

Service Valve Location

Charging valve locations will vary, but most of the time the high or low pressure fitting will be located at the compressor, receiver/drier (accumulator) or along the refrigerant lines. Always discharge, evacuate and recharge at the low side service fitting. On 1993–95 Navajo models, the high pressure service valve is located near the condenser on the high side line and the low side service valve is on top of the accumulator near the clutch cycling pressure switch.

System Discharging

R–12 refrigerant is a chlorofluorocarbon which, when mishandled, can contribute to the depletion of the ozone layer in the upper atmosphere. Ozone filters out harmful radiation from the sun. In order to protect the ozone layer, an approved R–12 Recovery/Recycling machine that meets SAE standard J1991 should be employed when discharging the system. Follow the operating instructions provided with the approved equipment exactly to properly discharge the system.

System Evacuating

If the air conditioning system has been opened to the atmosphere, it should be air and moisture free before being recharged with refrigerant. Moisture and air mixed with refrigerant will raise the compressor head pressure, possibly damage the system's components and will reduce the performance of the system. Moisture will boil at normal room temperature when exposed to a vacuum, the moisture then becomes a vapor and will be easily removed by the vacuum pump.

To evacuate or rid the system of air and moisture perform the following procedure:

1. Leak test the system and repair any leaks found.

2. Connect an approved charging station, Recovery/Recycling machine or manifold gauge set and vacuum pump to the discharge and suction ports. The red hose is normally connected to the discharge (high pressure) line, and the blue hose is connected to the suction (low pressure) line.

3. Open the discharge and suction ports and start the vacuum pump. If the pump is not able to pull at least 26 in. Hg vacuum, there is a leak that must be repaired before evacuation can occur.

4. Once the system has reached at least 26 in. Hg vacuum, allow the system to evacuate for at least 10 minutes. The longer the system is evacuated, the more contaminants will be removed.

5. Close all valves and turn the pump off. If the system loses more than 2 in. Hg vacuum after 15 minutes, there is a leak that should be repaired.

System Charging

1. Connect an approved charging station, Recovery/Recycling machine or manifold gauge set to the discharge and suction ports. The red hose is normally connected to the discharge (high pressure) line, and the blue hose is connected to the suction (low pressure) line.

2. Follow the instructions provided with the equipment and charge the system with the specified amount of refrigerant.

3. Perform a leak test.

SYSTEM COMPONENTS

Radiator

REMOVAL AND INSTALLATION

Except Navajo

1. Disconnect the negative terminal at the battery.
2. Drain the cooling system.
3. Disconnect the coolant reservoir hose.
4. Remove the fresh air duct, if equipped.
5. Remove the upper and lower radiator hoses.
6. Disconnect electric fan and thermo switch wire connector, if equipped.
7. Remove electric fan or clutch fan and cowling assembly.
8. Disconnect and plug automatic transaxle cooler lines, if equipped.
9. Remove radiator mounting brackets and bolts.
10. Remove radiator assembly.
To install:
11. Install the radiator assembly.
12. Connect the automatic transaxle cooler lines, if equipped.
13. Install the electric or clutch fan assembly.
14. Install the upper and lower radiator hose.
15. Install the fresh air duct, if equipped.
16. Connect the coolant reservoir hose.
17. Refill radiator with specified type and quantity of coolant.
18. Check the automatic transaxle fluid level, if equipped.
19. Reconnect the negative battery terminal.
20. Check cooling system for leaks.

Navajo

1. Disconnect the negative battery terminal.

NOTE: When the negative battery cable is disconnected and reconnected, some abnormal driveability symptoms may occur on restart. About 10 driving miles are needed for the ECU to re-establish the computer settings.

2. Drain the cooling system.
3. Disconnect the coolant reservoir hose.

4. Remove the radiator shroud 2 attaching screws.
5. Lift the shroud out of the lower retaining clips and drape it over the fan blades.
6. Loosen and remove the upper and lower hoses at the radiator.
7. Disconnect the transaxle cooler lines and support bracket, if equipped.
8. Remove the 2 radiator upper attaching screws.
9. Tilt the radiator rearward and lift upward to clear the radiator support and cooling fan.
To install:
10. Install the radiator assembly.
11. Connect the automatic transaxle cooling lines and support bracket, if equipped.
12. Install the upper and lower radiator hoses.
13. Install the radiator shroud.
14. Reconnect the coolant reservoir hose.
15. Refill radiator with specified type and quantity of coolant.
16. Check the automatic transaxle fluid level, if equipped.
17. Connect the negative battery terminal.
18. Check cooling system for leaks.

COOLING SYSTEM BLEEDING

Navajo

NOTE: Use the following procedure to remove all trapped air in the cooling system to ensure a complete fill and avoid the possibility of the engine overheating.

1. Ensure that the radiator drain plug is fully closed.
2. Fill the cooling system with a 50/50 mixture of the specified type of coolant.
3. Allow several minutes for coolant to flow through radiator and release any trapped air.
4. Install the radiator cap to the pressure relief position by turning the cap to the fully installed position and then backing off to the first stop to allow for any trapped air to be released.
5. Position the temperature and mode selection lever to the **MAXIMUM HEAT** position.

6. Start the vehicle and set the fast idle at 2000 rpm for approximately 3–4 minutes.

7. Turn the engine **OFF** and carefully remove the radiator cap.

8. Add coolant to bring the level up to the filler neck seat.

9. Install the cap to the pressure relief position.

10. Start the vehicle and run the engine at fast idle until the upper radiator hose is warm.

11. Turn the engine **OFF** and carefully remove the radiator cap.

12. Add coolant to bring the level up to the filler neck seat.

13. Install the cap to the fully installed position.

14. Remove the coolant reservoir cap and fill the reservoir with 1.1 quarts of the specified type of coolant.

Cooling Fan

TESTING

B2200, B2300, B2600i, B3000, B4000 and MPV

1. Disconnect the electric cooling fan connector.

2. Apply 12 volts to terminal **a** of fan motor connector and ground terminal **b**.

3. If the fan motor does not operate smoothly, replace the unit.

4. If the fan motor does operate smoothly, turn the ignition switch **ON**.

5. Measure the voltage between the terminals of the wire connector with the air conditioner and blower switch **ON**.

6. If there is not approximately 12 volts at the connector, test the fan relay.

REMOVAL AND INSTALLATION

B2200, B2300, B2600i, B3000 and B4000

1. Disconnect the negative battery terminal.

2. Drain the engine coolant.

3. Remove fan shroud, fan clutch and fan blades attaching bolts.

4. Installation is the reverse of the removal procedure.

MPV

1. Disconnect the negative battery terminal.

2. Remove the lower grille and the radiator grille.

3. Remove the hood lock assembly.

4. Disconnect the condenser fan connector.

5. Remove the condenser fan attaching bolts and remove the condenser fan.

6. Installation is the reverse of the removal procedure.

Condenser

REMOVAL AND INSTALLATION

B2200, B2300, B2600i, B3000 and B4000

1. Disconnect the negative battery terminal.

2. Properly discharge the air conditioning system.

3. Disconnect the compressor discharge line from the condenser at the spring lock coupling.

4. Disconnect the liquid line from the condenser at the spring lock coupling.

5. Remove 2 nuts from lower mounting studs.

6. Tilt top of radiator rearward.

7. Remove condenser attaching bolts and clips, and remove the condenser.

8. Installation is the reverse of the removal procedure. Use new O–rings at all fittings. If a new condenser is installed, add 1.4 – 1.9 oz. of new oil to the compressor during recharging. Evacuate, recharge and leak test the system.

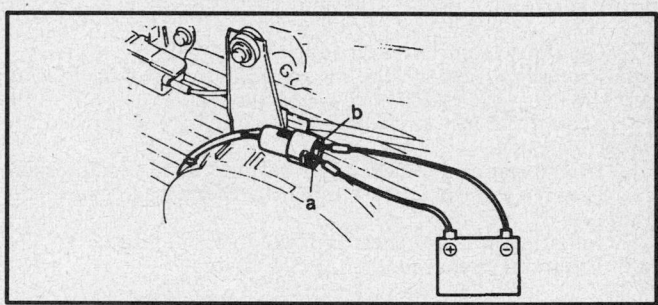

Condenser fan testing — MPV

MPV

1. Disconnect the negative battery terminal.

2. Properly discharge the air conditioning system.

3. Remove the lower grille and the radiator grille.

4. Remove the hood lock assembly.

5. Disconnect the condenser fan connector.

6. Remove the condenser fan attaching bolts and remove the condenser fan.

7. Disconnect the refrigerant high and low side pressure lines. Immediately cap all openings to minimize contamination.

8. Remove the condenser attaching bolts and remove the condenser.

9. Installation is the reverse of the removal procedure. Use new O–rings at all fittings. If installing a new condenser, add 1.0 oz. of new refrigerant oil to the compressor during recharge. Evacuate, recharge and leak test the system.

Navajo

1. Disconnect the negative battery terminal.

NOTE: When the negative battery cable is disconnected and reconnected, some abnormal driveability symptoms may occur on restart. About 10 driving miles are needed for the ECU to re-establish the computer settings.

2. Properly discharge the air conditioning system.

3. Remove 5 plastic retainers on top of the grille. Remove 2 screws attaching grilled to the head lamp housing.

4. Depress the spring tabs through the lower outboard grilled openings and detach the grilled from the head lamp housings and remove the grille.

5. Disconnect and plug the compressor discharge line at the condenser using the appropriate spring lock coupling tool.

6. Disconnect the condenser liquid line using the appropriate spring lock coupling tool. Immediately cap all openings.

7. Raise and support the vehicle safely. Remove the 2 attaching nuts at the lower mounting studs on the condenser.

8. Remove the upper radiator brackets and tilt the radiator rearward being careful not to damage the cooling fan or radiator core.

9. Remove the 2 bolts attaching the condenser to the radiator support. Remove the condenser assembly.

10. Installation is the reverse of the removal procedure.

11. Evacuate, recharge and leak test the system.

Compressor

REMOVAL AND INSTALLATION

1. Disconnect the negative battery terminal.

NOTE: On Navajo, when the negative battery cable is disconnected and reconnected, some abnormal driveability symptoms may occur on restart. About 10 driving miles are needed for the ECU to re-establish the computer settings.

2. On MPV, remove the air funnel.
3. Properly discharge the air conditioning system. Disconnect the magnetic clutch wire connector.
4. Loosen the lock nut and adjusting bolts and remove the compressor belt.
5. Disconnect and plug refrigerant lines at the compressor.
6. Remove the compressor mounting bolts and remove the compressor.
7. Installation is the reverse of the removal procedure.
8. Evacuate, recharge and test the system.

Receiver/Drier

REMOVAL AND INSTALLATION

B2200, B2300, B2600i, B3000, B4000 and MPV

1. Disconnect the negative battery terminal.
2. Properly discharge the air conditioning system.
3. Remove the radiator grille and lower grille (MPV).
4. On MPV, remove the right front parking light and headlight.
5. Disconnect the refrigerant lines at the receiver/drier. Immediately cap all openings to minimize system contamination.
6. Remove the receiver/drier attaching nuts and remove the receiver/drier.
7. Installation is the reverse of the removal procedure. Use new O-rings at the fittings. Evacuate, recharge and leak test.

Accumulator

REMOVAL AND INSTALLATION

Navajo

NOTE: The accumulator should be replaced whenever a major component of the system is replaced.

1. Disconnect the negative battery terminal.

NOTE: When the negative battery cable is disconnected and reconnected, some abnormal driveability symptoms may occur on restart. About 10 driving miles are needed for the ECU to re-establish the computer settings.

2. Properly discharge the air conditioning system.
3. Disconnect the wire connector from the pressure switch at the accumulator.
4. Remove the pressure switch, if required.
5. Disconnect and plug the refrigerant low pressure line using the appropriate spring lock coupling tool.
6. Using a backup wrench, loosen the accumulator to evaporator low pressure line.
7. Loosen the lower attaching screws holding the flanges of the case to the bracket and the evaporator inlet to the accumulator together.
8. Disconnect and plug the accumulator to the evaporator line.
9. Remove the bracket from the accumulator. Remove the accumulator. Drain and measure the oil in the accumulator.
10. Installation is the reverse of the removal procedure. Add the same amount of oil as drained from the accumulator, plus 2.0 oz. to the accumulator during installation. Evacuate, recharge, and leak test.

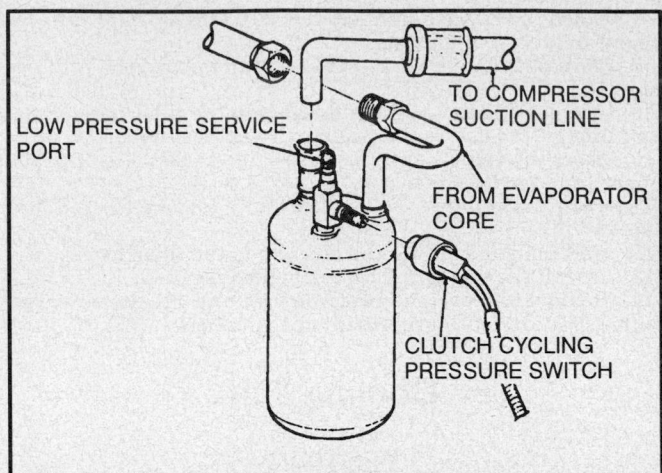

Accumlator assembly — Navajo

Evaporator

REMOVAL AND INSTALLATION

Except Navajo

1. Disconnect the negative battery terminal.
2. Properly discharge the air conditioning system.
3. Disconnect and plug the refrigerant lines at the evaporator.
4. Remove the grommets at the firewall.
5. Remove the glove box and, on MPV, the lower panel.
6. Remove the air flow ducts, if necessary.
7. Remove the evaporator unit drain hose.
8. Remove the seal plates from both sides of the evaporator unit.
9. Disconnect the air conditioning wiring harness and thermoswitch connector at the evaporator.
10. Remove the attaching bolts at the evaporator and remove the unit. Disassembly the unit as needed to remove the expansion valve and/or the evaporator core.
11. Installation is the reverse of the removal procedure. If installing a new evaporator core, add 3.0 oz. of new oil to the unit during installation. Use new O-rings at all fittings. Evacuate, recharge and leak test.

Navajo

1. Disconnect the negative battery terminal.

NOTE: When the negative battery cable is disconnected and reconnected, some abnormal driveability symptoms may occur on restart. About 10 driving miles are needed for the ECU to re-establish the computer settings.

2. Properly discharge the air conditioning system.
3. Disconnect the wire connector from the pressure switch at the accumulator. Remove the pressure switch.
4. Disconnect and plug the low pressure accumulator line using the appropriate spring lock coupling tool.
5. Using a backup wrench, disconnect and plug the evaporator inlet line.
6. Remove the attaching screws holding the vacuum reservoir and evaporator service cover to the evaporator case assembly. Move the reservoir aside, avoiding vacuum line damage.
7. Remove the 2 dash panel mounting nuts.
8. Remove the evaporator case service cover from the evaporator case assembly.
9. Remove the evaporator core and accumulator assembly from the vehicle.

10. Separate the evaporator core from the accumulator using 2 wrenches.

11. Installation is the reverse of the removal procedure. If installing a new evaporator core, add 3.0 oz. of oil to the unit during installation. Use new O–rings at appropriate fittings. Evacuate, recharge and leak test.

Expansion Valve

REMOVAL AND INSTALLATION

Except Navajo

1. Disconnect the negative battery terminal.
2. Properly discharge the air conditioning system.
3. Disconnect and plug the refrigerant lines at the evaporator.
4. Remove the grommet at the evaporator line connection.
5. Remove the glove box and lower panel.
6. Remove the air flow ducts, if required.
7. Remove the evaporator unit seal plates and remove the unit.
8. Remove evaporator securing clips.
9. Disassemble the unit.
10. Remove the thermo switch.
11. Remove the capillary tube from the outlet pipe.
12. Remove the expansion valve.
13. Installation is the reverse of the removal procedure. Use new O–rings at the fittings. Evacuate, recharge and leak test.

Fixed Orifice Tube

REMOVAL AND INSTALLATION

Navajo

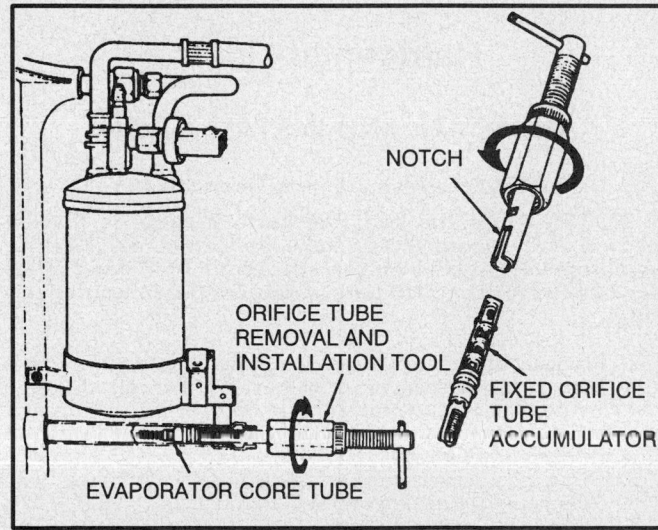

Fixed orifice tube removal – Navajo

1. Disconnect the negative battery terminal.

NOTE: When the negative battery cable is disconnected and reconnected, some abnormal driveability symptoms may occur on restart. About 10 driving miles are needed for the ECU to re–establish the computer settings.

2. Properly discharge the air conditioning system.
3. Disconnect and plug the lower evaporator inlet line.
4. Apply a small amount of refrigerant oil to the evaporator inlet to lubricate the orifice tube during removal.
5. Using a suitable tool (49 UN01 060, or equivalent), engage the 2 tangs on the orifice tube, being careful not to twist or rotate the tube as this might cause the tube to break off in the evaporator line.
6. Pull the orifice tube directly out. On some tools, a nut is used to secure the handle for removal by running the nut down against the core tube before pulling the orifice tube out.
7. If the tube breaks during removal, use a special extractor tool (49 UN01 061, or equivalent) to remove the remaining pieces.
8. Installation is the reverse of the removal procedure. Liberally apply clean refrigerant oil to the evaporator tube before installing the new orifice tube up to its stop. Use new O–rings. Evacuate, recharge and leak test.

Blower Motor

REMOVAL AND INSTALLATION

B2200 and B2600i

1. Disconnect the negative battery terminal.
2. Remove the right side kick panel cover and remove the ECU.
3. Remove the screws and remove the blower motor wire connector.
4. Remove the blower motor cover.
5. Remove the blower motor.
6. Installation is the reverse of the removal procedure.

B2300, B3000 and B4000

1. Disconnect the negative battery terminal.
2. Remove glove box, and remove ECU from blower case.
3. Disconnect blower motor and blower resistor connectors.
4. Loosen seal plate between blower case and heater case.
5. Remove blower case nuts and blower case.
6. Installation is the reverse of removal procedure.

MPV

1. Disconnect the negative battery terminal.
2. Remove the right side lower panel and undercover.
3. Disconnect the blower motor wire connector.
4. Remove the 3 blower motor attaching screws.
5. Remove the blower motor.
6. Installation is the reverse of the removal procedure.

Navajo

1. Disconnect the negative battery terminal.

NOTE: When the negative battery cable is disconnected and reconnected, some abnormal driveability symptoms may occur on restart. About 10 driving miles are needed for the ECU to re–establish the computer settings.

2. Remove the air cleaner. If equipped, remove the solenoid box cover in front of the blower motor (3 bolts).
3. Disconnect the wire harness connector from the blower motor.
4. Disconnect the blower motor cooling tube at the blower motor.

5. Remove the blower motor attaching screws.
6. Remove the blower motor from the blower housing.
7. Installation is the reverse of the removal procedure.

Blower Motor Resistor

REMOVAL AND INSTALLATION

Except Navajo

1. Disconnect the negative battery terminal.
2. Remove the glove box and lower panel, if required.
3. Disconnect the blower motor resistor wire connector.
4. Remove the attaching screw and remove the resistor.
5. Installation is the reverse of the removal procedure.

Navajo

1. Disconnect the negative battery terminal.

NOTE: When the negative battery cable is disconnected and reconnected, some abnormal driveability symptoms may occur on restart. About 10 driving miles are needed for the ECU to re-establish the computer settings.

2. Disconnect the wire connector from the blower motor resistor.
3. Remove the resistor attaching screws.
4. Remove the resistor assembly.
5. Installation is the reverse of the removal procedure.

Heater Core

REMOVAL AND INSTALLATION

Except Navajo

1. Disconnect the negative battery terminal.
2. Drain the engine coolant.
3. Disconnect heater core hoses.
4. Remove instrument panel, as follows:
   ● Remove transmission selector lever or knob.
   ● Remove center console.
   ● Remove the steering wheel.
   ● Remove the upper and lower steering column covers.
   ● Remove the instrument meter hood.
   ● Remove the instrument cluster assembly.
   ● Disconnect speedometer cable.
   ● Remove the air ducts.
   ● Remove the instrument hosing lower panels.
   ● Remove the glove box assembly.
   ● Remove heater control switch and cables, if required.
   ● Remove header and side trim, if required.
   ● Remove the center cap, the side covers and the center bracket bolts on the instrument panel.
   ● Remove the steering shaft bolts.
   ● Disconnect any necessary wire harness connectors.
   ● Remove the instrument panel.
5. Remove the seal plate.
6. Remove the attaching nuts, and the instrument panel attaching bracket.
7. Remove the heater unit.
8. Remove the attaching clips on heater unit and separate assembly.
9. Remove heater core.

To install:
10. Install the heater core.
11. Reattach heater case halves with clips.
12. Install the heater unit.
13. Install the seal plates.
   ● Install the instrument panel.
   ● Reconnect wire harness connectors.
   ● Install the steering shaft securing bolts.
   ● Install the center cap, the side covers and the center bracket bolts on the instrument panel.
   ● Install header and side trim, if removed.
   ● Install the heater control switch and cables.
   ● Install the glove box assembly.
   ● Install the instrument hosing lower panels.
   ● Install the heater ducts.
   ● Reconnect speedometer cable.
   ● Install instrument cluster and meter hood assembly.
   ● Install the upper and lower steering column covers.
   ● Install the steering wheel.
   ● Install the center console and the shift lever or knob.
14. Reconnect heater core hoses.
15. Reconnect the negative battery terminal.
16. Refill the cooling system with proper quantity and type of antifreeze.
17. Check the system for leaks.

Navajo

1. Disconnect the negative battery terminal.

NOTE: When the negative battery cable is disconnected and reconnected, some abnormal driveability symptoms may occur on restart. About 10 driving miles are needed for the ECU to re-establish the computer settings.

2. Drain the engine coolant.
3. Disconnect, remove and the plug the heater core hoses.
4. Remove the 4 screws attaching the heater core access cover to the plenum assembly located in the passenger compartment.
5. Remove the heater core cover.
6. Remove the heater core by pulling rearward and downward.
7. Installation is the reverse of the removal procedure.

Refrigerant Lines

REMOVAL AND INSTALLATION

1. Disconnect the negative battery terminal.

NOTE: When the negative battery cable is disconnected and reconnected, some abnormal driveability symptoms may occur on restart. About 10 driving miles are needed for the ECU to re-establish the computer settings.

2. Properly discharge the air conditioning system.
3. Remove chassis, engine or body parts, if required.
4. Using a backup wrench or the appropriate spring lock tool loosen, disconnect and immediately plug the refrigerant line. Discard all O-rings.
5. Disconnect wire connectors, if required.
6. Remove all attaching brackets and bolts.
7. Remove the refrigerant lines.
To install:
8. Apply a light coat of refrigerant oil to new O-rings.
9. Route refrigerant lines in original locations.
10. Use original securing brackets and bolts.
11. Evacuate, charge and check system for leaks.

Manual Control Head

REMOVAL AND INSTALLATION

B2200 and B2600i

1993

1. Disconnect the negative battery terminal.
2. Remove the instrument panel meter hood.
3. Remove the attaching screws, knobs and nuts.
4. Disconnect the air conditioner and the cigarette lighter connector.
5. Remove the center panel.
6. Remove the glove compartment.
7. Remove the attaching screws and disconnect the control head wire connectors.
8. Remove the control head assembly.
9. Disconnect the control cables.
10. Installation is the reverse of the removal procedure.

B2300, B3000 and B4000

1994

1. Disconnect negative battery terminal.
2. Remove ash tray receptacle and tray retainer.
3. Remove finish panel.
4. Disconnect vacuum lines and temperature cable.
5. Disconnect function cable.
6. Remove manual control head.
7. Installation is the reverse of the removal procedure.

1995

1. Disconnect negative battery terminal.
2. Remove finish panel.
3. Remove manual control mounting screws and manual A/C control head.
4. Disconnect all electrical connectors.
5. Disconnect function cable.
6. Installation is the reverse of the removal procedure.

MPV

1. Disconnect the negative battery terminal.
2. Remove the 2 lower side panels and the undercover.
3. Remove the steering column cover, if required.
4. Remove the instrument cluster assembly.
5. Remove the switch panel attaching nuts and washers.
6. Remove the switch panel.
7. Remove the attaching screws and remove the temperature control assembly.
8. Remove the center lower panel.
9. Remove the airflow mode attaching screws.
10. Remove the control assembly and disconnect the wire connectors.
11. Installation is the reverse of the removal procedure.

Navajo

1. Disconnect the negative battery terminal.

NOTE: When the negative battery cable is disconnected and reconnected, some abnormal driveability symptoms may occur on restart. About 10 driving miles are needed for the ECU to re-establish the computer settings.

2. Remove the ashtray from its retainer.
3. Disconnect the cigarette lighter wire connector.
4. Remove the 2 screws attaching the ashtray bracket to the instrument panel.

5. Remove the ashtray bracket from the instrument panel.
6. Carefully remove the finish panel from the instrument panel and cluster by pulling the panel straight back then up.
7. Disconnect the 4 X 4 transfer switch, if equipped.
8. Remove the 4 attaching screws at the control head.
9. Pull the control head assembly through the instrument panel opening far enough to allow removal of wire connectors.
10. Disconnect the vacuum hose harness.
11. Disconnect the control head cables.
12. Remove the control head assembly from the vehicle.

To install:
13. Connect the control cables to the control head.
14. Connect the vacuum hoses to the control head.
15. Connect the electrical wire connectors.
16. Install the control head assembly and secure with the 4 attaching screws.
17. Connect the 4 X 4 transfer switch, if equipped.
18. Attach finish panel to the instrument panel.
19. Install ashtray, cigarette lighter, wire connector and brackets to the instrument panel.
20. Reconnect the negative battery terminal.

Manual Control Cables

ADJUSTMENT

B2200 and B2600i

1993

1. To adjust airflow mode cable:
   • Set the airflow mode control lever to the **DEFROST** position.
   • Install the airflow mode cable with the shutter lever on the heater unit pushed fully downward.
   • Attach the securing clip.
   • Turn the blower switch to position **4** and make sure there are no air leaks from the center and floor area outlets.
2. To adjust the temperature control cable:
   • Set the temperature control lever to the **COLD** position.
   • Install the temperature control cable with the shutter lever on the heater unit pushed fully upward.
   • Attach the securing clip.
   • Make sure the temperature control lever moves fully from the **COLD** to **HOT** position.
3. To adjust the rec/fresh control cable:
   • Set the rec/fresh selector lever to the **RECIRCULATE** position.
   • Install the rec/fresh selector cable with the shutter lever on the blower unit pushed fully upward.
   • Make sure the rec/fresh selector cable moves fully from **RECIRCULATE** to the **FRESH** position.

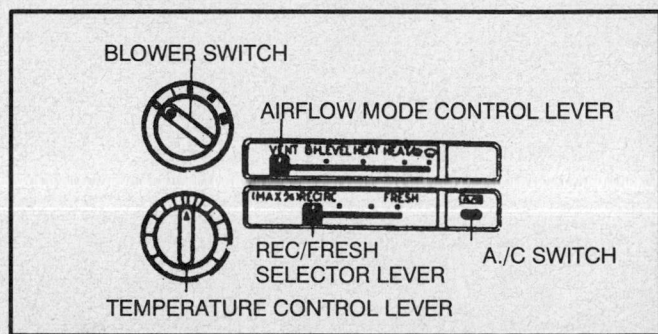

**Air conditioner and heater control head switches —
B2200 and B2600i**

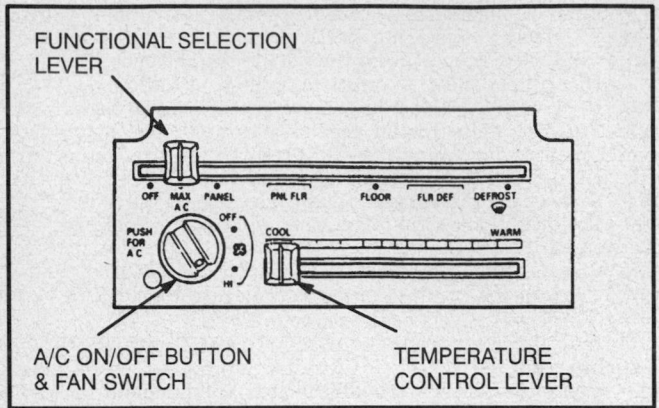

Air conditioner and heater control head switches – B2300, B3000, B4000 and Navajo (1994)

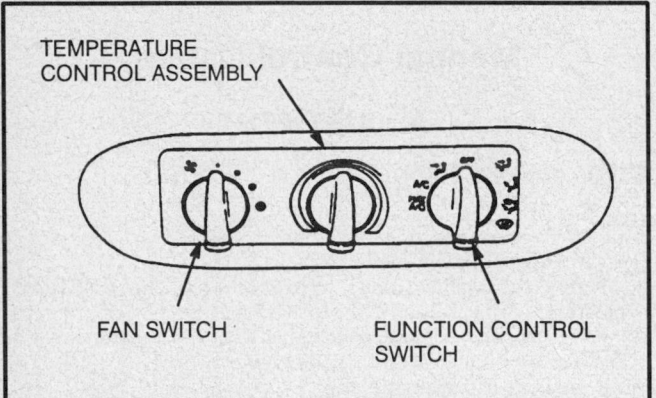

Air conditioner and heater control head switches – B2300, B3000, B4000 (1995)

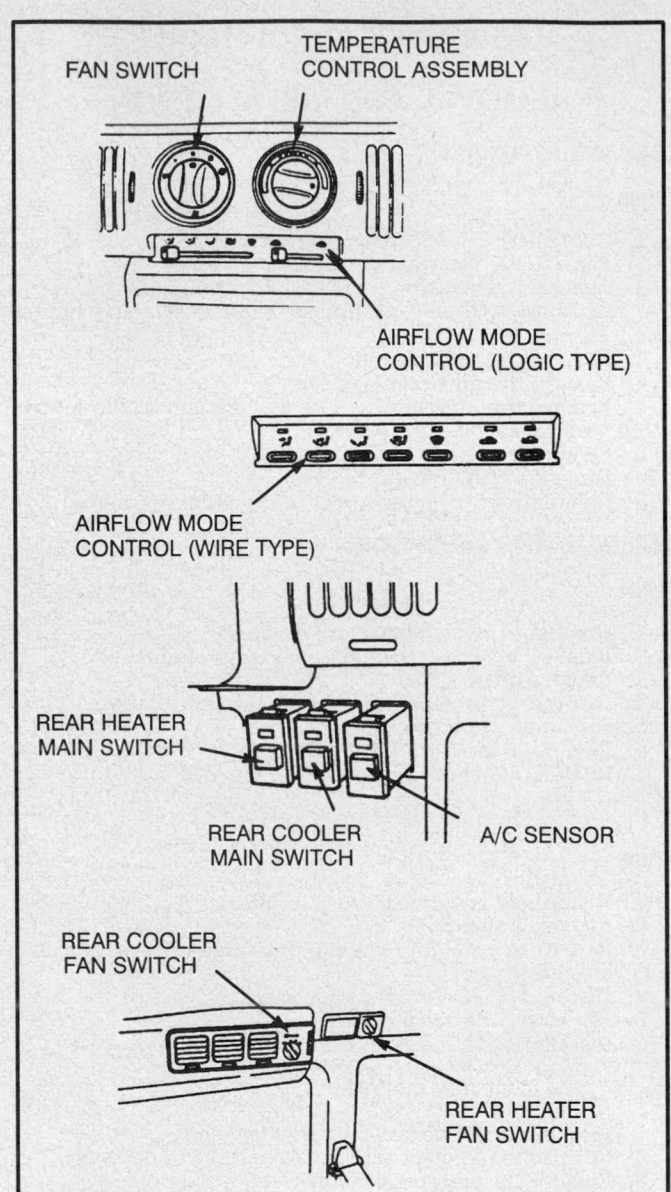

Air conditioner and heater control head switches – MPV (1994–95)

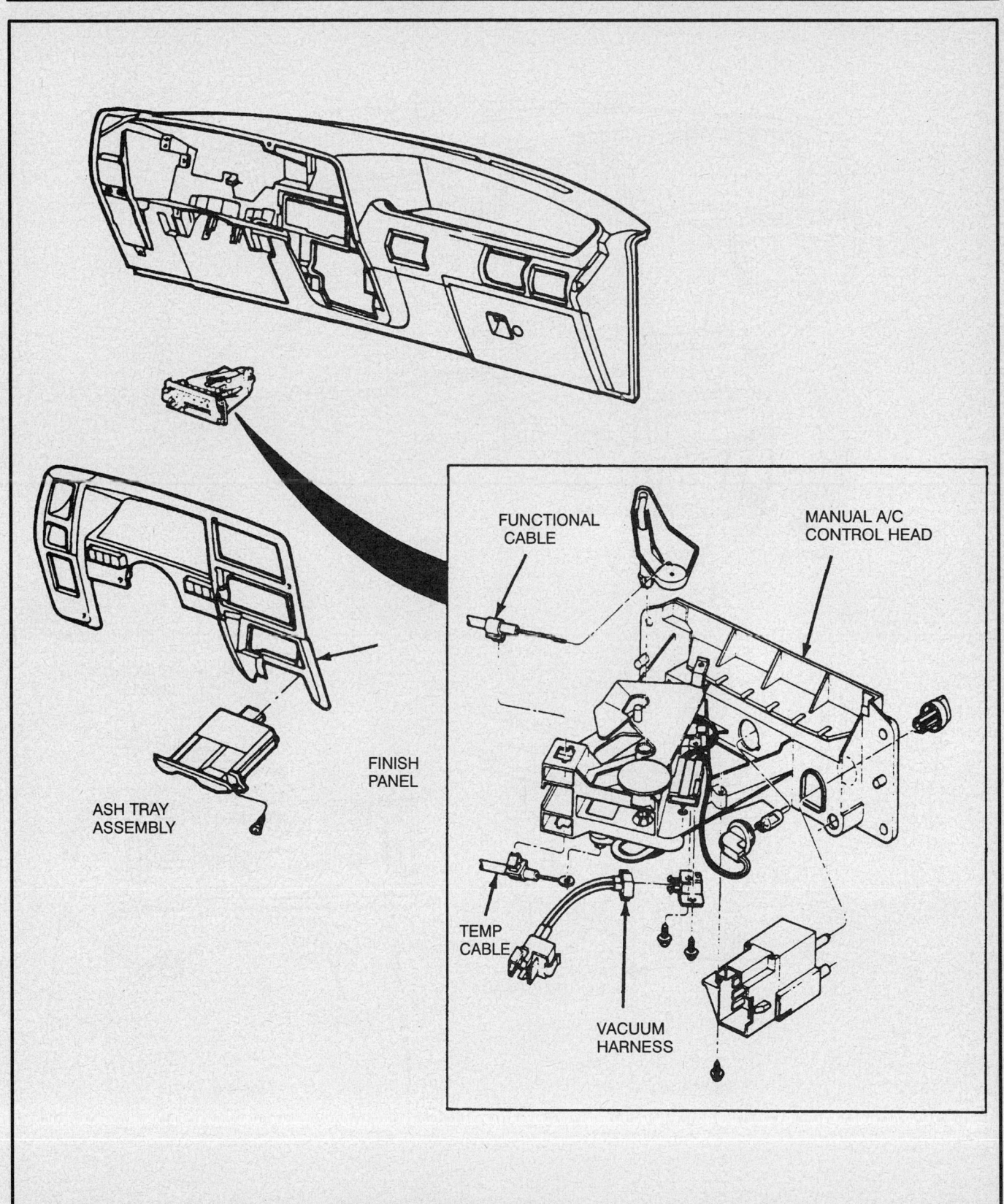

Manual A/C control head — B2300, B3000 and B4000 — 1994

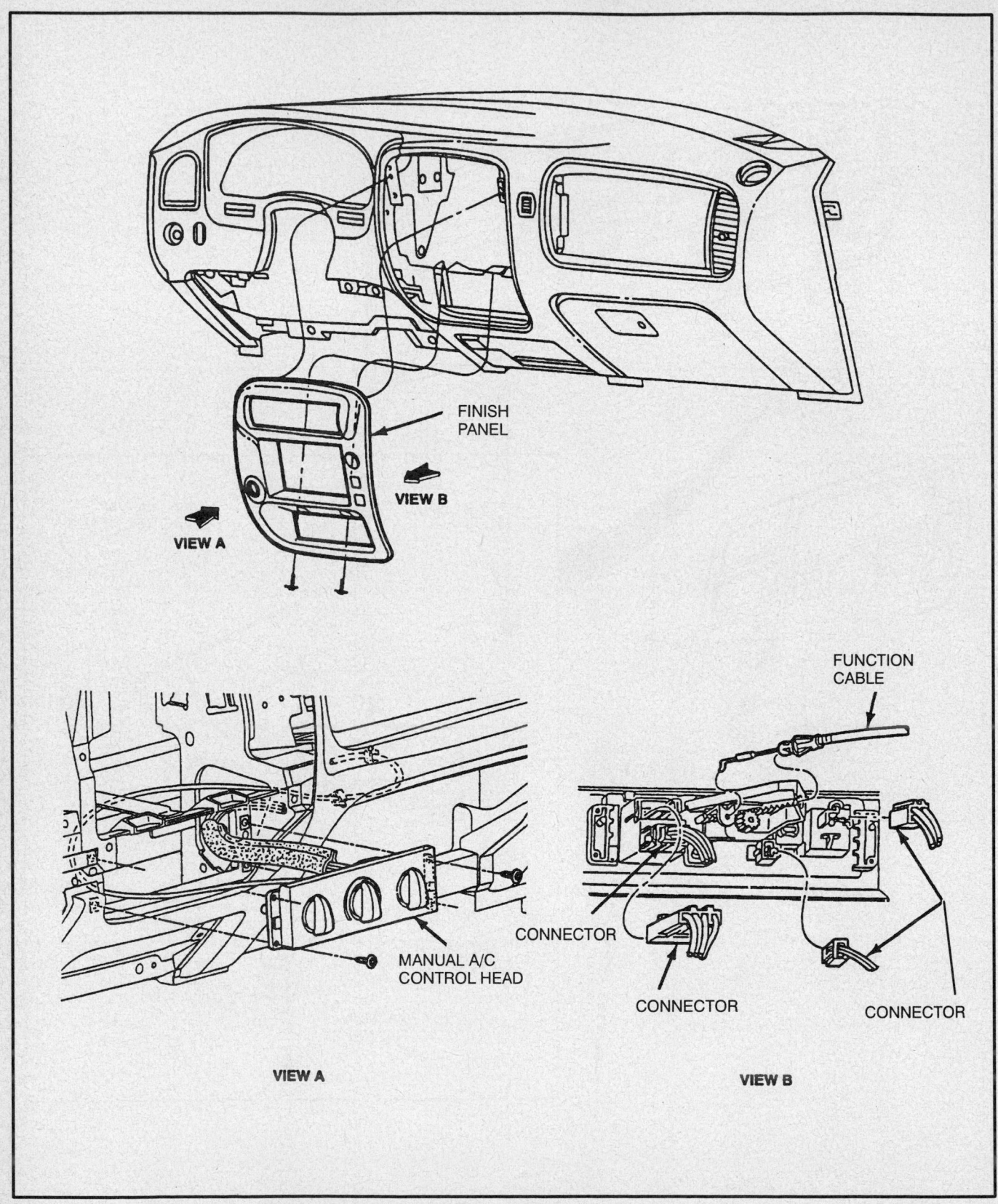

FINISH PANEL

VIEW B

VIEW A

FUNCTION CABLE

MANUAL A/C CONTROL HEAD

CONNECTOR

CONNECTOR

CONNECTOR

VIEW A

VIEW B

Manual A/C control head – B2300, B3000 and B4000 – 1995

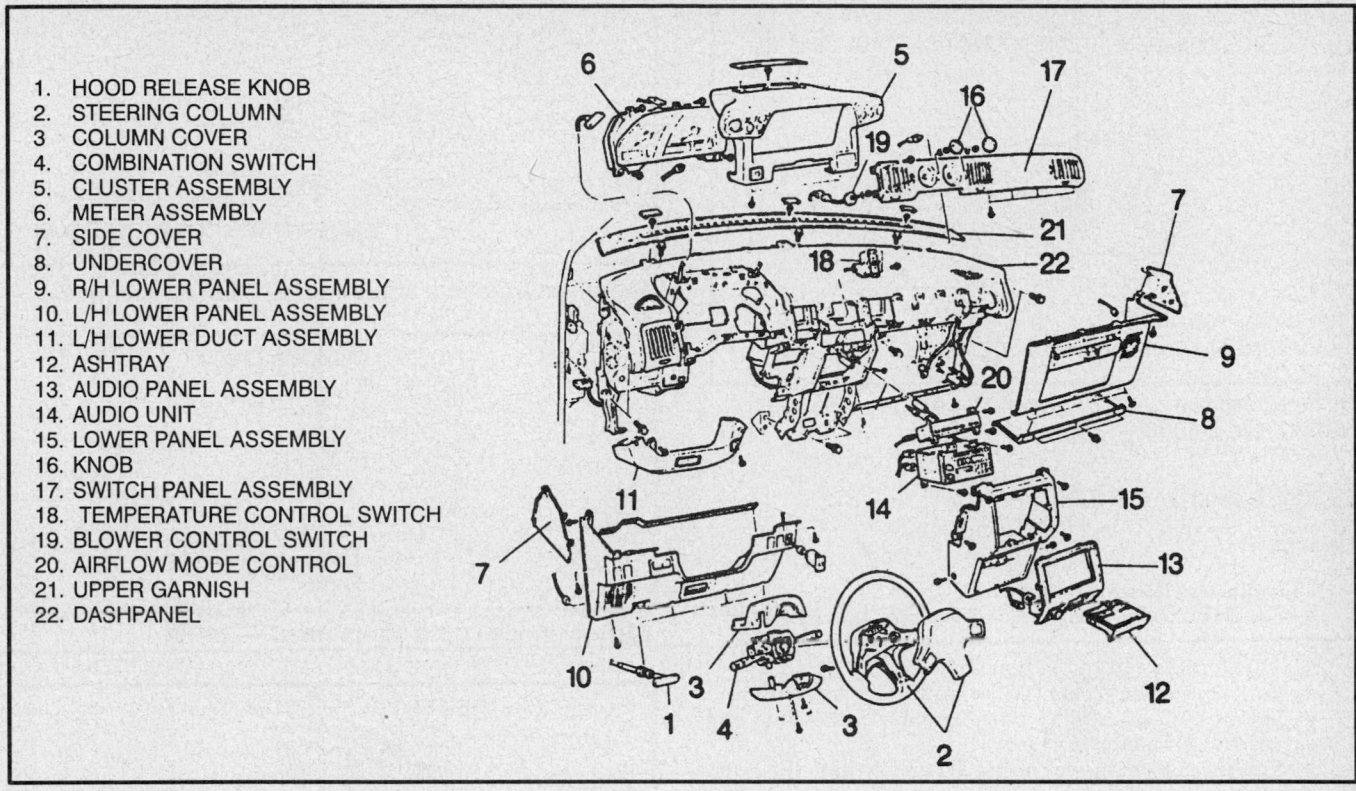

1. HOOD RELEASE KNOB
2. STEERING COLUMN
3. COLUMN COVER
4. COMBINATION SWITCH
5. CLUSTER ASSEMBLY
6. METER ASSEMBLY
7. SIDE COVER
8. UNDERCOVER
9. R/H LOWER PANEL ASSEMBLY
10. L/H LOWER PANEL ASSEMBLY
11. L/H LOWER DUCT ASSEMBLY
12. ASHTRAY
13. AUDIO PANEL ASSEMBLY
14. AUDIO UNIT
15. LOWER PANEL ASSEMBLY
16. KNOB
17. SWITCH PANEL ASSEMBLY
18. TEMPERATURE CONTROL SWITCH
19. BLOWER CONTROL SWITCH
20. AIRFLOW MODE CONTROL
21. UPPER GARNISH
22. DASHPANEL

Instrument panel assembly — MPV

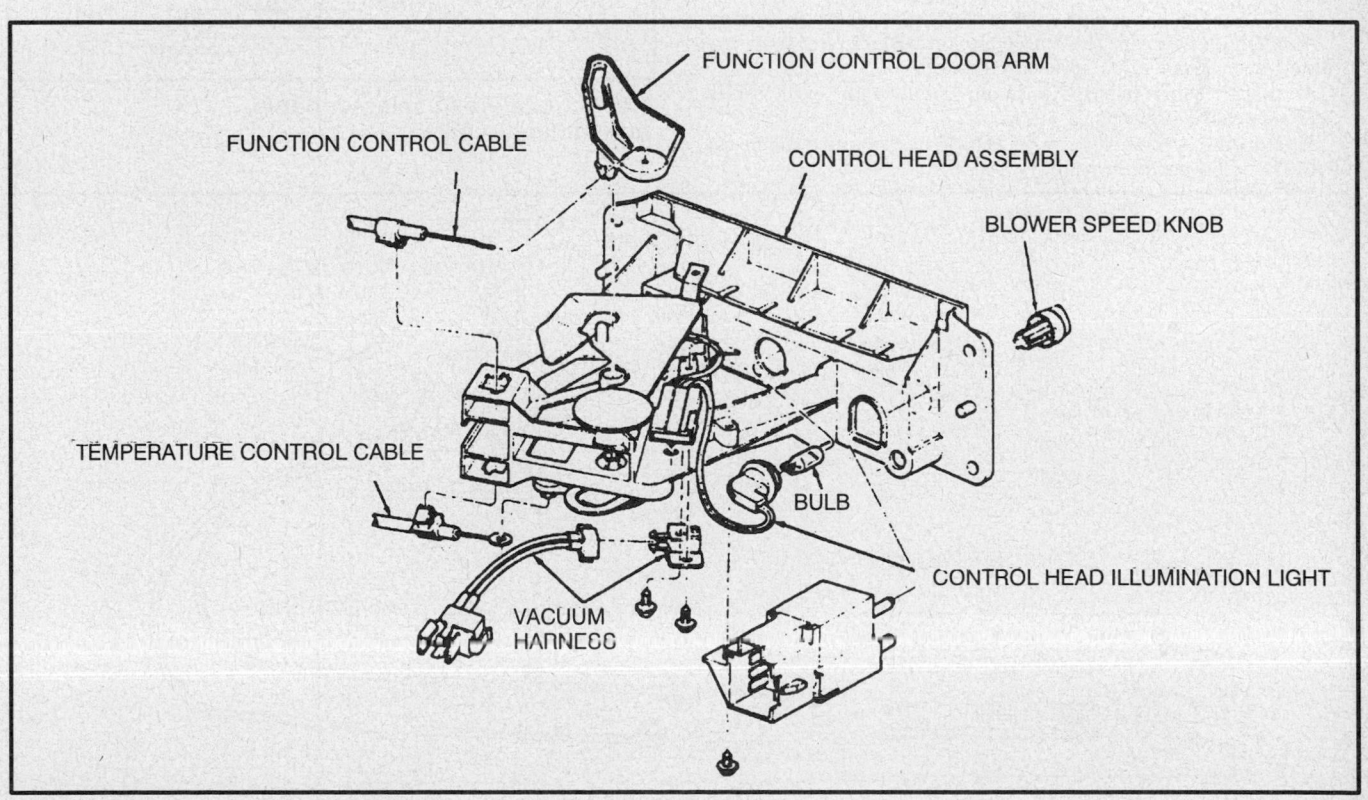

FUNCTION CONTROL DOOR ARM

FUNCTION CONTROL CABLE

CONTROL HEAD ASSEMBLY

BLOWER SPEED KNOB

TEMPERATURE CONTROL CABLE

BULB

CONTROL HEAD ILLUMINATION LIGHT

VACUUM HARNESS

Control head assembly — Navajo

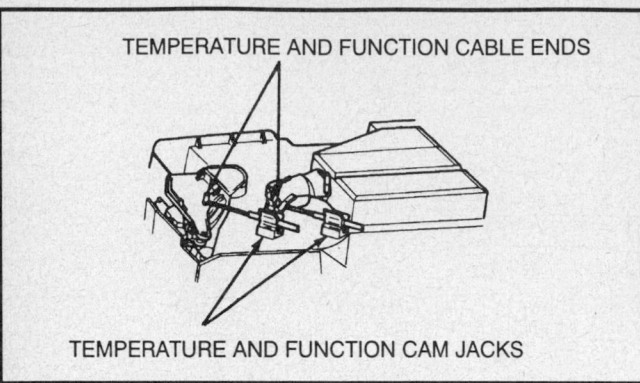

TEMPERATURE AND FUNCTION CABLE ENDS

TEMPERATURE AND FUNCTION CAM JACKS

Airflow and temperature control cables – B2300, B3000 and B4000 – 1995

B2300, B3000 and B4000

1994–95

1. To adjust airflow mode cable:
   • Set the airflow mode control lever to the **DEFROST** position.
   • Attach cable end to the function cam.
   • Pull on the cam jacket (White) until cam travel stops.
   • Install cable to clip by pushing cable jacket into clip from top until it snaps in place.
   • Run the system blower on **HIGH** and actuate the lever. Check for proper operation.
2. To adjust the temperature control cable:
   • Set the temperature cable lever to the **COLD** position and hold.
   • Attach the cable end wire to the temperature door cam.
   • push gently on the cable jacket (Black) to seat the blend door. Push until resistance is felt.
   • Install cable to clip by pushing cable jacket into clip from top until it snaps in place.
   • Run the system blower on **HIGH** and actuate the lever. Check for proper operation.

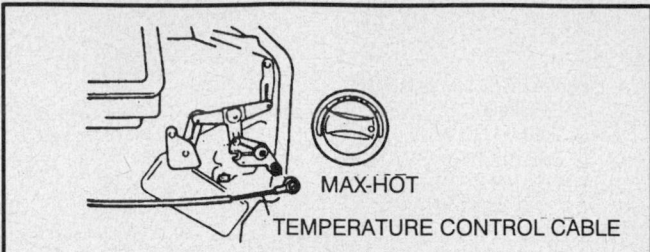

MAX-HOT

TEMPERATURE CONTROL CABLE

Temperature cable adjustment — MPV

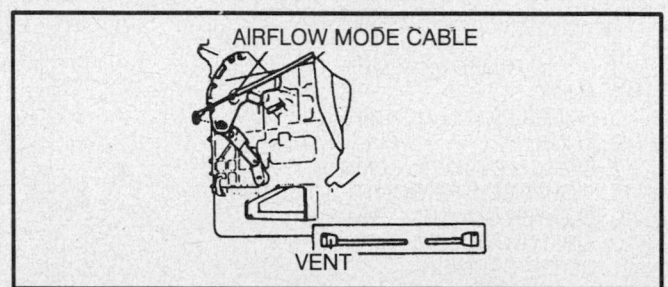

AIRFLOW MODE CABLE

VENT

Airflow mode cable adjustment — MPV

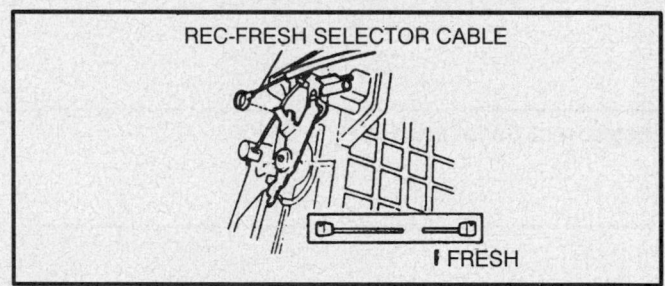

REC-FRESH SELECTOR CABLE

FRESH

Recirculate/Fresh selector cable adjustment — MPV

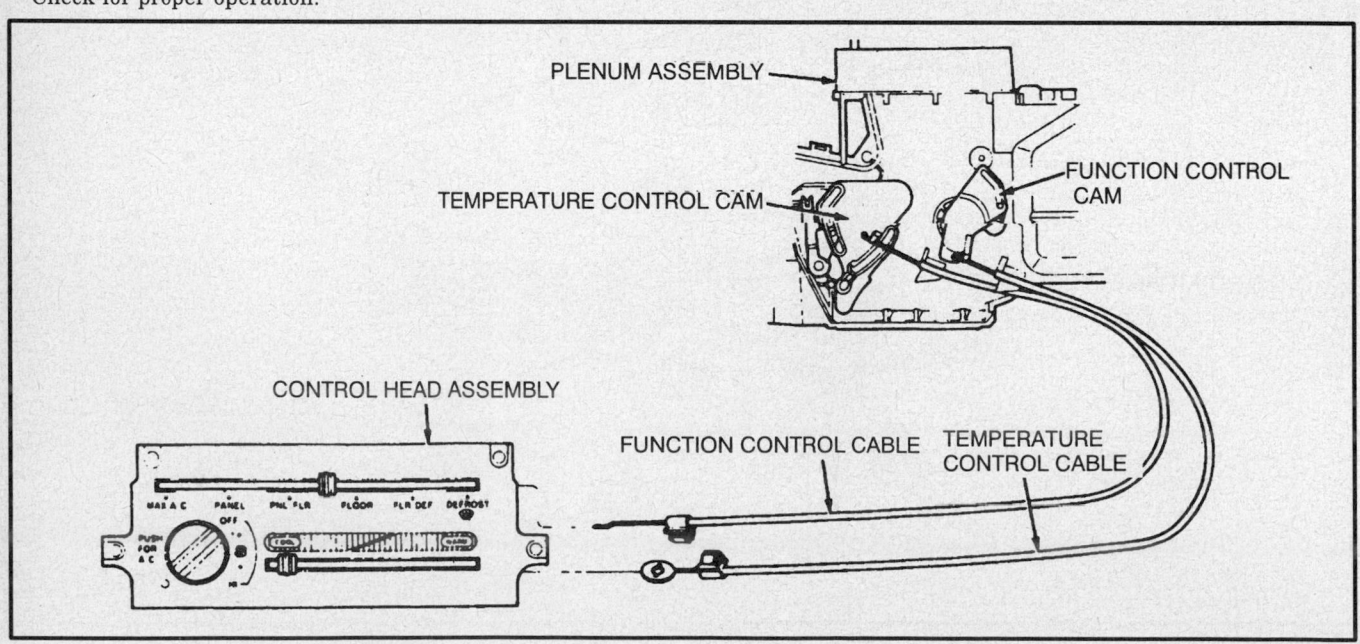

PLENUM ASSEMBLY

TEMPERATURE CONTROL CAM

FUNCTION CONTROL CAM

CONTROL HEAD ASSEMBLY

FUNCTION CONTROL CABLE

TEMPERATURE CONTROL CABLE

Control cable adjustment – Navajo

MPV

1. To adjust the temperature control cable:
   • Set the temperature control lever to the **MAX–HOT** position.
   • Install the cable and attach the clip with the heater unit shutter lever all the way to the right.
   • Make sure the temperature control lever moves easily from the **HOT** to **COLD** position.
2. To adjust airflow mode cable:
   • Set the airflow mode control lever to the **DEFROST** position.
   • Install the cable and attach the clip with the heater unit shutter lever at its closest point.
   • Make sure the temperature control lever moves easily from the **DEFROST** to the **VENT** position.
3. To adjust the rec/fresh control cable:
   • Set the rec/fresh selector lever to the **RECIRCULATE** position.
   • Install the cable and attach the clip with the blower unit shutter lever at its closest point.
   • Make sure the temperature control lever moves easily from the **RECIRCULATE** to the **FRESH** position.

Navajo

1. Disengage and allow the glove compartment door to hang free by squeezing the sides together.
2. Remove the cable from the securing clip and leave cable attached to the door cams.
3. To adjust the temperature control cables:
   • Set the temperature lever to the **COOL** position and hold.
   • Push gently on the black temperature cable until you feel resistance and the blend door seat.
   • Reattach the cable to the clip.
   • Make sure the temperature control lever moves easily from the **COOL** to the **WARM** position.
4. To adjust the function control cable:
   • Set the function selector lever to the **DEFROST** position and hold.
   • Pull the white function selector cable until there is resistance and the defrost door seats.
   • Reattach the cable to the clip.
   • Make sure the temperature control lever moves easily from the **DEFROST** to the **PANEL** or **MAX A/C** position.
5. Turn the ignition and blower switch **ON** and actuate the levers, checking that the temperature and function selectors are adjusted properly.

REMOVAL AND INSTALLATION

B2200, B2300, B2600i, B3000 and B4000

1. Disconnect the negative battery terminal.
2. Remove the instrument panel meter hood.
3. Remove the attaching screws, knobs and nuts.
4. Disconnect the air conditioner and the cigarette lighter connector.
5. Remove the center panel.
6. Remove the glove compartment.
7. Remove the attaching screws and disconnect the control head wire connectors.
8. Remove the control head assembly.
9. Disconnect the control cables at the control head and the heater unit.
10. Installation is the reverse of the removal procedure.

MPV

1. Disconnect the negative battery terminal.

2. Remove the 2 lower side panels and the undercover.
3. Remove the steering column cover, if required.
4. Remove the instrument cluster assembly.
5. Remove the switch panel attaching nuts.
6. Remove the switch panel.
7. Remove the attaching screws and remove the temperature control assembly.
8. Remove the center lower panel.
9. Remove the attaching screws and remove the airflow mode control assembly.
10. Disconnect the temperature control cable from the heater unit.
11. Disconnect the rec–fresh cable and airflow mode cable from the heater unit.
12. Installation is the reverse of the removal procedure.

Navajo

1. Disconnect the negative battery terminal.

NOTE: When the negative battery cable is disconnected and reconnected, some abnormal driveability symptoms may occur on restart. About 10 driving miles are needed for the ECU to re-establish the computer settings.

2. Remove the control head from the instrument panel.
3. Disengage and allow the glove compartment door to hang free by squeezing the sides together.
4. Remove the cables from the securing clips.
5. Remove the cables from the control cams noting how the cable ends are retained.
6. Remove the cables from the cable clips and the routing aids in the instrument panel.
7. Disconnect the cables from the control head assembly.
8. Installation is the reverse of the removal procedure.

Electronic Control Head

TESTING

MPV

1. Disconnect the negative battery terminal.
2. Remove the control head assembly.
3. Check each circuit as follows.
4. Checking REC–FRESH air selector circuit:
   • Supply 12 volts to terminals **h** and **g**.
   • Connect a resistance of 1k ohm between terminals **f** and **q**.
   • Ground terminal **o**, then measure the voltage between terminals **g** and **f**.
   • There should be approximately 12 volts at terminals **g** and **f**.
   • If not as specified, replace the electronic control head assembly.
   • Remove the 12 volt supply at terminals **g** and **h**.
   • With the recirculate switch pushed **ON**, there should be continuity between terminals **r** and **g**.
   • With the fresh switch pushed **ON**, there should be continuity between terminals **p** and **g**.
   • If not as specified replace the electronic control head assembly.
5. Checking airflow selector circuit:
   • Supply 12 volts to terminals **h** and **g**.
   • Connect a resistance of 1k ohm between terminals **n** and **g**.
   • Connect a jumper wire between terminals **l** and **g**.
   • There should be approximately 12 volts at terminals **n** and **g**.
   • If not as specified, replace the electronic control head assembly.

- Connect a resistance of 1k ohm between terminals **m** and **g**.
- Connect a jumper wire between terminals **j** and **g**.
- There should be approximately 12 volts at terminals **m** and **g**.
- If not as specified, replace the electronic control head assembly.
- Connect a resistance of 1k ohm between terminals **h** and **n**.
- There should be approximately 12 volts at terminals **n** and **g**.
- If not as specified, replace the electronic control head assembly.
- Connect a resistance of 1k ohm between terminals **h** and **m**.
- There should be approximately 12 volts at terminals **m** and **g**.
- If not as specified, replace the electronic control head assembly.
- Remove the 12 volt supply at terminals **g** and **h**.
- With the vent switch pushed **ON**, there should be continuity between terminals **b** and **g**.
- With the bi–level switch pushed **ON**, there should be continuity between terminals **a** and **g**.
- With the heat switch pushed **ON**, there should be continuity between terminals **d** and **g**.
- With the heat/defrost switch pushed **ON**, there should be continuity between terminals **c** and **g**.
- With the defrost switch pushed **ON**, there should be continuity between terminals **e** and **g**.

6. Checking indicator lights:
- Supply 12 volts to terminals **h** and **g**.
- Check for illumination of the indicator light as each switch is pushed.
- If any light fails to illuminate, replace the control assembly.
- Connect a jumper wire between terminals **h** and **s** and verify that the indicator lights dim.
- If not as specified, replace the control assembly.

7. Checking illumination lights:
- Supply 12 volts to terminals **h** and **g**.
- Connect a jumper wire between terminals **h** and **s**.
- Connect a jumper wire between terminals **g** and **t**.
- Check for illumination of the light, if there is no illumination replace the bulb.

8. Checking the air conditioning switch:
- With the switch **OFF**, there should be continuity between terminals **b** and **d**, and between terminals **f** and **h**.
- With the switch **ON**, there should be continuity between terminals **d** and **f**, and between terminals **c** and **h**, and between terminals **c** and **j**, and between terminals **h** and **j**.
- There should be continuity between terminals **h** and **i** in only one direction.
- If not as specified, replace the switch.

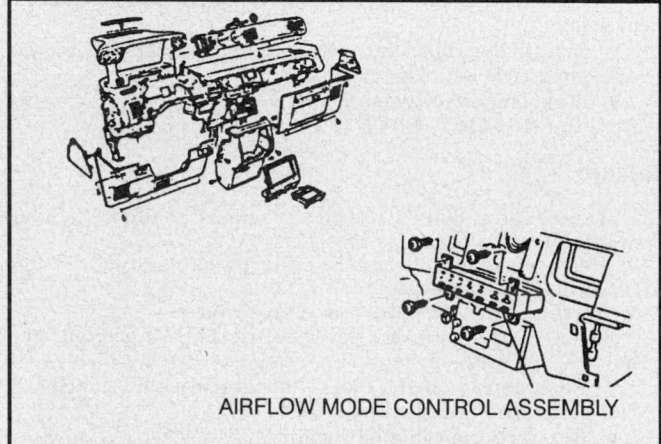

AIRFLOW MODE CONTROL ASSEMBLY

Electronic control head removal – MPV

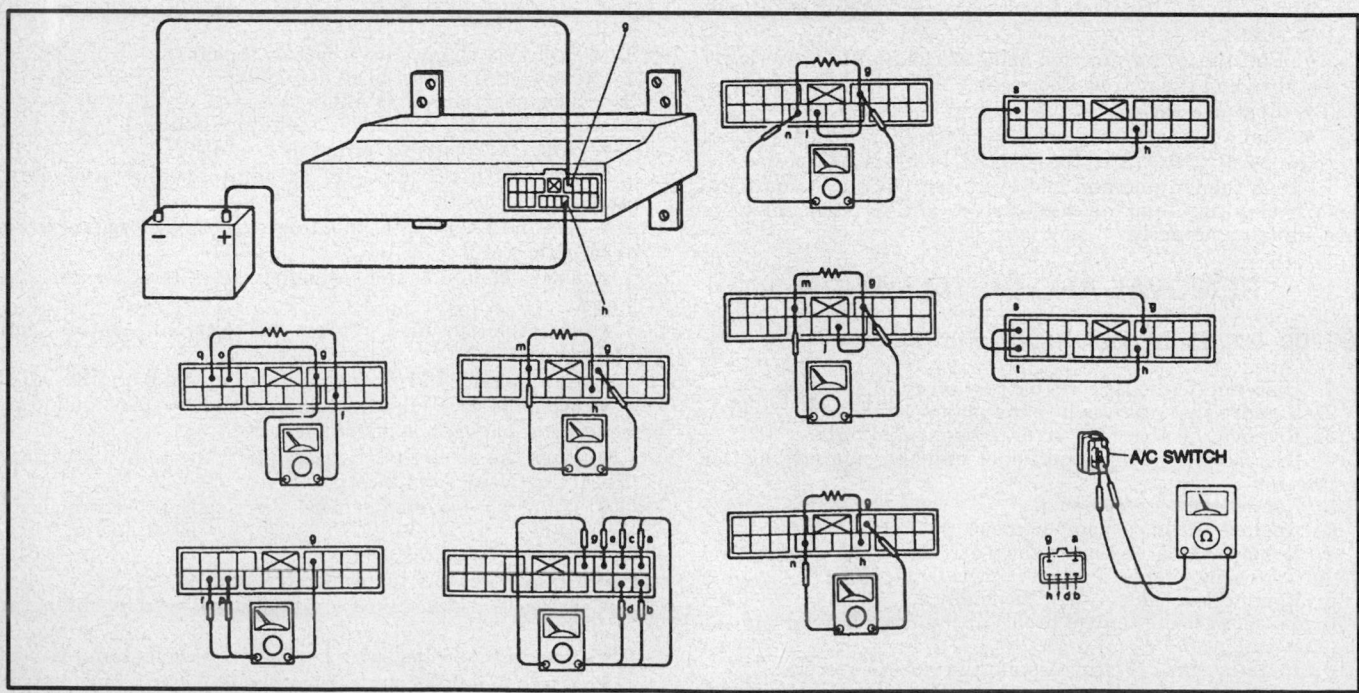

Electronic control head testing – MPV

REMOVAL AND INSTALLATION

MPV

1. Disconnect the negative battery terminal.
2. Remove the 2 lower side panels and the undercover.
3. Remove the steering column cover, if required.
4. Remove the instrument cluster assembly.
5. Remove the switch panel attaching nuts and washers.
6. Remove the switch panel.
7. Remove the attaching screws and remove the temperature control assembly.
8. Remove the center lower panel.
9. Remove the airflow mode control assembly attaching screws.
10. Remove the control assembly and disconnect the wire connectors.
11. Installation is the reverse of the removal procedure.

SENSORS AND SWITCHES

Pressure Switches

OPERATION

There are 2 styles of pressure switches being used, the first pressure switch, which switches the magnetic clutch ON or OFF as a result of irregularly high or low pressures of the refrigerant. The second is a pressure switch used on vehicles with automatic transmission to cycle ON and OFF the condenser fan according to system pressure. The pressure switches are located on the high side except the Navajo which has the switch located on the accumulator.

TESTING

Except Navajo

1. Disconnect the pressure switch wire connector from the receiver/drier or from the high pressure line.
2. Start the vehicle and turn the air conditioner **ON**.
3. Hook up the air conditioner gauges or charging station.
4. Check for 12 volts at the pressure switch wire connector.
5. If there is no voltage at either terminal of the wire connector, check the air conditioner relay.
6. Connect a jumper wire between the 2 terminals.
7. Check to see if compressor clutch engages or if condenser fan operates, if equipped.
8. If condenser fan and or compressor magnetic clutch fail to operate, check the unit and the wiring to the unit.
9. Check for continuity through the switch using an ohmmeter.
10. At system normal operating pressures, there should be continuity between the switch wire connector terminals.

Navajo

1. Connect an approved air conditioning charging station.
2. Start the engine and move the function selector lever to the **MAX-A/C**.
3. Set the blower speed switch to **MAX** and the temperature control lever to the extreme **COOL** position.
4. Observe that the compressor magnetic clutch disengages when system operating pressures drops to an approximate 24.5 psi.
5. Observe that the compressor magnetic clutch engages when system operating pressures reach approximately 43.5 psi or above.
6. If not as specified, replace the pressure switch.

REMOVAL AND INSTALLATION

1. Disconnect the negative battery terminal.

NOTE: On Navajo, when the negative battery cable is disconnected and reconnected, some abnormal driveability symptoms may occur on restart. About 10 driving miles are needed for the ECU to re-establish the computer settings.

2. Properly discharge the air conditioning system (not required on Navajo).
3. Remove radiator grille, if required.
4. Disconnect the pressure switch wire connector.
5. Using a wrench, remove the pressure switch.
6. Installation is the reverse of removal procedure.
7. If the air conditioning system pressure switch has a plastic base, hand tighten only.

Thermo Switch

OPERATION

If equipped, the thermo switch is mounted at the evaporator core outlet and senses the temperature of the cool air coming through the evaporator via capillary tube. Temperature signals are then input to the thermo switch. The thermo switch then opens or closes the circuit allowing 12 volt to flow to the pressure switch thus turning the magnetic clutch ON and OFF.

TESTING

Except Navajo

1. Disconnect negative battery terminal.
2. Remove the glove box and place a piece of cardboard over the blower air inlet to cause cooling process to speed up.
3. Run the engine at idle and set the A/C for **MAX COOL**.
4. Note that after a few minutes, the compressor should stop, indicating the switch has sensed a very low evaporator temperature.
5. For further testing, remove the thermo switch and place it in ice water.
6. Check continuity through the switch above freezing.
7. There should be no continuity through the switch when it reaches below 32°F (0°C).
8. Replace the thermo switch, if not as specified.

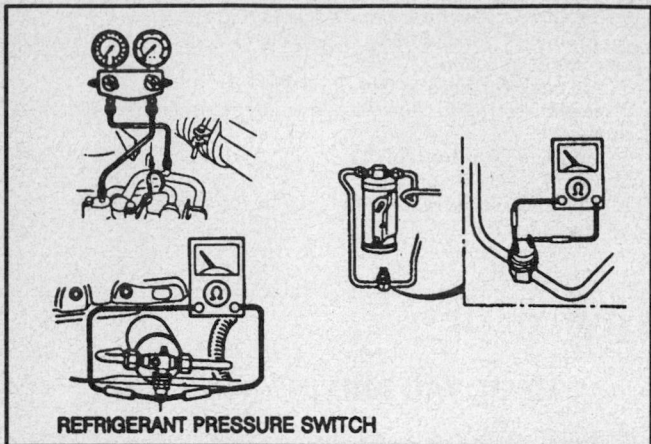

Pressure switch testing – B2200, B2300, B2600i B3000, B4000 and MPV

Magnetic Solenoid Valve

OPERATION

MPV with Rear System Only

The magnetic solenoid valve is mounted on the driver's side undercarriage, the solenoid is routed in the high pressure line. The solenoid is energized only when the rear main air conditioner switch is in the **ON** position, thus allowing the refrigerant to flow to the rear cooling system.

TESTING

MPV with Rear System Only

1. Disconnect the negative battery terminal.
2. Remove the grommet and disconnect the magnetic solenoid valve wire connector.
3. Measure the resistance between the wire connector terminals.
4. There should be approximately 20 ohms, if not as specified replace the solenoid valve.

REMOVAL AND INSTALLATION

MPV with Rear System Only

1. Disconnect the negative battery terminal.
2. Properly discharge the air conditioning system.
3. Remove the grommet and disconnect the magnetic solenoid valve wire connector.
4. Disconnect the refrigerant lines
5. Remove the attaching nut and remove the magnetic solenoid valve.
6. Installation is the reverse of the removal procedure.

Relays

OPERATION

Battery and load location may require that a switch be placed some distance from either component. This means a longer wire and a higher voltage drop. The installation of a relay between the battery and the load reduces the voltage drop. Because the switch controls the relay, this means amperage through the switch can be reduced.

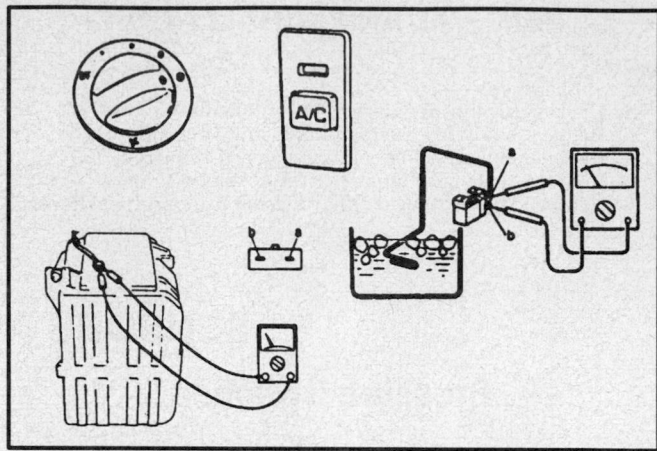

Thermo switch testing – 1993 B2200, B2600i 1993-95 and MPV

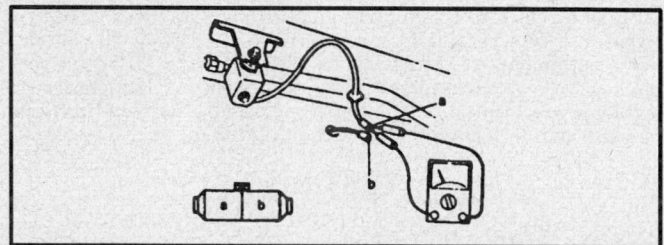

Magnetic solenoid valve testing – MPV

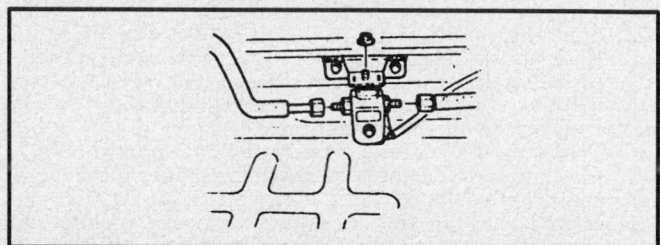

Magnetic solenoid valve removal – MPV

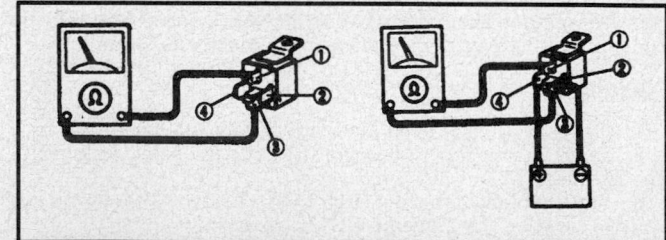

Air conditioning relay testing – B2200, B2300, B2600i, B3000 and B4000

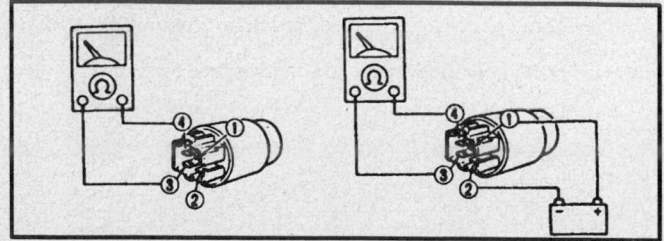

Air conditioning relay testing – MPV

TESTING

B2200, B2300, B2600i, B3000 and B4000

1. Disconnect the negative battery terminal.
2. Disconnect the relay wire connector.
3. Check that there is no continuity between terminals **1** and **3** of the relay.
4. If there is continuity, replace the relay.
5. Next apply 12 volts to terminal **4** and ground terminal **2**.
6. Check for continuity between terminals **1** and **3**.
7. If there is no continuity, replace the relay.

MPV

1. Disconnect the negative battery terminal.
2. Disconnect the relay wire connector.
3. Check that there is no continuity between terminals **3** and **4** of the relay.
4. If there is continuity, replace the relay.
5. Next apply 12 volts to terminal **1** and ground terminal **2**.
6. Check for continuity between terminals **3** and **4**.
7. If there is no continuity, replace the relay.

REMOVAL AND INSTALLATION

B2200, B2300, B2600i, B3000, B4000 and MPV

1. Disconnect negative battery terminal.
2. Locate relay and disconnect wire connector.
3. If required, remove attaching bolt and remove relay.
4. Installation is the reverse of the removal procedure.

Actuators

OPERATION

When the mode switch on the control head panel is depressed, an output signal corresponding to the depressed switch is issued to the mode actuator. The mode actuator, which then shifts to theselected position, performs opening and closing of the mode door and stops in the specified position.

TESTING

MPV

REC–FRESH SELECTOR DOOR

1. Disconnect the negative battery terminal.
2. Remove the right lower panel and the undercover.
3. Disconnect the REC–FRESH selector door actuator wire connector.
4. Apply 12 volts, the positive lead to terminal **g** and ground terminal **f** and the actuator motor should operate.

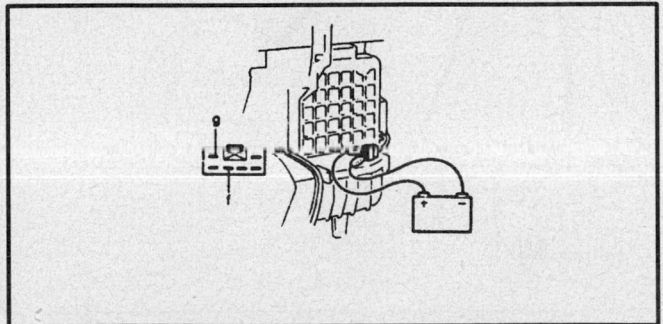

Recirculate/Fresh actuator testing – MPV

5. If not as specified, replace the actuator.

AIRFLOW MODE ACTUATOR

1. Disconnect the negative battery terminal.
2. Remove the driver's side lower panel.
3. Disconnect the airflow mode actuator wire connector.
4. Apply 12 volts, the positive lead to terminal **k** and ground terminal **i** and the motor should rotate to the **DEF** position.
5. Apply 12 volts, the positive lead to terminal **j** and ground terminal **k** and the motor should rotate to the **VENT** position.
6. If not as specified, replace the actuator.

REMOVAL AND INSTALLATION

1. Disconnect negative battery terminal.
2. Locate the actuator.
3. Remove the passenger or drivers side panel, if required.
4. Disconnect the actuator wire connector.
5. Remove actuator attaching screws.
6. Remove the actuator.
7. Installation is the reverse of the removal procedure.

Outside/Recirculating Air Door Vacuum Motor

OPERATION

Navajo

The Navajo the vacuum motor controls the recirculating/fresh air door movement by means of vacuum switch located on the control head. The vacuum motor is located on the right side heater plenum.

TESTING

1. Disconnect the negative battery terminal.

NOTE: When the negative battery cable is disconnected and reconnected, some abnormal driveability symptoms may occur on restart. About 10 driving miles are needed for the ECU to re-establish the computer settings.

2. Remove the glove box assembly.
3. Disconnect the vacuum connection at the vacuum motor.
4. Using a suitable vacuum pump, apply approximately 12 in. Hg of vacuum to the vacuum motor.
5. The vacuum pump should draw the recirculate/fresh door in and maintain the vacuum reading.
6. If as specified, check for vacuum with control head lever in recirculate or fresh position at vacuum motor.
7. If not as specified, replace the vacuum motor.

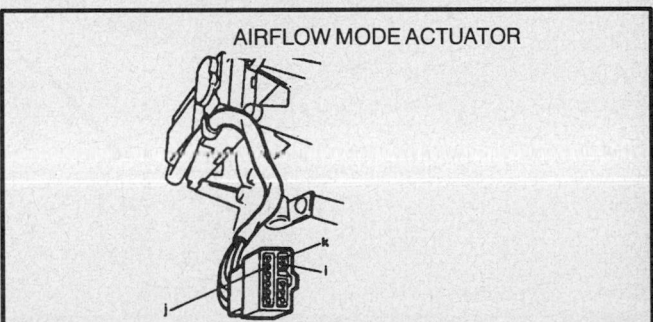

Airflow mode actuator testing – MPV

REMOVAL AND INSTALLATION

1. Disconnect the negative battery terminal.

NOTE: When the negative battery cable is disconnected and reconnected, some abnormal driveability symptoms may occur on restart. About 10 driving miles are needed for the ECU to re-establish the computer settings.

2. Remove the glove box assembly.
3. Disconnect the vacuum connection.
4. Remove the 2 screws attaching the vacuum motor to the plenum.
5. Remove the vacuum motor assembly.
6. Installation is the reverse of the removal procedure.

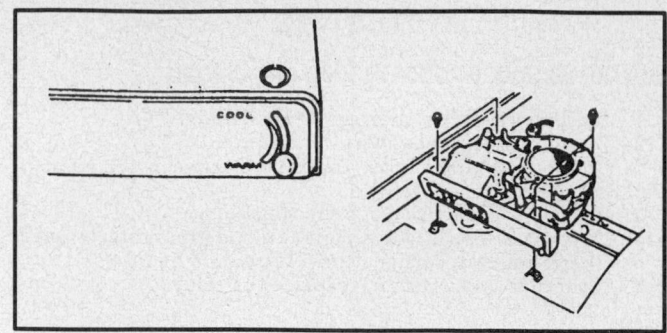

Component layout − MPV with rear A/C

REAR AUXILIARY SYSTEM

Evaporator

REMOVAL AND INSTALLATION

MPV

1. Disconnect the negative battery terminal.
2. Properly discharge the air conditioning system.
3. Remove the left rear side trim.
4. Disconnect the high and low pressure refrigerant lines. Cap the lines immediately to minimize system contamination.
5. Disconnect the rear cooling unit wire connectors.
6. Remove the rear cooling unit attaching nuts and bolts.
7. Remove the rear cooling unit case.
8. Disassemble the cooling unit.

9. Remove the evaporator core and expansion valve as a unit.
10. Disconnect the inlet and outlet pipes.
11. Remove the capillary tube from the outlet pipe.
12. Remove the expansion valve.

To install:

13. Attach the expansion valve to the evaporator core.
14. Attach the capillary tube from the outlet pipe.
15. Reconnect the inlet and outlet pipes.
16. Install the evaporator core and the expansion valve in the cooler unit. If installing a new evaporator core, add 1.7 oz. of new refrigerant oil to the unit during installation.
17. Reassemble the cooling unit.
18. Install the rear cooling unit using the attaching nuts and bolts.

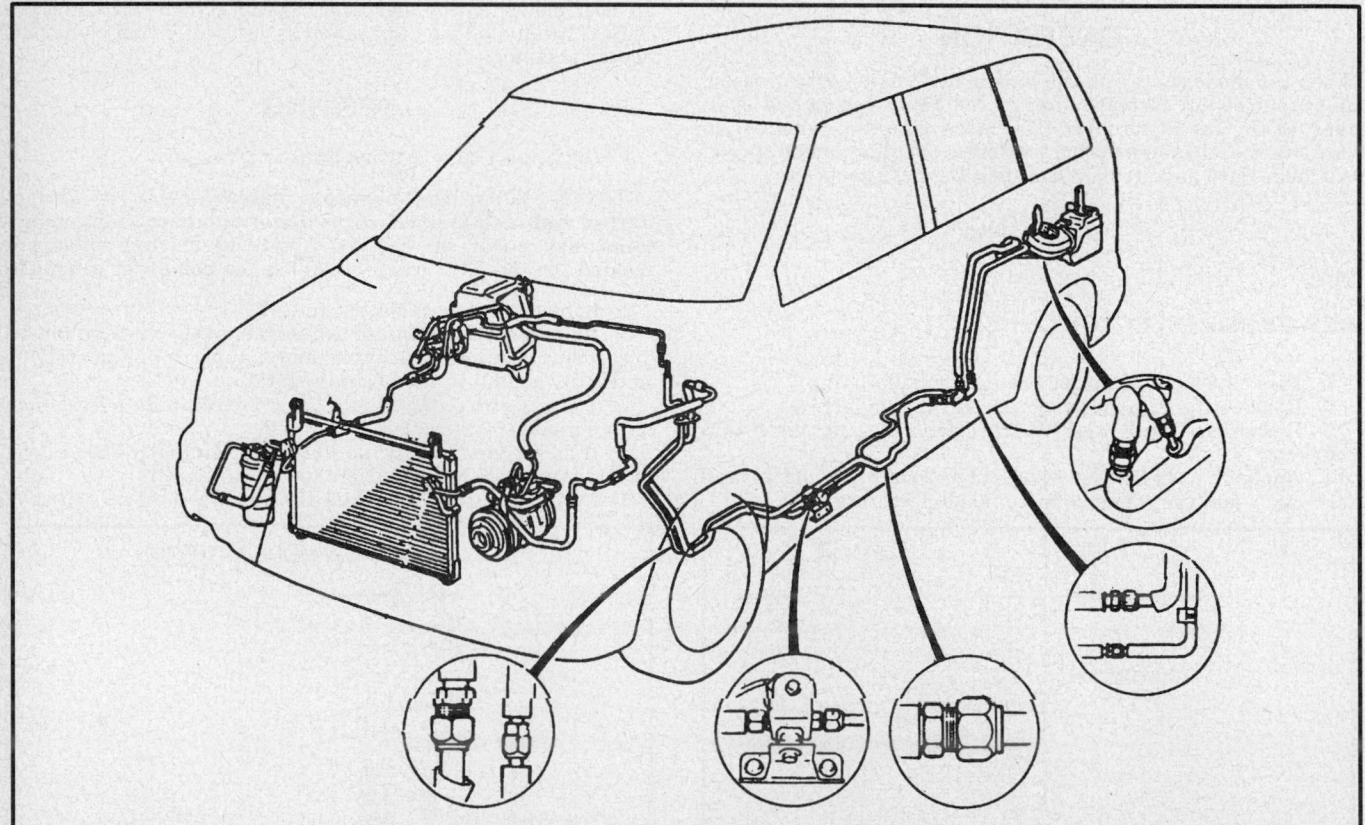

Rear auxiliary heater unit removal − MPV

19. Reconnect the rear cooling unit wire connectors.
20. Install the left rear side trim.
21. Reconnect the negative battery terminal.
22. Evacuate, recharge and leak test the rear cooling unit.

Expansion Valve

REMOVAL AND INSTALLATION

MPV

1. Disconnect the negative battery terminal.
2. Properly discharge the air conditioning system.
3. Remove the left rear side trim.
4. Disconnect the high and low pressure refrigerant lines. Cap the openings immediately.
5. Disconnect the rear cooling unit wire connectors.
6. Remove the rear cooling unit attaching nuts and bolts.
7. Remove the rear cooling unit case.
8. Disassemble the cooling unit.
9. Remove the evaporator core and expansion valve as a unit.
10. Disconnect the inlet and outlet pipes.
11. Remove the capillary tube from the outlet pipe.
12. Remove the expansion valve.
To install:
13. Attach the expansion valve to the evaporator core.
14. Attach the capillary tube from the outlet pipe.
15. Reconnect the inlet and outlet pipes.
16. Install the evaporator core and the expansion valve in the cooler unit.
17. Reassemble the cooling unit.
18. Install the rear cooling unit using the attaching nuts and bolts.
19. Reconnect the rear cooling unit wire connectors.
20. Install the left rear side trim.
21. Reconnect the negative battery terminal.
22. Evacuate, recharge and leak test the rear cooling unit.

Rear Cooling Unit Blower Motor

REMOVAL AND INSTALLATION

MPV

1. Disconnect the negative battery terminal.
2. Remove the left rear side trim.
3. Disconnect the blower unit wire connector.
4. Remove the blower unit attaching screws.
5. Remove the blower unit.
6. Installation is the reverse of the removal procedure.

Rear Cooling Unit Blower Motor Resistor

REMOVAL AND INSTALLATION

MPV

1. Disconnect the negative battery terminal.
2. Remove the left rear side trim.
3. Disconnect the blower motor resistor wire connector.
4. Remove the resistor attaching screw.
5. Remove the blower motor resistor.
6. Installation is the reverse of the removal procedure.

Refrigerant Lines

REMOVAL AND INSTALLATION

MPV

1. Disconnect the battery negative terminal.
2. Properly discharge the air conditioning system.
3. Remove chassis, engine or body parts, if required.
4. Using a backup wrench loosen, disconnect and immediately plug the refrigerant openings.
5. Disconnect wire connectors, if required.
6. Remove all attaching brackets and bolts.
7. Remove the refrigerant lines.
To install:
8. Apply a light coat of refrigerant oil to new O-rings.
9. Route refrigerant lines in original locations.
10. Use original securing brackets and bolts.
11. Evacuate, charge and check the air conditioning system for leaks.

Rear Heater Core

REMOVAL AND INSTALLATION

MPV

1. Disconnect the negative battery terminal.
2. Set the rear heater control knob to the warm position to open the water valve.
3. Properly drain the cooling system.
4. Remove the driver's seat.
5. Disconnect the heater hoses.
6. Disconnect the rear heater unit wire connector.
7. Remove the rear heater unit attaching bolts and remove the assembly.
8. Separate the heater unit case and remove the heater core.
9. Installation is the reverse of the removal procedure.

Rear Heater Blower Motor

REMOVAL AND INSTALLATION

MPV

1. Disconnect the negative battery terminal.
2. Set the rear heater control knob to the **WARM** position to open the water valve.
3. Drain the cooling system.
4. Remove the drivers seat.
5. Disconnect the heater hoses.
6. Disconnect the rear heater unit wire connector.
7. Remove the rear heater unit attaching bolts and remove the assembly.
8. Remove the blower motor attaching screws and remove the assembly.
9. Installation is the reverse of the removal procedure.

Rear Heater Unit Blower Motor Resistor

REMOVAL AND INSTALLATION

MPV

1. Disconnect the negative battery terminal.
2. Remove the drivers seat.
3. Disconnect the resistor wire connector.
4. Remove the attaching screw and remove the resistor.
5. Installation is the reverse of the removal procedure.

SYSTEM DIAGNOSIS CHARTS
AIR CONDITIONING DIAGNOSTIC CHART – B2200, B2300, B2600I, B3000, B4000 AND NAVAJO

**REFRIGERANT SYSTEM PRESSURE AND CLUTCH CYCLE TIMING EVALUATION CHART
FOR FIXED ORIFICE TUBE CYCLING CLUTCH SYSTEMS**

NOTE: Normal system conditional requirements must be maintained to properly evaluate refrigerant system pressures.
Refer to charts applicable to system under test.

HIGH (DISCHARGE) PRESSURE	LOW (SUCTION) PRESSURE	CLUTCH CYCLE TIME			COMPONENT — CAUSES
		RATE	ON	OFF	
HIGH	HIGH	CONTINUOUS RUN			CONDENSER — Inadequate Airflow.
HIGH	NORMAL TO HIGH				ENGINE OVERHEATING
NORMAL TO HIGH	NORMAL				AIR IN REFRIGERANT. REFRIGERANT OVERCHARGE (a). HUMIDITY OR AMBIENT TEMP. VERY HIGH (b).
NORMAL	HIGH				FIXED ORIFICE TUBE — Missing. O-Rings Leaking/Missing.
NORMAL	HIGH	SLOW	LONG	LONG	CLUTCH CYCLING SWITCH — High Cut-In.
NORMAL	NORMAL	SLOW OR NO CYCLE	LONG OR CONTINUOUS	NORMAL OR NO CYCLE	MOISTURE IN REFRIGERANT SYSTEM. EXCESSIVE REFRIGERANT OIL.
		FAST	SHORT	SHORT	CLUTCH CYCLING SWITCH — Low Cut-In or High Cut-Out.
NORMAL	LOW	SLOW	LONG	LONG	CLUTCH CYCLING SWITCH — Low Cut-Out.
NORMAL TO LOW	HIGH	CONTINUOUS RUN			COMPRESSOR — Low Pressure.
NORMAL TO LOW	NORMAL TO HIGH				A/C SUCTION LINE — Partially Restricted or Plugged (c).
NORMAL TO LOW	NORMAL	FAST	SHORT	NORMAL	EVAPORATOR — Low Airflow.
			SHORT TO VERY SHORT	NORMAL TO LONG	CONDENSER, FIXED ORIFICE TUBE, OR A/C LIQUID LINE — Partially Restricted or Plugged.
			SHORT TO VERY SHORT	SHORT TO VERY SHORT	LOW REFRIGERANT CHARGE.
			SHORT TO VERY SHORT	LONG	EVAPORATOR CORE — Partially Restricted or Plugged.
NORMAL TO LOW	LOW	CONTINUOUS RUN			A/C SUCTION LINE — Partially Restricted or Plugged (d). CLUTCH CYCLING SWITCH — Sticking Closed.
LOW	NORMAL	VERY FAST	VERY SHORT	VERY SHORT	CLUTCH CYCLING SWITCH — Cycling Range Too Close.
ERRATIC OPERATON OR COMPRESSOR NOT RUNNING		—	—	—	CLUTCH CYCLING SWITCH — Dirty Contacts or Sticking Open. POOR CONNECTION AT A/C CLUTCH CONNECTOR OR CLUTCH CYCLING SWITCH CONNECTOR. A/C ELECTRICAL CIRCUIT ERRATIC — See A/C Electrical Circuit Wiring Diagram. A/C PUSH BUTTON SWITCH — Not Depressed, Dirty Contacts or Open Circuit.

**ADDITIONAL POSSIBLE CAUSE COMPONENTS
ASSOCIATED WITH INADEQUATE COMPRESSOR OPERATION**

- COMPRESSOR CLUTCH Slipping • LOOSE DRIVE BELT
- CLUTCH COIL Open — Shorted or Loose Mounting.
- CLUTCH WIRING CIRCUIT — High Resistance, Open or Blown Fuse.

**ADDITIONAL POSSIBLE CAUSE COMPONENTS
ASSOCIATED WITH A DAMAGED COMPRESSOR**

- CLUTCH CYCLING SWITCH — Sticking Closed or Compressor Clutch Seized.
- SUCTION ACCUMULATOR DRIER — Refrigerant Oil Bleed Hole Plugged.
- REFRIGERANT LEAKS.

(a) Compressor may make noise on initial run. This is slugging condition caused by excessive liquid refrigerant.
(b) Compressor clutch may not cycle in ambient temperatures above 80°F depending on humidity conditions.
(c) Low pressure reading will be normal to high if pressure is taken at accumulator and if restriction is downstream of service access valve.
(d) Low pressure reading will be low if pressure is taken near the compressor and restriction is upstream of service access valve.

INSUFFICIENT COOLING DIAGNOSTIC CHART –
B2200, B2300, B2600I, B3000, B4000 AND NAVAJO

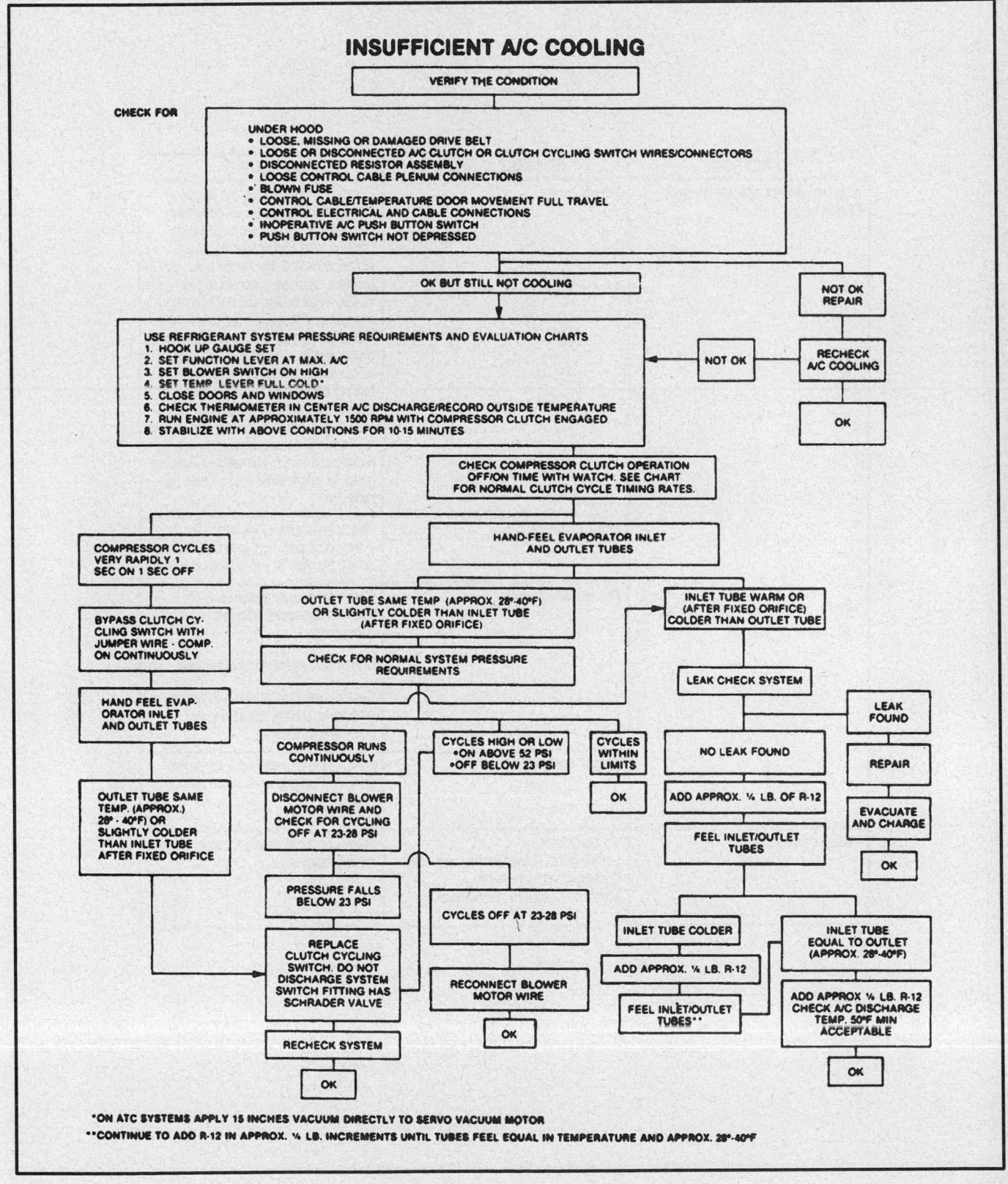

INSUFFICIENT A/C COOLING

VERIFY THE CONDITION

CHECK FOR

UNDER HOOD
- LOOSE, MISSING OR DAMAGED DRIVE BELT
- LOOSE OR DISCONNECTED A/C CLUTCH OR CLUTCH CYCLING SWITCH WIRES/CONNECTORS
- DISCONNECTED RESISTOR ASSEMBLY
- LOOSE CONTROL CABLE PLENUM CONNECTIONS
- BLOWN FUSE
- CONTROL CABLE/TEMPERATURE DOOR MOVEMENT FULL TRAVEL
- CONTROL ELECTRICAL AND CABLE CONNECTIONS
- INOPERATIVE A/C PUSH BUTTON SWITCH
- PUSH BUTTON SWITCH NOT DEPRESSED

OK BUT STILL NOT COOLING

NOT OK
REPAIR

USE REFRIGERANT SYSTEM PRESSURE REQUIREMENTS AND EVALUATION CHARTS
1. HOOK UP GAUGE SET
2. SET FUNCTION LEVER AT MAX. A/C
3. SET BLOWER SWITCH ON HIGH
4. SET TEMP. LEVER FULL COLD*
5. CLOSE DOORS AND WINDOWS
6. CHECK THERMOMETER IN CENTER A/C DISCHARGE/RECORD OUTSIDE TEMPERATURE
7. RUN ENGINE AT APPROXIMATELY 1500 RPM WITH COMPRESSOR CLUTCH ENGAGED
8. STABILIZE WITH ABOVE CONDITIONS FOR 10-15 MINUTES

NOT OK

RECHECK
A/C COOLING

OK

CHECK COMPRESSOR CLUTCH OPERATION
OFF/ON TIME WITH WATCH. SEE CHART
FOR NORMAL CLUTCH CYCLE TIMING RATES.

COMPRESSOR CYCLES
VERY RAPIDLY 1
SEC ON 1 SEC OFF

HAND-FEEL EVAPORATOR INLET
AND OUTLET TUBES

OUTLET TUBE SAME TEMP. (APPROX. 28°-40°F)
OR SLIGHTLY COLDER THAN INLET TUBE
(AFTER FIXED ORIFICE)

INLET TUBE WARM OR
(AFTER FIXED ORIFICE)
COLDER THAN OUTLET TUBE

BYPASS CLUTCH CY-
CLING SWITCH WITH
JUMPER WIRE - COMP.
ON CONTINUOUSLY

CHECK FOR NORMAL SYSTEM PRESSURE
REQUIREMENTS

LEAK CHECK SYSTEM

LEAK
FOUND

HAND FEEL EVAP-
ORATOR INLET
AND OUTLET TUBES

COMPRESSOR RUNS
CONTINUOUSLY

CYCLES HIGH OR LOW
•ON ABOVE 52 PSI
•OFF BELOW 23 PSI

CYCLES
WITHIN
LIMITS

NO LEAK FOUND

REPAIR

OUTLET TUBE SAME
TEMP. (APPROX.)
28° - 40°F) OR
SLIGHTLY COLDER
THAN INLET TUBE
AFTER FIXED ORIFICE

DISCONNECT BLOWER
MOTOR WIRE AND
CHECK FOR CYCLING
OFF AT 23-28 PSI

OK

ADD APPROX. ¼ LB. OF R-12

EVACUATE
AND CHARGE

FEEL INLET/OUTLET
TUBES

OK

PRESSURE FALLS
BELOW 23 PSI

CYCLES OFF AT 23-28 PSI

INLET TUBE COLDER

INLET TUBE
EQUAL TO OUTLET
(APPROX. 28°-40°F)

REPLACE
CLUTCH CYCLING
SWITCH. DO NOT
DISCHARGE SYSTEM
SWITCH FITTING HAS
SCHRADER VALVE

ADD APPROX. ¼ LB. R-12

RECONNECT BLOWER
MOTOR WIRE

ADD APPROX ¼ LB. R-12
CHECK A/C DISCHARGE
TEMP. 50°F MIN
ACCEPTABLE

FEEL INLET/OUTLET
TUBES**

RECHECK SYSTEM

OK

OK

OK

*ON ATC SYSTEMS APPLY 15 INCHES VACUUM DIRECTLY TO SERVO VACUUM MOTOR

**CONTINUE TO ADD R-12 IN APPROX. ¼ LB. INCREMENTS UNTIL TUBES FEEL EQUAL IN TEMPERATURE AND APPROX. 28°-40°F

BLOWER MOTOR AND VACUUM MOTOR DIAGNOSTIC CHART

CONDITION	POSSIBLE CAUSE	RESOLUTION
Blower does not operate properly. Check fuse.	Blower motor.	Connect a #10 gauge (or larger diameter) jumper wire directly from the positive battery terminal to the positive lead (orange wire) of the blower motor. If the motor runs, the problem must be external to the motor. If the motor will not run, connect a #10 gauge (or larger diameter) jumper wire from the motor black lead to a good ground. If the motor runs, the trouble is in the ground circuit. On vehicles with ground side switching, check the blower resistor, the blower switch and the harness connections. Service as required. If motor still will not run, the motor is inoperative and should be replaced.
	Blower resistor.	Check continuity of resistors for opens or shorts (self-powered test lamp). Service or replace as required.
	Blower wire harness.	Check for proper installation of harness connector terminal connectors. Check wire-to-terminal continuity. Check continuity of wires in harness for shorts, opens, abrasion, etc. Service as required.
	Blower switch(es).	Check blower switch(es) for proper contact. Replace switch(es) as required.
Vacuum motor system	Vacuum leak. Loose or disconnected vacuum hose. Damaged vacuum motor. Misrouted vacuum connections	Repair or repair system components, as required.

AIR CONDITIONING DIAGNOSTIC CHART

CONDITION	POSSIBLE CAUSE	RESOLUTION
Insufficient, erratic, or no heat or defrost.	Low radiator coolant level due to: Coolant leaks.	Check radiator cap pressure. Replace if below minimum pressure. Fill to specified coolant level. Pressure test for engine cooling system and heater system leaks. Service as required.

	Engine overheating.	Check radiator cap. Replace if below minimum pressure.
		
		Remove bugs, leaves, etc. from radiator or condenser fins.
		
		Check for:
		
		  Loose fan belt
		
		  Sticking thermostat
		
		  Incorrect ignition timing
		
		  Water pump impeller damage
		
		  Restricted cooling system
		
		Service as required.

	Loose fan belt.	Replace if cracked or worn and/or adjust belt tension.
	Thermostat.	Check coolant temperature at radiator filler neck. If under 170°F, replace thermostat.
	Plugged or partially plugged heater core.	Clean and backflush engine cooling system and heater core.
	Loose or improperly adjusted control cables.	Adjust to specifications.
	Kinked, clogged, collapsed, soft, swollen, or decomposed engine cooling system or heater system hoses.	Replace damaged hoses and backflush engine cooling system, then heater system, until all particles have been removed.
	Blocked air inlet.	Check cowl air inlet for leaves, foreign material, etc. Remove as required. Check internal blower inlet screen (on vehicles so equipped) for leaves and foreign material.

WIRING SCHEMATICS

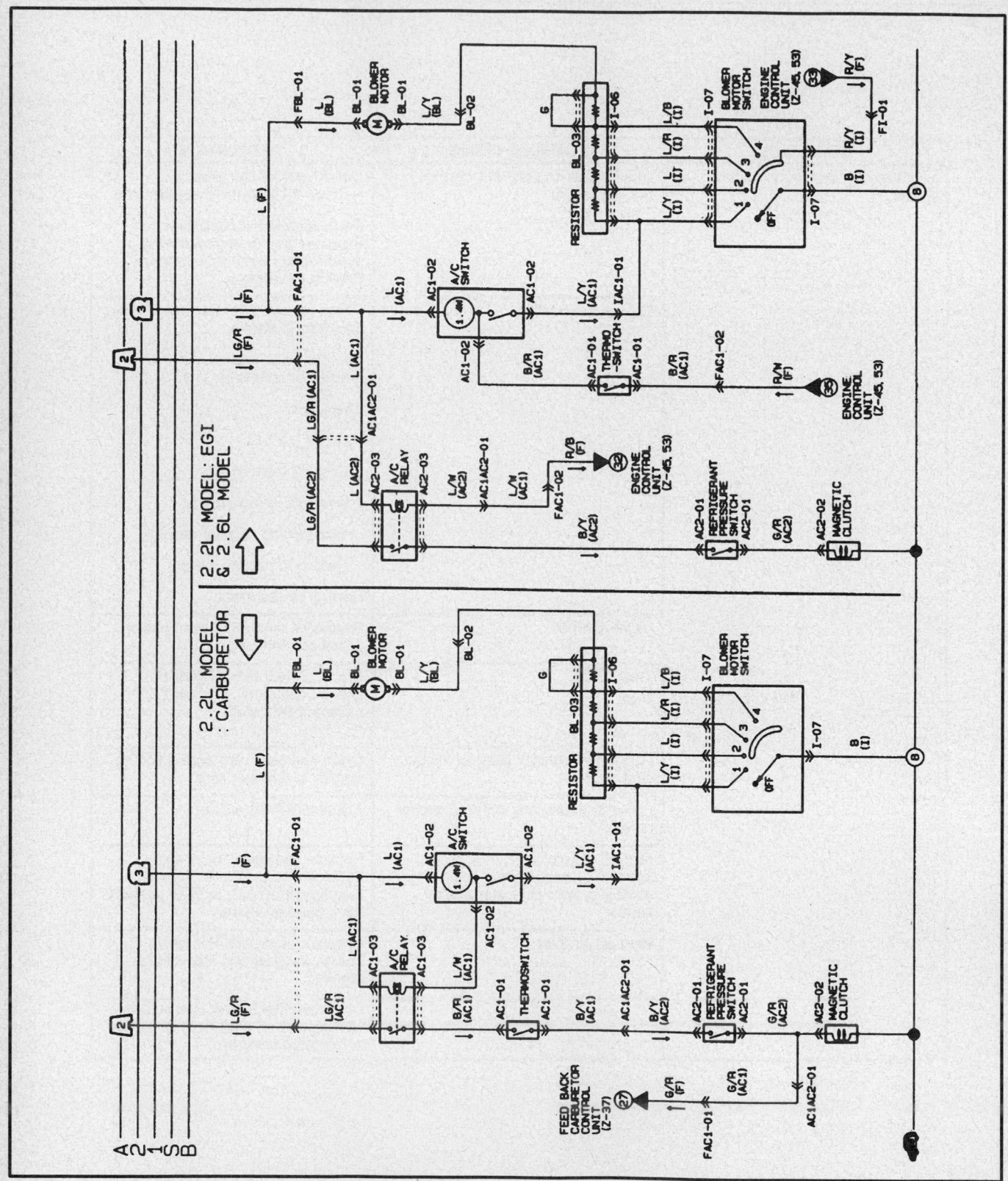

Air conditioning system wiring schematic—B2200 and B2600i — 1993

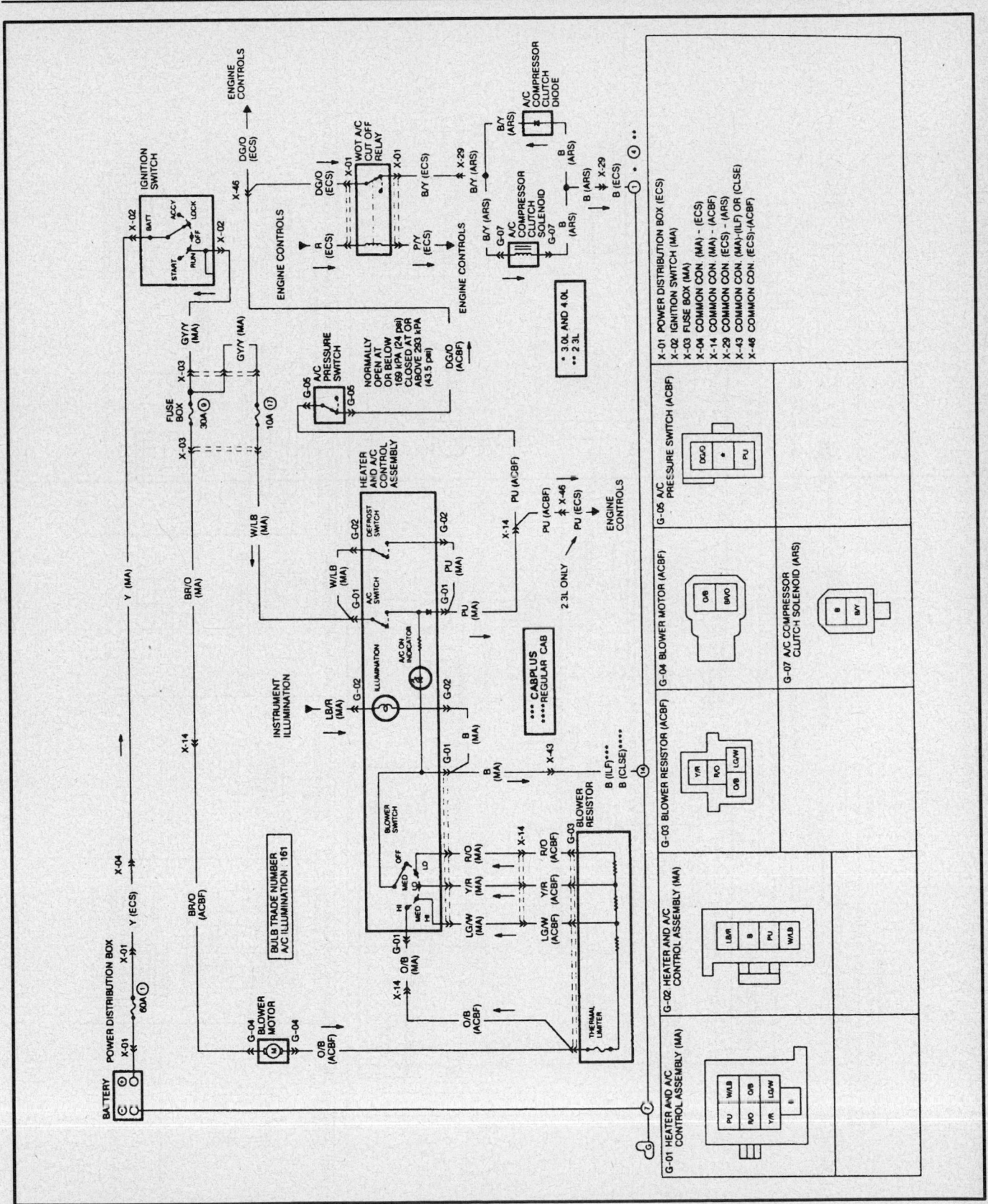

Air conditioning system wiring schematic — B2300, B3000 and B4000 — 1994

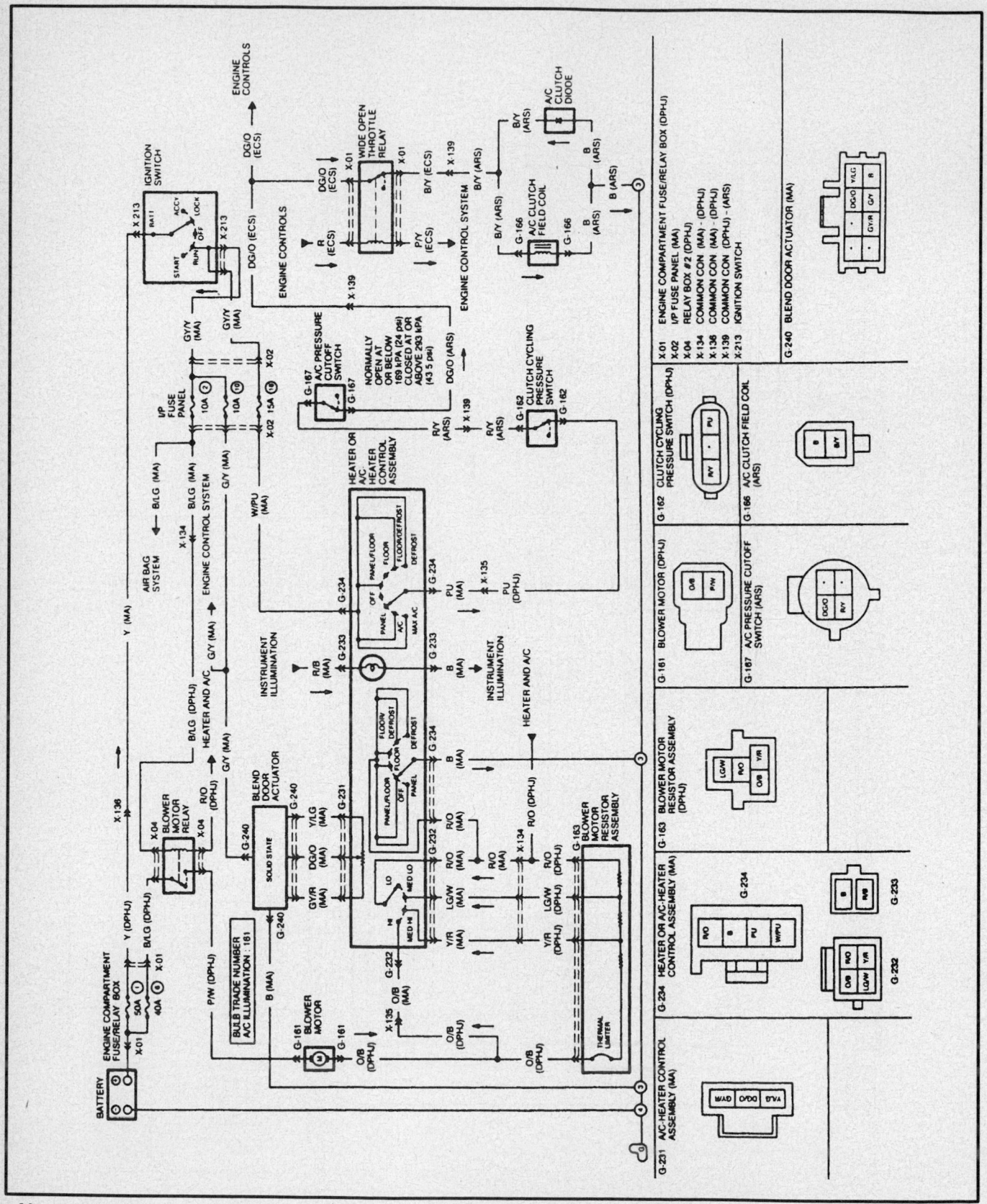

Air conditioning—heater system wiring schematic — B2300, B3000 and B4000 — 1995

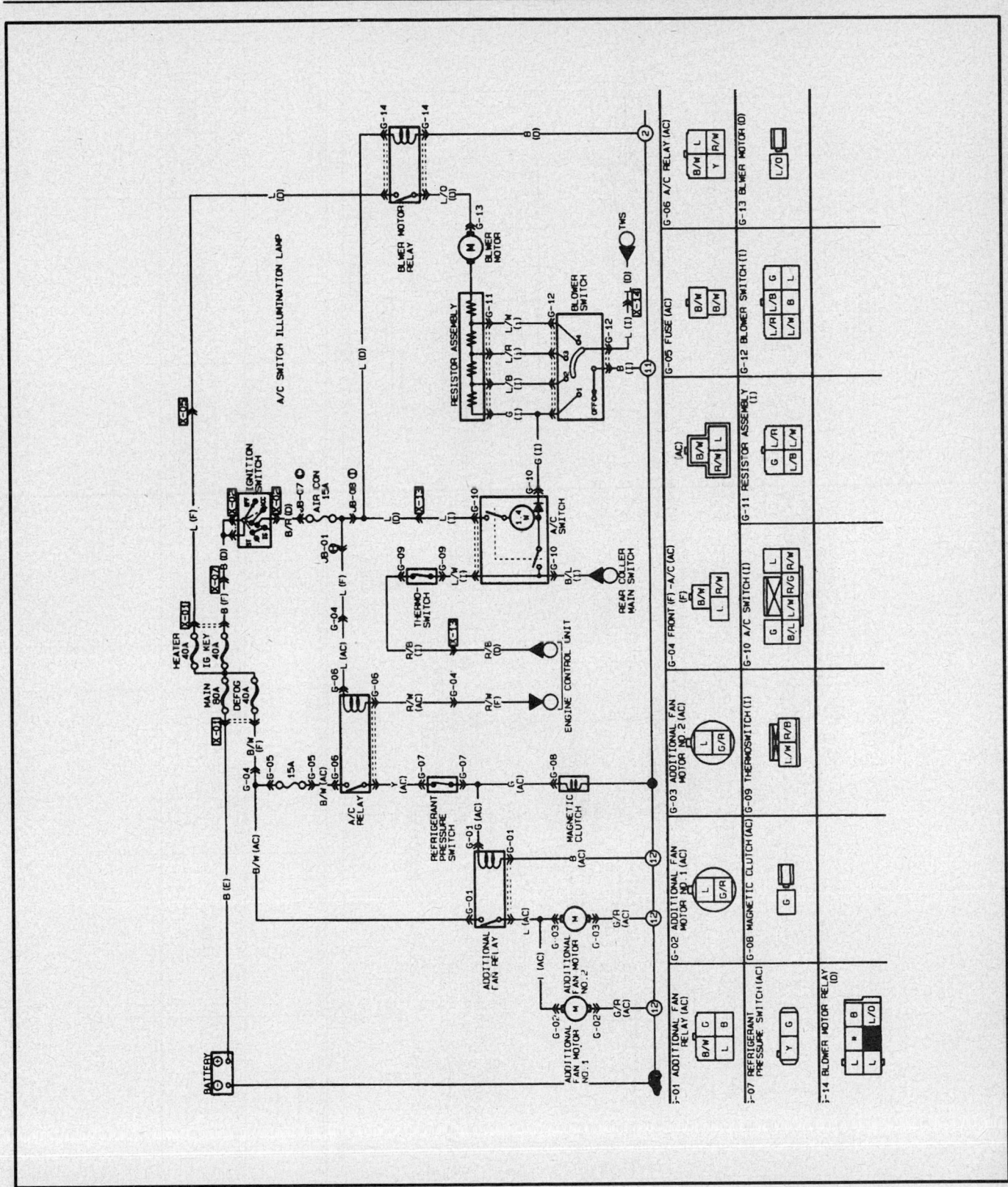

Air conditioning–heater system wiring schematic — MPV – 1993

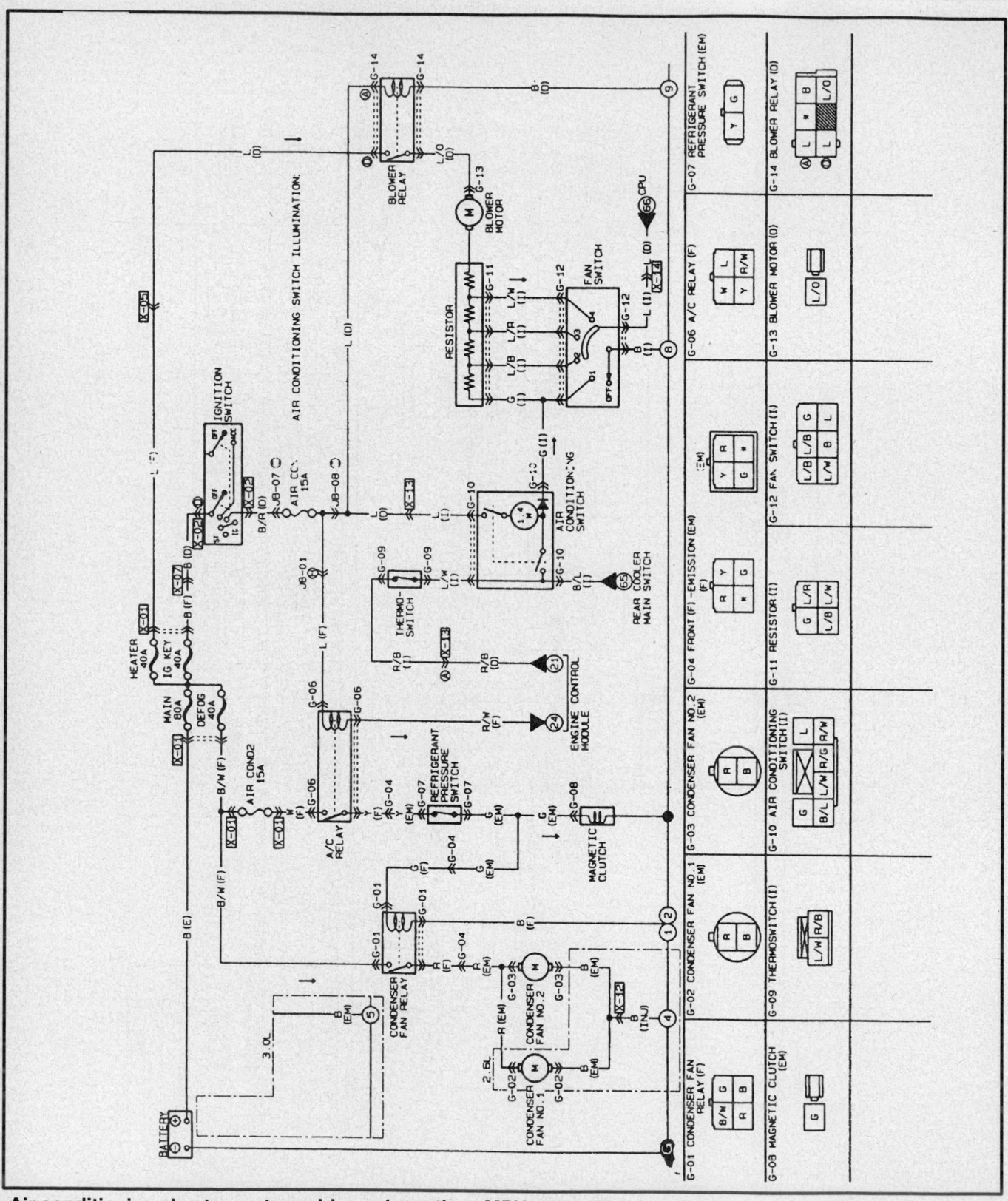

Air conditioning–heater system wiring schematic – MPV 1994–95

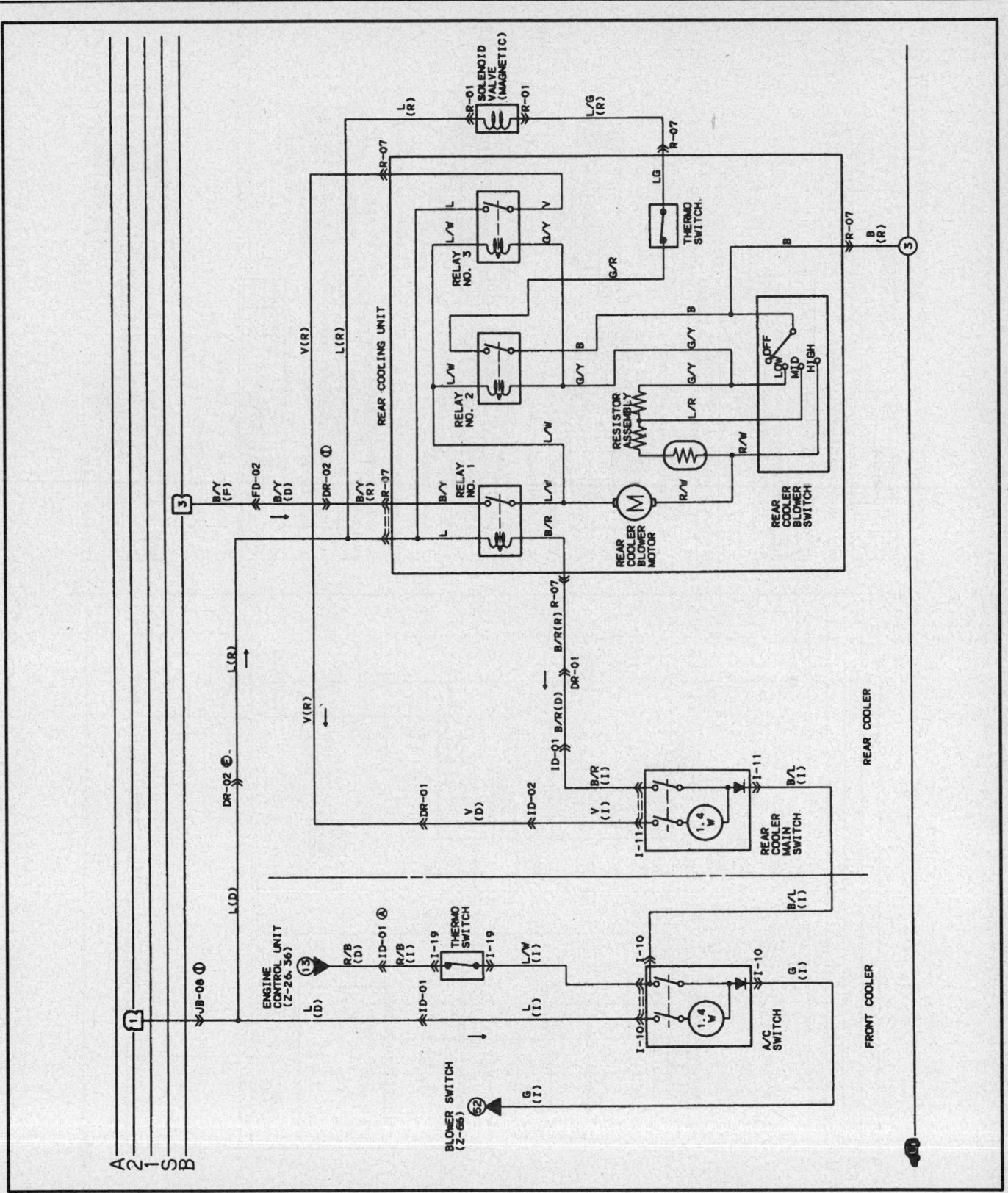

Auxiliary air conditioning wiring schematic – MPV – 1993

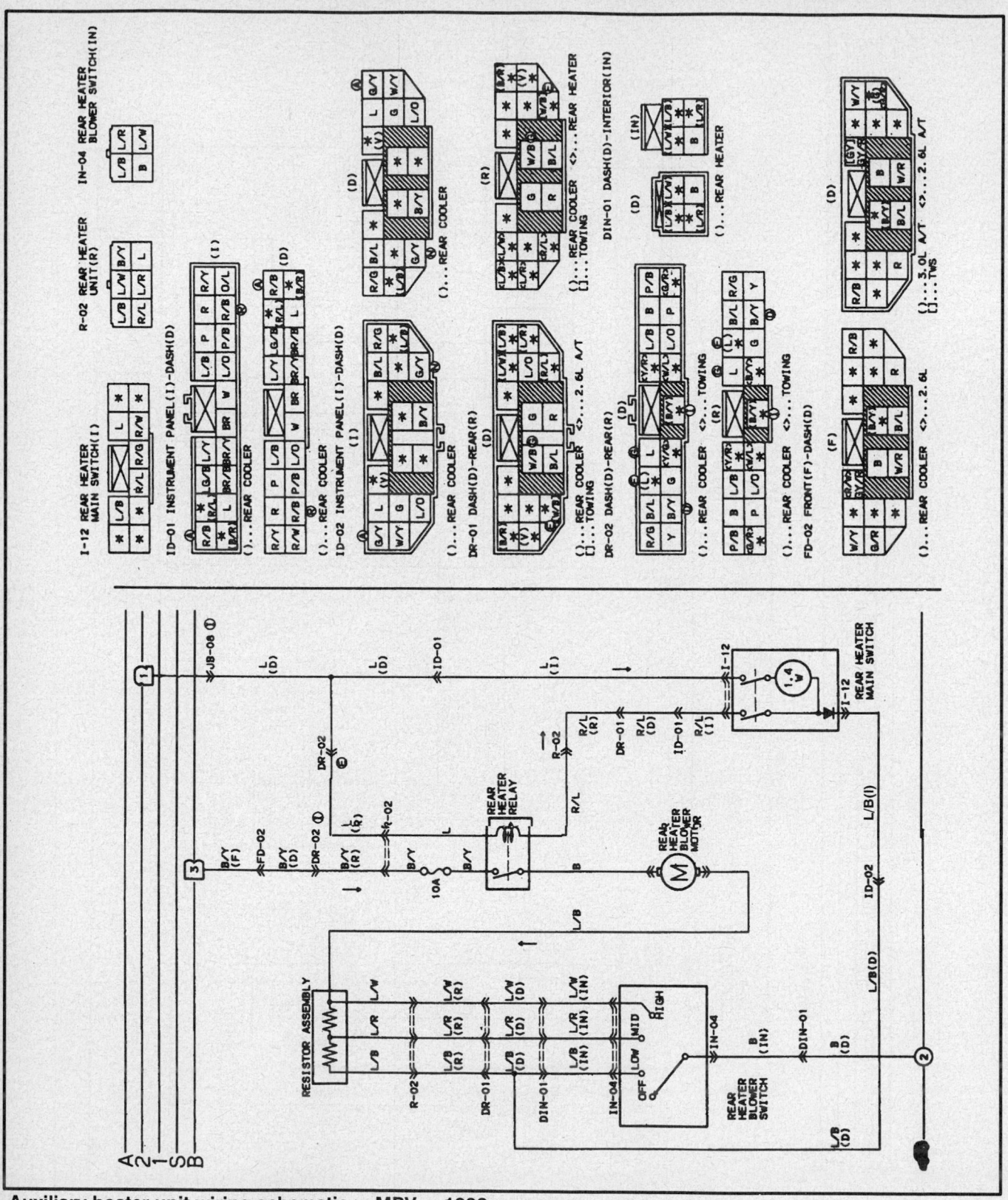

Auxiliary heater unit wiring schematic — MPV — 1993

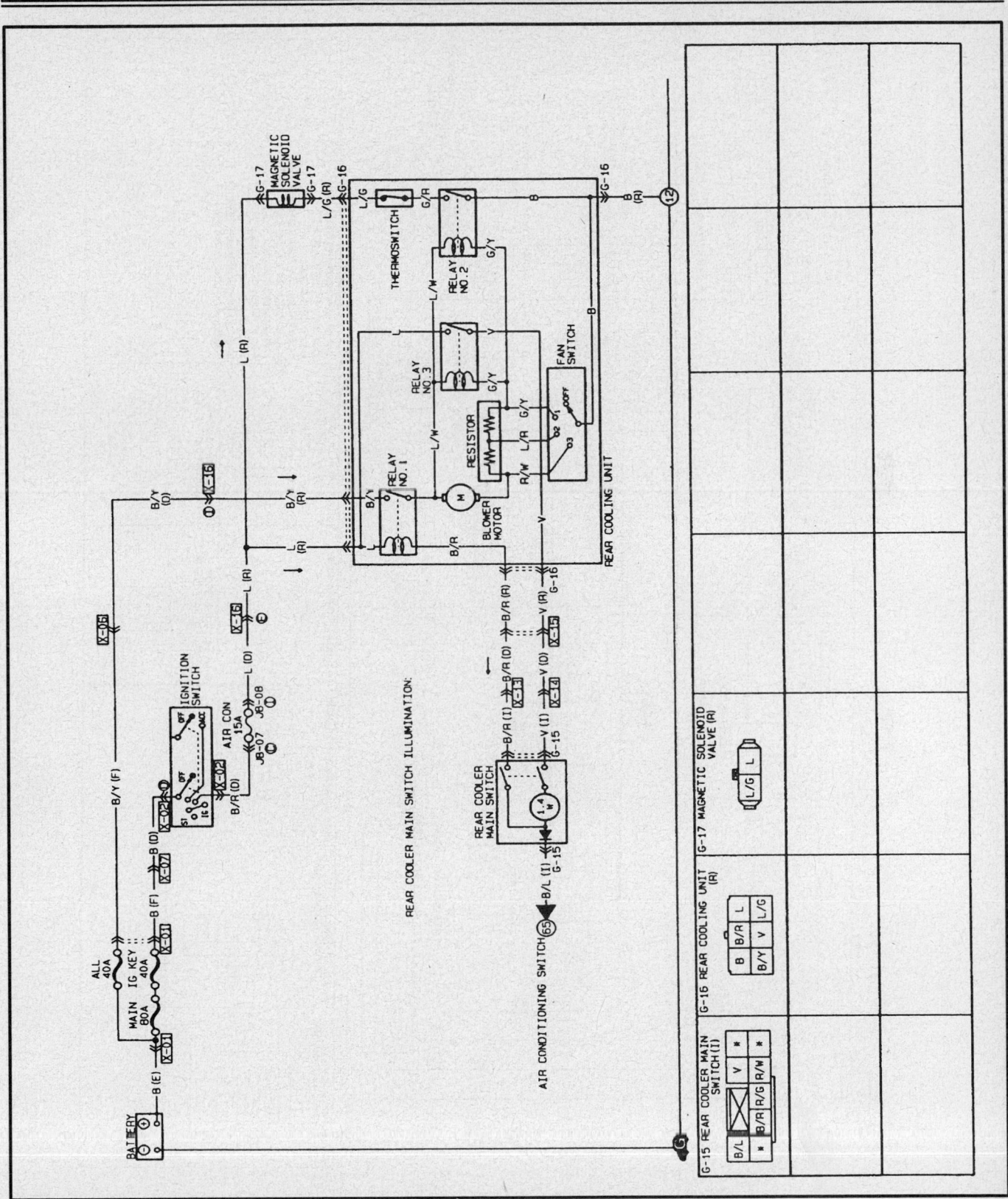

Air conditioning system wiring schematic — MPV rear except logical type 1994–95

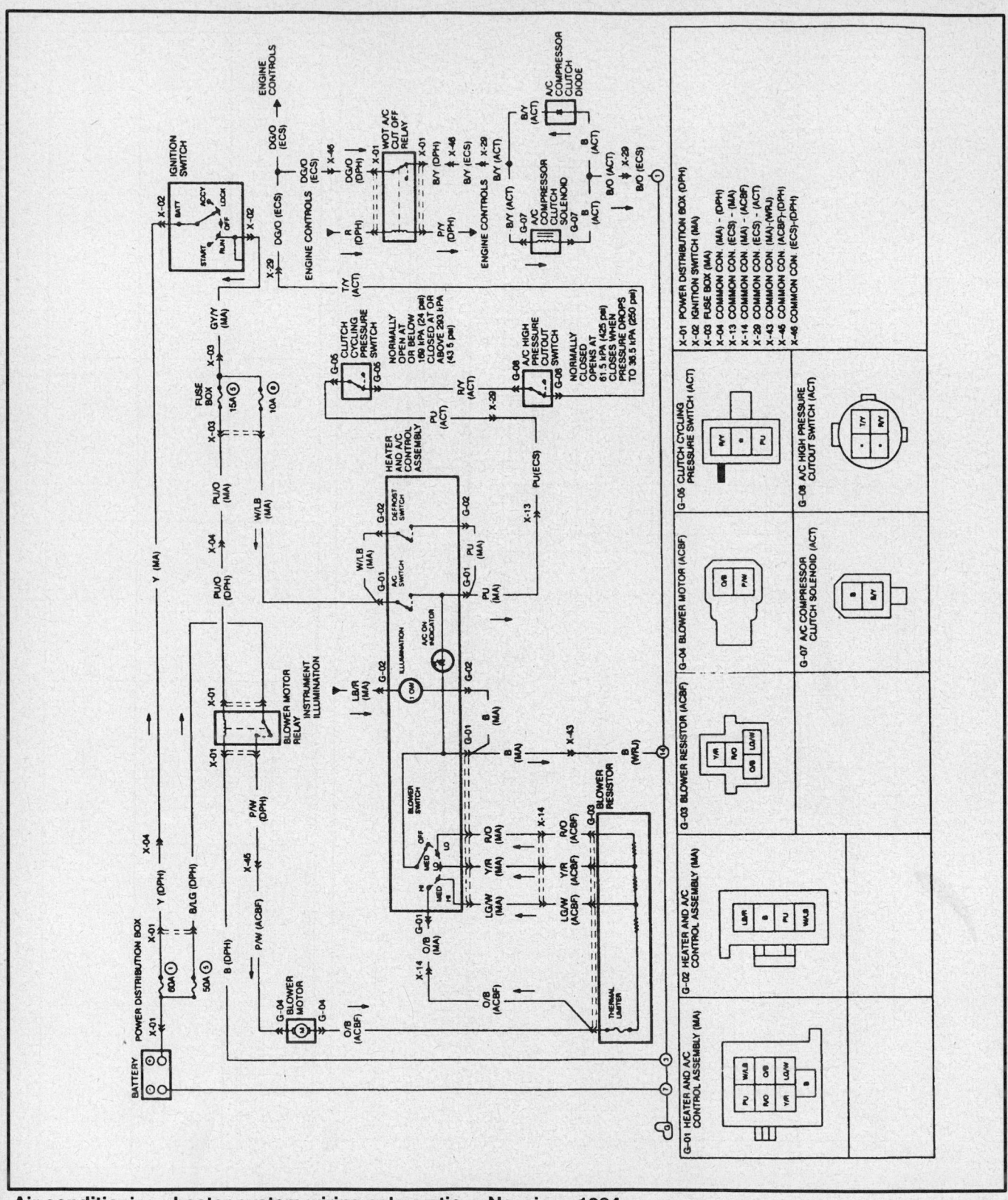

Air conditioning—heater system wiring schematic — Navajo — 1994

SPECIFICATIONS

ENGINE IDENTIFICATION

Year	Model	Engine Displacement Liters (cc)	Engine Series (ID/VIN)	Fuel System	No. of Cylinders	Engine Type
1993	190E	2.3 (2299)	M102	KE	4	102.985
	190E	2.6 (2599)	M103	KE	6	103.942
	300CE	3.2 (3199)	M104/EA52	HFM–SFI	6	104.992
	300CE	3.2 (3199)	M104/EA66	HFM–SFI	6	104.992
	300CE 4M	3.0 (2960)	M103	CIS–E	6	103.985
	300D 2.5L Turbo	2.5 (2497)	OM602	Diesel	5	602.962
	300E	3.2 (3199)	M104	HFM–SFI	6	104.992
	300E 2.8	2.8 (2803)	M104	HFM–SFI	6	104.942
	300SD	3.5 (3449)	OM603	Diesel	6	603.971
	300SE	3.2 (3199)	M104	LH	6	104.990
	300SL	3.0 (2962)	M104	LH–SFI	6	104.981
	300TE	3.2 (3199)	M104	HFM–SFI	6	104.992
	300TE 4M	3.0 (2960)	M103	CIS–E	6	103.985
	400E	4.2 (4196)	M119	LH–SFI	8	119.975
	400SEL	4.2 (4196)	M119	LH–SFI	8	119.971
	500E	5.0 (4973)	M119	LH–SFI	8	119.974
	500SEC	5.0 (4973)	M119/GAT0	LH–SFI	8	119.970
	500SEL	5.0 (4973)	M119/GA51	LH–SFI	8	119.970
	500SL	5.0 (4973)	M119/FA67	LH–SFI	8	119.972
	600SEC	6.0 (5987)	M120/GAT6	LH	12	120.980
	600SEL	6.0 (5987)	M120/GA57	LH	12	120.980
	600SL	6.0 (5987)	M120/FA76	LH–SFI	12	120.981
1994	C220	2.2 (2199)	M111	HFM–SFI	4	111.961
	C280	2.8 (2799)	M104	HFM–SFI	6	104.941
	E300	3.2 (3199)	M104/EA32	HFM–SFI	6	104.992
	E320	3.2 (3199)	M104/EA52	HFM–SFI	6	104.992
	E320	3.2 (3199)	M104/EA66	HFM–SFI	6	104.992
	E320	3.2 (3199)	M104/EA92	HFM–SFI	6	104.992
	E420	4.2 (4196)	M119	LH–SFI	8	119.975
	E500	5.0 (4973)	M119	LH–SFI	8	119.974
	S320	3.2 (3199)	M104	HFM–SFI	6	104.994
	S350	3.5 (3449)	OM603	EDS	6	603.971
	S420	4.2 (4196)	M119	LH–SFI	8	119.971
	S500	5.0 (4973)	M119/FA51	LH–SFI	8	119.970
	S500	5.0 (4973)	M119/GA70	LH–SFI	8	119.970
	S600	6.0 (5987)	M120/GA57	LH	12	120.980
	S600	6.0 (5987)	M120/GA76	LH	12	120.980
	SL320	3.2 (3199)	M104	HFM–SFI	6	104.991
	SL500	5.0 (4973)	M119	LH–SFI	8	119.972
	SL600	6.0 (5987)	M120	LH–SFI	12	120.981

ENGINE IDENTIFICATION

Year	Model	Engine Displacement Liters (cc)	Engine Series (ID/VIN)	Fuel System	No. of Cylinders	Engine Type
1995	C220	2.2 (2199)	M111	HFM–SFI	4	111.961
	C280	2.8 (2799)	M104	HFM–SFI	6	104.941
	E300	3.0 (2996)	OM606	EDS	6	606.910
	E320	3.2 (3199)	M104/EA32	HFM–SFI	6	104.992
	E320	3.2 (3199)	M104/EA52	HFM–SFI	6	104.992
	E320	3.2 (3199)	M104/EA66	HFM–SFI	6	104.992
	E320	3.2 (3199)	M104/EA92	HFM–SFI	6	104.992
	E420	4.2 (4196)	M119	LH–SFI	8	119.975
	S320	3.2 (3199)	M104	HFM–SFI	6	104.994
	S350	3.5 (3449)	OM603	EDS	6	603.971
	S420	4.2 (4196)	M119	LH–SFI	8	119.971
	S500	5.0 (4973)	M119/GA51	LH–SFI	8	119.970
	S500	5.0 (4973)	M119/GA70	LH–SFI	8	119.970
	S600	6.0 (5987)	M120/GA57	LH	12	120.980
	S600	6.0 (5987)	M120/GA76	LH	12	120.980
	SL320	3.2 (3199)	M104	HFM–SFI	6	104.991
	SL500	5.0 (4973)	M119	LH–SFI	8	119.972
	SL600	6.0 (5987)	M120	LH–SFI	12	120.981

CIS–E—Electronic Continuous Injection System
EDS—Electronic Diesel System
HFM–SFI—Hot Film Management–Sequential Fuel Injection
KE—Gasoline Injection System KE (continuous, electronic)
LH—Gasoline Injection System LH (air mass measurement with hot wire)
LH–SFI—Gasoline Injection System LH–Sequential Fuel Injection

REFRIGERANT CAPACITIES

Year	Model	Refrigerant (oz.)	Oil (fl. oz.)	Compressor Type
1993	190E	36.0	4.0①	Nippondenso①
	300E	38.4	4.0①	Nippondenso①
	300CE	38.4	4.0①	Nippondenso①
	300TE	38.4	4.0①	Nippondenso①
	300SE	35.2	5.4②	10PA20
	300E 4Matic	38.4	4.0①	Nippondenso①
	300TE 4Matic	38.4	4.0①	Nippondenso①
	300D Turbo	38.8	4.0	10PA17
	300SL	35.2	4.0	10PA17
	400E	35.2	4.0	10PA17
	400SE	35.2	5.4②	10PA20
	500SL	35.2	5.4②	10PA17
	500E	35.2	5.4②	10PA17
	500SEL	35.2	5.4②	10PA20
1994	C220	34	5.24②	6CA17
	C280	34	5.24②	6CA17

REFRIGERANT CAPACITIES

Year	Model	Refrigerant (oz.)	Oil (fl. oz.)	Compressor Type
1994	E300	33.5③	4.77②	10PA17
	E320	33.5③	4.77②	10PA17
	E420	33.5③	4.77②	10PA17
	E500	33.5③	4.77②	10PA17
	S320	42④	4.0②	10PA20
	S350	42④	4.0②	10PA20
	S420	42④	4.0②	10PA20
	S500	42④	4.0②	10PA20
	S600	42④	4.0②	10PA20
	SL320	33.5	4.77②	10PA17
	SL500	33.5	4.77②	10PA17
	SL600	33.5	4.77②	10PA17
1995	C220	34	5.24②	6CA17
	C280	34	5.24②	6CA17
	E300	33.5③	4.77②	10PA17
	E320	33.5③	4.77②	10PA17
	E420	33.5③	4.77②	10PA17
	S320	42④	5.4②	10PA20
	S350	42④	5.4②	10PA20
	S420	42④	5.4②	10PA20
	S500	42④	5.4②	10PA20
	S600	42④	5.4②	10PA20
	SL320	33.5	4.77②	10PA17
	SL500	33.5	4.77②	10PA17
	SL600	33.5	4.77②	10PA17

① Delco R-4 compressor may also be used on some models: 5.7 oz.
② With R134a refrigerant, PAG oil
③ With rear air conditioner: 40.6 oz.
④ With rear air conditioner: 49.4 oz.

AIR CONDITIONING BELT TENSION

Year	Model	Engine Liters (cc)	Belt Type	Specifications New	Specifications Used
1993	300E	3.0 (2962)	Serpentine	①	①
	300TE	3.0 (2962)	Serpentine	①	①
	300CE	3.0 (2962)	Serpentine	①	①
	300SE	3.0 (2962)	Poly-V	②	②
	300D Turbo	2.5 (2499)	Serpentine	①	①
	300SD	3.0 (2962)	Serpentine	①	①
	300SL	3.0 (2962)	Serpentine	①	①
	400E	4.0 (3988)	NA	NA	NA
	400SEL	4.0 (3988)	NA	NA	NA
	500SL	5.0 (4973)	Serpentine	①	①
	500E	5.0 (4973)	NA	NA	NA
	500SEL	5.0 (4973)	NA	NA	NA

AIR CONDITIONING BELT TENSION

Year	Model	Engine Liters (cc)	Belt Type	Specifications	
				New	Used
1993	600SL	6.0 (5924)	NA	NA	NA
	600SEL	6.0 (5924)	NA	NA	NA
	600SEC	6.0 (5924)	NA	NA	NA
1994	C220	2.2 (2199)	NA	NA	NA
	C280	2.8 (2799)	NA	NA	NA
	E320	3.2 (3199)	NA	NA	NA
	E420	4.2 (4196)	NA	NA	NA
	E500	5.0 (4973)	NA	NA	NA
	S320	3.2 (3199)	NA	NA	NA
	S350	3.5 (3449)	NA	NA	NA
	S420	4.2 (4196)	NA	NA	NA
	S500	5.0 (4973)	NA	NA	NA
	S600	6.0 (5987)	NA	NA	NA
	SL320	3.2 (3199)	NA	NA	NA
	SL500	5.0 (4973)	NA	NA	NA
	SL600	6.0 (5987)	NA	NA	NA
1995	C220	2.2 (2199)	NA	NA	NA
	C280	2.8 (2799)	NA	NA	NA
	E300	3.0 (2996)	NA	NA	NA
	E320	3.2 (3199)	NA	NA	NA
	E420	4.2 (4196)	NA	NA	NA
	S320	3.2 (3199)	NA	NA	NA
	S350	3.5 (3449)	NA	NA	NA
	S420	4.2 (4196)	NA	NA	NA
	S500	5.0 (4973)	NA	NA	NA
	S600	6.0 (5987)	NA	NA	NA
	SL320	3.2 (3199)	NA	NA	NA
	SL500	5.0 (4973)	NA	NA	NA
	SL600	6.0 (5987)	NA	NA	NA

NA—Not available.
① Equipped with automatic tensioner.
② Requires use of special Mercedes-Benz bolt tension gauge.

SYSTEM DESCRIPTION

General Information

Automatic Climate Control

Several models are equipped with an Automatic Climate Control (ACC) system which controls the cooling capacity electronically.

The ACC system operates on the same principle as the system used on the manually operated systems, except it is equipped with a control unit which utilizes various switches, sensors and vacuum motors.

Service Valve Location

300E, 300CE and 300TE

The service valve is located in the air conditioning pipe near the compressor.

System Discharging

R-12 refrigerant is a chlorofluorocarbon which, when released into the atmosphere, can contribute to the depletion of the ozone layer in the upper atmosphere. Ozone filters out harmful radiation from the sun. In order to protect the ozone layer, an approved R-12 recovery/recycling machine that meets SAE standards should be employed when discharging the system. Follow the operating instructions provided with the approved equipment exactly to properly discharge the system.

Some models use non-CFC R-134a. These systems are clearly identified with labeling on the refrigerant lines and/or information labels. Components coming in contact with R-134a cannot be used on R-12 refrigerant system and vice versa. Mixing R-12 and R-134a is not compatible in any amounts. Although R134a is a non-CFC refrigerant, the systems should be serviced only the approved, dedicated recovery/recycling equipment. Do not discharge any refrigerant directly into the atmosphere.

System Evacuating

If the air conditioning system has been opened to the atmosphere, it should be air and moisture free before being recharged with refrigerant. Moisture and air mixed with refrigerant will raise the compressor head pressure, possibly damage the system's components and will reduce the performance of the system. In addition, air and moisture in the system can lead to internal corrosion of the system components. Moisture will boil at normal room temperature when exposed to a vacuum. To evacuate or rid the system of air and moisture:

1. Leak test the system and repair any leaks found.
2. Connect an approved charging station, recovery/recycling machine or manifold gauge set and vacuum pump to the discharge and suction ports. The red hose is normally connected to the discharge (high pressure) line. The blue hose is connected to the suction (low pressure) line. If using a manifold gauge set, the center (usually yellow) hose is connected to the charging station or recovery/recycling machine.

3. Open the discharge and suction ports and start the vacuum pump. If the pump is not able to pull at least 26 in. Hg of vacuum there is a leak that must be repaired before evacuation can occur.
4. Once the system has reached at least 26 in. Hg of vacuum, allow the system to evacuate for at least 10 minutes. The longer the system is evacuated, the more moisture will be removed.
5. Close all valves and turn the pump off. If the system loses more than 2 in. Hg of vacuum after 15 minutes, there is a leak that should be repaired.

System Charging

1. Connect an approved charging station, recovery/recycling machine or manifold gauge set to the discharge and suction ports. The red hose is normally connected to the discharge (high pressure) line, and the blue hose is connected to the suction (low pressure) line. If using a manifold gauge set, the center (usually yellow) hose is connected to the charging station or recovery/recycling machine.
2. Follow the instructions provided with the equipment and charge the system with the specified amount of refrigerant.
3. Perform a leak test.

SYSTEM COMPONENTS

Radiator

REMOVAL AND INSTALLATION

1. Disconnect the negative battery cable. Remove the radiator cap.
2. Unscrew the radiator drain plug and drain the coolant from the radiator. If all of the coolant in the system is to be drained, move the heater controls to **WARM** and open the drain cocks on the engine block.
3. If equipped with an oil cooler, drain the oil from the cooler.
4. If equipped, loosen the radiator shell.
5. Loosen the hose clips on the top and bottom radiator hoses and remove the hoses from the connections on the radiator.
6. Unscrew and plug the bottom line on the oil cooler.
7. If equipped with an automatic transmission, unscrew and plug the lines on the transmission cooler.
8. Disconnect the right and left side rubber loops and pull the radiator up and from the body.
To install:
9. Inspect and replace any hoses which have become hardened or spongy.
10. Install the radiator shell and radiator, if the shell was removed, from the top and connect the top and bottom hoses to the radiator.
11. Bolt the shell to the radiator.
12. Attach the rubber loops or position the retaining spring, as applicable.
13. Position the hose clips on the top and bottom hoses.
14. Attach the lines to the oil cooler.
15. If equipped with an automatic transmission, connect the lines to the transmission cooler.
16. Move the heater levers to the **WARM** position and slowly add coolant, allowing air to escape.
17. Check the oil level and fill if necessary. Run the engine for about 1 minute at idle with the filler neck open.
18. Add coolant to the specified level. Install the radiator cap and turn it until it seats in the 2nd notch. Run the engine and check for leaks.

Cooling Fan

TESTING

300D Turbo, 300E, 300CE, 300TE, 300E 4Matic, 300TE 4Matic

1. Using a jumper wire, connect it to the 2 terminals of the pressure switch, located near the left inner fender well.
2. Turn the ignition switch **ON**; the fan should operate.
3. Check the fan's rotation, it should be clockwise; if the rotation is counterclockwise, reverse the 2-pole plug connector, located near the pressure switch.

REMOVAL AND INSTALLATION

190E

The vehicles are equipped with 2 fans: left and right.

1. Disconnect the negative battery cable.
2. Remove the front grille. Remove the bumper, if necessary.
3. Disconnect the electrical connectors. Remove the clamp that secures the wiring.
4. Remove the center strut in front of the condenser.
5. Loosen both cable straps from the condenser.
6. Remove the auxiliary fan-to-radiator support screws.
7. Remove the fan assemblies from the vehicle.
8. Installation is the reverse of the removal procedure.

300D Turbo, 300E, 300CE, 300TE, 300E 4Matic, 300TE 4Matic

1. Disconnect the negative battery cable.
2. At the left inner fender well, near the pressure switch, disconnect the fan's 2-pole electrical connector and loosen the cable clamp.
3. At the front of the vehicle, remove the fan to support screws and move the fan assembly forward to remove it.
4. If necessary, disconnect the guard screen and the mount from the fan assembly.
To install:
5. If removed, connect the guard screen and the mount to the fan assembly.

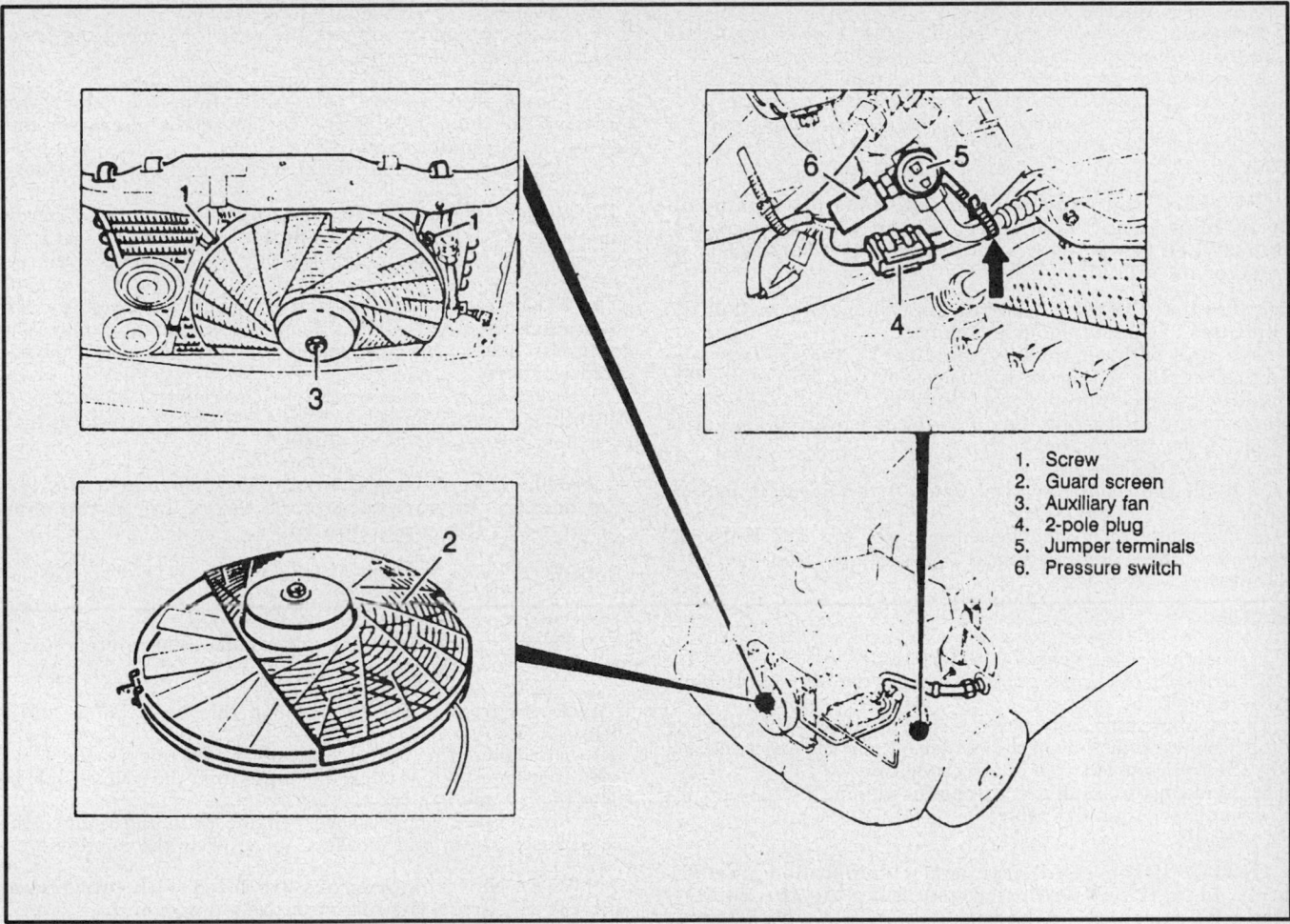

1. Screw
2. Guard screen
3. Auxiliary fan
4. 2-pole plug
5. Jumper terminals
6. Pressure switch

View of the auxiliary fan and related components—300E, 300CE and 300TE; other single fan systems similar

6. Position the fan assembly into the vehicle and secure it with the 2 screws.

7. At the left inner fender well, near the pressure switch, connect the fan's 2-pole electrical connector and tighten the cable clamp.

8. Connect the negative battery cable.

300SE

1. Disconnect the negative battery cable.

2. From the front left side of the vehicle, at the radiator supporting frame, disconnect the 2-pole electrical connector.

3. Disconnect the cable strap and expose the harness up to the auxiliary fan.

4. Remove the radiator support and crossmember screws.

5. Remove the stiffening strut-to-radiator support frame screw and the auxiliary fan from the vehicle.

6. Remove the auxiliary fan holder and protective grille.

To install:

7. Install the auxiliary fan holder and protective grille to the auxiliary fan.

8. Install the auxiliary fan to the vehicle and secure with the stiffening strut and radiator support frame screw.

9. Install the radiator support and crossmember screws.

10. Connect the cable strap and reposition the harness up to the auxiliary fan.

11. At the front left side of the vehicle, at the radiator supporting frame, connect the 2-pole electrical connector.

12. Connect the negative battery cable and check the fan operation.

Condenser

NOTE: Some models will use an air conditioning system charged with R-134a. These systems cannot have components, refrigerant or service equipment interchanged with R-12 systems.

REMOVAL AND INSTALLATION

190E

1. Disconnect the negative battery cable. Properly discharge the air conditioning system using recovery type equipment.

2. Remove the front bumper.

3. Remove the center brace between the cooling fans.

4. Remove the auxiliary fan mounting screws and place both fans to one side.

5. Detach the refrigerant lines from the condenser. Cap all openings to minimize contamination.

6. Remove the condenser mounting screws and carefully lift out the condenser.

7. Installation is the reverse of the removal procedure. Use new O-rings at refrigerant line connections. Evacuate, recharge and leak test the system.

300D Turbo, 300E, 300CE, 300TE, 300E 4Matic, 300TE 4Matic

1. Disconnect the negative battery cable.

2. Drain the cooling system. Discharge the air conditioning system using recovery type equipment.

3. Remove the radiator.

4. Loosen the lower air conditioning pipe-to-condenser clamp nut and separate the pipe from the condenser.

5. Loosen the upper air conditioning pipe-to-condenser fitting and separate the pipe from the condenser.

6. Remove the condenser-to-chassis clamp, 2 clips and lift the condenser from the vehicle.

To install:

NOTE: **If the condenser is not reinstalled immediately, blow it out with nitrogen and plug the connections. When replacing the condenser, fill it with 2/3 oz. of refrigerant oil.**

7. Position the condenser into the vehicle and install the condenser-to-chassis clamp and clips.

8. Install both air conditioning pipes to the condenser by lubricating the fitting with refrigerant oil. Torque the air conditioning pipe-to-condenser fitting to 11–13 ft. lbs. (15–18 Nm) and the air conditioning pipe-to-condenser clamp nut to 22–27 ft. lbs. (29–37 Nm).

9. Install the radiator.

10. Refill the cooling system. Connect the negative battery cable.

11. Evacuate, recharge, check for proper function and leakage; allow the engine to run at idle speed only for the 1st 4 minutes.

300SE

1. Disconnect the negative battery cable.

2. Drain the cooling system. Discharge the air conditioning.

3. Remove the radiator.

4. On applicable 300 series, remove the air conditioning pipe from the right side of the condenser and the air conditioning line from the left side of the condenser.

5. Remove the condenser-to-chassis clamp, 2 clips and lift the condenser from the vehicle.

To install:

NOTE: **If the condenser is not reinstalled immediately, blow it out with nitrogen and plug the connections. When replacing the condenser, fill it with 2/3 oz. of refrigerant oil.**

6. Position the condenser into the vehicle and install the condenser-to-chassis clamp and clips.

7. Using refrigerant oil, lubricate the O-rings and fitting threads.

8. Install both air conditioning pipes to the condenser by lubricating the fitting with refrigerant oil. Torque the air conditioning pipe-to-condenser fitting to 25–2 ft. lbs. (33–4 Nm), the air conditioning line-to-condenser to 11–13 ft. lbs. (15–18 Nm) and the air conditioning pipe-to-condenser clamp nut to 22–27 ft. lbs. (29–37 Nm).

9. Install the radiator.

10. Refill the cooling system. Connect the negative battery cable.

11. Evacuate, recharge, check for proper function and leakage; allow the engine to run at idle speed only for the 1st 4 minutes.

Compressor

NOTE: **Some models will use an air conditioning system charged with R-134a. These systems cannot have components, refrigerant or service equipment interchanged with R-12 systems.**

REMOVAL AND INSTALLATION

190E, 300D Turbo, 300E, 300CE, 300TE, 300E 4Matic, 300TE 4Matic

1. Disconnect the negative battery cable.

2. Discharge the air conditioning system.

3. Raise and safely support the vehicle. Remove the lower engine compartment panel.

4. Remove the radiator and engine cooling fan.

5. Loosen and remove the V-belt from the compressor (remove the collar bolt at the bottom of the alternator and swing the alternator upward).

6. Disconnect the 3-pole electrical connector from the compressor.

7. Remove the air conditioning pipes-to-compressor screw and separate the connector from the compressor; discard the O-rings. Using dummy plugs, plug the pipes and the compressor.

8. At the front of the compressor, remove the 2 compressor-to-bracket bolts. At the left side of the compressor, remove the compressor-to-engine bolts and lower the compressor from the vehicle.

9. Installation is the reverse of the removal procedure. If installing a new compressor, fill it with 4 oz. of refrigerant oil. Use new O-rings at the line fittings.

NOTE: **If replacing the compressor because of internal damage, be sure to replace the piping at the compressor and the expansion valve.**

300SE

1. Disconnect the negative battery cable.

2. Properly discharge the air conditioning system using recovery type equipment.

3. Slacken and remove the V-belt.

4. At the front of the torsion bar, remove 2 clamps and 4 self-locking nuts.

5. Disconnect the 3-pole connector at the compressor.

6. Disconnect the refrigerant pipes from the compressor; be sure to plug and cap the connectors.

7. Remove the compressor-to-engine bolts and remove the compressor. Drain and measure the oil from the compressor.

NOTE: **New compressors are filled with refrigerant oil. Slowly, drain the oil from the suction end.**

8. Installation is the reverse of the removal procedure. Install 4.5 oz. of new refrigerant oil into the compressor at the suction end if it is replaced. Evacuate, recharge and leak test the air conditioning system.

Receiver/Drier

NOTE: **Some models will use an air conditioning system charged with R-134a. These systems cannot have components, refrigerant or service equipment interchanged with R-12 systems.**

The receiver/drier is attached to the left fender well, near the pressure switches.

REMOVAL AND INSTALLATION

1. Disconnect the negative battery cable.

2. Properly, discharge the air conditioning system.

3. At the receiver/drier, disconnect the electrical connectors from the temperature switch and the pressure switch.

4. Remove both switches from the receiver/drier.

5. Disconnect and plug the air conditioning pipes from the receiver/drier.

6. Remove the receiver/drier-to-chassis screws and the receiver/drier; be sure to plug the connector openings.

7. Installation is the reverse of the removal procedure. If the receiver/drier is replaced, add approx. 1/3 oz. of refrigerant oil to the new unit. Use new O-rings at appropriate fittings. Evacuate, recharge and leak test the system.

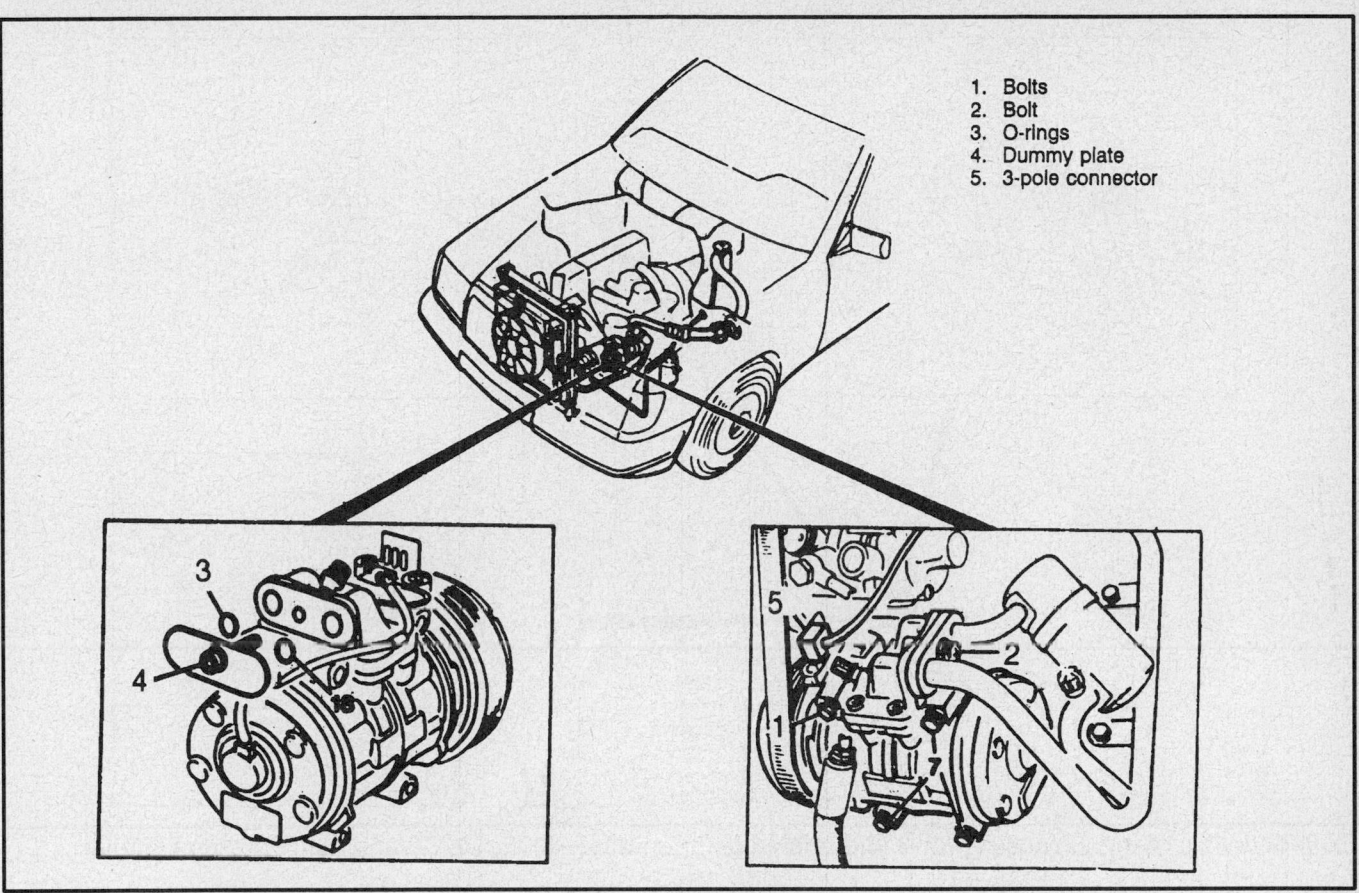

1. Bolts
2. Bolt
3. O-rings
4. Dummy plate
5. 3-pole connector

Compressor removal—models with M103 engine

Expansion Valve

NOTE: Some models will use an air conditioning system charged with R-134a. These systems cannot have components, refrigerant or service equipment interchanged with R-12 systems.

REMOVAL AND INSTALLATION

190E

1. Disconnect the negative battery cable.
2. Properly discharge the air conditioning system.
3. Remove the air inlet cover.
4. Remove the refrigerant pipes-to-expansion valve screw and pull the assembly from the expansion valve.
5. Remove the expansion valve-to-evaporator screws and the expansion valve.
6. Plug the opening of the expansion valve.
To install:
7. Using refrigerant oil, lubricate the O-rings on the evaporator pipes.
8. Install the expansion valve to the evaporator and torque the screws to 5–7 ft. lbs. (6–10 Nm).
9. Install the refrigerant pipes to the expansion valve and torque the screw to 5–9 ft. lbs. (7–13 Nm).
10. Connect the negative battery cable.
11. Evacuate and recharge the air conditioning system. To test for proper function and leakage; operate the engine, at idle, for the 1st 4 minutes.
12. Install the air inlet cover.

300D Turbo, 300E, 300CE, 300TE, 300E 4Matic, 300TE 4Matic

1. Disconnect the negative battery cable.
2. Discharge the air conditioning system.
3. In front of the brake master cylinder, loosen the clamp located on the air conditioning pipe.
4. At the cowl, above the power brake booster, remove the mount for the check valves.
5. At the cowl, remove the air conditioning pipes-to-expansion valve screw and separate the pipe connector from the expansion valve. Remove and discard both O-rings.
6. Remove the expansion valve screws and pull off the valve; be sure to plug the evaporator pipes and fittings with dummy plugs.
To install:
7. Using new seals, install the expansion valve and torque the bolts to 6–1.5 ft. lbs. (8–2 Nm).
8. Using new O-rings at the cowl, attach the pipe connector to the expansion valve and install the air conditioning pipes-to-expansion valve screw; torque the screw to 7–2 ft. lbs. (10–3 Nm).
9. At the cowl, above the power brake booster, install the mount for the check valves.
10. In front of the brake master cylinder, tighten the clamp located on the air conditioning pipe.
11. Connect the negative battery cable.
12. Evacuate and recharge the air conditioning system. To test for proper function and leakage; operate the engine, at idle, for the 1st 4 minutes.

300SE

1. Disconnect the negative battery cable.
2. Discharge the air conditioning system.

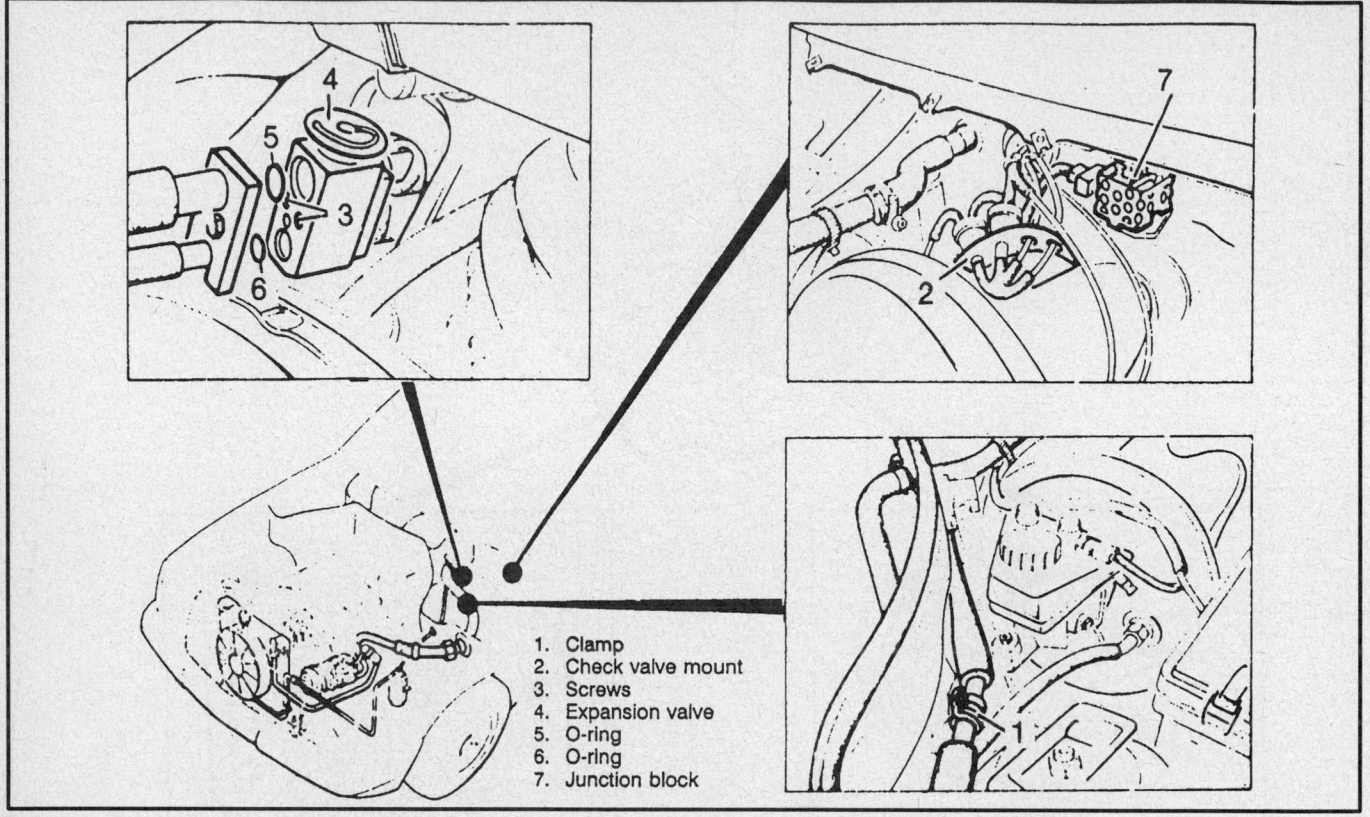

1. Clamp
2. Check valve mount
3. Screws
4. Expansion valve
5. O-ring
6. O-ring
7. Junction block

Exploded view of the expansion valve and related components—300E, 300CE and 300TE; others similar

3. Front under the left side of the instrument panel, remove the cover.
4. Open the expansion valve housing halfway.
5. Using a box wrench, loosen and remove the air conditioning hoses and pipes from the expansion valve.
6. Remove the expansion valve and plug the openings.

To install:
7. Using refrigerant oil, lubricate the expansion valve threads. Check the O-rings and replace, if necessary.
8. Connect and tighten the pressure hose-to-expansion valve to 11–13 ft. lbs. (15–18 Nm) and the suction hose-to-expansion valve to 22–27 ft. lbs. (29–37 Nm).
9. Connect the negative battery cable.
10. Evacuate and recharge the air conditioning system. To test for proper function and leakage; operate the engine, at idle, for the 1st 4 minutes.
11. Fasten the expansion valve to the housing.
12. Install the undercover to the instrument panel.

C220 and C280

1. Disconnect the negative battery cable.
2. Discharge the air conditioning system.
3. Remove the cover on the left and right air inlet.
4. Remove the air inlet.
5. Remove the wiper system.
6. Remove the water collector.
7. Remove the refrigerant pipes-to-expansion valve screw and pull the pipeline assembly from the expansion valve. Remove and discard the O-rings. Seal off the openings.
8. Remove the expansion valve screws and pull off the valve.
9. Installation is the reverse of the removal procedure. Torque the expansion valve screws to 5–7 ft. lbs. (6–10 Nm). Torque the refrigerant pipes-to-expansion valve screw to 5–9 ft. lbs. (7–13 Nm).

Blower Motor

REMOVAL AND INSTALLATION

190E

1. Disconnect the negative battery cable.
2. Remove the air intake cover.
3. Remove the bulkhead screws from both sides and move the bulkhead toward the engine as far as possible.
4. Remove the wiper arm.
5. Remove the wiper arm linkage screws and move the wiper linkage, with the wiper motor, aside.
6. On wiper systems with eccentric-sweep wiper, perform the following:
   • Open the wiper arm cover cap, remove the screw, and pull off the wiper arm.
   • Remove 5 nuts at the eccentric housing.
   • Pull the wiper system from the mountings and detach the wiring. Remove the wiper system.
7. Unclip the blower motor housing straps and lift the housing from the heater/air conditioning box.
8. Using a pointed tool, unclip the blower motor from the housing.
9. Pull off the flat plug and lift the blower motor from the housing.

To install:
10. Install the blower motor into the housing so the connections are pointing in the driving direction and the motor housing is held in the motor holder.
11. Refit the flat plug and clip the blower motor into the housing.
12. Install the upper heater/air conditioning box housing and secure with the straps.
13. Install the wiper linkage with the wiper motor.

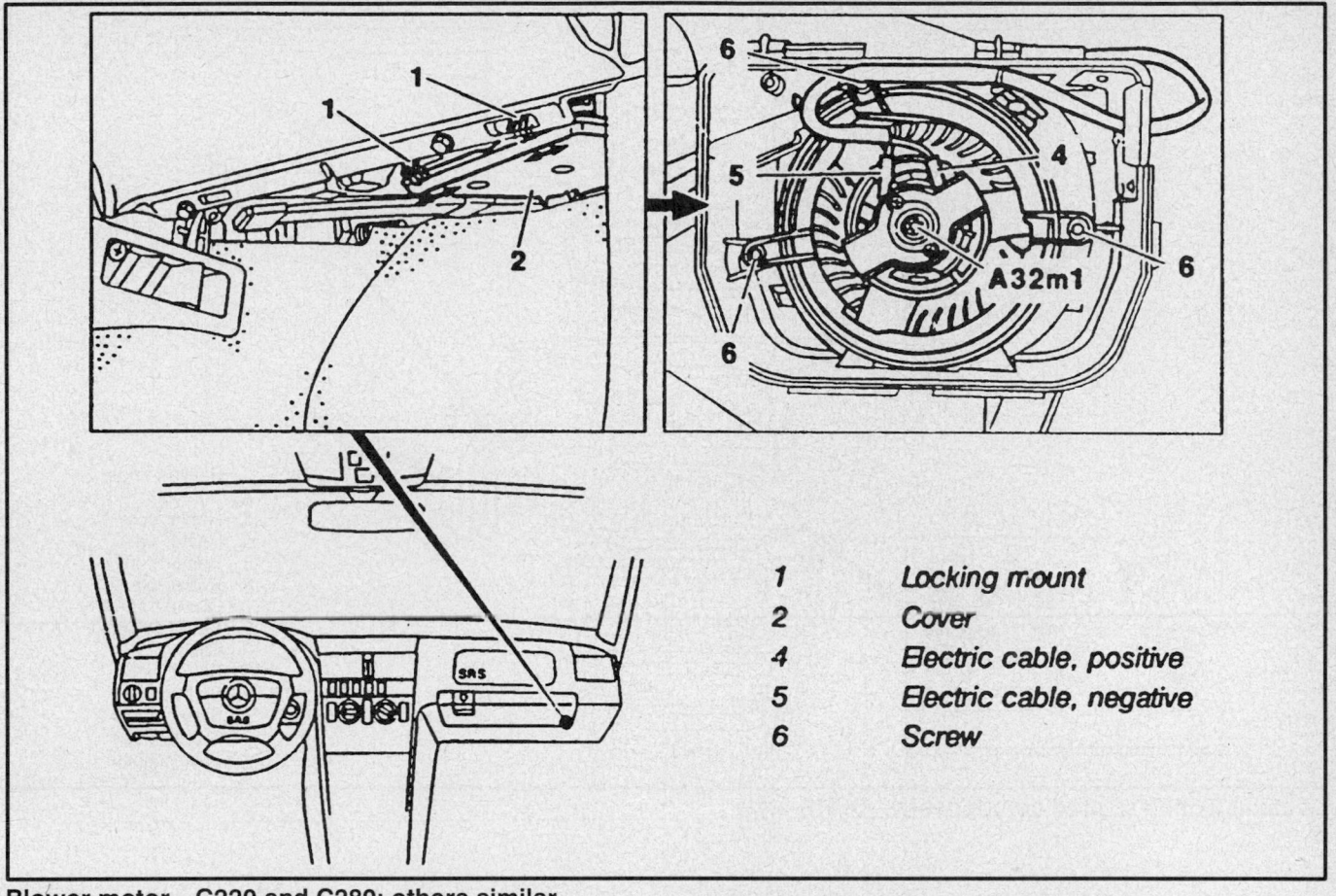

1   Locking mount
2   Cover
4   Electric cable, positive
5   Electric cable, negative
6   Screw

Blower motor—C220 and C280; others similar

14. Install the wiper arm.
15. Reposition the bulkhead and secure with the screws.
16. Install the air inlet cover.
17. Connect the negative battery cable. Test the blower motor for proper operation.

300D Turbo, 300E, 300CE, 300TE, 300E 4Matic, 300TE 4Matic

1. Disconnect the negative battery cable.
2. Remove the windshield wiper system.
3. Pull out the air temperature sensor from the upper heater/air conditioning box cover.
4. Remove the upper heater/air conditioning box cover clips and the cover.
5. Unclip the blower motor-to-heater/air conditioning box mounting strap.
6. Pull the blower motor from the heater/air conditioning box.

To install:
7. Install the blower motor into the heater/air conditioning box and secure with the mounting strap.
8. Install the upper cover to the heater/air conditioning box and secure with the clips.
9. Install the air temperature sensor into the upper heater/air conditioning box cover.
10. Install the windshield wiper system. Connect the negative battery cable.

300SE

1. Disconnect the negative battery cable.
2. Remove the air collector and dust filter.

3. Detach the electrical connectors
4. Remove 4 screws and lift out the blower assembly.
5. Installation is the reverse of the removal procedure.

NOTE: Blower assembly cannot be overhauled. If defective, it must be replaced as a unit with the bracket and electronic blower controller.

C220 and C280

1. Disconnect the negative battery cable.
2. Remove the cover under the right instrument panel.
3. Push the locking mounts to one side and fold the cover downwards.
4. Disconnect the electrical plug connection.
5. Remove the blower mounting screws.
6. Remove the blower together with blower regulator and electrical connection.
7. Installation is the reverse of the removal procedure.

Heater Core

REMOVAL AND INSTALLATION

190E

1. Disconnect the negative battery cable.
2. Drain the cooling system.
3. Remove the air intake cover.
4. Open the cable strap on the left side of the heater box and unscrew the cable connector screw.
5. Disconnect the blower switch electrical connector.
6. Disconnect the vacuum lines for the heater control switches and the electrical connectors for the switch lights.

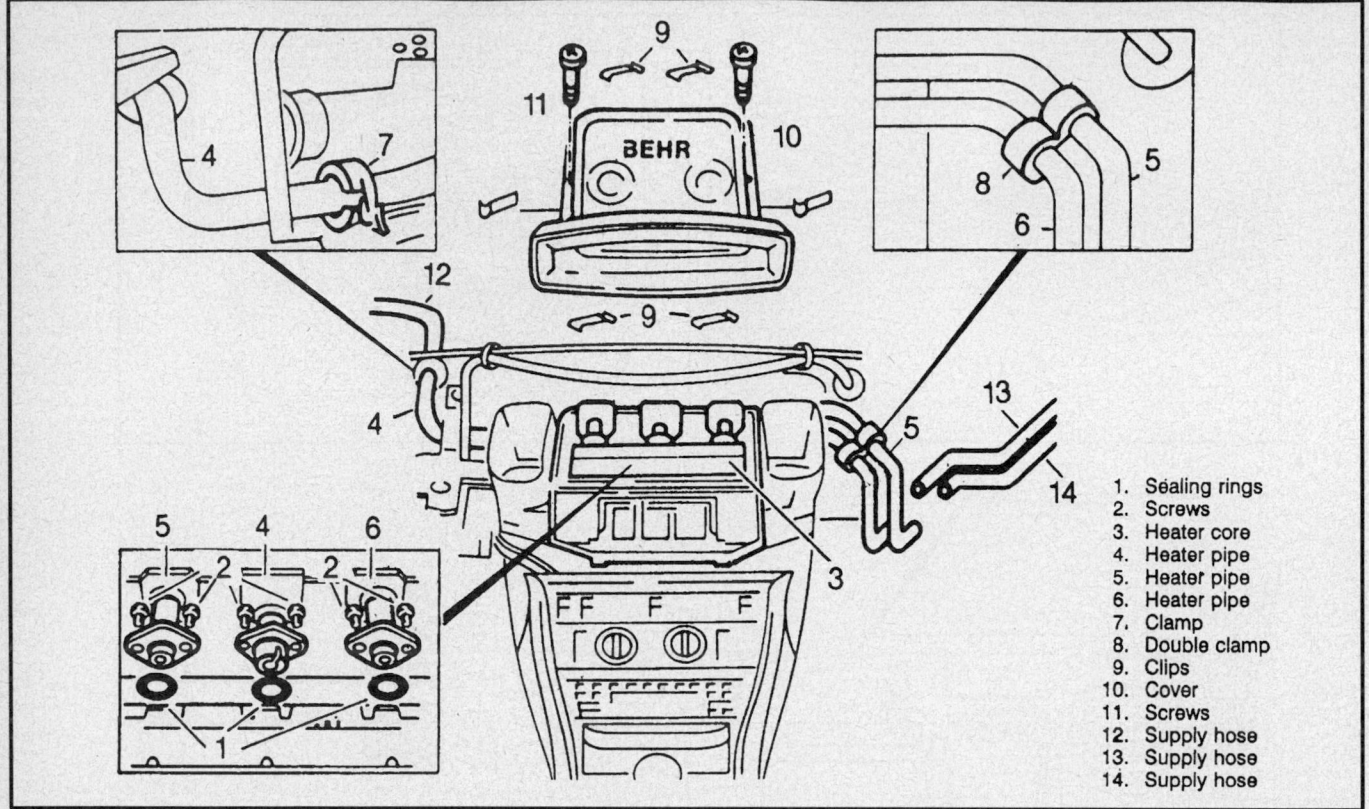

1. Sealing rings
2. Screws
3. Heater core
4. Heater pipe
5. Heater pipe
6. Heater pipe
7. Clamp
8. Double clamp
9. Clips
10. Cover
11. Screws
12. Supply hose
13. Supply hose
14. Supply hose

Heater box and related components—BEHR style

7. Remove the heater feed hose at the engine and place a container under the hose to catch excess coolant.

8. Remove the heater return hose.

9. Using compressed air, blow the residual coolant from the heater core.

10. At the heater box, remove the return flow pipe from the heater core and pull off the lateral nozzle air duct from the right side.

11. Remove the feed pipe from the heater core and pull off the lateral nozzle air duct from the left side. At the lower left, force the feed pipe holder from the angle bracket.

12. Remove the feed pipe, from below the air intake, and remove it rearward through the front wall.

13. Remove the heater box-to-chassis nuts.

14. At the control unit, disconnect the control wire from the actuator and the wire sheath from the lock.

15. Disconnect the control wire from the main air flap, disconnect the wire sheath from the clip and pull the actuating control wire from the heater box.

16. Pull the heater box out of the top of the vehicle.

17. From the heater box, remove the 3 cover-to-box screws and rivet; then, remove the cover.

18. From the left and right side defroster nozzles, lift the sealing rubber 1/2 way.

19. While pushing against the left side air flap, pull the air flap shaft partially out of the nozzle.

20. At the parting point of the box, disengage the top, lateral and bottom clamps.

21. Remove the legroom nozzles, with the connecting rod, from the heater box.

22. Separate the heater boxes at the parting line.

23. Remove the heater core-to-holding frame screws and remove the frame.

24. Remove the heater core from the heater box.

To install:

25. Insert the heater core into the heater box. Install the frame and secure with the screws.

26. Reassemble the heater box halves, install the legroom nozzles with the connecting rod and secure the box halves with the clips.

27. Install the air flap shaft into the defroster nozzle; make sure the flap bearings are correctly seated on the housing and the shaft lug engages the nozzle flap.

28. Reposition the defroster nozzle sealing rubber.

29. Install the heater box screws and rivet.

30. Install the heater box assembly into the vehicle.

31. Connect the control wire to the main air flap control and actuator.

32. Install the heater box-to-chassis nuts.

33. Install the feed pipe through the front wall and position it below the air intake.

34. At the lower left, force the feed pipe holder into the angle bracket. Install the lateral nozzle air duct to the left side and connect the feed pipe to the heater core.

35. Install the lateral nozzle air duct to the right side and connect the return flow pipe to the heater core, at the heater box.

36. Install the heater return hose and the heater feed hose.

37. Connect the vacuum lines for the heater control switches and the electrical connectors for the switch lights.

38. Connect the blower switch electrical connector.

39. Install the cable connector screw and secure the cable strap on the left side of the heater box.

40. Install the air intake cover.

41. Refill the cooling system. Connect the negative battery cable.

42. Start the engine, allow it to reach normal operating temperatures and check for leaks.

300D Turbo, 300E, 300CE, 300TE, 300E 4Matic, 300TE 4Matic

BEHR STYLE

1. Disconnect the negative battery cable.
2. Drain the cooling system.
3. Disconnect the hoses from the heater supply and return pipes. Using compressed air, blow the residual coolant from the heater core.
4. Remove the instrument panel.
5. Remove the upper heater box cover-to-heater box screws, 6 clips and the cover.
6. In the engine compartment, remove the heater supply pipe-to-chassis clamp.
7. From the top of the heater box, remove the heater supply and return pipes-to-heater core screws and swing the pipes away from the heater box.
8. Pull the heater core from the top of the heater box.
9. Clean any spilled coolant from inside the heater box.

To install:

10. Position the heater core into the heater box.
11. Using 3 new sealing rings, connect the heater supply and return pipes to the heater box.
12. In the engine compartment, install the heater supply pipe-to-chassis clamp.
13. Install the upper cover to the heater box, the 6 clips and the screws.
14. Install the instrument panel.
15. Connect the hoses to the heater supply and return pipes.
16. Refill the cooling system. Connect the negative battery cable.

VALEO STYLE

1. Disconnect the negative battery cable.
2. Drain the cooling system.
3. Disconnect the hoses from the heater supply and return pipes. Using compressed air, blow the residual coolant from the heater core.
4. Remove the instrument panel and the center console.
5. From the lower front of the heater box, pull off the temperature sensor heat exchanger, left and right 2-pole couplings.
6. Pull the air ducts from the bottom of the heater box.
7. From the front of the heater box, remove the crossmember and strut. From under the heater box, remove the bracket.
8. Loosen the ignition switch housing-to-steering column bolt. Turn the ignition key to position **1**, press the ignition switch housing locking button and pull the steering lock from the steering column.
9. Pull the air ducts from both sides of the heater box.
10. Remove the heater box-to-chassis nuts and pull the heater box from the firewall.
11. Disconnect the electrical connectors and clip from the blower motor. Disconnect the main air flap control cable from the heater box.
12. Remove the heater box retaining clips and pull the front case from the rear case. Remove the heater core from the heater case.
13. Remove the heater supply and return pipes-to-heater core screws and the pipes from the heater core.
14. Clean any spilled coolant from inside the heater box.

To install:

15. Using 3 new sealing rings, connect the heater supply and return pipes to the heater box.
16. Position the heater core into the heater box; make sure the rubber pipe grommets are seated properly.
17. Position the front case onto the heater box secure with the clips.
18. Connect the main air flap control cable to the heater box. Connect the electrical connectors and clip to the blower motor.

19. Using a new seal, position the heater box against the firewall and install the heater box-to-chassis nuts. Install the air ducts to both sides of the heater box.
20. Slide the steering lock into the steering column and tighten the bolt.
21. From under the heater box, install the bracket. At the front of the heater box, install the crossmember and strut.
22. Install the air ducts to the bottom of the heater box.
23. At the lower front of the heater box, install the temperature sensor heat exchanger, left and right 2-pole couplings.
24. Refill the cooling system. Connect the negative battery cable.
25. Install the center console and the instrument panel.
26. Connect the hoses to the heater supply and return pipes.

300SE

1. Disconnect the negative battery cable.
2. Discharge the air conditioning system.
3. Drain the cooling system. Detach and plug the heater hoses from the firewall tube connections.
4. Raise and support the vehicle. Remove the panel behind the front right side member.
5. Move both front seats rearward and cover. Remove the floormats from both sides of the vehicle.
6. Remove the instrument panel and the center console.
7. If equipped with ABS, remove the ABS control unit.
8. From the rear passenger compartment, remove the left and right air ducts and the air ducts from the transmission tunnel, on the driver's floor.
9. From the right side of the heater/air conditioning box, disconnect the 12-pole electrical connector for the temperature control.
10. Disconnect the 5-pole and 6-pole electrical connectors from the temperature dial and the 2-pole electrical connector from the temperature sensor, air volume and air distributing switch.
11. Disconnect the vacuum lines from the air volume switch.
12. Remove the heater/air conditioning box-to-stiffening strut screws.
13. Remove the cable straps from the blower motor housing. Loosen the main cable harness straps from the heater/air conditioning box.
14. Pull the right and left air ducts from the fresh air nozzles on the heater/air conditioning box.
15. From the heater/air conditioning box, perform the following procedures:
    - Disconnect the 2-pole electrical connectors from both temperature sensors.
    - Remove the electric lines cable connector screw.
    - Separate the electrical plug connector and unclip the coupling member from the holder.
16. Remove the expansion valve; be sure to plug the openings.
17. From both sides of the evaporator housing, remove the condensate drain hoses.
18. Remove the 2-pole electrical connector from the switch-over valve.
19. From the heater/air conditioning box, perform the following procedures:
    - Remove the lower heater/air conditioning box-to-holding angle bracket screws.
    - Remove the angle bracket-to-blower housing nut.
    - Remove the right side upper angle-to-chassis nut.
    - Remove the left side upper angle-to-chassis nut.
20. Pull the heater/air conditioning box rearward to disengage the heater pipes from the front wall.
21. Lift the heater/air conditioning box above the front passenger legroom and remove from the vehicle; be sure to keep the heater pipes vertical so coolant will not drain out.
22. Remove the evaporator housing and pull the heater core from the heater/air conditioning box.

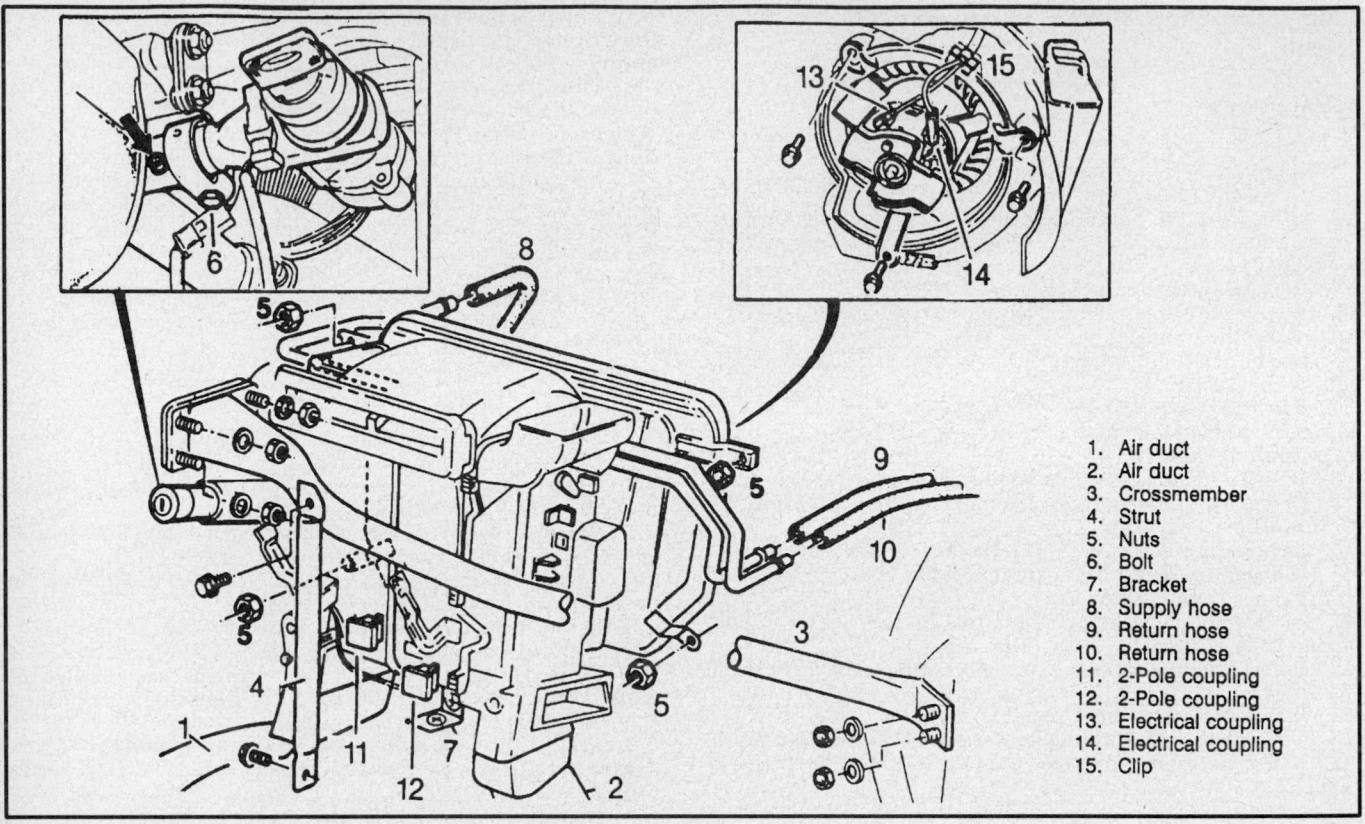

1. Air duct
2. Air duct
3. Crossmember
4. Strut
5. Nuts
6. Bolt
7. Bracket
8. Supply hose
9. Return hose
10. Return hose
11. 2-Pole coupling
12. 2-Pole coupling
13. Electrical coupling
14. Electrical coupling
15. Clip

View of the heater box and related components—VALEO style

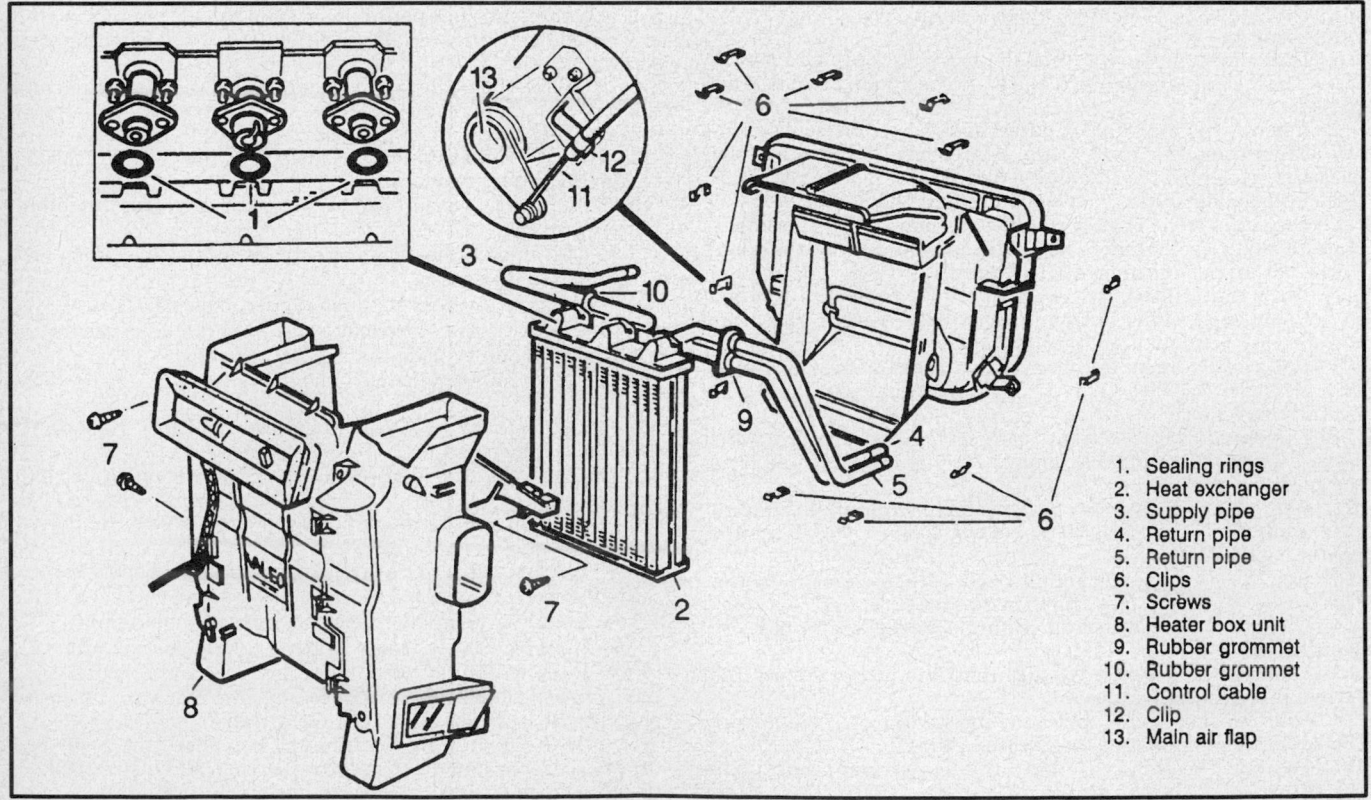

1. Sealing rings
2. Heat exchanger
3. Supply pipe
4. Return pipe
5. Return pipe
6. Clips
7. Screws
8. Heater box unit
9. Rubber grommet
10. Rubber grommet
11. Control cable
12. Clip
13. Main air flap

Exploded view of the heater box and components—VALEO style

To install:

NOTE: When assembling the cases, be sure to seal them especially well along the horizontal separating joint. Pay particular attention to the areas behind the expansion valve and temperature or blower control.

23. Install the heater core and the evaporator housing onto the heater/air conditioning box.
24. Install the heater/air conditioning box against the front wall and position the heater pipes through the front wall.
25. Connect the heater/air conditioning box to the left side upper angle bracket and screw.
26. Connect the heater/air conditioning box to the right side upper angle bracket and nuts.
27. Install the lower angle bracket with screws.
28. Connect the 2-pole electrical connector to the switch-over valve.
29. Install the condensate drain hoses to the heater/air conditioning box.
30. Using refrigerant oil, lubricate the O-rings and threads; then, connect the refrigerant lines to the expansion valve.
31. Connect the electric lines on the cable connector.
32. Connect the 2-pole electrical connectors to the temperature sensors.
33. Install both fresh air duct nozzles onto the heater/air conditioning box.
34. Install the main cable harness onto the heater/air conditioning box and secure with the cable straps.
35. Install the electric lines onto the blower housing and secure with the cable straps.
36. Mount the stiffening strut and screws.
37. Connect the vacuum lines to the air volume switch.
38. Connect the 2-pole, 5-pole and 6-pole electrical connectors onto the temperature dials. Connect the 2-pole connector onto the flow sensor switch and the air distributing switch.
39. Connect the 12-pole connector onto the electronic switch-gear.
40. Install both heater air ducts for the rear passenger compartment. Install the heater boxes.
41. If equipped with ABS, install the ABS control unit.
42. Fill the cooling system and check for leaks.
43. Install the center console and the instrument panel.
44. Install the both foot mats into the legroom.
45. Under the car, replace the side member panel, if removed.
46. Connect the negative battery cable.
47. Evacuate, recharge and leak test the air conditioning system. To test for proper function and leakage; operate the engine, at idle, for the 1st 4 minutes.

C220 and C280

1. Disconnect the negative battery cable.
2. Drain the cooling system.
3. Discharge the air conditioning system.
4. Remove the air inlet cover.
5. Remove the water collector.
6. Remove the series resistor for the heater blower.
7. Loosen the clamps on the hot water supply and return hoses and pull off the hoses. Seal off the openings.
8. Remove the instrument panel.
9. Remove the center console.
10. Remove the left and right floor covering.
11. Remove the front passenger airbag unit, if equipped.
12. Remove the jacket tube.
13. Remove the cable duct screws and loosen the cable duct.
14. Remove the bracket screws and bracket.
15. Remove the traverse pipe attaching bolts and nuts and remove the traverse pipe.
16. Disconnect the electrical cables at ground point.
17. Open the cable tie and remove the left and right rear air ducts.

18. Disconnect the vacuum lines at the cockpit separation point.
19. Remove the right ground strap.
20. Disconnect the plug connection for the blower motor.
21. Remove the air ducts to the left and right side outlets.
22. Remove the heater box.
23. Remove the screws and clips, and remove the cover.
24. Remove the screws and loosen the guide for the hot water supply pipe.
25. Remove the screws and loosen the hot water return pipe.
26. Detach the retaining clip for the hot water supply pipe.
27. Remove the heat exchanger together with the hot water pipes.
28. Remove the hot water pipe attaching screws and remove the pipes.
29. Installation is the reverse of the removal procedure.

Evaporator

NOTE: Some models will use an air conditioning system charged with R-134a. These systems cannot have components, refrigerant or service equipment interchanged with R-12 systems.

REMOVAL AND INSTALLATION

190E

1. Disconnect the negative battery cable.
2. Properly discharge the air conditioning system.
3. Remove the air intake cover.
4. Remove the bulkhead screws from both sides and move the bulkhead toward the engine as far as possible.
5. Remove the expansion valve.
6. Remove the blower motor.
7. Remove the lower blower motor housing screws and lift out the lower part of the housing.
8. Pull the temperature sensor from the guide tube.
9. Laterally, from left to right, remove the flange frame-to-evaporator housing clips and remove the flange frame.
10. Lift the evaporator, with the pan and drain hoses, from the evaporator housing.
To install:
11. Clean the evaporator and make sure the drain hoses are open.
12. Insert the evaporator into the pan. Insert the evaporator assembly, with the pan, into the evaporator housing.
13. Install the flange frame to the evaporator housing and secure with the clips.
14. Insert the temperature sensor into the guide tube up to the stop.
15. Install the lower part of the blower housing and secure with the screws.
16. Install the blower motor.
17. Unplug the refrigerant lines and connect them to the evaporator.
18. Install the expansion valve.
19. Reposition the bulkhead and secure with the screws.
20. Install the air inlet cover.
21. Connect the negative battery cable.
22. Evacuate and recharge the air conditioning system. To test for proper function and leakage; operate the engine, at idle, for the 1st 4 minutes.

300D Turbo, 300E, 300CE, 300TE, 300E 4Matic, 300TE 4Matic

1. Disconnect the negative battery cable.
2. Drain the cooling system. Discharge the air conditioning system.
3. Disconnect the heater hoses from the heater core.
4. In front of the brake master cylinder, loosen the clamp located on the air conditioning pipe.

5. At the cowl, above the power brake booster, remove the mount for the check valves.

6. At the cowl, remove the air conditioning pipes-to-expansion valve screw and separate the pipe connector from the expansion valve. Remove and discard both O-rings.

7. At the cowl, above the power brake booster, disconnect and pull out the fan motor lead from the junction block.

8. Remove the instrument panel and the center console.

9. Loosen and pull off both floor air ducts from the heater/air conditioning box.

10. From in front of the heater/air conditioning box, remove the crossmember and brace. From under the heater/air conditioning box, remove the box-to-chassis mount.

11. Loosen the ignition switch housing-to-steering column bolt. Turn the ignition key to position 1, press the ignition switch housing locking button and pull the steering lock from the steering column.

12. Pull the air ducts from both sides of the heater box.

13. From the lower front of the heater/air conditioning box, disconnect the heat exchanger temperature sensors, left and right 2-pole couplings, and the evaporator temperature sensor.

14. From the lower right of the heater/air conditioning box, disconnect the vacuum lines and the 2-pole connector from the switch-over valve and remove the valve.

15. Pull the left and right side air ducts from the nozzles of the heater/air conditioning box.

16. Remove the heater/air conditioning box-to-chassis nuts. Pull the outside air temperature sensor from the holder. Move the heater/air conditioning box down and outward.

17. Remove the heater/air conditioning box clips. At the top, remove the 4 cover-to-box screws and remove the cover.

18. At both sides of the box, remove the heater pipe clamps.

19. At the rear side of the box, disconnect the connecting rod from the fresh air recirculated air flap.

20. Remove both vacuum cylinders-to-chassis screws and the vacuum cylinder elements from the heater/air conditioning box.

21. Pull the heater core upward and out of the box.

22. Remove the 2 screws from the left and the right side parts. Pull the right side part out sightly and unclip the leg room flap joint. Remove both side parts.

23. Remove the upper 3 clips, from both sides of the heater/air conditioning box, and remove the upper section of the housing.

24. Remove the upper 3 clips, from both sides of the heater/air conditioning box, and the 1 from the center of the blower motor housing. On the left side of the box, near the evaporator air conditioning pipes, press the clip from the housing.

25. Pry the evaporator from the heater/air conditioning box.

To install:

26. Clean the inside of the evaporator housing.

27. If using a new evaporator, remove the screen from the old evaporator and glue it to the new one. If using a new evaporator, unscrew the expansion valve from the old evaporator; then, install new O-rings and the expansion valve onto the new evaporator.

28. Check and replace the bulkhead gasket, if necessary; add sealant to the sealing surface.

29. Position the evaporator into the heater/air conditioning box.

30. On the left side of the box, near the evaporator air conditioning pipes, press the clip into the housing. Install the upper 3 clips, onto both sides of the heater/air conditioning box, and the 1 from the center of the blower motor housing.

31. Install the upper section of the housing and press the upper 3 clips, onto both sides of the heater/air conditioning box.

32. Position both side parts onto the heater/air conditioning box and secure with the screws.

NOTE: When installing the right side part, re-clip the leg room flap joint.

33. Reposition the heater core into the box.

34. Reposition the vacuum cylinder elements into the heater/air conditioning box and install both vacuum cylinders-to-chassis screws.

35. At the rear side of the box, connect the connecting rod to the fresh air recirculated air flap.

36. At both sides of the box, install the heater pipe clamps.

37. Install the upper cover and the 4 screws. Re-clip the heater/air conditioning box clips.

38. Reposition the heater/air conditioning box, install the outside air temperature sensor into the holder and install the heater/air conditioning box-to-chassis nuts.

39. Install the left and right side air ducts onto the nozzles of the heater/air conditioning box.

40. Install the switch-over valve to the lower right of the heater/air conditioning box. Reconnect the vacuum lines and the 2-pole connector to the valve.

41. At the lower front of the heater/air conditioning box, connect the heat exchanger temperature sensors, left and right 2-pole couplings, and the evaporator temperature sensor.

42. Press the air ducts onto both sides of the heater box.

43. Slide the steering lock into the steering column and tighten the bolt.

44. From under the heater/air conditioning box, install the bracket. At the front of the heater box, install the crossmember and strut.

45. Install the air ducts to the bottom of the heater box.

46. Install the center console and the instrument panel.

47. At the cowl, above the power brake booster, connect the fan motor lead to the junction block.

48. Using new O-rings at the cowl, attach the pipe connector to the expansion valve and install the air conditioning pipes-to-expansion valve screw.

49. At the cowl, above the power brake booster, install the mount for the check valves.

50. In front of the brake master cylinder, tighten the clamp located on the air conditioning pipe.

51. Connect the heater hoses from the heater core.

52. Refill the cooling system. Connect the negative battery cable.

53. Evacuate and recharge the air conditioning system. To test for proper function and leakage; operate the engine, at idle, for the 1st 4 minutes.

300SE

1. Disconnect the negative battery cable.

2. Discharge the air conditioning system.

3. Drain the cooling system.

4. Remove the wiper system from the firewall. Remove the water collector near the wiper location.

5. Disconnect and plug the heater hoses from the heater core tubes at the firewall.

6. Disconnect the air conditioning lines from the connections at the expansion valve. Cap all openings immediately to minimize contamination.

7. Remove the air conditioning housing 3 retaining nuts at the firewall.

8. Disconnect the electrical connection on the blower support.

9. Remove the center console.

10. Remove the instrument panel.

11. Remove the mat from over the heater housing. Pull back the driver's side carpeting.

12. Remove the connections for the rear floor air ducts.

13. Remove the control unit for the belt tensioner and air bag.

14. Remove the ignition switch.

15. Remove the cross brace in front of the evaporator housing.

16. Disconnect other cables, wiring and air ducts which might interfere with the air conditioning unit removal.

17. Remove the expansion valve; be sure to plug the openings.

18. From both sides of the evaporator housing, remove the condensate drain hoses.

19. Remove the heater/air conditioning (evaporator) housing assembly. Lift the heater/air conditioning box above the front passenger legroom and remove from the vehicle; be sure to keep the heater pipes vertical so coolant will not drain out.

To install:

20. Clean and assembly the evaporator housing and pay special attention to the condensate drain connection.

NOTE: When assembling the cases, be sure to seal them especially well along the horizontal separating joint. Pay particular attention to the areas behind the expansion valve and temperature or blower control.

21. Install the heater/air conditioning box against the front wall and position the heater pipes through the front wall.

22. Connect the heater/air conditioning box to the mounting brackets.

23. Reattach all wiring, cables, ducting and other items as removed.

24. Install the instrument panel.

25. Install the center console.

26. In the engine compartment, reinstall the 3 air conditioner assembly retaining nuts.

27. Using refrigerant oil, lubricate the O-rings and threads; then, connect the refrigerant lines to the expansion valve.

28. Reattach the heater hoses.

29. Attach the blower wiring, install the water collector and the wiper assembly.

30. Fill the cooling system and check for leaks.

31. Connect the negative battery cable.

32. Evacuate, recharge and leak test the air conditioning system. To test for proper function and leakage; operate the engine, at idle, for the 1st 4 minutes.

C220 and C280

1. Disconnect the negative battery cable.

2. Drain the cooling system.

3. Discharge the air conditioning system.

4. Remove the cover on the left and right air inlet.

5. Remove the air inlet.

6. Remove the water collector.

7. Remove the expansion valve. Seal off the openings.

8. Loosen the clamps and pull off the hot water supply and return hoses. Seal off the openings.

9. Remove the instrument panel.

10. Remove the center console.

11. Remove the left and right floor covering.

12. Remove the front passenger airbag unit, if equipped.

13. Remove the jacket tube.

14. Remove the cable duct attaching screws and loosen the cable duct.

15. Remove the bracket attaching screws and bracket.

16. Remove the traverse pipe attaching screws and nuts and remove the pipe.

17. Remove the electrical cables at ground point.

18. Open the cable strap and remove the left and right rear air ducts.

19. Disconnect the vacuum lines at the cockpit separation point.

20. Remove the right ground strap.

21. Disconnect the blower motor electrical connection.

22. Remove the air ducts to the left and right side outlets.

23. Remove the air conditioner box.

24. Remove the heat exchanger.

25. Dismantle the valve block.

26. Pull off the vacuum lines on the vacuum actuator.

27. Remove the clips and disconnect the blower box from the air distributor box.

28. Remove the screw, loosen the gasket, and remove the upper section of the air distributor box.

29. Remove the evaporator.

30. Remove the expansion valve from the evaporator.

31. Installation is the reverse of the removal procedure.

Refrigerant Lines

REMOVAL AND INSTALLATION

NOTE: Some models will use an air conditioning system charged with R-134a. These systems cannot have components, refrigerant or service equipment interchanged with R-12 systems.

Removal of some additional components may be required on certain models to access the refrigerant lines, fittings or retaining clamps.

1. Disconnect the negative battery cable.

2. Discharge the air conditioning system.

3. At the cowl, remove the air conditioning pipes-to-expansion valve screw and separate the pipe connector from the expansion valve. Remove and discard both O-rings.

4. Remove the air conditioning pipes-to-compressor screw and separate the connector from the compressor; discard the O-rings. Using dummy plugs, plug the pipes and the compressor.

5. At the condenser, loosen the lower air conditioning pipe clamp nut and separate the pipe from the condenser.

6. Loosen the upper air conditioning pipe-to-condenser fitting and separate the pipe from the condenser.

7. Remove the air conditioning pipes from the vehicle.

To install:

8. Position the air conditioning pipes into the vehicle.

9. Using new O-rings at the cowl, attach the pipe connector to the expansion valve and install the air conditioning pipes-to-expansion valve screw; torque the screw to 7 ñ 2 ft. lbs. (10 ñ 3 Nm).

10. In front of the brake master cylinder, tighten the clamp located on the air conditioning pipe.

11. Using new O-rings lubricated with refrigerant oil, install them on the compressor and torque the air conditioning pipes connector-to-compressor bolt to 17 ± 1.7 ft. lbs. (23 ± 2.3 Nm).

12. Install both air conditioning pipes to the condenser by lubricating the fitting with refrigerant oil. Torque the air conditioning pipe-to-condenser fitting to 11–13 ft. lbs. (15–18 Nm) and the air conditioning pipe-to-condenser clamp nut to 22–27 ft. lbs. (29–37 Nm).

13. Connect the negative battery cable.

14. Evacuate and recharge the air conditioning system. To test for proper function and leakage; operate the engine, at idle, for the 1st 4 minutes.

Manual Control Head

REMOVAL AND INSTALLATION

300E, 300CE and 300TE

1. Disconnect the negative battery cable.

2. Remove the radio, then remove the ashtray with the control panel housing (bezel).

3. Pull the control knobs from the dials and levers on the manual control unit.

4. Remove the control switches-to-control unit nuts.

5. Remove the faceplate-to-control unit screws and the faceplate.

6. Remove the control unit-to-dash screws. If equipped, remove the control unit bulb(s).

7. Pull the control unit forward and disconnect the electrical, vacuum and cable connectors from the unit. Remove the control unit from the vehicle.

To install:

8. Install the control unit and connect the electrical, vacuum and cable connectors to it as removed.

9. If equipped with bulbs, install them.

10. Install the control unit to the dash and secure with the screws.

11. Position the faceplate and install the faceplate-to-control unit screws.

12. Install the control switches-to-control unit nuts.

13. Install the control panel bezel, ashtray and radio.

14. Refit the control knobs. Connect the negative battery cable and check the control switches operation.

C220 and C280

1. Remove the radio.

2. Pull off the control knobs.

3. Remove the hex nut under the right control knob.

4. Remove the cover attaching screws and remove the cover.

5. Remove the pushbutton control unit attaching screws and withdraw the control unit.

6. Disconnect the plug connection for the pushbutton control unit and the air volume switch.

7. Press off the locking lug, remove attaching screws and remove the air volume switch from the control unit.

8. Installation is the reverse of the removal procedure.

Electronic Control Head

REMOVAL AND INSTALLATION

190E

1. Disconnect the negative battery cable.

2. Pull outlets from the center of the instrument panel.

3. Remove the upper instrument panel-to-center console screws and push the console slightly downward.

4. Pull off the blower switch knob and pull the blower switch molding from the center console.

5. Disconnect the fresh air/recirculating air switch.

6. Using a pointed tool, lift clamp from both upper sides of the control head and pull the control head forward.

7. Disconnect both 12-pole electrical connectors from the control head and remove the control head.

8. To install, reverse the removal procedures. Connect the negative battery cable.

C220 and C280

1. Remove the radio.

2. Remove the cover attaching screws and remove the cover.

3. Unclip the switch block on the cover.

4. Remove the attaching screws and withdraw the pushbutton control unit.

5. Disconnect the left and right electrical connectors and remove the control unit.

6. Installation is the reverse of the removal procedure.

SENSORS AND SWITCHES

Circulating Pump

REMOVAL AND INSTALLATION

300E, 300CE and 300TE

1. Disconnect the negative battery cable.

2. Drain the cooling system to a level below the circulating pump.

3. Remove the coolant hose clamp and disconnect the hoses from the circulating pump.

4. Disconnect the 2-pole electrical connector from the circulating pump.

5. Remove the circulating pump bracket bolt and pull the pump from the vehicle.

To install:

6. Install the circulating pump and secure with the bolt.

7. Install the coolant hoses and tighten the clamps.

8. Connect the electrical connector to the circulating pump.

9. Refill the cooling system. Connect the negative battery cable.

C220 and C280

1. Disconnect the negative battery cable.

2. Drain off the pressure in the cooling system.

3. Remove the air cleaner.

4. Disconnect the electrical coupling on the hot water circulation pump.

5. Loosen the hose clamps on the hot water hoses and remove the hoses from the pump.

6. Remove the pump bracket attaching screws and remove the pump with bracket.

7. Disconnect the bracket from the hot water circulation pump.

8. Installation is the reverse of the removal procedure.

Duo Valve

REMOVAL AND INSTALLATION

300E, 300CE and 300TE

1. Disconnect the negative battery cable.

2. Release the pressure in the cooling system by loosening the radiator cap.

3. Disconnect the electrical connector from the duo valve.

4. Remove the heater hose clamps and pull the 3 hoses from the duo valve.

5. Press the rubber buffers from the duo valve brackets.

6. Remove the duo valve from the vehicle.

To install:

7. Install the duo valve and press the rubber buffers into the valve brackets.

8. Install the heater hoses and secure with the clamps.

9. Connect the electrical connector to the duo valve.

10. If necessary, top of the radiator and install the cap.

11. Connect the negative battery cable.

C220 and C280

1. Disconnect the negative battery cable.

2. Release the pressure in the cooling system by loosening the radiator cap.

3. Remove the cover above right of the components compartment.

4. Remove the electrical couplings from the control units.

5. Remove the attaching nuts from the unit support and remove the unit support.

6. Loosen the clamps on the hot water hoses and remove the hoses from the duo valve.

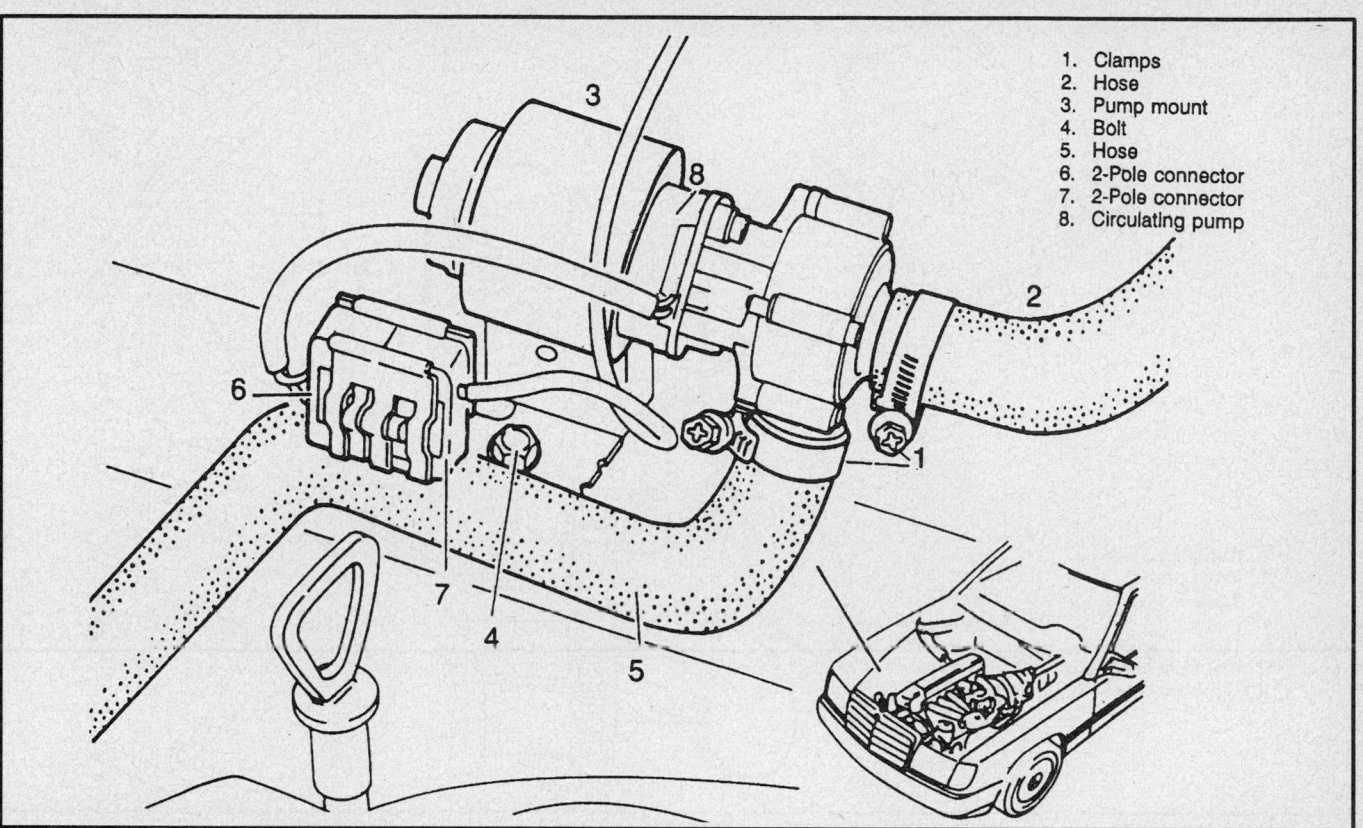

1. Clamps
2. Hose
3. Pump mount
4. Bolt
5. Hose
6. 2-Pole connector
7. 2-Pole connector
8. Circulating pump

View of the circulating pump—300E, 300CE and 300TE

7. Disconnect the electrical coupling on the duo valve.
8. Remove the nuts on the component panel.
9. Remove the duo valve with its bracket.
10. Remove the bracket from the duo valve.
11. Remove the rubber buffer on the duo valve.
12. Installation is the reverse of the removal procedure.

Air Flow Jet

The air flow jet is installed on vehicles without a sliding roof.

TESTING

300E, 300CE and 300TE

1. Turn the ignition switch **ON**.
2. Set the blower switch to **III** and the air distribution **DOWNWARD**.
3. Place a small square piece of paper on the temperature sensor interior air grid. If the paper adheres to the grid, the jet is functioning; if not, replace the jet.

REMOVAL AND INSTALLATION

300E, 300CE and 300TE

1. Disconnect the negative battery cable.
2. Position a cover under the heater box on the passenger's side to protect the interior.
3. Remove the instrument panel.
4. Pull the hoses from the air flow jet.

5. Loosen the air flow jet screw and pull the jet from it's mount.
To install:
6. Position the air flow jet onto it's mount and tighten the screw.
7. Push the hoses onto the air flow jet.
8. Install the instrument panel.
9. Connect the negative battery cable.

Interior Air Temperature Sensor

TESTING

1. Remove the temperature sensor from the dome light.
2. Place the sensor into an environmental oven and connect voltmeter to the electrical connectors.
3. Use the chart to determine if the resistance is acceptable to the temperature ranges.
4. If the sensor does not meet specifications, replace the sensor.

REMOVAL AND INSTALLATION

300E, 300CE and 300TE

1. Disconnect the negative battery cable.
2. Pull the dome light from the ceiling.
3. Disconnect the 2-pole electrical connector from the temperature sensor.
4. Disconnect the hose from the temperature sensor and remove the sensor from the vehicle.

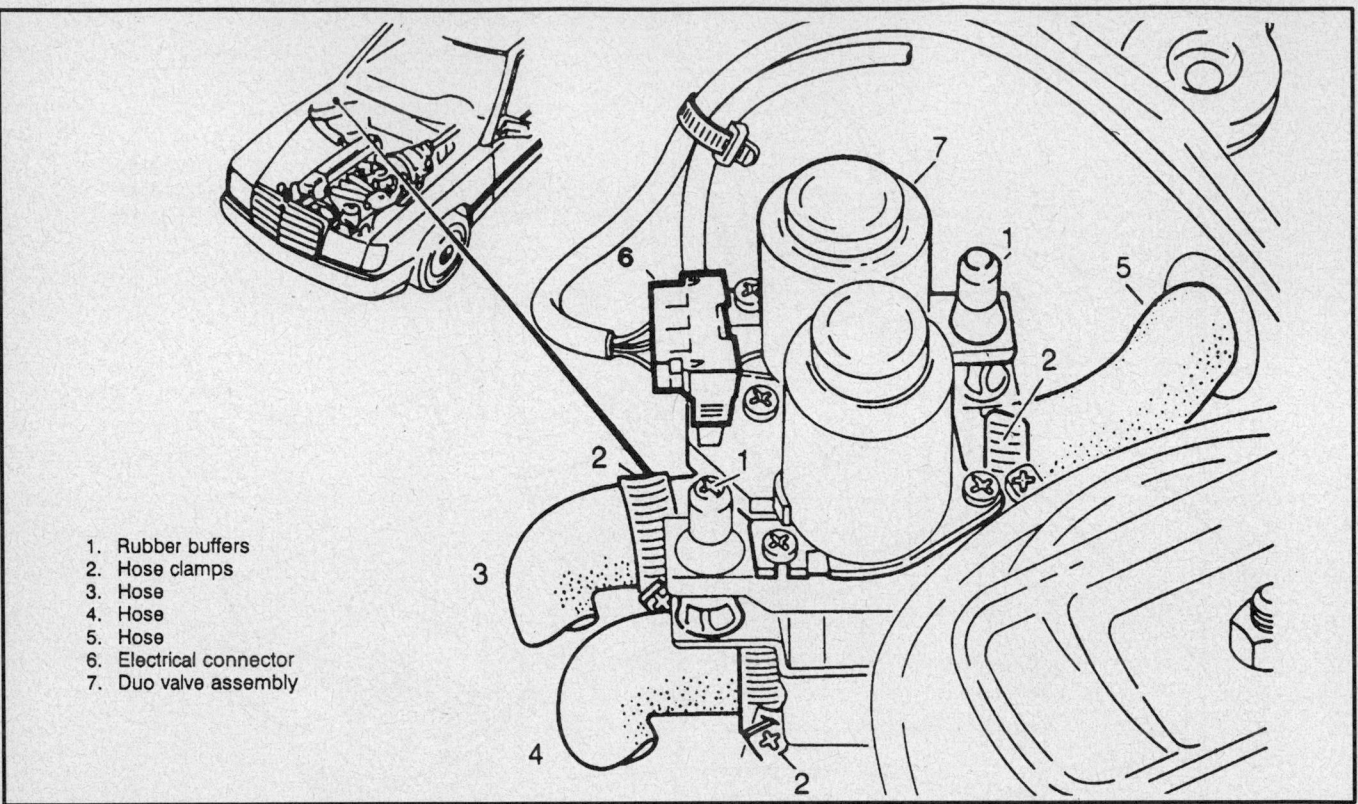

1. Rubber buffers
2. Hose clamps
3. Hose
4. Hose
5. Hose
6. Electrical connector
7. Duo valve assembly

View of the duo valve assembly—300E, 300CE and 300TE

Test values	
Sensor temperature in °C	Resistance in kΩ
+ 10	18.2 up to 21.5
+ 15	15.3 up to 17.2
+ 20	11.5 up to 13.5
+ 25	9.5 up to 10.5
+ 30	7.5 up to 8.5
+ 35	6.0 up to 7.0
+ 40	4.5 up to 5.5
+ 45	3.5 up to 4.5

Interior air temperature sensor test values—300E, 300CE and 300TE

To install:
5. Install the temperature sensor and connect the hose to it.
6. Connect the 2-pole electrical connector to the temperature sensor.
7. Install the dome light by inserting it on the right side.
8. Connect the negative battery cable.

Ventilation Blower

The ventilation blower is used for the temperature sensor interior air on vehicles equipped with a sliding roof.

TESTING

300E, 300CE and 300TE

1. Turn the ignition switch **ON**.
2. Place a 1 cm square. piece of paper on the temperature sensor interior air grid. If the paper adheres to the grid, the jet is functioning; if not, replace the jet.

REMOVAL AND INSTALLATION

300E, 300CE and 300TE

1. Disconnect the negative battery cable.
2. Remove the glove box.
3. Disconnect the hose from the blower.
4. Disconnect the 2-pole electrical connector from the blower.
5. Remove the blower.
To install:
6. Install the blower and connect the 2-pole electrical connector to the blower.
7. Connect the hose to the blower.
8. Install the glove box. Connect the negative battery cable.

Fresh/Recirc Air Switch-Over Valve

The fresh/recirc air switch over valve is located on the right side of the heater/air conditioning box near the glove box.

OPERATION

The switch-over valve is vacuum controlled and operates the fresh air/recirculated air flap.

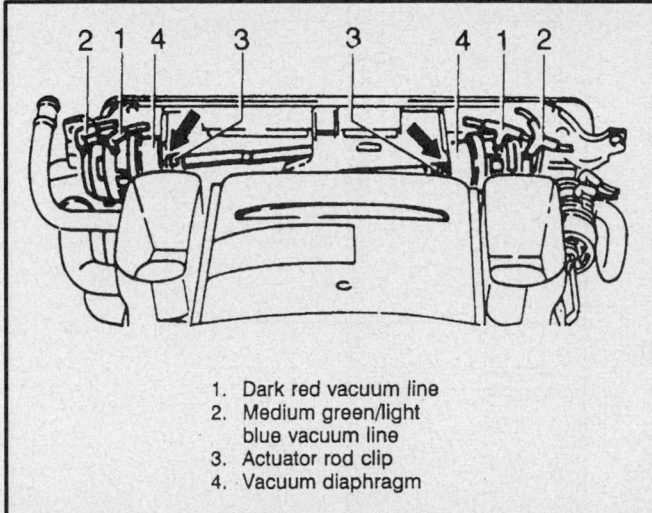

1. Dark red vacuum line
2. Medium green/light blue vacuum line
3. Actuator rod clip
4. Vacuum diaphragm

View of the left and right vacuum diaphragms—300E, 300CE and 300TE

REMOVAL AND INSTALLATION

1. Remove the glove box.
2. Disconnect the vacuum lines from the switch-over valve.
3. Disconnect the electrical connector from the switch-over valve
4. Remove the switch-over valve-to-heater/air conditioning box and remove the valve.
5. To install, reverse the removal procedures.

Vacuum Diaphragms

There are vacuum diaphragms located on the heater/air conditioning box.

OPERATION

The vacuum diaphragms control air flaps to change the air flow between fresh or recirculated.

REMOVAL AND INSTALLATION

1. Disconnect the negative battery cable.
2. Remove the instrument panel.
3. Disconnect the vacuum lines from the vacuum diaphragms.
4. At the vacuum diaphragm(s), open the actuation rod retaining clips and disconnect the rod(s) from the diaphragm(s).
5. Simultaneously, press downward and rotate the vacuum diaphragm to the right and remove it.
6. To install, reverse the removal procedures.
7. When connecting the vacuum lines, connect the dark red vacuum line to the side of the diaphragm and the medium green/light blue vacuum line to the rear of the diaphragm.

Air Distributor Switch

REMOVAL AND INSTALLATION

1. Disconnect the negative battery cable.

2. Remove the control unit from the console.
3. Loosen the bracket and pull the assembly forward.
4. Press the air distributor switch to the right and out of the rear of the bracket.
5. Press the adjusting off the rear of the air distributor switch and disconnect the cables; be careful not to kink the cables.
6. Disconnect the electrical connector from the rear of the switch.
To install:
7. Connect the electrical connector from the rear of the switch.
8. Reconnect the cables and slide the adjusting nuts onto the air distributor switch.
9. Press the air distributor switch into the bracket and to the right.
10. Install the bracket and tighten the screw.
11. Install the control unit onto the console. Connect the negative battery cable.

Air Distributor Switch Control Cables

REMOVAL AND INSTALLATION

300E, 300CE and 300TE

1. Disconnect the negative battery cable. Remove the air distributor switch.
2. Remove the lower cover at the front of the passenger's side.
3. Remove the instrument panel and the glove box.
4. Disconnect the control cable from the footwell air flap control lever.
5. Disconnect the control cable from the defroster nozzle control lever.
To install:
6. Connect the control cable to the defroster nozzle control lever.
7. Connect the control cable to the footwell air flap control lever.
8. Adjust the control cables, by turning the adjusting nuts, so the footwell air flaps and the defroster nozzles are fully closed with the air distributor switch in the **9 O'CLOCK** position.
9. Install the glove box and the instrument panel.
10. Install the lower cover at the front of the passenger's side.
11. Install the air distributor switch. Connect the negative battery cable.

Heat Exchanger Temperature Sensor

TESTING

1. Remove the temperature sensor(s) from the console.
2. Place the sensor into an environmental oven and connect voltmeter to the electrical connectors.
3. Use the chart to determine if the resistance is acceptable to the temperature ranges.
4. If the sensor does not meet specifications, replace the sensor.

REMOVAL AND INSTALLATION

1. Disconnect the negative battery cable.
2. Remove the control unit. Unclip the bracket.

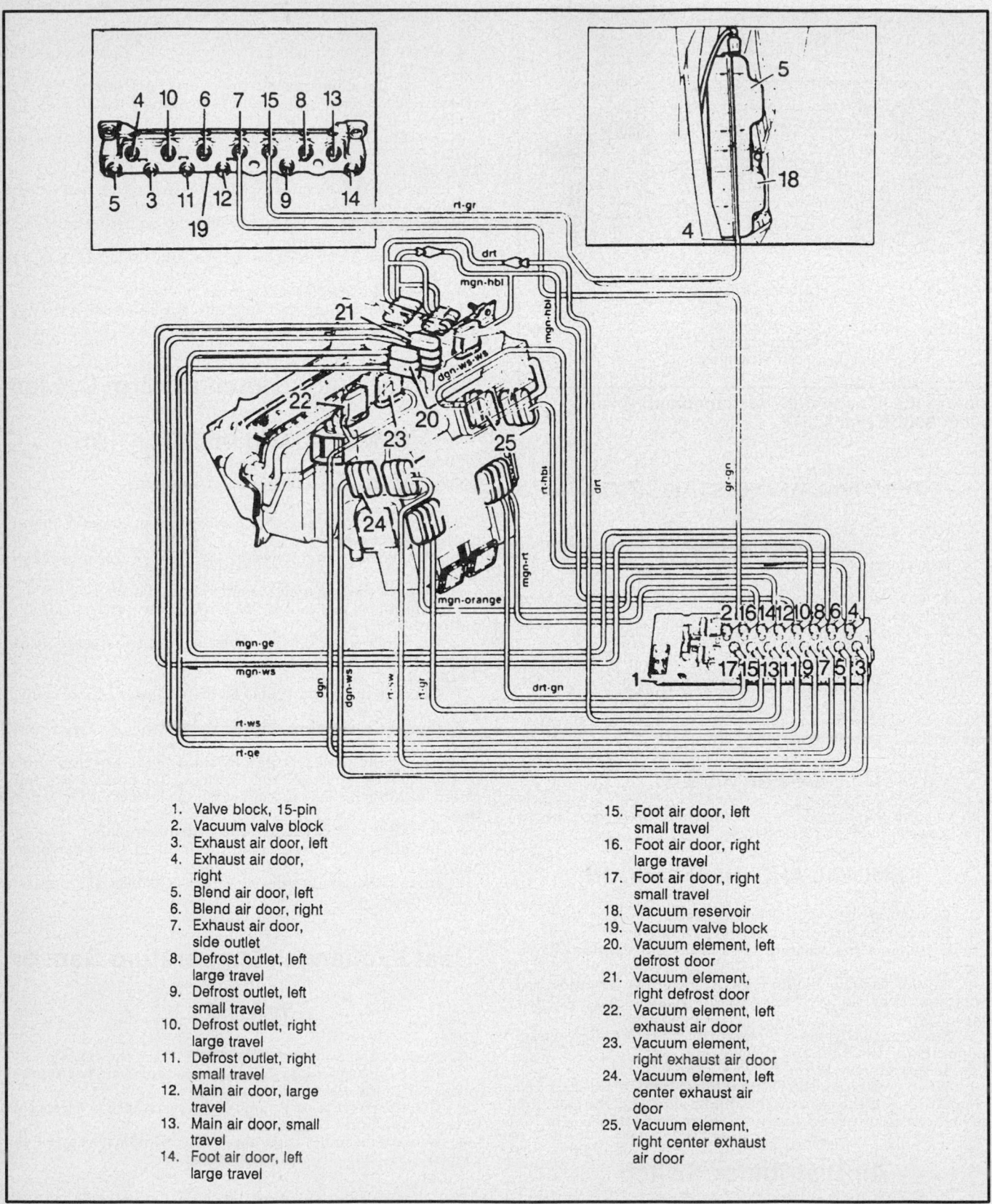

1. Valve block, 15-pin
2. Vacuum valve block
3. Exhaust air door, left
4. Exhaust air door, right
5. Blend air door, left
6. Blend air door, right
7. Exhaust air door, side outlet
8. Defrost outlet, left large travel
9. Defrost outlet, left small travel
10. Defrost outlet, right large travel
11. Defrost outlet, right small travel
12. Main air door, large travel
13. Main air door, small travel
14. Foot air door, left large travel

15. Foot air door, left small travel
16. Foot air door, right large travel
17. Foot air door, right small travel
18. Vacuum reservoir
19. Vacuum valve block
20. Vacuum element, left defrost door
21. Vacuum element, right defrost door
22. Vacuum element, left exhaust air door
23. Vacuum element, right exhaust air door
24. Vacuum element, left center exhaust air door
25. Vacuum element, right center exhaust air door

Vacuum circuit, vacuum diaphragms and vacuum connector block on automatic climate control systems

3. Disconnect both 2-pole electrical connectors from the temperature sensors.

4. Remove both temperature sensors from the dash.

To install:

5. Push both temperature sensors into the dash.

6. Connect both 2-pole electrical connectors to the temperature sensors.

7. Clip in the bracket. Install the control unit.

8. Connect the negative battery cable.

Pressure Switch

TESTING

300D Turbo, 300E, 300CE, 300TE, 300E 4Matic, 300TE 4Matic

1. Turn the ignition switch **ON**.

2. Using a jumper wire, jump the terminals of the auxiliary fan switch.

3. If the cooling fans do not come on, the problem is outside of the pressure switch.

4. Connect a high pressure gauge to the refrigerant line near the compressor.

5. Turn the air conditioning switch **ON**, the fresh/recirc air switch to **2**, and the fan switch to speed **4**.

6. Operate the engine at idle until the pressure on the gauge reaches about 22 bars (green switch) or 17 bars (red switch). Slowly increase engine speed, if necessary. If the auxiliary fan does not turn ON the pressure switch is defective.

7. To check the cutout pressure, operate the engine at idle until the gauge pressure reaches about 15 bars (green switch) or 12 bar (red switch), disconnect 1 plug from the pressure switch, if necessary. If the auxiliary fan does not switch OFF, the pressure switch is defective.

300SE

CUT-IN PRESSURE

1. Operate the engine and turn the air conditioning system **ON**; turn **ON** the blower motor and temperature dial.

2. If the compressor's electromagnetic clutch is not attracting, use a voltmeter to check for voltage at both terminals of the pressure switch; do not disconnect the electrical connectors.

3. If both terminals of the pressure switch are carrying voltage, check for:
   - A fault in the wire between the pressure switch and the electromagnetic clutch coil.
   - A defective electromagnetic clutch coil.

4. If only 1 terminal of the pressure switch are carrying voltage, check for:
   - Insufficiently charged air conditioning system.
   - Defective pressure switch.

5. To check the refrigerant level, perform the following procedures:
   - Pull the electrical connectors from the pressure switch and connect a jumper wire between them.
   - Operate the air conditioning system for 2–3 minutes.
   - With the electromagnetic clutch in operation, assure that the refrigerant flows without bubbles, past the sight glass.
   - If necessary, recharge the air conditioning system.

6. If the refrigerant level is adequate, the pressure switch is defective.

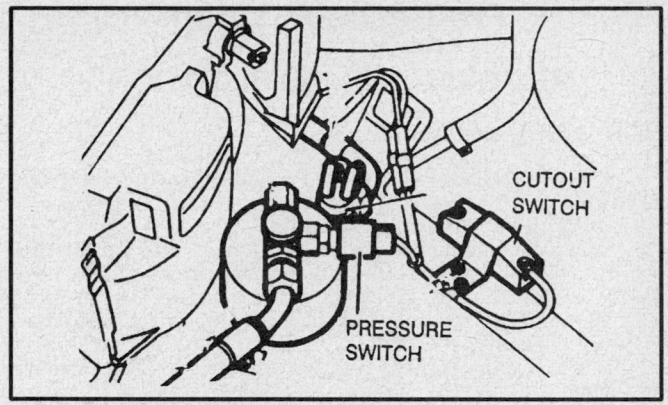

Showing pressure switch locations—300D Turbo, 300E, 300CE, 300TE, 300E 4Matic and 300TE 4Matic

CUT-OUT PRESSURE

1. After the cut-in pressure test has passed, connect an air conditioning pressure gauge to the pressure end of the service valve.

2. Disconnect both electrical connectors from the pressure switch and connect an ohmmeter to the pressure switch terminals.

3. Properly, discharge the air conditioning system by about 2 bars; at this point, the ohmmeter should register infinity.

REMOVAL AND INSTALLATION

300D, 300E, 300CE, 300TE, 300E 4Matic, 300TE 4Matic

AUXILIARY FAN SWITCH

1. Disconnect the negative battery cable.

2. Properly discharge the air conditioning system.

3. Disconnect the electrical connectors from both pressure switch.

4. Remove the pressure switch by screwing it from the fluid reservoir; be sure to plug the reservoir.

To install:

5. Using refrigerant oil, lubricate the O-ring and install the switch to the fluid reservoir; torque the switch to 7 ± 1.5 ft. lbs. (10 ± 2 Nm).

6. Connect both electrical connectors to pressure switch.

7. Using the proper procedure, evacuate and charge the air conditioning system.

8. Connect the negative battery cable.

9. Start the engine and allow it to run at idle for the 1st 4 minutes and check for leaks.

300SE

1. Disconnect the negative battery cable.

2. Properly, discharge the air conditioning system.

3. Disconnect the electrical connectors from the pressure switch.

4. Remove the pressure switch by screwing it from the receiver/drier; be sure to plug the reservoir.

To install:

5. Using refrigerant oil, lubricate the pressure switch threads and install the switch to the receiver/drier; torque the switch to 20 ± 4 Nm.

6. Connect both electrical connectors to pressure switch.

7. Using the proper procedure, evacuate and charge the air conditioning system.

8. Connect the negative battery cable.

9. Start the engine and allow it to run at idle for the 1st 4 minutes and check for leaks.

Pre-Resistor Group

REMOVAL AND INSTALLATION

300E, 300CE and 300TE

1. Position the hood vertically. Disconnect the negative battery cable.
2. On the left side, lift the hood-to-chassis seal.
3. Press the trim molding from the vehicle. Pull out the clip.
4. Remove the water drain-to-chassis screws and remove the water drain.
5. Disconnect the 2-pole and the 6-pole electrical connectors from the pre-resistor group.
6. Below the instrument panel on the driver's side, remove the cover.
7. From inside the vehicle, remove the pre-resistor group-to-chassis nuts.
8. Remove the pre-resistor group from the outside of the vehicle.

To install:

9. Position the pre-resistor group and secure with the nuts.
10. Below the instrument panel on the driver's side, install the cover.
11. Connect the 2-pole and the 6-pole electrical connectors to the pre-resistor group.
12. Insert the water drain into the drain pipe and secure with the screws.
13. Install the clip and press the trim molding onto the vehicle.
14. Refit the hood-to-chassis seal. Connect the negative battery cable.

Outside Air Temperature Sensor

The outside air temperature sensor is attached to the upper heater/air conditioning box and is located under the windshield wiper assembly on top of the cowl.

TESTING

1. Remove the outside air temperature sensor from the heater/air conditioning box.
2. Place the sensor into an environmental oven and connect voltmeter to the electrical connectors.
3. Use the chart to determine if the resistance is acceptable to the temperature ranges.

4. If the sensor does not meet specifications, replace the sensor.

REMOVAL AND INSTALLATION

300E, 300CE and 300TE

1. Disconnect the negative battery cable.
2. Remove the air inlet cover from the top of the cowl.
3. Pull off the vacuum lines from the servos for the main air valve.
4. Disconnect the 2-pole electrical connector from behind the glove box.
5. Pull the air temperature sensor from the heater/air conditioning box and pull the electrical cable through the cowl.
6. To install, reverse the removal procedure.

Evaporator Temperature Sensor

The evaporator temperature sensor is attached to the left side of the heater/air conditioning box.

TESTING

1. Remove the temperature sensor from the dome light.
2. Place the sensor into an environmental oven and connect voltmeter to the electrical connectors.
3. Use the chart to determine if the resistance is acceptable to the temperature ranges.
4. If the sensor does not meet specifications, replace the sensor.

REMOVAL AND INSTALLATION

300E, 300CE and 300TE

1. Disconnect the negative battery cable.
2. Remove the lower instrument panel cover from the left side.
3. Disconnect the cable strap.
4. Disconnect the 2-pole electrical connector from the evaporator temperature sensor.
5. Pull the temperature sensor from the heater/air conditioning box.
6. To install, reverse the removal procedures.
7. Connect the negative battery cable.

Test data

Sensor temperature in °C	Resistance in kΩ
0	8.1–9.9
+ 5	6.3–7.7
+ 10	5.0–6.0
+ 15	4.0–4.6
+ 20	3.1–3.9
+ 25	2.4–3.0
+ 30	1.9–2.3
+ 35	1.6–2.0
+ 40	1.4–1.6
+ 45	1.1–1.3

Outside air temperature sensor test values and evaporator temperature sensor test values—automatic climate control

Coolant Temperature Switch

OPERATION

The temperature switch sends a resistance value corresponding to the coolant temperature to the control unit. The control unit processes the value and switches the compressor OFF in 2 stages.

TESTING

300E, 300CE and 300TE

At the coolant temperature of 242°F (117°C) for a gasoline engine or 251°F (122°C) for a diesel engine, the switch ON period is reduced by 50 percent. The compressor is switched ON and OFF, in cycles: approx. 20 seconds ON and 20 seconds OFF. If the coolant temperature drops to 237°F (114°C) for a gasoline engine or to 251°F (122°C) for a diesel engine, the compressor is switched ON permanently.

At the coolant temperature of 248°F (120°C) for a gasoline engine or 262°F (128°C) for a diesel engine, the compressor is switched OFF completely. When the coolant temperature drops to 242°F (117°C) for a gasoline engine or 251°F (122°C) for a diesel engine, the compressor is switched on in cyclic operation.

SYSTEM DIAGNOSIS

Air Conditioning Diagnosis and Repair

The following diagnosis and repair procedures pertain to the air conditioning/automatic temperature control for models 300E, 300CE and 300TE.

Refrigerant compressor does not switch ON

1ST CAUSE

System not charged with sufficient quantity of refrigerant — possible leak or pressure switch defective.

REMEDY

1. Allow engine to run at idle.
2. Switch **ON** the function switch.
3. Disconnect both electrical connectors from the pressure switch, located on the fluid reservoir. Connect the electrical connectors to a new pressure switch.
4. If the compressor runs, check fluid level in air conditioner, eliminate leakage, if required.
5. If the fluid level is O.K., replace pressure switch.
6. If the compressor does not run, see cause 2.

2ND CAUSE

Malfunction in actuation from control unit or control panel to compressor shut-off control unit.

REMEDY

Check electrical components in air-conditioner automatic temperature control.

3RD CAUSE

Compressor shut-off not functioning.

REMEDY

Check compressor shut-off.

Imprecise customer complaint

TESTS

Check control quality and heating capacity.
   In the event of deviations from the nominal functions, check electrical components in air conditioner automatic temperature control.

Air Outlet Temperature Too Low When Maximum Heating State Required

1ST CAUSE

Circulation pump not running.

REMEDY

Check activation and current consumption (max. 0.8 amps) of circulation pump, replace circulation pump, if required.

2ND CAUSE

Duo valve defective

REMEDY

Check duo valve, replace, if required.

3RD CAUSE

Heat exchanger duty or defective.

REMEDY

Flush cooling system. Replace heat exchanger, if required.

Heater Does Not Heat Up Passenger Compartment To Temperature of Approx. 72°F (22°C) at Head Level With Adjustment Wheel Set to 72°F (22°C) and at Outside Temperature Below 0°C

1ST CAUSE

Electrical malfunction in system.

REMEDY

Check electrical components in air conditioner automatic temperature control and replace defective component, if required.

2ND CAUSE

Heat exchanger dirty or defective.

REMEDY

Flush heating system. Flush cooling system, if required, and replace heat exchanger, if required.

Heater Does Not Heat Up to Comfortable Temperature, Air Outlet Temperature Increases and Decreases Slowly at Regular Intervals

CAUSE

Ventilation of interior air temperature sensor not functioning properly.

REMEDY

Check ventilation fan for interior air temperature sensor. For this purpose switch **ON** ignition and position a small piece of paper approx. on grate for interior temperature sensor. The paper should remain in place. If not, remove glove box, check ventilation fan and replace it, if required.

Heater Only Heats Occasionally or Heats Continuously at Maximum Capacity.

1ST CAUSE

Discontinuity in one of the temperature sensors or leads.

REMEDY

Check electrical components in air-conditioner automatic temperature control and replace defective component, if required.

2ND CAUSE

Poor contact due to widened sockets.

REMEDY

Check all sockets from cable harness on control unit or control panel on temperature sensors (interior air, heat exchanger, outside air) and on duo valve individually and bend, as required.

Poor Refrigeration Capacity

1ST CAUSE

Coolant quantity in system too low.

REMEDY

Check system for leakage, replace fluid reservoir and refill system.

2ND CAUSE

Expansion valve sticks, is dirty or defective; therefore, vacuum too low or too high.

REMEDY

Replace expansion valve and fluid reservoir.

3RD CAUSE

Evaporator temperature sensor defective, therefore refrigerant compressor switches off too early.

REMEDY

Replace evaporator temperature sensor.

Refrigeration capacity decreases after longer period. Moreover air quantity from center and side nozzles decreases. Ice vapor comes out of center nozzles.

1ST CAUSE

Short circuit in evaporator temperature sensor.

REMEDY

Replace evaporator temperature sensor.

2ND CAUSE

Expansion valve defective.

REMEDY

Replace expansion valve.

Screeching noise from area of evaporator at idle immediately after refrigerant compressor switches on.

CAUSE

Expansion valve defective.

REMEDY

Replace expansion valve

SPECIFICATIONS

ENGINE IDENTIFICATION

Year	Model	Engine Displacement Liters (cc)	Engine Series Identification	Engine VIN	Fuel System	No. of Cylinders	Engine Type
1993	Diamante	3.0 (2972)	6G72	H	MPI	6	SOHC
	Diamante	3.0 (2972)	6G72	J	MPI	6	DOHC
	Eclipse	1.8 (1755)	4G37	B	MPI	4	SOHC
	Eclipse	2.0 (1997)	4G63	E	MPI	4	DOHC
	Galant	2.0 (1997)	4G63	G	MPI	4	SOHC
	Galant	2.0 (1997)	4G63	L	MPI	4	DOHC
	Mirage	1.5 (1468)	4G15	A	MPI	4	SOHC
	Mirage	1.8 (1834)	4G93	C	MPI	4	SOHC
	Precis	1.5 (1468)	G4DJ	N/A	MPI	4	N/A
	3000GT	3.0 (2972)	6G72	B	MPI	6	DOHC
	3000GT	3.0 (2972)	6G72	C	TURBO	6	DOHC
1994	Diamante	3.0 (2972)	6G72	H	MPI	6	SOHC
	Diamante	3.0 (2972)	6G72	J	MPI	6	DOHC
	Eclipse	1.8 (1755)	4G37	B	MPI	4	SOHC
	Eclipse	2.0 (1997)	4G63	E	MPI	4	DOHC
	Eclipse	2.0 (1997)	4G63	F	TURBO	4	DOHC
	Galant	2.4 (2351)	4G64	G	MPI	4	SOHC
	Galant	2.4 (2351)	4G64	L	MPI	4	DOHC
	Mirage	1.5 (1468)	4G15	A	MPI	4	SOHC
	Mirage	1.8 (1834)	4G93	C	MPI	4	SOHC
	Precis	1.5 (1468)	G4DJ	N/A	MPI	4	N/A
	3000GT	3.0 (2972)	6G72	J	MPI	6	DOHC
	3000GT	3.0 (2972)	6G72	K	TURBO	6	DOHC
1995	Diamante	3.0 (2972)	6G72	H	MPI	6	SOHC
	Diamante	3.0 (2972)	6G72	J	MPI	6	DOHC
	Eclipse	2.0 (1997)	420A	Y	MPI	4	DOHC
	Eclipse	2.0 (1997)	4G63	F	TURBO	4	DOHC
	Galant	2.4 (2351)	4G64	G	MPI	4	SOHC
	Mirage	1.5 (1468)	4G15	A	MPI	4	SOHC
	Mirage	1.8 (1834)	4G93	C	MPI	4	SOHC
	3000GT	3.0 (2972)	6G72	J	MPI	6	DOHC
	3000GT	3.0 (2972)	6G72	K	TURBO	6	DOHC

SOHC–Single Overhead Cam

DOHC–Dual Overhead Cams

MPI–Multi–Point Injection

REFRIGERANT CAPACITIES

Year	Model	Coolant (oz.)	Coolant Type	Compressor Oil (fl. oz.)	Compressor Type
1993	Diamante	34.2–37.7	R–12	5.4	Scroll type FX105V
	Diamante	26.1–27.9	R–134a	5.7	Scroll type MSC105
	Eclipse	33	R–12	2.7	Denso 10PA17
	Galant	33	R–12	N/A	Scroll type FX105V
	Mirage	26–30	R–12	4.4	Scroll type FX105V
	Precis	30	R–12	2.3–2.5	Sanden SD709
	3000GT	26–28	R–134a	5.4	Scroll type MSC105
1994	Diamante	34.2–37.7	R–12	5.4	Scroll type FX105V
	Diamante	26.1–27.9	R–134a	5.7	Scroll type MSC105
	Eclipse	33	R–12	2.7	Denso 10PA17
	Galant	26.1–27.5	R–134a	5.1–5.7	AX105VS
	Mirage	26–30	R–134a	4.4	Scroll type FX105V
	Precis	24–25	R–134a	5.8	Swash Plate FX15
	3000GT	26–28	R–134a	5.4	Scroll type MSC105
1995	Diamante	34.2–37.7	R–12	5.4	Scroll type FX105V
	Diamante	26.1–27.9	R–134a	5.7	Scroll type MSC105
	Eclipse	24.7–26.1	R–134a	3.4	Denso 10PA17C
	Eclipse ⑥	24.7–26	R–134a	5.7	Scroll type MSC105CVS
	Galant	26.1–27.5	R–134a	5.1	Scroll type MSC105CVS
	Mirage	26–30	R–134a	4.4	Scroll type FX105V
	3000GT	26–28	R–134a	5.4	Scroll type MSC105

AIR CONDITIONING BELT TENSION

Year	Model	Engine Liters (cc)	Belt Type	Specifications① New (lbs.)	Used (lbs.)
1993	Diamante	3.0 (2972) ④	Serpentine	0.24	0.24–0.35 ③
	Diamante	3.0 (2972) ⑤	Serpentine	0.15	0.16–0.22 ②
	Eclipse	1.8 (1755)	V–Belt	0.16–0.20	0.22–0.24
	Eclipse	2.0 (1997)	V–Belt	0.16–0.20	0.22–0.24
	Galant	2.0 (1997)	V–belt	0.20–0.21	0.23–0.28
	Mirage	1.5 (1468)	V–Belt	0.20–0.23	0.23–0.27
	Mirage	1.8 (1834)	V–Belt	0.22–0.24	0.27–0.30
	Precis	1.5 (1468)	V–Belt	0.20	0.25
	3000GT	3.0 (2972)	Serpentine	0.15	0.16–0.22 ②
1994	Diamante	3.0 (2972) ④	Serpentine	0.26–0.28	0.30–0.34
	Diamante	3.0 (2972) ⑤	Serpentine	0.14–0.16	0.16–0.20 ②
	Eclipse	1.8 (1755)	V–Belt	0.20–0.22	0.24–0.28
	Eclipse	2.0 (1997)	V–Belt	0.20–0.22	0.24–0.28
	Galant	2.4 (2351)	Serpentine	0.22–0.24	0.26–0.30
	Mirage	1.5 (1468)	V–belt	0.20–0.24	0.24–0.28
	Mirage	1.8 (1834)	V–Belt	0.22–0.24	0.27–0.30
	Precis	1.5 (1468)	V–Belt	N/A	0.34–0.42
	3000GT	3.0 (2972)	Serpentine	0.14–0.16	0.16–0.20

AIR CONDITIONING BELT TENSION

Year	Model	Engine Liters (cc)	Belt Type	Specifications① New (lbs.)	Used (lbs.)
1995	Diamante	3.0 (2972) ④	Serpentine	0.26–0.28	0.30–0.34
	Diamante	3.0 (2972) ⑤	Serpentine	0.14–0.16	0.16–0.20 ②
	Eclipse	2.0 (1997)	V–Belt	0.20–0.22	0.24–0.28
	Eclipse	2.0 (1997)	V–Belt	0.20–0.22	0.24–0.28
	Galant	2.4 (2351)	Serpentine	0.22–0.24	0.26–0.30
	Mirage	1.5 (1468)	V–belt	0.20–0.24	0.24–0.28
	Mirage	1.8 (1834)	Serpentine	0.22–0.24	0.27–0.30
	3000GT	3.0 (2972)	Serpentine	0.14–0.16	0.16–0.20

① inches of deflection at center of belt using 22 lbs. force

② Measured between idler pulley and crankshaft pulley

③ Measured between power steering pulley and tensioner pulley

④ SOHC–Single Overhead Cam

⑤ DOHC–Dual Overhead Cam

⑥ Turbo

SYSTEM DESCRIPTION

General Information

Eclipse, Galant, Mirage and Manual A/C 3000GT

The heater unit is located in the center of the vehicle with the blower housing and blend–air system. In the blend–air system, hot air and cool air are controlled by the blend–air damper to make a fine adjustment of the temperature. The heater system is also designed as a bi–level heater in which a separator directs warm air to the windshield or to the floor and cool air through the panel outlet.

The temperature inside the vehicle is controlled by means of the temperature control lever, the position of which determines the opening of the blend–air damper and the resulting mixing ratio of cool and hot air is used to control the outlet temperature.

All models use a 2 detent switch which is depressed one step for **ECONO** and a second step for **A/C**.

The air conditioning compressor coil will be energized when all of the following conditions are met:

1. The ignition switch is **ON**.
2. The blower motor switch is not in the **OFF** position.
3. The air conditioner switch is set in either the **ECONO** or **A/C** position.
4. The evaporator outlet air temperature sensor is reading at least 39°F (4°C).
5. The evaporator inlet air temperature sensor is reading at least 39°F (4°C).
6. Both dual pressure switch contacts are closed by refrigerant pressure above 30 psi on the low side and below 384 psi on the high side.
7. If equipped with a compressor refrigerant temperature sensor, the compressor discharge side refrigerant temperature must be less than 347°F (175°C).
8. If equipped with an engine coolant temperature switch, the engine coolant temperature must be less than 239°F (115°C).

9. If equipped with A/C belt lock controller, the difference between engine rpm and A/C belt rpm is less than 8% in any 3 second period.

Diamante and Full Auto A/C 3000GT

The fully automatic A/C system is standard on Diamante and is optionally equipped on 3000GT. In this system, signals from the various sensors are processed and controlled by the air conditioning control unit according to the set temperature. Thereafter, the system automatically controls the temperature of the air flow, the amount of air flow, the direction of air out-flow and the selection and direction of flow of either outside air or interior recirculated air through air door damper motors and potentiometers. An on–board diagnostic unit is used in troubleshooting the system.

Precis

The blend–air type system directs fresh air from the outside or inside recirculated air, by the use of air mixture dampers. These dampers are located within the air mixture chamber and control the amount of air passing through the heating and air conditioning systems. The air is then mixed accordingly and directed to the various outlets. The air damper doors are opened and closed by manual control cables or vacuum actuated devices. The cable–controlled system uses slide levers on the control panel, while vacuum–operated systems use dial type controls.

When the air conditioning switch is set to the **ON** position, the magnetic clutch on the compressor energizes. The following components are used to control compressor operation:

1. The magnetic clutch cycling switch, located on the receiver/drier, controls the on–off cycling of the compressor according to pressure within the system.
2. The engine coolant temperature switch senses high engine temperatures and will stop compressor operation.

3. An idle control system (integral to the engine ECU) is used to maintain engine idle speed when the compressor magnetic clutch is energized.

4. An air conditioning relay is located in the engine compartment and electrically controls current loads through the system. It is engaged when the A/C button is set to the **ON** position on the control panel.

Service Valve Location

Precis

The suction (low pressure) port is located either on the receiver/drier or on the rear of the compressor. The discharge (high pressure) port is located either on the discharge line near the compressor or on the rear of the compressor.

Eclipse, Galant and Mirage

The suction (low pressure) port is located on the compressor. The discharge (high pressure) port is located on the discharge line at the left front corner of the engine compartment.

Diamante and 3000GT

The suction (low pressure) port is located on the compressor. The discharge (high pressure) port is located on the discharge line near the compressor.

System Discharging

NOTE: R–12 refrigerant is a chlorofluorocarbon which, when mishandled, can contribute to the depletion of the ozone layer in the upper atmosphere. Ozone filters out harmful radiation from the sun. In order to protect the ozone layer, an approved R–12 Recovery/Recycling machine that meets SAE standard J1991 should be employed when discharging the system. Follow the operating instructions provided with the approved equipment exactly to properly discharge the system.

R–134a refrigerant is a non–chlorofluorocarbon with different chemical characteristics than R–12. Although it is designed to be less hazardous to the ozone layer of the atmosphere, it should still be discharged only into a recycling type machine and not vented to the atmosphere. Follow equipment manufacturer's instructions for this system. Use only dedicated equipment for R–134a systems. Avoid breathing R–134a vapors, as it can cause irritation. Never pressure test or leak test

R–134a service equipment with compressed air. Some mixtures of air and R–134a have been shown to be combustible, especially at higher pressures. Such a mixture may result in fire or explosion. Use appropriate cautions.

System Evacuating

If the air conditioning system has been opened to the atmosphere, it should be air and moisture free before being recharged with refrigerant. Moisture and air mixed with refrigerant will raise the compressor head pressure, possibly damage the system's components and will reduce the performance of the system. Moisture will boil at normal room temperature when exposed to a vacuum. To evacuate the system, perform the following procedure:

1. Leak test the system and repair any leaks found.

2. Connect an approved charging station, Recovery/Recycling machine or manifold gauge set and vacuum pump to the discharge and suction ports. The red hose is normally connected to the discharge (high pressure) line and the blue hose is connected to the suction (low pressure) line.

3. Open the discharge and suction ports and start the vacuum pump. If the pump is not able to pull at least 26 in. Hg of vacuum, there is a leak that must be repaired before evacuation can occur.

4. Once the system has reached at least 26 in. Hg of vacuum, allow the system to evacuate for at least 10 minutes. The longer the system is evacuated, the more contaminants will be removed.

5. Close all valves and turn the pump **OFF**. If the system loses more than 2 in. Hg of vacuum after 15 minutes, there is a leak that should be repaired.

System Charging

NOTE: Be sure to use dedicated equipment while charging systems using R–134a refrigerant.

1. Connect an approved charging station, Recovery/Recycling machine or manifold gauge set to the discharge and suction ports. The red hose is normally connected to the discharge (high pressure) line and the blue hose is connected to the suction (low pressure) line.

2. Follow the instructions provided with the equipment and charge the system with the specified amount of refrigerant.

3. Perform a leak test.

SYSTEM COMPONENTS

NOTE: Vehicles that are equipped with the Supplemental Inflatable Restraint or air bag system require additional service procedures. The air bag system must be disabled before performing service on or around the air bag, instrument panel components, wiring and sensors. Failure to follow safety and disabling procedures could result in accidental air bag deployment, possible personal injury and unnecessary air bag system repairs.

Radiator

REMOVAL AND INSTALLATION

1. Disconnect the negative battery cable and detach the fan motor plug.

2. Set temperature control to **HOT**, open radiator plug and drain the cooling system. Remove air intake ductwork, if needed.

3. Disconnect the overflow hose. If necessary, remove the overflow reservoir and bracket.

4. Disconnect the upper and lower radiator hoses.

5. Disconnect and plug the automatic transaxle cooler lines, if equipped.

6. Disconnect all electrical connectors to the electric cooling fan(s) and radiator sensors. Most of these connectors employ a waterproof connector. When disconnecting, make sure all parts of the connectors remain intact.

7. Remove the upper radiator mounts and/or mounting bolts and lift out the radiator assembly. On Mirage and 3000GT, it may be necessary to remove the radiator fan assembly prior to radiator removal.

8. Remove the radiator and condenser cooling fan(s).

To install:

9. Install cooling fans to radiator, if removed. Carefully install the radiator, mounts and retaining bolts.

10. Connect the automatic transaxle or transmission cooler lines, if equipped.

11. Connect all previously disconnected electrical connectors.

12. Install the upper and lower radiator hoses.

13. Install the overflow reservoir and hose.

14. Install any previously removed air intake ductwork.

15. Fill the radiator with coolant.

16. Connect the negative battery cable and check for leaks.

COOLING SYSTEM BLEEDING

Slowly fill the cooling system in the conventional manner until radiator is full. Also fill the reserve tank to the full mark. Install the radiator cap and start the engine. Warm the engine until the thermostat opens (upper radiator hose will be warm). Rev the engine 3 times and turn it **OFF**. Wait until the engine has cooled down, and then remove radiator cap and refill. Repeat the procedure until coolant level does not drop.

Electric Cooling Fans

TESTING

CAUTION

Make sure the key is in the OFF position when checking the electric cooling fan. If not, the fan could turn ON at any time, causing serious personal injury.

---

1. Disconnect the negative battery cable.

2. Disconnect the electrical plug from the fan motor harness.

3. Connect the appropriate terminals to the battery and make sure the fan runs smoothly, without abnormal noise or vibration.

4. Reconnect the negative battery cable.

REMOVAL AND INSTALLATION

1. Disconnect the negative battery cable.

2. Unplug the fan motor connector(s). Most of these connectors employ a waterproof connector. When disconnecting, make sure all parts of the connectors remain intact.

3. Remove the mounting screws. The radiator and condenser cooling fans are removable separately.

4. Remove the fan assembly and disassemble as required. On 3000GT, it may be necessary to remove the alternator prior to removing the cooling fan.

5. The installation is the reverse of the removal procedure.

6. Check the coolant level and refill as required.

7. Connect the negative battery cable and check for proper operation.

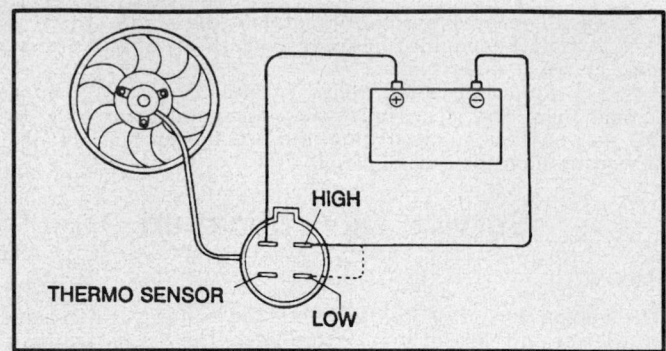

Radiator cooling fan check — Precis

Radiator cooling fan check — Mirage

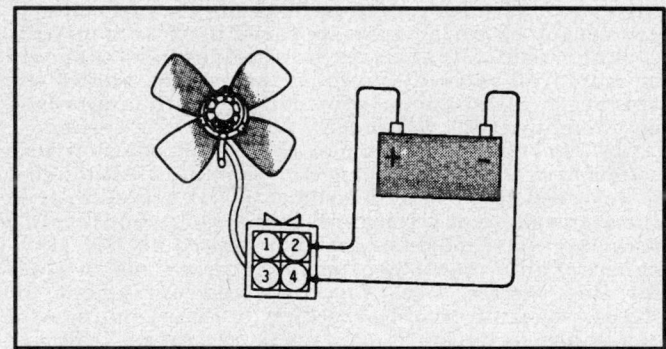

Radiator cooling fancheck — 1993–94 Eclipse

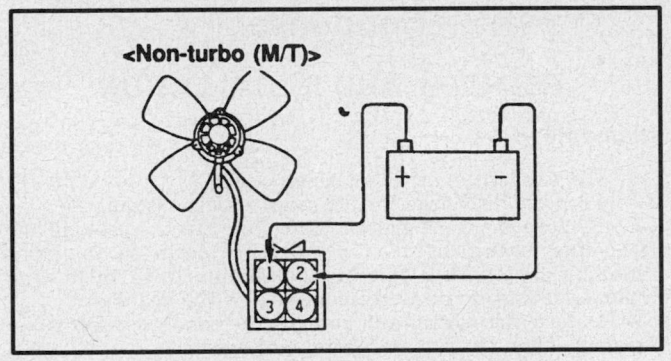

Radiator cooling fan check — 1995 Eclipse

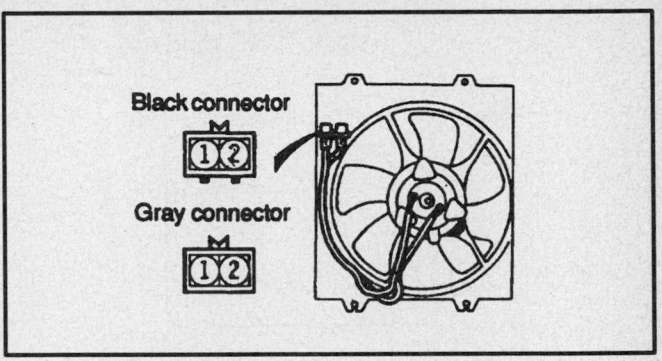

Condenser cooling fan check — Galant

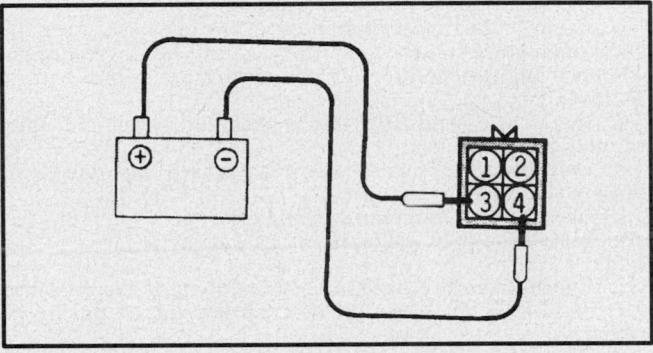

Condenser cooling fan check — 1993−94 Eclipse

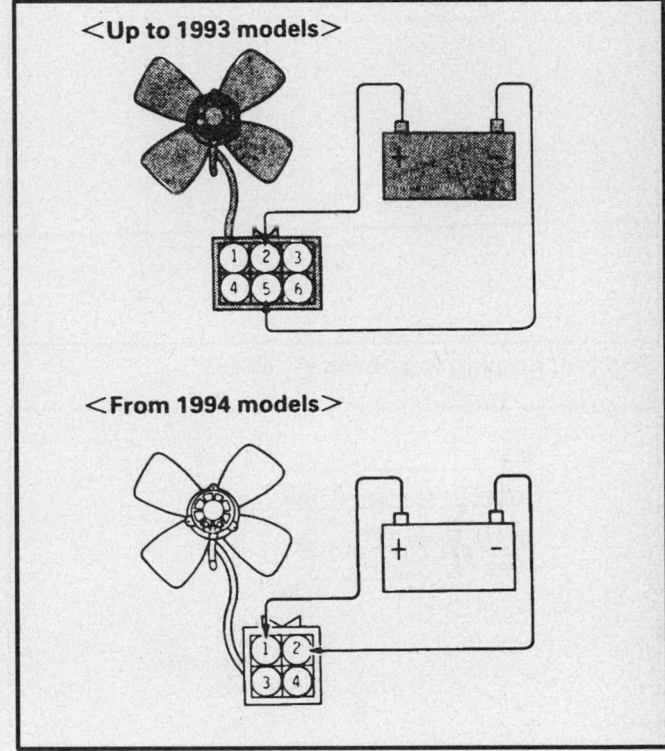

Radiator cooling fan check — Diamante

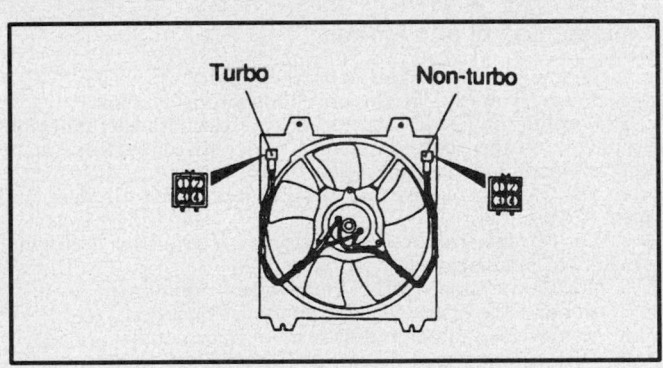

Condenser cooling fan check — 1995 Eclipse

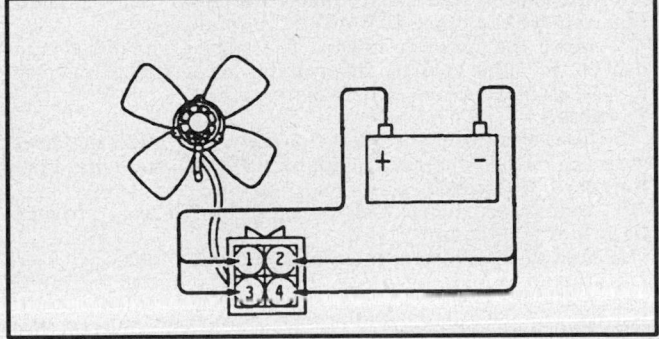

Radiator cooling fan check — Galant

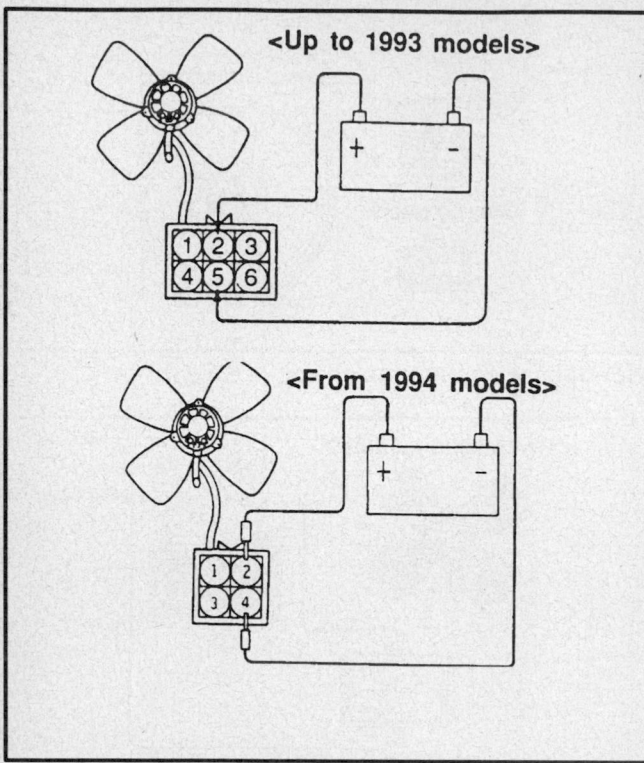

Radiator cooling fan check — 3000GT

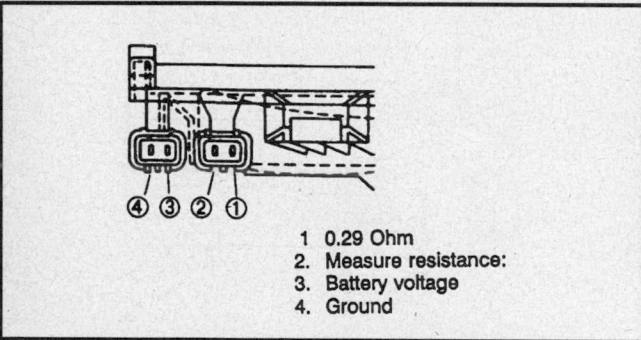

1. 0.29 Ohm
2. Measure resistance:
3. Battery voltage
4. Ground

Condenser cooling fan check — Diamante and 3000GT

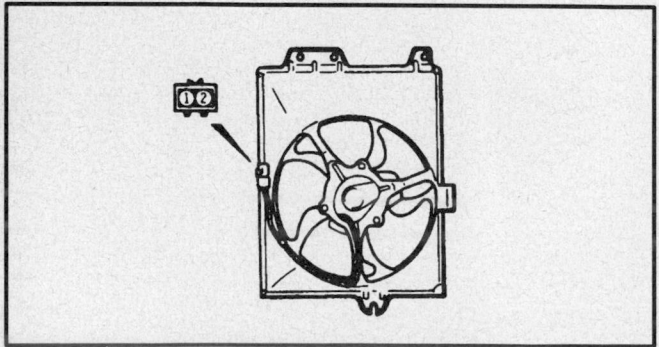

Condenser cooling fan check — Mirage

Condenser

REMOVAL AND INSTALLATION

Diamante

1. Disconnect the negative battery cable.
2. Properly discharge the air conditioning system.
3. Remove the front grille after taking out the parking and front side market lights. Carefully pry down on the grille retaining clips with a flat-blade tool to release them. Also remove the 2 grille reinforcements below the headlights.
4. Detach the wiring and remove the condenser fan motor assembly, then the radiator fan motor assembly.
5. Remove the 2 A/C refrigerant lines from the condenser, using appropriate wrenches to protect the fittings. Cap all openings to minimize contamination.
6. Remove the upper insulator mounting bolts, then the lower insulator/retainer and carefully lift out the condenser while moving the radiator slightly toward the engine.

To install:

7. Install the condenser and attach the lower and upper support insulators.
8. Using new lubricated O-rings, attach the refrigerant lines to the condenser.
9. Install both fan motor assemblies.
10. Install the front grille, then connect the negative battery cable.
11. Evacuate and recharge the A/C system. If the condenser was replaced, add 0.5 oz. of new refrigerant oil during the recharge.
12. Connect the negative battery cable and check the entire climate control system for proper operation and leaks.

Eclipse, Galant and Mirage

1. Disconnect the negative battery cable.
2. Properly discharge the air conditioning system.
3. Unplug the needed connector(s). Most of these connectors employ a waterproof connector. When disconnecting, make sure all parts of the connectors remain intact.
4. On Galant, remove air intake duct turbo air hose and pipe, if equipped.
5. On Mirage, remove the battery, battery tray and windshield washer reservoir.
6. On 1995 Eclipse Turbo, remove the radiator.
7. Remove the condenser fan motor assembly
8. Remove the upper radiator mounts or mounting bolts.
9. Disconnect the refrigerant lines from the condenser. Cover the exposed ends of the lines to minimize contamination.
10. On 1993 Galant, disconnect the power relay assembly, then remove the brace in front of the condenser.
11. Move the radiator toward the engine and lift the condenser from the vehicle. Inspect the lower rubber mounting insulators and replace, if necessary.

To install:

12. Lower the condenser into position and align the dowels with the lower mounting insulators. Install the bolts. Install the brace, if removed.
13. Using new lubricated O-rings, attach the refrigerant lines to the condenser
14. Install the radiator mounts and cooling fans.
15. Install remaining parts that were removed during the removal procedure.
16. Evacuate and recharge the air conditioning system. If the condenser was replaced, add 0.5 oz. of refrigerant oil for all

models, except 1995 Eclipse non–turbo which uses 1.35 oz. of refrigerant oil during the recharge.

17. Connect the negative battery cable and check the entire climate control system for proper operation and leaks.

Precis

1. Disconnect the negative battery cable.
2. Properly discharge the air conditioning system.
3. To disconnect the high pressure inlet hose from the condenser, perform the following:
   - Install the special tool 09977–33600 or equivalent, on the coupling.
   - Push the special tool onto the cage opening to release the female fitting from the garter spring.
   - Pull the fitting apart and remove the tool from the coupling.
   - Cover the exposed ends of the lines to minimize contamination.
4. Remove the grille assembly.
5. Remove the radiator.
6. Disconnect the outlet high pressure line from the condenser.
7. Remove the mounting bolts and remove the condenser from the vehicle.

To install:
8. Install the condenser and mounting bolts.
9. Replace the O–rings, lubricate and connect the suction line to the condenser.
10. Install the radiator.
11. Install the grille assembly.
12. To connect the discharge hose to the condenser, perform the following:
   - Check for a missing or damaged garter spring. Replace as necessary.
   - Thoroughly clean and dry the fittings, install a new O–ring and lubricate.
   - Assemble the fitting by pushing with a slight twisting motion.
   - To visually verify positive engagement, make sure the garter spring is over the flared end of the female fitting.
13. Fill the cooling system.
14. If the condenser was replaced, add 1.1 oz. of refrigerant oil during the recharge. Evacuate and recharge the system.
15. Connect the negative battery cable and check the entire climate control system for proper operation and leaks.

3000GT

1. Disconnect the negative battery cable.
2. Properly discharge the air conditioning system.
3. If equipped with automatic air conditioning system, remove the ductwork on top of the engine.
4. Remove the alternator.
5. Disconnect the electrical leads and then remove the condenser fan motor assembly.
6. Detach the electrical connections and remove the radiator fan motor assembly.
7. Remove the upper radiator/condenser insulator bolts.
8. Using two wrenches on the flare nut fittings, detach the high pressure A/C lines from the condenser. Discard the O–rings.
9. Move the radiator toward the engine and carefully lift out the condenser.

To install:
10. Position the condenser carefully into place and reattach the condenser A/C lines, using new, lubricated O–rings.
11. Install the upper radiator/condenser insulator bolts.
12. Reinstall both fan motor assemblies and reconnect their respective electrical connections.
13. Install the alternator and adjust the belt.
14. Reinstall the air duct work, as removed.

15. Properly evacuate and recharge the system. If the condenser was replaced, add 0.5 oz. of new refrigerant oil during the recharge.

16. Connect the negative battery cable and check the entire climate control system for proper operation and leaks.

Compressor

REMOVAL AND INSTALLATION

Diamante and 3000GT

1. Disconnect the negative battery cable.
2. Properly discharge the air conditioning system.
3. On 3000GT, if equipped with automatic air conditioning, remove the air ductwork on top of the engine as required for access to the compressor.
4. Remove the compressor drive belt.
5. Remove the condenser fan motor assembly (except Diamante with SOHC engine).
6. Disconnect the refrigerant lines from the compressor, discard O–rings, capping all openings to minimize contamination.
7. Detach the electrical connections from the compressor.
8. Remove the alternator drive belt and remove the alternator (except Diamante with SOHC engine).
9. Remove the compressor.

To install:
10. Check and adjust level of compressor oil. Install the compressor and torque the mounting bolts. Connect the clutch coil connector.
11. Reinstall the alternator (if removed) and adjust its drive belt.
12. Using new, lubricated O–rings, attach the A/C lines to the compressor.
13. Install the condenser fan motor, if removed.
14. Install and adjust the compressor drive belt.
15. Install the air ductwork as removed.
16. Evacuate and recharge the system.
17. Connect the negative battery cable and check the entire climate control system for proper operation and leaks.

Eclipse, Galant, Mirage and Precis

1. Disconnect the negative battery cable.
2. Properly discharge the air conditioning system.
3. On Eclipse and Precis, remove the distributor cap and wires.
4. On Galant and 1995 Eclipse non–turbo, remove the under cover side panel, if necessary.
5. On 1993–94 Eclipse 2.0L engine AWD, remove the center bearing bracket bolt.
6. Remove the tensioner pulley and bracket, then remove the compressor drive belt.
7. Disconnect the clutch coil connector and the refrigerant temperature connector, if equipped, from the compressor.
8. Disconnect the refrigerant lines from the compressor and discard the O–rings. Cover the exposed ends of the lines and openings to the compressor to minimize contamination.
9. Remove the compressor mounting bolts, compressor and bracket.

To install:
10. Check and adjust level of compressor oil. Install the compressor and torque the mounting bolts. Connect the clutch coil connector.
11. Using new lubricated O–rings, connect the refrigerant lines to the compressor.
12. Reattach the electrical connections.
13. Install the compressor belt and tensioner pulley. If removed, install the alternator belt. Adjust the belts to specifications.
14. Install the distributor cap and wires, if removed.

15. Install under cover side panel, if removed.
16. Install center bearing bracket bolt, if removed.
17. Evacuate and recharge the air conditioning system.
18. Connect the negative battery cable and check the entire climate control system for proper operation and leaks.

Receiver/Drier

REMOVAL AND INSTALLATION

NOTE: The receiver/drier must be replaced any time there is evidence of moisture in the system, if the system is left open for more than 24 hours, if the receiver/drier is plugged or if a major component (compressor, condenser, evaporator or refrigerant line) has been replaced.

1. Disconnect the negative battery cable.
2. Properly discharge the air conditioning system.
3. On Galant, remove the coolant reservoir tank.
4. Disconnect the electrical connector from the pressure switch on the receiver/drier.
5. On Eclipse, it may be necessary to remove the radiator and condenser cooling fan assemblies and remove the upper radiator insulators to gain access to receiver/drier in front of the condenser.
6. Disconnect the refrigerant lines from the receiver/drier assembly. Cover the exposed ends of the lines to minimize contamination.
7. On Galant, remove the receiver/drier cover.
8. Remove the mounting strap and the receiver/drier from its bracket. Remove the receiver/drier.
To install:
9. Assemble a new receiver/drier to its mounting strap and install. Install the cover on Galant.
10. Using new lubricated O-rings, connect the refrigerant lines to the receiver/drier.
11. Attach the connector to the pressure switch.
12. Install the coolant reservoir tank, if removed.
13. Evacuate and recharge the air conditioning system. If the receiver/drier was replaced, add 0.33 oz. of refrigerant oil during the recharge.
14. Connect the negative battery cable and check the entire climate control system for proper operation and leaks.

Expansion Valve

REMOVAL AND INSTALLATION

Diamante, Eclipse, Galant, Mirage and 3000GT

1. Disconnect the negative battery cable.

NOTE: If equipped with an air bag, wait for 1 minute to elapse before working inside the vehicle. The air bag system is set to deploy for a short period of time after the battery is disconnected.

2. Properly discharge the air conditioning system.
3. Remove the evaporator assembly and separate the upper and lower cases.
4. Remove the expansion valve from the evaporator lines using 2 wrenches to loosen the flared nut.
5. The installation is the reverse of the removal procedure. Use new lubricated O-rings when assembling.
6. Evacuate and recharge the air conditioning system.
7. Connect the negative battery cable and check the entire climate control system for proper operation and leaks.

Fixed Orifice Tube

REMOVAL AND INSTALLATION

Precis

NOTE: The fixed orifice tube in a non-serviceable part. The orifice tube is located within the liquid line near the evaporator and cannot be removed from the line. If the orifice tube is defective, the liquid line assembly must be replaced. The fixed orifice tube should also be replaced whenever the compressor is replaced.

1. Disconnect the negative battery cable.

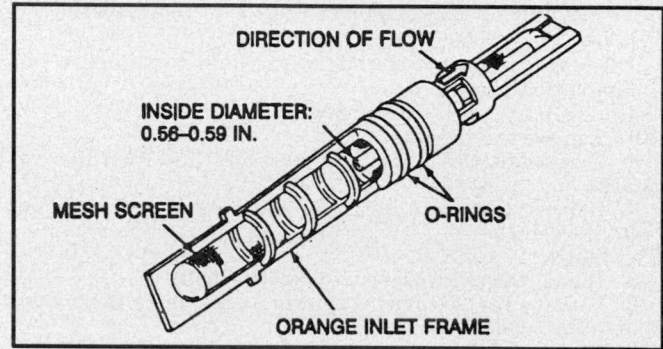

Fixed orifice tube — Precis

2. Properly discharge the air conditioning system.
3. Disconnect the liquid line from the evaporator and the condenser.
4. Remove the brackets retaining the liquid line in place and remove the line.
To install:
5. Using new lubricated O-rings, install the liquid line to the evaporator and condenser.
6. Secure the liquid line with the retaining brackets.
7. Evacuate and recharge the air conditioning system.
8. Connect the negative battery cable and check the entire climate control system for proper operation and leaks.

Blower Motor

REMOVAL AND INSTALLATION

Diamante

1. Disconnect the negative battery cable.
2. Remove the glove box assembly and the outer case.
3. Remove the passenger side lower instrument panel cover, the floor air duct and the reinforcement behind the glove box opening.
4. Remove the evaporator case mounting bolt (top) and nut (bottom). Remove the fresh/recirc air damper motor assembly.
5. Remove the Multi-port Fuel Injection (MFI) relay and control unit after detaching electrical connections.
6. Remove the small panel bracket on the right side.
7. Remove the blower assembly and disassemble on the bench as needed.
To install:
8. Reverse the removal procedure to install components. Connect the negative battery cable and check the entire climate control system for proper operation.

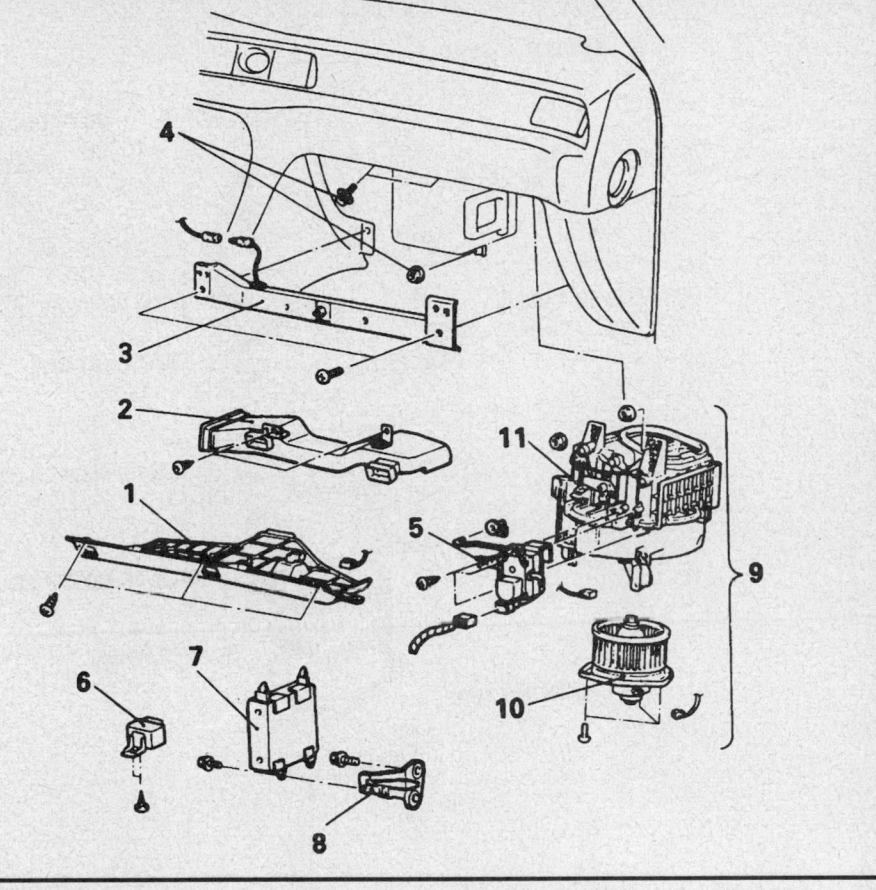

1. Right side lower cover
2. Floor duct
3. Glove box frame
4. Evaporator bolt and nut
5. Fresh/recirc air damper motor assembly
6. MFI control relay
7. MFI control unit
8. Right side lower bracket
9. Blower assembly
10. Blower motor
11. Blower case

Exploded view of the blower assembly — Diamante

Eclipse

1. Disconnect battery negative cable.
2. Remove the right side duct.
3. Remove the molded hose from the blower assembly.
4. For 1995 models, remove automatic compressor ECM.
5. Remove the blower motor assembly.
6. Remove the packing seal.
7. Remove the fan retaining nut and fan in order to replace the motor.

To install:

8. Check that the blower motor shaft is not bent and that the packing is in good condition. Clean all parts of dust, etc.
9. Assemble the motor and fan. Install the blower motor then connect the connector.
10. Install the automatic compressor ECM, if removed.
11. Install the molded hose. Install the duct.
12. Connect the negative battery cable and check the entire climate control system for proper operation

Mirage and Galant

1. Disconnect the negative battery cable.
2. Remove the glove box assembly and the speaker cover to the lower right of the glove box.
3. Remove the passenger side lower cowl side trim kick panel.
4. Remove the glove box frame along the top of glove box opening.
5. Remove the lap heater duct if obstructing access to blower assembly. If equipped with A/C, remove evaporator mounting nut.

6. Disconnect the electrical connector from the blower motor.
7. Remove the cooling tube from the blower assembly.
8. Remove the automatic compressor ECM.
9. Remove the blower motor assembly and disassemble on a workbench.

To install:

10. Assemble the motor and fan. Install the blower motor assembly and connect the wiring and cooling tube.
11. Install automatic compressor ECM.
12. Install the lap heater duct and evaporator mounting nuts, if removed.
13. Install the glove box frame, interior trim pieces and glove box assembly.
14. Connect the negative battery cable and check the entire climate control system for proper operation.

Precis

1. Disconnect the negative battery cable.
2. Remove the glove box assembly and the instrument panel cover around the glove box.
3. Disconnect the resistor and blower motor connectors.
4. Remove the motor cooling tube.
5. Remove the attaching screws and remove the blower assembly from the blower case and disassemble.

To install:

6. Position the blower motor into the blower case and install the attaching screws.
7. Install the cooling tube.
8. Connect the resistor and blower motor wire connector.

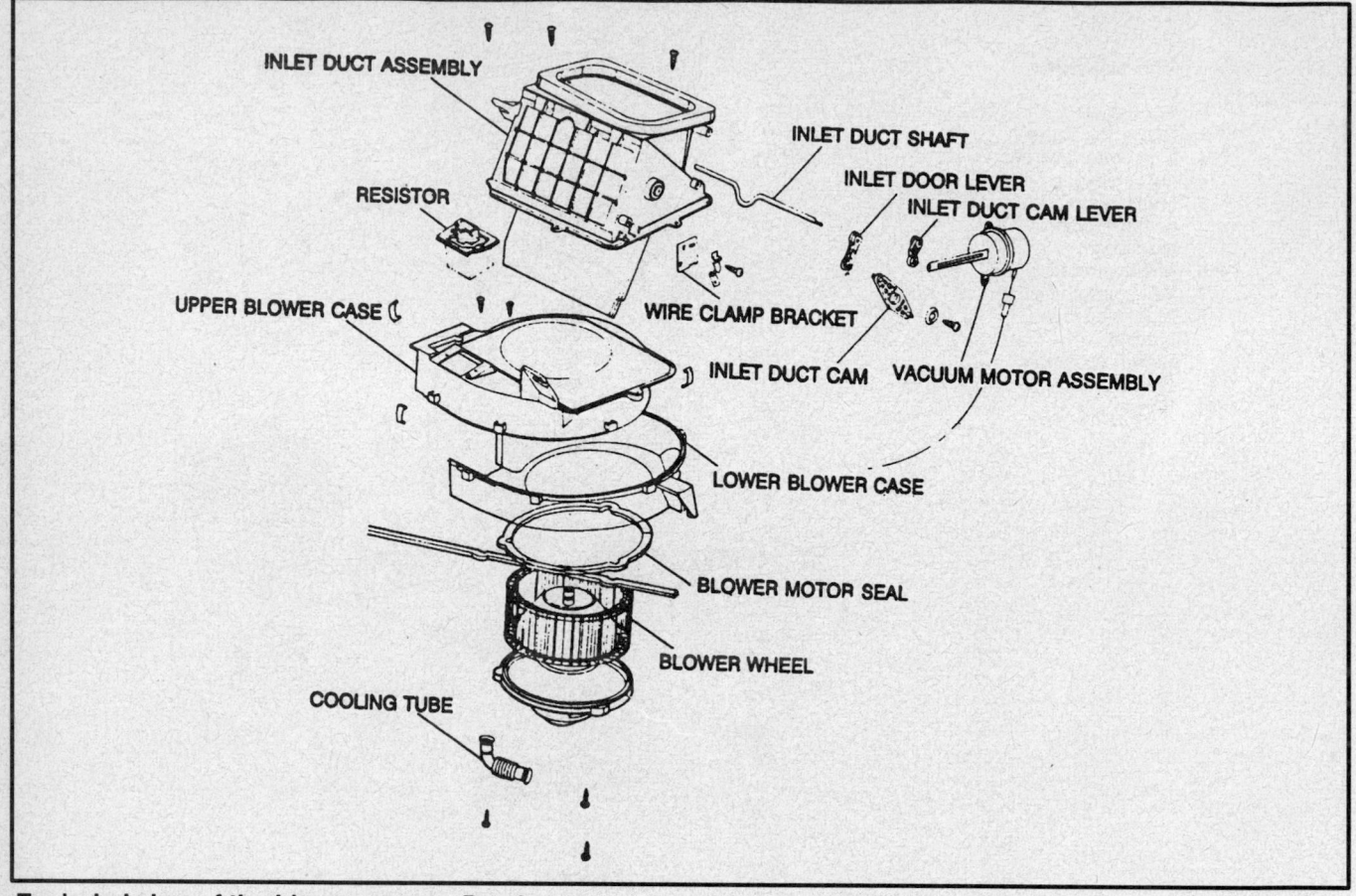

Exploded view of the blower case — Precis

9. Install the instrument panel under cover and glove box assembly.
10. Connect the negative battery cable and check the blower for proper operation.

3000GT

1. Disconnect the negative battery cable.
2. Remove the stopper, glove box, outer case, lower cover and bracket.
3. Remove the evaporator case mounting bolt and nut from the upper left corner and lower right corner of the case.
4. Detach the air selection control cable (or vacuum line if equipped with full automatic A/C).
5. Remove the frame piece at the right side.
6. Detach the electrical connector and remove the blower assembly.
7. Reverse removal procedure to install components. Check system for proper operation.

Blower Motor Resistor

REMOVAL AND INSTALLATION

Eclipse, Galant, Mirage, Precis and Manual A/C 3000GT

NOTE: If equipped with an air bag, wait for 1 minute to elapse before working inside the vehicle. The air bag system is set to deploy for a short period of time after the battery is disconnected.

1. Disconnect the negative battery cable.
2. Remove the glove box assembly. The resistor is accessible through the glove box opening and is mounted to the blower or evaporator case.
3. Disconnect the wire harness from the resistor.

4. Remove the mounting screws and remove the resistor.

5. The installation is the reverse of the removal procedure. Make sure the seal is intact when installing.

6. Connect the negative battery cable and check the entire climate control system for proper operation.

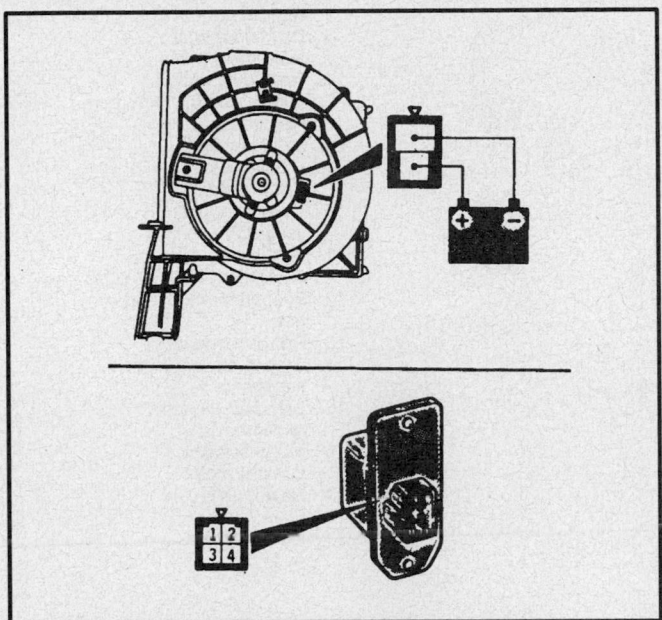

Checking blower motor and resistor — Mirage

TESTING

1. Using a digital volt/ohmmeter, check resistance values between terminals.

2. Values for 1995 Eclipse should be: 1.83 ohms between terminals **2** and **3**; 0.87 ohms between terminals **3** and **4**; and 0.31 ohms between terminals **1** and **3**.

3. Other models have similar resistance values.

Blower Motor Power Transistor

REMOVAL AND INSTALLATION

Diamante and Full Auto A/C 3000GT

NOTE: If equipped with an air bag, wait for 1 minute to elapse before working inside the vehicle. The air bag system is set to deploy for a short period of time after the battery is disconnected.

1. Disconnect the negative battery cable.

2. Remove the glove box assembly. The power transistor is accessible through the glove box opening and is mounted to the blower or evaporator case.

3. Disconnect the wire harness from the power transistor

4. Remove the mounting screws and remove the power transistor.

5. Reverse the removal procedure to install components.

6. Connect the negative battery cable and check the entire climate control system for proper operation.

Heater Core

REMOVAL AND INSTALLATION

Diamante

NOTE: If equipped with an air bag, wait for 1 minute after disconnecting the negative battery cable before working inside the vehicle. The air bag system is set to deploy for a short period of time after the battery is disconnected.

1. Disconnect negative battery cable.

2. Drain the coolant and disconnect the heater hoses from the core tubes at the firewall.

NOTE: To prevent damage to the air bag control unit during removal or installation of the floor console, avoid shocks or impact. Do not drop.

3. To remove the floor console, perform the following:
- Remove the floor console switch panel.
- Remove the retaining screws.
- Remove the floor console assembly.

4. Locate the rectangular plugs in the knee protector on either side of the steering column. Pry these plugs out and remove the screws.

5. Remove panel below glove box, then remove the right floor duct.

6. Remove the cover below the steering column and remove the two brackets behind the cover.

7. Remove the steering column cover.

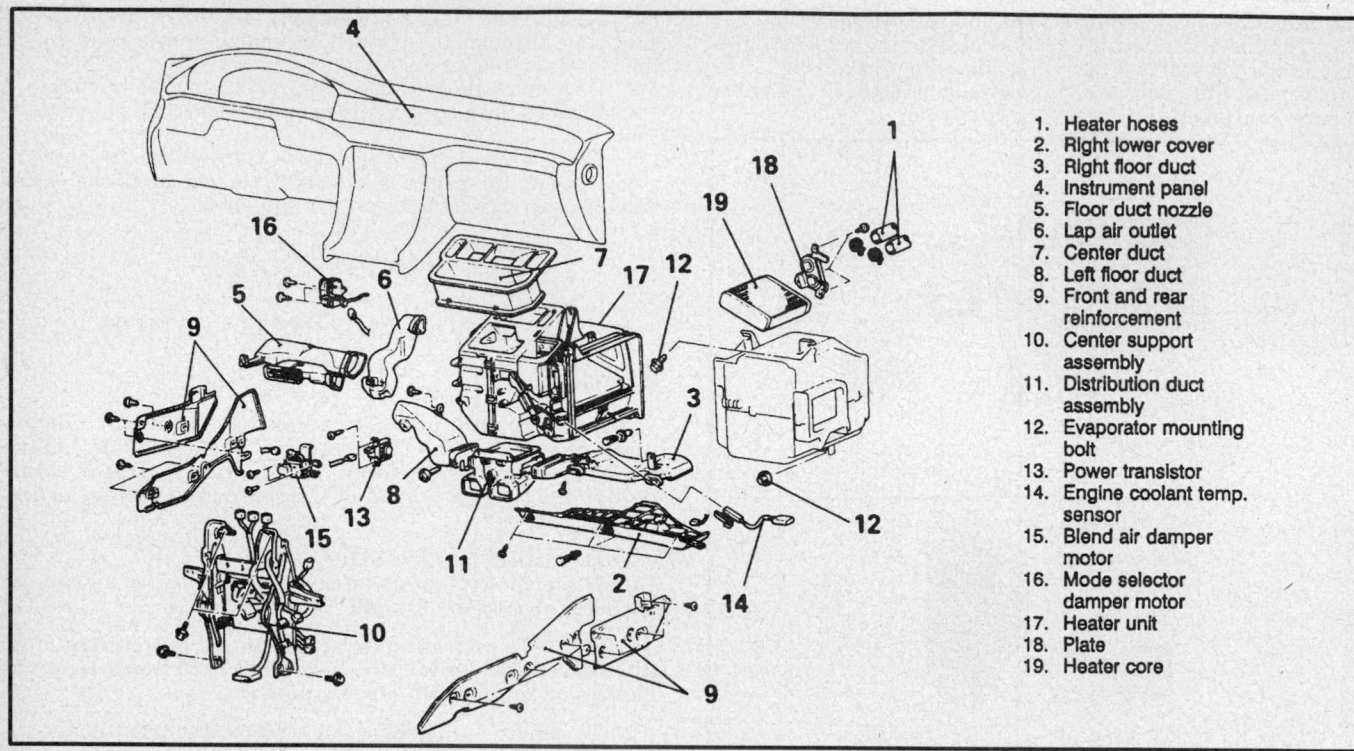

1. Heater hoses
2. Right lower cover
3. Right floor duct
4. Instrument panel
5. Floor duct nozzle
6. Lap air outlet
7. Center duct
8. Left floor duct
9. Front and rear reinforcement
10. Center support assembly
11. Distribution duct assembly
12. Evaporator mounting bolt
13. Power transistor
14. Engine coolant temp. sensor
15. Blend air damper motor
16. Mode selector damper motor
17. Heater unit
18. Plate
19. Heater core

Heater case and related components — Diamante

8. Remove the glove box assembly, outer case and glove box light switch.

9. Remove passenger side air bag module and disconnect harness connector, if equipped.

NOTE: The air bag module should be stored on a flat surface and placed so that the pad surface is facing upwards. Do not drop.

10. Remove the bezel around the radio panel, then remove the radio assembly.

11. Remove the cup holder.

12. Remove the speakers from the top of the instrument panel.

13. Remove the instrument cluster bezel and then the instrument cluster.

14. Remove the speedometer cable adapter locking piece, pull the speedometer cable slightly into the passenger compartment and remove the adapter.

15. Remove the steering column bolts and lower the column.

16. Detach the harness connectors at the lower left side of the instrument panel.

17. Remove the instrument panel mounting hardware and remove the instrument panel from the vehicle.

18. Remove the left floor duct nozzle, the left lap air duct, the upper center air duct and the left floor duct.

19. Remove the front and rear center reinforcements, then the center reinforcement assembly.

20. Remove the center distribution duct assembly.

21. Remove the evaporator case mounting bolt and nut to allow clearance for heater unit removal.

22. Detach and remove the power transistor, the heater coolant temperature sensor and the air mix and outlet selector damper motor assemblies.

23. Remove the heater unit.

24. Reverse removal procedure to install components. Check system for proper operation and leaks.

1993–94 Eclipse

1. Disconnect the negative battery cable.

2. Drain the coolant and disconnect the heater hoses from the core tubes at the firewall.

3. Properly discharge the air conditioning system and disconnect the refrigerant lines from the evaporator, if equipped. Cover the exposed ends of the lines to minimize contamination.

4. To remove the floor console, perform the following:
  • Remove the plugs, then the screws retaining the side covers and the small cover piece in front of the shifter.
  • Remove the shifter knob, (manual transmission), and the cup holder. Remove both small pieces of upholstery to gain access to retainer screws.
  • Disconnect both electrical connectors at the front of the console.
  • Remove the shoulder harness guide plates, if equipped.
  • Remove the retaining screws.
  • Remove the floor console assembly.

5. Locate the rectangular plugs in the knee protector on either side of the steering column. Pry these plugs out and remove the screws. Remove the screws from the hood lock release lever and the knee protector.

6. Remove the steering column covers.

7. Remove the instrument cluster bezel.

8. Remove the bezel around the radio panel, then remove the radio assembly.

9. Remove the center air outlet assembly by reaching through the grille and pushing the side clips out with a small flat-tipped tool while carefully prying the outlet free.

10. Pull the heater control knobs off and remove the heater control panel assembly.

11. Remove the glove box assembly.

12. Remove the instrument gauge cluster and the speedometer adapter by disconnecting the speedometer cable at the transaxle, pulling the cable slightly towards the vehicle interior, then giving a slight twist on the adapter to release it.

13. Remove the left and right speaker covers from the top of the instrument panel.

14. Remove the center plate below the heater controls.

15. Remove the heater control assembly.

16. Remove the lower air ducts.

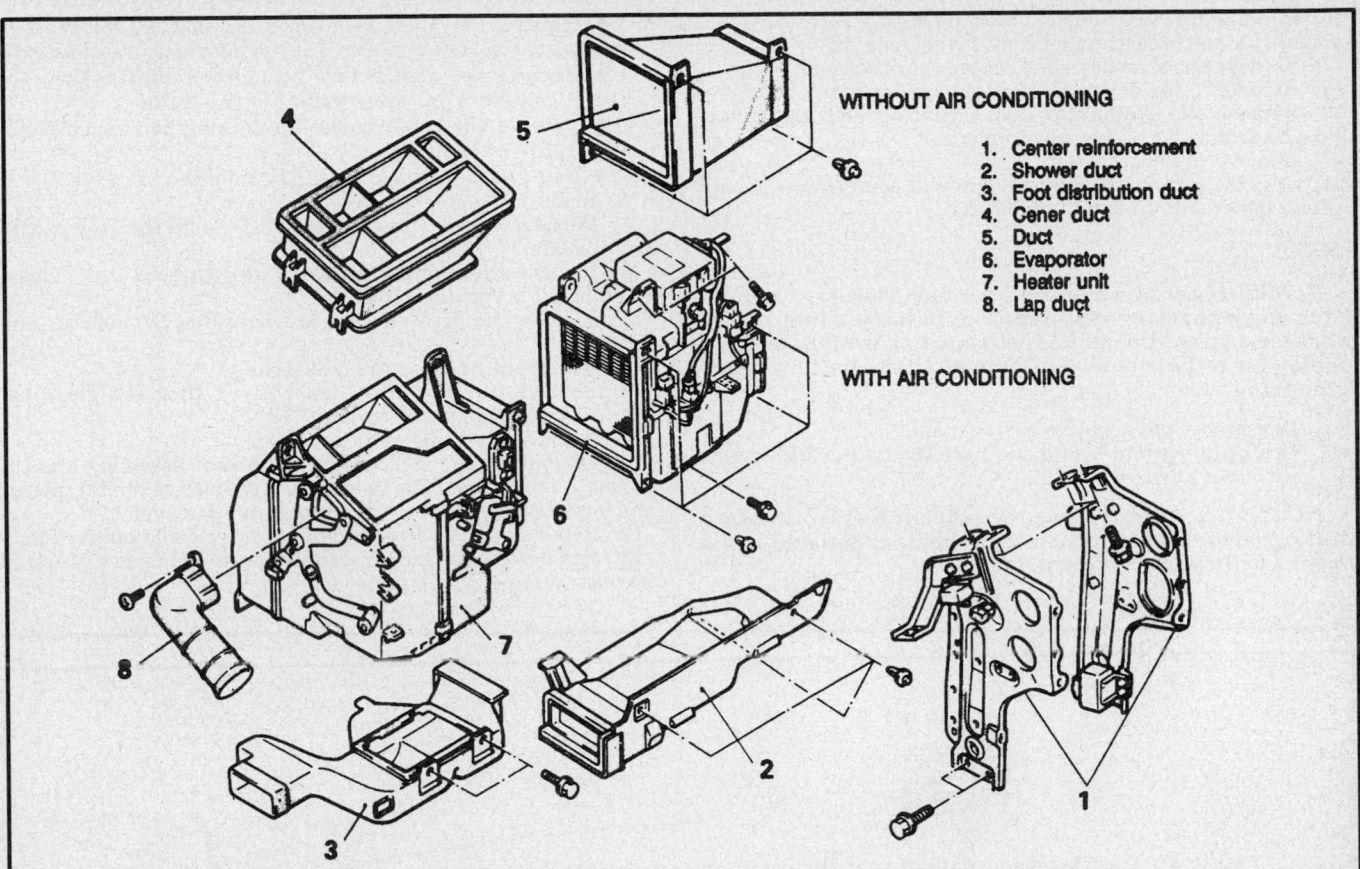

WITHOUT AIR CONDITIONING

1. Center reinforcement
2. Shower duct
3. Foot distribution duct
4. Cener duct
5. Duct
6. Evaporator
7. Heater unit
8. Lap duct

WITH AIR CONDITIONING

Heater case and related components — Eclipse

17. Remove the steering shaft support bolts and lower the steering column.
18. Remove the instrument panel mounting hardware and remove the instrument panel from the vehicle.
19. Remove both stamped steel center reinforcement pieces.
20. Remove the lower ductwork from the heater box.
21. Remove the upper center duct.
22. Vehicles without air conditioning will have a square duct in place of the evaporator; remove this duct if present. On vehicles with air conditioning, remove the evaporator assembly.
23. Remove the wiring harness connectors and the electronic control unit.
24. Remove the heater unit. To prevent bolts from falling inside the blower assembly, set the inside/outside air–selection damper to the position that permits outside air introduction.
25. Remove the cover plate around the heater tubes and remove the core fastener clips. Pull the heater core from the heater box, being careful not to damage the fins or tank ends.
26. Reverse removal procedure to install components. Check system for proper operation and leaks.

1995 Eclipse

NOTE: If equipped with an air bag, wait for 1 minute after disconnecting the negative battery cable before working inside the vehicle. The air bag system is set to deploy for a short period of time after the battery is disconnected.

1. Disconnect the negative battery cable.
2. Drain the coolant and disconnect the heater hoses from the core tubes at the firewall. Do not allow coolant to damage the vehicle speed sensor located below the heater hoses on non–turbo manual transmission vehicles.

NOTE: To prevent damage to the air bag control unit during removal or installation of the floor console, avoid shocks or impact. Do not drop.

3. To remove the floor console, perform the following:
   ● Remove center console trim panel.
   ● Remove the ashtray and cupholder assembly.
   ● Remove shift lever knob on manual transmission.
   ● Remove the retaining screws.
   ● Remove the floor console assembly.
4. Locate the rectangular plugs in the knee protector on either side of the steering column. Pry these plugs out and remove the screws.
5. Remove drivers side air bag assembly, steering wheel and passenger side air bag assembly.

NOTE: The air bag module should be stored on a flat surface with the pad facing upwards. Do not drop.

6. Remove the lap cooler duct and steering column covers.
7. Remove the instrument cluster bezel and then the instrument cluster.
8. Remove the radio.
9. Remove the glove box.
10. Remove passenger side air bag, storing on a flat surface with the pad facing upwards. Do not drop.
11. Remove the center air outlet assembly.
12. Remove hood release handle and lower cover.
13. Remove heater control assembly.
14. Remove front speakers and instrument panel switch.
15. Remove the steering shaft support bolts and lower the steering column.

16. Remove the instrument panel mounting hardware and remove the instrument panel from the vehicle.

17. Remove the stamped steel center reinforcement.

18. Remove lower ductwork from the heater box.

19. Remove the evaporator case mounting bolt and nut to allow clearance for heater unit removal.

20. Remove the heater unit.

21. Reverse removal procedure to install components. Check system for proper operation and leaks.

Galant

NOTE: If equipped with an air bag, wait for 1 minute after disconnecting the negative battery cable before working inside the vehicle. The air bag system is set to deploy for a short period of time after the battery is disconnected.

1. Disconnect the negative battery cable.

2. Drain the coolant and disconnect the heater hoses from the core tubes at the firewall.

NOTE: To prevent damage to the air bag control unit during removal or installation of the floor console, avoid shocks or impact. Do not drop.

3. To remove the floor console, perform the following:

• Remove the shift lever knob on manual transmission vehicles or the shift indicator plate on automatic transmissions.

• Remove the coin holder behind the shifter, then the center console trim cover in front of the shifter.

• Remove the center console retaining bolt cover plugs, then remove the bolts.

• Remove the console assembly, then the brackets.

4. Remove the steering column covers.

5. Remove the instrument cluster bezel and then the instrument cluster.

6. Remove the instrument panel switch, hood lock release handle and lower duct work.

7. Remove the driver's knee protector and left side air outlet cover.

8. Remove the center panel assembly.

9. Remove the glove box under cover, then the glove box and the right side panel cover.

10. Remove the radio and cupholder.

11. Disconnect the cables from the heater assembly and the blower, then pull out the heater control panel assembly, noting the location of the boss in the center reinforcement.

12. Remove cool air bypass damper lever cable connection..

13. Remove the passenger side air bag module and disconnect harness connector, if equipped.

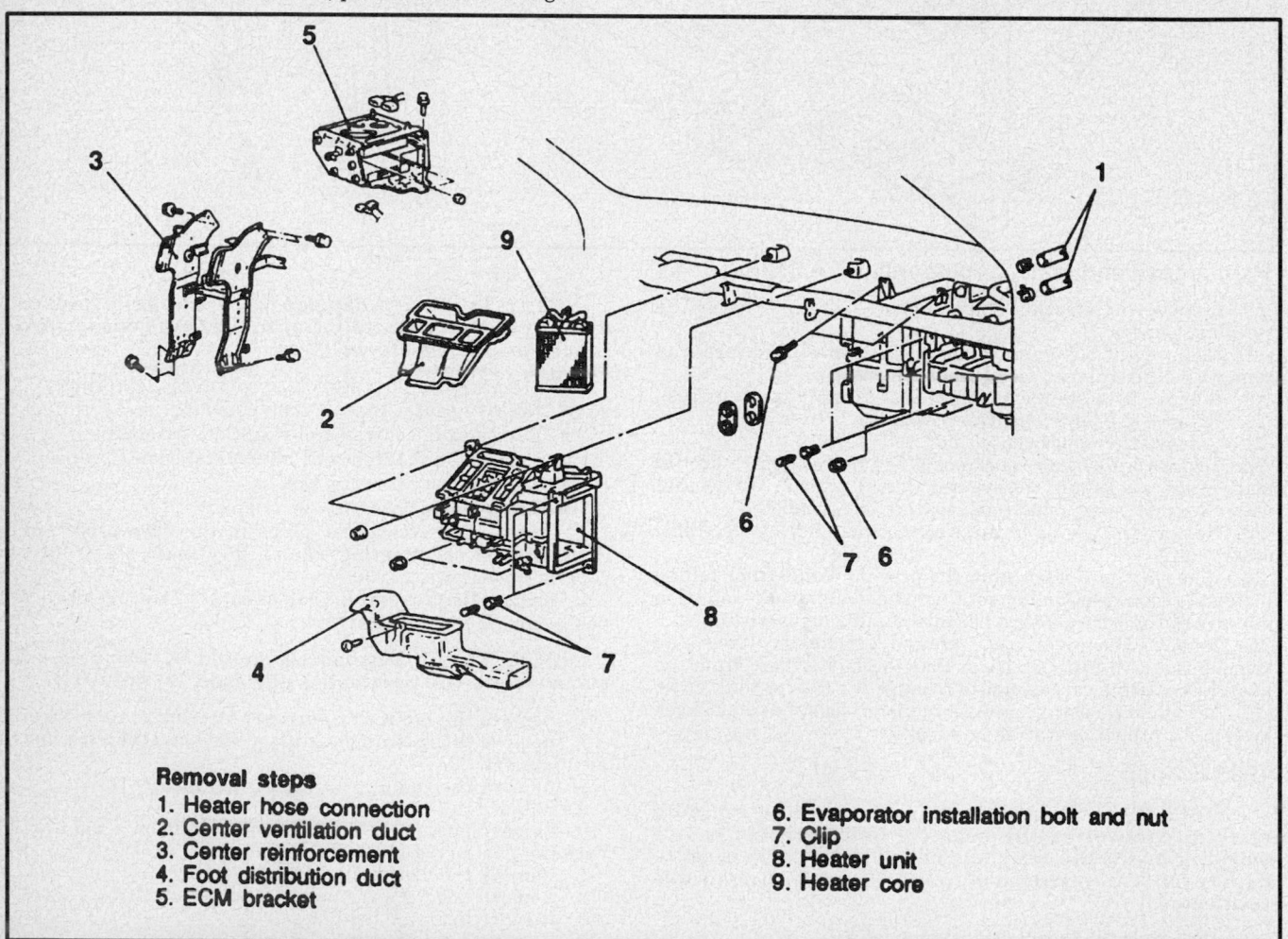

Removal steps

1. Heater hose connection
2. Center ventilation duct
3. Center reinforcement
4. Foot distribution duct
5. ECM bracket

6. Evaporator installation bolt and nut
7. Clip
8. Heater unit
9. Heater core

Heater case and related components — Galant

NOTE: The air bag module should be stored on a flat surface and placed so that the pad surface is facing upwards. Do not drop.

14. Remove the steering column bolts and lower the column.
15. Detach the harness connector at the lower left side of the instrument panel.
16. Remove the instrument panel mounting hardware and remove the instrument panel from the vehicle.
17. Remove the joint duct between the heater case and the blower assembly (on models without A/C).
18. Remove both stamped steel center reinforcement pieces
19. Remove the ECM bracket.
20. If equipped with A/C, remove the evaporator retaining nut and remove the heater case assembly. The heater core can now be removed from the case.
21. Reverse removal procedure to install components. Check system for proper operation and leaks.

Mirage

NOTE: If equipped with an air bag, wait for 1 minute after disconnecting the negative battery cable before working inside the vehicle. The air bag system is set to deploy for a short period of time after the battery is disconnected.

1. Disconnect the negative battery cable.
2. Drain the coolant and disconnect the heater hoses from the core tubes at the firewall.

NOTE: To prevent damage to the air bag control unit during removal or installation of the floor console, avoid shocks or impact. Do not drop.

3. To remove the floor console, perform the following:
   • Remove the floor console plate, if equipped and the screw behind the shift mechanism.
   • Remove the seat belt bezel and anchor from rear half of console.
   • Remove the bolts and lift out the rear console box assembly, if equipped.
   • Remove the shifter knob on manual transmission, then take out the front console bolts and remove the console.
   • Remove front console box assembly and bracket.
4. Remove the driver's knee protector and the steering column covers.
5. Remove the instrument cluster bezel and then the instrument cluster.
6. Remove the remote control mirror switch, rheostat or plug from the center panel, then the coin box or rear washer/wiper switch.
7. Remove the left side air outlet cover.
8. Remove the ashtray, the center panel assembly, (detach the air door cable from the heater housing), the radio assembly and the cup holder.
9. Remove the glove box under cover, then the glove box and the right side panel cover.

10. Remove the passenger side air bag module and disconnect harness connector, if equipped.

NOTE: The air bag module should be stored on a flat surface and placed so that the pad surface is facing upwards. Do not drop.

11. Disconnect the remaining cables from the heater assembly and the blower, then pull out the heater control panel assembly, noting the location of the boss in the center reinforcement.
12. Remove the steering column bolts and lower the column.
13. Remove the speedometer cable adapter locking piece, pull the speedometer cable slightly into the passenger compartment and remove the adapter.
14. Detach the harness connector at the lower left side of the instrument panel.
15. Remove the instrument panel mounting hardware and remove the instrument panel from the vehicle.
16. Remove the joint duct between the heater case and the blower assembly (on models without A/C).
17. Remove both stamped steel center reinforcement pieces.
18. If equipped with A/C, remove the evaporator retaining nut and remove the heater case assembly. The heater core can now be removed from the case.
19. Reverse removal procedure to install components. Check system for proper operation and leaks.

Precis

1. Disconnect the negative battery cable. If equipped with air conditioning, properly discharge system.
2. Set the temperature control lever to its **HOTTEST** position and drain the cooling system.
3. Disconnect the heater hoses and the evaporator drain hose, if equipped with A/C.
4. Remove the center console rear screws, rear half of console, shift knob, and front console screws. Lift the console and detach wiring connectors.
5. Remove the glove box, the center panel cover, and the right lower instrument panel section.
6. Remove the heater control panel, detaching cables or vacuum lines and wiring.
7. Remove the instrument panel center support bracket.
8. If equipped with air conditioning, remove the evaporator case.
9. Remove the rear heater duct. Loosen the heater unit retaining bolts and remove the heater unit.
To install:
10. Reassemble the heater core, if required.
11. Install the heater unit and tighten the mounting bolts.
12. Reattach the rear heater duct.
13. Install the evaporator case, if removed.
14. Install the instrument panel center support.
15. Install the heater control panel, reattaching control lines or cables and electrical connections.
16. Install the lower instrument panel section and the glove box.

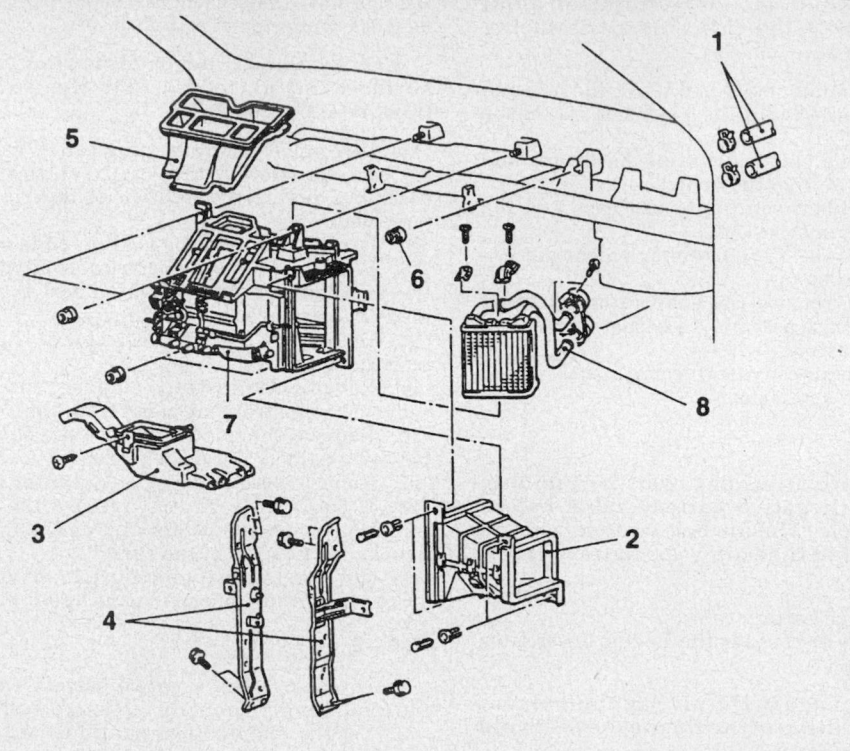

Removal steps

1. Heater hose connection
2. Joint duct
   <Vehicles without air conditioning>
3. Foot duct
4. Center reinforcement

5. Center ventilation duct
6. Evapolator installation nut
   <Vehicles with air conditioning>
7. Heater unit
8. Heater core

Heater case and related components — Mirage

17. Install the instrument panel center cover.
18. Connect the heater hoses and evaporator drain hose, if removed. Fill the cooling system.
19. If equipped with air conditioning, evacuate and recharge the air conditioning system.
20. Connect the negative battery cable and check the entire climate control system for proper operation and leaks.

3000GT

NOTE: If equipped with an air bag, wait for 1 minute after disconnecting the negative battery cable before working inside the vehicle. The air bag system is set to deploy for a short period of time after the battery is disconnected.

1. Disconnect the negative battery cable.
2. Drain the coolant and disconnect the heater hoses from the core tubes at the firewall.

NOTE: To prevent damage to the air bag control unit during removal or installation of the floor console, avoid shocks or impact. Do not drop.

3. To remove the floor console, perform the following:
   - Remove the cup holder and console plug.
   - Remove the rear console.
   - Remove the radio bezel and the radio.
   - Remove the switch bezel.
   - Remove the side covers and front console garnish.
   - Remove the shifter knob on manual transmission.

   - Remove the mounting screws and remove the console assembly.
4. Remove the hood lock release handle from the instrument panel.
5. Remove the interior and dash lights rheostat and switch bezel to its right.
6. Remove the driver's knee protector and the steering column covers.
7. Remove the glove box assembly and outer case.
8. On 1994–95 models, remove the passenger side air bag assembly.

NOTE: The air bag module should be stored on a flat surface with the pad surface facing upwards. Do not drop.

9. Remove the center air outlet assembly.
10. Remove the heater control assembly.
11. Remove the instrument cluster bezel and then the instrument cluster.
12. If equipped with front speakers, remove them. If not remove the plug in their place.
13. On 1993 models, remove the speedometer cable adapter (analog speedometer) by disconnecting the cable from the transaxle, removing the 2 side locking pins and pulling the cable slightly into the passenger compartment until adapter can be removed.
14. Disconnect the wiring harnesses on the right side of the instrument panel.

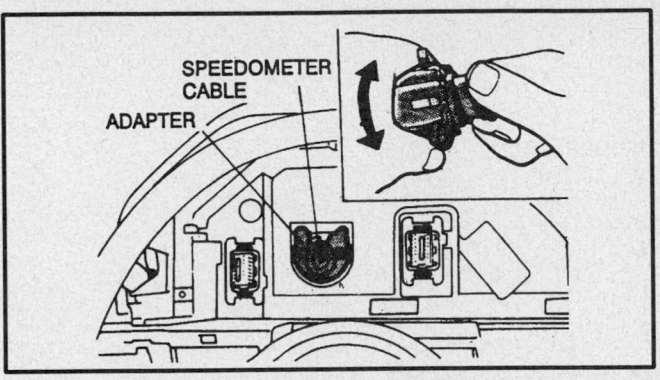

Typical removal of speedometer cable adapter

15. Remove the steering shaft support bolts and lower the steering column.

16. Remove the instrument panel mounting hardware and remove the instrument panel from the vehicle.

17. Remove both stamped steel center reinforcement pieces.

18. Remove the lower trim piece attached to the duct, then the floor ducts and lap duct.

19. If equipped with manual air conditioning, remove the evaporator case mounting bolt and nut to allow clearance for heater unit removal.

20. Remove the center duct above the heater unit.

21. Remove the heater unit. To prevent bolts from falling inside the blower assembly, set the inside/outside air–selection damper to the position that permits outside air introduction.

22. Remove the cover plate around the heater tubes and remove the core fastener clips. Pull the heater core from the heater box, being careful not to damage the fins or tank ends.

23. Reverse removal procedure to install components. Check system for proper operation and leaks.

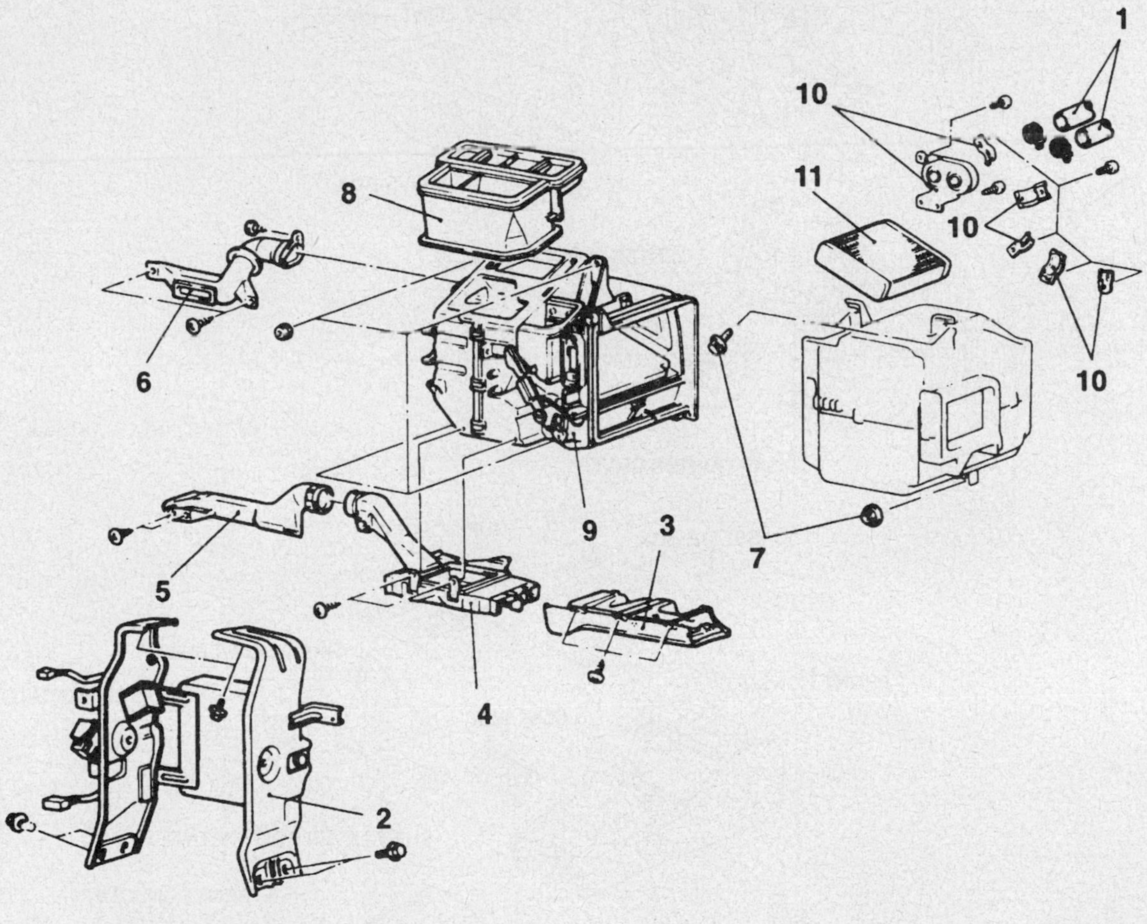

Removal steps

1. Water hoses connection
2. Center reinforcement
3. Under cover
4. Distribution duct (foot)
5. Foot shower duct
6. Lap cooler duct

7. Evaporator mounting bolt and nut <Vehicles with air conditioning>
8. Center duct
9. Heater unit
10. Plate
11. Heater core

Heater case and related components — 3000GT

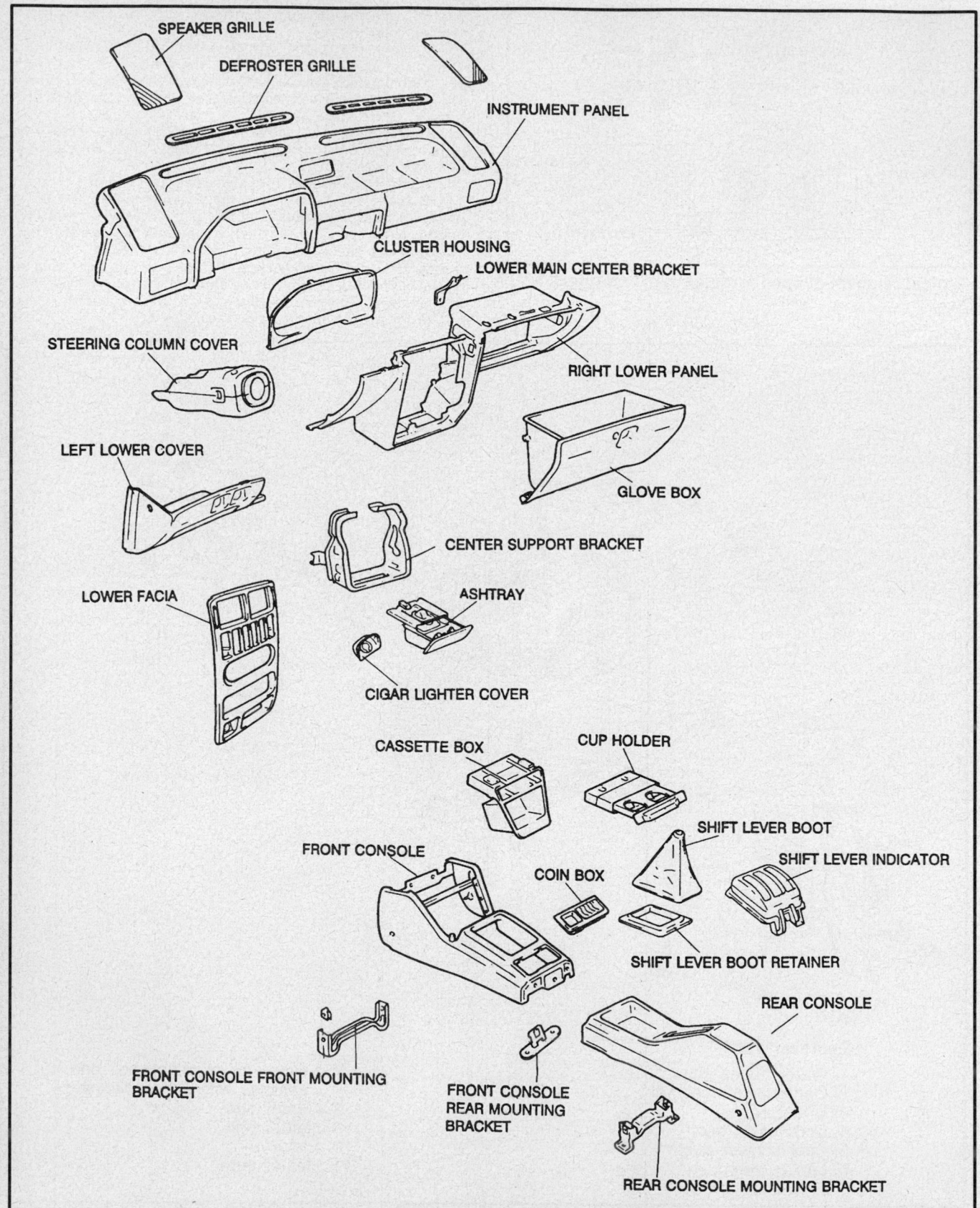

Floor console and instrument panel components — Precis

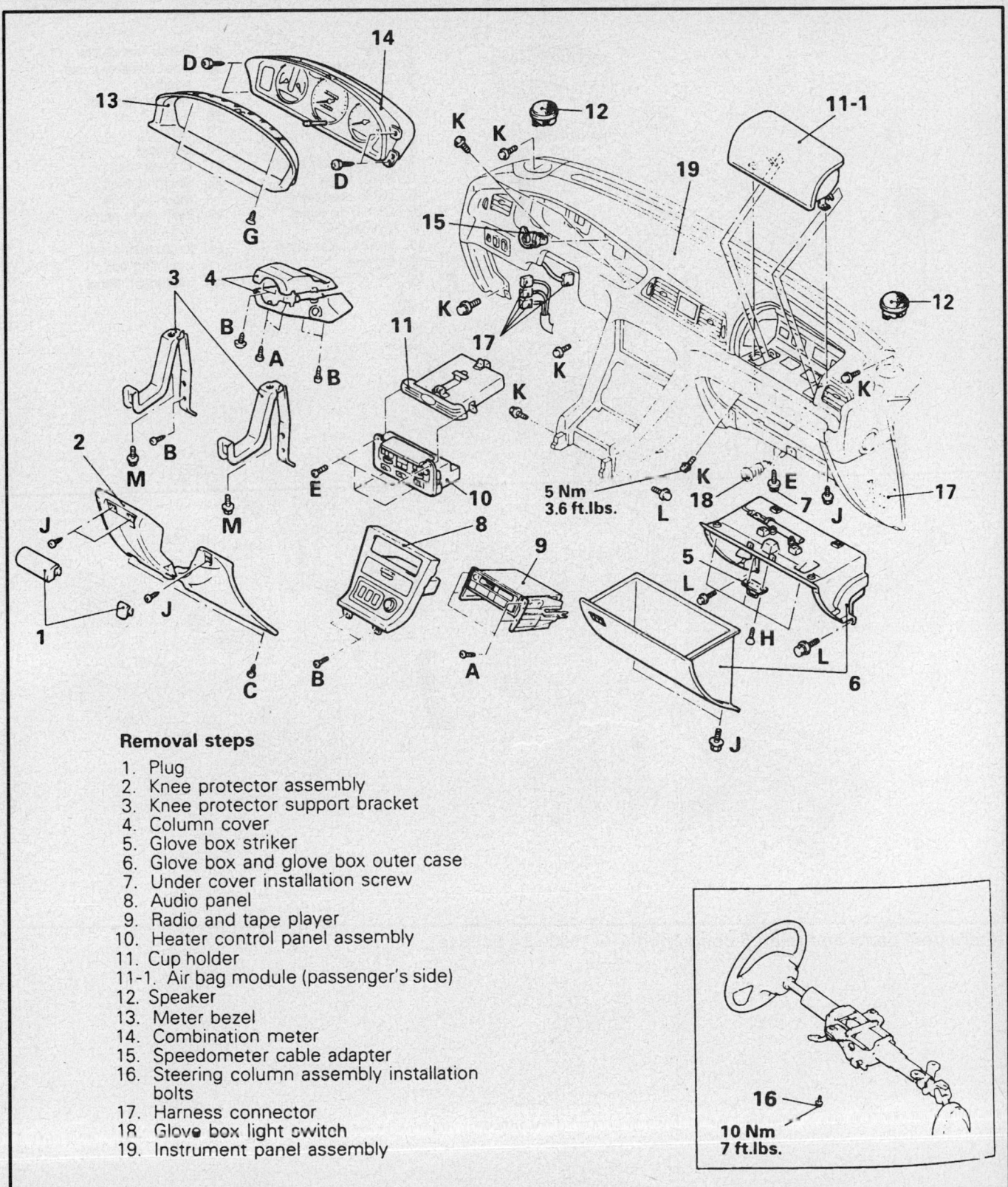

Removal steps

1. Plug
2. Knee protector assembly
3. Knee protector support bracket
4. Column cover
5. Glove box striker
6. Glove box and glove box outer case
7. Under cover installation screw
8. Audio panel
9. Radio and tape player
10. Heater control panel assembly
11. Cup holder
11-1. Air bag module (passenger's side)
12. Speaker
13. Meter bezel
14. Combination meter
15. Speedometer cable adapter
16. Steering column assembly installation bolts
17. Harness connector
18. Glove box light switch
19. Instrument panel assembly

10 Nm
7 ft.lbs.

Instrument panel and related components — 1994–95 Diamante

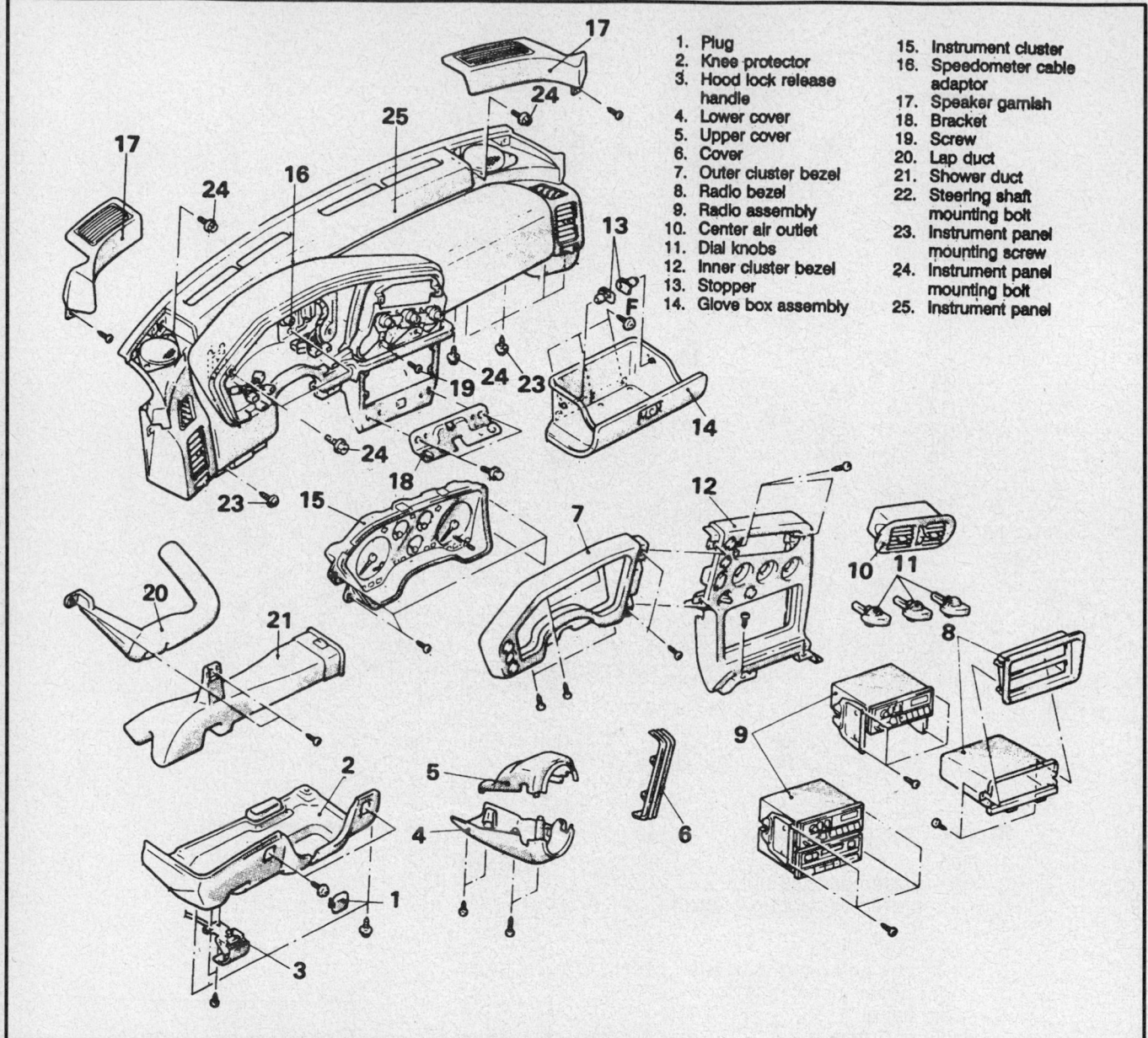

1. Plug
2. Knee protector
3. Hood lock release handle
4. Lower cover
5. Upper cover
6. Cover
7. Outer cluster bezel
8. Radio bezel
9. Radio assembly
10. Center air outlet
11. Dial knobs
12. Inner cluster bezel
13. Stopper
14. Glove box assembly
15. Instrument cluster
16. Speedometer cable adaptor
17. Speaker garnish
18. Bracket
19. Screw
20. Lap duct
21. Shower duct
22. Steering shaft mounting bolt
23. Instrument panel mounting screw
24. Instrument panel mounting bolt
25. Instrument panel

Instrument panel and related components — 1993–94 Eclipse

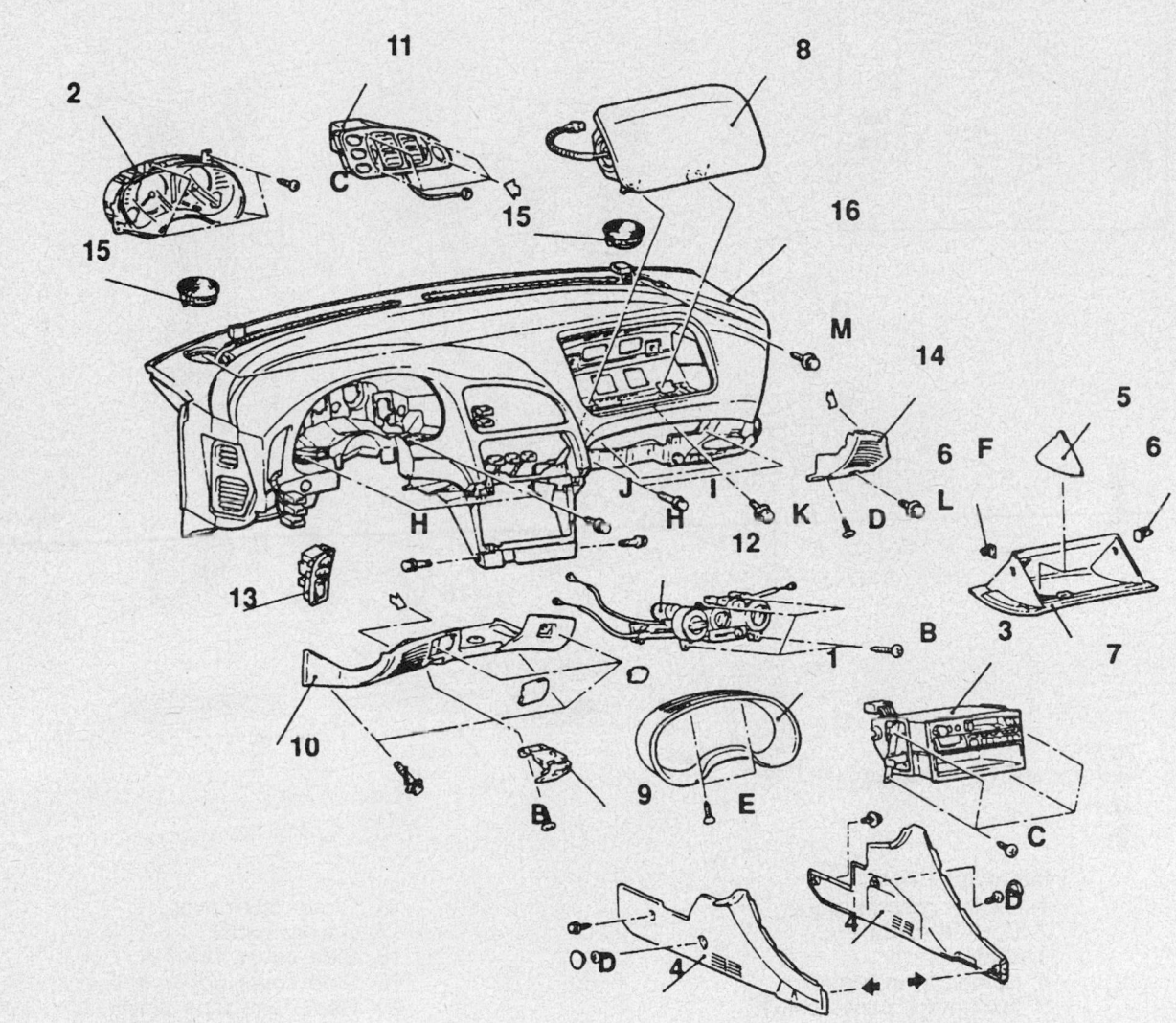

Instrument panel and related components — 1995 Eclipse

Removal steps

1. Meter bezel
2. Combination meter
3. Radio and tape player, and box
4. Console side cover
5. Sunglasses holder
6. Stopper
7. Glove box
8. Passenger's side air bag module assembly
9. Hood lock release handle
10. Instrument under cover L.H.
11. Center air outlet assembly
12. Heater control assembly
13. Instrument panel switch
14. Instrument under cover R.H.
15. Front speaker
16. Instrument panel assembly

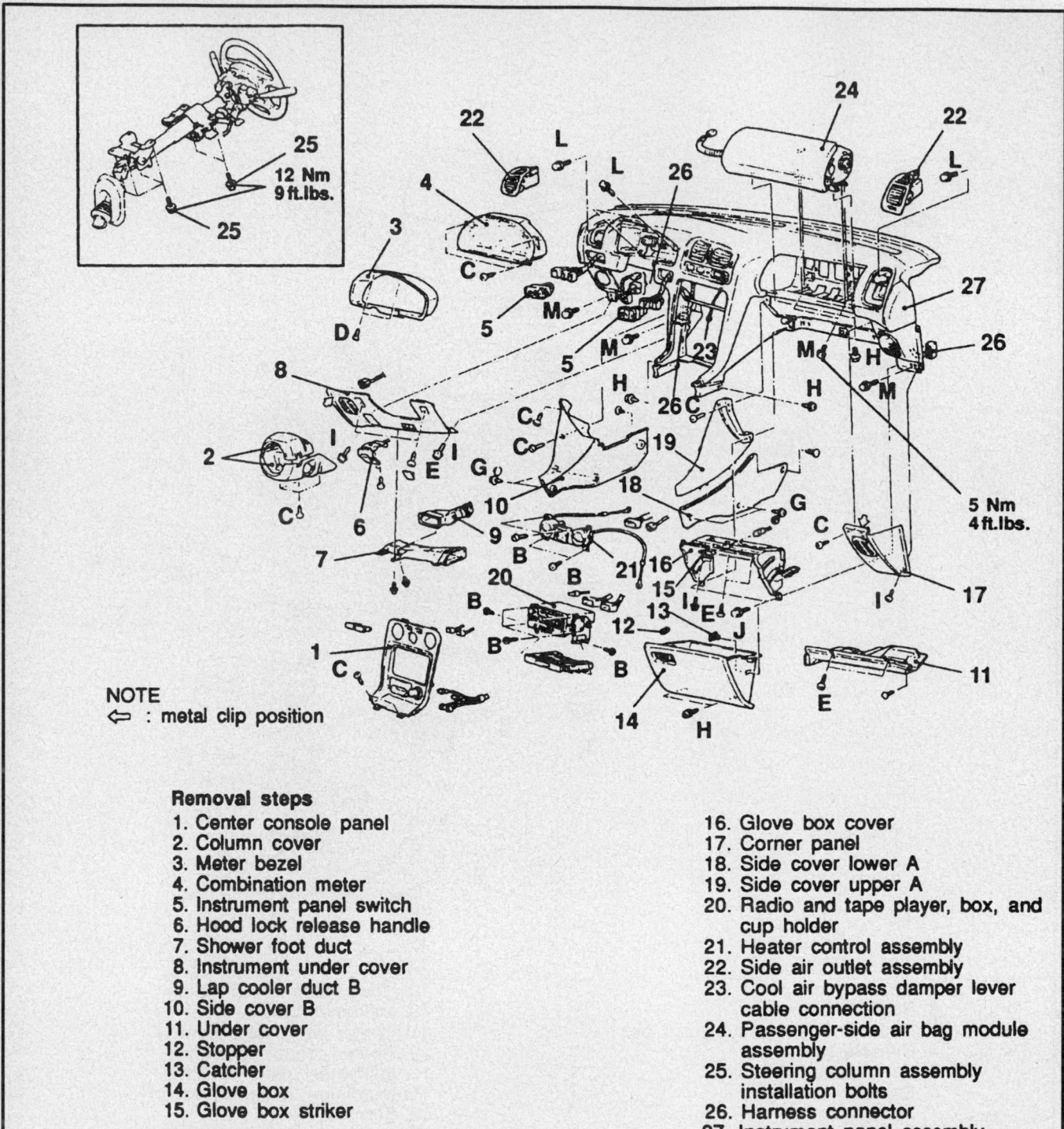

NOTE
⇦ : metal clip position

Removal steps
1. Center console panel
2. Column cover
3. Meter bezel
4. Combination meter
5. Instrument panel switch
6. Hood lock release handle
7. Shower foot duct
8. Instrument under cover
9. Lap cooler duct B
10. Side cover B
11. Under cover
12. Stopper
13. Catcher
14. Glove box
15. Glove box striker
16. Glove box cover
17. Corner panel
18. Side cover lower A
19. Side cover upper A
20. Radio and tape player, box, and cup holder
21. Heater control assembly
22. Side air outlet assembly
23. Cool air bypass damper lever cable connection
24. Passenger-side air bag module assembly
25. Steering column assembly installation bolts
26. Harness connector
27. Instrument panel assembly

Instrument panel and related components — Galant

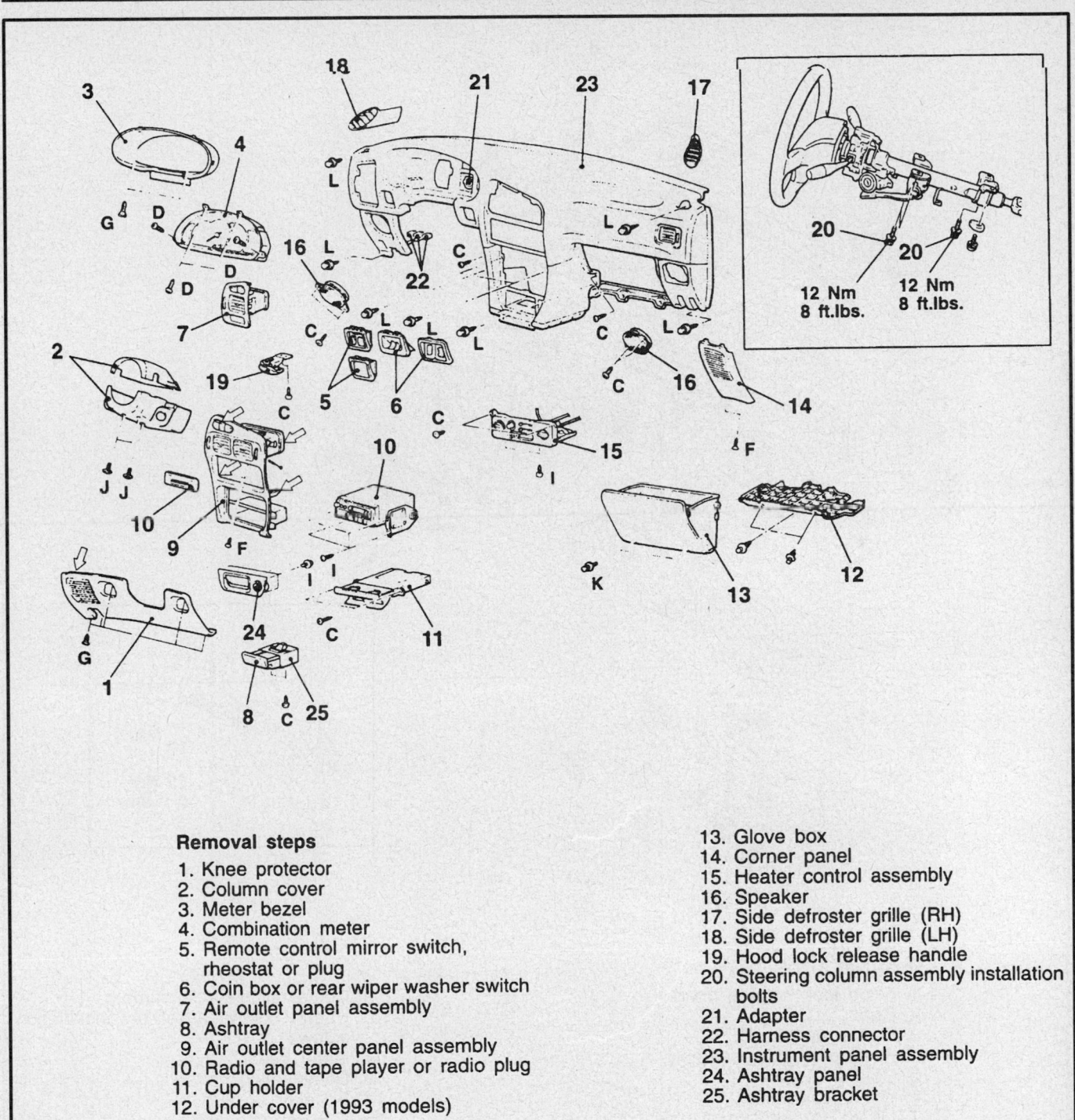

Removal steps

1. Knee protector
2. Column cover
3. Meter bezel
4. Combination meter
5. Remote control mirror switch, rheostat or plug
6. Coin box or rear wiper washer switch
7. Air outlet panel assembly
8. Ashtray
9. Air outlet center panel assembly
10. Radio and tape player or radio plug
11. Cup holder
12. Under cover (1993 models)
13. Glove box
14. Corner panel
15. Heater control assembly
16. Speaker
17. Side defroster grille (RH)
18. Side defroster grille (LH)
19. Hood lock release handle
20. Steering column assembly installation bolts
21. Adapter
22. Harness connector
23. Instrument panel assembly
24. Ashtray panel
25. Ashtray bracket

Instrument panel and related components — Mirage

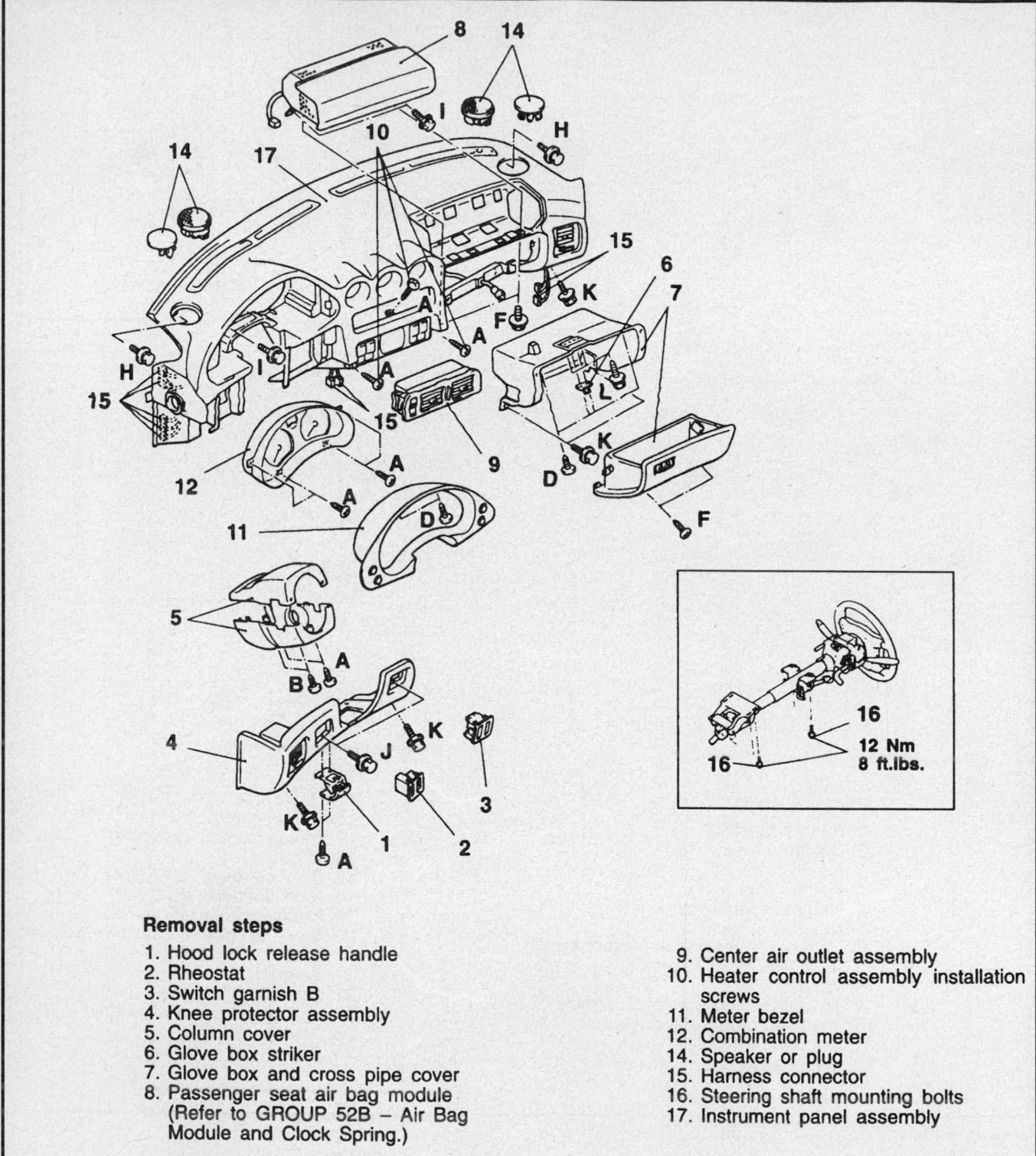

Removal steps

1. Hood lock release handle
2. Rheostat
3. Switch garnish B
4. Knee protector assembly
5. Column cover
6. Glove box striker
7. Glove box and cross pipe cover
8. Passenger seat air bag module
   (Refer to GROUP 52B – Air Bag
   Module and Clock Spring.)
9. Center air outlet assembly
10. Heater control assembly installation
    screws
11. Meter bezel
12. Combination meter
14. Speaker or plug
15. Harness connector
16. Steering shaft mounting bolts
17. Instrument panel assembly

Instrument panel and related components — 1994 3000GT

Evaporator

REMOVAL AND INSTALLATION

Diamante, Eclipse, Galant, Mirage and 3000GT

NOTE: If equipped with an air bag, wait for 1 minute to elapse before working inside the vehicle. The air bag system is set to deploy for a short period of time after the battery is disconnected.

1. Disconnect the negative battery cable.
2. Properly discharge the air conditioning system.
3. Disconnect the refrigerant lines from the evaporator connection on the engine side of the firewall. Discard all O-rings. Cap the exposed ends of the lines to minimize contamination.
4. On 3000GT, remove battery. Remove the condensation drain hose.
5. Remove the glove box assembly and any surrounding instrument panel trim on the right side.

6. Remove the supporting frame behind the glove box.
7. Remove the A/C control unit from the evaporator case, if equipped. Disconnect electrical connections as required.
8. Remove the evaporator mounting bolts and remove the evaporator assembly.
9. Disassemble the evaporator assembly and remove the expansion valve and evaporator core, as required.
10. Reverse removal procedure to install components. If evaporator was replaced, add 2 oz. of refrigerant oil, (except 1993–94 Eclipse, add 1 oz.) during the recharge.

Precis

1. Disconnect the negative battery cable.
2. Properly discharge the air conditioning system.
3. Disconnect the low pressure and high pressure lines from the evaporator fittings. Plug all openings to minimize contamination.
4. Remove the inlet and outlet pipe grommets.

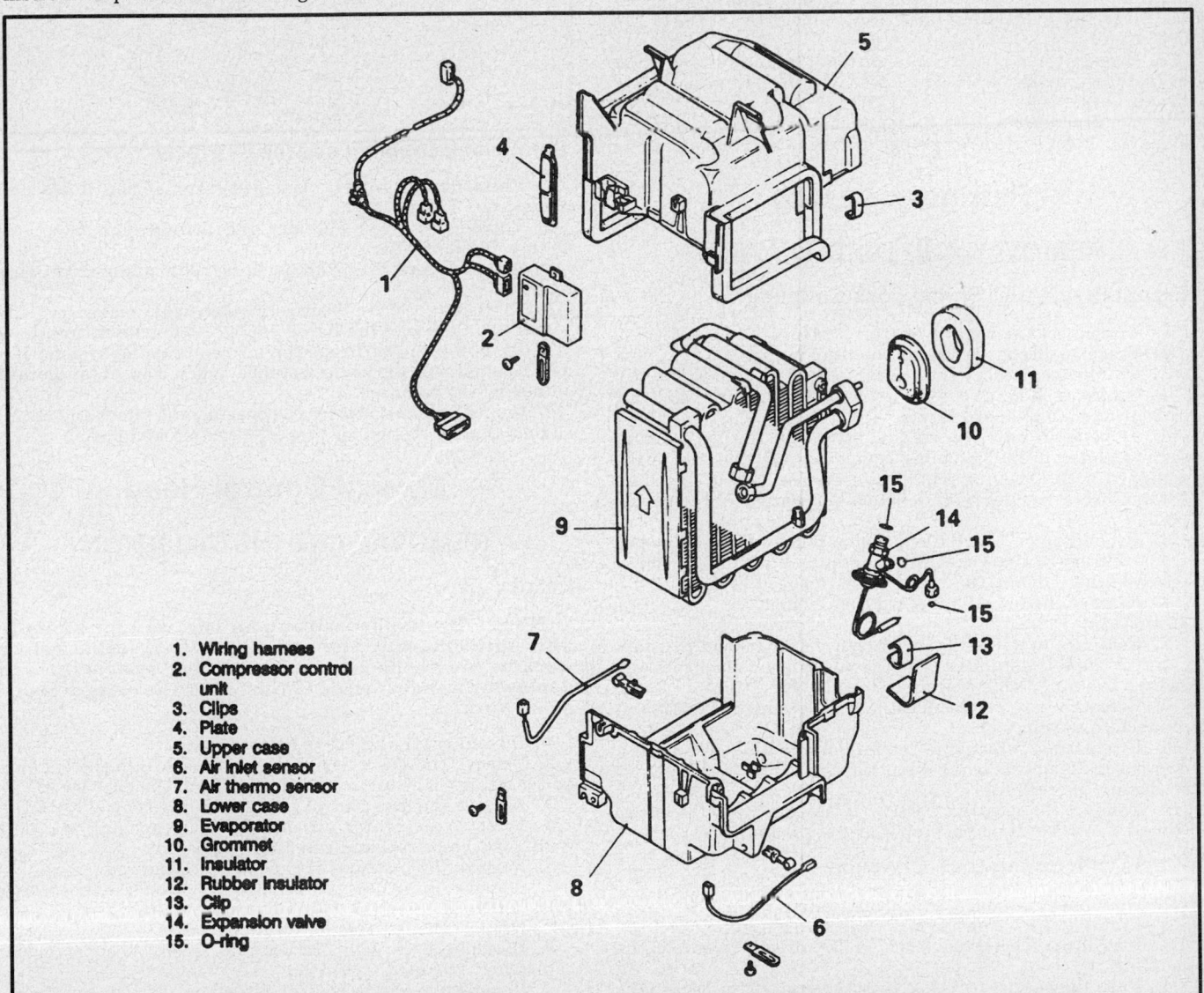

1. Wiring harness
2. Compressor control unit
3. Clips
4. Plate
5. Upper case
6. Air inlet sensor
7. Air thermo sensor
8. Lower case
9. Evaporator
10. Grommet
11. Insulator
12. Rubber insulator
13. Clip
14. Expansion valve
15. O-ring

Typical evaporator, expansion valve, case and related components. Assemblies may vary between vehicles

5. Remove the center console assembly rear screws, then rear half of the console. Remove the shift knob, then the front half of the console, detaching all wiring.

6. Remove the glove box assembly.

7. Remove the right lower instrument panel section, then the center panel cover.

8. Remove the blower motor assembly mounting bolts and remove the blower assembly.

9. Remove the evaporator assembly mounting bolts. Separate and remove the evaporator assembly from the heater assembly. Disassemble the unit on a workbench.

To install:

10. Thoroughly clean and dry the inside of the case and assemble. Position the evaporator assembly in place and install the mounting bolts.

11. Position the blower assembly in place and install the blower assembly mounting bolts.

12. Install the instrument panel center cover, the right lower section, and then the glove box.

13. Install the console assembly.

14. Coat the O-rings with compressor oil, install the grommet over the evaporator lines and connect the lines to the evaporator.

15. Evacuate and recharge the air conditioning system. If the evaporator was replaced, add 1.5 oz. of refrigerant oil during the recharge.

16. Connect the negative battery cable and check the entire climate control system for proper operation and leaks.

Refrigerant Lines

REMOVAL AND INSTALLATION

Except Precis with Spring Lock Coupling

1. Disconnect the negative battery cable.
2. Properly discharge the air conditioning system.
3. On Mirage, remove the windshield washer tank.
4. On 1993–94 Eclipse, remove the battery, reserve tank, air cleaner and air cleaner bracket.
5. Remove the nuts or bolts that attach the refrigerant lines sealing plates to the adjoining components. If the line is not equipped with a sealing plate, separate the flare connection. Always use a backup wrench when separating flare connections.
6. Depending on which line is being removed, the relay box (1993 Mirage), dual or triple pressure switch or coolant reserve tank (Galant) may have to be removed first.
7. Remove the line and discard the O-rings.

To install:

8. Coat the new O-rings with refrigerant oil and install. Connect the refrigerant lines to the adjoining components and tighten the nuts, bolts or flare connections.
9. Reinstall any components, air ductwork and electrical connectors as removed.
10. Evacuate and recharge the air conditioning system. If a new hose assembly is being installed, add 0.3 oz. of refrigerant oil during the recharge.
11. Connect the negative battery cable and check the entire climate control system for proper operation and leaks.

Precis with Spring Lock Coupling

1. Disconnect the negative battery cable.
2. Properly discharge the air conditioning system.
3. Install the special tool 09977–33600 or equivalent, on the coupling.
4. Push the special tool onto the cage opening to release the female fitting from the garter spring.
5. Pull the fitting apart and remove the tool from the coupling.

6. Cover the exposed ends of the lines to minimize contamination.

To install:

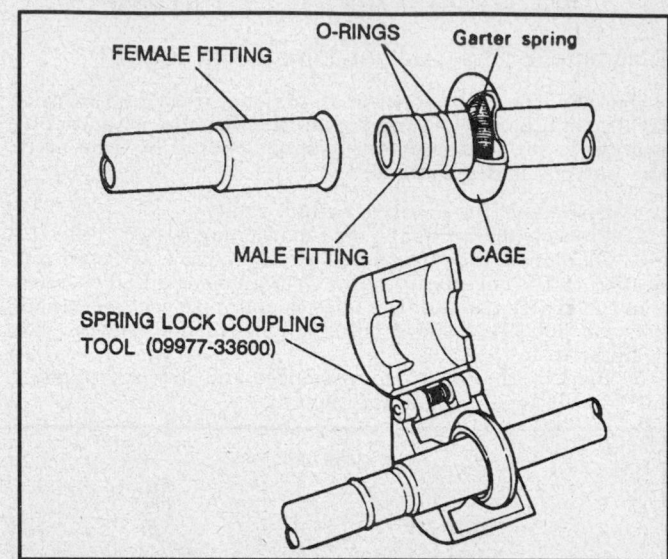

Spring lock coupling service — Precis

7. Check for a missing or damaged garter spring. Replace as necessary.
8. Thoroughly clean and dry the fittings, install a new O-ring and lubricate.
9. Assemble the fitting by pushing with a slight twisting motion.
10. To visually verify positive engagement, make sure the garter spring is over the flared end of the female fitting.
11. Evacuate and recharge the air conditioning system. If a new hose assembly is being installed, add 0.3 oz. of refrigerant oil during the recharge.
12. Connect the negative battery cable and check the entire climate control system for proper operation and leaks.

Manual Control Head

REMOVAL AND INSTALLATION

Eclipse

NOTE: If equipped with an air bag, wait for 1 minute after disconnecting the negative battery cable before working inside the vehicle. The air bag system is set to deploy for a short period of time after the battery is disconnected.

1. Disconnect the negative battery cable.
2. Remove the glove box assembly. Reach into the opening and disconnect the air selection cable from the door lever.
3. Remove the dial control knobs from the control head.
4. Remove the center air outlet by disengaging the tabs with a flat blade tool and carefully prying out.
5. Remove the instrument cluster bezel and radio bezel.
6. Remove the knee protector and lower the hood lock release handle.
7. Remove the left side lower duct work.
8. Disconnect the temperature and mode selection control cables from the heater housing.
9. Remove the heater control assembly.

To install:

10. Feed the control cable through the instrument panel, connect the connectors, install the control head assembly and secure with the screws.

11. Move the mode selection lever to the **DEFROST** position. Move the mode selection damper lever fully inward and connect the cable to the lever. Install the clip.

12. Move the temperature control lever to its **HOTTEST** position. Move the blend air damper lever fully downward and connect the cable to the lever. Install the clip.

13. Move the air selection control lever to the **RECIRC** position. Move the air selection damper fully inward and connect the cable to the lever. Install the clip.

14. Connect the negative battery cable and check the entire climate control system for proper operation.

15. Reverse the removal procedure to install the remaining interior pieces.

Galant

NOTE: If equipped with an air bag, wait for 1 minute after disconnecting the negative battery cable before working inside the vehicle. The air bag system is set to deploy for a short period of time after the battery is disconnected.

1. Disconnect the negative battery cable.
2. Remove the shift knob and shift lever boot on manual transmission.
3. Remove the center console panel.
4. Remove the hood lock release handle.
5. Remove the knee protector from beneath the steering column, the center panel and the floor air ducts.
6. Remove the heater control assembly.
7. Disconnect the mode selection control cable.
8. Note that once removed, the control lever assembly may be separated from the dial controls for inspection or replacement.

To install:

9. When reinstalling, make certain the lever assembly is connected to the dial panel before inserting the unit into the dash. Route the control cables to the heater case and install the retaining screws.

10. Set the temperature control knob to **MAX COOL**. Set the air mix damper lever at the bottom of the heater unit to the **MAX COOL** position, and install the cable to the lever pin. Push the outer cable in the direction of the arrow so that there is no looseness, and then secure it with the clip.

11. Set the knob for the air outlet changeover on the heater control assembly to the **DEF** position. Set the air outlet changeover damper lever of the heater unit to **DEF** position and install the cable to the lever pin. Push the outer cable in the direction of the arrow so that there is no looseness, and then secure it with the clip.

12. Connect the negative battery cable and check the entire climate control system for proper operation.

13. Reverse the removal procedure to install the remaining interior pieces.

Mirage

NOTE: If equipped with an air bag, wait for 1 minute after disconnecting the negative battery cable before working inside the vehicle. The air bag system is set to deploy for a short period of time after the battery is disconnected.

1. Disconnect the negative battery cable.
2. Remove the knee protector from beneath the steering column, the center panel and the floor air duct.
3. Remove the glove box assembly.
4. Disconnect the air, temperature and mode selection control cables from the heater housing.
5. Remove the heater control assembly, detaching electrical connectors as assembly is pulled from its mounting. Pull down

rear side of the assembly from under the instrument panel and pull assembly out at an angle.

6. Separate the control head from the left side first, then press out the lower and upper mounting brackets from behind the instrument panel.

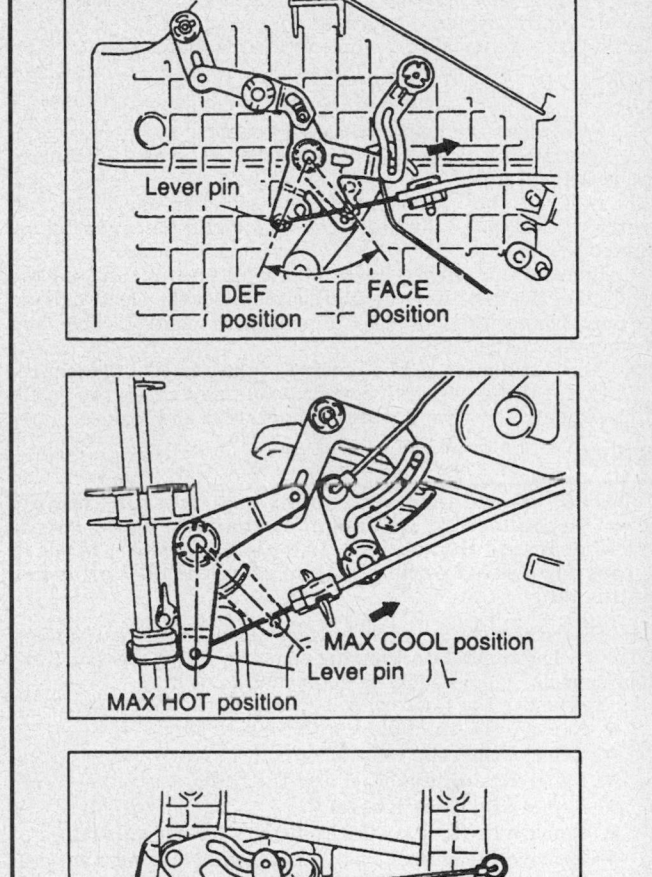

Adjusting air door cables — Mirage

7. Pull the control head out and disconnect the 3 connectors. Remove the control head assembly.

To install:

8. Feed the control cable through the instrument panel, connect the connectors, install the control head assembly and secure with the screws.

9. Set the knob for the air outlet changeover on the heater control assembly to the **DEF** position. Set the air outlet changeover damper lever of the heater unit to **DEF** position and install the cable to the lever pin. Push the outer cable in the direction of the arrow so that there is no looseness, and then secure it with the clip.

10. Set the temperature control knob on the heater control unit to **MAX HOT**. Set the air mix damper lever at the bottom of the heater unit to the **MAX HOT** position, and install the cable. Push the outer cable in the direction of the arrow so that there is no looseness, and then secure it with the clip.

11. Set the inside/outside air changeover lever to the **RECIRC** position. Set the inside/outside air changeover damper lever of the blower motor to the **RECIRC** position, and install the cable. Pull the outer cable in the direction of the arrow so that there is no looseness, and then secure it with the clip.

12. Connect the negative battery cable and check the entire climate control system for proper operation.

13. Reverse removal procedure to install components.

Precis

1. Disconnect the negative battery cable.

2. Remove the glove box. Remove the ashtray and remove the revealed screw.

3. Pull out the control assembly and disconnect the A/C switch (if equipped), the defroster switch and the cigar lighter connectors.

4. Remove the control head mounting screws and pull the unit out of the instrument panel. Disconnect the electrical and vacuum connectors and the temperature control cable and remove the control head.

5. The installation is the reverse of the removal procedure.

6. Connect the negative battery cable and check the entire climate control system for proper operation and leaks.

3000GT

NOTE: If equipped with an air bag, wait for 1 minute after disconnecting the negative battery cable before working inside the vehicle. The air bag system is set to deploy for a short period of time after the battery is disconnected.

1. Disconnect the negative battery cable. To prevent damage to the air bag control unit during removal or installation of the floor console, avoid shocks or impact. Do not drop.

2. To remove the floor console, perform the following:
   - Remove the cup holder and console plug.
   - Remove the rear console.
   - Remove the radio bezel and the radio.
   - Remove the switch bezel.
   - Remove the side covers and front console garnish.
   - Remove the shifter knob on manual transmission.
   - Remove the mounting screws and remove the console assembly.

3. Remove the glove box assembly and outer case.

4. Remove the hood lock release handle.

5. Remove the interior and dash lights rheostat and switch bezel to its right.

6. Remove the driver's knee protector and lower ventilation duct.

7. Remove the mode control cable and temperature control cable.

8. Remove center air outlet assembly by disengaging 2 clips accessible with a flat–blade tool through the fins.

9. Remove the heater control unit.

To install:

10. Feed the control cables through the instrument panel and route them in exactly the same position as before removal. Install the control head.

11. Install the center air outlet assembly.

12. Set the temperature lever to **HOT**, push the blend air door lever fully downward, then connect the cable.

13. Move mode lever to **DEFROST** position, pull the lower end of the mode door lever inward, then connect the cable.

14. Move the air selection lever to **RECIRC** position, move the air selection door lever against its stop, then connect the cable.

15. Connect the negative battery cable and check the entire climate control system for proper operation.

16. Reverse removal procedure to install components..

Manual Control Cables

ADJUSTMENT

All control cables are self–adjusting. If any cable is not functioning properly, try to move the affected lever to either extreme position, observe what may be binding and reposition the connecting link if possible. Also, check for proper routing and lubricate all moving parts. These cables cannot be disassembled. Replace if faulty.

Electronic Control Head

REMOVAL AND INSTALLATION

Diamante

NOTE: If equipped with an air bag, wait for 1 minute after disconnecting the negative battery cable before working inside the vehicle. The air bag system is set to deploy for a short period of time after the battery is disconnected.

1. Disconnect the negative battery cable.

NOTE: To prevent damage to the air bag control unit during removal or installation of the floor console, avoid shocks or impact. Do not drop.

2. To remove the floor console, perform the following:
   - Remove the floor console switch panel.
   - Remove the retaining screws.
   - Remove the floor console assembly.

3. Remove the center panel bezel and the air conditioning control trim piece.

4. Remove the air conditioning control panel assembly.

To install:

5. Reverse removal procedure to install components.

6. Connect the negative battery cable and check the entire climate control system for proper operation.

3000GT

NOTE: If equipped with an air bag, wait for 1 minute after disconnecting the negative battery cable before working inside the vehicle. The air bag system is set to deploy for a short period of time after the battery is disconnected.

1. Disconnect the negative battery cable.

NOTE: To prevent damage to the air bag control unit during removal or installation of the floor console, avoid shocks or impact. Do not drop.

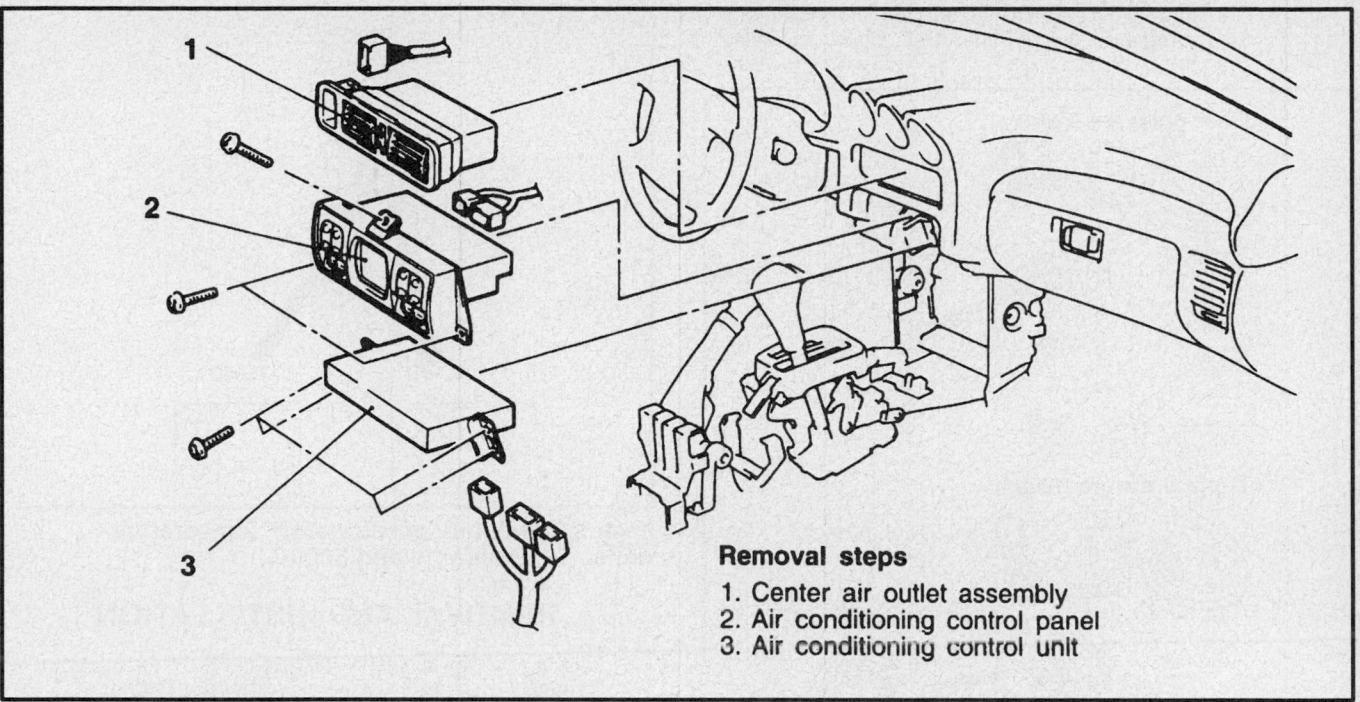

Removal steps
1. Center air outlet assembly
2. Air conditioning control panel
3. Air conditioning control unit

Removing electronic control head — 3000GT

2. To remove the floor console, perform the following:
- Remove the cup holder and console plug.
- Remove the rear console.
- Remove the radio bezel and the radio.
- Remove the switch bezel.
- Remove the side covers and front console garnish.
- Remove the shifter knob on manual transmission.
- Remove the mounting screws and remove the console assembly.

3. Remove the center air outlet assembly.
4. Remove the air conditioning control panel.
5. Remove the air conditioning control unit.
To install:
6. Reverse removal procedure to install components.
7. Connect the negative battery cable and check the entire climate control system for proper operation.

SENSORS AND SWITCHES

Dual Pressure Switch

OPERATION

All models use a dual pressure switch, except 1993 Mirage, which is a combination of a low pressure cut off switch and high pressure cut off switch. These functions will stop operation of the compressor in the event of either high or low refrigerant charge, preventing damage to the system. The switch is located near the sight glass on the refrigerant line on Eclipse, and on the receiver/drier on all other vehicles.

The dual pressure switch is designed to cut off voltage to the compressor coil when the pressure either drops below 30 psi or rises above 384 psi.

The 1993 Mirage with 1.8L engine uses a Triple Pressure Switch. The high and low pressure sensing operates as with the Dual Pressure Switch. This switch also has a third sensing element which monitors the medium pressure range as well.

TESTING

1. Check for continuity through the switch. Under all normal conditions, the switch should have continuity.
2. If the switch has no continuity, check for insufficient refrigerant charge or excessive pressures.
3. If neither of the above conditions exist and the switch has no continuity, replace the switch.

REMOVAL AND INSTALLATION

1. Disconnect the negative battery cable.
2. Properly discharge the air conditioning system.
3. Detach the electrical connector. Remove the switch from the refrigerant line or receiver/drier.
4. The installation is the reverse of the removal procedure.
5. Evacuate and recharge the air conditioning system.

6. Connect the negative battery cable and check the entire climate control system for proper operation. Check the system for leaks.

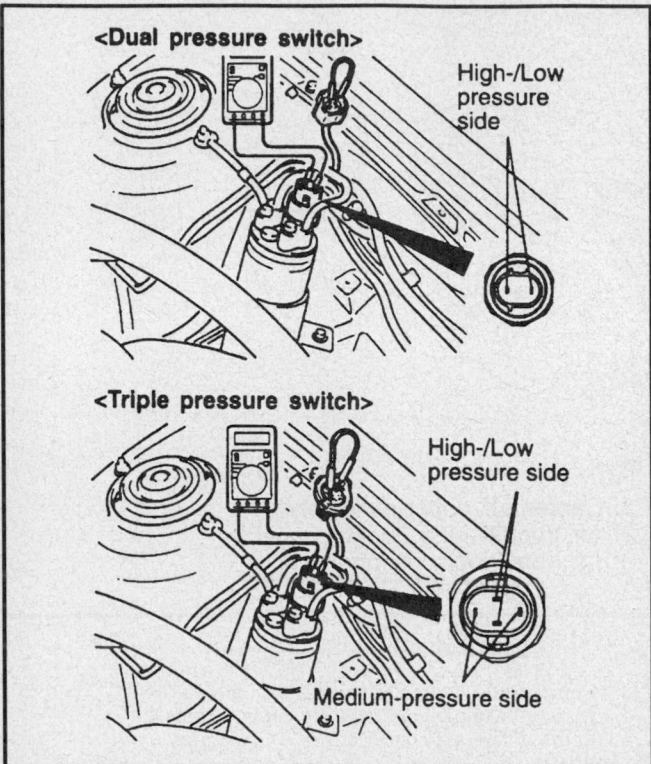

Dual and triple pressure switch — Mirage

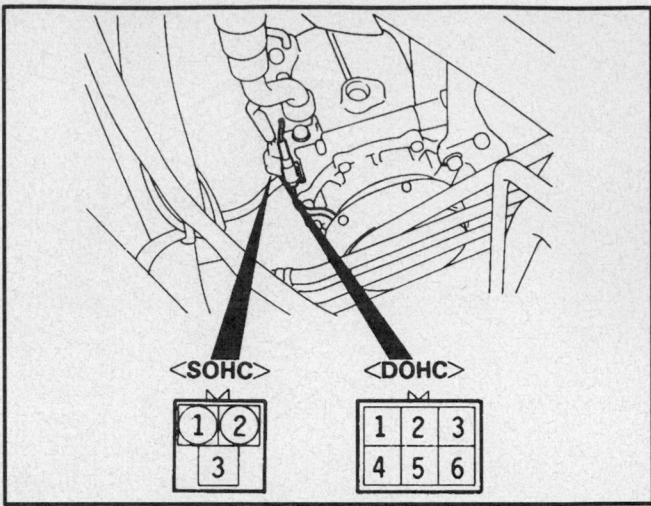

Testing continuity of refrigerant temperature sensor — Diamante and 3000GT

Refrigerant Temperature Sensor

OPERATION

Located on the rear of the compressor on Diamante, Mirage, Galant and 3000GT, the refrigerant temperature sensor detects the temperature of the refrigerant delivered from the compressor during operation. The switch is designed to cut off the compressor when the temperature of the refrigerant exceeds 347°F (175°C), preventing overheating. On the Diamante and 3000GT, the switch is mounted in combination with the compressor rpm sensor.

TESTING

1. Use an ohmmeter to check for continuity between the switch terminals **1** and **2**, when refrigerant temperature is below 293°F (145°C). On DOHC models check for continuity between terminals **3** and **4**. When refrigerant temperature exceeds 293°F (145°C), the switch opens and there should not be continuity.
2. If the sensor fails the test, replace the sensor.

REMOVAL AND INSTALLATION

1. Disconnect the negative battery cable.
2. Properly discharge the air conditioning system.
3. Disconnect the connector.
4. Remove the mounting screws and the sensor from the compressor.
5. Reverse removal procedure to install components. Use a new lubricated O–ring when installing.
6. Evacuate and recharge the air conditioning system.
7. Connect the negative battery cable and check the entire climate control system for proper operation and leaks.

Engine Coolant Temperature Switch/ Sensor

OPERATION

The engine coolant temperature is sensed by means of an on/off device (switch) or variable resistor (sensor), located on or near the thermostat housing or lower radiator. The engine coolant temperature switch contacts are designed to close above 185°F (85°C) which then energizes the radiator fan relay, causing the radiator fan to run.

The engine coolant temperature sensor is part of the emission control system. It varies the 5 volt reference signal from the ECM according to engine coolant temperature. The ECM then controls the radiator fan.

TESTING

1. If the switch is suspect, unplug and jump across the terminals in the connectors. The fan should run.
2. To test the switch, remove the switch from the engine. The switch should not have continuity at room temperature.

3. Place the switch in an oil or water bath and heat to at least 185°F (85°C).

4. The switch should have continuity when it reaches the above temperature.

REMOVAL AND INSTALLATION

1. Disconnect the negative battery cable.
2. Drain the engine coolant.
3. Unplug the connector.
4. Unscrew the switch from the thermostat housing.

To install:

5. Reverse removal procedure to install components. Use sealant on the threads when installing.
6. Refill the cooling system.
7. Connect the negative battery cable and check the entire climate control system for proper operation.

Compressor Revolution Sensor and Belt Lock Controller

OPERATION

On Diamante and 3000GT, an additional compressor cut off has been incorporated into the fully automatic air conditioning control system. The belt lock controller, located behind the glove box, is equipped with circuitry to detect belt slippage according to signals received from the compressor revolution sensor, mounted on the compressor and engine rpm. If the dif-ference in rpm exceeds 8% for more than 3 seconds, the belt lock controller will de-energize the magnetic clutch.

If the belt is audibly slipping or visually loose and the air conditioning will not work, try adjusting the belt tension to rule out this as a problem.

TESTING

1. Disconnect the negative battery cable.
2. Disconnect the compressor revolution sensor.
3. Measure the resistance between terminals **2** and **5** of the connector (center 2 terminals).
4. Normal resistance values are 370–440 ohms at 68°F (20°C).
5. Replace the sensor if not within specification.

REMOVAL AND INSTALLATION

Compressor Revolution Sensor

1. Disconnect the negative battery cable.
2. Properly discharge the air conditioning system
3. Remove the alternator, if required.
4. Remove the hold-down clamps and discard O-rings.
5. Remove thermostat and revolution pick-up sensor assembly from the compressor.
6. Reverse removal procedure to install components. Use new lubricated O-rings.
7. Evacuate and recharge the air conditioning system.
8. Connect the negative battery cable and check the entire climate control system for proper operation and leaks.

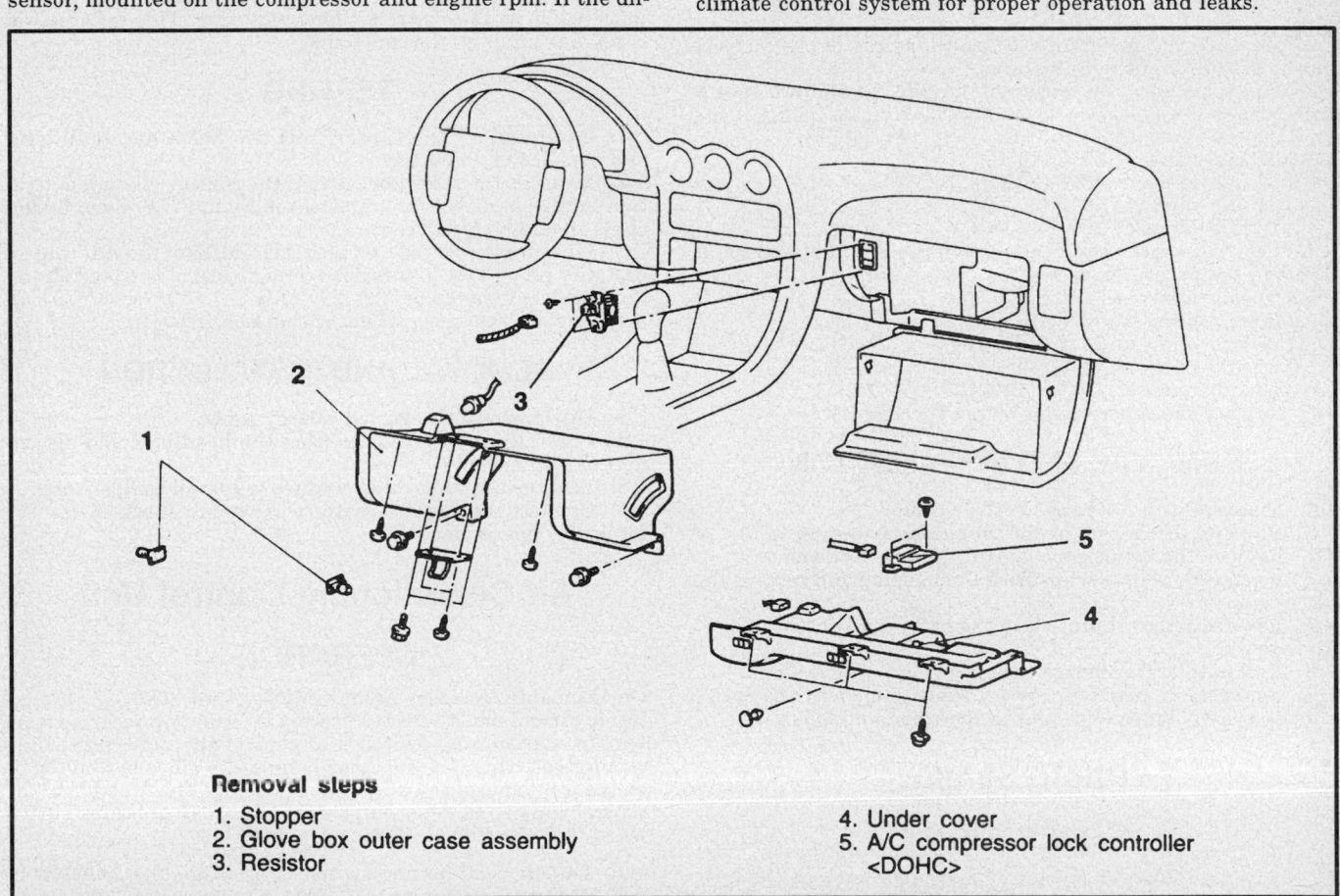

Removal steps
1. Stopper
2. Glove box outer case assembly
3. Resistor
4. Under cover
5. A/C compressor lock controller <DOHC>

Removing belt lock controller and testing RPM sensor — Diamante and 3000GT

Belt Lock Controller

1. Disconnect the negative battery cable.
2. Remove glove box and glove box outer case.
3. Remove the resistor or power transistor.
4. Remove the mounting screw, disconnect the connector and remove the controller.
5. Reverse removal procedure to install components.
6. Connect the negative battery cable and check the entire climate control system for proper operation.

Air Thermo and Air Inlet Sensors

OPERATION

These sensors function as cycling switches. Both sensors are located inside the evaporator housing. The air inlet sensor is normally on the right side of the housing and the air thermo sensor is normally on the left side. All vehicles, except Precis, use these sensors.

The air thermo sensor detects the temperature of the air in the passenger compartment and the air inlet sensor detects the temperature of the air coming into the cooling unit. The information is input to the auto compressor control unit and the information is processed, causing the compressor clutch to cycle.

TESTING

1. Disconnect the sensor connector near the evaporator case.
2. Measure the resistance across the wires of the suspect sensor at 2 different temperatures.
3. The resistance specifications for the air thermo sensor are:
   11.4 kilo–ohms at 32°F (0°C)
   7.32 kilo–ohms at 50°F (10°C)
   4.86 kilo–ohms at 68°F (20°C)
   3.31 kilo–ohms at 86°F (30°C)
   2.32 kilo–ohms at 104°F (40°C)
4. The resistance specifications for the air inlet sensor at different temperatures are:
   3.31 kilo–ohms at 32°F (0°C)
   2.00 kilo–ohms at 50°F (10°C)
   1.25 kilo–ohms at 68°F (20°C)
   0.81 kilo–ohms at 86°F (30°C)
   0.53 kilo–ohms at 104°F (40°C)
5. Replace the sensor if not within specifications.

REMOVAL AND INSTALLATION

1. Disconnect the negative battery cable.
2. Properly discharge the air conditioning system.
3. Remove the evaporator housing and then the covers.
4. Unclip the sensor wires from the housing and remove the sensor(s).
5. Reverse removal procedure to install components.
To install:
6. Evacuate and recharge the air conditioning system.
7. Connect the negative battery cable and check the entire climate control system for proper operation and leaks.

Photo Sensor

OPERATION

Diamante and 3000GT have a photo sensor (or ambient temperature sensor) to detect an increase in the outside air temperature and increase the speed of the blower motor. This will compensate for the increase in interior temperature due to the heat of the sunlight.

TESTING

With sunlight shining on the photo sensor, cover the sensor with your hand. If the speed of the blower decreases, then increases when sensor is exposed again, it is functioning properly.

REMOVAL AND INSTALLATION

3000GT

1. Disconnect the negative battery cable.
2. Open or remove the glove box, as required.
3. Disconnect the connector to the photo sensor.
4. Carefully pry the sensor from the instrument panel.
5. Reverse removal procedure to install components.
6. Connect the negative battery cable and check the sensor for proper operation.

Passenger Compartment Temperature Sensor

OPERATION

Diamante and 3000GT have a passenger compartment temperature sensor installed in the roof when equipped with an automatic climate control system. The function of this sensor is to detect the temperature of the passenger compartment, change the information into resistance values and provide the information to the controller for processing. This information is used as input by the controller.

TESTING

1. Carefully pry the sensor from the headliner, pull down and detach the connector.
2. Measure the resistance across the sensor. When temperature in the passenger compartment is about 77°F, about 4 kilo-ohms should be measured.
3. Measure the voltage across terminal **16** of the A/C control unit and ground when interior temperature is as noted above. Measurement should be 2.3–2.9 volts.
4. Replace the sensor if not within specifications.

REMOVAL AND INSTALLATION

1. Disconnect the negative battery cable.
2. Carefully pry the sensor from the headliner and disconnect the connector.
3. Reverse the removal procedure to install components.
4. Connect the negative battery cable and check the sensor for proper operation.

Air Conditioning Control Unit

OPERATION

On Diamante, Eclipse, Galant, Mirage and 3000GT, an electronic control unit is used to process information received from various sensors and switches to control the air conditioning compressor. The unit is located behind the glove box on top or on the front side of the evaporator housing. The function of the control unit is to send current to the dual pressure switch when the following conditions are met:

1. The air conditioning switch is in either the **ECONO** or **A/C** mode.
2. The refrigerant temperature sensor, if equipped, is reading 347°F (175°C) or less.

3. The air thermo and air inlet sensors are both reading at least 39°F (4°C).

TESTING

1. Disconnect the control unit connector.
2. Turn the ignition switch **ON**.
3. Turn the air conditioning switch **ON**.
4. Turn the temperature control lever too its **COOLEST** position.
5. Turn the blower switch to its **HIGHEST** position.
6. Follow the chart and probe the various terminals of the control unit connector under the specified conditions. This will rule out all possible faulty components in the system.
7. If all checks are satisfactory, replace the control unit. If not, check the faulty system or component.

REMOVAL AND INSTALLATION

1. Disconnect the negative battery cable.
2. Remove the glove box and locate the control module.
3. Disconnect the connector to the module and remove the mounting screws.
4. Remove the module from the evaporator housing.
5. The installation is the reverse of the removal installation.
6. Connect the negative battery cable and check the entire climate control system for proper operation.

Damper Control Motors

OPERATION

The Diamante and 3000GT with full auto air conditioning use electric motors to control the positioning of certain dampers. The inside/outside air select, blend air and mode select dampers are all controlled electronically. Motor position change is activated by signals sent by the air conditioning control unit.

TESTING

Damper Motors

Apply battery voltage to the proper connector terminals. Make sure the motor turns smoothly and quietly and no binding occurs. Reverse polarity and note that damper moves in the opposite direction. Be sure to cut off voltage when the door has reached its stop or if the motor does not rotate.

Blend Air Potentiometer

Connect an ohmmeter to the potentiometer terminals as shown and measure the resistance at the hottest (MH) and coolest (MC) positions. The resistance should gradually change as the damper is moved. At **MAX HOT** the reading should be about 0.2 kilo–ohms; at **MAX COOL** the reading should be about 4.8 kilo–ohms.

Mode Select Damper Potentiometer

Connect an ohmmeter to the potentiometer terminals and measure the resistance at the **FACE** and **FACE/DEF** positions. The resistance should gradually change as the damper is moved. At **DEF** position value should be about 0.2 kilo–ohms; at **FACE** position value should be about 4.8 kilo–ohms

REMOVAL AND INSTALLATION

Diamante and 3000GT

NOTE: If equipped with an air bag, wait for 1 minute after disconnecting the negative battery cable before working inside the vehicle. The air bag system is set to deploy for a short period of time after the battery is disconnected.

1. Disconnect the negative battery cable.
2. To gain access to the inside/outside (fresh/recirc) air selection damper motor, remove the glove box stopper and outer glove box case. Disconnect the connector, remove the screws and remove the air selection damper motor.
3. To gain access to the blend air damper motor:
   • Remove the floor console and radio assembly.
   • Remove the air conditioner control unit.
   • Remove the center air outlet.
   • Remove the air conditioning control head and the EPS control unit.
   • Remove the mounting screws and remove the motor.
4. To gain access to the mode select damper motor:
   • Remove the driver's side knee protector.
   • Remove the side console cover.
   • Remove the ductwork.
   • Remove the mounting screws and remove the motor.
5. Reverse removal procedure to install components.
6. Connect the negative battery cable and check the entire climate control system for proper operation.

Inspecting mode selection damper motor operation — 3000GT

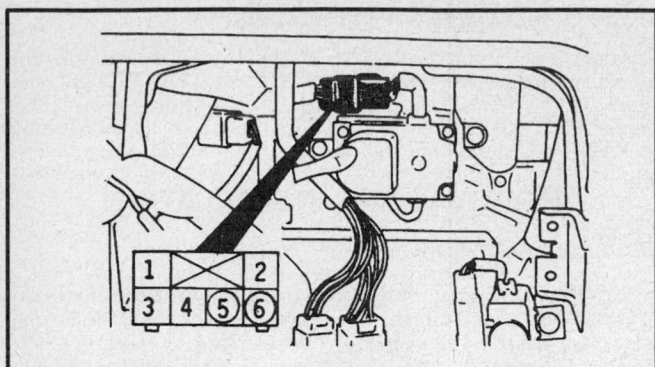

Testing mode selection damper potentiometer — 3000GT

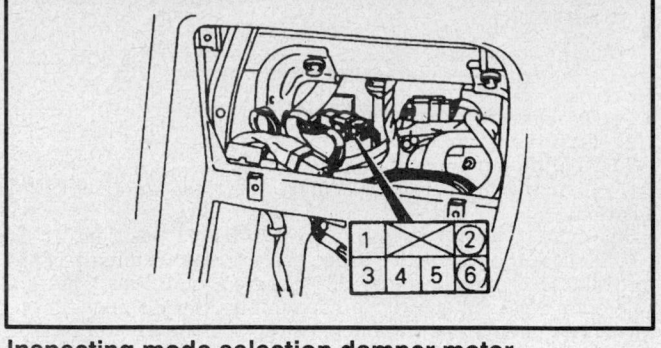

Inspecting mode selection damper motor operation — Diamante

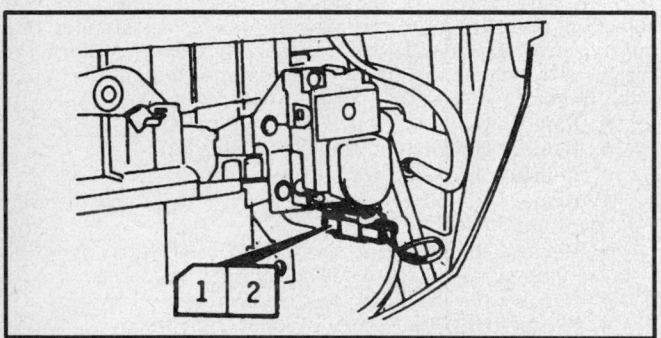

Checking fresh/recirc air damper motor — Diamante

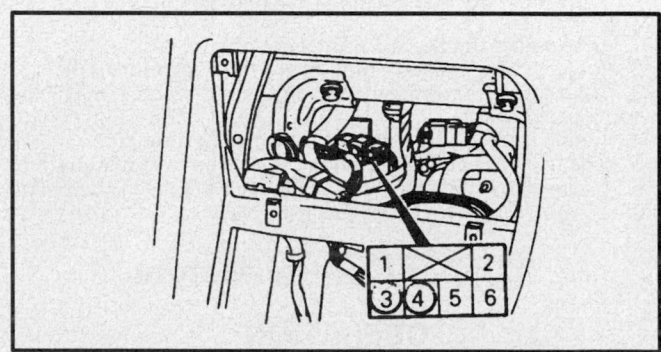

Inspecting mode selection damper potentiometer — Diamante

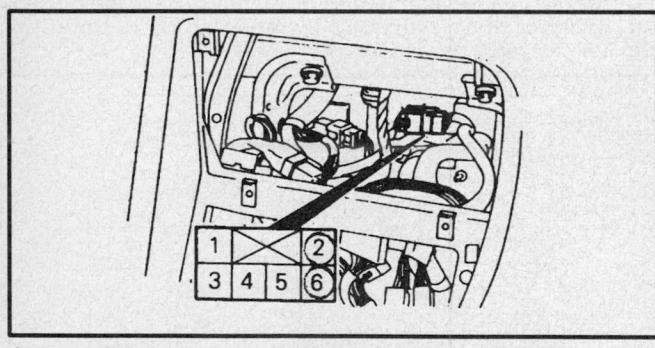

Inspecting blend air damper motor — Diamante

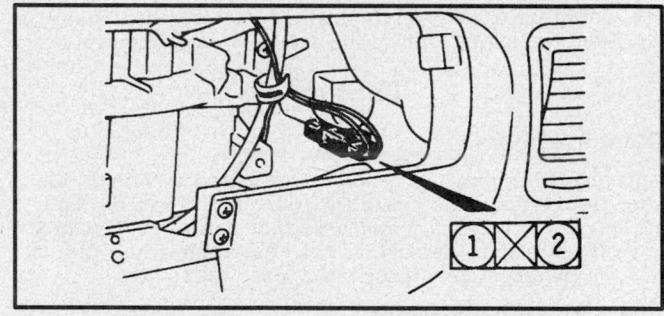

Inspecting air selection damper motor operation — 3000GT

Inspecting blend air damper potentiometer — Diamante

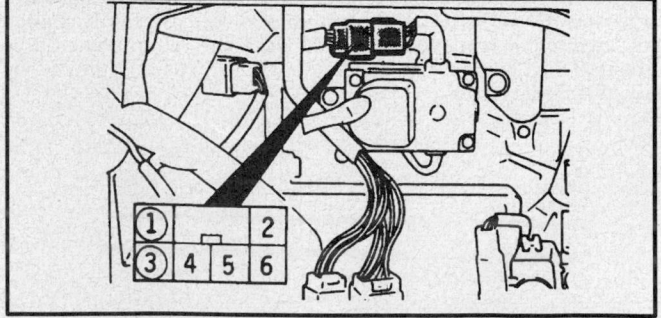

Inspecting blend air damper motor operation — 3000GT

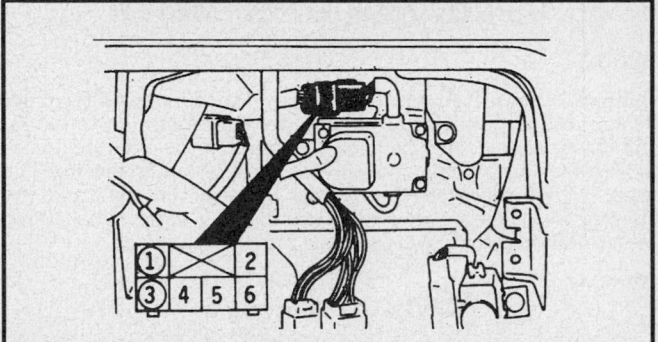

Testing blend air damper potentiometer — 3000GT   **Testing blend air damper potentiometer — 3000GT**

SYSTEM DIAGNOSIS

Air Conditioning Performance

PERFORMANCE TEST

Air temperature in the testing area must be at least 70°F (21°C) to ensure the accuracy of this test.

1. Connect a manifold gauge set to the system.
2. Set the controls to **RECIRC** or **MAX**, the mode lever to the **PANEL** position, temperature control level to the **COOLEST** position and the blower on its **HIGHEST** position.
3. Start the engine and adjust the idle speed to 1000 rpm with the compressor clutch engaged.
4. Allow the engine come to normal operating temperature and keep doors and windows closed.
5. Insert a thermometer in the left center panel outlet and operate the engine for 10 minutes. The clutch may cycle depending on the ambient conditions.
6. With the clutch engaged, compare the discharge air temperature to the performance chart.
7. If the values do not meet specifications, check system components for proper operation.

Air Conditioning Compressor

COMPRESSOR NOISE

Noises that develop during air conditioning operation can be misleading. A noise that sounds like serious compressor damage may only be a loose belt, mounting bolt or clutch assembly. Improper belt tension can also emit a noise that can be mistaken for more serious problems. Check and adjust all possible causes of the noise, including oil level, before replacing the compressor.

COMPRESSOR CLUTCH INOPERATIVE

1. Verify refrigerant charge and adjust if required.
2. Check for 12 volts at the clutch coil connection. If voltage is detected, check the coil.
3. If voltage is not detected at the coil, check the fuse or fusible link. If the fuse is not blown, check for voltage at the clutch relay. If voltage is not detected there, continue working backwards through the system's switches, etc. until an open circuit is detected.
4. Inspect all suspect parts and replace as required.

5. When the repair is complete, perform a complete system performance test.

CLUTCH COIL TESTING

1. Disconnect the negative battery cable.
2. Disconnect the compressor clutch connector.
3. Apply 12 volts to the wire leading to the clutch coil. If the clutch is operating properly, an audible click will occur when the clutch is magnetically pulled into the coil. If no click is heard, inspect the coil.
4. Check the resistance across the coil lead wire and ground. The specification is 3.4–3.8 ohms at approximately 70°F (20°C).
5. If not within specifications, replace the clutch coil.

Full Automatic Air Conditioning System

OPERATION

3000GT

The automatic system is equipped with self–diagnostic capabilities so the condition of the wire harnesses and components within the system can be analyzed. When the full automatic air conditioning system senses a malfunction, the fail–safe system is activated and a malfunction code is input to the electronic control unit. This information becomes output when the self–diagnostics connector is accessed. The connector is located behind the glove box or under the instrument panel to the left of the steering column on 3000GT.

USING MULTI–USE TESTER

3000GT

Mitsubishi's Multi–Use Tester MB991269 or MB991341 (or equivalent) in conjunction with the proper ROM pack can be used to check the system. To use the tester, connect the socket to the cigarette lighter and the connector to the vehicle's self–diagnosis check connector. Follow the manufacturer's instructions to set the tool and record the stored fault codes. Once the codes are recorded, check the faulty system(s) using the charts provided.

USING ANALOG VOLTMETER

3000GT

Connect a voltmeter across the ground terminal and terminal designated for the full automatic air conditioning system on the check connector. The code number for the malfunction is determined by counting sweeps of the voltmeter needle. The long sweeps represent the tenths digit of the code and the shorter sweeps represent the single digits. For example, 1 long sweep followed by 5 short sweeps indicates Code 15.

System Relays

OPERATION

Many of the systems within the air conditioning systems use relays to send current on its way and energize various components. The relays are positioned throughout the vehicle. All are conventional relays with internal contacts and a coil which pulls the contacts closed when energized.

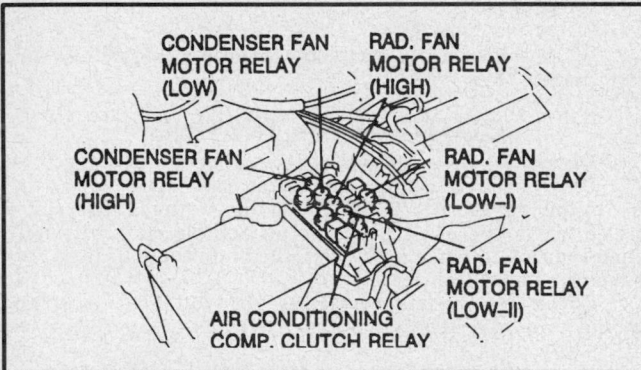

Relay block in right side of engine compartment — 1993 Diamante

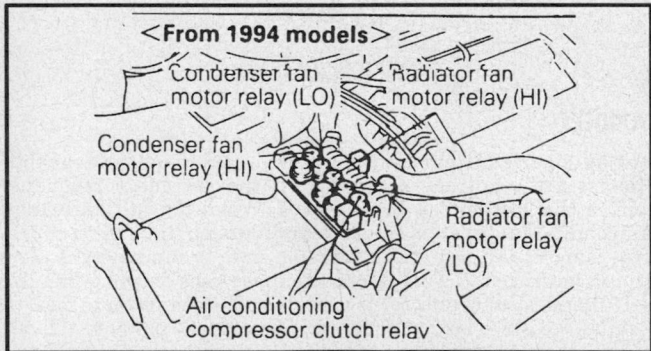

Relay block in right side of engine compartment — 1994–95 Diamante

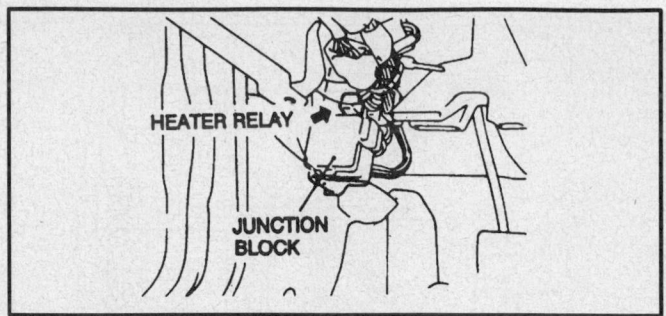

Heater relay under left side of instrument panel — Eclipse

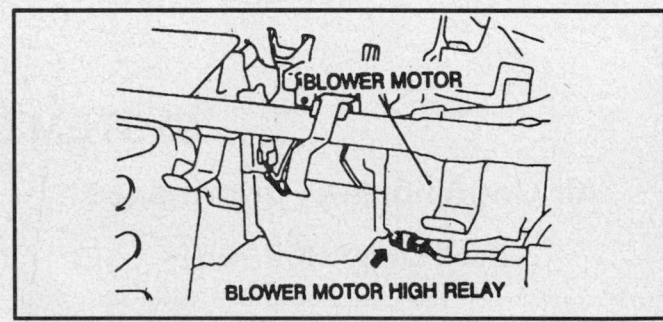

Blower motor relay near the heater unit — 1993–94 Eclipse

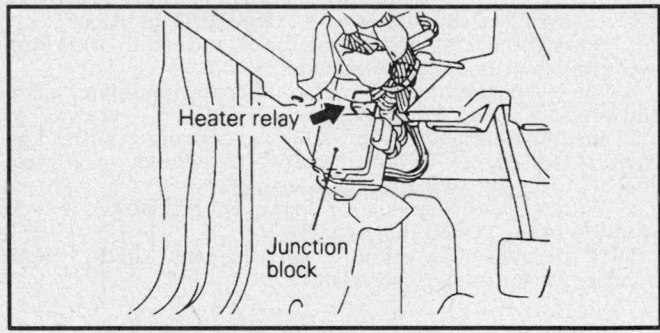

Heater relay under left side of dash — 1993–94 Eclipse

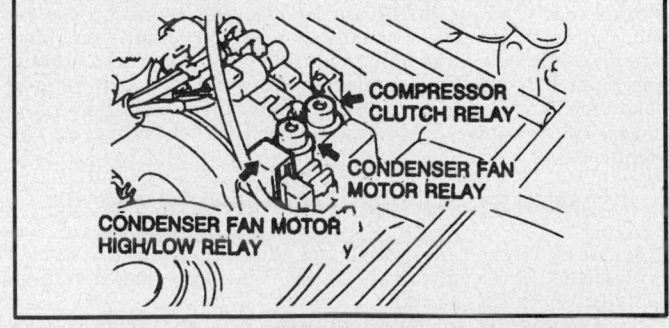

Relay block in right side of engine compartment — 1993–94 Eclipse

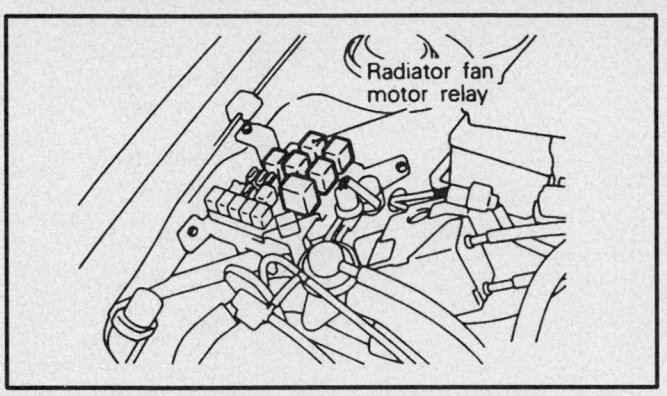

Relay block at the left side of engine compartment — 1993–94 Eclipse

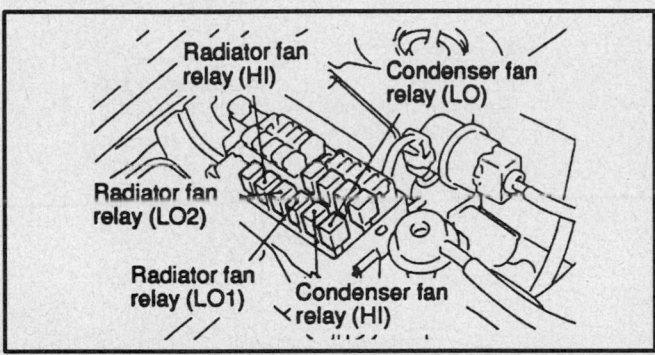

Relay block in right side of engine compartment — 1995 Eclipse turbo

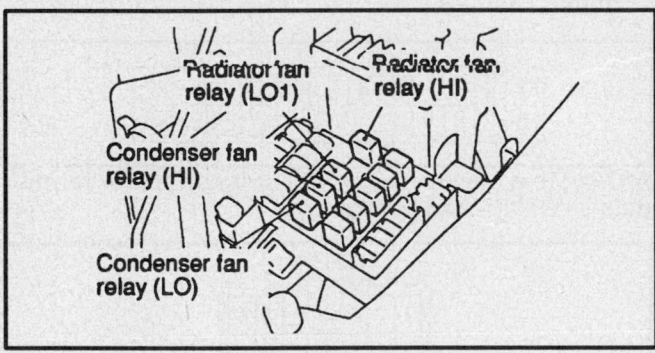

Relay block in left side of engine compartment — 1995 Eclipse non-turbo

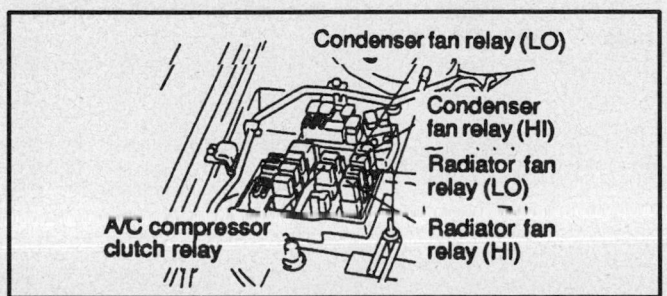

Relay block in right front of engine compartment — Galant

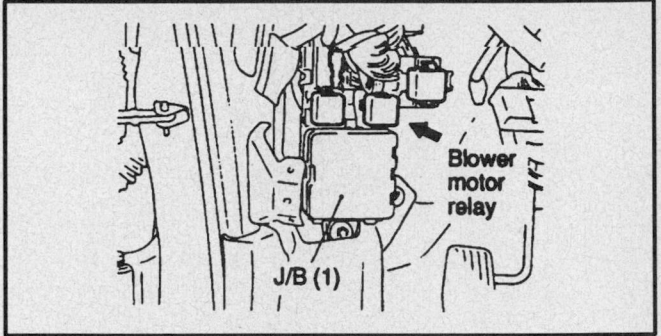

Relay block under left side of dash — Galant

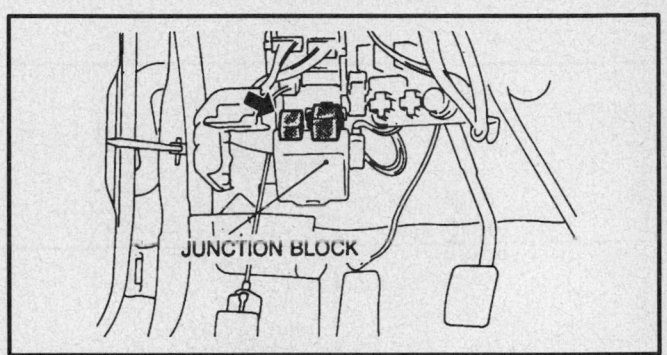

Blower motor relay under instrument panel — Mirage

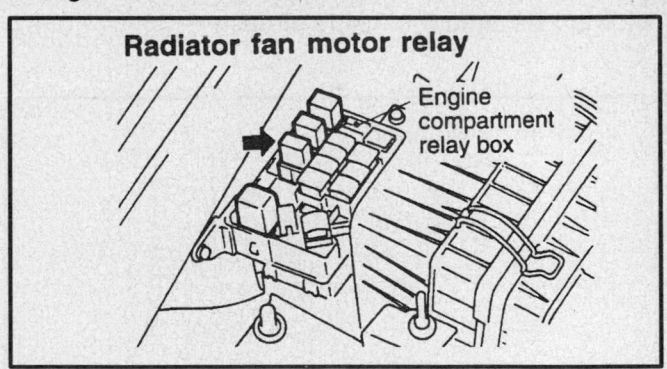

Radiator fan motor relay — Mirage

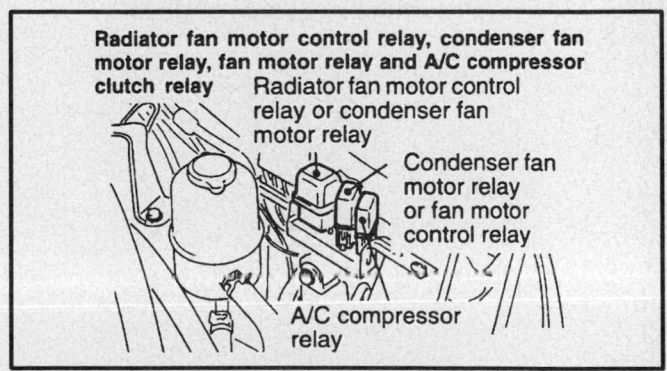

Condenser fan motor relay — Mirage

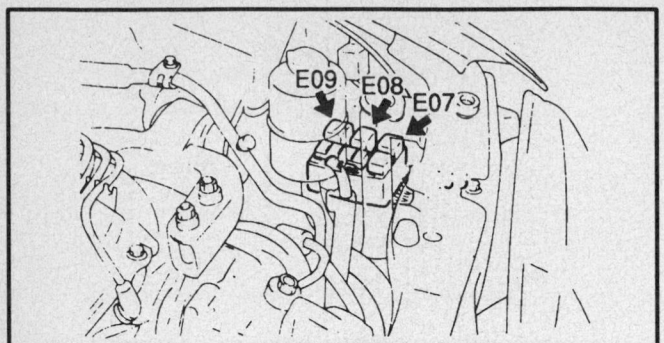

Condenser and fan motor relays — Precis

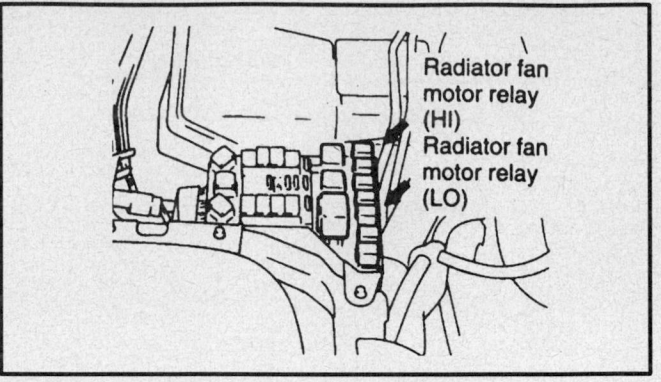

Radiator fan relays in right side of engine compartment — 3000GT

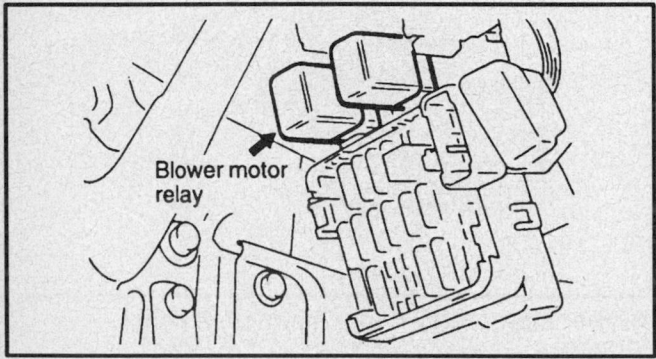

Blower relay under left side of dash — 3000GT

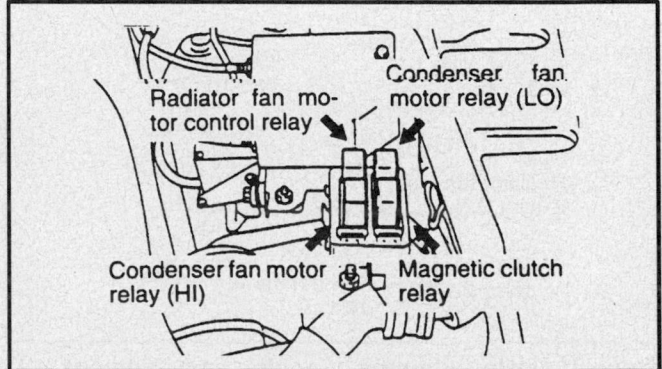

Relay block in left side of engine compartment — 3000GT full auto A/C

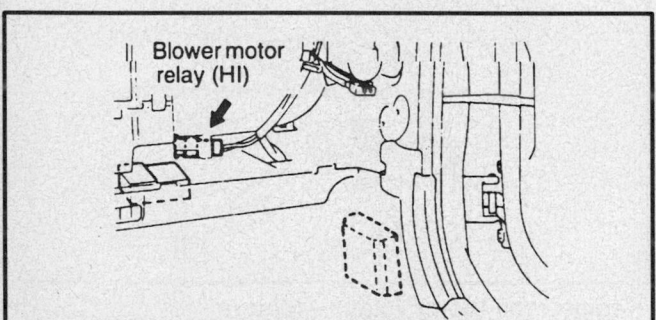

High blower relay under right side of dash — 3000GT

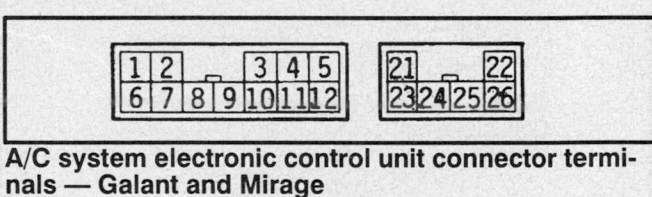

A/C system electronic control unit connector terminals — Galant and Mirage

A/C system electronic control unit connector terminals — 1993−94 Eclipse

A/C CONTROL UNIT DIAGNOSTICS — 1993–94 ECLIPSE

Terminal	Measurement item	Tester connection	Conditions		Specified value
1	Resistance	1–6	—		1,500±150 Ω at 25°C (77°F)
2	Voltage	2–3 2–8	Air conditioner switch	ON	System voltage
				OFF	0 V
3	Continuity	3-Ground	—		Continuity
4	Continuity	4-Ground	—		Continuity
5	Resistance	5–7	—		1,500±150 Ω at 25°C (77°F)
8	Continuity	8-Ground	—		Continuity
9	Voltage	9–3 9–8	Thermo sensor	OFF 78°C (172°F)	System voltage
				ON 85°C (185°F)	0 V
10	Voltage	10–3 10–8	ECONO switch	ON	System voltage
				OFF	0 V

A/C CONTROL UNIT DIAGNOSTICS — 1995 ECLIPSE TURBO

Terminal No.	Name of Signal	Condition	Terminal voltage
1	Automatic compressor ECM power supply	The ignition switch is ON	Battery positive voltage
2	Automatic compressor ECM power supply (ECONO mode)	When the ignition switch and the blower switch are ON, and the A/C switch has been turned to the first level	Battery positive voltage
6	A/C compressor clutch relay	When the compressor ON conditions are satisfied	Battery positive voltage
7	Automatic compressor ECM power supply (DRY mode)	When the ignition switch and the blower switch are ON, and the A/C switch has been turned to the second level	Battery positive voltage
8,9	Automatic compressor ECM ground	At all time	0V
21	Air inlet sensor	Sensor temperature is 25°C [1.5 kΩ]	Approx. 3V
22	Fin thermo sensor	Sensor temperature is 25°C [1.5 kΩ]	Approx. 3V
23	Air inlet sensor power supply	The ignition switch, blower switch and A/C switch are all ON	5V
26	Fin thermo sensor power supply	The ignition switch, blower switch and A/C switch are all ON	5V

A/C CONTROL UNIT DIAGNOSTICS — 1995 ECLIPSE NON-TURBO

Terminal No.	Name of Signal	Condition	Terminal voltage
5	Automatic compressor ECM power supply	The ignition switch is ON	Battery positive voltage
4	Automatic compressor ECM power supply (ECONO mode)	When the ignition switch and the blower switch are ON, and the A/C switch has been turned to the first level	Battery positive voltage
1	A/C compressor clutch relay	When the compressor ON conditions are satisfied	Battery positive voltage
13	Automatic compressor ECM power supply (DRY mode)	When the ignition switch and the blower switch are ON, and the A/C switch has been turned to the second level	Battery positive voltage
2	Automatic compressor ECM ground	At all time	0V
6	Air inlet sensor	Sensor temperature is 25°C [1.5 kΩ]	Approx. 3V
7	Fin thermo sensor	Sensor temperature is 25°C [1.5 kΩ]	Approx. 3V
14	Air inlet sensor power supply	The ignition switch, blower switch and A/C switch are all ON	5V
12	Fin thermo sensor power supply	The ignition switch, blower switch and A/C switch are all ON	5V

A/C CONTROL UNIT DIAGNOSTICS — GALANT

Terminal No.	Name of Signal	Condition	Terminal voltage
1	Automatic compressor ECM power supply	The ignition switch is ON	Battery positive voltage
2	Automatic compressor ECM power supply (ECONO mode)	When the ignition switch and the blower switch are ON, and the A/C switch has been turned to the first level	Battery positive voltage
6	A/C compressor clutch relay	When the compressor ON conditions are satisfied	Battery positive voltage
7	Automatic compressor ECM power supply (DRY mode)	When the ignition switch and the blower switch are ON, and the A/C switch has been turned to the second level	Battery positive voltage
8,9	Automatic compressor ECM ground	At all time	0V
21	Air thermo sensor	Sensor temperature is 25°C [1.0 kΩ]	Approx. 3V
22	Fin thermo sensor	Sensor temperature is 25°C [4.0 kΩ]	Approx. 3V
23	Air thermo sensor power supply	The ignition switch, blower switch and A/C switch are all ON	5V
26	Fin thermo sensor power supply	The ignition switch, blower switch and A/C switch are all ON	5V

A/C CONTROL UNIT DIAGNOSTICS — MIRAGE

Terminal No.	Name of Signal	Condition	Terminal voltage
1	Auto compressor control unit power supply	Ignition switch ON	Battery positive voltage
8	Auto compressor control unit earth	At all times	0V
7	Auto compressor control unit power supply (DRY mode)	When the ignition switch and the blower switch are ON, and the air conditioning switch has been turned to the second level	Battery positive voltage
2	Auto compressor control unit power supply (ECONO mode)	When the ignition switch and the blower switch are ON, and the air conditioning switch has been turned to the first level	Battery positive voltage
6	Air conditioning compressor clutch relay	When the compressor ON conditions are satisfied	Battery positive voltage
22	Air thermo sensor power supply	The ignition switch, blower switch and air conditioning switch are all ON	Approx. 3V
26	Air thermo sensor	At all times	0V

A/C CONTROL UNIT DIAGNOSTICS — 3000GT MANUAL A/C

Terminal No.	Signal	Conditions	Terminal voltage
8, 9	Auto compressor control unit ground	At all times	0V
1	Auto compressor control unit power supply	When ignition switch is ON	Battery positive voltage
6	Air conditioning compressor relay	When all conditions for switch-ON of the compressor are satisfied	Battery positive voltage
7	Air conditioning switch: A/C	When air conditioning switch pressed in to second step	Battery positive voltage
2	Air conditioning switch: ECONO	When air conditioning switch pressed in to first step	Battery positive voltage
21	Fin-thermo sensor ⊕	Ignition switch, blower switch and air conditioning switch: ON	Approx. 2.5V
22	Air-inlet sensor ⊕	Ignition switch, blower switch and air conditioning switch: ON	Approx. 1V
23	Fin-thermo sensor ⊖	Ignition switch, blower switch and air conditioning switch: ON Ambient temperature: 4°C (39°F)	0V
26	Air-inlet sensor ⊖	Ignition switch, blower switch and air conditioning switch: ON Ambient temperature: 4°C (39°F)	0V

A/C PERFORMANCE TEMPERATURE CHART — DIAMANTE AND 3000GT

Garage ambient temperature °C (°F)	21 (70)	26.7 (80)	32.2 (90)	37.8 (100)	43.3 (110)
Discharge air temperature °C (°F)	0.0 – 3.0 (32.0 – 37.4)	1.0 – 4.0 (33.8 – 39.2)	1.0 – 4.0 (33.8 – 39.2)	1.0 – 4.0 (33.8 – 39.2)	2.0 – 5.0 (35.6 – 41.0)
Compressor discharge pressure kPa (psi)	690 – 740 (98.1 – 105.3)	780 – 830 (110.9 – 118.1)	870 – 920 (123.7 – 130.9)	1,080 – 1,130 (153.6 – 160.7)	1,210 – 1,260 (172.1 – 179.2)
Compressor suction pressure kPa (psi)	130 – 190 (18.5 – 27.5)	130 – 190 (18.5 – 27.5)	130 – 190 (18.5 – 27.5)	130 – 190 (18.5 – 27.5)	130 – 190 (18.5 – 27.5)

A/C PERFORMANCE TEMPERATURE CHART — 1993–94 ECLIPSE

Garage ambient temperature °C (°F)	21 (70)	26.7 (80)	32.2 (90)	37.8 (100)	43.3 (110)
Discharge air temperature °C (°F)	2.0–8.0 (35.6–46.4)	2.0–8.0 (35.6–46.4)	2.0–8.0 (35.6–46.4)	4.0–11.0 (39.2–51.8)	6.0–14.0 (42.8–57.2)
Compressor discharge pressure kPa (psi)	900–1,300 (128–186)	1,000–1,400 (142–199)	1,100–1,500 (156–212)	1,300–1,700 (186–242)	1,500–1,900 (212–270)
Compressor suction pressure kPa (psi)	50–150 (7.1–21.3)	80–180 (11.4–25.6)	100–200 (14.2–28.4)	130–230 (18.5–32.7)	150–250 (21.3–35.6)

A/C PERFORMANCE TEMPERATURE CHART — 1995 ECLIPSE

Garage ambient temperature °C (°F)	20 (68)	25 (77)	35 (95)	40 (104)
Discharge air temperature °C (°F)	2.5–5.0 (37–41)	3.0–6.0 (37–43)	3.5–7.5 (38–46)	4.0–8.0 (39–46)
Compressor high pressure kPa (psi)	700–900 (101.6–130.6)	740–1,100 (107.4–159.6)	750–1,350 (108.8–195.4)	960–1,570 (139.3–227.8)
Compressor low pressure kPa (psi)	140 (20.3)	140–210 (20.3–30.5)	140–220 (20.3–31.9)	150–230 (21.8–33.4)

A/C PERFORMANCE TEMPERATURE CHART — 1994–95 GALANT

Garage ambient temperature °C (°F)	20 (68)	25 (77)	35 (95)	40 (104)
Discharge air temperature °C (°F)	2.5–4.5 (37–40)	2.5–4.5 (33–40)	4.0–6.5 (39–44)	6.5–9.0 (44–48)
Compressor high pressure kPa (psi)	765–960 (111.0–139.3)	765–960 (111.0–139.3)	1,325–1,420 (192.2–206.0)	1,570–1,765 (227.8–256.1)
Compressor low pressure kPa (psi)	40–135 (5.8–19.6)	40–135 (5.8–19.6)	80–175 (11.6–25.4)	155–255 (22.5–37.0)

A/C PERFORMANCE TEMPERATURE CHART — MIRAGE

Garage ambient temperature °C (°F)	21 (70)	26.7 (80)	32.2 (90)	37.8 (100)	43.3 (110)
Discharge air temperature °C (°F)	2.5 – 5.0 (36.5 – 41.0)	3.0 – 5.5 (37.4 – 41.9)	3.0 – 6.0 (37.4 – 42.8)	3.5 – 7.5 (38.3 – 45.5)	3.5 – 8.0 (38.3 – 46.4)
Compressor discharge pressure kPa (psi)	650 – 890 (92.5 – 126.6)	740 – 1,040 (105.3 – 147.9)	750 – 1,130 (106.7 – 160.7)	950 – 1,320 (135.1 – 187.7)	1,150 – 1,410 (163.6 – 200.5)
Compressor suction pressure kPa (psi)	140 – 210 (19.9 – 29.9)	140 – 210 (19.9 – 29.9)	140 – 210 (19.9 – 29.9)	150 – 220 (21.3 – 31.3)	150 – 220 (21.3 – 31.3)

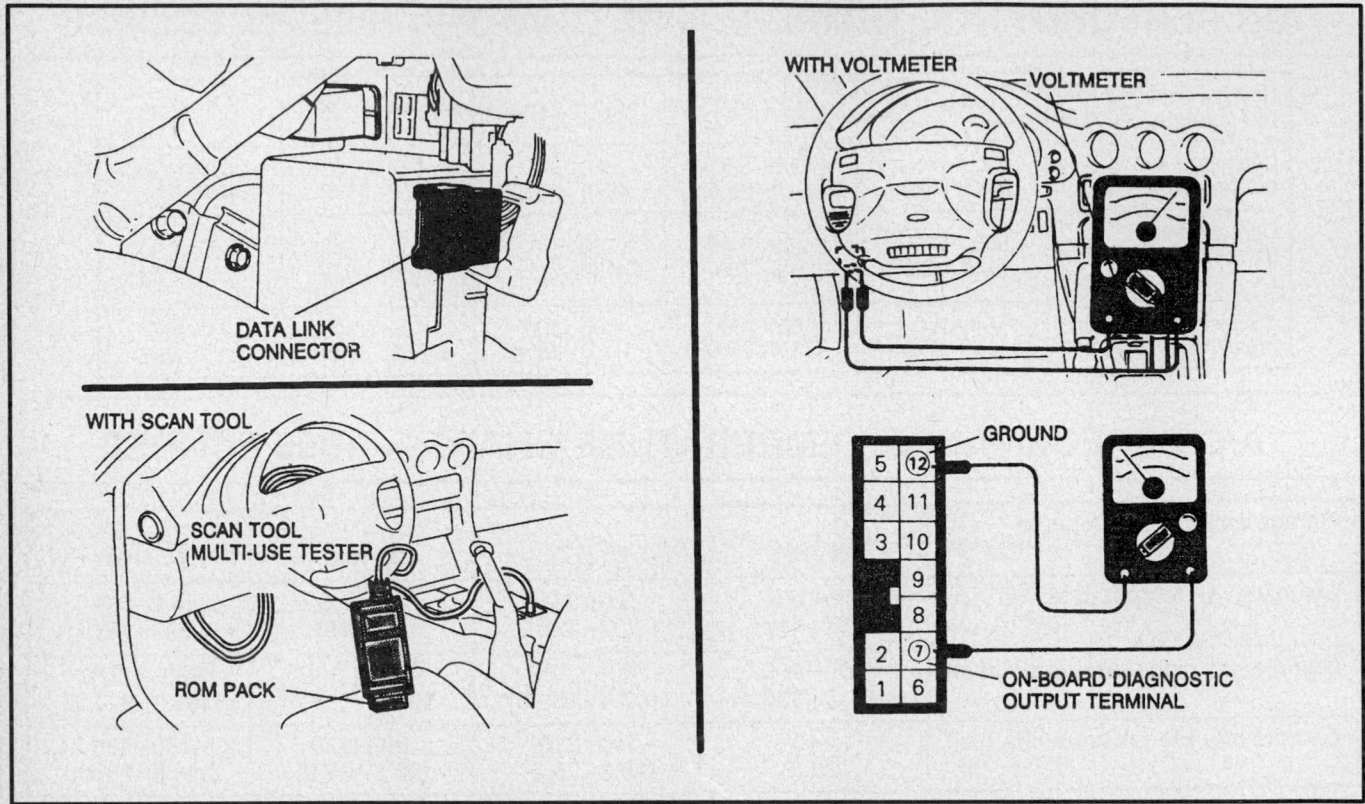

Self–diagnostics using scan tool or voltmeter — Diamante and 3000GT

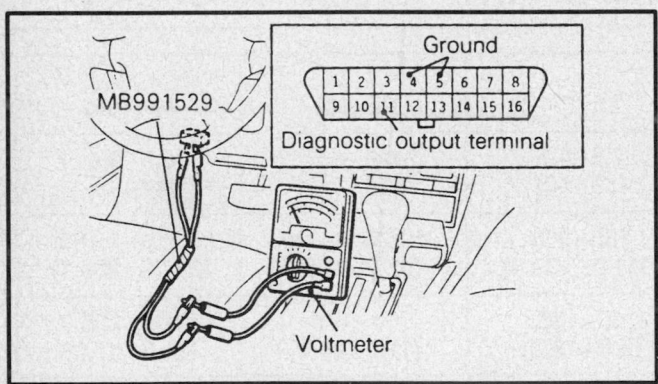

Self–diagnostic output terminal — 1994–95 Diamante and 3000GT

FULL AUTO A/C SELF–DIAGNOSTIC DISPLAY CODES — DIAMANTE AND 3000GT

No.	Display pattern (output codes) (use with voltmeter)	Cause	Fail safe
0	0.5 sec. / 3 sec. / 0.5 sec.	Normal	—
11	1.5 sec. 2 sec. 0.5 sec.	Open-circuited passenger compartment temperature sensor	Condition in which 25°C (77°F) is detected
12		Short-circuited passenger compartment temperature sensor	
13		Open-circuited air inlet sensor <1992 models> / Open-circuited ambience sensor <from 1993 models>	Condition in which 20°C (68°F) is detected
14		Shor-circuited air inlet sensor <1992 models> / Short-circuited ambience sensor <from 1993 models>	
21		Open-circuited fin thermo sensor	Condition in which –2°C (28°F) is detected
22		Short-circuited fin thermo sensor	
31		Open-circuited and short-circuited air mix damper potentiometer	MAX. HOT (Becomes MAX. COOL only when MAX. COOL is set.)
32		Open-circuited and short-circuited mode selector damper potentiometer	DEF. (Becomes FACE only when FACE mode is set.)
41		Defective air mix damper motor	—
42		Defective mode selector damper motor	—

NOTE: (1) If two or more abnormal conditions occur at the same time, the code numbers are alternately displayed, in order, repeatedly.
(2) The nature of the malfunction is entered and stored in the memory from the time the malfunction occurs until the ignition switch is next turned to OFF.

FULL AUTO A/C SELF—DIAGNOSTIC CODES — DIAMANTE AND 3000GT

Item no.	Inspection point	Method	Criteria		Probable cause	Remedy
			Normal	Abnormal		
11	Room-temperature sensor	Measure resistance of sensor when room temperature is 25°C (77°F).	Approx. 4 kΩ	Largely deviates from approx. 4 kΩ	Defective room-temperature sensor	Replace room-temperature sensor.
		Measure voltage across terminal ⑲ of air conditioner control unit and ground when room temperature is 25°C (77°F).	In approx. 2.3 – 2.9 V range	–	Open-circuited harness between room-temperature sensor and air conditioner control unit	Correct harness.
			–	Outside approx. 2.3 – 2.9 V range	Poor connection of air conditioner control unit connector or defective air conditioner control unit	Correct connector connection or replace air conditioner control unit.
13	Outside-air-temperature sensor	Measure resistance of sensor when ambient temperature is 25°C (77°F).	Approx. 4 kΩ	Largely deviates from approx. 4 kΩ	Defective outside-air sensor	Replace outside-air-temperature sensor.
		Measure voltage across terminal ⑥ of air control conditioner unit and ground when ambient temperature is 25°C (77°F).	In approx. 2.2 – 2.8 V range	–	Open-circuited harness between outside-air-temperature sensor and air conditioner control unit	Correct harness.
			–	Outside approx. 2.2 – 2.8 V range	Poor connection of air-conditioner control unit connector or defective air conditioner control unit	Correct connector connection or replace air conditioner control unit.
15	Water-temperature sensor	Measure resistance of sensor when water temperature is 22.5 to 30.5°C (57.6 to 86.9°F).	Conductive	Nonconductive	Defective water-temperature sensor	Replace water-temperature sensor.
		Measure voltage across terminal ⑧ of air conditioner control unit and ground when water temperature is 22.5 to 30.5°C (57.6 to 86.9°F).	Approx. 12 V	–	Open-circuited harness between water-temperature sensor and air control unit	Correct harness.
			–	Largely deviates from approx. 12 V	Poor connection of air conditioner control unit connector or defective air conditioner control unit	Correct connector connection or replace air conditioner control unit.
21	Air thermo sensor	Measure resistance of sensor when sensor's sensing temperature is 25°C (77°F).	Approx. 4 kΩ	Largely deviates from approx. 4 kΩ	Defective air thermo sensor	Replace air thermo sensor.
		Measure voltage across terminal ⑰ of air conditioner control unit and ground when sensor's sensing temperature is 25°C (77°F).	In approx. 2.3 – 2.9 V range	–	Open-circuited harness between air thermo sensor and air conditioner control unit	Correct harness.
			–	Outside approx. 2.3 – 2.9 V range	Poor connection of air conditioner control unit connector or defective air conditioner control unit	Correct connector connection or replace air conditioner control unit.
31	Air mix damper potentiometer				Defective air mix damper potentiometer	Replace air mix damper potentiometer.
		Measure voltage across terminal ⑤ of air conditioner control unit and ground when potentiometer is in MAX. COOL position.	In approx. 0.1 – 0.3 V range	–	Open-circuited harness between air mix damper potentiometer and air conditioner control unit	Correct harness.
			–	Outside approx. 0.1 – 0.3 V range	Poor connection of air conditioner control unit connector or defective air conditioner control unit	Correct connector connection or replace air conditioner control unit.
33	Outlet selector damper potentiometer				Defective outlet selector damper potentiometer	Replace outlet selector damper potentiometer.
		Measure voltage across terminal ⑥ of air conditioner control unit and ground when potentiometer is in FACE position.	In approx. 0.1 – 0.3 V range	–	Open-circuited harness between outlet selector damper potentiometer and air conditioner control	Correct harness.
			–	Outside approx. 0.1 – 0.3 V range	Poor connection of air conditioner control unit connector or defective air conditioner control unit	Correct connector connection or replace air conditioner control unit.

FULL AUTO A/C TROUBLESHOOTING BY SYMPTOM — DIAMANTE

No.	Sympton	Probable cause	Remedy
1	Air conditioning does not operate when the ignition switch in the ON position	Open-circuited power circuit harness	Correct harness.
		Defective compressor relay in relay box	Replace.
		Defective magnet clutch	Replace.
		Defective thermostat	Replace.
		Defective air conditioning engine coolant temperature switch	Replace.
		Defective dual pressure switch	Replace.
		Refrigerant leak	Charge refrigerant, correct leak.
		Excessive refrigerant	Discharge refrigerant.
		Defective control panel	Replace control panel.
		Defective belt lock controller <DOHC>	Replace belt lock controller.
		Defective air conditioning control unit	Replace air conditioning control unit.
		Defective engine control module	Replace engine control module.
2	Interior temperature does not raise (No warm air coming out).	Defective passenger compartment temperature sensor input circuit	Check on-board diagnostic output. Replace defective parts.
		Defective air mix damper potentiometer input circuit	
		Defective air mix damper drive motor	Replace air mix damper drive motor.
		Incorrect engagement of air mix damper drive motor lever and air mix damper	Engage correctly.
		Sticking air mix damper	Correct air mix damper.
		Open-circuited harness between air mix damper drive motor and air conditioning control unit	Correct harness.
		Defective control panel	Replace control panel.
		Defective air conditioning control unit	Replace air conditioning control unit.
3	Interior temperature does not lower (No cold air coming out).	Defective passenger compartment temperature sensor input circuit	Check on-board diagnostic output. Replace defective parts.
		Defective air inlet sensor input circuit <1992 models> Defective ambience sensor input circuit <from 1993 models>	
		Defective fin thermo sensor input circuit	
		Defective air mix damper potentiometer input circuit	
		Defective air mix damper drive motor	Replace air mix damper drive motor.

FULL AUTO A/C TROUBLESHOOTING BY SYMPTOM—DIAMANTE, CONT.

No.	Sympton	Probable cause	Remedy
3	Interior temperature does not lower (No cold air coming out)	Incorrect engagement of air mix damper drive motor lever and air mix damper	Engage correctly.
		Sticking air mix damper	Correct air mix damper.
		Open-circuited harness between air mix damper drive motor and air conditioning control unit	Correct harness.
		Open-circuited harness between photo sensor and air conditioning control unit	Correct harness.
		Defective air conditioning compressor clutch relay in the relay box	Replace.
		Refrigerant leak	Charge refrigerant, correct leak.
		Excessive refrigerant	Discharge refrigerant.
		Clogged receiver	Replace receiver.
		Clogged expansion valve	Replace expansion valve.
		Defective compressor	Replace compressor.
		Defective thermostat	Replace thermostat.
		Defective revolution pick up sensor	Replace revolution pick up sensor.
		Defective air inlet sensor <1992 models> Defective ambience sensor <from 1993 models>	Replace sensor.
		Defective air conditioning engine coolant temperature switch	Replace air conditioning engine coolant temperature switch.
		Defective magnetic clutch	Replace.
		Defective belt lock controller	Replace belt lock controller.
		Defective control panel	Replace control panel.
		Defective air conditioning control unit	Replace air conditionning control unit.
4	Blower motor does not rotate	Defective heater relay	Replace heater relay.
		Blown thermal fuse inside power transistor	Replace power transistor.
		Open-circuited harness between fuse and heater relay	Correct harness.
		Open-circuited harness between heater relay and blower motor	
		Open-circuited harness between power transistor and air conditioning control unit	Correct harness.
		Defective blower motor	Replace blower motor.
		Defective control panel	Replace control panel.
		Defective air conditioning control unit	Replace air conditioning control unit.

FULL AUTO A/C TROUBLESHOOTING BY SYMPTOM—DIAMANTE, CONT.

No.	Sympton	Probable cause	Remedy
5	Blower motor does not stop rotating.	Defective blower motor HI relay	Replace power relay.
		Defective power transistor	Replace power transistor.
		Short-circuited harness between blower motor relay and power transistor and air conditioning control unit	Correct harness.
		Defective control panel	Replace control panel.
		Defective air conditioning control unit	Replace air conditioning control unit.
6	Inside/outside-air selector damper does not operate.	Defective inside/outside-air selector drive motor	Replace inside/outside-air selector drive motor.
		Incorrect engagement of inside/outside-air selector drive motor and inside/outside-air selector damper	Engage correctly.
		Malfunctioning inside/outside-air selector damper	Correct inside/outside-air selector damper.
		Open-circuited harness between inside/outside-air selector motor and air conditioning control unit	Correct harness.
		Defective control panel	Replace control panel.
		Defective air conditioning control unit	Replace air conditioning control unit.
7	Outlet selector damper does not operate	Defective outlet selector damper potentiometer input circuit	Check on-board diagnostic output. Replace defective parts.
		Defective outlet selector drive motor	Replace outlet selector drive motor.
		Incorrect engagement of outlet selector drive motor and outlet selector damper	Engage correctly.
		Malfunctioning DEF.,FACE, and FOOT damper	Correct DEF., FACE, and FOOT damper.
		Open-circuited harness between outlet selector motor and control unit	Correct harness.
		Defective control panel	Replace control panel.
		Defective air conditioning control unit	Replace air conditioning control unit.
8	Condenser fan does not operate when the air conditioner is activated.	Defective condenser fan motor relay	Replace power relay.
		Defective condenser fan motor	Replace condenser fan motor.
9	Set temperature returns to 25°C (112°F) when the ignition switch is turned ON and OFF.	Open-circuited power circuit harness	Correct harness.
		Defective air conditioning control unit	Replace air conditioning control unit.

FULL AUTO A/C POWER CIRCUIT CHECK — DIAMANTE

1. Inspection of air conditioning control unit power source circuit

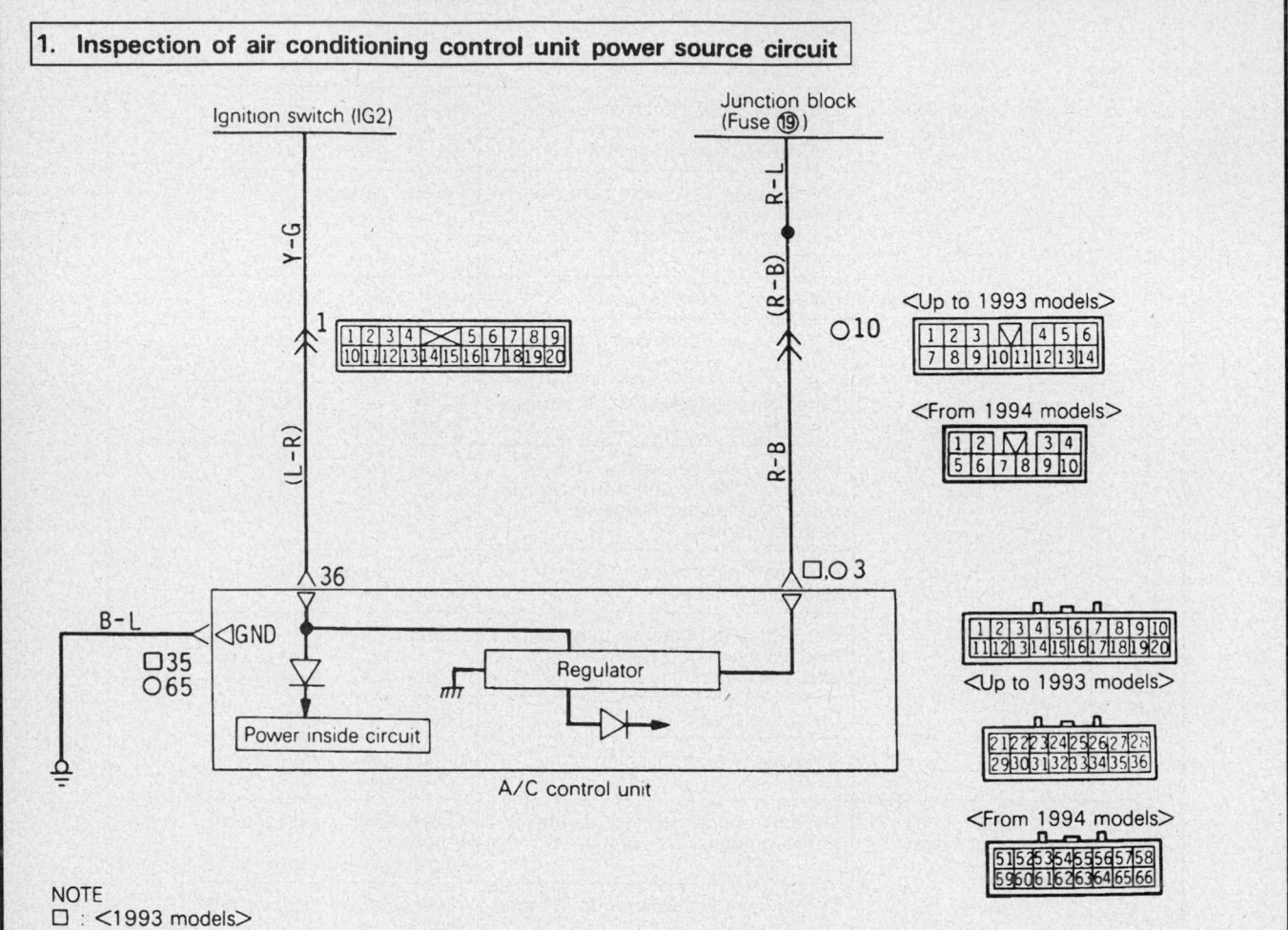

NOTE
□ : <1993 models>
○ : <From 1994 models>

Troubleshooting Hints

- Air conditioning control unit terminal voltage

Terminal No.	Signal name	Condition	Terminal voltage
3*2,*3	Back up power source	Normally	Battery positive voltage
36	A/C control unit power source	Ignition switch ON	Battery positive voltage
35*2 or 65*3	A/C control unit ground	Normally	0V

NOTE
*2: <1993 models>
*3: <From 1994 models>

POTENTIOMETER CIRCUIT CHECK — DIAMANTE

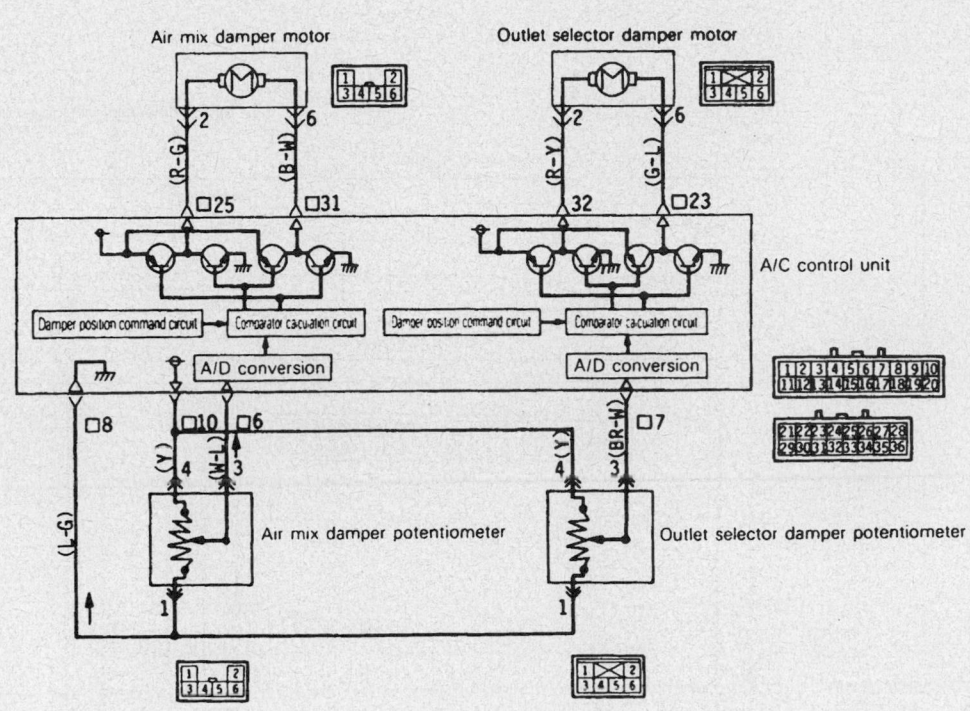

NOTE

□ : <From 1993 models>

Troubleshooting Hints

- Diagnosis
  No. 31 (Fix air mix damper at MAX. HOT position. However, fix at MAX. COOL position only when setting MAX. COOL.)
  No. 32 (Fix outlet selector damper at FACE position. However, fix at FACE position only when setting FACE mode.)

- Air conditioning control unit terminal voltages

Terminal No.	Signal name	Condition	Terminal voltage
6•2	Air mix damper potentiometer (input)	Air mix damper at MAX. COOL position	0.1–0.3V
		Air mix damper at MAX. HOT position	4.7–5.0V
7•2	Outlet selector damper potentiometer (input)	Outlet selector damper at FACE position	0.1–0.5V
		Outlet selector damper at DEF. position	4.7–5.0V
8•2	Air mix damper and outlet selector damper potentiometer (−)	Normally	0V
10•2	Sensor power source	Normally	4.8–5.2V

NOTE

•2: <From 1993 models>

INTERIOR TEMP. SENSOR, AIR INLET TEMP. SENSOR AND FIN THERMO SENSOR CHECKS — DIAMANTE

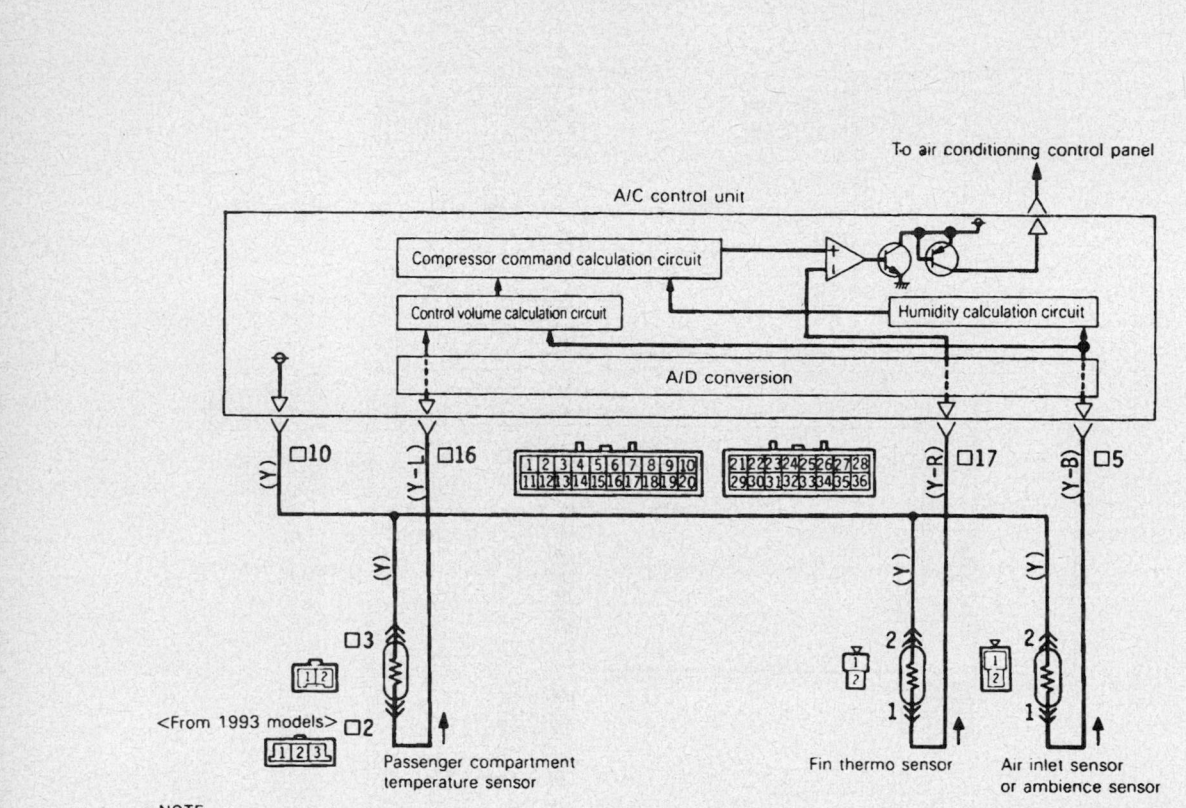

NOTE

□ : <From 1993 models>

Troubleshooting Hints

- Diagnosis
  No. 11, 12 [Fix passenger compartment temperature sensor input signal at 25°C (77°F).]
  No. 13, 14 [Fix ambience sensor[2] input signal at 20°C (68°F).]
  No. 21, 22 [Fix fin thermo sensor input signal at −2°C (28°F).]

- Air conditioning control unit terminal voltages.

Terminal No.	Signal name	Condition	Terminal voltage
5[2]	ambience sensor[2]	Temperature at sensor 25°C (77°F) (4 kΩ)	2.3–2.6V
10[2]	Sensor power source	Normally	4.8–5.2V
16[2]	Passenger compartment temperature sensor	Temperature at sensor 25°C (77°F) (4 kΩ)	2.5–2.7V
17[2]	Fin thermo sensor	Temperature at sensor 25°C (77°F) (4 kΩ) when air conditioning is OFF	2.5–2.7V

NOTE

[2]: <From 1993 models>

PHOTO SENSOR AND ENGINE COOLANT SENSOR CHECKS — DIAMANTE

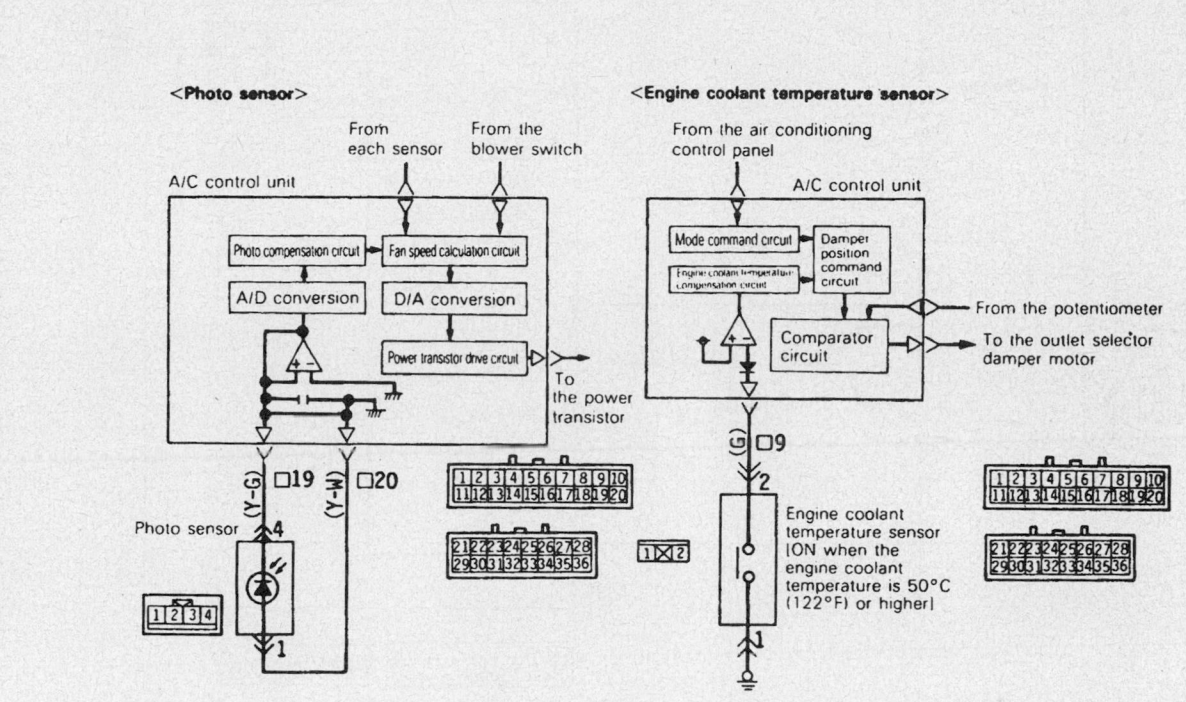

NOTE

☐ : <From 1993 models>

Troubleshooting Hints

Air conditioning control unit terminal voltages

Terminal No.	Signal name	Condition	Terminal voltage
19*2	Photo sensor ⊖	Normally	0V
20*2	Photo sensor ⊕	Illuminance 100,000 lux or more	−0.1 to −0.2V
		Illuminance less than 0 lux	0V
9*2	Engine coolant temperature sensor ⊕	Switch OFF [Engine coolant temperature less than 50°C (122°F)]	1.2V
		Switch ON [Engine coolant temperature 50°C (122°F) or higher]	0V

NOTE

*2: <From 1993 models>

POWER TRANSISTOR AND BLOWER MOTOR RELAY CHECKS — DIAMANTE

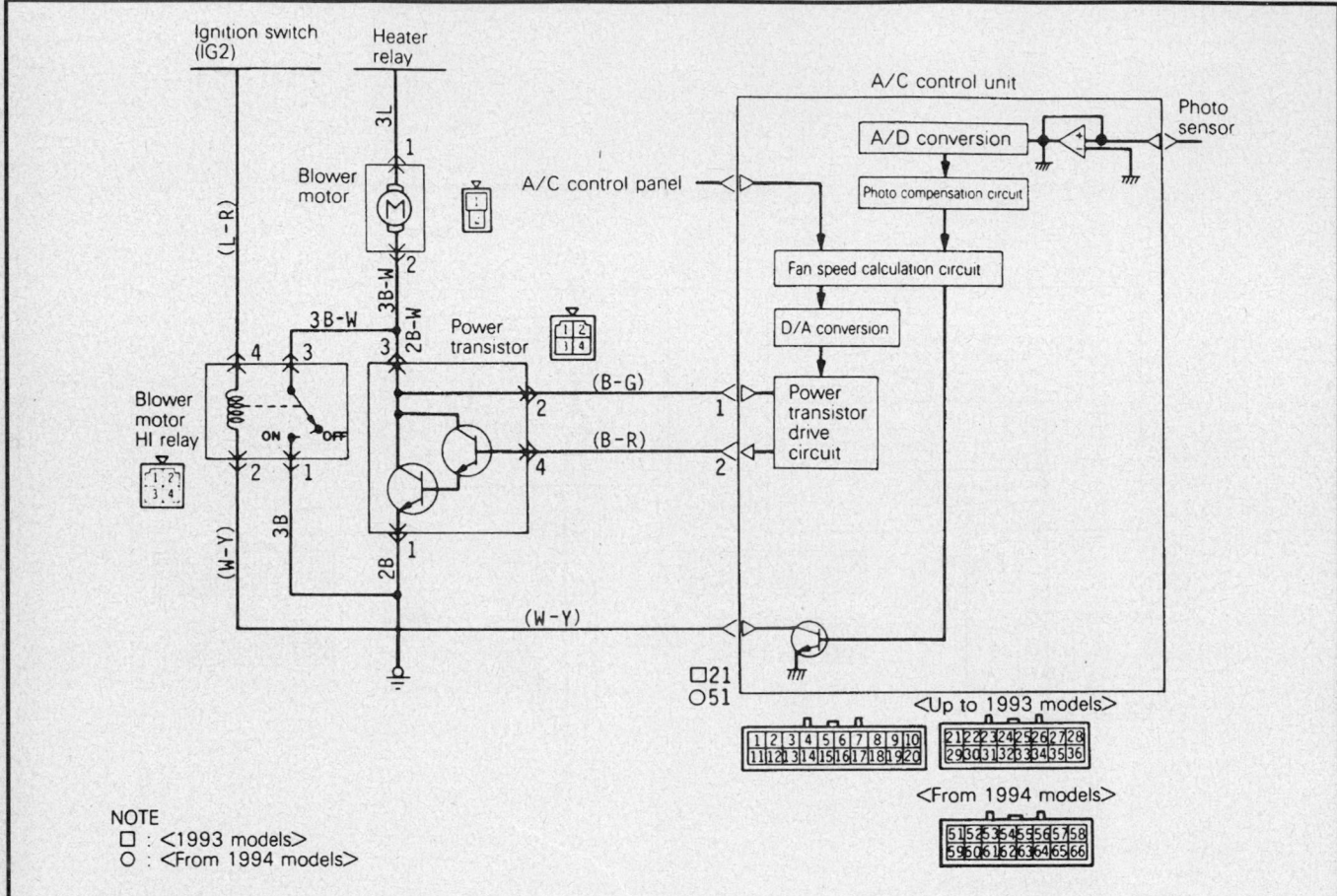

NOTE
□ : <1993 models>
○ : <From 1994 models>

Troubleshooting Hints

Air conditioning control unit terminal voltages

Terminal No.	Signal name	Condition	Terminal voltage
1	Power transister collector	Switch is turned OFF.	Battery positive voltage
		Switch is placed in LO.	Approx. 7V
		Switch is placed in HI.	0
2	Power transistor base	Blower switch is turned OFF.	0
		Blower switch is placed in LO.	Approx. 1.3V
		Blower switch is placed in HI.	Approx. 1.2V
21*2 or 51*3	Blower motor relay	Fan switch H is ON.	1.5V or less
		Fan switch in M, L, or OFF.	Battery positive voltage

NOTE

*2: <1993 models>
*3: <From 1994 models>

BELT LOCK CONTROLLER CIRCUIT CHECK — DIAMANTE

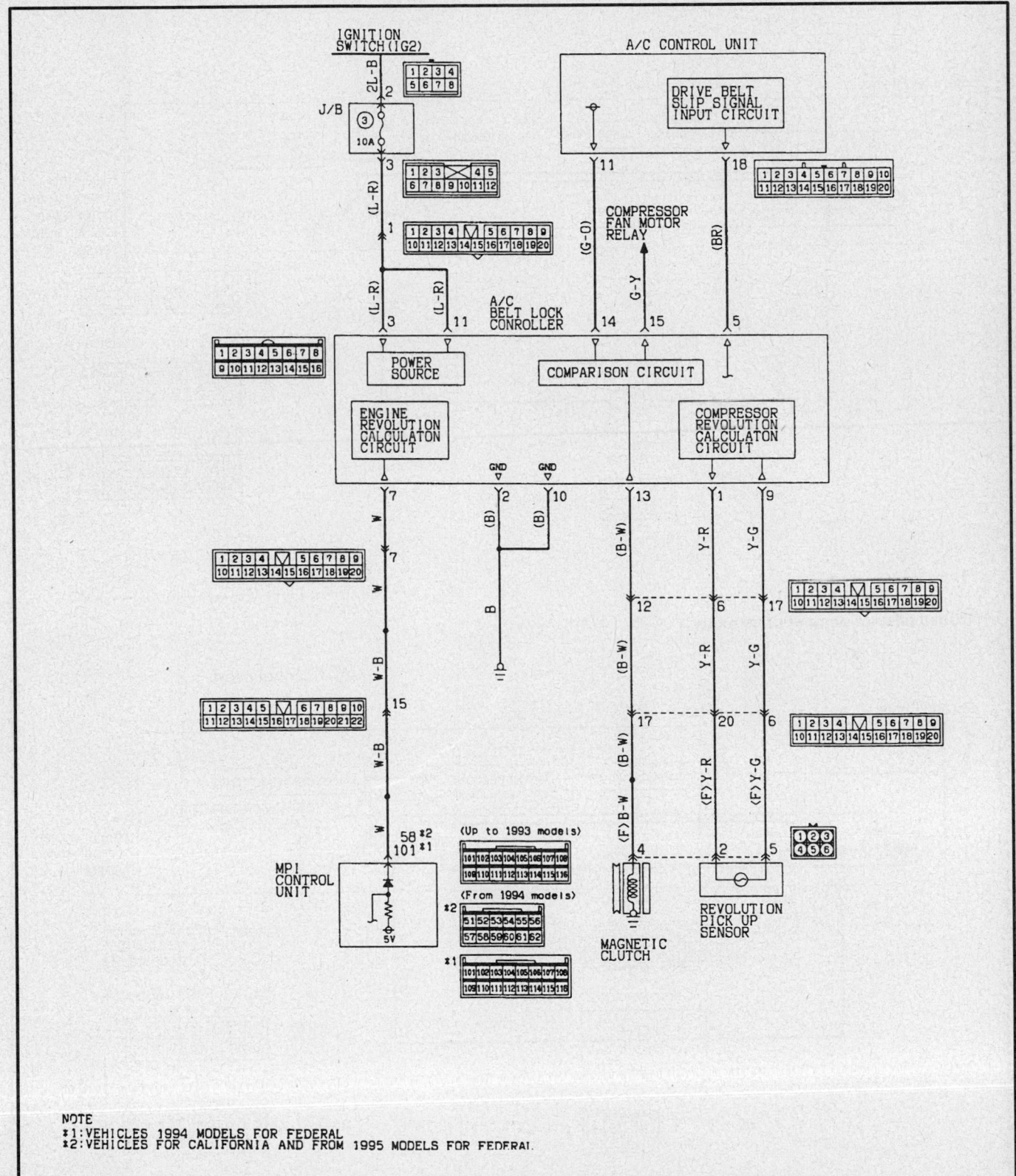

NOTE
‡1: VEHICLES 1994 MODELS FOR FEDERAL
‡2: VEHICLES FOR CALIFORNIA AND FROM 1995 MODELS FOR FEDERAL

DAMPER MOTOR CIRCUIT CHECK — DIAMANTE

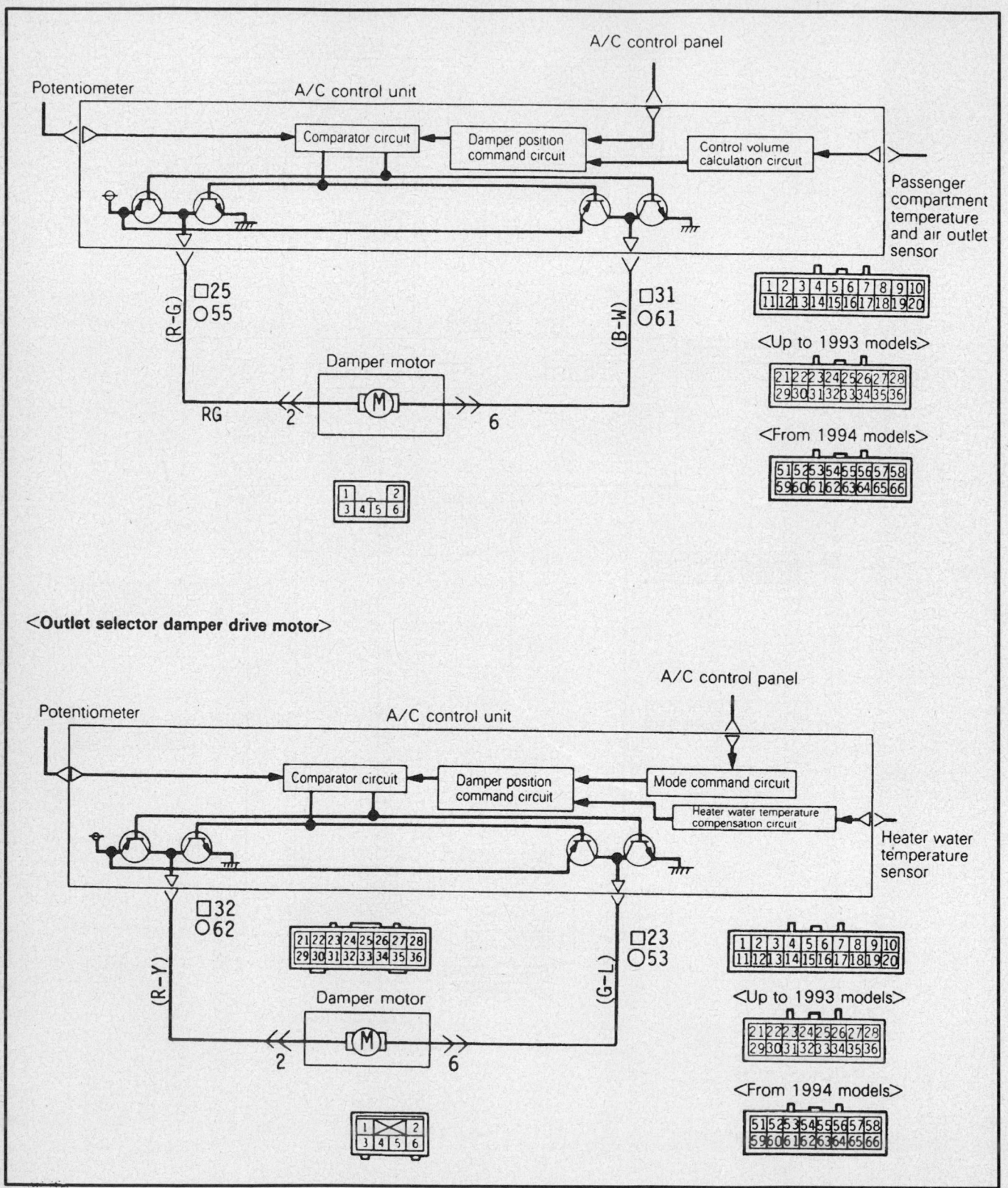

<Outlet selector damper drive motor>

FULL AUTO A/C TROUBLESHOOTING BY SYMPTOM — 3000GT

No.	Symptom	Probable cause	Remedy
1	Air conditioning does not operate when the ignition switch in the ON position.	Open-circuited power circuit harness	Correct harness.
		Defective control panel	Replace control panel.
		Defective air conditioning control unit	Check on-board diagnostic output.
		Defective magnetic clutch relay in relay box	Replace.
		Defective magnet clutch	Replace.
		Defective thermostat	Replace.
		Defective A/C engine coolant temperature switch for air conditioning cut off <Up to 1993 models>	Replace.
		Defective dual pressure switch	Replace.
		Refrigerant leak	Charge refrigerant, correct leak.
		Excessive refrigerant	Discharge refrigerant.
		Defective A/C compressor lock controller <DOHC>	Replace A/C compressor lock controller.
		Defective MFI control unit	Replace MFI control unit.
2	Interior temperature does not raise (No warm air coming out).	Defective interior temperature sensor input circuit	Check on-board diagnostic output. Replace defective parts.
		Defective blend air damper potentiometer input circuit	
		Defective blend air damper drive motor	Replace blend air damper drive motor.
		Incorrect engagement of blend air damper drive motor lever and blend air damper	Engage correctly.
		Sticking blend air damper	Correct blend air damper.
		Open-circuited harness between blend air damper drive motor and air conditioning control unit	Correct harness.
		Defective control panel	Replace control panel.
		Defective air conditioning control unit	Replace air conditioning control unit.
3	Interior temperature does not lower (No cold air coming out).	Defective interior temperature sensor input circuit	Check on-board diagnostic output. Replace defective parts.
		Defective air inlet sensor input circuit	
		Defective air thermo sensor input circuit	

FULL AUTO A/C TROUBLESHOOTING BY SYMPTOM — 3000GT, CONT.

No.	Symptom	Probable cause	Remedy
3	Interior temperature does not lower (No cold air coming out).	Defective blend air damper drive motor	Replace blend air damper drive motor.
		Incorrect engagement of blend air damper drive motor lever and blend air damper	Engage correctly.
		Sticking blend air damper	Correct blend air damper.
		Open-circuited harness between blend air damper drive motor and air conditioning control unit	Correct harness.
		Open-circuited harness between photo sensor and air conditioning control unit	Correct harness.
		Defective air-conditioning compressor relay in the relay box	Replace.
		Defective thermostat	Replace thermostat.
		Defective revolution pick up sensor <DOHC>	Replace revolution pick up sensor.
		Refrigerant leak	Charge refrigerant, correct leak.
		Excessive refrigerant	Discharge refrigerant.
		Clogged receiver	Replace receiver.
		Clogged expansion valve	Replace expansion valve.
		Defective compressor	Replace compressor.
		Defective air inlet sensor	Replace air inlet sensor.
		Defective magnetic clutch	Replace.
		Defective A/C compressor lock controller	Replace A/C compressor lock controller.
		Defective control panel	Replace control panel.
		Defective air conditioning control unit	Replace air conditioning control unit.
4	Blower motor does not rotate.	Defective blower motor	Replace blower motor.
		Blown thermal fuse inside air conditioning power transistor	Replace air conditioning power transistor.
		Defective blower motor relay	Replace blower motor relay.
		Open-circuited harness between fuse and blower motor relay	Correct harness.
		Open-circuited harness between blower motor relay and blower motor	Correct harness.
		Open-circuited harness between air conditioning power transistor and air conditioning control unit	Correct harness.
		Defective control panel	Replace control panel.
		Defective air conditioning control unit	Replace air conditioning control unit.

FULL AUTO A/C TROUBLESHOOTING BY SYMPTOM — 3000GT, CONT.

No.	Symptom	Probable cause	Remedy
5	Blower motor does not stop rotating.	Defective blower motor HI relay	Replace power relay.
		Short-circuited harness between blower motor relay and air conditioning power transistor air conditioning control unit	Correct harness.
		Defective control panel	Replace control panel.
		Defective air conditioning control unit	Replace air conditioning control unit.
		Defective air conditioning control unit	Replace air conditioning control unit.
		Defective air conditioning power transistor	Replace air conditioning power transistor.
6	Air selection damper does not operate.	Defective air selection drive motor	Replace air selection drive motor.
		Incorrect engagement of air selection drive motor damper	Engage correctly.
		Malfunctioning air selection damper	Correct air selection damper.
		Open-circuited harness between air selection motor and air conditioning control unit	Correct harness.
		Defective control panel	Replace control panel.
		Defective control panel	Replace control panel.
		Defective air conditioning control unit	Replace air conditioning control unit.
7	Mode selection damper does not operate.	Defective mode selection damper potentiometer input circuit	Check on-board diagnostic output. Replace defective parts.
		Defective mode selection drive motor	Replace mode selection drive motor.
		Incorrect engagement of mode selection drive motor and mode selection damper	Engage correctly.
		Malfunctioning DEF., FACE, and FOOT damper	Correct DEF., FACE, and FOOT damper.
		Open-circuited harness between mode selection motor and control unit	Correct harness.
		Defective control panel	Replace control panel.
		Defective air conditioning control unit	Replace air conditioning control unit.
8	Condenser fan does not operate when the air conditioning is activated.	Defective condenser fan motor relay	Replace power relay.
		Defective condenser fan motor	Replace condenser fan motor.

FULL AUTO A/C TROUBLESHOOTING BY SYMPTOM — 3000GT, CONT.

No.	Symptom	Probable cause	Remedy
9	Air-conditioning graphic display does not function correctly	Open-circuited harness between control panel and air conditioning control unit	Correct harness.
		Defective control panel	Replace control panel.
		Defective air conditioning control unit	Replace air conditioning control unit.
10	Air conditioning control panel blinks.	Wet compressor drive belt	Dry.
		Insufficient compressor drive belt tension	Check and adjust.
		Defective compressor drive belt	Replace.
		Defective compressor	Check and replace.
		Defective revolution pick-up sensor	Check and replace.
		Defective air conditioning switch	Replace air conditioning control panel.
		Defective A/C compressor lock controller	Replace A/C compressor lock controller.
		Defective air conditioning control unit	Replace air conditioning control unit.
		Defective MFI control unit	Replace MFI control unit.
11	Set temperature returns to 25°C (112°F) when the ignition switch is turned ON and OFF.	Open-circuited power circuit harness	Correct harness.
		Defective air conditioning control unit	Replace air conditioning control unit.

FULL AUTO A/C POWER CIRCUIT CHECK — 3000GT

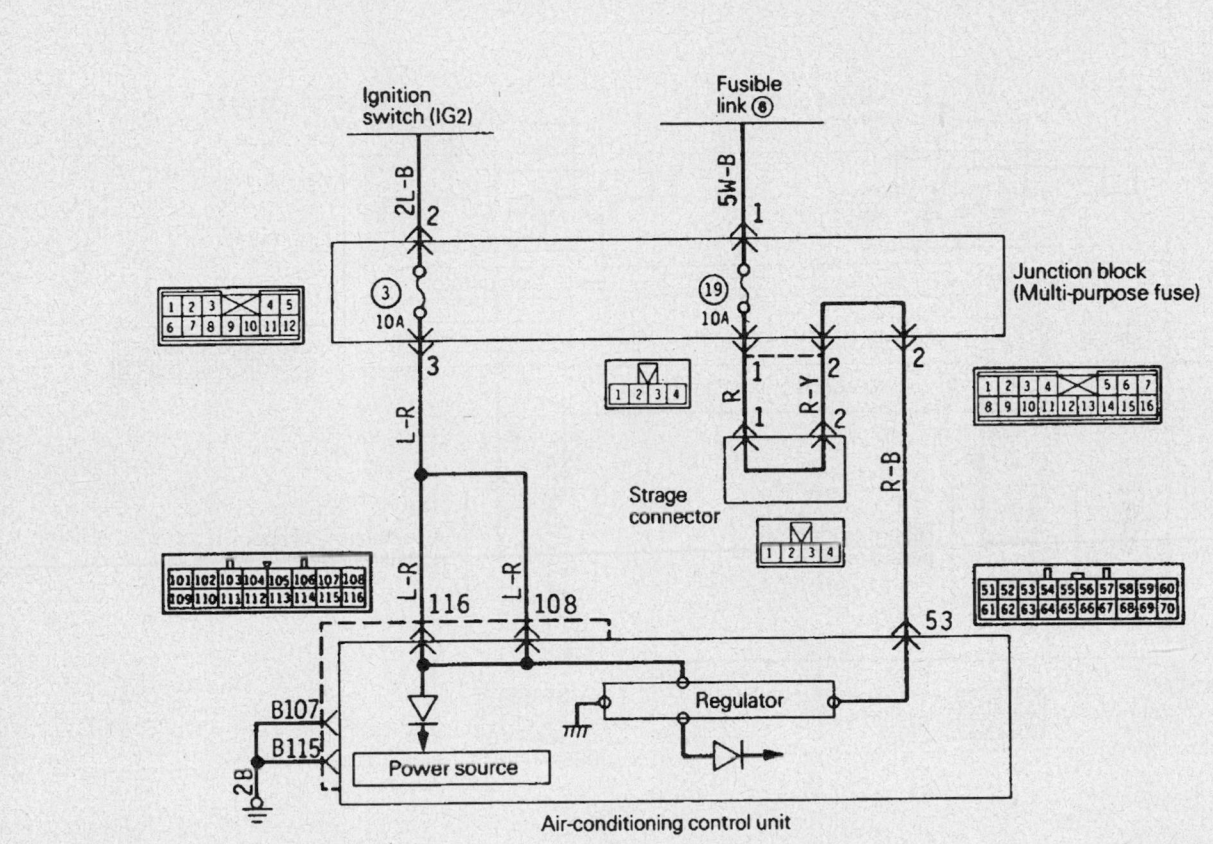

Troubleshooting Hints

● Air conditioning control unit terminal voltage

Terminal No.	Signal name	Condition	Terminal voltage
53	Backup power source	Normally	Battery positive voltage
108, 116	Air conditioning control unit power source	Ignition switch ON	Battery positive voltage
107, 115	Air conditioning control unit ground	Normally	0 V

POTENTIOMETER CIRCUIT CHECK — 3000GT

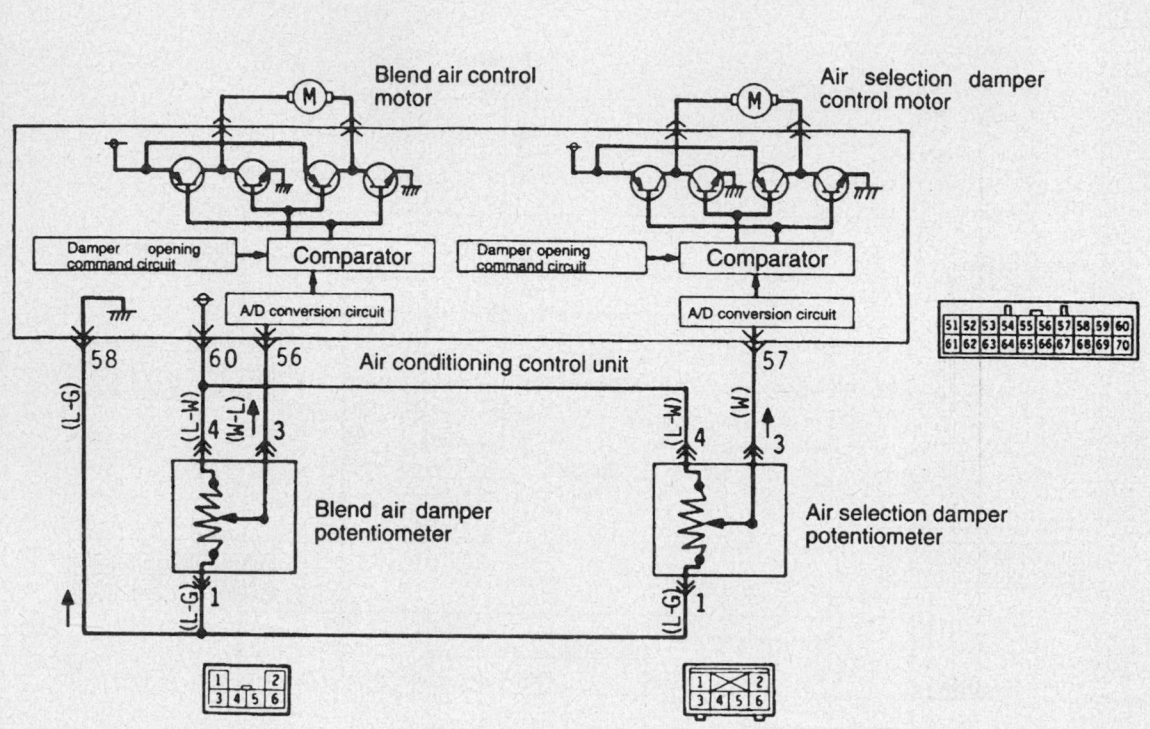

Troubleshooting Hints

- Diagnosis

    No. 31 (Fix blend air damper at MAX. HOT position, or at MAX. COOL position when it is at MAX. COOL position.)

    No. 32 (Fix air selection damper at FACE position, or at FACE position when it is at FACE position.)

- Air conditioning control unit terminal voltages

Terminal No.	Signal name	Condition	Terminal voltage
56	Blend air damper potentiometer (input)	Blend air damper at MAX. COOL position	0.1–0.3 V
		Blend air damper at MAX. HOT position	4.7–5.0 V
57	Mode selection damper potentiometer (input)	Air selection damper at FACE position	0.1–0.3 V
		Air selection damper at DEF. position	4.7–5.0 V
58	Blend air damper and mode selection damper potentiometer (−)	Normally	0 V
60	Sensor power source	Normally	4.8–5.2 V

COMPARTMENT TEMP. SENSOR, OUTSIDE AIR TEMP. SENSOR AND AIR THERMO SENSOR CIRCUIT CHECKS — 3000GT

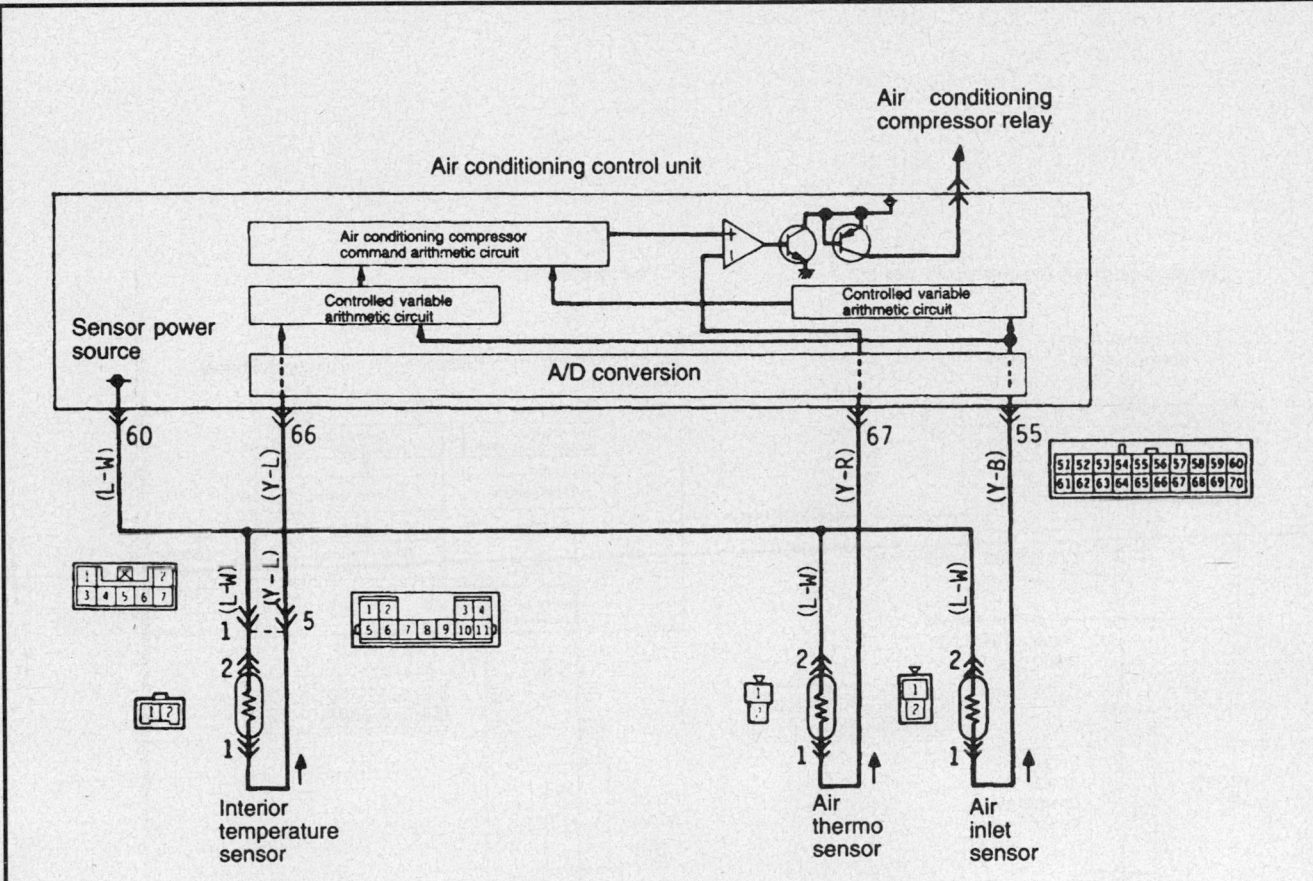

Troubleshooting Hints

● Diagnosis
    No. 11, 12 [Fix interior temperature sensor input signal at 25°C (77°F).]
    No. 13, 14 [Fix air inlet sensor input signal at 15°C (59°F).]
    No. 21, 22 [Fix air thermo sensor input signal at –2°C (–35.6°F).]

● Air conditioning control unit terminal voltages

Terminal No.	Signal name	Condition	Terminal voltage
55	Air inlet sensor	Temperature at sensor 25°C (77°F) (4 kΩ)	2.2–2.8 V
60	Sensor power source	Normally	4.8–5.2 V
66	Interior temperature sensor	Temperature at sensor 25°C (77°F) (4 kΩ)	2.0–2.9 V
67	Air thermo sensor	Temperature at sensor 25°C (77°F) (4 kΩ) when air conditioning is OFF	2.3–2.9 V

ENGINE COOLANT TEMP. SENSOR AND PHOTO SENSOR CIRCUIT CHECKS — 3000GT

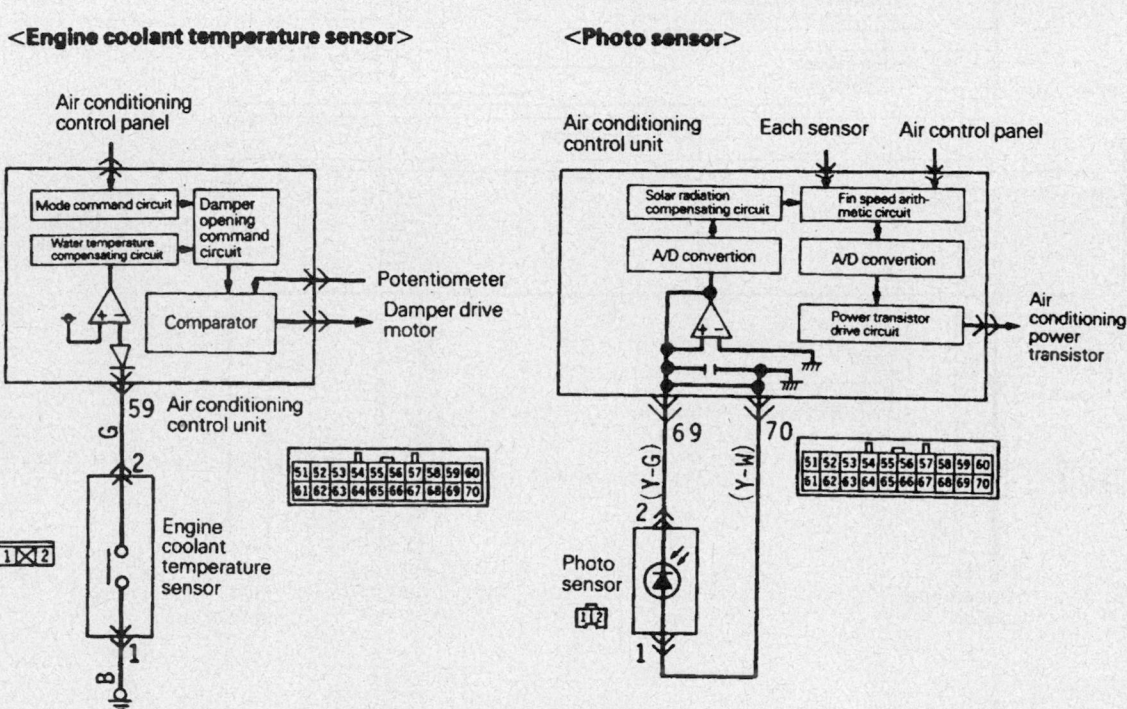

Troubleshooting Hints

● Air conditioning control unit terminal voltages

Terminal No.	Signal name	Condition	Terminal voltage
69	Photo sensor ⊖	Illuminance 100,000 lux or more	−0.1 to −0.2 V
		Illuminance less than 0 lux	0 V
70	Photo sensor ⊕	Normally	0 V
59	Engine coolant temperature sensor ⊕	Switch OFF [Engine coolant temperature less than 50°C (122°F)]	Battery positive voltage
		Switch ON [Engine coolant temperature 50°C (122°F) or higher]	0 V

POWER TRANSISTOR AND BLOWER MOTOR RELAY CHECKS — 3000GT

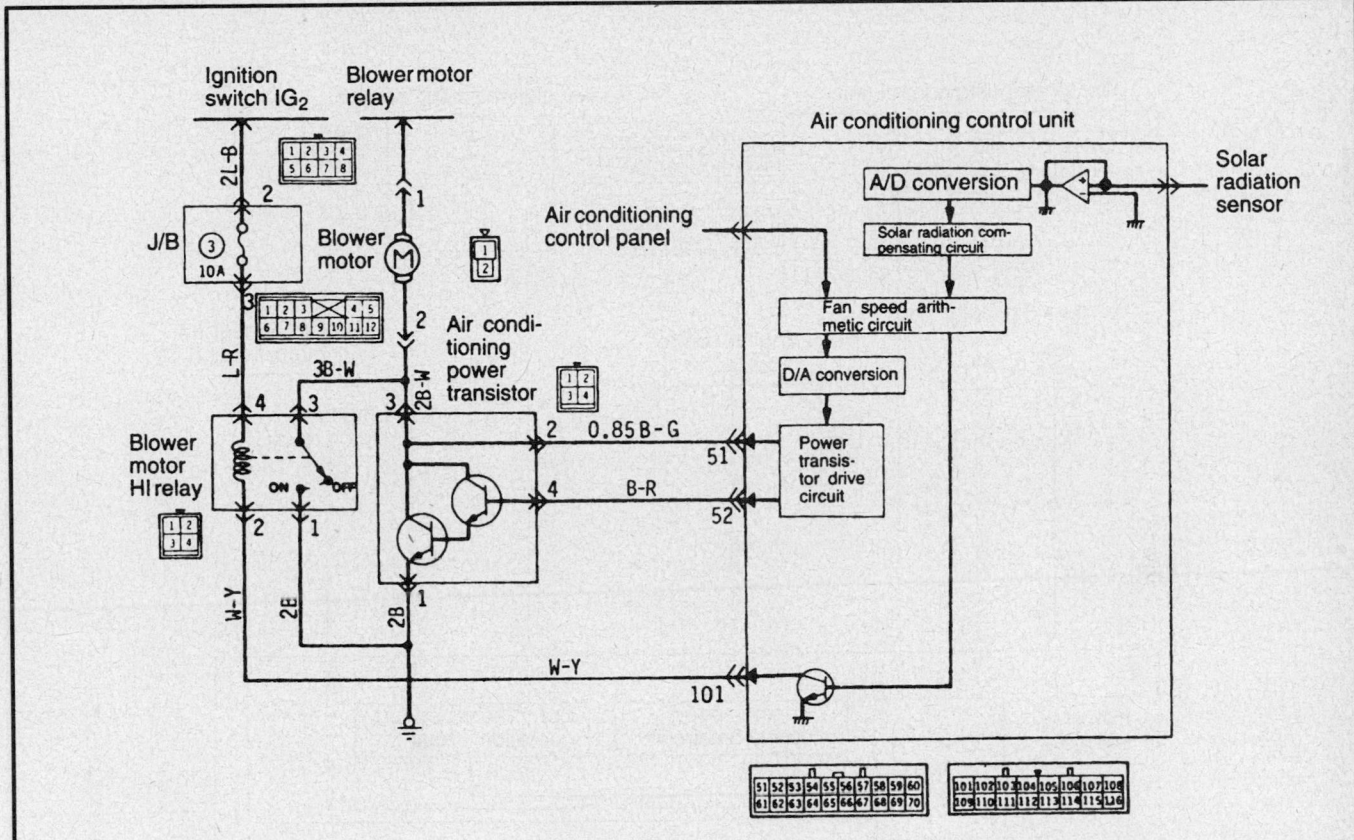

Troubleshooting Hints

- Air conditioning control unit terminal voltages

Terminal No.	Signal name	Condition	Terminal voltage
51	Air conditioning power transistor collector	Switch is turned OFF.	Battery positive voltage
		Switch is placed in LO.	Approx. 7 V
		Switch is placed in HI.	0 V
52	Air conditioning power transistor base	Blower switch is turned OFF.	0 V
		Blower switch is placed in LO.	Approx. 1.3 V
		Blower switch is placed in HI.	Approx. 1.2 V
101	Blower motor HI relay	Fan switch HI is ON.	1.5 V or less
		Fan switch in ME, LO, or OFF.	Battery positive voltage

BELT LOCK CONTROLLER CIRCUIT CHECK — 3000GT

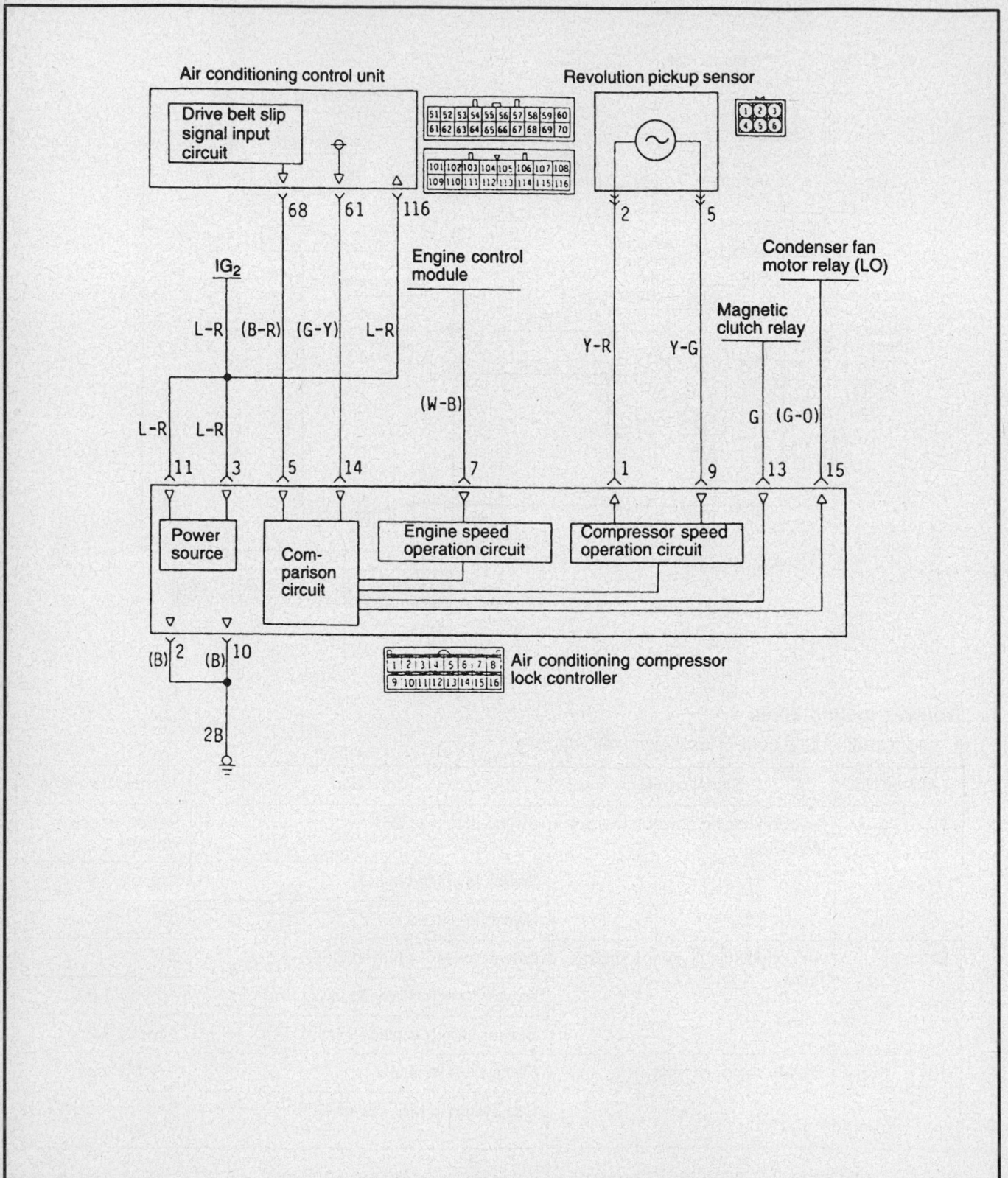

DAMPER MOTOR CIRCUIT CHECK — 3000GT

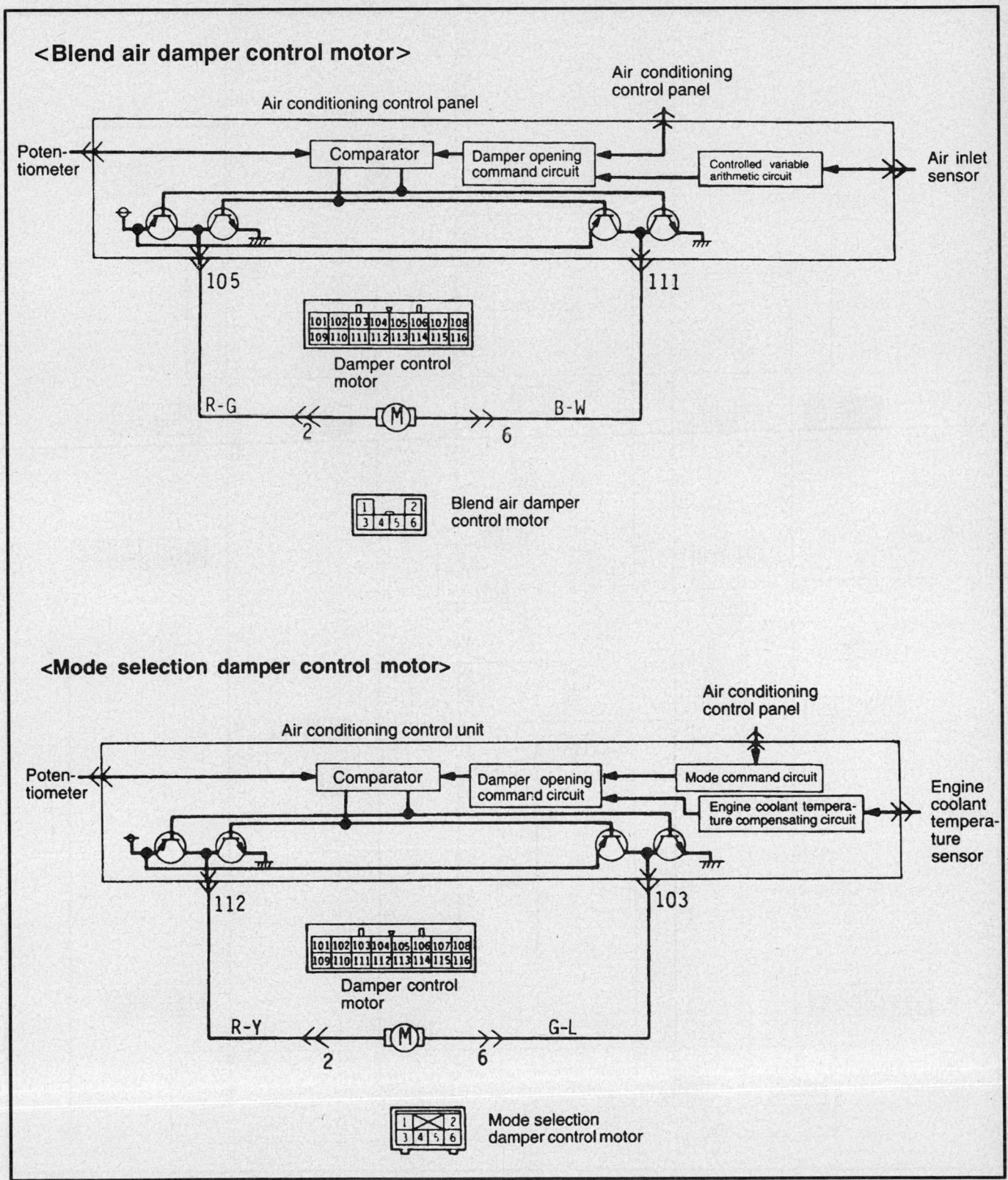

\<Blend air damper control motor\>

Air conditioning control panel

Air conditioning control panel

Poten-tiometer

Comparator

Damper opening command circuit

Controlled variable arithmetic circuit

Air inlet sensor

105   111

| 101 | 102 | 103 | 104 | 105 | 106 | 107 | 108 |
| 109 | 110 | 111 | 112 | 113 | 114 | 115 | 116 |

Damper control motor

R-G   2   (M)   6   B-W

| 1 | | 2 |
| 3 | 4 | 5 | 6 |

Blend air damper control motor

\<Mode selection damper control motor\>

Air conditioning control panel

Air conditioning control unit

Poten-tiometer

Comparator

Damper opening command circuit

Mode command circuit

Engine coolant temperature compensating circuit

Engine coolant temperature sensor

112   103

| 101 | 102 | 103 | 104 | 105 | 106 | 107 | 108 |
| 109 | 110 | 111 | 112 | 113 | 114 | 115 | 116 |

Damper control motor

R-Y   2   (M)   6   G-L

| 1 | | 2 |
| 3 | 4 | 5 | 6 |

Mode selection damper control motor

WIRING SCHEMATICS

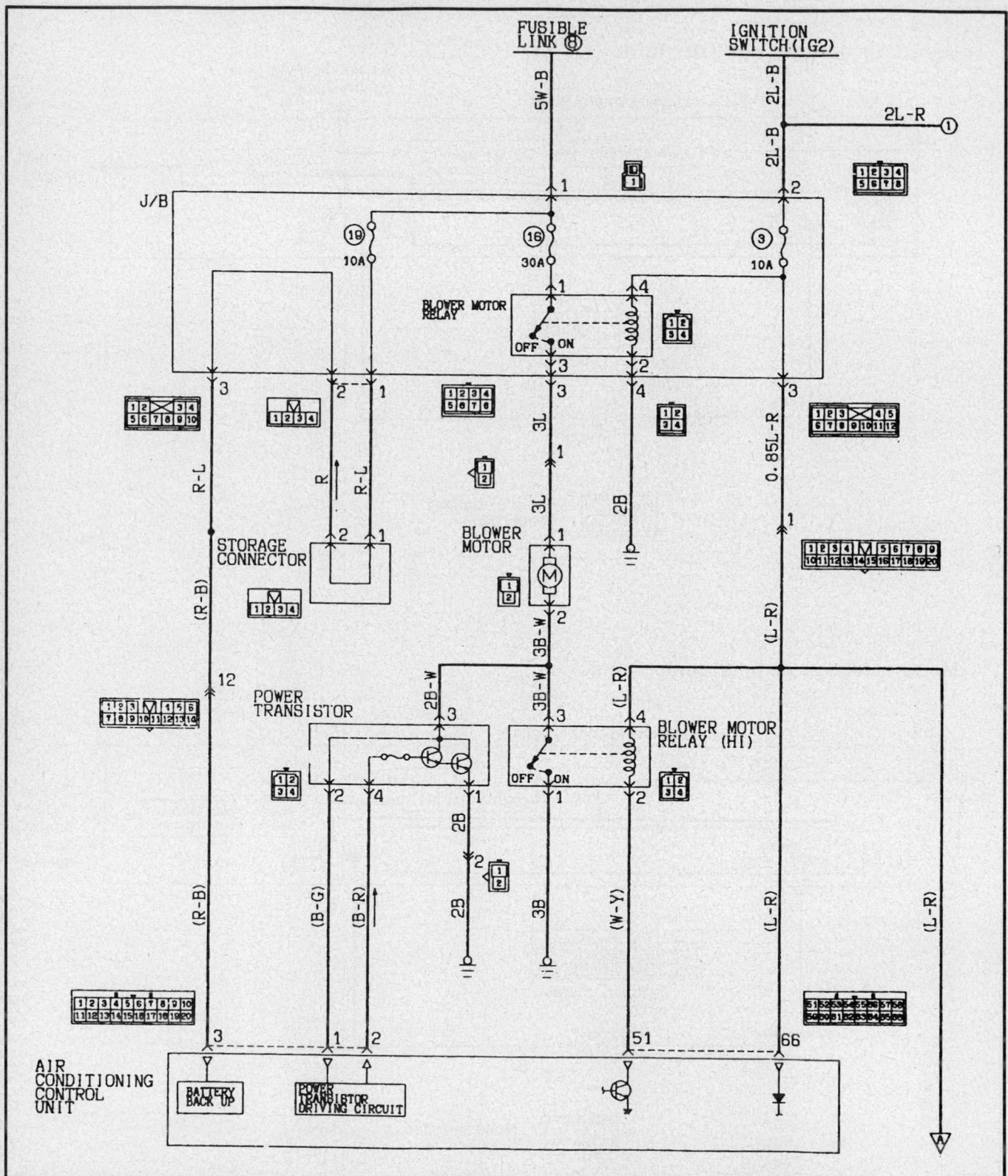

Wiring schematic — 1993 Diamante with SOHC engine

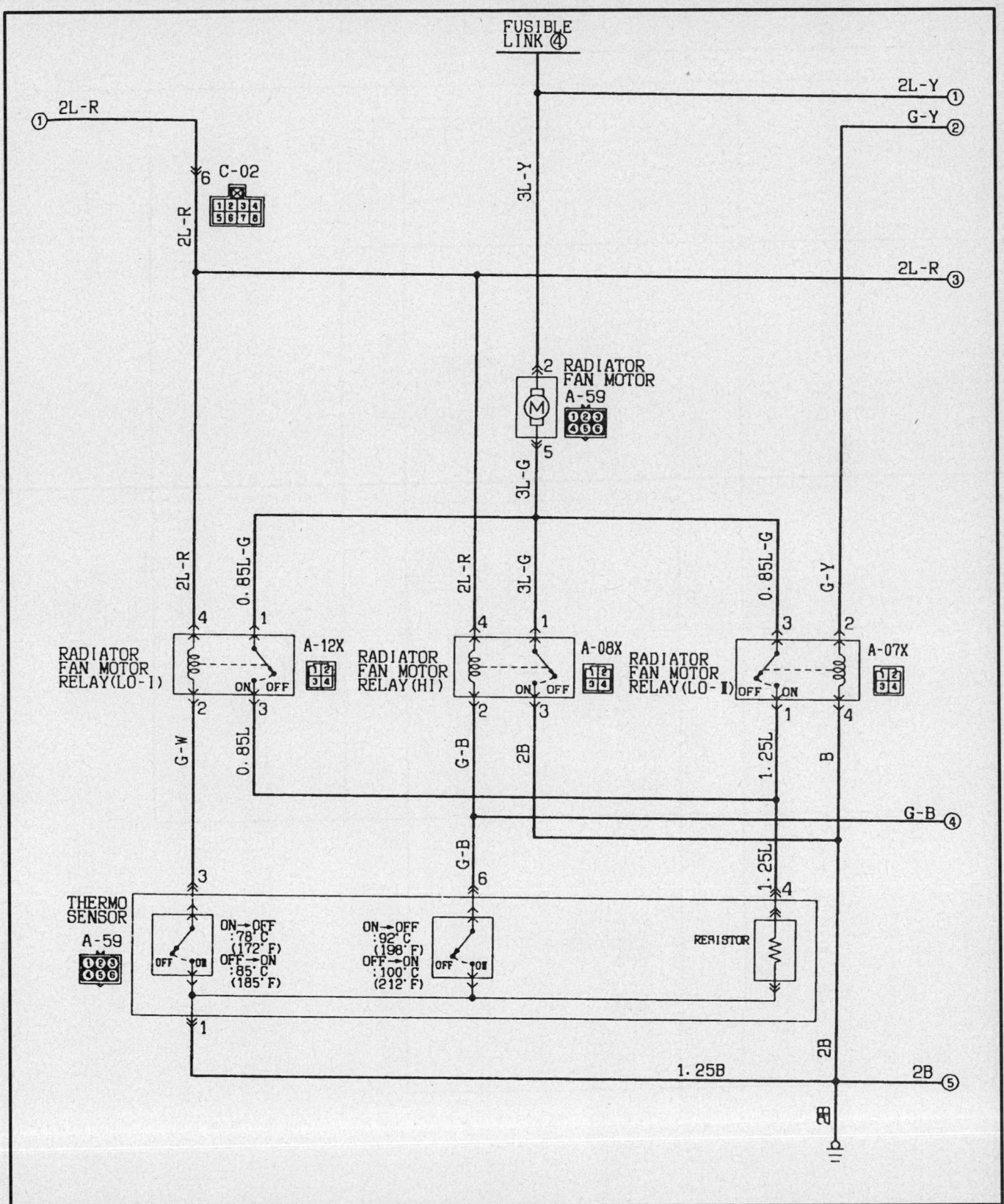

Wiring schematic — 1993 Diamante with SOHC engine, Cont.

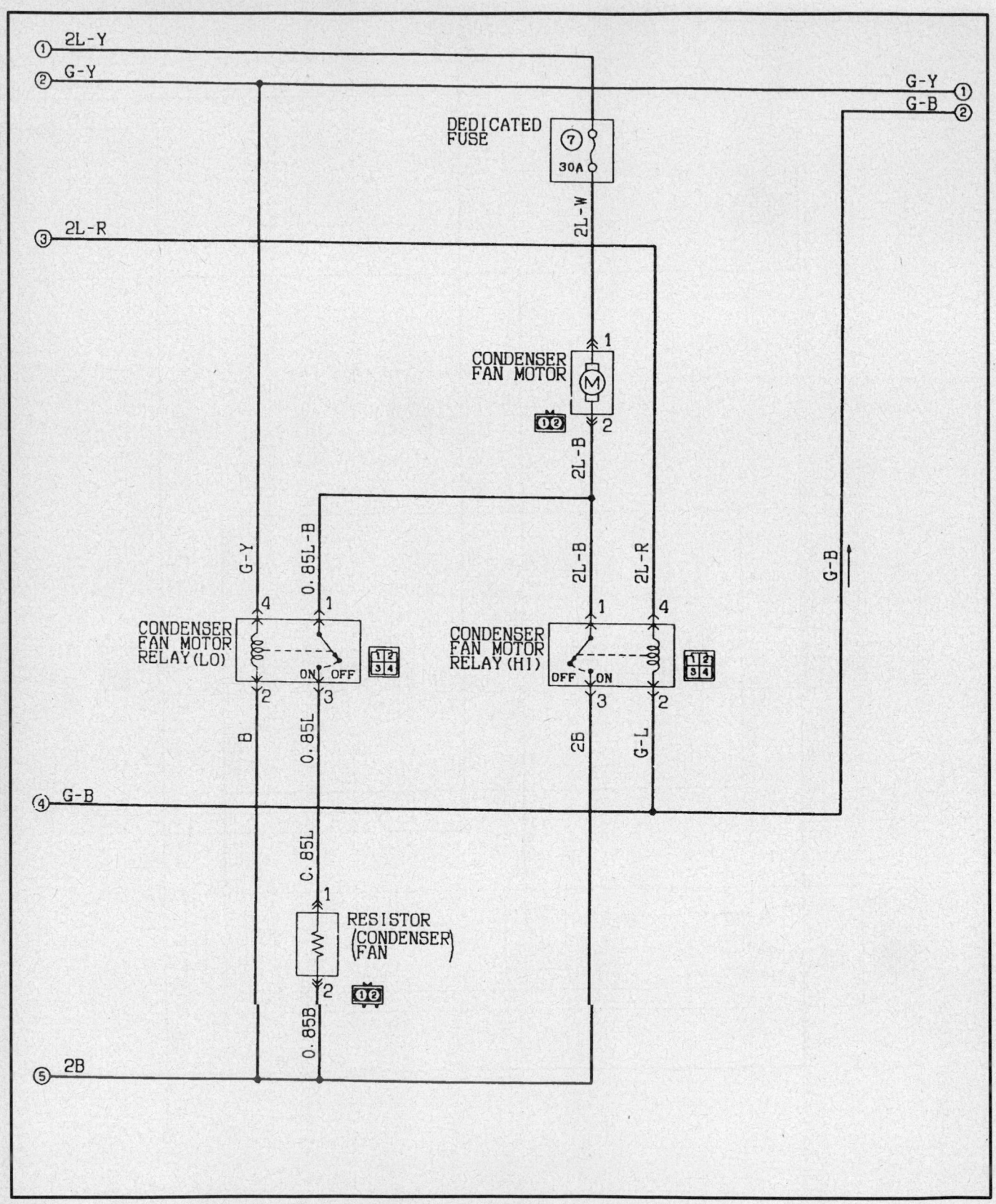

Wiring schematic — 1993 Diamante with SOHC engine, Cont.

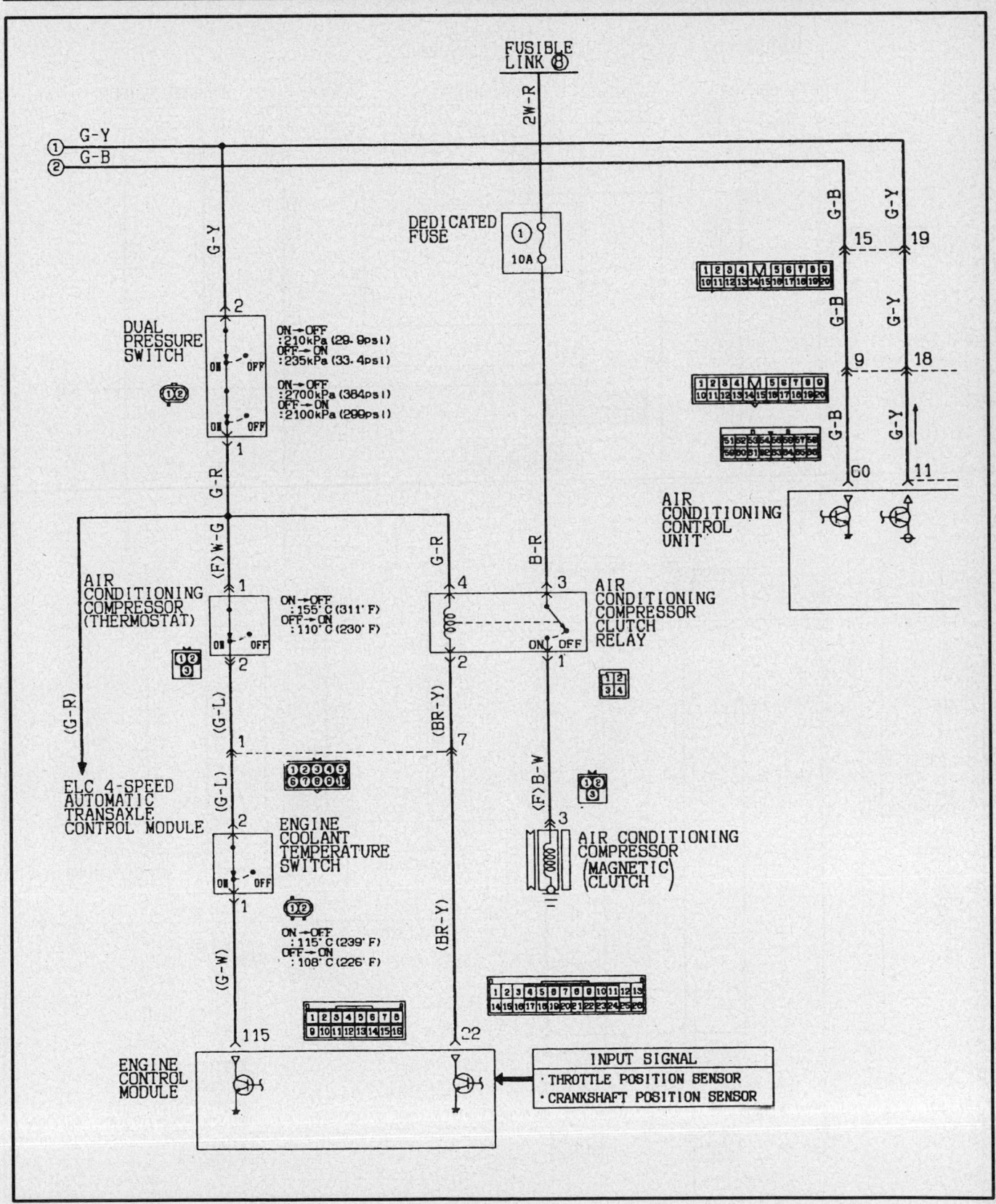

Wiring schematic — 1993 Diamante with SOHC engine, Cont.

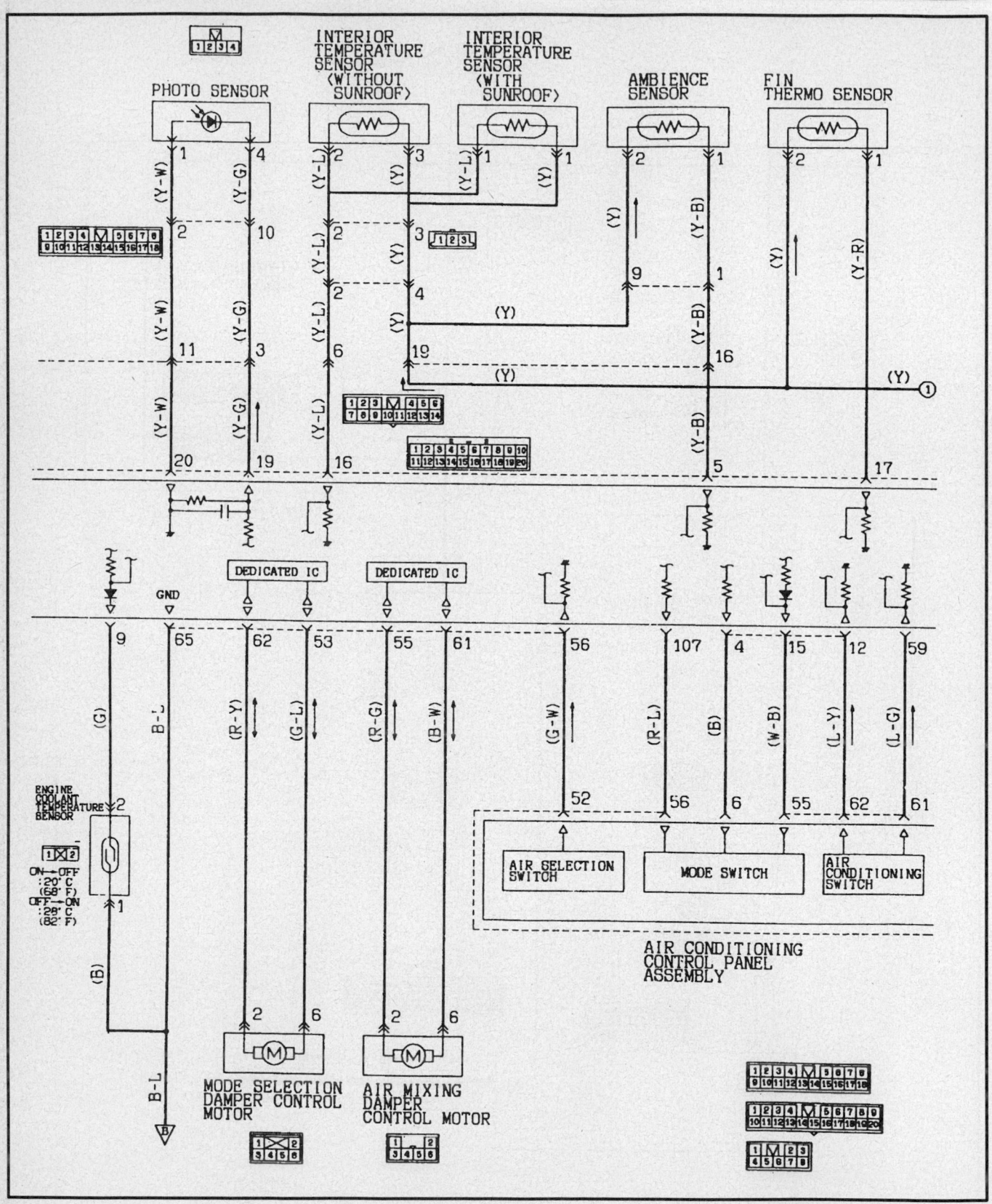

Wiring schematic — 1993 Diamante with SOHC engine, Cont.

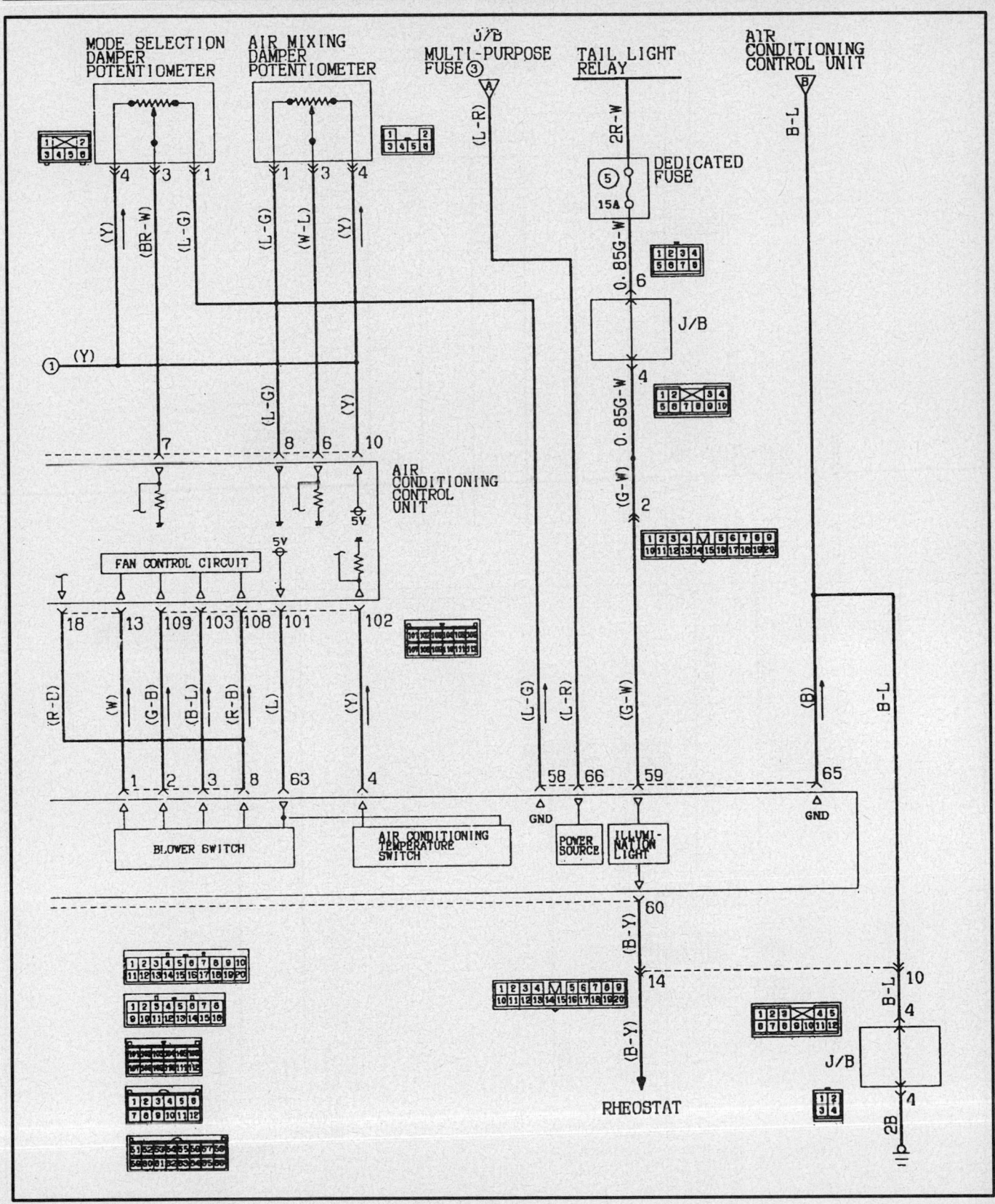

Wiring schematic — 1993 Diamante with SOHC engine, Cont.

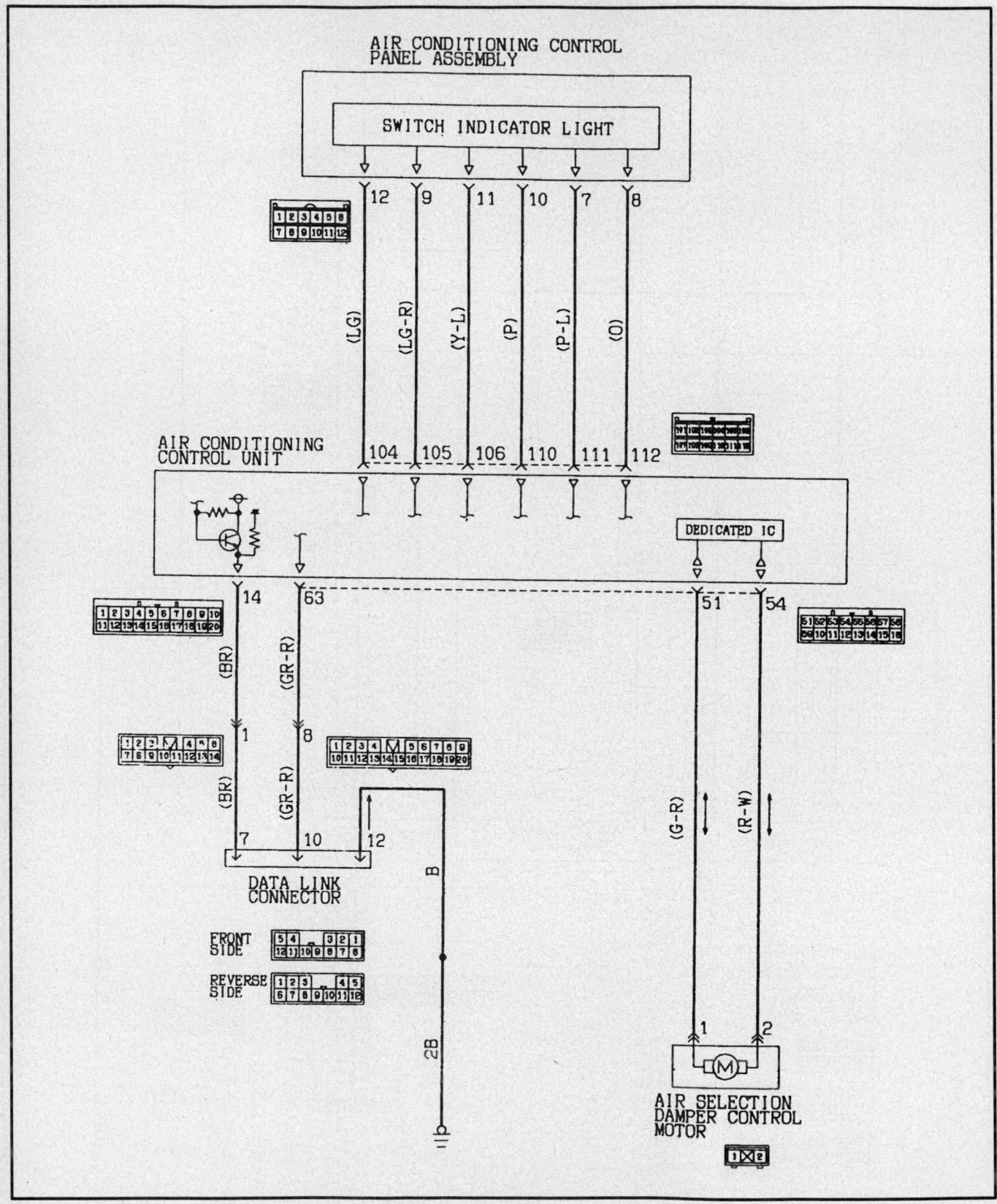

Wiring schematic — 1993 Diamante with SOHC engine, Cont.

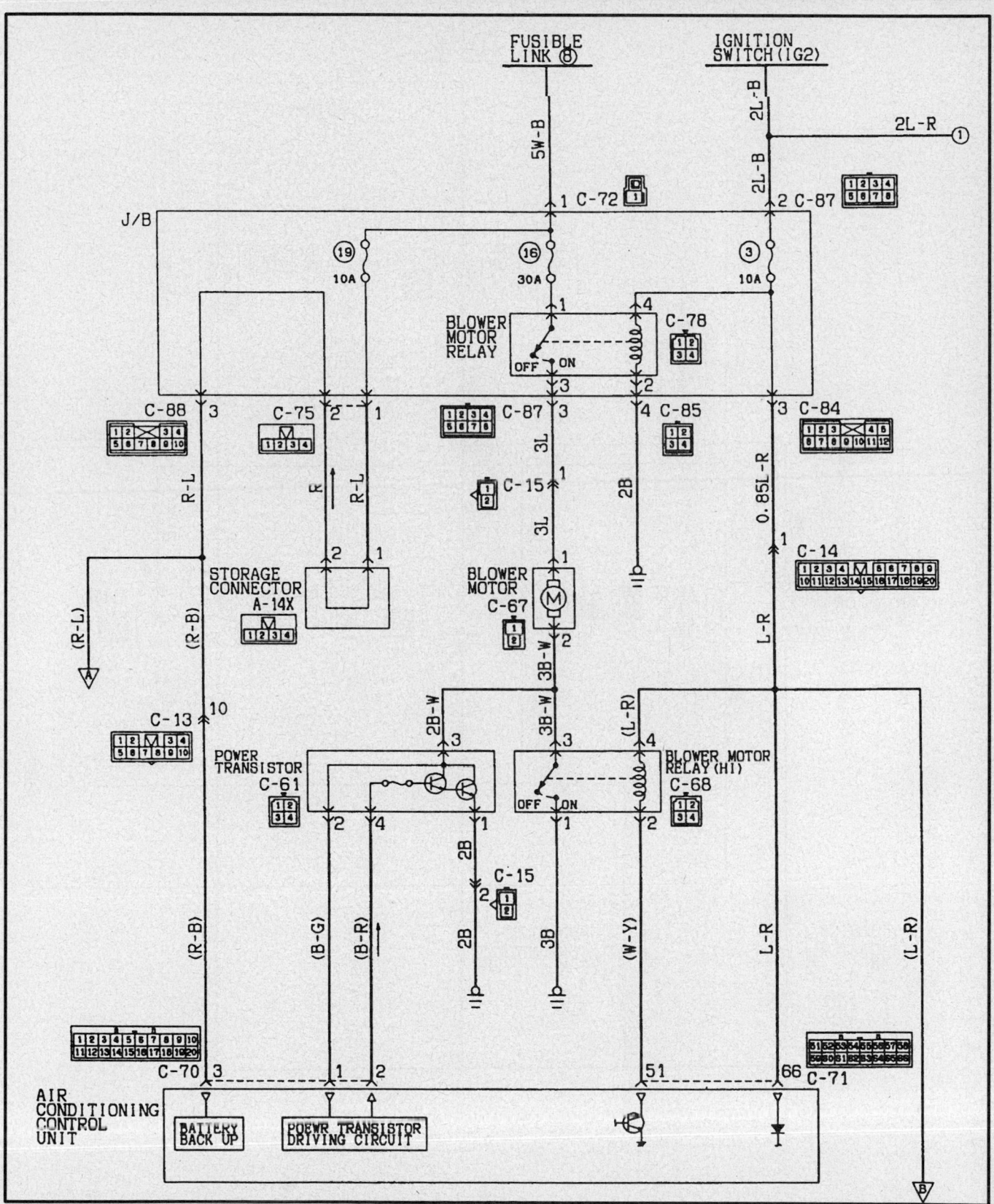

Wiring schematic — 1994-95 Diamante with SOHC engine

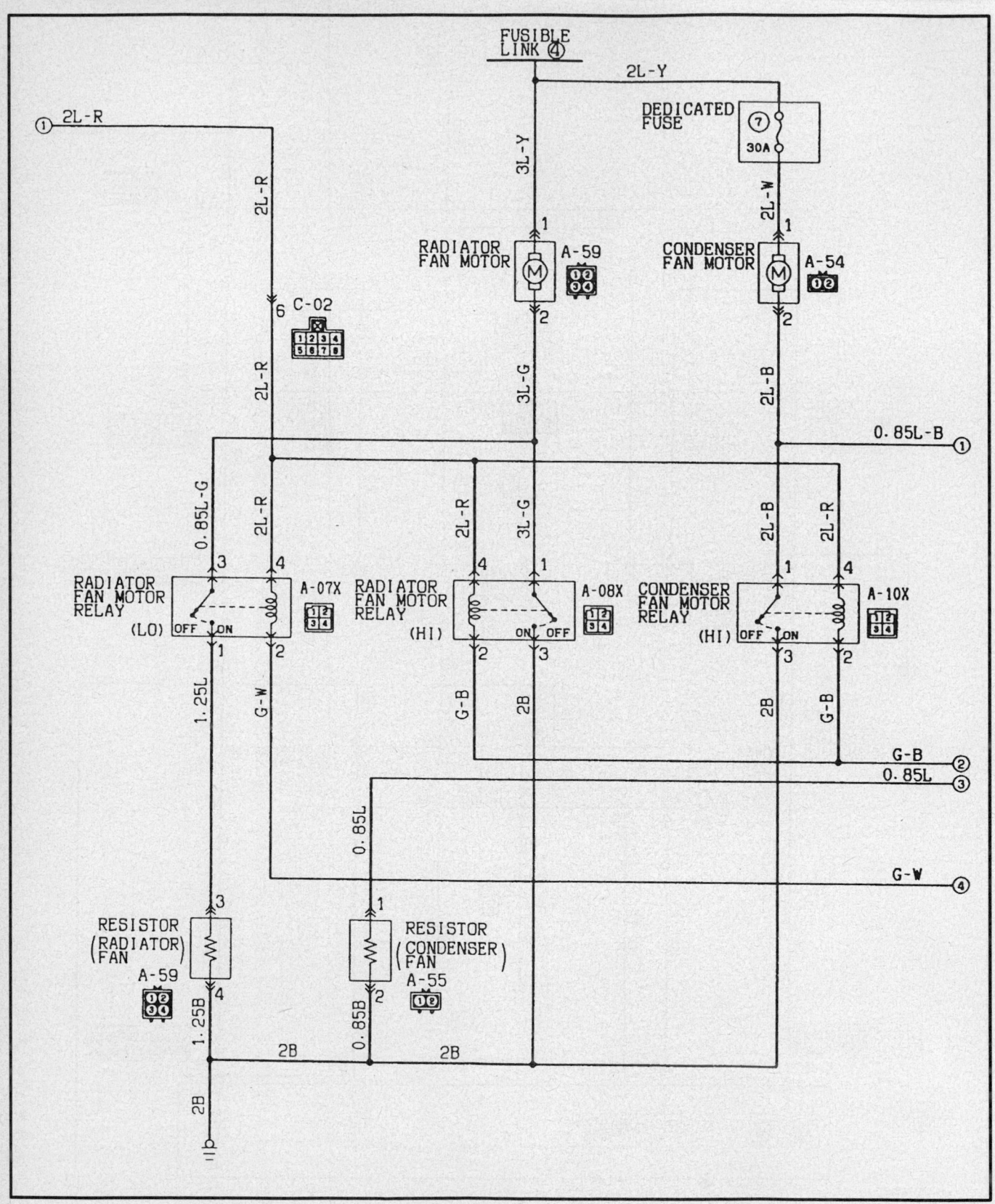

Wiring schematic — 1994—95 Diamante with SOHC engine, Cont.

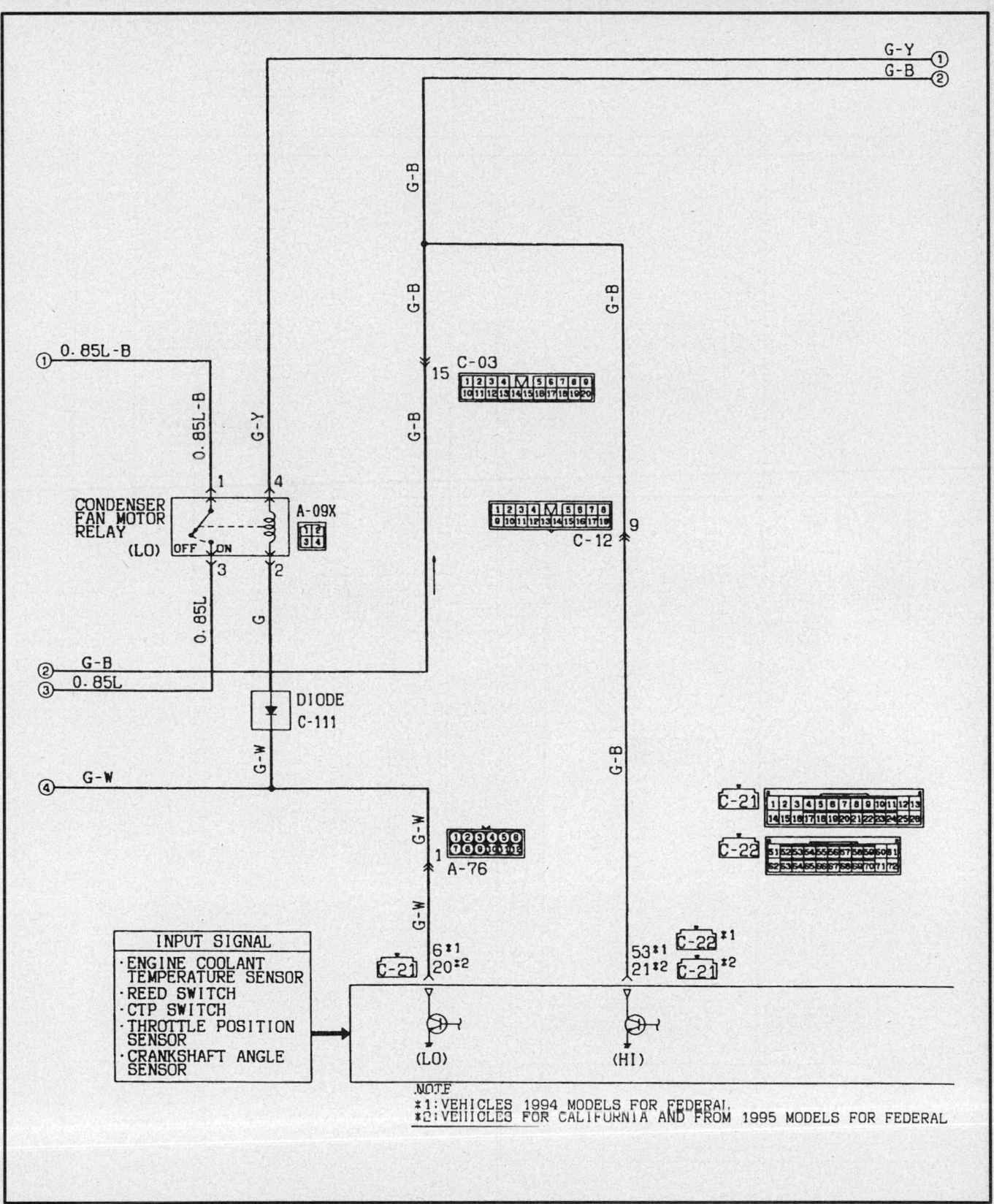

Wiring schematic — 1994–95 Diamante with SOHC engine, Cont.

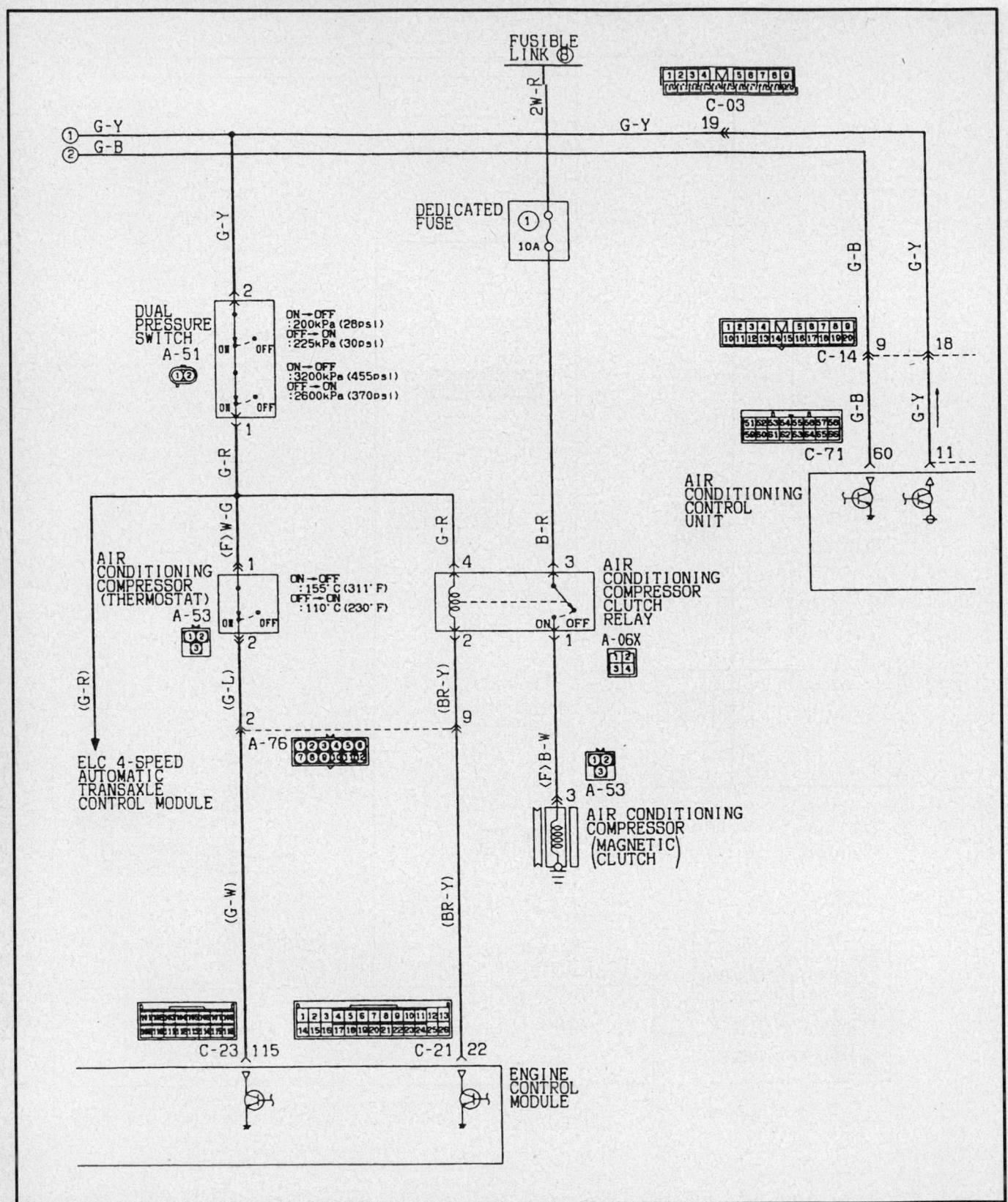

Wiring schematic — 1994–95 Diamante with SOHC engine, Cont.

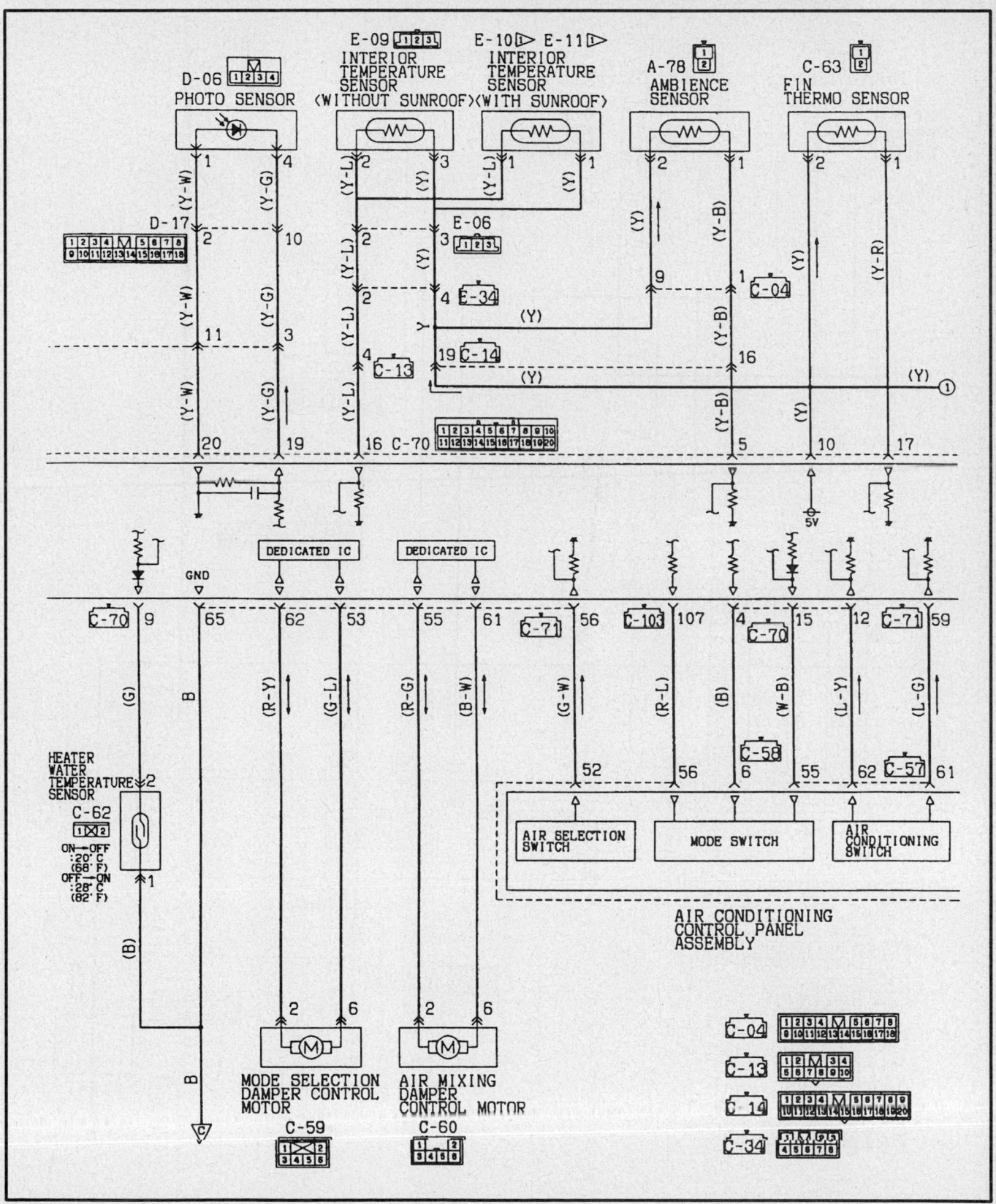

Wiring schematic — 1994–95 Diamante with SOHC engine, Cont.

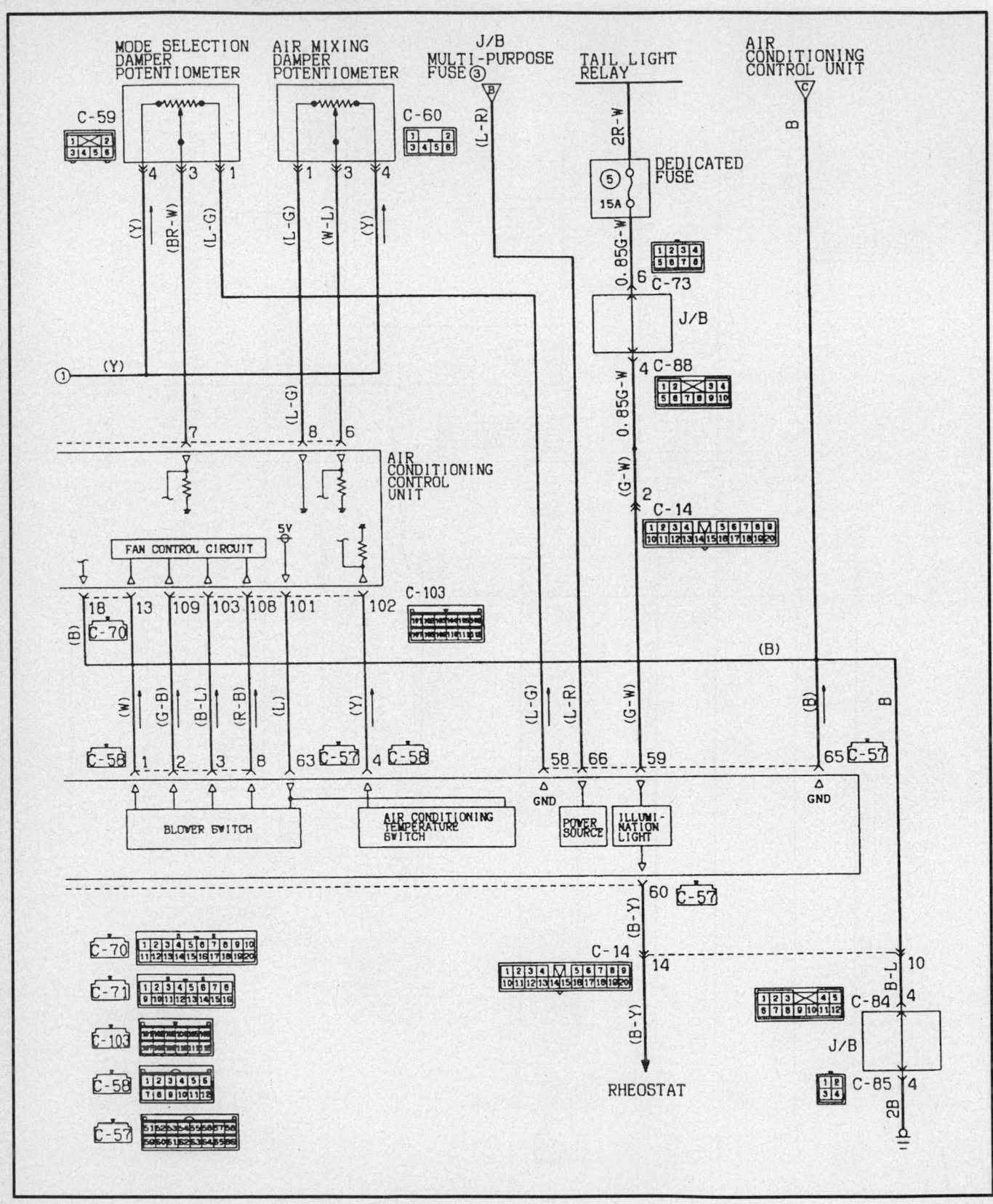

Wiring schematic — 1994–95 Diamante with SOHC engine, Cont.

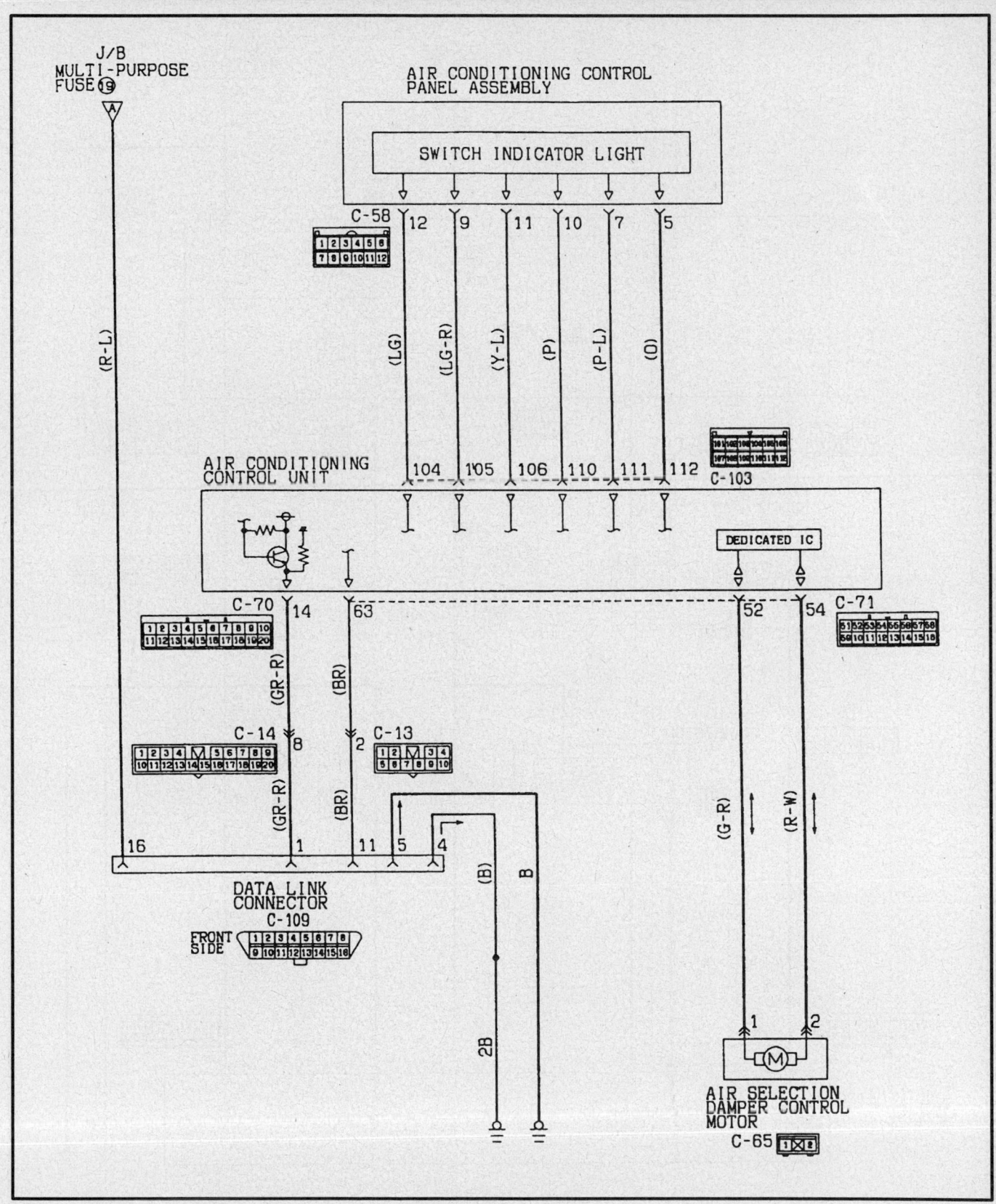

Wiring schematic — 1994–95 Diamante with SOHC engine, Cont.

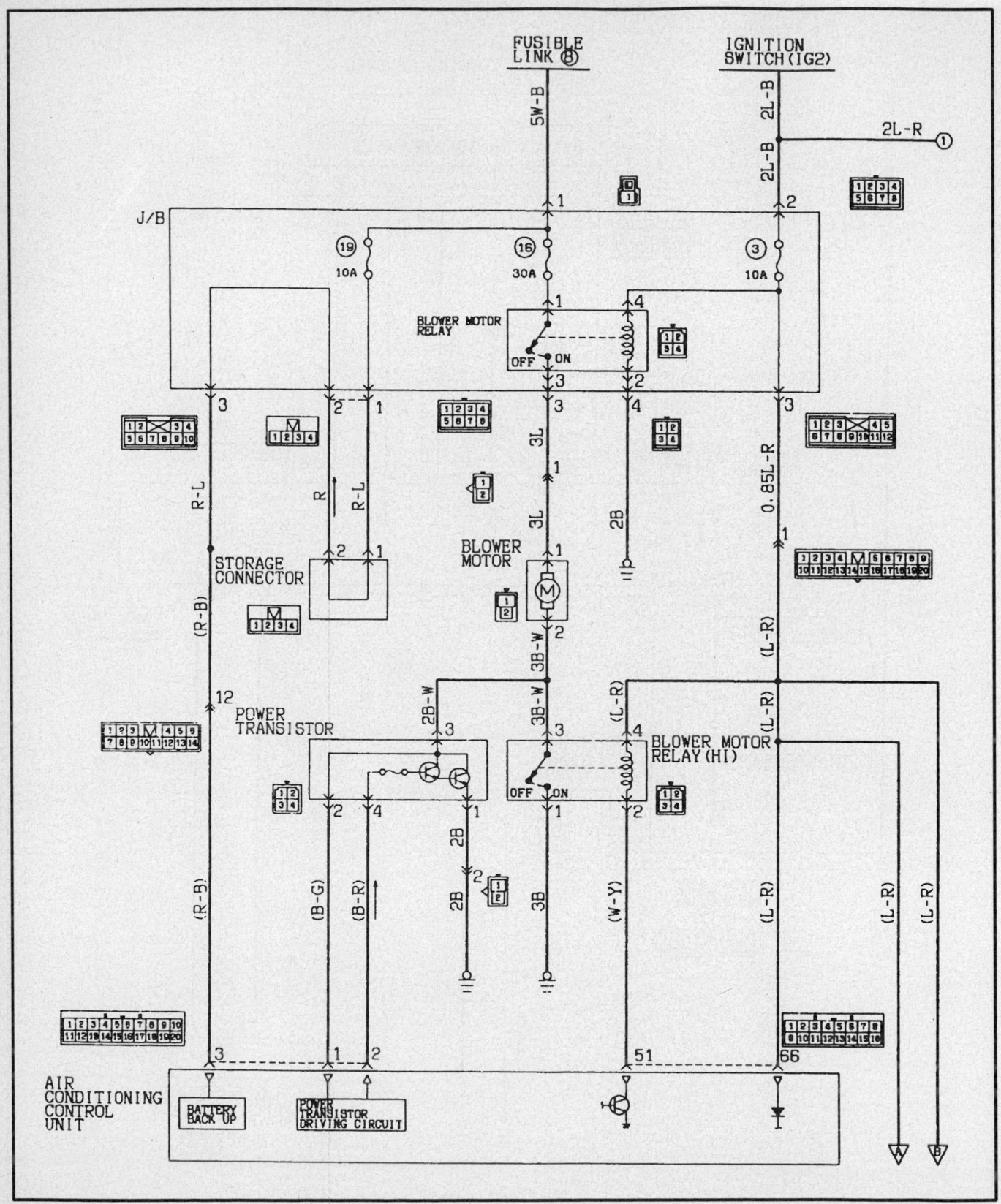

Wiring schematic — 1993 Diamante with DOHC engine

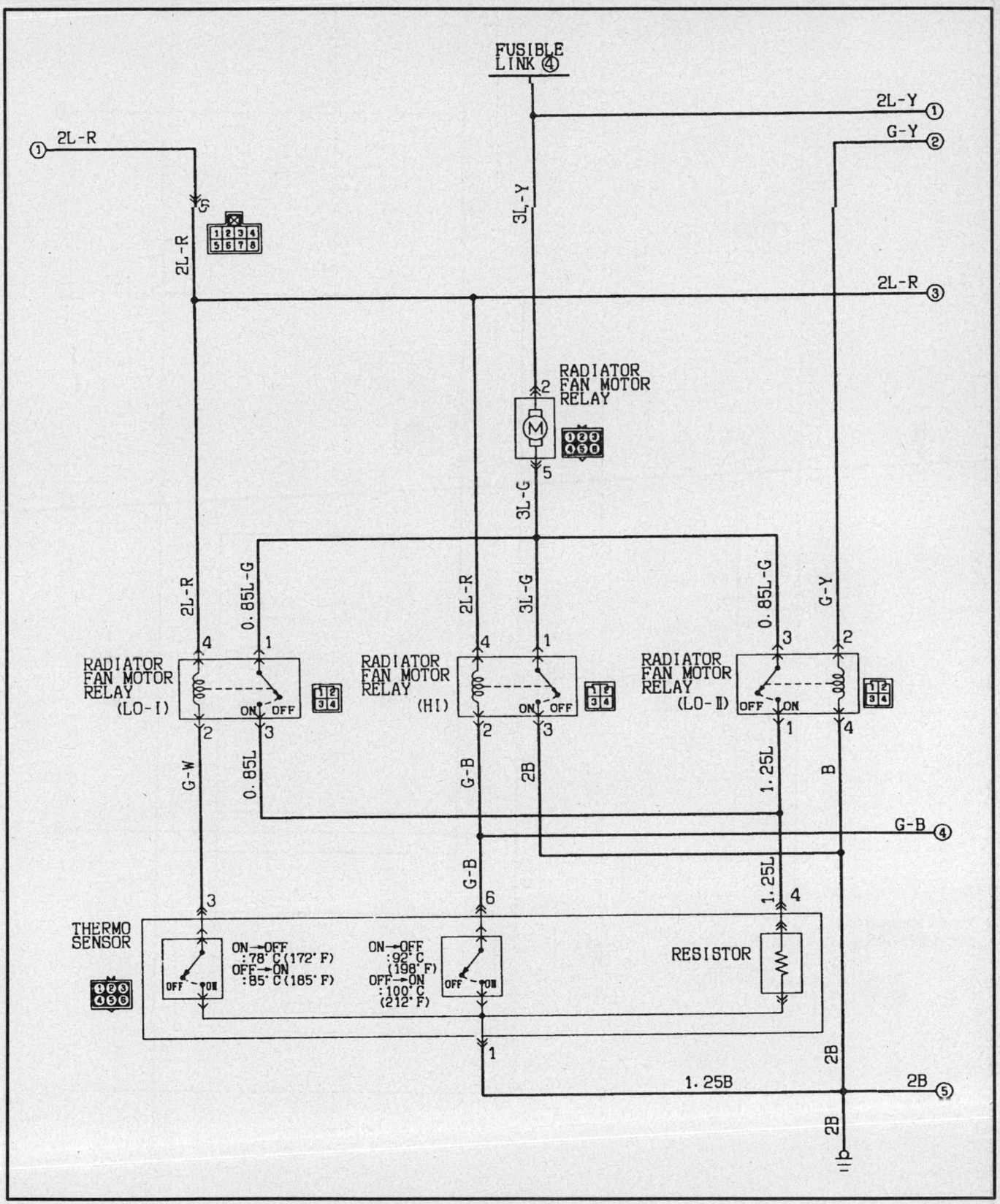

Wiring schematic — 1993 Diamante with DOHC engine, Cont.

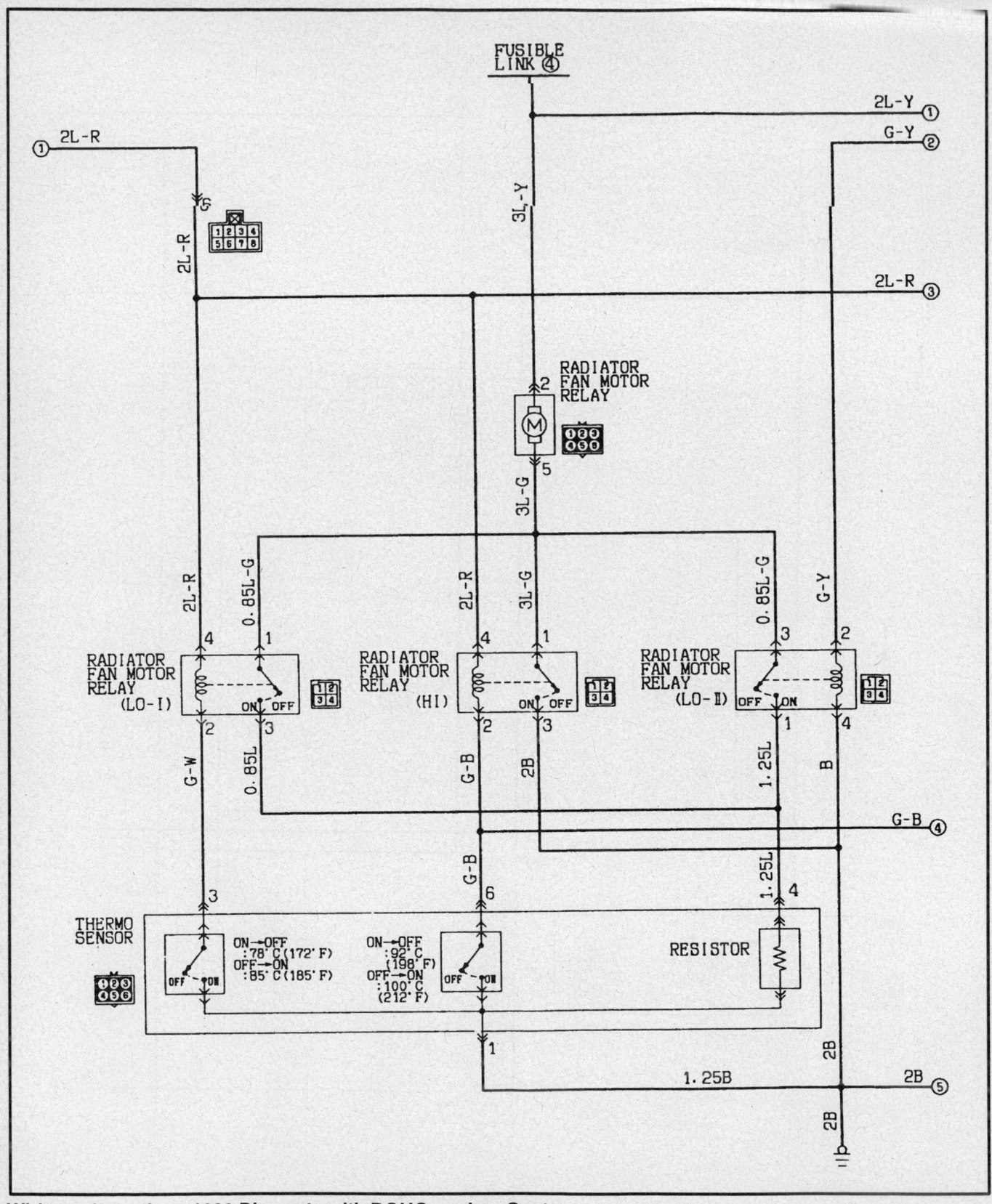

Wiring schematic — 1993 Diamante with DOHC engine, Cont.

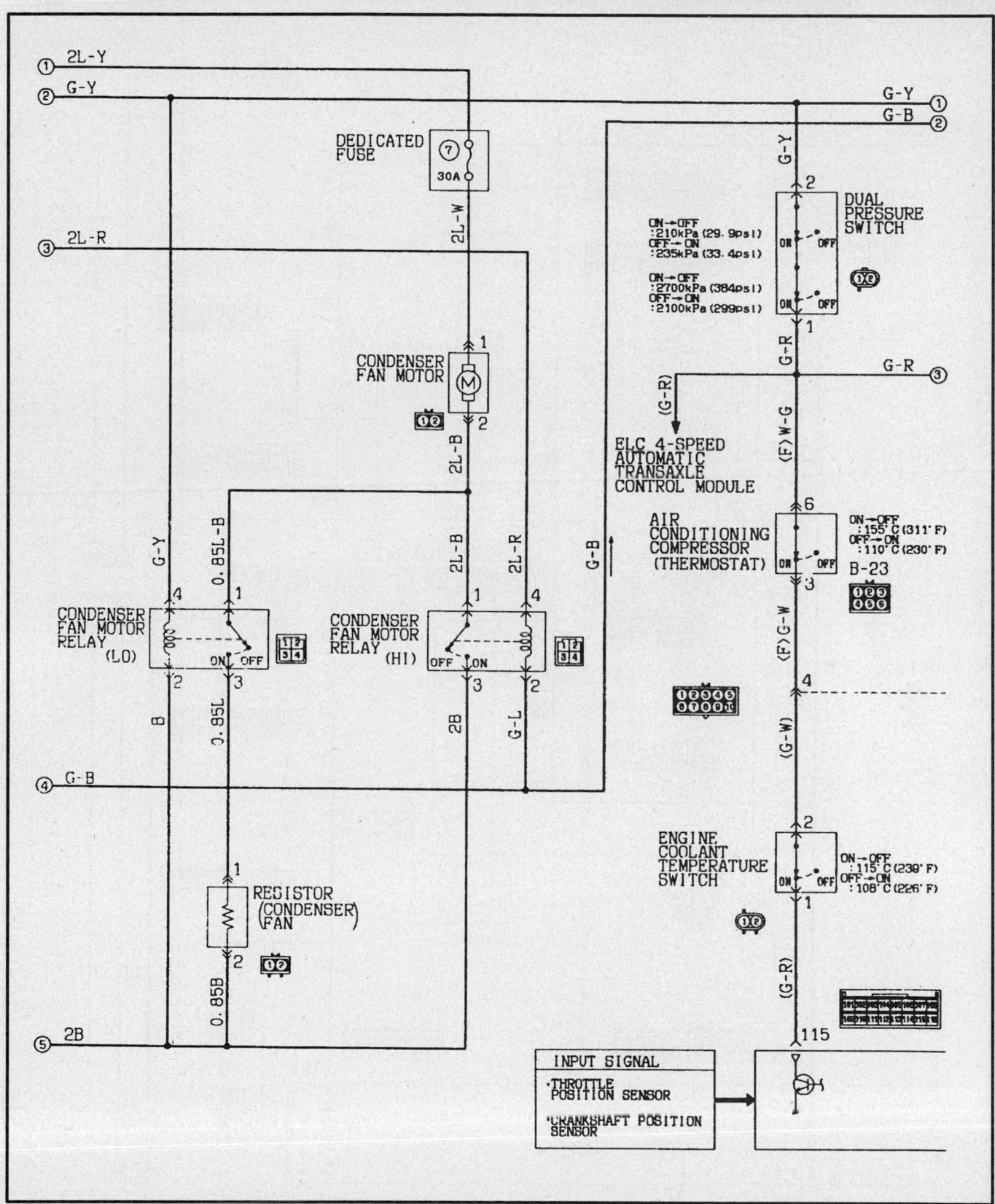

Wiring schematic — 1993 Diamante with DOHC engine, Cont.

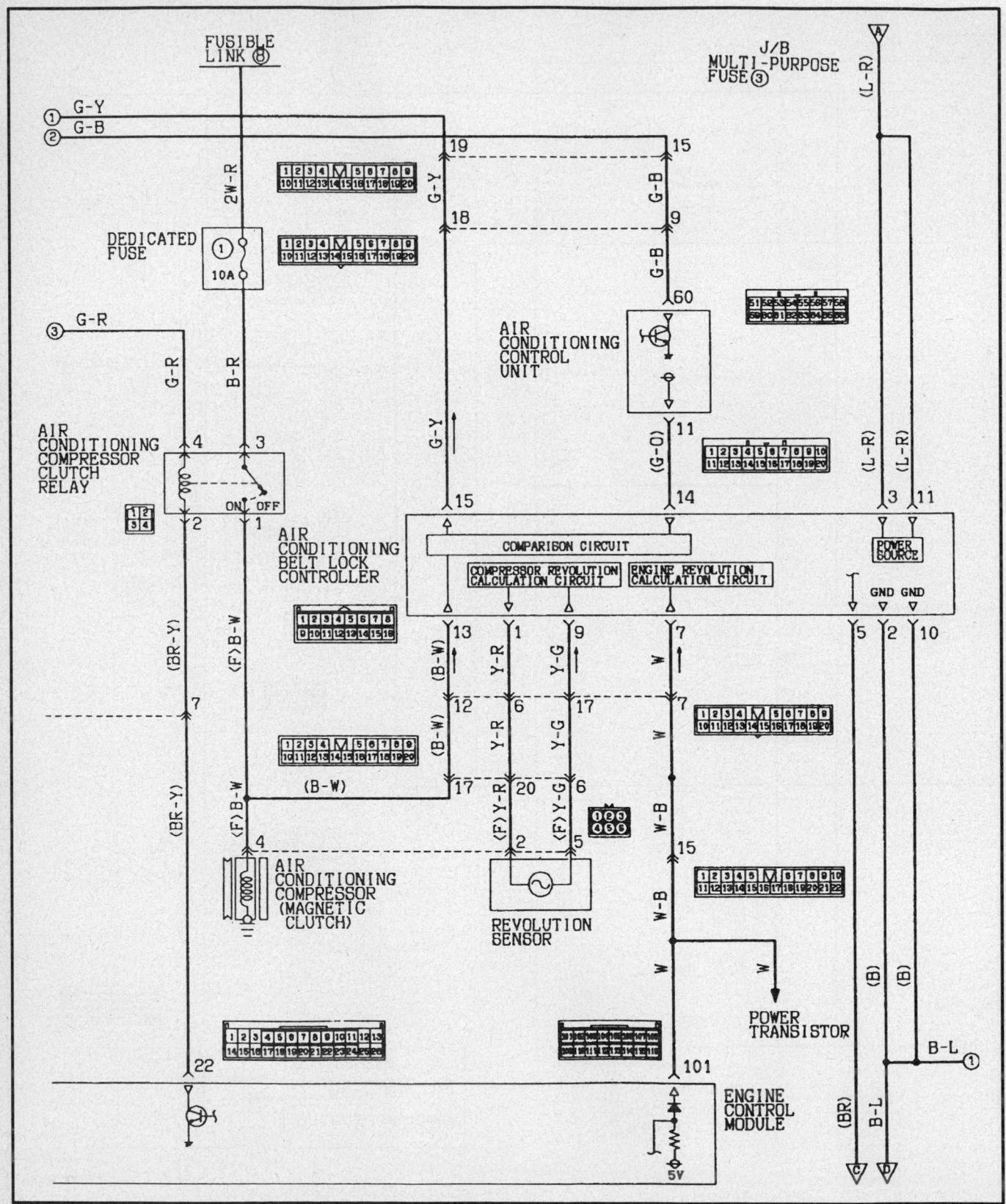

Wiring schematic — 1993 Diamante with DOHC engine, Cont.

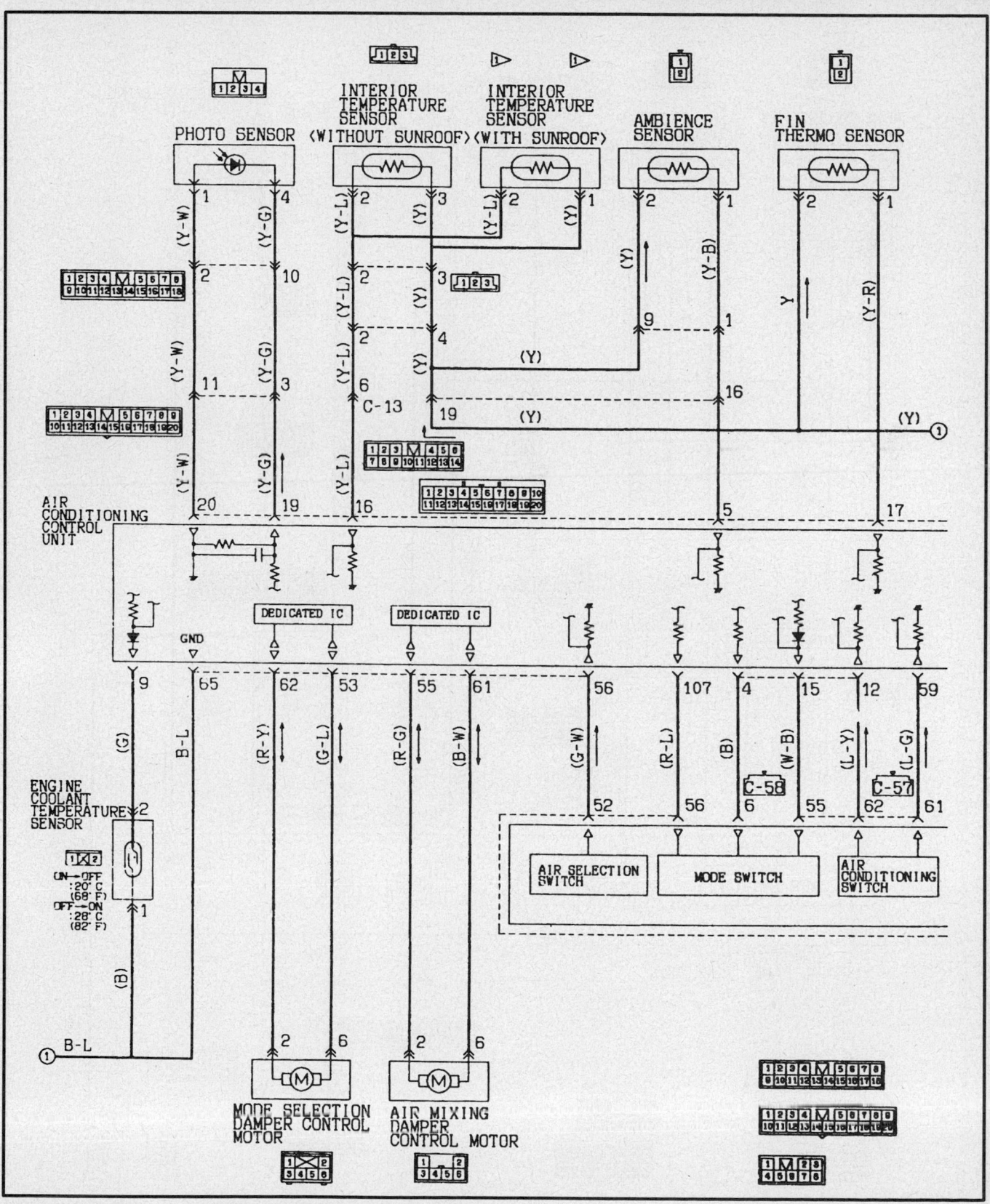

Wiring schematic — 1993 Diamante with DOHC engine, Cont.

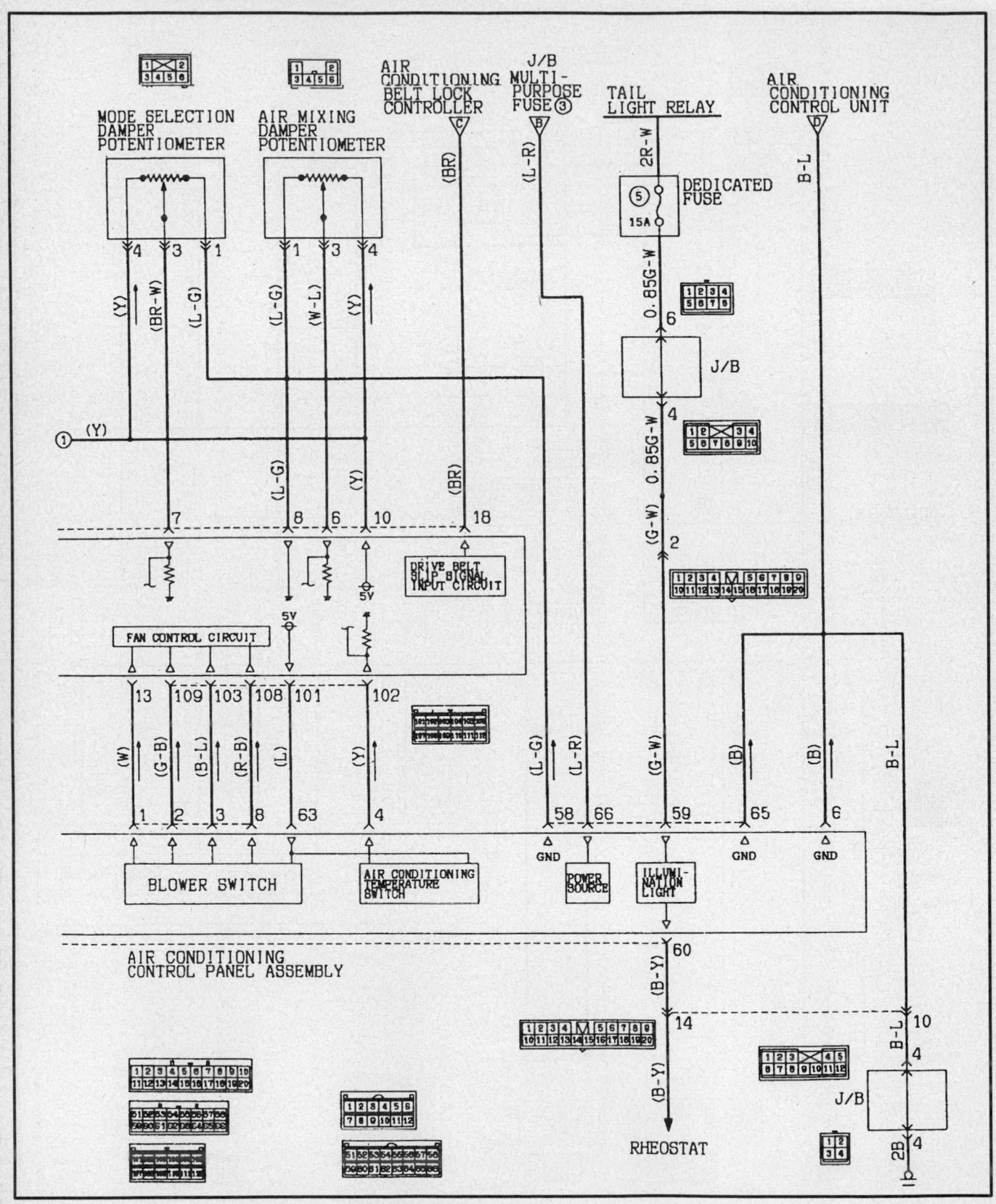

Wiring schematic — 1993 Diamante with DOHC engine, Cont.

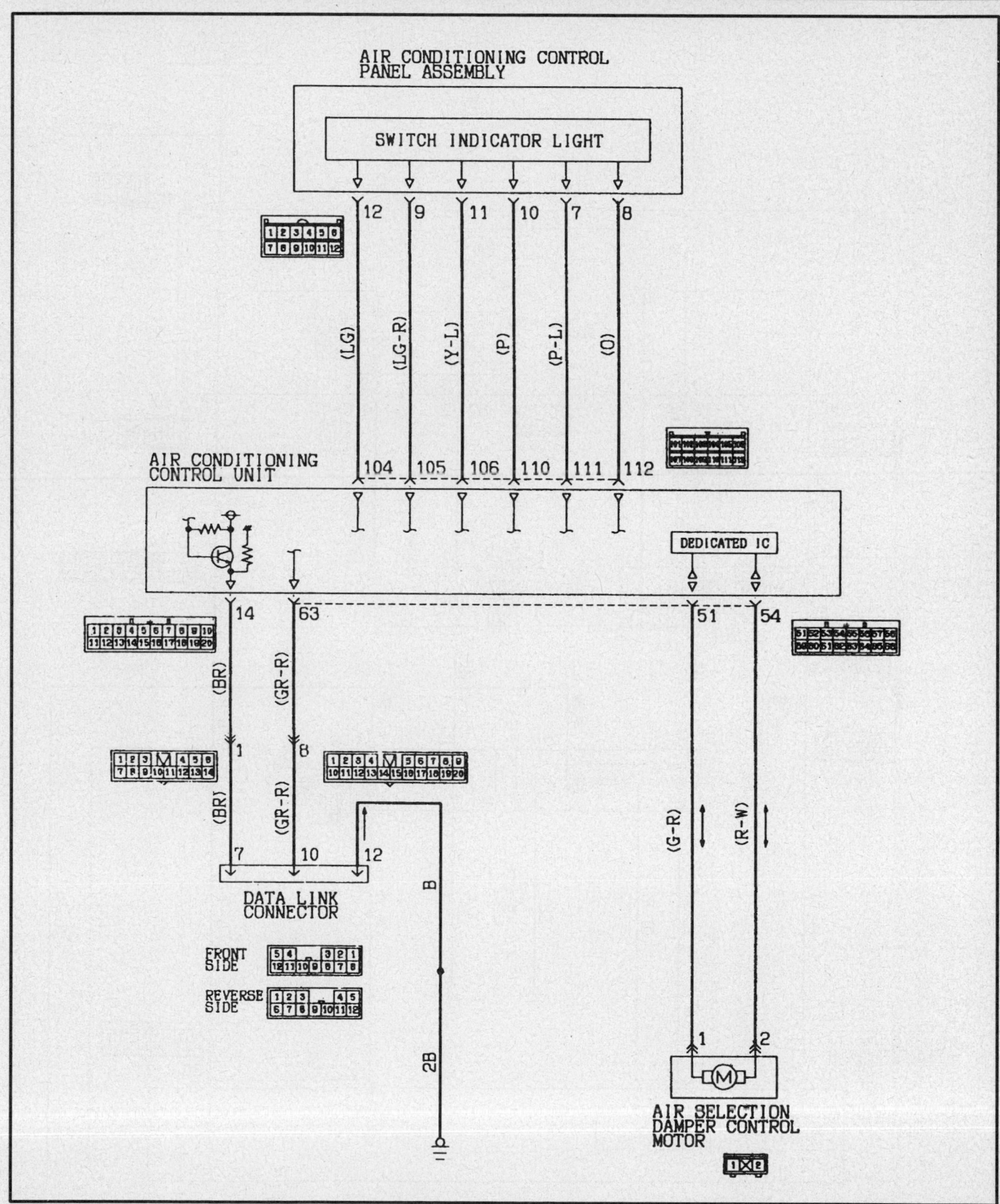

Wiring schematic — 1993 Diamante with DOHC engine, Cont.

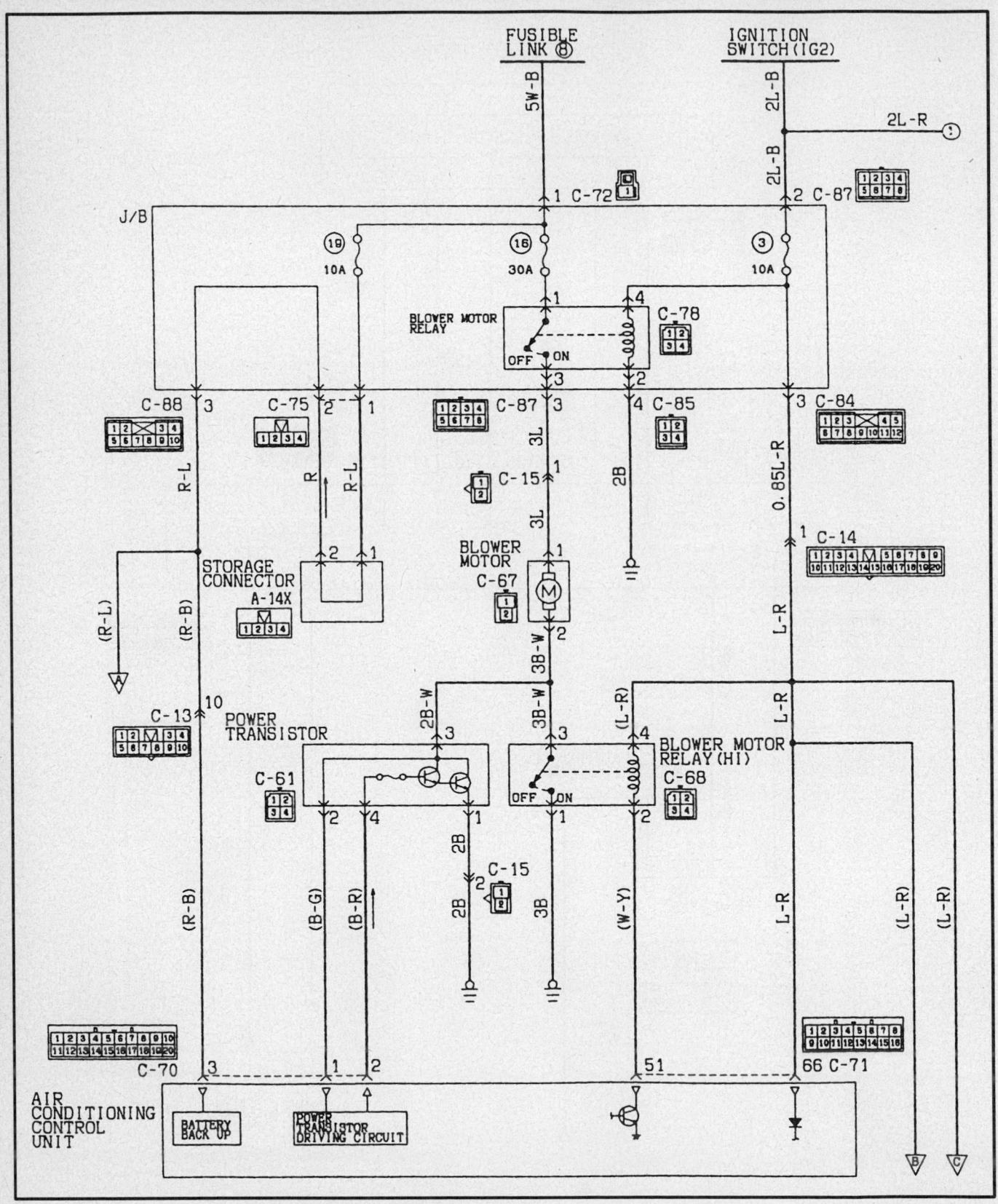

Wiring schematic — 1994–95 Diamante with DOHC engine

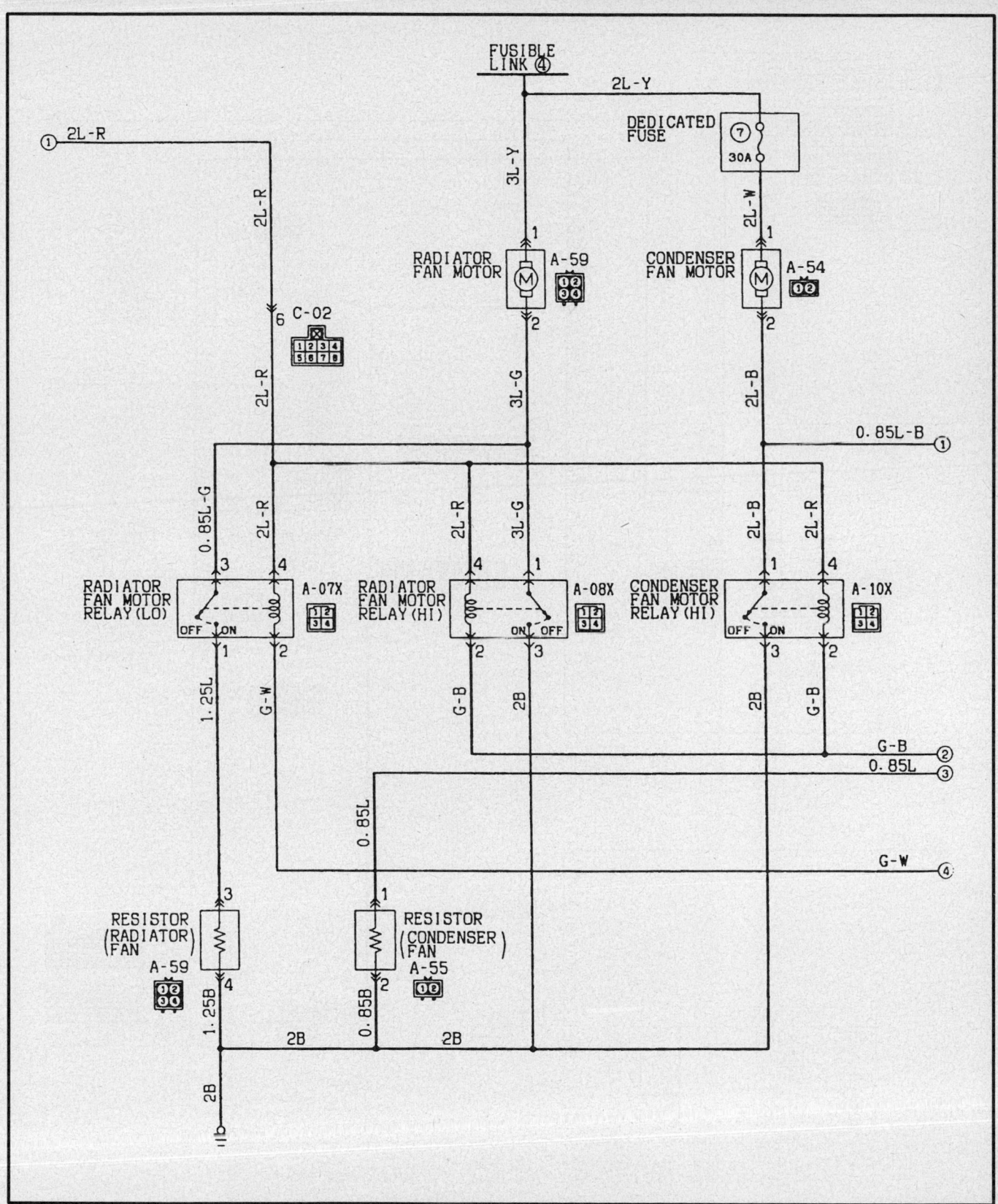

Wiring schematic — 1994–95 Diamante with DOHC engine, Cont.

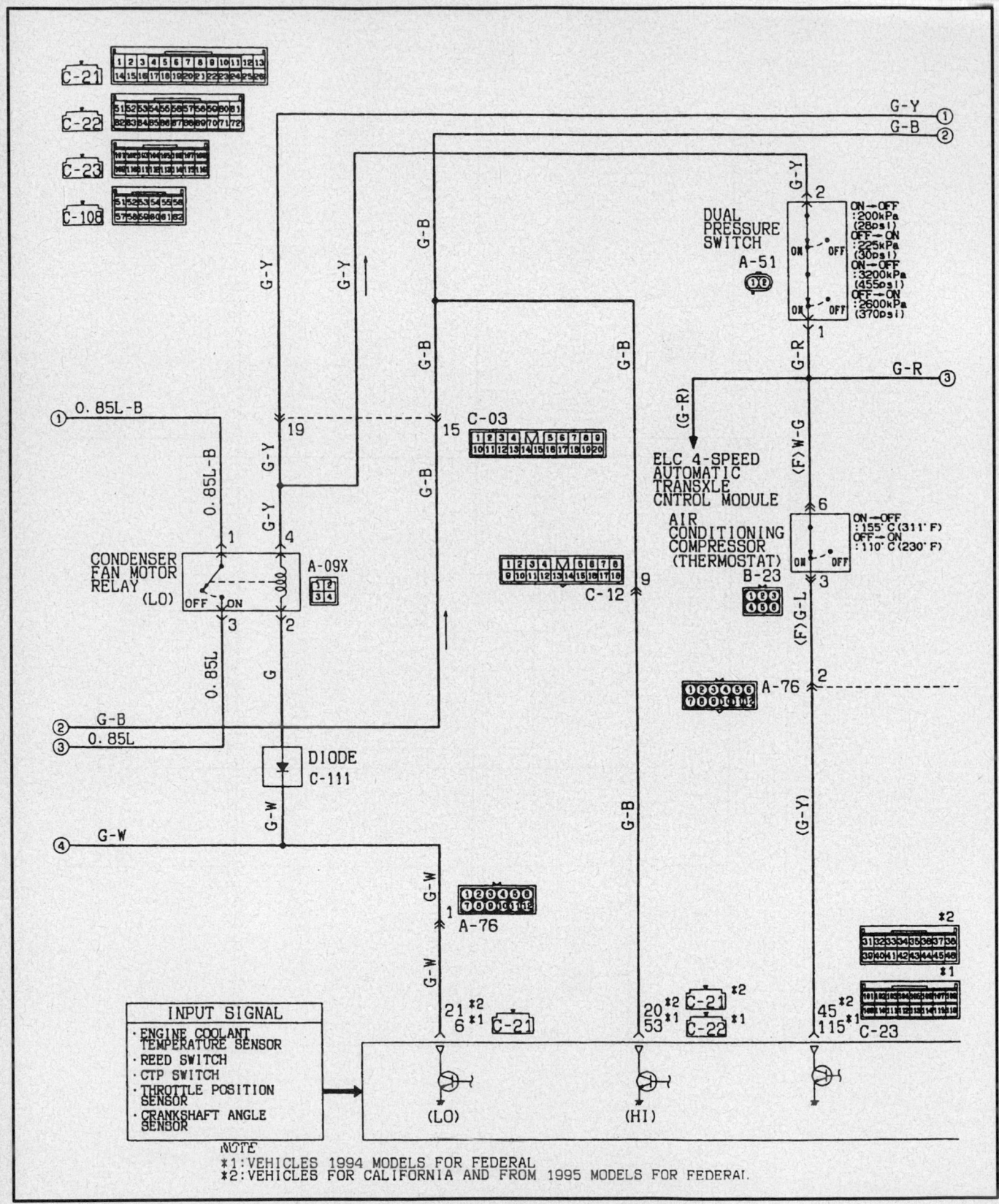

Wiring schematic — 1994-95 Diamante with DOHC engine, Cont.

NOTE:
*1: VEHICLES 1994 MODELS FOR FEDERAL
*2: VEHICLES FOR CALIFORNIA AND FROM 1995 MODELS FOR FEDERAL.

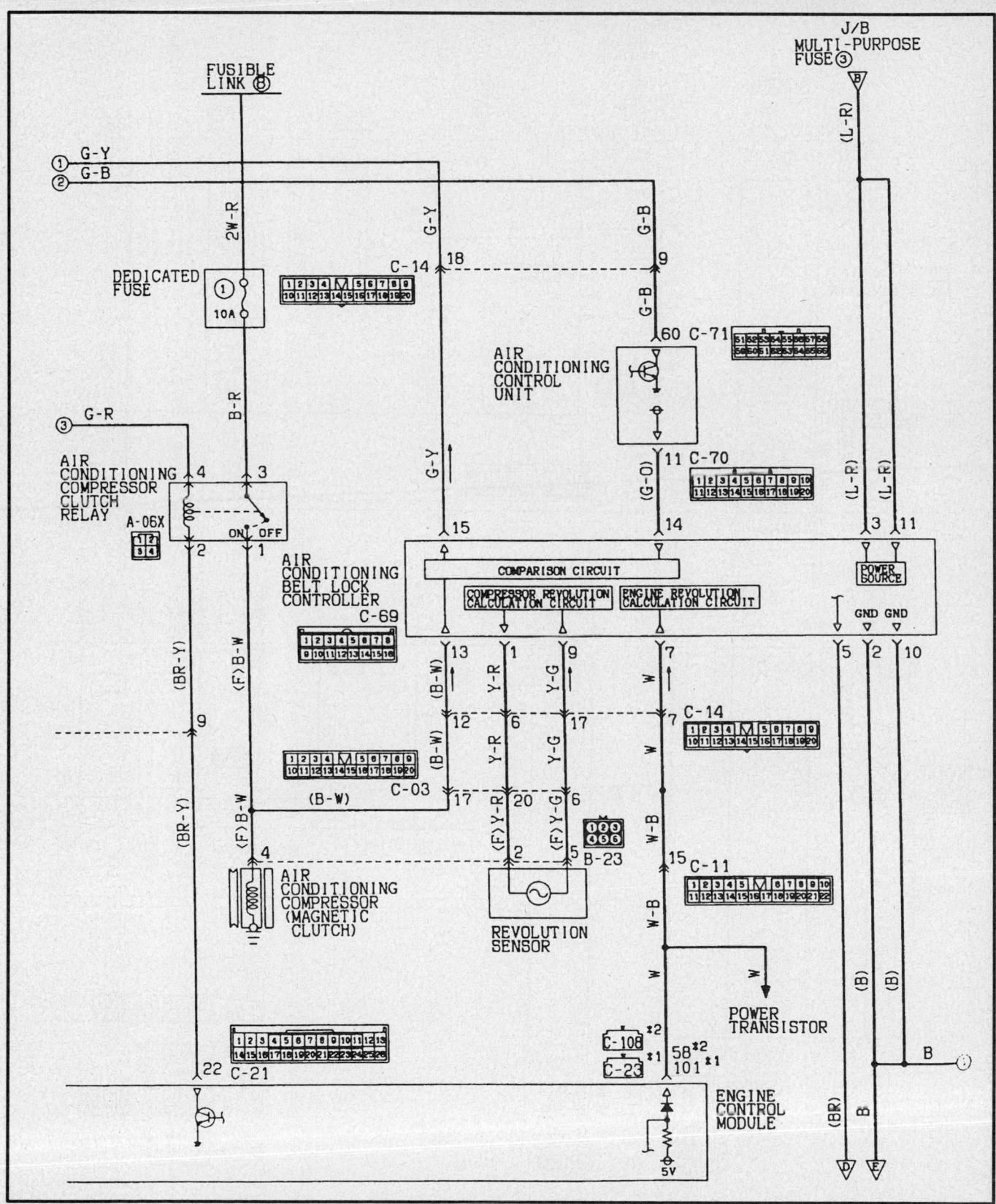

Wiring schematic — 1994–95 Diamante with DOHC engine, Cont.

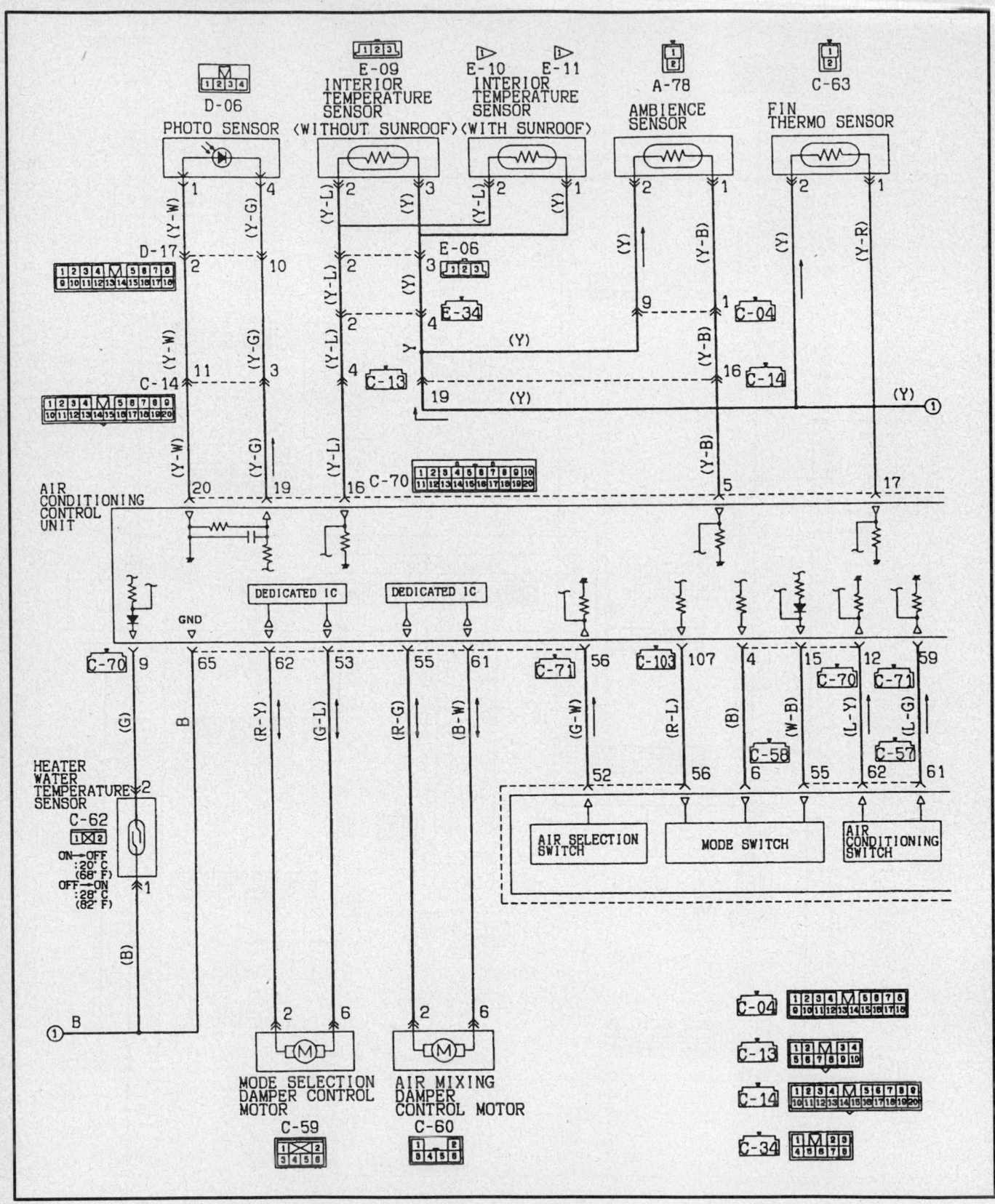

Wiring schematic — 1994–95 Diamante with DOHC engine, Cont.

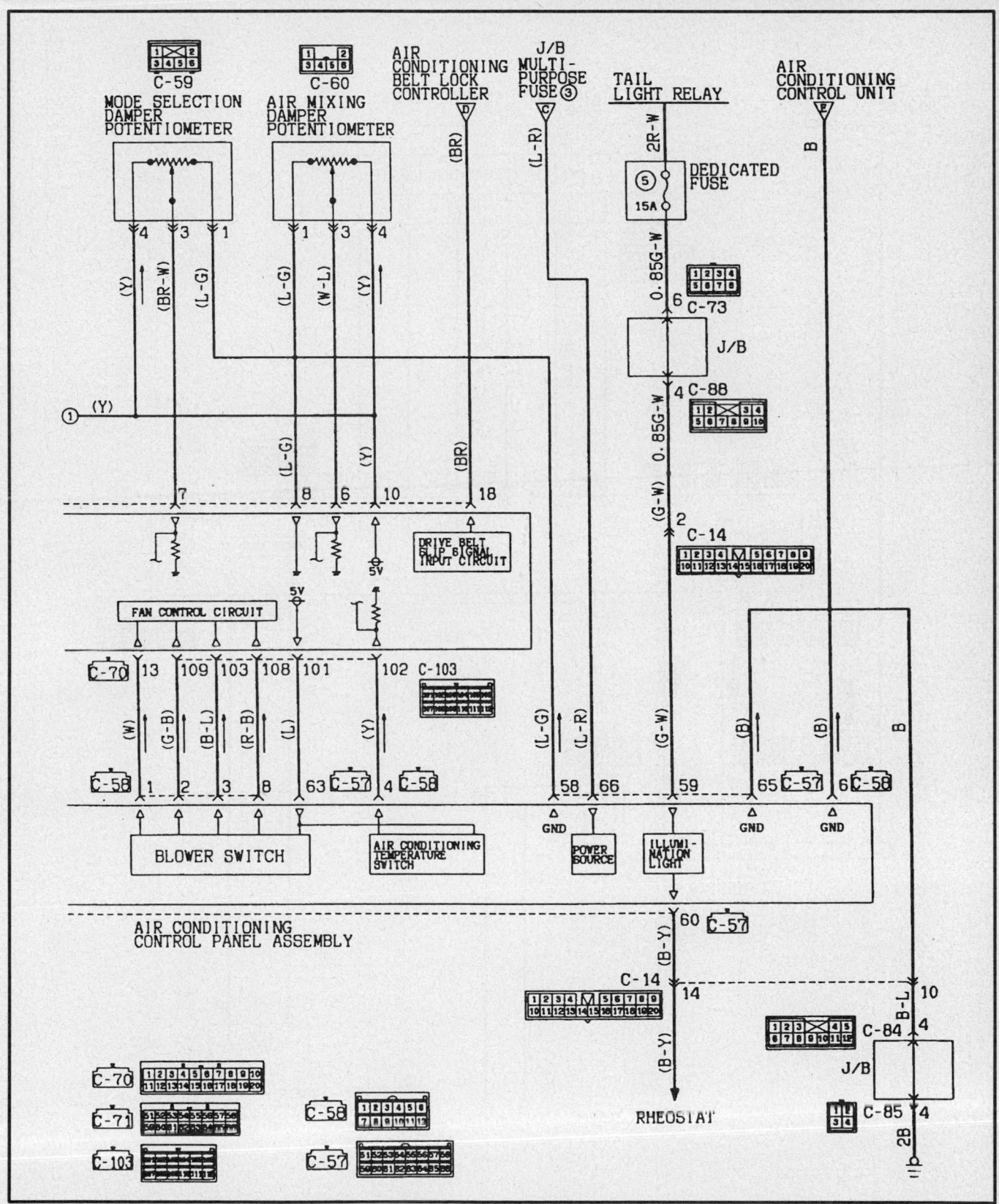

Wiring schematic — 1994–95 Diamante with DOHC engine, Cont.

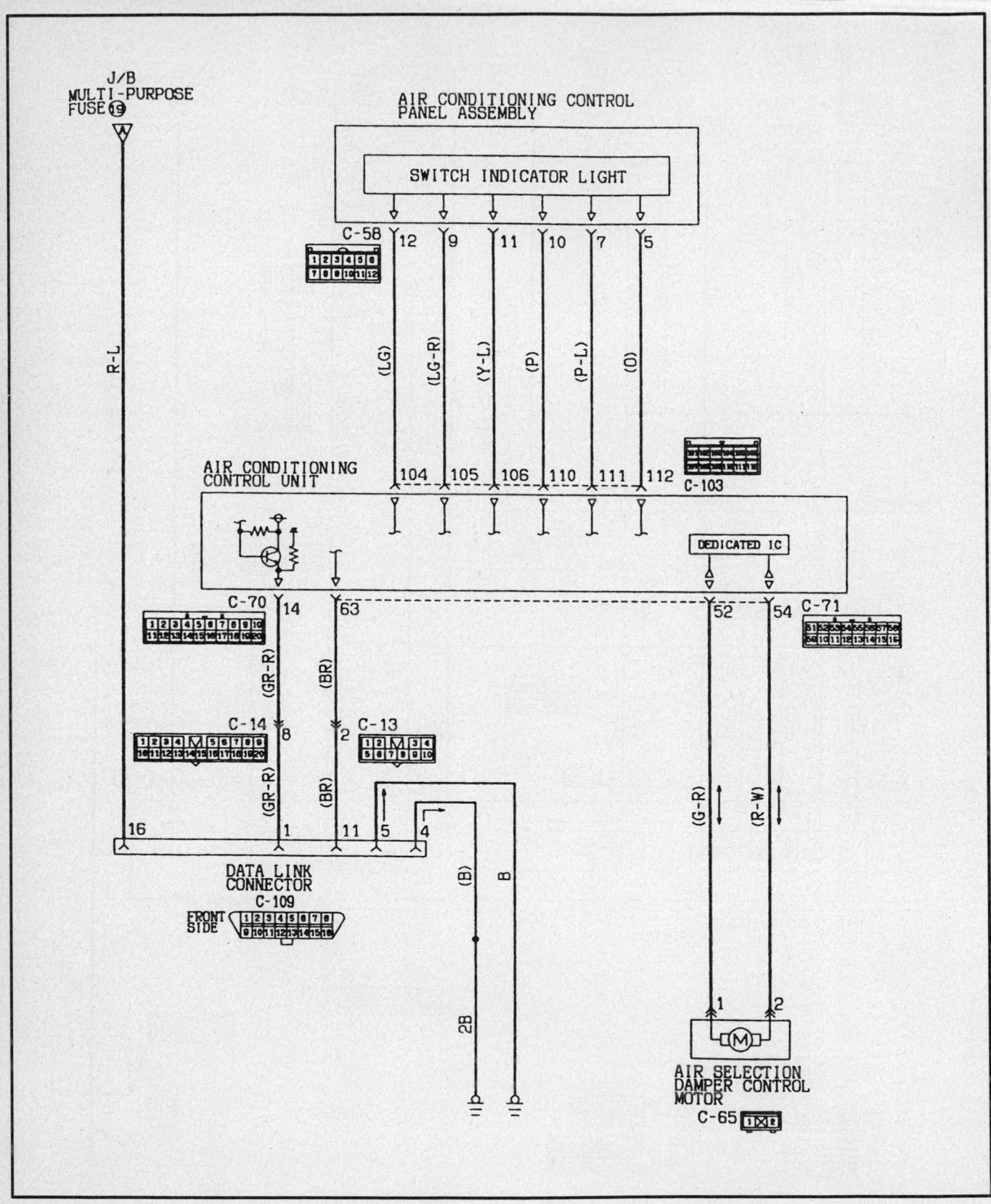

Wiring schematic — 1994–95 Diamante with DOHC engine, Cont.

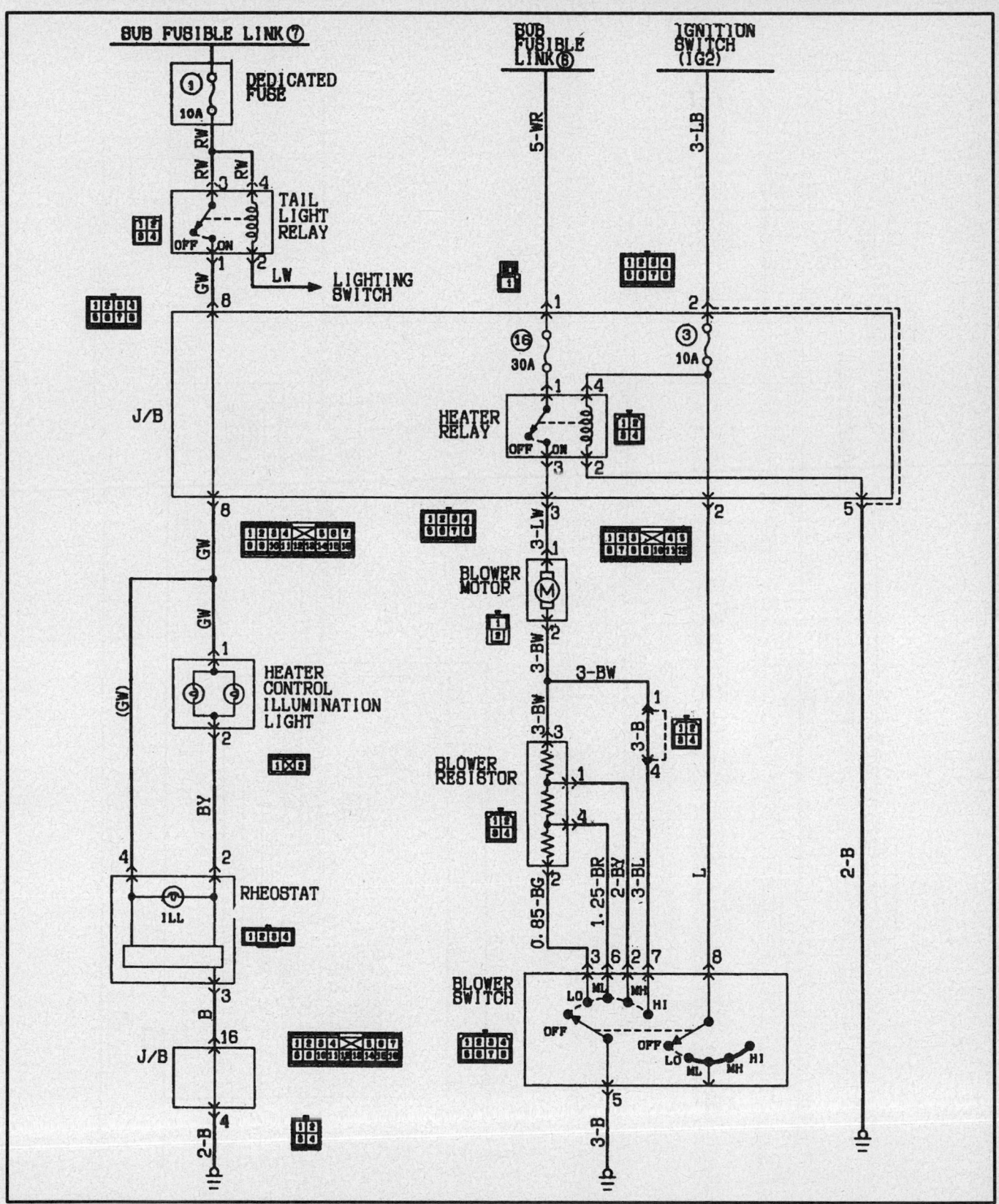

Wiring schematic — 1993–94 Eclipse with heater only

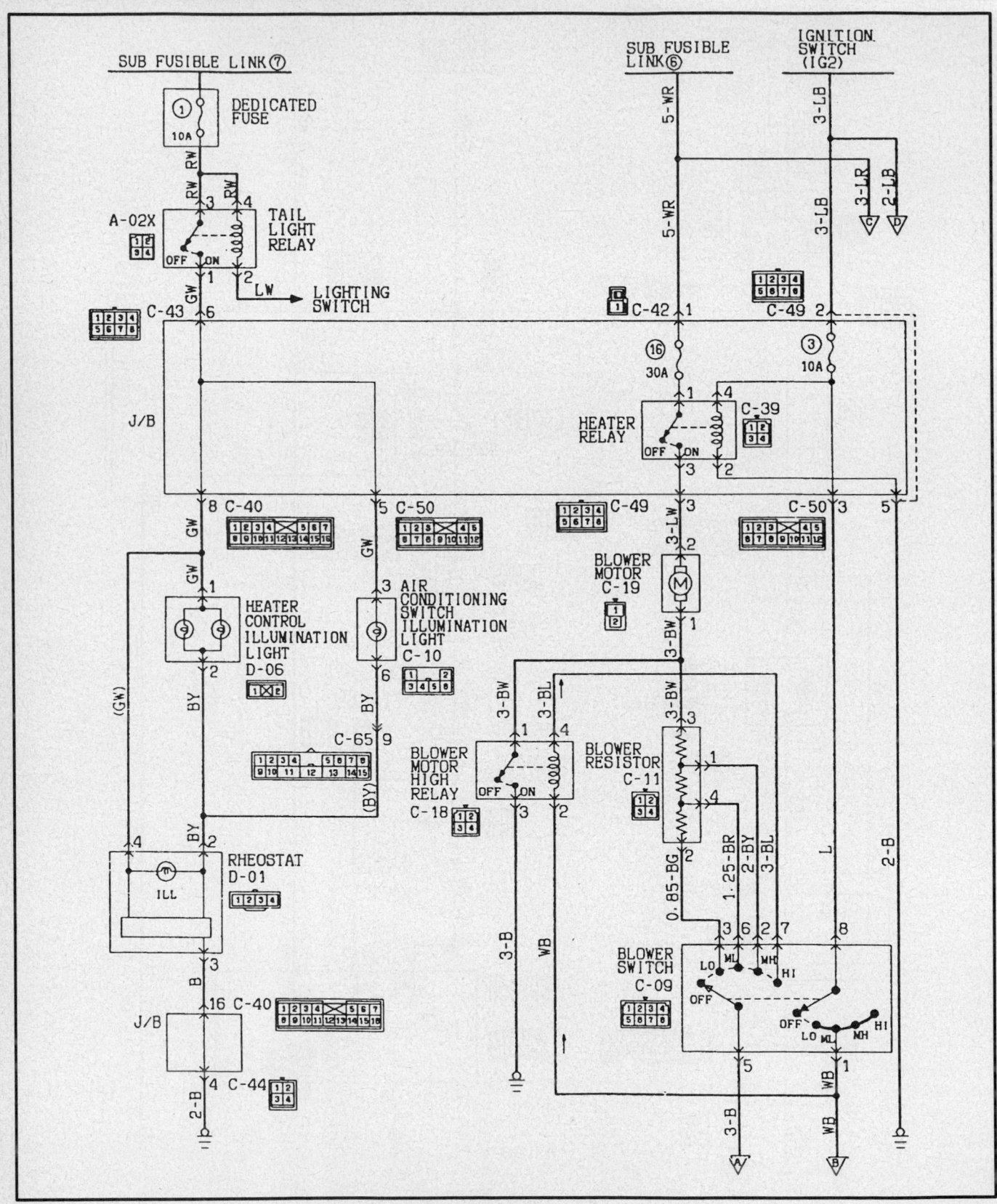

Wiring schematic — 1993—94 Eclipse with air conditioning

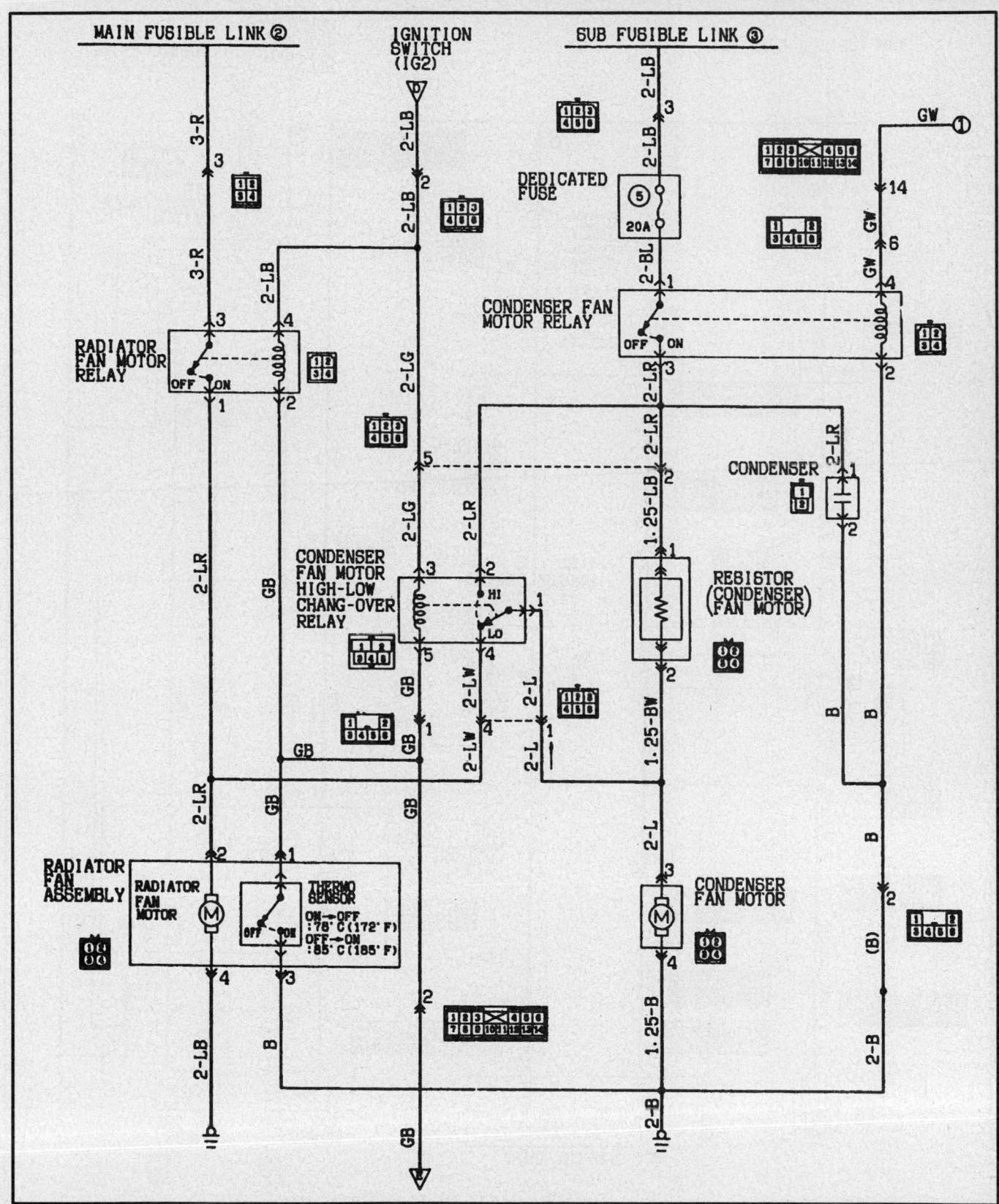

Wiring schematic — 1993–94 Eclipse with air conditioning, Cont.

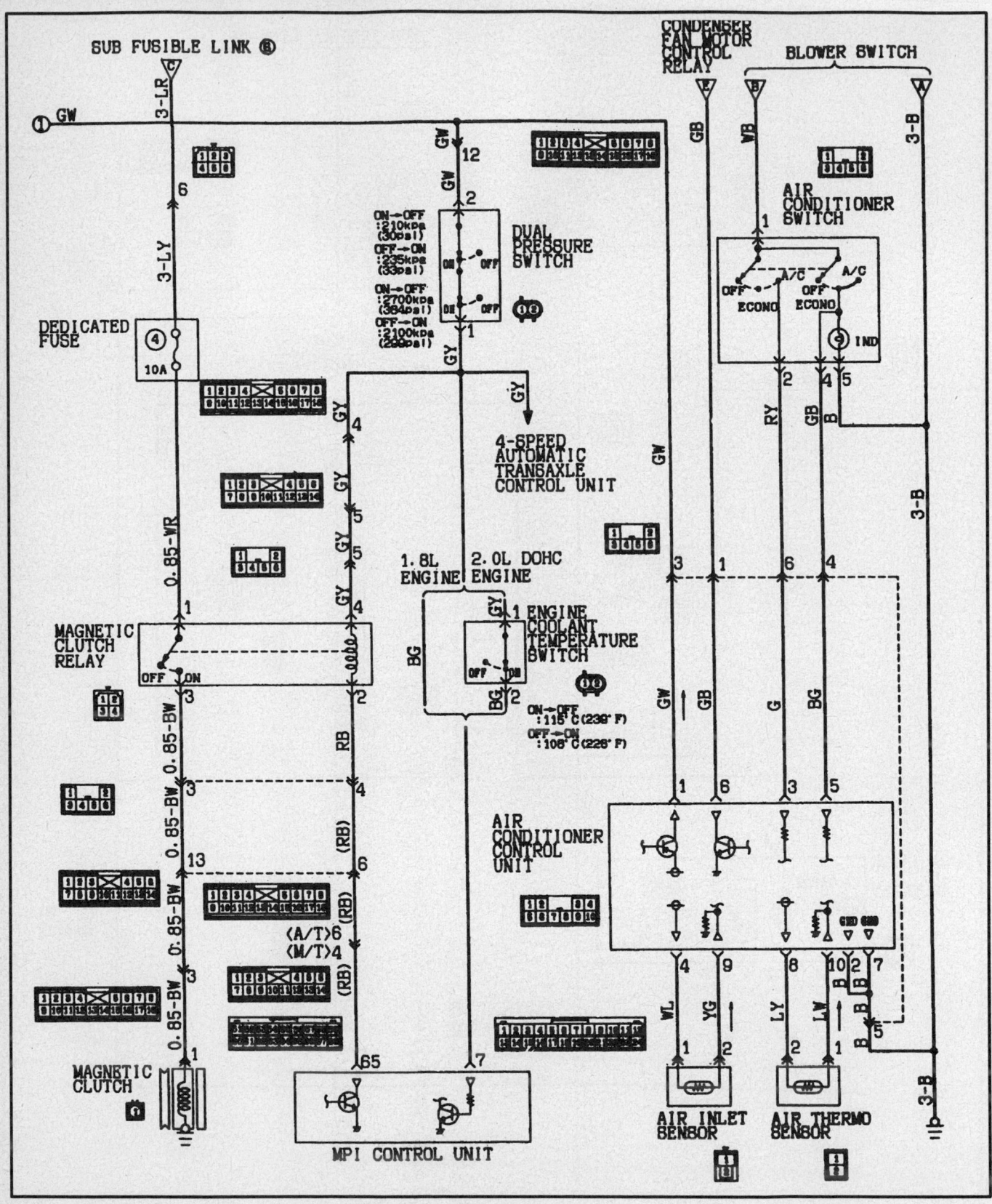

Wiring schematic — 1993–94 Eclipse with air conditioning, Cont.

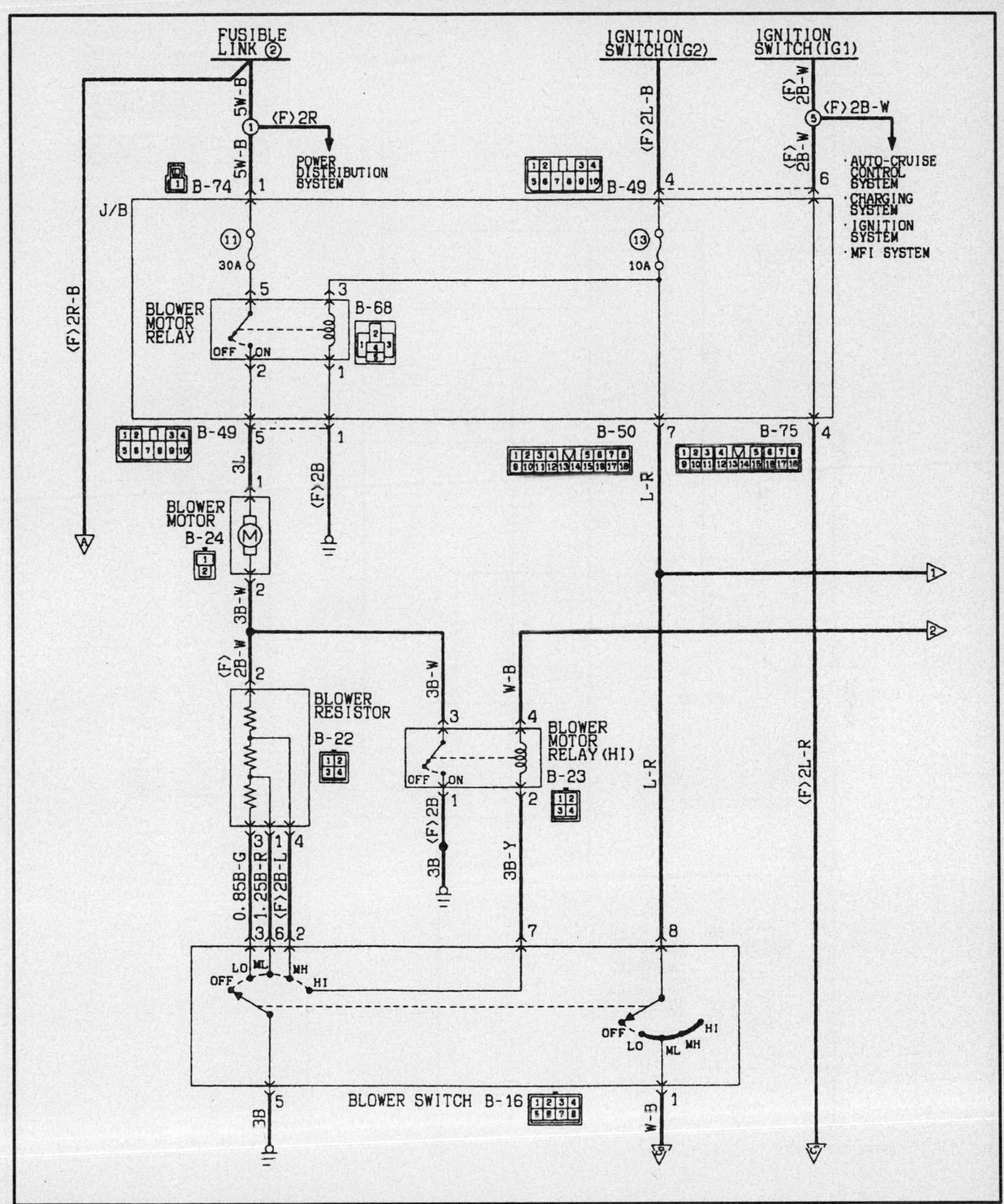

Wiring schematic — 1995 Eclipse non-turbo manual trans.

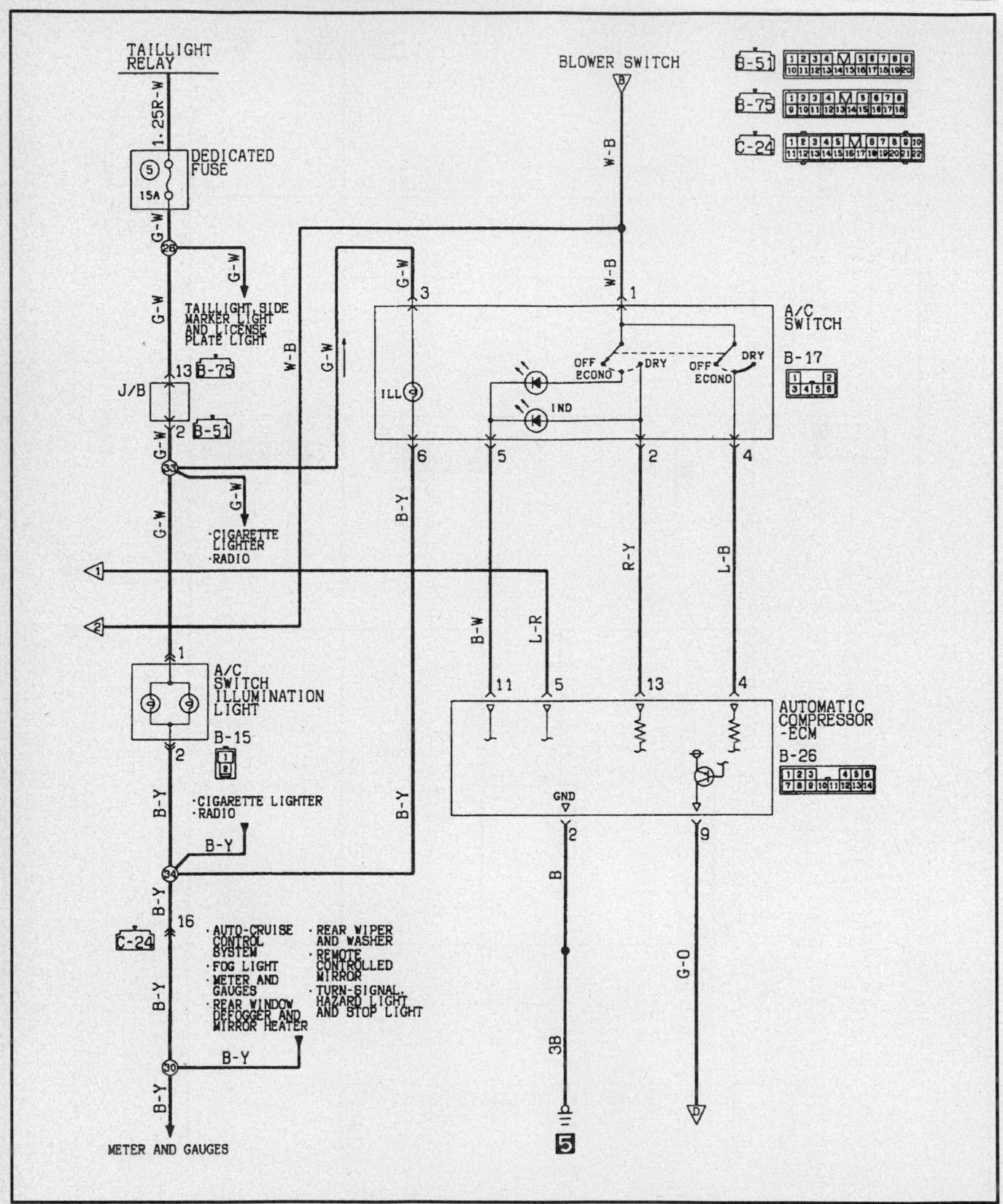

Wiring schematic — 1995 Eclipse non-turbo manual trans., Cont.

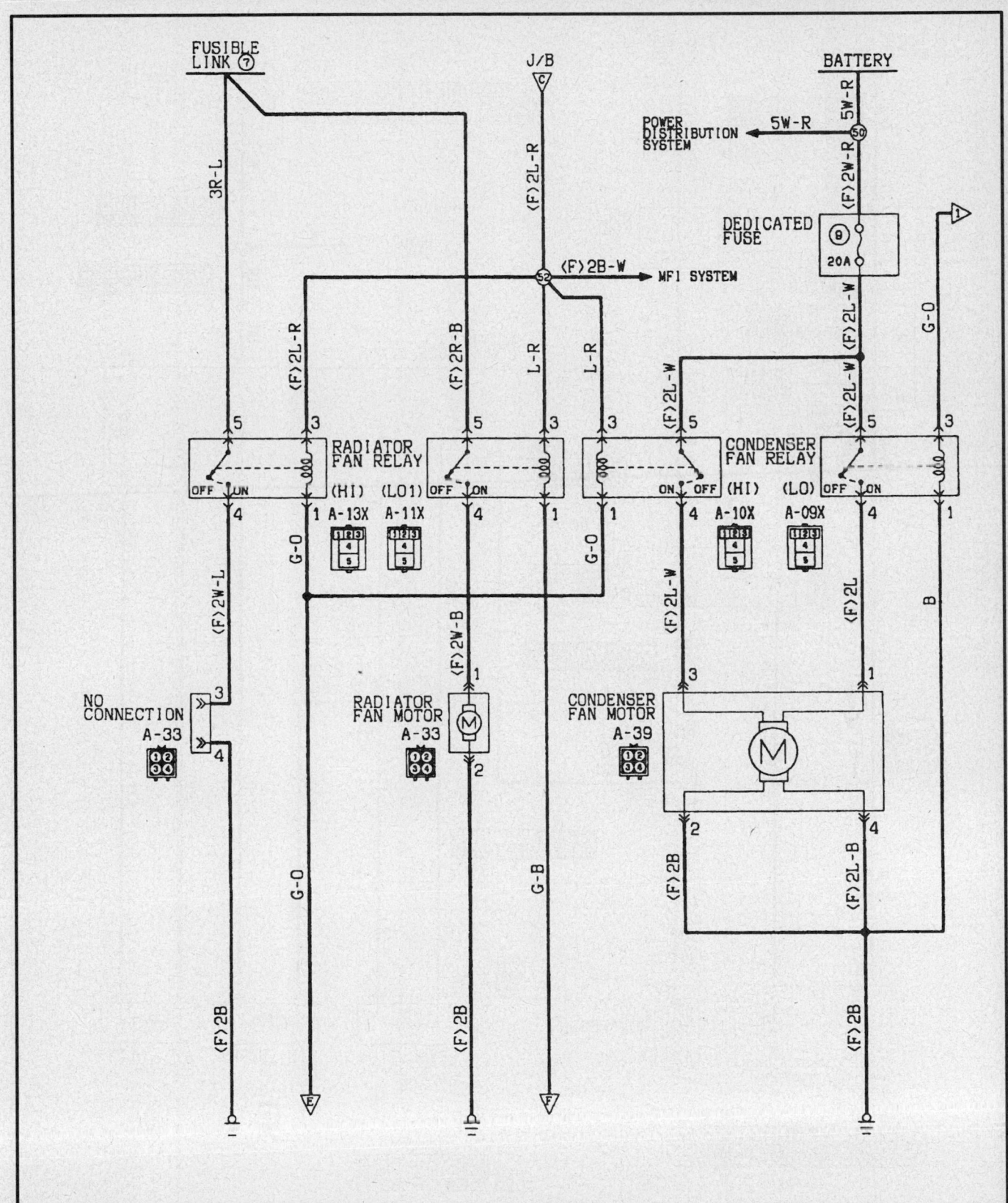

Wiring schematic — 1995 Eclipse non-turbo manual trans., Cont.

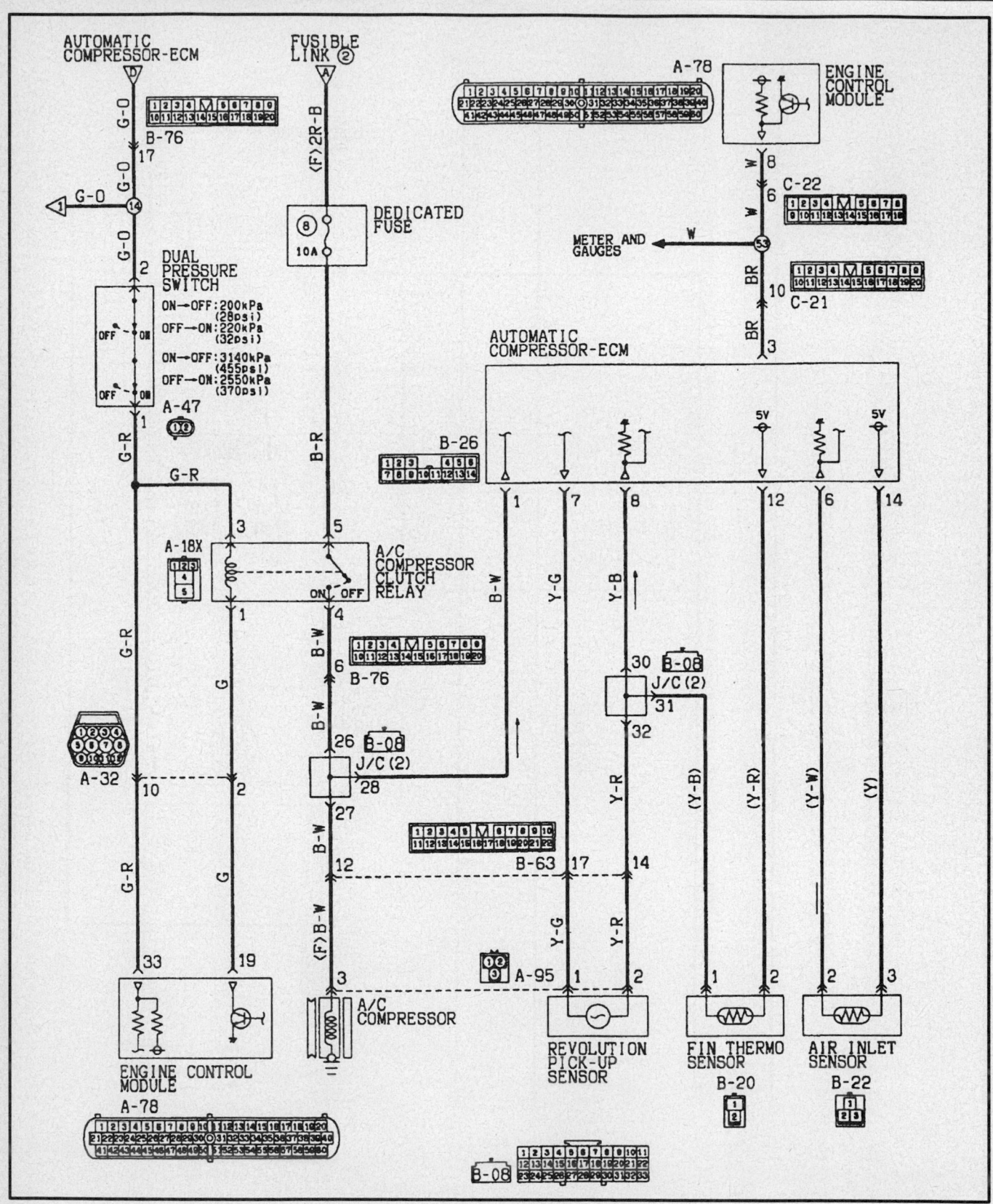

Wiring schematic — 1995 Eclipse non-turbo manual trans., Cont.

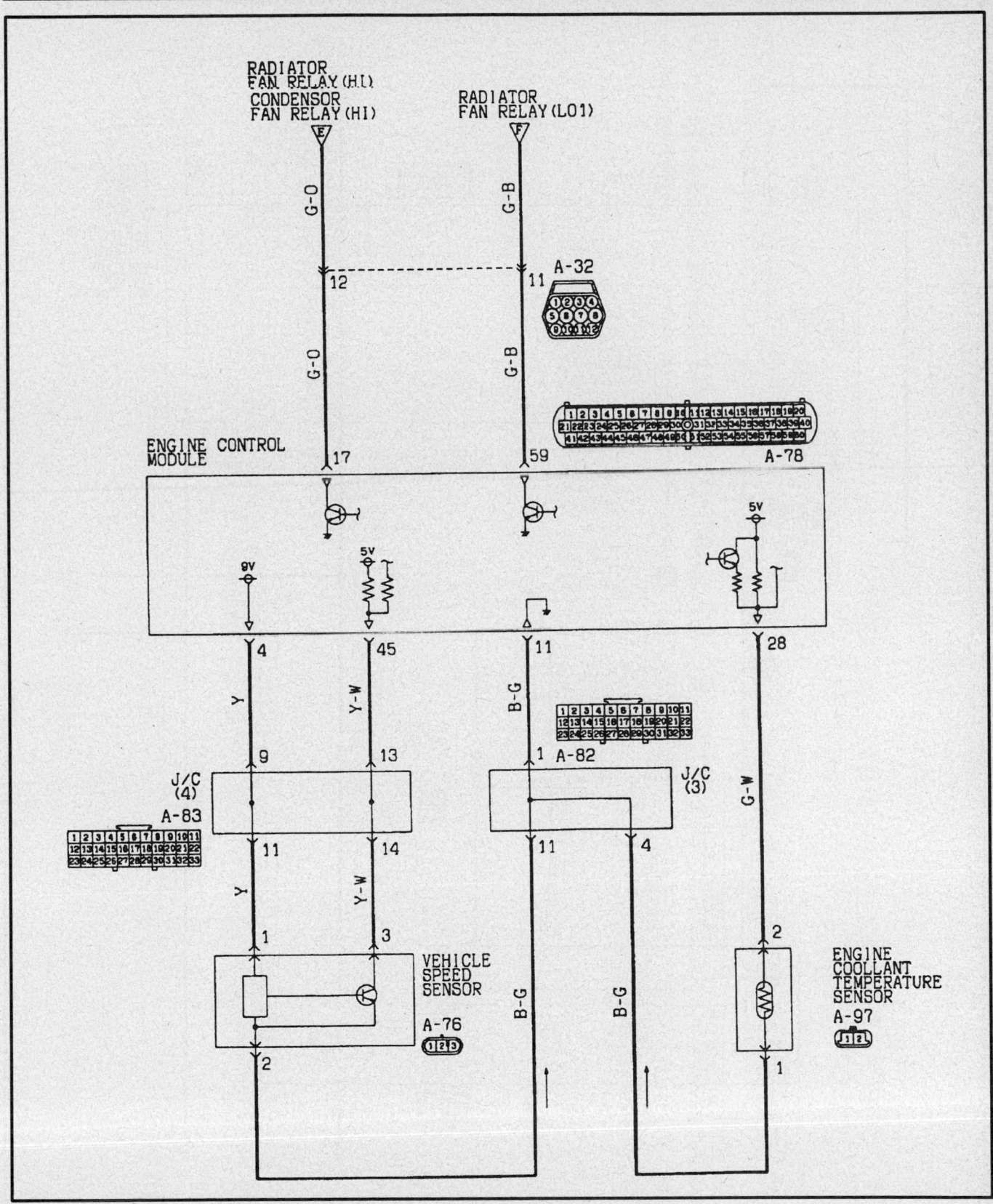

Wiring schematic — 1995 Eclipse non-turbo manual trans., Cont.

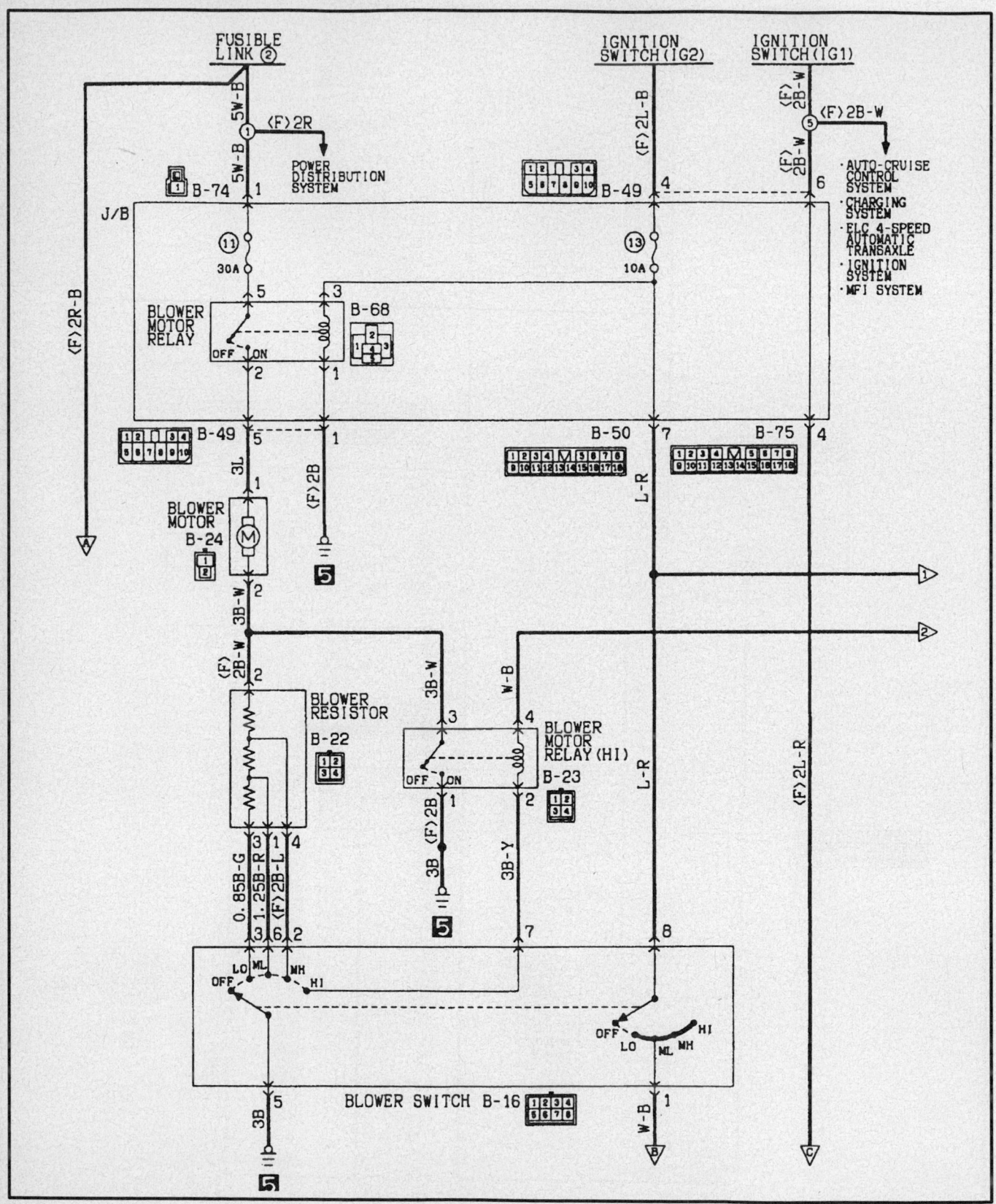

Wiring schematic — 1995 Eclipse non-turbo auto trans.

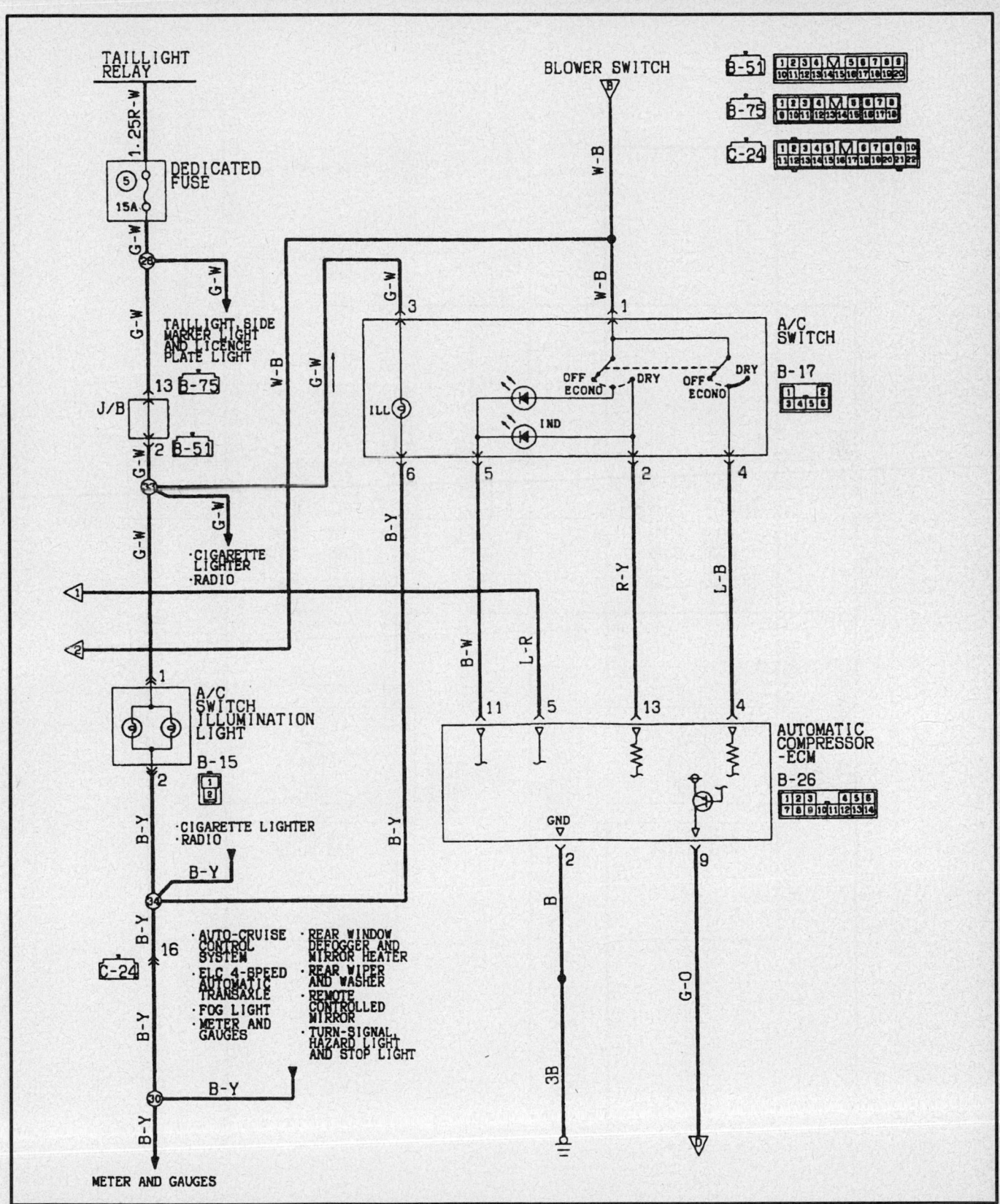

Wiring schematic — 1995 Eclipse non-turbo auto trans., Cont.

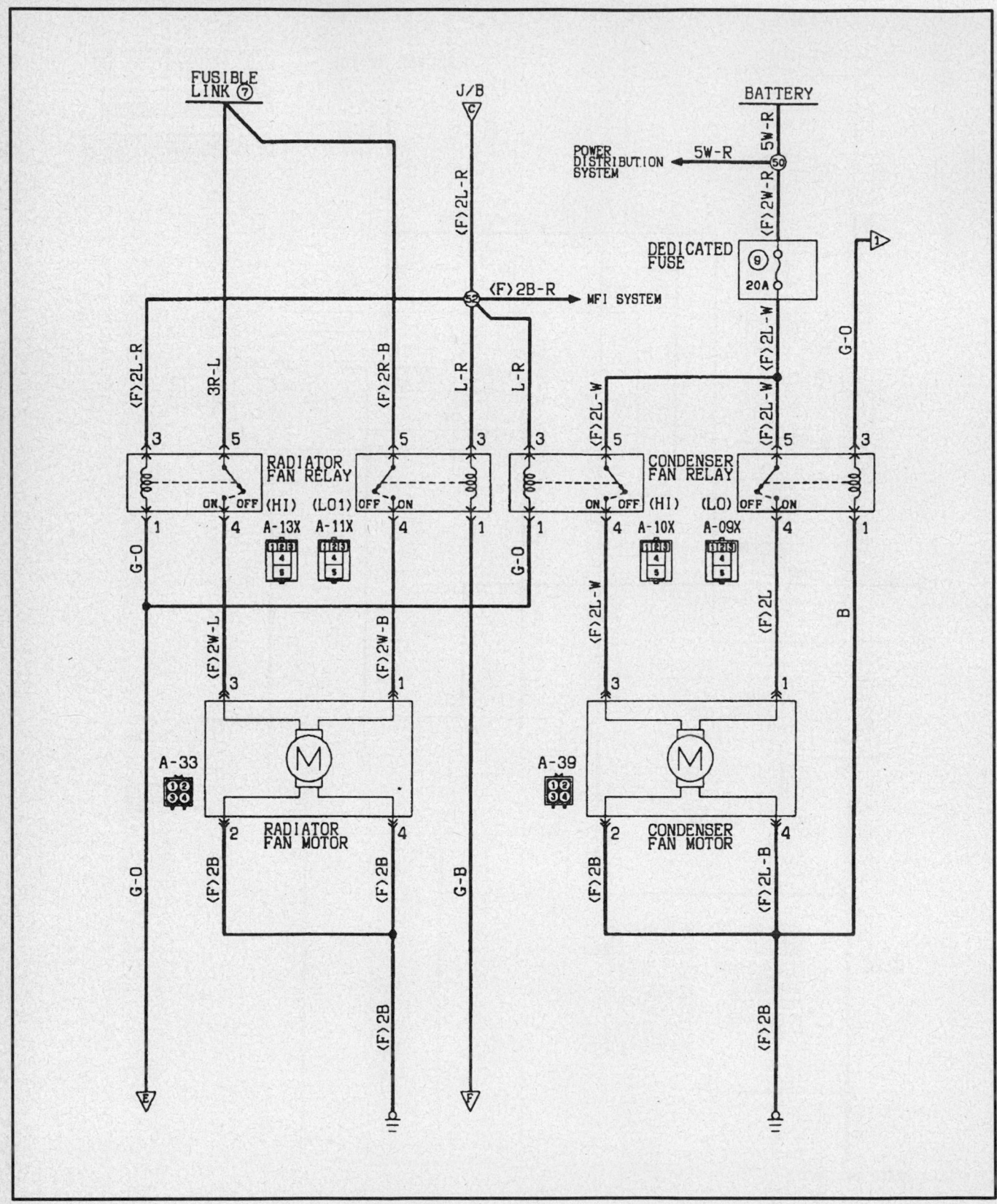

Wiring schematic — 1995 Eclipse non-turbo auto trans., Cont.

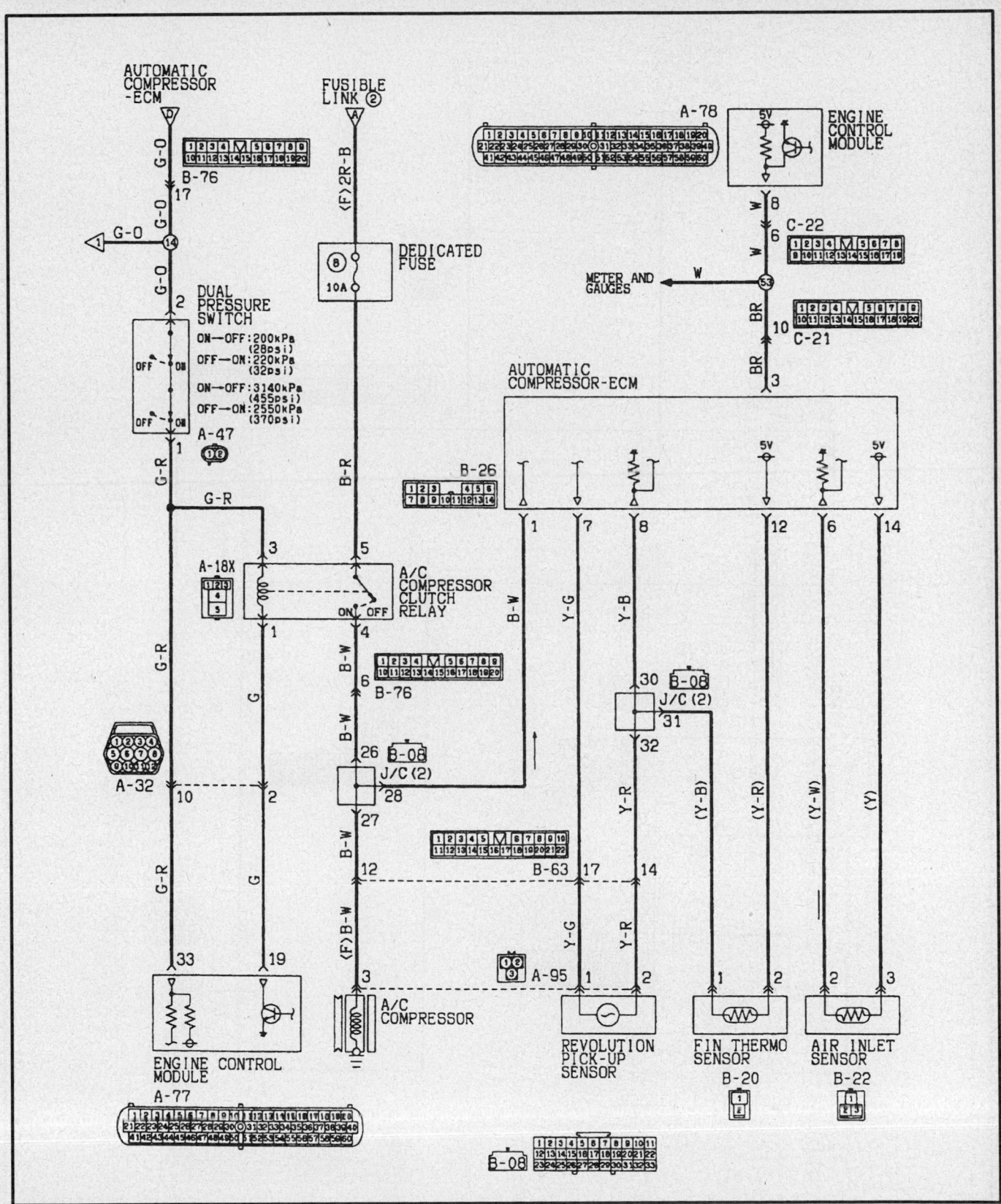

Wiring schematic — 1995 Eclipse non-turbo auto trans., Cont.

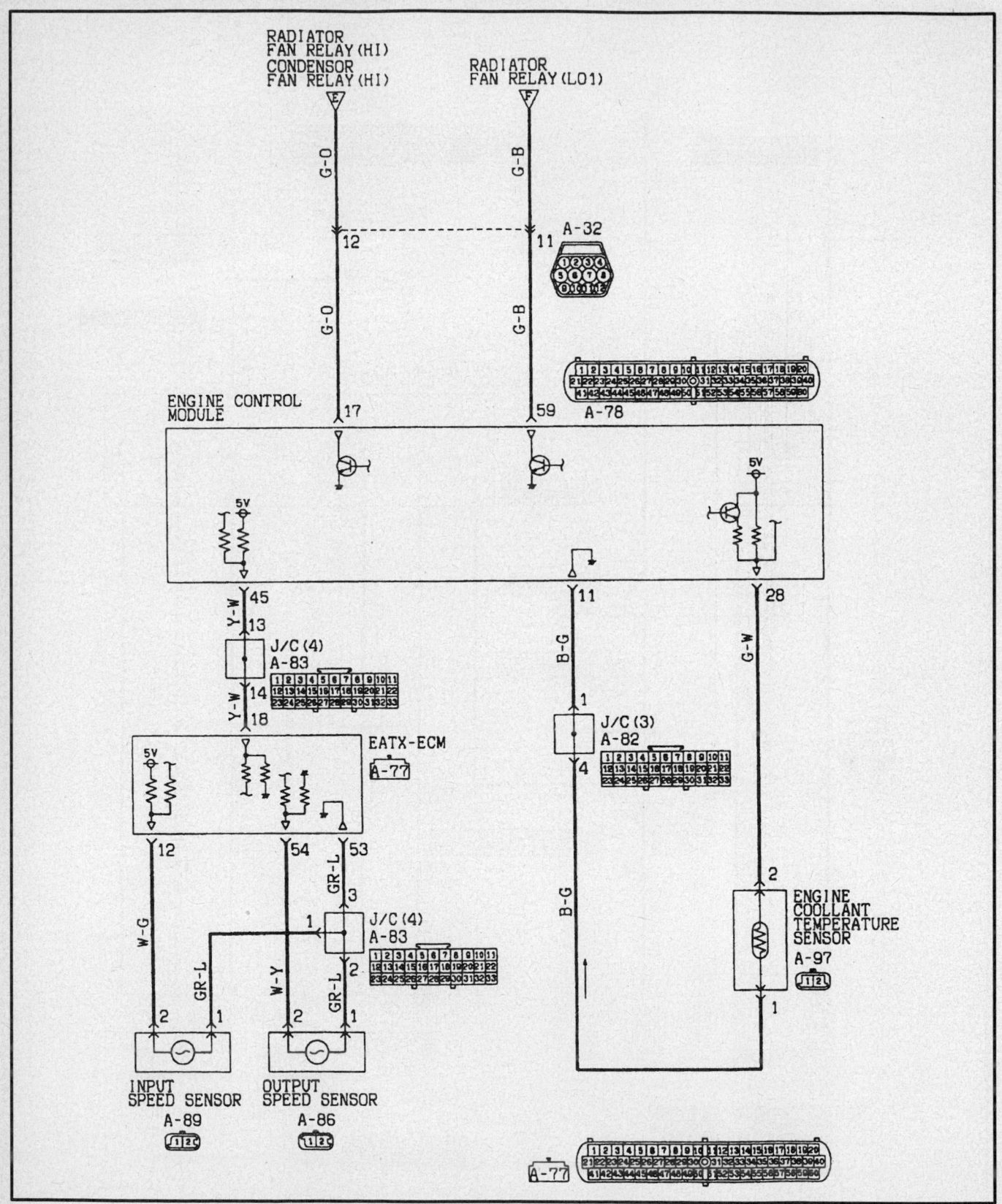

Wiring schematic — 1995 Eclipse non-turbo auto trans., Cont.

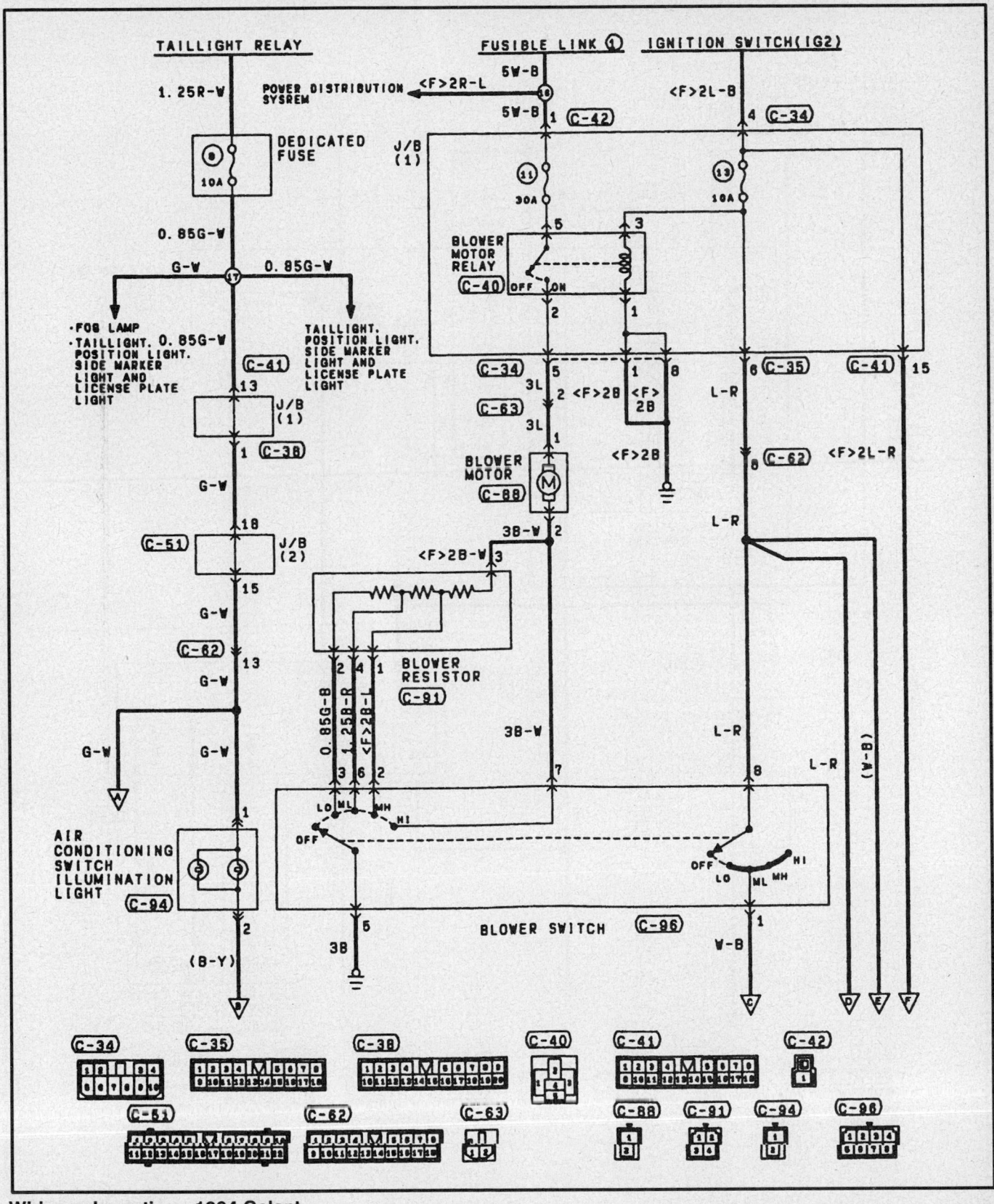

Wiring schematic — 1994 Galant

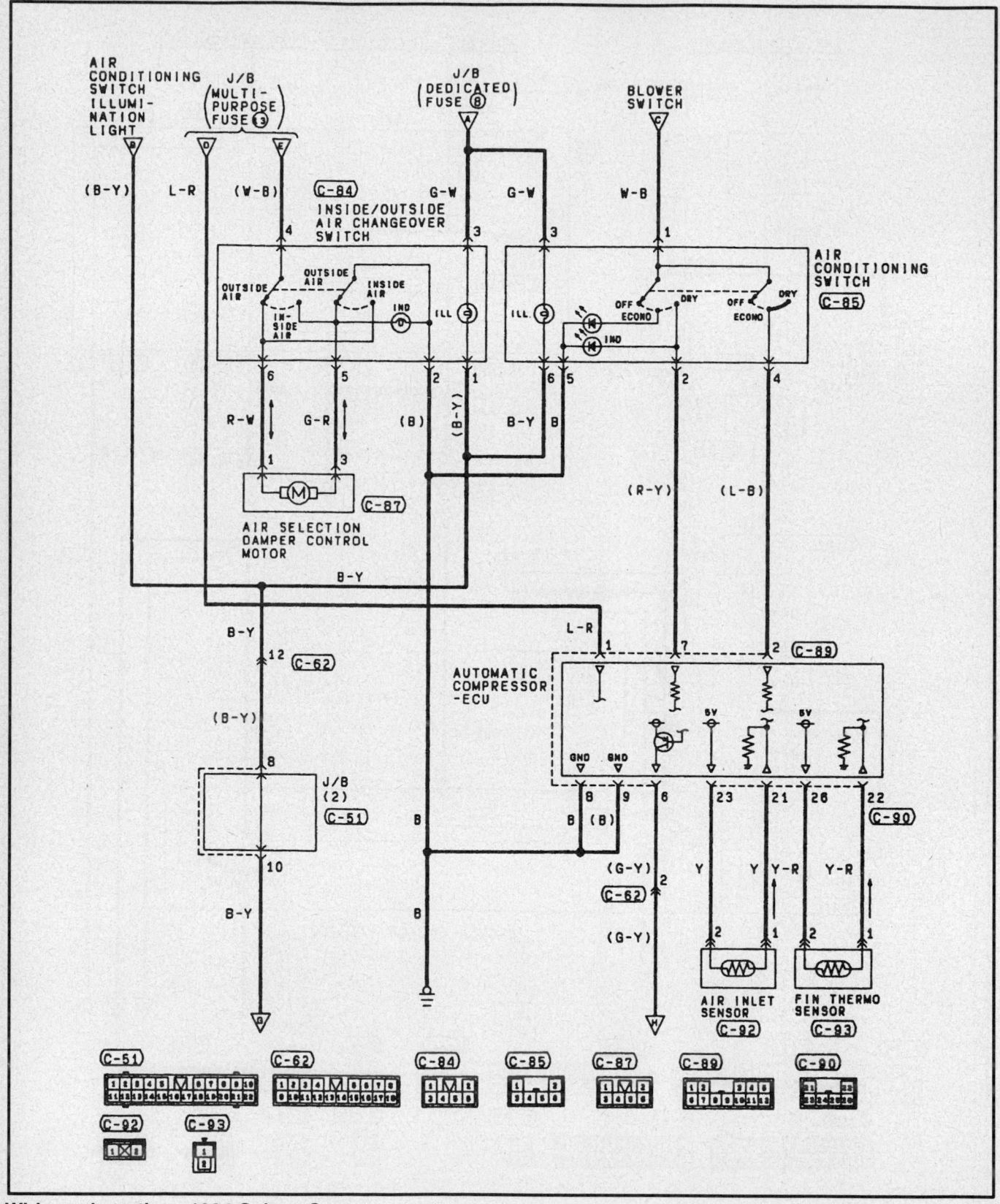

Wiring schematic — 1994 Galant, Cont.

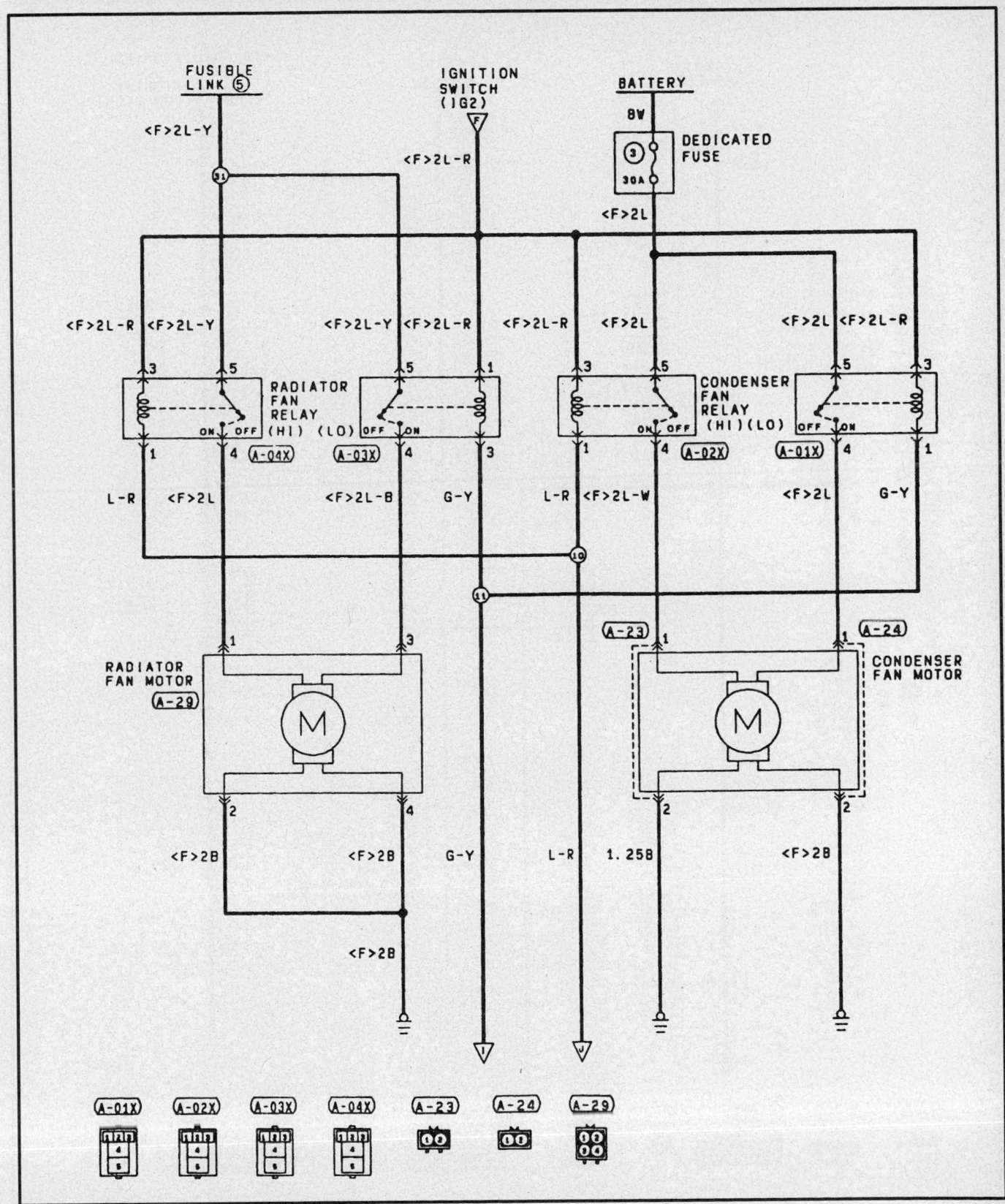

Wiring schematic — 1994 Galant, Cont.

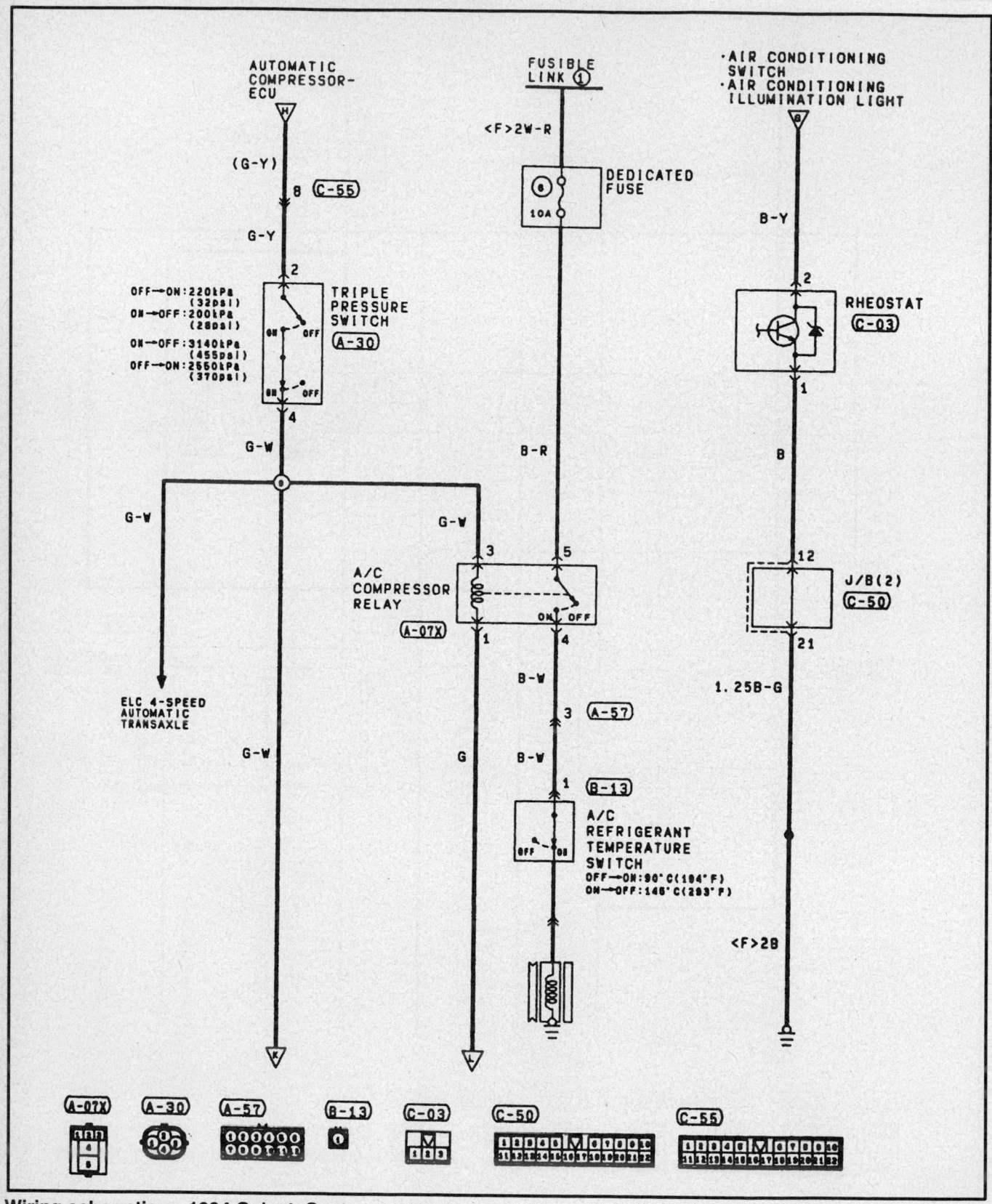

Wiring schematic — 1994 Galant, Cont.

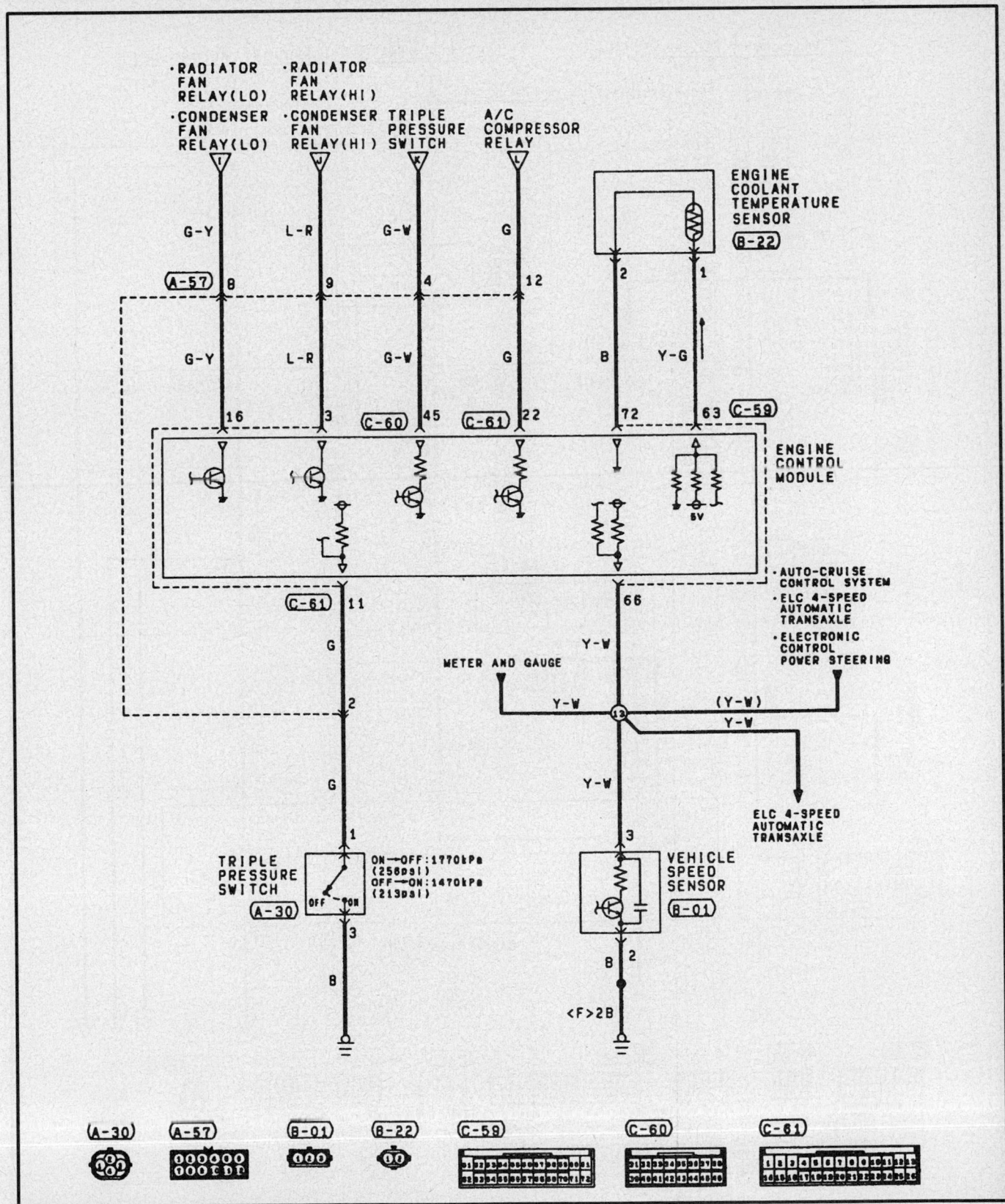

Wiring schematic — 1994 Galant, Cont.

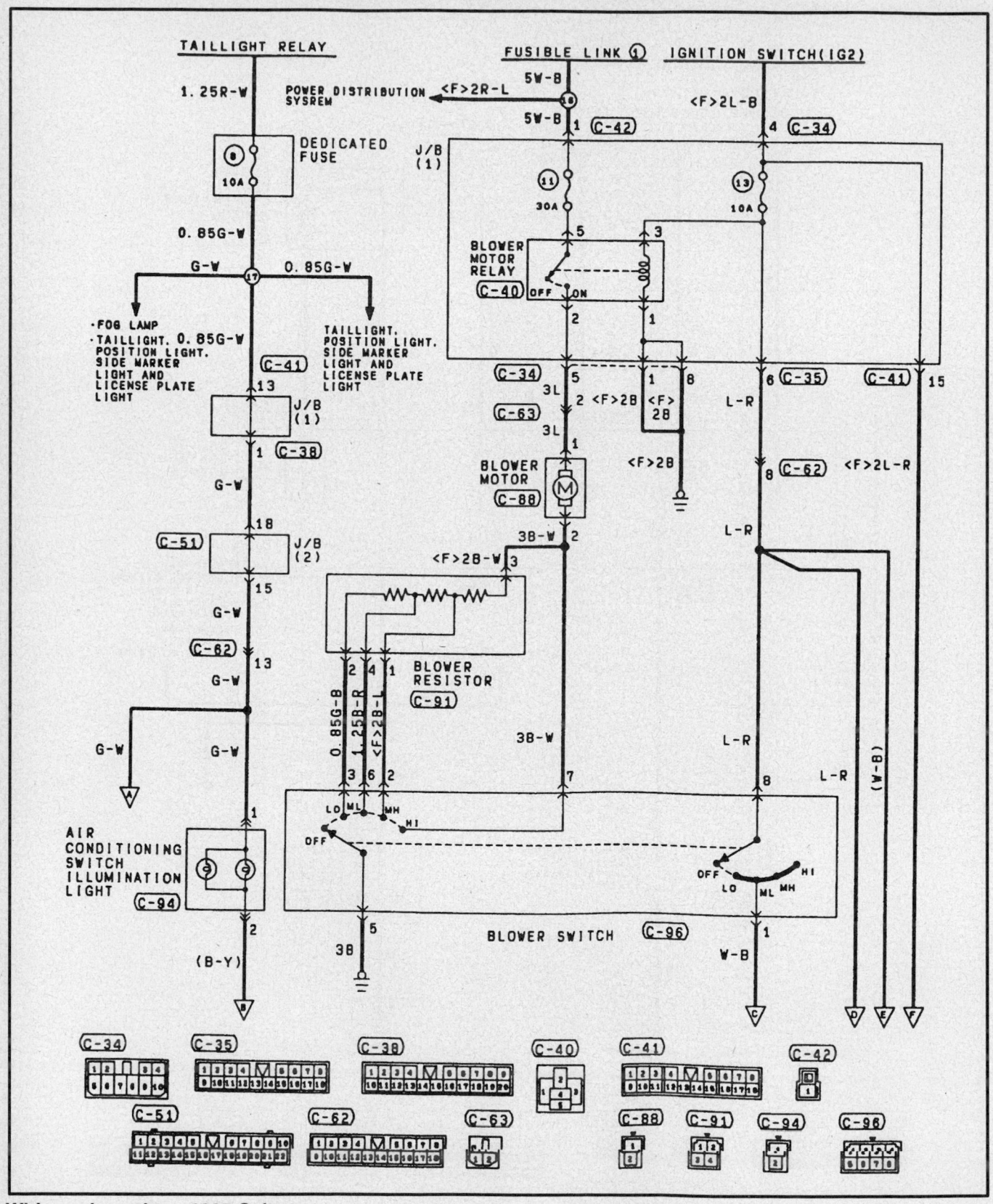

Wiring schematic — 1995 Galant

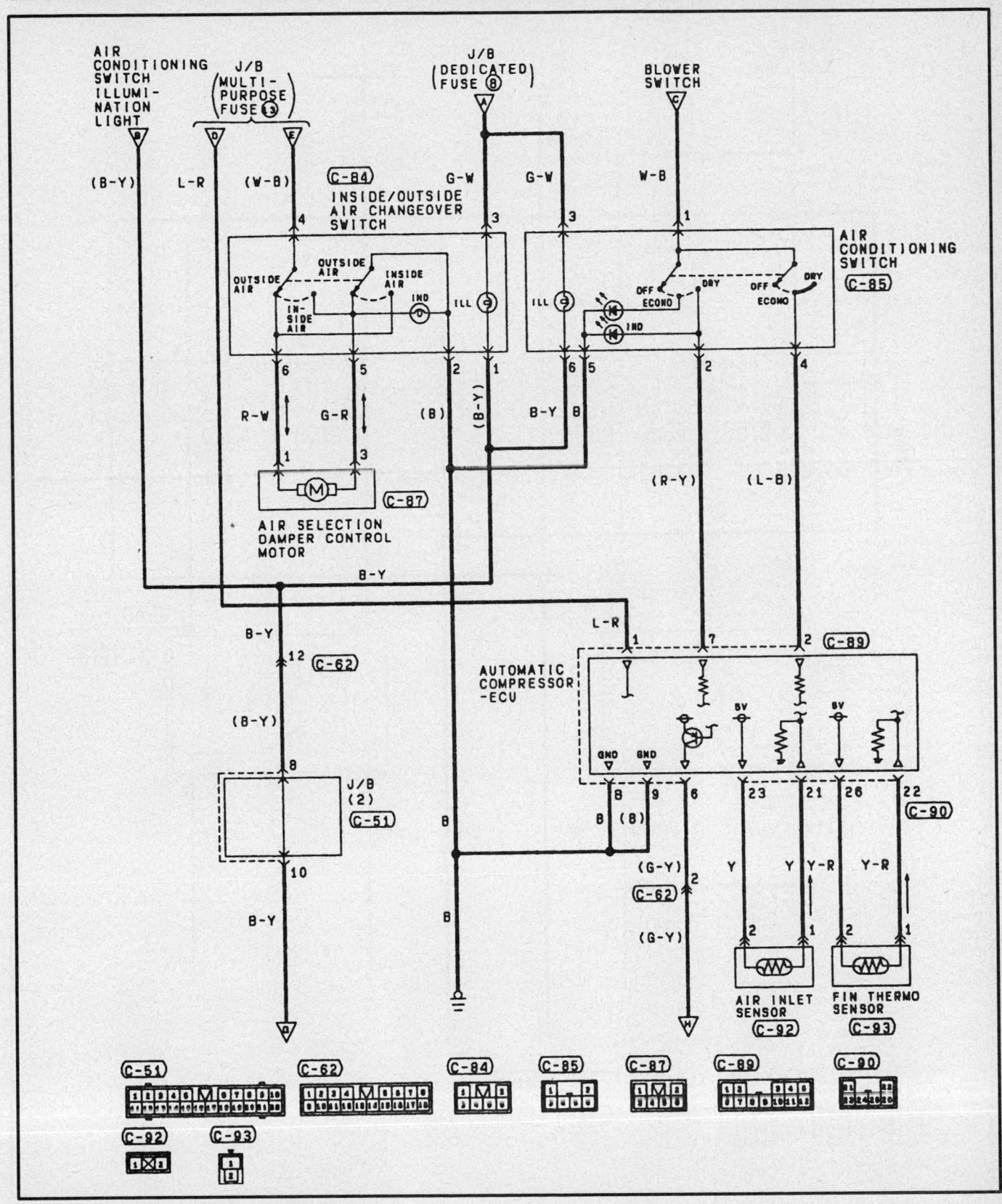

Wiring schematic — 1995 Galant, Cont.

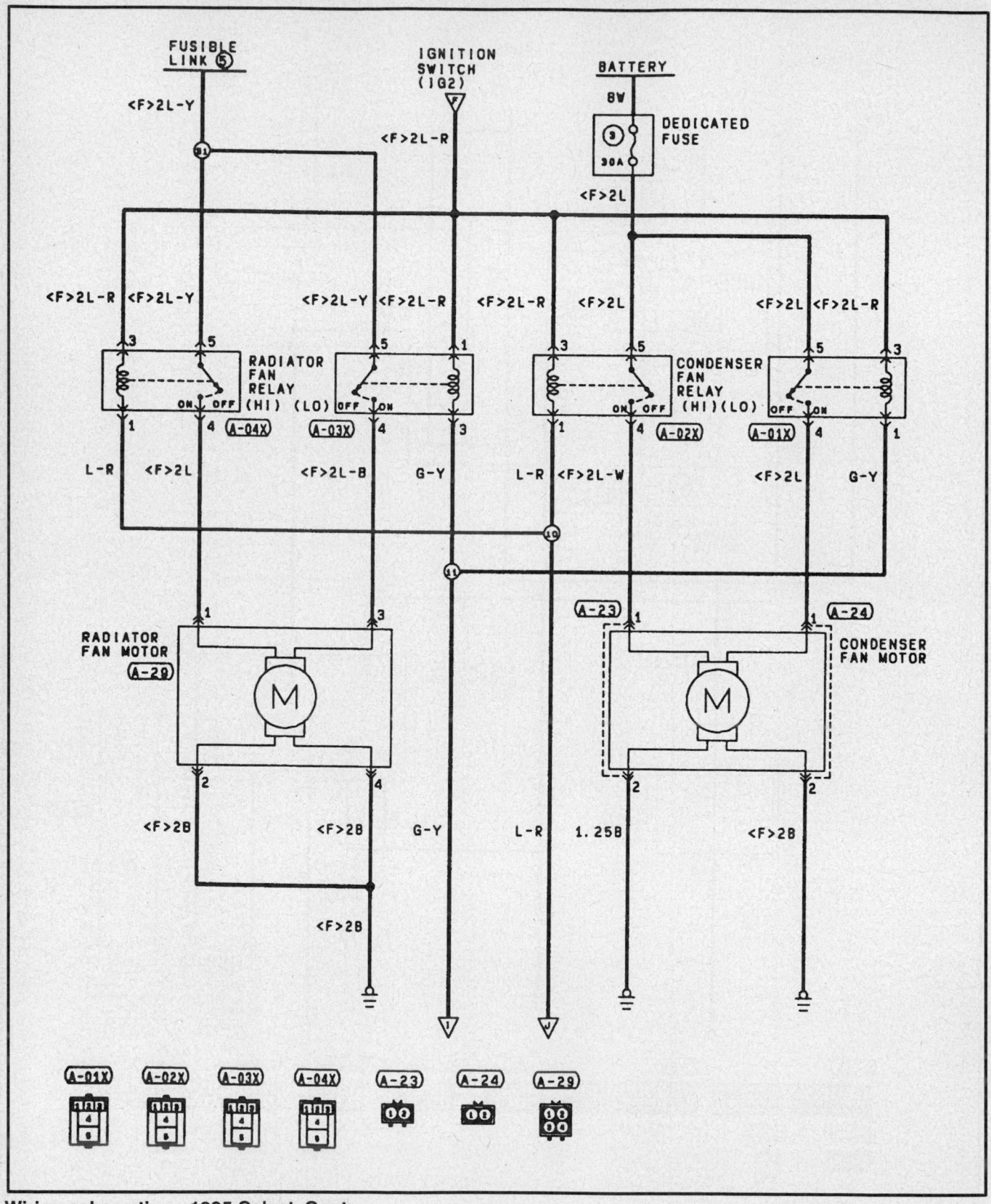

Wiring schematic — 1995 Galant, Cont.

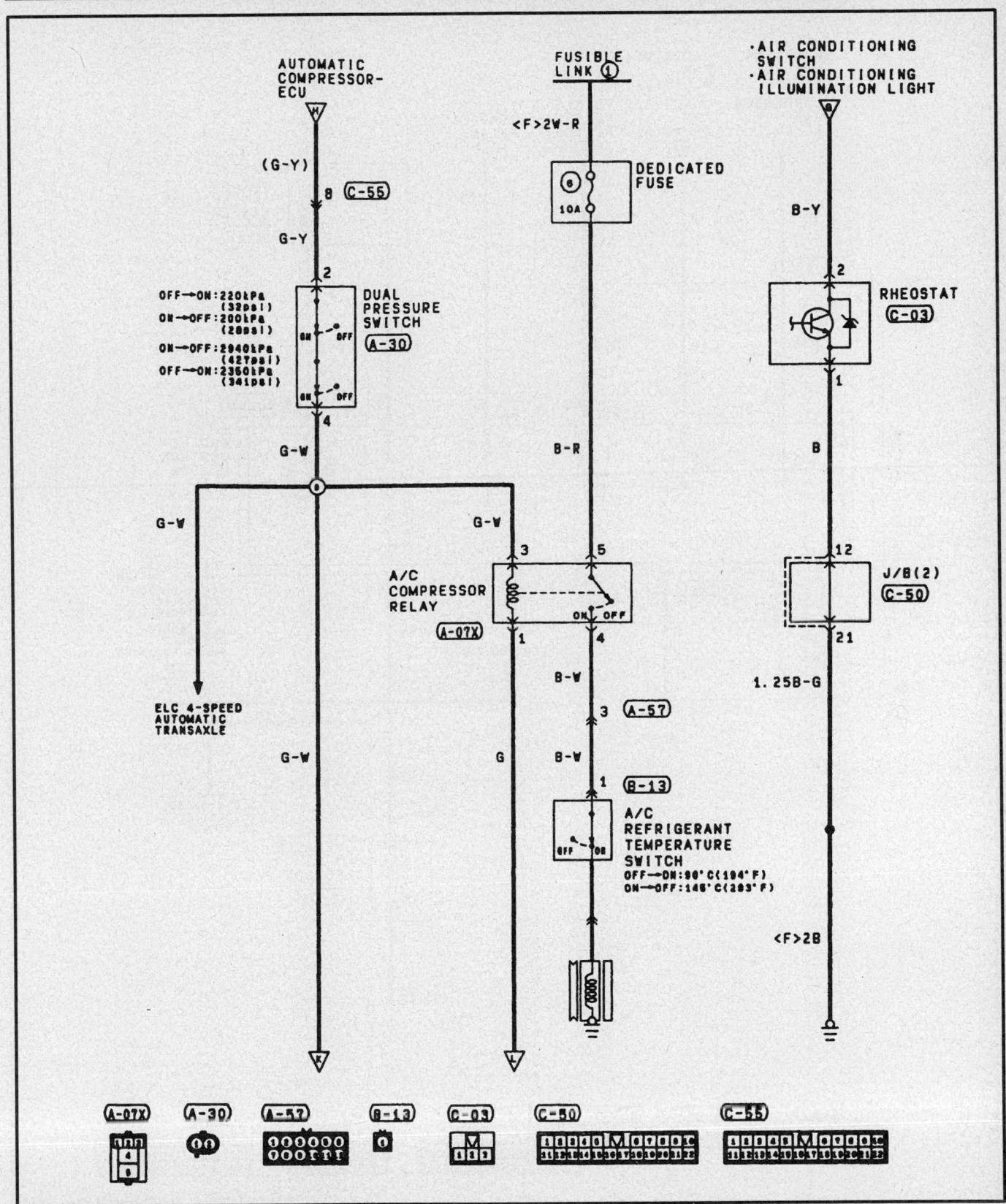

Wiring schematic — 1995 Galant, Cont.

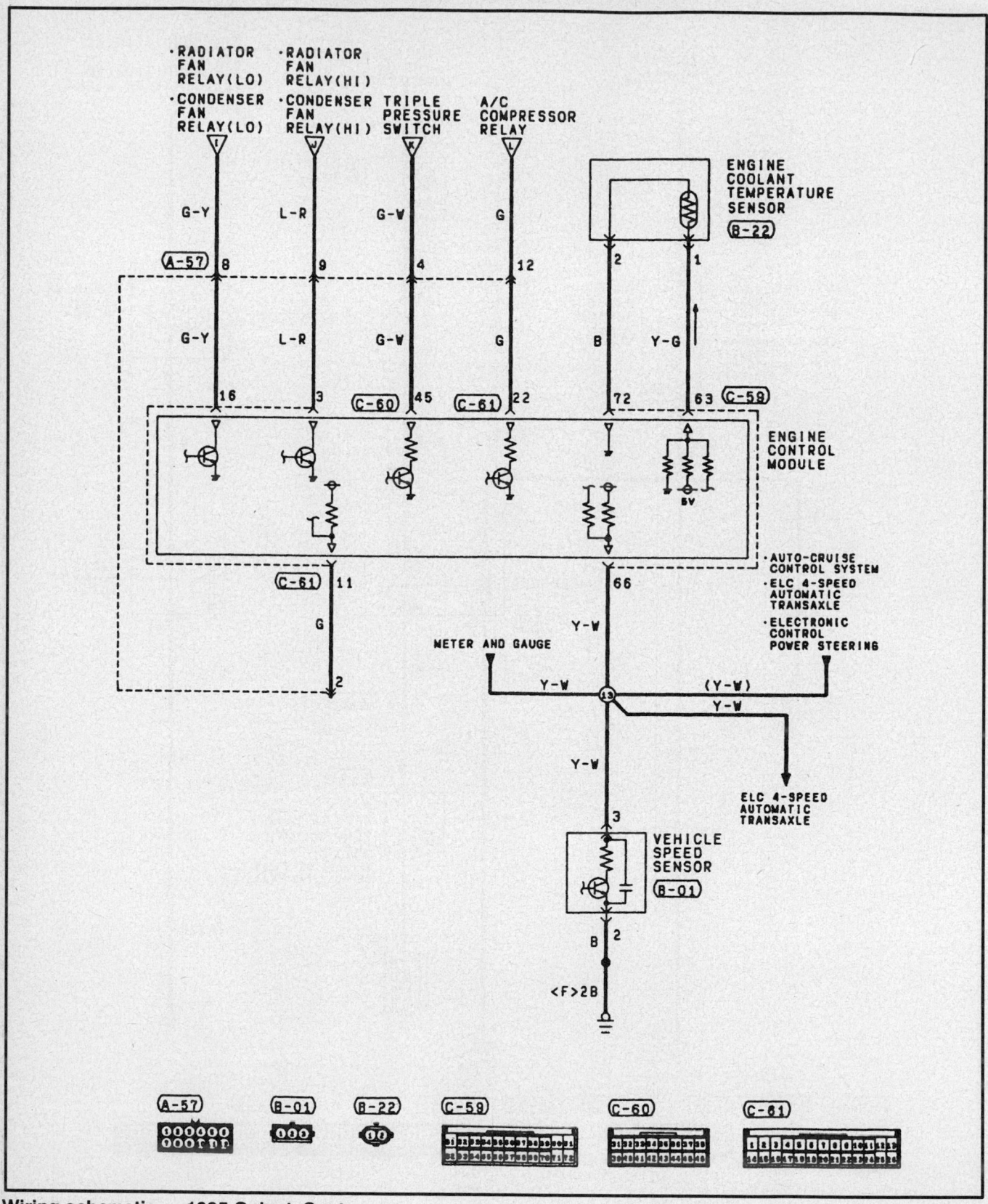

Wiring schematic — 1995 Galant, Cont.

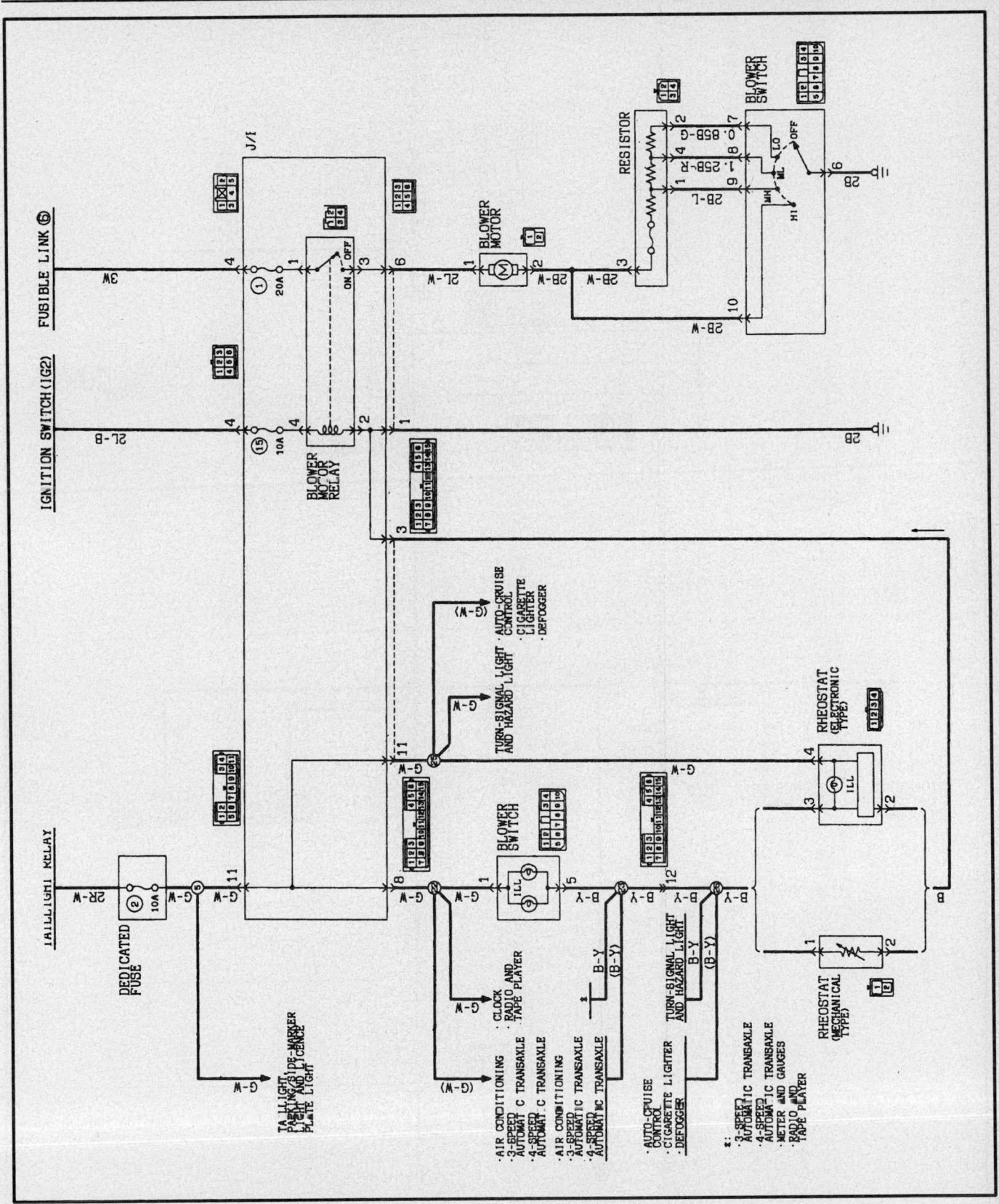

Wiring schematic — 1993 Mirage with heater only

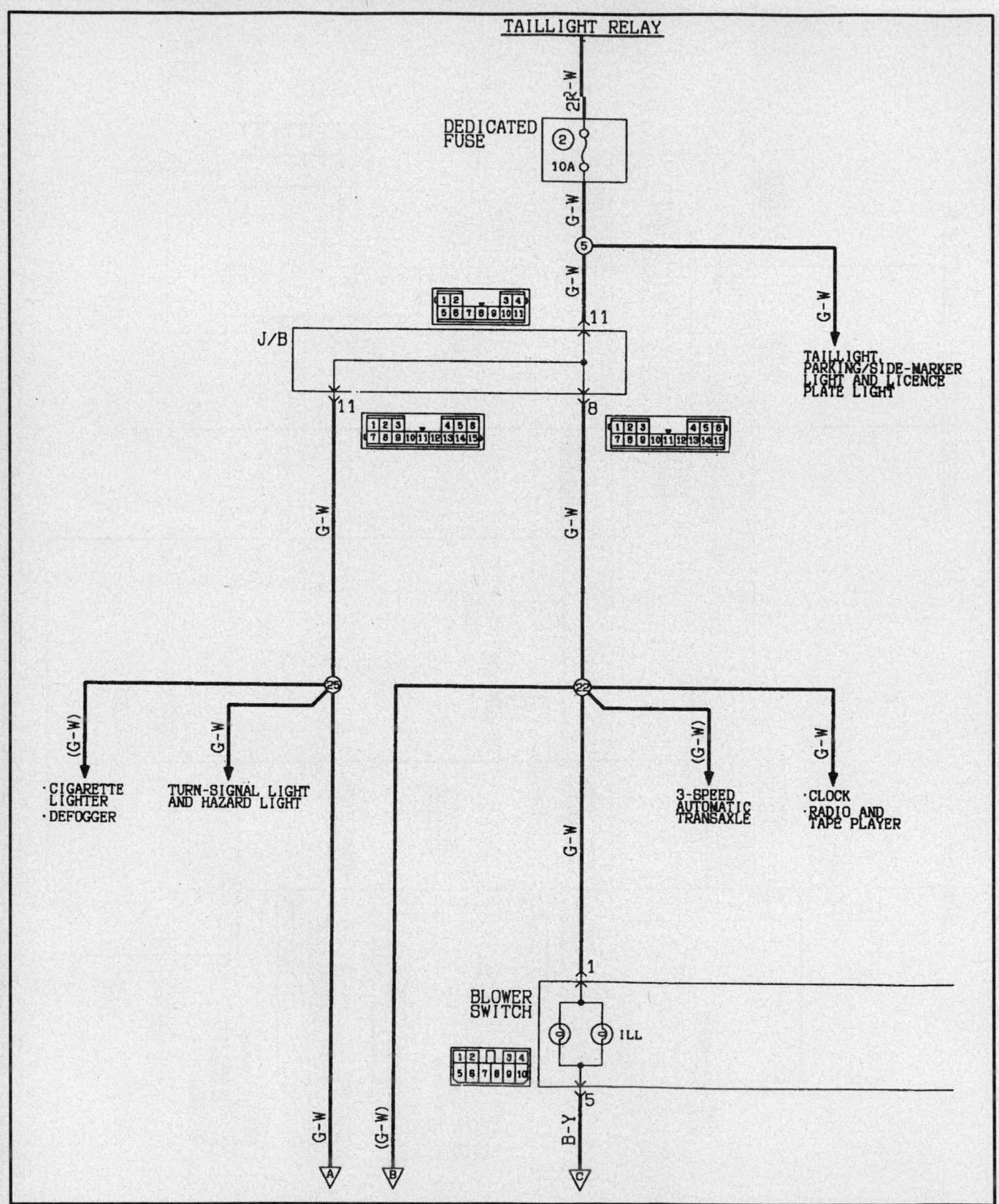

Wiring schematic — 1993 Mirage with 1.5L engine

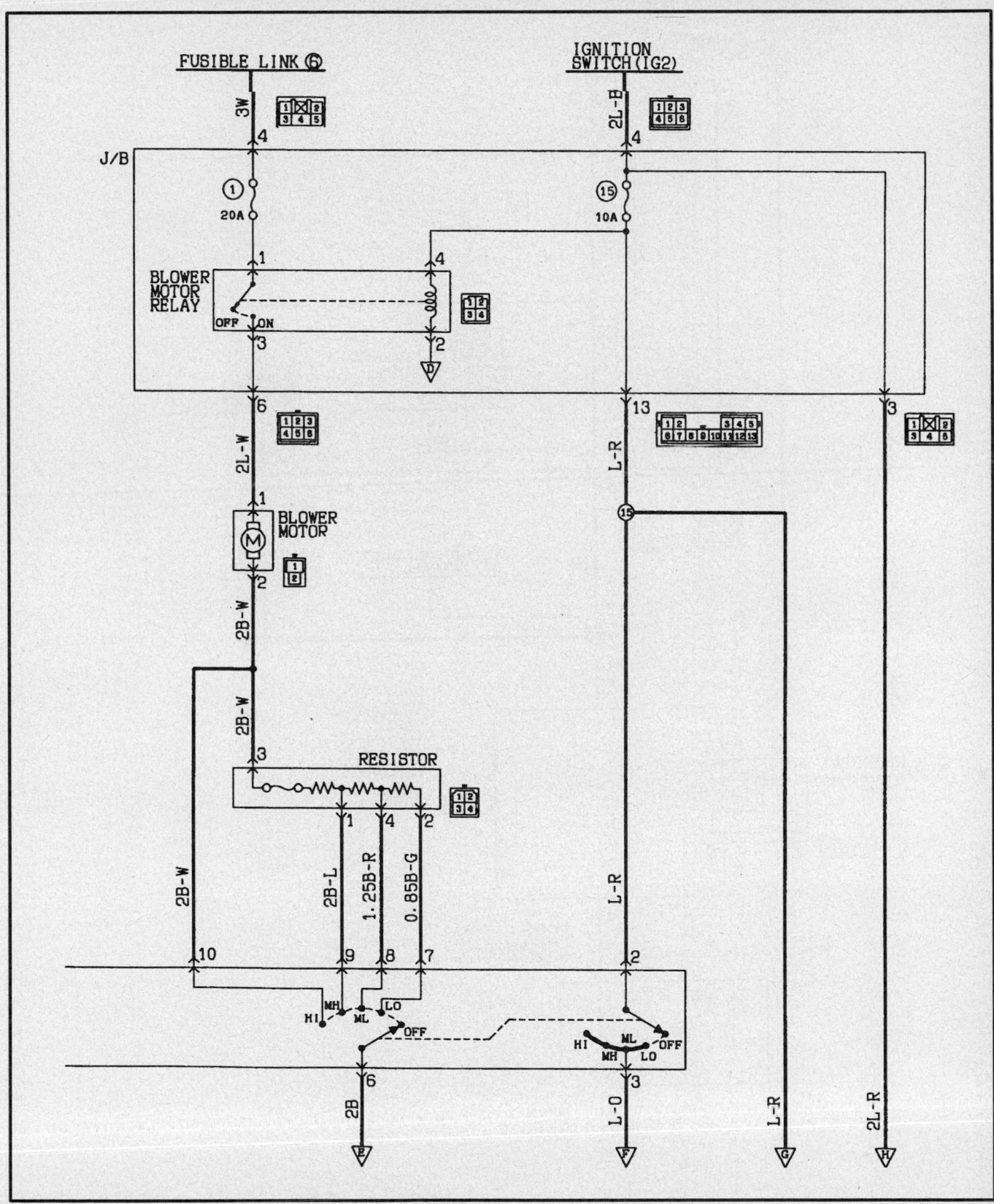

Wiring schematic — 1993 Mirage with 1.5L engine, Cont.

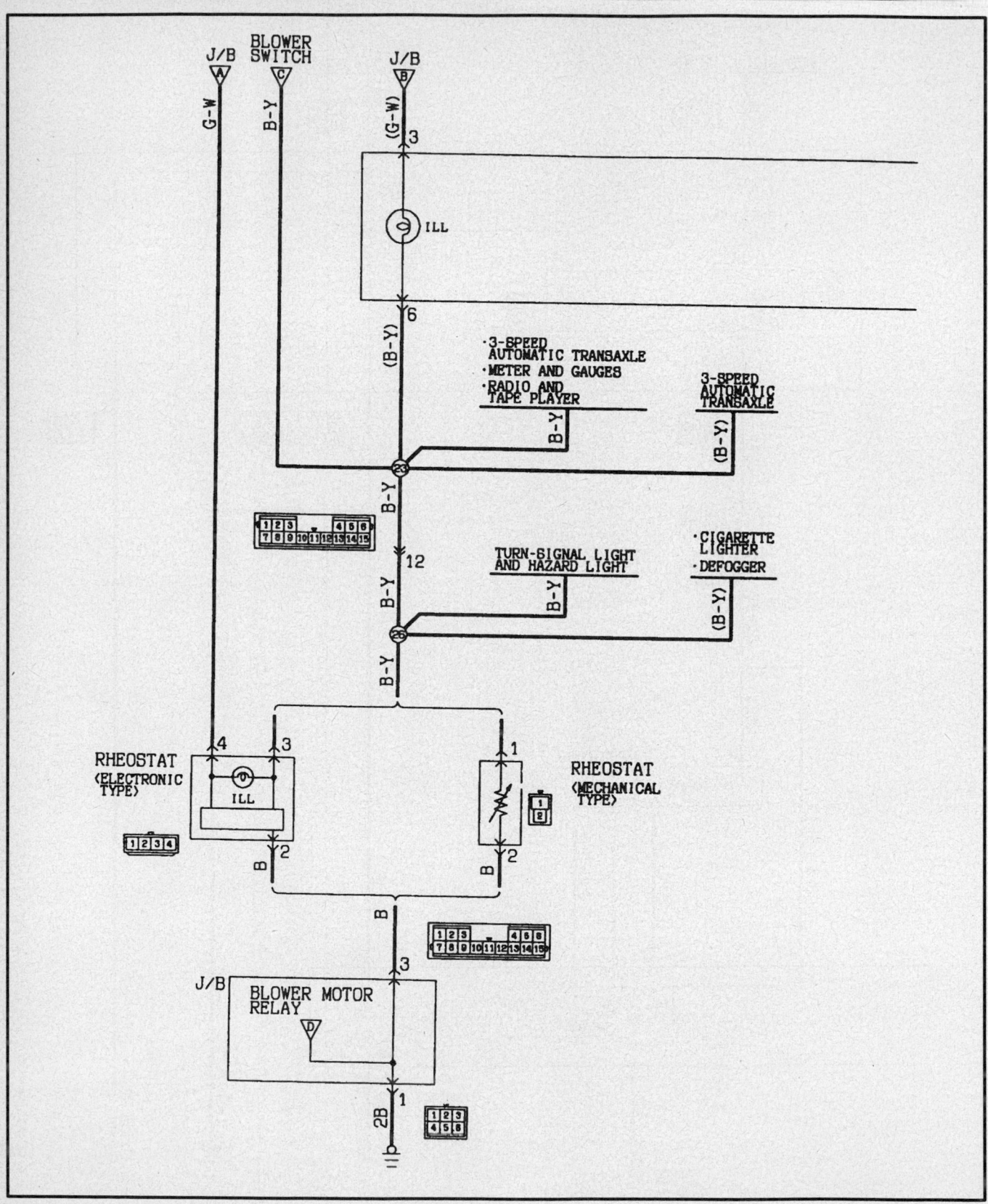

Wiring schematic — 1993 Mirage with 1.5L engine, Cont.

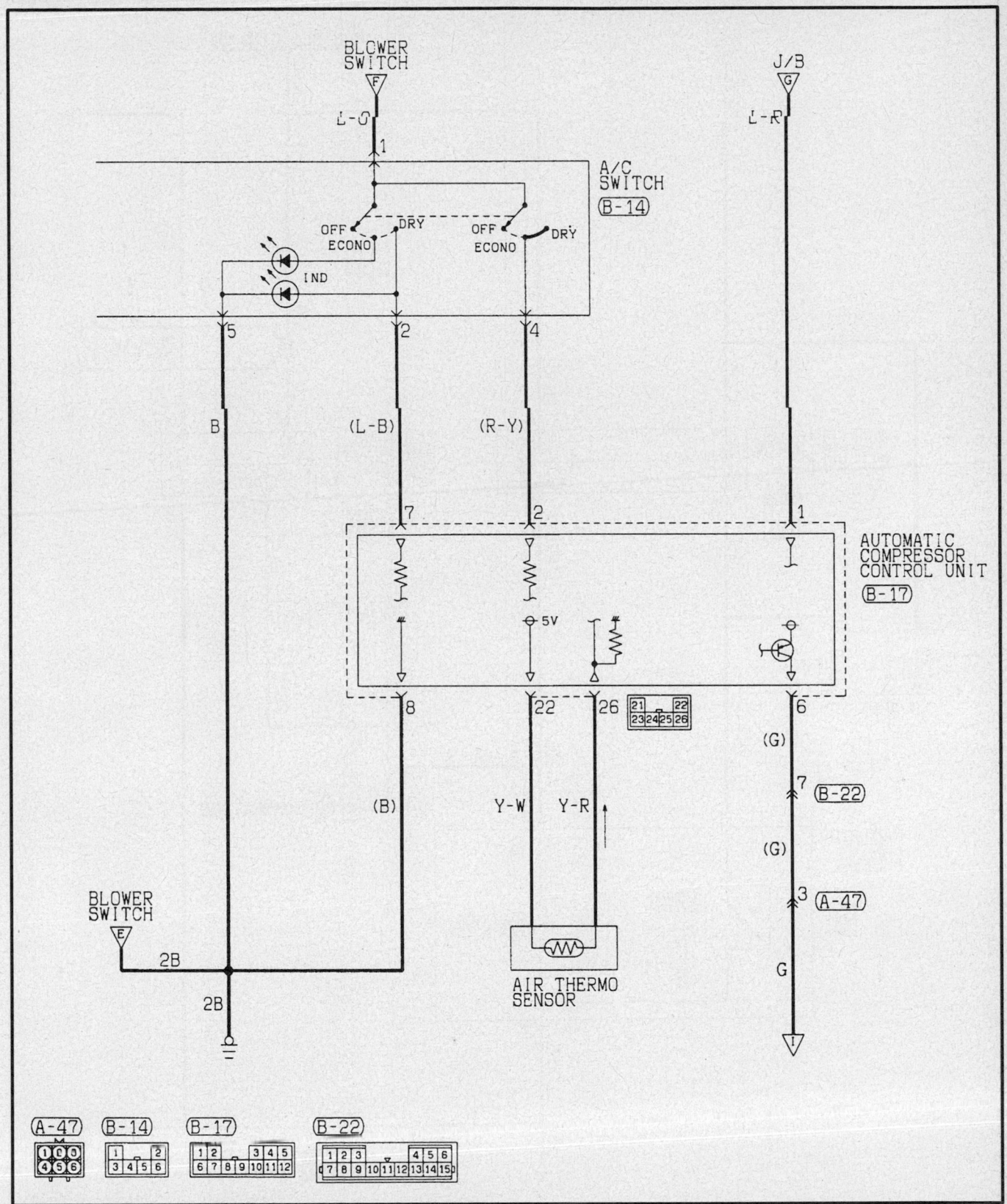

Wiring schematic — 1993 Mirage with 1.5L engine, Cont.

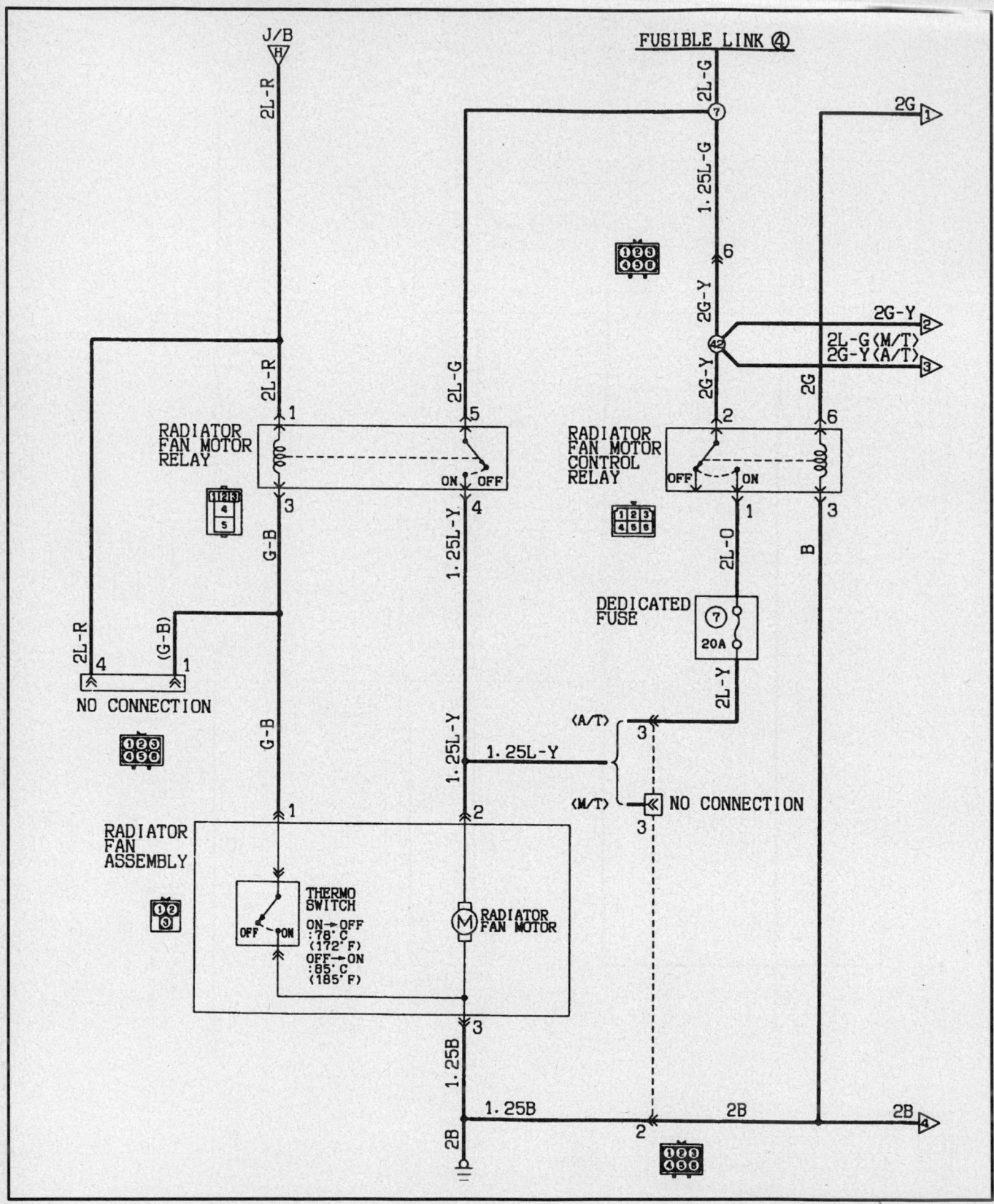

Wiring schematic — 1993 Mirage with 1.5L engine, Cont.

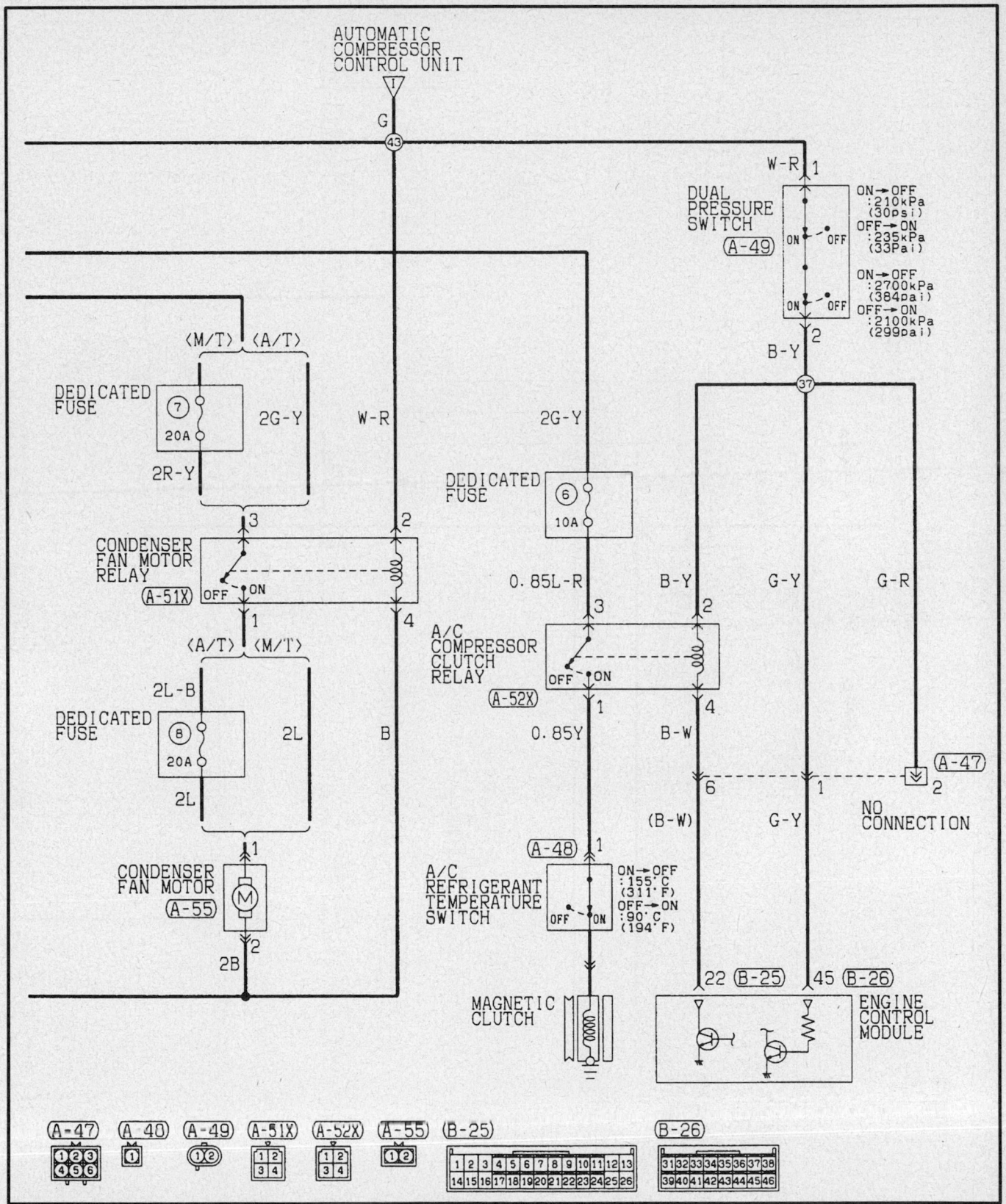

Wiring schematic — 1993 Mirage with 1.5L engine, Cont.

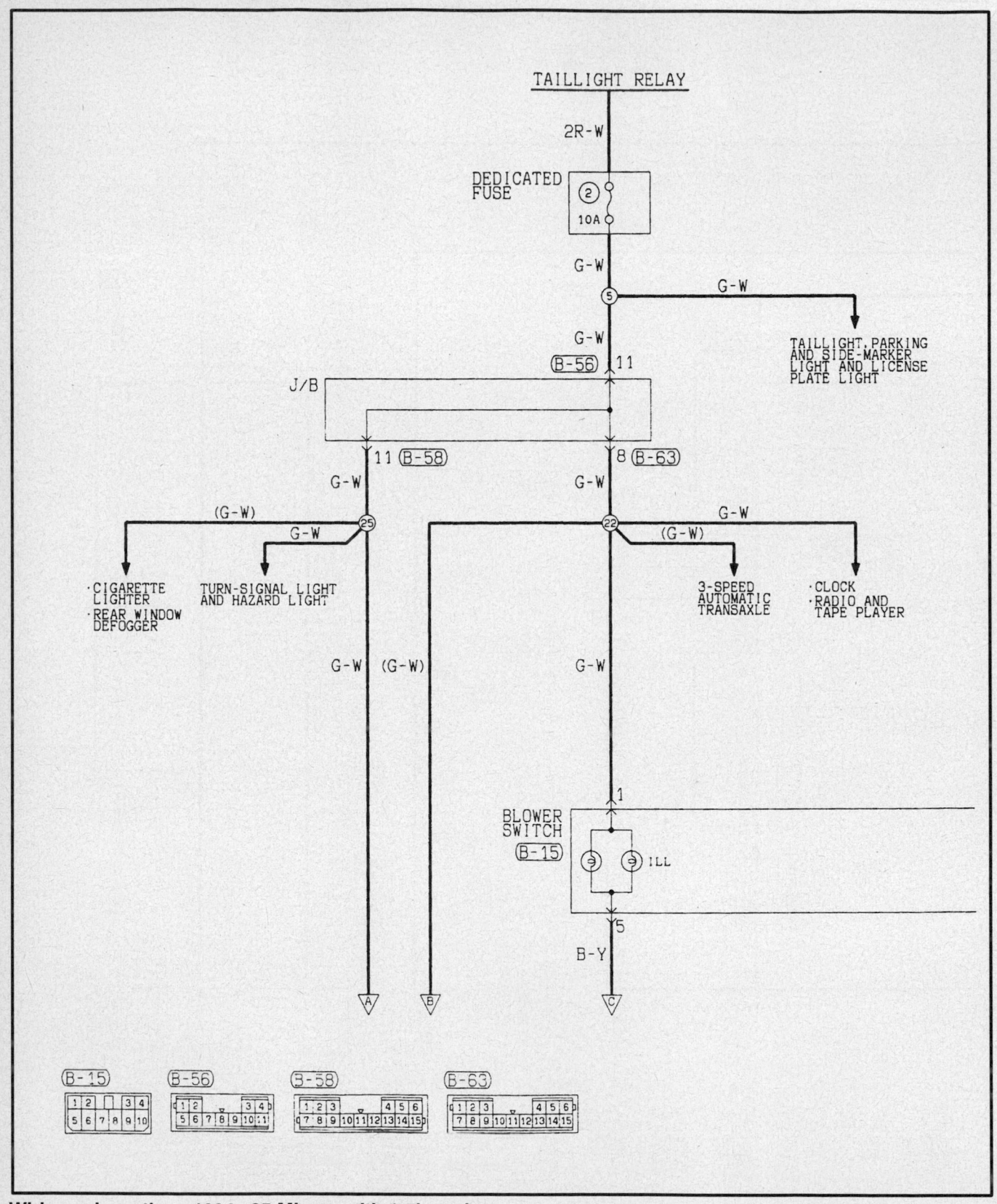

Wiring schematic — 1994–95 Mirage with 1.5L engine

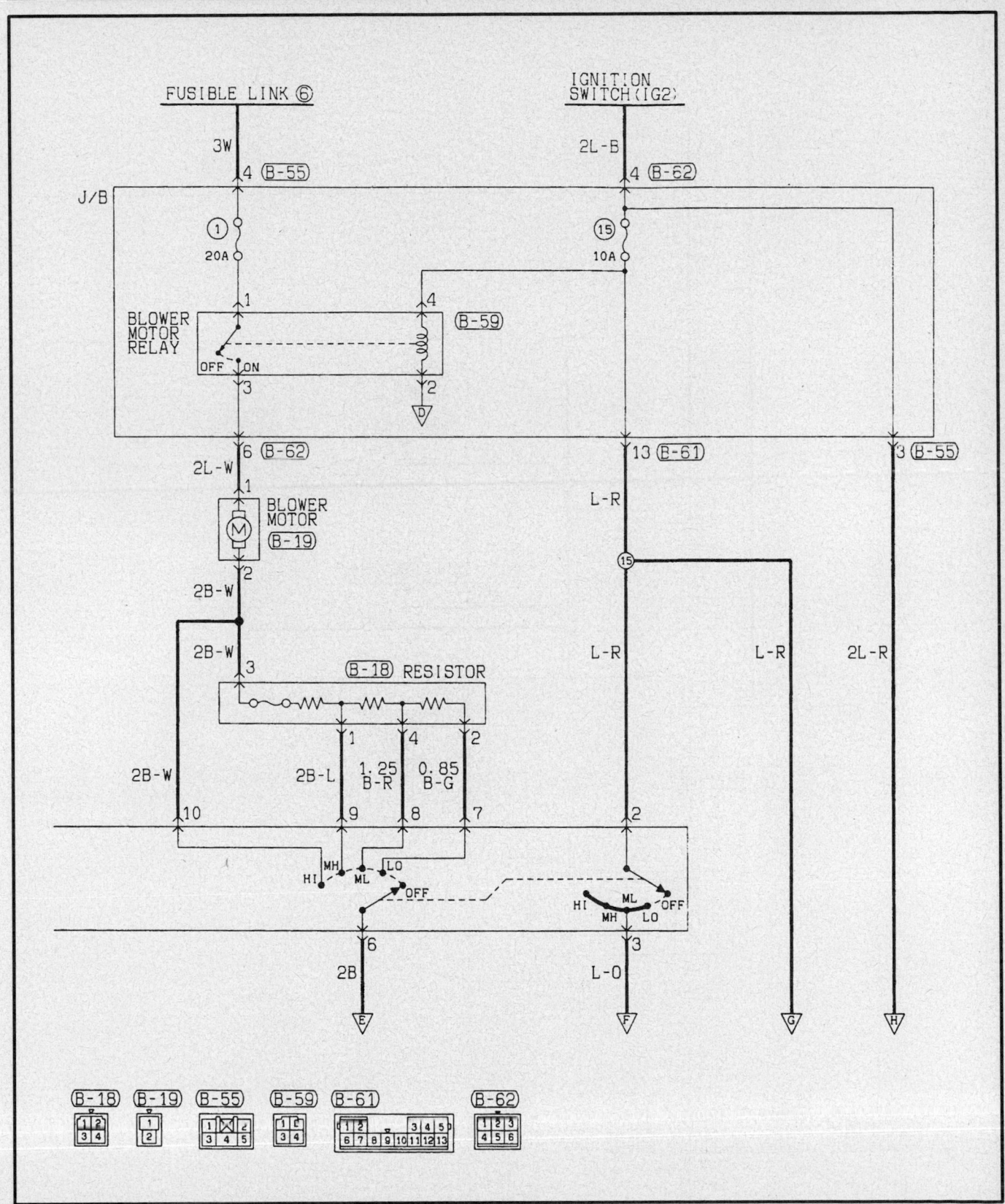

Wiring schematic — 1994–95 Mirage with 1.5L engine, Cont.

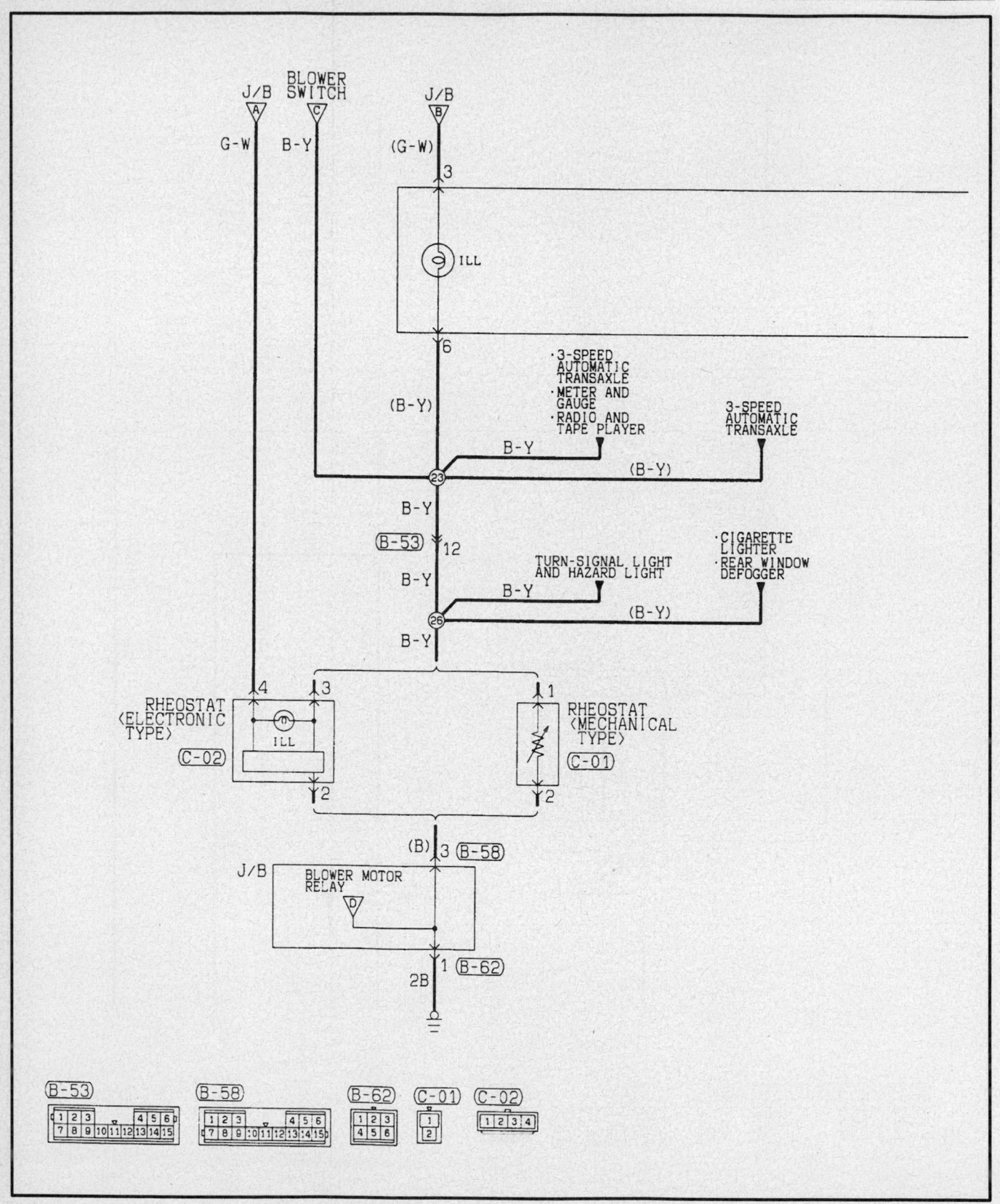

Wiring schematic — 1994–95 Mirage with 1.5L engine, Cont.

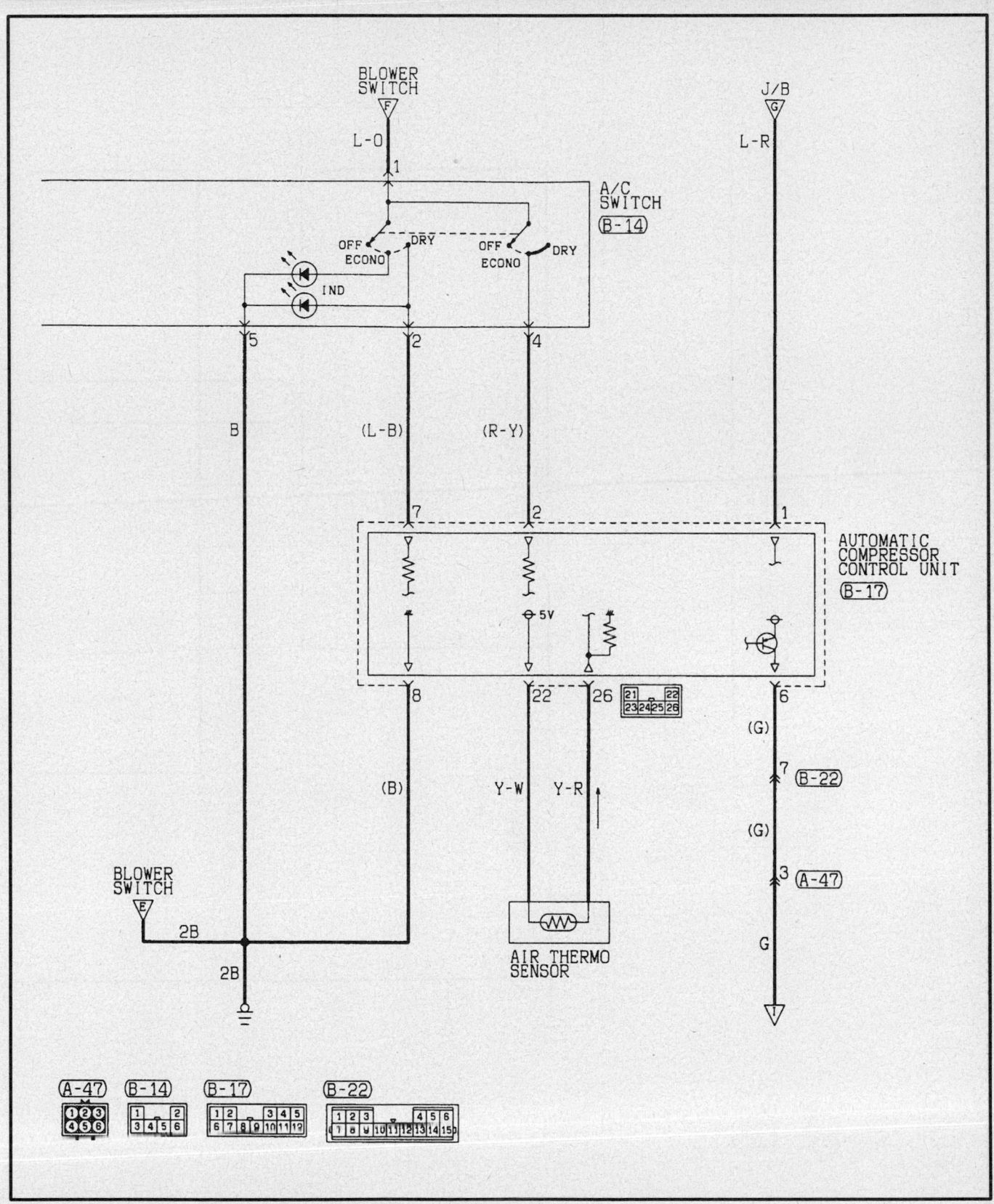

Wiring schematic — 1994–95 Mirage with 1.5L engine, Cont.

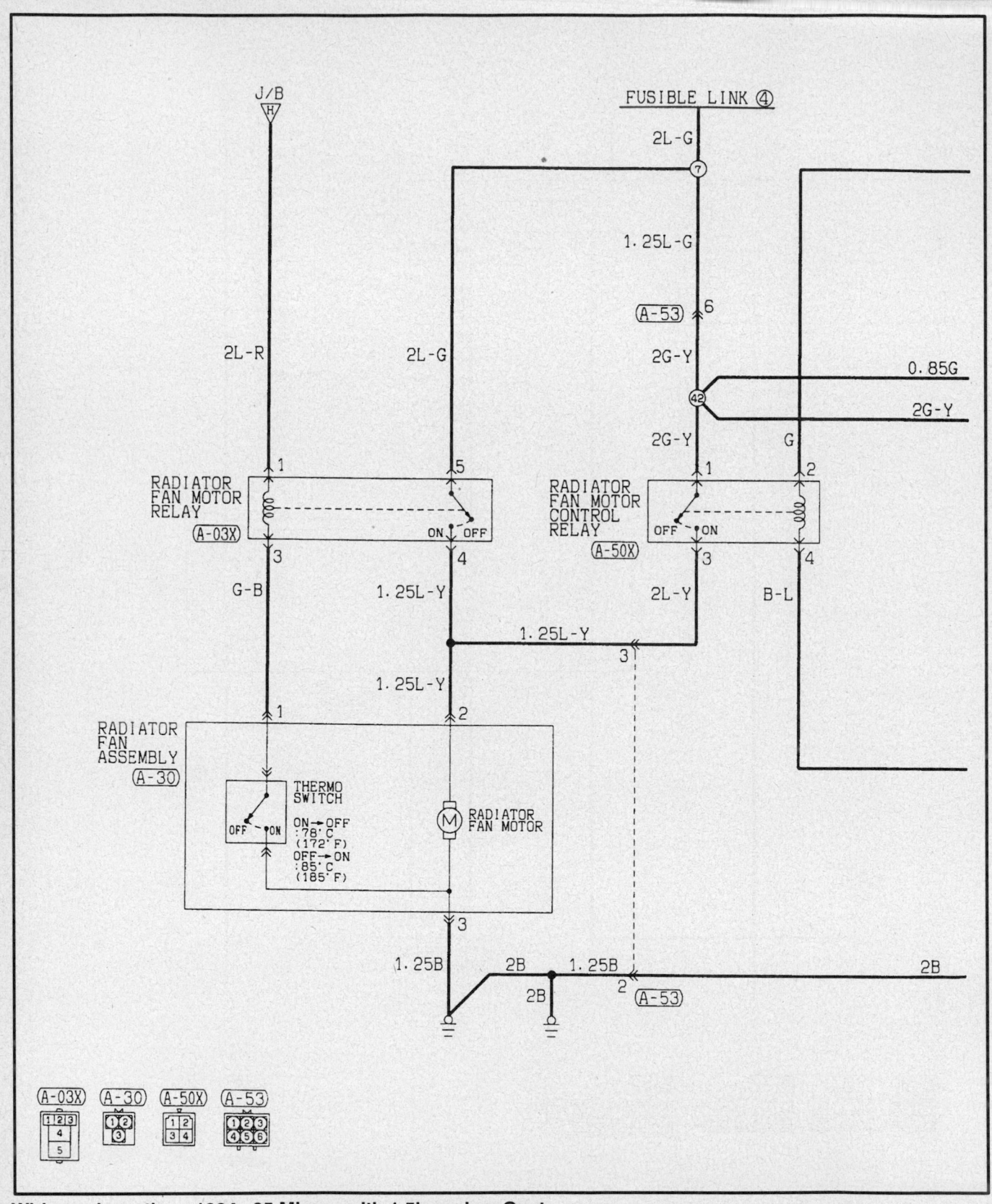

Wiring schematic — 1994–95 Mirage with 1.5L engine, Cont.

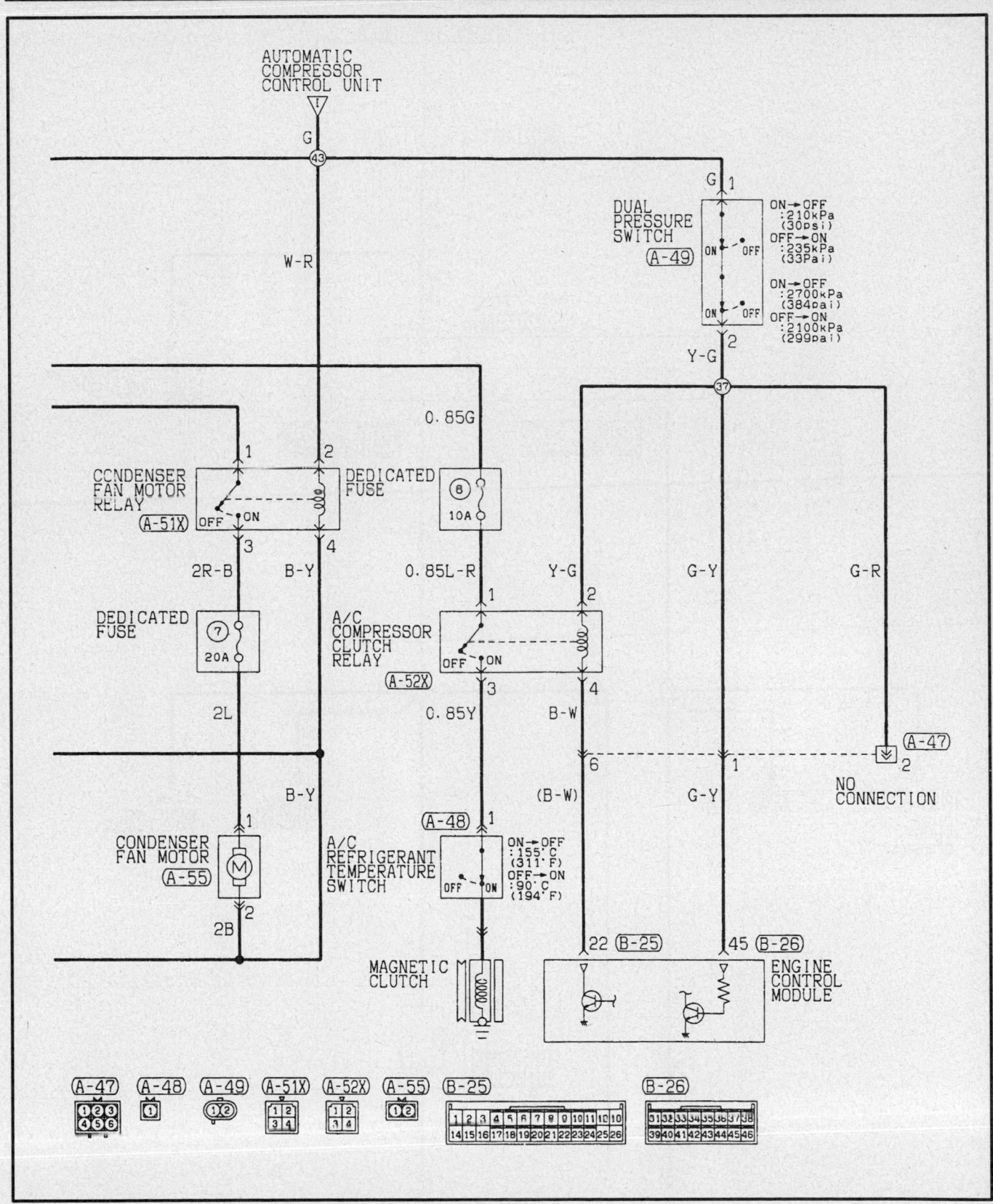

Wiring schematic — 1994–95 Mirage with 1.5L engine, Cont.

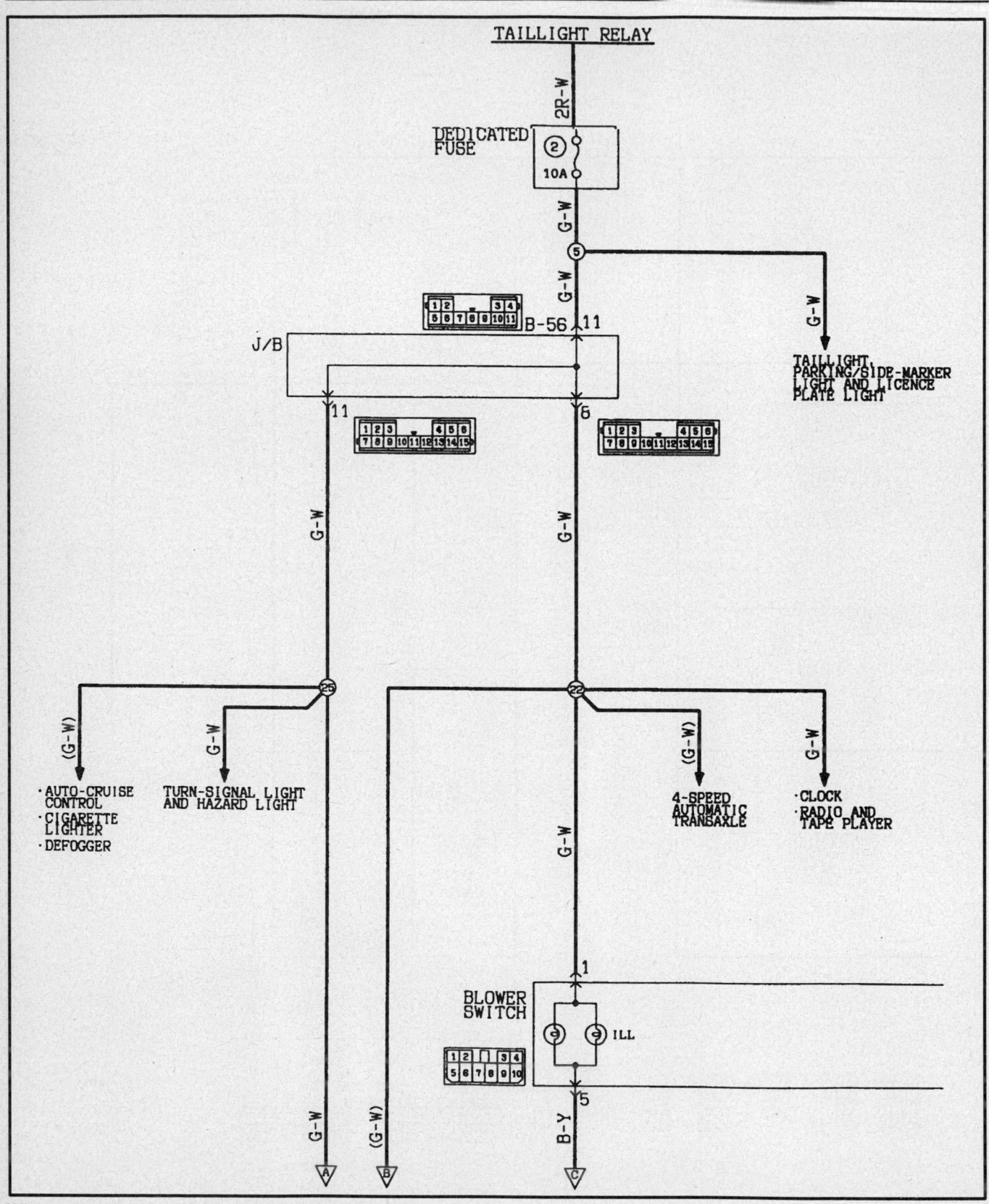

Wiring schematic — 1993 Mirage with 1.8L engine

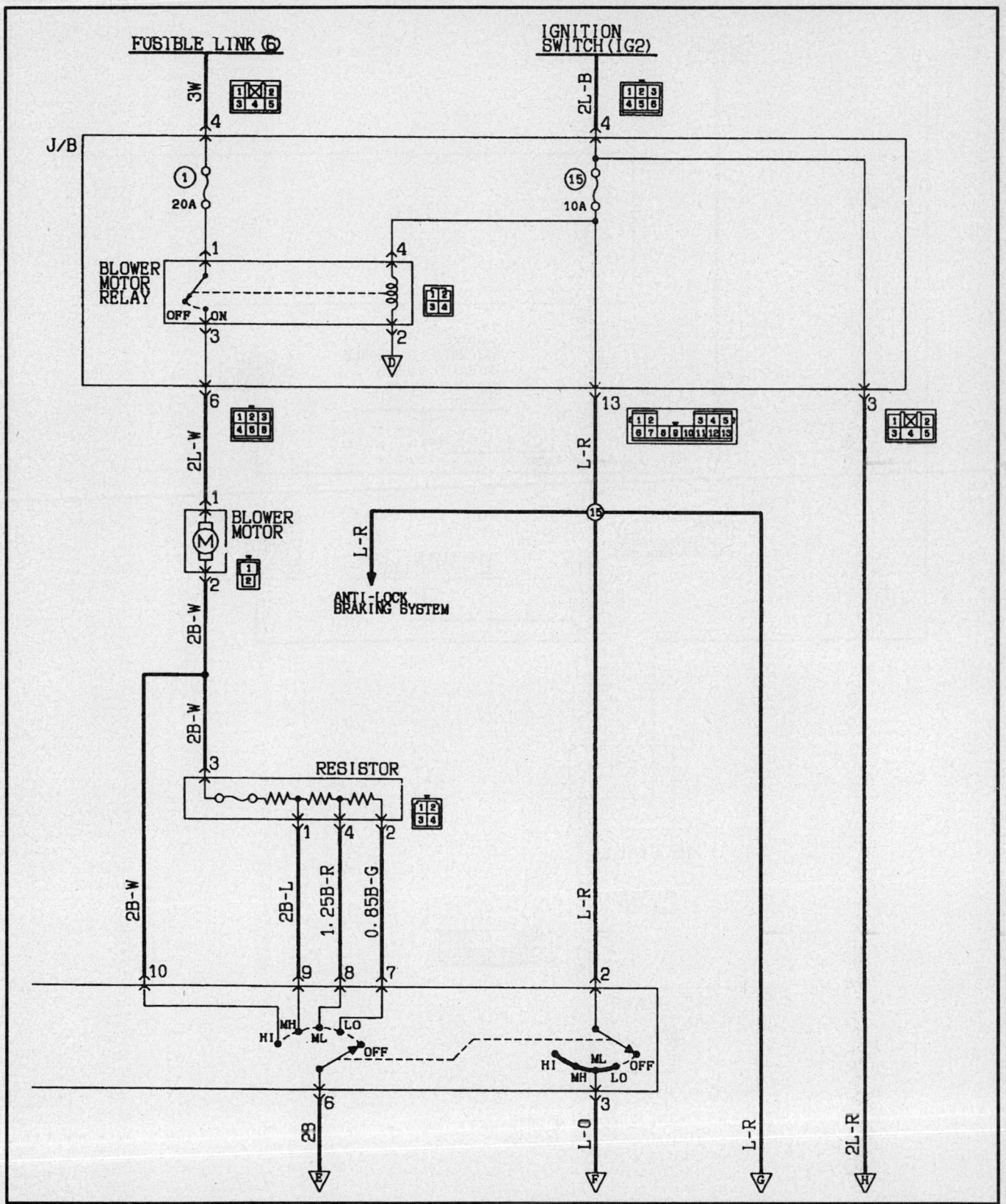

Wiring schematic — 1993 Mirage with 1.8L engine, Cont.

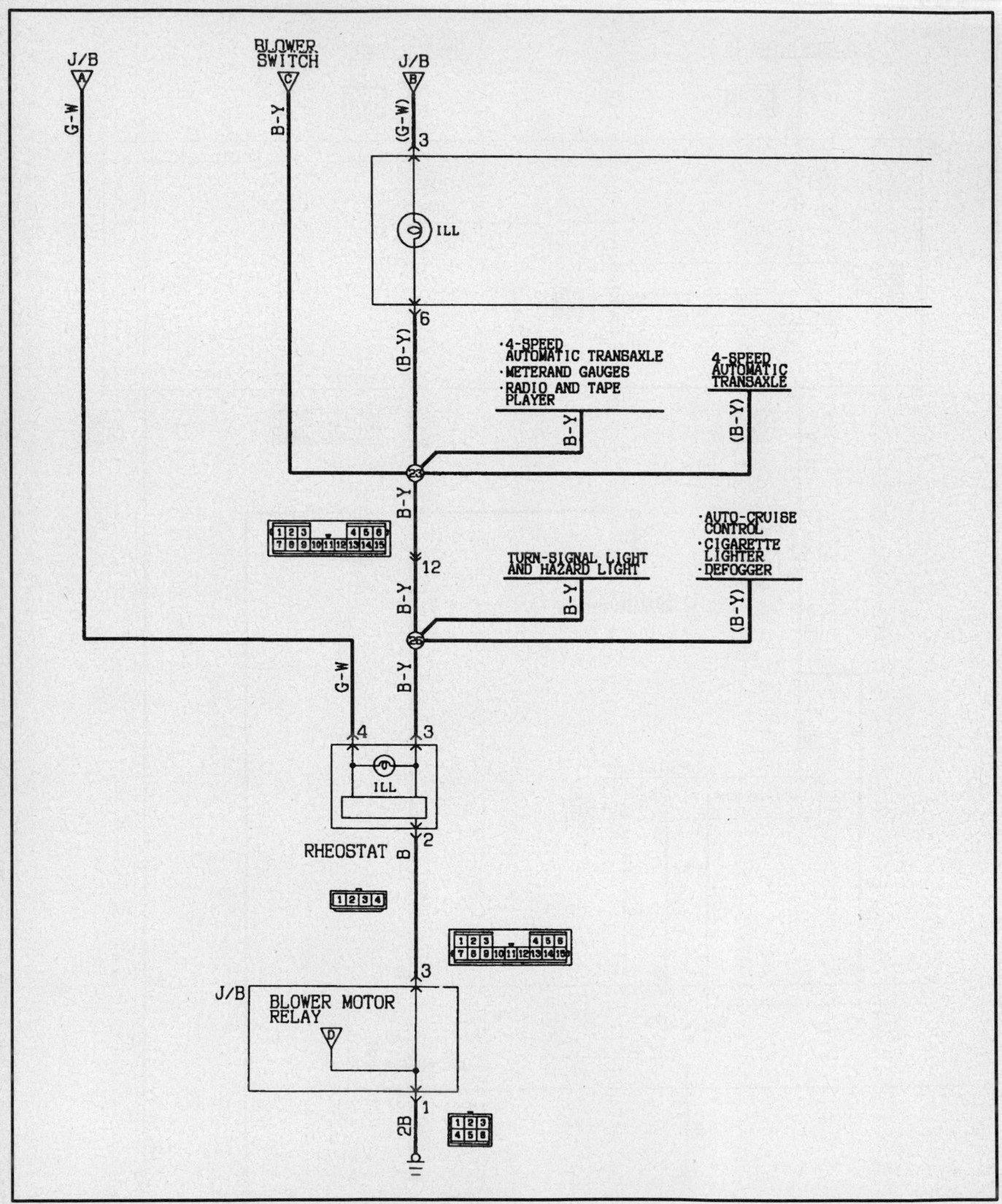

Wiring schematic — 1993 Mirage with 1.8L engine, Cont.

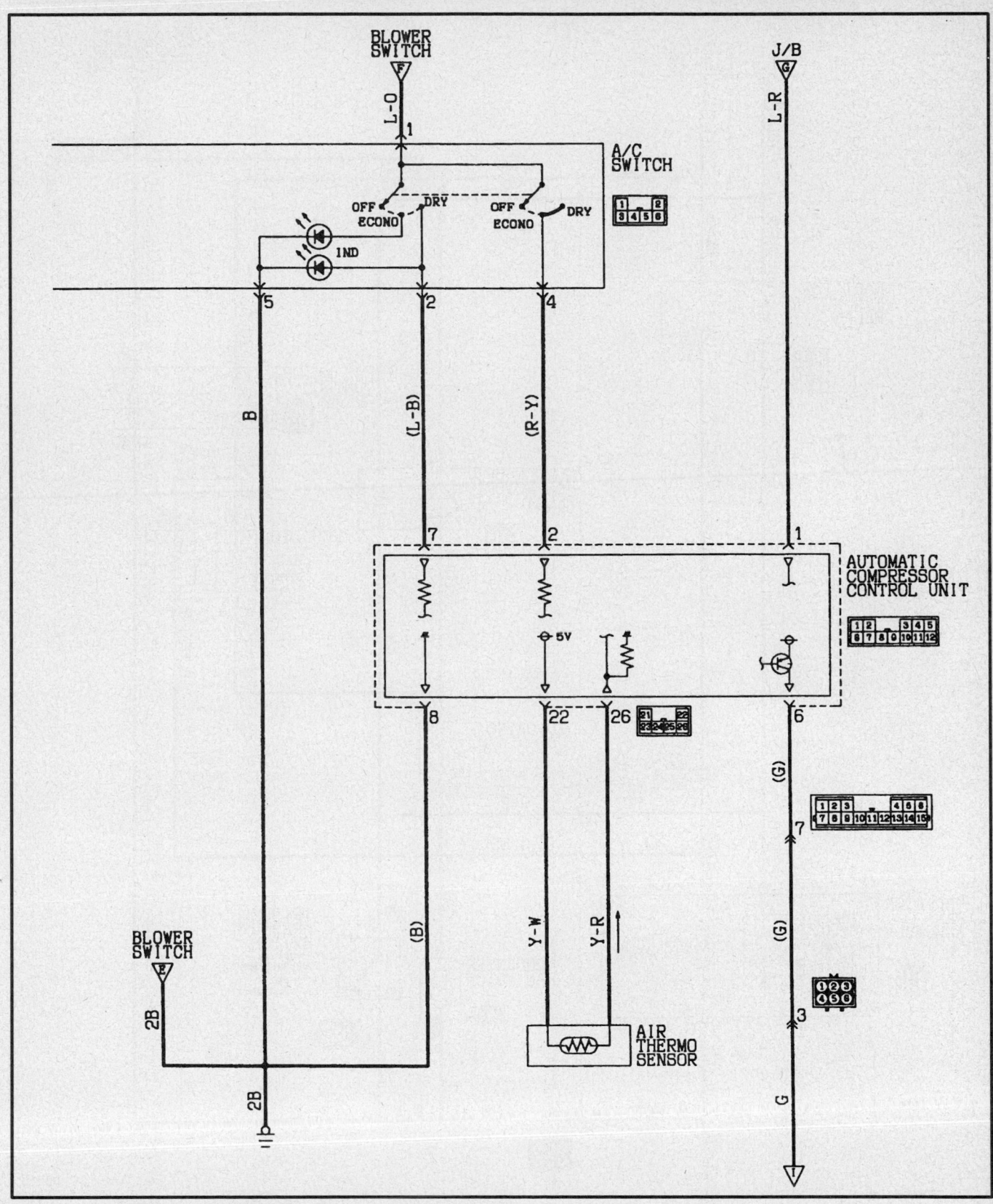

Wiring schematic — 1993 Mirage with 1.8L engine, Cont.

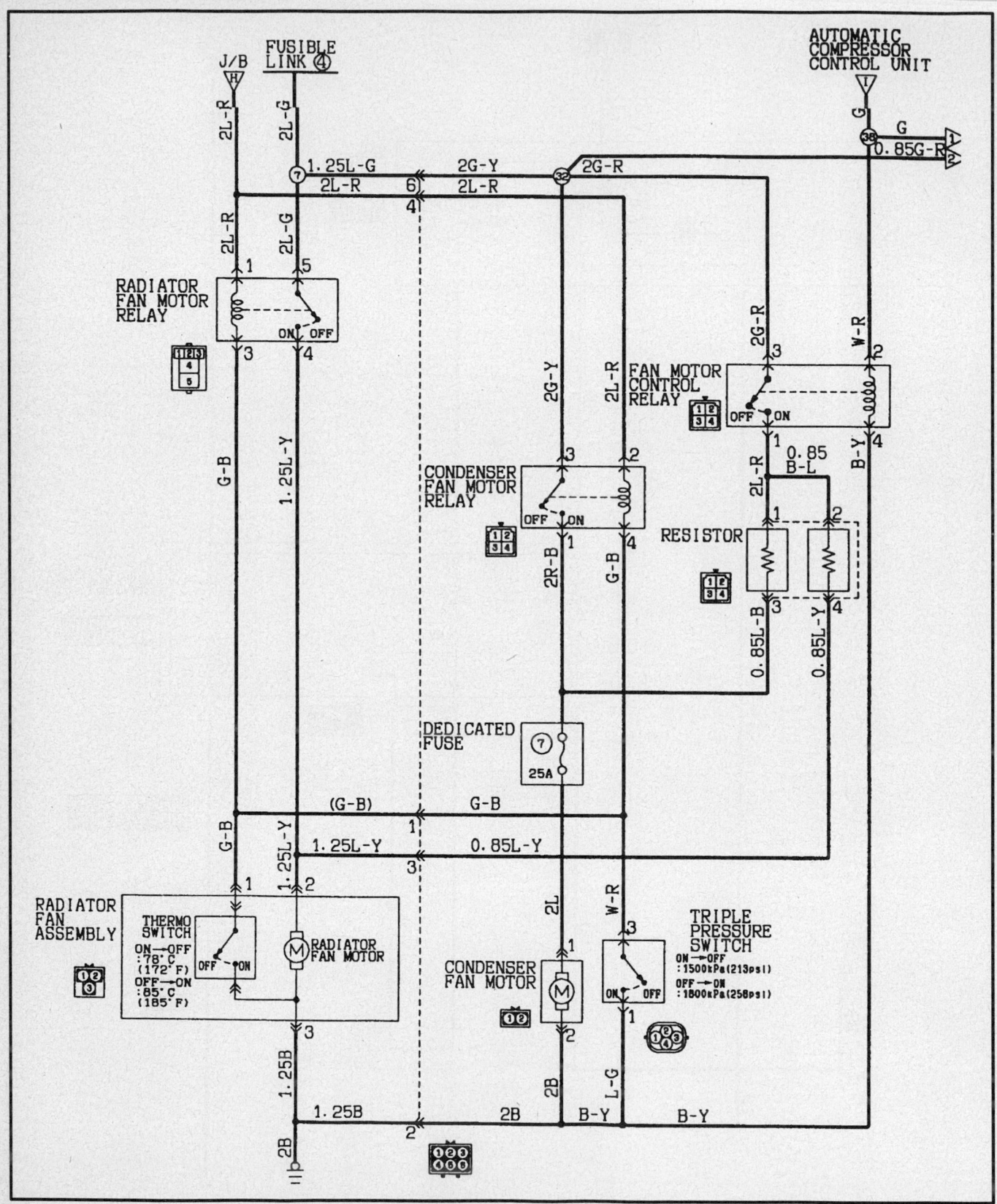

Wiring schematic — 1993 Mirage with 1.8L engine, Cont.

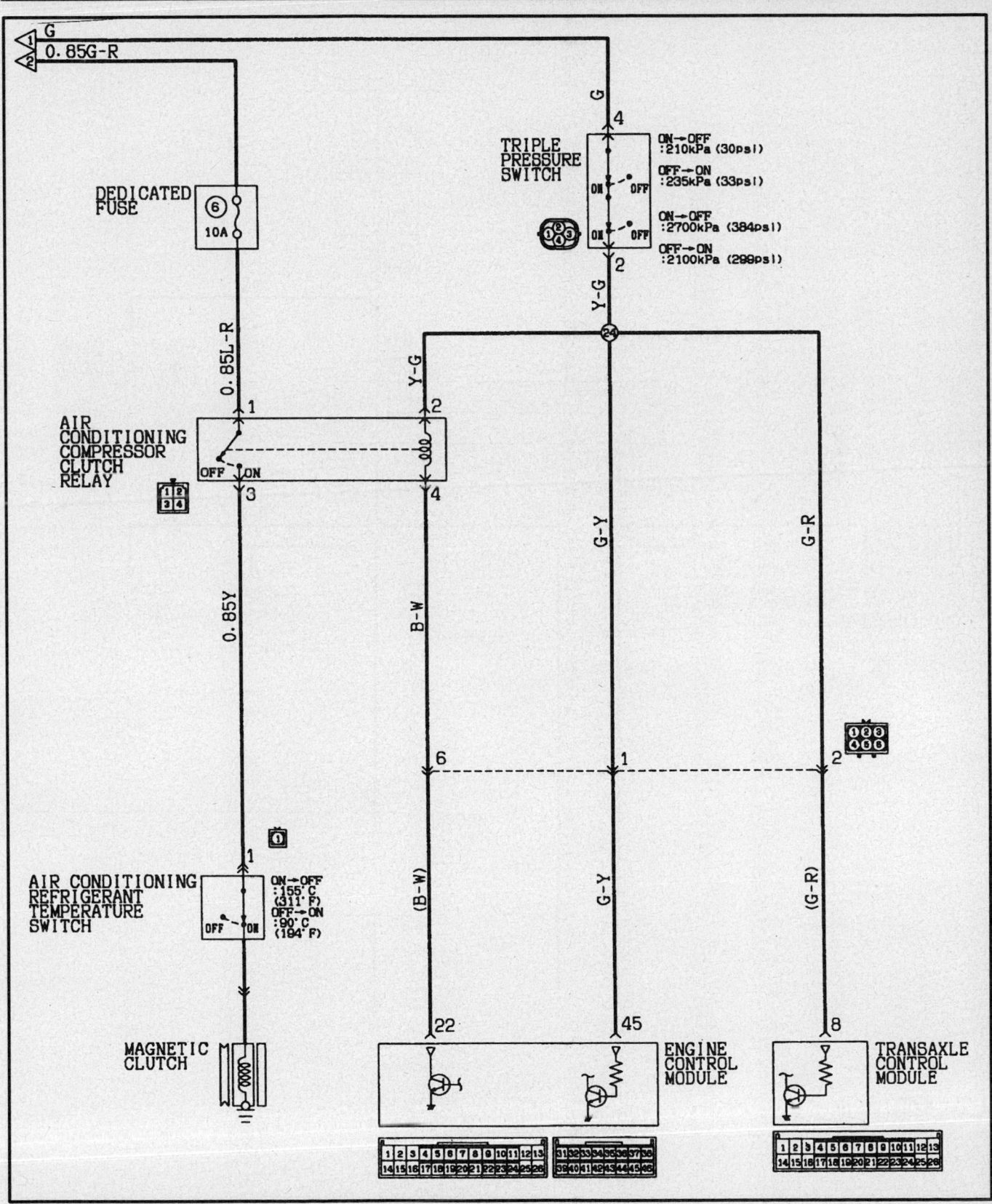

Wiring schematic — 1993 Mirage with 1.8L engine, Cont.

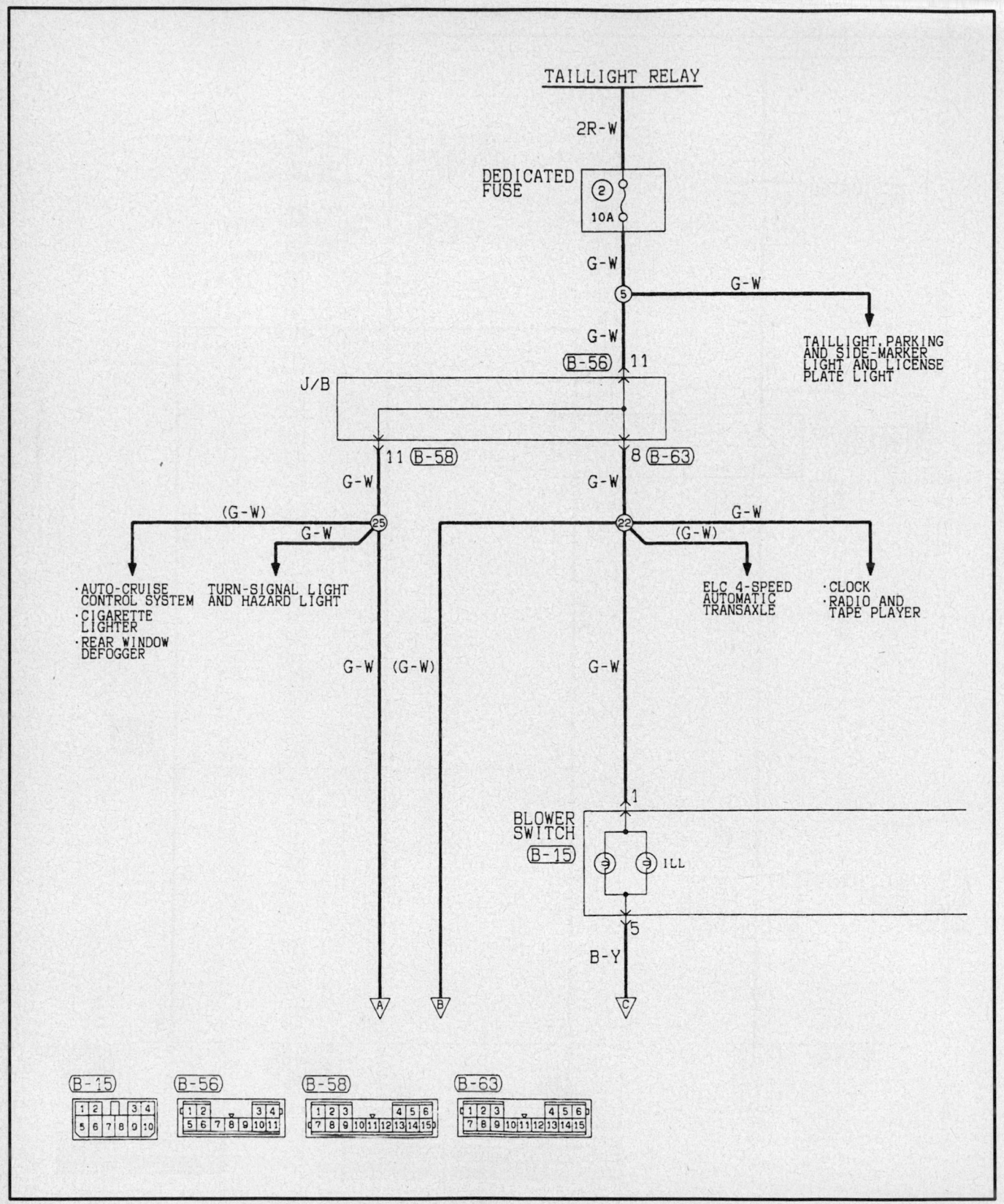

Wiring schematic — 1994-95 Mirage with 1.8L engine

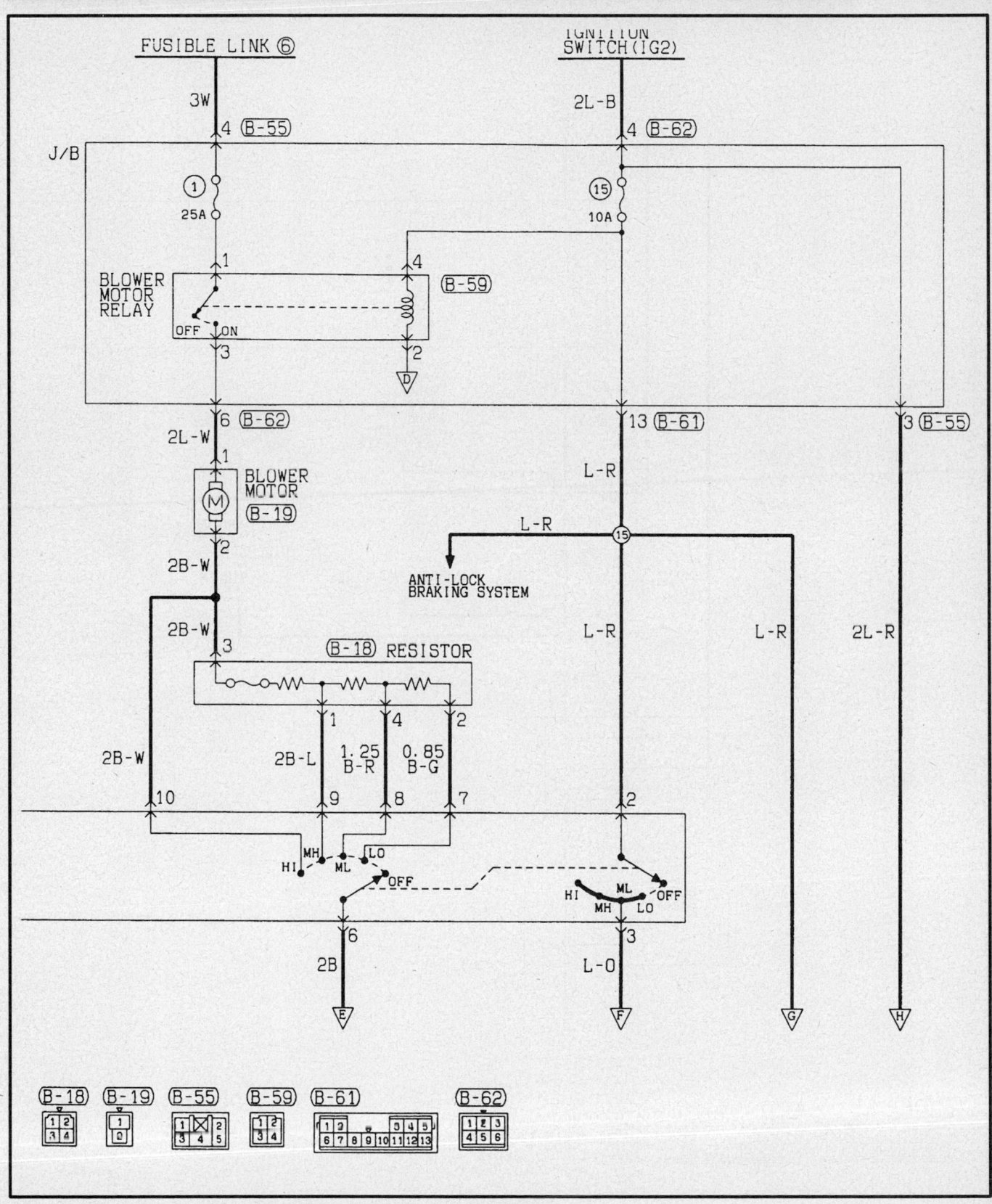

Wiring schematic — 1994–95 Mirage with 1.8L engine, Cont.

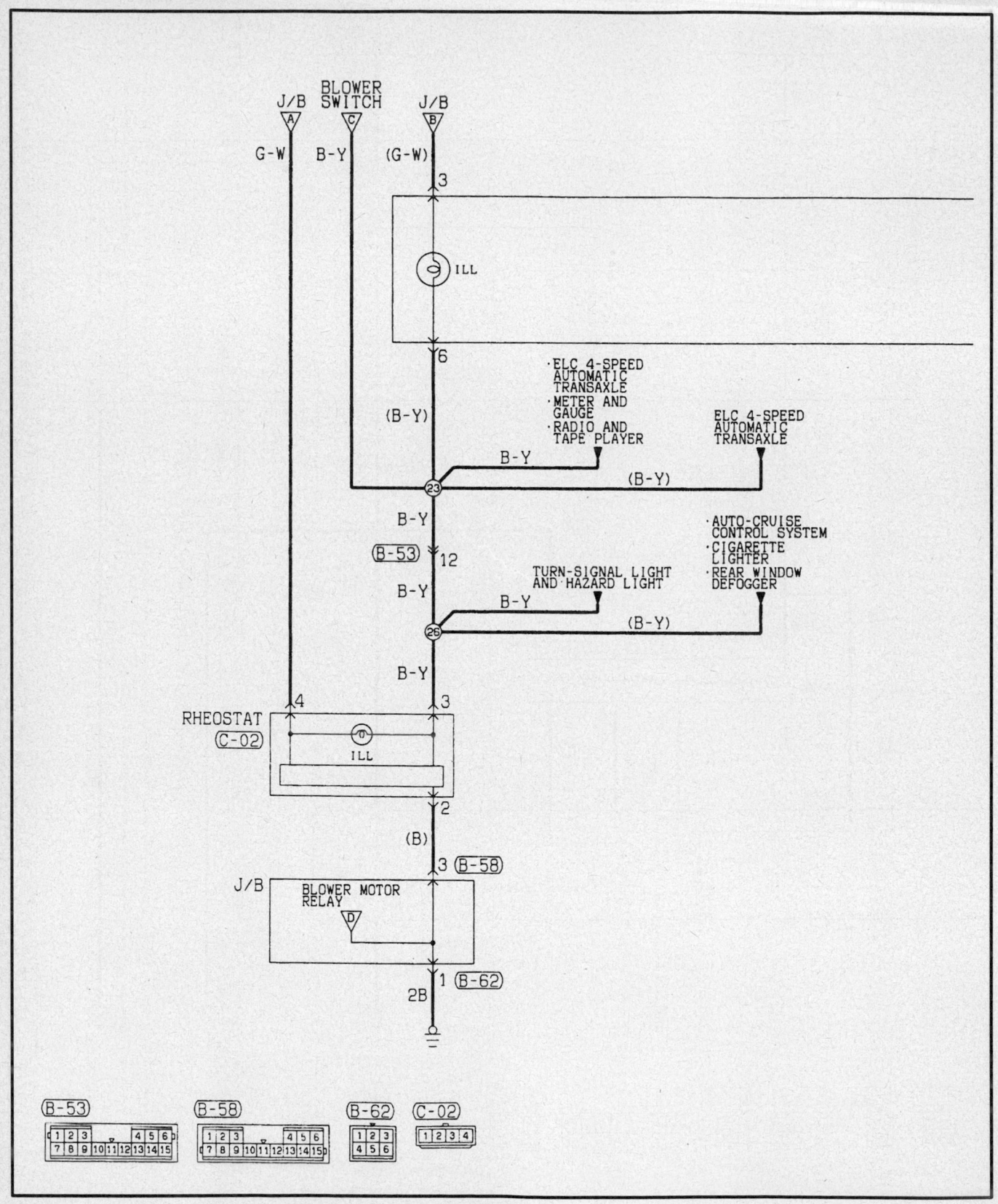

Wiring schematic — 1994–95 Mirage with 1.8L engine, Cont.

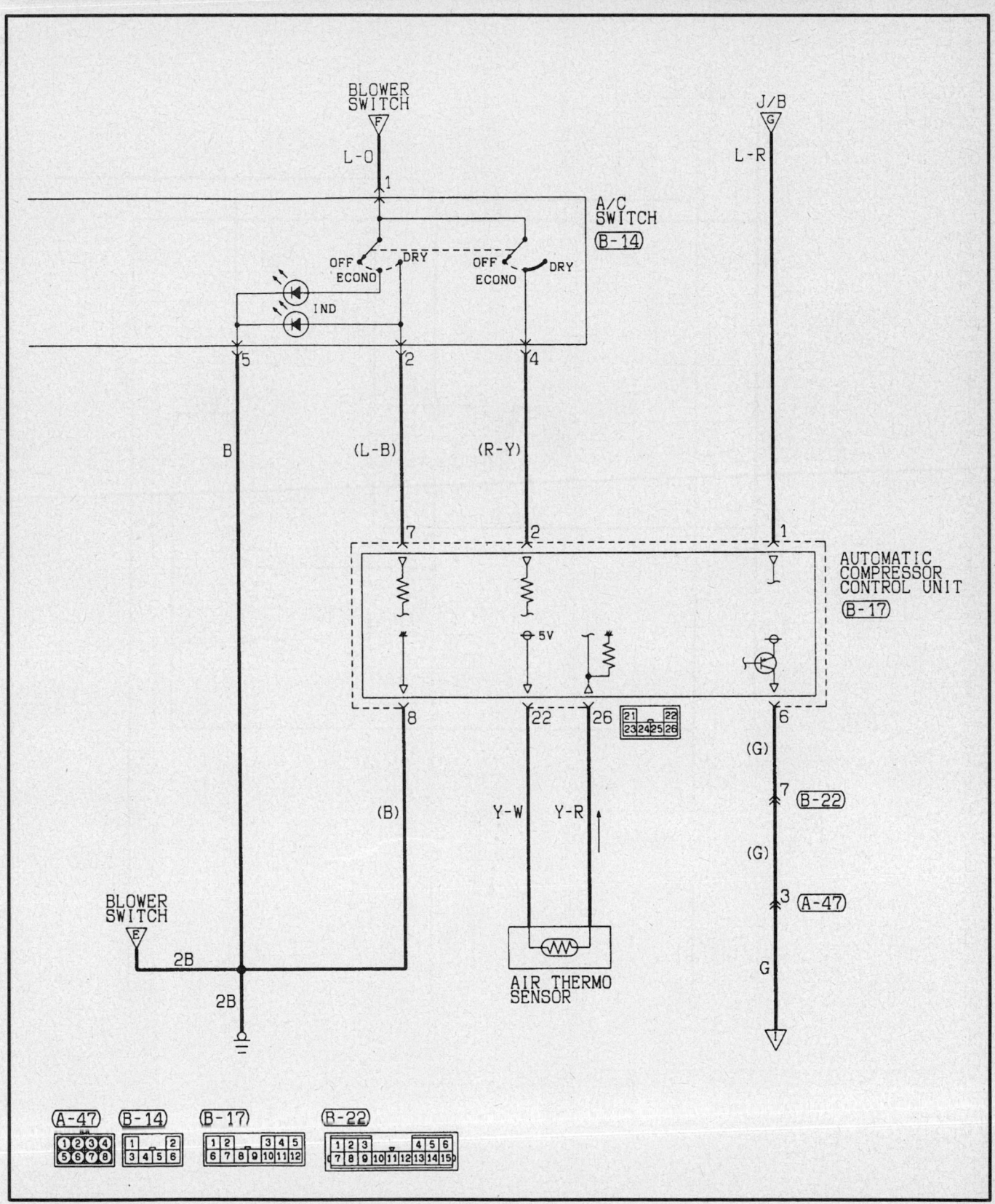

Wiring schematic — 1994–95 Mirage with 1.8L engine, Cont.

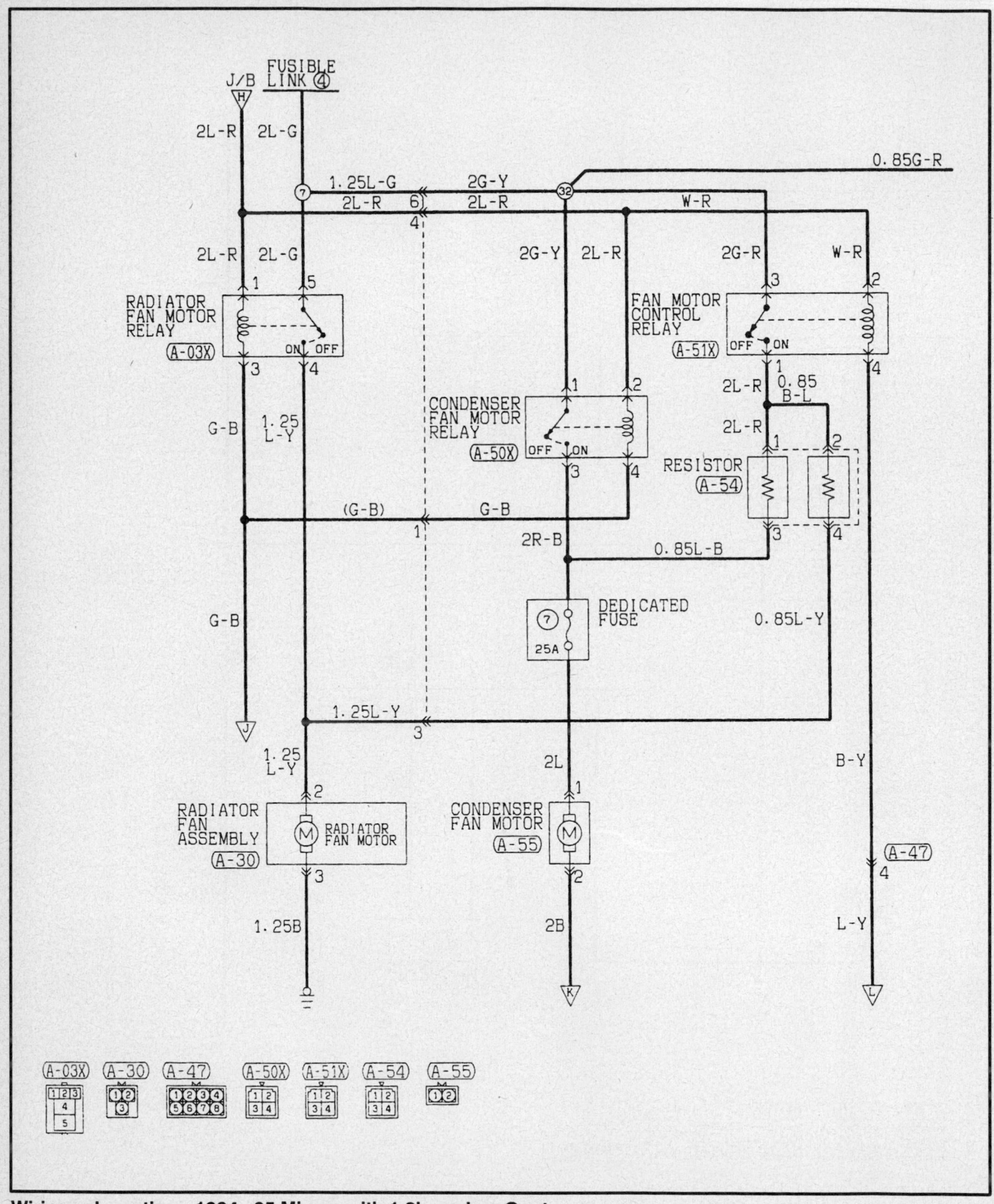

Wiring schematic — 1994–95 Mirage with 1.8L engine, Cont.

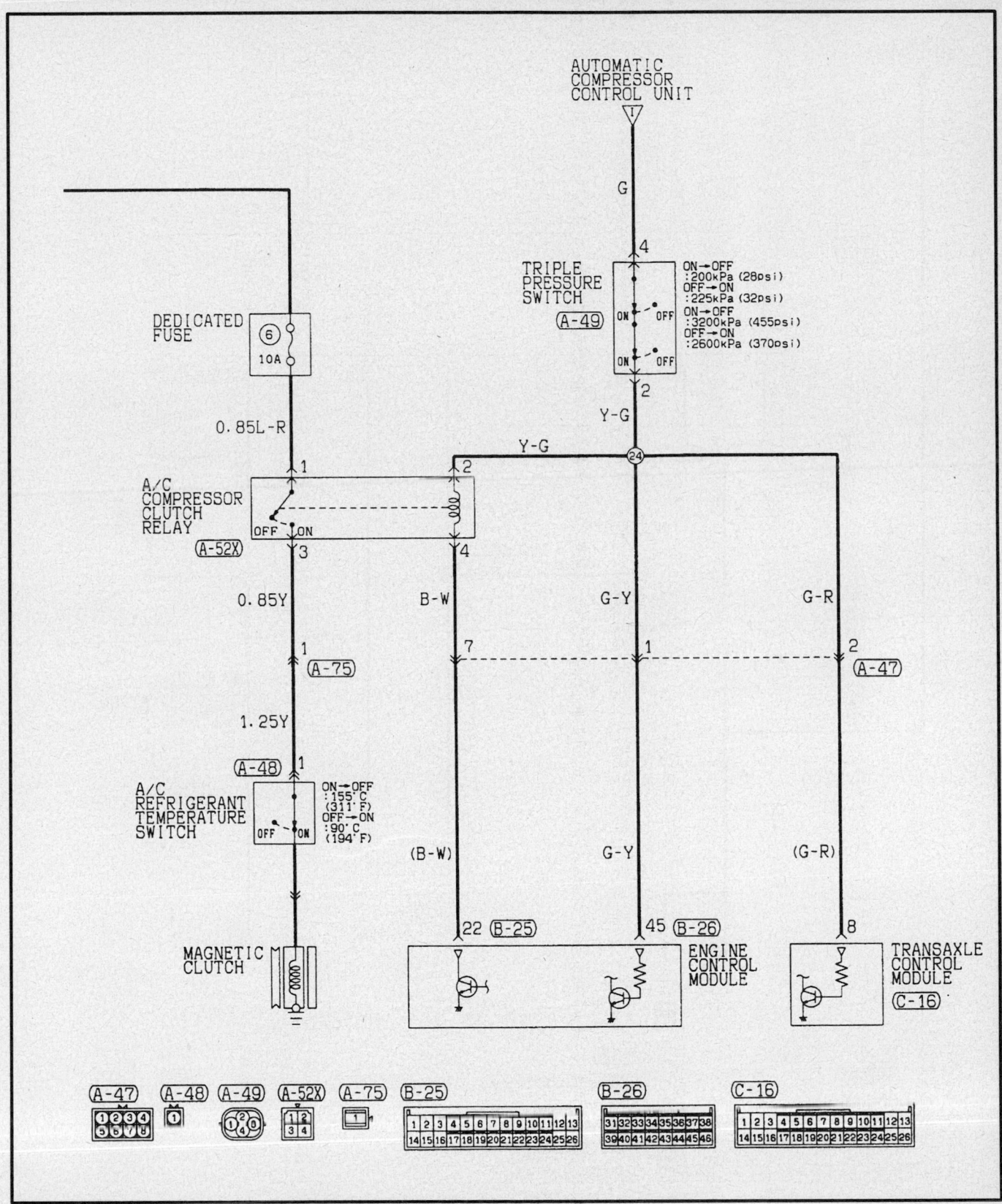

Wiring schematic — 1994—95 Mirage with 1.8L engine, Cont.

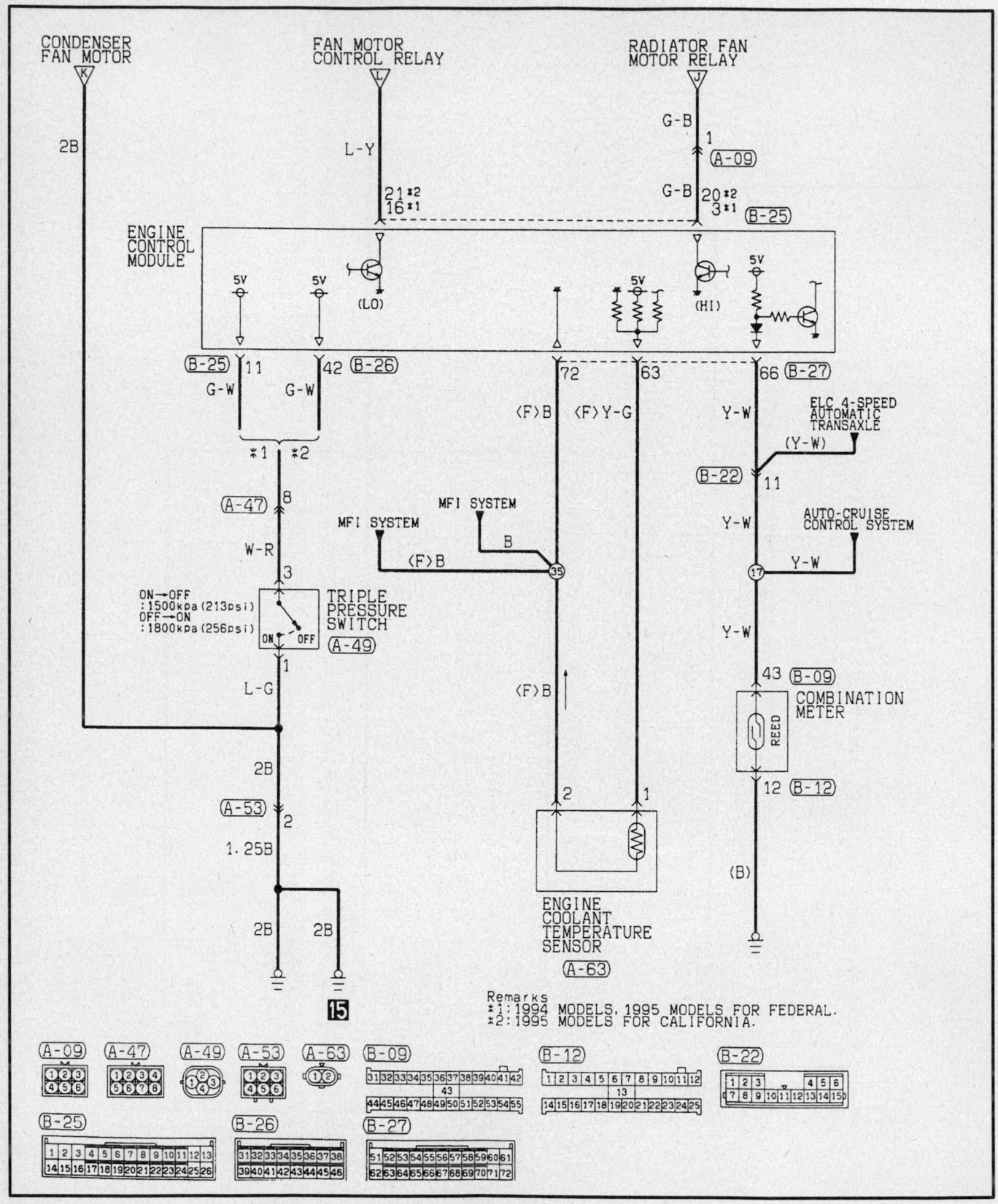

Wiring schematic — 1994–95 Mirage with 1.8L engine, Cont.

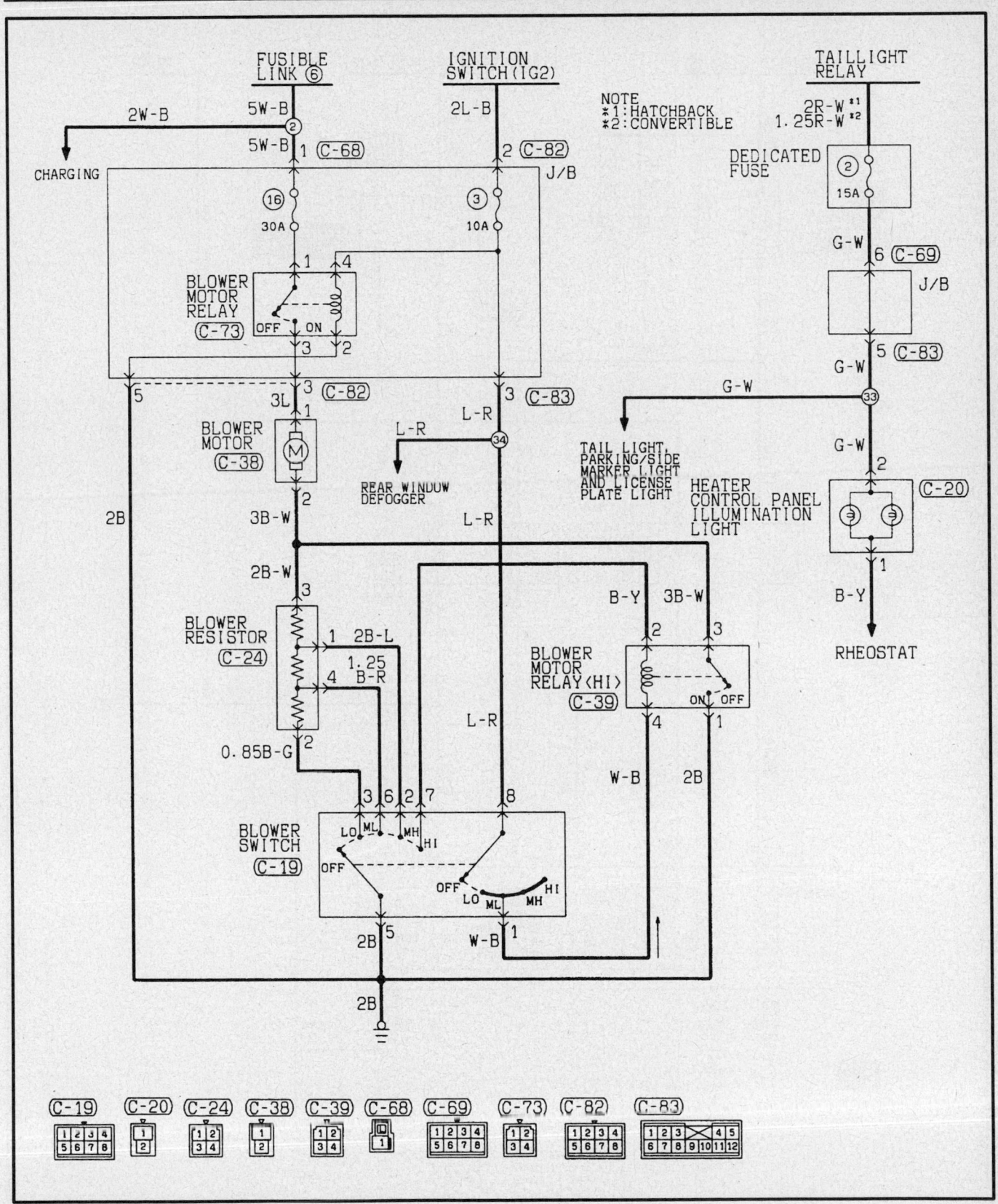

Wiring schematic — 3000GT

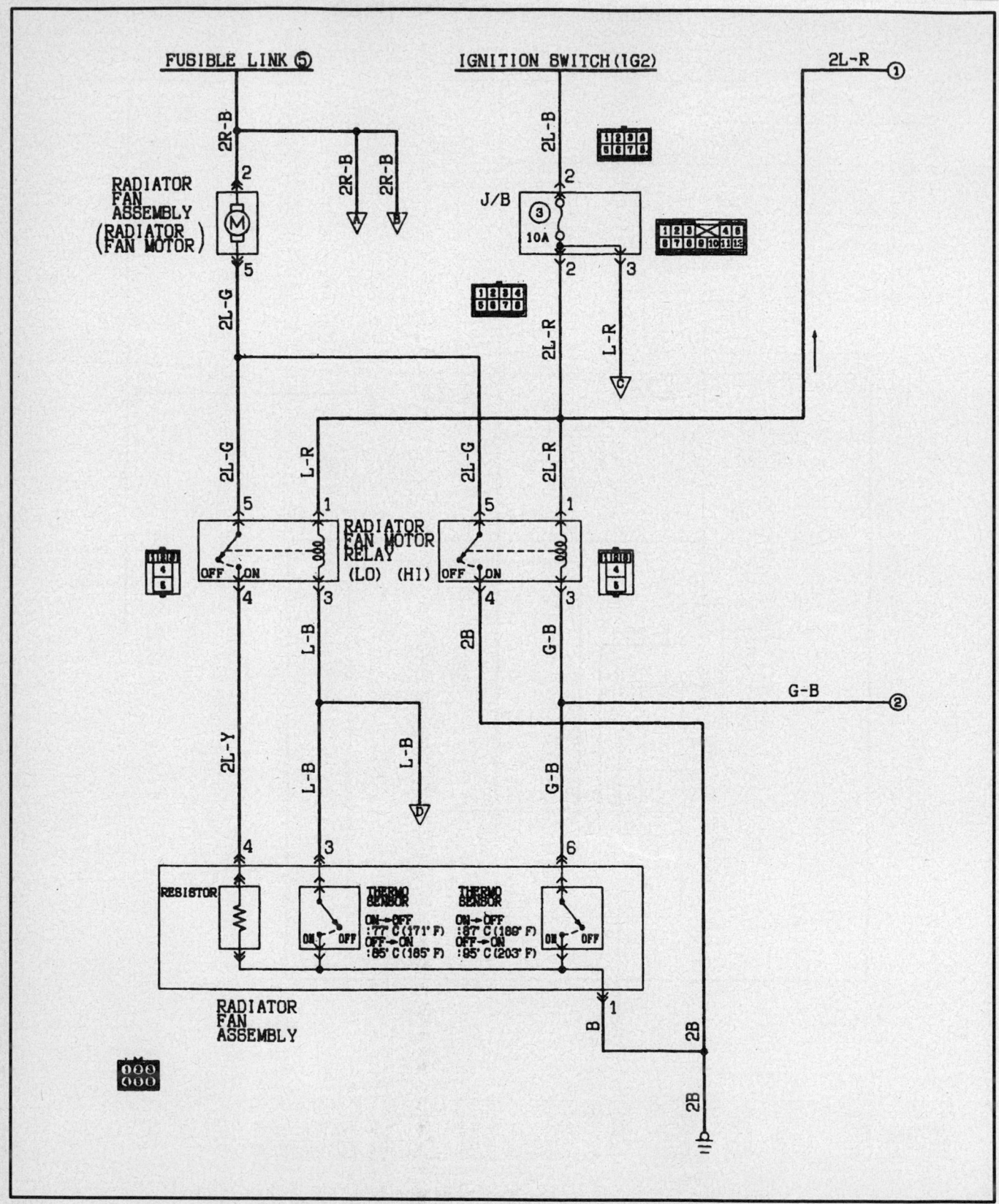

Wiring schematic — 1993 3000GT with manual air conditioning

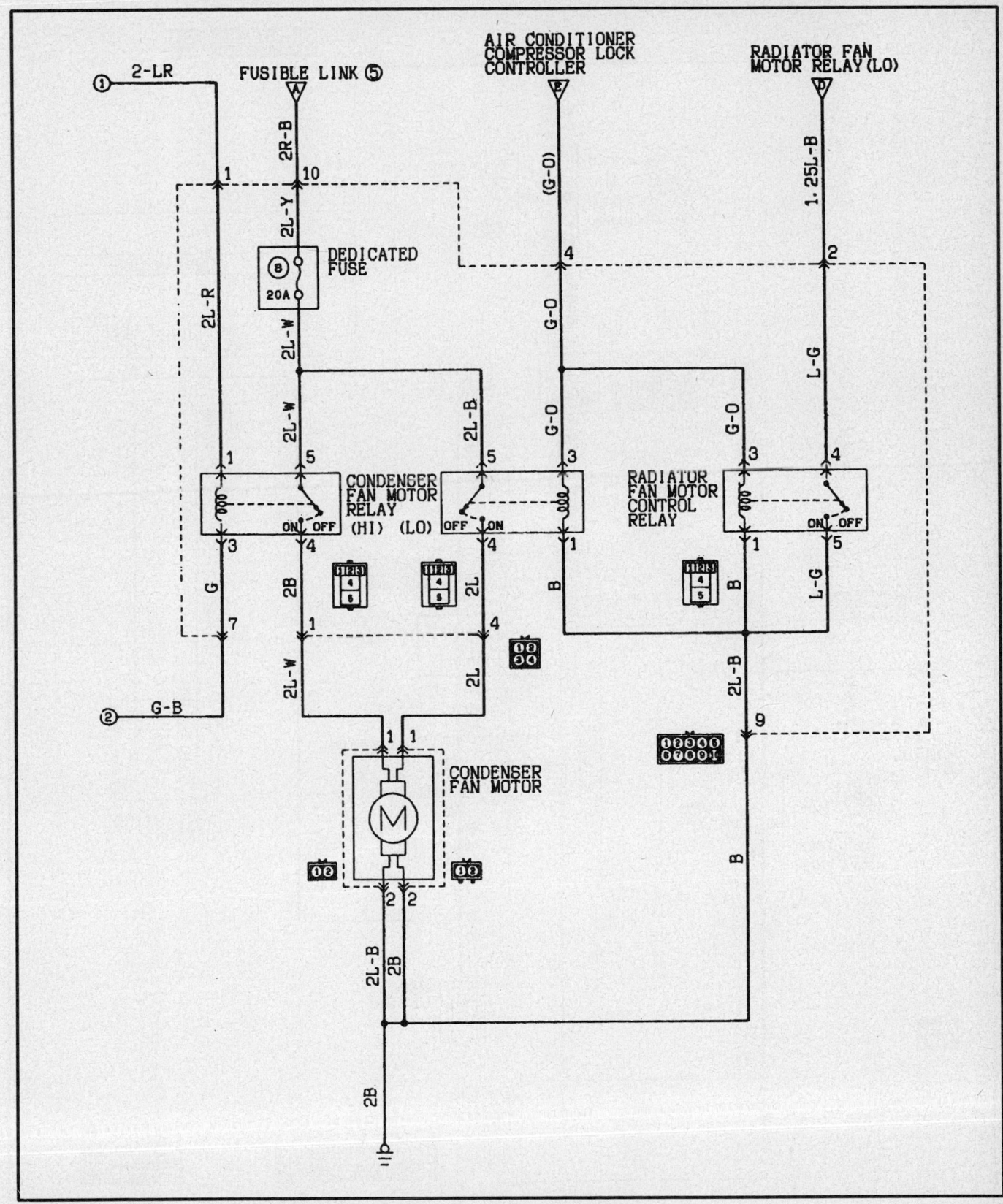

Wiring schematic — 1993 3000GT with manual air conditioning, Cont.

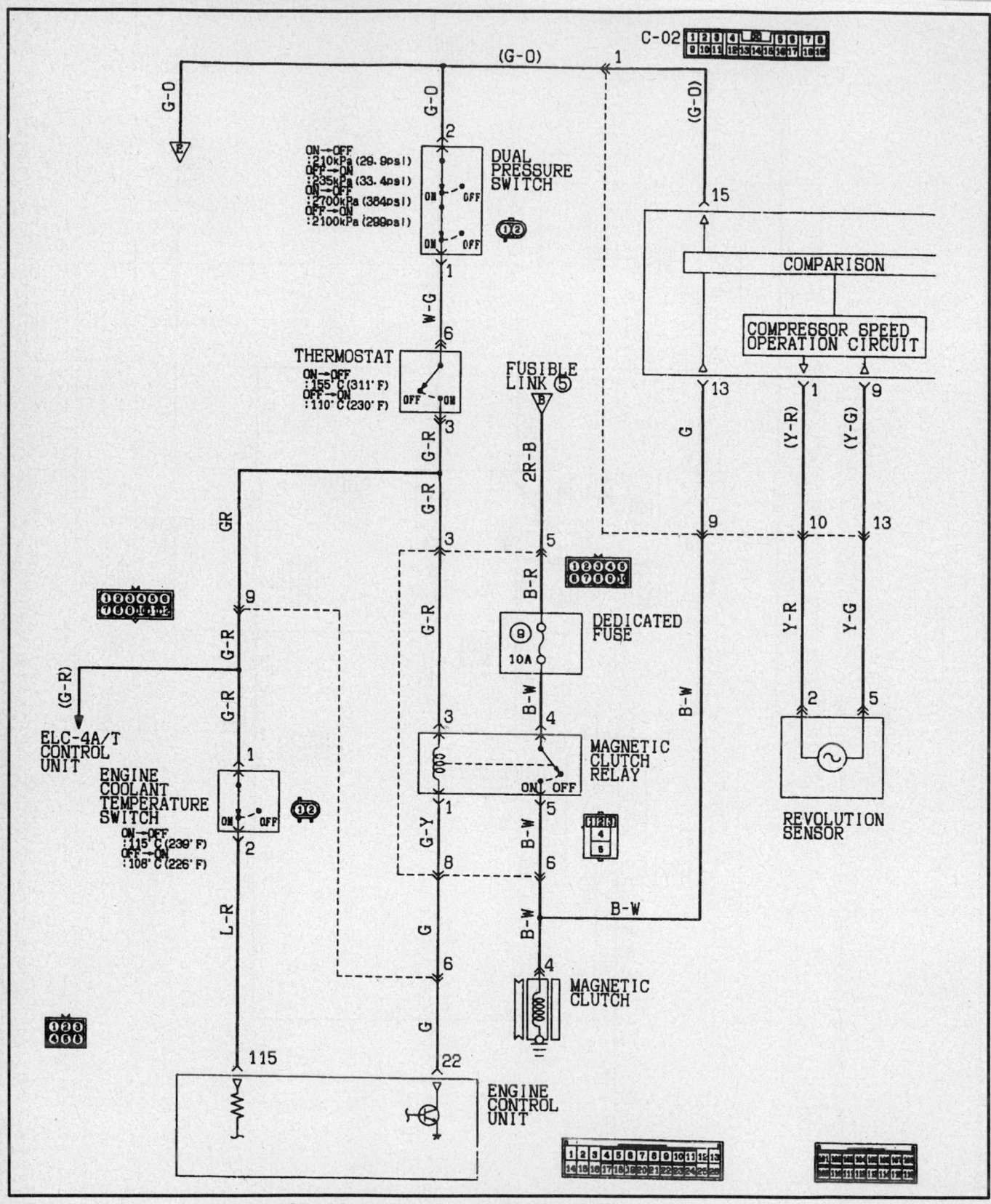

Wiring schematic — 1993 3000GT with manual air conditioning, Cont.

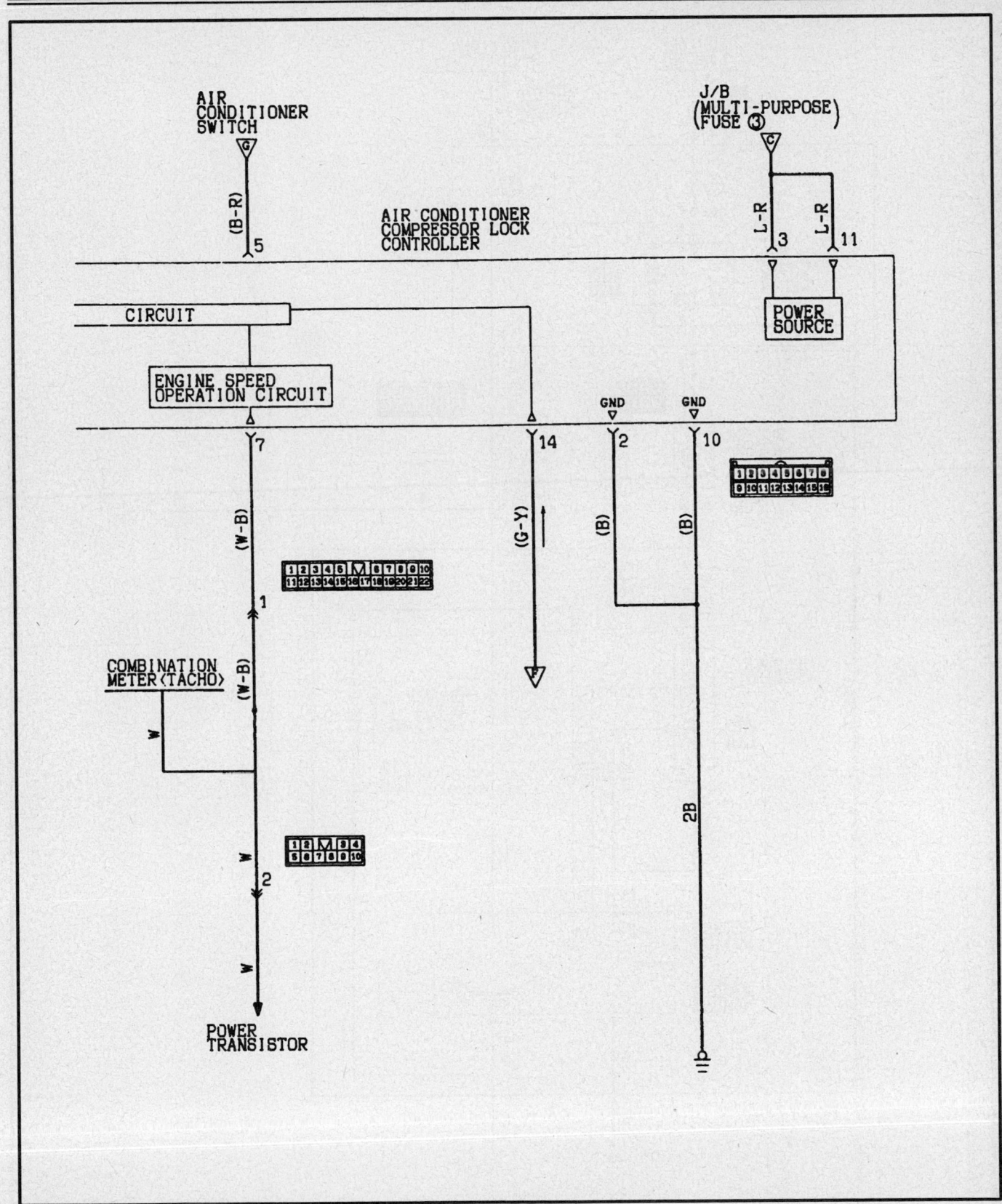

Wiring schematic — 1993 3000GT with manual air conditioning, Cont.

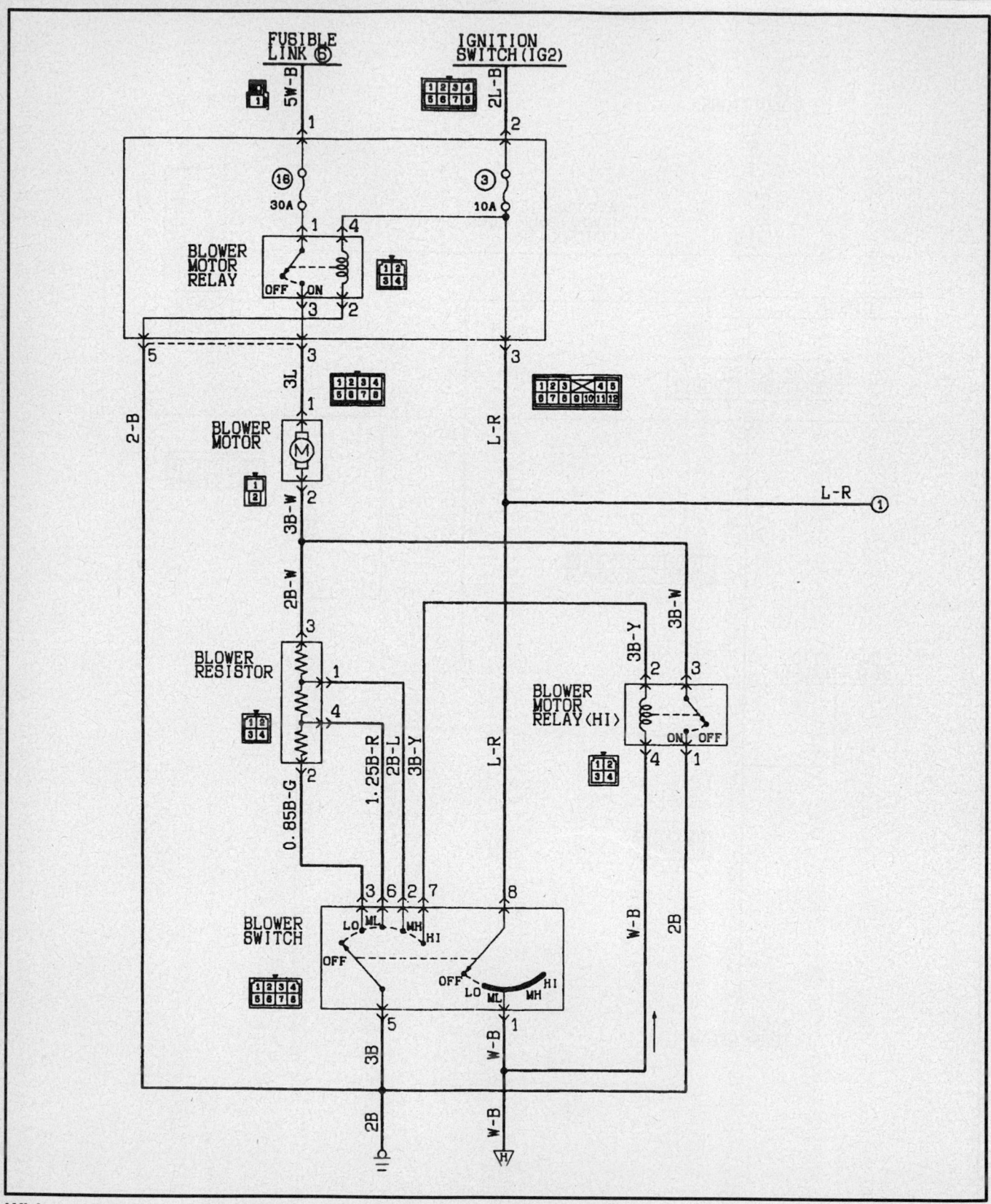

Wiring schematic — 1993 3000GT with manual air conditioning, Cont.

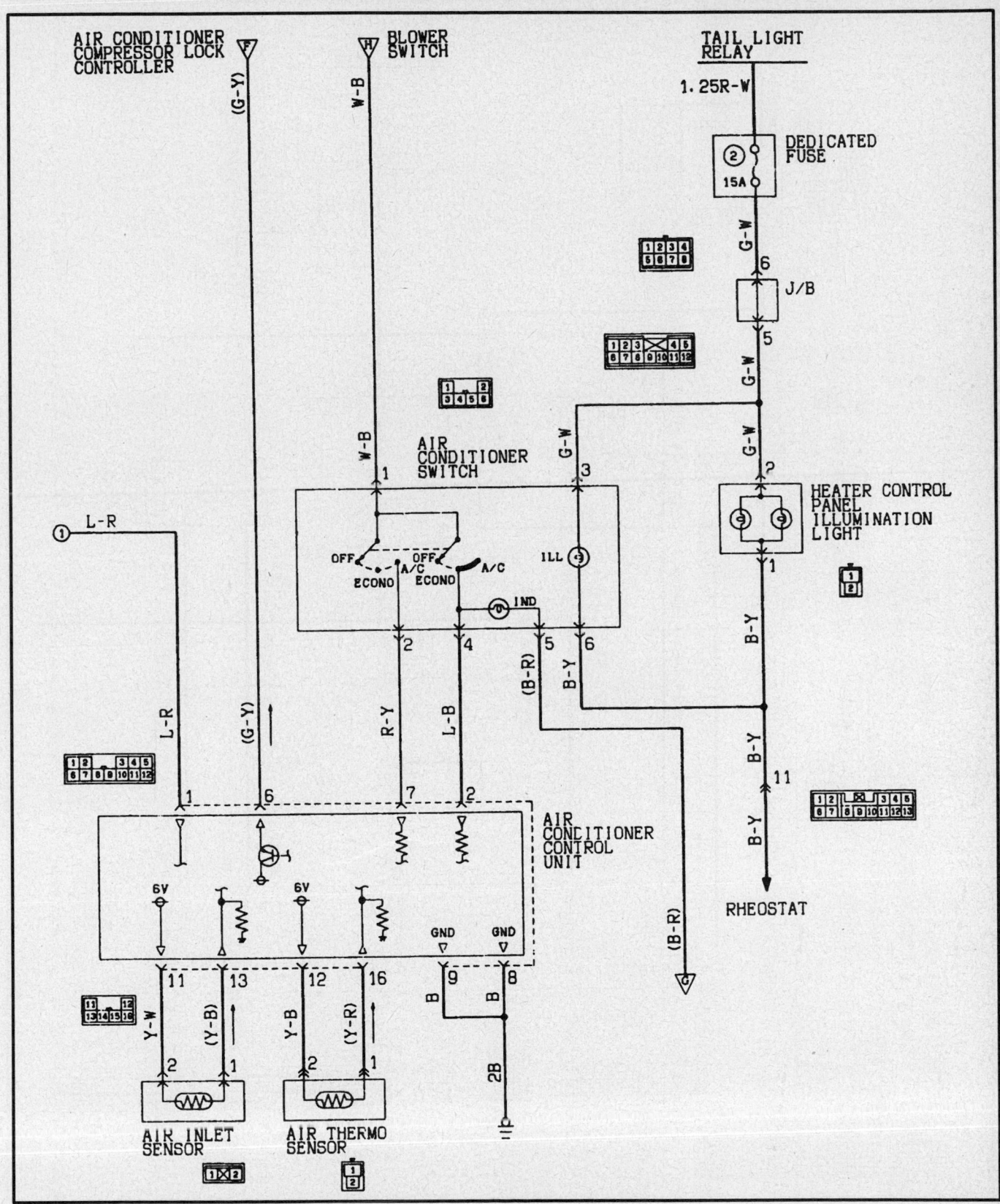

Wiring schematic — 1993 3000GT with manual air conditioning, Cont.

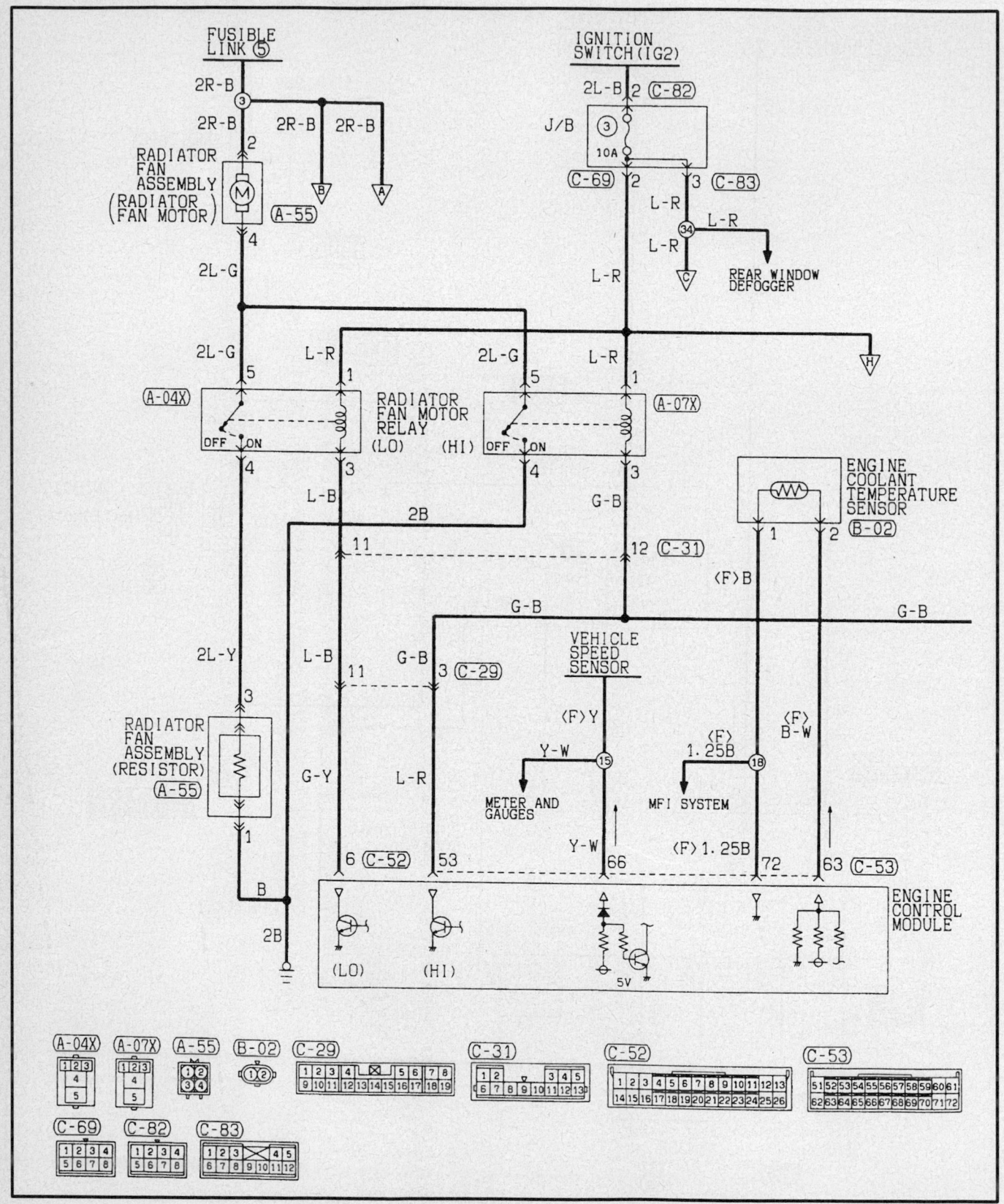

Wiring schematic — 1994–95 3000GT non-turbo (federal) with manual air conditioning

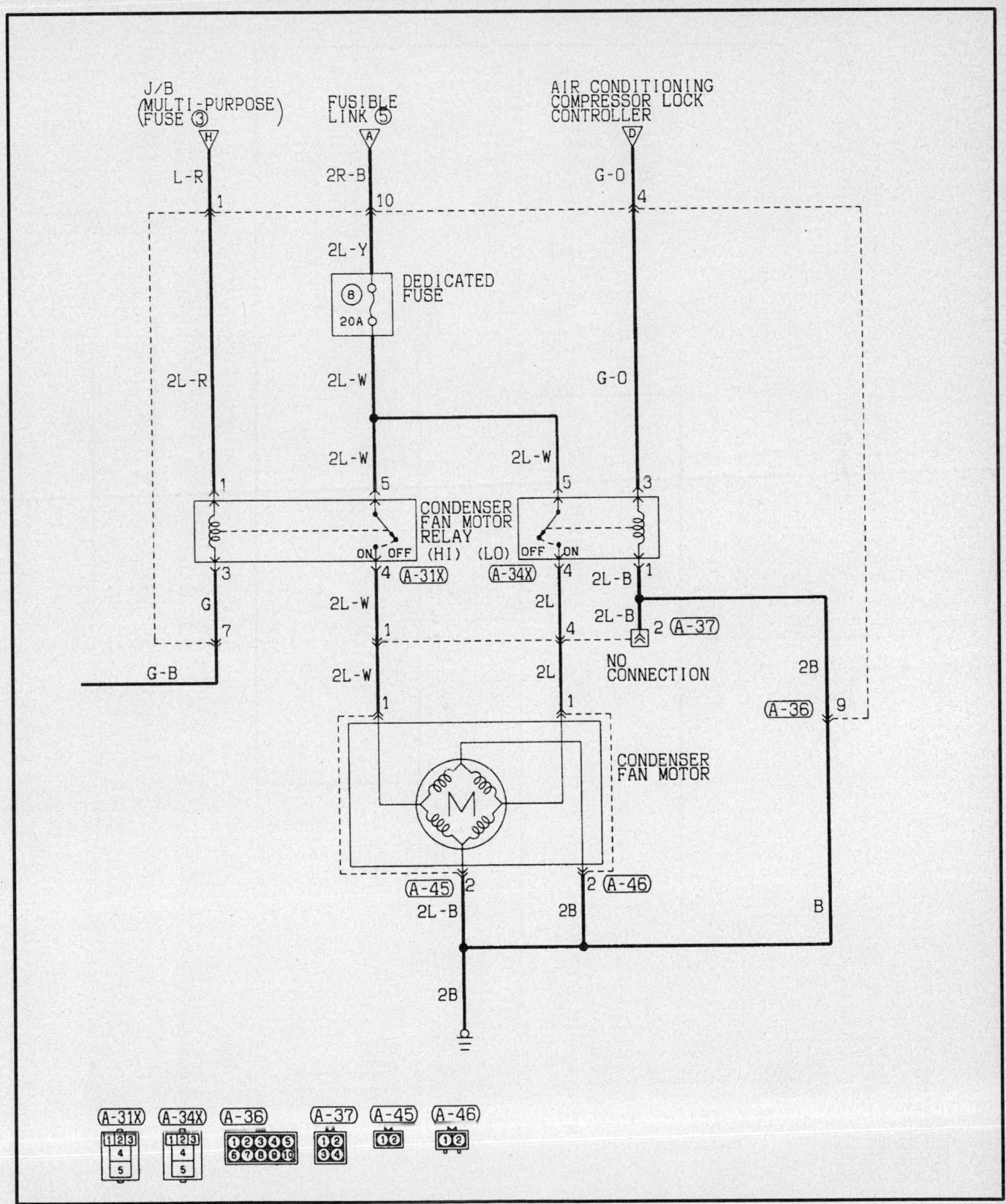

Wiring schematic — 1994—95 3000GT non-turbo (federal) with manual air conditioning, Cont.

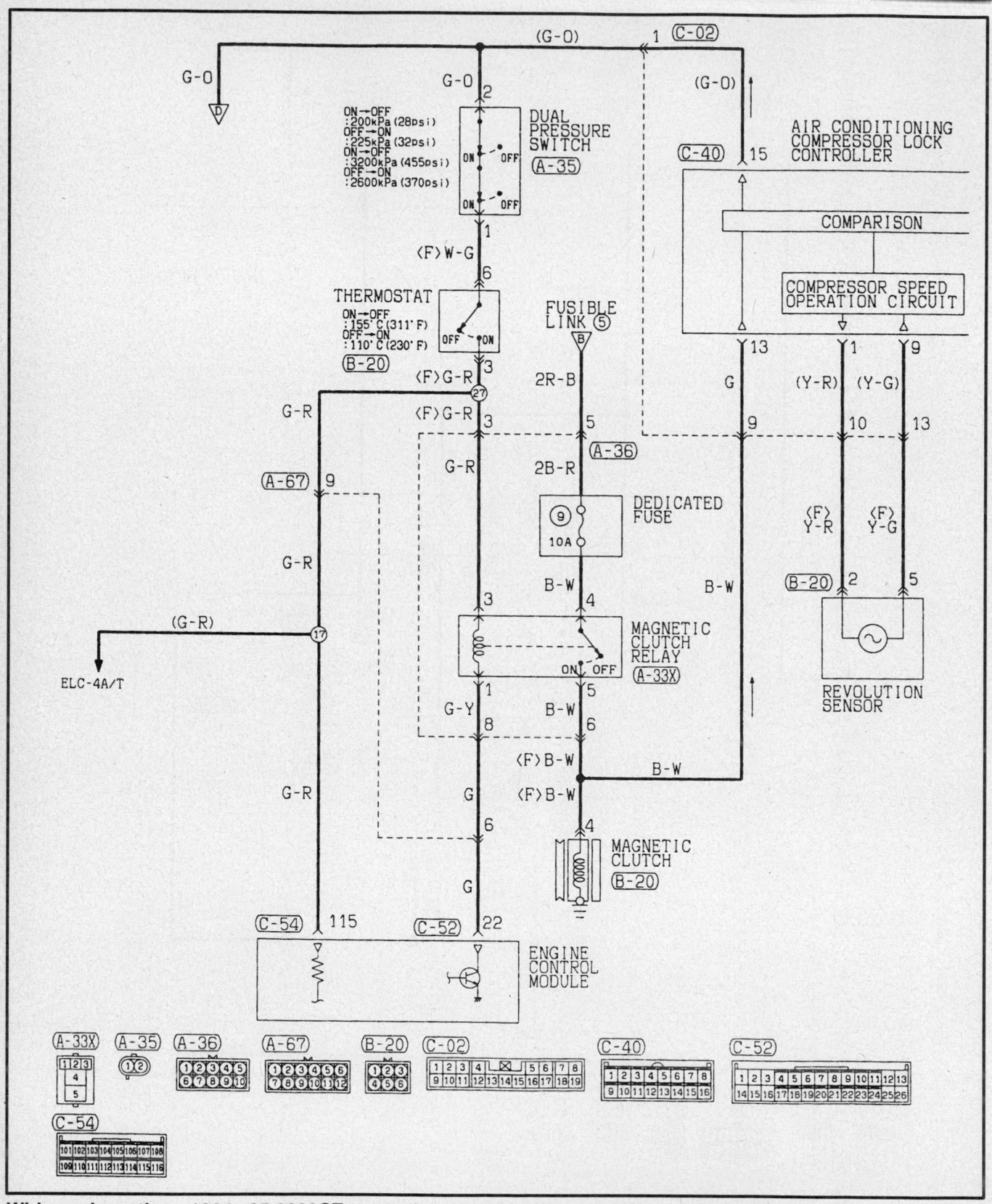

Wiring schematic — 1994–95 3000GT non-turbo (federal) with manual air conditioning, Cont.

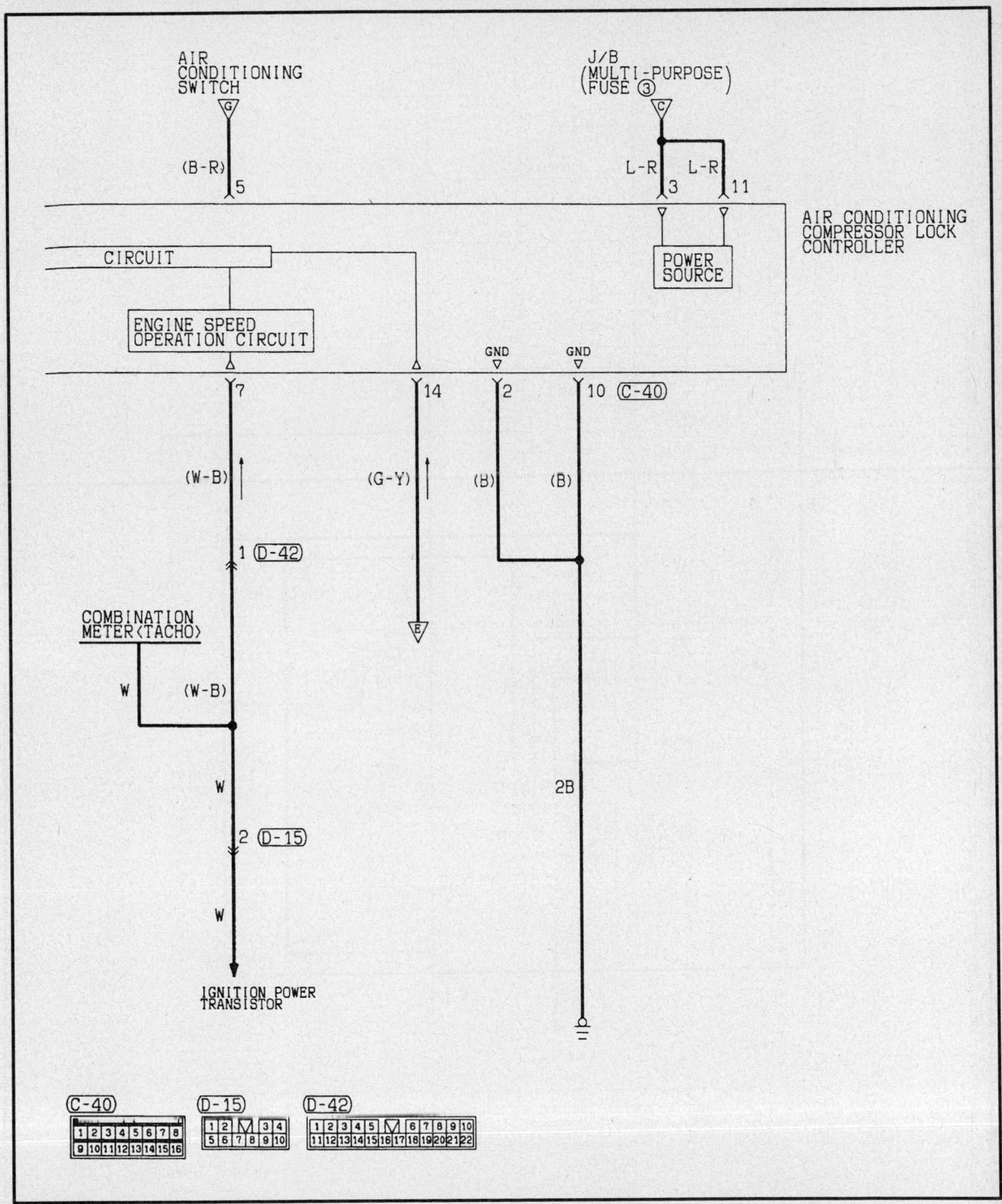

Wiring schematic — 1994–95 3000GT non-turbo (federal) with manual air conditioning, Cont.

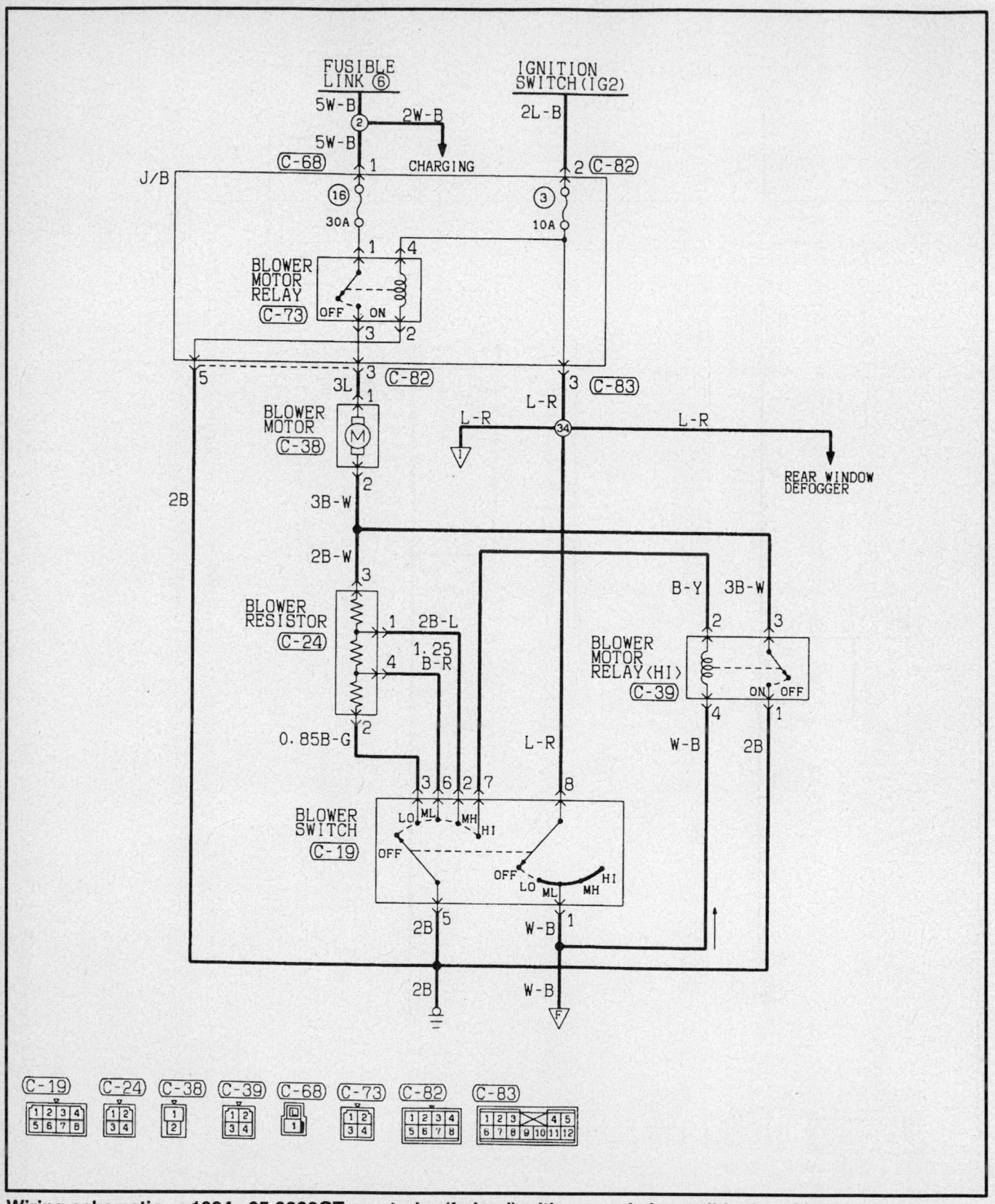

Wiring schematic — 1994–95 3000GT non-turbo (federal) with manual air conditioning, Cont.

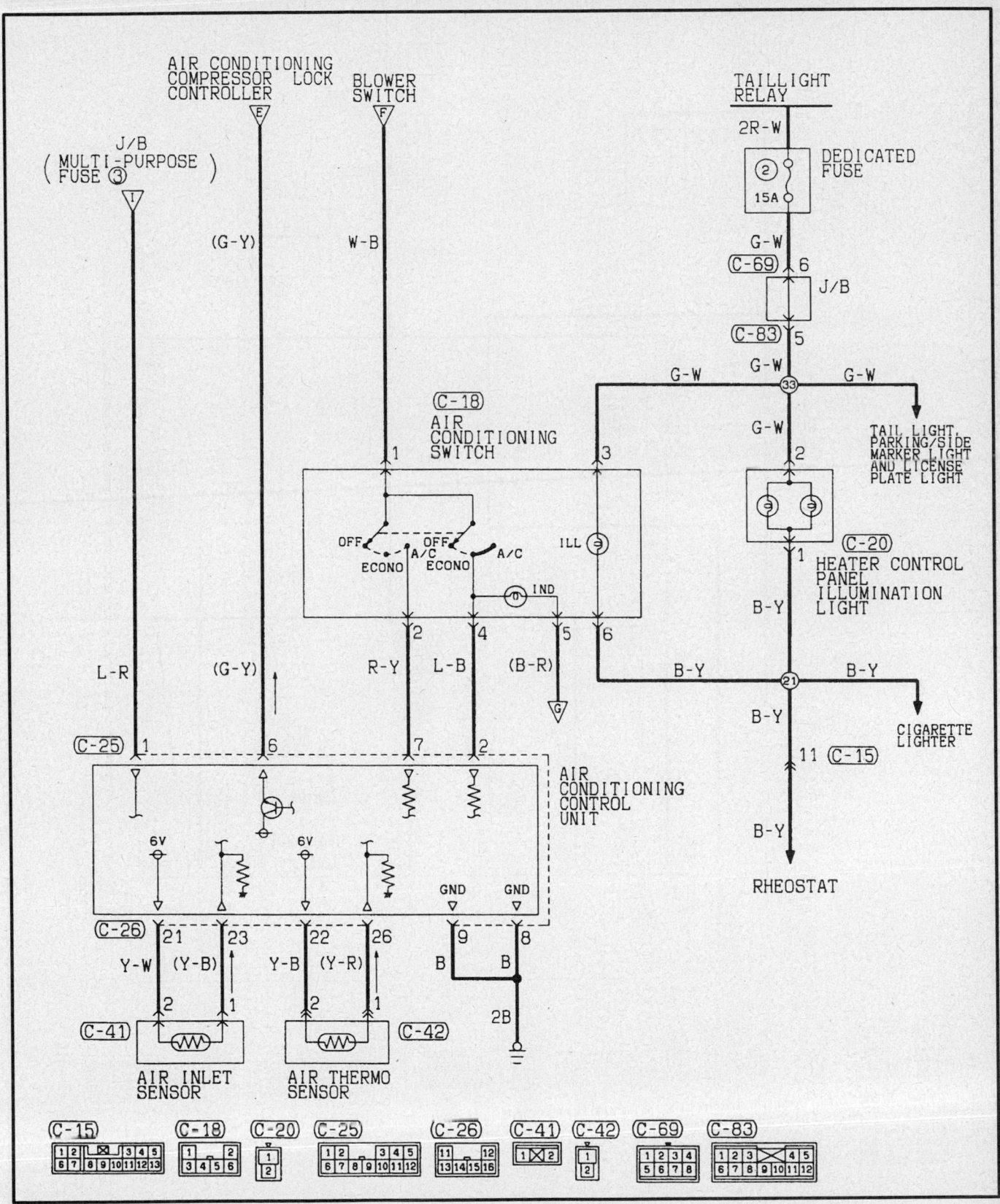

Wiring schematic — 1994−95 3000GT non-turbo (federal) with manual air conditioning, Cont.

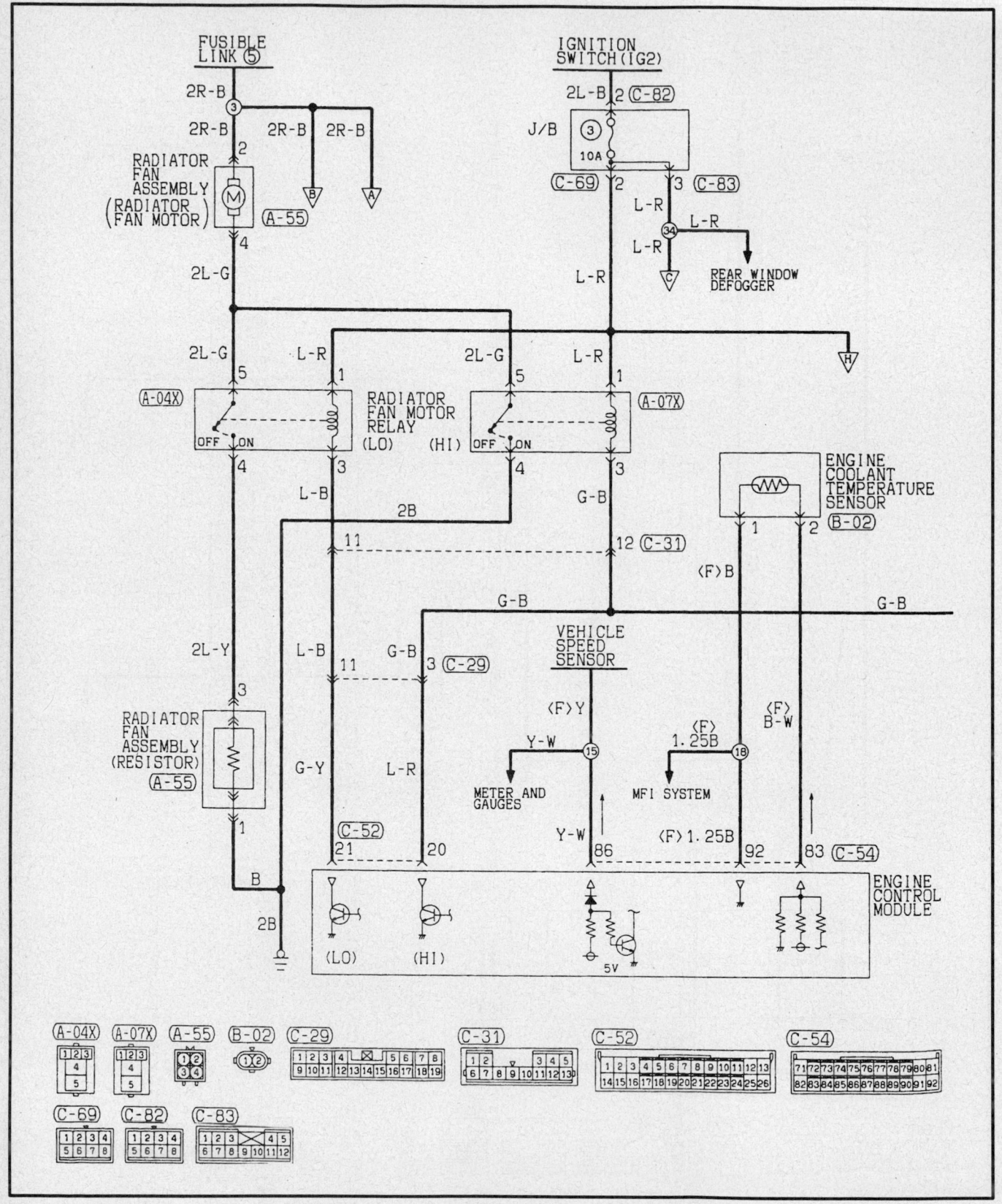

Wiring schematic — 1994–95 3000GT turbo (all) and nonturbo (california) with manual air conditioning

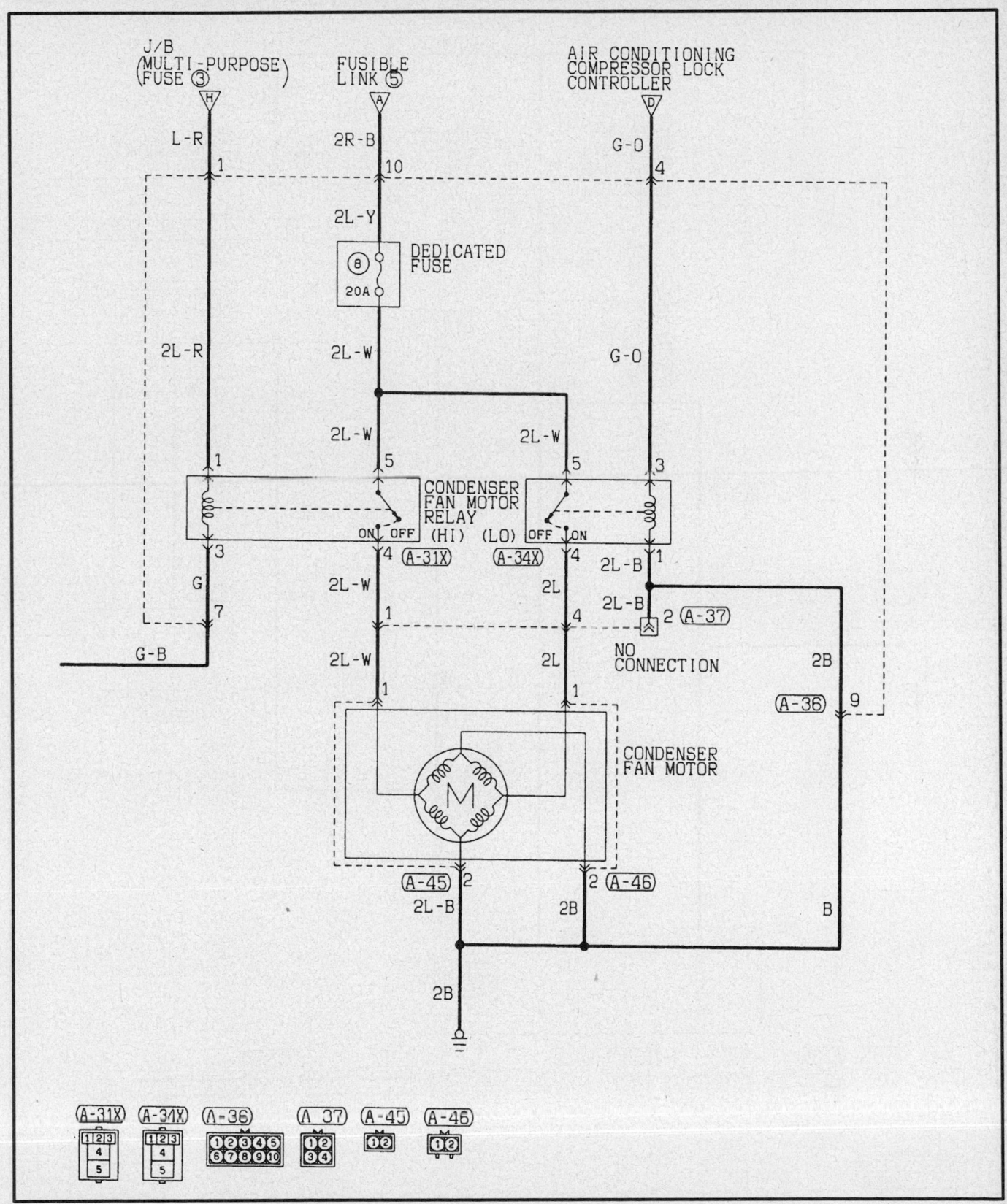

Wiring schematic — 1994–95 3000GT turbo (all) and nonturbo (california) with manual air conditioning, Cont.

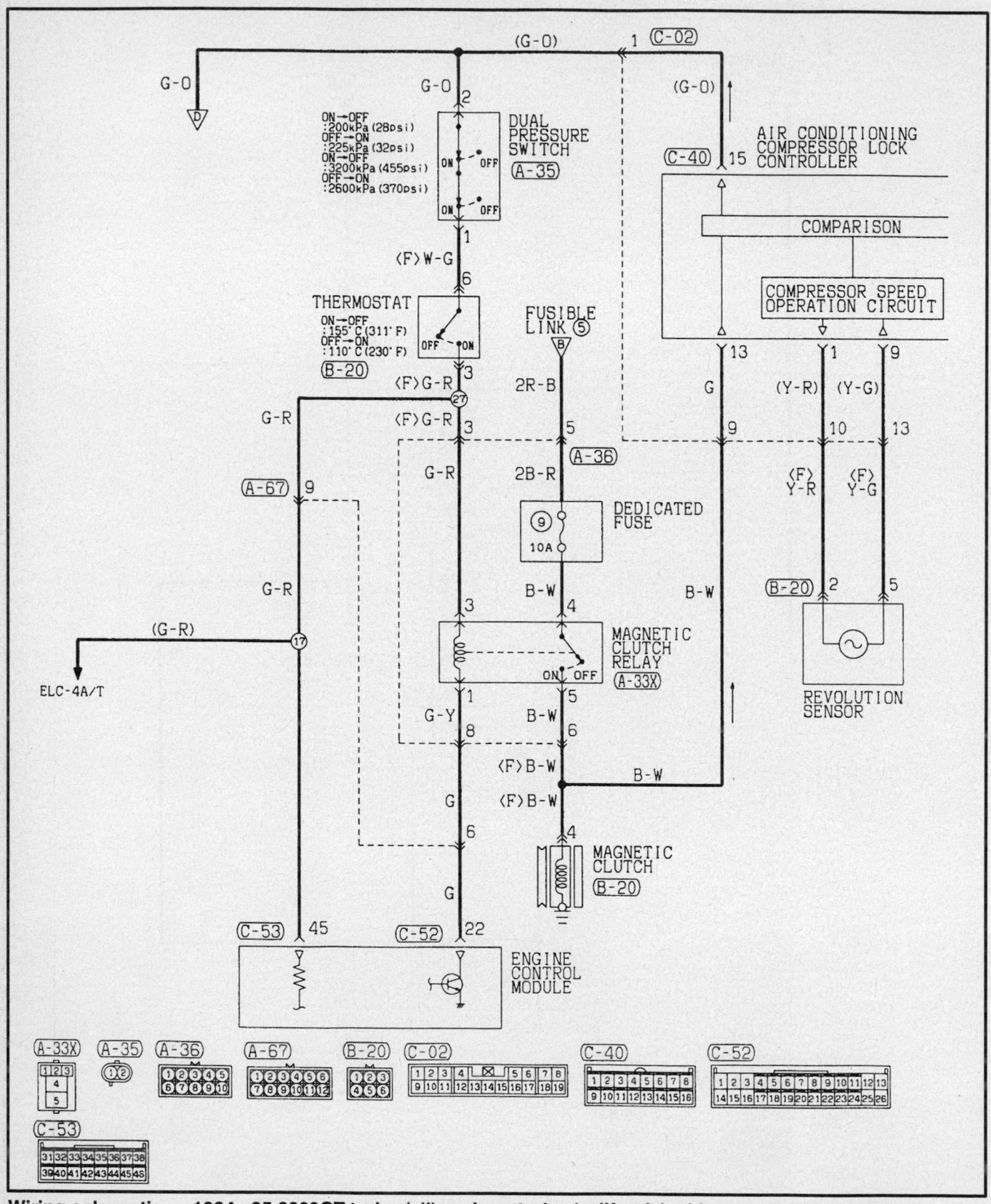

Wiring schematic — 1994–95 3000GT turbo (all) and nonturbo (california) with manual air conditioning, Cont.

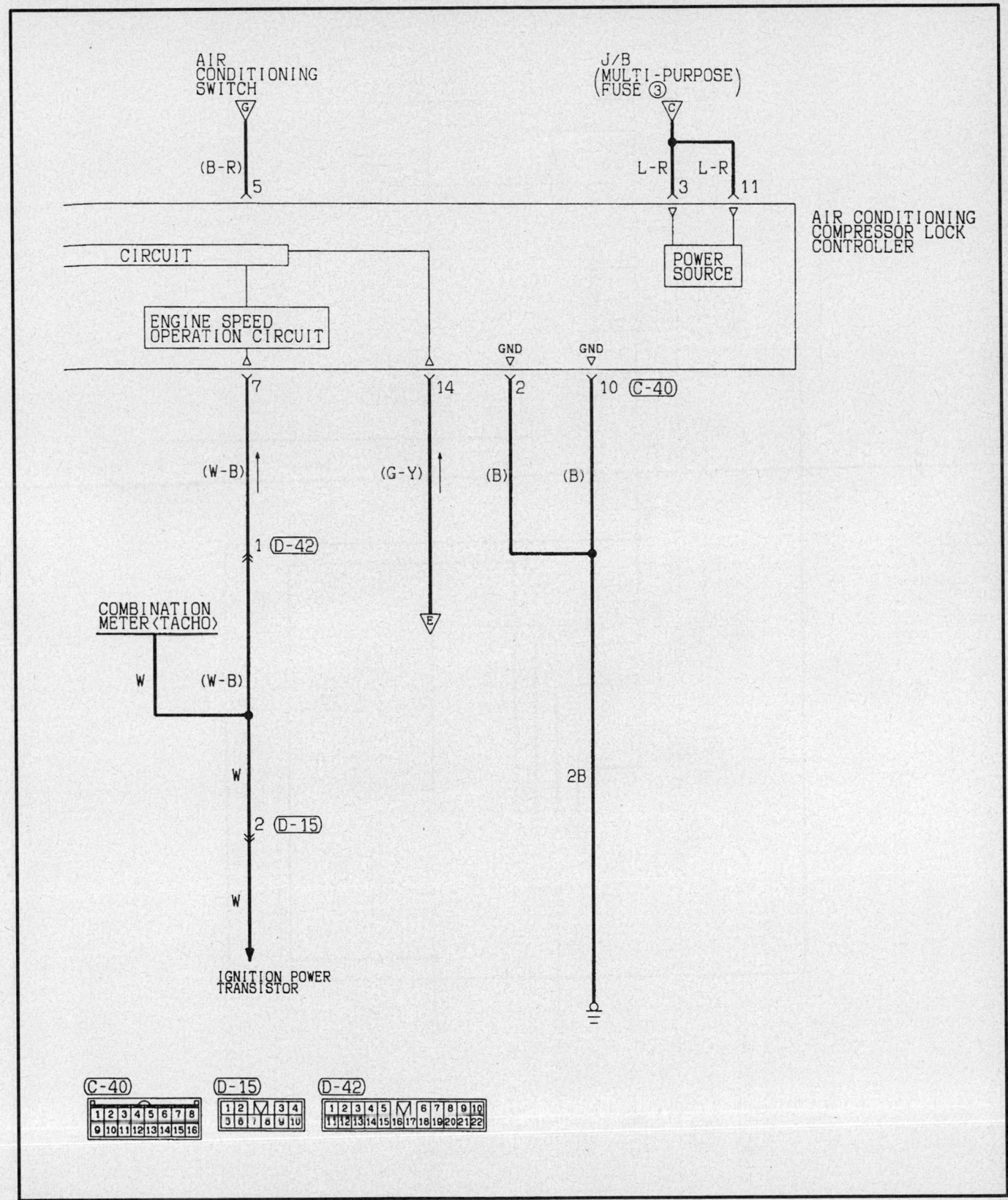

Wiring schematic — 1994—95 3000GT turbo (all) and nonturbo (california) with manual air conditioning, Cont.

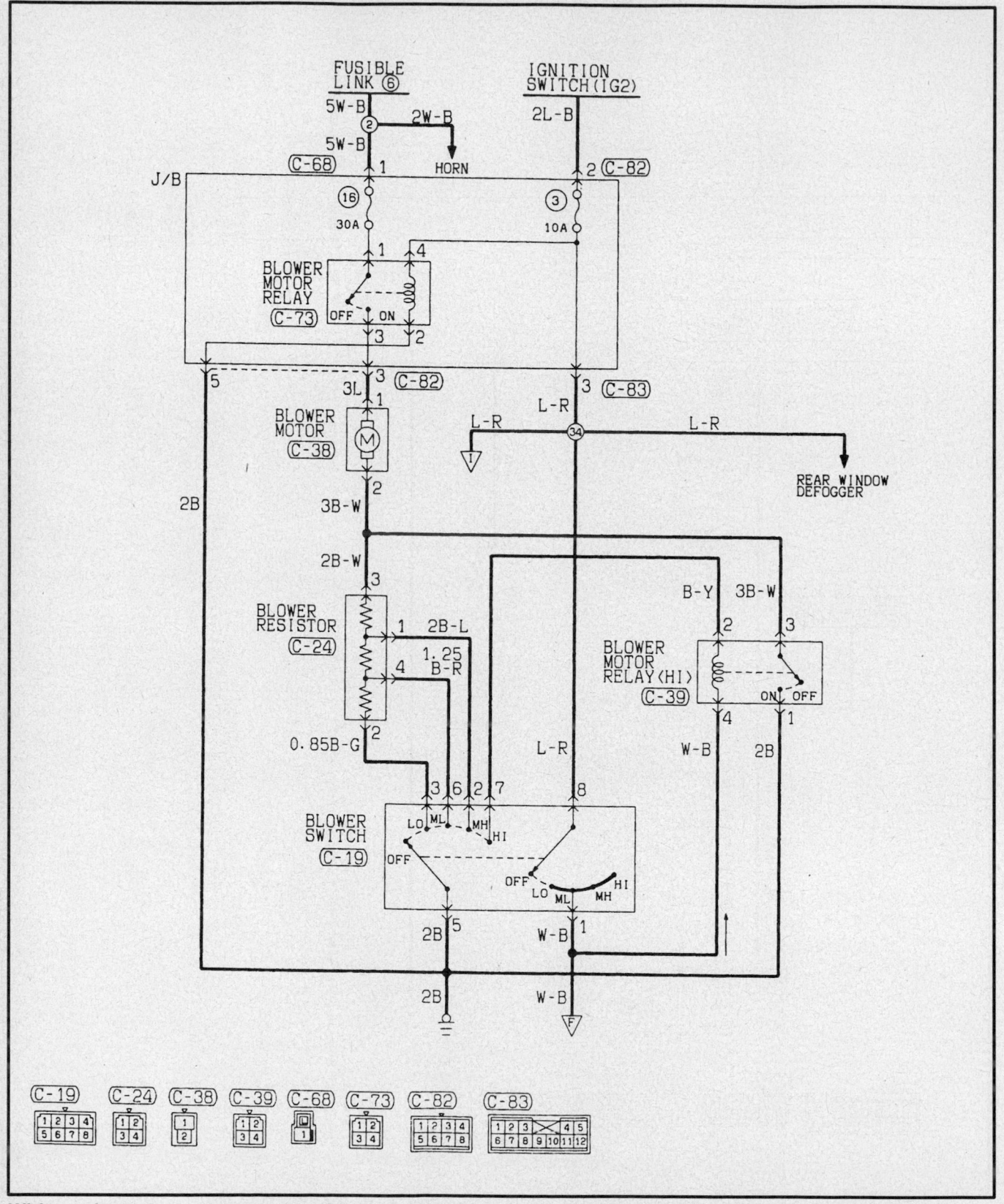

Wiring schematic — 1994-95 3000GT turbo (all) and nonturbo (california) with manual air conditioning, Cont.

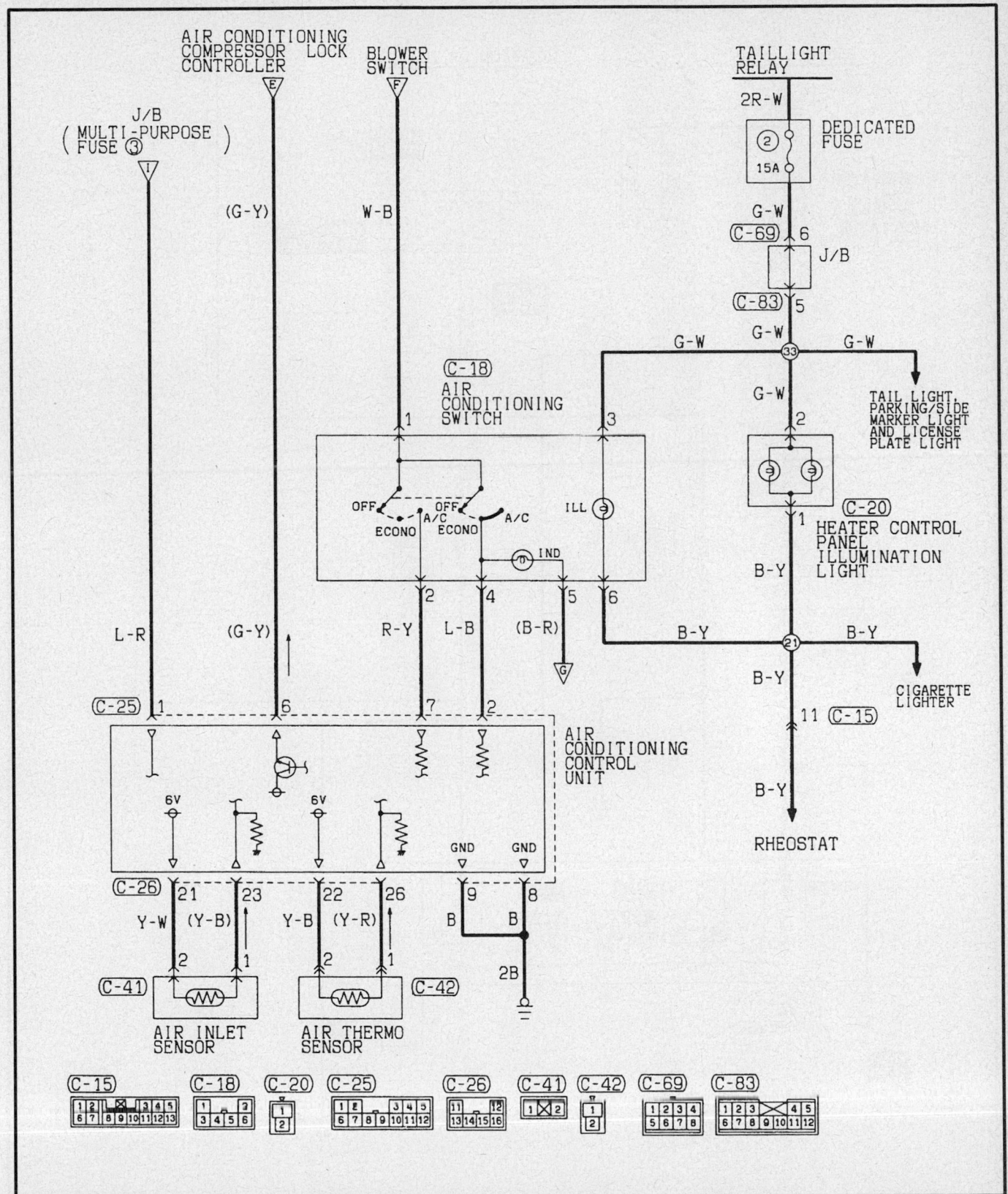

Wiring schematic — 1994-95 3000GT turbo (all) and nonturbo (california) with manual air conditioning, Cont.

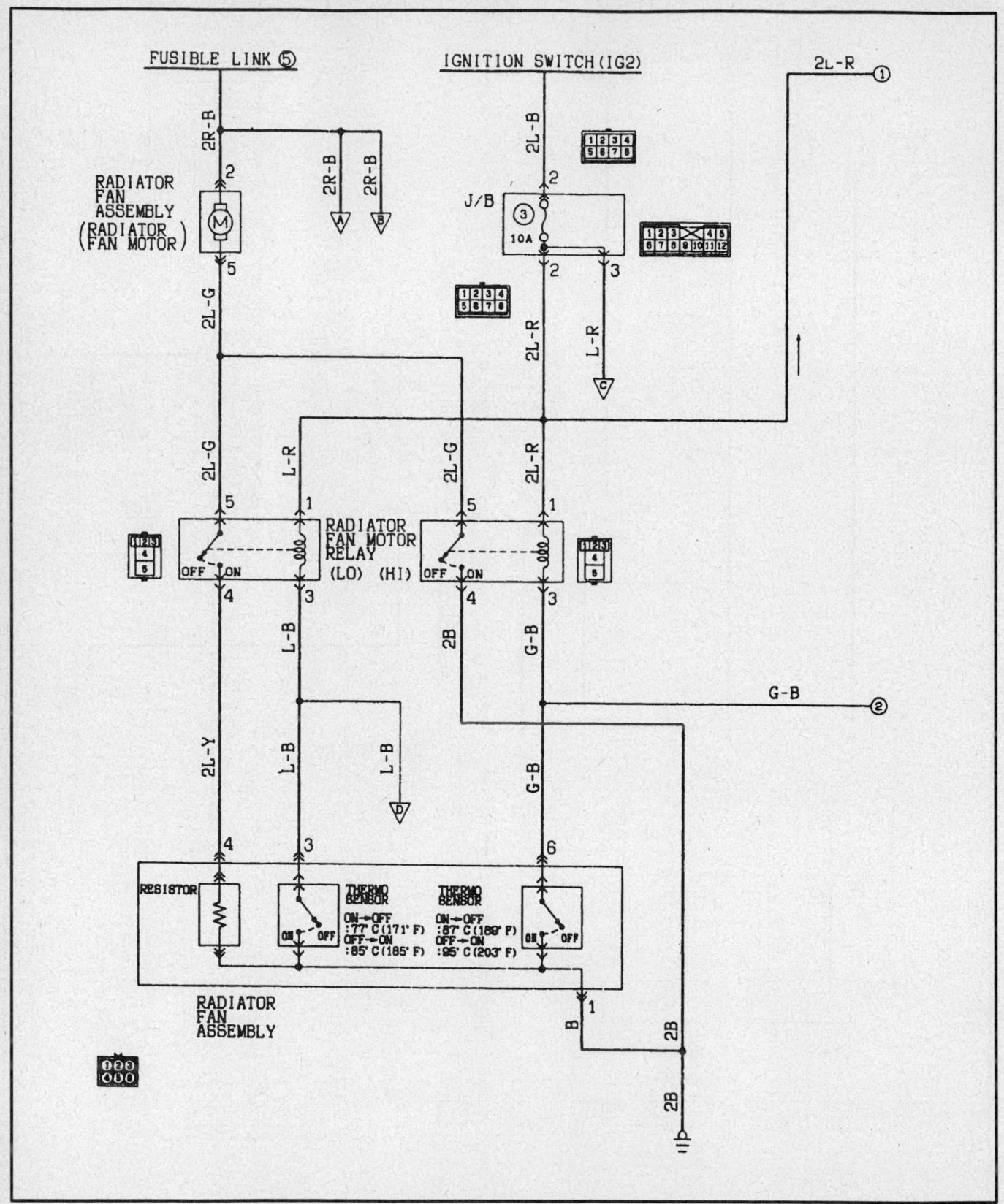

Wiring schematic — 1993 3000GT with full auto air conditioning

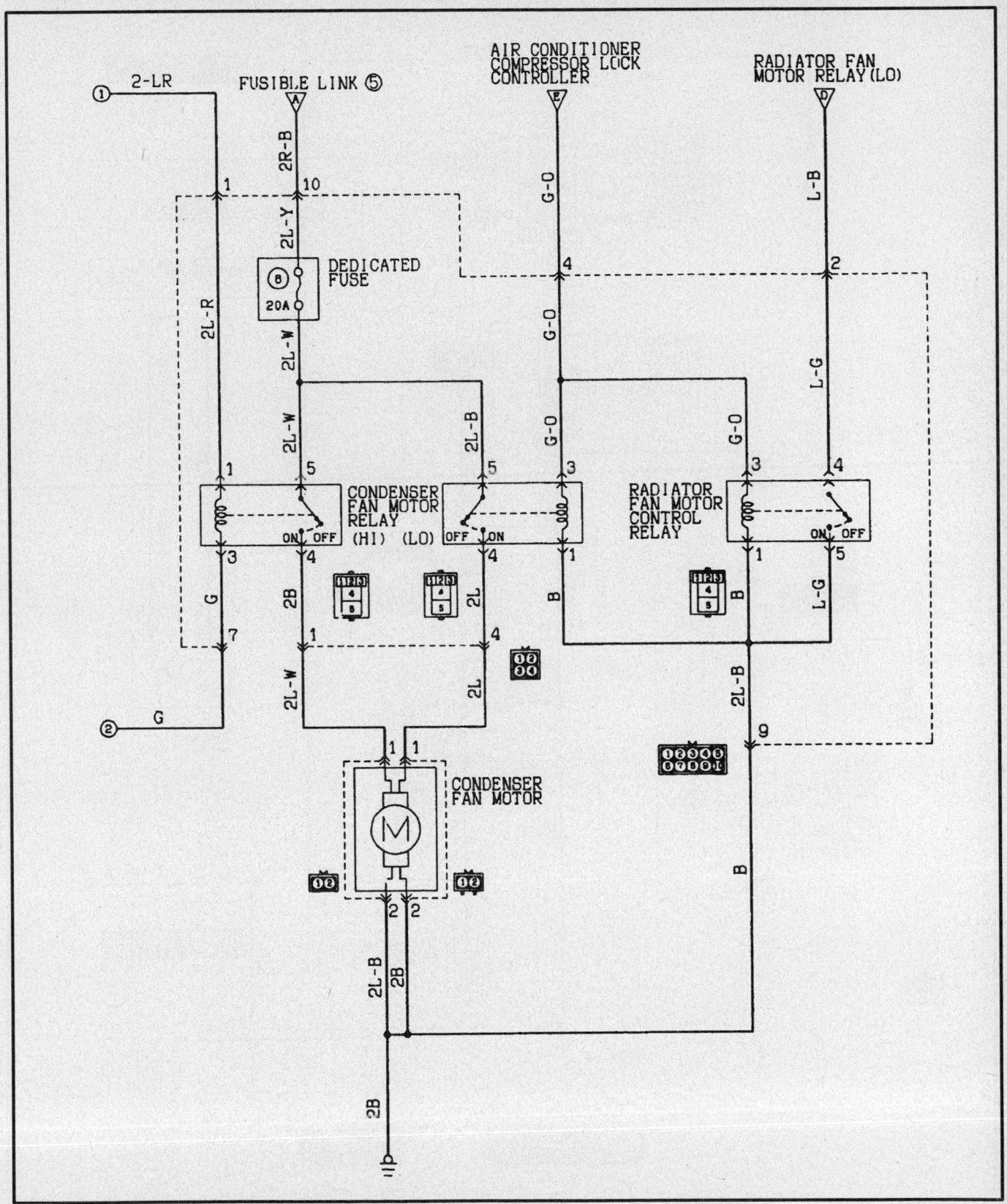

Wiring schematic — 1993 3000GT with full auto air conditioning, Cont.

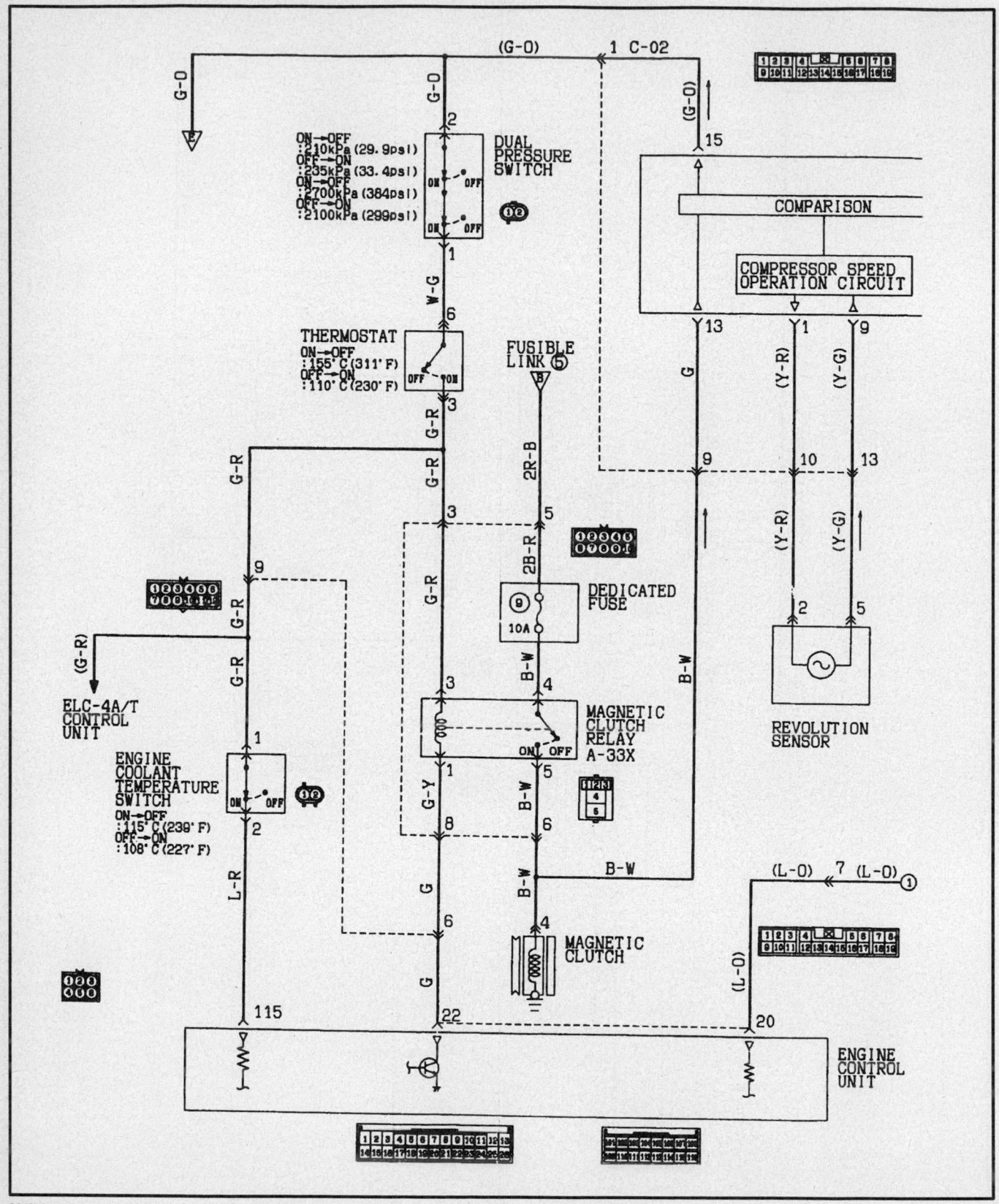

Wiring schematic — 1993 3000GT with full auto air conditioning, Cont.

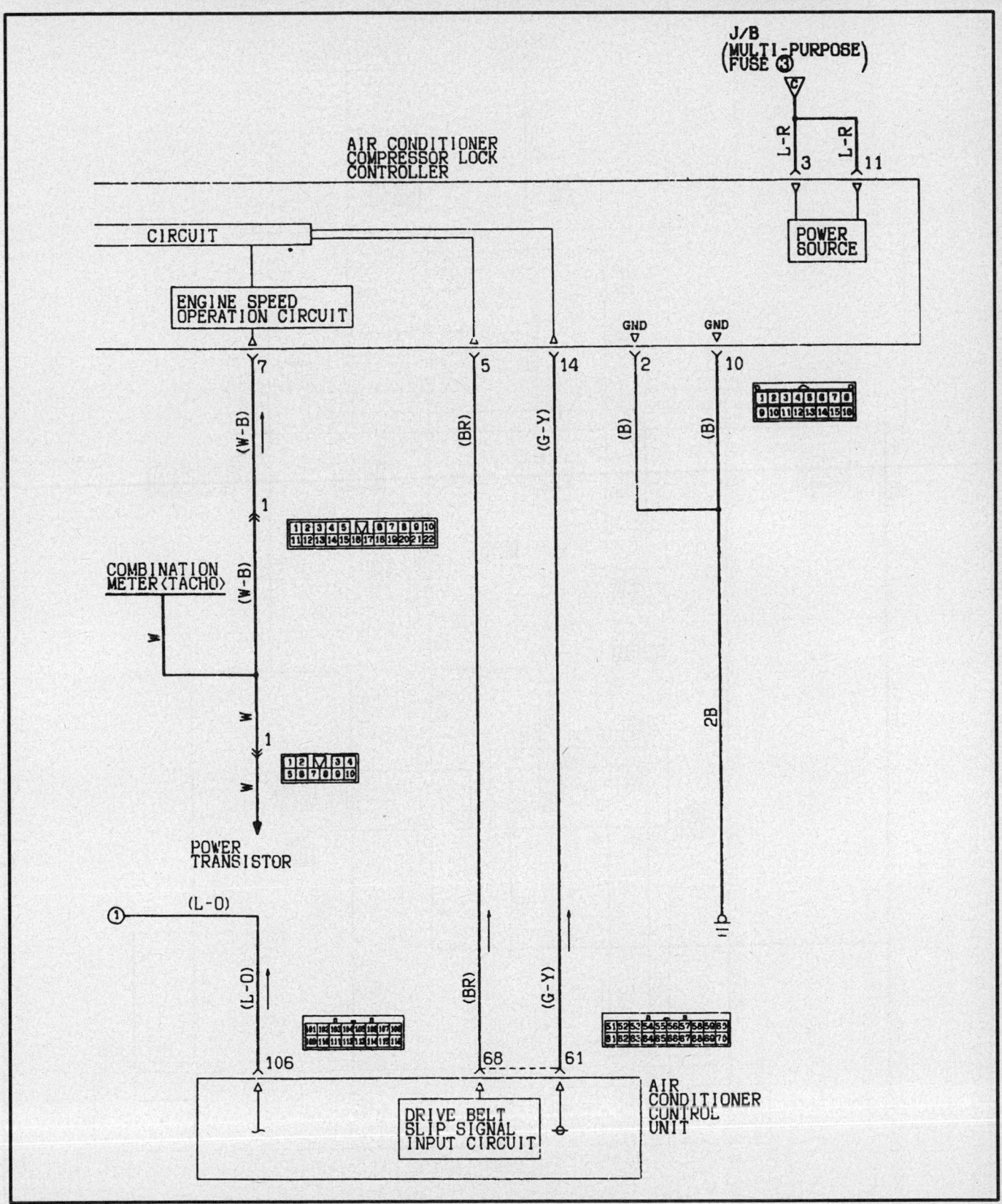

Wiring schematic — 1993 3000GT with full auto air conditioning, Cont.

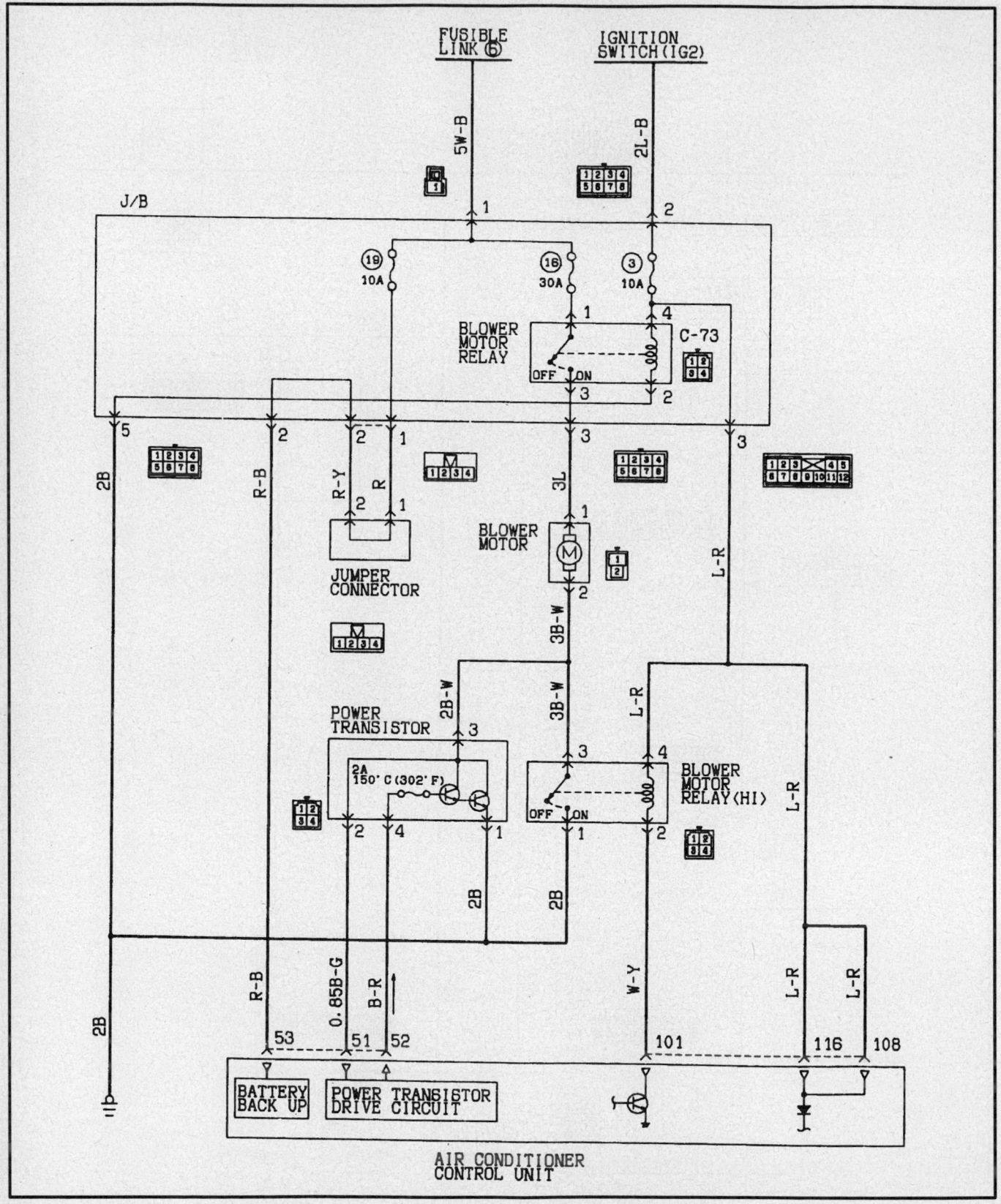

Wiring schematic — 1993 3000GT with full auto air conditioning, Cont.

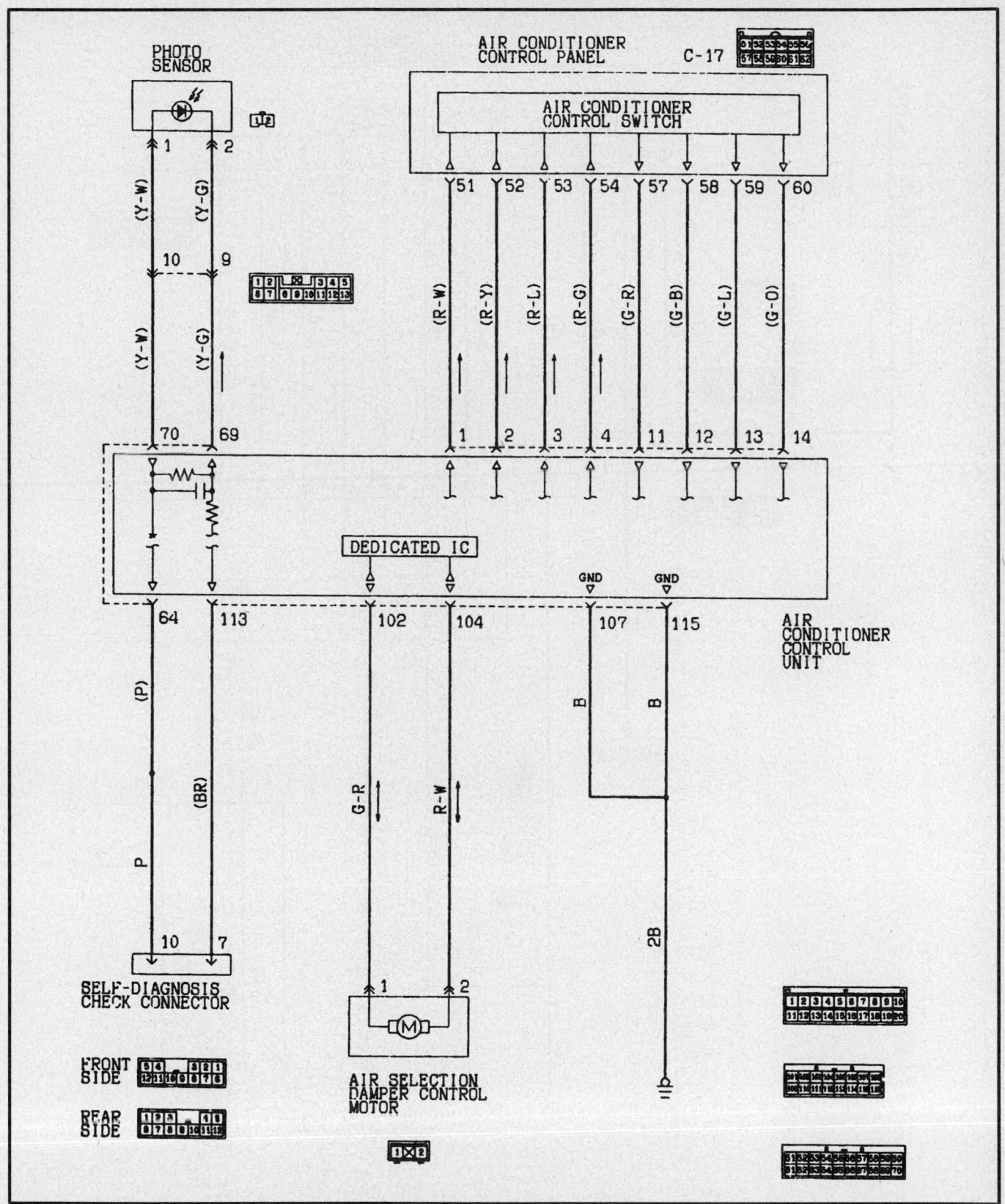

Wiring schematic — 1993 3000GT with full auto air conditioning, Cont.

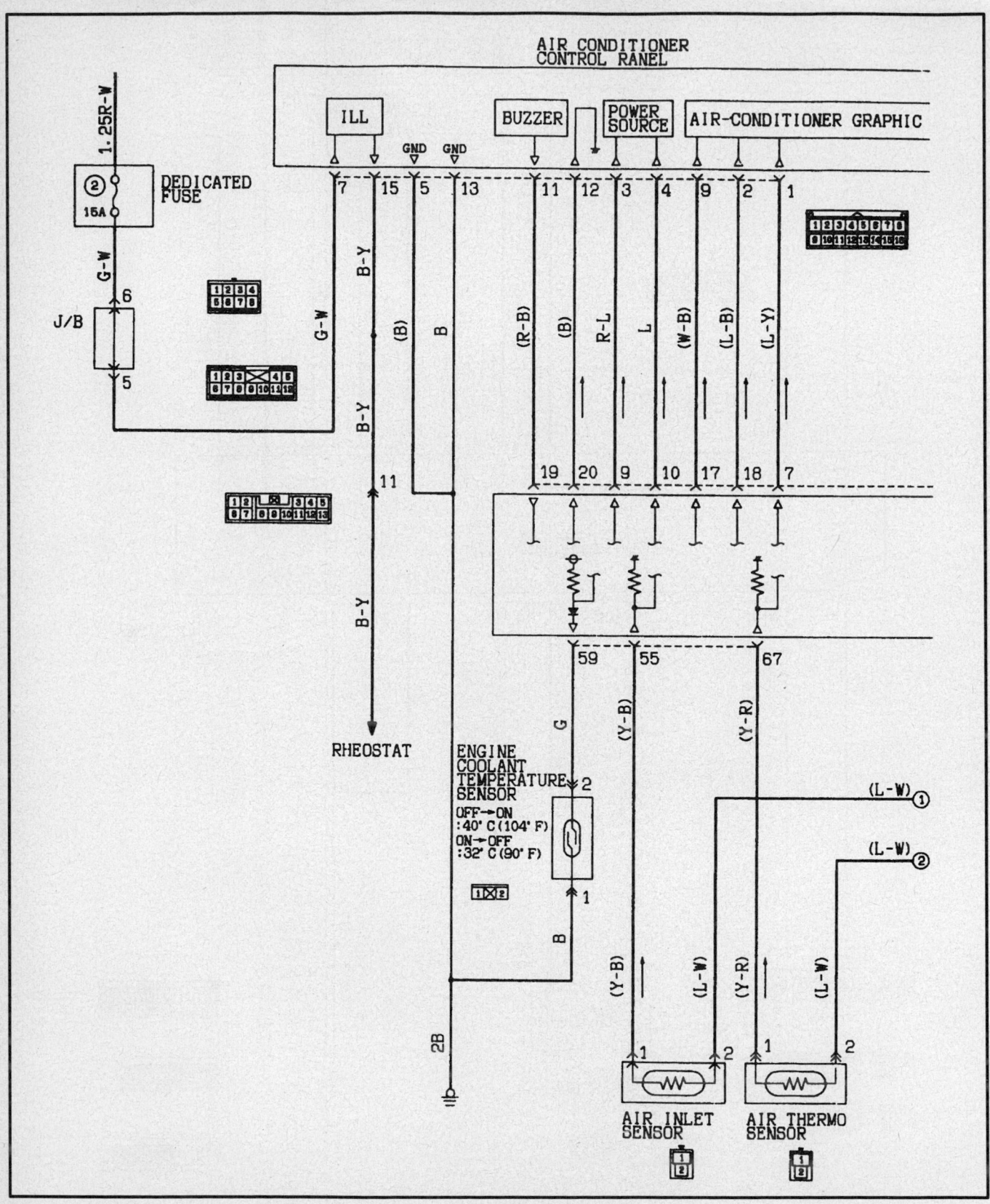

Wiring schematic — 1993 3000GT with full auto air conditioning, Cont.

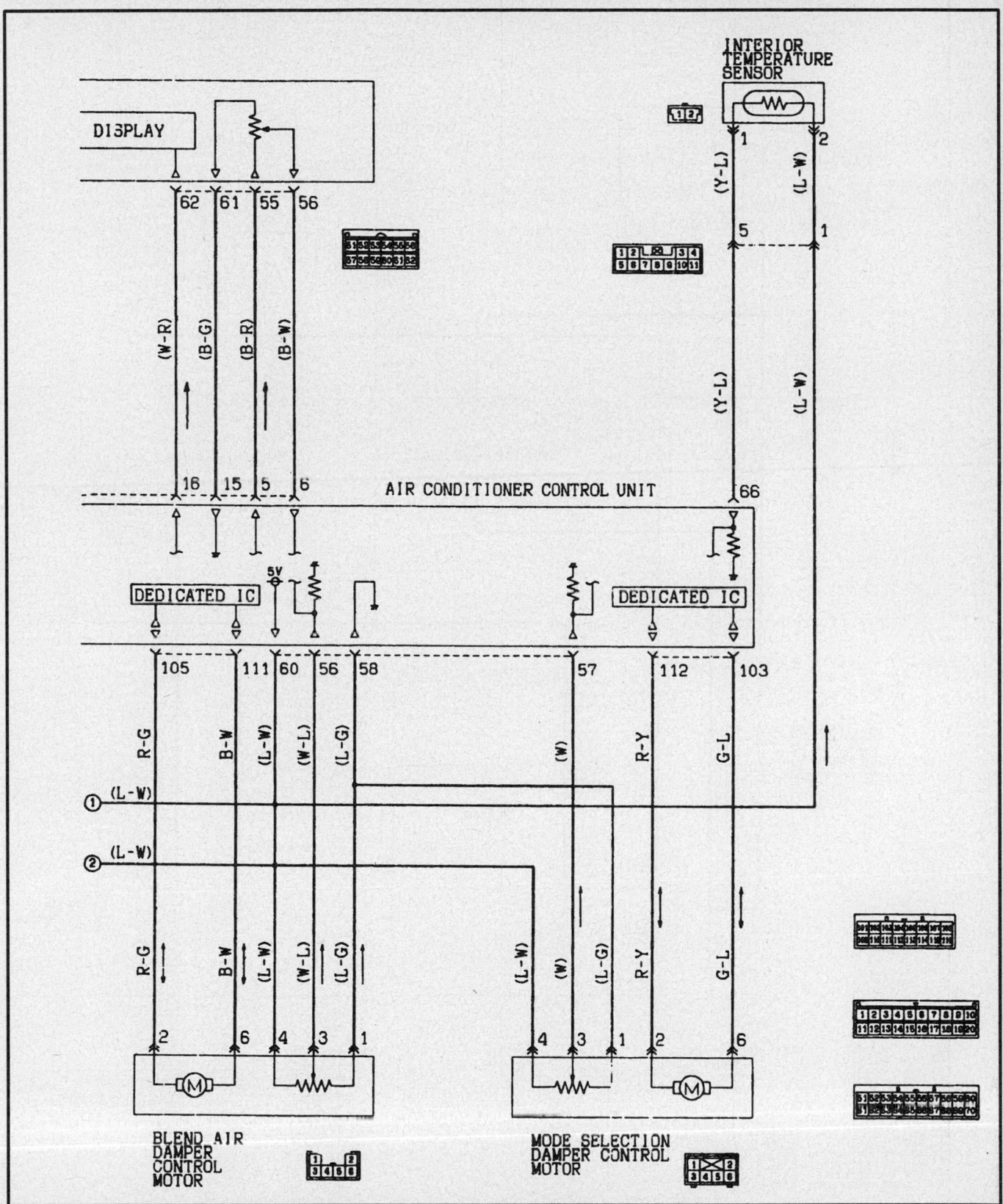

Wiring schematic — 1993 3000GT with full auto air conditioning, Cont.

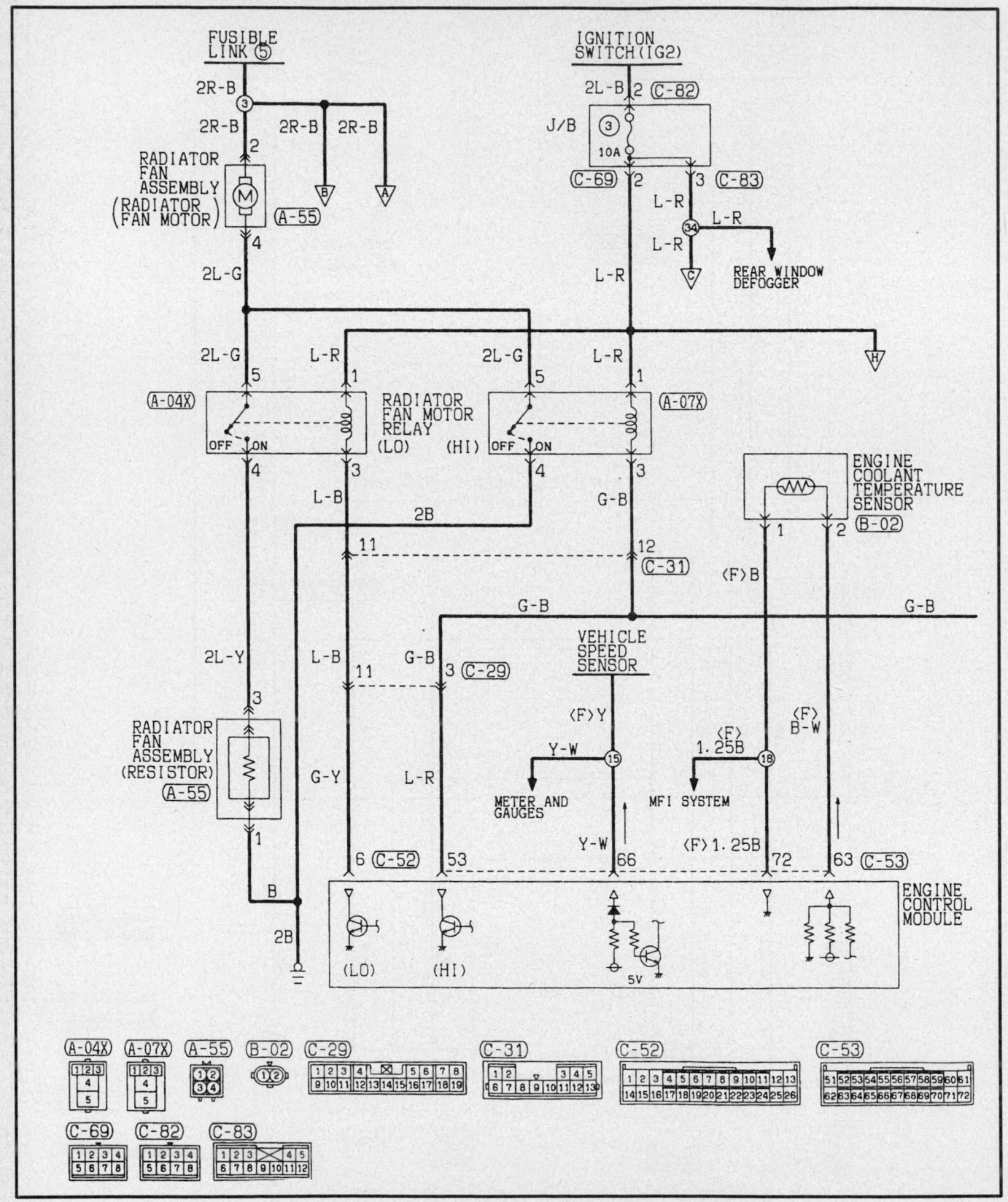

Wiring schematic — 1994–95 3000GT non-turbo (federal) with full auto air conditioning

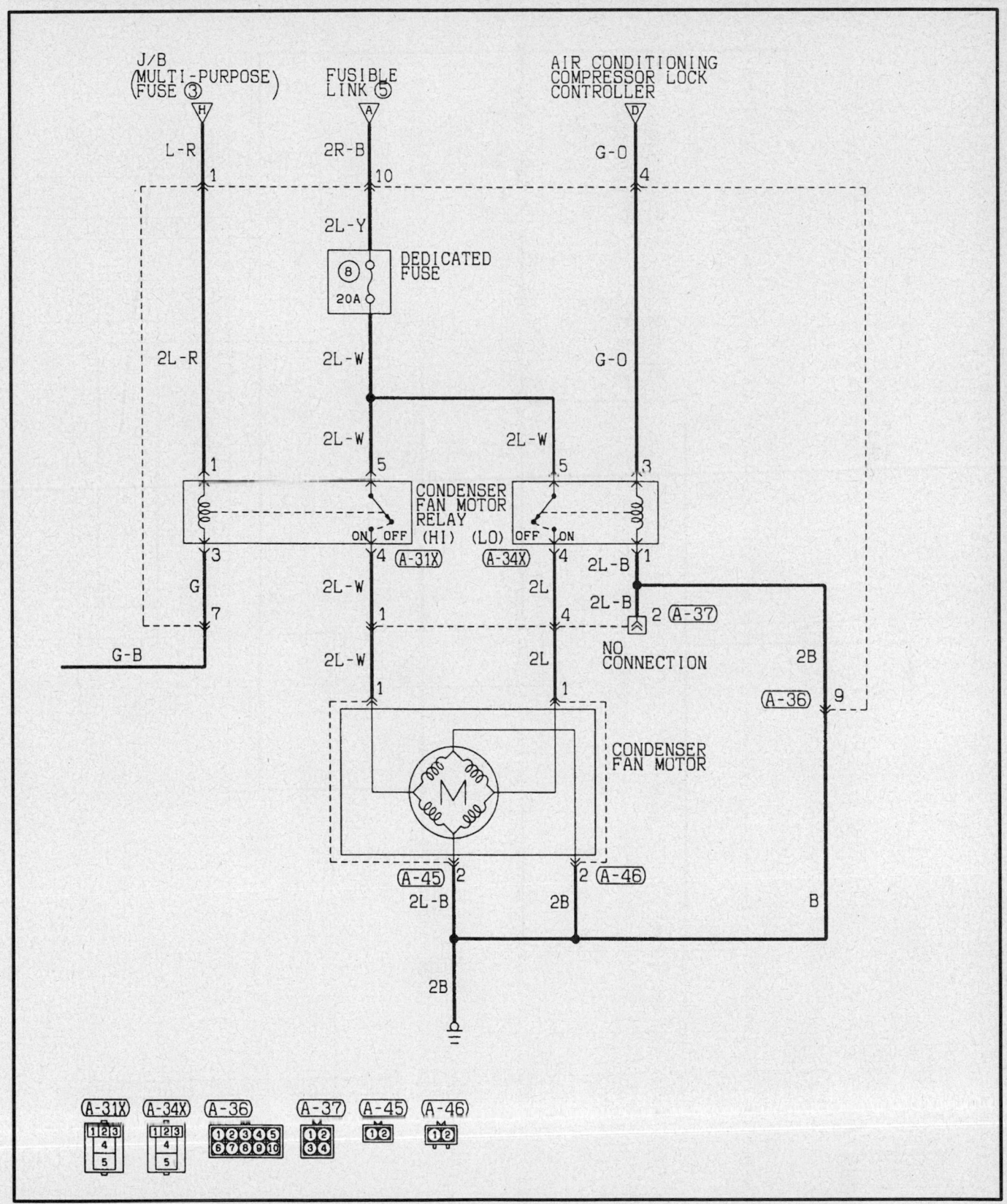

Wiring schematic — 1994—95 3000GT non-turbo (federal) with full auto air conditioning, Cont.

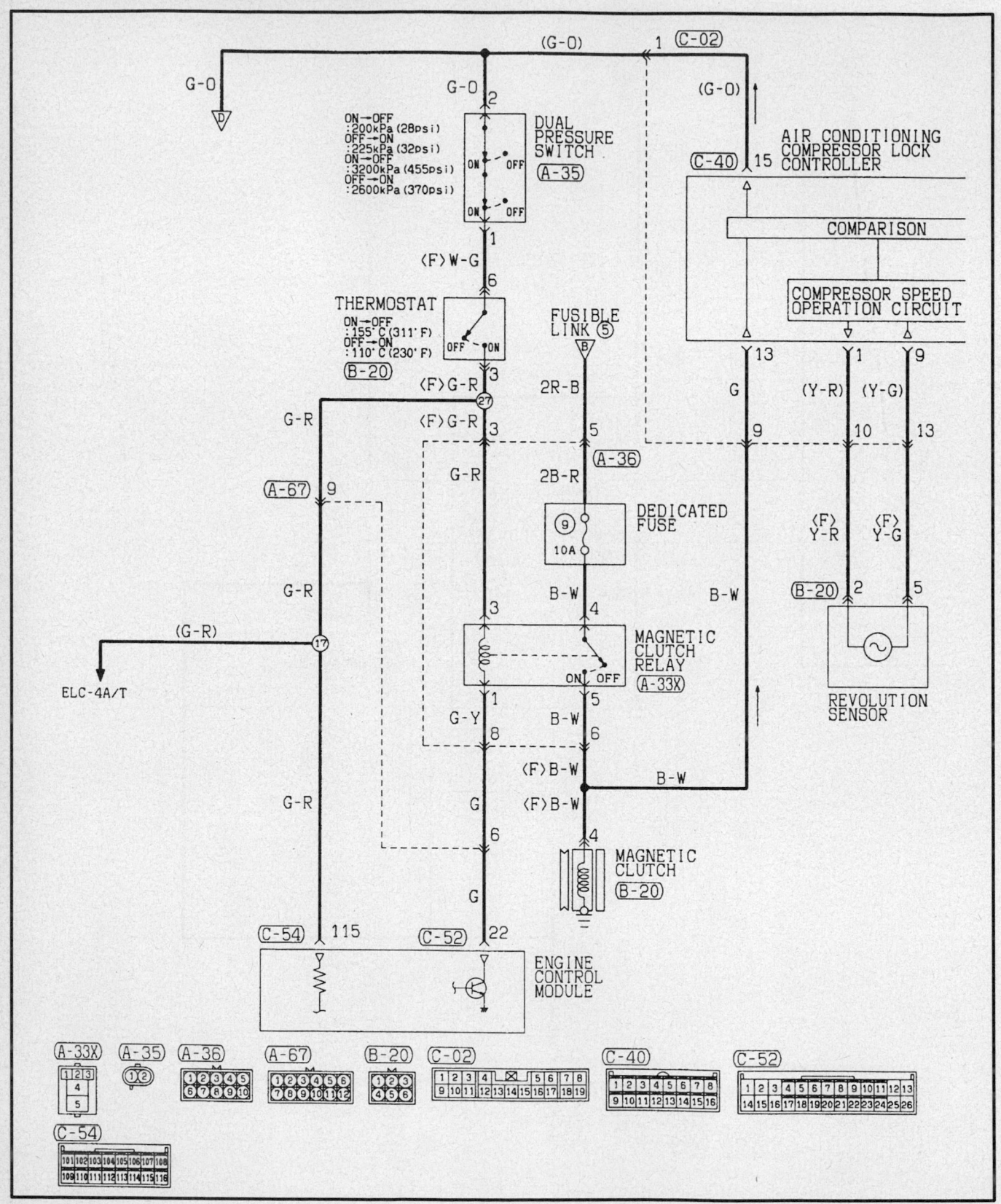

Wiring schematic — 1994–95 3000GT non-turbo (federal) with full auto air conditioning, Cont.

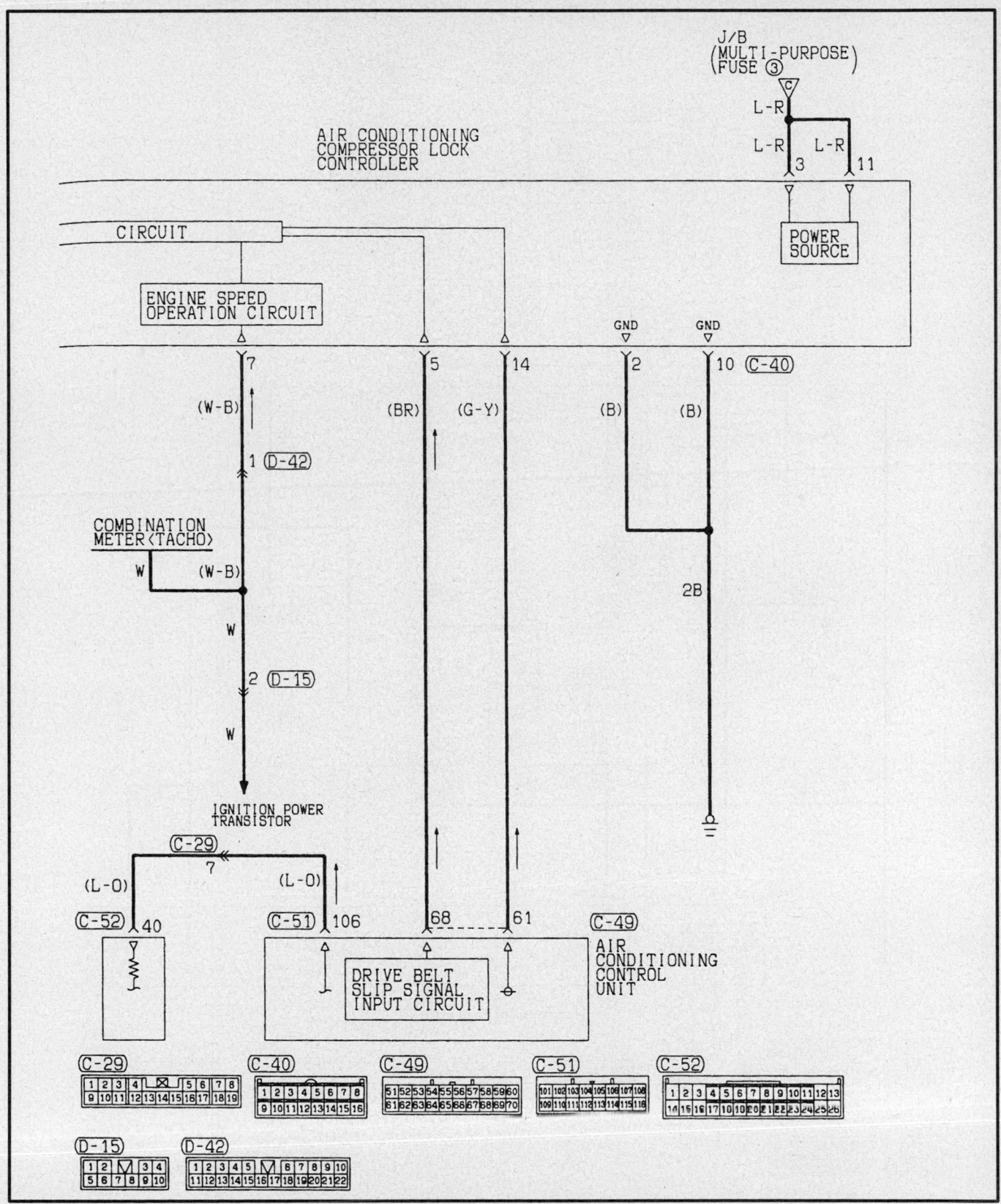

Wiring schematic — 1994-95 3000GT non-turbo (federal) with full auto air conditioning, Cont.

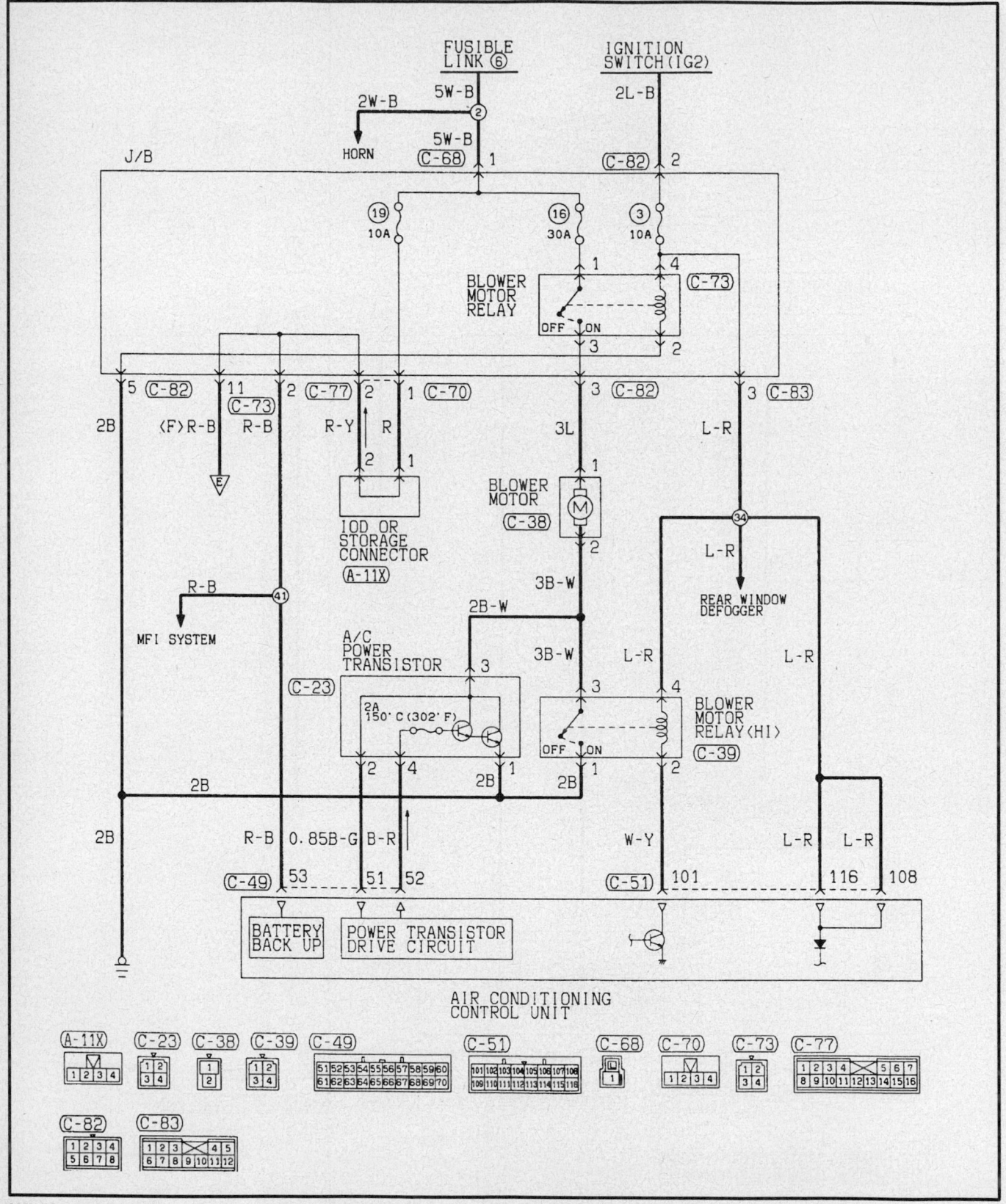

Wiring schematic — 1994—95 3000GT non-turbo (federal) with full auto air conditioning, Cont.

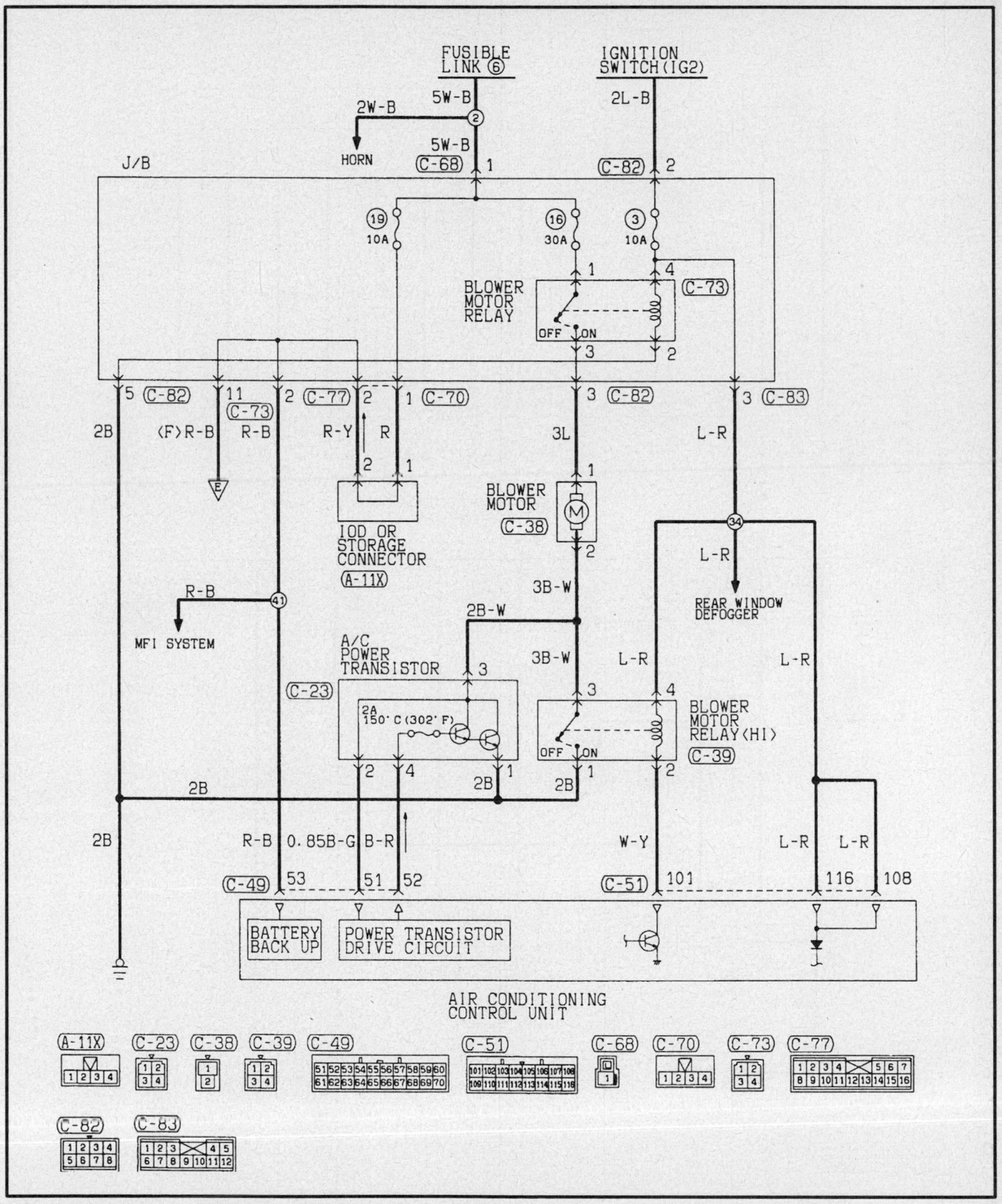

Wiring schematic — 1994–95 3000GT non-turbo (federal) with full auto air conditioning, Cont.

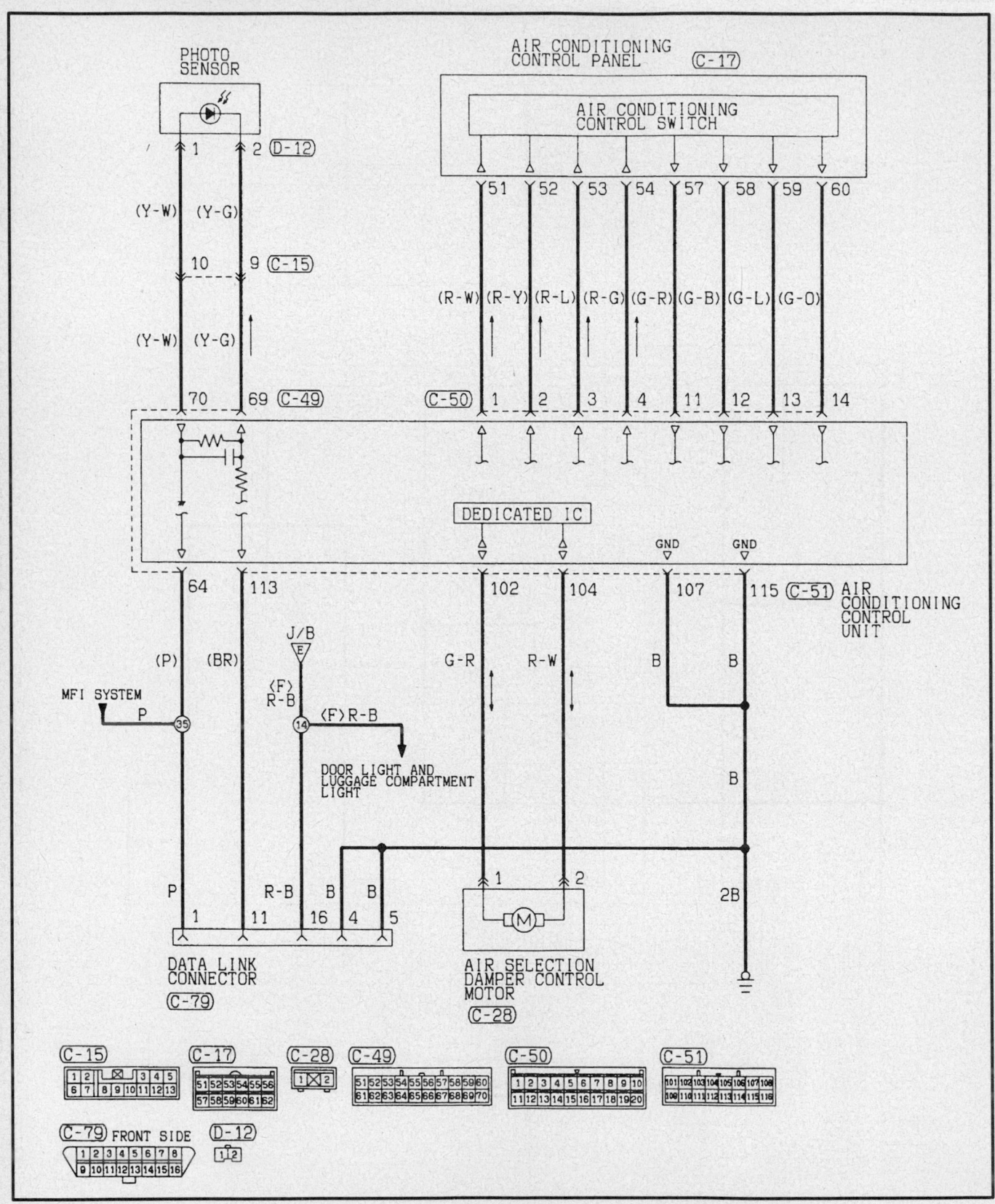

Wiring schematic — 1994–95 3000GT non-turbo (federal) with full auto air conditioning, Cont.

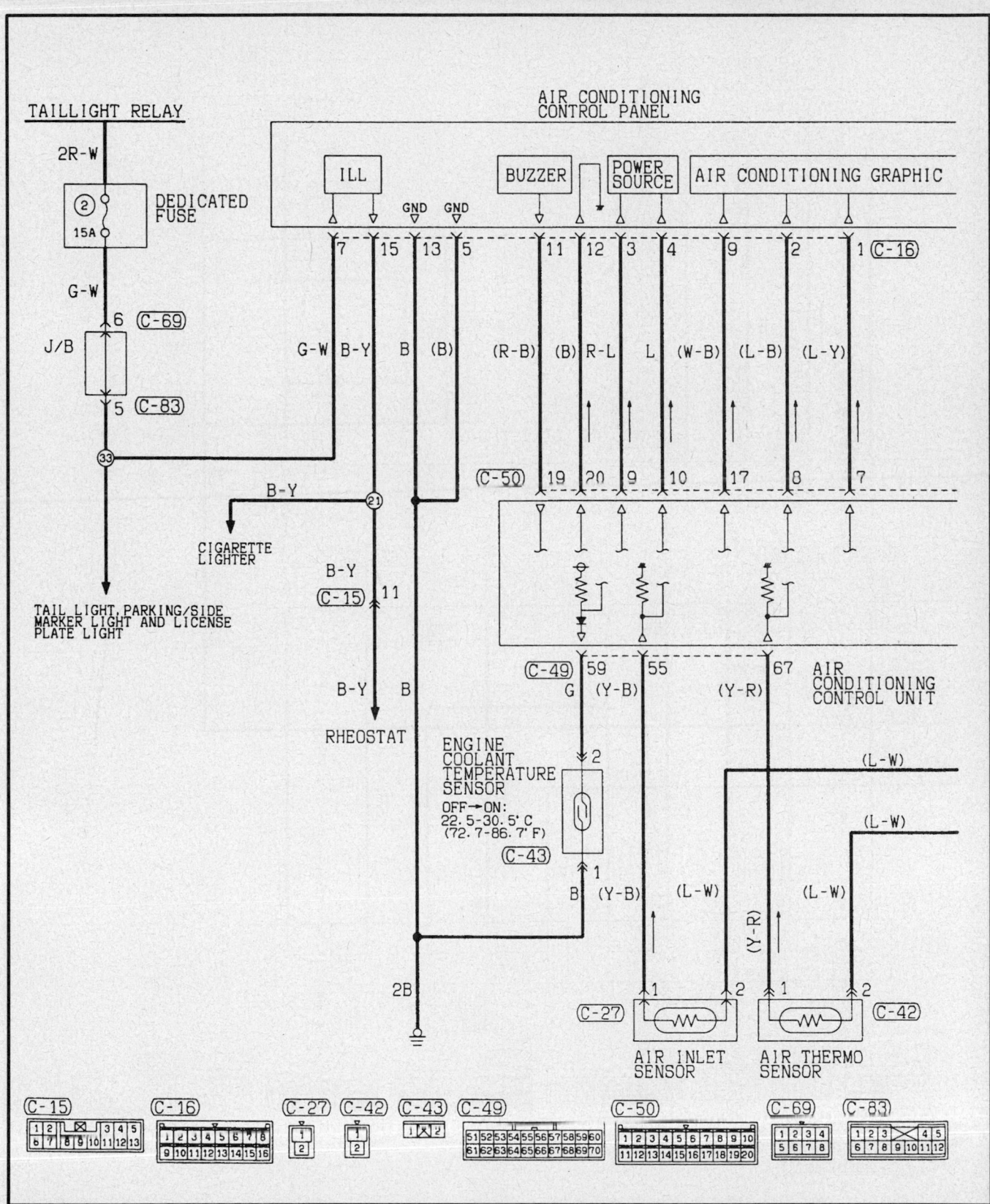

Wiring schematic — 1994-95 3000GT non-turbo (federal) with full auto air conditioning, Cont.

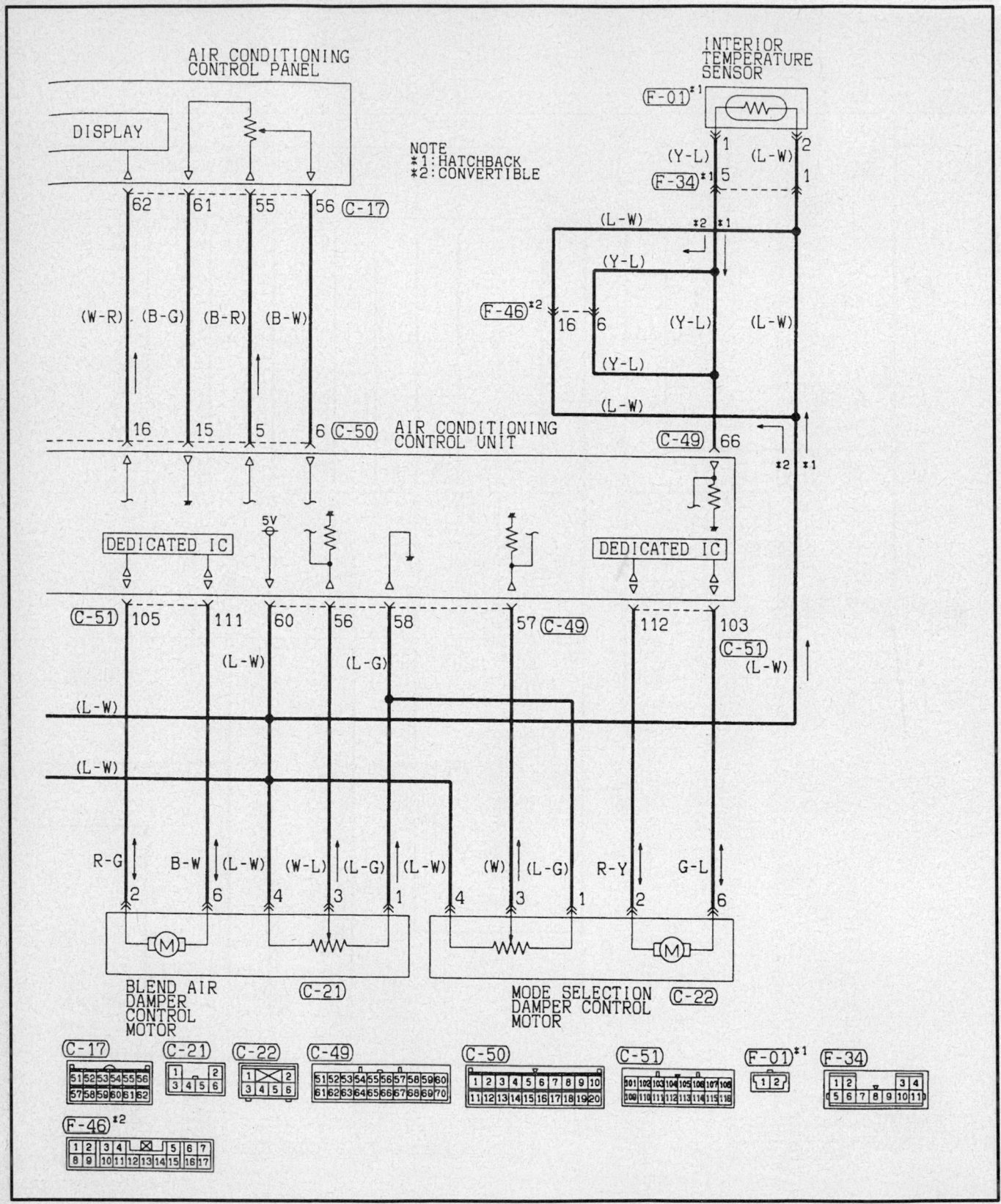

Wiring schematic — 1994—95 3000GT non-turbo (federal) with full auto air conditioning, Cont.

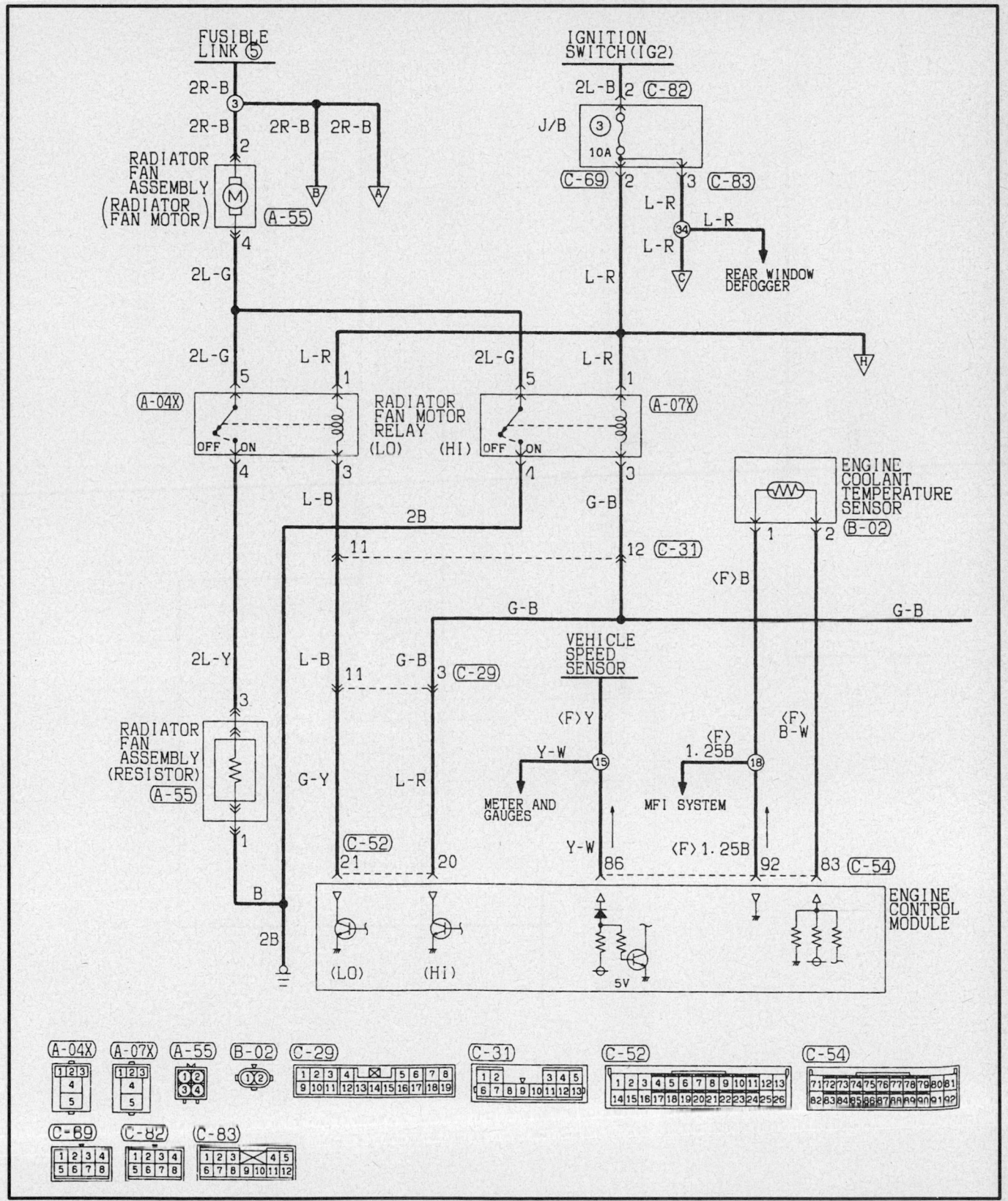

Wiring schematic — 1994–95 3000GT turbo (all) and non-turbo (california) with full auto air conditioning

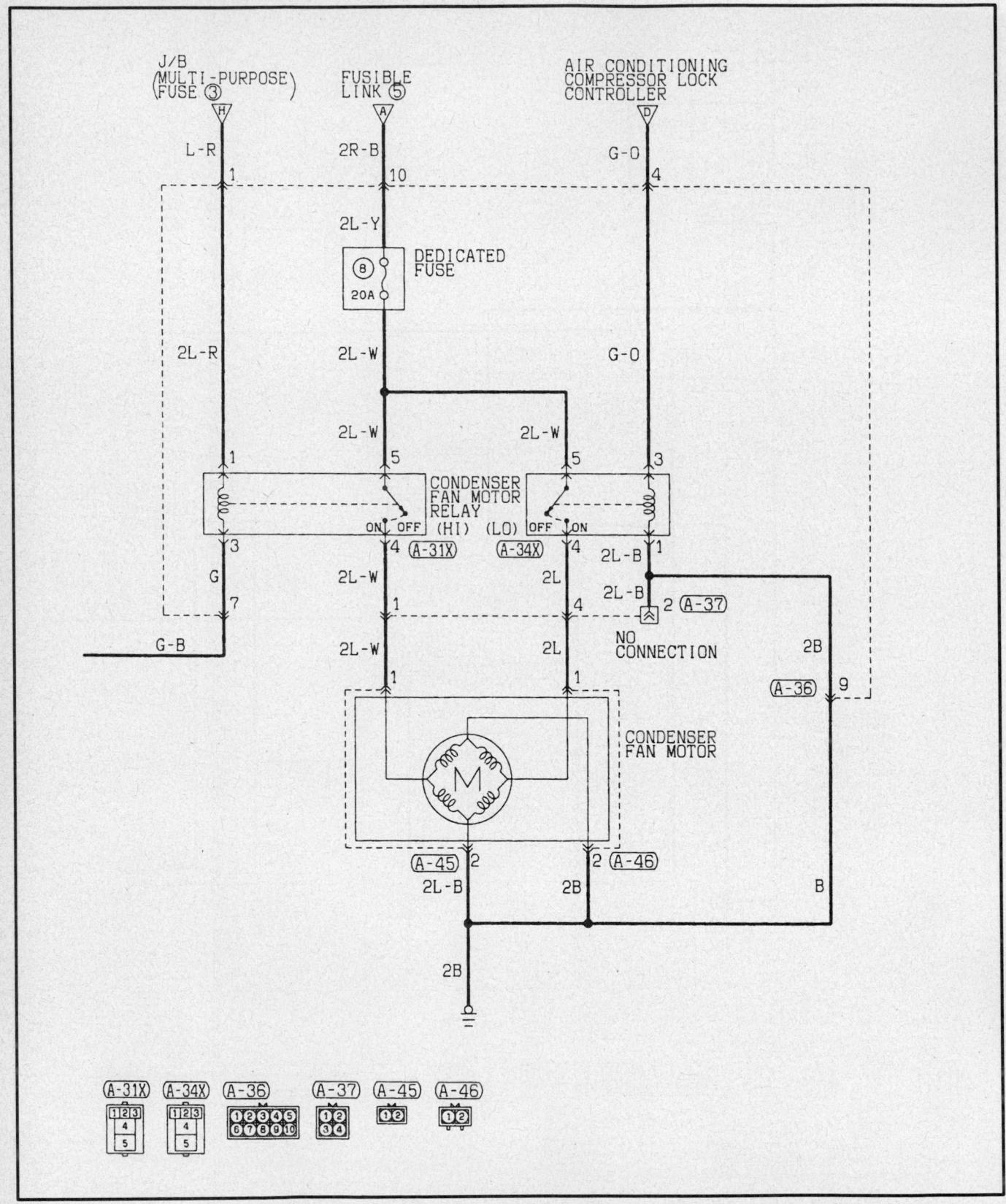

Wiring schematic — 1994–95 3000GT turbo (all) and non-turbo (california) with full auto air conditioning, Cont.

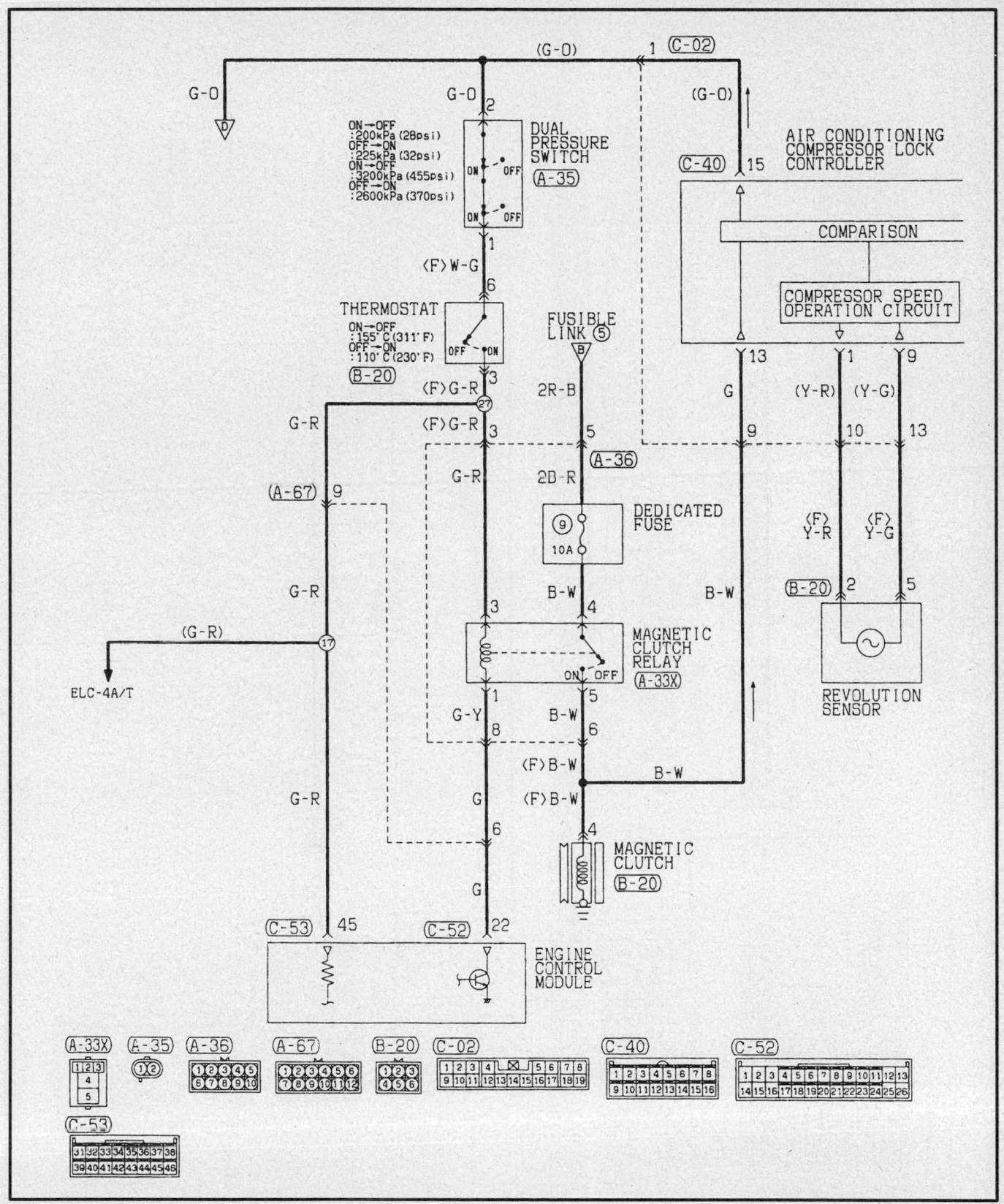

Wiring schematic — 1994–95 3000GT turbo (all) and non-turbo (california) with full auto air conditioning, Cont.

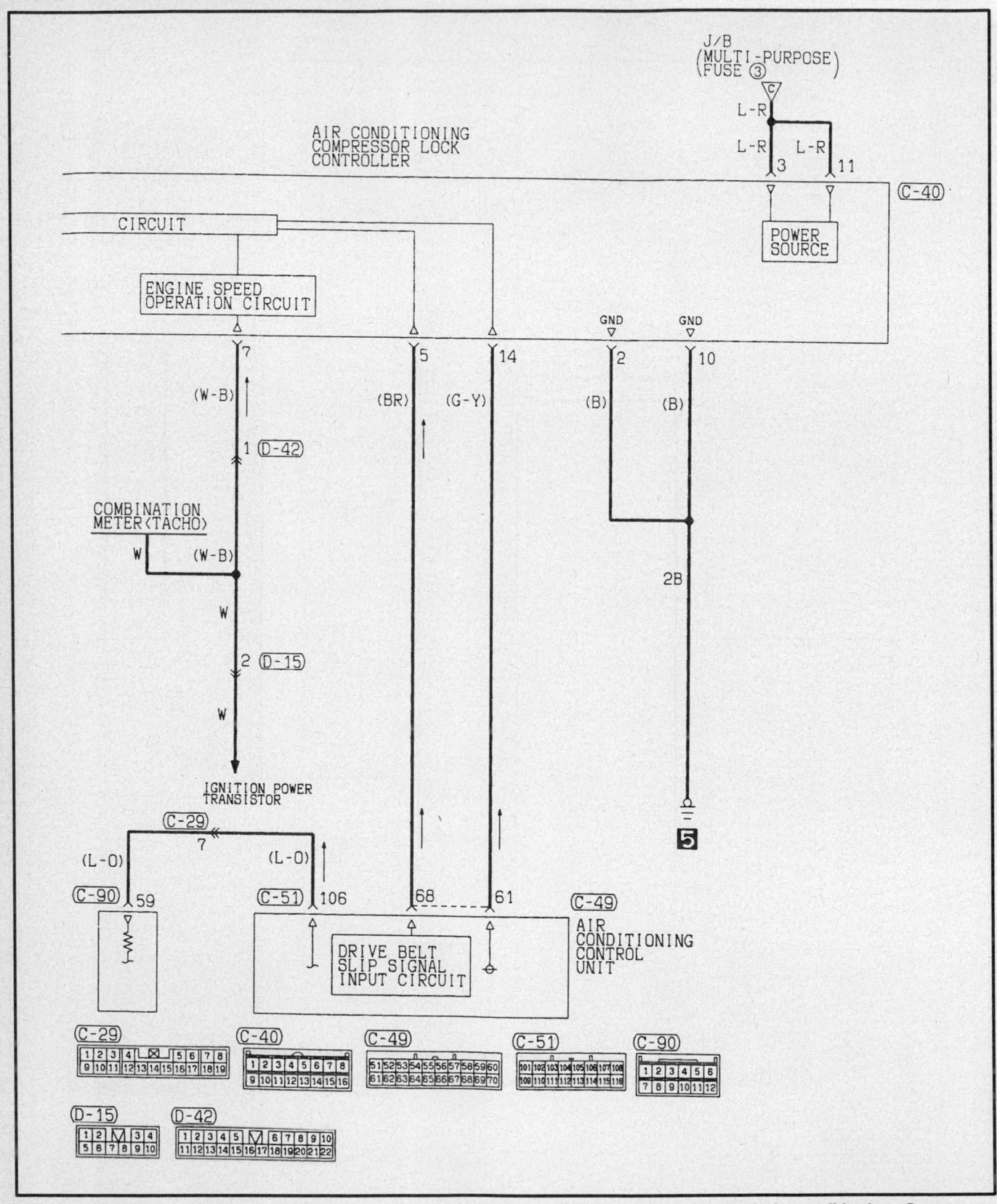

Wiring schematic — 1994–95 3000GT turbo (all) and non-turbo (california) with full auto air conditioning, Cont.

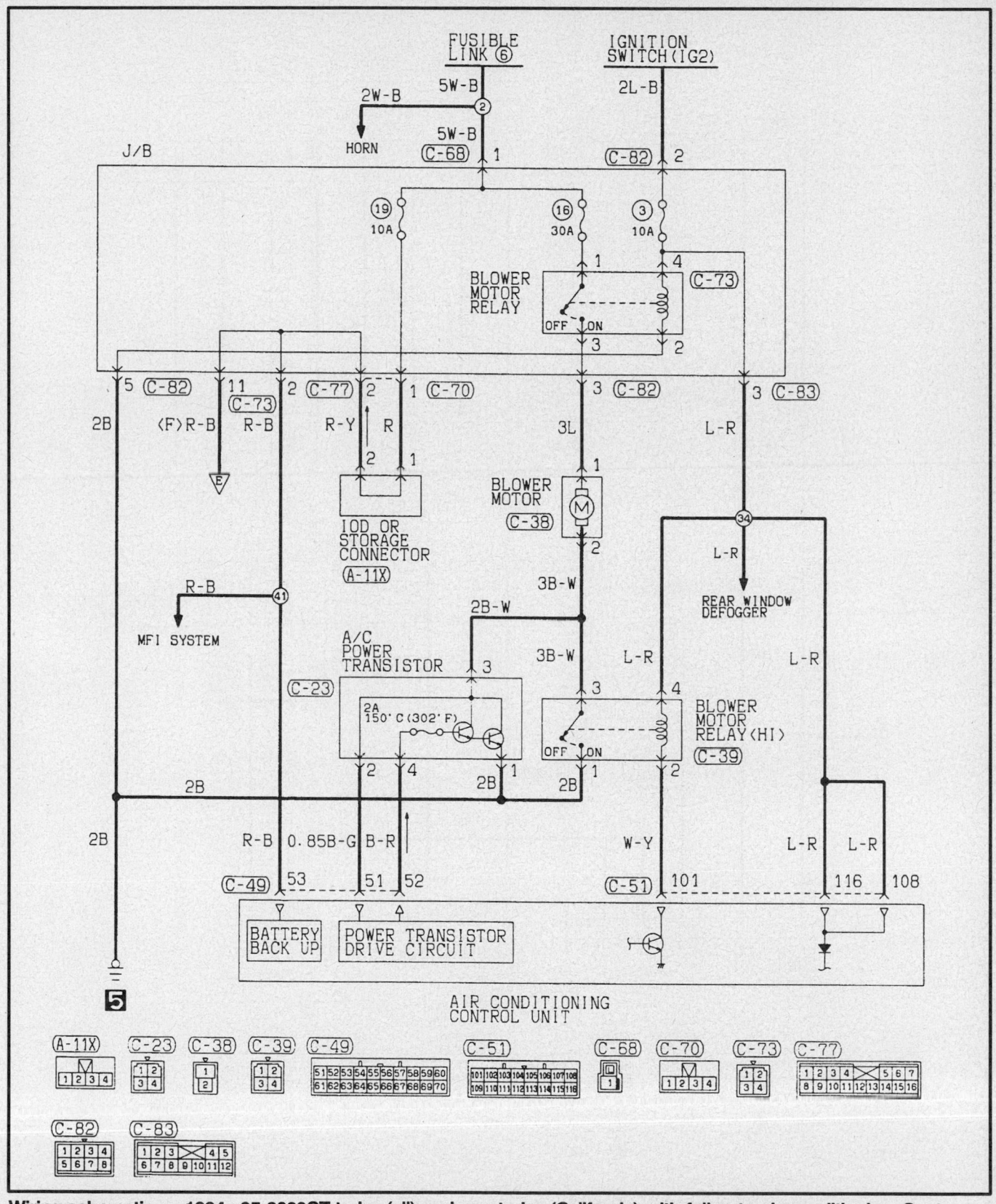

Wiring schematic — 1994–95 3000GT turbo (all) and non-turbo (California) with full auto air conditioning, Cont.

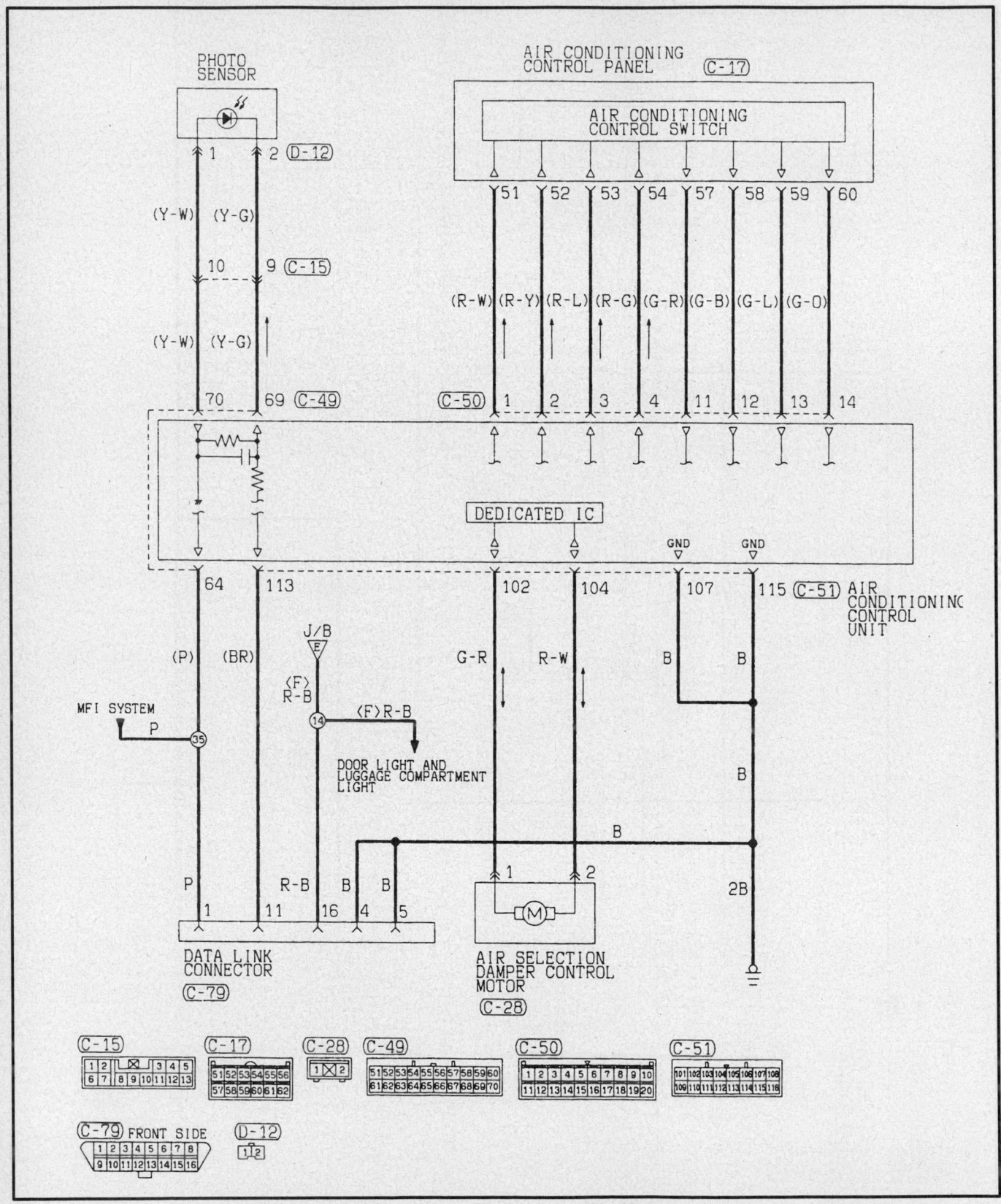

Wiring schematic — 1994–95 3000GT turbo (all) and non-turbo (california) with full auto air conditioning, Cont.

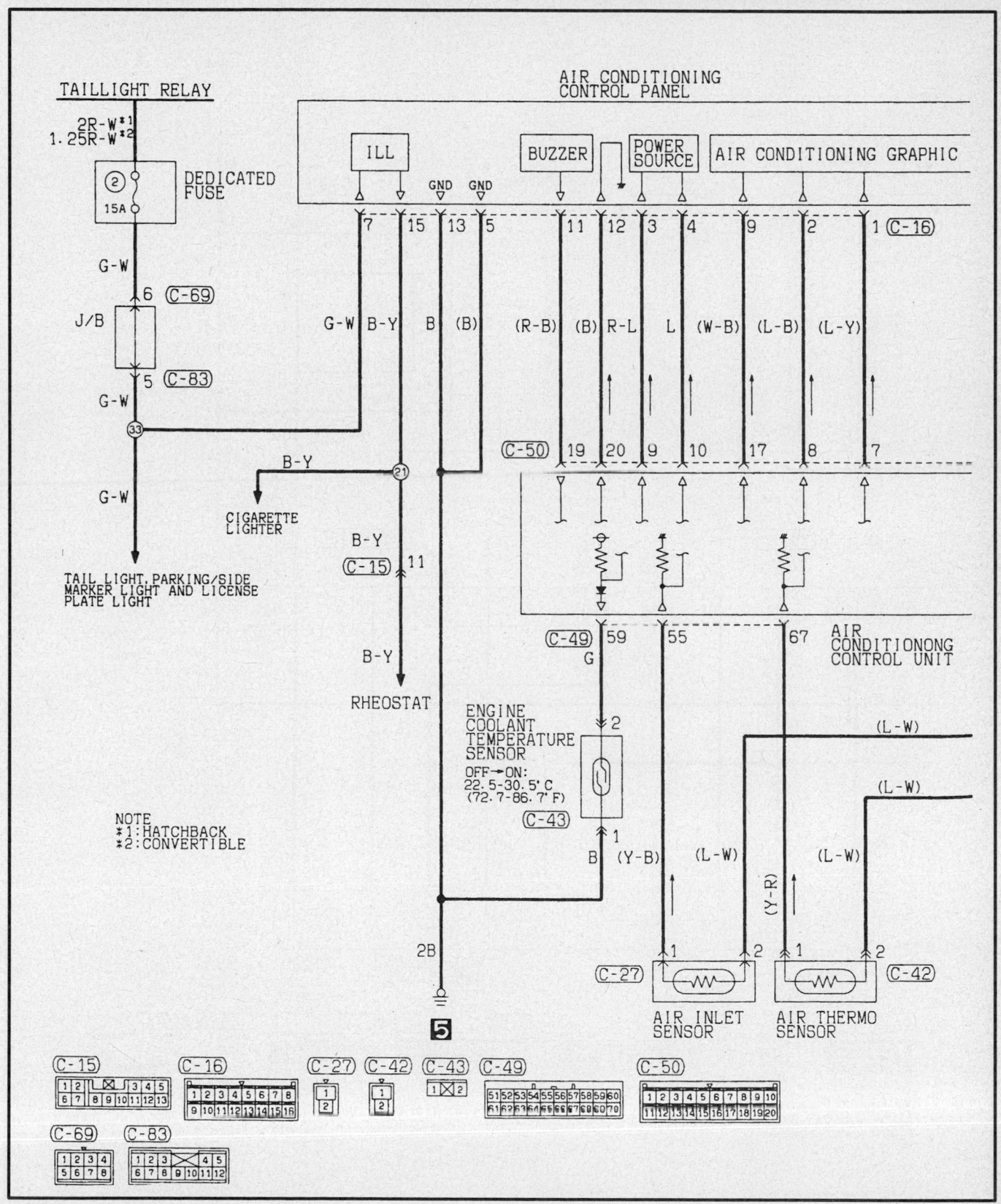

Wiring schematic — 1994—95 3000GT turbo (all) and non-turbo (california) with full auto air conditioning, Cont.

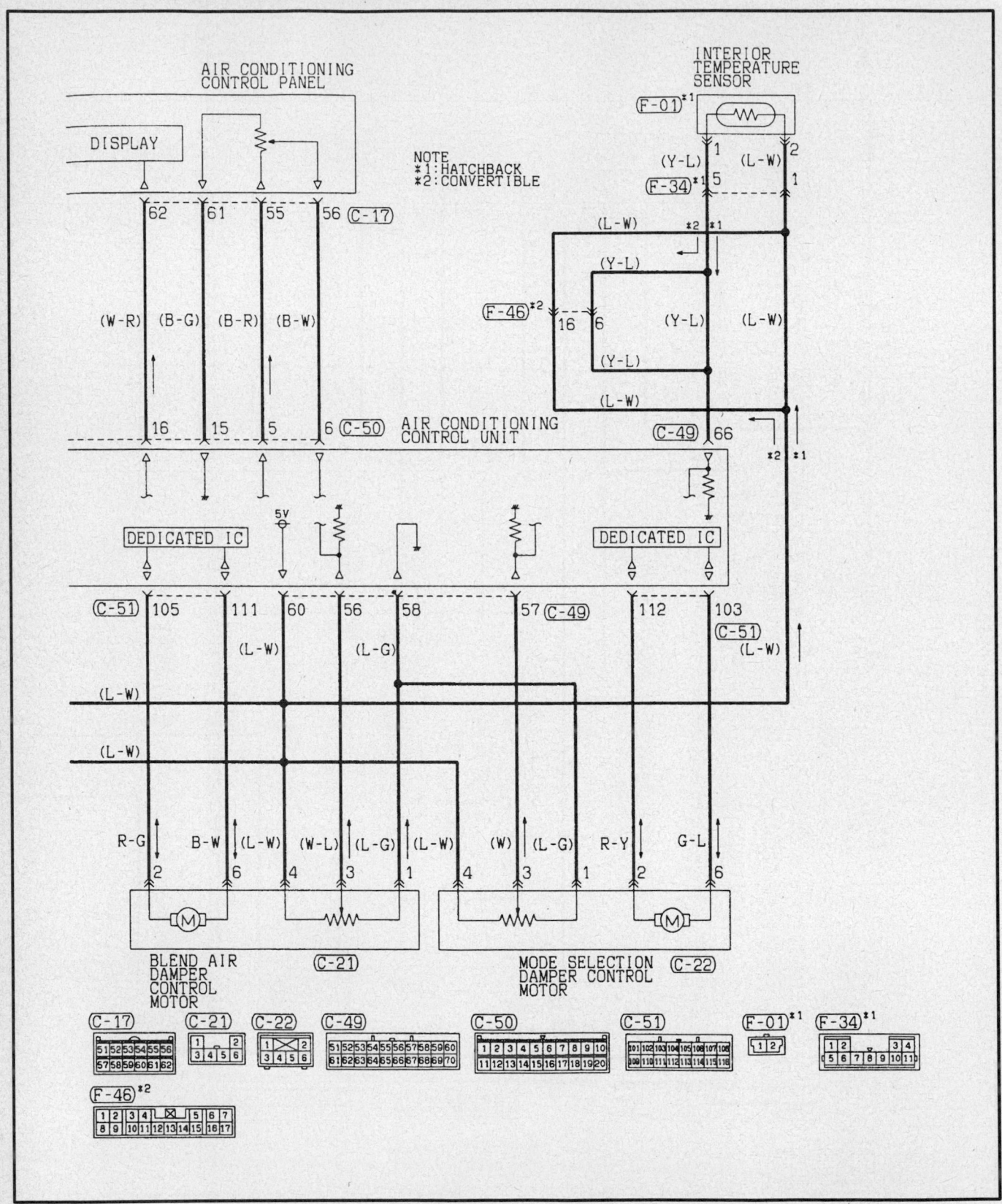

Wiring schematic — 1994–95 3000GT turbo (all) and non-turbo (california) with full auto air conditioning, Cont.

SPECIFICATIONS

ENGINE IDENTIFICATION

Year	Model	Engine Displacement Liters (cc)	Engine Series (ID/VIN)	Fuel System	No. of Cylinders	Engine Type
1993	Montero	3.0 (2972)	6G72	MPI	6	OHC
	Pick-up ①	2.4 (2350)	4G64	MPI	4	SOHC
	Pick-up ②	3.0 (2972)	6G72	MPI	6	OHC
	Expo	1.8 (1834)	4G93	MPI	4	SOHC
	Expo	2.4 (2350)	4G64	MPI	4	SOHC
1994	Montero	3.0 (2972)	6G72	MPI	6	SOHC
	Montero	3.5 (3497)	6G74	MPI	6	DOHC
	Pick-Up [1]	2.4 (2350)	4G64	MPI	4	OHC
	Pick-Up [2]	3.0 (2972)	6G72	MPI	6	OHC
	Expo	1.8 (1834)	4G93	MPI	4	SOHC
	Expo	2.4 (2350)	4G64	MPI	4	SOHC
1995	Montero	3.0 (2972)	6G72	MPI	6	SOHC
	Montero	3.5 (3497)	6G74	MPI	6	DOHC
	Pick-Up①	2.4 (2350)	4G64	MPI	4	OHC
	Pick-Up②	3.0 (2972)	6G72	MPI	6	OHC
	Expo	1.8 (1834)	4G93	MPI	4	SOHC
	Expo	2.4 (2350)	4G64	MPI	4	SOHC

OHC—Overhead Cam
SOHC—Single overhead Cam
DOHC—Dual overhead Cam
MPI—MultiPoint Injection
① RWD
② 4WD

REFRIGERANT CAPACITIES

Year	Model	Refrigerant (oz.)	Coolant Type	Compressor Oil (fl. oz.)	Compressor Type
1993	Montero	28	R12	2.7	Denso 10PA15
	Pick-Up	30	R12	4.4	FX80
	Expo①	30	R12	3.4	Denso 10PA15
	Expo②	30	R12	2.7	Denso 10PA15
1994	Montero	21–23	R134a	2.0–3.2	Denso 10PA15
	Pick-Up	26–28	R134a	4.1–4.8	Denso 10PA15
	Expo①	26.8	R134a	3.4–4.8	MSC 90C
	Expo②	26.8	R134a	2.0–3.2	Denso 10PA15
1995	Montero	21–23	R134a	2.0–3.2	Denso 10PA15
	Pick-Up	26–28	R134a	4.1–4.8	Denso 10PA15
	Expo①	26.8	R134a	3.4–4.8	MSC 90C
	Expo②	26.8	R134a	2.0–3.2	Denso 10PA15

① 1.8 Engine
② 2.4 Engine

AIR CONDITIONING BELT TENSION

Year	Model	Engine Liters (cc)	Belt Type	Specifications① New (lbs.)	Specifications① Used (lbs.)
1993	Montero	3.0 (2972)	V Belt	0.20–0.24	0.26–0.30
	Pick-Up	2.4 (2350)	V Belt	0.33–0.39	0.33–0.39
	Pick-Up	3.0 (2972)	V Belt	0.33–0.39	0.33–0.39
	Expo	1.8 (1834)	Serpentine	0.22–0.24	0.27–0.30
	Expo	2.4 (2350)	Serpentine	0.17–0.19	0.21–0.24
1994	Montero	3.0 (2972)	V Belt	0.26–0.32	0.35
	Montero	3.5 (3497)	V Belt	0.20–0.24	0.26–0.30
	Pick-Up	2.4 (2350)	V Belt	N/A	0.33–0.39
	Pick-Up	3.0 (2972)	V Belt	N/A	0.33–0.39
	Expo	1.8 (1834)	Serpentine	0.22–0.24	0.27–0.30
	Expo	2.4 (2350)	Serpentine	0.17–0.19	0.21–0.24
1995	Montero	3.0 (2972)	V Belt	0.26–0.32	0.35
	Montero	3.5 (3497)	V Belt	0.20–0.24	0.26–0.30
	Pick-Up	2.4 (2350)	V Belt	N/A	0.33–0.39
	Pick-Up	3.0 (2972)	V Belt	N/A	0.33–0.39
	Expo	1.8 (1834)	Serpentine	0.22–0.24	0.27–0.30
	Expo	2.4 (2350)	Serpentine	0.17–0.19	0.21–0.24

① Inches of deflection at center of belt using 22lbs. force

SYSTEM DESCRIPTION

General Information

The heater unit is located behind the center of the instrument panel with the blower housing and blend–air system. In the blend–air system, hot air and cool air are controlled by blend–air damper to make fine adjustments of temperature. The heater system is also designed as a bi–level heater in which a separator directs warm air to the windshield or to the floor and cool air through the panel outlet.

The temperature inside the vehicle is controlled by means of the temperature control lever, the position of which determines the opening of the blend–air damper and the resulting mixing ratio of cool and hot air is used to control the outlet temperature.

The air conditioning compressor coil will be energized when all of the following conditions are met:

1. The air conditioner switch on the control head is depressed.
2. The blower motor switch is not in the OFF position.
3. The low pressure or dual pressure switch is reading at least 30 psi (206 kPa) pressure.
4. The thermistor is sensing at least 37.4°F (3°C).
5. The engine coolant temperature sensor is reading less than 235°F (113°C).
6. On vehicles equipped with a compressor refrigerant temperature sensor, the compressor discharge side refrigerant temperature must be less than 347°F (175°C).

Service Valve Locations

The suction (low pressure side) service valve is located on the compressor on all vehicles. The discharge (high pressure side) service valve is located either on the compressor or near the compressor on the discharge line. A test of the system with the manifold gauge set attached to the service valves can reveal if system is operating properly, low on refrigerant or may have other faults.

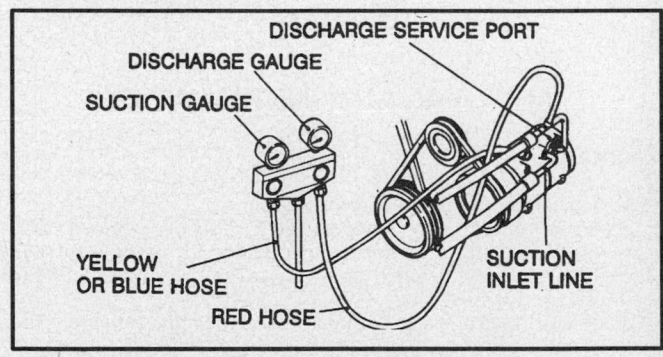

A/C service gauges connected to service ports

System Discharging

NOTE: R–12 refrigerant is a chloroflourocarbon which, when mishandled, can contribute to the depletion of the ozone layer in the upper atmosphere. Ozone filters out harmful radiation from the sun. In order to protect the ozone layer, an approved R–12 Recovery/Recycling machine that meets SAE standard J1991 should be employed when discharging the system. Follow the operating instructions provided with the approved equipment exactly to properly discharge the system.

R–134a refrigerant is a non–chloroflourocarbon with different chemical characteristics than R–12. Although it is designed to be less hazardous to the ozone layer of the atmosphere, it should still be discharged only into a recycling type machine and not vented to the atmosphere. Follow equipment manufacturer's instructions for this system. Use only dedicated equipment for R–134a systems. Avoid breathing R–134a vapors, as it can cause irritation. Never pressure test or leak test R–134a service equipment with compressed air. Some mixtures of air and R–134a have been shown to be combustible, especially at higher pressures. Such a mixture may result in fire or explosion. Use appropriate cautions.

System Evacuating

If the air conditioning system has been opened to the atmosphere, it should be air and moisture free before being recharged with refrigerant. Moisture and air mixed with refrigerant will raise the compressor head pressure, possibly damage the system's components and will reduce the performance of the system. Moisture will boil at normal room temperature when exposed to a vacuum. To evacuate the system, perform the following procedure:

1. Leak test the system and repair any leaks found.

2. Connect an approved charging station, Recovery/Recycling machine or manifold gauge set and vacuum pump to the discharge and suction ports. The red hose is normally connected to the discharge (high pressure) line and the blue hose is connected to the suction (low pressure) line.

3. Open the discharge and suction ports and start the vacuum pump. If the pump is not able to pull at least 26 in. Hg of vacuum, there is a leak that must be repaired before evacuation can occur.

4. Once the system has reached at least 26 in. Hg of vacuum, allow the system to evacuate for at least 10 minutes. The longer the system is evacuated, the more contaminants will be removed.

5. Close all valves and turn the pump **OFF**. If the system loses more than 2 in. Hg of vacuum after 15 minutes, there is a leak that should be repaired.

System Charging

NOTE: Be sure to use dedicated equipment while charging systems using R–134a refrigerant.

1. Connect an approved charging station, Recovery/Recycling machine or manifold gauge set to the discharge and suction ports. The red hose is normally connected to the discharge (high pressure) line and the blue hose is connected to the suction (low pressure) line.

2. Follow the instructions provided with the equipment and charge the system with the specified amount of refrigerant.

3. Perform a leak test.

SYSTEM COMPONENTS

Some vehicles are equipped with the Supplemental Inflatable Restraint or air bag system. The air bag system must be disabled before performing service on or around the air bag, instrument panel components, wiring and sensors. Failure to follow safety and disabling procedures could result in accidental air bag deployment, possible personal injury and unnecessary air bag system repairs.

Radiator

REMOVAL AND INSTALLATION

Montero

1. Disconnect negative battery cable.
2. Move temperature lever to **HOT** position, remove radiator cap, open drain plug and drain coolant. If using antifreeze recycling equipment, follow manufacturer's recommended procedures for draining.
3. If equipped with automatic transmission, remove under cover from radiator, then detach oil cooler hose.
4. Remove the air cleaner case.
5. Remove the upper radiator hose.
6. Remove the radiator fan shroud by removing 2 mounting bolts on each side.
7. Detach the reserve tank overflow hose, then take off the reserve tank.
8. Detach the upper end of the lower radiator hose, carefully lift out the radiator, then remove the lower hose.
To install:
9. Reattach lower end of the lower radiator hose, then position radiator into vehicle. Connect the upper end of the lower radiator hose.
10. Install the reserve tank and overflow hoses.

11. Position and attach the radiator fan shroud and attach radiator mounting bolts on each side.
12. Reinstall the upper radiator hose.
13. If equipped with automatic transmission, reattach the oil cooler line and install the lower cover.
14. Reinstall the air cleaner case.
15. Tighten drain plug and refill the system with coolant.
16. Connect the negative battery cable, run the vehicle until the thermostat opens, fill the radiator completely and check the automatic transmission fluid level, if necessary.
17. Check for leaks. Once the vehicle has cooled, recheck the coolant level.

Pick-up

1. Disconnect the negative battery cable.
2. Move temperature lever to **HOT** position, remove radiator cap, radiator plug and drain the coolant. Check for proper procedures on antifreeze recycling equipment.
3. Remove overflow hose.
4. Remove the upper and lower radiator hoses.
5. Remove radiator shroud assembly (2.4L engines have 2–piece shroud; 3.0L engine has 1–piece shroud and lower shroud plate which must be removed).
6. If equipped with automatic transmission, detach and plug the oil cooler line.
7. Remove the radiator.
8. Remove the overflow tube and the reserve tank.
To install:
9. Reattach reserve tank and overflow tube.
10. Carefully lower radiator into position and install attaching screws.
11. Connect the automatic transmission cooler hoses, if equipped.
12. Install the shroud assembly.
13. Connect the lower and upper hoses, then the coolant reserve tank hose.

14. Tighten drain plug and refill the system with coolant.

15. Connect the negative battery cable, run the vehicle until the thermostat opens, fill the radiator completely and check the automatic transmission fluid level, if equipped.

16. Check for leaks. Once the vehicle has cooled, recheck the coolant level.

Expo

1. Disconnect the negative battery cable.

2. Move the temperature lever to full **HOT** position.

3. Remove the radiator drain plug and cap. If using antifreeze recycling equipment, following manufacturer's draining instructions.

4. Remove the overflow tube from the radiator and reserve tank.

5. Remove the upper and lower radiator hoses.

6. Detach and plug the oil cooler line if equipped with automatic transmission.

7. Remove the radiator fan connector.

8. Remove the 2 upper radiator insulators.

9. Detach the 2 lower insulator mounting screws and carefully lift out the radiator assembly.

10. If equipped with A/C, remove the condenser fan motor assembly, detach the engine coolant temperature switch connector, remove the fan motor assembly.

11. Remove the radiator fan, fan motor and fan shroud.

To install:

12. Install the fan shroud, fan motor and fan.

13. On models with A/C, reattach the fan motor assembly and attach coolant switch connector, and install the condenser fan motor assembly.

14. Reattach the resistor assembly to the fan shroud.

15. Carefully lower the radiator assembly into place on the 2 lower insulators.

16. Attach the radiator fan connector and the condenser fan connector (if equipped).

17. Reconnect the automatic transmission cooler line, if disconnected.

18. Replace the lower and upper radiator hoses.

19. Reposition the reserve tank and attach the overflow tube.

20. Close drain plug and refill the system with coolant (follow manufacturer's instructions if using an antifreeze recycling machine).

21. Connect the negative battery cable, run the vehicle until the thermostat opens, fill the radiator completely and check the automatic transmission fluid level.

22. Check for leaks. Once the vehicle has cooled, recheck the coolant level.

Electric Cooling Fan

An electric condenser cooling fan and radiator cooling fan are mounted side–by–side on the radiator on Expo models. Each can be removed separately.

On Montero, an electric condenser cooling fan is mounted in front of the condenser and a thermal clutch type fan is attached directly to the water pump pulley.

The condenser on Pick–Up is cooled by the thermo–clutch type fan attached directly to the water pump pulley.

TESTING

─────── CAUTION ───────

Make sure the key is in the OFF position when checking the electric cooling fan. If not, the fan could turn ON at any time, causing serious personal injury.

Montero

1. Disconnect condenser fan motor connector and ground terminal **1**.

2. Apply battery voltage directly to terminal **2**.

3. Fan should turn smoothly without binding or noise.

4. Remove battery voltage and ground wires from connector, reattach connector to fan motor.

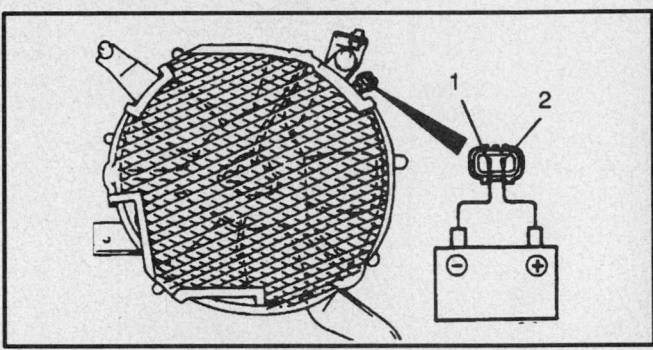

Checking condenser fan operation—Montero

Expo

1. Disconnect the negative battery cable.

2. Disconnect the condenser cooling fan connector.

3. Ground terminal **1**, then apply battery voltage to terminal **2**.

4. Make sure the fan runs smoothly, without abnormal noise or vibration.

5. Reconnect condenser cooling fan connector. Connect the negative battery cable.

REMOVAL AND INSTALLATION

Montero

1. Disconnect the negative battery cable.

2. Remove grille by removing 3 top and 3 bottom screws.

3. Disconnect the condenser fan connector.

4. Remove the fan assembly mounting bolts and take assembly out through grille opening.

5. The installation is the reverse of the removal procedure.

6. Connect the negative battery cable and check the fan for proper operation.

Expo

1. Disconnect the negative battery cable. Then detach fan connector and remove resistor from mounting.

2. Remove 2 upper mounting bolts and 1 lower mounting bolt attaching condenser fan shroud to radiator. Lift condenser fan assembly out of vehicle.

3. Remove 3 screws holding fan to motor assembly and remove fan.

4. Remove 3 mounting bolts holding center cover to back of shroud.

5. The installation is the reverse of the removal procedure.

6. Connect the negative battery cable and check the fan for proper operation.

Condenser

REMOVAL AND INSTALLATION

Montero

1. Disconnect the negative battery cable.

2. Properly discharge the air conditioning system following equipment manufacturer's procedures.

3. Remove the radiator grille by detaching 3 top and 3 bottom screws.

4. Remove the hood latch bracket and hood latch stay.

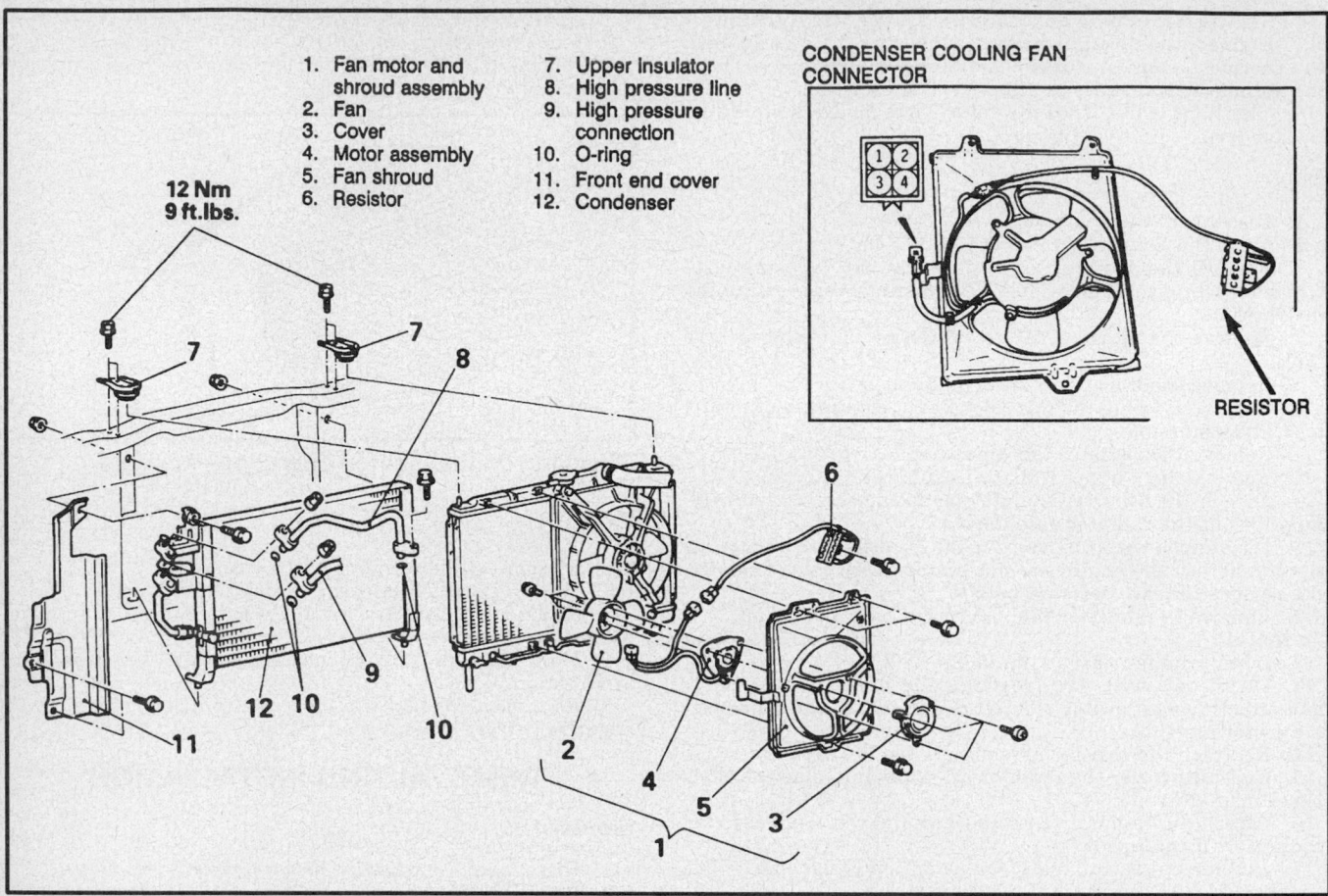

1. Fan motor and shroud assembly
2. Fan
3. Cover
4. Motor assembly
5. Fan shroud
6. Resistor
7. Upper insulator
8. High pressure line
9. High pressure connection
10. O-ring
11. Front end cover
12. Condenser

12 Nm
9 ft.lbs.

CONDENSER COOLING FAN CONNECTOR

RESISTOR

Condenser and fan assembly—Expo

5. Remove transmission oil cooler mounting bolt (for automatic transmission models), then remove engine oil cooler mounting bolts and brackets.

6. Remove condenser mounting side bolt. Using proper wrenches, disconnect and remove condenser high pressure line from across lower front of condenser.

7. Remove additional line connected to receiver/drier. Detach the receive/drier bracket and remove the receiver/drier.

8. Disconnect the fan motor connector and remove the fan motor assembly through the grille opening.

9. Detach additional high pressure line fitting near top of condenser and remove the attaching bracket.

10. Carefully remove the condenser, then detach the headlight side seal, frame side seal and the under seal.

To install:

11. Reattach the under seal, frame side seal and headlight side seal to the condenser.

12. Reposition the condenser.

13. Position high pressure line near top of condenser by installing the attaching bracket and reconnect line to condenser line, using new O-ring coated with clean refrigerant oil.

14. Install the condenser fan motor assembly and attach the connector.

15. Install receiver/drier, using new O-rings coated with clean refrigerant oil when reattaching high pressure line to receiver/drier. If receiver/drier is replaced, add 0.25 oz. of refrigerant oil during recharging.

16. Reinstall condenser side mounting bolt, then install engine oil cooler bracket and (if equipped) transmission oil cooler mounting bolt.

17. Install hood latch stay and bracket mounting bolt, then install grille with 3 upper and 3 lower mounting bolts.

18. Follow appropriate procedures to evacuate and recharge air conditioning system. Run system to ensure proper operation. Perform leak test, especially around condenser and condenser fittings.

Pick-Up

1. Disconnect the negative battery cable.

2. Properly discharge the air conditioning system.

3. Remove the grille assembly removing 3 screws across the top, 2 clips at each upper corner and 5 clips across the grille lower edge.

4. Using appropriate wrenches, remove the receiver/drier bracket holding receiver/drier to condenser. Remove the receiver/drier.

5. Cover the exposed ends of the refrigerant lines to minimize contamination.

6. Remove the condenser mounting bolts and remove the condenser through the grille opening.

To install:

7. Install the condenser with its mounting bolts.

8. Using new, lubricated O-rings, connect the refrigerant lines to the condenser and install receiver/drier. If installing a new receiver/drier, add 0.25 oz. of refrigerant oil during recharging.

9. Install the grille assembly.

10. Evacuate and recharge the air conditioning system. If the condenser was replaced, add 0.5 oz. of refrigerant oil during the recharge.

11. Connect the negative battery cable and check the entire climate control system for proper operation and leaks.

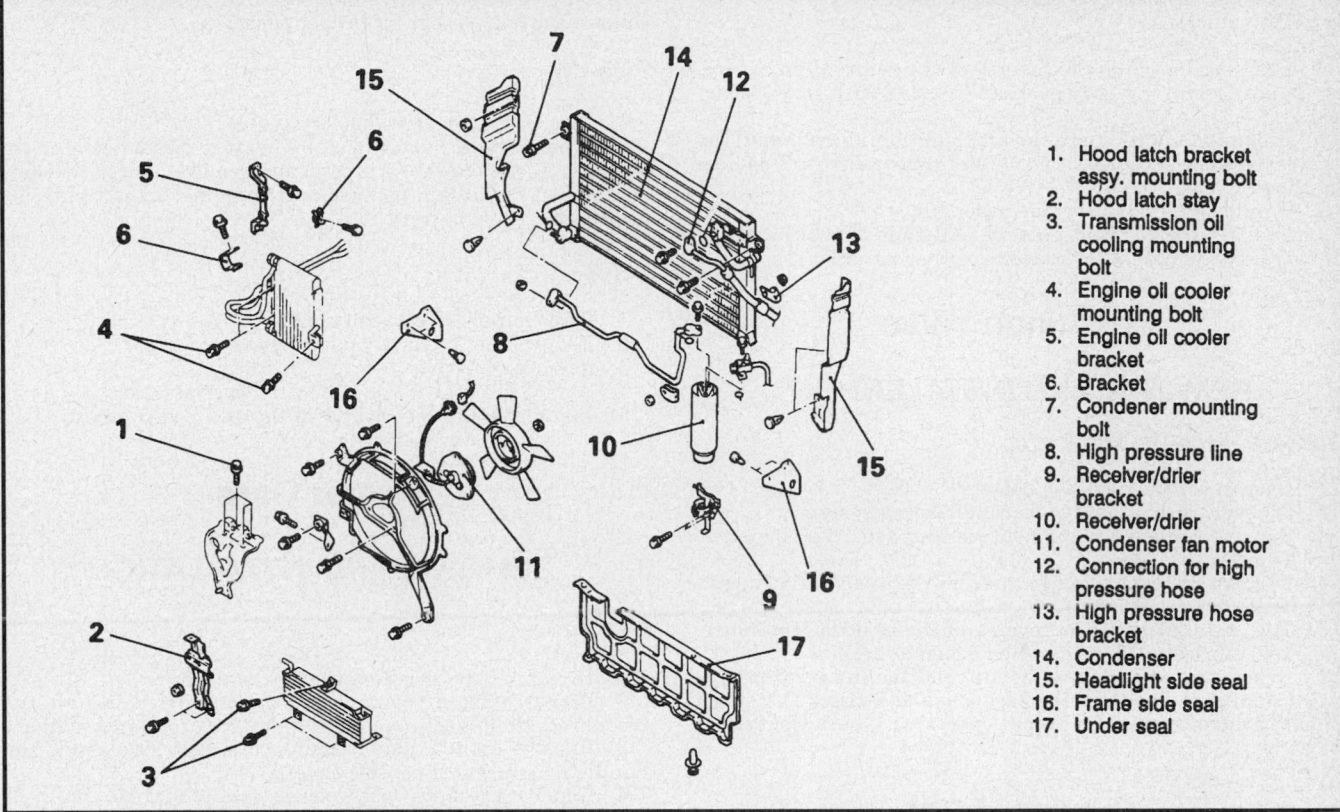

1. Hood latch bracket assy. mounting bolt
2. Hood latch stay
3. Transmission oil cooling mounting bolt
4. Engine oil cooler mounting bolt
5. Engine oil cooler bracket
6. Bracket
7. Condener mounting bolt
8. High pressure line
9. Receiver/drier bracket
10. Receiver/drier
11. Condenser fan motor
12. Connection for high pressure hose
13. High pressure hose bracket
14. Condenser
15. Headlight side seal
16. Frame side seal
17. Under seal

Condenser, receiver/drier and cooling fan—Montero

Expo

1. Disconnect the negative battery cable.
2. Properly discharge the air conditioning system.
3. Remove the grille assembly by removing the mounting screws and clips top and bottom.
4. Using 2 flare nut wrenches, disconnect the refrigerant lines from the condenser. Cover the exposed ends of the lines to minimize contamination.
5. Remove the condenser mounting bolts from the back side of the condenser, and remove the condenser through the grille opening.

To install:

6. Install the condenser and secure with its mounting bolts.
7. Using new, lubricated O-rings, connect the refrigerant lines to the condenser.
8. Retattach the grille assembly.
9. Evacuate and recharge the air conditioning system. If the condenser was replaced, add 1 oz. of refrigerant oil during the recharge.
10. Connect the negative battery cable and check the entire climate control system for proper operation and leaks.

Compressor

REMOVAL AND INSTALLATION

Montero, Pick-Up and Expo

1. Disconnect the negative battery cable.
2. Properly discharge the air conditioning system.
3. On Montero, to gain clearance, remove battery, battery tray and radiator shroud.
4. On Expo with 1.8L engine, remove the left lower panel cover near compressor.

5. On all models, relieve the tension and remove the compressor drive belt from the clutch pulley. Disconnect the electrical connector from the temperature/pressure switch on the compressor.
6. Disconnect the refrigerant lines from the compressor and discard the O-rings. Cover the exposed ends of the lines and openings to the compressor to minimize contamination.
7. Remove the compressor mounting bolts, compressor and bracket.

To install:

8. Check and adjust level of compressor oil. Install the compressor mounting bracket and mounting bolts. Connect the clutch coil connector.
9. Using new, lubricated O-rings, connect the refrigerant lines to the compressor.
10. Wrap the drive belt around the pulley and adjust to specification, using tensioner bolt.
11. On Expo with 1.8L engine, replace the lower left cover or on Montero, replace radiator shroud, battery tray and battery.
12. Evacuate and recharge the air conditioning system.
13. Connect the negative battery cable and check the entire climate control system for proper operation and leaks.

Receiver/Drier

REMOVAL AND INSTALLATION

Montero, Pick-Up and Expo

1. Disconnect the negative battery cable.
2. Properly discharge the air conditioning system.
3. On Montero and Pick-Up, remove the grille assembly to gain access to receiver.
4. On all models, disconnect the refrigerant lines from the receiver/drier assembly. Cover the exposed ends of the lines to minimize contamination.

5. Remove the mounting bolts and remove the receiver/drier from the vehicle.
To install:
6. The installation is the reverse of the removal procedure, using new O–rings at fittings. Coat O–rings with clean refrigerant oil.
7. Evacuate and recharge the air conditioning system. If the receiver/drier was replaced, add 0.25 oz. of refrigerant oil during the recharge.
8. If removed, reinstall grille assembly.
9. Connect the negative battery cable and check the entire climate control system for proper operation and leaks.

Expansion Valve

REMOVAL AND INSTALLATION

Montero, Pick-Up and Expo

1. Disconnect the negative battery cable.
2. Properly discharge the air conditioning system.
3. Remove the evaporator housing and separate the upper and lower cases.
4. Remove the expansion valve from the evaporator lines.
To install:
5. The installation is the reverse of the removal procedure. Use new, lubricated O–rings when assembling.
6. Evacuate and recharge the air conditioning system.
7. Connect the negative battery cable and check the entire climate control system for proper operation. Check the system for leaks.

Blower Motor

REMOVAL AND INSTALLATION

Montero

1. Disconnect the negative battery cable.
2. Remove the floor air outlet duct.
3. Working under the blower housing, disconnect the blower connector, remove blower motor mounting screws and lower the blower motor out of the assembly.
4. Installation is the reverse of the removal procedure.

Pick-Up and Expo

1. Disconnect negative battery cable.
2. On Expo, remove lap air duct, glove box, blower resistor, speaker fascia and glove box frame.
3. On all models, from under the right side of the instrument panel, remove blower motor mounting screws, lower the motor assembly and detach the blower motor wiring.
4. When installing, be sure mounting gasket is in good shape and properly positioned.
5. Reconnect negative battery cable.

Blower Motor Resistor

REMOVAL AND INSTALLATION

Montero

1. Disconnect the negative battery cable.
2. Remove the floor air duct.
3. Disconnect the wire harness from the resistor.
4. Remove the mounting screws and remove the resistor.
5. The installation is the reverse of the removal procedure. Make sure the seal is intact when installing.

6. Connect the negative battery cable and check the entire climate control system for proper operation.

Pick-Up

1. Disconnect negative battery cable.
2. From behind blower motor housing, disconnect resistor wiring, remove mounting screws and remove blower resistor.
3. When installing, be sure wiring connector is tight. Reconnect negative battery cable.

Expo

1. Remove negative battery cable.
2. Remove lap air duct beneath glove box.
3. Remove glove box.
4. Detach resistor wiring, then remove resistor.
5. Installation is the reverse of the removal procedure.

Heater Core

REMOVAL AND INSTALLATION

Montero

1. Disconnet the negative battery cable.
2. Properly drain coolant from system. If using an antifreeze recycling machine, follow manufacturer's instructions.
3. Remove switch panel, connectors, left side trim, shift handle(s) and center console covers.
4. Remove the hood lock release handle and the fuel filler door lock release handle.
5. Remove the lower left instrument panel cover and then the right speaker cover.
6. Remove the glove box stopper, then take out the glove box by detaching 2 lower retaining screws.
7. Remove the heater control assembly and radio cover panel, then detach and remove the control assembly and radio.
8. Remove the plug from the top rear of the instrument cluster bezel, remove 2 retaining screws from the front of the bezel and remove the cluster assembly with bezel.
9. Detach the instrument cluster.
10. Remove the speedometer cable adapter from the instrument cluster.
11. Remove upper and lower covers from steering column.
12. Remove the clock or clock opening plate from the instrument panel, then take off the fascia for the right and left defroster outlets.
13. Remove the door mirror control switch.
14. Take out both front speakers.
15. Remove the instrument panel lighting rheostat, then remove the rear wiper switch and the door lock switch.
16. Detach the blend air door cable.
17. Disconnet the wiring harness connector from the steering column multi–function switch, then remove the steering column retaining bolts and lower the steering column clear of the instrument panel.
18. Remove 9 retaining bolts and instrument panel.
19. Remove the connection for the water hoses from the firewall side.
20. Remove both floor air ducts and the lap air duct from the left side of the housing assembly.
21. If equipped with A/C, remove the evaporator housing mounting bolt from the top left of the housing and the mounting nut from the lower edge of the housing. If not equipped with A/C, remove right side attaching duct.
22. Remove the center air duct assembly (intake/defrost duct).
23. Unscrew 4 screws and remove the center reinforcement piece.

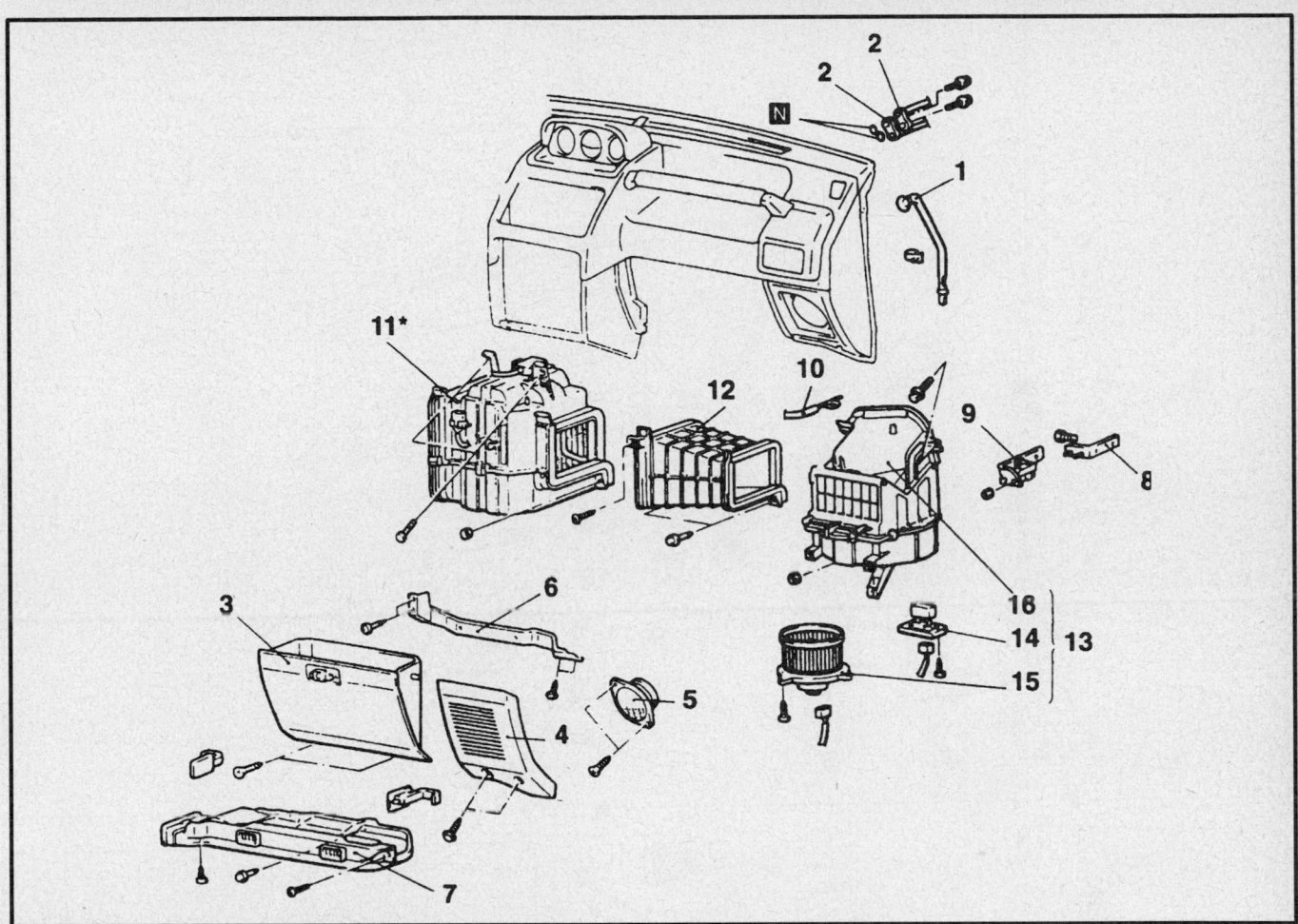

Blower motor and related components—Montero

24. Take out 2 top retaining bolts and 2 bottom edge retaining nuts and take out the heater assembly.

25. The heater core can now be extracted through the top opening of the heater assembly housing.

To install:

26. Carefully insert the heater core into the housing and remount the housing with 2 bolts at top and 2 nuts and bottom.

27. Install the center reinforcement bracket.

28. Install the upper center intake/defroster duct.

29. Install right side attaching duct or evaporator mounting bolt and nut as removed.

30. Attach the lap air outlet, then both floor air ducts.

31. Attach both heater hoses at firewall connection.

32. Position and attach the instrument panel assembly.

33. Raise steering column to position and install attaching bolts, then reconnect multi-function switch connector.

34. Attach blend air door control cable.

35. Reinstall the door lock switch, rear wiper switch and lighting rheostat.

36. Install both front speakers.

37. Install the door mirror control switch, replace the defroster duct covers and install the clock (or clock cover).

38. Position and attach the top and bottom steering column covers.

39. Attach the speedometer cable adapter to the back of the combination meter cluster, position the cluster, install the cluster bezel assembly, and replace the bezel top screw plug.

40. Install the radio assembly and heater control assembly, and attach the center panel cover.

41. Attach the glove box and stopper, then replace the right and left speaker covers.

42. Position and attach the fuel filler release handle and the hood lock release handle.

43. Install the floor console assembly and connectors.

44. Refill the cooling system, attach negative battery cable, and check system operation.

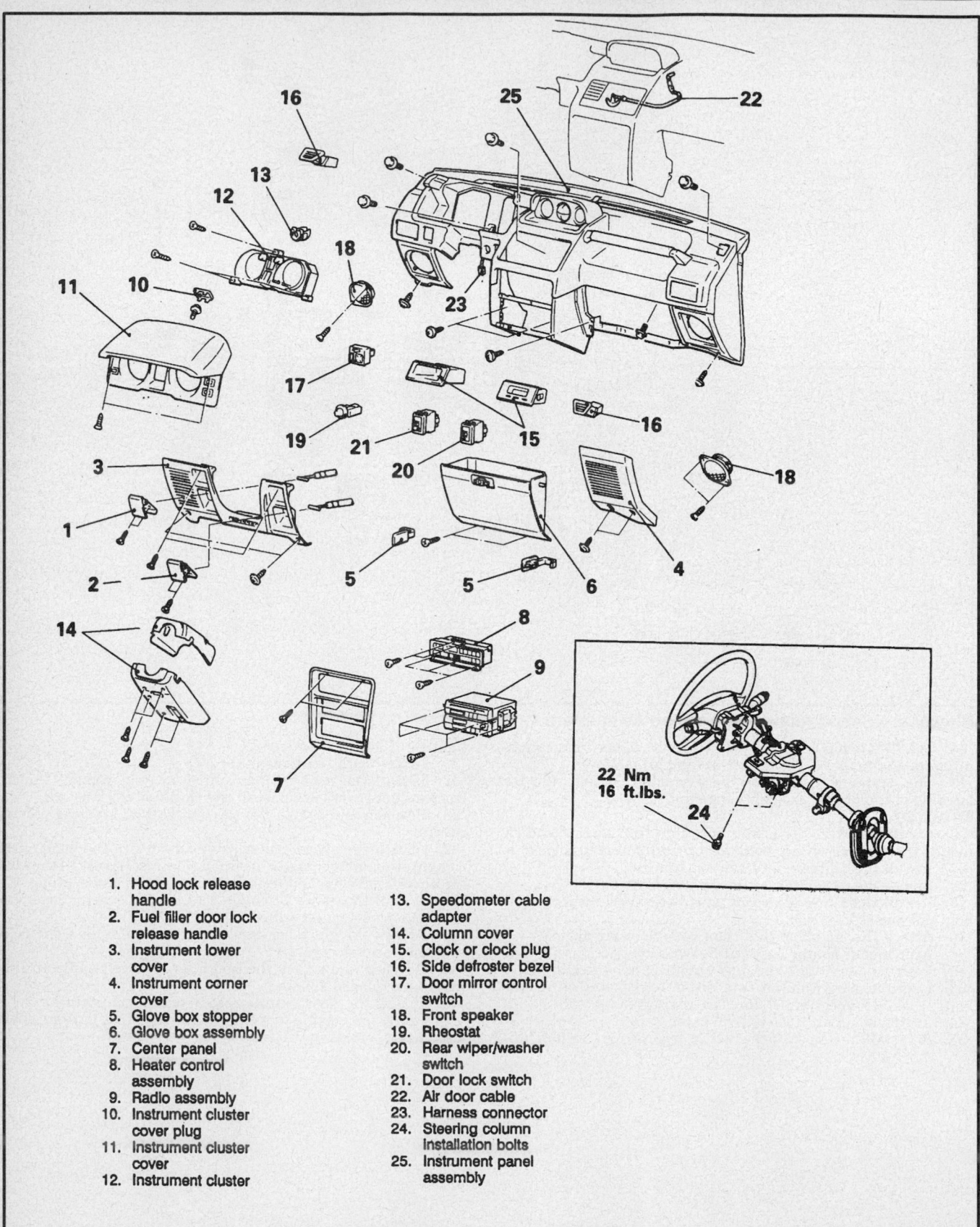

1. Hood lock release handle
2. Fuel filler door lock release handle
3. Instrument lower cover
4. Instrument corner cover
5. Glove box stopper
6. Glove box assembly
7. Center panel
8. Heater control assembly
9. Radio assembly
10. Instrument cluster cover plug
11. Instrument cluster cover
12. Instrument cluster
13. Speedometer cable adapter
14. Column cover
15. Clock or clock plug
16. Side defroster bezel
17. Door mirror control switch
18. Front speaker
19. Rheostat
20. Rear wiper/washer switch
21. Door lock switch
22. Air door cable
23. Harness connector
24. Steering column installation bolts
25. Instrument panel assembly

Exploded view of the instrument panel—Montero

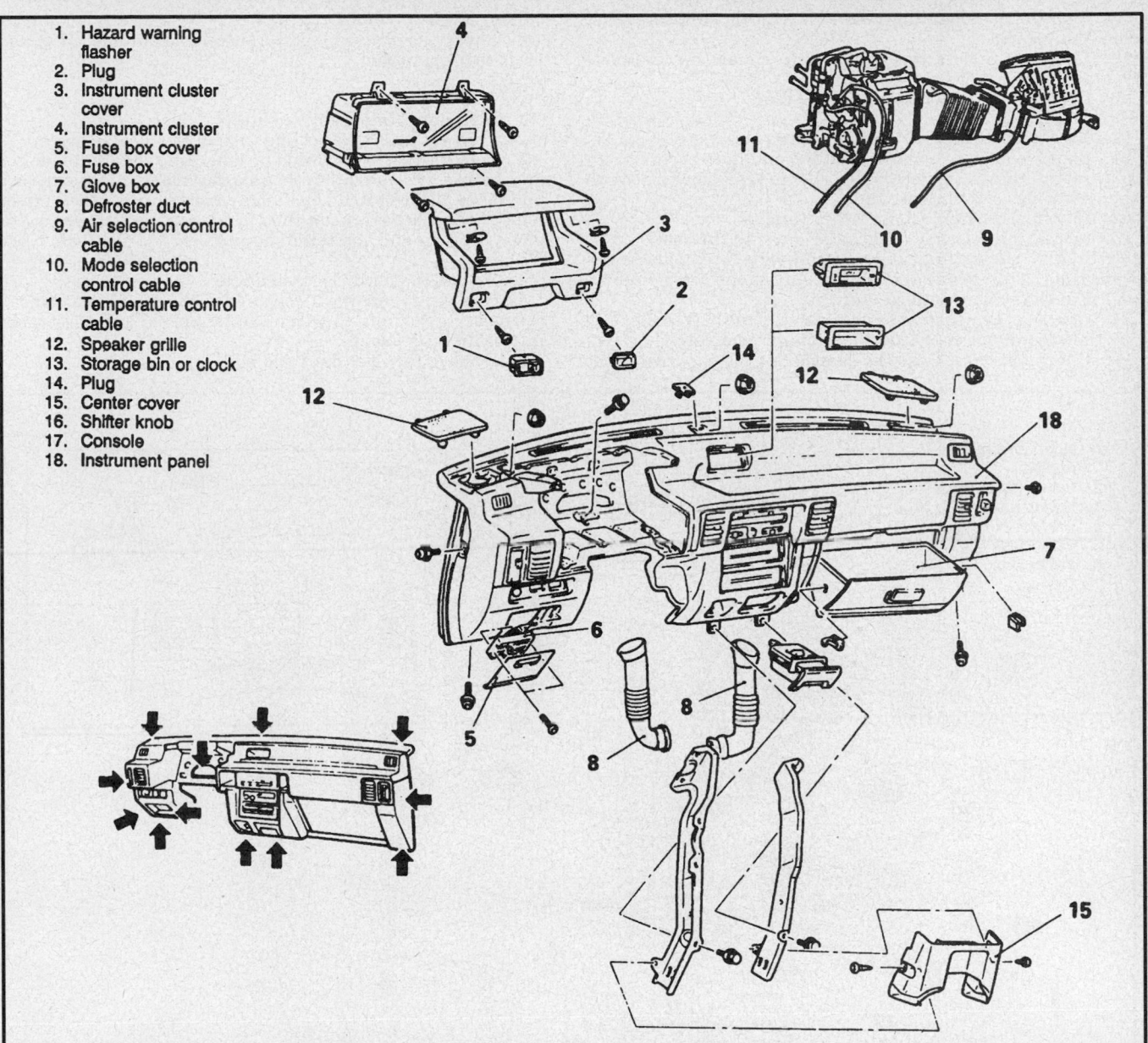

1. Hazard warning flasher
2. Plug
3. Instrument cluster cover
4. Instrument cluster
5. Fuse box cover
6. Fuse box
7. Glove box
8. Defroster duct
9. Air selection control cable
10. Mode selection control cable
11. Temperature control cable
12. Speaker grille
13. Storage bin or clock
14. Plug
15. Center cover
16. Shifter knob
17. Console
18. Instrument panel

Exploded view of the instrument panel—Pick-Up

Pick-Up

1. Disconnect the negative battery cable.
2. Drain the coolant. Follow all manufacturer's instructions when using antifreeze recycling equipment. Disconnect the heater hoses from the core tubes on engine side of firewall.
3. Remove the hazard flasher switch and the matching switch or cover on the other side of the column by gently prying from bottom with a trim stick. Remove the instrument cluster cover and instrument cluster, disconnecting the instrument connectors during removal.
4. Remove the fuse box cover, fuse box retaining screws and position the fuse box aside.
5. Remove the glove box assembly by detaching side retaining clips.
6. Remove the defroster ducts from each side of the heater housing assembly.
7. Label and disconnect the air, mode and temperature control cables.

8. Remove the front speaker grilles by gently prying at spring clip area on lower left and lower right sides.
9. Remove the parcel box or clock from center of instrument panel, as equipped.
10. Remove the nut cover from the top center of the instrument panel by reaching through the clock opening, depressing the side retaining clip and pressing upward.
11. Remove the cover from lower center of the panel.
12. Remove the shifter knob and floor console assembly, if equipped.
13. Move the tilt steering column down as far as it will go.
14. Remove the instrument panel retaining nuts and bolts and carefully remove the instrument panel from the vehicle, detaching all harnesses and cables.
15. Remove the duct from the right side of the heater case.
16. Remove the defroster duct from the top center of the heater case.
17. Remove the center reinforcement braces.

18. Remove the mounting nuts and remove the heater case from the vehicle.
19. Remove the hose cover, joint hose clamp and the plate from the case.
20. Remove the heater core from the case.

To install:

21. Install the heater core to the heater case.
22. Install the plate, joint hose clamp and hose cover.
23. Install the assembled heater case to the vehicle. Connect the heater hoses to the core tubes.
24. Install the center reinforcement braces.
25. Install the defroster and center ducts to the case.
26. Install the instrument panel and all related parts in reverse order of the removal sequence. Adjust the control cables.
27. Fill the system with coolant.
28. Connect the negative battery cable, run the vehicle until the thermostat opens and fill the radiator completely.
29. Check for leaks. Once the vehicle has cooled, recheck the coolant level.
30. Check the entire climate control system and all gauges for proper operation.

Expo

1. Disconnect the negative battery cable.
2. Properly drain the cooling system and heater hoses.
3. Remove the floor console by detaching the front side covers, taking off the shifter handle for manual transmission, pulling up the 3-switch panel (disconnect wiring), then removing the retaining screws at the console corners, 1 in the switch panel opening and the retaining nuts for the seat belt brackets.
4. Detach the hood release handle.
5. Gently pry out the 2 plugs from the panel just beneath the steering column, then remove this panel and the bracket just behind the panel.
6. Remove the floor duct and both lap ducts.

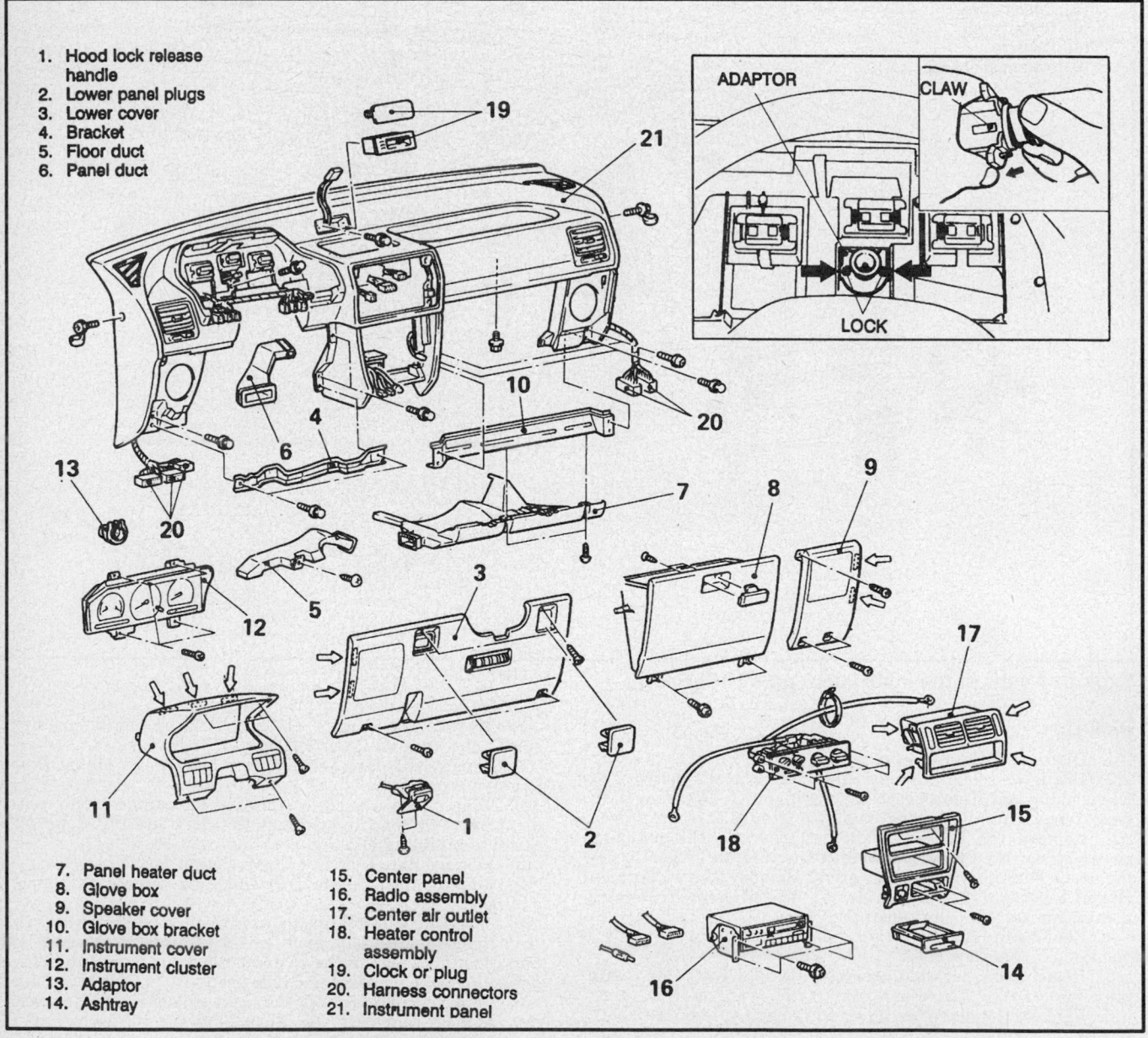

1. Hood lock release handle
2. Lower panel plugs
3. Lower cover
4. Bracket
5. Floor duct
6. Panel duct

ADAPTOR   CLAW

LOCK

7. Panel heater duct
8. Glove box
9. Speaker cover
10. Glove box bracket
11. Instrument cover
12. Instrument cluster
13. Adaptor
14. Ashtray
15. Center panel
16. Radio assembly
17. Center air outlet
18. Heater control assembly
19. Clock or plug
20. Harness connectors
21. Instrument panel

Exploded view of the instrument panel—Expo

7.   Remove the 2 glove box retaining screws beneath the box and pull glove box out and around the stopper.

8.   Remove the right side speaker cover.

9.   Remove the bracket behind the glove box opening.

10.   Remove the cover from the instrument cluster by taking out the 3 retaining screws and noting 3 metal clips on upper back side of cover.

11.   Detach and take out the instrument cluster.

12.   The adapter in the center of the instrument cluster is removed by taking out the locking collar (2 screws), pulling the speedometer cable slightly toward the steering wheel, then detach the rear of the adapter from the cable. Now turn the adapter until the notched section (claw) is lined up with the tab on the cable section. Slide the adapter rearward and off.

13.   Pull out the ashtray, remove the center panel cover, then detach and take out the radio assembly.

14.   To remove the center air outlet assembly, disengage the clip on the lower section of the assembly. Now, insert a flat–bladed tool between outlet fins to disengage the spring clips at the top corners of the assembly, and take out the assembly.

15.   Label the cables, disconnect them and remove the heater control panel.

16.   Remove the clock or clock plug from the top center of the instrument panel.

17.   Detach the harness connectors from under both sides of the instrument panel. Now, remove the retaining screws and carefully take out the instrument panel.

18.   Disconnect heater hoses from engine side of firewall.

19.   Pop out the 2 clips holding the joint duct between the heater case and blower assembly and remove the duct.

20.   If equipped with A/C, remove the vertical plate subassembly and the 2 nuts retaining the evaporator assembly.

21.   Remove the 2 center reinforcements.

22.   Disconnect and remove the A.B.S. control unit assembly.

23.   Remove the rear heater duct connection., the floor air duct and the defroster duct.

24.   If so equipped, detach and remove the automatic transmission control unit.

25.   Remove the heater case and the heater hose plate. Remove the heater core from the case.

To install:

26.   Install heater core into the case, replace the heater hose plate and position and install the heater case assembly.

27.   If removed, attach and install the automatic transmission control unit.

28.   Install the defroster, floor and rear duct assemblies.

29.   Connect and install the A.B.S. control unit.

30.   Install the 2 center reinforcements.

31.   On A/C equipped models, replace the nuts and clips to the evaporator assembly.

32.   Reconnect the joint duct between the blower and heater case using retaining clips.

33.   Reattach the heater hoses.

34.   Reposition and install the instrument panel and reconnect the harness connectors.

35.   Install the clock or clock plug in top of the instrument panel.

36.   Connect the cables and install the heater control assembly, then install the center air outlet assembly over the heater control.

37.   Connect and install the radio assembly, attach the center panel and then the ashtray.

38.   Reverse the removal procedure to install the adapter.

39.   Connect and install the instrument cluster, then replace the cluster cover.

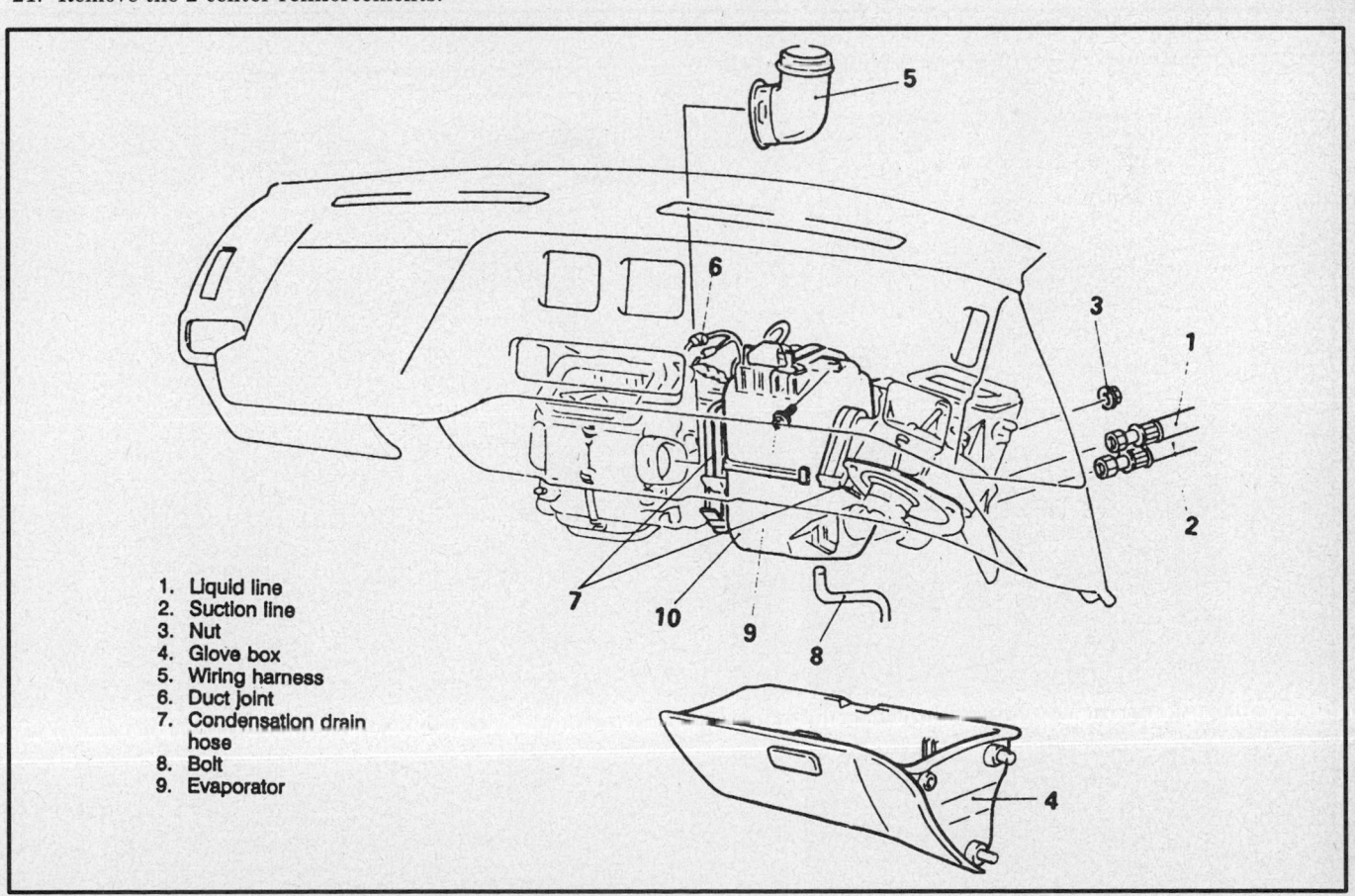

1. Liquid line
2. Suction line
3. Nut
4. Glove box
5. Wiring harness
6. Duct joint
7. Condensation drain hose
8. Bolt
9. Evaporator

Evaporator case and related components—Pick-Up

40. Install the bracket behind the glove box, then the right speaker cover, and the glove box, paying attention to the glove box stopper during installation.
41. Install the remaining air ducts.
42. Reattach the support bracket beneath the steering column opening.
43. Replace the cover beneath the steering column and install the 2 plugs at the top corners of this panel.
44. Reattach the hood release handle.
45. Reconnect the negative battery cable, refill the cooling system and operate the system to check for proper cooling and heating.

Evaporator

REMOVAL AND INSTALLATION

Montero, Pick-Up and Expo

1. Disconnect the negative battery cable.
2. Properly discharge the air conditioning system.
3. Use 2 wrenches to disconnect the liquid and suction lines from the evaporator fittings at the firewall. On Pick-up, remove the retaining nut located just above the hoses. On Montero and Expo, remove the condensation drain hose.
4. On Expo, remove the heater duct outlet below the glove box. On all models, remove the glove box assembly.
5. On Montero and Expo, remove the right speaker cover. On Pick–Up, remove the defroster duct.
6. On Montero and Expo, remove the bracket behind the glove box, then remove the right floor air duct (Montero only).

7. On Pick-Up, remove the duct joint between the evaporator housing and the heater housing. Also remove the drain line from beneath the evaporator case.
8. On all models, disconnect the electrical harness connector and any cables running to the evaporator case.
9. Remove the retaining bolts or clips and pull evaporator case out.
10. Disassemble the evaporator case and remove the evaporator.

To install:

11. Install the evaporator to the case and assemble. Carefully install the assembled case into the vehicle and tighten the mounting bolts and nuts.
12. Connect the condensation drain hose to the case (Pick-Up).
13. Reattach electrical connections or cables which may have been detached from the evaporator case.
14. On Pick–Up, install the duct joint between the evaporator and heater cases, ensuring a slight clearance on either side of the case.
15. Install the defroster duct (Pick-Up).
16. On all models, install the glove box bracket, if removed, then the glove box and right speaker cover.
17. In the engine compartment, install the drain hose and retaining nut if not already done during installation.
18. Using new lubricated O–rings, connect the refrigerant lines to the evaporator fittings.
19. Evacuate and recharge the air conditioning system. If the evaporator was replaced, add 1.4 oz. of refrigerant oil during the recharge.
20. Connect the negative battery cable and check the entire climate control system for proper operation and leaks.

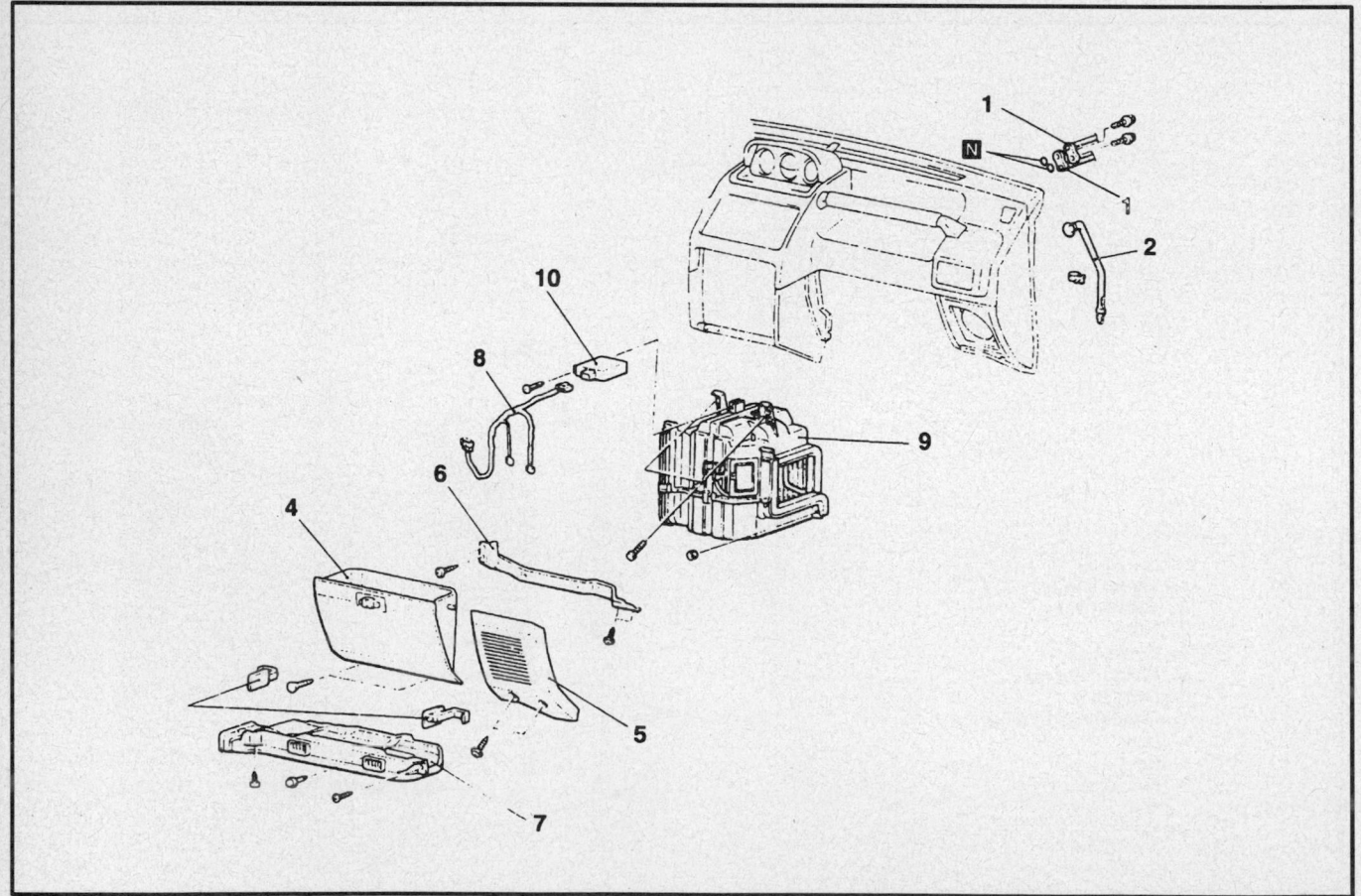

Evaporator case and related components—Montero

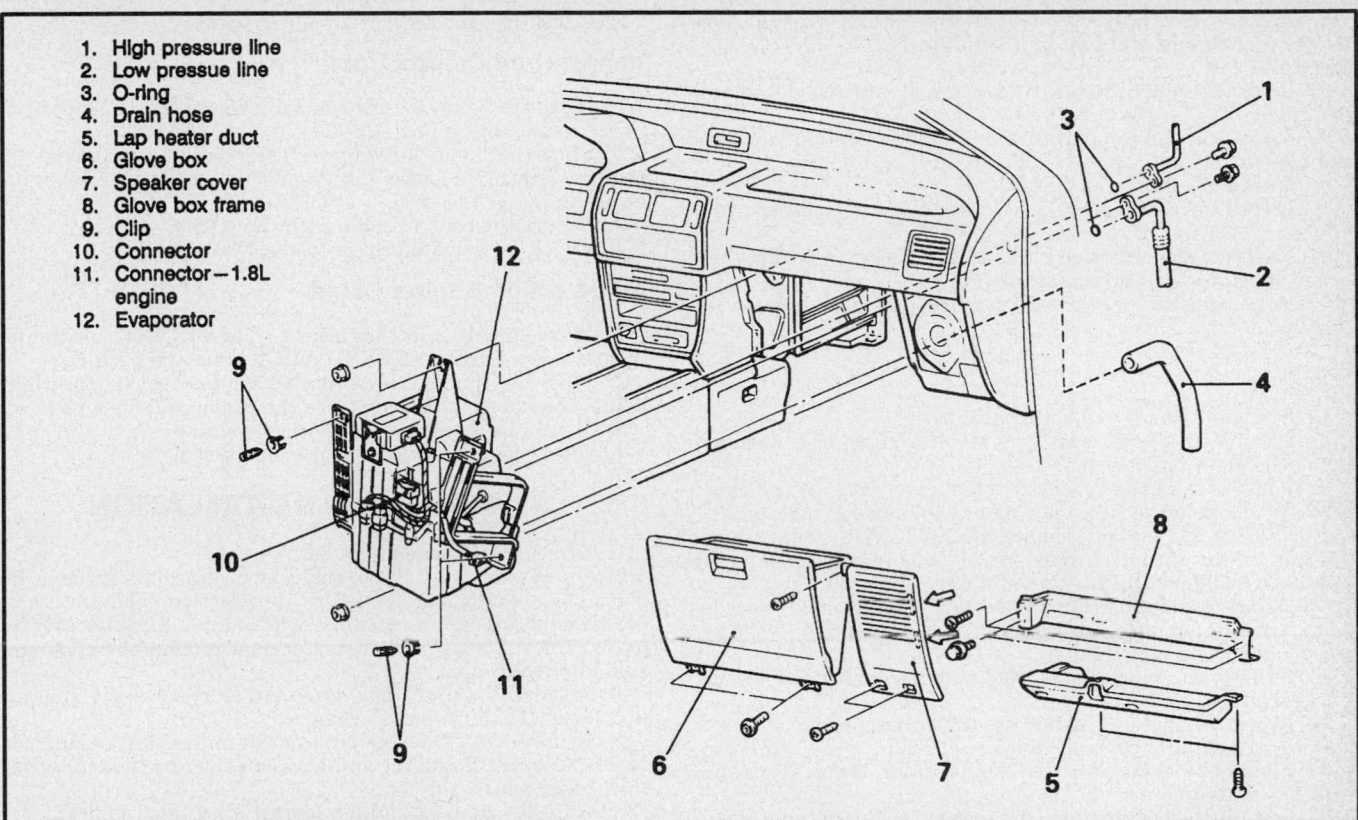

1. High pressure line
2. Low pressue line
3. O-ring
4. Drain hose
5. Lap heater duct
6. Glove box
7. Speaker cover
8. Glove box frame
9. Clip
10. Connector
11. Connector – 1.8L engine
12. Evaporator

Evaporator case and related components – Expo

Refrigerant Lines

REMOVAL AND INSTALLATION

1. Disconnect the negative battery cable.
2. Properly discharge the air conditioning system.
3. Separate the flare connection. Always use a backup wrench when separating flare connections. If the line is equipped with a sealing plate, remove the nuts or bolts that attach the refrigerant lines sealing plates to the adjoining components.
4. Always cap the connections of the component and the line to prevent contamination. Remove the line and discard the O-rings.

To install:

5. Coat the new O-rings with refrigerant oil and install. Connect the refrigerant lines to the adjoining components and tighten the nuts, bolts or flare connections.
6. Evacuate and recharge the air conditioning system.
7. Connect the negative battery cable and check the entire climate control system for proper operation. Check the system for leaks.

Manual Control Head

REMOVAL AND INSTALLATION

Montero

1. Disconnect the negative battery cable.
2. Remove the stoppers from the glove box and lower the glove box down to provide access to the back of the control panel.

3. Label and detach the air selection cable from the blower housing and the temperature control cable from the heater housing.
4. Remove the cover from beneath the steering column and remove the lap air duct and the left side floor duct.
5. Detach the air mode cable from the air door.
6. Remove the center panel cover, then the control headassembly with cables attached. Disassemble as required.

To install:

7. Reposition control panel and cables back into opening and attach, then install the center cover.
8. Make sure the mode lever is in **DEFROST** position and door damper lever is pressed down, then reattach the air mode control cable to the air door lever.
9. Install the left floor duct and lap air duct, then replace the lower cover beneath the steering column.
10. Reconnect the air selection with the lever in the **RE-CIRC** position and the door damper lever pressed inward. Then move the temperature lever to the **HOT** position and blend air lever pressed downward to attach the temperature control cable.
11. Lift and attach the glove box assembly to its stoppers.
12. Reconnect the negative battery cable. Adjust the control cables if required. Check system operation.

Pick-Up

1. Disconnect the negative battery cable.
2. Remove the glove box stoppers and lower the glove box. Reach inside opening and remove the air selection cable from the blower housing.
3. Remove the knobs from the control panel. Remove the center panel lower retaining screws, then use a trim stick to disengage the top edge of the panel.
4. Remove the defroster duct from under the left side of the instrument panel to gain access to the control cables on the heater housing. Label and disconnect the mode selection cable and the temperature control cable.

5. Remove the control head, disconnecting wiring from blower switch and A/C switch (if equipped).

To install:

6. Reattach switch wiring, then position and attach the control head.

7. Reconnect the temperature and mode selection cables to the control head.

8. Install the defroster duct.

9. Install the center panel, then reposition the control panel knobs.

10. Reattach the selection cable to the blower housing, then raise the glove box and install its stoppers.

11. Reconnect the negative battery cable. Check system operation.

Expo

1. Disconnect negative battery cable.

2. Remove the duct from beneath the glove box, then remove the glove box assembly.

3. Remove the hood release handle, then take off the panel beneath the steering column. Remove the left lap air duct.

4. Remove the ashtray, then the center panel, radio assembly and center air outlet (note spring clips inside top of outlet panel accessible with flat–bladed tool through the fins).

5. Detach the fresh/recirc air control cable from its door lever, then the temperature cable from its damper, and the air mode cable from its door.

6. Pull out the control assembly and disconnect any wiring.

To install:

7. Attach wiring and install the control assembly.

8. Reattach all 3 control cables.

9. Install the center air outlet, the radio, the center panel and the ashtray.

10. Install the left lap duct, the instrument panel under cover and the hood release handle.

11. Install the glove box assembly and the right lap air duct.

12. Reattach the negative battery cable. Check the system operation.

Manual Control Cables

ADJUSTMENT

Mode Selection Control Cable

1. Move the control lever to the **DEFROST** position.

2. Move the damper lever all the way inward and attach the cable with its retaining clip, ensuring the cable has no slack.

3. Check for smooth and proper operation.

Temperature Control Cable

1. Move the temperature control lever to the **HOT** position (move to far left on Pick-Up).

2. With the blend air damper lever pulled up against the stopper, adjust the outer cable tension so the inner cable has no slack.

3. Secure the control cable with the clamp.

4. Check for smooth and proper operation.

Air Selection Control Cable

1. Move the air selection lever to the **RECIRC** position on Montero and Expo; to **FRESH AIR** position on Pick-Up.

2. With the damper lever pulled all the way to the right, adjust the outer cable tension so the inner cable has no slack.

3. Secure the control cable with the clamp.

4. Check for smooth and proper operation.

REMOVAL AND INSTALLATION

1. Disconnect the negative battery cable.

2. On Montero and Expo, cables are accessible through the glove box opening. On Pick-Up, air selection cable is accessible through glove box opening, while other 2 cables may require removal of left side defroster duct remove the passenger side lap heater duct.

3. Remove the glove box assembly or remove the stoppers and lower the glove box as required.

4. Remove the center panel, remove control knobs, and control head bezel. Some retaining screws may be hidden by garnish plugs which pop out.

5. Note the routing and disconnect all control cables.

6. Remove the screws retaining the control head to the instrument panel, then pull the control head out and disconnect all wiring connectors.

7. Remove the control head from the vehicle. Disconnect the cables from the control head.

To install:

8. Feed the control cables through instrument panel opening in exactly the same position as before removal. Connect the wiring and install the control head. Secure with its retaining screws.

9. Reconnect the cables to their respective levers and doors.

10. Install the control head bezel, knobs and center panel.

11. Install the glove box assembly and lap heater duct if removed.

12. Connect the negative battery cable and check the entire climate control system for proper operation.

SENSORS AND SWITCHES

Dual Pressure Switch

OPERATION

The Montero and Pick-ups which use R-134A refrigerant use a dual pressure switch, located on the line near the receiver/drier, which is a combination of a low pressure cut off switch and high pressure cut off switch. These functions will stop operation of the compressor in the event of either high or low refrigerant charge, preventing damage to the system. The switch is located on the refrigerant line near the receiver drier.

The dual pressure switch is designed to cut off voltage to the compressor coil when the pressure either drops below 30 psi or rises above 384 psi on R-12 systems. Cut off points are 28 psi and 455 psi for R-134a systems.

TESTING

1. Check for continuity through the switch. Under all normal conditions, the switch should be continuous.

2. If the switch is open, check for insufficient refrigerant charge or excessive pressures.

3. If neither of the above conditions exist and the switch is open, replace the switch.

4. Pressure and continuity can be verified with manifold gauge set attached while reading ohmmeter. Switch should be **ON** (have continuity) between 30–384 psi for R–12 systems. If not, replace the switch.

REMOVAL AND INSTALLATION

1. Disconnect the negative battery cable.

2. Properly discharge the air conditioning system.

3. Remove the switch from the refrigerant line and cap all openings.

4. The installation is the reverse of the removal installation, using a new O–ring lubricated with clean refrigerant oil.

5. Evacuate and recharge the air conditioning system.

6. Connect the negative battery cable and check the entire climate control system for proper operation. Check the system for leaks.

Low Pressure Cut Off Switch

OPERATION

Pickup with R–12 have a low pressure cut off switch to monitor the refrigerant gas pressure. It is connected in series with the compressor and will turn off voltage to the compressor clutch coil when the monitored pressure drops below 30 psi, which could damage the compressor. The switch is located near the receiver/drier in the high pressure line. It is a sealed unit that must be replaced if faulty.

TESTING

1. Disconnect the switch connector and use a jumper wire between terminals inside the connector boot.

2. Press the A/C switch and blower switch **ON**, then turn the ignition switch to **ON** but do not start engine. Listen for the compressor clutch to engage.

3. If the compressor clutch does not engage, inspect the system for an open circuit (faulty fin thermostat, temperature switch or fuse).

4. If the clutch engages, connect an air conditioning manifold gauge to the system.

5. Read the low pressure gauge. The low pressure cut off switch should complete the circuit at pressures of at least 30 psi. Check the system for leaks if the pressures are too low. Make corrective action.

6. If the pressures are normal, remove the jumper and connect the switch to the boot connector. With ignition turned to **ON** and clutch does not engage, discharge the system and replace the switch.

REMOVAL AND INSTALLATION

1. Disconnect the negative battery cable.

2. Properly discharge the air conditioning system.

3. Unplug the boot connector from the switch.

4. Using an oil pressure sending unit socket, remove the switch from the line at the receiver/drier.

To install:

5. Seal the threads of the new switch with teflon tape.

6. Install the switch to the receiver/drier and connect the boot connector.

7. Evacuate and recharge the system, adding 0.5 oz. of refrigerant oil. Check for leaks.

8. Check the switch for proper operation.

Triple Pressure Switch

Used on Expo models, this switch detects excessively low pressure (**OFF** at 30 psi; **ON** at 33 psi), excessively high pressure (**OFF** at 384 psi; **ON** at 299 psi), and medium operating pressures (**OFF** at 199 psi; **ON** at 256 psi). The switch is located on the receiver/drier.

TESTING

1. Remove the switch connector and attach an ohmmeter to the high and low pressure side terminals (2 opposing terminals across the narrowest part of the switch). Place a jumper between the corresponding terminals on the disconnected wiring.

2. Install a manifold gauge set to the high pressure side service valve and the low side service valve. Start the engine and operate the system.

3. At normal operating pressures, there is continuity between the terminals. If not, replace the switch.

REMOVAL AND INSTALLATION

1. Disconnect the negative battery cable.

2. Properly discharge the air conditioning system.

3. Unplug the boot connector from the switch.

4. Using an oil pressure sending unit socket, remove the switch from the receiver/drier.

To install:

5. Seal the threads of the new switch with teflon tape.

6. Install the switch to the receiver/drier and connect the boot connector.

7. Evacuate and recharge the system, adding 0.5 oz. of refrigerant oil. Check for leaks.

8. Check the switch and system for proper operation.

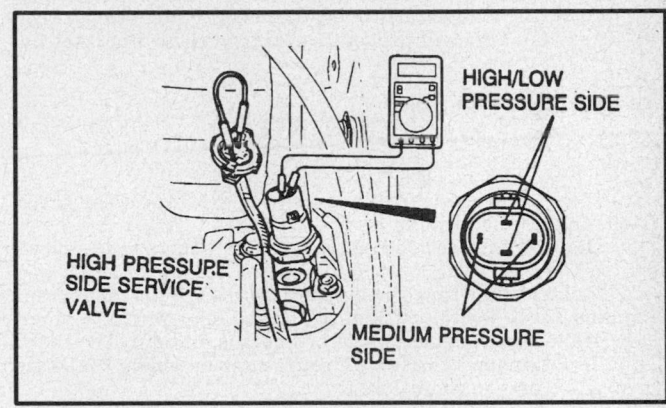

Checking triple pressure switch—Expo

Engine Coolant Temperature Switch

OPERATION

The engine coolant temperature switch, located on or near the thermostat housing, is connected in series with the compressor clutch relay. The switch is designed to cut off the compressor when the engine coolant temperature rises above 233°F (115°C), preventing engine overheating when the supply of cooling air is not sufficient for both the radiator and condenser.

TESTING

1. If the switch is suspect, unplug and jump across the terminals in the connectors with switch still in place.

2. Set and A/C and blower switches to the **ON** position. Then turn the ignition switch to **ON**. Listen for the compressor clutch to engage. If it does not, the fin thermistor, low pressure switch, wiring connection or fuse may be faulty. If clutch engages, replace the switch.

3. An on–bench test may be made as follows: Remove the switch and place it in an oil bath. Heat the oil and check continuity. There should be continuity until reaches at least 233°F (108°C). The switch should close above this temperature.

REMOVAL AND INSTALLATION

1. Disconnect the negative battery cable. Drain out some of the coolant.

2. Unplug the connector.

3. Unscrew the switch from the thermostat housing.

4. The installation is the reverse of the removal installation. Use sealant on the threads when installing.

5. Refill the cooling system.

6. Connect the negative battery cable and check the entire climate control system for proper operation.

Thermistor

OPERATION

On all models, evaporator freeze up is controlled by a thermistor (air inlet sensor). The body of the thermistor assembly is mounted to the evaporator case and the probe is inserted to the evaporator fins. The thermistor is connected in parallel to the A/C control unit which will cut off voltage to the compressor when the temperature of the evaporator drops below 37.4°F (3°C). This will prevent freezing of the evaporator fins.

TESTING

1. If the compressor will not engage, disconnect the thermistor connector and jump across the wires.

2. Depress the air conditioning switch and turn the blower switch **ON**.

3. Momentarily turn the ignition switch ON, without cranking, and listen for the click of the clutch engaging.

4. If the clutch engages, the problem is probably the thermistor. If not, inspect the low pressure switch, wiring connection or fuse for proper condition.

REMOVAL AND INSTALLATION

1. Disconnect the negative battery cable.

2. Properly discharge the air conditioning system.

3. Remove the evaporator case.

4. Disassemble the evaporator case and unclip the thermistor probe from the evaporator fins.

5. Remove the thermistor from the case.

To install:

6. Assemble the evaporator case assembly. Make sure the thermistor probe is securely clipped to the evaporator fin.

7. Apply sealant to the hole in the lower case where the wires pass through.

8. Install the evaporator case to the vehicle.

9. Evacuate and recharge the air conditioning system.

10. Connect the negative battery cable and check the entire climate control system for proper operation and leaks.

System Relays

OPERATION

Many of the systems within the air conditioning systems use relays to send current on its way and energize various components. The relays are positioned throughout the vehicle. All are conventional relays with internal contacts and a coil which pulls the contacts closed when energized.

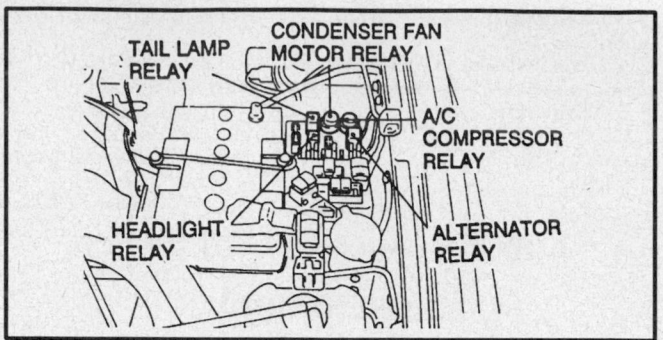

A/C relays located in engine compartment — Montero

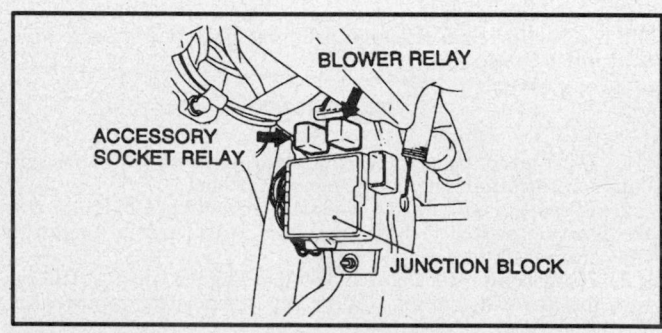

A/C relays located under left side of instrument panel — Montero

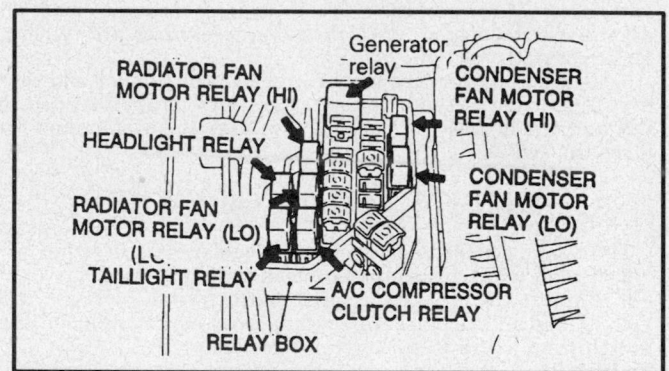

Condenser, compressor and fan relays — Expo

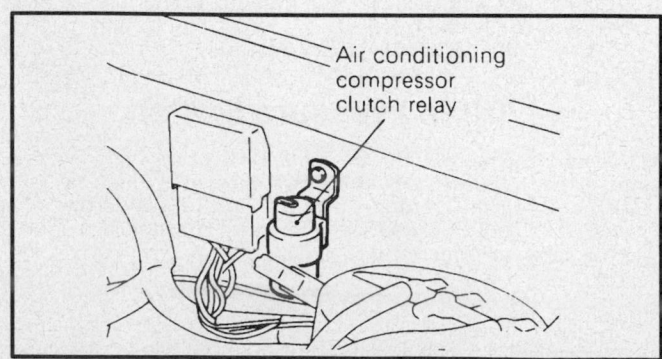

A/C relay located in engine compartment — Pick-Up

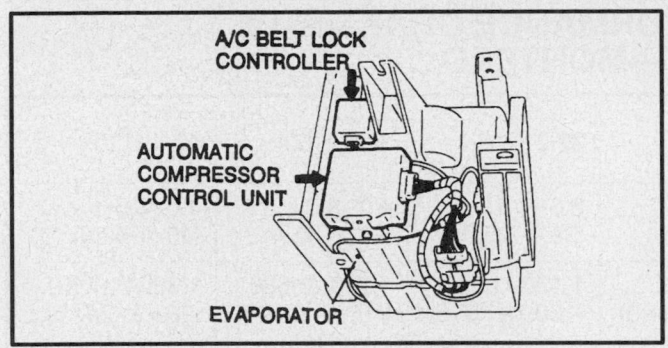

A/C control unit on evaporator case — Expo

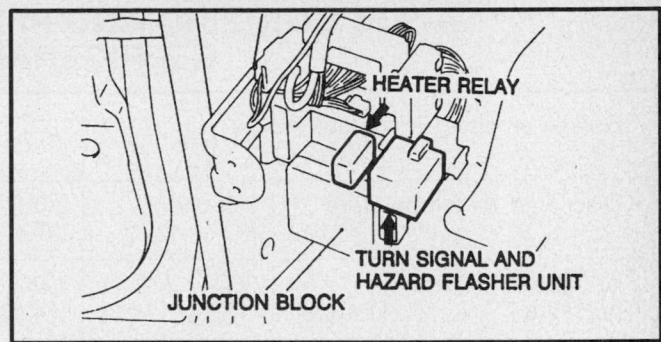

Heater relay location of firewall — Typical

SYSTEM DIAGNOSIS

Air Conditioning Performance

PERFORMANCE TEST

Air temperature in the testing area must be at least 70°F (21°C), but not in the direct sunlight, to ensure the accuracy of this test.

1. Connect a manifold gauge set to the system.
2. Start the engine. Set the controls to **RECIRC** or **MAX**, the mode lever to the **PANEL** position, temperature control level to the coolest position and the blower on its highest position.
3. Rev engine until idle is 1000 rpm with the compressor clutch engaged.
4. Allow the engine come to normal operating temperature and keep doors and windows closed and hood open.
5. Insert a thermometer in the left center panel outlet and operate the engine for 10 minutes. The clutch may cycle depending on the ambient conditions.
6. With the clutch engaged, compare the discharge air temperature to the performance chart.
7. If the values do not meet specifications, check system components for proper operation.

AIR CONDITIONING PERFORMANCE CHART R-12 REFRIGERANT—EXPO

Garage ambient temperature °C (°F)	21 (70)	26.7 (80)	32.2 (90)	37.8 (100)	43.3 (110)
Discharge air temperature °C (°F)	2.5–7.5 (36.5–45.5)	2.5–8.0 (36.5–46.5)	3.0–8.0 (37.4–46.5)	3.5–8.0 (38.3–46.5)	3.5–8.0 (38.3–46.5)
Compressor discharge pressure kPa (psi)	850–900 (121.0–128.1)	1,000–1,070 (142.3–152.3)	1,100–1,150 (156.5–163.6)	1,250–1,320 (177.9–187.8)	1,350–1,400 (192.1–199.2)
Compressor suction pressure kPa (psi)	130–310 (18.5–27.0)	140–310 (19.9–27.0)	140–320 (19.9–28.5)	160–320 (22.8–28.5)	165–320 (23.5–29.9)

AIR CONDITIONING PERFORMANCE CHART R-12 REFRIGERANT—PICK-UP

Garage ambient temperature °C (°F)	21 (70)	26.7 (80)	32.2 (90)	37.8 (100)	43.3 (110)
Discharge air temperature °C (°F)	2.8–4.4 (37–40)	3.3–5.0 (38–41)	3.9–5.6 (39–42)	4.4–7.2 (40–45)	4.4–7.8 (40–46)
Compressor discharge pressure kPa (psi)	758–1,310 (110–190)	896–1,517 (130–220)	1,103–1,793 (160–260)	1,310–1,999 (190–290)	1,517–2,206 (220–320)
Compressor suction	131–165	138–179	145–186	152–193	159–200

AIR CONDITIONING PERFORMANCE CHART R-12 REFRIGERANT—MONTERO

Garage ambient temperature °C (°F)	21 (70)	26.7 (80)	32.2 (90)	37.8 (100)	43.3 (110)
Discharge air temperature °C (°F)	3.0–6.0 (37.4–42.8)	3.0–7.0 (37.4–44.6)	3.5–7.5 (38.3–45.5)	4.0–8.0 (39.2–46.4)	4.5–8.5 (40.1–47.3)
Compressor discharge pressure kPa (psi)	980–1,230 (139.4–174.9)	1,050–1,300 (149.3–184.9)	1,130–1,380 (160.7–196.3)	1,270–1,580 (180.6–224.7)	1,330–1,740 (189.2–247.5)
Compressor suction pressure kPa (psi)	120–220 (17.1–31.3)	120–230 (17.1–32.7)	130–240 (18.5–34.1)	150–270 (21.3–38.4)	170–280 (24.2–39.8)

AIR CONDITIONING PERFORMANCE CHART R-134a—MONTERO

Garage ambient temperature °C (°F)	21 (70)	26.7 (80)	32.2 (90)	37.8 (100)	43.3 (110)
Discharge air temperature °C (°F)	3.0–6.0 (37.4–42.8)	3.0–7.0 (37.4–44.4)	3.5–7.5 (38.3–45.5)	4.0–8.0 (39.2–46.4)	4.5–8.5 (40.1–47.3)
Compressor discharge pressure kPa (psi)	961–1,402 (139–203)	1,029–1,471 (149–213)	1,108–1,549 (161–225)	1,245–1,745 (181–253)	1,304–1,902 (189–276)
Compressor suction pressure kPa (psi)	98–216 (14–31)	98–226 (14–33)	108–235 (16–34)	137–265 (20–38)	157–275 (23–40)

Air Conditioning Compressor

COMPRESSOR NOISE

Noises that develop during air conditioning operation can be misleading. A noise that sounds like serious compressor damage may only be a loose belt, mounting bolt or clutch assembly. Improper belt tension can also emit a noise that can be mistaken for more serious problems. Check and adjust all possible causes of the noise, including oil level, before replacing the compressor.

COMPRESSOR CLUTCH INOPERATIVE

1. Verify refrigerant charge and add if required.
2. Check for 12 volts at the clutch coil connection. If voltage is detected, check the coil. If voltage is not detected at the coil, check the fuse or fusible link. If the fuse is not blown, check for voltage at the clutch relay. If voltage is not detected there, continue working backwards through the system's switches, etc. until an open circuit is detected.
3. Inspect all suspect parts and replace as required.
4. When the repair is complete, perform a complete system performance test.

CLUTCH COIL TESTING

1. Disconnect the negative battery cable.
2. Disconnect the compressor clutch connector.
3. Apply 12 volts to the wire leading to the clutch coil. If the clutch is operating properly, an audible click will occur when the clutch is magnetically pulled into the coil. If a click is not heard, inspect the coil.
4. Check the resistance across the coil lead wire and ground. The specification is 3.4–3.8 ohms at approximately 70°F (20°C).
5. If not within specifications, replace the clutch coil.

WIRING SCHEMATICS

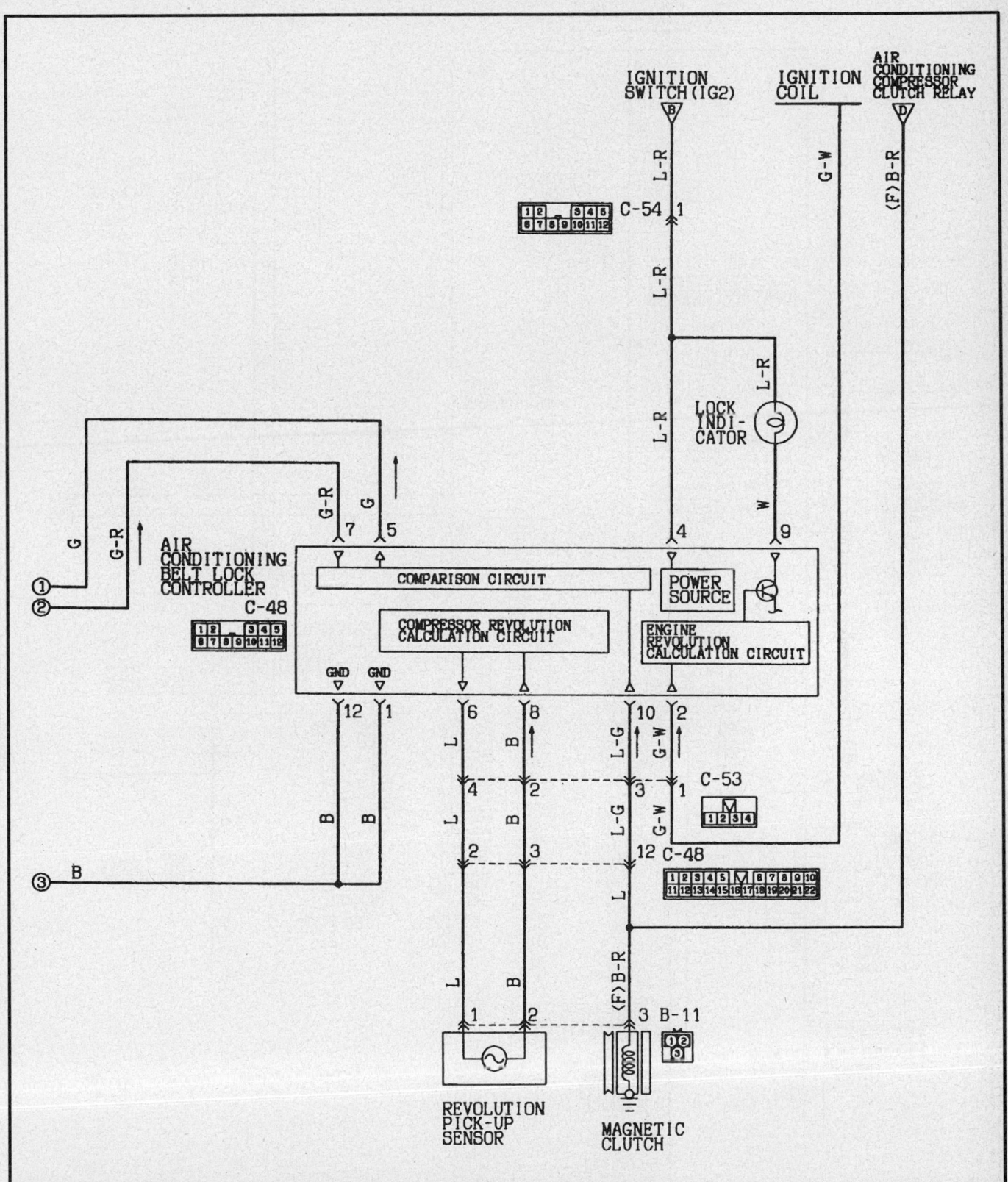

Air conditioning system wiring schematic—1993 Expo with 1.8L engine

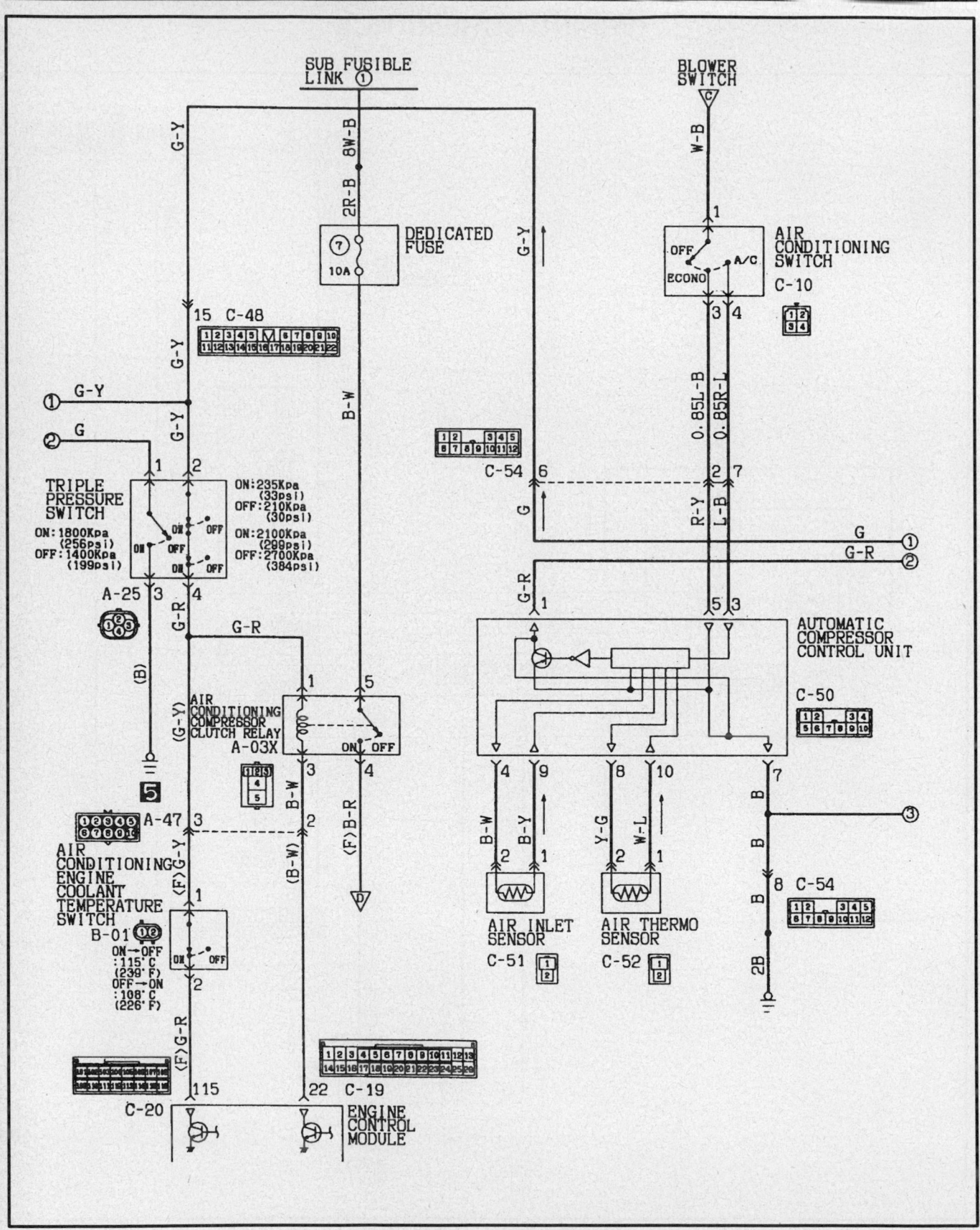

Air conditioning system wiring schematic—1993 Expo with 1.8L engine, Cont.

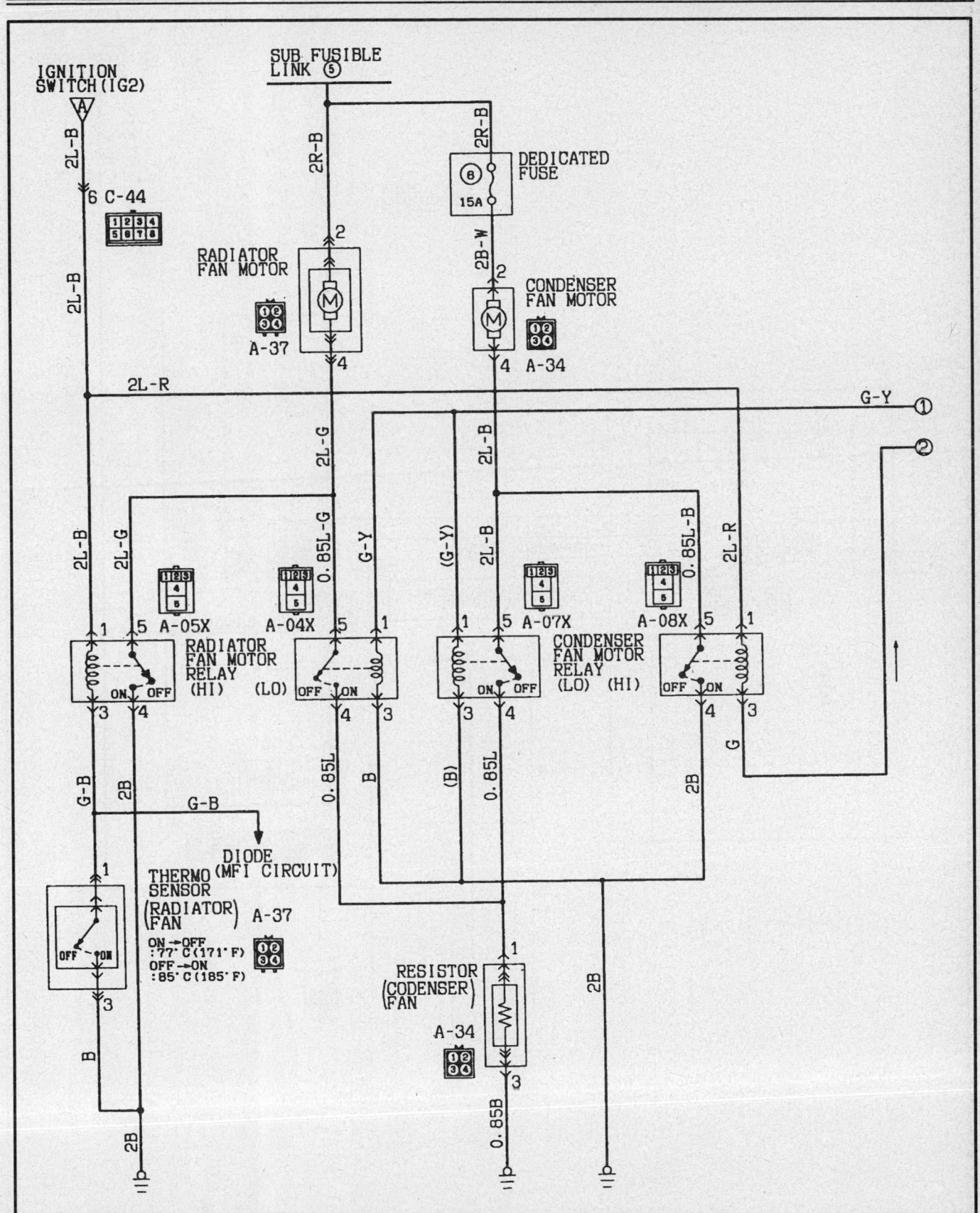

Air conditioning system wiring schematic—1993 Expo with 1.8L engine, Cont.

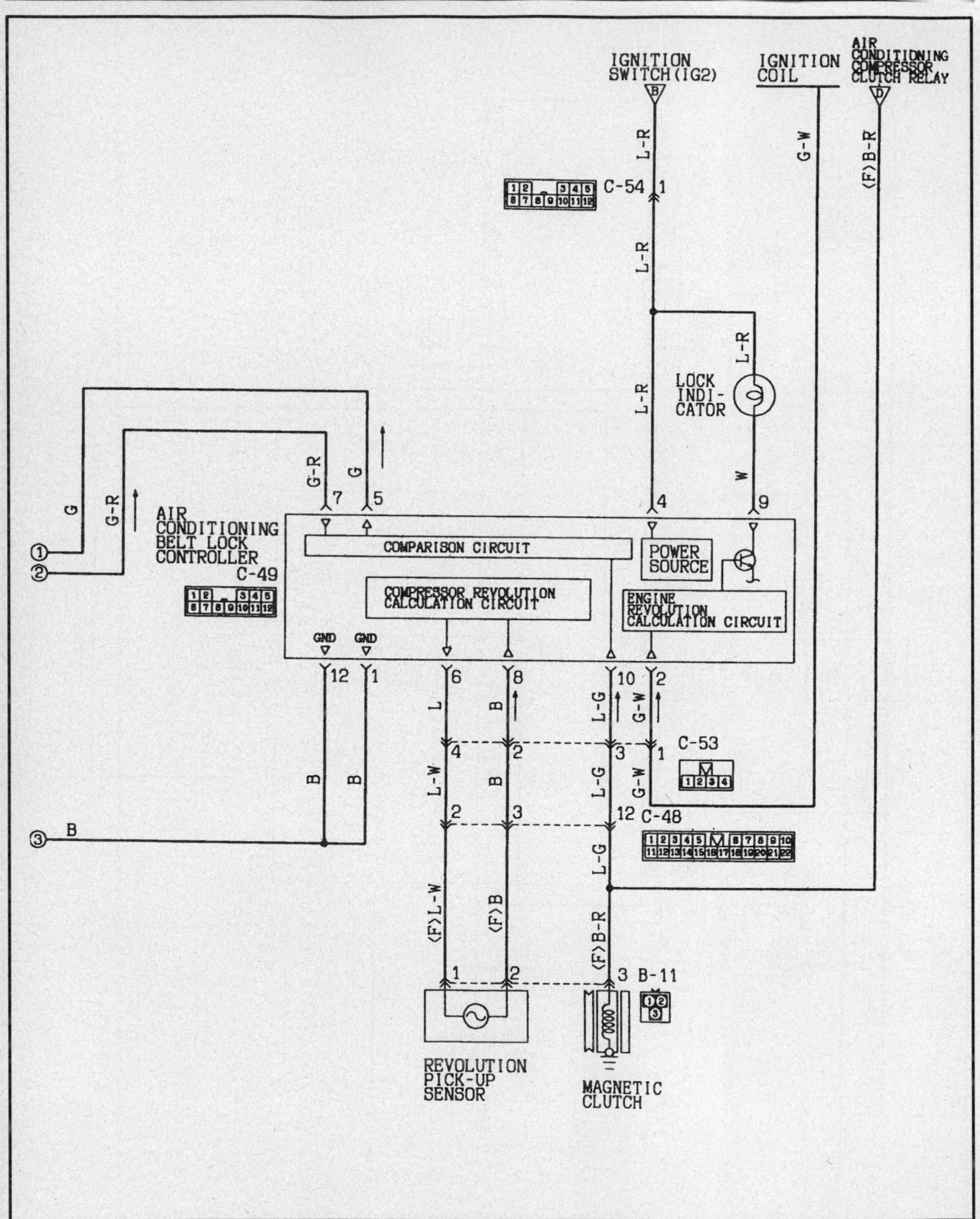

Air conditioning system wiring schematic—1993 Expo with 1.8L engine, Cont.

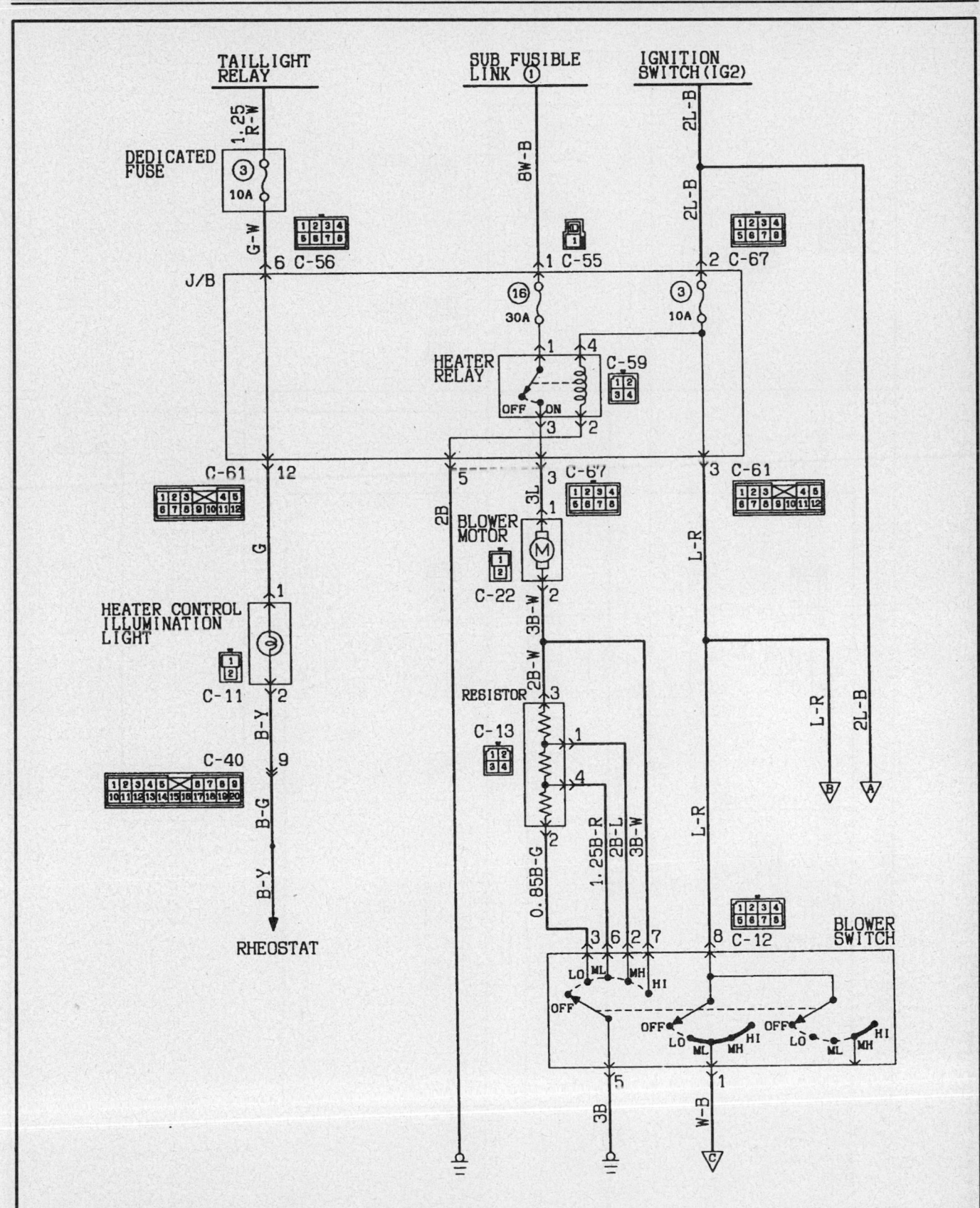

Air conditioning system wiring schematic—1993 Expo with 2.4L engine

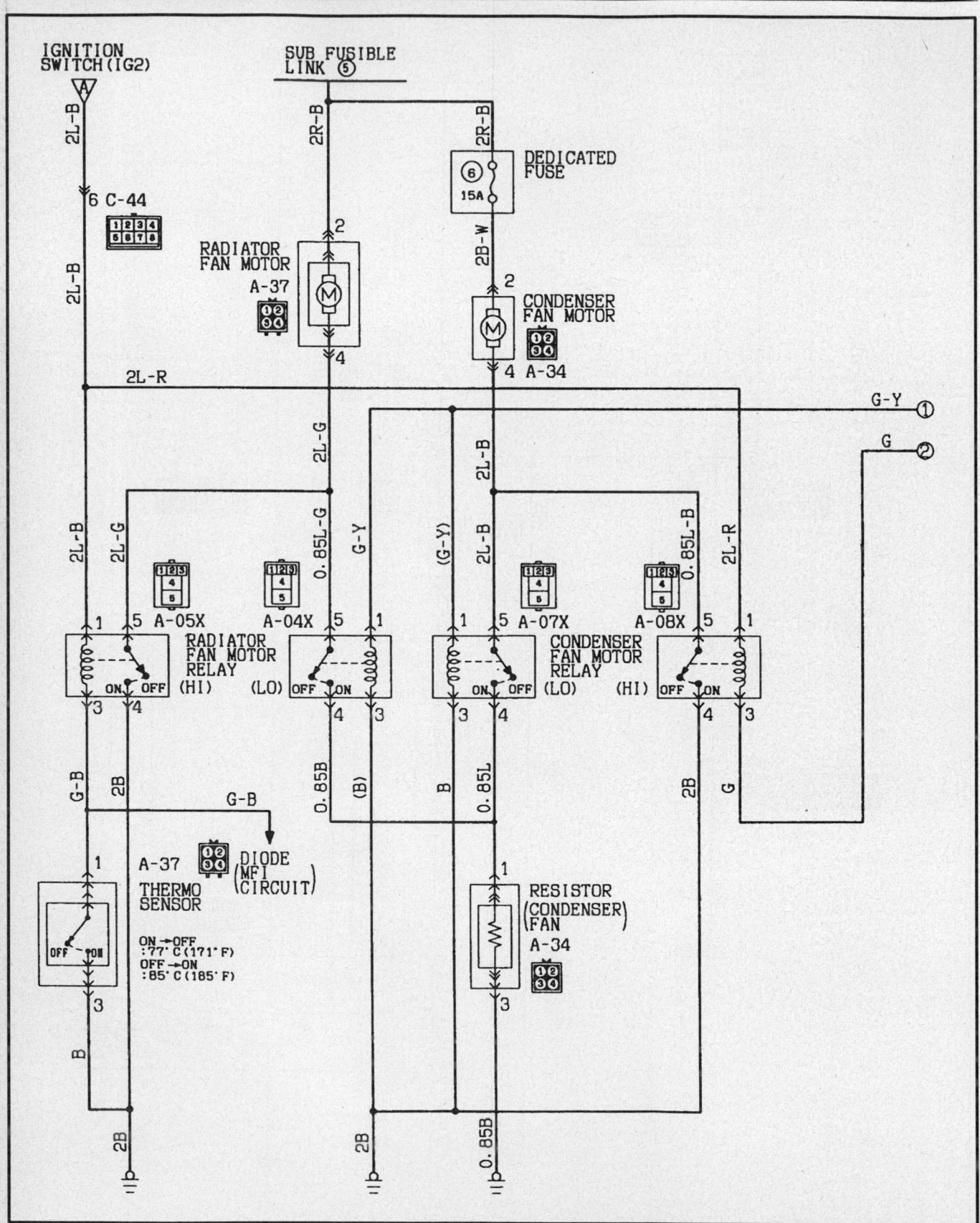

Air conditioning system wiring schematic—1993 Expo with 2.4L engine, Cont.

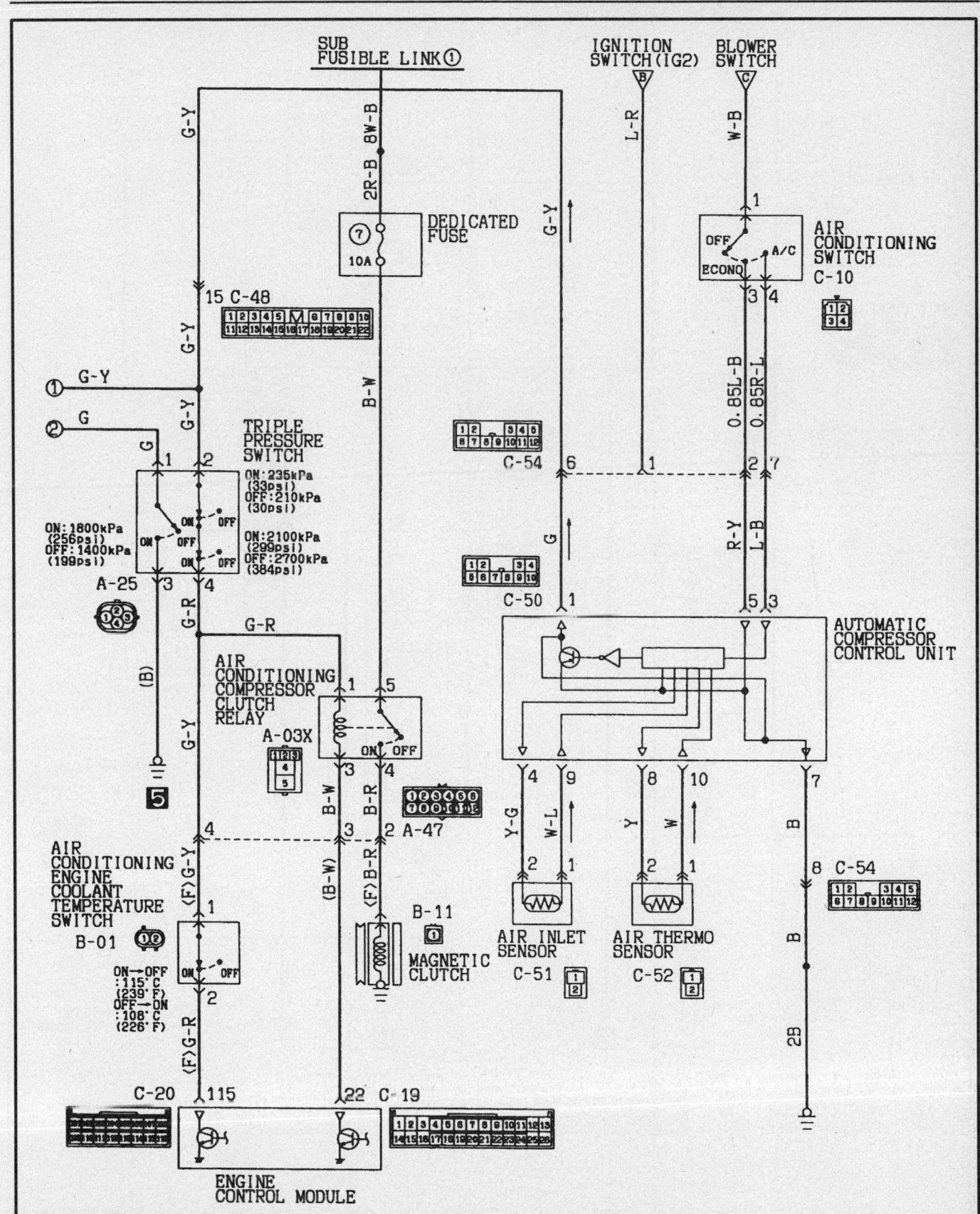

Air conditioning system wiring schematic—1993 Expo with 2.4L engine, Cont.

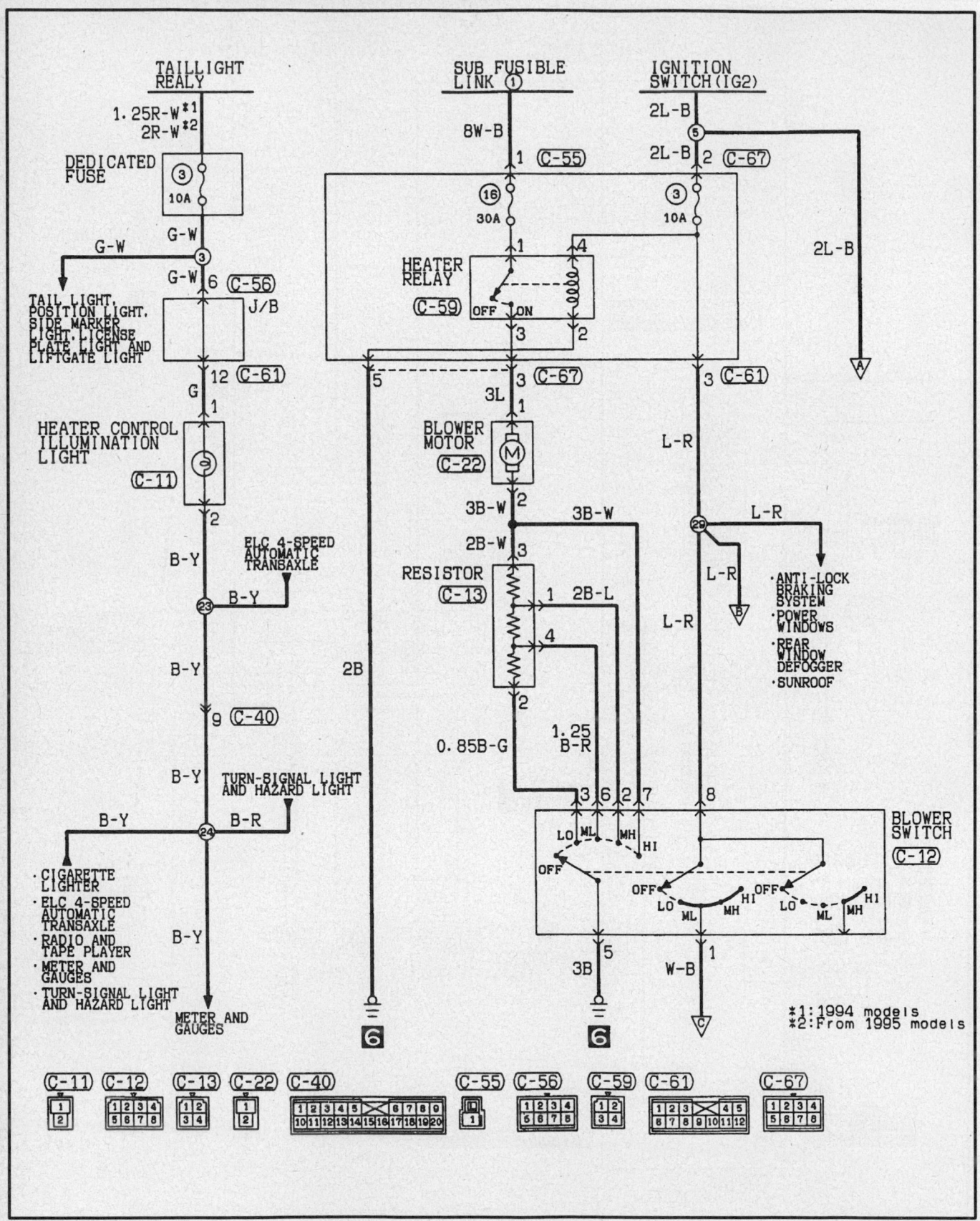

Heater system wiring schematic—1994–95 Expo with 1.8L engine

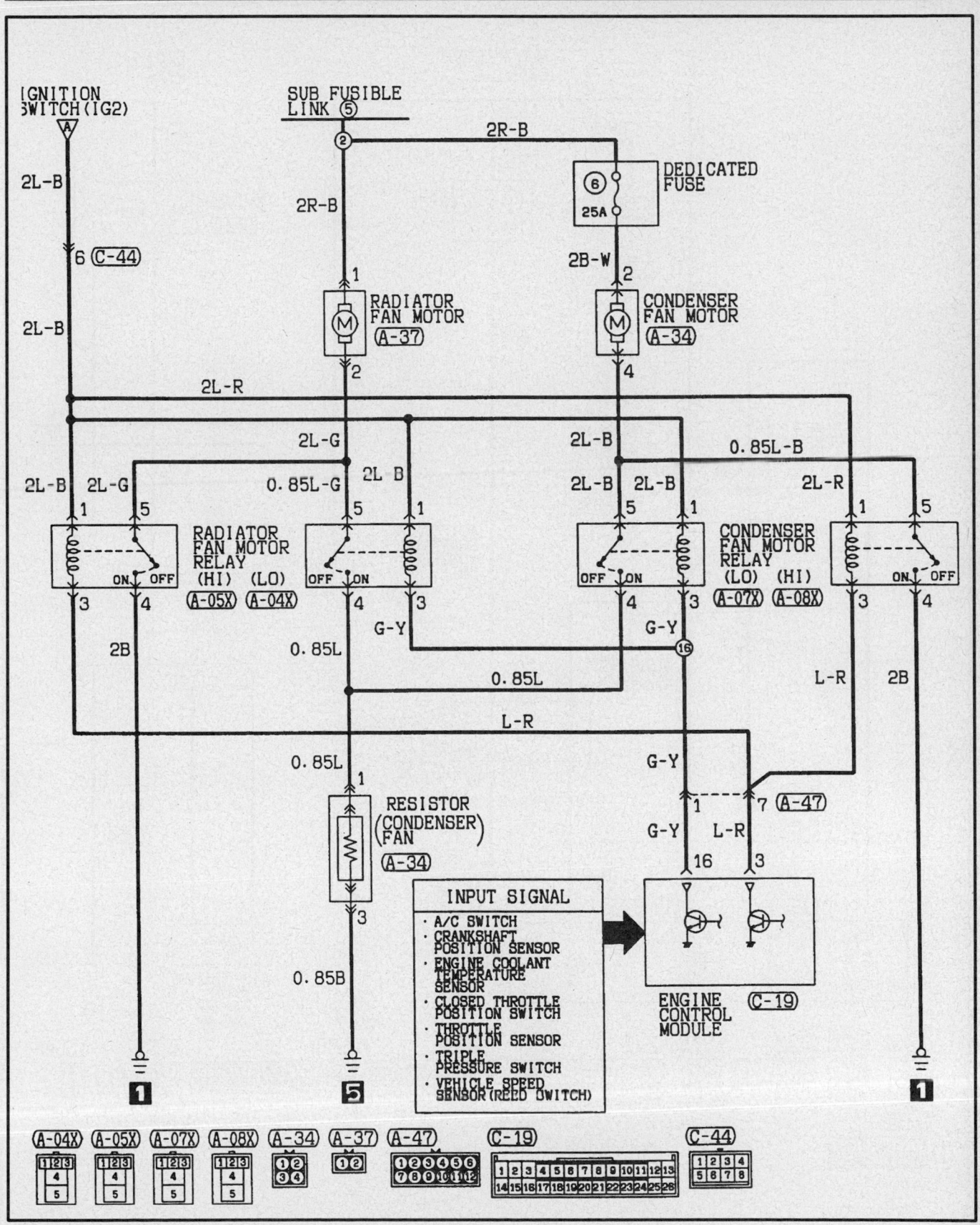

Air conditioning system wiring schematic—1994–95 Expo with 1.8L engine

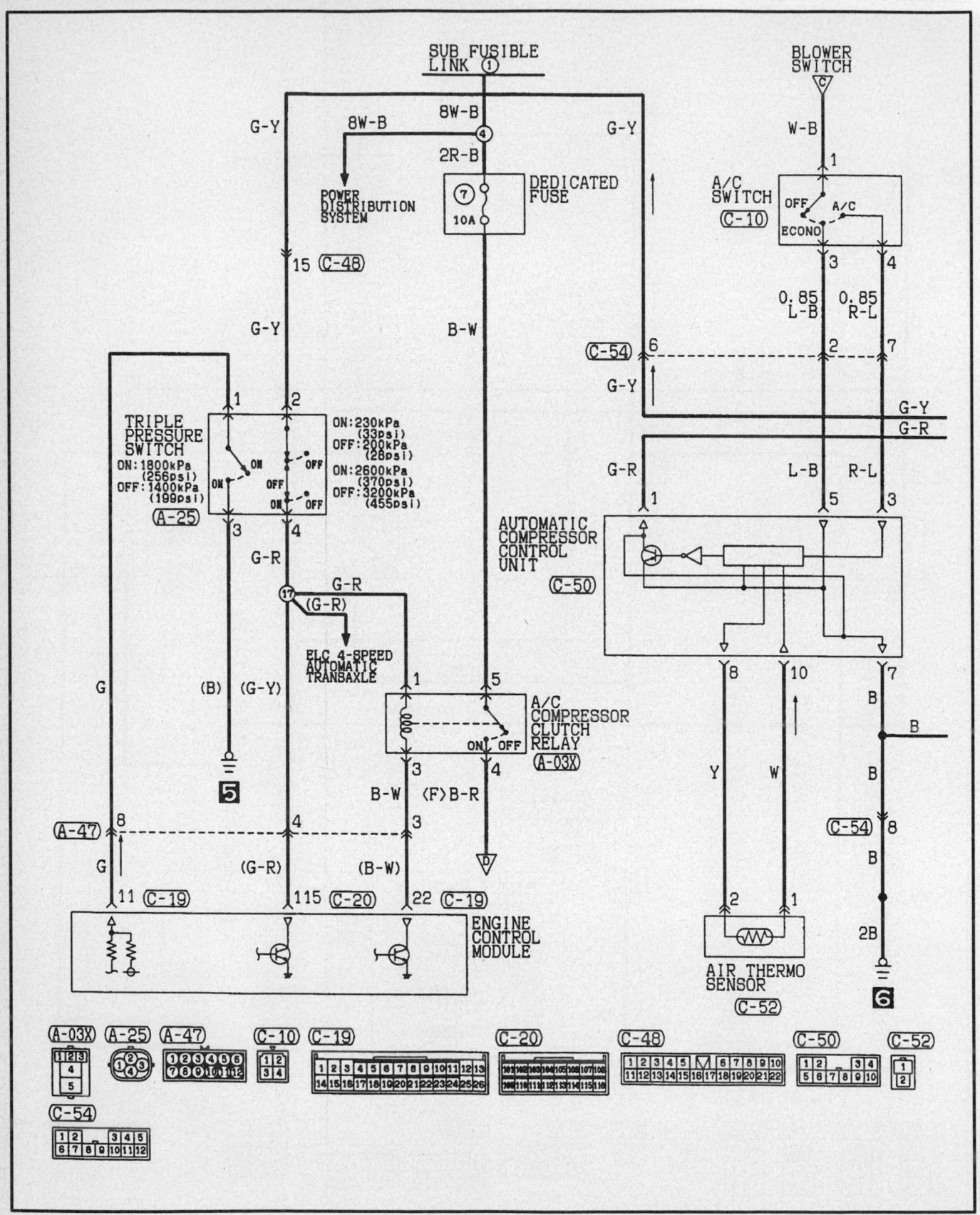

Air conditioning system wiring schematic—1994–95 Expo with 1.8L engine, Cont.

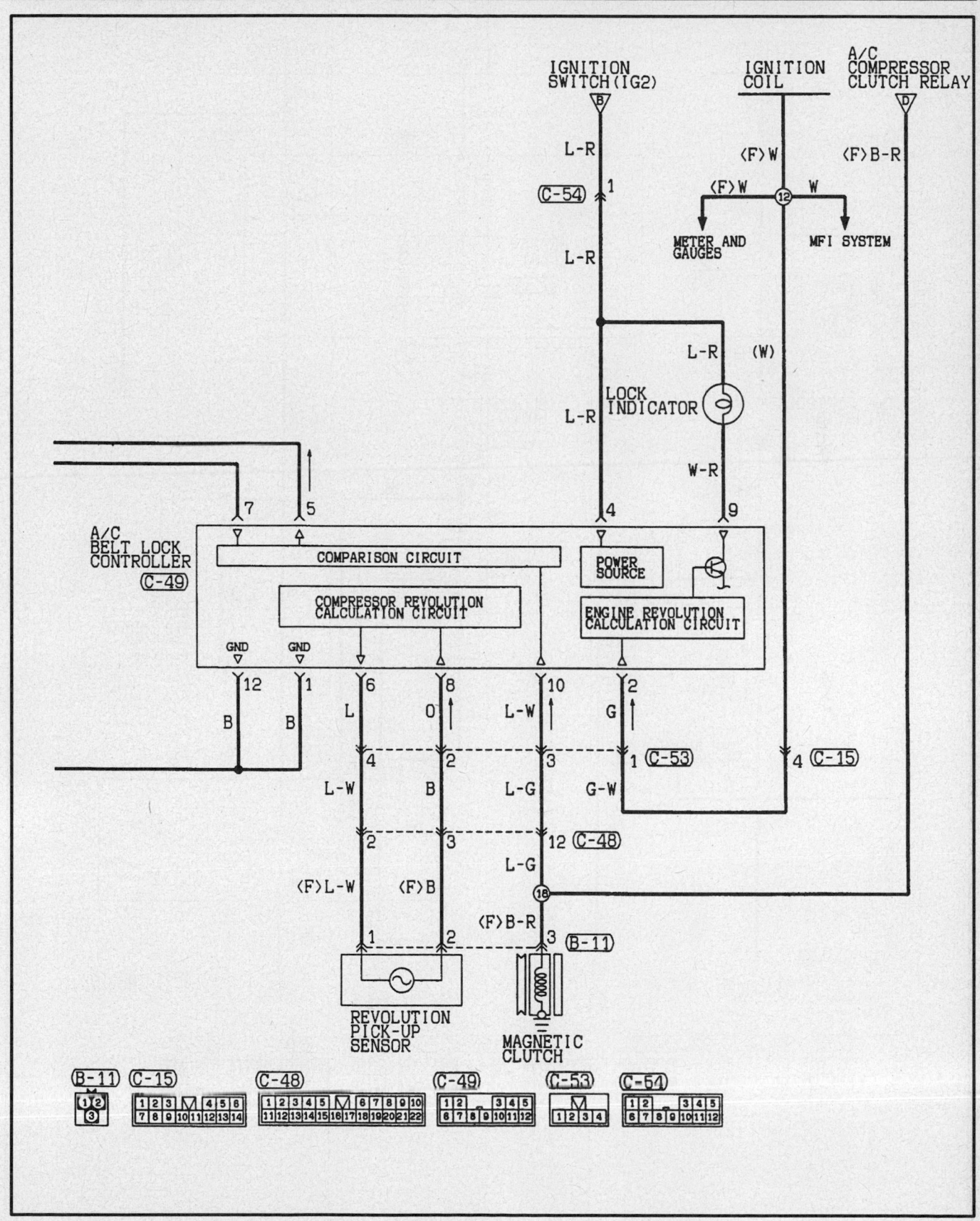

Air conditioning system wiring schematic—1994–95 Expo with 1.8L engine, Cont.

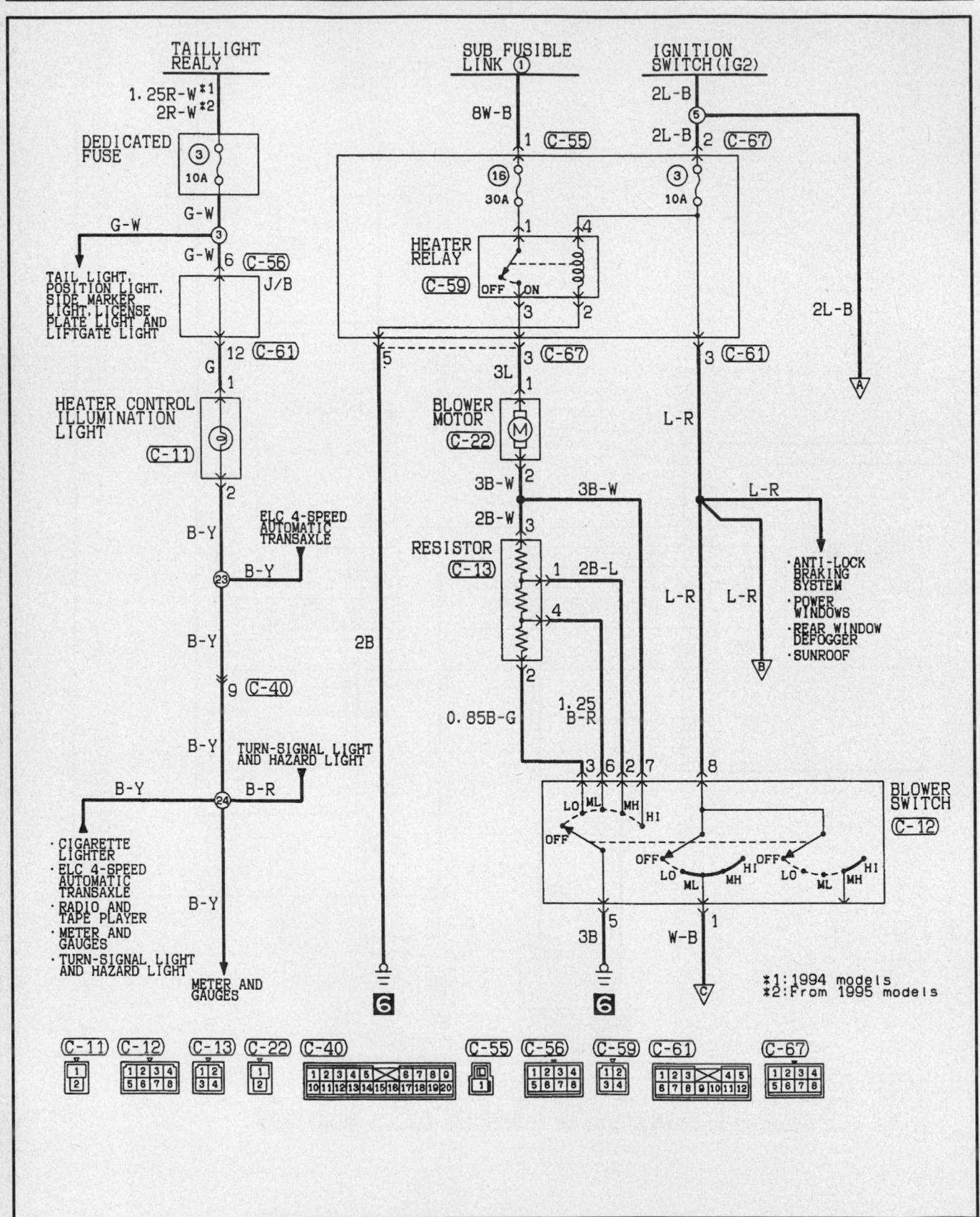

Heater system wiring schematic—1994–95 Expo with 2.4L engine

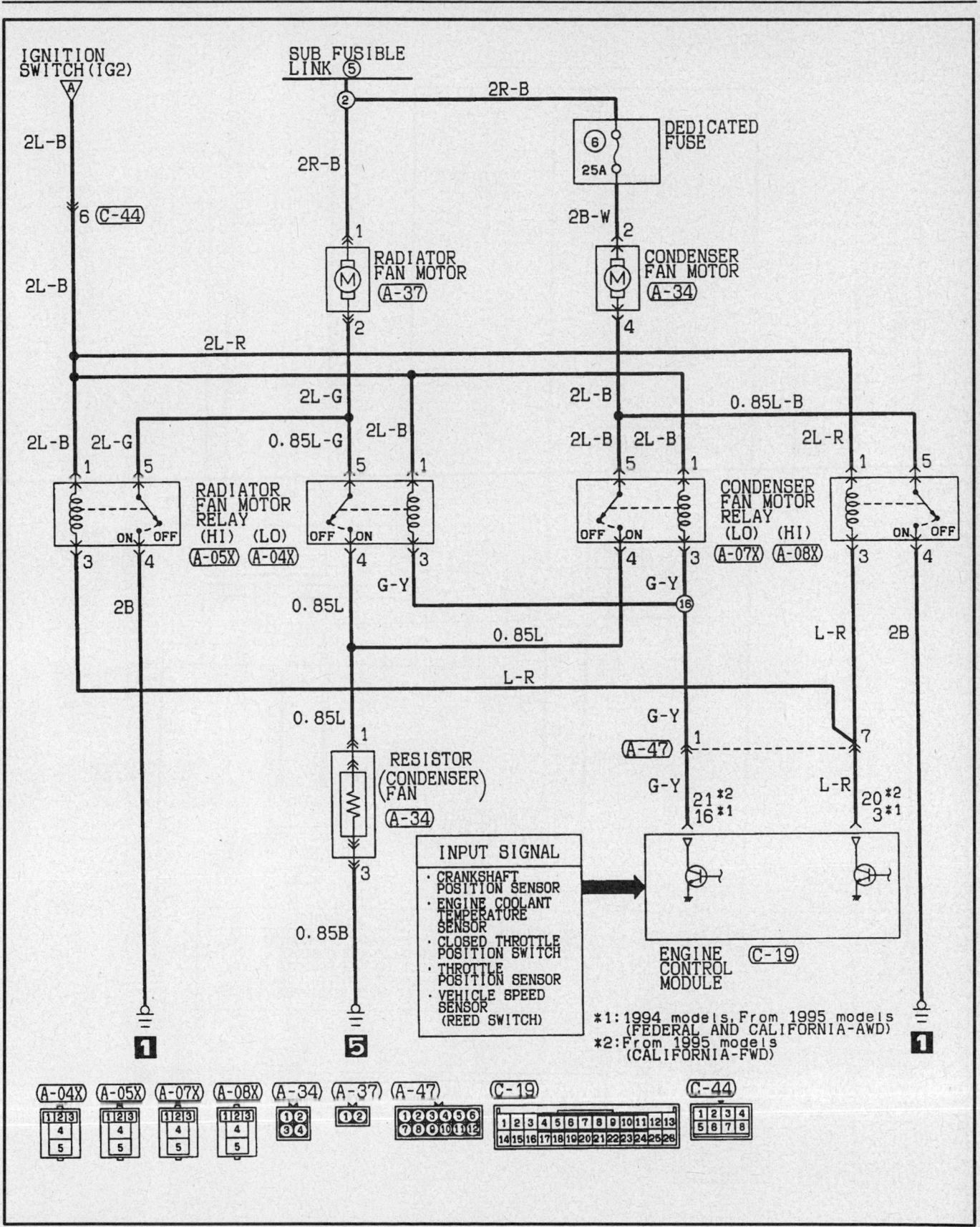

Air conditioning system wiring schematic—1994–95 Expo with 2.4L engine

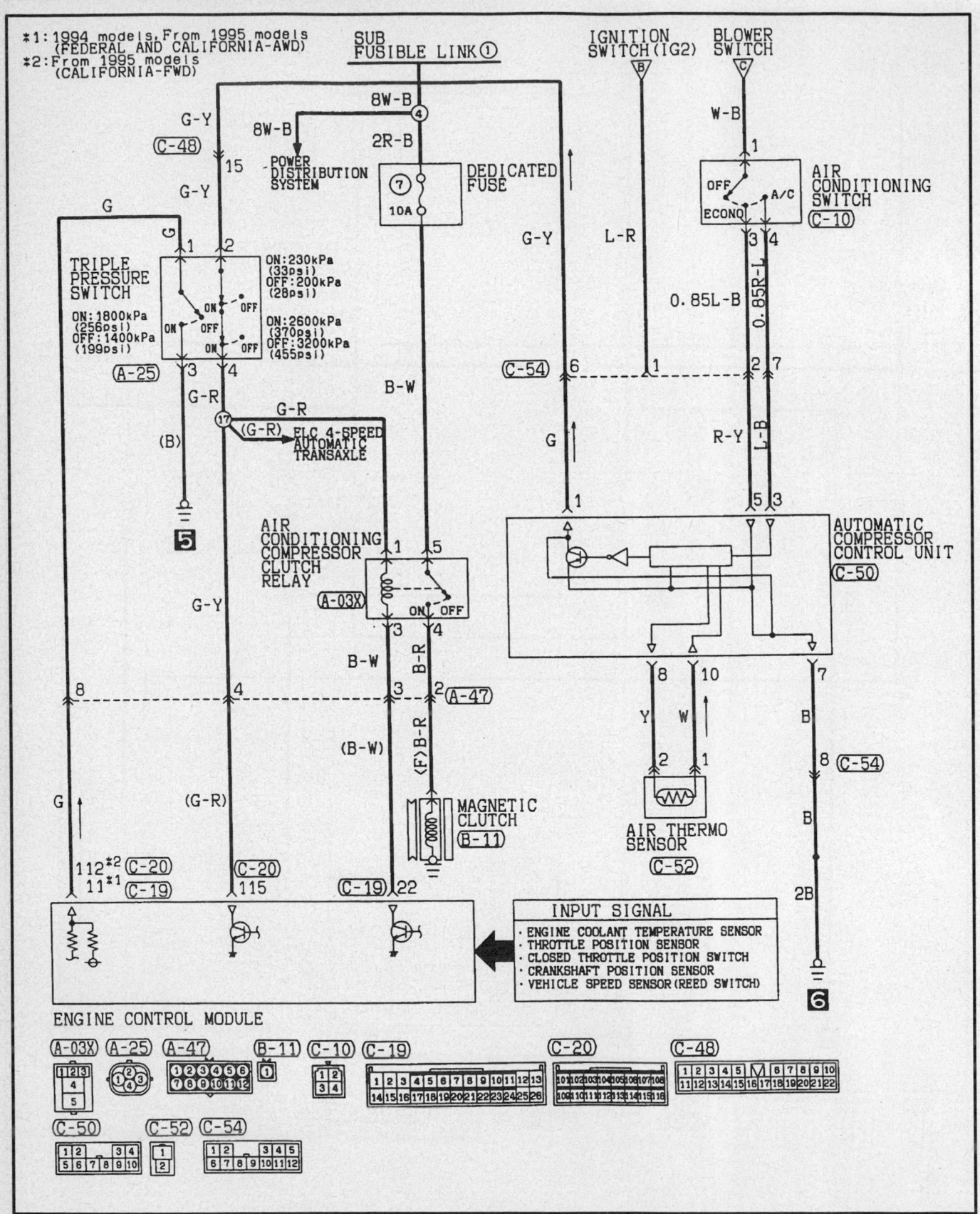

Air conditioning system wiring schematic—1994–95 Expo with 2.4L engine, Cont.

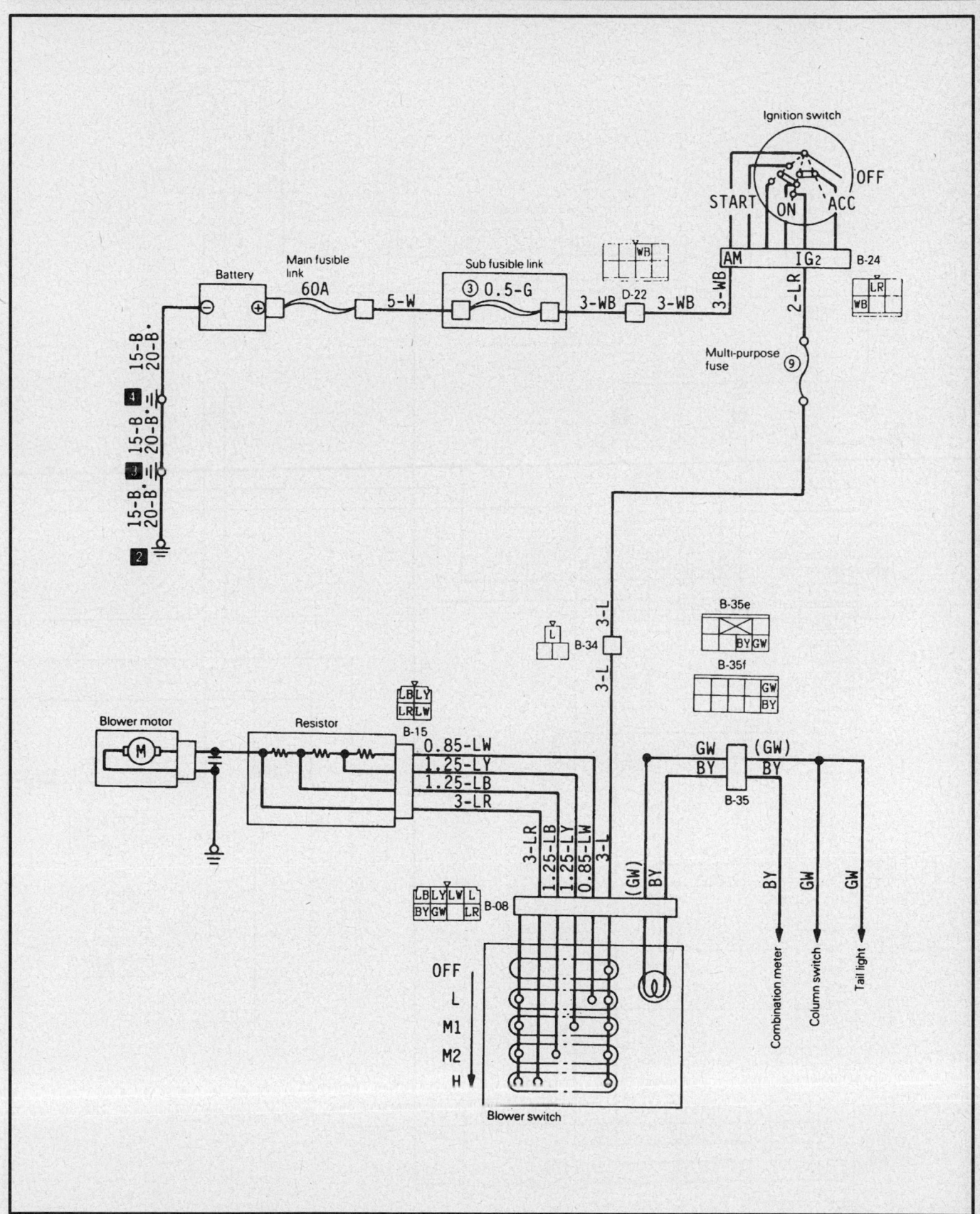

Heater system wiring schematic—Pick-Up

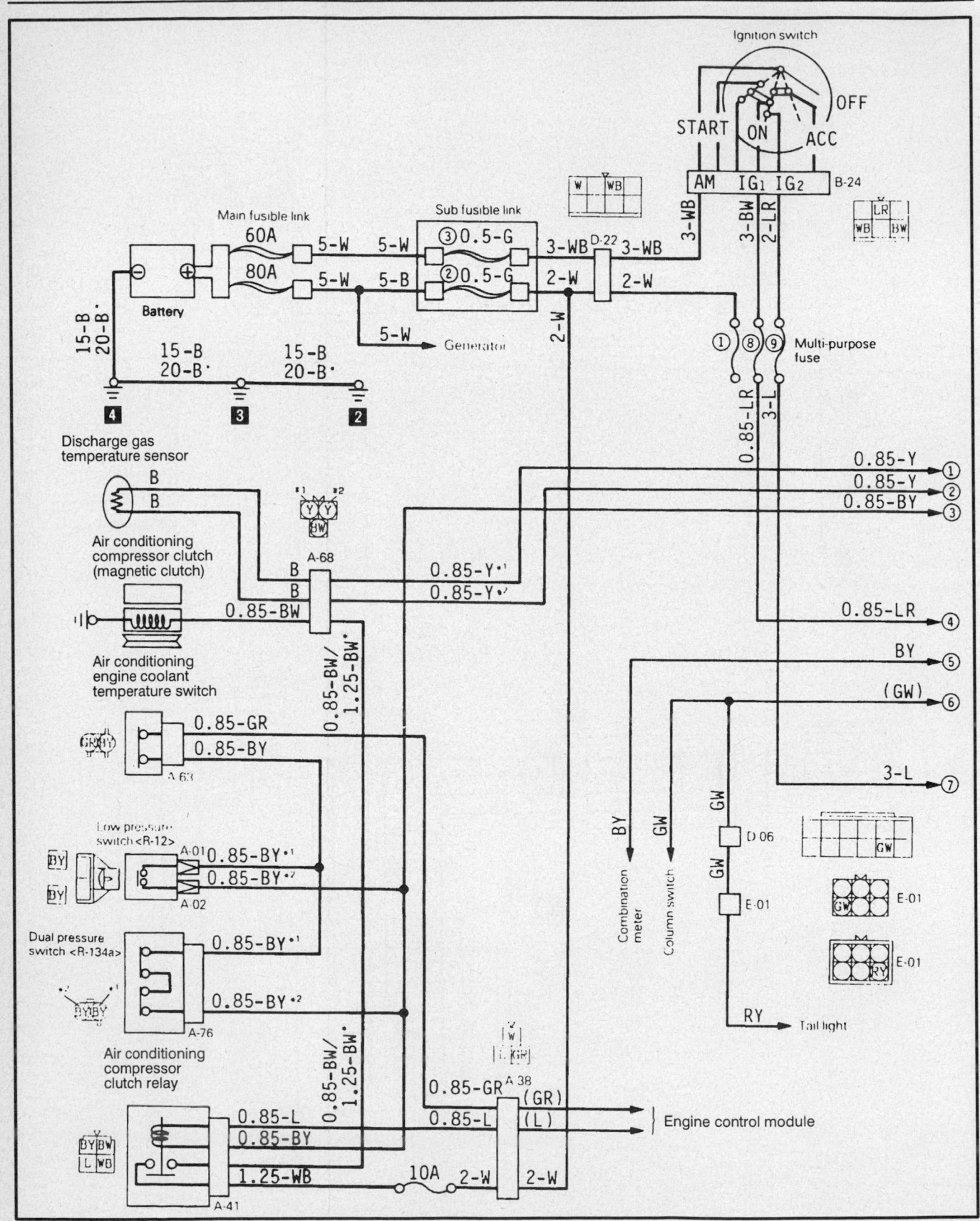

Air conditioning system wiring schematic—Pick-Up

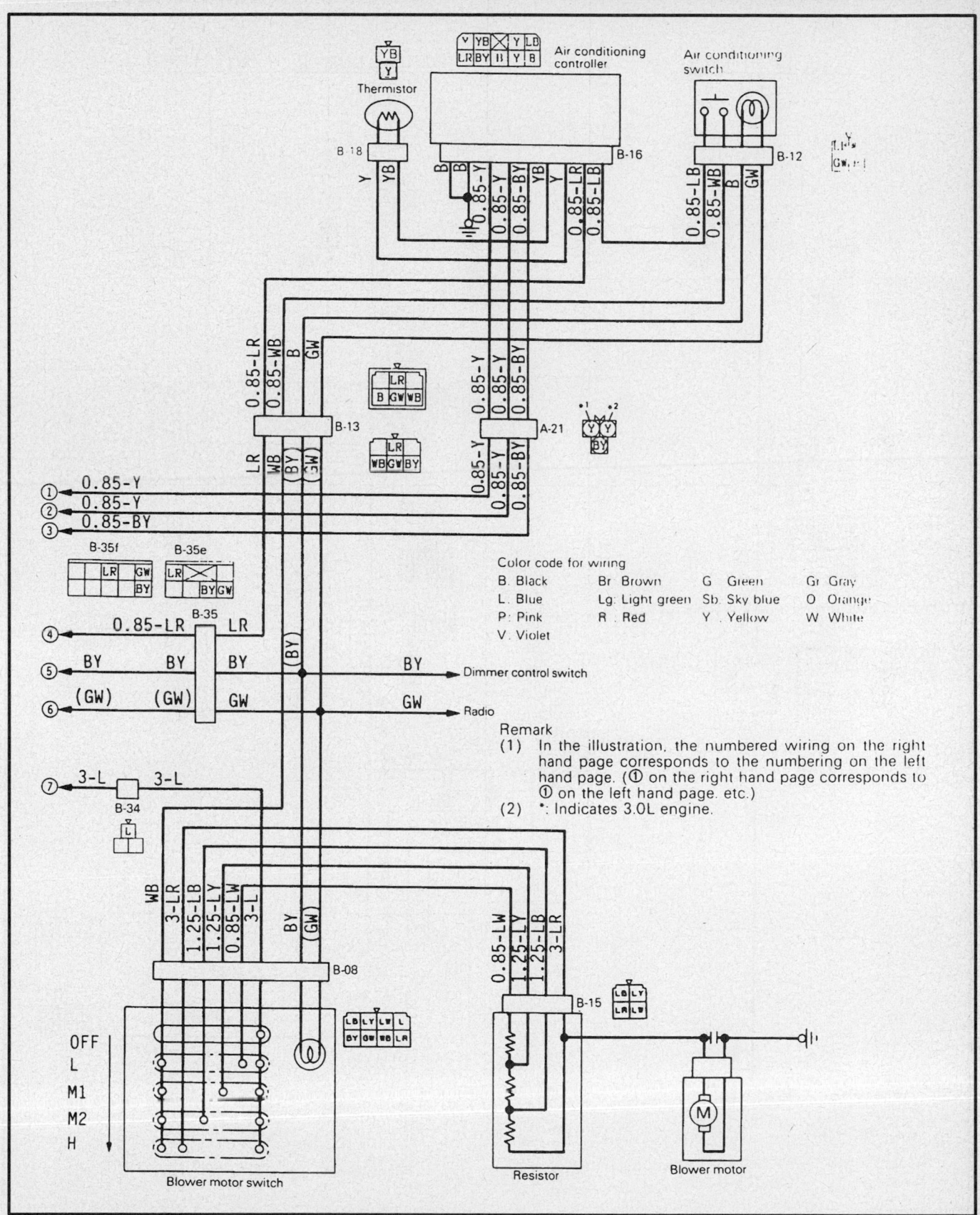

Air conditioning system wiring schematic—Pick-Up, Cont.

Color code for wiring

B: Black   Br: Brown   G: Green   Gr: Gray
L: Blue   Lg: Light green   Sb: Sky blue   O: Orange
P: Pink   R: Red   Y: Yellow   W: White
V: Violet

Remark
(1) In the illustration, the numbered wiring on the right hand page corresponds to the numbering on the left hand page. (① on the right hand page corresponds to ① on the left hand page. etc.)
(2) *: Indicates 3.0L engine.

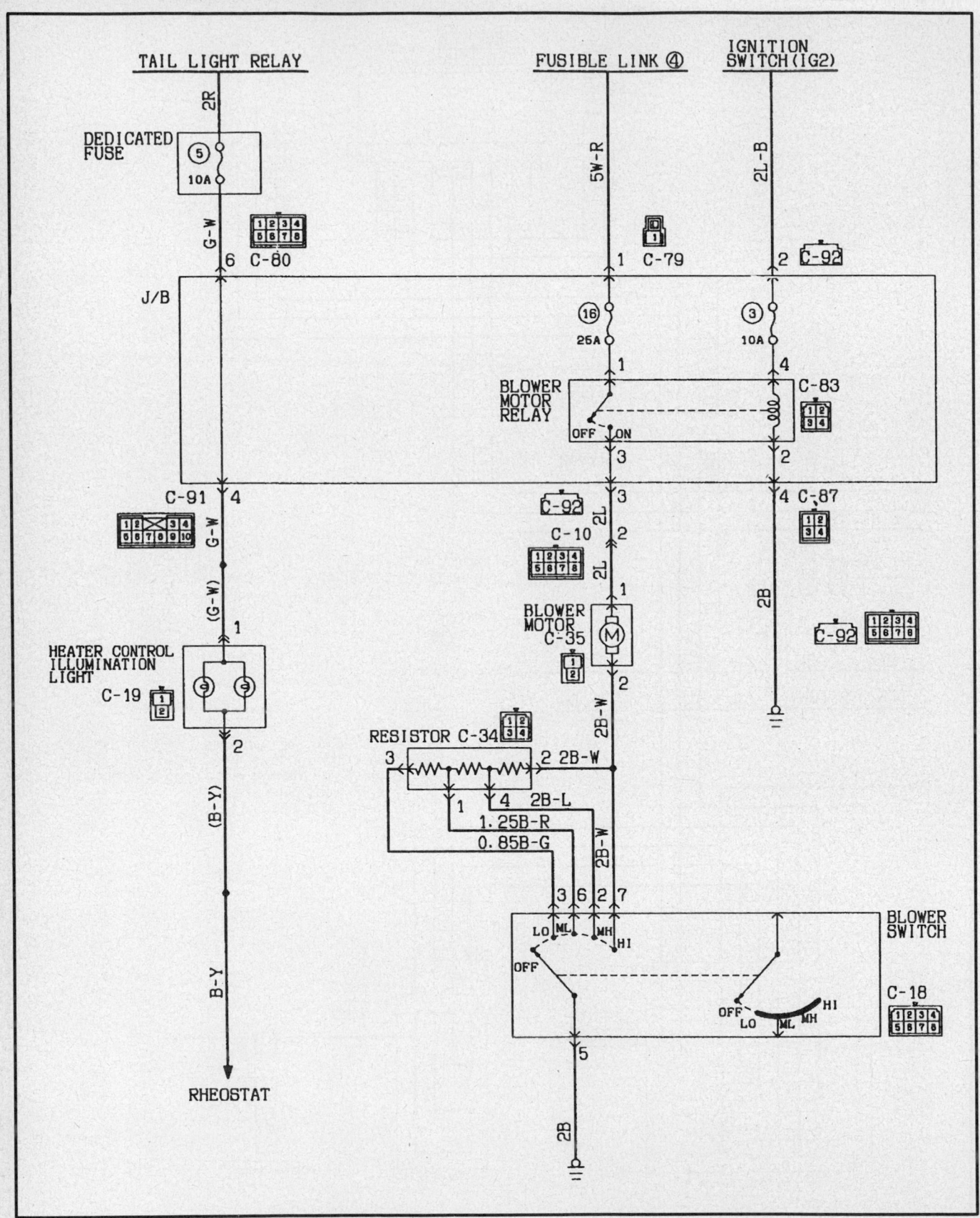

Heater system wiring schematic—1993 Montero

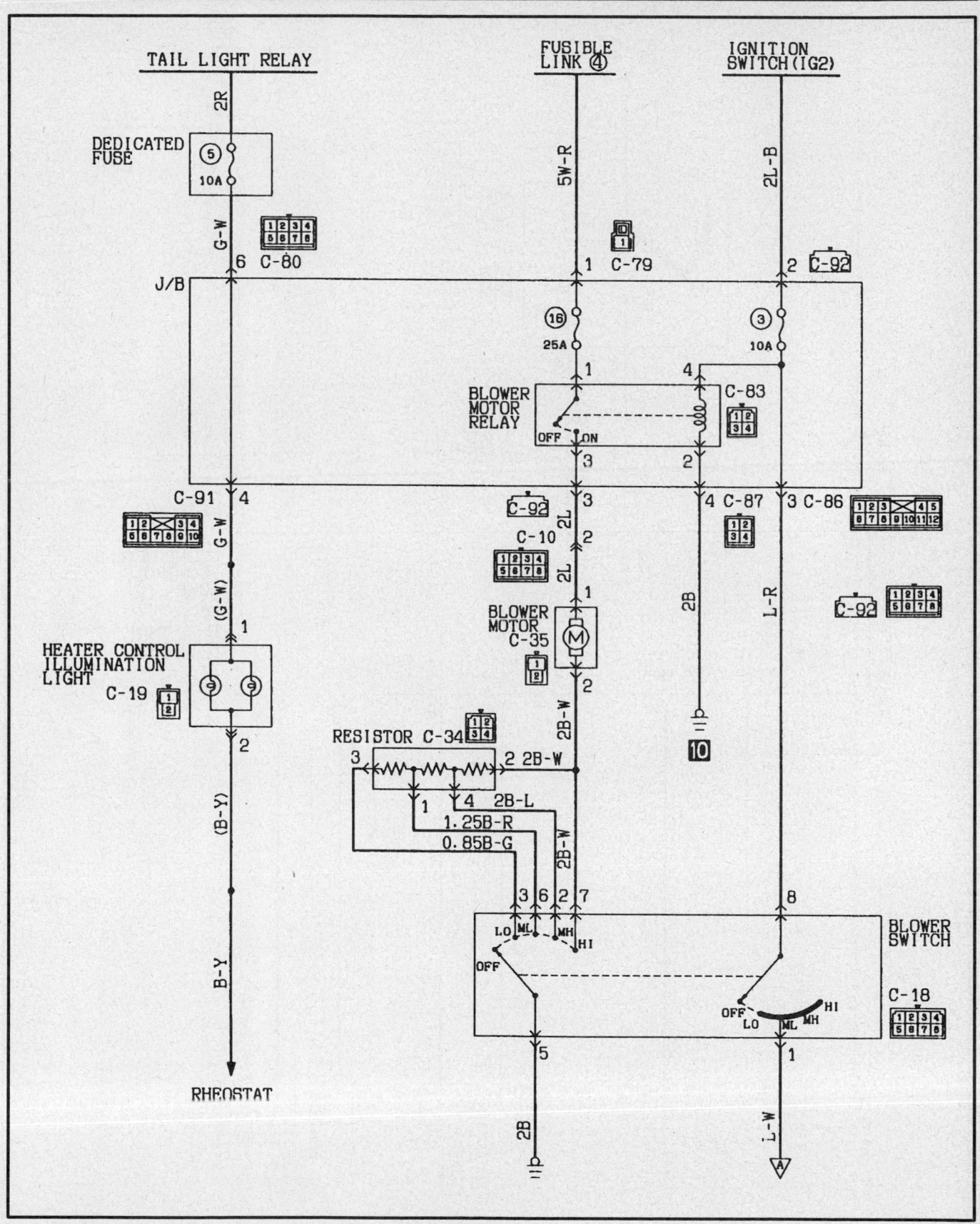

Air conditioning system wiring schematic—1993 Montero

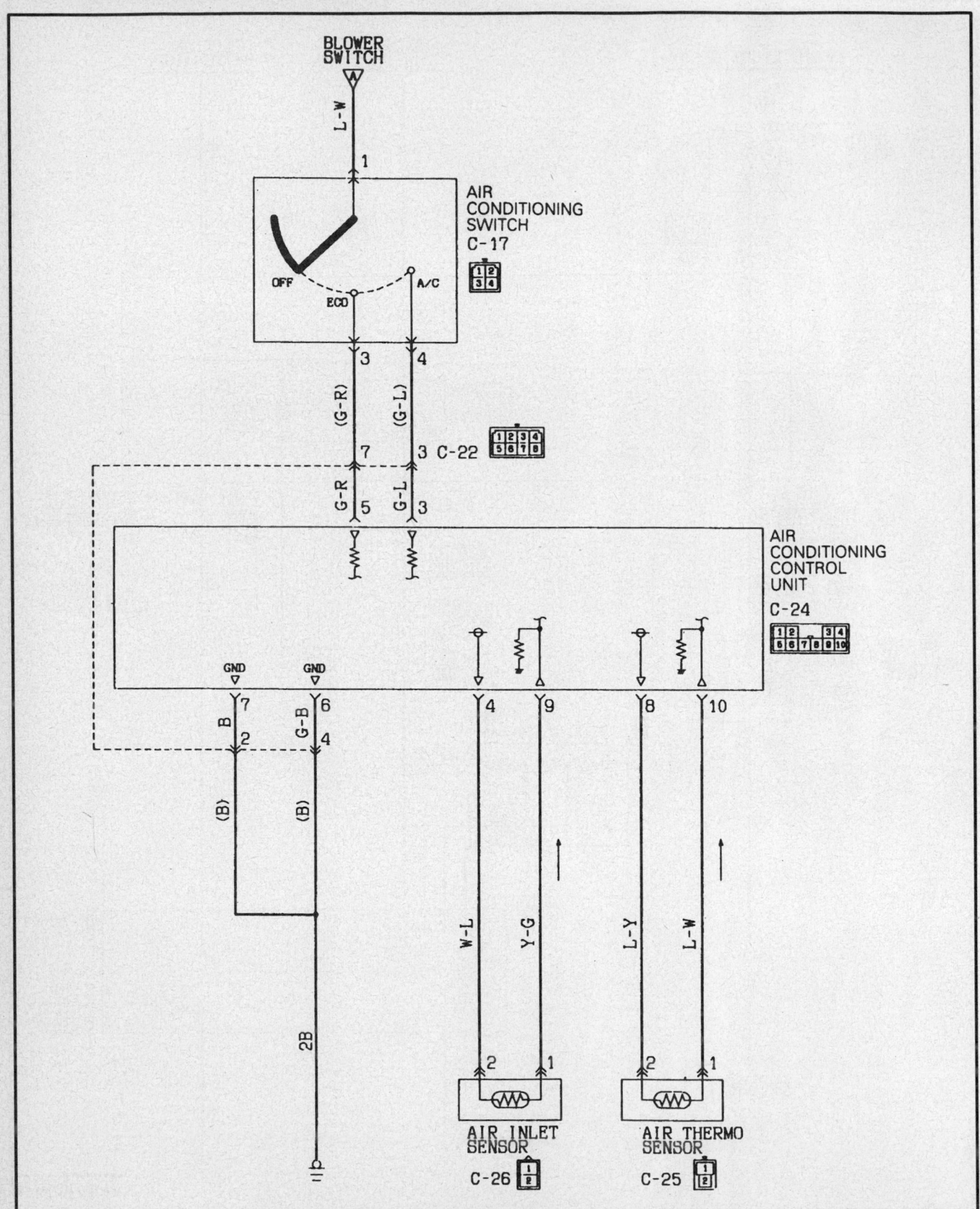

Air conditioning system wiring schematic—1993 Montero, Cont.

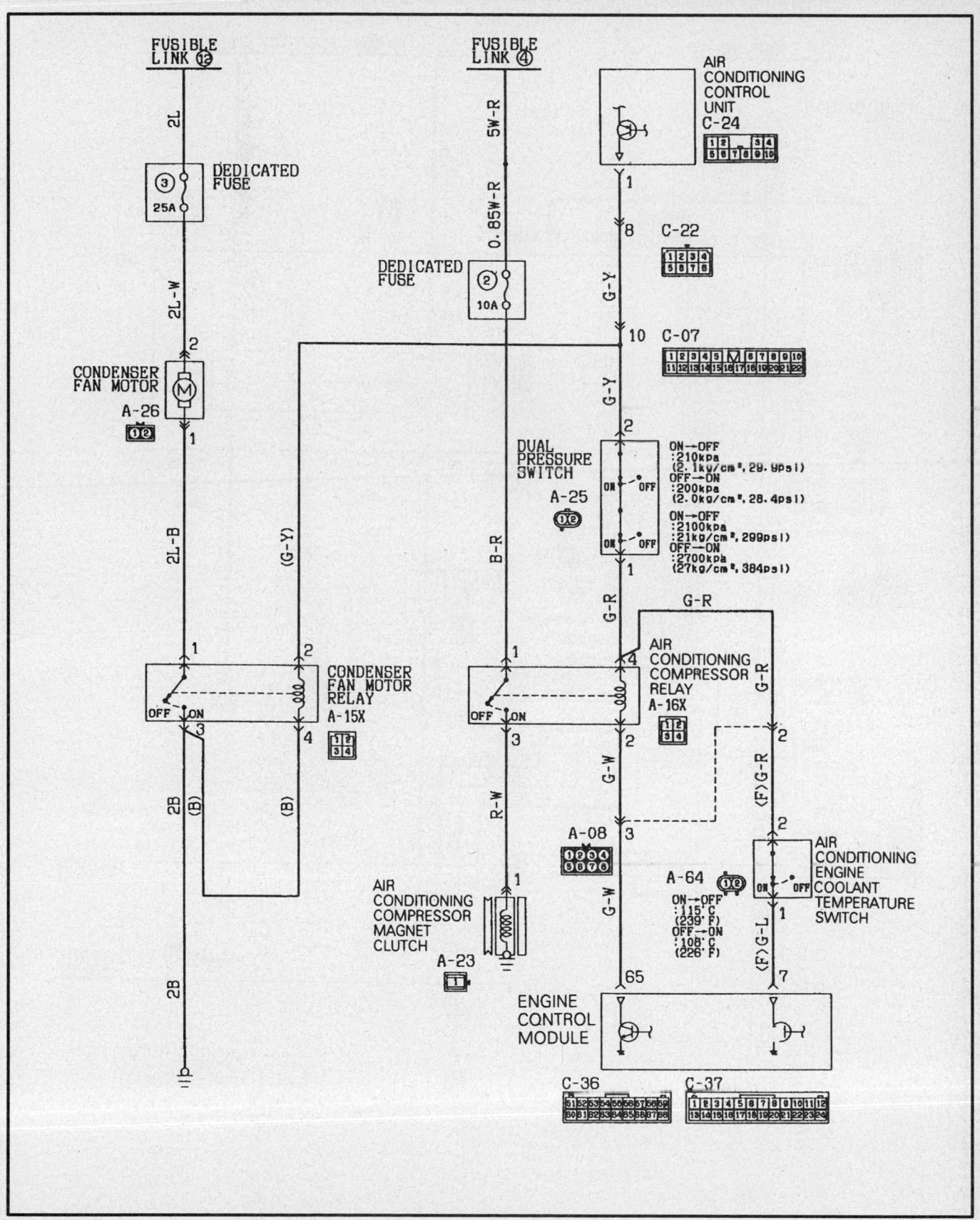

Air conditioning system wiring schematic—1993 Montero, Cont.

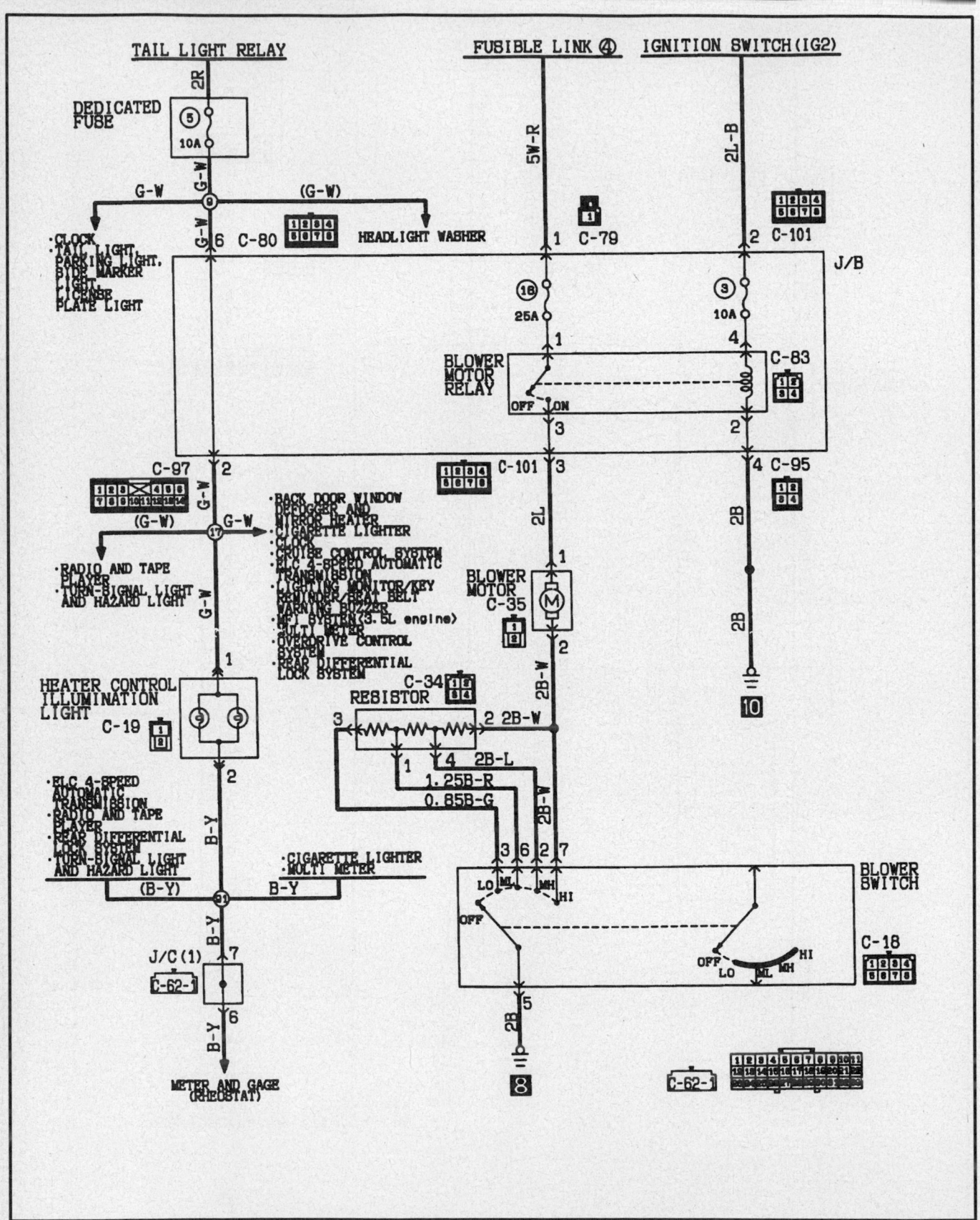

Heater system wiring schematic—1994–95 Montero

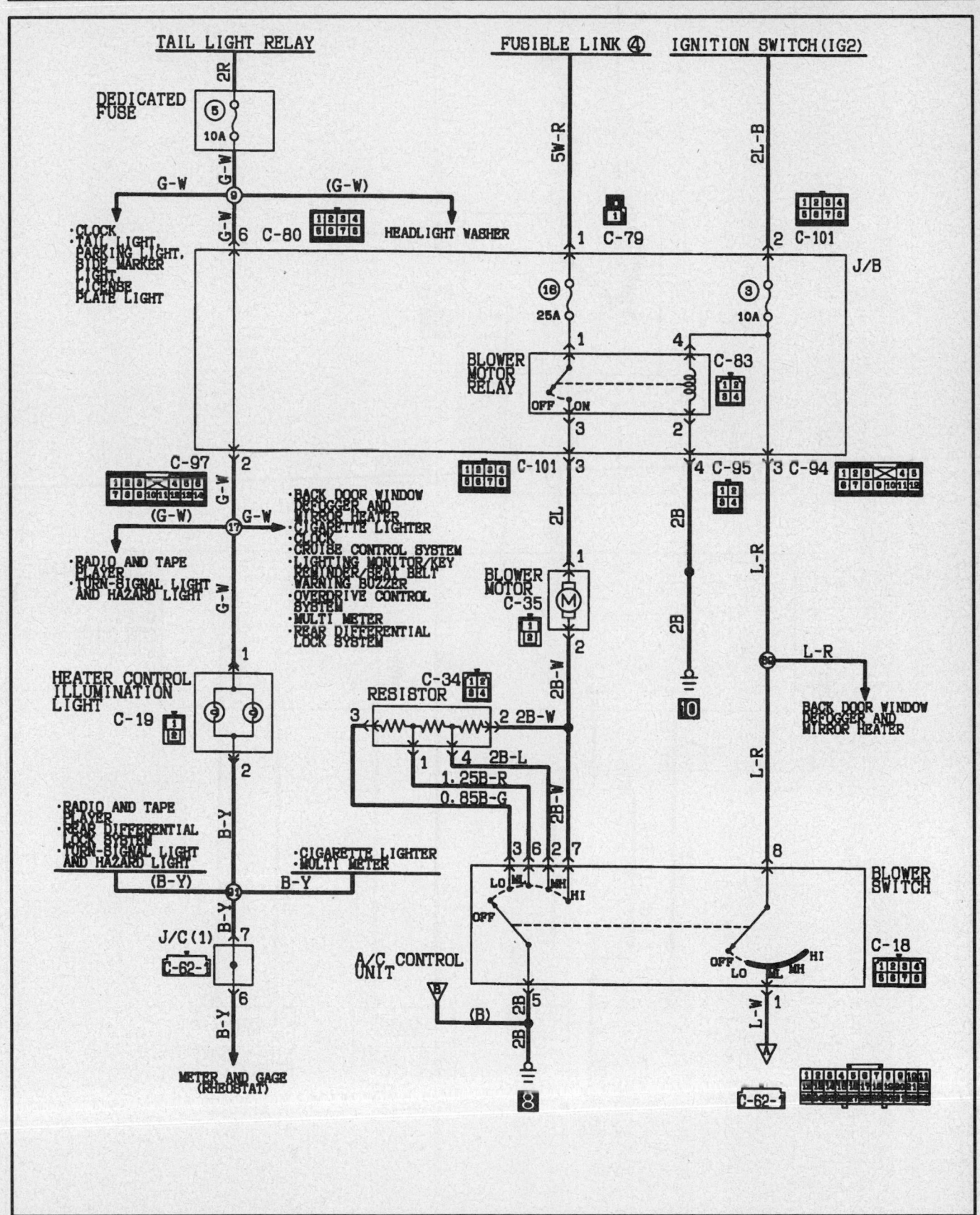

Air conditioning system wiring schematic—1994–95 Montero with 3.0L 12 valve engine

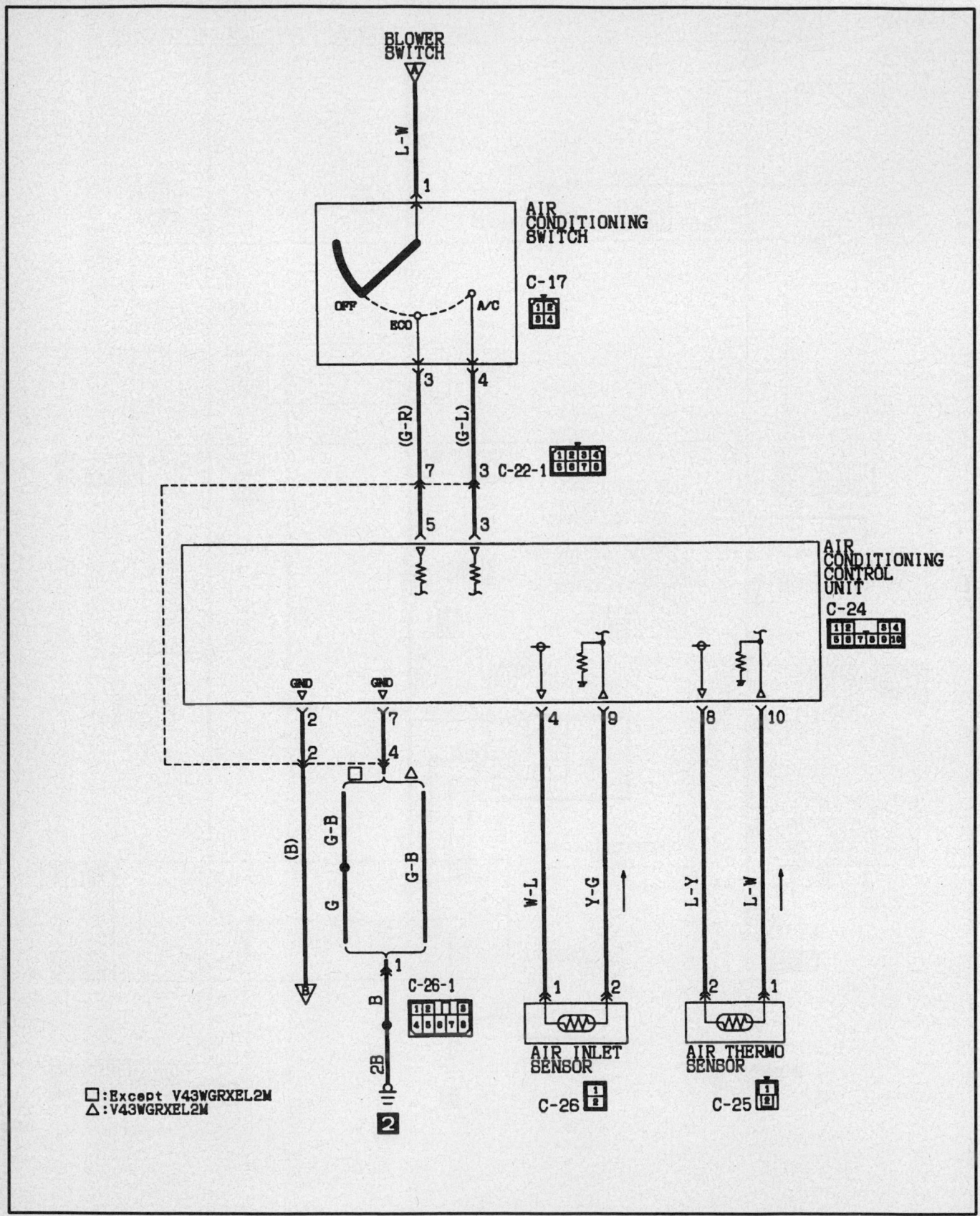

Air conditioning system wiring schematic—1994–95 Montero with 3.0L 12 valve engine, Cont.

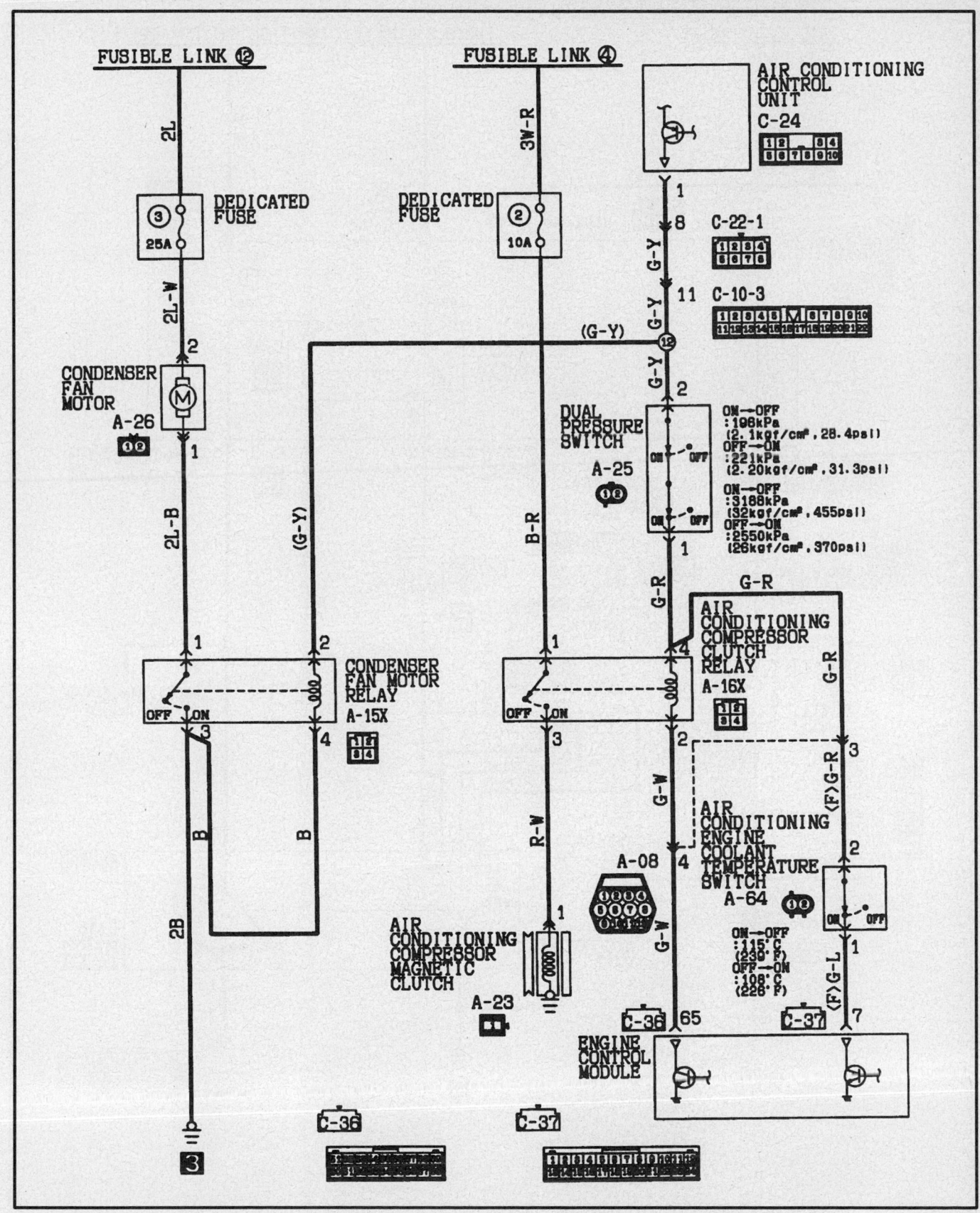

FUSIBLE LINK ⑫

FUSIBLE LINK ④

AIR CONDITIONING CONTROL UNIT C-24

C-22-1

C-10-3

DEDICATED FUSE ③ 25A

DEDICATED FUSE ② 10A

CONDENSER FAN MOTOR A-26

(G-Y)

DUAL PRESSURE SWITCH A-25

ON→OFF :196kPa (2.1kgf/cm², 28.4psi)
OFF→ON :221kPa (2.20kgf/cm², 31.3psi)

ON→OFF :3188kPa (32kgf/cm², 455psi)
OFF→ON :2550kPa (26kgf/cm², 370psi)

AIR CONDITIONING COMPRESSOR CLUTCH RELAY A-16X

CONDENSER FAN MOTOR RELAY A-15X

AIR CONDITIONING ENGINE COOLANT TEMPERATURE SWITCH A-64

ON→OFF :115°C (239°F)
OFF→ON :108°C (226°F)

AIR CONDITIONING COMPRESSOR MAGNETIC CLUTCH A-23

A-08

C-36

C-37

ENGINE CONTROL MODULE

C-36

C-37

Air conditioning system wiring schematic—1994—95 Montero with 3.0L 12 valve engine, Cont.

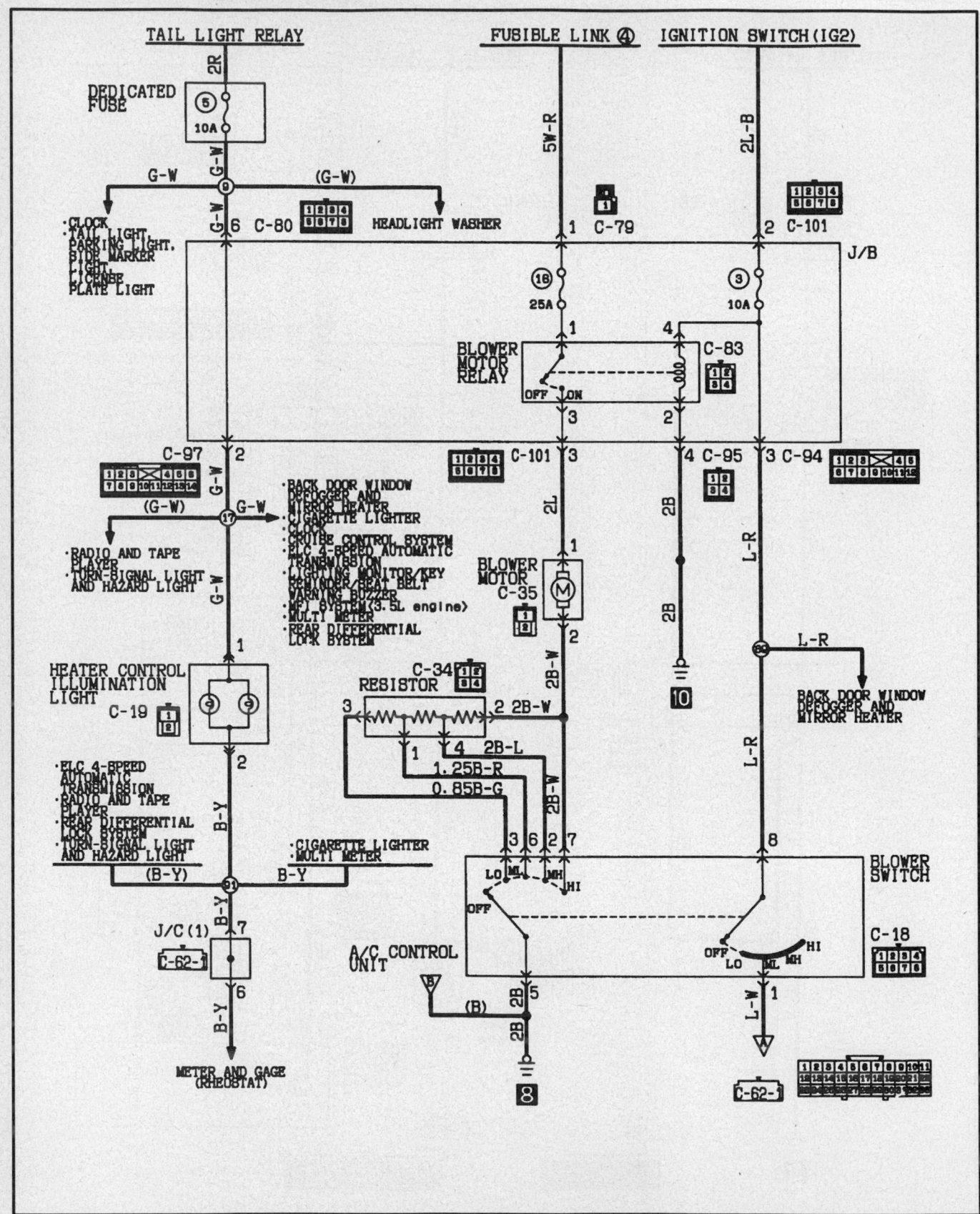

Air conditioning system wiring schematic—1994 Montero with 3.5L engine

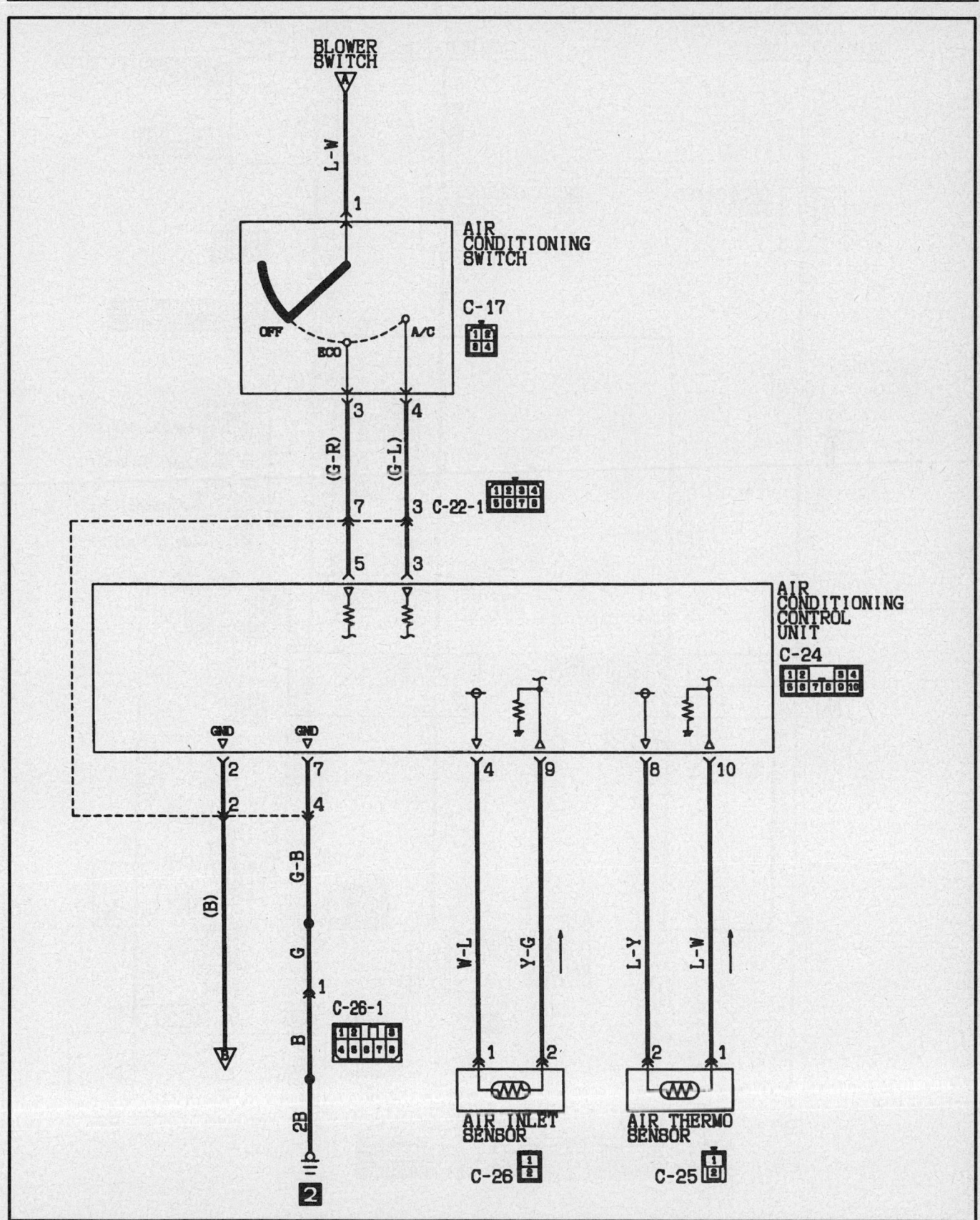

Air conditioning system wiring schematic—1994 Montero with 3.5L engine, Cont.

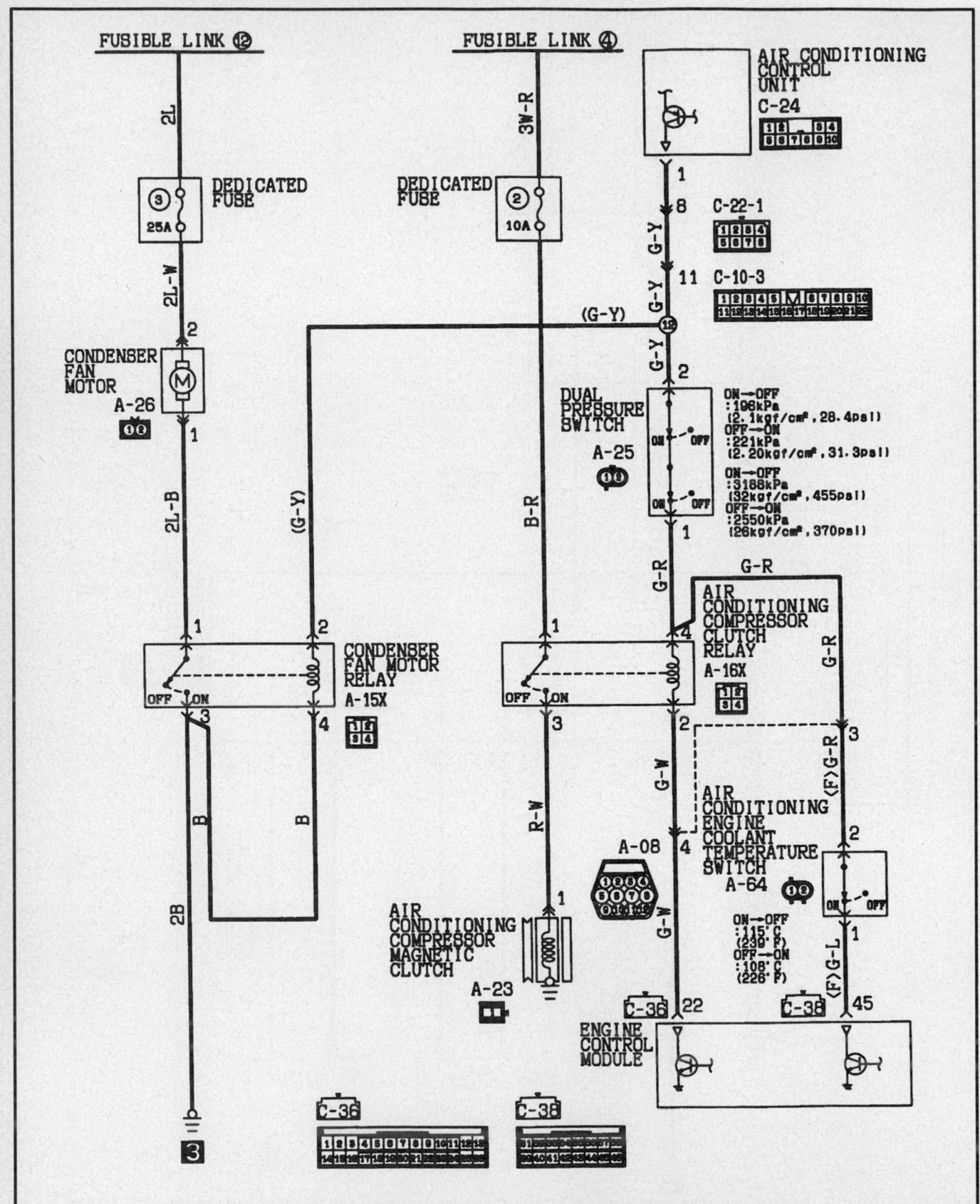

Air conditioning system wiring schematic—1994 Montero with 3.5L engine, Cont.

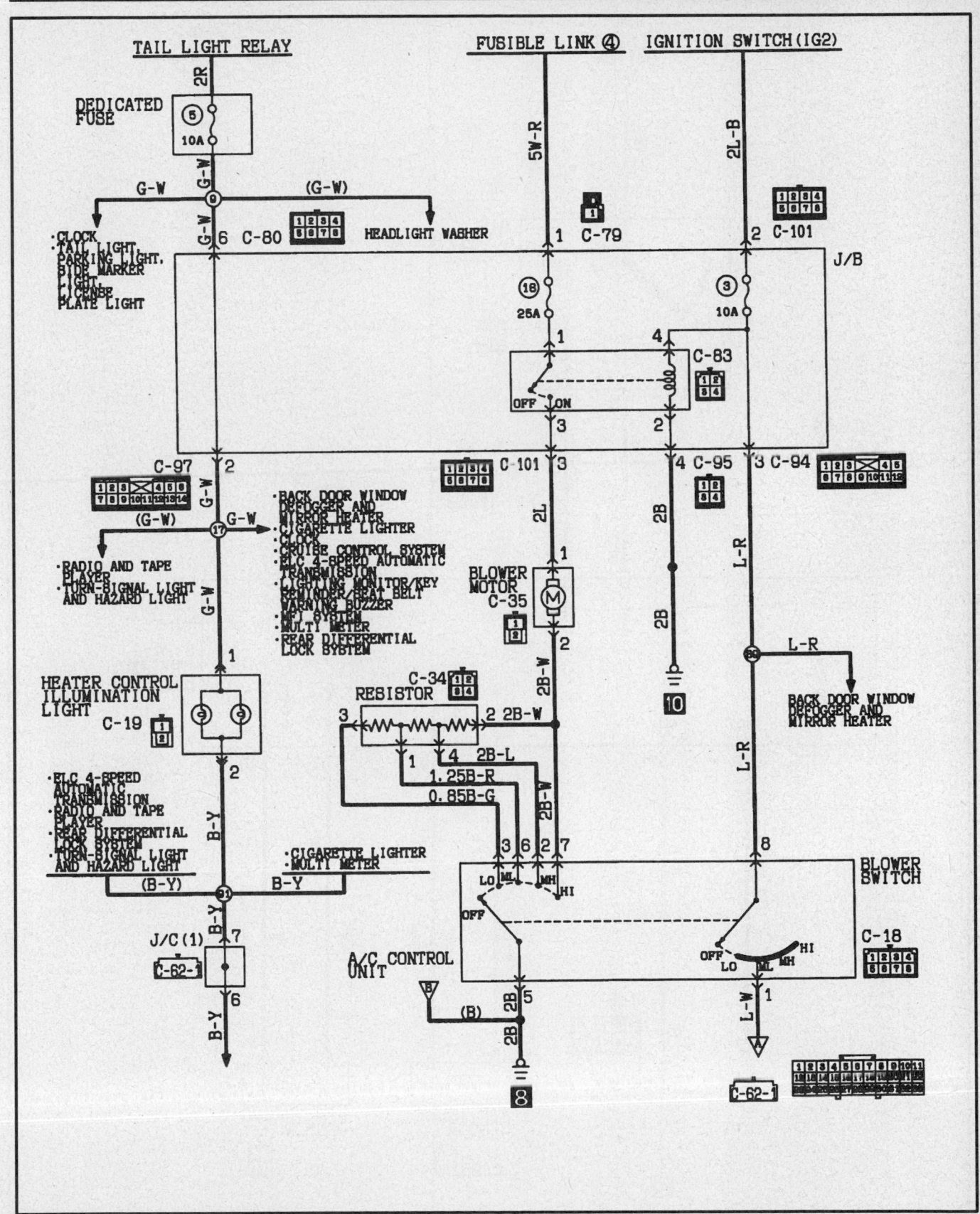

Air conditioning system wiring schematic—1995 Montero with 3.0L 24–valve or 3.5L engine

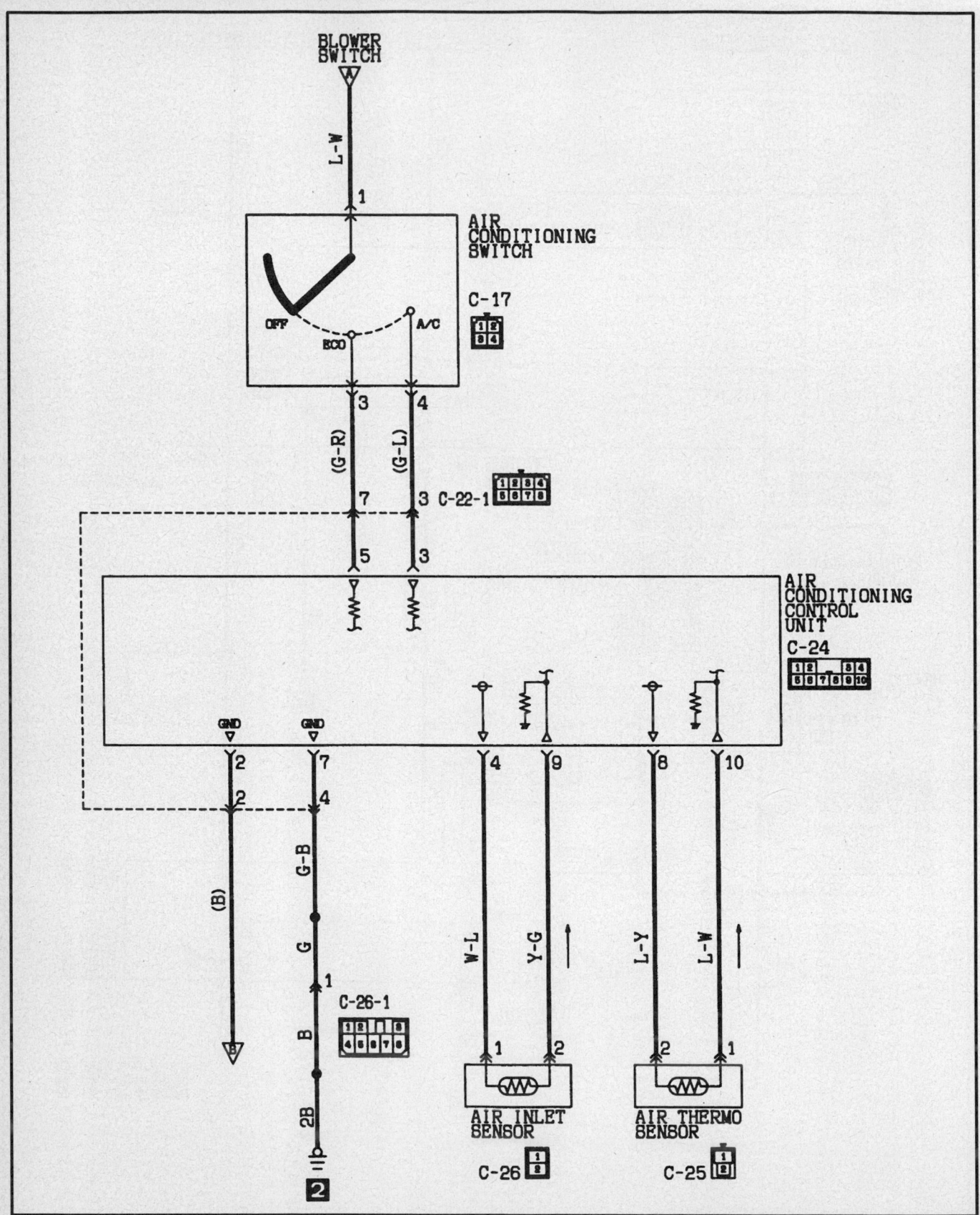

Air conditioning system wiring schematic—1995 Montero with 3.0L 24-valve or 3.0L engine

SPECIFICATIONS

ENGINE IDENTIFICATION

Year	Model	Engine Displacement Liters (cc)	Engine Series (ID/VIN)	Fuel System	No. of Cylinders	Engine Type
1993	240SX	2.4 (2389)	KA24DE	MFI	4	SOHC
	300ZX	3.0 (2960)	VG30DE	MFI	6	DOHC
	300ZX	3.0 (2960)	VG30DETT	MFI	6	DOHC–Twin Turbo
	Maxima	3.0 (2960)	VG30E	MFI	6	SOHC
	Maxima	3.0 (2960)	VE30DE	MFI	6	DOHC
	Sentra	1.6 (1597)	GA16DE	MFI	4	DOHC
	NX	1.6 (1597)	GA16DE	MFI	4	DOHC
	Sentra	2.0 (1998)	SR20DE	MFI	4	DOHC
	NX	2.0 (1998)	SR20DE	MFI	4	DOHC
	Altima	2.4 (2389)	KA24DE	MFI	4	DOHC
1994	240ZX	2.4 (2389)	KA24DE	MFI	4	DOHC
	300ZX	3.0 (2960)	VG30DE	MFI	6	DOHC
	300ZX	3.0 (2960)	VG30DETT	MFI	6	DOHC–Twin Turbo
	Maxima	3.0 (2960)	VG30E	MFI	6	SOHC
	Maxima	3.0 (2960)	VE30DE	MFI	6	DOHC
	Sentra	1.6 (1597)	GA16DE	MFI	4	DOHC
	Sentra	2.0 (1998)	SR20DE	MFI	4	DOHC
	Altima	2.4 (2389)	KA24DE	MFI	4	DOHC
1995	200SX	1.6 (1597)	GA16DE	MFI	4	DOHC
	200SX	2.0 (1998)	SR20DE	MFI	4	DOHC
	240SX	2.4 (2389)	KA24DE	MFI	4	DOHC
	300ZX	3.0 (2960)	VG30DE	MFI	6	DOHC
	300ZX	3.0 (2960)	VG30DETT	MFI	6	DOHC–Twin Turbo
	Maxima	3.0 (2960)	VG30DE	MFI	6	DOHC
	Sentra	1.6 (1597)	GA16DE	MFI	4	DOHC
	Altima	2.4 (2389)	KA24DE	MFI	4	DOHC

MFI – Multiport Fuel Injection
SOHC – Single Overhead Cam
DOHC – Dual Overhead Cam

REFRIGERANT CAPACITIES

Year	Model	Refrigerant Type	Refrigerant (oz.)	Oil① (fl. oz.)	Compressor Type
1993	240SX②	R-12	29.0–32.0	8.0	V5
	300ZX②	R-12	26.5–30.0	6.8	DKS–16H
	Maxima	R-134a	30.0–33.4	6.8	DKS–16H
	NX ②	R-12	23.0–26.4	6.8	DKV–14D
	Sentra②	R-12	23.0–26.4	6.8	DKV–14D
	Altima	R-134a	24.6–28.1	6.8	DKV–14C

REFRIGERANT CAPACITIES

Year	Model	Refrigerant Type	Refrigerant (oz.)	Oil① (fl. oz.)	Compressor Type
1994	240SX②	R–12	29.0–32.0	8.0	V5
	300ZX	R–134a	19.4–22.9	6.8	DKS–16H
	Maxima	R–134a	30.0–33.4	6.8	DKS–16H
	Sentra	R–134a	21.1–24.6	6.8	DKV–14D
	Altima	R–134a	24.6–28.1	6.8	DKV–14C
1995	200SX, Sentra	R–134a	21.1–24.6	6.8	DKV–14D
	240SX②	R–12	29.0–32.0	8.0	V5
	300ZX	R–134a	19.4–22.9	6.8	DKS–16H
	Maxima	R–134a	27.3–29.1	6.8	V6
	Altima	R–134a	24.6–28.1	6.8	DKV–14C

① Total oil capacity of the system.
② Systems use R–12 refrigerant and standard air conditioning oil; do not mix in any amount with R-134a refrigerant or its special oil.

AIR CONDITIONING BELT TENSION

Year	Model	Engine Liters (cc)	Belt Type	Specifications	
				New (lbs.)①	Used (lbs.)①
1993	240SX	2.4 (2389)	Poly–V	0.26–0.30	0.30–0.34
	300ZX	3.0 (2960)	Poly–V	0.28–0.31	0.31–0.35
	Maxima	3.0 (2960) (SOHC)	Poly–V	0.16–0.24	0.20–0.28
	Maxima	3.0 (2960) (DOHC)	Poly–V	0.20–0.24	0.22–0.26
	Sentra	1.6 (1597)	Poly–V	0.20–0.28	0.24–0.31
	NX	1.6 (1597)	Poly–V	0.20–0.28	0.24–0.31
	Sentra	2.0 (1998)	Poly–V	0.28–0.31	0.31–0.35
	NX	2.0 (1998)	Poly–V	0.28–0.31	0.31–0.35
	Altima	2.4 (2389)	Poly–V	0.24–0.28	0.28–0.31
1994	240SX	2.4 (2389)	Poly–V	0.26–0.30	0.30–0.34
	300ZX	3.0	Poly–V	0.28–0.31	0.31–0.35
	Maxima	3.0 (SOHC)	Poly–V	0.16–0.24	0.20–0.28
	Maxima	3.0 (DOHC)	Poly–V	0.20–0.28	0.22–0.26
	Sentra	1.6	Poly–V	0.20–0.28	0.24–0.31
	Sentra	2.0	Poly–V	0.26–0.30	0.28–0.31
	Altima	2.4	Poly–V	0.24–0.28	0.28–0.31
1995	200SX, Sentra	1.6	Poly–V	0.20–0.24	0.24–0.26
	200SX	2.0	Poly–V	0.26–0.30	0.28–0.31
	240SX	2.4 (2389)	Poly–V	0.26–0.30	0.30–0.34
	300ZX	3.0	Poly–V	0.28–0.31	0.31–0.35
	Maxima	3.0	Poly–V	0.15–0.16	0.17–0.18
	Altima	2.4	Poly–V	0.24–0.28	0.28–0.31

① Inches of deflection at mid–point of belt run.
SOHC – Single Overhead Cam Engine
DOHC – Dual Overhead Cam Engine

SYSTEM DESCRIPTION

General Information

240SX

The 240SX utilizes R-12 refrigerant. A manually operated air conditioning and heating system is used. The control panel can either be a lever type connected through cables to the key air doors, or a push button type which uses electrical connections and door motors. To activate and protect the system a series of relays energize the compressor and the condenser fan. A dual pressure switch provides compressor cut-off in the event of extremely high or low pressure on the high side of the system. A variable displacement compressor is used also.

300ZX

Beginning in 1994, the 300ZX uses R-134a, non-CFC refrigerant. Either manual or automatic air conditioning is used. A dual pressure switch provides compressor cut-off in the event of extremely high or low pressure on the high side of the system. A suction throttle valve is used on automatic A/C systems to prevent evaporator freeze-up. Additionally, a thermo control amplifier will cycle the compressor on and off to prevent evaporator freeze-up. A fast idle control device, controlled through the engine control computer, provides idle increase when A/C is ON or if engine temperatures rise (to improve engine cooling).

Maxima and Altima

R-134a, non-CFC refrigerant, is used. Like the 300ZX, either manual or automatic air conditioning systems are used. As part of the protection system a triple pressure switch (which monitors high, low and medium pressures) and thermo control amplifier are used to stop compressor operation under certain extreme conditions. Both systems utilize an FICD solenoid. Maxima uses a V-6 variable displacement compressor to provide varying refrigerant control in response to the required cooling capacity.

Sentra and 200SX

Beginning in 1994, the Sentra and 200SX use R-134a, non-CFC refrigerant. A manual air conditioning system with either lever type or push button type control panel is used. In 1995, the Sentra and 200SX use a combination push button/control knob control panel. A dual pressure switch, evaporator thermo control amplifier, FICD solenoid and relays for the compressor clutch and cooling fans are used.

Service Valve Location

200SX and Sentra

The low pressure valve is near the firewall, the high pressure valve is in the high pressure line between the condenser and the evaporator.

240SX

Both valves are near the compressor or the high pressure valve is near the condenser.

300ZX

Both valves are near the firewall on the right fender. Models also have the sight glass near the high service valve.

Altima

The low pressure valve is near the firewall, the high pressure valve is at the condenser.

Maxima

The low pressure valve is at the compressor or on later models, in the low pressure line between the compressor and evaporator. The high pressure valve is at or near the condenser.

Special Precautions

1. All refrigerant service work must be done with the proper recycling equipment. Carefully follow the manufacturer's instructions for use of that equipment. Do not allow any refrigerant to discharge to the air.
2. Any amount of water will make the system less effective. When any part of the system has been removed, plug or cap the lines to prevent moisture from the air entering the system. When installing a new component, do not uncap the fittings until ready to attach the lines.
3. When assembling a fitting, always use a new O-ring and lightly lubricate the fitting with compressor oil. Be careful not to apply lubricant to threaded portions of connections.
4. When a compressor is removed, do not leave it on its side or upside down for more than 10 minutes. The oil may leak into the low pressure chamber.
5. The proper amount of oil must be maintained in the system to prevent compressor damage and to maintain system efficiency. Be sure to measure and adjust the amount of oil removed or added to the system, especially when replacing the compressor.
6. CFC-12 (R-12) refrigerant and HFC-134a (R-134a) refrigerant, and their respective lubrication oils, are not compatible, and must never be mixed in any amount. Mixing of the refrigerants or their lubrication oils may cause system failure.

System Discharging

1. Install adapter valves to the vehicle service valves and/or connect the refrigerant recycling equipment according to the manufacturer's instructions.
2. Open both the adapter or manifold valves slowly to prevent excess oil loss. Allow the refrigerant to stop flowing before going on to the next step.

System Evacuating

1. Open both the high and low pressure valves and run the vacuum pump for more than 5 minutes. The gauges should stabilize at 29.13–29.92 in. (740–760mm) Hg vacuum.
2. Close the valves and turn the pump OFF. Check to see that the vacuum gauges remain stable. If the gauge on the low pressure side moves 3.94 in. (100mm) Hg in about 10 minutes, the system will discharge itself in about one month.
3. If the system will not hold vacuum, first check that the service equipment is properly connected and in good working order. If any connections in the system have been disturbed, make sure they have been properly reconnected. Be sure to use new lightly oiled O-rings and that the fitting is not over torqued.
4. If the system holds vacuum, open the valves and run the pump for more than 20 minutes. Close the valves, then turn the pump OFF.

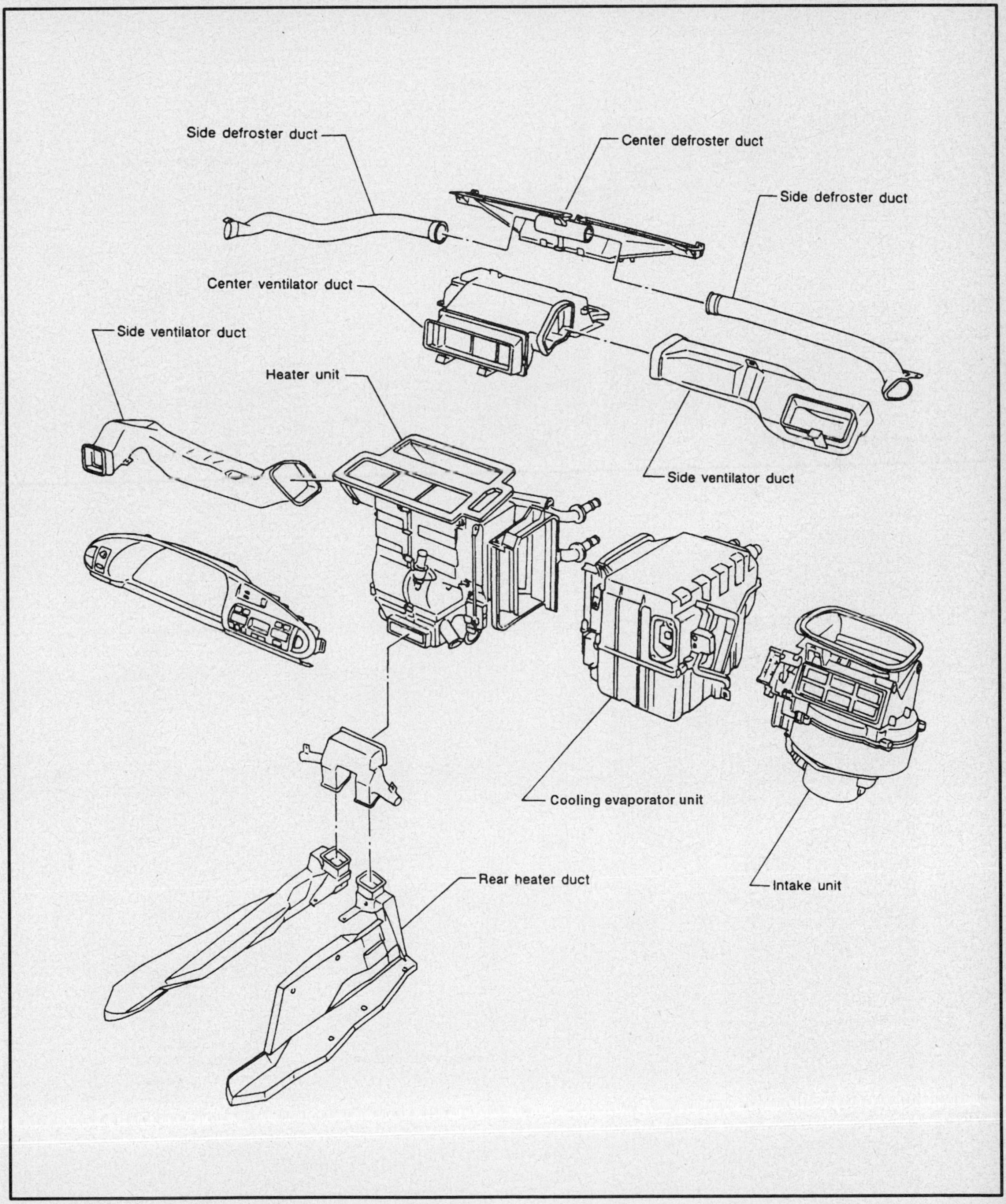

Side defroster duct

Center defroster duct

Side defroster duct

Center ventilator duct

Side ventilator duct

Heater unit

Side ventilator duct

Cooling evaporator unit

Rear heater duct

Intake unit

Heating and air conditioning components—Altima

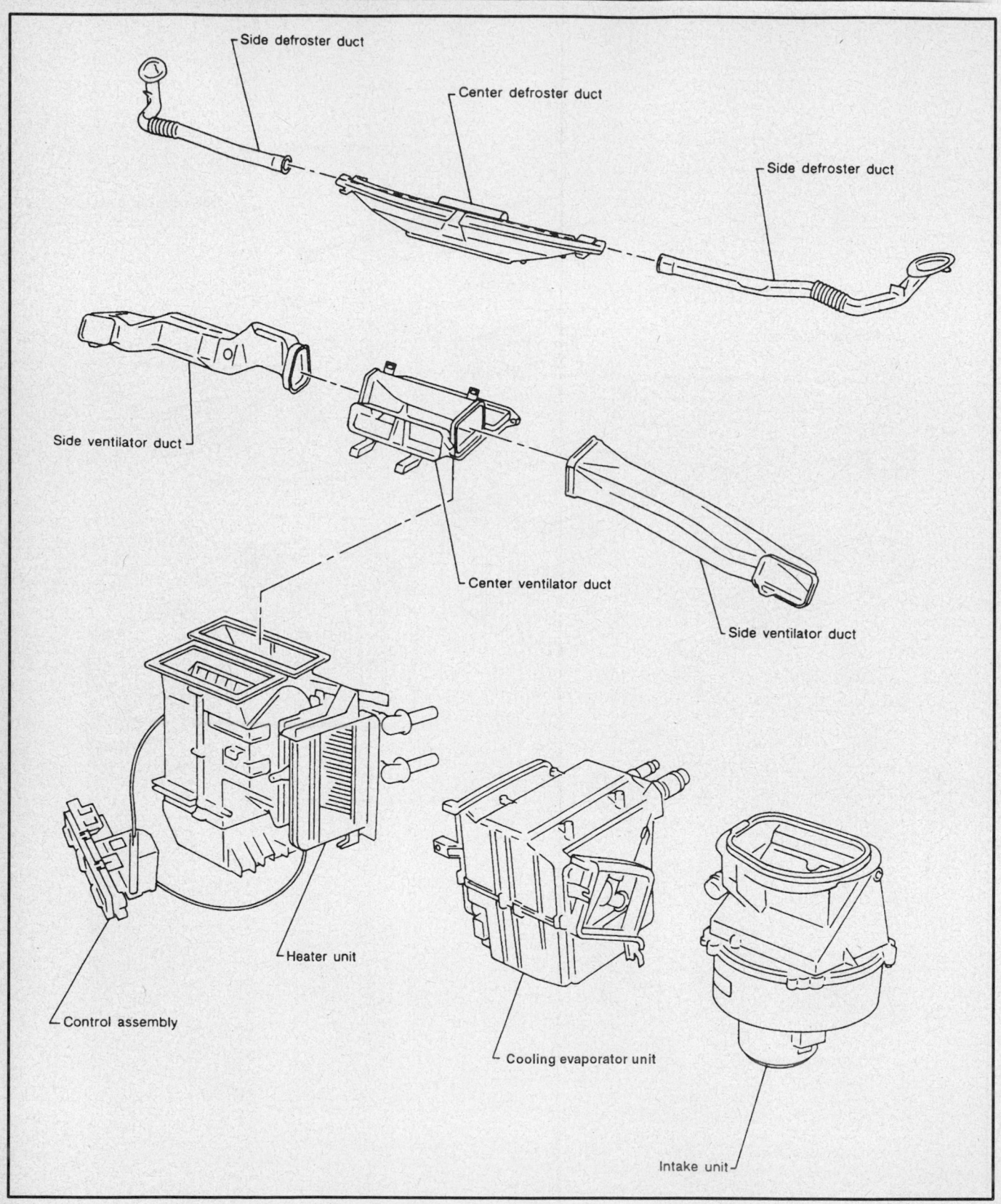

- Side defroster duct
- Center defroster duct
- Side defroster duct
- Side ventilator duct
- Center ventilator duct
- Side ventilator duct
- Heater unit
- Control assembly
- Cooling evaporator unit
- Intake unit

Heating and air conditioning components—Sentra and 200SX

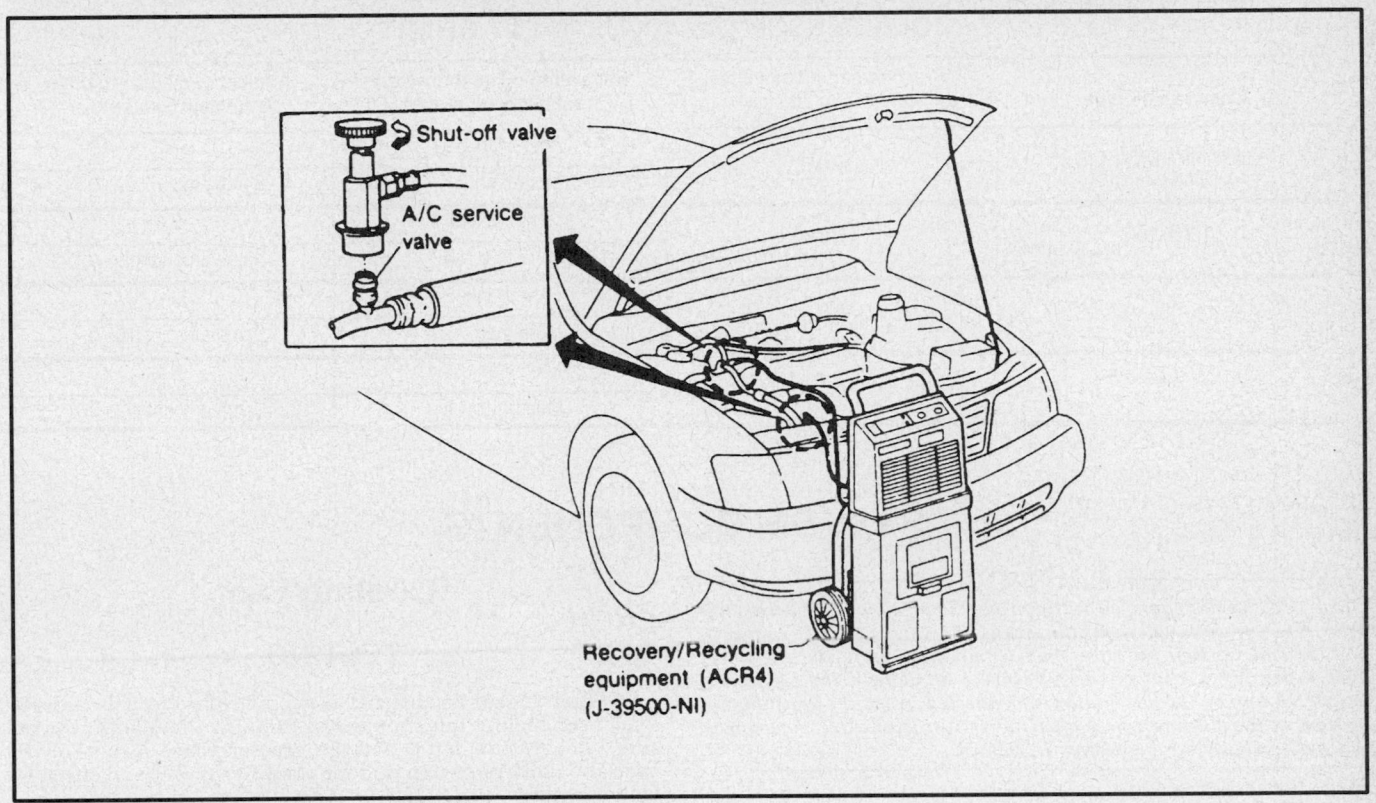

Shut-off valve

A/C service valve

Recovery/Recycling equipment (ACR4) (J-39500-NI)

Typical service connections—200SX and Sentra shown

System Charging

1. Always use recycling/charging station equipment. The equipment in use will determine the charging procedure. Carefully follow the manufacturer's instructions and add the correct amount of refrigerant as noted in the specifications chart. Never add refrigerant through the high pressure service valve.

2. If charging directly from the refrigerant container, add refrigerant to the low pressure side until it slows or stops flowing. Start the engine, set the controls to maximum cooling and, with the refrigerant can upright, continue to flow the refrigerant into the low pressure side until the specified amount has been added.

3. With the system fully charged and with the correct oil level in the compressor, run the air conditioner at the FULL COLD setting for more than 5 minutes.

4. Stop the engine and immediately check the system for leaks using a suitable leak detector. Be sure to check at every line fitting, the service valves, the pressure switch at the receiver/drier, at the compressor shaft seals, bolt holes and clutch, and the pressure and temperature relief valves.

5. To check the evaporator and valves inside the vehicle, insert the leak detector probe into the water drain hose for more than 10 minutes. Leaking refrigerant is heavier than air and will seek the lower exit, so always look for leaks at the lowest point.

Compressor Oil Service

The compressor is lubricated with a special oil that circulates with the refrigerant when the system is operating and drops out of the refrigerant when the system is stopped. Insufficient or incorrect oil will cause damage to the compressor. Too much oil will impair the system's cooling ability. When installing new parts of the system or a new compressor, the oil quantity must be adjusted.

NOTE: Systems with R-134a use a special refrigerant oil which is different from the oil used with R-12. Be sure to use the correct oil type for the specific refrigerant application.

1. If a new compressor is being installed, drain the oil out of the old unit and measure it.

2. Adjust the quantity of oil in the new compressor according to the chart given.

3. From the oil drained from the old compressor, drain the corresponding amount of oil from the new compressor.

4. New compressors usually come with the full amount of oil, so it is necessary to remove oil to maintain the right system level.

5. If installing another major system component, add oil as follows:
- evaporator: 2.5 oz.
- Condenser: 2.5 oz.
- Receiver/drier: 0.2 oz.

6. If a large oil leak is indicated, make the necessary repairs, add 1.0 oz. of oil, then run the system at idle speed set for full cooling for about 10 minutes. Stop the engine and drain the oil from the compressor to measure how much oil to add.

COMPRESSOR OIL ADJUSTMENT CHART

Compressor Type	Pre–charged oil quantity in new compressor	Recovered oil quantity (oz.) from old compressor	Amount of oil (oz.) to drain from new compressor
DKV–14C, DKV–14D	6.8	Less than 2.4	3.7
		More than 2.4	Same amount plus 0.7
DKS–16H	6.8	Less than 4.4	2.4
		More than 4.4	Same amount plus 0.7
V5	8.0	Less than 3.2	5.1
		More than 3.2	Same amount plus 0.7
V6	8.5	Less than 3.4	5.4
		More than 3.4	Same amount plus 0.7

SYSTEM COMPONENTS

―――――― CAUTION ――――――
Some vehicles are equipped with air bag supplemental restraint systems. The system is still active for about 10 minutes after disconnecting the battery. Wait for more than 10 minutes before starting work and do not use a memory saver. If power is required for diagnostic work, the air bag module can be disconnected inside the panel in the bottom of the steering wheel after the system is inactive. Reconnect the module before reconnecting the battery.

NOTE: When removing any component of the refrigerant system, properly discharge the refrigerant into recovery equipment. Do not vent the refrigerant into the air.

Radiator and Cooling Fan

REMOVAL AND INSTALLATION

1. Disconnect the negative battery cable. Do not use a memory saver. On vehicles with theft-protected radios, make sure the owner's reset code is available.
2. Remove the apron under the front of the engine, if equipped, and drain the cooling system.
3. Remove or disconnect the reservoir tank and bracket, and remove the upper and lower hoses from the radiator.
4. Disconnect the temperature switch and electric fan connectors.
5. On vehicles with automatic transmissions, disconnect and plug the transmission cooling lines.
6. On rear wheel drive vehicles with electric fans, it should be possible to remove the fans and shroud as an assembly. To remove the radiator, remove the upper radiator retaining bolts and lift the unit up and out.
To install:
7. Set the lugs on the bottom of the radiator into the rubber mounts on the body and secure the unit with the upper mounting bolts.
8. Install the shrouding and fans.
9. Connect the automatic transmission cooling lines and the reservoir tank with all coolant hoses.
10. Fill the cooling system and look for leaks before installing the remaining parts.
11. Plug in all the electrical connectors for the fan(s) and temperature switches.
12. Connect the battery and start the engine to bleed the cooling system and check for leaks.

Cooling Fan

TESTING

1. When the air conditioner is running, the electric radiator/condenser cooling fan should also run. On the 300ZX, the engine temperature must also be greater than 95°C (203°F). Turn the ignition switch and air conditioner **ON** and check for fan operation.
2. If the fan does not run, disconnect the plug to the fan and check for 12 volts between one of the terminals and ground. If voltage is present, test the fan with jumper wires from the battery.
3. If there is no voltage reaching the fan, locate the fan relay on the underhood relay panel. With the ignition and air conditioning both **ON**, there should be 12 volts between 2 of the terminals and ground.
4. Turn the air conditioner **OFF** to see which terminal looses voltage. That one will be the relay switching circuit, which is controlled by the engine control computer. The other terminal should still have voltage from the battery.
5. If the voltages to the relay are correct, the relay is faulty. If there is no battery voltage to the relay, check the wiring from the thermoswitch in the cooling system.
6. On some vehicles, the engine computer activates the fan relay. If no battery voltage is present at the relay with the air conditioner **ON**, check the wiring from the engine computer. Also check the temperature sensor and the thermoswitch in the cooling system.

REMOVAL AND INSTALLATION

1. Disconnect the negative battery cable. Do not use a memory saver. On vehicles with theft-protected radios, make sure the owner's reset code is available.
2. Remove the apron under the front of the engine, if equipped. Drain about 2 quarts from the cooling system.
3. Disconnect the reservoir tank and upper hose from the radiator.
4. Disconnect the temperature switch and electric fan connectors, if equipped.
5. On some vehicles, it should be possible to remove the fans and shroud as an assembly.
To install:
6. Mount the fan on the shroud and install the shroud.
7. Reconnect the switch and fan wiring.
8. Connect the hoses and refill the cooling system.

9. Install any ducts or covers that were removed and start the engine to check for coolant leaks and proper fan operation.

Condenser

REMOVAL AND INSTALLATION

NOTE: Refer to the Refrigerant Capacities chart or the vehicle's air conditioner identification label for the correct refrigerant to use. Be sure not to intermix components, refrigerant, oil or service equipment on vehicles using different refrigerant systems.

1. Disconnect the negative battery cable. Do not use a memory saver. On vehicles with theft-protected radios, make sure the owner's reset code is available.
2. On 240SX, remove the engine air inlet duct, air filter assembly and the radiator top mounting bracket.
3. On some front wheel drive vehicles, the radiator can be pushed towards the rear far enough to remove the condenser without disconnecting the engine coolant hoses. Unbolt the upper radiator mounts and tilt the top of the radiator back.
4. If the radiator must be removed, remove the apron under the front of the engine, if equipped, and drain the cooling system. Disconnect and plug the oil cooling hoses on automatic transmission models, then remove the radiator.
5. Properly discharge the refrigerant and disconnect and cap the pressure lines from the condenser. If the receiver/drier is bolted to the condenser, unbolt it before lifting the condenser out.
To Install:
6. Installation is the reverse of removal. When installing the condenser, be sure to use new O-ring seals and lightly lubricate them with compressor oil.
7. Do not over torque the fittings or they will be distorted and leak. Those secured with bolts are torqued to 5–8 ft. lbs. (8–11 Nm) for bolts with 10mm heads or 7–9 ft. lbs. (10–12 Nm) for bolts with 12mm heads.

Compressor

REMOVAL AND INSTALLATION

NOTE: Refer to the Refrigerant Capacities chart or the vehicle's air conditioner identification label for the correct refrigerant to use. Be sure not to intermix components, refrigerant, oil or service equipment on vehicles using different refrigerant systems.

1. Properly discharge the air conditioning system using recovery equipment.
2. On some models, the compressor is more easily removed from under the vehicle.
3. On 300ZX, remove the engine under cover, the front stabilizer bar, and the idler pulley. Remove the air pipes and hoses for access.
4. On other models, it may be necessary to remove the the alternator and/or the idler pulley.
5. Disconnect the pressure lines and plug them.
6. Loosen or remove the drive belt and remove the compressor.
7. Installation is the reverse of removal. Be sure to tighten the bolt to specification.

Receiver/Drier

REMOVAL AND INSTALLATION

NOTE: Refer to the Refrigerant Capacities chart or the vehicle's air conditioner identification label for the correct refrigerant to use. Be sure not to intermix components, refrigerant, oil or service equipment on vehicles using different refrigerant systems.

1. On all models, the receiver/drier is on or near the condenser. Properly discharge the system using recovery equipment.
2. Disconnect the pressure switch.
3. Disconnect the refrigerant lines and cap them to prevent moisture from entering the system.
4. Unbolt and remove the receiver/drier.
To Install:
5. Installation is the reverse of removal. Be sure to use new O-rings and gaskets.
6. Do not over torque the fittings or they will be distorted and leak. Those secured with bolts are torqued to 5–8 ft. lbs. (8–11 Nm).

Expansion Valve

REMOVAL AND INSTALLATION

NOTE: Refer to the Refrigerant Capacities chart or the vehicle's air conditioner identification label for the correct refrigerant to use. Be sure not to intermix components, refrigerant, oil or service equipment on vehicles using different refrigerant systems.

The expansion valve on all models is in the same housing with the evaporator inside the vehicle. The evaporator, which is between the blower and the heater, can be removed without removing the heater core.

1. Disconnect the negative battery cable and wait for at least 10 minutes while the airbag system de-energizes. Do not use a memory saver. Then, properly discharge the system using refrigerant recovery equipment and disconnect and plug the evaporator line fittings at the firewall.
2. The blower motor and housing must be removed first. Removing the glove compartment makes this easier. On some vehicles, the expansion valve can be accessed once the blower housing is removed.
3. Installation is the reverse of removal. Make sure the seals between the housings are in good condition, replace as necessary. Always use new O-rings on the refrigerant line fittings.

Blower Motor

REMOVAL AND INSTALLATION

1. The blower can be removed without removing the housing. Disconnect the negative battery cable first.
2. If necessary, remove the glove compartment to gain access. On most vehicles, it is possible to squeeze the sides of the door to let it fall open beyond the normal stops.
3. Disconnect the wiring and remove the mounting bolts to lower the motor out.
4. Installation is the reverse of removal. The resistor or speed control amplifier is mounted on the evaporator housing and is accessible without removing the blower.

Heater Core

REMOVAL AND INSTALLATION

200SX and Sentra

1. Disconnect the negative battery cable. If equipped with air bag system, wait 10 minutes for the system to fully de-energize before proceeding. Do not use a memory saver.
2. Set the **TEMP** lever to the maximum **HOT** position and drain the engine coolant.
3. Disconnect the heater hoses at the engine compartment.
4. Remove the instrument panel assembly. On some models, it will be necessary to remove the instrument panel reinforcement.
5. Remove the heater control assembly.
6. If equipped with air conditioning, separate the heating unit from the cooling unit. If heater only, detach the heater-to-blower housing air duct from the side of the heater housing.
7. Remove the heater unit assembly.
8. On some models the heater unit is not a serviceable component. On serviceable units, remove the case clips and split the case. Remove the core.

To install:

9. On serviceable units, install the heater core and assemble the heater case halves. Use new gaskets and seals as required. Always check the operation of the air mix door when reattaching the heater case halves.
10. Mount the heater unit and connect it the cooling unit, if equipped.
11. Install the heater control assembly.
12. Install the instrument panel reinforcement (if applicable) and the instrument panel.
13. Connect the heater hoses. Use new grommets, as required.
14. Fill and bleed the cooling system.
15. Connect the negative battery cable.

240SX and 300ZX

1. Disconnect the negative battery cable. If the vehicle has an air bag system, wait more than 10 minutes for the system to fully de-energize before starting any further work. Do not use a memory saver.
2. With the **TEMP** lever set to the **HOT** position, drain the cooling system.
3. Disconnect the heater hoses from the driver's side of the heater unit.
4. Remove the console box and the floor mats.
5. Remove the instrument panel lower covers from both the driver's and passenger's sides of the vehicle. Remove the lower cluster lids.
6. Remove the left side ventilator duct. On 240SX, detach the defroster duct from the upper center heater unit opening.
7. Remove the panel from the back side of the steering wheel and disconnect the air bag connector.
8. Remove the radio, equalizer and stereo cassette deck, as required.
9. Remove the instrument panel-to-transmission tunnel stay.
10. Remove the rear heater duct from the floor of the vehicle.
11. Remove the center ventilator duct.
12. Remove the left and right side ventilator ducts from the lower heater outlets.
13. Disconnect and label the wiring harness connections.
14. Separate the heating unit. Remove the 2 screws at the bottom sides of the heater unit and the 1 screw at the top of the unit and remove the unit together with the heater control assembly.
15. Separate the heater case halves and slide the core from the case.

To install:

16. Install the heater core and assemble the heater case halves. Use new gaskets and seals, as required.
17. Mount the heater unit/control assembly and install the upper and lower attaching screws.
18. Plug in the wiring harness connectors.
19. Connect the left and right side ducts to the lower heater outlets.
20. Connect the center ventilator duct.
21. Connect the rear heater duct.
22. Attach the instrument panel-to-transmission stay.
23. Install the cassette deck, equalizer and radio.
24. On 240SX, connect the upper defroster duct to the upper center heater opening. Connect the left side ventilator duct.
25. Install the lower cluster lids and lower instrument panel covers.
26. Install the floor mats and console box.
27. Install the front seats. Torque the seat bolts to 32–41 ft. lbs. (43–55 Nm).
28. Connect the heater hoses. Use new grommets as required.
29. Fill the cooling system to the proper level.
30. On vehicles with an air bag, reconnect the module at the steering wheel, then connect the negative battery cable.

Altima

1. Disconnect the negative battery cable. If equipped with an airbag system, wait 10 minutes for the system to de-energize before proceeding. Do not use a memory saver.
2. Set the **TEMP** lever to the maximum **HOT** position and drain the engine coolant.
3. Disconnect the heater hoses at the engine compartment.
4. Remove the driver's side instrument panel trim assembly.
5. Detach the left side ventilator duct, if required.
6. Remove the core cover and remove the core.

To install:

7. Install the core and cover. Use new seals and gaskets, as required.
8. Install the control and heater valve levers. Connect the air mix door control cable. Install the side ventilator duct and the attachment to the right air duct or evaporator housing.
9. Install the driver's side panel trim.
10. Connect the heater hoses to the core. Use new grommets, as required.
11. Fill and bleed the cooling system.
12. Connect the negative battery cable.

Maxima

1. Disconnect the negative battery cable. If equipped with an airbag, wait at least 10 minutes for the system to fully de-energize before proceeding. Do not use a memory saver.
2. Set the **TEMP** lever to the **HOT** position.
3. Drain the cooling system.
4. Disconnect the heater hoses from the driver's side of the heater unit.
5. Remove the front floor mats.
6. Remove the instrument panel lower covers from both the driver's and passenger's sides of the vehicle.
7. Remove the left side ventilator duct.
8. Remove the instrument panel.
9. Remove the rear heater duct from the floor of the vehicle.
10. Disconnect the wiring harness connectors.
11. Separate the heating unit from the cooling unit. Remove the 2 screws at the bottom sides of the heater unit and the 1 screw from the top of the unit. Lift out the heater together with the heater control assembly.
12. Remove the center vent cover and heater control assembly, loosening the clips and screws.
13. Remove the screws securing the door shafts.

14. Remove the clips from the case and split the case. Remove the core.

15. Separate the heater case halves and slide the core from the case.

To install:

16. Install the heater core and assemble the heater case halves. Use new gaskets and seals, as required.

17. Install the door shaft retaining screws.

18. Install the heater control assembly and center vent cover.

19. Mount the heater unit/control assembly and install the upper and lower attaching screws.

20. Plug in the wiring harness connectors.

21. Install the rear heater duct.

22. Install the instrument panel.

23. Install the left side ventilator duct.

24. Install the instrument panel lower covers.

25. Install the floor mats.

26. Connect the heater hoses. Use new grommets, as required.

27. Fill the cooling system to the proper level.

28. Connect the negative battery cable.

Evaporator

REMOVAL AND INSTALLATION

The evaporator, which is between the blower and the heater, can be removed without removing the heater core.

1. Disconnect the negative battery cable. If equipped with an airbag system, wait 10 minutes for the system to fully de-energize before proceeding. Do not use a memory saver. Properly discharge the air conditioning system using recovery equipment and disconnect and plug the evaporator and pressure line fittings at the firewall.

2. The blower motor and housing must be removed first. Removing the glove compartment makes this easier. On some vehicles, the expansion valve can be accessed once the blower housing is removed.

3. On some models it may be necessary to remove the center console. On vehicles with an air bag, some of the wiring for that system is in the console. Take care when removing and installing the center console in order not to disturb the wiring, connectors or sensors in the area.

4. Remove the panel from the back side of the steering wheel and disconnect the air bag connector.

5. Remove the electrical connectors and air ducts which may interfere. Remove the evaporator cover or remove the evaporator housing.

To install:

6. Installation is the reverse of removal. Make sure the seals between the housings are in good condition, replace as necessary.

7. On vehicles with an air bag, reconnect the module at the steering wheel, then connect the negative battery cable. Evacuate, recharge and leak test the system.

Manual Control Head

REMOVAL AND INSTALLATION

200SX, Altima, Maxima and Sentra

1. If the vehicle has a theft protected radio, obtain the owner's security code and disconnect the negative battery cable. If equipped with an airbag system, wait 10 minutes for the system to de-energize before proceeding. Do not use a memory saver.

2. Remove the center console bezel and/or the heater control bezel as required.

3. Detach the temperature control cable and the fresh vent cable at the heater housing.

4. If all the cables are unclipped at their lower end, the control assembly should come straight out once the screws are removed. Carefully unplug the wires.

5. When disassembling the unit for repair, most of the fasteners are plastic clips which can be easily pried apart. Be careful not to break the tabs. The knobs on the front can be removed with pliers but wrap a rag around the knob to keep from scratching the finish.

6. Installation is the reverse of removal. Connect the battery and test the system.

240SX

1. If the vehicle has a theft protected radio, obtain the owner's security code and disconnect the negative battery cable. If equipped with an airbag system, wait 10 minutes for the system to de-energize before proceeding. Do not use a memory saver.

2. Remove the radio.

3. Remove the screws and lift the control unit out far enough to disconnect the cables and wiring.

4. When disassembling the unit for repair, all fasteners are plastic clips which can be easily pried apart. Be careful to not break the tabs. The knobs on the front can be removed with pliers but wrap a rag around the knob to keep from scratching the finish.

5. Installation is the reverse of the removal procedure.

300ZX

1. If the vehicle has a theft protected radio, obtain the owner's security code and disconnect the negative battery cable. If equipped with an airbag system, wait 10 minutes for the system to de-energize before proceeding. Do not use a memory saver.

2. Remove the 2 screws from the bottom of the control pod and carefully remove the controls far enough to disconnect the wiring.

3. Installation is the reverse of removal.

Push Button Control Panel Cables and Actuators

ADJUSTMENTS

Mode Door Motor

1. Move the side link by hand and hold the mode door in the **VENT** mode (**DEF** mode on Altima and Maxima).
2. Install the mode door motor on the heater unit and connect it to the wiring harness.
3. Turn the ignition switch to **ON**. Attach the mode door motor rod to the side link rod holder.
4. Turn the defroster switch to **ON**. Check that the side link operates at the fully open position.
5. Also, turn the vent switch to **ON** and check that the side link operates at the fully open position.

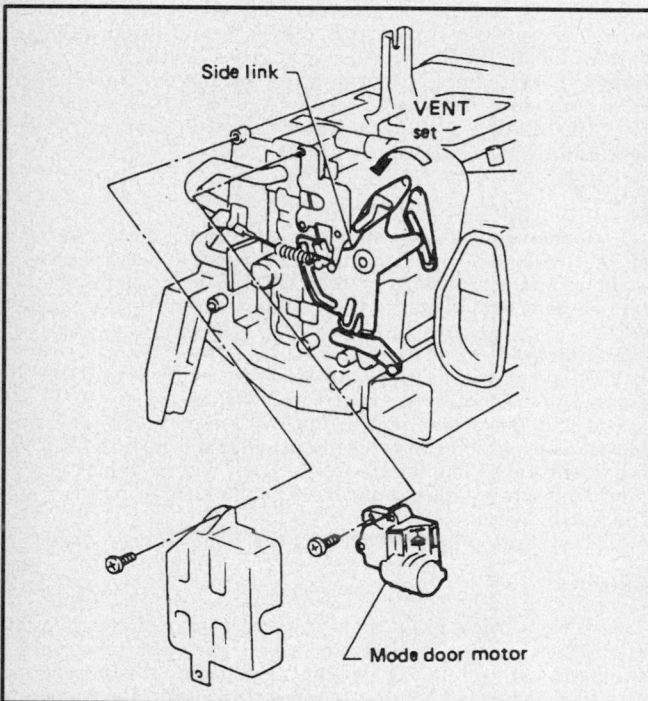

Mode door linkage adjustment—push button control

Air Intake Door Motor

ALTIMA, SENTRA (EXCEPT 1995) AND MAXIMA

1. Connect the intake door motor wiring connector before installing the intake door motor.
2. Turn the ignition switch to **ON**. Turn the recirculation switch to **ON**.
3. Install the intake door motor on the intake unit. Install the intake door lever.
4. Set the intake door rod in the **REC** position and fasten the door rod to the holder on the intake door lever.

5. Check that the intake door operates properly when the recirculation switch is turned **ON** and **OFF**.

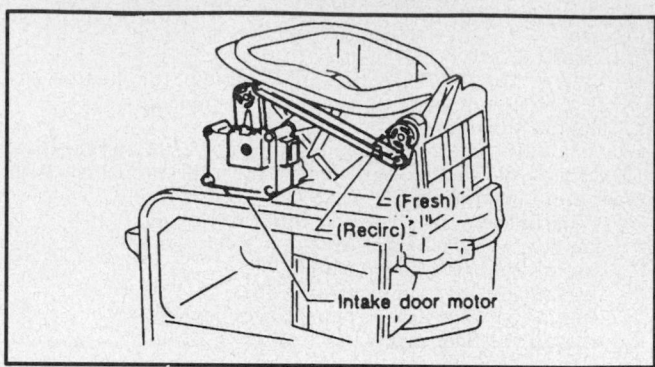

Air intake door adjustment—Maxima shown

Air Intake Door Motor

200SX, 300ZX AND SENTRA (1995)

1. Install the intake door motor on the intake unit and attach the harness connector.
2. Turn the ignition switch **ON**. Turn the recirculation switch to **ON**.
3. On 300ZX, install the intake door lever, set the intake door rod in the **REC** position and fasten the door rod to the holder on the intake door lever.
4. Check that the intake door operates properly when the recirculation switch is turned **ON** and **OFF**.

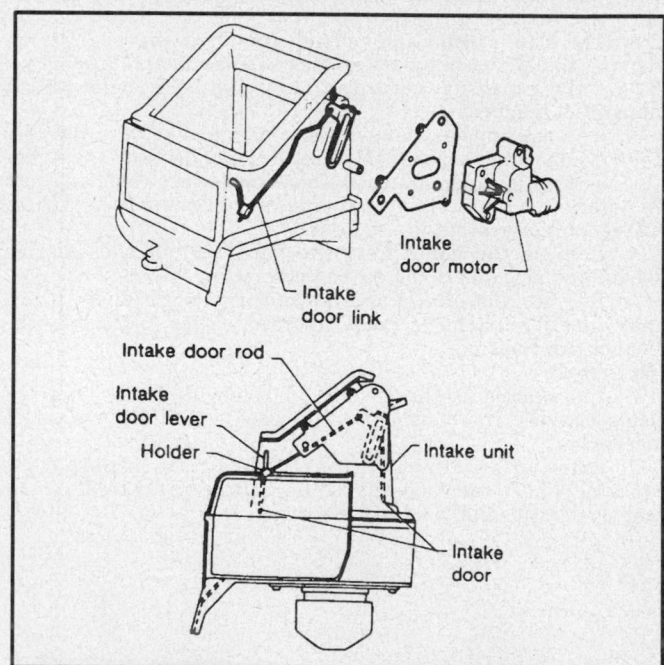

Air intake door adjustment—300ZX shown

Air Mix Door Motor And Water Valve

1. Install the air mix door motor on the heater unit and attach the harness connector
2. Turn the ignition switch **ON**. Set the temperature control to the **FULL-COLD** position.
3. Hold the air mix doors in the **FULL-COLD** position and attach the door link to the air mix motor rod.
4. Check to make sure the air mix door operates correctly as the temperature control is cycled from **COLD** to **HOT**.
5. Set the temperature control to the **FULL-COLD** position. Rotate the water valve to the **FULL-COLD** position (fully closed). Attach the cable to the water valve and clamp the cable in position.
6. Check to make sure the water valve operates correctly as the temperature control is cycled from **COLD** to **HOT**.

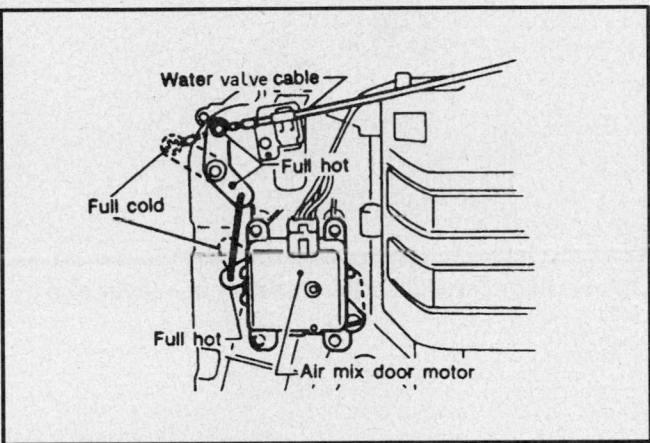

Air mix door motor—Maxima shown

Fresh Vent (Bi-level) Motor

ALTIMA AND MAXIMA

1. Connect the fresh vent door motor wiring connector before installing the fresh vent door motor.
2. Turn the ignition switch to **ON**. Install the fresh vent door motor on the heater unit. Install the fresh vent door rod to the fresh vent door link rod holder.
3. Check that the fresh vent door operates properly when the bi-level switch is turned **ON** and **OFF** with the temperature control set in the **MIDDLE** position.

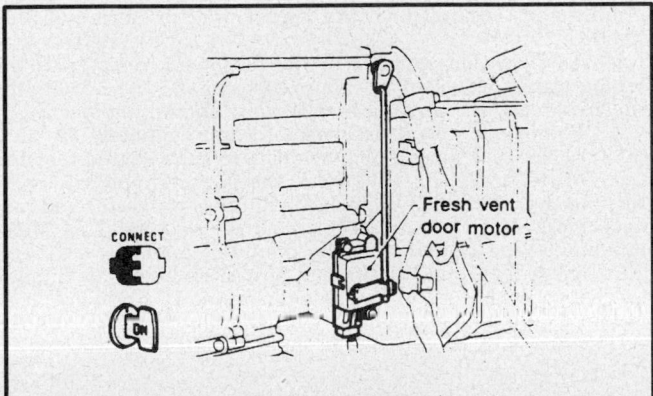

Fresh vent door motor—Altima shown

Temperature Control Cable

200SX AND SENTRA

1. With the cable detached from the air mix door lever, move the temperature control lever to **HOT**.
2. Set the air mix door lever in the **FULL HEAT** position and attach the cable to the air mix door lever.
3. Pull on the outer cable case to remove any cable slack, then clamp the cable in position.

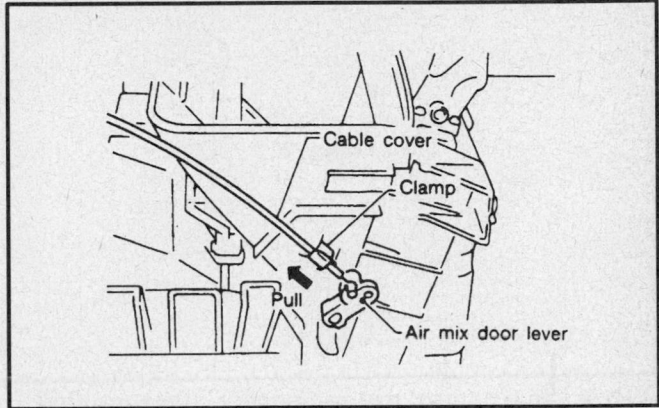

Temperature control cable adjustment—200SX and Sentra

Lever Control Panel Cables and Actuators

ADJUSTMENT

If the cable needs adjusting, remove the E-ring and take the cable from the clamp and linkage.

Air (Mode) Control Cable

1. Move the air control lever to the **DEFROST** position to set the side link in the defrost mode.
2. Hook the cable to the door lever, the gently pull the outer cable case away from the door lever to remove any slack. Clamp the cable in place.

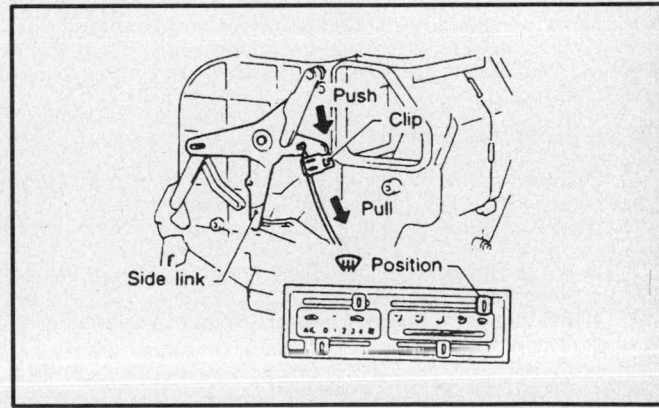

Air (mode) control cable adjustment—control lever

Water Valve Control Rod

1. To adjust the control rod, disconnect the temperature control cable from the door lever.
2. Move the air mix door lever and the valve link lever all the way in the direction that would pull the rod toward the valve lever.
3. Gently pull the rod so there is about 0.080 in. (2mm) gap between the rod and valve lever and secure the rod at the door lever.

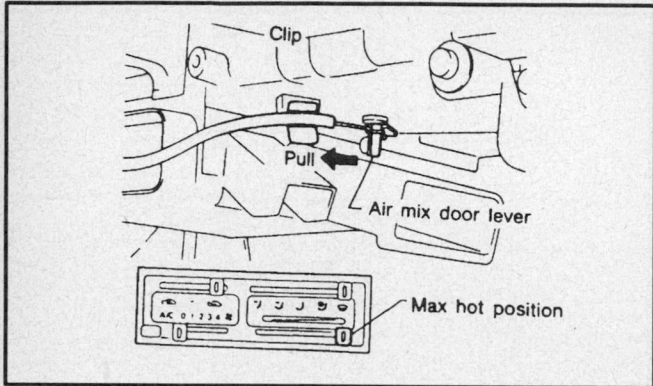

Water valve control rod adjustment—lever control

Temperature Control Cable

1. With the cable detached from the air mix door lever, move the temperature control lever to **HOT**.

2. Set the air mix door lever in the full heat position and attach the cable to the air mix door lever.
3. Pull on the outer cable case to remove any cable slack, then clamp the cable in position.

Intake Door Control Cable

1. Move the control lever to the **FRESH** position.
2. Attach the cable and take up the slack in the housing before securing it with the clip.

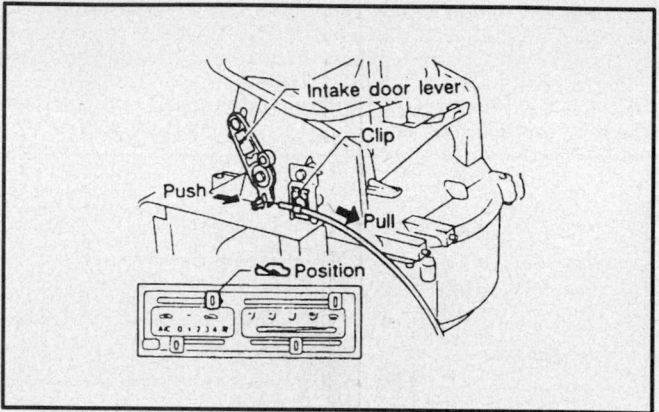

Intake door control cable adjustment—lever control

SENSORS AND SWITCHES

TESTING

Dual Pressure Switch

1. Disconnect the connector from the switch and attach an ohmmeter to the switch terminals.
2. Attach a manifold gauge set so system pressures can be read.
3. If system pressure is below 22–29 psi or above 356–412 psi, the switch should be **OFF** and no continuity should exist.
4. At pressures between these extremes, the switch will be **ON** and continuity will exist. If switch does not respond as noted, replace it.

Triple Pressure Switch

1. Disconnect the connector from the switch and attach an ohmmeter to the appropriate switch terminals.
2. Attach a manifold gauge set so system pressures can be read.
3. Refer to the appropriate chart for the terminal connections and system pressures.
4. If switch operation does not correspond to the chart values, replace it.

Compressor Thermal Protector

1. Disconnect the connector from the thermal protector switch and attach an ohmmeter to the switch terminals.

2. If the temperature of the compressor exceeds approximately 293°F (145°C) the switch is off and there should be no continuity. At lower temperatures the switch is open and continuity should exist. If switch does not respond as noted, replace it.

Thermo Control Amp

1. Run the engine and operate the air conditioning system.
2. With the harness still connected to the thermo control amp, connect a voltmeter from the harness side between a ground and terminal **C** of the amp connector (terminal **2** on Maxima).
3. Install a thermometer in the outlet air register. If the temperature decreases to approximately 37°F (2.5°C), the thermo amp will turn OFF and 12 volts should register.
4. When temperature increases to approximately 39–41°F (4–5°C), the amp should be ON and zero volts should register.
5. With the system OFF, check the power supply circuit by turning the ignition **ON**, detach the harness connector and connect a voltmeter to harness terminal **A** (terminal **3** on Maxima) and a good ground.; 12 volts should be read.
6. The body ground circuit can be checked with an ohmmeter between the center harness terminal **B** (terminal **1** on Maxima) and a body ground. With the ignition **OFF** and the A/C switch and fan switch **ON**, there should be continuity.

TRIPLE-PRESSURE SWITCH

	Terminals	High-pressure side line pressure kPa (kg/cm², psi)	Operation	Continuity
Low-pressure side	① – ④	Increasing to 157–226 (1.6–2.3, 23–33)	ON	Exists.
		Decreasing to 152.0–201.0 (1.55–2.05, 22.0–29.2)	OFF	Does not exist.
Medium-pressure side*	② – ③	Increasing to 1,422–1,618 (14.5–16.5, 206–235)	ON	Exists.
		Decreasing to 1,128–1,422 (11.5–14.5, 164–206)	OFF	Does not exist.
High-pressure side	① – ④	Increasing to 1,667–2,059 (17–21, 242–299)	ON	Exists.
		Decreasing to 2,452–2,844 (25–29, 356–412)	OFF	Does not exist.

* For cooling fan morot operation.

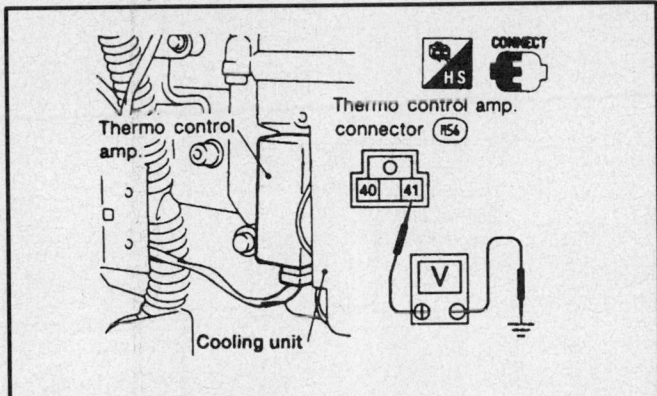

Testing the thermo control amplifier—except Maxima

Engine Temperature Switch

1. Disconnect the connector from the switch terminal on the thermostat housing. Attach an ohmmeter to the switch terminals.
2. When the engine coolant temperature decreases to or is below 185–195°F (85–91°C), the switch should be **OFF** and no continuity should exist.
3. When the coolant temperature increases to 198–208°F (92–98°C), the switch will be on and continuity should exist.

Auto Amplifier Power Supply Check (Automatic A/C)

1. Check the power supply circuit for the auto amp with the ignition switch **ON**.
2. Detach the auto amp harness connector and connect a voltmeter from the harness side. Measure the voltage between the indicated terminals and a body ground. Each should measure 12 volts. Test the following terminals:
- 300ZX, terminals **40**, **41** and **60**.
- Altima, terminals **11**, **12** and **16**.
- Maxima, terminal **1** of the Auto Amplifier (BCM) connector and terminal **3** of the Control Unit connector.

3. Turn the ignition **OFF**. With the harness still disconnected, connect an ohmmeter to the harness side between the indicated terminals and a body ground. Continuity should exist. Test the following terminals:
- 300ZX, terminals **55** and **33**.
- Altima, terminal **20**.
- Maxima, terminal **8** of the Control Unit connector.

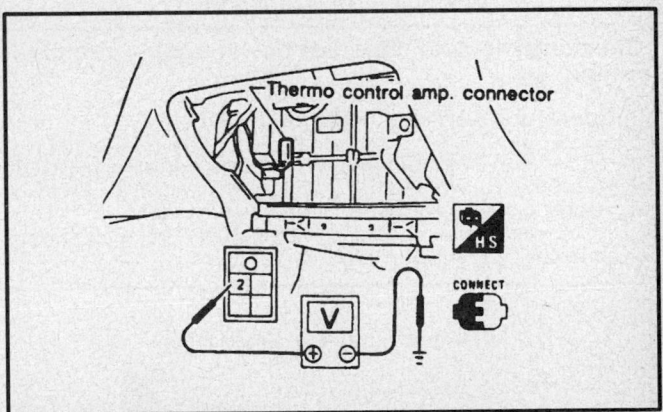

Testing the thermo control amplifier—Maxima

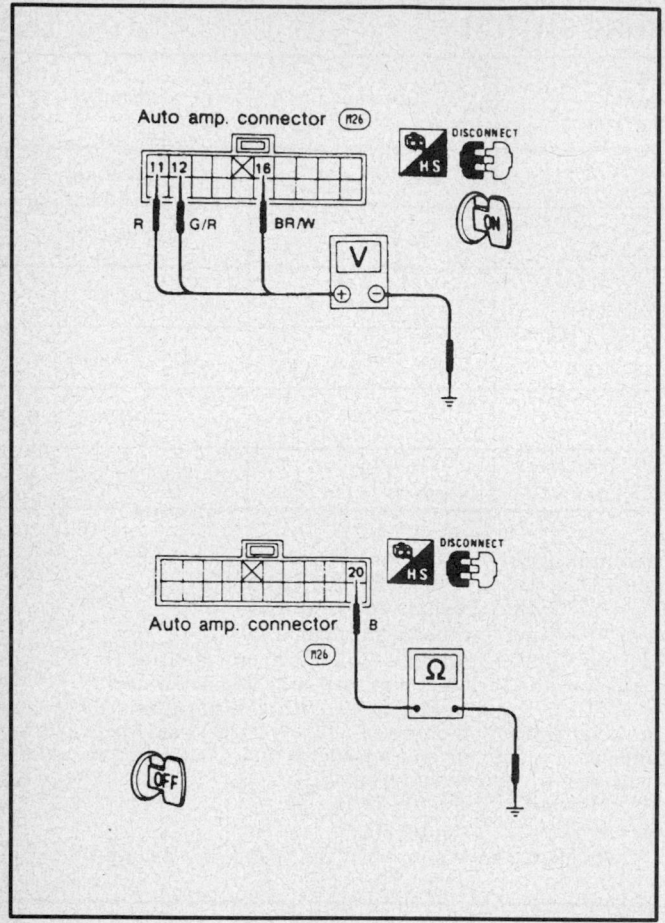

Checking the auto amplifier power supply circuit—Altima

Temperature Sensors (Automatic A/C)

1. After disconnecting the desired temperature sensor (ambient, intake, in-vehicle, floor duct, or defrost duct), attach an ohmmeter between the sensor harness terminals.

2. The resistance should correspond to the temperatures given in the appropriate chart.

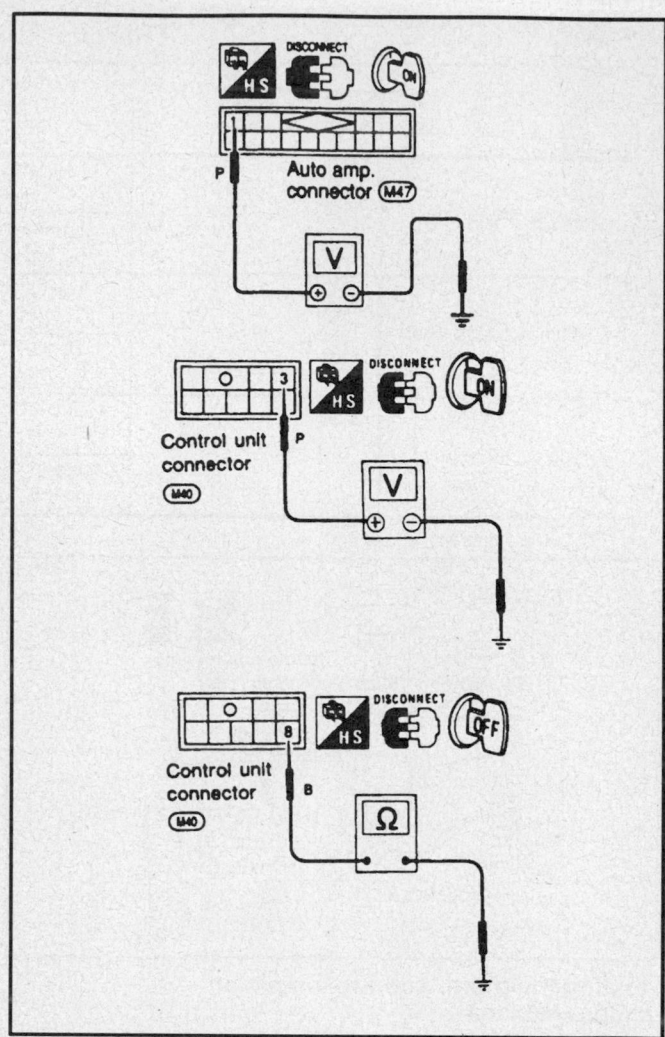

Checking the auto amplifier power supply circuit—Maxima

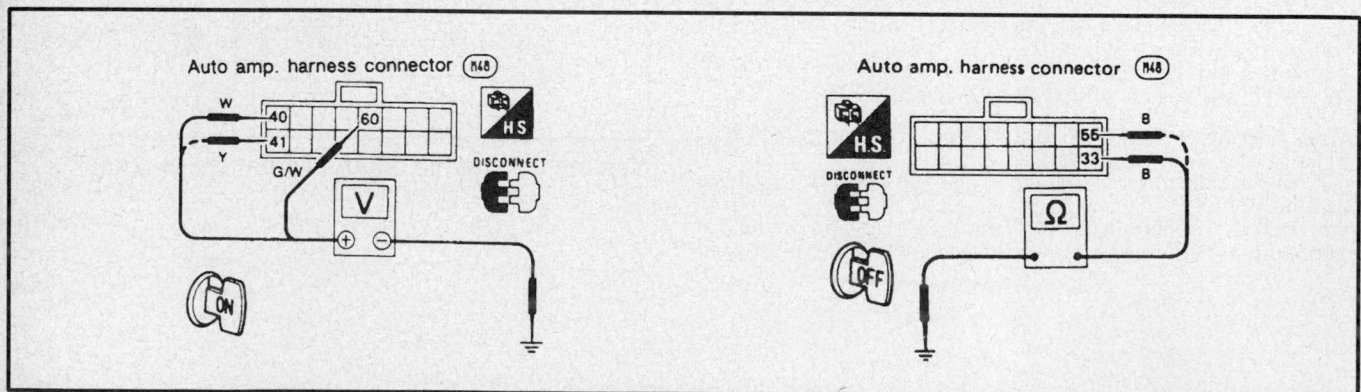

Checking the auto amplifier power supply circuit—300ZX

AUTO A/C SENSOR RESISTANCE CHART— ALTIMA AND MAXIMA

Temperature °C (°F)	Resistance kΩ
–15 (5)	12.73
–10 (14)	9.92
–5 (23)	7.80
0 (32)	6.19
5 (41)	4.95
10 (50)	3.99
15 (59)	3.24
20 (68)	2.65
25 (77)	2.19
30 (86)	1.81
35 (95)	1.51
40 (104)	1.27
45 (113)	1.07

AUTO A/C SENSOR RESISTANCE CHART— 300ZX

Temperature °C (°F)	Resistance kΩ
5 (41)	13.11
10 (50)	10.18
15 (59)	7.96
20 (68)	6.29
25 (77)	5.00
30 (86)	4.01
35 (95)	3.24
40 (104)	2.63
45 (113)	2.15
50 (122)	1.77
55 (131)	1.47
60 (140)	1.22
65 (149)	1.02
70 (158)	0.86
75 (167)	0.73
80 (176)	0.62

SYSTEM DIAGNOSIS

System Performance Testing

1. Vehicle must be in a well ventilated area where the engine can be safely run at 1500 rpm, preferably not in direct sunlight. Open the hood to help engine cooling.
2. With driver's window open, doors closed and hood open, operate the system set for full cooling of recirculated air, blower fan on **HIGH** speed. On manual systems, set the mode control to **VENT** and blower on **HIGH** speed.
3. Operate the system for more than 10 minutes, then use a thermometer to measure the air outlet temperature at the center dash vent.

4. With a relative humidity of 50–60 percent, the outlet air temperature should be about 30–35°F (18–23°C) cooler than the outside air. The system effectiveness will decrease as the humidity increases.
5. The following chart assumes a relative humidity of 50–70 percent. The compressor discharge and suction pressures will increase with higher outside air temperature and humidity.

AUTOMATIC CONTROL SYSTEM

300ZX

1. Start the engine.

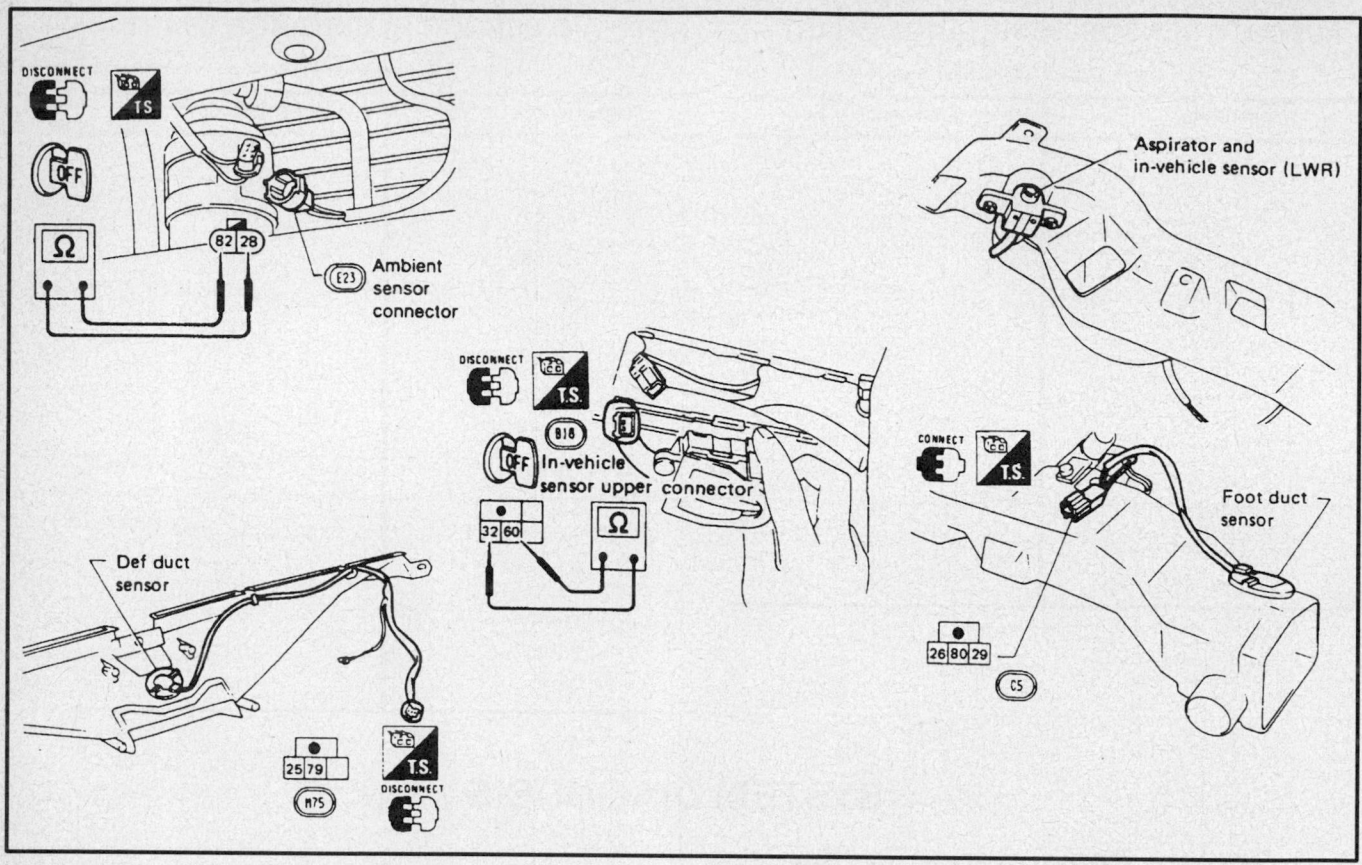

Testing the ambient, In-vehicle and defroster sensors—300ZX shown

2. Press and hold both the **AUTO** and **OFF** switches for at least 5 seconds.

3. The self-diagnostic mode is canceled if the **OFF** switch is pressed separately or if the engine is turned **OFF**.

4. Moving from one diagnostic step to the next is done by pressing only the **AUTO** switch when required.

5. The codes will be displayed in the lower portion of the display panel (code monitor). The upper half of the display (data monitor) will provide data information for each code.

6. By pressing either **FAN** or **MODE** switch, the code monitor will change to the next code and the data monitor will also change.

7. Rather than a series of code numbers, the 300ZX uses existing symbols used on the display panel for code representation when in the self-diagnostic mode. These are shown in the appropriate diagnostic chart. Use this information to make appropriate circuit, ground and component checks to pinpoint the system problem.

Maxima

1. Be sure the fresh vent lever is in the **OFF** position. Start the engine and, within 5 seconds of starting, press and hold the **OFF** switch for at least 5 seconds.

2. The system will then cycle through a series of self-diagnostic routines before registering on the control panel display.

3. The self-diagnostic process can be exited at any time by either pressing the **AUTO** button or turning the engine **OFF**.

4. Shifting from one step to another is accomplished by pushing the temperature control "up" arrow (warmer) or the "down" arrow (cooler).

5. Additionally, shifting from Step 5 in the diagnostic chart to auxiliary mechanism is accomplished by pushing the fan switch.

PERFORMANCE CHART TEST READINGS (PSI)

	Ambient Temp (degrees F)	High Pressure Side (PSI)	Low Pressure Side (PSI)
240SX	68		
	77	108–132	26–31
	86	128–158	23–38
	95	151–185	24–31
1993 300 ZX, Sentra	68	88–132	26–36
	77	118–166	27–37
	86	148–203	28–38
	95	179–237	32–46
300ZX (except 1993)	68	149–181	26–32
	77	162–199	27–33
	86	195–237	32–39
	95	228–279	39–48
1994 Sentra	68		
	77	129–182	24–40
	86	162–193	26–43
	95	195–262	27–46
1995 Sentra, 200SX	68	146–191	16–30
	77	179–232	17–33
	86	213–273	20–38
	95	274–314	23–47
Maxima (except 1995)	68	108–164	11–21
	77	151–213	16–27
	86	193–262	21–33
	95	236–310	26–39
Maxima (1995)	68	114–151	20–24
	77	142–189	20–24
	86	169–225	21–26
	95	199–262	23–27
Altima	68	121–159	18–23
	77	152–198	20–26
	86	178–235	22–29
	95	182–249	24–33

NOTE: Above readings assume a relative humidity of 50–70%

A/C DIAGNOSIS: INSUFFICIENT COOLING

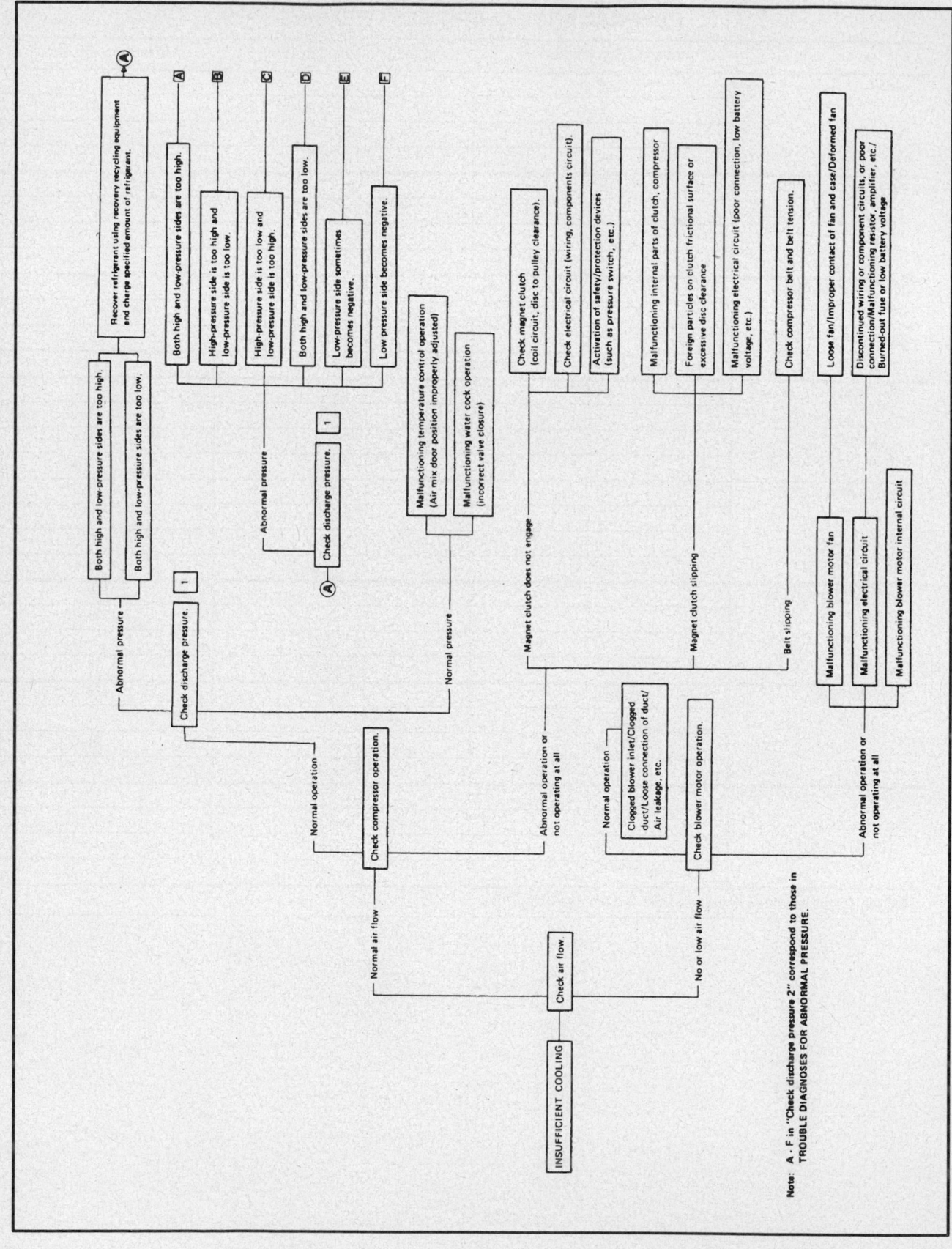

Note: A - F in "Check discharge pressure 2" correspond to those in TROUBLE DIAGNOSES FOR ABNORMAL PRESSURE.

AUTO. A/C SELF–DIAGNOSTIC STEP CHART—300ZX CONT'D

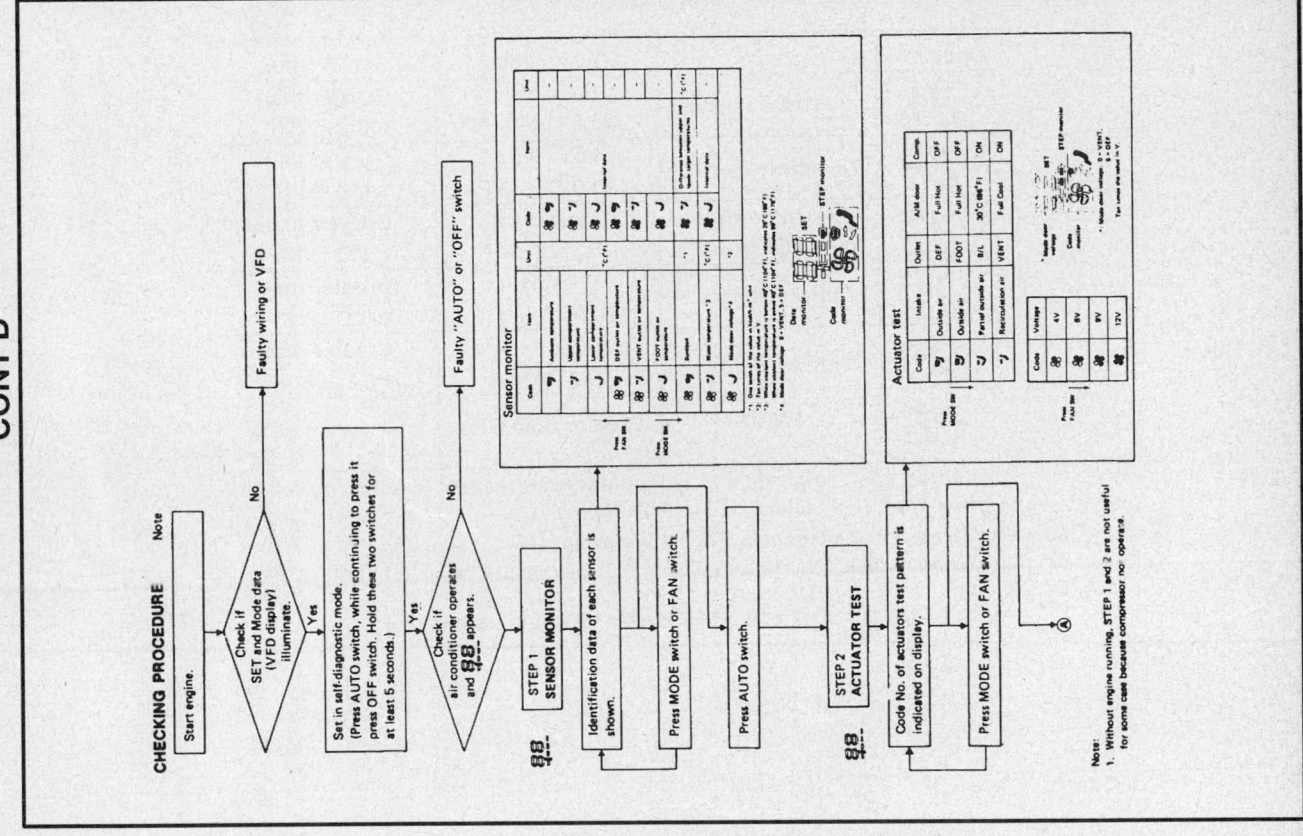

AUTO. A/C SELF–DIAGNOSTIC STEP CHART—300ZX

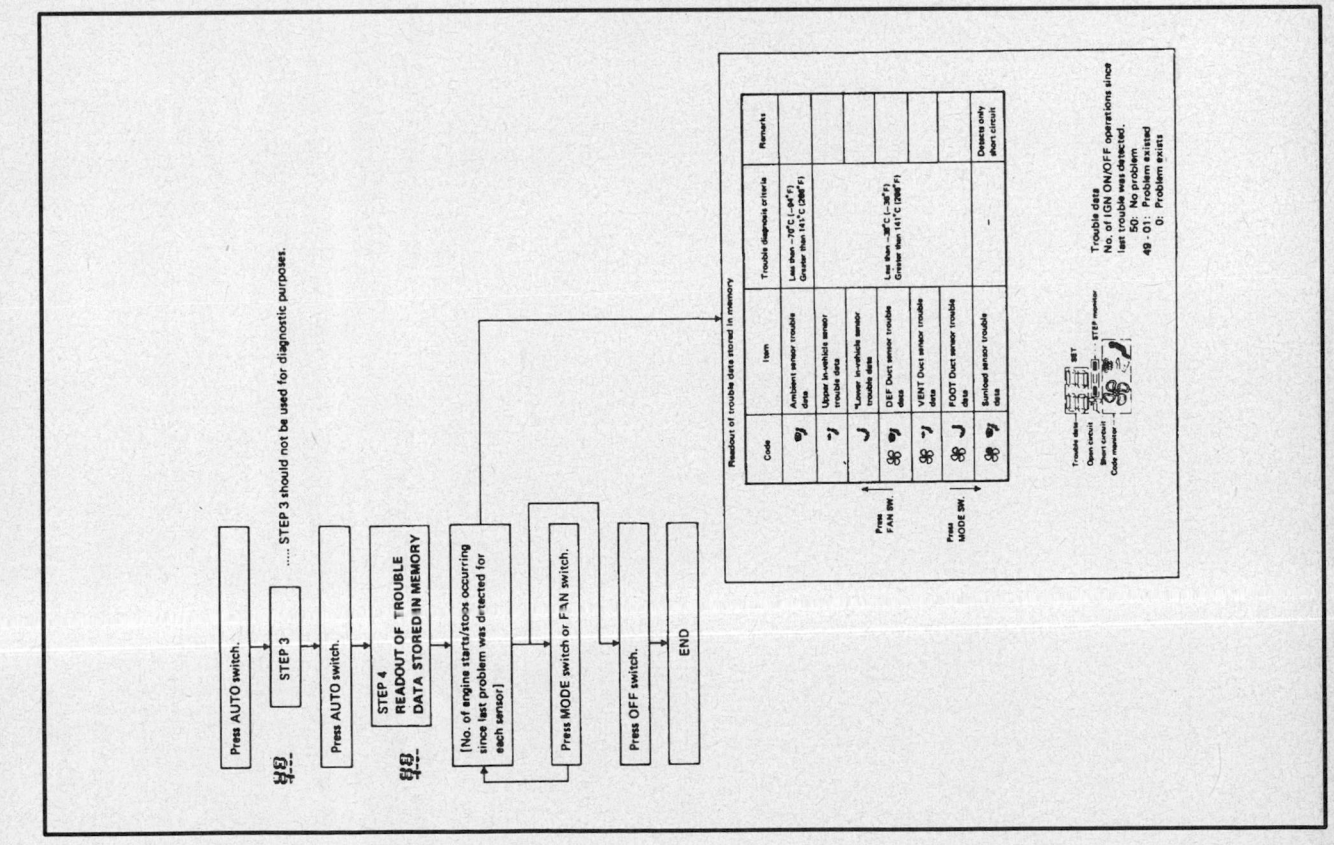

AUTO. A/C SENSOR CIRCUIT RESISTANCE CHART—ALTIMA AND MAXIMA

Code No.	Sensor	Open circuit	Short circuit
21	Ambient sensor	Less than −41.9°C (−43°F)	Greater than 100°C (212°F)
22	In-vehicle sensor	Less than −41.9°C (−43°F)	Greater than 100°C (212°F)
23	Thermal transmitter*3	Less than −25.6°C (−14°F)	Greater than 150°C (302°F)
24	Intake sensor	Less than −41.9°C (−43°F)	Greater than 100°C (212°F)
25	Sunload sensor*2	Less than 0.01515 mA	Greater than 0.545 mA
26	PBR*1	Greater than 50%	Less than 30%

*1: "50%" and "30%" refer to percentage with respect to full stroke of air mix door. (Full cold: 0%, Full hot: 100%)

*2: **Conduct self-diagnosis STEP 2 under sunshine.**
When conducting indoors, direct light (more than 60W) at sunload sensor.

*3: **Conduct self-diagnosis STEP 2 after warming up engine.**

AUTO. A/C SELF–DIAGNOSTIC STEP CHART—MAXIMA

CHECKING PROCEDURE

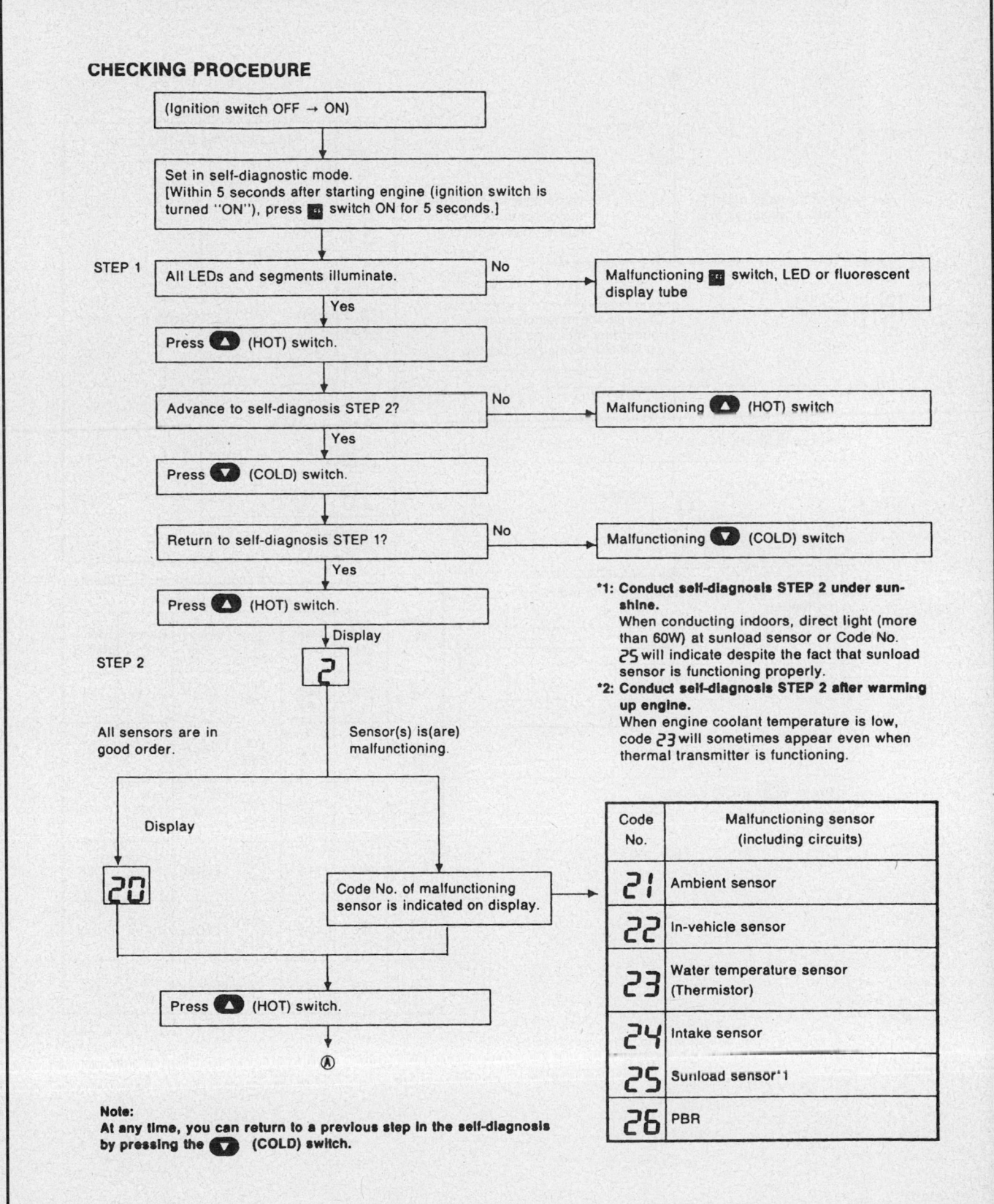

(Ignition switch OFF → ON)

Set in self-diagnostic mode.
[Within 5 seconds after starting engine (ignition switch is turned "ON"), press ■ switch ON for 5 seconds.]

STEP 1

All LEDs and segments illuminate. — No → Malfunctioning ■ switch, LED or fluorescent display tube

Yes

Press ▲ (HOT) switch.

Advance to self-diagnosis STEP 2? — No → Malfunctioning ▲ (HOT) switch

Yes

Press ▼ (COLD) switch.

Return to self-diagnosis STEP 1? — No → Malfunctioning ▼ (COLD) switch

Yes

Press ▲ (HOT) switch.

Display

STEP 2 `2`

All sensors are in good order.   Sensor(s) is(are) malfunctioning.

Display

`20`   Code No. of malfunctioning sensor is indicated on display.

Press ▲ (HOT) switch.

Ⓐ

Note:
At any time, you can return to a previous step in the self-diagnosis by pressing the ▼ (COLD) switch.

*1: **Conduct self-diagnosis STEP 2 under sunshine.**
When conducting indoors, direct light (more than 60W) at sunload sensor or Code No. `25` will indicate despite the fact that sunload sensor is functioning properly.

*2: **Conduct self-diagnosis STEP 2 after warming up engine.**
When engine coolant temperature is low, code `23` will sometimes appear even when thermal transmitter is functioning.

Code No.	Malfunctioning sensor (including circuits)
`21`	Ambient sensor
`22`	In-vehicle sensor
`23`	Water temperature sensor (Thermistor)
`24`	Intake sensor
`25`	Sunload sensor*1
`26`	PBR

AUTO. A/C SELF–DIAGNOSTIC STEP CHART—MAXIMA, CONT'D

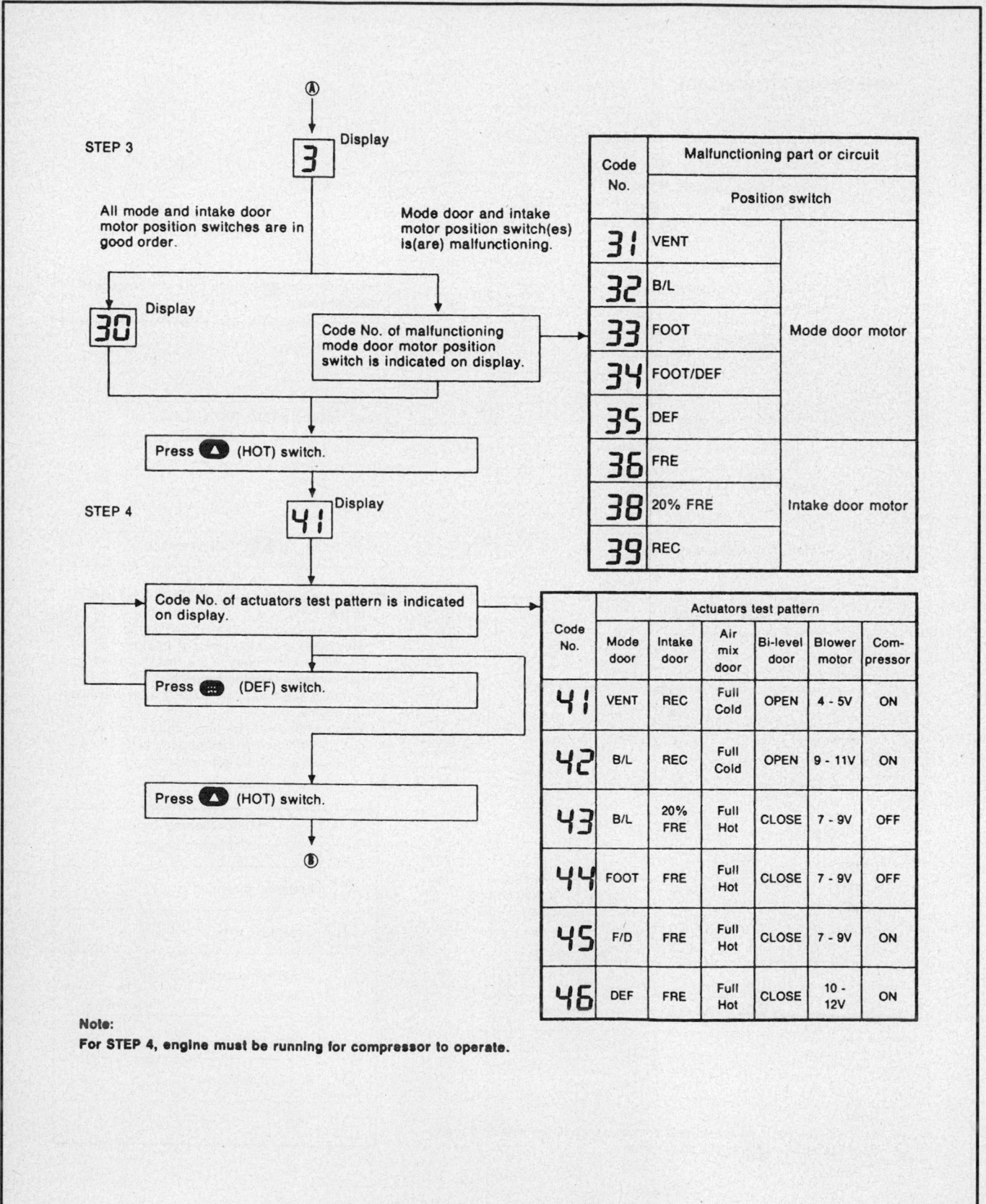

Code No.	Malfunctioning part or circuit		
	Position switch		
31	VENT		
32	B/L		
33	FOOT		Mode door motor
34	FOOT/DEF		
35	DEF		
36	FRE		
38	20% FRE		Intake door motor
39	REC		

STEP 3

Display: **3**

All mode and intake door motor position switches are in good order.

Mode door and intake motor position switch(es) is(are) malfunctioning.

Display: **30**

Code No. of malfunctioning mode door motor position switch is indicated on display.

Press ▲ (HOT) switch.

STEP 4

Display: **41**

Code No. of actuators test pattern is indicated on display.

Press ⦂⦂⦂ (DEF) switch.

Press ▲ (HOT) switch.

Code No.	Actuators test pattern					
	Mode door	Intake door	Air mix door	Bi-level door	Blower motor	Com-pressor
41	VENT	REC	Full Cold	OPEN	4 - 5V	ON
42	B/L	REC	Full Cold	OPEN	9 - 11V	ON
43	B/L	20% FRE	Full Hot	CLOSE	7 - 9V	OFF
44	FOOT	FRE	Full Hot	CLOSE	7 - 9V	OFF
45	F/D	FRE	Full Hot	CLOSE	7 - 9V	ON
46	DEF	FRE	Full Hot	CLOSE	10 - 12V	ON

Note:
For STEP 4, engine must be running for compressor to operate.

AUTO. A/C SELF–DIAGNOSTIC STEP CHART—MAXIMA, CONT'D

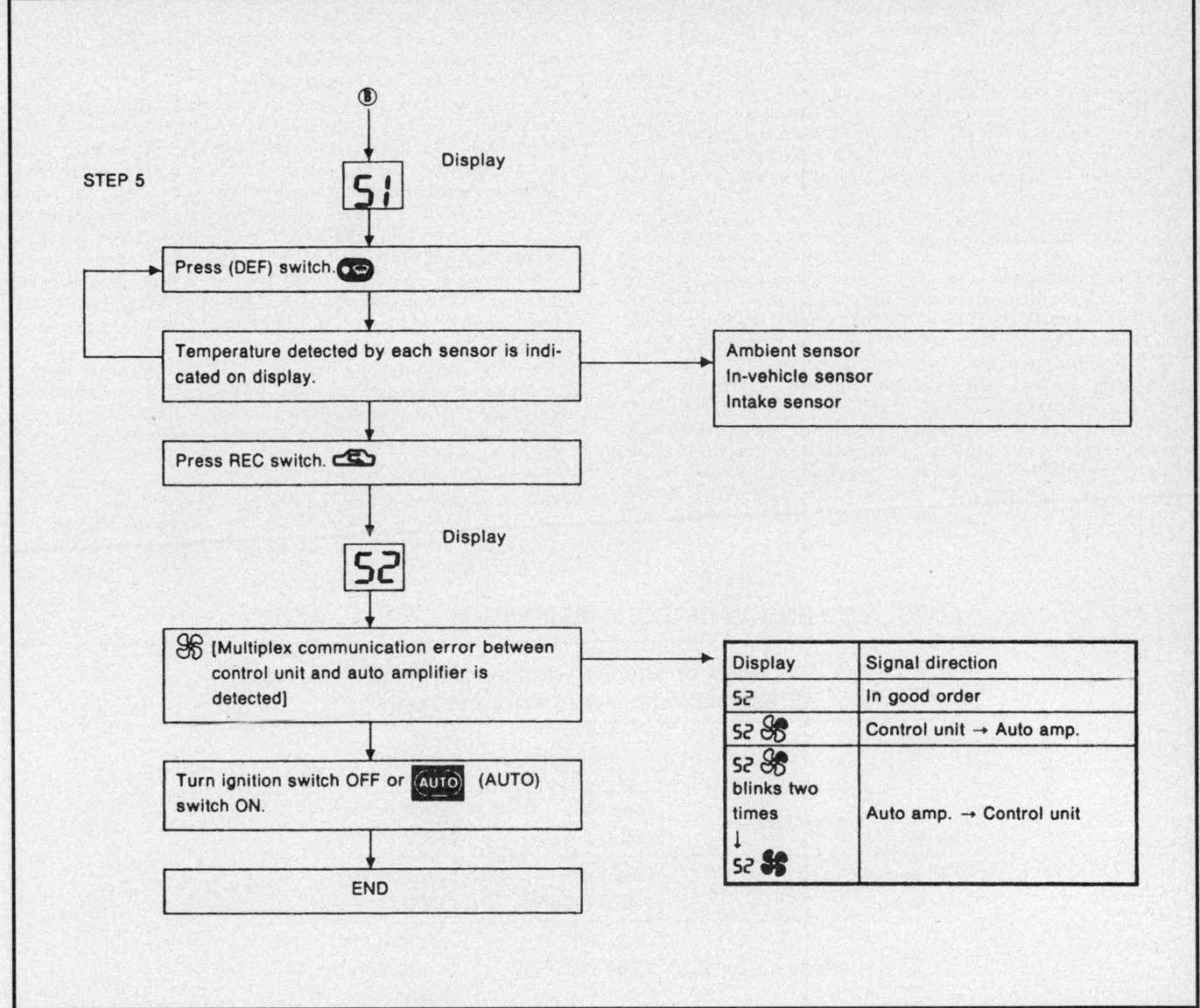

6. The self-diagnostic process will result in a display of any trouble codes which are in the computer memory. As they are displayed, record each code for further reference. The codes signal faults with sensors, mode doors or actuators.

7. The self-diagnostic steps occur as follows:
  • Step 1 checks the LED and segments to be sure these are in good order.
  • Step 2 check each sensor circuit for open or short circuit. If all sensors are okay, a 20 will be displayed. If a sensor is malfunctioning the corresponding code blinks on display, with a short circuit indicated by a "–" (minus sign) in front of the code. If more than one sensor is bad, each code will blink twice.
  • The sensors or circuits are considered malfunctioning when the input signal corresponds with any of the conditions shown in the appropriate chart.
  • Step 3 checks the mode door position. If all doors are okay, 30 will be displayed. Refer to the appropriate diagnostic chart for door malfunction codes.
  • Step 4 check the operation of each actuator.

  • Step 5 checks the temperature being detected by the sensors. When the **DEFROST** button is pressed once, the display temperature will be for the ambient sensor.
  • Then, as the **DEFROST** button is pressed again, the in-vehicle sensor temperature will display. If the **DEFROST** button is pressed again, the intake sensor temperature signal will display. The fourth time the **DEFROST** button is pushed, the display returns to the original 5 for the Step 5 sequence.
  • The auxiliary mechanism is the temperature setting trimmer that compensates for differences between the temperature setting as selected (digitally displayed) and the temperature actually felt by the driver in a range of + 6°F (+ 3°C).
  • To operate the trimmer, when in Step 5, press the **FAN** switch to set the auxiliary mode. Then, press the "Up" (warmer) arrow and "Down" (colder) arrow as desired. The temperature will change at a rate of 1°F (0.5°C) each time a switch is pressed.

Altima

1. Be sure the fresh vent lever is in the **OFF** position. Start the engine and, within 5 seconds of starting, press and hold the **OFF** switch for at least 5 seconds.

2. The system will then cycle through a series of self-diagnostic routines before registering on the control panel display.

3. The self-diagnostic process can be exited at any time by either pressing the **AUTO** button or turning the engine OFF.

4. Shifting from one step to another is accomplished by pushing the temperature control "up" arrow (warmer) or the "down" arrow (cooler).

5. Additionally, shifting from Step 5 in the diagnostic chart to auxiliary mechanism is accomplished by pushing the fan switch.

6. The self-diagnostic process will result in a display of any trouble codes which are in the computer memory. As they are displayed, record each code for further reference. The code signal faults with sensors, mode doors or actuators.

7. The self-diagnostic steps occur as follows:

- Step 1 checks the LED and segments to be sure these are in good order.

- Step 2 check each sensor circuit for open or short circuit. If all sensors are okay, a **20** will be displayed. If a sensor is malfunctioning the corresponding code blinks on display, with a short circuit indicated by a blinking **ECON** indicator. If more than one sensor is bad, each code will blink twice.

- The sensors or circuits are considered malfunctioning when the input signal corresponds with any of the conditions shown in the appropriate chart.

- Step 3 checks the mode door position. If all doors are okay, **30** will be displayed. Refer to the appropriate diagnostic chart for door malfunction codes.

- Step 4 check the operation of each actuator. When the **DEFROST** button is pressed once, **42** will display for the Vent door. Each time the **DEFROST** button is pressed again, the next number will display in order (41 through 46). Make a visual and audio check of the operation of each door.

- Step 5 checks the temperature being detected by the sensors. When the **DEFROST** button is pressed once, the display temperature will be for the ambient sensor.

- Then, as the **DEFROST** button is pressed again, the in-vehicle sensor temperature will display. If the **DEFROST** button is pressed again, the display returns to the original **5** for the Step 5 sequence.

- The auxiliary mechanism is the temperature setting trimmer that compensates for differences between the temperature setting as selected (digitally displayed) and the temperature actually felt by the driver in a range of + 6°F (+ 3°C).

- To operate the trimmer, when in Step 5, press the **FAN** switch to set the auxiliary mode. Then, press the "Up" (warmer) arrow and "Down" (colder) arrow as desired. The temperature will change at a rate of 1°F (0.5°C) each time a switch is pressed.

AUTO. A/C SENSOR CIRCUIT RESISTANCE CHART—ALTIMA

If a circuit is opened or shorted, display shows its code No. when input corresponds with any of following conditions.

Code No.	Sensor	Open circuit	Short circuit
21	Ambient sensor	Less than −50°C (−58°F)	Greater than 75°C (167°F)
22	In-vehicle sensor	Less than −50°C (−58°F)	Greater than 75°C (167°F)
25	Sunload sensor*2	Less than 48.84 W/m² (42 kcal)	Greater than 1,640 W/m² (1,410 kcal)
26	PBR*1	Greater than 50%	Less than 30%

*1: "50%" and "30%" refer to percentage with respect to full stroke of air mix door. (Full cold: 0%, Full hot: 100%)

*2: **Conduct self-diagnosis STEP 2 under sunshine.**
When conducting indoors, direct light (more than 60W) at sunload sensor.

AUTO. A/C SELF–DIAGNOSTIC STEP CHART—ALTIMA

AUTO. A/C SELF–DIAGNOSTIC STEP CHART—ALTIMA CONT'D

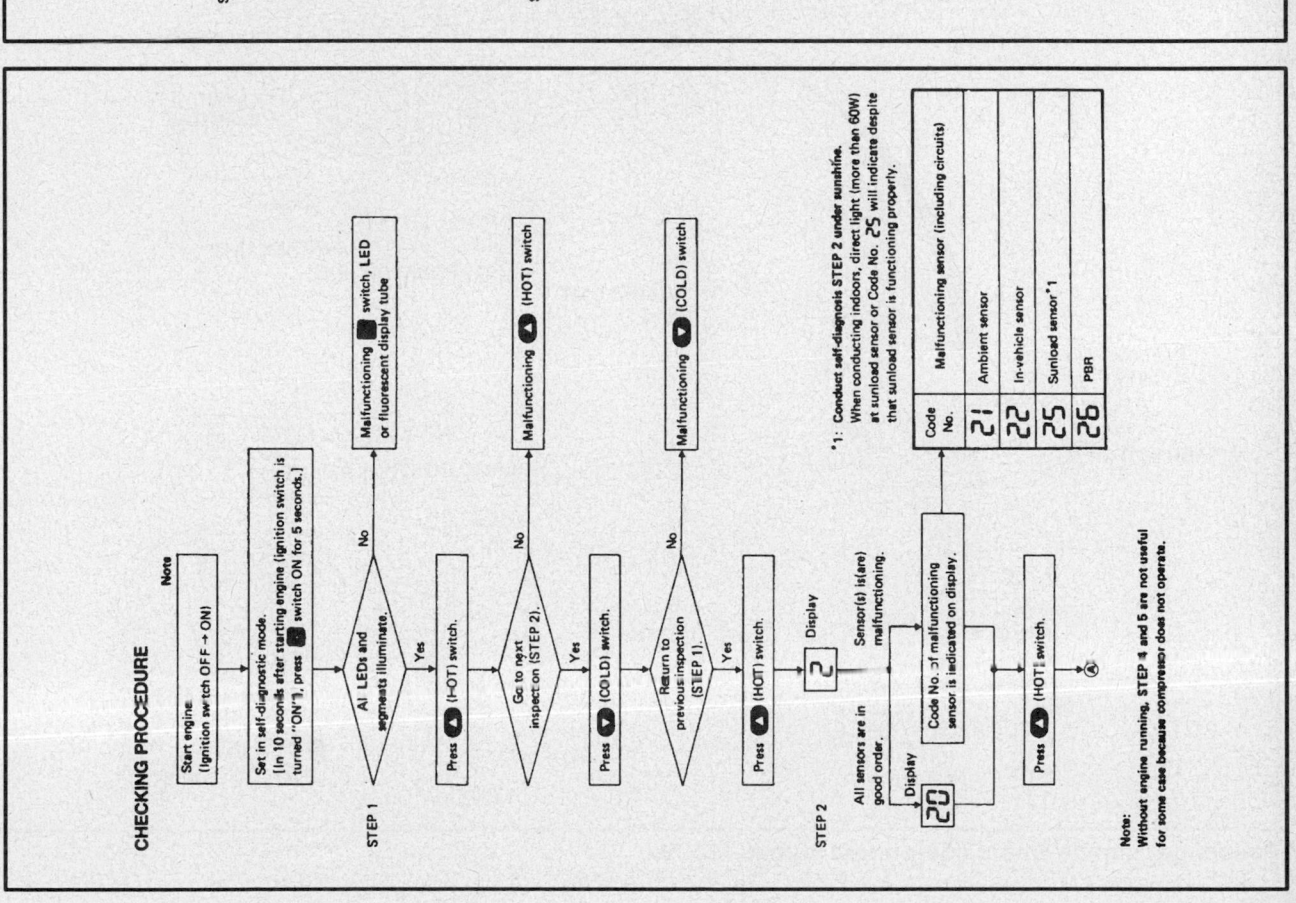

STEP 3 — Mode and intake door motor position switch(es) is(are) malfunctioning.

Code No.	Malfunctioning mode and intake door motor position switch (including circuits)
31	VENT
32	B/L
34	FOOT
35	FOOT/DEF
36	DEF
37	REC
38	20% FRE
39	FRE

STEP 4 — Code No. of actuators test pattern is indicated on display.

Actuators test pattern

Code No.	Mode door	Intake door	Air mix door	Fresh vent door	Blower motor	Com-pressor
41	VENT	REC	Full Cold	Open	4 - 5V	ON
42	B/L	REC	Full Cold	Open	9 - 11V	ON
43	B/L	20% FRE	Full Hot	Close	7 - 9V	ON
44	FOOT	FRE	Full Hot	Close	7 - 9V	OFF
45	F/D	FRE	Full Hot	Close	7 - 9V	OFF
46	DEF	FRE	Full Hot	Close	10 - 12V	ON

STEP 5 — Temperature detected by each sensor is indicated on display.

Ambient sensor
In-vehicle sensor

Turn ignition switch OFF or (AUTO) switch ON.

END

CHECKING PROCEDURE

Note

Start engine.
(Ignition switch OFF → ON)

Set in self-diagnostic mode.
[In 10 seconds after starting engine (ignition switch is turned "ON"), press ▮ switch ON for 5 seconds.]

STEP 1 — All LEDs and segments illuminate.

Malfunctioning ▮ switch, LED or fluorescent display tube

Malfunctioning ▲ (HOT) switch

Malfunctioning ▼ (COLD) switch

STEP 2 — Sensor(s) is(are) malfunctioning.

Code No.	Malfunctioning sensor (including circuits)
21	Ambient sensor
22	In-vehicle sensor
25	Sunload sensor*1
26	PBR

*1: Conduct self-diagnosis STEP 2 under sunshine. When conducting indoors, direct light (more than 60W) at sunload sensor or Code No. 25 will indicate despite that sunload sensor is functioning properly.

Note:
Without engine running, STEP 4 and 5 are not useful for some case because compressor does not operate.

COMPONENT LAYOUTS

The following figures provide component layouts for all the main components, switches, sensors and relays on each Nissan model. Use these locations for service and diagnostic help, accompanied by the Wiring Schematics.

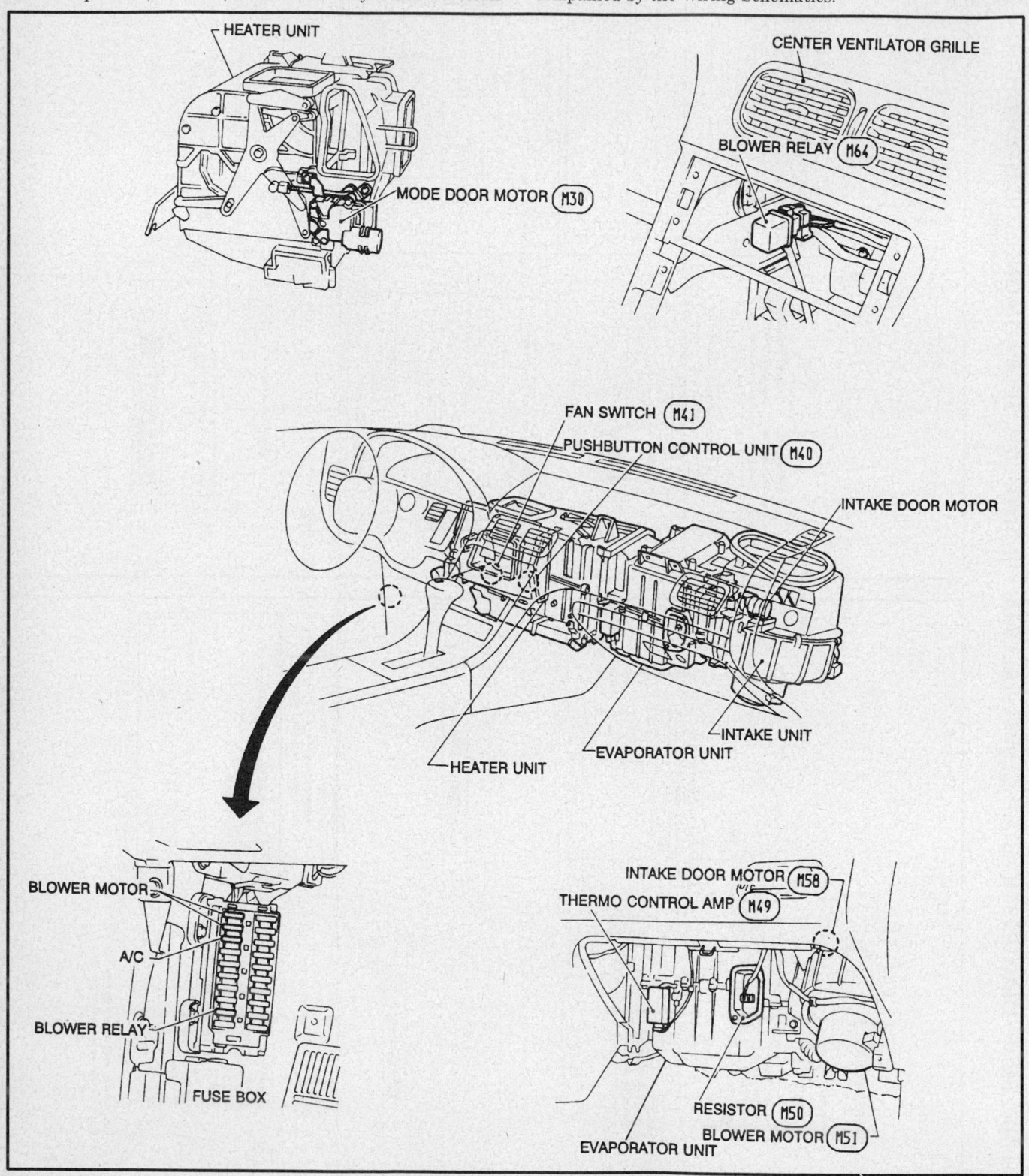

Passenger compartment component layout—240SX

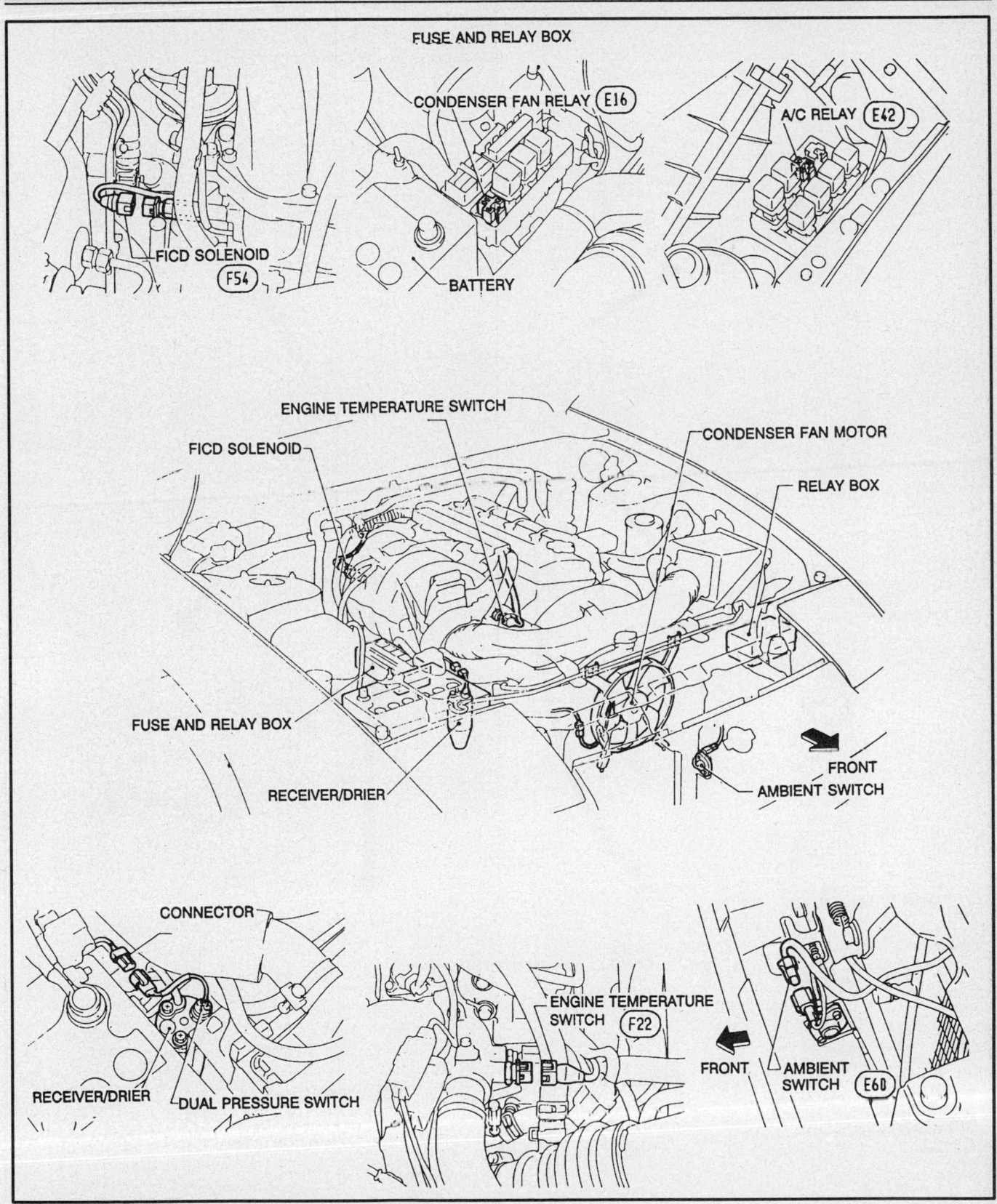

Engine compartment component layout—240SX

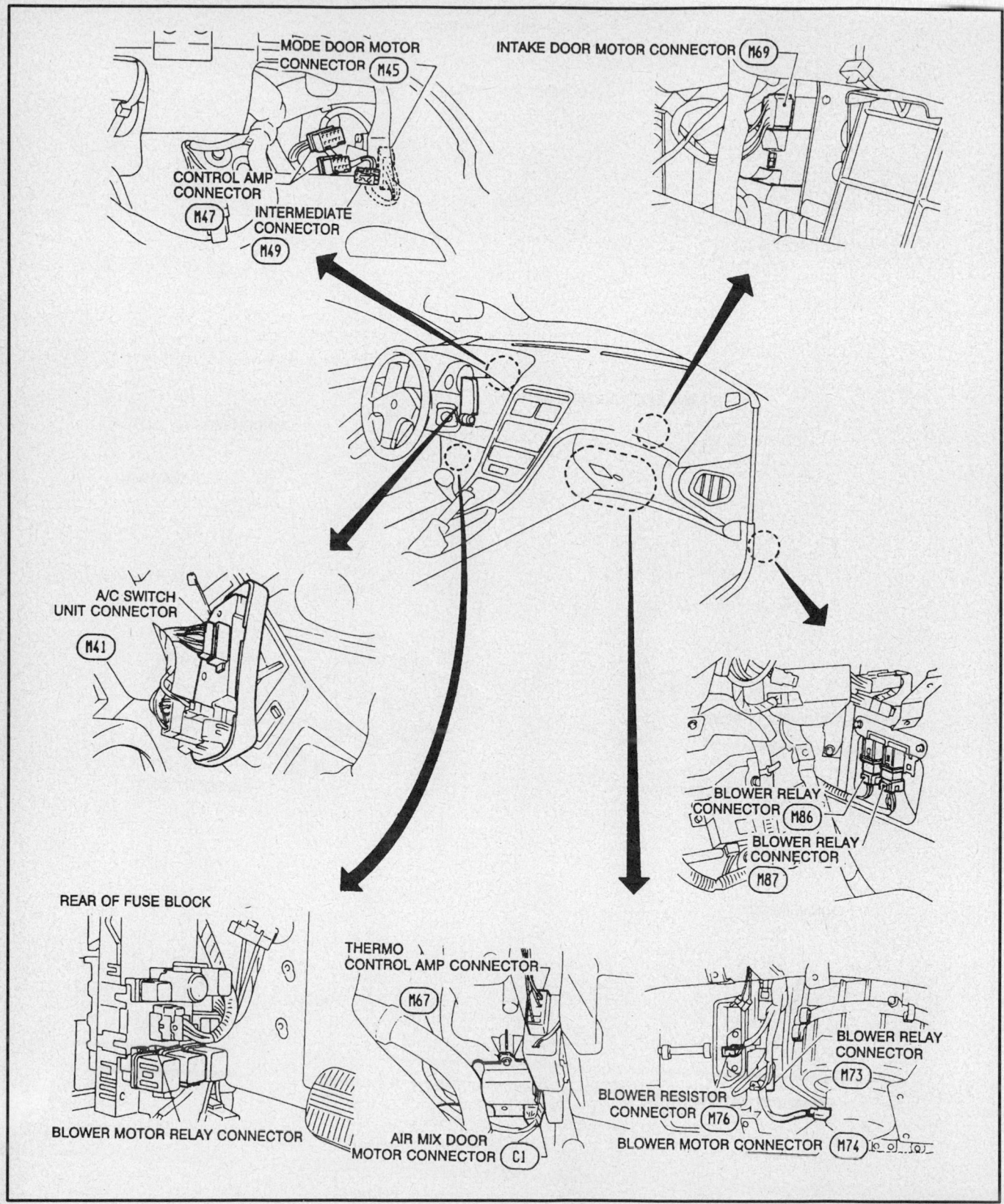

Passenger compartment component layout—300ZX (except 1995)

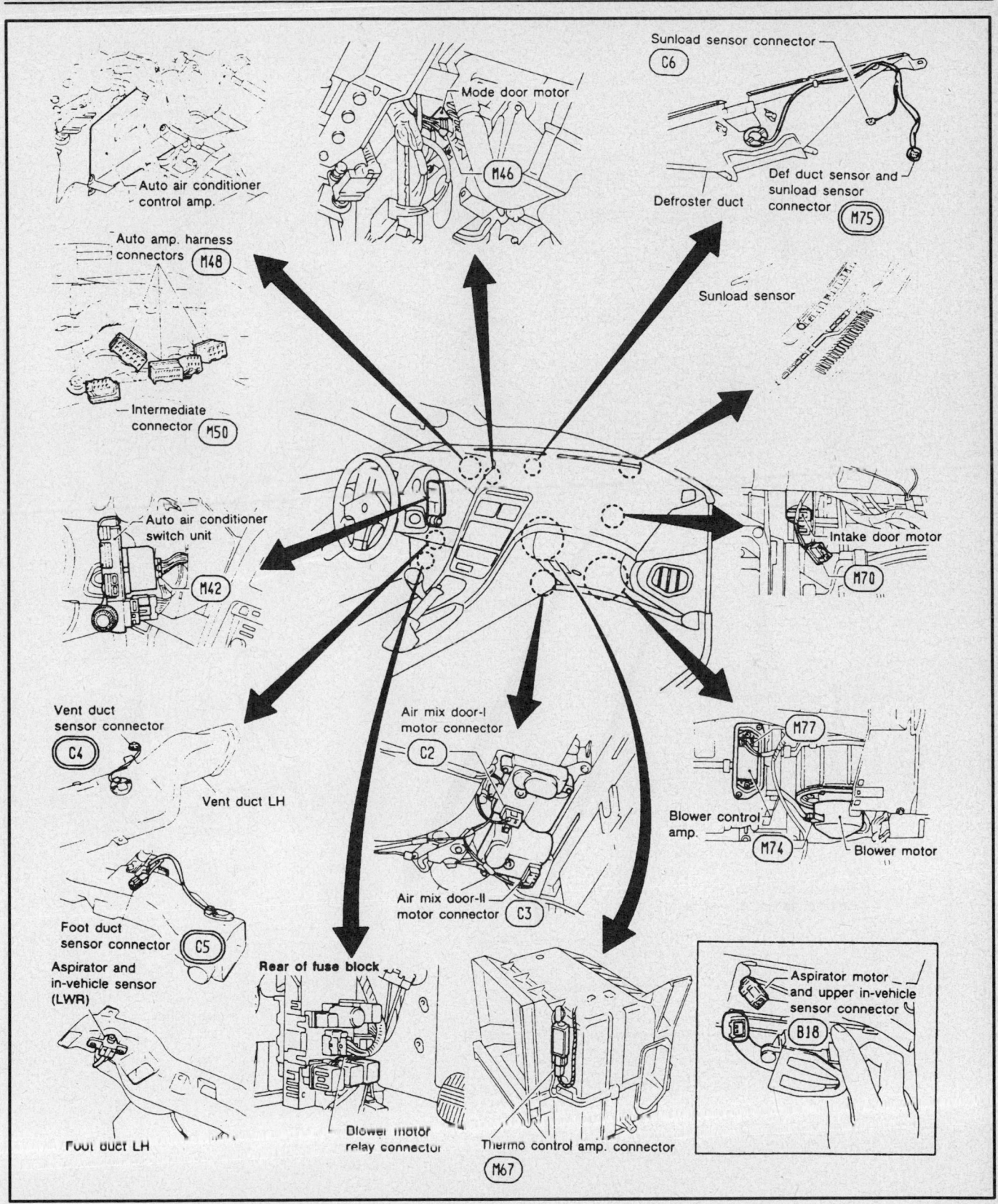

Sunload sensor connector C6

Mode door motor M46

Def duct sensor and sunload sensor connector M75

Defroster duct

Auto air conditioner control amp.

Auto amp. harness connectors M48

Intermediate connector M50

Sunload sensor

Auto air conditioner switch unit M42

Intake door motor M70

Vent duct sensor connector C4

Air mix door-I motor connector C2

Vent duct LH

M77

Blower control amp.

M74

Blower motor

Foot duct sensor connector C5

Air mix door-II motor connector C3

Aspirator and in-vehicle sensor (LWR)

Rear of fuse block

Aspirator motor and upper in-vehicle sensor connector B18

Foot duct LH

Blower motor relay connector

Thermo control amp. connector M67

Passenger compartment component layout—1995 300ZX

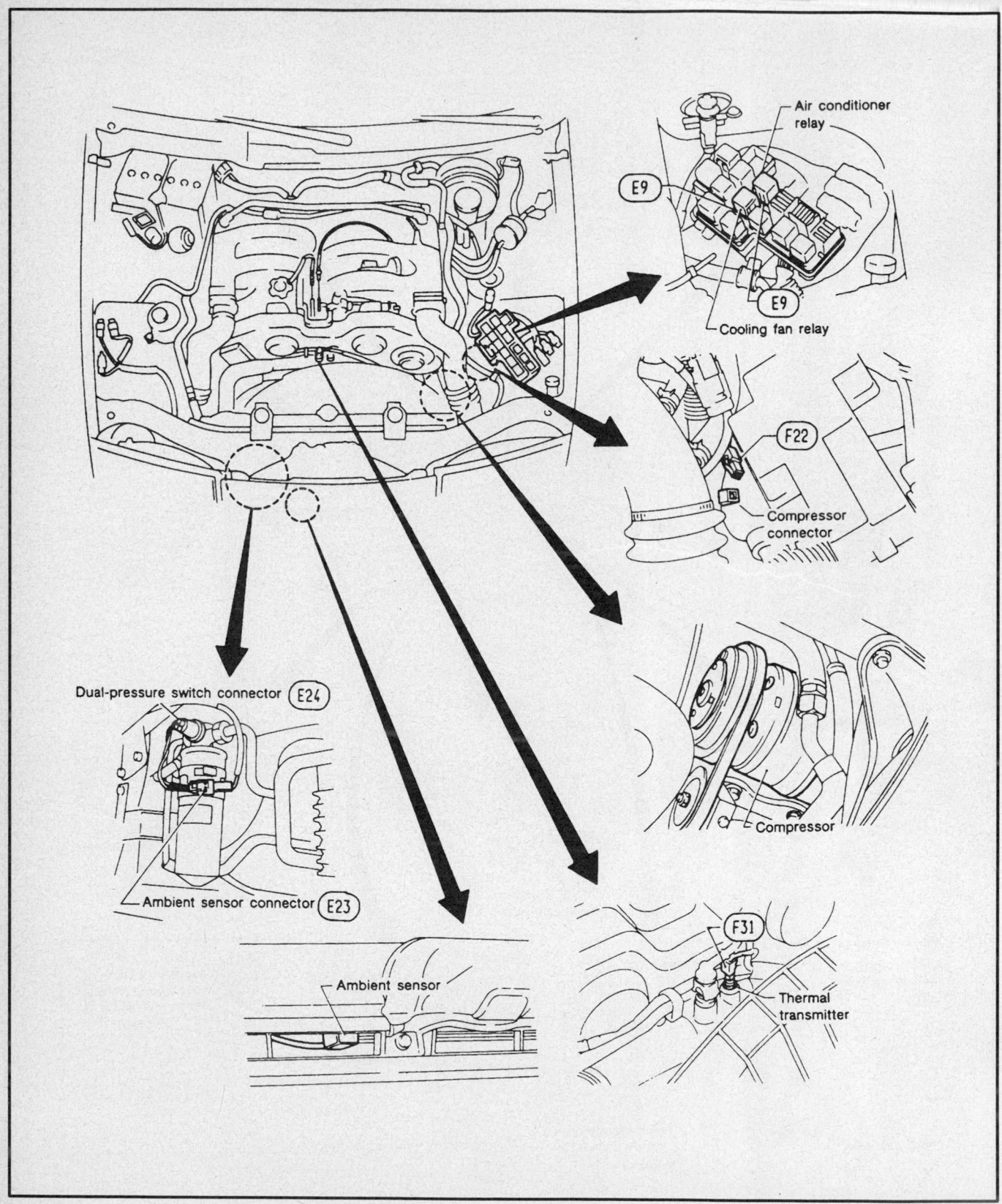

Air conditioner relay

E9

Cooling fan relay

F22

Compressor connector

Compressor

Dual-pressure switch connector E24

Ambient sensor connector E23

Ambient sensor

F31

Thermal transmitter

Engine compartment component layout—300ZX

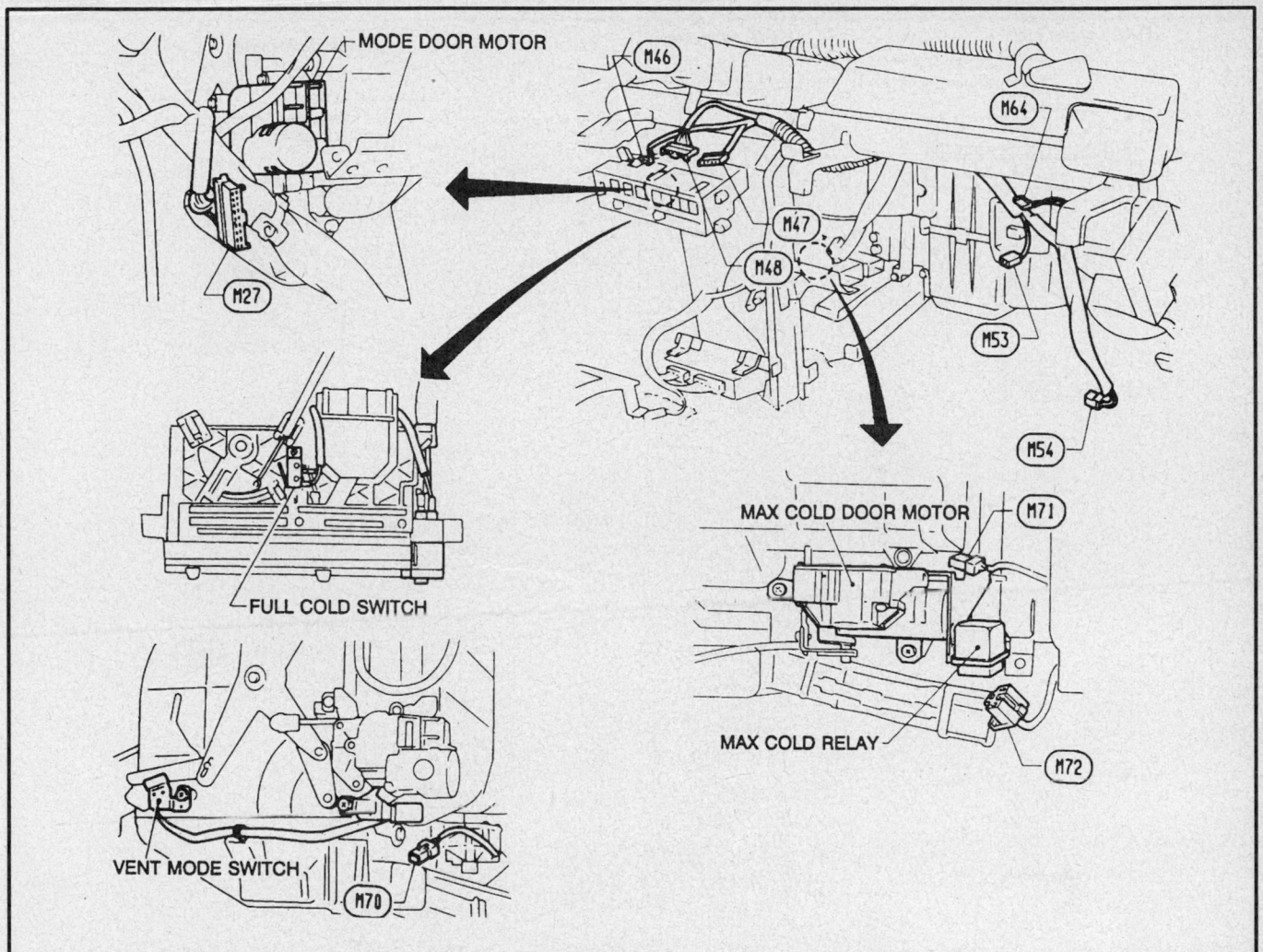

MODE DOOR MOTOR

M46

M64

M27

M47

M48

M53

M54

FULL COLD SWITCH

MAX COLD DOOR MOTOR — M71

MAX COLD RELAY

M72

VENT MODE SWITCH

M70

Passenger compartment component layout—1993 Maxima

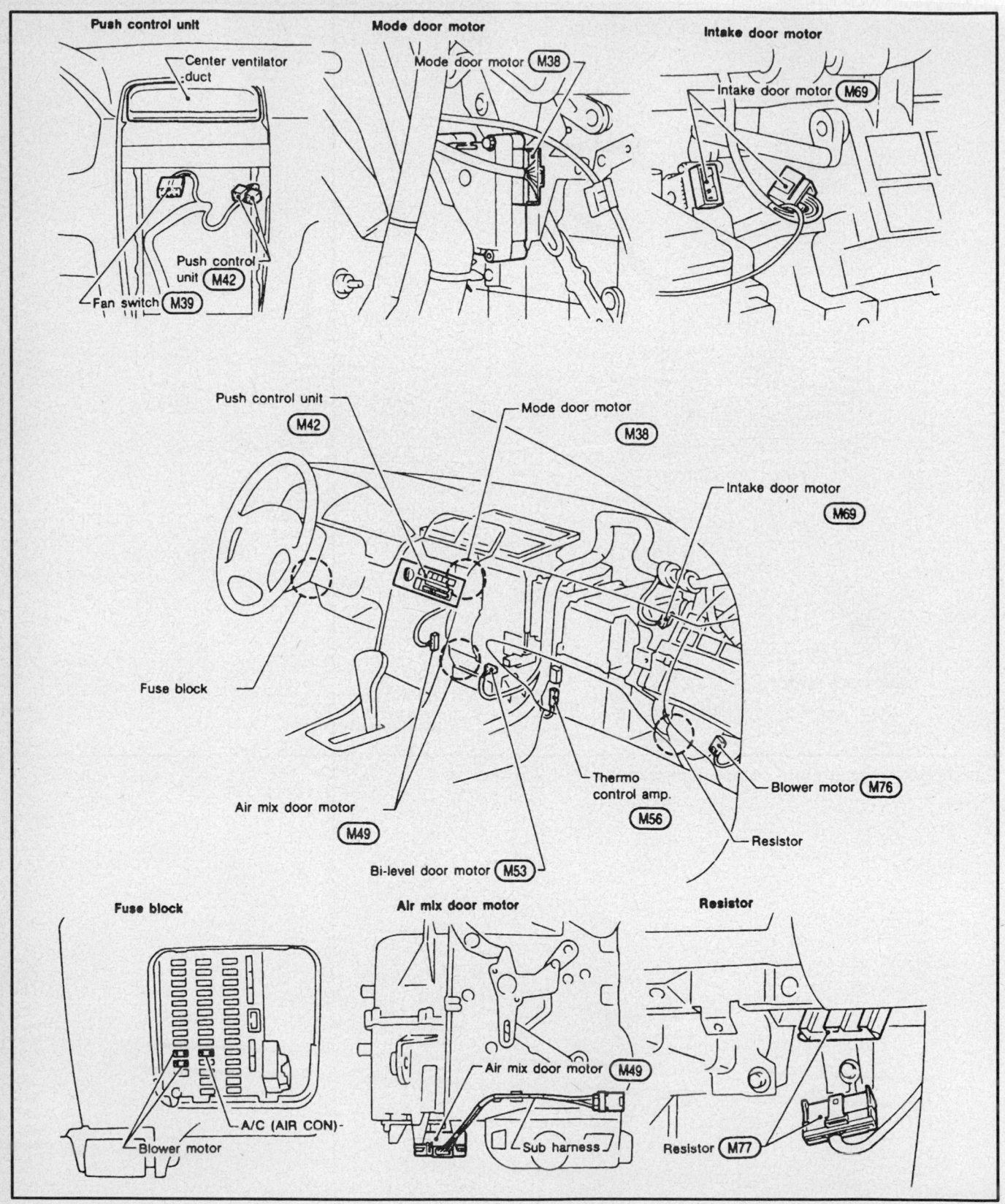

Push control unit

Center ventilator duct

Push control unit M42

Fan switch M39

Mode door motor

Mode door motor M38

Intake door motor

Intake door motor M69

Push control unit M42

Mode door motor M38

Intake door motor M69

Fuse block

Air mix door motor M49

Bi-level door motor M53

Thermo control amp. M56

Blower motor M76

Resistor

Fuse block

A/C (AIR CON)

Blower motor

Air mix door motor

Air mix door motor M49

Sub harness

Resistor

Resistor M77

Passenger compartment component layout—Maxima (except 1993)

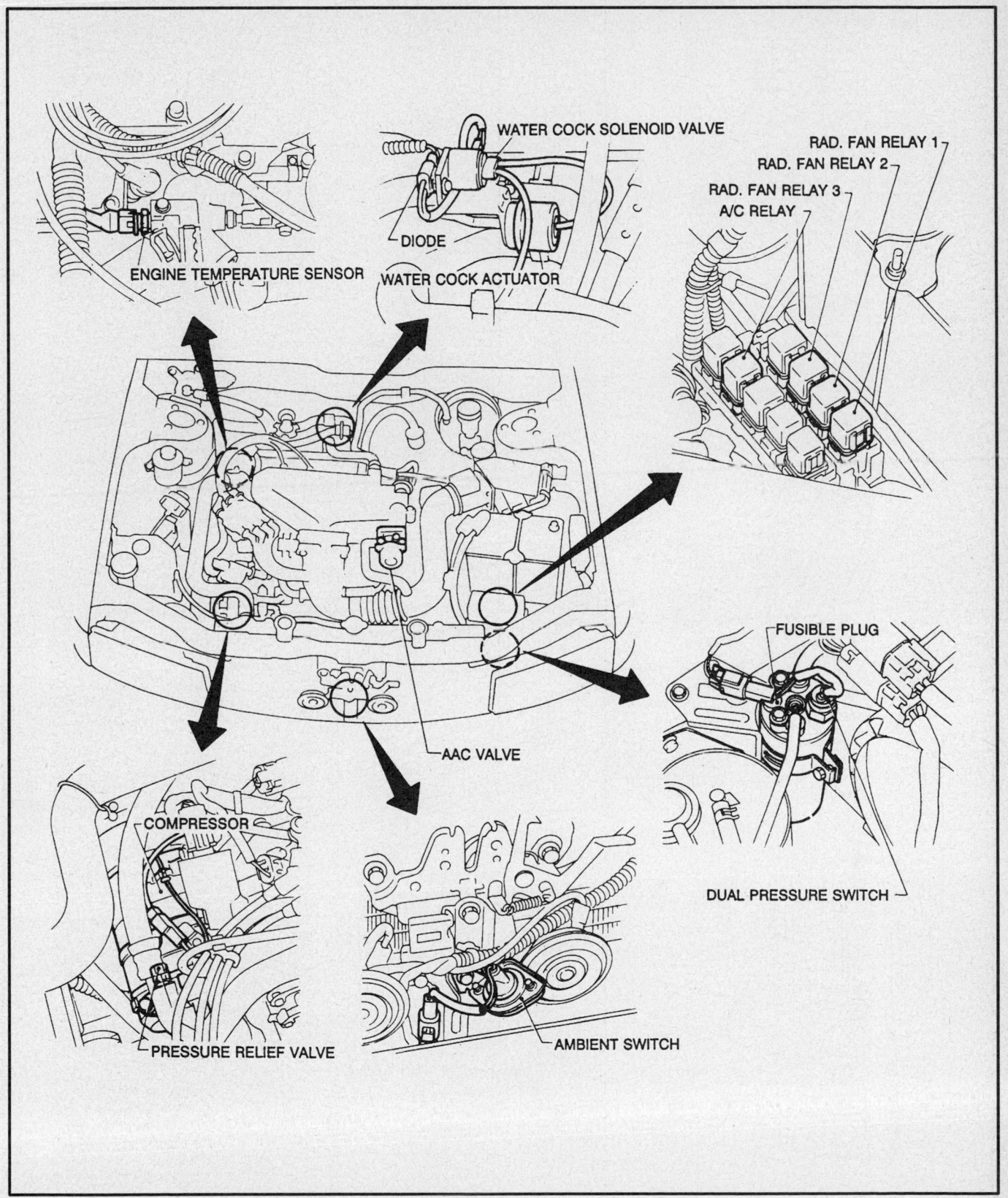

Engine compartment component layout—1993 Maxima

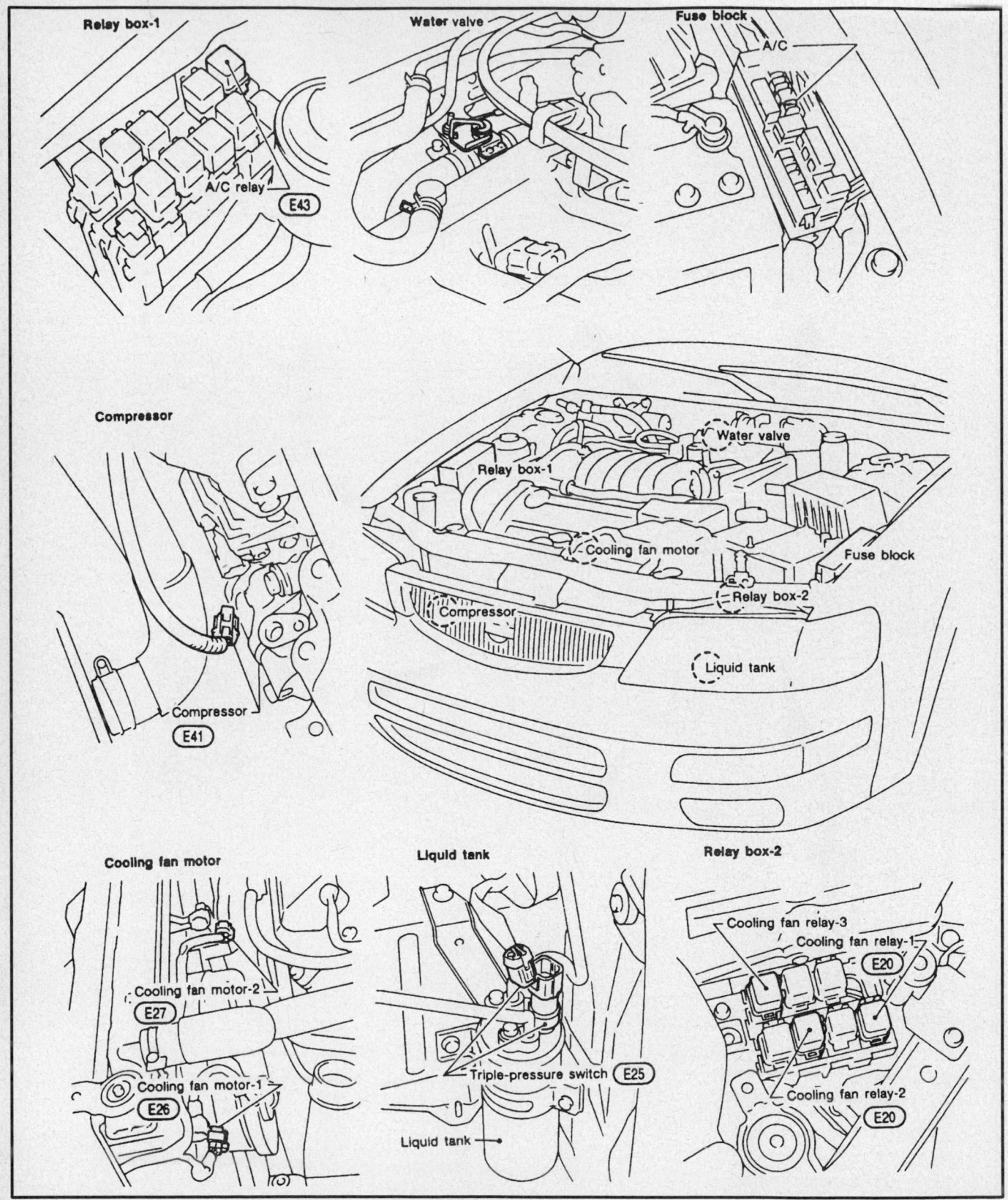

Engine compartment component layout—Maxima (except 1993)

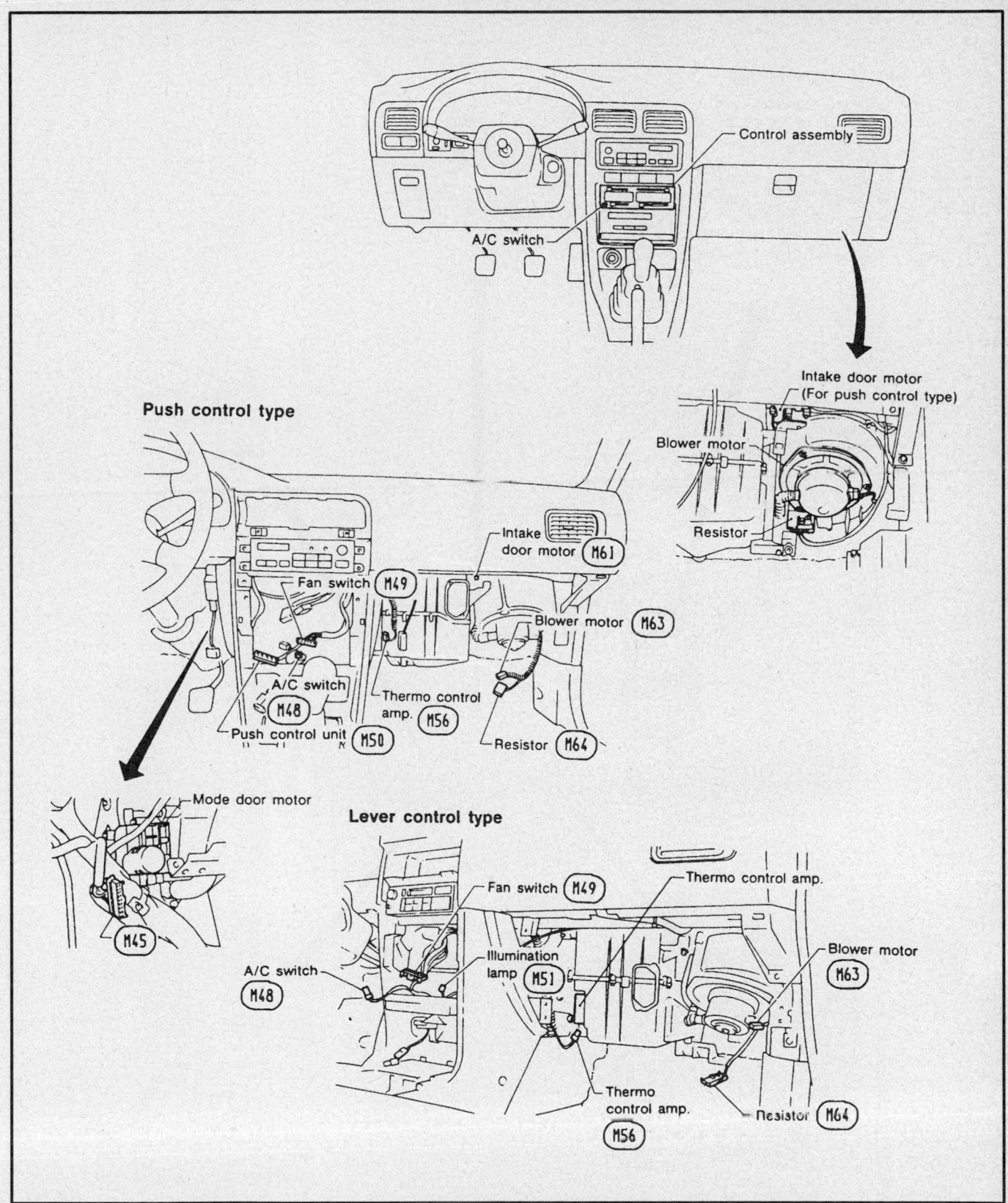

Push control type

Lever control type

Passenger compartment component layout—Sentra (except 1995)

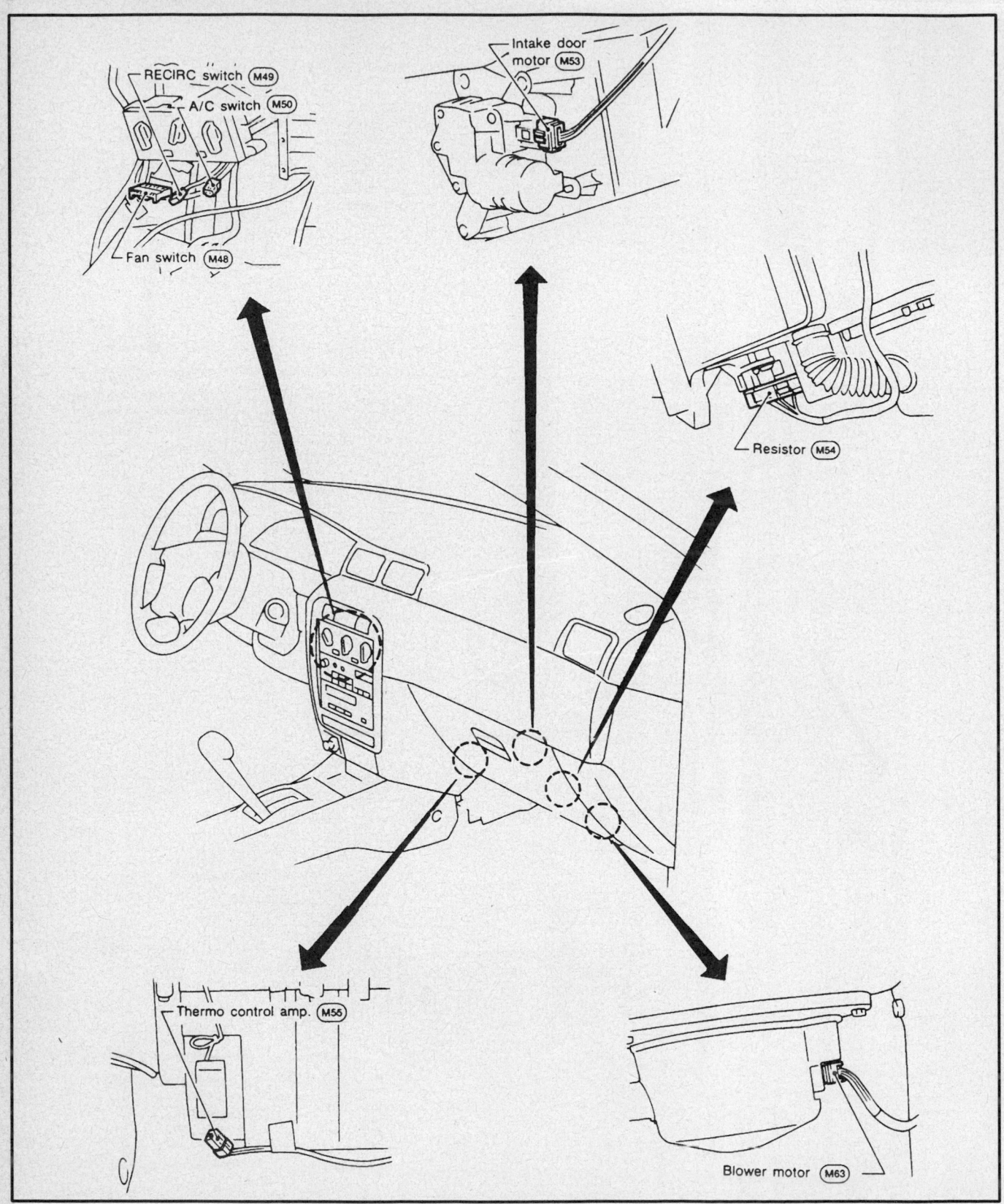

RECIRC switch (M49)
A/C switch (M50)
Fan switch (M48)
Intake door motor (M53)
Resistor (M54)
Thermo control amp. (M55)
Blower motor (M63)

Passenger compartment component layout—1995 Sentra and 200SX

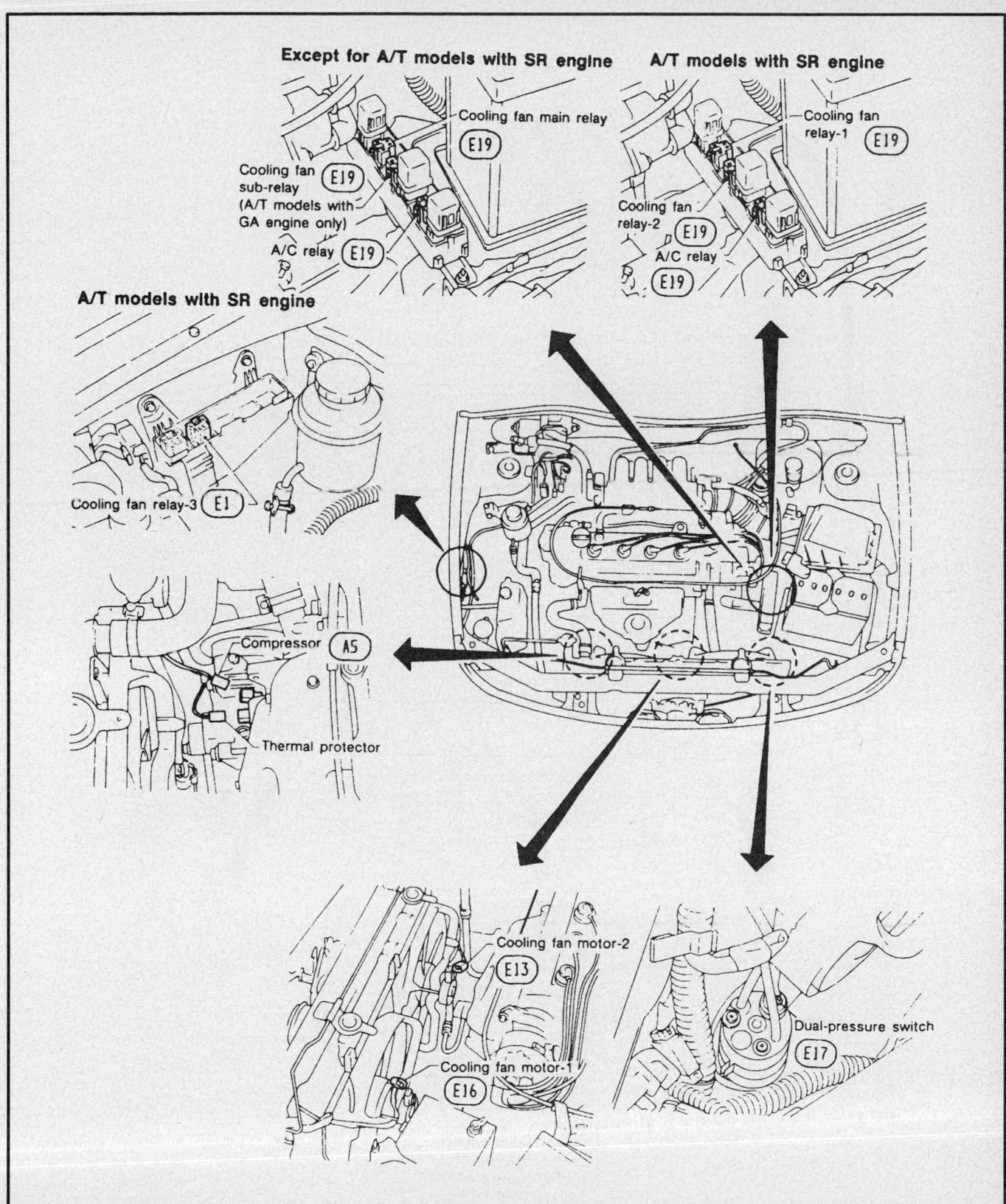

Except for A/T models with SR engine

Cooling fan main relay E19

Cooling fan sub-relay (A/T models with GA engine only) E19

A/C relay E19

A/T models with SR engine

Cooling fan relay-1 E19

Cooling fan relay-2 E19

A/C relay E19

A/T models with SR engine

Cooling fan relay-3 E1

Compressor A5

Thermal protector

Cooling fan motor-2 E13

Cooling fan motor-1 E16

Dual-pressure switch E17

Engine compartment component layout—Sentra (except 1995)

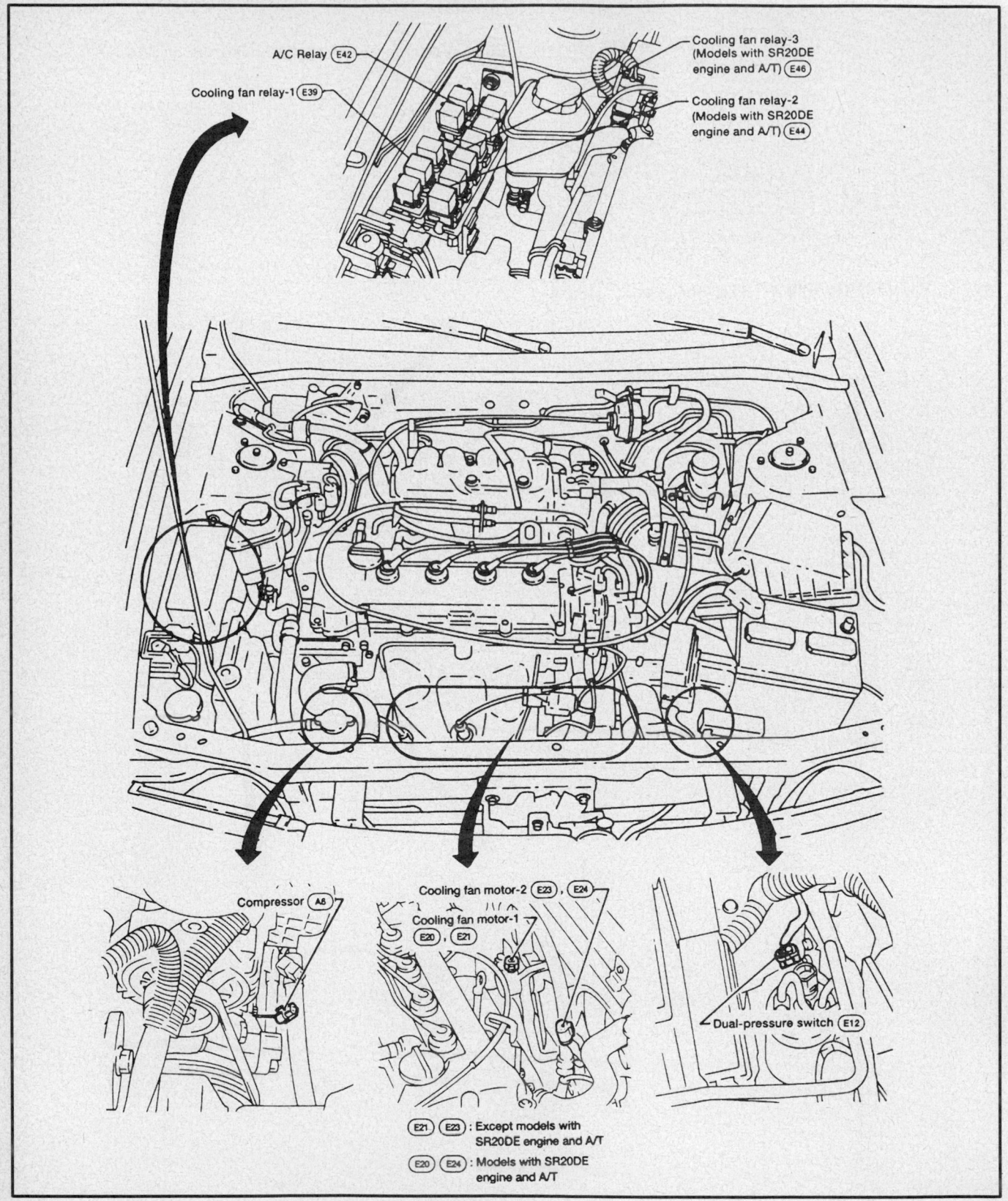

A/C Relay (E42)

Cooling fan relay-1 (E39)

Cooling fan relay-3
(Models with SR20DE
engine and A/T) (E46)

Cooling fan relay-2
(Models with SR20DE
engine and A/T) (E44)

Compressor (A8)

Cooling fan motor-2 (E23), (E24)
Cooling fan motor-1 (E20), (E21)

Dual-pressure switch (E12)

(E21) (E23) : Except models with
SR20DE engine and A/T

(E20) (E24) : Models with SR20DE
engine and A/T

Engine compartment layout—1995 Sentra and 200SX

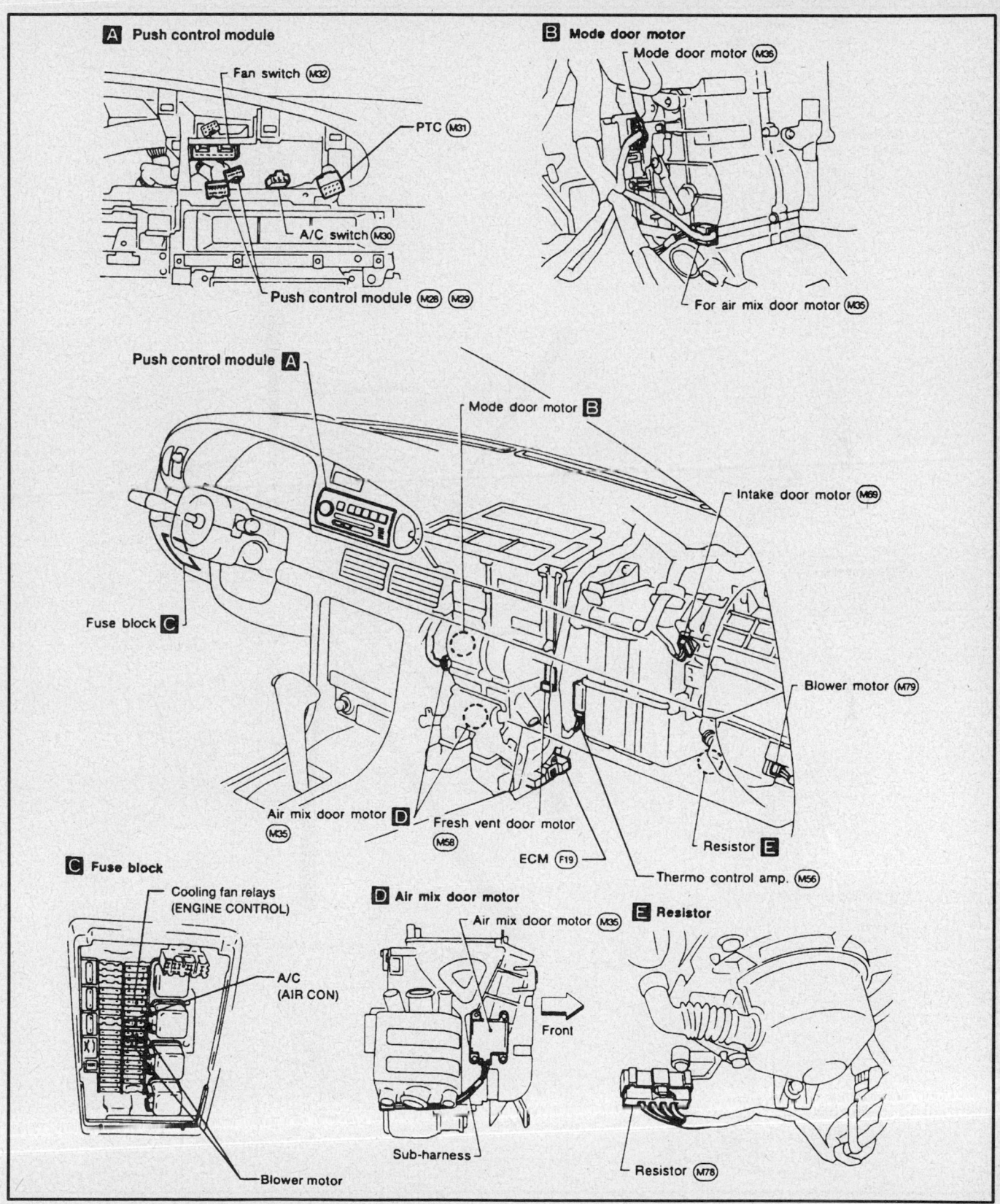

A Push control module

Fan switch (M32)

PTC (M31)

A/C switch (M30)

Push control module (M28) (M29)

B Mode door motor

Mode door motor (M36)

For air mix door motor (M35)

Push control module **A**

Mode door motor **B**

Intake door motor (M69)

Blower motor (M79)

Fuse block **C**

Air mix door motor **D** (M35)

Fresh vent door motor (M58)

ECM (F19)

Resistor **E**

Thermo control amp. (M56)

C Fuse block

Cooling fan relays (ENGINE CONTROL)

A/C (AIR CON)

Blower motor

D Air mix door motor

Air mix door motor (M35)

Front

Sub-harness

E Resistor

Resistor (M78)

Passenger compartment component layout—Altima

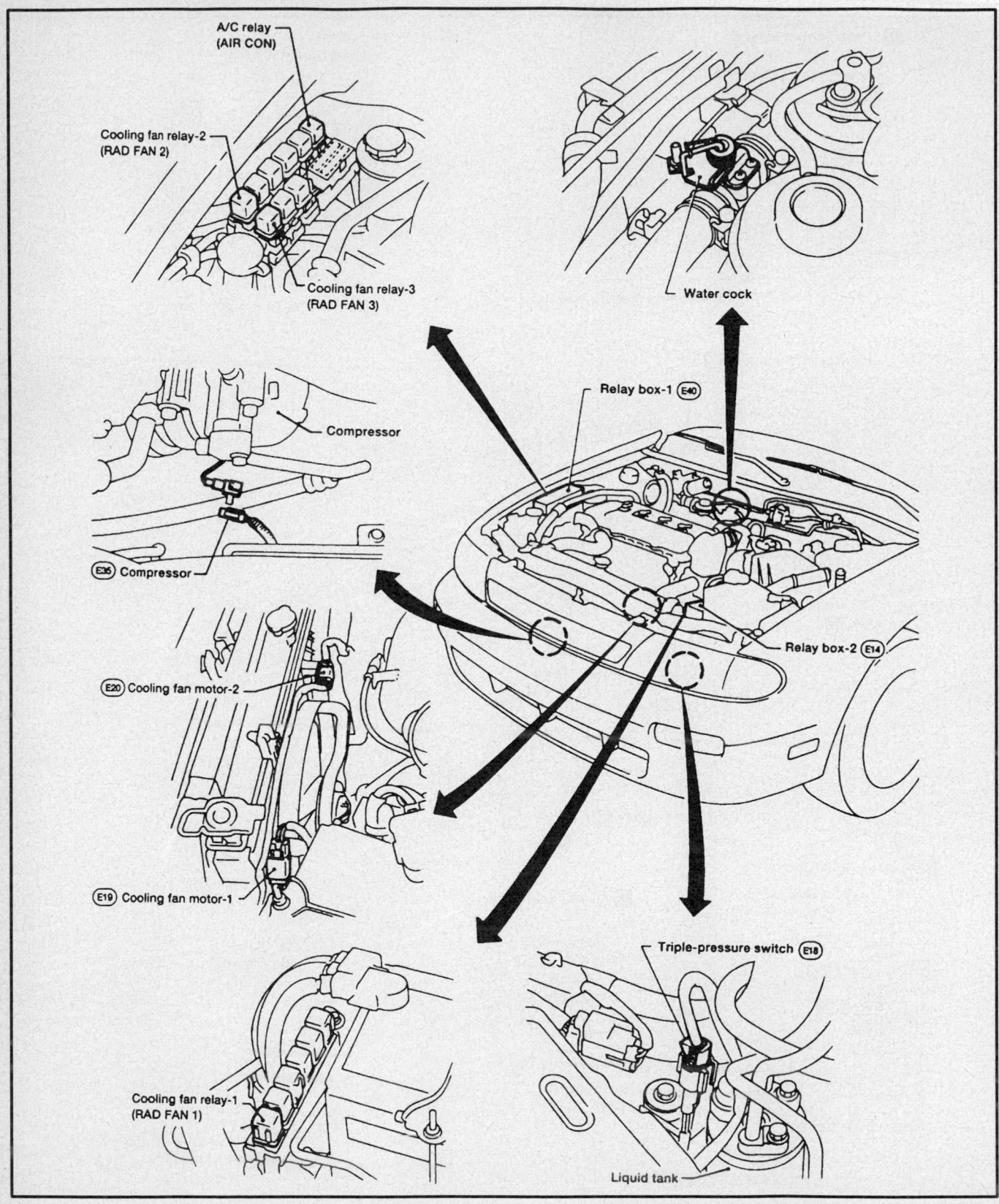

Engine compartment component layout—Altima

WIRING SCHEMATIC

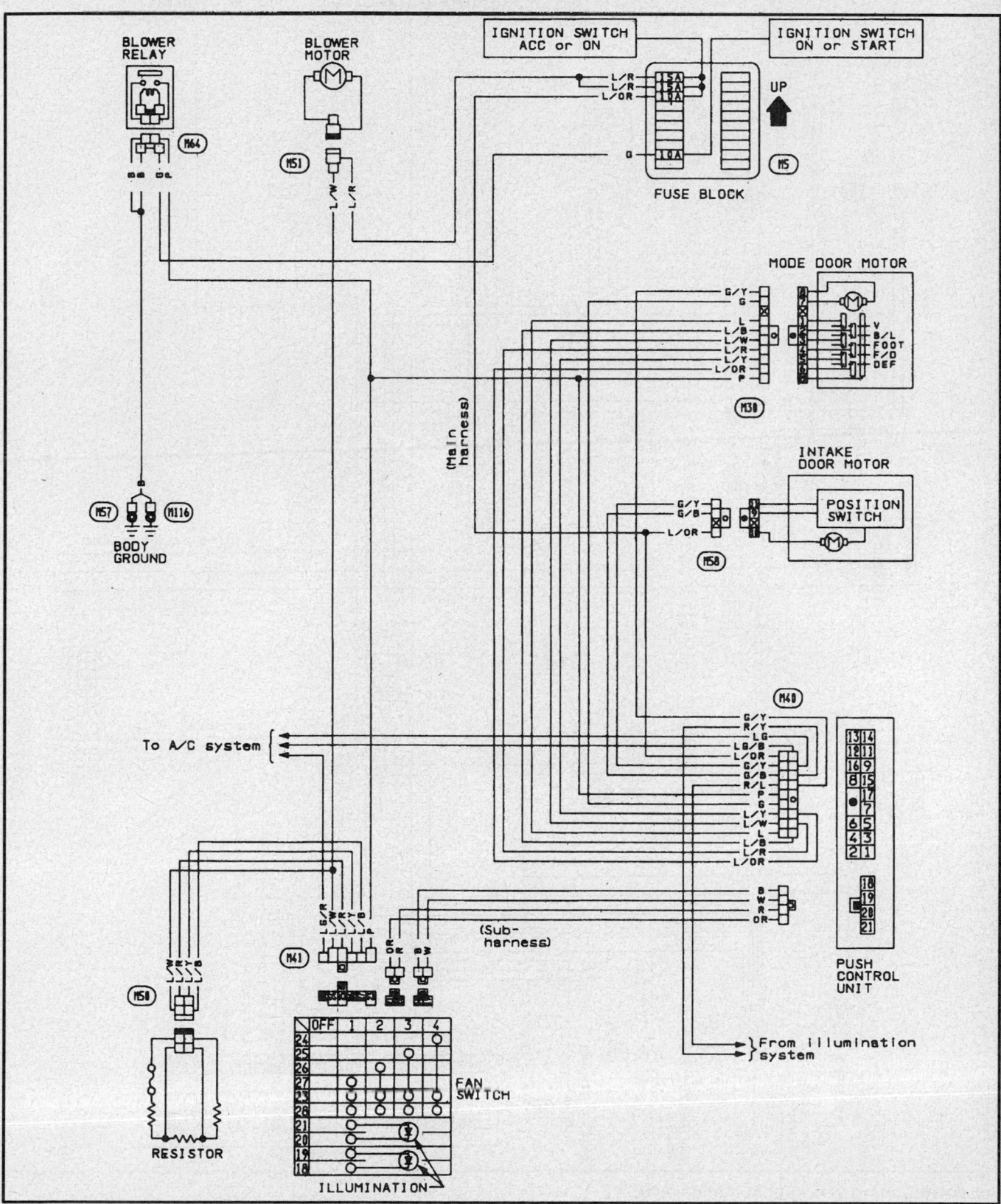

Heater only wiring schematic—240SX

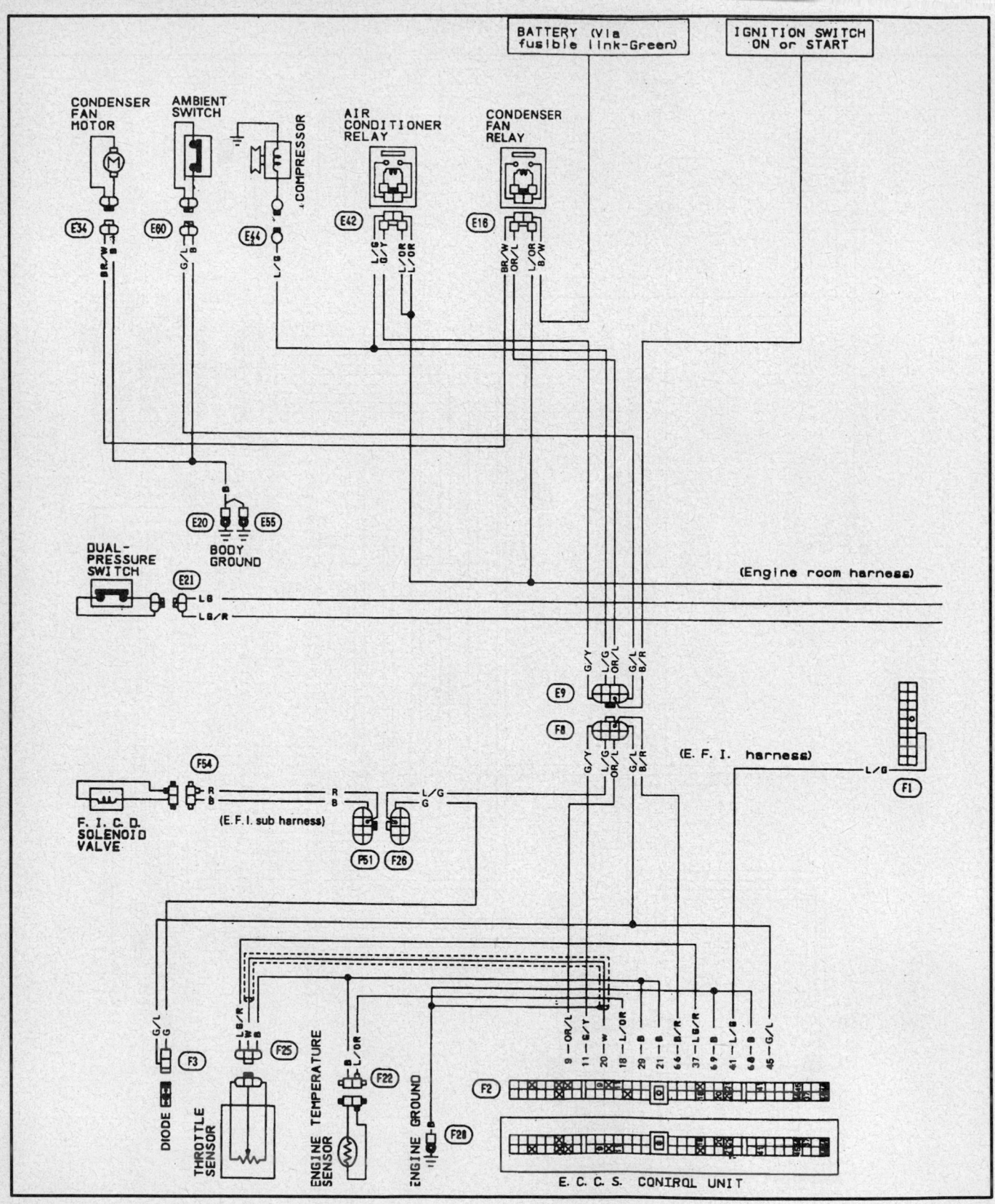

Air conditioning wiring schematic—240SX

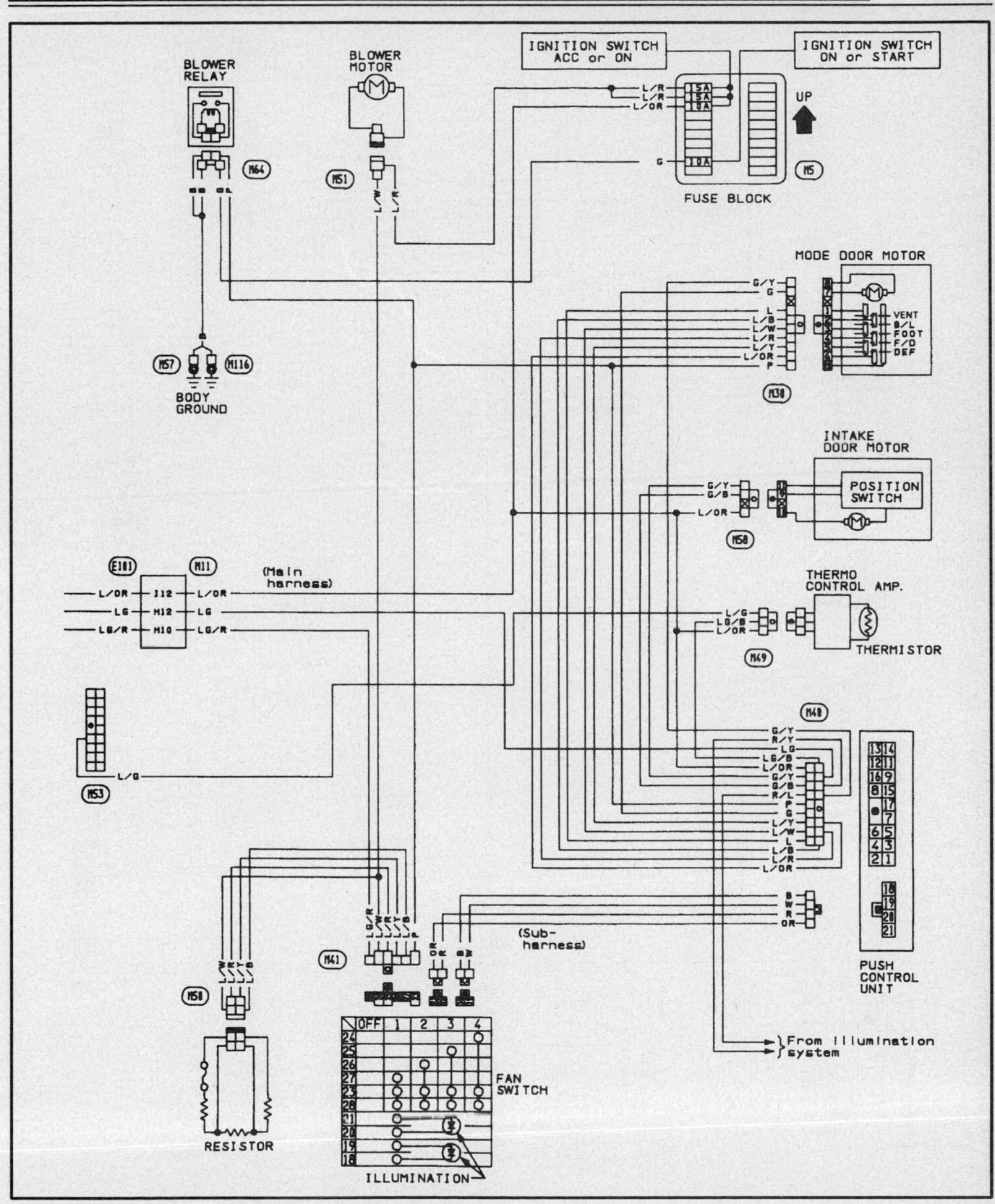

Air conditioning wiring schematic—240SX, Cont'd

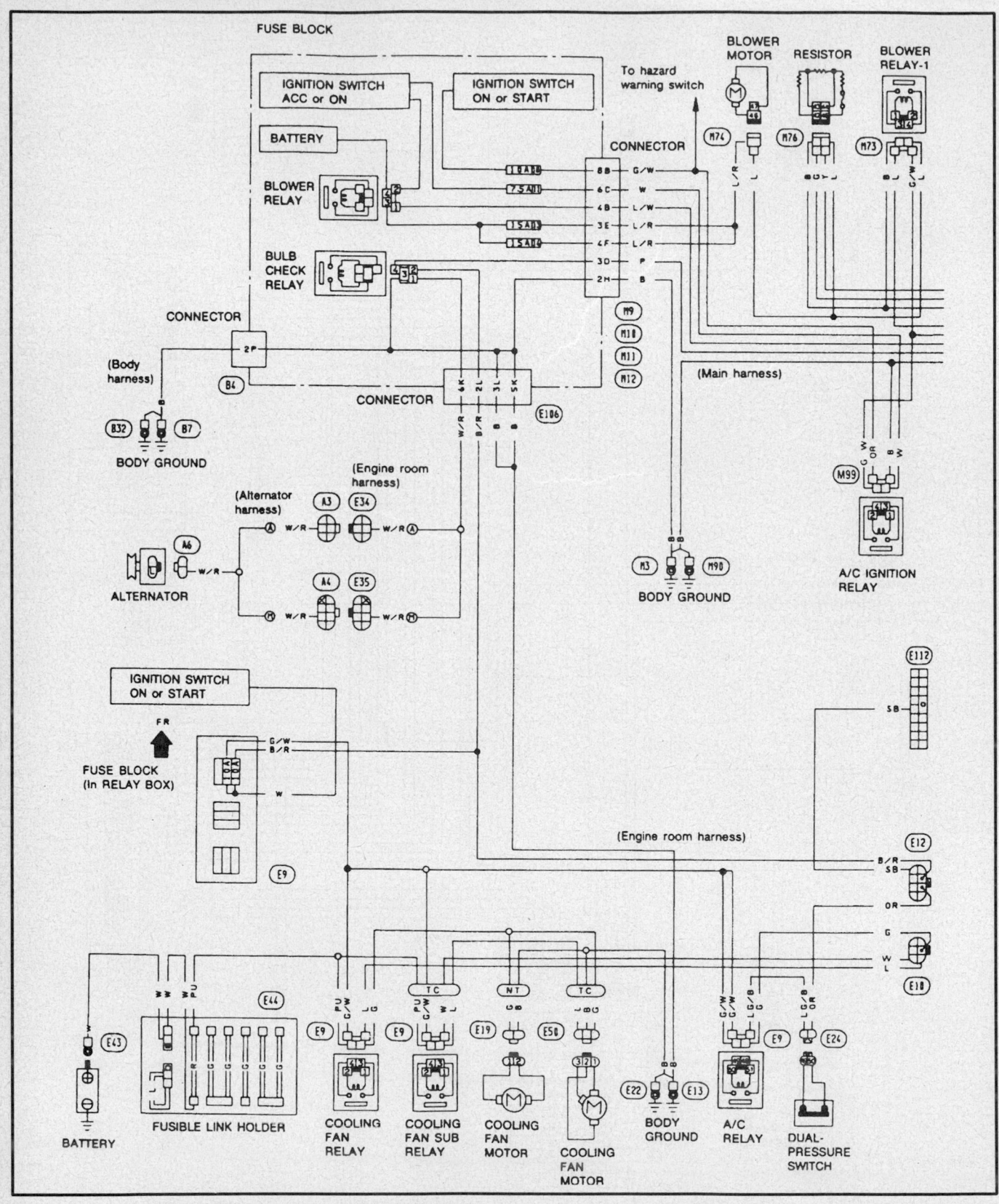

Manual air conditioning wiring schematic—300ZX

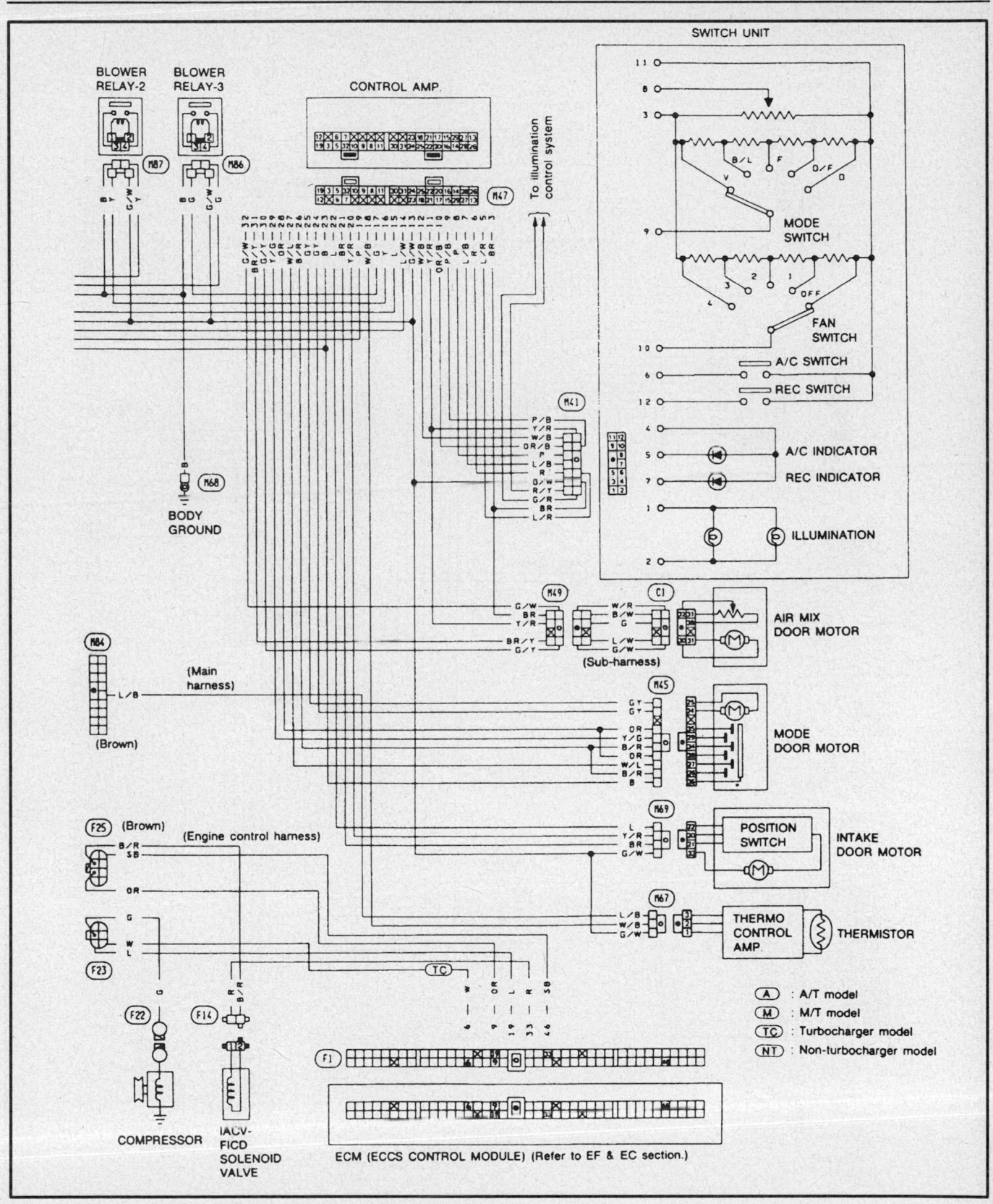

Manual air conditioning wiring schematic—300ZX, Cont'd

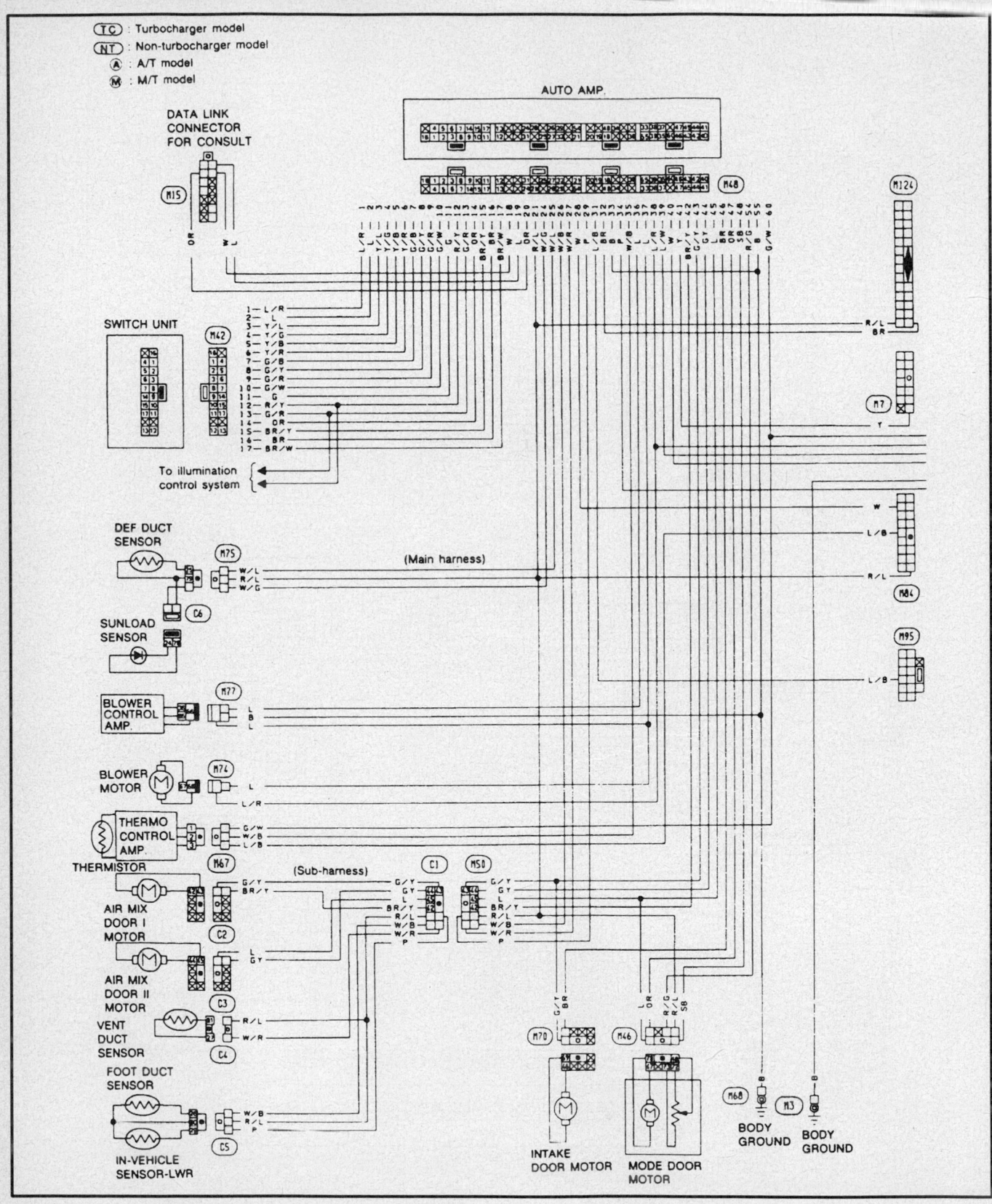

Automatic air conditioning wiring schematic—300ZX

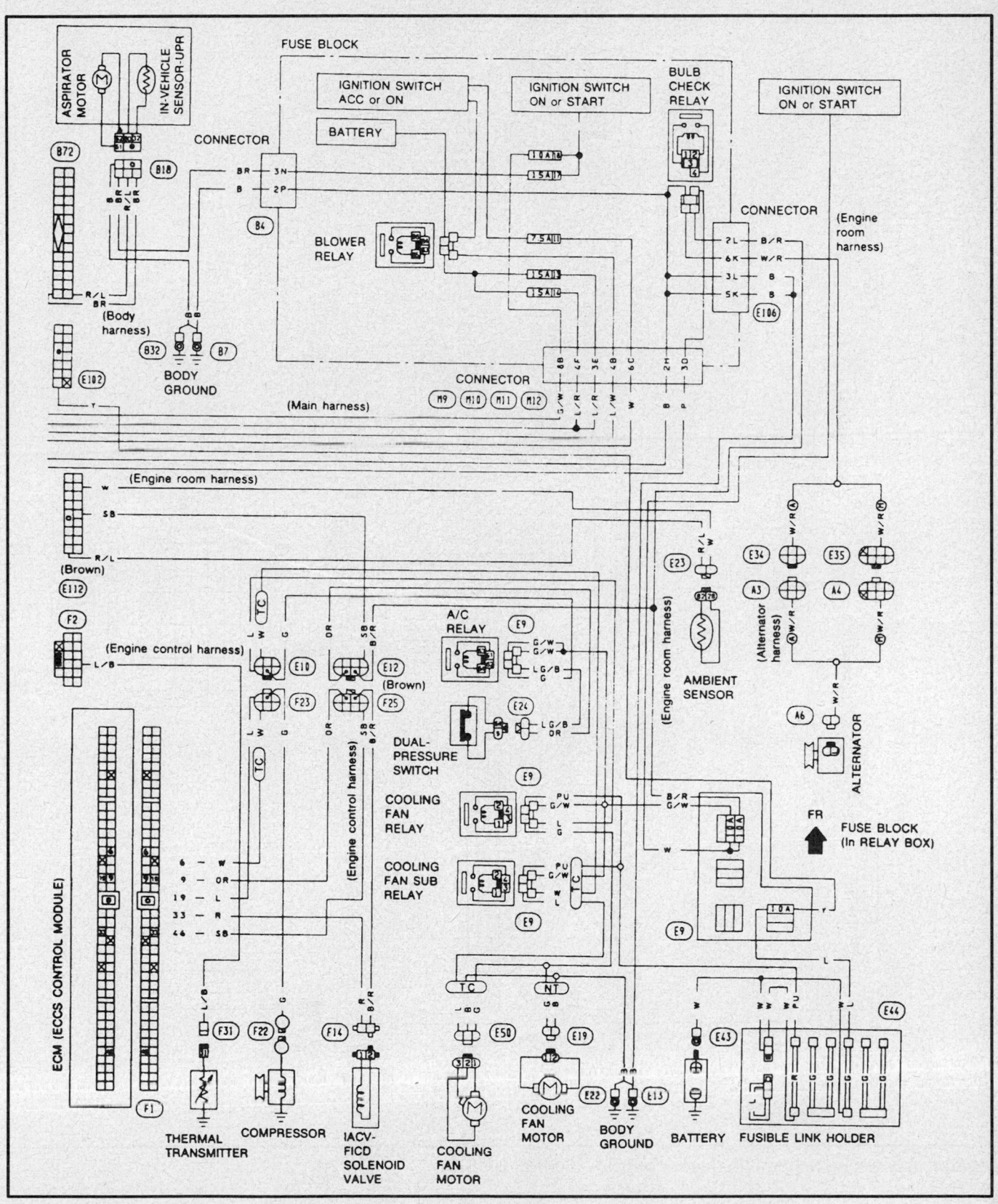

Automatic air conditioning wiring schematic—300ZX, Cont'd

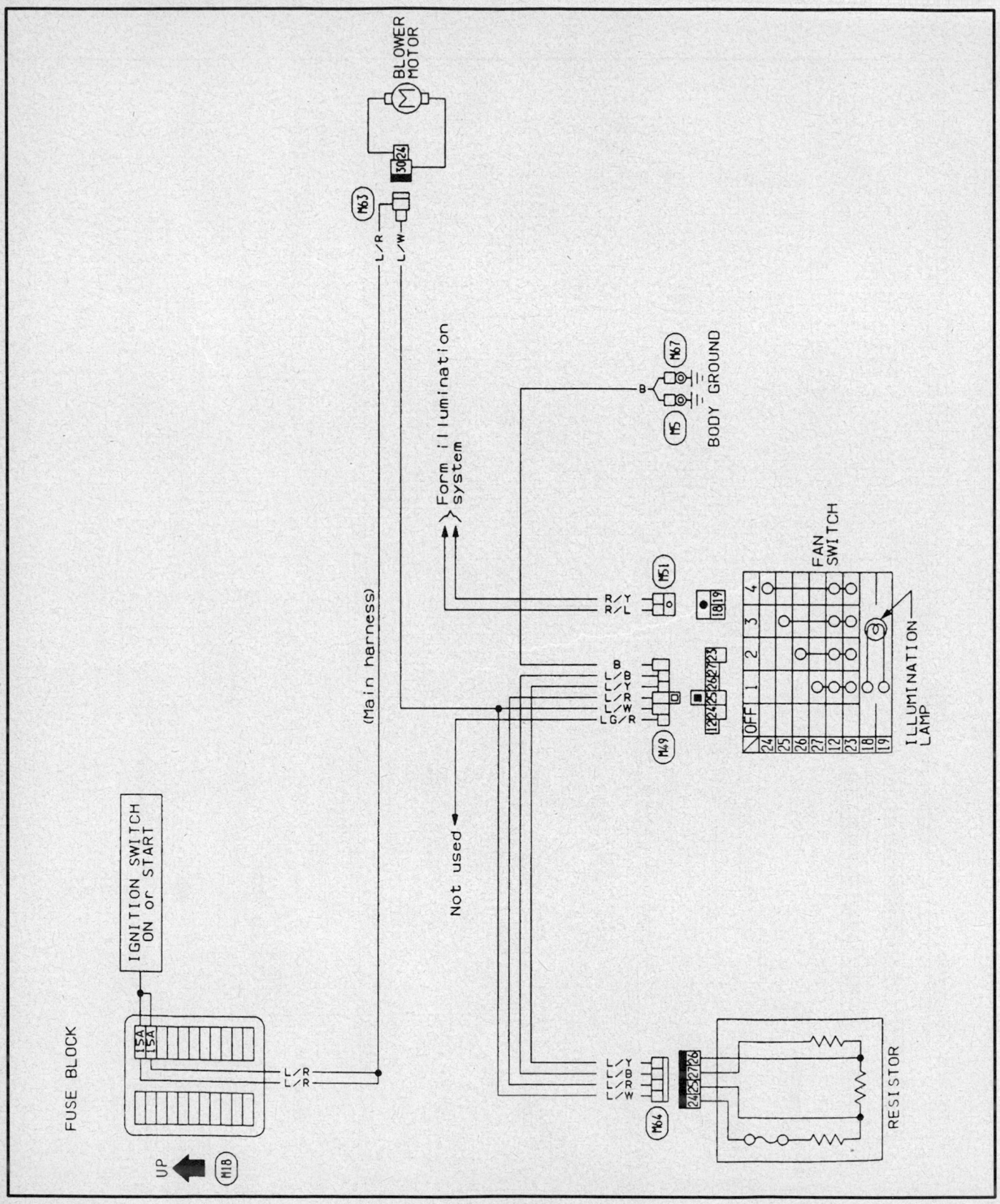

Heater only wiring schematic (lever control)—Sentra, 200SX

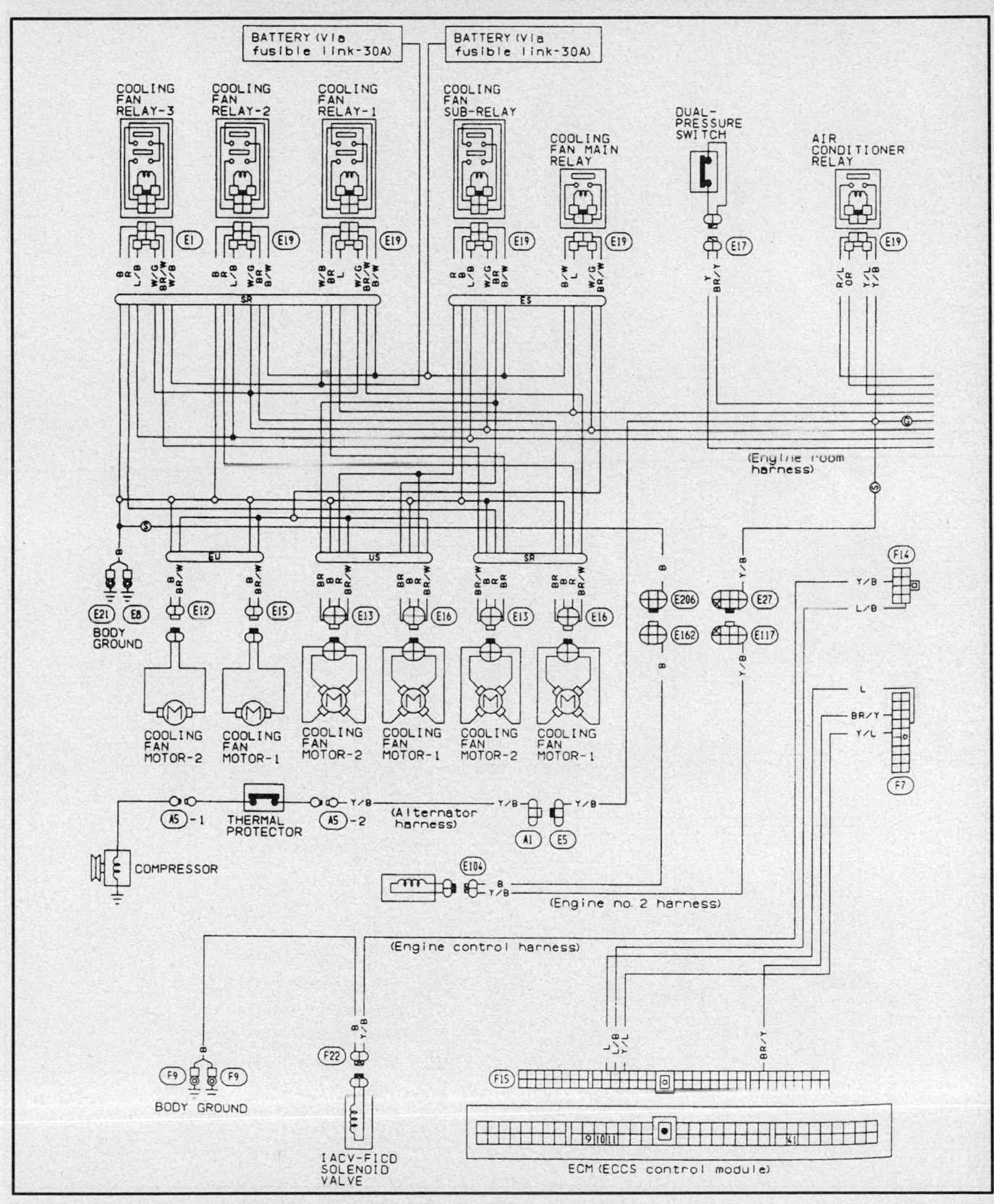

Air conditioning wiring schematic (lever control)—Sentra (except 1995)

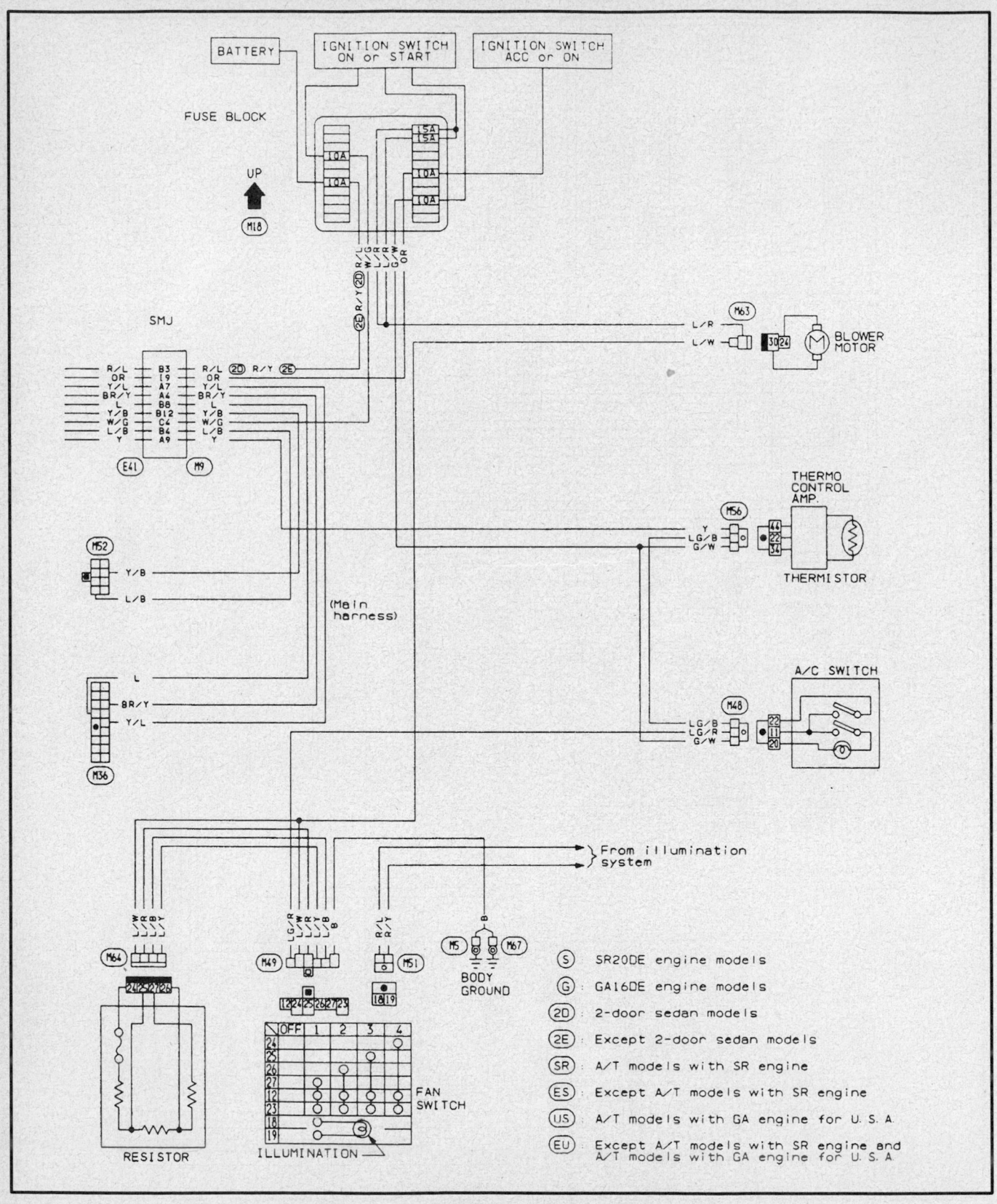

Air conditioning wiring schematic (lever control)—Sentra (except 1995), Cont'd

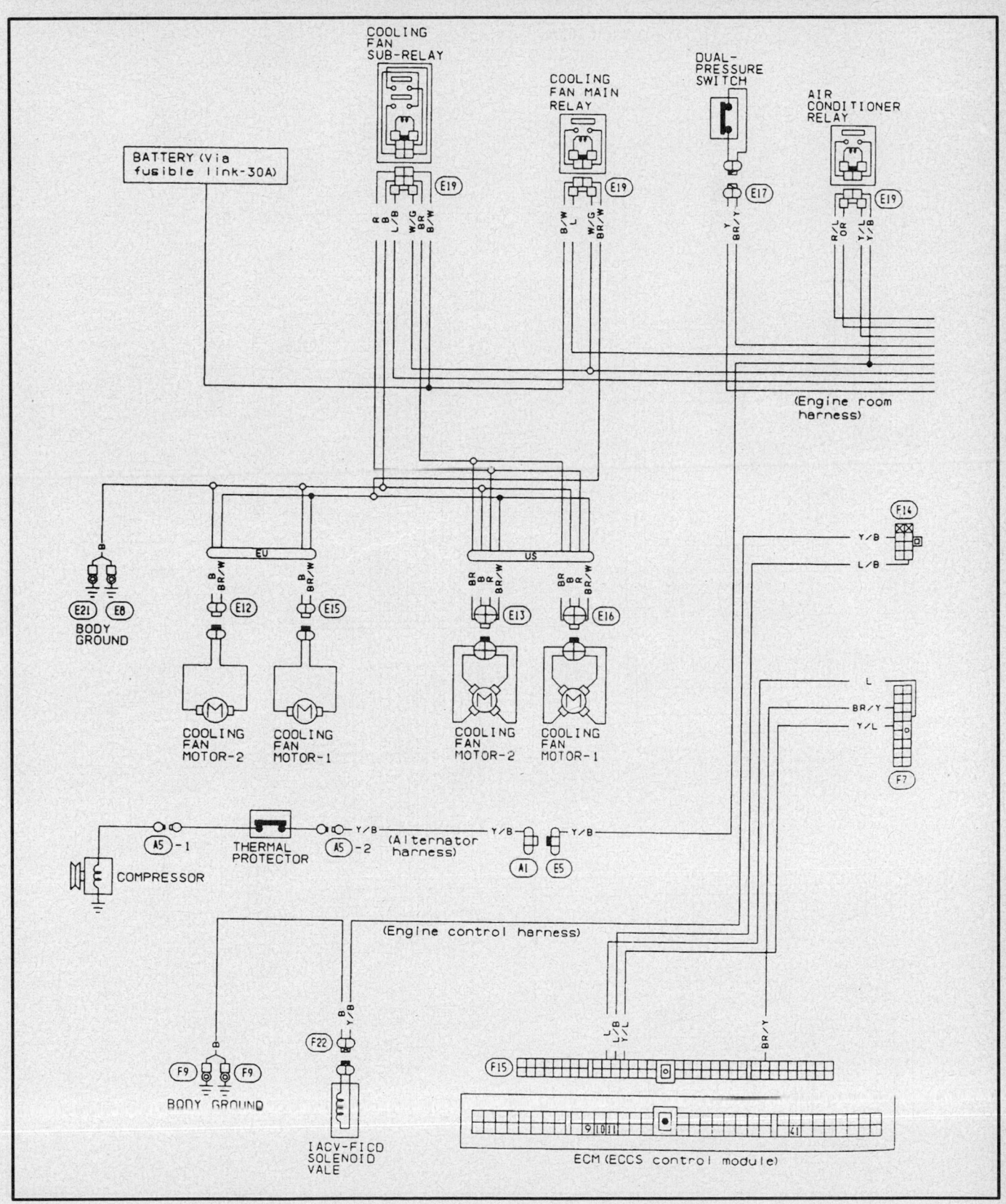

Air conditioning wiring schematic (push button control)—Sentra (except 1995)

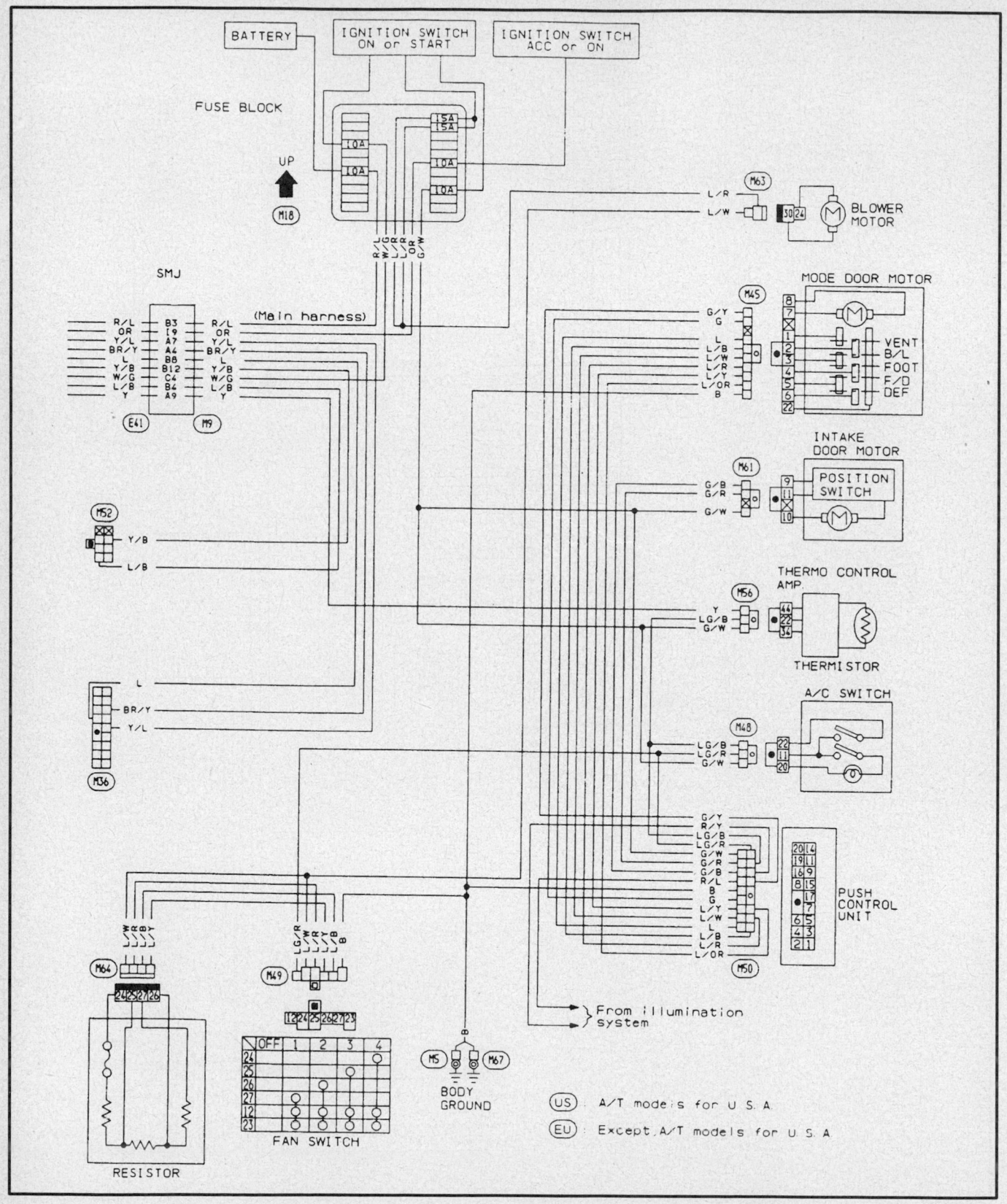

Air conditioning wiring schematic (push button control)—Sentra (except 1995), Cont'd

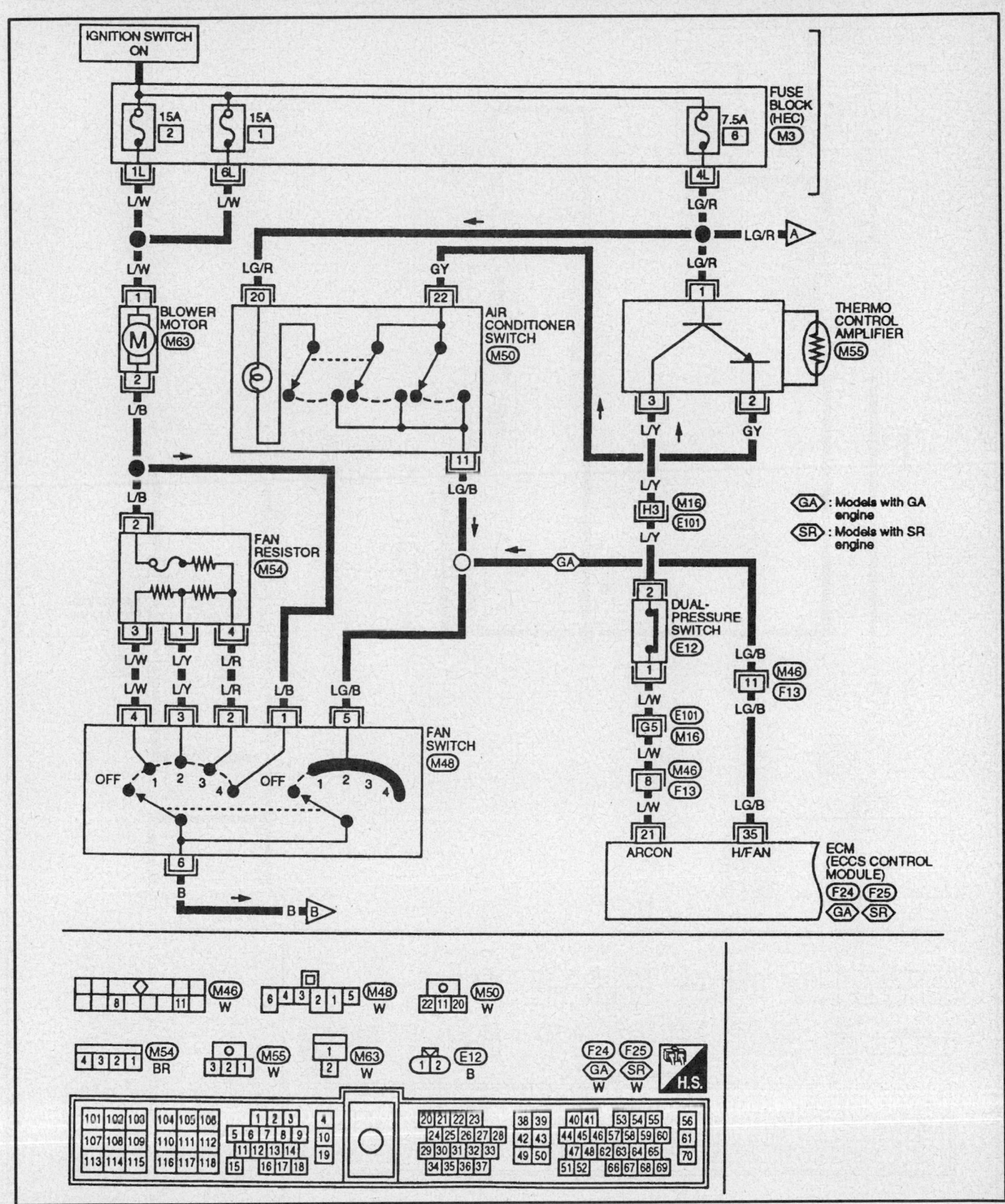

Air conditioning wiring schematic—1995 Sentra, 200SX

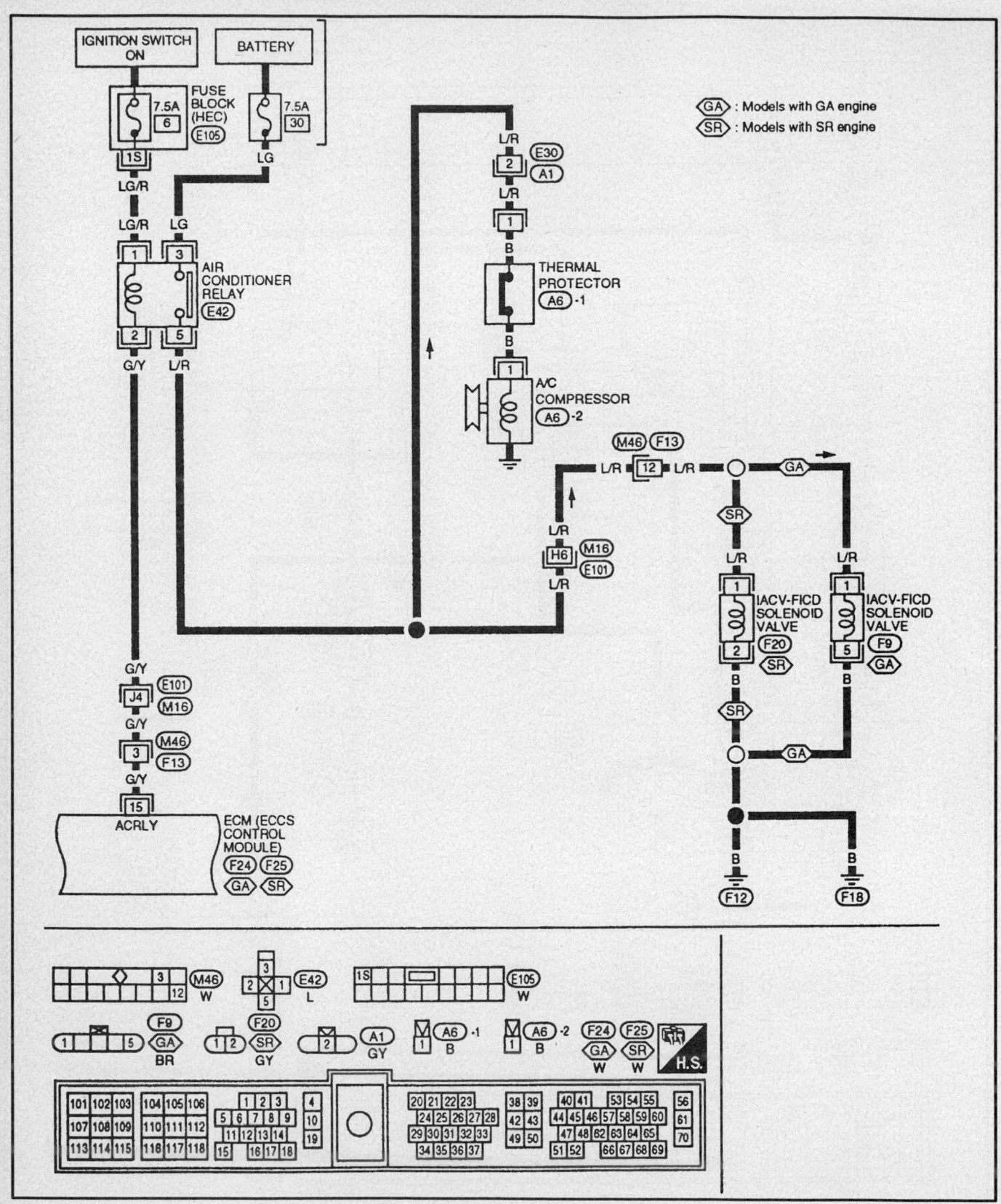

Air conditioning wiring schematic—1995 Sentra, 200SX, Cont'd

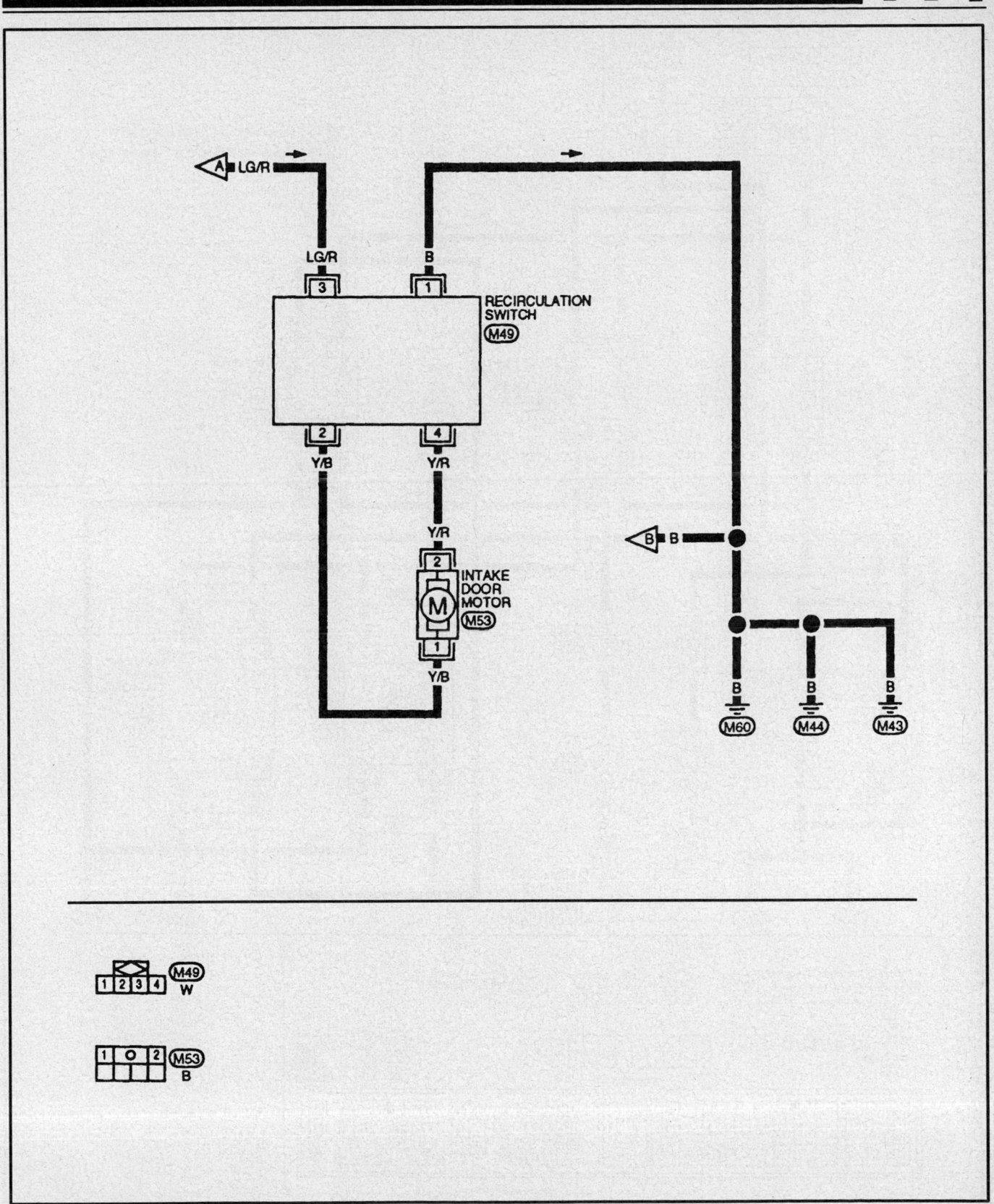

Air conditioning wiring schematic—1995 Sentra, 200SX. Cont'd

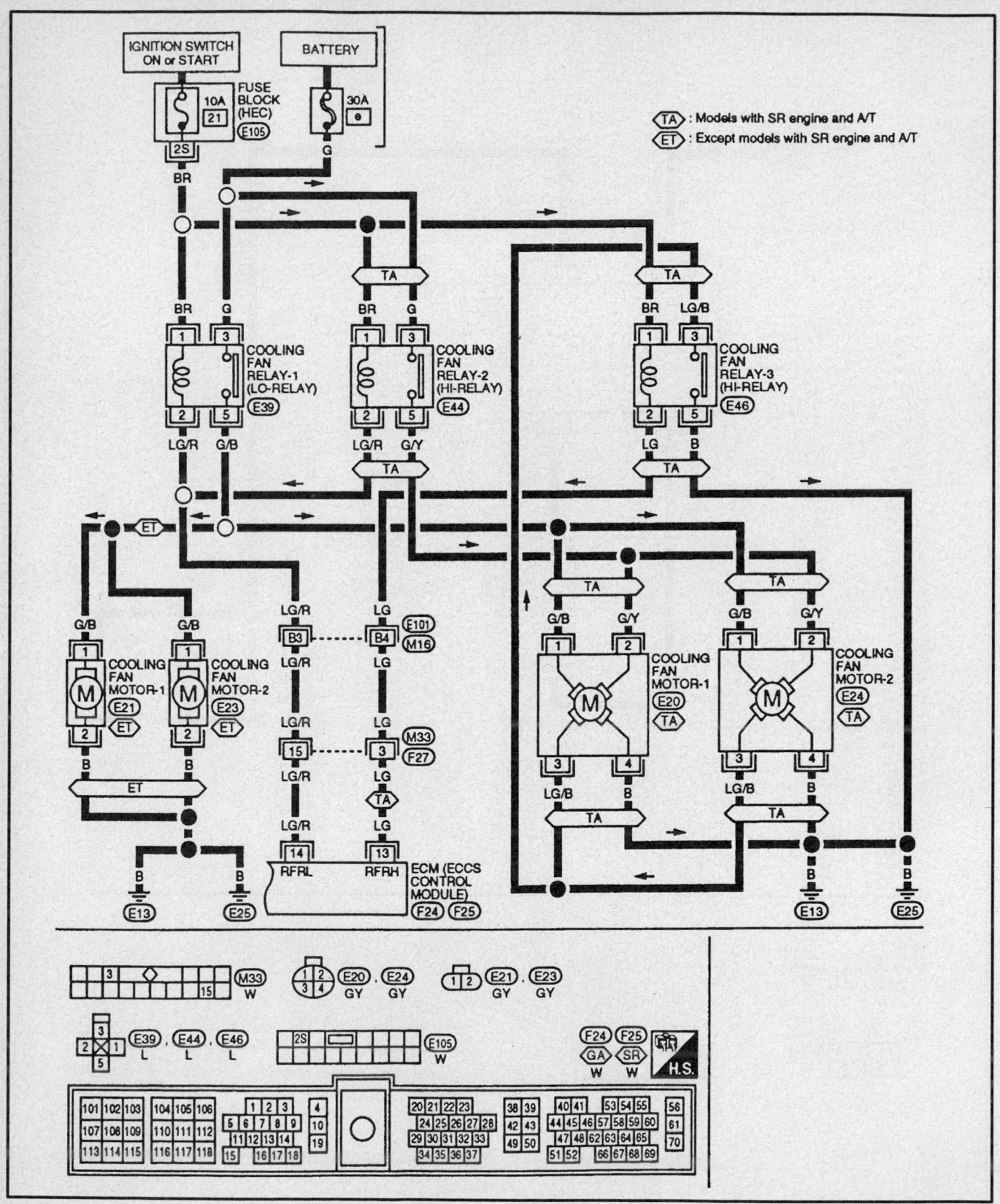

Air conditioning wiring schematic—1995 Sentra, 200SX, Cont'd

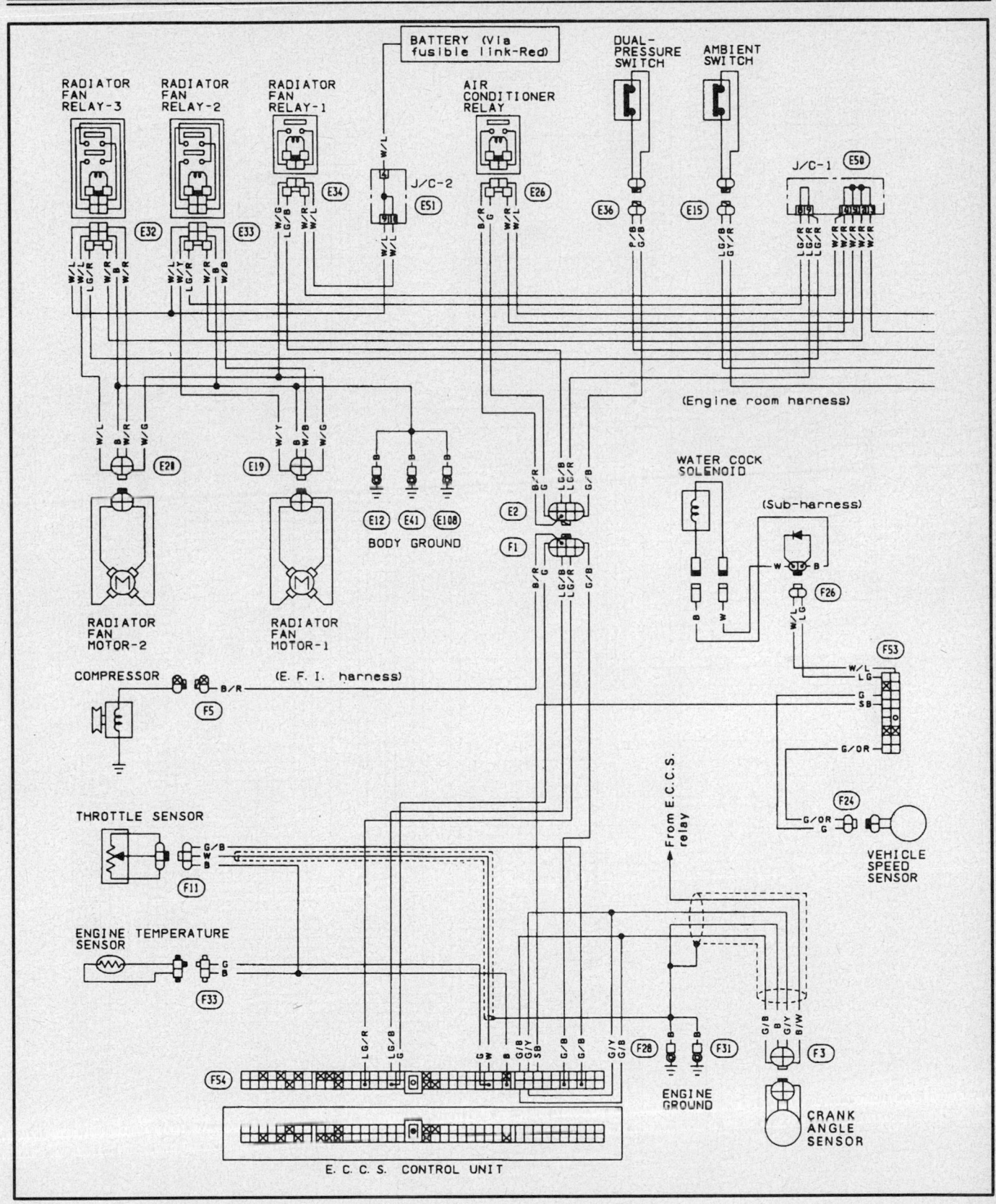

Manual air conditioning wiring schematic—Maxima with VG engine (SOHC)

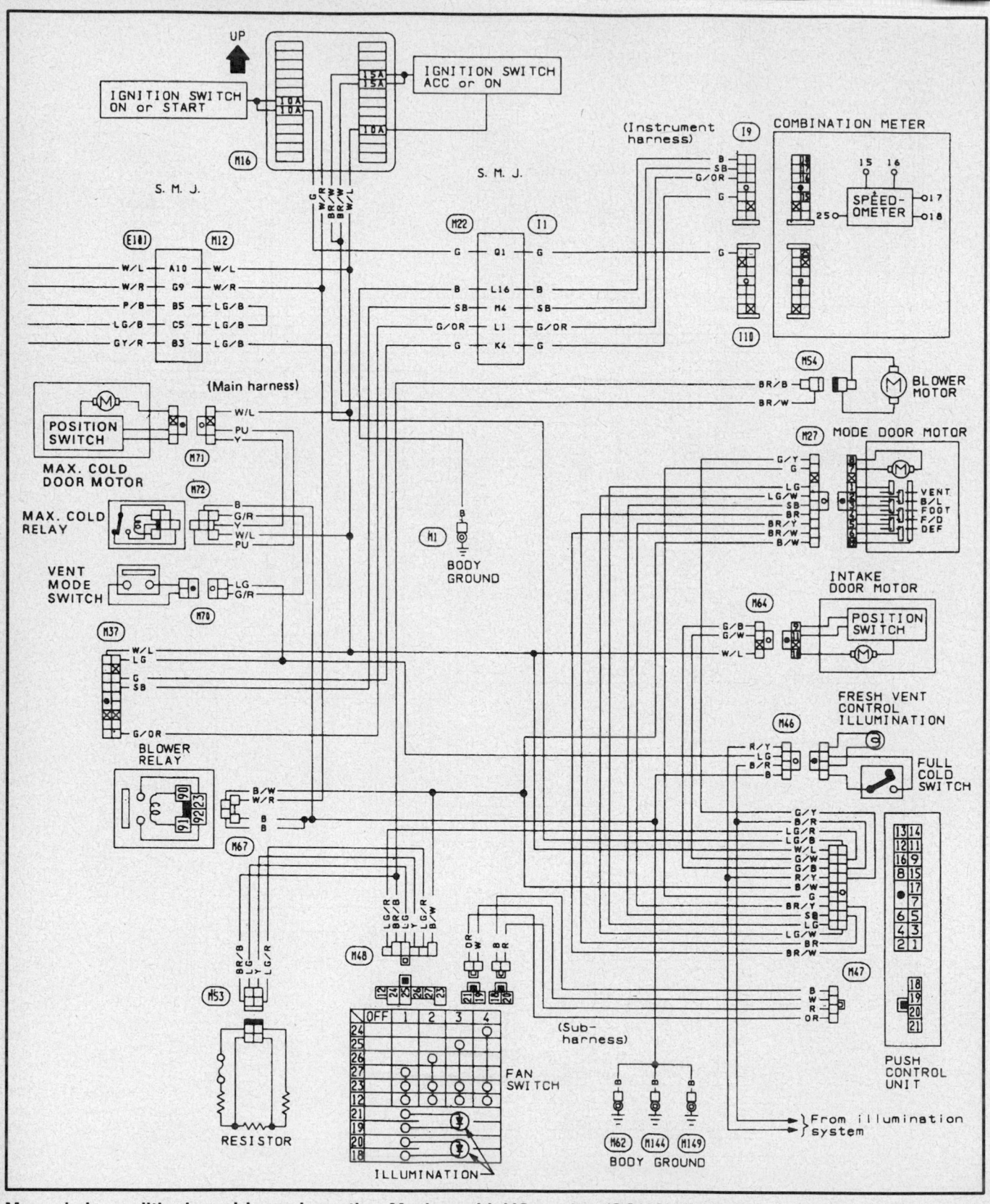

Manual air conditioning wiring schematic—Maxima with VG engine (SOHC), Cont'd

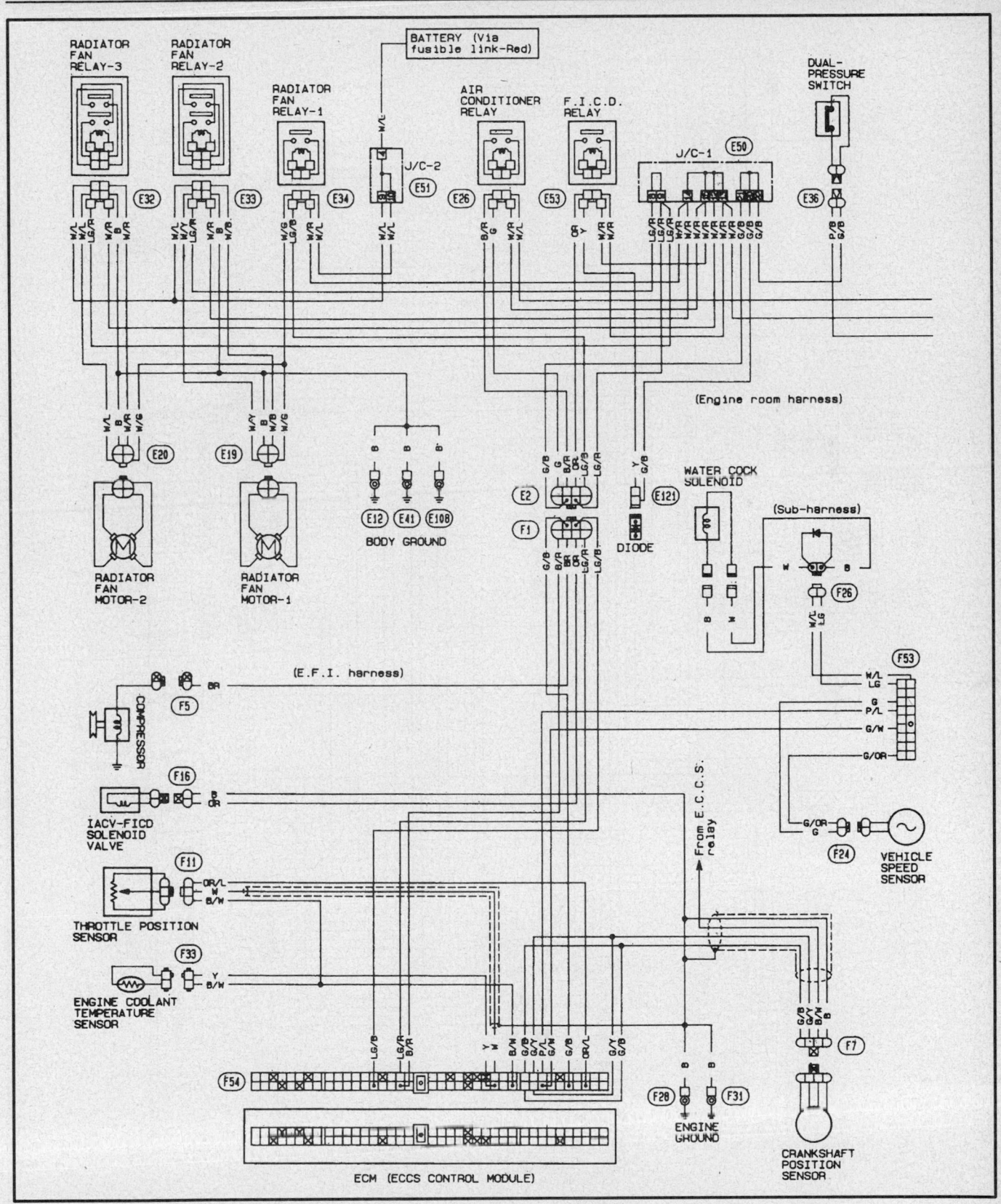

Manual air conditioning wiring schematic—Maxima with VE engine (DOHC)

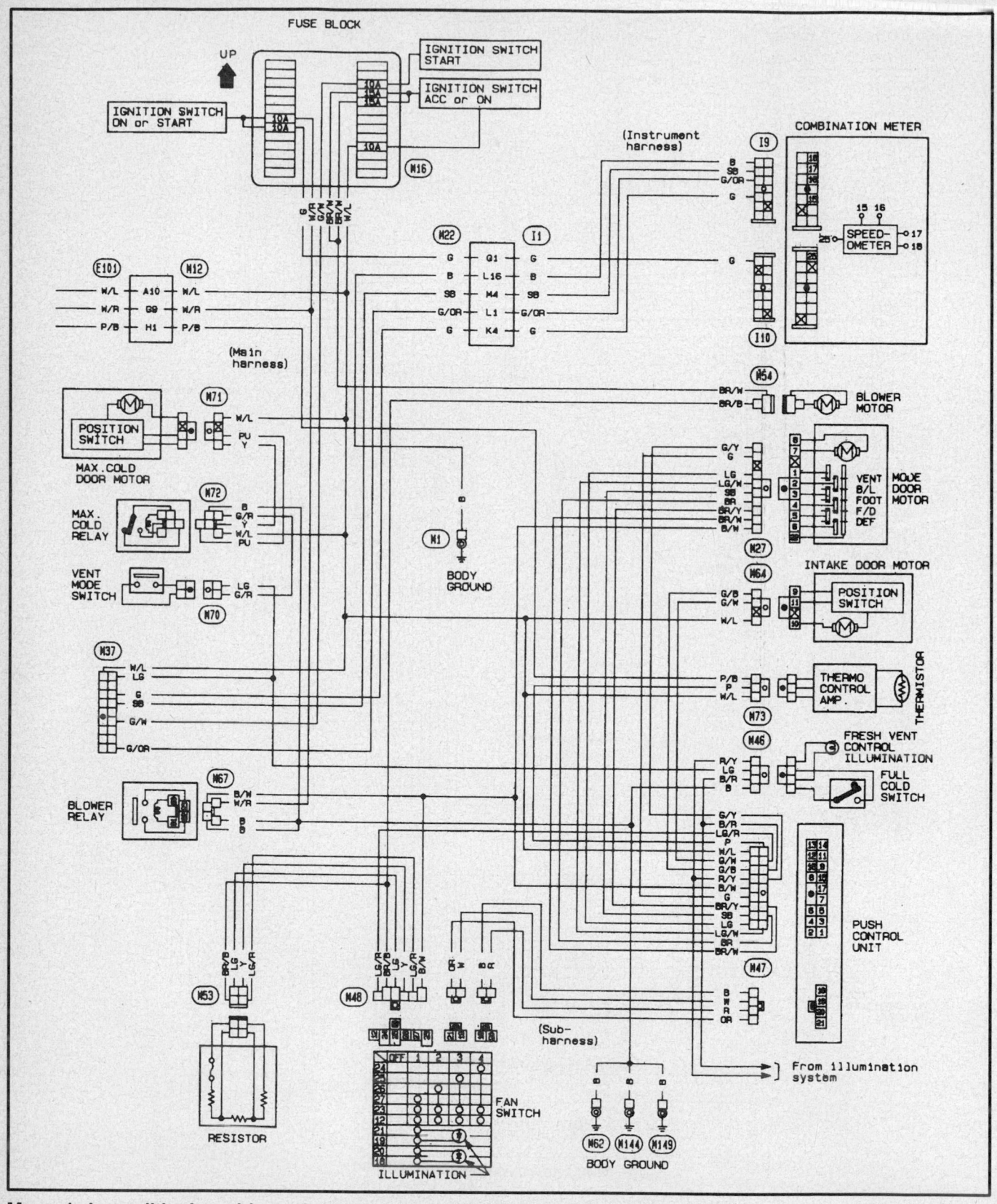

Manual air conditioning wiring schematic—Maxima with VE engine (DOHC), Cont'd

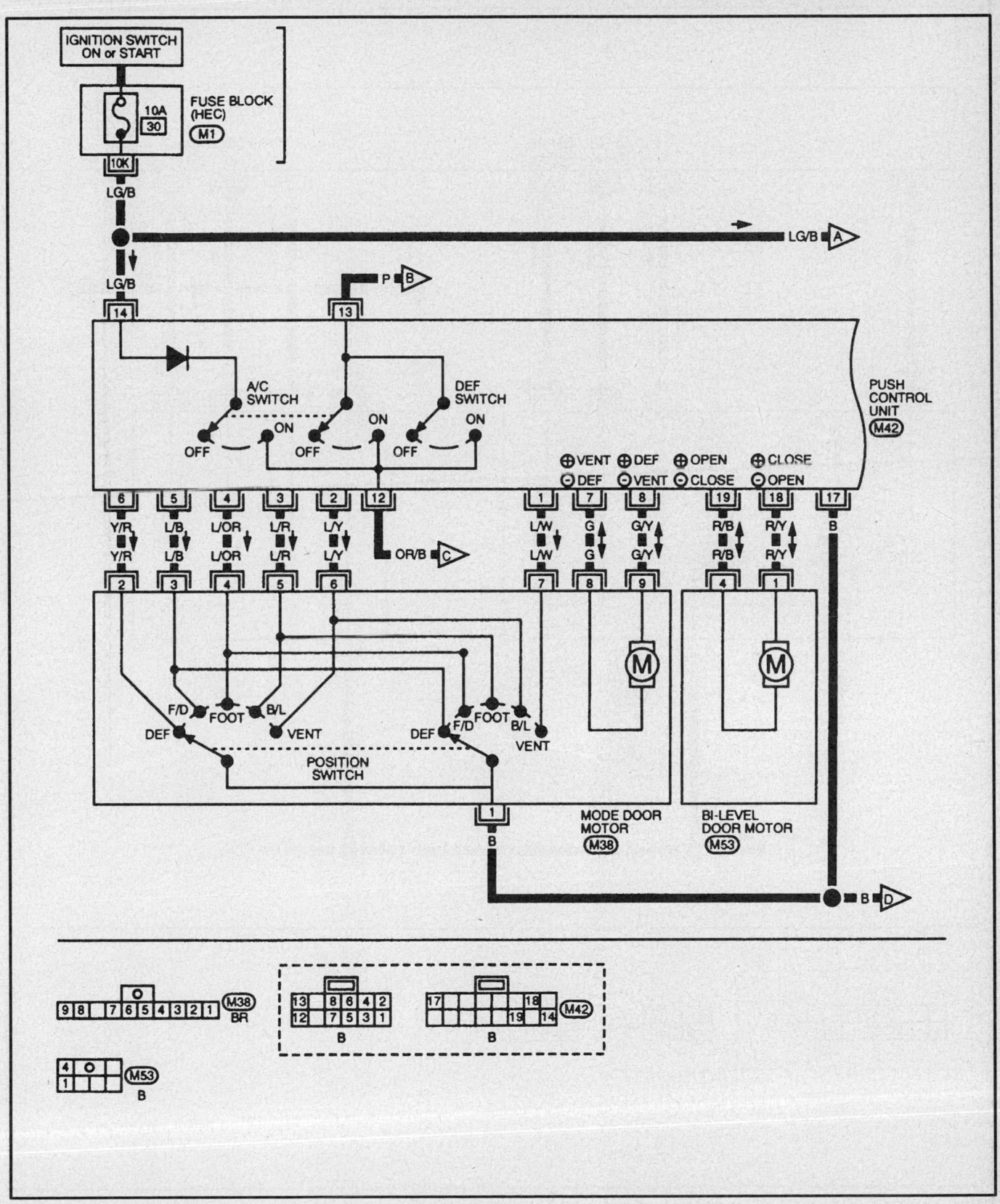

Manual air conditioning wiring schematic—1995 Maxima

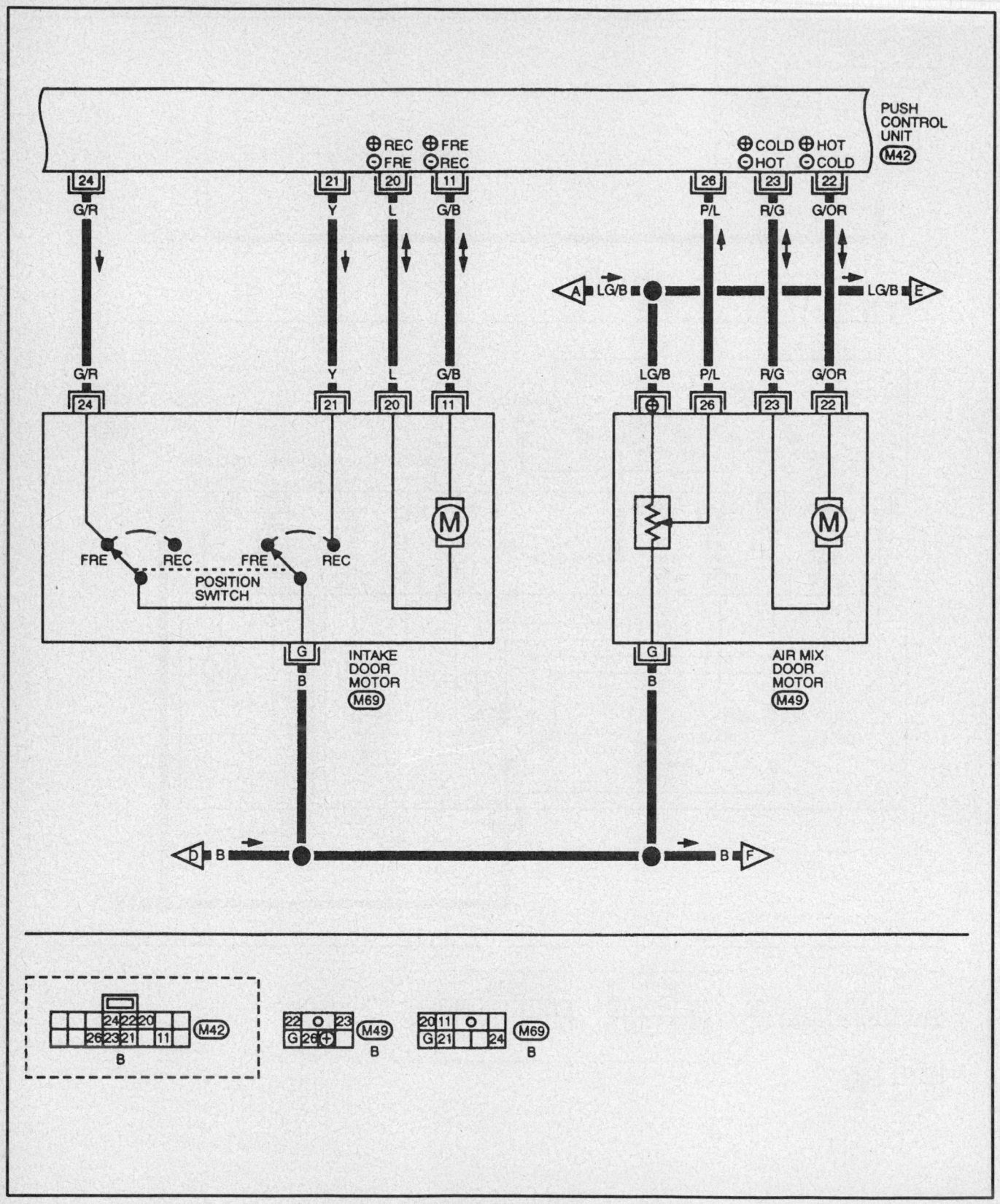

Manual air conditioning wiring schematic—1995 Maxima, Cont'd

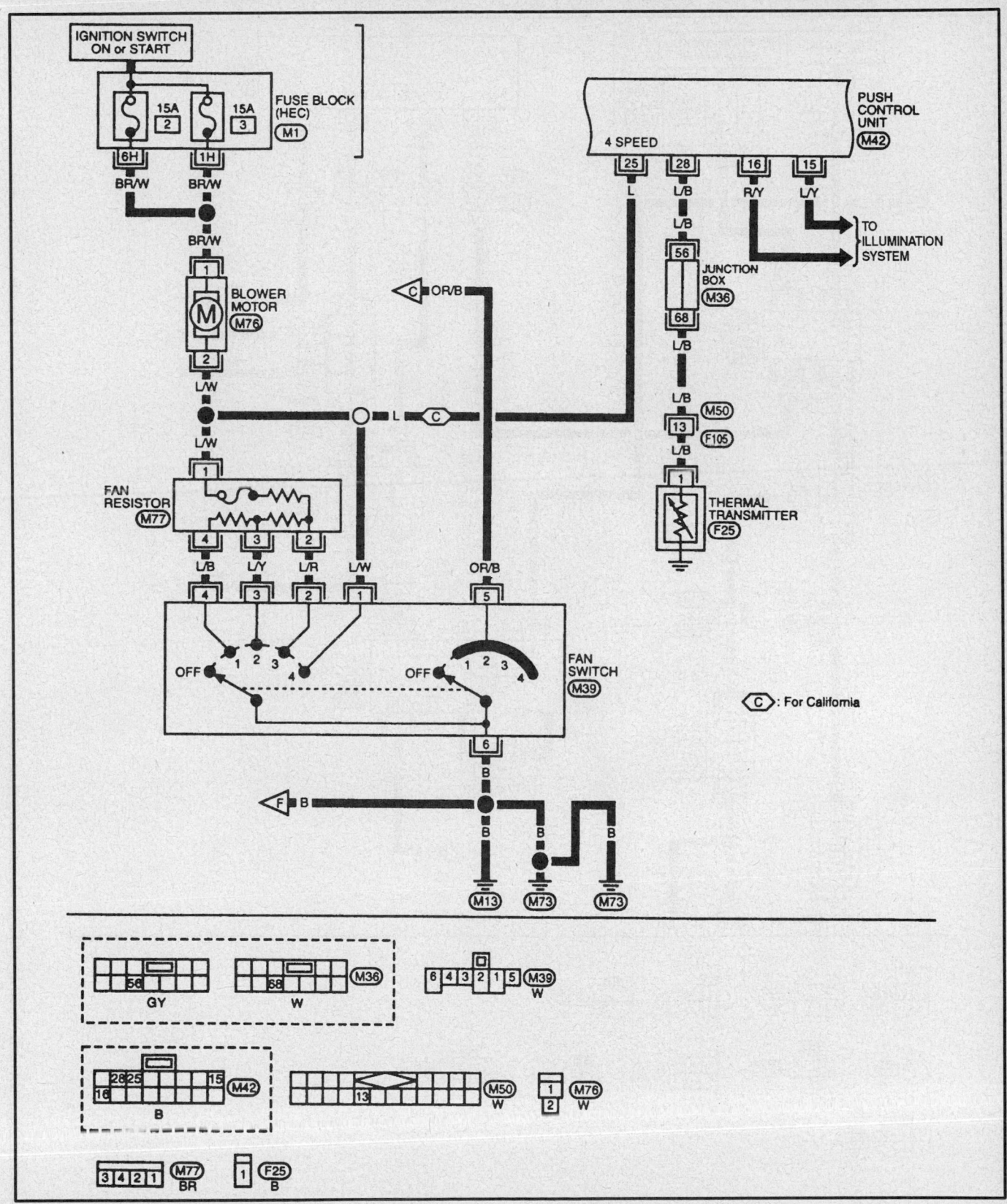

Manual air conditioning wiring schematic—1995 Maxima, Cont'd

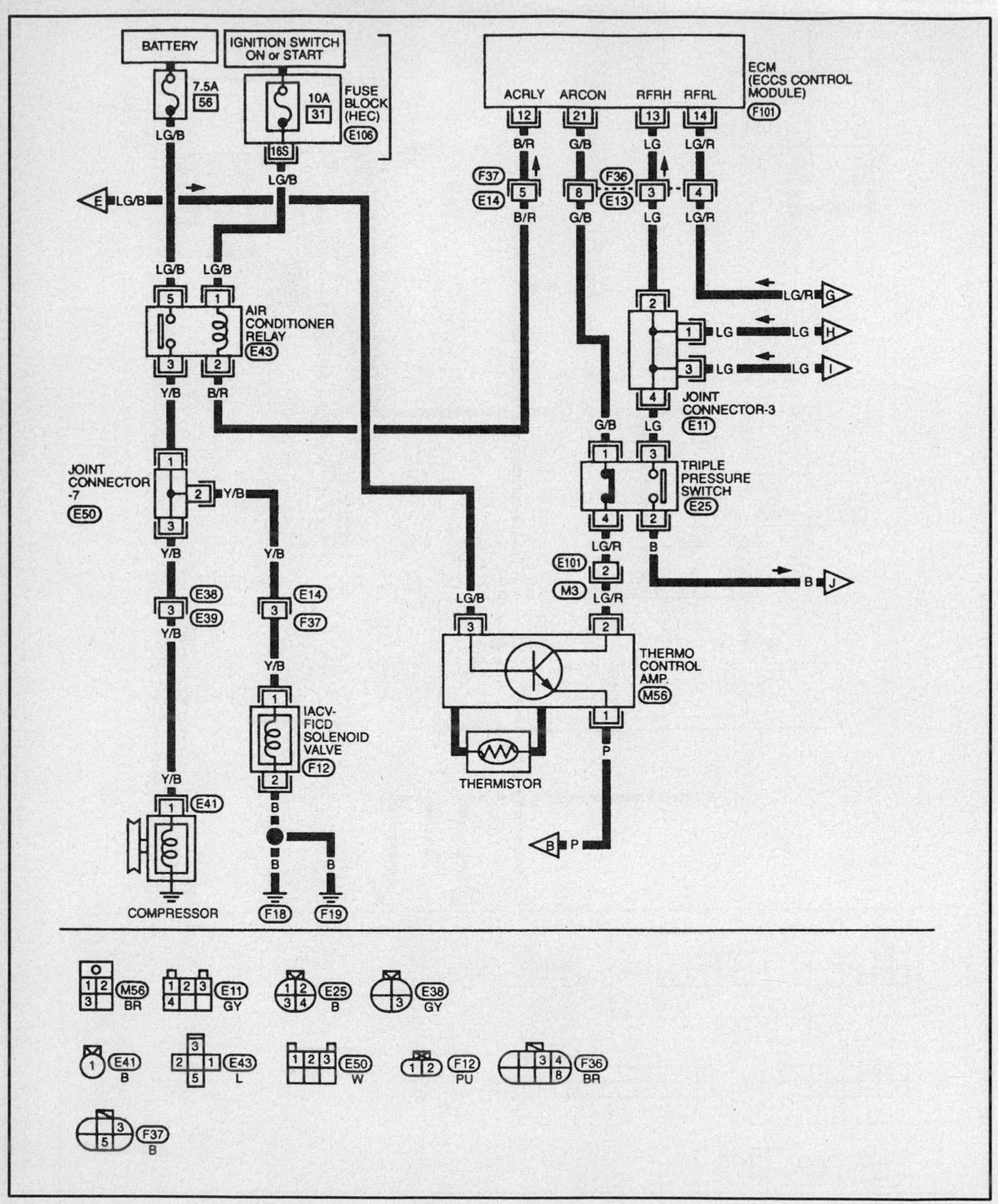

Manual air conditioning wiring schematic—1995 Maxima, Cont'd

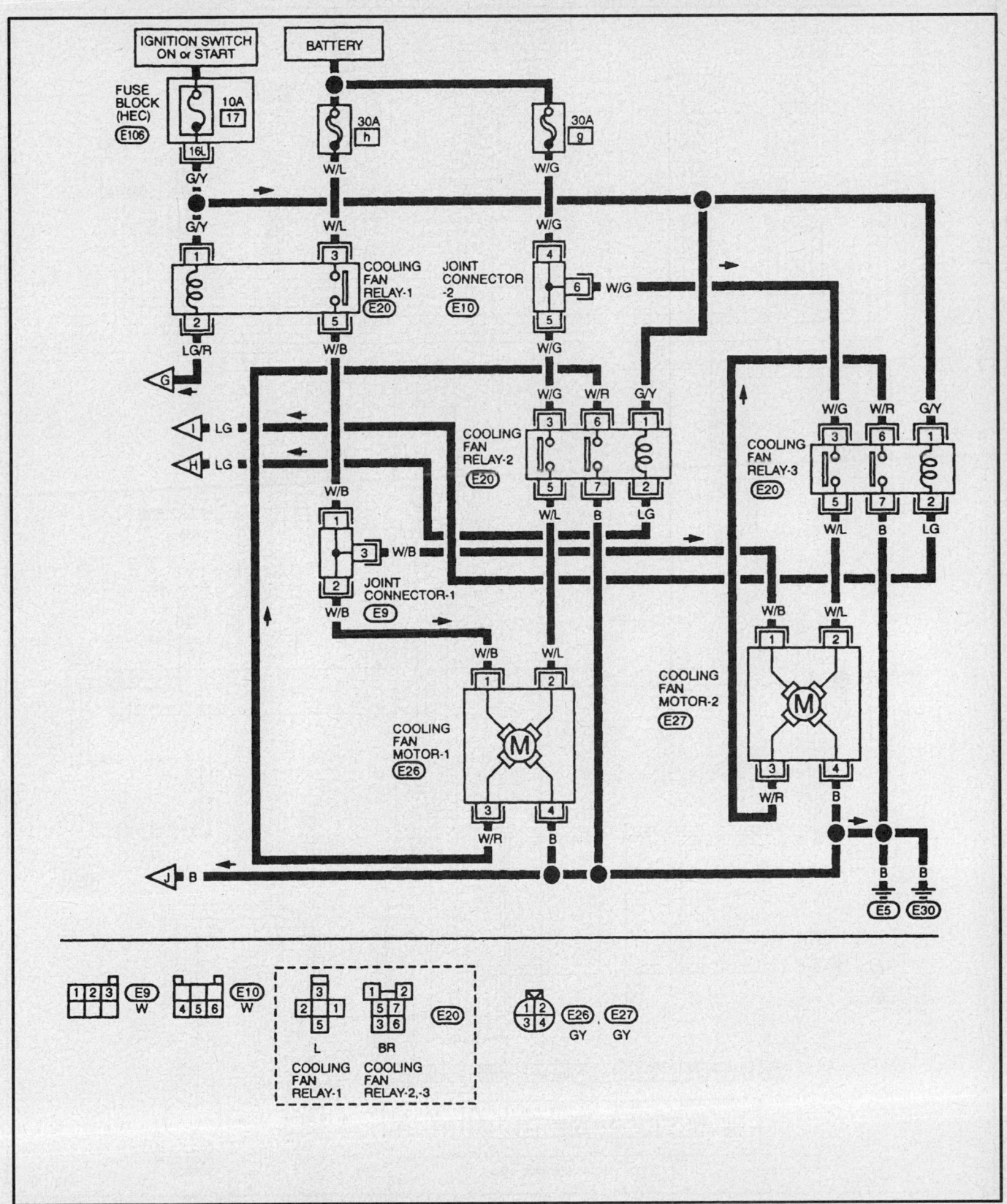

Manual air conditioning wiring schematic—1995 Maxima, Cont'd

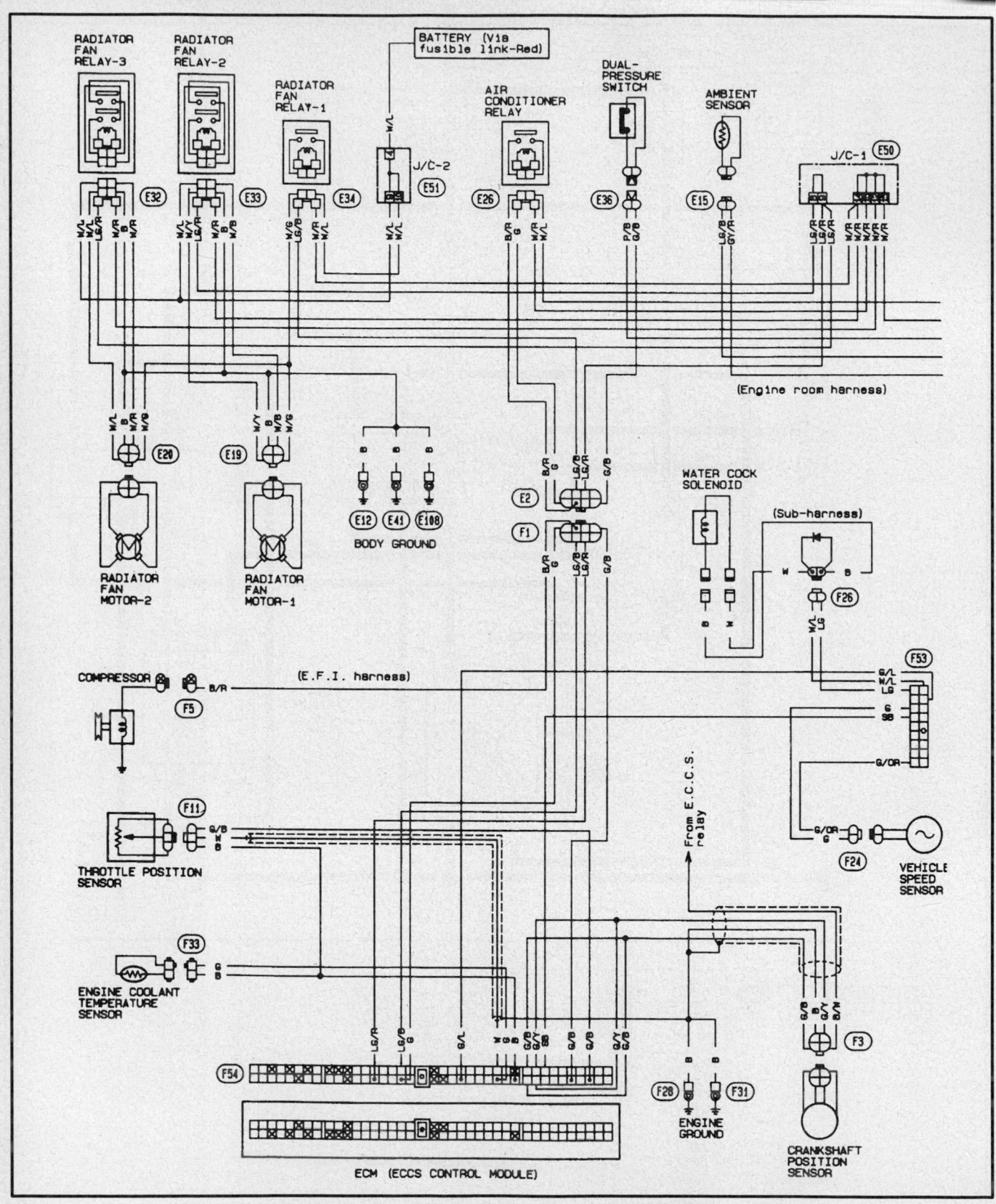

Automatic air conditioning wiring schematic—Maxima with VG engine (SOHC)

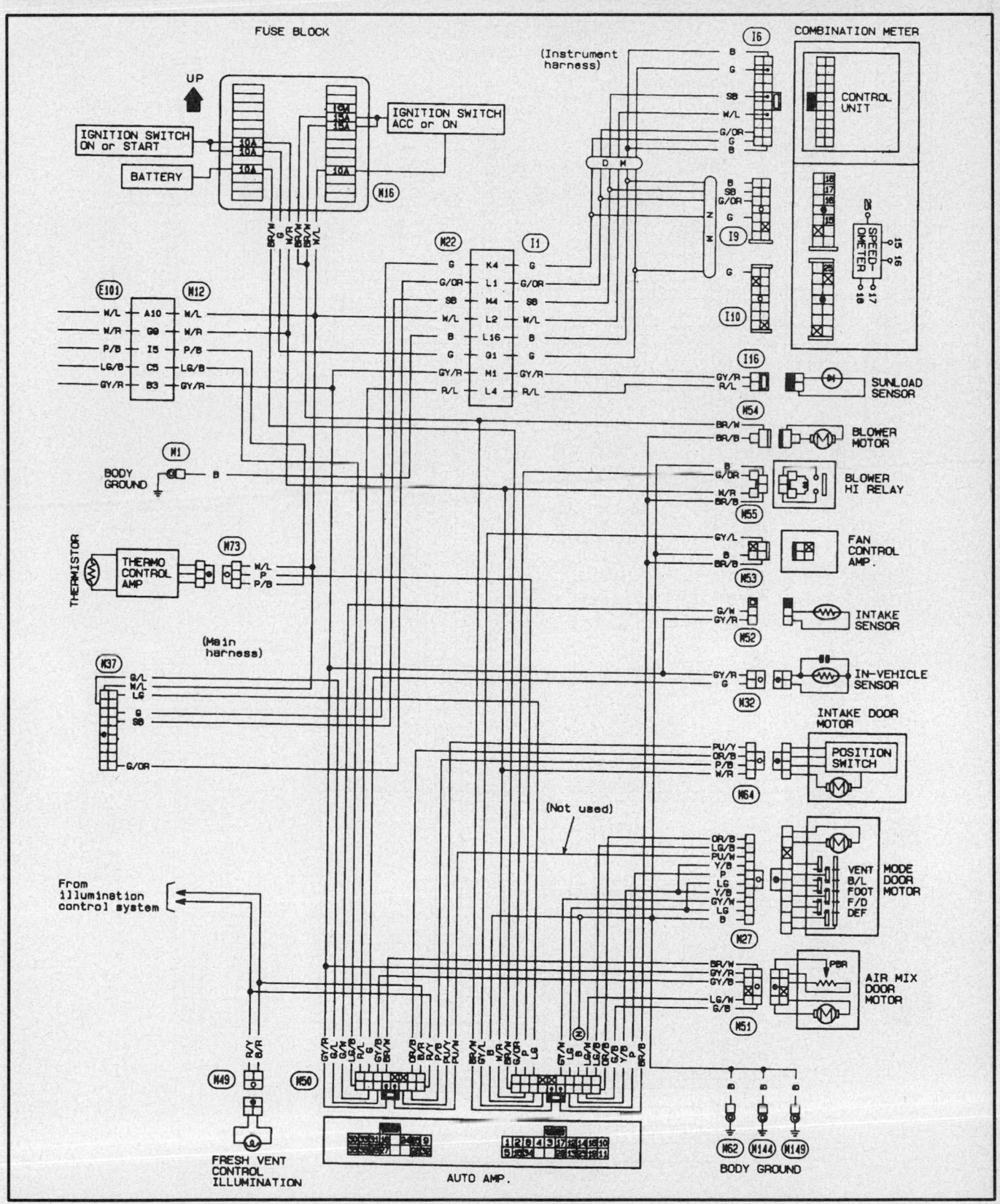

Automatic air conditioning wiring schematic—Maxima with VG engine (SOHC), Cont'd

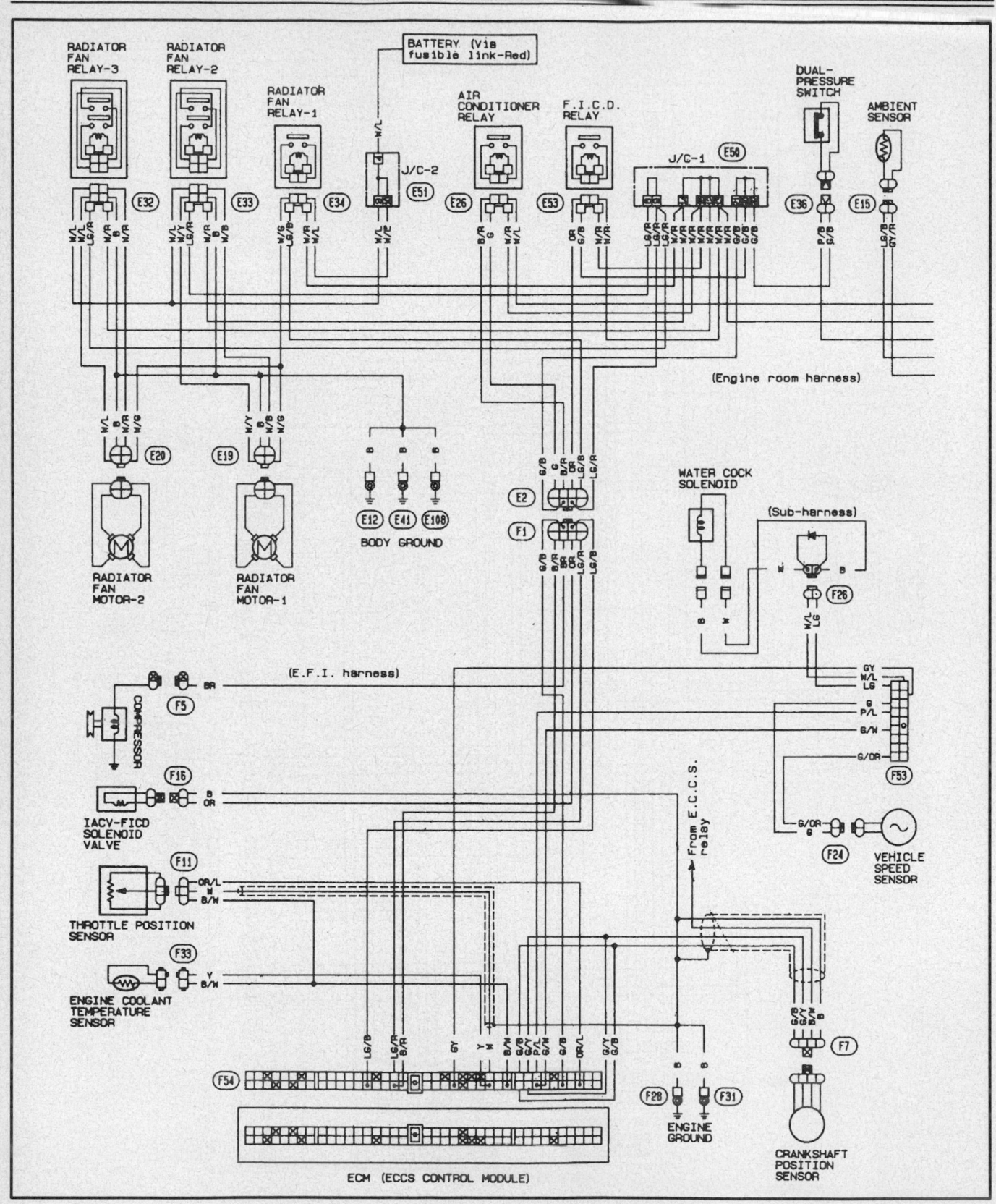

Automatic air conditioning wiring schematic—Maxima with VE engine (DOHC)

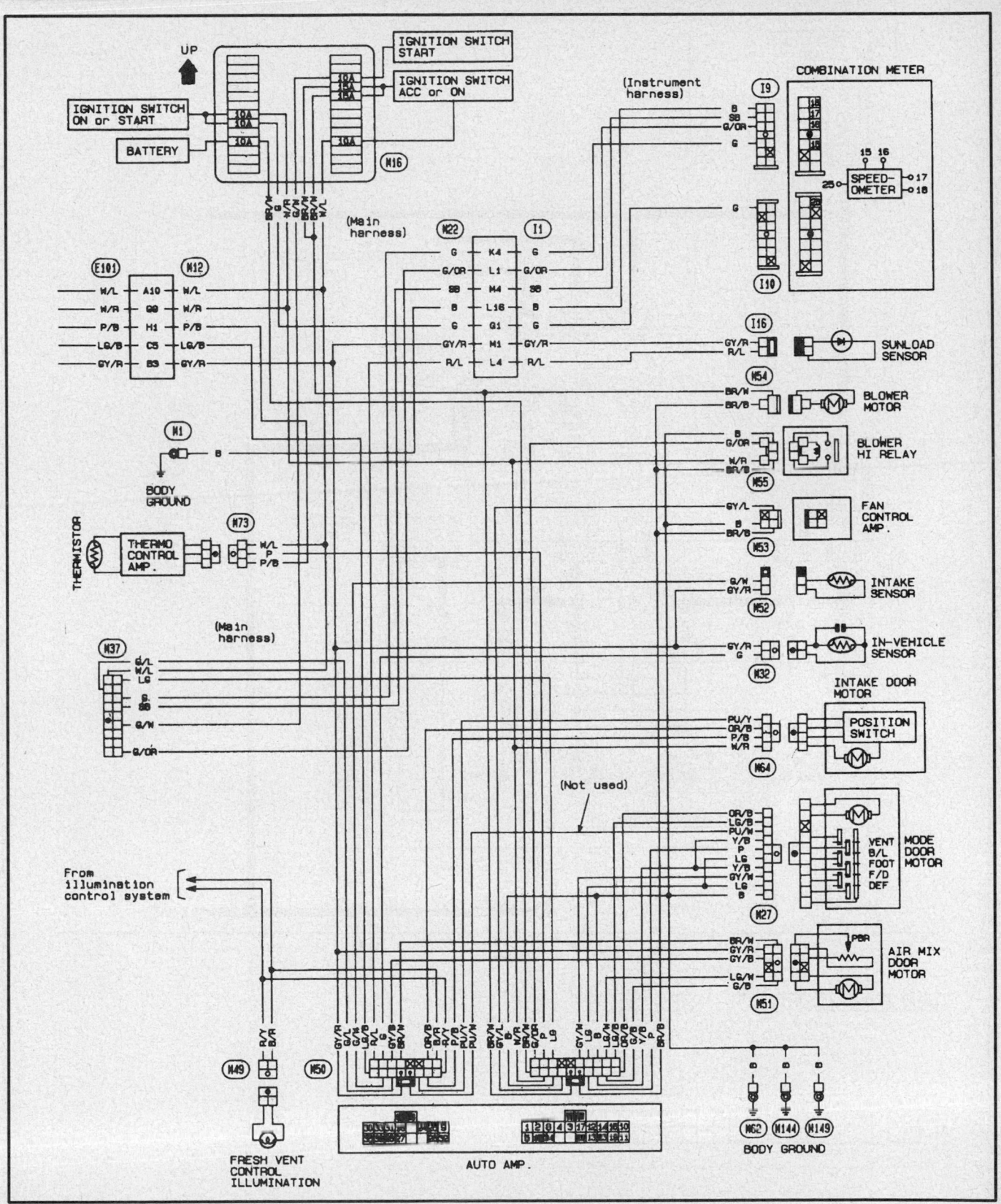

Automatic air conditioning wiring schematic—Maxima with VE engine (DOHC), Cont'd

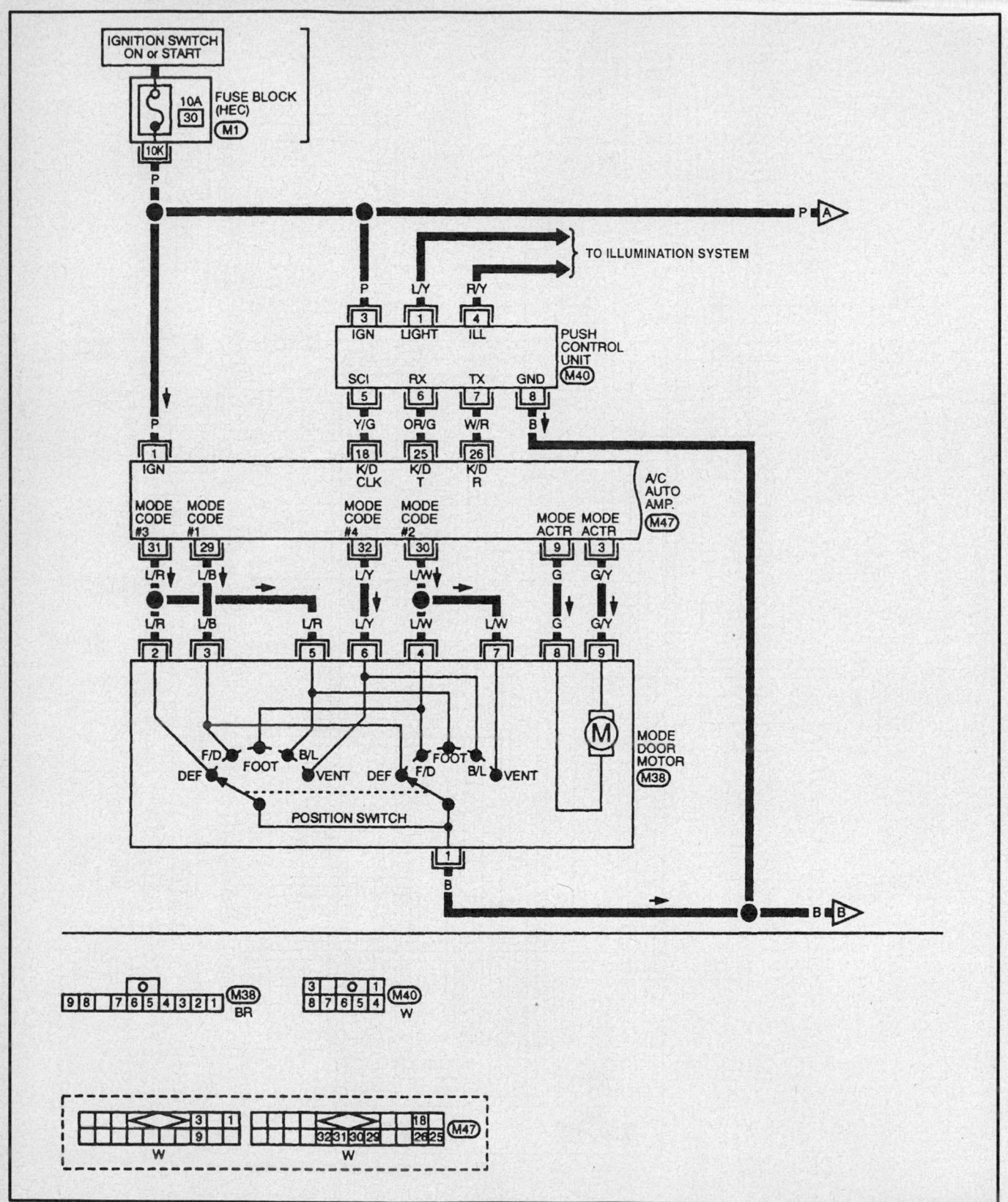

Automatic air conditioning wiring schematic—1995 Maxima

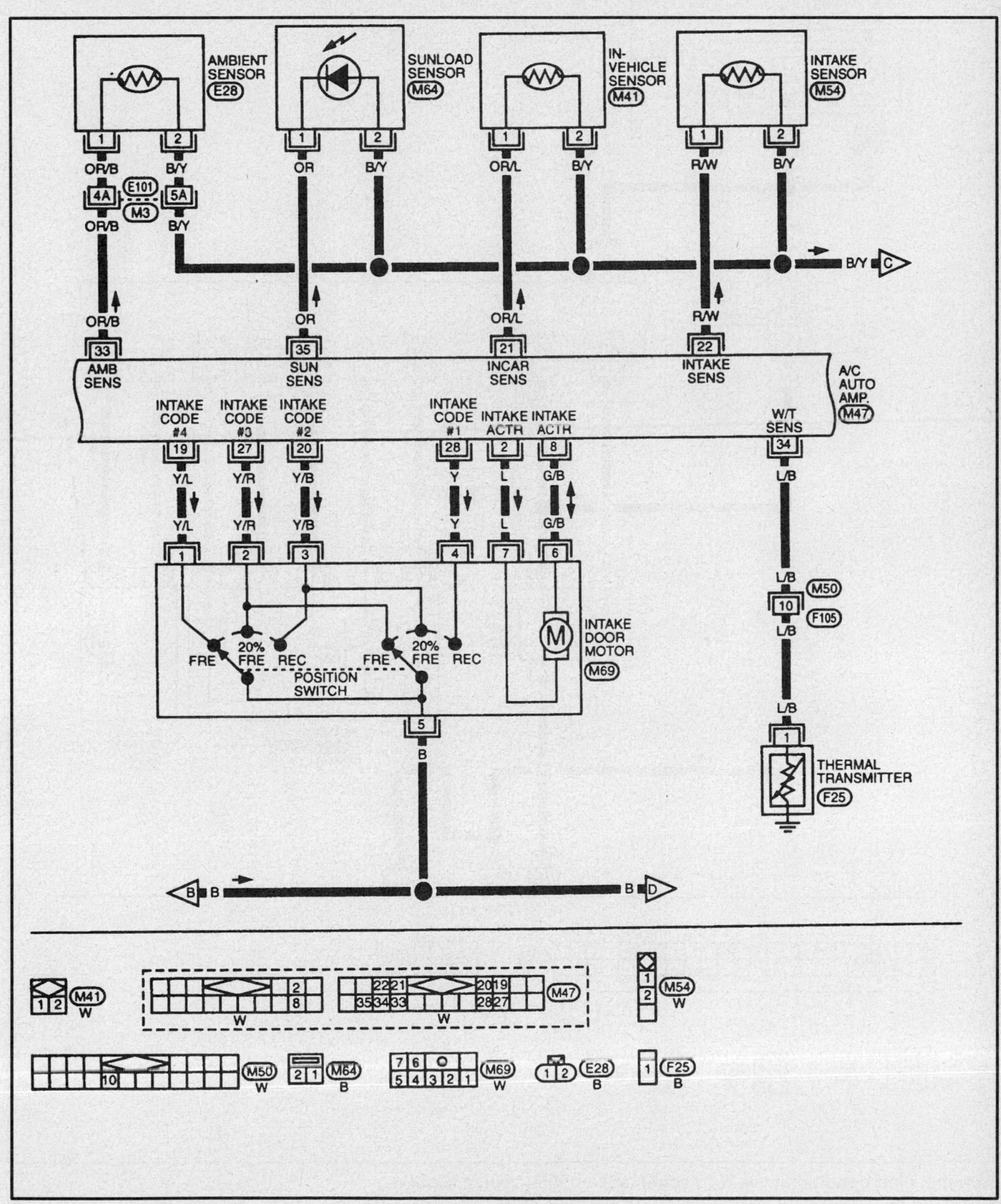

Automatic air conditioning wiring schematic—1995 Maxima, Cont'd

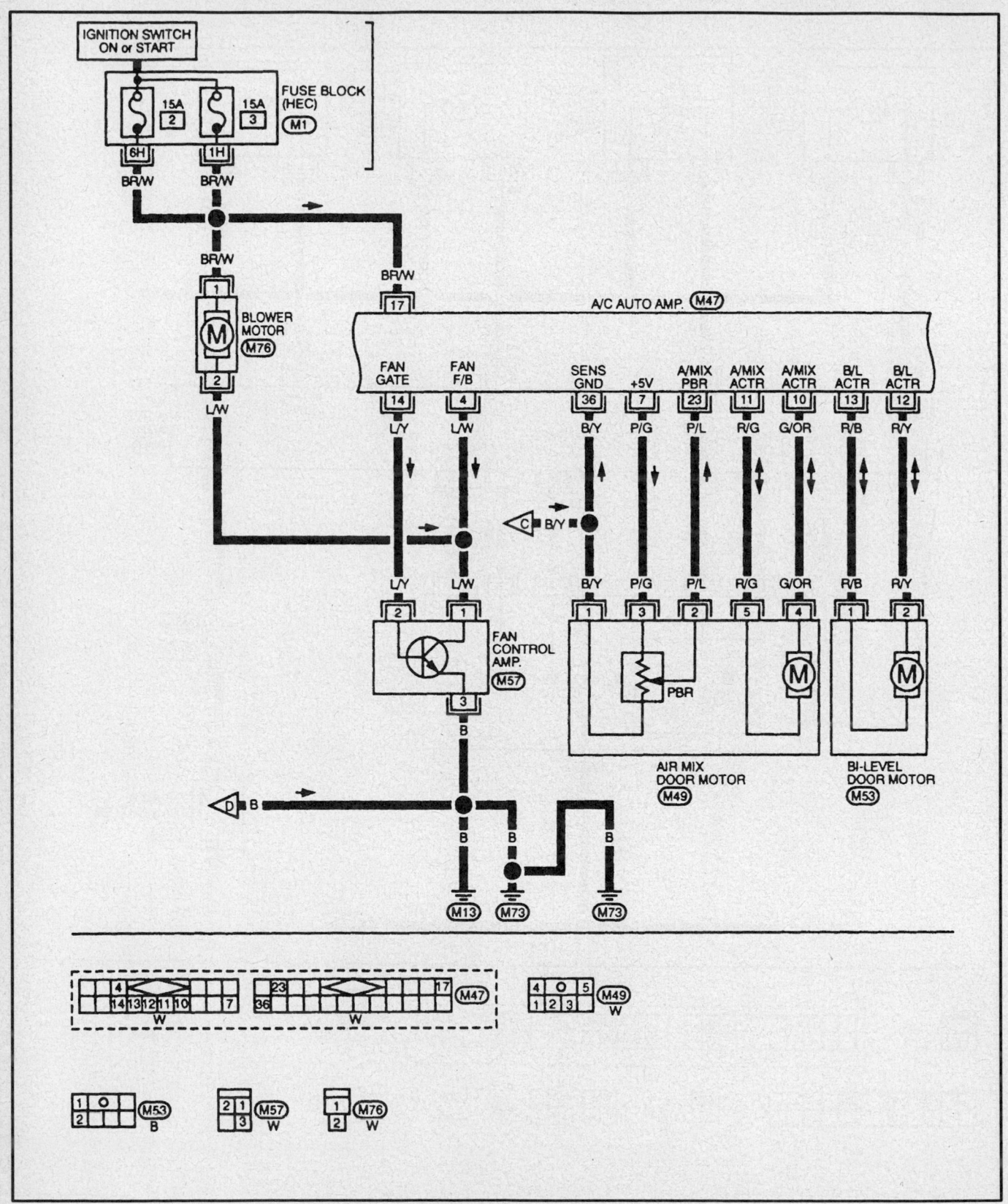

Automatic air conditioning wiring schematic—1995 Maxima, Cont'd

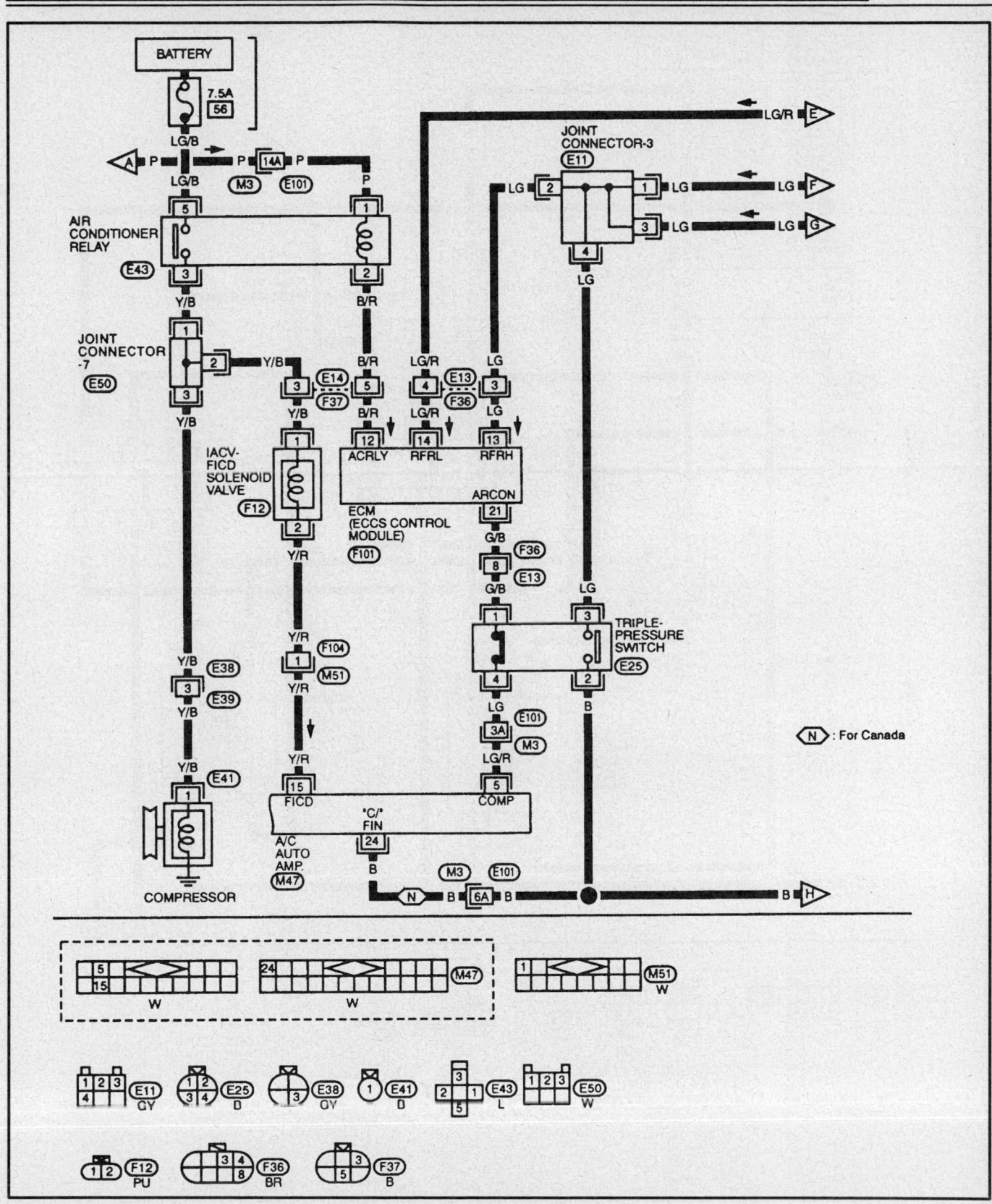

Automatic air conditioning wiring schematic—1995 Maxima, Cont'd

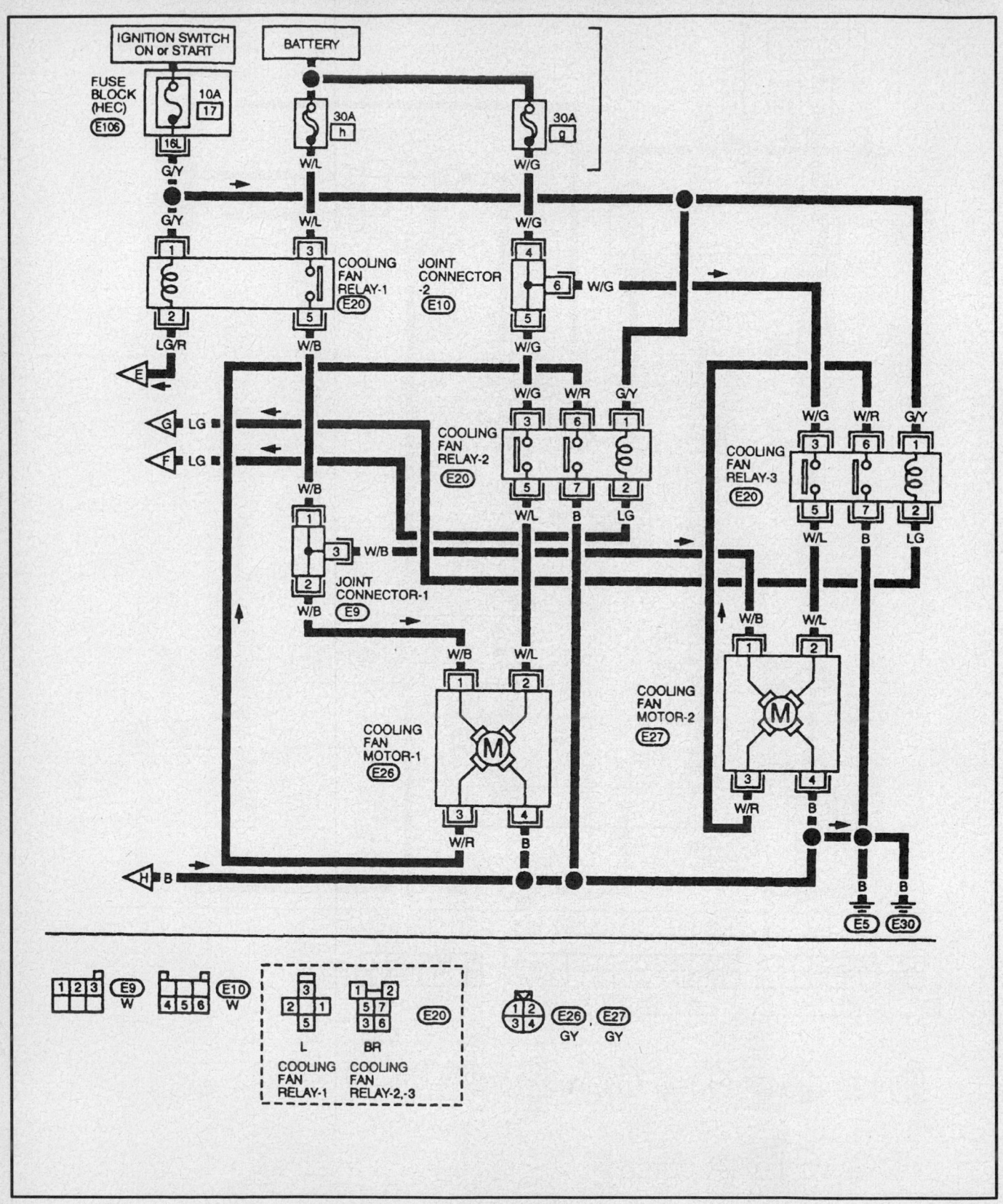

Automatic air conditioning wiring schematic—1995 Maxima, Cont'd

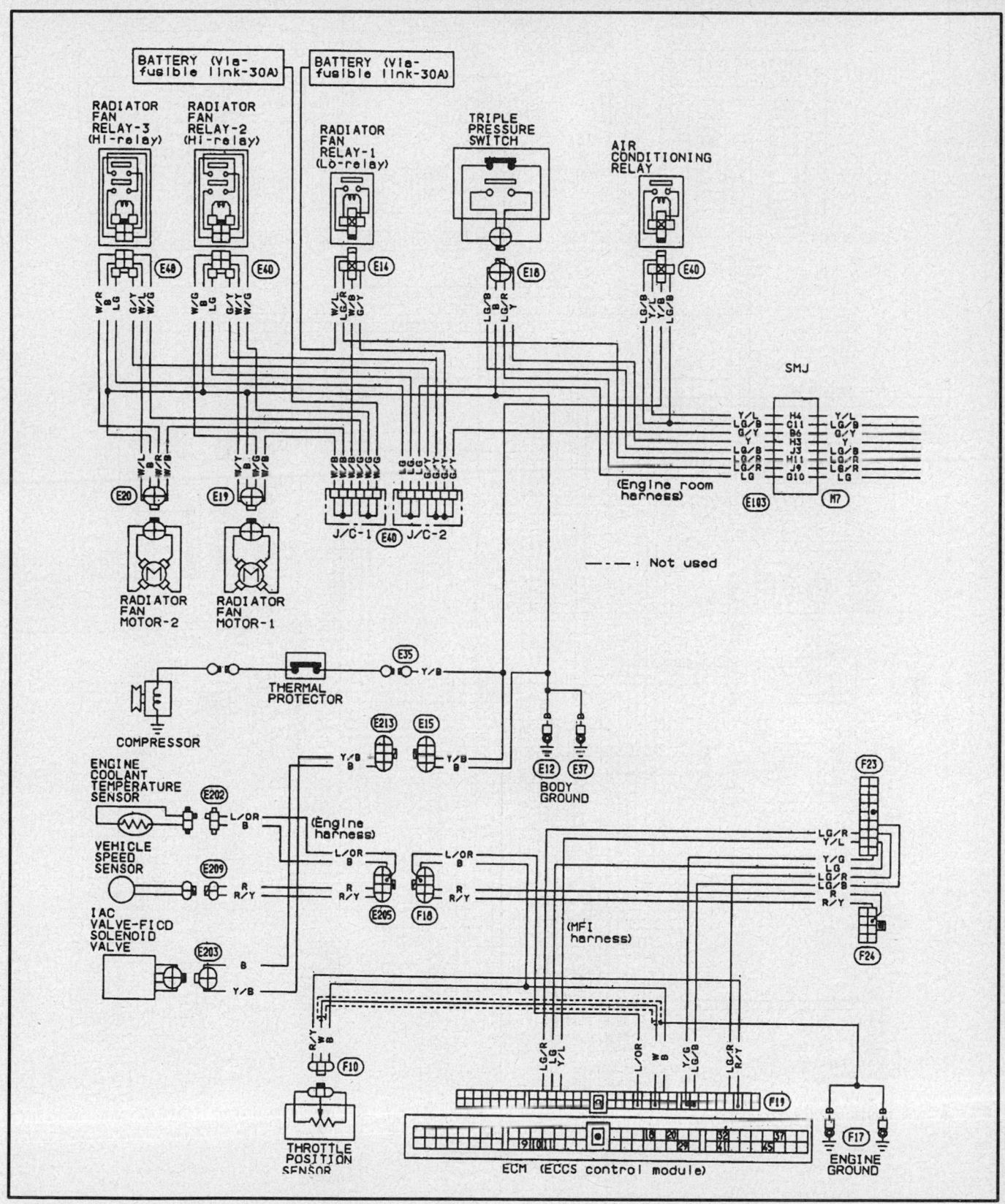

Manual air conditioning wiring schematic — Altima

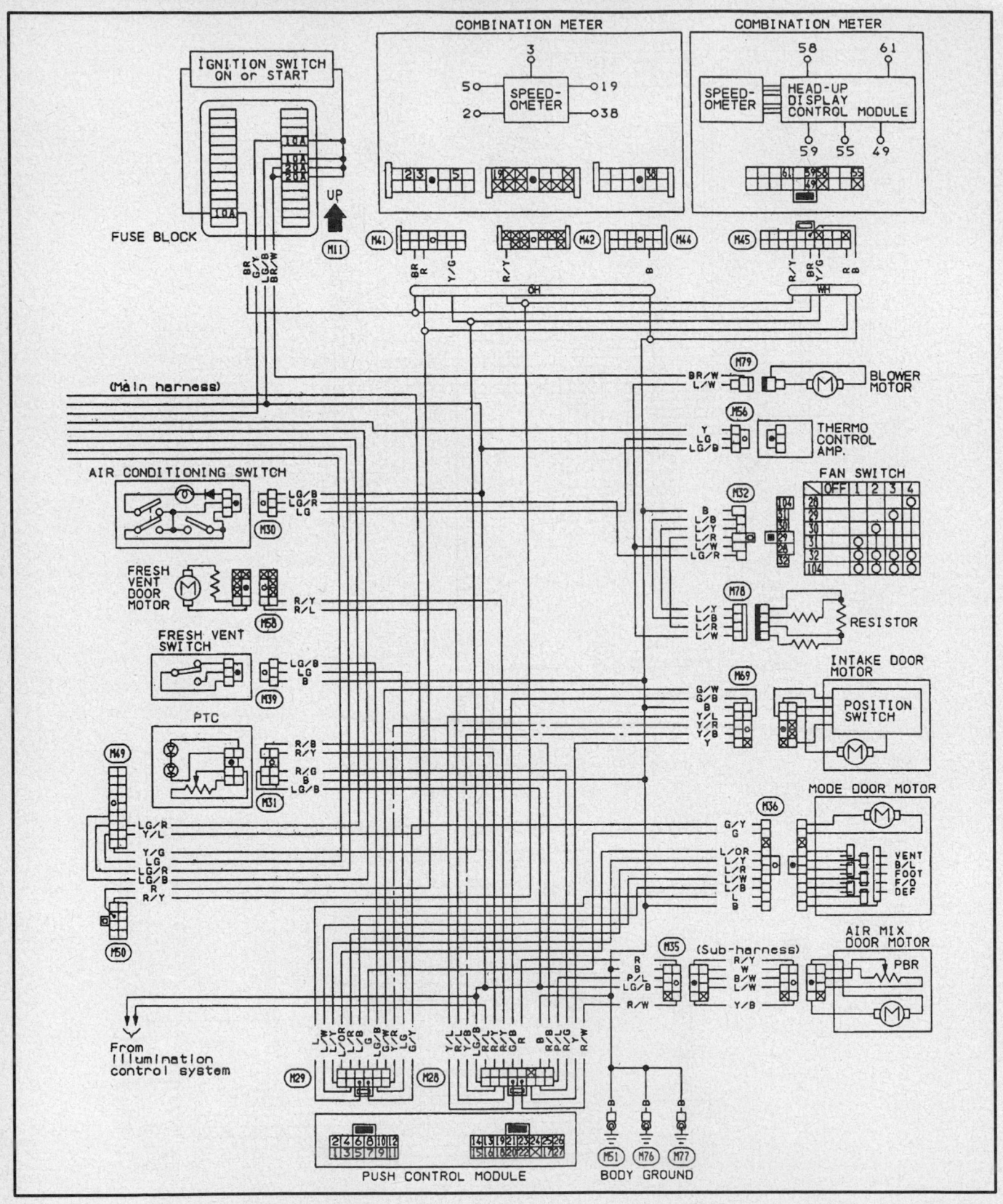

Manual air conditioning wiring schematic—Altima, Cont'd

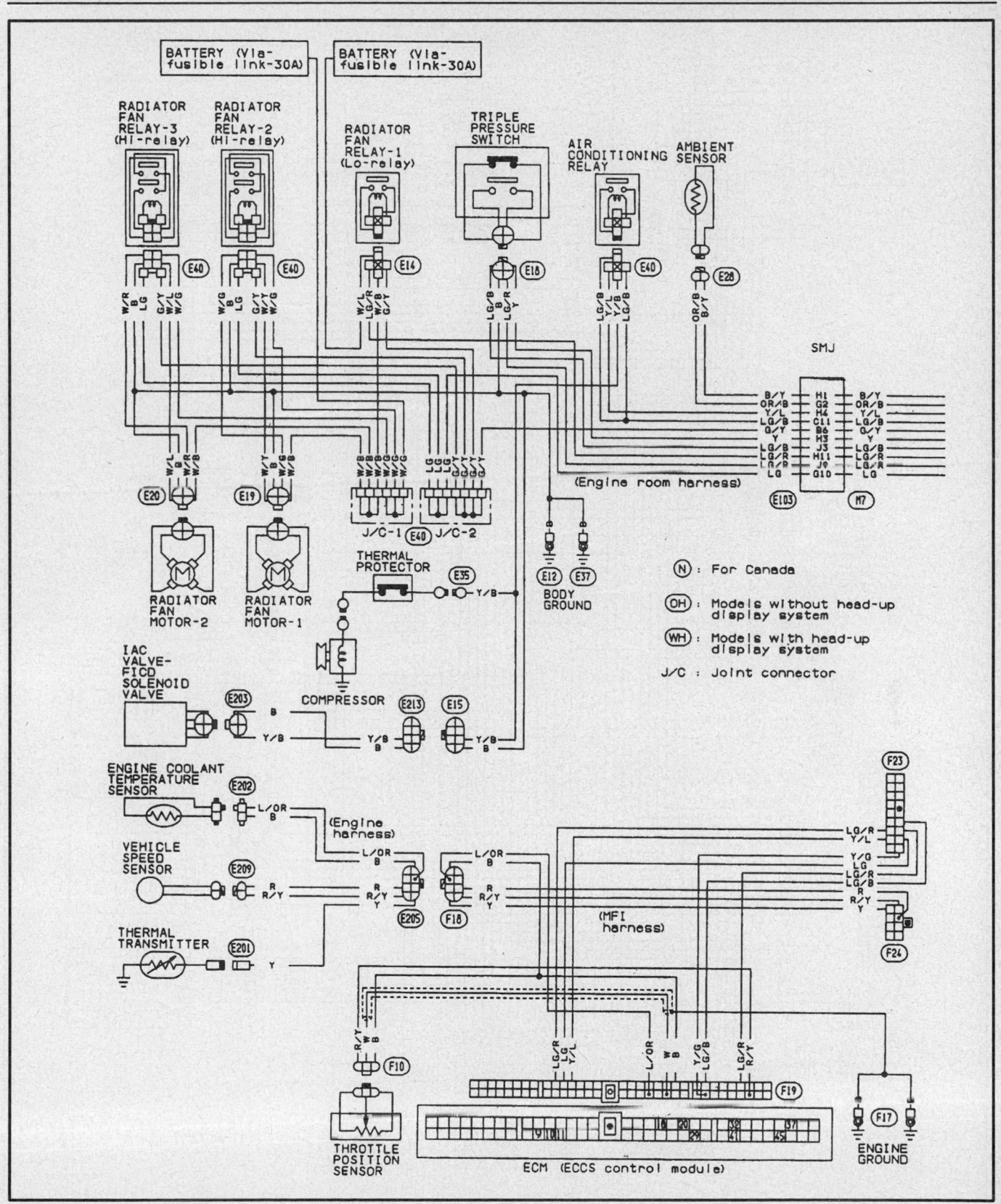

Automatic air conditioning wiring schematic—Altima

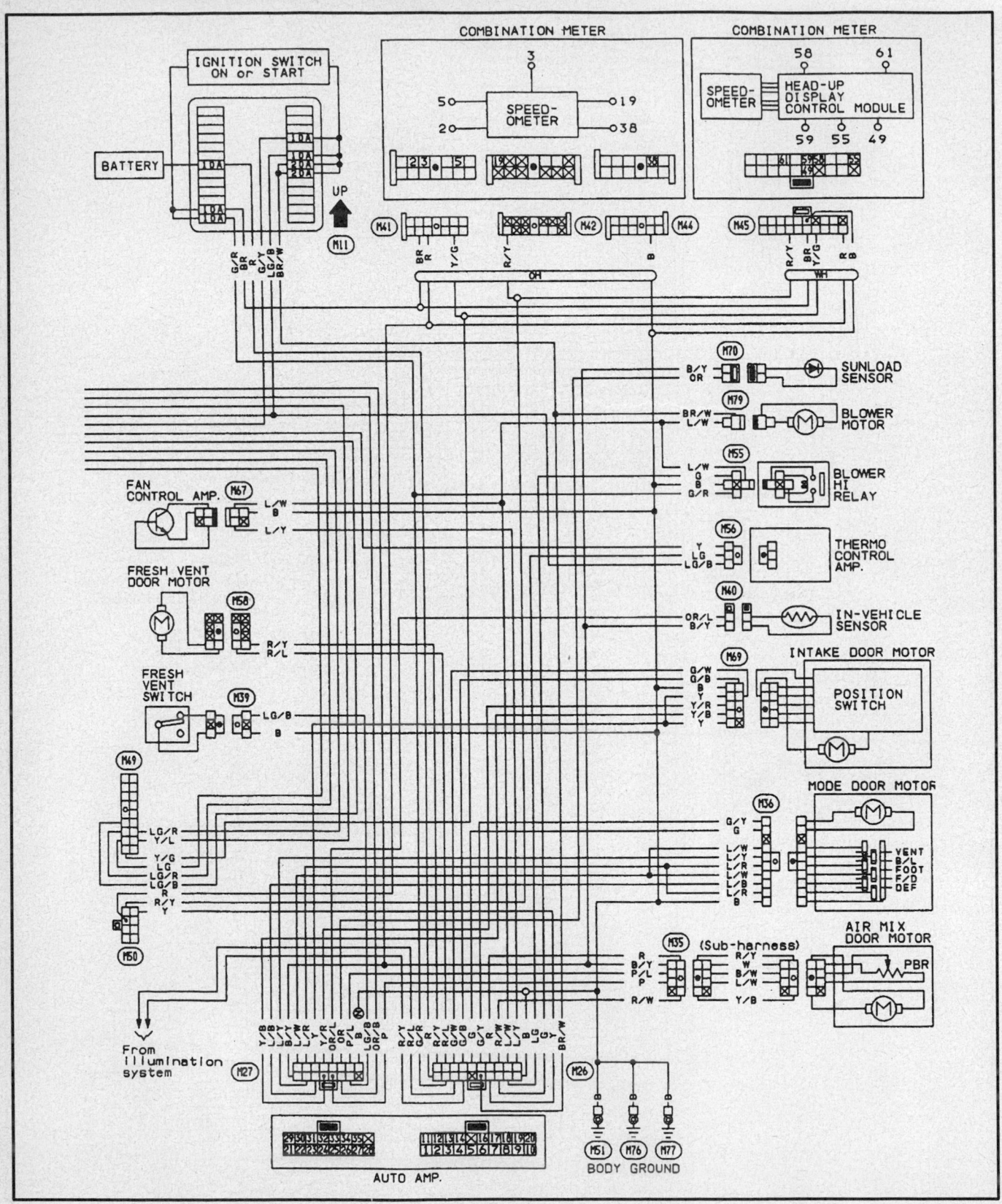

Automatic air conditioning wiring schematic—Altima, Cont'd

SPECIFICATIONS

ENGINE IDENTIFICATION

Year	Model	Engine Displacement Liters (cc)	Engine Series (ID/VIN)	Fuel System	No. of Cylinders	Engine Type
1993	Pick-Up	2.4 (2389)	K24E	EFI	4	SOHC
	Pick-Up	3.0 (2960)	VG30E	EFI	6	DOHC
	Pathfinder	3.0 (2960)	VG30E	EFI	6	DOHC
	Quest	3.0 (2960)	VG30E	EFI	6	DOHC
1994	Pick-Up	2.4 (2389)	K24E	EFI	4	SOHC
	Pick-Up	3.0 (2960)	VG30E	EFI	6	DOHC
	Pathfinder	3.0 (2960)	VG30E	EFI	6	DOHC
	Quest	3.0 (2960)	VG30E	EFI	6	DOHC
1995	Pick-Up	2.4 (2389)	K24E	EFI	4	SOHC
	Pick-Up	3.0 (2960)	VG30E	EFI	6	DOHC
	Pathfinder	3.0 (2960)	VG30E	EFI	6	DOHC
	Quest	3.0 (2960)	VG30E	EFI	6	DOHC

EFI – Electronic fuel injection
DOHC–Dual overhead cam
SOHC – Single overhead cam

REFRIGERANT CAPACITIES

Year	Model	Refrigerant (oz.)	Oil (fl. oz.)	Compressor Type
1993	Pick-Up	26.5–30.0	6.8	DKV–14C
	Pathfinder	26.5–30.0	6.8	DKV–14C
	Quest (front A/C only)*	36.0	7.0	FX–15
	Quest (front & rear A/C)*	56.0	10.0	FX15
1994	Pick-Up	26.5–30.0	6.8	DKV–14C
	Pathfinder	26.5–30.0	6.8	DKV–14C
	Quest (front A/C only)*	36.0	7.0	FS–10
	Quest (front & rear A/C)*	56.0	10.0	FS–10
1995	Pick-Up	26.5–30.0	6.8	DKV–14C
	Pathfinder	26.5–30.0	6.8	DKV–14C
	Quest (front A/C only)*	36.0	7.0	FS–10
	Quest (front & rear A/C)*	56.0	10.0	FS–10

* System uses R–12 refrigerant – all others use
  R–134a refrigerant and corresponding oil.

AIR CONDITIONING BELT TENSION

Year	Model	Engine Liters (cc)	Belt Type	Specifications New (lbs.)	Used (lbs.)
1993	Pick-Up	2.4	V–belt	0.31–0.39	0.39–0.47
	Pick-Up	3.0	V–belt	0.28–0.35	0.35–0.43
	Pathfinder	3.0	V–belt	0.28–0.35	0.35–0.43
	Quest	3.0	Poly–V	0.16–0.24	0.20–0.28
1994	Pick-Up	2.4	A–type	0.28–0.35	0.35–0.43
	Pick-Up	3.0	A–type	0.28–0.35	0.35–0.43
	Pathfinder	3.0	A–type	0.28–0.35	0.35–0.43
	Quest	3.0	Poly–V	0.16–0.24	0.20–0.28
1995	Pick-Up	2.4	A–type	0.28–0.35	0.35–0.43
	Pick-Up	3.0	A–type	0.28–0.35	0.35–0.43
	Pathfinder	3.0	A–type	0.28–0.35	0.35–0.43
	Quest	3.0	Poly–V	0.16–0.24	0.20–0.28

SYSTEM DESCRIPTION

General Information

In 1993, the Pathfinder and Pick-Up air conditioning systems began using non-CFC R-134a as a refrigerant. In 1994 the Quest also began using this type of refrigerant. Specific type of refrigerant oil is also used with this system.

Pathfinder and Pick-Up

These models use either a manually controlled air conditioning system or an automatic air conditioning system. Both systems share the same basic components of the system, plus operating switches, sensors and protection devices such as a dual pressure switch, thermo control amplifier, fan control relays, compressor control relay and a blower relay.

On automatic systems, an ambient temperature sensor, in-vehicle temperature sensor, sunload sensor, and heater water temperature sensor are added. These provide input signals to the auto amplifier which processes the inputs and provides output signals to the air mix door and blower motor.

The Automatic Temperature Control (ATC) system is different from the one used in the Nissan cars in that the Potentiometer Temperature Control (PTC) lever adjusts a calibrated resistor, which feeds the control demand to the amplifier. The resulting signal is read by the amplifier which will control blower fan speed and move the air mix door, which has a second adjustable resistor. By keeping these 2 signals mathematically balanced, the amplifier will maintain the selected temperature. Other information used in the calculation is outside and inside air temperatures, engine coolant temperature, sun load and compressor on signal. There is no on-board diagnostic function with this system, but it can be tested with a standard volt/ohmmeter.

Quest

Quest uses a recycling clutch fixed orifice tube, instead of an expansion valve. In addition, an accumulator, located on the low side of the system takes the place of the traditional receiver/drier. The compressor is in this type of system is "cycled" in order to maintain the proper refrigerant pressures required by the system.

This model offers a front-only or front and rear air conditioning systems. The rear system has its own temperature and blower controls. It also has a separate heater core, evaporator core and blower motor in its own housing in the rear of the vehicle. Refrigerant and heater lines from the engine compartment are routed along the vehicle under-carriage.

System protection is provided by separate high pressure and low pressure switches. The low pressure switch is mounted on the accumulator. The high pressure switch is mounted on the back of the compressor. Both sense the pressure in the system and will stop compressor operation in the event of extremely high or extremely low operating pressure.

Service Valve Location

Pathfinder and Pick-Up

1. On vehicles with the V6 engine, both service valves are on the refrigerant lines close to the compressor.
2. On vehicles with the 4 cylinder engine, the high pressure valve is in the high pressure line between the compressor and condenser. The low pressure valve is on the low pressure line at the firewall, near the driver's side.

Quest

Both valves are located in the right front of the engine compartment, with the high side valve near the condenser and the low side valve just above the brake master cylinder.

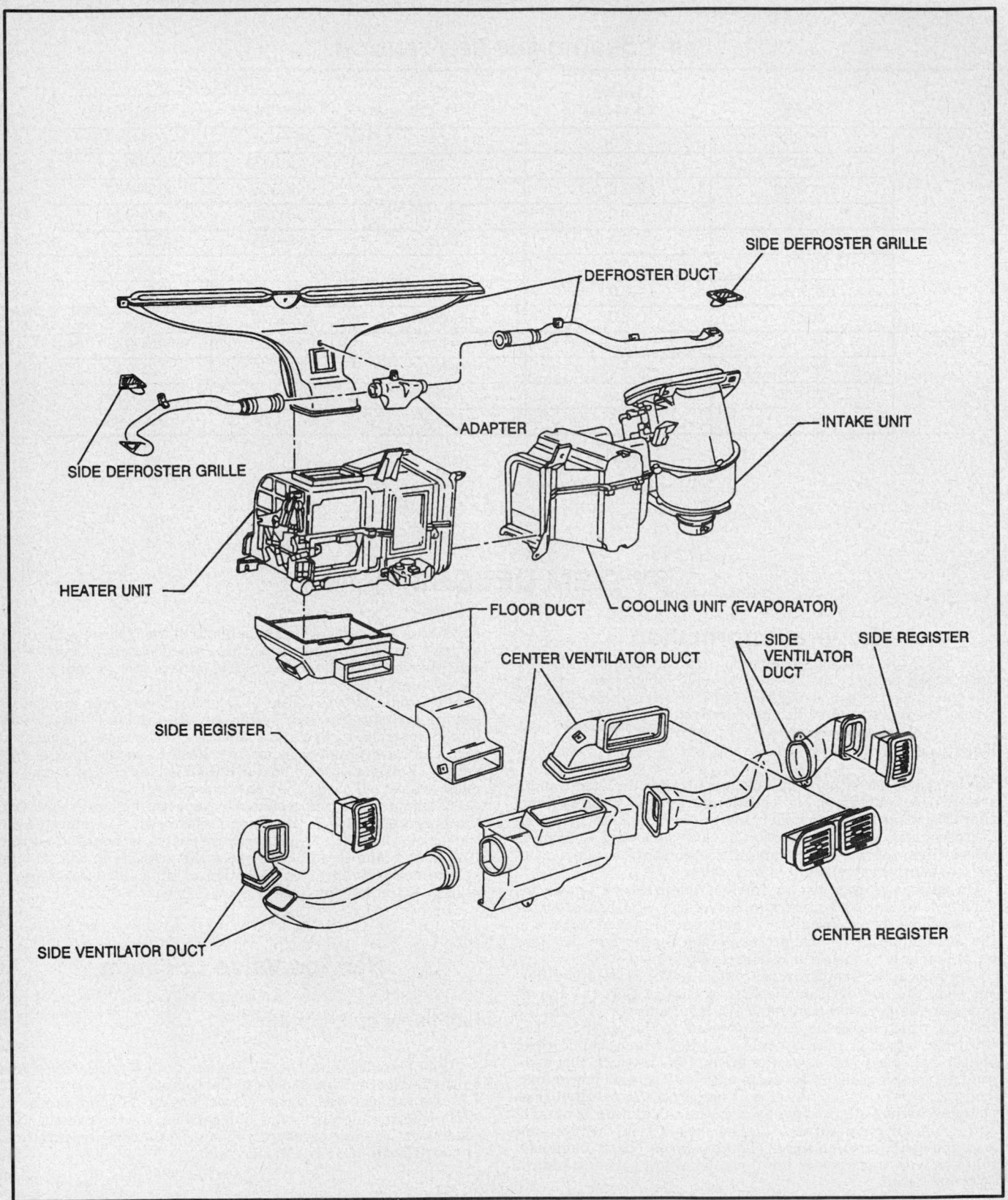

SIDE DEFROSTER GRILLE

DEFROSTER DUCT

SIDE DEFROSTER GRILLE

ADAPTER

INTAKE UNIT

SIDE DEFROSTER GRILLE

HEATER UNIT

COOLING UNIT (EVAPORATOR)

FLOOR DUCT

SIDE REGISTER

CENTER VENTILATOR DUCT

SIDE VENTILATOR DUCT

SIDE REGISTER

SIDE VENTILATOR DUCT

CENTER REGISTER

Air conditioning system components—Quest

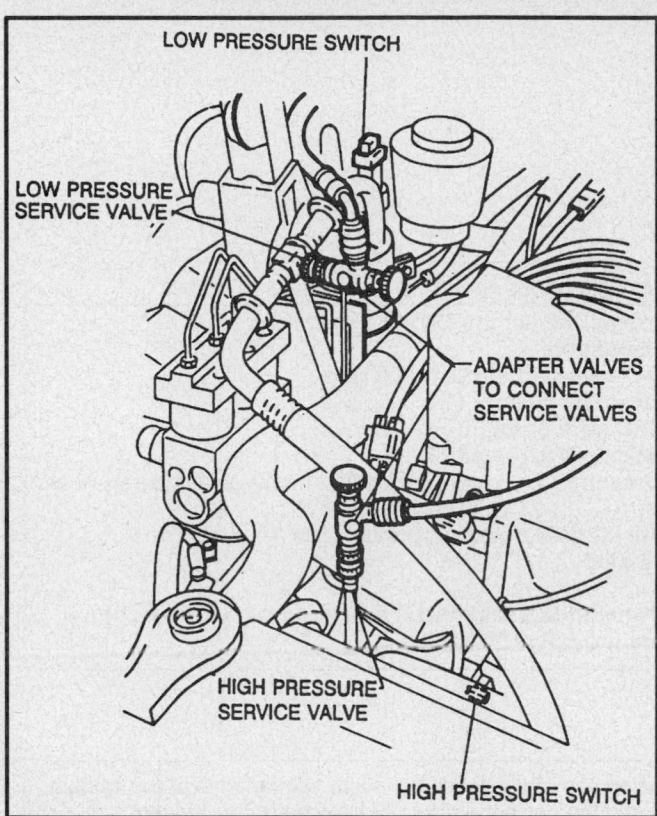

LOW PRESSURE SWITCH

LOW PRESSURE
SERVICE VALVE

ADAPTER VALVES
TO CONNECT
SERVICE VALVES

HIGH PRESSURE
SERVICE VALVE

HIGH PRESSURE SWITCH

Service Valve locations—Quest

Special Precautions

1. All refrigerant service work must be done with the proper recycling equipment. Carefully follow the manufacturer's instructions for use of that equipment. Do not allow the refrigerant to discharge to the air.
2. Any amount of water will make the system less effective. When any part of the system has been removed, plug or cap the lines to prevent moisture from the air entering the system. When installing a new component, do not uncap the fittings until ready to attach the lines.
3. When assembling a fitting, always use a new O-ring and lightly lubricate the fitting with compressor oil.
4. When a compressor is removed, do not leave it on its side or upside down for more than 10 minutes. The oil may leak into the pumping chamber.
5. The proper amount of oil must be maintained in the system to prevent compressor damage and to maintain system efficiency. Be sure to measure and adjust the amount of oil removed or added to the system, especially when replacing the compressor.
6. On systems using R-134a refrigerant, note that this refrigerant and R-12 are not compatible in any amounts. Mixing of the 2 different refrigerants will result in compressor failure. Avoid using equipment or components that could possibly mix these incompatible chemicals.

System Discharging

1. Install adapter valves to the vehicle service valves and connect the refrigerant recycling equipment according to the manufacturer's instructions.

2. Open both the adapter or manifold valves slowly to prevent excess oil loss. Proceed with recycling of the refrigerant according to the manufacturers instructions. Do not discharge the refrigerant into the atmosphere.

System Evacuating

1. Open both the high and low pressure valves and run the vacuum pump for more than 5 minutes. The gauges should stabilize at 29.13–29.92 in. (740–760mm) Hg vacuum.
2. Close the valves and turn the pump **OFF**. Check to see that the vacuum gauges remain stable. If the gauge on the low pressure side moves 3.94 in. (100mm) Hg vacuum in about 10 minutes, the system will discharge itself in about 1 month.
3. If the system will not hold vacuum, first check that the service equipment is properly connected and in good working order. If any connections in the vehicle system have been disturbed, make sure they have been properly reconnected. Be sure to use new lightly oiled O-rings and that the fitting is not over torqued.
4. If the system holds vacuum, open the valves and run the pump for more than 20 minutes. Close the valves, then turn the pump **OFF**.

System Charging

Use only SAE approved recycling equipment. Carefully follow the manufacturer's instructions and add the correct amount of R-12 or R-134a as dictated by the type of system and as noted in the specifications chart. Never add refrigerant through the high pressure service valve.

Compressor and Component Oil Service

NOTE: Systems using R-134a refrigerant also use a specific oil which is different from the oil used with R-12 systems. Use only the correct oil application for each system.

The compressor is lubricated with a special oil that circulates with the refrigerant when the system is operating and drops out of the refrigerant when the system is stopped. Insufficient oil will cause damage to the compressor but too much oil will inhibit the system's cooling ability. When installing new parts or a new compressor, the oil quantity must be adjusted.

1. Discharge refrigerant into refrigerant recovery/recycling equipment. Measure lubricant discharged into the recovery/recycling equipment.
2. Drain the lubricant from the "old" compressor into a graduated container and record the amount of lubricant drained.
3. Drain the lubricant from the "new" compressor into a separate clean container.
4. Measure an amount of the new lubricant equal to that drained from the "old" compressor, and add this lubricant to the "new" compressor through the suction port opening.
5. Measure an amount of the new lubricant equal to that recovered during discharging, and add this lubricant to the "new" compressor through the suction port opening.
6. If the accumulator also needs to be replaced, add an additional 0.2 fl. oz. of lubricant at this time.

NOTE: Do not add this 0.2 fl. oz. of lubricant if only replacing the compressor

7. If installing another major system component, add oil as noted in the "Compressor and Component Oil Service" chart.

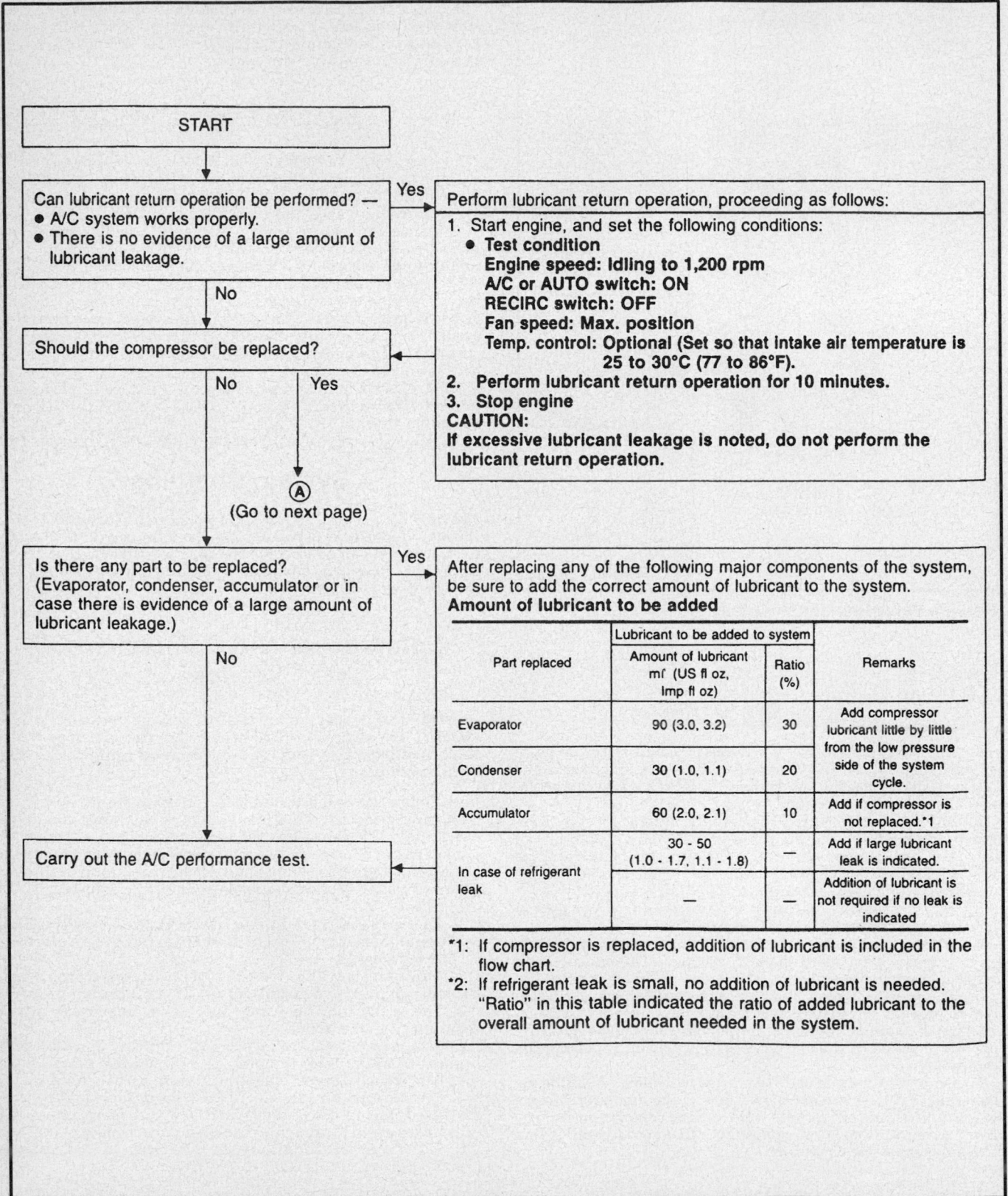

```
                    ┌─────────────────────┐
                    │        START        │
                    └─────────────────────┘
                              │
                              ▼
┌──────────────────────────────────────┐  Yes  ┌──────────────────────────────────────────┐
│ Can lubricant return operation be     │──────▶│ Perform lubricant return operation,       │
│ performed? —                          │       │ proceeding as follows:                    │
│ ● A/C system works properly.          │       └──────────────────────────────────────────┘
│ ● There is no evidence of a large     │
│   amount of lubricant leakage.        │
└──────────────────────────────────────┘
                    │ No
                    ▼
┌──────────────────────────────────────┐
│ Should the compressor be replaced?    │
└──────────────────────────────────────┘
          │ No          │ Yes
                        ▼
                       (A)
               (Go to next page)
```

Perform lubricant return operation, proceeding as follows:

1. Start engine, and set the following conditions:
   ● **Test condition**
     Engine speed: Idling to 1,200 rpm
     A/C or AUTO switch: ON
     RECIRC switch: OFF
     Fan speed: Max. position
     Temp. control: Optional (Set so that intake air temperature is
     25 to 30°C (77 to 86°F).
2. **Perform lubricant return operation for 10 minutes.**
3. **Stop engine**
CAUTION:
If excessive lubricant leakage is noted, do not perform the
lubricant return operation.

```
┌──────────────────────────────────────┐  Yes
│ Is there any part to be replaced?     │──────▶
│ (Evaporator, condenser, accumulator   │
│ or in case there is evidence of a     │
│ large amount of lubricant leakage.)   │
└──────────────────────────────────────┘
                    │ No
                    ▼
┌──────────────────────────────────────┐
│ Carry out the A/C performance test.   │◀──────
└──────────────────────────────────────┘
```

After replacing any of the following major components of the system, be sure to add the correct amount of lubricant to the system.
Amount of lubricant to be added

Part replaced	Lubricant to be added to system		Remarks
	Amount of lubricant mℓ (US fl oz, Imp fl oz)	Ratio (%)	
Evaporator	90 (3.0, 3.2)	30	Add compressor lubricant little by little from the low pressure side of the system cycle.
Condenser	30 (1.0, 1.1)	20	
Accumulator	60 (2.0, 2.1)	10	Add if compressor is not replaced.*1
In case of refrigerant leak	30 - 50 (1.0 - 1.7, 1.1 - 1.8)	—	Add if large lubricant leak is indicated.
	—	—	Addition of lubricant is not required if no leak is indicated

*1: If compressor is replaced, addition of lubricant is included in the flow chart.
*2: If refrigerant leak is small, no addition of lubricant is needed. "Ratio" in this table indicated the ratio of added lubricant to the overall amount of lubricant needed in the system.

Compressor and component oil service—lubricant quantity

1. Discharge refrigerant into refrigerant recovery/recycling equipment. Measure lubricant discharged into the recovery/ recycling equipment.
2. Drain the lubricant from the "old" (removed) compressor into a graduated container and record the amount of lubricant drained.
3. Drain the lubricant from the "new" compressor into a separate, clean container.
4. Measure an amount of the new lubricant equal to that drained from the "old" compressor, and add this lubricant to the "new" compressor through the suction port opening.
5. Measure an amount of the "new" lubricant equal to that recovered during discharging, and add this lubricant to the "new" compressor through the suction port opening.
6. If the accumulator (liquid tank) also needs to be replaced, add an additional 5 mℓ (0.2 US fl oz, 0.2 Imp fl oz) of lubricant at this time.
   Do not add this 5 mℓ (0.2 US fl oz, 0.2 Imp fl oz) of lubricant if only replacing the compressor.

Lubricant adjusting procedure for compressor replacement

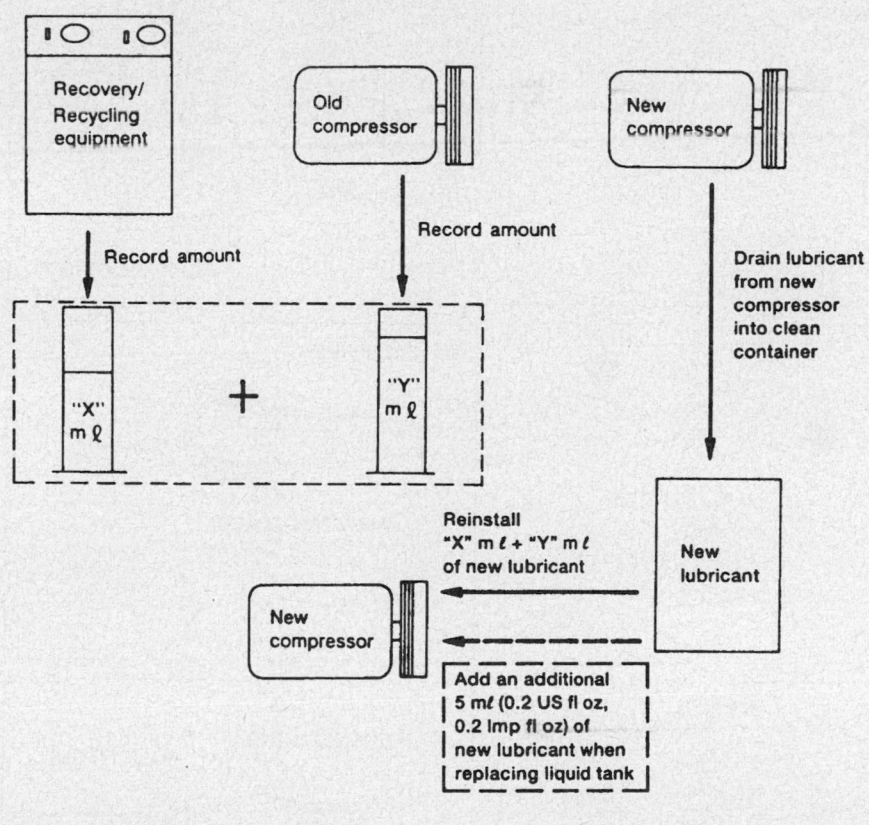

Compressor and component oil service—lubricant quantity

Spring Lock Coupling

Quest

Quest uses a special spring lock coupling on many of its refrigerant line connections. A special removal tool is needed.

1. Discharge the air conditioning system using recovery equipment.
2. Fit the spring lock coupling special tool to the coupling, close the tool and push it into the open side of the cage to expand the garter spring and release the female fitting.

3. Pull the fitting apart and remove the special tool.
To install:
4. Check that the garter spring is in the cage of the male fitting. If the spring is damaged carefully replace it.
5. Clean the ends of the fittings and install new (specified type) O-rings lubricated with clean refrigerant oil.
6. Install the plastic indicator ring into the cage opening, if the ring is to be used.
7. Fit the female fitting to the male fitting and push until the garter spring snaps over the flared end of the female fitting (the plastic indicator will snap out of the cage, indicating engagement).

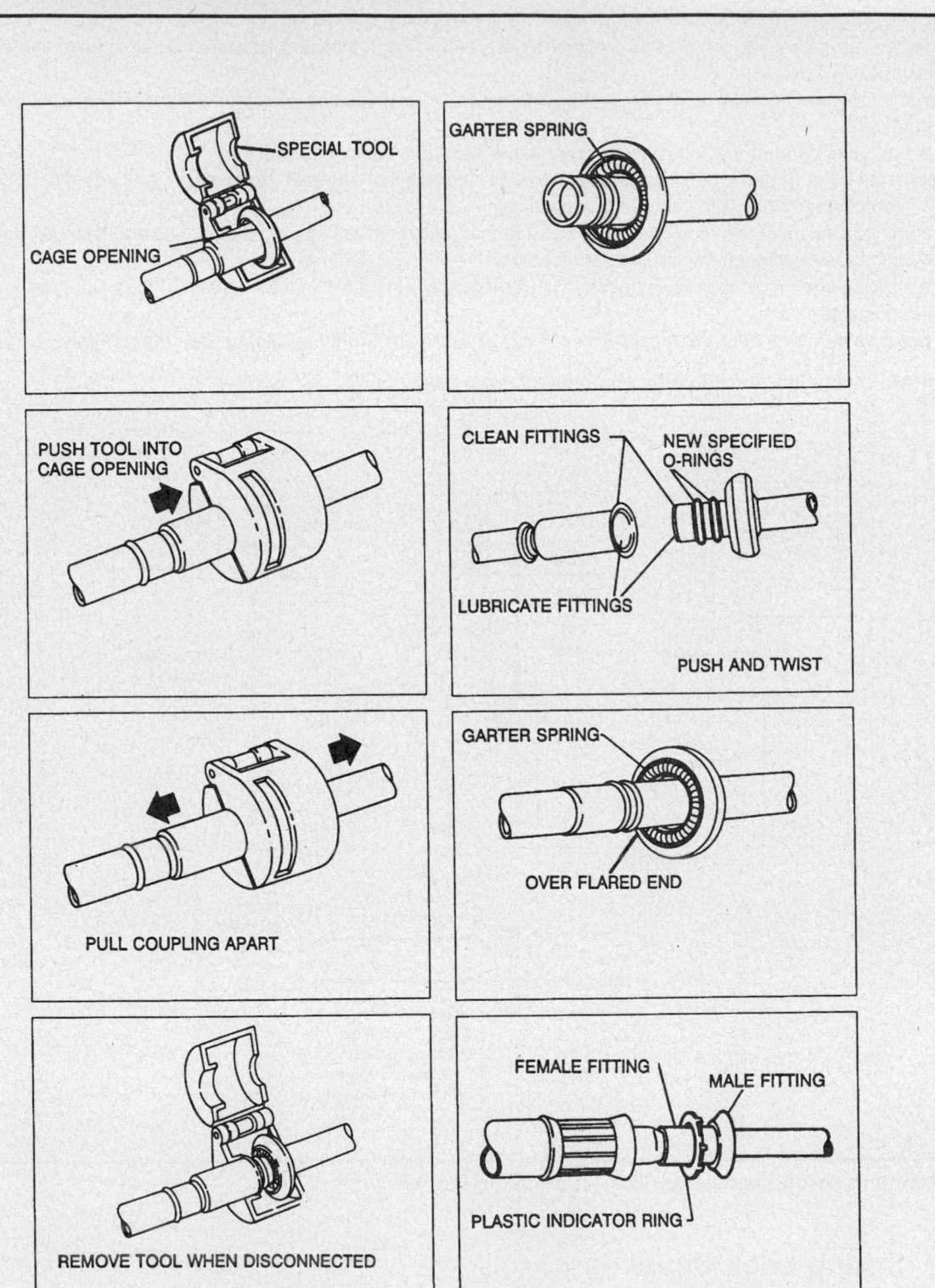

SPECIAL TOOL

CAGE OPENING

GARTER SPRING

PUSH TOOL INTO CAGE OPENING

CLEAN FITTINGS

NEW SPECIFIED O-RINGS

LUBRICATE FITTINGS

PUSH AND TWIST

PULL COUPLING APART

GARTER SPRING

OVER FLARED END

REMOVE TOOL WHEN DISCONNECTED

FEMALE FITTING

MALE FITTING

PLASTIC INDICATOR RING

Spring lock coupling disconnect/connect procedures—Quest

SYSTEM COMPONENTS

NOTE: When removing any component of the refrigerant system, properly discharge the refrigerant into recovery equipment. Do not vent the refrigerant into the air.

Radiator and Cooling Fan

REMOVAL AND INSTALLATION

1. Disconnect the negative battery cable. On vehicles with theft-protected radios, make sure the owner's reset code is available.
2. Drain the cooling system. Remove the engine under cover. On 2.4L engines, remove the reservoir tank and hose.
3. Remove upper and lower hoses from the radiator.
4. On Quest, disconnect the temperature switch and fan connectors, and remove the right bolt from the fuse box and move the box aside.
5. On vehicles with automatic transmissions, disconnect and plug the transmission cooling lines.
6. Remove the lower fan shroud (Pathfinder and Pick-Up).
7. To remove the radiator, remove the upper radiator retaining bolts and lift the unit up and out.
To install:
8. Set the lugs on the bottom of the radiator into the rubber mounts on the body and secure the unit with the upper mounting bolts.
9. Install the fan shroud. On Quest, reattach the fuse box.
10. Connect the automatic transmission cooling lines and all coolant hoses with the reservoir tank.
11. Fill the cooling system and look for leaks before installing the remaining parts.
12. Plug in all the electrical connectors for the fan and temperature switches.
13. Connect the battery and start the engine to bleed the cooling system and check for leaks.

Electric Cooling Fan

TESTING

Quest

The electric cooling fan (radiator) is controlled by outputs from the Engine Control Module (ECM). The module responds to input signals from the vehicle speed sensor, the engine coolant temperature sensor and the air conditioning switch ("ON" signal). The fan operates as follows:

A/C SWITCH "OFF"

- When the engine coolant temperature is less than 201°F (94°C), the fan will not operate.
- Between 203–210°F (95–99°C), the fan operates at low speed.
- Between 212–219°F (100–104°C), the fan is on low speed if vehicle speed is less than 12 mph. If vehicle speed is more than 20 mph, the fan is on high speed at these temperatures.
- When engine coolant temperature exceeds 221°F (105°C), the fan operates at high speed.

A/C SWITCH "ON"

- With coolant temperature 201°F (24°C) or less and vehicle speed 68 mph or more, the fan is off.
- At the same temperature above, but with vehicle speed under 68 mph, the fan will be on at low speed.
- When coolant temperature is between 203–219°F (95–104°C) and vehicle speed is under 12 mph, the fan is off.

- At the same temperature above, but with vehicle speed over 12 mph, the fan is on at high speed.
- With engine coolant temperature over 220°F (105°C), fan is on at high speed at any engine speed.

NOTE: A/C clutch will not engage below 50°F (10°C) ambient temperatures.

REMOVAL AND INSTALLATION

Quest

1. Disconnect the negative battery cable. If the upper radiator will interfere and require removal, partially drain the cooling system, then disconnect the hose.
2. Detach the cooling fan connector and remove any wiring or hoses that may be clipped to the fan shroud.
3. Remove the fan assembly bolts and lift the assembly out of the vehicle.
4. Installation is the reverse of the removal assembly.

Condenser and Receiver/Drier

REMOVAL AND INSTALLATION

NOTE: Systems using R-134a refrigerant and corresponding refrigerant oil. Use only the refrigerant, oil, components and service equipment specified for these applications.

Quest

1. Disconnect the negative battery cable. On vehicles with theft-protected radios, make sure the owner's reset code is available.
2. The radiator may have to be removed first, or the mounting bolts removed so the radiator can be moved to provide clearance for the condenser removal. Remove the apron under the front of the engine, if equipped, and drain the cooling system.
3. Disconnect and plug the oil cooling hoses on automatic transmission models, then remove the fan(s) and radiator.
4. Properly discharge the air conditioning system into recovery equipment, disconnect and cap the pressure lines from the condenser.
5. Installation is the reverse of removal. When installing the condenser, be sure to use new O-ring seals and lightly lubricate them with compressor oil.
6. Do not over torque the fittings or they will be distorted and leak.

Pathfinder and Pick-Up

1. Properly discharge the air conditioning system using recovery type equipment.
2. Remove the coolant reservoir tank and the side marker lamps.
3. Remove the front grille (5 fasteners).
4. Remove the harness clip from the hood lock stay, if equipped (press out). Remove the hood lock stay plate and brace.
5. Detach the high pressure hose from the condenser and from the receiver/drier. Cap all openings immediately.
6. Remove the 2 condenser mounting bolts and remove the condenser.
To install:
7. If installing a replacement condenser, add oil according to the procedure given under "Compressor and Component Oil Service."
8. Position the condenser and attach the high pressure lines, using new O-rings.

9. Install the hood lock stay plate and brace.
10. Install the front grille, the side market lights and the coolant reservoir.
11. Evacuate, recharge and leak test the system.

Compressor

REMOVAL AND INSTALLATION

1. Properly discharge the system using refrigerant recovery equipment. Disconnect the pressure lines and plug them.
2. On some models, it may be easier to remove the compressor from under the vehicle.
3. Unplug the connectors and loosen the drive belt. A belt tensioner pulley with an adjusting bolt is under the compressor on the 4 cylinder engine or next to the compressor on the V6 engine.
4. On Pathfinder and Pick-Up with V6 engines, remove the alternator for clearance, then continue removal of the compressor.
5. Remove the pivot bolts and lift the compressor out. Do not leave the compressor on end or upside down for more than a few minutes or the oil may run into the cylinders.
6. Installation is the reverse of removal. Be sure to tighten the belt to specification, do not over tighten or bearing damage will result.

Blower Motor

REMOVAL AND INSTALLATION

1. The blower can be removed without removing the housing. The resistor is mounted on the evaporator housing and is accessible without removing the blower. On vehicles with theft protected radios, obtain the owner's security code.
2. If necessary, remove the glove compartment to gain access. On most vehicles, it is possible to squeeze the sides of the door to let it fall open beyond the normal stops.

3. Disconnect the wiring and remove the mounting bolts to lower the motor out.
4. Installation is the reverse of the removal procedure.

Heater Core

REMOVAL AND INSTALLATION

Pick-Up and Pathfinder

1. Disconnect the negative battery cable. On vehicles with theft protected radios, obtain the owner's security code.
2. Set the TEMP lever to the maximum **HOT** position and drain the engine coolant.
3. Disconnect the heater hoses at the engine compartment.
4. It is necessary to remove the entire dash board. Start by removing the ashtray and remove the screws holding the center console face cover. Remove the cover, heater controls, radio and center vent.
5. Disconnect the control cables and wiring as needed and remove the dash board.
6. Disconnect the ducts and remove the heater unit. Remove the case clips and split the case to remove the core.
To install:
7. Install the heater core and assemble the heater case halves. Use new gaskets and seals as required. Always check for smooth operation of the air mix door when re-attaching the heater case halves.
8. Install the heater unit and use a new gasket to connect it to the cooling unit.
9. Install the instrument panel.
10. Install the heater control assembly, center vent and radio.
11. Adjust the heater controls and air flow doors as required.
12. Connect the heater hoses and re-fill the cooling system.
13. Connect the negative battery cable and start the engine to test the system.

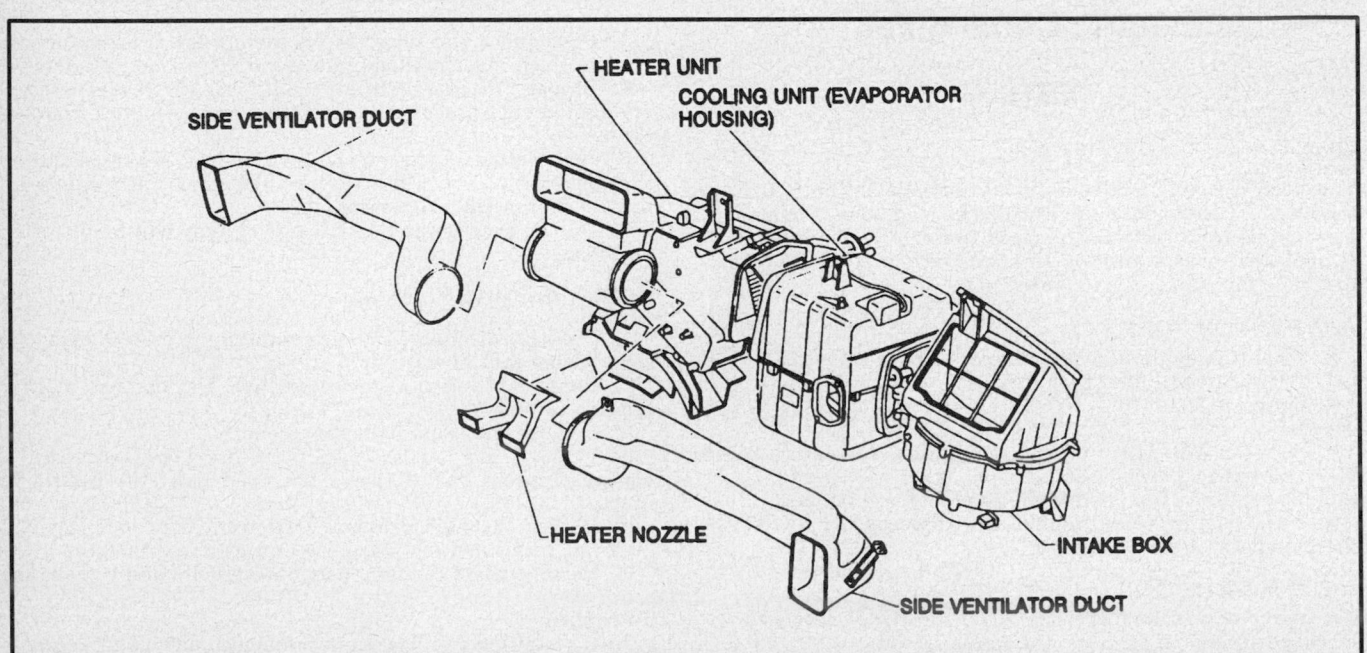

Pick-Up and Pathfinder heater/air conditioner assembly

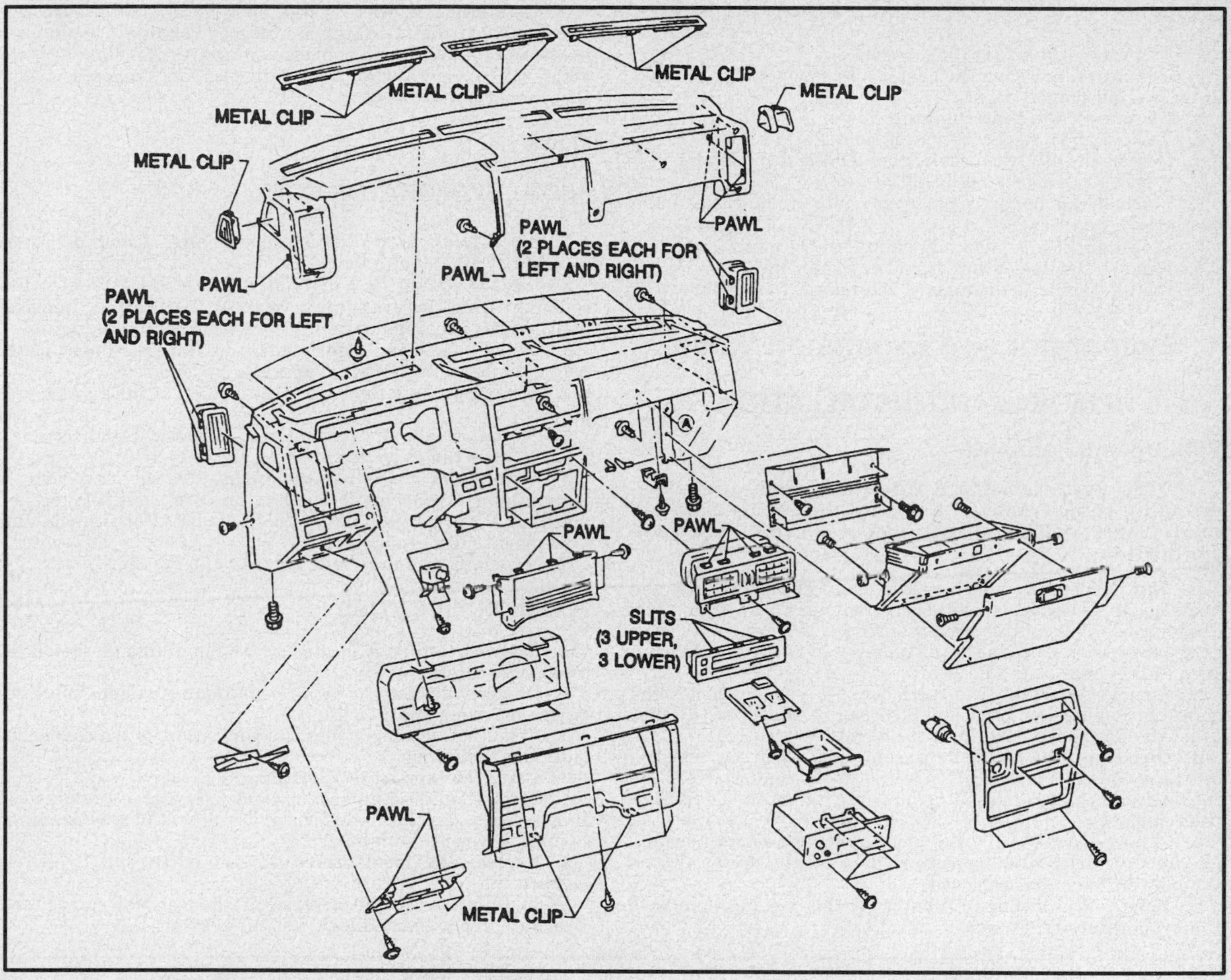

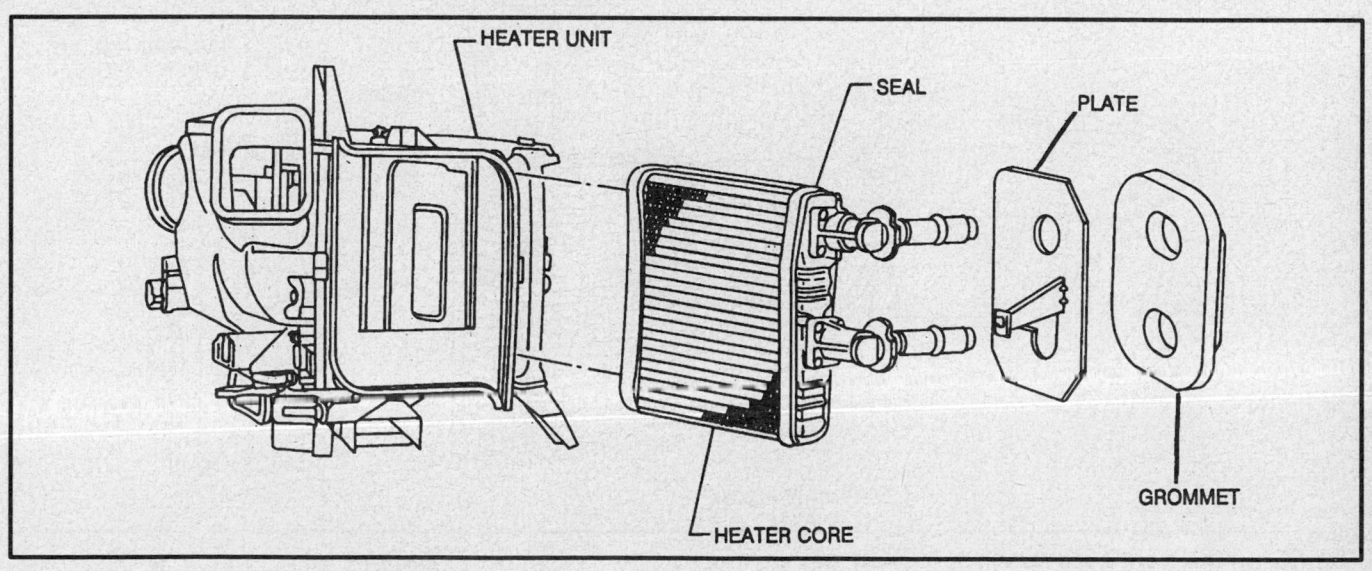

METAL CLIP · **METAL CLIP** · **METAL CLIP** · **METAL CLIP** · **METAL CLIP**

PAWL · **PAWL (2 PLACES EACH FOR LEFT AND RIGHT)** · **PAWL** · **PAWL**

PAWL (2 PLACES EACH FOR LEFT AND RIGHT)

PAWL · **PAWL**

SLITS (3 UPPER, 3 LOWER)

PAWL

METAL CLIP

Pick-Up and Pathfinder dash board assembly must be removed to remove the heater unit

HEATER UNIT

SEAL

PLATE

HEATER CORE

GROMMET

Removing the heater core—Quest

Quest

1. Properly drain the cooling system.
2. Disconnect and plug the heater hoses from the core tubes in the engine compartment.
3. Disconnect the heater unit air ducts.
4. Remove the 2 heater retaining bolts.
5. Detach the electrical connectors for the door motors.
6. Remove the heater assembly.
7. Remove the heater pipe cover plate, then remove the heater core retainer.
8. Disconnect the heater core shutoff valve control rod.
9. Remove the heater core from the heater unit.
10. Installation is the reverse of the removal procedure.

Evaporator and Expansion Valve

REMOVAL AND INSTALLATION

Pick-Up and Pathfinder

NOTE: Systems using R-134a refrigerant and corresponding refrigerant oil. Use only the refrigerant, oil, components and service equipment specified for these applications.

1. The evaporator, which is between the blower and the heater, can be removed without removing the heater core. Properly discharge the system using refrigerant recovery equipment, then disconnect and plug the evaporator and pressure line fittings at the firewall.
2. Remove the glove compartment. On some vehicles the sides of the glove compartment door can be squeezed together to let the door open down past the stops.
3. Disconnect the wiring for the blower fan resistor, which is on the evaporator housing. There is also a connector for the thermo control amplifier on the housing, either on the front or the top right.
4. If necessary, remove the blower motor and its housing. On some vehicles, the expansion valve can be accessed once the blower housing is removed.
5. Remove the cooling unit and split the housing to remove the evaporator and expansion valve.

6. Installation is the reverse of removal. Make sure the seals between the housings are in good condition, replace as necessary. If installing a replacement evaporator core, add the additional refrigerant oil as specified under "Compressor and Component Oil Servicing".

Quest

FRONT EVAPORATOR CORE

1. Properly discharge the air conditioning system using recovery/recycling equipment.
2. Use the spring lock disconnect procedure to detach the couplings from the evaporator tubes at the firewall. Immediately cap all openings to minimize system contamination.
3. Remove the lower right panel from the instrument panel assembly for access to the evaporator housing.
4. Remove the air duct from the heater to the right panel outlet.
5. Disconnect the blower motor and electrical connector.
6. Remove the evaporator.
7. Installation is the reverse of the removal procedure. If installing a replacement evaporator core, add the proper amount of refrigerant oil as noted under "Compressor and Component Oil Servicing".
8. Evacuate, recharge and leak test the system.

FIXED ORIFICE TUBE

The fixed orifice tube is located in the liquid line on the outlet side of the condenser.
1. Properly discharge the air conditioning system using recovery/recycling equipment.
2. Remove any components blocking access to the condenser outlet line coupling.
3. Using the spring-lock disconnect procedure and special tool detach the liquid line at the condenser and at the firewall. Immediately cap the condenser and evaporator tube openings to minimize contamination.
4. Replace the fixed orifice tube or entire liquid line as needed.
5. Installation is the reverse of the removal procedure. Evacuate, recharge and leak test the system.

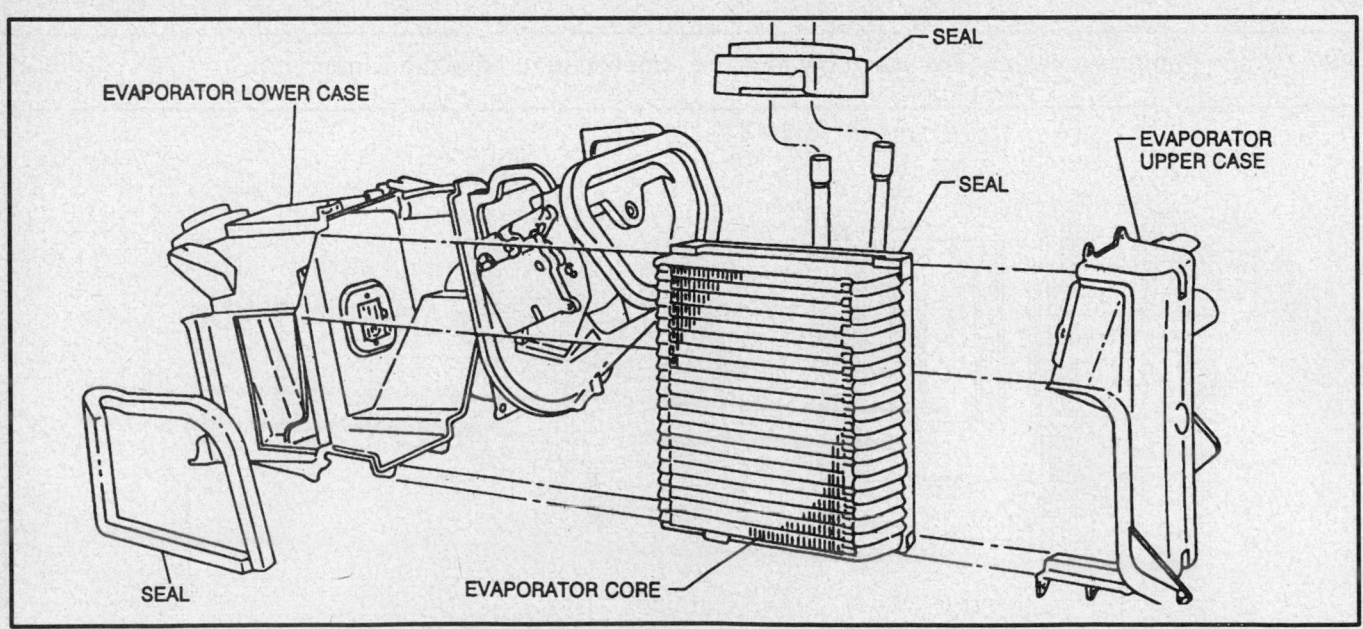

Removing the front evaporator core—Quest

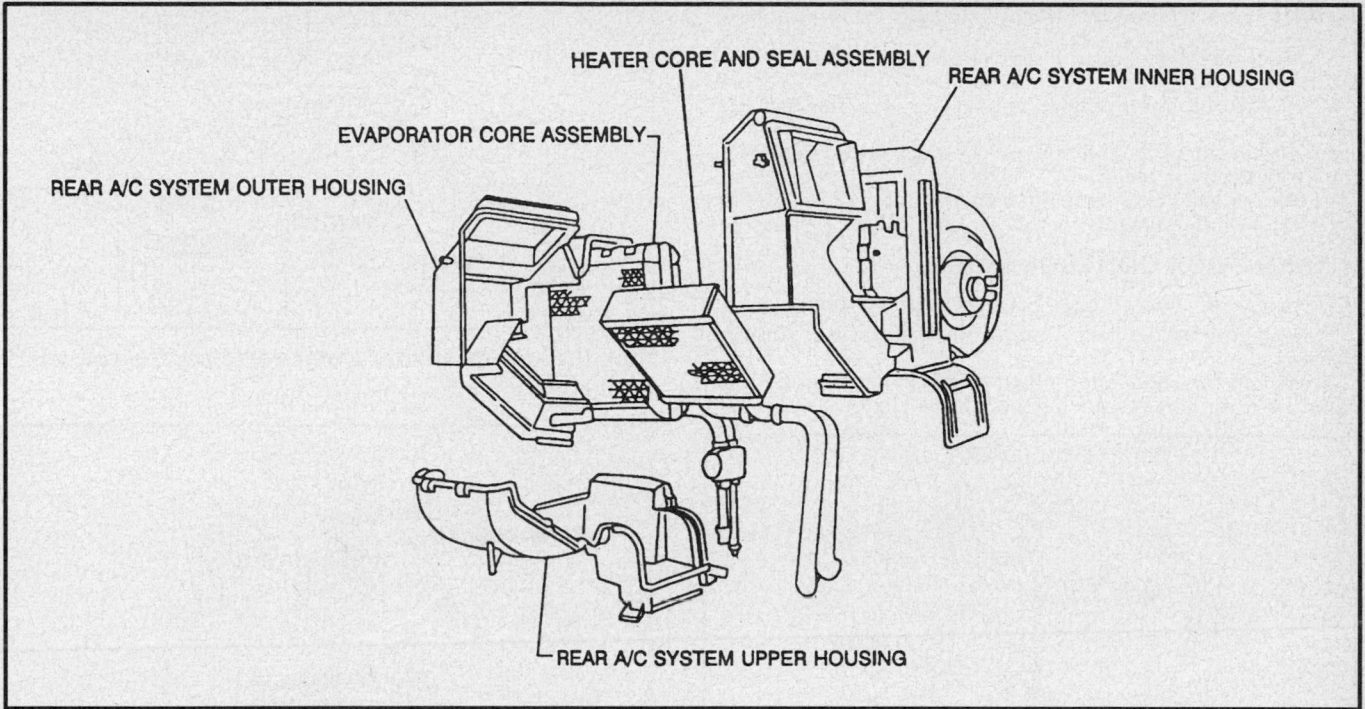

HEATER CORE AND SEAL ASSEMBLY

REAR A/C SYSTEM INNER HOUSING

EVAPORATOR CORE ASSEMBLY

REAR A/C SYSTEM OUTER HOUSING

REAR A/C SYSTEM UPPER HOUSING

Rear heater-air conditioning system components—Quest

REAR EVAPORATOR CORE AND HEATER CORE

1. Properly discharge the air conditioning system using recovery/recycling equipment.
2. Remove the driver's side rear trim panel and remove the bolts retaining the heating/air conditioning housing in place.
3. Remove the upper housing and the outer housing.
4. Remove the evaporator core and the heater core.
5. Installation is the reverse of the removal procedure. If installing a new evaporator core, add the indicated amount of new refrigerant oil as specified in "Compressor and Component Oil Servicing". Evacuate, recharge, and leak test the system.

Manual System Controls

REMOVAL AND INSTALLATION

1. Disconnect the negative battery cable. If the vehicle has a theft protected radio, obtain the owner's security code.
2. Working under the dash, disconnect the control cables on either side of the heater assembly and unclip them from the housing.
3. If necessary, remove the ashtray assembly to gain access to the screws for the center console bezel.
4. Remove the radio.
5. If all the cables are disconnected at their lower end, the control assembly should come straight out once the screws are removed. Carefully unplug the wires.
6. When disassembling the unit for repair, most of the fasteners are plastic clips which can be easily pried apart. Be careful not to break the tabs. The knobs on the front can be removed with pliers but wrap a rag around the knob to keep from scratching the finish.
7. Installation is the reverse of removal. Adjust the control cables and connect the battery to test the system.

ADJUSTMENTS

Pathfinder and Pick-Up

If the linkage has been disassembled, it should be adjusted as an assembly rather than trying to adjust only one part. First adjust the rods, then connect and adjust the cables to the linkage.

VENTILATOR DOOR CONTROL ROD

1. Viewed from the driver's side, disconnect the cable and rotate the side link fully clockwise.
2. With the upper and lower door levers pushed down, connect the lower rod first, then the upper rod.

DEFROSTER DOOR CONTROL ROD

1. Rotate the side link fully counterclockwise.
2. Push the defroster door lever towards the firewall and connect the rod.

AIR CONTROL CABLE

1. Rotate the side link fully clockwise.
2. With the control lever in the **DEFROST** position, hook the cable to the side link.
3. Take up the slack in the cable housing by pushing it gently away from the firewall and secure the housing.

WATER VALVE CONTROL ROD

1. To adjust the control rod, disconnect the temperature control cable from the air mix door lever.
2. The valve end of the rod is attached to the valve link lever with a wire loop. With the rod loose at the air mix door end, move the air mix door lever and the valve link lever all the way in the direction that would pull the rod away from the valve link lever.
3. Gently pull the rod so there is about 0.080 in. (2mm) gap between the rod and valve lever and secure the rod at the door lever.

TEMPERATURE CONTROL CABLE

1. Move the temperature control lever to the full **COLD** position.
2. Rotate the air mix door linkage towards the full **HOT** position.
3. Attach the cable and take up the slack in the cable housing away from the lever.
4. Secure the cable housing with the clip and operate the lever to check for smooth operation.

INTAKE DOOR CONTROL CABLE

1. Move the control lever to the **RECIRCULATE** position.
2. Move the intake door lever all the way towards the cable housing clip.
3. Attach the cable and pull the slack in the housing away from the lever before securing it with the clip.

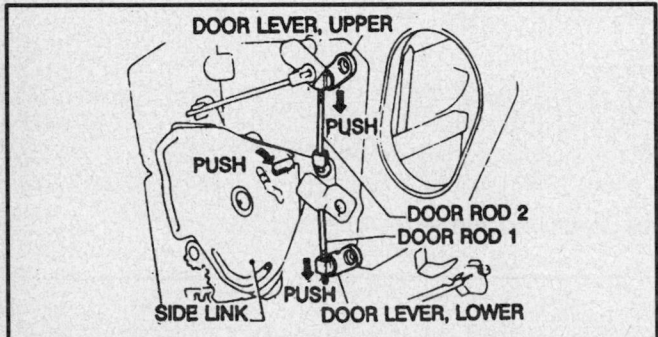

Pick-Up and Pathfinder ventilator door control rod adjustment

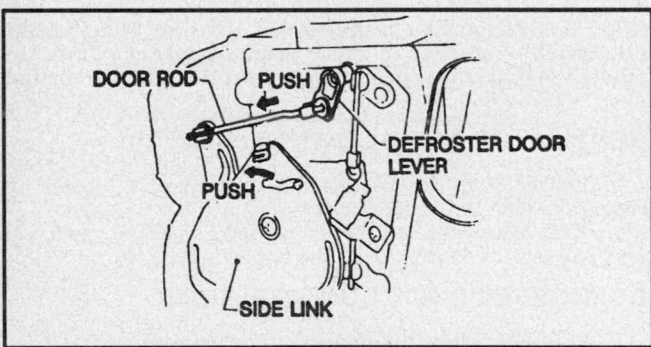

Pick-Up and Pathfinder defroster door control rod adjustment

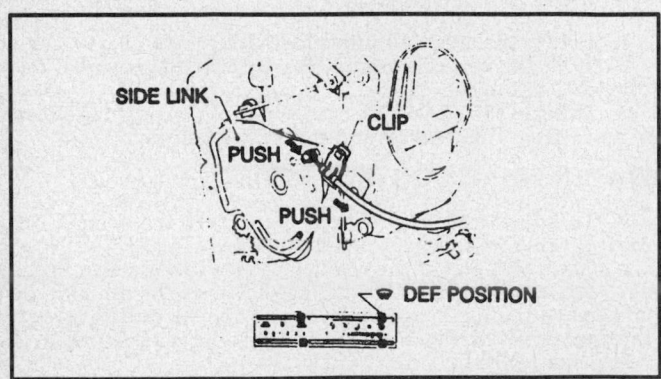

Pick-Up and Pathfinder air control cable adjustment

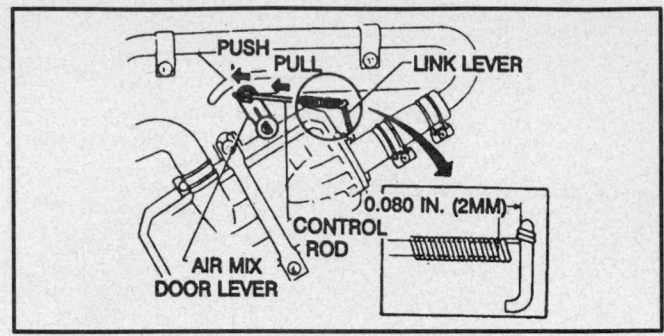

Pick-Up and Pathfinder water valve control rod adjustment

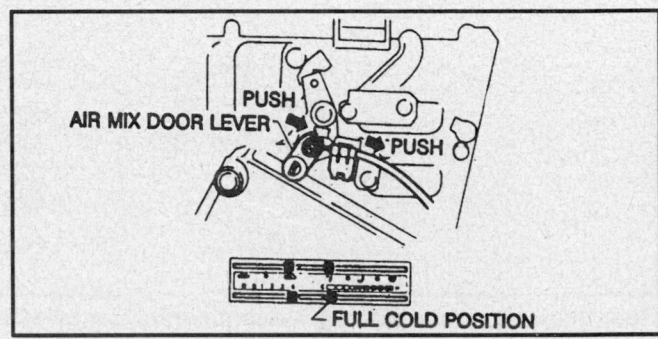

Pick-Up and Pathfinder temperature control cable adjustment

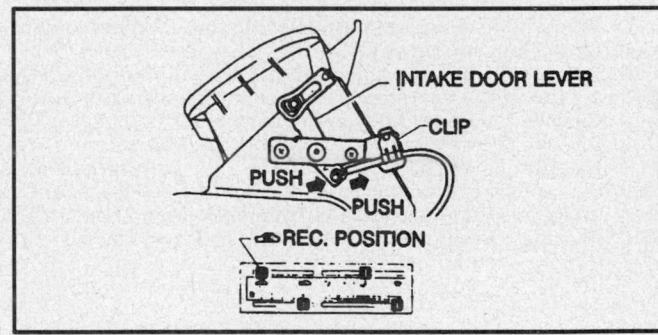

Pick-Up and Pathfinder intake door control cable adjustment

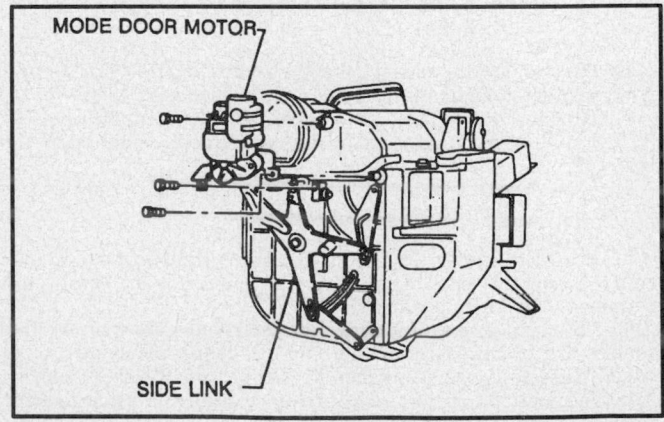

Mode door linkage adjustment—Quest

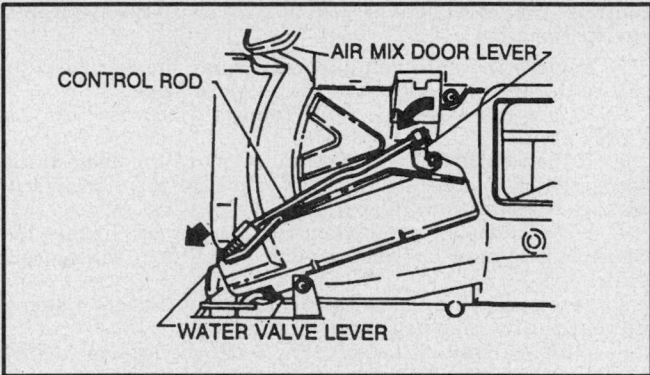

Water valve control rod adjustment—Quest

AIR CONTROL CABLE

1. Put the air control lever in the **DEFROST** position.
2. Working from the driver's side, rotate the side link fully clockwise.
3. Attach the cable to the link and pull the cable housing away from the cable end.
4. Secure the housing and operate the lever to check for smooth operation.

WATER VALVE CONTROL ROD

1. With the temperature control cable disconnected, push the air mix door lever towards the firewall.
2. With the rod loose at the air mix door end, move the valve link lever all the way towards the firewall.
3. The rod is attached to the valve with a wire loop. Gently pull the rod so there is about 0.080 in. (2mm) gap between the rod and valve lever and secure the rod at the door lever. Operate the lever by hand to check for smooth operation.

TEMPERATURE CONTROL CABLE

1. Set the control lever in the full **COLD** position.
2. With the air mix door in the full hot position, attach the cable and take up the slack in the housing away from the door lever.
3. Secure the housing and operate the lever to check for smooth operation.

INTAKE DOOR CONTROL CABLE

1. Set the control lever to the **RECIRCULATE** position.
2. Move the control link towards the cable housing clamp.
3. Attach the cable, take up the slack away from the link and secure the cable housing.

Quest

MODE DOOR

1. Move the side link by hand and hold the mode door in the **DEFROST** position.
2. If detached, install the mode door motor on the heater unit and connect it to the body harness.

3. Turn the ignition switch to **ON** and turn the DEF switch to **ON**.
4. Adjust the length and attach the mode door motor rod to the side link rod holder.
5. Turn the VENT switch to **ON**. Check that the side link operates at the fully open position. Also turn the DEF switch **ON** to check that the side link operates at the fully open position.

WATER VALVE CONTROL ROD

1. First, disconnect the temperature control rod from the air mix door lever.
2. Connect the water valve control rod to the water valve lever.
3. Push the control rod away from the air mix door lever and hold this position.
4. Move the air mix door by hand toward the maximum cold position (door lever will turn counterclockwise and the door will completely cover the heater core).
5. While holding both the rod and the door, adjust the length of the rod and connect it to the air mix door lever. Check for proper operation.
6. Adjust the temperature control rod.

TEMPERATURE CONTROL ROD

1. Install the air mix door motor on the heater unit and connect it to the main harness.
2. Turn the ignition switch to **ON**.
3. Turn the temperature control knob to maximum cold setting.
4. Move the air mix door by hand to the maximum **COLD** position (completely covering the heater core), and hold it.
5. Adjust the length of the temperature control rod and connect it to the air mix door lever. Check for proper operation.

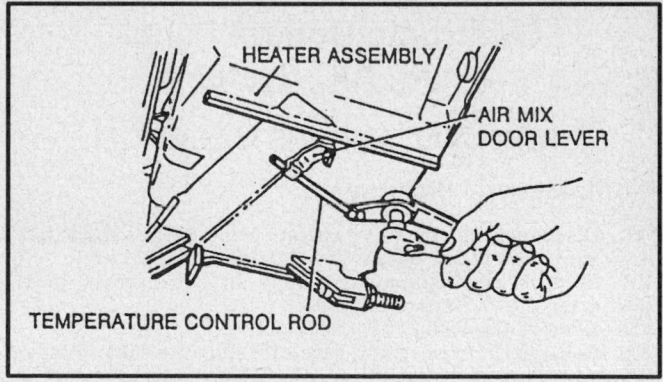

Temperature control rod adjustment—Quest

INTAKE DOOR

1. Connect the intake door motor harness connector before installing the connector on the door motor.
2. Turn the ignition to **ON** and turn the recirculate switch to **ON**.
3. Install the intake door lever and the intake door motor.
4. Set the intake door rod in the **RECIRC** position and attach the door rod to the holder.
5. Check that the intake door operates properly when the RECIRC switch in turned **ON** and **OFF**.

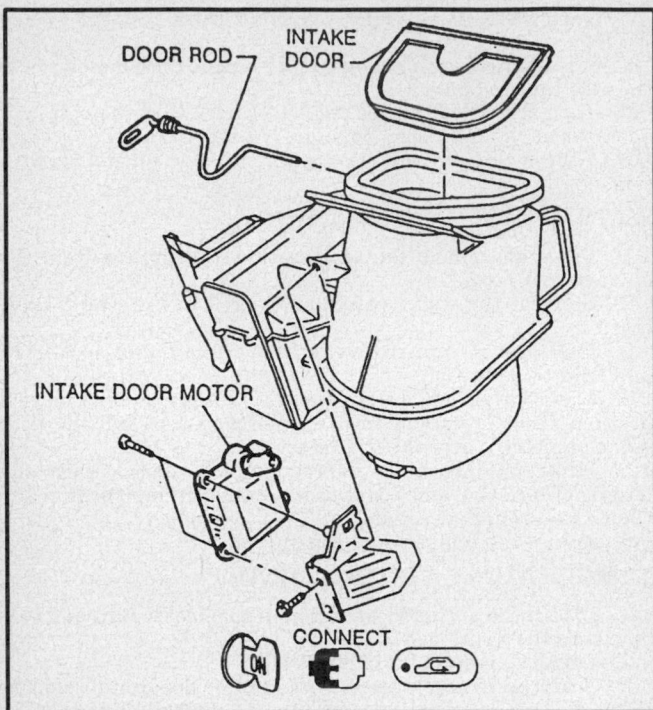

Intake air door motor—Quest

Electronic Control Panel
(Auto. A/C System)

REMOVAL AND INSTALLATION

Pathfinder and Pick-Up

1. Disconnect the negative battery cable. If the vehicle has a theft protected radio, obtain the owner's security code.
2. Remove the ashtray assembly to gain access to the screws for the center console bezel.
3. Remove the radio.
4. Remove the screws and carefully slide the control assembly straight out far enough to carefully unplug the wires.
5. When disassembling the unit for repair, most of the fasteners are plastic clips which can be easily pried apart. Be careful not to break the tabs. The knobs on the front can be removed with pliers but wrap a rag around the knob to keep from scratching the finish.
6. Installation is the reverse of the removal procedure. Reconnect the battery and test the system before installing the radio and console bezel.

ADJUSTMENTS

Pick-Up and Pathfinder

MODE DOOR MOTOR

The mode door determines the air flow through the air distribution system depending on the mode selected (vent, defrost, etc.). The door linkage is located on the left side of the housing and is controlled by a motor. The motor has a built-in position sensor and will stop at the position called for by the controls. The adjustment procedure starts with the motor linkage disconnected.

1. Remove the auto amplifier and relay bracket from the side of the heating unit, above the accelerator pedal.
2. Rotate the side link fully counter clockwise into the **VENT** position.
3. If the rods have been disconnect, move the doors to the vent position and secure the rods. Operate the side link by hand to check for smooth operation.
4. With the motor installed on the housing but linkage disconnected, connect the motor wiring and turn the ignition switch **ON**.
5. Set the controls to the **VENT** mode, let the motor stop at its vent position and attach the linkage.
6. With the ignition switch **ON**, cycle the system to **DEF** and check the operation of the linkage.

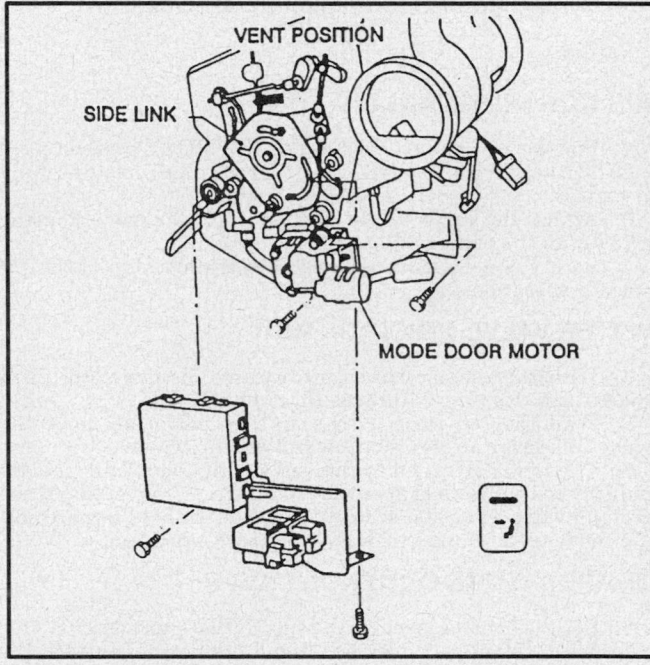

Pick-Up and Pathfinder mode door motor adjustment (with auto. A/C)

AIR MIX DOOR MOTOR

1. With the motor installed but the rod disconnected, connect the wiring.
2. Near the hood latch in the front of the vehicle, disconnect the ambient temperature sensor and jumper the terminals together.
3. Set the temperature control lever to the full **COLD** position and turn the ignition switch **ON**.
4. The motor will stop at the full **COLD** position. Move the linkage to that position by hand and secure the rod.
5. Move the temperature control lever to full **HOT** position and check the linkage for smooth operation. Remember to reconnect the temperature sensor.

AIR INTAKE DOOR

1. With the door motor removed but wiring connected, turn the ignition switch to **ACC** and make sure the recirculate button is **OFF**.
2. Hold the door in the fresh air position and install the motor.
3. Switch the recirculate button **ON** and **OFF** to check for smooth operation of the door.

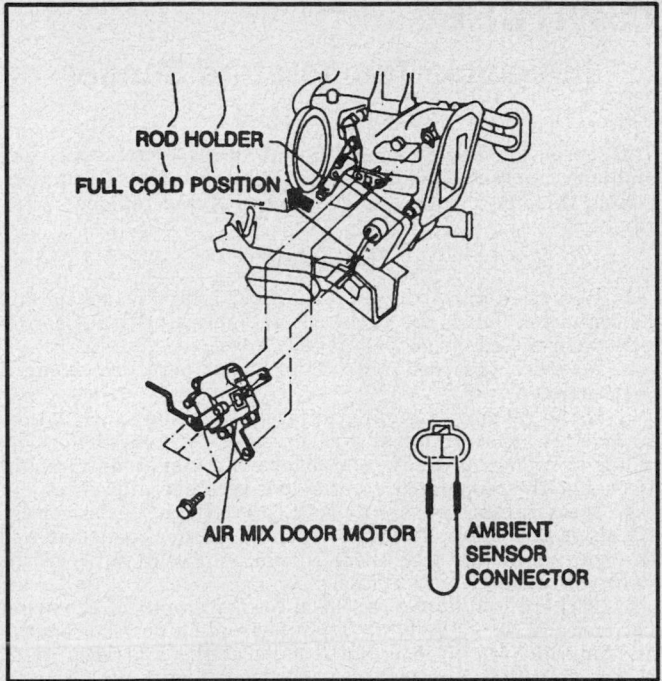

Pick-Up and Pathfinder air mix door motor adjustment (with auto. A/C)

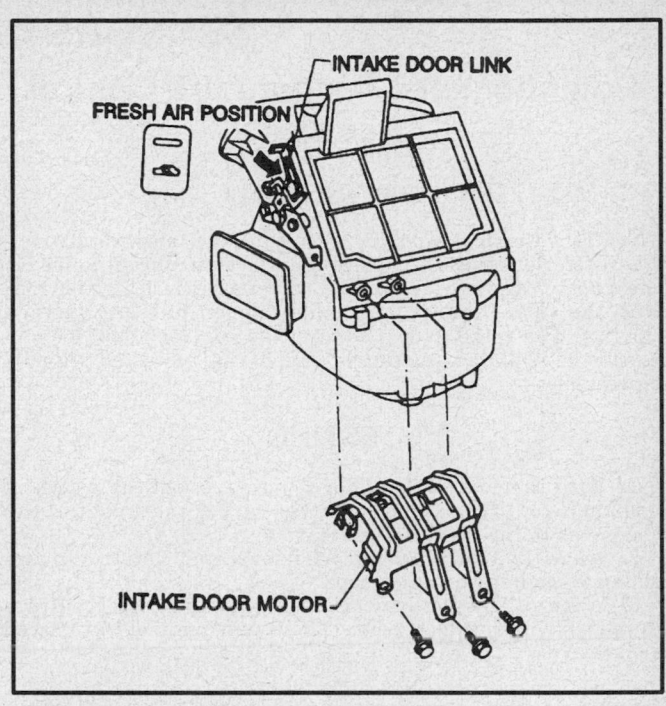

Pick-Up and Pathfinder air intake door motor adjustment (with auto. A/C)

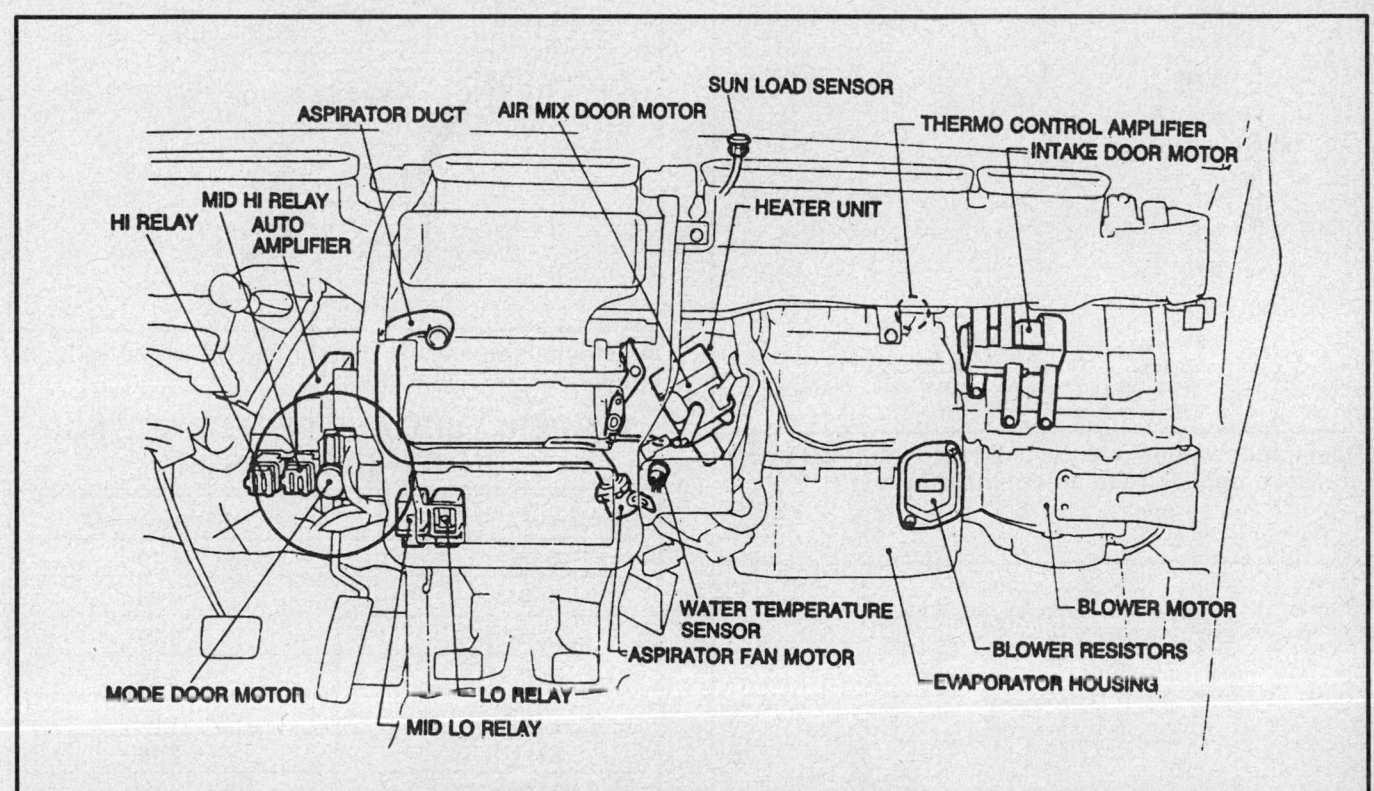

Pick-Up and Pathfinder automatic air conditioning system components

SENSORS AND SWITCHES

Potentiometer Temperature Control Resistor

OPERATION

The PTC resistor is adjusted by moving the temperature control lever. Selecting a temperature selects an output value for the resistor that the amplifier will mathematically balance with the values from all the other temperature and position sensors. The resistor is built into the control amplifier and cannot be replaced separately, but it can be tested with an ohmmeter.

TESTING

1. With the control amplifier removed, touch the probes of an ohmmeter to the connector on the back of the amplifier. Set the meter to the 1000 ohm scale.
2. Move the temperature control lever and compare the resistance reading with the graph.
3. Some slight error may exist but a faulty resistor will produce an obviously bad reading. The resistor cannot be replaced separately.

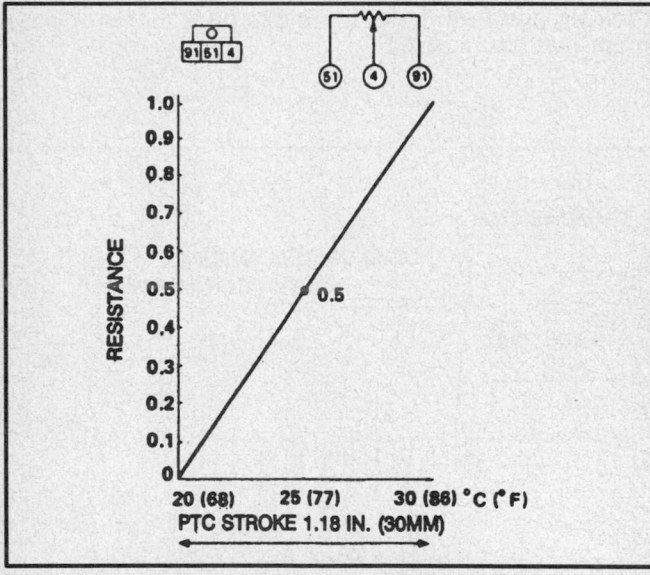

Resistance values over lever position for PTC in the control amplifier, read at terminals 91 and 4

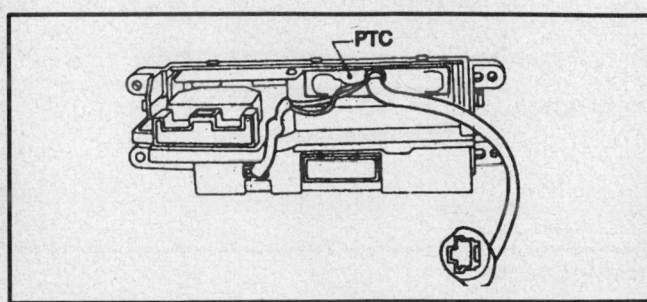

The PTC has its own wiring harness

In-Vehicle Temperature Sensor

OPERATION

The sensor converts temperature into a resistance which the amplifier can read. It is in the left side of the control amplifier, behind the small grille and can be tested and replaced separately.

TESTING

1. With the control amplifier removed, locate the sensor and its connector. Touch the probes of an ohmmeter to the terminals, with the meter on the 10,000 ohm scale.
2. Measure the resistance and the temperature, using a thermometer.
3. If the reading is greatly different from the specification, remove the sensor and test it at other temperatures before deciding to replace it. Use a cold drink container or a drop light to change the temperature but do not immerse the sensor.
4. If the sensor appears to work correctly, check the voltage supply to the sensor. With the control amplifier connected and the ignition switch **ON**, there should be 5 volts between the **yellow/blue** wire and ground.
5. If there is no voltage, check for continuity of the wires between the sensor and auto amplifier and for power output at the amplifier. If there is not 5 volts at the amplifier itself, chances are that other sensors are also not working.

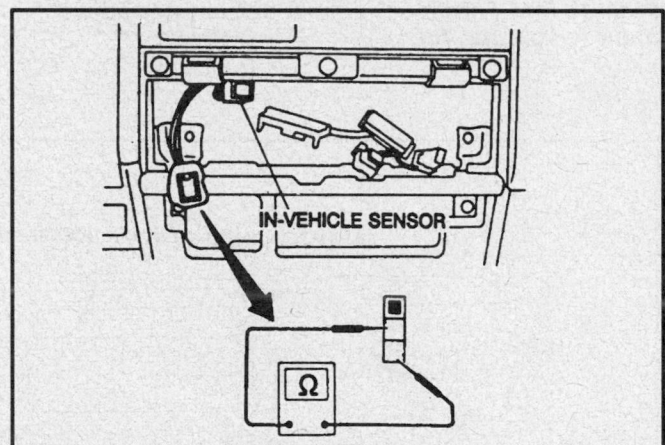

In-vehicle temperature sensor can be tested with an ohmmeter and a thermometer

TEMPERATURE AND RESISTANCE FOR IN-VEHICLE SENSOR

Temperature °C (°F)	Resistance kΩ
0 (32)	6.19
5 (41)	4.95
10 (50)	3.99
15 (59)	3.24
20 (68)	2.65
25 (77)	2.19
30 (86)	1.81
35 (95)	1.51
40 (104)	1.27

Aspirator Motor

OPERATION

There is a small fan mounted in front of the heater unit which runs whenever the ignition is ON. This fan draws inside air past the in-vehicle temperature sensor through a duct leading up to the sensor. It can be replaced separately but it may be necessary to remove the radio to gain access.

TESTING

1. Before removing or disconnecting anything, turn the ignition switch **ON** and hold a lighted cigarette or other source of smoke up to the small grille in front of the in-vehicle sensor. The smoke should be drawn into the grille. If not, turn the air conditioner system **ON** and set it for automatic operation.

2. If the smoke does not flow into the sensor grille, locate the connector for the motor under the right side of the center console. Un-plug the connector and check for voltage.

3. If there is voltage to the motor, remove it for bench testing or replacement. If there is no voltage, use the wiring diagram to trace the fault.

Ambient Air Sensor

OPERATION

This sensor converts temperature into an electrical resistance which the auto amplifier can read. It operates in a much different range than the in-vehicle sensor and they are not interchangeable. The sensor and connecter are mounted under the hood, near the secondary latch.

TESTING

1. Disconnect the sensor and connect an ohmmeter set on the 10,000 ohm scale.

2. Measure the resistance and the temperature, using a thermometer.

3. If the reading is greatly different from the specification, test the sensor at other temperatures before deciding to replace it. Use a cold drink container or a drop light to change the temperature but do not immerse the sensor.

4. If the sensor appears to work correctly, check the voltage supply to the sensor. With the control amplifier connected and the ignition switch **ON**, there should be 5 volts between the **yellow** wire and ground.

5. If there is no voltage, check for continuity of the wires between the sensor and auto amplifier and for power output at the amplifier. If there is not 5 volts at the amplifier itself, chances are that other sensors are also not working.

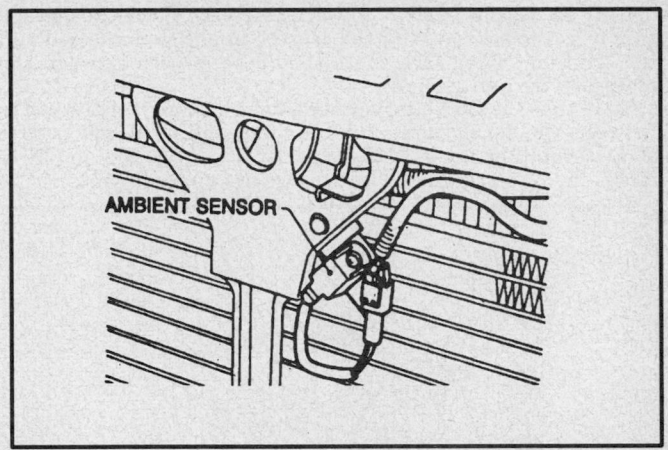

Ambient sensor under the hood is a different range than the In-vehicle sensor

TEMPERATURE AND RESISTANCE FOR AMBIENT SENSOR

Temperature °C (°F)	Resistance kΩ
−20 (−4)	9.93
−10 (14)	5.57
0 (32)	3.26
10 (50)	1.98
20 (68)	1.25
25 (77)	1.00
30 (86)	0.81
40 (104)	0.54

Sun Load Sensor

OPERATION

The sensor is a diode which converts light to a current that is fed to the auto amplifier. There the current is processed for use by the control amplifier. The sun load sensor is mounted in the defroster outlet vent, held by plastic spring clips on the sensor body.

TESTING

1. Above the accelerator pedal, un-plug the auto amplifier connectors.

2. Measure the voltage between terminal **6** of the large connector and terminal **5** of the smaller connector or between terminal **6** and ground.

3. Changing the light that strikes the sun load sensor should change the voltage and the current it puts out. A very bright light is required to see a change in output.

4. If the sensor appears to work correctly, check the voltage supply to the sensor. With the control amplifier connected and the ignition switch **ON**, there should be 5 volts between the **orange** wire and ground.

5. If there is no voltage, check for continuity of the wires between the sensor and auto amplifier, and for power output at the amplifier itself. If there is not 5 volts at the amplifier itself, chances are that other sensors are also not working.

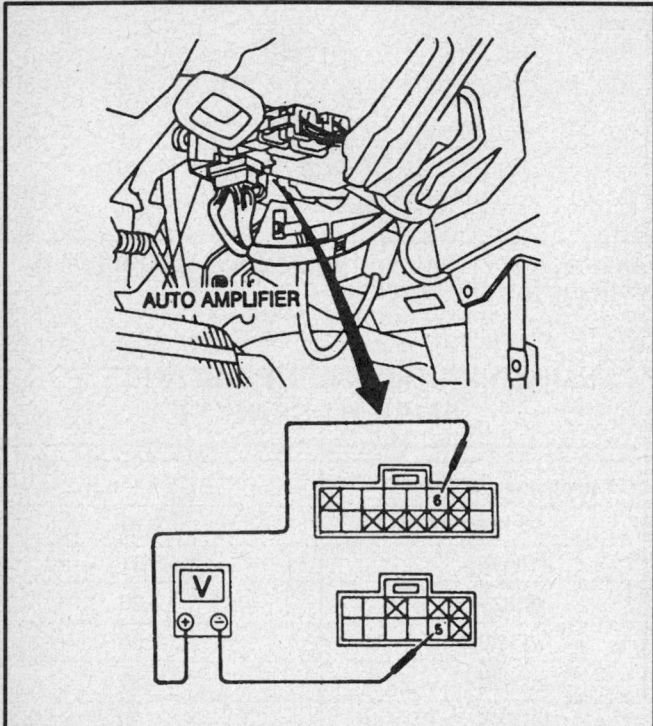

Measure the voltage at the auto amplifier connectors to test the sun load sensor, compare the readings to the chart

CURRENT AND VOLTAGE OUTPUT FOR SUNLOAD SENSOR

Input current mA	Output voltage V
0	5.00
0.1	4.09
0.2	3.18
0.3	2.27
0.4	1.36
0.5	0.45

Water Temperature Sensor

OPERATION

The sensor is mounted to the right side of the heater core and converts engine coolant temperature into an electrical resistance which the auto amplifier can read. It is dedicated to this system and not connected to any other system. This sensor op-

erates through the micro-switch and is out of the control loop when the system is in **VENT** or **DEF** modes.

TESTING

1. Disconnect the sensor and connect an ohmmeter set on the 10,000 ohm scale.

2. Measure the resistance and the temperature, using a thermometer.

3. If the reading is greatly different from the specification, remove the sensor and test it at other temperatures before deciding to replace it. Use a cold drink container or a drop light to change the temperature but do not immerse the sensor.

4. If the sensor appears to work correctly, check the voltage supply to the sensor. With the control amplifier connected and the ignition switch **ON**, there should be 5 volts between the **yellow/red** wire and ground.

5. If there is no voltage, check for continuity of the wires between the sensor, the micro switch and the auto amplifier and for power output from the amplifier. If there is not 5 volts at the amplifier itself, chances are that other sensors are also not working.

The water temperature sensor is on the right side of the heater core

TEMPERATURE RESISTANCE FOR WATER TEMPERATURE SENSOR

Temperature °C (°F)	Resistance kΩ
0 (32)	3.99
10 (50)	2.54
20 (68)	1.67
30 (86)	1.12
40 (104)	0.78
50 (122)	0.55
60 (140)	0.40
70 (158)	0.29
80 (176)	0.22

Micro-Switch

OPERATION

The switch is on the left side of the heater and is activated by the side link. When the controls are set for **VENT** or **DEF**, the micro switch shorts the water temperature sensor circuit and the full 5 volts is returned to the auto amplifier. With the water temperature sensor out of the control loop, temperature control is manual even with the fan switch in the **AUTO** position.

TESTING

1. Turn the ignition switch **ON** and put the system controls in **VENT** mode.

2. Disconnect the micro-switch and check for continuity between terminals **10** and **93**. Make sure there is no continuity between terminals **10** and **52** or between **52** and **93**.

3. Put the system controls in **FOOT** mode and check for continuity between terminals **10** and **52**. Make sure there is no continuity between **10** and **93**.

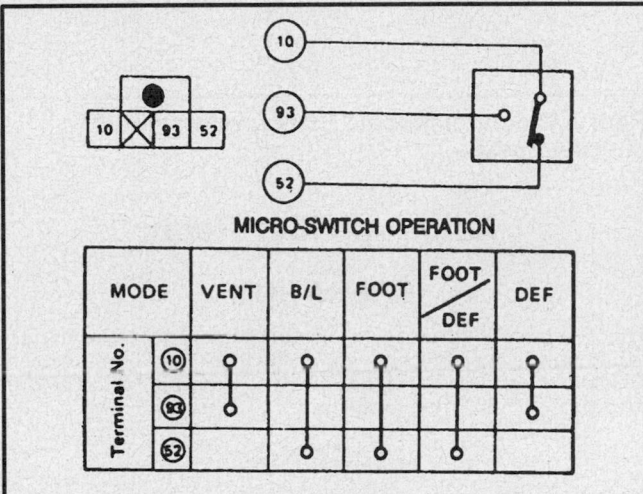

Micro-switch testing schematic

Dual Pressure Switch

OPERATION

The switch is mounted in the top of the receiver/drier. Its function is to turn the compressor clutch off if the refrigerant pressure in the high side is too high or too low. It can only be properly tested when gauges are connected to the service valves. Replacing the switch requires discharging the refrigerant from the system into recovery equipment.

TESTING

1. When pressure is decreasing, the switch should open (compressor off) when high side pressure is 26–31 psi. or close (compressor on) when pressure gets down to 270–327 psi.

2. When pressure is increasing, the switch should close (compressor on) when high side pressure is 26–34 psi or open (compressor off) when pressure is 356–412 psi.

3. If all other tests indicate a faulty dual pressure switch, disconnect the wiring and jumper the terminals to simulate a closed switch. If the compressor clutch operates, make sure the refrigerant pressures are correct before replacing the switch.

Low Pressure Switch

TESTING

Quest

1. With a manifold gauge set attached to the system, and using an ohmmeter at the low pressure switch terminals, check for continuity.

2. When low side pressure decreases to 24 psi, the low pressure switch should turn OFF and no continuity should exist.

3. When low side pressure increases to or above 47 psi, the switch should open and continuity should exist.

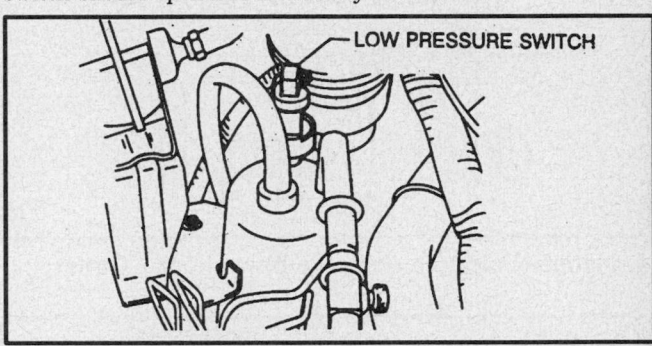

Low pressure switch location for testing—Quest

High Pressure Switch

TESTING

Quest

1. With a manifold gauge set attached to the system, and using an ohmmeter at the low pressure switch terminals, check for continuity.

2. When high side pressure increases to 404 psi, the switch should turn **OFF** and no continuity should exist.

3. When high side pressure decreases to 250 psi or lower, the switch should turn **ON** and continuity should exist.

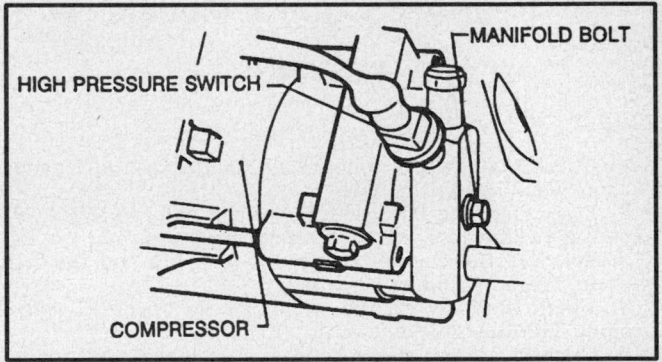

High pressure switch location for testing—Quest

Front A/C Control Module

TESTING

Quest

1. Check the power supply circuit for the A/C control module with the ignition **ON**.

2. Disconnect the A/C control module harness connector, and connect a voltmeter from the harness side connectors.

3. Measure voltage from ground to terminal **1**. There should be 12 volts.

4. Measure voltage from ground to terminal **28**. There should be 12 volts.

5. Turn the ignition **OFF** to check the body ground circuit.

6. Attach an ohmmeter on the harness side of the connector between terminal **8** and ground and between terminal **38** and ground. In both cases, there should be continuity.

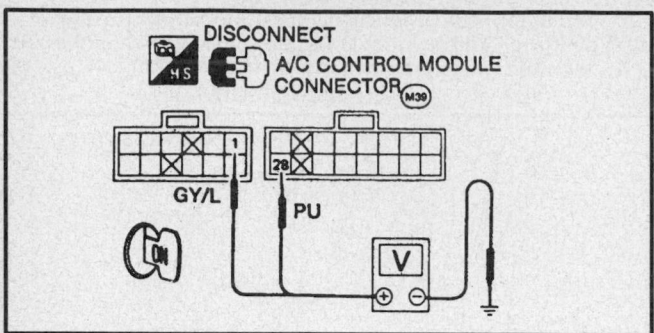

A/C control module power supply check—Quest

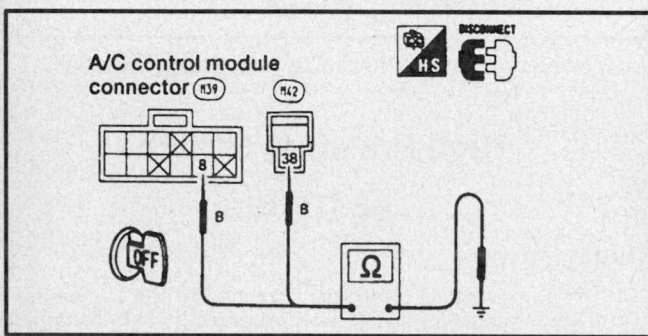

A/C control module body ground circuit check—Quest

Rear A/C Control Module

TESTING

Quest

1. Check the power supply circuit for the rear A/C control module with the ignition **ON**.
2. Disconnect the rear module harness and connect a voltmeter at the harness side of the connector.
3. Measure the voltage between terminal **1** and the body ground. There should be 12 volts.
4. Check the body ground circuit for the rear A/C control module with the ignition switch **OFF**.
5. Connect an ohmmeter between terminal **4** and ground. There should be continuity.

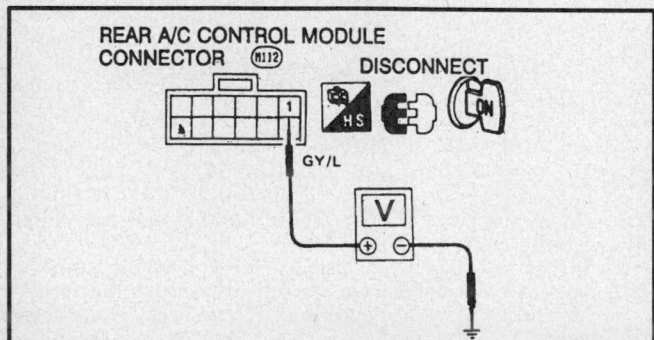

Rear A/C control module power supply check—Quest

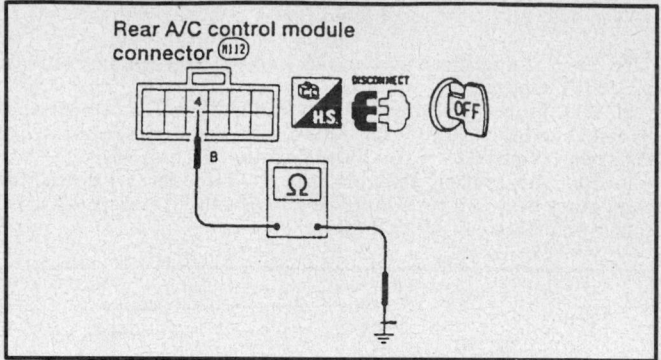

Rear A/C control module body ground circuit check—Quest

Auto Amplifier Relay

OPERATION

The relay is mounted to the inner fender near the battery. When the blower fan and air conditioner are both switched **ON**, the relay closes to signal the auto amplifier that the compressor clutch has been activated.

TESTING

1. Turn the ignition switch, the air conditioner and the blower fan **ON**.
2. Un-plug the relay connector and check for 12 volts between 2 of the terminals and ground.
3. If voltage is reaching the connector, plug the connector in and listen or feel for the relay activating.
4. If the relay does activate but no voltage passes through to the other terminals, the relay contacts are faulty and the relay must be replaced.

Compressor and Fan Relays

OPERATION

On the right inner fender near the firewall, there are 2 relays. The front one is for the blower fan, the rear is for the compressor clutch. When the main blower fan relay is activated by turning the fan switch **ON**, power is supplied to one of the other 4 relays inside the vehicle, depending on the position of the switch. The high and middle high speed relays are near the auto amplifier. The middle low and low speed relays are behind the radio. Each relay is activated by the fan switch and completes a circuit to the fan resistor mounted on the front of the evaporator housing. The compressor relay is activated by the engine computer through the dual pressure switch and the thermo control amplifier.

1. Turn the ignition switch, the air conditioner and the blower fan **ON**.
2. Un-plug the relay connector and check for 12 volts between 2 of the terminals and ground.
3. If voltage is reaching the connector, plug the connector in and listen or feel for the relay activating. If no voltage is reaching the connector, make sure the fan switch is in the correct position for the relay being tested.
4. If the relay does activate but no voltage passes through to the other terminals, the relay contacts are faulty and the relay must be replaced.

Type	Outer view	Circuit	Connector symbol and connection	Case color
1T				BLACK
1M				BLUE
2M				BROWN
1M·1B				GRAY

System relay color and terminal identification for testing

Air Mix Door Position Sensor

OPERATION

The sensor is a Potentiometer Balance Resistor (PBR) built into the air mix door motor. A voltage is supplied to terminal No. 2 on the motor and a variable resistor returns a portion of the voltage to the amplifier from terminals 3 and 5. The amplifier interprets the return voltage as a door position.

TESTING

1. With all wiring connected and the air mix door in the full cold position, there should be 5 volts between terminal **2** and ground. There should be 12 volts between terminal **12** and ground. If not, check the wiring and power supplies from the auto amplifier.

2. With the air mix door in full cold position, there should be 0 volts between terminals **3** and **5** at the door motor connector.

3. Move the temperature control lever to a warmer position and see that the voltage between terminals **3** and **5** increases to 5 volts as the door position reaches full **HOT**.

4. A faulty resistor unit cannot be repaired, the door motor must be replaced.

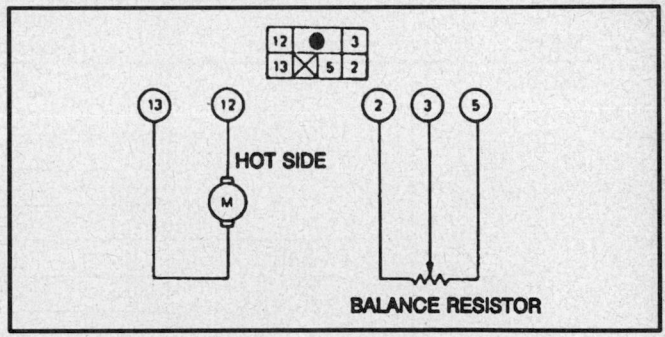

Power balance resistor and motor connections for testing air mix door position sensor

Thermo Control Amplifier

OPERATION

This amplifier is mounted on top of the evaporator housing on the blower motor side. Its function is to prevent ice build-up on the evaporator by turning the compressor relay off when the housing air temperature is near freezing. It can be considered a temperature controlled solid state relay, normally closed.

TESTING

1. With the ignition switch and air conditioner **OFF**, unplug the connector at the dual pressure switch on the receiver/drier. Check for continuity of the **green/orange** wire between the dual pressure switch and the thermo amplifier.

2. Reconnect the dual pressure switch, turn the air conditioner and ignition **ON** and, at the thermo amplifier connector, check for 8–9 volts between the **green/orange** wire and ground. With the ignition **OFF**, check for continuity between the **green/blue** wire and ground.

3. If these tests show correct results, the thermo amplifier will allow the compressor to run. If ice builds up in the evaporator housing, the thermo amplifier will not turn the compressor off as required. This amplifier cannot be repaired.

Auto Amplifier

OPERATION

The auto amplifier supplies power to all the sensors, reads the return signal and the temperature control lever position and operates the blower fan relays and air mix door motor. The amplifier also sends a signal to the engine control computer when compressor operation is required. The engine computer turns on the air conditioner relay and the Auxiliary Air Control (AAC) valve to increase idle speed. The auto amplifier program includes the ability to average the input from the sun load sensor, so sudden changes like driving in and out of shady areas will not cause sudden oscillations in air conditioner output. If the system is in **AUTO** mode when the engine is started in cold weather, the auto amplifier will run the blower fan at low speed until the heater core temperature is at least 120°F (50°C).

TESTING

1. First check the fuses. With the ignition switch **ON**, make sure power is available to the auto amplifier at terminal No. 1 on the smaller connector. Terminal No. **17** on the same connector is the amplifier ground. Also check for power going to the control unit at terminal No. **34** and a good ground at terminal No. **37**.

2. Check that each temperature sensor is getting a steady 5 volts from the amplifier and that each sensor is returning a steady voltage. If supply voltage is not steady, the amplifier is faulty. The return voltage should be less than supply and should also be steady.

3. If the system can be operated in manual mode but not automatic and the voltages to and from the amplifier are correct, this does not necessarily mean the amplifier is faulty. Be sure all other components of the system are correct before replacing the auto amplifier.

SYSTEM DIAGNOSIS

SYSTEM PERFORMANCE TESTING

1. Vehicle must be in a well ventilated area where the engine can be safely run at 1500 rpm, preferably not in direct sunlight. Open the hood to help engine cooling.

2. With windows open, operate the system on **MAXIMUM A/C** (recirc), blower fan on **HIGH** speed, air coming from the **FACE** vents.

3. Operate the system for more than 10 minutes, then use a thermometer to measure the air outlet temperature at the center dash vent.

4. Use the Temperature/Pressure chart for system performance check. The chart is for a relative humidity of 50–70 percent. The compressor discharge and suction pressures will increase with higher outside air temperature and humidity.

TEMPERATURE/PRESSURE CHART

Vehicle	Engine	Outside Temperature	High Side Pressure (psi)	Low Side Pressure (psi)
Pick-Up	2.4L	68	137–168	17–24
		77	162–196	20–28
		86	188–228	23–33
		95	213–260	27–37
		104	236–290	31–41
	3.0L	68	145–173	13–20
		77	176–210	17–26
		86	205–247	23–31
		95	235–284	27–37
		104	264–321	33–43

TEMPERATURE/PRESSURE CHART, Cont'd

Vehicle	Engine	Outside Temperature	High Side Pressure (psi)	Low Side Pressure (psi)
Pathfinder	2.4L	68	137–168	17–24
		77	162–196	20–28
		86	188–228	23–33
		95	213–260	27–37
		104	236–290	31–41
	3.0L	68	145–173	13–20
		77	176–210	17–26
		86	205–247	23–31
		95	235–284	27–37
		104	264–321	33–43
Quest	3.0L	68	100–195	22–46
		77	119–220	22–46
		86	145–245	22–46
		95	161–280	22–46
		104	215–340	22–46

COMPONENT LAYOUTS

The following figures provide component layouts for all the main components, switches, sensors and relays on Nissan Truck model. Use these location illustrations, accompanied by the wiring schematics, for service and diagnostic help.

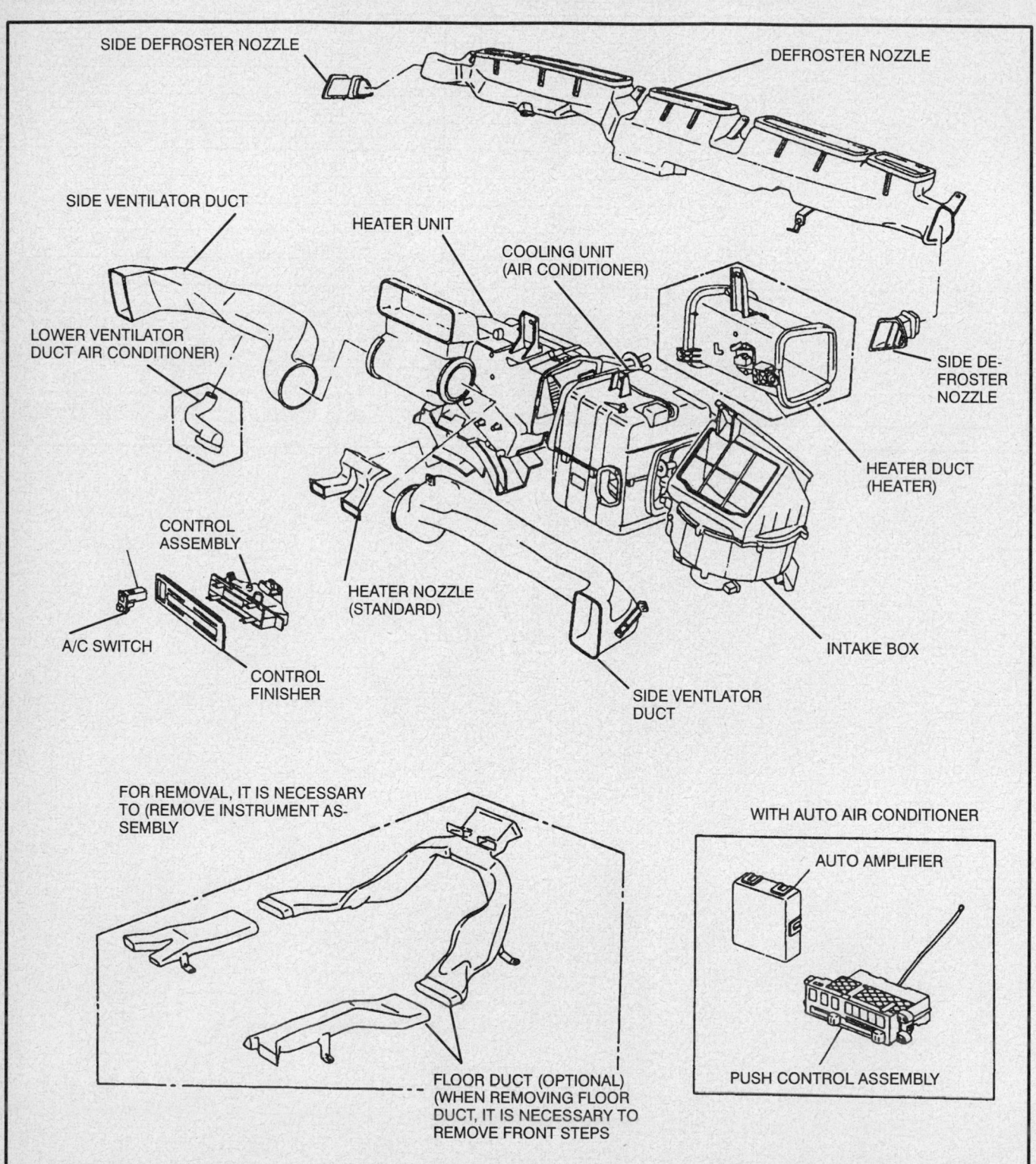

SIDE DEFROSTER NOZZLE

DEFROSTER NOZZLE

SIDE VENTILATOR DUCT

HEATER UNIT

COOLING UNIT (AIR CONDITIONER)

SIDE DE-FROSTER NOZZLE

LOWER VENTILATOR DUCT AIR CONDITIONER)

HEATER DUCT (HEATER)

CONTROL ASSEMBLY

A/C SWITCH

CONTROL FINISHER

HEATER NOZZLE (STANDARD)

SIDE VENTLATOR DUCT

INTAKE BOX

FOR REMOVAL, IT IS NECESSARY TO (REMOVE INSTRUMENT ASSEMBLY

WITH AUTO AIR CONDITIONER

AUTO AMPLIFIER

FLOOR DUCT (OPTIONAL) (WHEN REMOVING FLOOR DUCT, IT IS NECESSARY TO REMOVE FRONT STEPS

PUSH CONTROL ASSEMBLY

Component layout—Pathfinder

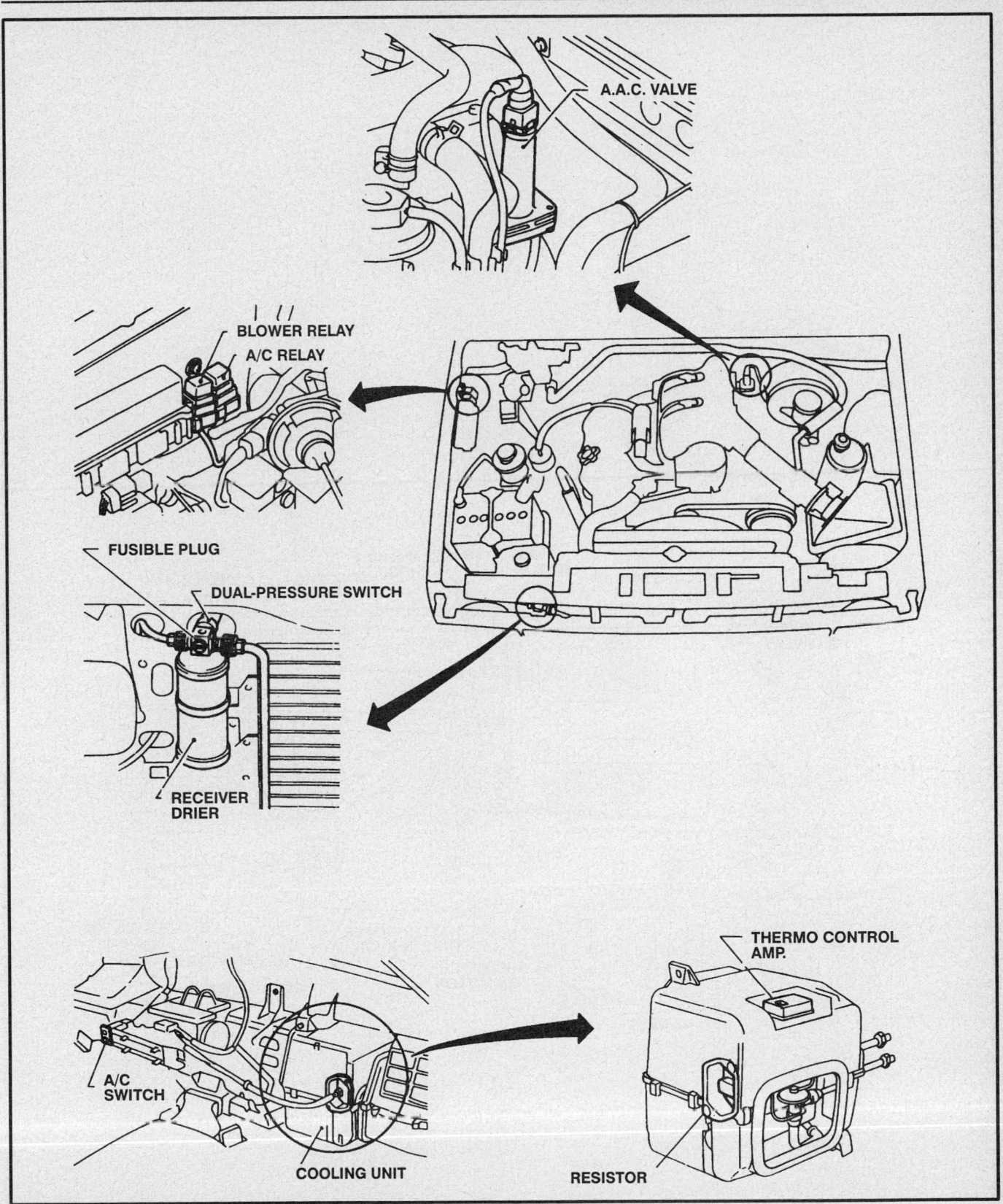

A.A.C. VALVE

BLOWER RELAY
A/C RELAY

FUSIBLE PLUG

DUAL-PRESSURE SWITCH

RECEIVER DRIER

THERMO CONTROL AMP.

A/C SWITCH

COOLING UNIT

RESISTOR

Manual air conditioning system component layout—Pathfinder and Pick-Up

PASSENGER COMPARTMENT

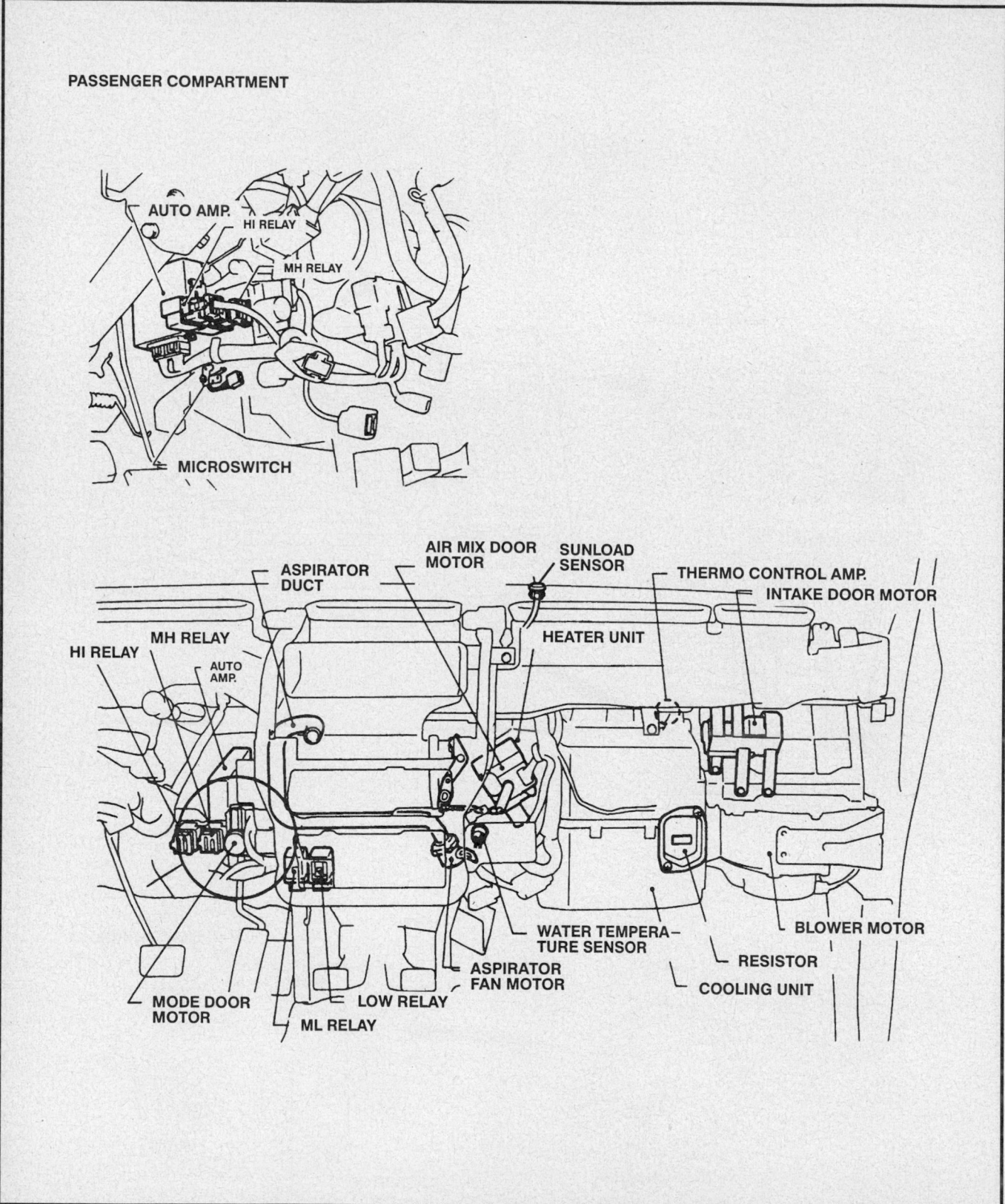

Automatic air conditioning system passenger compartment component layout—Pathfinder and Pick-Up

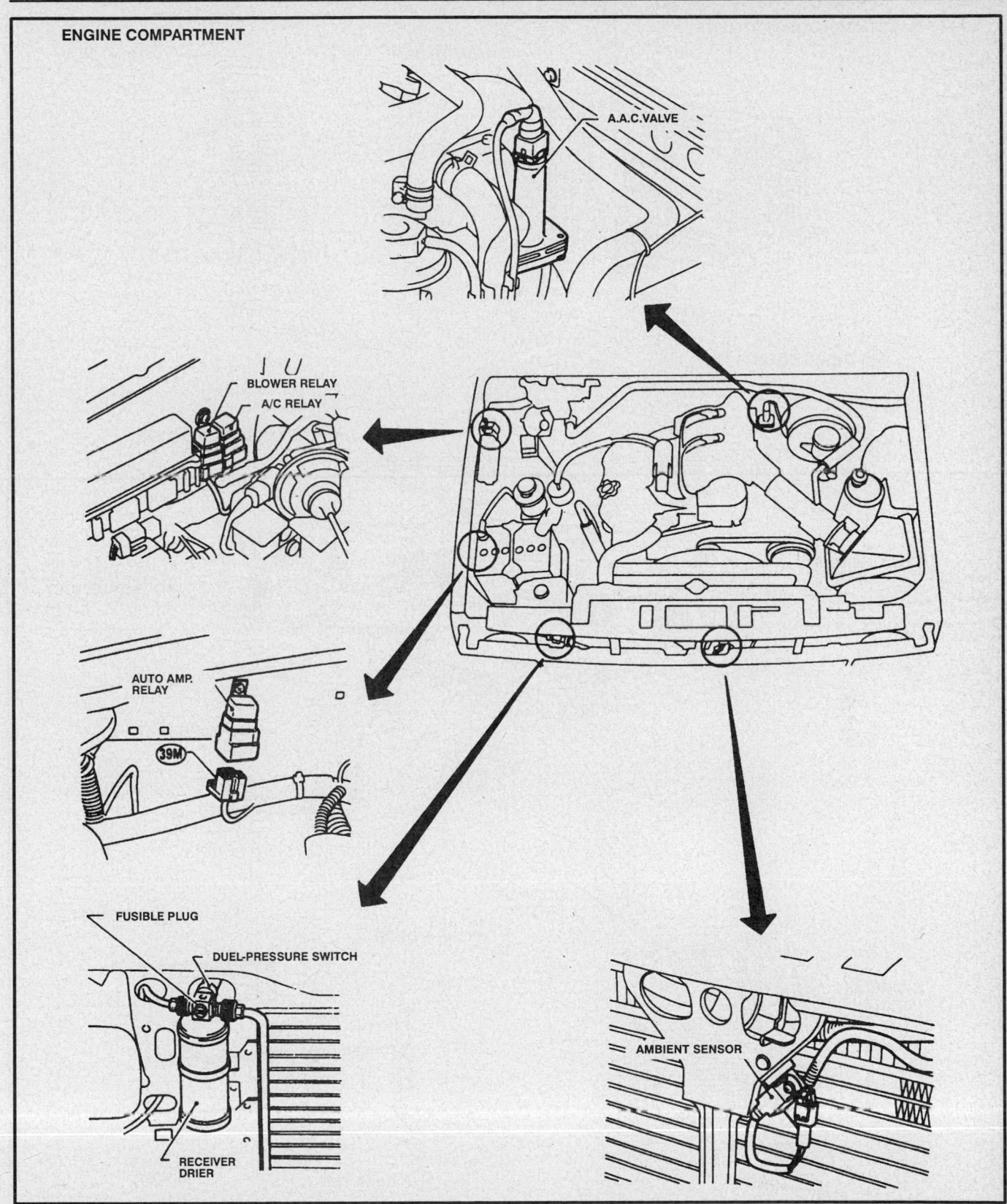

ENGINE COMPARTMENT

A.A.C.VALVE

BLOWER RELAY
A/C RELAY

AUTO AMP.
RELAY

39M

FUSIBLE PLUG

DUEL-PRESSURE SWITCH

RECEIVER
DRIER

AMBIENT SENSOR

Automatic air conditioning system engine compartment component layout—Pathfinder and Pick-Up

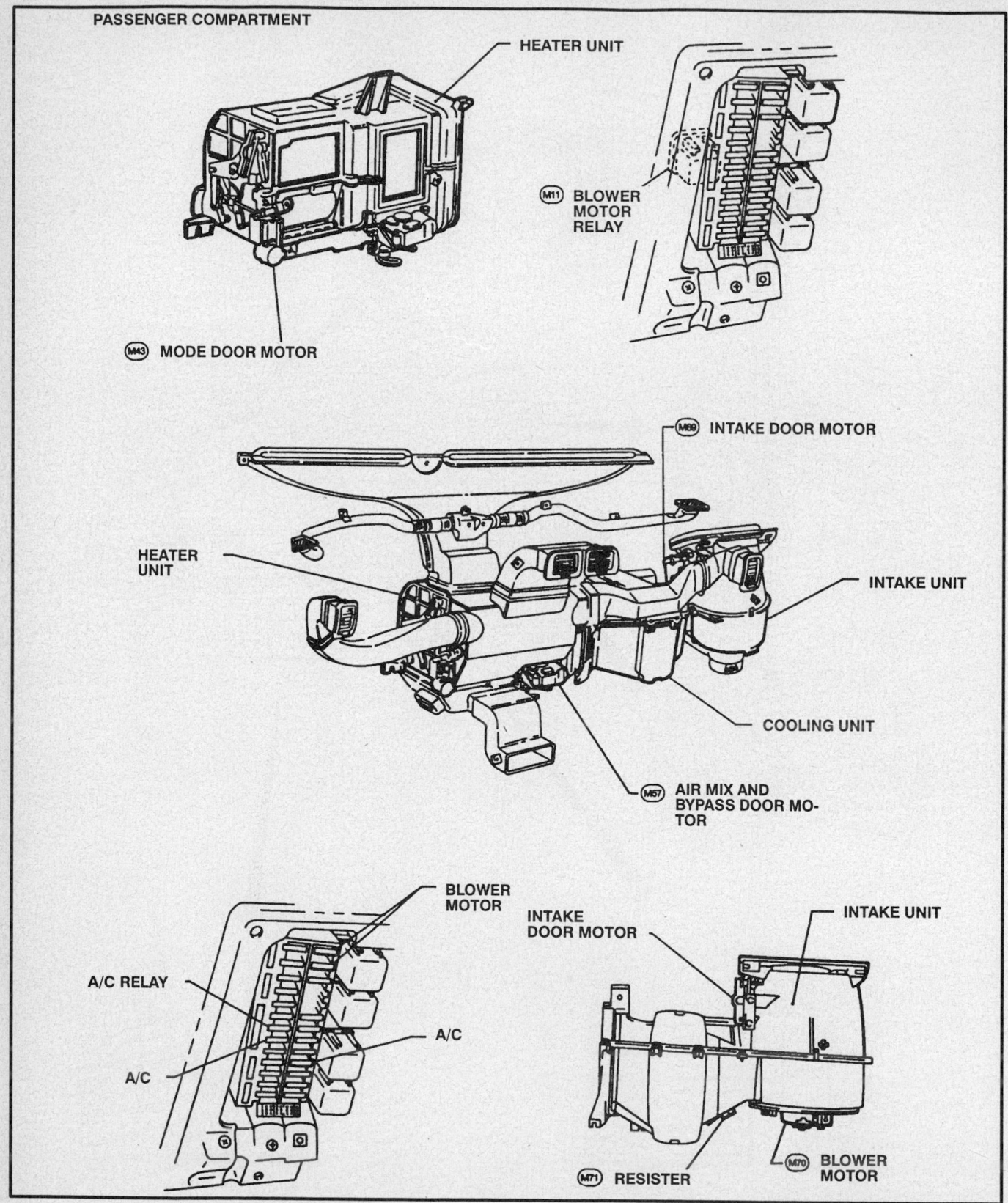

PASSENGER COMPARTMENT

HEATER UNIT

M11 BLOWER MOTOR RELAY

M43 MODE DOOR MOTOR

M69 INTAKE DOOR MOTOR

HEATER UNIT

INTAKE UNIT

COOLING UNIT

M57 AIR MIX AND BYPASS DOOR MOTOR

BLOWER MOTOR

A/C RELAY

A/C

A/C

INTAKE DOOR MOTOR

INTAKE UNIT

M71 RESISTER

M70 BLOWER MOTOR

Air conditioning system passenger compartment component layout—Quest

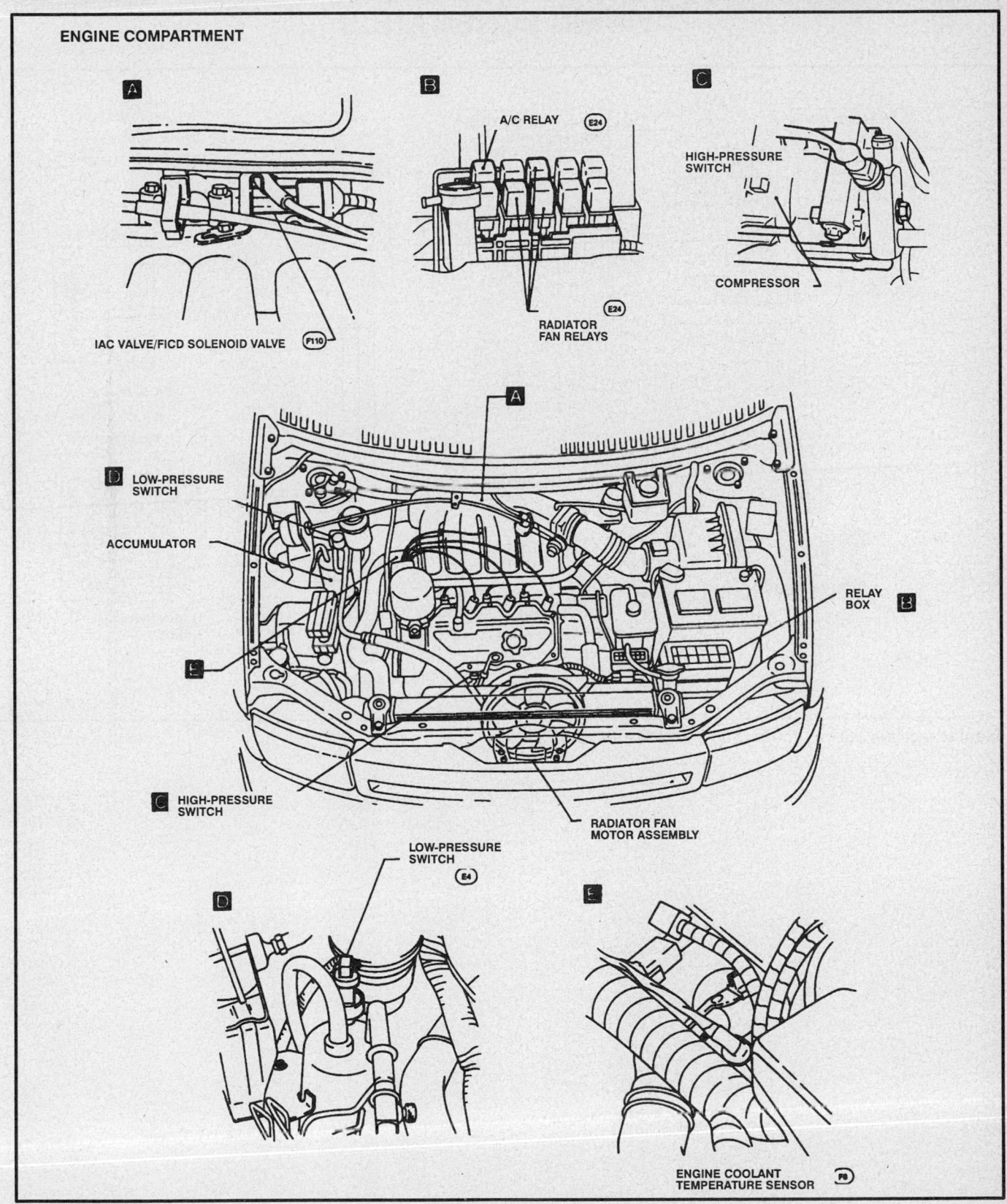

ENGINE COMPARTMENT

A

IAC VALVE/FICD SOLENOID VALVE F110

B

A/C RELAY E24

RADIATOR
FAN RELAYS E24

C

HIGH-PRESSURE
SWITCH

COMPRESSOR

A

D LOW-PRESSURE
SWITCH

ACCUMULATOR

E

RELAY
BOX B

C HIGH-PRESSURE
SWITCH

RADIATOR FAN
MOTOR ASSEMBLY

LOW-PRESSURE
SWITCH E4

D

ENGINE COOLANT
TEMPERATURE SENSOR F8

E

Air conditioning system engine compartment component layout—Quest

WIRING SCHEMATICS

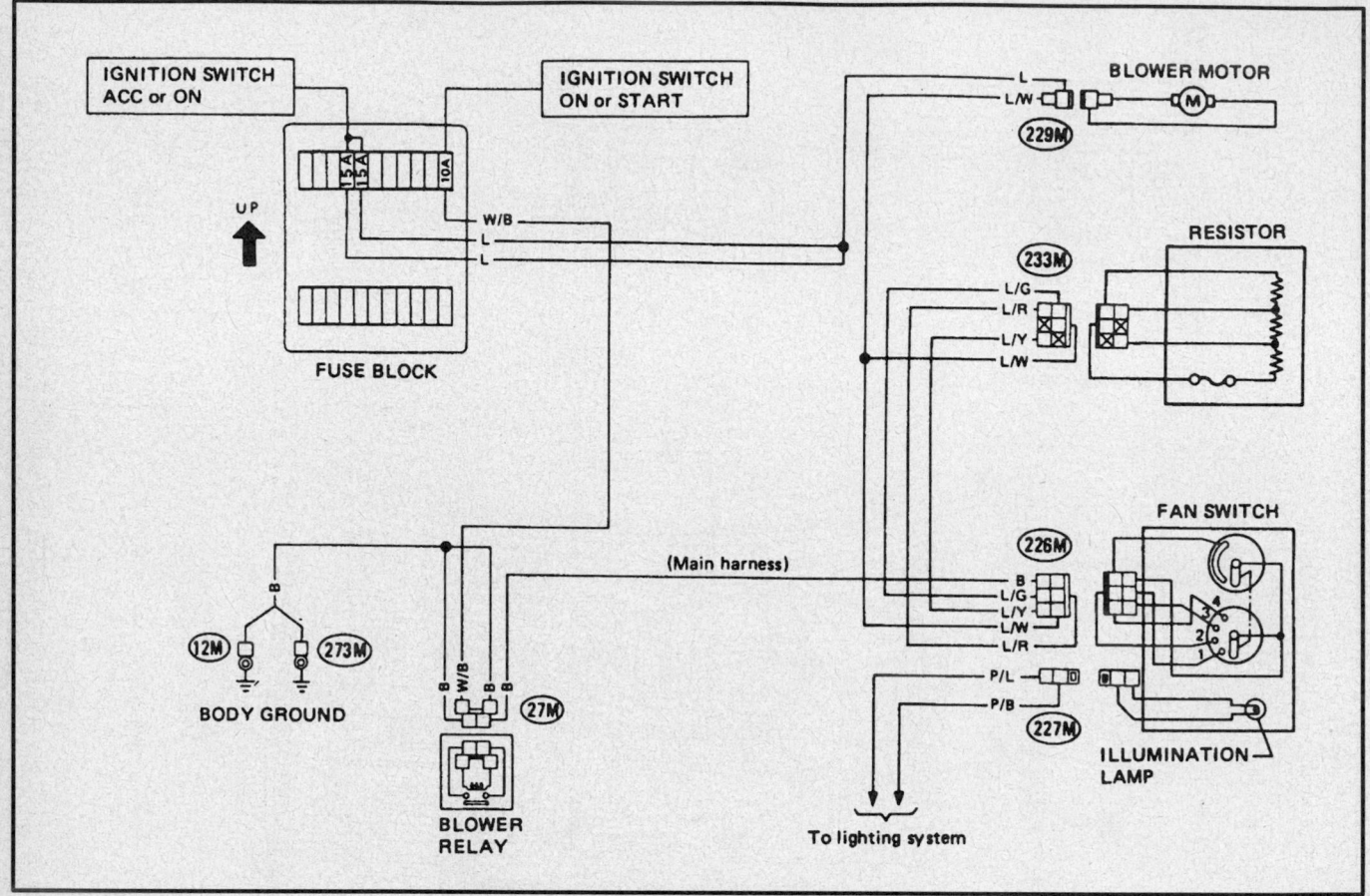

Heater system wiring schematic—Pathfinder and Pick-Up

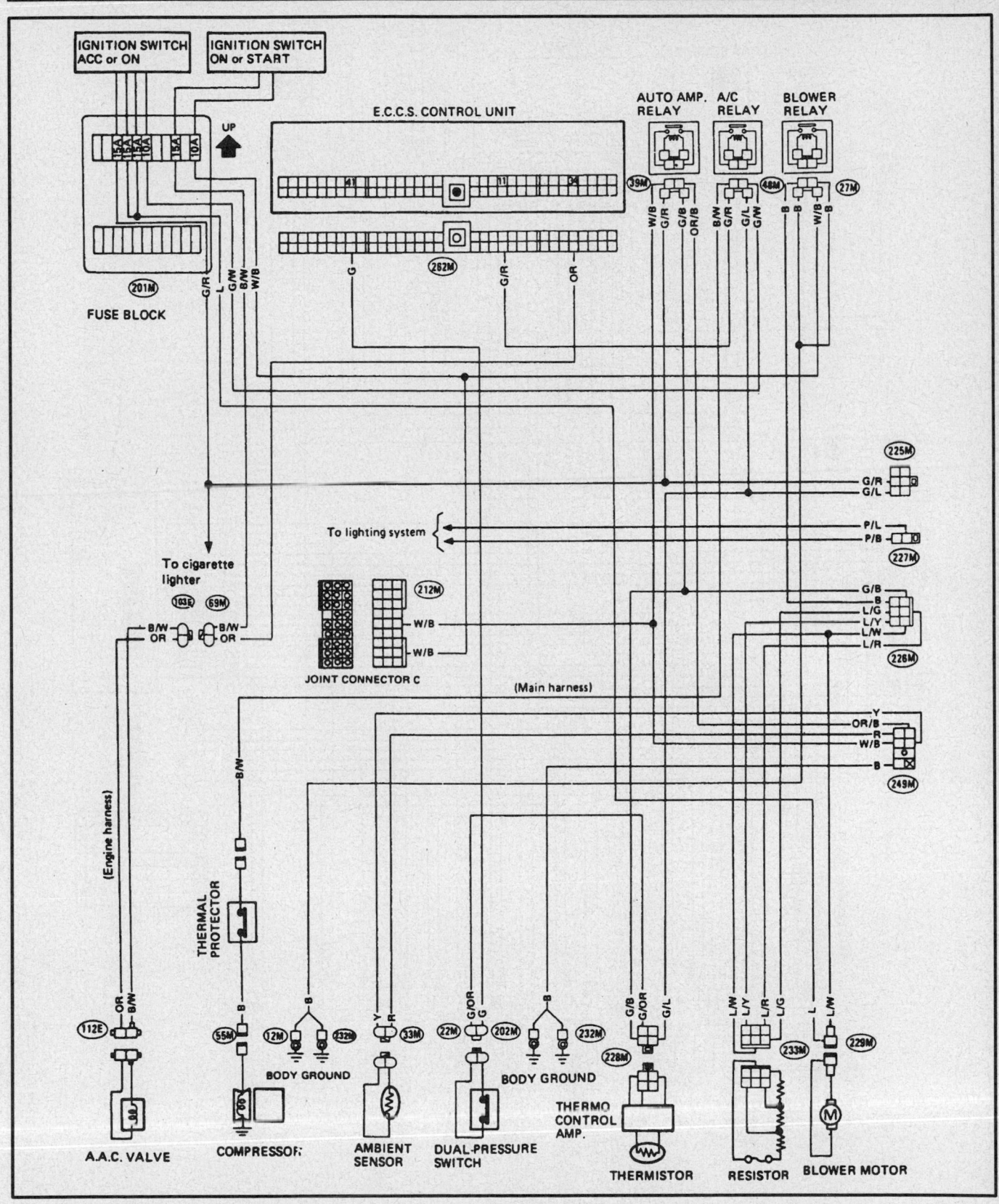

Automatic air conditioning system wiring schematic—Pathfinder and Pick-Up

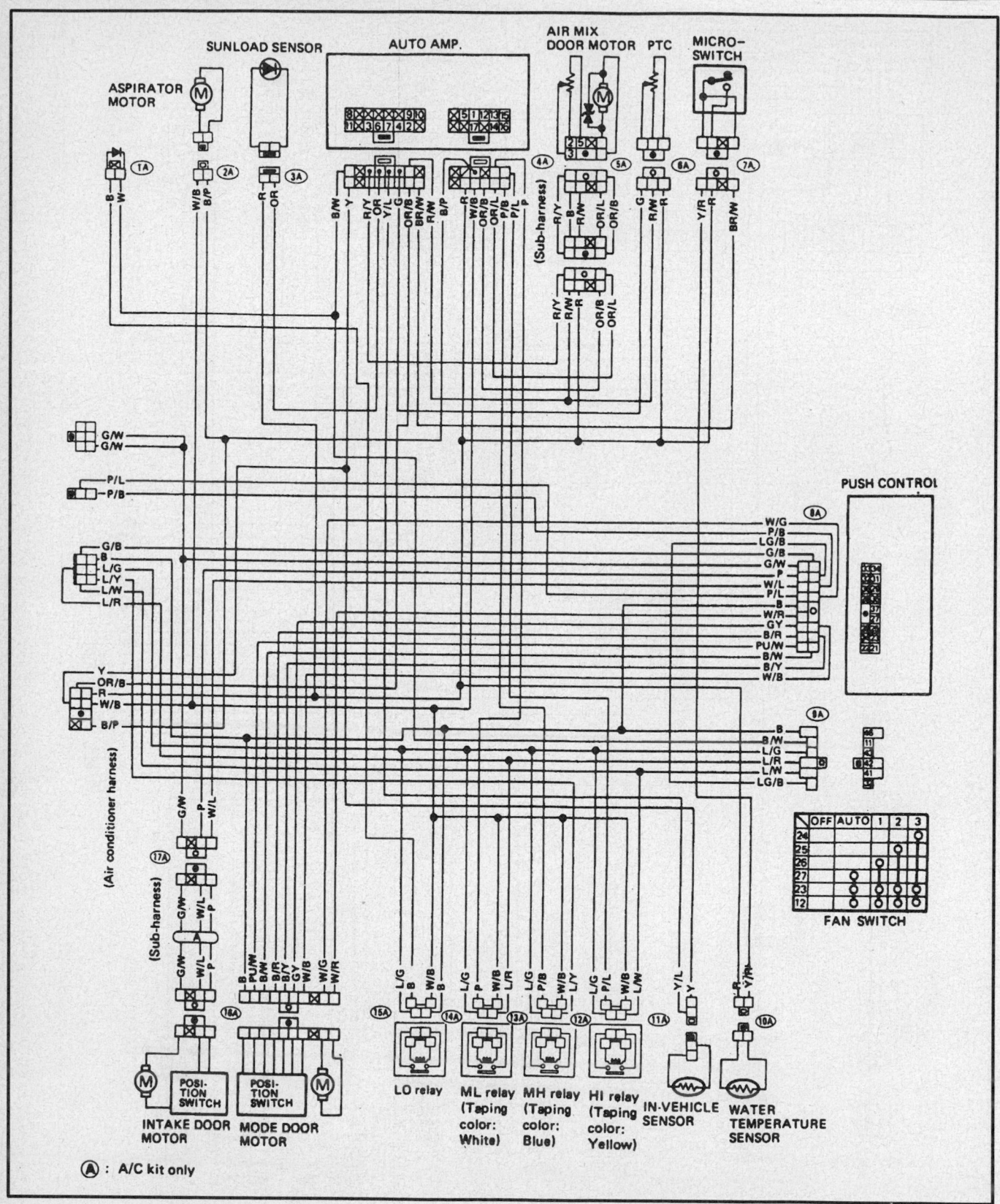

Automatic air conditioning system wiring schematic—Pathfinder and Pick-Up, Cont'd.

Ⓐ : A/C kit only

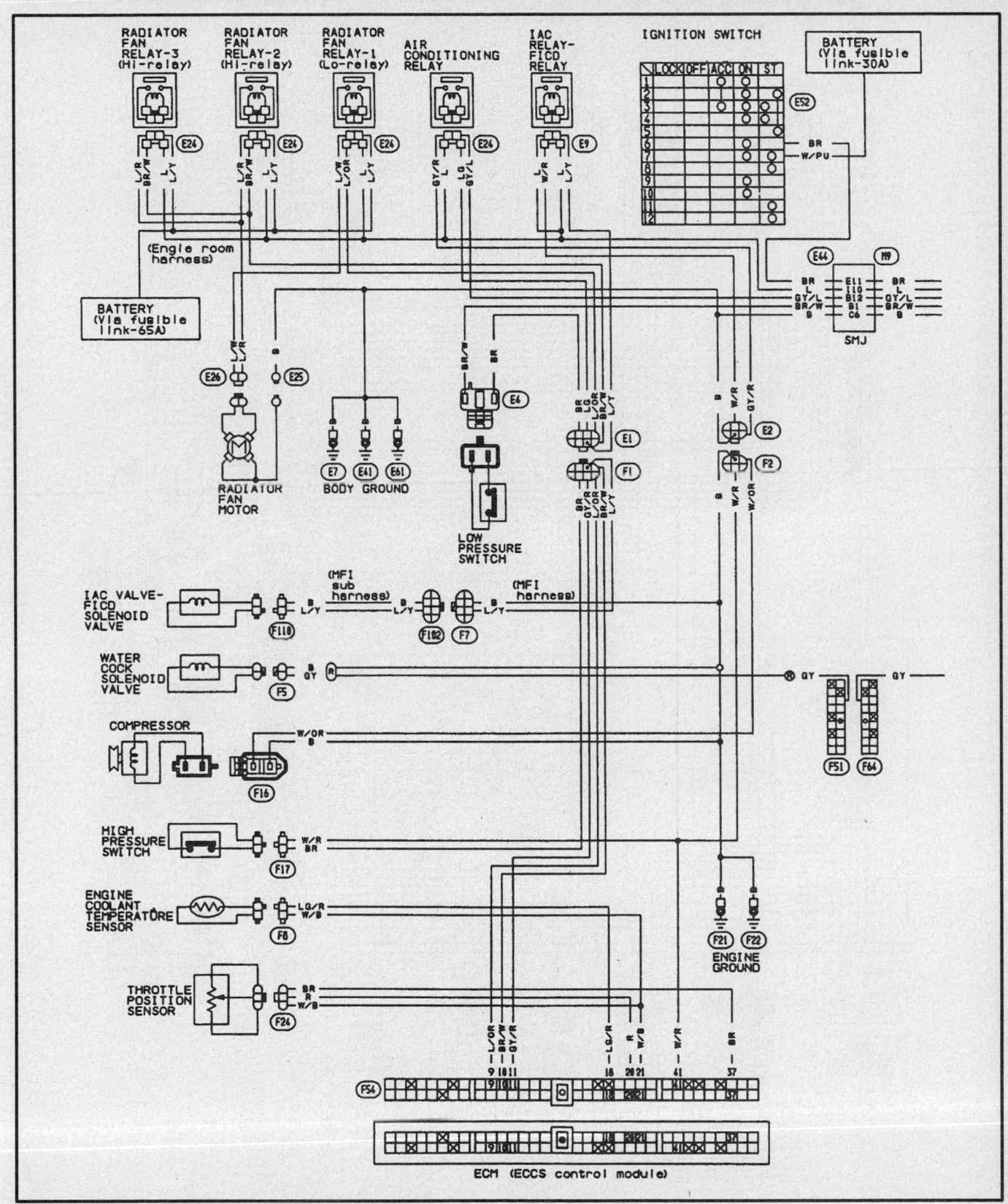

Air conditioning system wiring schematic—Quest

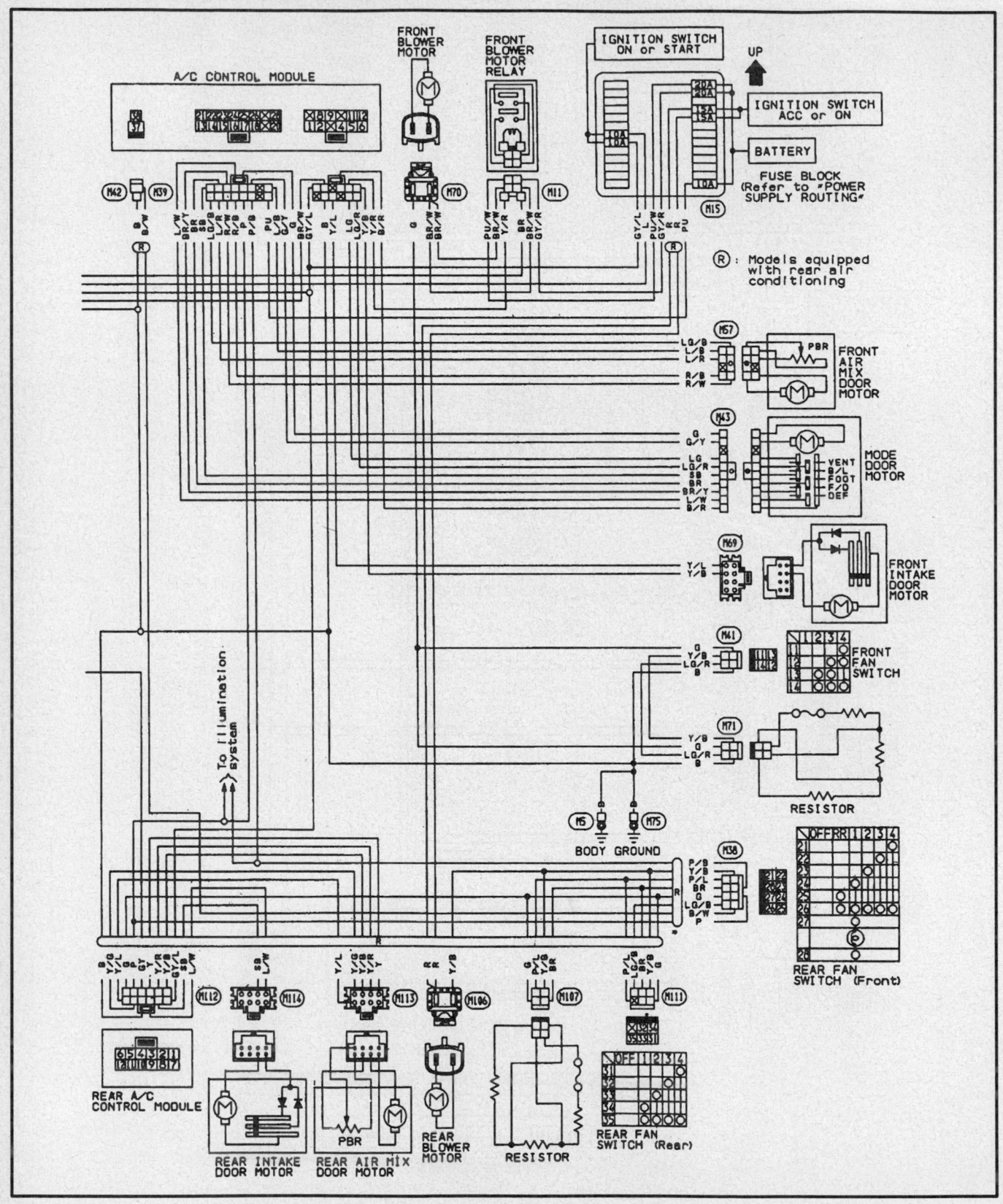

Air conditioning system wiring schematic—Quest, Cont'd.

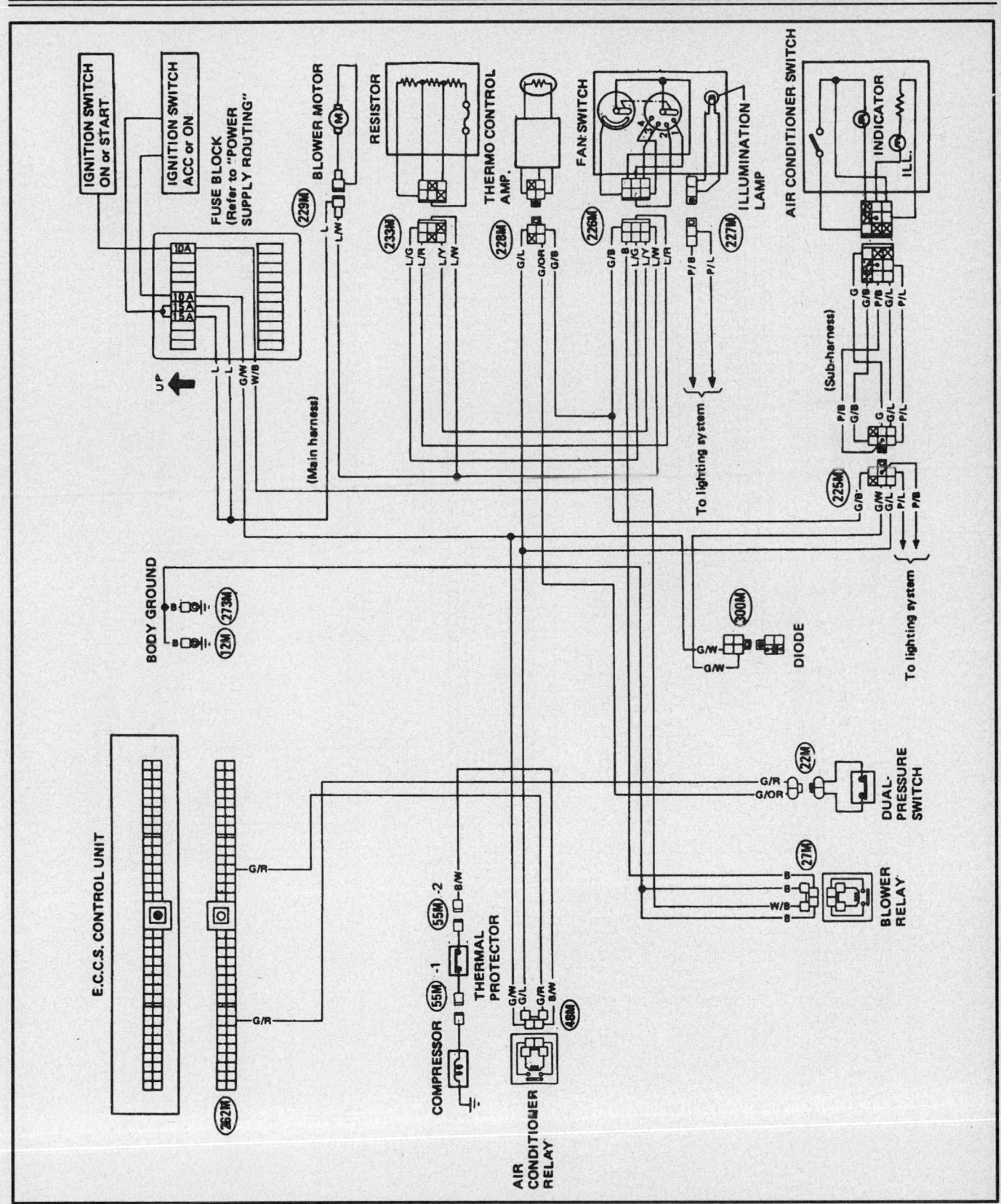

Manual air conditioning system wiring schematic—Pathfinder and Pick-Up 1993

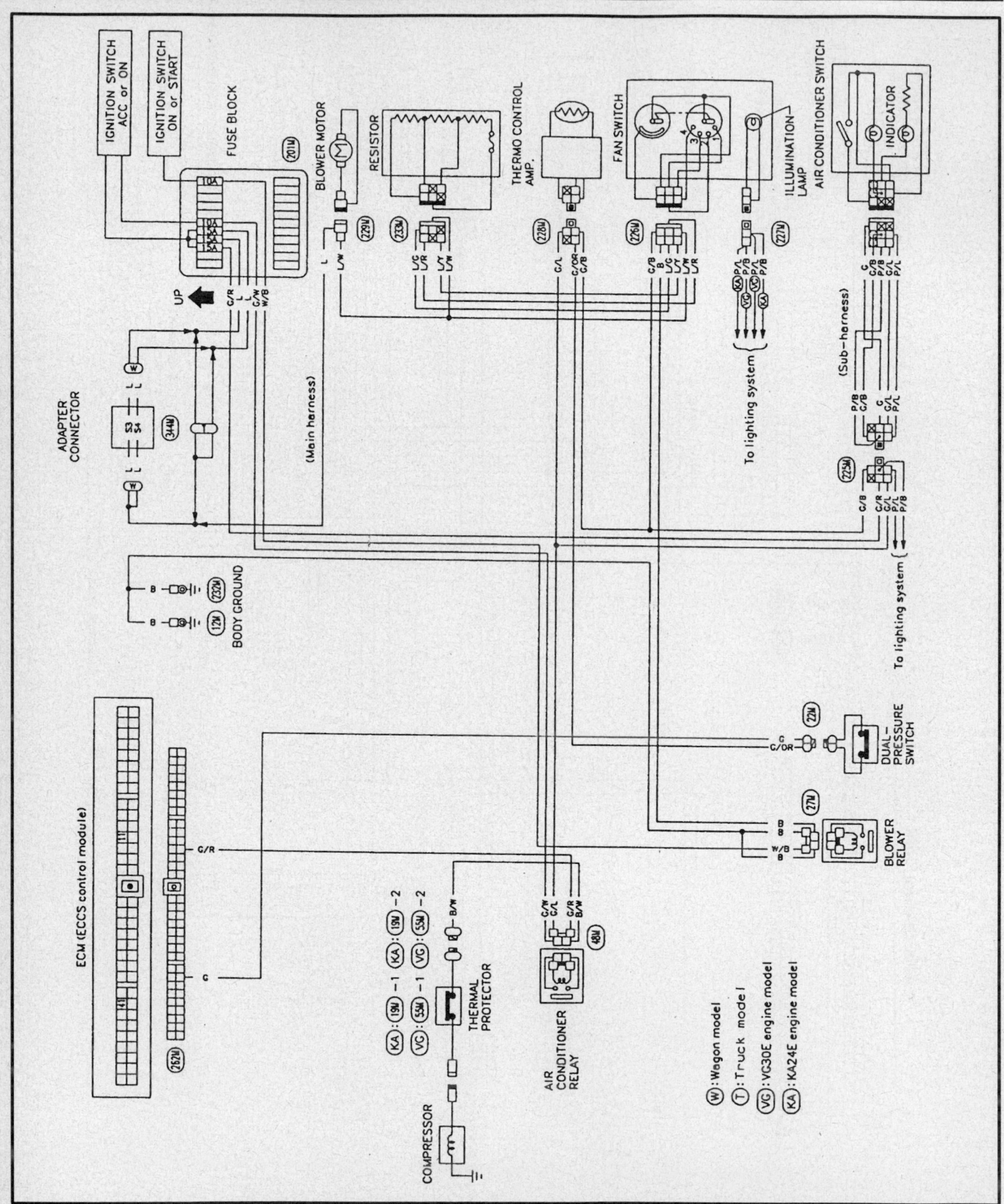

Manual air conditioning system wiring schematic—Pathfinder and Pick-Up 1994–95

SPECIFICATIONS

ENGINE IDENTIFICATION

Year	Model	Engine Displacement Liters (cc)	Engine Series (ID/VIN)	Fuel System	No. of Cylinders	Engine Type
1993	911 Carrera 2 ①	3.6 (3600)	M64/01	DME	6	SOHC
	911 Carrera 4 ②	3.6 (3600)	M64/01	DME	6	SOHC
	911 RS	3.6 (3600)	M64/01	DME	6	③
	911 Turbo	3.6 (3600)	930/69	KE	6	③
1994	911 Carrera	3.6 (3600)	M64/05/06	DME	6	③
	911 Speedster	3.6 (3600)	M64/01/02	DME	6	③
	911 Turbo	3.6 (3598)	M64/50	KE	6	③

SOHC—Single Overhead Cam
DME—Digital Motor Electronic Fuel Injector
KE—Bosch Electronics CIS Fuel Injection

① Includes Carrera 2 Coupe, Targa Cabriolet
② Includes Carrera 4 Coupe, Targa Cabriolet
③ Air cooled 6 cyl. horizontally opposed, rear mounted

REFRIGERANT CAPACITIES

Year	Model	Refrigerant (oz.)	Oil (fl. oz.)	Compressor Type
1993	911 Carrera 2 ①	35.0–40.0	4.7–5.0	R–134
	911 Carrera 4 ①	35.0–40.0	4.7–5.0	R–134
	911 RS	35.0–40.0	4.7–5.0	R–134
	911 Turbo	35.0–40.0	4.7–5.0	R–134
1994	911 Carrera	35.0–40.0	4.7–5.0	R–134
	911 Speedster	35.0–40.0	4.7–5.0	R–134
	911 Turbo	35.0–40.0	4.7–5.0	R–134

① Includes Carrera 2 Coupe, Targa Cabriolet
② Includes Carrera 4 Coupe, Targa Cabriolet

AIR CONDITIONING BELT TENSION

Year	Model	Engine Liters (cc)	Belt Type	Specifications New (lbs.)	Specifications Used (lbs.)
1993	911 Carrera 2 ①	3.6 (3600)	V–Belt	5.0	5.0
	911 Carrera 4 ②	3.6 (3600)	V–Belt	5.0	5.0
	911 RS	3.6 (3600)	V–Belt	5.0	5.0
	911 Turbo	3.3 (3299)	Ribbed	5.0	5.0
1994	911 Carrera	3.6 (3600)	V–Belt	5.0	5.0
	911 Speedster	3.6 (3600)	V–Belt	5.0	5.0
	911 Turbo	3.6 (3598)	Ribbed	5.0	5.0

① Includes Carrera 2 Coupe, Targa Cabriolet
② Includes Carrera 4 Coupe, Targa Cabriolet
③ Millimeters of deflection at center of belt using moderate thumb pressure

SYSTEM DESCRIPTION

General Information

The automatic A/C–heater system regulates the interior temperature by using temperature sensors and a temperature control knob. The system consists of:

- An A/C–heater control unit.
- An air distribution housing with 2 front mounted A/C–heater blowers.
- A blower final stage.
- Air distribution flaps and flap drive motors.
- A temperature sensor.
- A compressor.
- An evaporator.

Supplemental Restraint System

Before starting any service procedures on components, especially under the instrument panel and near the steering column, the air bag system must be disabled. To disable the system, disconnect the negative battery cable and wait 20 minutes for the air bag system to de–energize. Failure to follow this procedure could result in possible air bag deployment, personal injury or otherwise unneeded air bag system repairs.

To activate the air bag system, reconnect the negative battery cable and turn the ignition switch to **ON**. The air bag light on the instrument panel should come ON for about 5 seconds and then go OFF. If the air bag light fails to come ON, remains ON longer than 5 seconds or comes ON while driving, the air bag system needs servicing.

Service Valve Locations

The high–side service valve is on the discharge line and the low–side service valve is on the low side refrigerant line where both lines connect to the compressor.

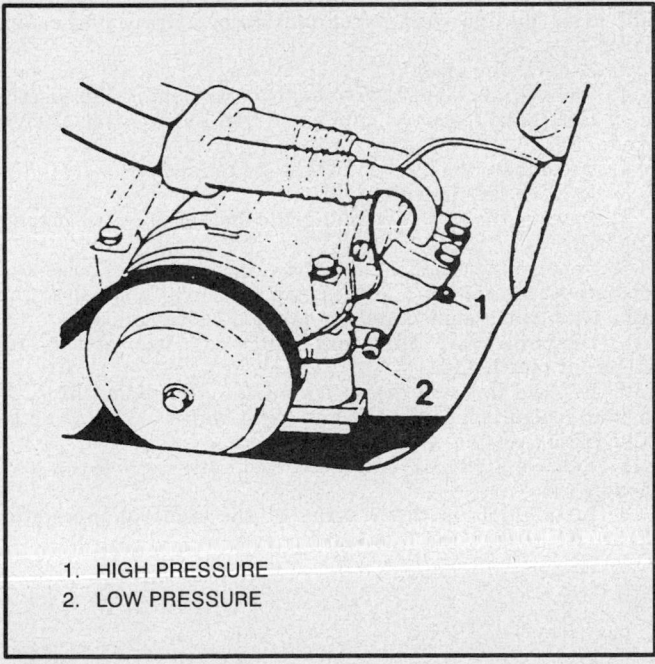

1. HIGH PRESSURE
2. LOW PRESSURE

Service valve locations — 911

System Discharging

Connect an approved refrigerant recovery/recycle system to the vehicle's air conditioning system and operate as instructed by the refrigerant recovery/recycle system manufacturer. Never vent R–12 or R–134a refrigerant directly to the atmosphere.

System Evacuating

Any time the air conditioning system has been exposed to the atmosphere, such as during a repair or installation, the system must be evacuated using a vacuum pump. If the system has been opened for several days, the receiver/drier should be replaced.

3. Connect the gauge set to the appropriate high and low side fittings and connect the center hose to the vacuum pump inlet.

4. Start the pump and open both gauge valves. Run the pump for 15 minutes. Close the valves and stop the pump. The low pressure gauge should read about 27–30 in. Hg vacuum and remain steady with the valve closed.

NOTE: If the low side pressure gauge does not reach more than 27–30 in. Hg vacuum in 15 minutes, there is a leak in the air conditioning system. Check and repair as necessary.

5. If there are no leaks, open the valve and continue to pump for at least another 15 minutes, then close the valves, stop the pump and disconnect the center charging hose.

System Charging

Always wear eye protection and gloves while charging the air conditioning system. The air conditioning system may be charged with refrigerant by either vapor or liquid methods. If the system is overcharged, the compressor will be damaged.

1. Connect an approved charging station, recovery/recycling machine or manifold gauge set to the service valves. The red hose is normally connected to the discharge (high pressure) line, and the blue hose is connected to the suction (low pressure) line.

2. Follow the equipment manufacturer's instructions provided with the equipment and charge the system to the specified amount of refrigerant.

3. Perform a leak test.

SYSTEM COMPONENTS

Condenser

REMOVAL AND INSTALLATION

Front

1. Disconnect the negative battery cable and wait 20 minutes for the air bag system to de–energize.
2. Properly discharge the air conditioning system refrigerant using an approved refrigerant recovery/recycling equipment.
3. Disconnect the air conditioner hoses. Cap all open fittings immediately to prevent contamination.
4. Remove the stone guard screws.
5. Remove the condenser with the stone guard.
6. Installation is the reverse of the removal procedure. Evacuate, charge and leak test the system.

Rear

1. Disconnect the negative battery cable and wait 20 minutes for the air bag system to de–energize.
2. Properly discharge the air conditioning system refrigerant using an approved refrigerant recovery/recycling equipment.
3. Remove the mounting bracket from the center plate.
4. Loosen the screws on the compressor compartment cover hinges.
5. Disconnect the air conditioner hoses. Cap all open fittings immediately to prevent contamination.
6. Remove the condenser.
7. Installation is the reverse of the removal procedure. Evacuate, charge and leak test the system.

Compressor

REMOVAL AND INSTALLATION

1. Disconnect the negative battery cable and wait 20 minutes for the air bag system to de–energize.
2. Properly discharge the air conditioning system refrigerant using an approved refrigerant recovery/recycling equipment.
3. Disconnect the air conditioner hoses. Cap all open fittings immediately to prevent contamination.
4. Remove the belt tensioner bolt and the compressor belt.
5. Remove the compressor plate bolts and the compressor.
6. Installation is the reverse of the removal procedure. Evacuate, charge and leak test the system.

Expansion Valve

REMOVAL AND INSTALLATION

1. Disconnect the negative battery cable and wait 20 minutes for the air bag system to de–energize.
2. Properly discharge the air conditioning system refrigerant using an approved refrigerant recovery/recycling equipment.

3. Disconnect the air conditioner hoses. Cap all open fittings immediately to prevent contamination.
4. Remove the A/C–heater unit.
5. Remove the insulating tape from the expansion valve.
6. Remove the capillary tube holder.
7. Remove the air conditioner line and the pressure switch from the expansion valve.
8. Remove the expansion valve nut from the evaporator and remove the expansion valve.
9. Installation is the reverse of the removal procedure. Evacuate, charge and leak test the system.

Receiver/Drier

REMOVAL AND INSTALLATION

1. Disconnect the negative battery cable and wait 20 minutes for the air bag system to de–energize.
2. Properly discharge the air conditioning system refrigerant using an approved refrigerant recovery/recycling equipment.
3. Disconnect the air conditioner refrigerant lines. Cap all open fittings immediately to prevent contamination.
4. Open the hose clamps completely and remove the receiver/drier.
5. Installation is the reverse of the removal procedure. Evacuate, charge and leak test the system.

Air Conditioner–Heater Unit

REMOVAL AND INSTALLATION

1. Disconnect the negative battery cable and wait 20 minutes for the air bag system to de–energize.
2. Properly discharge the air conditioning system refrigerant using an approved refrigerant recovery/recycling equipment.
3. Remove the tank.
4. Remove the upper cover of the A/C–heater and disconnect the central electric connector. Set the central electric aside.
5. Disconnect the blower final stage connector.
6. Remove the firewall.
7. Remove the fresh air inlet grille and unscrew the mounting bolts.
8. Remove the condensation and rain water drain hoses and disconnect the refrigerant lines from the expansion valve. Cap all open fittings immediately to prevent contamination.
9. Disconnect the refrigerant switch connector and the refrigerant pipe holder.
10. Remove the side nozzle air guides, the radio, the A/C–heater control head, the left and right warm air guide necks and disconnect the electrical connectors.
11. Remove the mounting screws and nuts. Remove the A/C–heater unit.
12. Installation is the reverse of the removal procedure. Evacuate, charge and leak test the system.

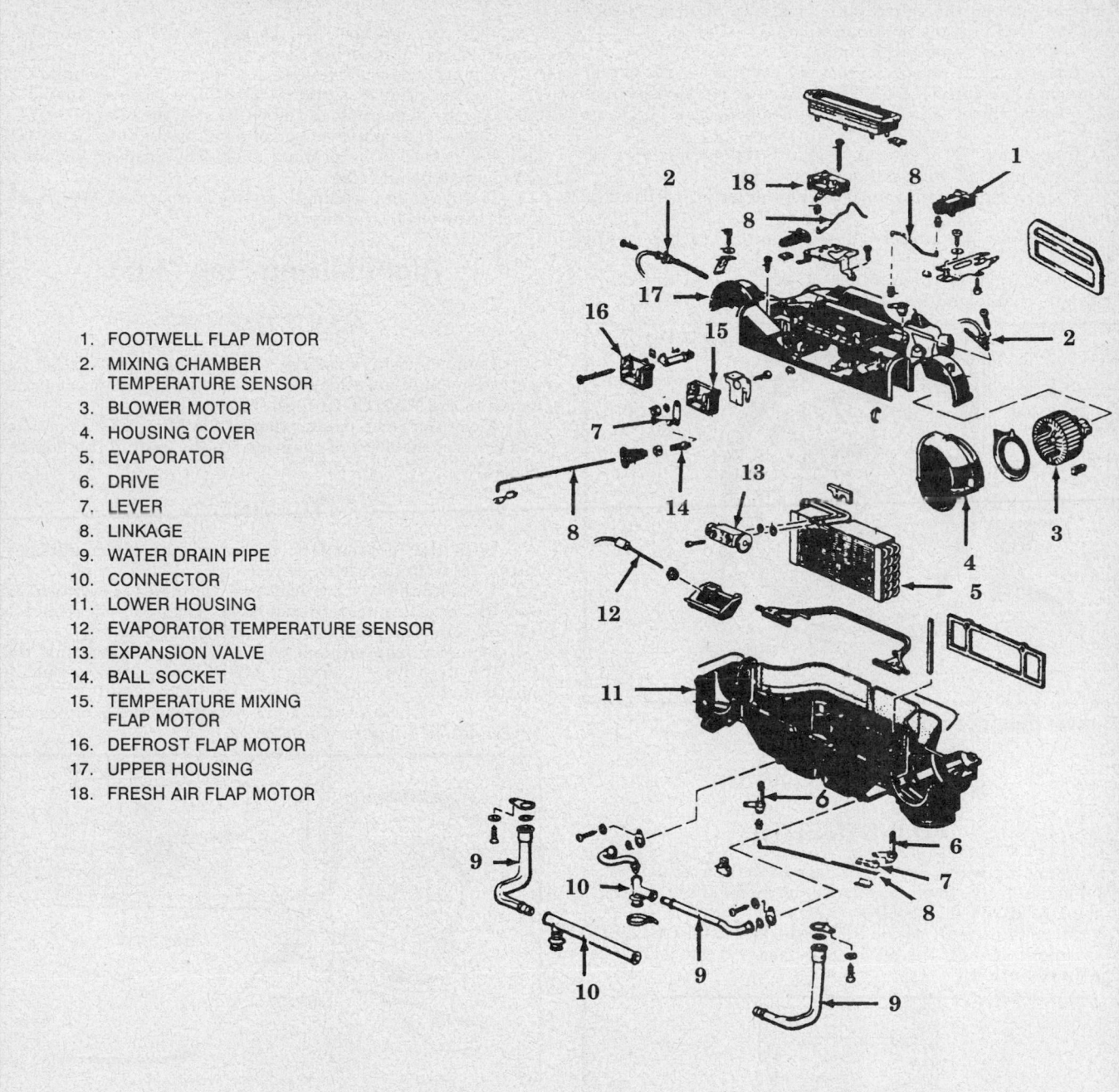

1. FOOTWELL FLAP MOTOR
2. MIXING CHAMBER
   TEMPERATURE SENSOR
3. BLOWER MOTOR
4. HOUSING COVER
5. EVAPORATOR
6. DRIVE
7. LEVER
8. LINKAGE
9. WATER DRAIN PIPE
10. CONNECTOR
11. LOWER HOUSING
12. EVAPORATOR TEMPERATURE SENSOR
13. EXPANSION VALVE
14. BALL SOCKET
15. TEMPERATURE MIXING
    FLAP MOTOR
16. DEFROST FLAP MOTOR
17. UPPER HOUSING
18. FRESH AIR FLAP MOTOR

Air conditioning–heater unit exploded view—911

Blower Motors

REMOVAL AND INSTALLATION

1. Disconnect the negative battery cable and wait 20 minutes for the air bag system to de–energize.

2. Properly discharge the air conditioning system refrigerant using an approved refrigerant recovery/recycling equipment.

3. Remove the tank.

4. Remove the upper cover of the A/C–heater and disconnect the central electric connector. Set the central electric aside.

5. Disconnect the blower final stage connector.

6. Remove the firewall.

7. To remove the right side blower motor, disconnect the blower motor connector and remove it from the holder, remove the motor cover clamps and the motor cover. Continue with Step 9.

8. To remove the left side blower motor, disconnect the expansion tank and the refrigerant lines. Cap all open fittings immediately to prevent contamination.

9. If equipped, remove the air filters.

10. Install part "A" of special tool 9512 (Puller) on the blower motor shaft and turn CLOCKWISE. Ensure that the openings in the blower wheel are aligned with the openings in the housing.

11. Install part "B" of special tool 9512 (Puller) over part "A" and install part "C" wing nut onto the shaft.

12. Tighten the wing nut until the blower motor is free of the housing.

13. Disconnect the blower motor connector and remove the blower motor.

14. Installation is the reverse of the removal procedure. Evacuate, charge and leak test the system.

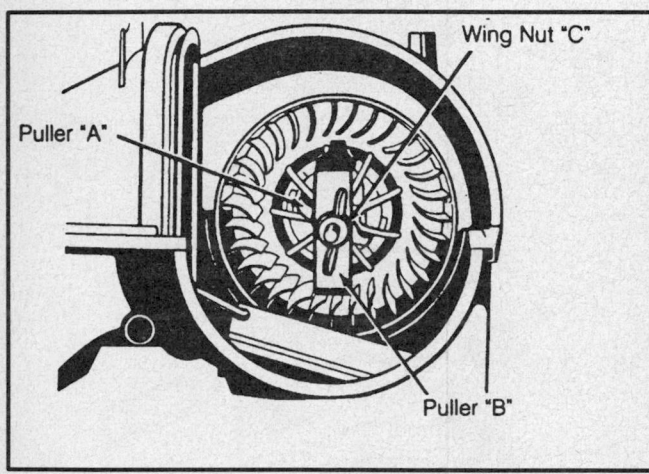

Blower motor removal

Defrost Flap Motor

ADJUSTMENTS

1. Connect positive battery voltage to the defrost flap motor pin **4** and negative to pin **5**. Ensure the motor smoothly moves to the **DEFROST CLOSED** position.

2. Move the defrost nozzle flap to the **DEFROST CLOSED** position and connect the drive of the motor to the joint of the flap and secure it.

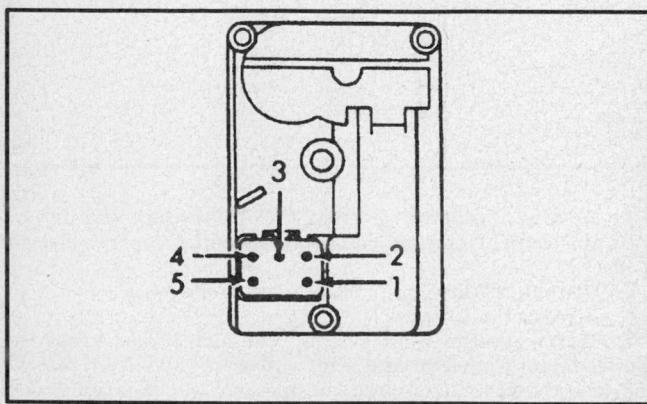

Flap motor terminal identification

TESTING

1. With the ignition **ON**, backprobe the air conditioner–heater control unit wiring connector.

2. Connect the positive lead of a voltmeter to terminal **G26** and the negative to terminal **G18**. The reading should be 0.2–5.0 volts depending on the position of the motor.

3. Connect the positive lead of a voltmeter to terminal **G13** and the negative to terminal **G18**. The reading should be approximately 5.0 volts.

4. If the voltage readings are not as specified, replace the air conditioner–heater regulator.

Right Mixing Flap Motor

ADJUSTMENTS

1. Connect positive battery voltage to the right mixing flap motor pin **5** and negative to pin **4**. Ensure the motor smoothly moves to the **MAX COLD** position.

2. Move the right mixing flap to the **MAX COLD** position and connect the drive of the motor to the joint of the flap and secure it.

TESTING

1. With the ignition **ON**, backprobe the air conditioner–heater control unit wiring connector.

2. Connect the positive lead of a voltmeter to terminal **G8** and the negative to terminal **G18**. The reading should be 0.2–5.0 volts depending on the position of the motor.

3. Connect the positive lead of a voltmeter to terminal **G13** and the negative to terminal **G18**. The reading should be approximately 5.0 volts.

4. If the voltage readings are not as specified, replace the air conditioner–heater regulator.

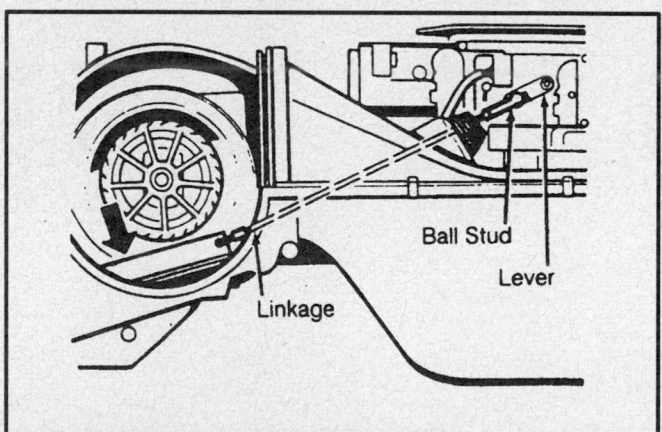

Temperature mixing flap adjustment

Left Mixing Flap Motor

ADJUSTMENTS

1. Connect positive battery voltage to the left mixing flap motor pin **4** and negative to pin **5**. Ensure the motor smoothly moves to the **MAX COLD** position.

2. Move the left mixing flap to the **MAX COLD** position and connect the drive of the motor to the joint of the flap and secure it.

TESTING

1. With the ignition **ON**, backprobe the air conditioner–heater control unit wiring connector.
2. Connect the positive lead of a voltmeter to terminal **G25** and the negative to terminal **G18**. The reading should be 0.2–5.0 volts depending on the position of the motor.
3. Connect the positive lead of a voltmeter to terminal **G13** and the negative to terminal **G18**. The reading should be approximately 5.0 volts.
4. If the voltage readings are not as specified, replace the air conditioner–heater regulator.

Footwell Flap Motor

ADJUSTMENTS

1. Connect positive battery voltage to the footwell flap motor pin **5** and negative to pin **4**. Ensure the motor smoothly moves to the **FOOTWELL FLAPS CLOSED** position.

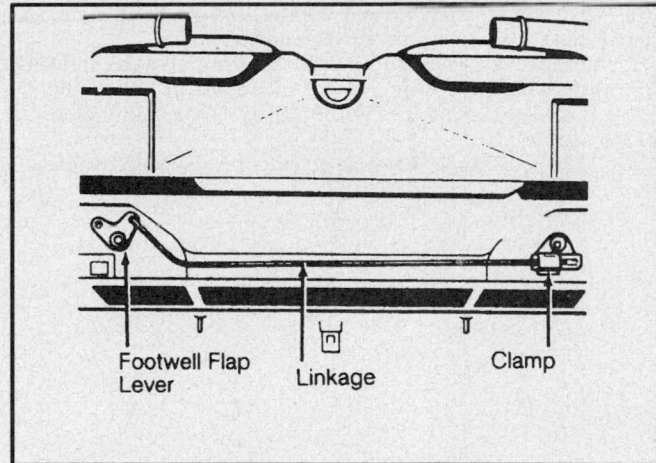

Footwell Flap
Lever   Linkage   Clamp

Footwell flap adjustment

2. Move the footwell flaps to the **FOOTWELL FLAPS CLOSED** position and engage the linkage onto the lever and secure it with a clamp.

TESTING

1. With the ignition **ON**, backprobe the air conditioner–heater control unit wiring connector.
2. Connect the positive lead of a voltmeter to terminal **G27** and the negative to terminal **G18**. The reading should be 0.2–5.0 volts depending on the position of the motor.
3. Connect the positive lead of a voltmeter to terminal **G13** and the negative to terminal **G18**. The reading should be approximately 5.0 volts.
4. If the voltage readings are not as specified, replace the air conditioner–heater regulator.

Fresh Air Flap Motor

TESTING

1. With the ignition **ON**, backprobe the air conditioner–heater control unit wiring connector.
2. Connect the positive lead of a voltmeter to terminal **G20** and the negative to terminal **G18**. The reading should be 0.2–5.0 volts depending on the position of the motor.
3. Connect the positive lead of a voltmeter to terminal **G13** and the negative to terminal **G18**. The reading should be approximately 5.0 volts.
4. If the voltage readings are not as specified, replace the air conditioner–heater regulator.

SENSORS AND SWITCHES

Air Mix Chamber Temperature Sensors

TESTING

Left Mix Chamber Temperature Sensor

1. With the ignition turned **OFF**. Disconnect the air conditioner–heater control unit wiring connector.
2. Measure the resistance between terminals **G18** and **G23**. The resistance should be 30.6–34.7 kilo-ohms at 32°F (0°C), 9.5–10.5 kilo-ohms at 77°F (25°C) or 3.4–3.8 kilo-ohms at 122°F (50°C).
3. If the resistance is not as specified, replace the sensor.

Right Mix Chamber Temperature Sensor

1. With the ignition turned **OFF**. Disconnect the air conditioner–heater control unit wiring connector.
2. Measure the resistance between terminals **G18** and **G24**. The resistance should be 30.6–34.7 kilo-ohms at 32°F (0°C), 9.5–10.5 kilo-ohms at 77°F (25°C) or 3.4–3.8 kilo-ohms at 122°F (50°C).
3. If the resistance is not as specified, replace the sensor.

Rear Fan Temperature Sensor

1. With the ignition turned **OFF**. Disconnect the air conditioner–heater control unit wiring connector.
2. Measure the resistance between terminals **G18** and **G10**. The resistance should be 28.8–36.4 kilo-ohms at 32°F (0°C),

9.0–11.0 kilo-ohms at 77°F (25°C) or 3.1–4.0 kilo-ohms at 122°F (50°C).

3. If the resistance is not as specified, replace the sensor.

Evaporator Temperature Sensor

1. With the ignition turned **OFF**. Disconnect the air conditioner–heater control unit wiring connector.

2. Measure the resistance between terminals **G18** and **G22**. The resistance should be 8.8–9.2 kilo-ohms at 32°F (0°C) or 2.6–2.9 kilo-ohms at 77°F (25°C).

3. If the resistance is not as specified, replace the sensor.

Oil Cooler Temperature Sensor

1. With the ignition turned **OFF**. Disconnect the air conditioner–heater control unit wiring connector.

2. Measure the resistance between terminals **G18** and **G12**. The resistance should be 3.6–4.0 kilo-ohms at 140°F (60°C), 1.4–1.6 kilo-ohms at 185°F (85°C) or 0.9–1.0 kilo-ohms at 212°F (100°C).

3. If the resistance is not as specified, replace the sensor.

TESTING

Left Mix Chamber Temperature Sensor

1. With the ignition turned **OFF**. Disconnect the air conditioner–heater control unit wiring connector.

2. Measure the resistance between terminals **G18** and **G23**. The resistance should be 30.6–34.7 kilo-ohms at 32°F (0°C), 9.5–10.5 kilo-ohms at 77°F (25°C) or 3.4–3.8 kilo-ohms at 122°F (50°C).

3. If resistance is not as specified replace the sensdor.

Right Air Mix Chamber Temperature Sensor

1. With the ignition turned **OFF**. Disconnect the air conditioner–heater control unit wiring connector.

2. Measure the resistance between terminals **G18** and **G12**. The resistance should be 3.6–4.0 kilo-ohms at 140°F (60°C), 1.4–1.6 kilo-ohms at 185°F (85°C) or 0.9–1.0 kilo-ohms at 212°F (100°C).

3. If the resistance is not as specified, replace the sensor.

Evaporator Temperature Sensor

1. With the ignition turned **OFF**. Disconnect the air conditioner–heater control unit wiring connector.

2. Measure the resistance between terminals **G18** and **G12**. The resistance should be 8.8–9.2 kilo-ohms at 32°F (0°C) or 2.6–2.9 kilo-ohms at 77°F (25°C).

3. If the resistance is not as specified, replace the sensor.

Rear Fan Temperature Sensor

1. With the ignition turned **OFF**. Disconnect the air conditioner–heater control unit wiring connector.

2. Measure the resistance between terminals **G18** and **G10**. The resistance should be 28.8–36.4 kilo-ohms at 32°F (0°C), 9.0–11.0 kilo-ohms at 77°F (25°C) or 3.1–4.0 kilo-ohms at 122°F (50°C).

3. If the resistance is not as specified, replace the sensor.

Oil Cooler Temperature Sensor Circuit

1. With the ignition turned **OFF**. Disconnect the air conditioner–heater control unit wiring connector.

2. Measure the resistance between terminals **G18** and **G12**. The resistance should be 3.6–4.0 kilo-ohms at 140°F (60°C), 1.4–1.6 kilo-ohms at 185°F (85°C) or 0.9–1.0 kilo-ohms at 212°F (100°C).

3. If the resistance is not as specified, replace the sensor.

SPECIFICATIONS

ENGINE IDENTIFICATION

Year	Model	Engine Displacement Liters (cc)	Engine Series (ID/VIN)	Fuel System	No. of Cylinders	Engine Type
1993	900 3DR, 4DR	2.1 (2119)	B212i	EFI	4	DOHC-16V
	900S	2.1 (2119)	B212i	EFI	4	DOHC-16V
	900 Turbo	2.0 (1985)	B202	EFI	4	DOHC-16V
	900 T-Convertible	2.0 (1985)	B202	EFI	4	DOHC-16V
	900 S-Convertible	2.0 (1985)	B202	EFI	4	DOHC-16V
	9000CS	2.0 (2290)	B202	EFI	4	DOHC-16V
	9000CSE	2.3 (2290)	B234	EFI	4	DOHC-16V
	9000CD	2.3 (2290)	B234	EFI	4	DOHC-16V
	9000CDE	2.3 (2290)	B234	EFI	4	DOHC-16V
	9000 CD-Turbo	2.3 (2290)	B234L	EFI	4	DOHC-16V
1994	900 Cpe, 5-dr, Conv	2.0 (1985)	B206L	EFI	4	DOHC-16V
	900 Cpe, 5-dr, Conv	2.3 (2290)	B234i	EFI	4	DOHC-16V
	900 Cpe, 5-dr, Conv	2.5 (2498)	B258	EFI	6	DOHC-24V
	9000 CD/CS	2.3 (2290)	B234	EFI	4	DOHC-16V
	9000 CD-Turbo	2.3 (2290)	B234	EFI	4	DOHC-16V
1995	900 Cpe, 5-dr, Conv	2.0 (1985)	B204L	EFI	4	DOHC-16V
	900 Cpe, 5-dr, Conv	2.3 (2290)	B234i	EFI	4	DOHC-16V
	900 Cpe, 5-dr, Conv	2.5 (2498)	B258	EFI	6	DOHC-24V
	9000CS	2.3 (2990)	B234LPT	EFI	4	DOHC-16V
	9000CSE/Aero	2.3 (2290)	B234	EFI	4	DOHC-16V
	9000CSE	3.0 (2961)	B308	EFI	6	DOHC-24V
	9000CDE	3.0 (2961)	B308	EFI	6	DOHC-24V

DOHC–Dual Overhead Cam
EFI–Electronic Fuel Injection

REFRIGERANT CAPACITIES

Year	Model	Refrigerant (oz.)	Oil (fl. oz.)	Compressor Type
1993	900 3DR, 4DR	39.5	4.4	Sanden SD510
	900S	39.5	4.4	Sanden SD510
	900 Turbo	39.5	4.4	Sanden SD510
	900 T-Convertible	39.5	4.4	Sanden SD510
	900 S-Convertible	39.5	4.4	Sanden SD510
	9000CS	39.5	4.4	Sanden SD510
	9000CSE	39.5	4.4	Sanden SD510
	9000 CD	39.5	4.4	Sanden SD510
	9000 CDE	39.5	4.4	Sanden SD510
	9000 CD-Turbo	39.5	4.4	Sanden SD510
1994	900 Coupe	25.6–28.2	6.8	Seiko-Seiki SS121 DN1
	900 5-door	25.6–28.2	6.8	Seiko-Seiki SS121 DN1
	900 Convertible	25.6–28.2	6.8	Seiko-Seiki SS121 DN1

REFRIGERANT CAPACITIES

Year	Model	Refrigerant (oz.)	Oil (fl. oz.)	Compressor Type
1994	9000 CD, CS	25.6–28.2	6.8	Seiko-Seiki SS121 DN1
	9000 CD-Turbo	25.6–28.2	6.8	Seiko-Seiki SS121 DN1
1995	900 Coupe	25.6–28.2	6.8	Seiko-Seiki SS121 DN1
	900 5-door	25.6–28.2	6.8	Seiko-Seiki SS121 DN1
	900 Convertible	25.6–28.2	6.8	Seiko-Seiki SS121 DN1
	9000 Aero	25.6–28.2	6.8	Seiko-Seiki SS121 DN1
	9000 CS	25.6–28.2	6.8	Seiko-Seiki SS121 DN1
	9000 CSE	25.6–28.2	6.8	Seiko-Seiki SS121 DN1
	9000 CDE	25.6–28.2	6.8	Seiko-Seiki SS121 DN1

AIR CONDITIONING BELT TENSION

Year	Model	Engine Liters (cc)	Belt Type	Specifications New	Specifications Used
1993	900 3DR, 4DR	2.1 (2119)	V-Belt	110–130②	75–85②
	900S	2.1 (2119)	V-Belt	110–130②	75–85②
	900 Turbo	2.0 (1985)	V-Belt	3/16①	3/16①
	900 T-Convertible	2.0 (1985)	V-Belt	3/16①	3/16①
	900 S-Convertible	2.0 (1985)	V-Belt	3/16①	3/16①
	9000CS	2.3 (2290)	Serpentine	110–130②	75–85②
	9000CSE	2.3 (2290)	Serpentine	110–130②	75–85②
	9000 CD	2.3 (2290)	Serpentine	110–130②	75–85②
	9000 CDE	2.3 (2290)	Serpentine	110–130②	75–85②
	9000 CD Turbo	2.3 (2290)	Serpentine	110–130②	75–85②
1994	900 Cpe, 5-dr, Conv	2.0 (1985)	Serpentine	③	③
	900 Cpe, 5-dr, Conv	2.3 (2290)	Serpentine	③	③
	900 Cpe, 5-dr, Conv	2.5 (2498)	Serpentine	③	③
	9000 CD/CS	2.3 (2290)	Serpentine	③	③
	9000 CD-Turbo	2.3 (2290)	Serpentine	③	③
1995	900 Cpe, 5-dr, Conv	2.0 (1985)	Serpentine	③	③
	900 Cpe, 5-dr, Conv	2.3 (2290)	Serpentine	③	③
	900 Cpe, 5-dr, Conv	2.5 (2498)	Serpentine	③	③
	9000 CS	2.3 (2290)	Serpentine	③	③
	9000 CSE, Aero	2.3 (2290)	Serpentine	③	③
	9000 CSE	3.0 (2961)	Serpentine	③	③
	9000 CDE	3.0 (2961)	Serpentine	③	③

① Inches of deflection at midpoint of belt using 10 lbs. of force.
② Reading obtained using appropriate belt tension gauge.
③ Automatic belt tensioner.

SYSTEM DESCRIPTION

General Information

900

The climate control system used in the Saab 900 is a filtered fresh-air system. Air enters through a grille in the cowl, passes through the filter and goes through the heating and ventilation unit to the passenger cabin. Stale air exits the cabin through an exhaust vent behind the rear bumper on the right side. The system is available as a manual heating and ventilating system, a manual heating and ventilating system with air conditioning or an automatic climate control (ACC) system.

9000

The climate control system used in the Saab 9000 is an electronic automatic climate control (ACC) system. In automatic mode, the system will maintain any preset temperature between 62.6°F (17°C) and 80.6°F (27°C). The system can also be operated in manual mode.

Supplemental Restraint System

INSTRUCTIONS

When any service is performed around the supplemental restraint system (air bag) components or wiring, the system must be disabled to prevent accidental deployment.

DISABLING

1. Disconnect the negative battery cable.
2. Remove the air bag fuse from the main fuse box.
3. Disconnect the air bag control module.

ACTIVATING

1. Connect the air bag control module.
2. Install the air bag fuse in the main fuse box.
3. Connect the negative battery cable.
4. Turn ignition switch to **ON**. After 6 to 10 seconds, **SRS** lamp on instrument panel will come on for 3 to 4 seconds.

Service Valve Locations

The high-pressure service valve is located on top of the receiver/drier. The low-pressure service valve is on an extension tube in front of the battery.

System Discharging

───── CAUTION ─────

Under no circumstances should draining and filling equipment for R134a refrigerant be used for R12 refrigerant, and vice-versa. Small amounts of the wrong refrigerant or the wrong compressor oil can cause chemical reactions which will damage both the servicing equipment and the air conditioning system.

1. Connect the manifold gauge high pressure hose to the high pressure service valve.
2. Connect the manifold gauge low pressure hose to the low pressure service valve.

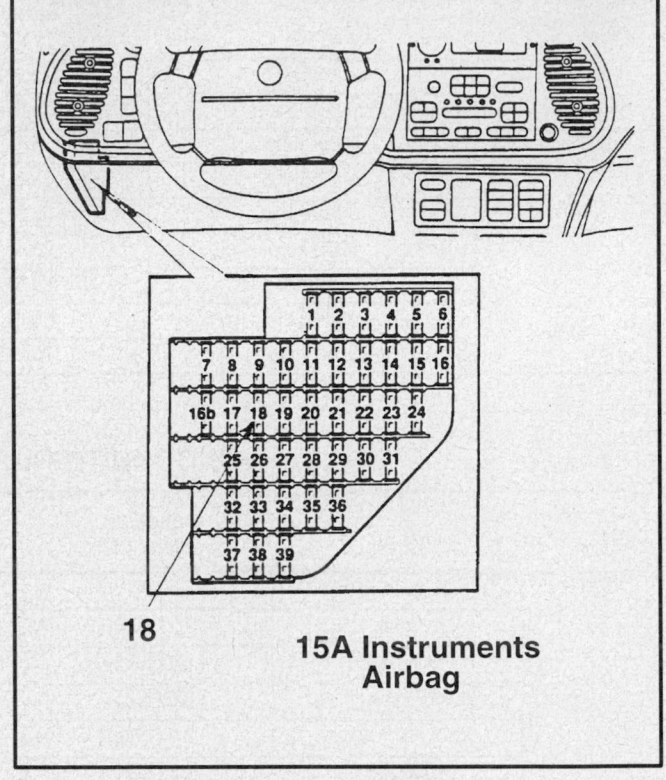

Airbag fuse location—1994–95 900

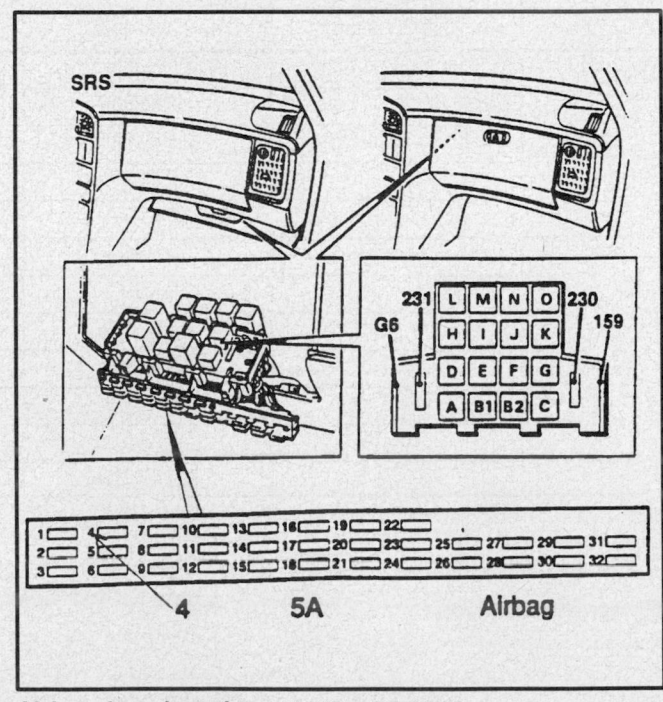

Airbag fuse location—1994–95 9000

1 Knee guard, driver's side
2 Steering wheel center pad
3 Passenger side airbag
4 Knee guard, passenger side
5 Control module
6 Seat belt tensioner

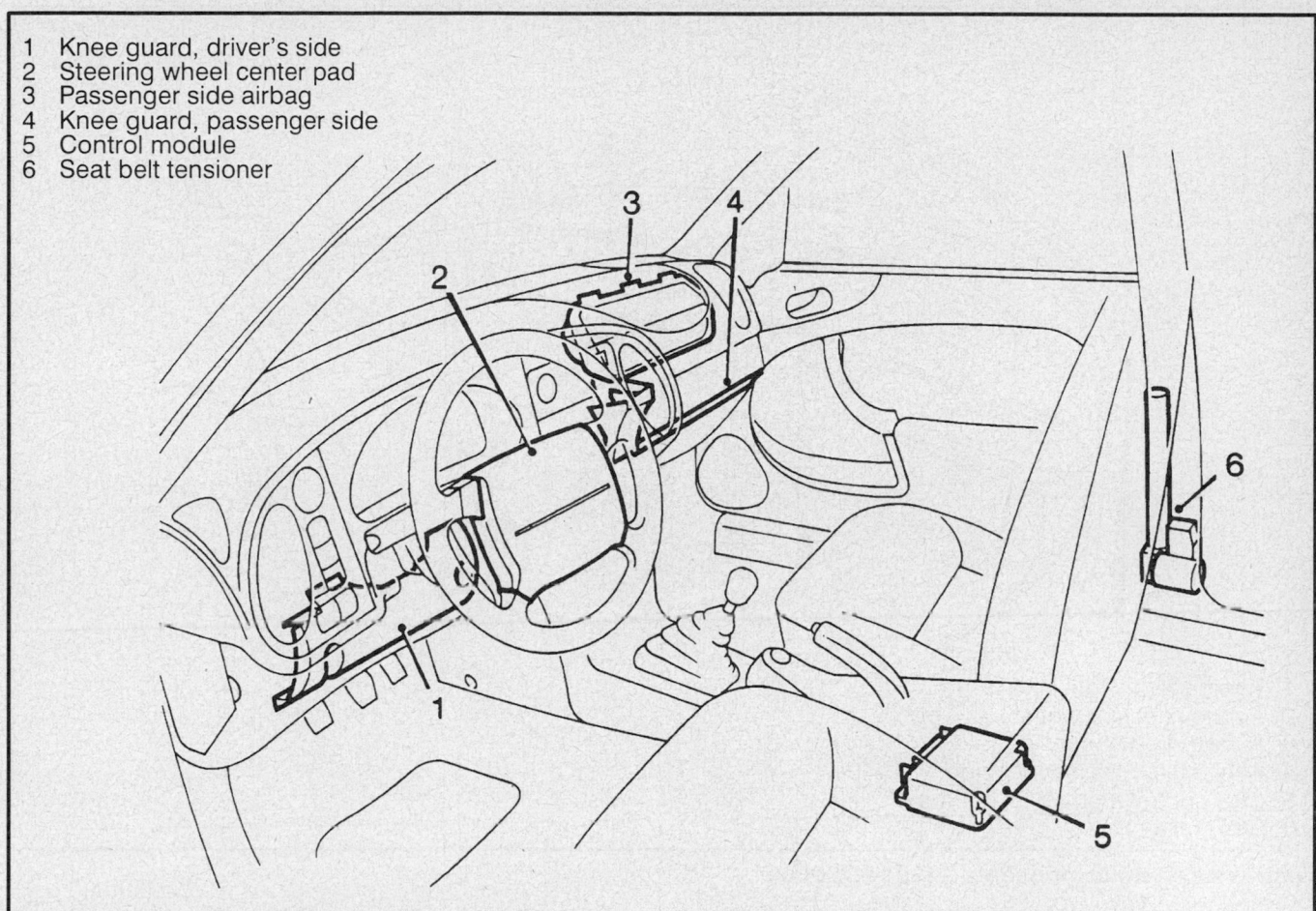

Restraint system components—1994—95 900

NOTE: Do not apply refrigerant oil to the seat of the connection. To prevent releasing refrigerant, use charging hoses with a stop valve when installing the manifold gauge set to the service valves on the refrigerant lines. If using a stop valve, close the valve prior to connecting the hoses to the service valves.

3. Connect the center manifold gauge hose to a recovery machine.
4. Operate the recovery machine.
5. Open both high and low pressure hand valves of the manifold gauge set.

NOTE: When operating the recovery machine, always follow the directions given in the instruction manual for the machine. After recovery, the amount of refrigerant oil removed must be measured and the same amount added into the system when recharging.

6. Stop the recovery machine when discharging has been completed.
7. Remove the manifold gauge set and replace the service valve caps.

System Evacuating

NOTE: Before charging the system with refrigerant, be sure to completely evacuate the system.

1. Properly connect a manifold gauge set to the service valves.
2. Discharge the refrigerant from the system according to the proper procedure but leave the high and low pressure manifold gauge hoses connected to the service valves.
3. Connect the center hose of the manifold gauge set to a vacuum pump.
4. Open both the high and low pressure hand valves and run the vacuum pump.

NOTE: If opening the low pressure hand valve pulls the high pressure gauge into the vacuum range, there is no blockage in the system.

5. After 10 minutes or more, check that the low pressure gauge indicates 29.53 in. Hg or more of vacuum.

NOTE: If the reading is not 29.53 in. Hg or more of vacuum, close both the high and low hand valves of the manifold gauge set and stop the vacuum pump. Then, check the system for leaks and repair, as necessary.

6. Close both the high and low hand valves and stop the vacuum pump.
7. Leave the system in this condition for 5 minutes or longer and check that there is no change in the gauge indicator.

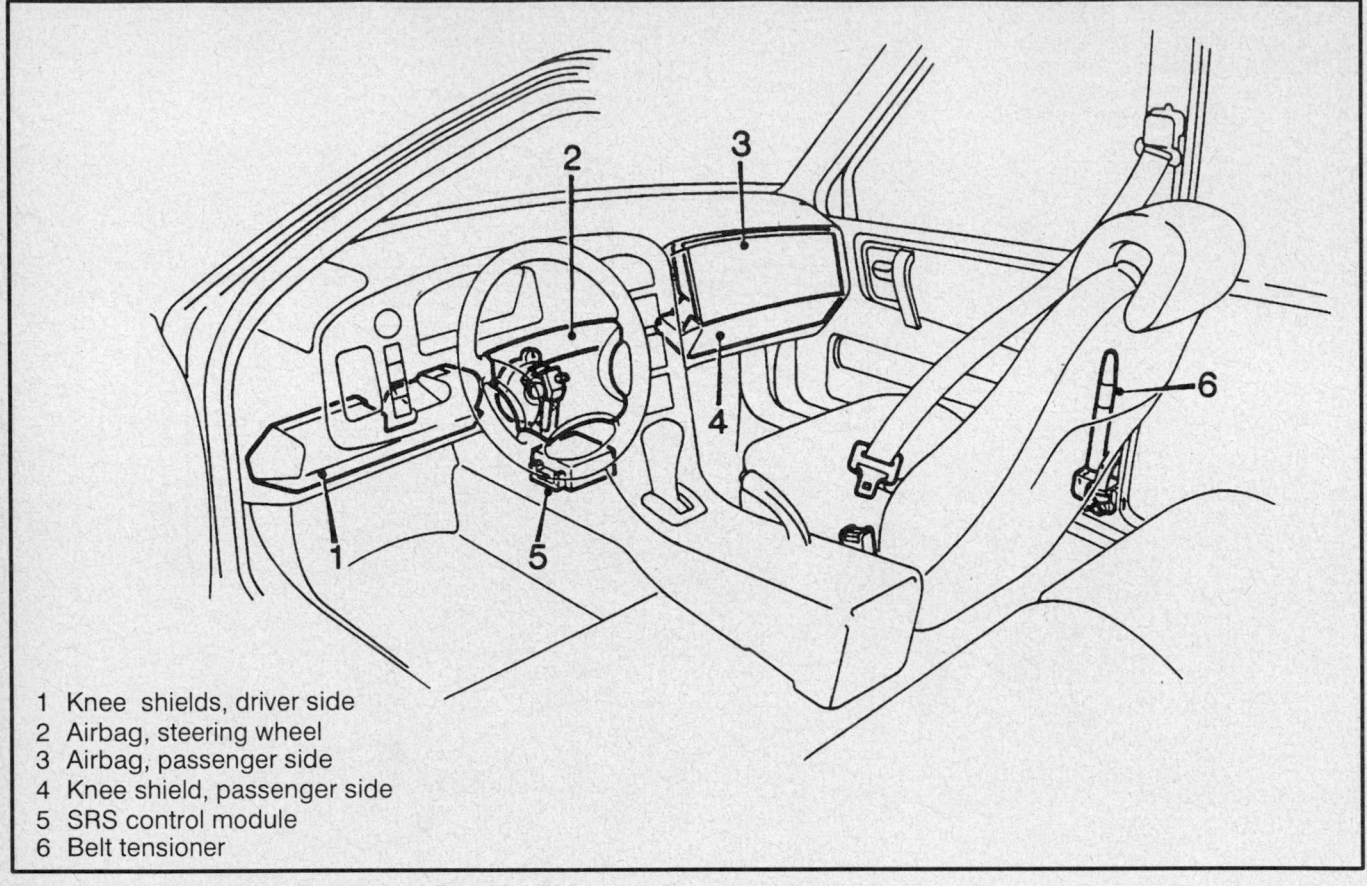

1 Knee shields, driver side
2 Airbag, steering wheel
3 Airbag, passenger side
4 Knee shield, passenger side
5 SRS control module
6 Belt tensioner

Restraint system components—1994—95 9000

System Charging

Use only approved recharging/recycling service equipment. The use of small cans is not recommended as adequate control of refrigerant charge. Always follow equipment manufacturers instructions for recharging the system.

SYSTEM COMPONENTS

Charge Air Cooler

REMOVAL AND INSTALLATION

1994—95 900

1. Release the 2 grille snap-in lugs. Lift the grille up and away from the 2 locating pins and out of the vehicle.
2. Disconnect and remove the horn.
3. Remove the direction indicators and headlamps as follows:
   • Remove the direction indicator retaining bolt and lift out the direction indicator.
   • Remove the 3 headlamp retaining bolts.
   • Lift the headlamp away from the vehicle and disconnect the headlamp connectors. Remove the headlamp.
4. Raise and safely support the vehicle.
5. Remove the 13 retaining bolts from the right- and left-side spoiler skirts.
6. Remove the screws retaining the fender liners to the bumper ends.
7. Pull the fender liners aside to gain access to the outer spoiler retaining bolts. Remove the bolts.
8. Remove the spoiler middle retaining bolt.

9. Unsnap the 4 snap fasteners on each spoiler section and pull the spoiler sections forward to remove.
10. Disconnect the ambient air temperature sensor and the headlamp washer hose.
11. Remove the 2 bumper mounting bolts and pull the bumper forward.
12. Disconnect the hoses from the charge air cooler.
13. Remove the screws and the charge air cooler.
To install:
14. Position the charge air cooler, ensuring that the plastic foam seams and rubber bushings on the left side are correctly positioned.
15. Attach the charge air cooler hoses and tighten the attaching screws.
16. Push the bumper into position and install the 2 bumper mounting bolts.
17. Connect the ambient air temperature sensor and the headlamp washer hose.
18. Install the spoiler skirts by reversing the removal procedure.
19. Remove the supports and lower the vehicle.
20. Connect the electrical connectors and install the headlamps and direction indicators by reversing the removal procedure.
21. Install the horn and the grille.

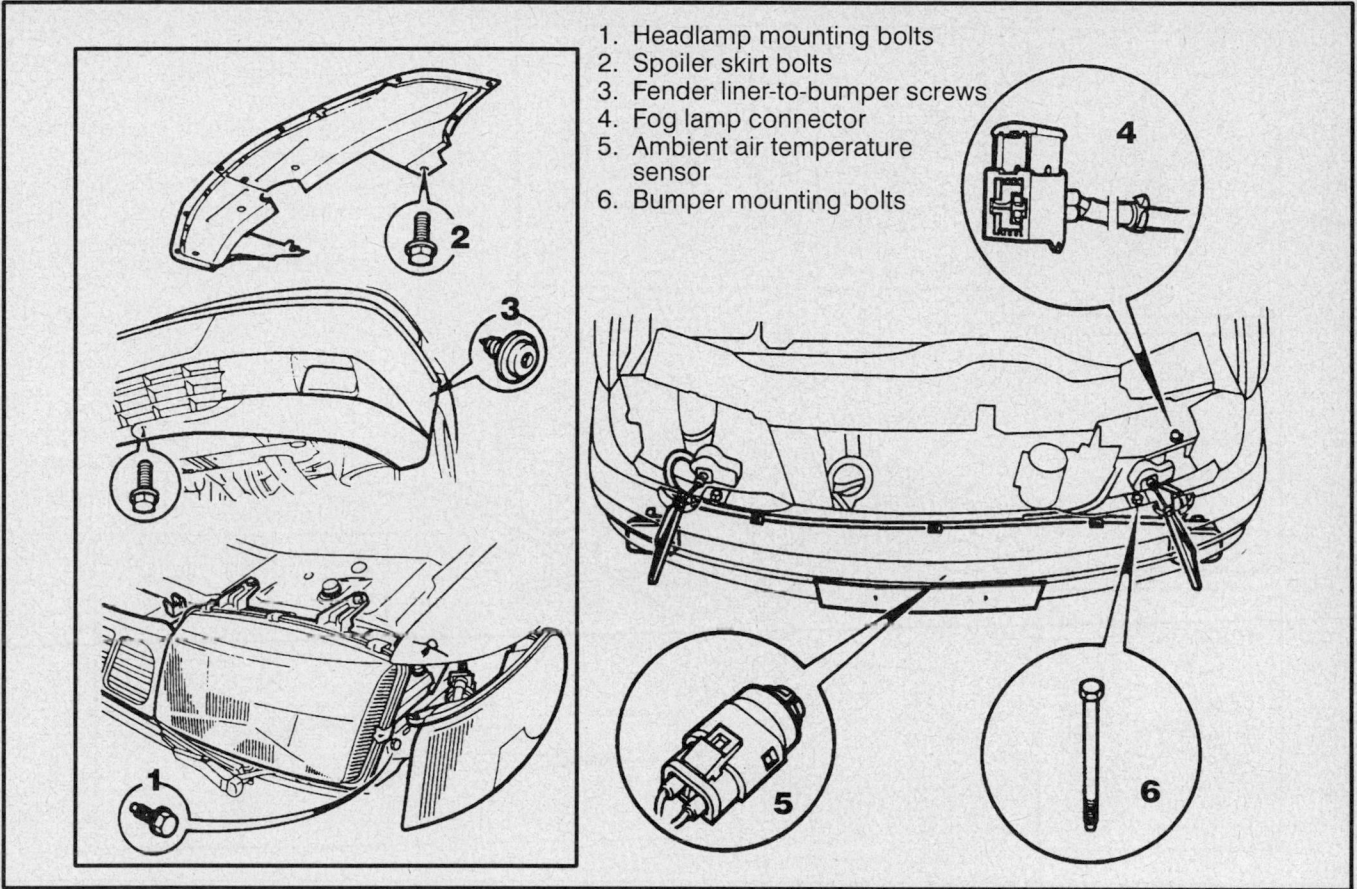

1. Headlamp mounting bolts
2. Spoiler skirt bolts
3. Fender liner-to-bumper screws
4. Fog lamp connector
5. Ambient air temperature sensor
6. Bumper mounting bolts

Charge air cooler access—1994–95 900

Radiator

REMOVAL AND INSTALLATION

1994–95 900

1. On Turbo models, remove the charge air cooler.
2. On non-Turbo models, release the 2 grille snap-in lugs. Lift the grille up and away from the 2 locating pins and out of the vehicle.
3. Release the engine oil cooler (if installed) and position it away from the radiator, ensuring that the oil cooler lines are not damaged.
4. Separate the air conditioning condenser from the radiator.
5. Disconnect and remove the battery. Remove the battery tray.
6. Properly drain the coolant.

NOTE: Removing the lid from the coolant expansion tank will allow the coolant to drain faster.

7. On Turbo models, remove the bypass hose together with the intake hose.
8. On 4-cylinder models, disconnect the upper radiator hoses at the radiator.
9. On 6-cylinder models, completely remove the upper radiator hoses.
10. Disconnect the radiator fan electrical connectors.
11. Release the servo pump oil line and the radiator breather hose clips from the radiator crossmember and turn the oil line to one side.

12. Remove the 2 radiator fan assembly attaching screws. Lift the fan assembly from the vehicle.
13. On automatic transmission models, carefully disconnect the transmission oil cooler lines. Remove the screw attaching the oil cooler lines to the radiator and plug the connections to prevent leakage and contamination.
14. Disconnect the lower radiator hose at the radiator.
15. Remove the clamps attaching the radiator to the radiator crossmember.
16. Raise the radiator slightly and release the air conditioner compressor cable clips.
17. Lift the radiator out of the vehicle.

To install:

18. Lubricate the rubber radiator mounting bushings with petroleum jelly and position the radiator on the bushings.
19. Attach the air conditioner compressor cable clips.
20. Push the radiator down on the mounting bushings and install the radiator-to-crossmember attaching clips.
21. On automatic transmission models, unplug and connect the transmission cooler line fittings. Torque the fittings to 18.5 ft. lbs. (25 Nm).
22. Secure the transmission cooler lines to the radiator with 1 screw.
23. Tighten the radiator drain plug to 3 ft. lbs. (4 Nm).
24. Connect the lower radiator hose to the radiator.
25. Position and secure the radiator fan assembly with 2 screws. Connect the radiator fan electrical connector.
26. Attach the radiator breather hose clips and the servo pump oil line clamp to the radiator crossmember.
27. On 6-cylinder models, install the upper radiator hoses.
28. On 4-cylinder models, connect the upper radiator hoses at the radiator.

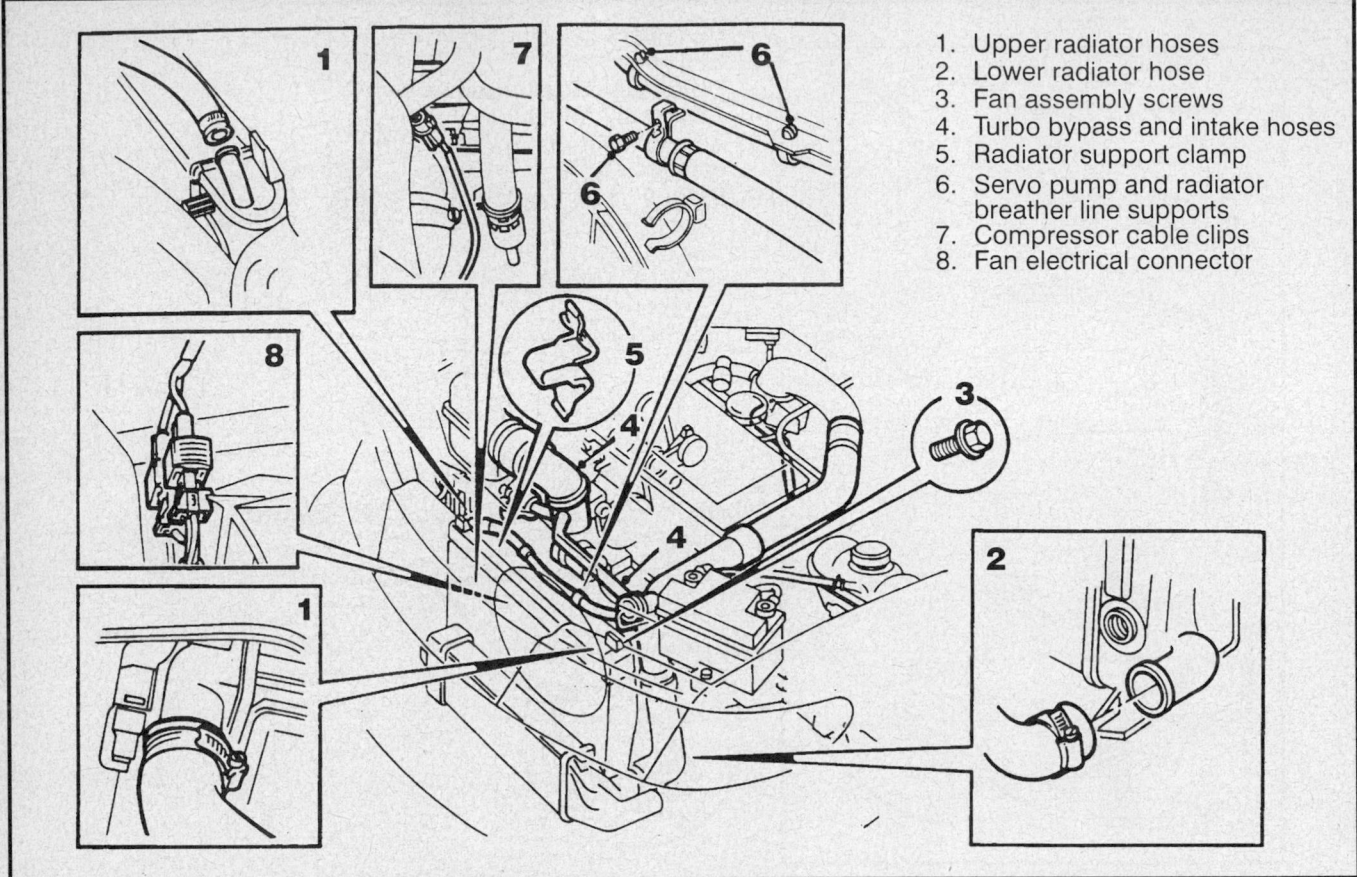

1. Upper radiator hoses
2. Lower radiator hose
3. Fan assembly screws
4. Turbo bypass and intake hoses
5. Radiator support clamp
6. Servo pump and radiator breather line supports
7. Compressor cable clips
8. Fan electrical connector

Radiator removal and installation—1994–95 900

29. On Turbo models, install the bypass hose together with the intake hose.
30. Fill the system with coolant and test for leaks.
31. Install the battery tray and battery.
32. On automatic transmission models, check the transmission fluid level and add fluid if necessary.
33. Position and secure the air conditioning condenser.
34. Position and secure the engine oil cooler (if installed).
35. On non-Turbo models, install the grille.
36. On Turbo models, install the charge air cooler.
37. Bleed the cooling system.

9000

1. Loosen the expansion tank pressure cap.
2. Raise and safely support the vehicle.
3. Remove the center air deflector.
4. Properly drain the coolant.
5. Remove the 2 air conditioning condenser lower retaining bolts.
6. Remove the supports and lower the vehicle.
7. Disconnect the upper coolant hose at the radiator.
8. Remove the air cleaner air intake tube (if necessary).
9. Remove the air conditioning condenser upper retaining bolt.
10. On Turbo models, disconnect the boost pressure control valve cables and remove the boost pressure control valve from the bracket on the radiator fan assembly.
11. Disconnect the electrical connectors from the radiator fan and the thermostatic switch.
12. Remove the top bolt from the oil cooler (if installed).

Loosen the 2 bottom bolts and separate the oil cooler from the radiator.
13. Disconnect the breather hose and the lower coolant hose from the radiator.
14. Remove the ignition coil mounting (if necessary).
15. On automatic transmission models, carefully disconnect the transmission fluid cooler lines. Plug the fittings to prevent leakage and contamination.
16. Remove the bolt securing the radiator to the radiator crossmember. Lift the radiator from the vehicle.
To install:
17. Position the oil cooler (if installed) in front of the air conditioning compressor.

NOTE: Ensure that the oil cooler lines are positioned correctly.

18. Install the radiator in the rubber radiator mountings.
19. Push the radiator down and install the upper radiator-to-radiator crossmember bolt.
20. On automatic transmission models, connect the transmission fluid cooler lines. Torque the fittings to 18.5 ft. lbs. (25 Nm).
21. Attach the oil cooler (if installed) to the radiator.
22. Connect the breather hose and the lower coolant hose to the radiator.
23. On Turbo models, install the boost pressure control valve on the radiator fan housing and connect the control valve cables.
24. Attach the ignition coil mount to the radiator crossmember (if removed).
25. Connect the radiator fan and thermostatic switch electrical connectors.

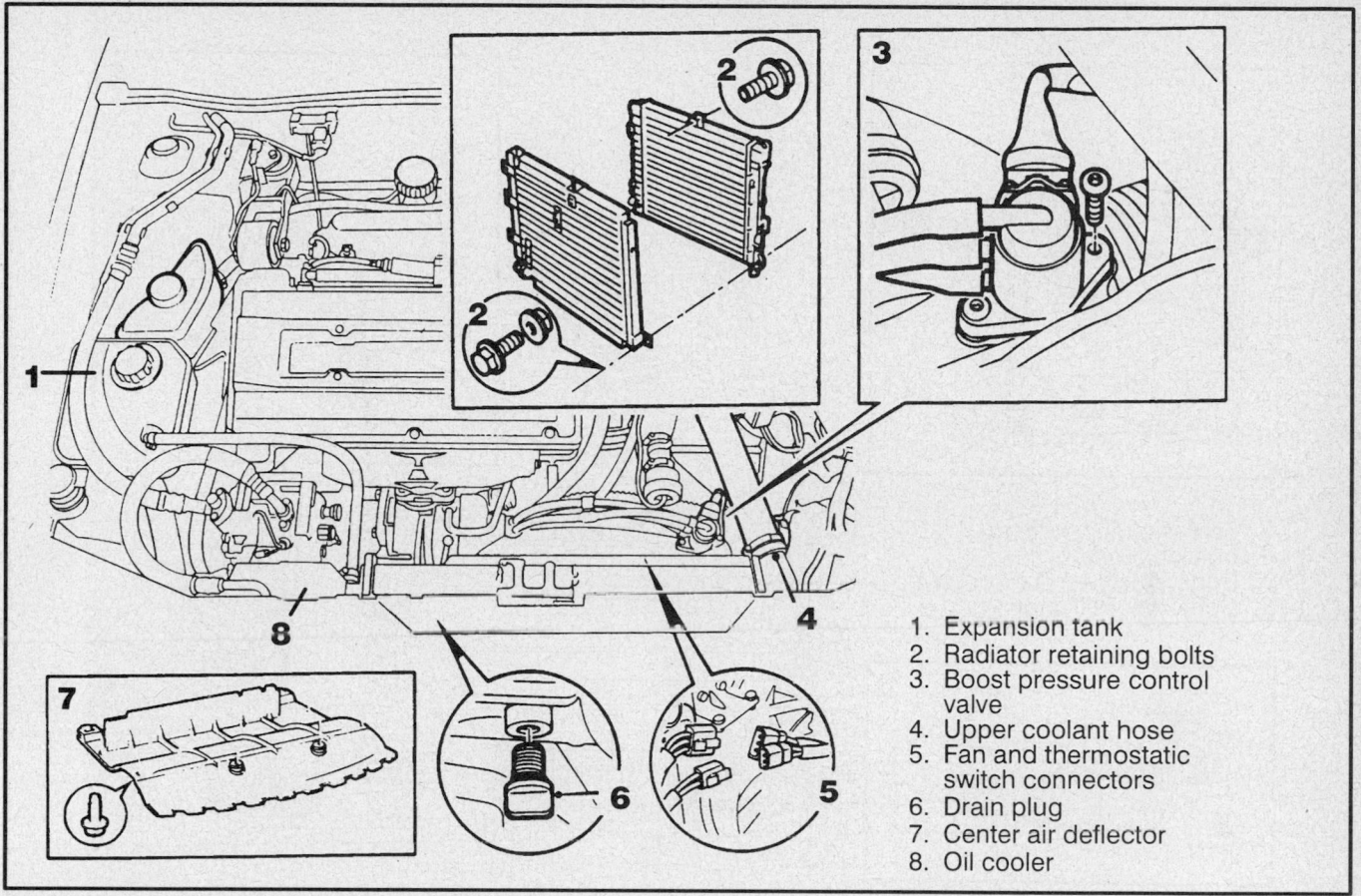

1. Expansion tank
2. Radiator retaining bolts
3. Boost pressure control valve
4. Upper coolant hose
5. Fan and thermostatic switch connectors
6. Drain plug
7. Center air deflector
8. Oil cooler

Radiator removal and installation—9000

26. Connect the upper coolant hose to the radiator.
27. Install the air conditioning condenser upper retaining bolt.
28. Install the air cleaner air intake tube (if removed).
29. Raise and safely support the vehicle.
30. Install the 2 air conditioning condenser lower retaining bolts.
31. Install the drain plug. Hand tighten only.
32. Install the center air deflector.
33. Remove the supports and lower the vehicle.
34. Fill the system with coolant and test for leaks.
35. On automatic transmission models, check the transmission fluid level and add fluid if necessary.
36. Fill the expansion tank with coolant and install the pressure cap.
37. Bleed the cooling system.

COOLING SYSTEM BLEEDING

1. Fill the cooling system to the **MAX** level.
2. Install the pressure cap.
3. Run the engine, preferably at varying speeds, until the radiator fan starts.
4. Remove the pressure cap and add coolant to the **MAX** level.
5. Repeat steps 2, 3 and 4 three times.
6. Turn off the engine and add coolant to the **MAX** level if necessary.

Electric Cooling Fan

REMOVAL AND INSTALLATION

1994–95 900

1. Disconnect and remove the battery.
2. Remove the battery tray.
3. Disconnect the radiator fan electrical connector.
4. Release the servo pump oil line and the radiator breather hose clips from the radiator crossmember and turn the oil line to one side.
5. Remove the 2 radiator fan assembly attaching screws. Lift the fan assembly from the vehicle.
6. Installation is the reverse of the removal procedure.

9000

1. Disconnect the radiator fan electrical connection.
2. Disconnect the ignition coil **HT** lead (if installed) at the distributor cap.
3. On Turbo models, disconnect the boost pressure control valve electrical connector and remove the boost pressure control valve from the radiator fan housing. Move the boost pressure control valve to one side.
4. Remove the 2 upper retaining screws from the radiator fan housing. Bend the fan housing slightly to allow access to the radiator fan cable assembly retaining clip.
5. Release the radiator fan cable assembly from the retaining clip.
6. Raise and safely support the vehicle.

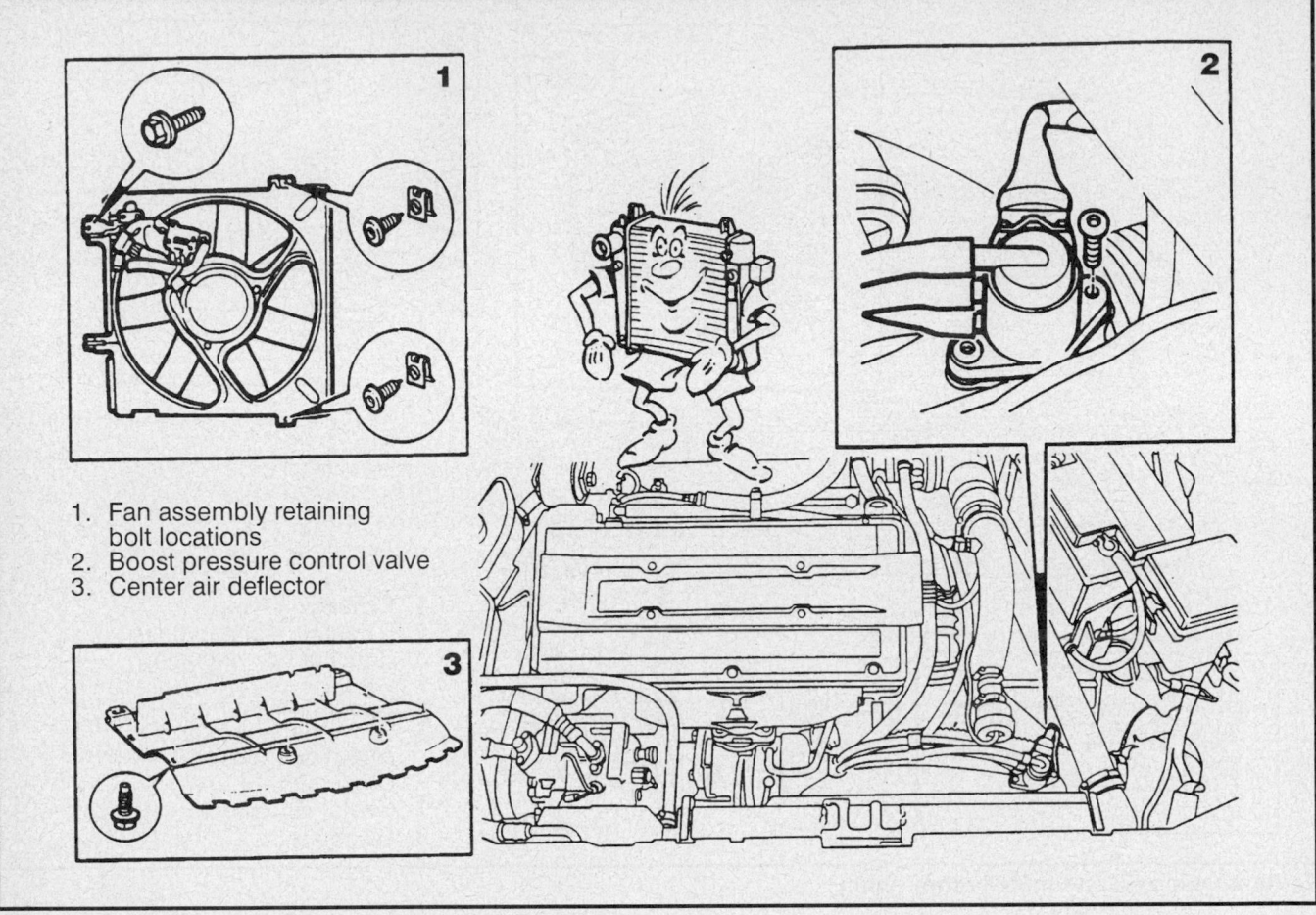

1. Fan assembly retaining bolt locations
2. Boost pressure control valve
3. Center air deflector

Radiator cooling fan removal and installation—9000

7. Remove the center air deflector.
8. Remove the lower retaining screw from the radiator fan housing.
9. Remove the supports and lower the vehicle.
10. Lift the fan assembly from the vehicle.
11. Installation is the reverse of the removal procedure.

Condenser

REMOVAL AND INSTALLATION

1994–95 900

1. Properly discharge the refrigerant. Observe all safety precautions.
2. On Turbo models, remove the charge air cooler and the duct between the charge air cooler and the intake manifold.
3. On non-Turbo models, release the 2 grille snap-in lugs. Lift the grille up and away from the 2 locating pins and out of the vehicle.
4. On non-Turbo models, disconnect and remove the horn.
5. On non-Turbo models, remove the left side direction indicator and headlamp as follows:
 • Remove the direction indicator retaining bolt and lift out the direction indicator.
 • Remove the 3 headlamp retaining bolts.

 • Lift the headlamp away from the vehicle and disconnect the headlamp connector. Remove the headlamp.
6. Disconnect the receiver pressure switch electrical connector(s).
7. Remove the bolt from the receiver PAD connector. Plug the openings to prevent entry of dirt and moisture.
8. Remove the 2 condenser retaining bolts and lift the condenser together with the receiver from the vehicle.
9. Installation is the reverse of the removal procedure. Use new O-rings lubricated with clean refrigerant oil at the PAD connector and torque the PAD connector bolt to 6.6 ft. lbs. (9 Nm).

1993 9000

1. Properly discharge the refrigerant. Observe all safety precautions.
2. Remove the grille retaining screws and lift the grille from the vehicle.
3. Detach and remove the front spoiler.
4. Disconnect condenser cooling fan electrical connectors and remove condenser cooling fan (if equipped).
5. Carefully disconnect the condenser inlet and outlet fittings and cap or plug the openings to prevent entry of dirt and moisture.
6. Raise and safely support the vehicle.
7. Working under the vehicle, remove the condenser support bolts. Remove the condenser from below.
8. Installation is the reverse of the removal procedure.

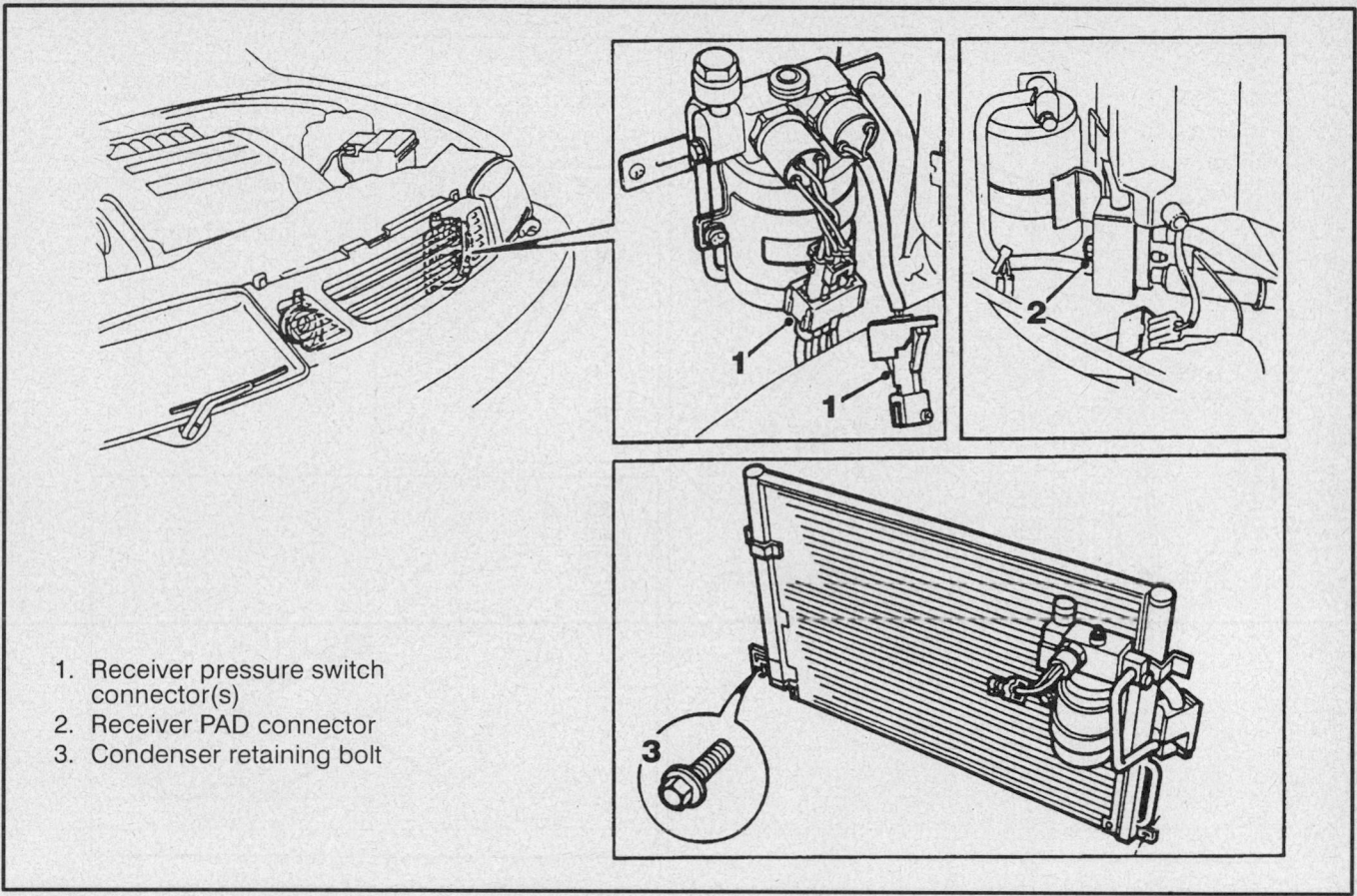

1. Receiver pressure switch connector(s)
2. Receiver PAD connector
3. Condenser retaining bolt

Condenser removal and installation—1994–95 900

Compressor

REMOVAL AND INSTALLATION

1993 900

1. Properly discharge the refrigerant. Observe all safety precautions.
2. Loosen the adjusting link and remove the compressor belt.
3. Disconnect the compressor electrical connectors.
4. Disconnect the high- and low-pressure lines from the compressor. Plug the openings to prevent entry of dirt and moisture.
5. Remove the 4 compressor retaining bolts and lift the compressor from the vehicle.
6. Installation is the reverse of the removal procedure.
7. Leak test, evacuate and recharge the system.

1994–95 900

1. Properly discharge the refrigerant. Observe all safety precautions.
2. On Turbo models, remove the turbo air intake manifold.
3. Remove the compressor drive belt and disconnect the compressor electrical connector.
4. Disconnect the high- and low-pressure hoses at the compressor. Plug the openings to prevent entry of dirt and moisture.
5. On 4-cylinder, non-Turbo models, remove the compressor retaining bolts and lift the compressor out of the vehicle.

6. On Turbo and 6-cylinder models:
   • Remove the upper 2 compressor retaining bolts.
   • Raise and safely support the vehicle.
   • Remove the air shield in front of the wheel housing.
   • Remove the lower compressor retaining bolt and lower the compressor under the oil cooler lines.
To install:
7. Adjust the oil level in the compressor.

NOTE: A new service replacement Seiko-Seiki SS121 DN1 compressor contains 6.8 oz. (200 ml) of refrigerant oil. Prior to installing the replacement compressor, drain the refrigerant oil from the removed compressor into a calibrated container. Then, drain the refrigerant oil from the new compressor into a clean calibrated container. Measure the amount of oil drained from the removed compressor and pour the same amount of clean oil back into the new compressor.

8. Installation is the reverse of the removal procedure. Use new O-rings, lubricated with clean refrigerant oil, on the low- and high-pressure line fittings. Torque the fittings to 14.8 ft. lbs. (20 Nm).
9. Leak test, evacuate and recharge the system.

1993 9000

1. Disconnect the negative battery cable.
2. Properly discharge the refrigerant. Observe all safety precautions.
3. Disconnect the high- and low-pressure lines from the compressor. Plug the openings to prevent entry of dirt and moisture.

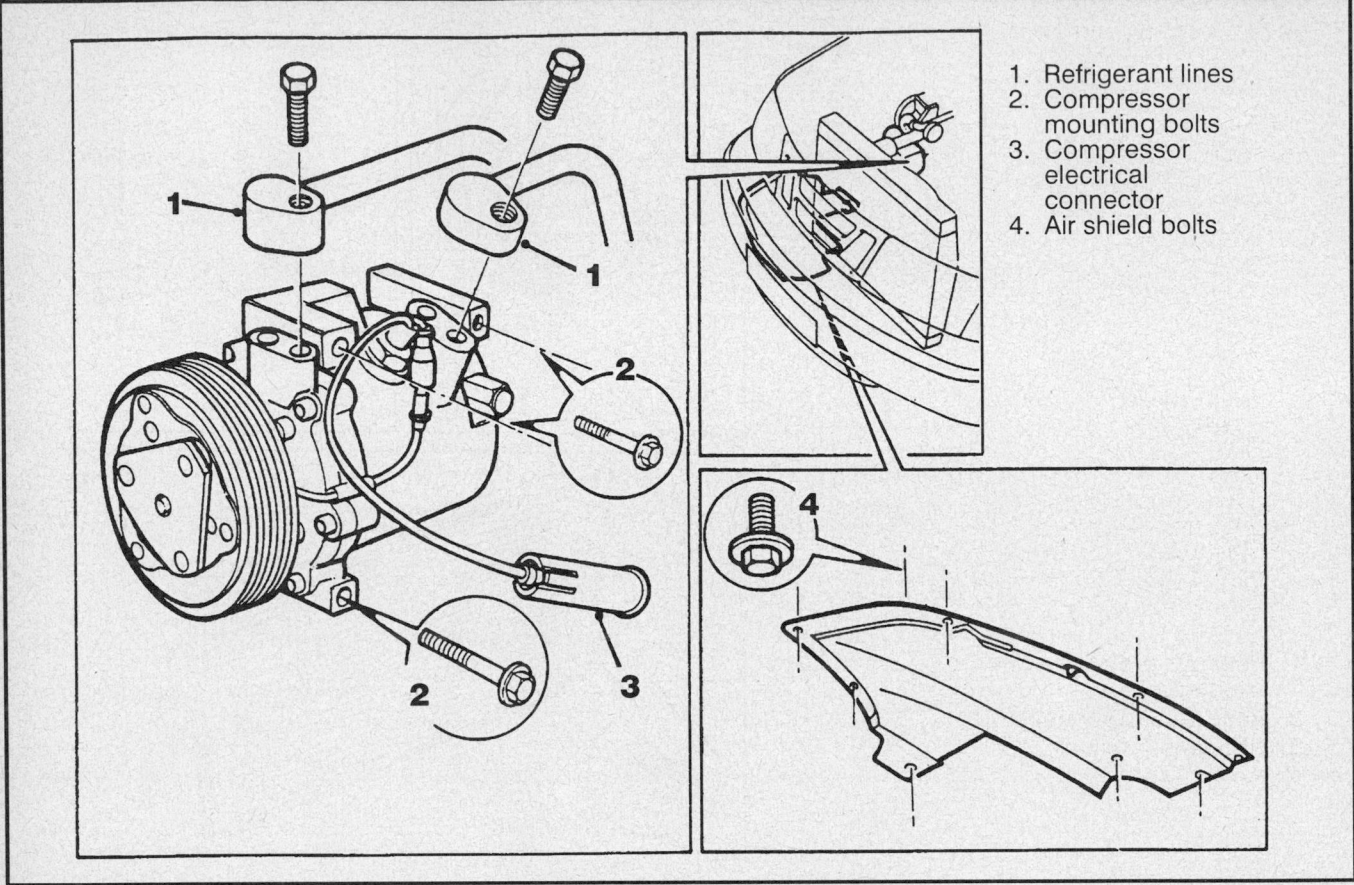

1. Refrigerant lines
2. Compressor mounting bolts
3. Compressor electrical connector
4. Air shield bolts

Compressor removal and installation—1994—95 900

NOTE: **The power steering reservoir can be bent aside to allow access to the refrigerant line connections.**

4. Disconnect the compressor clutch electrical connectors.
5. Remove the plastic cover from the right headlight.
6. Loosen the belt tensioner and remove the compressor belt.
7. Remove the belt tensioner pulley from the compressor and set the pulley aside.
8. Remove the compressor bolts and carefully lift the compressor from the vehicle.
9. Installation is the reverse of the removal procedure. Torque the compressor mounting bolts to 15–19 ft. lbs. (20–25 Nm) and the line connections to 53–80 inch lbs. (6–9 Nm).
10. Leak test, evacuate and recharge the system.

Receiver/Drier

NOTE: **Whenever a major component is being replaced in an air conditioning system or whenever an air conditioning system has been open to the atmosphere for an extended period of time, the receiver/drier should be replaced.**

REMOVAL AND INSTALLATION

1994—95 900

1. Properly discharge the refrigerant. Observe all safety precautions.

2. Release the 2 grille snap-in lugs and lift the grille up and out of the vehicle.
3. Disconnect the electrical connector(s) for the pressure switch(es).
4. Disconnect the lines from the receiver/drier. Plug the openings to prevent entry of dirt and moisture.
5. Loosen the receiver/drier bracket bolt and lift the receiver/drier out of the bracket.
6. Remove and save the pressure switch(es).
7. Installation is the reverse of the removal procedure. Use new O-rings, lubricated with clean refrigerant oil, at all pressure fittings. Torque the line connector bolts to 6.6 ft. lbs. (9 Nm).
8. Leak test, evacuate and recharge the system.

1993 9000

1. Disconnect the negative battery cable.
2. Properly discharge the refrigerant. Observe all safety precautions.
3. Remove the evaporator cover and disconnect the pressure switch electrical connectors.
4. Pull rubber molding and grommet out of the way and disconnect the refrigerant line fittings.
5. Disconnect the fitting at the expansion valve.
6. Remove the screw securing the receiver/drier and remove the receiver/drier.
7. Installation is the reverse of the removal procedure.
8. Leak test, evacuate and recharge the system.

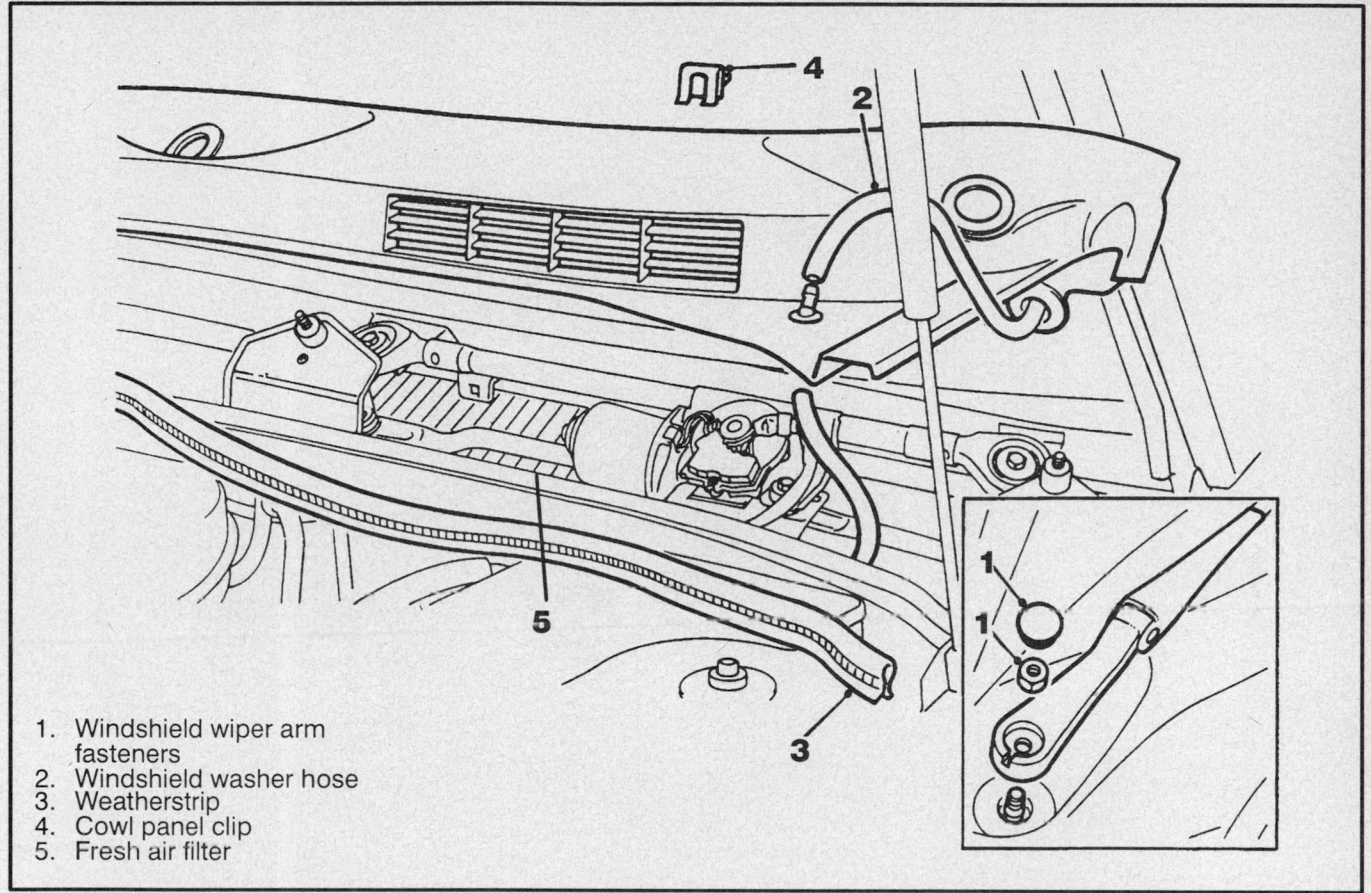

1. Windshield wiper arm
   fasteners
2. Windshield washer hose
3. Weatherstrip
4. Cowl panel clip
5. Fresh air filter

Fresh air filter access—1994—95 900

Fresh Air Filter

REMOVAL AND INSTALLATION

1994—95 900

1. Remove windshield wiper arms.
2. Disconnect the windshield washer hose at the cowl panel.
3. Remove the rubber weatherstrip from the cowl panel.
4. Remove the cowl panel retaining clip.
5. Raise the cowl panel slightly and disconnect the windshield washer hose from the underside. Remove the cowl panel.
6. Disconnect the windshield wiper motor electrical connector.
7. Remove the windshield wiper spindle guides.
8. Remove the 3 windshield wiper mechanism attaching bolts and lift the wiper mechanism out of the vehicle.
9. Release and lift out the fresh air filter.
10. Installation is the reverse of the removal procedure.

Blower Motor

REMOVAL AND INSTALLATION

1993 900

1. Disable the supplemental restraint system (air bag).
2. Remove the steering wheel and both speaker/defroster grilles.

3. Remove the 4 instrument cluster retaining screws.
4. Tilt the instrument cluster rearward and disconnect the electrical and vacuum connectors. Remove the instrument cluster.
5. Remove the upper instrument panel trim panel screws; then remove the instrument panel trim panel screws from under the glove compartment. Remove the instrument panel trim panel.
6. Disconnect the blower motor electrical connector.
7. Remove the 3 blower motor retaining screws and remove the blower motor.
8. Installation is the reverse of the removal procedure.

1994—95 900

1. Remove the fresh air filter.
2. Disconnect the blower motor electrical connector.
3. Remove the fresh air filter frame.
4. Remove the blower motor cover.
5. Remove the electrical connector attaching screw.
6. Remove the 2 blower motor attaching screws and lift the blower motor and blower fan from the vehicle.
7. Installation is the reverse of the removal procedure.

1993 9000

1. Disconnect the negative battery cable.
2. Remove the hood.
3. Remove the windshield wiper arms.
4. Remove the windshield wiper motor and air conditioning evaporator cover panels.
5. Disconnect the blower motor control unit electrical connector.

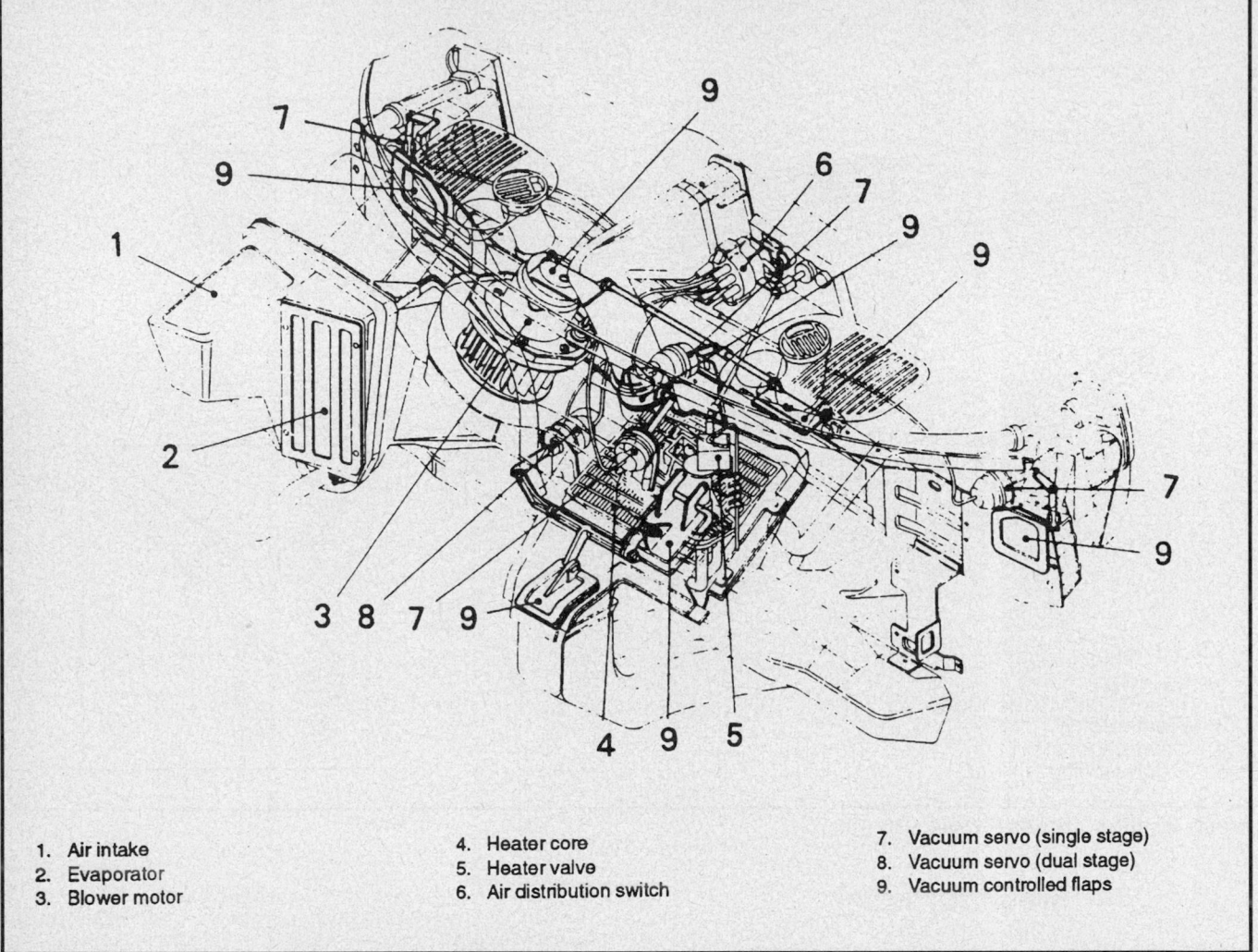

1. Air intake
2. Evaporator
3. Blower motor

4. Heater core
5. Heater valve
6. Air distribution switch

7. Vacuum servo (single stage)
8. Vacuum servo (dual stage)
9. Vacuum controlled flaps

Air conditioning component locations—1993 900

6. Remove the cowl cover panel seal and the signal converter.

7. Remove the cowl cover panel.

8. Remove the electronic ignition control unit mounting bolts and move the ignition unit to one side.

9. Remove the 4 cowl lead-through panel screws and remove the lead-through panel.

10. Disconnect the windshield wiper electrical connector and remove the windshield wiper mechanism.

11. Drain the cooling system, remove the coolant hose grommets and disconnect the coolant hose quick-disconnect couplings at the heater core.

12. Remove the cruise control vacuum pump mounting screws and push the pump aside.

13. Remove the evaporator retaining screws and the refrigerant hose retaining clips.

14. Disconnect the temperature control cable from the temperature valve.

15. Remove the engine bracket from the right rear corner of the engine compartment.

16. Remove the rear motor-mount nut. Using an engine sling attached to the rear engine-lift hook, carefully tilt the engine forward.

17. Carefully lift the evaporator, release the blower motor mounting clips and tilt the blower motor assembly to lift out.

18. Installation is the reverse of the removal procedure. During installation, ensure that all components are properly aligned and all clips are securely attached.

Heater Core

REMOVAL AND INSTALLATION

1993 900

1. Disconnect the negative battery cable.

2. Properly drain the cooling system.

3. Disconnect the heater hoses at the heater valve fittings. Plug the ends of the fittings on the valve.

4. Disable the supplemental restraint system (air bag) if installed.

5. Remove the lower steering column cover.

6. Remove the storage console (if installed) as follows:

● Remove the ashtray and the ashtray bracket.

● Remove the console attaching bolt through the ashtray opening.

● Remove the gauges and radio components (if installed) from the storage console.

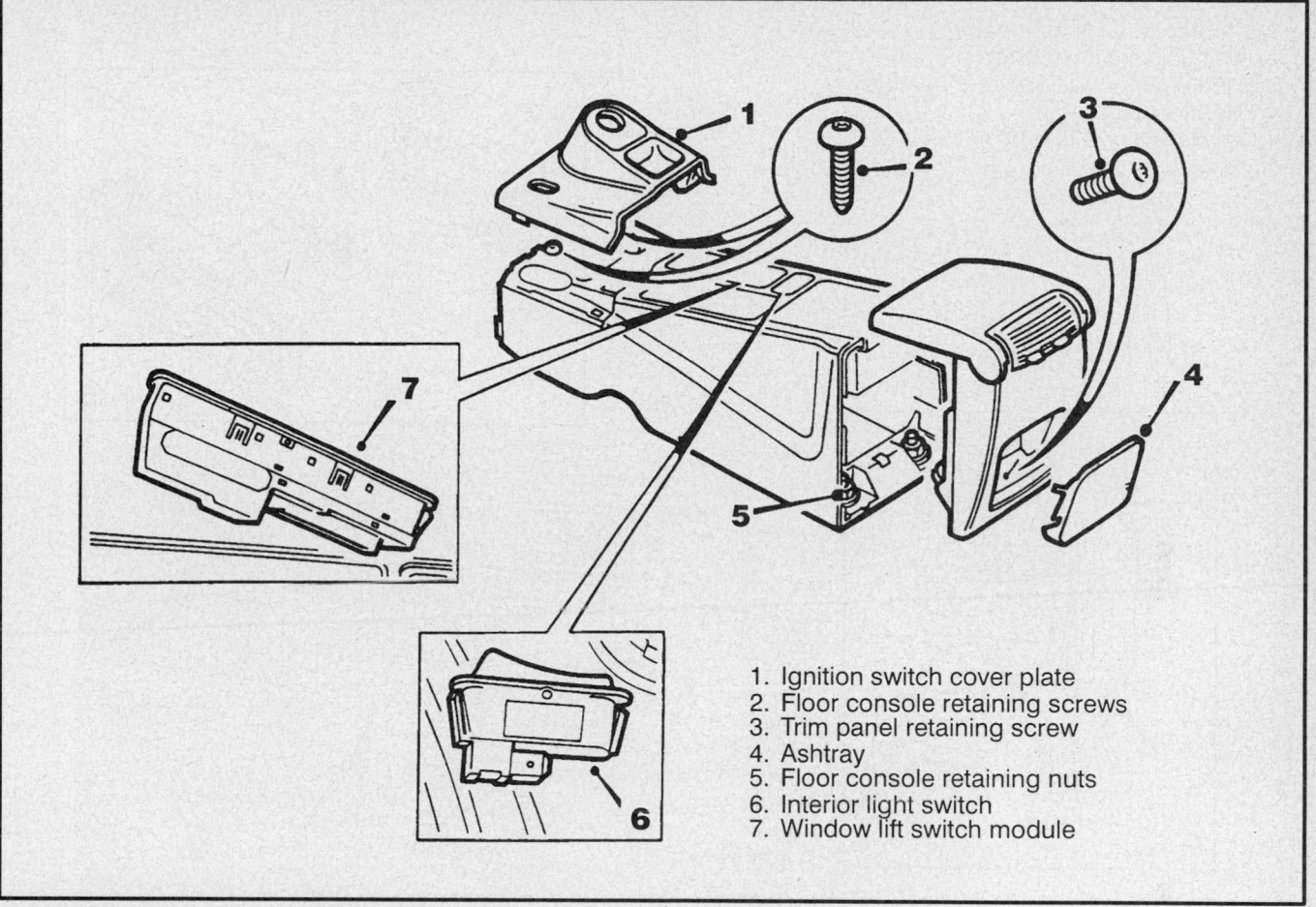

1. Ignition switch cover plate
2. Floor console retaining screws
3. Trim panel retaining screw
4. Ashtray
5. Floor console retaining nuts
6. Interior light switch
7. Window lift switch module

Floor console removal and installation—1994–95 900

• Remove the 6 console attaching screws and remove the console.

7. Remove the lower instrument panel pad as follows:

• In the engine compartment, remove the 2 lower instrument panel pad nuts, which are located near the door hinges.

• Remove the ashtray and the ashtray bracket.

• Remove the lower instrument panel pad center bolt through the ashtray opening and remove the pad.

8. Remove the left speaker and defroster grille.

9. Slide the heater control rod forward to disengage the control knob, then backward to disconnect the heater valve.

10. Remove the air diffuser ducts from the heater core case.

11. Remove the screws from the lower section of the heater core case and separate the lower and upper sections.

12. Disconnect the return spring from the brake pedal and depress the pedal slightly to allow the heater valve to clear the steering column.

13. Lower the heater core together with the heater valve assembly from the vehicle.

14. Carefully remove the capillary tube from the heater core.

15. Remove the 4 heater valve attaching screws and separate the heater valve from the heater core.

16. Installation is the reverse of the removal procedure. Use new O-rings between the heater valve and the heater core. Bleed the cooling system.

1994–95 900

1. Properly drain the cooling system.

2. Disconnect the heater water hoses at the firewall in the engine compartment.

3. Blow any remaining coolant from the heater core with compressed air.

4. Remove the glove compartment retaining screws, bolt, quick-release pin and bracket catch. Pull the glove compartment out partway to disconnect the lamp; then remove the glove compartment.

5. Remove the floor console as follows:

• Apply the handbrake.

• Remove the ignition switch cover plate by loosening the left front corner first and working around the plate counterclockwise. Disconnect the ignition switch lighting connector.

• Remove the rear ashtray. Remove the rear trim panel retaining screw and trim panel.

• Remove the floor console retaining screws and nuts.

• Pull the floor console to the rear and lift to gain access to the window lift and interior light switch connectors.

• Remove and disconnect the window lift and interior light switches.

• Lift and remove the floor console.

6. Remove the center console side panel screws and remove both side panels.

7. On manual transmission models, release the shift lever boot clips and remove the boot.

8. Reach in through side panel openings and push out the heating and air conditioning control panel.

9. Disconnect the electrical and mechanical connectors (as applicable) and remove the heating and air conditioning control panel.

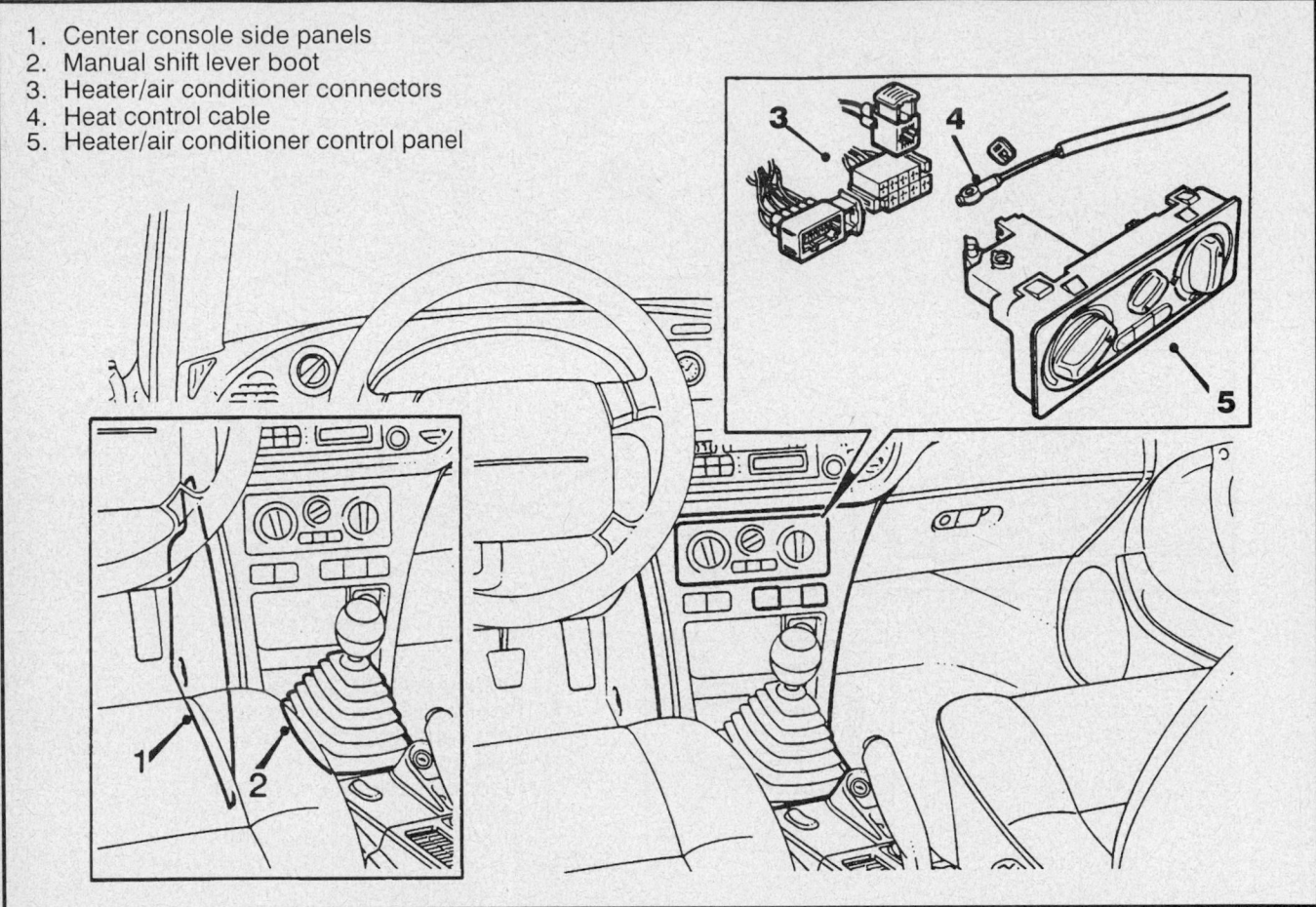

1. Center console side panels
2. Manual shift lever boot
3. Heater/air conditioner connectors
4. Heat control cable
5. Heater/air conditioner control panel

Center console removal and installation—1994−95 900

10. Disconnect the center console electrical connectors.
11. Remove the center console-to-instrument panel quick-release pins.
12. Remove the center console.
13. Cut the tie-wraps and remove the rear air ducts.
14. Open the heater core case.
15. Disconnect the hoses from the heater core.
16. Remove the toggle clips at the sides of the heater core case.
17. Pull the heater hoses down and lift out the heater core.
18. Installation is the reverse of the removal procedure. On 6-cylinder models, bleed the cooling system after the installation is complete.

1993 9000

1. Remove the blower motor assembly.
2. Properly drain the cooling system.
3. Release the quick-disconnect fittings.
4. Disconnect the heater hoses at the heater core.
5. Lift the evaporator core enough to allow the heater core to clear the opening.
6. Remove the heater core.
7. Installation is the reverse of the removal procedure. Use new O-rings at the quick-disconnect fittings.

Evaporator

REMOVAL AND INSTALLATION

1993 900

1. Properly discharge the refrigerant. Observe all safety procedures.
2. Disconnect the refrigerant lines from the expansion vavle and the evaporator. Plug the openings to prevent entry of dirt and moisture.
3. Remove the 2 upper evaporator cover bolts and remove the upper section of the evaporator cover.
4. Remove the servo pump.
5. Remove the 4 evaporator mounting bolts and remove the evaporator.
6. Installation is the reverse of the removal procedure. Torque the expansion valve/evaporator connection to 15–20 ft. lbs. (21–27 Nm), the receiver/expansion valve line connector to 10–15 ft. lbs. (14–20 Nm) and the evaporator/compressor line connection to 21–29 ft. lbs. (28–39 Nm).

1994−95 900

1. Properly discharge the refrigerant. Observe all safety precautions.
2. Remove the glove compartment retaining screws, bolt, quick-release pin and bracket catch. Pull the glove compartment out partway to disconnect the lamp; then remove the glove compartment.

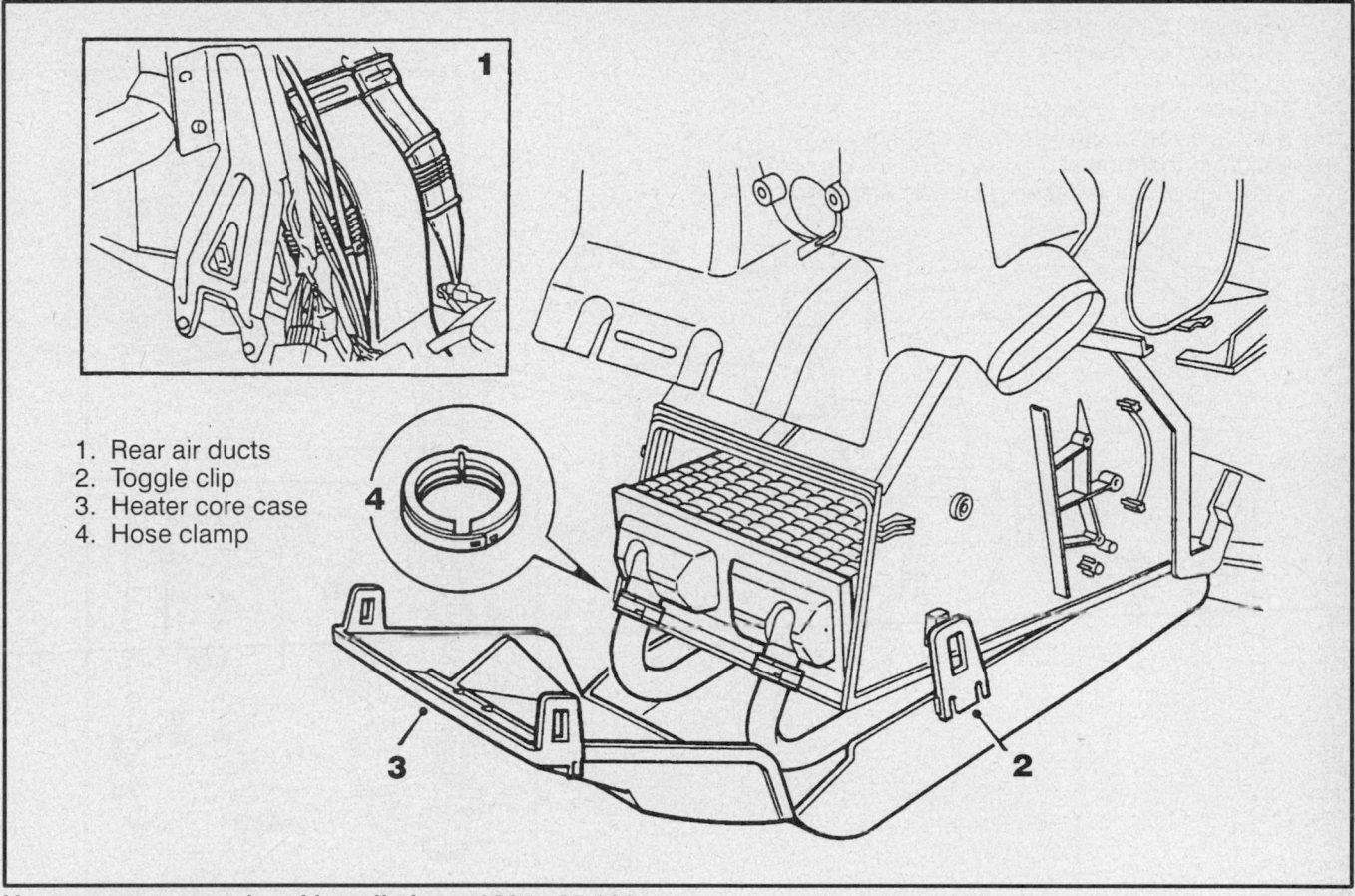

1. Rear air ducts
2. Toggle clip
3. Heater core case
4. Hose clamp

Heater core removal and installation—1994–95 900

3. Remove the center console side panel.
4. On models with passenger supplemental restraint system (air bag), disable the supplemental restraint system. Remove the passenger side knee guard.
5. Remove the floor and side air diffuser ducts.
6. On automatic transmission models, remove the transmission control module from the bracket in the engine compartment and let the control module hang from its cables. Remove the 3 bracket retaining bolts and remove the bracket.
7. Disconnect the instrument panel wiring, open the tie-wraps and bend the cable sets to one side.
8. Fold back the carpet and remove the protective cover.
9. On automatic climate control models, remove the fan control unit.
10. Loosen the anti-frost thermostat attaching nut and remove the end cover from the climate control unit.

NOTE: The attachment clips may be broken off the climate control unit end cover if necessary, and the end cover reattached with screws.

11. On 4-cylinder models, remove the screws connecting the air conditioning lines PAD connection at the expansion valve.
12. On 6-cylinder models, remove the screws securing the expansion valve and remove the expansion valve.
13. Plug the openings to prevent entry of dirt and moisture.

NOTE: If the evaporator is constructed with one-piece tubes between the evaporator and the lead-through in the bulkhead, the tubes must be cut before removal and a new evaporator must be fitted.

14. Disconnect the anti-frost thermostat connector and sen-

sor. Remove the anti-frost thermostat sensor.

—— **CAUTION** ——

If it is necessary to cut the evaporator tubes, use plate shears. Sawing or filing will contaminate the system with metal particles.

15. If necessary, cut the evaporator tubes, using plate shears.
16. Pull the evaporator out of the climate control unit.
17. Installation is the reverse of the removal procedure. Use new O-rings lubricated with clean refrigerant oil. Torque at the expansion valve is 44 inch lbs. (5 Nm) and torque at the connector block is 14.8 ft. lbs. (20 Nm).

1993 9000

1. Disconnect the negative battery cable.
2. Remove the hood.
3. Remove the windshield wiper arms.
4. Remove the windshield wiper motor and air conditioning evaporator cover panels.
5. Properly discharge the refrigerant. Observe all safety precautions.
6. Remove the cowl cover panel seal and the signal converter.
7. Remove the cowl cover panel.
8. Remove the electronic ignition control unit mounting bolts and move the ignition unit to one side.
9. Remove the 4 cowl lead-through panel screws and remove the lead-through panel.

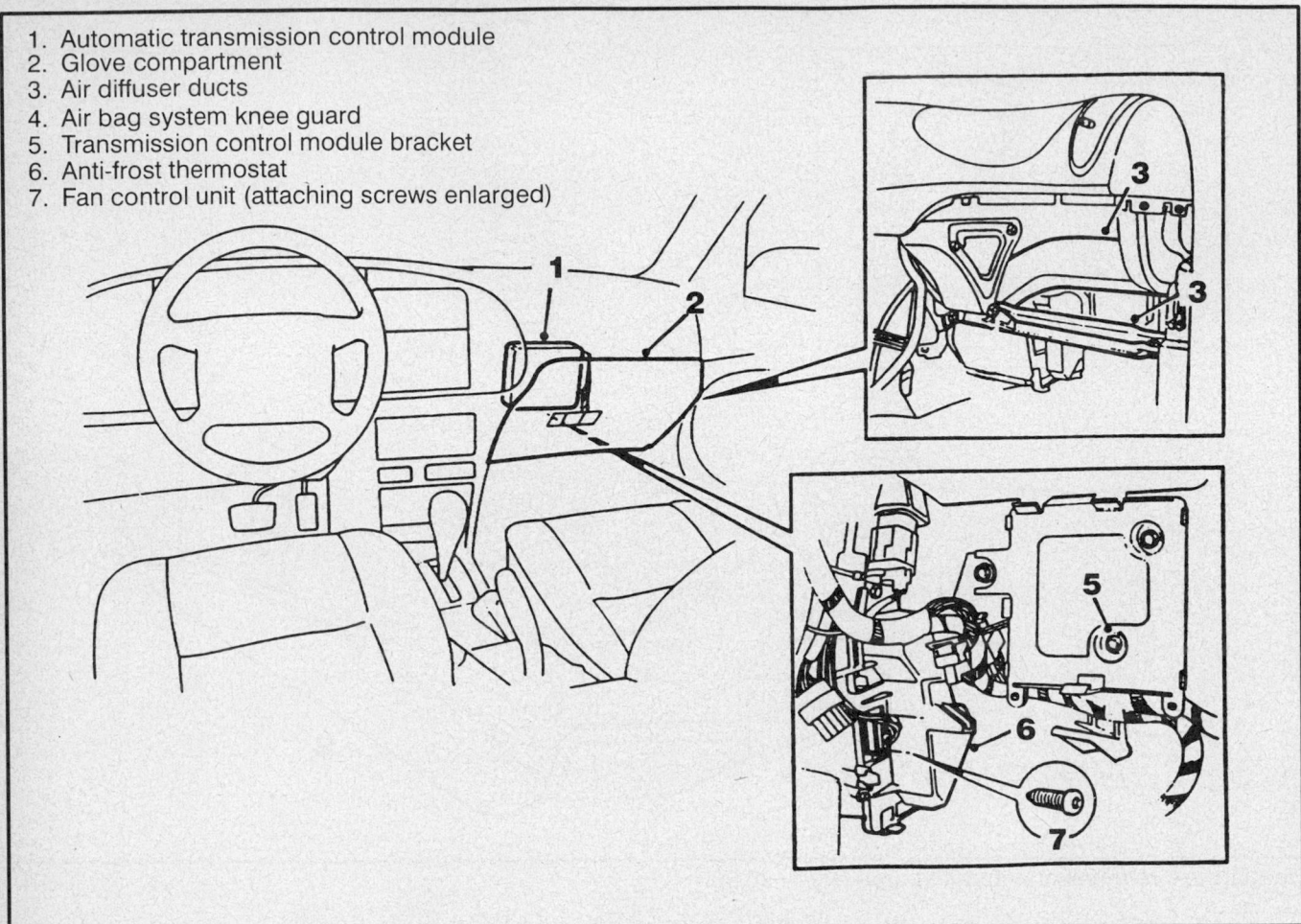

1. Automatic transmission control module
2. Glove compartment
3. Air diffuser ducts
4. Air bag system knee guard
5. Transmission control module bracket
6. Anti-frost thermostat
7. Fan control unit (attaching screws enlarged)

Evaporator core access—1994–95 900

10. Disconnect the windshield wiper electrical connector and remove the windshield wiper mechanism.
11. Remove the cruise control vacuum pump mounting screws and push the pump aside.
12. Remove the evaporator retaining screws and the refrigerant hose retaining clips.
13. Remove the engine bracket from the right rear corner of the engine compartment.
14. Remove the rear motor-mount nut. Using an engine sling attached to the rear engine-lift hook, carefully tilt the engine forward.
15. Loosen the receiver/drier inlet and evaporator outlet fittings.
16. Demount the power steering reservoir. Position the reservoir off to the side.
17. Disconnect the fan control unit, air recirculation valve actuator, anti-freeze thermostat and receiver/drier pressure switch connectors.
18. Carefully move the evaporator assembly toward the center of the vehicle.
19. Remove the evaporator together with the fresh air filter, the receiver/drier and the expansion valve.
20. Remove the fresh air filter, the receiver/drier and the expansion valve.
21. Remove insulation to expose sensor probe attaching clips.
22. Disconnect the capillary tube and expansion valve.
23. Remove the anti-frost thermostat and recirculation valve actuator.
24. Cut through the evaporator case flange gasket. Release

the fasteners, lift off the upper half of the case and remove the evaporator core.
25. Installation is the reverse of the removal procedure. Torque the receiver/drier lines to 13–19 ft. lbs. (18–25 Nm) and the expansion valve to 27–53 inch lbs. (3–6 Nm).

Refrigerant Lines

WARNING: Be sure not to intermix components, refrigerant, oil or service equipment from R-12 systems with R-134a systems.

REMOVAL AND INSTALLATION

1. Disconnect the negative battery cable.
2. Properly discharge the air conditioning system.
3. Remove the nuts or bolts that attach the refrigerant line sealing plates to the adjoining components. If the lines are connected with flare nuts, use a backup wrench when disassembling. Cover the exposed ends of the lines to minimize contamination.
4. Remove the lines and discard the gaskets or O-rings.
To install:
5. Coat the new gaskets or O-rings with clean refrigerant oil and install. Connect the refrigerant lines to the adjoining components and tighten the nuts or bolts.
6. Evacuate and recharge the air conditioning system.
7. Connect the negative battery cable and check the entire climate control system for proper operation and leaks.

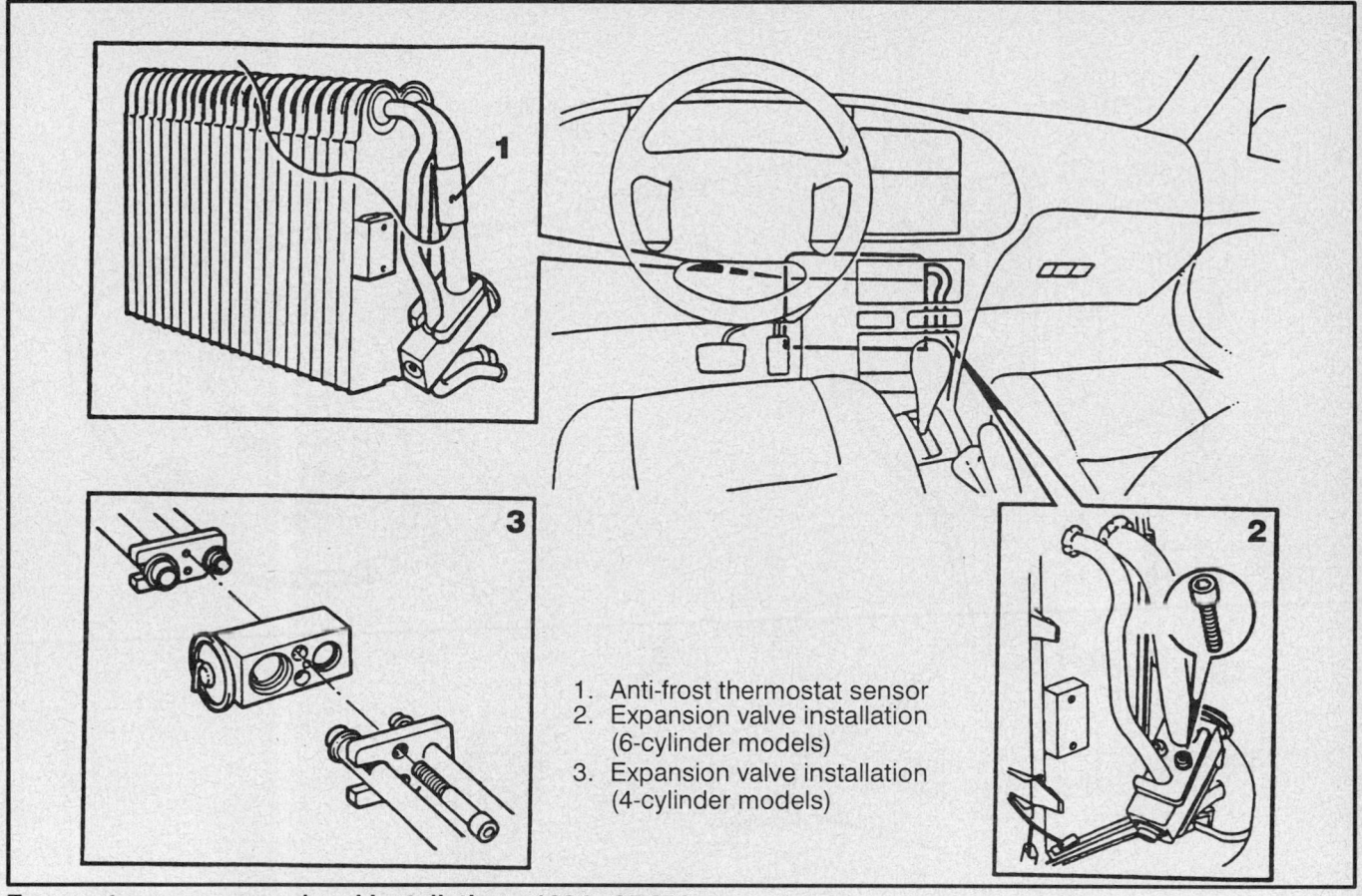

1. Anti-frost thermostat sensor
2. Expansion valve installation (6-cylinder models)
3. Expansion valve installation (4-cylinder models)

Evaporator core removal and installation—1994–95 900

REFRIGERANT LINE CONNECTOR TORQUE VALUES		
Connector Location	1993 ft. lbs. (Nm)	1994–95 ft. lbs. (Nm)
Compressor Low Pressure	16–20 (22–27)	14.8 (20)
Compressor High Pressure	16–20 (22–27)	14.8 (20)
Evaporator Low Pressure	21–29 (28–39)	25.1 (34)①
Evaporator High Pressure	10–15 (14–20)	14.8 (20)①
Condenser Inlet	15–21 (21–28)	6.6 (9)
Receiver/drier	10–15 (14–20)	6.6 (9)

① Block and in-line connectors. For PAG type, torque to 6.6 ft. lbs. (9 Nm).

Manual Climate Control Panel

REMOVAL AND INSTALLATION

1994–95 900

1. Remove the panel on the right side of the center console.
2. Remove the control shaft.
3. Press the control panel out from the rear.
4. Disconnect the electrical and vacuum harness connectors.
5. Disconnect the control cable from the panel.
6. Installation is the reverse of the removal procedures.

Control Cable

REMOVAL AND INSTALLATION

1994–95 900

1. Remove the climate control panel.
2. Remove the two control cable lower retaining clips.
3. Remove the control cable.

To install:

4. Connect the control cable to the climate control panel.
5. Install the climate control panel.
6. Connect the control cable to the air-blending flap lever.
7. Turn the temperature control knob to full cooling.
8. Hold the temperature control knob securely while pushing the air-blending flap lever forward as far as possible.
9. Secure the cable sheathing to the climate control unit with the retaining clip.
10. Test to ensure that the temperature control knob can be turned to both end positions without springing back.
11. Install the panel on the right side of the console.

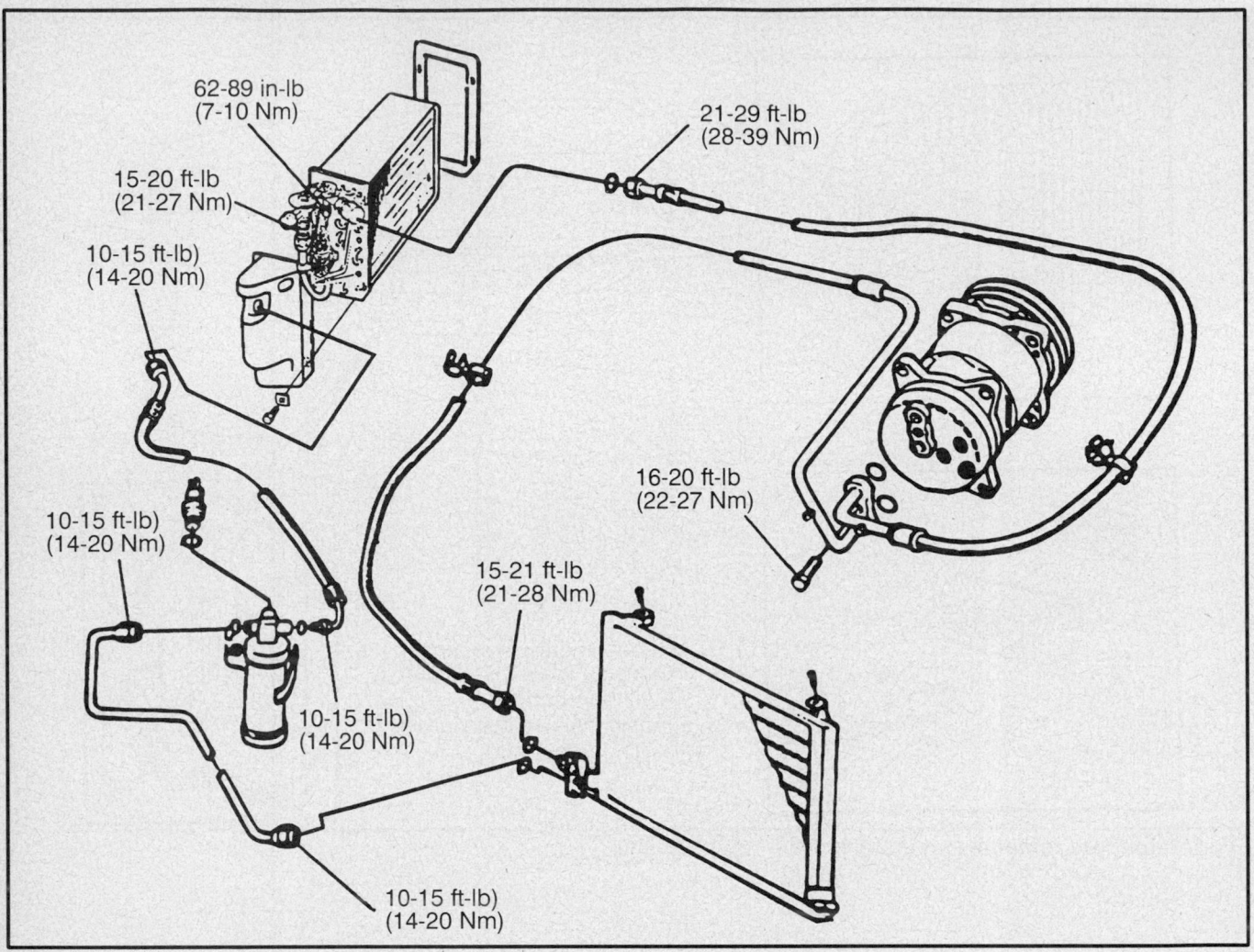

Refrigerant line connector torque values—1993 900

Torque values shown in diagram:
- 62-89 in-lb (7-10 Nm)
- 15-20 ft-lb (21-27 Nm)
- 10-15 ft-lb) (14-20 Nm)
- 10-15 ft-lb) (14-20 Nm)
- 10-15 ft-lb) (14-20 Nm)
- 10-15 ft-lb) (14-20 Nm)
- 15-21 ft-lb (21-28 Nm)
- 21-29 ft-lb (28-39 Nm)
- 16-20 ft-lb (22-27 Nm)

Control Shaft

REMOVAL AND INSTALLATION

1. Remove the panel on the right side of the console.
2. Telescope and remove the control shaft.
3. Installation is the reverse of the removal procedure.

Automatic Climate Control System Control Panel

REMOVAL AND INSTALLATION

1. Turn the ignition switch to **OFF**.
2. On 9000, remove the ashtray.
3. On 9000, release the ashtray holder upper locking tabs and pull the ashtray holder forward.
4. On 900, remove the 2 outer buttons below the automatic climate control (ACC) system control panel.
5. Press the automatic climate control (ACC) system control panel out from behind.
6. Disconnect the 39-pin electrical connector.
To install:
7. Connect the 39-pin electrical connector.

8. Install the ACC system control panel.
9. On 9000, install ashtray holder and the ashtray.
10. On 900, connect and install the 2 outer buttons below the ACC system control panel.

NOTE: Read the stored diagnostic codes before calibrating the control panel. The calibration process erases all stored diagnostic codes.

11. Calibrate the ACC system by pressing the **AUTO** and **VENT** buttons at the same time.

Automatic Climate Control Unit

REMOVAL AND INSTALLATION

1994—95 900

1. Disable the supplemental restraint system (air bag).
2. Properly discharge the refrigerant. Observe all safety precautions.
3. Properly drain the coolant.
4. Disconnect the air conditioning lines and heater hoses.
5. Using compressed air, blow coolant out of the heater core.
6. Remove the condensate drain tube.

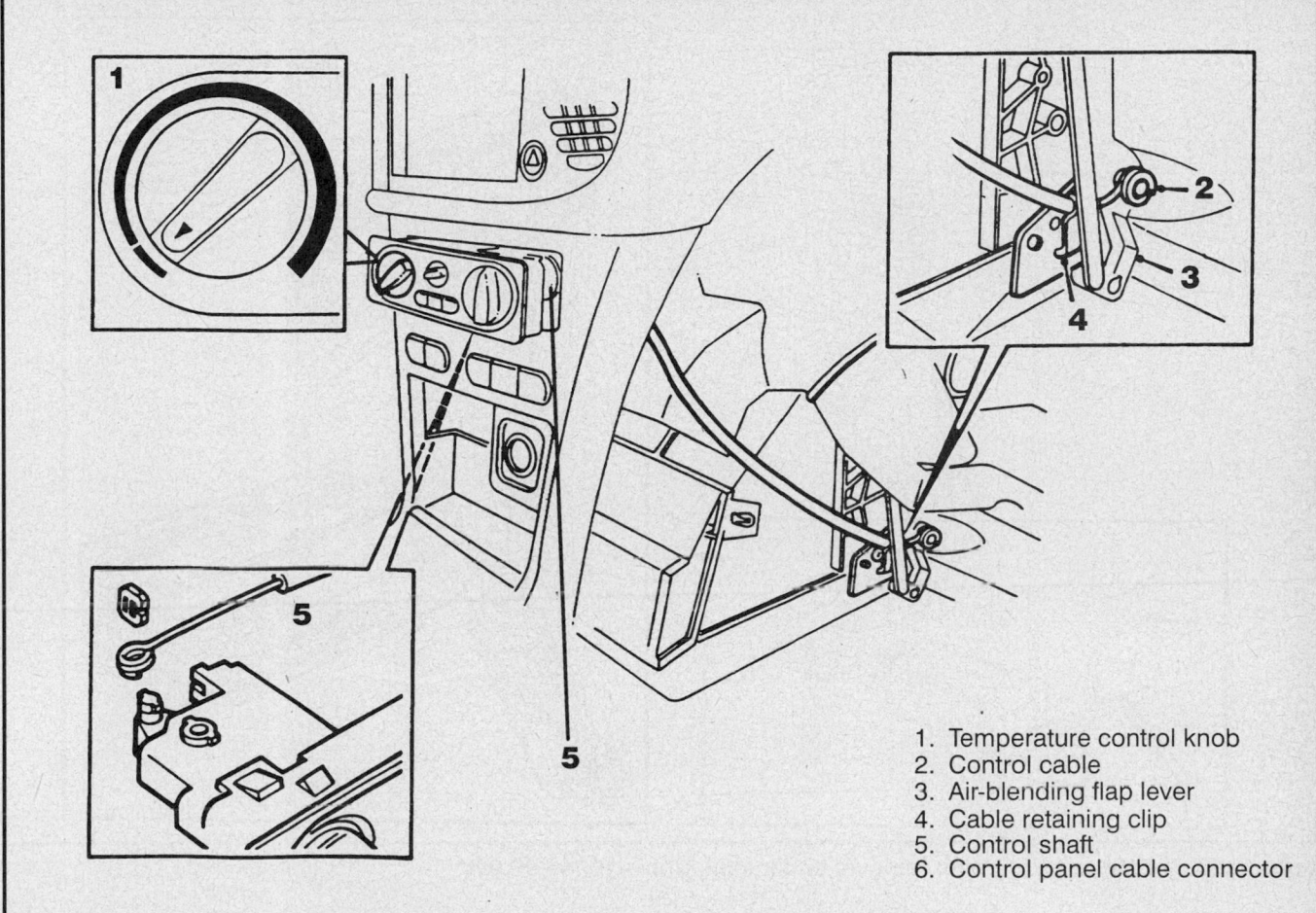

1. Temperature control knob
2. Control cable
3. Air-blending flap lever
4. Cable retaining clip
5. Control shaft
6. Control panel cable connector

Control cable removal and installation—1994—95 900

7. Pull the steering wheel out as far as possible.
8. Remove the air bag retaining screws on the underside of the steering wheel.
9. Lift the airbag away from the steering wheel and disconnect the air bag electrical connector.
10. Disconnect the horn connector.
11. Turn the steering wheel to the straight ahead position.
12. Loosen, but do not remove, the steering column nut. Rock the steering wheel loose, remove the nut and connectors and lift the steering wheel off the column.
13. Remove the steering column shroud retaining screws and remove the shroud.
14. On the column-mounted control stalks, press in the 2 retaining clips and pull the units straight out. Unplug the control stalk electrical connectors.
15. Remove the diagnostic socket from below the left side of the instrument panel.
16. Remove the lower instrument panel screws and quick-release pins. Lift out the lower instrument panel.
17. Press the forks on the radio face panel outward to release the catches. Pull the radio out, disconnect the electrical and antenna connectors and set the radio aside.
18. Remove the storage compartment, if installed.
19. Using a screwdriver, remove the radio contact box.
20. Release the extraction screws, pull out the auxiliary instrument panel and disconnect the auxiliary panel electrical connector.

21. Remove the light switch and the headlamp beam control switch by pressing out from behind.
22. Remove the instrument cluster trim panel retaining screws. Release the side retaining clips and lift out the trim panel.
23. Disconnect all panel electrical connectors and remove the instrument cluster trim panel.
24. Remove the glove compartment retaining screws, bolt, catch and quick-release pin. Pull the glove compartment out to disconnect the glove compartment light. Remove the glove compartment.
25. Remove the A-pillar moldings and trim.
26. Using a screwdriver, remove the speaker grilles.
27. Pull the sun sensor slightly rearward, lift up and disconnect the sun sensor connector (if equipped).
28. Disconnect the alarm system (if equipped).
29. Remove the defroster cover/instrument panel retaining nut.
30. Release the defroster cover edge clips and remove the defroster cover.
31. Remove the main instrument cluster retaining screws. Pull out, disconnect and remove the main instrument cluster.
32. Remove the tie-wraps to release the wiring harness under the instrument panel.

NOTE: The passenger side tie-wrap can be opened.

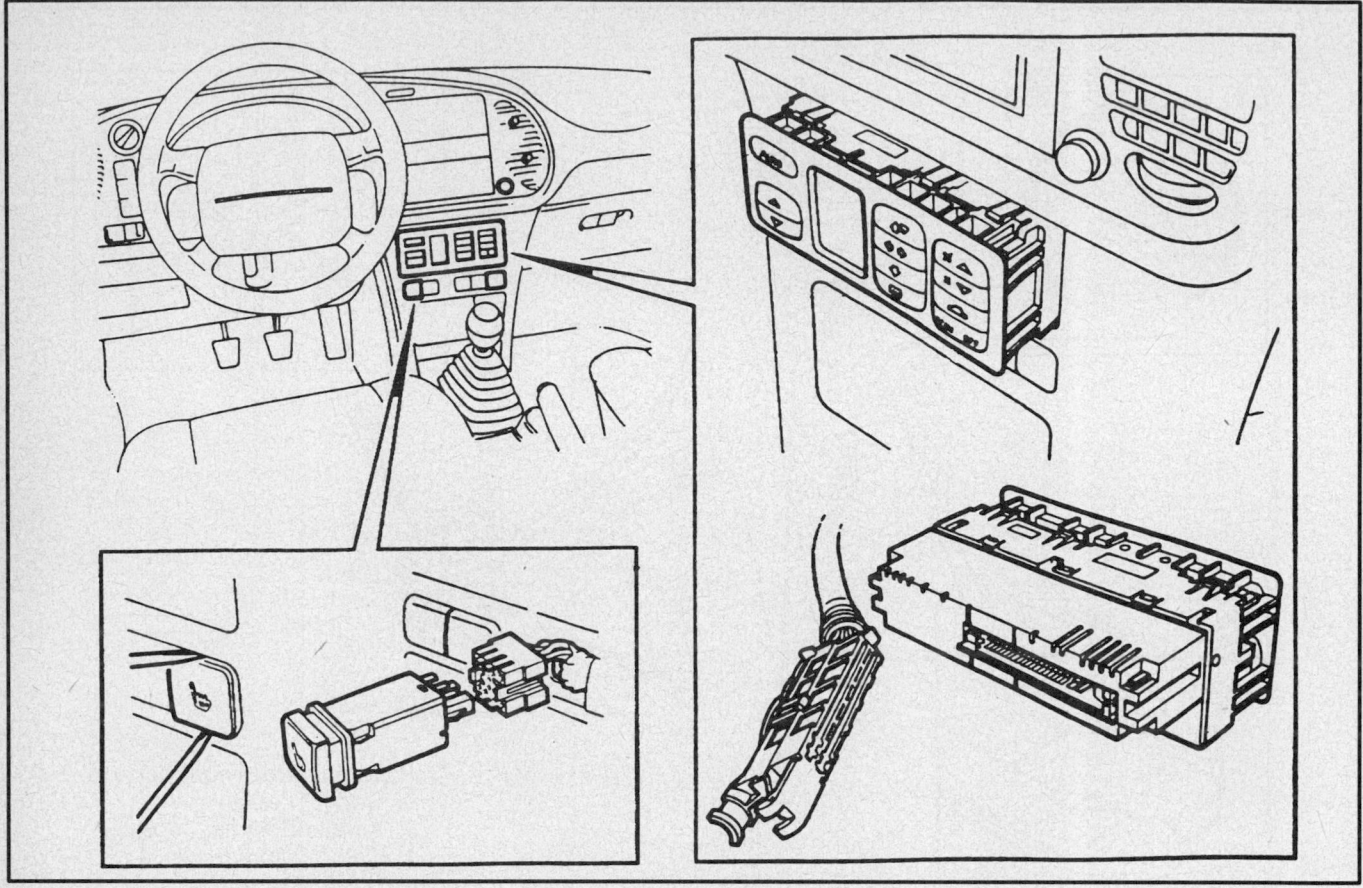

Automatic climate control panel removal and installation—1994–95 900

33. Remove the driver side floor air duct.
34. Remove the 2 fuse holder retaining screws and let the fuse holder hang free.
35. Remove the instrument panel retaining bolts from the A-pillar.
36. Remove the air conditioning control panel.
37. Remove the quick-release pins securing the instrument panel to the center console.
38. Disconnect and remove the passenger side air bag (if equipped).
39. Remove the right and center air vent ducts.
40. Remove the right speaker cable tie-wraps and disconnect the speaker.
41. Remove the instrument panel retaining bolts on each side of the speakers.
42. Remove the instrument panel.
43. Remove the floor console as follows:
   • Apply the handbrake.
   • Remove the ignition switch cover plate by loosening the left front corner first and working around the plate counterclockwise. Disconnect the ignition switch lighting connector.
   • Remove the rear ashtray. Remove the rear trim panel retaining screw and trim panel.
   • Remove the floor console retaining screws and nuts.
   • Pull the floor console to the rear and lift to gain access to the window lift and interior light switch connectors.
   • Remove and disconnect the window lift and interior light switches.
   • Lift and remove the floor console.
44. On manual transmission models, release the shift lever boot clips and remove the boot.
45. Disconnect the center console electrical connectors.
46. Remove the center console.
47. Cut the tie-wraps and remove the rear air ducts.
48. Remove the driver side knee guard.
49. Remove the fresh air filter.
50. Remove the instrument panel crossmember retaining nuts and bolts.
51. Remove the support on the driver side of the climate control unit.
52. If equipped with a passenger side air bag, remove the passenger side knee guard.
53. Disconnect the steering wheel pad and horn connectors.
54. Remove the steering gear pinch bolt.
55. Remove the bolt and the 2 nuts from the steering column support. Remove the steering column.

NOTE: Do not separate the steering column.

56. Remove the 4 nuts securing the angular supports at the top of the pedal assembly and fold out the angular supports.
57. Fold out the instrument panel crossmember.
58. Remove the 2 screws securing the main fuse box to the instrument panel crossmember.
59. Note the cable position for reference during installation and remove the instrument panel crossmember.
60. Disconnect the climate control unit and blower motor connectors.
61. Remove the 4 climate control unit-to-fresh air filter attaching screws.
62. Remove the climate control unit attaching screw near the heater hose connections.

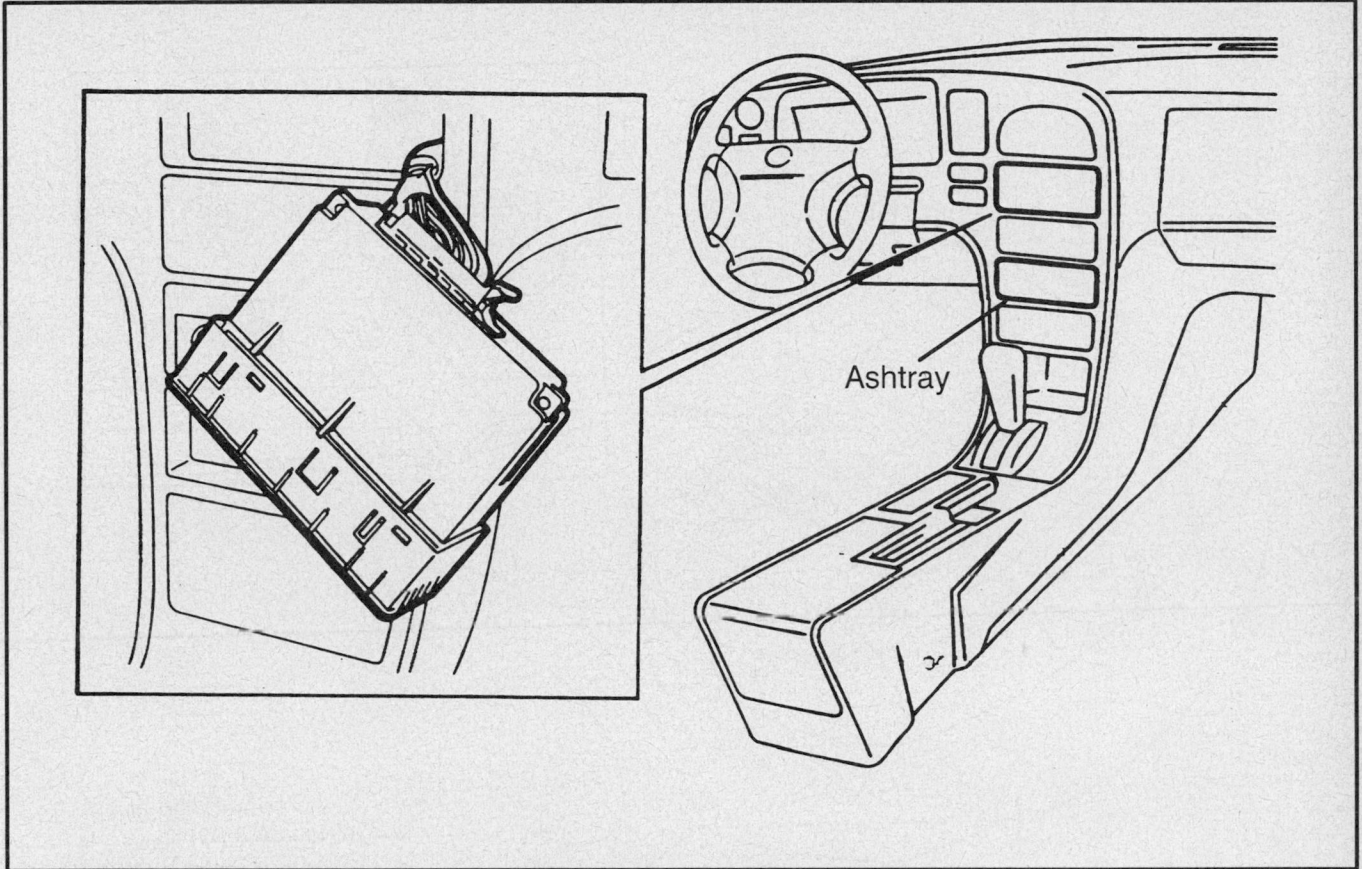

Ashtray

Automatic climate control panel removal and installation—1995 9000

63. Lift out the climate control unit.
To install:
64. Installation is the reverse of the removal procedure. Use new O-rings lubricated with clean refrigerant oil. If installed, toreque nut on passenger side air bag stay to 15 ft. lbs. (20 Nm). Ensure steering column shaft and tube assembly are at neutral center.
65. Fill and bleed the cooling system.
66. Leak test, evacuate and charge the air conditioning system.
67. Test the system for proper operation.

Expansion Valve

REMOVAL AND INSTALLATION

1993 900

1. Properly discharge the refrigerant. Observe all safety precautions.
2. Remove the 2 evaporator case upper retaining bolts.
3. Remove the upper portion of the evaporator case.
4. Disconnect and plug the inlet line.
5. Disconnect the compensating tube from the outlet line.
6. Peel back the insulating tape and remove the capillary tube from the clip.
7. Remove the expansion valve.
8. Installation is the reverse of the removal procedure.

1994—95 900

1. Properly discharge the refrigerant. Observe all safety precautions.

2. On 4-cylinder models, raise and safely support the vehicle.
3. On 6-cylinder models, gain access to the evaporator case.
4. Remove the bolts securing the expansion valve.
5. Remove the expansion valve and plug the lines to prevent entry of dirt and moisture.
6. Installation is the reverse of the removal procedure.

1993 9000

1. Disconnect the negative battery cable.
2. Properly discharge the refrigerant. Observe all safety precautions.
3. Remove the evaporator case cover.
4. Remove cowl panel in engine compartment.
5. Peel off the insulating wrap.
6. Remove the capillary tube retaining clip.
7. Disconnect the capillary tube. Plug the openings to prevent entry of dirt and moisture.
8. Disconnect the expansion valve fittings and plug the lines.
9. Remove the expansion valve.
10. Installation is the reverse of the removal procedure.

Anti-Frost Thermostat

REMOVAL AND INSTALLATION

1994—95 900

1. Gain access to the evaporator core.
2. Remove the anti-frost thermostat attaching nut.
3. Remove the insulating wrap and the clip from the thermal sensor.

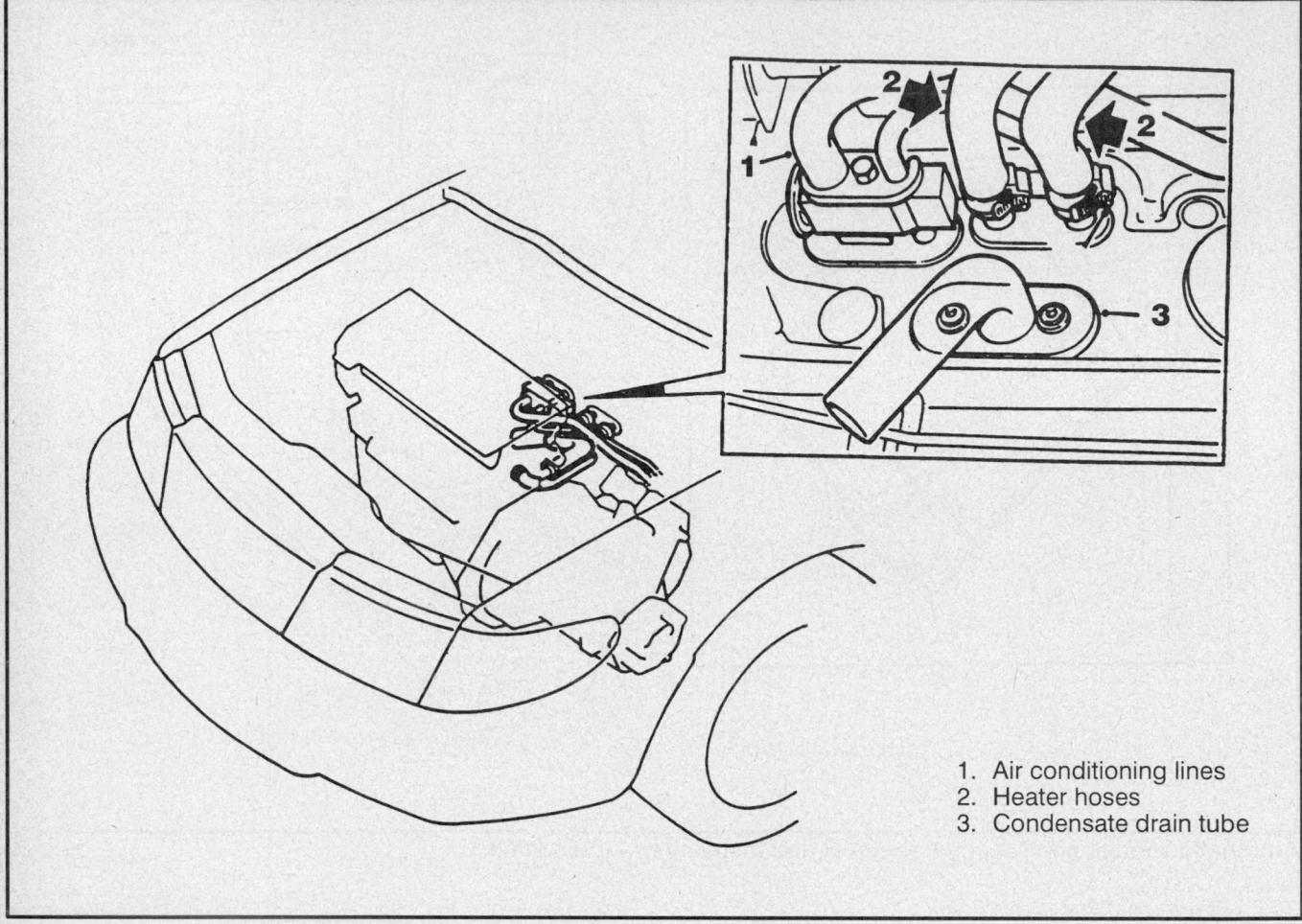

1. Air conditioning lines
2. Heater hoses
3. Condensate drain tube

Lower cowl heating and air conditioning connections—1994–95 900

4. Disconnect the anti-frost thermostat connector.
5. Remove the anti-frost thermostat.
6. Installation is the reverse of the removal procedure.

1993 9000

1. Properly discharge the refrigerant. Observe all safety precautions.
2. Remove the evaporator case cover.
3. Disconnect the anti-frost thermostat connector.
4. Remove the anti-frost thermostat.
5. Installation is the reverse of the removal procedure.

Function Control Motors

OPERATION

The airflow control doors are operated either by vacuum actuators (1993 900) or by electric stepper motors (9000, 1994–95 900). Vacuum actuators are controlled from a vacuum manifold/switch on the control panel. Stepper motors receive signals from the automatic climate control (ACC) system, based on input from the ACC control panel and various sensors.

REMOVAL AND INSTALLATION

1994–95 900
RECIRCULATION DOOR

1. Remove the glove compartment retaining screws, bolt, catch and quick-release pin. Pull the glove compartment out to disconnect the glove compartment light. Remove the glove compartment.
2. Disconnect the recirculation motor connector.
3. Release the 4 catches and disconnect the recirculation motor shaft from the flap lever.

NOTE: If the shaft is in the bottom position, use a screwdriver to crack the link at the fracture notch.

4. Remove the recirculation motor.
5. Installation is the reverse of the removal procedure.

AIR DISTRIBUTOR

1. Remove the Automatic Climate Control (ACC) system control module.
2. Remove the 2 stepper motor retaining screws.
3. Disconnect the stepper motor electrical connector.
4. Remove the stepper motor.
5. Installation is the reverse of the removal procedure.

NOTE: To calibrate the ACC sytem, press the AUTO and OFF buttons at the same time. Since calibration will erase previously stored trouble codes, the codes should be read and recorded before calibration is accomplished.

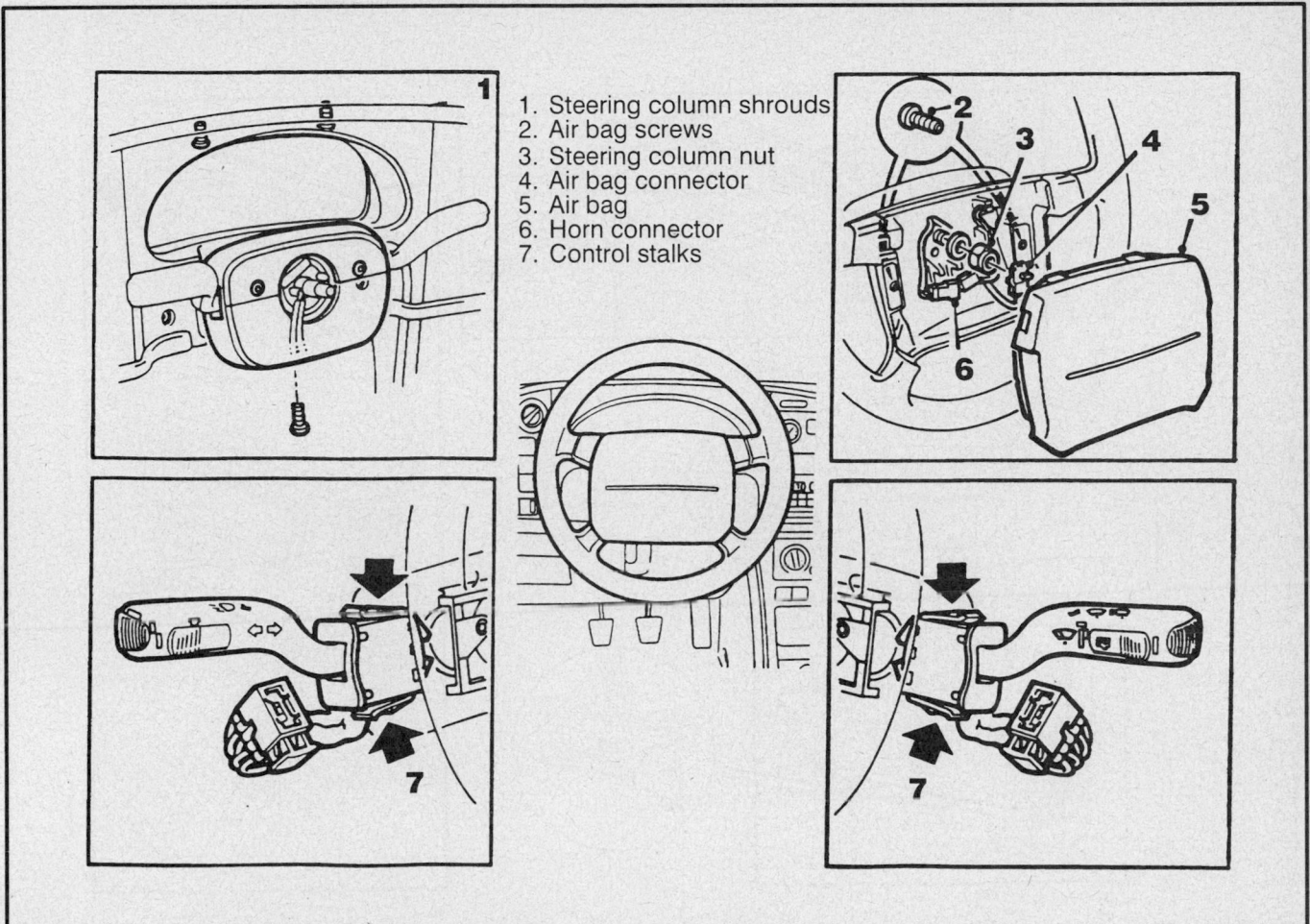

1. Steering column shrouds
2. Air bag screws
3. Steering column nut
4. Air bag connector
5. Air bag
6. Horn connector
7. Control stalks

Steering wheel removal and installation—1994—95 900

AIR BLENDING DOOR

1. Remove the glove comparment retaining screws, bolt, quick-release pin and bracket catch. Pull the glove compartment out partway to disconnect the lamp; then remove the glove compartment.
2. Remove the right side panel from the center console.
3. Remove the right side floor air duct.
4. Remove the 2 stepper motor retaining screws.
5. Disconnect the stepper motor electrical connector.
6. Installation is the reverse of the removal procedure.

1993 9000

1. Remove the A-pillar trim panels and speaker grilles.

2. Remove the instrument panel upper trim panel retaining screws.
3. Disconnect and remove the solar sensor and the instrument panel upper trim panel.
4. Remove the glove compartment. Allow the fuse panel to fall forward.
5. Remove the right side floor and defroster ducts.
6. Disconnect the sensor and stepper motor connectors.
7. Remove the sensor together with the sensor bracket.
8. Remove the stepper motor mounting screws.
9. Remove the stepper motor.
10. Installation is the reverse of the removal procedure.

SENSORS AND SWITCHES

Temperature Sensing
OPERATION

Blend-air Sensor

The blend-air sensor is a thermistor with a pointed tip, inserted into the right floor air distribution duct. The electrical resistance of the sensor varies inversely with the temperature of the air in the duct. Input from this sensor determines the position of the air blending door.

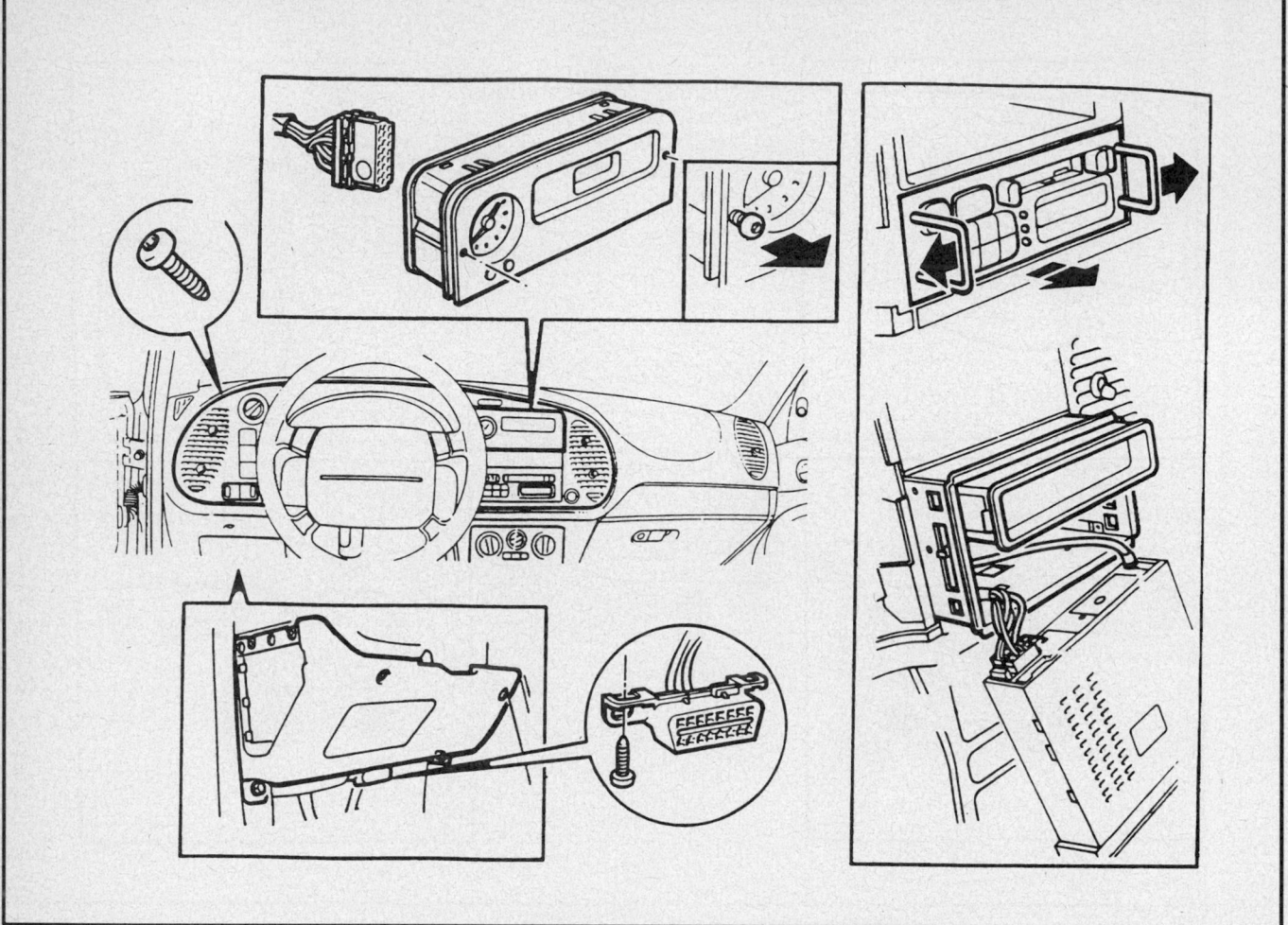

Instrument panel removal and installation—1994–95 900

In-Car Sensor

The in-car sensor is mounted in the instrument panel below the ACC module. An integral suction fan draws air from the passenger cabin across a thermistor which provides input to the control unit. Inputs from this sensor are used to help determine the position of the air blending door and the speed of the blower motor.

Solar Sensor

The solar sensor is positioned on the top of the instrument panel. A photo diode, the solar sensor provides solar radiation input to the control unit. Input from this sensor is a factor in determining the speed of the blower motor.

REMOVAL AND INSTALLATION

1994–95 900

BLEND-AIR SENSOR

1. Remove the glove compartment retaining screws, bolt, quick-release pin and bracket catch. Pull the glove compartment out partway to disconnect the lamp; then remove the glove compartment.

2. Remove the right side panel from the center console.
3. Remove the right side floor air duct.
4. Detach and withdraw the blend-air sensor.
5. Disconnect the electrical connector and press out the blend-air sensor leads.
6. Installation is the reverse of the removal procedure.

IN-CAR SENSOR

1. Remove the Automatic Climate Control (ACC) system control module.
2. Press the buttons beside the in-car sensor, grasp the in-car sensor cover and pull out.
3. Using a small prybar, carefully release the sensor retaining catches.
4. Press the sensor inward, disconnect and remove the sensor through the control module opening.
5. Installation is the reverse of the removal procedure.

NOTE: Previously stored trouble codes will be cleared during calibration. Read and record any trouble codes before calibrating.

6. Calibrate the ACC system by pressing the **AUTO** and **OFF** buttons at the same time.

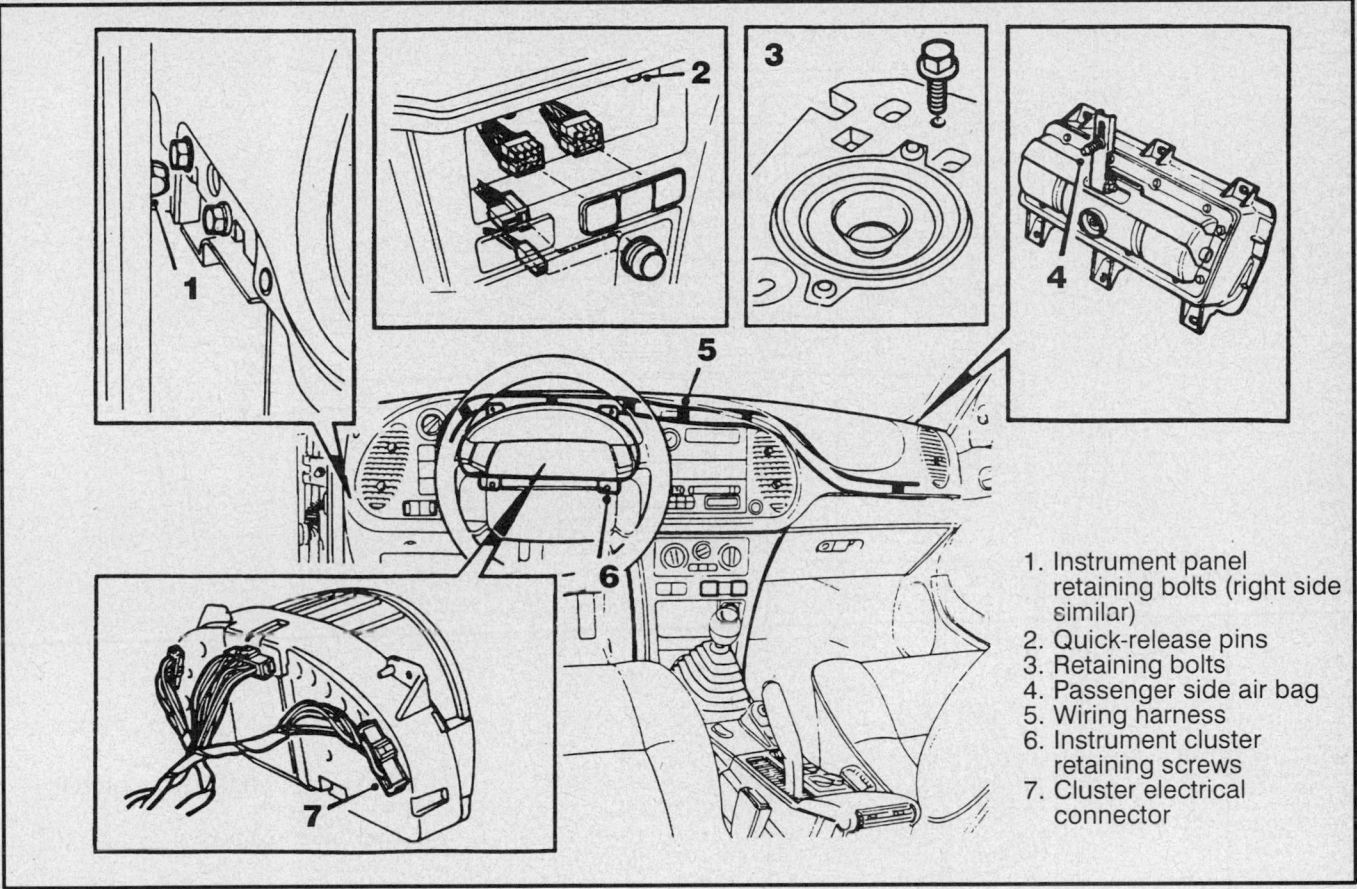

Instrument cluster removal and installation—1994–95 900

1. Instrument panel retaining bolts (right side similar)
2. Quick-release pins
3. Retaining bolts
4. Passenger side air bag
5. Wiring harness
6. Instrument cluster retaining screws
7. Cluster electrical connector

SOLAR SENSOR

1. Slide the solar sensor cover rearward.
2. Lift the cover and disconnect the sensor electrical connector.
3. Press the sensor against the cover and turn the sensor counterclockwise.
4. Installation is the reverse of the removal procedure.

1993 9000

BLEND-AIR SENSOR

1. Disconnect the negative battery cable.
2. Remove the glove compartment. Allow the fuse panel to fall forward.
3. Disconnect the blend-air sensor electrical connector and push the connector through the blend-air actuator bracket.
4. Remove the blend-air sensor.
5. Installation is the reverse of the removal procedure.

IN-CAR SENSOR

1. Remove the Automatic Climate Control (ACC) system control panel
2. Remove the in-car sensor grille.
3. Insert two screwdrivers through the grille opening and carefully push the sensor into the instrument panel cavity.
4. Disconnect the sensor and remove it through the control panel opening.
5. Installation is the reverse of the removal procedure.

SOLAR SENSOR

1. Disconnect the negative battery cable.

2. Carefully separate the door trim seals from the A-pillars.
3. Remove the A-pillar trim panels and speaker grilles.
4. Remove the instrument panel upper trim panel retaining screws.
5. Disconnect and remove the solar sensor and the instrument panel upper trim panel.
6. Separate the solar sensor from the trim panel.
7. Installation is the reverse of the removal procedure.

Pressure Sensing

OPERATION

A 3-stage pressure sensor is installed on the receiver/drier. It has the following functions:

• It allows the compressor to work at temperatures as low as 32°F (0°C). The system pressure at this temperature is approximately 29 psi (2 bar).

• It turns the engine cooling fan ON when the system pressure reaches approximately 239 psi (16.5 bar) and OFF when the system pressure drops to approximately 181 psi (12.5 bar).

• It breaks the electrical circuit to the compressor if the system pressure rises above 435 psi (30 bar) and restores the circuit when the system pressure falls to approximately 348 psi (24 bar).

An additional pressure sensor is installed on vehicles for hot-climate countries. This sensor turns ON the second stage of the blower motor when pressure in the system exceeds 319 psi (22 bar).

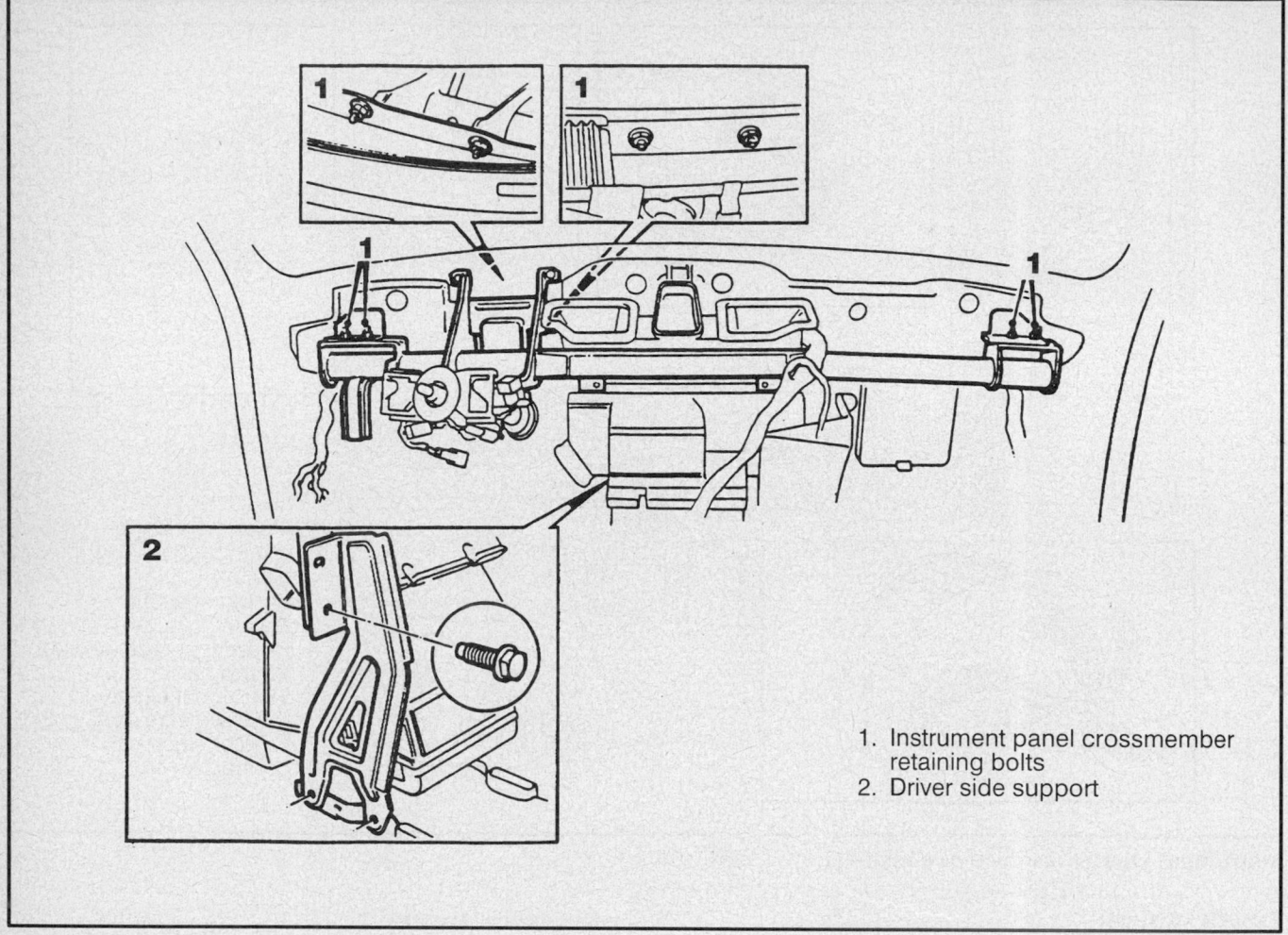

1. Instrument panel crossmember retaining bolts
2. Driver side support

Instrument panel bracing—1994–95 900

REMOVAL AND INSTALLATION

1. Disconnect the negative battery cable.
2. Properly discharge the refrigerant. Observe all safety precautions.
3. Gain access to the receiver/drier.

4. Disconnect the electrical connector and unscrew the sensor/switch. Plug the opening to prevent entry of dirt and moisture.
5. Installation is the reverse of the removal procedure. Use new O-rings lubricated in clean refrigerant oil. Leak test, evacuate and charge the system.

SYSTEM DIAGNOSIS

Self-test

The self-test function detects abnormal conditions in the AUTOMATIC CLIMATE CONTROL (ACC) system and automatically provides default values in the event of system or component failure. Fault codes are stored by the ACC system and can be read with an ISAT diagnostic tester.

SELF-TEST FAULT CODES

Code	Function or component
B1343	Solar sensor Open circuit or shorted to battery positive

Code	Function or component
B1347	Mixed-air sensor Shorted to ground
B1348	Mixed-air sensor Open circuit or shorted to battery positive
B1352	Indoor temperature sensor Shorted to ground
B1353	Indoor temperature sensor Open circuit or shorted to battery positive

SELF-TEST FAULT CODES – CONT'D

Code	Function or component
B1355	Power for ventilation fan motor and indoor temperature sensor Shorted to ground
B1360	Keypad faulty
B1493	A/C system Shorted to ground
B1498	Electrically heated rear window Shorted to ground
B1515	Common sensor ground shorted to battery positive
B1605	Control module Internal control module fault
B1675	Air distribution flap motor Driver stage faulty
B1676	Recirculation flap motor Driver stage faulty
B1677	Heater flap motor Driver stage faulty
B2402	Stepping motor for air distribution damper Shorted to ground
B2403	Stepping motor for air distribution damper Open circuit
B2404	Stepping motor for air distribution damper Shorting between connections or to battery positive
B2405	Air distribution damper loose
B2406	Air distribution damper jammed
B2413	Motor for recirculation damper Open circuit
B2414	Motor for recirculation damper Short circuited
B2422	Fan test voltage Shorted to ground
B2423	Fan test voltage Shorted to battery positive

SELF-TEST FAULT CODES – CONT'D

Code	Function or component
B2426	Fan control voltage Overload
B2427	Fan control voltage Shorted to ground
B2428	Fan control voltage Shorted to battery positive
B2492	Stepping motor for air blending damper Shorted to ground
B2493	Stepping motor for air blending damper Open circuit
B2494	Stepping motor for air blending damper Shorting between connections
B2495	Air blending damper hose
B2496	Air blending damper jammed

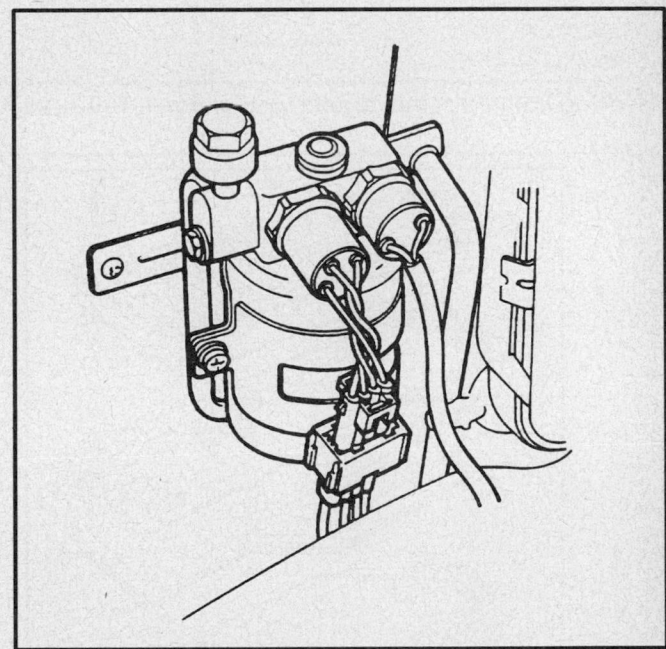

Receiver/drier with normal and hot-climate pressure sensors—1994–95 900

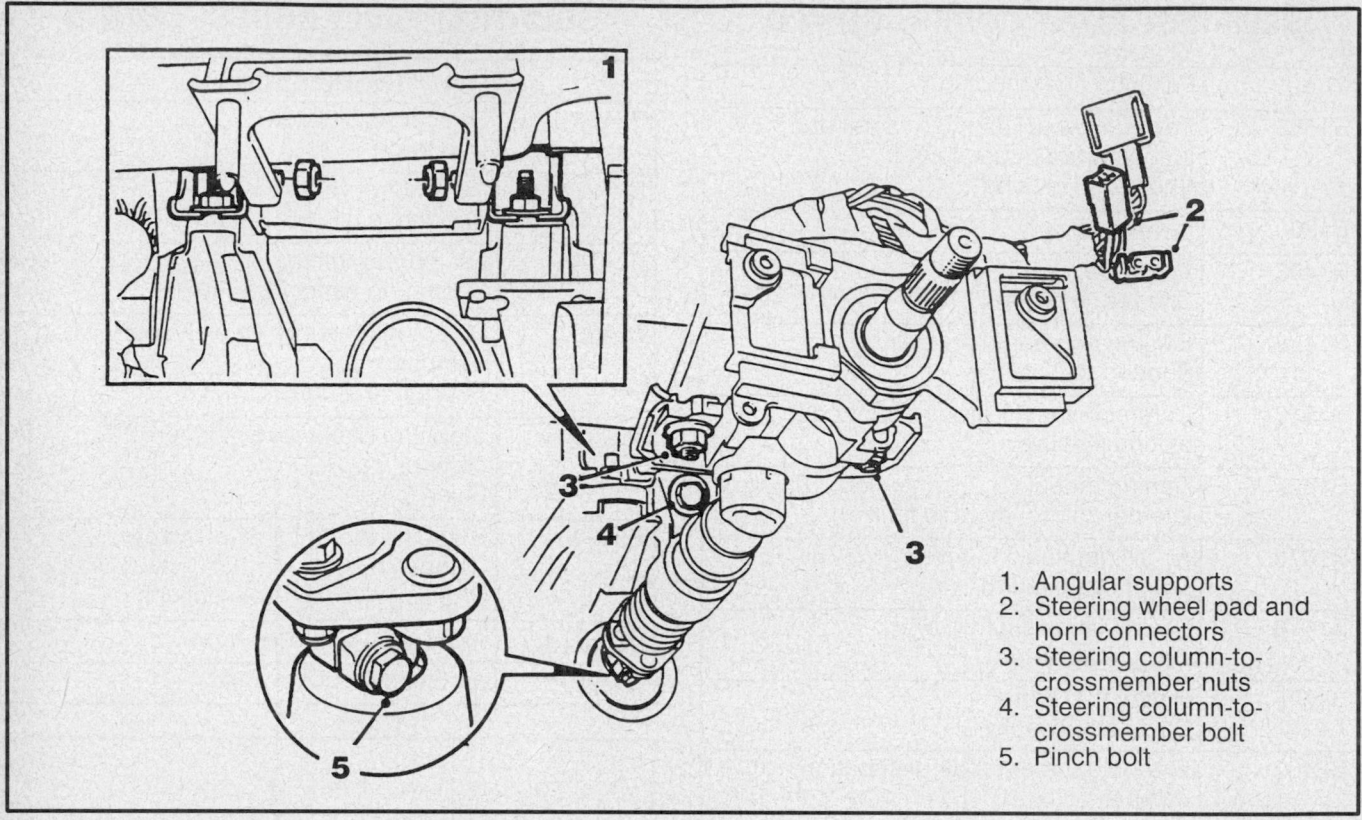

1. Angular supports
2. Steering wheel pad and horn connectors
3. Steering column-to-crossmember nuts
4. Steering column-to-crossmember bolt
5. Pinch bolt

Steering column removal and installation—1994–95 900

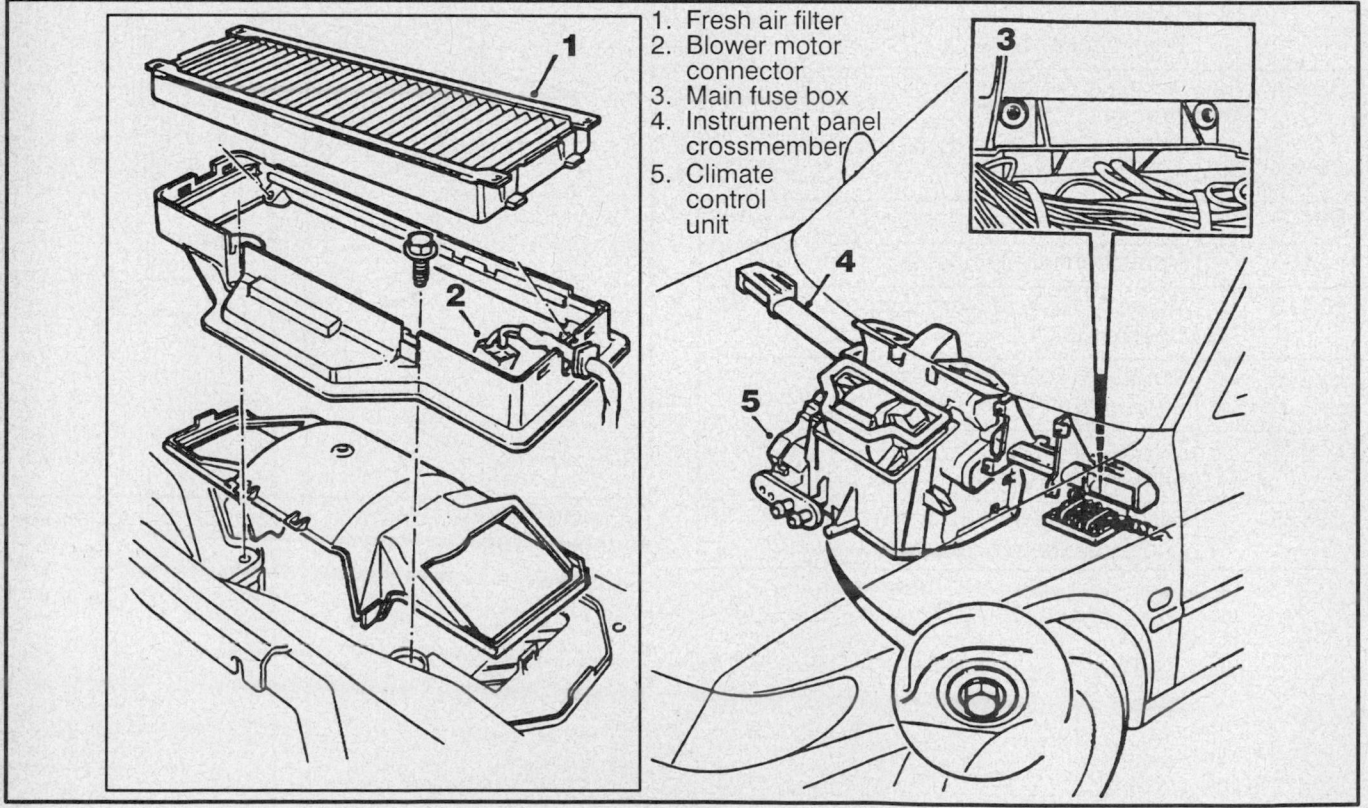

1. Fresh air filter
2. Blower motor connector
3. Main fuse box
4. Instrument panel crossmember
5. Climate control unit

Climate control unit removal and installation—1994–95 900

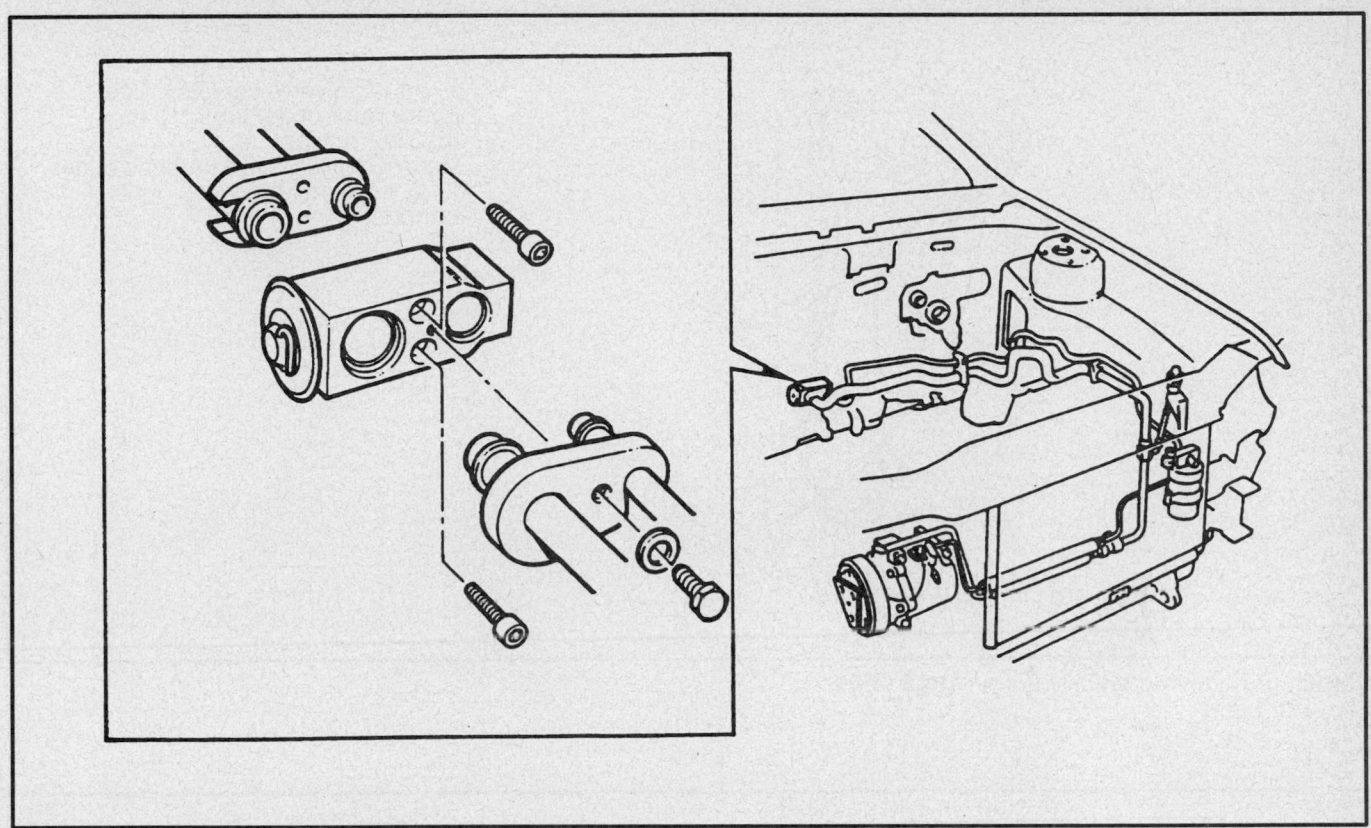

Expansion valve on 4-cylinder models—1994–95 900

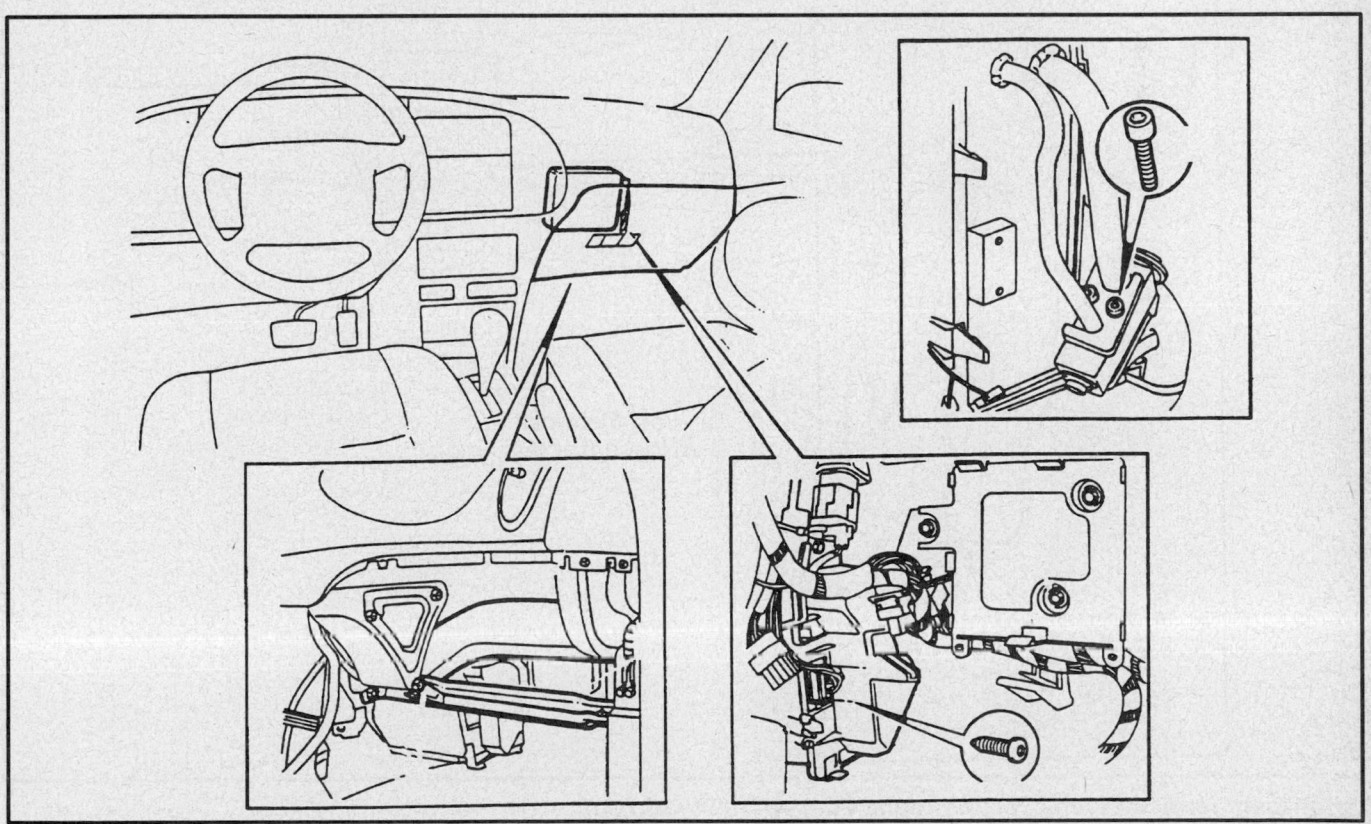

Expansion valve on 6-cylinder models—1994–95 900

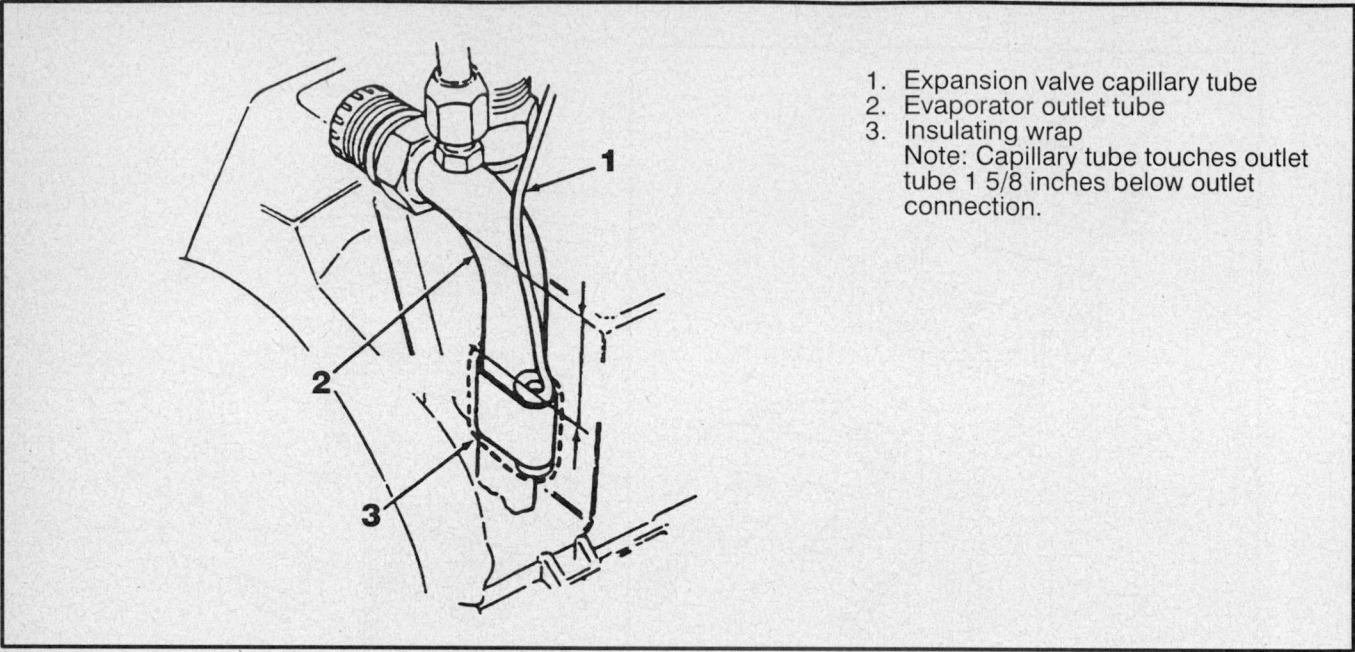

1. Expansion valve capillary tube
2. Evaporator outlet tube
3. Insulating wrap
Note: Capillary tube touches outlet tube 1 5/8 inches below outlet connection.

Expansion valve capillary tube—1993 9000

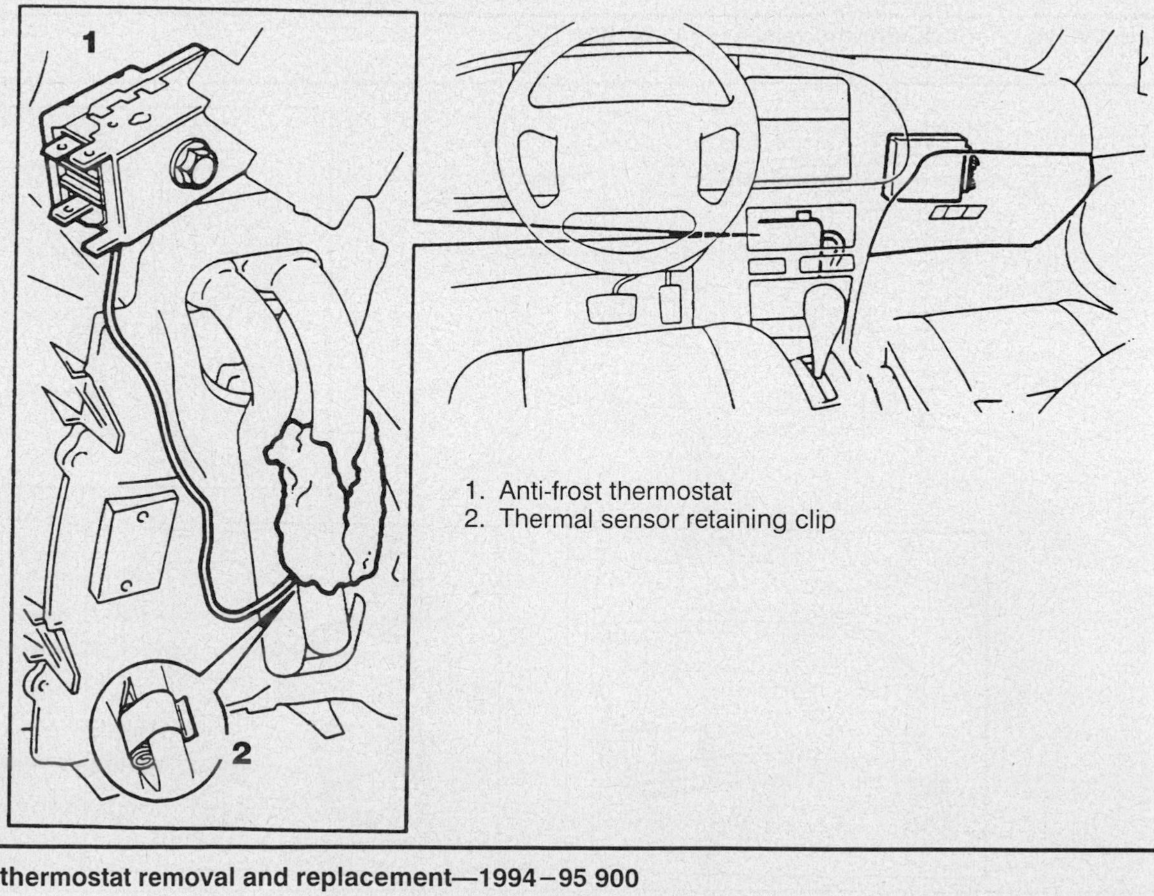

1. Anti-frost thermostat
2. Thermal sensor retaining clip

Anti-frost thermostat removal and replacement—1994–95 900

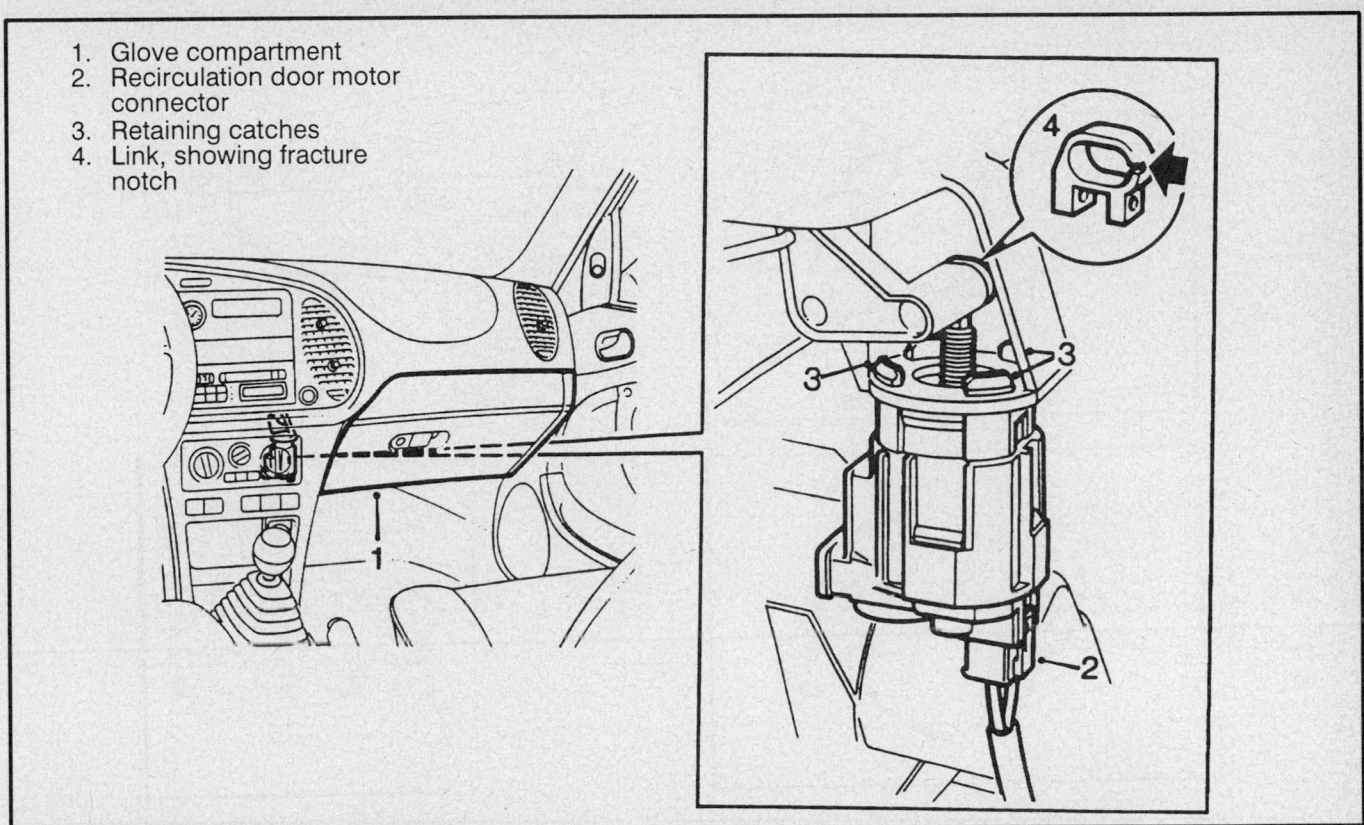

1. Glove compartment
2. Recirculation door motor connector
3. Retaining catches
4. Link, showing fracture notch

Recirculation door motor—1994–95 900

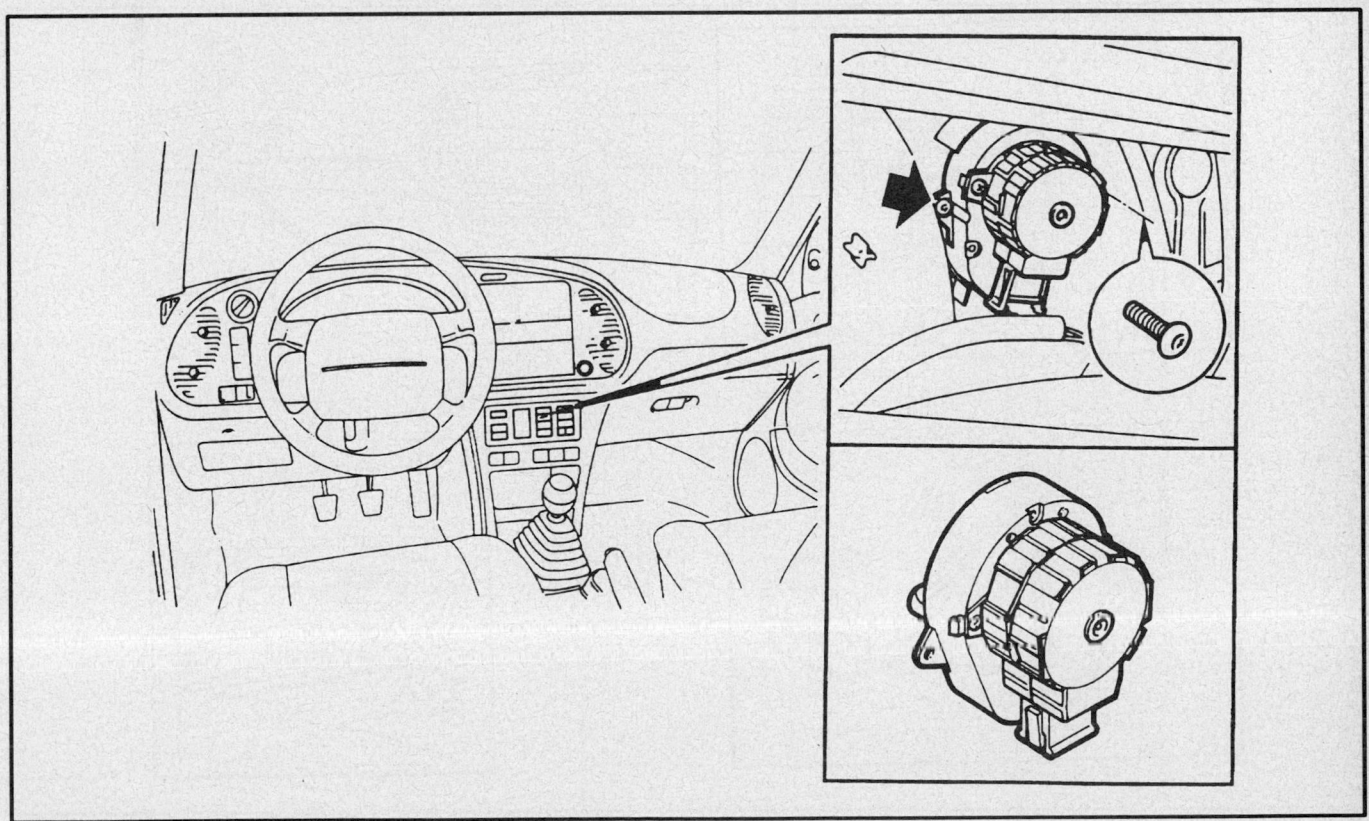

Air distributor door stepper motor—1994–95 900

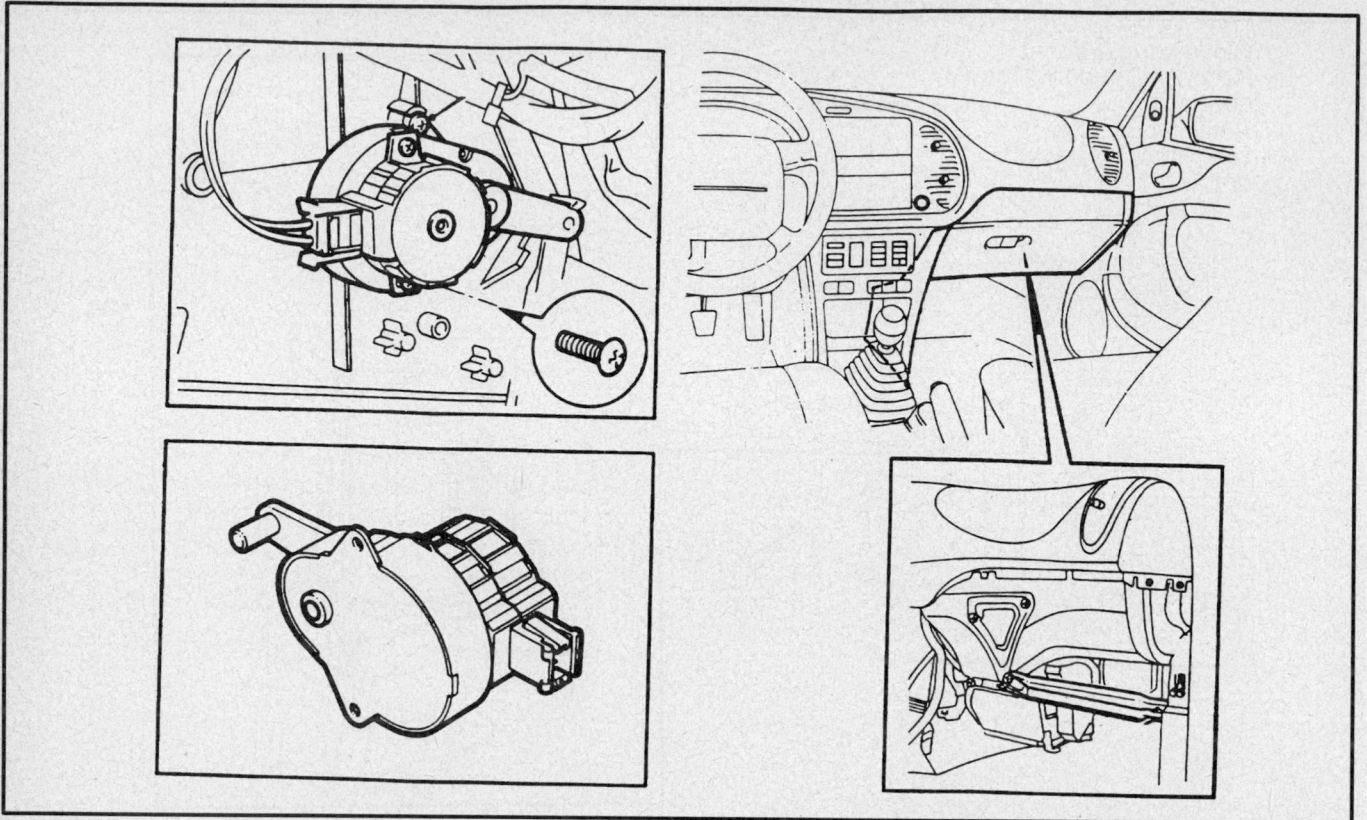

Air blending door stepper motor—1994–95 900

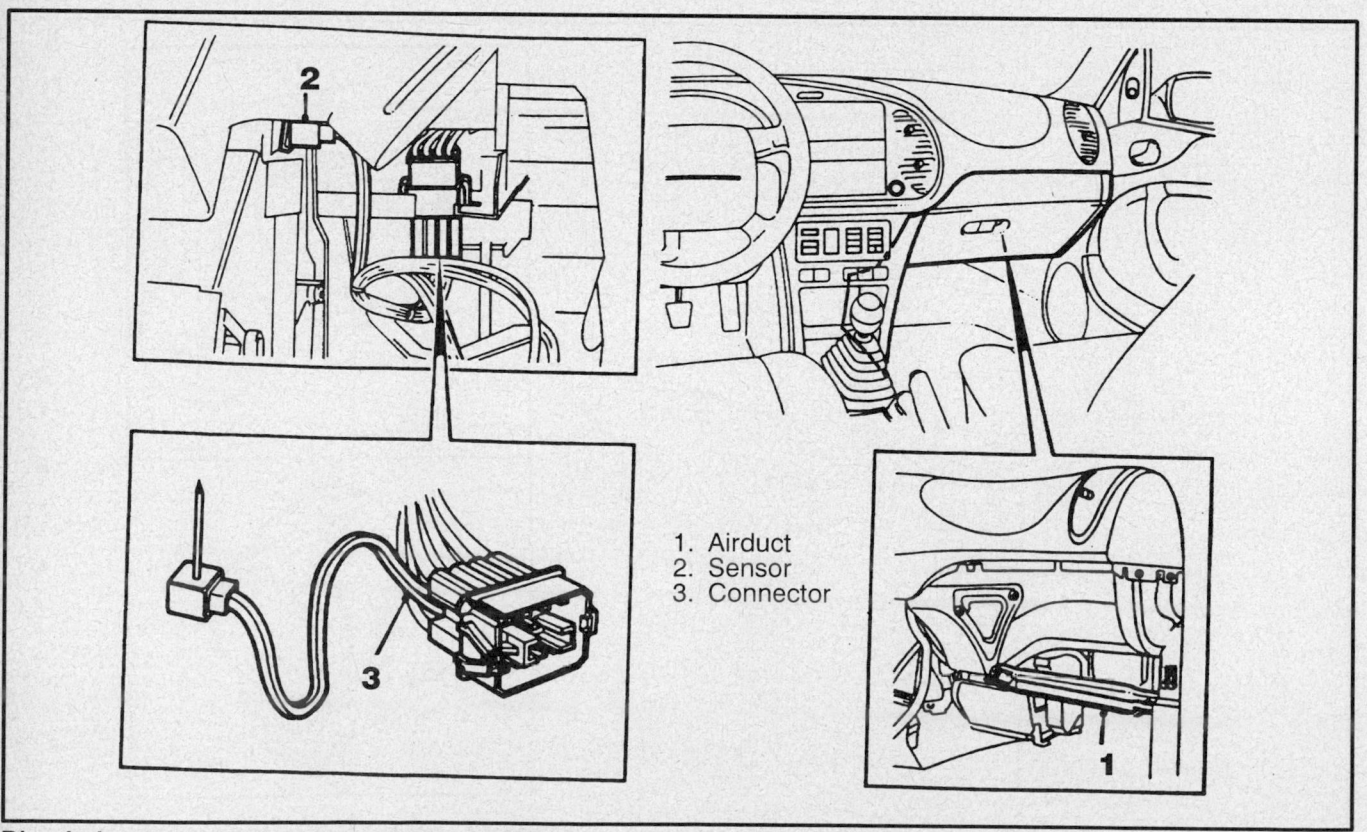

1. Airduct
2. Sensor
3. Connector

Blend-air temperature sensor—1994–95 900

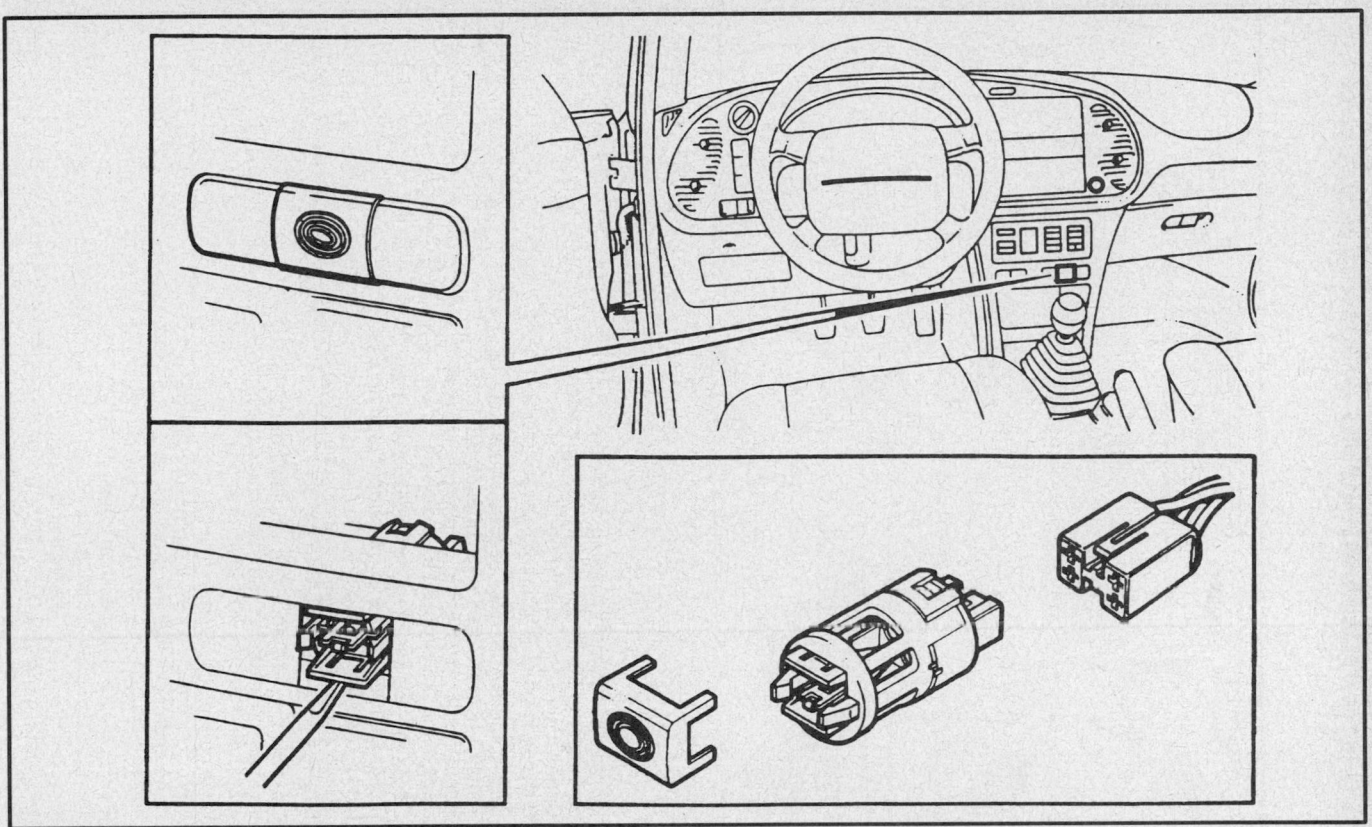

In-car temperature sensor—1994–95 900

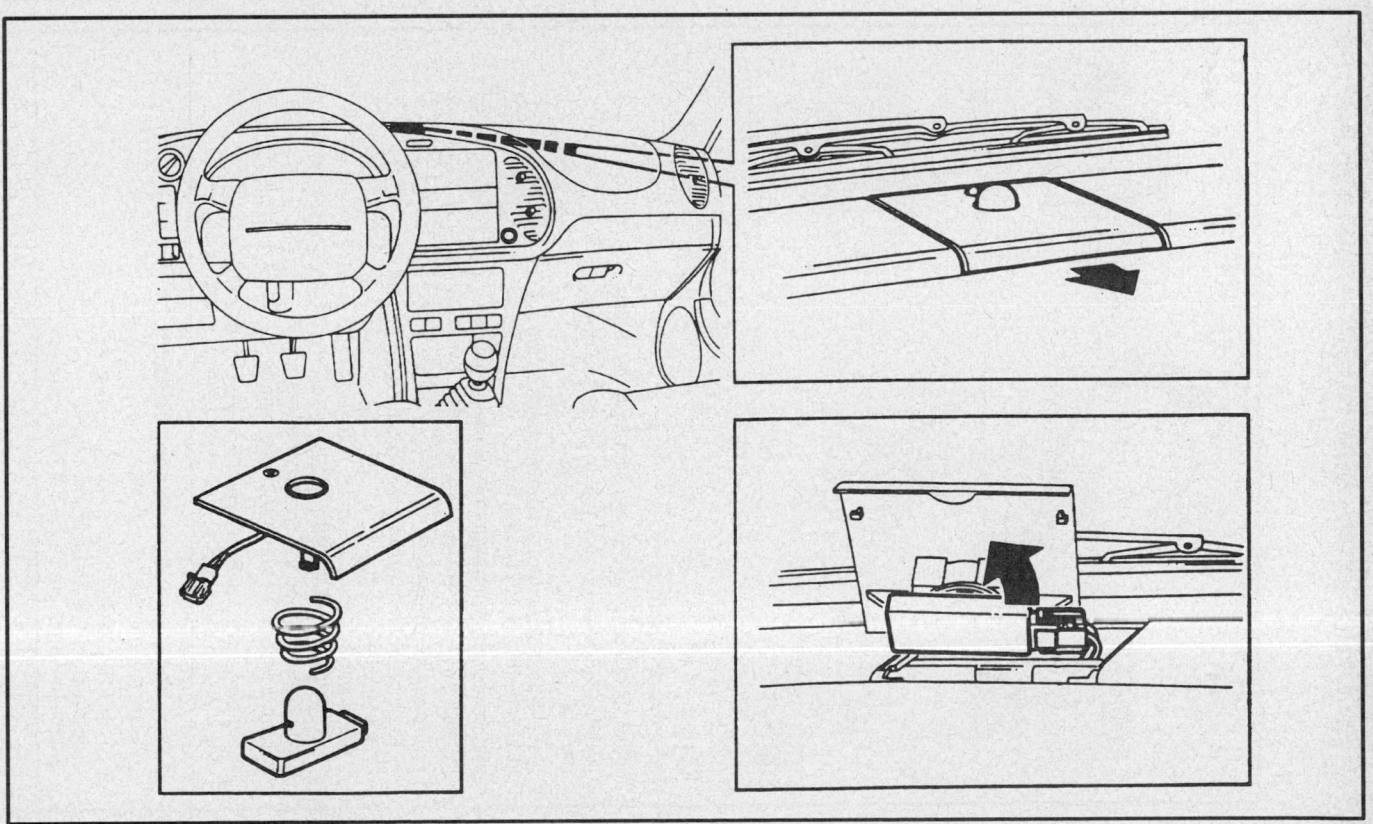

Solar sensor—1994–95 900

A/C SYMPTOM DIAGNOSIS—1994–95 900, CONT'D

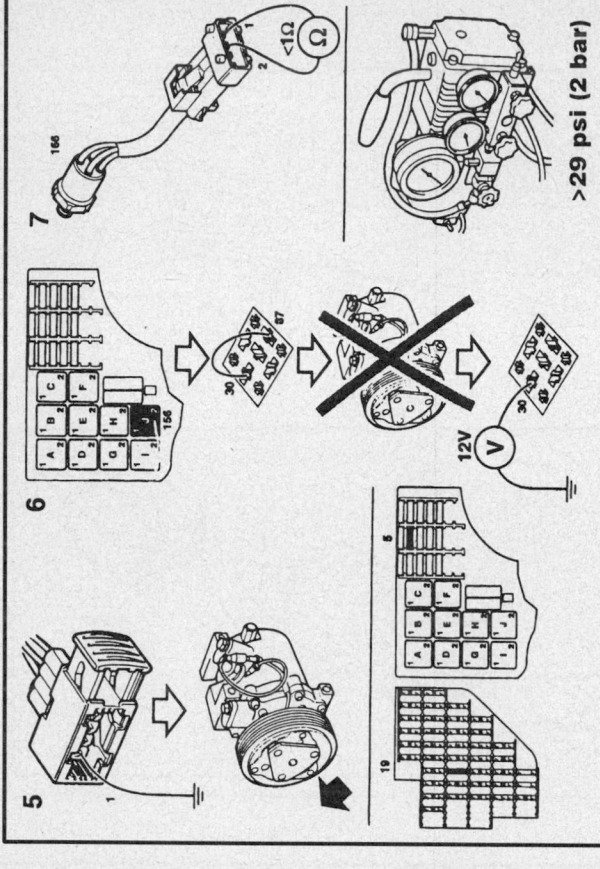

>29 psi (2 bar)

5. Remove the grille and unplug the 4-pin connector of the three-stage pressure switch. Connect pin 1 to a good ground. Proceed to point 7 if the compressor starts.

   If the compressor does not start, check fuse 19 in fuse holder 22A in the dashboard and fuse 5 in fuse holder 342A in the engine bay. If these fuses are intact, proceed to point 6.

6. Check the A/C relay (156) on position J in relay holder 342B by connecting a jumper lead across pins 30 and 87.
   If the compressor still fails to start, check that battery positive is applied to pin 30.

7. Measure the resistance across pins 1 and 2 in the male connector of the three-stage pressure switch. It should be less than 1 ohm.

   If it is correct, proceed to point 8.
   If it is not correct, connect a pressure-gauge stand and check that the pressure is higher than 29 psi (2 bar).

   If the pressure is higher than 29 psi (2 bar), change the pressure switch.
   If it is not, there is probably insufficient refrigerant in the system.

A/C SYMPTOM DIAGNOSIS—1994–95 900

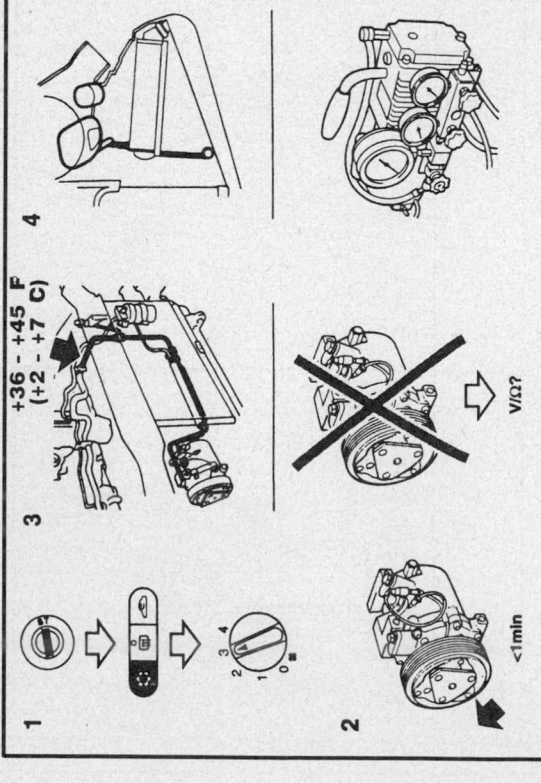

+36 – +45 F
(+2 – +7 C)

<1min

No or poor cooling

Check the following before you start fault diagnosis:

- that the compressor drive belt is intact and does not slip
- that the flow of air through the air ducts to the indoor interior is not obstructed
- that the flow of air through the condenser is not obstructed

1. Cars with manual A/C:
   Start the engine, press the A/C button and start the ventilation fan.
   Cars with ACC:
   Press the AUTO button.

2. Open the bonnet and check whether the compressor starts up within one minute.

3. If the compressor is in operation, check whether the low-pressure line is cold (36 – 45°F (2 – 7 C)). If it is, proceed to point 4.
   If the compressor does not start, the fault is electrical. Proceed to point 5.

4. If the low-pressure line is cold, check the operation of the air-blending flap.
   If the low-pressure line is not cold, connect a pressure-gauge stand.

A/C SYMPTOM DIAGNOSIS—1994—95 900 CONT'D

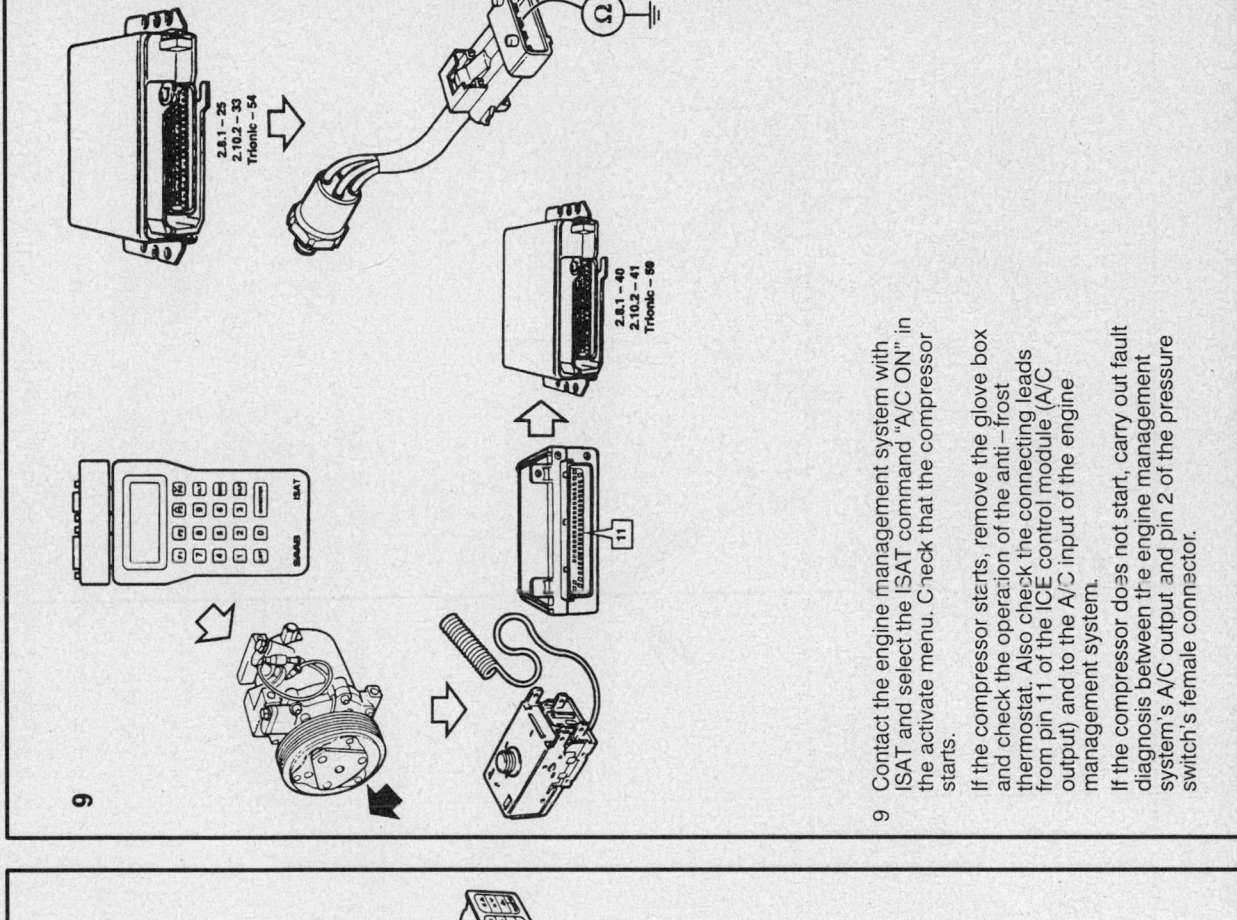

9 Contact the engine management system with ISAT and select the ISAT command "A/C ON" in the activate menu. Check that the compressor starts.

If the compressor starts, remove the glove box and check the operation of the anti—frost thermostat. Also check the connecting leads from pin 11 of the ICE control module (A/C output) and to the A/C input of the engine management system.

If the compressor does not start, carry out fault diagnosis between the engine management system's A/C output and pin 2 of the pressure switch's female connector.

A/C SYMPTOM DIAGNOSIS—1994—95 900, CONT'D

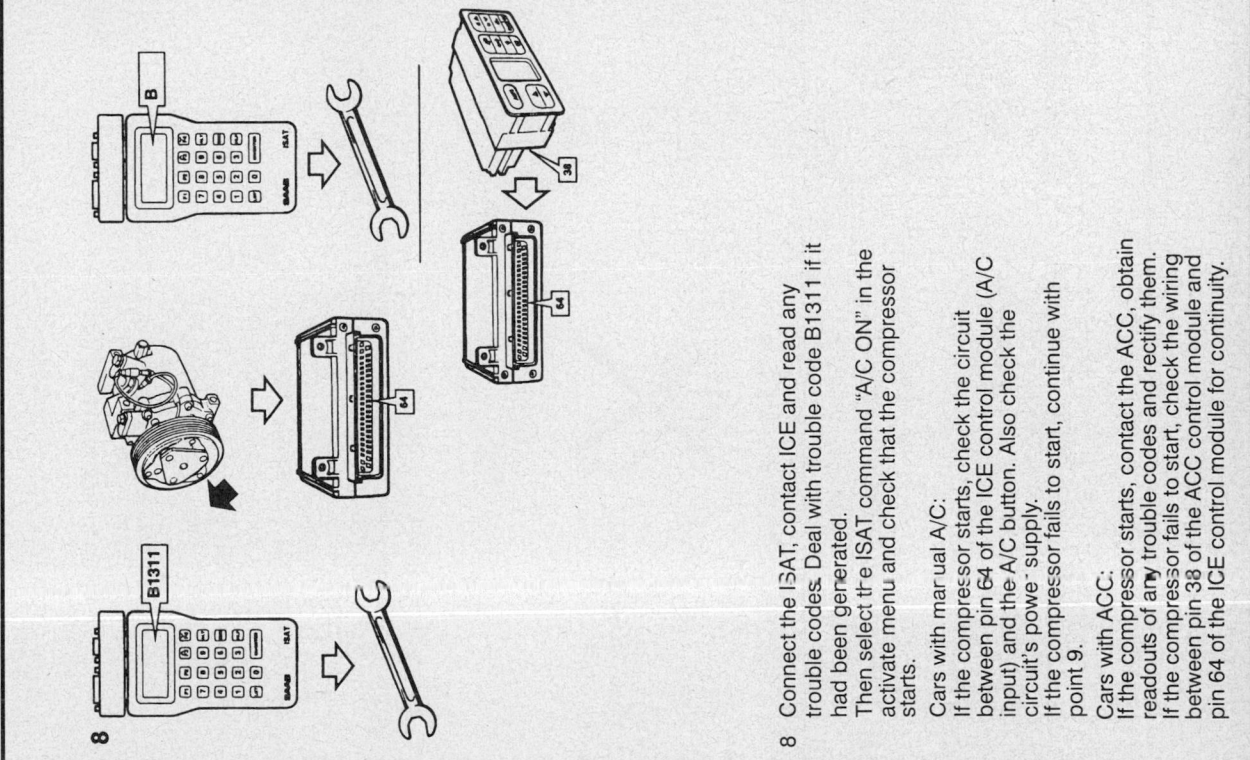

8 Connect the ISAT, contact ICE and read any trouble codes. Deal with trouble code B1311 if it had been generated.

Then select the ISAT command "A/C ON" in the activate menu and check that the compressor starts.

Cars with manual A/C:
If the compressor starts, check the circuit between pin 64 of the ICE control module (A/C input) and the A/C button. Also check the circuit's power supply.
If the compressor fails to start, continue with point 9.

Cars with ACC:
If the compressor starts, contact the ACC, obtain readouts of any trouble codes and rectify them.
If the compressor fails to start, check the wiring between pin 38 of the ACC control module and pin 64 of the ICE control module for continuity.

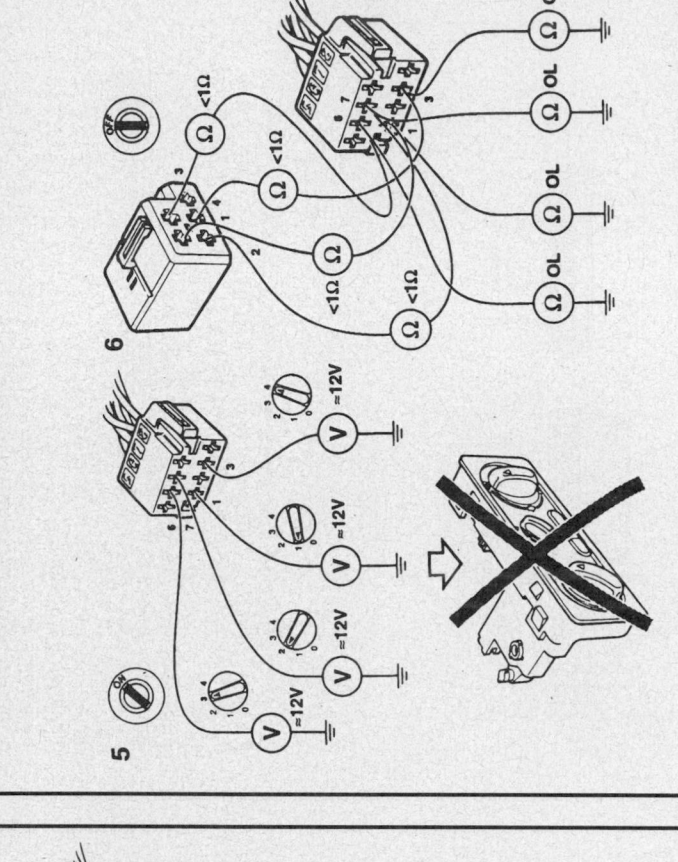

HEATER SYMPTOM DIAGNOSIS—1994–95 900

5 Check the voltage on the following pins at the rear of the control panel's 8-pin connector. Readings should be taken with the fan connector unplugged and the control panel connector plugged in.

- Fan speed 1 should give a reading of 12 V on pin 1
- Fan speed 2 should give a reading of 12 V on pin 7
- Fan speed 3 should give a reading of 12 V on pin 6
- Fan speed 4 should give a reading of 12 V on pin 3

  Change the control panel if any reading is incorrect.

6 Check the leads for shorting/continuity if correct readings were obtained when carrying out point 5 but not when carrying out point 4.

---

1 Check fuse 3 and that it is live.

2 Unplug the 8-pin connector from the rear of the control panel and check whether pin 2 of the connector is live.

3 Check the wiring between pin 2 of the control panel and fuse 3 for continuity/shorting.

4 Unplug the fan's connector and check the voltage as shown below:

- Fan speed 1 should give a reading of 12 V on pin 1 (RD/WH)
- Fan speed 2 should give a reading of 12 V on pin 2 (WH)
- Fan speed 3 should give a reading of 12 V on pin 4 (GN)
- Fan speed 4 should give a reading of 12 V on pin 3 (YE)

  Also check whether the resistance across pin 5 and a good grounding point is <0.1 ohm.
  Try fitting a new fan resistor if all readings are correct.

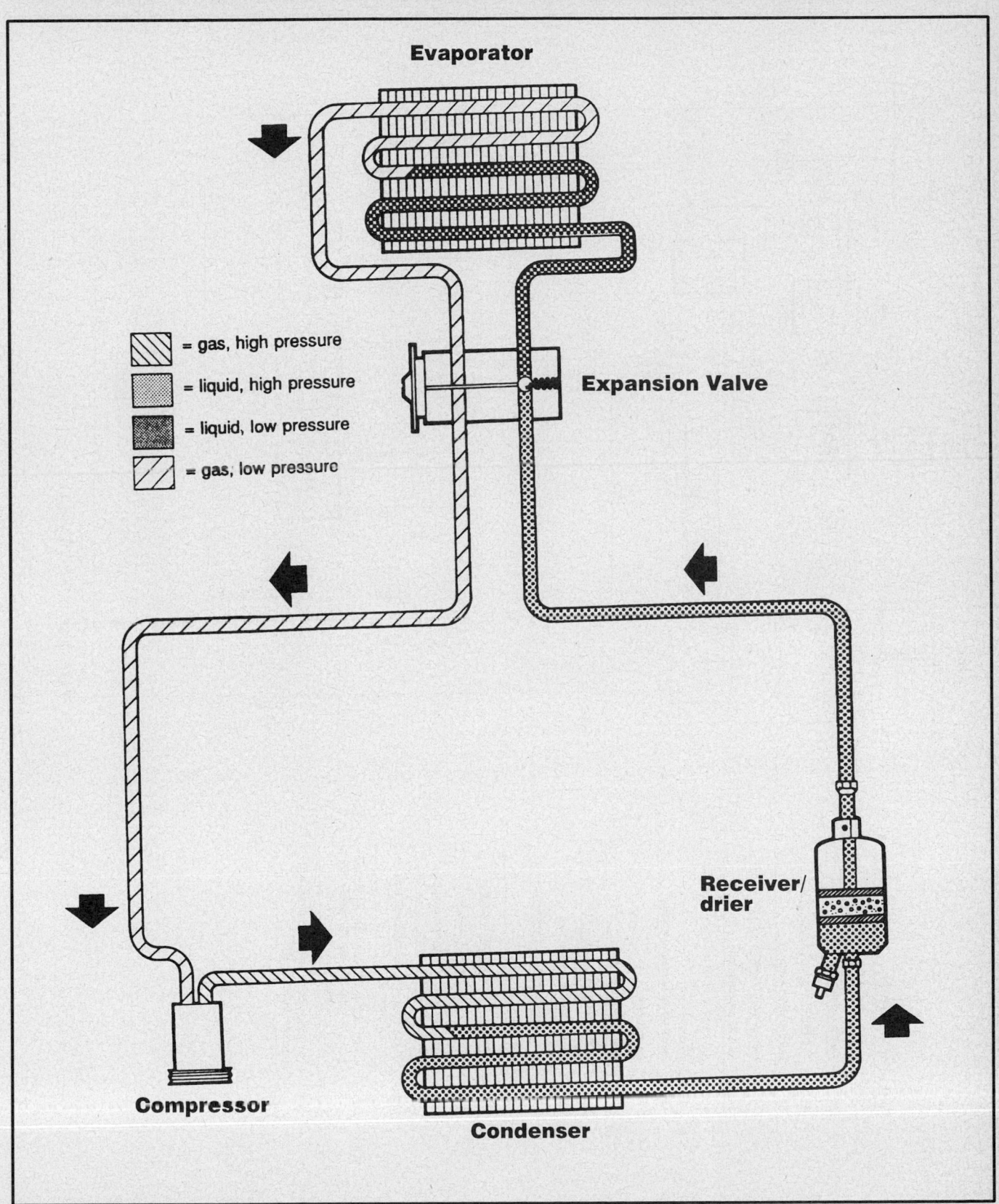

Air conditioning system schematic

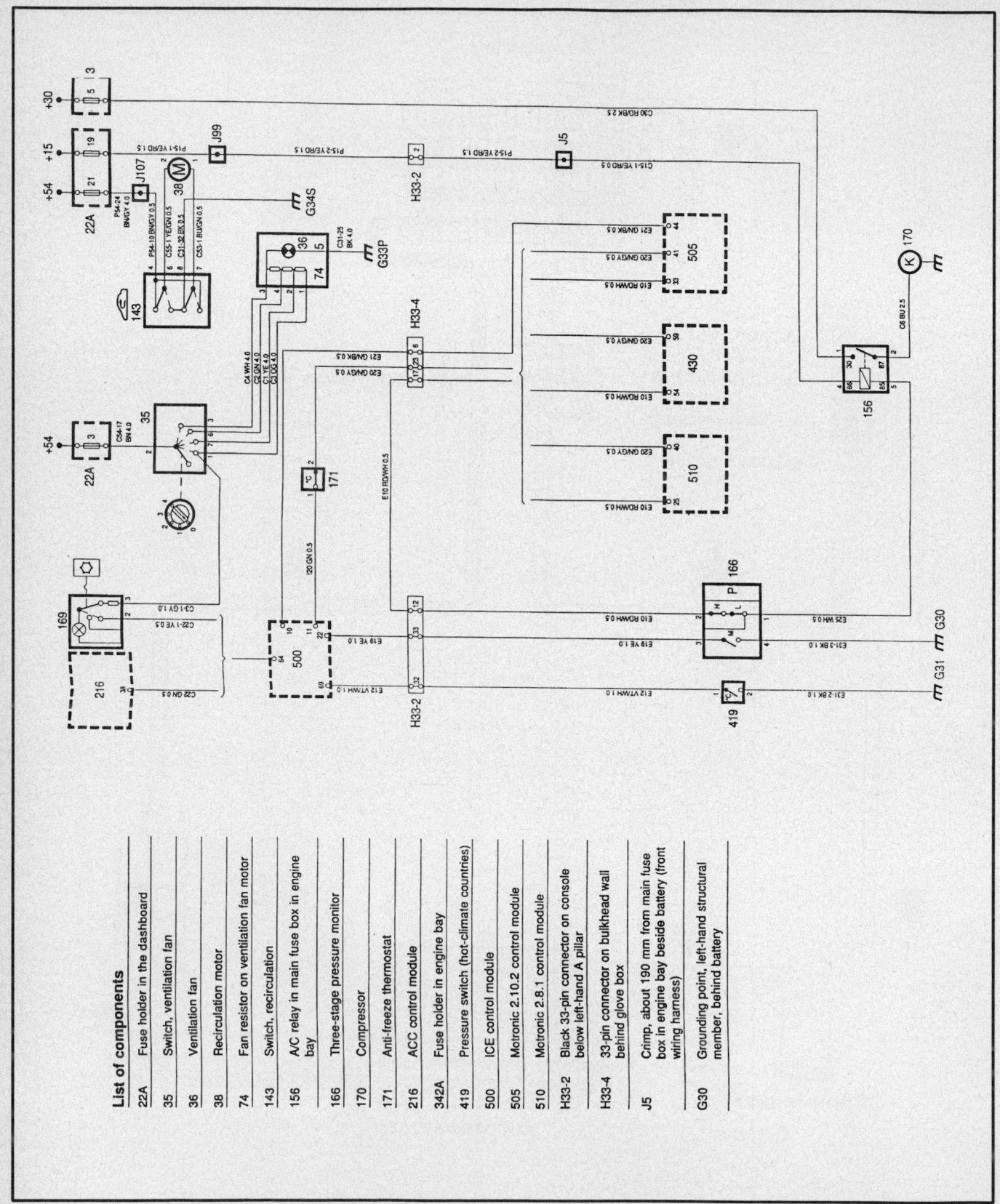

Manual air conditioning wiring diagram—1994–95 900

List of components

22A	Fuse holder in the dashboard
35	Switch, ventilation fan
36	Ventilation fan
38	Recirculation motor
74	Fan resistor on ventilation fan motor
143	Switch, recirculation
156	A/C relay in main fuse box in engine bay
166	Three-stage pressure monitor
170	Compressor
171	Anti-freeze thermostat
216	ACC control module
342A	Fuse holder in engine bay
419	Pressure switch (hot-climate countries)
500	ICE control module
505	Motronic 2.10.2 control module
510	Motronic 2.8.1 control module
H33-2	Black 33-pin connector on console below left-hand A pillar
H33-4	33-pin connector on bulkhead wall behind glove box
J5	Crimp, about 190 mm from main fuse box in engine bay beside battery (front wiring harness)
G30	Grounding point, left-hand structural member, behind battery

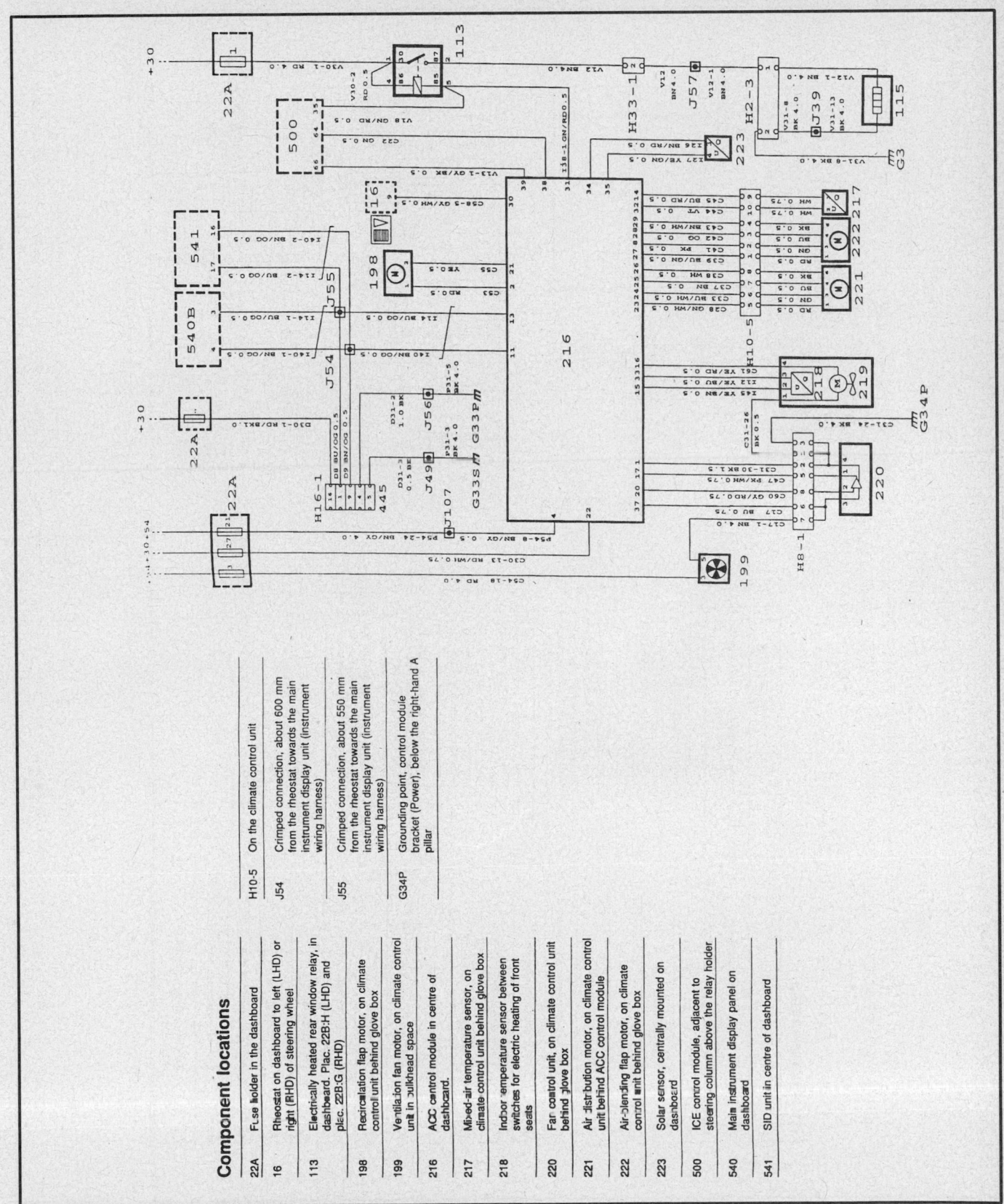

Component locations

H10-5	On the climate control unit
J54	Crimped connection, about 600 mm from the rheostat towards the main instrument display unit (instrument wiring harness)
J55	Crimped connection, about 550 mm from the rheostat towards the main instrument display unit (instrument wiring harness)
G34P	Grounding point, control module bracket (Power), below the right-hand A pillar

22A	Fuse holder in the dashboard
16	Rheostat on dashboard to left (LHD) or right (RHD) of steering wheel
113	Electrically heated rear window relay, in dashboard. Plac. 22B:H (LHD) and plac. 22B:G (RHD)
198	Recirculation flap motor, on climate control unit behind glove box
199	Ventilation fan motor, on climate control unit in bulkhead space
216	ACC control module in centre of dashboard.
217	Mixed-air temperature sensor, on climate control unit behind glove box
218	Indoor temperature sensor between switches for electric heating of front seats
220	Fan control unit, on climate control unit behind glove box
221	Air distribution motor, on climate control unit behind ACC control module
222	Air-blending flap motor, on climate control unit behind glove box
223	Solar sensor, centrally mounted on dashboard
500	ICE control module, adjacent to steering column above the relay holder
540	Main instrument display panel on dashboard
541	SID unit in centre of dashboard

Automatic air conditioning wiring diagram—1994–95 900

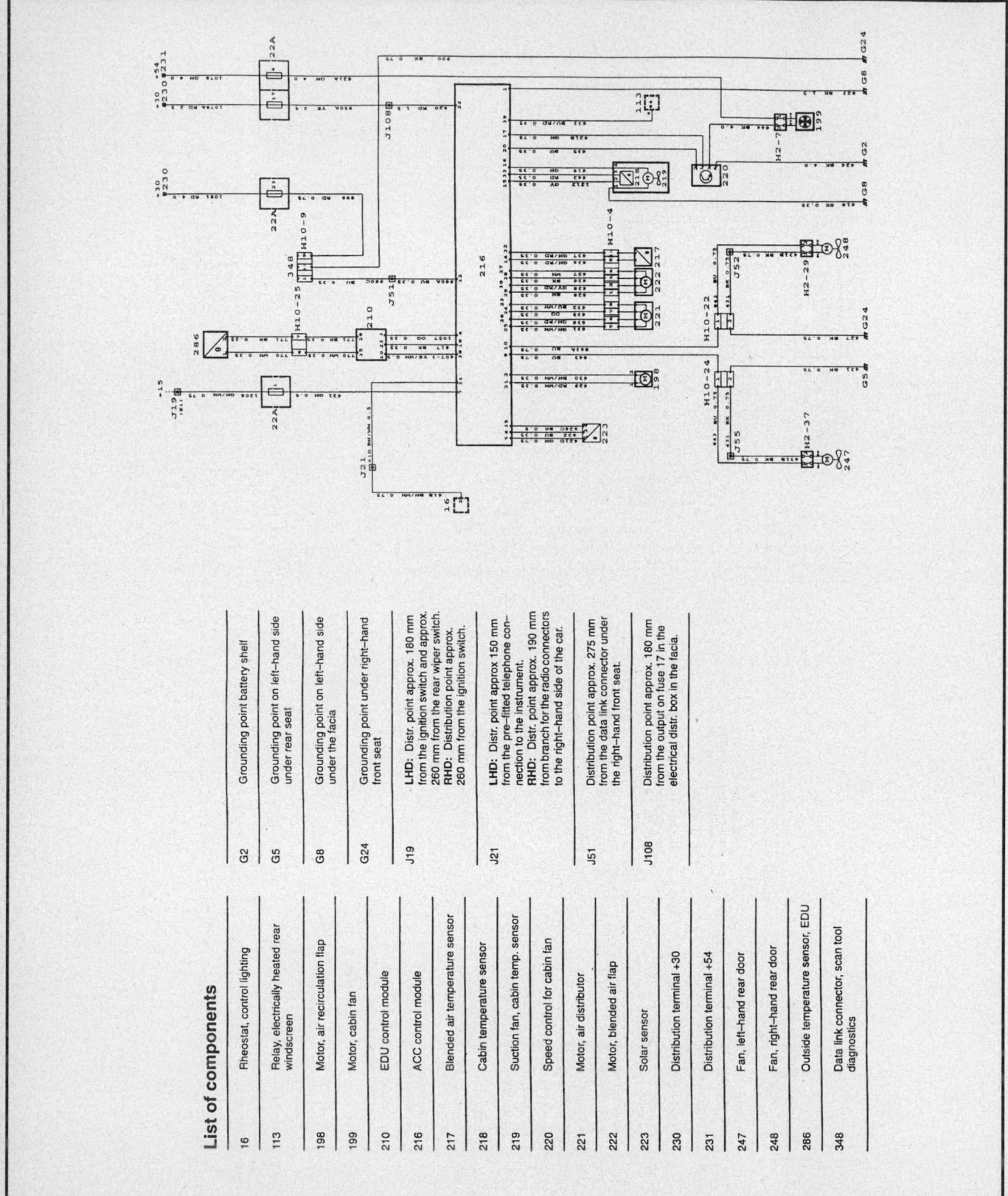

List of components

16	Rheostat, control lighting
113	Relay, electrically heated rear windscreen
198	Motor, air recirculation flap
199	Motor, cabin fan
210	EDU control module
216	ACC control module
217	Blended air temperature sensor
218	Cabin temperature sensor
219	Suction fan, cabin temp. sensor
220	Speed control for cabin fan
221	Motor, air distributor
222	Motor, blended air flap
223	Solar sensor
230	Distribution terminal +30
231	Distribution terminal +54
247	Fan, left-hand rear door
248	Fan, right-hand rear door
286	Outside temperature sensor, EDU
348	Data link connector, scan tool diagnostics

G2	Grounding point battery shelf
G5	Grounding point on left-hand side under rear seat
G8	Grounding point on left-hand side under the facia
G24	Grounding point under right-hand front seat
J19	LHD: Distr. point approx. 180 mm from the ignition switch and approx. 260 mm from the rear wiper switch. RHD: Distribution point approx. 260 mm from the ignition switch.
J21	LHD: Distr. point approx 150 mm from the pre-fitted telephone connection to the instrument. RHD: Distr. point approx. 190 mm from branch for the radio connectors to the right-hand side of the car.
J51	Distribution point approx. 275 mm from the data link connector under the right-hand front seat.
J108	Distribution point approx. 180 mm from the output on fuse 17 in the electrical distr. box in the facia.

Automatic air conditioning wiring diagram—1995 9000

SPECIFICATIONS

ENGINE IDENTIFICATION

Year	Model	Engine Displacement Liters (cc)	Engine Series (ID/VIN)	Fuel System	No. of Cylinders	Engine Type
1993	Legacy	2.2 (2212)	6	MPFI	4	OHC
	Loyale	1.8 (1810)	4①	SPFI②	4	OHC
	Justy	1.2 (1207)	7③	MPFI	3	OHC
	SVX	3.3 (3318)	3	MPFI	6	DOHC
1994	Impreza	1.8 (1820)	2①	MPFI	4	SOHC
	Impreza	2.2 (2212)	NA	MPFI	4	SOHC
	Legacy	2.2 (2212)	6	MPFI	4	SOHC
	Loyale	1.8 (1810)	4①	SPFI②	4	OHC
	Justy	1.2 (1207)	7③	MPFI	3	SOHC
	SVX	3.3 (3318)	3	MPFI	6	DOHC
1995	Impreza	1.8 (1820)	2①	MPFI	4	SOHC
	Impreza	2.2 (2212)	NA	MPFI	4	SOHC
	Legacy	2.2 (2212)	6	MPFI	4	SOHC
	SVX	3.3 (3318)	3	MPFI	6	DOHC

OHC – Overhead Cam
DOHC – Dual Overhead Cam
SPFI – Single-Port Fuel Injection
MPFI – Multi-Port Fuel Injection

① Vin 4 = 2WD; Vin 5 = 4WD
② Turbo models are equipped with MPFI
③ Vin 7 = 2WD; Vin 8 = 4WD
NA – Not Available

REFRIGERANT CAPACITIES

Year	Model	Refrigerant (oz.)	Oil (fl. oz.)	Compressor Type
1993	Legacy	29-32	3.2	Calsonic V5-15C
	Legacy	29-32	2.4	Zexel DKS-15CH
	Loyale	28	2.4	Hitachi
	Justy	①	①	①
	SVX	23	2.4	②
1994	Impreza	23-26	6.1	Zexel Rotary Vane
	Legacy	29-32	3.2	Calsonic V5-15C
	Legacy	29-32	2.4	Zexel DKS-15CH
	Loyale	28	2.4	Hitachi
	Justy	①	①	①
	SVX	23	2.4	②
1995	Impreza	23-26	6.1	Zexel Rotary Vane
	Legacy	29-32	3.2	Calsonic V5-15C
	SVX	23	2.4	②

① Justy is not equipped with A/C system
② Type not specified by manufacturer

AIR CONDITIONING BELT TENSION

Year	Model	Engine Liters (cc)	Belt Type	Specifications New	Used
1993	Legacy	2.2 (2212)	Poly-V	0.30-0.34	0.35-0.39
	Loyale	1.8 (1810)	V-Belt	0.30-0.34	0.30-0.34
	Justy	1.2 (1207)	①	①	①
	SVX	3.3 (3318)	Poly-V	0.24-0.27	0.28-0.31
1994	Impreza	1.8 (1820)	V-Belt	0.30-0.34	0.30-0.34
	Impreza	2.2 (2212)	Poly-V	0.30-0.34	0.35-0.39
	Legacy	2.2 (2212)	Poly-V	0.30-0.34	0.35-0.39
	Loyale	1.8 (1810)	V-Belt	0.30-0.34	0.30-0.34
	Justy	1.2 (1207)	①	①	①
	SVX	3.3 (3318)	Poly-V	0.24-0.27	0.28-0.31
1995	Impreza	1.8 (1820)	V-Belt	0.30-0.34	0.30-0.34
	Impreza	2.2 (2212)	Poly-V	0.30-0.34	0.35-0.39
	Legacy	2.2 (2212)	Poly-V	0.30-0.34	0.35-0.39
	SVX	3.3 (3318)	Poly-V	0.24-0.27	0.28-0.31

① Justy is not equipped with an A/C system

SYSTEM DESCRIPTION

General Information

HEATING SYSTEM

The heating and ventilating systems consist of a control unit, heater unit, blower assembly, connecting heater ducts and heater hoses. Fresh air from the outside is introduced into the passenger compartment through the center and side ventilator grilles when the ventilator fan is operated.

Fresh outside air can also be introduced through the side vents on the driver side and passenger side, by ram pressure produced while the vehicle is in motion. A high performance heating system is adopted. All vehicles are equipped with a front side window defroster and some vehicles are further equipped with the rear heater duct.

AIR CONDITIONING SYSTEM

When the mode control switch is set at **A/C–MAX**, **A/C–LO** or **DEF** positions the air conditioner microswitch will be turned on. In this condition, when the blower switch is turned **ON**, USA vehicles, or when the blower motor and air conditioner switch are turned **ON**, Canadian vehicles the blower relay and air conditioner relay will activate. This in turn causes the blower motor, Fast Idle Control Device (FICD) and compressor clutch to activate. This in turn activates the pressure switch main fan control or the thermo switch, causing the main fan to activate.

When either the high–low pressure switch or the thermostat activates, all air conditioning circuits, except the blower motor, will deactivate. In this condition, when the temperature of the coolant in the radiator is high enough and the thermo switch turns on, the radiator main fan will activate. When refrigerant pressure exceeds the specified value with the air conditioning switch to **ON**, the main fan will activate to help cool the condenser.

Service Valve Location

The low pressure service port is located on the suction hose connection, near the compressor.

The high pressure service port is located at the rear of the compressor, on the metal portion of the flexible hose.

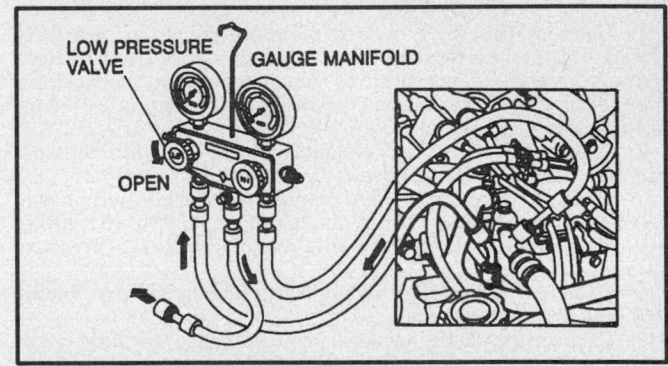

Service valve locations with manifold gauge set connected – Legacy

System Discharging

The pressurized refrigerant inside the system must be discharged to a pressure approaching atmospheric pressure prior to evacuating refrigerant inside system. This operation should be made to permit safe removal when replacing system components.

1. Always use approved recovery/recycling equipment meeting current SAE standards.
2. Always follow the equipment manufacturer's instructions to assure complete and safe discharging.

NOTE: Never vent or discharge refrigerant directly to the atmosphere. To help protect the atmosphere ozone layer from destruction by CFCs found in air conditioning refrigerant, follow instructions to keep refrigerant in a closed–loop system.

System Evacuating

1. Disconnect the negative battery cable.
2. Discharge the refrigerant from system.
3. When refrigerant has been discharged to a pressure approaching atmospheric pressure, connect center charging hose to a vacuum pump.
4. Close both valves of manifold gauge fully. Start vacuum pump.
5. Open low pressure valve of the manifold gauge and evacuate the old refrigerant from system.
6. When the low pressure gauge reading has reached to approximately 19.69 in. Hg vacuum, slowly open high pressure valve.
7. When pressure inside system has dropped to 27.95 in. Hg vacuum, fully close both of valves of manifold gauge and stop vacuum pump. Allow the system to remain in this state for 5–10 minutes and confirm that the reading does not rise.

NOTE: The low pressure gauge reads lower by 0.98 in. Hg vacuum per a 1000 ft. elevation. Perform evacuation according to the following observation: The rate of ascension of the low pressure gauge, should be less than 0.98 in. Hg vacuum within 5 minutes. If system leakage is suspected, perform a leak test.

Leak Testing

If the pressure rises or the specified negative pressure can not be obtained, there is a leak in the system. In this case, immediately charge system with refrigerant and repair the leak described in the following.

1. Confirm that both valves of manifold gauge are fully closed and then disconnect center charging hose from vacuum pump. Connect center hose to can tap in place of vacuum pump. Attach refrigerant can top and pass refrigerant to manifold gauge.
2. Loosen the connection of center fitting of manifold gauge to purge air from center hose.
3. Open low pressure valve of manifold gauge and charge refrigerant into system. After 1 can, about 0.09 lb. (0.4 kg) of refrigerant has been charged into system close low pressure valve.
4. Check for refrigerant leakage with a leak detector. Repair any leakage as it is found.
5. Confirm that both valves of manifold gauge are fully closed and change center charging hose from can tap to vacuum pump.
6. Open high and low pressure valves and operate a vacuum pump to evacuate the refrigerant from the system. When the pressure in system has dropped to 27.95 in Hg vacuum, fully close both valvesof the manifold gauge. Remove the manifold gauge set.

System Charging

NOTE: The following procedure is given in case charging by individual cans is required. However, current practices suggest using only approved recovery/recycling service equipment meeting current SAE standards. Follow equipment manufacturer's instructions to assure accurate, complete and safe system charging. If charging with small cans, use the following procedures.

Hitachi and Panasonic Systems

1. Install a manifold gauge to the system.

NOTE: Be sure to purge air from the high and low pressure charging hoses. If air is mixed with refrigerant in system, evacuation of system should be performed.

2. Attach center charging hose of manifold gauge to refrigerant can through can tap. Break seal of refrigerant can to allow refrigerant to enter manifold gauge. Loosen charging hose at the center fitting of manifold gauge and purge air from inside charging hose.
3. On Hitachi system, open high and low pressure valves of manifold gauge and charge refrigerant into system. On Panasonic system, open only the high pressure valve of the manifold gauge.

NOTE: When refrigerant charging speed is slow, immerse refrigerant can in water heated to a temperature of about 104°F (40°C). However, note that this is dangerous when water is hot.

─────────── **CAUTION** ───────────
Under any circumstances the refrigerant can must not be warmed in water heated to a temperature of over 126°F (52°C). A blow torch or stove must never be used to warm the can.
──────────────────────────────────

NOTE: When charging liquid refrigerant into the system, with the can turned upside down to reduce charging time, charge it only through high pressure valve, but not through low pressure valve.

4. On Hitachi system only, if refrigerant charging speed slows down, charge it while running the compressor for ease of charging. After performing Steps 13 above, proceed with charging system in the following order.

NOTE: After completion of charging, the compressor should always be turned several times manually.

5. On both systems, shut off high pressure valve of manifold gauge. Remember, on the Panasonic system, the low pressure valve is kept closed.

─────────── **CAUTION** ───────────
Never charge refrigerant through the high pressure side of system, when the engine is running. This will force refrigerant back into refrigerant can and the can may explode.
──────────────────────────────────

6. Run the engine at idle speed.
7. Set temperature control dial or lever at **MAX** cool and fan switch at **MAX** speed.
8. On Hitachi system, charge refrigerant while controlling low pressure gauge reading a 40 psi or less by turning in or out low pressure valve of manifold gauge. On the Panasonic system, charge refrigerant into the system through the low pressure valve after difference of pressure between low and high pressure gauge appears. Repeat from Step 7 when difference of pressure between low and high pressure gauges does not appear after 1 minute of operation. It is not possible to charge refrigerant withoutpressure difference between low and high pressure gauges.
9. When refrigerant can is empty, fully close both valves of manifold gauge and replace refrigerant can with a new one. Before opening the manifold gauge valve to charge refrigerant from the new can, be sure to purge air from inside charging hose.

10. Charge the specified amount of refrigerant into system by weighing charged refrigerant with scale. Overcharging will cause discharge pressure to rise.

NOTE: **Measure the amount of charged refrigerant with a scale. Make a note of the amount charged for can. The presence of bubbles in sight glass of receiver/drier is an unsuitable method of checking the amount of refrigerant charged in system. The state of the bubbles in sight glass should only be used forchecking whether the amount of charged refrigerant is small or not. The amount of charged refrigerant can be correctly judged by means of discharge pressure.**

11. After the specified amount of refrigerant has been charged into system, close manifold gauge valves. Detach the charging hoses from the service valves of system. Be sure to install valve cap on service valve.
12. Confirm that there are no leaks in system by checking with a leak detector.

NOTE: **Conducting a performance test prior to removing the manifold gauge is a good service operation.**

Diesel Kiki System

1. Install manifold gauge to system.

NOTE: **Be sure to purge air from the high and low pressure charging hoses. If air is mixed with refrigerant in system, evacuation of system should be performed.**

2. Attach center charging hose of manifold gauge to refrigerant can through can tap. Break seal of refrigerant can to allow refrigerant to enter manifold gauge. Loosen the charging hose at the center fitting of manifold gauge and purge air from inside charging hose.
3. Open only the low pressure valve of the manifold gauge to charge the refrigerant into the system.

NOTE: **When refrigerant charging speed is slow, immerse refrigerant can in water heated to a temperature of about 104°F (40°C). However, note that this is dangerous when water is hot.**

————————CAUTION————————
Under any circumstances, the refrigerant can must not be warmed in water heated to a temperature of over 126oF (52oC). A blow torch or stove must never be used to warm up the can.
————————————————————

4. Should the refrigerant charging speed slow down, charge it with the engine running and the compressor engaged.
5. After having completed Steps 1–3, proceed with the charging in the following manner:
6. Run the engine at idling speed.
7. Set temperature control dial or lever at **MAX** cool and fan switch at **MAX** speed. Charge refrigerant into the system.
8. When refrigerant can is empty, fully close both valves of manifold gauge and replace refrigerant can with a new one. Before opening manifold gauge valve to charge refrigerant from anew can, be sure to purge air from inside charging hose.
9. Charge a maximum 2.0 lbs. (0.9 kg) of refrigerant into system. Weigh the charged refrigerant with scale. Overcharging will cause discharge pressure to rise.

NOTE: **Measure the amount of charged refrigerant with a scale. Make a note of the amount charged from the can. The presence of bubbles in sight glass of receiver/drier is an unsuitable method of checking the amount of refrigerant charged in system. The state of the bubbles in sight glass should only beused for checking**

whether the amount of charged refrigerant is small or not. The amount of charged refrigerant can be correctly judged by means of discharge pressure.

10. After the refrigerant has been charged into system, close manifold gauge valves. The detach charging hoses from service valves of system. Be sure on install valve cap to service valve.
11. Confirm that there are no leaks in system by checking with a leak detector.

NOTE: **Conducting a performance test prior to removing the manifold gauge is a good service operation.**

Calsonic System

1. Install manifold gauge to system.

NOTE: **Be sure to purge air from the high and low pressure charging hoses. If air is mixed with refrigerant in system, evacuation of system should be performed.**

2. Attach center charging hose of manifold gauge to refrigerant can through can tap. Break seal of refrigerant can to allow refrigerant to enter manifold gauge. Loosen the charging hose at the center fitting of manifold gauge and purge air from inside charging hose.
3. Open only the high pressure valve of the manifold gauge to charge the refrigerant into the system.

NOTE: **If charging liquid refrigerant into the system with the can turned upside down to reduce charging time, charge it only through the high pressure service valve only. After manually.**

4. When the low pressure gauge reading reaches 14 psi, approximately 1.0 lb. (98 kPa) of refrigerant has been charged into the system. Completely close the high pressure valve of the manifold gauge and stop the charging.
5. If charging the system through the low pressure side, proceed as follows:
6. With the engine off, open the lower pressure valve of the manifold gauge and charge the refrigerant through the system.
7. When the refrigerant charging speed slows down, close the high pressure valve of the manifold gauge and open the low pressure.
8. Start the engine, set temperature control dial or lever at **MAX** cool and fan switch at **MAX** speed. Charge refrigerant into the system.
9. Charge the system until the bubbles in the sight glass is clear.

NOTE: **Keep in mind, air conditioning systems that utilize a recycling clutch, produce bubbles in the sight glass when the clutch engages. Allow 5 seconds after the clutch engages to determine if bubbles continue. If so, add refrigerant to clear the sight glass.**

————————CAUTION————————
Never charge refrigerant through the high pressure side of the system. This will force refrigerant back into the refrigerant can and may cause the can to explode.
————————————————————

10. Charge the refrigerant while controlling the low pressure gauge reading at 40 psi. (275 kPa) or less by turning the low pressure valve at the manifold gauge.
11. When the refrigerant can is empty, fully close both valves of manifold gauge and replace refrigerant can with a new one. Before opening manifold gauge valve to charge refrigerant from a new can, be sure to purge air from inside charging hose.

12. Charge a maximum 2.0 lbs. (0.9 kg) of refrigerant into system. Weigh the charged refrigerant with scale. Overcharging will cause discharge pressure to rise.

NOTE: Measure the amount of charged refrigerant with a scale. Make a note of the amount charged for can. The presence of bubbles in sight glass of receiver/drier is an unsuitable method of checking the amount of refrigerant charged in system. The state of the bubbles in sight glass should only be used for checking whether the amount of charged refrigerant is small or not. The amount of charged refrigerant can be correctly judged by means of discharge pressure.

13. After the refrigerant has been charged into system, close manifold gauge valves. The detach charging hoses from service valves of system. Be sure to install valve cap to service valve.
14. Confirm that there are no leaks in system by checking with a leak detector.

NOTE: Conducting a performance test prior to removing the manifold gauge is a good service operation.

Compressor and Component Oil Level Adjustment

When replacing the compressor, condenser, evaporator or receiver/drier, adjustments to the refrigerant oil level need to be made to compensate for lost oil in the oil component or due to system leak. First, stabilize the system if it is operable.

SYSTEM OIL STABILIZATION

1. Start the engine and run it at 1500 rpm.
2. Set the air conditioning switch to **ON**.
3. Set the air mode to **RECIRCULATE**.
4. Set the blower to **HIGH** speed.
5. The ambient air temperature should be 80°F (27°C).
6. Operate the system for 10 minutes.
7. Stop the engine. Then, slowly, using proper equipment, discharge the system.
8. After the component replacement and/or repairs are made, add new refrigerant oil to the component according to the "Refrigerant Oil Adjustment Chart."

REFRIGERANT OIL ADJUSTMENT CHART

Component	Oil to be Added (oz.)				
	Calsonic	Diesel-Kiki	Hitachi	Panasonic	Zexel
Compressor	2.9	2.4	2.4	2.4	2.4
Evaporator	2.9	2.4	2.4	2.0	2.4
Condenser	2.9	1.7	1.7	1.4	1.7
Receiver/Drier	0.2	None	None	None	None
Large Leak	1.4	1.7	1.7	1.4	1.7

SYSTEM COMPONENTS

Radiator

REMOVAL AND INSTALLATION

Impreza and Legacy

1. Disconnect the cables and remove the battery.
2. Properly drain the cooling system.
3. Disconnect both radiator hoses from the engine. Prepare to catch remaining coolant.
4. Remove the V–belt cover.
5. Remove the fan connectors.
6. Remove the radiator brackets. Slightly lift the radiator, slide it to the left, detach the automatic transaxle cooler hoses, and remove the radiator from the vehicle.
7. The cooling fans can be removed at the bench.
8. Installation is the reverse of the removal procedure. Open the air vent plug on the radiator during refilling.

Loyale and Justy

1. Disconnect the negative battery cable and drain the cooling system (on Justy, place a hose through the hole in the under cover for draining).
2. Disconnect the inlet and outlet hoses from the engine side.
3. Disconnect the overflow hose from the radiator.

4. Disconnect the fan motor connectors.
5. Remove the radiator mounting brackets.
6. If equipped with automatic transaxle, disconnect the cooler lines and plug.
7. Remove the radiator from the vehicle.
8. Installation is the reverse of the removal procedure.

SVX

1. Disconnect the cables and remove the battery.
2. Raise and properly support the vehicle. Remove the engine under cover.
3. Properly drain the cooling system.
4. Disconnect the radiator hose from the water pump. Disconnect and plug the automatic transaxle hose from the pipe (if equipped).
5. Lower the vehicle. Remove the radiator fan motor connectors. Remove the coolant reservoir hose.
6. Remove the V–belt cover.
7. Disconnect the upper radiator hose from the water pipe.
8. Remove the radiator upper bracket and remove the radiator.
9. Installation is the reverse of the removal procedure. After initially filling the cooling system, run the engine to normal operating temperature at 2,000–3,000 rpm for 5 minutes.

When engine cools down, remove the radiator cap and adjust the coolant level.

Cooling Fan

TESTING

1. Disconnect the negative battery cable.
2. Disconnect the cooling fan electrical connector.
3. Apply a 12 volt source between the positive and negative terminals of the fan motor connector. The fan should operate.
4. While the fan is in operation, take notice to any abnormal noises, vibrations or fan–to–shroud interference.
5. If the fan motor is inoperative, inspect the connector and harness leading from the fan motor, for damage.
6. If the fan motor checks good, test the thermo–sensor.
7. Connect the negative battery cable.

REMOVAL AND INSTALLATION

1. Disconnect the negative battery cable.
2. Disconnect the fan motor lead connector from the harness connector.
3. On Legacy, remove the overflow reservoir tank.
4. Loosen the lower shroud–to–radiator mounting bolts.
5. Remove the upper shroud–to–radiator mounting bolts.
6. Lift the fan and motor assembly out and remove.
7. Remove the fan motor–to–shroud retaining nuts and separate the fan and motor assembly from the shroud.
8. Remove the fan–to–motor retaining nuts and separate the fan from the motor.
To install:
9. Assemble the fan and motor assembly. Prior to installing the retaining nuts, apply a coat of sealant to the threads and install.

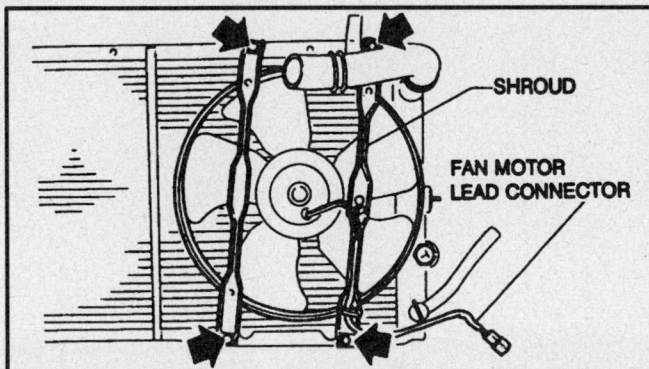

SHROUD

FAN MOTOR LEAD CONNECTOR

Removal and installation of cooling fan assembly — Loyale

10. Assemble the fan/motor assembly to the shroud and install the retaining nuts. Spin the fan and insure that there is no fan–to–shroud interference.
11. Lower the fan shroud assembly in position to the lower mounting bolts.
12. Install the upper shroud mounting bolts.
13. Secure the fan assembly in place with the lower mounting bolts.
14. Connect a 12 volt source to the fan motor lead wire connector and check for noises, vibrations or fan interference.
15. Connect the fan motor connector to the harness connector.
16. Connect the negative battery cable. Start the engine and test the fan operation.

Condenser

REMOVAL AND INSTALLATION

1. Disconnect the negative battery cable.
2. Safely discharge the air conditioning system.
3. Remove the front grille, the radiator bracket and the hood stay.
4. If equipped with an air guide, remove it from the radiator support.
5. Disconnect the pipe connections and cap all openings.
6. Remove the condenser–to–radiator mounting bolts and remove the condenser.
To install:
7. Lower the condenser in place to the radiator and install the mounting bolts.
8. Prior to connecting the condenser piping, apply refrigerant oil to the O–ring seals.
9. Connect the condenser piping to the condenser.
10. If equipped with an air guide, install it to the radiator support, stay and other components as removed.
11. Install the front grille and the lower bracket attachment.
12. Evacuate, charge and leak test the air conditioning system.
13. Connect the negative battery cable. Start the engine and test air conditioning system.

Compressor

REMOVAL AND INSTALLATION

Impreza and Legacy

DIESEL KIKI/ZEXEL AND CALSONIC

1. Disconnect the negative battery cable.
2. Properly discharge the refrigerant using recovery/recycling equipment.
3. Remove the low pressure hose, then the high pressure hose and plug the openings on both. Take care not to allow the O–ring to be loss when removing the hose connections.
4. Remove the retaining bolts from the alternator and compressor belt cover and remove the belt cover.
5. Loosen the lock bolt on the alternator bracket, turn the adjustment bolt and remove the alternator drive belt.
6. Loosen the lock bolt on the idler pulley, turn the adjustment bolt and remove the compressor drive belt.
7. Disconnect the alternator harness connector from the alternator.
8. Disconnect the compressor wire connector from the harness connector.
9. On the Calsonic system, remove the compressor–to–lower bracket mounting bolts and remove the lower bracket. Remove the compressor–to–upper bracket mounting bolts and remove the compressor from the engine.
10. On Diesel Kiki system, remove the compressor–to–bracket mounting bolts and remove the compressor from the engine.
To install:
11. On the Diesel Kiki system, position the compressor to the mounting bracket and install the retaining bolts. Torque the retaining bolts to 17–31 ft. lbs. (23–42 Nm).
12. On the Calsonic system, position the compressor to the upper bracket and install the retaining bolts. Install the lower bracket to the compressor and install the retaining bolts. Torque the retaining bolts to 17–31 ft. lbs. (23–42 Nm).

13. Connect the compressor wire connector to the harness connector.

14. Plug the alternator connector to the alternator.

15. Install the compressor drive belt and adjust the belt tension. Tighten the pulley lock bolt to 1731 ft. lbs. (23–42 Nm).

16. Install the alternator drive belt and adjust the belt tension. Tighten the pulley lock bolt to 17–31 ft. lbs. (23–42 Nm).

17. Apply compressor oil to the outside edges of the O–rings and connect the high pressure hose and low pressure hoses to the compressor. Torque the retaining bolts to: 10–18 ft. lbs. (14–25 Nm) for Diesel Kiki system and 7–14 ft. lbs. (10–20 Nm) for Calsonic system.

18. Install the drive belt cover over the alternator and compressor pulleys.

19. Connect the negative battery cable.

20. Recharge the refrigerant and test the system operation.

Loyale

HITACHI

1. Disconnect the negative battery cable.

2. Remove the spare tire.

3. Remove the pulser and connector from the compressor.

4. Remove the fan shroud.

5. Discharge the refrigerant using recovery/recycling equipment.

6. Remove the low pressure hose then the high pressure hose and plug the openings on both.

7. Remove the alternator drive belt and upper compressor bracket. Remove the condenser fan assembly, then the rear V–belt and idler pulley.

8. Remove the compressor and compressor lower bracket as an assembly.

9. Remove the compressor from the vehicle.

10. Installation is the reverse of the removal procedure. Be sure to adjust the compressor oil level as described in this article. Evacuate, recharge and leak test the system.

PANASONIC

1. Disconnect the negative battery cable.

2. Remove the spare tire.

3. Discharge the refrigerant using a air conditioning manifold gauge set.

4. Remove the low pressure hose then the high pressure hose and plug the openings on both. Take care not to allow the O–ring to be loss when removing the hose connections.

5. Remove the fan shroud retaining bolts and remove the fan shroud.

6. Remove the condenser fan assembly.

7. Loosen the idler pulley locknut.

8. Loosen the compressor bolts, move the compressor forward and remove the compressor drive belt.

9. Disconnect the compressor connector from the harness connector, then remove the compressor from the engine.

To install:

10. Install the compressor on the compressor bracket and install the mounting bolts.

11. Place the drive belt over the crankshaft, power steering, oil pump, water pump, idler and compressor pulleys.

12. Adjust the drive belt tension by changing the idler pulley position.

13. Connect the compressor wire connector to the harness connector.

14. Assemble the condenser fan to the fan drive and install the assembly to the water pump.

15. Apply compressor oil to the outside edges of the O–rings and connect the high pressure hose, then the low pressure hose to the compressor.

16. Install the radiator fan shroud. Connect the negative battery cable.

17. Recharge the refrigerant and test the air conditioning system.

18. Install the spare tire.

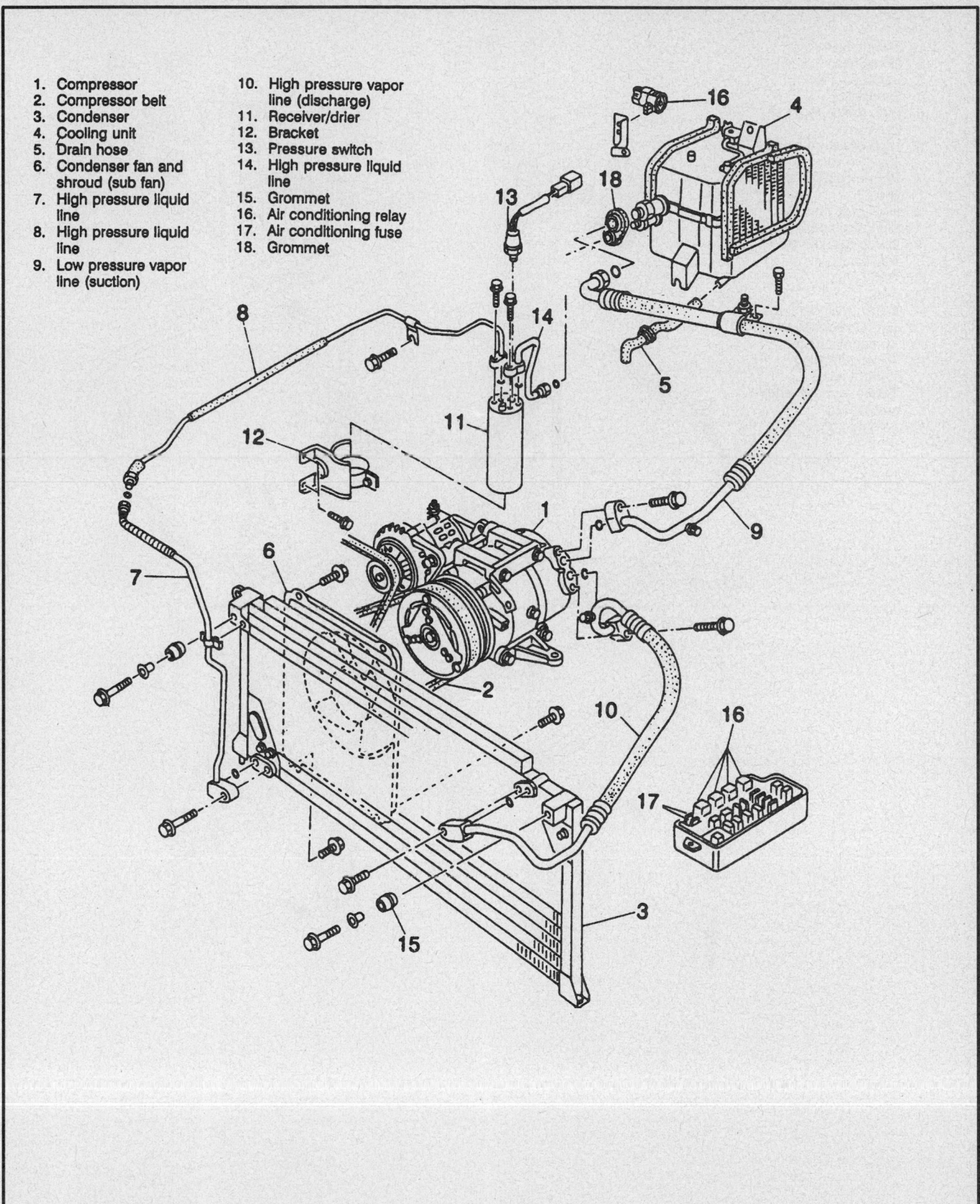

1. Compressor
2. Compressor belt
3. Condenser
4. Cooling unit
5. Drain hose
6. Condenser fan and shroud (sub fan)
7. High pressure liquid line
8. High pressure liquid line
9. Low pressure vapor line (suction)
10. High pressure vapor line (discharge)
11. Receiver/drier
12. Bracket
13. Pressure switch
14. High pressure liquid line
15. Grommet
16. Air conditioning relay
17. Air conditioning fuse
18. Grommet

Exploded view of the air conditioning system – Calsonic (Typical)

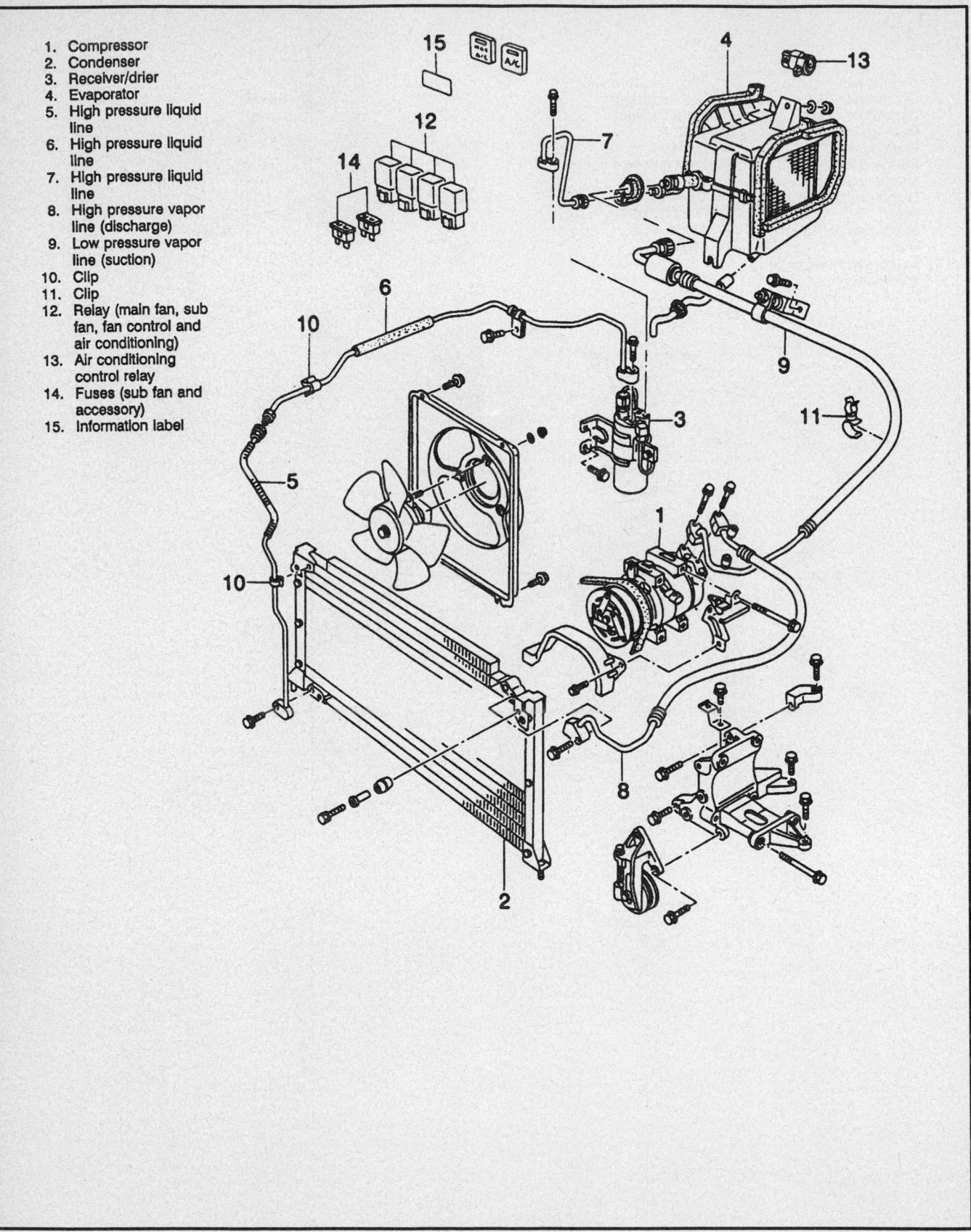

1. Compressor
2. Condenser
3. Receiver/drier
4. Evaporator
5. High pressure liquid line
6. High pressure liquid line
7. High pressure liquid line
8. High pressure vapor line (discharge)
9. Low pressure vapor line (suction)
10. Clip
11. Clip
12. Relay (main fan, sub fan, fan control and air conditioning)
13. Air conditioning control relay
14. Fuses (sub fan and accessory)
15. Information label

Exploded view of the air conditioning system – Diesel Kiki (Typical)

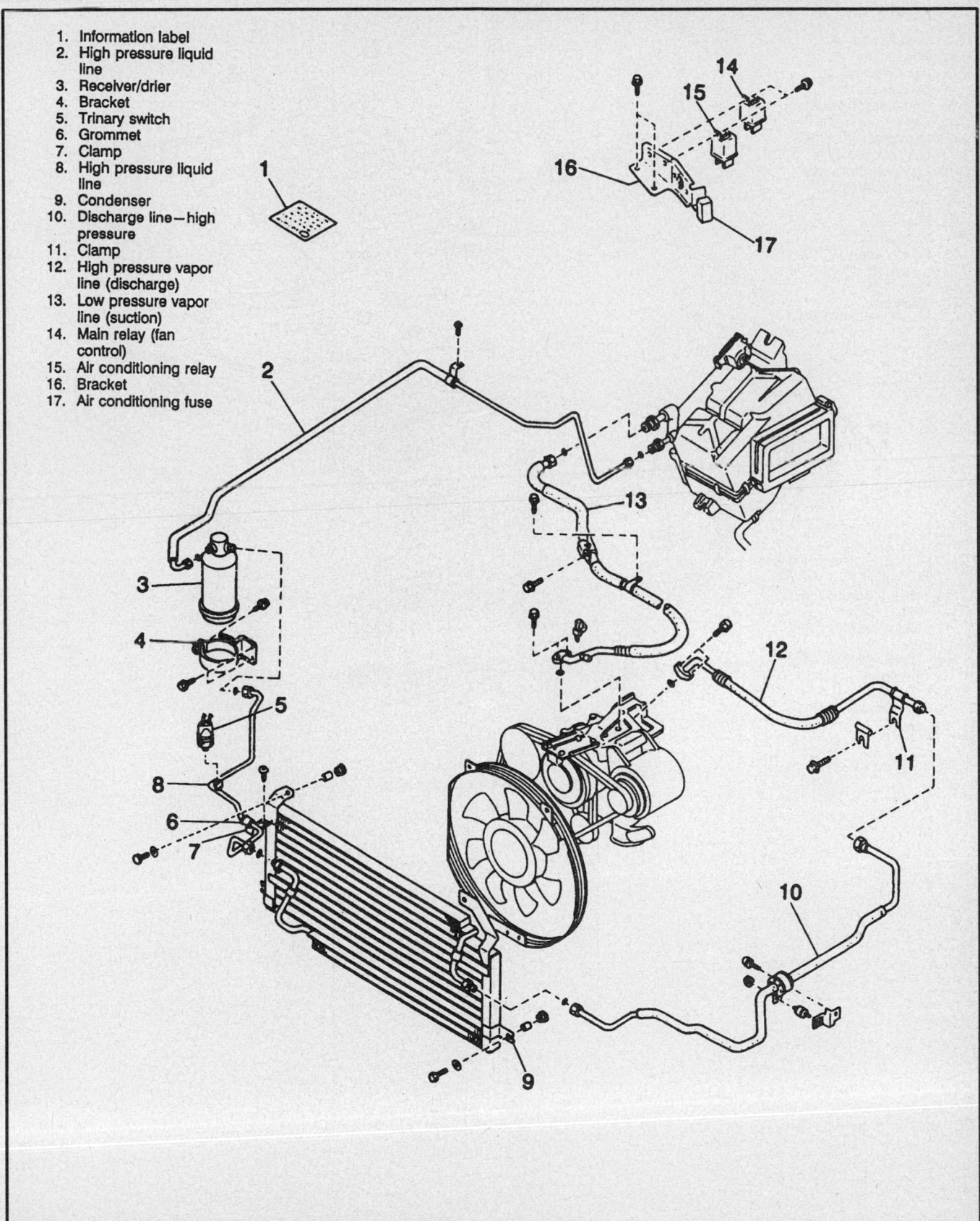

1. Information label
2. High pressure liquid line
3. Receiver/drier
4. Bracket
5. Trinary switch
6. Grommet
7. Clamp
8. High pressure liquid line
9. Condenser
10. Discharge line—high pressure
11. Clamp
12. High pressure vapor line (discharge)
13. Low pressure vapor line (suction)
14. Main relay (fan control)
15. Air conditioning relay
16. Bracket
17. Air conditioning fuse

Exploded view of the air conditioning system — Hitachi (Typical)

1. Compressor
2. Condenser
3. Receiver/drier
4. Condenser fan
5. Compressor bracket
6. Belt
7. High pressure vapor line (discharge)
8. Low pressure vapor line (suction)
9. Relay
10. Idler pulley
11. Evaporator
12. Drain hose
13. Grommet
14. Grommet
15. Grommet

16. High pressure liquid line
17. High pressure liquid line
18. Discharge line—high pressure
19. Shroud
20. Thermostat control
21. Band

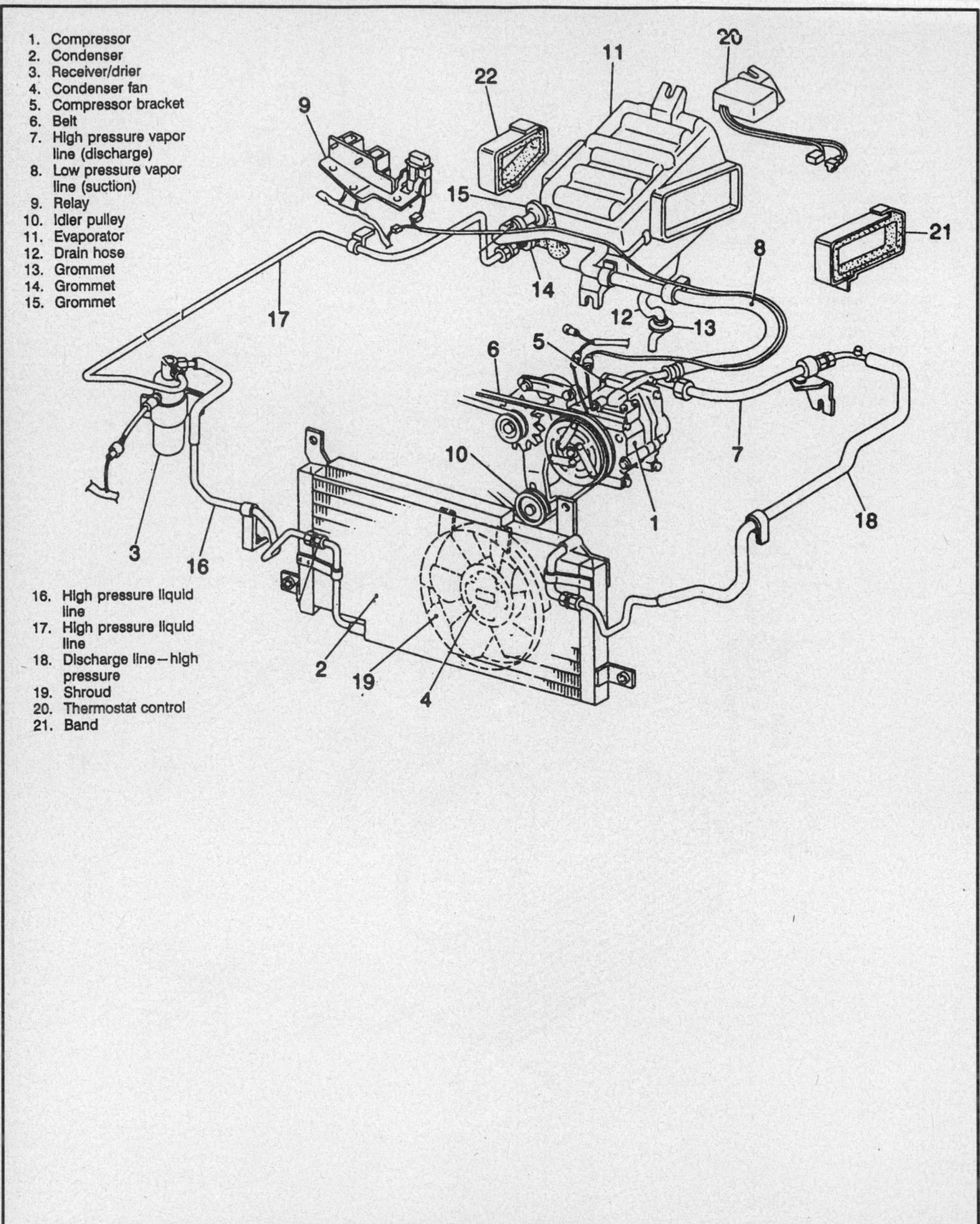

Exploded view of the air conditioning system – Panasonic (Typical)

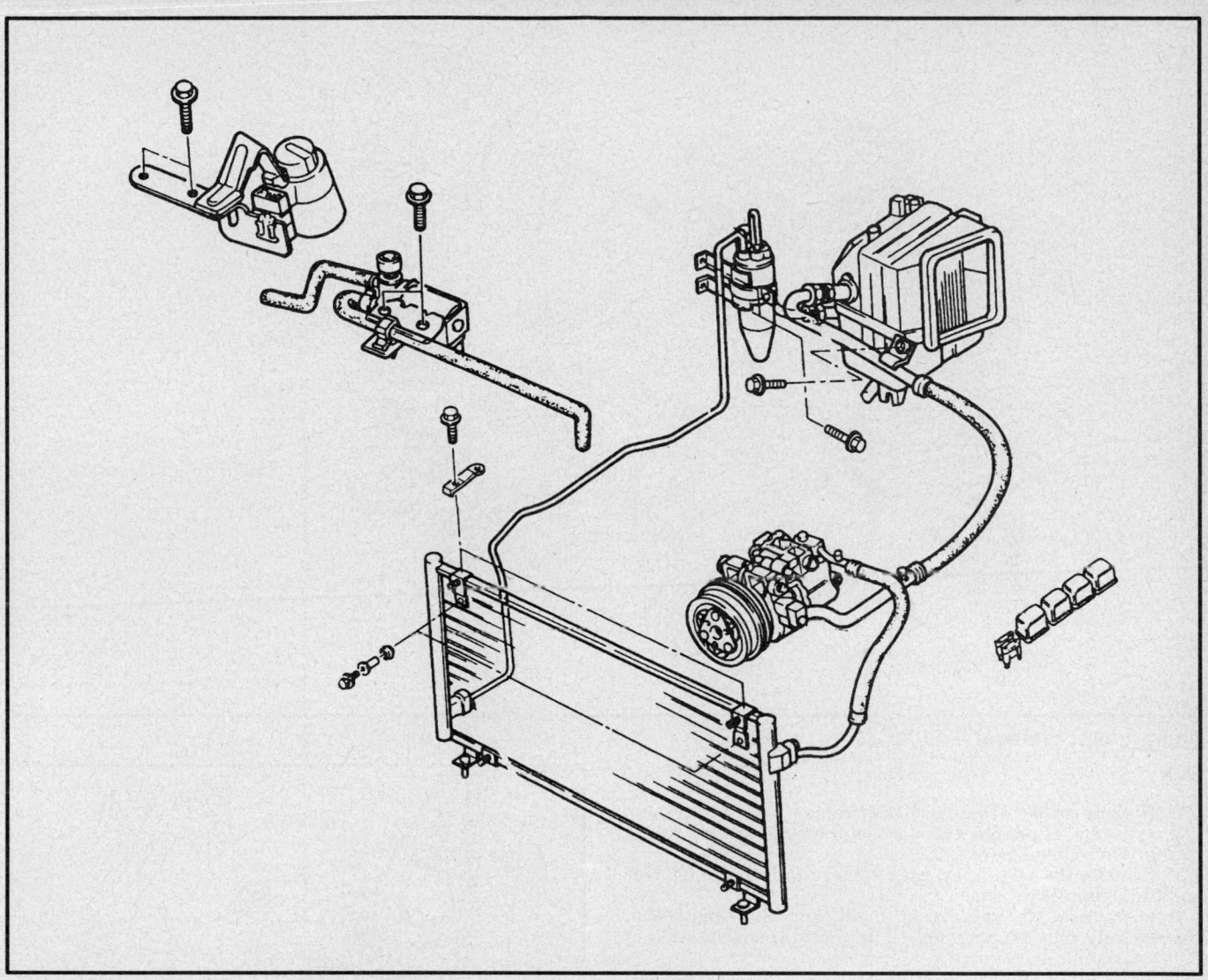

Exploded view of the air conditioning system – Zexel Rotary Vane

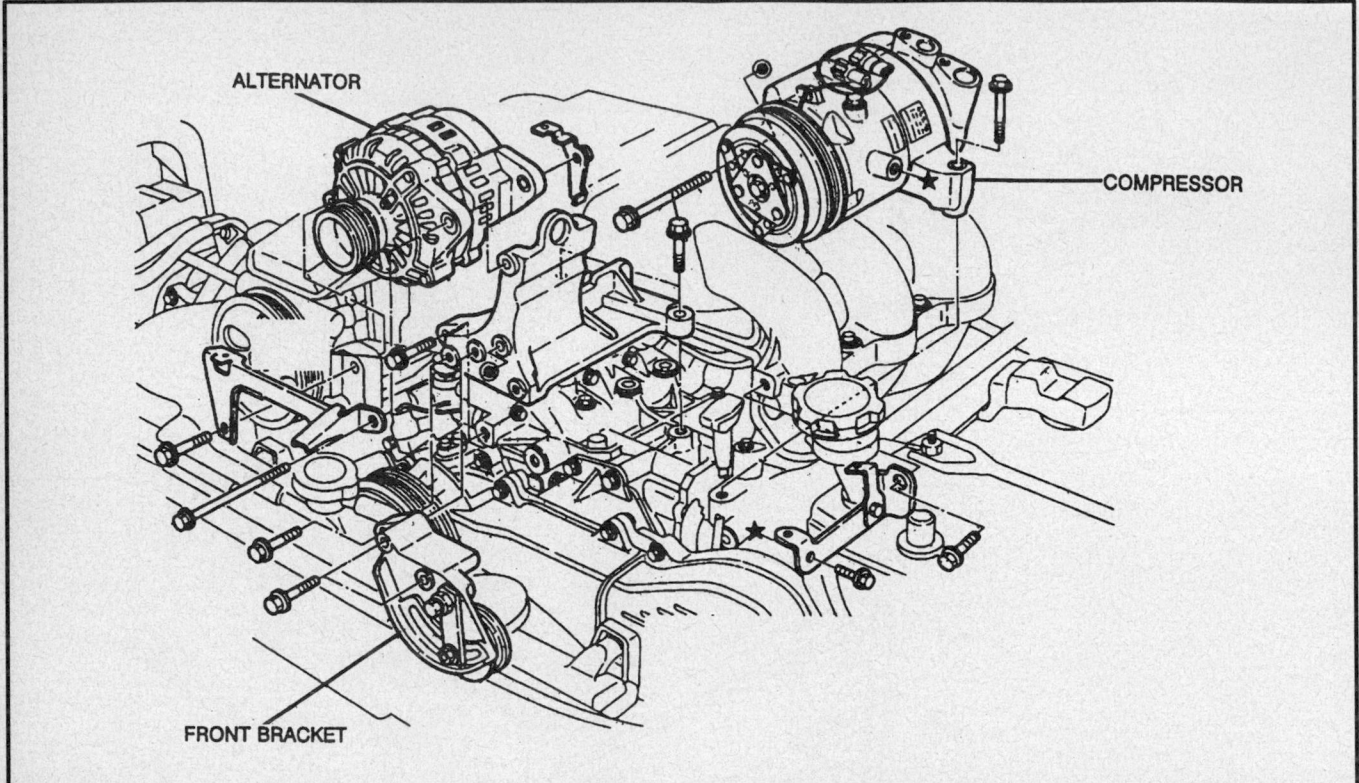

ALTERNATOR

COMPRESSOR

FRONT BRACKET

Compressor removal – SVX

SVX

1. Disconnect the negative battery cable.
2. Properly discharge the air conditioning system using recovery/recycling equipment.
3. Remove the belt cover, then remove the alternator belt and the compressor belt.
4. Disconnect the refrigerant lines from the compressor. Immediately plug all openings to minimize contamination of the system and components.
5. Detach the alternator harness, then remove the belt cover bracket and the alternator.
6. Detach the compressor harness connector.
7. Remove the idler pulley, then remove the compressor sub–bracket, the upper bracket and then the compressor.
8. Installation is the reverse of the removal procedure. Be sure to adjust the compressor oil as described in this article. The alternator and compressor mounting bolts are tightened to 23-29 ft. lbs. (31-39 Nm).

Receiver/Drier

REMOVAL AND INSTALLATION

1. Disconnect the negative battery cable.
2. Discharge the air conditioning system using recovery/recycling equipment.
3. Remove the evaporator canister and place it aside.
4. Disconnect the harness connector from the pressure switch.
5. Disconnect the receiver/drier inlet and outlet pipes. Cap or plug the openings immediately.
6. Plug the openings at the receiver/drier immediately.

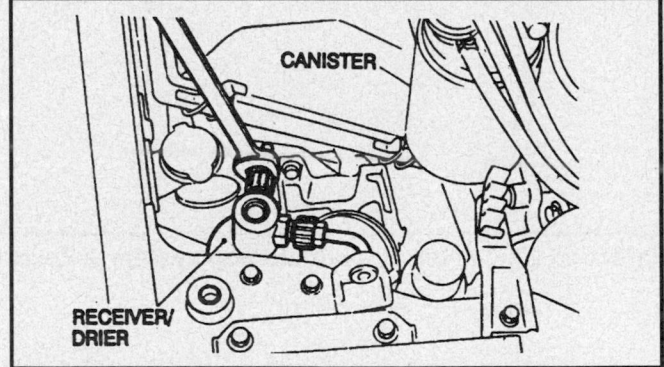

CANISTER

RECEIVER/
DRIER

Removal and installation of the receiver/drier – Loyale

NOTE: Keep in mind, the receiver/drier incorporates a desiccant filter. If the moisture is allowed to inner the drier, it must be replaced. The openings must be plugged immediately.

7. Remove the mounting bolts and remove the receiver/drier.
To install:
8. Position the receiver/drier into mounting bracket and install the retaining bolts. Torque the bolts to 4-7 ft. lbs. (5-4 Nm).
9. Remove the caps from the receiver hoses and from the receiver openings. Connect the inlet and outlet pipes immediately. Torque the receiver/drier hose connections to the following:

- Hitachi and Panasonic systems: 7–14 ft. lbs. (10–20 Nm).
- Diesel Kiki and Calsonic: 4-7 ft. lbs. (5-9 Nm).
10. Evacuate, leak test and charge the system.

Expansion Valve

—CAUTION—

If vehicle is equipped with an airbag system, after disconnecting the negative battery cable, wait at least 10 minutes before proceeding with further work to allow time for the airbag system to fully de–energize and prevent accidental deployment of the airbag.

REMOVAL AND INSTALLATION

NOTE: In order to remove the expansion valve, the evaporator must be removed and disassembled.

1. Disconnect the negative battery cable.
2. Discharge the refrigerant system.
3. Remove the evaporator assembly from the vehicle.
4. Remove the evaporator upper and lower case half retaining clamps. Separate the upper and lower case halves from the evaporator.

NOTE: The thermostat capillary is inserted into evaporator fin, at a specified position. Take note to this location prior to removing it.

5. Remove the thermostat retaining screws. While holding the thermostat, carefully remove the capillary from the evaporator fins and remove the thermostat.
6. Remove the insulation from the evaporator discharge pipe wrapping the expansion valve capillary tube.
7. Remove the clamp securing the capillary tube on the side of the discharge pipe.
8. Disconnect the inlet pipe from the expansion valve.
9. Disconnect the expansion valve from the evaporator fitting and remove the expansion valve.
To install:

NOTE: During the installation of the expansion valve, use all new O-rings at the pipe joints. Coat the O-rings with clean refrigerant oil.

10. Install the expansion valve to the evaporator fitting; do not tighten the fitting at this time.
11. Install the expansion valve so the capillary tubing is routed in its original position.
12. Install the expansion valve capillary tube, on the discharge pipe and secure it in place with the retaining clamp.
13. Wrap the capillary tube and discharge pipe with new insulator tape.
14. Connect the inlet pipe to the expansion valve. Torque the following:
    Inlet fitting–to–expansion valve: 7–14 ft.lbs. (10–22 Nm).
    Evaporator–to–expansion valve: 7–14 ft. lbs.(10–20 Nm).
    Expansion valve sensing tube–to–discharge pipe: 5–9 ft.lbs. (7–13 Nm).
15. Place the evaporator into the lower case half.
16. Install the thermostat to the upper case and insert the capillary into the evaporator fins.

NOTE: When installing the thermostat, insert the capillary tube end into the 4th core fin and to a depth of 1.2 in., on the left side of the evaporator.

17. Install the upper case half and secure with the retaining clips.

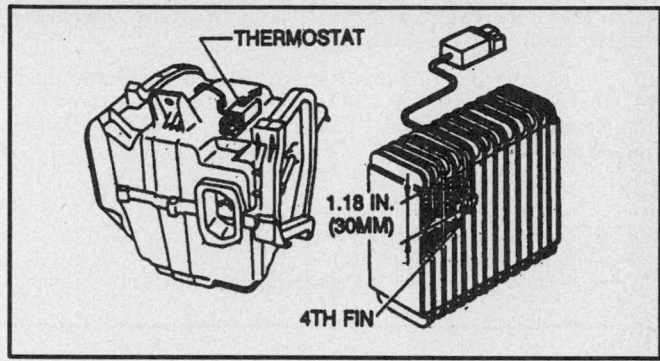

Insallation position of the thermostat capillary

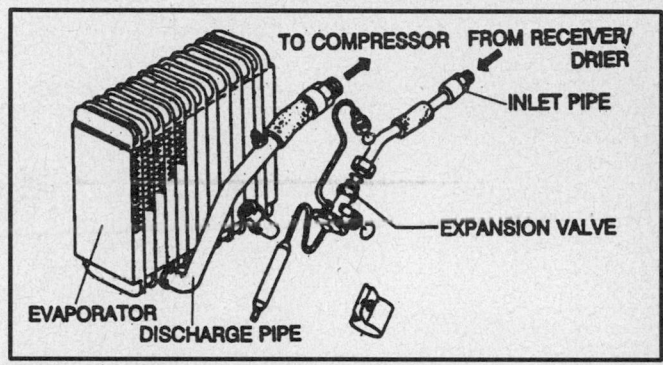

Removal and installation of the expansion valve

18. Install the evaporator assembly into the vehicle.
19. Connect the negative battery cable.
20. Evacuate, charge and test the system.

Blower Motor

REMOVAL AND INSTALLATION

Except SVX

1. Disconnect the negative battery cable.
2. Remove the lower right trim panel retaining screws and remove the trim panel (Loyale).
3. On all except Justy, remove the glove box or glove pocket and frame.
4. Vehicles without air conditioning, remove the heater duct.
5. If equipped with air conditioning, separate the blower assembly from the evaporator unit.
6. Disconnect the blower vacuum hose from the instrument panel vacuum hose.
7. Disconnect the motor harness and resistor harness.
8. Remove the blower motor mounting bolts and nuts.
9. Remove the ventilation duct bracket and remove the blower motor from the vehicle.
To install:
10. Install the blower motor assembly and ventilation duct bracket under the dash. Install the retaining nuts and bolts. Torque the bolts and nuts to 4-7 ft. lbs. (5-9 Nm).
11. Connect the blower motor harness and resistor harness.
12. Connect the vacuum hose to instrument panel vacuum hose.

NOTE: The vacuum hose fitting must be a greater length than, 0.31 in. (8 mm).

13. Vehicles without air conditioning, install the heater duct.
14. Install the glove box, trim panel and retaining screws.
15. Connect the negative battery cable. Test the blower motor operation.

SVX

1. Disconnect the negative battery cable.
2. Remove the glove box unit.
3. Remove 3 bolts from the steering suport beam.
4. Loosen the nut securing the passenger side airbag module, if equipped.
5. Remove the nut and the passenger side airbag module bracket.
6. Disconnect the passenger airbag module connector at the harness.
7. Remove the 4 screws securing the passenger side airbag module.
8. Disconnect the blower motor harness connector.
9. Remove the heating and cooling hoses.
10. Remove the blower motor mounting nuts.
11. Remove the blower motor assembly.
12. Installation is the reverse of the removal procedure.

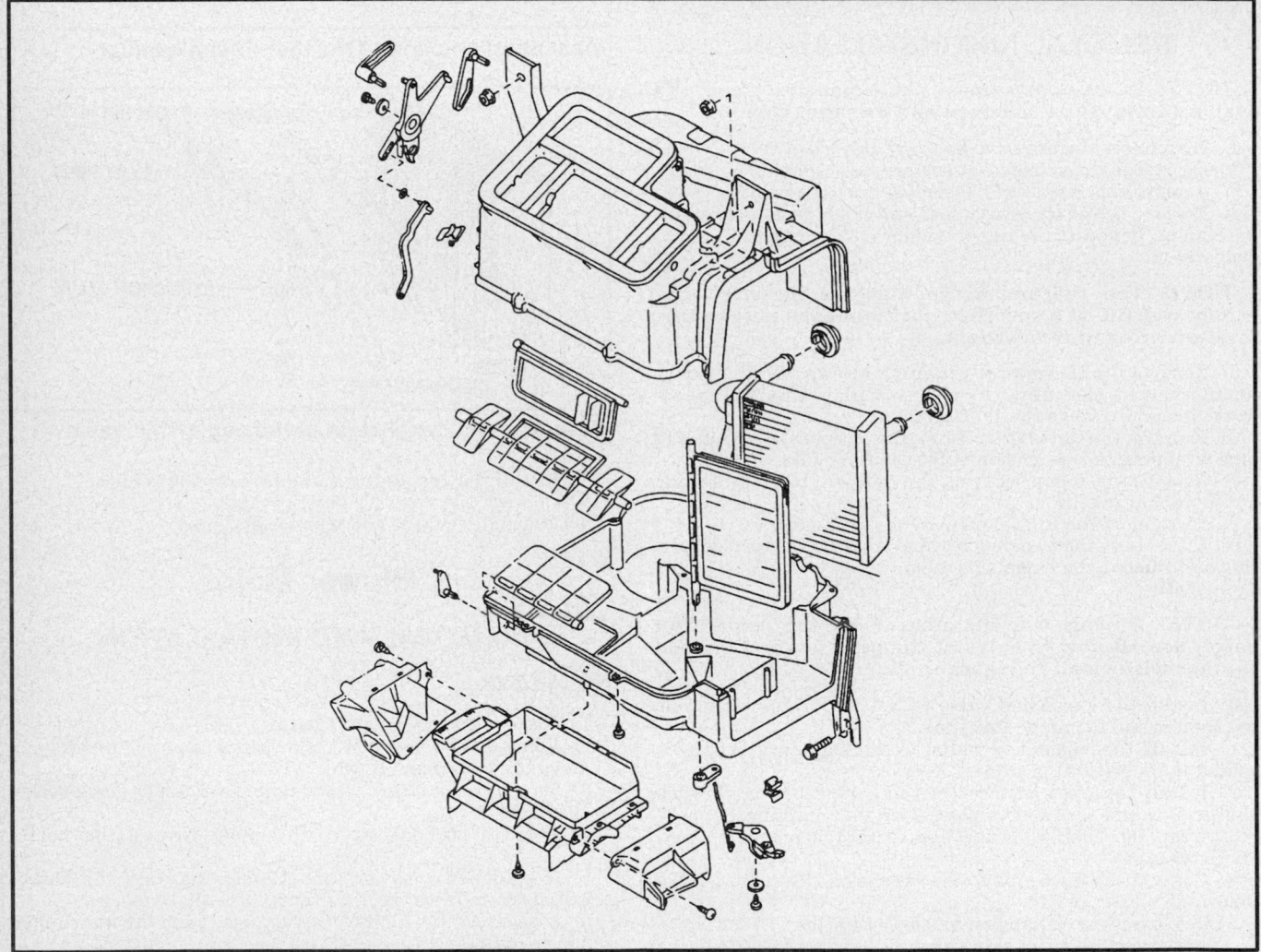

Exploded view of the heater assembly – Impreza

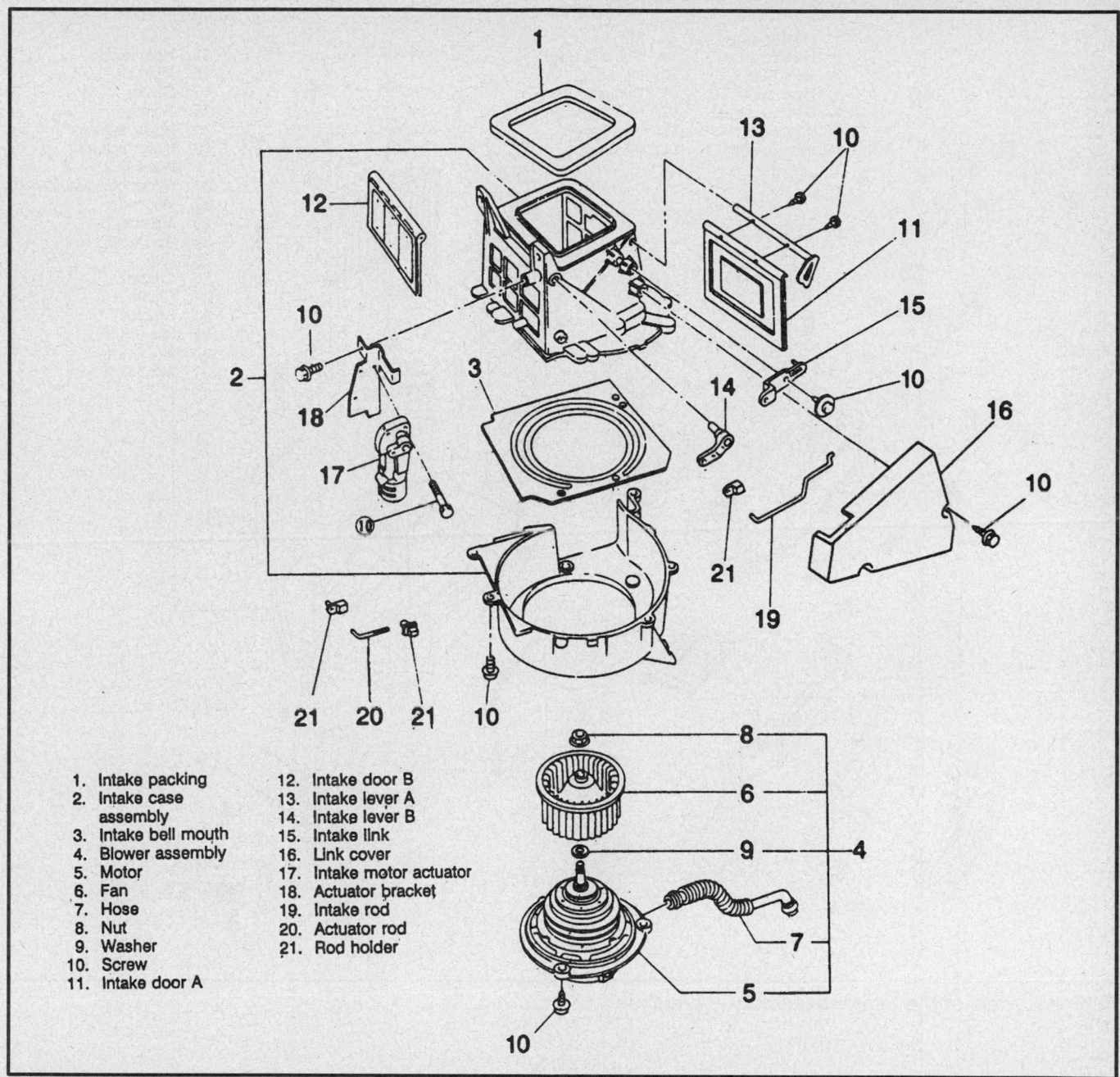

1. Intake packing
2. Intake case assembly
3. Intake bell mouth
4. Blower assembly
5. Motor
6. Fan
7. Hose
8. Nut
9. Washer
10. Screw
11. Intake door A
12. Intake door B
13. Intake lever A
14. Intake lever B
15. Intake link
16. Link cover
17. Intake motor actuator
18. Actuator bracket
19. Intake rod
20. Actuator rod
21. Rod holder

Exploded view of the blower motor and ventilator assembly (Typical)

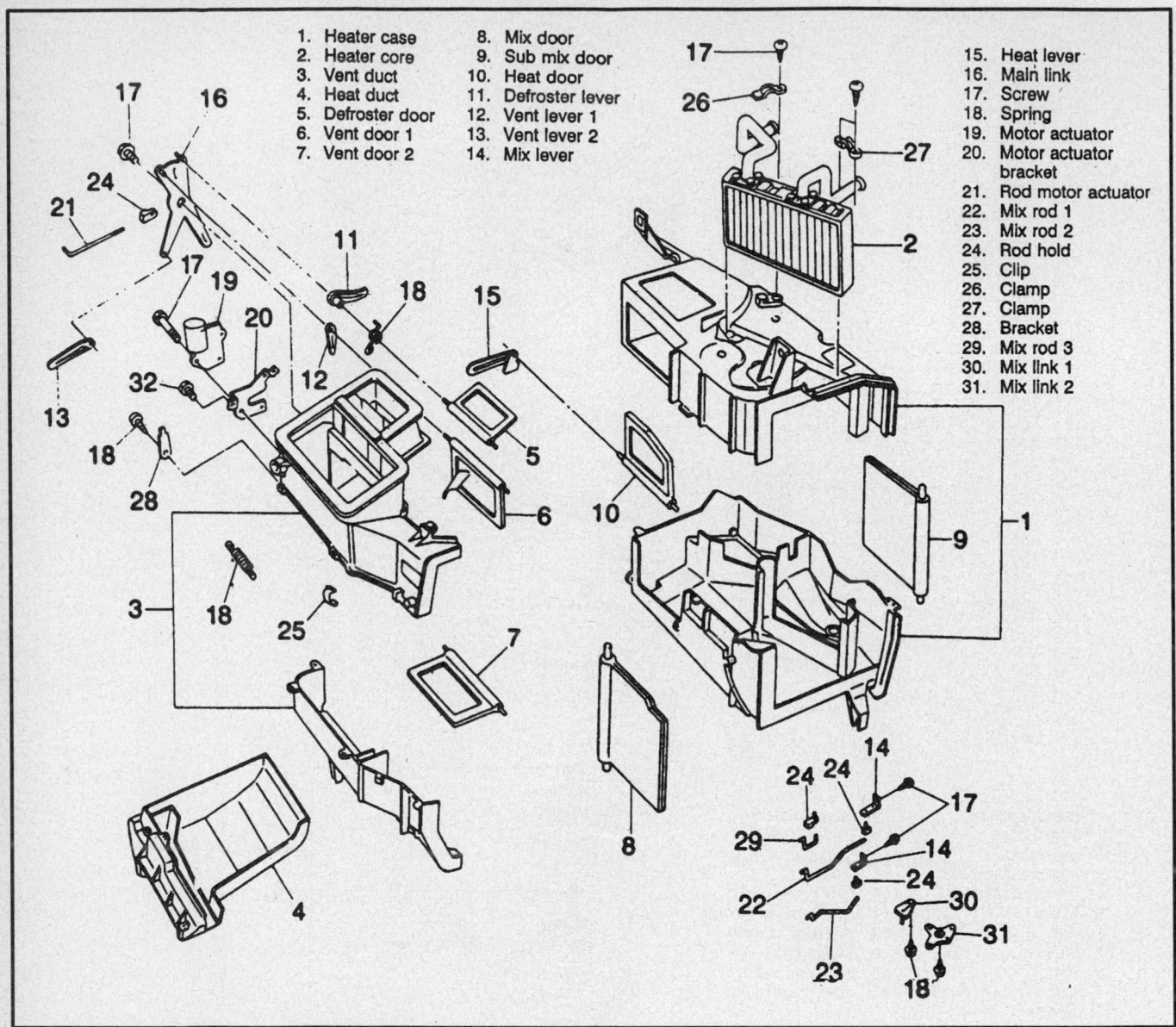

1. Heater case
2. Heater core
3. Vent duct
4. Heat duct
5. Defroster door
6. Vent door 1
7. Vent door 2
8. Mix door
9. Sub mix door
10. Heat door
11. Defroster lever
12. Vent lever 1
13. Vent lever 2
14. Mix lever
15. Heat lever
16. Main link
17. Screw
18. Spring
19. Motor actuator
20. Motor actuator bracket
21. Rod motor actuator
22. Mix rod 1
23. Mix rod 2
24. Rod hold
25. Clip
26. Clamp
27. Clamp
28. Bracket
29. Mix rod 3
30. Mix link 1
31. Mix link 2

Exploded view of the heater assembly — Legacy

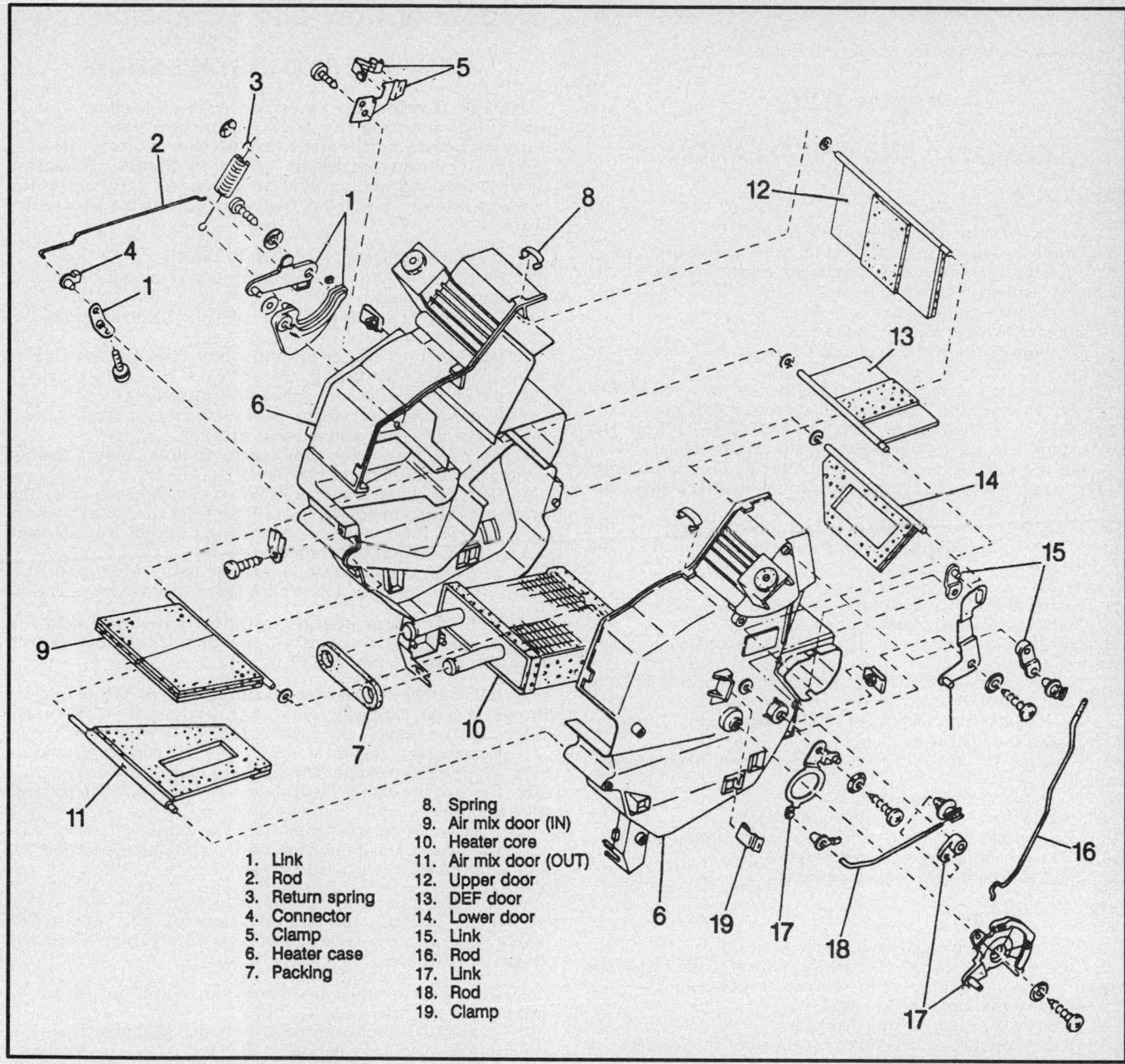

1. Link	8. Spring	
2. Rod	9. Air mix door (IN)	
3. Return spring	10. Heater core	
4. Connector	11. Air mix door (OUT)	
5. Clamp	12. Upper door	
6. Heater case	13. DEF door	
7. Packing	14. Lower door	
	15. Link	
	16. Rod	
	17. Link	
	18. Rod	
	19. Clamp	

Exploded view of the heater assembly – Justy

Blower Motor Resistor

REMOVAL AND INSTALLATION

NOTE: On Justy, the resistor is inside the blower duct, therefore, removal of the blower unit is required. On all other models, proceed as below.

1. Disconnect the negative battery cable.
2. Remove the glove box unit.
3. Disconnect the resistor wire connector from the resistor.

4. Remove the resistor retaining screws and remove the resistor from the heater case.
To install:
5. Position the resistor assembly in the heater case opening and install the retaining screws.

NOTE: When installing a replacement resistor, the new resistor must be the equivalent and specified applicable to the blower unit. Do not apply sealer to the resistor board mounting surface.

6. Connect the resistor harness connector to the resistor.

7. Install the glove box unit. Connect the negative battery cable.
8. Check the blower for proper operation.

Heater Core

REMOVAL AND INSTALLATION

Except SVX

1. Disconnect the negative battery cable.
2. Drain the engine coolant through the radiator drain plug.
3. Disconnect the heater hoses in the engine compartment. Drain the coolant from the hoses.
4. Remove the radio box or console.
5. Remove the instrument panel.
6. Disconnect the heater control cables and the fan motor harness.
7. Disconnect the duct between the heater unit and blower assembly. Remove the right and left defroster nozzles.
8. Remove the heater assembly mounting bolts from the heater unit. Lift up and out on the heater unit and remove.
9. On the Legacy and SVX, discharge the air conditioning system and remove the evaporator assembly, then remove the heater assembly.
10. With the heater assembly out the vehicle, remove the heater core tube retaining clamps and lift the core from the heater case.
To install:
11. Install the heater core into the heater case. Secure it in place with the retaining clamps and screws.
12. Install the heater assembly to its mounting position under the dash.
13. Install the mounting bolts. Torque the mounting bolts to 4-7 ft. lbs. (5-9 Nm).
14. On Legacy and SVX, install the evaporator assembly, then install the heater assembly.
15. Connect the heater control cables and fan motor harness connectors.
16. Install the instrument panel.
17. Install the radio and console assemblies.
18. Connect the heater hoses in the engine compartment.
19. Fill the cooling system with coolant.
20. Connect the negative battery cable.

SVX

1. Disconnect the negative battery terminal.
2. Drain the engine coolant. Drain as much coolant from the heater as possible, and plug the disconnected hose.
3. Remove the instrument panel.
4. Remove the steering support beam.
5. Disconnect the door actuator connectors from the heater unit.
6. Remove the aspirator hose.
7. Remove the evaporator.
8. Remove the heater core.
9. Installation is the reverse of the removal procedure.

Evaporator Core and Expansion Valve

REMOVAL AND INSTALLATION

NOTE: If vehicle is equipped with an airbag system, after disconnecting the negative battery cable, wait 10 minutes before performing any further work while system fully de-energizes in order to avoid accidental deployment. All airbag system wiring is yellow. Do not use electrically powered test equipment on these circuits.

1. Disconnect the negative battery cable.
2. Properly discharge the refrigerant system using recovery/recycling equipment.
3. Disconnect the low pressure line from the evaporator outlet fitting. Cap the fitting.
4. Disconnect the high pressure line from the evaporator inlet fitting. Cap the fitting.
5. Remove the inlet and outlet pipe grommets.
6. Remove the instrument panel lower cover (Loyale) and remove the glove box and support bracket.
7. On SVX, remove the time control unit and detach the fan control amplifier harness connector.
8. Disconnect the air conditioning wire harness from the evaporator. Disconnect the drain hose from the evaporator.
9. Remove the evaporator mounting nut and bolt. Remove the evaporator from the vehicle.
10. Remove the upper and lower case half retaining clamps. Separate the upper and lower case halves from the evaporator.

NOTE: The thermostat capillary is inserted into the evaporator fin at a specified position. Take note to this location prior to removing it.

11. Remove the thermostat retaining screws. While holding the thermostat, carefully remove the capillary from the evaporator fins and remove the thermostat.
12. Remove the insulation from the evaporator discharge pipe wrapping the expansion valve capillary tube.
13. Remove the clamp securing the capillary tube on the side of the discharge pipe.
14. Disconnect the inlet pipe from the expansion valve.
15. Disconnect the expansion valve from the evaporator fitting and remove the expansion valve.
To install:

NOTE: During the installation of the expansion valve, use all new O-rings at the pipe joints. Coat the O-rings with clean refrigerant oil.

16. Install the expansion valve to the evaporator fitting; do not tighten the fitting at this time.
17. Install the expansion valve so the capillary tubing is routed in its original position.
18. Install the expansion valve capillary tube, on the discharge pipe and secure it in place with the retaining clamp.
19. Wrap the capillary tube and discharge pipe with new insulator tape.

20. Connect the inlet pipe to the expansion valve. Torque the following:
Inlet fitting–to–expansion valve: 7–14 ft. lbs. (10–20 Nm).
Evaporator–to–expansion valve: 7–14 ft. lbs. (10–20 Nm).
Expansion valve sensing tube–to–discharge pipe: 5–9 ft. lbs. (7–13 Nm).
21. Place the evaporator into the lower case half.
22. Install the thermostat to the upper case and insert the thermistor into the evaporator fins.

NOTE: When installing the thermostat, insert the capillary tube end into the 4th core fin and to a depth of 1.2 in., on the left side of the evaporator.

23. Install the upper case half and secure with the retaining clips.
24. Install the evaporator assembly under the dash and into the mounting position. Install the retaining nut and bolt.
25. Adjust the position of the evaporator assembly so the inlet and outlet connections are aligned with the heater and blower unit connections.
26. On SVX, connect the fan control amplifier harness and install the time control unit.
27. Install the drain hose. Connect the air conditioning wire harness.
28. Install the inlet and outlet pipe grommets.

29. Install the glove box and the lower support bracket.
30. Connect the suction hose to the evaporator inlet fitting.
31. Connect the discharge hose to the evaporator outlet fitting.
32. Connect the negative battery cable.
33. Evacuate, charge and test the system.

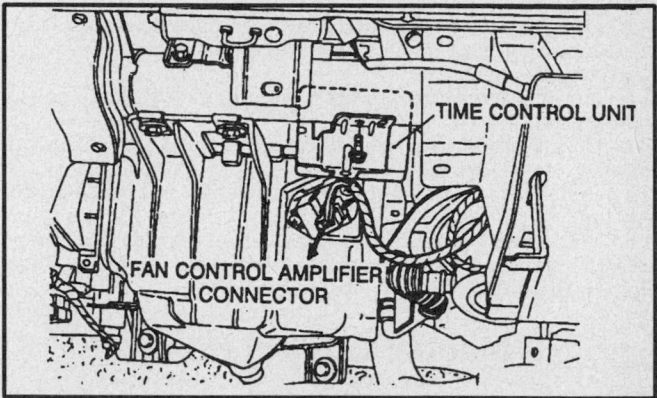

Component removal for evaporator removal – SVX

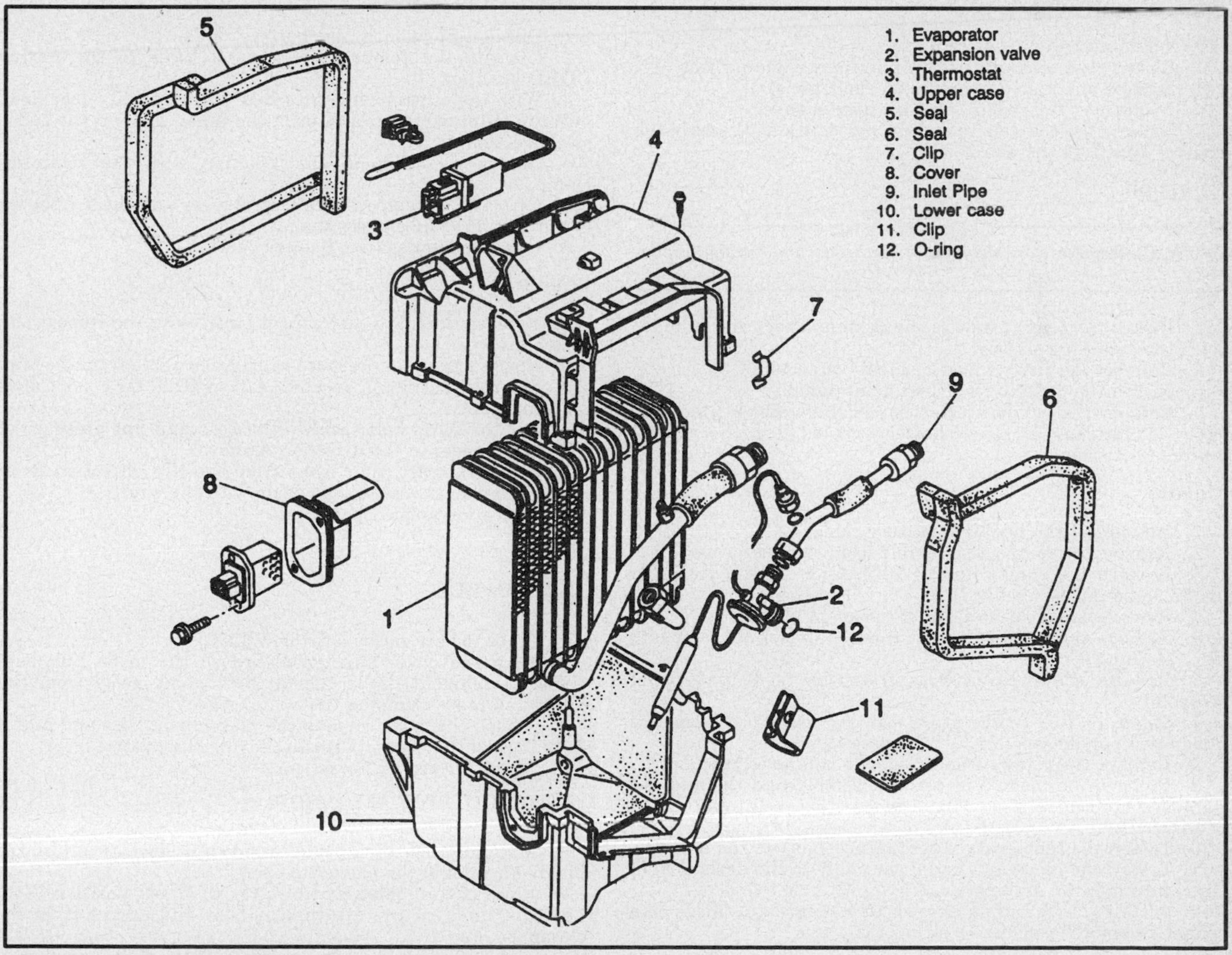

1. Evaporator
2. Expansion valve
3. Thermostat
4. Upper case
5. Seal
6. Seal
7. Clip
8. Cover
9. Inlet Pipe
10. Lower case
11. Clip
12. O-ring

Exploded view of the evaporator and related components

Refrigerant Lines

REMOVAL AND INSTALLATION

1. When disconnecting or connecting refrigerant lines, always use 2 wrenches.
2. Use protective plugs and plug each open line, to prevent contamination and moisture from entering the lines and related components.
3. Never use compressed air. Use only new O–rings during installation.
4. Coat the new O–ring with compressor oil prior to installation.
5. Install the O–ring against the shoulder to ensure proper seating.
6. When connecting 2 lines together, insert the tube section into the union and tighten the retaining nut by hand. Then, tighten the nut to 21–33 ft. lbs. (31–44 Nm).

Manual Control Head

REMOVAL AND INSTALLATION

Impreza and Legacy

1. Disconnect the negative battery cable.
2. Remove the temperature cable from the heater unit.
3. Remove the instrument cluster facia panel.
4. Disconnect the control unit harness connectors.
5. Remove the control unit retaining screws and remove the control unit from the dash.

To install:

──────────────── CAUTION ────────────────
DO NOT attempt to move the link off the heater unit during installation.
──

6. Install the control unit to the dash and secure it in place with the retaining screws.
7. Connect the control unit harness connectors.
8. Install the facia to the instrument panel.
9. Connect the temperature control cable to the heater unit.
10. Connect the negative battery cable. Test the control switch operation.

Loyale

1. Disconnect the negative battery cable.
2. Remove the temperature cable from the heater unit.
3. Remove the control knobs DEF, OFF, TEMP, from the mode and panel assembly.
4. Remove the facia from the instrument cluster.
5. Remove the heater control from the visor by removing the retaining screws.
6. Remove the vacuum hose from the mode pad panel assembly.
7. Separate the temperature control assembly from the mode and panel assembly by loosening the screws.
8. Remove the screws from the mode and panel assembly.
9. Remove the mode and panel assembly and the and the temperature control assembly.

To install:

10. Install the temperature control assembly to the dash.
11. Install the mode and panel assembly to the dash. Install the bulbs into the assembly.
12. Install the retaining screws and secure the mode and panel assembly in place.

13. Install the vacuum hose to the mode pad panel assembly.
14. Install the heater control to the visor and secure it in place with the retaining screws.
15. Install the instrument cluster facia panel.
16. Install controls knobs to the panel assembly.
17. Connect the temperature cable to the heater unit.
18. Connect the negative battery cable. Test the control switch operation.

Justy

1. Pull the knobs from the control levers.
2. Remove the center pocket and reach through this opening and push the heater control panel from its backing.
3. Remove radio knobs and remove the facia plate.
4. Remove the center panel around the control panel.
5. Remove the control unit screws and pull the unit out to detach the control cables and fan switch connector.
6. Installation is the reverse of the removal procedure.

Manual Control Cables

ADJUSTMENT

Impreza and Legacy

1. Disconnect the negative battery cable.
2. Operate the temperature control lever to the **FULL COLD** position.
3. With the control cable attached to the air mix door link, pull the outer cable out and push the inner cable in the opposite direction.
4. Secure the cable in this position with the retaining clamp.
5. Operate the temperature control lever and check freedom of movement at full stroke range.
6. Connect the negative battery cable.

Loyale

1. Remove the lower instrument panel trim and remove the fuse box.
2. Remove the ram pressure ventilation cable from the clip.
3. Set the ventilation lever to **A/C** (**VENT OFF** for Canadian models).
4. Set the inner cable end to the boss and put pressure of the control lever in the direction **A** shown.
5. Pull the outlet cable away from the clip (direction **B**) to remove any slack. Attach the cable with the clip.
6. Check for proper operation.

Justy

MODE CABLE

1. Place the air outlet lever in **VENT**.
2. Turn the mode link downward so the mode link boss (cable attachment) is at the farthest point away from the flush–mounted clamp on the heater case.
3. Attach the mode cable to the attachment boss and pull it fully toward the clamp (without moving the control lever).
4. Check for proper operation.

INSIDE/OUTSIDE AIR CABLE

1. Manually set the inside/outside air door to allow the inside air inlet of the blower to open.
2. Place the air inlet control lever to **CIRC** position. Connect the cable on the attachment boss and secure it in the clamp.

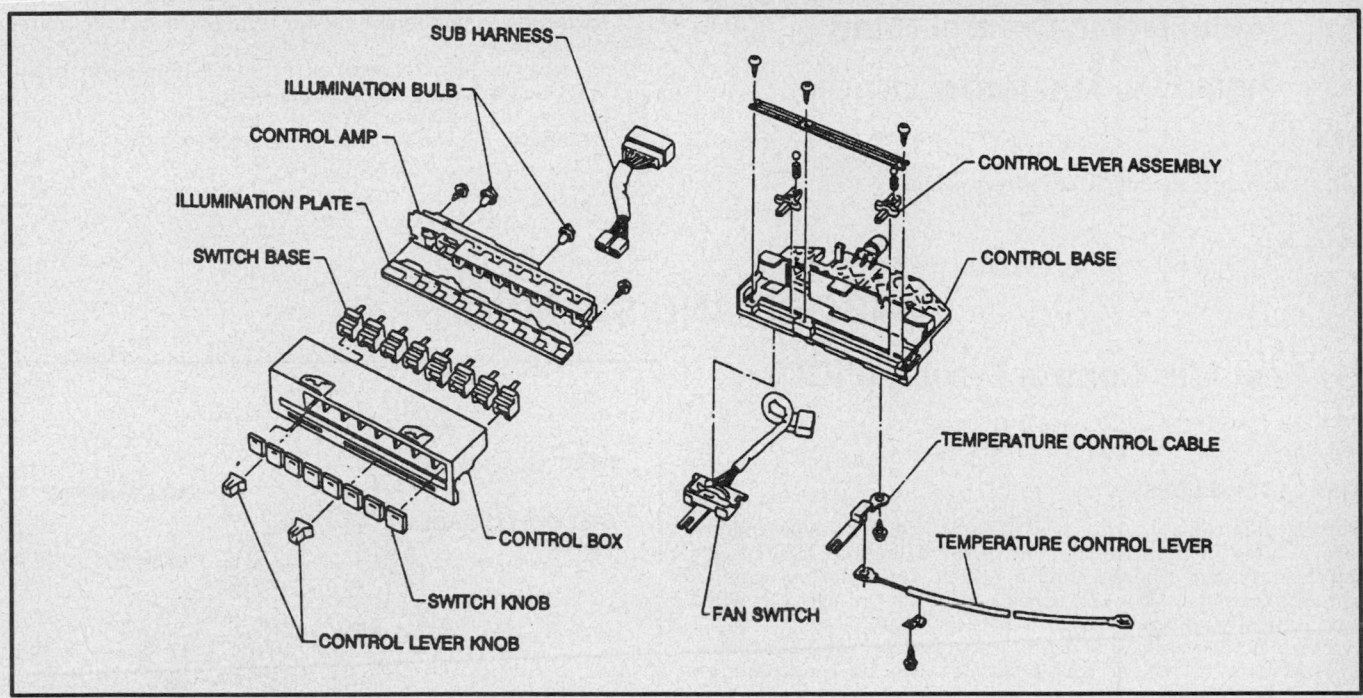

Exploded view of the temperature control unit – Legacy

3. Pull firmly on the cable toward the heater case to remove any slack (without moving the blower link). Check the cable attachment.

AIR MIX CABLE

1. Place the temperature control lever in **HOT**.
2. Turn the air mix link downward so the cable attaching boss in farthest from the cable clamp on the heater case.
3. Attach the cable on the attachment boss, put it in the clamp and pull the cable toward the clamp (without moving the control link).
4. Recheck that the cable is fully on the boss.

REMOVAL AND INSTALLATION

Impreza and Legacy

1. Disconnect the negative battery cable.
2. Remove the instrument cluster facia retaining screws and remove the facia from the dash.
3. Disconnect the clip securing the control cable to the control lever and lift the cable from the lever.
4. From the heater unit, remove the temperature cable retaining clamp and disconnect the cable from the mix door link.
5. Remove the cable from under the dash.
To install:
6. Install the new cable under the dash and route it up to the temperature control unit.
7. Connect the cable to the control lever. Adjust as required and install the retaining clip.
8. Install the instrument visor and the retaining screws.
9. Connect the opposite end of the control cable to the mix door link at the heater unit. Adjust, as required.
10. Connect the negative battery cable.

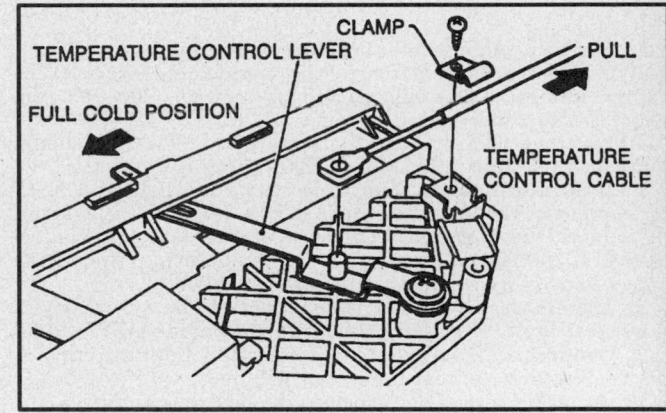

Temperature control cable connection and adjustment – Legacy

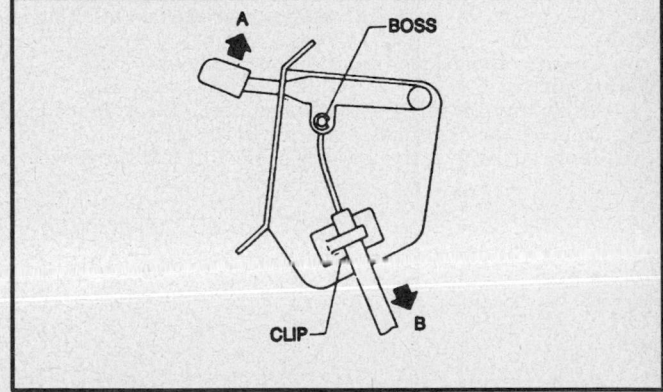

Adjusting the ram pressure ventilation cable - Loyale

Electronic Control Head

REMOVAL AND INSTALLATION

SVX

1. Disconnect the negative battery cable.

2. Remove the instrument cluster facia panel and the center air outlet grille.
3. Remove the control unit attaching screws, detach the aspirator duct and the control panel wiring.
4. Remove the control unit.
5. Installation is the reverse of the removal procedure.

SENSORS AND SWITCHES

Fast Idle Control Device (FICD)

OPERATION

Impreza and Loyale

The fast idle control device is of the solenoid valve type and is incorporated in the throttle body of the SPFI and MPFI fuel injection system. This system operates when the air conditioner is turned on. The idle speed need not be adjusted. It will automatically adjust its self to a 800–900 rpm.

The fast idle control device is controlled by the Electronic Control Unit (ECU), activated through the air conditioning compressor circuit.

TESTING

1. Start the engine and allow it to warm up.
2. Connect a tachometer to the engine and observe the engine idle rpm. The idle should be between 700–800 rpm when the air conditioning system is off.
3. Energize the air conditioning system. The idle should automatically adjust its self to a 800–900 rpm.
4. If the idle does not change, connect a test light and check for current at the fast idle control device. If current is evident, disconnect the electrical connector at the fast idle control device. If the fast idle control device is operating, the engine rpm will drop when the compressor is engaged.
5. If there was no change in rpm, the fast idle control device may be at fault. To confirm this, turn the engine **OFF**.
6. Connect a 12 volt source directly to it intermittently. A noticeable clicking from the device will be heard if the device is working. If there is no response, the device is defective.

REMOVAL AND INSTALLATION

1. Disconnect the negative battery cable.
2. Disconnect the electrical connector at the fast idle control device.
3. Unscrew the device from the throttle body.
To install:
4. Screw the fast idle control device to the throttle body.
5. Connect the electrical connector to the device.
6. Connect the negative battery cable and test the device.

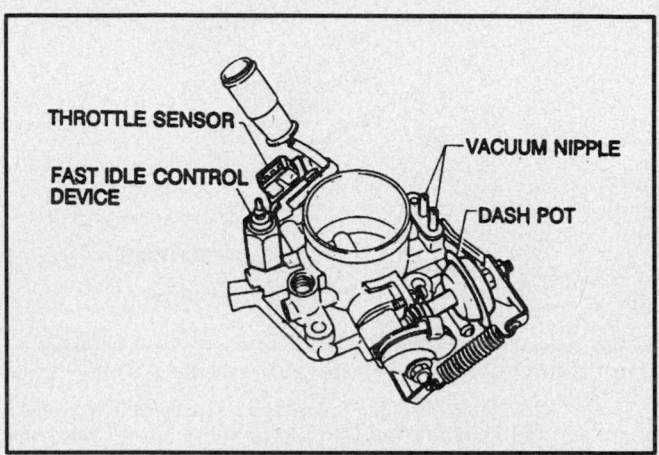

Location of the Fast Idle Control Device (FICD)

Pulser Amplifier

OPERATION

Loyale

Whenever the compressor rpm drops below a specific value, the belt protection system quickly turns off the magnetic clutch of the compressor. This allows the operation to the alternator, water pump and power steering units to operate normally and also prevents breakage or damage to the compressor belt.

To control the belt protection system, the ratio of the compressor rpm to the engine rpm is monitored by a pulse amplifier. When the compressor rpm drops more than 20–25 percent below the normal rpm, the systems determines if the compressor is locked and turns off the magnetic clutch of the compressor.

When the systems detected a locked compressor and turned the air conditioning system off, the magnetic clutch will remain off until the air conditioning switch is turned off and turned on again.

TESTING

1. Start the engine. Turn the air conditioning switch, blower switch and high/low switch, to the **ON** positions.

2. Disconnect the 2 pin pole connector from the pulser amplifier.

3. Observe the compressor magnetic clutch reaction, it should turn off.

4. If not, perform a continuity test of the wiring circuit from the amplifier to the negative side of the ignition coil.

5. If continuity does not exist, the wiring circuit is faulty.

6. If continuity exits, disconnect the wire at the air conditioning relay exciting coil, leading to the amplifier. If the magnetic clutch turns off the amplifier is at fault.

7. If the magnetic clutch remains on, the relay is at fault.

REMOVAL AND INSTALLATION

1. Disconnect the negative battery cable.
2. Remove the glove box and pocket assembly.
3. Remove the front shelf.
4. Disconnect the harness connector at the pulser amplifier.
5. Remove the amplifier–to–evaporator retaining bolt and remove the amplifier.

To install:

6. Install the pulser amplifier to the evaporator and install the retaining bolt.
7. Connect the harness connector to the amplifier.
8. Install the front shelf.
9. Install the glove box and pocket assembly.
10. Connect the negative battery cable.

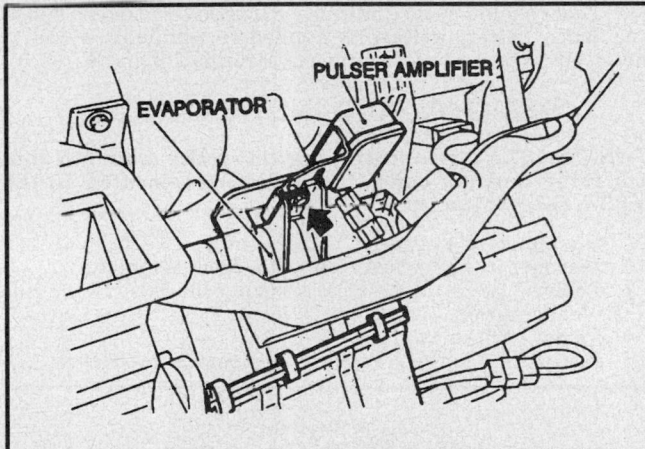

Removal and installation of the pulsar amplifier

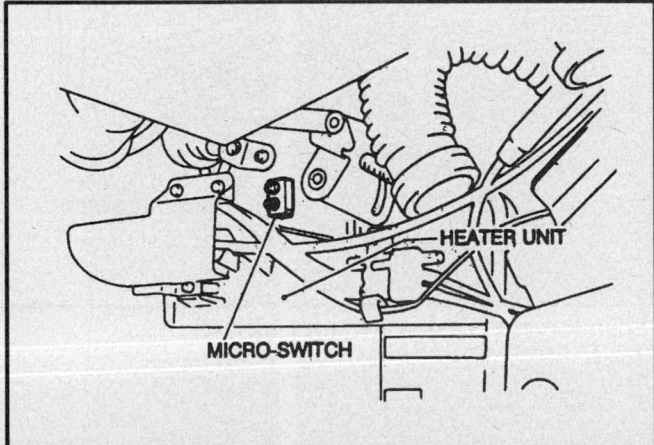

Location of the micro–switch – Loyale

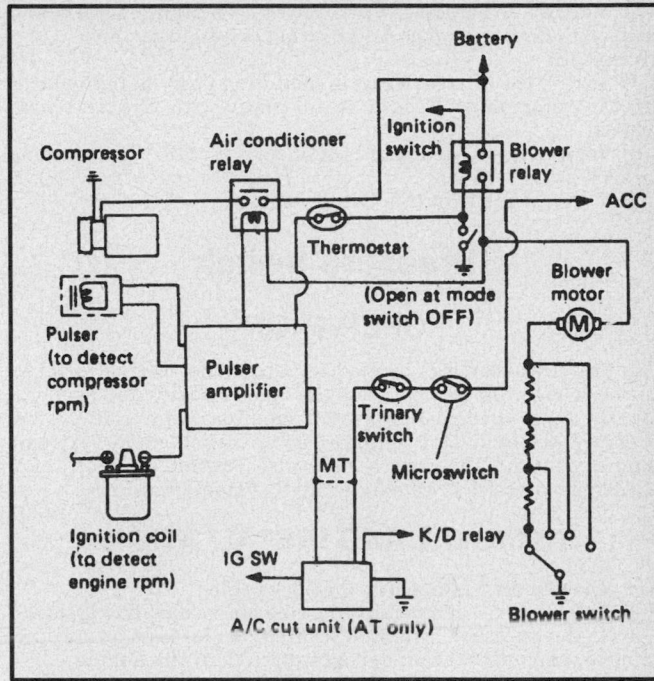

Pulsar amplifier (belt protection system) schematic

Micro–Switch

OPERATION

Loyale

When the mode control lever is set to **A/C MAX**, **A/C** or **DEF** positions, the micro–switch for the air conditioning system, is turned **ON**. When the blower switch is turned on, the blower relay, the air conditioning relay and the sub–fan relay will activate. This in turn causes the blower motor, the Fast Idle Control Device (FICD) and compressor clutch to activate.

Thermo Control Amplifier

OPERATION

Impreza

The thermo control amplifier disconnects the magnet clutch circuit to prevent the evaporator from becoming frosted, when the temperature of the evaporator fin drops close to 36°F (2°C). As the evaporator is cooled, the thermistor (located on the evaporator fin) interrupts the BASE current of the amplifier. This de–energizes the A/C relay coil, which in turn disconnects the magned clutch circuit.

REMOVAL AND INSTALLATION

Loyale

1. Disconnect the negative battery cable.
2. The micro–switch is located on the left side of the heater unit.
3. Remove the lower left instrument trim panel retaining screws. Remove the trim panel.

4. Remove the micro–switch bracket retaining screws and remove the micro–switch and bracket, as an assembly.

To install:

5. Install the micro–switch in mounting position to the heater/evaporator unit. Secure it in place with the retaining screws.

6. Install the lower trim panel and install the retaining screws.

7. Connect the negative battery cable.

Pressure Switch

OPERATION

The pressure switch is located on either the receiver/drier or on the refrigerant line between the receiver/drier and evaporator. On some models, the switch monitors high side system pressure and will stop compressor operation under extreme conditions. And the switch may also control condenser fan operation to assist in cooling at high system pressures.

REMOVAL AND INSTALLATION

1. Disconnect the negative battery cable.
2. Discharge the refrigerant from the air conditioning system.
3. If the pressure switch is located on the refrigerant line, remove the charcoal canister and place it on the engine.
4. Disconnect the pressure switch and harness connections.
5. Unscrew the pressure switch from the refrigerant line and remove.
6. If the pressure switch located on the receiver/drier, disconnect the harness connector and unclip the harness from its mounting point.
7. Unscrew the pressure switch from the receiver/drier and remove.

To install:

8. If the pressure switch located on the receiver/drier; thread the pressure switch into the receiver/drier.
9. Connect the harness connector and secure the harness in place, to the receiver/drier.
10. If the pressure switch located on the refrigerant line; thread the pressure switch into refrigerant line.
11. Connect the harness and pressure switch connections.
12. Place the charcoal canister in the mounting bracket ase-cure it in place.
13. Connect the negative battery cable.
14. Evacuate and recharge the refrigerant in the system.

Relay and Fuses

TESTING

NOTE: The air conditioning, fan control and condenser relays are all checked using an ohm meter. Specified resistance readings will determine the relays condition.

AIR CONDITIONING OR FAN CONTROL RELAY

Hitachi and Panasonic

1. Remove the relay from the vehicle.

2. Measure the resistance between terminals **3** and **4**. In the case of the Hitachi relay, the resistance reading should be approximately 80 ohms and in the case of the Panasonic relay, approximately 90 ohms.

3. There should be no continuity between terminals **1** and **2**.

4. When battery voltage is applied to terminals **3** and **4**, there should be continuity between terminals **1** and **2**.

AIR CONDITIONING MAIN FAN, SUB FAN AND FAN CONTROL RELAYS

Diesel-kiki/Zexel and Calsonic

1. Remove the relay from the vehicle.
2. Measure the resistance between terminals **1** and **2** It should be approximately 100 ohms.
3. There should be no continuity between terminals **3** and **4**.
4. When battery voltage is applied to terminals **1** and **2**, there should be continuity between terminals **3** and **4**.

AIR CONDITIONING CUT RELAY

Diesel Kiki and Calsonic

1. Remove the relay from the vehicle.
2. Measure the resistance between terminals **1** and **2** It should be approximately 100 ohms.
3. There should be no continuity between terminals **3** and **4**.
4. When battery voltage is applied to terminals **1** and **2**, there should be continuity between terminals **3** and **4**.

REMOVAL AND INSTALLATION

NOTE: The air conditioning relay, the main fan control relay and air conditioner fuse are located in the engine compartment.

1. Disconnect the negative battery cable.
2. Disconnect the harness connector from the relay.
3. Remove the retaining bolts securing the relay to the side of the fender apron.
4. Remove the relay.
5. Installation is the reverse of the removal procedure.

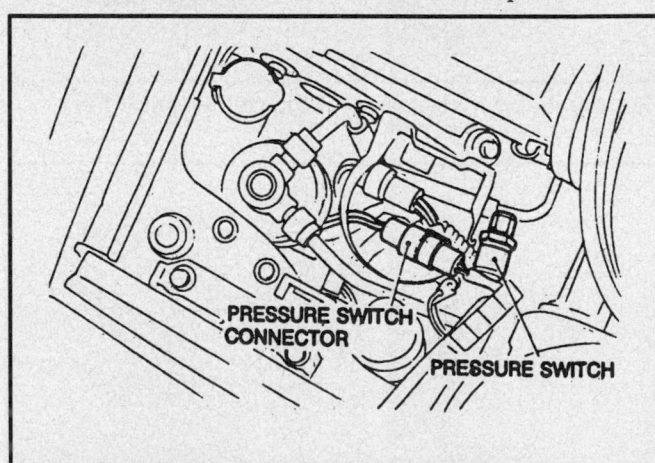

Location of pressure switch (Typical)

Evaporator outlet air temperature °C (°F)	Thermo control amp. operation
2.5 – 3.5 (36.5 – 38.3)	Turns OFF
3.5 – 5.5 (38.3 – 41.9)	Turns ON

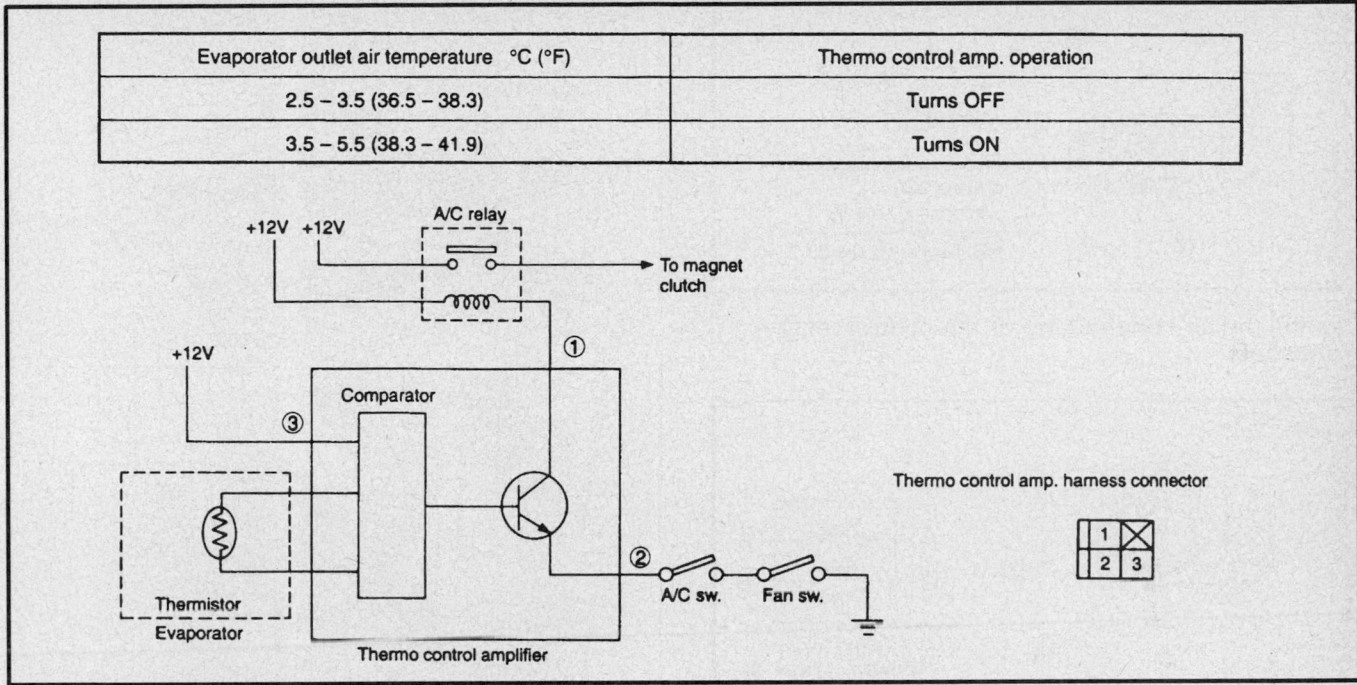

Thermo control amplifier operation – Impreza

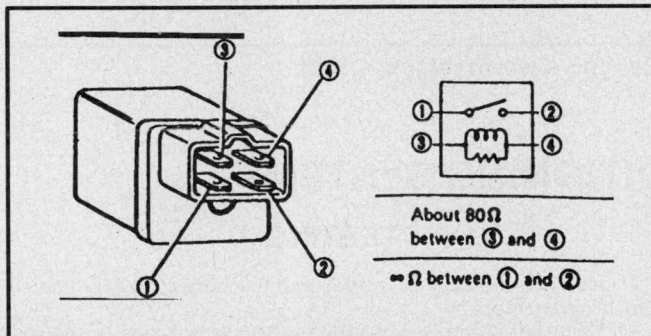

Testing the air conditioning or fan control relay – Hitachi

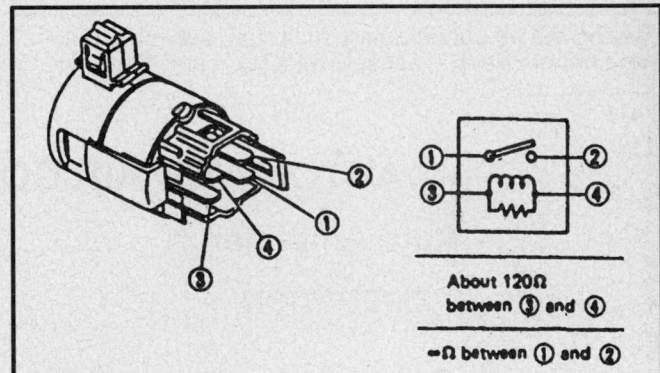

Testing the air conditioning cut out relay – Diesel Kiki and Calsonic

Location of the relays and fuses – Legacy

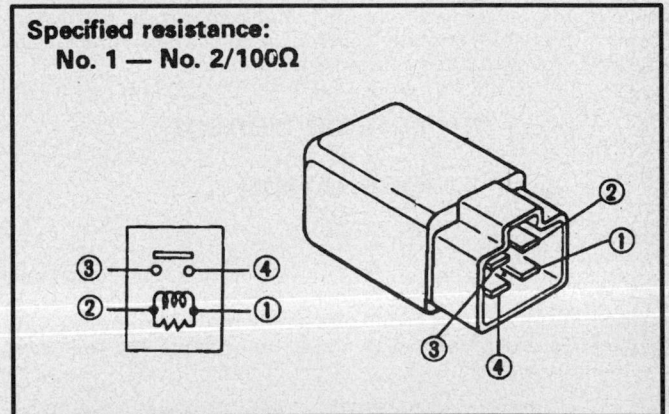

Location of the system fuses and relays – SVX

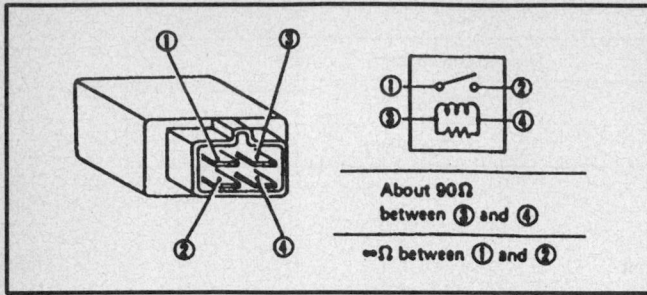

Testing the air conditioning or fan control relay – Panasonic

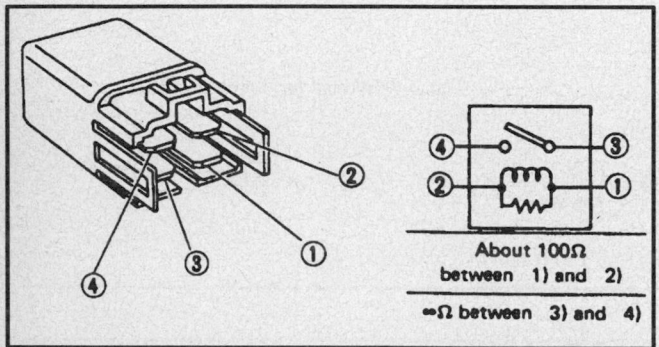

Testing the air conditioning, main fan, sub–fan and fan control relays – Diesel–Kiki/Zexel and Calsonic

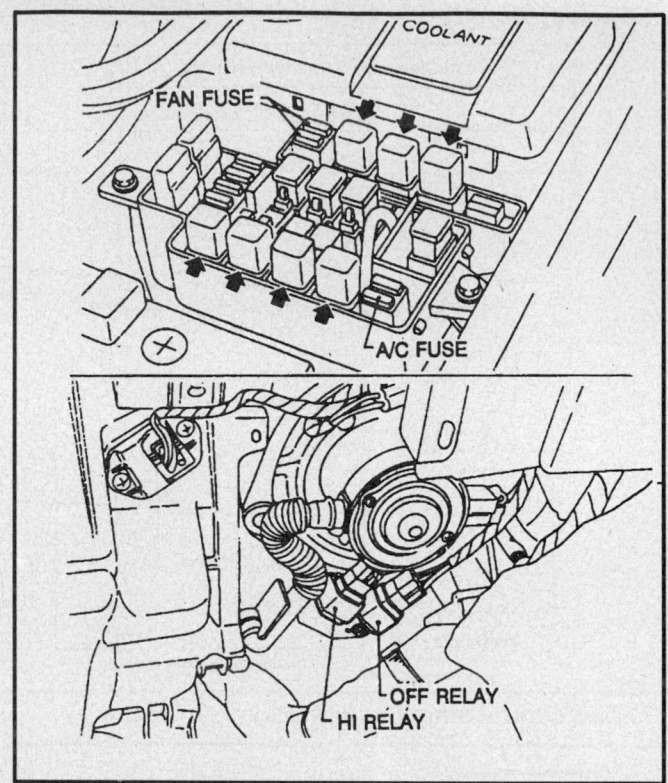

Testing system relays – SVX

AUTOMATIC AIR CONDITIONING SYSTEM

Auto Amplifier

OPERATION

SVX

The auto amplifier, located on the control panel assembly, performs computation based on signals from each switch, sensor and engine control unit. It compares the results and the PBR (potentiometric balance resistor) signal. It then commands the door motor, fan control amplifier and compressor solenoidactuator, thus automatically controlling air outlet, intake, temperature, quantity and compressor operation.

In–Vehicle Sensor

OPERATION

SVX

The sensor is installed on the left side of the control panel and detects the temperature of the interior air. This air is constantly drawn over the sensor by the aspirator. The air temperature is converted to a resistance value and then sent to the auto amplifier.

TESTING

1. Remove the auto amplifier and disconnect the in–vehicle sensor connector.
2. Using an ohmmeter attached to the sensor side of the connector, check the switch for continuity at various temperatures:
   50°F (10°C): 6.0 kilo–ohms
   68°F (20°C): 3.75 kilo–ohms
   77°F (25°C): 3.0 kilo–ohms
   86°F (30°C): 2.42 kilo–ohms
   104°F (40°C): 1.06 kilo–ohms
3. Then, using a voltmeter and with the ignition switch **ON**, measure the voltage at the in–vehicle sensor connector.
4. Between terminal **1** and ground or between terminals **1** and **2**, there should be about 5 volts.

Ambient Sensor

OPERATION

SVX

The ambient sensor is installed on the hood lock stay. It detects the temperature of the ambient air and converts the temperature to a resistance value which is sent to the auto amplifier.

TESTING

1. Disconnect the ambient sensor connector.

2. Using an ohmmeter, check the resistance of the sensor at various temperatures:

50°F (10°C): 6.0 kilo–ohms
68°F (20°C): 3.75 kilo–ohms
77°F (25°C): 3.0 kilo–ohms
86°F (30°C): 2.42 kilo–ohms
104°F (40°C): 1.06 kilo–ohms

3. Then, using a voltmeter and with the ignition switch **ON**, check voltage signal between terminal **2** and a body ground or between terminals **1** and **2**.

4. The voltage signal should be about 5 volts in both cases.

Sunload Sensor

OPERATION

SVX

The sunload sensor detects the intensity of sunlight in the passenger compartment. It is installed on the upper left side of the instrument panel. The diode converts the solar radiator into a current value, which is sent as a voltage signal to the auto amplifier.

Evaporator Sensor

OPERATION

SVX

The evaporator sensor is installed on the evaporator assembly case on the heater side. It converts the temperature of air flowing to the heater unit to a resistance value after passing through the evaporator. It sends this signal to the auto amplifier.

TESTING

1. Remove the glove box.
2. Disconnect the BM2 connector (refer to the diagnostic charts for terminal identification).
3. Turn the ignition switch **ON**.
4. Using an ohmmeter attached to terminals **11** and **13** on the harness side of the connector, measure the resistance, depending on actual temperature:

50°F (10°C): 4.01 kilo–ohms
68°F (20°C): 2.67 kilo–ohms
77°F (25°C): 2.20 kilo–ohms
86°F (30°C): 1.83 kilo–ohms
104°F (40°C): 1.28 kilo–ohms

FAN CONTROL AMPLIFIER

OPERATION

SVX

The fan control amplifier is installed on the cooling unit. It receives the base current from the auto amplifier, and control the voltage applied to the fan motor.

TESTING

1. Remove the glove box.
2. Detach the fan control amplifier connector. Turn the ignition switch and the AUTO switch **ON**.
3. Set the fan speed to **HI**. Using a voltmeter on the harness side of the connector, place one probe on terminal **2** and the other on body ground. There should be a maximum of 1.0 volt.
4. Set the fan speed to **LOW/MED** and check the voltage again, it should now be about 12 volts. Move the terminal probe to terminal **1** and keep the other on the body ground. The reading should be 1.02.0 volts.
5. Reattach the fan control amplifier connector.
6. With the ignition switch **ON**, measure the voltage by back–probing at terminal **1** and placing the other probe to a body ground.
7. With the AUTO switch **ON** and the fan at **HI**, there should be 0 volts.
8. With the fan switch moved to **LOW/MED**, the reading should be 1.0–2.0 volts.
9. Turn the ignition switch and AUTO switch **OFF**.
10. Detach the fan control amplifier connector.
11. Using an ohmmeter, check the resistance between terminal **4** and a body ground. It should be 0 ohms.

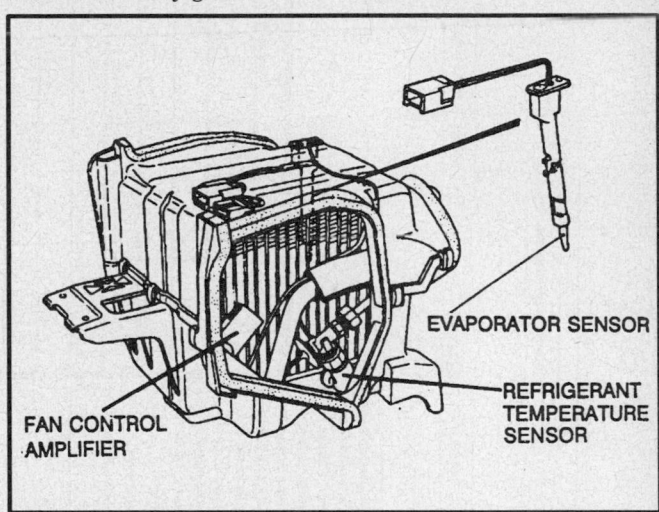

Location of evaporator sensor, fan control amplifier, and refrigerant temperature sensor – SVX

SYSTEM DIAGNOSIS

GENERAL AIR CONDITIONING SYSTEM DIAGNOSIS

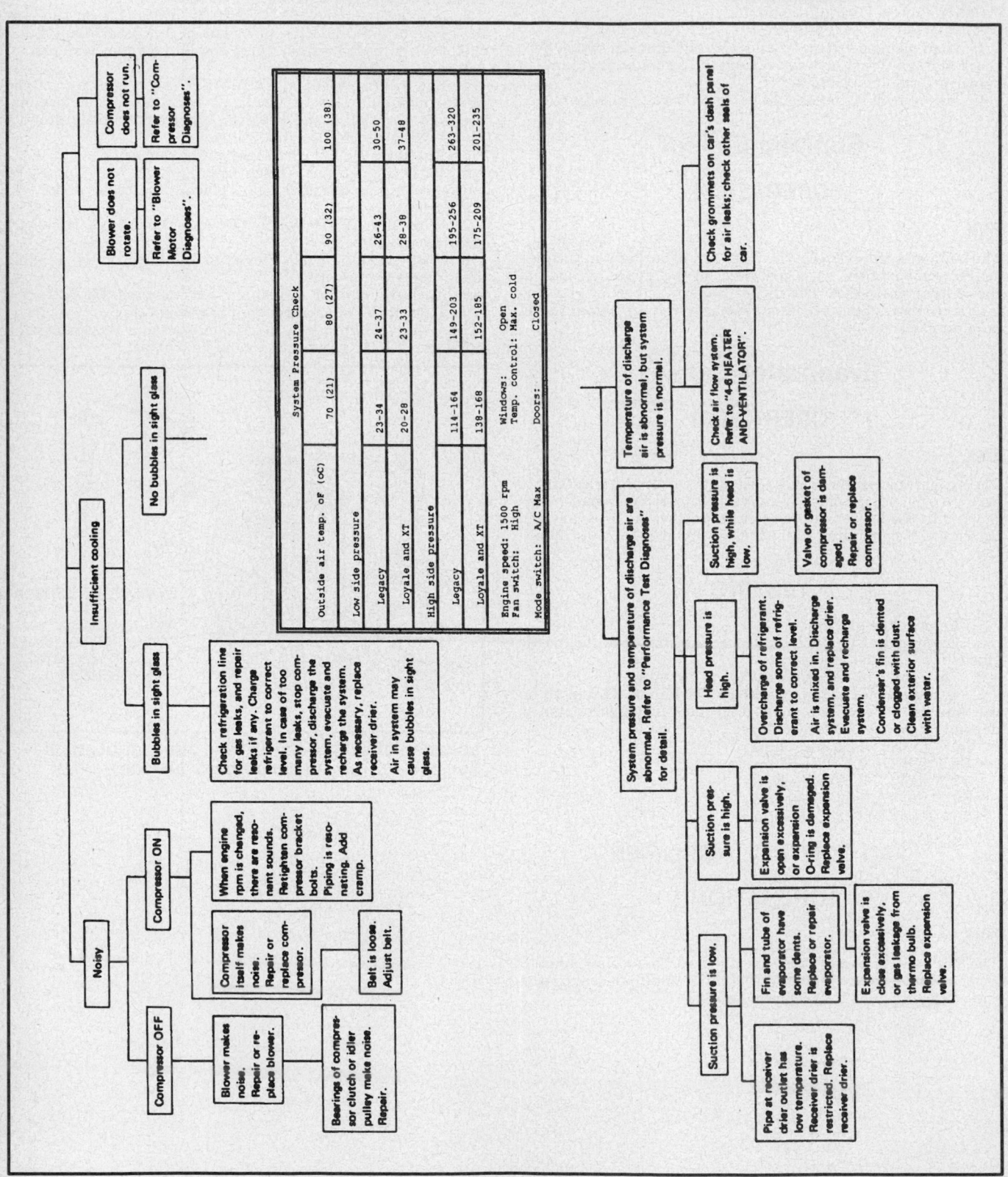

System Pressure Check

Outside air temp. °F (°C)	70 (21)	80 (27)	90 (32)	100 (38)
Low side pressure				
Legacy	23–34	24–37	26–43	30–50
Loyale and XT	20–28	23–33	28–38	37–48
High side pressure				
Legacy	114–164	149–203	195–256	263–320
Loyale and XT	138–168	152–185	175–209	201–235

Engine speed: 1500 rpm
Fan switch: High
Mode switch: A/C Max
Windows: Open
Temp. control: Max. cold
Doors: Closed

Noisy

- **Compressor OFF**
  - Blower makes noise. Repair or replace blower.
  - Bearings of compressor clutch or idler pulley make noise. Repair.
- **Compressor ON**
  - Compressor itself makes noise. Repair or replace compressor.
  - When engine rpm is changed, there are resonant sounds. Retighten compressor bracket bolts. Piping is resonating. Add cramp.
  - Belt is loose. Adjust belt.

Insufficient cooling

- **Bubbles in sight glass**
  - Check refrigeration line for gas leaks, and repair leaks if any. Charge refrigerant to correct level. In case of too many leaks, stop compressor, discharge the system, evacuate and recharge the system. As necessary, replace receiver drier.
  - Air in system may cause bubbles in sight glass.
- **No bubble in sight glass**
- **Blower does not rotate** — Refer to "Blower Motor Diagnoses".
- **Compressor does not run.** — Refer to "Compressor Diagnoses".

System pressure and temperature of discharge air are abnormal. Refer to "Performance Test Diagnoses" for detail.

- Suction pressure is low.
  - Pipe at receiver drier outlet has low temperature. Receiver drier is restricted. Replace receiver drier.
  - Fin and tube of evaporator have some dents. Replace or repair evaporator.
  - Expansion valve is close excessively, or gas leakage from thermo bulb. Replace expansion valve.
- Suction pressure is high.
  - Expansion valve is open excessively, or expansion O-ring is damaged. Replace expansion valve.
- Head pressure is high.
  - Overcharge of refrigerant. Discharge some of refrigerant to correct level.
  - Air is mixed in. Discharge system, and replace drier. Evacuate and recharge system.
  - Condenser's fin is dented or clogged with dust. Clean exterior surface with water.
- Suction pressure is high, while head is low.
  - Valve or gasket of compressor is damaged. Repair or replace compressor.

Temperature of discharge air is abnormal, but system pressure is normal.

- Check air flow system. Refer to "4-6 HEATER AND VENTILATOR".
- Check grommets on car's dash panel for air leaks; check other seals of car.

BLOWER MOTOR DIAGNOSIS – LOYALE

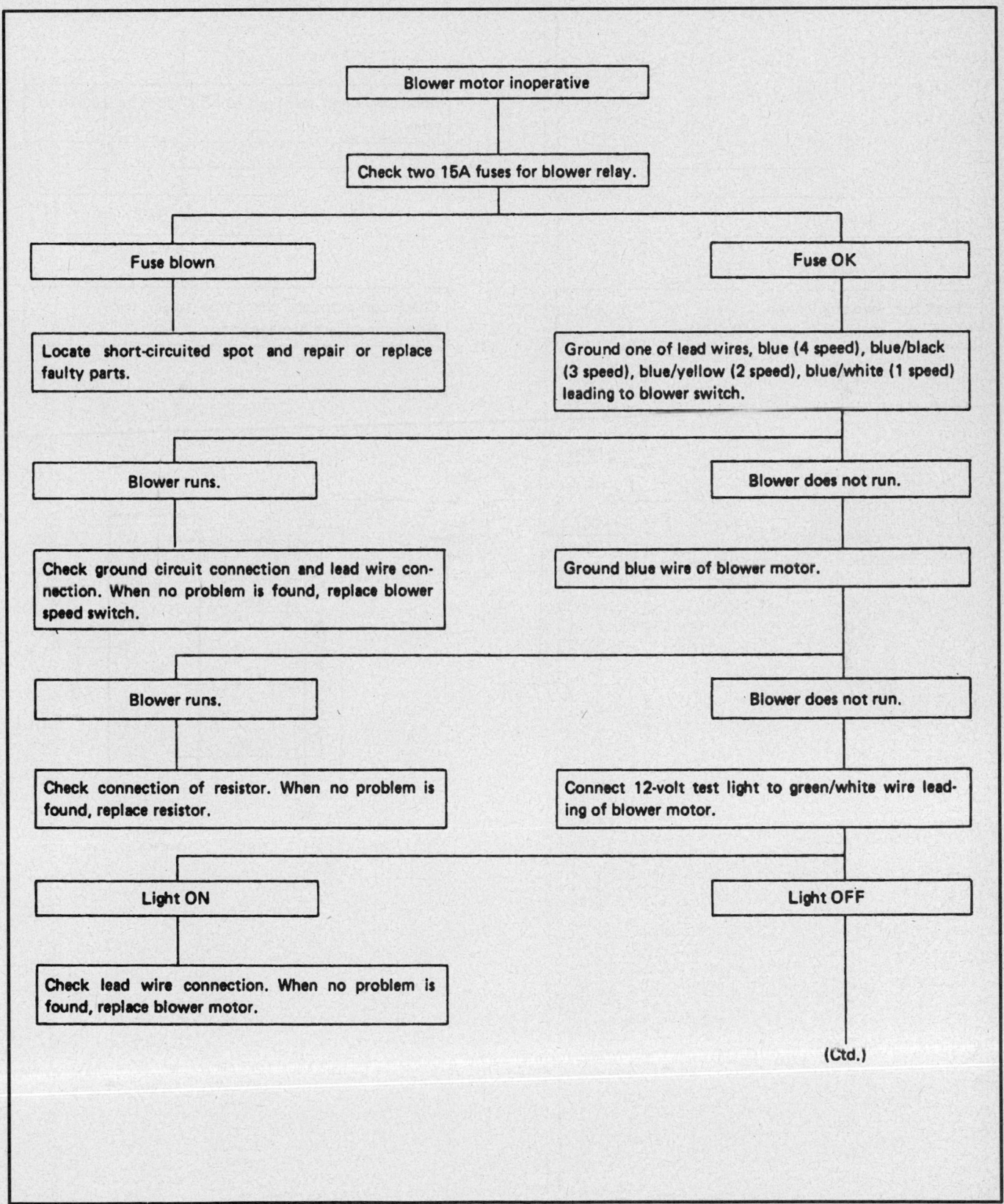

Blower motor inoperative

Check two 15A fuses for blower relay.

Fuse blown

Locate short-circuited spot and repair or replace faulty parts.

Fuse OK

Ground one of lead wires, blue (4 speed), blue/black (3 speed), blue/yellow (2 speed), blue/white (1 speed) leading to blower switch.

Blower runs.

Check ground circuit connection and lead wire connection. When no problem is found, replace blower speed switch.

Blower does not run.

Ground blue wire of blower motor.

Blower runs.

Check connection of resistor. When no problem is found, replace resistor.

Blower does not run.

Connect 12-volt test light to green/white wire leading of blower motor.

Light ON

Check lead wire connection. When no problem is found, replace blower motor.

Light OFF

(Ctd.)

BLOWER MOTOR DIAGNOSIS – LOYALE CONT'D

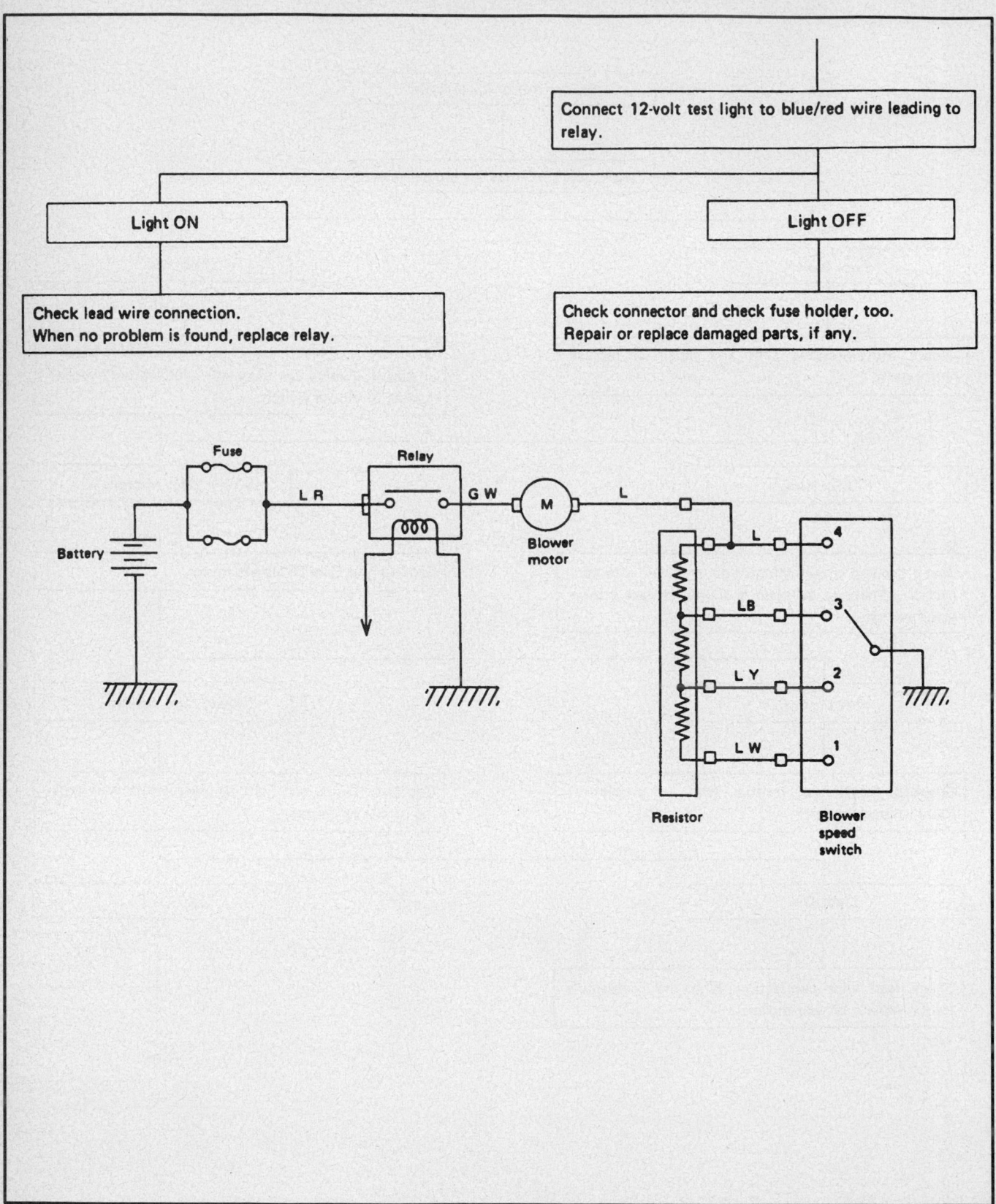

Connect 12-volt test light to blue/red wire leading to relay.

Light ON

Check lead wire connection.
When no problem is found, replace relay.

Light OFF

Check connector and check fuse holder, too.
Repair or replace damaged parts, if any.

Fuse

Relay

L R

G W

Blower motor

L

Battery

Resistor

L

LB

LY

LW

4

3

2

1

Blower speed switch

BLOWER MOTOR DIAGNOSIS – LEGACY

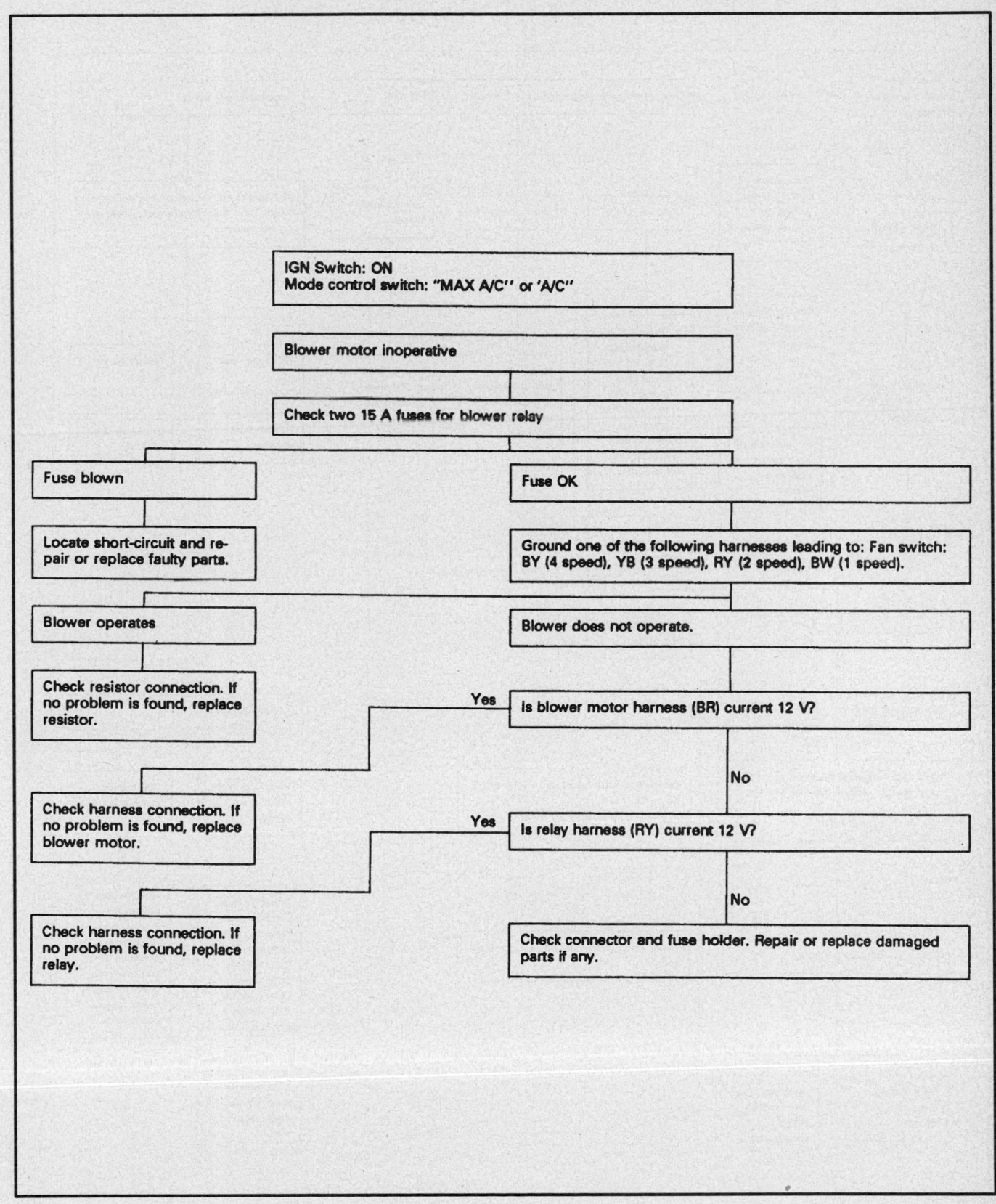

IGN Switch: ON
Mode control switch: "MAX A/C'' or 'A/C''

Blower motor inoperative

Check two 15 A fuses for blower relay

Fuse blown

Locate short-circuit and re-pair or replace faulty parts.

Blower operates

Check resistor connection. If no problem is found, replace resistor.

Check harness connection. If no problem is found, replace blower motor.

Check harness connection. If no problem is found, replace relay.

Fuse OK

Ground one of the following harnesses leading to: Fan switch: BY (4 speed), YB (3 speed), RY (2 speed), BW (1 speed).

Blower does not operate.

Yes — Is blower motor harness (BR) current 12 V?

No

Yes — Is relay harness (RY) current 12 V?

No

Check connector and fuse holder. Repair or replace damaged parts if any.

COMPRESSOR DIAGNOSIS – LEGACY AND LOYALE

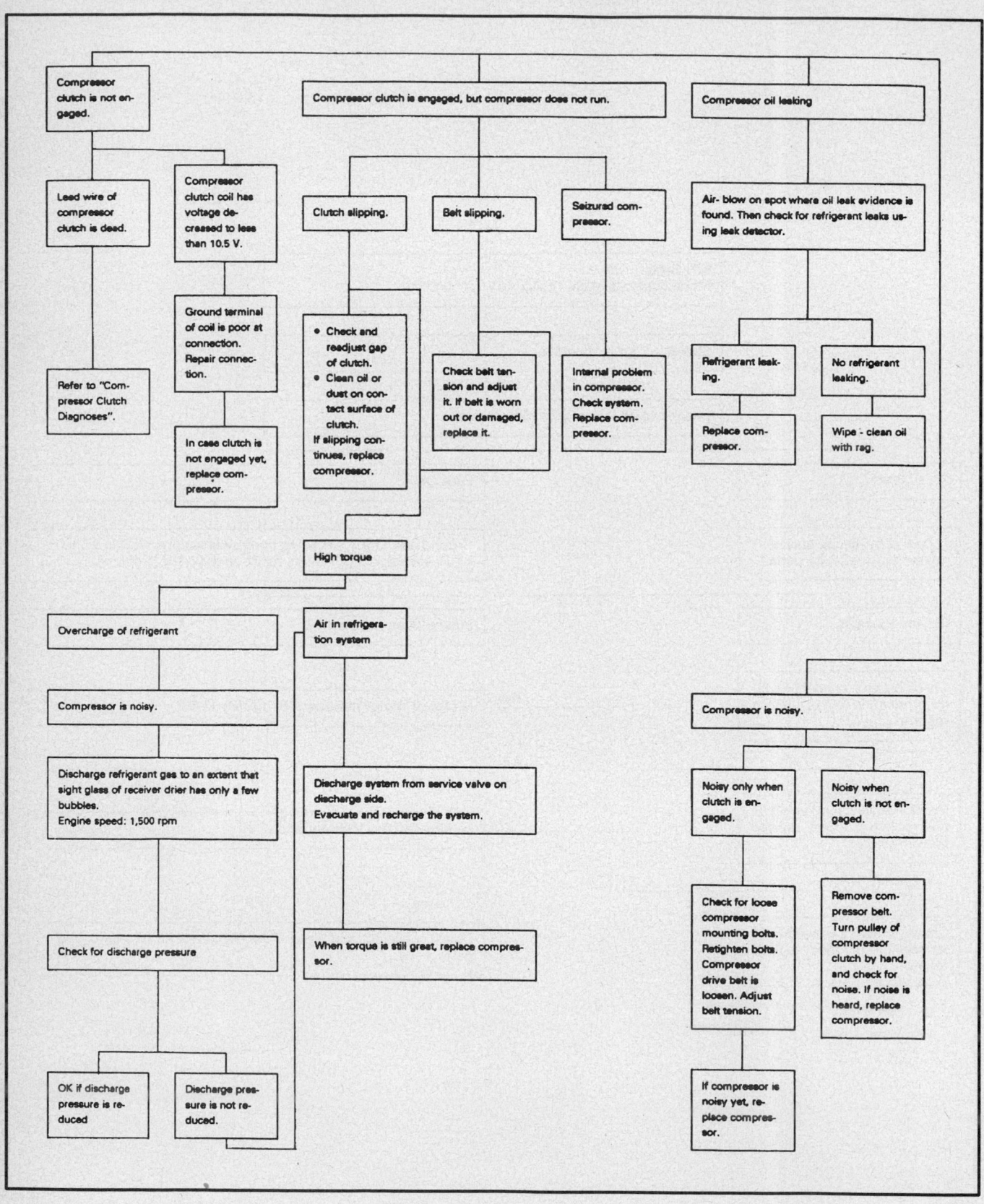

COMPRESSOR CLUTCH DIAGNOSIS – LEGACY

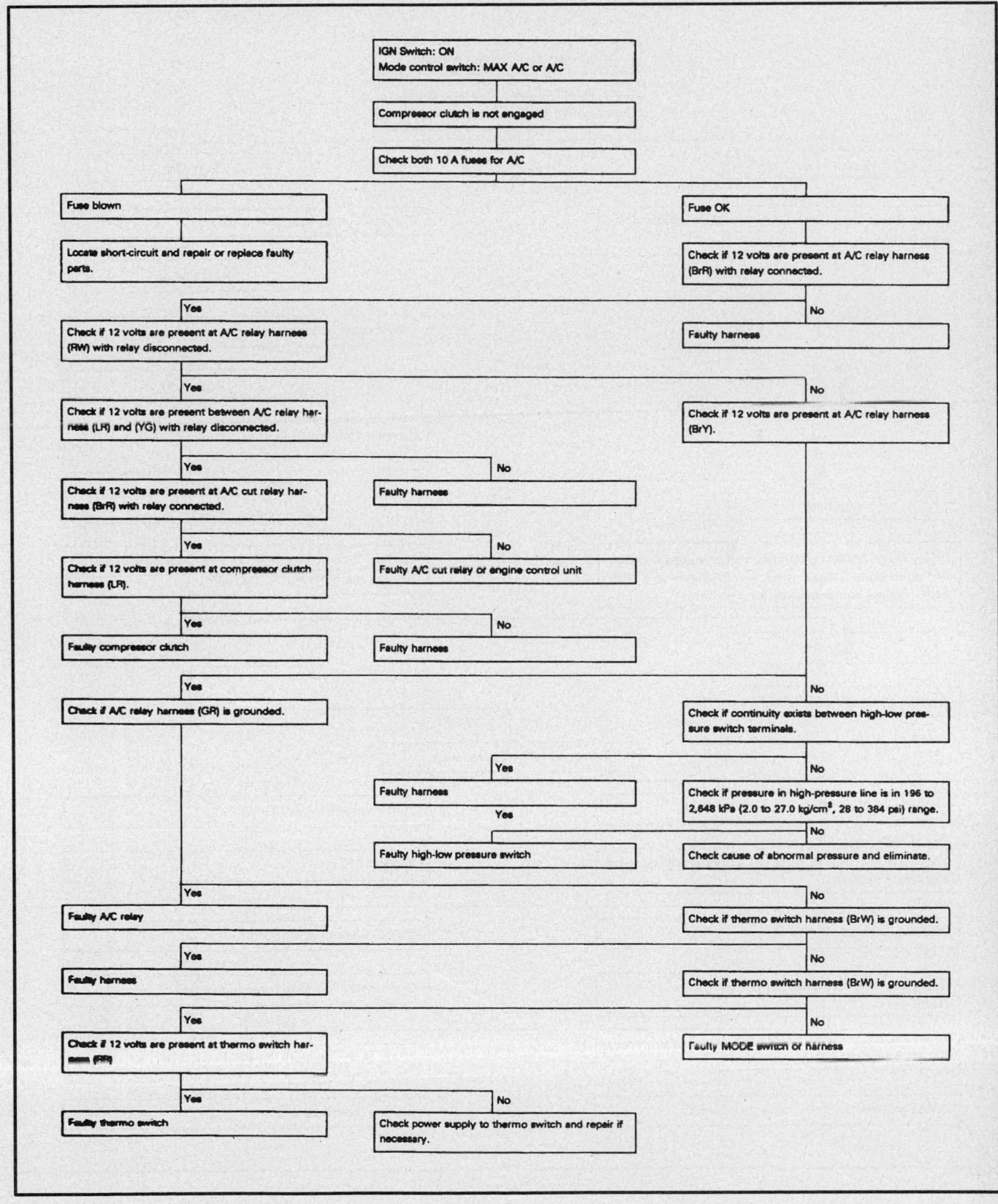

IGN Switch: ON
Mode control switch: MAX A/C or A/C

Compressor clutch is not engaged

Check both 10 A fuses for A/C

Fuse blown

Locate short-circuit and repair or replace faulty parts.

Yes

Check if 12 volts are present at A/C relay harness (RW) with relay disconnected.

Yes

Check if 12 volts are present between A/C relay harness (LR) and (YG) with relay disconnected.

Yes

Check if 12 volts are present at A/C cut relay harness (BrR) with relay connected.

Yes

Check if 12 volts are present at compressor clutch harness (LR).

Yes

Faulty compressor clutch

Yes

Check if A/C relay harness (GR) is grounded.

Yes

Faulty A/C relay

Yes

Faulty harness

Yes

Check if 12 volts are present at thermo switch harness (RR)

Yes

Faulty thermo switch

No

Check power supply to thermo switch and repair if necessary.

Fuse OK

Check if 12 volts are present at A/C relay harness (BrR) with relay connected.

No

Faulty harness

No

Check if 12 volts are present at A/C relay harness (BrY).

No

Faulty harness

No

Faulty A/C cut relay or engine control unit

No

Faulty harness

No

Check if continuity exists between high-low pressure switch terminals.

Yes

Faulty harness

No

Check if pressure in high-pressure line is in 196 to 2,648 kPa (2.0 to 27.0 kg/cm^2, 28 to 384 psi) range.

Yes

Faulty high-low pressure switch

No

Check cause of abnormal pressure and eliminate.

No

Check if thermo switch harness (BrW) is grounded.

No

Check if thermo switch harness (BrW) is grounded.

No

Faulty MODE switch or harness

COMPRESSOR CLUTCH DIAGNOSIS – LOYALE WITH HITACHI SYSTEM

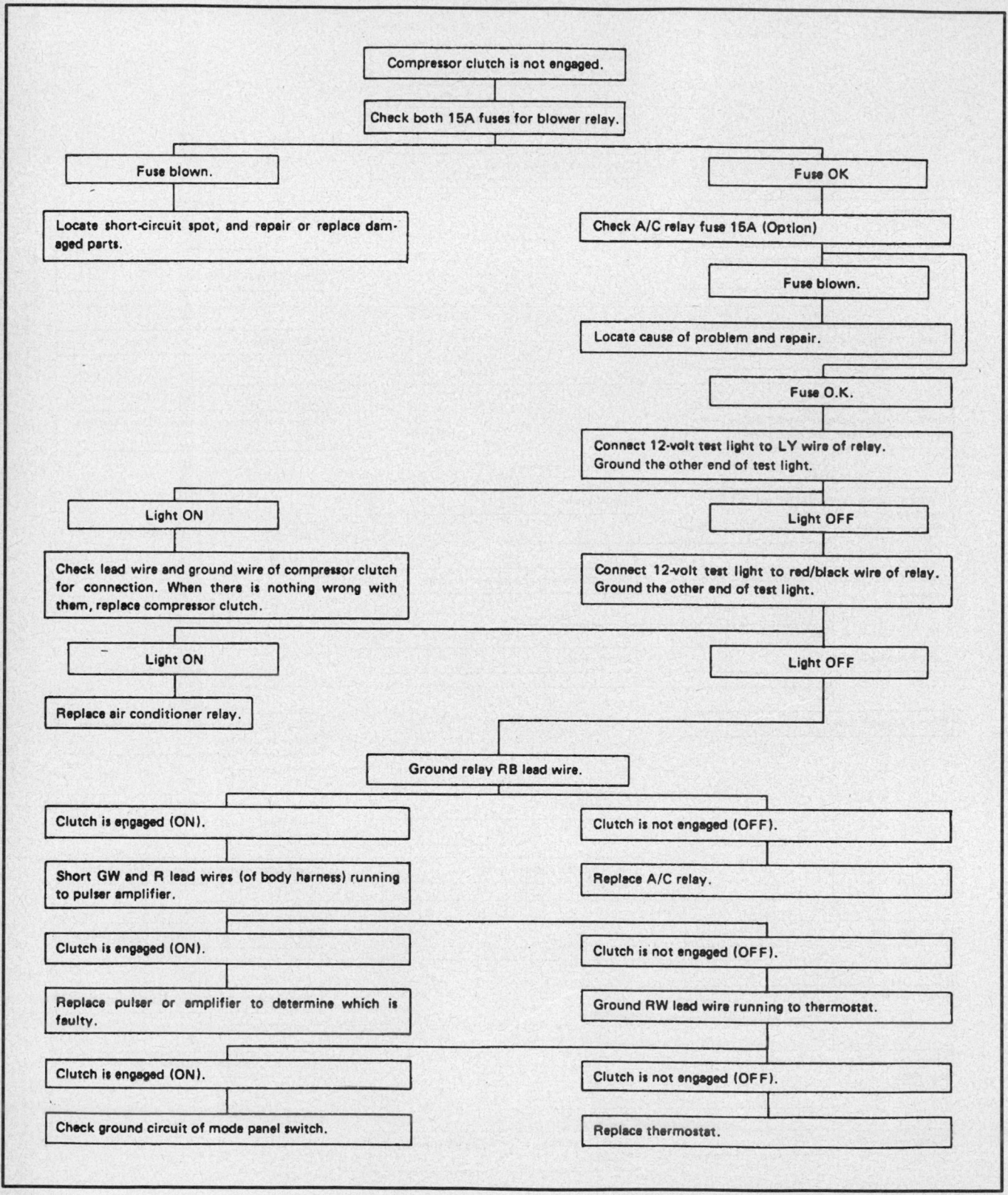

Compressor clutch is not engaged.

Check both 15A fuses for blower relay.

Fuse blown.

Locate short-circuit spot, and repair or replace damaged parts.

Fuse OK

Check A/C relay fuse 15A (Option)

Fuse blown.

Locate cause of problem and repair.

Fuse O.K.

Connect 12-volt test light to LY wire of relay. Ground the other end of test light.

Light ON

Check lead wire and ground wire of compressor clutch for connection. When there is nothing wrong with them, replace compressor clutch.

Light OFF

Connect 12-volt test light to red/black wire of relay. Ground the other end of test light.

Light ON

Replace air conditioner relay.

Light OFF

Ground relay RB lead wire.

Clutch is engaged (ON).

Short GW and R lead wires (of body harness) running to pulser amplifier.

Clutch is engaged (ON).

Replace pulser or amplifier to determine which is faulty.

Clutch is engaged (ON).

Check ground circuit of mode panel switch.

Clutch is not engaged (OFF).

Replace A/C relay.

Clutch is not engaged (OFF).

Ground RW lead wire running to thermostat.

Clutch is not engaged (OFF).

Replace thermostat.

COMPRESSOR CLUTCH DIAGNOSIS – LOYALE WITH PANASONIC SYSTEM

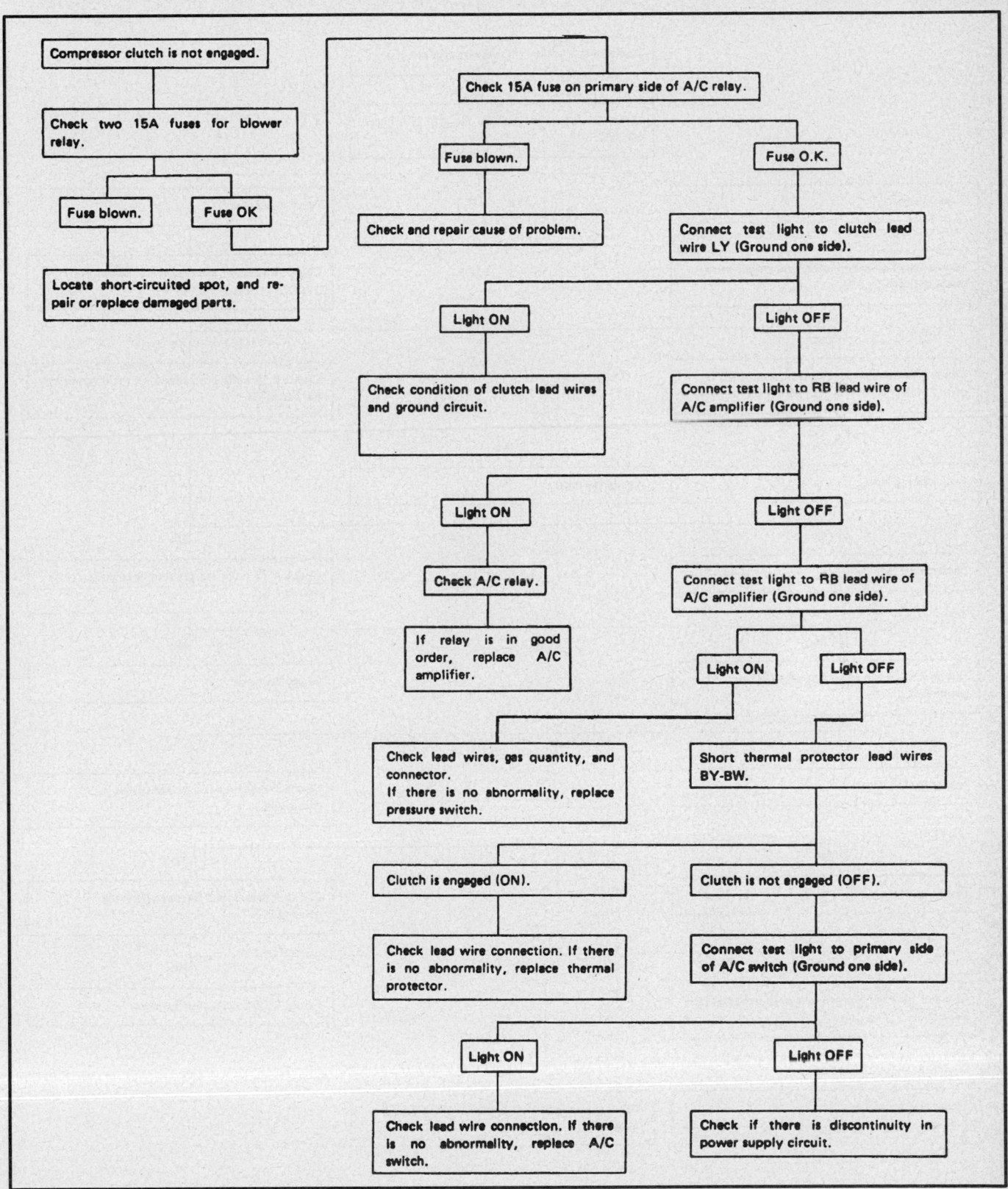

RADIATOR MAIN FAN DIAGNOSIS – LEGACY

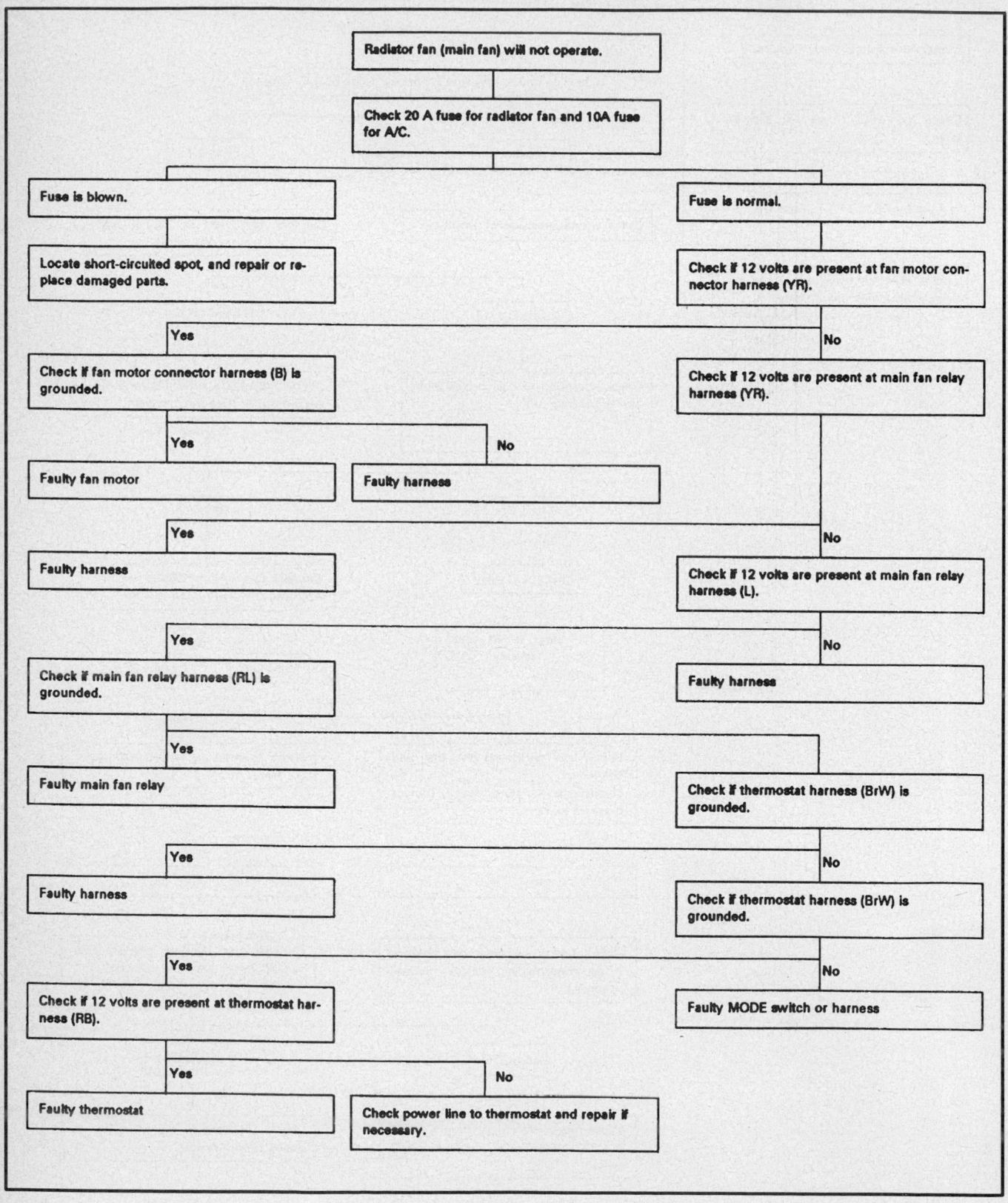

Radiator fan (main fan) will not operate.

Check 20 A fuse for radiator fan and 10A fuse for A/C.

Fuse is blown.

Locate short-circuited spot, and repair or replace damaged parts.

Yes

Check if fan motor connector harness (B) is grounded.

Yes — Faulty fan motor
No — Faulty harness

Yes — Faulty harness

Yes

Check if main fan relay harness (RL) is grounded.

Yes — Faulty main fan relay

Yes — Faulty harness

Yes

Check if 12 volts are present at thermostat harness (RB).

Yes — Faulty thermostat
No — Check power line to thermostat and repair if necessary.

Fuse is normal.

Check if 12 volts are present at fan motor connector harness (YR).

No

Check if 12 volts are present at main fan relay harness (YR).

No

Check if 12 volts are present at main fan relay harness (L).

No — Faulty harness

Check if thermostat harness (BrW) is grounded.

No

Check if thermostat harness (BrW) is grounded.

No — Faulty MODE switch or harness

RADIATOR MAIN FAN DIAGNOSIS – LOYALE

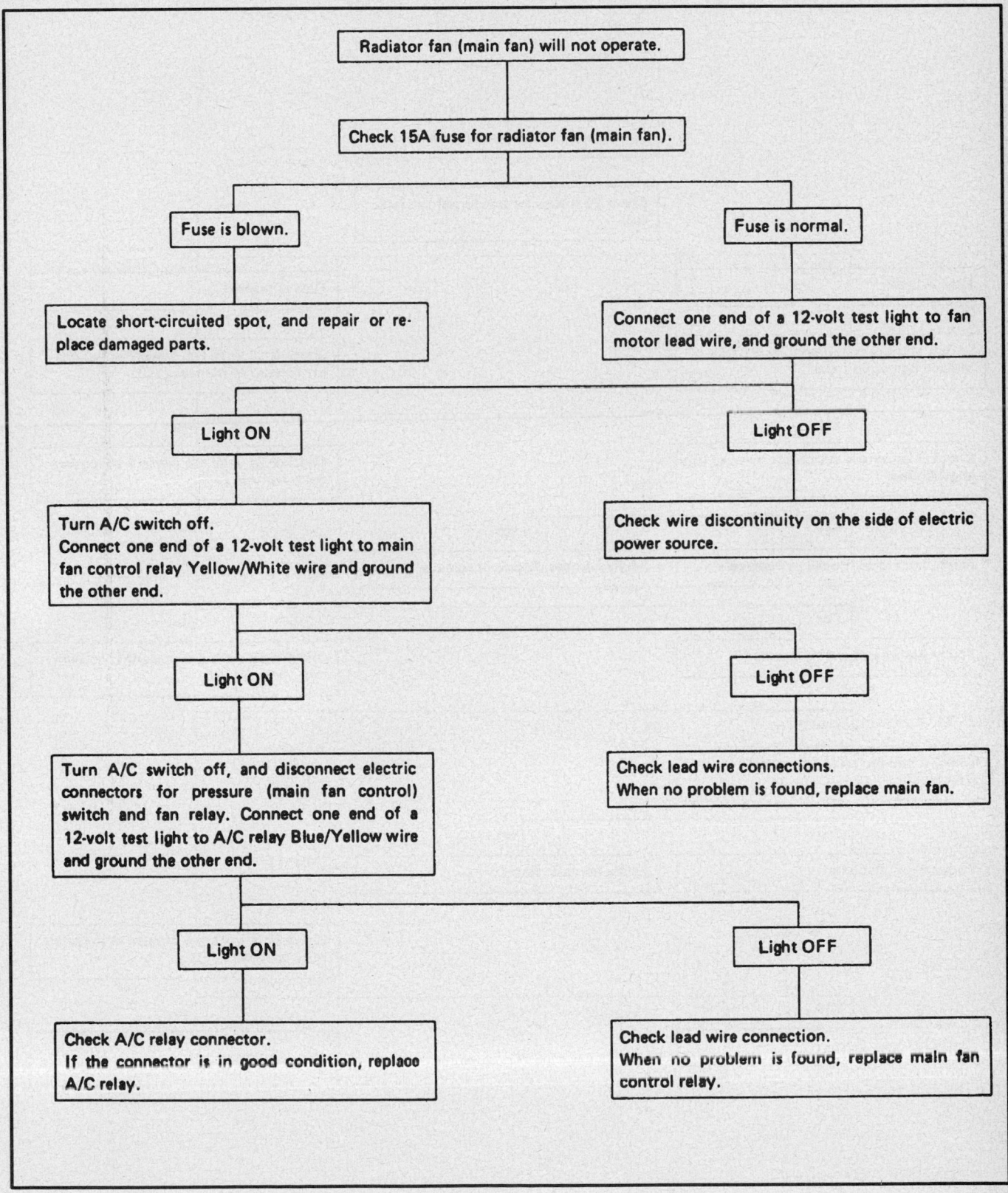

Radiator fan (main fan) will not operate.

Check 15A fuse for radiator fan (main fan).

Fuse is blown.

Fuse is normal.

Locate short-circuited spot, and repair or replace damaged parts.

Connect one end of a 12-volt test light to fan motor lead wire, and ground the other end.

Light ON

Light OFF

Turn A/C switch off.
Connect one end of a 12-volt test light to main fan control relay Yellow/White wire and ground the other end.

Check wire discontinuity on the side of electric power source.

Light ON

Light OFF

Turn A/C switch off, and disconnect electric connectors for pressure (main fan control) switch and fan relay. Connect one end of a 12-volt test light to A/C relay Blue/Yellow wire and ground the other end.

Check lead wire connections.
When no problem is found, replace main fan.

Light ON

Light OFF

Check A/C relay connector.
If the connector is in good condition, replace A/C relay.

Check lead wire connection.
When no problem is found, replace main fan control relay.

CONDENSER SUB FAN DIAGNOSIS (1) − LEGACY

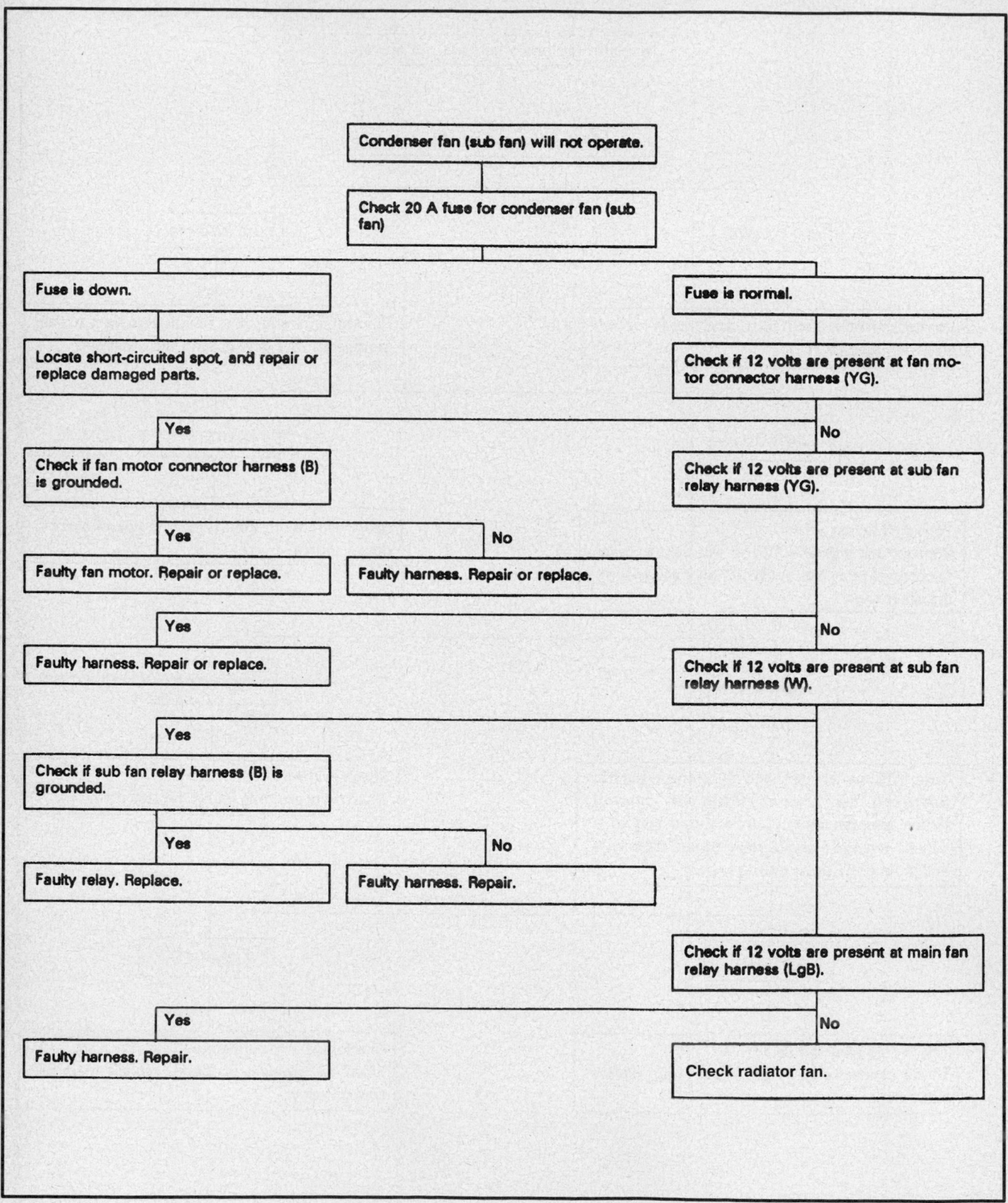

Condenser fan (sub fan) will not operate.

Check 20 A fuse for condenser fan (sub fan)

Fuse is down.

Locate short-circuited spot, and repair or replace damaged parts.

Fuse is normal.

Check if 12 volts are present at fan motor connector harness (YG).

Yes — Check if fan motor connector harness (B) is grounded.

No — Check if 12 volts are present at sub fan relay harness (YG).

Yes — Faulty fan motor. Repair or replace.

No — Faulty harness. Repair or replace.

Yes — Faulty harness. Repair or replace.

No — Check if 12 volts are present at sub fan relay harness (W).

Yes — Check if sub fan relay harness (B) is grounded.

Yes — Faulty relay. Replace.

No — Faulty harness. Repair.

Check if 12 volts are present at main fan relay harness (LgB).

Yes — Faulty harness. Repair.

No — Check radiator fan.

CONDENSER SUB FAN DIAGNOSIS (2) – LEGACY

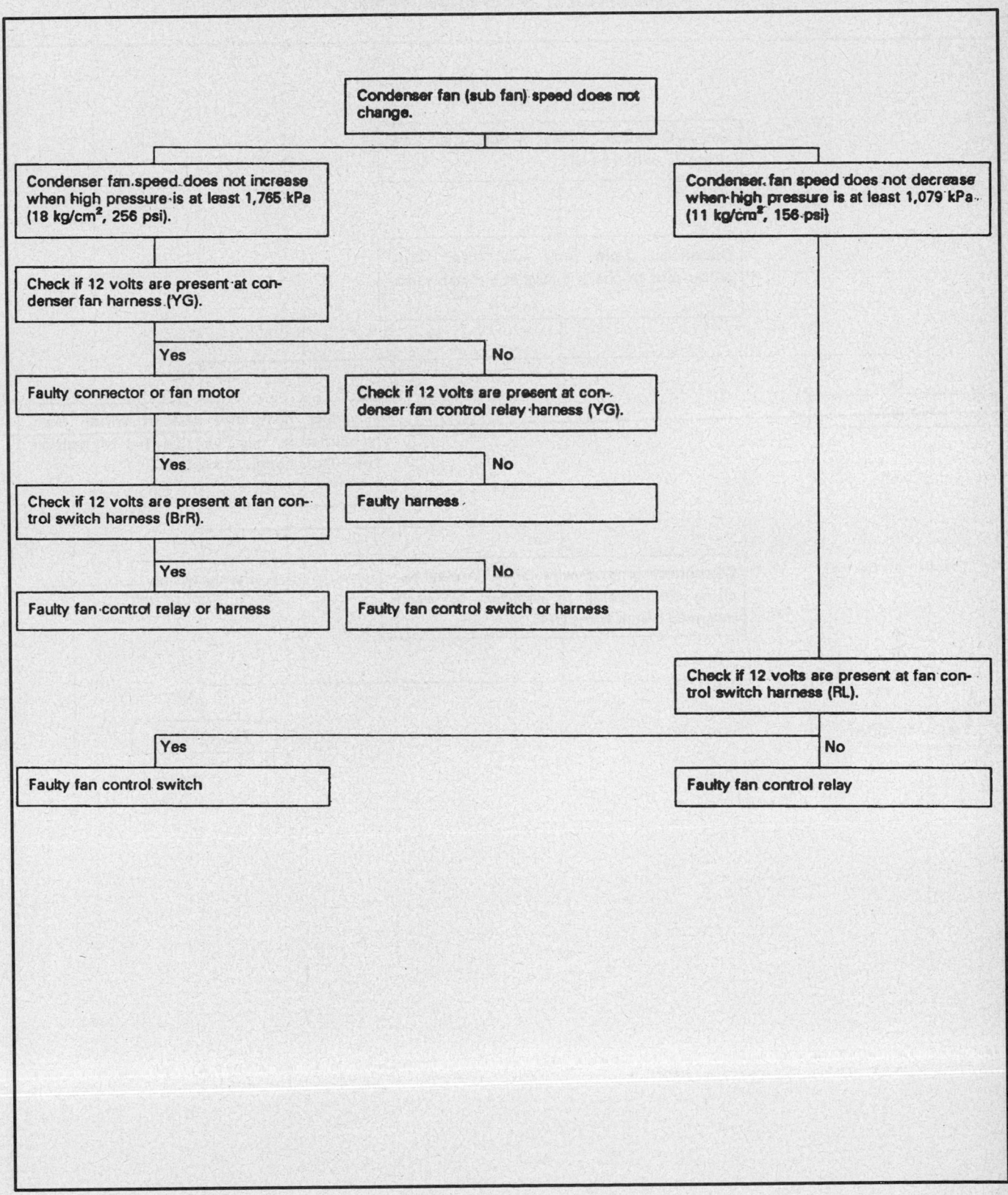

Condenser fan (sub fan) speed does not change.

Condenser fan speed does not increase when high pressure is at least 1,765 kPa (18 kg/cm², 256 psi).

Condenser fan speed does not decrease when high pressure is at least 1,079 kPa (11 kg/cm², 156 psi)

Check if 12 volts are present at condenser fan harness (YG).

Yes → Faulty connector or fan motor

No → Check if 12 volts are present at condenser fan control relay harness (YG).

Yes → Check if 12 volts are present at fan control switch harness (BrR).

No → Faulty harness

Yes → Faulty fan control relay or harness

No → Faulty fan control switch or harness

Check if 12 volts are present at fan control switch harness (RL).

Yes → Faulty fan control switch

No → Faulty fan control relay

PULSER AND RELATED CIRCUIT DIAGNOSIS – LOYALE WITH HITACHI SYSTEM ONLY

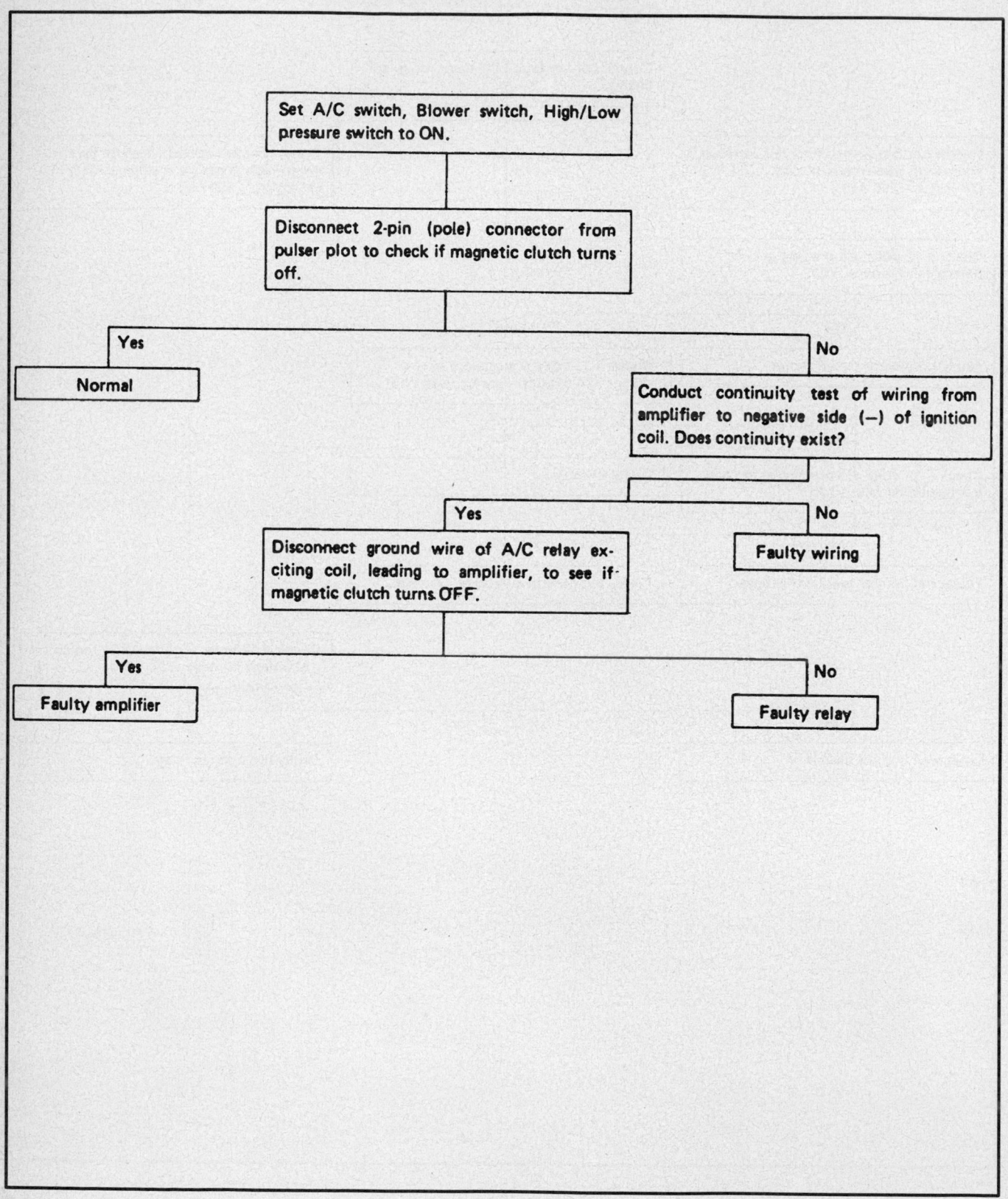

PULSER AND RELATED CIRCUIT DIAGNOSIS – LOYALE WITH HITACHI SYSTEM ONLY, CONT'D

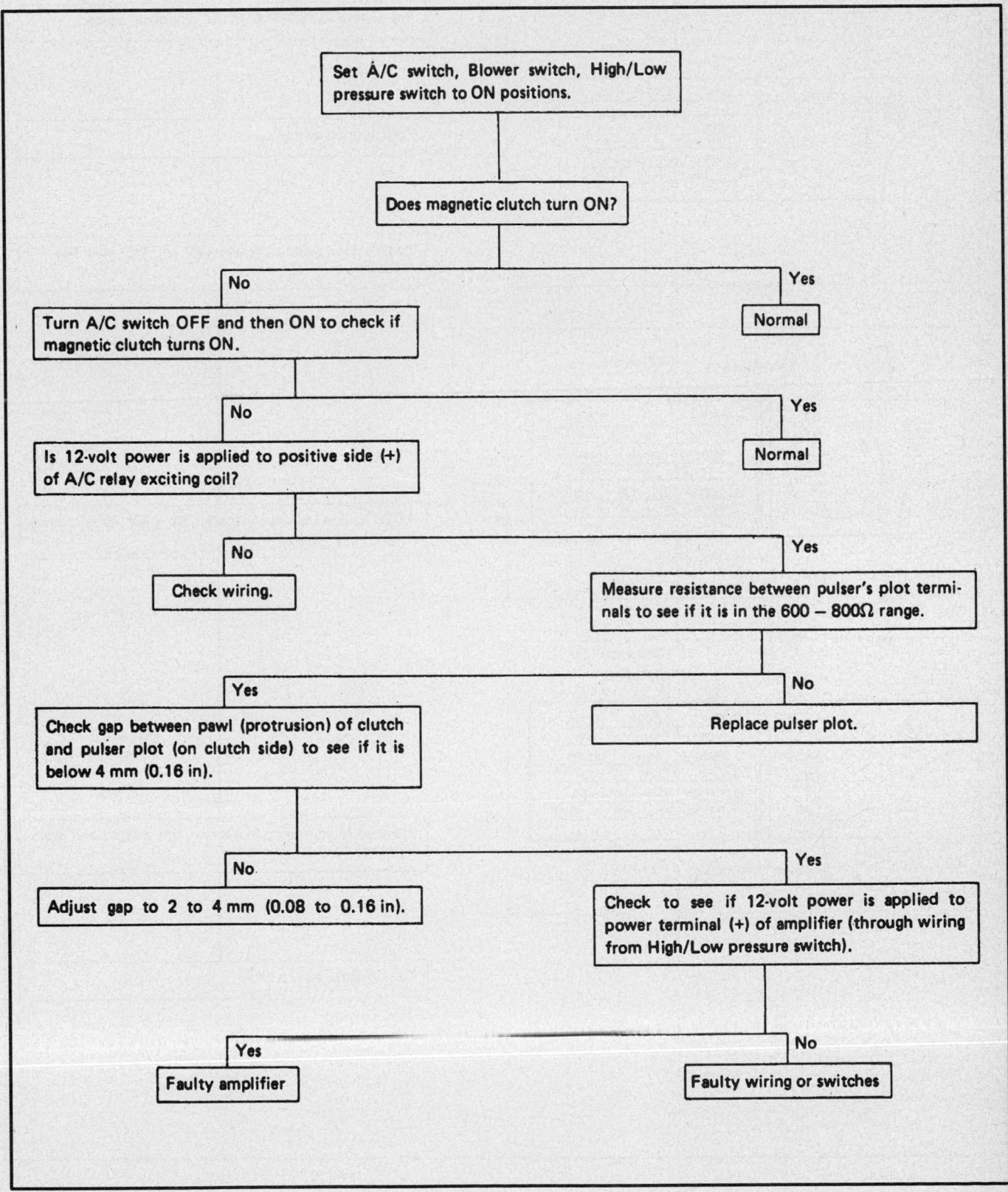

Set A/C switch, Blower switch, High/Low pressure switch to ON positions.

Does magnetic clutch turn ON?

No → Turn A/C switch OFF and then ON to check if magnetic clutch turns ON.

Yes → Normal

No → Is 12-volt power is applied to positive side (+) of A/C relay exciting coil?

Yes → Normal

No → Check wiring.

Yes → Measure resistance between pulser's plot terminals to see if it is in the 600 – 800Ω range.

Yes → Check gap between pawl (protrusion) of clutch and pulser plot (on clutch side) to see if it is below 4 mm (0.16 in).

No → Replace pulser plot.

No → Adjust gap to 2 to 4 mm (0.08 to 0.16 in).

Yes → Check to see if 12-volt power is applied to power terminal (+) of amplifier (through wiring from High/Low pressure switch).

Yes → Faulty amplifier

No → Faulty wiring or switches

CLEARING SELF-DIAGNOSIS CODES — SVX WITH AUTO. A/C

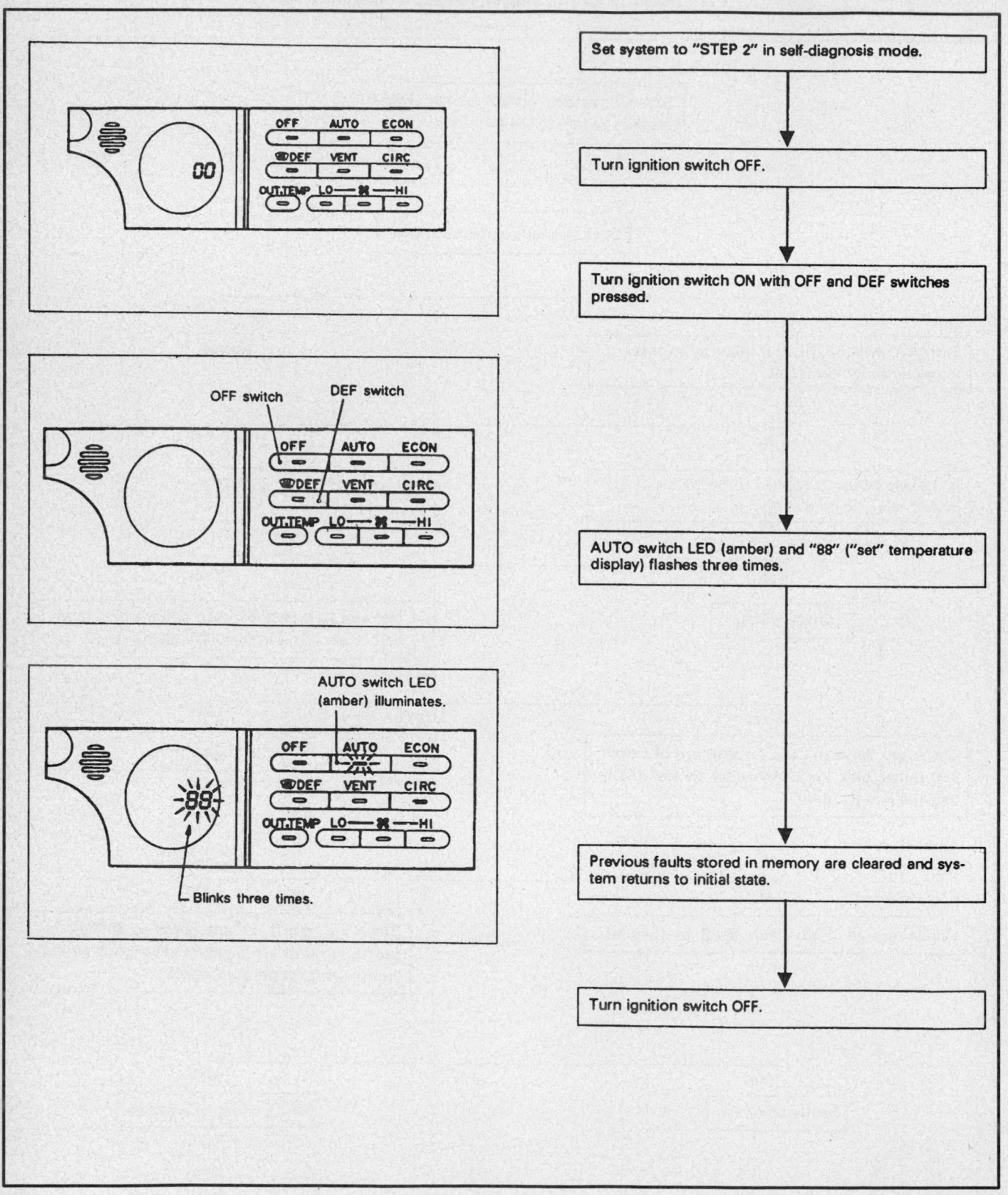

Set system to "STEP 2" in self-diagnosis mode.

↓

Turn ignition switch OFF.

↓

Turn ignition switch ON with OFF and DEF switches pressed.

↓

AUTO switch LED (amber) and "88" ("set" temperature display) flashes three times.

↓

Previous faults stored in memory are cleared and system returns to initial state.

↓

Turn ignition switch OFF.

ENTERING SELF-DIAGNOSTICS – SVX WITH AUTO. A/C

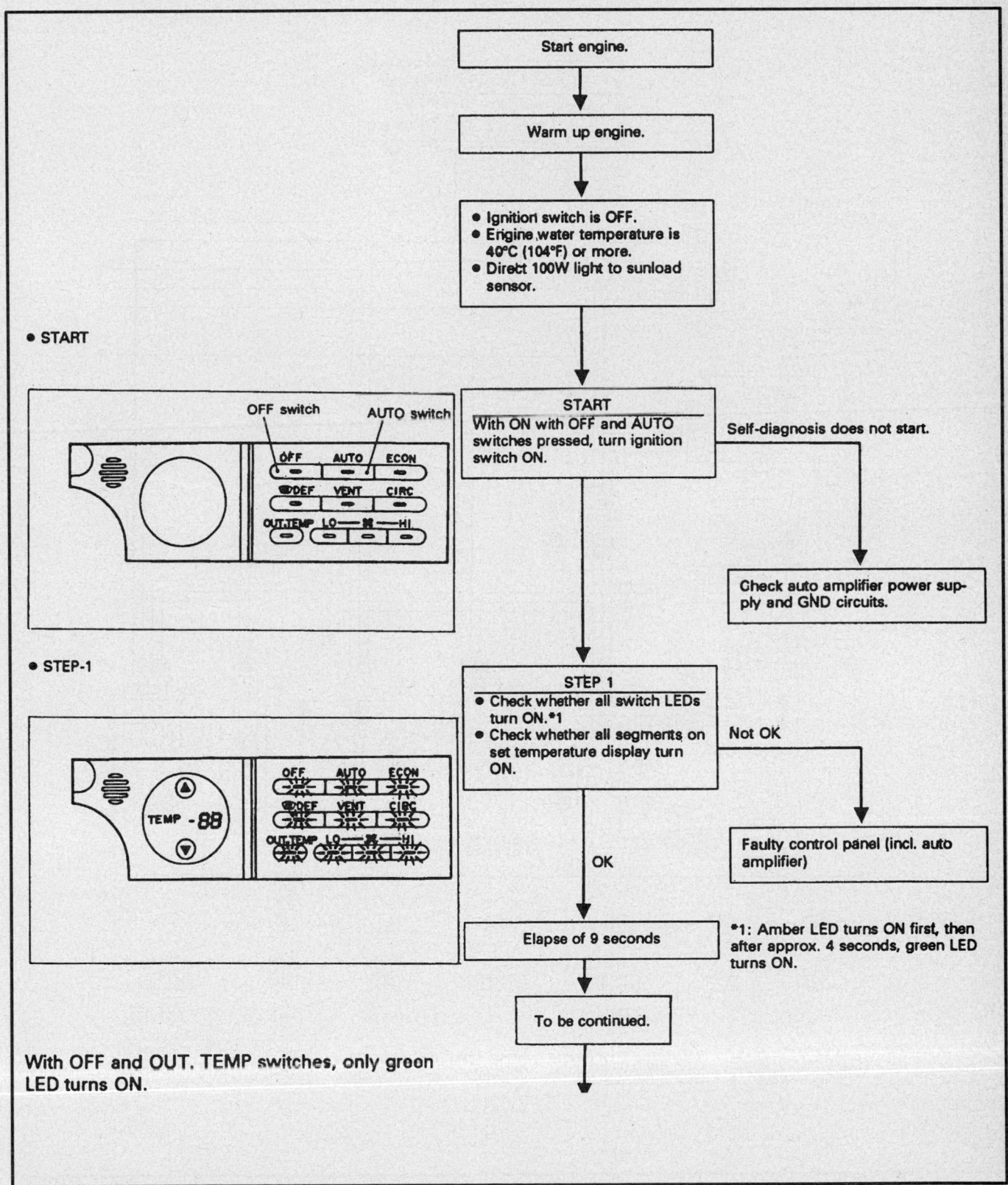

Start engine.

Warm up engine.

- Ignition switch is OFF.
- Engine water temperature is 40°C (104°F) or more.
- Direct 100W light to sunload sensor.

● START

START
With ON with OFF and AUTO switches pressed, turn ignition switch ON.

Self-diagnosis does not start.

OFF switch   AUTO switch

OFF   AUTO   ECON
DEF   VENT   CIRC
OUT.TEMP LO — ☒ — HI

Check auto amplifier power supply and GND circuits.

● STEP-1

STEP 1
- Check whether all switch LEDs turn ON.*1
- Check whether all segments on set temperature display turn ON.

Not OK

TEMP -**88**

OFF   AUTO   ECON
DEF   VENT   CIRC
OUT.TEMP LO — ☒ — HI

Faulty control panel (incl. auto amplifier)

OK

Elapse of 9 seconds

*1: Amber LED turns ON first, then after approx. 4 seconds, green LED turns ON.

To be continued.

With OFF and OUT. TEMP switches, only green LED turns ON.

WIRING SCHEMATICS

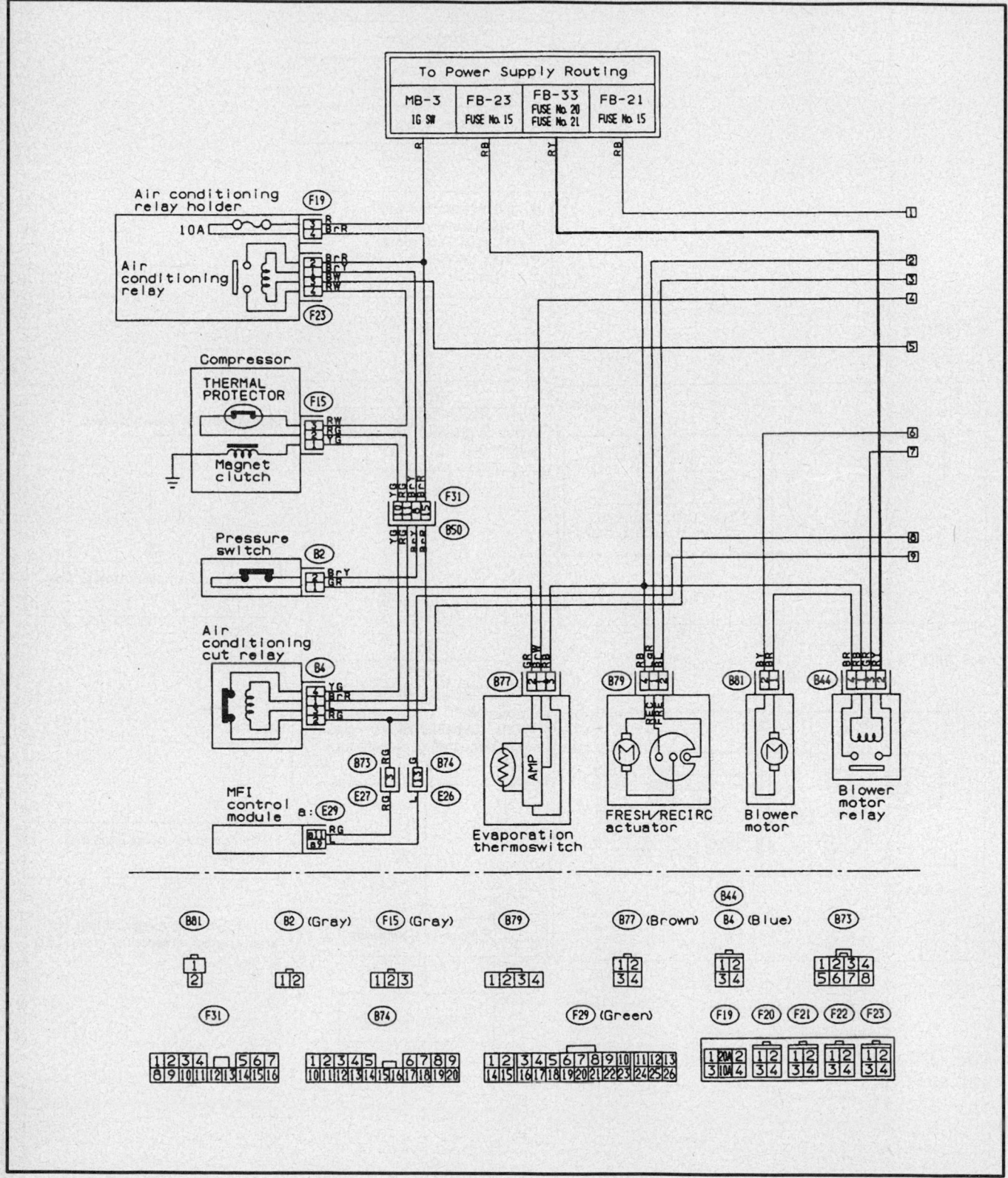

Air conditioning system wiring schematic – Impreza

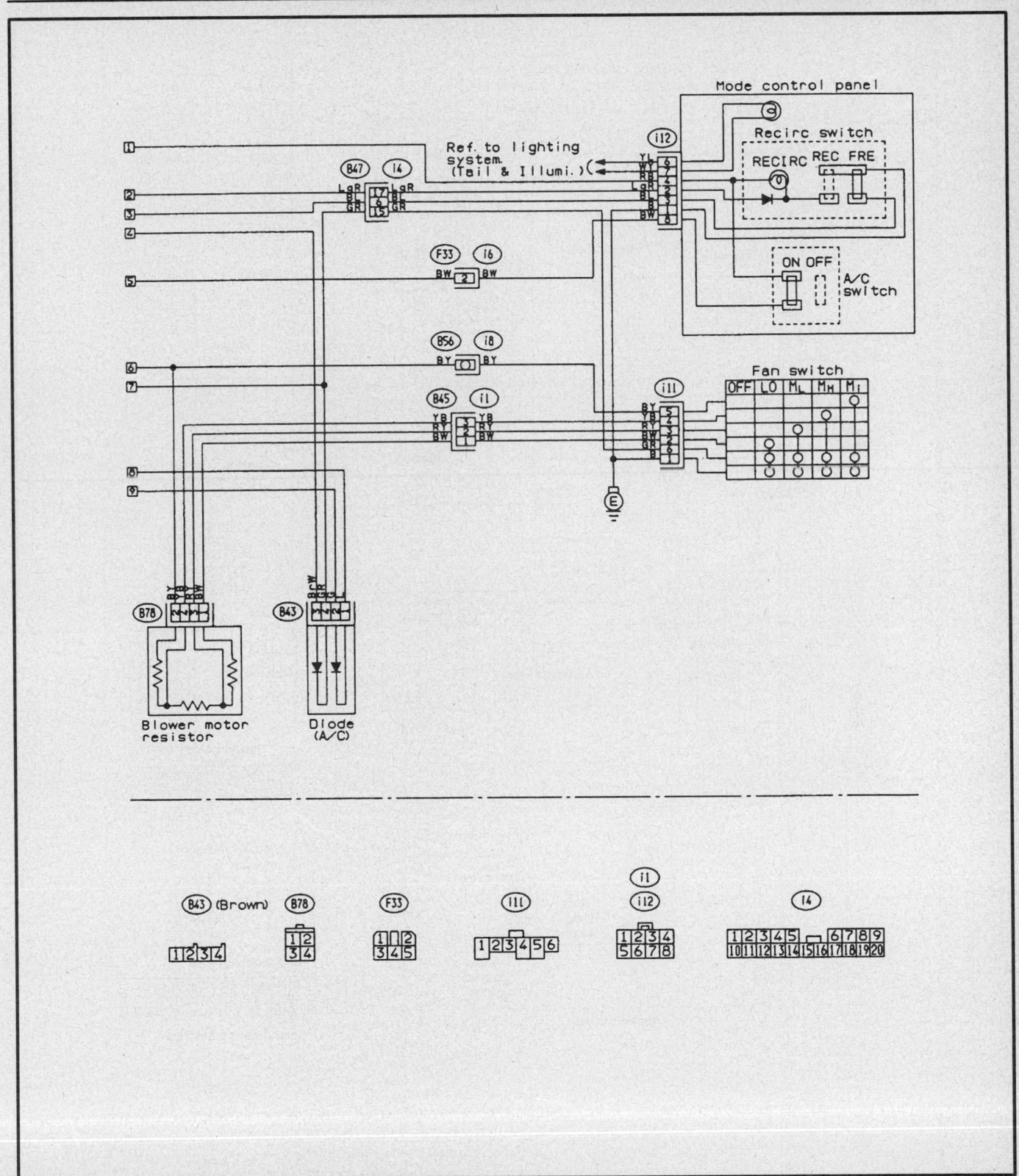

Air conditioning system wiring schematic — Impreza, Cont'd

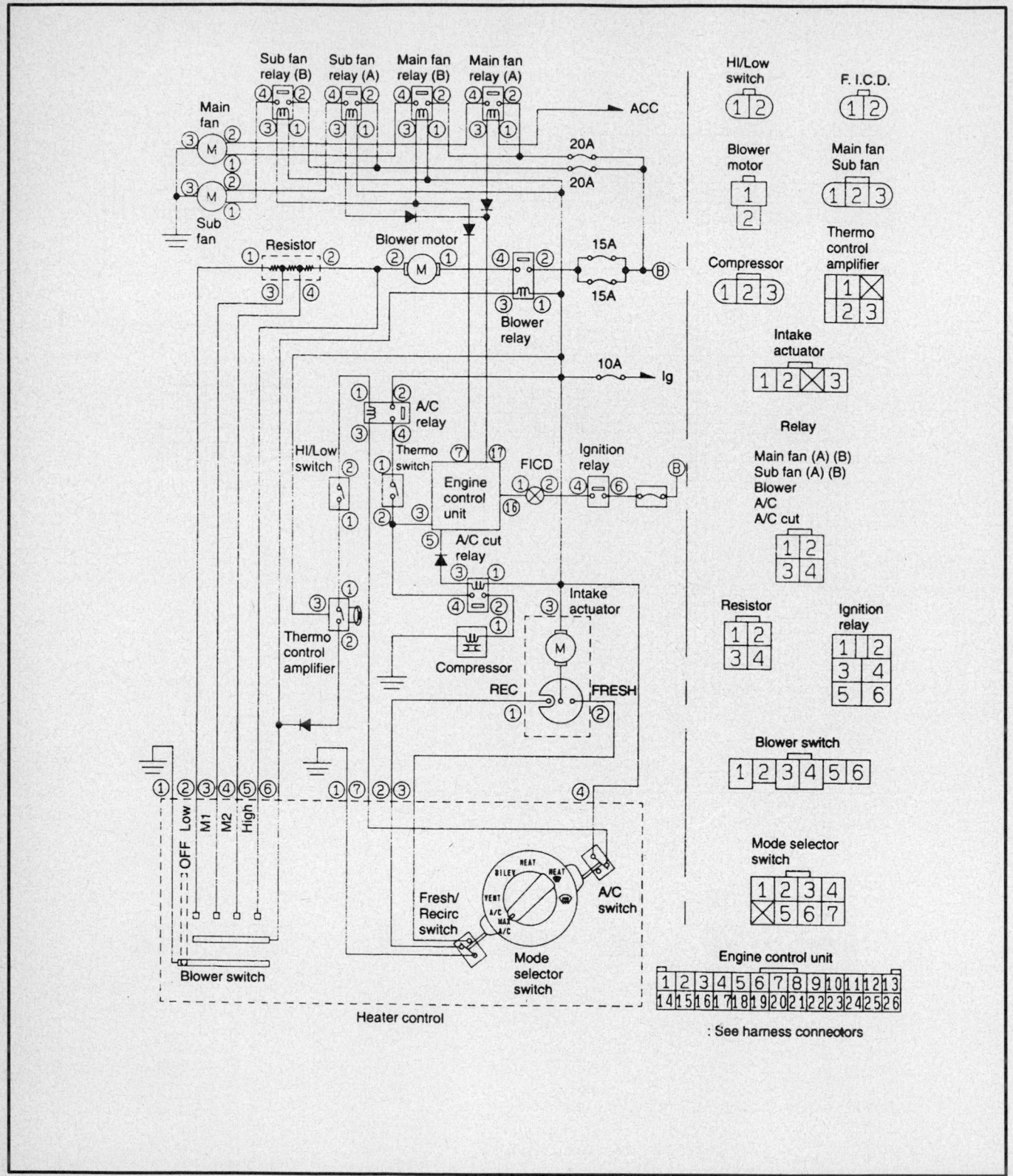

Air conditioning compressor control system – Impreza

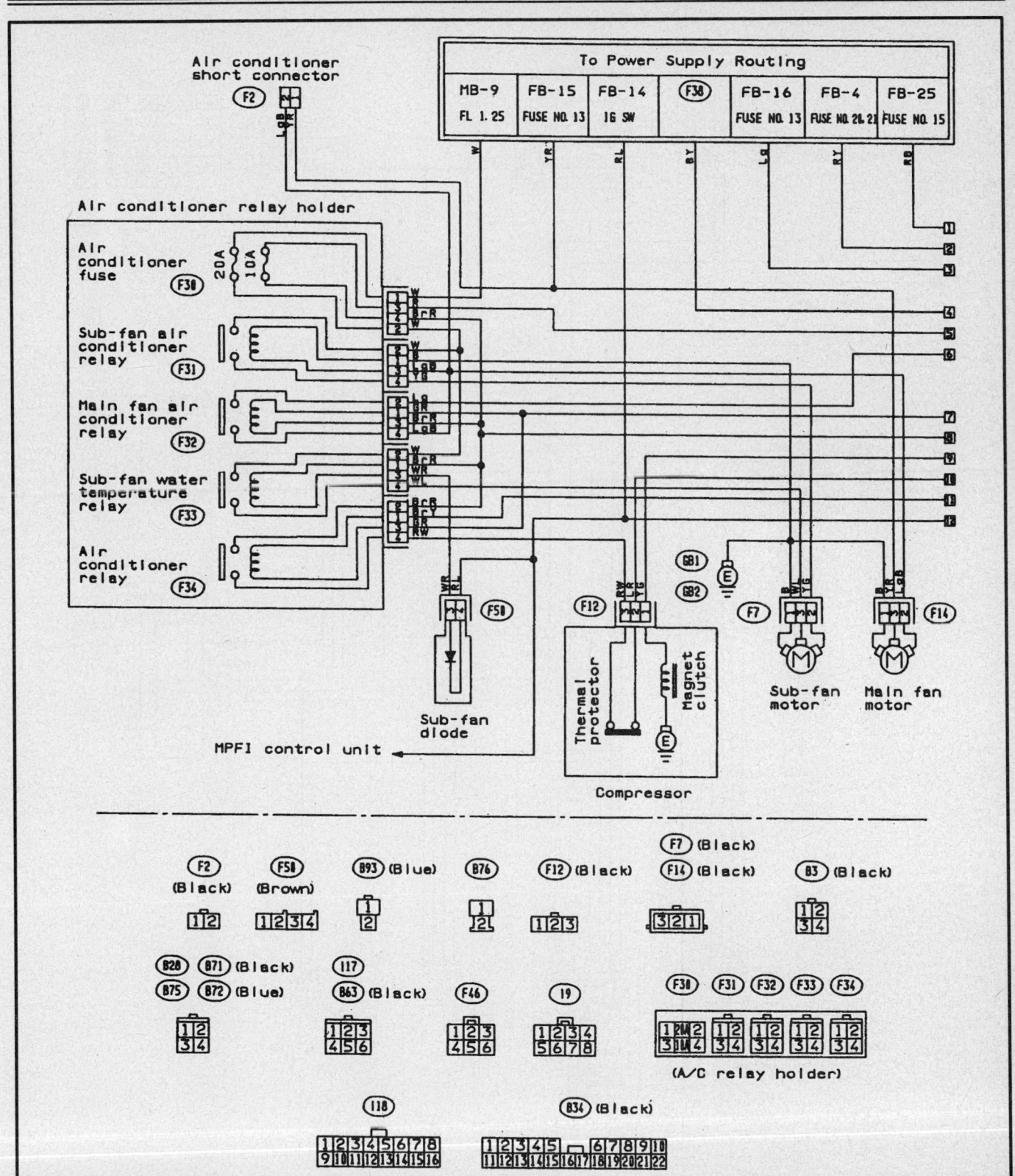

Air conditioning system wiring schematic – 1993 Legacy

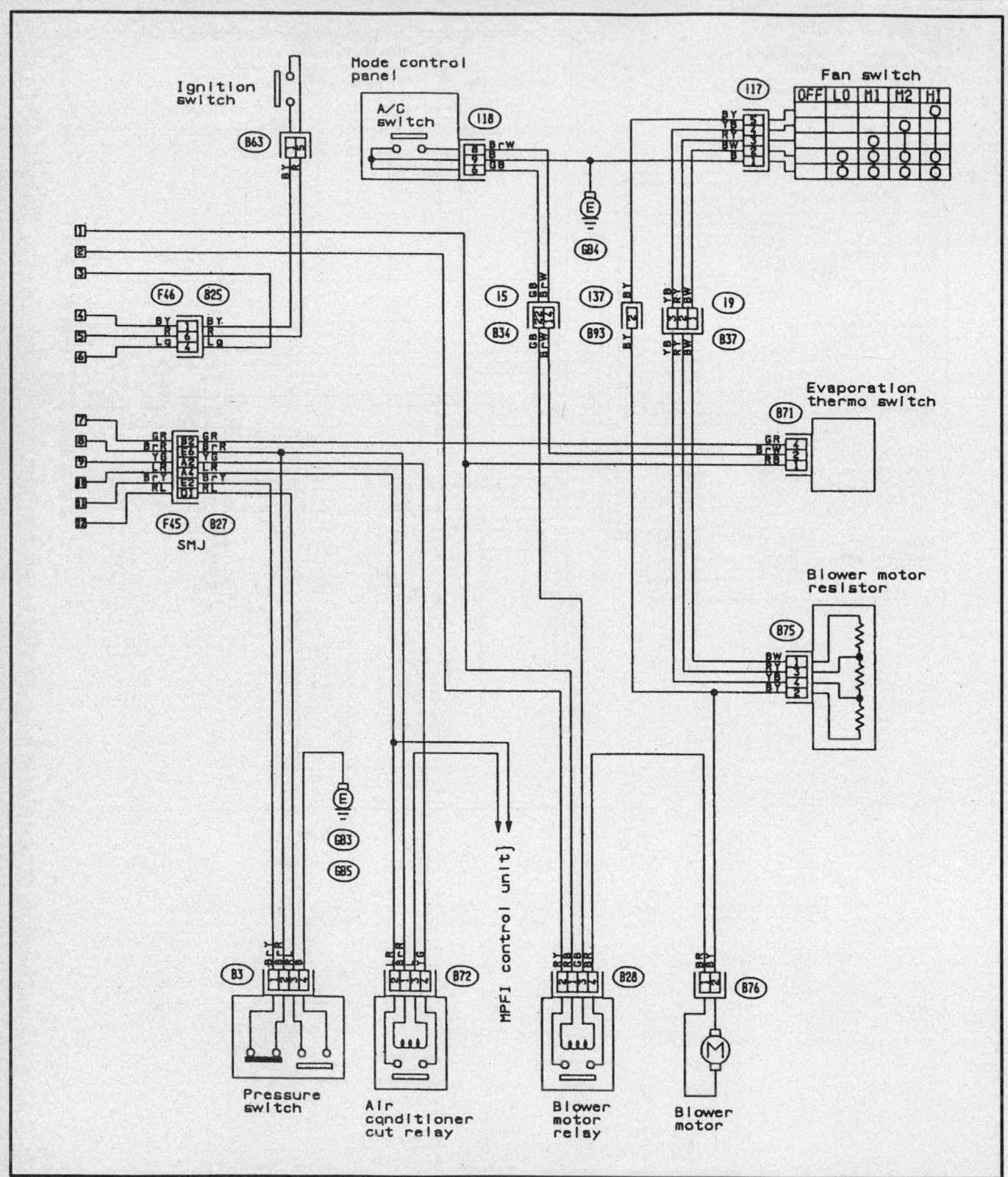

Air conditioning system wiring schematic — 1993 Legacy, Cont'd

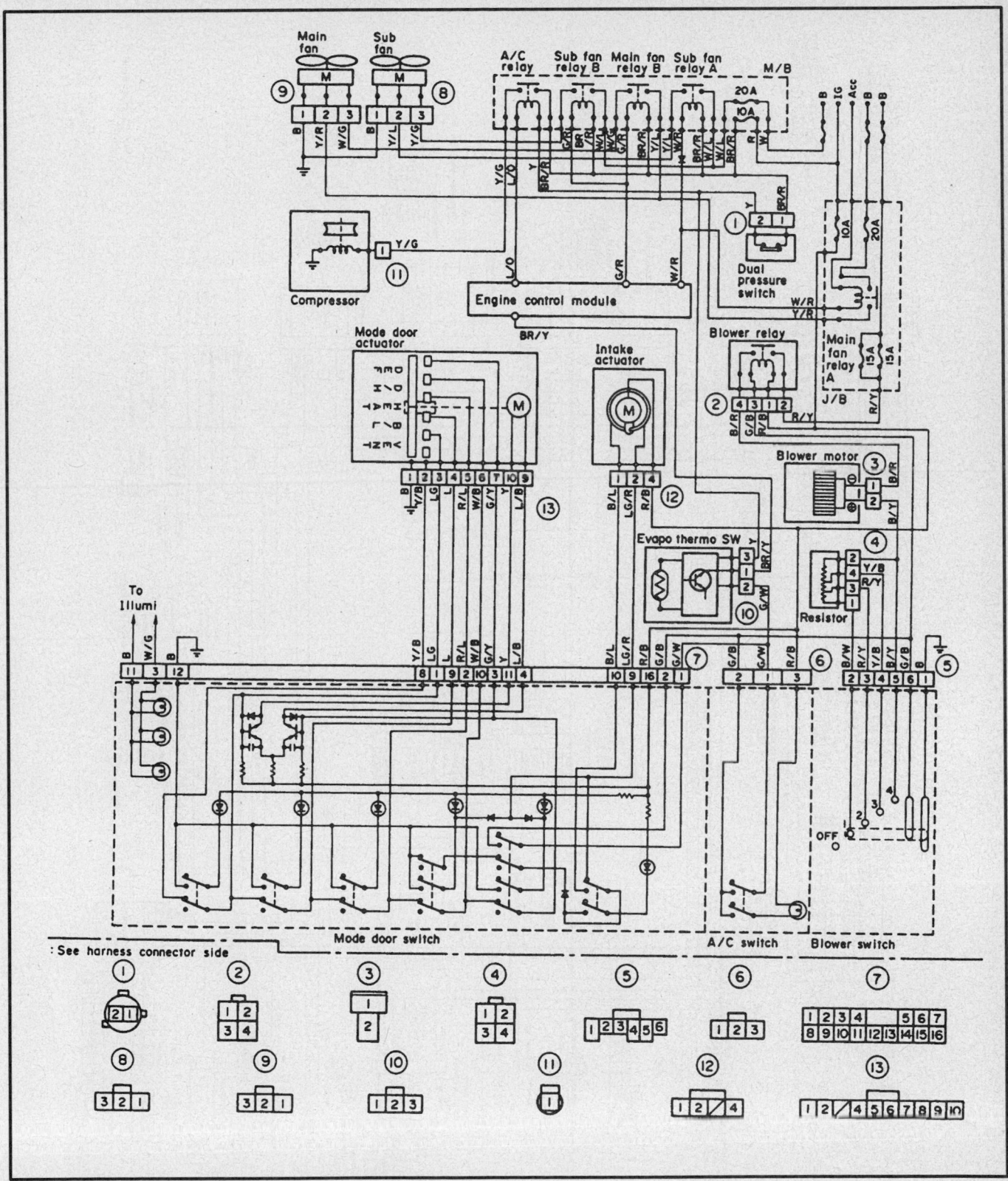

Air conditioning system wiring schematic – 1994-95 Legacy

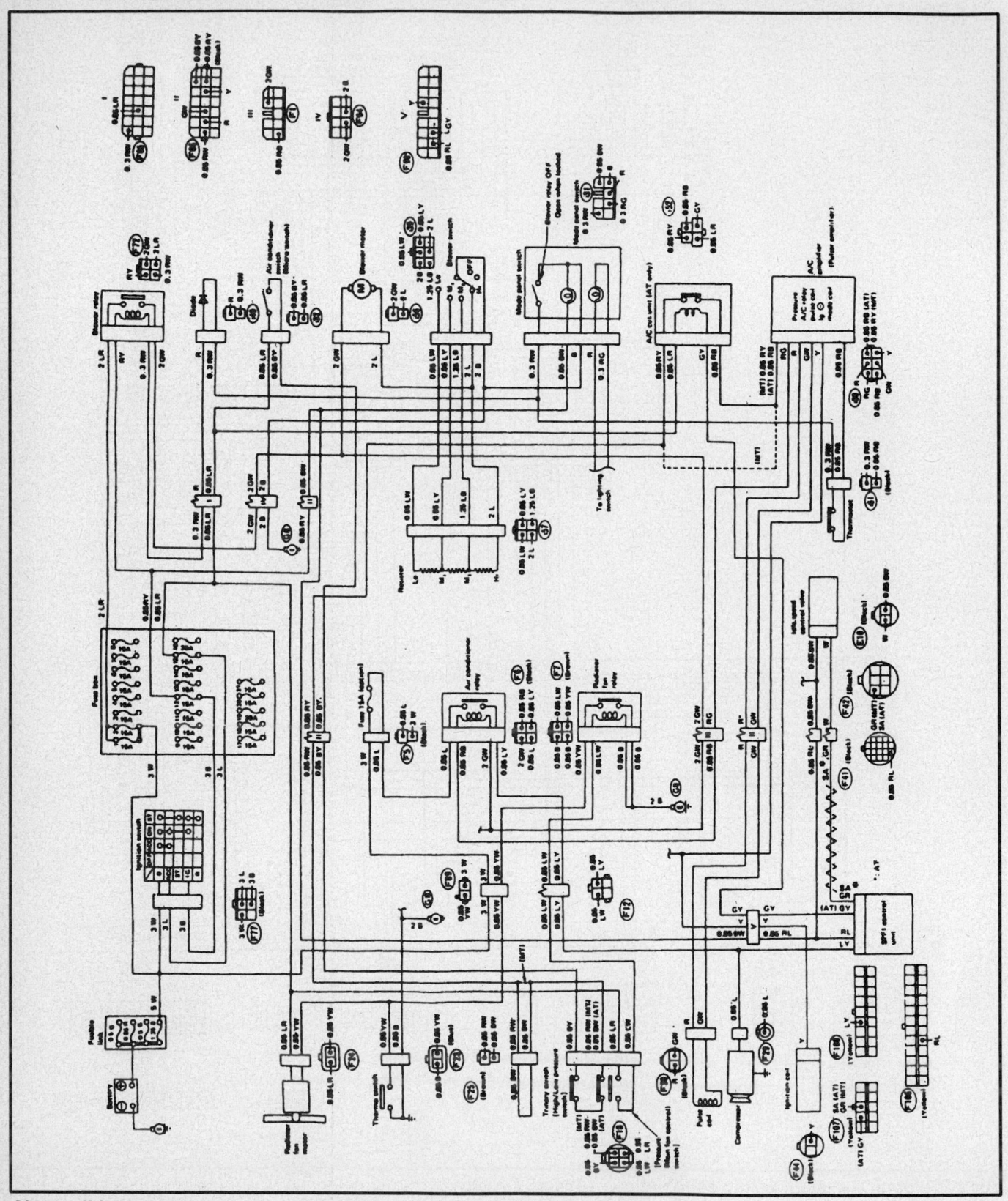

Air conditioning system wiring schematic – Loyale with Hitachi system

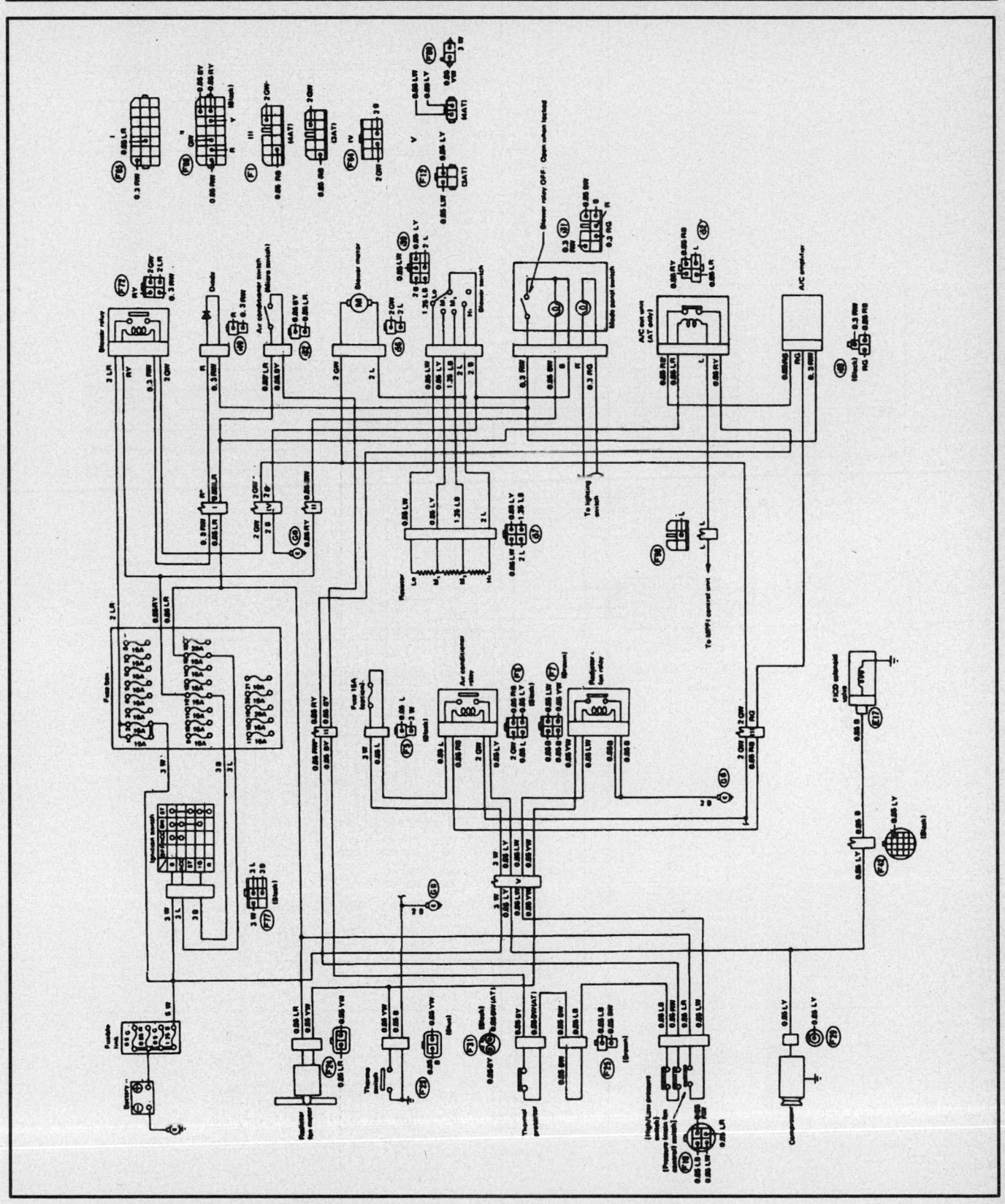

Air conditioning system wiring schematic — Loyale with Panasonic system

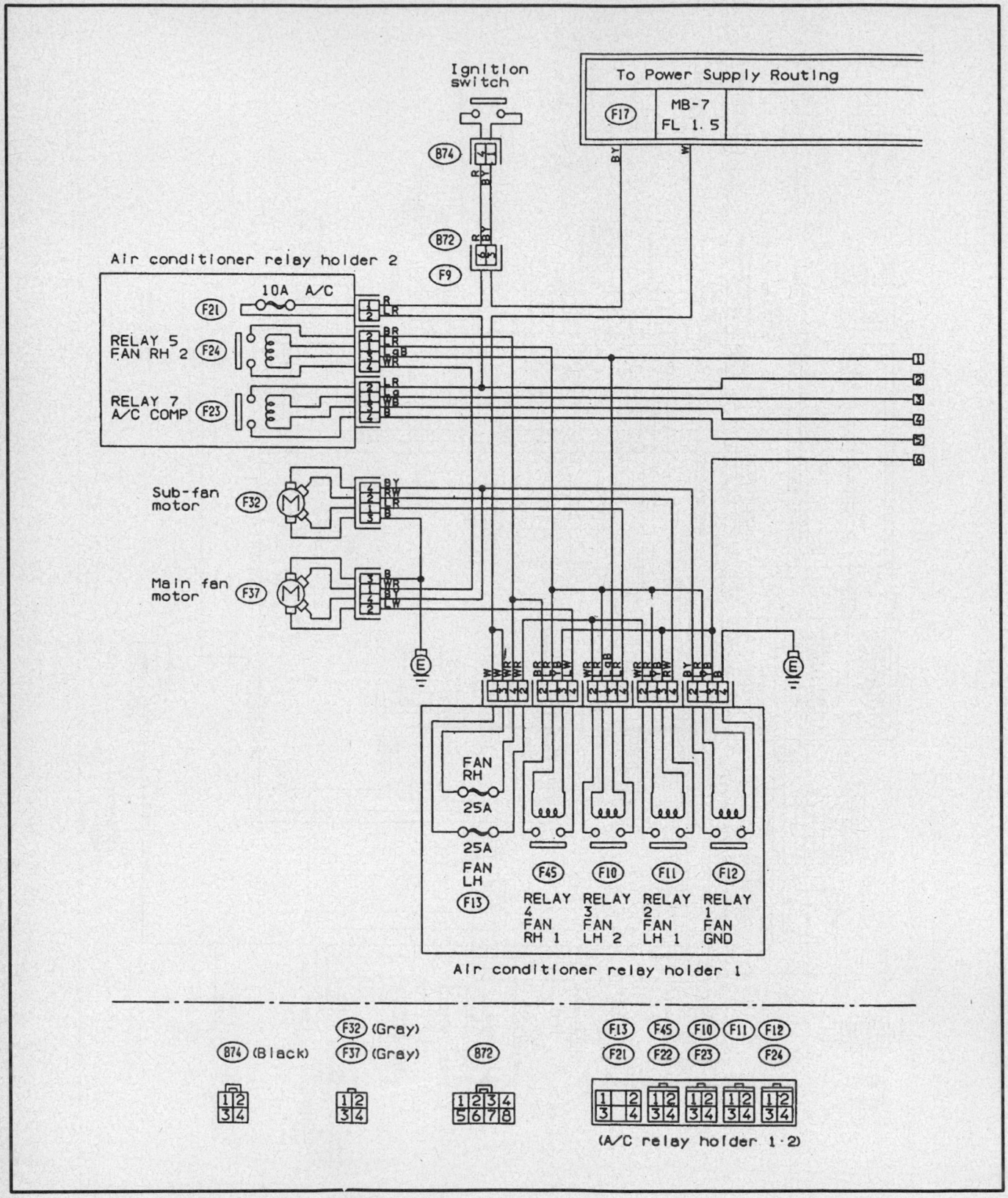

Air conditioning system wiring schematic — SVX

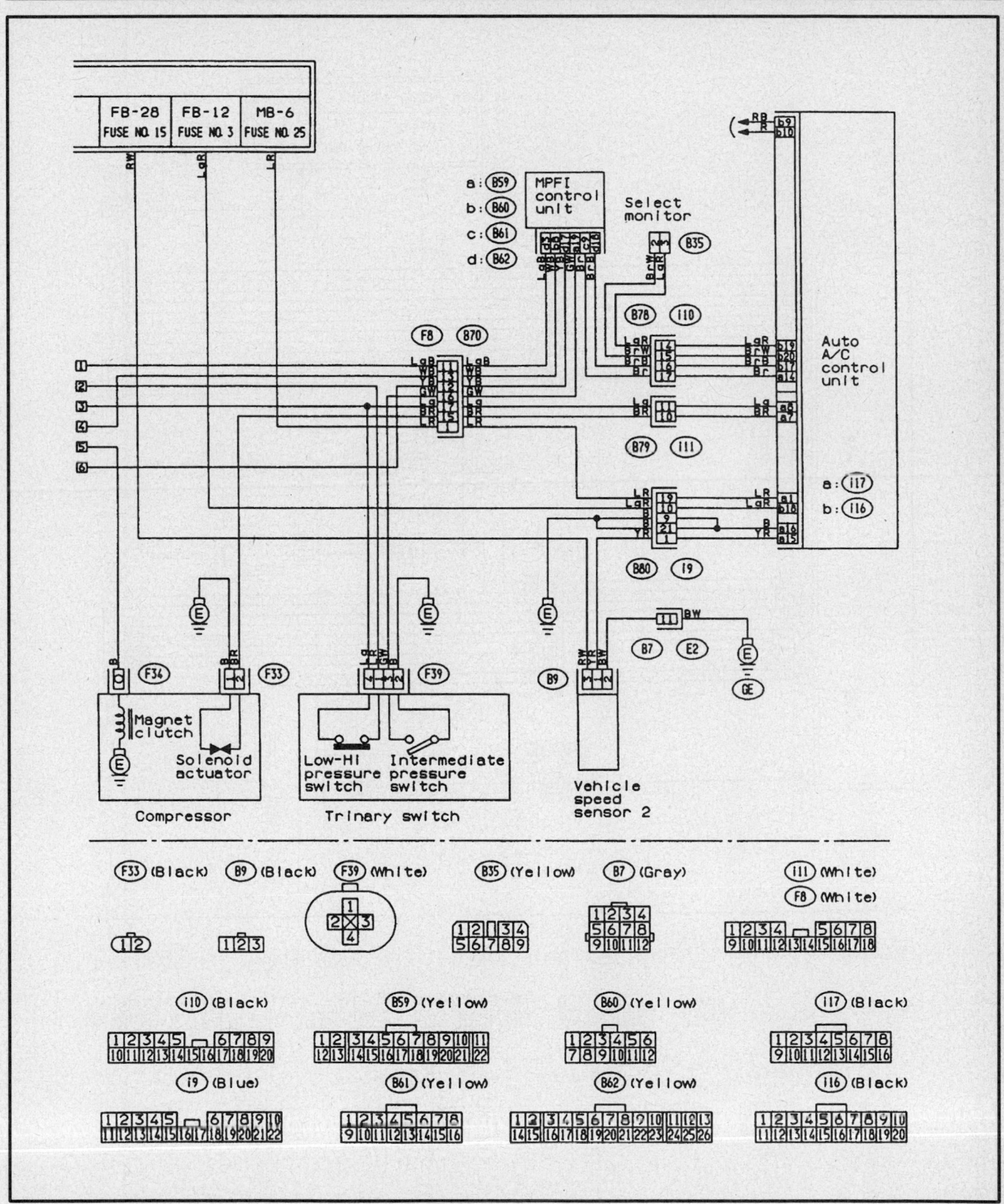

Air conditioning system wiring schematic — SVX, Cont'd

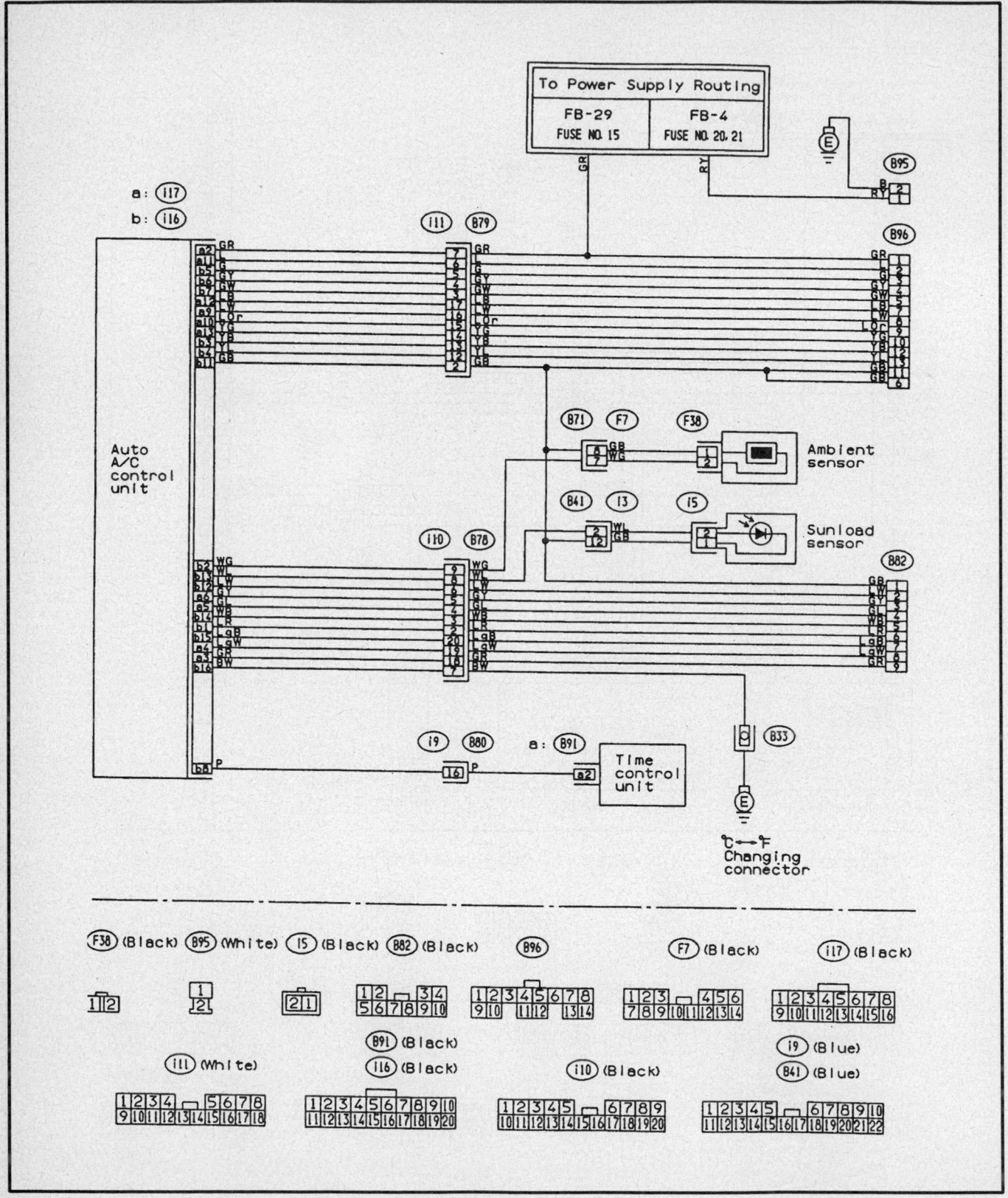

Air conditioning system wiring schematic – SVX, Cont'd

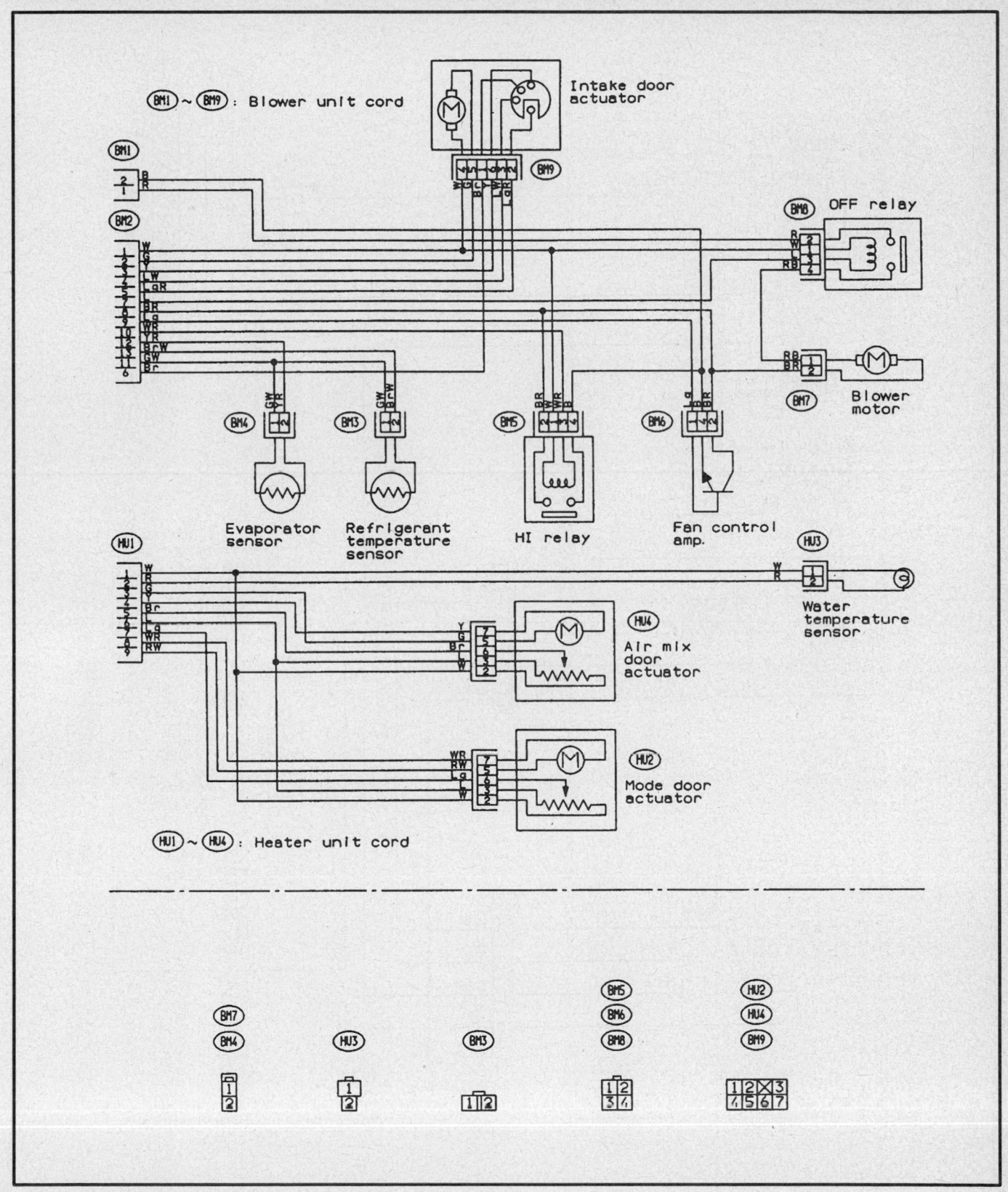

Air conditioning system wiring schematic — SVX, Cont'd

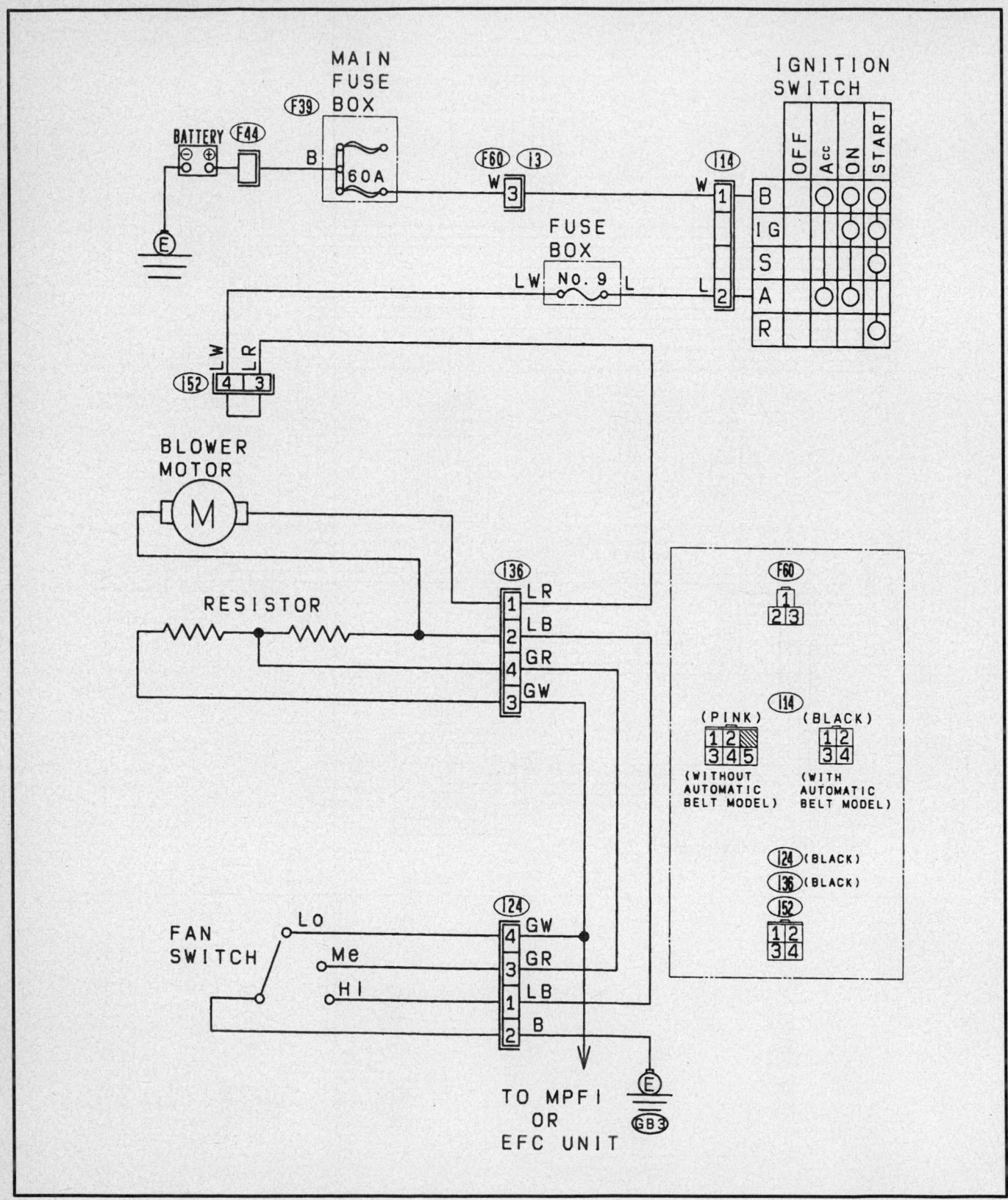

Air conditioning system wiring schematic — Justy

SPECIFICATIONS

ENGINE IDENTIFICATION

Year	Model	Engine Displacement Liters (cc)	Fuel System	No. of Cylinders	Engine Type
1993	Samurai	1.3	TBI	4	SOHC
	Sidekick	1.6	TBI	4	SOHC
	Sidekick	1.6	PFI	4	SOHC
	Swift	1.3	TBI	4	SOHC
	Swift	1.3	PFI	4	SOHC
1994	Samurai	1.3	TBI	4	SOHC
	Sidekick	1.6	TBI	4	SOHC
	Sidekick	1.6	PFI	4	SOHC
	Swift	1.3	TBI	4	SOHC
	Swift	1.3	PFI	4	SOHC

REFRIGERANT CAPACITIES

Year	Model	Refrigerant (oz.)	Oil (fl. oz.)	Compressor Type
1993	Samurai	18	2.0-3.4	Nippondenso
	Sidekick	21.0-23.0	2.0-3.4	Nippondenso
	Sidekick	21.0-23.0	2.0-3.4	Nippondenso
	Swift	18	2.0-3.4	Nippondenso
	Swift	18	2.0-3.4	Nippondenso
1994	Samurai	NA	NA	Nippondenso
	Sidekick	21.2	6.1①	Nippondenso
	Sidekick	21.2	3.7-6.1②	Nippondenso
	Swift	NA	NA	Nippondenso
	Swift	NA	NA	Nippondenso

① R-134a Refrigerant
② R-12 Refrigerant
NA – Not Available

AIR CONDITIONING BELT TENSION

Year	Model	Engine Liters (cc)	Belt Type	Belt Tension Specifications	
				New (lbs.)	Used (lbs.)
1993	Samurai	1.3	NA	0.4-0.47	NA
	Sidekick	1.6	NA	0.24-0.35	NA
	Swift	1.3	NA	0.31-0.41①	NA
	Swift	1.3	NA	0.21-0.27②	NA
1994	Samurai	1.3	NA	0.24-0.35	NA
	Sidekick	1.6	NA	0.24-0.35	NA
	Swift	1.3	NA	0.31-0.39	NA

① With Power Steering
② Without Power Steering
NA – Not Available

SYSTEM DESCRIPTION

General Information

The heater unit is located in the vehicle beneath the instrument panel. The heater system delivers fresh or recirculated air to direct warm air through the vents to either the windshield, floor or the panel outlets. The air conditioning system is designed to be activated in combination with a separate air conditioning switch installed in the control assembly and the fan speed switch. The systems, depending on model application, use a variety of devices such as relays for controlling the heater, blower, and compressor operation, and a dual pressure switch to monitor system operating pressures and stop compressor operation when extremely high or low pressure is sensed. Also used are a thermistor, and a fast idle control device.

SERVICE VALVE LOCATION

Charging valve locations will vary, but most of the time the high or low pressure fitting will be located at the compressor, receiver/drier or along the refrigerant lines. Always discharge, evacuate and recharge at the low side service fitting.

SYSTEM DISCHARGING

R-12 refrigerant is a chloroflourocarbon which, when mishandled, can contribute to the depletion of the ozone layer in the upper atmosphere. Ozone filters out harmful radiation from the sun. In order to protect the ozone layer, an approved R-12 Recovery/Recycling machine that meets SAE standard J1991 should be employed when discharging the system. Follow the operating instructions provided with the approved equipment exactly to properly discharge the system.

Vehicles that use R-134a refrigerant in the air conditioning system have been introduced as an alternative to the ozone depleting R-12 systems. Systems which use the R-134a type of refrigerant will have warning labels affixed to the components in the system.

R-12 and R-134a systems require different types of lubricating oil. Components, refrigerant, oil and charging/evacuation equipment must never be interchanged between system types.

SYSTEM EVACUATING

If the air conditioning system has been opened to the atmosphere, it should be air and moisture free before being recharged with refrigerant. Moisture and air mixed with refrigerant will raise the compressor head pressure, possibly damage the system's components and will reduce the performance of the system. Moisture will boil at normal room temperature when exposed to a vacuum, the moisture then becomes a vapor and will be easily removed by the vacuum pump.

1. Leak test the system and repair any leaks found.
2. Connect an approved charging station, recovery/recycling machine or manifold gauge set and vacuum pump to the discharge and suction ports, following the instructions for the particular units in use.
3. Open the discharge and suction ports and start the vacuum pump. If the pump is not able to pull at least 26 in. Hg vacuum, there is a leak that must be repaired before evacuation can occur.
4. Once the system has reached at least 26 in. Hg vacuum, allow the system to evacuate for at least 10 minutes. The longer the system is evacuated, the more contaminants will be removed.
5. Close all valves and turn the pump off. If the system loses more than 2 in. Hg vacuum after 15 minutes, there is a leak that should be repaired.

SYSTEM CHARGING

1. Connect an approved charging station, recovery/recycling machine or manifold gauge set to the discharge and suction ports. Follow the manufacturer's instructions for the correct hookup and use of the equipment.
2. Charge the system with the specified amount of refrigerant.
3. Perform a leak test.

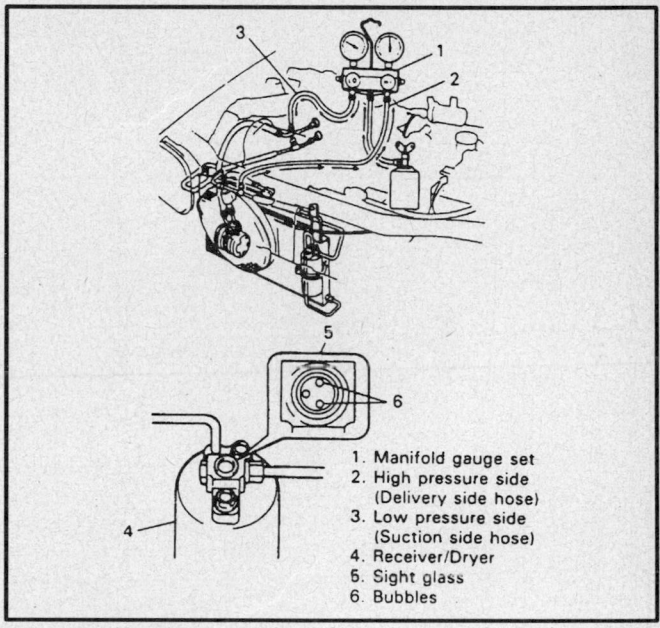

1. Manifold gauge set
2. High pressure side (Delivery side hose)
3. Low pressure side (Suction side hose)
4. Receiver/Dryer
5. Sight glass
6. Bubbles

Manifold Gauge Hookup

OIL LEVEL CHECKING

The total oil capacity is distributed with the refrigerant throughout the air conditioning system. To return the maximum amount of oil to the compressor for checking during Removal and Installation or replacement of the compressor, perform the following procedure, provided that the system has not ruptured and the compressor is functional.

NOTE: If the compressor cannot be run, remove the compressor and drain the oil, adding the amounts as noted below, then reinstall the compressor (same or replacement) and make any other necessary repairs, and perform the following procedure and recheck and adjust oil accordingly.

1. Set the A/C switch to **ON**. Turn the blower motor to the **HIGH** position.
2. Start the engine and run the compressor for more than 20 minutes between 800–1000 rpm.
3. Stop the engine, then perform appropriate repairs. When replacing key system components, additional new refrigerant oil needs to be added to the parts being installed:
   - Condenser—0.7–1.0 oz.
   - Receiver/drier 0.4 oz.
4. If replacing the compressor or if low oil level is suspect, drain the oil from the compressor into a calibrated container. Check the oil for any contamination.

NOTE: The new, replacement compressor is furnished with a full capacity of oil. This oil should be drained and the compressor reinstalled with an equal amount of oil as was drained from the old compressor.

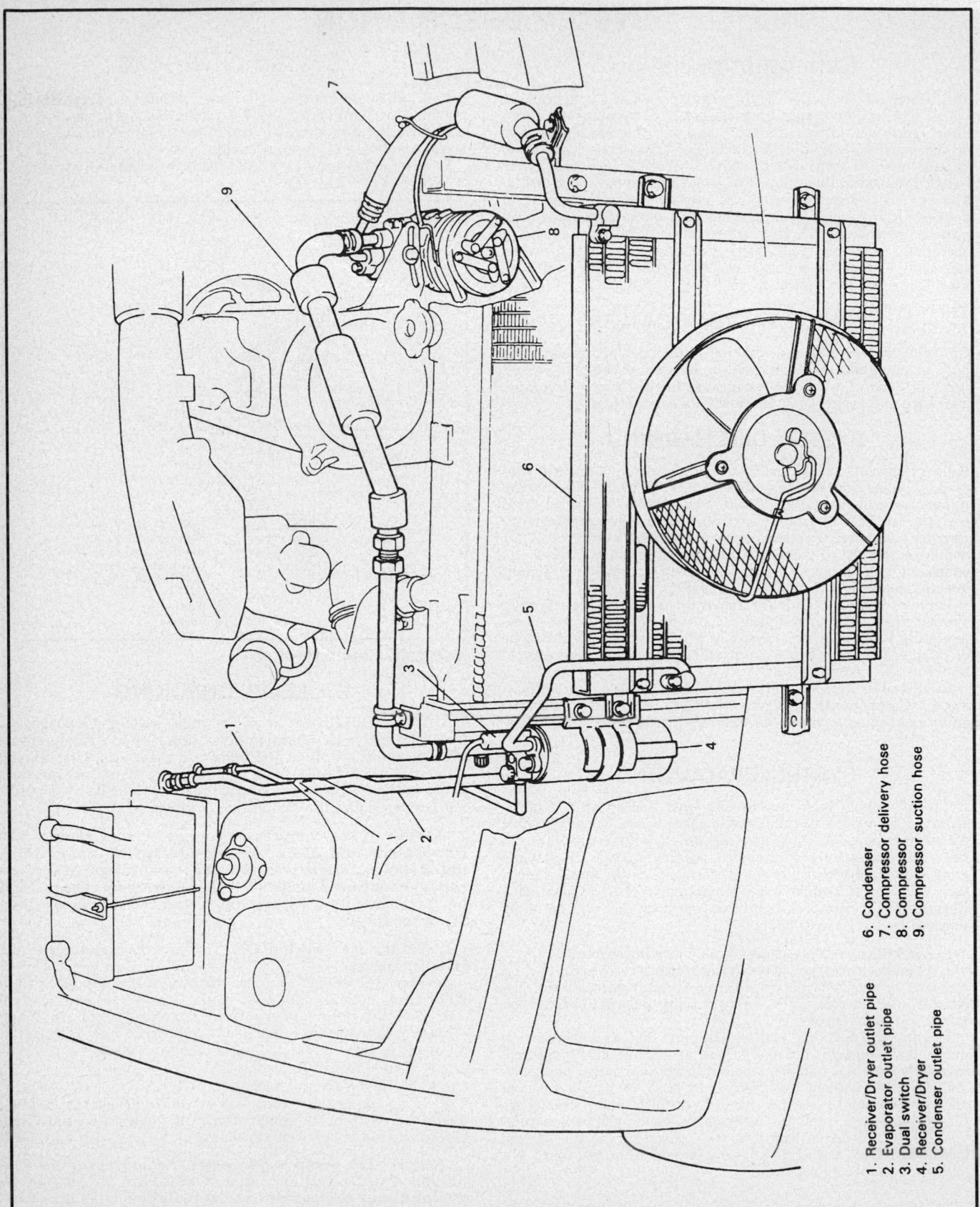

1. Receiver/Dryer outlet pipe
2. Evaporator outlet pipe
3. Dual switch
4. Receiver/Dryer
5. Condenser outlet pipe
6. Condenser
7. Compressor delivery hose
8. Compressor
9. Compressor suction hose

Air Conditioning System Components — Samurai, others similar

SYSTEM COMPONENTS

Radiator

REMOVAL AND INSTALLATION

1. Disconnect the negative battery cable.
2. Drain the cooling system by loosing the drain plug in the radiator
3. Remove the automatic transmission cooling lines from the radiator if the vehicle is so equipped.
4. If necessary, remove the cooling fan/clutch and radiator shroud.
5. Disconnect the reservoir tank hose, along with the upper and lower radiator hoses.
6. Loosen and remove the radiator attaching bolts and remove the radiator.
7. Installation is the reverse of the removal process. Make sure to properly warm up the vehicle and check the coolant level.

Condensor

REMOVAL AND INSTALLATION

1. Properly discharge the air condition system using an approved refrigerant recovery/recycling system.
2. On Samurai and Sidekick, remove the front grille. On Swift, remove the front bumper.
3. Disconnect the refrigerant lines from the condenser fittings and cap to prevent the entry of contamination.
4. On Samurai and Sidekick, it will be necessary to remove the condenser cooling fan assembly.
5. On Swift, disconnect and plug the receiver/drier outlet pipe above the condenser. Remove the condenser, cooling fan and receiver drier as an assembly.
6. The installation procedure is the opposite of the removal process. Make sure to use new O–rings that have been lightly coated with refrigerant oil. When replacing the condenser, be sure to add 0.7 to 1.0 oz. of the correct refrigerant oil to the new condenser.

Compressor

REMOVAL AND INSTALLATION

1. Properly discharge the air conditioner system.
2. Disconnect and cap the refrigerant lines along with the inlet and outlet ports on the compressor.
3. Disconnect the compressor clutch wiring connector.
4. Loosen and remove the compressor drive belt.
5. Loosen and remove the compressor mounting bolts and remove the compressor from the vehicle.
6. Installation is the opposite of the removal process. If installing a new compressor, make sure to measure and install the correct amount of oil into the system. Make sure to use new O–rings that have been lightly coated with refrigerant oil on any connections which were taken apart. Evacuate and recharge the system. Check for leaks.

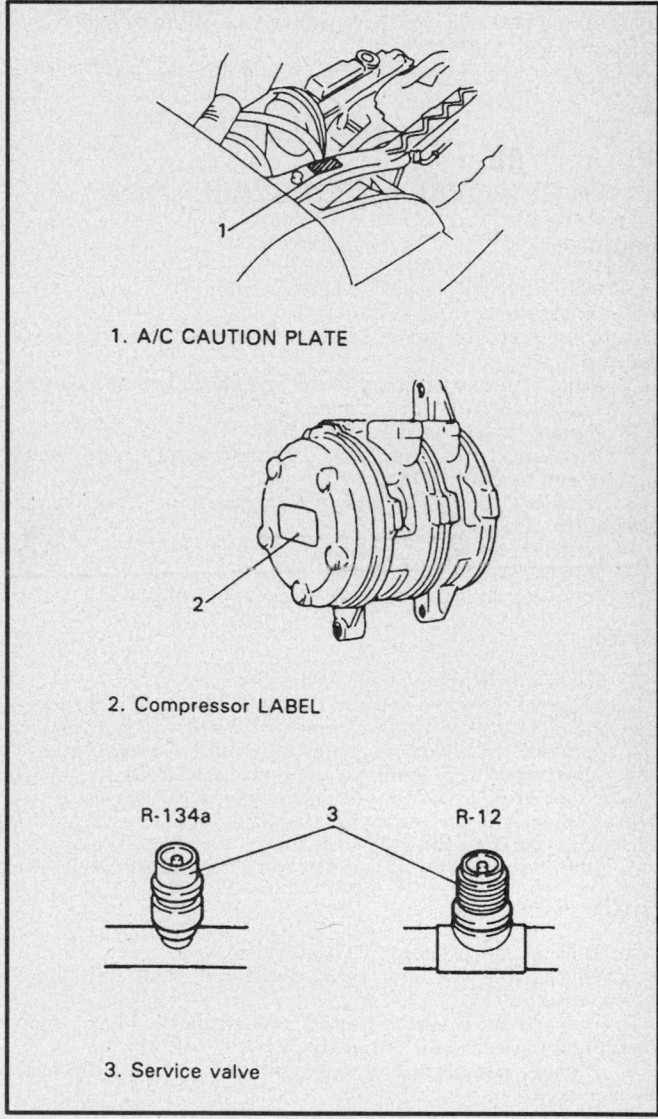

1. A/C CAUTION PLATE

2. Compressor LABEL

R-134a   3   R-12

3. Service valve

Typical Caution Labels and Service Valve Fittings

Receiver/Drier

REMOVAL AND INSTALLATION

1. Properly discharge the air conditioning system.
2. Disconnect the liquid lines from the inlet and outlet fittings.

3. Loosen the receiver/drier from the holder and remove it from the vehicle.

4. Installation is the opposite of the removal process. When installing a new receiver/drier, add 0.4 oz. of the proper type of refrigerant oil to the system.

5. Evacuate and recharge the system and check it for leaks.

Blower Motor

REMOVAL AND INSTALLATION

Samurai

1. Disconnect the negative battery cable.
2. Drain the cooling system.
3. Disconnect the heater inlet and outlet hoses at the heater pipes.
4. Remove the instrument panel and speedometer assembly.
5. Loosen the front door stopper screws.
6. Remove the steering column holder.
7. Disconnect the electrical connectors for the heater blower and blower resistor.
8. Loosen and remove the heater case nut on the engine side of the firewall.
9. Remove the heater assembly.
10. Remove the heater blower.
11. Installation is the reverse of the removal process.

Sidekick

1. Disconnect the negative battery cable.
2. Remove the glove box and the glove box support brackets.
3. Remove the electrical connector from the blower motor.
4. Remove the electrical connector from the blower motor.
5. Disconnect the fresh air control cable from the blower motor case and position it out of the way of the blower motor.
6. Remove the blower motor mounting screws and pull the blower motor from the blower housing.
7. Installation is the reverse of the removal process.

Swift

1. Disconnect the negative battery cable.
2. Disconnect the electrical connector from the blower motor resistor.
3. Remove the fresh air control cable from the blower motor housing and position it out of the way.
4. Remove the glove box upper panel to gain access to the blower motor.
5. Remove the blower motor.
6. Installation is the reverse of the removal process.

Blower Motor Resistor

REMOVAL AND INSTALLATION

1. Disconnect the negative battery cable.
2. Disconnect the electrical connector to the blower motor resistor.
3. Remove the screws which attach the blower motor resistor to the blower motor case and remove the blower motor resistor.
4. Installation is the reverse of the removal process.

Heater Core

REMOVAL AND INSTALLATION

Samurai

1. Disconnect the negative battery cable.
2. Drain the cooling system.
3. Disconnect the heater inlet and outlet hoses at the heater pipes.
4. Remove the instrument panel and speedometer assembly.
5. Loosen the front door stopper screws.
6. Remove the steering column holder.
7. Disconnect the electrical connectors for the heater blower and blower resistor.
8. Loosen and remove the heater case nut on the engine side of the firewall.
9. Remove the heater assembly.
10. Remove the heater blower.
11. Remove the screws and clips which hold the heater housing halves together and separate the cases.
12. Remove the heater core from the heater housing.
13. Installation is the reverse of the removal process.

Sidekick

1. Disconnect the negative battery cable.
2. Drain the cooling system and remove the heater hoses from the inlet and outlet pipes of the heater core.
3. Remove the steering wheel.
4. Remove the instrument panel, speedometer and glove box assemblies to gain access to the heater assembly.
5. Disconnect the electrical connectors and control cables that connect to the heater housing.
6. Remove the heater housing mounting bolts and remove it from the vehicle.
7. Remove the attaching screws and clips which hold the heater housing together and separate the housing to gain access to the heater core.
8. Installation is the opposite of the removal process.

Swift

1. Disconnect the negative battery cable.
2. Drain the cooling system and disconnect the two heater hoses from the heater core inlet and outlet pipes.
3. Remove the console box.
4. Disconnect the electrical wires and control cables from the heater housing.
5. Disconnect the steering joint upper bolt and remove the steering column unit from the vehicle.
6. Remove the speedometer assembly , left and right speaker covers, hood opening cable and center garnish from the dash.
7. Remove the dashboard mounting bolts and the dashboard being careful to protect it from damage.
8. Remove the heater assembly mounting bolts and nuts.
9. Remove the heater assembly from the vehicle.
10. Remove the screws and clips that hold the heater case halves together and split the cases to gain access to the heater core.
11. Installation is the reverse of the removal process.

Evaporator Assembly

REMOVAL AND INSTALLATION

1. Disconnect the negative battery cable.
2. Discharge the air conditioning system using an approved refrigerant recovery/recycling system.
3. Disconnect the fresh air control cable from the blower motor housing.
4. On Swift, disconnect the blower motor and blower motor resistor connectors.
5. On Sidekick and Swift, remove the glove box.
6. Remove the blower motor unit.
7. On Swift, disconnect the air conditioning amplifier and thermistor wires.
8. Disconnect and cap the refrigerant lines that connect to the evaporator and remove the evaporator from the vehicle.
9. Installation is the reverse of the removal process. Always use new O–rings lightly coated with refrigerant oil when reassembling the system.

Expansion Valve

REMOVAL AND INSTALLATION

1. Remove the evaporator unit.
2. Remove the screws that hold the upper and lower evaporator cases together.
3. Locate the expansion valve and loosen the line fittings.
4. Being careful not to tear any foam insulating material, remove the expansion valve from the evaporator core.
5. Installation is the reverse of the removal process. Always use new O–rings lightly coated with refrigerant oil when reassembling the system.

Refrigerant lines

1. Disconnet the negative battery cable.
2. Properly discharge the air conditioning using an approved refrigerant recovery/recycling system.
3. Disconnect the refrigerant lines using two wrenches to prevent damage to the lines and fittings.
4. Remove all attaching brackets and clips along with other parts that are in the way.
5. Remove the refrigerant line.

6. Installation is the reverse of the removal process. Always use new O–rings lightly coated with refrigerant oil when reinstalling parts.
7. Evacuate, recharge and leak test the system.

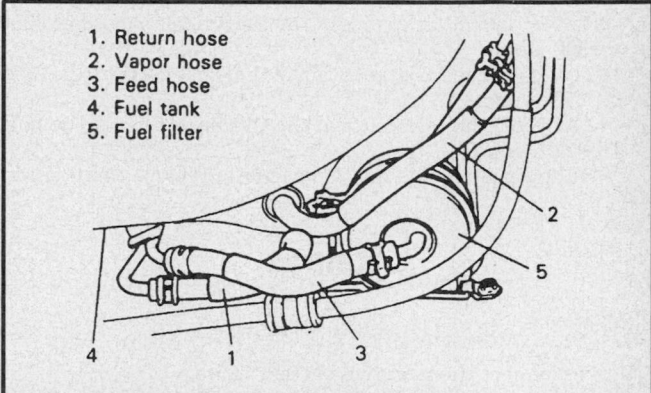

1. Return hose
2. Vapor hose
3. Feed hose
4. Fuel tank
5. Fuel filter

A/C Hose Routing – Suzuki Samurai

Control Cables

ADJUSTMENTS

Mode Control Cable

1. Move the control lever to the ventilation position.
2. Put the outer cable into the control lever cable guide and clamp securely.
3. Push the mode control door lever to the fully open position, which will put the cable in the proper position.

Temperature Control Cable

1. Move the control lever to the maximum cooling position.
2. Push the temperature control door lever to the full counterclockwise position which will adjust the cable to the proper position.

Fresh Air Control Cable

1. Move the control lever to the fresh air position.
2. Push the fresh air control door lever fully clockwise, which will adjust the cable to the proper position.

SENSORS AND SWITCHES

Vacuum Switching Valve

To prevent the engine from stalling or overheating, the Vacuum Switching Valve (VSV) increases engine speed by opening or closing according to a signal sent from the air conditioning amplifier. When the VSV is open, the intake manifold receives air through the VSV and also the idle port and ISC solenoid valve.

TESTING

1. Using an ohmmeter, check for continuity between the terminals on the VSV. The ohmmeter reading should be 24–30 ohms. There should be no continuity between the terminals and the valve body.

2. Connect 12 volts to the VSV terminals. Air should flow freely in one port and out the other. There should be no air flow when the battery is not connected.

Thermistor

The thermistor is installed inside the evaporator case. When the evaporator temperature drops below 32°F, the thermistor will send a signal to the air conditioning amplifier which will cause the compressor to shut off until the temperature increases.

TESTING

1. Disconnect the thermistor electrical connector at the evaporator case and connect an ohmmeter to the thermistor leads. Verify that the resistance is within the specified limits.
- At 32°F, the resistance of the thermistor should be 4200 to 5000 Ohms.
- At 50°F, the resistance of the thermistor should be 2800 to 3200 Ohms.
- At 70°F, the resistance of the thermistor should be 1800 to 2000 Ohms.

2. If the resistance is not as specified, replace the thermistor.

Relays

TESTING

1. Disconnect the negative battery cable.
2. Remove the electrical relay and test for continuity between the voltage coil terminals and no continuity between the contact point terminals.
3. When battery voltage is applied to the voltage coil terminals, there should be continuity between the contact point terminals.
4. If the relay is not functioning correctly, it should be replaced.

Dual Pressure Switch

The dual pressure switch stops the air conditioning compressor operation when the refrigerant pressure falls below or rises above normal operating ranges to prevent damage to the air conditioning system. The switch is installed on the high pressure line near the receiver/drier.

TESTING

1. Connect a manifold gauge set to the air conditioning service ports. Start the engine and turn the air conditioning on. Verify that the system operating pressures are within normal ranges.
2. Disconnect the electrical terminal to the dual pressure switch.
3. Connect an ohmmeter across the terminals of the dual pressure switch.
4. If the air conditioning system pressure should fall below approximately 30 psi or rise above approximately 383 psi, there should be no continuity. Within the low and high pressures, there should be continuity. If the switch does not function within these parameters, replace it.

Removal and Installation

1. Properly discharge the air conditioning system using an approved refrigerant recovery/recycling unit following the manufacturer's instructions.
2. Disconnect the electrical connector at the dual pressure switch and remove the dual pressure switch.
3. Installation is the reverse of the removal process. Make sure to use new O-rings lightly coated with refrigerant oil when reinstalling parts. Evacuate, recharge and leak test the system.

Relays

TESTING

Fan and Air Conditioning Switch

TESTING

Check for continuity between the fan switch terminals as indicated.

Samurai
- At position **I**, there should be continuity between the Light Green and Blue/White wires.
- At position **II**, there should be continuity between the Light Green, Blue/White and Blue Yellow wires.
- At position **III**, there should be continuity between the Light Green, Blue/White and Blue wires.

Sidekick and Swift
- At position **I**, there should be continuity between the Light Green and Pink/Black wires.
- At position **II**, there should be continuity between the Light Green, Pink/Black and Pink/Blue wires.
- At position **III**, there should be continuity between the Light Green, Pink/Black and Pink/Green wires.
- At position **IV**, there should be continuity between the Light Green, Pink/Black and Pink wires.

Blower Resistor

TESTING

Samurai

The blower motor resistor is located on the left side of the heater case. Disconnect the electrical connector at the resistor and use an ohmmeter to check the continuity between the Blue/White and Blue wire terminals. If there is no continuity between the wires, replace the resistor.

Sidekick and Swift

The blower motor resistor is located in the lower front housing of the blower housing case. Remove the electrical harness plug and measure the resistance between the terminals as indicated. The terminal identification numbers are molded into the resistor block. If resistance is not as specified, replace the resistor.

Sidekick
- Between terminals **H** and **LO**, the resistance should be **1.8** ohms.
- Between terminals **H** and **M1**, the resistance should be **1.0** ohms.
- Between terminals **H** and **M2**, the resistance should be **0.5** ohms.

Swift
- Between terminals **H** and **LO**, there should be continuity.
- Between terminals **H** and **M1**, there should be continuity.
- Between terminals **H** and **M2**, there should be continuity.

SPECIFICATIONS

ENGINE IDENTIFICATION

Year	Model	Engine Displacement Liters (cc)	Engine Series ID	Fuel System	No. of Cylinders	Engine Type
1993	Camry	2.2 (2164)	5S-FE	EFI	4	DOHC
	Camry	3.0 (2952)	3VZ-FE	EFI	6	DOHC
	Celica	1.6 (1587)	4A-FE	EFI	4	DOHC
	Celica	2.0 (1998)	3S-GTE	EFI	4	DOHC, Turbo
	Celica	2.2 (2164)	5S-FE	EFI	4	DOHC
	Corolla	1.6 (1587)	4A-FE	EFI	4	DOHC
	Corolla	1.8 (1762)	7A-FE	EFI	4	DOHC
	MR2	2.0 (1998)	3S-GTE	EFI	4	DOHC, Turbo
	MR2	2.2 (2164)	5S-FE	EFI	4	DOHC
	Paseo	1.5 (1495)	5E-FE	EFI	4	DOHC
	Tercel	1.5 (1457)	3E-E	EFI	4	SOHC
1994	Camry	2.2 (2164)	5S-FE	EFI	4	DOHC
	Camry	3.0 (2952)	1MZ-FE	EFI	6	DOHC
	Celica	1.8 (1762)	7A-FE	EFI	4	DOHC
	Celica	2.2 (2164)	5S-FE	EFI	4	DOHC
	Corolla	1.6 (1587)	4A-FE	EFI	4	DOHC
	Corolla	1.8 (1762)	7A-FE	EFI	4	DOHC
	MR2	2.0 (1998)	3S-GTE	EFI	4	DOHC, Turbo
	MR2	2.2 (2164)	5S-FE	EFI	4	DOHC
	Paseo	1.5 (1495)	5E-FE	EFI	4	DOHC
	Supra	3.0 (2592)	2JZ-GE	EFI	6	DOHC
	Supra	3.0 (2592)	2JZ-GTE	EFI	6	DOHC, Turbo
	Tercel	1.5 (1457)	3E-E	EFI	4	SOHC
1995	Avalon	3.0 (2995)	1MZ-FE	EFI	6	DOHC
	Camry	2.2 (2164)	5S-FE	EFI	4	DOHC
	Camry	3.0 (2952)	1MZ-FE	EFI	6	DOHC
	Celica	1.8 (1762)	7A-FE	EFI	4	DOHC
	Celica	2.2 (2164)	5S-FE	EFI	4	DOHC
	Corolla	1.6 (1587)	4A-FE	EFI	4	DOHC
	Corolla	1.8 (1762)	7A-FE	EFI	4	DOHC
	MR2	2.0 (1998)	3S-GTE	EFI	4	DOHC, Turbo
	MR2	2.2 (2164)	5S-FE	EFI	4	DOHC
	Paseo	1.5 (1495)	5E-FE	EFI	4	DOHC
	Supra	3.0 (2592)	2JZ-GE	EFI	6	DOHC
	Supra	3.0 (2592)	2JZ-GTE	EFI	6	DOHC, Turbo
	Tercel	1.5 (1457)	3E-E	EFI	4	SOHC

DOHC–Dual Overhead Cam
SOHC–Single Overhead Cam
EFI–Electronic Fuel Injection

REFRIGERANT CAPACITIES

Year	Model	Refrigerant (oz.)	Oil (fl. oz.)	Compressor Type
1993	Camry	32-35	①	Nippondenso
	Celica	24-27	①	Nippondenso
	Corolla	24-28	①②	③
	Cressida	27-28	①	Nippondenso
	MR2	28-30	①	Nippondenso
	Paseo	25-28	①	Nippondenso
	Supra	22-27	①	Nippondenso
	Tercel	25-28	①	Nippondenso
1994	Camry	28-32	①	Nippondenso
	Celica	21-25	①	Nippondenso
	Corolla	25-28	①②	Nippondenso
	MR2	25-26	①	Nippondenso
	Paseo	23-26	①	Nippondenso
	Supra	23-27	①	Nippondenso
	Tercel	23-26	①	Nippondenso
1995	Avalon	28-32	①	Nippondenso
	Camry	28-32	①	Nippondenso
	Celica	21-25	①	Nippondenso
	Corolla	23-26	①②	Nippondenso
	MR2	25-26	①	Nippondenso
	Paseo	23-26	①	Nippondenso
	Supra	23-26	①	Nippondenso
	Tercel	21-25	①	Nippondenso

① Drain and measure amount recovered; replace same amount.
② Manufacturer recommends different oils per engine: Densooil 7, 4A-GE; Densooil 6, 4A-FE. Use recommended oils or equivalent per application.
③ Nippondenso (4A-FE) or Rotary (4A-GE).

AIR CONDITIONING BELT TENSION

Year	Model	Engine Liters (cc)	Belt Type	Specifications	
				New ①	Used ②
1993	Camry	2.2 (2164)	Poly-V	140-190	100-120
	Camry	3.0 (2692)	Poly-V	140-190	65-110
	Celica	1.6 (1587)	Poly-V	135-185	80-120
	Celica	2.0 (1998)	Poly-V	155-175	70-100
	Celica	2.2 (2164)	Poly-V	155-175	70-100
	Corolla	1.6 (1587)	Poly-V②	140-180	80-100
	Corolla	1.8 (1762)	Poly-V③	140-180	80-100
	MR2	2.0 (1998)	Poly-V	135-185	80-100
	MR2	2.2 (2164)	Poly-V	135-185	80-100
	Paseo	1.5 (1495)	Poly-V	135-185	80-100
	Tercel	1.5 (1497)	Poly-V	135-185	80-100

AIR CONDITIONING BELT TENSION

Year	Model	Engine Liters (cc)	Belt Type	Specifications New ①	Used ②
1994	Camry	2.2 (2164)	Poly-V	139-191	99-121
	Camry	3.0 (2952)	Poly-V	139-191	66-110
	Celica	1.8 (1762)	Poly-V	155-175	100-120
	Celica	2.2 (2164)	Poly-V	120-140	60-80
	Corolla	1.6 (1587)	Poly-V②	140-180	80-120
	Corolla	1.8 (1762)	Poly-V③	140-180	80-120
	MR2	2.0 (1998)	Poly-V	135-185	75-125
	MR2	2.2 (2164)	Poly-V	135-185	75-125
	Paseo	1.5 (1495)	Poly-V	135-185	80-120
	Supra	3.0 (2952)	Poly-V	* Auto Tensioner	* Auto Tensioner
	Tercel	1.5 (1457)	Poly-V	135-185	80-120
1995	Avalon	3.0 (2952)	Poly-V	143-187	66-110
	Camry	2.2 (2164)	Poly-V	139-191	99-121
	Camry	3.0 (2952)	Poly-V	139-191	66-110
	Celica	1.8 (1762)	Poly-V	170-180	95-135
	Celica	2.2 (2164)	Poly-V	135-185	80-120
	Corolla	1.6 (1587)	Poly-V②	135-185	80-120
	Corolla	1.8 (1762)	Poly-V③	135-185	80-120
	MR2	2.0 (1998)	Poly-V	135-185	80-120
	MR2	2.2 (2164)	Poly-V	135-185	80-120
	Paseo	1.5 (1495)	Poly-V	135-185	80-120
	Supra	3.0 (2952)	Poly-V	* Auto Tensioner	* Auto Tensioner
	Tercel	1.5 (1457)	Poly-V	135-185	80-120

① Measurement is pounds of tension, using appropriate tensioner gauge.
② Measured between compressor and crank pulley.
③ Measured between compressor and idler pulley.

SYSTEM DESCRIPTION

General Information

The blend-air type heater system is used on all models. The blend-air method on vehicles without air conditioning uses a controlled flow system with the engine coolant flow controlled through the heater core, with the use of a heater coolant shut-off valve. The temperature of the heated air entering the passenger compartment is controlled by regulating the quantity of air which flows through the heater core air passages or fins. This heated air then blends with a controlled amount of cool fresh air which by-passes the heater core. The air flow for the heating system is through the cowl air intake and into the heating system. Defroster operation is controlled by the air control lever and cable or vacuum servo motor, moving the defroster damper to direct heated air to the defroster outlets.

The air conditioning system is designed to cycle a compressor on and off to maintain the desired cooling within the passenger compartment. Passenger compartment comfort is maintained by the temperature lever located on the control head.

The system is also designed to prevent the evaporator from freezing.

When an air conditioning mode is selected, electrical current is sent to the compressor clutch coil. On most models, the compressor is equipped with a cut-off solenoid which will shut the compressor off momentarily under certain conditions. These include wide-open throttle and low idle speeds. The switches on the control head are used to control the operation of the air conditioning system.

Avalon, Camry, Celica and Supra may also be equipped with automatic air conditioning systems. A series of temperature sensors provide signals through the A/C amplifier which in turn controls the electronic door actuators to position temperature, mode and blower speeds to achieve and maintain operator set temperature.

Service Valve Location

There are 2 service access gauge port valves on the system. The high pressure discharge port is located in the discharge line. This port may require the use of a high pressure gauge adapter. The other service port (low pressure side) is located on the low pressure side of the system or on the compressor.

On most vehicles, the letter **D** (discharge side) marked near the compressor service valve side indicates the high pressure side. The letter **S** (suction side) indicates the low pressure side.

NOTE: To prevent release of refrigerant always use stop valves when installing the manifold gauge set to the service valves.

System Discharging

R-12 refrigerant is a chlorofluorocarbon which, when mishandled, can contribute to the depletion of the ozone layer in the upper atmosphere. Ozone filters out harmful radiation from the sun. In order to protect the ozone layer, an approved R-12 recovery/recycling machine that meets SAE standard J1991 should be employed when discharging the system. Follow the operating instructions provided with the approved equipment exactly to properly discharge the system.

All 1994-95 air conditioner systems use R-134a refrigerant and polyalkyleneglycol refrigerant oil, which are not compatible with R-12 refrigerant and mineral oil. Do not attempt to use R-12 servicing equipment or tools on an R-134a system as damage will result.

System Evacuating

If the air conditioning system has been opened to the atmosphere, it should be air and moisture free before being recharged with refrigerant. Moisture and air mixed with refrigerant will raise the compressor head pressure, possibly damage the system's components and will reduce the performance of the system. To evacuate the system, perform the following procedure:

1. Leak test the system and repair any leaks found.
2. Connect an approved charging station, recovery/recycling machine or manifold gauge set and vacuum pump to the discharge and suction ports. The red hose is normally connected to the discharge (high pressure) line and the blue hose is connected to the suction (low pressure) line.

3. Open the discharge and suction ports and start the vacuum pump. If the pump is not able to pull at least 26 in. Hg of vacuum, there is a leak that must be repaired before evacuation can occur.

4. Once the system has reached at least 26 in. Hg of vacuum, allow the system to evacuate for at least 30 minutes. The longer the system is evacuated, the more contaminants will be removed.

5. Close all valves and turn the pump off. If the system loses more than 2 in. Hg of vacuum after 15 minutes, there is a leak that should be repaired.

System Charging

1. Connect an approved charging station, recovery/recycling machine, to the discharge and suction ports. The red hose is normally connected to the discharge (high pressure) line and the blue hose is connected to the suction (low pressure) line.
2. Follow the instructions provided with the equipment and charge the system with the specified amount of refrigerant.
3. Perform a leak test.

ADDING REFRIGERANT OIL

It is imperative that the specified type and quantity of refrigerant oil be maintained in a refrigerant system for proper operation. A surplus of oil, the wrong oil viscosity or insufficient oil will cause refrigerant system problems. Insufficient oil or the wrong oil results in poor lubrication and possible compressor damage. A surplus of oil allows too much oil to circulate with the refrigerant, causing the cooling capacity of the system to be reduced.

When it is necessary to replace a component in the refrigerant system, certain procedures must be followed to assure that the total oil charge on the system is correct after the new part is installed. During normal air conditioning operation some refrigerant oil is circulated through the system with the refrigerant and some is retained in the compressor. If certain components of the system are removed for replacement some of the refrigerant oil will go with the component. To maintain the original total oil charge, it is necessary to compensate for the oil loss by adding oil to the system with the replacement part.

SYSTEM COMPONENTS

Radiator

REMOVAL AND INSTALLATION

Avalon, Camry with 1MZ-FE engine

——————— CAUTION ———————

If vehicle is equipped with an air bag system, when ignition is turned to LOCK and negative battery cable is disconnected, do not work inside the passenger compartment for at least 30 seconds to give the SRS (air bag supplemental restraint system) a chance to become fully disarmed.

1. Disconnect the negative battery cable. Drain engine coolant.
2. On Canadian model, disconnect relay block from battery hold-down clamp.

3. Remove battery and tray and disconnect the cruise control actuator.
4. Disconnect radiator hoses and automatic transmission oil cooler hoses.
5. Disconnect the cruise control actuator wire from the No. 1 cooling fan shroud.
6. Remove the two upper supports and lift out the radiator and cooling fans assembly.
7. Remove the two lower supports, oil cooler hoses, lower radiator hose and cooling fans.
To install:
8. Install the cooling fans, lower radiator hose, oil cooler hoses and two lower supports.
9. Install radiator assembly and two upper supports. Connect cruise control actuator wire to the No. 1 cooling fan shroud.
10. Connect the radiator hoses and automatic transmission oil cooler hoses.

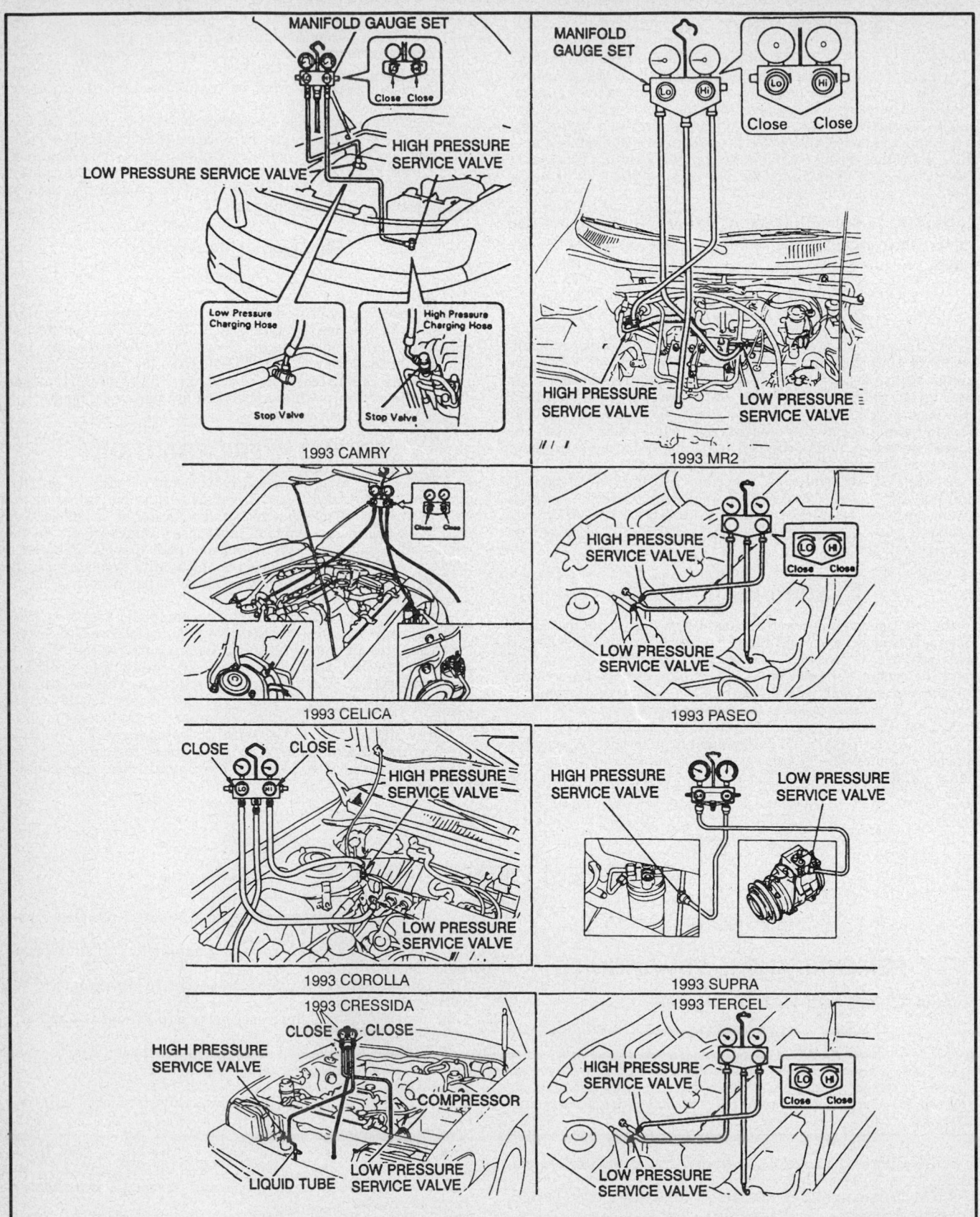

Service valve locations — 1993 models

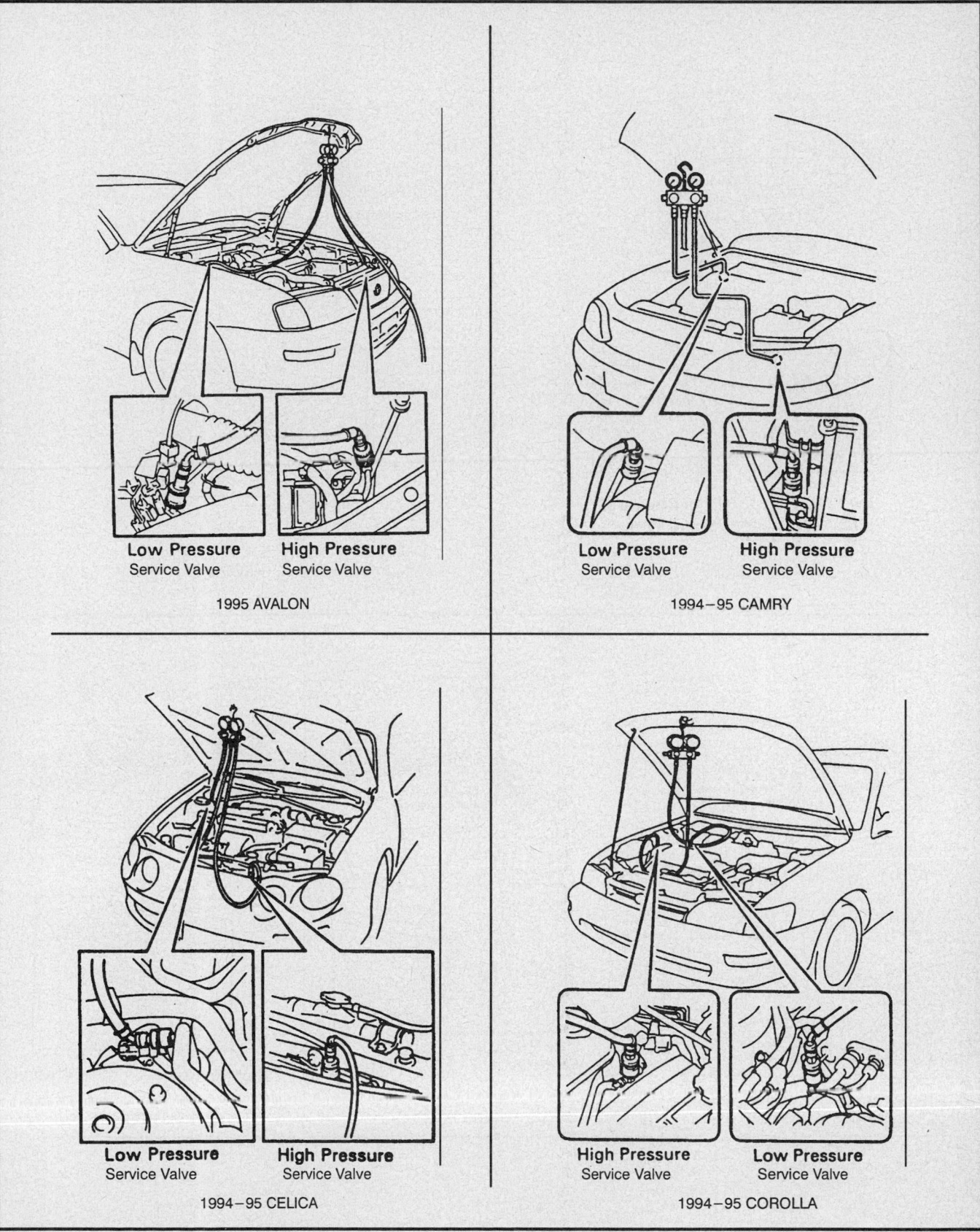

Low Pressure Service Valve **High Pressure** Service Valve

1995 AVALON

Low Pressure Service Valve **High Pressure** Service Valve

1994–95 CAMRY

Low Pressure Service Valve **High Pressure** Service Valve

1994–95 CELICA

High Pressure Service Valve **Low Pressure** Service Valve

1994–95 COROLLA

Service valve locations – 1994-95 models

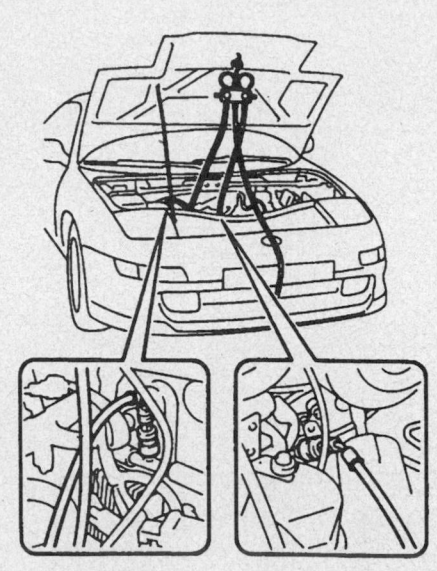

Low Pressure
Service Valve

High Pressure
Service Valve

1994–95 MR2

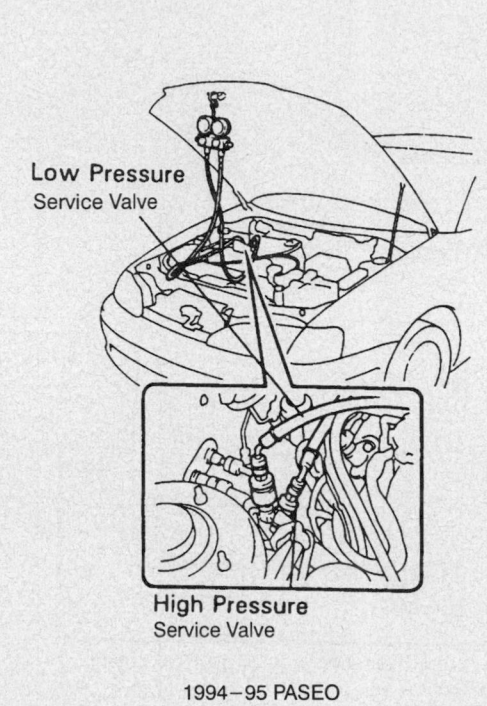

Low Pressure
Service Valve

High Pressure
Service Valve

1994–95 PASEO

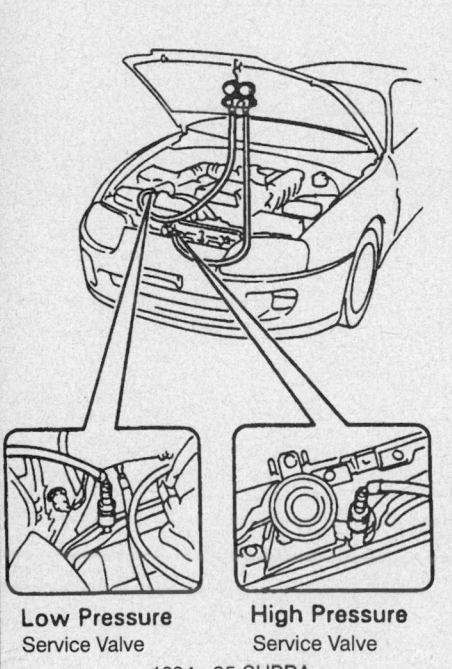

Low Pressure
Service Valve

High Pressure
Service Valve

1994–95 SUPRA

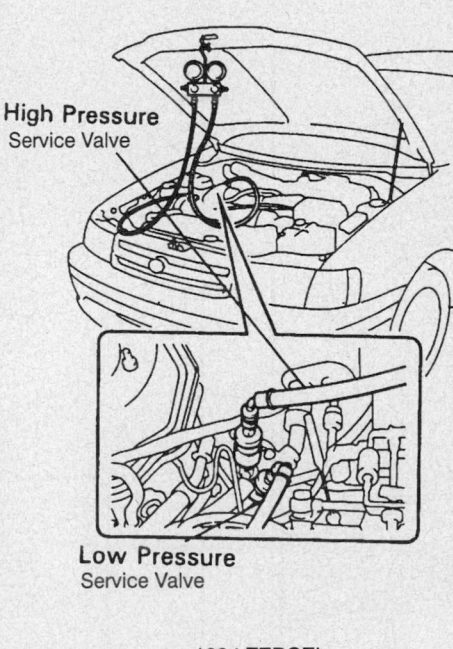

High Pressure
Service Valve

Low Pressure
Service Valve

1994 TERCEL

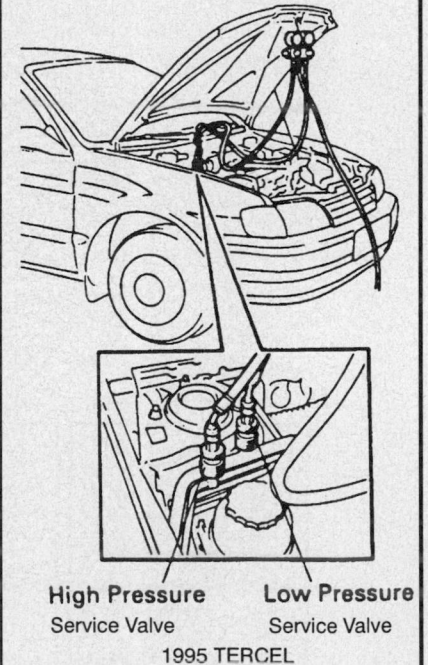

High Pressure
Service Valve

Low Pressure
Service Valve

1995 TERCEL

Service valve locations – 1994-95 models Cont'd

11. Install tray, battery and connect the cruise control actuator.

12. On Canadian model, connect the relay block to the battery hold-down clamp.

13. Reconnect the battery cable, fill the engine with coolant. Start the engine and check for leaks. Check all fluid levels as necessary.

Camry with 5S-FE engine

———————— CAUTION ————————

If vehicle is equipped with an air bag system, when ignition is turned to LOCK and negative battery cable is disconnected, do not work inside the passenger compartment for at least 30 seconds to give the SRS (air bag supplemental restraint system) a chance to become fully disarmed.

1. Disconnect the negative battery cable. Drain engine coolant.

2. On 1993 models, remove the cruise control actuator cover, and disconnect the water temperature switch.

3. Disconnect the coolant reservoir hose and all radiator hoses.

4. Disconnect the cooling fan motor electrical connections.

5. If equipped with automatic transaxle, disconnect the oil cooler lines.

6. Remove the radiator supports and remove the radiator assembly with the electrical cooling fans from the vehicle. Then remove the fans from the radiator assembly.

To install:

7. Install the electrical cooling fans to the radiator assembly. Install the radiator assembly in the vehicle and check that the rubber cushions are in the correct position.

8. If equipped with automatic transaxle, connect the oil cooler lines.

9. Connect the cooling fan motor electrical connections and the water temperature switch. Connect the radiator hoses and reservoir hose.

10. Install the cruise control cover, igniter and bracket assembly, ignition coil and battery, as removed.

11. Reconnect the battery cable, fill (bleed cooling system) the engine with coolant. Start the engine and check for leaks. Check all fluid levels as necessary.

Camry with 3VZ-FE engine

———————— CAUTION ————————

If vehicle is equipped with an air bag system, when ignition is turned to LOCK and negative battery cable is disconnected, do not work inside the passenger compartment for at least 30 seconds to give the SRS (air bag supplemental restraint system) a chance to become fully disarmed.

1. Disconnect the negative battery cable. Properly drain the cooling system.

2. Remove the cruise control actuator cover. Disconnect the hydraulic cooling fan system pressure hose from the fan motor. Plug the hose. Discard the gasket.

3. Disconnect the upper radiator hose, the coolant reserve hose and the hydraulic motor return hose (from the fan motor connection).

4. Working under the car, remove the engine cover. Detach the lower radiator hose and the oil cooler hoses if equipped with automatic transaxle.

5. Remove the 2 radiator support brackets from the top of the radiator and lift out the radiator with the fan motor assembly attached.

6. The fan can now be separated from the radiator.

To install:

7. Assemble the fan to the radiator and position the assembly in place and secure with the 2 radiator supports on top.

8. Under the car, reattach the oil cooler hoses (A/T) and the lower radiator hose. Install the engine cover.

9. Attach the return line to the fan motor. Attach the coolant reserve hose and upper radiator hose.

10. Install a new gasket and attach the pressure line to the fan motor. Install the cruise control actuator cover.

11. Fill the cooling system. Attach the negative battery cable. Bleed and top off the hydraulic system for the cooling fan. Check system operation at normal operating temperatures and adjust fluid levels.

Celica

———————— CAUTION ————————

If vehicle is equipped with an air bag system, when ignition is turned to LOCK and negative battery cable is disconnected, do not work inside the passenger compartment for at least 30 seconds to give the SRS (air bag supplemental restraint system) a chance to become fully disarmed.

1. Disconnect the negative battery cable. Remove the engine undercover. Drain engine coolant.

2. On the 3S-GTE and 5S-FE engines, disconnect the water temperature switch connector.

3. If equipped with ABS, remove the ABS control relay from the radiator support assembly. On the 3S-GTE engine, remove the air duct at the alternator.

4. Remove the engine relay box from the battery.

5. Remove the upper radiator support seal (7 clips and 3 screws).

6. Disconnect the coolant reservoir hose and all radiator hoses.

7. Disconnect the cooling fan motor electrical connection.

8. If equipped with automatic transaxle, disconnect the oil cooler lines. Remove the radiator assembly with the electrical cooling fan from the vehicle. Remove the electrical cooling fan from the radiator assembly, as necessary.

To install:

9. Install the electrical cooling fan to the radiator assembly. Install the radiator assembly in the vehicle and check that the rubber cushions are in the correct position.

10. If equipped with automatic transaxle, connect the oil cooler lines.

11. Connect the cooling fan motor electrical connection. Connect the radiator hoses and reservoir hose. Install the upper radiator support seal assembly.

12. Install the engine relay box to the battery, if necessary. On the 3S-GTE engine install the alternator air duct.

13. If equipped with ABS, install the ABS control relay to the radiator support assembly.

14. On the 3S-GTE and 5S-FE engines, connect the water temperature switch electrical connector.

15. Install the engine undercover, reconnect the negative battery cable, fill (bleed cooling system) the engine with coolant. Start the engine and check for leaks. Check all fluid levels as necessary.

Corolla

———————— CAUTION ————————

If vehicle is equipped with an air bag system, when ignition is turned to LOCK and negative battery cable is disconnected, do not work inside the passenger compartment for at least 30 seconds to give the SRS (air bag supplemental restraint system) a chance to become fully disarmed.

1. Disconnect the negative battery cable.

2. Drain engine coolant.

3. If equipped with automatic transaxle, disconnect the oil cooler lines.

4. Disconnect the coolant reservoir hose and all radiator hoses.

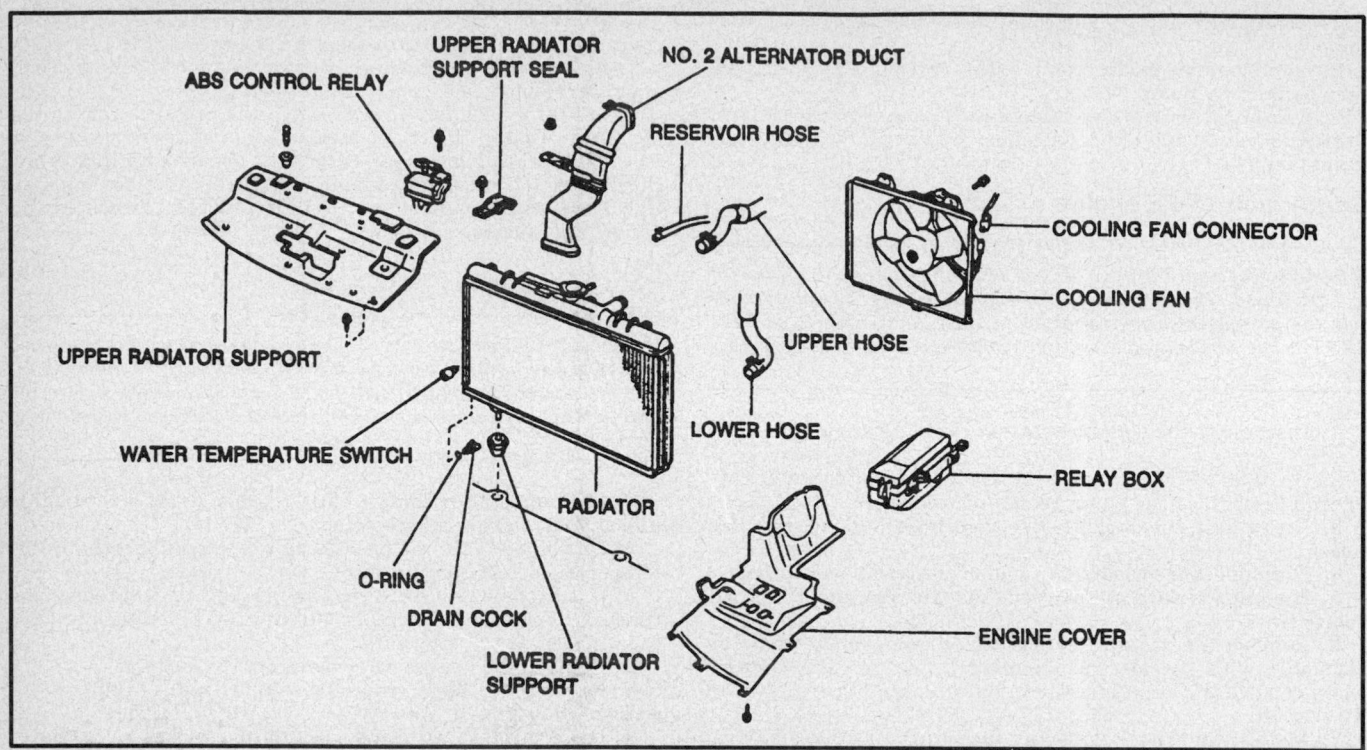

ABS CONTROL RELAY

UPPER RADIATOR SUPPORT SEAL

NO. 2 ALTERNATOR DUCT

RESERVOIR HOSE

COOLING FAN CONNECTOR

COOLING FAN

UPPER RADIATOR SUPPORT

UPPER HOSE

WATER TEMPERATURE SWITCH

LOWER HOSE

RADIATOR

RELAY BOX

O-RING

DRAIN COCK

LOWER RADIATOR SUPPORT

ENGINE COVER

Exploded view radiator assembly – Celica

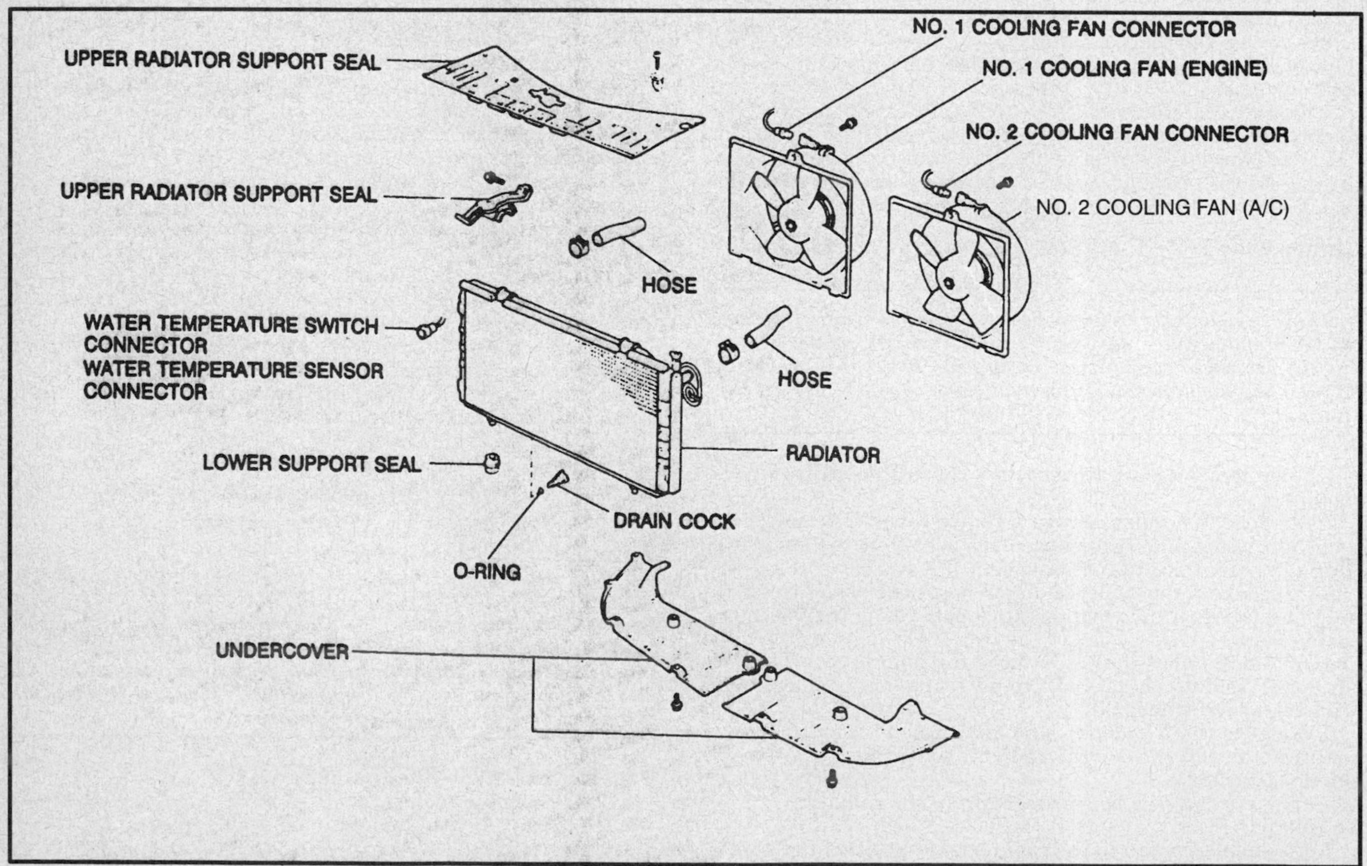

UPPER RADIATOR SUPPORT SEAL

NO. 1 COOLING FAN CONNECTOR

NO. 1 COOLING FAN (ENGINE)

UPPER RADIATOR SUPPORT SEAL

NO. 2 COOLING FAN CONNECTOR

NO. 2 COOLING FAN (A/C)

HOSE

WATER TEMPERATURE SWITCH CONNECTOR
WATER TEMPERATURE SENSOR CONNECTOR

HOSE

RADIATOR

LOWER SUPPORT SEAL

DRAIN COCK

O-RING

UNDERCOVER

Exploded view radiator assembly – MR2

5. Disconnect the cooling fan motor electrical connection.

6. Remove the radiator supports, then take out the radiator with the electrical cooling fan attached.

To install:

7. Install the electrical cooling fan to the radiator assembly. Install the radiator assembly in the vehicle and check that the rubber cushion supports are in the correct position.

8. Connect the cooling fan motor electrical connection. Connect the radiator hoses and reservoir hose.

9. If removed, reattach the automatic transaxle cooling lines.

10. Reconnect the negative battery cable and fill (bleed cooling system) the engine with coolant. Start the engine and check for leaks. Check all fluid levels, as necessary.

MR2

───────── CAUTION ─────────

If vehicle is equipped with an air bag system, when ignition is turned to LOCK and negative battery cable is disconnected, do not work inside the passenger compartment for at least 30 seconds to give the SRS (air bag supplemental restraint system) a chance to become fully disarmed.

1. Disconnect the negative battery cable.

2. Remove the front luggage undercover. Drain engine coolant.

3. Remove the upper radiator support seal assembly (7 clips).

4. Disconnect the radiator hoses. Remove the front hood lock assembly.

5. Disconnect the radiator cooling fan electrical connectors.

6. Disconnect water temperature sensor or switch electrical connection.

7. Remove the radiator upper supports and lift out the radiator assembly with the electrical cooling fans attached.

8. Remove the electrical cooling fans from the radiator assembly, as necessary.

To install:

9. Install the electrical cooling fans to the radiator assembly. Install the radiator assembly in the vehicle and check that the rubber cushions are in the correct position.

10. Reconnect water temperature sensor electrical connection and cooling fans electrical connections.

11. Install the front hood lock assembly.

12. Connect the radiator hoses. Reconnect the negative battery cable and fill (bleed cooling system) the engine with coolant. Start the engine and check for leaks.

13. Install upper radiator support seal and front luggage undercover.

Paseo and Tercel

───────── CAUTION ─────────

If vehicle is equipped with an air bag system, when ignition is turned to LOCK and negative battery cable is disconnected, do not work inside the passenger compartment for at least 30 seconds to give the SRS (air bag supplemental restraint system) a chance to become fully disarmed.

1. Disconnect the negative battery cable.

2. Remove the right and left engine under covers.

3. Properly drain the coolant.

4. Remove the air intake connector (3 bolts), disconnect the electric cooling fan connector, and detach the overflow and radiator hoses.

5. If equipped with automatic transaxle, disconnect and plug the oil cooler lines.

6. Remove the upper supports and lift out the radiator assembly with the cooling fan attached.

To install:

7. Position radiator assembly and attach upper supports.

8. Reconnect oil cooler lines, hoses, electrical connections and air intake, as removed.

9. Install the lower covers, attach the battery cable, refill the cooling system, and check for proper operation.

Supra

───────── CAUTION ─────────

If vehicle is equipped with an air bag system, when ignition is turned to LOCK and negative battery cable is disconnected, do not work inside the passenger compartment for at least 30 seconds to give the SRS (air bag supplemental restraint system) a chance to become fully disarmed.

1. Disconnect the negative battery cable. Drain engine coolant.

2. Disconnect condenser fan motor electrical connection.

3. Disconnect the coolant reservoir hose and all radiator hoses.

4. If equipped with automatic transaxle, disconnect and plug the oil cooler lines. Remove the radiator supports. Remove the radiator assembly with the condenser fan from the vehicle.

5. Remove the condenser fan from the radiator assembly, as necessary.

To install:

6. Install the condenser fan to the radiator assembly. Install the radiator assembly in the vehicle and check that the rubber cushions are in the correct position.

7. If equipped with automatic transaxle, connect the oil cooler lines.

8. Connect the condenser fan motor electrical connection. Connect the radiator hoses and reservoir hose.

9. Reconnect the negative battery cable, fill (bleed cooling system) the engine with coolant. Start the engine and check for leaks. Check all fluid levels, as necessary.

COOLING SYSTEM FILLING AND BLEEDING

Except MR2

1. Be sure all drain cocks are tightly closed.

2. Slowly fill the cooling system with coolant. Run the engine and set the heater temperature control to full heat. Check for leaks.

3. Stop the engine and add coolant to radiator until the level reaches the proper level.

4. Fill the coolant into the reservoir tank to the "FULL" mark.

MR2

NOTE: When preforming this service procedure the vehicle must be level. Also set the heater control level to HOT position.

1. Remove the spare tire, the front luggage compartment trim and the upper radiator support seal.

2. Connect suitable service hoses to the radiator air drain and heater valve. Suspend the opposite end of the radiator air service hose upward connected to the hood stay.

3. Suspend the opposite end of the hose connected to the heater air bleeder valve to the underside of the hood. Be sure not to close-off or pinch any of the tubes.

4. Open the radiator and heater air bleeder valves about 3 turns.

5. Pour the coolant into the water filler. When the coolant level in the service hoses stops dropping, close the air drain plugs of the radiator and heater. Close the radiator cap to the first stop.

6. Start the engine and run it at fast idle for approximately 3 minutes and then shut off the engine. Repeat previous steps and add more coolant as needed to stabilize coolant level.

7. Completely tighten the radiator cap and fill the reservoir tank to the "FULL" mark.

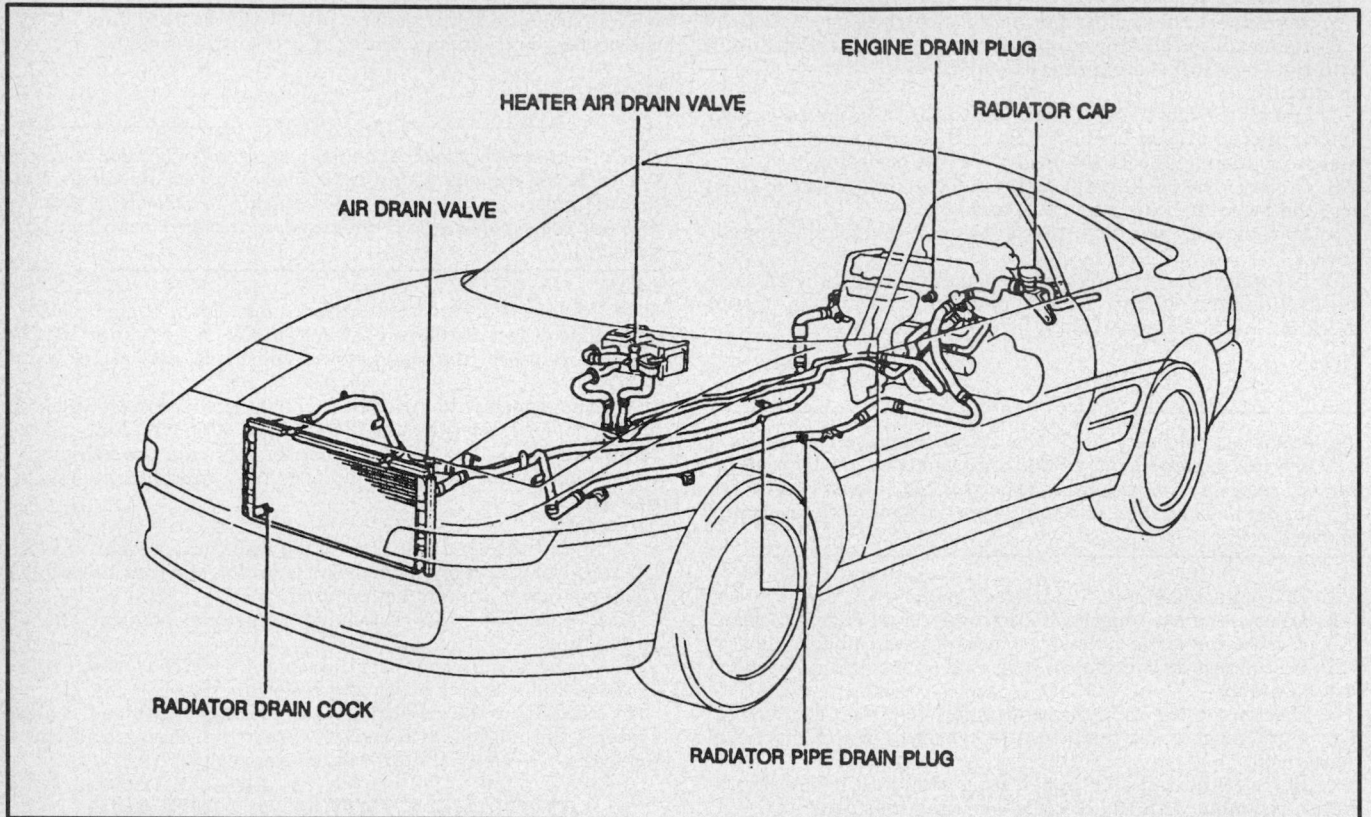

Cooling circuit – MR2

8. Remove service hoses, install radiator seal, luggage compartment trim and spare tire.

HYDRAULIC COOLING FAN SYSTEM BLEEDING

Camry with 3VZ-FE engine

1. Check fluid level in cooling fan system reservoir tank. If low, add ATF Dexron® II fluid to appropriate "HOT" or "COLD" mark on tank.
2. To bleed the system, place a jumper wire between terminals **OP1** and **E1** of the check connector.
3. Start the engine without depressing the accelerator. Let engine run for several seconds. Any air in the system will rise through the tank.
4. Continue to run the engine until all bubbling or foaming in the reservoir tank stops. Adjust the fluid level if needed.

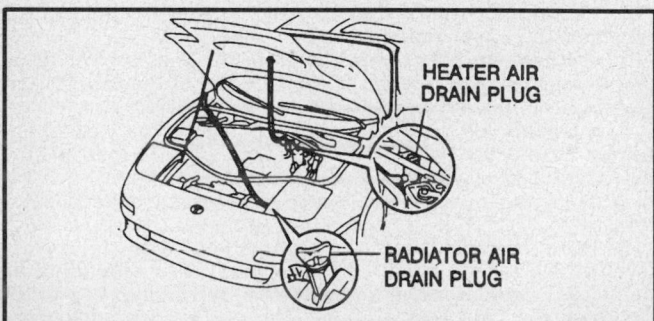

Service hose attachment and location of air bleed plugs – MR2

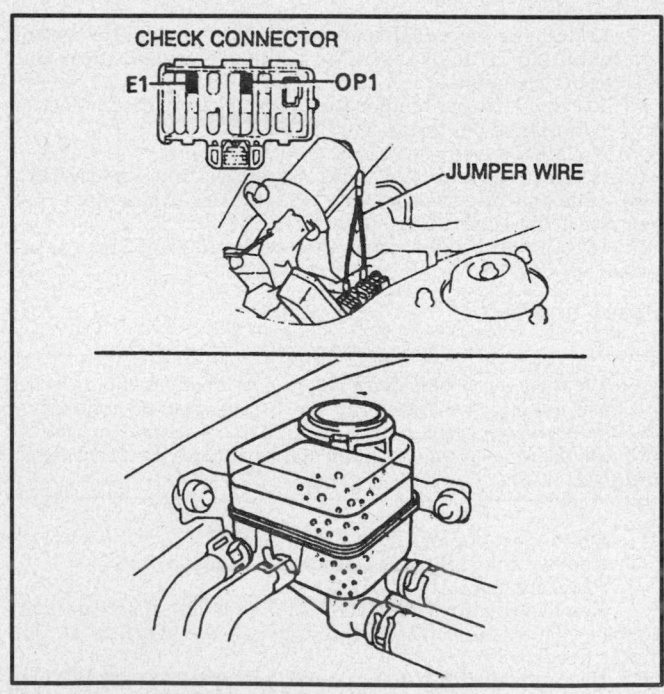

Bleeding hydraulic cooling fan system – 1993 Camry with 3VZ-FE engine

COOLING FAN AMPERAGE TEST

Model & Application	1993	1994	1995
Avalon			
1MZ-FE engine	N/A	N/A	6.1-7.3
Camry			
3VZ-FE engine	①	N/A	N/A
5S-FE engine	5.8-7.4	5.7-7.7	6.0-7.4
1MZ-FE engine	N/A	①	6.0-7.4
Celica			
3S-GTE engine	8.8-10.8	N/A	N/A
4A-FE & 5S-FE engine	5.8-7.4	6.0-7.4	6.0-7.4
7A-FE engine	N/A	6.0-7.4	6.0-7.4
Corolla			
4A-FE engine	5.8-7.4	6.0-7.4	6.0-7.4
4A-GE engine	5.8-7.4	N/A	N/A
7A-FE engine	N/A	6.0-7.4	6.0-7.4
MR2			
5S-FE engine	5.8-7.4	5.8-7.4	6.0-7.4
3S-GTE engine	N/A	5.8-7.4	6.0-7.4
MR2 engine compartment fan	3.1-4.3	3.1-4.3	3.1-4.3
Paseo			
5S-FE engine	8-11	8-11	8-11
Supra			
7M-GE engine	6.0-7.4	N/A	N/A
7M-GTE engine	6.0-7.4	N/A	N/A
2JZ-GE engine	N/A	6.0-7.4	6.0-7.4
2JZ-GTE engine	N/A	6.0-7.4	6.0-7.4
Tercel			
3E-FE engine	8-11	8-11	8-11

① Model was an electronically operated
   hydraulic engine cooling fan system.

Electric Cooling Fan

TESTING—ELECTRIC ENGINE COOLING FAN

Avalon, Camry, Celica, Corolla, MR2, Paseo, Tercel

LOW TEMPERATURE CONDITION (BELOW 181°F)

1. Turn the ignition switch **ON**. Check that the fan stops. If the fan runs, then check the cooling fan relay and water temperature switch. Check for a separated connector or severed wire between the cooling fan relay and water temperature switch.
2. Disconnect the water temperature switch connector and check that the fan rotates.
3. If the fan does not rotate, check the cooling fan relay, fan motor, ignition or engine main relay and fuse. Check for a short circuit between the cooling fan relay and water temperature switch.
4. Reconnect the water temperature switch connector.

HIGH TEMPERATURE CONDITION (ABOVE 194-201°F)

1. Start the engine and raise the engine coolant temperature. On dual fan systems, fan should operate at low speed when temperature is between 185-194°F. Above 194-199°F (201°F for Paseo and Tercel), single fan system should operate and dual fan system should turn at high speed.
2. Confirm that the fan rotates; if it does not rotate, replace the water temperature switch.

TESTING—ELECTRONICALLY CONTROLLED HYDRAULIC FAN

Camry with 3VZ-FE engine

1. Disconnect the union bolt and remove the gasket from the pressure line connection at the hydraulic motor. Plug the line.

NOTE: This is a pressure line; watch for any residual pressure bleed as you remove the line. Take precautions.

2. Connect the gauge side of a pressure gauge to the pressure hose and the valve side of the gauge to the hydraulic motor connection.
3. Be sure air conditioning is off. Bleed system if required. Place a jumper wire between terminals **OP1** and **E1** of the check connector.

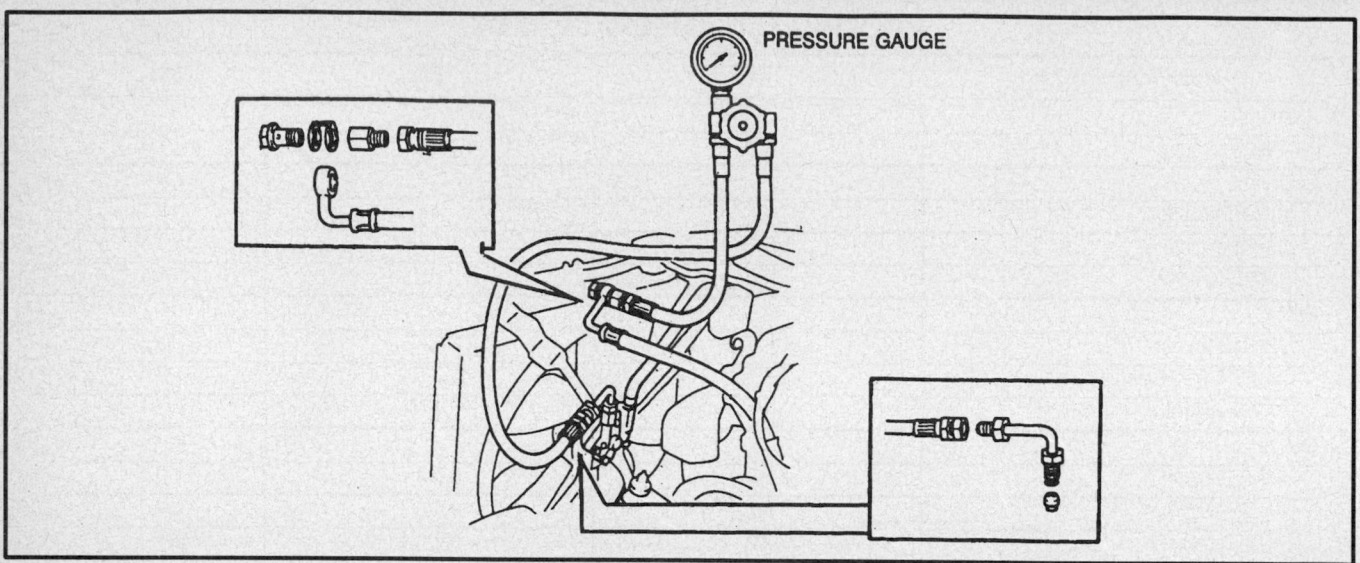

Pressure gauge attachment for cooling system check — 1993 Camry with 3VZ-FE engine

PRESSURE GAUGE

COOLING FAN ECU

THROTTLE POSITION SENSOR

IGNITER

OIL FILTER

HYDRAULIC PUMP (P/S PUMP)

A/C PRESSURE SWITCH

HYDRAULIC MOTOR

WATER TEMPERATURE SWITCH

OIL COOLER

CONDENSER

COOLING FAN

COOLING FAN ECU

HYDRAULIC MOTOR

SOLENOID VALVE

HYDRAULIC PUMP

P/S PUMP

P/S GEAR HOUSING

RADIATOR

OIL FILTER

OIL COOLER

RESERVOIR TANK

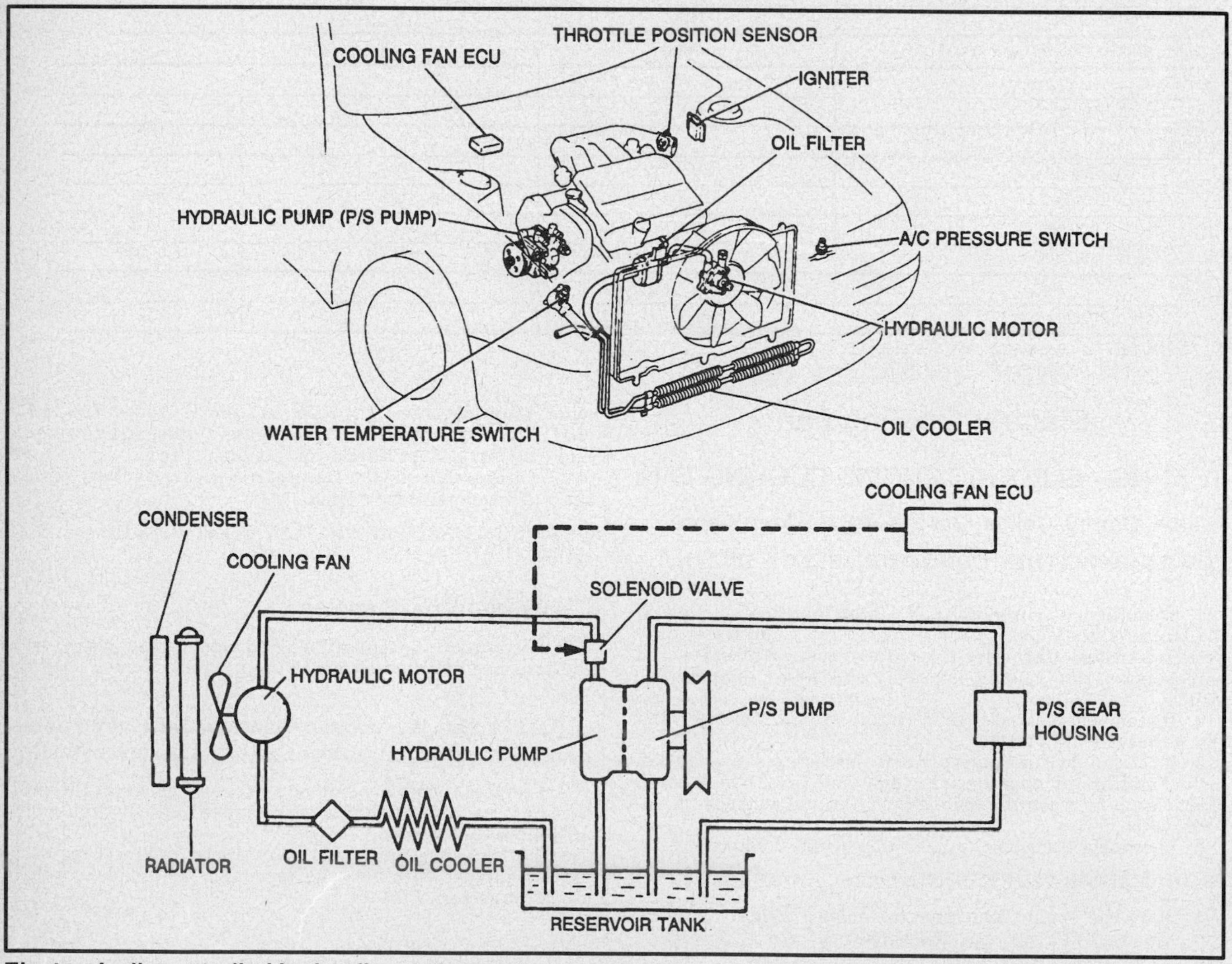

Electronically controlled hydraulic cooling system components — 1993 Camry with 3VZ-FE engine

4. Start the engine and run at 2,000 rpm until hydraulic system fluid is at normal operating temperature (158-195°F).

5. With engine at idle, system pressure should be 142-284 psi.

6. Remove the jumper wire from the check connector and watch that system pressure decreases.

7. If system does not respond as indicated, check for leaks, ensure system oil filter is not plugged, and that solenoid valve is operating (7.6-8.0 ohms resistance at solenoid terminals). Check for proper continuity and voltage signals at cooling fan ECU, mounted behind the glove box.

Fan Motor Load Test

1. Connect the battery and the ammeter to the fan motor connector (complete circuit).

2. Check to see that the motor rotates smoothly. On a single and dual fan assemblies check for the standard amperage specification. Refer to the standard amperage (use these specifications for fan motor load test) specification chart, as required.

3. If any of the above specifications are not as specified, replace the fan motor assembly.

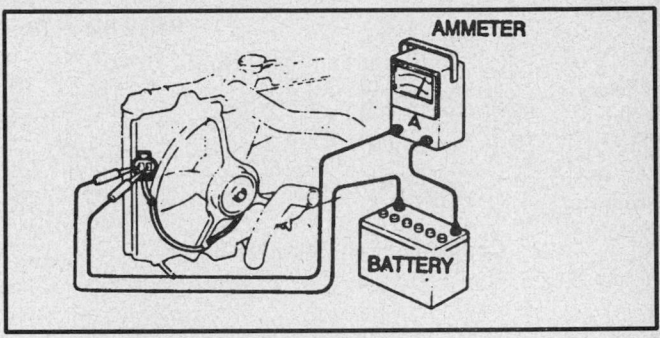

Fan motor load test connections

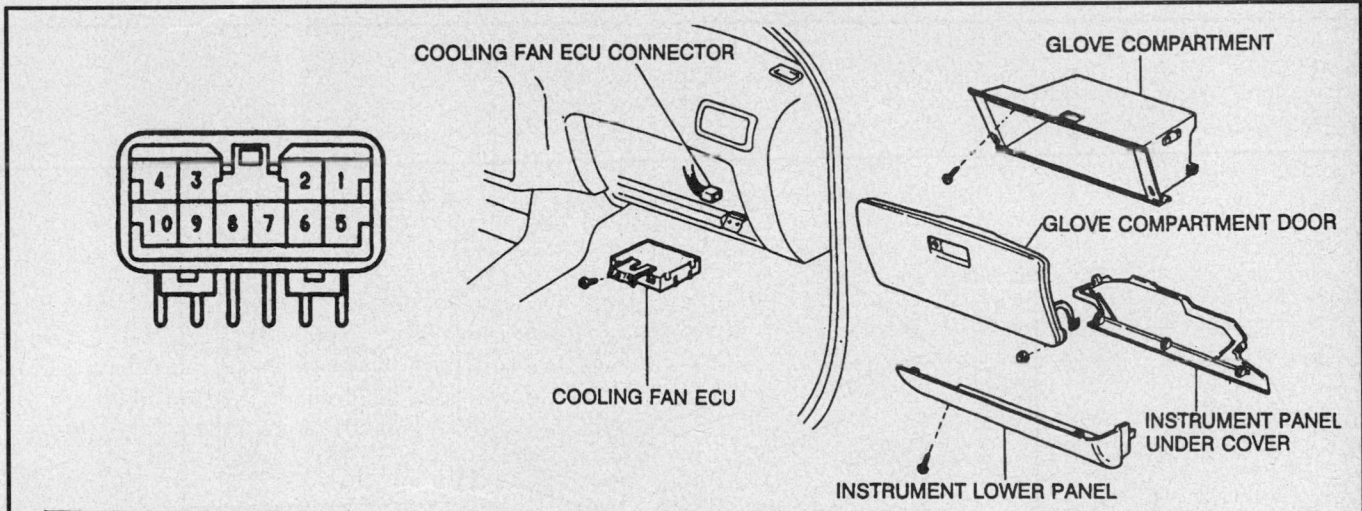

Check for	Tester connection	Condition	Specified value
Voltage	1 – Ground	Ignition switch ON	Battery voltage
Resistance	2 – 3	Solenoid valve at cold (25°C (77°F))	7.6 – 8.0 Ω
Continuity	4 – Ground		Continuity
Continuity	5 – Ground	Throttle valve open	No continuity
		Throttle valve closed	Continuity
Continuity	8 – Ground	A/C pressure SW connector disconnected	No continuity
		A/C pressure SW connector connected	Continuity
Resistance	9 – 10	Coolant temperature at 80°C (176°F)	1.48 – 1.58 kΩ

Inspecting hydraulic cooling fan ECU — 1993 Camry with 3VZ-FE engine

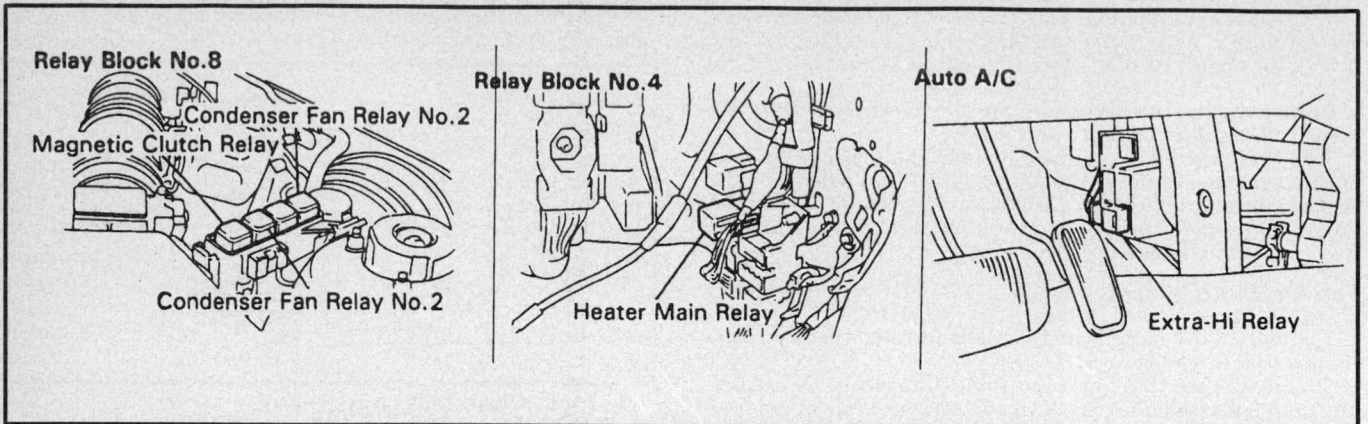

Relay Block No.8
Condenser Fan Relay No.2
Magnetic Clutch Relay
Condenser Fan Relay No.2

Relay Block No.4
Heater Main Relay

Auto A/C
Extra-Hi Relay

Location of electric cooling fan components — Avalon

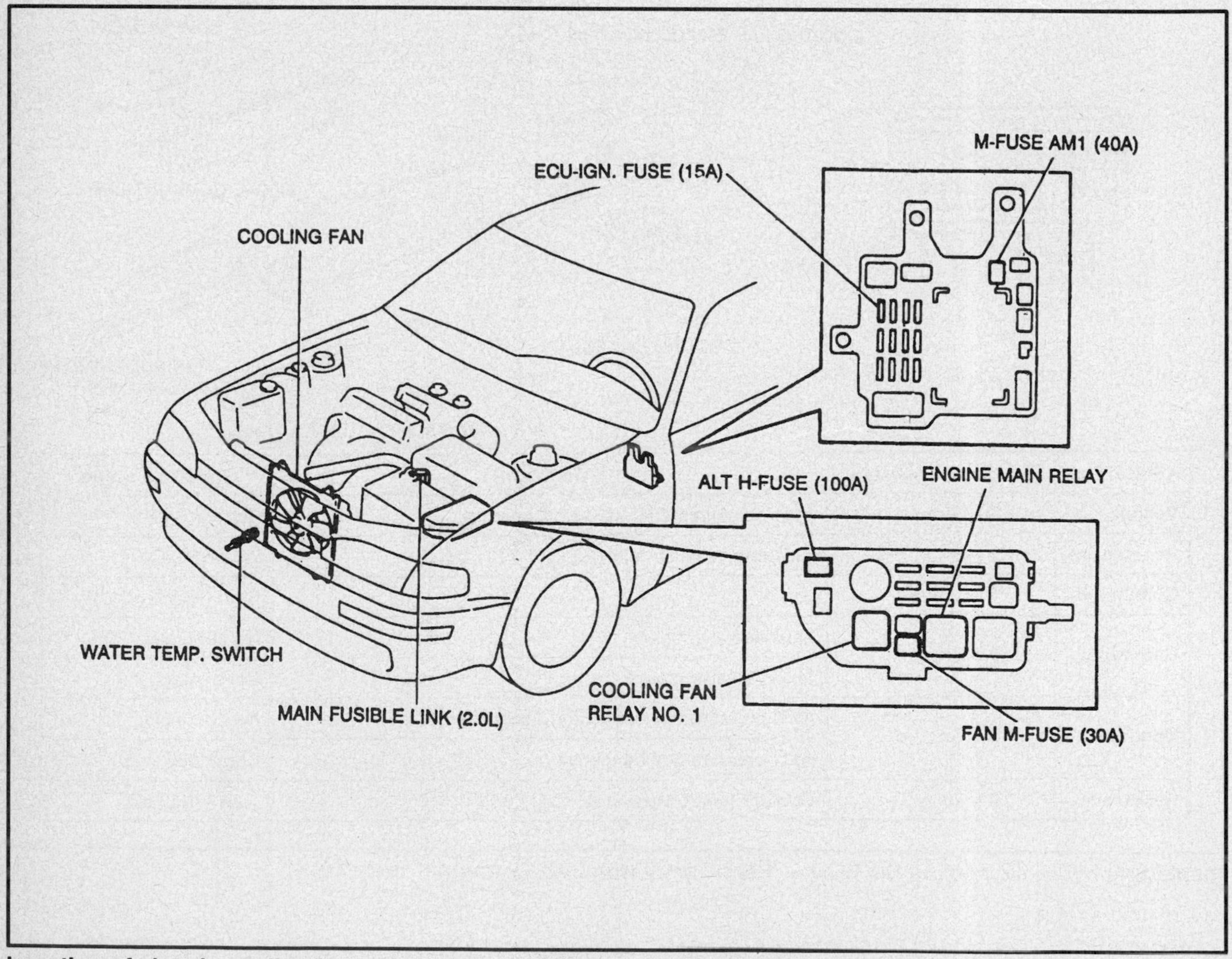

COOLING FAN

ECU-IGN. FUSE (15A)

M-FUSE AM1 (40A)

ALT H-FUSE (100A)

ENGINE MAIN RELAY

WATER TEMP. SWITCH

MAIN FUSIBLE LINK (2.0L)

COOLING FAN RELAY NO. 1

FAN M-FUSE (30A)

Location of electric cooling fan components — 1993 Camry with 5S-FE engine

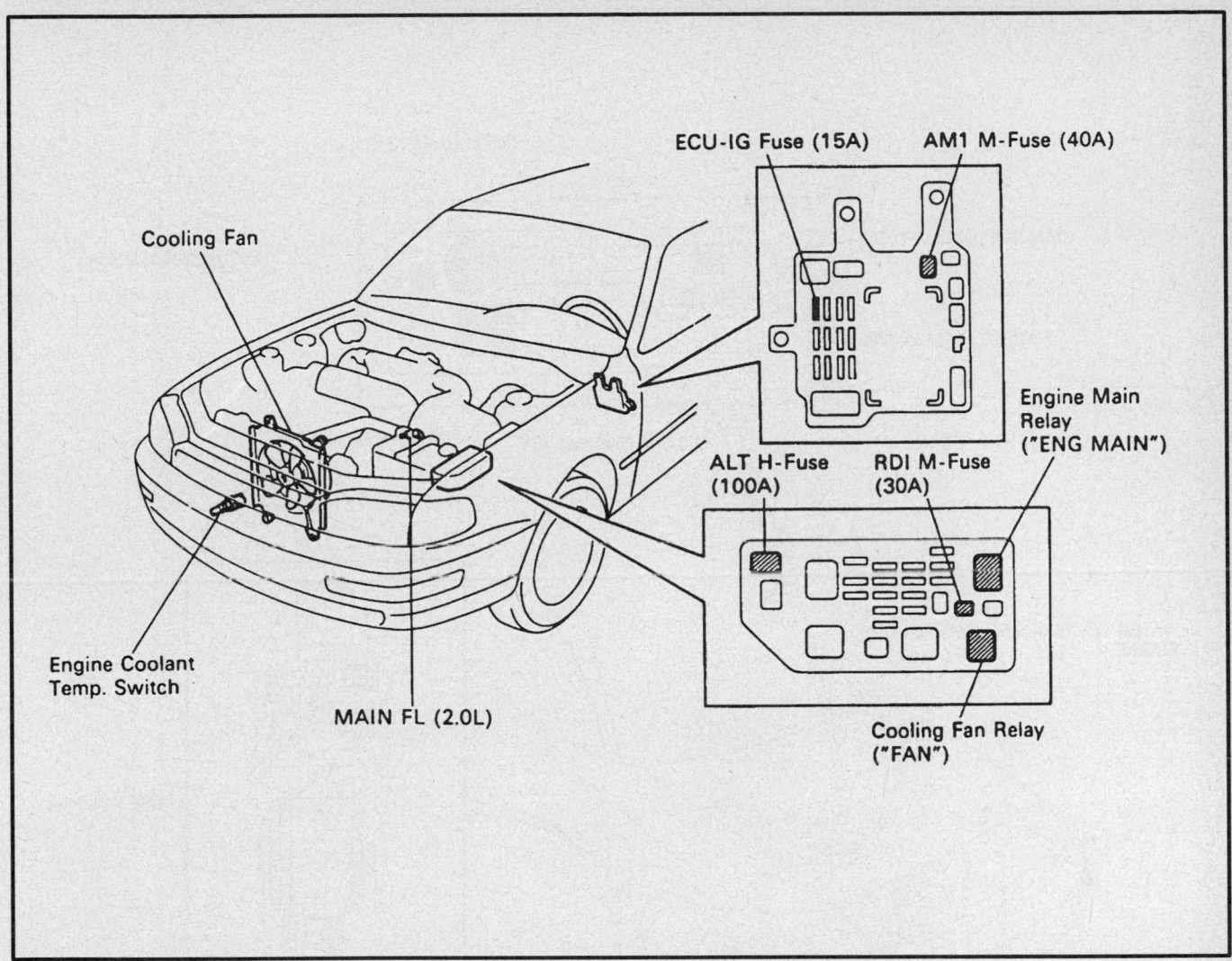

Location of electric cooling fan components — 1994-95 Camry with 5S-FE engine

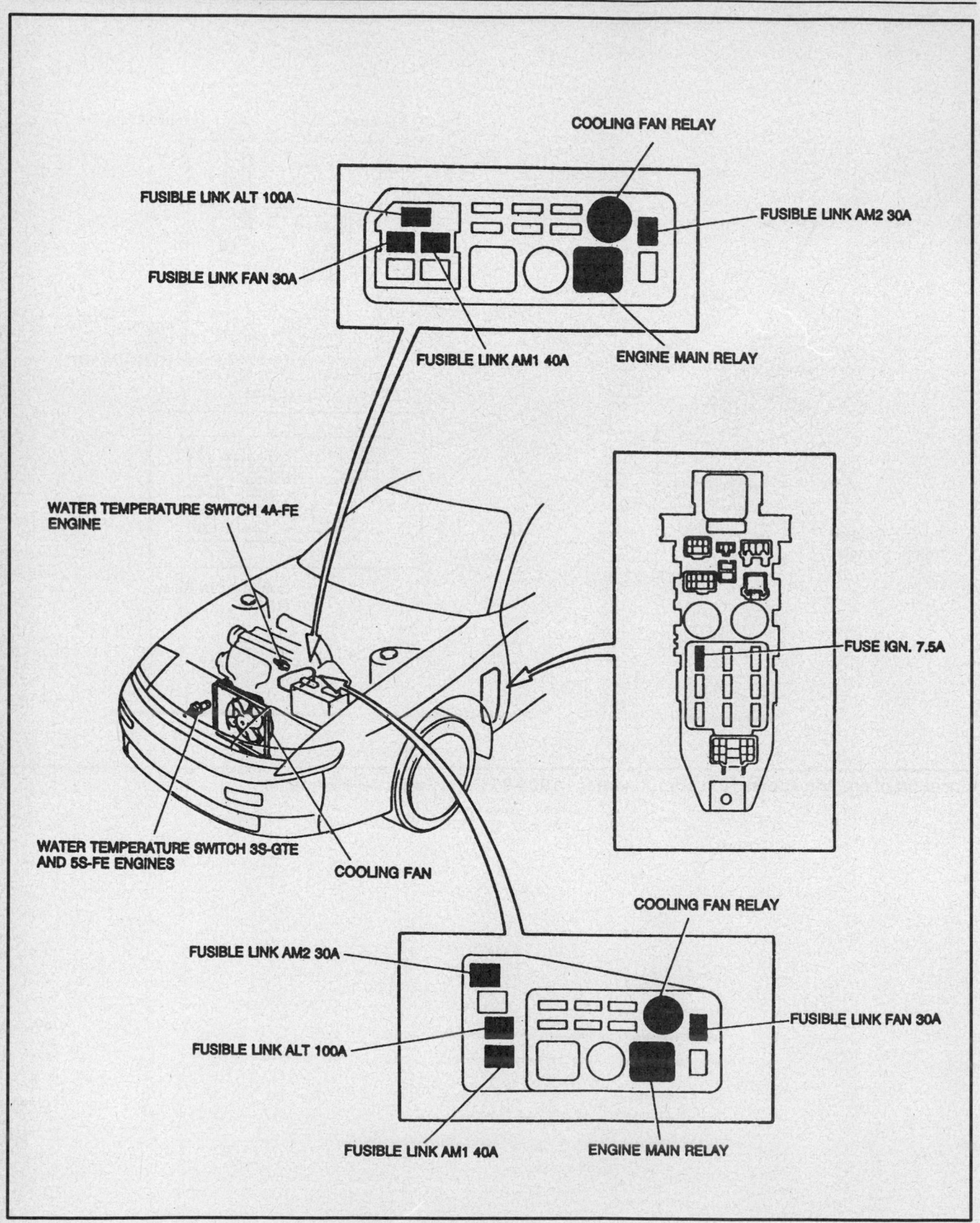

COOLING FAN RELAY

FUSIBLE LINK ALT 100A

FUSIBLE LINK AM2 30A

FUSIBLE LINK FAN 30A

FUSIBLE LINK AM1 40A

ENGINE MAIN RELAY

WATER TEMPERATURE SWITCH 4A-FE ENGINE

FUSE IGN. 7.5A

WATER TEMPERATURE SWITCH 3S-GTE AND 5S-FE ENGINES

COOLING FAN

COOLING FAN RELAY

FUSIBLE LINK AM2 30A

FUSIBLE LINK FAN 30A

FUSIBLE LINK ALT 100A

FUSIBLE LINK AM1 40A

ENGINE MAIN RELAY

Location of electric cooling fan components — 1993 Celica

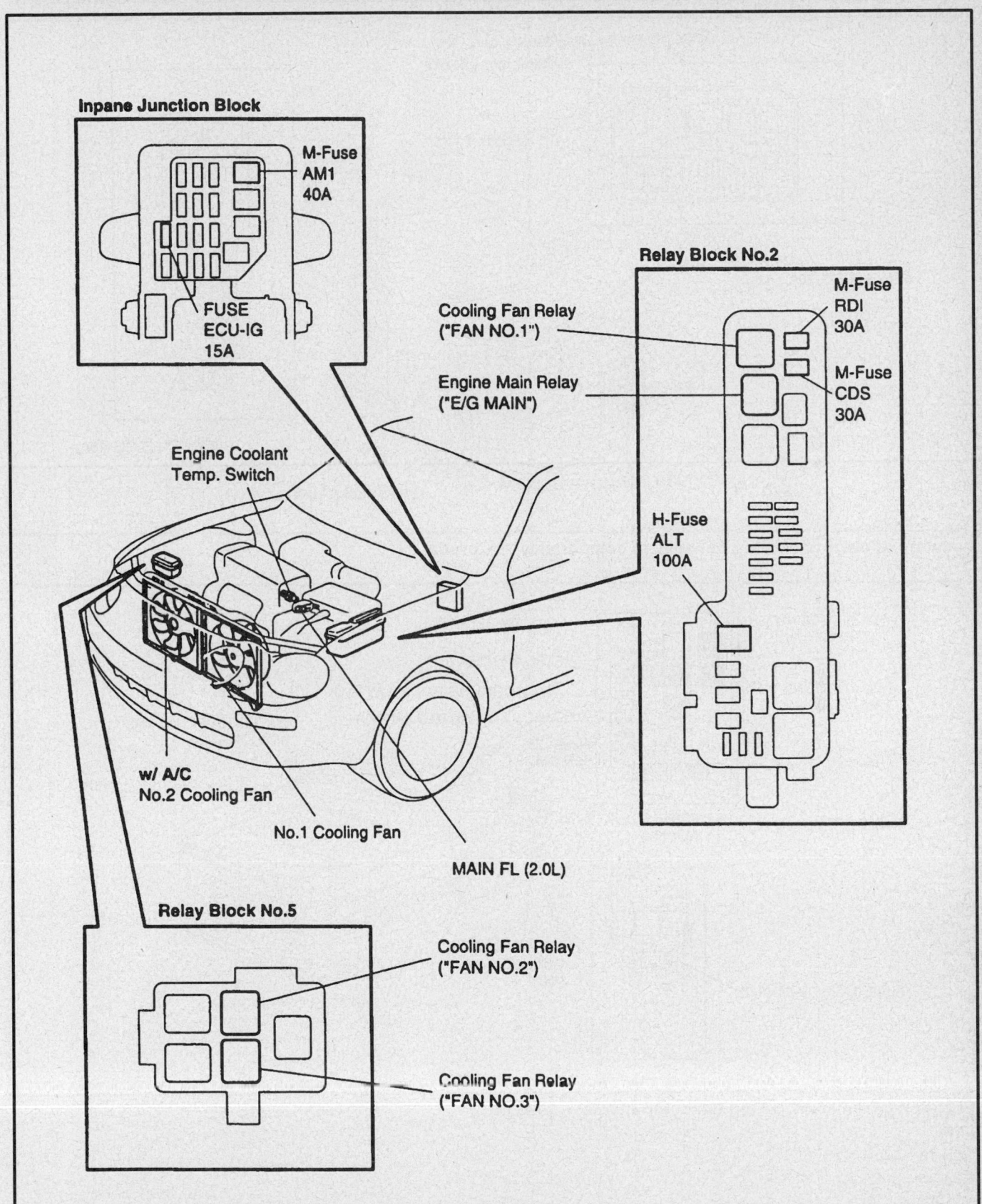

Inpane Junction Block

M-Fuse
AM1
40A

FUSE
ECU-IG
15A

Relay Block No.2

Cooling Fan Relay
("FAN NO.1")

Engine Main Relay
("E/G MAIN")

M-Fuse
RDI
30A

M-Fuse
CDS
30A

H-Fuse
ALT
100A

Engine Coolant
Temp. Switch

w/ A/C
No.2 Cooling Fan

No.1 Cooling Fan

MAIN FL (2.0L)

Relay Block No.5

Cooling Fan Relay
("FAN NO.2")

Cooling Fan Relay
("FAN NO.3")

Location of electric cooling fan components — 1994-95 Celica

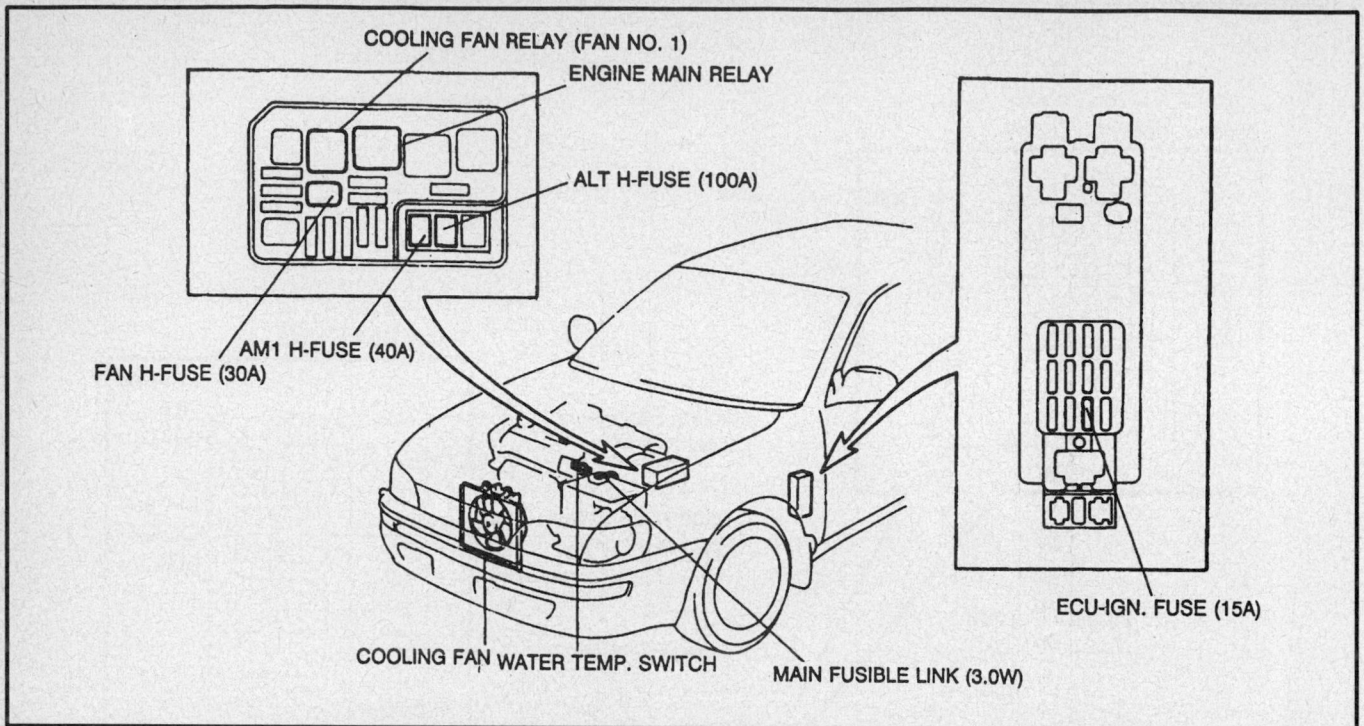

COOLING FAN RELAY (FAN NO. 1)

ENGINE MAIN RELAY

ALT H-FUSE (100A)

AM1 H-FUSE (40A)

FAN H-FUSE (30A)

COOLING FAN WATER TEMP. SWITCH

MAIN FUSIBLE LINK (3.0W)

ECU-IGN. FUSE (15A)

Location of electric cooling fan system components — Corolla

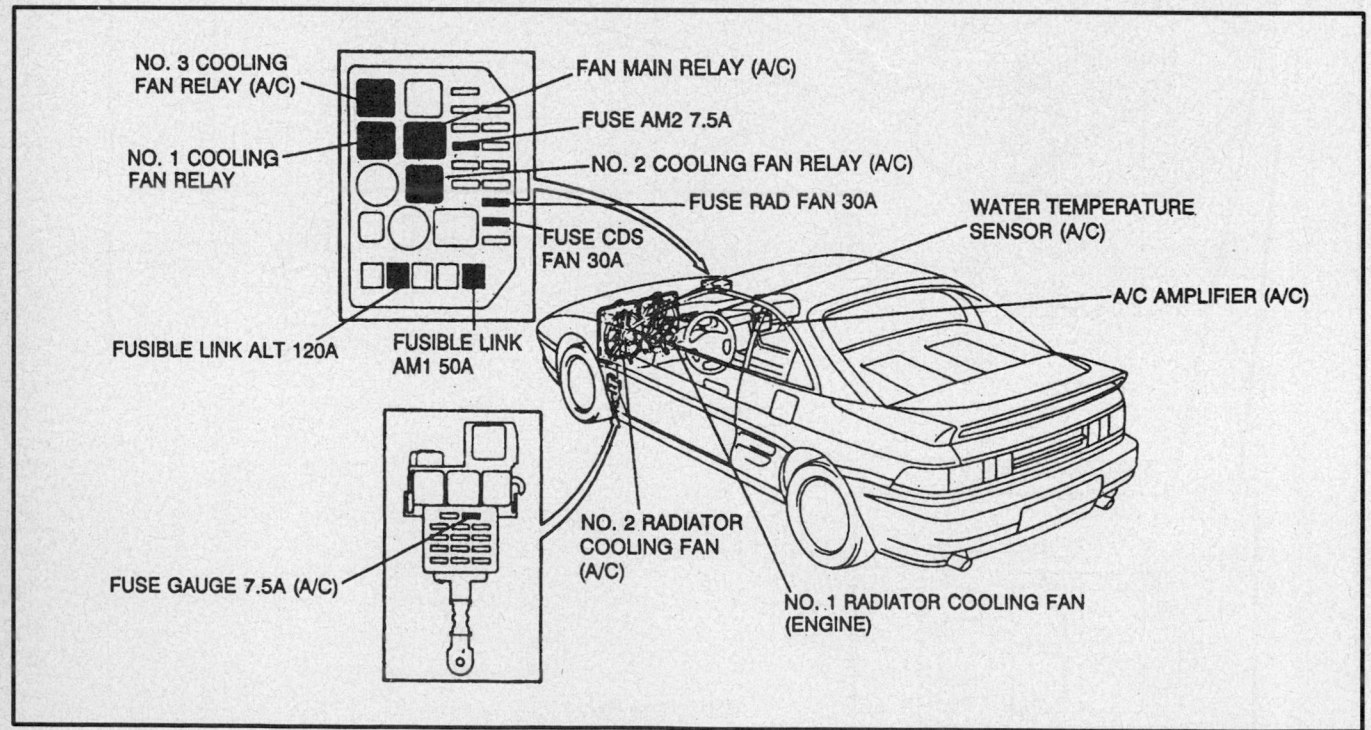

NO. 3 COOLING FAN RELAY (A/C)

NO. 1 COOLING FAN RELAY

FUSIBLE LINK ALT 120A

FUSIBLE LINK AM1 50A

FUSE GAUGE 7.5A (A/C)

FAN MAIN RELAY (A/C)

FUSE AM2 7.5A

NO. 2 COOLING FAN RELAY (A/C)

FUSE RAD FAN 30A

FUSE CDS FAN 30A

WATER TEMPERATURE SENSOR (A/C)

A/C AMPLIFIER (A/C)

NO. 2 RADIATOR COOLING FAN (A/C)

NO. 1 RADIATOR COOLING FAN (ENGINE)

Location of radiator cooling fan components — 1993 MR2

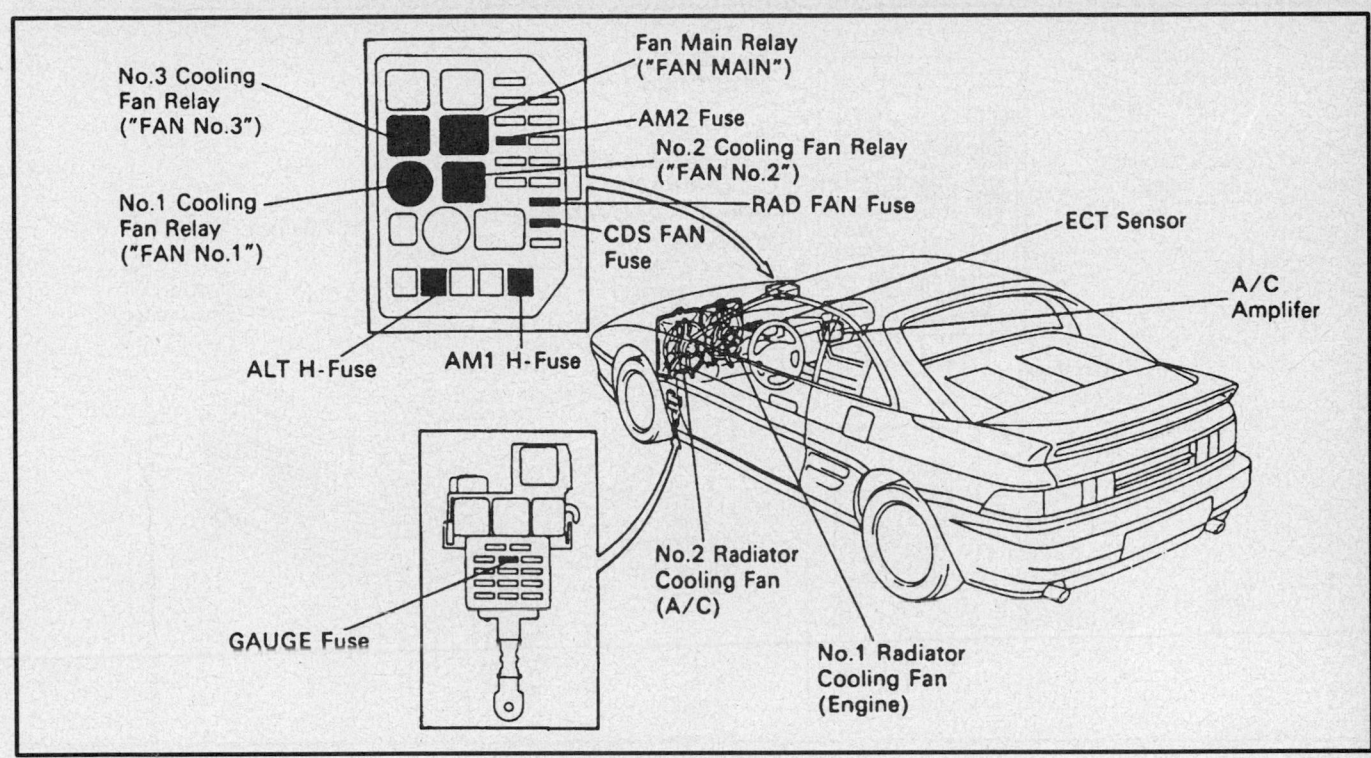

Location of electric cooling fan components – 1994-95 MR2

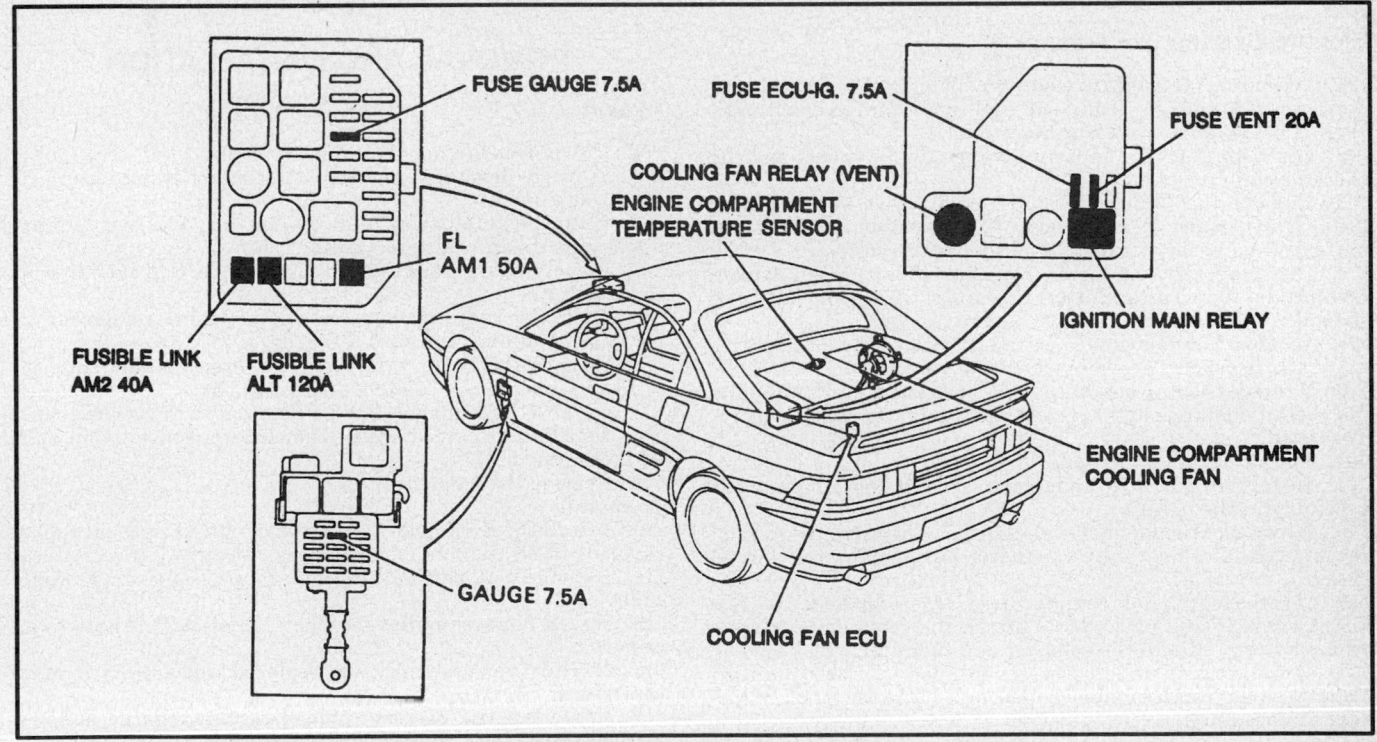

Location of cooling fan components – 1993 MR2 with 3S-GTE engine

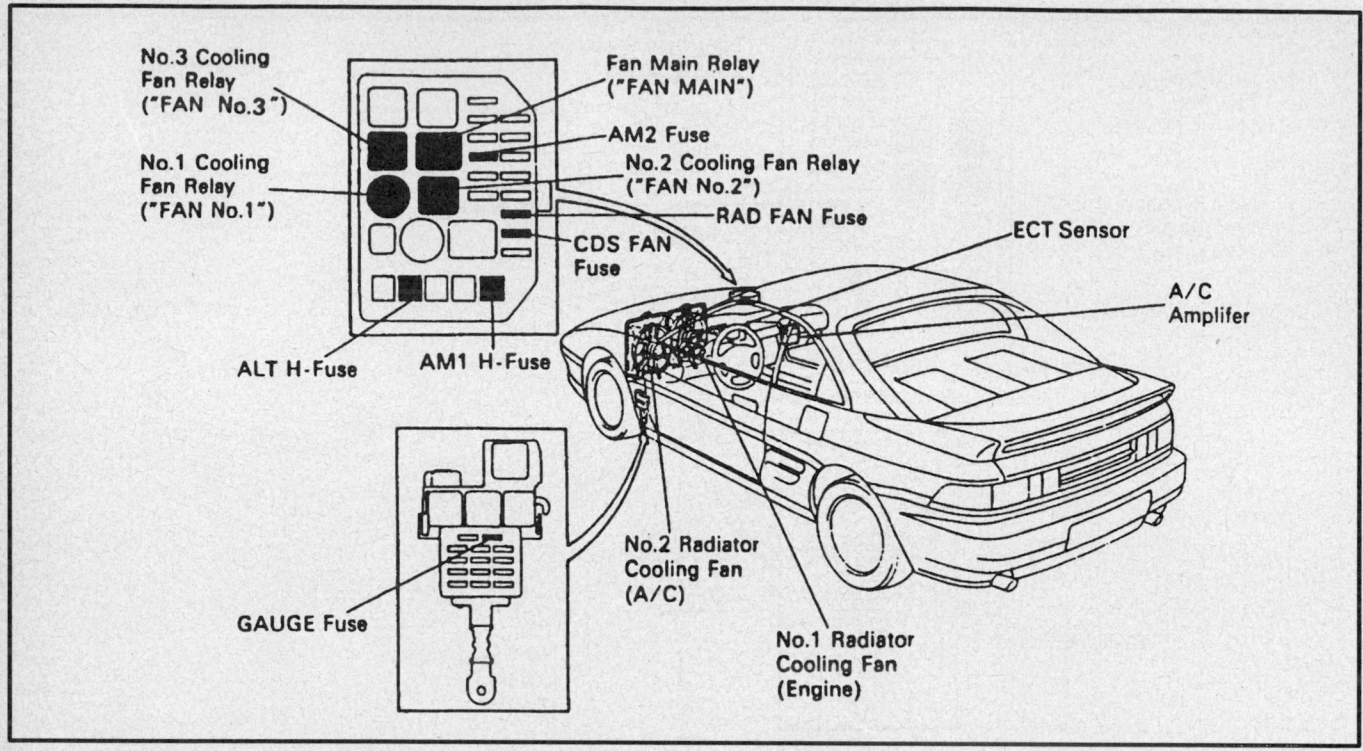

No.3 Cooling Fan Relay ("FAN No.3")

Fan Main Relay ("FAN MAIN")

No.1 Cooling Fan Relay ("FAN No.1")

AM2 Fuse

No.2 Cooling Fan Relay ("FAN No.2")

RAD FAN Fuse

CDS FAN Fuse

ECT Sensor

A/C Amplifer

ALT H-Fuse

AM1 H-Fuse

GAUGE Fuse

No.2 Radiator Cooling Fan (A/C)

No.1 Radiator Cooling Fan (Engine)

Location of cooling fan components — 1994-95 MR2 with 3S-GTE engine

REMOVAL AND INSTALLATION

Electric Cooling Fan Assembly

1. Disconnect the negative battery cable. Remove engine undercover, if equipped. Drain the cooling system at least until level is below upper radiator hose.
2. On MR2, remove the front luggage under covers and the radiator support cover.
3. Remove the radiator hose, reservoir hose and reservoir tank, if necessary. Remove relay box assembly from battery, battery, if necessary, solenoid and fuel pump resistor.
4. Disconnect the fan motor electrical connector. On Avalon, disconnect the cruise control actuator wire from the fan shroud.
5. Remove the fan motor assembly retaining bolts and remove the fan motor assembly from the vehicle.
6. Remove the fan, spacer, if equipped, and nut. Remove the fan motor, bushings and screws from the fan motor assembly.

To install:

7. Install fan to fan motor.
8. Install fan motor to fan motor assembly. Install fan motor assembly in the vehicle.
9. Reconnect the fan motor electrical connection. On Avalon, reconnect the cruise control actuator wire to the fan shroud clamp.
10. If removed, install radiator hose, reservoir hose and reservoir tank. Install battery and attach the relay box assembly to the battery. Install the solenoid and fuel pump resistor.
11. Install engine undercover, if equipped. Connect negative battery cable. Refill engine coolant and bleed the cooling system, if necessary.

Condenser

REMOVAL AND INSTALLATION

Avalon

1. Disconnect the negative battery cable.
2. Properly discharge the air conditioning system using recovery equipment.
3. Remove radiator fan and cooling fan. Remove radiator upper mounts and radiator grille.
4. Remove refrigerant system connections. Cap open fittings immediately.
5. Push the radiator towards enging. Push condenser towards the radiator and pull upwards.
6. Remove the battery, upper cover, brackets and supports to clear access to the condenser connections.
7. On 1993 3.0L models (3VZ-FE), remove the cooling fan.
8. Detach refrigerant lines from the condenser. Cap open fittings immediately.
9. Remove the condenser.

To install:

10. Install the condenser to the vehicle. Make sure all rubber cushions fit on the mounting flanges correctly.
11. Reconnect all refrigerant lines. Replace O-rings, as applicable.
12. Install fan assemblies, brackets, supports and battery, as removed.
13. If condenser assembly was replaced, add 1.4–1.7 fl. oz. of compressor oil.
14. Reconnect the battery cable. Evacuate, charge and test refrigerant system. check system for leaks.

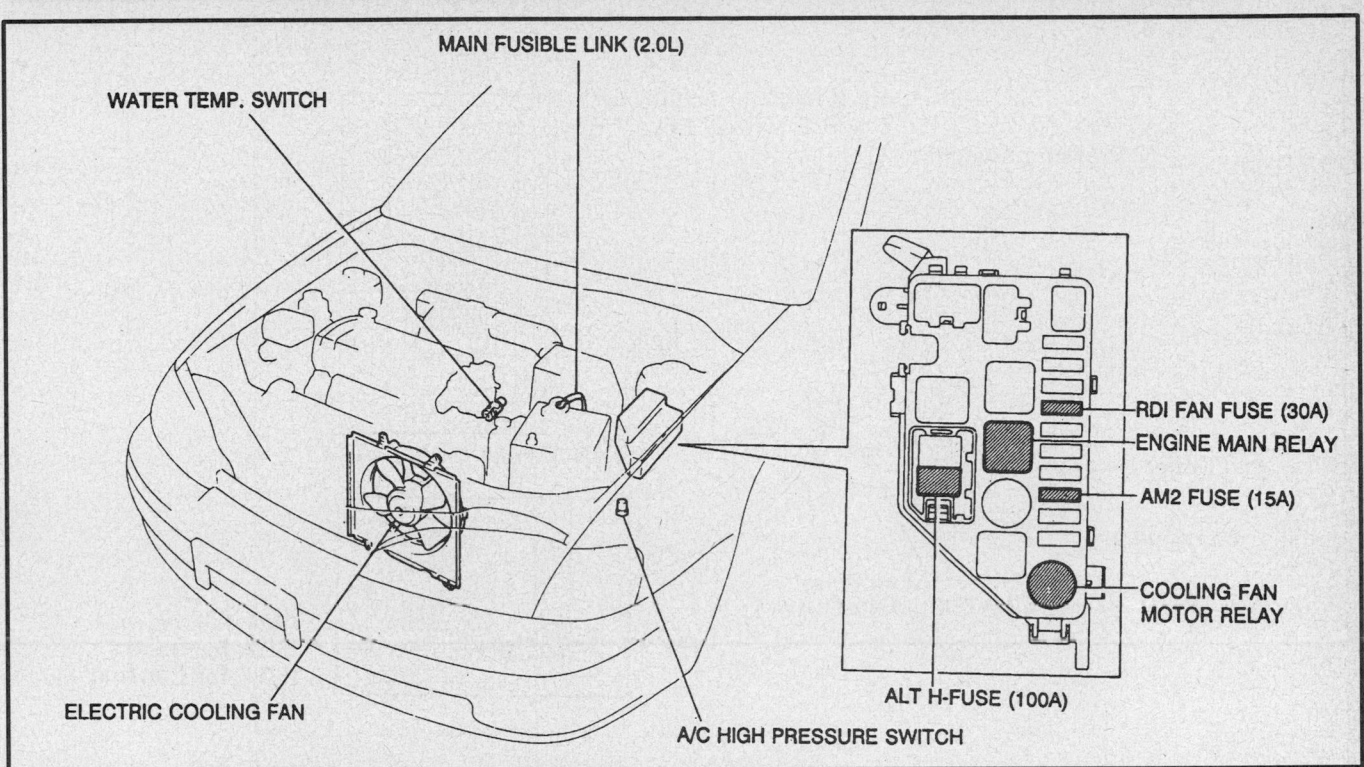

MAIN FUSIBLE LINK (2.0L)

WATER TEMP. SWITCH

RDI FAN FUSE (30A)
ENGINE MAIN RELAY
AM2 FUSE (15A)
COOLING FAN MOTOR RELAY

ELECTRIC COOLING FAN

A/C HIGH PRESSURE SWITCH

ALT H-FUSE (100A)

Location of electrical cooling fan system components – 1993 Paseo

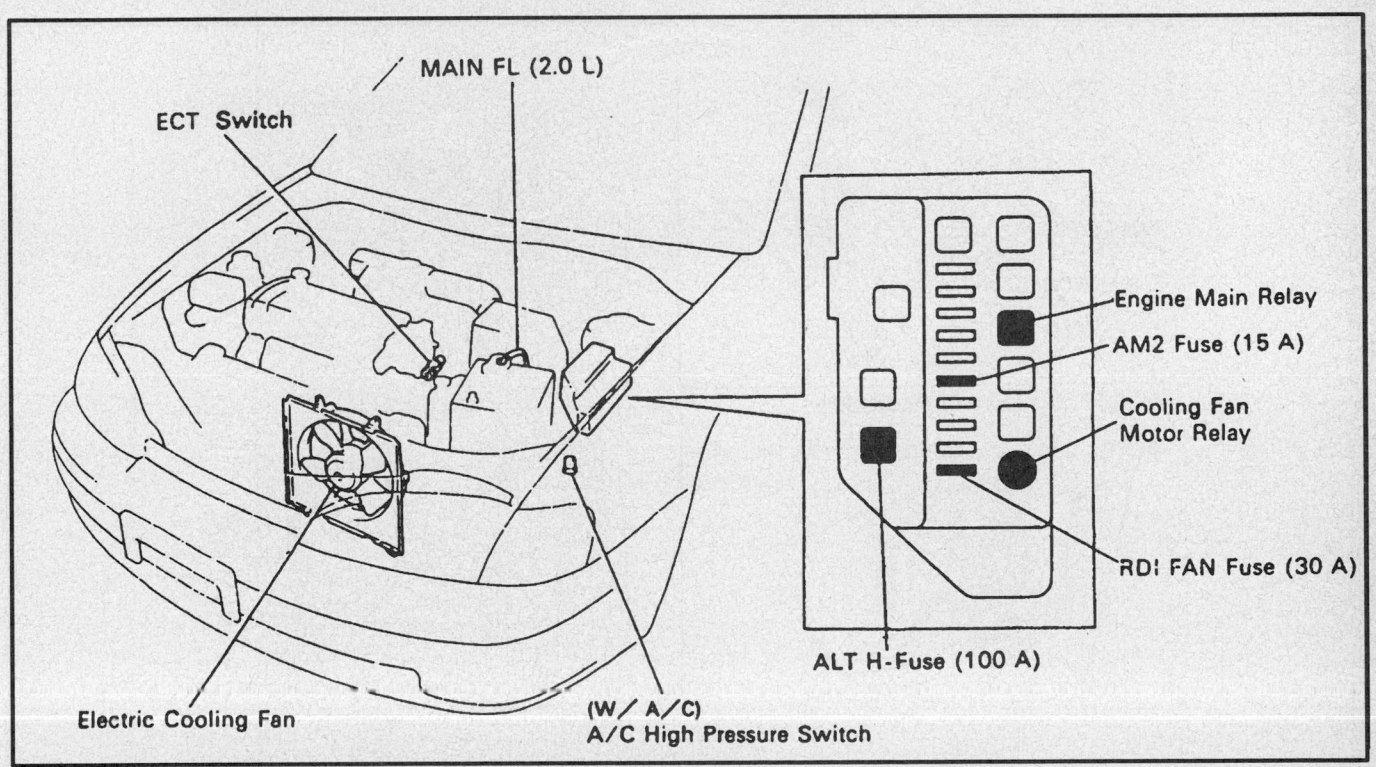

MAIN FL (2.0 L)

ECT Switch

Engine Main Relay

AM2 Fuse (15 A)

Cooling Fan Motor Relay

RDI FAN Fuse (30 A)

Electric Cooling Fan

(W/ A/C)
A/C High Pressure Switch

ALT H-Fuse (100 A)

Location of electrical cooling fan components – 1994-95 Paseo

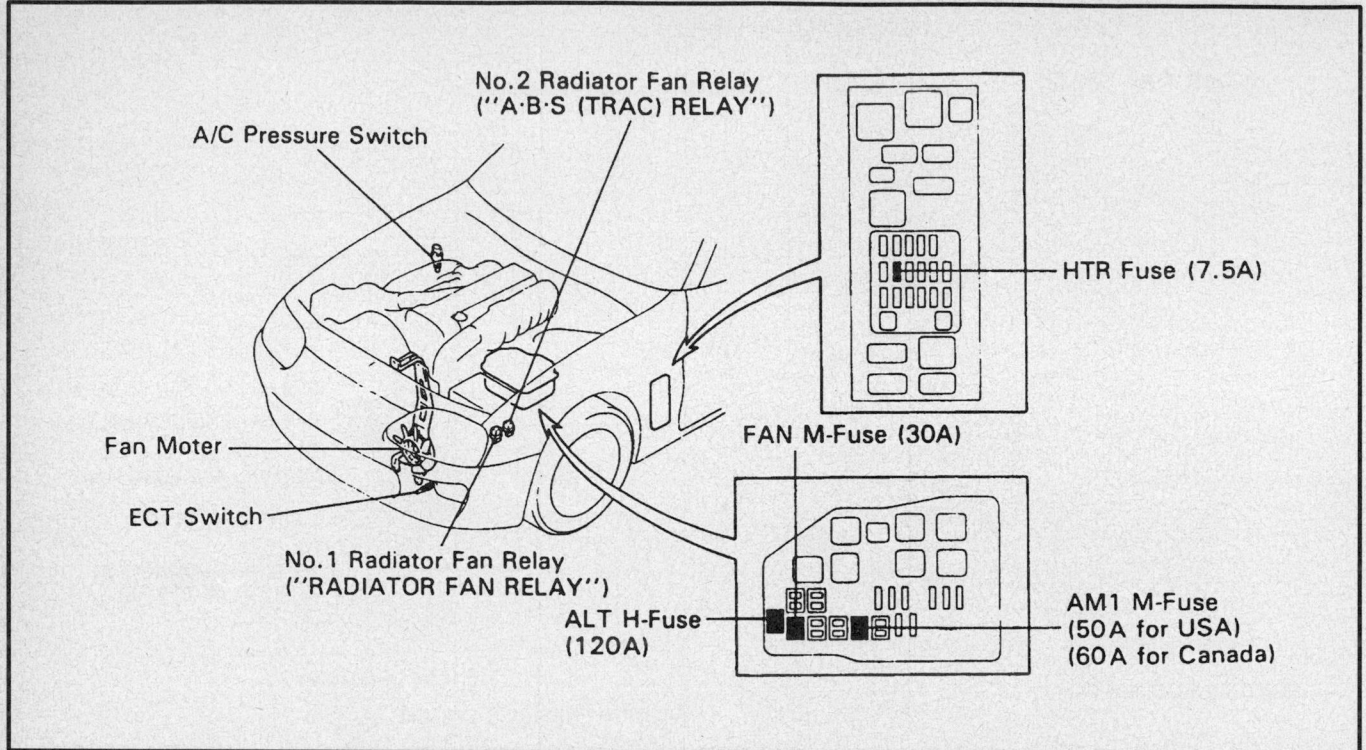

Location of electric cooling fan components – 1994-95 Supra

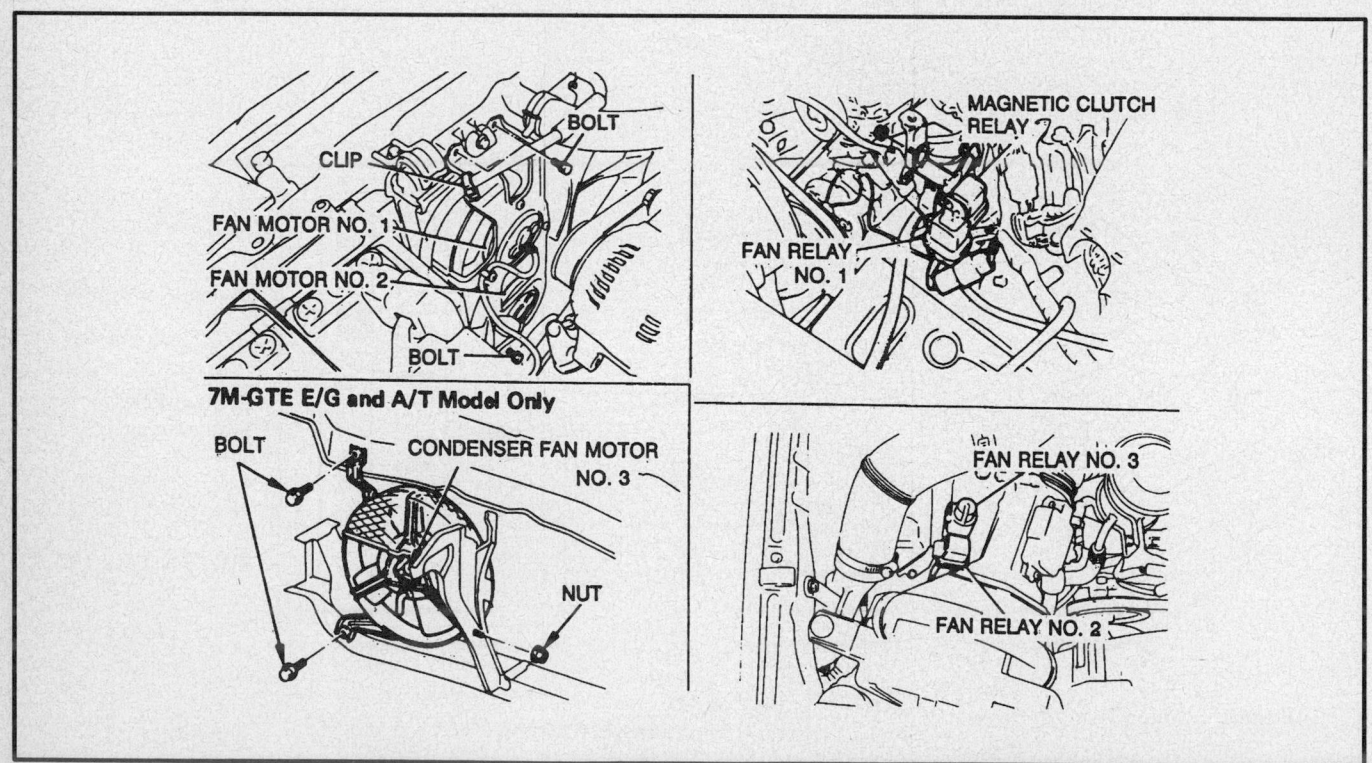

Electric cooling fan system components – 1993 Supra

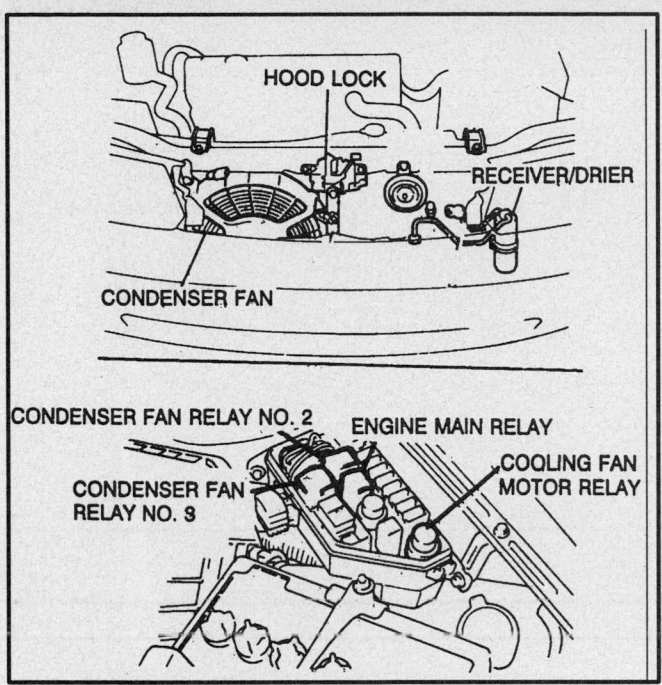

**Electric cooling fan system components –
1993 Tercel**

Camry

1. Disconnect the negative battery cable.
2. Properly discharge the air conditioning system using recovery equipment.
3. Remove the radiator grille, upper radiator mounts, radiator cooling fan and cooling fan.
4. Remove condenser.
To install:
5. Install condenser to the vehicle. Make sure all rubber cushions fit on the mounting flanges.
6. Reconnect the refrigerant connections. Replace O-rings, if required.
7. Install radiator grille, upper radiator mounts, radiator fan and cooling fan.
8. Reconnect battery cable. Evacuate, charge and test refrigerant system. Check system for leaks.

Celica and Corolla

1. Disconnect the negative battery cable.
2. Recover refrigerant (discharge system) from refrigeration system.
3. Remove engine undercover (Celica). Remove the front grille assembly. Remove the hood lock (Corolla), center brace and horns.
4. On Corolla, remove front bumper assembly and oil cooler (leave hoses attached), if equipped.
5. Remove the condenser fan assembly. On 1993 Corolla, remove the oxygen sensor (located left of the radiator cap).
6. Remove all refrigerant system connections. Cap open fittings immediately.

7. Remove the condenser.
To install:
8. Install the condenser to the vehicle. Make sure all rubber cushions fit on the mounting flanges correctly.
9. Reconnect all refrigerant system connections. Replace O-rings, if required.
10. Install fan, center brace, hood lock and horns.
11. On Corolla install oil cooler and oxygen sensor (if removed) and front bumper assembly.
12. Install front grille and engine undercover.
13. If condenser assembly was replaced, add 1.4–1.7 fl. oz. of compressor oil.
14. Reconnect battery cable. Evacuate, charge and test refrigerant system. Check system for leaks.

Paseo and Tercel

1. Disconnect the negative battery cable.
2. Properly discharge the air conditioning system using recovery equipment.
3. Remove the front grille assembly. Remove the hood lock, center brace and horns. Remove the receiver/drier assembly.
4. Remove the front bumper assembly.
5. Remove the condenser fan assembly.
6. Remove all refrigerant system connections. Cap open fittings immediately.
7. Remove the ambient sensor from below the receiver/drier location. Remove the condenser.
To install:
8. Install the condenser to the vehicle. Make sure all rubber cushions fit on the mounting flanges correctly. Install ambient sensor.
9. Reconnect all refrigerant system connections. Replace O-rings, if required.
10. Install front grille assembly, hood lock and center brace.
11. Install the horn, receiver, bumper and fan assembly.
12. Install oil cooler.
13. If condenser assembly was replaced, add 1.4–1.7 fl. oz. of compressor oil.
14. Reconnect the battery cable. Evacuate, charge and test refrigerant system. Check system for leaks.

MR2

1. Disconnect the negative battery cable.
2. Properly discharge the air conditioning system, using recovery equipment.
3. Remove condenser cover and condenser retaining bracket assemblies.
4. Disconnect refrigerant lines from the condenser. Cap open fittings immediately.
5. Remove the 2 retaining bolts and lift out the condenser.
To install:
6. Install the condenser to the vehicle. Make sure all rubber cushions fit on the mounting flanges correctly.
7. Reconnect all refrigerant system connections. Replace O-rings, if required.
8. Install condenser retaining bracket assemblies and cover.
9. If condenser assembly was replaced, add 1.4–1.8 fl. oz. of compressor oil.
10. Reconnect the battery cable. Evacuate, charge and test refrigerant system. Check system for leaks.

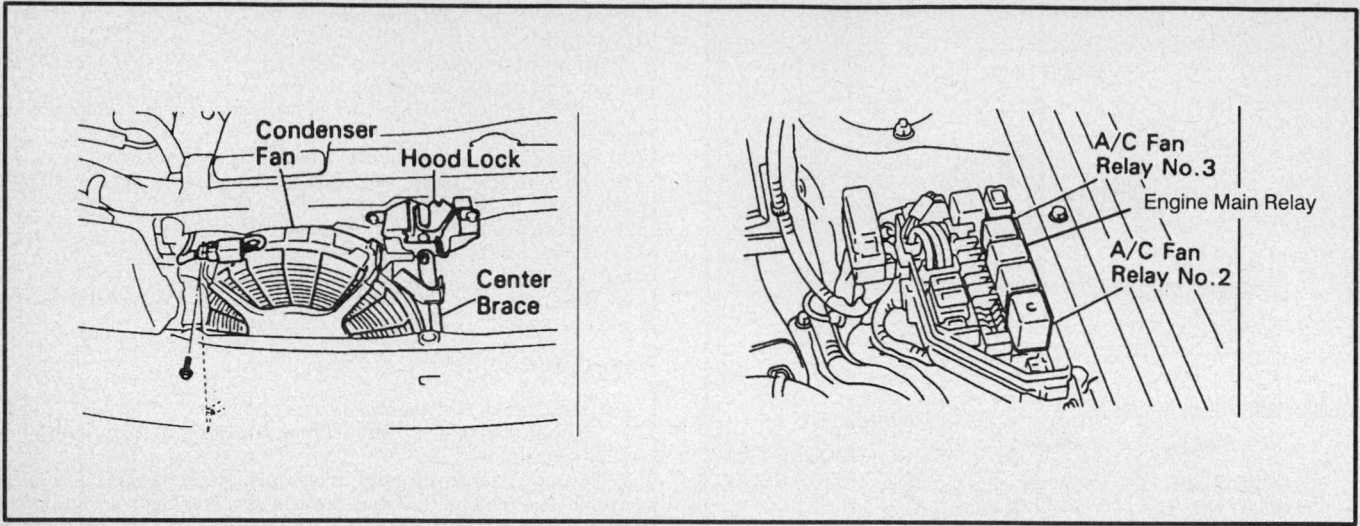

Location of electric cooling fan components – 1994 Tercel

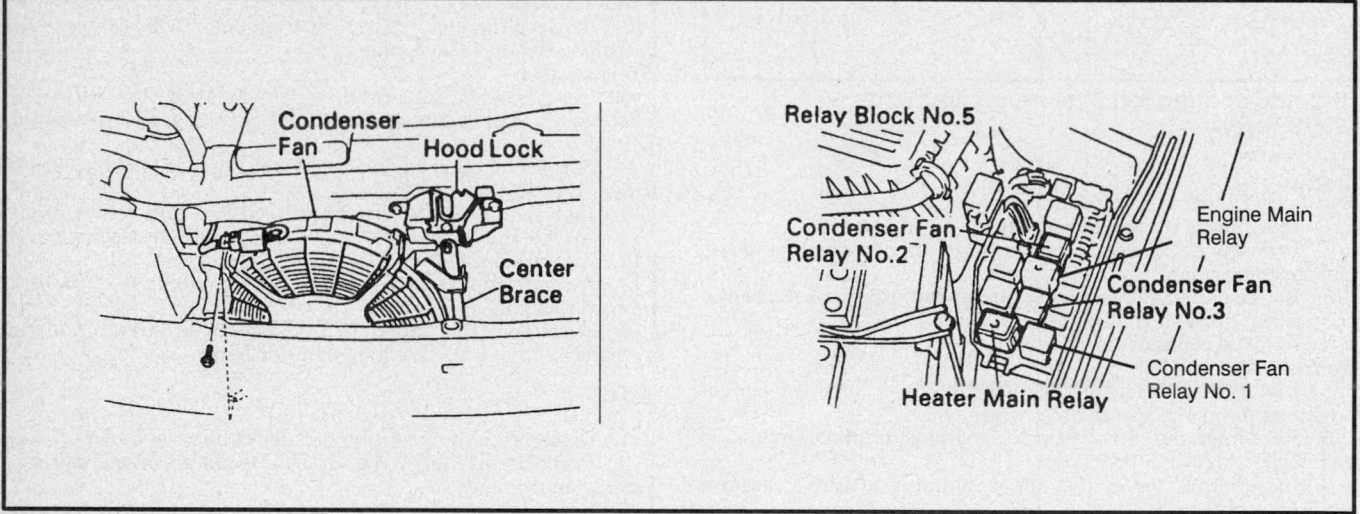

Location of electric cooling fan components – 1995 Tercel

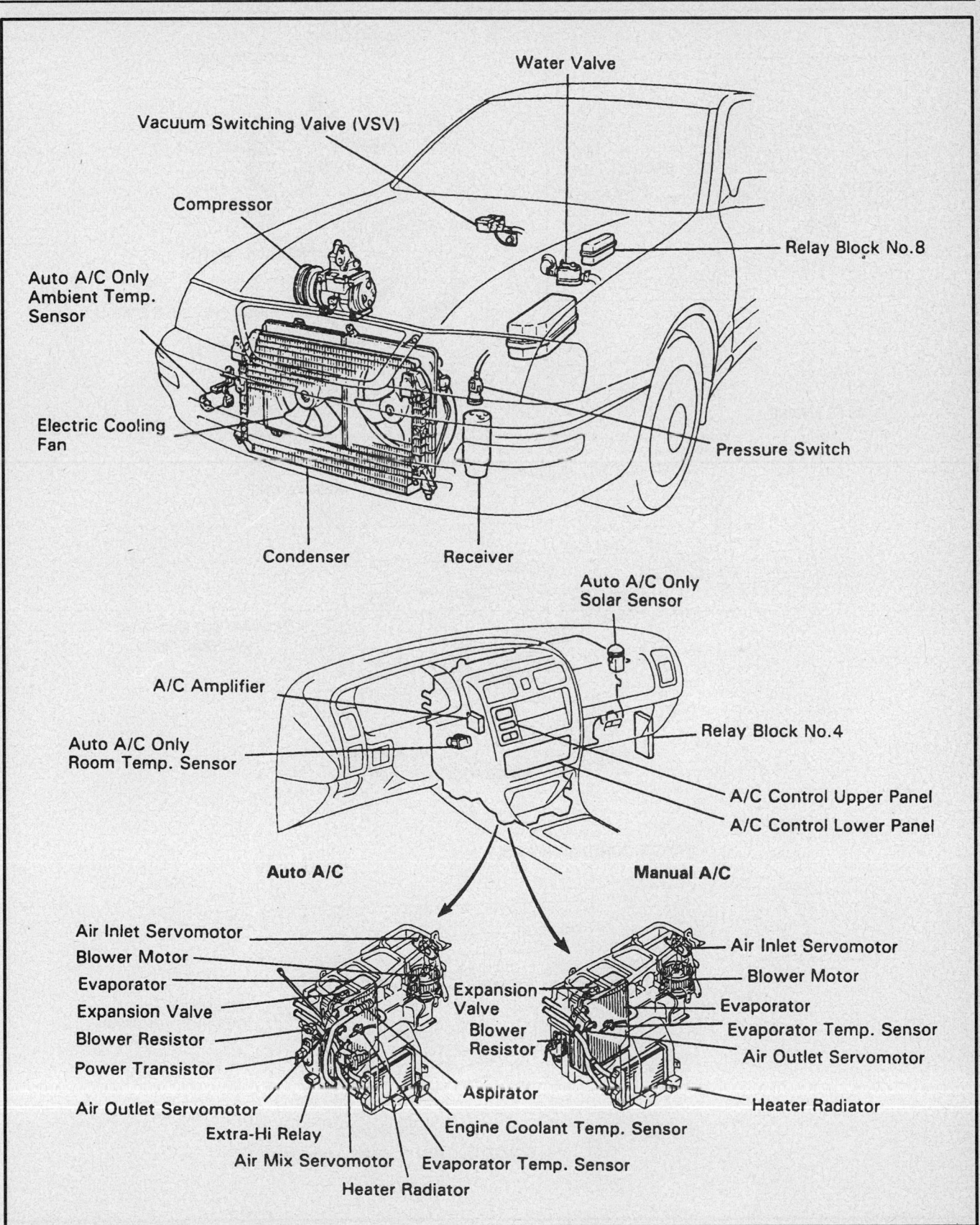

Air conditioning system components — Avalon

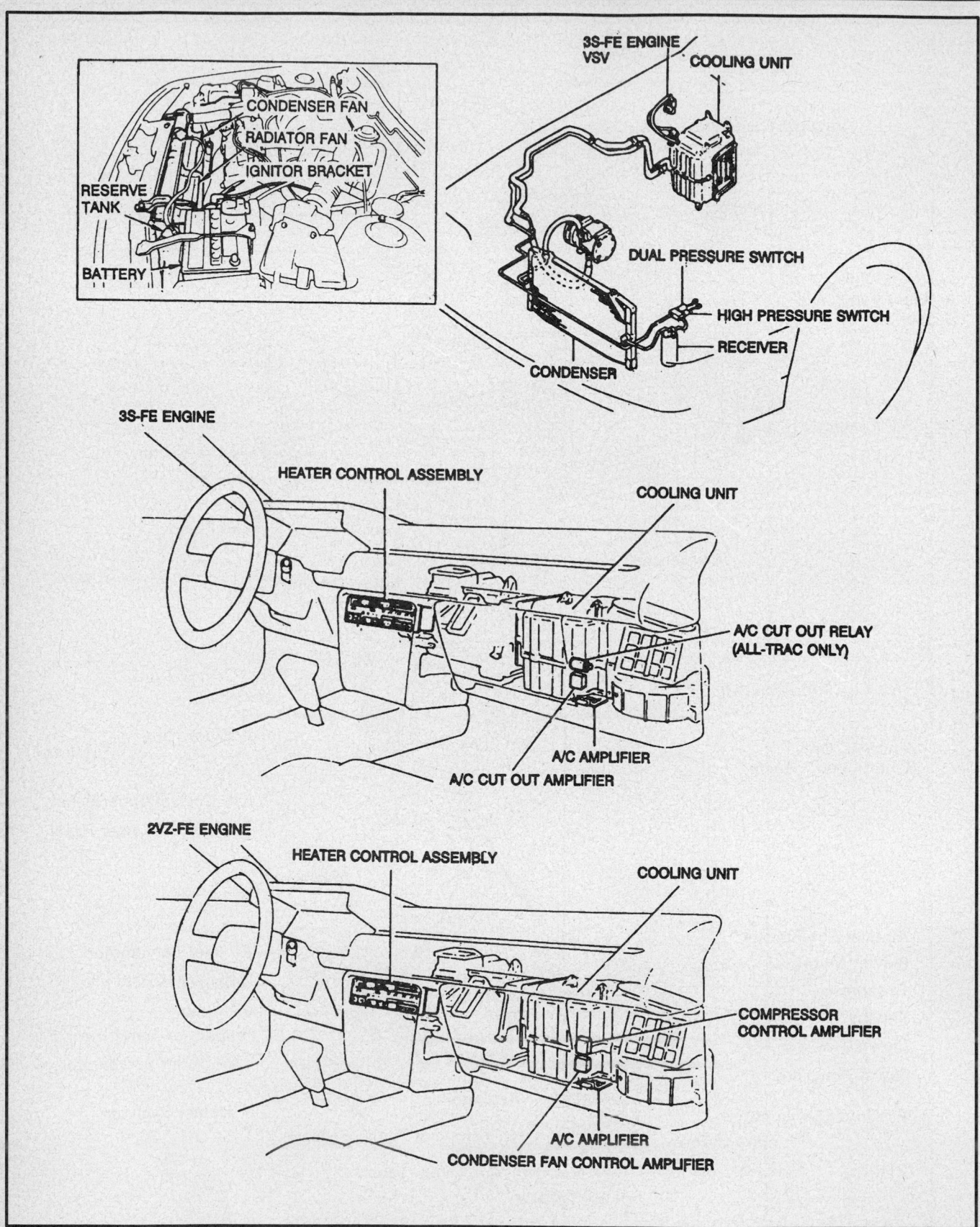

CONDENSER FAN
RADIATOR FAN
IGNITOR BRACKET
RESERVE TANK
BATTERY

3S-FE ENGINE VSV
COOLING UNIT
DUAL PRESSURE SWITCH
HIGH PRESSURE SWITCH
RECEIVER
CONDENSER

3S-FE ENGINE
HEATER CONTROL ASSEMBLY
COOLING UNIT
A/C CUT OUT RELAY (ALL-TRAC ONLY)
A/C AMPLIFIER
A/C CUT OUT AMPLIFIER

2VZ-FE ENGINE
HEATER CONTROL ASSEMBLY
COOLING UNIT
COMPRESSOR CONTROL AMPLIFIER
A/C AMPLIFIER
CONDENSER FAN CONTROL AMPLIFIER

Air conditioning system components – 1993 Camry

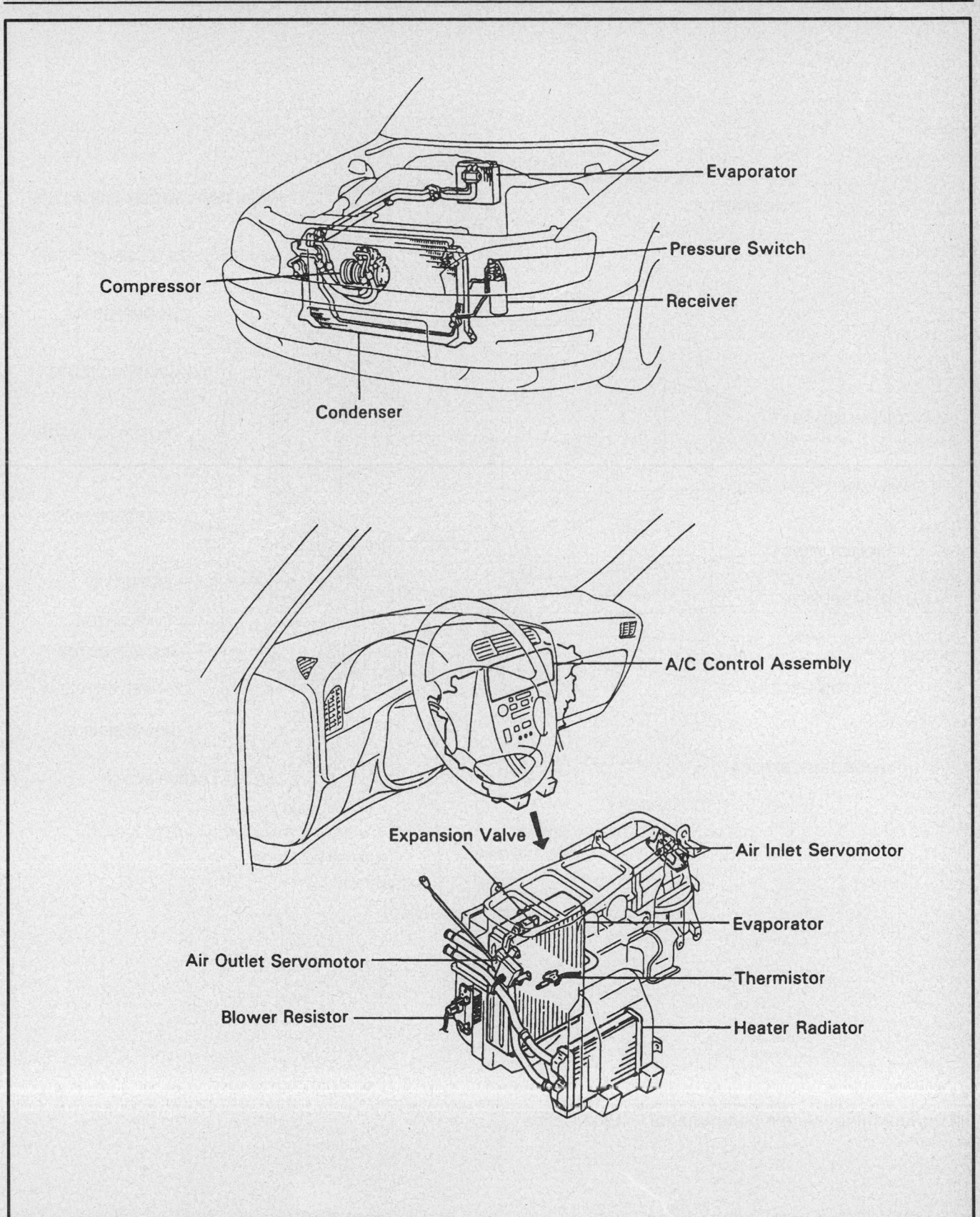

Evaporator

Pressure Switch

Compressor

Receiver

Condenser

A/C Control Assembly

Expansion Valve

Air Inlet Servomotor

Air Outlet Servomotor

Evaporator

Blower Resistor

Thermistor

Heater Radiator

Air conditioning system components – 1994-95 Camry

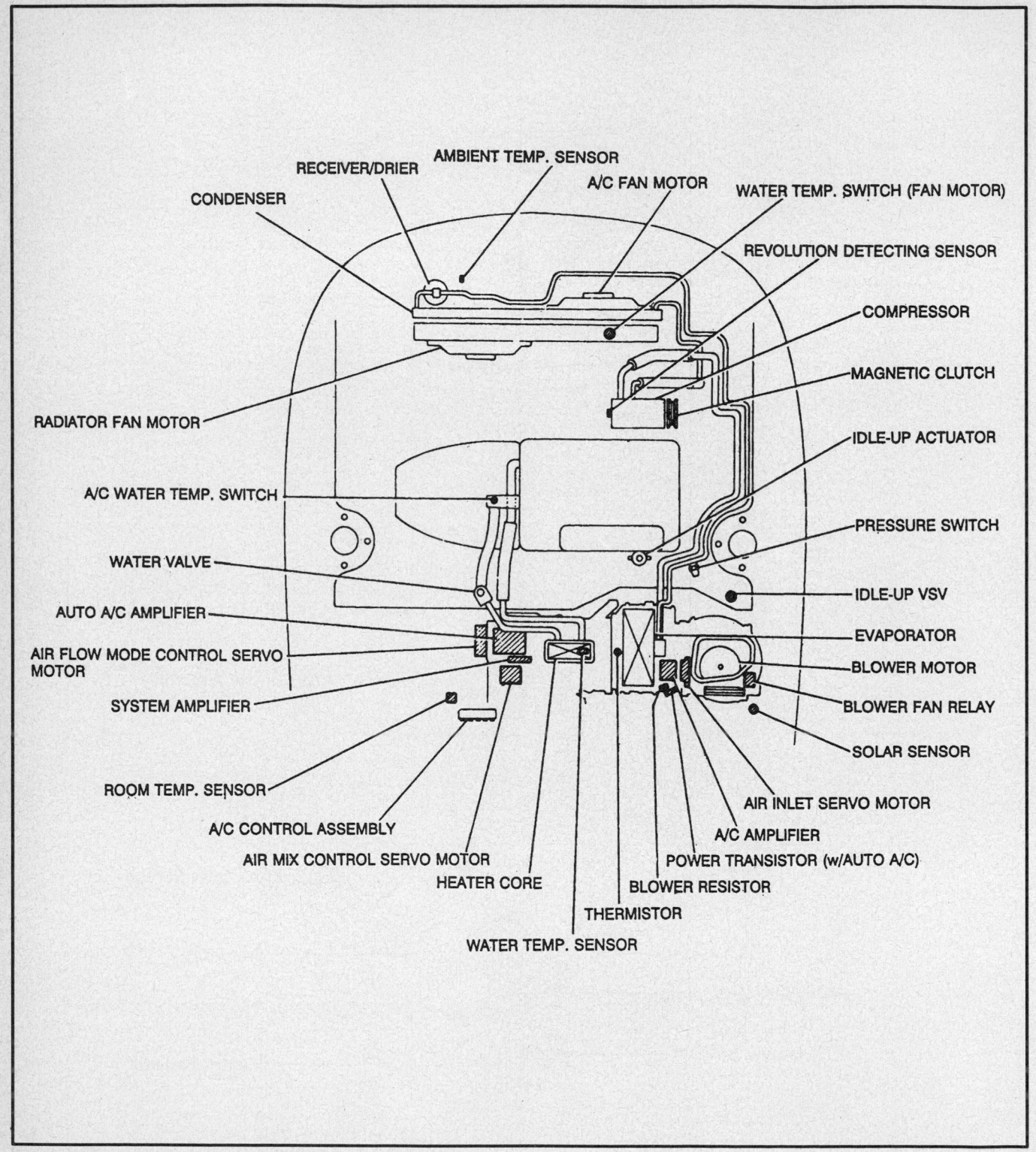

CONDENSER

RECEIVER/DRIER

AMBIENT TEMP. SENSOR

A/C FAN MOTOR

WATER TEMP. SWITCH (FAN MOTOR)

REVOLUTION DETECTING SENSOR

COMPRESSOR

MAGNETIC CLUTCH

RADIATOR FAN MOTOR

IDLE-UP ACTUATOR

A/C WATER TEMP. SWITCH

PRESSURE SWITCH

WATER VALVE

IDLE-UP VSV

AUTO A/C AMPLIFIER

EVAPORATOR

AIR FLOW MODE CONTROL SERVO MOTOR

BLOWER MOTOR

SYSTEM AMPLIFIER

BLOWER FAN RELAY

SOLAR SENSOR

ROOM TEMP. SENSOR

AIR INLET SERVO MOTOR

A/C CONTROL ASSEMBLY

A/C AMPLIFIER

AIR MIX CONTROL SERVO MOTOR

POWER TRANSISTOR (w/AUTO A/C)

HEATER CORE

BLOWER RESISTOR

THERMISTOR

WATER TEMP. SENSOR

Air conditioning system components – 1993 Celica

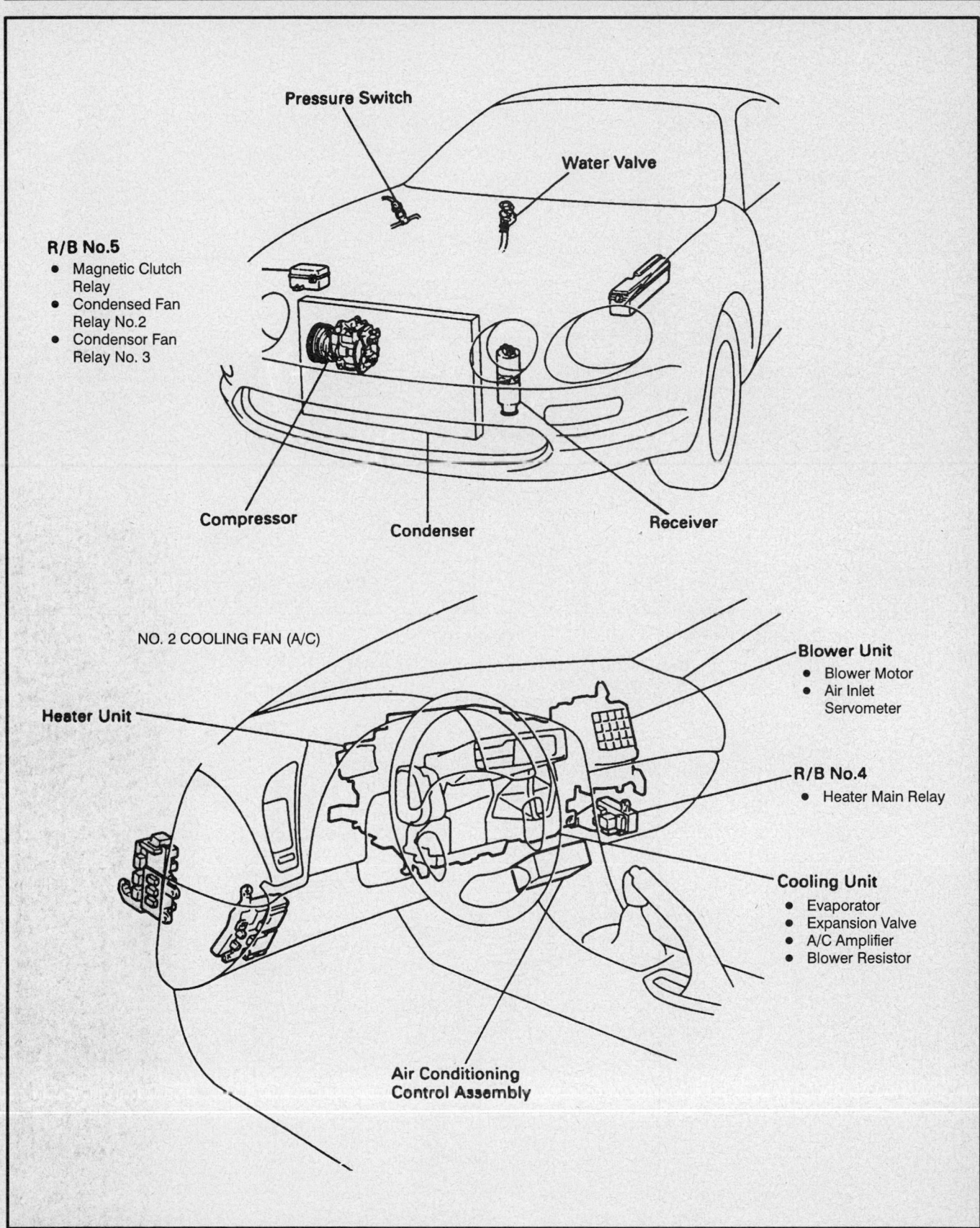

Pressure Switch

Water Valve

R/B No.5
- Magnetic Clutch Relay
- Condensed Fan Relay No.2
- Condensor Fan Relay No. 3

Compressor

Condenser

Receiver

NO. 2 COOLING FAN (A/C)

Heater Unit

Blower Unit
- Blower Motor
- Air Inlet Servometer

R/B No.4
- Heater Main Relay

Cooling Unit
- Evaporator
- Expansion Valve
- A/C Amplifier
- Blower Resistor

Air Conditioning Control Assembly

Air conditioning system components — 1994-95 Celica

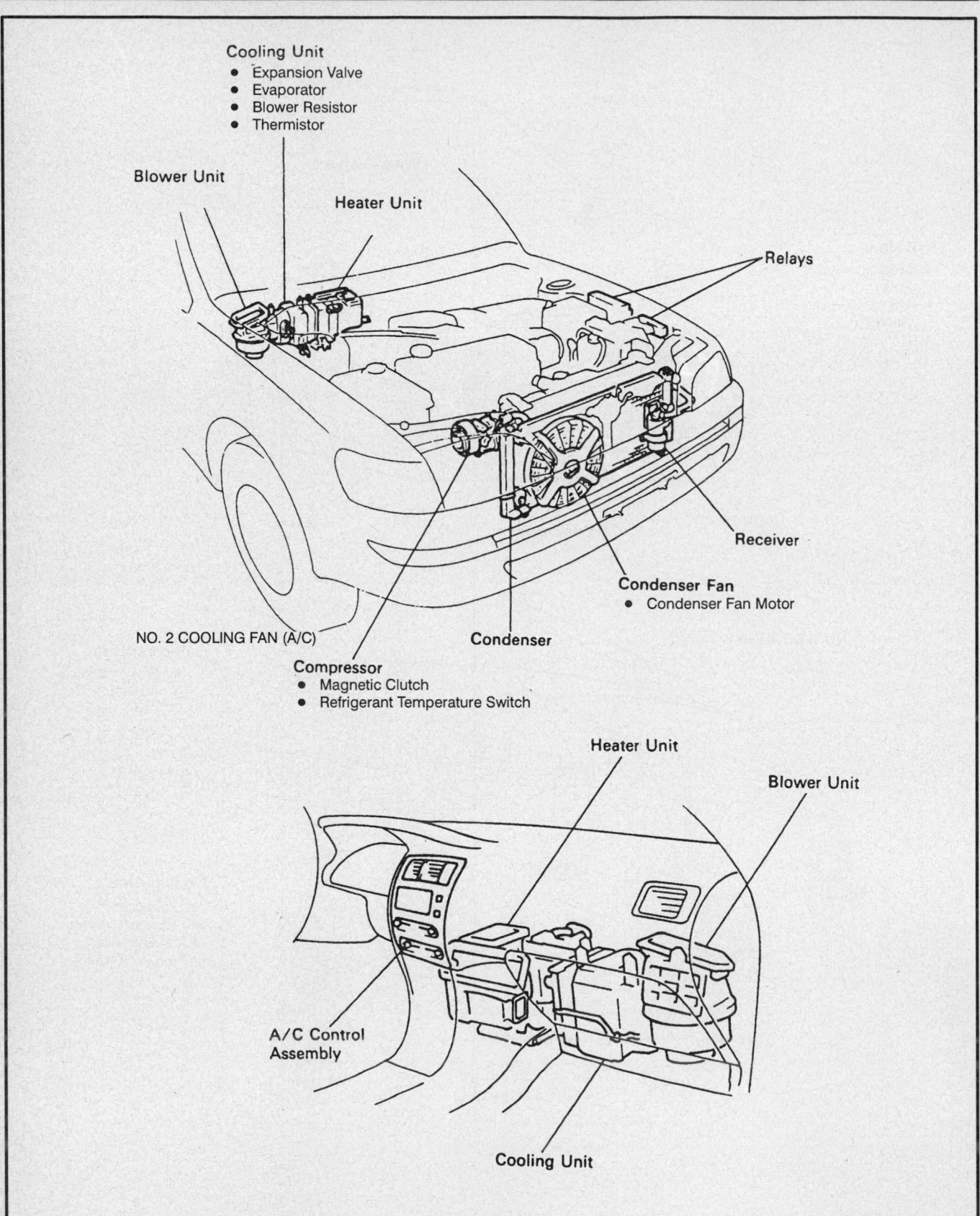

Cooling Unit
- Expansion Valve
- Evaporator
- Blower Resistor
- Thermistor

Blower Unit

Heater Unit

Relays

Receiver

Condenser Fan
- Condenser Fan Motor

NO. 2 COOLING FAN (A/C)

Condenser

Compressor
- Magnetic Clutch
- Refrigerant Temperature Switch

Heater Unit

Blower Unit

A/C Control Assembly

Cooling Unit

Air conditioning system components – 1994-95 Corolla

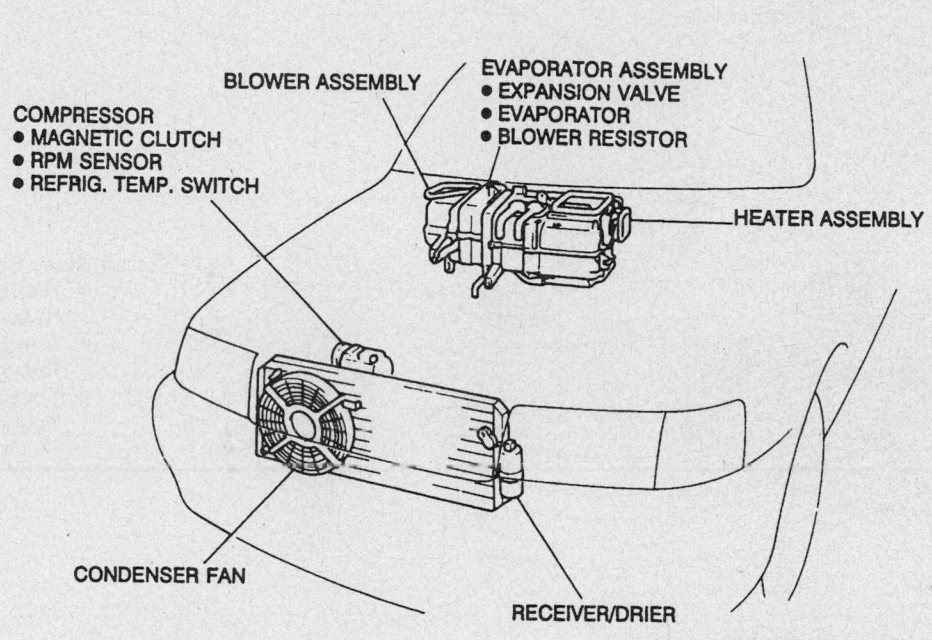

COMPRESSOR
- MAGNETIC CLUTCH
- RPM SENSOR
- REFRIG. TEMP. SWITCH

BLOWER ASSEMBLY

EVAPORATOR ASSEMBLY
- EXPANSION VALVE
- EVAPORATOR
- BLOWER RESISTOR

HEATER ASSEMBLY

CONDENSER FAN

RECEIVER/DRIER

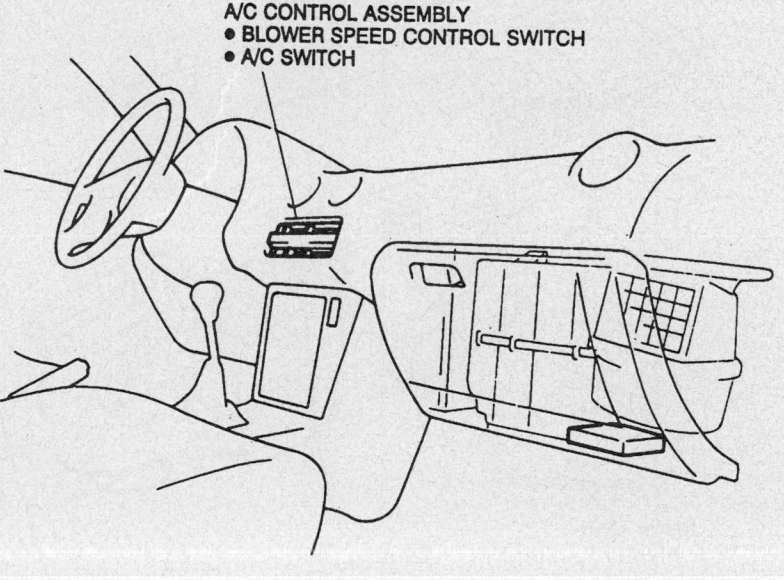

A/C CONTROL ASSEMBLY
- BLOWER SPEED CONTROL SWITCH
- A/C SWITCH

Air conditioning system components — Paseo

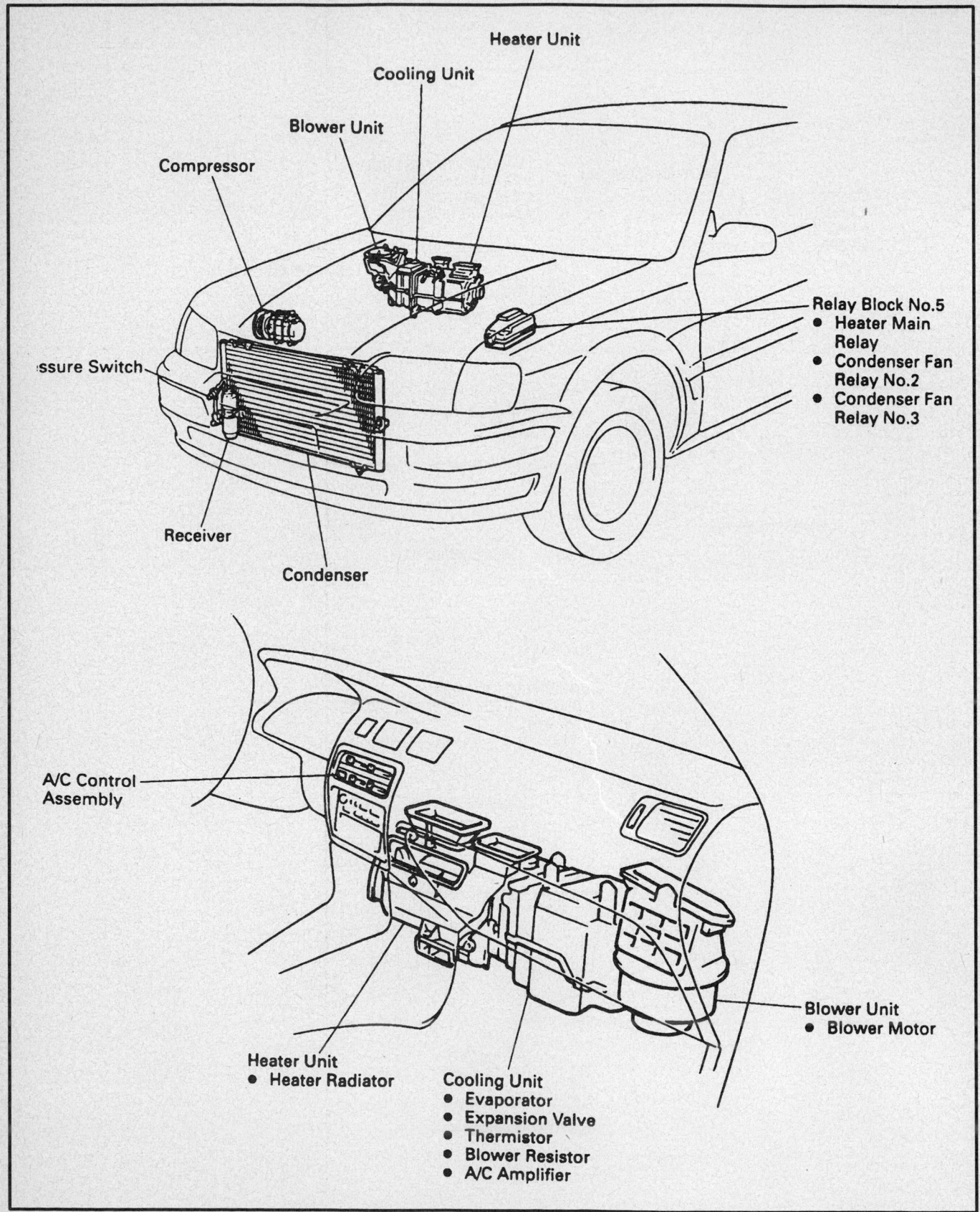

Heater Unit

Cooling Unit

Blower Unit

Compressor

Relay Block No.5
- Heater Main Relay
- Condenser Fan Relay No.2
- Condenser Fan Relay No.3

ssure Switch

Receiver

Condenser

A/C Control Assembly

Blower Unit
- Blower Motor

Heater Unit
- Heater Radiator

Cooling Unit
- Evaporator
- Expansion Valve
- Thermistor
- Blower Resistor
- A/C Amplifier

Air conditioning system components — 1995 Tercel

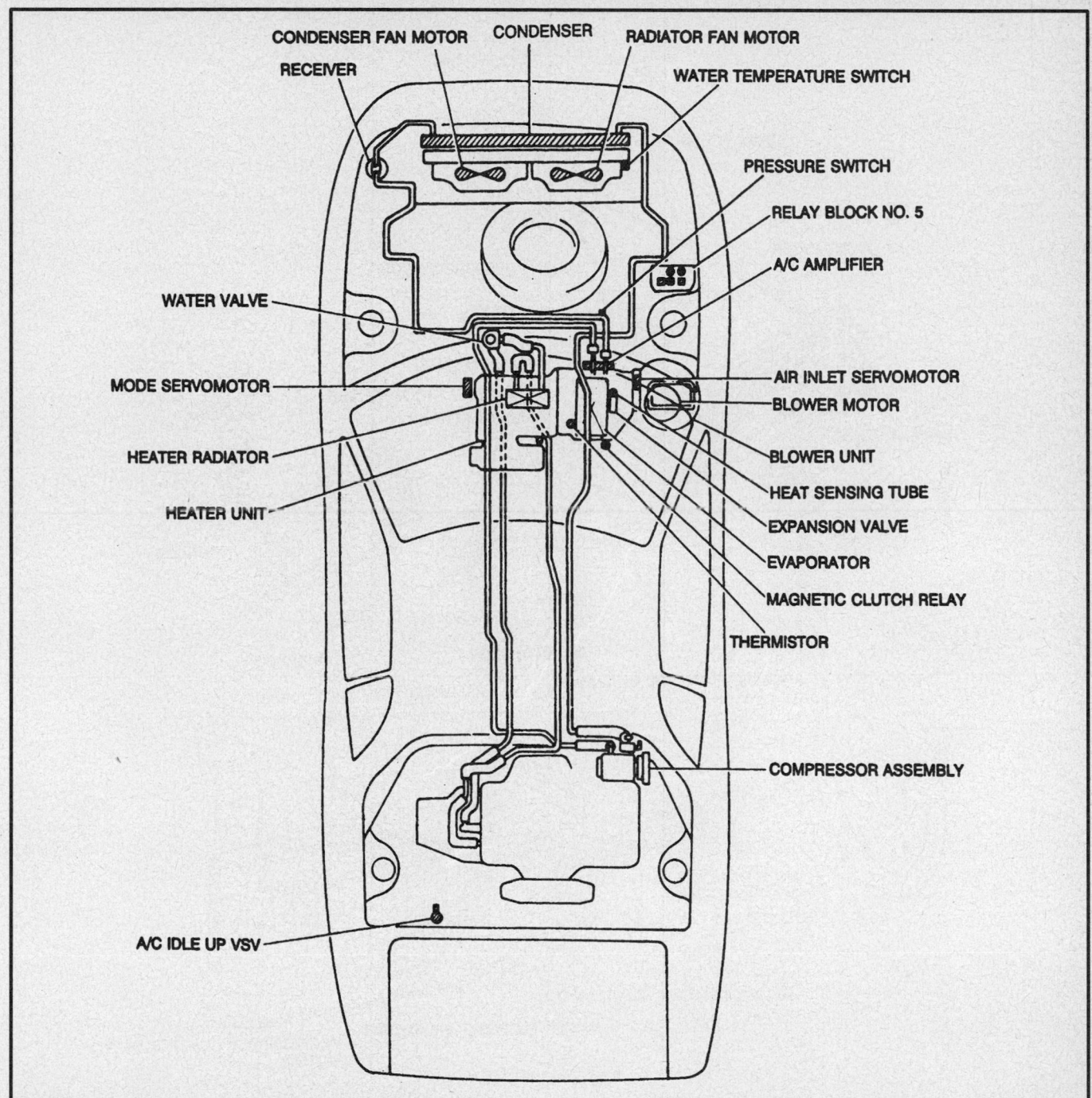

Air conditioning system components – MR2

Supra

1. Disconnect the negative battery cable.
2. Properly discharge the air conditioning system using recovery equipment.
3. Remove the air cleaner duct and air cleaner. On turbocharged engines, remove turbocharger air hose clamp and push hose toward engine side.

4. On all models, remove the front bumper. Remove the radiator support upper seal.
5. Remove receiver. Disconnect all refrigerant system connections. Cap open fittings immediately. Remove condenser.

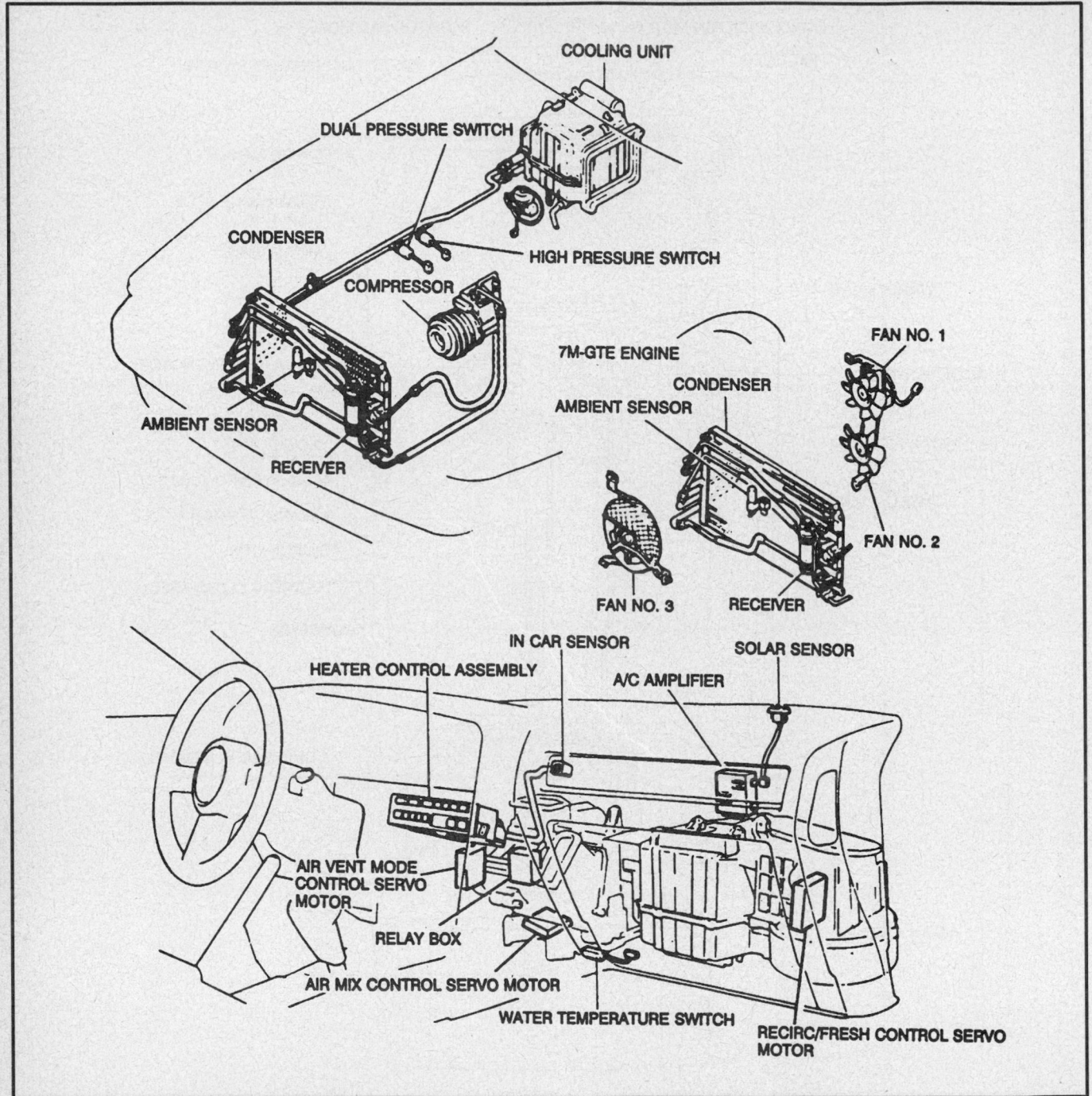

Air conditioning system components — 1993 Supra

To install:

6. Install condenser to the vehicle. Make sure all rubber cushions fit on the mounting flanges correctly.

7. Reconnect all refrigerant system connections. Replace O-rings, if required. Install receiver.

8. Install radiator support upper seal and front bumper.

9. Install air cleaner and air cleaner duct. On turbocharged engines, reconnect the turbocharger air hose and clamp.

10. If condenser assembly was replaced, add 1.4–1.7 fl.oz. of compressor oil.

11. Reconnect battery cable. Evacuate, charge and test refrigerant system. Check system for leaks.

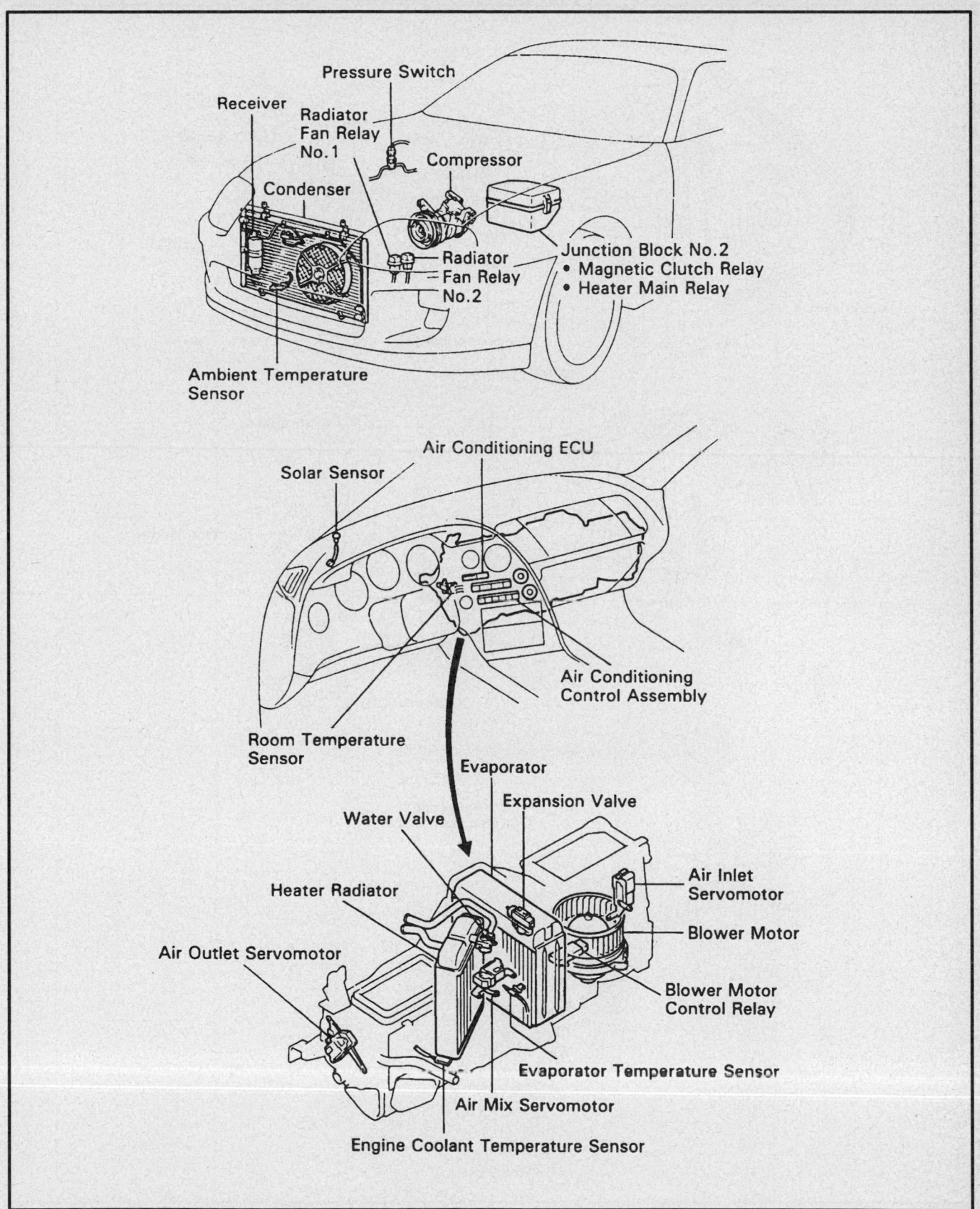

Air conditioning system components – 1994-95 Supra

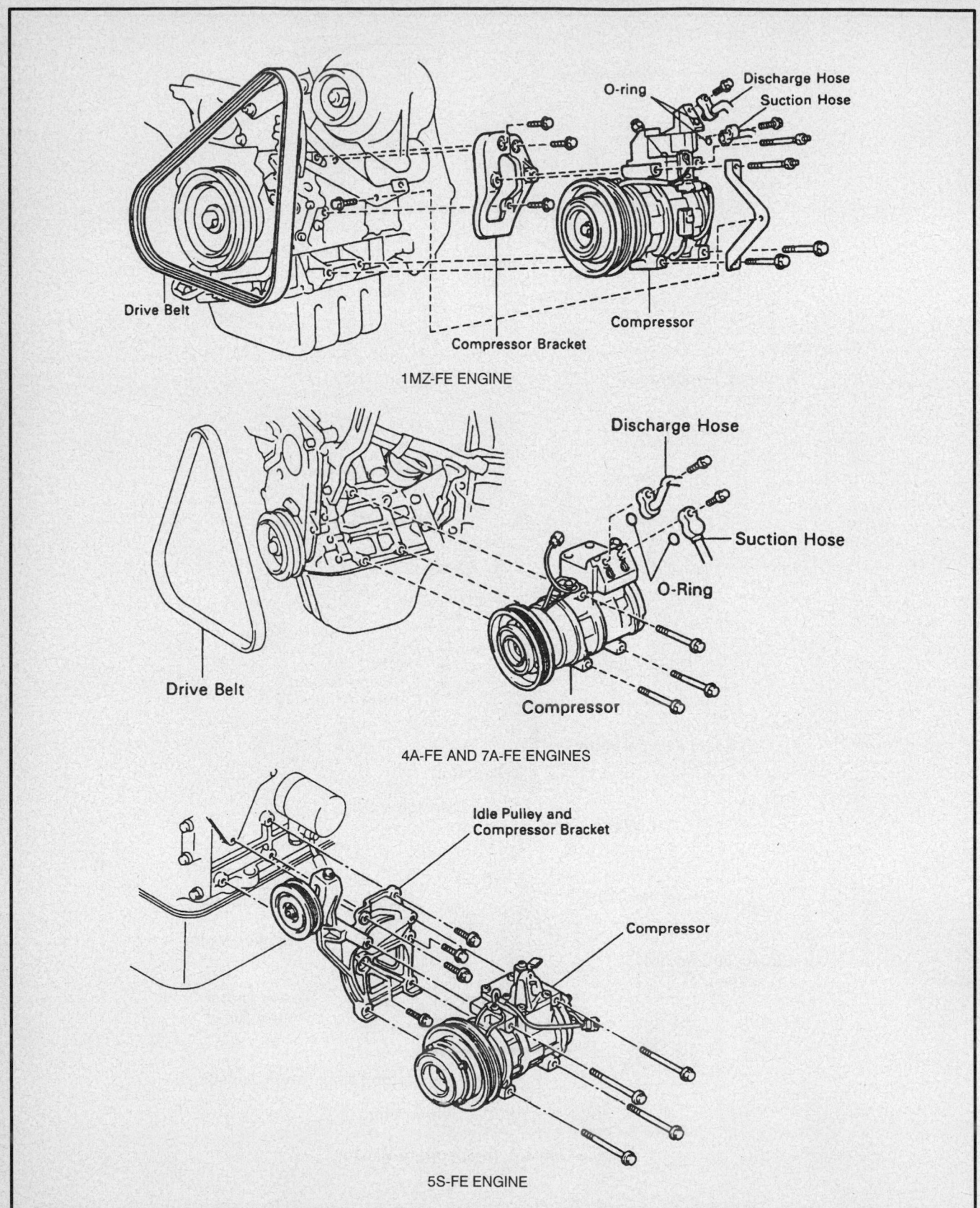

1MZ-FE ENGINE

4A-FE AND 7A-FE ENGINES

5S-FE ENGINE

Compressor removal and installation — 1MZ-FE, 4A-FE, 7A-FE and 5S-FE, others similar

Compressor

REMOVAL AND INSTALLATION

1. Run the engine at idle with the air conditioning on for approximately 10 minutes. Stop the engine and properly discharge the system. Disconnect the negative battery cable.
2. Remove the following specific items:
- On MR2, Paseo and Tercel, remove engine under cover.
- On Corolla, remove the washer reserve tank.
- On Camry with 3VZ-FE engine, remove the battery, battery bracket and remove the engine cooling fan.
- On Supra, remove the battery, battery bracket and the power steering pump.

3. Disconnect electrical connector for magnetic clutch, temperature switch and revolution sensor.
4. Disconnect the air conditioning hoses from the compressor service valves. Cap open fittings immediately.
5. Loosen the compressor mounting bolts. Remove the compressor drive belt. Remove the compressor mounting bolts. Remove the compressor from the vehicle.

To install:
6. Install compressor with mounting bolts. Install drive belt.
7. Reconnect hoses to the compressor service valves.
8. Connect electrical connector to magnetic clutch, temperature switch and revolution sensor.
9. Reinstall specific items as removed to access compressor.
10. Reconnect the battery cable. Evacuate, recharge and test refrigerant system. Check system for leaks.

Receiver/Drier

REMOVAL AND INSTALLATION

1. Disconnect the negative battery cable.
2. Properly discharge the air conditioning system, using recovery type equipment.
3. Remove the following specific items:
- On 1994–95 Celica, remove the coolant reservoir tank.
- On Corolla, remove the grille and the horn.
- On MR2, remove left fender liner and engine under cover.
- On Paseo and Tercel, remove the grille.
- On 1994–95 Supra, remove the front bumper and radiator support upper seal.

4. Disconnect lines from the receiver/drier. Cap open fittings immediately. Remove the receiver from the receiver/drier holder assembly. Remove the receiver/drier.

To install:
5. Install receiver in receiver/drier and holder assembly. Reconnect lines to the receiver.
6. Install the specific items as removed per vehicle.
7. If receiver assembly was replaced, add 0.7 fl. oz. of compressor oil.
8. Reconnect the battery cable. Evacuate, recharge and test refrigerant system. Check system for leaks.

Expansion Valve

REMOVAL AND INSTALLATION

NOTE: On all Toyota vehicles the cooling unit or evaporator assembly must be removed before the expansion valve

can be replaced. Refer to the cooling unit or evaporator assembly service procedures.

Blower Motor

REMOVAL AND INSTALLATION

NOTE: The air conditioning assembly is integral with the heater assembly (including the blower motor). In some cases it may be necessary to remove the Cooling Unit assembly or package tray to remove the blower motor.

Avalon

1. Disconnect the negative battery cable.

――――――― CAUTION ―――――――
If vehicle is equipped with an air bag system, when ignition is turned to LOCK and negative battery cable is disconnected, do not work inside the passenger compartment for at least 30 seconds to give the SRS (air bag supplemental restraint system) a chance to become fully disarmed.
――――――――――――――――――――――――

2. Remove the lower finish panel. Disconnect connector and remove the blower motor.

To install:
3. Install blower motor to vehicle. Reconnect connector and install the lower finish panel.
4. Check the blower motor for proper operation at all speeds.

Camry

1. Disconnect the negative battery cable.

――――――― CAUTION ―――――――
If vehicle is equipped with an air bag system, when ignition is turned to LOCK and negative battery cable is disconnected, do not work inside the passenger compartment for at least 30 seconds to give the SRS (air bag supplemental restraint system) a chance to become fully disarmed.
――――――――――――――――――――――――

2. Remove the glove box.
3. Remove the ECU and bracket and the relay block wiring harness and bracket.
4. Remove the air duct between the blower motor assembly and the heater assembly. Disconnect the blower motor wire connector at the blower motor case.
5. Disconnect the air source selector control cable at the blower motor assembly or servo control lines.
6. Remove air conditioning amplifier and wiring, if necessary.
7. Remove the mounting screws attaching the blower motor to the blower case, remove the blower motor assembly from the vehicle.

To install:
8. Clean blower motor housing of all dirt, leaves etc. before installation. Install the blower motor assembly in the vehicle.
9. Install air conditioning amplifier and wiring, as necessary. Reconnect all control cables and route servo control lines, as necessary.
10. Reconnect all electrical components and connections and install duct work.
11. Install glove box and reconnect the negative battery cable.
12. Check the blower motor for proper operation at all speeds after installation.

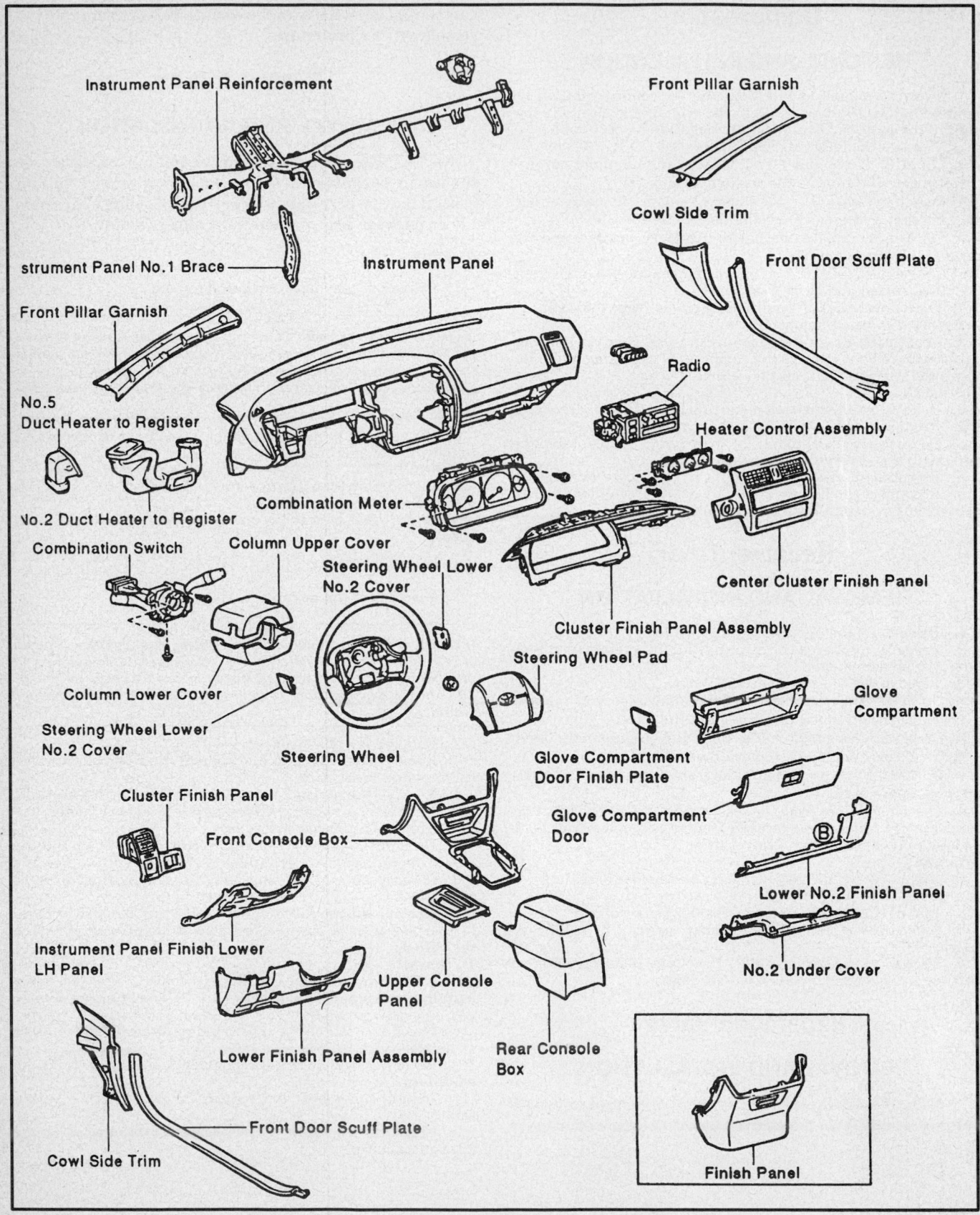

Exploded view of instrument panel for heater component removal — Avalon

Celica, MR2 and Supra

1. Disconnect the negative battery cable.

──────────── CAUTION ────────────

If vehicle is equipped with an air bag system, when ignition is turned to LOCK and negative battery cable is disconnected, do not work inside the passenger compartment for at least 30 seconds to give the SRS (air bag supplemental restraint system) a chance to become fully disarmed.

───────────────────────────────

2. Remove the glove box and any instrument panel trim which may restrict access to the blower assembly. On 1994–95 Supra, remove door sill and pull back carpet.
3. Disconnect the blower motor control cable, if equipped. Remove all related electrical components, as necessary, to gain access for blower motor assembly. Unplug the multi-connector.
4. Detach the blower housing from the heater or evaporator housing, as equipped. Loosen the mounting screws and withdraw the blower assembly.
5. Installation is the reverse order of the service removal procedure. Make sure to clean blower motor housing of all dirt, leaves etc. before installation. Check the blower motor for proper operation at all speeds after installation.

Corolla

1. Disconnect the negative battery cable.

──────────── CAUTION ────────────

If vehicle is equipped with an air bag system, when ignition is turned to LOCK and negative battery cable is disconnected, do not work inside the passenger compartment for at least 30 seconds to give the SRS (air bag supplemental restraint system) a chance to become fully disarmed.

───────────────────────────────

2. Remove the glove box assembly and disconnect the blower motor connector.
3. Remove the blower motor.
To install:
4. Place the blower in position, making sure it is properly aligned within the case. Install the retaining screws. Connect the wiring to the motor.
5. Install the glove box assembly.
6. Connect the battery cable. Evacuate and recharge the air conditioning system. Make a complete system operating check.

Paseo and Tercel

1. Disconnect the negative battery cable.

──────────── CAUTION ────────────

If vehicle is equipped with an air bag system, when ignition is turned to LOCK and negative battery cable is disconnected, do not work inside the passenger compartment for at least 30 seconds to give the SRS (air bag supplemental restraint system) a chance to become fully disarmed.

───────────────────────────────

2. Remove the A/C amplifier.
3. Disconnect the electrical from the blower motor.
4. Remove the blower motor assembly.
To install:
5. Make sure to clean blower motor housing of all dirt, leaves etc. before installation.
6. Install the blower motor assembly.
7. Reconnect the electrical connector to the blower motor.
8. Install the A/C amplifier.
9. Reconnect the negative battery cable. Check the blower motor for proper operation at all speeds after installation.

Blower Motor Resistor

REMOVAL AND INSTALLATION

1. Disconnect the negative cable.
2. Disconnect the electrical connector from the blower resistor assembly.
3. Remove mounting screw and remove the blower resistor assembly from the case.
4. Installation is the reverse of the service removal procedure. Reconnect the negative battery cable. Check the blower motor for proper operation at all speeds after installation.

Heater Core

REMOVAL AND INSTALLATION

NOTE: **The air conditioning assembly is integral with the heater assembly (including the heater core). In some cases it may be necessary to remove the Cooling Unit assembly.**

Avalon

1. Disconnect the negative battery cable. Drain cooling system. Properly discharge the air conditioning system using recovery equipment.

──────────── CAUTION ────────────

If vehicle is equipped with an air bag system, when ignition is turned to LOCK and negative battery cable is disconnected, do not work inside the passenger compartment for at least 30 seconds to give the SRS (air bag supplemental restraint system) a chance to become fully disarmed.

───────────────────────────────

2. Remove the instrument panel by removing the following:
• pillar trim, door sill plate, hood lock release lever and cowl side trim.
• steering wheel.
• steering column cover and combination switch.
• lower finish panels, fuse box bolt, heater ducts, parking brake release lever, under cover and glove box door.
• glove compartment, center instrument panel, radio and heater control assembly.
• On floor shift models, remove upper console panel, rear console box and front console box.
• On column shift models, remove finish panel.
• On all models, remove steering column, instrument bezel assembly and combination meter.
• detach electrical connectors, junction box bolts and panel retaining bolts. Lift out the panel and remove instrument panel reinforcement.
3. Remove evaporator assembly as described in this article.
4. Remove water valve control cable guide, three clamps and pull out heater core.
To install:
5. Install heater core to vehicle, three clamps and water valve control cable guide.
6. Install evaporator assembly as described in this article.
7. Install the instrument panel in the reverse of the removal procedure.
8. Connect the battery cable. Refill the cooling system. Evacuate and recharge the air conditioning system. Leak test and check the entire system operation.

Camry

1. Disconnect the negative battery cable. Drain the cooling system.

CAUTION

If vehicle is equipped with an air bag system, when ignition is turned to LOCK and negative battery cable is disconnected, do not work inside the passenger compartment for at least 30 seconds to give the SRS (air bag supplemental restraint system) a chance to become fully disarmed.

---

2. Remove the heater housing side cover (left side of housing).
3. Remove the 3 clamps from the heater pipes.
4. Disconnect the heater pipes and slide the heater core out of the housing.

To install:

5. Install the heater core into the heater housing, make sure to clean heater housing of all dirt, leaves etc. before installation.
6. Attach the heater pipes to the core, then install the clamps to retain the pipes.
7. Install the heater housing side cover.
8. Refill the cooling system. Attach the battery cable and test the system operation, especially watching for leaks.

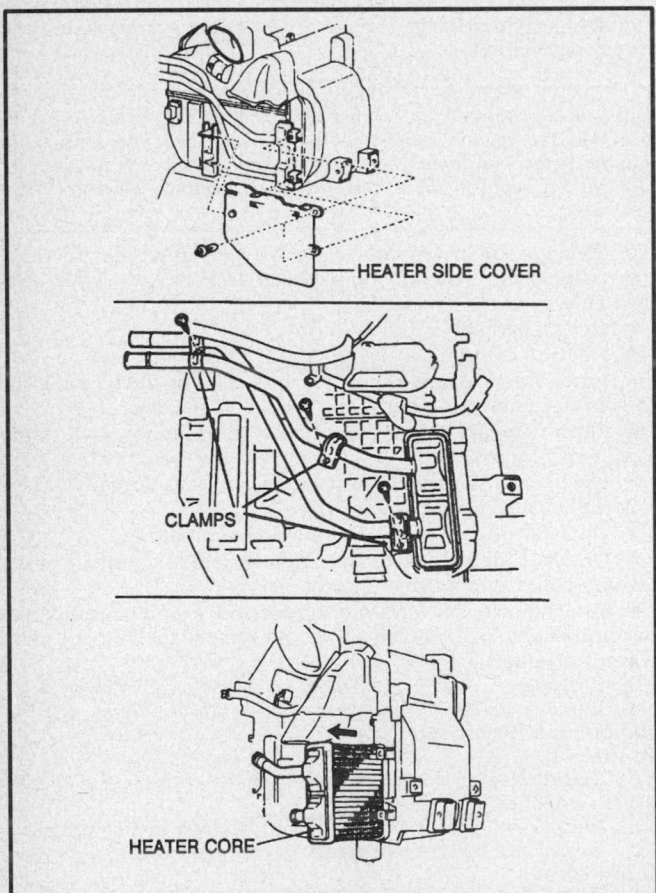

Heater core removal – 1993 Camry

Celica and Supra

1. Disconnect the negative battery cable. Drain the cooling system.

CAUTION

If vehicle is equipped with an air bag system, when ignition is turned to LOCK and negative battery cable is disconnected, do not work inside the passenger compartment for at least 30 seconds to give the SRS (air bag supplemental restraint system) a chance to become fully disarmed.

---

2. Remove the console by removing the shift knob, wiring connector, and console attaching screws.
3. Remove the package tray, if equipped, and all necessary surrounding components blocking access to the heater.
4. Remove the center air outlet, the A/C amplifier, if equipped, and wiring harness.
5. Remove vacuum and/or electrical connections from the heater housing.
6. Remove the air duct between the evaporator and heater or between the blower and heater. Remove all remaining ducts blocking removal of heater assembly.
7. Disconnect the heater hoses at the firewall or at the rear of the heater housing.
8. Position all remaining wiring and cables away from the heater housing.
9. Detach the heater housing from the evaporator housing and remove the heater housing from the vehicle.

To install:

10. Install the heater housing to the vehicle, reconnecting the unit to the evaporator and reattaching all wiring and cables.
11. Install all hoses, ductwork and instrument panel and console components as removed.
12. Connect the battery cable. Refill the cooling system. Operate the system and check for leaks.

Corolla and Tercel

1. Disconnect the negative battery cable. Drain cooling system. Properly discharge the air conditioning system using recovery type equipment.

CAUTION

If vehicle is equipped with an air bag system, when ignition is turned to LOCK and negative battery cable is disconnected, do not work inside the passenger compartment for at least 30 seconds to give the SRS (air bag supplemental restraint system) a chance to become fully disarmed.

---

2. Remove the instrument panel by removing the following:
- pillar trim and door sill plate.
- steering wheel.
- steering column cover, rear center console, hood release handle, panel trim below steering column, combination switch, glove box door and lower instrument panel.
- center console bezel, then the heater-A/C control panel and the radio assembly.
- instrument cluster bezel and instrument cluster.
- front console, left side bezel and switch assembly, left side heater duct and the small right side defroster nozzle.
- passenger side airbag assembly if equipped.
- detach electrical connectors, junction block bolts (2), and 8 panel retaining bolts. Lift out the panel.
3. Remove the evaporator assembly as described in this article.
4. Remove the heater hoses from the heater tubes. Remove the grommets from the heater tubes at the firewall.
5. Remove the instrument panel reinforcement braces.
6. Remove the heater duct and defroster nozzle.
7. Remove the heater assembly (4 nuts).

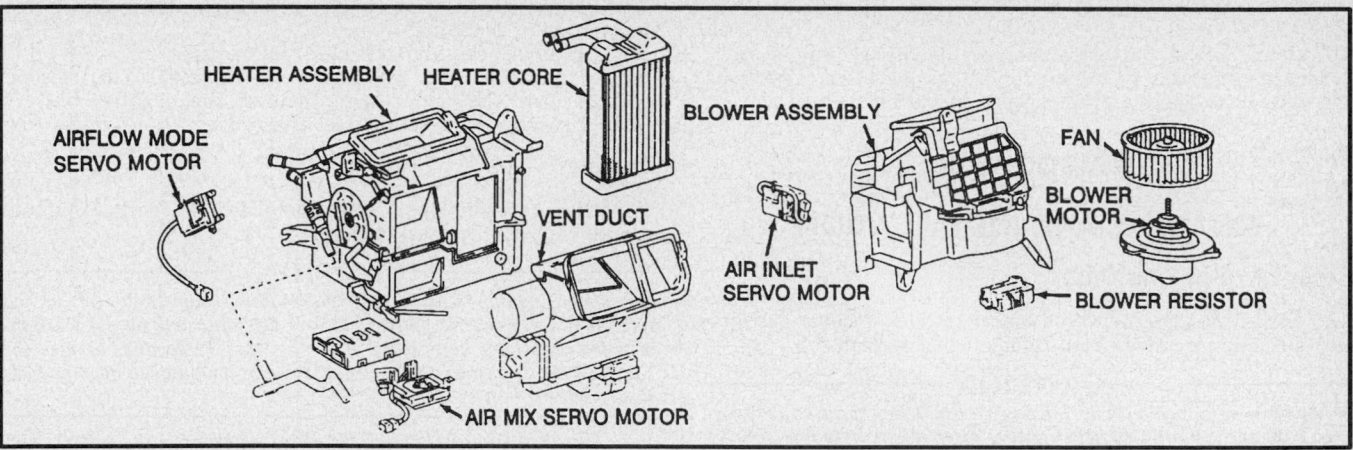

Exploded view of the heater assembly – Celica

To install:

8. Clean heater housing of all dirt, leaves etc. before installation. Install the heater core into the case, position the case halves and secure with retaining screws and clips.

9. Install the heater assembly to its mounting.

10. Reattach the heater and defroster ducts. Install the reinforcement braces.

11. Install the heater tube grommet and attach the heater hoses to the tubes.

12. Reinstall the evaporator assembly.

13. Install the instrument panel in reverse of the removal procedure.

14. Connect the battery cable. Refill the cooling system. Evacuate and recharge the air conditioning system. Leak test and check entire system operation.

MR2

NOTE: Removal of the heater assembly may be facilitated by the removal of the instrument panel, center console or front seat(s).

1. Disconnect the negative battery cable. Disconnect the heater hose at the engine compartment.

─────── CAUTION ───────

If vehicle is equipped with an air bag system, when ignition is turned to LOCK and negative battery cable is disconnected, do not work inside the passenger compartment for at least 30 seconds to give the SRS (air bag supplemental restraint system) a chance to become fully disarmed.

2. Remove the clips retaining the lower part of the heater unit case, then remove the lower part of the case.

3. Using a suitable tool, carefully pry open the lower part of the heater unit case.

4. Remove the heater core assembly from the heater unit case.

To install:

5. Install the heater core into the heater housing, make sure to clean heater housing of all dirt, leaves etc. before installation. Install lower heater unit case.

6. Reconnect the heater hose and refill the coolant system.

7. Connect the negative battery cable. Refill the coolant. Bleed cooling system. Start the engine and check heater system for proper operation.

Paseo

1. Disconnect the negative battery cable. Properly drain the cooling system and discharge the air conditioning system using recovery type equipment.

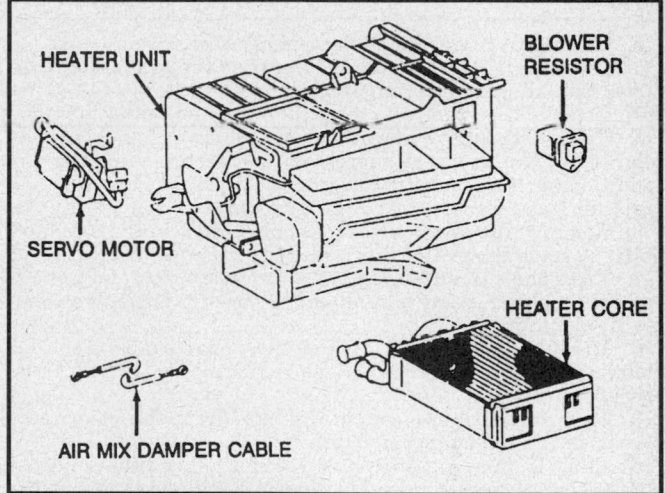

Disassembled view of the heater assembly – MR2

2. Remove the instrument panel by removing the following components:

- front pillar trim and door sill plate.
- steering wheel and column covers.
- console assembly.
- hood release handle.
- trim panel below steering column.
- combination switch from steering column.
- instrument cluster bezel and instrument cluster assembly.
- glove box.
- center panel bezel, radio, console over shift lever, clock and heater-A/C control panel.
- heater duct and junction block from left side.
- 3 retaining nuts and 1 bolt and remove the panel.

3. Remove the evaporator assembly as described in this article.

4. Detach the heater hoses from the heater core tubes. Plug the hoses and tubes to prevent coolant leakage.

5. Remove the 2 center braces, then remove the heater assembly. The heater core can be removed on the bench.

To install:

6. Clean the heater housing of debris prior to assembling the heater core. Install the center braces.

7. Install the heater hoses.

8. Reinstall the evaporator assembly.

9. Install the instrument panel in reverse of removal procedure.
10. Connect the battery cable. Refill the cooling system. Evacuate and recharge the air conditioning system. Check entire system for leaks and for proper operation.

Evaporator

REMOVAL AND INSTALLATION

Except Avalon and Camry

1. Disconnect the negative battery cable. Recover refrigerant (discharge system) from refrigeration system.

CAUTION

If vehicle is equipped with an air bag system, when ignition is turned to LOCK and negative battery cable is disconnected, do not work inside the passenger compartment for at least 30 seconds to give the SRS (air bag supplemental restraint system) a chance to become fully disarmed.

---

2. On Supra, remove the charcoal canister.
3. Disconnect the refrigerant lines from the evaporator core pipes. Cap all openings immediately.
4. Remove the grommets from the inlet and outlet fittings.
5. Remove the glove box assembly and lower panel trim, as required. Disconnect all necessary connectors and the air conditioning harness. On Paseo and Tercel, remove the A/C amplifier. On Supra, remove the EFI and ABS computer.
6. Remove the evaporator assembly attaching nuts and bolts. Remove the evaporator assembly from the vehicle.
7. Place the assembly on a suitable work bench and remove control amplifier, relay assemblies or power transistor assembly if so equipped.
8. Using suitable tools, remove the upper evaporator case clamps and retaining screws. Remove thermistor with thermistor holder.
9. Remove the lower evaporator case from the evaporator core. Remove the evaporator core.
10. Remove the heat insulator (heat sensing tube) and the clamp from the outlet tube. Disconnect the liquid line from the inlet fitting of the expansion valve.
11. Disconnect the expansion valve from the inlet fitting of the evaporator. Remove the expansion valve.

NOTE: Before installing the evaporator, check the evaporator fins for blockage. If the fins are clogged, clean them with compressed air. Never use water to clean the evaporator. Check the fittings for cracks and or scratches and replace, as necessary.

To install:
12. Connect the expansion valve to the inlet fitting of the evaporator and torque it to 17 ft. lbs. Be sure the O-ring is positioned on the tube fitting.
13. Connect the liquid line tube to the inlet fitting on the expansion valve. Torque the nut to 10 ft. lbs.
14. Install the clamp and heat insulator (heat sensing tube) to the outlet tube.
15. Install the upper and lower cases on the evaporator. Install the thermistor. Install control amplifier, relay assemblies or power transistor assembly, if equipped.
16. Install the air conditioning wiring harness to the evaporator assembly and all other necessary components.
17. Install the evaporator assembly in the vehicle. Be careful not to pinch the wiring harness while installing the evaporator assembly. Install the EFI and ABS computers (Supra).
18. Install the glove box assembly and the grommets on the inlet and outlet fittings.
19. Connect the liquid line to the evaporator inlet fittings and torque to 10 ft. lbs.

20. Connect the suction tube to the evaporator outlet fitting and torque to 24 ft. lbs.
21. On Supra, reinstall the charcoal canister.
22. If the evaporator was replaced, add 1.4–1.7 oz. of compressor oil to the compressor. Connect the negative battery cable. Evacuate, charge and test the refrigeration system.

Avalon

1. Disconnect the negative battery cable. Properly discharge the air conditioning system.

CAUTION

If vehicle is equipped with an air bag system, when ignition is turned to LOCK and negative battery cable is disconnected, do not work inside the passenger compartment for at least 30 seconds to give the SRS (air bag supplemental restraint system) a chance to become fully disarmed.

---

2. Remove the glove compartment, instrument under cover, ECM and ECU with bracket.
3. Remove the blower unit.
4. Disconnect the refrigerant lines. Cap open fittings immediately.
5. Remove the thermistor and evaporator cover. Pull out the evaporator.
To install:
6. Install the evaporator, evaporator cover and thermistor. Reconnect the refrigerant lines. Replace O-rings as necessary.
7. Install the blower unit, the ECU with bracket, the ECM, instrument under cover and glove compartment.
8. Connect the battery cable. Evacuate and recharge the air conditioning system. Check the system for proper operation.

Camry

1. Disconnect the negative battery cable. Properly discharge the air conditioning system.

CAUTION

If vehicle is equipped with an air bag system, when ignition is turned to LOCK and negative battery cable is disconnected, do not work inside the passenger compartment for at least 30 seconds to give the SRS (air bag supplemental restraint system) a chance to become fully disarmed.

---

2. Drain the cooling system. Disconnect the cable from the water valve and the heater hoses from the heater core pipes at the firewall. Plug the hoses and pipes to prevent coolant leakage.
3. Remove the instrument panel by removing the following:
- front pillar trim, door sill plates and door opening covers.
- hood release handle (2 screws), and remove kick panels.
- steering column cover.
- bezel around shift lever, then the rear console box.
- coin box and the panel trim below the steering column.
- combination switch from the steering column.
- glove box and lower trim.
- front console box, then the center panel bezel.
- instrument cluster bezel and instrument cluster.
- instrument panel air outlets from both sides.
- radio assembly and the heater-A/C control assembly.
- heater duct and right side defroster nozzle.
- remove the instrument panel and wiring connectors, then remove the 2 center braces.
4. Remove the blower assembly as described in this article.
5. Detach the refrigerant lines from the block joint at the firewall. Plug all openings to minimize contamination.
6. Remove the rear floor air ducts from the evaporator housing. Remove the side heater core protector plate.
7. Detach the connectors and remove 3 nuts and take out the evaporator assembly.

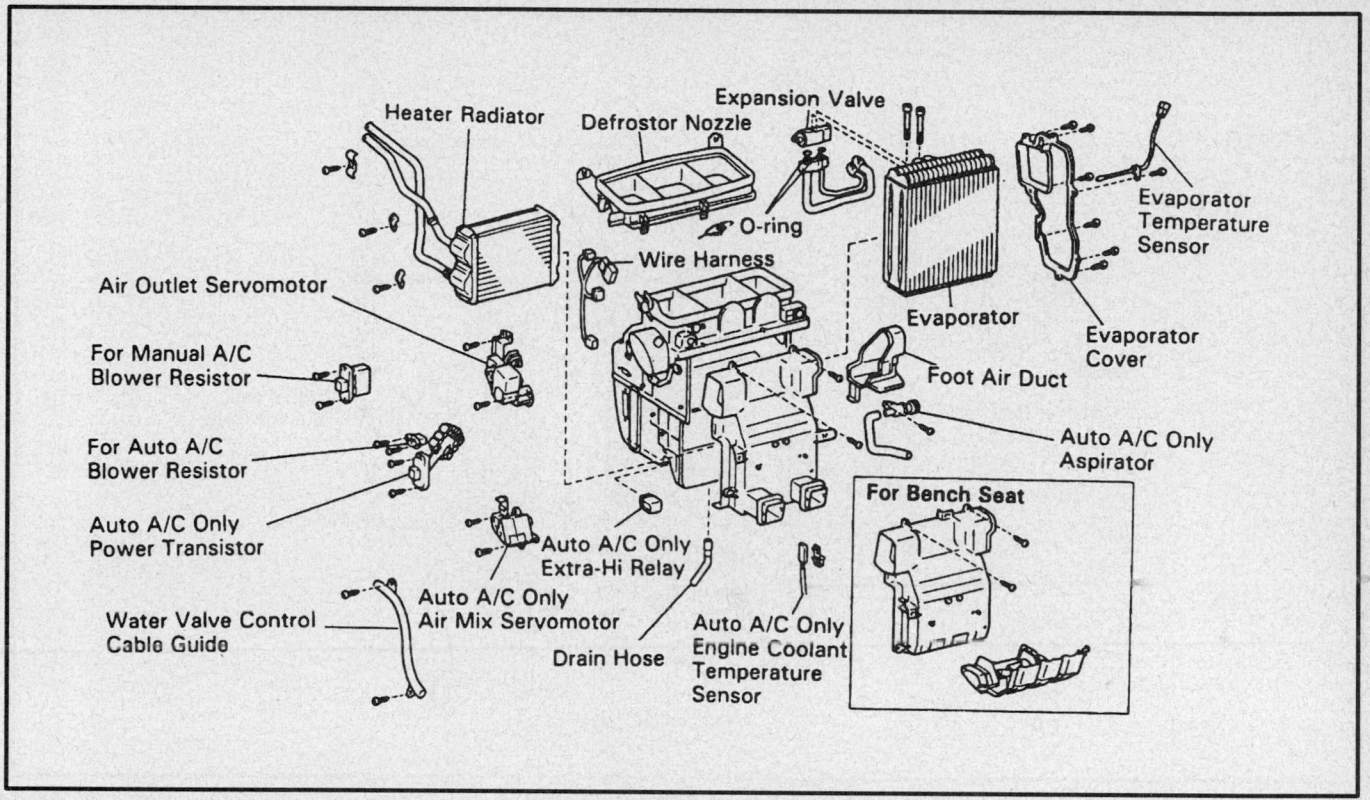

Exploded view of evaporator assembly – Avalon and 1994-95 Camry

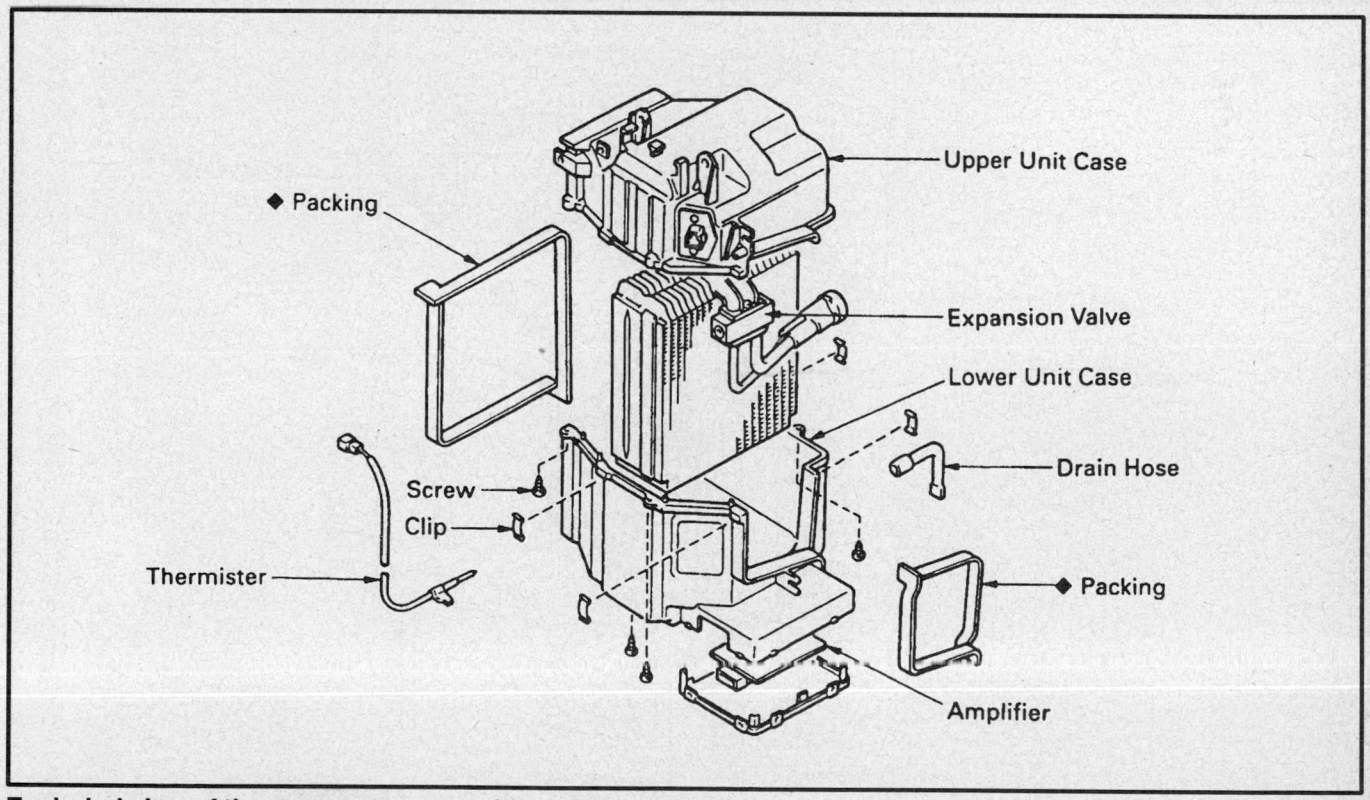

Exploded view of the evaporator assembly – 1994-95 Celica

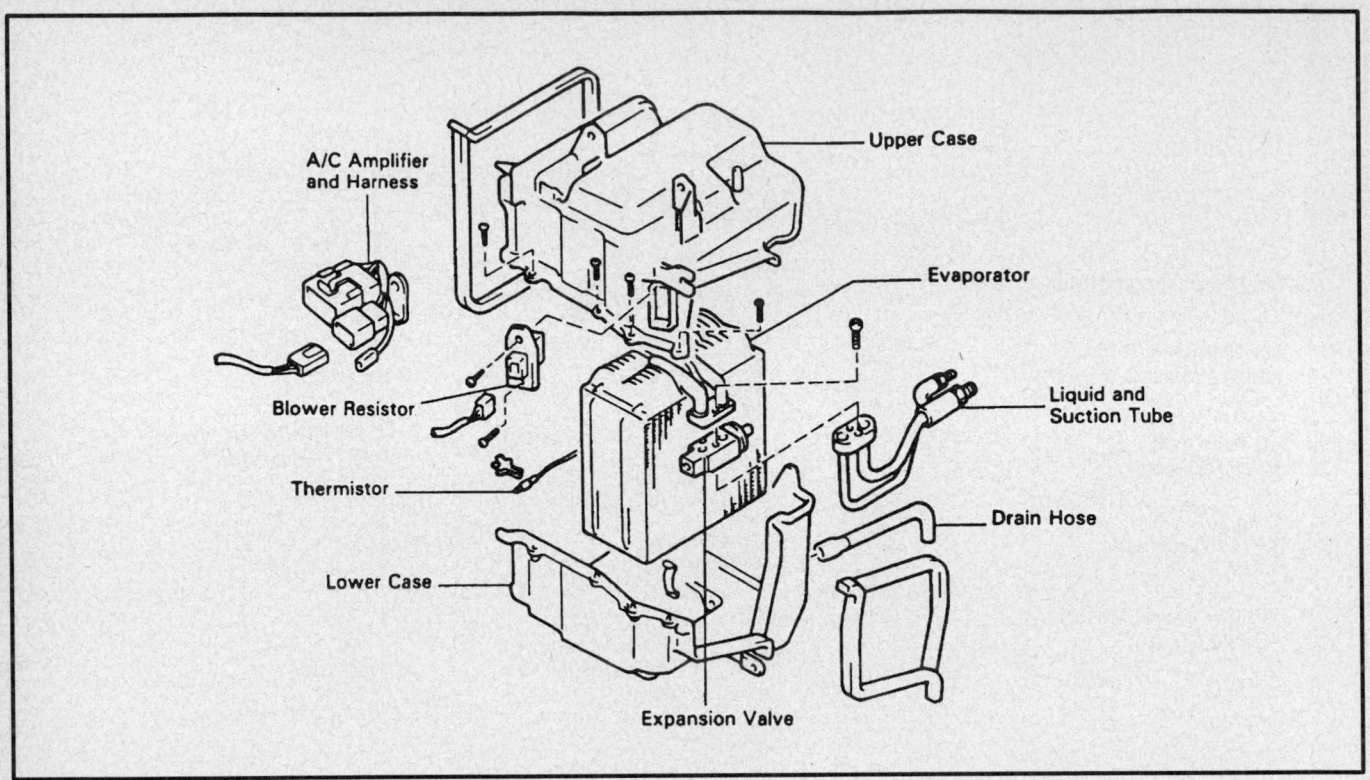

A/C Amplifier and Harness

Upper Case

Evaporator

Blower Resistor

Liquid and Suction Tube

Thermistor

Drain Hose

Lower Case

Expansion Valve

Exploded view of the evaporator assembly — 1994-95 Corolla

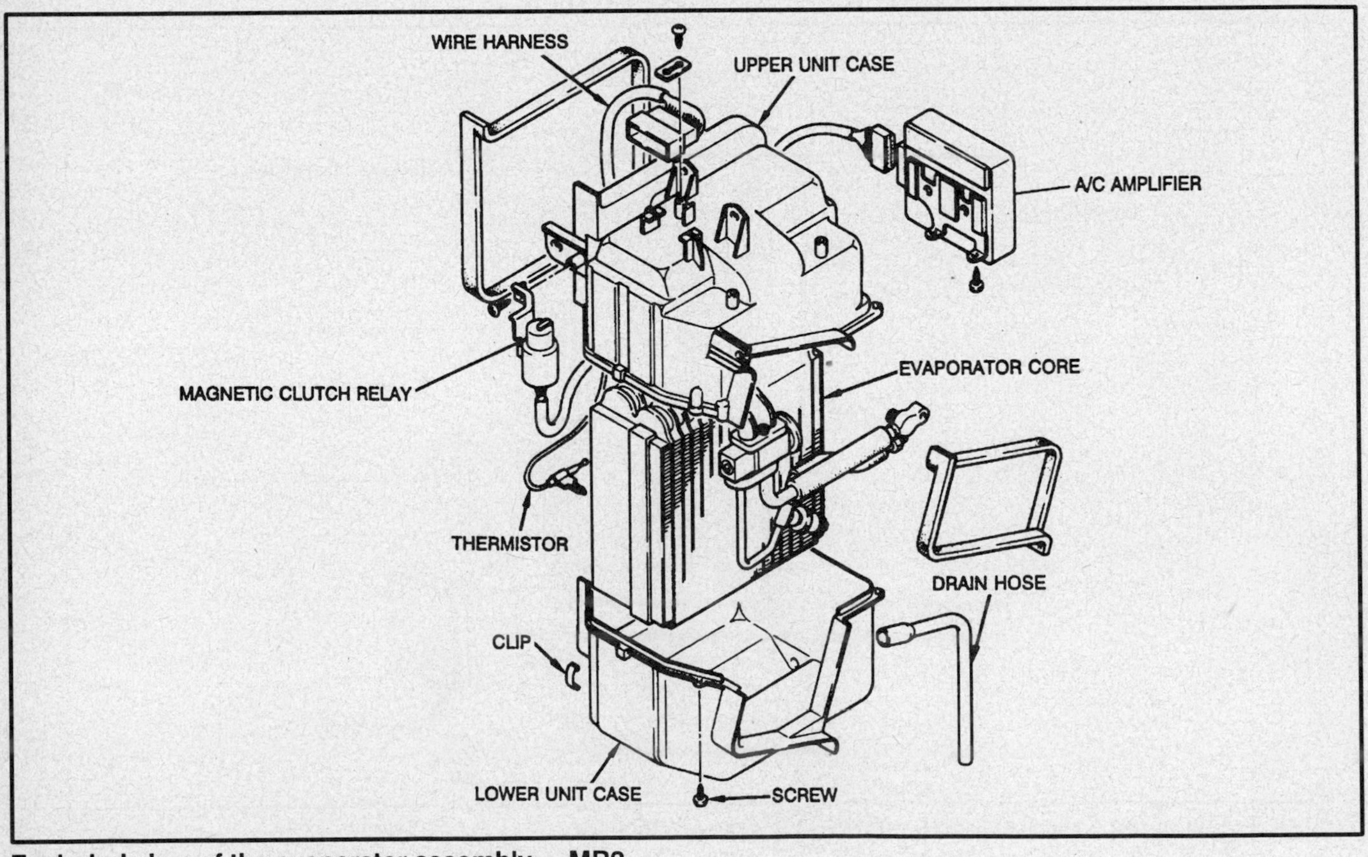

WIRE HARNESS

UPPER UNIT CASE

A/C AMPLIFIER

MAGNETIC CLUTCH RELAY

EVAPORATOR CORE

THERMISTOR

DRAIN HOSE

CLIP

LOWER UNIT CASE

SCREW

Exploded view of the evaporator assembly — MR2

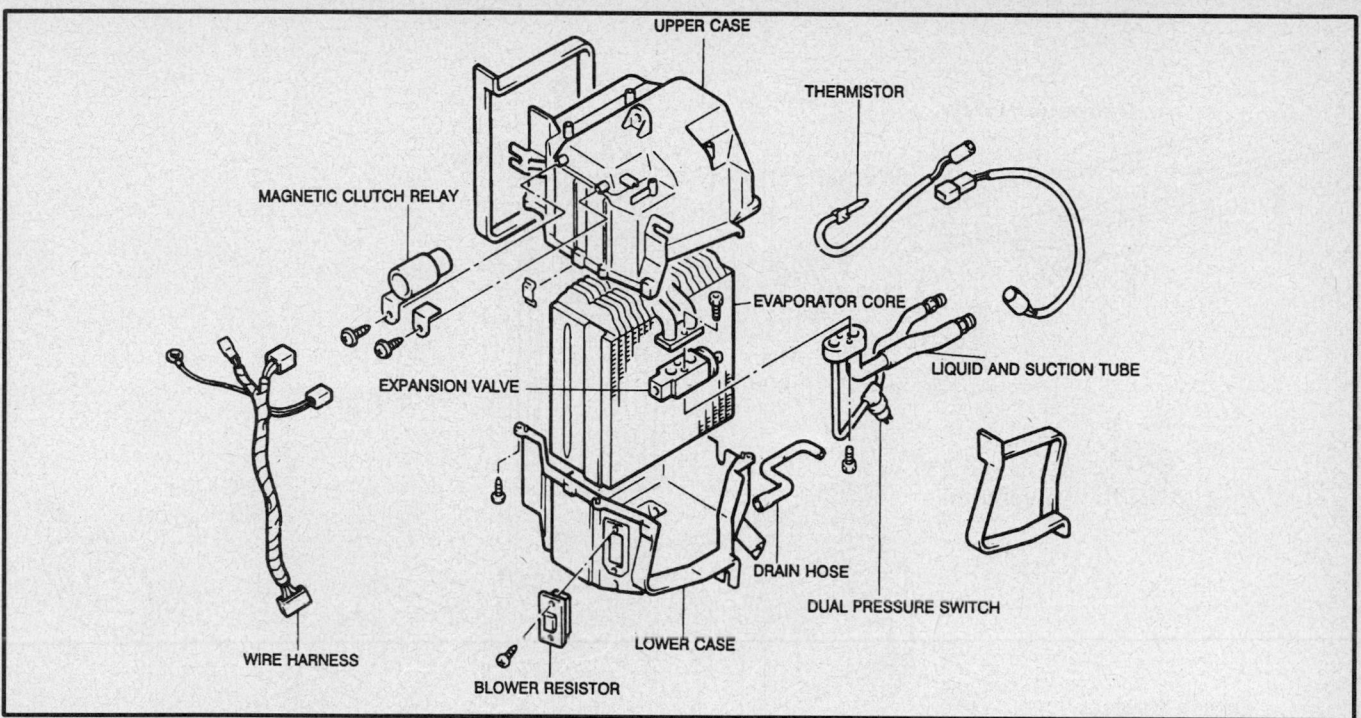

UPPER CASE

THERMISTOR

MAGNETIC CLUTCH RELAY

EVAPORATOR CORE

EXPANSION VALVE

LIQUID AND SUCTION TUBE

DRAIN HOSE

DUAL PRESSURE SWITCH

WIRE HARNESS

LOWER CASE

BLOWER RESISTOR

Exploded view of the evaporator assembly — Paseo

To install:

8. Position the unit in position and install retaining nuts. Reattach connectors.
9. Install the side plate and reattach the rear floor ducts.
10. Reattach the refrigerant lines to the block joint.
11. Install the blower assembly.
12. Install the instrument panel by reversing the removal procedure.
13. Attach the heater hoses, then the cable at the water valve.
14. Connect the battery cable. Refill the cooling system. Evacuate and recharge the air conditioning system. Check system operation. Check for leaks.

Refrigerant Lines

REMOVAL AND INSTALLATION

1. Disconnect the negative battery cable.
2. Recover refrigerant (discharge system) from refrigeration system.
3. Replace faulty line or hose. Always replace O-rings.
4. Connect the negative battery cable. Evacuate, charge and test the refrigeration system.

Manual Control Head

REMOVAL AND INSTALLATION

───────── CAUTION ─────────
If vehicle is equipped with an air bag system, when ignition is turned to LOCK and negative battery cable is disconnected, do not work inside the passenger compartment for at least 30 seconds to give the SRS (air bag supplemental restraint system) a chance to become fully disarmed.

AIR CONDITIONING SWITCH (LEVER TYPE)

1. Disconnect the negative battery cable.
2. Remove the control panel bezel, if necessary. Remove the air conditioning switch.
3. Install air conditioning switch. Install the bezel, if removed. Reconnect negative battery cable.
4. Check system for proper operation.

AIR CONDITIONING SWITCH (PUSHBUTTON TYPE)

1. Disconnect the negative battery cable. Remove the control panel from the instrument panel, detaching harness connector.
2. Remove air conditioning switch.
3. Installation is the reverse of the removal procedure.
4. Check system for proper operation.

CONTROL PANEL ASSEMBLY

1. Disconnect the negative battery cable.
2. Remove the center panel bezel. Pull the knobs from the panel controls, take out 4 retaining screws and pull heater-A/C control panel from the center panel.
3. Detach the control cable(s). Disconnect the electrical connector.
4. Install in reverse of the removal procedure.

Camry, Celica, Corolla, Paseo, Tercel

BLOWER SPEED CONTROL SWITCH

1. Disconnect the negative battery cable.
2. Remove the control plate.
3. Remove the center cluster finish panel.
4. Remove the ash tray, radio assembly and all connections (Tercel and Paseo).
5. Remove the light from the air conditioning control assembly. Remove the blower switch from the rear of the air conditioning control assembly. Disconnect the electrical connector to switch. Remove the blower speed control switch.

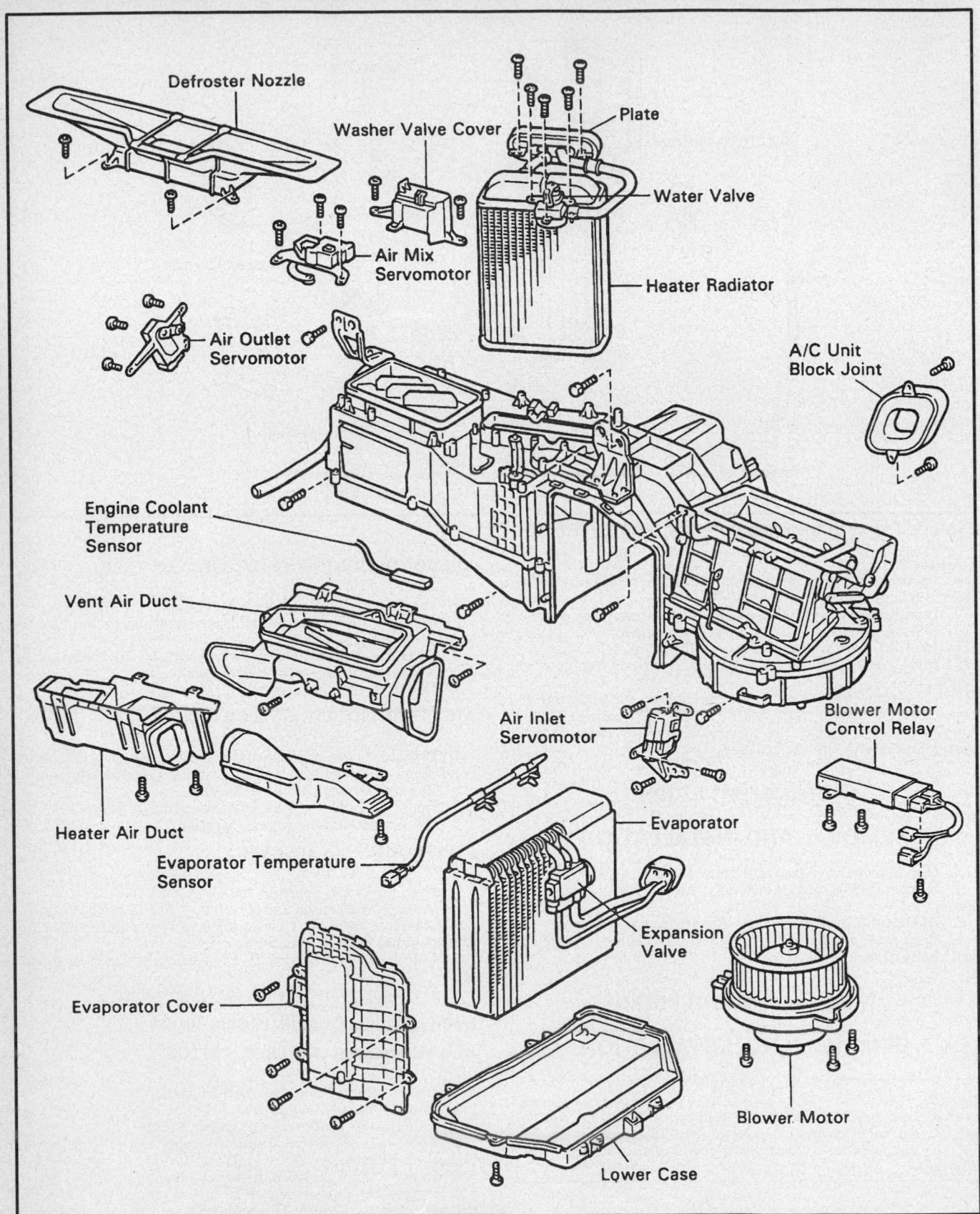

Defroster Nozzle

Washer Valve Cover

Plate

Water Valve

Air Mix Servomotor

Heater Radiator

Air Outlet Servomotor

A/C Unit Block Joint

Engine Coolant Temperature Sensor

Vent Air Duct

Heater Air Duct

Air Inlet Servomotor

Blower Motor Control Relay

Evaporator Temperature Sensor

Evaporator

Expansion Valve

Evaporator Cover

Lower Case

Blower Motor

Exploded view of evaporator assembly — 1994-95 Supra

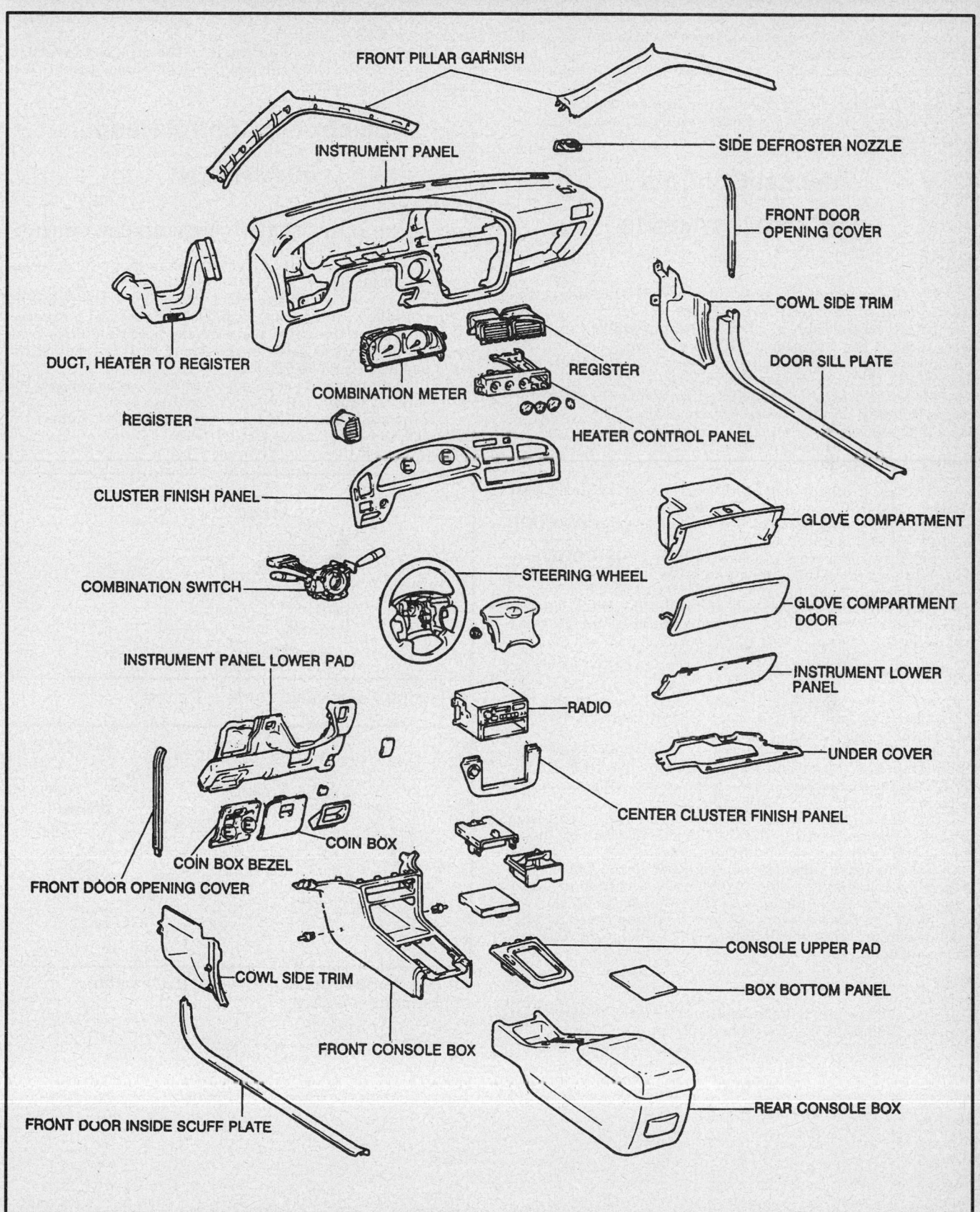

FRONT PILLAR GARNISH

INSTRUMENT PANEL

SIDE DEFROSTER NOZZLE

FRONT DOOR OPENING COVER

COWL SIDE TRIM

DOOR SILL PLATE

DUCT, HEATER TO REGISTER

COMBINATION METER

REGISTER

HEATER CONTROL PANEL

REGISTER

CLUSTER FINISH PANEL

GLOVE COMPARTMENT

GLOVE COMPARTMENT DOOR

COMBINATION SWITCH

STEERING WHEEL

INSTRUMENT LOWER PANEL

INSTRUMENT PANEL LOWER PAD

RADIO

UNDER COVER

COIN BOX

CENTER CLUSTER FINISH PANEL

COIN BOX BEZEL

FRONT DOOR OPENING COVER

CONSOLE UPPER PAD

BOX BOTTOM PANEL

COWL SIDE TRIM

FRONT CONSOLE BOX

REAR CONSOLE BOX

FRONT DOOR INSIDE SCUFF PLATE

Exploded view of the instrument panel — 1993 Camry

To install:

6. Install the blower speed control switch to the air conditioning control assembly.

7. Install ash tray, radio assembly and all connections (Tercel and Paseo).

8. Install center cluster finish panel and control plate.

9. Reconnect the negative battery cable. Check system for proper operation.

Manual Controls

CABLE ADJUSTMENTS

Avalon

1. Set the temperature control dial to **COOL** position. Set the water valve lever to **COOL** position.

2. Install control cable and lock the clamp while pushing the outer cable in the direction of **COOL** position.

3. Set the mix damper and the control dial to **COOL** position. Install the control cable and lock the clamp.

4. Move the control levers left and right and check for stiffness or binding through the full range of the levers. Test control cable operation.

Camry and Celica

1. Set the air inlet damper and control lever to the **FRESH** position. Install the cable and lock the clamp.

2. Set the air mix damper and control lever to the **COOL** position. Install and lock the cable.

3. Set the water valve and control lever to the **COOL** position. While pushing the outer cable in the direction of **COOL** position, clamp the outer cable to the water valve bracket.

4. Move the control levers left and right and check for stiffness or binding through the full range of the levers. Test control cable operation.

Corolla, Paseo and Tercel

1. Set the air inlet damper and control lever to the **RECIRC** position (pull damper lever toward cable). Install the control cable and lock the cable clamp.

2. Set the mode selector damper (on Paseo and Tercel, push lever away from cable) and control lever to the **DEF** position (**FACE** on Paseo and Tercel). Install the control cable and lock it in place.

3. Set the air mix damper (on Paseo and Tercel, pull lever toward cable) and control lever to the **COOL** position. Install the control cable and lock it in place.

4. Set the water valve and control lever to the **COOL** position. While pushing the outer cable in the direction of **COOL** position, clamp the outer cable to the water valve bracket.

5. Move the control levers left and right and check for stiffness or binding through the full range of the levers. Test control cable operation.

MR2

1. Set the air mix damper and control lever to the **COOL** position. Clamp the control cable in place.

2. Adjust the water valve. Set the water valve and control lever to the **COOL** position.

3. While pushing the outer cable in the direction of **COOL** position, clamp the outer cable to the water valve bracket. Test control cable operation.

Electronic Control Head

ADJUSTMENT

1993 Supra

AUTOMATIC TEMPERATURE CONTROL SERVO MOTOR

1. Disconnect the short circuit connector. Make short terminals **1** and **3** for test.

2. Place the temperature control lever at 77°F position. Run engine at idle. Turn on blower switch to the **AUTO** position.

3. Verify that the guide plate on the servo motor is positioned at the mark **O** between the **R** and **W**. If not, adjust the servo motor position as follows:

4. If the guide plate position is over the **W** area connect the red/green and brown/yellow wires together.

5. If the guide plate position is over the **R** area connect the red/green and white/black wire harness.

6. Reconnect the short circuit connector.

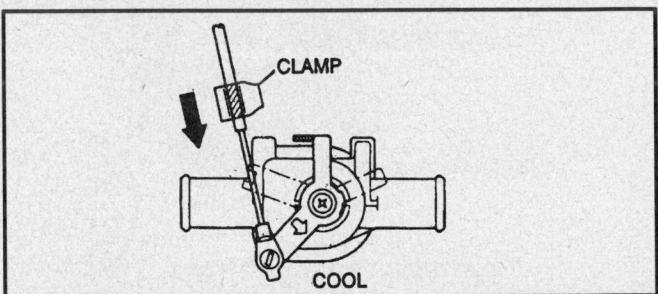

Adjusting water valve cable – Camry

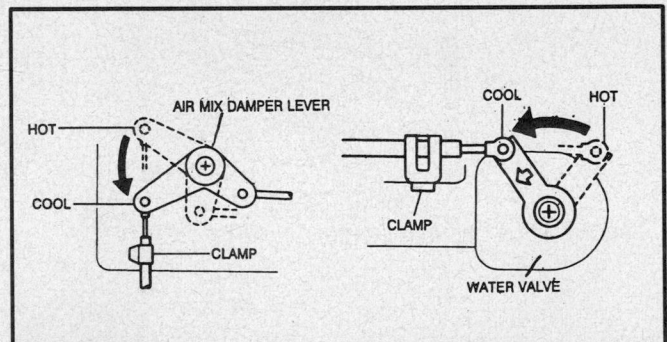

Air mix damper cable and water valve cable adjustment – Celica

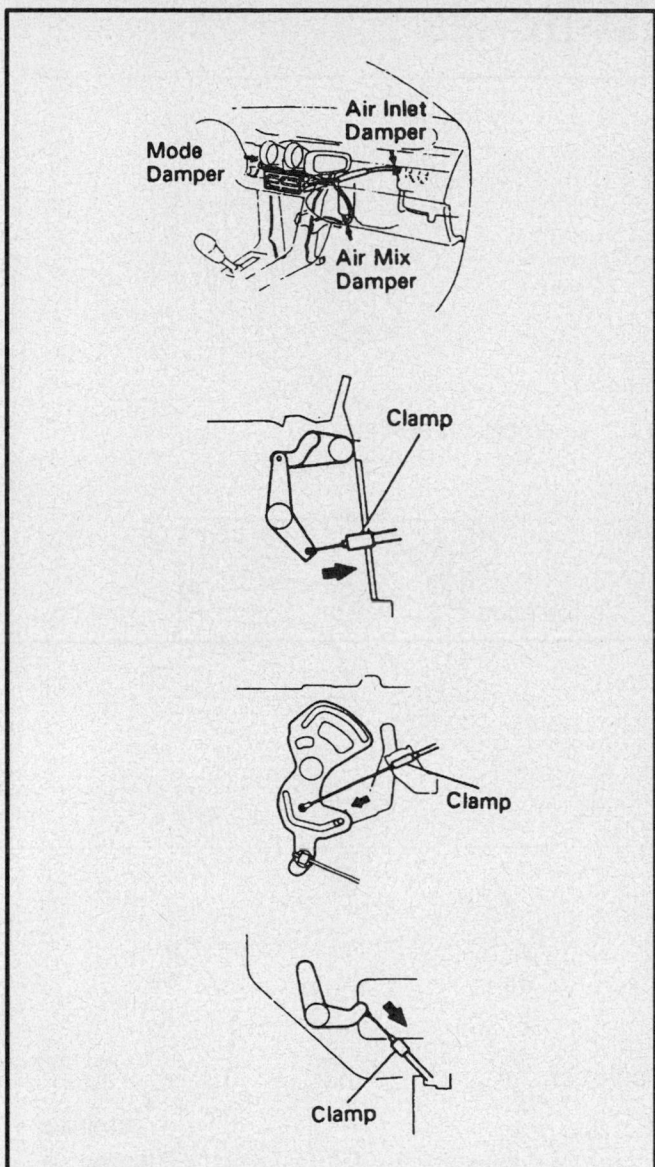

Adjusting air inlet damper, mode damper, air mix damper and water valve control cables – Paseo and Tercel

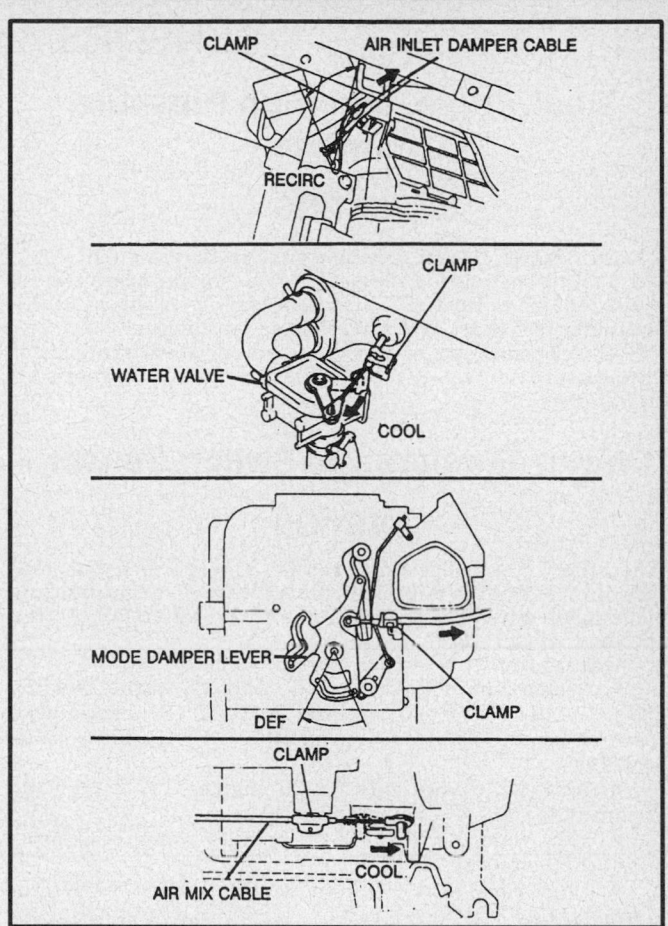

Adjusting air inlet damper, mode damper, air mix damper and water valve control cables – Corolla

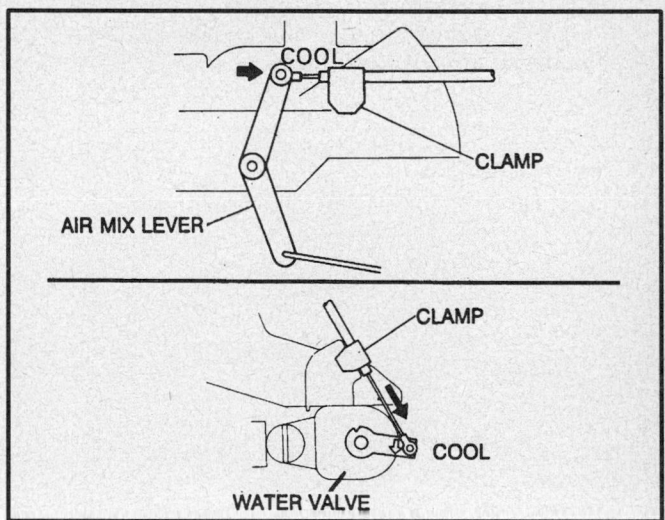

Adjusting air mix damper and water valve control cables – MR2

SENSORS AND SWITCHES

Dual, Triple, and High Pressure Switch

TESTING

1. Disconnect electrical connector of pressure switch.
2. Install manifold gauge set. With engine operating at about 2000 rpm, turn A/C switch on and off as shown in the continuity test chart and observe gauge readings.
3. Check continuity between the appropriate 2 terminals of the pressure switch. Refer to pressure switch diagnosis illustrations.

Water Temperature Switch/Sensor

TESTING

When the water temperature reaches the specified temperature the continuity is broken. Check that the continuity is made again when the temperature of the water falls to the specified temperature.

Check continuity of switch. Replace as necessary.
- Avalon and 1995 Camry with 1MZ-FE engine—switch No. 1 208°F OFF (no continuity); 190°F ON (continuity), switch No. 2 199°F ON (continuity); 181°F OFF (no continuity)
- 1994–95 Camry with 5S-FE engine—199°F OFF (no continuity); 181°F ON (continuity)
- 1994 Camry with 1MZ-FE engine—check resistance: 1.48-1.59 ohms at 176°F
- 1993 Celica—212°F OFF (no continuity); 203°F ON (continuity)
- 1994–95 Celica—199°F OFF (no continuity); 181°F ON (continuity)
- 1993 Corolla—radiator fan: white switch—194°F OFF (no continuity); 181°F ON (continuity)
- 1993 Corolla—A/C cutout: blue switch—217°F OFF (no continuity); 208°F ON (continuity)

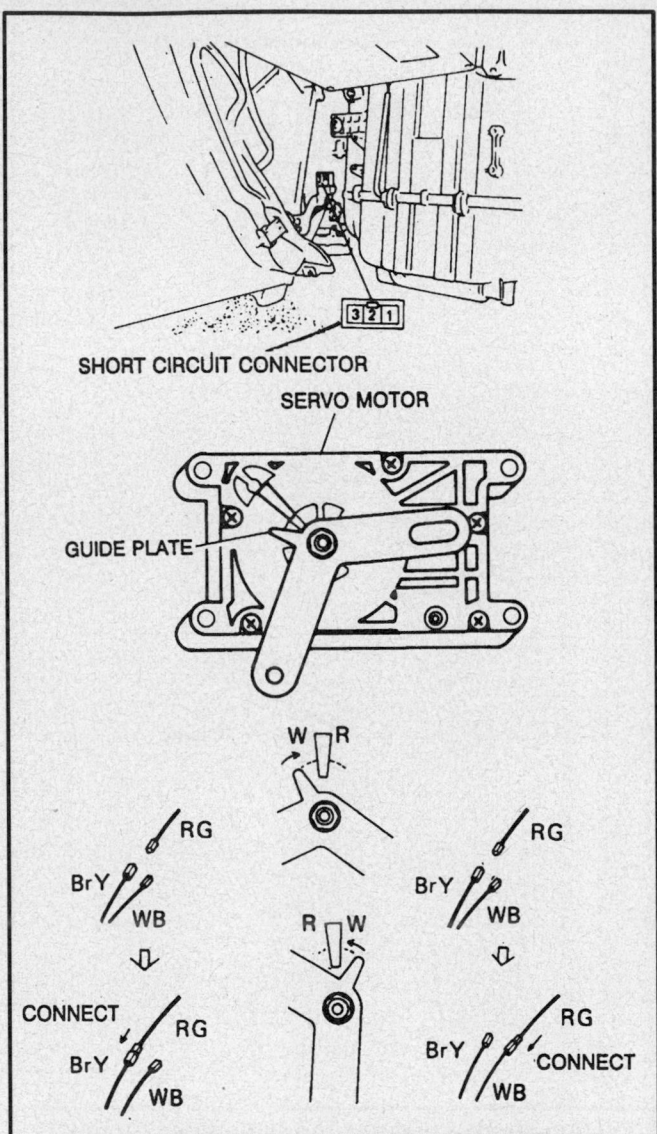

Adjusting automatic temperature control panel servo motor – 1993 Supra

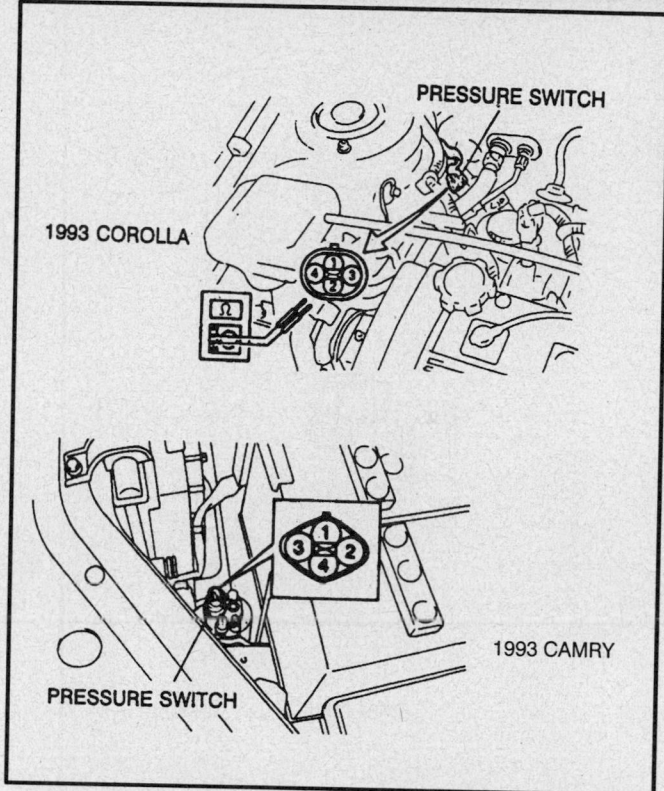

1993 COROLLA

PRESSURE SWITCH

1993 CAMRY

PRESSURE SWITCH

1993 Dual and high pressure switch testing (models not shown have only a 2-terminal connector)

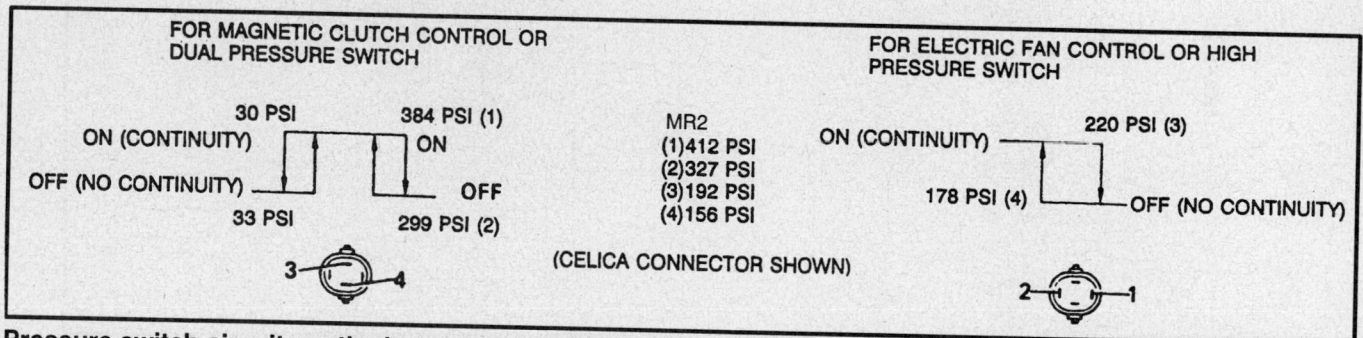

FOR MAGNETIC CLUTCH CONTROL OR DUAL PRESSURE SWITCH

30 PSI   384 PSI (1)
ON (CONTINUITY)   ON
OFF (NO CONTINUITY)   OFF
33 PSI   299 PSI (2)

3 — 4

MR2
(1) 412 PSI
(2) 327 PSI
(3) 192 PSI
(4) 156 PSI

(CELICA CONNECTOR SHOWN)

FOR ELECTRIC FAN CONTROL OR HIGH PRESSURE SWITCH

ON (CONTINUITY) — 220 PSI (3)
178 PSI (4) — OFF (NO CONTINUITY)

2 — 1

Pressure switch circuit continuity testing – 1993 models

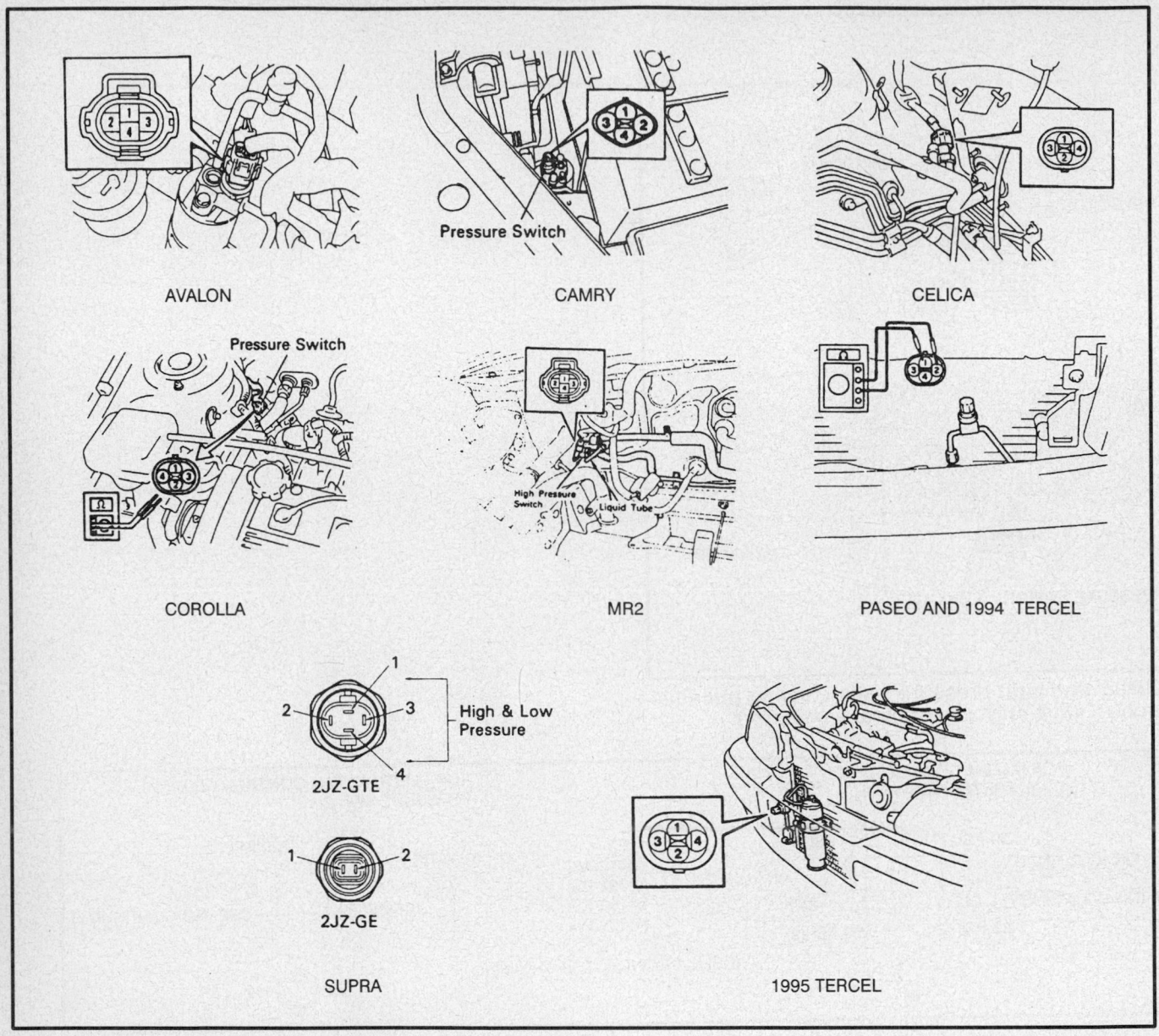

Dual and high pressure switch testing — 1994-95 models

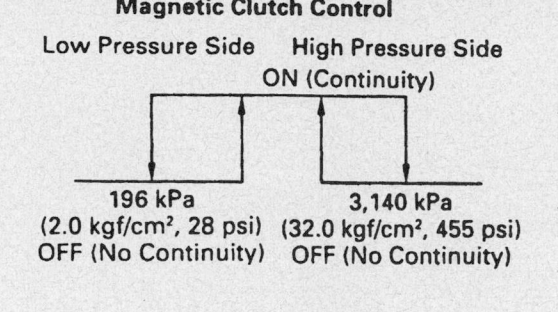

Magnetic Clutch Control

Low Pressure Side   High Pressure Side
ON (Continuity)

196 kPa
(2.0 kgf/cm², 28 psi)
OFF (No Continuity)

3,140 kPa
(32.0 kgf/cm², 455 psi)
OFF (No Continuity)

1994	Camry, Celica, MR2, Supra	4	1
	Corolla	2	1
	Paseo, Tercel	1	2
1995	Avalon, Camry, Celica, MR2, Paseo, Supra, Tercel	4	1
	Camry, Celica, MR2, Supra	2	1

Magnetic Clutch Control Testing Pin Numbers

Cooling Fan Control

1,520 kpa
(15.5 kgf/cm², 220 psi)

ON
(Continuity)

OFF
(No Continuity)

1,226 kpa
(12.5 kgf/cm², 178 psi)

1994	Camry, Celica, MR2	2	3
	Corolla	3	4
1995	Avalon, Camry, Celica, MR2, Paseo, Tercel	2	3
	Corolla	3	4

Cooling Fan Control Testing Pin Numbers

Pressure switch testing – 1994-95 models

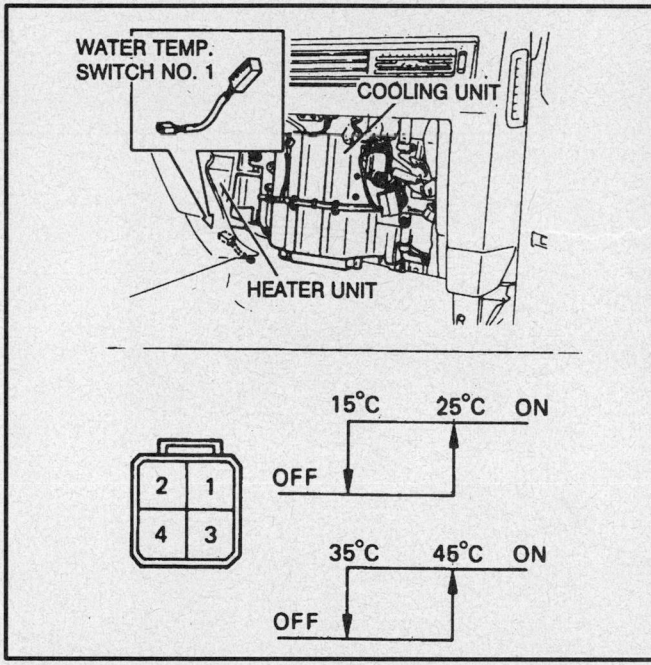

Testing water temperature switch No. 1 – Supra

- 1994–95 Corolla—199°F OFF (no continuity); 181°F ON (continuity)
- MR2—check resistance: 1.05 kilo-ohms at 203°F; 1.19 kilo-ohms at 194°F; 1.35 kilo-ohms at 185°F. If resistance value is not as specified, replace.
- 1994–95 Paseo and 1994 Tercel— 201°F OFF (no continuity); 181°F ON (continuity)
- 1995 Tercel—194°F OFF (no continuity); 181°F ON (continuity)

- 1993 Supra—switch #1 on bottom of heater unit: refer to illustration; switch #2 on thermostat housing (turbo engine only)—234°F OFF (no continuity) 225°F ON (continuity); switch # 3 on thermostat housing—212°F OFF (no continuity), 203°F ON (continuity).
- 1994–95 Supra— 207°F OFF (no continuity); 190°F ON (continuity).

Air Conditioning Relays

TESTING

1. Remove cover of relay box. Disconnect the negative battery cable.
2. Remove the relay. Inspect relay for continuity when relay switch is closed. If continuity is not as specified, replace the relay.

Thermistor

TESTING

───── CAUTION ─────

If vehicle is equipped with an air bag system, when ignition is turned to LOCK and negative battery cable is disconnected, do not work inside the passenger compartment for at least 30 seconds to give the SRS (air bag supplemental restraint system) a chance to become fully disarmed.

1. Disconnect the negative battery cable and remove the glove box to access the thermistor. With the thermistor still installed, use an ohmmeter and measure the resistance at the connector (resistance 1500 ohms at 77°F).
2. Place the thermistor in cold water. While varying the temperature of the water measure the resistance at the connector. The colder the water the higher the resistance (MAX. 5500 ohms at 30°F water temperature).

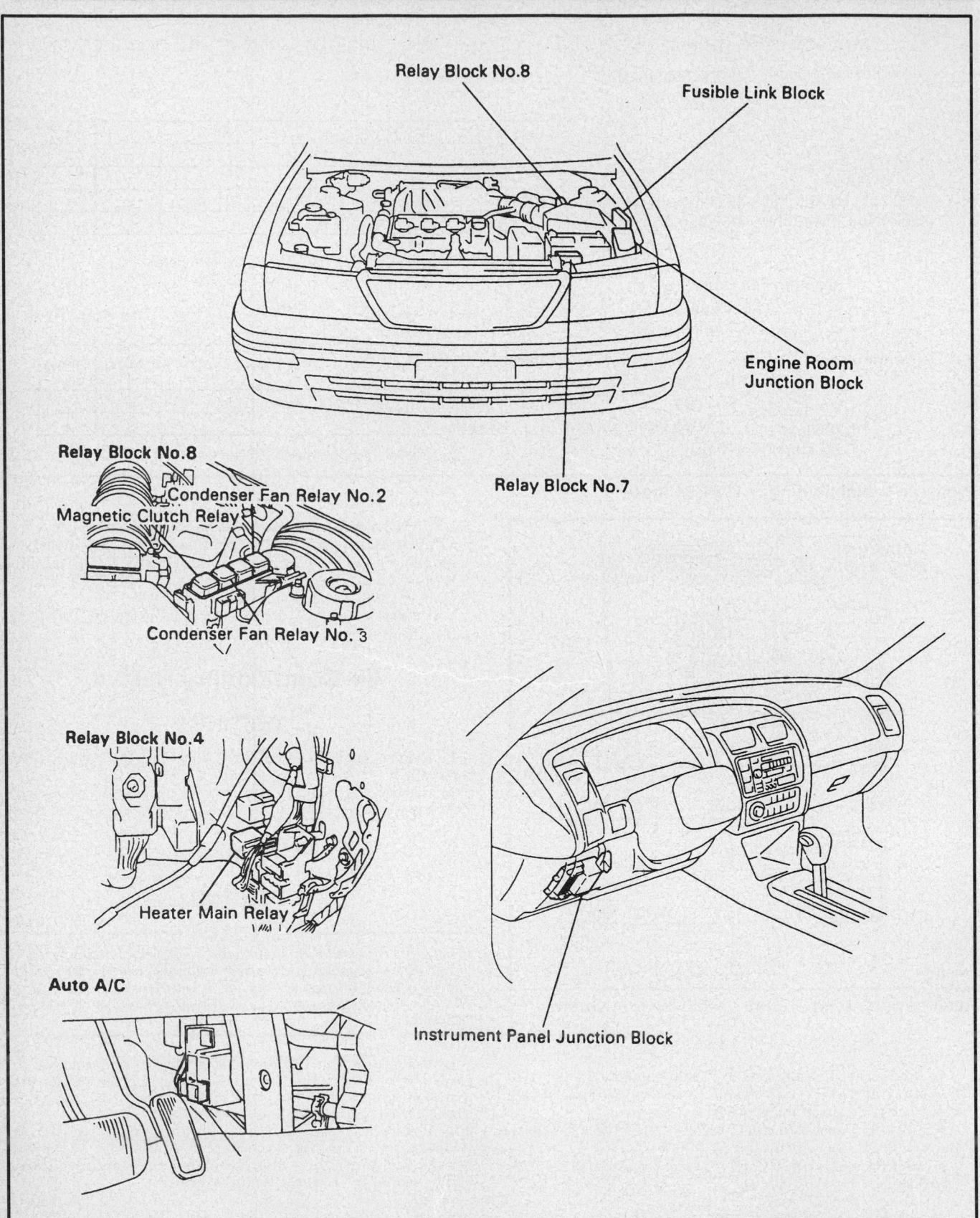

Relay Block No.8

Fusible Link Block

Engine Room Junction Block

Relay Block No.7

Relay Block No.8

Condenser Fan Relay No. 2

Magnetic Clutch Relay

Condenser Fan Relay No. 3

Relay Block No.4

Heater Main Relay

Auto A/C

Instrument Panel Junction Block

Location of system relays — Avalon

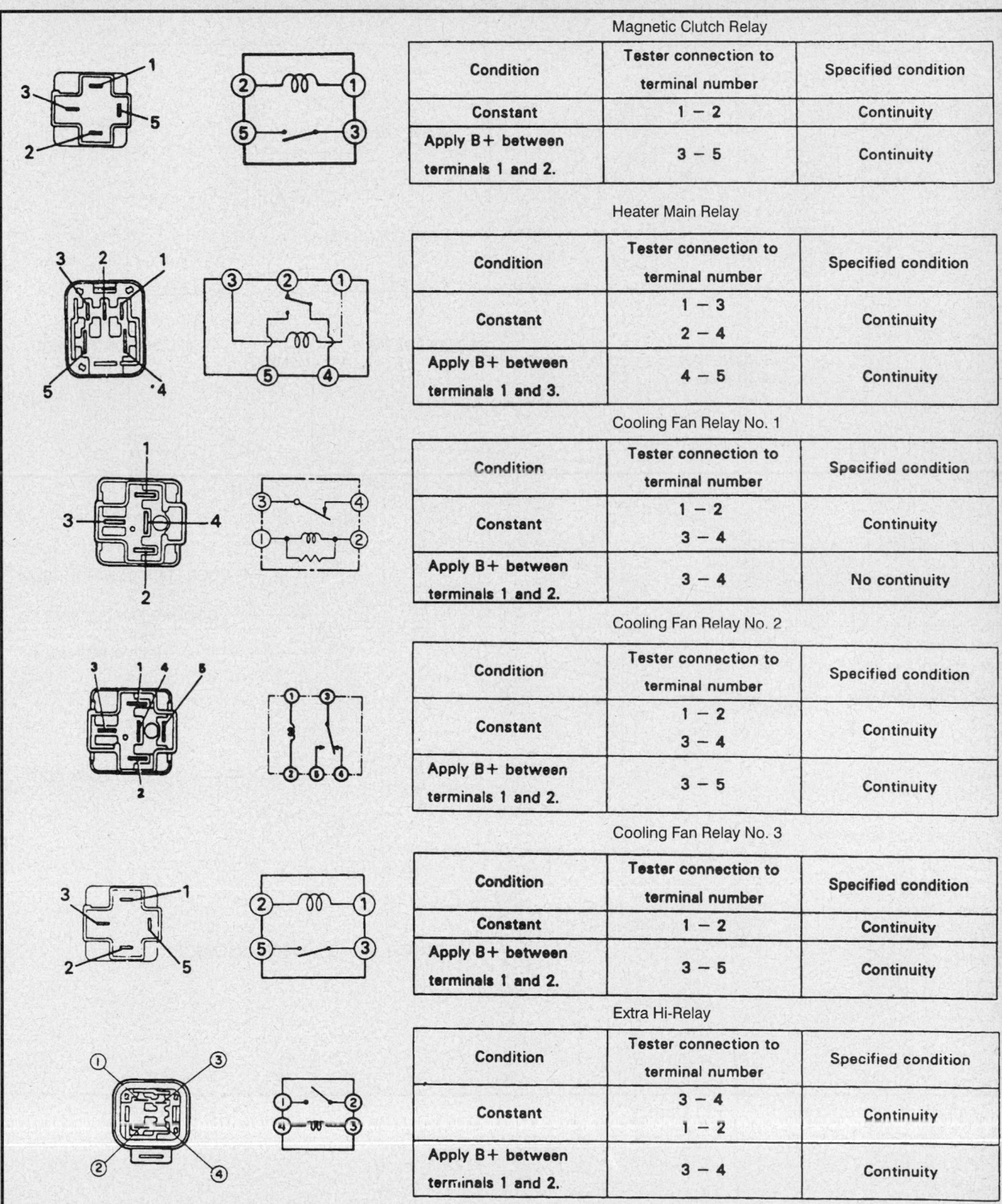

Magnetic Clutch Relay

Condition	Tester connection to terminal number	Specified condition
Constant	1 − 2	Continuity
Apply B+ between terminals 1 and 2.	3 − 5	Continuity

Heater Main Relay

Condition	Tester connection to terminal number	Specified condition
Constant	1 − 3 2 − 4	Continuity
Apply B+ between terminals 1 and 3.	4 − 5	Continuity

Cooling Fan Relay No. 1

Condition	Tester connection to terminal number	Specified condition
Constant	1 − 2 3 − 4	Continuity
Apply B+ between terminals 1 and 2.	3 − 4	No continuity

Cooling Fan Relay No. 2

Condition	Tester connection to terminal number	Specified condition
Constant	1 − 2 3 − 4	Continuity
Apply B+ between terminals 1 and 2.	3 − 5	Continuity

Cooling Fan Relay No. 3

Condition	Tester connection to terminal number	Specified condition
Constant	1 − 2	Continuity
Apply B+ between terminals 1 and 2.	3 − 5	Continuity

Extra Hi-Relay

Condition	Tester connection to terminal number	Specified condition
Constant	3 − 4 1 − 2	Continuity
Apply B+ between terminals 1 and 2.	3 − 4	Continuity

Relay continuity testing − Avalon

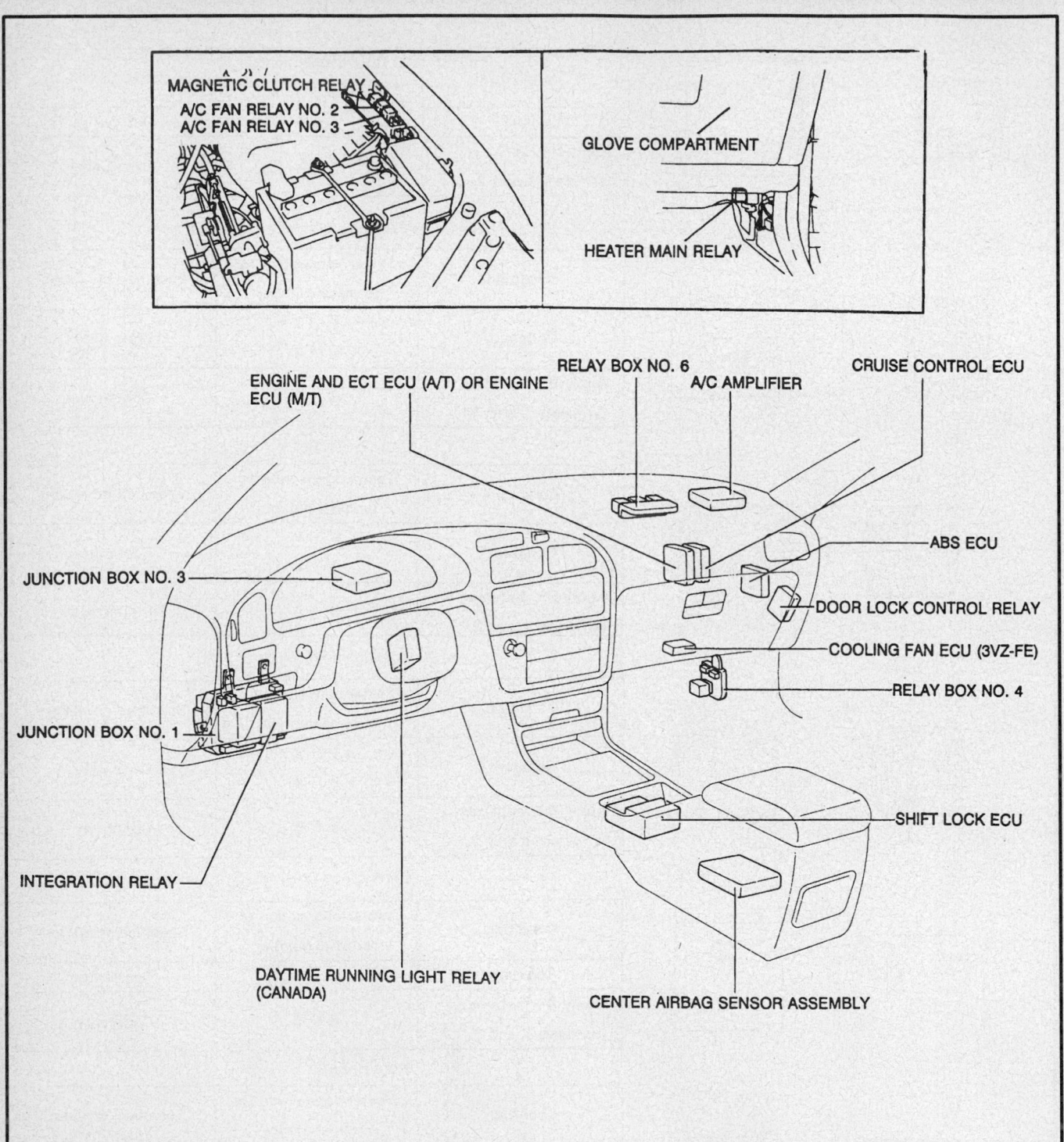

MAGNETIC CLUTCH RELAY
A/C FAN RELAY NO. 2
A/C FAN RELAY NO. 3

GLOVE COMPARTMENT

HEATER MAIN RELAY

ENGINE AND ECT ECU (A/T) OR ENGINE ECU (M/T)

RELAY BOX NO. 6

A/C AMPLIFIER

CRUISE CONTROL ECU

JUNCTION BOX NO. 3

ABS ECU

DOOR LOCK CONTROL RELAY

COOLING FAN ECU (3VZ-FE)

RELAY BOX NO. 4

JUNCTION BOX NO. 1

INTEGRATION RELAY

SHIFT LOCK ECU

DAYTIME RUNNING LIGHT RELAY (CANADA)

CENTER AIRBAG SENSOR ASSEMBLY

Location of system relays – 1993 Camry

MAGNETIC CLUTCH RELAY

Terminal / Condition	1	2	3	4
Constant	○———	——coil——	———	———○
Apply battery voltage to terminal 1 and 4.		○———	———○	

HEATER MAIN RELAY

Terminal / Condition	1	2	3	4	5
Constant	○———	——coil——	———○		
		○———	———	———○	
Apply battery voltage to terminal 1 and 3.				○———	———○

FAN RELAY NO. 2

Terminal / Condition	1	2	3	4	5
Constant	○———	——coil——	———○		
			○———	———	———○
Apply battery voltage to terminal 1 and 4.	○———	———○			

FAN RELAY NO. 3

Terminal / Condition	1	2	3	4
Constant	○———	——coil——	———	———○
Apply battery voltage to terminal 1 and 4.		○———	———○	

Relay continuity testing – 1993 Camry

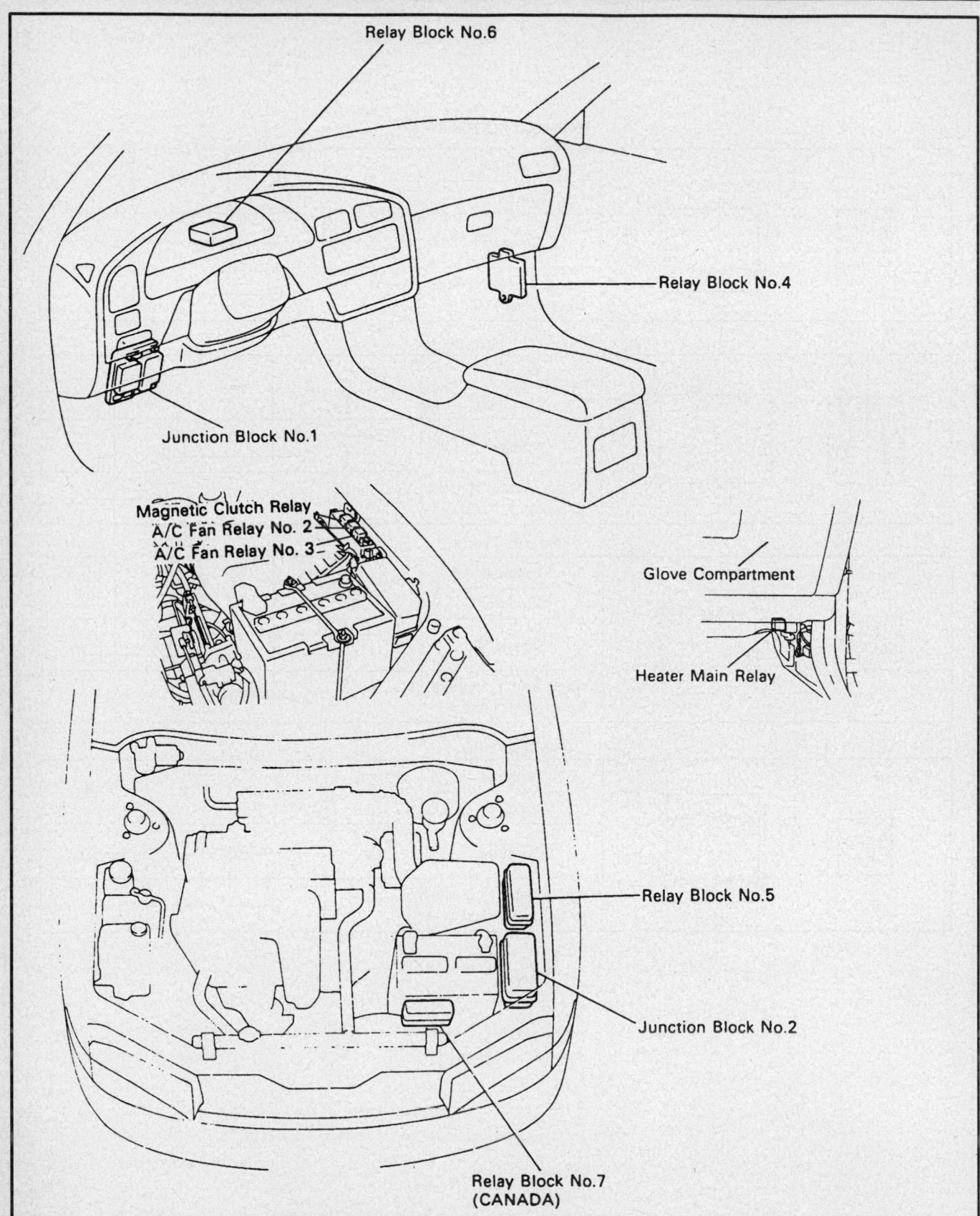

Relay Block No.6

Relay Block No.4

Junction Block No.1

Magnetic Clutch Relay
A/C Fan Relay No. 2
A/C Fan Relay No. 3

Glove Compartment

Heater Main Relay

Relay Block No.5

Junction Block No.2

Relay Block No.7
(CANADA)

Location of system relays — 1995 Camry

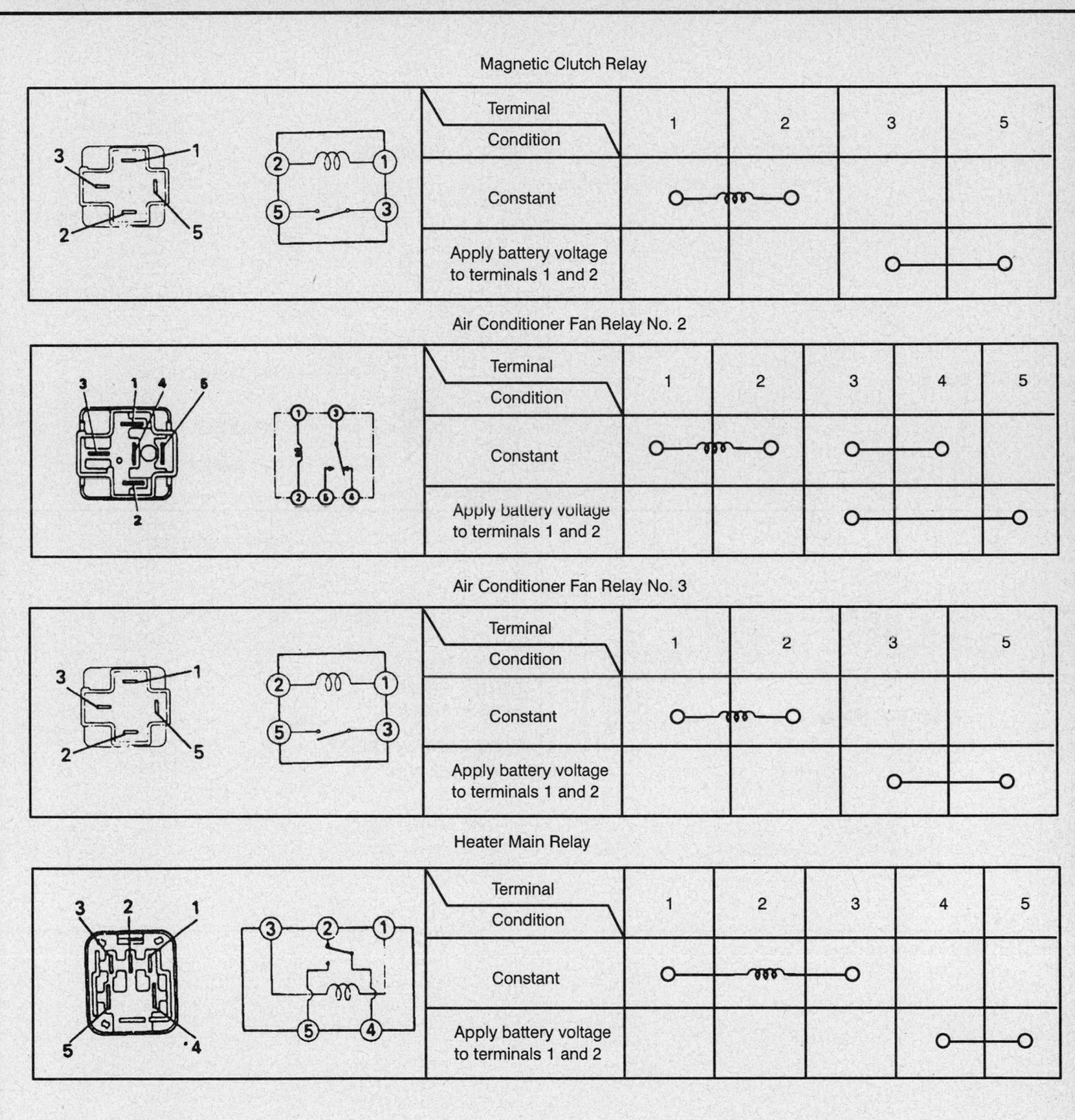

Magnetic Clutch Relay

Terminal Condition	1	2	3	5
Constant		⚬—coil—⚬		
Apply battery voltage to terminals 1 and 2			⚬———⚬	

Air Conditioner Fan Relay No. 2

Terminal Condition	1	2	3	4	5
Constant	⚬—coil—⚬		⚬———⚬		
Apply battery voltage to terminals 1 and 2			⚬———⚬		

Air Conditioner Fan Relay No. 3

Terminal Condition	1	2	3	5
Constant	⚬—coil—⚬			
Apply battery voltage to terminals 1 and 2			⚬———⚬	

Heater Main Relay

Terminal Condition	1	2	3	4	5
Constant	⚬—coil—⚬				
Apply battery voltage to terminals 1 and 2				⚬———⚬	

Relay continuity testing – 1995 Camry

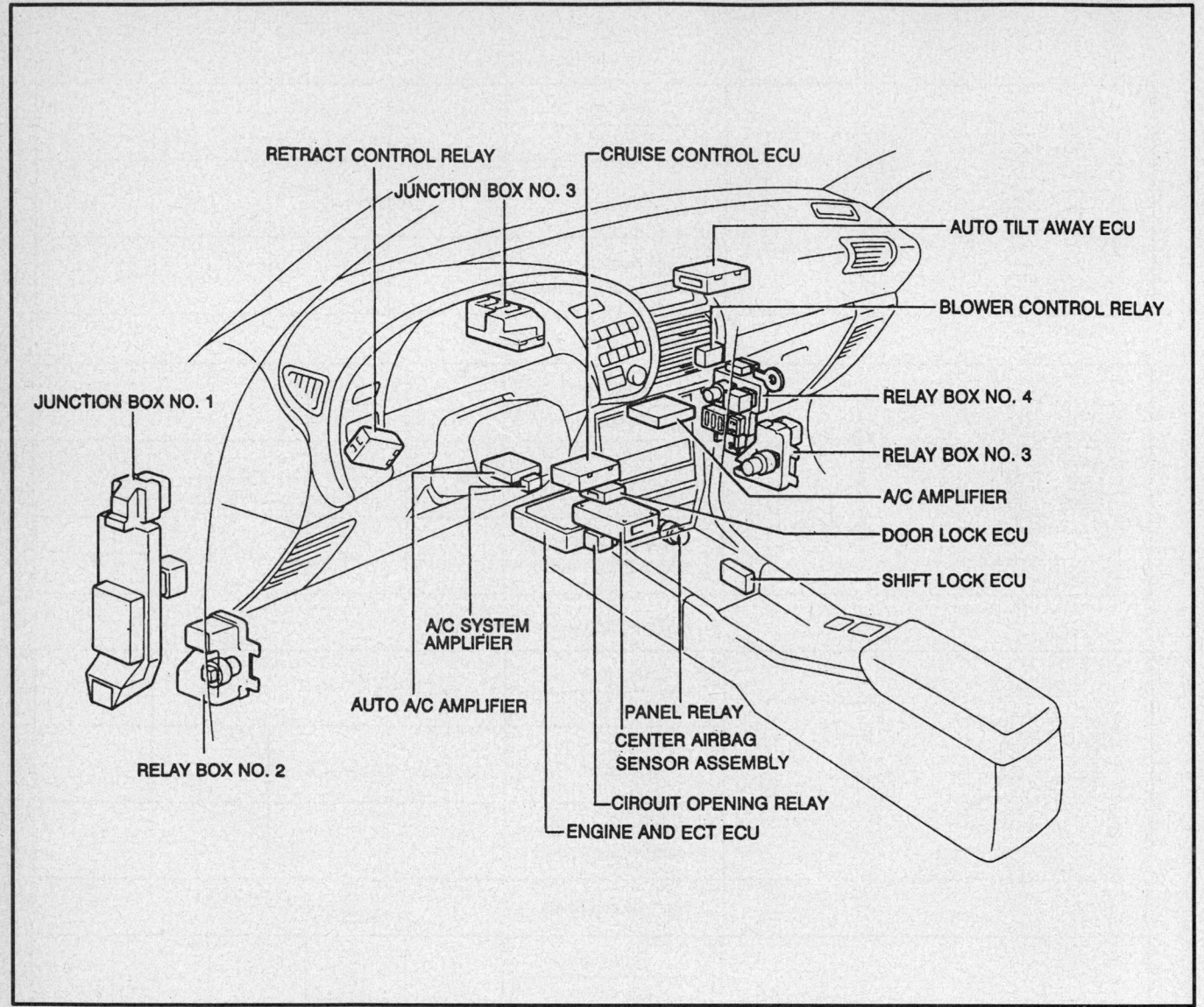

Location of system relays – Celica

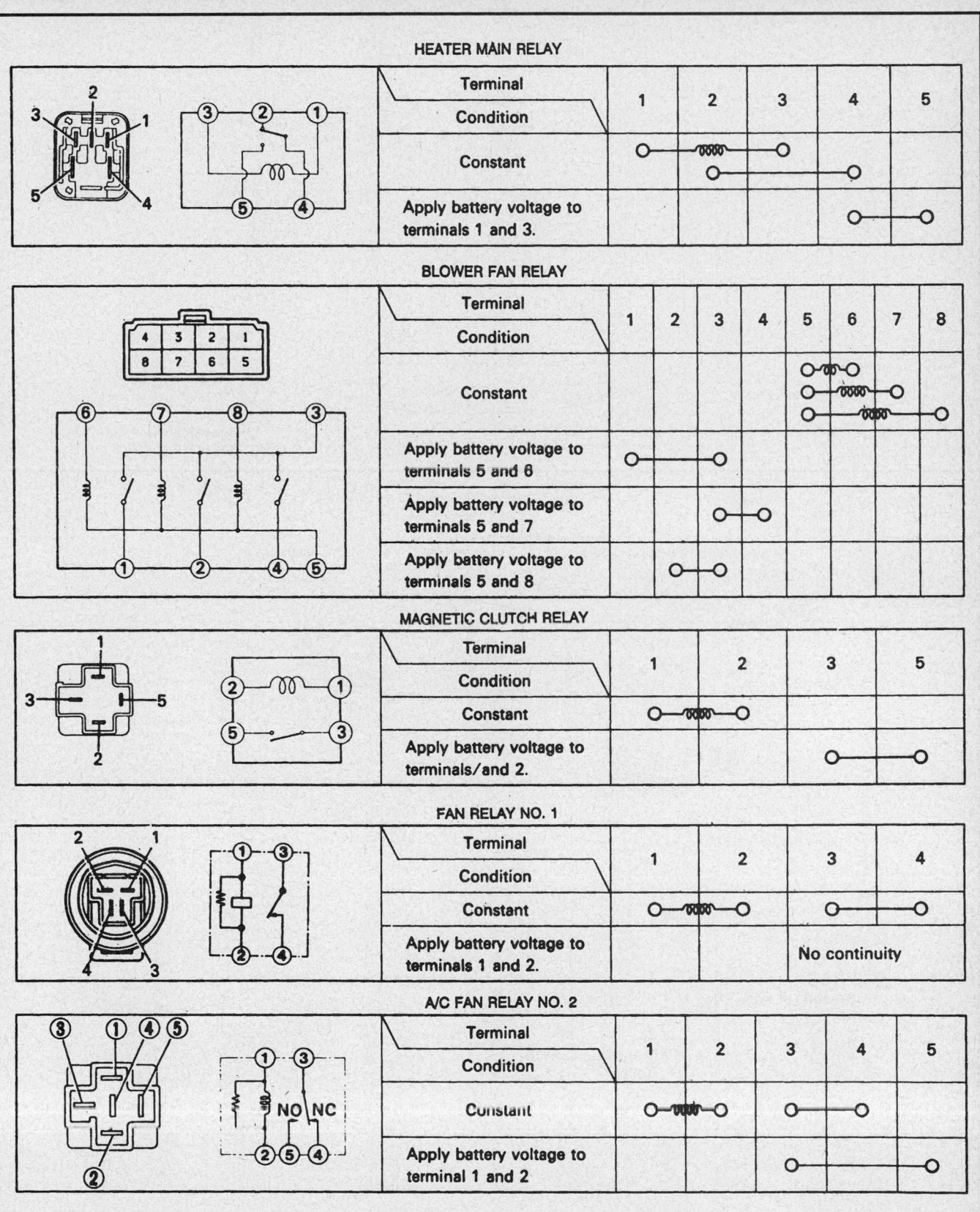

HEATER MAIN RELAY

Terminal Condition	1	2	3	4	5
Constant	o—⟋⟋⟋—o		o		
		o——————o			
Apply battery voltage to terminals 1 and 3.				o——o	

BLOWER FAN RELAY

Terminal Condition	1	2	3	4	5	6	7	8
Constant					o—⟋⟋⟋—o			
					o——⟋⟋⟋——o			
					o——⟋⟋⟋——o			
Apply battery voltage to terminals 5 and 6	o————o							
Apply battery voltage to terminals 5 and 7			o——o					
Apply battery voltage to terminals 5 and 8		o——o						

MAGNETIC CLUTCH RELAY

Terminal Condition	1	2	3	5
Constant	o—⟋⟋⟋—o			
Apply battery voltage to terminals/and 2.			o——o	

FAN RELAY NO. 1

Terminal Condition	1	2	3	4
Constant	o—⟋⟋⟋—o		o——o	
Apply battery voltage to terminals 1 and 2.			No continuity	

A/C FAN RELAY NO. 2

Terminal Condition	1	2	3	4	5
Constant	o—⟋⟋⟋—o		o——o		
Apply battery voltage to terminal 1 and 2			o——o		

Relay continuity testing – Celica

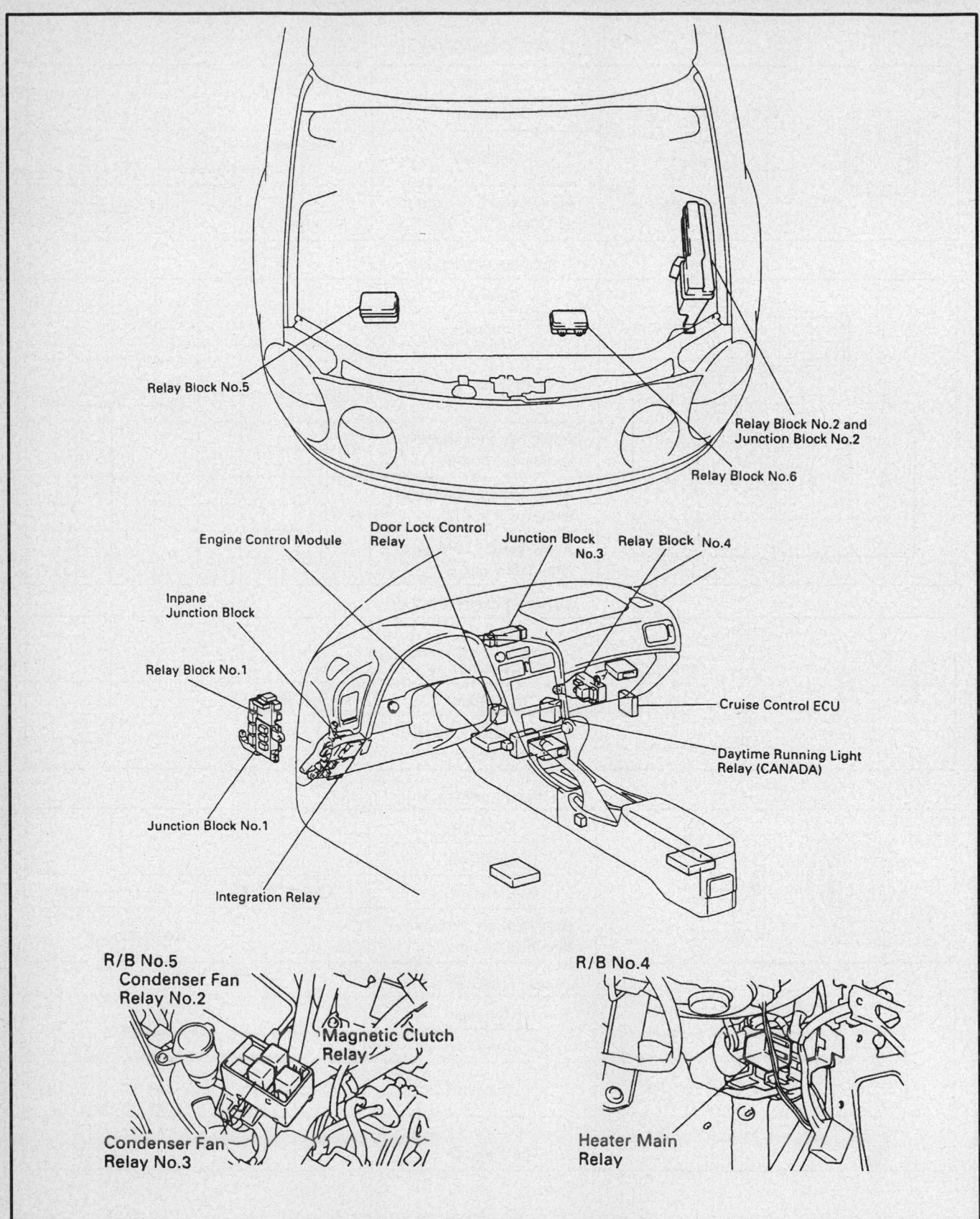

Relay Block No.5

Relay Block No.2 and Junction Block No.2

Relay Block No.6

Engine Control Module

Door Lock Control Relay

Junction Block No.3

Relay Block No.4

Inpane Junction Block

Relay Block No.1

Cruise Control ECU

Daytime Running Light Relay (CANADA)

Junction Block No.1

Integration Relay

R/B No.5
Condenser Fan Relay No.2

Magnetic Clutch Relay

Condenser Fan Relay No.3

R/B No.4

Heater Main Relay

Location of system relays – 1994-95 Celica

Magnetic Clutch Relay

Terminal Condition		1	2	3	5
Constant		⊙〰〰⊙			
Apply battery voltage to terminals 1 and 2				⊙——⊙	

Heater Main Relay

Terminal Condition		1	2	3	4	5
Constant		⊙——〰〰——⊙	⊙		⊙	
Apply battery voltage to terminals 1 and 3					⊙——⊙	

Condenser Fan Relay No. 2

Terminal Condition		1	2	3	4	5
Constant		⊙——〰〰——⊙		⊙——⊙		
Apply battery voltage to terminals 1 and 2					⊙——⊙	

Condenser Fan Relay No. 3

Terminal Condition		1	2	3	5
Constant		⊙——〰〰——⊙			
Apply battery voltage to terminals 1 and 2				⊙——⊙	

Relay continuity testing – 1994-95 Celica

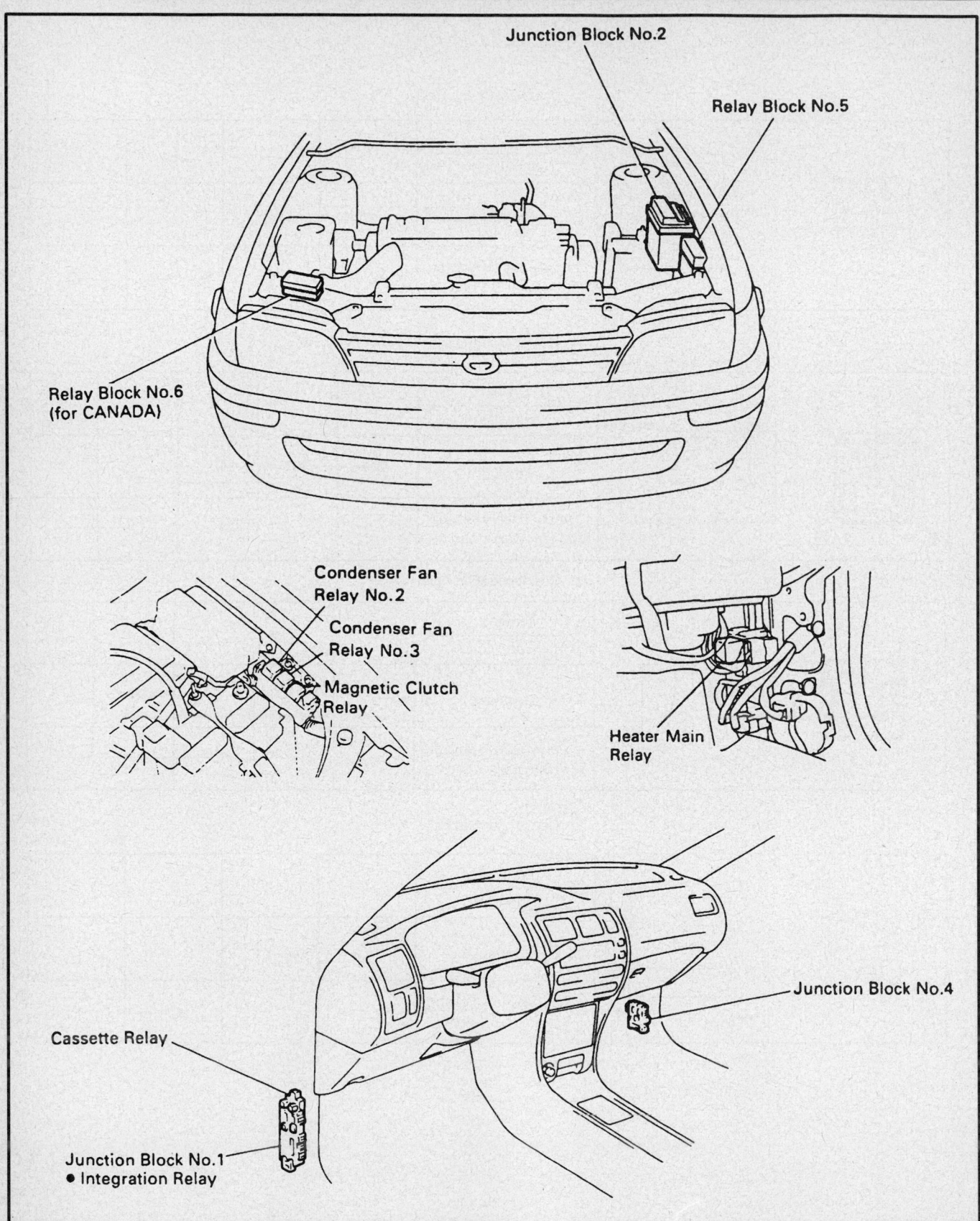

Junction Block No.2

Relay Block No.5

Relay Block No.6
(for CANADA)

Condenser Fan
Relay No.2

Condenser Fan
Relay No.3

Magnetic Clutch
Relay

Heater Main
Relay

Junction Block No.4

Cassette Relay

Junction Block No.1
• Integration Relay

Location of system relays – 1993-95 Corolla

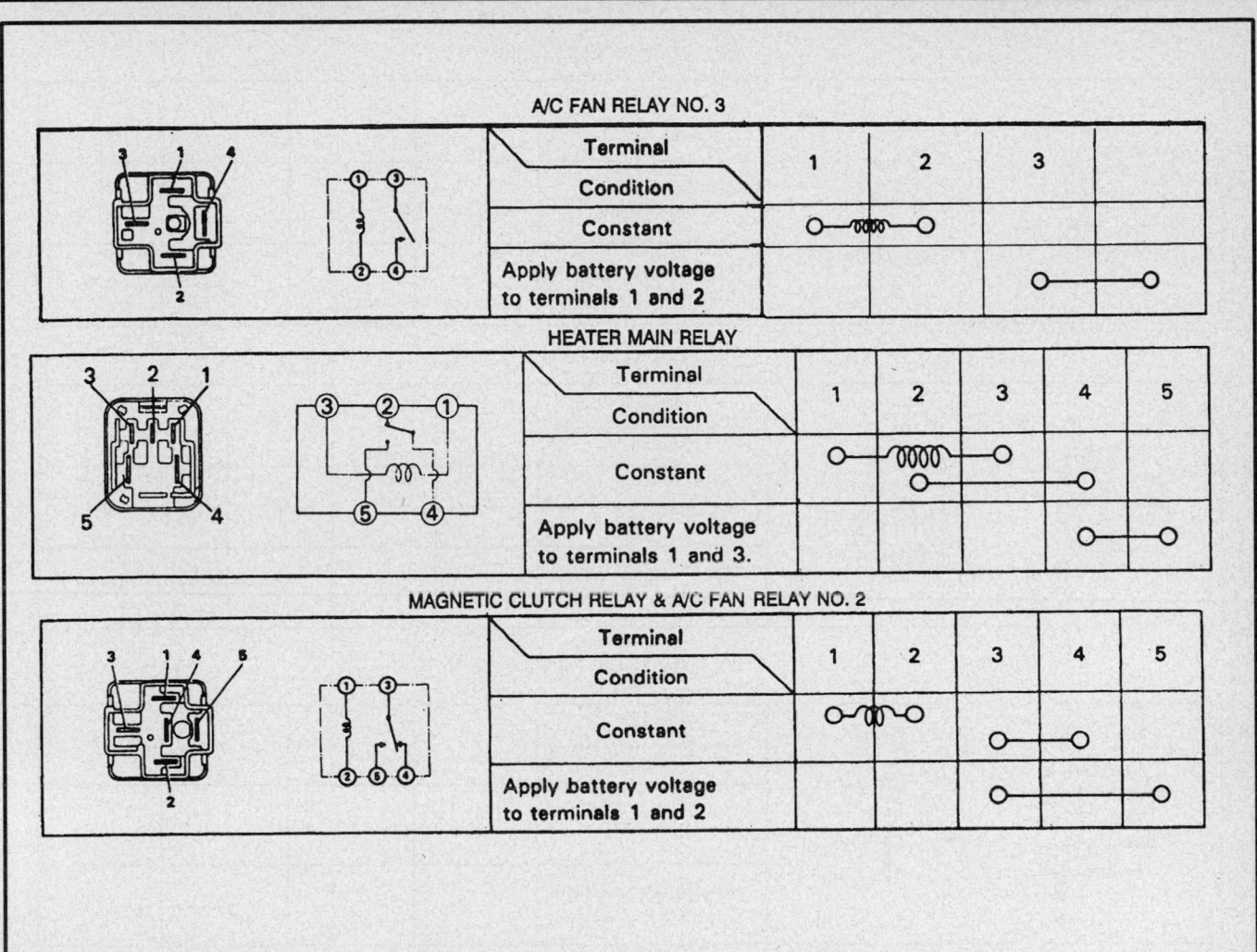

A/C FAN RELAY NO. 3

Terminal / Condition	1	2	3	
Constant	○─wwww─○			
Apply battery voltage to terminals 1 and 2			○──────○	

HEATER MAIN RELAY

Terminal / Condition	1	2	3	4	5
Constant	○─wwww─○	○──────○			
Apply battery voltage to terminals 1 and 3.				○──────○	

MAGNETIC CLUTCH RELAY & A/C FAN RELAY NO. 2

Terminal / Condition	1	2	3	4	5
Constant	○─wwww─○	○──────○			
Apply battery voltage to terminals 1 and 2			○──────○		

Relay continuity testing – 1993 Corolla

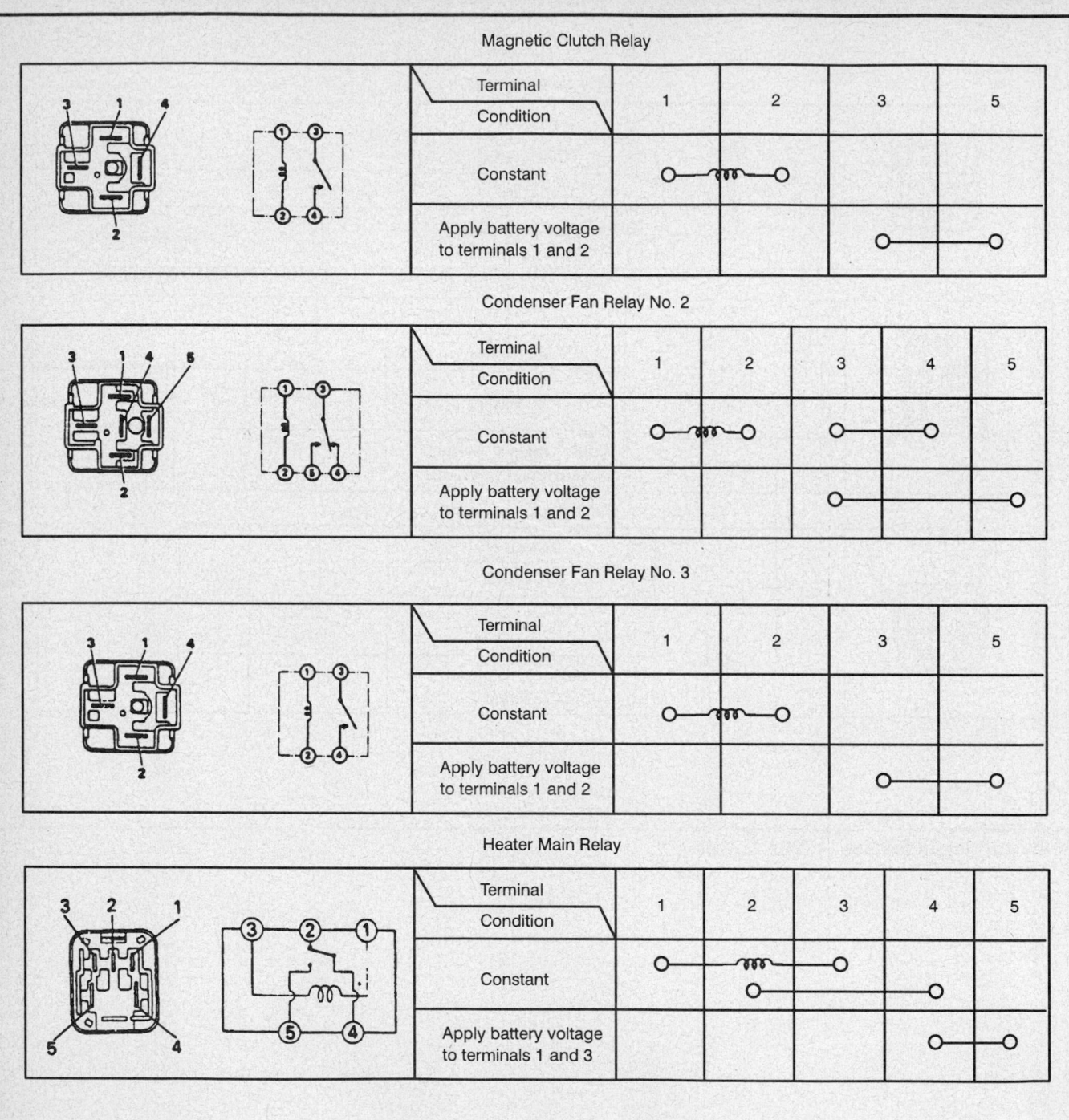

Magnetic Clutch Relay

Terminal / Condition	1	2	3	5
Constant	o—coil—o			
Apply battery voltage to terminals 1 and 2			o——o	

Condenser Fan Relay No. 2

Terminal / Condition	1	2	3	4	5
Constant	o—coil—o		o——o		
Apply battery voltage to terminals 1 and 2			o——o		

Condenser Fan Relay No. 3

Terminal / Condition	1	2	3	5
Constant	o—coil—o			
Apply battery voltage to terminals 1 and 2			o——o	

Heater Main Relay

Terminal / Condition	1	2	3	4	5
Constant	o—coil—o			o——o	
Apply battery voltage to terminals 1 and 3				o——o	

Relay continuity testing — 1994-95 Corolla

Location of system relays – 1993 Paseo and Tercel

HEATER MAIN RELAY

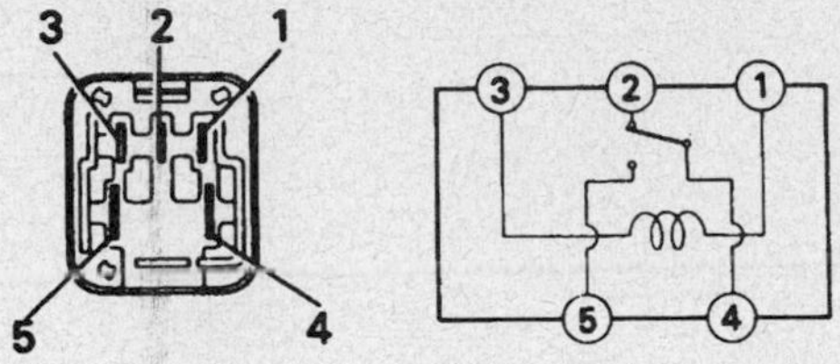

Terminal / Condition	1	2	3	4	5
Constant	O——⦚⦚⦚⦚——O		O		
		O			O
Apply battery voltage to terminals 1 and 3.				O——O	

CONDENSER FAN RELAY NO. 2

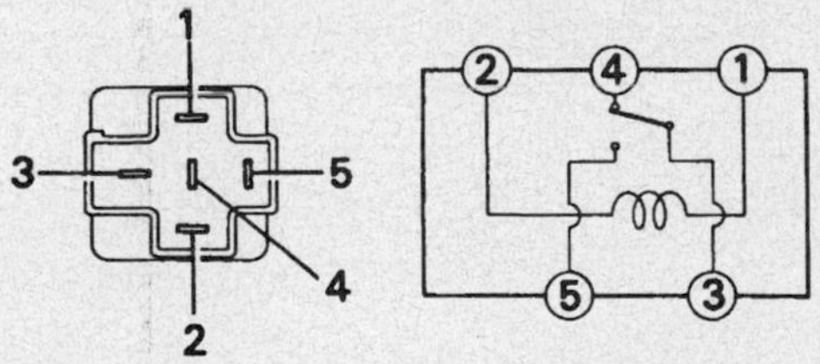

Terminal / Condition	1	2	3	4	5
Constant	O——⦚⦚⦚⦚——O				
		O——O			
Apply battery voltage to terminals 1 and 2.				O——O	

CONDENSER FAN RELAY NO. 3

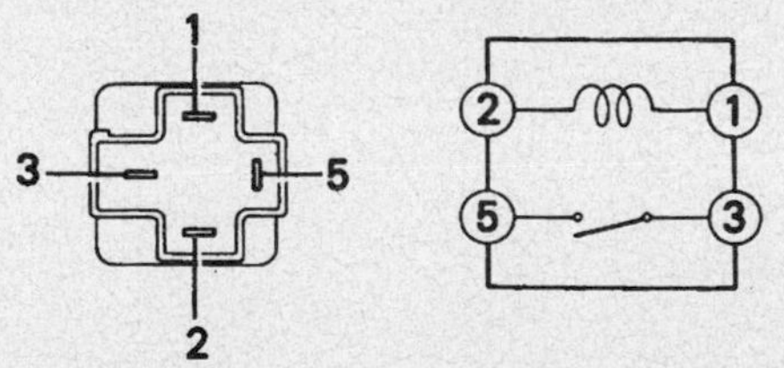

Terminal / Condition	1	2	3	5
Constant	O——⦚⦚⦚⦚——O			
Apply battery voltage to terminals 1 and 2.			O——O	

MAGNETIC CLUTCH RELAY

Terminal / Condition	1	2	3	4
Constant	O——⦚⦚⦚⦚——O		O	
Apply battery voltage to terminals 1 and 3.		O——O		

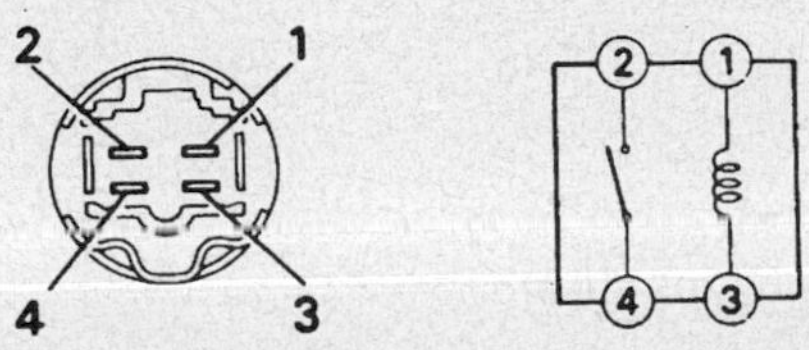

Relay continuity testing – 1993 Paseo and Tercel

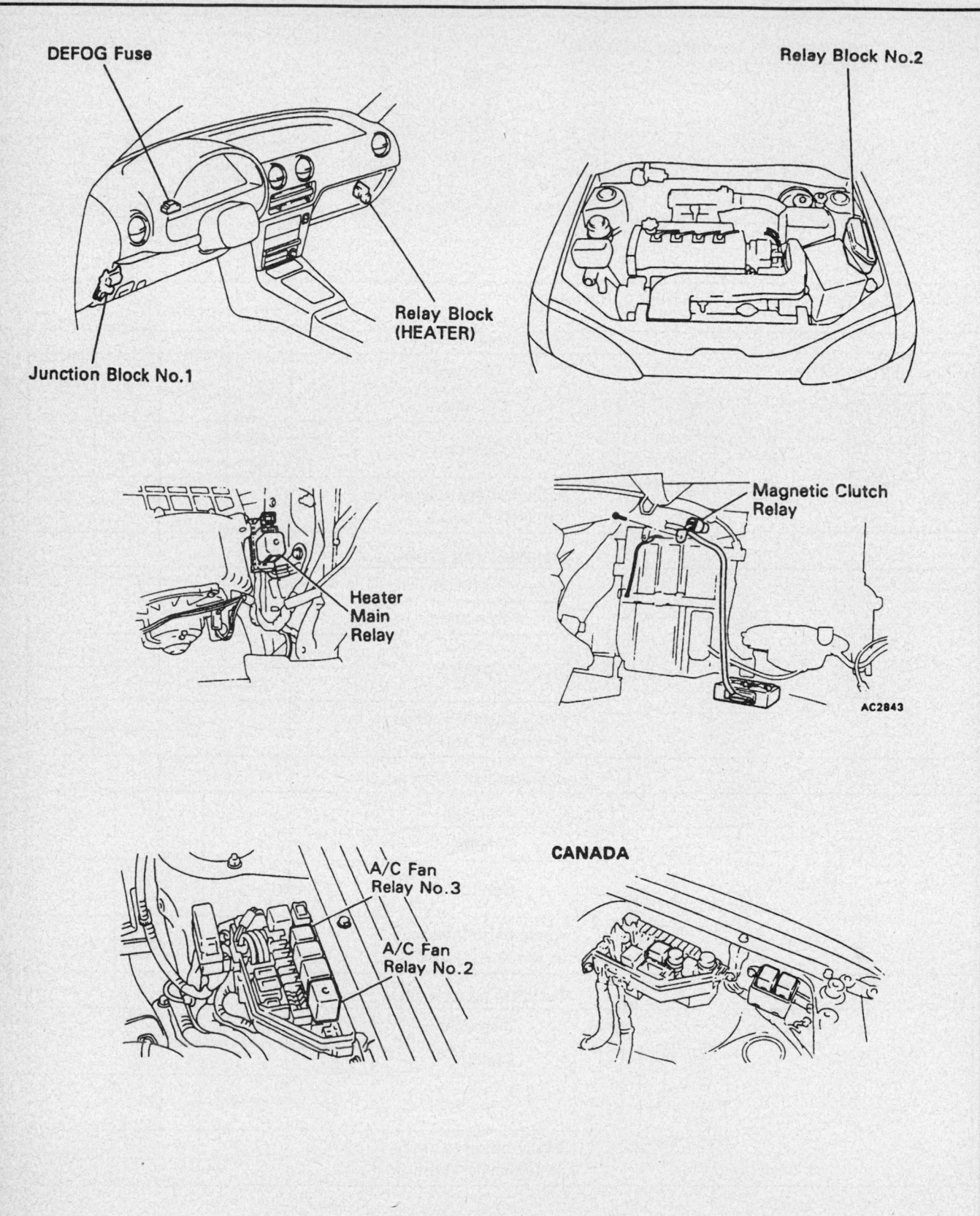

Location of system relays – 1994 Paseo, 1994 Tercel similar

Heater Main Relay & Condenser Fan Relay No. 2

Terminal / Condition	1	2	3	4	5
Constant		○——www——○	○		
		○—————————————○			
Apply battery voltage to terminals 1 and 3				○————○	

Magnetic Clutch Relay & Condenser Fan & Condenser Fan Relay No. 3

Terminal / Condition	1	2	3	5
Constant	○——www——○		○	
Apply battery voltage to terminals 1 and 3		○—————————————○		○

Condenser Fan Relay No. 2 (CANADA)

Terminal / Condition	1	2	3	4	5
Constant	○——www——○		○————○		
Apply battery voltage to terminals 1 and 2				○————○	

Condenser Fan Relay No. 3 (CANADA)

Terminal / Condition	1	2	3	5
Constant	○——www——○			
Apply battery voltage to terminals 1 and 2			○————————○	

Relay continuity testing – 1994 Paseo and Tercel

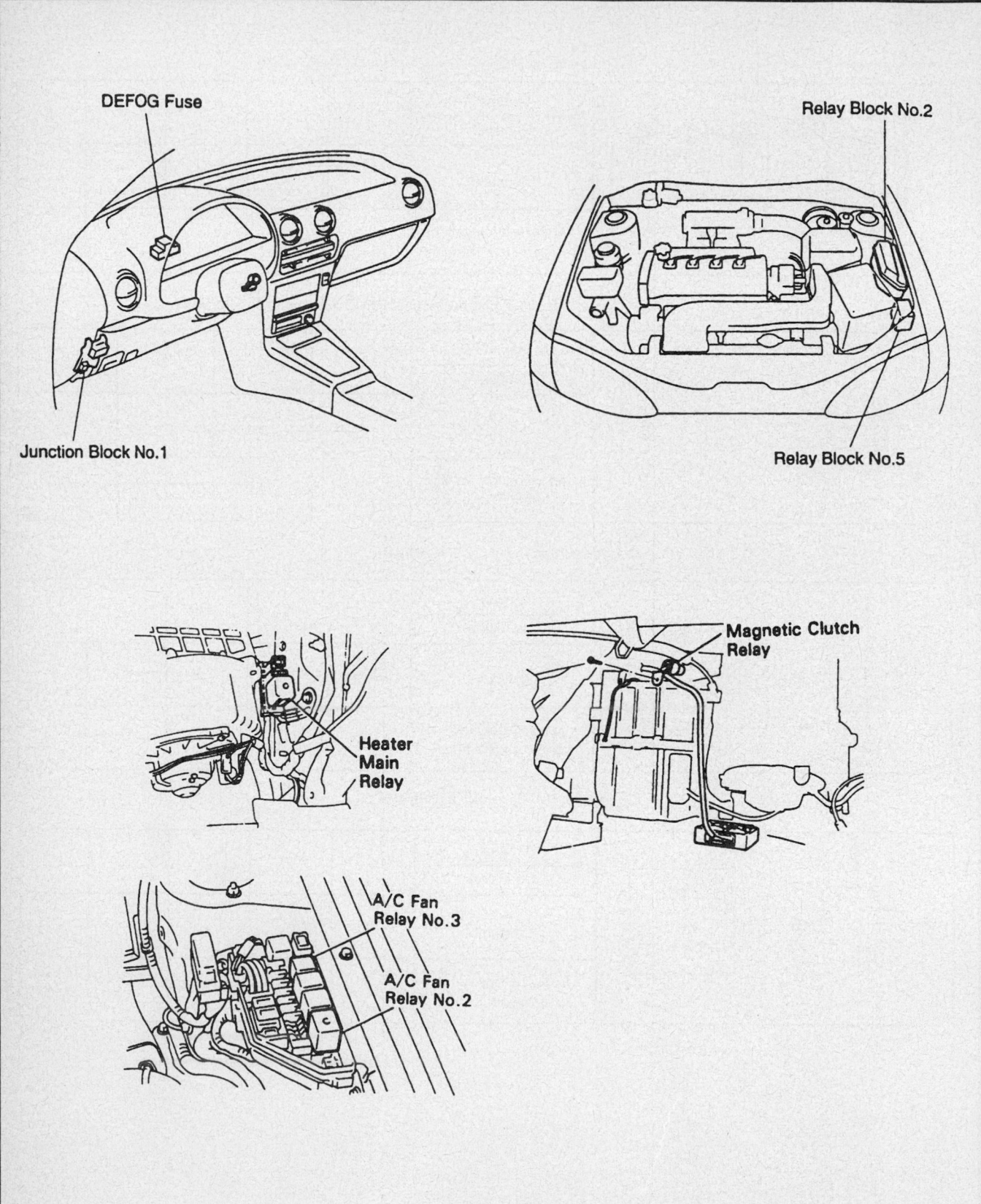

DEFOG Fuse

Junction Block No.1

Relay Block No.2

Relay Block No.5

Heater Main Relay

Magnetic Clutch Relay

A/C Fan Relay No.3

A/C Fan Relay No.2

Location of system relays – 1995 Paseo

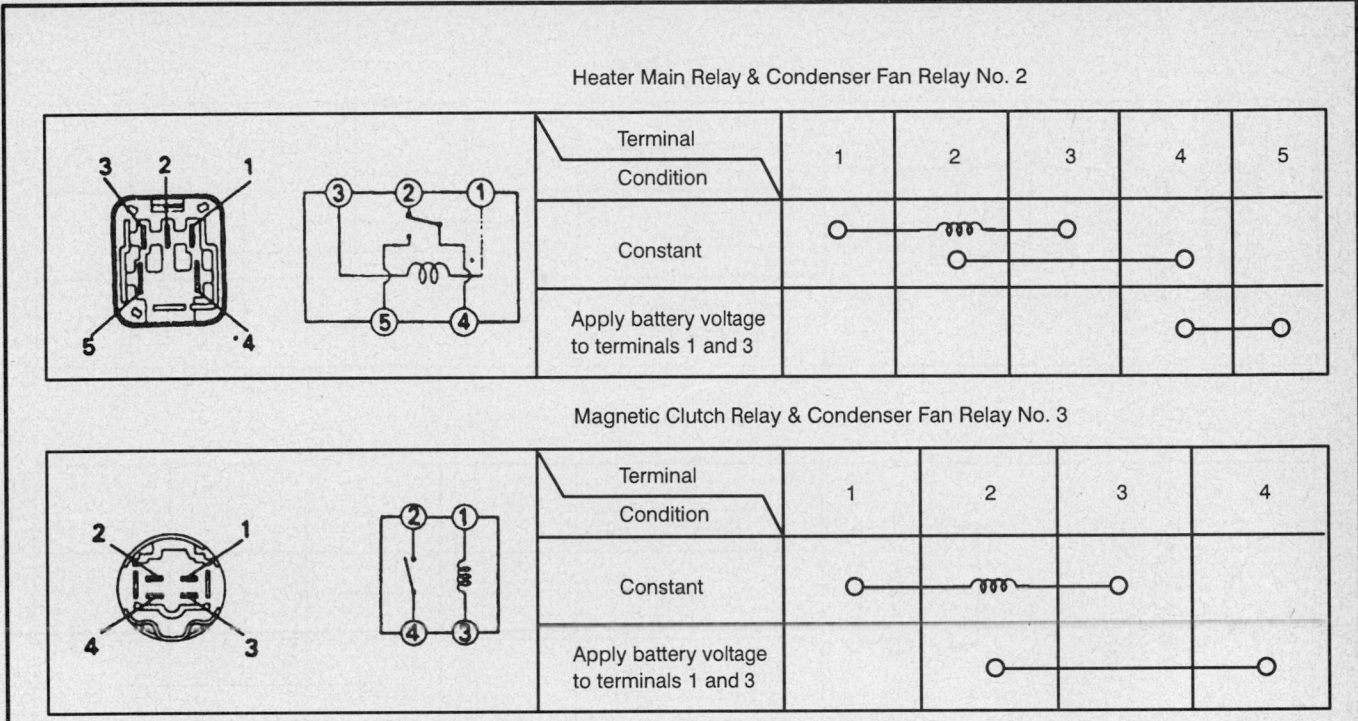

Heater Main Relay & Condenser Fan Relay No. 2

Terminal Condition	1	2	3	4	5
Constant	○━━━	～～～	━━○ ○━━━	━━○	
Apply battery voltage to terminals 1 and 3				○━━━	━━○

Magnetic Clutch Relay & Condenser Fan Relay No. 3

Terminal Condition	1	2	3	4
Constant	○━━━	～～～	━━○	
Apply battery voltage to terminals 1 and 3	○━━━		━━○	

Relay continuity testing — 1995 Paseo

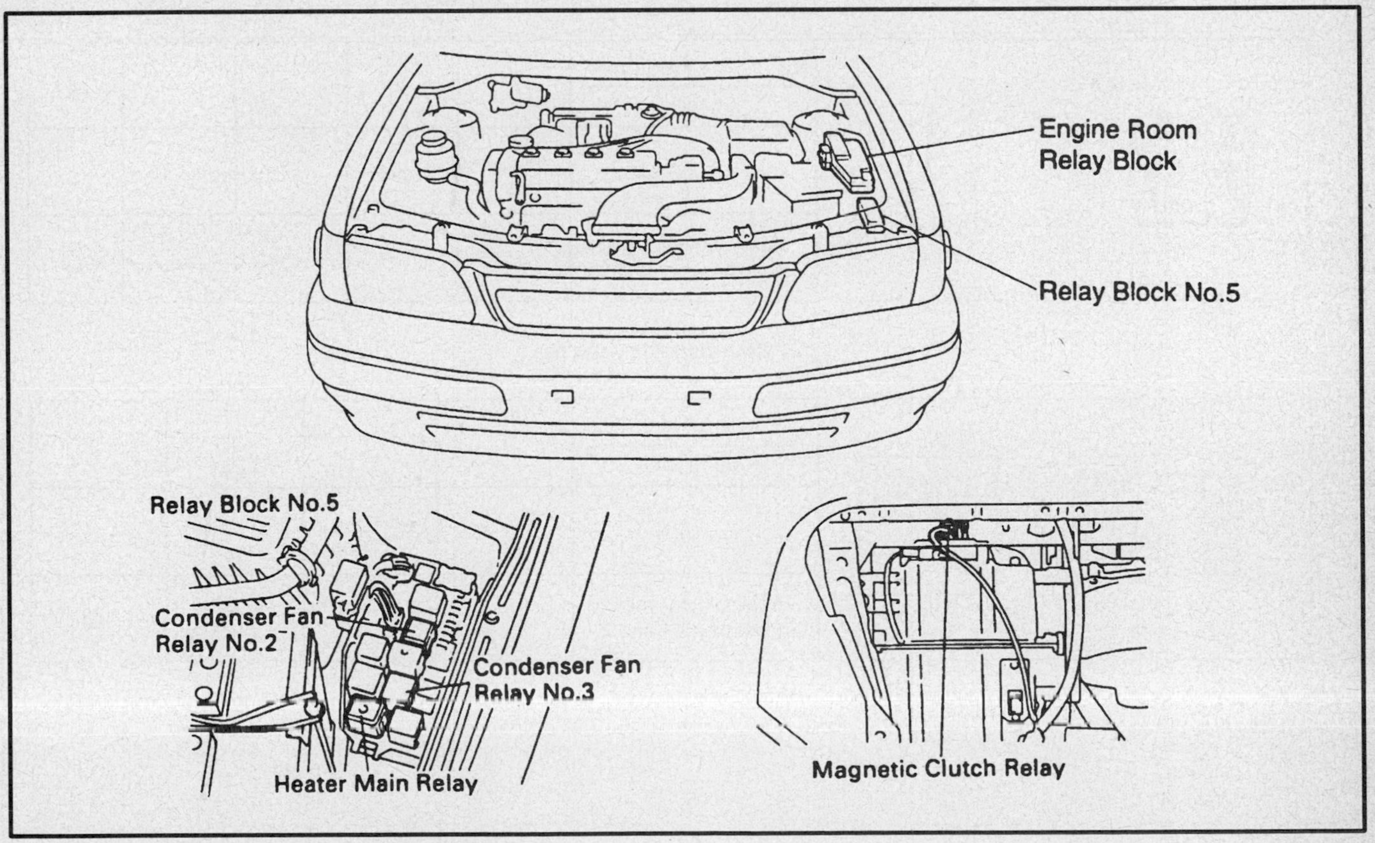

Engine Room
Relay Block

Relay Block No.5

Relay Block No.5

Condenser Fan
Relay No.2

Condenser Fan
Relay No.3

Heater Main Relay

Magnetic Clutch Relay

Location of system relays — 1995 Tercel

Heater Main Relay

Terminal / Condition	1	2	3	4	5
Constant	O——coil——O (1-2-3)			O——O (2-4)	
Apply battery voltage to terminals 1 and 3				O——O (4-5)	

Magnetic Clutch Relay Continuity

Terminal / Condition	1	2	3	5
Constant	O——O (1-3)			
Apply battery voltage to terminals 1 and 3		O——O (2-5)		

Condenser Fan Relay No. 2

Terminal / Condition	1	2	3	4	5
Constant	O——coil——O (1-2)		O——O (3-4)		
Apply battery voltage to terminals 1 and 2			O——O (3-5)		

Condenser Fan Relay No. 3

Terminal / Condition	1	2	3	5
Constant	O——coil——O (1-2)			
Apply battery voltage to terminals 1 and 2			O——O (3-5)	

Relay continuity testing – 1995 Paseo

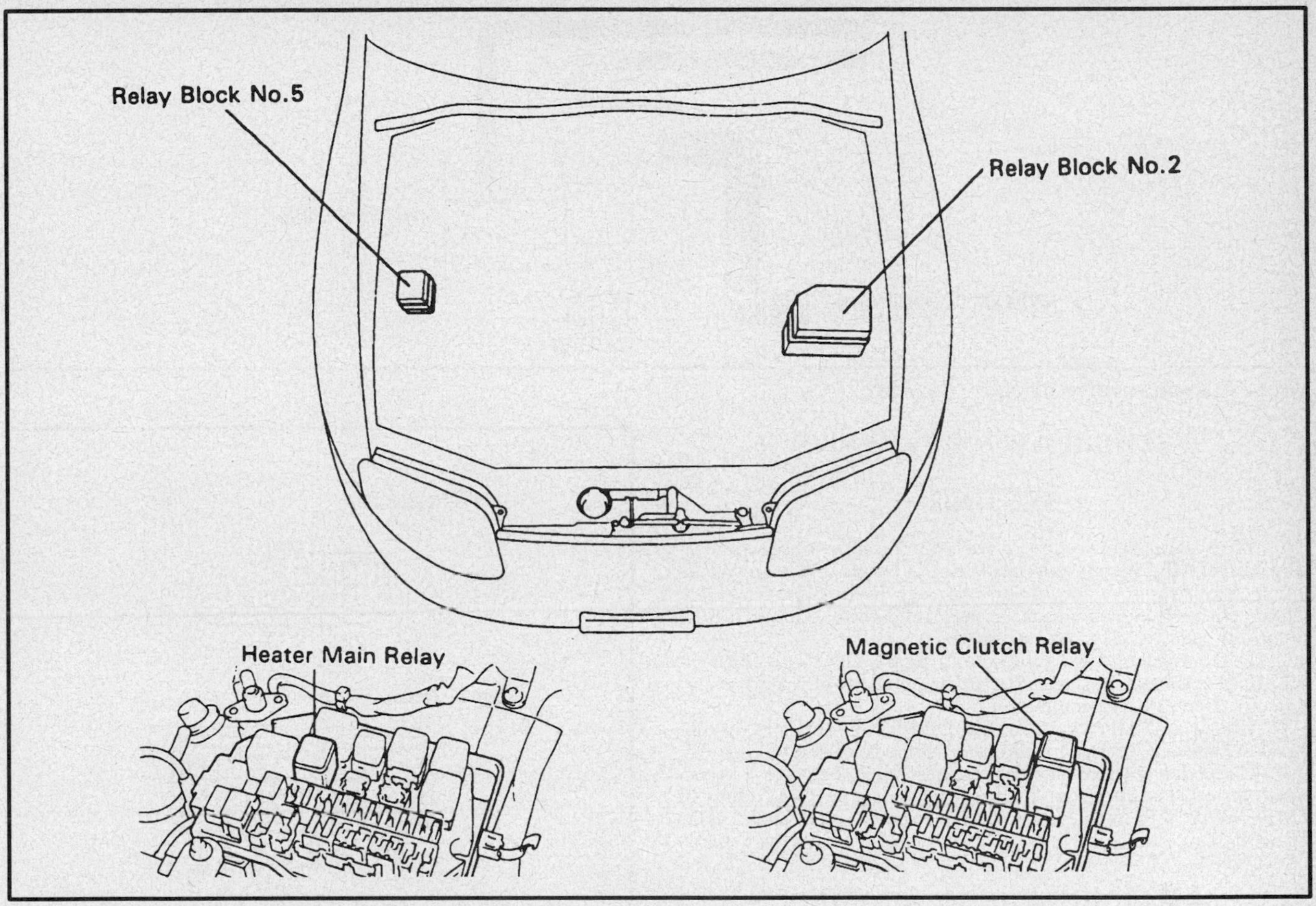

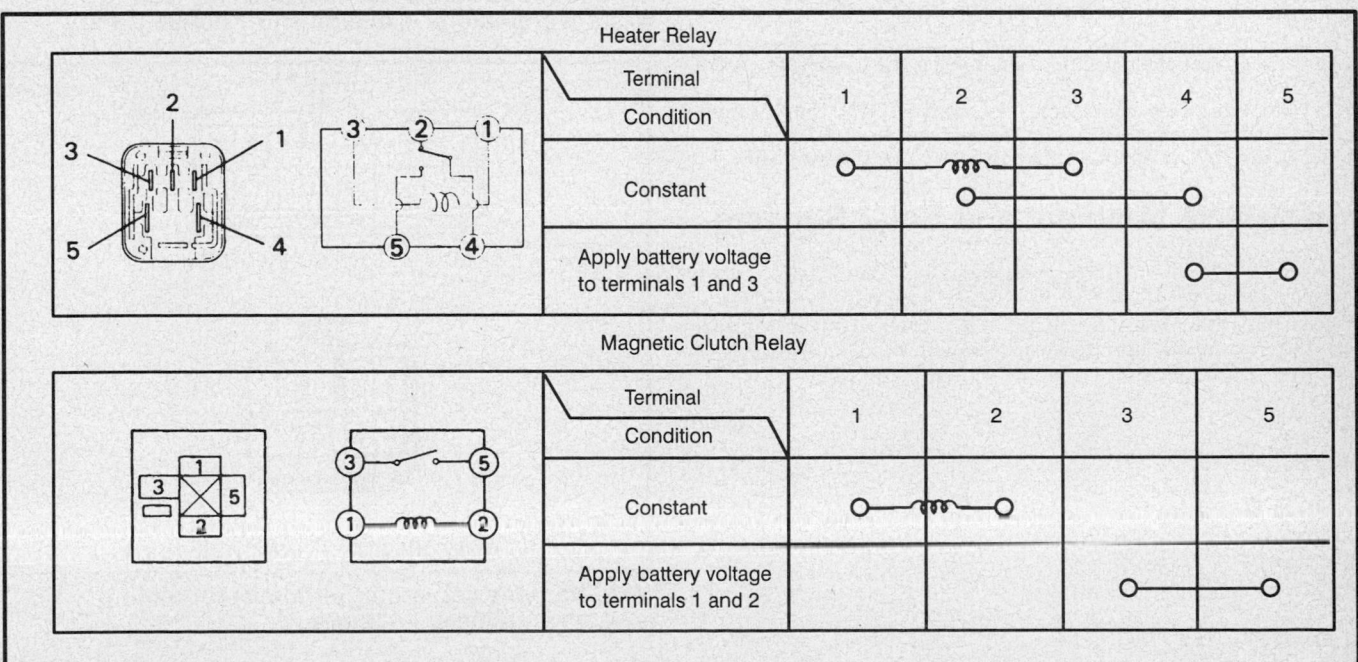

Location of system relays – 1994-95 Supra

Heater Relay

Terminal / Condition	1	2	3	4	5
Constant	O—	—ʘʘʘ—	—O		
		O—	——	—O	
Apply battery voltage to terminals 1 and 3				O—	—O

Magnetic Clutch Relay

Terminal / Condition	1	2	3	5
Constant	O—	—ʘʘʘ—O		
Apply battery voltage to terminals 1 and 2			O—	—O

Relay continuity testing – 1994-95 Supra

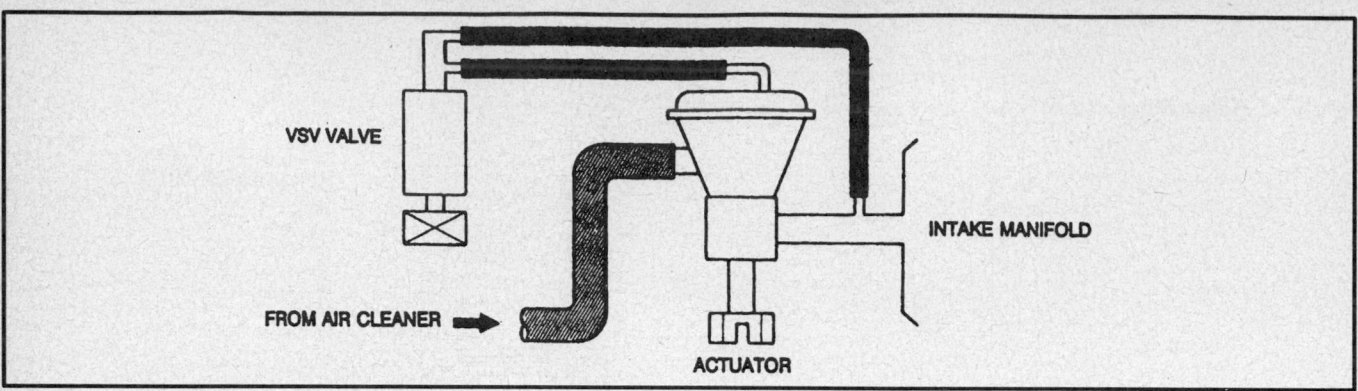

Vacuum switch valve circuit – typical

Vacuum Switching Valve

TESTING

1. With valve removed from the vehicle, note which connection is from the intake manifold. Apply battery voltage to the valve terminals and blow air into the non-manifold connection. Check that air comes out of the manifold connection but does not come out the filter (if equipped).

2. Disconnect battery voltage and again blow into the non-manifold connection. Check that air comes out of the filter but not out the manifold connection.

3. Check valve for short circuit. Check that there is no continuity between each terminal and the body of the valve.

4. Check for open circuit measure resistance between 2 terminals. On 1993 models, the specified resistance is 37–44 ohms at 68°F. On 1994–95 models, the specified resistance is 30–34 ohms at 68°F. If resistance valve is not as specified, replace the valve.

Air Conditioning Amplifier

TESTING

1. Disconnect the amplifier and inspect the connector on the wire harness side.

2. Constant test conditions are ignition **ON** temperature control lever **MAX. COOL** and blower switch in **HI** position.

3. If the circuit is not as specified, replace the amplifier.

In-Vehicle, Ambient and Solar Sensors

TESTING

Check the sensor resistance. If there is a open circuit in the sensor the system will operate at a maximum condition (full hot or cold).

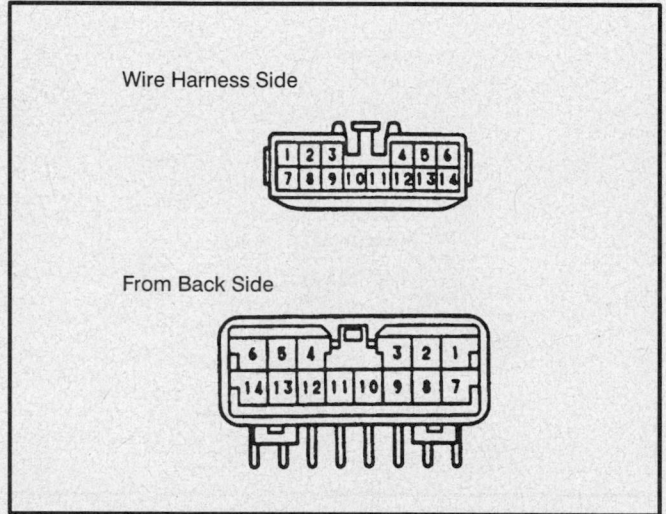

Wire harness connector terminals for testing system amplifiers – Avalon and 1994-95 Camry

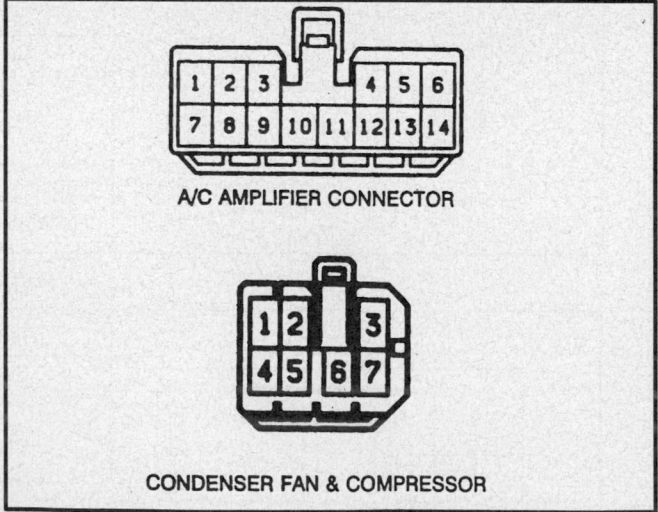

Wire harness connector terminals for testing system amplifiers – Camry

INSPECTION OF AIR CONDITIONING AMPLIFIER CIRCUIT – AVALON (MANUAL AIR CONDITIONER), 1995 CAMRY

Tester connection to termianl number	Condition	Specified condition
5 – Ground	Constant	Continuity
1 – ECM terminal AC1	Constant	Continuity
7 – ECM terminal ACT	Constant	Continuity
14 – 13	Constant	Approx. 115 Ω at 20 °C (68 °F)
9 – 13	Constant	1.5 kΩ at 20 °C (68 °F)
4 – Ground	Ignition switch ON	Approx. 10 to 14 v
4 – Ground	Ignition switch OFF	No voltage
8 – Ground	A/C switch ON	Battery positive voltage
8 – Ground	A/C switch OFF	No voltage
10 – Ground	A/C switch ON	Battery positive voltage
10 – Ground	A/C switch OFF	No voltage
12 – Ground	A/C switch ON	Battery positive voltage
12 – Ground	A/C switch OFF	No voltage

BACK PROBE INSPECTION

Tester connection to terminal number	Condition	Specified condition
2 – Ground	Refrigerant pressure 196 – 3,410 kPa	Battery positive voltage
2 – Ground	Refrigerant pressure less than 196 kPa or more than 3,140 kPa	No voltage

INSPECTION OF AIR CONDITIONING AMPLIFIER CIRCUIT – 1994 CAMRY

Tester connection to terminal number	Condition	Specified Condition
5 – Ground	Constant	Continuity
1 – ECM terminal ACA	Constant	Continuity
7 – ECM terminal ACT	Constant	Continuity
9 – 13	Constant	1.5 kΩ at 20 °C (68 °F)
14 – 13	Constant	Approx. 115 Ω at 20 °C (68 °F)
12 – Ground	Turn A/C switch ON	Battery positive voltage
12 – Ground	Turn A/C switch OFF	Approx. 10 – 14 v
4 – Ground	Start the engine	Approx. 10 – 14 v
4 – Ground	Stop the engine	No voltage
10 – Ground	Turn A/C switch ON	Battery positive voltage
10 – Ground	Turn A/C switch OFF	No voltage
8 – Ground	Turn A/C switch ON	Battery positive voltage
8 – Ground	Turn A/C switch OFF	No voltage

INSPECTION OF AIR CONDITIONING AMPLIFIER CIRCUIT – 1993 CAMRY

Check for	Tester connection	Condition	Specified value
Continuity	5 – ground	Constant	Continuity
Resistance	9 – 13	Constant	1.5 KΩ at 25 °C (77°F)
	14 – 13	Constant	Approx. 115 Ω at 20°C (68°F)
Voltage	12 – ground	Turn A/C switch on	Battery voltage
		Turn A/C switch off	No voltage
	4 – ground	Start the engine	Approx. 10 – 14 V
		Stop the engine	No voltage
	2 – ground	Turn A/C switch on	Battery voltage
		Turn A/C switch off	No voltage
	10 – ground	Turn A/C switch on	Battery voltage
		Turn A/C switch off	No voltage
	8 – ground	Turn A/C switch on	Battery voltage
		Turn A/C switch off	No voltage

INSPECTION OF AIR CONDITIONING AMPLIFIER CIRCUIT – 1993 CELICA

Check for	Tester connection	Condition	Specified value
Continuity	•¹ 2 – ground	Engine coolant less than 95°C (203°F)	Continuity
		Engine coolant more than 100°C (212°F)	No continuity
	15 – ground	Constant	Continuity
Resistance	•¹ 5 – ground	Constant	Approx. 12 Ω
	9 – 14	Constant	Approx. 115 Ω
	16 – 14	Constant	Approx. 15 kΩ at 25°C (77°F)
Voltage	1 – ground	Turn A/C switch on.	Battery voltage
		Turn A/C switch off.	No voltage
	3 – ground	Turn A/C switch on.	Battery voltage
		Turn A/C switch off.	No voltage
	6 – ground	Turn A/C switch on	Battery voltage
		Turn A/C switch off.	No voltage
	8 – ground	Constant	Battery voltage
	13 – ground	Turn A/C switch on.	Battery voltage
		Turn A/C switch off.	No voltage
	18 – ground	Start the engine.	Approx. 10 to 14 V
		Stop the engine.	No voltage

•¹: with Variable Volume Control Mechanism Compressor

Continuity	1 – 6	Constant	Continuity
	9 – ground	Constant	Continuity
Resistance•¹	5 – 2	Constant	Approx. 3 kΩ
	5 – 10	Constant	Approx. 6 kΩ
	11 – 10	Constant	1.2 – 4.8 kΩ
	12 – 2	Temp switch turned to MAX COOL	Approx. 3 kΩ
Voltage	7 – ground	Constant	Battery voltage

•¹: without AUTO A/C models

Voltage	3 – ground	Temp. control switch turned to MAX HOT	Approx. 0 V•¹
		Temp. control switch turned to MAX COOL	Approx. 5 V
	4 – ground	Temp. control switch turned to MAX HOT	Approx. 5 V
		Temp. control switch turned to MAX COOL	Approx. 0 V•¹

•¹: Voltage becomes 0 V when switch is turned, then soon returns to 5 V.

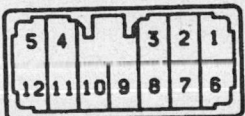

INSPECTION OF AIR CONDITIONING AMPLIFIER CIRCUIT – 1994-95 CELICA

Tester connection to terminal number	Condition	Specified condition
6 – Ground	Constant	Continuity
11 – 15	Constant	1.5 KΩ at 20 °C (68 °F)
15 – 16 (5S–FE Engine)	Constant	Approx. 115 Ω at 20 °C (68 °F)
7 – Ground	Constant	1.2 KΩ at 20 °C (68 °F)
10 – Ground	A/C switch on	Battery positive voltage
10 – Ground	A/C switch off	No voltage
12 – Ground	A/C switch on	Battery positive voltage
12 – Ground	A/C switch off	No voltage
14 – Ground	Constant	Battery positive voltage
5 – Ground	Constant	Approx. 10 – 14 V

BACK PROBE INSPECTION

Tester connection to terminal number	Condition	Specified Condition
2 – Ground	Refrigeration pressure 2.0 – 32 kgf/cm³	Battery positive voltage
2 – Ground	Refrigeration pressure less than 2.0 – 32 kgf/cm³ or more	No voltage

Wire Harness Side

From Back Side

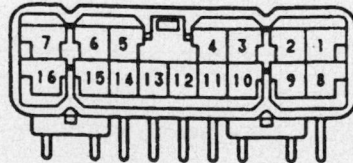

INSPECTION OF AUTO A/C AMPLIFIER CIRCUIT – 1993 CELICA, 1993 SUPRA

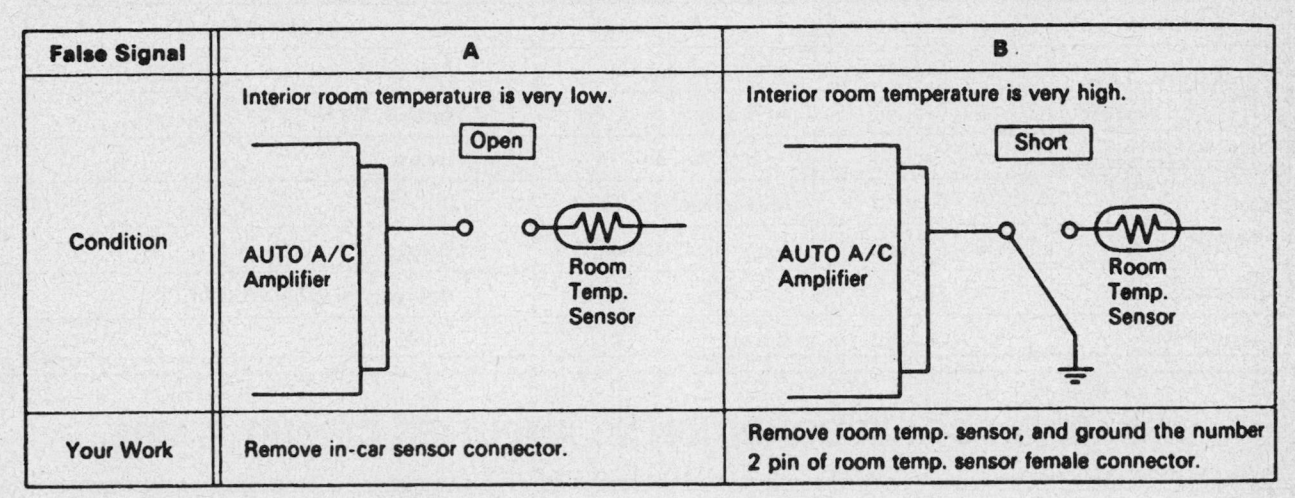

False Signal	A	B
Condition	Interior room temperature is very low. **Open** — AUTO A/C Amplifier, Room Temp. Sensor	Interior room temperature is very high. **Short** — AUTO A/C Amplifier, Room Temp. Sensor
Your Work	Remove in-car sensor connector.	Remove room temp. sensor, and ground the number 2 pin of room temp. sensor female connector.

Condition: Setting Temperature is at 25°C (77°F)

System Main Parts	False Signal	Motion			
Air Mix Control Servomotor	A	Air mix control servo motor shaft moves towards max-hot side.			
	B	Air mix control servo motor shaft moves towards max-cool side.			
Air Flow Mode Control Servomotor		Air Vent Mode Damper			
		VENT	BI-LEVEL	HEAT	DEF
	A	Close	Close	Open	Close
	B	Open	Close	Close	Close
Blower Motor	A	Blower motor rotates at high speed.			
	B				
Water Valve	A	OPEN			
	B	CLOSE			
FRE/REC Control Servomotor	FRE Switch ON	Fresh air is ventilated.			
	REC Switch ON	Recirculation air is ventilated.			

INSPECTION OF AIR CONDITIONING AMPLIFIER CIRCUIT – 1993 COROLLA

Check for	Tester Connection	Condition	Specified Value
Voltage	1 – Ground	Ignition switch on	Approx. 10 to 14 V
	5 – Ground	A/C switch on	Approx. 10 to 14 V
	7 – Ground	A/C switch on	Below 1 V
	9 – Ground	Magnetic clutch on	0 V
	8 – Ground	Magnetic clutch on	Below 1V
Resistance	4 – 10	Constant	Approx. 1.5 kΩ at 25°C (77°F)
Continuity	4 – Ground	Constant	Continuity

INSPECTION OF AIR CONDITIONING AMPLIFIER CIRCUIT – MR2

Check for	Tester connection	Condition		Specified value
Continuity	8 – Engine control ECU terminal A/C	Constant		Continuity
	13 – Ground	Constant		Continuity
Resistance	3 – Ground	Constant		Continuity
	9 – 15	Engine coolant condition	85°C (185°F)	Approx. 1.35 kΩ
			90°C (194°F)	Approx. 1.19 kΩ
			95°C (203°F)	Approx. 1.05 kΩ
	14 – 17	Ambient temperature at 25°C (77°F)		Approx. 1.5 kΩ
Voltage	1 – Ground	Ignition switch position	LOCK or ACC	No voltage
			ON	Battery voltage
	2 – Ground	Ignition switch position	LOCK or ACC	No voltage
			ON	Battery voltage
	4 – Ground	ECON switch position with ignition switch ON	OFF	No voltage
			ON	Battery voltage
	6 – Ground	A/C switch position with ignition switch ON	OFF	No voltage
			ON	Battery voltage
	7 – Ground	Ignition switch position	LOCK or ACC	No voltage
			ON	Battery voltage
	10 – Ground	Ignition switch position	LOCK or ACC	No voltage
			ON	Battery voltage
	11 – Ground	Ignition switch position	LOCK or ACC	No voltage
			ON	Battery voltage
	18 – Ground	Engine condition	Running	Approx. 10 to 14 v
			Stopped	No voltage

INSPECTION OF AIR CONDITIONING AMPLIFIER CIRCUIT – 1994-95 MR2

Tester connection to terminal number	Condition	Specified condition (Continuity)
1 – Ground	Constant	Continuity
2 – ECM terminal AC1 (5S–FE)	Constant	Continuity
6 – Ground	Constant	Continuity
10 – ECM terminal ACT	Constant	Continuity
9 - 18	Engine coolant condition 85 °C (185 °F)	Approx. 1.35 KΩ
9 - 18	Engine coolant condition 90 °C (194 °F)	Approx. 1.19 KΩ
9 - 18	Engine coolant condition 95 °C (203 °F)	Approx. 1.05 KΩ
12 – 16	Constant	1.5 KΩ at 20 °C (68 °F)
5 – Ground	Engine condition stopped	No voltage
5 – Ground	Engine condition running	Battery positive voltage
7 – Ground	Ignition switch position OFF	No voltage
7 – Ground	Ignition switch position ON	Battery positive voltage
11 – Ground	A/C switch position OFF	No voltage
11 – Ground	A/C switch position ON	Battery positive voltage
15 – Ground	Constant	Battery positive voltage

BACK PROBE INSPECTION

Tester connection to terminal number	Condition	Specified condition (Voltage)
3 – Ground	Refrigerant pressure 196 – 3,140 kPa	Battery positive voltage
3 – Ground	Refrigerant pressure less than 196 or more than 3,140 kPa	No voltage
8 – Ground	Refrigerant pressure 1,520 kPa or more	Battery positive voltage
8 – Ground	Refrigerant pressure less than 1,520 kPa	No voltage

Wire Harness Side   From Back Side

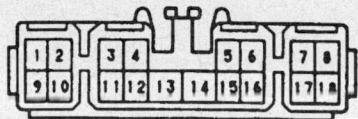

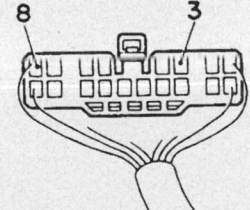

INSPECTION OF AIR CONDITIONING AMPLIFIER CIRCUIT – TERCEL (POWER STEERING) AND PASEO

Check for	Tester Connection	Condition	Specified Value
Voltage	1 – Ground	Start the engine	Approx. 10 to 14 V
		Stop the engine	No voltage
	8 – Ground	A/C switch on	Battery voltage
		A/C switch off	No voltage
	7 – Ground	Blower switch on	Battery voltage
		Blower switch off	No voltage
Resistance	2 – 13	Constant	Approx. 1.5 kΩ at 25°C (77°F)
	9 – 13	Constant	Approx. 240 Ω
Continuity	5 – 7	Constant	Continuity
	12 – Ground	Constant	Continuity

INSPECTION OF AIR CONDITIONING AMPLIFIER CIRCUIT – TERCEL (W/O POWER STEERING)

Check for	Tester Connection	Condition	Specified Value
Voltage	1 – Ground	Start the engine	Approx. 10 to 14 V
		Stop the engine	No voltage
	8 – Ground	A/C switch on	Battery voltage
		A/C switch off	No voltage
	7 – Ground	Blower switch on	Battery voltage
		Blower switch off	No voltage
Resistance	2 – 12	Constant	Approx. 1.5 kΩ at 25°C (77°F)
Continuity	5 – 7	Constant	Continuity
	12 – Ground	Constant	Continuity

INSPECTION OF AIR CONDITIONING AMPLIFIER CIRCUIT – 1995 PASEO

Tester connection to terminal number	Condition	Specified value (Voltage)
7 – Ground	Blower switch ON	Battery positive voltage
7 – Ground	Blower switch OFF	No voltage
8 – Ground	A/C switch ON	Battery positive voltage
8 – Ground	A/C switch OFF	No voltage
Tester connection to terminal number	Condition	Specified value (Resistance)
2 – 13	Constant	Approx. 1.5 kΩ at 25°C (77°F)
9 – 13	Constant	Approx. 240 Ω
Tester connection to terminal number	Condition	Specified value (Continuity)
5 – 7	Constant	Continuity
12 – Ground	Constant	Continuity

USA (California)

Tester connection to terminal number	Condition	Specified value (Voltage)
2 – Ground	Blower switch ON	Battery positive voltage
2 – Ground	Blower switch OFF	No voltage
7 – Ground	A/C switch ON	Battery positive voltage
7 – Ground	A/C switch OFF	No voltage
Tester connection to terminal number	Condition	Specified value (Resistance)
8 – 12	Constant	Approx. 1.5 kΩ at 25°C (77°F)
10 – 12	Constant	Approx. 240 Ω
Tester connection to terminalnumber	Condition	Specified value (Continuity)
5 – Ground	Constant	Continuity

California

INSPECTION OF AIR CONDITIONING AMPLIFIER CIRCUIT – 1995 TERCEL (WITH POWER STEERING)

Tester connection to terminal number	Condition	Specified condition
5 – Ground	Constant	Continuity
1 – Ground	Constant	Continuity
6 – Ground	Constant	Continuity
1 – ECM terminal AC1	Constant	Continuity
6 – ECM terminal ACT	Constant	Continuity
8 – 12	Constant	Approx. 1.5 kΩ at 25 °C (77 °F)
7 – Ground	A/C switch ON	Battery positive voltage
7 – Ground	A/C switch OFF	No voltage
9 – Ground	A/C switch ON	Battery positive voltage
9 – Ground	A/C switch OFF	No voltage
11 – Ground	Constant	Battery positive voltage

BACK PROBE INSPECTION

Tester connection to terminal number	Condition	Specified condition
2 – Ground	Refrigeration pressure 196 – 3,140 kPa	Battery positive voltage
2 – Ground	Refrigeration pressure less than 196 or more than 3,140 kPa	No voltage

Wire harness side

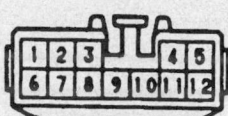

From back side

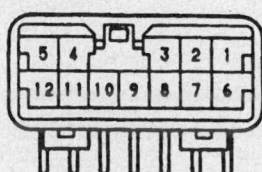

INSPECTION OF AIR CONDITIONING AMPLIFIER CIRCUIT – 1995 TERCEL (WITHOUT POWER STEERING)

Tester connection to terminal number	Condition	Specified condition
4 – Ground	Constant	Continuity
6 – ECM terminal ACT	Constant	Continuity
8 – ECM terminal AC1	Constant	Continuity
6 – 10	Constant	Approx. 1.5 kΩ at 25 °C (77 °F)
5 – Ground	A/C switch ON	Battery positive voltage
5 – Ground	A/C switch OFF	No voltage
9 – Ground	Ignition switch ON	Battery positive voltage
9 – Ground	Ignition switch OFF	No voltage
7 – Ground	A/C switch ON	Battery positive voltage
7 – Ground	A/C switch OFF	No voltage

BACK PROBE INSPECTION

Tester connection to terminal number	Condition	Specified condition
1 – Ground	Refrigeration pressure 196 – 3,140 kPa	Battery positive voltage
1 – Ground	Refrigeration pressure less than 196 or more than 3,140 kPa	No voltage

• Wire Harness Side   From Back Side

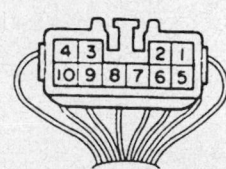

INSPECTION OF AMPLIFIER CIRCUIT – 1994-95 SUPRA (MANUAL AIR CONDITIONER)

Check for	Tester connection	Condition	Specified value
Continuity	10 – Ground	Constant	Continuity
Voltage	2 – 10	Turn A/C switch on.	Battery voltage
		Turn A/C switch off.	No voltage
Resistance	6 – 9	Constant	Approx. 1.5 kΩ at 25°C (77°F)

INSPECTION OF AIR CONDITIONING AMPLIFIER CIRCUIT – AVALON
(AUTOMATIC AIR CONDITIONER)

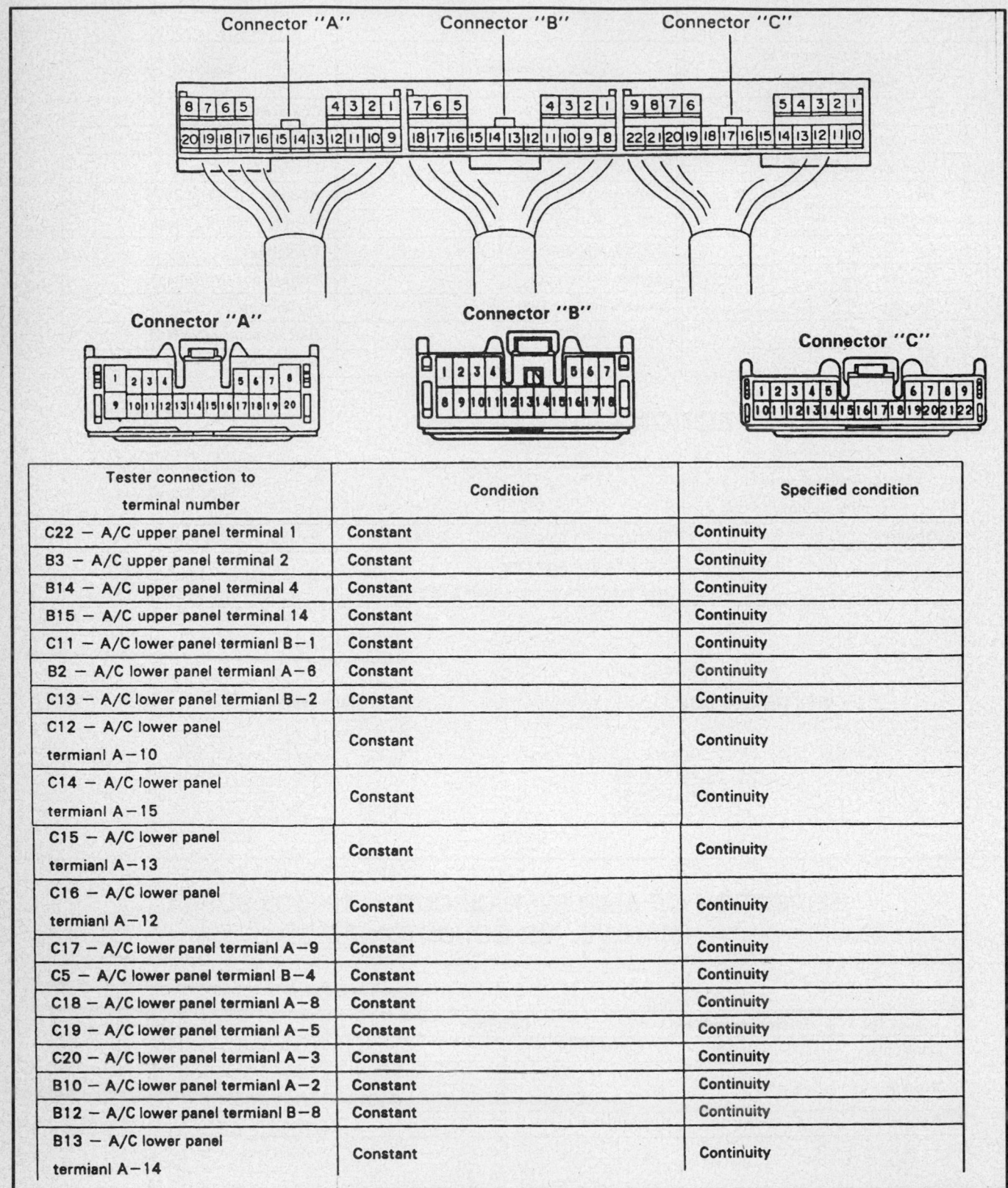

Tester connection to terminal number	Condition	Specified condition
C22 – A/C upper panel terminal 1	Constant	Continuity
B3 – A/C upper panel terminal 2	Constant	Continuity
B14 – A/C upper panel terminal 4	Constant	Continuity
B15 – A/C upper panel terminal 14	Constant	Continuity
C11 – A/C lower panel termianl B–1	Constant	Continuity
B2 – A/C lower panel termianl A–6	Constant	Continuity
C13 – A/C lower panel termianl B–2	Constant	Continuity
C12 – A/C lower panel termianl A–10	Constant	Continuity
C14 – A/C lower panel termianl A–15	Constant	Continuity
C15 – A/C lower panel termianl A–13	Constant	Continuity
C16 – A/C lower panel termianl A–12	Constant	Continuity
C17 – A/C lower panel termianl A–9	Constant	Continuity
C5 – A/C lower panel termianl B–4	Constant	Continuity
C18 – A/C lower panel termianl A–8	Constant	Continuity
C19 – A/C lower panel termianl A–5	Constant	Continuity
C20 – A/C lower panel termianl A–3	Constant	Continuity
B10 – A/C lower panel termianl A–2	Constant	Continuity
B12 – A/C lower panel termianl B–8	Constant	Continuity
B13 – A/C lower panel termianl A–14	Constant	Continuity

INSPECTION OF AIR CONDITIONING AMPLIFIER CIRCUIT – AVALON (AUTOMATIC AIR CONDITIONER) CONT'D

Tester connection to terminal number	Condition	Specified condition
A6 – Ground (Canada Only)	Constant	Continuity
C10 – Metar ECU terminal 6	Constant	Continuity
A4 – Timer ECU terminla 13	Constant	Continuity
A20 – Ground	Constant	Continuity
B8 – ECM terminal ACT	Constant	Continuity
A4 – ECM terminal AC1	Constant	Continuity
A14 – A15	Constant	Continuity
A2 – A11	Constant	Continuity
C3 – A18	Solar sensor subject to electrical light	Continuity
C3 – A18	Cover solar sensor by a cloth	No continuity
B1 – A19	Constant	Approx. 165 – 205 Ω at 25 °C (77 °F)
C8 – A19	Constant	Approx. 1.5 kΩ at 25 °C (77 °F)
C9 – A19	Constant	Approx. 5.0 kΩ at 25 °C (77 °F)
C7 – A19	Constant	Approx. 1.7 kΩ at 25 °C (77 °F)
C6 – A19	Constant	Approx. 1.7 kΩ at 25 °C (77 °F)
A5 – Ground	Constant	Battery positive voltage
A16 – Ground	Ignition switch ACC	Battery positive voltage
A8 – Ground	Ignition switch ON	Battery positive voltage
A8 – Ground	Ignition switch OFF	No voltage
A3 – Ground	Ignition switch ON	Battery positive voltage
A3 – Ground	Ignition switch OFF	No voltage
A10 – Ground	Ignition switch ON	Battery positive voltage
A10 – Ground	Ignition switch OFF	No voltage
B5 – Ground	Mode switch FACE	Battery positive voltage
B5 – Ground	Mode switch B/L	Battery positive voltage
B7 – Ground	Mode switch FOOT	Battery positive voltage
B8 – Ground	Mode switch FOOT/ DEF	Battery positive voltage
B18 – Ground	Mode switch DEF	Battery positive voltage

FROM BACKSIDE

Tester connection to terminal number	Condition	Specified condition
C2 – Ground	Refrigeration pressure 196 – 3,140 kPa	Continuity
C2 – Ground	Refrigeration pressure less than 196 kPa or more than 3,140 kPa	No continuity
A12 – Ground	Air inlet switch FRESH	Battery positive voltage
A13 – Ground	Air inlet switch RECIRC	Battery positive voltage

INSPECTION OF AIR CONDITIONING AMPLIFIER CIRCUIT – 1994-95 SUPRA
(AUTOMATIC AIR CONDITIONER)

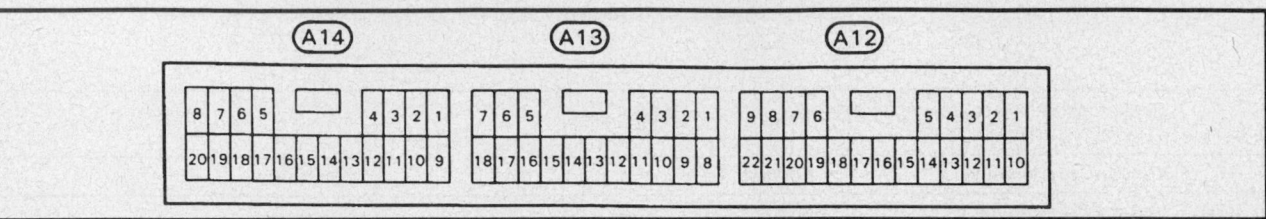

Terminal No.	Symbol	Tester Connection	Wiring Color	Condition	Standard Value
A12-1	L-B/L	A12-1↔A14-9	BR-W↔W-B	IG ON. B/L mode switch: OFF→ON	10~14 V → Below 1.0 V
A12-2	L-FACE	A12-2↔A14-9	G↔W-B	IG ON. FACE mode switch: OFF→ON	10~14 V → Below 1.0 V
A12-3	L-M1	A12-3↔A14-9	P-B↔W-B	IG ON. Fan speed dial: LO→M1	10~14 V → Below 1.0 V
A12-4	L-DEF	A12-4↔A14-9	R-Y↔W-B	IG ON. DEF mode switch: OFF→ON	10~14 V → Below 1.0 V
A12-6	L-AUTO	A12-6↔A14-9	R-B↔W-B	IG ON. AUTO switch: OFF→ON	10~14 V → Below 1.0 V
A12-7	A/C-IN	A12-7↔A14-9	L↔W-B	IG ON. A/C compressor: ON→OFF	10~14 V → Below 1.0 V
A12-8	MDEF	A12-8↔A14-9	Y-L↔W-B	IG ON. Mode control switch: FACE→DEF	Below 1.0 V → 10~14 V
A12-9	MFAC	A12-9↔A14-9	W↔W-B	IG ON. Mode control switch: DEF→FACE	Below 1.0 V → 10~14 V
A12-10	L-F/D	A12-10↔A14-9	BR↔W-B	IG ON. F/D mode switch: OFF→ON	10~14 V → Below 1.0 V
A12-11	L-FOOT	A12-11↔A14-9	Y↔W-B	IG ON. FOOT mode switch: OFF→ON	10~14 V → Below 1.0 V
A12-12	L-HI	A12-12↔A14-9	LG↔W-B	IG ON. Fan speed dial: LO→HI	10~14 V → Below 1.0 V
A12-13	L-LO	A12-13↔A14-9	R↔W-B	IG ON. Fan speed dial: HI→LO	10~14 V → Below 1.0 V
A12-14	L-M2	A12-14↔A14-9	B-W↔W-B	IG ON. Fan speed dial: LO→M2	10~14 V → Below 1.0 V
A12-15	L-M3	A12-15↔A14-9	P↔W-B	IG ON. Fan speed dial: LO→M3	10~14 V → Below 1.0 V
A12-16	L-RDEF	A12-16↔A14-9	V↔W-B	IG ON. Rear DEF switch: OFF→ON	10~14 V → Below 1.0 V
A12-17	L-REC	A12-17↔A14-9	LG-B↔W-B	IG ON. REC mode switch: OFF→ON	10~14 V → Below 1.0 V
A12-18	L-FRS	A12-18↔A14-9	GR↔W-B	IG ON. FRS mode switch: OFF→ON	10~14 V → Below 1.0 V
A12-19	L-A/C	A12-19↔A14-9	B↔W-B	IG ON. A/C switch: OFF→ON	10~14 V → Below 1.0 V
A12-20	ACC	A12-20↔A14-9	L-R↔W-B	Turn ignition switch ACC	10~14 V
A12-21	IGN	A12-21↔A14-9	B-W↔W-B	Start the engine	Pulse signal
A12-22	LOCK-IN	A12-22↔A13-9	G-Y↔V-W	IG ON. A/C compressor: ON	Pulse signal
A13-1	MC	A13-1↔A14-9	R-Y↔W-B	Temperature set: MAX. HOT→MAX. COOL	Below 1.0 V → 10~14 V
A13-2	S5	A13-2↔A14-9	BR-W↔W-B	Always	4.5~5.5 V

INSPECTION OF AIR CONDITIONING AMPLIFIER CIRCUIT – 1994-95 SUPRA (AUTOMATIC AIR CONDITIONER) (CONT.)

Terminal No.	Symbol	Tester Connection	Wiring Color	Condition	Standard Value
A13-3	MH	A13-3↔A14-9	V↔W-B	Temperature set: MAX. COOL→MAX. HOT	Below 1.0 V → 10~14 V
A13-5	TR	A13-5↔A13-9	Y-L↔V-W	Cabin temp.: 25°C (77°F)/40°C (104°F)	1.8~2.2 V/ 1.2~1.6 V
A13-6	TAM	A13-6↔A13-9	P-B↔V-W	Cabin temp.: 25°C (77°F)/40°C (104°F)	1.3~1.8 V/ 0.8~1.3 V
A13-7	TE	A13-7↔A13-9	L-Y↔V-W	Evapo. Ambient Temp.: 0°C (32°F)/15°C (59°F)	2.0~2.4V/1.4~1.8V
A13-9	SG	A13-9↔Body GND	V-W↔Body GND	Always	Below 1 Ω
A13-11	SPD	A13-11↔A14-9	P↔W-B	Turn the propeller shaft slowly.	10~14 V → Below 1.0 V
A13-14	PSW	A13-14↔A14-9	L-Y↔W-B	Normal A/C pressure	Below 1.0 V
A13-16	TW	A13-16↔A13-9	LG-R↔V-W	Engine coolant temp.: 0°C (32°F)/40°C (104°F)	2.8~3.2 V/ 1.8~2.2 V
				Engine coolant temp.: 70°C (158°F)	0.9~1.3 V
A13-17	TS	A13-17↔A13-9	Y-G↔V-W	Sensor subjected to electric light	0.8↔4.3 V
				Sensor covered by a cloth	Below 0.8 V
A13-18	TP	A13-18↔A13-9	G-W↔V-W	Temperature set: MAX. COOL→MAX. HOT	3.7~4.3 V → 0.8~1.2 V
A14-6	MGC	A14-6↔A14-9	L-R↔W-B	A/C compressor: ON → OFF	Below 1.0 V → 10~14 V
A14-7	+B	A14-7↔A14-9	W-R↔W-B	Always	10~14 V
A14-8	IG	A14-8↔A14-9	R-L↔W-B	Turn ignition switch IG	10~14 V
A14-9	GND	A14-9↔Body GND	W-B↔Body GND	Always	Below 1Ω
A14-10	TPM	A14-10↔A13-9	LG↔V-W	IG ON. Mode control switch: FACE→DEF	3.7 V~4.3 V → 0.8~1.2 V
A14-11	TSET	A14-11↔A13-9	L-B↔V-W	IG ON. Temperature set: MAX.HOT→MAX.COOL	Below 0.3 V → Over 4.7 V
A14-15	BLW	A14-15↔A14-9	L↔W-B	IG ON. Fan speed: LO→HI	Approx. 1 V → Approx. 2 V
A14-16	HR	A14-16↔A14-9	L-W↔W-B	IG ON. OFF switch: ON mode→ OFF mode / Mode control switch: DEF	Below 1.0 V → 10~14 V
A14-17	MR/F	A14-17↔A14-9	GR↔W-B	During cool-down on AUTO after hot soak	Below 1.0 V
A14-18	RDEF	A14-18↔A14-9	B↔W-B	IG ON. Rear DEF switch: OFF→ON	10~14 V → Below 1.0 V *
A14-19	MREC	A14-19↔A14-9	G-R↔W-B	IG ON. Air inlet control switch: FRS→REC	10~14 V → Below 1.0 V
A14-20	MFRS	A14-20↔A14-9	G↔W-B	IG ON. Air inlet control switch: REC→FRS	10~14 V → Below 1.0 V

* After 15 minutes, ON mode will change to OFF mode automatically.

Air Inlet (Fresh/Recirc) Servo Motor

TESTING

Avalon, Camry, 1993 Celica and 1993 MR2

1. With battery voltage applied to terminal **1** and ground at terminal **3** check that the lever moves smoothly from **RECIRC** to **FRESH**.
2. With battery voltage applied to terminal **1** and ground at terminal **3** check that the lever moves smoothly from **FRESH** to **RECIRC**.
3. If operation is not as specified, replace the servo motor.

1994—95 Celica

1. With battery voltage applied to terminal **1** and ground at terminal **3** check that the lever moves smoothly from **RECIRC** to **FRESH**.
2. With battery voltage applied to terminal **1** and ground at terminal **2** check that the lever moves smoothly from **FRESH** to **RECIRC**.
3. If operation is not as specified, replace the servo motor.

1994—95 MR2

1. With battery voltage applied to terminal **3** and ground at terminal **4** check that the lever moves smoothly from **RECIRC** to **FRESH**.
2. With battery voltage applied to terminal **1** and ground at terminal **4** check that the lever moves smoothly from **FRESH** to **RECIRC**.
3. If operation is not as specified, replace the servo motor.

1994—95 Supra

1. With battery voltage applied to terminal **2** and ground at terminal **3** check that the lever moves smoothly from **RECIRC** to **FRESH**.
2. With battery voltage applied to terminal **2** and ground at terminal **5** check that the lever moves smoothly from **FRESH** to **RECIRC**.
3. If operation is not as specified, replace the servo motor.

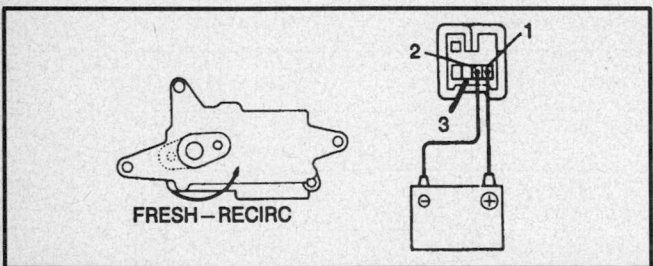

Air inlet (fresh/recirc) servo motor testing – Camry shown

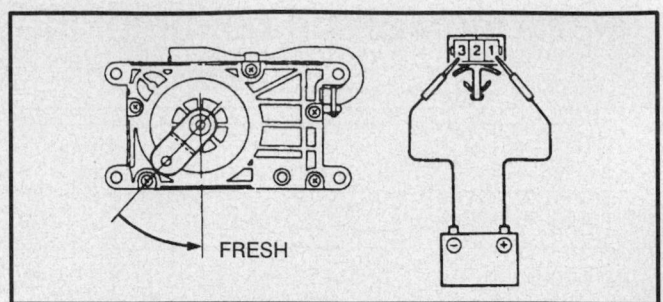

Air inlet (fresh/recirc) servo motor testing – 1994-95 Celica

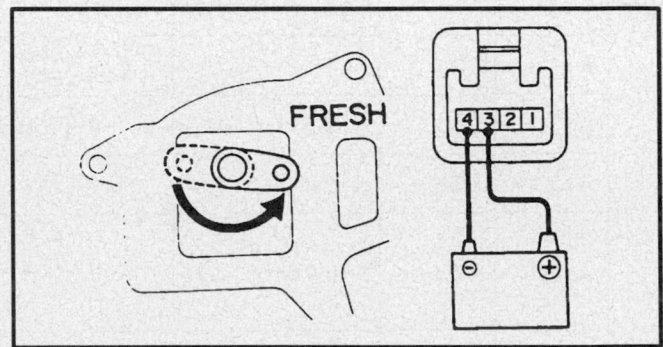

Air inlet (fresh/recirc) servo motor testing – 1994-95 MR2

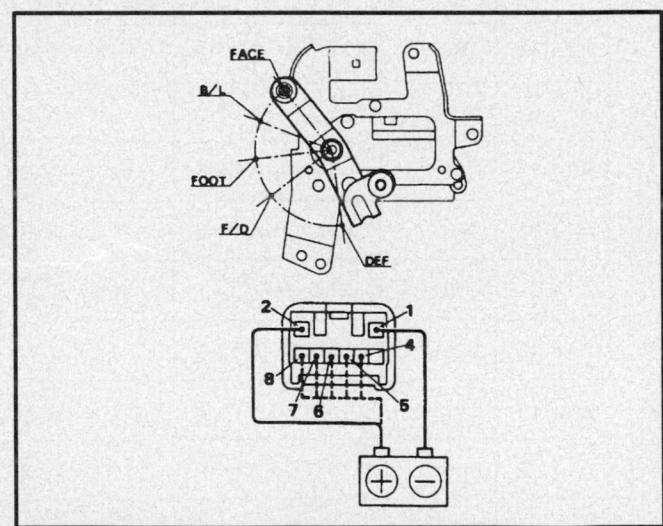

Air outlet servo motor testing – Avalon

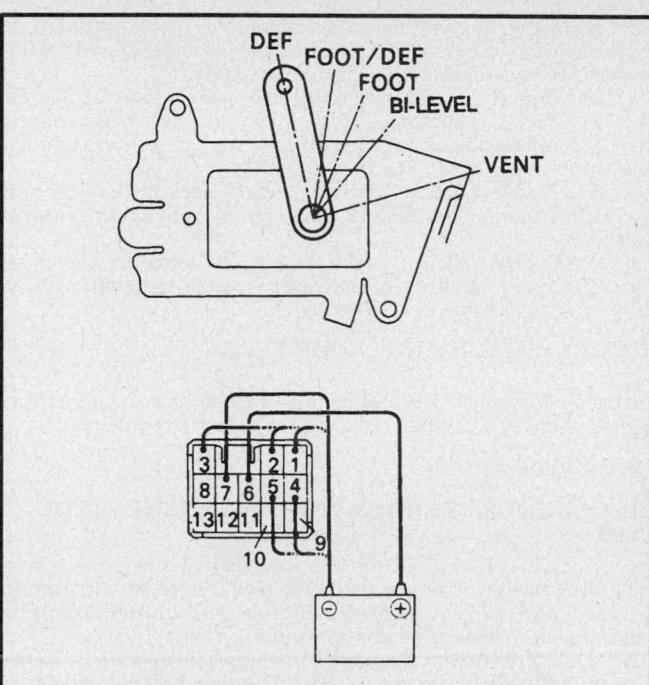

Testing air outlet (mode) servo motor – MR2

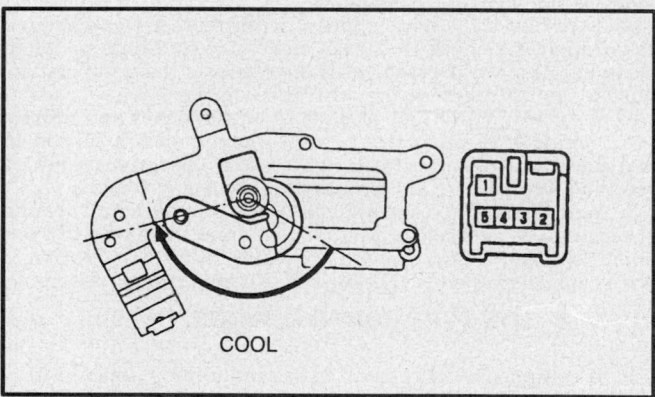

Air mix servo motor testing – Avalon

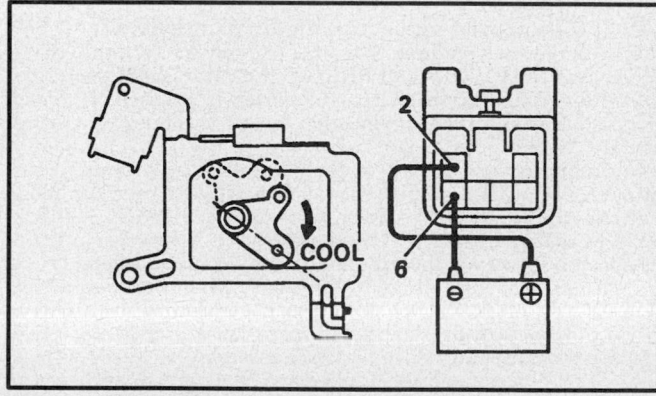

Air mix servo motor testing – Celica

Air Outlet (Mode) Servo Motor

TESTING

Avalon

1. Connect battery voltage to terminal **2** and the ground to terminal **1**.
2. As negative lead is moved to each terminal, servo motor arm should move as follows:
- Terminal **4**: Face
- Terminal **5**: B/L
- Terminal **6**: Foot
- Terminal **7**: Foot/Def
- Terminal **8**: Def
3. If operation is not as specified, replace the servo motor.

Camry and 1993 Celica

1. Connect battery voltage to terminal **6** and the ground to terminal **7**.
2. As negative lead is moved to each terminal, servo motor arm should move as follows:
- Terminal **1**: Def (Camry); Vent (Celica)
- Terminal **2**: Foot/Def (Camry); Bi-Lev (Celica)
- Terminal **3**: Foot (Camry); Foot 2 (Celica)
- Terminal **4**: Bi-Lev (Camry); Foot/Def (Celica)
- Terminal **5**: Face (Camry); not used (Celica)
- Terminal **7**: not used (Camry); Def (Celica)
- Terminal **8**: not used (Camry); Foot 1 (Celica)
3. If operation is not as specified, replace the servo motor.

1994–1995 Celica

1. Connect battery voltage to terminal **6** and the ground to terminal **7**.
2. As negative lead is moved to each terminal, servo motor arm should move as follows:
- Terminal **1**: Face
- Terminal **2**: B/L
- Terminal **3**: Foot
- Terminal **4**: Foot/Def
- Terminal **5**: Def
3. If operation is not as specified, replace the servo motor.

MR2

1. Connect battery voltage to terminal **6** and ground to terminal **7**.
2. As ground lead is moved to each terminal, note that door moves as noted:
- Terminal **1**: Vent
- Terminal **2**: Bi-Lev
- Terminal **3**: Foot
- Terminal **4**: Foot/Def
- Terminal **5**: Def

Air Mix (Temperature) Control Servo Motor

TESTING

Avalon

Connect battery voltage to terminal **1** and ground to terminal **2**. Check that servo motor lever moves from **HOT** to **COOL**.

Celica

Connect battery voltage to terminal **2** and ground to terminal **6**. Check that servo motor lever moves from **HOT** to **COOL**.

Air Conditioning Control Assembly

TESTING

Avalon

ROTARY SWITCH AND PUSHBUTTON TYPE

1. Connect battery voltage to terminal **C-1** and ground to terminals **C-2** check that the illumination blub lights. If no light appears, check illumination blub.
2. With battery voltage applied to terminal **C-1** and ground to terminals **C-6** and **C-7** check that the FRESH and RECIRC indicators light alternately each time the air inlet control switch is pressed. If operation is not as specified, replace the air conditioning control upper panel.
3. Check the continuity of the panel switches as shown in the respective test chart. If continuity is not as shown, replace the control assembly.

PUSHBUTTON TYPE CONTROL PANEL

1. Connect battery positive lead to terminal **B-14** and ground to terminal **B-6** and check that the illumination blub lights. If no light appears, check the illumination blub.
2. Connect battery positive lead to terminal **A-7** and the ground to terminal **A-1**. Push each of the mode buttons and check that the indicator lights up. If operation is not as specified, replace the air conditioning control lower panel.
3. Keeping these same connections, push each of the blower speed control buttons and check that each indicator lights up. If operation is not as specified, replace the air conditioning control lower panel.
4. Connect battery positive lead to terminal **A-7** and the ground to terminal **B-6**. Check that the AUTO indicator lights up. If operation is not as specified, replace the air conditioner control lower panel.
5. Check the continuity of the panel switches as shown in the respective test chart. If continuity is not as specified, replace the air conditioner control lower panel.
6. Check that the resistance between terminals **B-11** and **B-5** is approximately 3000 ohms. Check that the resistance between terminals **B-4** and **B-5** increases from zero ohms to approximately 3000 ohms when the temperature control dial is gradually turned from HOT to COOL. If operation is not as specified, replace the air conditioner control lower panel.
7. Connect battery positive lead to terminal **C-9** and the ground to terminal **C-2**. Check that the air conditioner indicator illuminates. If operation is not as specified, replace the air conditioner control upper panel.
8. Connect battery positive lead to terminal **C-9** and ground to terminals **C-4** and **C-14**. Check that the FRESH and RECIRC indicators light up. If operation is not as specified, replace the air conditioner control upper panel.
9. Connect battery positive lead to terminal **C-6** and ground to terminal **C-7**. Move battery positive lead to terminal **C-8**. Check that the mode indicator dims. If operation is not as specified, replace the air conditioner control upper panel.

Camry

ROTARY SWITCH AND PUSHBUTTON TYPE

1. Connect battery positive lead to terminal **A-12** and the ground to terminal **A-4**. Push A/C button in and check that it lights up. If not, replace the control assembly.

2. Move the battery negative connection to terminal **A-1**. Push each mode button and be sure each one lights when depressed. If not, replace the control assembly.
3. Keeping these same connections, check that "FRESH" and "RECIRC" indicators light alternately each time the air inlet control button is pressed. If not, replace the control assembly.
4. Now move battery voltage lead to terminal **A-14** and check that the mode indicator dims. If not, replace the control assembly.
5. Check the continuity of the panel switches as shown in the respective test chart. If continuity is not as shown, replace the control assembly.

ROTARY SWITCH AND LEVER TYPE

Perform continuity check of each switch as shown. If performance is not as specified, replace the respective switch.

1993 Celica

DIAL BLOWER SPEED SWITCH AND PUSHBUTTON TYPE

1. With battery voltage applied to terminal **A-18** and ground at terminal **A-17** check that the illumination bulb lights. If no light appears check illumination bulb.
2. With battery voltage applied to terminal **A-1** and ground at terminal **A-2** check that the FRESH and RECIRC indicators light alternately each time the air inlet control switch button is pressed. If operation is not as specified, replace the air conditioning control assembly.
3. With battery voltage applied to terminal **A-1** and ground at terminal **A-2** check that each mode buttons lights up when mode buttons are pressed in. If operation is not as specified, replace the air conditioning control assembly.
4. With battery voltage applied to terminal **A-1** and ground at terminal **A-15** push the air conditioning switch button in and check that the indicator lights up. If operation is not as specified, replace the air conditioning control assembly.
5. With battery voltage applied to terminal **A-1** and ground at terminal **A-2** connect a positive lead from the battery to terminal **A-3** and check that the indicators dim. If operation is not as specified, replace the air conditioning control assembly.

PUSHBUTTON TYPE CONTROL PANEL

1. If equipped with automatic air conditioning apply battery voltage to terminal **A-5** and ground at terminal **B-1** or **B-5** check that the FRESH (**B-1**) and RECIRC (**B-5**) indicators light. If operation is not as specified, replace the air conditioningcontrol assembly.
2. If not equipped with automatic air conditioning apply battery voltage to terminal **A-5** and ground at terminal **C-10** check that the FRESH and RECIRC indicators light each time (alternately) the air inlet control switch is pressed. If operation is not as specified, replace the air conditioning control assembly.
3. Apply battery voltage to terminal **A-5** and ground at terminal **C-10** check that each mode buttons lights up when mode buttons (apply ground to these terminals **A-8** FACE, **A-9** B/L, **A-24** FOOT and **B-7** AUTO) are pressed in. If operation is not as specified, replace the air conditioning control assembly.
4. Apply battery voltage to terminal **A-5** and ground at terminal **C-10** check that each blower speed indicators light up when buttons are pressed in. If operation is not as specified, replace the air conditioning control assembly.
5. With battery voltage applied to terminal **A-5** and ground at terminal **C-11** push the air conditioning switch button in and check that the indicator lights up. If operation is not as specified, replace the air conditioning control assembly.
6. With battery voltage applied to terminal **A-5** and ground at terminal **C-10** connect a positive lead from the battery to

terminal **A-6** and check that the indicators dim. If operation is not as specified, replace the air conditioning control assembly. Refer to wiring schematics, as necessary.

1994—95 Celica

DIAL BLOWER SPEED SWITCH AND PUSHBUTTON TYPE

1. With battery voltage applied to terminal **A-8** and ground at terminal **A-21** check that the illumination bulb lights. If no light appears check illumination bulb.
2. With battery voltage applied to terminal **A-19** and ground at terminal **A-22** check that the FRESH and RECIRC indicators light alternately each time the air inlet control switch

button is pressed. If operation is not as specified, replace the air conditioning control assembly.

3. With battery voltage applied to terminal **A-19** and ground at terminal **A-22** check that each mode buttons lights up when mode buttons are pressed in. If operation is not as specified, replace the air conditioning control assembly.
4. With battery voltage applied to terminal **A-19** and ground at terminal **A-18** push the air conditioning switch button in and check that the indicator lights up. If operation is not as specified, replace the air conditioning control assembly.
5. With battery voltage applied to terminal **A-19** and ground at terminal **A-21** and **A-22** connect a positive lead from the battery to terminal **A-8** and check that the indicators dim. If operation is not as specified, replace the air conditioning control assembly.

A/C SWITCH CONTINUITY

Terminal Switch Position	C-1	C-11	Illumination	
			C-7	C-8
OFF			○――⌇⌇⌇――○	
ON	○――――○			

Connector "C"

AUTO A/C SWITCH CONTINUITY

Terminal Switch Position	A-1	A-2	A-8	B-1
OFF		○―――――○		
ON	○―――――――――――○			

Connector "B" Connector "A"

MODE CONTROL SWITCH CONTINUITY

Terminal Switch Position	A-1	A-3	A-4	B-3	B-9	B-10
FACE	○―――――――――――○					
B/L	○――――――――――――――――――○					
FOOT	○――――――――――――――――――――――○					
FOOT/DEF	○―――――――――○					
DEF	○――――○					

Connector "B" Connector "A"

Pushbutton control panel testing — Avalon

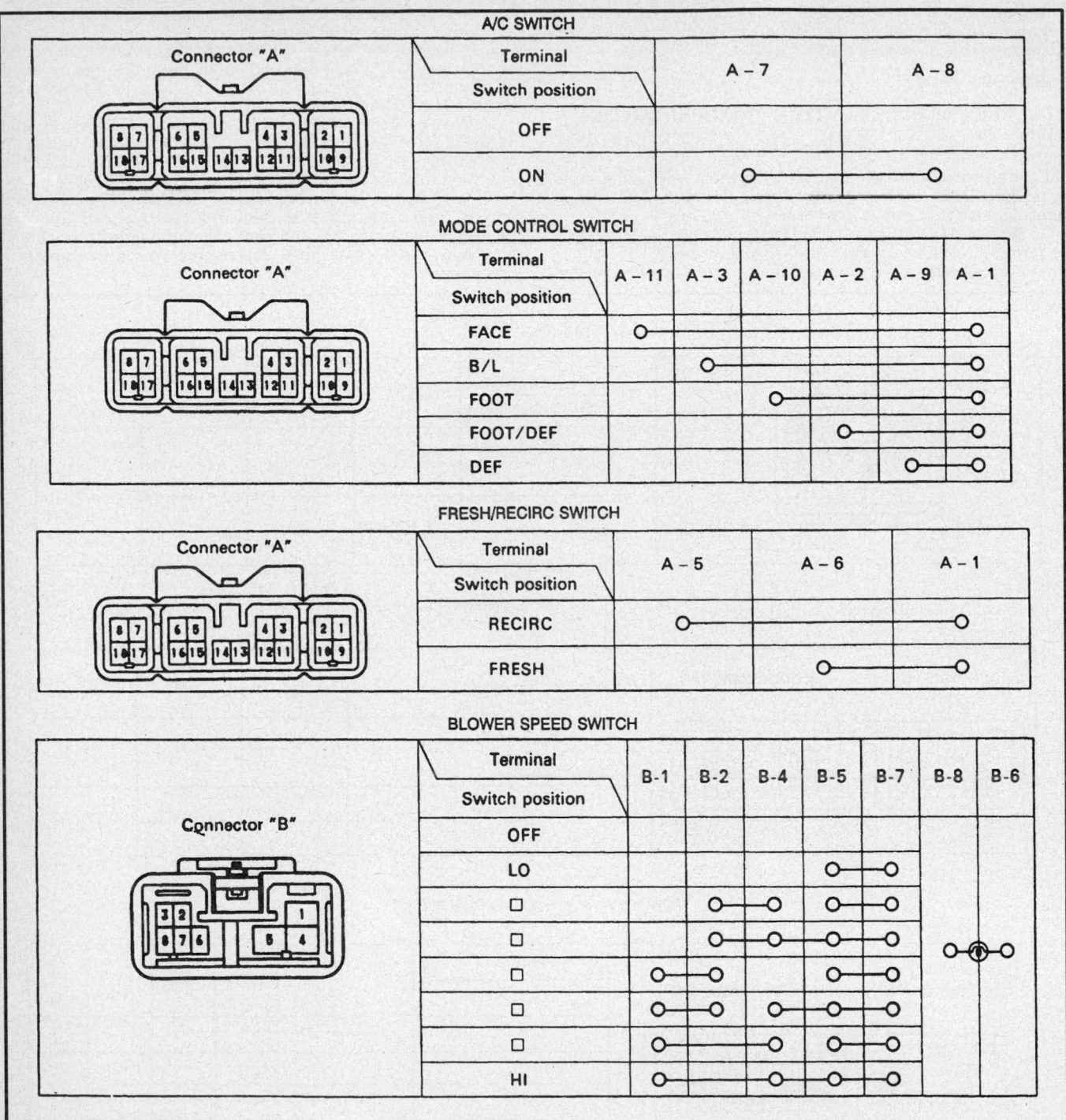

A/C SWITCH

Terminal / Switch position	A – 7	A – 8
OFF		
ON	o———	———o

Connector "A"

MODE CONTROL SWITCH

Terminal / Switch position	A – 11	A – 3	A – 10	A – 2	A – 9	A – 1
FACE	o					o
B/L		o				o
FOOT			o			o
FOOT/DEF				o		o
DEF					o———o

Connector "A"

FRESH/RECIRC SWITCH

Terminal / Switch position	A – 5	A – 6	A – 1
RECIRC	o		o
FRESH		o———	———o

Connector "A"

BLOWER SPEED SWITCH

Terminal / Switch position	B-1	B-2	B-4	B-5	B-7	B-8	B-6
OFF							
LO				o———o		
□		o———o		o———o		
□		o———o	o	o———o		
□	o———o			o———o		
□	o———o	o	o	o———o		
□	o———o		o	o———o		
HI	o		o	o———o		

Connector "B"

Rotary and puhbutton control panel testing – 1993 Camry

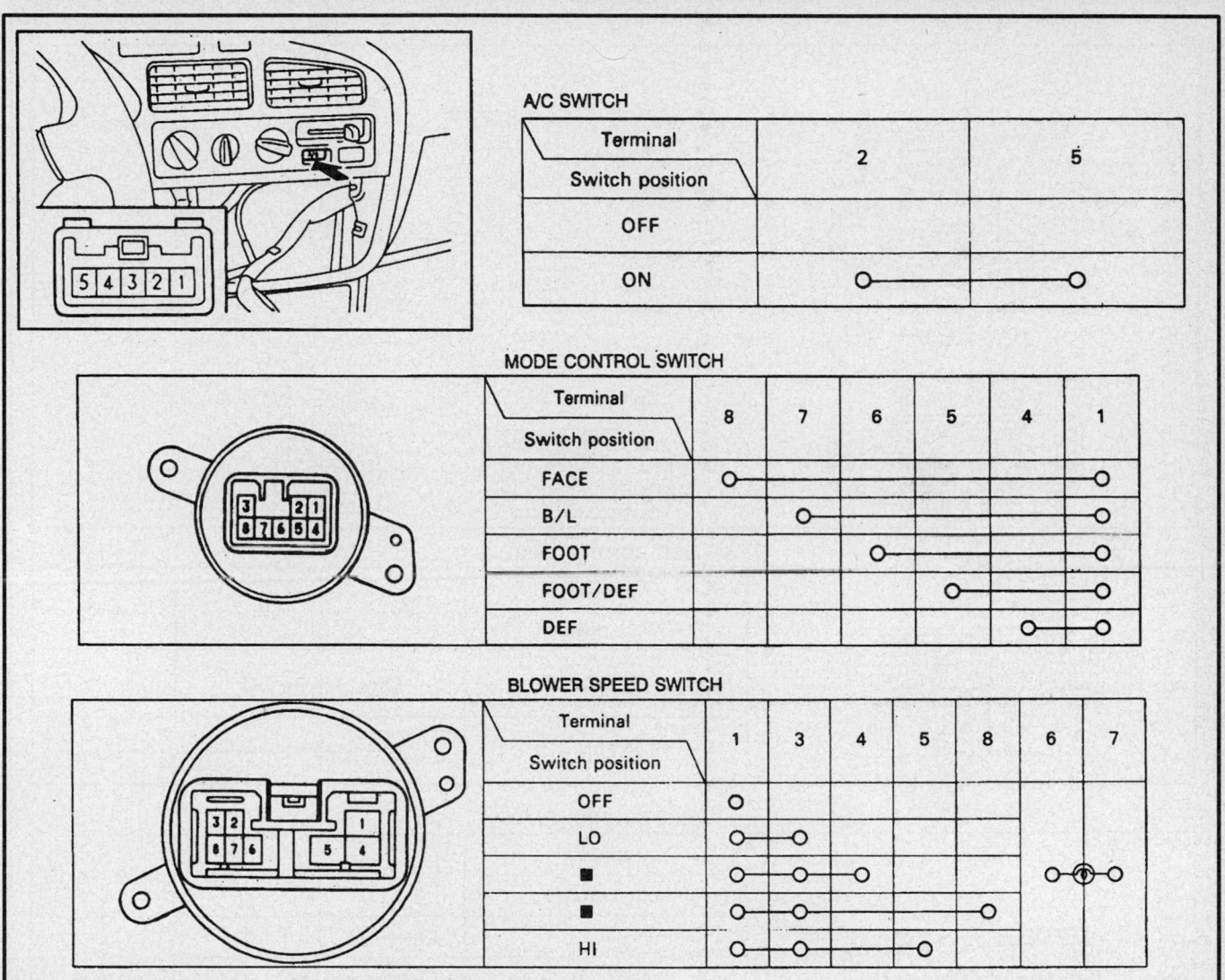

A/C SWITCH

Terminal / Switch position	2	5
OFF		
ON	o—————o	

MODE CONTROL SWITCH

Terminal / Switch position	8	7	6	5	4	1
FACE	o——————————————————o
B/L		o————————————————o
FOOT			o—————————————o
FOOT/DEF				o————————o
DEF					o——————o

BLOWER SPEED SWITCH

Terminal / Switch position	1	3	4	5	8	6	7
OFF	o						
LO	o——o					
■	o——o——o			o—(⟲)—o
■	o——o——————o		
HI	o——o————o			

Rotary and pushbutton control panel testing – 1993 Camry

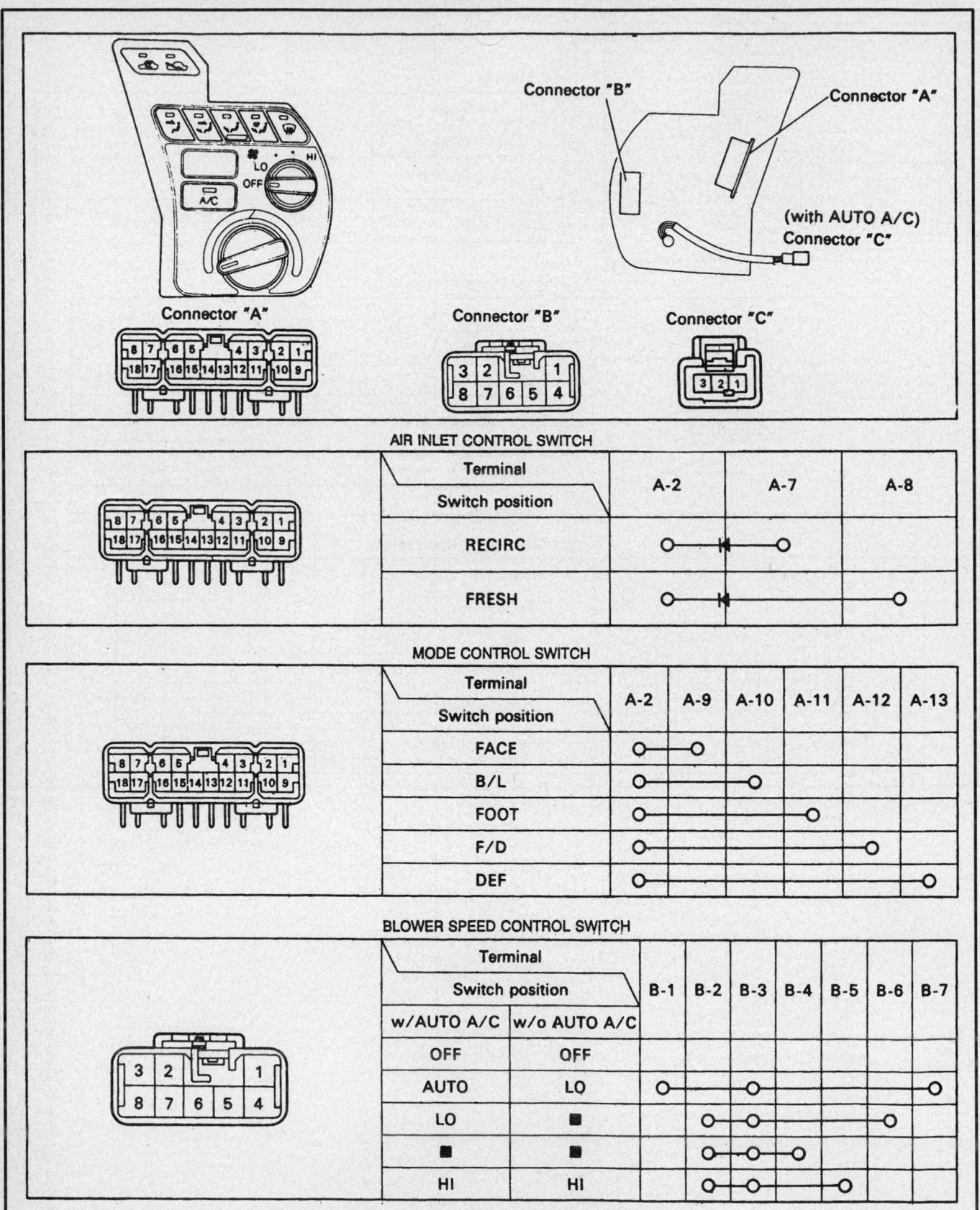

AIR INLET CONTROL SWITCH

Terminal / Switch position	A-2	A-7	A-8
RECIRC	O——◁——O		
FRESH	O——◁—————————O		O

MODE CONTROL SWITCH

Terminal / Switch position	A-2	A-9	A-10	A-11	A-12	A-13
FACE	O——O					
B/L	O————O					
FOOT	O————————O					
F/D	O————————————O					
DEF	O————————————————O					

BLOWER SPEED CONTROL SWITCH

w/AUTO A/C	w/o AUTO A/C	B-1	B-2	B-3	B-4	B-5	B-6	B-7
OFF	OFF							
AUTO	LO	O		O				O
LO	■		O	O			O	
■	■		O	O	O			
HI	HI		O	O		O		

Dial blower speed switch and pushbutton type control panel testing – Celica

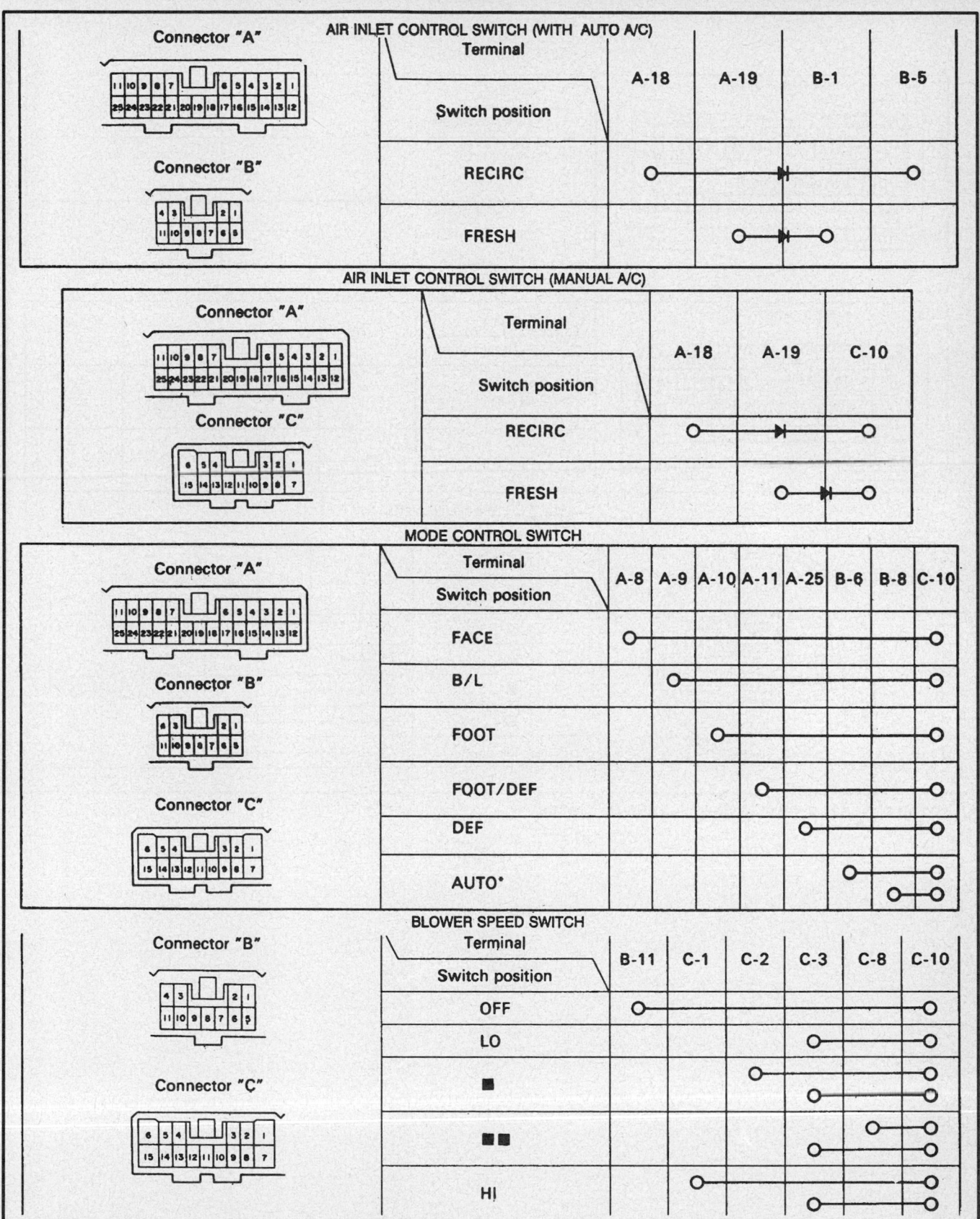

AIR INLET CONTROL SWITCH (WITH AUTO A/C)

Terminal / Switch position	A-18	A-19	B-1	B-5
RECIRC	○———————	——▷|——	——————○	
FRESH	○————	—|◁—○		

AIR INLET CONTROL SWITCH (MANUAL A/C)

Terminal / Switch position	A-18	A-19	C-10
RECIRC	○————	—◁|——————○	
FRESH	○————	—|◁—○	

MODE CONTROL SWITCH

Terminal / Switch position	A-8	A-9	A-10	A-11	A-25	B-6	B-8	C-10
FACE	○——————————————————○							○
B/L		○———————————————○						○
FOOT			○—————————————○					○
FOOT/DEF				○————————————○				○
DEF					○——————————○			○
AUTO*						○——————○		○
							○————○	

BLOWER SPEED SWITCH

Terminal / Switch position	B-11	C-1	C-2	C-3	C-8	C-10
OFF	○——————————————————————○					○
LO				○——————————○		○
■			○——————————○			○
				○————————○		○
■ ■					○————○		○
			○————————○			○
HI		○————————————○				○
				○————————○		○

Pushbutton type control panel testing — Celica

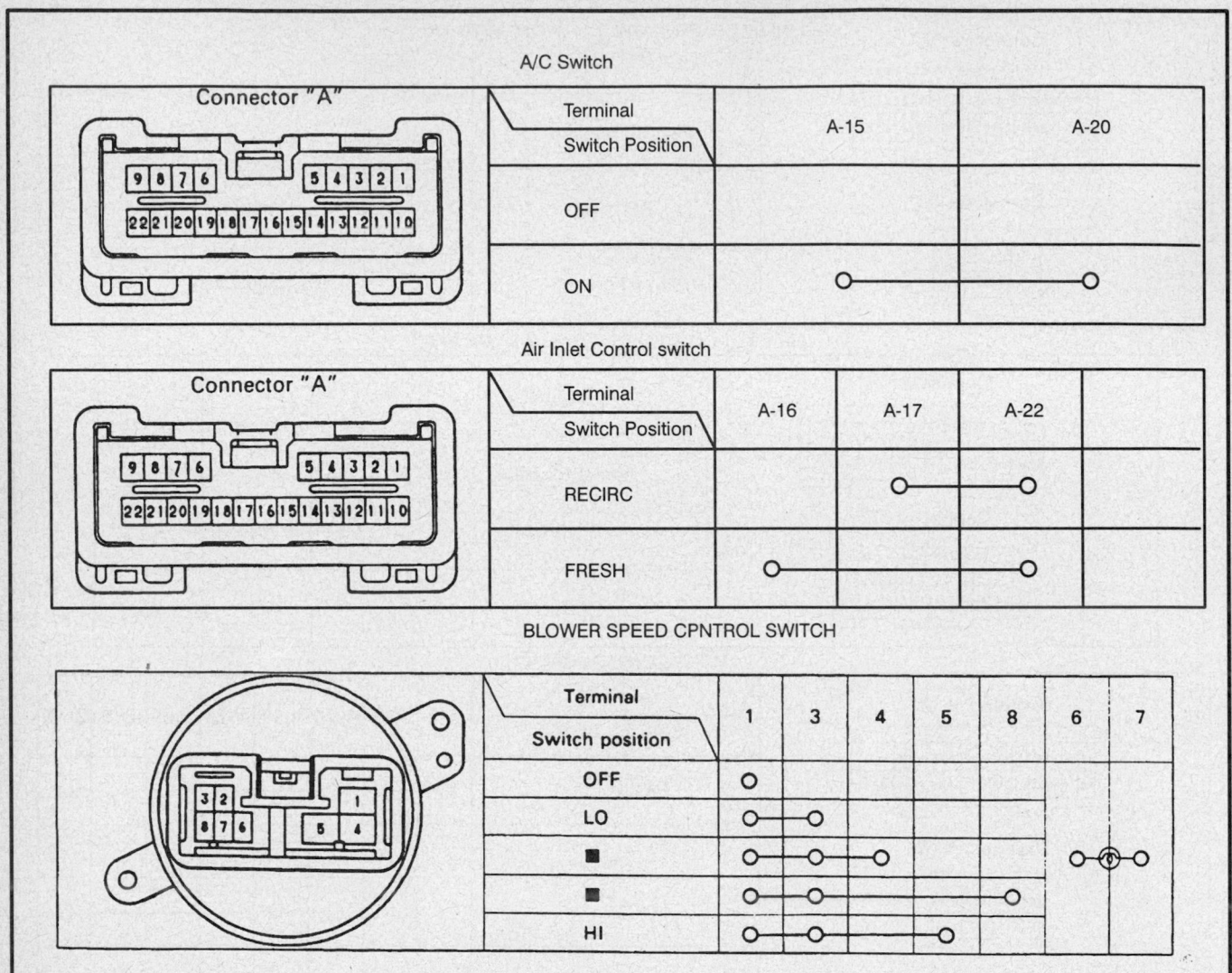

A/C Switch

Connector "A"	Terminal / Switch Position	A-15	A-20
	OFF		
	ON	○——————○	

Air Inlet Control switch

Connector "A"	Terminal / Switch Position	A-16	A-17	A-22	
	RECIRC		○——○		
	FRESH	○—————————○			

BLOWER SPEED CPNTROL SWITCH

Terminal / Switch position	1	3	4	5	8	6	7
OFF	○						
LO	○——○						
■	○——○——○				○—◉—○	
■	○——○—————————○					
HI	○——○——————————○				

A/C control panel switch testing – 1994-95 Celica

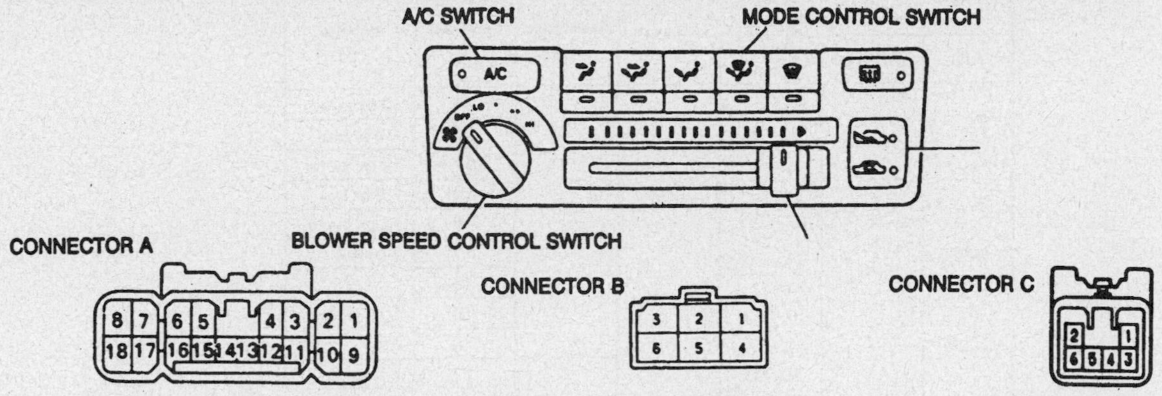

A/C SWITCH   MODE CONTROL SWITCH

BLOWER SPEED CONTROL SWITCH

CONNECTOR A

CONNECTOR B

CONNECTOR C

AIR INLET CONTROL SWITCH

Connector "A"

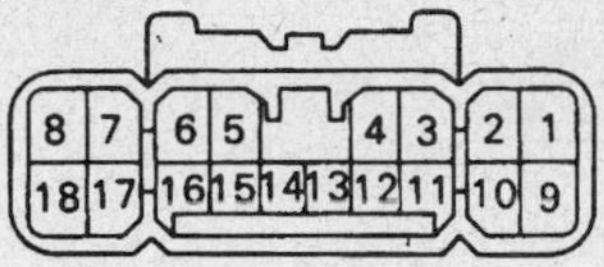

Terminal / Switch position	A-1	A-9	A-15
FRESH (Free)	o	▶|	o
RECIRC (Pushed in)		o—◀—o	

MODE CONTROL SWITCH

Connector "A"

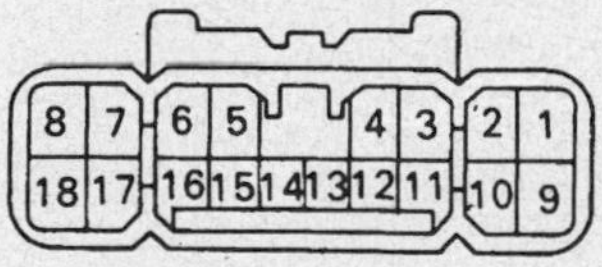

Terminal / Switch position	A-4	A-5	A-12	A-13	A-14	A-15
FACE			o			o
B/L				o		o
FOOT	o					o
FOOT/DEF		o				o
DEF					o	o

BLOWER CONTROL SWITCH

Connector "B"

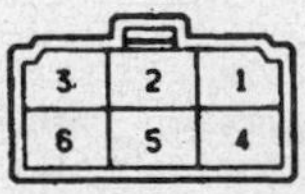

Terminal / Switch position	B-1	B-2	B-3	B-4	B-6
OFF					
LO				o	o
■		o		o	o
■ ■	o			o	o
HI	o			o	o

A/C SWITCH

Connector "C"

Terminal / Switch position	C-3	C-5	C-6
OFF			
A/C		o	o

A/C control panel switch testing — MR2

Control Button				Resistance (Ω)	Terminal Ⓐ	Voltage (V)
A/C	FRS/REC	Mode Control	Blower Speed			
OFF	FRS	AUTO	AUTO	620	14	12 or more
					15	1.5 or less
					17	12 or more
					18	1.0 or less
					8	12 or more
					7	1 or less
					19	
					16	12 or more
					6	
				70	12	1.5 or less
					3	1 or less
					13	12 or more
					4	12 or more
ON	REC			620	14	1 or less
					17	1,5 or less
					15	
			OFF	70	12	12 or more
					3	
			LO		12	
			M		13	1 or less
					4	
			HI	620	13	12 or more
		DEF			6	1 or less
					18	12 or more
					7	
		F/D			16	1 or less
					6	12 or more
		FOOT			19	1 or less
					16	12 or more
		BI-LEVEL			7	1 or less
					19	12 or more
		FACE			8	1 or less
					7	12 or more
		AUTO	AUTO		18	1 or less
					7	1 or less

RESISTANCE Ⓐ

Control Button				Resistance (Ω)	Terminal Ⓐ	Voltage (V)
A/C	FRS/REC	Mode Control	Blower Speed			
ON	REC	AUTO	AUTO	620	8	1 or less
					7	12 or more
OFF					19	1 or less
					8	12 or more

Automatic air conditioning control panel switch testing — 1993 Supra

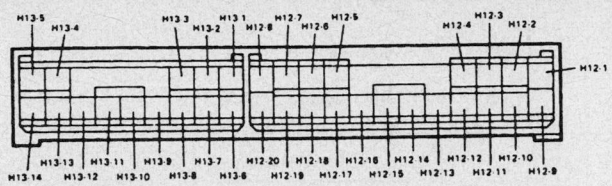

Switch	SW1 H13-7	SW2 H13-2	SW3 H12-13	SW4 B13-9	SW5 H13-10	SW6 B13-1	SW7 H12-16
OFF	○						○
R/F		○					○
DEF			○				○
FOOT	○					○	
F/D		○				○	
A/C			○			○	
RDEF	○				○		
FACE		○			○		
FAND⁻			○		○		
AUTO	○			○			
B/L		○		○			
FAND⁺			○	○			

FAND⁻: Turn fan speed dial counterclockwise.
FAND⁺: Turn fan speed dial clockwise.

A/C control panel switch testing – 1994-95 Supra

A/C Switch Continuity

Connector "C"

Terminal / Switch Position	C-9	C-11	Illumination C-10	C-8
OFF			○––〰––○	
ON	○–––––○			

Mode Control Switch Continuity

Connector "A"

Switch Position	A-1	A-4	A-5	A-6	A-7	A-8
FACE	○					○
B/L	○				○	
FOOT	○			○		
FOOT/DEF	○		○			
DEF	○	○				

Blower Speed Control Switch Continuity

Connector "B"

Terminal / Switch position	1	3	4	5	8	Illumination 6	7
OFF	○						
LO	○––○						
■ (M1)	○––○––○					○––⊗––○	
■ (M2)	○––○			○			
HI	○––○		○				

Rotary and puhbutton control panel testing – Avalon

MR2

1. With battery voltage applied to terminal **A-18** and ground at terminal **A-8** check that the illumination bulb lights. If no light appears check illumination bulb.

2. With battery voltage applied to terminal **A-10** and ground at terminal **A-15** check that the FRESH and RECIRC indicators light alternately each time the air inlet control switch button is pressed. Then connect a positive lead from the battery to terminal **A-3** and check that the indicator dims. If operation is not as specified, replace the air conditioning control assembly.

3. With battery voltage applied to terminal **A-10** and ground at terminal **A-15** check that each mode buttons lights up when mode buttons are pressed in. Then connect a positive lead from the battery to terminal **A-3** and check that the indicator dims. If operation is not as specified, replace the air conditioning control assembly.

4. With battery voltage applied to terminal **C-1** and ground at terminal **C-4** check that the illumination lights up. If illumination does not light up test bulb.

5. With battery voltage applied to terminal **C-5** and ground at terminal **C-2** push air conditioning switch button in and check that the indicator lights. Then connect battery voltage to terminal **C-3** and check that the indicators dim. If operation is not as specified, replace the air conditioning switch.

1993 Supra

1. Measure output voltage by connecting battery voltage to terminal **1** and **2** and ground to terminal **10**.

2. Connect the negative lead from the voltmeter to terminal **10** and the positive lead to each terminal with the indicated resistance.

3. Check that the output voltage is as shown in the chart. Confirm that each indicator light is operational when the button is pushed.

1994−95 Supra

Check continuity of control panel switches as shown in the chart. If continuity is not as shown, replace switch.

WIRING SCHEMATICS

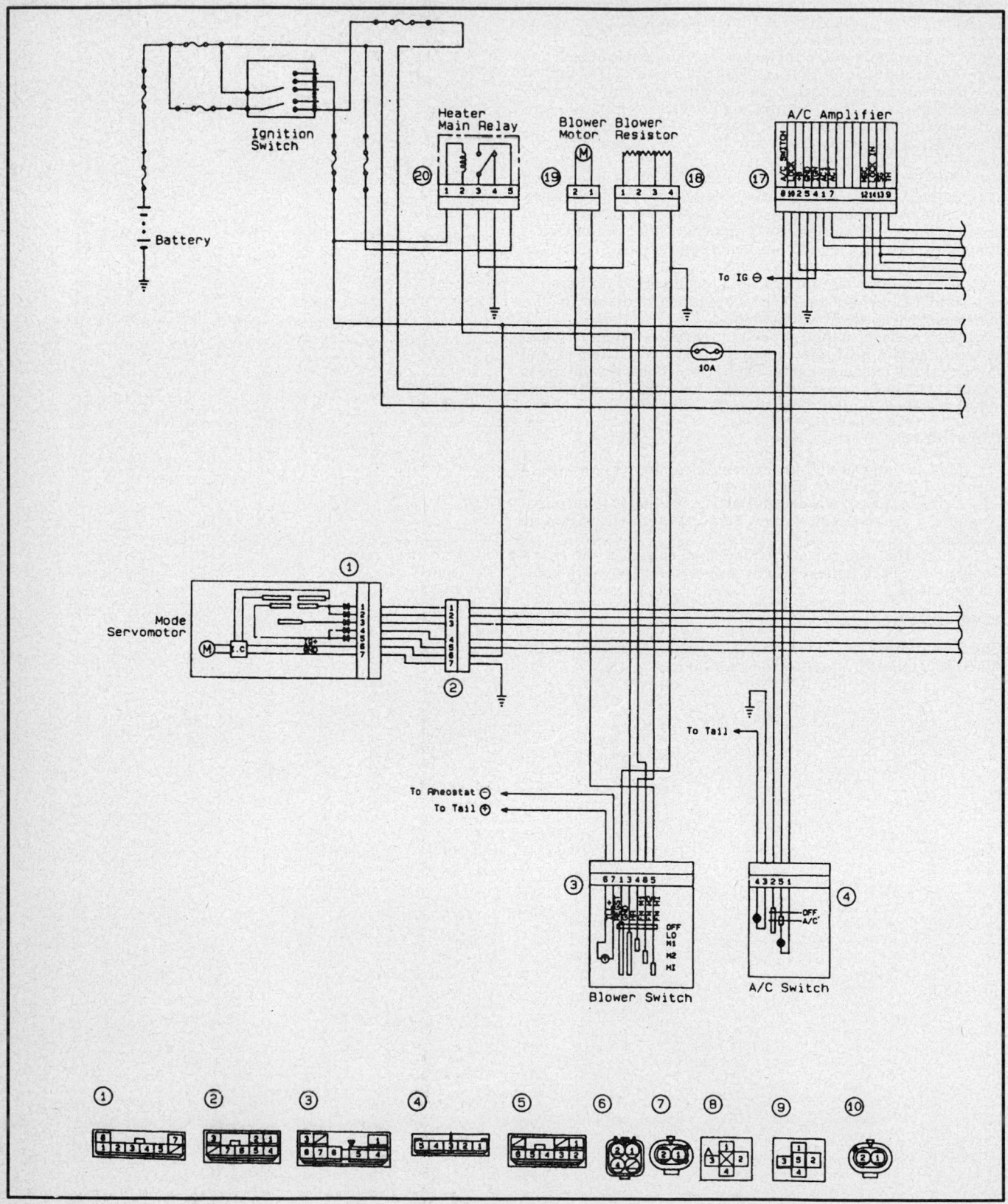

Air conditioning wiring schematic – 1993 Camry 5S-FE engine (lever type)

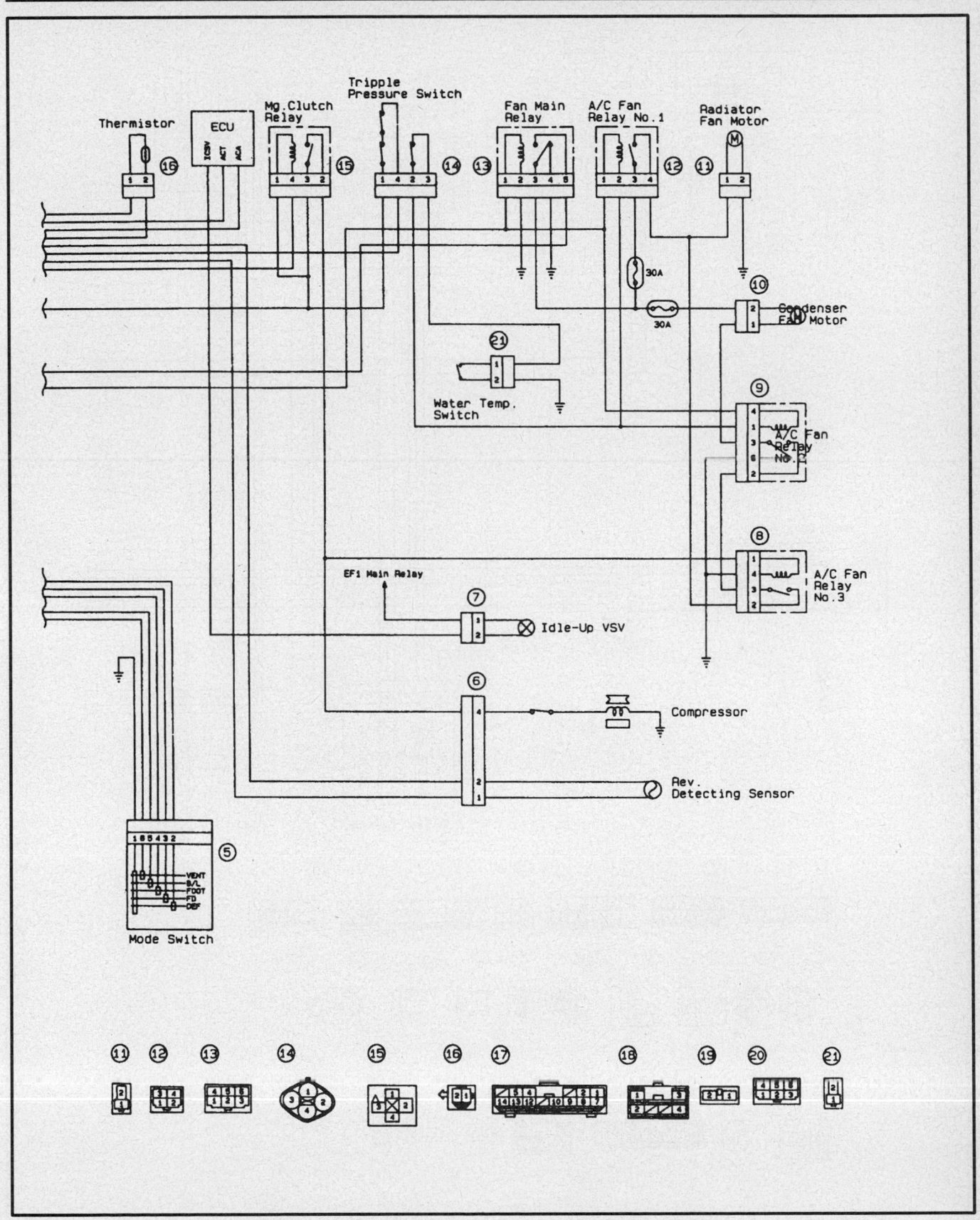

Air conditioning wiring schematic – 1993 Camry 5S-FE engine (lever type), Cont'd

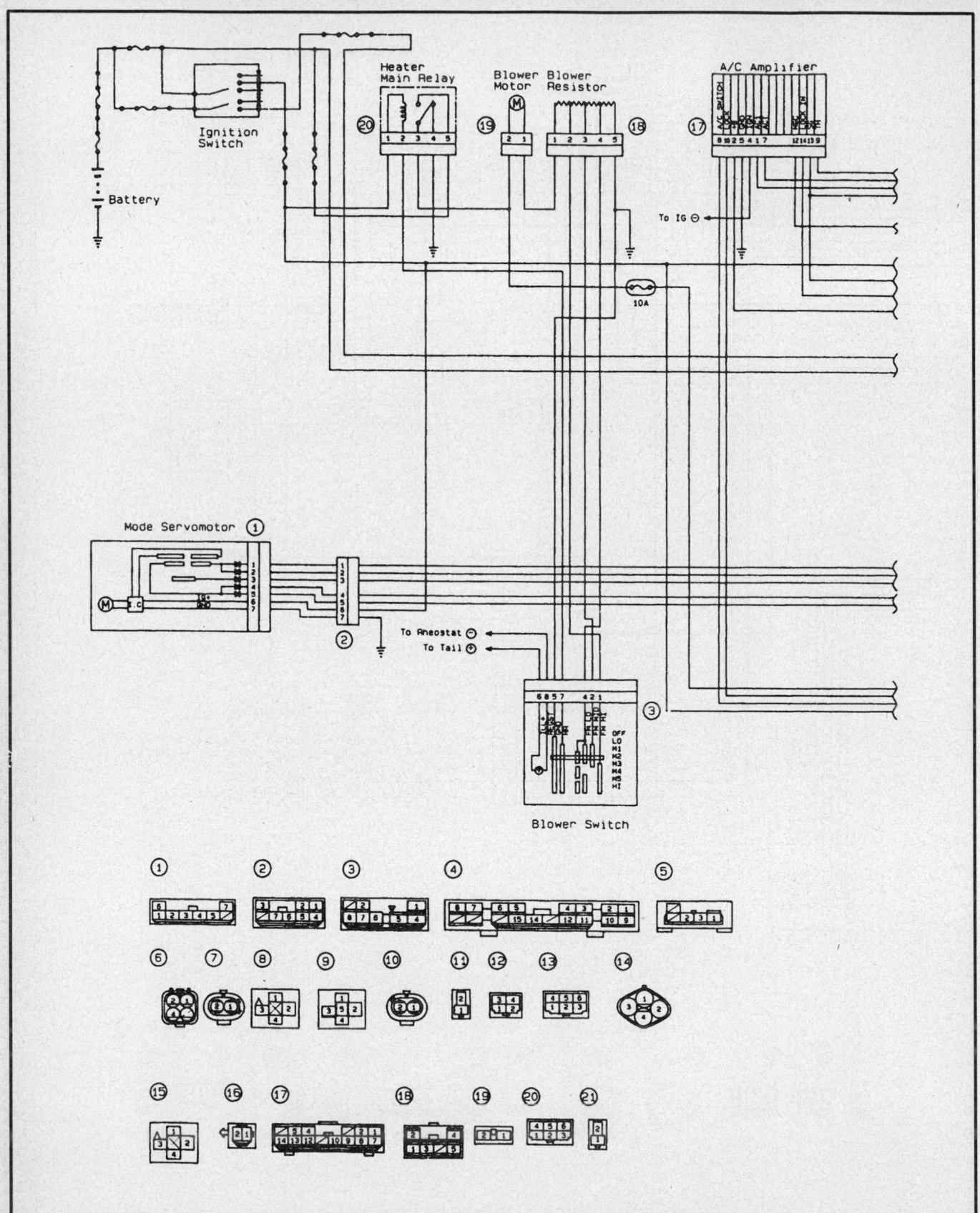

Air conditioning wiring schematic – 1993 Camry 5S-FE engine (pushbutton type)

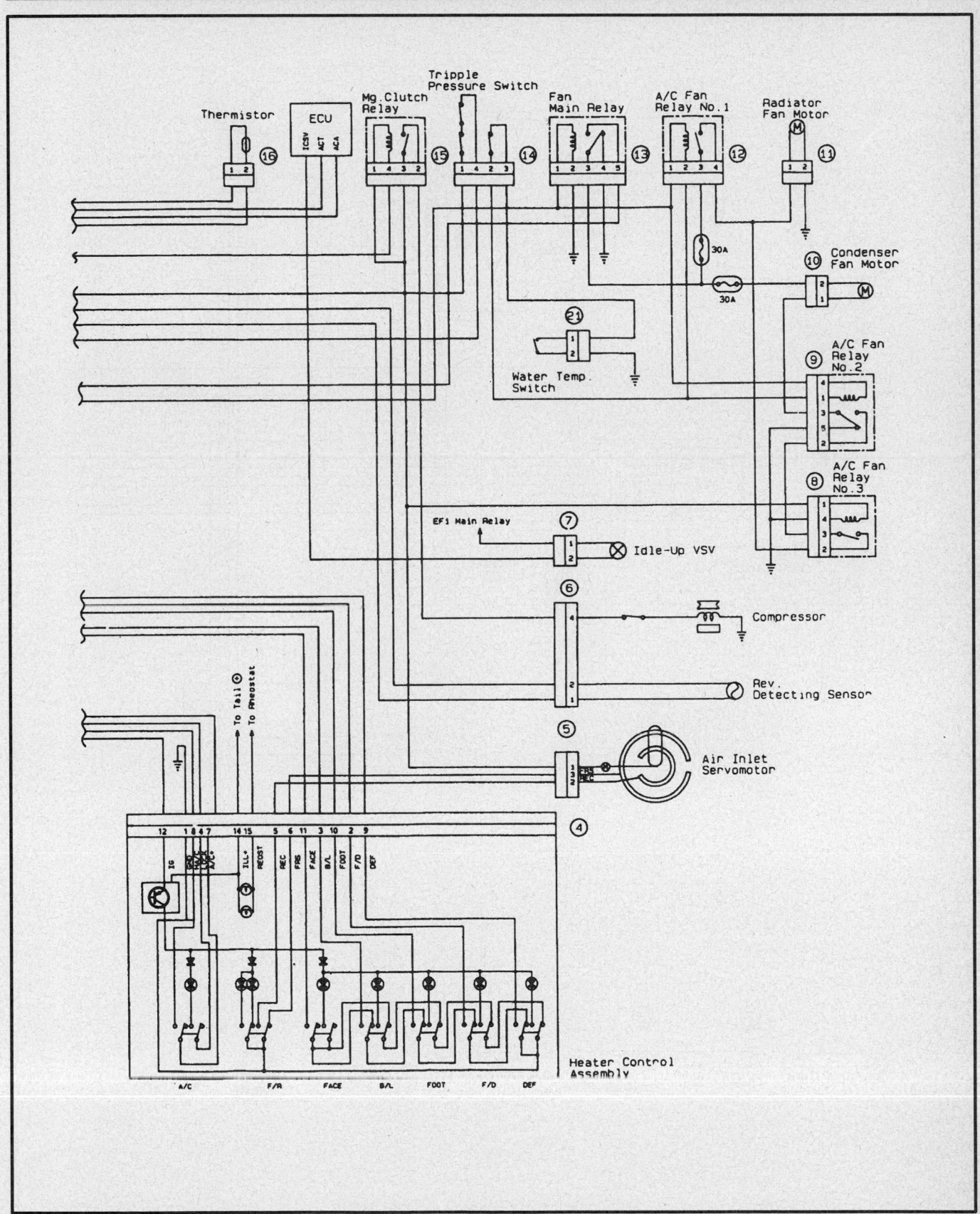

Air conditioning wiring schematic – 1993 Camry 5S-FE engine (pushbutton type) – Cont'd

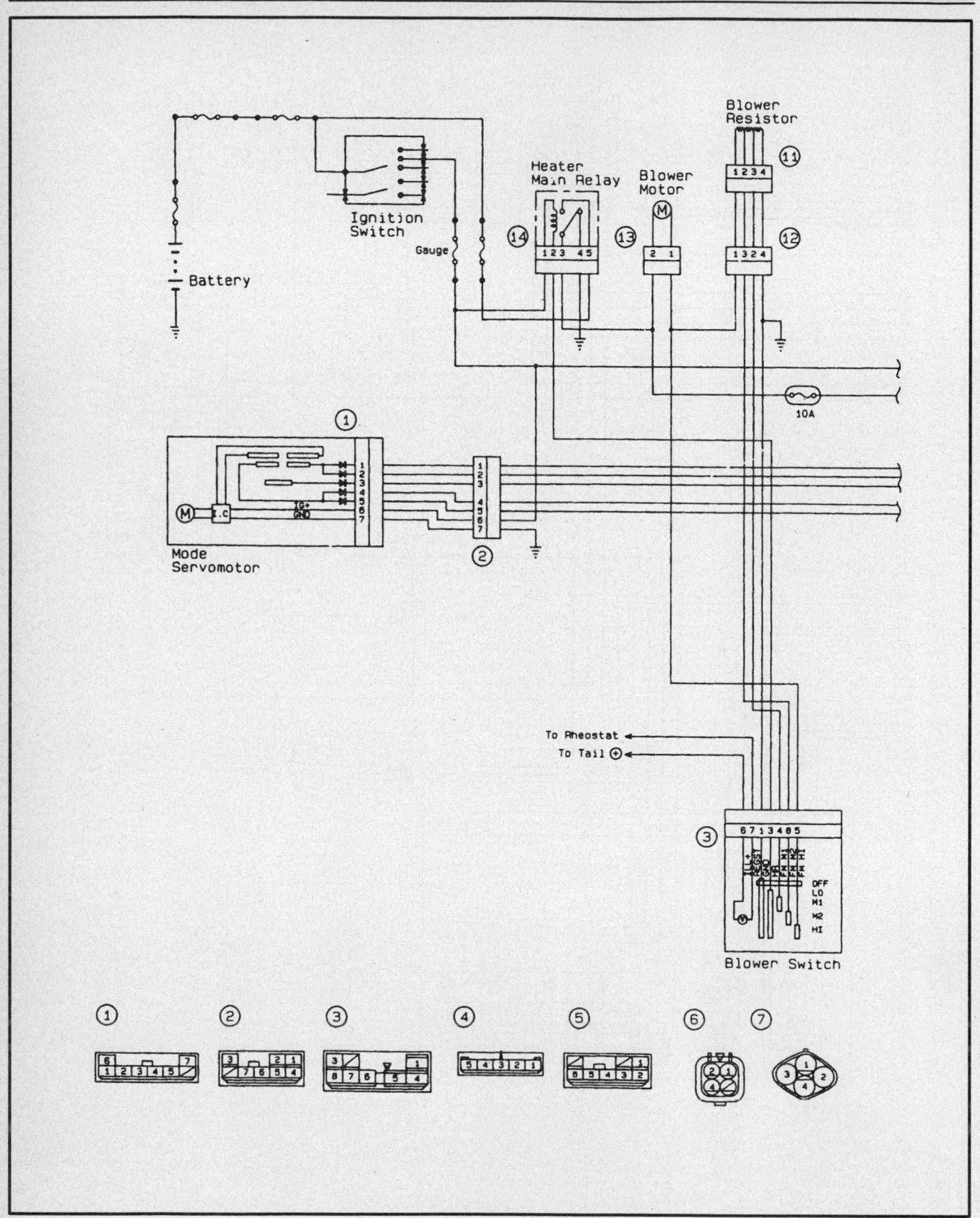

Air conditioning wiring schematic — 1993 Camry 3VZ-FE engine (lever type)

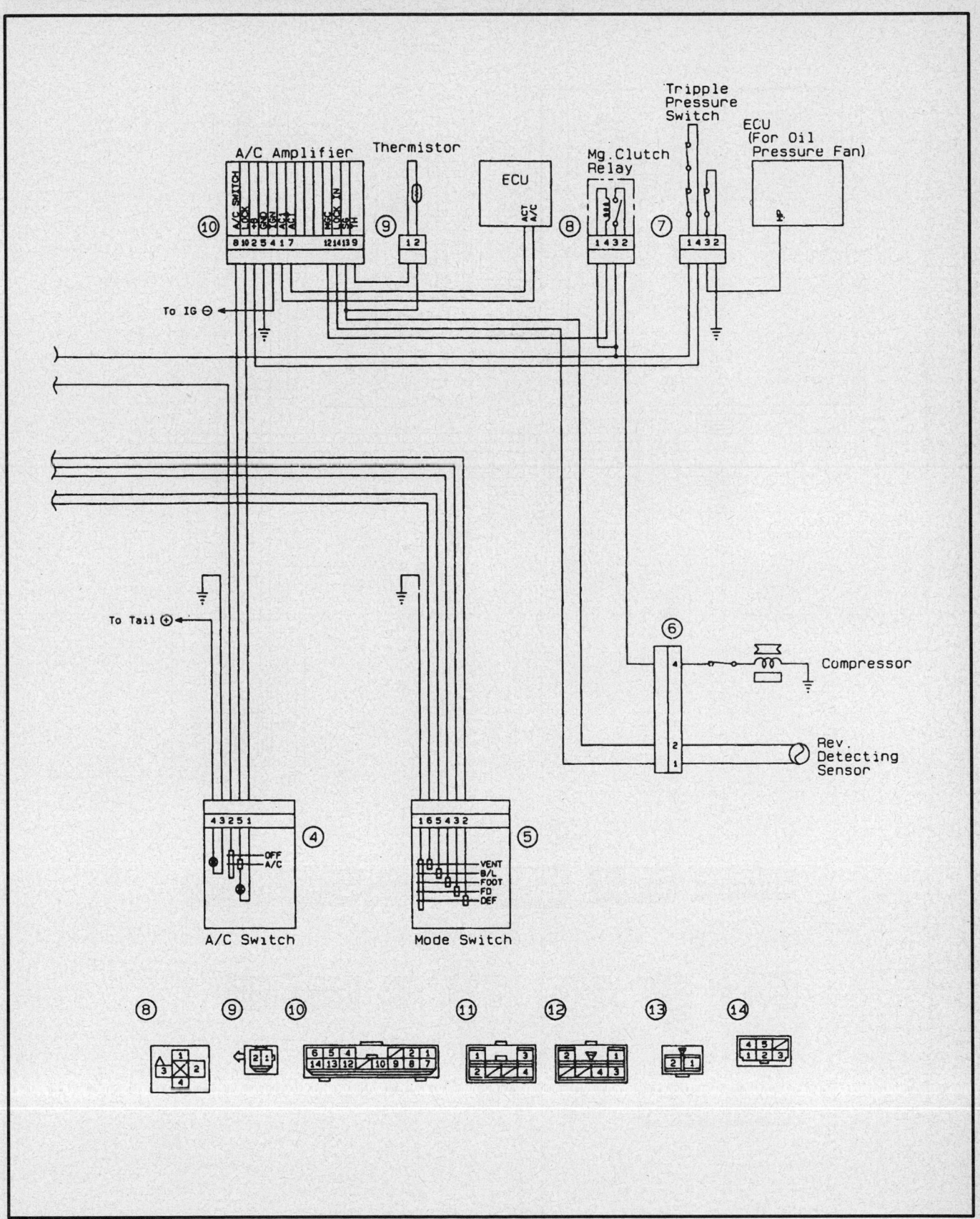

Air conditioning wiring schematic — 1993 Camry 3VZ-FE engine (lever type) — Cont'd

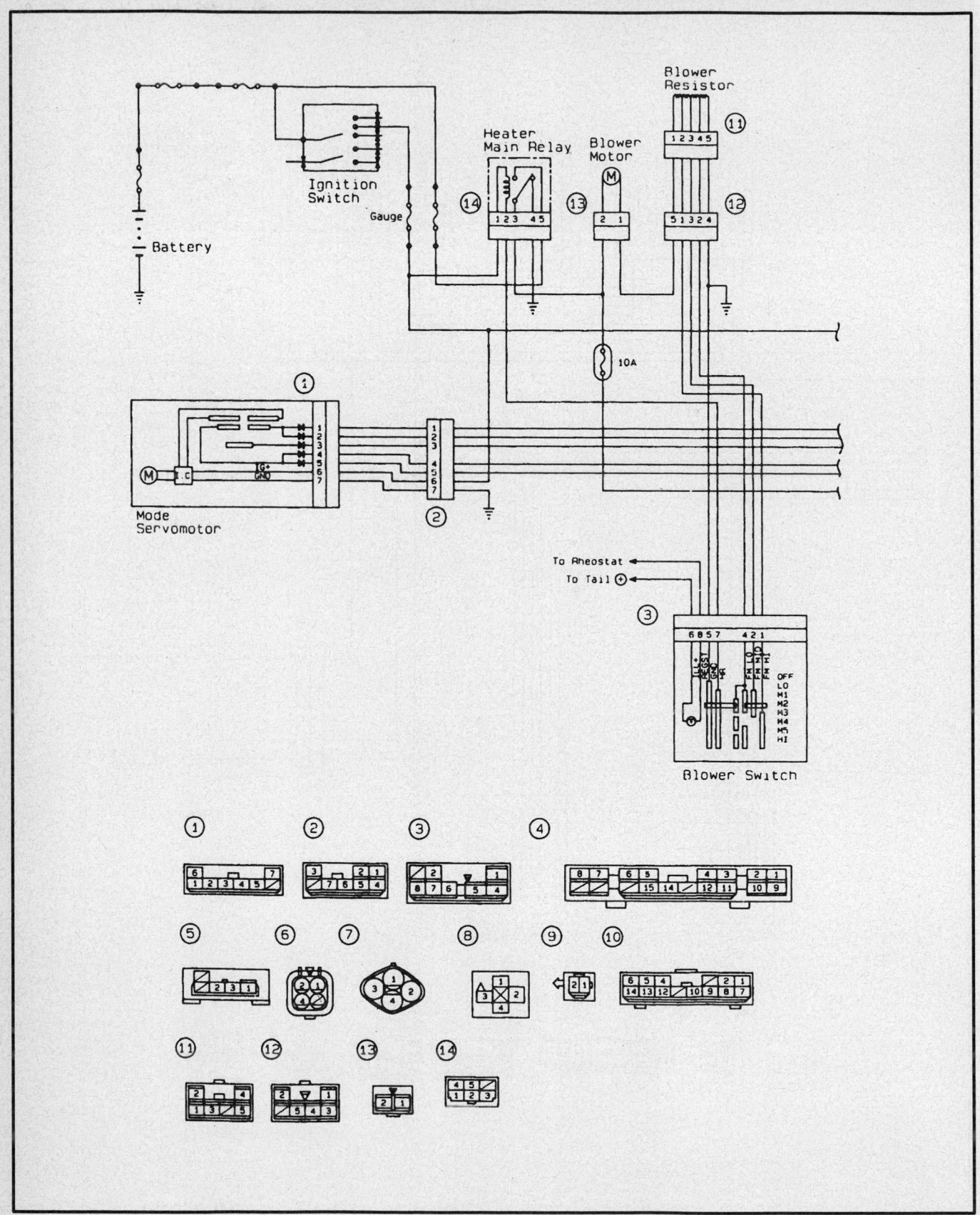

Air conditioning wiring schematic – 1993 Camry 3VZ-FE engine (pushbutton type)

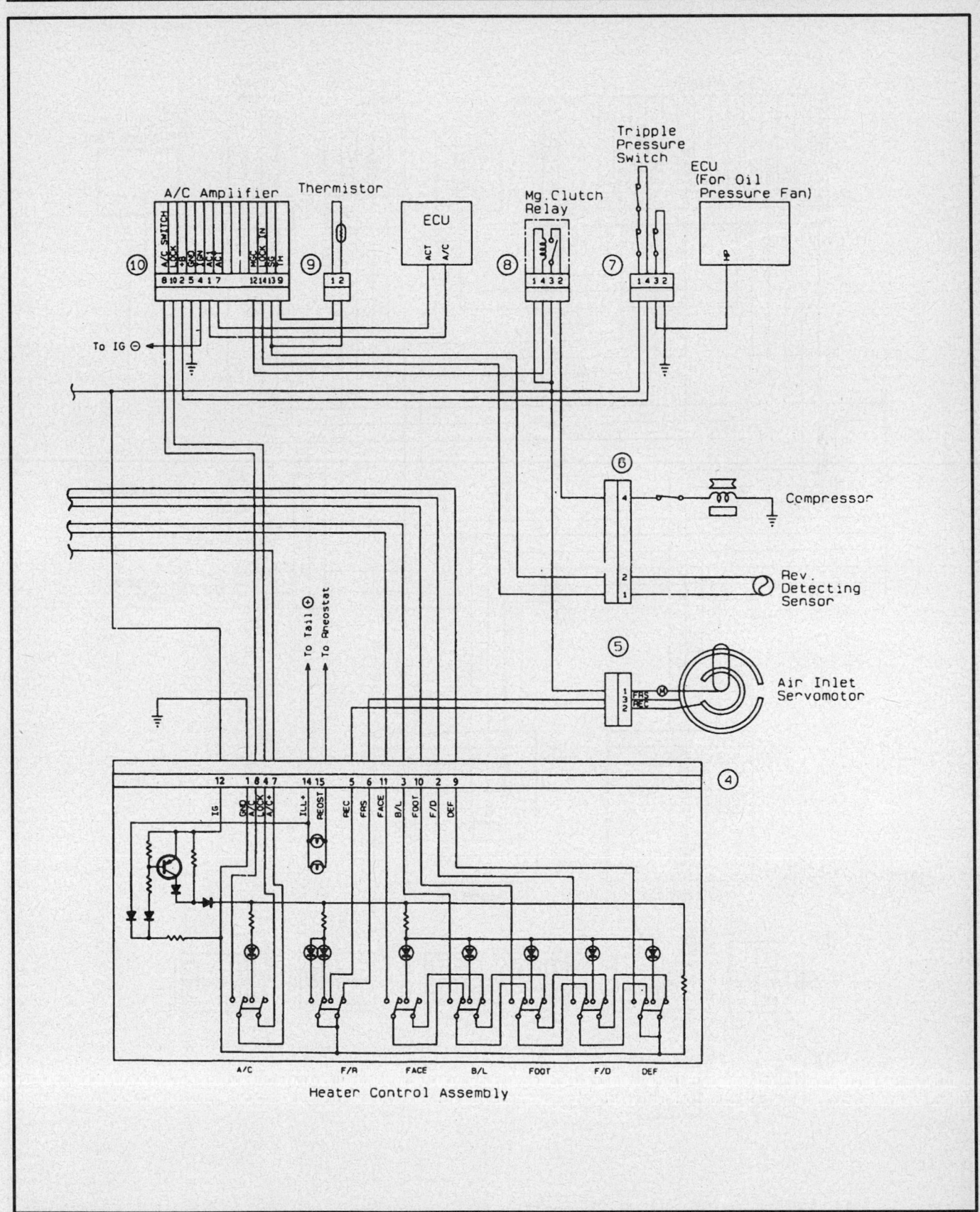

Air conditioning wiring schematic – 1993 Camry 3VZ-FE engine (pushbutton type), Cont'd

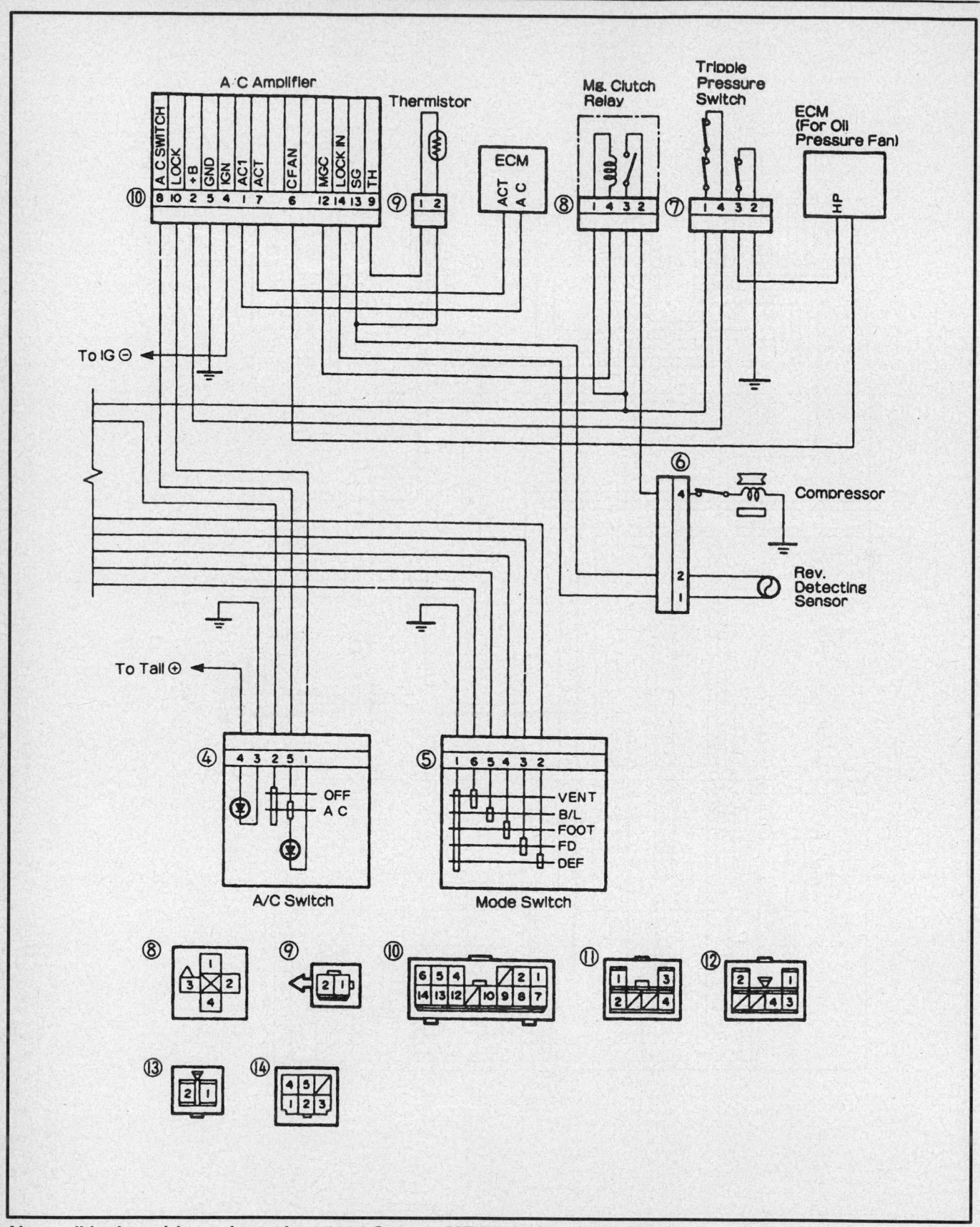

Air conditioning wiring schematic – 1994 Camry 1MZ-FF engine (lever type)

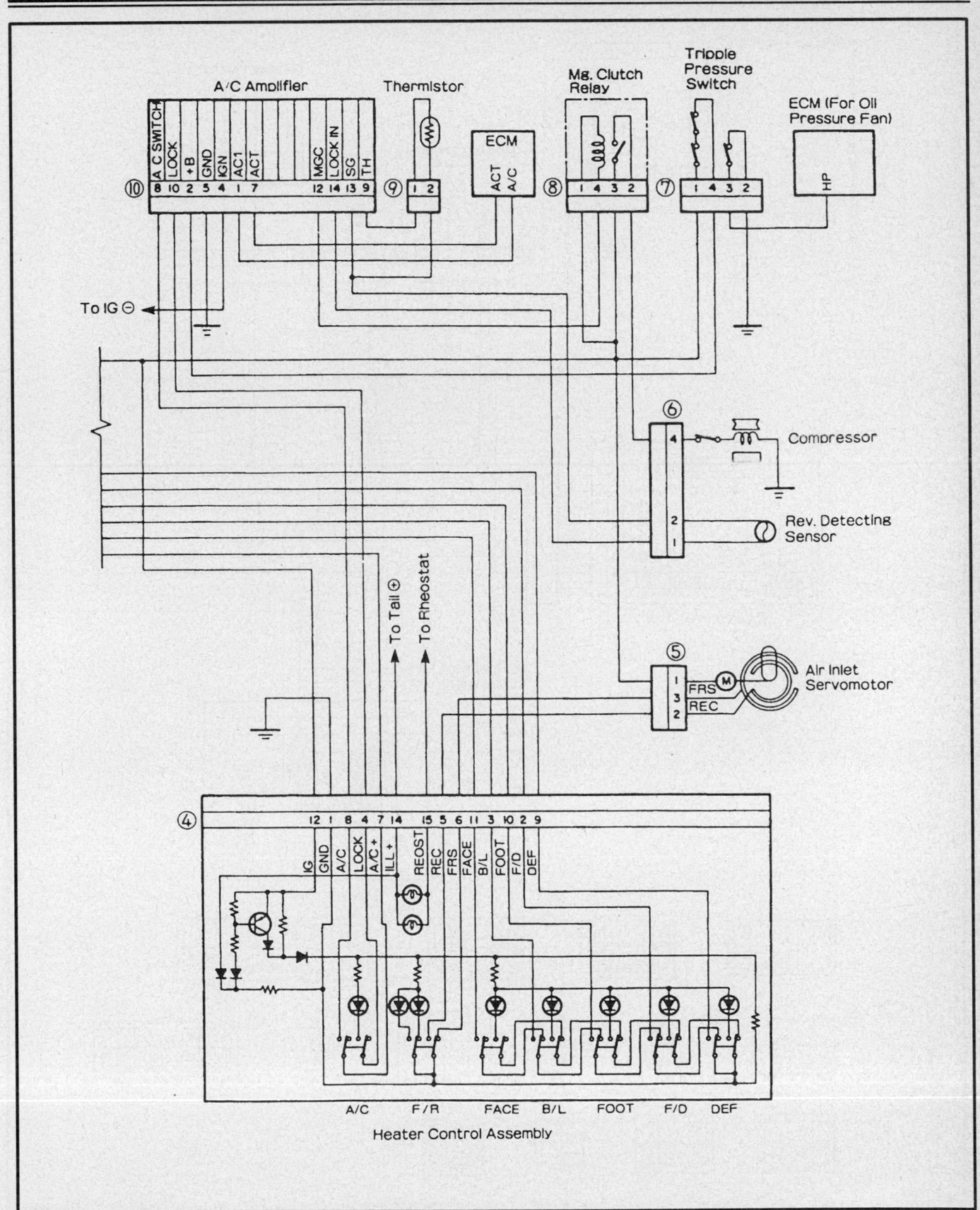

Air conditioning wiring schematic — 1994 Camry 1MZ-FF engine (lever type) Cont'd

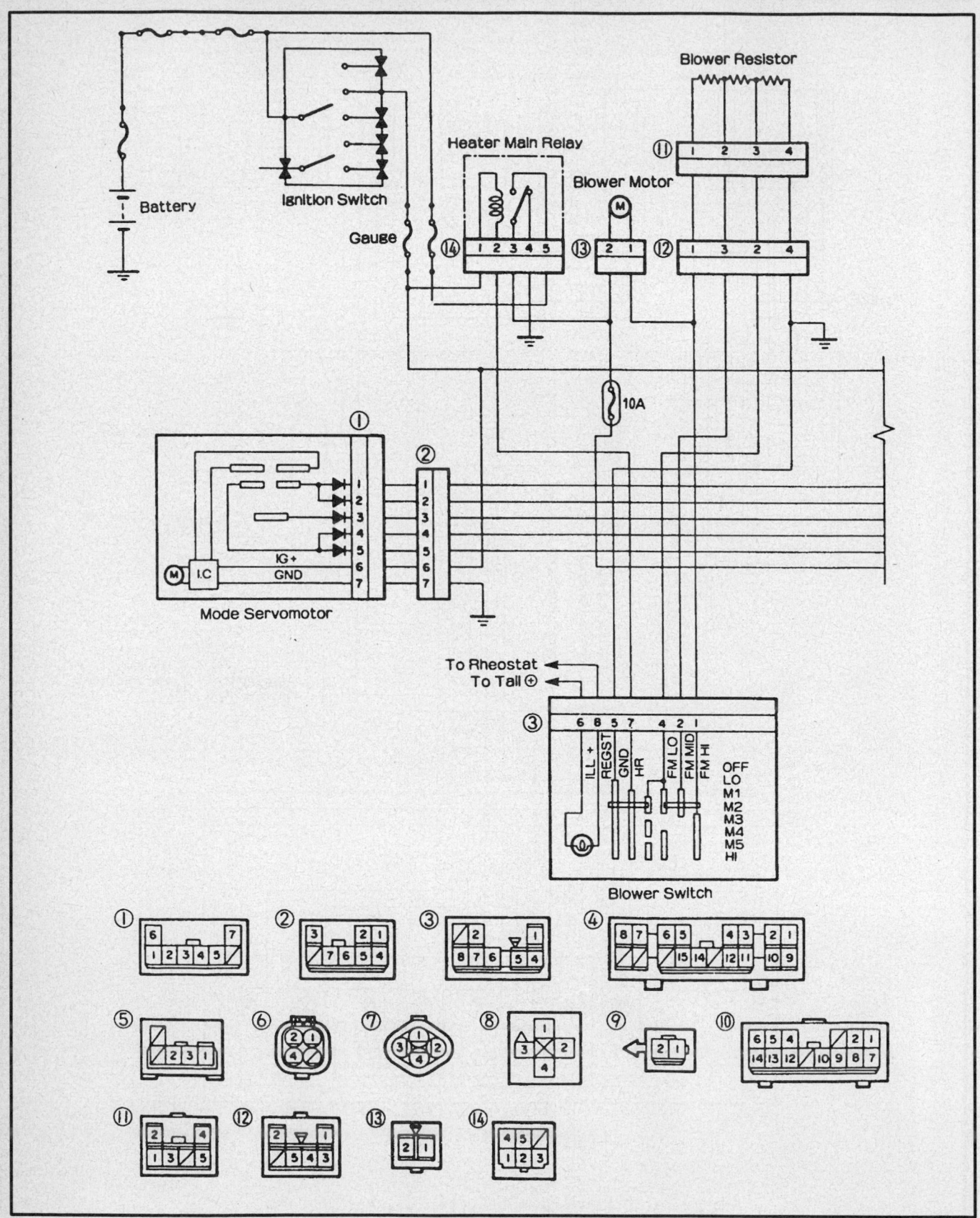

Air conditioning wiring schematic – 1994 Camry 1MZ-FF engine (pushbutton type)

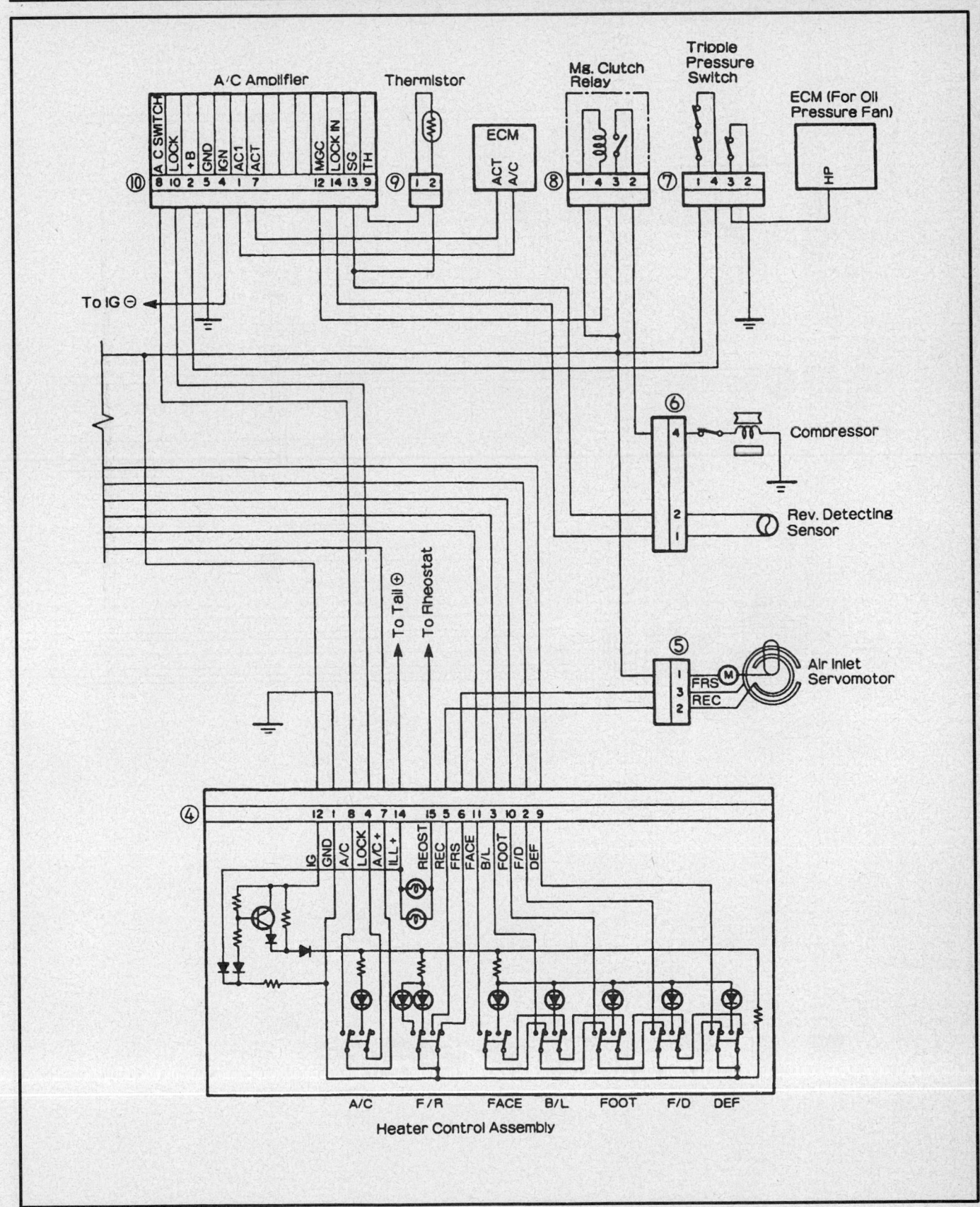

Air conditioning wiring schematic — 1994 Camry 1MZ-FF engine (pushbutton type), Cont'd

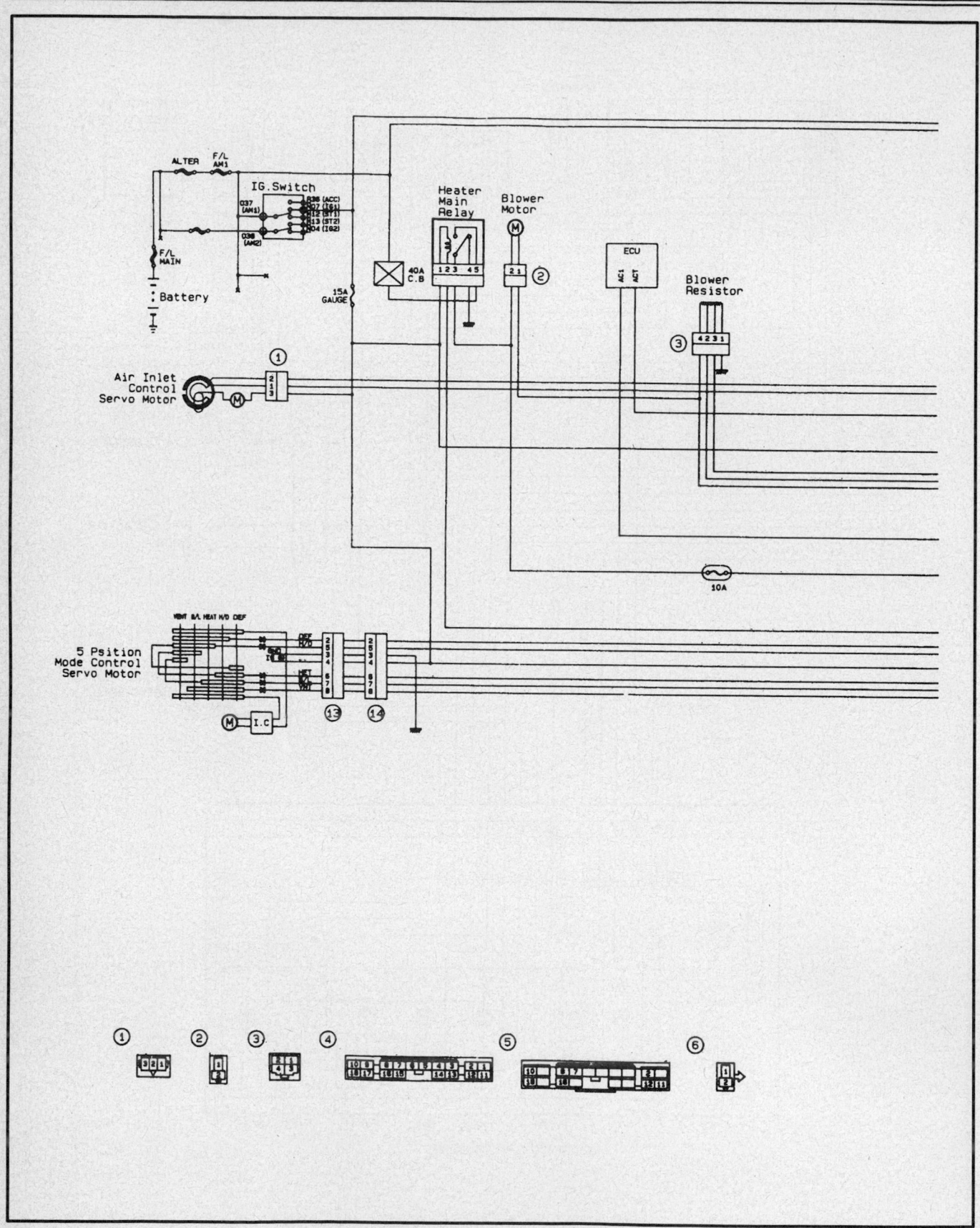

Air conditioning wiring schematic – 1993 Celica with manual A/C system

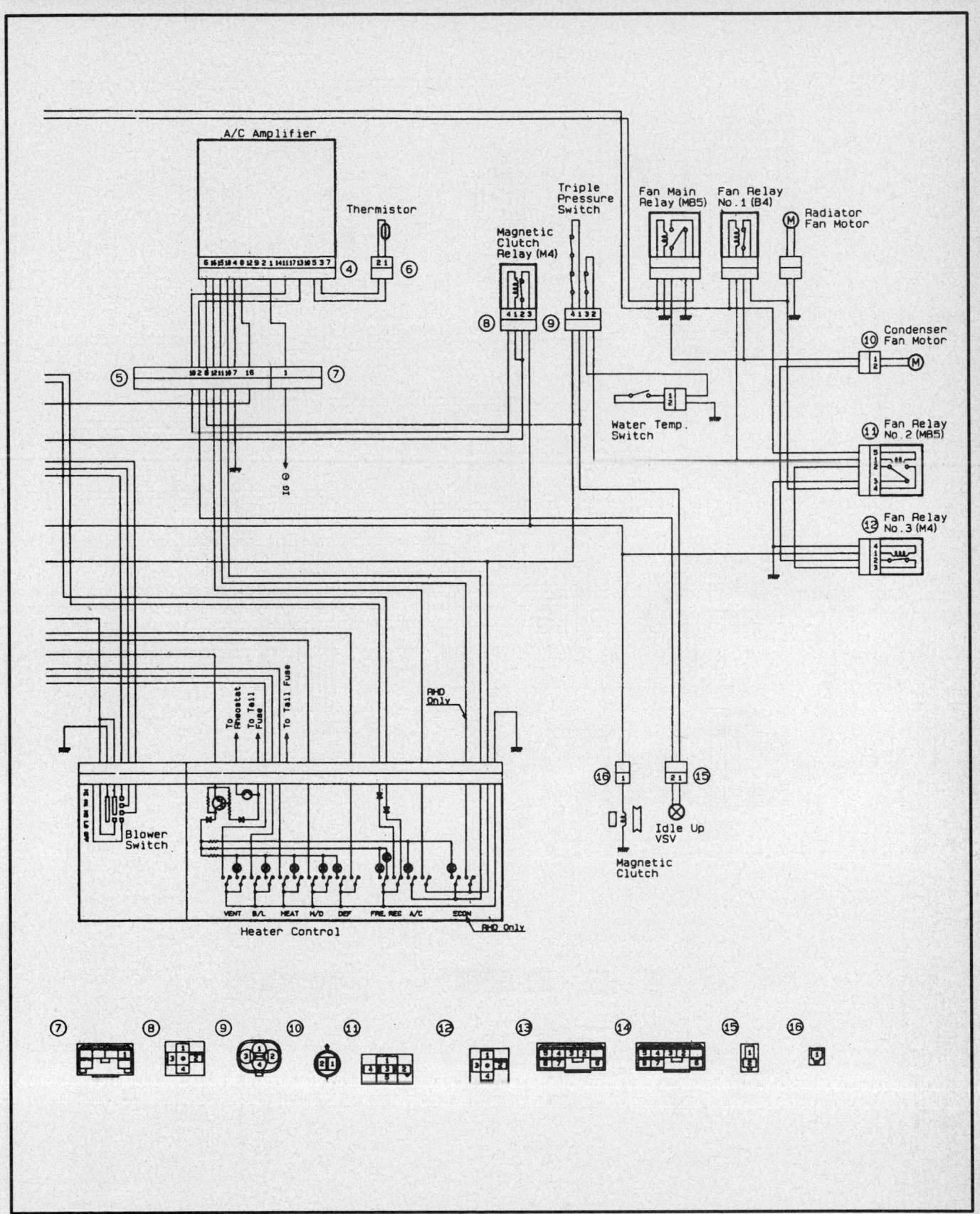

Air conditioning wiring schematic – 1993 Celica with manual A/C system, Cont'd

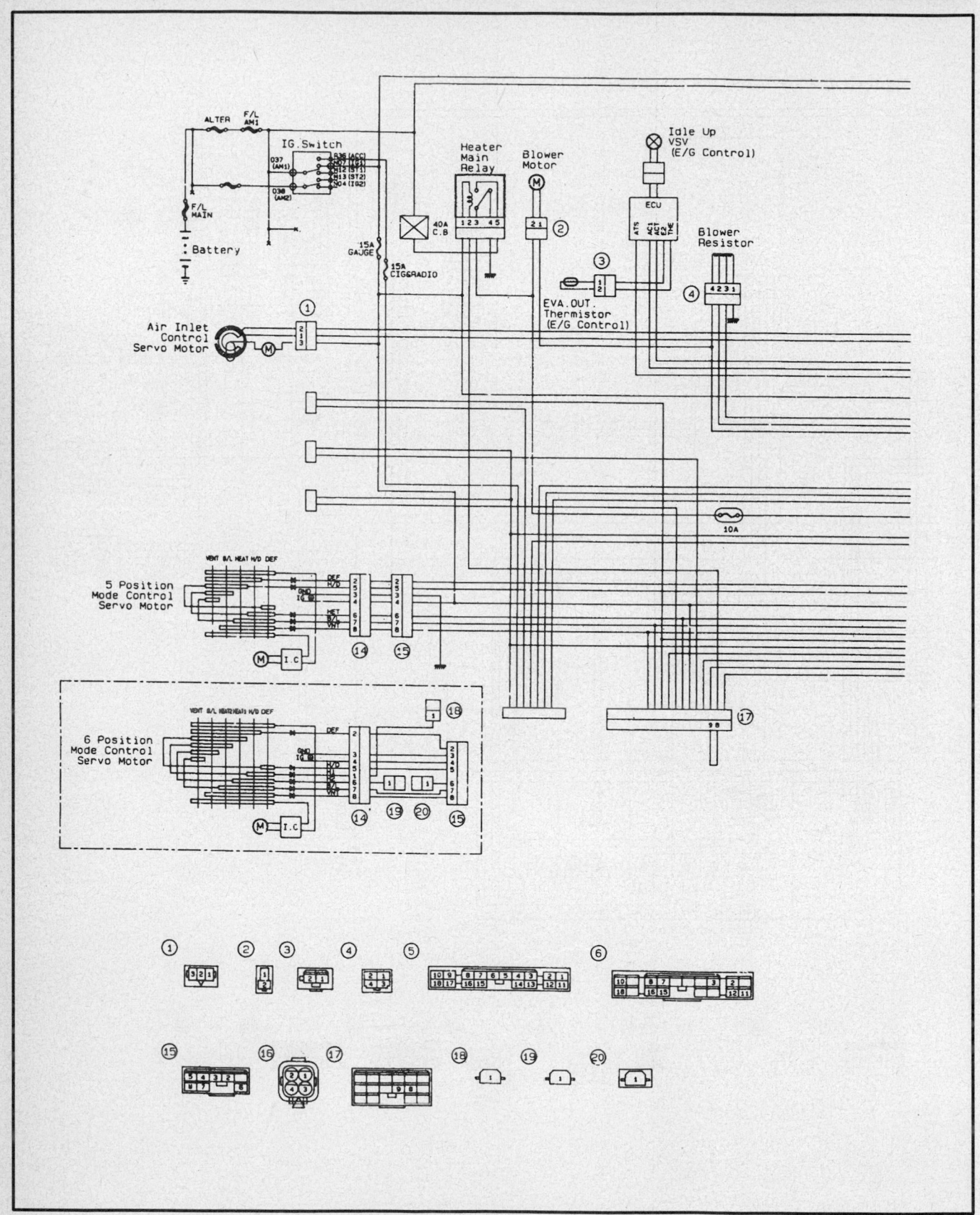

Air conditioning wiring schematic – 1993 Celica with automatic A/C system

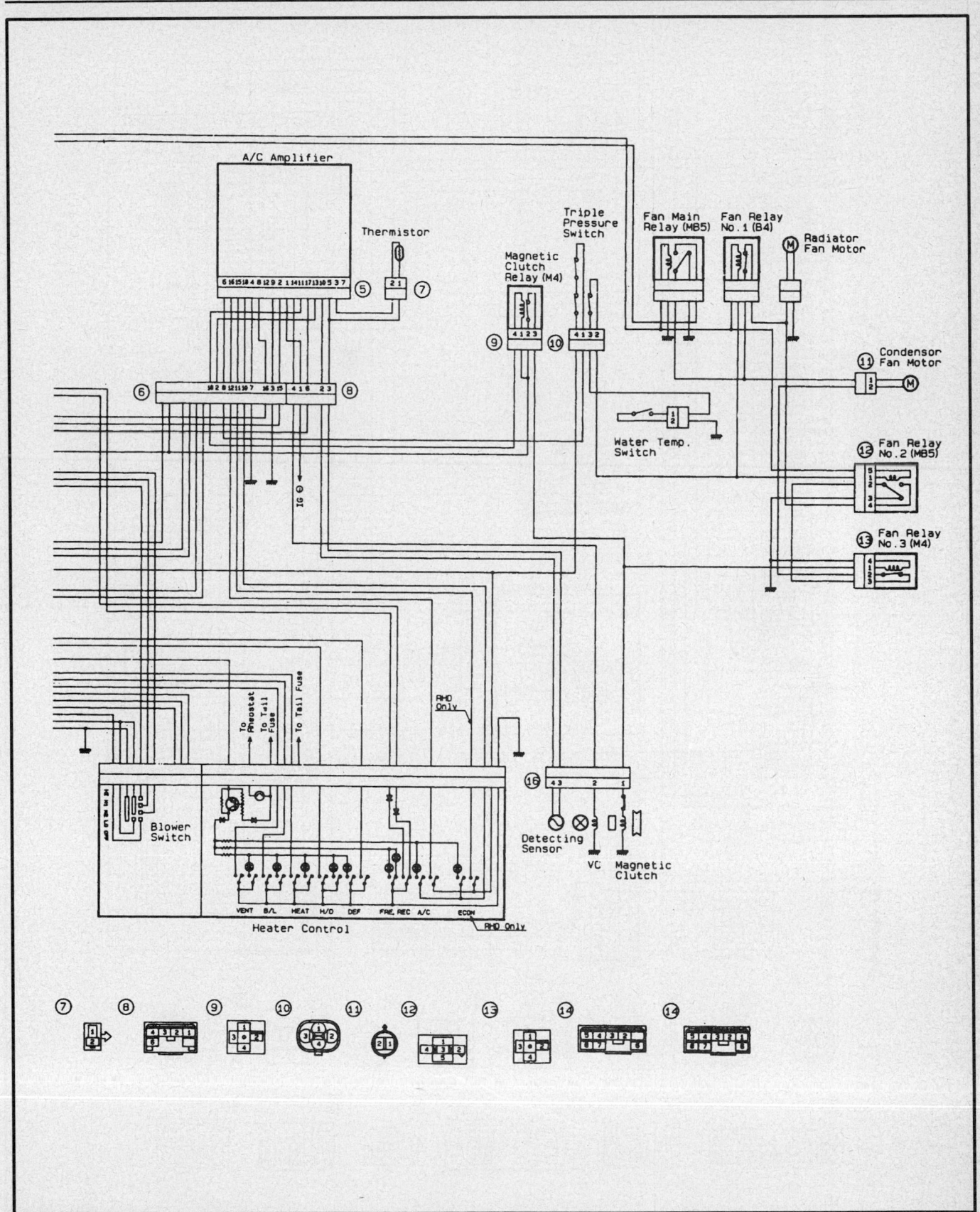

Air conditioning wiring schematic — 1993 Celica with automatic A/C system, Cont'd

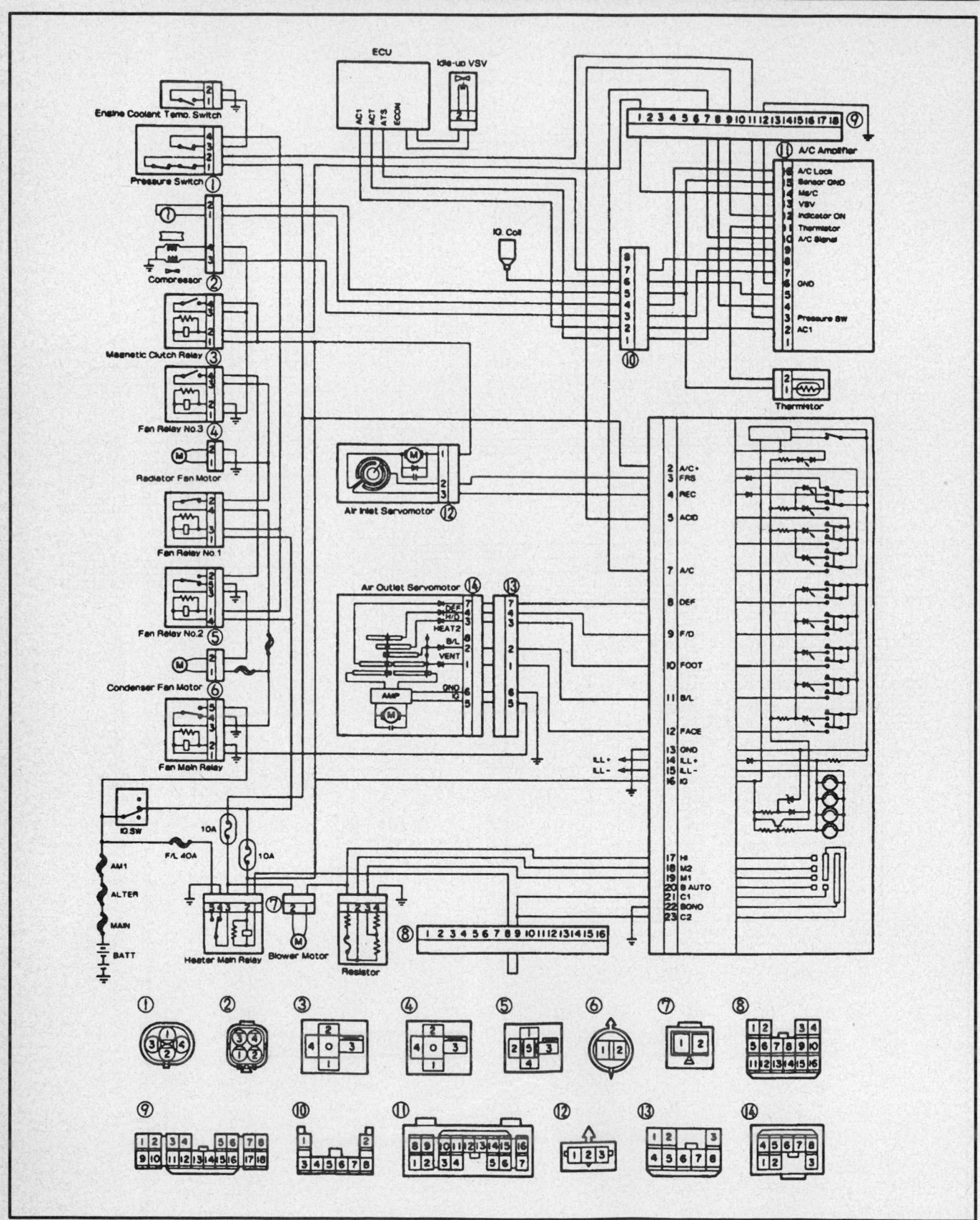

Air conditioning wiring schematic – 1994-95 Celica with 5S-FE engine

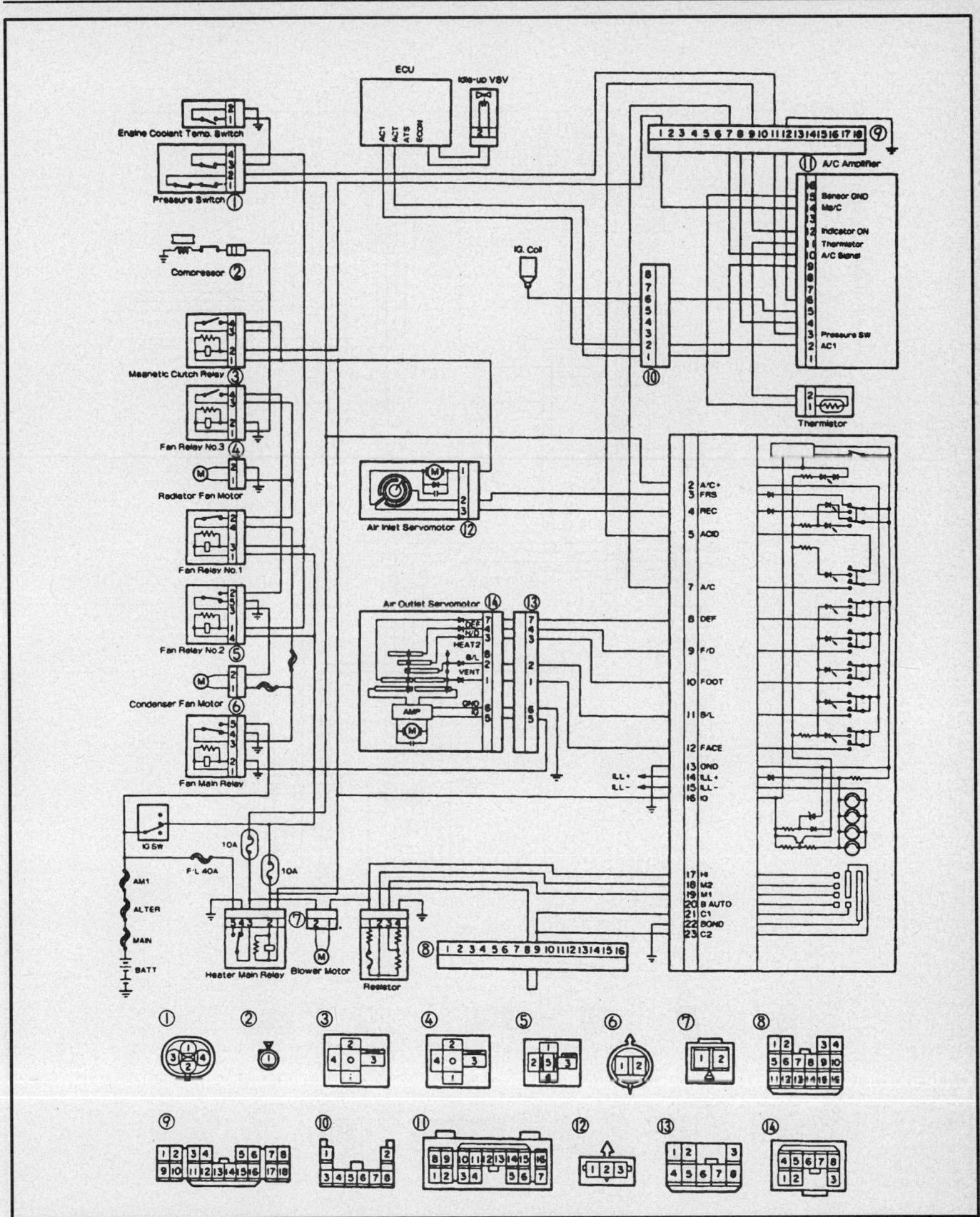

Air conditioning wiring schematic — 1994-95 Celica with 7A-FE engine

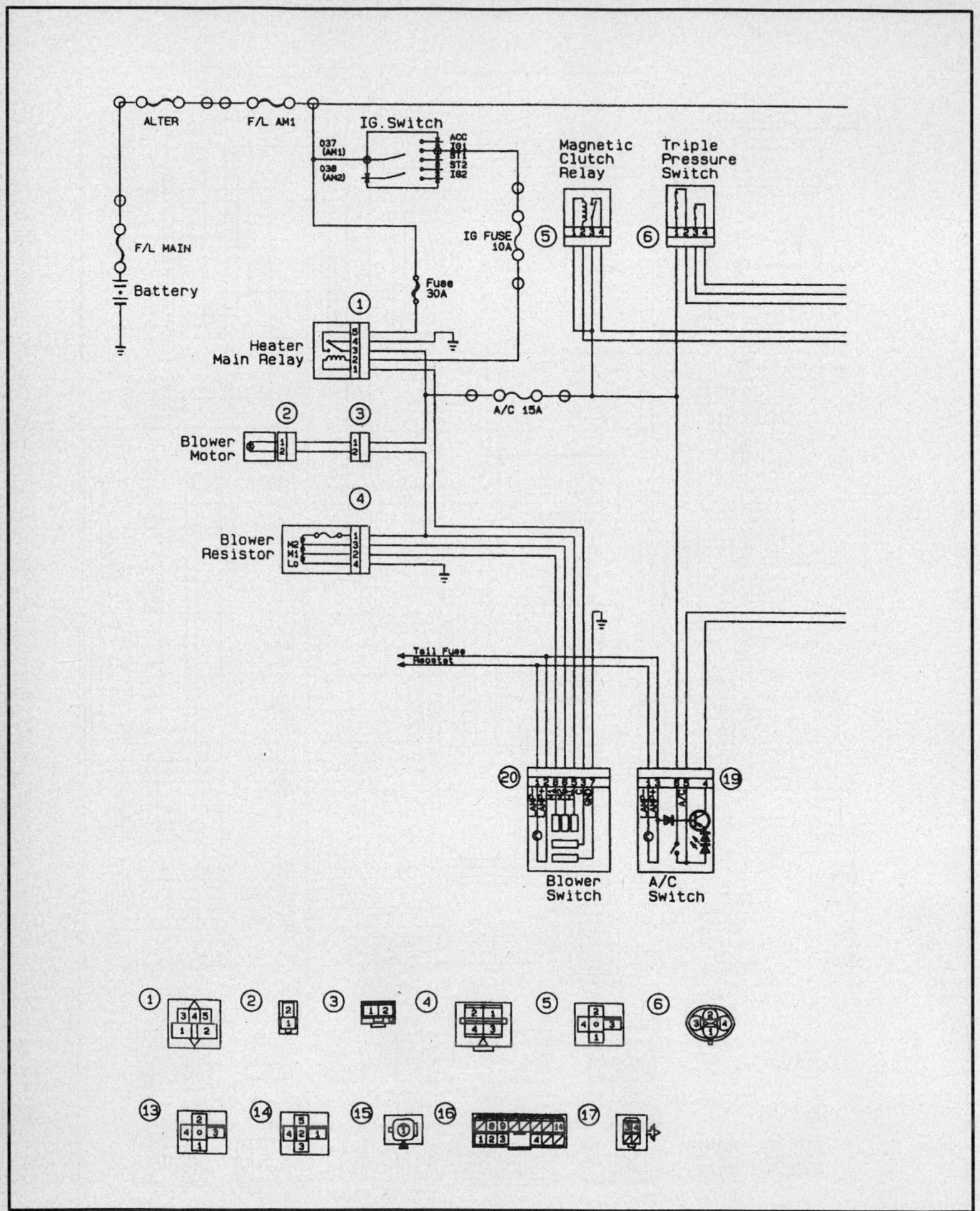

Air conditioning wiring schematic – 1993 Corolla

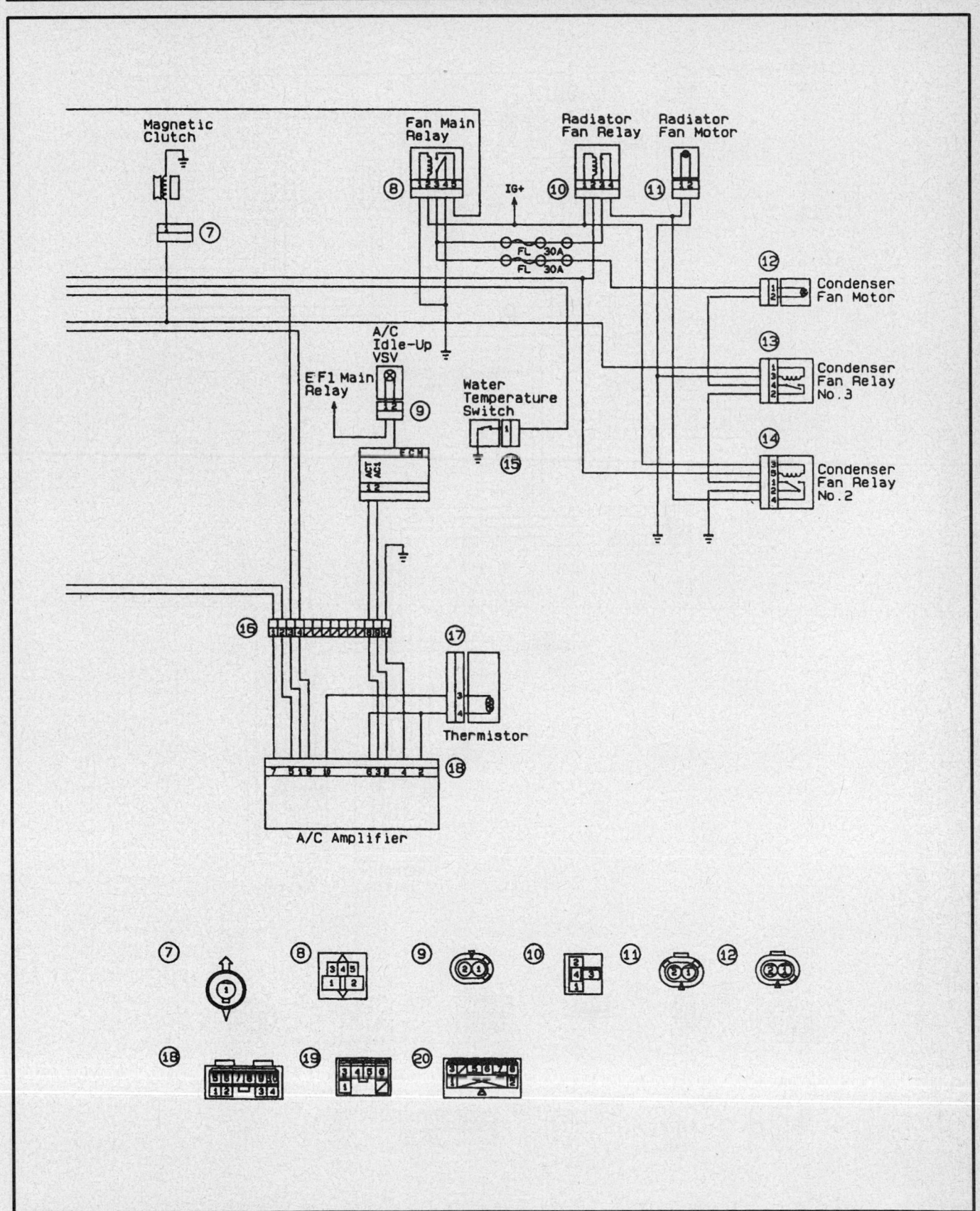

Air conditioning wiring schematic — 1993 Corolla, Cont'd

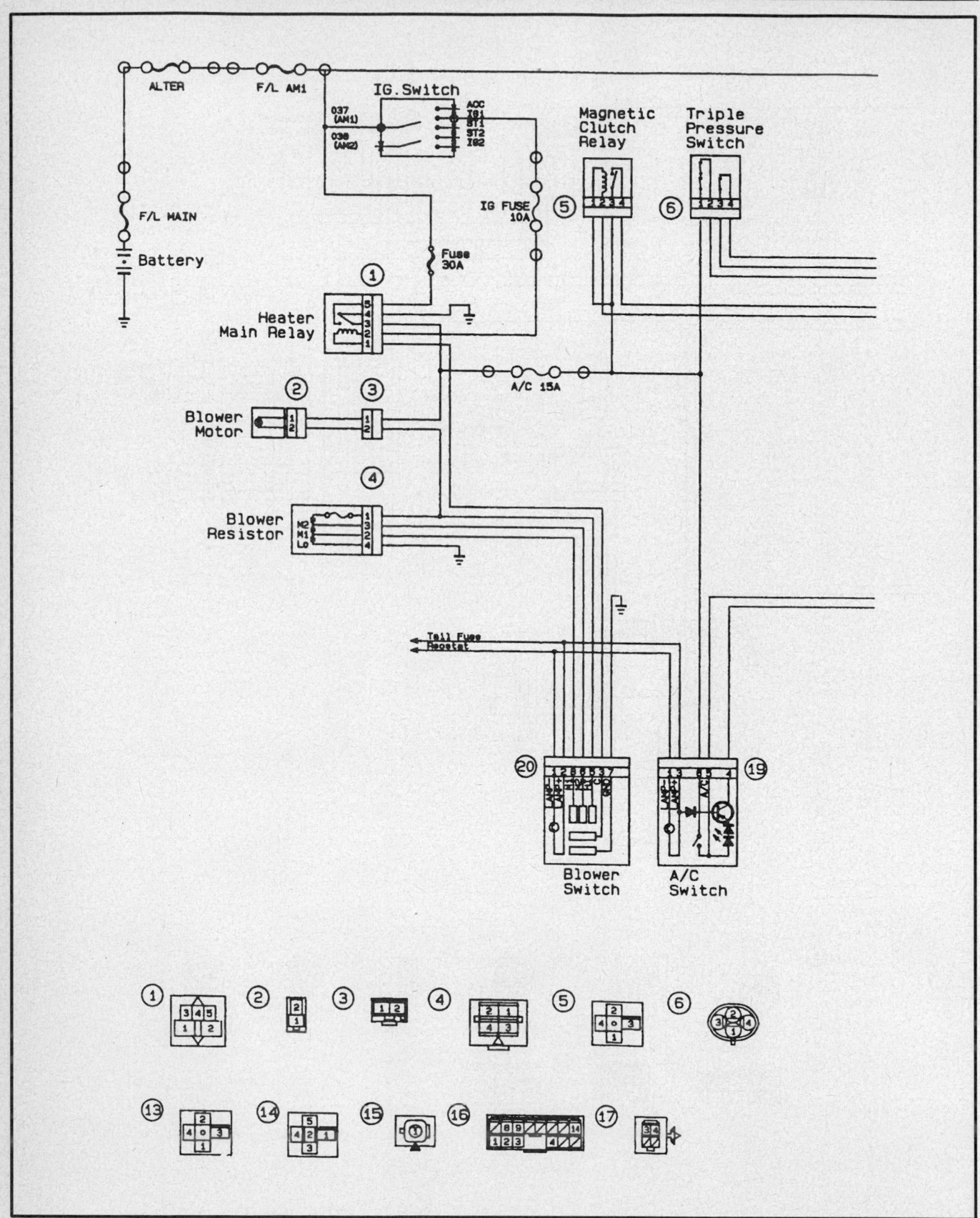

Air conditioning wiring schematic — 1994 Corolla

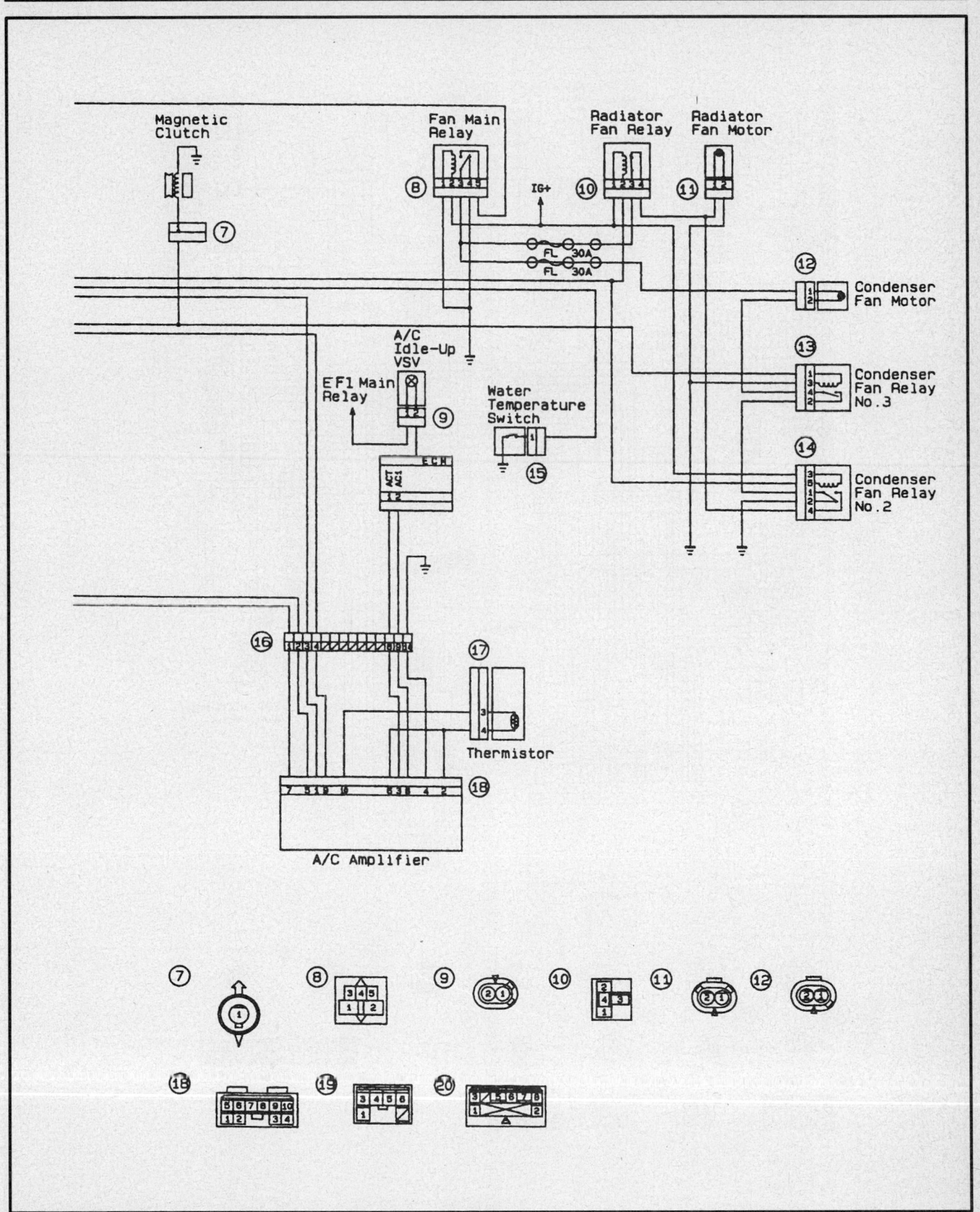

Air conditioning wiring schematic – 1994 Corolla, Cont'd

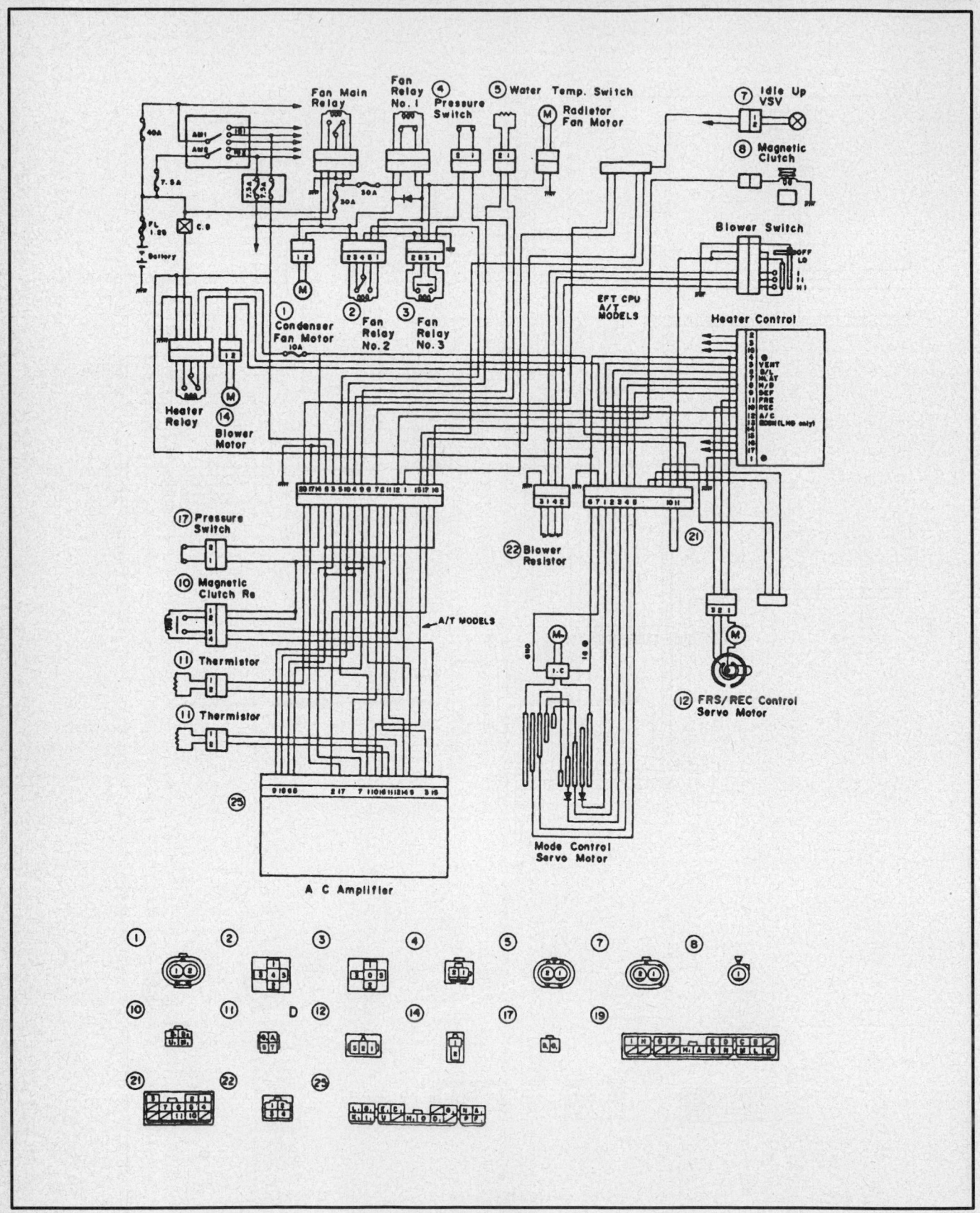

Air conditioning wiring schematic — 1993 MR2 5S-FE engine

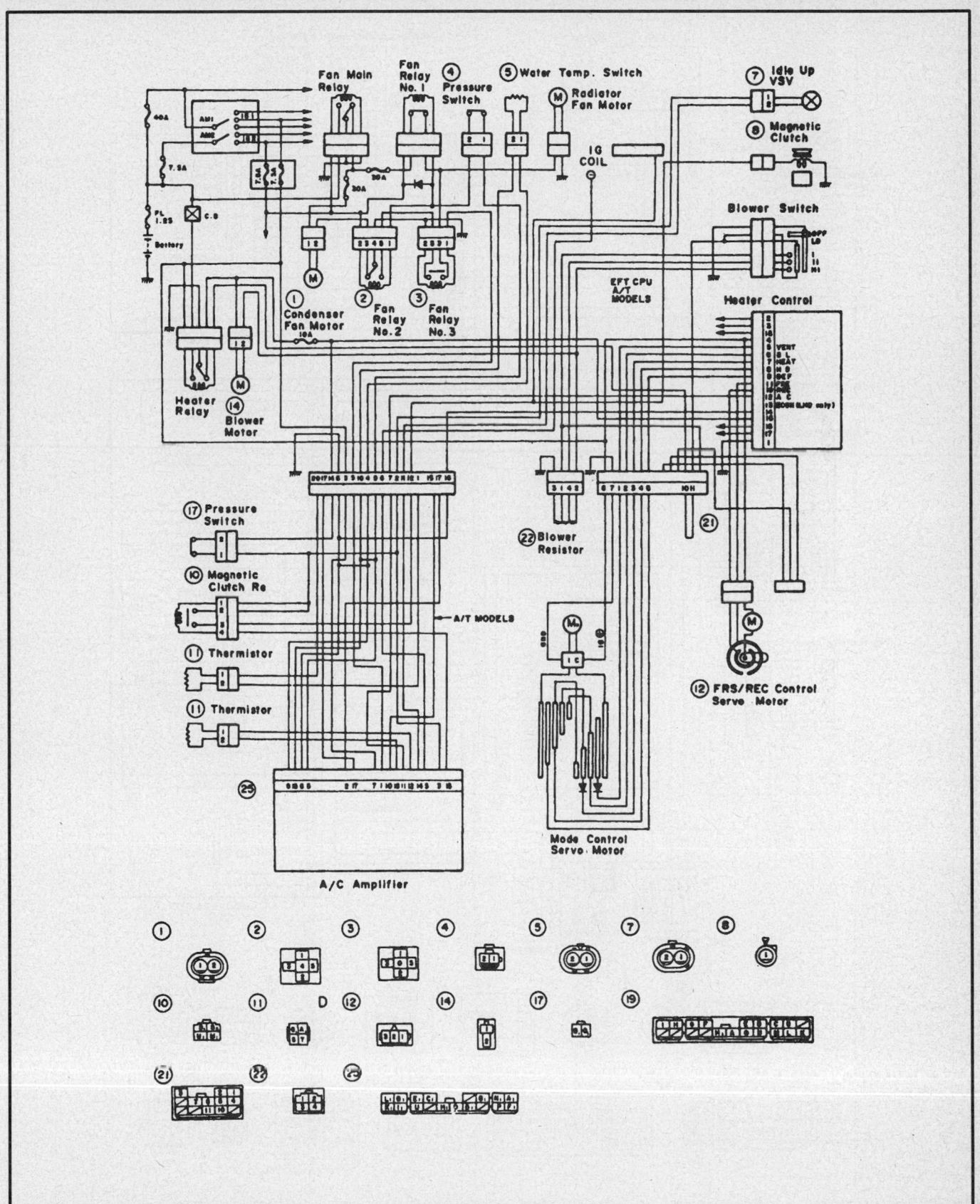

Air conditioning wiring schematic – 1993 MR2 3S-GTE (turbo) engine

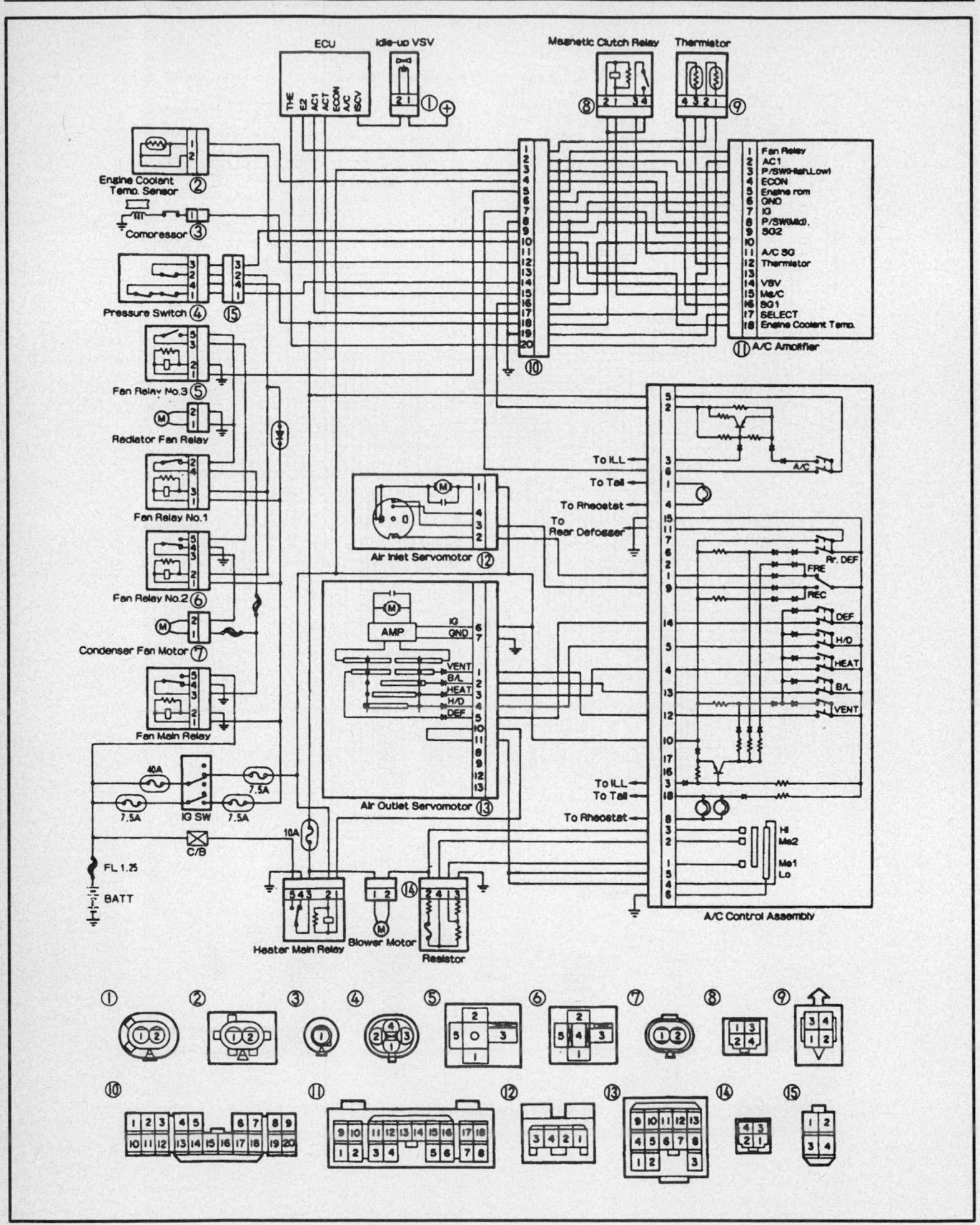

Air conditioning wiring schematic — 1994 MR2 5S-FE

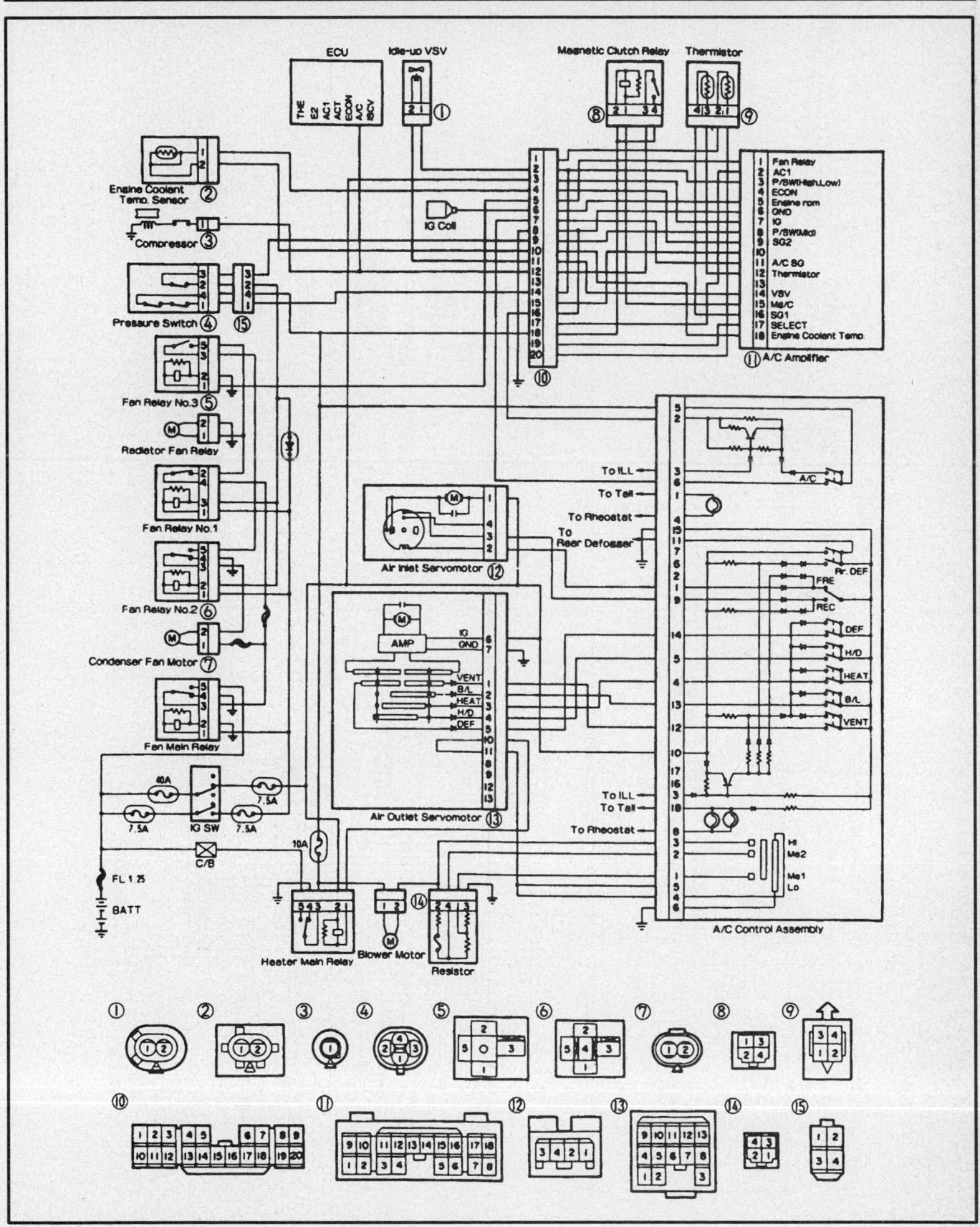

Air conditioning wiring schematic – 1994 MR2 3S-FE

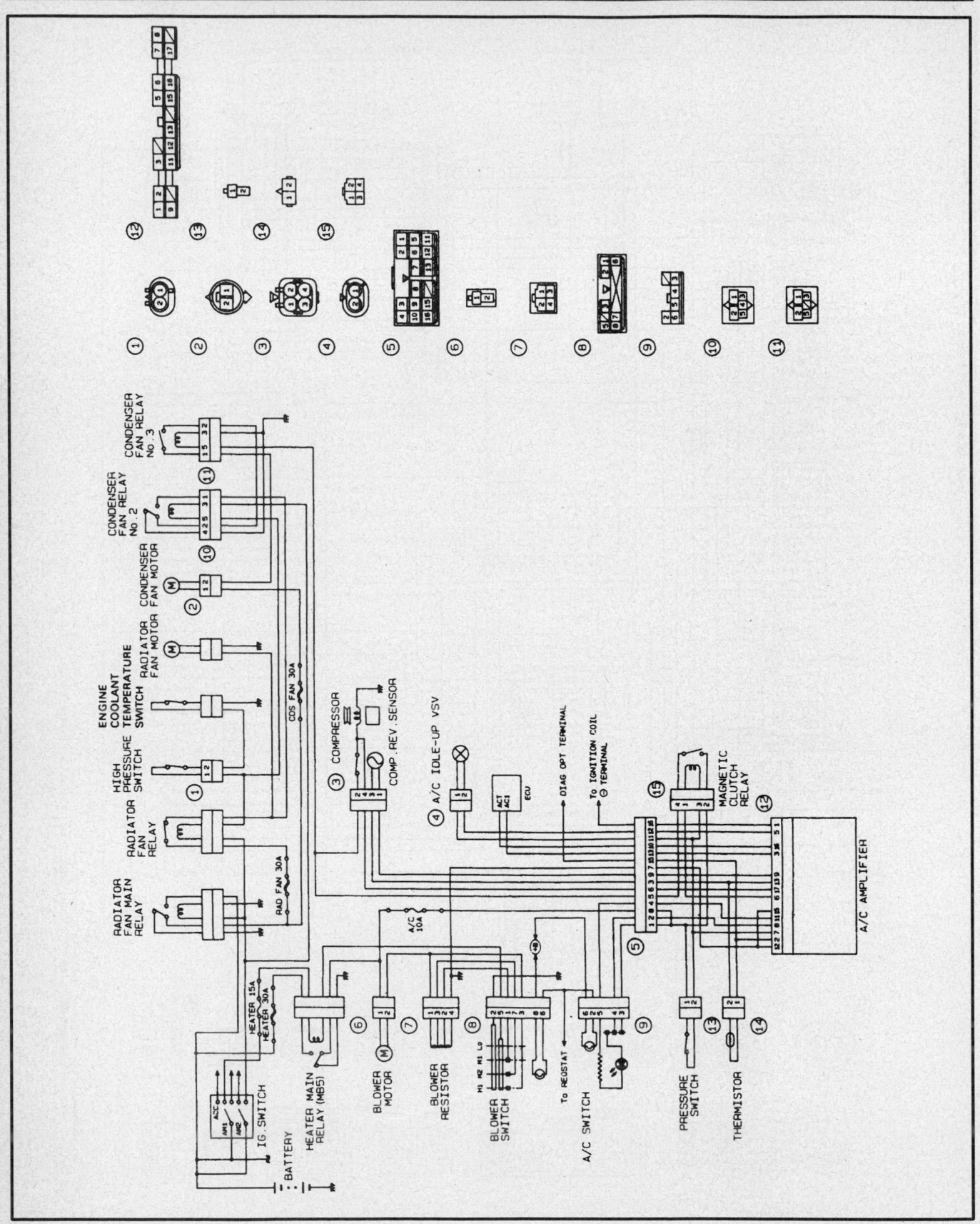

Air conditioning wiring schematic – 1993 Paseo

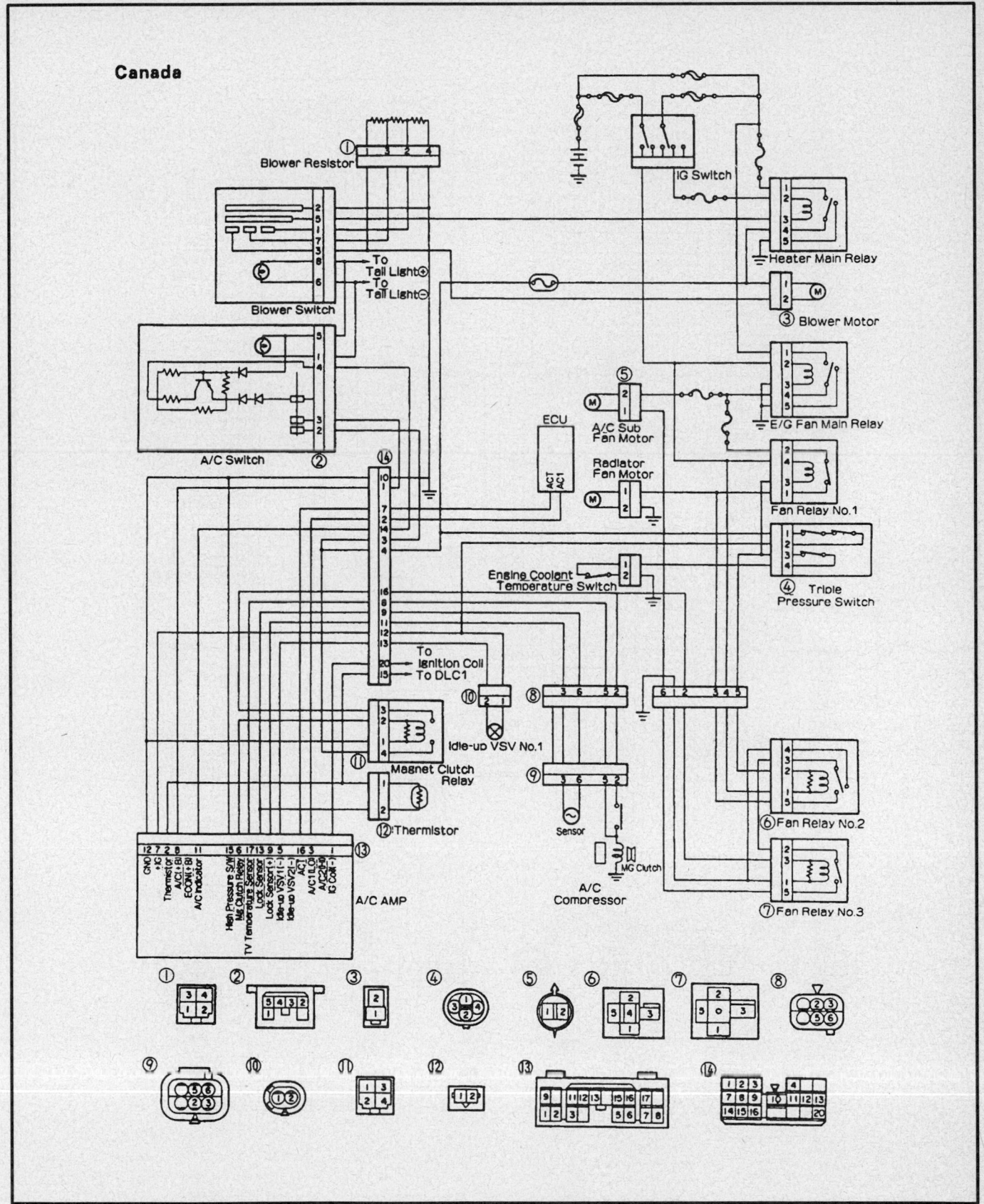

Canada

Air conditioning wiring schematic – 1994 Paseo Canada, 1994 Tercel Canada

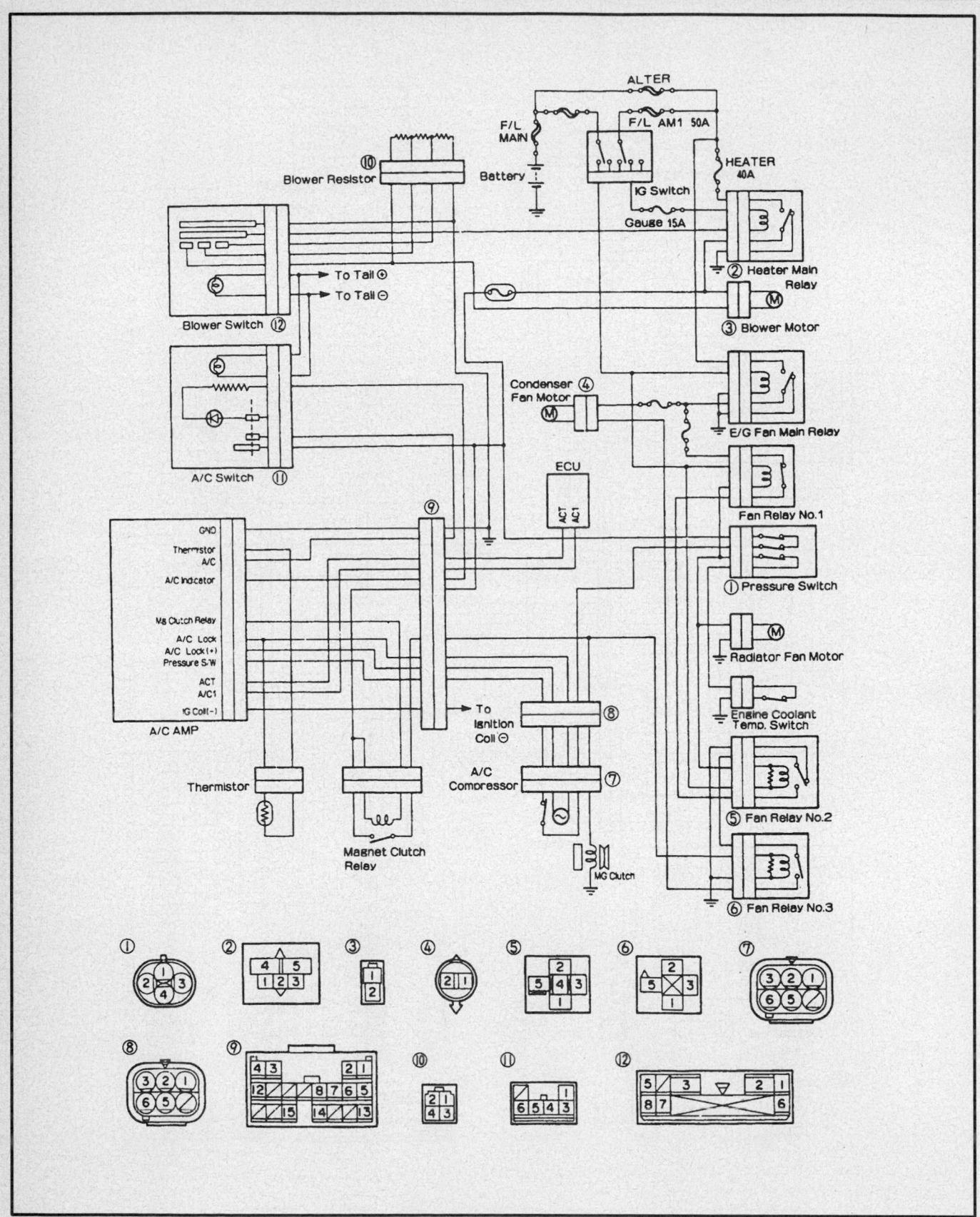

Air conditioning wiring schematic – 1995 Paseo California

SPECIFICATIONS

ENGINE IDENTIFICATION

Year	Model	Engine Displacement Liters (cc)	Engine Series (ID/VIN)	Fuel System	No. of Cylinders	Engine Type
1993	Land Cruiser	4.5 (4477)	1FZ–FE	EFI	6	DOHC
	Pick–Up	2.4 (2366)	22R–E	EFI	4	OHC
	Pick–Up	3.0 (2959)	3VZ–E	EFI	6	OHC
	Previa	2.4 (2366)	2TZ–FE	EFI	4	DOHC
	T100	3.0 (2959)	3VZ–E	EFI	6	OHC
	4Runner	2.4 (2366)	22R–E	EFI	4	OHC
	4Runner	3.0 (2959)	3VZ–E	EFI	6	OHC
1994	Land Cruiser	4.5 (4477)	1FZ–FE	EFI	6	DOHC
	Pick–Up	2.4 (2366)	22R–E	EFI	4	OHC
	Pick–Up	3.0 (2959)	3VZ–E	EFI	6	OHC
	Previa	2.4 (2366)	2TZ–FE	EFI	4	DOHC
	T100	3.0 (2959)	3VZ–E	EFI	6	OHC
	4Runner	2.4 (2366)	22R–E	EFI	4	OHC
	4Runner	3.0 (2959)	3VZ–E	EFI	6	OHC
1995	Land Cruiser	4.5 (4477)	1FZ–FE	EFI	6	DOHC
	Pick–Up	2.4 (2366)	22R–E	EFI	4	OHC
	Pick–Up	3.0 (2959)	3VZ–E	EFI	6	OHC
	Previa	2.4 (2366)	2TZ–FE	EFI	4	DOHC
	T100	3.4 (3378)	3RZ–FE	EFI	6	DOHC
	T100	2.7 (2693)	5VZ–FE	EFI	4	OHC
	4Runner	2.4 (2366)	22R–E	EFI	4	OHC
	4Runner	3.0 (2959)	3VZ–E	EFI	6	OHC

OHC–Overhead Cam   DOHC–Dual Overhead Cams
OHV–Overhead Valves   EFI–Electronic Fuel Injection

REFRIGERANT CAPACITIES

Year	Model	Refrigerant (oz.)	Oil (fl. oz.)	Compressor Type
1993	Land Cruiser	30–33	①	R–12
	Pick–Up	24–29	①	R–12
	Previa	32–35②	①	R–12
	T100	22–24	①	R134a③
	4Runner	27–30	①	R–12
1994	Land Cruiser	28–32	①	R134a③
	Pick–Up	25–28	①	R–12
	Previa	30–34④	①	R134a③
	T100	22–24	①	R134a③
	4Runner	23–26	①	R134a③

REFRIGERANT CAPACITIES

Year	Model	Refrigerant (oz.)	Oil (fl. oz.)	Compressor Type
1995	Land Cruiser	28–32	①	R134a③
	Pick–Up	19–22	①	R134a③
	Previa	30–34④	①	R134a③
	T100	22–24	①	R134a③
	4Runner	23–26	①	R134a③

① Drain and measure amount during compressor removal; replace same amount.
② With rear air conditioning system; 40.5-44.0 oz.
③ Systems with R-134a require special refrigerant oil; do not use or mix with oil used in R-12 systems.
④ With rear air conditioning system: 39-42 oz.

AIR CONDITIONING BELT TENSION

Year	Model	Engine Liters (cc)	Belt Type	Specifications New (lbs.)	Used (lbs.)
1993	Land Cruiser	4.5 (4477)	V	100–150	60–100
	Pick–Up	2.4 (2366)	V & Poly–V	100–150	60–100
	Pick–Up	3.0 (2959)	V & Poly–V	100–150	60–100
	Previa	2.4 (2366)	Poly–V	120–160	100–140
	T100	3.0 (2959)	V	100–150	60–100
	4Runner	2.4 (2366)	V & Poly–V	100–150	60–100
	4Runner	3.0 (2959)	V & Poly–V	100–150	60–100
1994	Land Cruiser	4.5 (4477)	V	100–150	60–100
	Pick–Up	2.4 (2366)	V	100–150	60–100
	Pick–Up	3.0 (2959)	V	100–150	60–100
	Previa	2.4 (2366)	Poly–V	139–191	66–110
	T100	3.0 (2959)	V	100–150	60–100
	4Runner	2.4 (2366)	V	100–150	60–100
	4Runner	3.0 (2959)	V	100–150	60–100
1995	Land Cruiser	4.5 (4477)	V	100–150	60–100
	Pick–Up	2.4 (2366)	V	100–150	60–100
	Pick–Up	3.0 (2959)	V	100–150	60–100
	Previa	2.4 (2366)	Poly–V	139–191	66–110
	T100	2.7 (2693)	Poly–V	135–185	80–120
	T100	3.4 (3378)	Poly–V	135–185	80–120
	4Runner	2.4 (2366)	V	100–150	60–100
	4Runner	3.0 (2959)	V	100–150	60–100

SYSTEM DESCRIPTION

General Information

All vehicles use a blend-air type fresh air system regulates the temperature of the air in the cab. Control operation is by a combination of manual cable control and electrical switches.

On some vehicles, the compressor is equipped with a cut-off solenoid which will momentarily shut off the compressor under certain conditions such as wide-open throttle and low idle speeds.

In order for the compressor clutch to be activated, a series of components must be energized. For example, the ignition switch must be **ON**, the blower switch must be **ON**, also causing the heater relay to switch **ON**. The air conditioning switch must be **ON**, causing the air conditioning amplifier to turn **ON**. The low pressure switch must be **ON**, indicating system pressure is more than 30 psi. The Vacuum Switching Valve (VSV) must go **ON**, resulting in the idle up signal. After all of these condition have been met, the magnetic clutch should turn ON.

The Land Cruiser is optionally equipped with a rear heater system.

Previa vehicles may use both a front and rear heating and cooling system. The Previa is also equipped with an ice box assembly in the center console. This ice box is a separate cooling unit with its own blower, evaporator, expansion valve and thermistor, but it is tied into the same refrigerant lines and electrical circuit as the vehicle's front and rear heater-A/C system.

4Runner also has a heater blower motor and air outlet located in the rear console to provide additional heating to the rear compartment.

NOTE: Some models uses an air conditioning system charged with R-134a, non-CFC refrigerant. This refrigerant cannot be mixed in any amount with R-12, nor can R-12 system refrigerant oil be used in this system. Be careful to inspect and use only the correct refrigerant and refrigerant oil for each system.

Service Valve Locations

Land Cruiser, Pick-Up, and 4Runner service valves are located on the compressor. Previa and T100 service valves are located on the high and low pressure lines near the firewall.

System Discharging

Refrigerant R-12 containing CFCs for automobile air conditioners is believed to cause harm by depleting the ozone layer which helps protect the earth from the ultraviolet rays of the sun.

For this reason, it is necessary to prevent the release of refrigerant to the atmosphere and to use the minimum amount of new refrigerant when servicing the air conditioner. New equipment is available to recover and recycle used refrigerant. It should be used when discharging the system for service, when moisture or air gets into the system or when excess refrigerant must be removed. To prevent release of refrigerant, use charging hoses with stop valves when installing the manifold gauge set to the service valves.

NOTE: Always use a dedicated set of manifold gauges and other equipment to prevent the mixing of R-134a and R-12 refrigerants and oils.

When handling the recovery machine, always follow the manufacturer's recommended practices. After refrigerant recovery, the amount of compressor oil removed must be measured and the same amount added to the system.

System Evacuating

To prevent release and wasteful use of refrigerant, evacuate air with care from the refrigeration system. Do not evacuate before recovering refrigerant in the system.

The use of a refrigerant recovery machine is recommended. After the refrigerant has been recovered, follow the manufacturer's recommendation to pump down the system to evacuate air and moisture. This can often be done without changing any of the hose hookups.

NOTE: The same vacuum pump can be used for both R-12 and R-134a systems, by using the correct adapters for hook-up.

System Flushing

System flushing is recommended if there has been a failure of the compressor. Metal chips may be distributed through the system which should be removed by flushing.

Use care not to allow refrigerant to escape into the atmosphere. The use of a refrigerant recovery machine is recommended. After the refrigerant has been recovered, follow the manufacturer's recommendation to evacuate the system, flush it and prepare the system to receive a fresh charge of refrigerant and oil. Always use a proper refrigerant suitable for flushing and for the type of ystem being flushed. In most cases of compressor failure, the receiver must also be replaced.

System Charging

When charging the system, use caution when handling the refrigerant and all hose connections. Use care not to allow refrigerant to escape into the atmosphere. If there is not enough refrigerant gas in the system, there likely won't be enough oil to properly lubricate the compressor, leading to unit burnout. Always make sure the system has sufficient oil.

NOTE: Take precautions to ensure using proper equipment, refrigerant and refrigerant oil dedicated to the refrigerant system type.

If the valve on the high pressure side is opened, refrigerant flows in the reverse direction and on some systems, could cause the service can to rupture. Open and close the valve on the low pressure side only.

Do not overfill the system with refrigerant. This can cause inadequate cooling, poor fuel economy, engine overheating, etc. Most vehicles have a sight glass somewhere in the system, usually on or near the receiver. This helps determine if the refrigerant charge is sufficient.

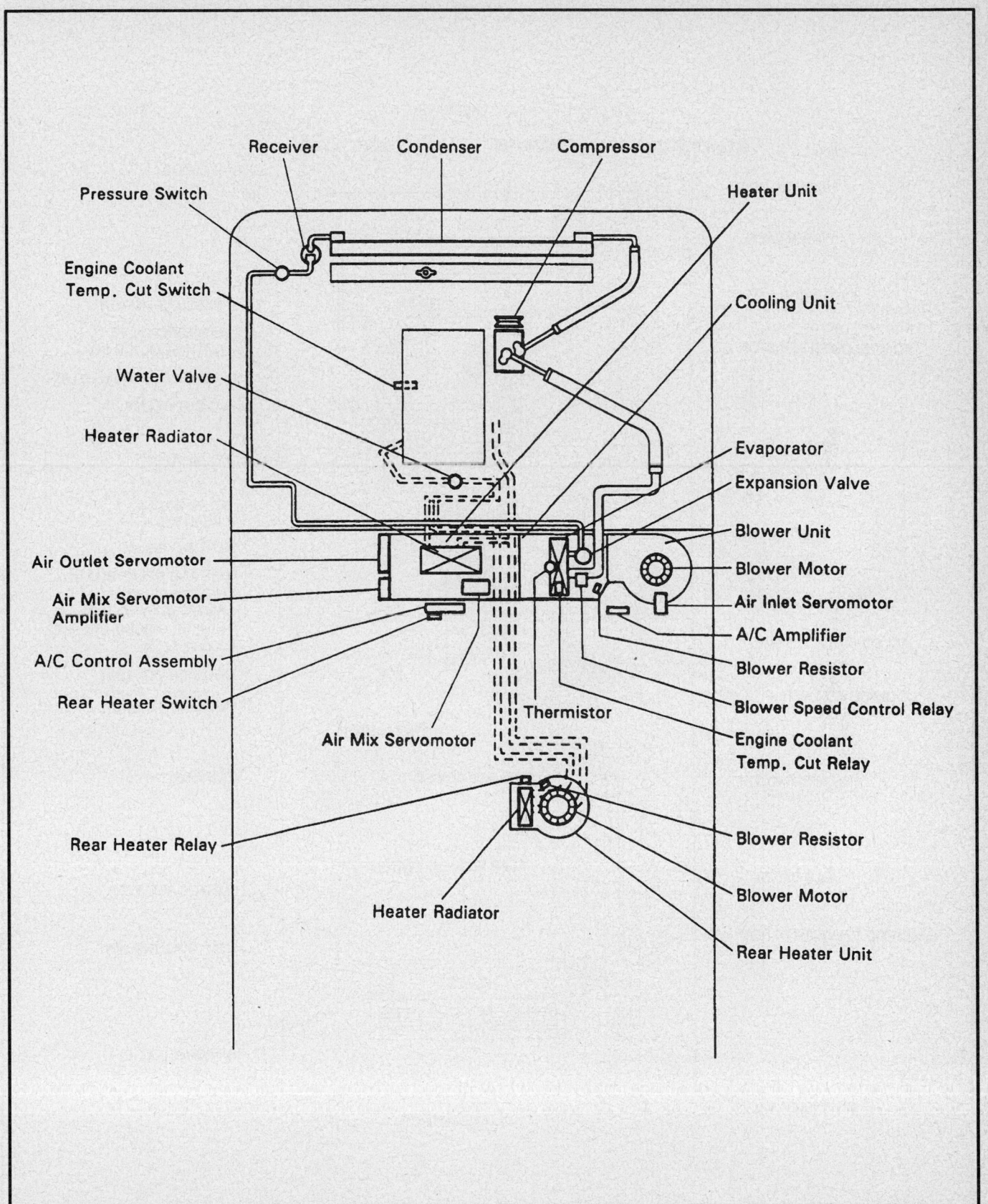

Receiver

Condenser

Compressor

Pressure Switch

Heater Unit

Engine Coolant
Temp. Cut Switch

Cooling Unit

Water Valve

Heater Radiator

Evaporator

Expansion Valve

Blower Unit

Air Outlet Servomotor

Blower Motor

Air Mix Servomotor
Amplifier

Air Inlet Servomotor

A/C Amplifier

A/C Control Assembly

Blower Resistor

Rear Heater Switch

Blower Speed Control Relay

Engine Coolant
Temp. Cut Relay

Air Mix Servomotor

Thermistor

Rear Heater Relay

Blower Resistor

Blower Motor

Heater Radiator

Rear Heater Unit

Land Cruiser heater–A/C system components

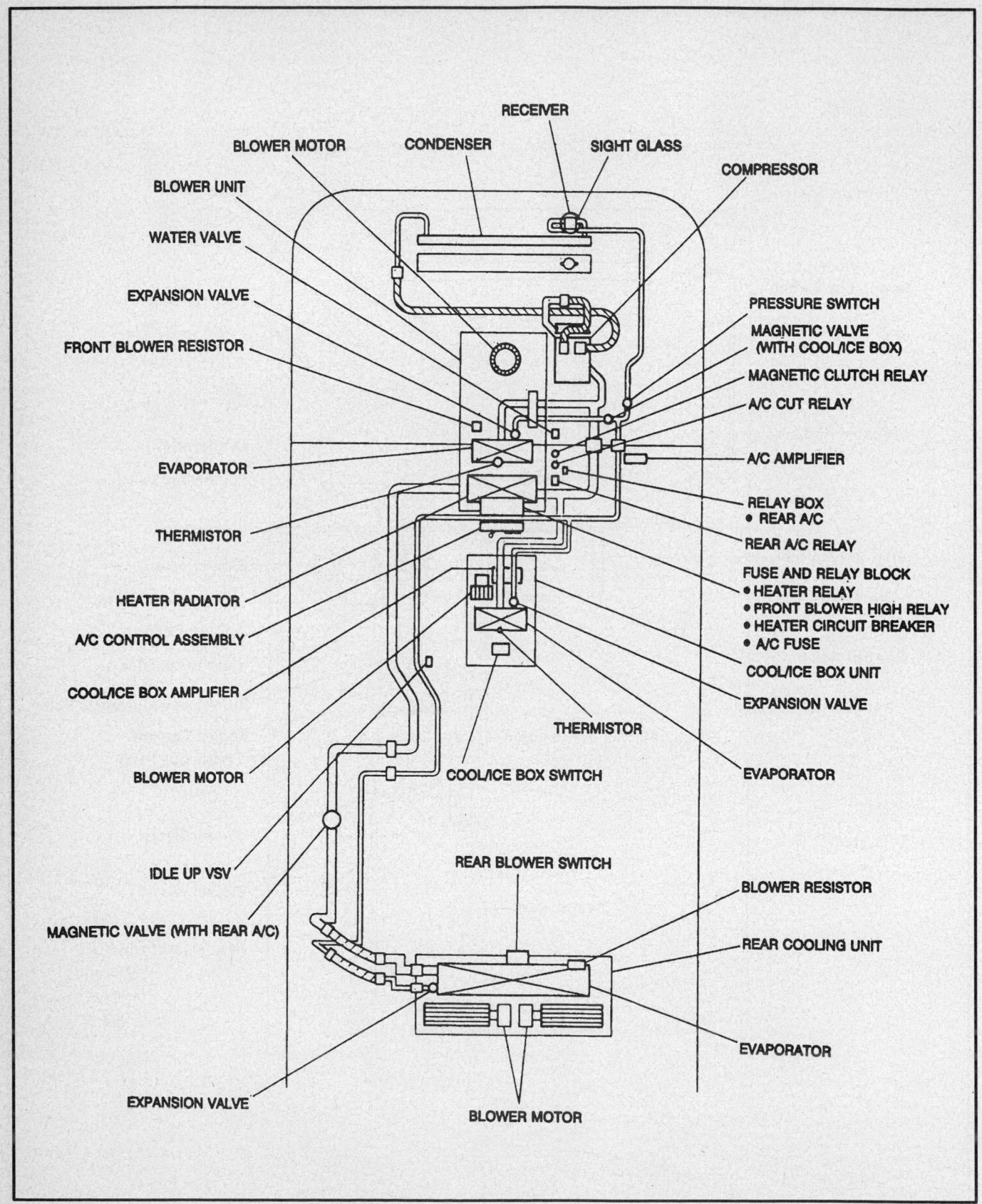

Previa heater–A/C components with rear system

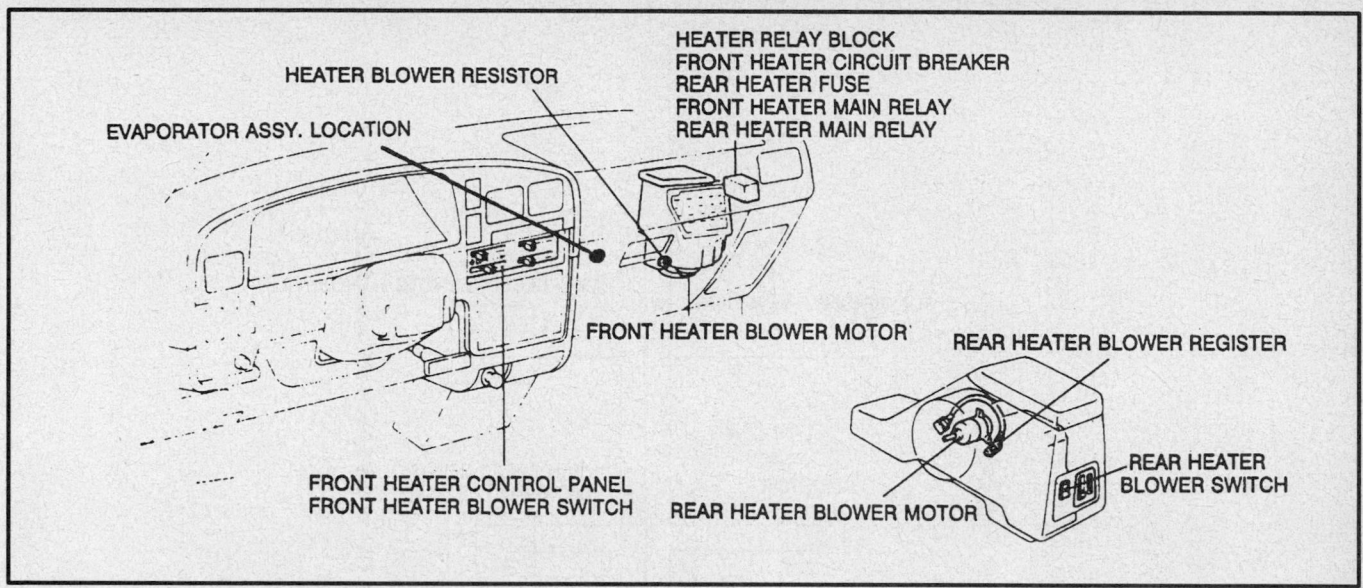

4Runner—A/C system with rear heater

SYSTEM COMPONENTS

Radiator

REMOVAL AND INSTALLATION

1. Disconnect the negative battery cable. Properly drain the cooling system.
2. Perform the following specific operations:
   ● On Land Cruiser remove the grille (5 screws and clip), reservoir hose and tank, and battery with case.
   ● On Pick-Up and 4Runner, remove the air intake duct (22R- E engine), the fan shrouds (with A/C) and the engine under cover.
   ● On Previa, remove the air intake duct and the engine under cover.
   ● On T100, remove the engine under cover.
3. Disconnect the radiator hoses. Disconnect the turbocharger water hose, if equipped.
4. Disconnect the automatic transmission cooling lines, if equipped. Be prepared to catch some transmission fluid that will likely run out.
5. On some models, it may be necessary to remove the power steering and air conditioning belts, the fan with fluid coupler and water pump pulley.
6. Remove the radiator assembly.
To install:
7. Installation is the reverse of the removal procedure.
8. Refill cooling system, warm engine, check fluid level at external reservoir.

COOLING SYSTEM BLEEDING & CHECKING

1. Coolant level should be checked at the remote reservoir. Full and Low level indicators are on the reservoir tank.
2. Coolant should be added to the reservoir. Never open the radiator cap when the system is hot.
3. After the engine has been idling for at least 10 minutes with the heater temperature control fully open, add coolant to the reservoir tank up to the **FULL** level. Securely tighten the reservoir tank cap.
4. Run the engine at about 2000–3000 rpm for 5 minutes, then stop the engine.
5. After the coolant level drops, remove the reservoir tank cap and add coolant up to the **FULL** mark. Securely tighten the reservoir cap. Start the engine and check for leaks.

Cooling Fan

TESTING

4Runner

The 4Runner uses a condenser fan, two relays a resistor and a high pressure (on the line near the receiver/drier) to assist system cooling by activating the fan when high pressure is sensed and/or the A/C switch is **ON**. The fan operates at two speeds under the conditions as shown in the chart.

CONDENSER FAN OPERATING CHART (4RUNNER)

A/C Switch	Magnetic Clutch	Refrigerant Pressure	Fan Motor Speed
OFF or ON	OFF	Less than approx. 178 psi,	Off
		More than approx. 220 psi,	Off
ON	ON	Less than approx. 178 psi	Low
		More than approx. 220 psi	High

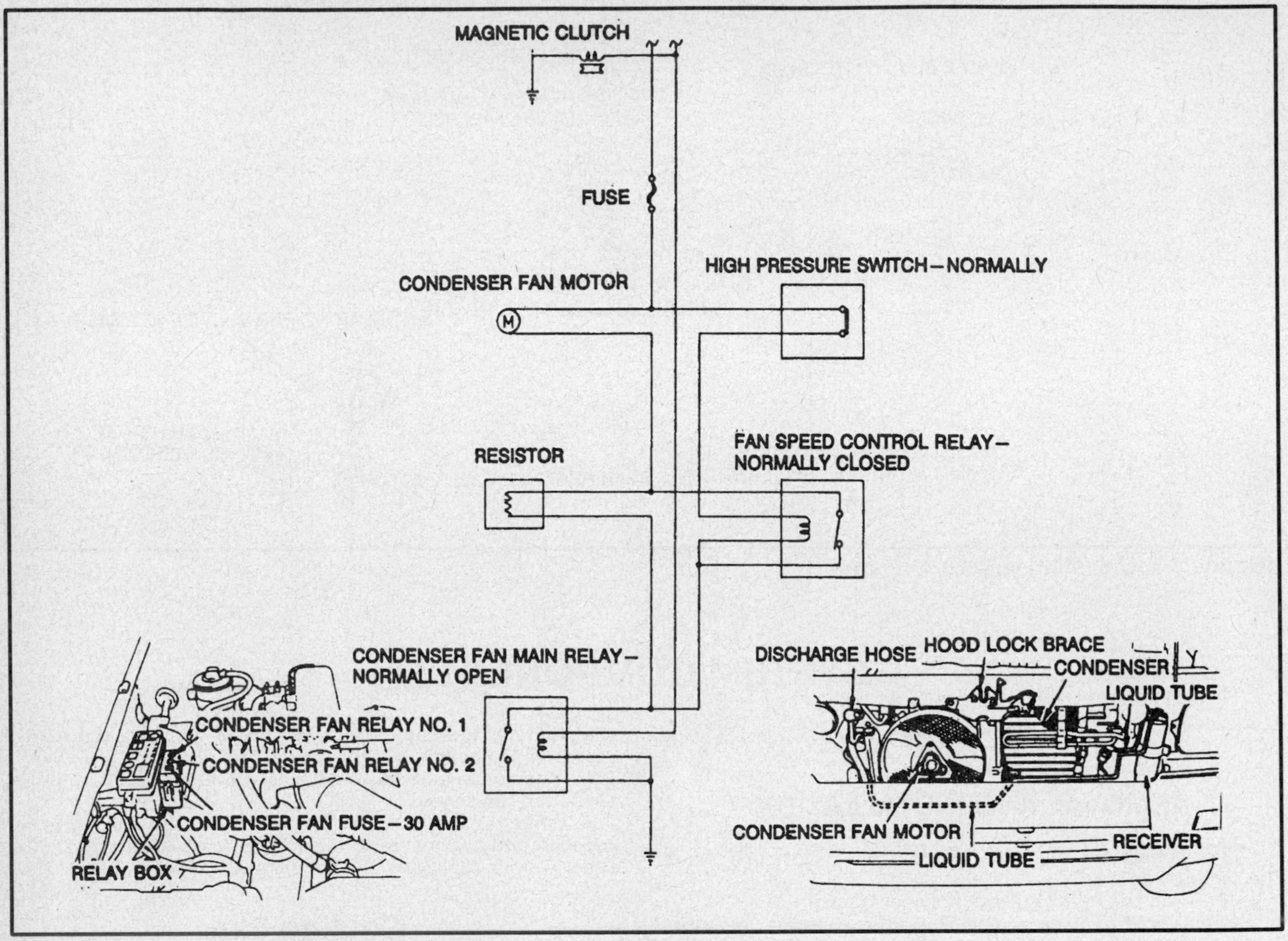

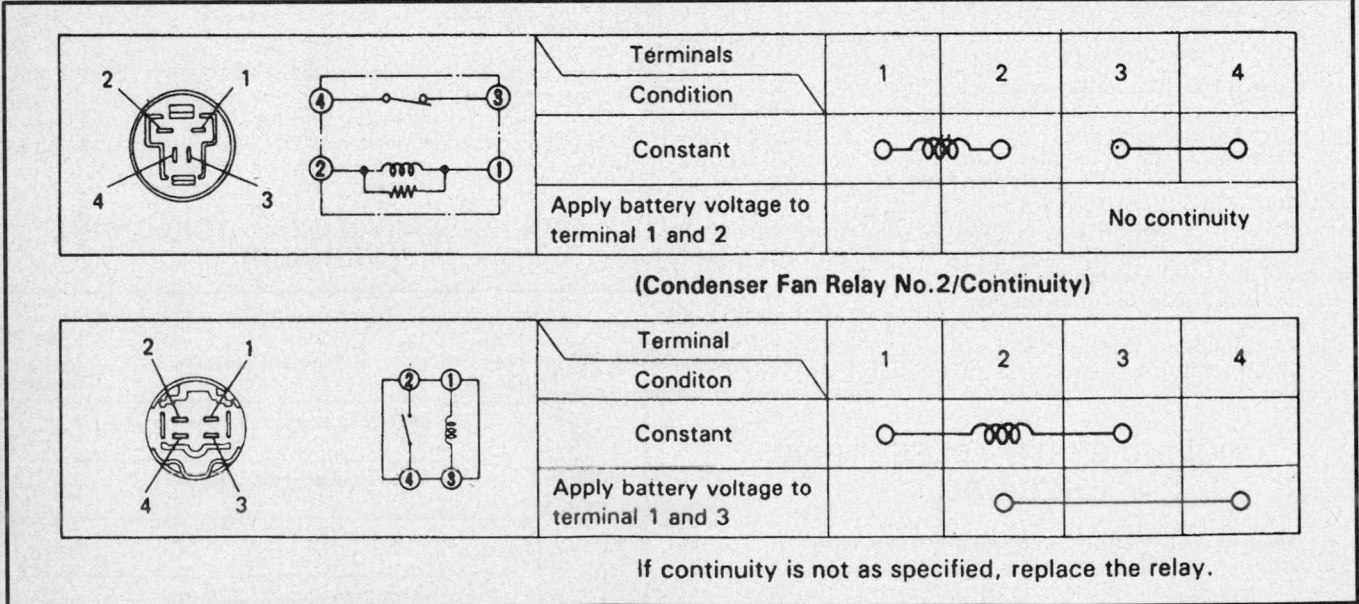

4Runner condenser fan component location, and wiring circuit

MAGNETIC CLUTCH

FUSE

CONDENSER FAN MOTOR   HIGH PRESSURE SWITCH—NORMALLY

RESISTOR   FAN SPEED CONTROL RELAY—
NORMALLY CLOSED

CONDENSER FAN MAIN RELAY—
NORMALLY OPEN

CONDENSER FAN RELAY NO. 1
CONDENSER FAN RELAY NO. 2
CONDENSER FAN FUSE—30 AMP
RELAY BOX

DISCHARGE HOSE HOOD LOCK BRACE
CONDENSER
LIQUID TUBE

CONDENSER FAN MOTOR   RECEIVER
LIQUID TUBE

Terminals Condition	1	2	3	4
Constant	○—ⱳⱳ—○		○——○	
Apply battery voltage to terminal 1 and 2			No continuity	

(Condenser Fan Relay No.2/Continuity)

Terminal Conditon	1	2	3	4
Constant	○	○—ⱳⱳ—○		
Apply battery voltage to terminal 1 and 3		○——○		

If continuity is not as specified, replace the relay.

4Runner condenser fan relay schematic — 1993

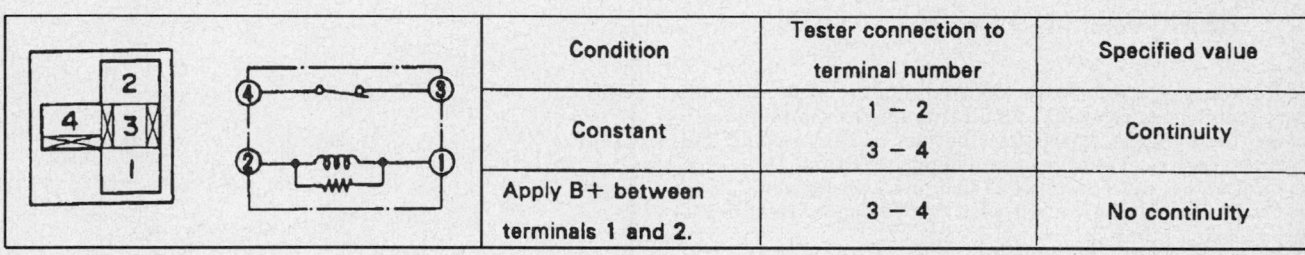

		Condition	Tester connection to terminal number	Specified value
		Constant	1 − 2 3 − 4	Continuity
		Apply B+ between terminals 1 and 2.	3 − 4	No continuity

		Condition	Tester connection to terminal number	Specified value
		Constant	1 − 2	Continuity
		Apply B+ between terminals 1 and 2.	3 − 5	Continuity

4Runner condenser fan relay schematic — 1994−95

CONDENSER FAN MOTOR

1. Disconnect the negative battery cable.
2. Disconnect the electric plug from the fan motor.
3. Apply battery voltage to the connector on the fan motor. The motor should run smoothly, drawing no more than 8.0 - 0.7 amps.
4. If operation is not as specified, replace the fan motor.

CONDENSER FAN MOTOR RESISTOR

1. To check the resistor, use an ohmmeter. It should be 0.6–0.06 ohm at room temperature.
2. If out of specification, replace the resistor.

CONDENSER FAN HIGH PRESSURE SWITCH

1. Disconnect the negative battery cable.
2. Disconnect the connector from the high pressure switch and install a continuity tester at the switch terminals.
3. Check for continuity when the fan is on and no continuity with fan off.
4. Install a manifold gauge set. Reconnect the negative battery cable and operate the system. The fan should be OFF when the refrigerant pressure is below 178 psi or over 220 psi, and the A/C control switch is either OFF or ON.
5. The fan should be ON when the refrigerant pressure is below approximately 178 psi, and both the magnetic clutch and air conditioning switch are ON. The fan should run at LOW speed. When the refrigerant pressure is above 220 psi, and both the magnetic clutch and air conditioning switch are ON, the fan should run at HIGH speed.
6. If readings are not as specified, replace the high pressure switch after disconnecting the negative battery terminal, properly discharging the air conditioning system. Install new switch, evacuate and recharge the system.
7. Retest switch operation. Reconnect the negative battery cable and check system operation.

Condenser

REMOVAL AND INSTALLATION

1. Properly discharge the refrigeration system using a refrigerant recovery system.
2. Remove the following specific items:
   ● On Land Cruiser, remove the hood lock brace and center brace.
   ● On Pick-Up, remove the front grille and hood lock brace.
   ● On T100, remove the grille, horn, hood lock and center brace.
   ● On 4Runner, remove the clearance lights, grille, hood lock brace and condenser fan motor.
3. On Pick-Up and Previa, disconnect the liquid line from the receiver/drier. On all models, disconnect the lines to the condenser and immediately cap all openings to minimize system contamination.
4. Remove the retaining bolts and remove the condenser from the vehicle. Be careful not to damage the radiator or the condenser fins.

To install:

5. Installation is the reverse of the removal procedure. Evacuate, charge and test the system. If a new condenser has been used, additional refrigerant oil must be added:1.4–1.7 oz. on all models except 1993 4Runner and 1995 Land Cruiser; 0.7 oz. on 1993 4Runner and 1.4 oz. on 1995 Land Cruiser.

NOTE: Be sure to utilize equipment, refrigerant and oil dedicated to the refrigerant system type.

Compressor

REMOVAL AND INSTALLATION

1. Run engine at idle with air conditioning on for 10 minutes to stabilize refrigerant and oil throughout the system.
2. Shut off engine. Disconnect battery negative cable and detach the electrical lead from the magnetic clutch.
3. On Land Cruiser, remove the engine under cover.
4. On Pick-Up and 4Runner with the V6 engine remove the power steering pump.
5. Properly discharge the refrigeration system using a refrigerant recovery system.
6. Disconnect the 2 hoses from the compressor service valves and cap immediately to keep dirt and moisture out of the rest of the system.
7. Remove the fan shroud (Pick-Up and 4Runner), remove the compressor drive belt and remove the compressor mounting bolts. Lift the compressor from the vehicle.
To install:
8. Installation is the reverse of the removal procedure. Evacuate, charge and test the system. If a new compressor has been used, additional refrigerant oil must be added, the same amount as drained and measured from the old compressor.

NOTE: Be sure to utilize equipment, refrigerant and oil dedicated to the refrigerant system type.

Receiver/Drier

REMOVAL AND INSTALLATION

1. Disconnect the negative battery cable. Properly discharge the air conditioning system using a refrigerant recovery system.
2. Remove the grille on T100 and the grille and clearance lights 4Runner.
3. Disconnect and cap the 2 hoses from the receiver/drier.
4. Remove the receiver from the vehicle.
To install:
5. Installation is the reverse of the removal procedure. Evacuate, charge and test the system. If a new receiver has been used, additional refrigerant oil must be added, generally approximately 3/4 ounce.

NOTE: Be sure to utilize equipment, refrigerant and oil dedicated to the refrigerant system type.

Expansion Valve

REMOVAL AND INSTALLATION

1. The expansion valve is located inside the evaporator housing. The evaporator assembly must be removed to access the expansion valve. Follow procedure outlined in this article.
2. Remove the expansion valve by disconnecting the liquid tube from the inlet fitting of the valve. Remove the packing and heat sensing bulb.

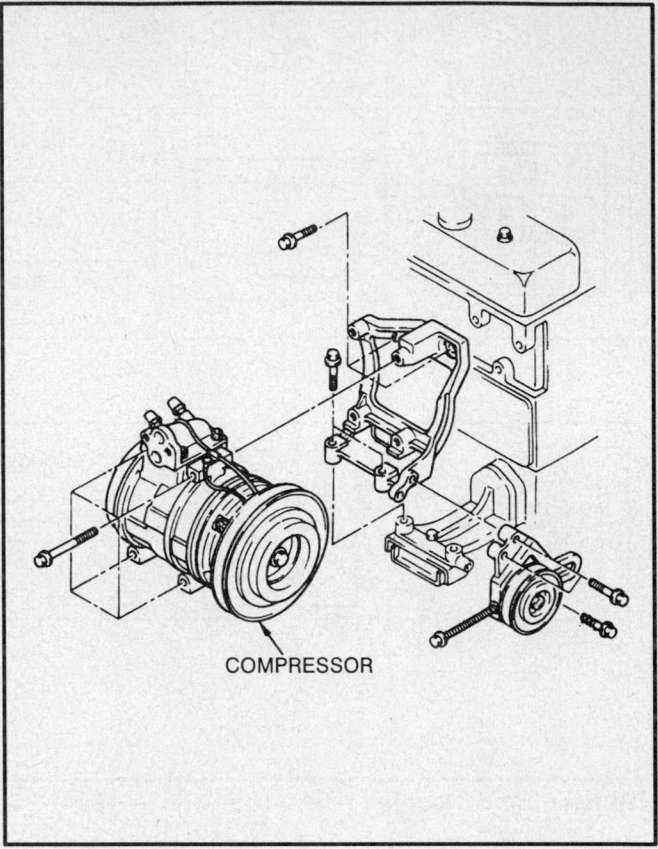

Air conditioning compressor installation—Land Cruiser shown

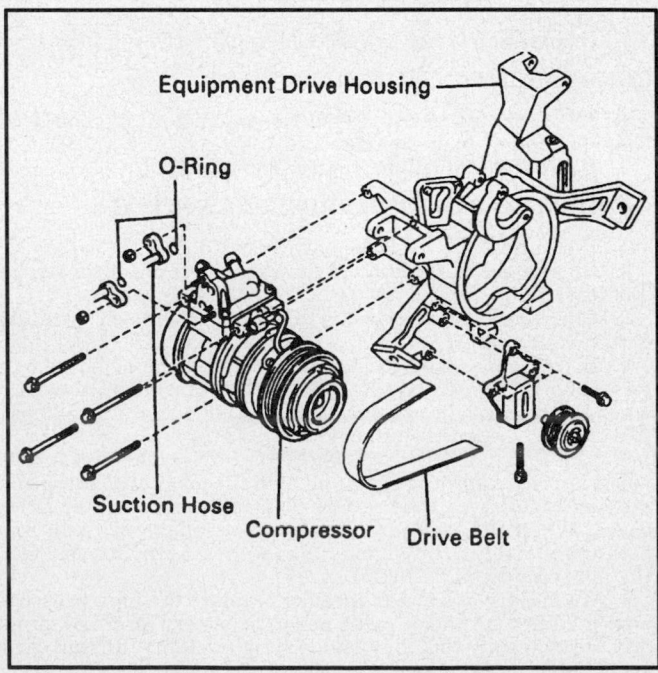

Air conditioning compressor installation—Previa

To install:

3. Installation is the reverse of the removal procedure. Make sure the expansion valve and thermistor are in the proper places for accurate heat sensing. Check electrical contacts for corrosion.

4. Evacuate, charge and test the system. If a new evaporator has been used, additional refrigerant oil must be added, about 3/4 ounce.

NOTE: Be sure to utilize equipment, refrigerant and oil dedicated to the refrigerant system type.

Blower Motor

REMOVAL AND INSTALLATION

Land Cruiser

1. Disconnect the negative battery cable. Properly discharge the air conditioning system, using recovery equipment.

2. The instrument panel requires removal. Remove the steering wheel. Mask off the windshield pillars above the panel for protection.

3. Remove the steering column covers (5 screws). Detach the hood and fuel door release handles from the panel.

4. Remove the lower panel beneath the steering column (4 screws). Remove the heater duct in this area.

5. Remove the combination switch from the steering column, detaching the electrical connectors. Remove the turn signal bracket.

6. Pull off the choke knob end (manual transmission), remove the ashtray, and remove the instrument cluster trim panel (6 screws). Remove the instrument cluster, disconnecting speedometer and gauge connections.

7. Pull the knobs off the climate control panel and remove the 4 retaining screws. Pull the control panel out and support it out of the way.

8. Remove the radio assembly, disconnecting the wiring and cable.

9. Remove the front console box (4 screws).

10. Remove the speaker grille and speaker from the panel. Remove the glove box (2 screws below the door).

11. Remove 2 retaining screws, disconnect the wiring, and take out the ECU assembly.

12. Remove 10 bolts and 6 screws securing the instrument panel and remove the panel from the vehicle.

13. Detach the connectors and retaining bolts and lower the steering column to the floor.

14. Remove the instrument panel reinforcement (2 screws at each end).

15. Remove the evaporator assembly, following procedures described in this article.

16. Detach the connector from the blower motor and the connector from the air inlet servo motor. Remove the bolt and 2 nuts holding the blower unit and remove it from the vehicle.

To install:

17. Reinstall the blower motor assembly. Follow procedures to properly install the evaporator assembly.

18. Install the instrument panel reinforcement, raise and attach the steering column and connectors.

19. Position and secure the instrument panel.

20. Install the ECU, then the glove box and speaker.

21. Install the console box, then replace the radio and climate control panel.

22. Install the instrument cluster, trim, knobs, panels and other items as removed.

23. Evacuate and recharge the system. Reconnect the negative battery cable. Test the entire system for proper operation.

Pick-Up, T100 and 4Runner

1. Disconnect the negative battery cable.

2. It may be necessary to remove the entire heater assembly to access the blower motor. If so, drain cooling system, disconnect heater hoses at firewall, remove any duct or trim work interfering and detach the heater assembly from the vehicle.

3. If blower can be removed directly from the heater assembly while in the vehicle, it may be necessary to remove the glove box door or assembly.

4. Disconnect the wiring and, if equipped, the heater cooling tube from the blower motor.

5. Remove the screws retaining the blower motor to the heater assembly case. Remove the blower motor.

6. Install in reverse of removal procedure, replacing any gaskets or seals as needed.

Previa

1. Disconnect the negative battery cable. Remove the intake air duct.

2. From the firewall side, remove the retaining screws and disconnect electrical leads and remove the blower motor from the vehicle.

3. To install, reverse removal procedure.

Blower Motor Resistor

REMOVAL AND INSTALLATION

1. The blower motor resistor is mounted on or near the blower motor. Examine the installation to see if the heater case or blower motor must be removed to access the blower motor resistor.

2. Disconnect the battery negative cable.

3. If the assembly does not need to be removed, locate and remove the blower motor resistor mounting screws. Disconnect the electrical connector. Remove the resistor from the cooling case.

4. If the either the evaporator assembly or heater assembly must be removed to access the blower motor, properly discharge the air conditioning system or drain the cooling system as required.

5. Disconnect and cap the refrigerant lines from the evaporator tubes at the firewall or disconnect the heater hoses from the firewall.

6. Remove the glove box and surrounding components as needed, then remove the assembly.

7. Disassemble the unit case. Remove the blower motor resistor.

To install:

8. Installation is the reverse of the removal process. Test the motor before final assembly. Replace any sealing material that may have been disturbed at disassembly.

9. Check electrical contacts for corrosion, especially around the motor resistor connector.

10. If the air conditioning system has been opened to remove the cooling unit, evacuate, charge and test the system. If the cooling system was drained, properly refill the system.

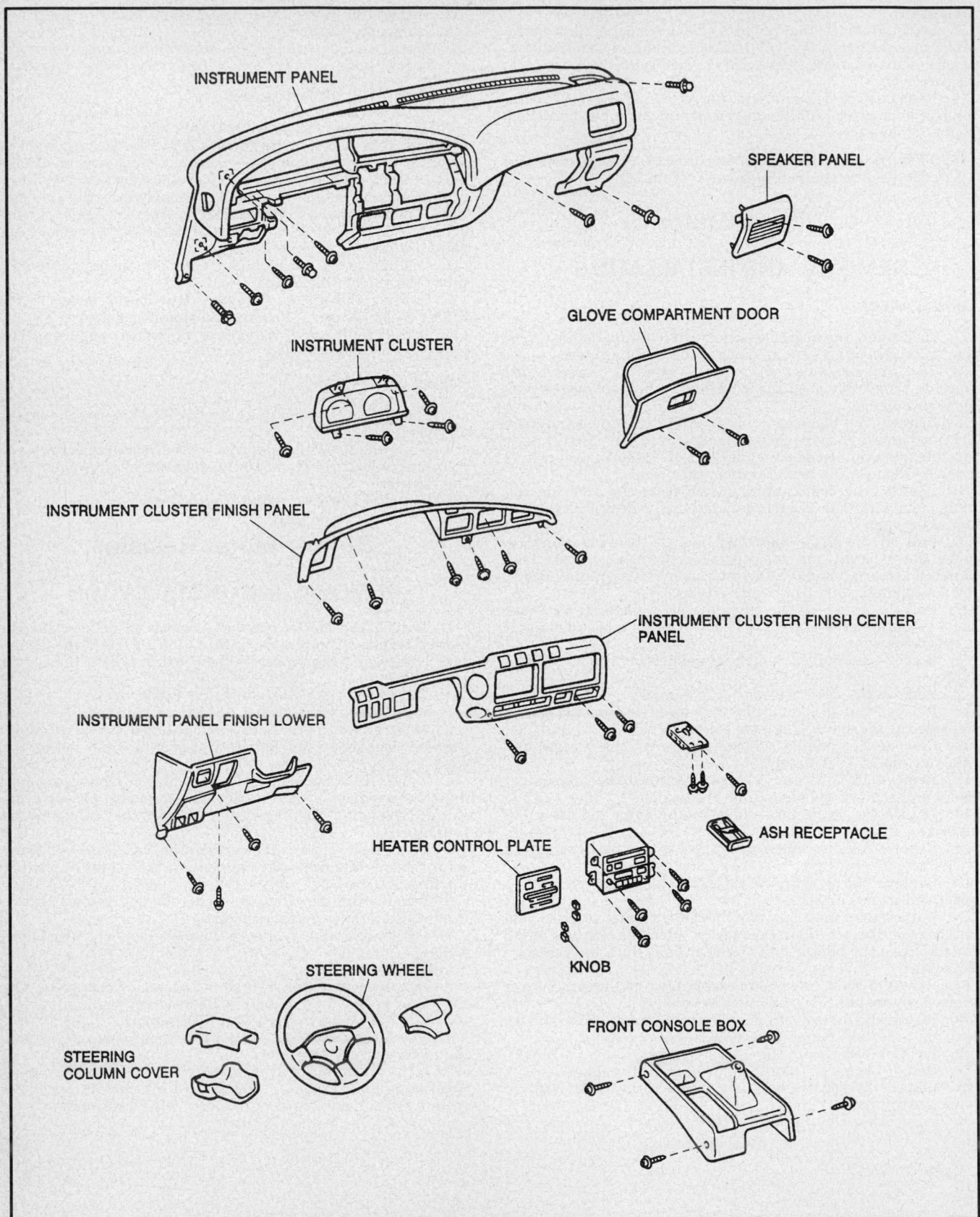

INSTRUMENT PANEL

SPEAKER PANEL

GLOVE COMPARTMENT DOOR

INSTRUMENT CLUSTER

INSTRUMENT CLUSTER FINISH PANEL

INSTRUMENT CLUSTER FINISH CENTER PANEL

INSTRUMENT PANEL FINISH LOWER

ASH RECEPTACLE

HEATER CONTROL PLATE

KNOB

STEERING WHEEL

STEERING COLUMN COVER

FRONT CONSOLE BOX

Exploded view of Land Cruiser instrument panel for blower motor removal

Heater Core

REMOVAL AND INSTALLATION

Land Cruiser

1. Disconnect the negative battery cable. Properly discharge and capture the refrigerant from the air conditioning system. Properly drain and capture the coolant from the cooling system. Disconnect the heater hoses from the connections at the firewall.
2. Disconnect the suction and discharge lines from the manifold fittings on the firewall and continue with the removal of the evaporator assembly as described in this article.
3. The instrument panel requires removal. Remove the steering wheel. Mask off the windshield pillars above the panel for protection.
4. Remove the steering column covers (5 screws). Detach the hood and fuel door release handles from the panel.
5. Remove the lower panel beneath the steering column (4 screws). Remove the heater duct in this area.
6. Remove the combination switch from the steering column, detaching the electrical connectors. Remove the turn signal bracket.
7. Pull off the choke knob end (manual transmission), remove the ashtray, and remove the instrument cluster trim panel (6 screws). Remove the instrument cluster, disconnecting speedometer and gauge connections.
8. Pull the knobs off the climate control panel and remove the 4 retaining screws. Pull the control panel out and support it out of the way.
9. Remove radio assembly, disconnecting wiring and cable.
10. Remove the front console box (4 screws).
11. Remove the speaker grille and speaker from the panel. Remove the glove box (2 screws below the door).
12. Remove 2 retaining screws, disconnect the wiring, and take out the ECU assembly.
13. Remove 10 bolts and 6 screws securing the instrument panel and remove the panel from the vehicle.
14. Remove heater duct. Remove steering column bolts, detach harness connectors and lower steering column to floor.

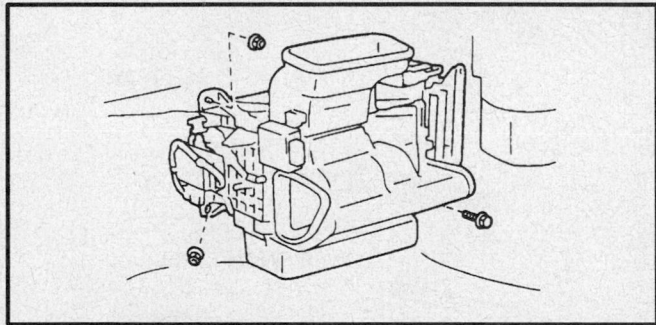

Removing heater unit—Land Cruiser

15. Remove the instrument panel reinforcements (2 screws at each end).
16. Remove the center defroster nozzle (3 screws near the base of the windshield).
17. Remove 2 nuts and a screws holding the heater unit and remove it from the vehicle. Remove the heater core.
To install:
18. Install the heater core to the housing and install the housing in the vehicle.
19. Install the center defroster nozzle, the instrument panel reinforcement, reattach the steering column and connectors, and reattach the heater duct.

20. Position and secure the instrument panel.
21. Install the ECU, then the glove box and speaker.
22. Install the console box, then replace the radio and climate control panel.
23. Install the instrument cluster, trim, knobs, panels and other items as removed.

NOTE: When installing the heater hoses, push hose onto the tube only to the second ridge, then install the hose clamp with the clamp at 12 o'clock position.

24. Evacuate and recharge the system. Refill the cooling system. Reconnect the negative battery cable. Test the entire system for proper operation.

Pick-Up and 4Runner

1. Disconnect the negative battery terminal.
2. Drain the cooling system.
3. Remove the glove box, the defroster hoses, the air damper, the air duct and the 2 side defroster ducts.
4. Disconnect the control unit cables and electrical connections from the heater assembly.
5. Disconnect the heater hoses from the core tubes.
6. Remove the retaining bolts and take out the heater unit. At this point, the core may be removed from the case.
To install:
7. Installation is the reverse of the removal procedure. Make sure the heater hoses are in good condition, and that all cable controls are in place.
8. Refill cooling system and check for leaks.

T100

1. Disconnect the negative battery cable. Properly discharge and capture the refrigerant from the air conditioning system.
2. Disconnect the suction and discharge lines from the tube connections at the firewall. Cap all openings immediately to minimize contamination. Remove the grommets around the tubes.
3. Remove the evaporator drain pipe grommet.
4. Remove the glove box door (2 screws), the lower trim panel, and the door reinforcement.
5. Remove the evaporator housing assembly (4 screws and 1 nut) after detaching the electrical connectors.
6. Properly drain and capture the fluid from the cooling system. Detach the heater hoses from the heater core tubes at the firewall. Remove the pipe grommets.
7. Remove the instrument panel, starting with the front pillar trim, the door scuff plates and the cowl side trim.
8. Remove the steering wheel, the column cover, the hood lock release lever (detach from the panel only), the lower panel trim and the combination switch on the column.
9. Remove the lower center instrument panel cover. Remove the heater control knobs and gently pry off the finish panel.
10. Remove the radio assembly, disconnect the climate control panel cables from the heater unit, then remove the climate control assembly.
11. Remove 2 screws now accessible in the center panel, then pry the panel off gently (tape the screwdriver tip first).
12. Remove the instrument cluster trim and the cluster.
13. Remove the small center air outlet register, the left side heater duct, then the glove box reinforcement and the two center braces.
14. Detach the instrument panel wiring harness connectors, remove the 2 bolts from the instrument panel on either side of the steering column location, and remove the instrument panel assembly with remaining components attached.

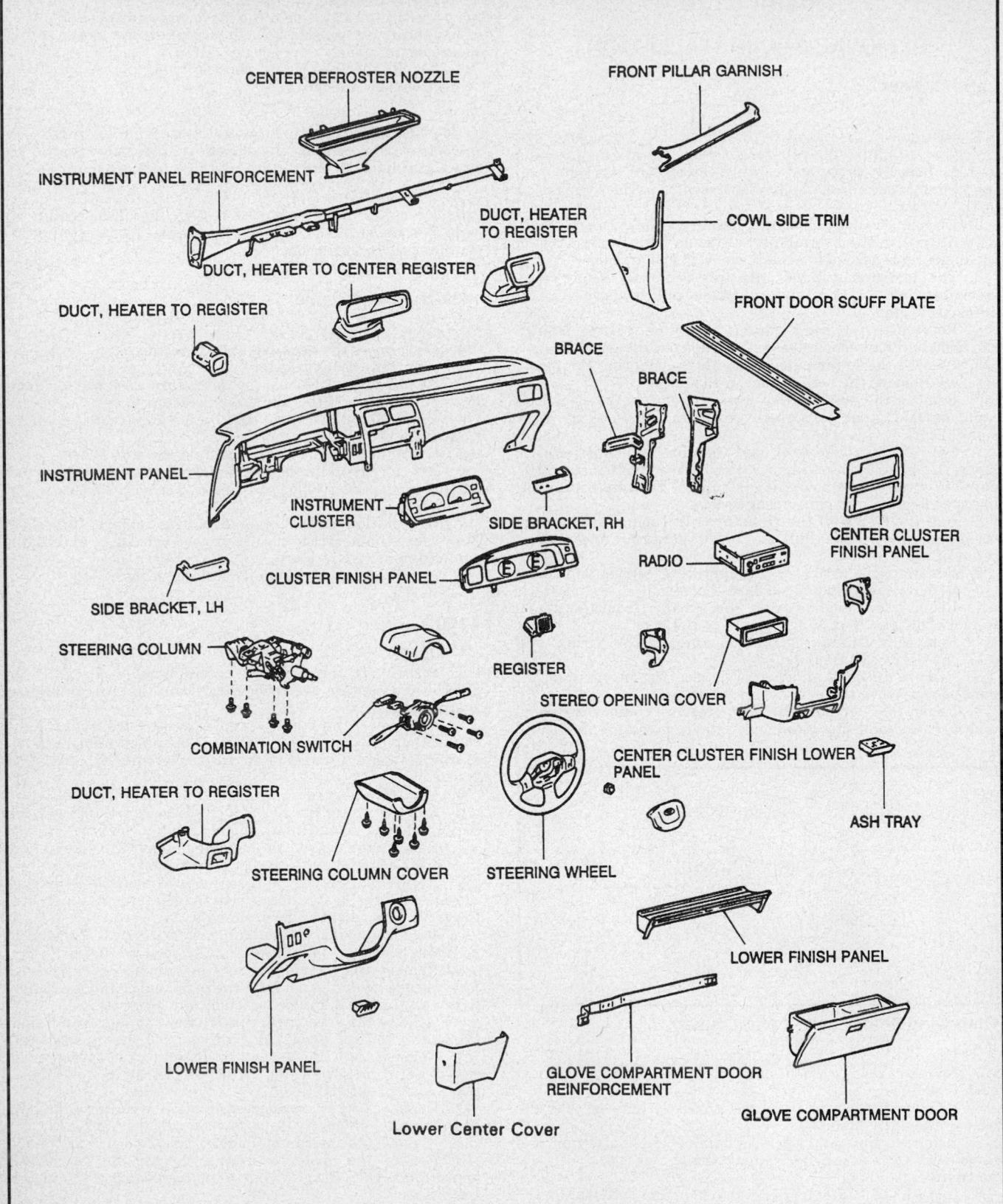

Exploded view of instrument panel—T100

15. Remove the right side, center and floor air ducts.

16. Remove 2 bolts and 1 nut holding the heater assembly in place and remove the assembly from the vehicle. Heater core can be removed on the bench.

To install:

17. Assembly the heater core and install the assembly to the vehicle. Reattach the air ducts as removed.

18. Install the instrument panel assembly, attaching the wiring harnesses.

19. Install the center braces, glove box reinforcement, left heater duct and small center air outlet register.

20. Install the instrument cluster and trim panel.

21. Reattach cables and connections and install the climate control panel, the radio and the center panel trim.

22. Install the steering column and column components, as removed.

23. Install the evaporator assembly, making all connections. Install the glove box, reinforcement and trim.

24. Reattach the heater hoses and air conditioning lines as removed from the connections at the firewall.

25. Refill the cooling system. Evacuate and recharge the air conditioning system with R-134a refrigerant and any appropriate refrigerant oil as needed.

26. Connect the battery cable. Operate and check the air conditioning and heating systems.

Evaporator

REMOVAL AND INSTALLATION

Land Cruiser, Pick-Up, T100, 4Runner

1. Disconnect the battery negative terminal.

2. Discharge the refrigeration system using a refrigerant recovery system.

3. Disconnect the refrigerant lines from the cooling unit inlet and outlet fittings and cap immediately to keep dirt and moisture out of the rest of the system. Also remove the plate or grommets at the tube fittings on the firewall.

4. Remove the glove box. On Land Cruiser, remove the engine control module (ECM) from its mounting above the evaporator assembly. On T100, remove panel lower center trim and glove box reinforcement.

5. Detach electrical connectors from the evaporator housing. Remove evaporator assembly retaining nuts and screws. Remove assembly from the vehicle.

6. Evaporator case may be disassembled by removing the external electrical components, as equipped, separating the case halves and removing the evaporator core.

To install:

7. Reassemble the evaporator assembly and reposition in the vehicle and install the 3 screws and 2 nuts.

8. Reconnect electrical connections to the evaporator assembly and install the ECM, if removed. Install the glove box and related components, as removed.

9. Install the plate at the evaporator core tubes on the firewall, then reconnect the refrigerant lines.

10. If a new evaporator core was installed, add 1.4-1.7 oz. of new refrigerant oil to the compressor during recharge.

11. Connect the battery cable. Evacuate and recharge the system.

NOTE: Be sure to utilize equipment, refrigerant and oil dedicated to the refrigerant system type.

Previa

1. Disconnect the negative battery cable. Properly discharge and recover air conditioning system refrigerant.

2. Inside the engine compartment, remove the air intake duct for the heater-A/C system. Remove the blower motor.

3. Detach any electrical connectors from the evaporator or blower housing that may interfere with removal.

4. Disconnect and plug the refrigerant lines from the evaporator tubes at the firewall.

5. Remove the 2 nuts and 1 bolt holding the evaporator cover to the firewall. Remove the evaporator from the vehicle.

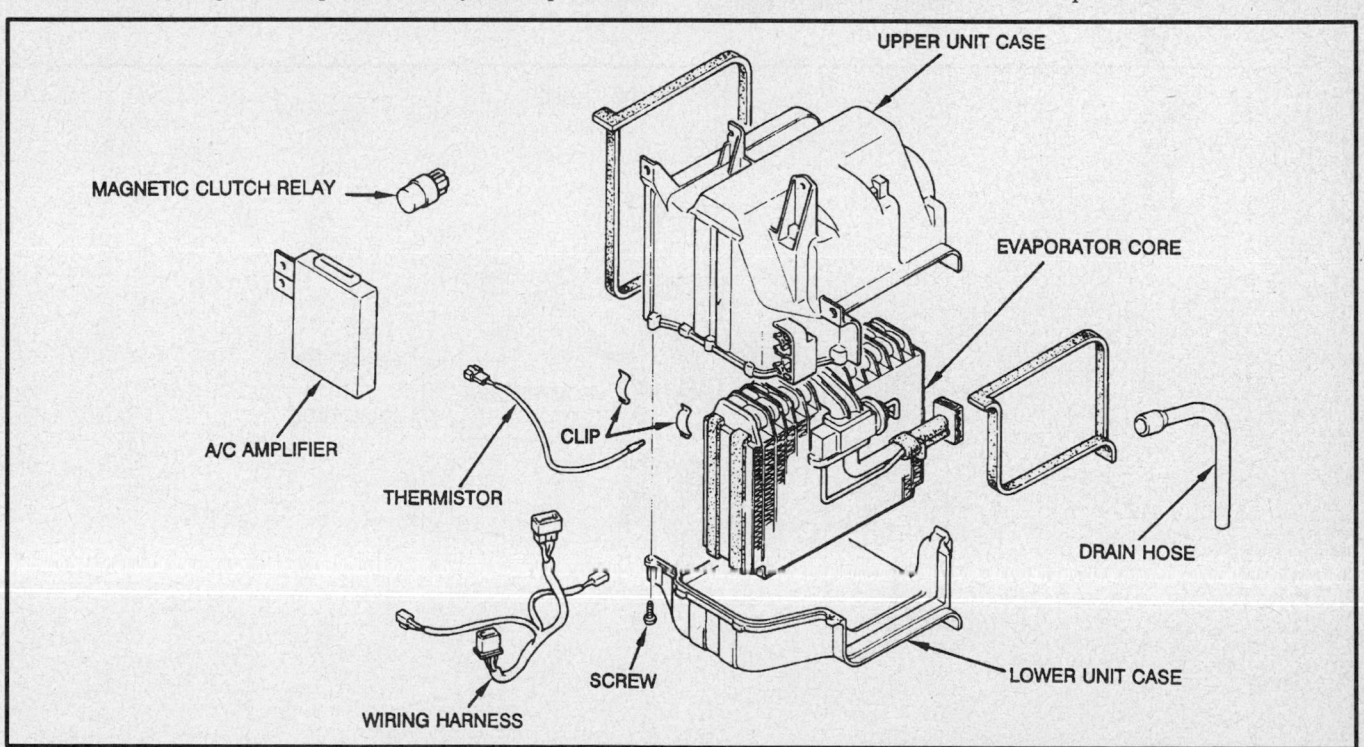

Exploded view of evaporator assembly—Land Cruiser shown; Pick—Up, T100 and 4Runner similar

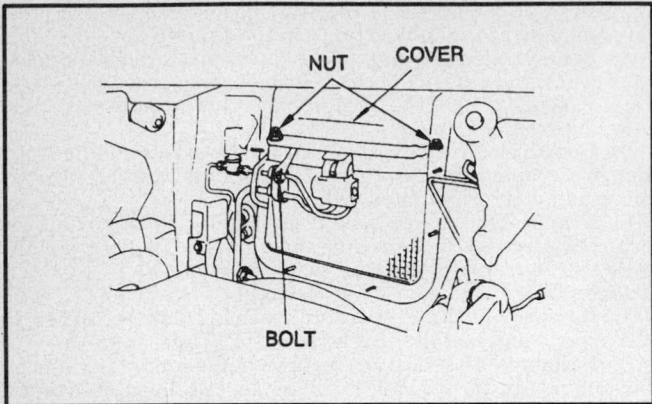

Showing location of retaining bolts and screws to remove evaporator—Previa

6. The thermistor and expansion valve should be removed and transferred if new evaporator core is being installed.
To install:
7. With expansion valve and thermistor attached, position the evaporator into the vehicle and install the cover nuts and bolt.
8. Reconnect the refrigerant lines, attach electrical connectors and install the blower motor.
9. Install the air intake duct, reconnect the battery cable, then evacuate and recharge the system. If a new evaporator core was installed, add 1.4-1.7 oz. of new refrigerant oil during the recharge.

Refrigerant Lines

REMOVAL AND INSTALLATION

1. Discharge the refrigeration system using a refrigerant recovery system, if possible.

2. Disconnect the faulty refrigerant line. Cap the open fittings immediately to keep dirt and moisture out of the rest of the system.
3. When installing new refrigerant lines, measure the diameter of the tube. On the tubes measuring 0.31 in. or approximately 3/8 in., torque the fittings to 10 ft. lbs. On tubes measuring 0.50 in or approximately 1/2 in., torque the fittings to 17 ft. lbs. On tubes measuring 0.62 in. or approximately 5/8 in., torque the fittings to 24 ft. lbs. Generally a small torque wrench is used with a crow's foot adapter to torque air conditioning fittings. When tightening these fittings, apply a few drops of compressor oil to the O-ring fittings for easy tightening. Tighten the nut using 2 wrenches to avoid twisting the tube.
4. Evacuate, charge and test the system.

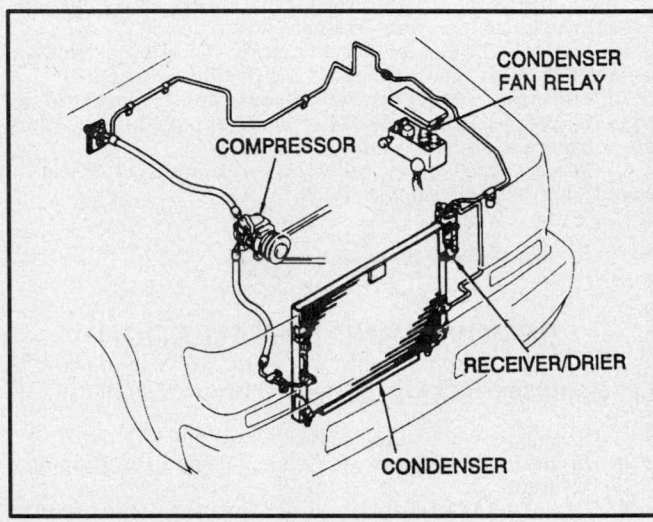

Refrigerant line routing—Land Cruiser

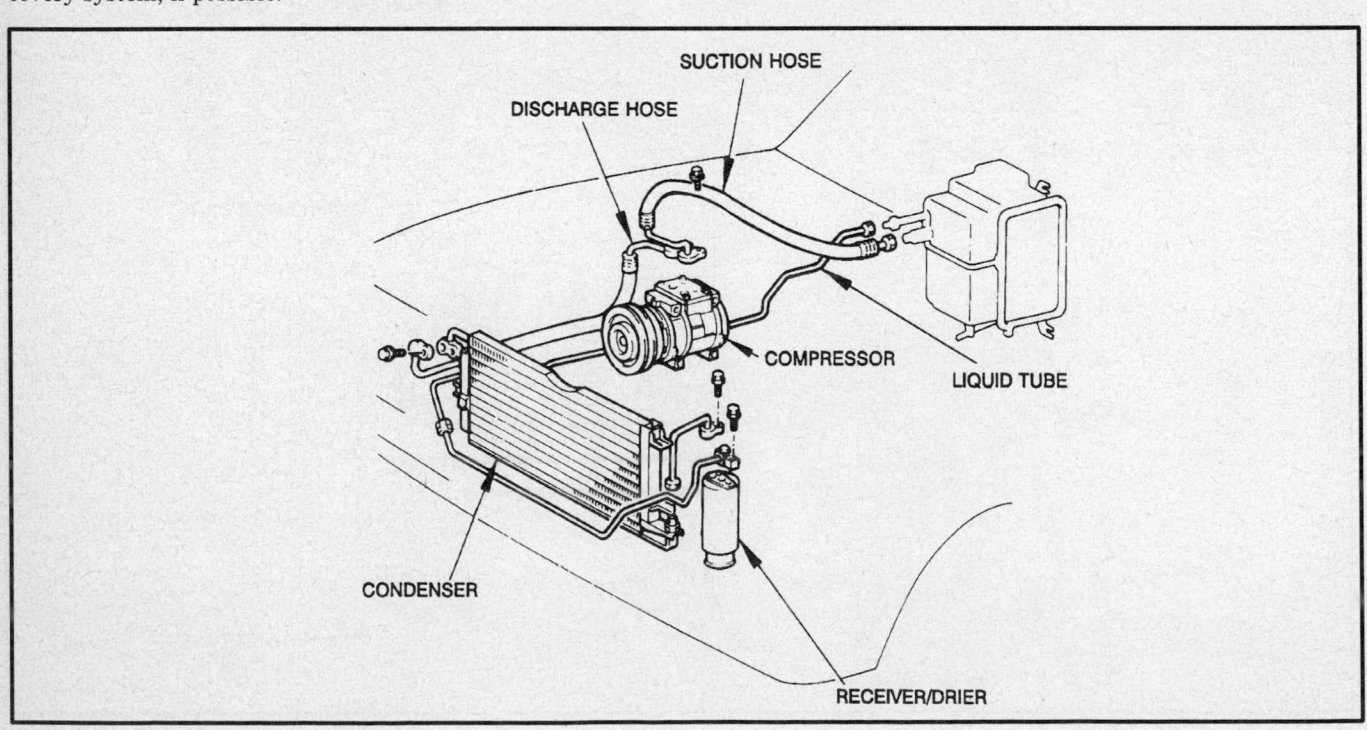

Refrigerant line routing—Pick-Up

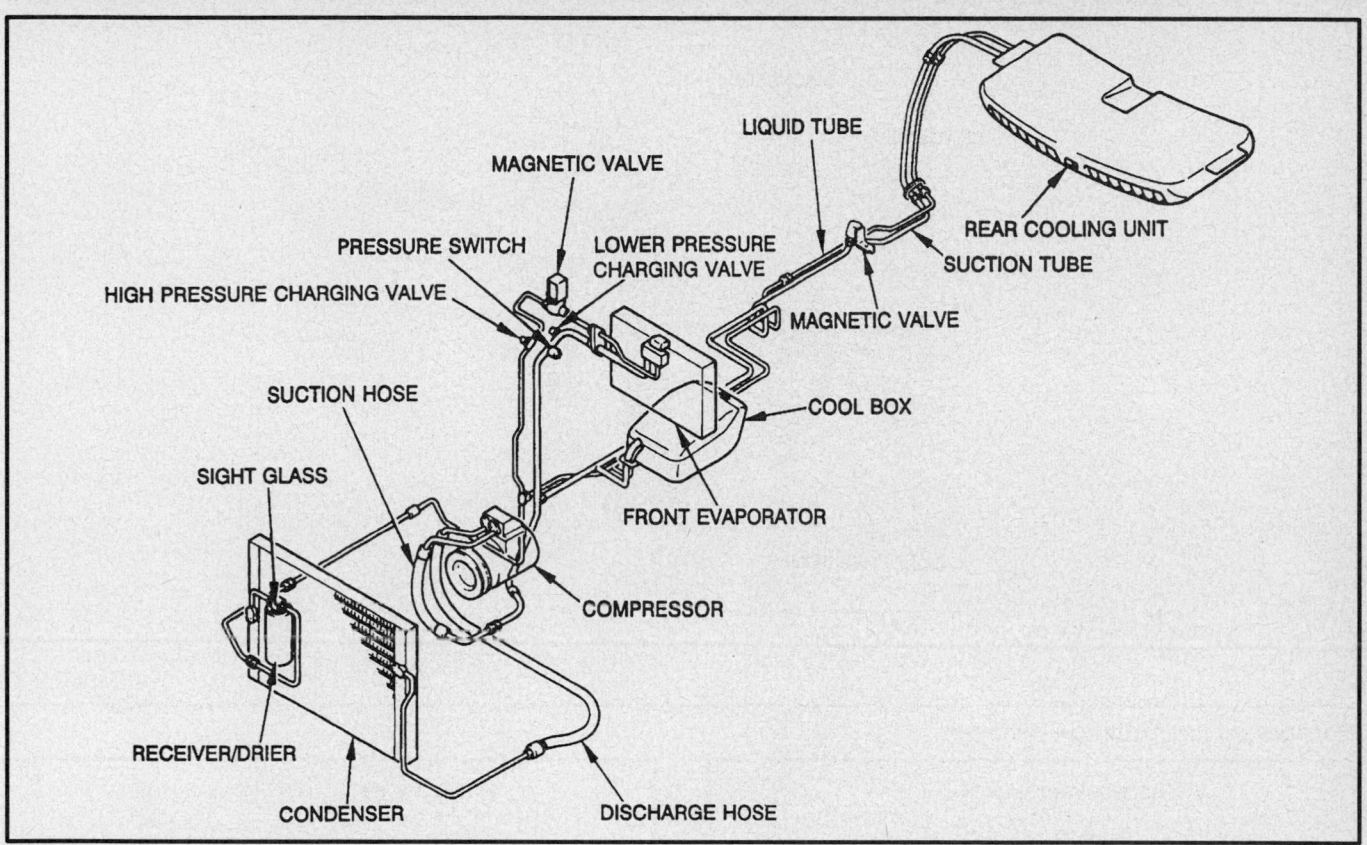

Refrigerant line routing—Previa

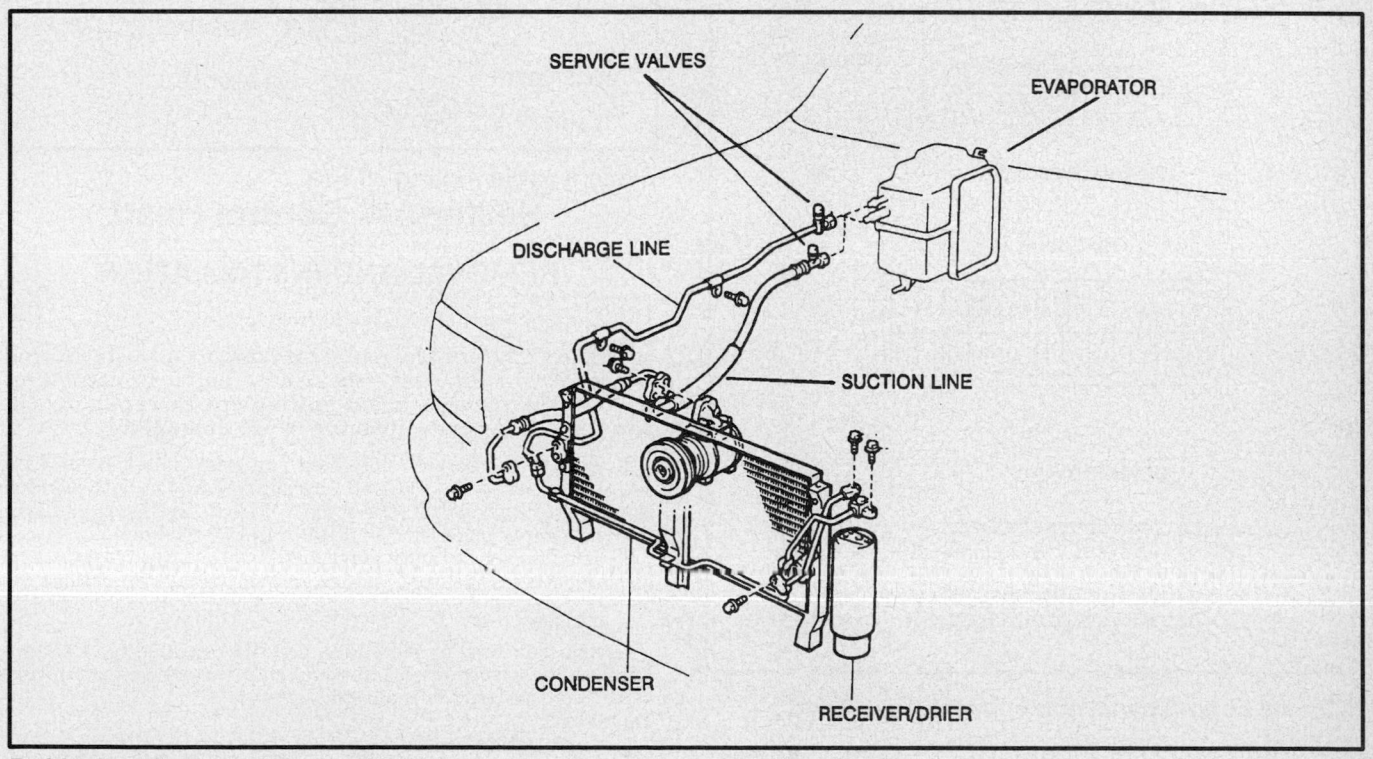

Refrigerant line routing—T100

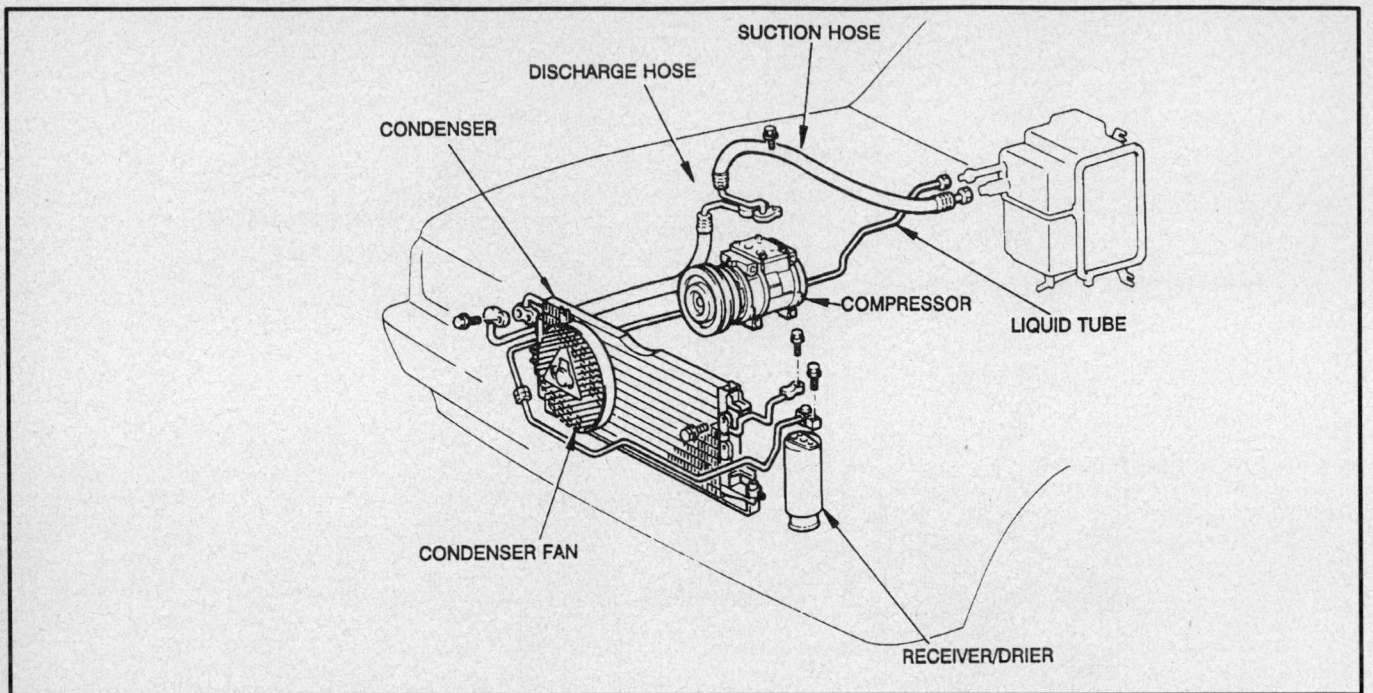

Refrigerant line routing—4Runner

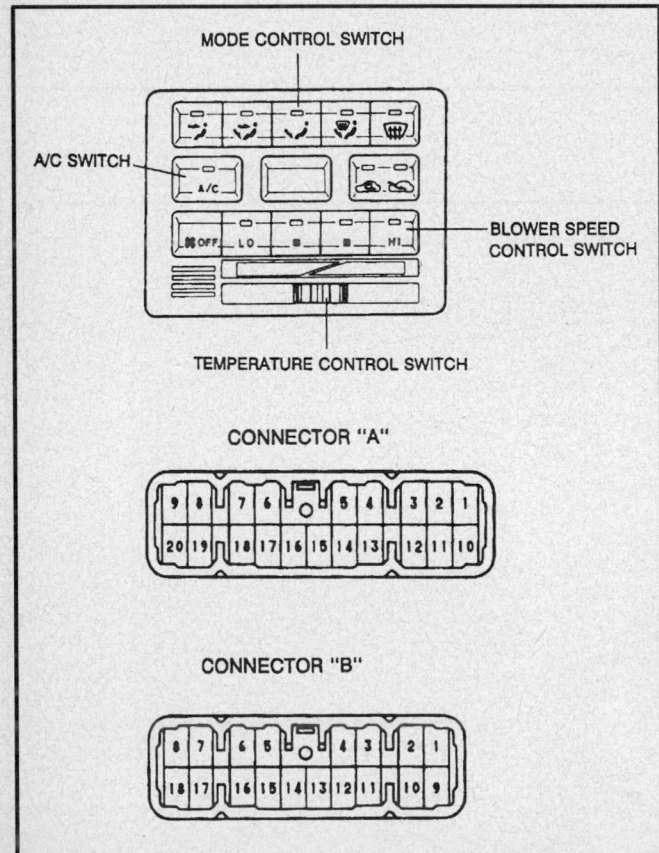

Climate control panel and connectors — Land Cruiser

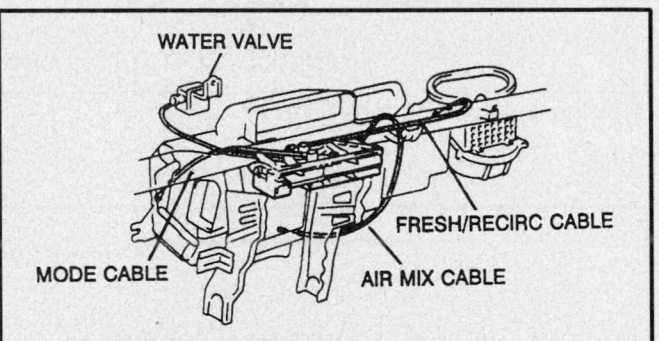

System cable routing—T100

Heater-A/C Control Head

REMOVAL AND INSTALLATION

1. Disconnect the negative battery cable.

NOTE: The control panel on Land Cruiser is an electric control unit. Only the water valve is cable controlled. Use caution when pulling out or replacing the panel so electrical connector is not damaged.

2. Locate the screws that hold the trim panel around the heater control head. Pull off the control knobs, if needed to remove the trim panel. On some vehicles, the surround trim may be simply pried off. On T100, remove cupholder.

3. If necessary, remove glove box to access control cables for disconnecting; otherwise, cables and electrical connections can be disconnected as control assembly is pulled from the instrument panel.

4. The heater control head is usually retained by 4 screws. Remove these screws and disconnect any electrical connectors as the control head is removed.

To install:

5. Installation is the reverse of the removal procedure. Securely fasten all control connections. Tighten screws securely to prevent rattles.

6. Adjust cables as needed. Reconnect battery cable and test operation.

TESTING

Land Cruiser

SWITCH ILLUMINATION TESTS

1. With the control panel connector detached (as during removal), apply direct battery voltage to the terminals and make any switch settings as noted for each test that follows.

2. On connector "A", connect the positive battery lead to **13** and the negative lead to **3** and watch that panel bulb lights. If not, test the bulb directly with an appropriate tested and replace if defective.

3. To check the air inlet control switch, on connector "A", connect the positive battery lead to **9** and the negative lead to **8**. Push in air inlet control button. **FRESH** or **RECIRC** indicator should light.

4. Push in the same button again. The indicator should go off and the other indicator light should come on. Move the positive lead to terminal **13** and indicator light should dim. If not, test the bulb directly with an appropriate tested and replace if defective.

5. To check the mode control switch, use connectors "A" and "B". Connect the positive lead to terminal **A-9** and the negative lead to terminal **B-16**. Push in each mode button and check that their lights operate when button is depressed.

6. Now connect the positive lead to **A-13** and check that the indicator dims. If not, test the bulb directly with an appropriate tested and replace if defective.

7. To test the blower speed control switch, use both connectors. Attach positive lead to **A-9** and the negative lead to **B-16**. As each blower speed button is depressed, its light should light. Connect the positive lead to **A-13** and watch the indicator dim. If not, test the bulb directly with an appropriate tested and replace if defective.

8. Check the A/C switch light by connecting the positive lead to **A-9** and the negative lead to **B-18**. With button depressed, indicator should light up. Move the positive lead to **A-13** and watch indicator dim. If not, test the bulb directly with an appropriate tested and replace if defective.

SWITCH CONTINUITY TESTS

1. Check the air inlet control switch, mode control switch and blower speed control switch continuity. Using an appropriate circuit tester, check switch continuity as noted in each chart. If continuity is not as indicated, replace the climate control assembly.

2. To check continuity of A/C switch, check that there is continuity between terminals **B-6** and **B-17** intermittently each time the A/C switch button is depressed. Replace the control assembly if not as specified.

3. To check the temperature control switch continuity, measure resistance between **B-1** and **B-2**. It should be about 3.0 kilo ohms.

4. Now check resistance between **B-1** and **B- 3**. Resistance should increase from 0.0 kilo ohm to about 3.0 kilo ohms as temperature knob is turned from cold to hot position. If not as specified, replace A/C control assembly.

Manual Control Cables

ADJUSTMENT

NOTE: Of the following adjustments, only the water valve cable adjustment applies to Land Cruiser; other dampers are controlled electrically.

1. Move the control levers left and right and check for stiffness and binding through the full range of the levers.

2. To adjust the **air inlet damper control cable**, set the control panel lever to **FRESH** position, the damper lever as noted, then lock cable in place with the adjusting clip:
   - Damper lever cable attaching point moved toward cable adjustment clamp—T100.
   - Damper lever cable attaching end pulled away from the adjustment clamp—Pick-Up, Previa and 4Runner.

3. To adjust the **air mix damper control cable**, set the air control lever to the **COOL** position (**WARM** on T100). Set the air damper door lever as described, then lock cable in place with the adjusting clip:
   - Damper lever cable attaching end pushed away from cable clamp—T100.
   - Cable attaching end of lever pulled toward the adjusting clip—Pick-Up, Previa and 4Runner.

4. To adjust the **water valve control cable**, set the control panel lever to the **COOL** position (**WARM** on T100), set the valve lever as noted and lock the cable in place with the adjusting clip:
   - Push the cable connecting end of the lever on the water valve away from the cable clamp—Land Cruiser, Pick-Up and 4Runner.
   - Push the cable connecting end of the lever on the water valve toward the adjusting clamp—Previa, T100

5. To adjust the **mode damper control cable**, set the control panel lever to the **VENT** position on Previa or **DEF** position on Pick-Up and T100. Adjust the damper lever position as noted, and lock the cable in place with the adjusting clip:
   - Rotate the mode damper lever clockwise and install the control cable—Previa.
   - Push the cable attaching end and lever assembly away from the adjustment clip—Pick-Up, T100 and 4Runner.

6. To adjust the **side vent duct control cable** on Previa, set the side vent duct and the mode control lever to the **VENT** position. Move the cable attaching end of the driver's side cable lever away from the adjustment clip and lock the cable in place with the clamp. On the passenger's side, move the cable attaching end of the damper lever toward the cable adjustment clip. Lock the cable with the clip.

7. To adjust the **rear heat damper control cable** on Previa, set the rear panel control lever to **RR HEAT**. Move the damper lever cable attaching end toward the cable adjusting clip. Lock the cable in place with the clip.

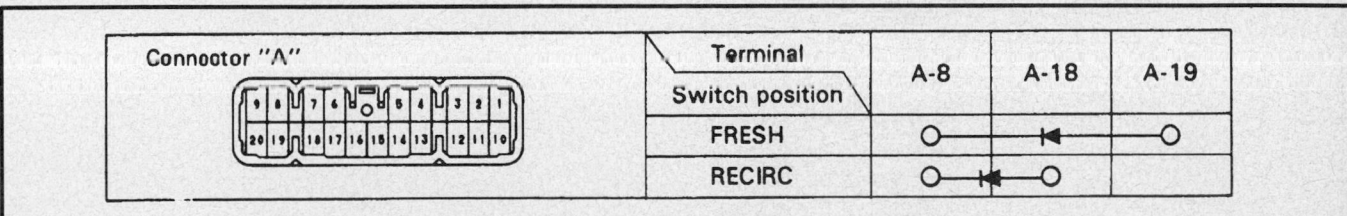

Connector "A"	Terminal Switch position	A-8	A-18	A-19
	FRESH	○	◁	○
	RECIRC	○	▷	○

Air inlet switch continuity test - Land Cruiser

Connector "A"

Connector "B"

Terminal / Switch position	A-1	A-10	B-9	B-10	B-13	B-16
OFF		○——————————————————————○				○
LO	○——○					○
(M1)			○——————————————————————○			○
(M2)				○————————————○		○
HI					○————○	○

Blower speed switch continuity test chart — Land Cruiser

Connector "A"

Connector "B"

Terminal / Switch position	A-7	A-11	A-12	A-14	B-4	B-11	B-16
FACE				○——————————————————————————————○			○
BI-LEVEL			○——○				○
FOOL	○——○						○
FOOT-DEF					○————————————○		
DEF		○——○					○

Mode control switch continuity test chart

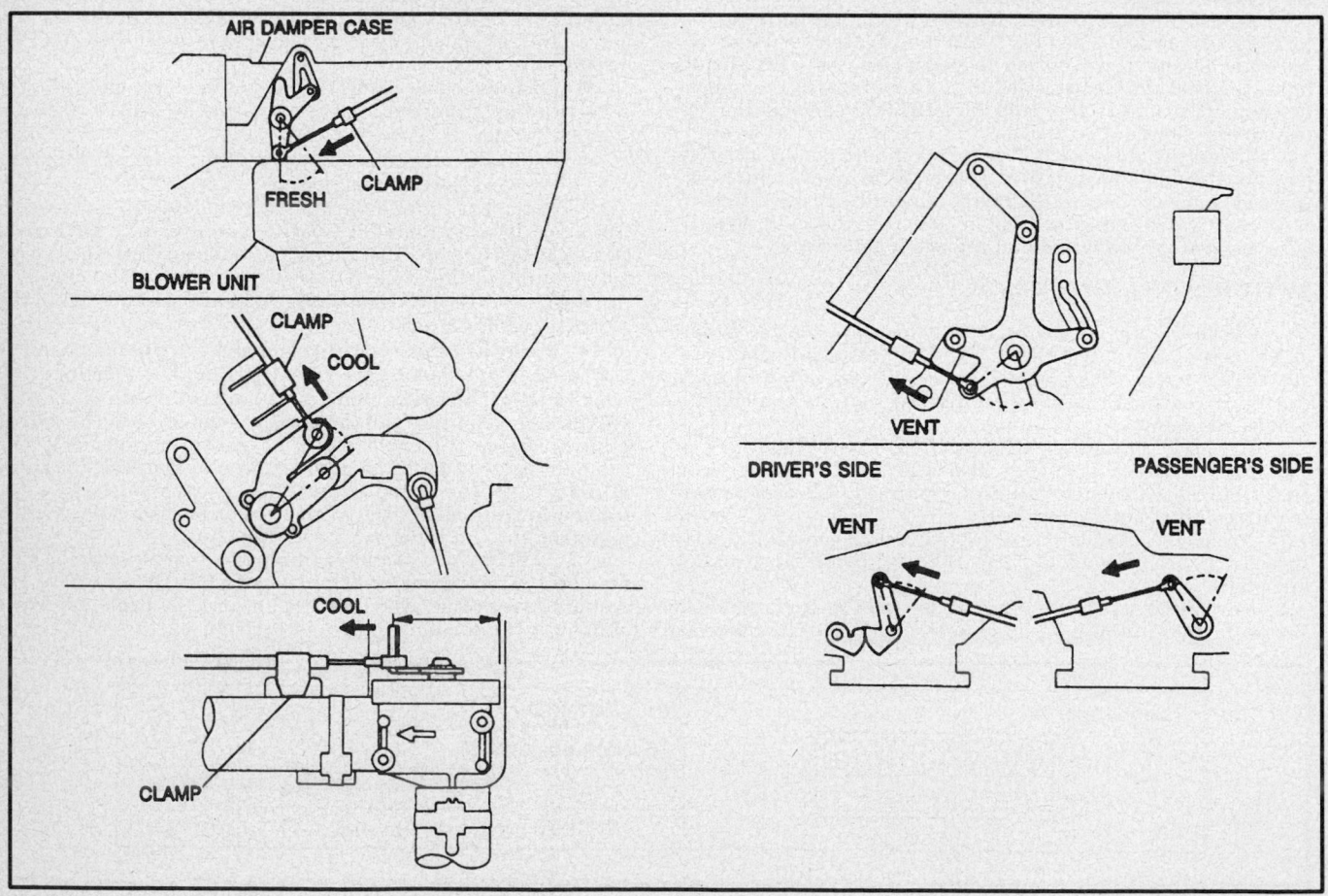

AIR DAMPER CASE

CLAMP

FRESH

BLOWER UNIT

CLAMP

COOL

COOL

CLAMP

VENT

DRIVER'S SIDE   PASSENGER'S SIDE

VENT   VENT

Control cable adjusting points—Previa shown

SENSORS AND SWITCHES

Air Conditioner Switch

OPERATION

The air conditioner switch is basically an ON/OFF switch. The primary tests are simply continuity checks.

TESTING

Using an ohmmeter, check for continuity for each switch terminal shown in the table. If there is no continuity, replace the air conditioning switch.

REMOVAL AND INSTALLATION

1. Disconnect the battery negative cable.

2. Most air conditioning switches clip into the instrument panel. The panel trim plate may have to be removed first. Use a suitable small, flat bladed prying tool. Wrap tape around the end of the tool to prevent scratching the instrument panel face. Pry the switch from the panel. In some cases, the switch can be pushed out from the back although the glove box or other obstruction may have to be removed.

3. Disconnect the electrical connector and test the switch terminals for continuity.

To install:

4. Reconnect the electrical connector and push the switch into place until it clicks.

5. Reconnect the negative battery terminal and test switch.

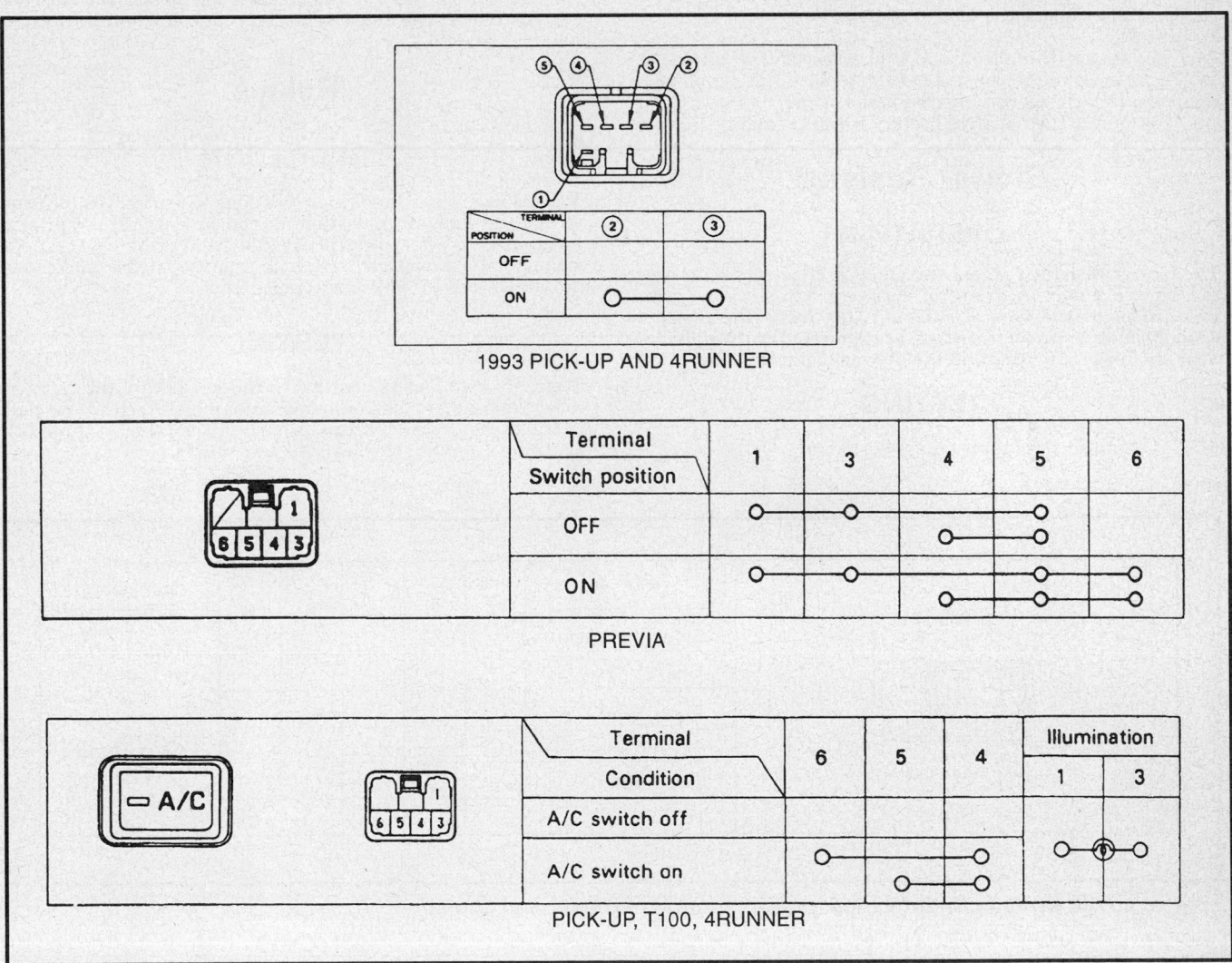

1993 PICK-UP AND 4RUNNER

PREVIA

PICK-UP, T100, 4RUNNER

Air conditioning switch continuity testing—all models, except Land Cruiser

Blower Speed Switch

OPERATION

The blower speed switch feeds power to the blower resistor and the relay.

TESTING

Using an ohmmeter, check for continuity for each switch terminal as shown. If there is no continuity, replace the blower speed switch.

REMOVAL AND INSTALLATION

1. Disconnect the battery negative cable.
2. Blower speed switches are integrated into the climate control panel. Remove the panel trim and adjacent components. Pull the control panel out, disconnect the electrical connections and remove the blower switch.
To install:
3. Reconnect the electrical connector and position the switch to the climate control panel. Replace the panel, other components, as removed, the the panel trim.
4. Reconnect the negative battery terminal and test switch.

Blower Resistor

OPERATION

The blower resistor reduces the amount of power being fed to the blower motor. A group of resistors, often wound metal coils, impedes the flow of current. This heats the resistors. Usually blower motor resistors are mounted in the air duct near the blower motor or on the blower motor housing.

TESTING

1. Disconnect the battery negative cable.

2. Locate the resistor and remove the electrical connector. Some resistors may be tested in place, others may need to be removed to access the terminals. Most blower resistors are secured to their mounting by 1 or 2 screws which can be removed to take out the resistor.
3. Test the resistor terminals for continuity.
To install:
4. Reinstall the resistor, if it was removed and connect the electrical connector.
5. Reconnect the negative battery terminal and test system.

REMOVAL AND INSTALLATION

1. Disconnect the battery negative cable.
2. Locate the resistor and remove the electrical connector. Most blower resistors are secured to their mounting by 1 or 2 screws which are removed to take out the resistor.
To install:
3. Install the resistor and connect the electrical connector.
4. Reconnect the negative battery terminal and test system.

Relays

OPERATION

Toyotas use relays in various locations to control the functions of heating and air conditioning components. Their primary function is to act as a switching device, taking lower current signals from a control switch to operate higher current requirement motors or other components.

TESTING

Tests are confined to continuity checks. Locate the relay, remove from its socket and using an ohmmeter, check for continuity at each relay terminal shown in the table. If there is no continuity, replace the relay.

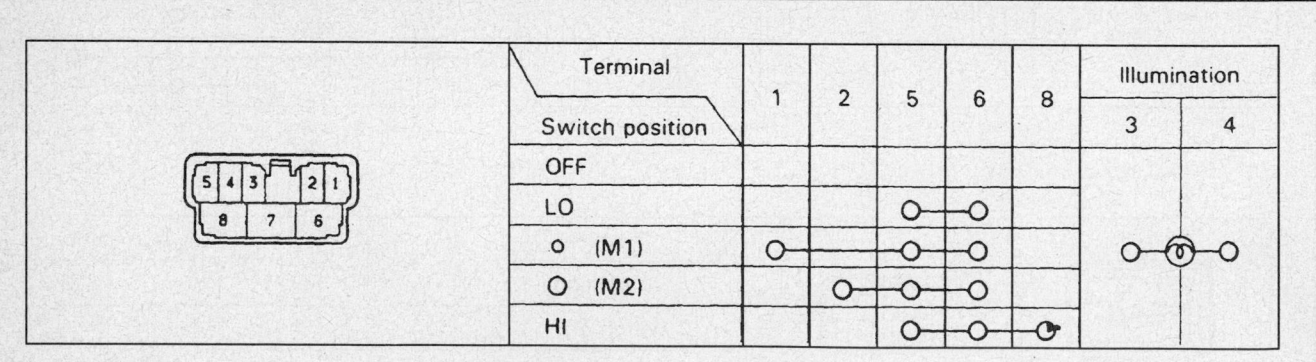

Blower speed switch continuity testing—all models, except Land Cruiser

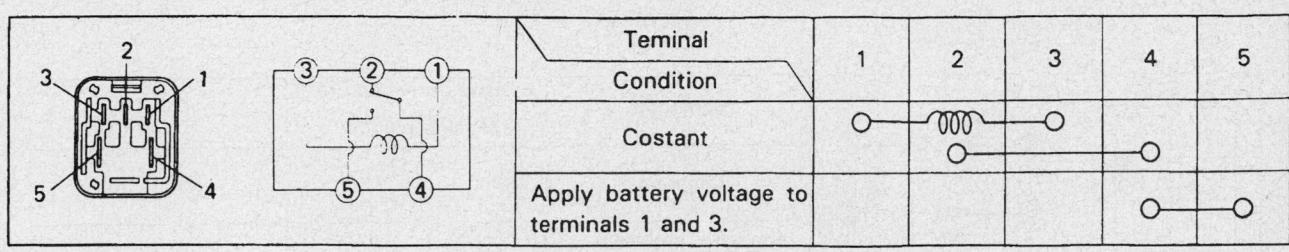

HEATER RELAY—LAND CRUISER, PICK-UP, T100 AND 4RUNNER

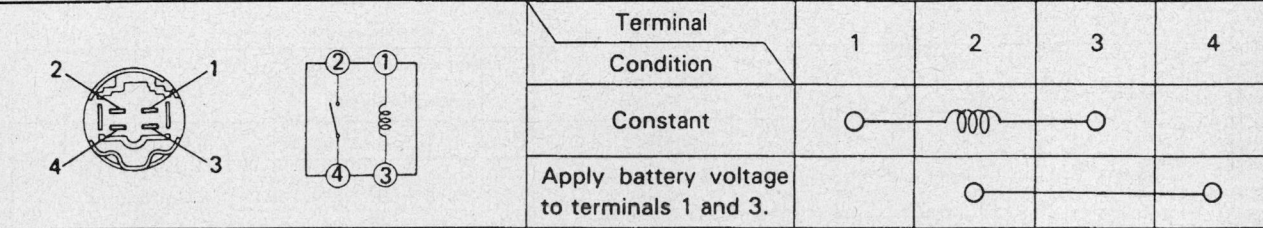

MAGNETIC CLUTCH RELAY—LAND
CRUISER AND PICK-UP
ENGINE TEMP. A/C CUT RELAY—1993
LAND CRUISER
CONDENSER FAN RELAY #2—4RUNNER

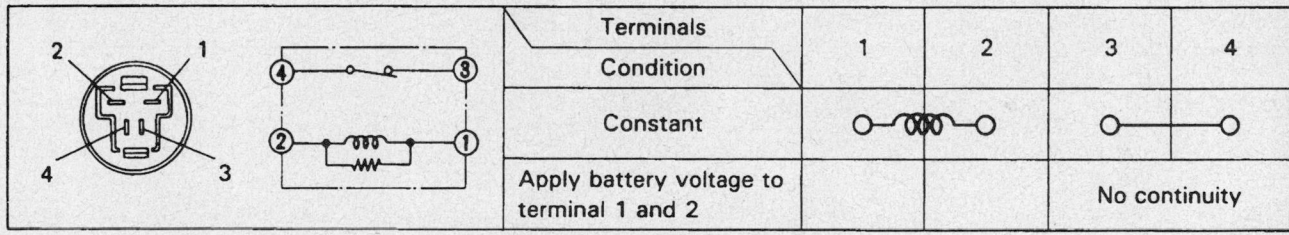

CONDENSER FAN RELAY #1—4RUNNER

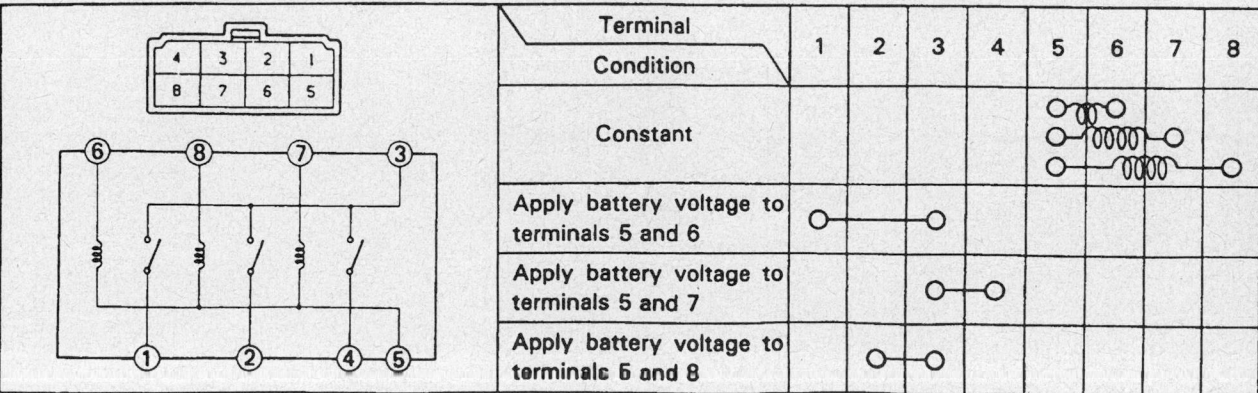

BLOWER SPEED CONTROL RELAY— 1993 LAND CRUISER

Relay continuity testing—except Previa

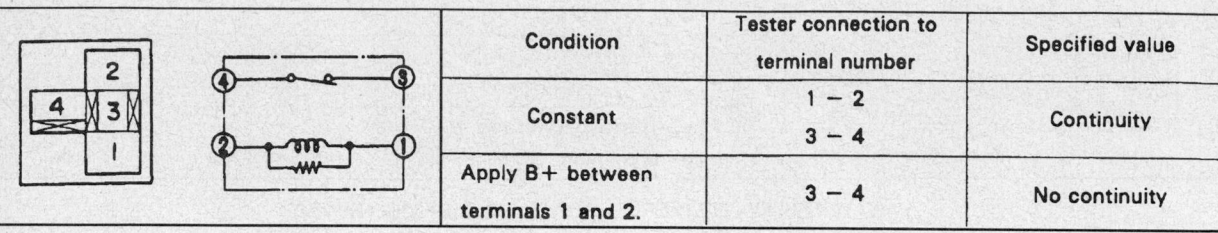

	Condition	Tester connection to terminal number	Specified value
	Constant	1 – 2 3 – 4	Continuity
	Apply B+ between terminals 1 and 2.	3 – 4	No continuity

	Condition	Tester connection to terminal number	Specified value
	Constant	1 – 2	Continuity
	Apply B+ between terminals 1 and 3.	3 – 5	Continuity

Relay continuity testing—except Previa cont'd

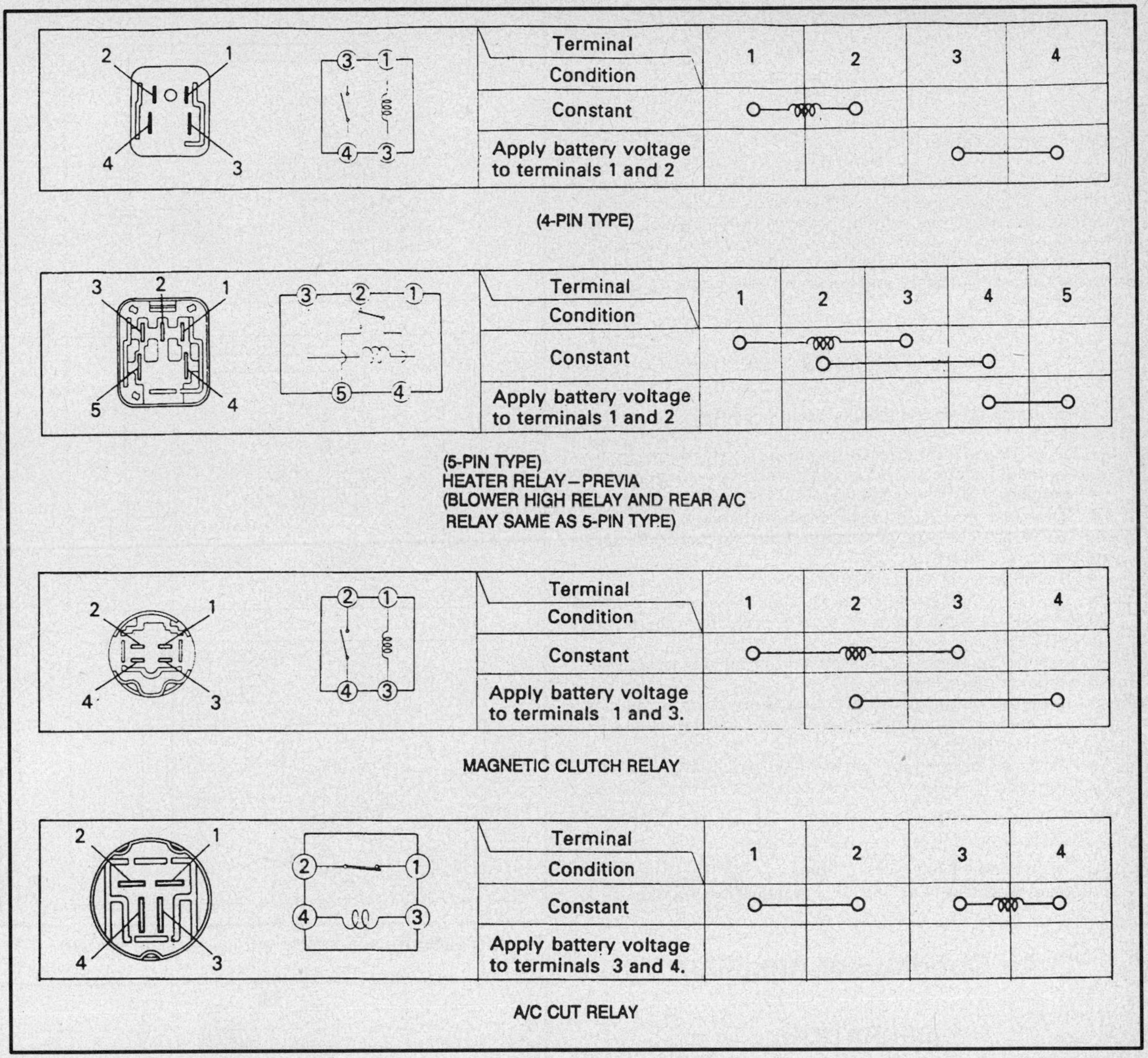

(4-PIN TYPE)

Terminal / Condition	1	2	3	4
Constant	○——coil——○			
Apply battery voltage to terminals 1 and 2			○———○	

(5-PIN TYPE)
HEATER RELAY — PREVIA
(BLOWER HIGH RELAY AND REAR A/C
RELAY SAME AS 5-PIN TYPE)

Terminal / Condition	1	2	3	4	5
Constant	○	——coil——○	○	○	
Apply battery voltage to terminals 1 and 2				○———○	

MAGNETIC CLUTCH RELAY

Terminal / Condition	1	2	3	4
Constant	○——coil——○			
Apply battery voltage to terminals 1 and 3.		○———○		

A/C CUT RELAY

Terminal / Condition	1	2	3	4
Constant	○———○		○——coil——○	
Apply battery voltage to terminals 3 and 4.				

Relay continuity testing—Previa

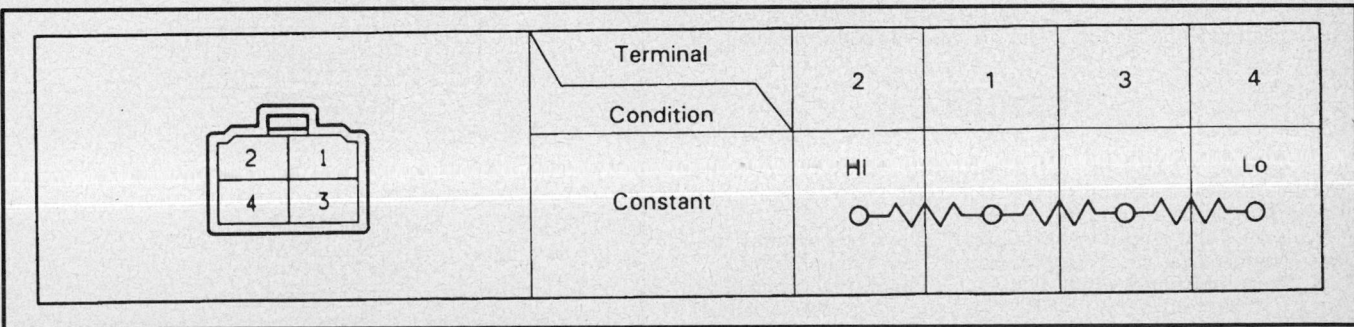

Terminal / Condition	2	1	3	4
Constant	HI	○—www—○—www—○—www—○		Lo

Blower resistor continuity testing—all models

Vacuum Switching Valve (VSV)

OPERATION

Except Land Cruiser

The VSV is a load sensing device, monitoring engine vacuum. At times of heavy engine load, in this case, when the air conditioning is turned on, the switch responds to the change in engine vacuum and sends an electric signal to the engine management computer. The computer compares this information with that of other sensors and sends an idle up signal to the engine fuel system.

TESTING

1. Disconnect the vacuum hoses and the electrical connector from the VSV.
2. Check the vacuum circuits inside the valve blowing air into the vacuum connector ports in the following sequence:
   - Connect VSV electrical terminals to battery voltage.
   - Blow into pipe **A** (input from throttle body) and check that air comes out pipe **B** (output to air cleaner), but does not come out filter **C**.
   - Disconnect the battery.
   - Blow into pipe **B** and check that air comes out the filter **C** but does not come out pipe **A**. If a problem is found, replace the VSV.
3. Check for an electrical short circuit or an open circuit using the following procedure:
   - Using an ohmmeter, check that there is no continuity between each terminal and the VSV body. If there is a problem, replace the VSV.
   - Using an ohmmeter, measure the resistance between the 2 terminals of the VSV. It should read in the following approximate ranges:

   > Pick-Up and 4Runner—37–42 ohms

   > Previa and T100—32 ± 2 ohms
4. If resistance is not as specified, replace the VSV.

Air Conditioner Amplifier

OPERATION

The amplifier is located on the evaporator assembly housing on all models except Previa. On Previa, it is located in the center ice box housing. On Land Cruiser, the unit is located externally to the evaporator housing. On Pick-Up, T100 and 4Runner, the amplifier is housed in a slot on the evaporator housing.

TESTING

1. Amplifier tests are primarily voltage and continuity checks. Use the following charts to identify both the pin number of the connector and the specified values.
2. Access the amplifier through the glove box opening (except Previa). Disconnect the connector from the amplifier.
3. Turn ignition switch **ON**, set temperature control to **MAX COOL** and blower to **HI**. Test the connector terminals on the wire harness side.
4. If circuit tests as specified in the appropriate chart, replace the amplifier.

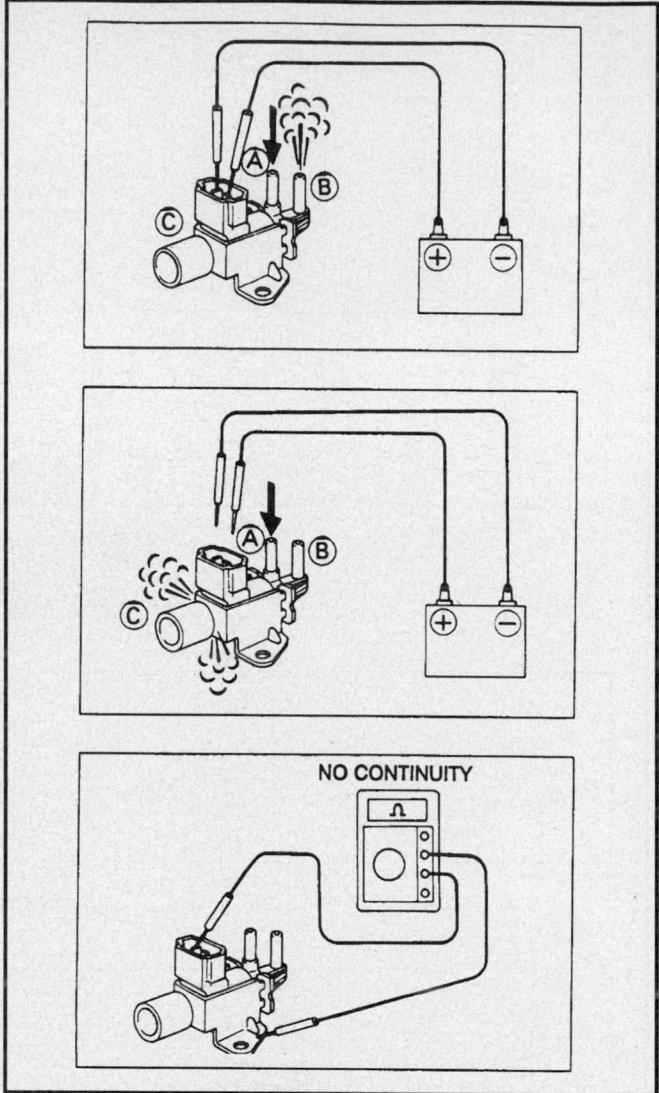

Testing vacuum switching valve—Previa shown

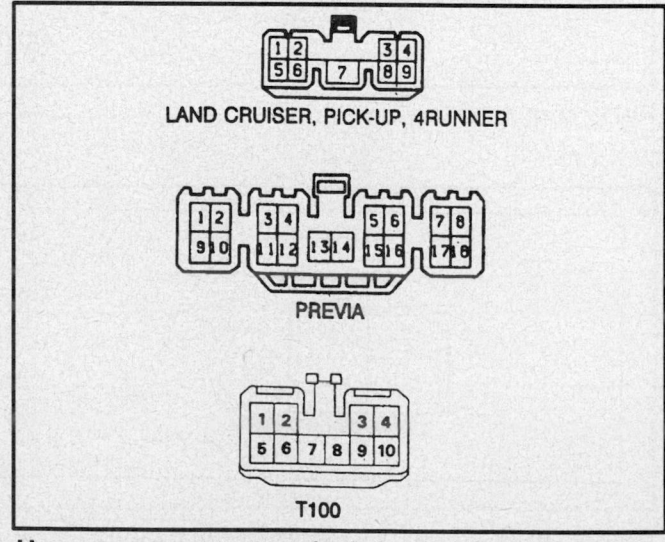

Harness connector terminals for testing A/C amplifier

A/C AMPLIFIER TEST CHART—LAND CRUISER

Check for	Tester connection	Condition	Specified value
Continuity	6 — Ground	Constant	Continuity
	8 — 9	Constant	Continuity
Voltage	2 — 6	Turn A/C switch on.	Battery voltage
		Turn A/C switch off.	No voltage
	3 — 6	Turn A/C switch on.	Battery voltage
		Turn A/C switch off.	No voltage
	5 — 6	Start the engine.	Approx. 10 to 14 V
		Stop the engine.	No voltage
Resistance	9 — 6	Constant	Approx. 1.5 kΩ at 25°C (77°F)

A/C AMPLIFIER TEST CHART—PICK-UP

Check for	Tester connection	Condition	Specified value
Continuity	7 — 8	Constant	Continuity
	8 — Ground	Constant	Continuity
Voltage	3 — 8	Turn A/C switch on.	Battery voltage
		Turn A/C switch off.	Battery voltage
	4 — 8	Turn A/C switch on.	Battery voltage
		Turn A/C switch off.	No voltage
	6 — 8	Start the engine.	Approx. 10 to 14 V
		Stop the engine.	No voltage
	8 — 9	Turn A/C switch on.	Battery voltage
		Turn A/C switch off.	Battery voltage
Resistance	5 — 8	Constant	Approx. 1.5 kΩ at 25°C (77°F)
	2 — 5	MAX COOL	Approx. 0 Ω
		MIN COOL	Approx. 3 kΩ

A/C AMPLIFIER TEST CHART—PICK-UP

Tester connection to terminal number	Condition	Specified value (Continuity)
7 — Ground	Constant	Continuity
1 — ECM terminal ACV	Constant	Continuity

Tester connection to terminal number	Condition	Specified value (Resistance)
2 — 5	Temperature control lever MAX COOL	Approx. 0 Ω
2 — 5	Temperature control lever MIN	Approx. 3 Ω
5 — 8	Constant	Approx. 1.5 kΩ at 25 °C (77 °F)
7 — 8	Constant	Approx. 3.8 Ω at 25 °C (77 °F)

Tester connection to terminal number	Condition	Specified value (Voltage)
4 — Ground	A/C switch ON	Battery positive voltage
4 — Ground	A/C switch OFF	No voltage
6 — Ground	Ignition switch ON	Approx. 10 to 14 v
6 — Ground	Ignition switch OFF	No Voltage

A/C AMPLIFIER TEST CHART—4RUNNER

Check for	Tester connection	Condition	Specified value
Continuity	8 — Ground	Constant	Continuity
Voltage	3 — 8	Turn A/C switch on.	Battery voltage
		Turn A/C switch off.	Battery voltage
	4 — 8	Turn A/C switch on.	Battery voltage
		Turn A/C swtich off.	No voltage
	6 — 8	Start the engine.	Approx. 10 to 14 V
		Stop the engine.	No voltage
	8 — 9	Turn A/C switch on.	Battery voltage
		Turn A/C switch off.	Battery voltage
Resistance	5 — 8	Constant	Approx. 1.5 kΩ at 25°C (77°F)
	2 — 5	MAX COOL	Approx. 3 kΩ
		MIN COOL	Approx. 0 Ω
	7 — 8	Constant	Approx. 3.6 Ω

A/C AMPLIFIER TEST CHART—4RUNNER

Tester connection to terminal number	Condition	Specified value (Continuity)
7 – 8	Constant	Continuity
8 – Ground	Constant	Continuity
Tester connection to terminal number	**Condition**	**Specified value (Voltage)**
3 – 8	Turn A/C switch ON	Battery positive voltage
3 – 8	Turn A/C switch OFF	Battery positive voltage
4 – 8	Turn A/C switch ON	Battery positive voltage
4 – 8	Turn A/C switch OFF	No voltage
6 – 8	Start the engine.	Approx. 10 to 14 V
6 – 8	Stop the engine.	No voltage
8 – 9	Turn A/C switch ON	Battery positive voltage
8 – 9	Turn A/C switch OFF	Battery positive voltage
Tester connection to terminal number	**Condition**	**Specified value (Resistance)**
2 – 5	MAX. COOL	Approx. 0 Ω
2 – 5	MIN. COOL	Approx. 3 kΩ
5 – 8	Constant	Approx. 1.5 kΩ at 25 °C (77 °F)

A/C AMPLIFIER TEST CHART—PREVIA

Check for	Tester connection	Condition		Specified value
Continuity	1 – 2	Constant		Continuity
	11 – Groung	A/C switch position	ON	Continuity
			OFF	No continuity
	12 – Ground	Rear blower switch position	ON	Continuity
			OFF	No continuity
	13 – Ground	Constant		Continuity
	17 – *2	Constant		Continuity
Resistance	1 – 15	Constant		Approx. 1.5 kΩ
	3 – 7	Constant		Approx. 60 Ω
	4 – 8	Constant		Approx. 20 Ω
Voltage	4 – Ground	Ignition switch position	LOCK, ACC or START	No voltage
			ON	Battery voltage
	5 – Ground	Ignition switch position	LOCK, ACC or START	No voltage
			ON	Battery voltage
	6 – Ground	Ignition switch position	LOCK, ACC or START	No voltage
			ON	Battery voltage
	12 – Ground	Engine condition	Running	Battery voltage
			Stopped	No voltage

A/C AMPLIFIER TEST CHART—PREVIA

Tester connection to terminal number	Condition	Specified Condition
6 — Ground	Constant	Continuity
7 — Ground	Rear blower switch position OFF	No continuity
7 — Ground	Rear blower switch position ON	Continuity
10 — Ground	Front A/C switch position OFF	No continuity
10 — Ground	Front A/C switch position ON	Continuity
16 — Cool box amplifier terminal 2	Constant	Continuity
4 — 15	Constant	Approx. 15 kΩ at 25 °C (85 °F)
12 — 13	Constant	Approx. 20 Ω at 25 °C (85 °F)
12 — 14	Constant	Approx. 60 Ω at 25 °C (85 °F)
3 — Ground	Ignition switch position LOCK or ACC	No voltage
3 — Ground	Ignition switch position ON	Battery positive voltage
7 — Ground	Engine condition Stopped	No voltage
7 — Ground	Engine condition Running	Battery positive voltage
8 — Ground	Ignition switch position LOCK or ACC	No voltage
8 — Ground	Ignition switch position ON	Battery positive voltage
1 — Ground	Ignition switch position LOCK or ACC	No voltage
1 — Ground	Ignition switch position ON	Battery positive voltage

A/C AMPLIFIER TEST CHART—T-100

Check for	Tester Connection	Condition	Specified Value
Voltage	1 — Ground	Ignition switch on	Approx. 10 to 14 V
	5 — Ground	A/C switch on	Approx. 10 to 14 V
	7 — Ground	A/C switch on	Below 1 V
	9 — Ground	Magnetic clutch on	0 V
	8 — Ground	Magnetic clutch on	Below 1V
Resistance	4 — 10	Constant	Approx. 1.5 kΩ at 25°C (77°F)
Continuity	4 — Ground	Constant	Continuity

A/C AMPLIFIER TEST CHART—T100

Tester connection to terminal number	Condition	Specified condition
8 — Ground	Constant	Continuity
1 — ECM terminal ACT	Constant	Continuity
9 — ECM terminal AC1	Constant	Continuity
7 — Ground	A/C switch ON	Continuity
7 — Ground	A/C switch OFF	No continuity
2 — 6	Constant	1.5 kΩ at 25 °C (77 °F)
4 — Ground	A/C switch ON	Battery positive voltage
4 — Ground	A/C switch OFF	No voltage

REAR AUXILIARY SYSTEM

Expansion Valve

REMOVAL AND INSTALLATION

Previa

The expansion valve can be accessed only after the rear A/C assembly is removed and disassembled.

DENSO TYPE

1. Disconnect the negative battery cable. Remove the right and left air inlet and outlet grilles.
2. Remove the filter and the lower case cover.
3. Remove the rear air conditioning switch.
4. Discharge the refrigeration system using a refrigerant recovery system.
5. Disconnect the refrigerant lines from the cooling unit inlet and outlet fittings and cap immediately to keep dirt and moisture out of the rest of the system.
6. Remove the evaporator assembly.
7. Using an hex wrench, remove 2 bolts and lift off the expansion valve.

To install:

8. Installation is the reverse of the removal procedure. Install the expansion valve.
9. Install the blower assembly, electrical components and assemble the cooler case.
10. Install the filter and grilles. Evacuate and recharge the system.

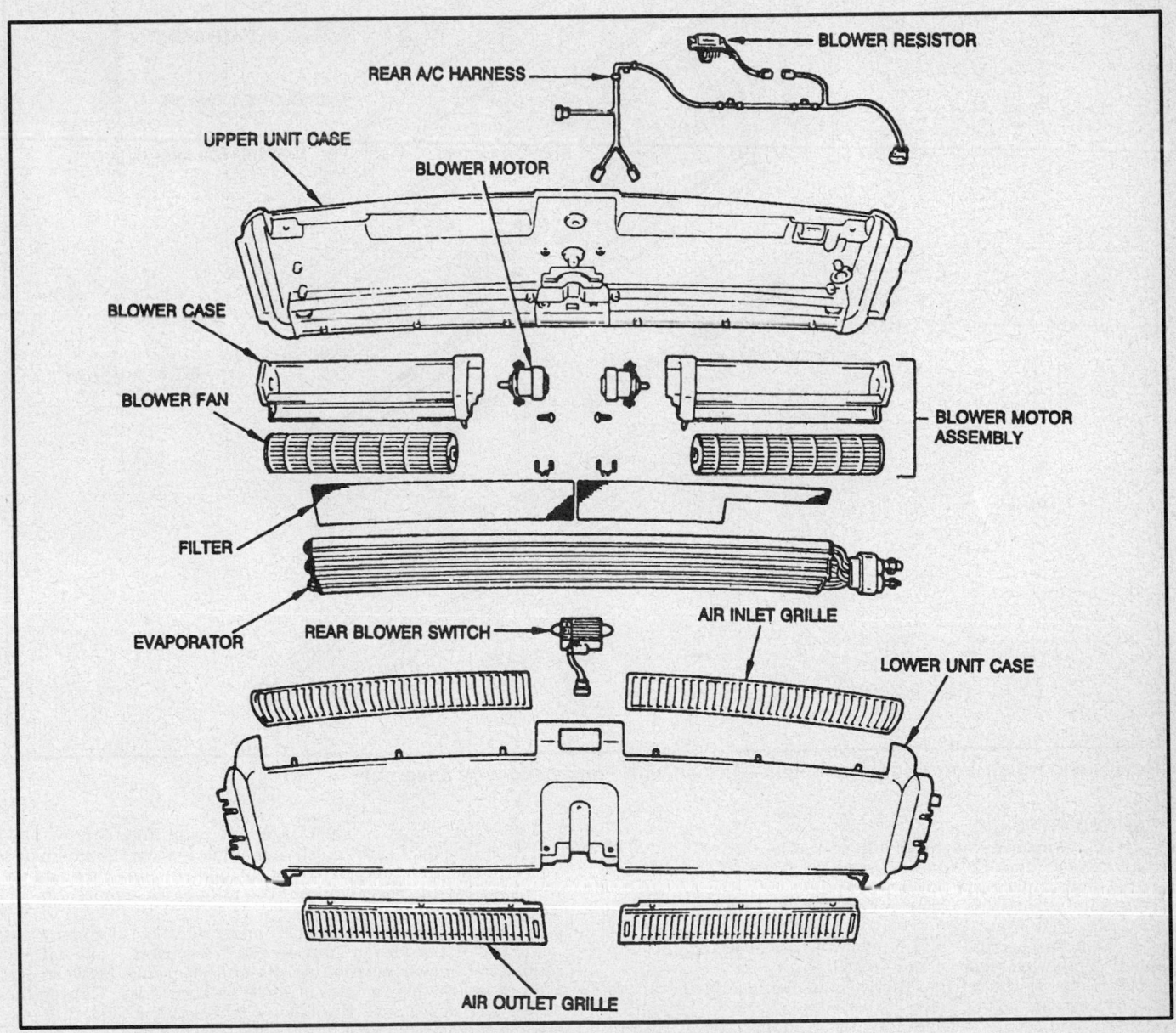

Rear auxiliary air conditioning system—Previa with Denso type assembly

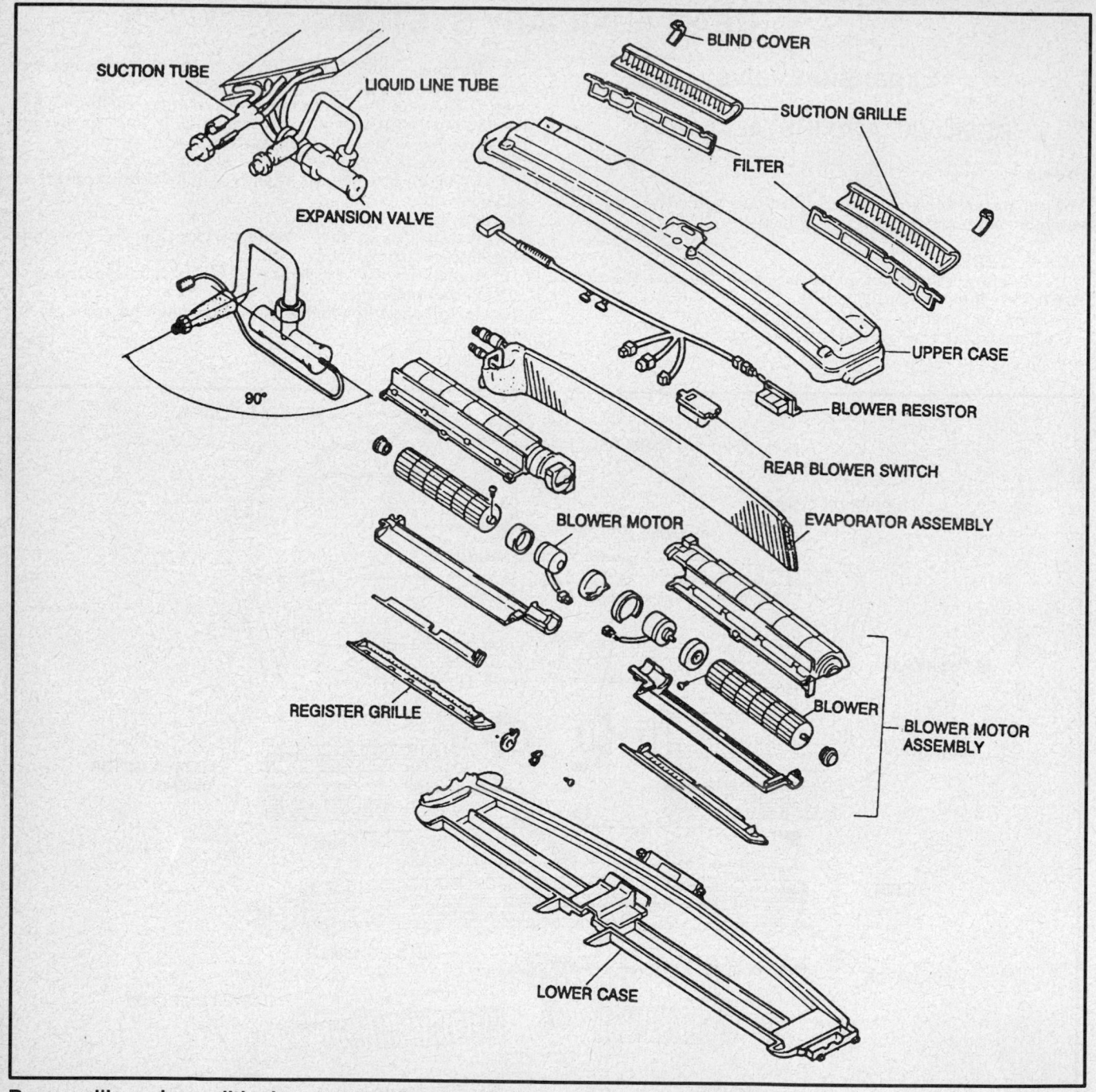

Rear auxiliary air conditioning system—Previa with Panasonic type assembly

PANASONIC TYPE

1. Disconnect the negative battery cable.
2. Remove the 12 screws and lift off the right and left grilles and filters from the lower case.
3. Empty the drain. Then remove the 9 screws and remove the lower case.
4. Remove the right and left blower motor assemblies. Remove the blower resistor and switch.
5. Discharge the refrigeration system using a refrigerant recovery system.
6. Disconnect the refrigerant lines from the cooling unit inlet and outlet fittings and cap immediately to keep dirt and moisture out of the rest of the system.

7. Remove the evaporator assembly by pulling out.
8. Remove the heat protective insulators from the expansion valve and suction tube. Separate the heat-sensing tube and remove the expansion valve from the inlet of the evaporator.

To install:

9. Temporarily assemble the blower wheel to the motor assembly. Put the blower unit on the lower case. Take care to adjust the blower position so the end clearance between the blower and the blower case is equal on both sides. Tighten the screw and make sure the blower wheel turns smoothly. Assemble the blower upper case to the lower case.
10. Connect the liquid line tube to the expansion valve and, using a crow's foot wrench, torque the nut to 10 ft. lbs. Con-

nect the expansion valve to the inlet fitting of the evaporator and torque to 17 ft. lbs. Connect the heat sensing tube to the suction line and reattach the heat insulators around the expansion valve.

11. Install the evaporator to the upper case.
12. Install the switch and the blower motor assemblies to the upper case.
13. Install the lower case, the filters and grilles. Connect the drain hoses. Evacuate and recharge the system.

Rear Blower Motor

REMOVAL AND INSTALLATION

Previa

DENSO TYPE
1. Disconnect the negative battery cable. Remove the right and left air inlet and outlet grilles.
2. Remove the filter and the lower case cover.
3. Remove the rear A/C switch.
4. Discharge the refrigeration system using a refrigerant recovery system.
5. Remove the evaporator assembly.
6. Remove the left and right blower assemblies.
To install:
7. Installation is the reverse of the removal procedure. Assemble the blower wheels to the motors, if removed. Install the blower resistor, if removed. Install the blower and motor assemblies to the upper case.
8. Install the evaporator assembly to the upper case. Install the rear blower switch.
9. Install the lower case to the upper case. Install the filter and grilles.
10. Evacuate and recharge the system.

PANASONIC TYPE
1. The motor assemblies can be removed without removing the entire cooling system. Remove the 12 screws and lift off the right and left grilles and filters.
2. Empty the drain. Then remove the 9 screws and remove the lower case.
3. Remove the right and left blower motor assemblies by removing the 3 screws on each assembly and disconnecting the electrical connector. Disengage the 8 retaining pawls and remove the blower assembly.
To install:
4. Installation is the reverse of the removal procedure. Assemble the blower motor assemblies.
5. Install the lower case. Make sure the drains are properly installed.
6. Install the grilles and filters.

Land Cruiser

1. Disconnect the negative battery cable.
2. Remove the right front seat.
3. Disconnect the blower motor and rear heater relay connections. Remove 1 bolt and take out the relay.
4. Remove 4 screws and take off the blower side cover. Remove 1 bolt and 7 screws to take off the blower upper cover with the motor attached. Separate the motor from the cover.
5. Reverse removal procedure to install the blower motor.

Blower Motor Resistor

REMOVAL AND INSTALLATION

Previa
DENSO TYPE
1. Remove the blower motor as described above.
2. Disconnect the resistor connection, remove the 2 retaining screws and take out the blower resistor.
3. Installation is the reverse of the removal procedure.

Evaporator

REMOVAL AND INSTALLATION

Previa
DENSO TYPE
1. Disconnect the negative battery cable. Remove the right and left air inlet and outlet grilles.
2. Remove the filter and the lower case cover.
3. Remove the rear air conditioning switch.
4. Discharge the refrigeration system using a refrigerant recovery system.
5. Disconnect the refrigerant lines from the cooling unit inlet and outlet fittings and cap immediately to keep dirt and moisture out of the rest of the system.
6. Remove the evaporator assembly.
To install:
7. Installation is the reverse of the removal procedure.
8. Install the blower assembly, electrical components and assemble the cooler case.
9. Install the filter and grilles. Evacuate and recharge the system.

PANASONIC TYPE
1. Disconnect the negative battery cable.
2. Remove the 12 screws and lift off the right and left grilles and filters.
3. Empty the drain. Then remove the 9 screws and remove the lower case.
4. Remove the right and left blower motor assemblies. Remove the blower resistor and switch.
5. Discharge the refrigeration system using a refrigerant recovery system.
6. Disconnect the refrigerant lines from the cooling unit inlet and outlet fittings and cap immediately to keep dirt and moisture out of the rest of the system.
7. Remove the evaporator assembly by pulling out.
To install:
8. Installation is the reverse of the removal procedure. Temporarily assemble the blower wheel to the motor assembly. Put the blower unit on the lower case. Take care to adjust the blower position so the end clearance between the blower and the blower case is equal on both sides. Tighten the screw and make sure the blower wheel turns smoothly. Assemble the blower upper case to the lower case.
9. Connect the liquid line tube to the expansion valve and, using a crow's foot wrench, torque the nut to 10 ft. lbs. Connect the expansion valve to the inlet fitting of the evaporator and torque to 17 ft. lbs. Connect the heat sensing tube to the suction line and reattach the heat insulators around the expansion valve.
10. Install the evaporator to the upper case.
11. Install the switch and the blower motor assemblies to the upper case.
12. Install the lower case, the filters and grilles. Connect the drain hoses. Evacuate and recharge the system.

Refrigerant Lines

REMOVAL AND INSTALLATION

1. Discharge the refrigeration system using a refrigerant recovery system, if possible.
2. Disconnect the faulty refrigerant line. Cap open fittings immediately to keep moisture out of the rest of the system.
3. Some interior trim panels may need to be removed to take out the damaged section of refrigerant line. Due to high pressures always replace lines with new ones of equal quality.

4. When installing new refrigerant lines, measure the diameter of the tube. On the tubes measuring 0.31 in. or approximately 3/8 in., torque the fittings to 10 ft. lbs. On tubes measuring 0.50 in. or approximately 1/2 in., torque the fittings to 17 ft. lbs. On tubes measuring 0.62 in. or approximately 5/8 in., torque the fittings to 24 ft. lbs. Generally a small torque wrench is used with a crow's foot adapter to torque air conditioning fittings. When tightening these fittings, apply a few drops of compressor oil to the O-ring fittings for easy tightening. Tighten the nut using 2 wrenches to avoid twisting the tube.
5. Evacuate, charge and test the system.

SYSTEM DIAGNOSTICS

Troubleshooting by Symptom

NOTE: Following each symptom below, the items listed to check are in order of priority of most likely to cause the problem listed. Not all items listed are applicable to every model. Where applicable, front system checks are listed separately from rear system checks.

NO BLOWER OPERATION

Front System

Check heater circuit breaker, fusible link, heater relay, blower speed control switch, blower control relay, blower motor, blower resistor, circuit wiring (including grounds).

Rear System

Check rear A/C fuse, rear A/C relay, rear A/C switch, rear blower motor, circuit wiring (including grounds).

NO BLOWER CONTROL

Front System

Check blower high relay, blower speed control switch, blower speed control relay, blower resistor, circuit wiring (including grounds).

Rear System

Check rear A/C switch, rear blower resistor, circuit wiring (including grounds).

NO AIR FLOW MODE CONTROL OR AIR INLET CONTROL

Check drive belt tension, A/C control assembly, air inlet servomotor, air outlet servomotor.

INSUFFICIENT AIR FLOW

Front System

Check heater relay, blower motor, blower resistor, circuit wiring (including grounds), air inlet for blockage, evaporator core clogged or frosted, heater unit or duct for leak, heater core, A/C amplifier.

Rear System

Check rear A/C filter, rear blower relay, rear blower motor, rear blower resistor, circuit wiring (including grounds), air inlet for blockage, rear evaporator core clogged or frosted.

NO COOL AIR COMES OUT

Check refrigerant level, drive belt tension, A/C fuse, check system with manifold gauge set, front A/C thermistor, A/C cut relay, front expansion valve, clutch relay, compressor clutch, pressure switch, water valve, compressor, climate control panel/cable adjustment, A/C switch, air mix servomotor, A/C amplifier, front evaporator core, rear expansion valve, rear evaporator core, circuit wiring (including grounds).

COOL AIR COMES OUT INTERMITTENTLY

Check refrigerant level, drive belt tension, system operation check with manifold gauge set, receiver/drier (excessive moisture in system—expansion valve may be freezing), compressor, A/C amplifier, front A/C thermistor, circuit wiring and grounds.

COOL AIR COMES OUT ONLY AT HIGH ENGINE SPEED

Check refrigerant level, drive belt tension, system operation check with manifold gauge set, air in system, condenser, compressor.

INSUFFICIENT COOLING

Check refrigerant level, drive belt tension, system operation check with manifold gauge set, condenser, receiver/drier, water valve cable adjustment, engine coolant temperature A/C cut switch, air mix servomotor, expansion valve (front or rear), air or excessive oil in system, A/C amplifier, thermistor, evaporator core (front or rear), clutch relay, magnetic clutch, compressor.

NO WARM AIR COMES OUT

Check engine coolant volume, heater fuse, heater relay, water valve, climate control panel/cable adjustments, air mix servomotor, heater core, wiring and grounds.

AIR TEMPERATURE CONTROL NOT FUNCTIONING

Check water valve and adjustment, heater core, climate control panel/cable adjustments, air mix servomotor, wiring and grounds.

NO ENGINE IDLE UP WITH A/C ON

A/C vacuum switching valve, A/C amplifier.

NOTE: When checking systems which uses R-134a refrigerant, do not use same test gauges and hoses used with R-12 systems. Contamination, improper operation or system damage could result from any mix of R-12 with R-134a or the system oils.

TROUBLESHOOTING WITH GAUGES

This is a method in which the trouble is located by using a manifold gauge. Read the manifold gauge pressure when the following conditions are established:

(a) Temperature at the air inlet is 30 — 35°C (86 — 95°F)

(b) Engine running at 1,500 rpm

(c) Blower fan speed switch set at high speed

(d) Temperature control lever set at cool side

HINT: It should be noted that the gauge indications may vary slightly due to ambient temperature conditions.

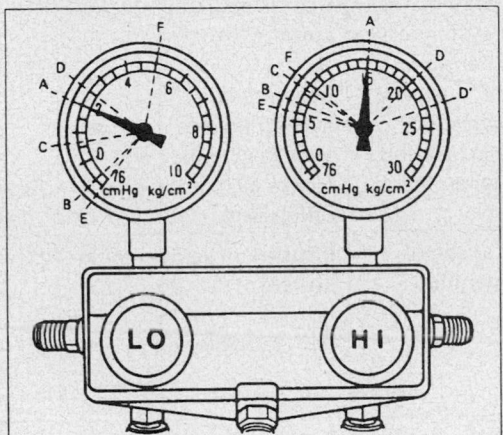

NORMALLY FUNCTIONING REFRIGERATION SYSTEM

Gauge reading:

Low pressure side
1.5 — 2.0 kg/cm^2
(21 — 28 psi, 147 — 196 kPa)

High pressure side
14.5 — 15.0 kg/cm^2
(206 — 213 psi, 1,422 — 1,471 kPa)

Each pointer of manifold gauge point to position A.

No.	Trouble	Condition	Position of Pointers
1	Moisture present in refrigeration system	Periodically cools and then fails to cool	Between A and B
2	Insufficient refrigerant	Insufficient cooling	C
3	Poor circulation of refrigerant	Insufficient cooling	C
4	Refrigerant overcharge or insufficient cooling of condenser	Does not cool sufficiently	D
5	Expansion valve improperly mounted, heat sensing tube defective (Opens too wide)	Insufficient cooling	D
6	Air present in refrigeration system	Does not cool sufficiently	Low is D High is D'
7	Refrigerant does not circulate	Does not cool (Cools from time to time in some cases)	E
8	Insufficient compression	Does not cool	F

TROUBLESHOOTING WITH GAUGES, CONT.

No.	Symptom seen in refrigeration system	Probable cause	Diagnosis	Remedy
1	During operation, pressure at low pressure side sometimes becomes a vacuum and sometimes normal	Moisture entered in refrigeration system freezes at expansion valve orifice and temporarily stops cycle, but normal state is restored after a time when the ice melts	Drier in oversaturated state ↓ Moisture in refrigeration system freezes at expansion valve orifice and blocks circulation of refrigerant	(1) Replace receiver and drier (2) Remove moisture in cycle through repeated vacuum purging (3) Charge refrigerant to proper amount
2	Pressure low at both low and high pressure sides Bubbles seen in sight glass Insufficient cooling performance	Gas leakage at some place in refrigeration system	Insufficient refrigerant in system ↓ Refrigerant leaking	(1) Check with leak tester and repair (2) Charge refrigerant to proper amount
3	Pressure low at both low and high pressure sides Frost on tubes from receiver to unit	Refrigerant flow obstructed by dirt in receiver	Receiver clogged	Replace receiver
4	Pressure too high at both low and high pressure sides	Unable to develop sufficient performance due to excessive refrigerant in system Condenser cooling insufficient	Excess refrigerant in cycle → refrigerant overcharged Condenser cooling insufficient → condenser fins clogged or fan motor faulty	(1) Clean condenser (2) Check fan motor operation (3) If (1) and (2) are normal, check refrigerant amount HINT: Vent out refrigerant through gauge manifold low pressure side by gradually opening valve.
5	Pressure too high at both low and high pressure sides Frost or large amount of dew on piping at low pressure side	Trouble in expansion valve or heat sensing tube not installed correctly Refrigerant flow out	Excessive refrigerant in low pressure piping ↓ Expansion valve opened too wide	(1) Check heat sensing tube installed condition (2) If (1) is normal, test expansion valve in unit (3) Replace if defective

TROUBLESHOOTING WITH GAUGES, CONT.

No.	Symptom seen in refrigeration system	Probable cause	Diagnosis	Remedy
6	Pressure too high at both low and high pressure sides	Air entered refrigeration system	Air present in refrigeration system ↓ Insufficient vacuum purging	(1) Replace receiver and drier (2) Check compressor oil to see if dirty or insufficient (3) Vacuum purge and charge new refrigerant
7	Vacuum indicated at low pressure side, very low pressure indicated at high pressure side

Frost or dew seen on piping before and after receiver and drier or expansion valve | Refrigerant flow obstructed by moisture or dirt in refrigerant freezing or adhering to expansion valve orifice

Refrigerant flow obstructed by gas leakage from expansion valve | Expansion valve orifice clogged ↓ Refrigerant does not flow | Allow to stand for some time and then restart operation to determine if trouble is caused by moisture or dirt.

If caused by dirt, remove expansion valve and clean off dirt by blowing with air. If unable to remove dirt, replace valve.

Vacuum purge and charge new refrigerant to proper amount.

For gas leakage from heat sensing tube, replace expansion valve. |
| 8 | Pressure too high at low pressure side
Pressure too low at high pressure side | Internal leak in compressor | Compression defective ↓ Valve leaking or broken sliding parts (Piston, cylinder, gasket, etc.) broken | Repair or replace compressor |

* HINT at No.6
These gauge indications are shown when the refrigeration system has been opened and the refrigerant charged without vacuum purging.

WIRING SCHEMATICS

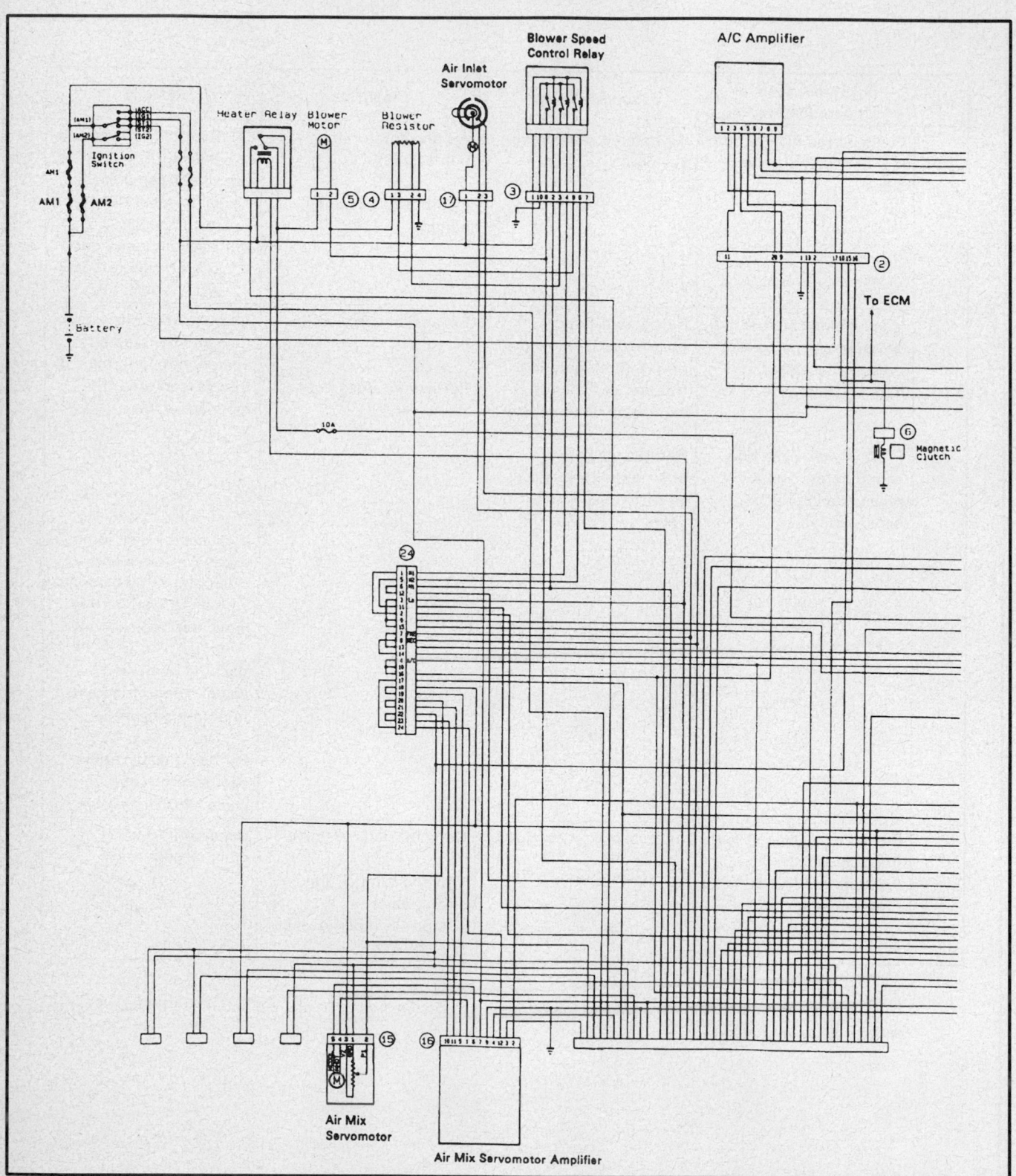

Heater wiring schematic—1993–94 Land Cruiser

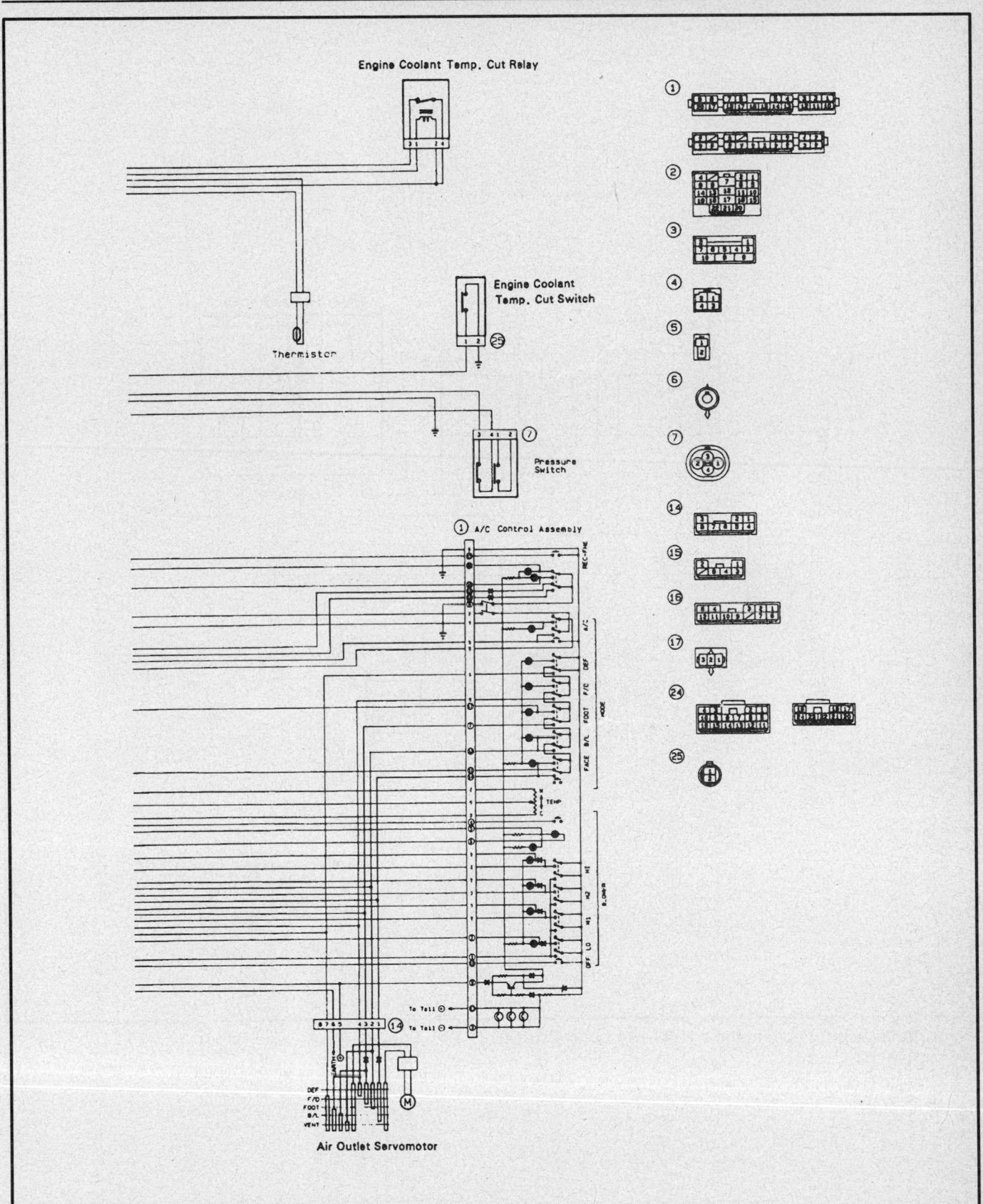

Heater wiring schematic—1993–94 Land Cruiser

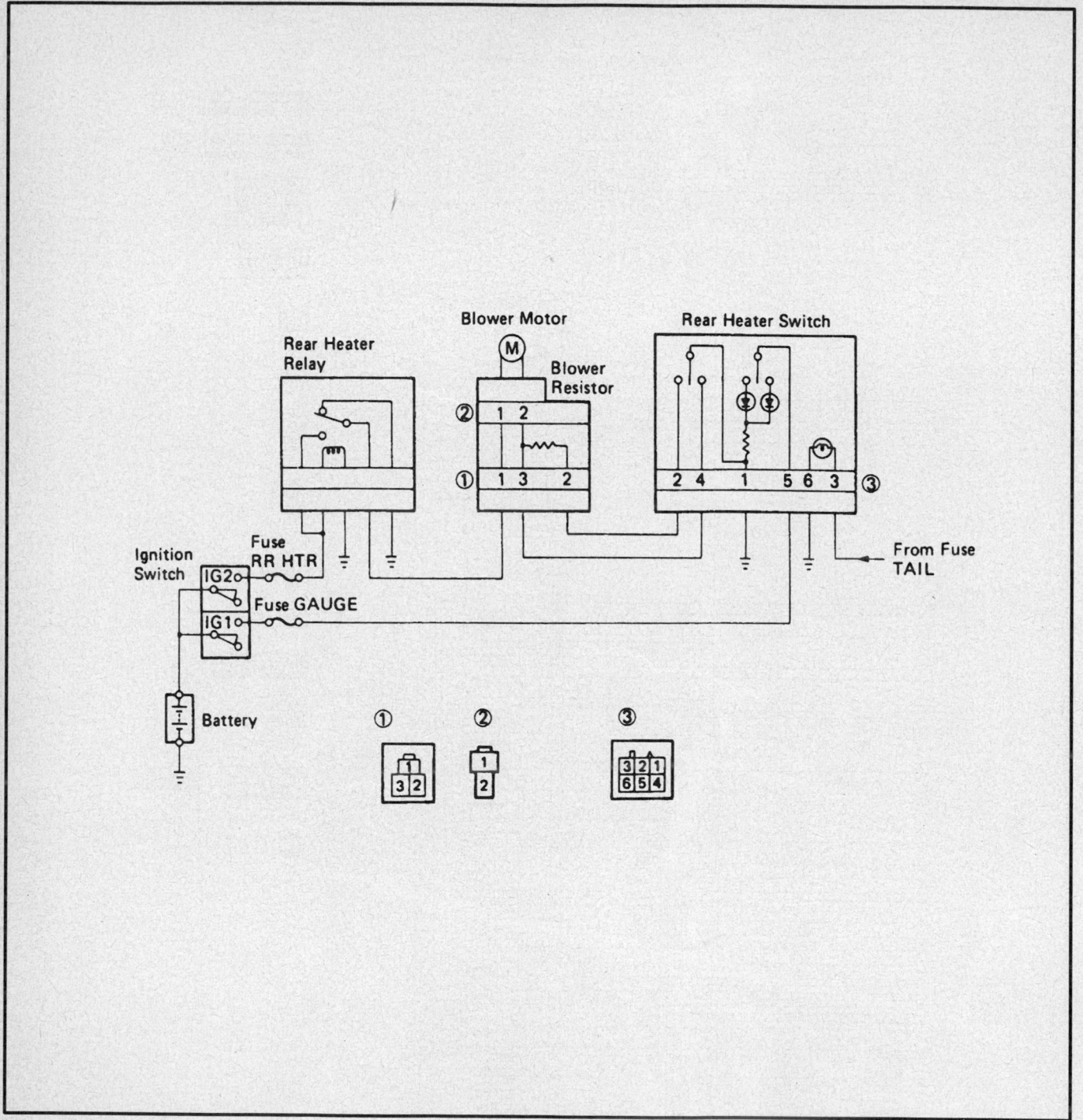

Rear heater wiring schematic—1993–94 Land Cruiser

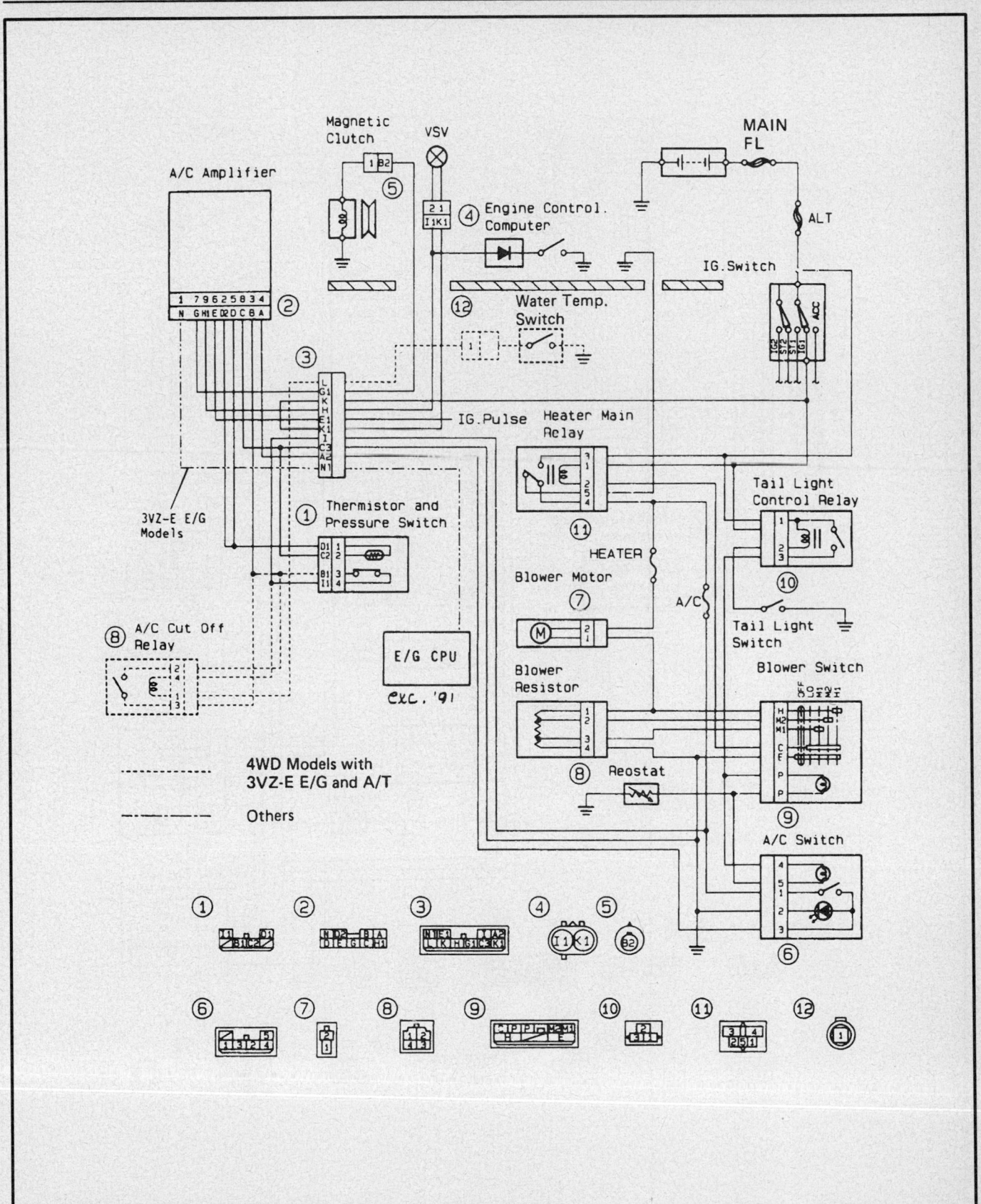

Heater-air conditioning system wiring schematic—1993-94 Pick-Up

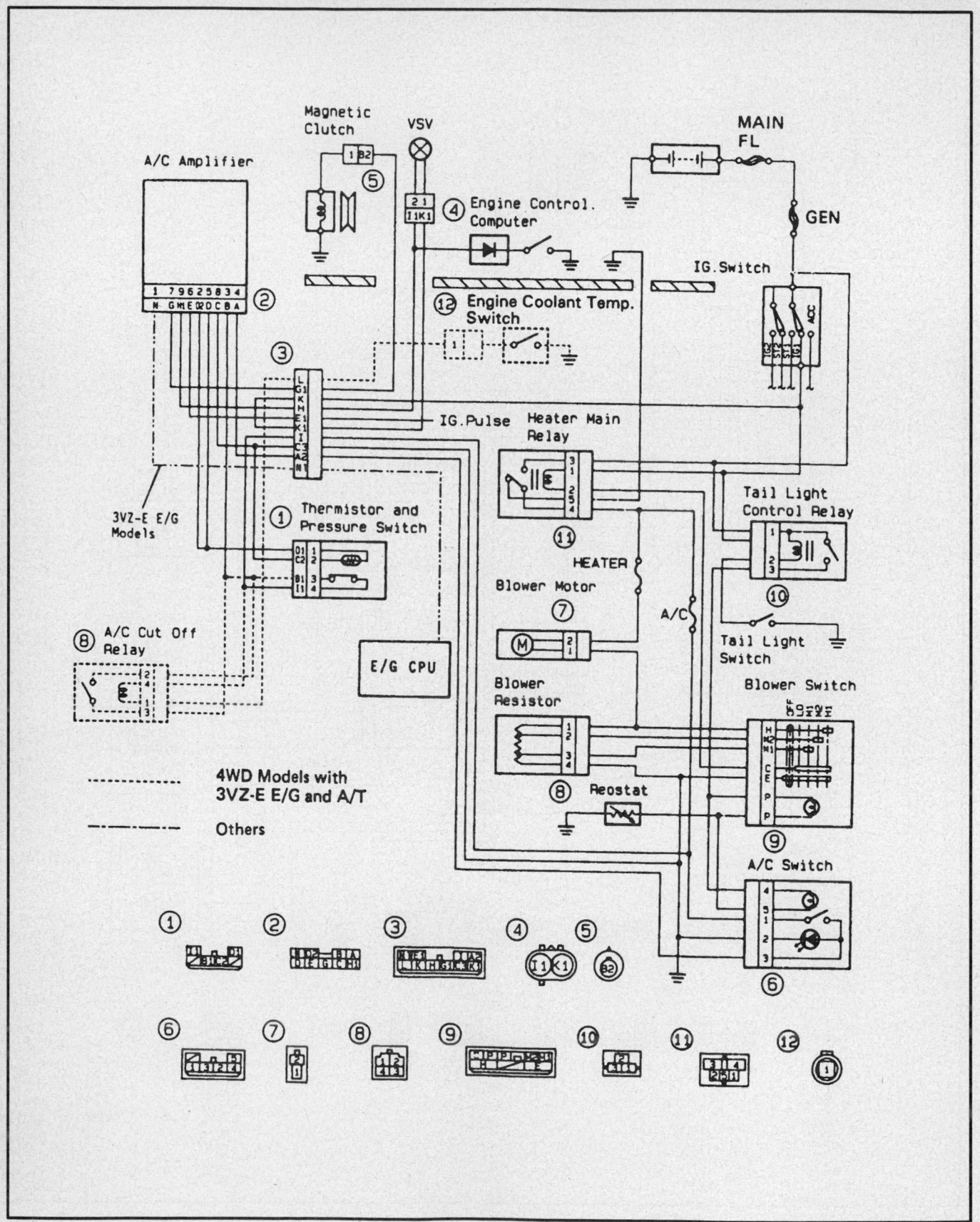

Heater-air conditioning system wiring schematic — 1995 Pick-up

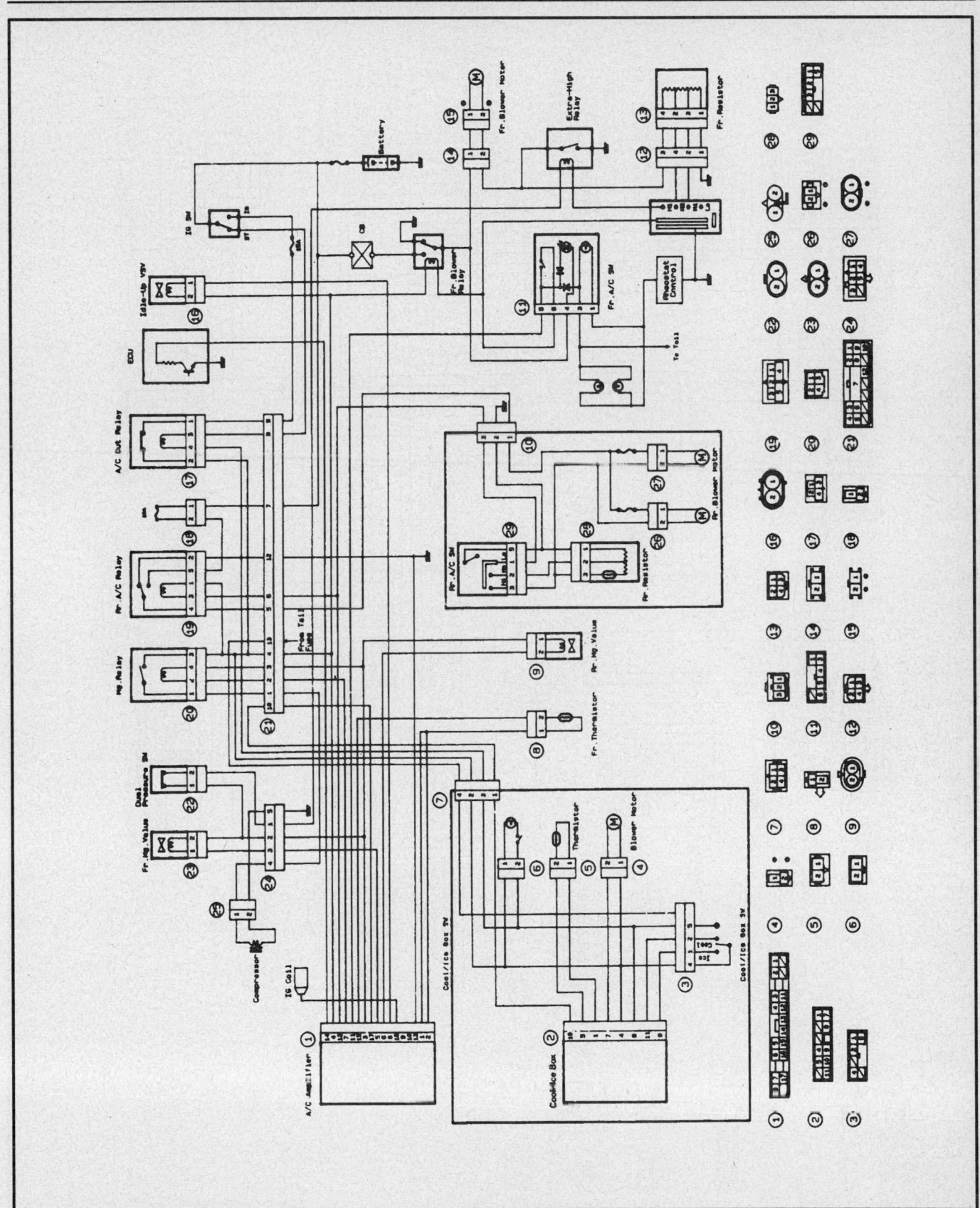

Heater-air conditioning system wiring schematic—1993–94 Previa with rear auxiliary system

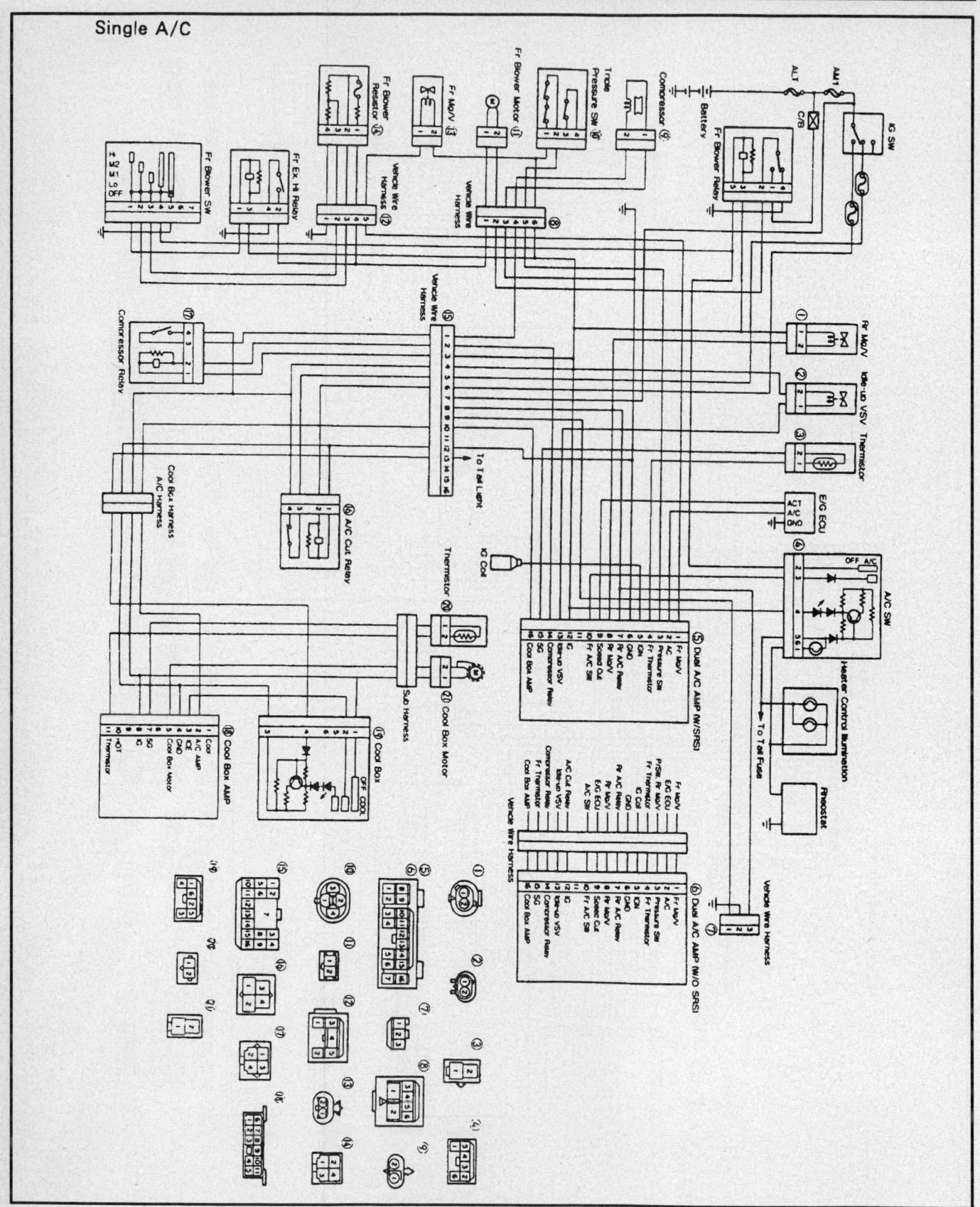

Heater-air conditioning system wiring schematic (Single A/C)—1994 Previa

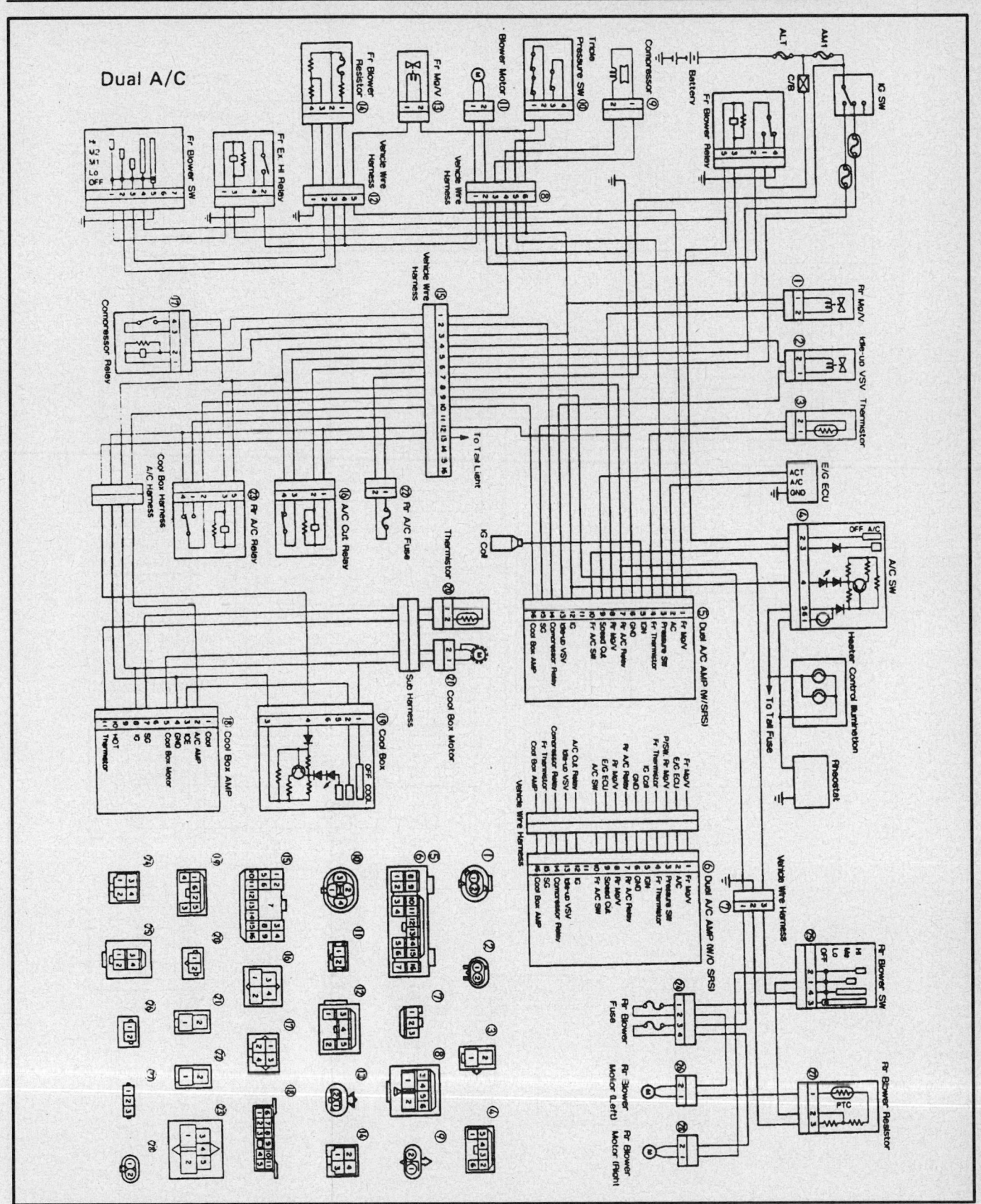

Heater-air conditioning system wiring schematic (Dual A/C)—1994 Previa

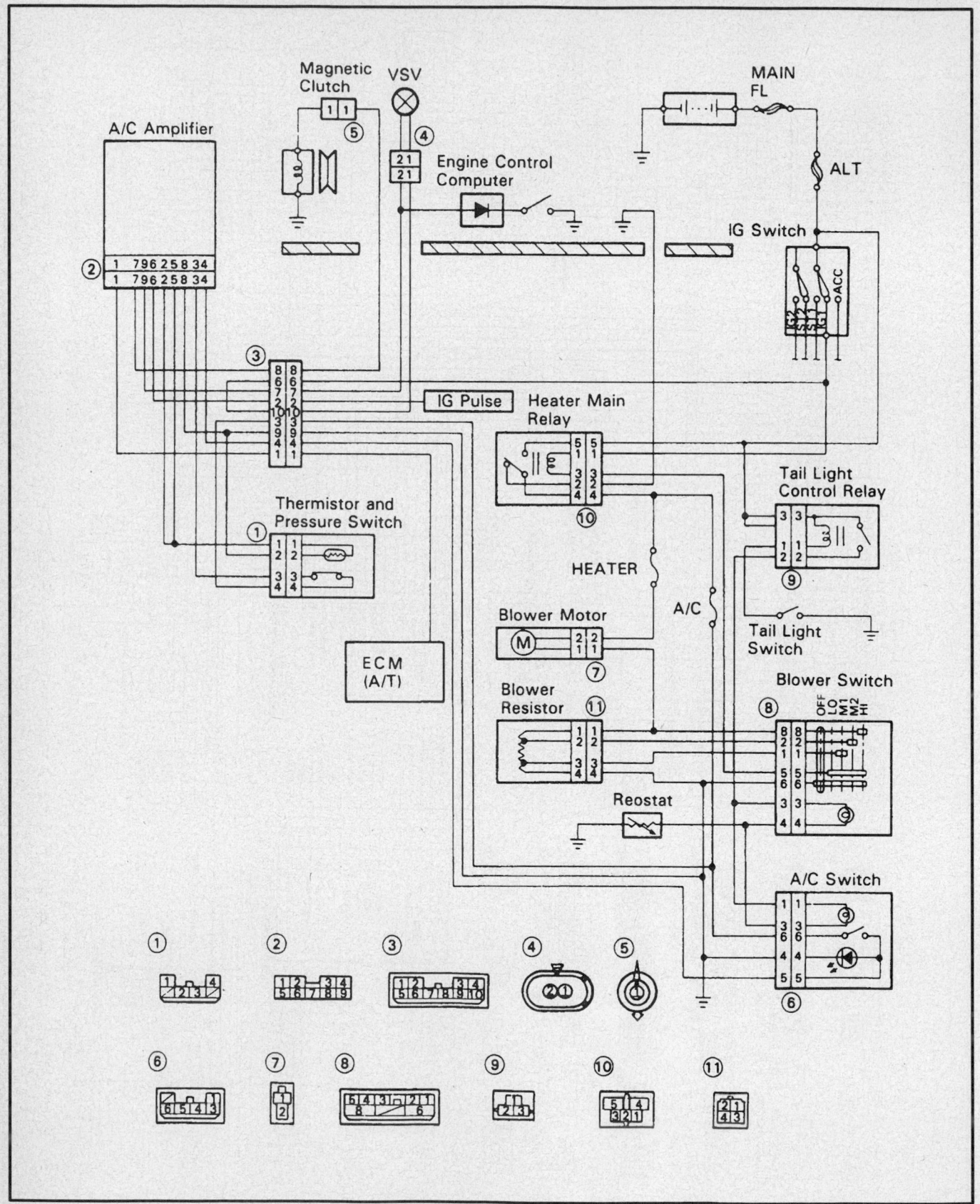

Heater-air conditioning system wiring schematic—1993-94 T100

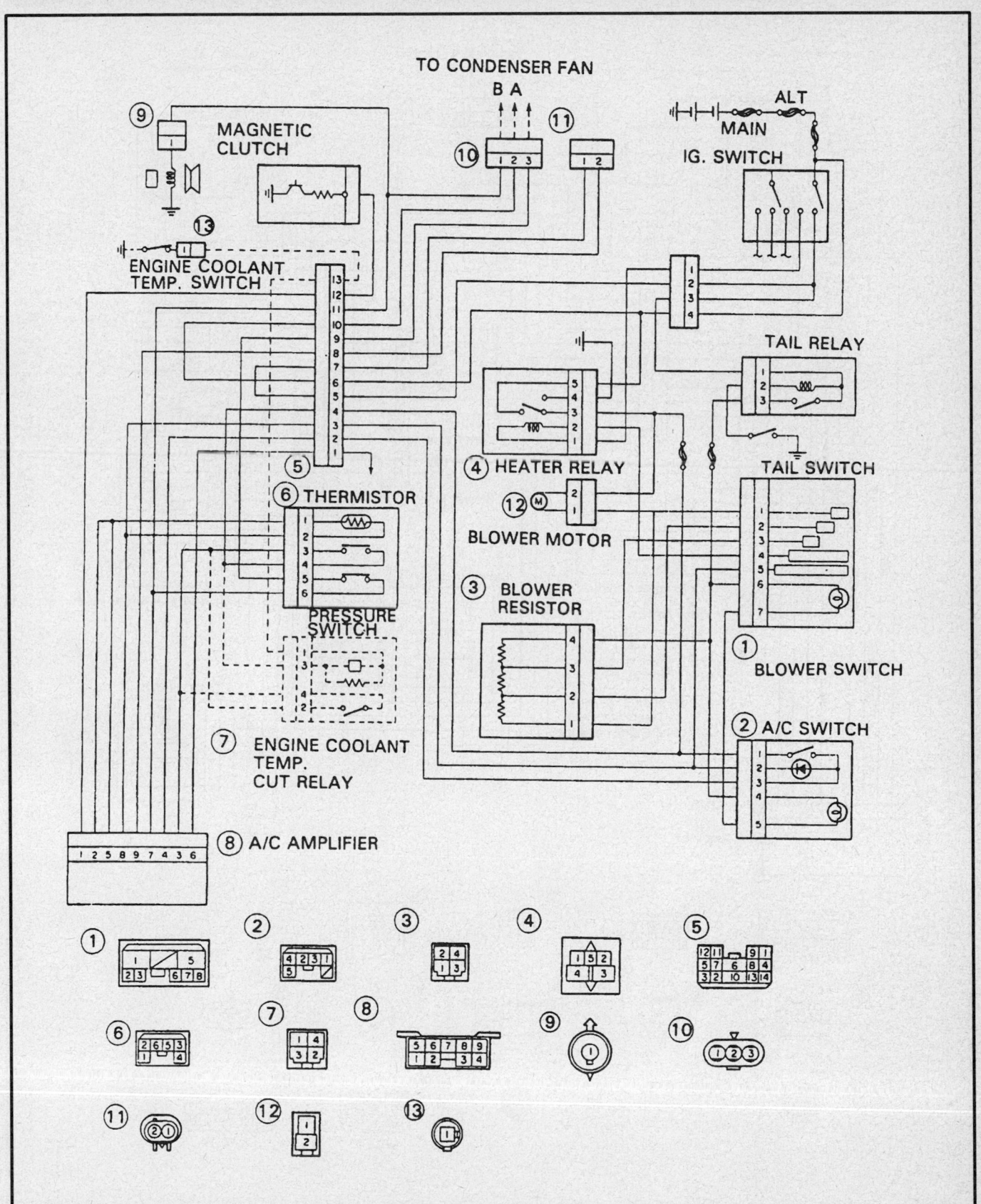

Heater-air conditioning system wiring schematic—1994 4Runner

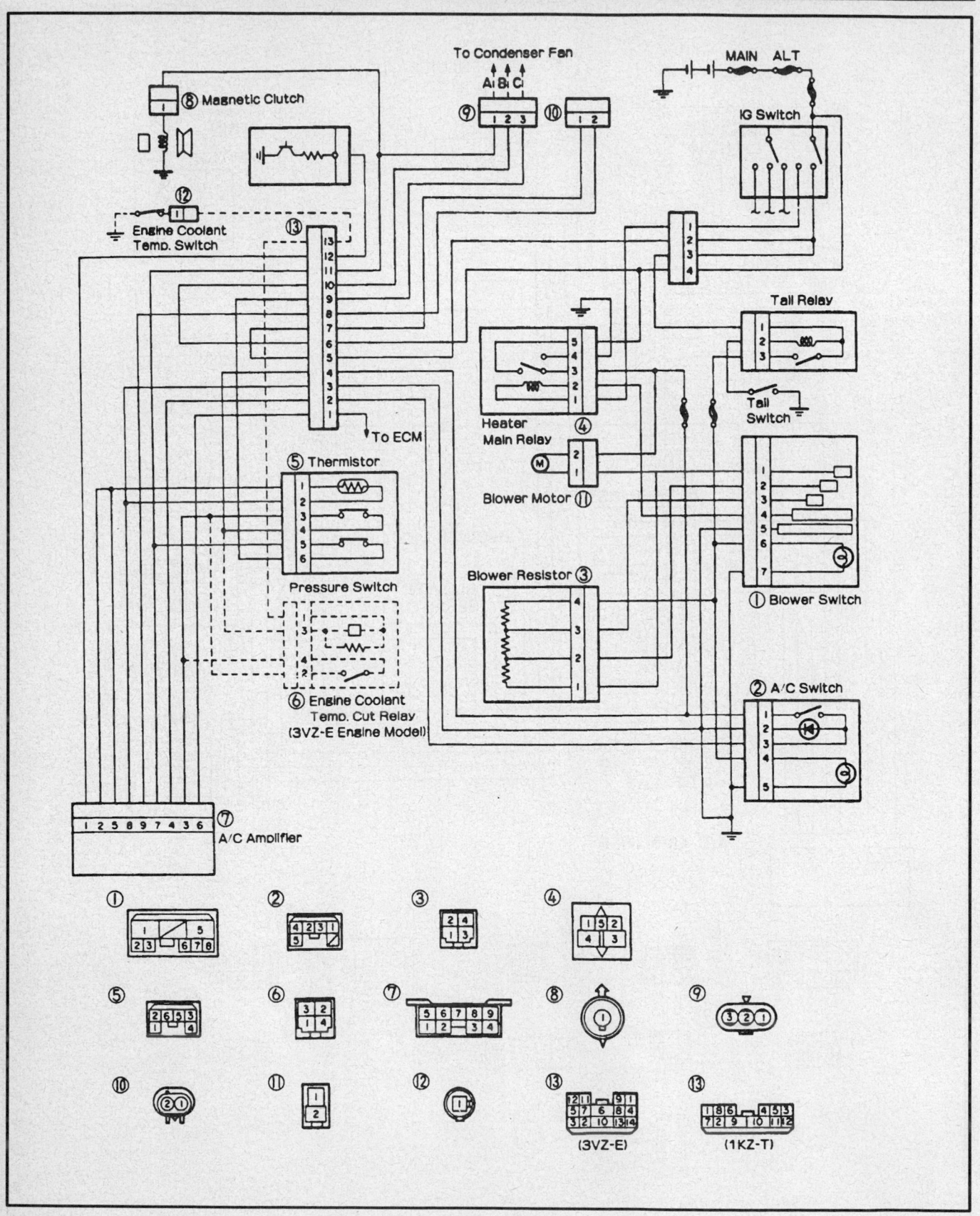

Heater-air conditioning system wiring schematic—1995 4Runner

SPECIFICATIONS

ENGINE IDENTIFICATION

Year	Model	Engine Displacement Liters (cc)	Engine Series (ID/VIN)	Fuel System	No. of Cylinders	Engine Type
1993	Cabriolet	1.8 (1780)	2H	AFC–Digifant	4	SOHC
	Corrado SLC	1.8 (1780)	PG	AFC–Digifant	4	SOHC
	Corrado VR6 ①	2.8 (2778)	AAA	CIS–E Motronic	4	SOHC
	Fox	1.8 (1780)	UN	EFI	4	SOHC
	Fox	1.8 (1780)	ABG	AFC–Digifant	4	SOHC
	Golf GL	1.8 (1780)	RV	AFC–Digifant	4	SOHC
	Golf GTI	1.8 (1780)	RV,PF	AFC–Digifant	4	SOHC
	Golf GTI 16V	2.0 (1984)	9A	CIS–E Motronic	4	DOHC
	Jetta Diesel	1.6 (1588)	ME	Diesel Inj.	4	SOHC
	Jetta GL, Carat	1.8 (1780)	RV,PF	AFC–Digifant	4	SOHC
	Jetta GLI 16V	2.0 (1984)	9A	CIS–E Motronic	4	DOHC
	Passat	2.0 (1984)	9A	CIS–E Motronic	4	DOHC
	Passat GLX	2.8 (2778)	NA	CIS–E Motronic	6	DOHC
	Eurovan	2.5 (2480)	NA	EFI	6	SOHC
1994	Corrado	2.8 (2778)	NA	AFC–Digifant	6	DOHC
	Golf III	2.0 (1984)	NA	CIS–E Motronic	4	SOHC
	Golf III GTI	2.8 (2778)	NA	AFC–Digifant	6	DOHC
	Jetta III	2.0 (1984)	NA	CIS–E Motronic	4	SOHC
	Jetta III GLX	2.8 (2778)	NA	AFC–Digifant	6	DOHC
	Passat GLX	2.8 (2778)	NA	CIS–E Motronic	6	DOHC
	Eurovan	2.5 (2480)	NA	EFI	6	SOHC
1995	Cabrio	2.0 (1984)	NA	CIS–E Motronic	4	SOHC
	Golf III	2.0 (1984)	NA	CIS–E Motronic	4	SOHC
	GTI VR6	2.8 (2778)	SLG	AFC–Digifant	6	SOHC
	Jetta III	2.0 (1984)	NA	CIS–E Motronic	4	SOHC
	Jetta III GLX	2.8 (2778)	NA	AFC–Digifant	6	SOHC
	Passat	2.8 (2778)	—	CIS–E Motronic	6	SOHC
	Eurovan	2.5 (2480)	—	EFI	6	SOHC

NA–Not available
① Canada
DOHC–Dual Overhead Cam
SOHC–Single Overhead Cam
EFI–Electronic Fuel Injection

AFC–Air Flow Control
CIS–E–Continuous Injection System-Electronic

REFRIGERANT CAPACITIES

Year	Model	Refrigerant (oz.)	Oil (fl. oz.)	Compressor Type
1993	Cabriolet	38–42	4.6	Sanden
	Corrado	37–40	4.6	Sanden
	Fox	37–40	8.0	Nippondenso
	Golf	37–40	8.0	Nippondenso
	Jetta	37–40	4.6	Sanden

REFRIGERANT CAPACITIES

Year	Model	Refrigerant (oz.) ①	Oil (fl. oz.)	Compressor Type
1993	Passat	39–42	3.9	Sanden
	Eurovan	32–35 ②	4.6 ②	Sanden
1994	Corrado	34–37	3.9	Sanden
	Golf III & GTI	27–30	3.9	Sanden
	Jetta III & GLX	27–30	3.9	Sanden
	Passat GLX	39–42	3.9	Sanden
	Eurovan	32–35 ②	4.6 ②	Sanden
1995	Cabrio	NA	NA	NA
	Golf III	27–30	3.9	Sanden
	GTI VR6	27–30	3.9	Sanden
	Jetta III & GLX	27–30	3.9	Sanden
	Passat	39–42	3.9	Sanden
	Eurovan	32–35 ②	4.6 ②	Sanden

NA–Not available
① Some replacement compressors are supplied with a full charge of oil for the entire system. Check the compressor oil quantity prior to installation.
② If equipped with 2 evaporators, refrigerant capacity is 46–49 oz. and refrigerant oil capacity is 8.1 oz.

AIR CONDITIONING BELT TENSION

Year	Model	Engine Liters (cc)	Belt Type	Specifications ① New (lbs.)	Specifications ① Used (lbs.)
1993	Cabriolet	1.8 (1780)	V–Belt	3/16–3/8"	3/16–3/8"
	Corrado	1.8 (1780)	V–Belt	②	②
	Corrado ③	2.8 (2778)	V–Belt	②	②
	Fox	1.8 (1780)	V–Belt	3/16–3/8"	3/16–3/8"
	Golf GL, GTI	1.8 (1780)	V–Belt	3/16–3/8"	3/16–3/8"
	Golf GTI 16V	2.0 (1984)	V–Belt	3/16–3/8"	3/16–3/8"
	Jetta Diesel	1.6 (1588)	V–Belt	3/16–3/8"	3/16–3/8"
	Jetta GL, Carat	1.8 (1780)	V–Belt	3/16–3/8"	3/16–3/8"
	Jetta GLI 16V	2.0 (1984)	V–Belt	3/16–3/8"	3/16–3/8"
	Passat	2.8 (2778)	V–Belt	②	②
	Eurovan	2.5 (2480)	V–Belt	②	②
1994	Corrado	2.8 (2778)	Ribbed	②	②
	Golf III	2.0 (1984)	V–Belt	3/16–3/8"	3/16–3/8"
	Golf III GTI	2.8 (2778)	Ribbed	②	②
	Jetta III	2.0 (1984)	V–Belt	3/16–3/8"	3/16–3/8"
	Jetta III GLX	2.8 (2778)	Ribbed	②	②
	Passat GLX	2.0 (2778)	Ribbed	②	②
	Eurovan	2.5 (2480)	V–Belt	②	②
1995	Cabrio	2.0 (1984)	V–Belt	②	②
	Golf III	2.0 (1984)	V–Belt	3/16–3/8"	3/16–3/8"
	GTI VR6	2.8 (2778)	Ribbed	②	②
	Jetta III	2.0 (1984)	V–Belt	3/16–3/8"	3/16–3/8"

AIR CONDITIONING BELT TENSION

Year	Model	Engine Liters (cc)	Belt Type	Specifications ① New (lbs.)	Used (lbs.)
1995	Jetta III GLX	2.8 (2778)	Ribbed	②	②
	Passat	2.8 (2778)	V–Belt	②	②
	Eurovan	2.5 (2480)	V–Belt	②	②

① Deflection with thumb pressure at midpoint of longest belt run.
② Automatic tensioner used; no adjustment.
③ Canada

SYSTEM DESCRIPTION

General Information

Cabriolet

Cabriolet uses a manually controlled heater–air conditioning-system. The control levers on the instrument panel direct vacuum signals to the various doors and heater valve to operate the components according to the selected setting. The heater core and evaporator core share the same housing. The expansion valve uses a capillary tube inserted in the evaporator coils to monitor evaporator temperature and control the amount of refrigerant entering the evaporator to prevent freezing.

Fox

The system is vacuum operated from levers on the control panel. The control panel consists of 2 parts. The upper part control vacuum distribution. The lower part is for temperature control and contains a vacuum switch for the air recirculation door servo.

Corrado, Golf, Golf III, GTI, Jetta and Jetta III

These models use a blend air systems. These models also have the 2-part control panel for vacuum and for temperature regulation. System protection is provided by a pressure switch which monitors high side system pressure and will stop compressor operation is pressure falls below 17 psi or if it rises above about 464 psi. The switch is mounted on a Schrader type valve to allow removal without system discharge.

Passat

Passat uses dial type controls on the panel. A combination of cables and vacuum connections are used to set air door and temperature operations. The blower, evaporator core and heater core are all in the same housing assembly. An A/C relay energizes the compressor when the A/C switch is pressed and the vehicle system temperatures are within normal range. This system also uses an evaporator thermostat controlled from the control panel and with a capillary tube in the evaporator coils. Like the other systems, a dual-pressure switch protects the compressor from excessively high or low pressures. The expansion valve is of the H-valve design and is covered with a protective insulation to help maintain proper operation. An ambient temperature switch is used to prevent compressor engagement when outside air is below 45°F (7°C).

Service Valve Locations

The service valves are of the schrader type. Locations of the service valves may be in 2 areas depending upon the vehicle. On most vehicles, they are located on the high and low pressure hoses. On others, they may be located on the air conditioning compressor suction and discharge ports.

R-134a Safety Precautions

Systems use R-134a non-CFC refrigerant. These systems use similar components as previous R-12 systems; however, the components cannot be interchanged between systems. R-134a system components, including O-rings, hoses, compressor, etc., are identified by a green label, green stripe or lettering **R-134a**. Use only R-134a applicable replacement components.

R-134a is a colorless gas. When viewed through the sight glass it may appear milky due to the mixture of the refrigerant and PAG refrigerant oil.

- Work only in a well-ventilated area.
- Always use a dedicated set of equipment for servicing R-134a systems so you do not intermix any amounts of refrigerants or oils between R-12 and R-134a systems.
- Always use approved service equipment meeting SAE standard J1991 or newer (such as Kent-Moore ACR-4, or equivalent).
- Always wear appropriate safety protection during refrigerant service operations.
- Do not vent R-134a refrigerant to the open air.
- Do not warm refrigerant containers except by setting them in a pan of warm water.
- Although R-134a is non-flammable, always keep it away from open flames (poisonous gas will form).
- Never introduce compressed air into any R-134a container or capped off air conditioning system component.
- Do not steam clean condensers or evaporators; use only cold water or compressed air.
- Use only a halogen type leak detector with R-134a systems.
- When flushing the system or component, use only nitrogen and compressed air. Do not use R-11 as a flushing agent.

System Discharging

1. Disconnect the negative battery cable.
2. Use only an approved recovery/recycling type air conditioning station for discharging. Do not allow refrigerant to be discharged to the atmosphere.
3. Follow the equipment manufacturer's instructions to properly discharge the system.
4. Disconnect the lead from the compressor clutch to prevent accidental system operation during or after discharging.
5. When the air conditioning system has been completely discharged, measure the amount of oil that collected in the can.
6. This measured amount of oil, must be added to the refrigerant system before it is recharged.

NOTE: Always add new refrigerant oil, never the oil that had been collected from the system.

7. Component replacement or repairs can now be accomplished. Do not allow the system to remain open for any length of time.

8. Reconnect the compressor clutch lead. Connect the negative battery cable.

System Flushing

The system or components may be flushed after discharge. Flush a component anytime the system has been open for extended periods, if there has been compressor failure, or if you suspect there are any impurities, additional moisture or old refrigerant oil present. Be sure to flush if you are unclear how much refrigerant oil is in the system. This is critical to ensure proper operation and life of the system after recharge. You should also flush the system if you are unable to pull a constant vacuum during evacuation or a leak-free system (excessive moisture is likely present). Note the following when flushing:

• Use only compressed air and nitrogen to flush the components.

• DO NOT blow compressed air and nitrogen through the compressor or expansion valve.

• Only blow compressed air and nitrogen through disconnected, free flowing components.

• Always flush components in the opposite direction of the normal refrigerant flow.

• Do not use R-11 as a flushing agent.

• After disconnecting the component to be flushed, cap the openings of the components remaining in the system, but do not cap the component to be flushed.

• Flush the evaporator through the low pressure line with the high pressure line removed.

• If any component has dark, thick deposits that cannot be removed with compressed air, replace the component (light gray deposits are normal).

• Always replace the receiver/drier and expansion valve after flushing.

System Evacuating

Whenever the system has been opened to the atmosphere, the system must be evacuated to remove all air and moisture that has accumulated in the system.

1. Disconnect the negative battery cable.

2. Connect the manifold gauge set to the compressor and to the discharge service ports. Connect the center (charging) hose to a vacuum pump service port.

3. Open both manifold gauge valves.

4. Start the vacuum pump and operate it until the evaporator suction gauge reads at least 26 in. Hg vacuum.

5. If at least 26 in. Hg of vacuum cannot be reached, either the system has a leak or the vacuum pump is defective.

6. If the vacuum pump is okay, charge the system with at least 14 oz. (397g) of refrigerant, leak test and repair all leaks.

7. Discharge and evacuate the system again.

8. Before starting the engine, be sure the air conditioner is OFF.

9. Turn the compressor manually about 10 times, then start the engine. Let it idle for a few minutes before turning on the A/C system or raising the engine idle. Operate the system for about 5 minutes.

10. Turn the manifold gauge valves to their closed position and stop the vacuum pump.

11. Observe the evaporator suction valve for at least 2–5 minutes. The vacuum gauge reading must remain constant.

12. Connect the negative battery cable.

NOTE: If the vacuum level falls off, the system has a leak and must be repaired before charging. Properly discharge the system, then recharge with at least 14 fl. oz. (397g) of refrigerant. Leak test the system and repair as required. Retest with the vacuum pump.

System Charging

After evacuating the system and being sure no leakage exists, charge in the following manner:

1. Connect an approved charging station or recovery/recycling machine to the discharge and suction ports. The red hose is normally connected to the discharge (high pressure) line. The blue hose is normally connected to the suction (low pressure) line.

2. Follow the charging equipment manufacturer's instructions and charge the system with the specified amount of refrigerant, use system pressure readings and the sight glass for additional determination of proper charge level.

3. After system recharge, manually rotate the compressor about 10 turns before starting the engine. Only start the engine with the air conditioner OFF. Once the idle speed has stabilized, A/C can be switched ON. Let engine run at idle for about 2 minutes before raising the engine speed.

———————— **CAUTION** ————————

Do not attempt to charge the system on the high pressure side, the high system pressure could be transferred into the charging cans and cause them to explode.

Air Bag System Disabling

If equipped with an air bag, the system must be disabled prior to working on components which require the removal of the steering column, instrument panel or related components which could affect the airbag system.

1. To disable the air bag system, disconnect the negative battery cable and tape it to be sure it is insulated from accidental grounding.

2. Wait at least 20 minutes for the system to completely becomedisabled before beginning work inside the passenger compartment.

SYSTEM COMPONENTS

Radiator
REMOVAL AND INSTALLATION

1. Disconnect the negative battery cable and drain the cooling system.

2. Disconnect the inlet and outlet hoses from the engine side.

3. If equipped with a radiator cover, remove the retaining bolts and remove it.

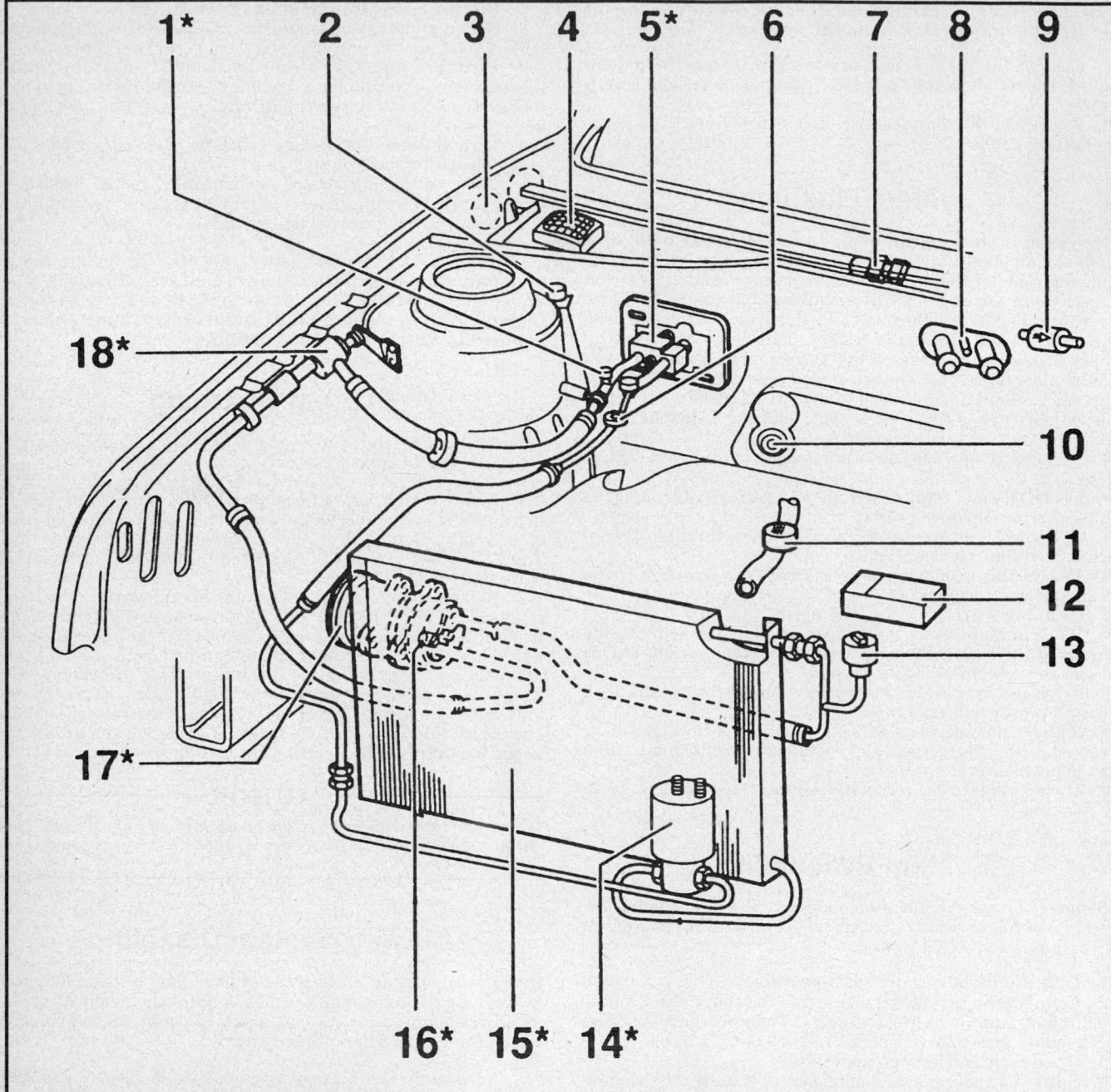

* DISCHARGE A/C SYSTEM BEFORE REMOVING

1. LOW PRESSURE SERVICE VALVE
2. FRESH AIR/RECIRCULATING FLAP 2-WAY VALVE
3. VACUUM RESERVOIR
4. AIR INTAKE GRILLE
5. EXPANSION VALVE
6. SIGHT GLASS
7. AMBIENT TEMPERATURE SWITCH
8. HEATER CORE CONNECTIONS
9. CHECK VALVE

10. EVAPORATOR WATER DRAIN
11. A/C THERMAL SWITCH AND THIRD SPEED COOLANT FAN
12. COOLANT FAN CONTROL
13. A/C PRESSURE SWITCH
14. RECEIVER/DIRER
15. CONDENSER
16. PRESSURE RELIEF VALVE
17. A/C CLUTCH
18. DAMPER

Showing air conditioning component layout—Corrado

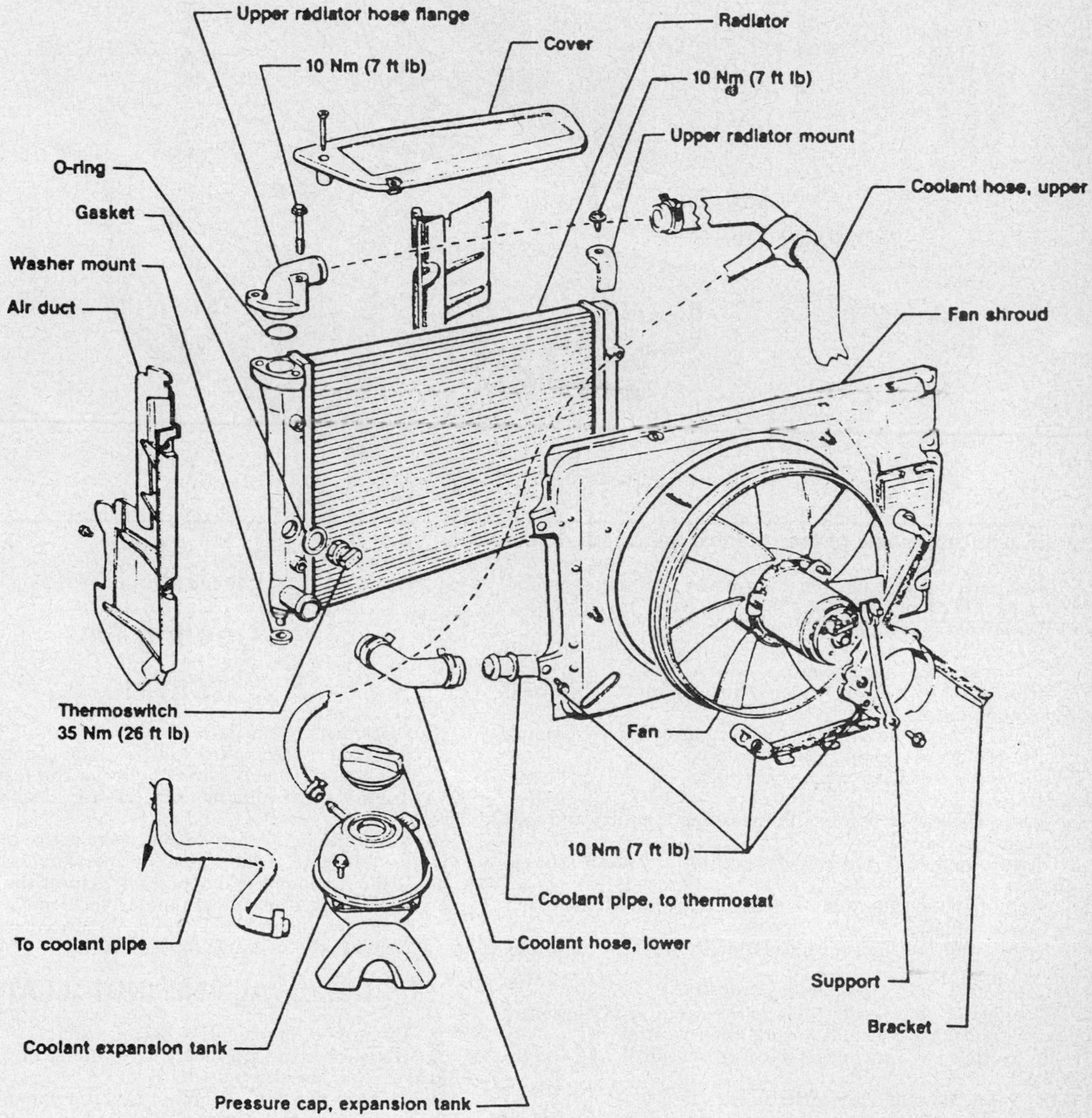

Upper radiator hose flange

10 Nm (7 ft lb)

Cover

Radiator

10 Nm (7 ft lb)

O-ring

Upper radiator mount

Gasket

Coolant hose, upper

Washer mount

Air duct

Fan shroud

Thermoswitch
35 Nm (26 ft lb)

Fan

10 Nm (7 ft lb)

To coolant pipe

Coolant pipe, to thermostat

Coolant hose, lower

Support

Bracket

Coolant expansion tank

Pressure cap, expansion tank

NOTE

Ensure that no coolant hoses or lines touch the knock sensor. This could dampen the sensor and diminish the signal.

Exploded view of radiator and cooling fan components—Corrado with 1.8L engine

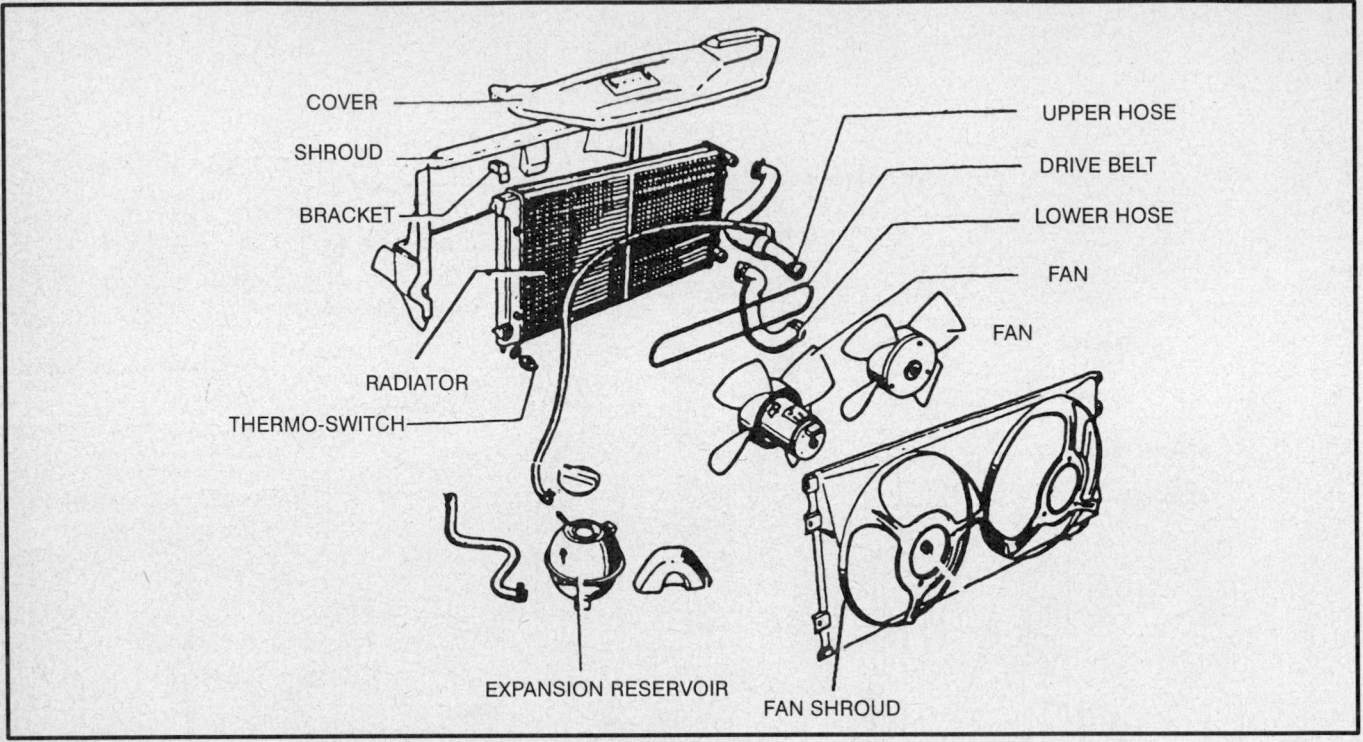

COVER
SHROUD
BRACKET
RADIATOR
THERMO-SWITCH
EXPANSION RESERVOIR
UPPER HOSE
DRIVE BELT
LOWER HOSE
FAN
FAN
FAN SHROUD

Typical exploded view of the radiator and related components

4. Disconnect electrical connector at the radiator temperature sensor. Disconnect the overflow hose from the radiator.
5. Disconnect the fan motor connectors.
6. Remove the fan and shroud assembly retaining bolts and lift the fan shroud assembly out.
7. If equipped with automatic transaxle, disconnect the cooler lines and plug.
8. Remove the radiator upper mounting bracket retaining bolts and remove the mounting brackets.
9. Remove the radiator from the vehicle.
To install:
10. Lower the radiator into the mounting position and seat the mounting cushions.
11. Install the radiator mounting brackets and secure the radiator in place.
12. If equipped with automatic transaxle, connect the cooler lines to the radiator.
13. Install the fan and shroud assembly and the retaining bolts.
14. Connect the fan motor connectors.
15. Connect electrical connector to the radiator temperature sensor. Connect the overflow hose to the radiator.
16. If equipped with a radiator cover, install it and the retaining bolts.
17. Connect the inlet and outlet hoses.
18. Refill the cooling system with coolant. Fill the overflow reservoir tank to the upper level.
19. Connect the negative battery cable.
20. Start the engine and allow it to warm up 5–10 minutes at 2000–3000 rpm.

NOTE: Observe the radiator fan to ensure that it activates when the engine temperature has reach approximately 212°F (100°C) and will cut off at approximately 194°F (90°C).

21. Shut the engine OFF and allow it to cool sufficiently, where it is safe to remove the radiator cap.
22. If the coolant level has dropped below the filler neck, top off the coolant level.

23. Install the radiator cap and the vent plug.

Cooling Fan

TESTING

1. Disconnect the negative battery cable.
2. Disconnect the cooling fan electrical connector.
3. Apply and 12 volt source between the positive an negative terminals of the fan motor connector. The fan should operate.
4. While the fan is in operation, take notice to any abnormal noises, vibrations or fan-to-shroud interference.
5. If the fan motor is inoperative, inspect the connector and harness leading from the fan motor, for damage.
6. If the fan motor checks good, test the thermo-sensor.
7. Connect the negative battery cable.

REMOVAL AND INSTALLATION

1. Disconnect the negative battery cable.
2. Disconnect the fan motor wire connector and remove the harness from the shroud.
3. Remove the fan shroud-to-radiator mounting bolts and lift the fan assembly out.
4. Remove the fan motor-to-shroud retaining nuts and separate the shroud and fan assembly.
5. Remove the fan-to-motor retaining nuts and separate the fan from the motor.
To install:
6. Assemble the fan and motor assembly. Prior to installing the retaining nuts, apply a coat of sealant to the threads and install.
7. Assemble the fan to the shroud and install the retaining nuts. Spin the fan and insure that there is no fan-to-shroud interference.
8. Position the fan and shroud assembly to the radiator and install the retaining bolts. Torque the bolts to 7 ft. lbs. (10 Nm).

9. Connect and 12 volt source to the fan lead wire connector and check for noises, vibrations or fan interference.

10. Secure the fan lead wire to the shroud and connect it to the harness connector.

11. Connect the negative battery cable. Start the engine and test fan operation.

Condenser

REMOVAL AND INSTALLATION

Cabriolet, Fox, Golf, Jetta and Passat

1. Drain the cooling system. Disconnect the upper and lower radiator hoses. Properly discharge the air conditioning system using an approved recovery station.

2. Remove the shroud and electric cooling fan from the radiator and move them towards the engine.

3. If the equipped with an automatic transmission, remove the fluid cooling lines at the radiator.

4. Remove the retaining bolts or nuts from the top and bottom of the radiator and remove the radiator.

NOTE: The battery may be removed to gain additional working clearance.

5. Disconnect the inlet and outlet lines at the condenser. Cap or plug the opening immediately.

6. Remove the retaining bolts or nuts from the condenser and carefully lift the condenser from the front of the vehicle.
To install:

7. Carefully install the condenser into the vehicle.

8. Connect the inlet and outlet lines to the condenser.

9. Install the radiator and secure with the nuts/bolts.

10. If the equipped with an automatic transmission, install the fluid cooling lines to the radiator.

11. Install the shroud and electric cooling fan to the radiator.

12. Install the upper and lower radiator hoses and refill the cooling system.

13. Install a new receiver/drier.

14. Evacuate and recharge the air conditioning system. Check for leaks.

15. Add the correct amount of refrigerant oil to the condenser. Evacuate and charge the air conditioning system. Verify the system operates correctly.

NOTE: Some replacement condensers are supplied with a full charge of nitrogen. If the gas is not heard escaping when the component is first opened, it may be leaking.

Corrado, Golf III, GTI and Jetta III

1. Obtain the radio security code for resetting after the procedure is complete. Disconnect the negative battery cable, then the positive cable and remove the battery.

2. Properly discharge the air conditioning system using an approved recovery station for R-134a systems.

3. Remove the front lock support and the grille. Remove the seal from around the radiator and condenser.

4. Remove the front bumper, bumper cross support, and front air deflectors.

5. Disconnect the refrigerant lines from the condenser and cap all openings immediately.

6. Remove the condenser mounting bolts and carefully remove the condenser.
To install:

7. Installation is the reverse of the removal procedure. Be sure the seal is properly in place around the condenser and radiator.

8. Evacuate and recharge the air conditioning system. Perform a leak test.

9. Reinstall the battery, enter the radio security code. Perform a system operation check.

Compressor

REMOVAL AND INSTALLATION

Fox

The compressor is located under the front of the vehicle.

1. Disconnect the negative battery cable.

2. Properly discharge the air conditioning system using recovery type equipment.

3. Raise and safely support the vehicle.

4. Disconnect both the suction and the discharge lines from the compressor head. Cap or plug the openings immediately.

5. At the crankshaft pulley, loosen the tensioner plate nuts and remove the drive belt.

NOTE: The crankshaft pulley contains shims for the drive belt adjustment, if a new belt is installed, it may be necessary to remove or add shims accordingly.

6. Disconnect the electrical connection from the magnetic pulley terminal.

7. Remove the compressor-to-bracket retaining bolts and the compressor from the engine.
To install:

8. Position the compressor to the mounting bracket and install the compressor-to-bracket retaining bolts. Torque to 28 ft. lbs. (38 Nm).

9. Remove the tensioner plate and outer split pulley half from the crankshaft pulley.

10. Install the drive belt, the split pulley half and the tensioner plate. To adjust the drive belt tension, remove or add shims to the assembly until the deflection is 3/16–3/8 in. (5–10mm) between the pulleys. Install any extra shims between the outer split pulley and tensioner plate.

11. Torque the tensioner plate-to-crankshaft nuts to 15 ft. lbs. (20 Nm).

12. Connect the electrical connection to the magnetic pulley terminal.

13. Connect both the suction and the discharge lines to the compressor.

14. If the system has been opened for a long time, or if the compressor has been replaced due to internal failure, install a new receiver/drier at this time.

15. Connect the negative battery cable.

16. Evacuate and charge the air conditioning system.

17. Verify that the oil level is correct in the compressor and the system is operating correctly.

NOTE: Some replacement compressors come with a full charge of oil adequate for the entire system.

Cabriolet, Golf, Jetta and Passat

1. Disconnect the negative battery cable.

2. Properly discharge the air conditioning system using recovery type equipment.

3. Remove the electrical connector from the magnetic clutch terminal.

4. Disconnect both the suction and the discharge lines from the compressor head. Cap or plug the opening immediately.

5. Loosen the adjusting bolts on compressor bracket, to provide slack in the drive belt. Remove the drive belt.

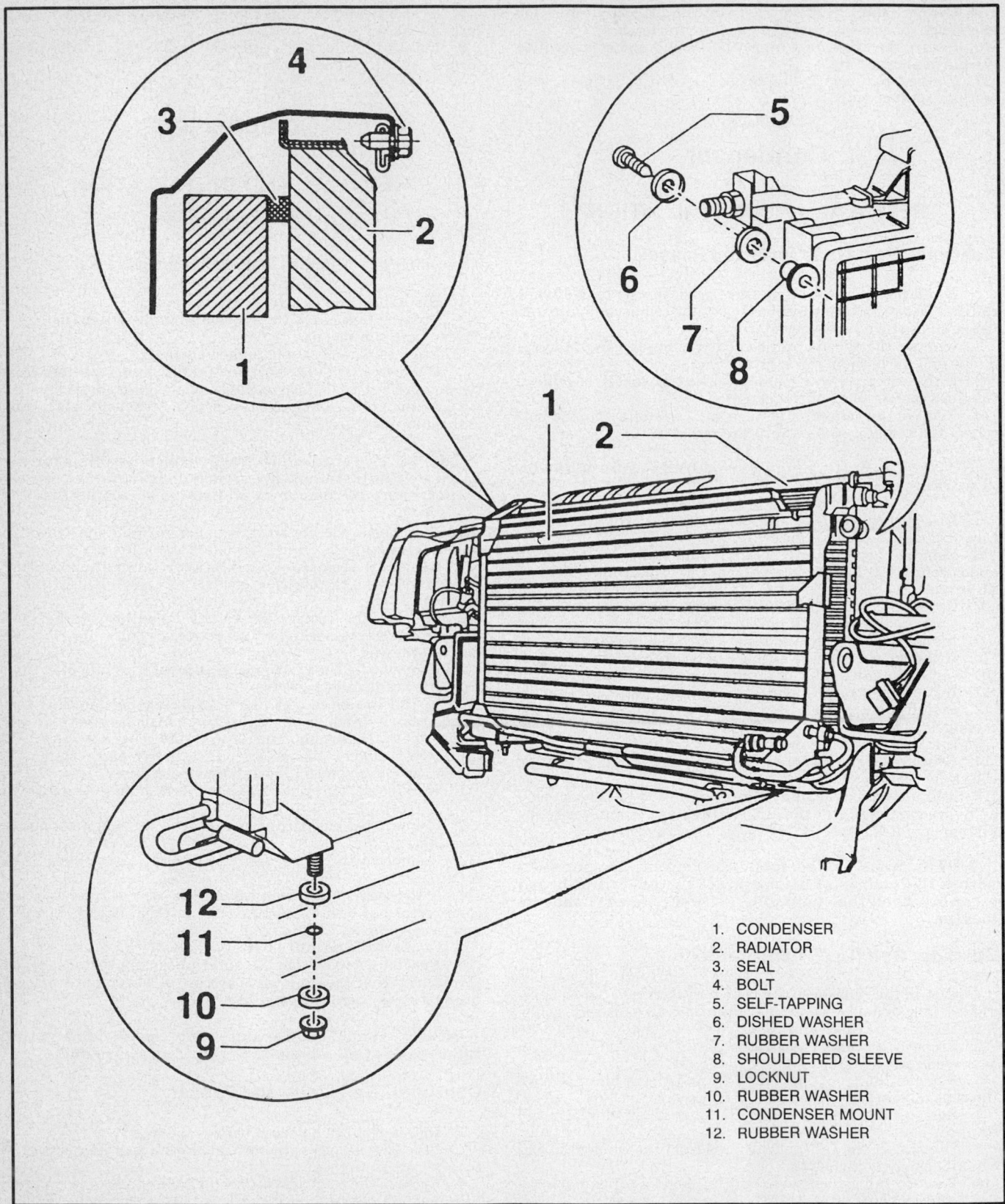

1. CONDENSER
2. RADIATOR
3. SEAL
4. BOLT
5. SELF-TAPPING
6. DISHED WASHER
7. RUBBER WASHER
8. SHOULDERED SLEEVE
9. LOCKNUT
10. RUBBER WASHER
11. CONDENSER MOUNT
12. RUBBER WASHER

Removing the condenser—Corrado shown

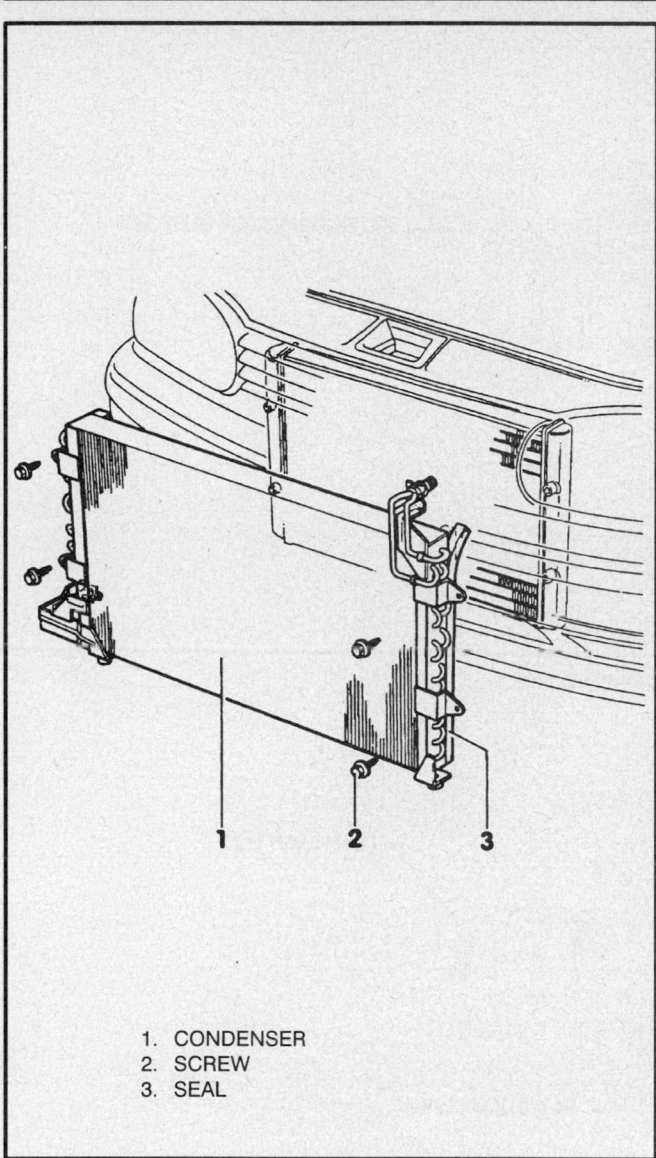

1. CONDENSER
2. SCREW
3. SEAL

Condenser removal—Golf III, GTI and Jetta III

6. Remove the alternator drive belt.
7. Remove the compressor retaining bolt from the bracket. Remove the compressor from the engine brackets.
To install:
8. Install the compressor to the engine brackets and the bolt.
9. Install the drive belts. Adjust to a deflection of 5/16–3/8 in.(8–10mm) between the compressor and the crankshaft pulley.
10. Install the electrical connector to the magnetic clutch terminal.
11. Connect both the suction and the discharge lines to the compressor head.
12. Verify that the compressor has the correct level of refrigerant oil.

NOTE: Some replacement compressors come with a full charge of oil adequate for the entire system.

13. Connect the negative battery cable.

14. Evacuate and charge the air conditioning system.
15. Verify that the system operates properly.

Corrado, Golf III, GTI, Jetta III and Passat

1. Disconnect the negative battery cable.
2. Properly discharge the air conditioning system using recovery type equipment.
3. Disconnect both the suction and the discharge lines from the compressor head. Cap or plug the openings immediately.
4. Loosen the idler pulley adjustment bolt, to relax the tension on the drive belt. Remove the drive belt from the compressor pulley.
5. Disconnect the electrical connection from the magnetic pulley terminal.
6. On 2.8L engine, remove the front bumper and the right headlight housing to gain access for removing the ribbed drive belt and alternator.
7. Remove the compressor-to-bracket retaining bolts and remove the compressor from the engine.

NOTE: In some instances, to ease removal and installation, the brackets or part of the brackets can be removed with the compressor or taken from the compressor when on the bench and installed before installation of the compressor.

To install:
8. Install the compressor to the engine and the compressor-to-bracket retaining bolts. Tighten the mounting bolts to 18 ft. lbs. (25 Nm).
9. Connect the electrical connection to the magnetic pulley terminal.
10. On 2.8L engine, reinstall the drive belt, alternator, right headlight cover and front bumper.
11. On 1.8L engine, install the drive belt on the compressor pulley. Adjust the drive belt deflection to 3/16–3/8 in. (8–10mm) between the compressor and the crankshaft pulley. Tighten the idler pulley adjustment bolt.
12. Connect both the suction and the discharge lines to the compressor head.
13. Connect the negative battery cable.
14. Evacuate and charge the air conditioning system.
15. Verify that the oil level is correct in the compressor and the system is operating correctly.

Receiver/Drier

REMOVAL AND INSTALLATION

1. Disconnect the negative battery cable.
2. Discharge the refrigerant from the system.

NOTE: After discharging the system, measure the amount of refrigerant oil that was lost with the refrigerant; it must be replaced at the time of reassembly.

3. Disconnect the liquid lines from the receiver/drier inlet and outlet fittings; be sure to plug or cap the openings.
4. Loosen the clamps and remove the receiver/drier from its mounting bracket.
5. Install the receiver/drier into the mounting bracket and secure with the clamps.
6. Connect the liquid line pipes from the receiver/drier inlet and outlet fittings.
7. Evacuate and charge the air conditioning system.
8. Connect the negative battery cable.

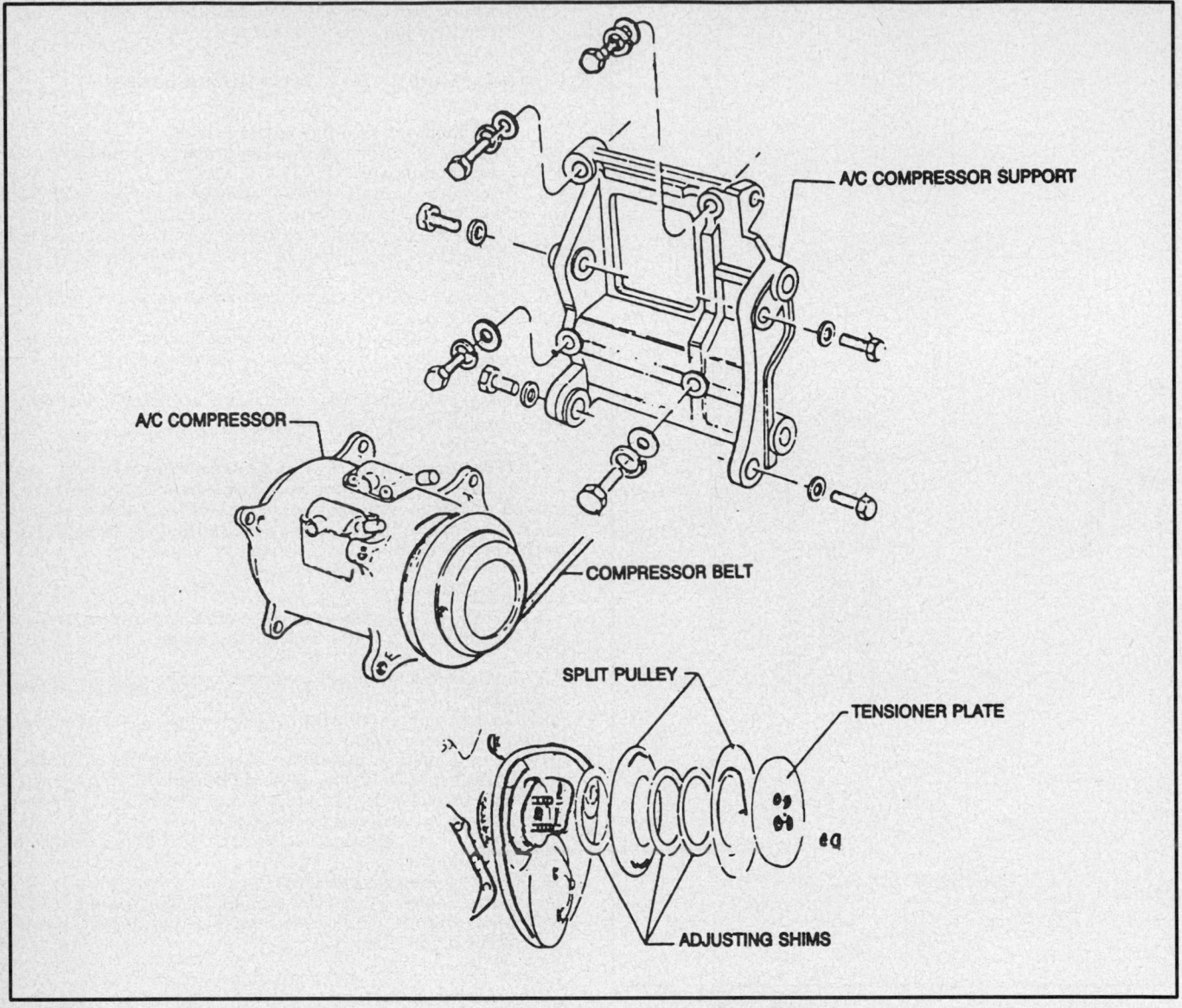

A/C COMPRESSOR SUPPORT

A/C COMPRESSOR

COMPRESSOR BELT

SPLIT PULLEY

TENSIONER PLATE

ADJUSTING SHIMS

Exploded view of the compressor and the crankshaft tensioner pulley—Fox

9. Verify the air conditioning system operates correctly.

Expansion Valve

REMOVAL AND INSTALLATION

The expansion valve is located within the evaporator housing assembly, with the evaporator core. Some systems use a standard type expansion valve and sensing bulb on the outlet line; other systems use an H-valve style.

Fox

1. Disconnect the negative battery cable.
2. If equipped with a console, remove it.
3. Properly discharge the air conditioning system using recovery type equipment.
4. Disconnect the evaporator inlet and outlet pipes and cap or plug the openings immediately.

5. Disconnect the water drain tube from the bottom of the evaporator housing.
6. Separate and lower the evaporator housing from the air conditioning/heater housing, then, remove it from the vehicle.
7. Separate the evaporator from the evaporator housing.
8. Disassemble the expansion valve from the evaporator.

To install:

9. Assemble the expansion valve to the evaporator.
10. Assemble the evaporator, be sure the sensing bulb is tightly secured to the evaporator outlet line, and assemble the evaporator housing and install it in the vehicle.
11. Connect the air conditioning pipes to the evaporator and the water drain tube to the evaporator housing.
12. Evacuate, recharge and leak test the air conditioning system.
13. If equipped with a console, install it.
14. Connect the negative battery cable.
15. Verify the air conditioning system is operating correctly.

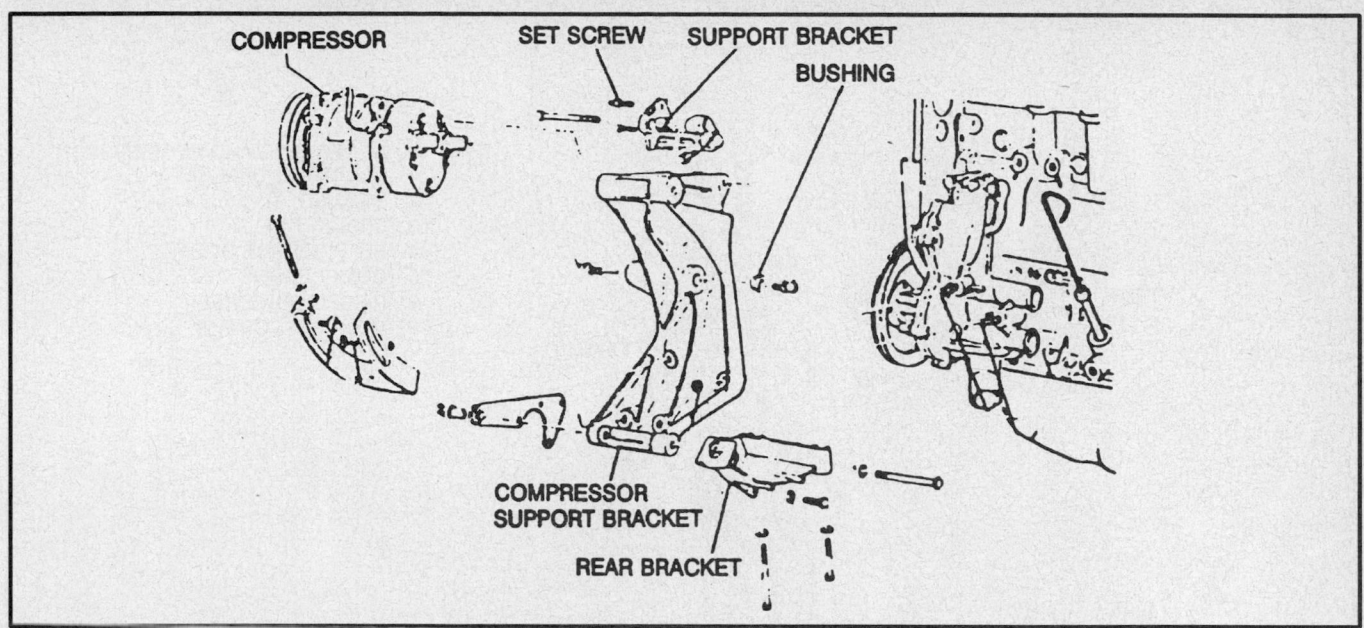

Compressor removal and installation—Cabriolet, Golf, GTI, Jetta and Passat

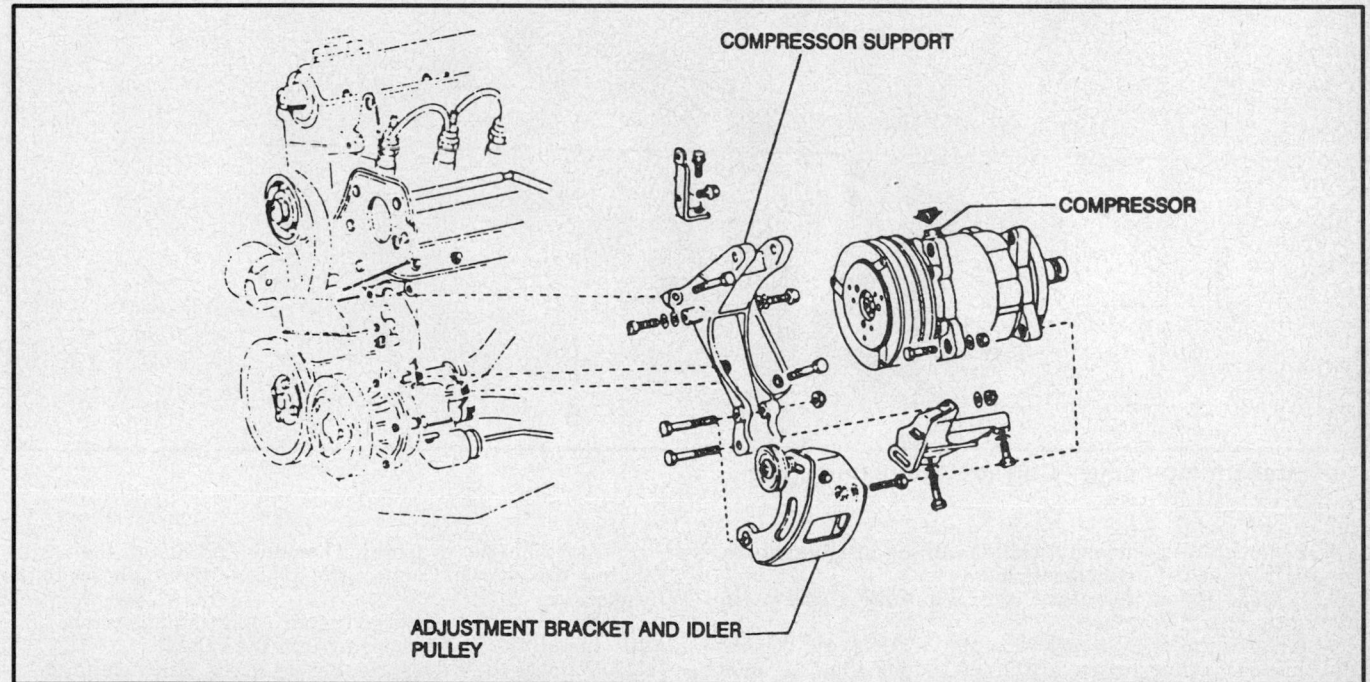

Compressor removal and installation with diesel engine

Golf, Golf III, GTI, Jetta, Jetta III and Passat

NOTE: If equipped with an air bag system, disconnect and tape the negative battery cable. Wait at least 20 minutes before removing instrument panel components on or near the air bag steering column location or passenger side location.

On some applications, the H-valve may be located on the engine compartment side of the firewall and requires system discharge, insulation removal and refrigerant fine fitting disconnect. If H-valve is inside the evaporator housing, perform the procedure given below.

1. Remove the instrument panel using the following procedures:

- Disconnect the negative battery cable.
- Remove the steering wheel.
- Remove the gear shift lever knob, the boot and the console.
- Remove the knee bar and the lower instrument panel trays.
- Remove the steering column cover and disconnect the steering column switches.
- Remove the temperature control unit levers, knob and bezel. Remove the instrument panel face plate and the radio.
- Remove the headlight switch and bezel.
- From under the rear defogger switch, remove the blank switch cover to expose the instrument cluster retaining screw.

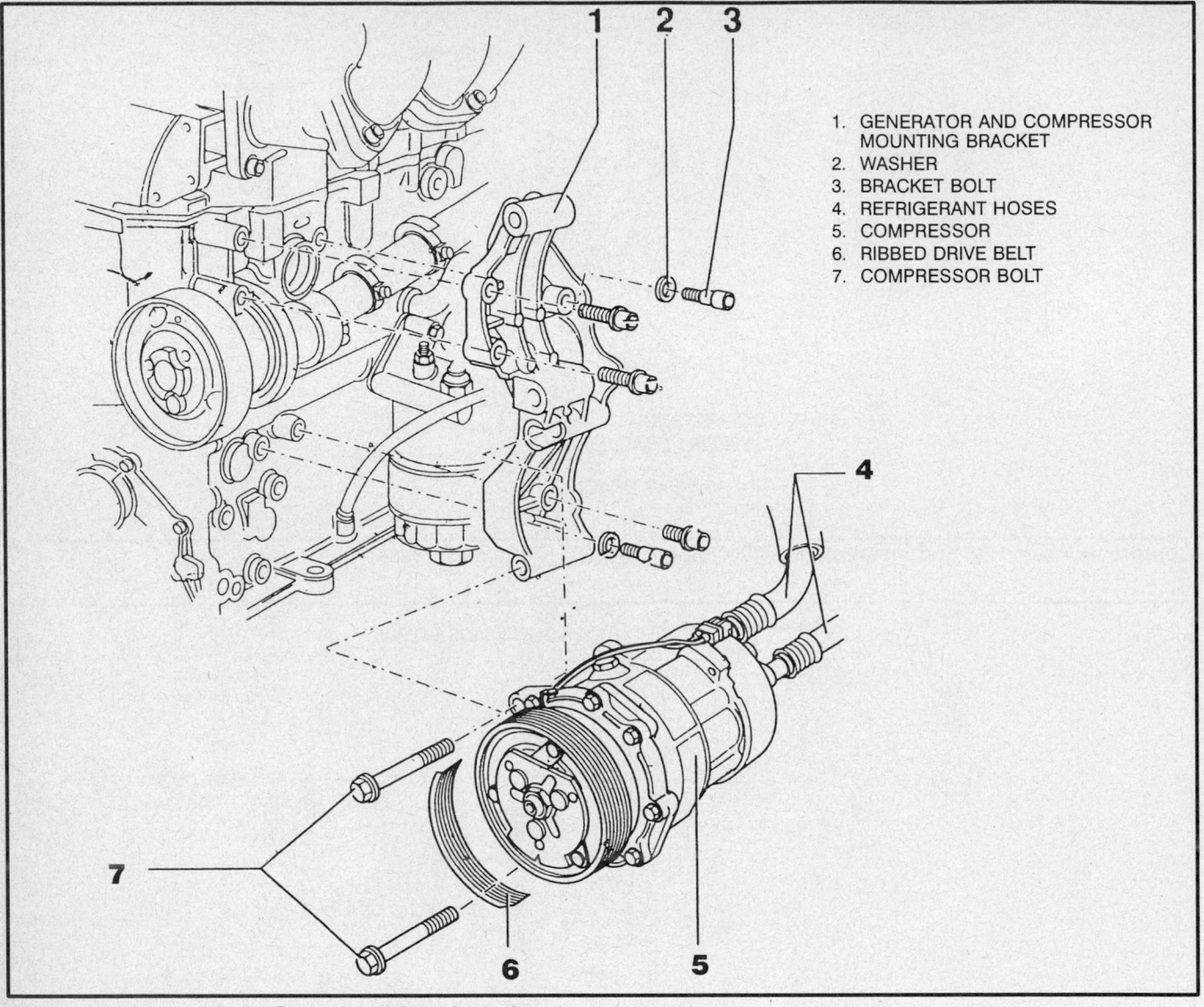

1. GENERATOR AND COMPRESSOR MOUNTING BRACKET
2. WASHER
3. BRACKET BOLT
4. REFRIGERANT HOSES
5. COMPRESSOR
6. RIBBED DRIVE BELT
7. COMPRESSOR BOLT

Compressor mounting—Corrado with 2.8L engine

- Remove the speedometer cable from the instrument cluster and remove the instrument cluster.
- Remove the temperature control retaining screws and move the control head back.
- Remove the relay panel from the bracket and separate the electrical connectors from the left side of the instrument panel.
- Remove the glove box and the plenum water drain tray.
- Remove the instrument panel–to–chassis fasteners, partially remove the panel and disconnect the electrical connectors from the right side of the panel.
- Remove the instrument panel from the vehicle.
2. Drain the cooling system to a level below the heater core and discharge the air conditioning system safely.
3. Disconnect the cables from the evaporator housing. Remove the heater housing wiring, the vacuum hoses, the heater hoses, the evaporator hoses and the cables.
4. Remove the heater/evaporator housing from the vehicle.
5. Separate the halves of the evaporator housing and remove the evaporator.
6. Disassemble the expansion valve from the evaporator.
7. Assemble the expansion valve to the evaporator.

8. Assemble the evaporator housing and install the assembly into the vehicle. Connect the air conditioning hoses to the evaporator.
9. Evacuate and recharge the air conditioning system.
10. Install the heater housing into the vehicle.
11. Connect the cables, the heater hoses, the vacuum hoses and the electrical connectors.
12. Refill the cooling system and check for leaks.
To install:
13. Install the instrument panel using the following procedures:
- Install the instrument panel into the vehicle. Connect the electrical connectors to the right side of the panel and secure the instrument panel to the chassis.
- Install the glove box and the plenum water drain tray.
- Install the electrical connectors to the left side of the instrument panel and the relay panel to the bracket.
- Move the control head forward and install the temperature control retaining screws.
- Install the instrument cluster and the speedometer cable to the instrument cluster.

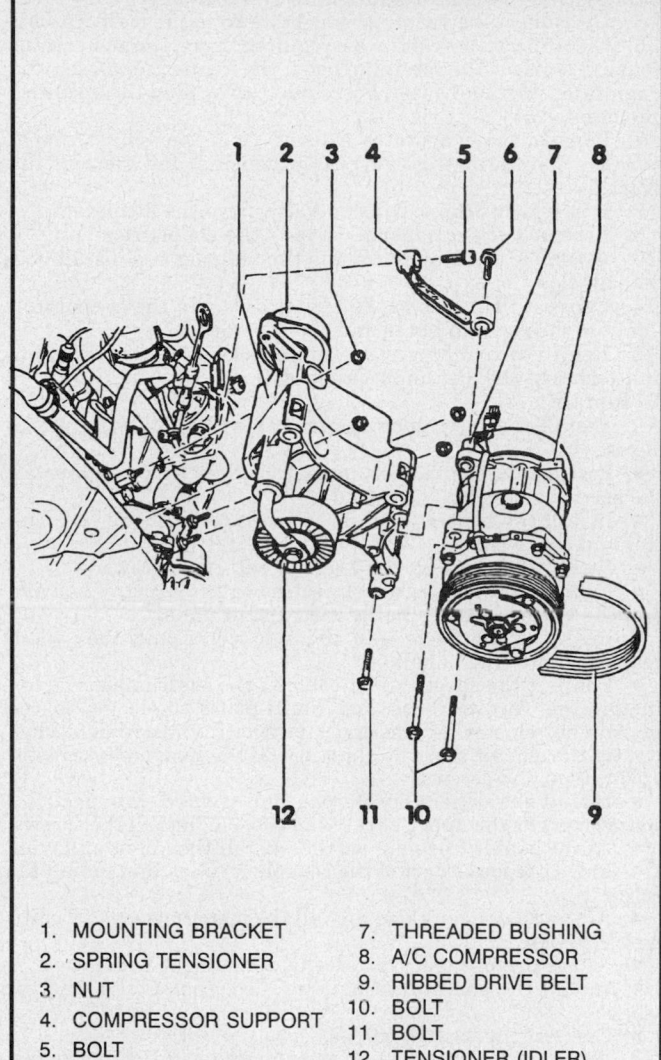

1.	MOUNTING BRACKET	7.	THREADED BUSHING
2.	SPRING TENSIONER	8.	A/C COMPRESSOR
3.	NUT	9.	RIBBED DRIVE BELT
4.	COMPRESSOR SUPPORT	10.	BOLT
5.	BOLT	11.	BOLT
6.	BOLT	12.	TENSIONER (IDLER) PULLEY

Compressor mounting—Golf III, and Jetta III with 4 cylinder engine

- Install the headlight switch and bezel.
- Install the instrument panel face plate and the radio. Install the temperature control unit levers, knob and bezel.
- Install the steering column cover and the steering column switches.
- Install the knee bar and the lower instrument panel trays.
- Install the gear shift lever knob, the boot and the console.
- Install the steering wheel. Connect the battery cable.

14. Verify the cooling system and the air conditioning system is operating correctly.

Cabriolet and Corrado

NOTE: If equipped with an air bag system, disconnect and tape the negative battery cable. Wait at least 20 minutes before removing instrument panel components on or near the air bag steering column location or passenger side location.

1.	MOUNTING BRACKET	7.	A/C COMPRESSOR
2.	WASHER	8.	RIBBED DRIVE BELT
3.	BOLT	9.	BOLTS
4.	BOLT	10.	BOLT
5.	BOLT	11.	WASHER
6.	BOLT		

Compressor mounting—Golf III, GTI and Jetta III with V6 engine

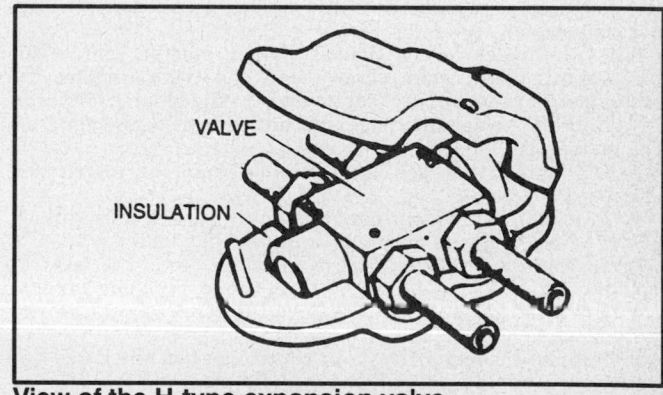

View of the H-type expansion valve

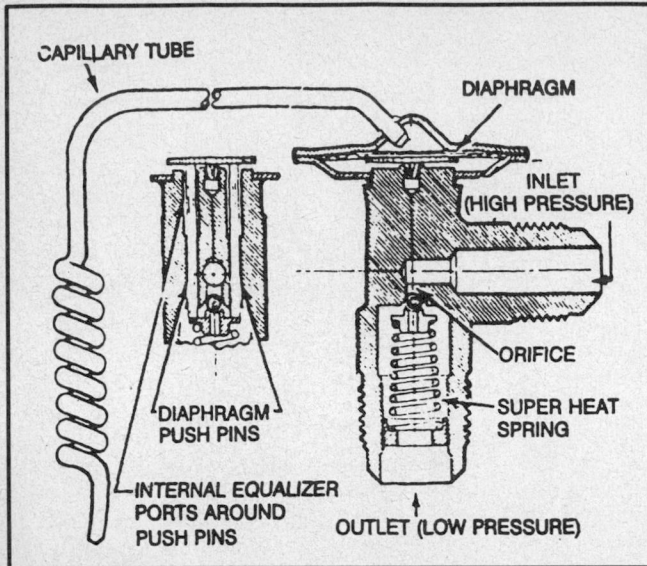

Cross-section of the typical expansion valve

On some applications, the H-valve may be located on the engine compartment side of the firewall and requires system discharge, insulation removal and refrigerant fine fitting disconnect. If H-valve is inside the evaporator housing, perform the procedure given below.

1. Remove the instrument panel using the following procedures:
- Disconnect the battery cable.
- Remove the steering wheel. Tilt the shelf downward, remove the screws and remove the shelf.
- From the driver's side, remove the instrument panel cover-to-instrument panel screws, pry out the clips and pull the cover downward.
- From the passenger's side, remove the shelf-to-instrument panel screws and the shelf. Pry out the lower instrument panel cover-to-instrument panel clips and pull the cover from the guides.
- At the console, remove the screws and pull the lower part of the console rearward.
- From the heater/fresh air control, remove the knobs and trim.
- From the upper part of the console, remove the screws and pull the upper part of the console out slightly. Disconnect the electrical connectors from the console and remove the upper console pan.
- At the upper part of the instrument cluster, remove the instrument cluster trim screws and the trim. Remove the instrument cluster(center) screw and tip the cluster forward.
- Pull off the vacuum hose and multi-point connector from the instrument cluster.
- Disconnect the speedometer cable from the instrument cluster.
- From the instrument panel, push the switch forward (out of the panel), pull the air ducts from the side vents.
- Disconnect the electrical connectors from the ashtray housing and the wiring harness from the instrument panel.
- Open the glove box and remove the screws from the center, left and right sides.
- Pull out the heater/fresh air control, pry off the E-clip and disconnect the flap cable. Remove the control.
- Remove the instrument panel-to-chassis screws and clips. Remove the instrument panel from the vehicle.

2. Drain the cooling system to a level below the heater core.

3. From the inside the vehicle, disconnect the heater hoses from the heater core, plug the opening on both the core and hoses and remove the heater core.

4. Discharge the air conditioning system safely.

5. Disconnect the vacuum connectors from the fresh air box.

6. Disconnect the cables as required from the evaporator housing. Remove the retaining bolts, the heater core hoses, the evaporator inlet and outlet hoses and cap or plug the openings immediately.

7. Remove the evaporator housing from the vehicle. Separate the halves of the evaporator housing and remove the evaporator.

8. Disassemble the expansion valve from the evaporator.

9. Assemble the expansion valve to the evaporator.

10. Assemble the evaporator and the housing and install it in the vehicle.

11. Connect the hoses to the heater core and the evaporator. Connect the vacuum hoses and the control cables.

12. Refill the cooling system and check for leaks. Evacuate and recharge the air conditioning system.

To install:

13. Install the instrument panel using the following procedures:
- Position the instrument panel into the vehicle and install the screws and clips.
- Install the heater/fresh air control, connect the flap control and the E-clip.
- Install the glove box and secure with the screws.
- Connect the electrical connectors to the ashtray housing and the wiring harness to the instrument panel.
- Push the air ducts into the side vents and the switch rearward (into the panel).
- Connect the speedometer cable to the instrument cluster. Install the vacuum hose and multi-point connector to the instrument cluster. At the upper part of the instrument cluster, tip the cluster rearward and install the instrument cluster screw, trim and screws.
- Install the upper console pan and connect the electrical connectors. At the upper part of the console, install the screws.
- At the heater/fresh air control, install the knobs and trim.
- Move the lower part of the console forward and install the screws.
- At the passenger's side, install the instrument panel cover and the shelf.
- At the driver's side, install the instrument panel cover.
- Install the shelf and tilt it upward. Install the steering wheel.
- Connect the battery cables.

14. Verify the cooling system and the air conditioning system is operating correctly.

Blower Motor

REMOVAL AND INSTALLATION

NOTE: If equipped with an air bag system, disconnect and tape the negative battery cable. Wait at least 20 minutes before removing instrument panel components on or near the air bag steering column location or passenger side location.

Fox

1. Disconnect the negative battery cable.

2. Remove the front cover sealing gasket and the water deflector.

3. Loosen the fresh air housing cover retaining clips and remove the front fresh air housing cover.

4. If equipped with air conditioning, remove the lock and disconnect the air distribution flap levers.

5. Remove the rear fresh air housing cover.

6. If equipped with air conditioning, disconnect the vacuum hoses from the vacuum motor and the grommets at the bottom of the fresh air housing.

7. Disconnect the resistor and the thermal circuit breaker from the support.

8. Loosen the blower motor mounting screws and disconnect the electrical terminals, if equipped with air conditioning.

9. Remove the bottom of fresh air housing covers.

10. Remove the fresh air housing cover.

11. Rotate the blower motor towards the front of the vehicle and remove it from the housing.

To install:

12. Position the blower motor in the housing, rotate it rearward and lower it into position.

13. Install the fresh air housing covers.

14. Install the blower motor mounting screws and connect the electrical terminals, if equipped with air conditioning.

15. Install and connect the thermal circuit breaker and resistor.

16. If equipped with air conditioning, connect the vacuum hoses to the vacuum motor and the grommets at the bottom of the fresh air housing.

17. Install the fresh air housing cover.

18. If equipped with air conditioning, connect the air distribution flap levers and install the lock.

19. Install the front fresh air housing cover and tighten the fresh air housing cover retaining clips.

20. Remove the front cover sealing gasket and the water deflector.

21. Install the negative battery cable and check the operation of the blower motor.

Cabriolet and Corrado

1. Disconnect the negative battery cable.

2. Remove the fresh air recirculation housing and gasket from the heater box, located at the cowl.

3. Disconnect the electrical connector and remove the series resistor holder from the blower motor.

4. Remove the blower motor from the heater box.

To install:

5. Position the blower motor in the heater box.

6. Install the series resistor holder onto the blower motor to secure it.

7. Install the fresh air recirculation housing and gasket.

8. Connect the negative battery cable.

9. Check the blower motor operation.

Golf, GTI, Jetta and Passat

1. Disconnect the negative battery cable.

2. Disconnect the electrical connectors from the blower motor.

3. Disengage the retaining lug.

4. Rotate the blower motor clockwise and lower it from the housing.

To install:

5. Raise the blower motor into position and turn it counterclockwise to lock it into place.

6. Engage the retaining lug.

7. Connect the electrical connectors at the blower motor.

8. Connect the negative battery cable and test the blower motor operation.

Golf III, GTI and Jetta III

1. Disconnect the negative battery cable.

2. Remove the glove compartment.

NOTE: The blower motor resistor can be removed at this time if needed.

3. Remove the electrical connector from the blower motor.

4. Remove 5 blower motor housing screws and lower the blower motor from the housing.

5. Installation is the reverse of the removal procedure.

NOTE: If the resistor was removed, a proper sealant must be applied to the mating surface before resistor installation.

Heater Core

REMOVAL AND INSTALLATION

NOTE: If equipped with an air bag system, disconnect and tape the negative battery cable. Wait at least 20 minutes before removing instrument panel components on or near the air bag steering column location or passenger side location.

Fox

1. Disconnect the negative battery cable.

2. Remove the instrument panel. Remove console, if equipped.

3. Drain the cooling system to a level below the heater core.

4. From the inside the vehicle, disconnect the heater hoses from the heater core, plug the opening on both the core and hoses and remove the heater core.

5. Disconnect the cables, as required from the heater housing. Remove the retaining bolts, the heater housing from the vehicle.

6. Separate the halves of the heater housing and remove the heater core.

To install:

7. Assemble the heater core into the heater housing and install it in the vehicle.

8. Connect the hoses to the heater core and the control cables to the housing.

9. Refill the cooling system and check for leaks.

10. Install the instrument panel and the console, if equipped.

11. Verify the cooling system is operating correctly.

Cabriolet and Corrado

1. Remove the instrument panel using the following procedures:

• Disconnect the battery cable.

• Remove the steering wheel. Tilt the shelf downward, remove the screws and remove the shelf.

• From the driver's side, remove the instrument panel cover-to-instrument panel screws, pry out the clips and pull the cover downward.

• From the passenger's side, remove the shelf-to-instrument panel screws and the shelf. Pry out the lower instrument panel cover-to-instrument panel clips and pull the cover from the guides.

• At the console, remove the screws and pull the lower part of the console rearward.

• From the heater/fresh air control, remove the knobs and trim.

• From the upper part of the console, remove the screws and pull the upper part of the console out slightly. Disconnect the electrical connectors from the console and remove the upper console pan.

• At the upper part of the instrument cluster, remove the instrument cluster trim screws and the trim. Remove the instrument cluster center screw and tip the cluster forward.

• Pull off the vacuum hose and multi-point connector from the instrument cluster.

• Disconnect the speedometer cable from the instrument cluster.

• From the instrument panel, push the switch forward, out of the panel. Pull the air ducts from the side vents.

• Disconnect the electrical connectors from the ashtray housing and the wiring harness from the instrument panel.

• Open the glove box and remove the screws from the center, left and right sides.

• Pull out the heater/fresh air control, pry off the E-clip and disconnect the flap cable. Remove the control.

• Remove the instrument panel-to-chassis screws and clips. Remove the instrument panel from the vehicle.

2. Properly drain the cooling system.

3. From the inside the vehicle, disconnect the heater hoses from the heater core, plug the opening on both the core and hoses and remove the heater core.

NOTE: If the unit has a core cover on the side, remove the cover and pull the core from the housing.

To install:

4. Position the heater core into the heater box, connect the heater hoses and install the core cover, if equipped.

5. Refill the cooling system and check for leaks.

6. Install the instrument panel using the following procedures:

• Position the instrument panel into the vehicle and install the screws and clips.

• Install the heater/fresh air control, connect the flap control and the E-clip.

• Install the glove box and secure with the screws.

• Connect the electrical connectors to the ashtray housing and the wiring harness to the instrument panel.

• Push the air ducts into the side vents and the switch rearward into the panel.

• Connect the speedometer cable to the instrument cluster. Install the vacuum hose and multi-point connector to the instrument cluster. At the upper part of the instrument cluster, tip the cluster rearward and install the instrument cluster screw, trim and screws.

• Install the upper console pan and connect the electrical connectors. At the upper part of the console, install the screws.

• At the heater/fresh air control, install the knobs and trim.

• Move the lower part of the console forward and install the screws.

• At the passenger's side, install the instrument panel cover and the shelf.

• At the driver's side, install the instrument panel cover.

• Install the shelf and tilt it upward. Install the steering wheel.

• Connect the battery cables.

7. Inspect the operation of the heater and the controls.

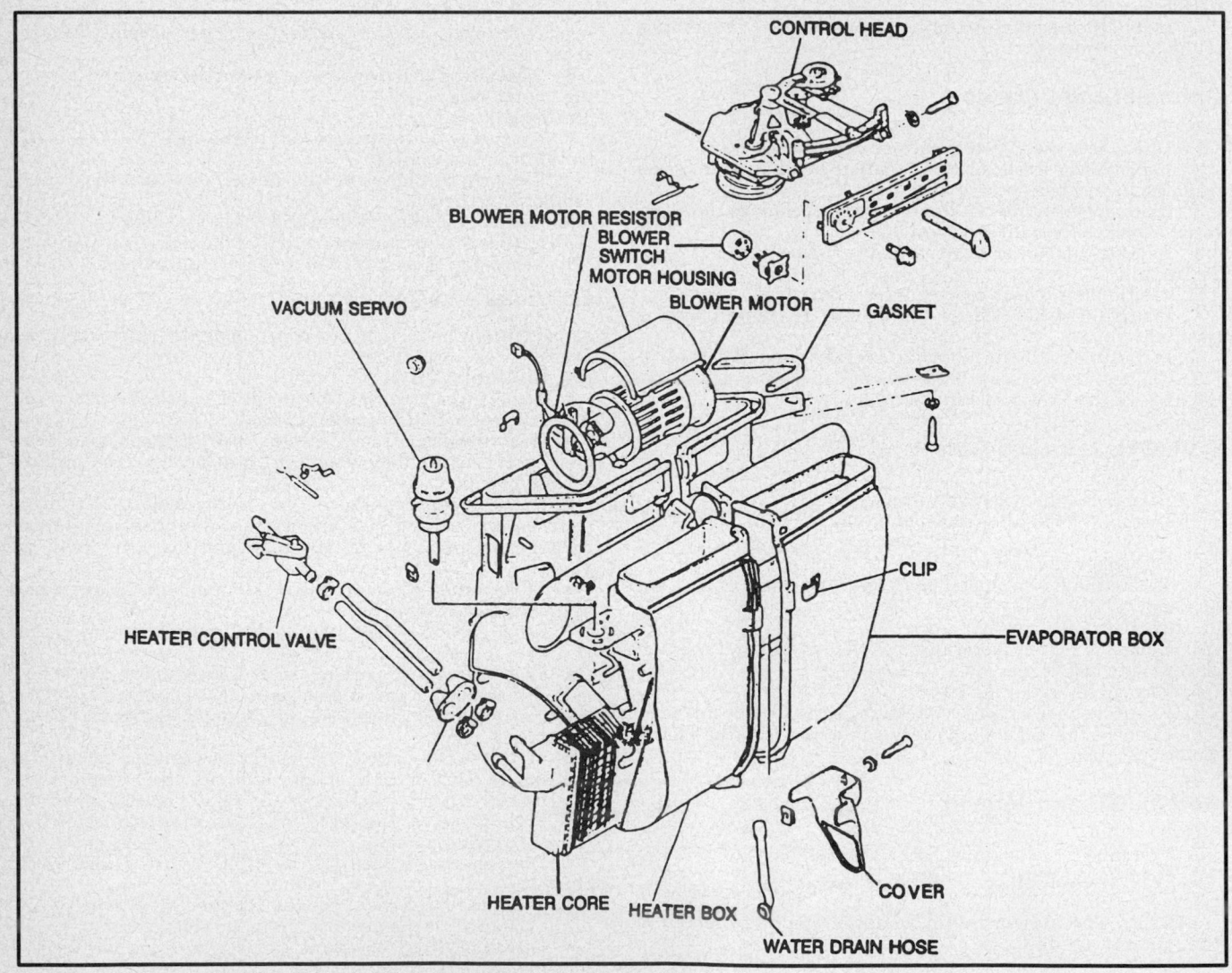

Exploded view of the heater/evaporator assembly—Cabriolet

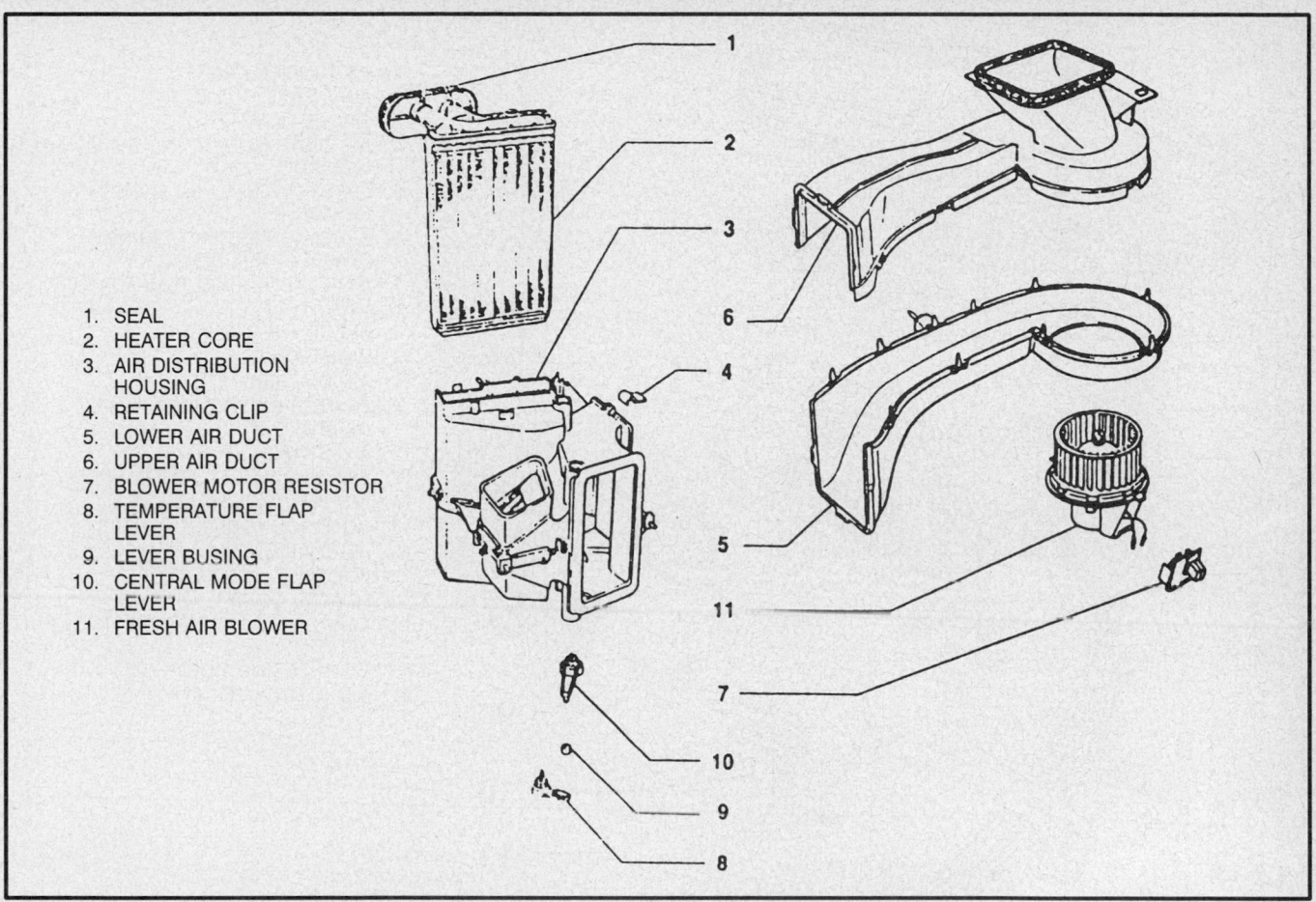

1. SEAL
2. HEATER CORE
3. AIR DISTRIBUTION HOUSING
4. RETAINING CLIP
5. LOWER AIR DUCT
6. UPPER AIR DUCT
7. BLOWER MOTOR RESISTOR
8. TEMPERATURE FLAP LEVER
9. LEVER BUSING
10. CENTRAL MODE FLAP LEVER
11. FRESH AIR BLOWER

Exploded view of the heater assembly—Corrado

Golf, Jetta and Passat

NOTE: On some Golf III and Jetta III models, there may be poor air distribution to the floor and/or the control knobs may be stiff to operate in some positions. This condition is likely caused by improper meshing of the air door gears. If this complaint is present, note the air door gear position during the removal and installation and make adjustment as needed.

1. Remove the instrument panel using the following procedures:
● Disconnect the negative battery cable.
● Remove the steering wheel.
● Remove the gear shift lever knob, the boot and the console.
● Remove the knee bar and the lower instrument panel trays.
● Remove the steering column cover and disconnect the steering column switches.
● Remove the temperature control unit levers, knob and bezel. Remove the instrument panel face plate and the radio.
● Remove the headlight switch and bezel.
● From under the rear defogger switch, remove the blank switch cover to expose the instrument cluster retaining screw.
● Remove the speedometer cable from the instrument cluster and the instrument cluster.
● Remove the temperature control retaining screws and move the control head back.

● Remove the relay panel from the bracket and separate the electrical connectors from the left side of the instrument panel.
● Remove the glove box and the plenum water drain tray.
● Remove the instrument panel–to–chassis fasteners, partially remove the panel and disconnect the electrical connectors from the right side of the panel.
● Remove the instrument panel from the vehicle.
2. Properly drain and recover the coolant.
3. Remove the heater housing wiring, the vacuum hoses, the heater hoses and the cables.
4. Remove the heater housing from the vehicle. Remove the core cover and pull the core from the housing.
To install:
5. Install the core into the housing and replace the cover. Install the heater housing into the vehicle.
6. Connect the cables, the heater hoses, the vacuum hoses and the electrical connectors.
7. Refill the cooling system and check for leaks.
8. Install the instrument panel using the following procedures:
● Install the instrument panel into the vehicle. Connect the electrical connectors to the right side of the panel and secure the instrument panel to the chassis.
● Install the glove box and the plenum water drain tray.
● Install the electrical connectors to the left side of the instrument panel and the relay panel to the bracket.
● Move the control head forward and install the temperature control retaining screws.

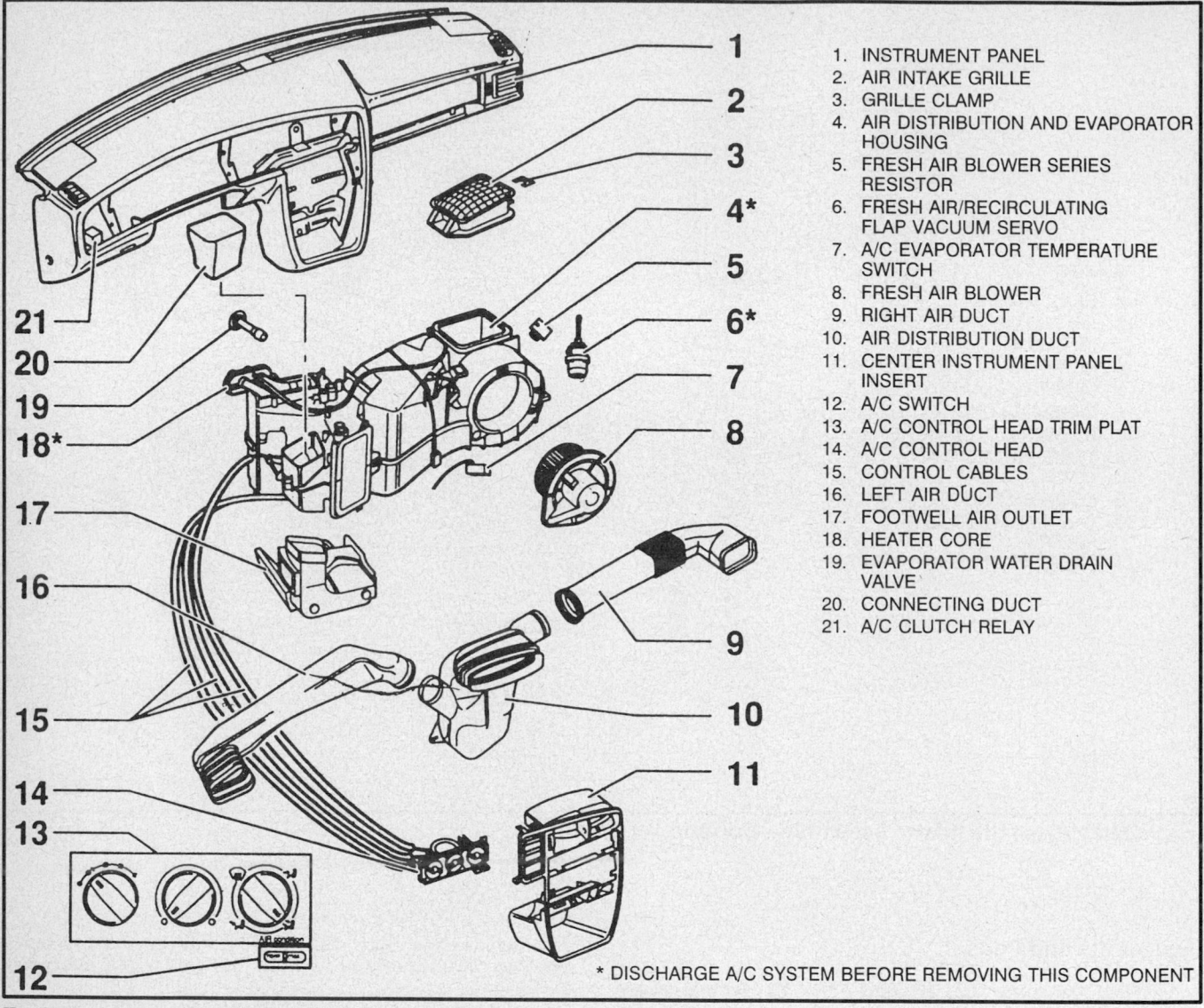

1. INSTRUMENT PANEL
2. AIR INTAKE GRILLE
3. GRILLE CLAMP
4. AIR DISTRIBUTION AND EVAPORATOR HOUSING
5. FRESH AIR BLOWER SERIES RESISTOR
6. FRESH AIR/RECIRCULATING FLAP VACUUM SERVO
7. A/C EVAPORATOR TEMPERATURE SWITCH
8. FRESH AIR BLOWER
9. RIGHT AIR DUCT
10. AIR DISTRIBUTION DUCT
11. CENTER INSTRUMENT PANEL INSERT
12. A/C SWITCH
13. A/C CONTROL HEAD TRIM PLAT
14. A/C CONTROL HEAD
15. CONTROL CABLES
16. LEFT AIR DUCT
17. FOOTWELL AIR OUTLET
18. HEATER CORE
19. EVAPORATOR WATER DRAIN VALVE
20. CONNECTING DUCT
21. A/C CLUTCH RELAY

* DISCHARGE A/C SYSTEM BEFORE REMOVING THIS COMPONENT

Exploded view of the heater and air conditioner assembly—Corrado

- Install the instrument cluster and the speedometer cable to the instrument cluster.
- Install the headlight switch and bezel.
- Install the instrument panel face plate and the radio. Install the temperature control unit levers, knob and bezel.
- Install the steering column cover and the steering column switches.
- Install the knee bar and the lower instrument panel trays. Install the gear shift lever knob, the boot and the console.
- Install the steering wheel. Connect the battery cable.
9. Inspect the heating system operation.

Golf III, GTI and Jetta III

1. Disconnect the negative battery cable.
2. Remove the instrument panel, but do not disassemble farther than shown in the appropriate illustration.
3. Remove the housing support bracket.
4. Disconnect the heater hoses at the firewall and plug the openings to prevent coolant spills.
5. Remove the heater and evaporator housing assembly. The heater housing may be removed separately. If the evaporator housing is also removed, the air conditioning system

must be properly discharged first, then refrigerant lines must the disconnected and capped at the firewall.
6. Disassemble the housing and remove or replace the heater core.
To install:
7. Installation is the reverse of the removal procedure

Evaporator

REMOVAL AND INSTALLATION

NOTE: **If equipped with an air bag system, disconnect and tape the negative battery cable. Wait at least 20 minutes before removing instrument panel components on or near the air bag steering column location or passenger side location.**

Fox

1. If equipped with a console, remove it.
2. Properly discharge the air conditioning system using recovery type equipment.

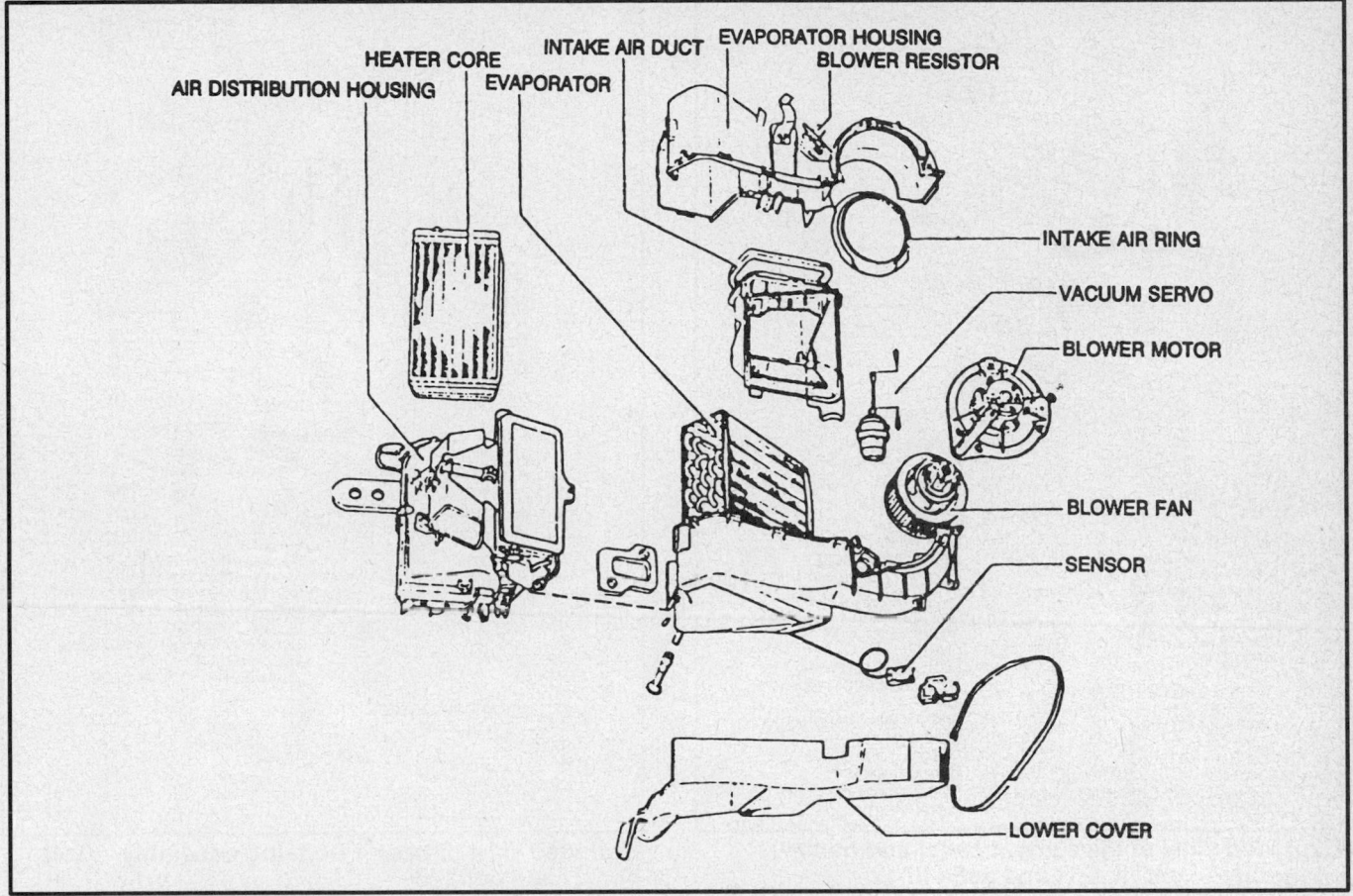

Exploded view of the heater assembly—Golf, Jetta and Passat

3. Disconnect the evaporator inlet and outlet pipes and cap or plug the openings immediately.

4. Disconnect the water drain tube from the bottom of the evaporator housing.

5. Separate and lower the evaporator housing from the air conditioning/heater housing, then, remove it from the vehicle.

6. Separate the evaporator from the evaporator housing.

To install:

7. Assemble the evaporator to the evaporator housing and install it in the vehicle.

8. Connect the air conditioning pipes to the evaporator and the water drain tube to the evaporator housing.

9. Connect the negative battery cable.

10. Evacuate, recharge and leak test the air conditioning system.

11. If equipped with a console, install it.

12. Verify the air conditioning system is operating correctly.

Cabriolet

1. Remove the instrument panel using the following procedures:

• Disconnect the battery cable.

• Remove the steering wheel. Tilt the shelf downward, remove the screws and remove the shelf.

• From the driver's side, remove the instrument panel cover-to-instrument panel screws, pry out the clips and pull the cover downward.

• From the passenger's side, remove the shelf-to-instrument panel screws and the shelf. Pry out the lower instrument panel cover-to-instrument panel clips and pull the cover from the guides.

• At the console, remove the screws and pull the lower part of the console rearward.

• From the heater/fresh air control, remove the knobs and trim.

• From the upper part of the console, remove the screws and pull the upper part of the console out slightly. Disconnect the electrical connectors from the console and remove the upper console pan.

• At the upper part of the instrument cluster, remove the instrument cluster trim screws and the trim. Remove the instrument cluster(center) screw and tip the cluster forward. Pull off the vacuum hose and multi-point connector from the instrument cluster. Disconnect the speedometer cable from the instrument cluster.

• From the instrument panel, push the switch forward out of the panel, pull the air ducts from the side vents.

• Disconnect the electrical connectors from the ashtray housing and the wiring harness from the instrument panel.

• Open the glove box and remove the screws from the center, left and right sides.

• Pull out the heater/fresh air control, pry off the E-clip and disconnect the flap cable. Remove the control.

• Remove the instrument panel-to-chassis screws and clips. Remove the instrument panel from the vehicle.

2. Properly drain and recover coolant from the cooling system.

3. From the inside the vehicle, disconnect the heater hoses from the heater core, plug the opening on both the core and hoses and remove the heater core.

4. Properly discharge the air conditioning system using recovery type equipment.

5. Disconnect the vacuum connectors from the fresh air box.

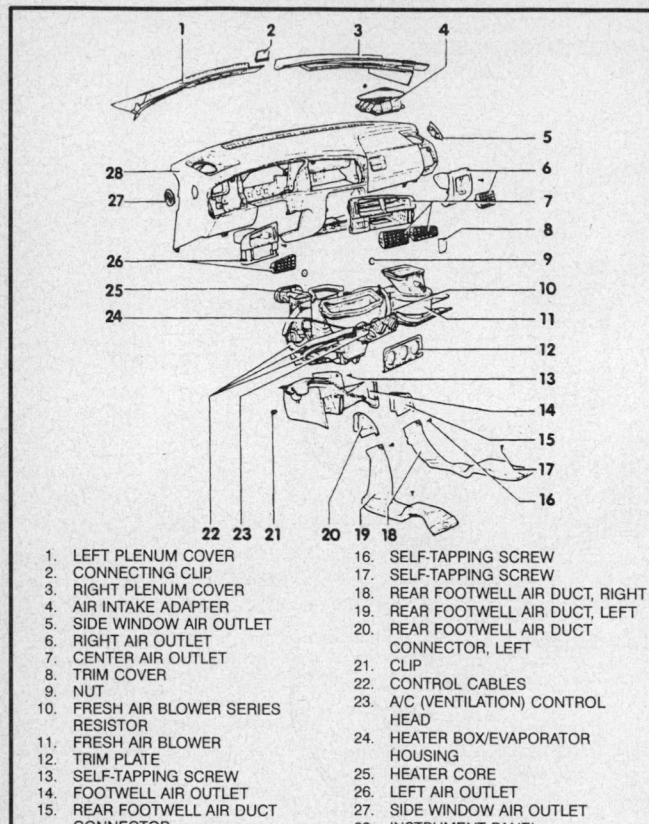

1. LEFT PLENUM COVER
2. CONNECTING CLIP
3. RIGHT PLENUM COVER
4. AIR INTAKE ADAPTER
5. SIDE WINDOW AIR OUTLET
6. RIGHT AIR OUTLET
7. CENTER AIR OUTLET
8. TRIM COVER
9. NUT
10. FRESH AIR BLOWER SERIES RESISTOR
11. FRESH AIR BLOWER
12. TRIM PLATE
13. SELF-TAPPING SCREW
14. FOOTWELL AIR OUTLET
15. REAR FOOTWELL AIR DUCT CONNECTOR
16. SELF-TAPPING SCREW
17. SELF-TAPPING SCREW
18. REAR FOOTWELL AIR DUCT, RIGHT
19. REAR FOOTWELL AIR DUCT, LEFT
20. REAR FOOTWELL AIR DUCT CONNECTOR, LEFT
21. CLIP
22. CONTROL CABLES
23. A/C (VENTILATION) CONTROL HEAD
24. HEATER BOX/EVAPORATOR HOUSING
25. HEATER CORE
26. LEFT AIR OUTLET
27. SIDE WINDOW AIR OUTLET
28. INSTRUMENT PANEL

Exploded view of instrument panel and heater assembly—Golf III, GTI and Jetta III

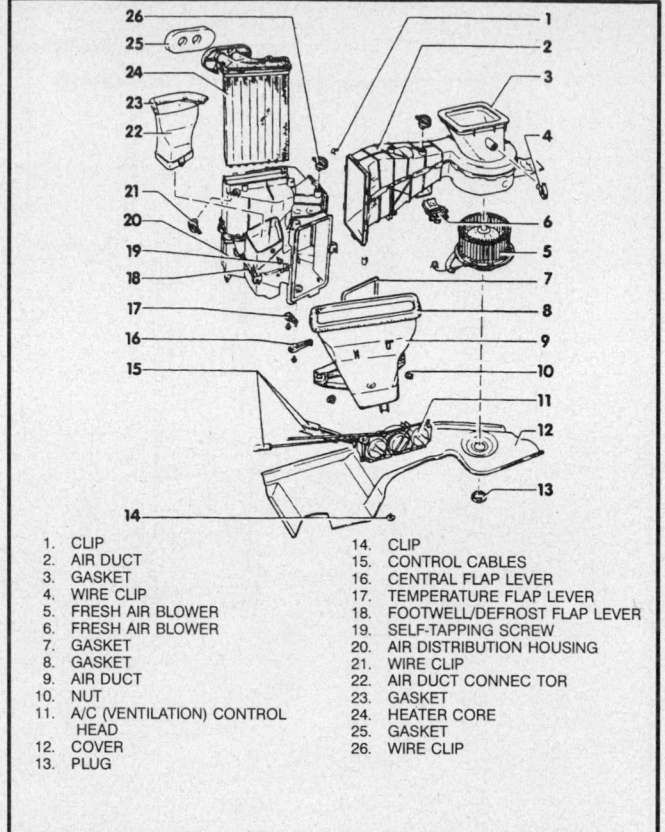

1. CLIP
2. AIR DUCT
3. GASKET
4. WIRE CLIP
5. FRESH AIR BLOWER
6. FRESH AIR BLOWER
7. GASKET
8. GASKET
9. AIR DUCT
10. NUT
11. A/C (VENTILATION) CONTROL HEAD
12. COVER
13. PLUG
14. CLIP
15. CONTROL CABLES
16. CENTRAL FLAP LEVER
17. TEMPERATURE FLAP LEVER
18. FOOTWELL/DEFROST FLAP LEVER
19. SELF-TAPPING SCREW
20. AIR DISTRIBUTION HOUSING
21. WIRE CLIP
22. AIR DUCT CONNECTOR
23. GASKET
24. HEATER CORE
25. GASKET
26. WIRE CLIP

Exploded view of heater housing assembly—Golf III, GTI and Jetta III

6. Disconnect the cables as required from the evaporator housing. Remove the retaining bolts, the heater core hoses, the evaporator inlet and outlet hoses and cap or plug the openings immediately.

7. Remove the evaporator housing from the vehicle. Separate the halves of the evaporator housing and remove the evaporator.

To install:

8. Assemble the evaporator and the housing and install it in the vehicle. If the evaporator core is replaced, add 0.7 oz. additional refrigerant oil during recharge.

9. Connect the hoses to the heater core and the evaporator. Connect the vacuum hoses and the control cables.

10. Refill the cooling system and check for leaks. Evacuate, recharge and leak test the air conditioning system.

11. Install the instrument panel using the following procedures:
   • Position the instrument panel into the vehicle and install the screws and clips.
   • Install the heater/fresh air control, connect the flap control and the E-clip.
   • Install the glove box and secure with the screws.
   • Connect the electrical connectors to the ashtray housing and the wiring harness to the instrument panel.
   • Push the air ducts into the side vents and the switch rearward (into the panel).
   • Connect the speedometer cable to the instrument cluster. Install the vacuum hose and multi-point connector to the instrument cluster. At the upper part of the instrument cluster, tip the cluster rearward and install the instrument cluster screw, trim and screws.
   • Install the upper console pan and connect the electrical connectors. At the upper part of the console, install the screws.
   • At the heater/fresh air control, install the knobs and trim.

   • Move the lower part of the console forward and install the screws.
   • At the passenger's side, install the instrument panel cover and the shelf.
   • At the driver's side, install the instrument panel cover.
   • Install the shelf and tilt it upward. Install the steering wheel.
   • Connect the battery cable.

12. Verify the cooling and the air conditioning systems are operating correctly.

Corrado

1. Disconnect the negative battery cable. Properly discharge the air conditioning system using approved recovery equipment. Drain the cooling system.

2. Disconnect the refrigerant lines from the connections at the firewall. Cap openings immediately. Disconnect the heater hoses at the firewall.

3. Remove the locking cable from the steering lock housing, if equipped.

4. Remove the instrument panel, starting with the front storage trays:
   • Remove the shelf screws and plastic nuts, then pull out the right side tray.
   • Turn the rotating clips of the side of the driver's tray and pullout this tray.
   • Remove the oval head screw at the left end of the instrument panel tray, remove the remaining screws and take off the instrument panel cover.

5. Remove the steering wheel.

6. Remove the instrument cluster trim plate by prying off the cover cap and removing the 4 screws.

7. Pry out the side vents with a flat-bladed prybar.

8. Remove the radio.

9. Pry off the center panel trim plate, remove the retaining screws beneath it and pull out the cassette storage box.

10. Pull the knobs off the climate control panel and pull off the sliding levers.

11. Pry off the trim plate and remove the control panel. Finish removing the retaining screws inside the cavity and remove the complete center trim plate.

12. Remove the steering column cover and switch assembly.

13. Pry off the cover caps from each side end of the instrument panel and remove the hex bolts.

14. Unscrew the nut from the back of the center panel opening and remove the nuts from the underside of the instrument panel beneath the windshield area (use a mirror to see the locations).

15. Pull the instrument panel slightly forward, disconnect the harnesses and cables and remove the instrument panel.

16. Remove the air intake grille, seal and clamp from on top of the blower motor housing.

17. Remove the heater-evaporator housing, with the controls and cables attached.

18. If needed, the air ducts can now be removed.

19. Disassemble the evaporator housing and remove the evaporator core.

To install:

20. Reassemble the evaporator core into the housing. Be sure to add 0.8 oz. (24 ml) of new refrigerant oil to the evaporator during installation.

21. Reinstall air ducts as removed.

22. Install the heater-evaporator housing. Be sure the cables are properly routed and not kinked or bent.

23. Install the air intake seal, grille and clamp on the blower motor housing.

24. Position the instrument panel and reattach the harnesses and cables. Loosely install the hex nuts at either end of the panel. Reinstall the nuts to the underside of the panel and at the back of the center panel opening. Tighten the hex nuts.

25. Reinstall the remaining components in reverse of the removal procedure. When installing the driver's side storage tray, be sure the push locating pins are fully seated in the retainers.

26. Reattach the heater hoses and air conditioning lines at the firewall.

27. Fill the cooling system. Evacuate and recharge the air conditioning system. Perform a leak check.

28. Connect the negative battery cable. Start the engine and let it idle for a few minutes, then perform a check of all systems and components, looking for leaks or improper operation.

Golf, Jetta, and Passat

1. Remove the instrument panel using the following procedures:

- Disconnect the negative battery cable.
- Remove the steering wheel.
- Remove the gear shift lever knob, the boot and the console.
- Remove the knee bar and the lower instrument panel trays.
- Remove the steering column cover and disconnect the steering column switches.
- Remove the temperature control unit levers, knob and bezel. Remove the instrument panel face plate and the radio.
- Remove the headlight switch and bezel.
- From under the rear defogger switch, remove the blank switch cover to expose the instrument cluster retaining screw.
- Remove the speedometer cable from the instrument cluster and the instrument cluster.
- Remove the temperature control retaining screws and move the control head back.
- Remove the relay panel from the bracket and separate the electrical connectors from the left side of the instrument panel.
- Remove the glove box and the plenum water drain tray.

- Remove the instrument panel-to-chassis fasteners, partially remove the panel and disconnect the electrical connectors from the right side of the panel.
- Remove the instrument panel from the vehicle.

2. Properly drain the cooling system. Properly discharge the air conditioning system using recovery type equipment.

3. Disconnect the cables from the evaporator housing. Remove the heater housing wiring, the vacuum hoses, the heater hoses, the evaporator hoses and the cables.

4. Remove the heater/evaporator housing from the vehicle.

5. Separate the halves of the evaporator housing and remove the evaporator.

To install:

6. Assemble the evaporator housing and install the assembly into the vehicle. Connect the air conditioning hoses to the evaporator.

7. If the evaporator core was replaced, add 0.7 oz. (21 ml) additional refrigerant oil during recharge. Evacuate, recharge and leak test the air conditioning system.

8. Install the heater housing into the vehicle.

9. Connect the cables, the heater hoses, the vacuum hoses and the electrical connectors.

10. Refill the cooling system and check for leaks.

11. Install the instrument panel using the following procedures:

- Install the instrument panel into the vehicle. Connect the electrical connectors to the right side of the panel and secure the instrument panel to the chassis.
- Install the glove box and the plenum water drain tray.
- Install the electrical connectors to the left side of the instrument panel and the relay panel to the bracket.
- Move the control head forward and install the temperature control retaining screws.
- Install the instrument cluster and the speedometer cable to the instrument cluster.
- Install the headlight switch and bezel.
- Install the instrument panel face plate and the radio. Install the temperature control unit levers, knob and bezel.
- Install the steering column cover and the steering column switches.
- Install the knee bar and the lower instrument panel trays.
- Install the gear shift lever knob, the boot and the console.
- Install the steering wheel. Connect the battery cable.

12. Verify the cooling and the air conditioning system are operating correctly.

Golf III, GTI and Jetta III

NOTE: On some Golf III and Jetta III models, there may be poor air distribution to the floor and/or the control knobs may be stiff to operate in some positions. This condition is likely caused by improper meshing of the air door gears. If this complaint is present, note the air door gear position during the removal and installation and make adjustment as needed.

1. Disconnect the negative battery cable. Properly discharge the air conditioning system using approved recycling equipment.

2. Disconnect and cap the refrigerant lines at the firewall connector.

3. Remove the instrument panel

4. Remove the housing support bracket.

5. Properly drain the cooling system. Disconnect the heater hoses at the firewall and plug the openings to prevent coolant spills.

6. Remove the heater and evaporator housing assembly.

7. Disassemble the housing and remove or replace the evaporator core.

To install:

8. Installation is the reverse of the removal procedure. Seal grooves and mating surfaces o both housing halves with silicone sealer.

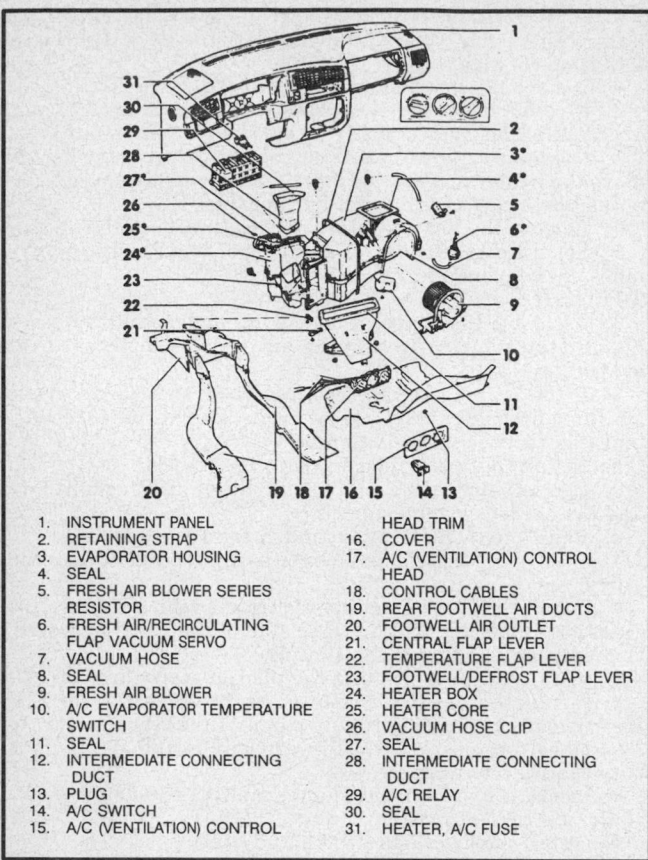

1. INSTRUMENT PANEL
2. RETAINING STRAP
3. EVAPORATOR HOUSING
4. SEAL
5. FRESH AIR BLOWER SERIES RESISTOR
6. FRESH AIR/RECIRCULATING FLAP VACUUM SERVO
7. VACUUM HOSE
8. SEAL
9. FRESH AIR BLOWER
10. A/C EVAPORATOR TEMPERATURE SWITCH
11. SEAL
12. INTERMEDIATE CONNECTING DUCT
13. PLUG
14. A/C SWITCH
15. A/C (VENTILATION) CONTROL HEAD TRIM
16. COVER
17. A/C (VENTILATION) CONTROL HEAD
18. CONTROL CABLES
19. REAR FOOTWELL AIR DUCTS
20. FOOTWELL AIR OUTLET
21. CENTRAL FLAP LEVER
22. TEMPERATURE FLAP LEVER
23. FOOTWELL/DEFROST FLAP LEVER
24. HEATER BOX
25. HEATER CORE
26. VACUUM HOSE CLIP
27. SEAL
28. INTERMEDIATE CONNECTING DUCT
29. A/C RELAY
30. SEAL
31. HEATER, A/C FUSE

Exploded view of instrument panel and air conditioning components—Golf III, GTI and Jetta III

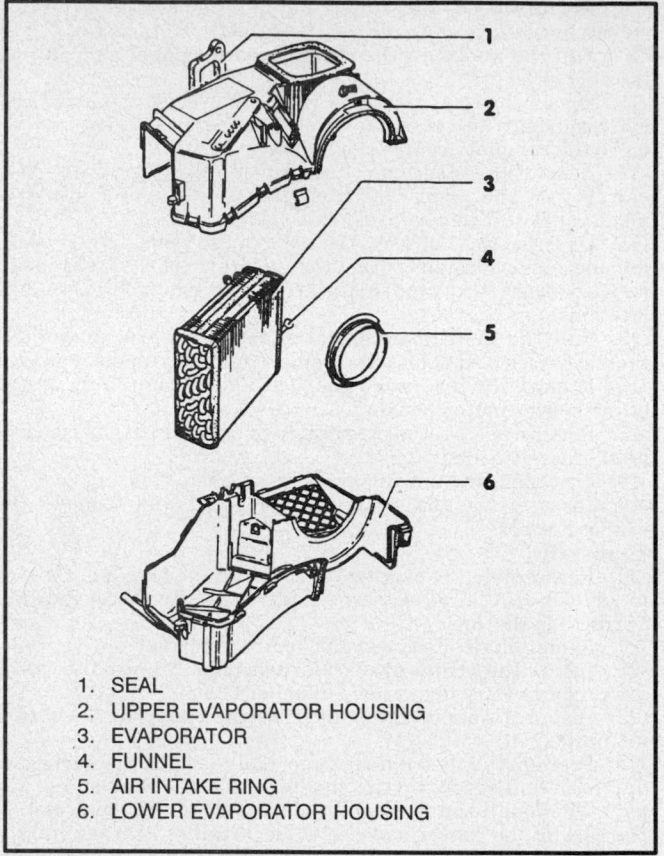

1. SEAL
2. UPPER EVAPORATOR HOUSING
3. EVAPORATOR
4. FUNNEL
5. AIR INTAKE RING
6. LOWER EVAPORATOR HOUSING

Exploded view of the evaporator housing—Golf III, GTI and Jetta III

Refrigerant Lines

REMOVAL AND INSTALLATION

1. Disconnect the negative battery cable.
2. Properly discharge the air conditioning system using recovery type equipment.
3. Unscrew the desired line from its adjoining component. If the lines are connected with flare nuts, use a back–up wrench when disassembling. Cover the exposed ends of the lines to minimize contamination.
4. Remove the lines and discard the O-rings.
To install:
5. Coat the O-rings with refrigerant oil and install. Connect the refrigerant lines to the adjoining components and tighten.
6. Add 0.3 oz. (9 ml) of additional refrigerant oil for each refrigerant line replaced. Evacuate, recharge and leak test the air conditioning system.
7. Connect the negative battery cable and check the entire climate control system for proper operation and leaks.

Manual Control Head

REMOVAL AND INSTALLATION

1. Disconnect the negative battery cable.
2. Remove the instrument panel bezel.
3. Remove the radio, if necessary.

4. Remove the manual control head retaining screws and pull the unit out of the instrument panel. On models so equipped, note depth position of capillary tube for thermostat in the evaporator on removal for proper reinstallation.
5. Disconnect all electrical connections, actuating cables and vacuum hoses from the unit and remove from the instrument panel.
6. The installation is the reverse of the removal procedure.
To install:
7. Check that the capillary tube from the control panel, if equipped, is properly inserted into the evaporator coils to the depth as removed.
8. Connect the negative battery cable and check the entire climate control system for proper operation.

Manual Control Cables

ADJUSTMENT

Except Golf III, GTI and Jetta III

1. Disconnect the negative battery cable.
2. Operate the temperature control lever to the **FULL COLD** position.
3. With the control cable attached to the air mix door link, pull the outer cable out and push the inner cable in the opposite direction.
4. Secure the cable in this position with the retaining clamp.
5. Operate the temperature control lever and check freedom of movement at full stroke range.

6. Connect the negative battery cable.

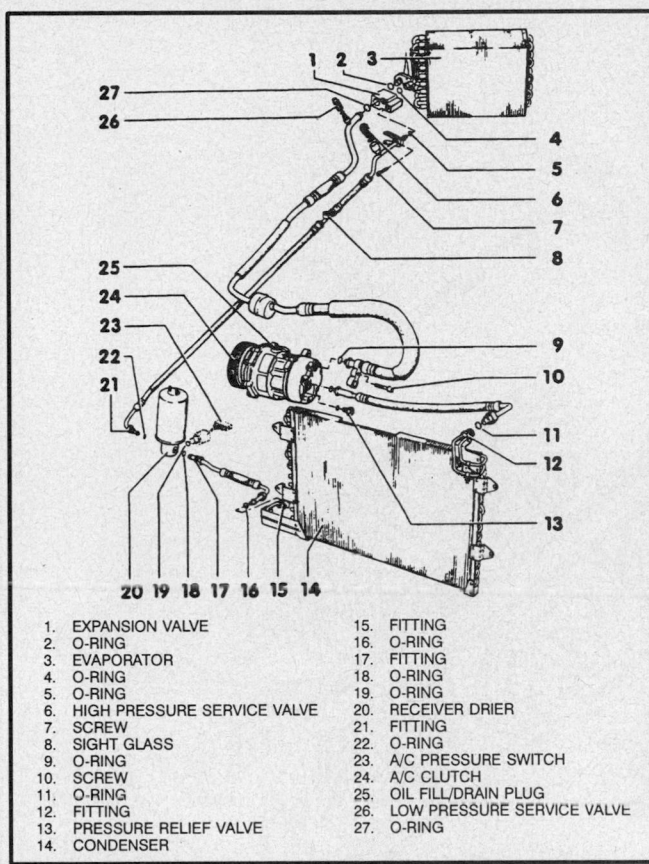

1.	EXPANSION VALVE	
2.	O-RING	
3.	EVAPORATOR	
4.	O-RING	
5.	O-RING	
6.	HIGH PRESSURE SERVICE VALVE	
7.	SCREW	
8.	SIGHT GLASS	
9.	O-RING	
10.	SCREW	
11.	O-RING	
12.	FITTING	
13.	PRESSURE RELIEF VALVE	
14.	CONDENSER	
15.	FITTING	
16.	O-RING	
17.	FITTING	
18.	O-RING	
19.	O-RING	
20.	RECEIVER DRIER	
21.	FITTING	
22.	O-RING	
23.	A/C PRESSURE SWITCH	
24.	A/C CLUTCH	
25.	OIL FILL/DRAIN PLUG	
26.	LOW PRESSURE SERVICE VALVE	
27.	O-RING	

Refrigerant line routing and air conditioning system components—Golf III, GTI and Jetta III

Golf III, GTI and Jetta III

MAIN SHUT–OFF FLAP CABLE

1. With control panel installed in instrument panel, adjust the blower control knob to stop at position O.
2. Connect the main shut-off flap cable (black sleeve) to the main shut-off flap lever. Push the lever toward the cable clip to its stop.
3. Hold the lever in this position and install the sleeve into the retaining clip.

TEMPERATURE FLAP CABLE

1. With the control panel installed in the instrument panel, adjust the temperature control knob to full COLD.
2. Connect the temperature flap cable (blue sleeve) to the temperature flap lever. Push the lever away from the retaining clip to its stop.
3. Hold the lever in this position and insert the cable sleeve into the retaining clip.

FLOOR/DEFROST FLAP CABLE

1. With the control panel installed in the instrument panel, adjust the air flow distribution knob to the DEFROST position.
2. Connect the floor/def cable (black sleeve) to the floor/def flap lever. Push the lever toward the cable clip until it stops.
3. Hold the lever in this position and insert the cable sleeve into the retaining clip.

CENTRAL FLAP CABLE

1. With the control panel installed in the instrument panel, adjust the air flow distribution knob to the VENT position.
2. Connect the central flap cable (black sleever) to the central flap lever. Push the lever away from the cable clip until it stops.
3. Holding this position, insert the cable sleeve into the retaining clip.

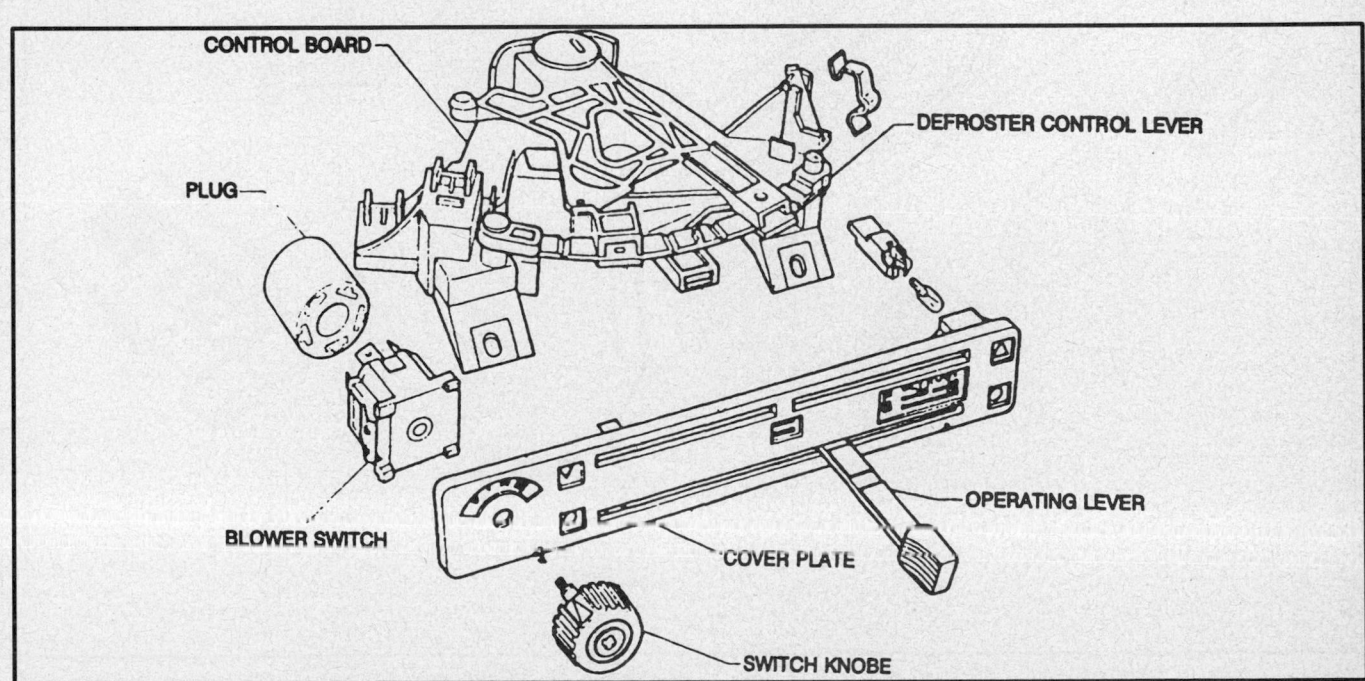

Exploded view of the control head—Cabriolet

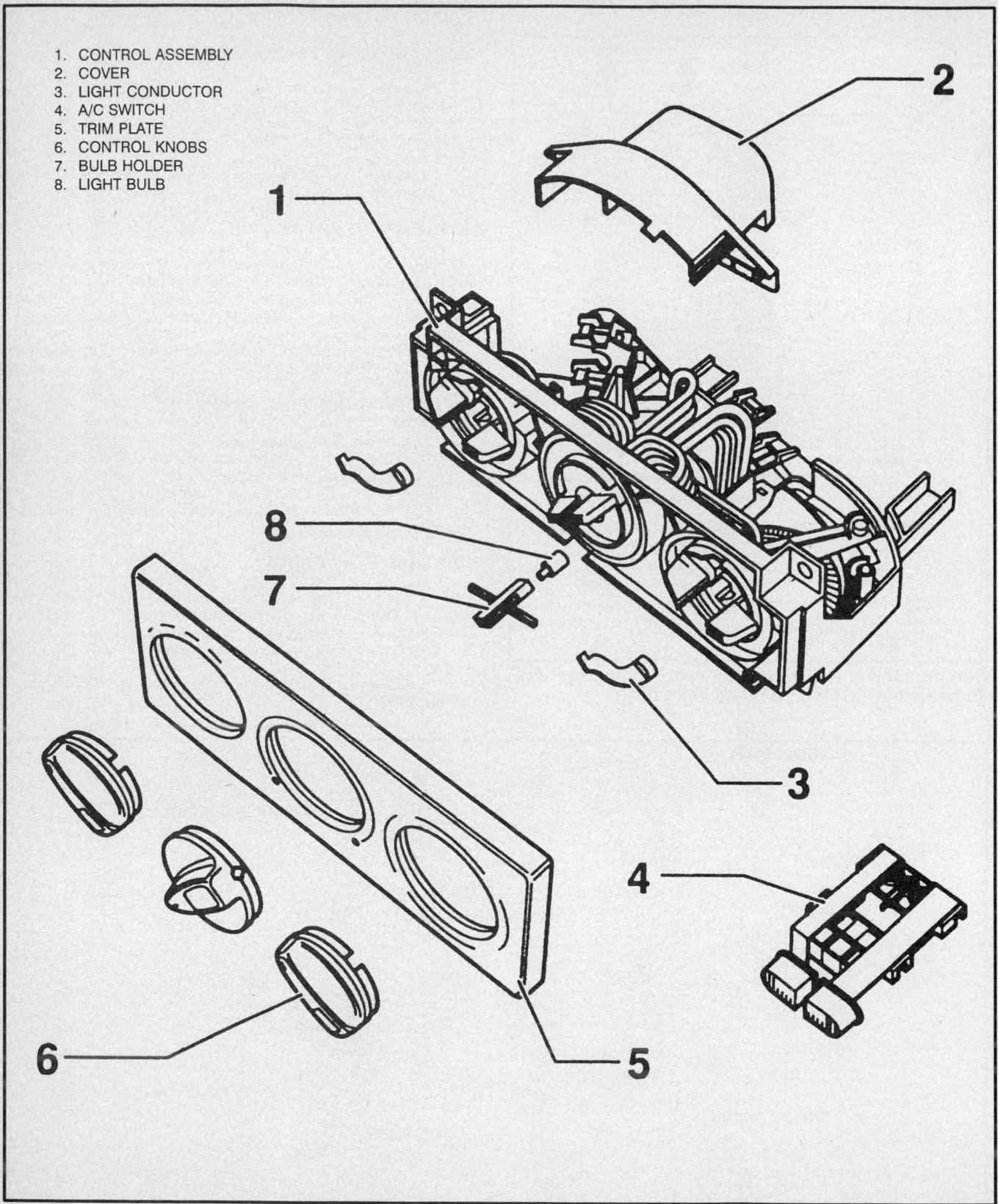

1. CONTROL ASSEMBLY
2. COVER
3. LIGHT CONDUCTOR
4. A/C SWITCH
5. TRIM PLATE
6. CONTROL KNOBS
7. BULB HOLDER
8. LIGHT BULB

Exploded view of the control head—Corrado

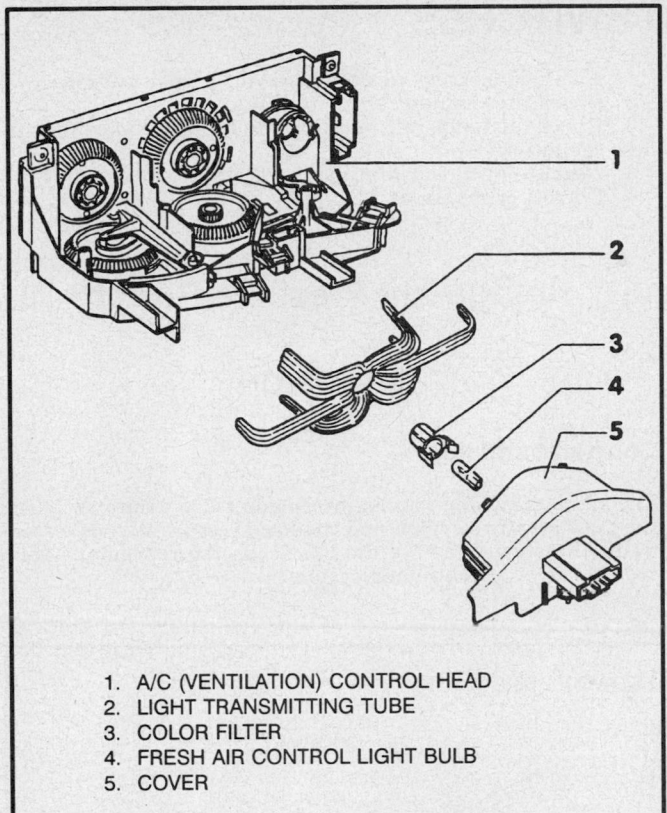

1. A/C (VENTILATION) CONTROL HEAD
2. LIGHT TRANSMITTING TUBE
3. COLOR FILTER
4. FRESH AIR CONTROL LIGHT BULB
5. COVER

Exploded view of the control head—Golf III, GTI and Jetta III

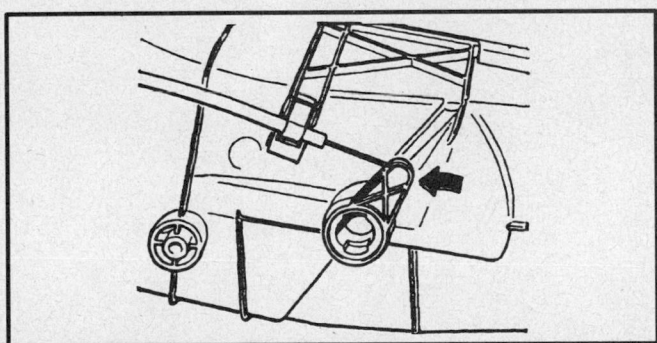

Adjusting main shut-off flap control cable—Golf III, GTI and Jetta III

REMOVAL AND INSTALLATION

1. Disconnect the negative battery cable.
2. Remove the necessary bezel in order to gain access to the control head.
3. Remove the screws that fasten the control head to the instrument panel.
4. Pull the unit out and disconnect the temperature control cable.
5. Disconnect the cable end from the air conditioning housing.

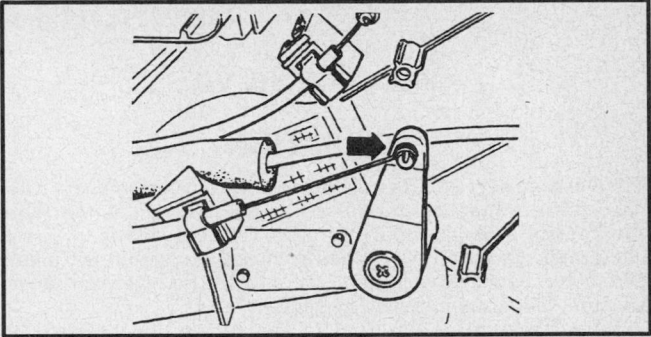

Adjusting the temperature flap control cable—Golf III, GTI and Jetta III

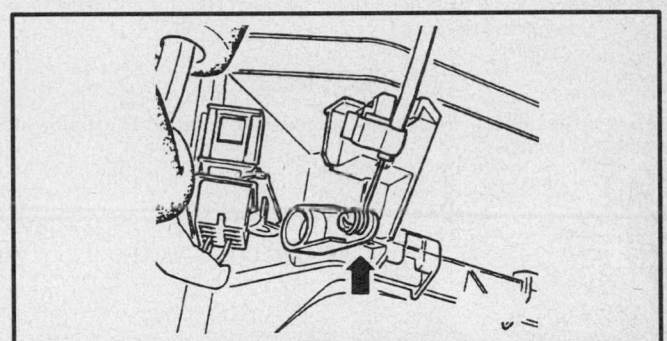

Adjusting floor/defrost flap control cable—Golf III, GTI and Jetta III

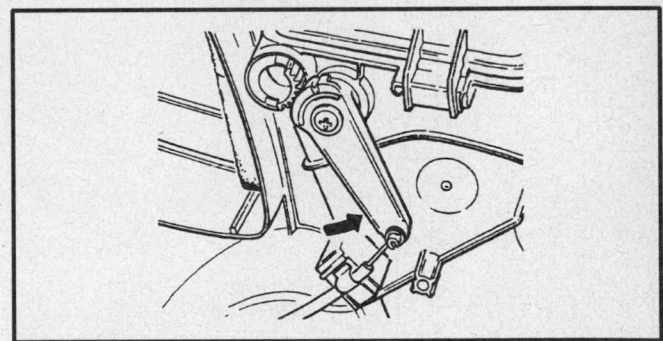

Adjusting central flap control cable—Golf III, GTI and Jetta III

6. Take note of the cable's routing and remove the from the vehicle.
To install:
7. Install the cable by routing it in exactly the same position as it was prior to removal.
8. Connect the self-adjusting clip to the door crank and secure the cable.
9. Connect the upper end of the cable to the control head.
10. Place the temperature lever on the coolest side of its travel. Allowing the self-adjusting clip to slide on the cable, rotate the door counterclockwise by hand until it stops.
11. Cycle the lever back and forth a few times to make sure the cable moves freely.
12. Connect the negative battery cable and check the entire climate control system for proper operation.

SENSORS AND SWITCHES

Vacuum Servo

OPERATION

The vacuum servo opens and closes the ventilation doors when vacuum in admitted or relieved at the vacuum servo. When the control switch is move to each selector position, various vacuum ports are either opened or closed. An adjoining linkage connected between vacuum servo and to the lever of the ventilation door transmits the movement.

When vacuum is admitted to the servo, the internal diaphragm contracts, pulling on the linkage. This action will open the ventilation door. When vacuum is relieved from the servo, the internal diaphragm expands to normal position, in turn allows the linkage and door lever to move in the opposite position, closing the door.

TESTING

If the ventilation doors are inoperative inspect the following possibilities:

1. Check connecting vacuum hoses for proper routing.
2. Check the vacuum servos for leaks.
3. Check the temperature control unit and the vacuum harness connector.
4. Check that the air distribution doors are not binding.
5. Correct or repair, as required.

Refrigerant Pressure Switch

OPERATION

Cabriolet and Fox

The air conditioning system incorporates 2 pressure switches; the high pressure switch and the low pressure switch. Essentially, these switches are used to sense the refrigerant pressure of the air conditioning system.

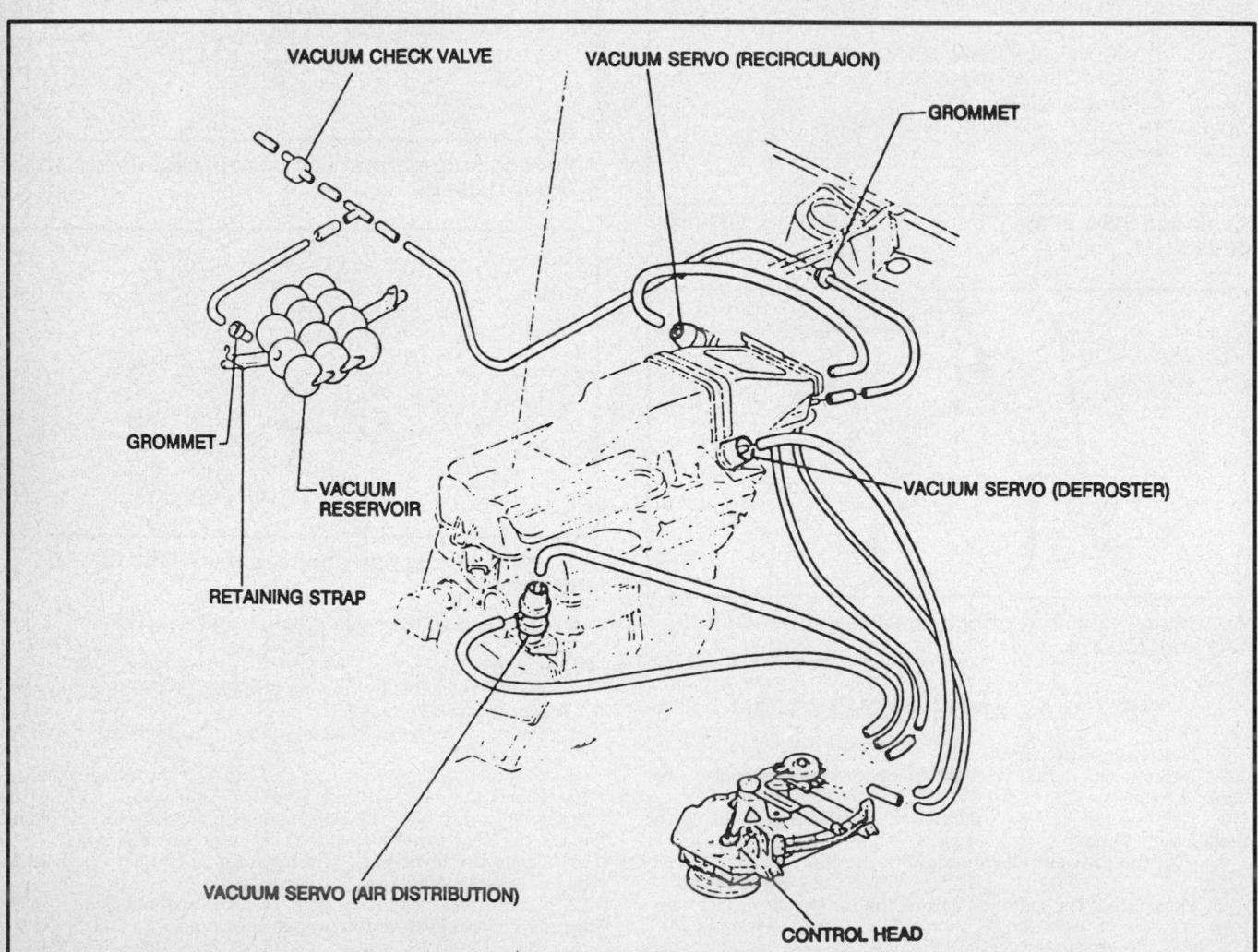

Vacuum control system hose routing—Cabriolet

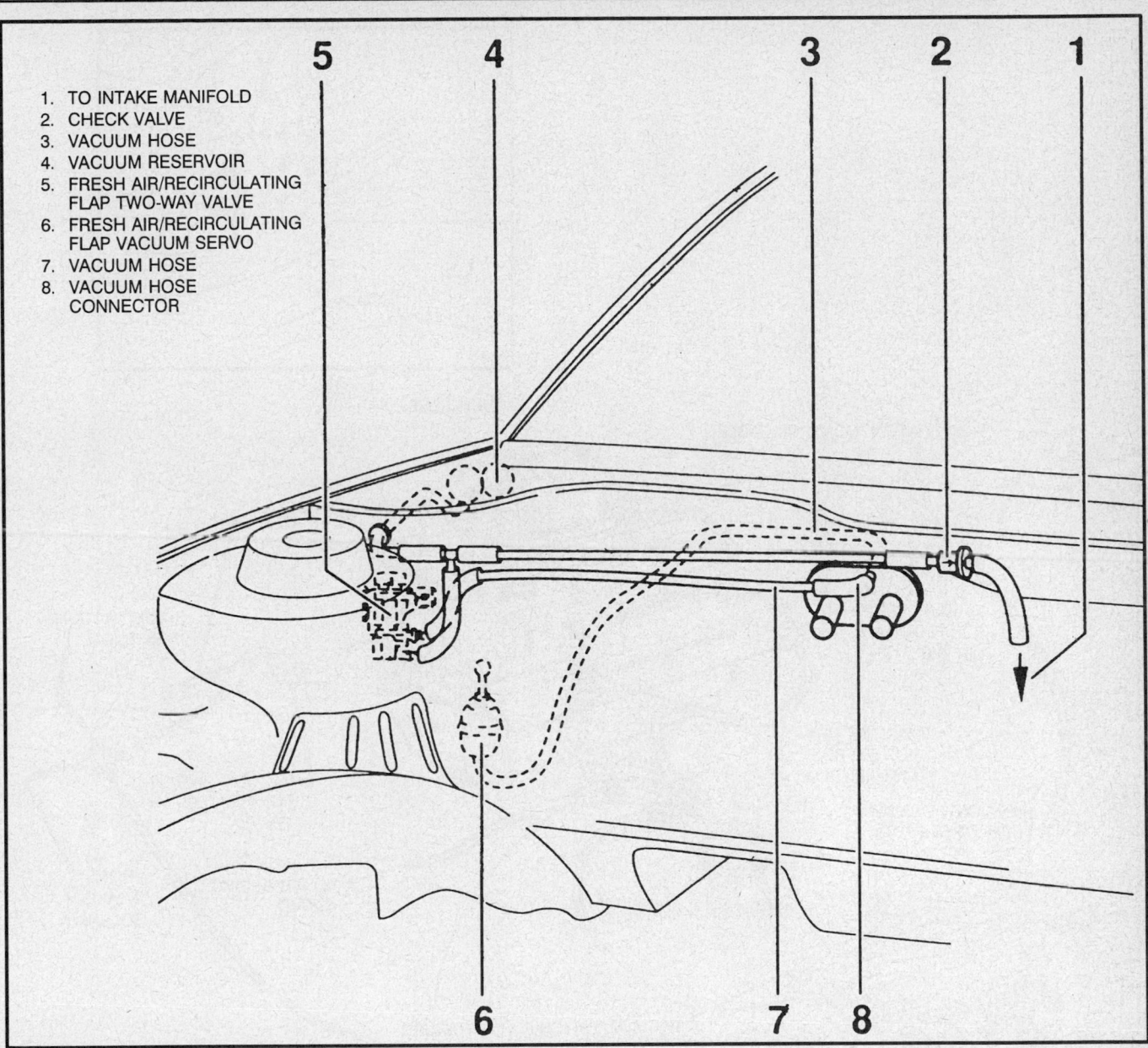

1. TO INTAKE MANIFOLD
2. CHECK VALVE
3. VACUUM HOSE
4. VACUUM RESERVOIR
5. FRESH AIR/RECIRCULATING
   FLAP TWO-WAY VALVE
6. FRESH AIR/RECIRCULATING
   FLAP VACUUM SERVO
7. VACUUM HOSE
8. VACUUM HOSE
   CONNECTOR

Vacuum hose routing—Corrado

The low pressure switch monitors the refrigerant pressure on the suction side of the system. The low pressure switch turns off voltage to the compressor clutch coil when the pressure drops to a level that may damage the compressor.

The high pressure switch monitors the refrigerant pressure on the discharge side. When the discharge pressure moves in excess of 200–210 psi., the high pressure switch closes the circuit and will cause the condenser fan to activate. When the pressure drops between, 164-174 psi. the high pressure switch opens the circuit, cutting the fan off.

Corrado, Golf, Jetta and Passat

These models use a dual–pressure combined high and low pressure protection in one switch. It is mounted on the high pressure line, usually near the condenser and senses either extremely low pressure as with a loss of refrigerant or extremely high pressure as with a blockage or compressor malfunction

and will stop compressor operation. The switch is mounted on a Schrader type valve and therefore does not require system discharge for removal.

TESTING

If the system is low on refrigerant and the compressor clutch doesnot engage, unplug the low pressure switch or dual pressure switch connector and jump the terminals. If the clutch engages, the switch is operating properly. Check for low refrigerant charge or compressor malfunction.

If the system pressures are nominal and the compressor clutch does not engage, unplug the switch and jump the terminals. If the compressor engages, the switch is faulty and should be replaced. If the compressor clutch still does not engage, check the terminals for battery voltage and/or a possible open circuit.

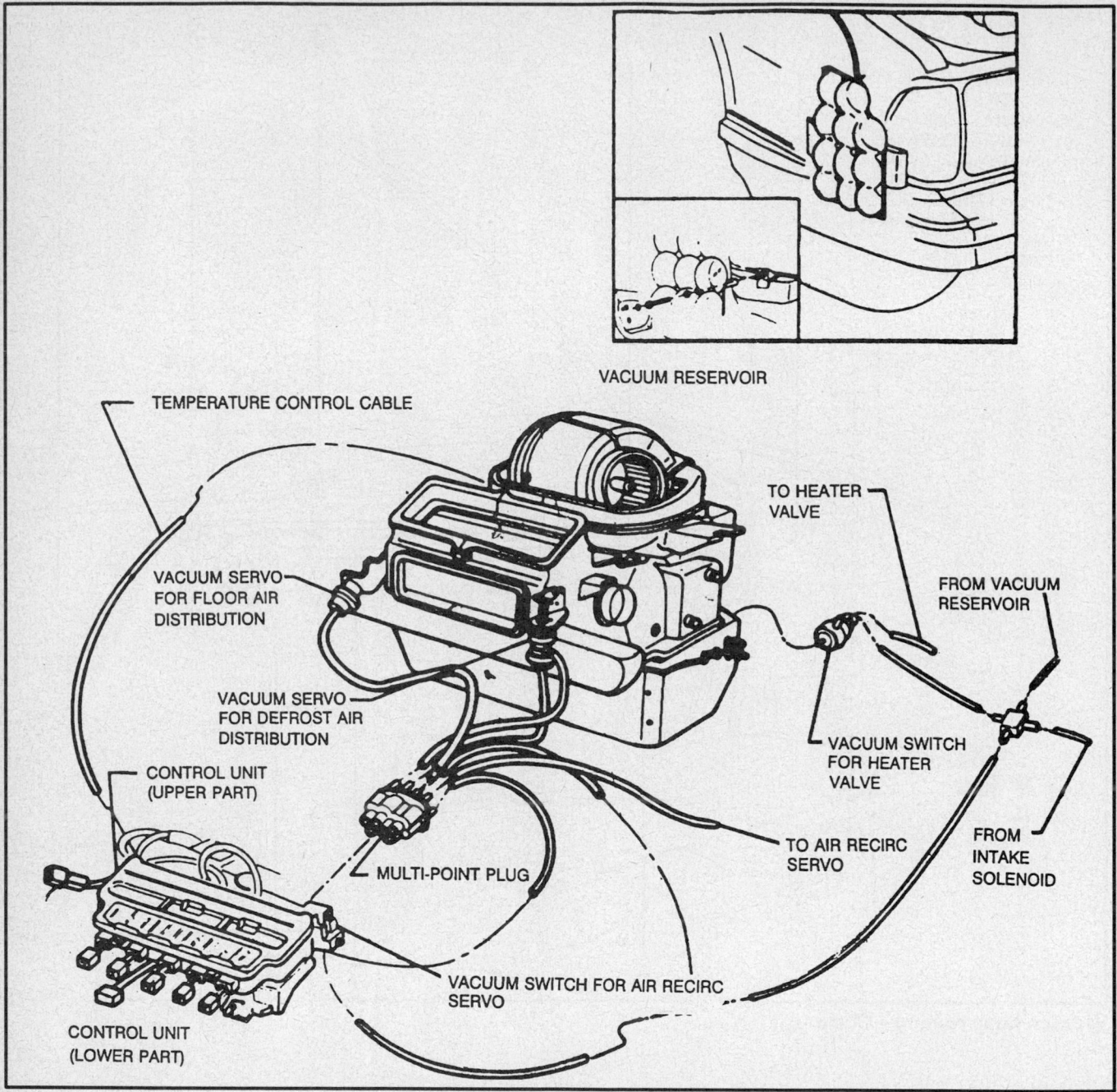

VACUUM RESERVOIR

TEMPERATURE CONTROL CABLE

TO HEATER VALVE

FROM VACUUM RESERVOIR

VACUUM SERVO FOR FLOOR AIR DISTRIBUTION

VACUUM SWITCH FOR HEATER VALVE

VACUUM SERVO FOR DEFROST AIR DISTRIBUTION

FROM INTAKE SOLENOID

CONTROL UNIT (UPPER PART)

TO AIR RECIRC SERVO

MULTI-POINT PLUG

VACUUM SWITCH FOR AIR RECIRC SERVO

CONTROL UNIT (LOWER PART)

Vacuum hose routing—Fox and Passat

If the high pressure exceeds specified limits and the condenser fan does not activate, disconnect the high pressure switch or dual pressure switch connector and jump the terminals. If the fan operates, the switch is faulty. If the fan is still inoperative, test the condenser fan and circuit.

REMOVAL AND INSTALLATION

Cabriolet, Fox, Vanagon

The individual pressure switches are threaded into the refrigerant into the refrigerant lines.

1. Disconnect the negative battery cable.
2. Properly discharge the air conditioning system.
3. Unplug the connector from the switch.
4. Unscrew the switch from the component on which it is mounted.

To install:

5. Seal the threads of the new switch with teflon tape.
6. Install the switch and connect the connector.
7. Evacuate and recharge the system. Check for leaks.
8. Check the switch for proper operation.

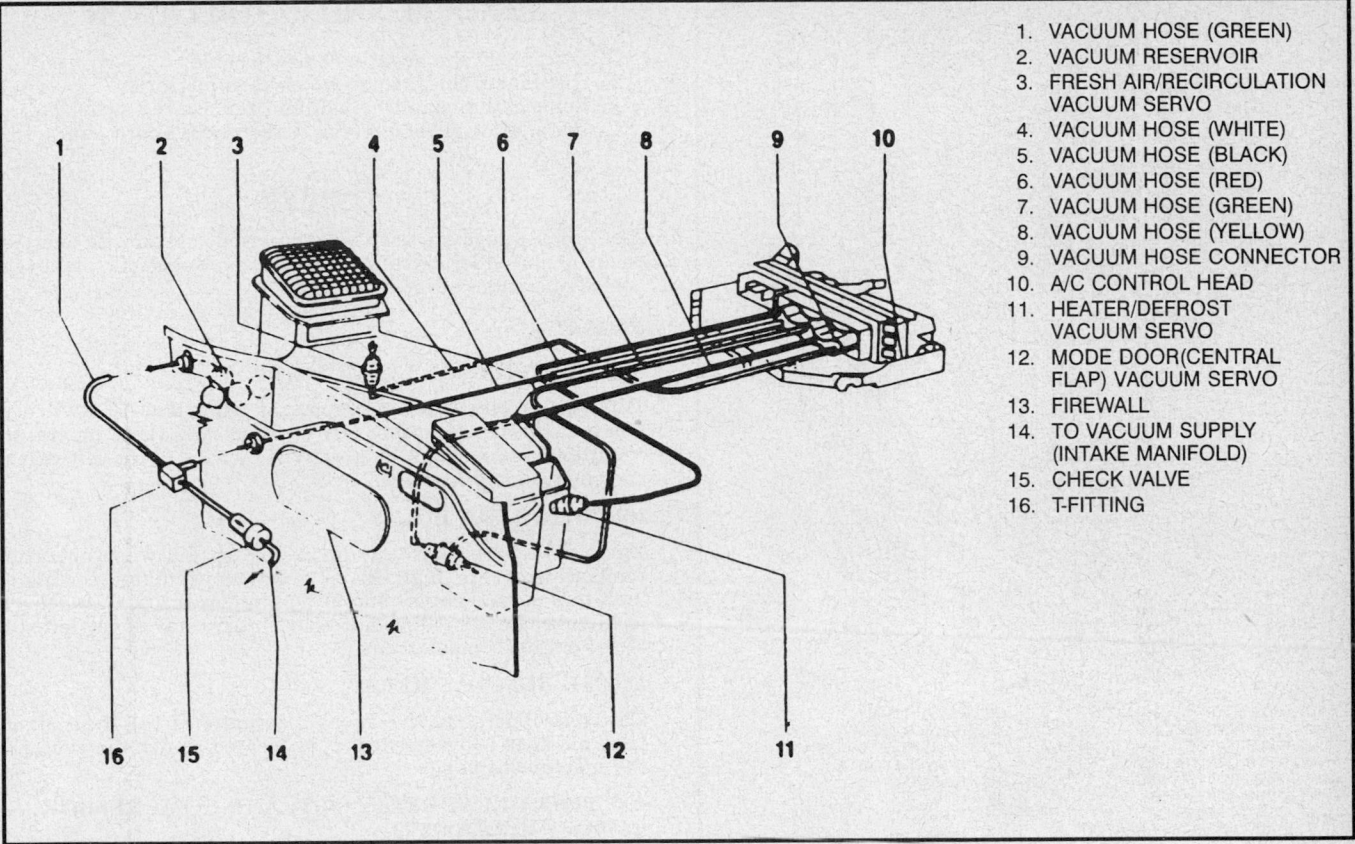

1. VACUUM HOSE (GREEN)
2. VACUUM RESERVOIR
3. FRESH AIR/RECIRCULATION VACUUM SERVO
4. VACUUM HOSE (WHITE)
5. VACUUM HOSE (BLACK)
6. VACUUM HOSE (RED)
7. VACUUM HOSE (GREEN)
8. VACUUM HOSE (YELLOW)
9. VACUUM HOSE CONNECTOR
10. A/C CONTROL HEAD
11. HEATER/DEFROST VACUUM SERVO
12. MODE DOOR(CENTRAL FLAP) VACUUM SERVO
13. FIREWALL
14. TO VACUUM SUPPLY (INTAKE MANIFOLD)
15. CHECK VALVE
16. T-FITTING

View of the hose layout—Golf, GTI and Jetta

Cooling Fan Thermo-Switch

OPERATION

The thermo–switch senses the radiator coolant temperature. When the radiator coolant temperature is between 201–226°F, the thermo–switch sends current to the cooling fan relay, in turn the relay activates the cooling fan.

When the coolant temperature drops between 183–206°F, the thermo–switch will cut the current flow to the coolant fan relay, thus causing the fan stop.

TESTING

If the coolant fan fails to come on when the radiator temperatures are between 201-226°F or operates continuously, the thermo-switch may be at fault.

1. Start the engine and allow it to warm to approximately 226°F; if the fan does not come ON, disconnect connector at the thermo-switch. Touch the connector to ground. The fan should operate.
2. If the cooling fan activates, the thermo-switch is defective. If the cooling fan does not activate, use a test light to check continuity at the thermo-switch connector. If current exist, test the cooling fan relay.
3. If the coolant fan runs continuously without cutting off,disconnect the connector at the thermo-switch. If the fan cuts OFF, the thermo-switch is defective.
4. If the fan still continues to operate; disconnect the connector at the cooling fan relay. The fan should stop, thus indicating the relay is at fault.

REMOVAL AND INSTALLATION

The thermo-switch is threaded into the side of the radiator tank, on the lower left side or in to the engine block.

1. Allow the engine to cool sufficiently.
2. Disconnect the negative battery cable.
3. Drain the cooling system.
4. Disconnect the electrical connector at the thermo-switch.
5. Unscrew the thermo-switch from the radiator.
To install:
6. Install the switch and torque to 11 ft. lbs. (15 Nm).
7. Connect the electrical connector to the switch.
8. Fill the cooling system. Connect the negative battery cable.
9. Start the engine and allow it to warm up. Top off the cooling system, as required.

Ambient Temperature Switch

Passat uses an ambient temperature switch which will not allow compressor operation if the outside temperature is too cold. This prevent premature wear on the compressor under severe conditions. It also prevents cold, conditioned air from blowing in the passenger compartment unnecessarily. The switch closes above 45°F (7°C) and opens below 30°F (–1°C). The switch is normally located near the front grille.

TESTING

1. Using an appropriate circuit tester on the ohm scale, check for switch continuity.

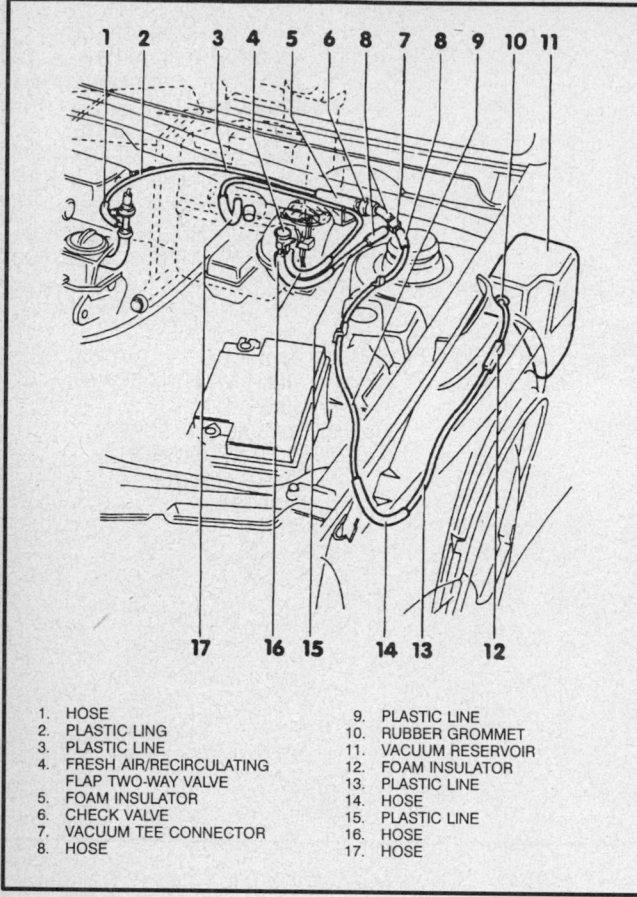

1. HOSE
2. PLASTIC LING
3. PLASTIC LINE
4. FRESH AIR/RECIRCULATING FLAP TWO-WAY VALVE
5. FOAM INSULATOR
6. CHECK VALVE
7. VACUUM TEE CONNECTOR
8. HOSE
9. PLASTIC LINE
10. RUBBER GROMMET
11. VACUUM RESERVOIR
12. FOAM INSULATOR
13. PLASTIC LINE
14. HOSE
15. PLASTIC LINE
16. HOSE
17. HOSE

Vacuum hose routing—Golf III, GTI and Jetta III

2. Observe fan operation.
3. Disconnect the switch connector and probe the terminals. There should be continuity if the temperature is above 45°F (7°C).

REMOVAL AND INSTALLATION

1. Disconnect the negative battery cable.
2. Disconnect the switch electrical connector.
3. Remove the mounting bolt and remove the switch.
4. Installation is the reverse of the removal procedure.

Relays

A series of relays are used on the various systems to energize components under certain conditions or to cut off component operations under severe conditions.

Passat

A/C COMPRESSOR CLUTCH RELAY

This relay energizes the compressor when the A/C switch in **ON** and the fan is in any **ON** position, and the temperature conditions are normal. This relay is located at the left rear of the engine compartment.

RADIATOR FAN RELAY

This relay energizes the radiator cooling fan when operating temperatures are high. This assists in radiator cooling to maintain normal engine operating temperatures. This relay is located beside the A/C compressor clutch relay at the left rear of the engine compartment.

FRESH AIR FLAP RELAY

This relay energizes the solenoid actuator at the fresh air intake air door when needed. It is located under the center of the instrument panel.

A/C TIME DELAY RELAY (M/T) AND COMPRESSOR CUTOFF RELAY (A/T)

This relay, used on manual transaxle equipped models, provides at time delay for compressor operation under certain downshift operating conditions to provide additional power to the engine when needed. It is located behind the center console.

The compressor cutoff relay is used on automatic transaxle equipped models to stop compressor operation when the transaxle is kicked down into low gear, such as for passing, or in wide open throttle so maximum engine power is available. This relay will also be behind the center console.

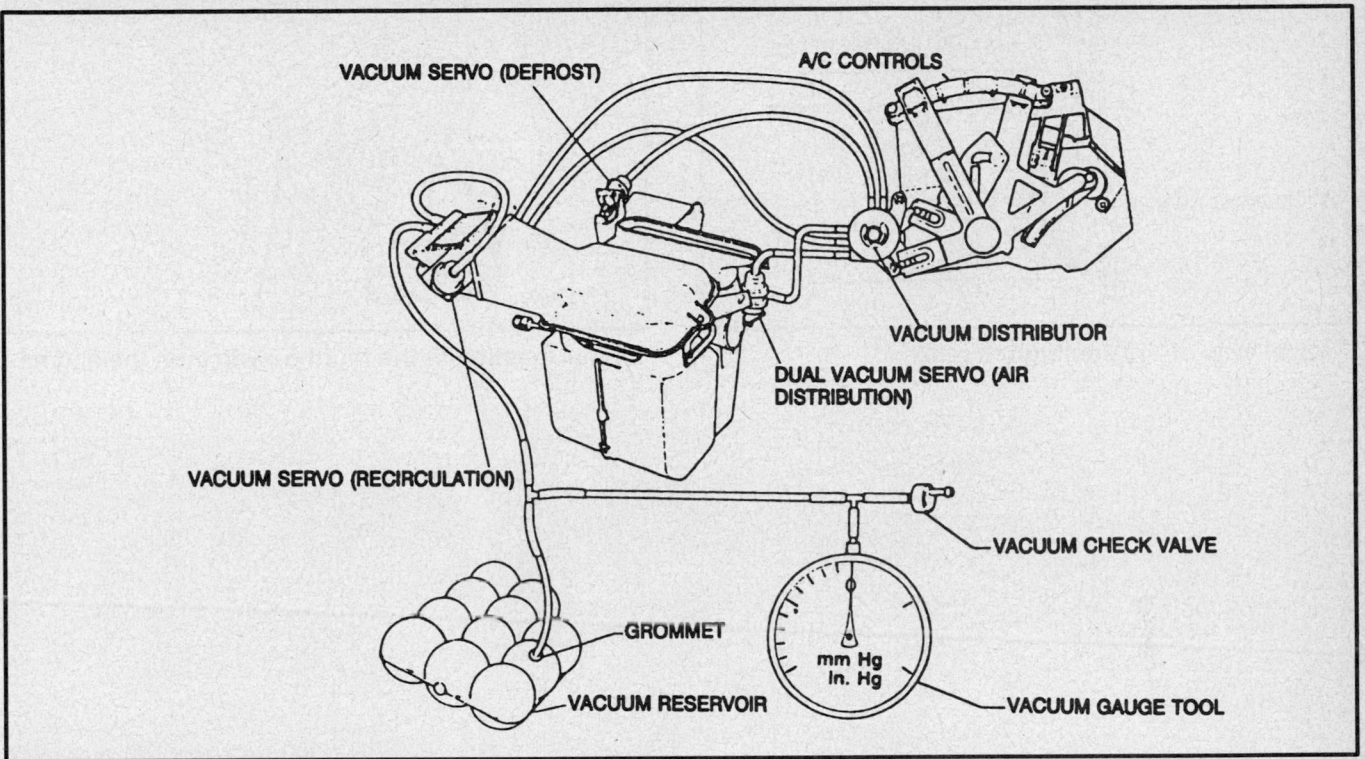

VACUUM SERVO (DEFROST)

A/C CONTROLS

VACUUM DISTRIBUTOR

DUAL VACUUM SERVO (AIR DISTRIBUTION)

VACUUM SERVO (RECIRCULATION)

VACUUM CHECK VALVE

GROMMET

mm Hg
In. Hg

VACUUM RESERVOIR

VACUUM GAUGE TOOL

Checking the vacuum system with a vacuum gauge tool

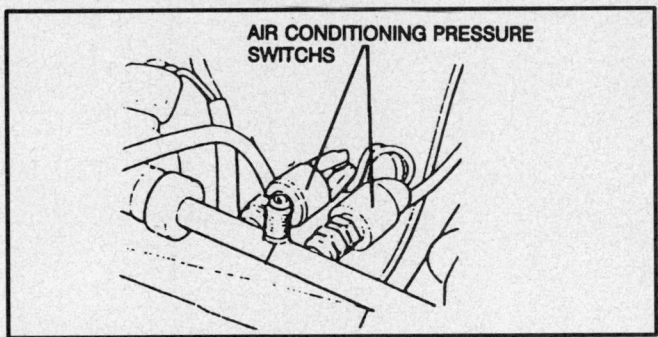

AIR CONDITIONING PRESSURE SWITCHS

View of the refrigerant pressure switches—Cabriolet, Fox and Vanagon

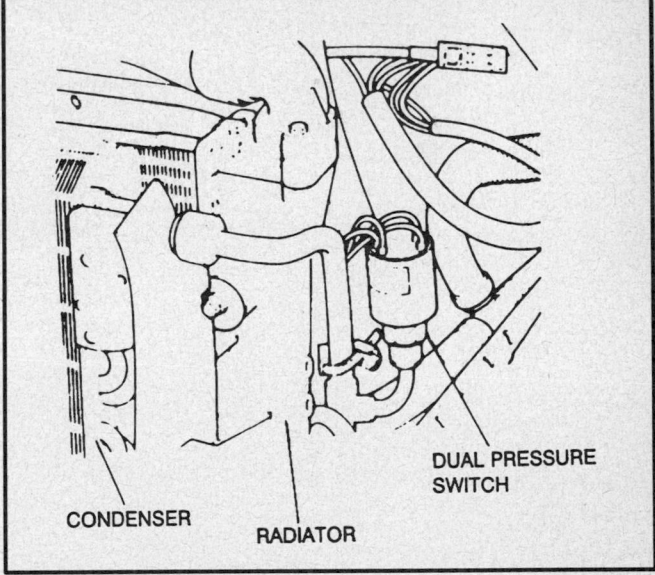

DUAL PRESSURE SWITCH

CONDENSER

RADIATOR

View of the dual pressure switch—Corrado, Golf, GTI, Jetta and Passat

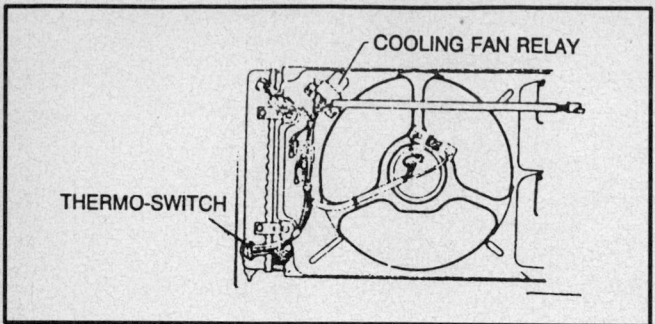

Typical view of the cooling fan relay

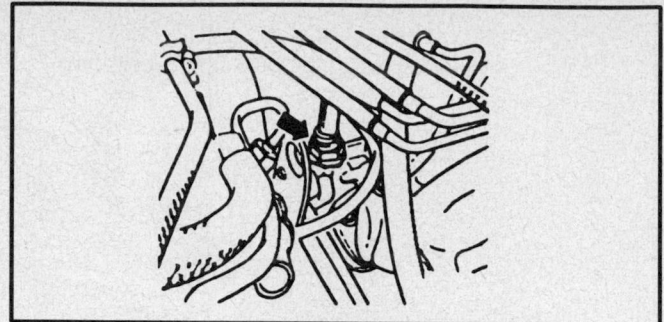

Typical location of the thermo-switch on the engine

SPECIFICATIONS

ENGINE IDENTIFICATION

Year	Model	Engine Displacement Liters (cc)	Engine Series (ID/VIN)	Fuel System	No. of Cylinders	Engine Type
1993	240 Series	2.3L (2316)	B230F	Bosch LH 2.4	4	SOHC
	850 Series	2.4L (2382)	B5254S	Bosch LH 3.2	5	DOHC
	940 Series	2.3L (2316)	B230F	Bosch LH 2.4	4	SOHC
	960 Series	2.9L (2922)	B6304S	Motronic 1.8	6	DOHC
1994	850 Series	2.4L (2382)	B5254S	Bosch LH 3.2	5	DOHC
	940 Series	2.3L (2316)	B230F	Bosch LH 2.4	4	SOHC
	960 Series	2.9L (2922)	B6304S	Motronic 1.8	6	DOHC
1995	850 Series	2.4L (2382)	B5254S	Bosch LH 3.2	5	DOHC
	940 Series	2.3L (2316)	B230F	Bosch LH 2.4	4	SOHC
	960 Series	2.9L (2922)	B6304S	Motronic 1.8	6	DOHC

DOHC – Dual Overhead Cam
SOHC – Single Overhead Cam

REFRIGERANT CAPACITIES

Year	Model	Refrigerant (oz.)	Oil (fl. oz.)	Compressor Type
1993	240 Series	46.4	①	①
	850 Series	26	6.76	Zexel DKS-15CH
	940 Series	31	②	②
	960 Series	31	②	②
1994	850 Series	26	6.76	Zexel DKS-15CH
	940 Series	31	②	②
	960 Series	31	②	②
1995	850 Series	26	6.76	Zexel DKS-15CH
	940 Series	31	②	②
	960 Series	31	②	②

① Delco 6 6 cyl. – 10.4 oz.,
   Diesel-KiKi YA15 – 6.8 oz.
   Sankyo/Sanden SD510 – 4.6 oz.
② Delco R4 – 6.0 oz.
   Sankyo/Sanden SD510 – 4.6 oz.
   Sankyo/Sanden SD709 – 8.1 oz.
   York AZ10 – 10.1 oz.

AIR CONDITIONING BELT TENSION

Year	Model	Engine Liters (cc)	Belt Type	Specifications New (lbs.)	Specifications Used (lbs.)
1993	240 Series	2.3L (2316)	V–Belt	0.2–0.4	0.2–0.4
	850 Series	2.4L (2382)	Serpentine	②	②
	940 Series	2.3L (2316)	V–Belt	①	①
	960 Series	2.9L (2922)	Serpentine	②	②
1994	850 Series	2.4L (2382)	Serpentine	②	②
	940 Series	2.3L (2316)	V–Belt	①	①
	960 Series	2.9L (2922)	Serpentine	②	②
1995	850 Series	2.4L (2382)	Serpentine	②	②
	940 Series	2.3L (2316)	V–Belt	①	①
	960 Series	2.9L (2922)	Serpentine	(2)	(2)

① Delco compressor: 0.04–0.08 in. deflection, Diesel–Kiki compressor: 0.2–0.4 in. deflection, Sankyo/Sanden compressor: 0.2–0.4 in. deflection, York compressor: 0.1–0.4 in. deflection

② Automatic tensioner used, no adjustment required.

SYSTEM DESCRIPTION

General Information

All air conditioning equipped models use R–134a refrigerant in the system. The components of the system are virtually the same as with previous R–12 systems, but cannot be intermixed.

The heater core and blower motor are contained in the heater box (fresh air housing) located in the passenger compartment under the dashboard. The blower fan is of a turbine design and is accessible from under the dash. The heater core is mostly accessible through the removal and disassembly of the heater box.

The 240 Series is equipped with either heater only or manual air conditioning system (combined unit heating and air conditioning). The 850 and 940 Series will have the manual air conditioning system standard and Automatic or Electronic Climate Control (ACC or ECC) as optional equipment. The 960 Series has ECC as standard equipment. The control panels vary slightly according to the type of system used.

240 Series

Two Climate Units (CU) are used and are of common construction, one for the use of a heating system only and the other for the use of both a heating unit and an air conditioning unit combined. The removal and installation of the heating system components and the air conditioning/heating system components are basically the same for both systems.

850, 940 and 960 Series

Two types of climate control units are used, the Manual Climate Control (MCC) and the Automatic or Electronic Climate Control (ACC or ECC). The difference in the units lie in the components of each system and whether the controls are operated manually or by electronic feedback. The MCC air doors are cable controlled and the ECC doors are electric motor controlled.

With the MCC unit, the passenger compartment is kept at a preset temperature regardless of the ambient temperature.

The unit is set at the control panel, but is controlled by a programmer located behind the instrument controlled unit. However, the wiring, vacuum and air flow schematics are different from the other units.

The ECC system incorporates a self–diagnosis function; faults are indicated by a series of flashing codes when the A/C button is pushed. The control unit is programmed to make the best operating selection if a fault is detected. If a fault is detected, the unit ignores the faulty signal and selects an alternative pre–programmed value. The control unit is also designed to prevent the delivery of faulty outputs. The presence of a fault(s) is indicated by flashing of the A/C button. In the workshop, any such fault code may be identified by setting the controls to a specified configuration. The absence of a fault code is not a guarantee that the system is fault–free.

The ECC control module detects the control panel setting and receives information from various sensors connected in the system. The module also receives a signal from the engine management system when the A/C relay is activated, verifying the engine is running and the A/C system can be switched ON. The damper door motors and fan speed power stage controller react quickly to assure temperature setting and air volume are correct, and also provide feedback if there are any faults indicated in the system.

Service Valve Location

York Compressor System

NOTE: Since these systems are equipped with R–134a refrigerant, be sure to use dedicated service equipment with proper connectors. Do not use a gauge set or other equipment previously used on R–12 equipped systems.

The service valve location for high pressure side is at compressor's DISCH valve. The service valve location for the low pressure side is at compressor's SUCTION valve.

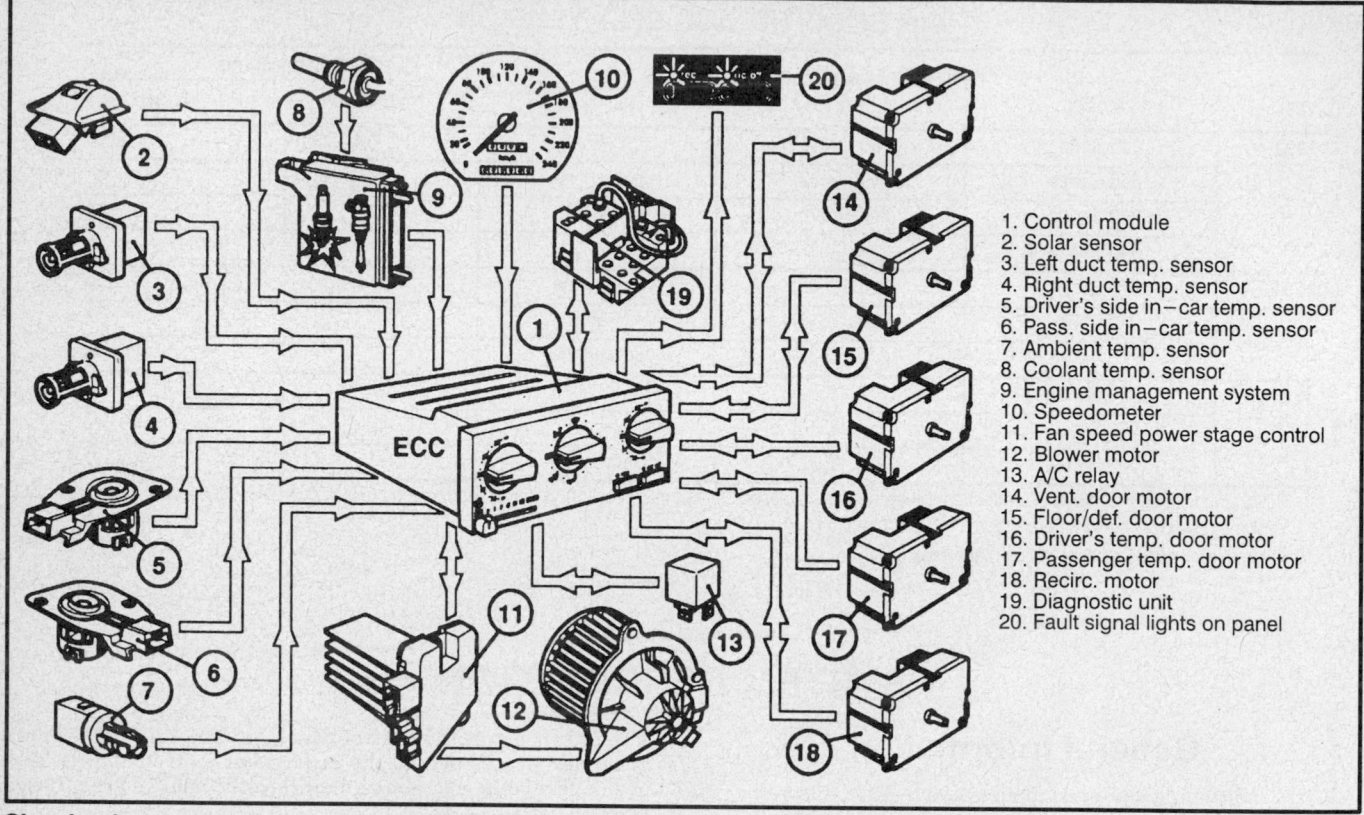

Showing input and output relationship of components on electronic climate control system—850 Series shown

1. Control module
2. Solar sensor
3. Left duct temp. sensor
4. Right duct temp. sensor
5. Driver's side in–car temp. sensor
6. Pass. side in–car temp. sensor
7. Ambient temp. sensor
8. Coolant temp. sensor
9. Engine management system
10. Speedometer
11. Fan speed power stage control
12. Blower motor
13. A/C relay
14. Vent. door motor
15. Floor/def. door motor
16. Driver's temp. door motor
17. Passenger temp. door motor
18. Recirc. motor
19. Diagnostic unit
20. Fault signal lights on panel

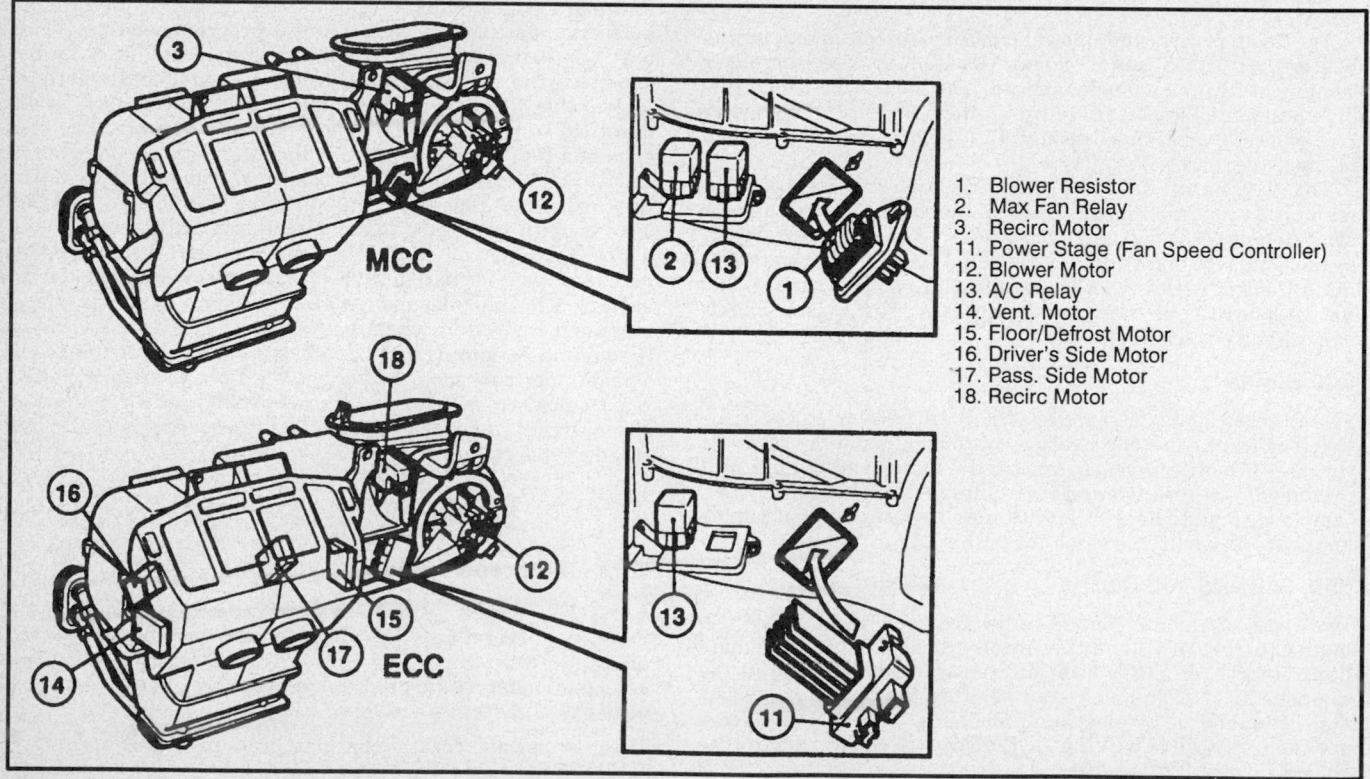

Showing component differences between manual and electronic systems—850, 940 and 960 models

1. Blower Resistor
2. Max Fan Relay
3. Recirc Motor
11. Power Stage (Fan Speed Controller)
12. Blower Motor
13. A/C Relay
14. Vent. Motor
15. Floor/Defrost Motor
16. Driver's Side Motor
17. Pass. Side Motor
18. Recirc Motor

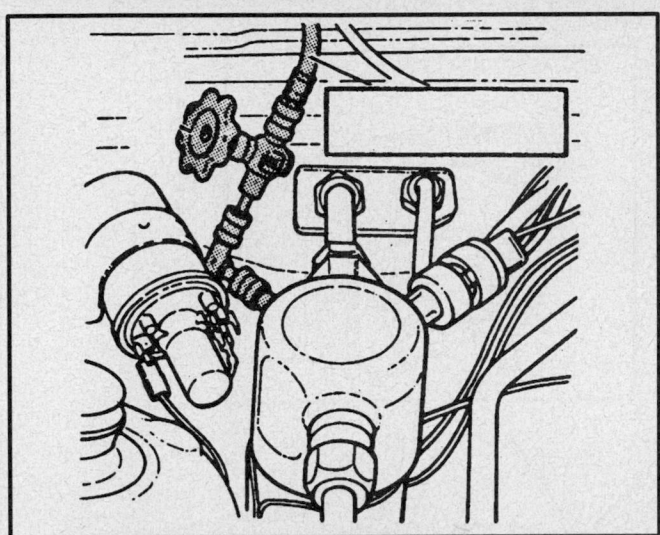

Low side service port location on York compressors

Except York Compressor System

The high pressure service valve is located on the compressor. The low pressure service valve is located on the receiver/drier assembly.

System Discharging

Although R–134a is a non–CFC refrigerant, it should not be vented to the open air. Always use an approved Recovery/Recycling machine that meets SAE standard J1991 should be employed when discharging the system. Follow the operating instructions provided with the approved equipment exactly to properly discharge the system and recover the refrigerant.

System Evacuating

If the air conditioning system has been opened to the atmosphere, it should be air and moisture free before being recharged with refrigerant. Moisture and air mixed with refrigerant will raise the compressor head pressure, possibly damage the system's components and will reduce the performance of the system. To evacuate the system, perform the following procedure:

1. Leak test the system and repair any leaks found.
2. Connect an approved charging station, Recovery/Recycling machine or manifold gauge set and vacuum pump to the discharge and suction ports. The red hose is normally connected to the discharge (high pressure) line and the blue hose is connected to the suction (low pressure) line.
3. Open the discharge and suction ports and start the vacuum pump. If the pump is not able to pull at least 26 in. Hg of vacuum, there is a leak that must be repaired before evacuation can occur.
4. Once the system has reached at least 26 in. Hg of vacuum, allow the system to evacuate for at least 30 minutes. The longer the system is evacuated, the more contaminants will be removed.
5. Close all valves and turn the pump OFF. If the system loses more than 2 in. Hg of vacuum after 15 minutes, there is a leak that should be repaired.

System Charging

1. Connect an approved charging station, Recovery/Recycling machine or manifold gauge set to the discharge and suction ports. The red hose is normally connected to the discharge (high pressure) line and the blue hose is connected to the suction (low pressure) line.
2. Follow the instructions provided with the equipment and charge the system with the specified amount of refrigerant.
3. Perform a leak test.

Air Bag Servicing Information

240 Series

Servicing components or troubleshooting wiring requires disabling the air bag/Supplemental Restraint System (SRS) first. This must be done to avoid accidental deployment of the air bag.

1. Disconnect and cover the negative battery cable.
2. Disconnect only the yellow SRS connector. The connector is located under the carpet on the driver's side of the console.

――――――――― CAUTION ―――――――――
Do not disconnect the connector at the SRS crash sensor (under the driver's seat) or the air bag will deploy.
―――――――――――――――――――――――――――

3. Reconnect this connector (and any others detached during repairs) after completing service.

NOTE: The connectors for the SRS have gold–plated terminal pins. If these pins are detached or the lead is detached from the connector, they cannot be repaired or spliced. Replace the harness or component if this happens.

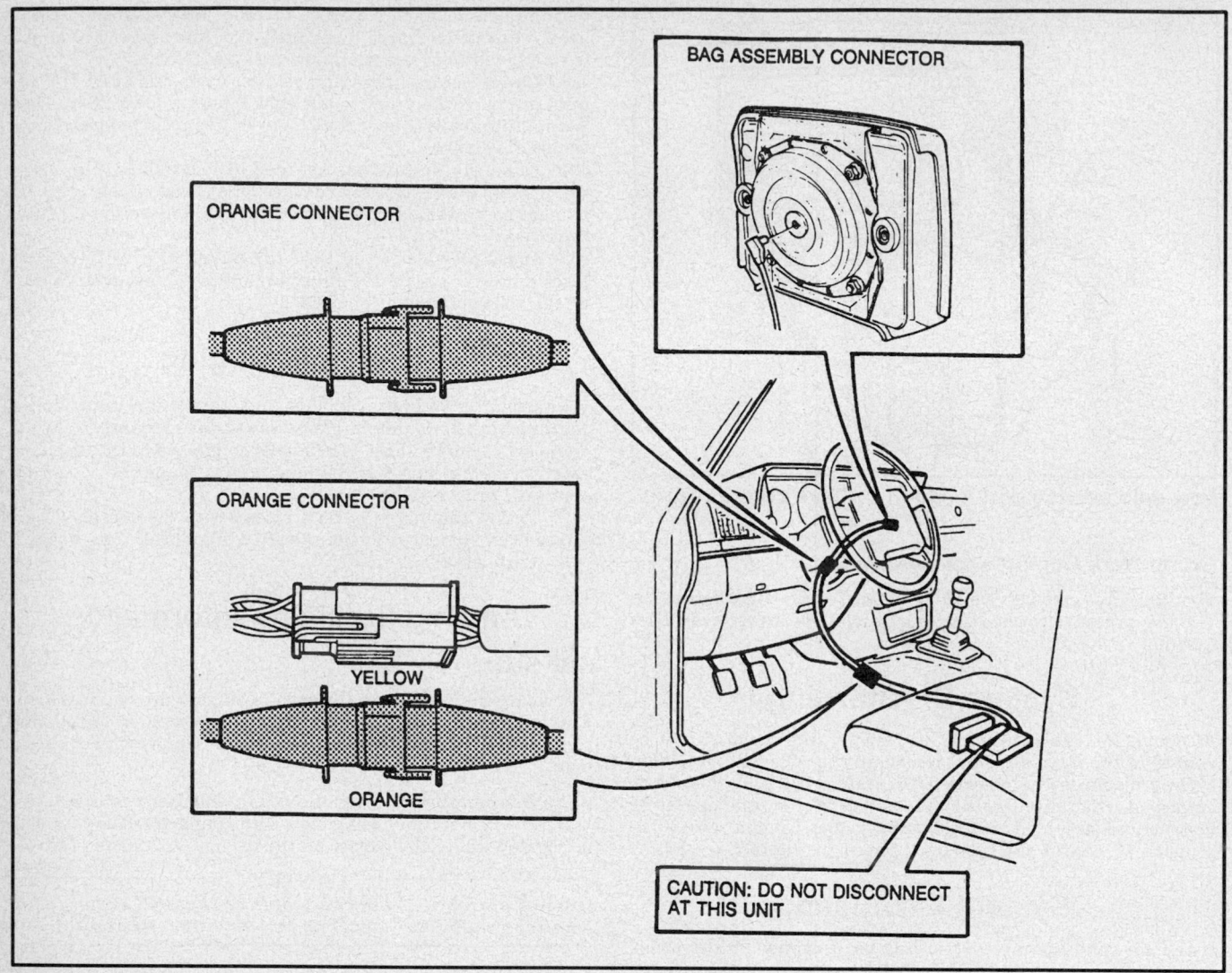

ORANGE CONNECTOR

ORANGE CONNECTOR

YELLOW

ORANGE

BAG ASSEMBLY CONNECTOR

CAUTION: DO NOT DISCONNECT
AT THIS UNIT

Supplemental restraint system (air bag) disconnect location—240 Series

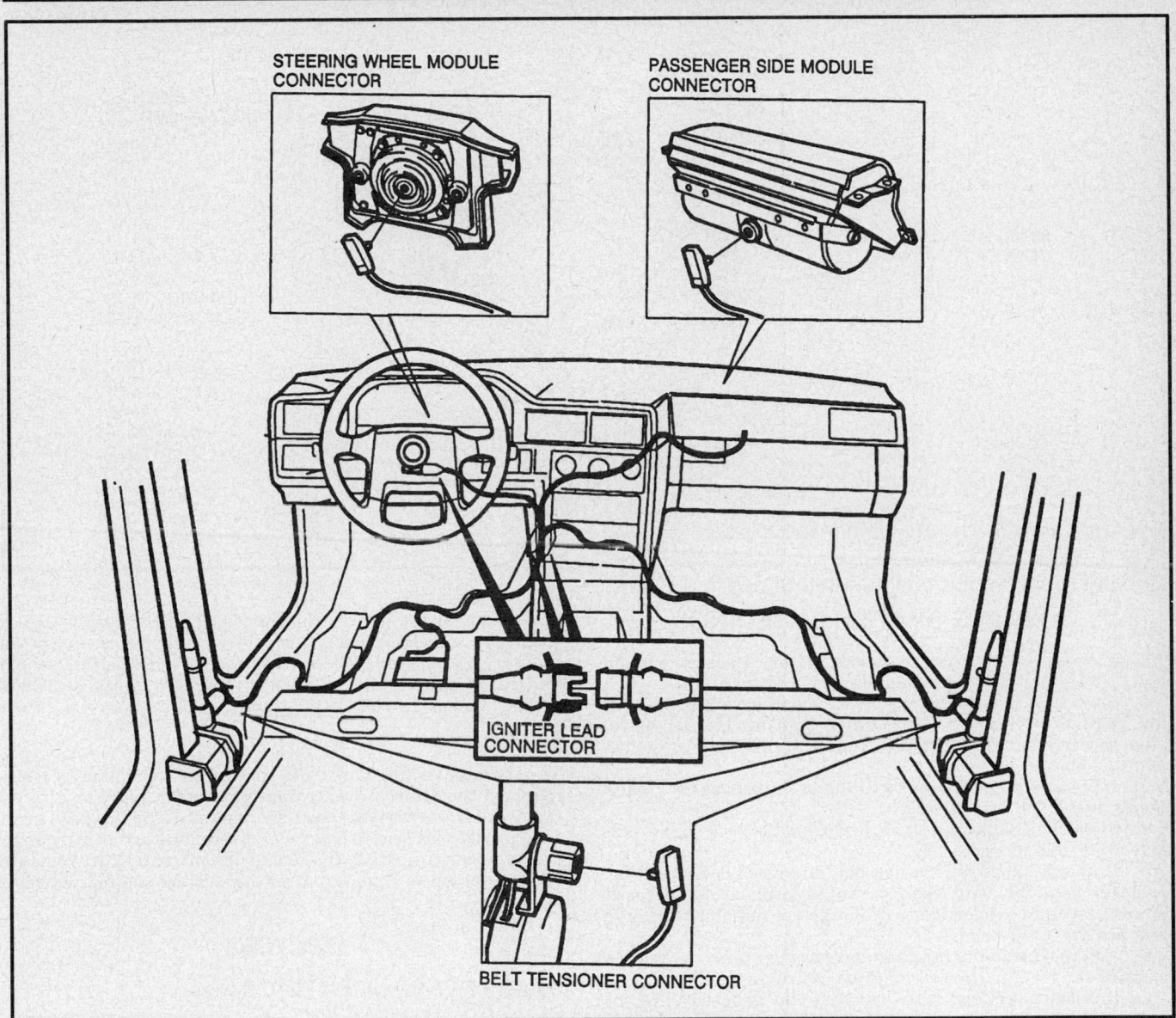

STEERING WHEEL MODULE CONNECTOR

PASSENGER SIDE MODULE CONNECTOR

IGNITER LEAD CONNECTOR

BELT TENSIONER CONNECTOR

Supplemental Restraint System (air bag) disconnect location—940 and 960 Series

SYSTEM COMPONENTS

Radiator

REMOVAL AND INSTALLATION

1. Disconnect the negative battery cable. Drain engine coolant.

2. Remove the expansion tank assembly. Remove upper and lower radiator hoses.

3. Disconnect all electrical connection at radiator assembly.

4. If equipped with automatic transmission disconnect the oil cooler lines. Remove the radiator and fan shroud retaining bolts. Remove the radiator assembly from the vehicle.

To install:

5. Install the radiator and fan shroud assembly in the vehicle. Note the correct placement of the radiator is essential for proper operation check that the rubber cushions if equipped are in the correct position.

6. If equipped, with automatic transmission reconnect the automatic transmission oil cooler lines.

7. Connect all electrical connection at radiator assembly.

8. Install the expansion tank assembly. Reconnect the upper and lower radiator hoses.

9. Reconnect the negative battery cable, fill (bleed cooling system) the engine with coolant. Start the engine and check for leaks. Check all fluid levels, as necessary.

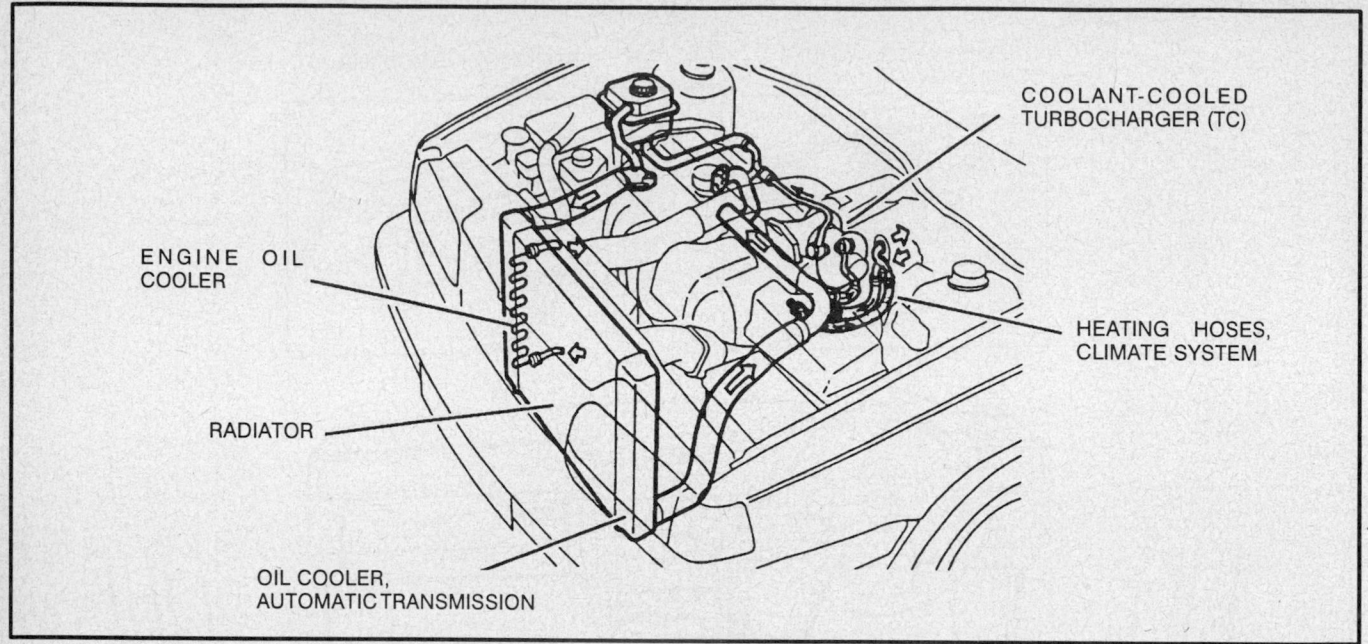

COOLANT-COOLED TURBOCHARGER (TC)

ENGINE OIL COOLER

HEATING HOSES, CLIMATE SYSTEM

RADIATOR

OIL COOLER, AUTOMATIC TRANSMISSION

Cooling system components—850 Series

COOLING SYSTEM BLEEDING

1. To release the air in the cooling system, loosen the union bolt (air bleeder valve) if equipped.
2. Slowly fill the cooling system with coolant when the coolant begins to come out of the union bolt (air bleeder valve) stop pouring and close the air drain valve. Torque the union bolt (air bleeder valve).
3. Add coolant to radiator until the level reaches the proper level. Install the radiator cap.
4. Start the engine and check for leaks. Recheck the coolant level and refill as necessary.
5. If not equipped with union bolt (air bleed valve), fill the radiator assembly and open cooling system at furthermost point from engine (open lower drain cock in radiator to remove trapped air if necessary).
6. Add coolant to the radiator and recovery tank as required to raise the level to the full mark as indicated (cold).
7. Run the engine with the radiator cap removed until the engine reaches correct operating temperature. Add coolant to the radiator until the level reaches the proper level. Install the radiator cap after coolant bubbling subsides. Fill the coolant into the reservoir tank to the FULL mark.

Cooling Fan

240 Series

The cooling fan is control by a thermal switch in the lower radiator hose or on the radiator and by a relay. When temperature of engine coolant reaches a preset temperature, the thermal switch closes and energizes the cooling fan via the relay.

940 Series

The cooling fan is controlled by the fuel system Bosch LH–Jetronic 2.4 electronic control unit and pressure sensors

mounted near the front of the condenser. If the system uses a Regina type fuel/ignition control system, the fan is control via pressure sensors and a relay. The sensor is a thermal switch located in the coolant expansion tank. It closes at 239°F (115°C) and starts the fan operation.

960 Series

The radiator cooling fan is a 2–speed unit controlled by a signal from the Motronic control unit via a fan relay or directly by one of the 2 pressure switches mounted in the high pressure refrigerant line. When coolant temperature is high when the engine is turned off, the Motronic control unit will operate the fan for up to 5 minutes more to reduce engine temperature.

TESTING

System Functional Test—240 Series

1. Turn ignition to the **ON** position.
2. Connect the 2 wires at thermal switch to each other. The electric fan should run.
3. If cooling fan does not operate, run direct power source and ground to isolate electric fan operation. If fan operates check wiring and relay for cooling fan circuit.

Checking Radiator Thermal Switch Operation

1. Check radiator switch operation with ohmmeter across switch terminals.
2. Place switch in water bath. Contacts should be closed when water temperature is above 190–200°F (88–93°C).
3. Contacts of switch should open when water temperature is 180–188°F (82–86°C).

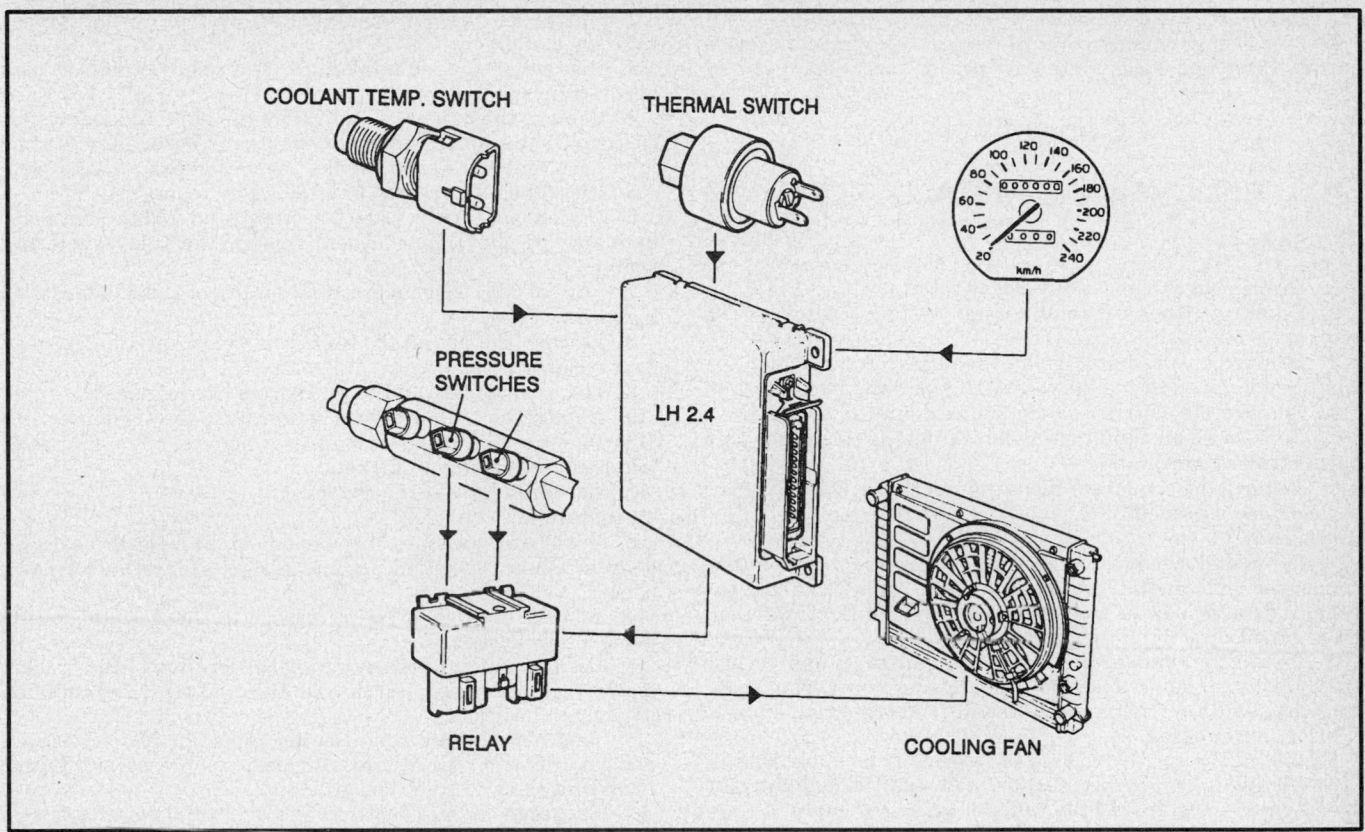

Electric cooling fan control via Bosch LH—Jetronic 2.4 control unit—940 Series

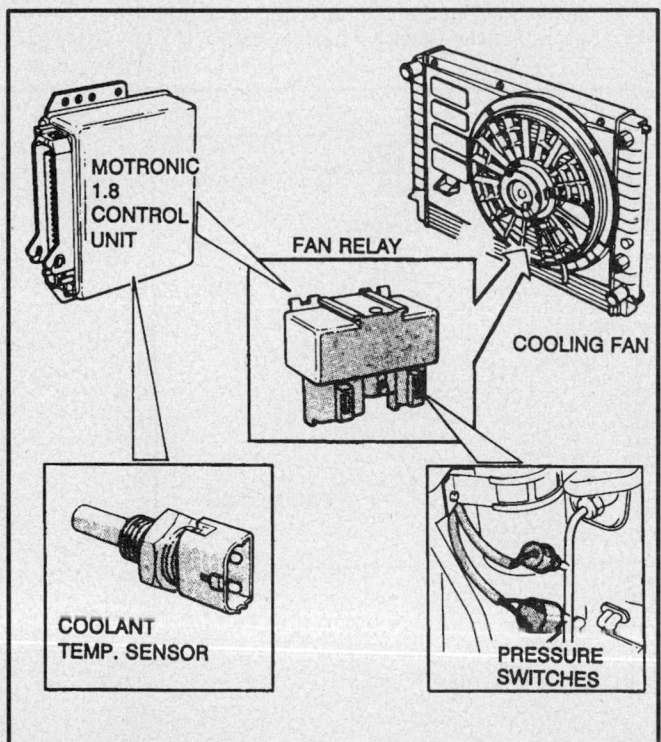

Electric cooling fan control via Motronic 1.8 control unit—960 Series

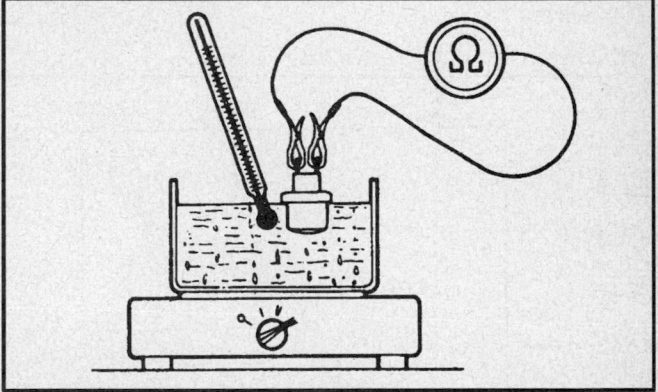

Testing radiator thermal switch

REMOVAL AND INSTALLATION

1. Disconnect the negative battery cable. Remove engine undercover, as necessary.
2. Disconnect the fan motor electrical connector.
3. Remove the fan motor assembly retaining bolts and remove the fan motor assembly from the vehicle.
4. Remove the fan, spacer if equipped and nut. Remove the fan motor, bushings and screws from the fan motor assembly.
To install:
5. Install fan to fan motor.
6. Install fan motor to fan motor assembly. Install fan motor assembly in the vehicle.

7. Reconnect the fan motor electrical connection.

8. Install engine undercover as necessary. Connect negative battery cable and check system for proper operation.

Condenser

REMOVAL AND INSTALLATION

240 Series

1. Disconnect the negative battery cable.

2. Discharge the air conditioning system, using proper recovery equipment.

3. Remove the radiator grille, headlight frames and the right headlight. Remove the center stay and the horn bracket.

4. Remove the electric cooling fan assembly, if equipped.

5. Remove all air conditioning lines from the condenser. Cap open fittings immediately.

6. Remove the condenser mounting retaining bolts. Remove the condenser assembly.

To install:

7. Drain and measure the amount of refrigerant oil from the condenser and install the same amount of new oil in the replacement condenser (except systems with York compressor; oil is added directly to the compressor).

8. Install the condenser (transfer any air seals and be sure they are fit to their correct position). Using new O-ring seals, lubricated with refrigerant oil, install the refrigerant lines to the condenser assembly.

9. Install the electric cooling fan assembly as applicable.

10. Install horn bracket, center stay, right headlight, and headlight frames. Install the radiator grille assembly.

11. Reconnect the battery cable. Evacuate, charge and test refrigerant system.

850 Series

1. Disconnect the negative battery cable.

2. Discharge the air conditioning system, using proper recovery equipment.

3. Disconnect the air intake hose and remove the hose connector from the fan cover.

4. Remove the diagnostic unit from the fan control unit box. Disconnect the control unit box air intake hoses. Remove the inlet hose connector from the fan cover (2 clips).

5. Disconnect the relays from the relay casing.

6. Disconnect the fan cover (4 screws) and fold the fan cover back toward the engine. Then, remove the relay shelf and spacers.

7. Remove the cover plate from on top of the condenser (3 Torx screws).

8. Remove the air intake unit from below the condenser (2 Torx screws).

9. Disconnect and cap the pipes from the condenser.

10. Detach the high pressure sensor from the condenser.

11. Remove the 4 upper condenser screws, then the lower left–hand screw and 2 brackets.

12. Carefully lift out the condenser.

To install:

13. Drain and measure the amount of oil from the old condenser. Replace the same amount of new oil into the new condenser.

14. Install the high pressure sensor to the new condenser, using a new gasket.

15. Position the condenser, noting the location of the bracket for the high pressure hose between the condenser and radiator. Attach the brackets.

16. Reattach the air conditioning pipes for the condenser, using new O-rings lubricated with clean compressor oil. Torque the connections of 15 ft. lbs. (20 Nm).

17. Recharge the air conditioning system and test the system for leaks.

18. Reinstall the air intake unit, upper cover pate, the fan cover, relay shelf, diagnostic unit and intake hoses.

19. Reconnect the negative battery cable.

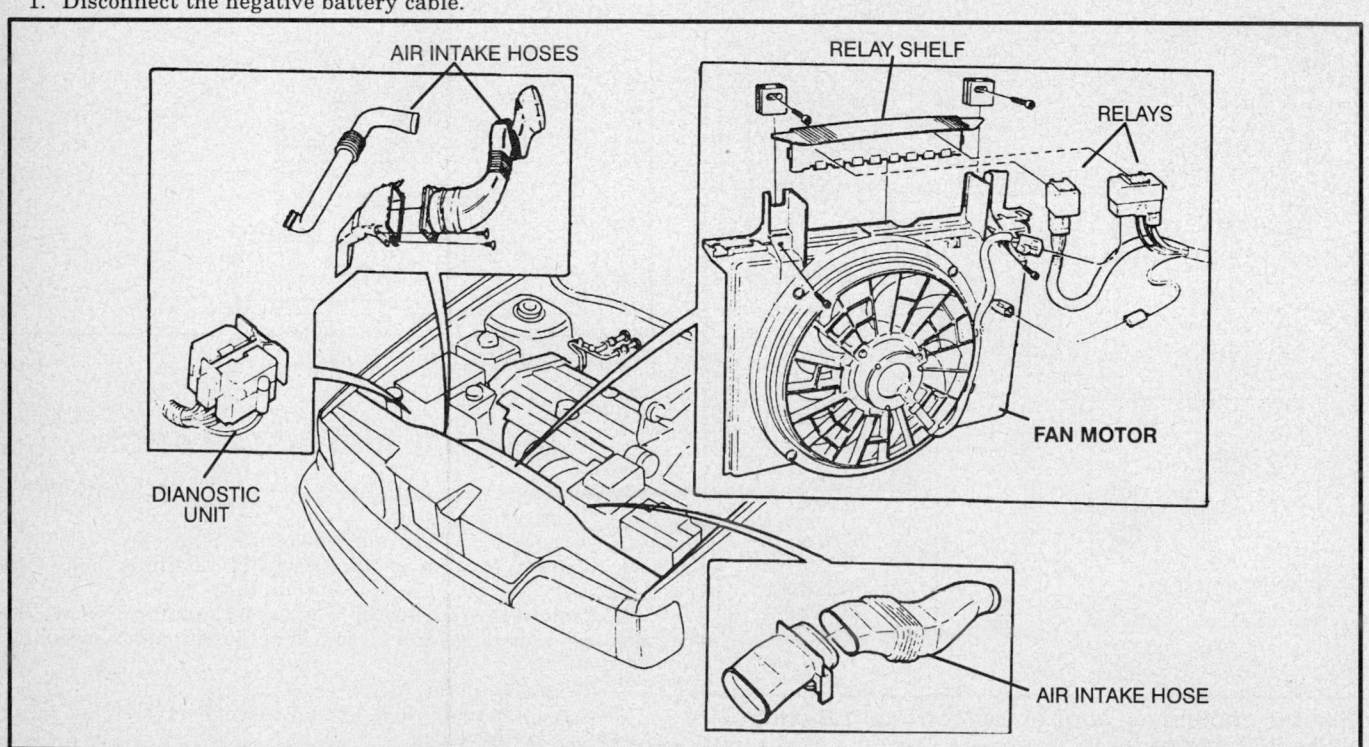

Removing the fan components—850 Series

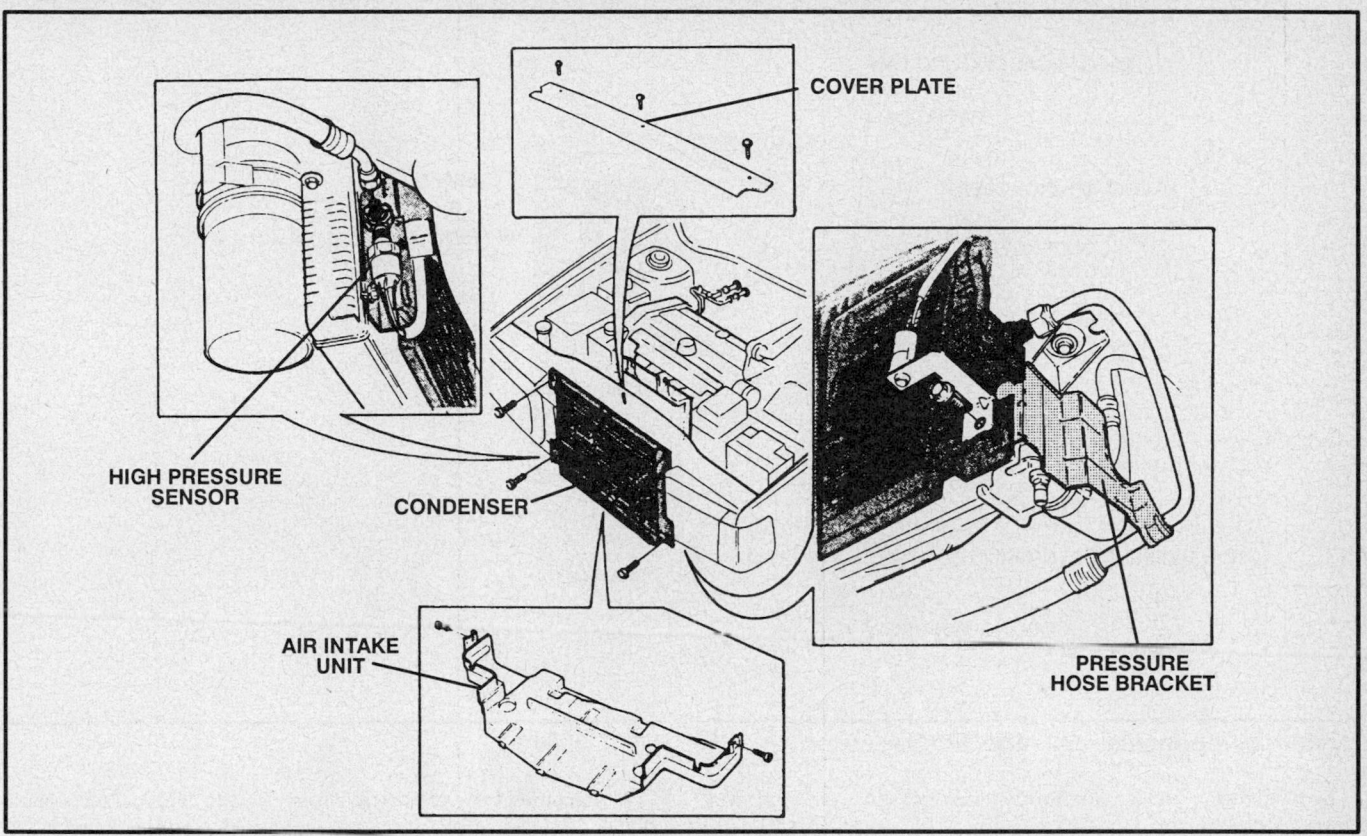

Removing the condenser and related components—850 Series

940 and 960 Series

1. Disconnect the negative battery cable.
2. Recover refrigerant (discharge system) from refrigeration system.
3. Remove the radiator grille, the support stay from in front of the condenser and the upper radiator mounting bolts.
4. Remove the hood release cable from the upper radiator mounting crossmember.
5. Remove the air seal from the upper radiator cross member.
6. Remove the upper condenser retaining screws and the upper radiator crossmember. From under the bumper, remove the air guide panel.
7. Recover refrigerant (discharge system) from refrigeration system.
8. Remove all refrigerant system connections from the condenser. Cap open fittings immediately.
9. Remove the lower condenser nuts and the condenser assembly from the vehicle.
To install:
10. Drain and measure the amount of refrigerant oil from the condenser and install the same amount of new oil in the replacement condenser.
11. Install the condenser (transfer air seals and be sure to install them in the correct position). Using new O-ring seals, lubricated with refrigerant oil, install the lines to the condenser.
12. Install the lower air guide panel under the bumper and the upper air guide panel to the upper radiator member.
13. Install the hood release cable to the upper radiator member.
14. Install the upper radiator member, the stay support in front of the condenser and the radiator grille.

15. Reconnect the negative battery cable.
16. Evacuate, charge and test refrigerant system. Check system for leaks.

Compressor

REMOVAL AND INSTALLATION

Except York Compressors and 850 Series

1. Disconnect the negative battery cable.
2. Recover refrigerant (discharge system) from refrigeration system.
3. Remove all refrigerant system connections from the compressor. Cap open fittings immediately.
4. Loosen the compressor and mounting brackets bolts. Disconnect the electrical connector from the compressor.
5. Remove the drive belt from the compressor, the mounting bolts and the compressor assembly.
To install:
6. Drain the refrigerant oil from the compressor and measure so the same amount of new oil can be installed in the compressor, if replacing the unit.
7. Mount the compressor on the mounting brackets and install the mounting bolts. Install compressor assembly.
8. Immediately upon opening the service connection ports, attach the hoses and tighten securely.
9. Install the drive belt. Adjust the drive belt so it is not possible to depress it by more than 0.2–0.4 in. for Sankyo and Kiki or 0.04–0.08 in. for Delco at the middle of the longest belt span between pulleys.
10. Connect the negative battery cable.

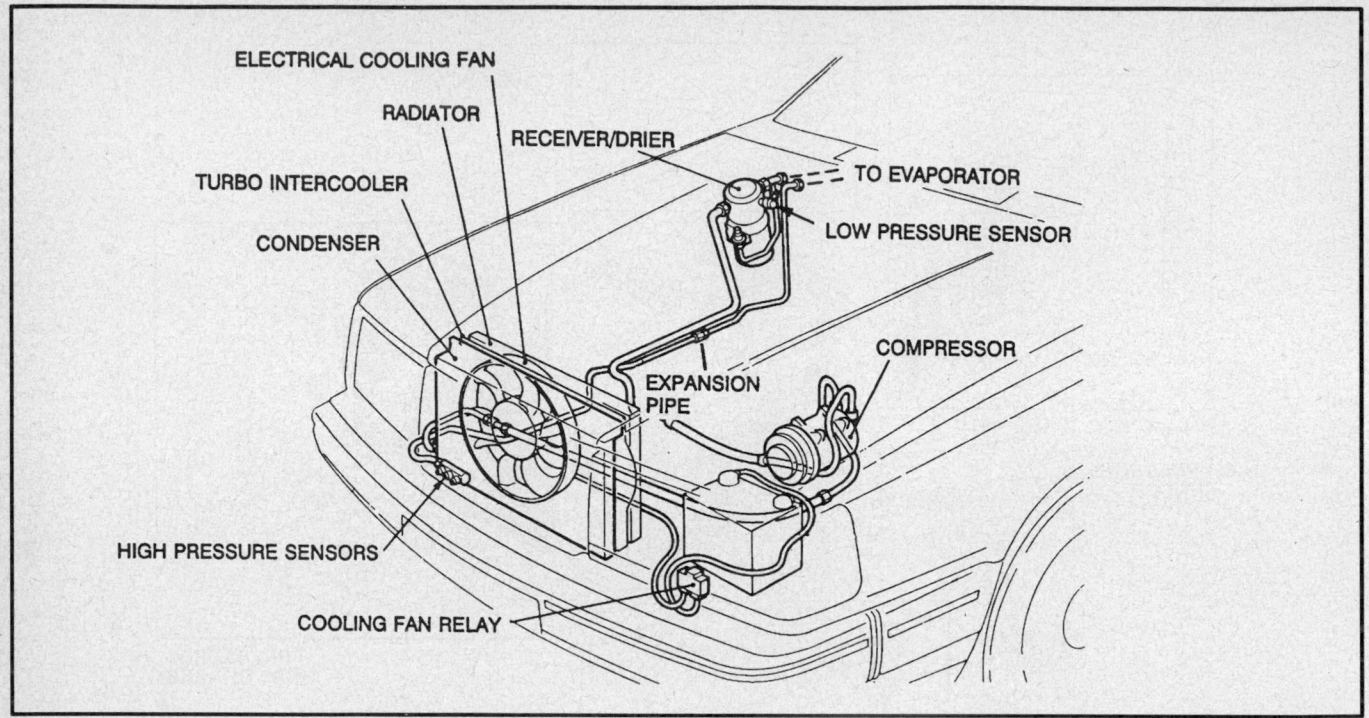

System components—940 and 960 Series

11. Evacuate, check for proper refrigerant oil level and charge the system.
12. Start the engine, allow it to reach normal operating temperatures and the check the system operation.

York Compressor System

1. Disconnect the negative battery cable.
2. Properly recover refrigerant (discharge system) from refrigeration system, using an approved recovery system.
3. Disconnect the suction and discharge service valves from the compressor head. Cap open fittings immediately.
4. At the crankshaft pulley, loosen the tensioner plate nuts and remove the drive belt.
5. Disconnect the electrical connection from compressor assembly.
6. Remove the compressor–to–bracket retaining bolts and the compressor assembly.
To install:
7. Drain the refrigerant oil from the compressor and measure so the same amount can be installed in the compressor, if replacing the unit.
8. Install compressor assembly. Install the compressor–to–bracket retaining bolts and torque to 28 ft. lbs.
9. Remove the tensioner plate and outer split pulley half from the crankshaft pulley.
10. Install the drive belt, the split pulley half and the tensioner plate. To adjust the drive belt tension, remove or add shims to the assembly until the deflection is 0.1–0.4 in. between the pulleys. Install any extra shims between the outer split pulley and tensioner plate.
11. Torque the tensioner plate–to–crankshaft nuts to 15 ft. lbs. (20 Nm).

12. Reconnect the electrical connection to compressor assembly.
13. Connect both the suction and the discharge service lines to the compressor assembly.
14. Connect the negative battery cable.
15. Evacuate, check for proper refrigerant oil level and recharge the air conditioning system.

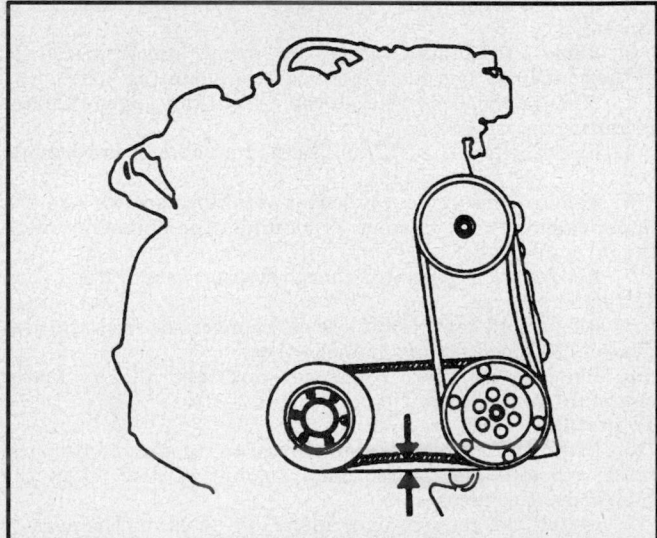

Drive belt tension measurement location—York compressor

16. Start the engine, allow it to reach normal operating temperatures and the check the system operation.

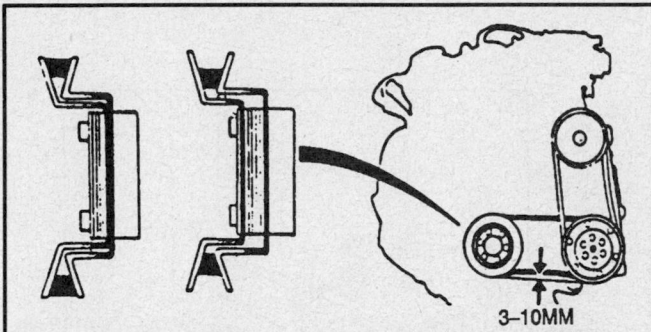

Adjusting the compressor drive belt—York compressor

850 Series (Zexel Compressor)

1. Disconnect the negative battery cable.
2. Recover refrigerant (discharge system) from refrigeration system.
3. Disconnect the air intake hose and remove the hose connector from the fan cover.
4. Remove the diagnostic unit from the fan control unit box. Disconnect the control unit box air intake hoses. Remove the inlet hose connector from the fan cover (2 clips).
5. Disconnect the relays from the relay casing.
6. Disconnect the 4 fan cover screws and then, remove the relay shelf and spacers.
7. Disconnect the 2–pin connector from the fan relay on 1–pin connector from the fan motor.
8. Remove the fan cover.
9. Protect the radiator with a suitable cover, then disconnect the air conditioning hose pipes from the compressor. Cap all openings immediately.
10. Disconnect the snap connectors from the receiver–drier. Cap open hose fittings immediately.
11. Remove the right side headlamp casing and then remove the receiver–drier bracket screw.
12. Remove the air guide from beneath the radiator (2 Torx screws).
13. Remove the receiver–drier and bracket.
14. Using a 3/8 socket, loosen the drive belt tensioner to remove the serpentine drive belt.
15. Detach the compressor clutch wire and the temperature sensor wire. Remove 2 screws from the compressor brackets.
16. Lift out the compressor.
To install:
17. Switch the brackets and pipe connection flange to the new compressor and torque the bracket screws to 30 ft. lbs. (40 Nm) and the compressor flange bolts to 18 ft. lbs. (24 Nm).
18. Use new O-rings, lubricated with new refrigerant oil, when making all pipe connections. Reverse the remaining removal procedure to complete installation.
19. Check and adjust the compressor oil level as required.

Receiver/Drier

REMOVAL AND INSTALLATION

240, 940 and 960 Series

1. Disconnect the negative battery cable.

2. Recover refrigerant (discharge system) from refrigeration system.
3. Disconnect, cap or plug the refrigerant lines to the receiver/drier assembly.
4. Disconnect the electrical connector from the receiver/drier pressure sensor.
5. Remove the receiver/drier from the bracket.

NOTE: Before replacement of a new receiver/drier, drain the refrigerant oil from the old unit, measure the amount of oil and add the same amount of new oil into the new receiver/drier assembly.

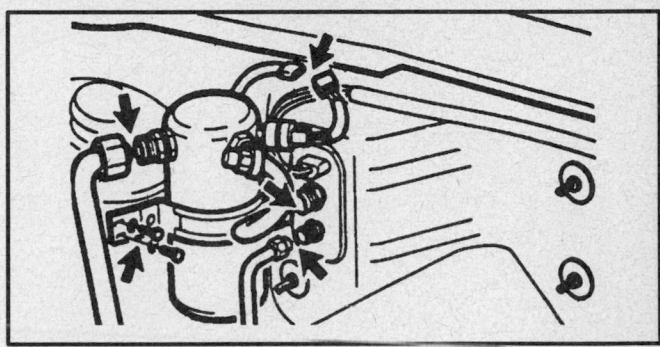

Remove the receiver/drier assembly—except 850 Series

To install:
6. Install the receiver/drier assembly into the bracket.
7. Connect the electrical connector to the receiver/drier pressure sensor.
8. Remove the line caps and install the refrigerant lines to the receiver/drier assembly.
9. Evacuate, check for proper refrigerant oil level and charge the air conditioning system.
10. Connect the negative battery cable.
11. Start the engine, allow it to reach normal operating temperatures and check the system operation.

850 Series

NOTE: This procedure also covers replacement of the suction pipe from the receiver/drier. If replacing only the suction pipe, follow this procedure, except do not change the receiver–drier unless the system has been opened for a substantial time or if there was a leak or failure in the system. Always use new O-rings at all connections.

1. Disconnect the negative battery cable.
2. Properly discharge the air conditioning refrigerant using a recovery type system.
3. Disconnect the air intake hose from behind the grille, remove the diagnostic units and intake air hoses from the front left side of the engine compartment.
4. Disconnect the relays and cables from the fan cover. Remove 4 fan cover screws and remove the relay casing and spacers.
5. Disconnect the 2–pin connector from the fan relay and the 1–pin connector from the fan motor. Remove the fan cover.
6. Properly cover the radiator to protect it during receiver/drier removal.
7. Disconnect the suction (low side) pipe connection from the compressor.
8. Disconnect the snap–on connections from the receiver/drier (special Volvo tool 5472, or equivalent, may be required).

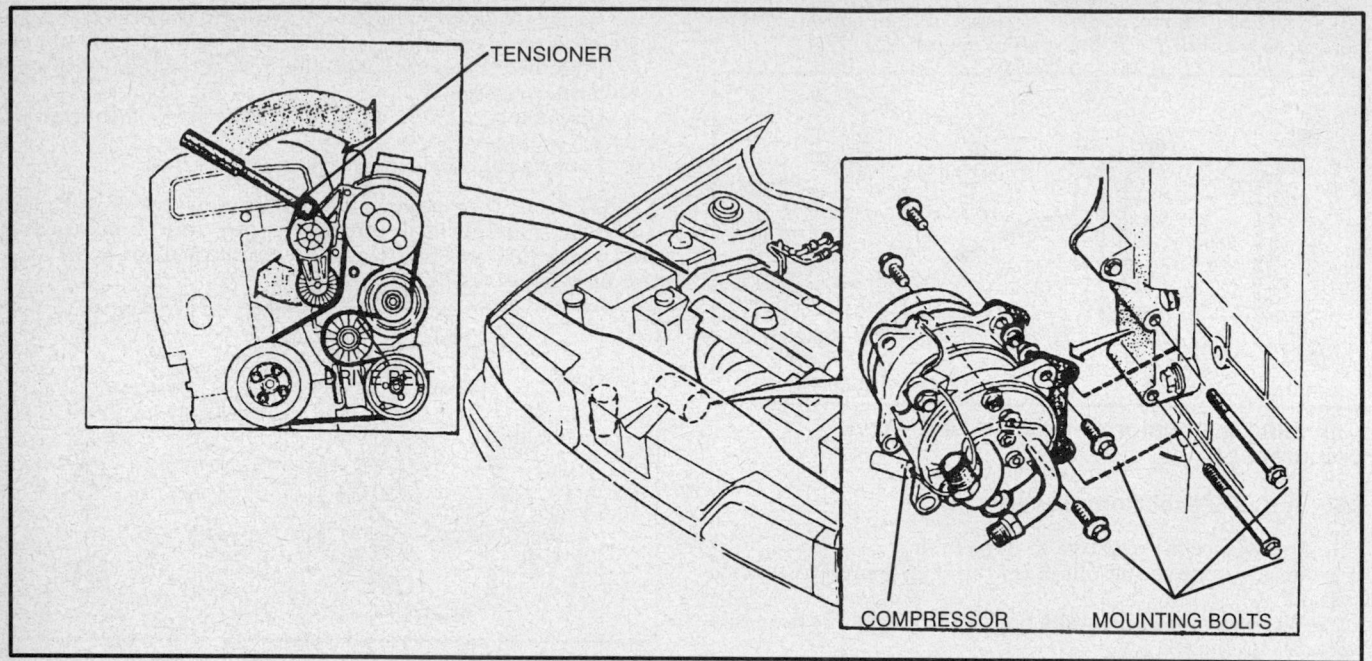

TENSIONER

DRIVE BELT

COMPRESSOR   MOUNTING BOLTS

Removing compressor and drive belt—850 Series

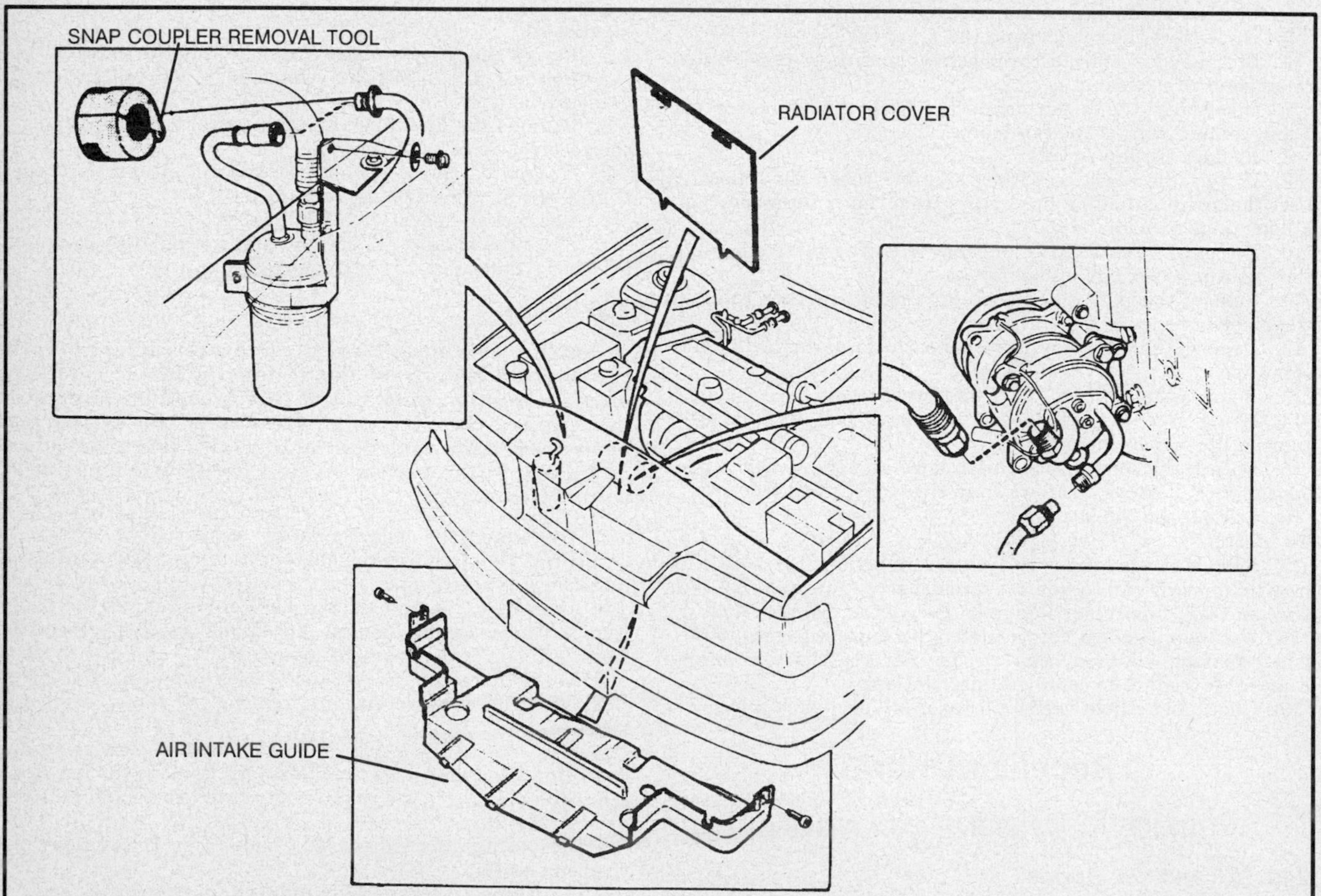

SNAP COUPLER REMOVAL TOOL

RADIATOR COVER

AIR INTAKE GUIDE

Removing the receiver/drier—850 Series

9. Remove the receiver–drier bracket screw, then remove the air intake guide from beneath the radiator. Leave the bracket suspended from the side member while removing the receiver/drier.

To install:

10. Install in the reverse of the removal procedure. Always use new O-rings at all connections. Be sure the receiver/drier is properly aligned so the hose connections fit without strain.

11. Recharge the air conditioning system and check for leaks.

Expansion Valve

REMOVAL AND INSTALLATION

NOTE: The 240 Series are equipped with an expansion valve. The 940, 960 and 850 Series are equipped with a fixed orifice tube.

240 Series

1. Disconnect the negative battery cable.

2. Properly recover refrigerant (discharge system) from the air conditioning system.

3. Remove the right side sound proofing panel from under the glove box. Remove the console side panel from the right side.

4. Remove the evaporator cover and the evaporator outlet insulation.

5. Remove the expansion valve from the evaporator tube.

6. Carefully remove the capillary tube with the expansion valve. Using new O-rings lubricated with refrigerant oil, carefully install the expansion valve and the capillary tube.

7. Installation is the reverse of the removal procedure. Evacuate, check for proper refrigerant oil level and charge the system. Check the system for proper operation.

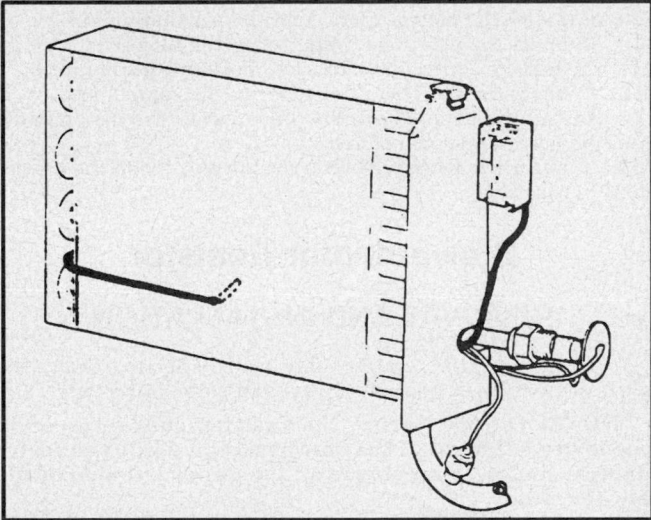

Expansion valve location—240 Series

Fixed Orifice Tube

REMOVAL AND INSTALLATION

NOTE: The orifice tube is located in the evaporator inlet and regulates the amount of refrigerant flowing into the evaporator assembly.

940 and 960 Series

1. Disconnect the negative battery cable. Properly recover the refrigerant (discharge system) from the air conditioning system.

2. Remove the inlet tube from the evaporator, separate the rubber and remove the fix orifice tube.

3. Lubricate the tube with refrigerant oil, position the short filtered end (outlet filter) towards the evaporator and install the tube assembly.

4. Reconnect the negative battery cable. Evacuate, check for proper refrigerant oil level and charge the system. Check the system for proper operation.

850 Series

NOTE: When removing or replacing refrigerant pipes or hoses, remove the pipe between the evaporator and the receiver/drier first.

1. Disconnect the negative battery cable, then properly discharge the air conditioning system using an approved recovery station.

2. Disconnect the coolant overflow chamber (connection is beneath the chamber), then move the chamber onto the engine temporarily.

3. Disconnect the pressure sensing switch on the pipe at the firewall.

4. Disconnect the right side headlight cover and remove the control unit box air intake hoses.

5. Remove the receiver/drier bracket screw for clearance, disconnect the snap coupling at both ends of the low side refrigerant pipe (tool 5472, or equivalent, may be required), then remove the refrigerant pipe from between the evaporator and receiver/drier. Cap all openings immediately.

6. Detach the liquid (low side) pipe connection at the condenser and disconnect the snap coupler at the middle of the line (tool 5385, or equivalent, may be required).

7. Mark the position of the pipe pieces before separating them. Separate the flange connection and use needle–nose pliers to carefully pull out the expansion valve.

To install:

8. Use new O-rings when making pipe connections. When replacing the pipe between the evaporator and receiver/drier, remove the drier bottle plug first.

9. Be sure to reposition the pressure sensing switch on the refrigerant line.

10. Replace all other components in reverse of the removal procedure.

NOTE: If the system was leaking before the repairs or has been opened for an extended period of time, the receiver/drier should also be replaced.

11. Recharge the air conditioning system and check for leaks.

Blower Motor

REMOVAL AND INSTALLATION

240 Series

1. Disconnect the negative battery cable.
2. Remove the sound insulation and side panels on both sides of the radio, if equipped.
3. Remove the control panel and center console.
4. Remove or disconnect as required, the center air vents, the cable and electrical connectors from the clock, the glove compartment and air ducts for the center air vents.
5. From the right side, remove the air ducts and disconnect the vacuum hoses from the shutter actuators.
6. Fold back the floor mat, remove the rear floor duct screw and move the duct aside.
7. Remove the outer blower motor casing and the blower motor wheel.

NOTE: It may be necessary to remove the support from under the glove compartment in order to remove the blower motor casing.

8. Disconnect the blower motor switch from the center console and the electrical leads from the switch.
9. From the left side, disconnect the air ducts and the vacuum hoses from the shutter actuators.
10. Remove or disconnect the inner blower motor casing, the vacuum hose from the rear floor shutter actuator, the electrical connector and the blower motor. Should the blower motor need to be replaced, a modified replacement unit is available. Certain modifications must be done and instructions are included with the new assembly.

To install:

11. Clean heater housing of all dirt, leaves etc. before installation. Install the blower motor, the electrical connector, the vacuum hose to the rear floor shutter actuator and the inner blower motor casing.
12. Install the blower motor wheel and the outer blower motor casing.
13. Install the rear floor air duct and the floor mat.
14. At the left side, connect the air ducts and the vacuum hoses to the shutter actuators.
15. Connect the electrical leads to the blower motor switch and the switch to the center console.
16. At the right side, install the air ducts and connect the vacuum hoses to the shutter actuators.
17. Install or connect as required the center air vents, the cable and electrical connectors to the clock, the glove compartment and air ducts for the center air vents.
18. Install the control panel and center console.
19. Install the sound insulation and side panels to both sides of the radio.
20. Reconnect the negative battery cable. Check system for proper operation.

850 Series

1. Disconnect the negative battery cable.
2. From the right side, remove the side kick panel, the lower glove box panel and the glove box.
3. Disconnect the electrical connector and the mounting bracket from the blower motor housing.
4. Disconnect the electrical connector and cable duct from the blower motor.
5. Remove the blower motor–to–housing screws and the motor.

To install:

6. Clean heater housing of all dirt, leaves etc. before installation. Install the rubber seal to the blower motor and install assembly.
7. Connect the cable duct and electrical connector to the blower motor and the positive terminal to the housing.
8. Connect the negative battery cable and check all blower motor speeds.
9. Install the glove box and the lower panel.

940 and 960 Series

1. Disconnect the negative battery cable.
2. Remove the lower glove box panel.
3. From the right side, remove the instep molding.
4. Remove the panel from above the control unit; be careful not damage it upon removal.
5. Disconnect the electrical connector from the control unit.
6. Remove the control unit–to–bracket bolts and the control unit. Remove the bracket–to–chassis bolts and the bracket.
7. Disconnect the electrical connector from the blower motor.
8. Remove the ventilation pipe, the blower motor–to–housing screws and the blower motor.

To install:

9. Clean heater housing of all dirt, leaves etc. before installation. Install the blower motor and the ventilation pipe.
10. Connect the electrical connector to the blower motor.
11. Install the control unit bracket and the control unit.
12. Connect the electrical connector to the control unit.
13. Install the panel above the control unit, the instep panel and the lower glove box panel.
14. Connect the negative battery cable and check the blower motor operation.

Blower Motor Resistor

REMOVAL AND INSTALLATION

1. Disconnect the negative cable. On 850 Series, remove the glove compartment door (4 screws) and panel (4 screws).

NOTE: On 850 Series, the resistor connector is on the lower left front of the blower motor, while the recirc damper motor connector is on the upper left side of the blower motor.

2. Disconnect the electrical connector from the blower resistor assembly.
3. Remove mounting screw and remove the blower resistor assembly from the case.

4. Installation is the reverse of the service removal procedure. Reconnect the negative battery cable. Check the blower motor for proper operation at all speeds after installation.

NOTE: Some vehicles may be prone to increased fan noise in fan speed No. 1. This is due to too high a fan speed. Noise level can be lowered by installing an additional resistor in series with the positive lead of the fan switch.

Heater Core

REMOVAL AND INSTALLATION

NOTE: On some vehicles equipped with Automatic Climate Control, a thermal switch is located on the outlet hose from the heater core. It switches on and starts the fan motor only when the water temperature exceeds approximately 95°F (35°C). This prevents cold air from being blown into the passenger compartment during winter. The thermal switch is bypassed in the defrost position.

240 Series

1. Disconnect the negative battery cable. Drain cooling system.
2. Move the heater controls to the **CLOSED** position.
3. Remove the sound proofing and side panels from both sides of the center dash console.
4. Remove the radio and the center control panel. Disconnect any necessary cables and move the panel aside.
5. Remove the glove box assembly and the strip below the right air vent by carefully prying it off with a small prybar.
6. Remove the steering wheel casing (column cover) and disconnect the choke control with the cover plate.
7. Remove the strip from under the left air vent, the instrument panel lighting intensity and the light switch knobs; do not remove the switch.
8. Remove the speedometer drive cable and any electrical connectors from the instrument panel cover plate and the cover plate.
9. Remove the storage compartment, the center air vents and the instrument panel frame.
10. From the left side, disconnect the windshield wiper connectors.
11. Disconnect the air duct between the heater and the center air vents.
12. Disconnect the electrical connector from the glove box courtesy light and the rubber straps from the defroster vents.
13. Remove the dashboard unit from the dash assembly, as necessary.
14. Remove or disconnect the rear floor air duct screws and lower the duct slightly.
15. Remove or disconnect the following:
   - The lower heater mount screws.
   - The vacuum hose from the vacuum tank.
   - The cable from the control valve.
   - The upper and lower center console screws.
   - The center support screws located on the console.
   - The fan motor ground electrical connector.
   - The inlet hose from the control valve.
16. Disconnect the upper hose from the heater core tube and the vacuum hoses from the shutter actuators.
17. Loosen the upper housing screws.
18. From the right side, disconnect the vacuum hoses from the shutter actuators.
19. Disconnect and remove the air ducts.

20. Disconnect the hoses from the vacuum tank. Remove the rear floor duct screws and lower the duct slightly.
21. Remove the upper and lower console screws and position it aside.
22. Remove the right support screws and the support.
23. Disconnect the electrical connector from the heater fan switch and the positive lead.
24. Disconnect the REC shutter vacuum hose from the control panel.
25. Disconnect the input vacuum hose from the T connection–to–floor shutter actuators.
26. Remove the upper heater housing retaining assembly screws and remove the assembly from the vehicle.
27. Place the assembly on a cleared area and remove or disconnect the following:
   - The upper hose from the heater core.
   - The air inlet rubber seal from the top of the housing.
   - The REC shutter clips, from the left side.
   - The rubber seals from both defroster vents.
   - All outer blower motor casing clips and the casing from the assembly.
28. Remove the blower motor wheel locking clips (from both sides) and the blower motor wheels.
29. Remove the heater core drain hose and the vacuum tank assembly. The vacuum tank bracket screws from the left side. The REC shutter spring and heater housing clips.
30. Remove the blower motor screws and the heater control valve capillary tube from the T joint.
31. Pull the heater housing apart from the middle.
32. Remove the blower motor and the heater core assembly.
To install:
33. Install the blower and heater core in the housing assembly. Make sure that the fan motor is correctly positioned in the housing. Install fan motor hose.
34. Using butyl sealant or equivalent coat mating surface of the heater housing and assemble the case.
35. Install the heater control valve capillary tube to the T joint and the blower motor screws.
36. Install the heater housing clips and REC shutter spring. At the left side, install vacuum tank assembly, the vacuum tank bracket screws and the heater core drain hose.
37. Install the blower motor wheel and the blower motor wheel locking clips to both sides.
38. Install or connect the following items:
   - The outer blower motor casing clips to the assembly.
   - The rubber seals to both defroster vents.
   - The REC shutter clips to the left side.
   - The air inlet rubber seal to the top of the housing.
   - The upper hose to the heater core.
39. Install the heater assembly into the vehicle.

NOTE: Before installation, be sure all sealing flanges are correctly sealed to prevent air leakage during the system operation.

40. Install the upper housing retaining screws.
41. Connect the REC shutter vacuum hose to the control panel.
42. Connect the electrical connector to the heater fan switch and the positive lead. Install protective cover.
43. Install the right support and console.
44. Install the heater assembly lower mount and the rear floor duct. Connect the hoses to the vacuum tank.
45. Install the air ducts. At the right side, connect the vacuum hoses to the shutter actuators.
46. Connect the upper hose to the heater core tube and the vacuum hoses to the shutter actuators.
47. Install or connect the following items:
   - The inlet hose to the control valve.

- The fan motor ground electrical connector.
- The console center support and the center console screws.
- The cable to the control valve.
- The vacuum hose to the vacuum tank.
- The lower heater mount screws.

48. Install the rear floor air and the dashboard unit to the dash assembly.

49. Connect the electrical connector to the glove box courtesy light and the rubber straps to the defroster vents.

50. Connect the windshield wiper connectors, the air duct between the heater housing and the center air vents.

51. Install the instrument panel, the storage compartment, the center air vents and the instrument panel frame.

52. Install the speedometer cable and any electrical connectors to the instrument panel.

53. Install the strip from under the left air vent, the instrument panel lighting intensity and the light switch knobs.

54. Install the steering wheel casing and connect the choke control with the cover plate.

55. Install the glove box assembly and the strip below the right air vent.

56. Install the center control panel and the radio.

57. Install the sound proofing and side panels to both sides of the center dash console.

58. Move the heater controls to the **OPEN** position.

59. Refill the cooling system. Connect the negative battery cable.

60. Start the engine, allow it to reach normal operating temperatures and check for leaks. Check system for proper operation.

850 Series

NOTE: The heater core can be replaced without removing the evaporator housing.

1. Pinch off the heater hoses at the firewall with suitable clamps. This will avoid the need to drain the cooling system.

2. Remove the left and right sound panels from beneath the instrument panel.

3. Bend back the carpet, then remove the panels from both sides of the center console under the instrument panel.

4. Remove the amplifier and bracket from the center console, if equipped.

5. Detach the drain hose from the floor board.

6. Remove the 4 screws holding the heater core housing to the air duct.

7. Place an absorbent cloth or paper beneath the heater hoses at the connection to the heater housing. Remove the flange screw at the heater hose connection. Detach the heater hoses.

8. Disconnect the heater housing by pulling toward the gearshift while twisting slightly upward. Remove it to one side when free of the rest of the climate control housing.

9. Remove 4 screws and take the heater core out of the heater core housing.

To install:

10. Install the heater core and housing in reverse of the removal procedure, except do not install the amplifier, bracket or center covers until the system has been checked. Use new O-rings at the heater hose connections.

11. Top off any coolant lost during the removal steps. Start the engine, operate the heater and check for leaks.

12. Install the amplifier, bracket and center cover plates.

940 and 960 Series with ACC or MCC

NOTE: The following procedure is also for vehicles equipped with Manual or Automatic Climate Control systems.

1. Disconnect the negative battery cable.

2. Drain the cooling system. Disconnect the heater hoses from the heater core assembly.

3. Remove the ashtray, the ashtray holder, the cigarette lighter and console's storage compartment.

4. Remove the console assembly from the gearshift lever and the parking brake.

5. Disconnect the electrical connector. Remove the rear ashtray, the console and light.

6. Remove the screws beneath the plastic cover in the bottom of the storage compartment and the parking brake console.

7. From the left side of the passenger compartment, remove the panel from under the dashboard.

8. Pull down the floor mat and remove the side panel screws, front and rear edge.

9. From the right side of the passenger compartment, remove the panel from under the glove compartment and the glove compartment box with lighting.

10. Pull down the floor mat on the right side and remove the side panel screws, front and rear edge.

11. Remove the radio compartment assembly screws.

12. Remove the screws from the heater control, the radio compartment assembly console and the control panel.

13. Loosen the heater control head assembly retaining screws and remove the assembly and mount from the dash.

14. Remove the center dash panel, the distribution duct screw and the air duct–to–panel vents/distribution duct screws.

15. Remove the screws holding the air ducts top–to–rear seats and the air distribution duct section–to–rear seat ducts.

16. Remove the vacuum hoses from the vacuum motors and the hose from the aspirator, if equipped with an ACC unit.

17. Remove the distribution unit housing from the vehicle.

18. Remove the retaining clips and the heater core assembly.

19. If the vacuum motors must be replaced, remove the panel from the distribution unit and replace the vacuum motor.

To install:

20. Clean heater core housing of all dirt, leaves etc. before installation. Install the heater core assembly and the retaining clips.

21. Install the distribution unit into the vehicle.

22. Connect the vacuum hoses to the vacuum motors and the hose to the aspirator, if equipped with an ACC unit.

23. Install the air ducts top–to–rear seats and the air distribution duct section–to–rear seat ducts.

24. Install the center dash panel, the distribution duct screw and the air duct–to–panel vents/distribution duct screws.

25. Install the heater control head assembly unit and the mount to the dash.

26. Install the heater control, the radio compartment console and the control panel.

27. Install the radio compartment screws.

28. At the right side of the passenger compartment, install the panel under the glove compartment and the glove compartment box with lighting.

29. Install the side panel screws, front and rear edge.

30. At the left side of the passenger compartment, install the panel under the dashboard.

31. Install the plastic cover in the bottom of the storage compartment and the parking brake console.

32. Connect the electrical connector. Install the rear ashtray, the console and light.

33. Install the console assembly to the gearshift lever and the parking brake.

34. Install the ashtray holder, the ashtray, the cigarette lighter and console's storage compartment.

35. Reconnect the heater core hoses. Refill the cooling system and charge the air conditioning system.

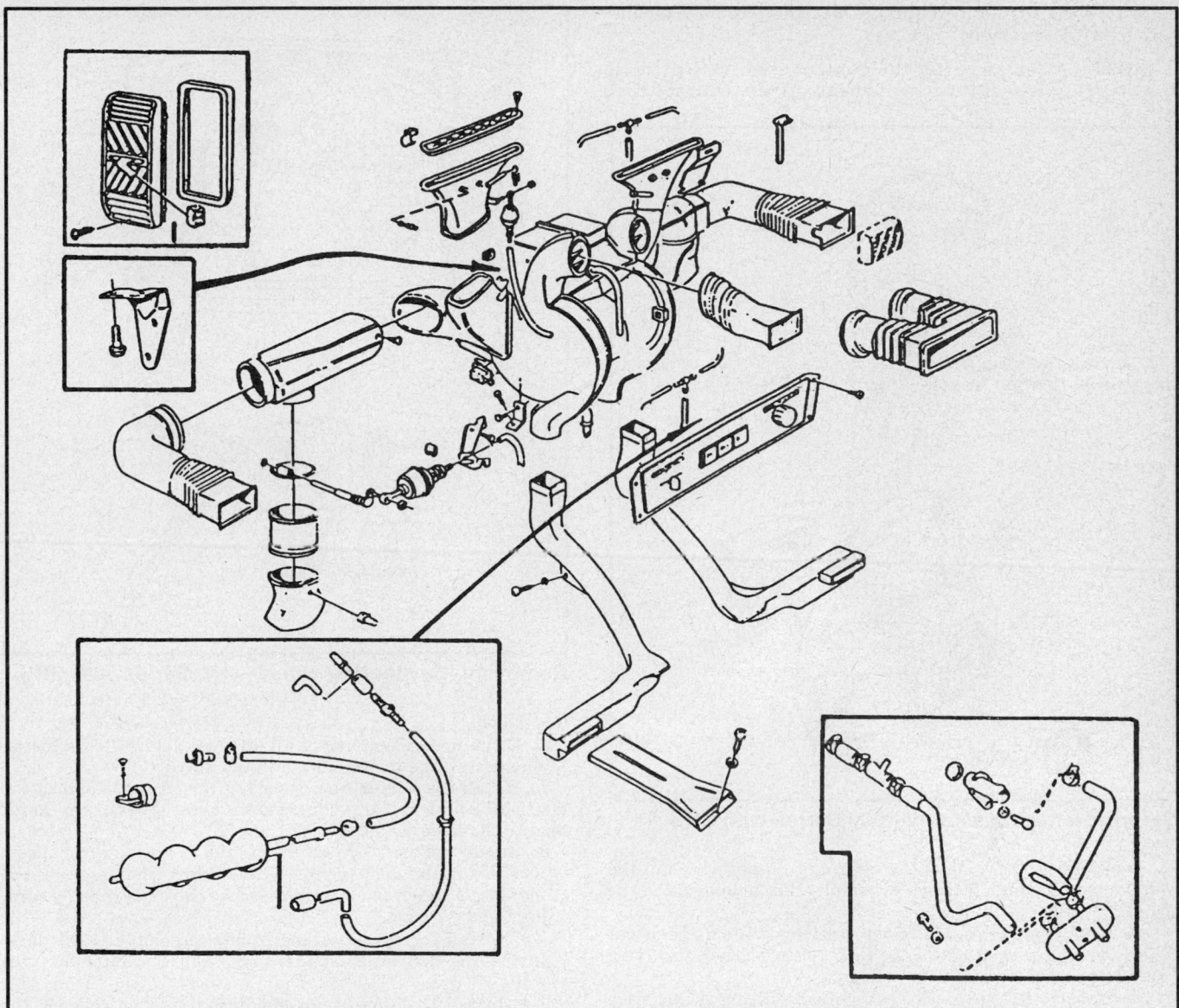

Heater unit with air conditioning—240 Series

36. Connect the negative battery cable. Start the engine, allow it to reach normal operating temperatures. Check system for proper operation.

940 and 960 Series with ECC

NOTE: The following procedure is also for vehicles equipped with the Electronic Climate Control (ECC) system.

1. Disconnect the negative battery cable.

2. Drain cooling system. Disconnect the heater hoses from the heater core assembly. Remove the heater core cover plate.

3. Remove the dashboard by performing the following procedures:

- From the right side, remove the lower glove box panel, the glove box, the footwell panel and the A post panel. Disconnect the solar sensor electrical connector and cut the cable ties.

- From the left side, remove the lower steering wheel sound–proofing, the knee bolster (leave bracket attached to bolster), the footwell panel and the A post panel.

- From the left side, remove the defroster grille, the plastic fuse box screws, the ashtray, the dashboard–to–center console screws, the parking brake–to–console screws (move console rearward) and the lower center console screws (located below the ashtray).

NOTE: Before performing the next procedure, be sure the front wheels are in the straight ahead position.

- If an SRS equipped vehicle, remove the steering column adjuster (Allen), the steering column covers, the air bag assembly (Torx), the steering wheel center bolt, the plastic tape label screw from the steering wheel hub (use the lock screw, label attached, to lock the contact reel through the steering wheel hub hole) and lift off the steering wheel.

Remove the contact reel and the steering column combination switch assembly.

NOTE: After securing the contact reel, do not turn the steering wheel for it will shear off the contact reel pin.

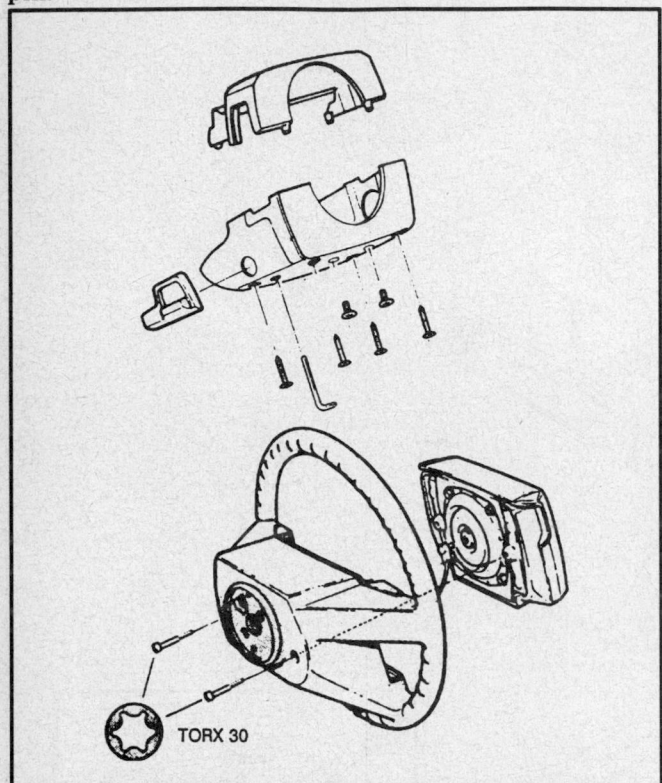

TORX 30

Steering wheel assembly—900 Series with SRS

● From the left side of the steering column, push out the light switch panel. Remove the small trim moldings and the light switch.

● From the right side of the steering column, push out the switch panel. Remove the ECC control panel, the radio console and the small trim molding.

● Remove the outer air vent grille by lifting it upwards, grasp it at the bottom and pull it upwards to release it. Remove the instrument panel cover–to–dash screws and the cover.

● Remove the combined instrument assembly–to–dash screws and the assembly; disconnect any electrical connectors and/or vacuum hoses.

● From the rear of the dashboard, cut the cable ties.

● At the dashboard–to–firewall area, turn the retaining clip 1/3 turn (to release), pull the dash out slightly and pass the fuse box through the opening. Disconnect the cable harnesses from the dashboard and carefully lift it from the vehicle.

4. From the left side of the heater housing, remove the lower duct. Disconnect the vacuum hoses from the diaphragms and the electrical connector. Remove the heater core cover–to–housing screws and the cover.

5. Remove the heater core–to–housing bracket and carefully remove the heater core.

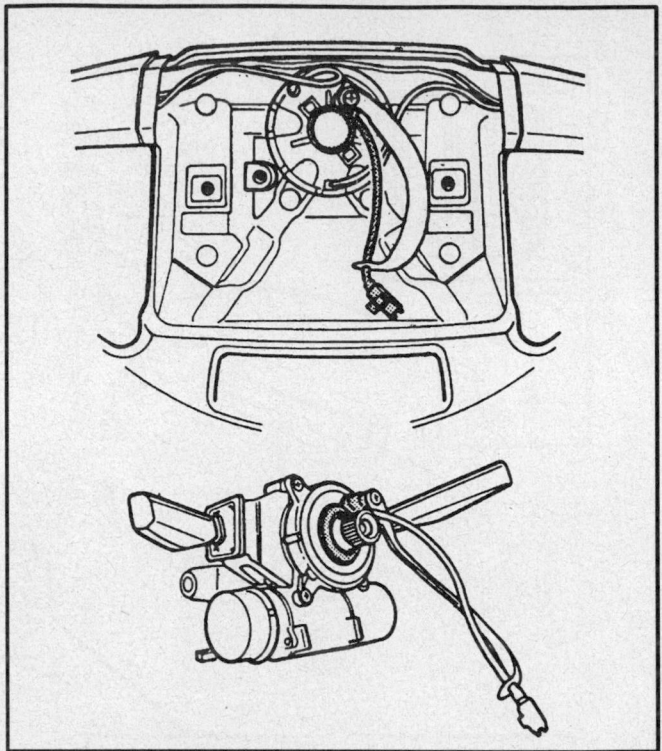

Removing the steering wheel—900 Series with SRS

To install:

6. Clean heater housing of all dirt and debris before installation. Install the heater core and the bracket.

7. Install the heater core cover to the housing. Connect the electrical connector and the vacuum hoses. Install the lower duct to the housing assembly.

8. Install the dash by performing the following procedures:

● Install the dash, connect the cable harnesses, pass the fuse box through the opening. Secure the dash clips by turning them 1/3 turn.

● Install the combined instrument assembly to the dash. Install the instrument panel cover and the outer air vent grille.

● Install the small trim molding, the radio console, the ECC control panel and the right side switch panel.

● At the left side of the steering column, install the light switch, the small trim moldings and the light switch panel.

● If an SRS equipped vehicle, install the steering column combination switch assembly and the contact reel. Install the steering wheel and remove the lock screw. Install the steering wheel center bolt, the air bag assembly and the steering column adjuster.

● If not an SRS equipped vehicle, install the steering column combination switch assembly, the steering column covers, the steering wheel adjustment assembly and the steering wheel.

● At the left side, install the lower center console screw, the parking brake–to–console screws, the dashboard–to–center console screws, the ashtray, the plastic fuse box screws and the defroster grille.

- At the left side, install the A post panel, the footwell panel, the knee bolster (with bracket) and the lower steering wheel sound–proofing.
- At the right side, connect the solar sensor electrical connector, install the A post panel, the footwell panel, the glove box and the lower glove box panel.

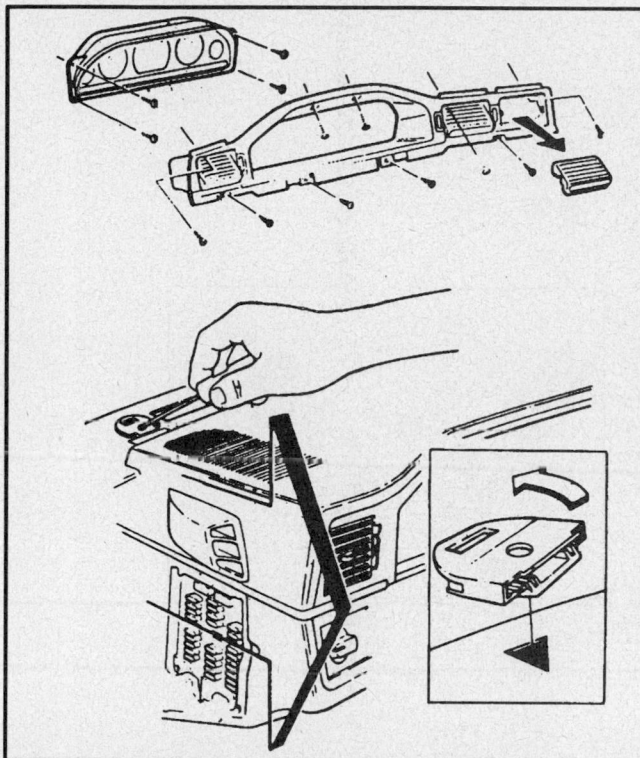

Remove the dashboard assembly—900 Series

9. Install the heater core cover plate and connect the heater hoses to the heater core.
10. Refill the cooling system. Connect the negative battery cable.
11. Start the engine, allow it to reach normal operating temperatures. Check the heater operation and the system for leaks.

Evaporator

REMOVAL AND INSTALLATION

240 Series

1. Disconnect the negative battery cable. Properly recover refrigerant (discharge system) from the air conditioning system.
2. Remove the glove box, panel below the glove box and side panel next to heater assembly. Remove the right side defroster vent and duct.
3. Remove the expansion valve. Remove the insulation and evaporator cover assembly.
4. Remove all refrigerant system connections. Cap open fittings immediately. Remove the evaporator assembly.
To install:
5. Installation is the reverse of the service removal procedure. Install new evaporator seal (insulation) and O-rings at refrigerant system connections. Evacuate, recharge and test refrigerant system. Check system for leaks.

850 Series

NOTE: This procedure requires removal of the dashboard assembly and removes the entire climate control system assembly which is necessary to remove the evaporator.

1. Disconnect the negative battery cable. Properly discharge and recover the refrigerant from the air conditioning system.
2. From the engine compartment side, detach the windshield wiper nuts, wiper well cover panel screws, wiper well, wiper motor lower and left mountings, and outer dashboard mounting screws.
3. Remove the steering wheel hub plate and steering wheel nuts. Mark the wheel position on the shaft for proper realignment. Remove the steering wheel, carefully noting the air bag components so they are not damaged or deployed.
4. Remove the steering column cover (4 screws). Remove the combination switch connector.
5. Remove the left and right soundproofing (3 screws) and remove the defroster side cover (1 screw).
6. Remove the left and right speaker covers and both speakers (2 Torx screws each). Detach the speaker connectors.
7. Remove the 3 dashboard mounting screws from each end of the dashboard.
8. If equipped with ECC, remove the radio assembly. Push up the locking button on the underside of the ECC control module and push the module loose from behind. Remove the control module and detach the connector.
9. If equipped with MCC, remove the knobs from the climate control panel, remove 2 screws from the control panel front and remove the panel bezel. Remove the fan switch and A/C connector. Remove the 4 screws and take out the control panel. Remove the radio.
10. On all systems, remove 4 screws from the cigarette lighter compartment, detach the connector and take out the compartment.
11. Carefully lift out the dashboard.
12. Disconnect the snap connectors from the refrigerant pipes at the evaporator (special tools 5385 and 5472 or equivalent are needed). Immediately cap all openings.
13. Remove the refrigerant lines cover plate and rubber gasket from the firewall.
14. Attach suitable clamps to the heater hoses near the firewall to avoid loss of coolant. Detach quick–release couplings for hoses by pressing the catches together and pulling the hoses out. Plug the hose openings.
15. Remove the cover plate and rubber gasket from the firewall.
16. Detach the following connectors: fan motor, recirc damper motor and fan resistor. Remove the cable duct from the fan motor and remove the connectors from the bracket.
17. Remove the double relay assembly from near the fan motor.
18. Open the climate control box and remove the connector for the lighting control. Replace the control box cover.
19. From the center console, remove the ashtray (2 screws) and cigarette light bracket (2 screws). Remove the 4 screws holding the console to the floor.
20. Put the gear lever in neutral, apply the hand brake, and remove the hand brake opening cover plate. Lift the console up and forward to remove it.
21. Remove the cover panels from each side of the climate control assembly. Remove the screw holding the floor duct to the center support.
22. Remove the climate control amplifier and bracket. Remove the drain hose from the floor.

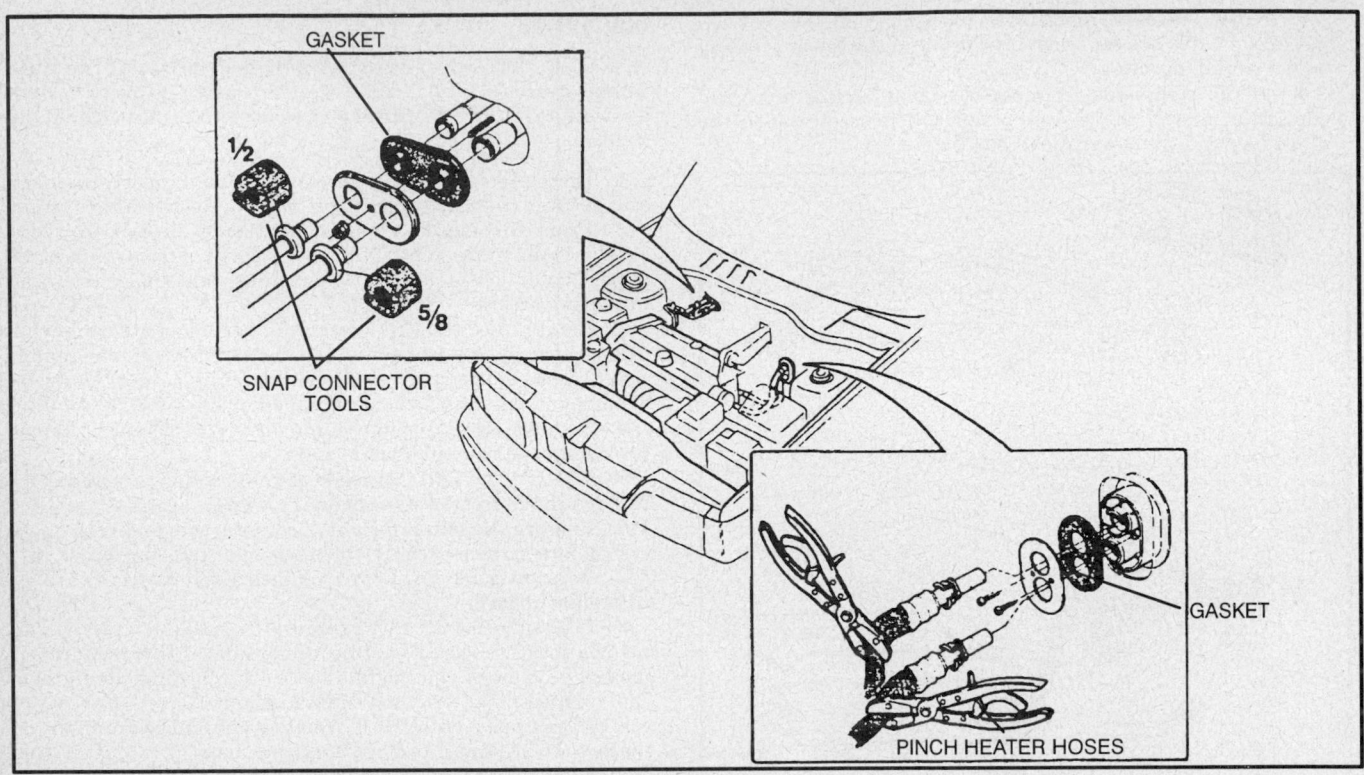

Removing the refrigerant lines and heater hoses—850 Series

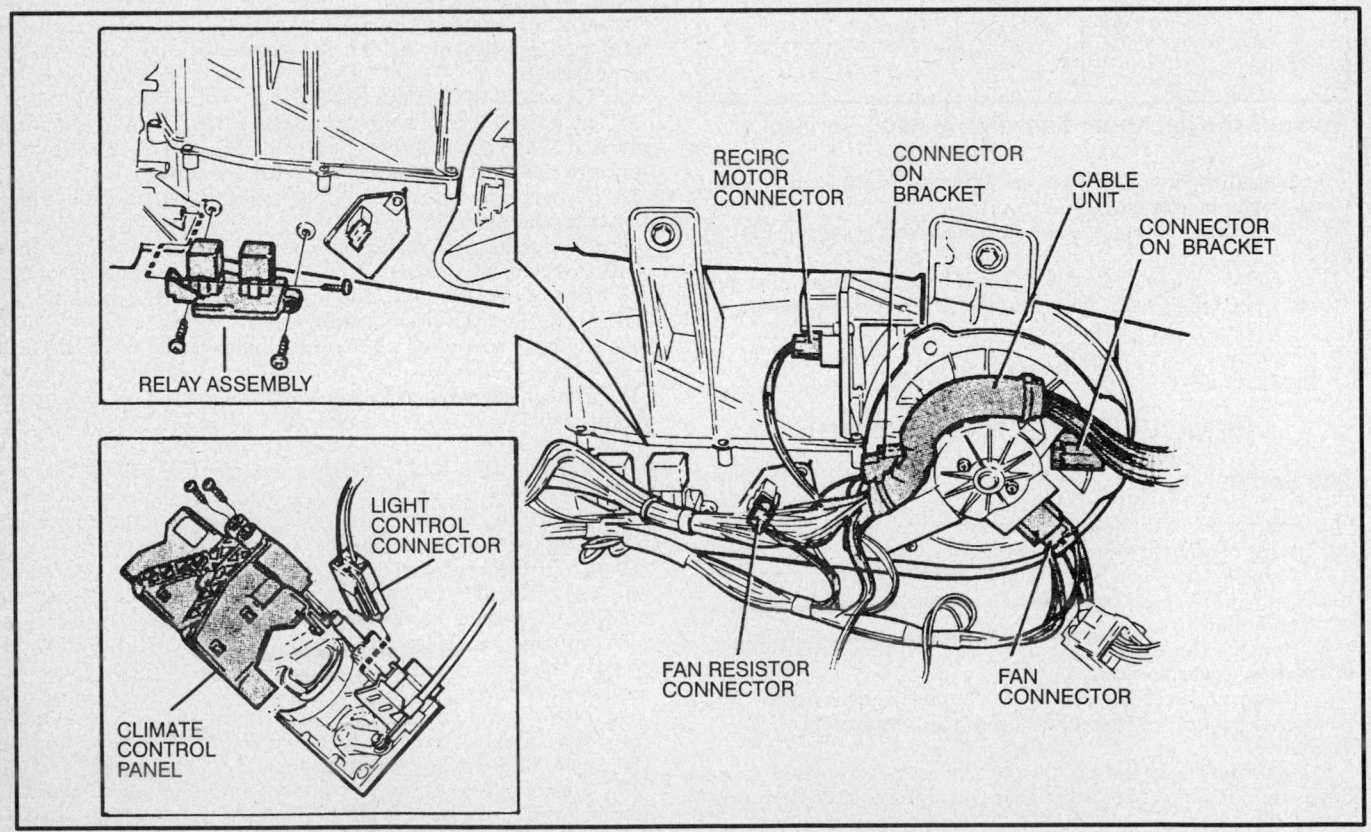

Detaching connections during climate control assembly removal—850 Series

23. On MCC systems, disconnect the cable from the right–hand temperature door.

24. If equipped with cruise control, detach the screw from the cruise control vacuum cylinder and the climate control unit.

25. Remove the 4 screws holding the climate control unit in place and carefully lift out the unit.

26. Remove the screws and clips holding the evaporator housing in place, remove the cover and take out the evaporator.

To install:

27. Replace the evaporator and cover gasket.

28. Install the climate control unit.

29. Reinstall the cruise control vacuum cylinder, cable at the right air door (MCC), drain hose, climate control amplifier and bracket, and floor duct.

30. Install the center side covers. Reinstall the center console in reverse of the removal procedure.

31. Install and reconnect the relay assembly, control lighting connector and other connectors around the fan motor as removed.

32. Reinstall the dashboard by reversing the removal steps.

33. Reattach the heater hoses and refrigerant lines at the firewall.

34. Refill the cooling system as needed. Recharge the air conditioning system. Start the engine and operate the heating and cooling system, checking for leaks and proper operation.

940 and 960 Series

MANUAL LEVER AND AUTOMATIC CLIMATE CONTROL TYPE SYSTEMS

1. Disconnect the negative battery cable.

2. Recover refrigerant (discharge system) from refrigeration system.

3. Remove the glove box and panel below the glove box assembly.

4. Remove all refrigerant system connections. Cap open fittings immediately.

5. Remove the right side instep molding and panel covering the control unit.

6. Remove the control unit and mounting bracket.

7. Remove all electrical connections and 2 lower screws of fan housing. Remove the evaporator housing cover from the assembly. Remove the evaporator assembly.

To install:

8. Transfer rubber seal and filter to evaporator. Apply sealer to lower casing and position the evaporator in the assembly. Install evaporator housing cover.

9. Reconnect all electrical connections. Position wiring harness to housing cover.

10. Install control unit and bracket. Install panel and right side instep molding.

11. Install the glove box and panel below the glove box assembly.

12. Reconnect the negative battery cable. Evacuate, charge and test refrigerant system. Check system for leaks.

Removing the evaporator—850 Series

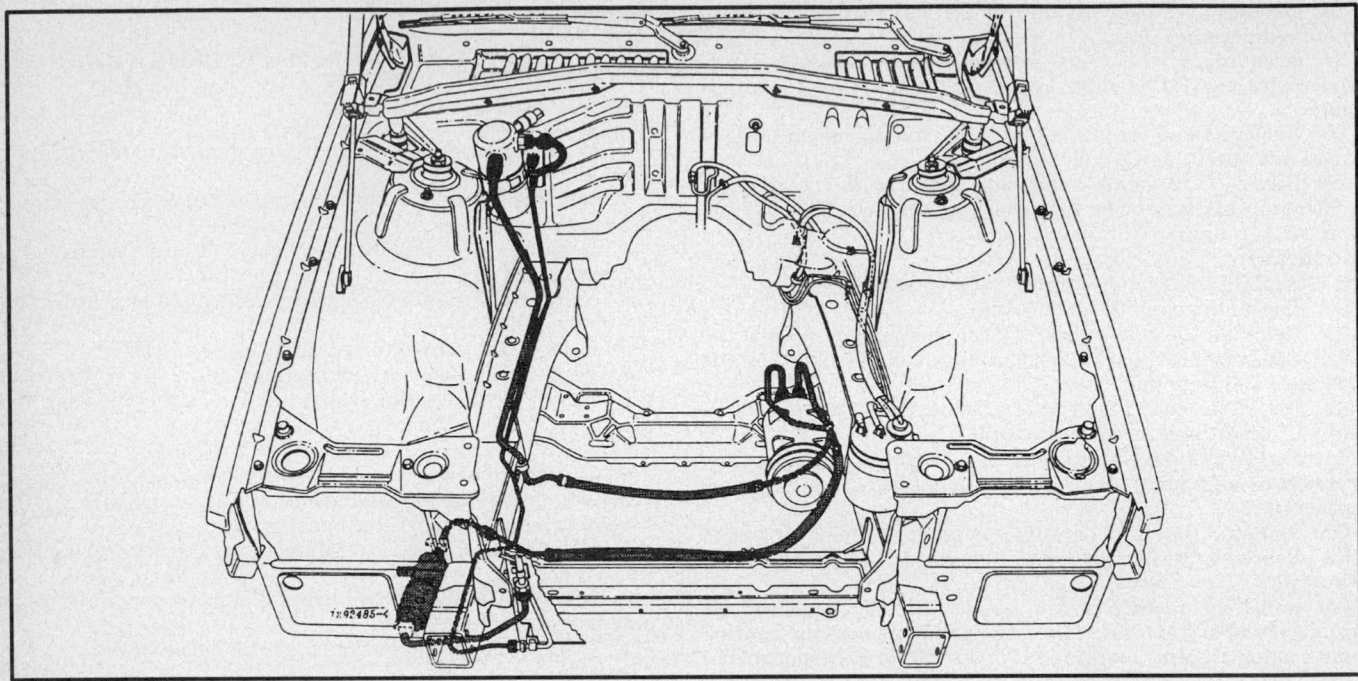

Refrigerant line routing—940 Turbo

ELECTRONIC CLIMATE CONTROL TYPE SYSTEM

1. Disconnect the negative battery cable. Recover refrigerant (discharge system) from refrigeration system.
2. Disconnect the electrical connector and unscrew the receiver/drier from the wheel house.
3. Disconnect the electrical connectors from the firewall. Remove the cover plate and the foam rubber seal.
4. From the right side, remove the lower glove box panel and the glove box.
5. Disconnect the vacuum lines from the tank and remove the evaporator cover. Remove the evaporator assembly from the housing.

To install:

6. Installation is the reverse of the service removal procedure. Install new evaporator seal (insulation) and O-rings at refrigerant system connections. Evacuate, charge and test refrigerant system. Check system for leaks.

Refrigerant Lines

REMOVAL AND INSTALLATION

240, 940 and 960 Series

1. Disconnect the negative battery cable. Recover refrigerant (discharge system) from refrigeration system.
2. Remove and replace defective line. Install new O-rings, as required.
3. Reconnect the negative battery cable. Evacuate, charge and test refrigerant system. Check system for leaks.

850 Series

1. Disconnect the negative battery cable. Properly discharge and recover the refrigerant.

2. Disconnect the air intake hoses from both sides of the radiator to gain access.
3. Remove the diagnostic connector boxes. Remove the fan cover (4 screws) and the relay casing and spacers. Detach the 2–pin connector from the fan relay and the 1–pin connector from the fan motor. Remove the fan cover.
4. Cover the radiator, disconnect the refrigerant line from the compressor. Cap the openings immediately.
5. Remove the line from the condenser and/or receiver/drier connection. Cap the openings immediately.
6. Remove the coolant reservoir from its mounting and lay it aside on the engine.
7. Disconnect the pipe from the condenser. Detach the snap couplings from the connection at the middle of the engine compartment (this is the location of the expansion tube).

To install:

8. Reinstall the pipes and hoses in reverse of the removal procedure, using new O-rings lubricated with clean refrigerant oil. Recharge the system and check for leaks.

Manual Control Head

REMOVAL AND INSTALLATION

240 Series

1. Disconnect the negative battery cable.
2. Remove the sound proofing and side panels from both sides of the center dash console.
3. Remove the radio assembly. Remove the center control panel. Position the control assembly as far forward as possible.
4. Remove the lever knob, cable from lever and control assembly.
5. Install is the reverse of the service removal procedure. Adjust cable as necessary.

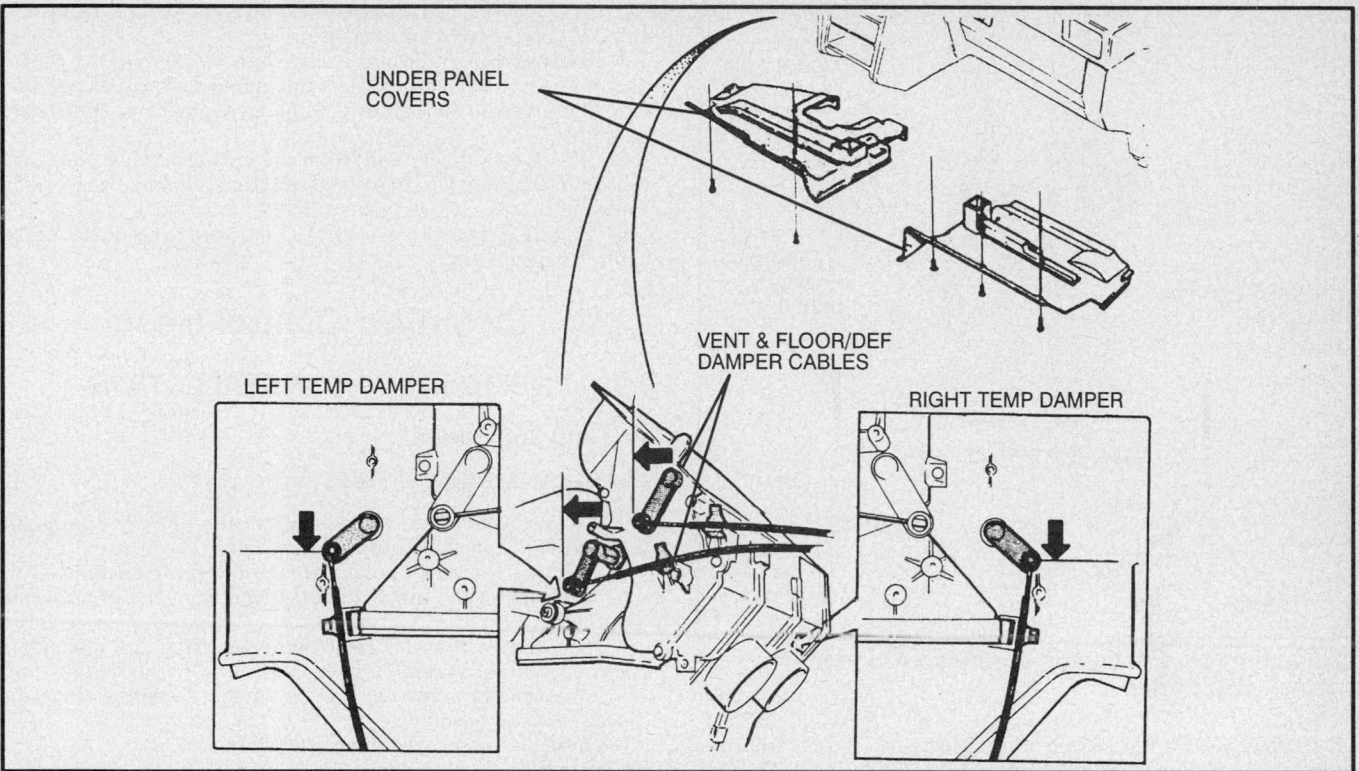

UNDER PANEL COVERS

VENT & FLOOR/DEF DAMPER CABLES

LEFT TEMP DAMPER

RIGHT TEMP DAMPER

Adjusting the temperature cables, vent cable and floor/defrost cable—850 Series

850 Series

1. Be sure both covers are removed from beneath the instrument panel. Disconnect the cables from the back of the climate control unit.

2. Remove the knobs and fan switch button from the control panel. Remove the panel cover.

3. Remove the fan switch and recirc–A/C switch from the control panel. Remove 4 screws and take out the control panel.

4. Remove the back cover from the control panel and detach the light connector.

5. Press the cable clip with pliers and disconnect the cables. Take out the control panel.

To install:

6. Install the light connector and the back cover of the control panel. Position the panel in place.

7. Move the Vent control cable arm and attach the cable so the sleeve end is 17mm from the clip. Set the Floor/Def cable arms and attach the cable ends so the end of the sleeve is flush with the clip.

8. Be sure the cable sleeves are pressed tightly into the clips. Reinstall the rest of the cover plate and knobs for the control panel.

940 and 960 Series

1. Disconnect the negative battery cable.

2. Remove the trim panel. Remove the control assembly from the dashboard.

3. Disconnect control cable clip, vacuum connections and electrical connections, as equipped.

4. Install is the reverse of the service removal procedure. Adjust cable, as necessary.

Manual Control Cables

ADJUSTMENT

240, 940 and 960 Series

Make sure the air mix shutter assembly touches both end stops when the control cable is moved between **COOL** and **WARM** positions on the manual control head assembly.

850 Series

NOTE: Before adjusting the control wires, try adjusting the lower attachment of the cable at the climate control unit.

1. Remove the left and right covers from beneath the instrument panel (remove only one side cover if only that side is being adjusted).

2. To adjust either side temperature damper cable, disconnect the cable sleeve from its clip, turn the left temperature damper to 0. Then, push the lever as far down as it will go, and push the cable sleeve into the clip.

3. To adjust the Vent and Floor/Def damper cables, set the control to **DEFROST** (12 o'clock) and push the Vent and Floor/Def levers to the end position. Push the cable sleeves into their clips.

4. Be sure both covers are removed from beneath the instrument panel. Disconnect the cables from the back of the climate control unit.

5. Remove the knobs and fan switch button from the control panel. Remove the panel cover.

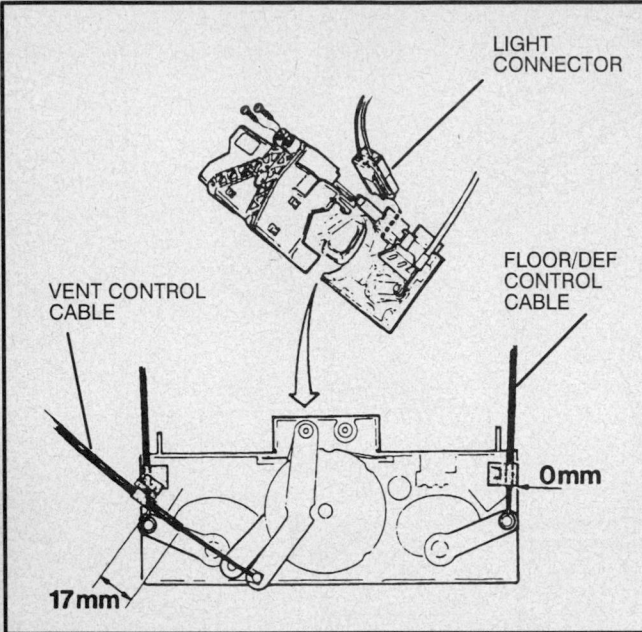

LIGHT CONNECTOR

FLOOR/DEF CONTROL CABLE

VENT CONTROL CABLE

0mm

17mm

Adjusting control cables on the control panel arms—850 Series

6. Remove the fan switch and recirc–A/C switch from the control panel. Remove 4 screws and take out the control panel.

7. Remove the back cover from the control panel and detach the light connector.

8. Press the cable clip with pliers and disconnect the cables. Move the vent control cable arm and attach the cable so the sleeve end is 17mm from the clip. Set the Floor/Def cable arms and attach the cable ends so the end of the sleeve is flush with the clip.

9. Be sure the cable sleeves are pressed tightly into the clips.

10. Reinstall the light connector and the back cover of the panel. Install the control panel in reverse of the removal procedure. Check control operations.

REMOVAL AND INSTALLATION

240 Series

1. Disconnect the negative battery cable.

2. Remove the sound proofing and side panels from both sides of the center dash console.

3. Remove the radio assembly. Remove the center control panel. Position the control assembly as far forward as possible.

4. Remove the (upper end) cable from lever on the control assembly.

5. Disconnect (lower end) from the unit assembly. Note location and position for correct installation. Remove the control cable.

6. Install is the reverse of the removal procedure. Adjust cable, as necessary.

Electronic Control Head

REMOVAL AND INSTALLATION

940 and 960 Series

PROGRAMMER ASSEMBLY

1. Disconnect the negative battery cable. Remove the panel beneath the glove box and the glove box.

2. Remove the outer panel vents and the air ducts.

3. Disconnect the air mix shutter rod from the programmer assembly.

4. Disconnect the electrical connector from the left side of the programmer assembly.

5. Remove the clips for the vacuum hose connections and disconnect the hoses.

6. Remove the programmer assembly.

To install:

7. Install the programmer assembly.

8. Connect the electrical connector to the left side of the programmer and connect the junction.

9. Install the control rod (air mix rod) and adjust as follows:
  • Start the engine to obtain vacuum, if necessary.
  • Set the temperature dial to **MAX HEAT** on the thumbwheel. Pull control rod until it reaches end position. Secure rod to programmer assembly.

10. Install the air ducts and panel vents.

11. Install the glove box unit and the lower panels.

12. Reconnect the negative battery cable. Check system for proper operation.

SENSORS AND SWITCHES

Control Panel Temperature Sensor (ACC)

OPERATION

The purpose of the control panel temperature sensor is to energize the fan motor at temperatures above 64°F (18°C). At temperatures below 64°F (18°C) and if engine temperature is below 93°F (34°C), the fan motor will not start. This to prevent cold air from being blown into the passenger compartment.

TESTING

To test the control panel temperature sensor use a volt–amp meter, check that current only flows through the sensor at temperatures above 65°F (18°C) and the sensor cuts the current off at temperatures below 65°F (18°C).

REMOVAL AND INSTALLATION

1. Disconnect the negative battery cable. Remove the control head panel and pull the control head away from the dash.

2. Disconnect the temperature sensor plug electrical connections.

3. Remove the temperature sensor from control head assembly.

4. Installation is the reverse of the service removal procedure.

Thermal Switch (ACC)

OPERATION

The purpose of the thermal switch, located in the "T" connection of the heater hose, is to switch on the heater fan at coolant temperatures above 93°F (34°C). This is done to prevent cold air from being blown into the passenger compartment before the heater assembly has had time to warm up. It is important that the switch is connected at all times. Otherwise, the heater fan will not operate until the temperature of the passenger compartment reaches 64°F (18°C).

TESTING

To test the thermal switch use a volt–amp meter, check that current only flows through the switch at temperatures between 86–104°F (30–40°C) and the switch cuts the current off at a temperature of 50°F (10°C).

REMOVAL AND INSTALLATION

1. Disconnect the negative battery cable. Drain cooling system.

2. Disconnect electrical connection at switch.

3. Remove the thermal switch from the "T" connection on the water hose.

4. Installation is the reverse of the service removal procedure. Refill cooling system.

In-Vehicle Temperature Sensor (ACC and ECC)

OPERATION

The purpose of the in–vehicle temperature sensor is to monitor the vehicle inside compartment air temperature. The in–vehicle temperature sensor is located behind the glovebox on 940 and 960 Series and behind the passenger grab handle on 850 Series.

TESTING

To test the in–vehicle temperature sensor use a volt–amp meter, check that current passes through the sensor. If not, replace sensor.

REMOVAL AND INSTALLATION

850 Series

1. Be sure the ignition switch is **OFF**.

2. Remove the grab handle (2 screws). Bend back the instrument panel B–post and pull back the cover by bending out the corner of the inside cover.

3. Remove the connection from the sensor. Remove 2 screws holding the sensor in place and remove it.

4. Installation is the reverse of the removal procedure.

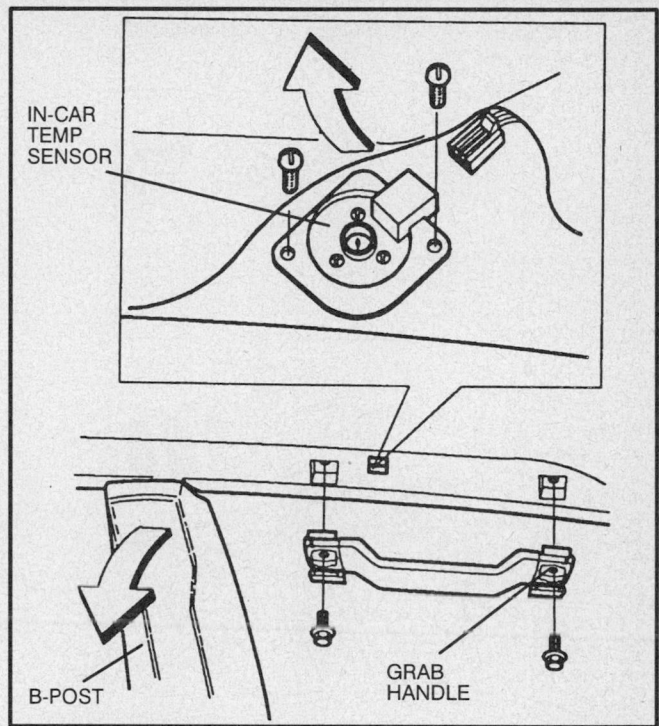

Removing in-car temperature sensor—850 Series

940 and 960 Series

1. Disconnect the negative battery cable. Remove the panel from under the glove box assembly.

2. Remove the glove box unit.

3. Disconnect the air hose and electrical connector from the sensor.

4. Remove the retaining clip and remove the sensor.

5. Installation is the reverse of the service removal procedure.

Ambient Temperature Sensor (ACC and ECC)

OPERATION

The purpose of the ambient temperature sensor is to monitor the air temperature (outside air) at the heater assembly. The ambient temperature sensor is located on the heater housing assembly near the fan motor (940 and 960 Series) or on the passenger side of the air intake grille in the engine compartment (850 Series).

TESTING

At 68–73°F (20–23°C) (room temperature), with the ignition switch turned **ON**, check the resistance across sensor with an ohmmeter. The resistance must be 30–40 ohms. If the reading is 65–100 ohms, the sensor is defective and must be replaced. The higher the room temperature, the lower the resistance value.

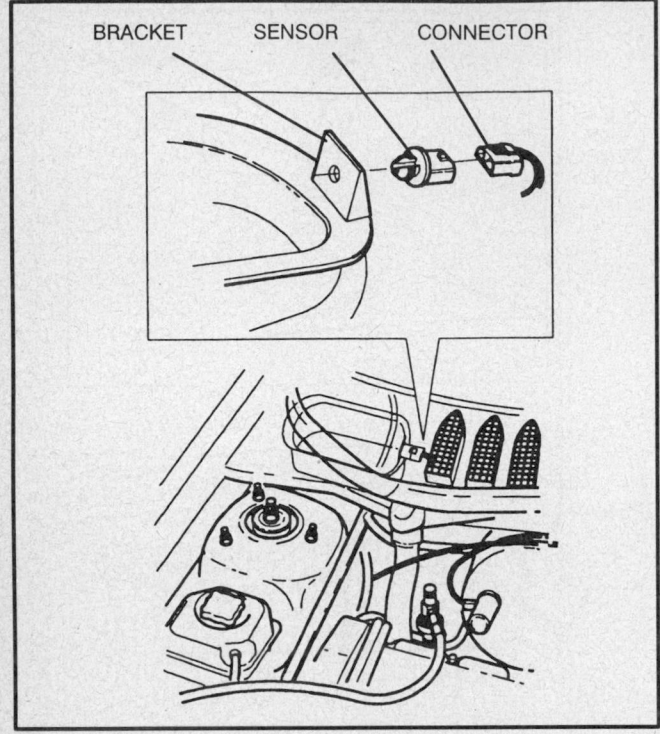

Remove ambient (outside) air temperature sensoring—850 Series

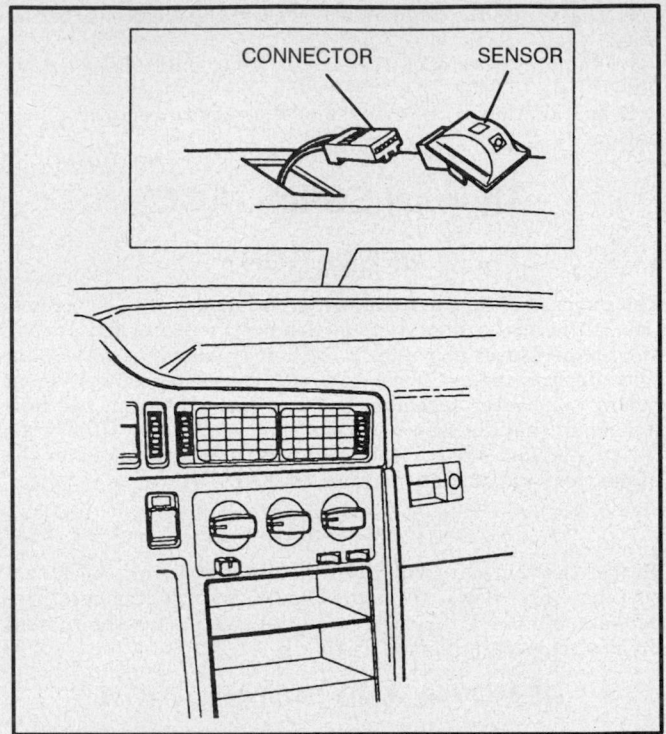

Removing the solar sensor—850 Series

REMOVAL AND INSTALLATION

1. Disconnect the negative battery cable. Remove the panel beneath the glove box and the glove box assembly.
2. Disconnect the sensor electrical connector. Remove the screws and the sensor from housing.
3. Installation is the reverse of the service removal procedure.

Duct Temperature Sensor

OPERATION

850 Series

The purpose of the duct temperature sensors is to provide a feedback signal to the control module to make adjustments if air temperature in the ducts is not as selected on the control panel. One sensor is located in each of the right and left ducts to either side of the climate control panel.

REMOVAL AND INSTALLATION

850 Series

1. Be sure the ignition switch is **OFF**. Remove the climate control panel.
2. Remove the sound panels beneath the instrument panel and remove the glove compartment assembly.

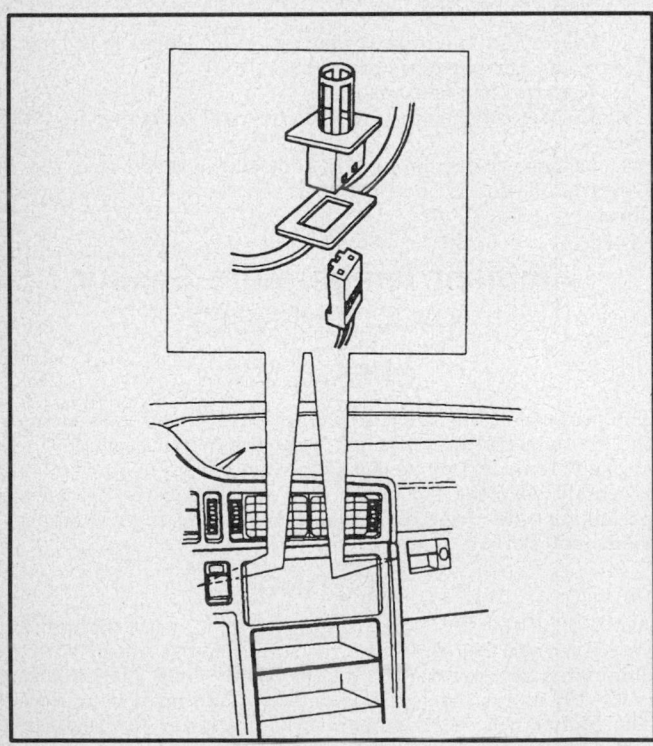

Removing the duct temperature sensors—850 Series

3. Detach the electrical connector from the duct temperature sensor. Cut the retaining tie strap and pull the duct temperature sensor downward from the duct.

4. Installation is the reverse of the removal procedure.

Solar Sensor

OPERATION

The solar sensor determines the intensity of the sunlight coming into the passenger compartment and provides and signal to the climate control module to adjust operation as needed to maintain interior temperature. The sensor is located on top of the dashboard at the base of the windshield. On 850 Series, the sensor is combined with the security alarm diode.

REMOVAL AND INSTALLATION

1. Be sure ignition switch is **OFF**. Use a small, flat–bladed tool and carefully pry the solar sensor loose from the instrument panel.

2. Disconnect the electrical connector from the sensor.

3. Installation is the reverse of the removal procedure.

SYSTEM DIAGNOSIS

Self–Diagnostics/Electronic Climate Control

FAULT TRACING

The ECC system incorporates a self–diagnosis function; faults are indicated by a series of flashing codes when the A/C button is depressed. The control unit is programmed to make the best of the situation if a fault is detected. If a fault is detected, the unit ignores the faulty signal and selects and alternative pre–programmed value; it is also designed to prevent the delivery of faulty codes.

A fault(s) is indicated by flashing of the A/C button; however, the absence of a fault code is not a guarantee the system is fault free.

FAULT INDICATION TO DRIVER

The driver is warned of a fault when the ignition switch is turned ON and the A/C button flashes continually. On 850 Series there is an LED indicator above both the A/C and RECIRC switches which will flash to indicate a fault has been noted. Further indication of the fault's seriousness is provided when the engine is started:

1. A serious fault will cause the A/C button to flash continuously, while the engine is running.

2. Less serious fault will cause the A/C button to flash for 20 seconds, after the engine has been started.

RETRIEVING FAULT CODES

850 Series

Fault codes are read on the diagnostic control unit located in the right front corner of the engine compartment. The unit has a light which flashes in conjunction with the number of the code.

Fault codes are 3–digits and the flashes from the diagnostic unit correspond, in sequence, to each digit of the code. For example, code 2–3–1 would flash 2 times, pause, flash 3 times, pause, and flash 1 time.

Codes are flashed one code at a time. To search for more codes, depress the button after each code to go to the next one. Codes are retrieve in numerical ascending order. When the first code is repeated, there are no more codes in the system.

1. Be sure the ignition switch is **OFF**. Remove the top from the diagnostic connector unit.

2. Connect the selector cable from side A of the unit to output pin **1** on side B.

3. Turn the ignition switch to **ON**. Depress the button on side A of the unit and count and write down the number of flashes shown.

4. Depress the button to retrieve the next code. When the first code is repeated, there are no more fault codes in the system.

5. Perform appropriate system repairs. Delete the fault code(s).

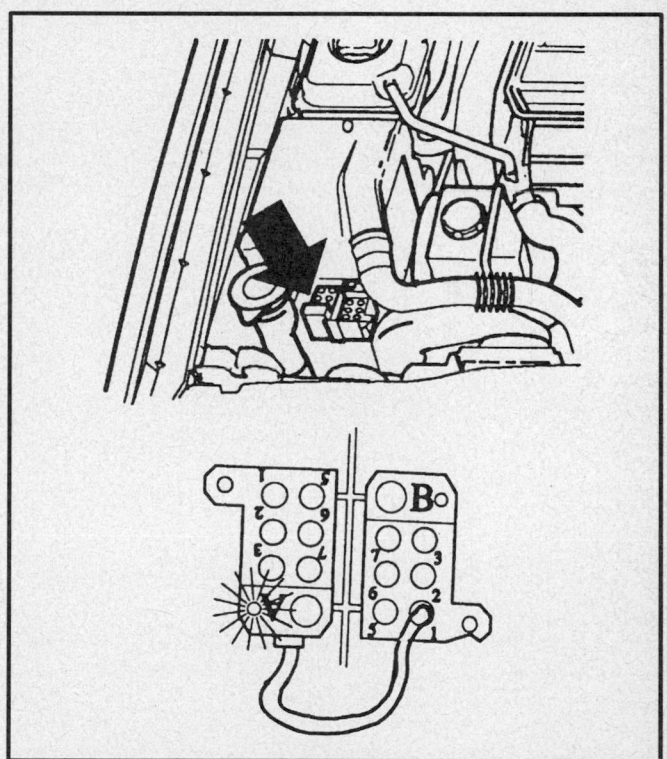

Showing location of diagnostic control unit and connection for retrieving fault codes—850 Series

940 and 960 Series

1. Before retrieving a fault code, the following conditions must be met:
   - Start and operate the engine.
   - Set fan control to **AUTO**.
   - Set the air distribution control to **VENT**.
   - Set the temperature control to **MAX COOLING**.

● Depress the **RECIRC** switch and release the A/C switch.

2. Focus a strong lamp (not fluorescent tube) on the solar sensor (located on the right side of the dash).

NOTE: If a lamp is not used, a fault code will be displayed, even if the system is fault–free. If a lamp is not used, the ignition switch must be turned OFF before the next code retrieval; otherwise, the fault code will still be present.

3. To report a fault code, depress and release the A/C button within 5 seconds.

NOTE: The first fault code should be retrieved about 5 seconds after starting the engine; this will allow the self–diagnosis function time to operate and the voltage to stabilize.

4. Since each fault code consists of 3 digits, they will be displayed as follows:
● The first digit is indicated by 1 or 2 flashes.
● After an interval, the second digit is indicated by 1–6 flashes.
● After another interval, the third digit is indicated by 1–9 flashes.
● Assemble the flashed digits into the fault code number.

NOTE: Only 3 fault codes can be stored at a time and only 1 fault code will be reported upon request; perform a number of request to be sure that all potential faults are reported.

5. If several fault codes are present, they will be reported in a rolling manner.

6. When the ignition switch is turned **OFF**, the fault codes will be removed from the memory.

7. Perform the appropriate repairs.

DELETING FAULT CODES

850 Series

NOTE: All fault codes must be read at least once before they can be deleted.

1. Be sure the selector cable is connected from side A of the diagnostic unit to output pin **1** on side B.

2. Turn the ignition switch to **ON**. Press the button on side A and hold it down for at least 5 seconds. Release the button and the LED will come ON.

3. Press the button again while the LED is ON and hold it down for another 5 seconds. The fault codes are now deleted.

4. To check that all codes were deleted, turn the ignition to **OFF**, then back to **ON**. Press the button and count the flashes.

5. If the Code 1–1–1 flashes, this indicates all codes have been cleared.

6. If another code appears, continue to press the button to determine how many codes remain. Be sure all repairs have been made, then repeat the delete process.

DIAGNOSTIC TROUBLE CODES—850 SERIES

Diagnostic trouble code (DTC)	Cause
1-1-1	No fault found by diagnostic system
1-2-1	Outside temperature sensor ground (GND) short
1-2-2	Outside temperature sensor open circuit or shorted to 12 V
1-2-3	Driver's side passenger compartment temperature sensor GND short
1-2-4	Driver's side passenger compartment temperature sensor open circuit or short to 12 V
1-2-5	Passenger side passenger compartment temperature sensor GND short
1-2-6	Passenger side passenger compartment temperature sensor open circuit or shorted to 12 V
1-3-1	Left-hand duct temperature sensor short to ground
1-3-2	Left-hand duct temperature sensor open-circuit or short to 12 V supply
1-3-3	Right-hand duct temperature sensor short to groun
1-3-4	Right-hand duct temperature sensor open-circuit or short to 12 V supply
1-3-5	Engine temperature no frequency signal
1-4-1	Driver's side temperature switch faulty control signal
1-4-3	Passenger side temperature switch faulty control signal
1-4-5	Air distribution switch faulty control signal
1-5-1	Fan speed sensor faulty control signal
1-5-2	Control signal from fan speed signal GND short
2-1-1	Driver's side damper motor position sensor open circuit or short to 12 V
2-1-2	Driver's side damper motor position sensor GND short
2-2-1	Passenger's side damper motor position sensor open circuit or short to 12 V
2-2-2	Passenger's side damper motor position sensor GND short
2-3-1	Ventilation damper motor position sensor open circuit or short to 12 V
2-3-2	Diagnostic trouble code (DTC) Ventilation damper motor position sensor GND short
2-3-3	Floor-defrost damper motor position sensor open circuit or short to 12 V
2-3-4	Floor-defrost damper motor position sensor GND short
2-3-5	Recirculation damper motor position sensor open circuit or short to 12 V
2-3-6	Recirculation damper motor position sensor GND short
3-1-1	Driver's side damper motor shorted to GND or 12 V
3-1-2	Passenger's side damper motor shorted to GND or 12 V
3-1-3	Ventilation damper motor shorted to GND or 12 V
3-1-4	Floor/defrost damper motor shorted to GND or 12 V
3-1-5	Recirculation damper motor shorted to GND or 12 V
3-2-1	Driver's side damper motor active too long
3-2-2	Passenger side damper motor active too long
3-2-3	Ventilation damper motor active too long
3-2-4	Floor/defrost damper motor active too long
3-2-5	Recirculation damper motor active too long
4-1-1	Passenger compartment fan overcurrent or seized fan
4-1-2	Driver's side passenger compartment temperature sensor intake fan GND short

DIAGNOSTIC TROUBLE CODES—850 SERIES, CONT.

4-1-3	Driver's side passenger compartment temperature sensor intake fan, no control voltage
4-1-4	Driver's side passenger compartment temperature sensor intake fan seized
4-1-5	Passenger side passenger compartment temperature sensor fan GND short
4-1-6	Passenger side passenger compartment temperature sensor intake fan, no control voltage
4-1-7	Passenger side passenger compartment temperature sensor intake fan seized
4-1-8	Power stage, no control signal
4-1-9	Power stage giving faulty diagnostic signal
4-2-0	Control unit fault in program memory
5-1-1	Self-adjustment damper motor limit positions not carried out

DIAGNOSTIC FAULT CODE CHART—940 AND 960 SERIES

Faults and fault codes

Note: Fault may be caused by defective component or the wiring

Fault	Code	Fault class*
Outside temperature sensor (on fan casing)	121	A
– Short-circuit to ground	121	A
– Open-circuit or short-circuit to +12 V	122	A
Interior temperature sensor (in roof light)		
– Short-circuit to ground	131	A
– Open-circuit or short-circuit to +12 V	132	A
Water temperature sensor (beside heat exchanger)		
– Short-circuit to ground	141	M
– Open-circuit or short-circuit to +12 V	142	M
Alternator		
– D+signal level fault in alternator	151	A
Solar sensor (in loudspeaker grille)	161	I
N.B. Illuminate the device with a lamp, otherwise the fault will be reported even if the sensor is intact.		
Servo motor/potentiometer		
– Open-circuit or short-circuit to ground	211	A
– Short-circuit to +12 V	212	A
Servo motor drive		
– Pin 17 or 18 incorrectly connected to +12 V supply	213	A
Servo motor		
– Failure to operate within 10 s (due to seizure of arm or interruption in electrical supply)	214	A
ECC controls		
– Faulty temperature control	231	A
Fan motor		
– Starting current excessive (motor runs sluggishly or seizes) ..	233	A
Power unit		
– Incorrect connection of +12 V supply		
Output affected:		
Water valve	241	A
Bi-level (B/L)	242	A
Vent	243	A
Rec	244	A
Defroster	245	A
Floor	246	A
Fan, max. speed relay	247	A
Compressor	248	A
Radiator fan relay	249	A
Fault-free	111	

* Fault class: A = serious fault
M = less serious fault
I = no fault indication to driver

SYSTEM DIAGNOSTIC CHART—AUTOMATIC CLIMATE CONTROL

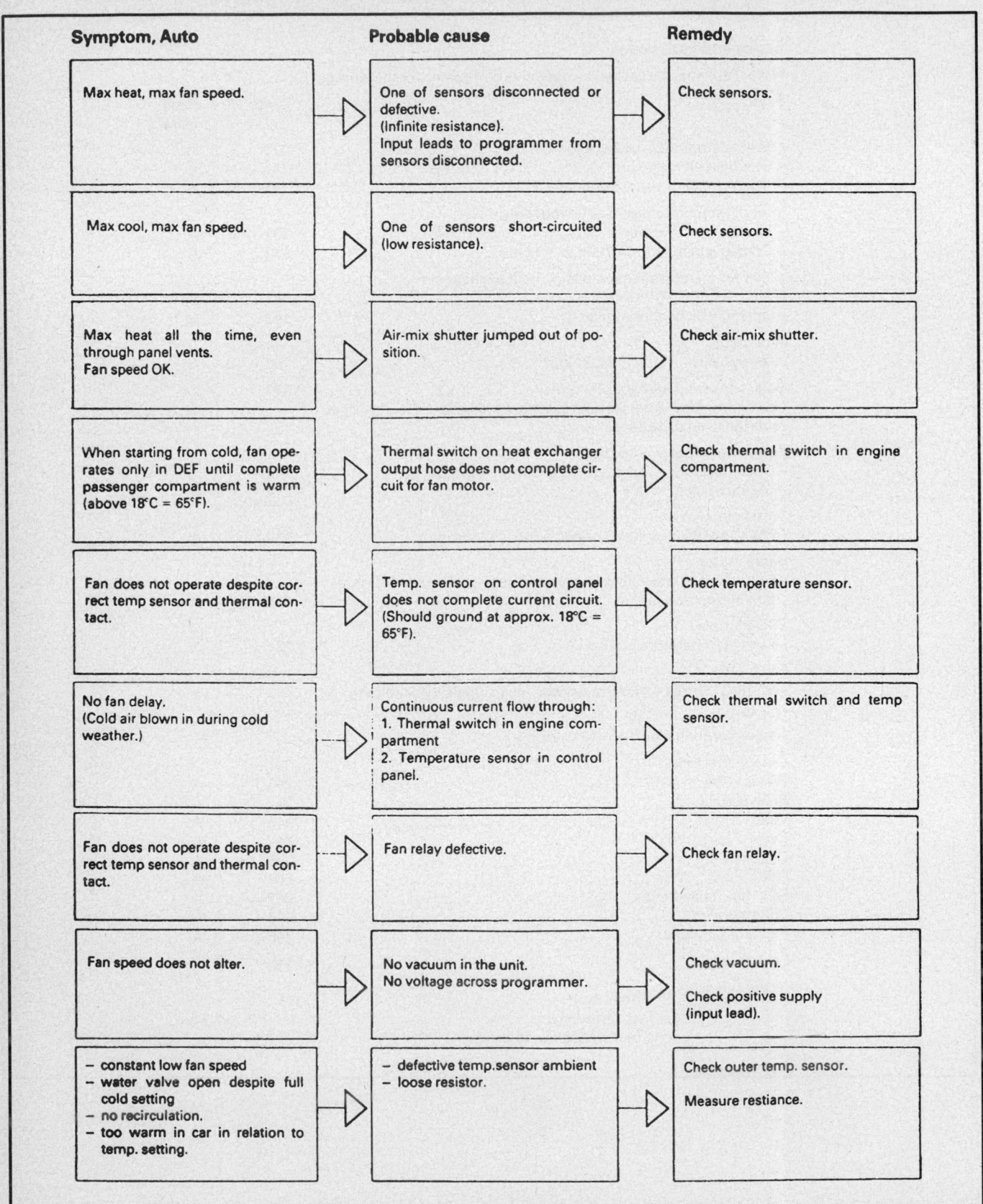

Symptom, Auto	Probable cause	Remedy
Max heat, max fan speed.	One of sensors disconnected or defective. (Infinite resistance). Input leads to programmer from sensors disconnected.	Check sensors.
Max cool, max fan speed.	One of sensors short-circuited (low resistance).	Check sensors.
Max heat all the time, even through panel vents. Fan speed OK.	Air-mix shutter jumped out of position.	Check air-mix shutter.
When starting from cold, fan operates only in DEF until complete passenger compartment is warm (above 18°C = 65°F).	Thermal switch on heat exchanger output hose does not complete circuit for fan motor.	Check thermal switch in engine compartment.
Fan does not operate despite correct temp sensor and thermal contact.	Temp. sensor on control panel does not complete current circuit. (Should ground at approx. 18°C = 65°F).	Check temperature sensor.
No fan delay. (Cold air blown in during cold weather.)	Continuous current flow through: 1. Thermal switch in engine compartment 2. Temperature sensor in control panel.	Check thermal switch and temp sensor.
Fan does not operate despite correct temp sensor and thermal contact.	Fan relay defective.	Check fan relay.
Fan speed does not alter.	No vacuum in the unit. No voltage across programmer.	Check vacuum. Check positive supply (input lead).
– constant low fan speed – water valve open despite full cold setting – no recirculation. – too warm in car in relation to temp. setting.	– defective temp.sensor ambient – loose resistor.	Check outer temp. sensor. Measure restiance.

GENERAL AIR CONDITIONING DIAGNOSTIC CHART

No cooling	Poor cooling	Intermittent cooling	Noise	Possible cause	Remedy
				Electrical faults:	
X				Blown fuse	Check fuses (see wiring diagram)
X				Poor connection or short (compressor does not operate)	Check all cables
X				Compressor coupling burnt	Replace coupling
X				Fan motor (blower), does not operate	Check cables and motor
	X	X		Fan motor (blower), poor operation (loose or cracked motor)	Check/replace
		X	X	Broken or poor connection in compressor clutch winding (clutch moves in and out)	Replace clutch
			X	Fan motor screeches or contacts fan shroud	Check
				Mechanical faults	
X	X		X	Drive belt too loose or cracked	Tension or replace belt.
X	X			Heater control valve leaks in "COOL"	Check valve.
	X			Air ducts blocked	Check and clean
	X			Air inlet in front of windscreen/shield blocked	Check and clean
			X	Clutch bearing worn or off-centre	Replace bearing.
	X		X	Compressor worn or loose	Recondition compressor.
			X	Low oil level in compressor (260) (warm underneath)	Drain system. Measure amount of oil in compressor. Must be at least 1.5 dl (0.3 US pint). Refit compressor. Replace drying agent in receiver/dryer and refit system.
				System faults	
X				Evaporator thermostat does not disengage compressor.	Check/replace thermostat.
X				Expansion valve stuck in open position	Replace.
X				Leakage	Top-up system. Find leakage and repair.
X				Blocked hose or component	Check flow through each component
X				No refrigerant in system	Add refrigerant.
	X			Air flow through condenser blocked	Clean condenser
	X			Evaporator blocked on air cooling side	Clean off dirt etc.

No cooling	Poor cooling	Intermittent cooling	Noise	Possible cause	Remedy
	X			Evaporator thermostat incorrectly adjusted	Check thermostat.
	X		X	Insufficient refrigerant (whistling noise from evaporator near expansion valve, bubbles in sight glass)	Drain and refill system.
	X			Expansion valve capillary tube damaged.	Replace.
	X			Receiver/dryer blocked	Replace.
	X	X		Moisture in system. Cooling capacity good at start (few minutes) then poor. Or poor operation at high ambient temperatures	Drain system, replace receiver/dryer or drying agent, fill with refrigerant. See page 167
	X			Air in system (bubbles in sight glass)	Drain system, replace receiver/dryer or drying agent, fill with refrigerant.
		X		Ice on evaporator air cooling side (thermostat adjusted too low or fan not operating)	Check evaporator thermostat. Test with fan on
		X		Loose evaporator thermostat	Check/replace.
		X		Poor contact between expansion valve capillary tube and evaporator outlet or poor insulation	Check
		X		Too large a difference between off and on for evaporator thermostat	Replace.
			X	System overfull causes crashing noise or vibrations from high pressure lines, clicking noise from compressor, excessive compressor pressure and suction pressure, hissing noise from expansion valve, bubbles or vapour in sight glass. If compressor valves damaged by overfilling, compressor pressure will be too low	Drain System. Refill
			X	Moisture in system, can cause noise from expansion valve	Drain system, replace/receiver/dryer or drying agent, fill with refrigerant.

REFRIGERANT SYSTEM PRESSURE TESTING CHART

Fault tracing   Pressure testing

A separate pressure gauge kit or the pressure gauges on the filling station (5143) should be used for the following tests.

Low pressure side	High pressure side	Cause	Remedy
Low	Normal	1. Expansion valve blocked or seized in closed position. 2. Expansion valve capillary tube damage – liquid loss. 3. Moisture in system, causes ice in expansion valve.	1. Remove blockage. Replace valve if necessary. 2. Replace expansion valve. 3. Drain system. Replace receiver/dryer. Evacuate system and fill.
Low	Low	1. Not enough refrigerant. No bubbles in sight glass, pressure gauge readings very low. Possibly no refrigerant in sight glass. This can cause large leakage. Expansion valve can be blocked or seized in open position.	1. Drain system, Evacuate and fill. 2. Replace expansion valve. Fill system.
Low	High	1. Blockage in receiver/dryer or connecting pipes.	1. Replace. Remove blockage.
High	Normal	1. Expansion valve seized in open position. 2. Expansion valve coil against evaporator outlet, loose or poorly insulated. 3. Not enough refrigerant. Possibly bubbles in sight glass.	1. Replace. 2. Secure coil and insulate. 3. Drain system. Evacuate and fill.
High	Low	1. Defective compressor.	1. Repair/replace. Replace receiver/dryer.
Normal – High	High	1. Too much refrigerant. 2. No cold air reaches condenser. 3. Blockage in high pressure side. 4. Engine radiator overheated. 5. Air in system. Poor evacuation and filling of refrigerant.	1. Drain system. Evacuate and fill. 2. Remove obstruction. Check cooling fan and belts. 3. Remove blockage. 4. Improve cooling. 5. Drain system. Replace receiver/dryer. Evacuate and fill according to instructions.
Normal	Normal	1. Moisture in system, occasional formation of ice. Low pressure side pressure varies. Cooling ability OK in cool conditions but poor or non existent in hot weather.	1. Drain system. Replace receiver/dryer. Evacuate and fill according to instructions.

WIRING SCHEMATICS

MASTER LEGEND FOR SCHEMATICS AND COMPONENT IDENTIFICATION

This is a master legend to be used with all Volvo schematic and figures to identify components by the Volvo numbering system.

1/1	Battery
2/10	ECC power unit
2/22	A/C relay
2/24	Max fan relay
2/30	Overload relay
2/48	A/C blocking relay
3/1	Ignition switch
3/2	Light switch
3/54	RECIRC and A/C switches
3/55	A/C panel lights
3/56	Heater fan switch
3/57	Climate control panel
4/4	Rheostat
4/6	ECC control module
4/10	Ign control module (EZK DI)
4/21	TCU control module
4/23	Heater controls
4/30	ECC control module
4/31	Fan motor power module
4/41	MFI control module (Fenix)
4/45	MFI control module (LH 3.2)
5/1	Combined instrument
6/26	Alternator
6/27	Throttle control servo motor
6/28	Fan motor
6/35	Optional heater
6/45	Driver temp door motor
6/46	Pass temp door motor
6/47	Floor/def door motor
6/48	Recirc door motor
6/49	Vent door motor
7/9	Eng coolant temp sensor
7/10	In−car sensor
7/11	Ambient temp sensor

7/12	Solar sensor
7/41	A/C high press sensor
7/53	A/C low press sensor
7/59	Lt duct temp sensor
7/60	Rt duct temp sensor
7/64	Driver side in−car sensor
7/65	Pass side in−car sensor
7/68	Solar sensor/alarm LED
7/83	A/C high press sensor
8/2	ECC solenoids
8/3	A/C solenoid
11	Fuse box
15/1	Positive terminal
15/2	30−rail in elect distribution
17/7	Diagnostic unit socket A
17/10	Diagnostic unit socket B
20/18	Blower motor resistor
24/1	14−pin instr pnl conn (firewall)
24/2	53−pin firewall harness conn
24/10	2−pin htr−A/C conn (firewall)
24/11	10−pin A/C conn (firewall)
24/12	4−pin htr−A/C harness conn (f/w)
24/13	53−pin instr pnl harness conn (f/w)
24/15	14−pin lt door sill harness conn
31	Grounds (all "31" numbers)
C2	53−pin instr pnl lt harness conn
C3	53−pin instr pnl rt harness conn
C19	2−pin instr pnl conn
C51	8−pin eng harness conn
C54	Eng harness conn
C154	Cooling fan harness conn
C160	6−pin instr pnl conn
C161	1−pin conn at firewall
C162	2−pin lt B−post conn
C163	2−pin conn (diesel)
C/EB	4−pin A/C hi press sensor conn
D1	4−pin inst. pnl conn

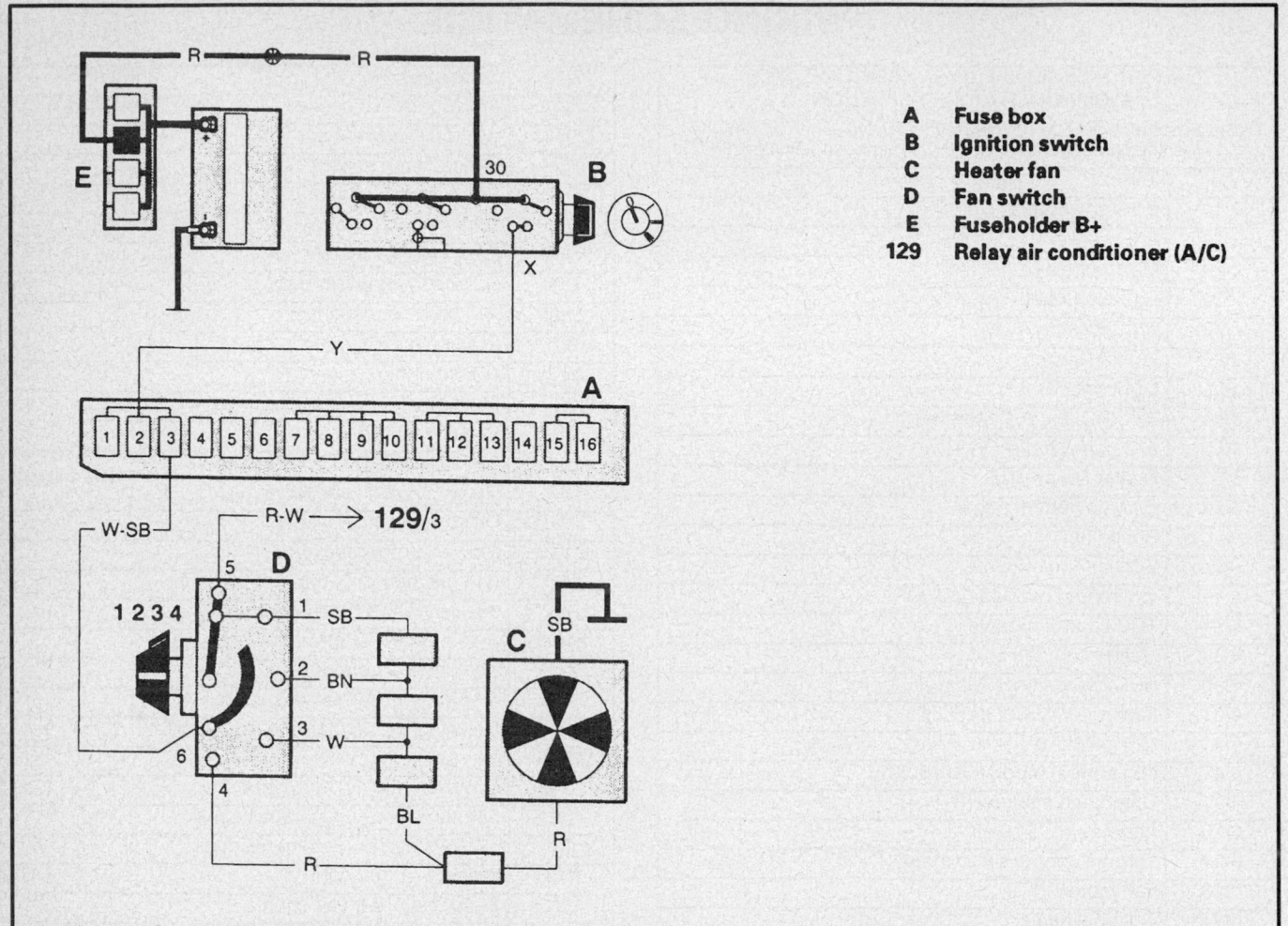

A	Fuse box
B	Ignition switch
C	Heater fan
D	Fan switch
E	Fuseholder B+
129	Relay air conditioner (A/C)

Heater system wiring schematic—240 Series

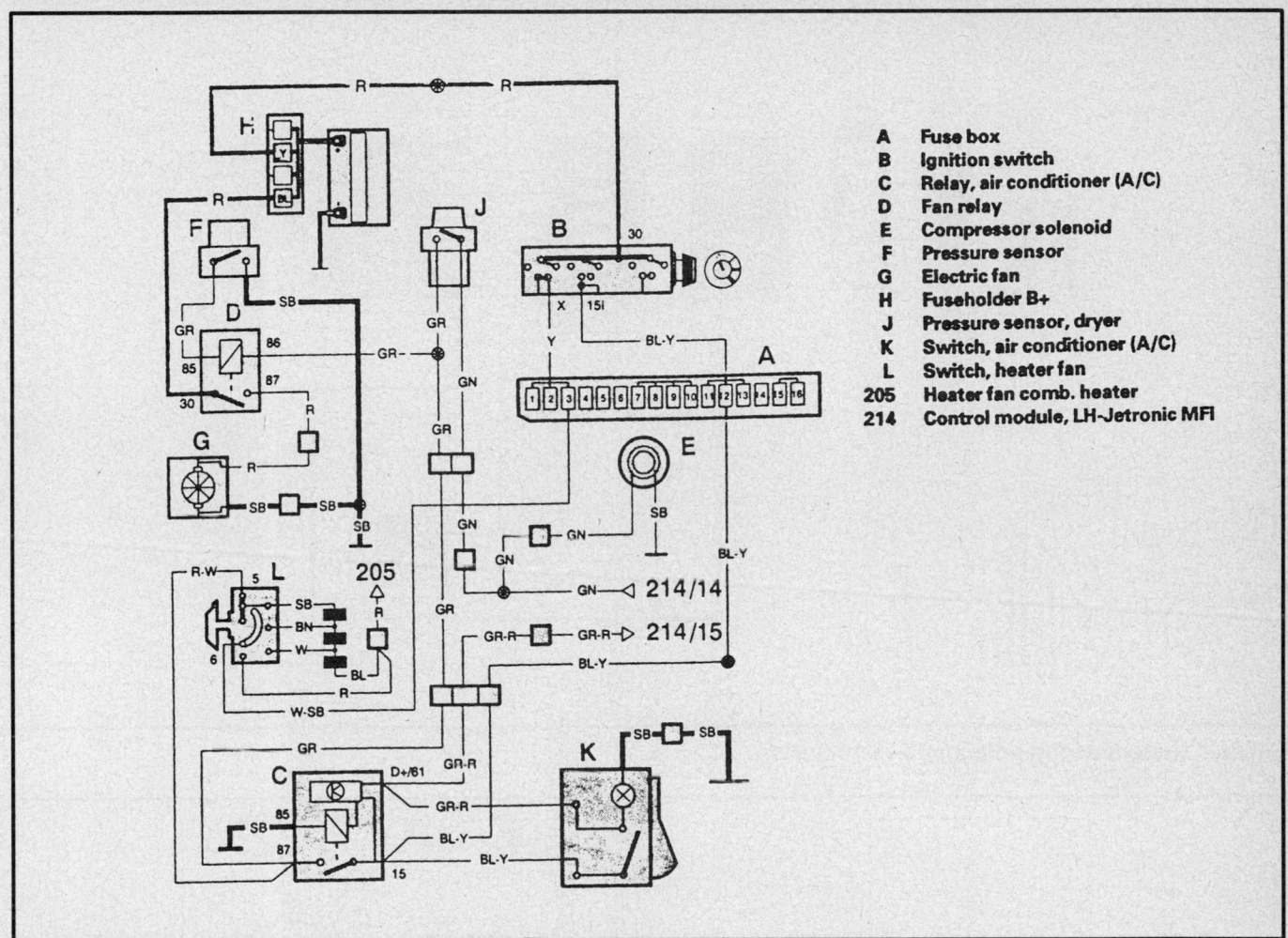

A	Fuse box
B	Ignition switch
C	Relay, air conditioner (A/C)
D	Fan relay
E	Compressor solenoid
F	Pressure sensor
G	Electric fan
H	Fuseholder B+
J	Pressure sensor, dryer
K	Switch, air conditioner (A/C)
L	Switch, heater fan
205	Heater fan comb. heater
214	Control module, LH-Jetronic MFI

Air conditioning system wiring schematic—240 Series

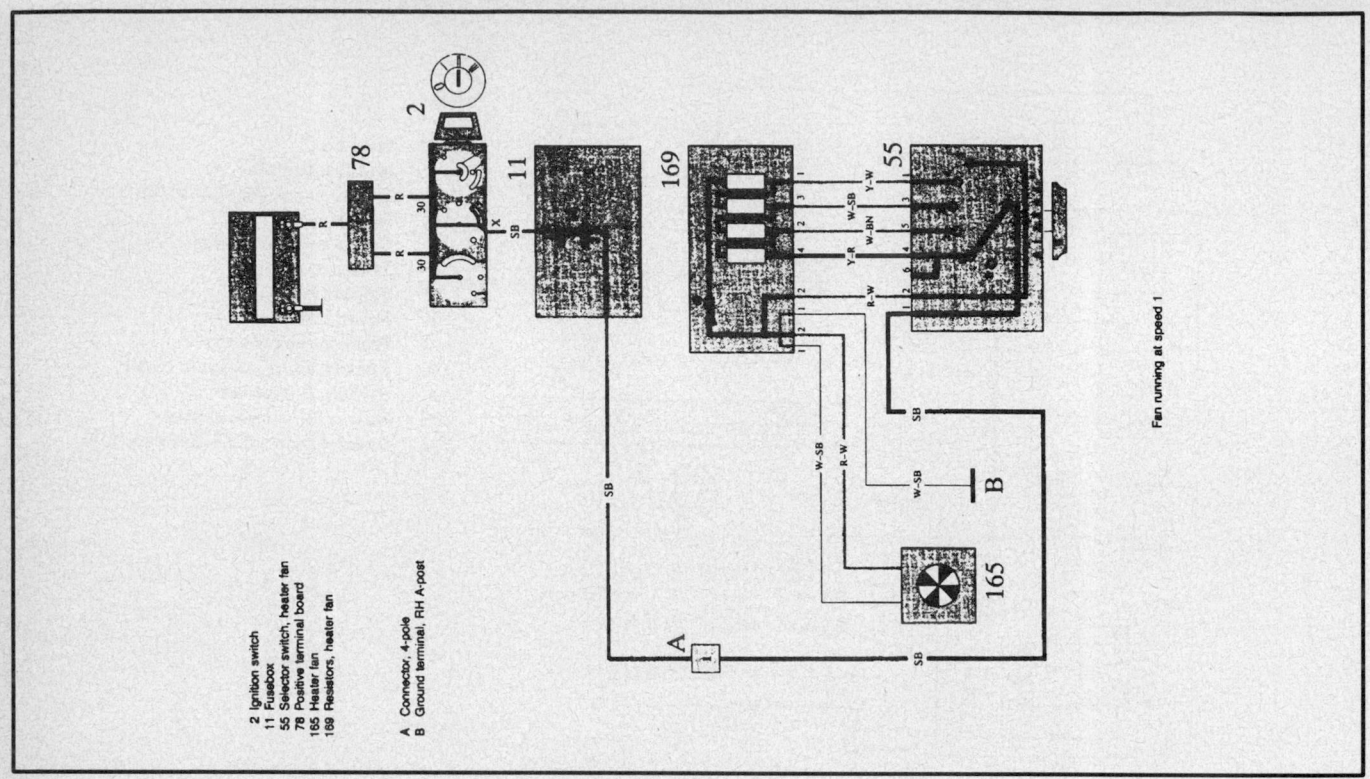

Heater system wiring schematic—940 Series

Key:
2 Ignition switch
11 Fusebox
55 Selector switch, heater fan
78 Positive terminal board
165 Heater fan
169 Resistors, heater fan

A Connector, 4-pole
B Ground terminal, RH A-post

Fan running at speed 1

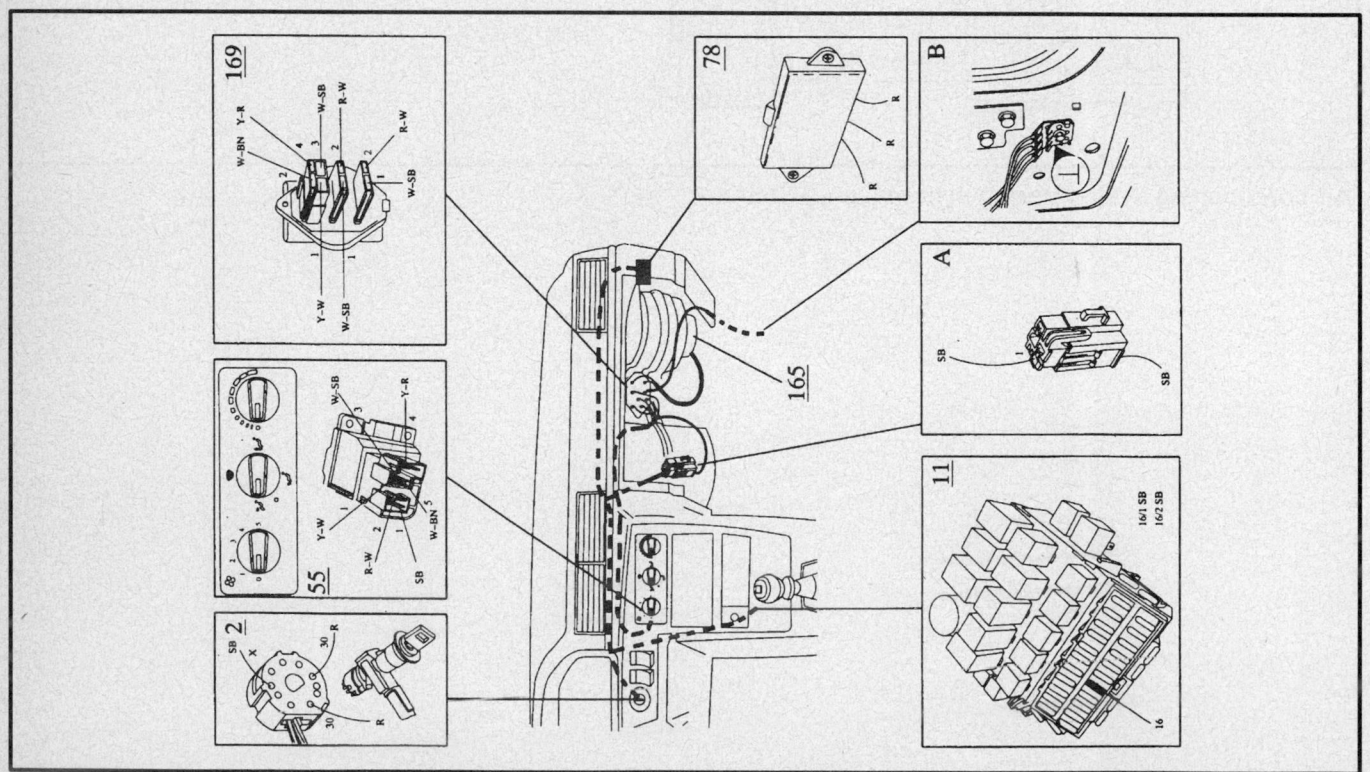

Heater system component locations—940 Series

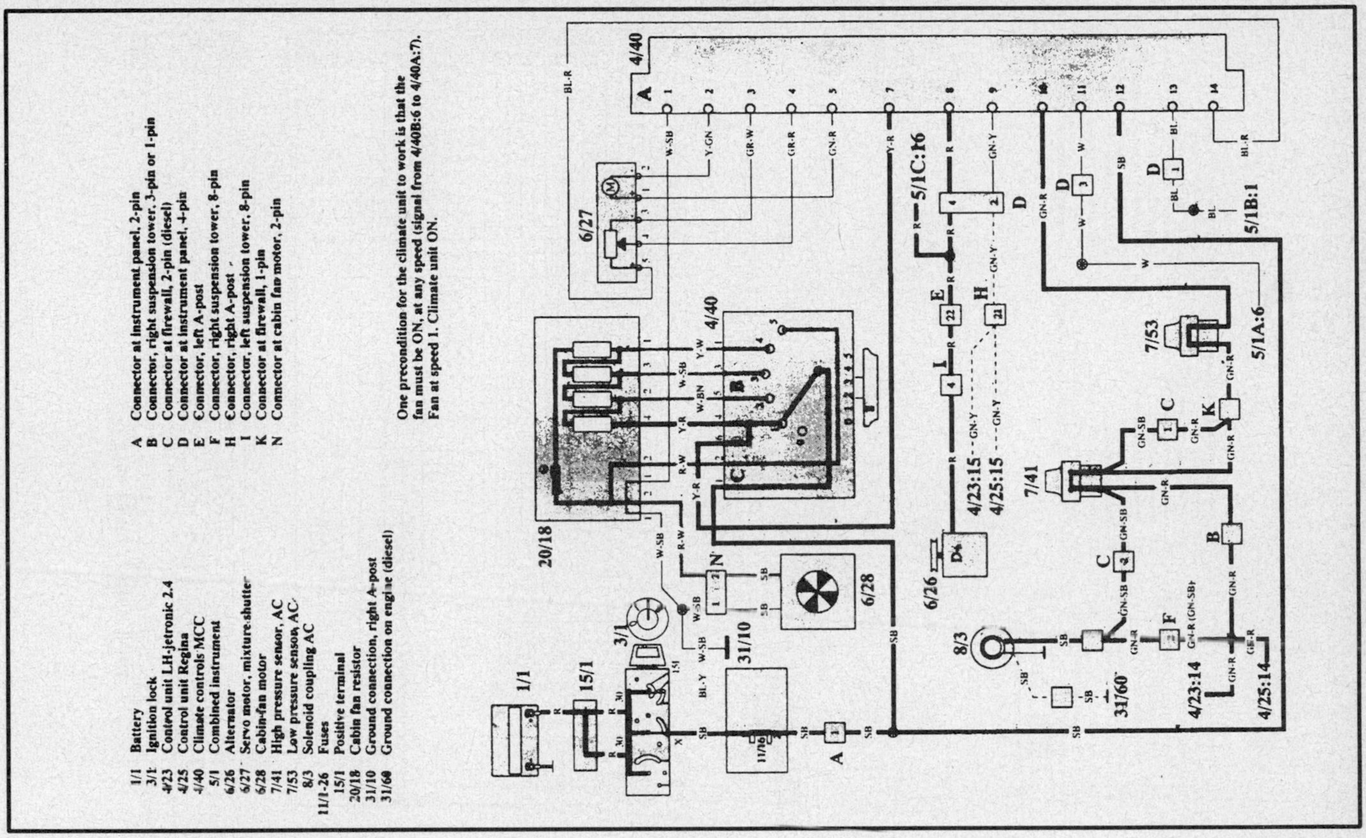

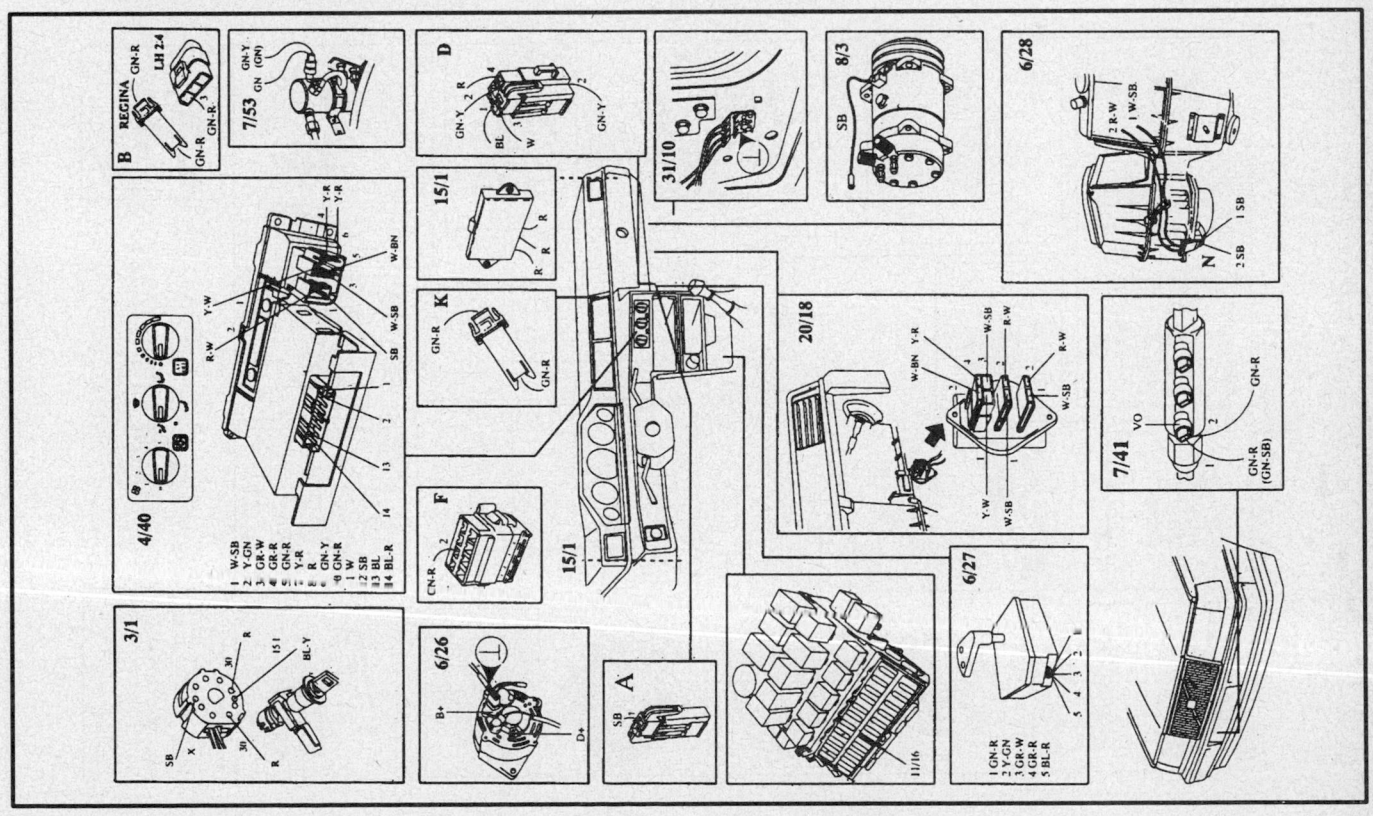

Manual air conditioning system wiring schematic—1993–94 940 Series

A	Connector at instrument panel, 2-pin
B	Connector, right suspension tower, 3-pin or 1-pin
C	Connector at firewall, 2-pin (diesel)
D	Connector at instrument panel, 4-pin
E	Connector, left A-post
F	Connector, right suspension tower, 8-pin
H	Connector, right A-post
I	Connector, left suspension tower, 8-pin
K	Connector at firewall, 1-pin
N	Connector at cabin fan motor, 2-pin

One precondition for the climate unit to work is that the fan must be ON, at any speed (signal from 4/40B:6 to 4/40A:7). Fan at speed 1. Climate unit ON.

1/1	Battery
3/1	Ignition lock
4/23	Control unit LH-Jetronic 2.4
4/25	Control unit Regina
4/40	Climate controls MCC
5/1	Combined instrument
6/26	Alternator
6/27	Servo motor, mixture-shutter
6/28	Cabin-fan motor
7/41	High pressure sensor, AC
7/53	Low pressure sensor, AC
8/3	Solenoid coupling, AC
11/1-26	Fuses
15/1	Positive terminal
20/18	Cabin fan resistor
31/10	Ground connection, right A-post
31/60	Ground connection on engine (diesel)

Manual air conditioning system component locations—1993–94 940 Series

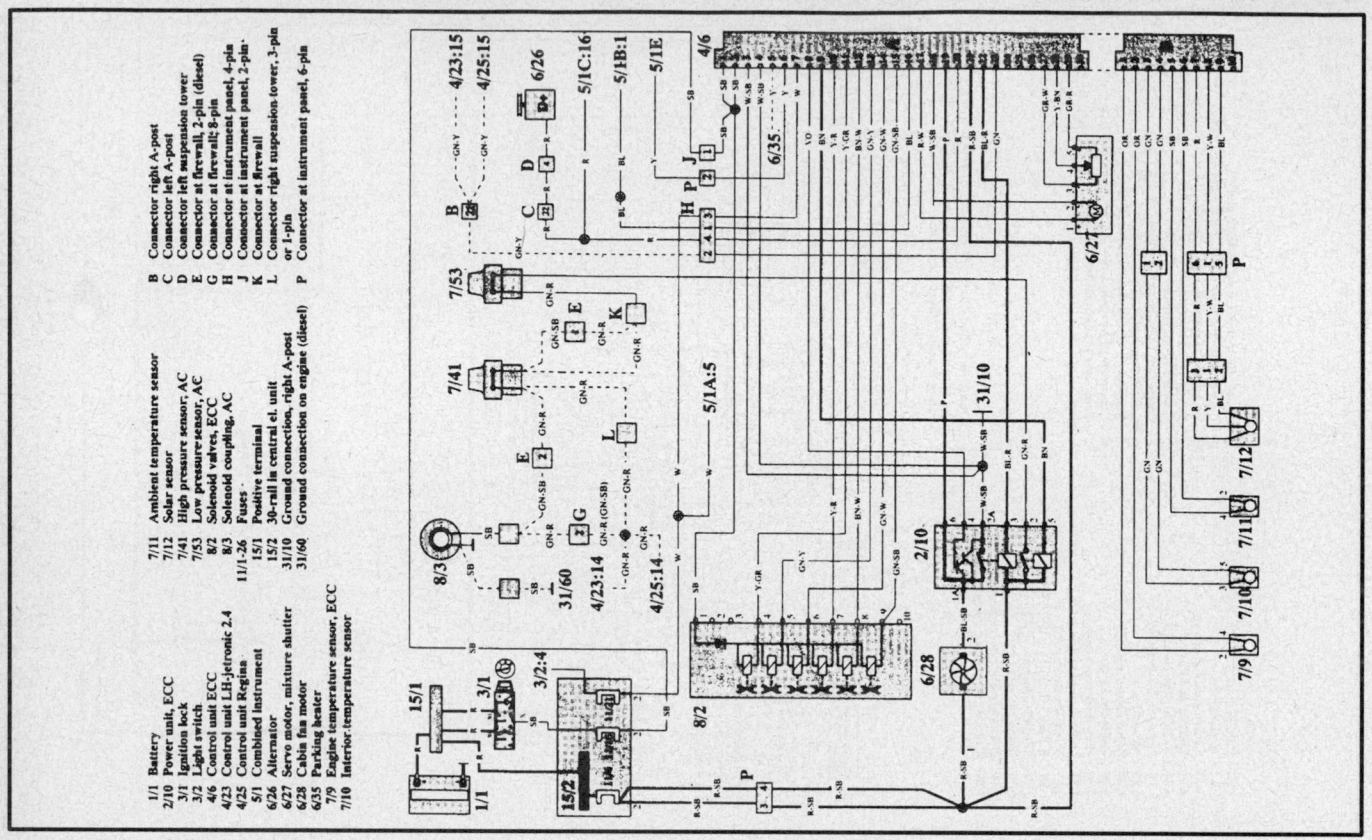

Electronic climate control system wiring schematic—1993–95 940 Series

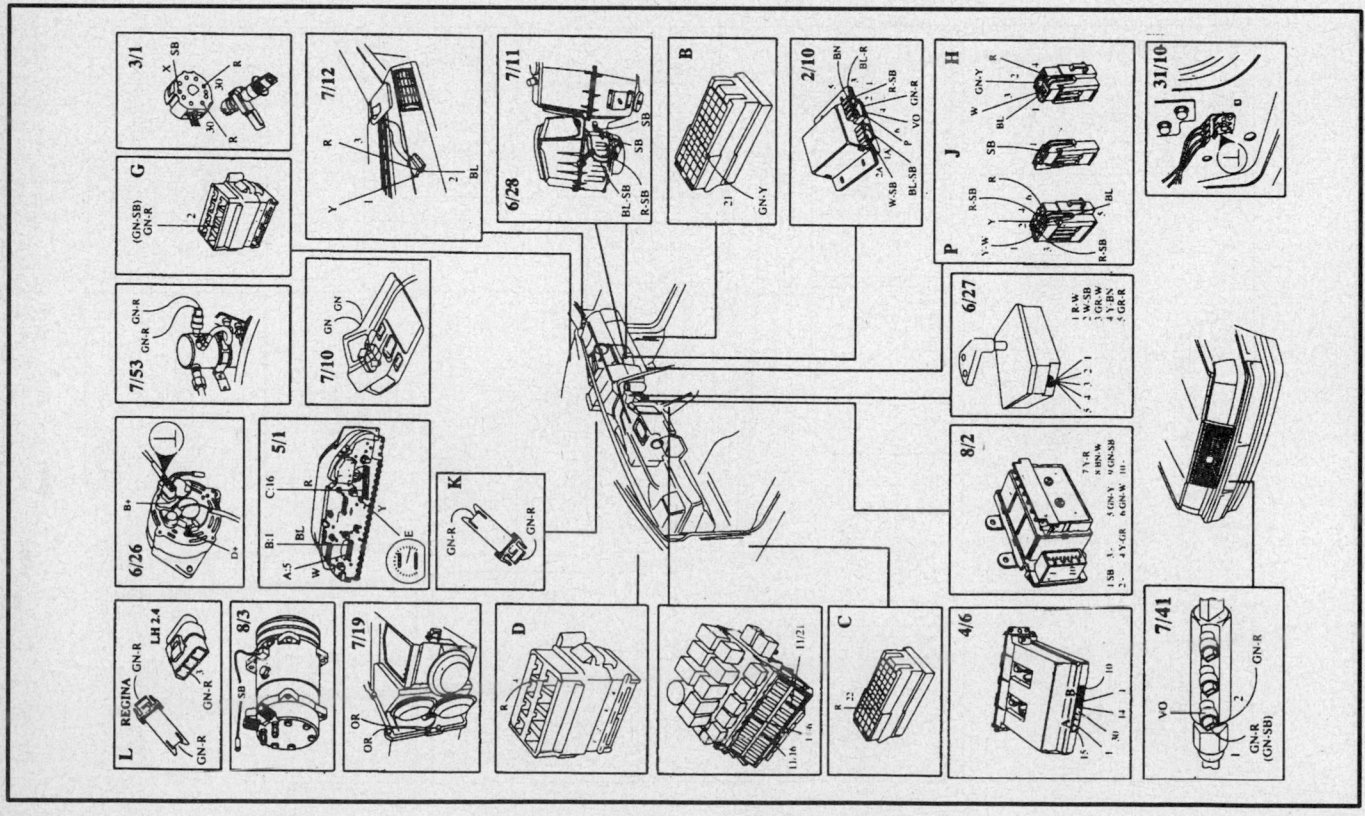

Electronic climate control system component locations—1993–95 940 Series

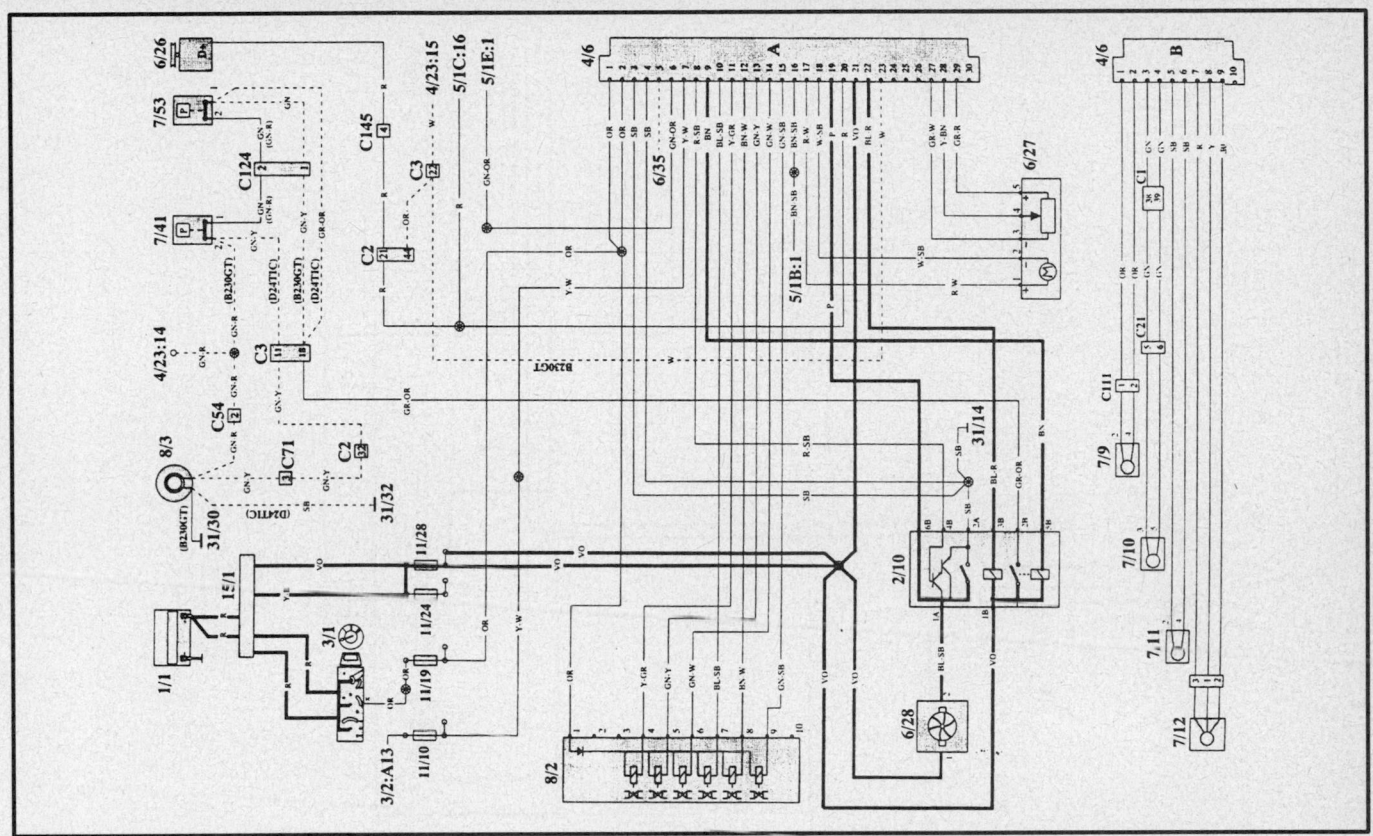

Electronic climate control system wiring schematic—1993–94 960 Series with B204FT engine

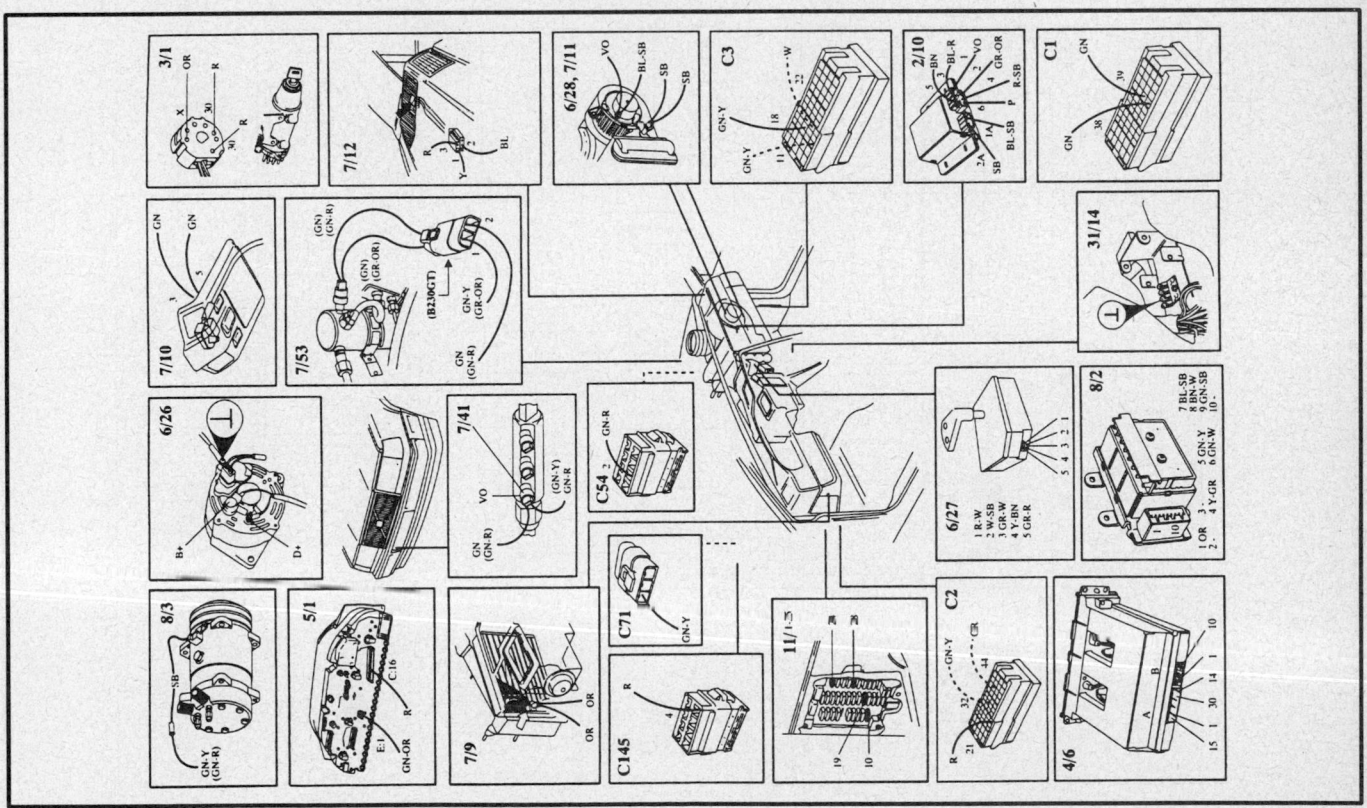

Electronic climate control system component locations—1993–94 960 Series with B204FT engine

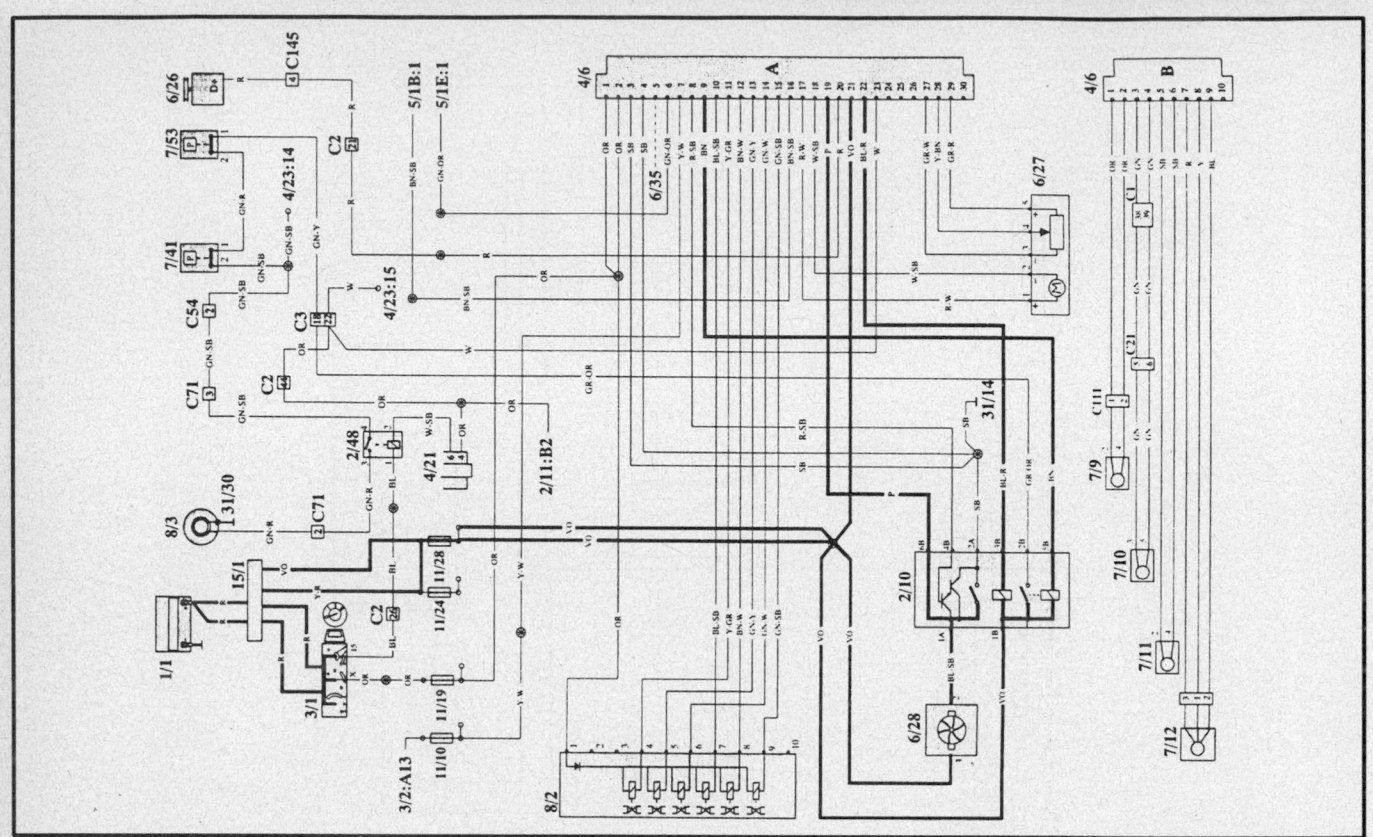

Electronic climate control system wiring schematic—1993—94 960 Series with B230GT engine

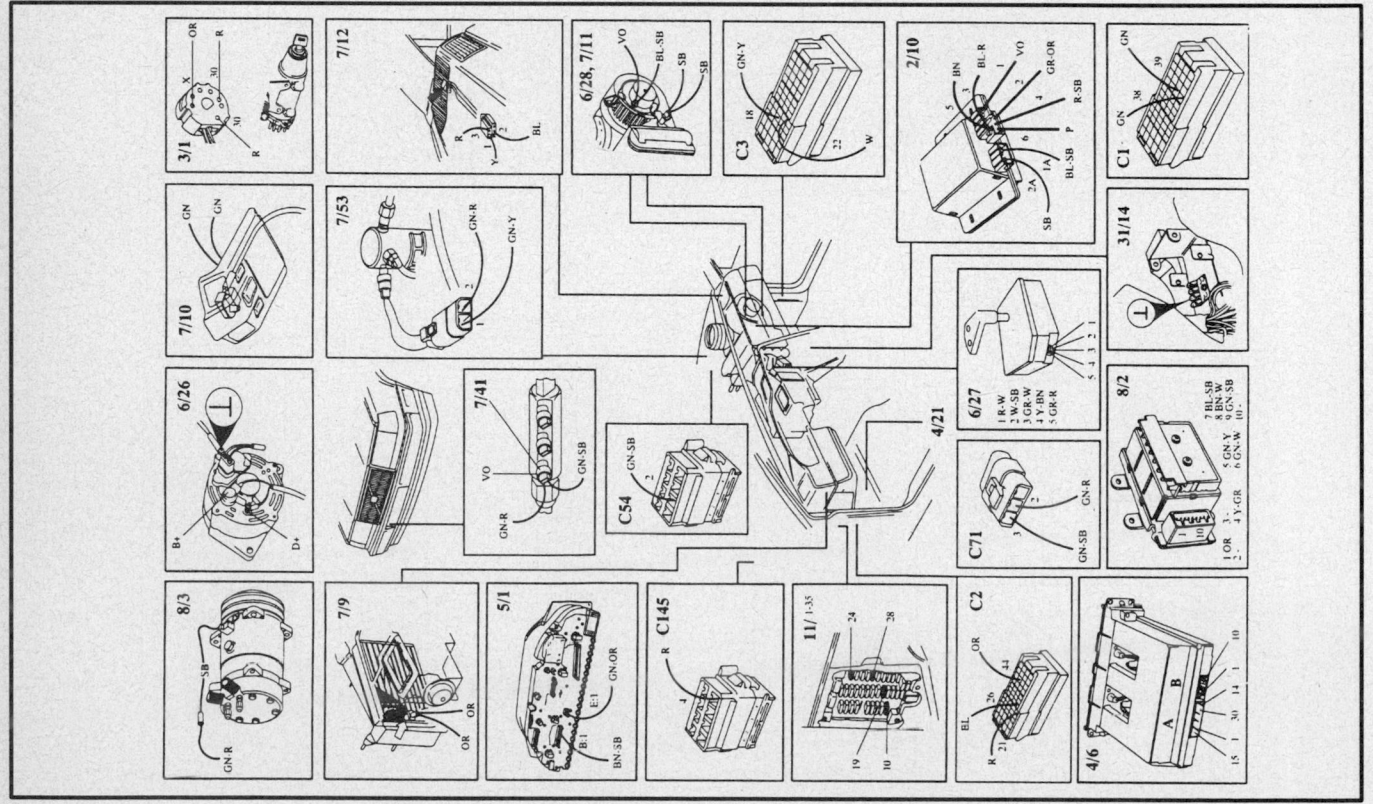

Electronic climate control system component locations—1993—94 960 Series with B230GT engine

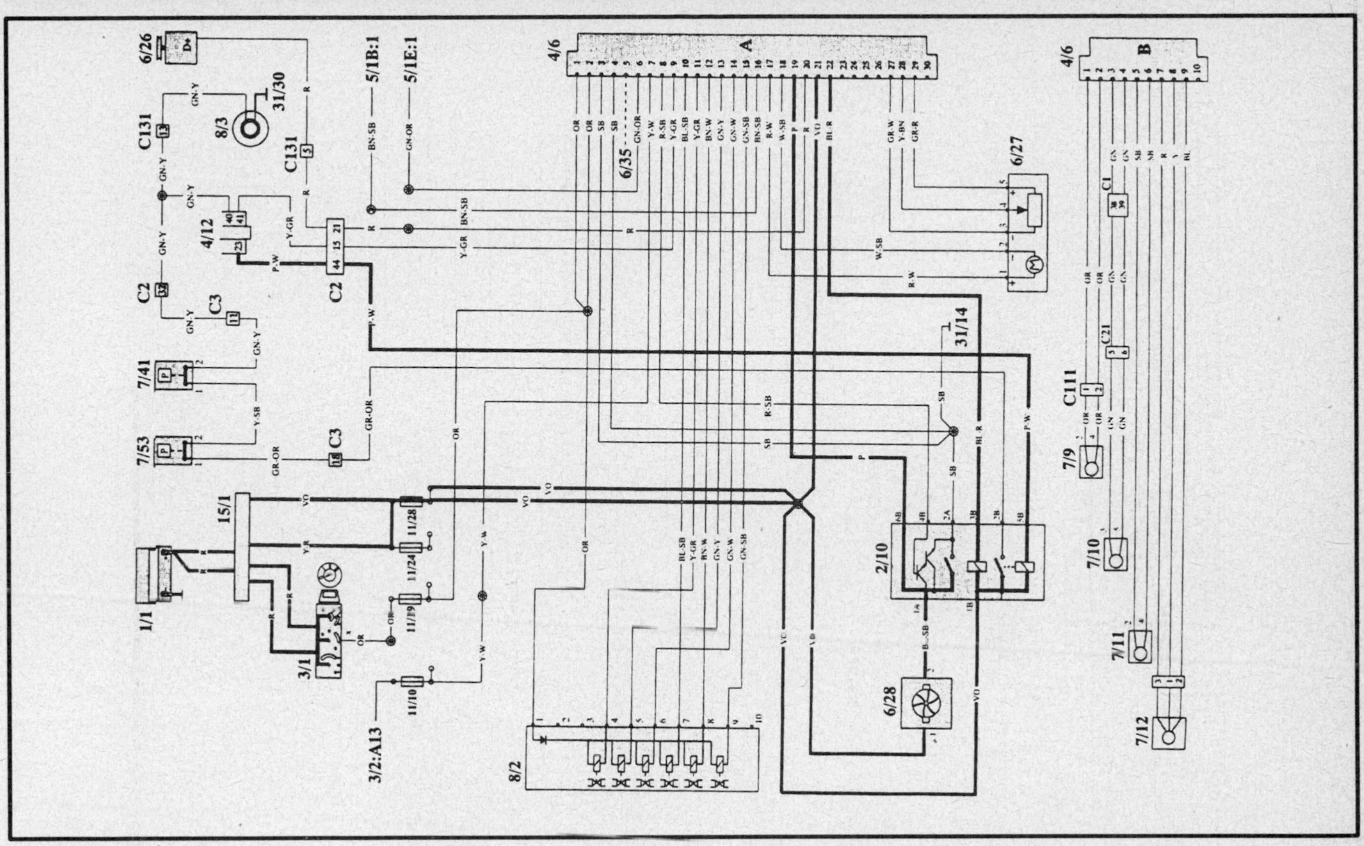

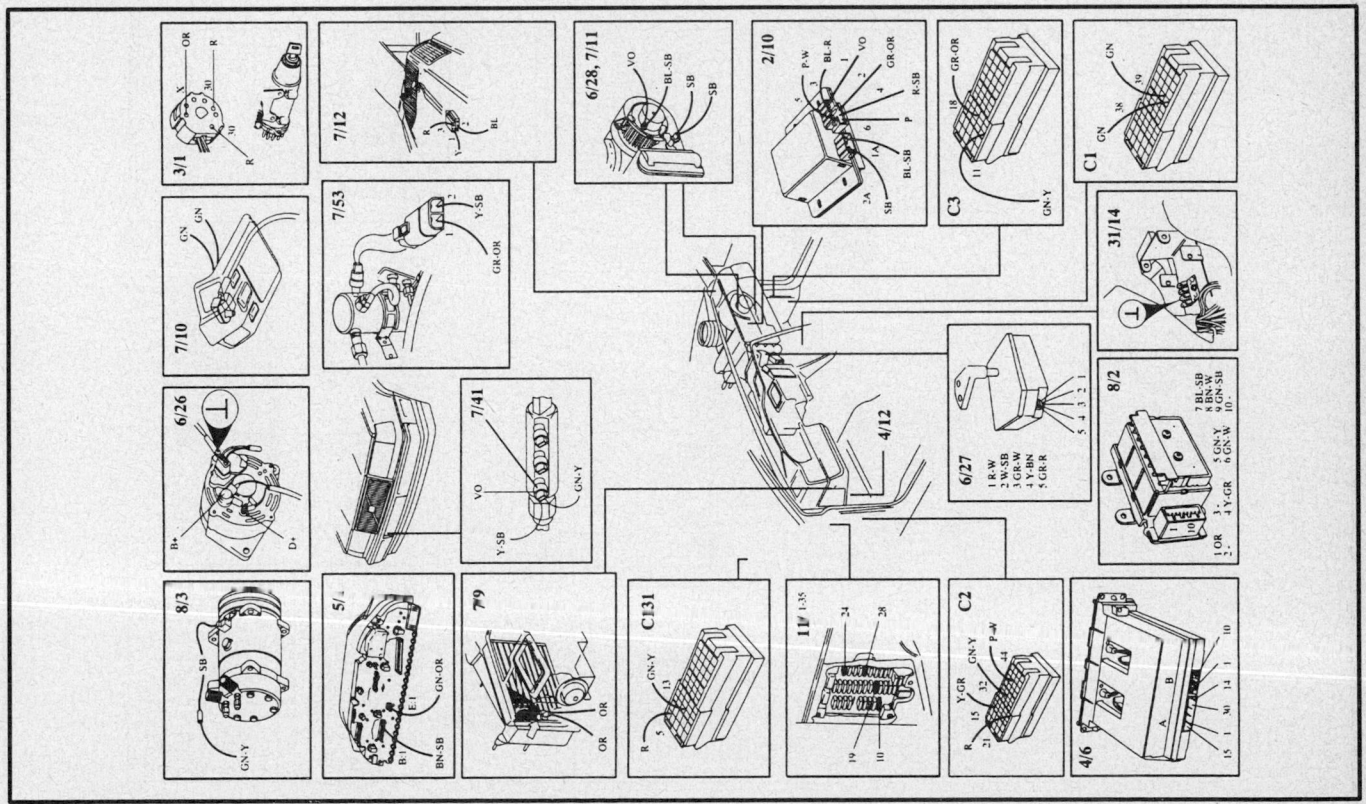

Electronic climate control system wiring schematic—1993–94 960 Series with B6304 engine

Electronic climate control system component locations—1993–94 960 Series with B6304 engine

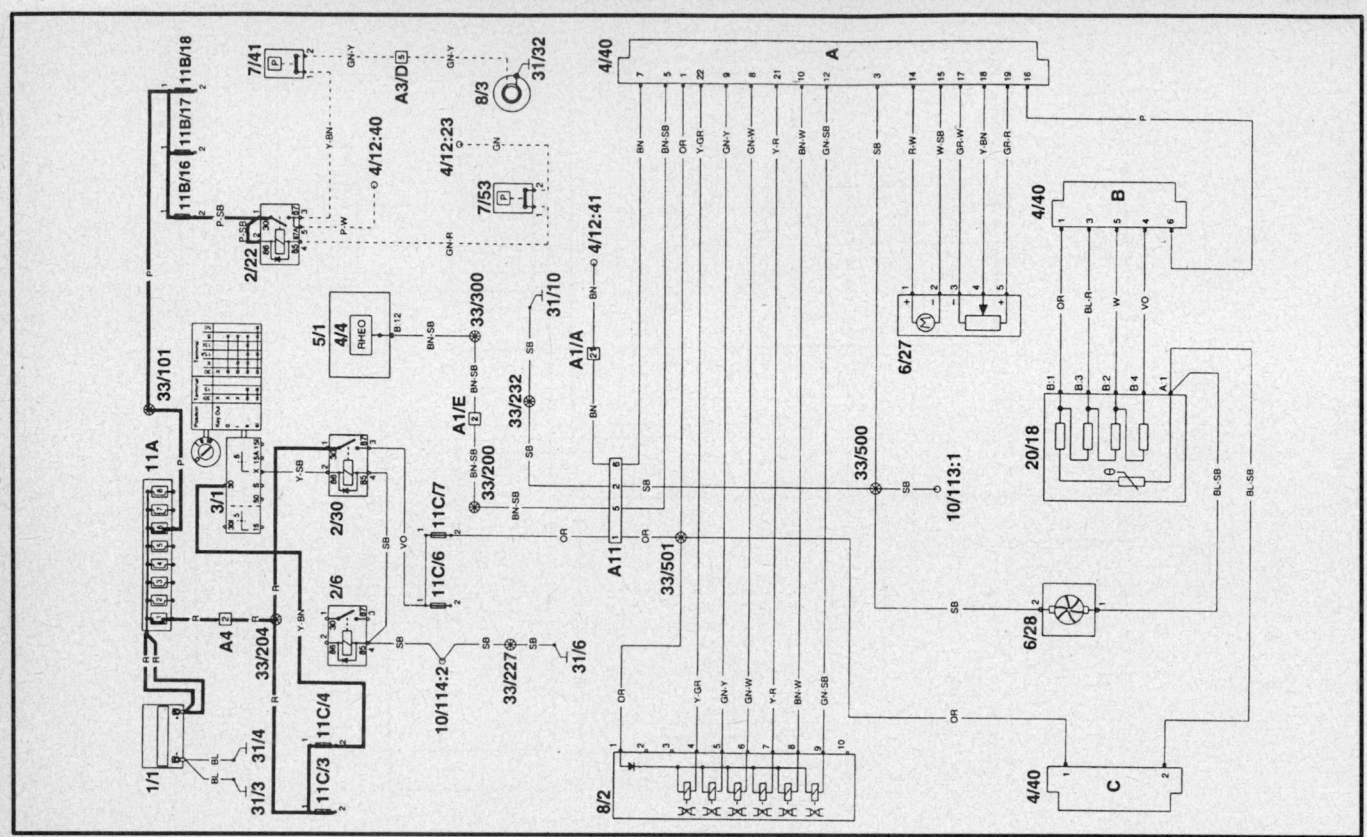

Manual climate control system wiring schematic—1995 960 Series

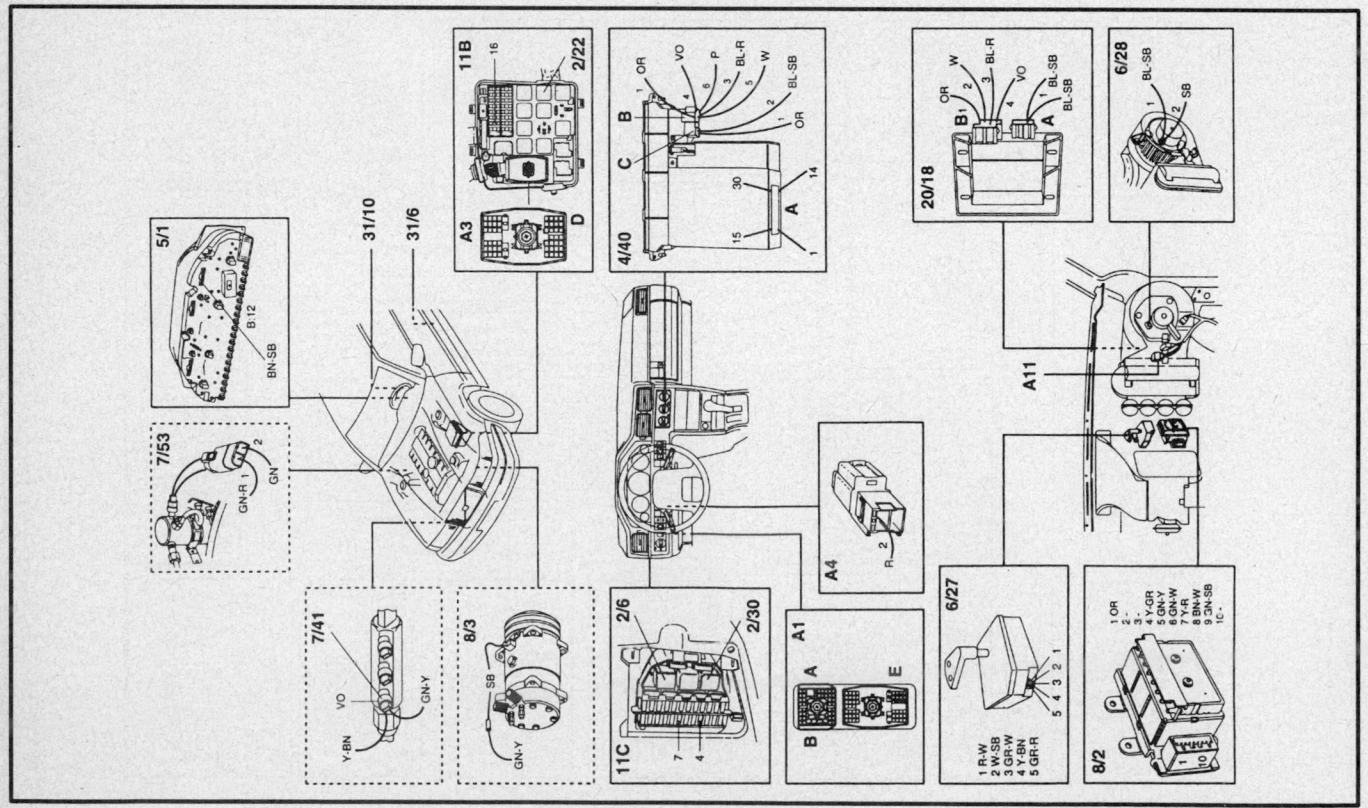

Manual climate control system component locations—1995 960 Series

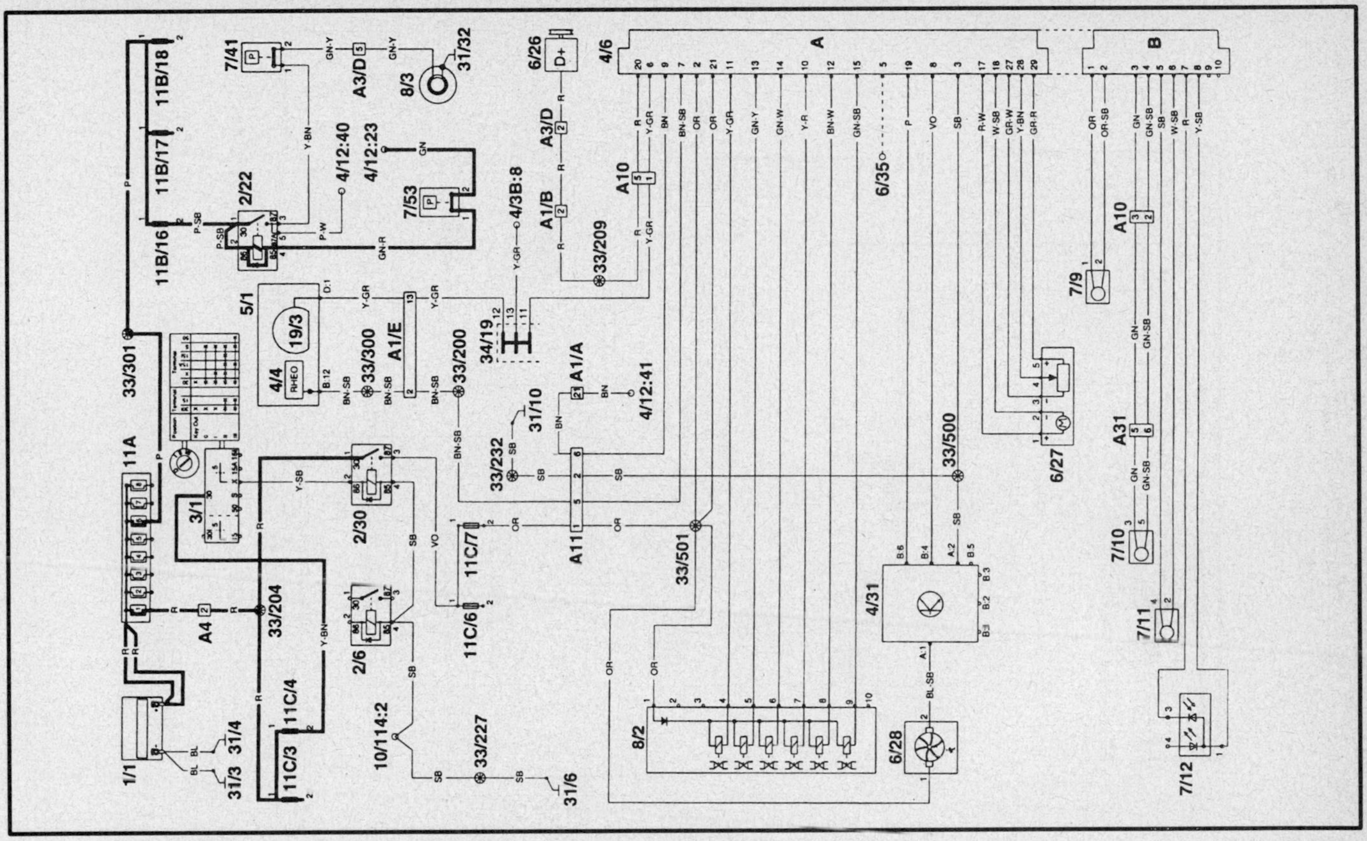

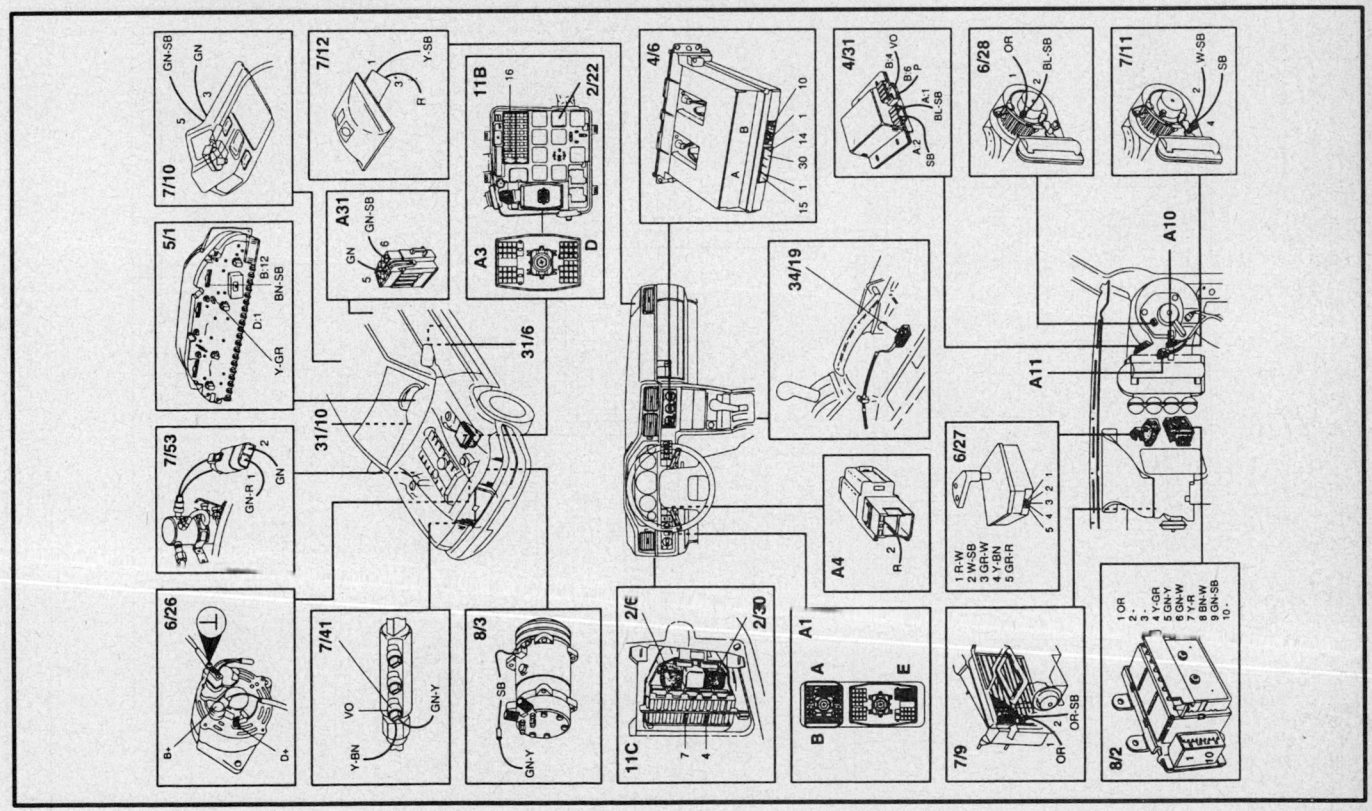

Electronic climate control system wiring schematic—1995 960 Series

Electronic climate control system component locations—1995 960 Series

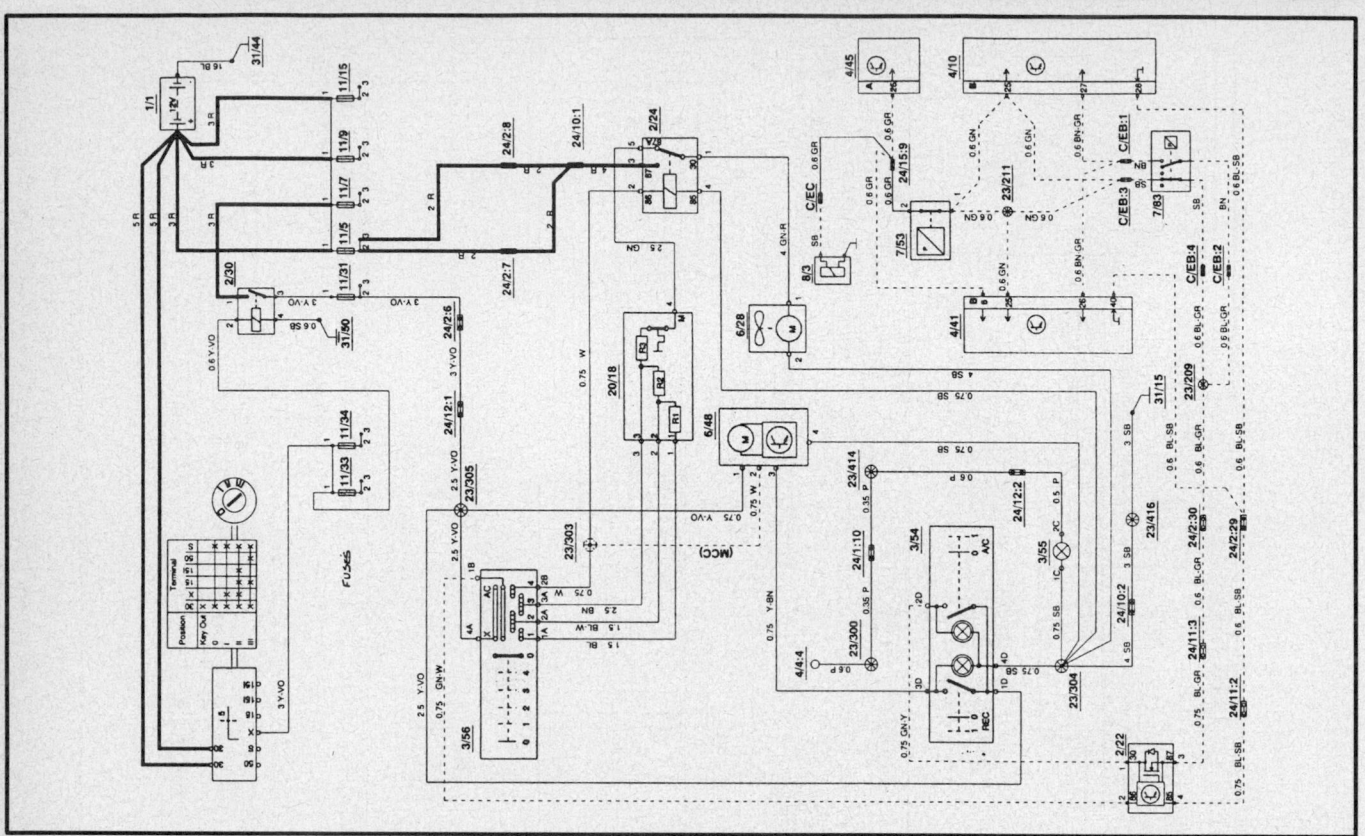

Manual air conditioning system wiring schematic—1993 850 Series

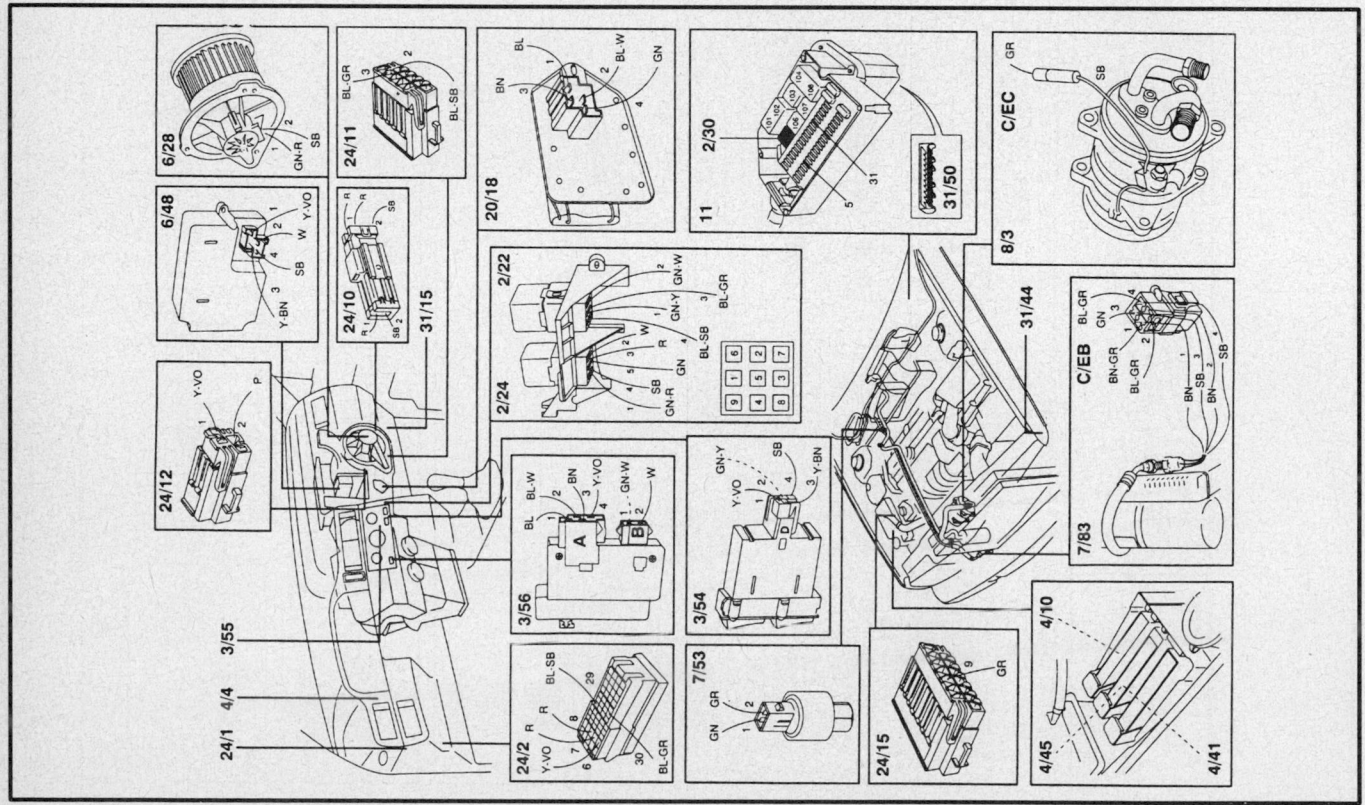

Manual air conditioning system component locations—1993 850 Series

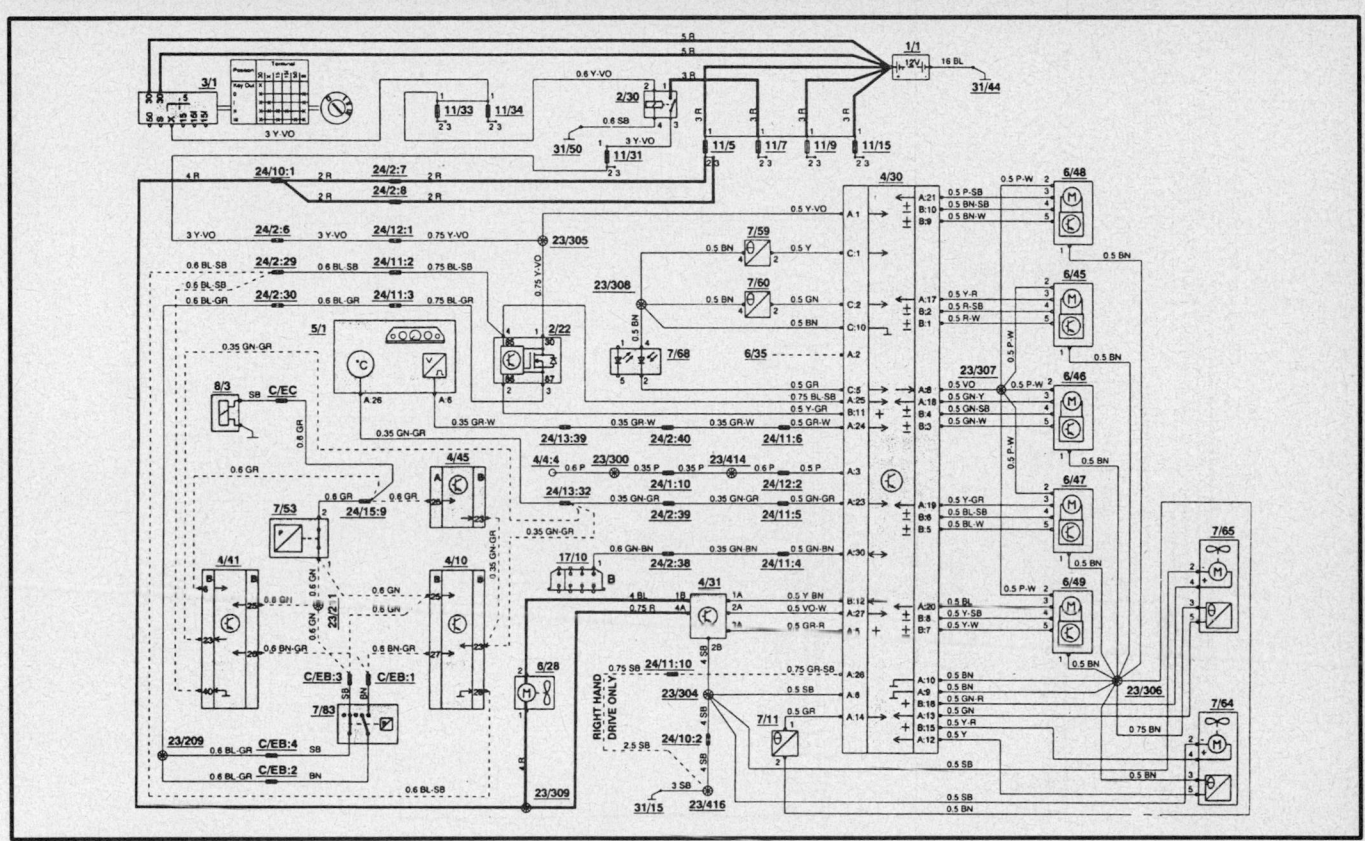

Electronic climate control system wiring schematic—1993 850 Series

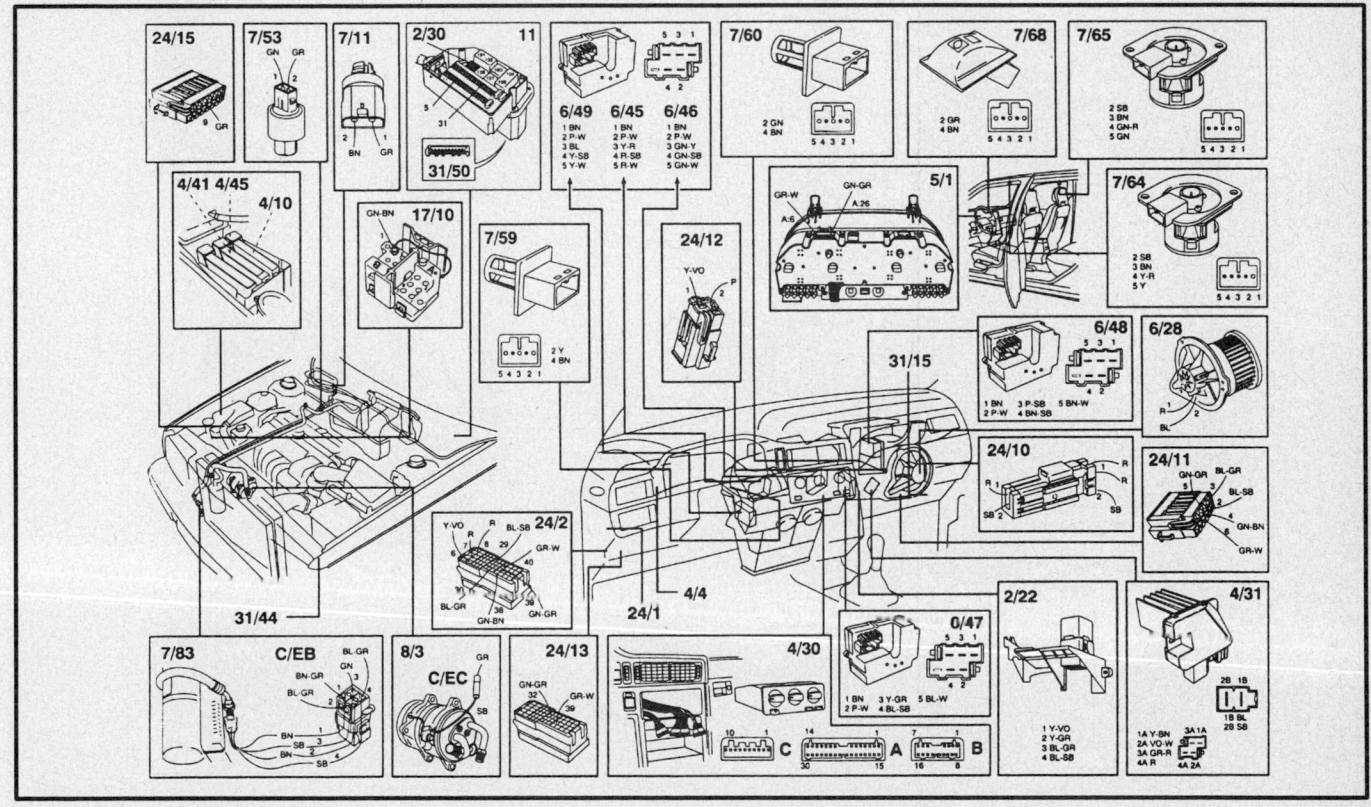

Electronic climate control system component locations—1993 850 Series

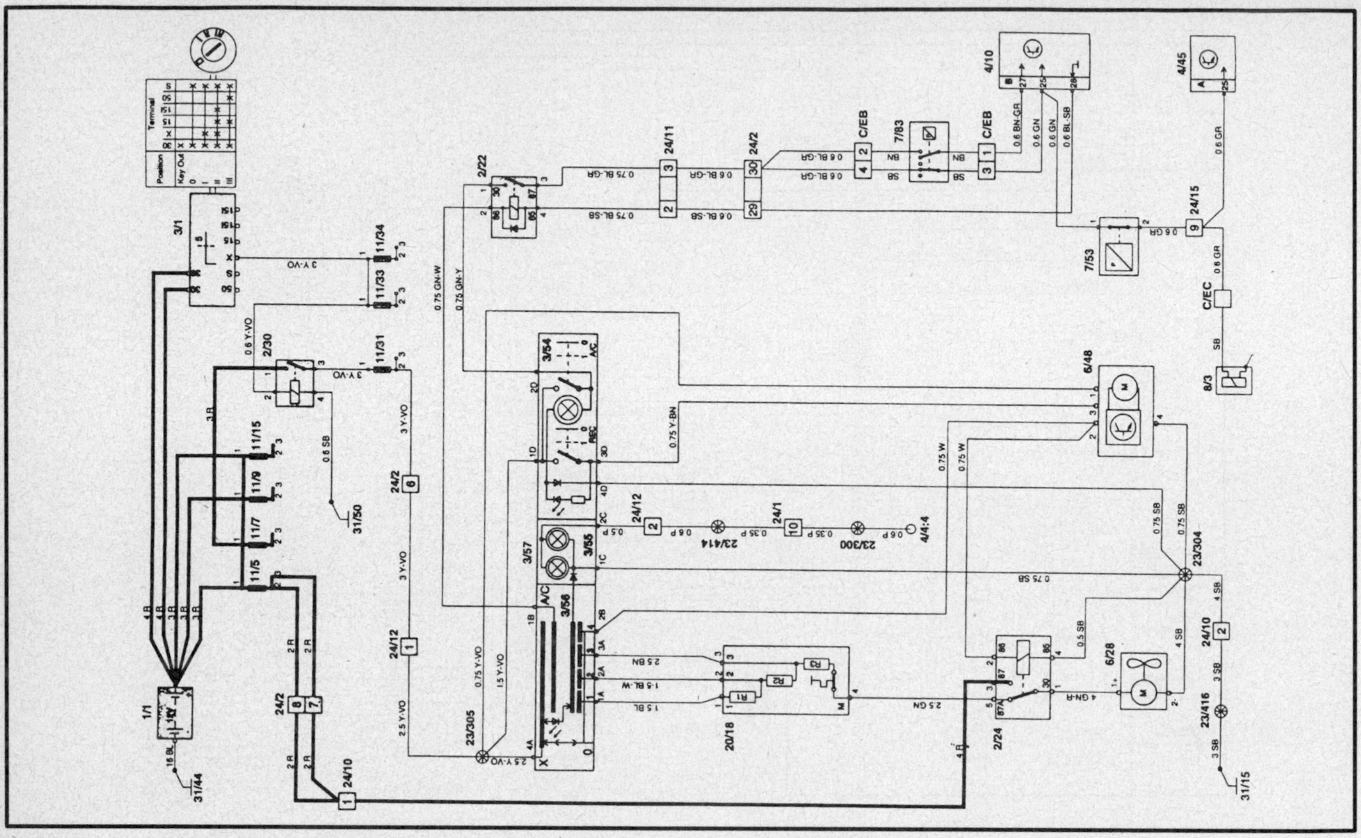

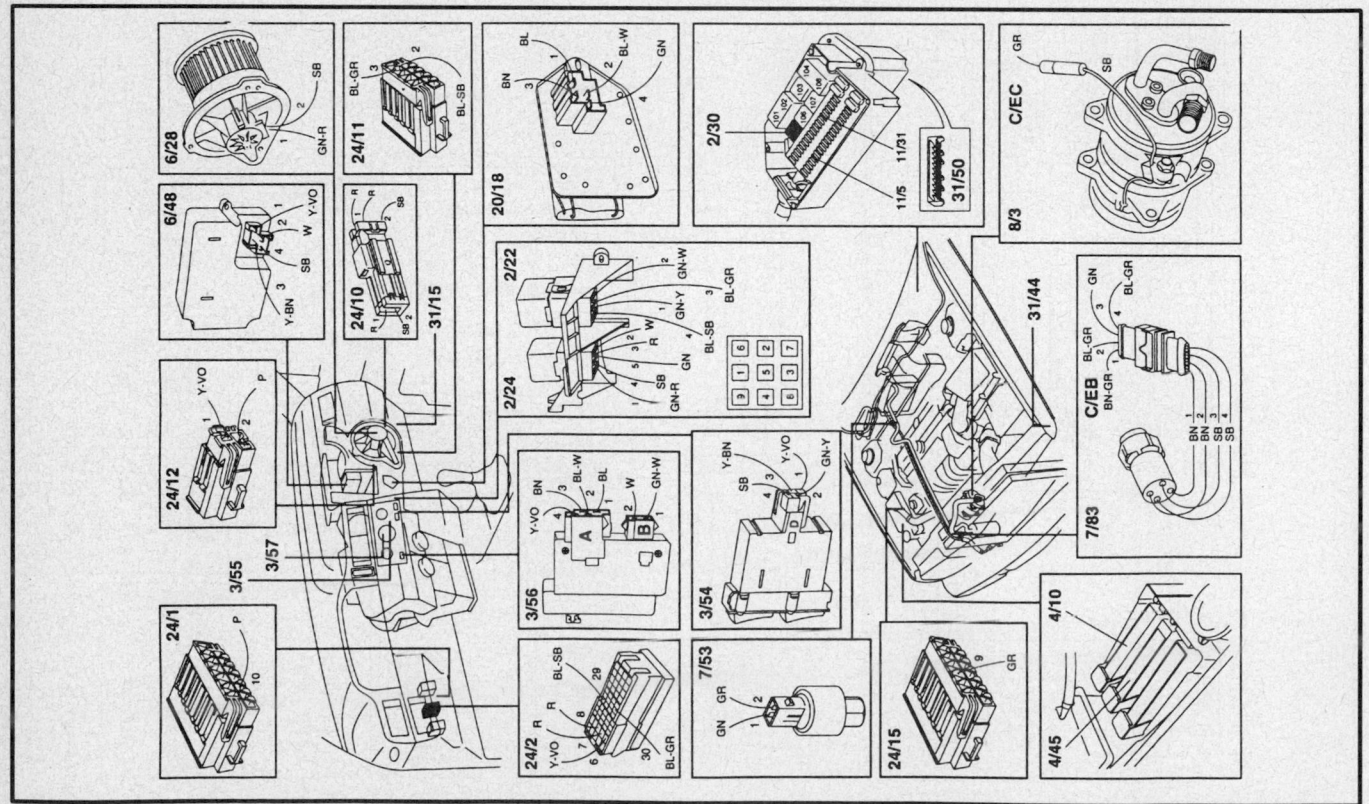

Manual air conditioning system wiring schematic—1994–95 850 Series with Bosch LH 3.2

Manual air conditioning system component locations—1994–95 850 Series with Bosch LH 3.2

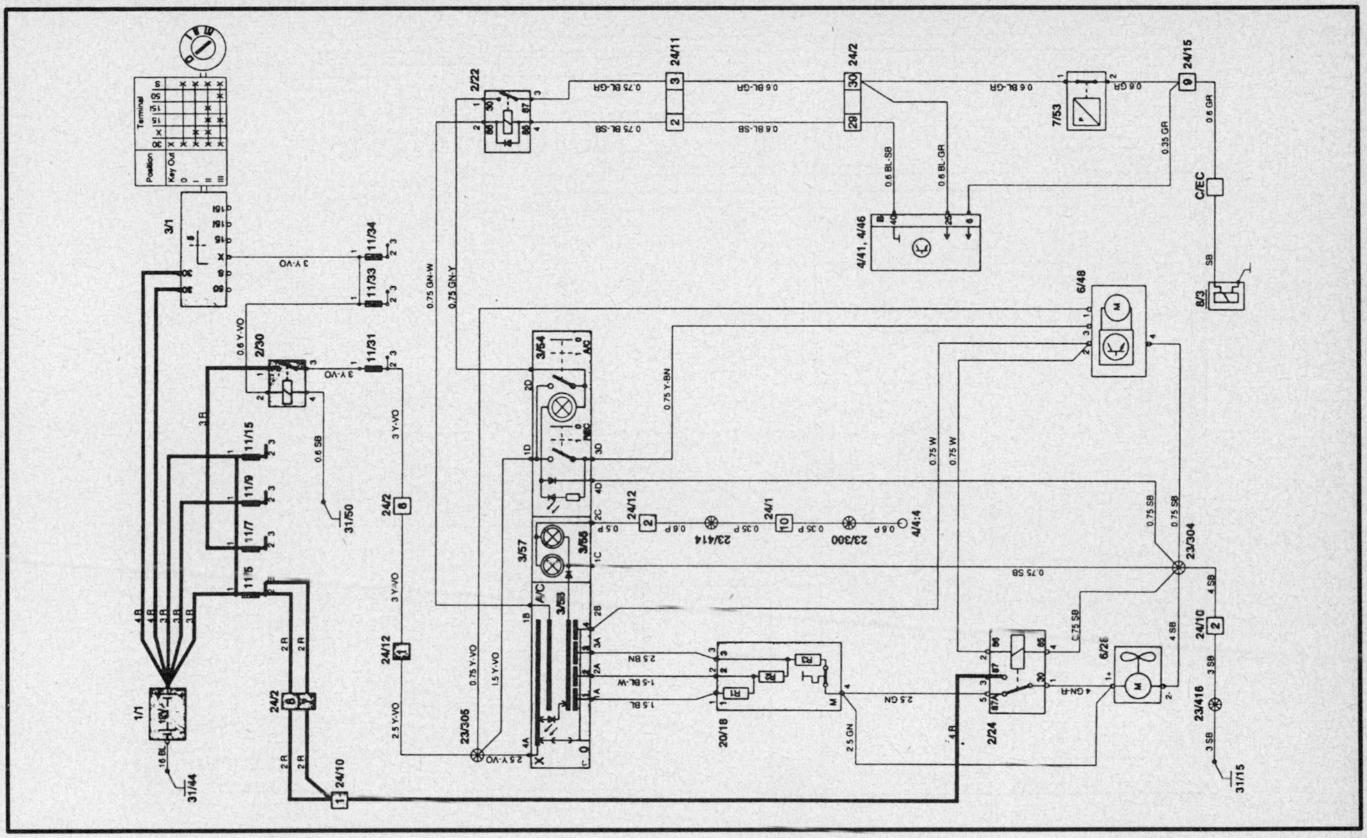

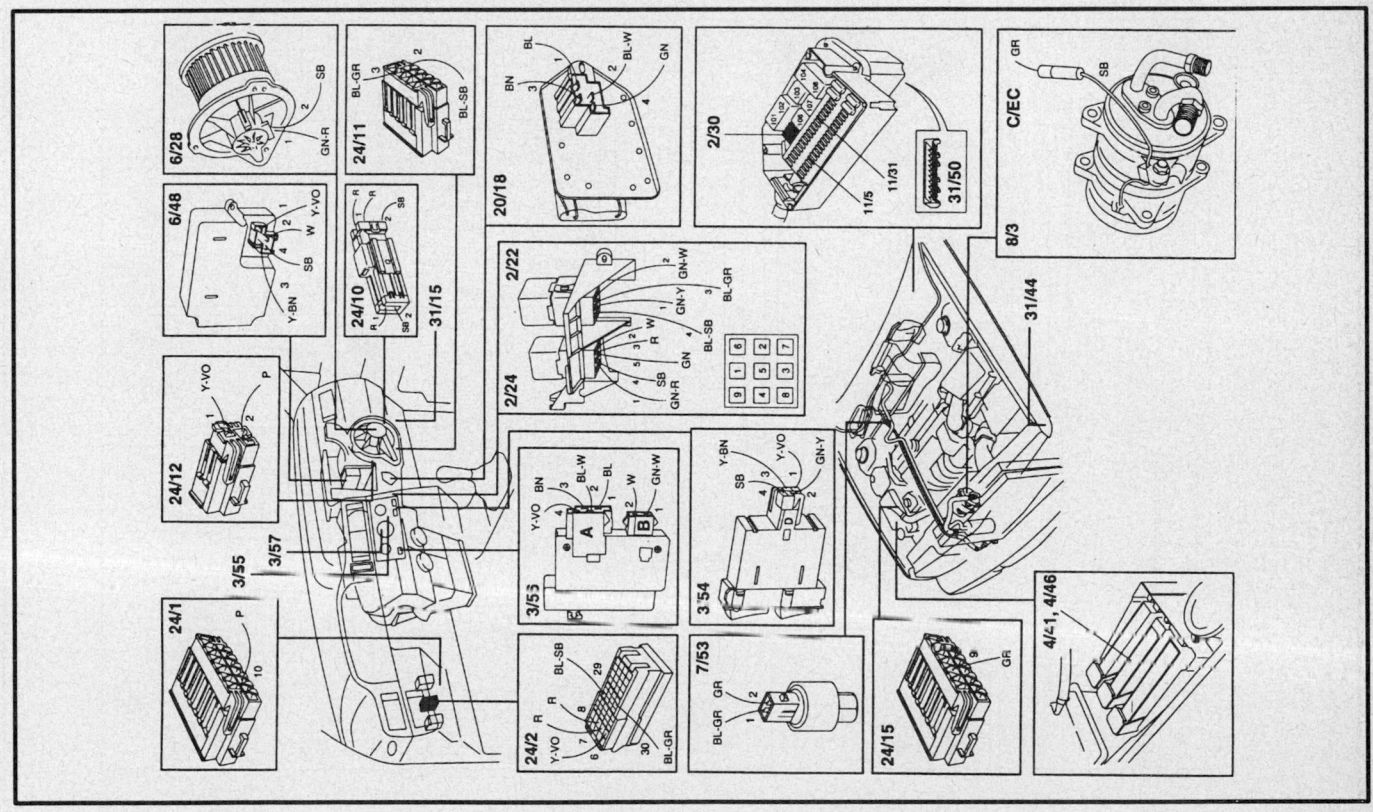

Manual air conditioning system wiring schematic—1994–95 850 Series with Fenix 5.2 or Motronic 4.3

Manual air conditioning system component locations—1994–95 850 Series with Fenix 5.2 or Motronic 4.3

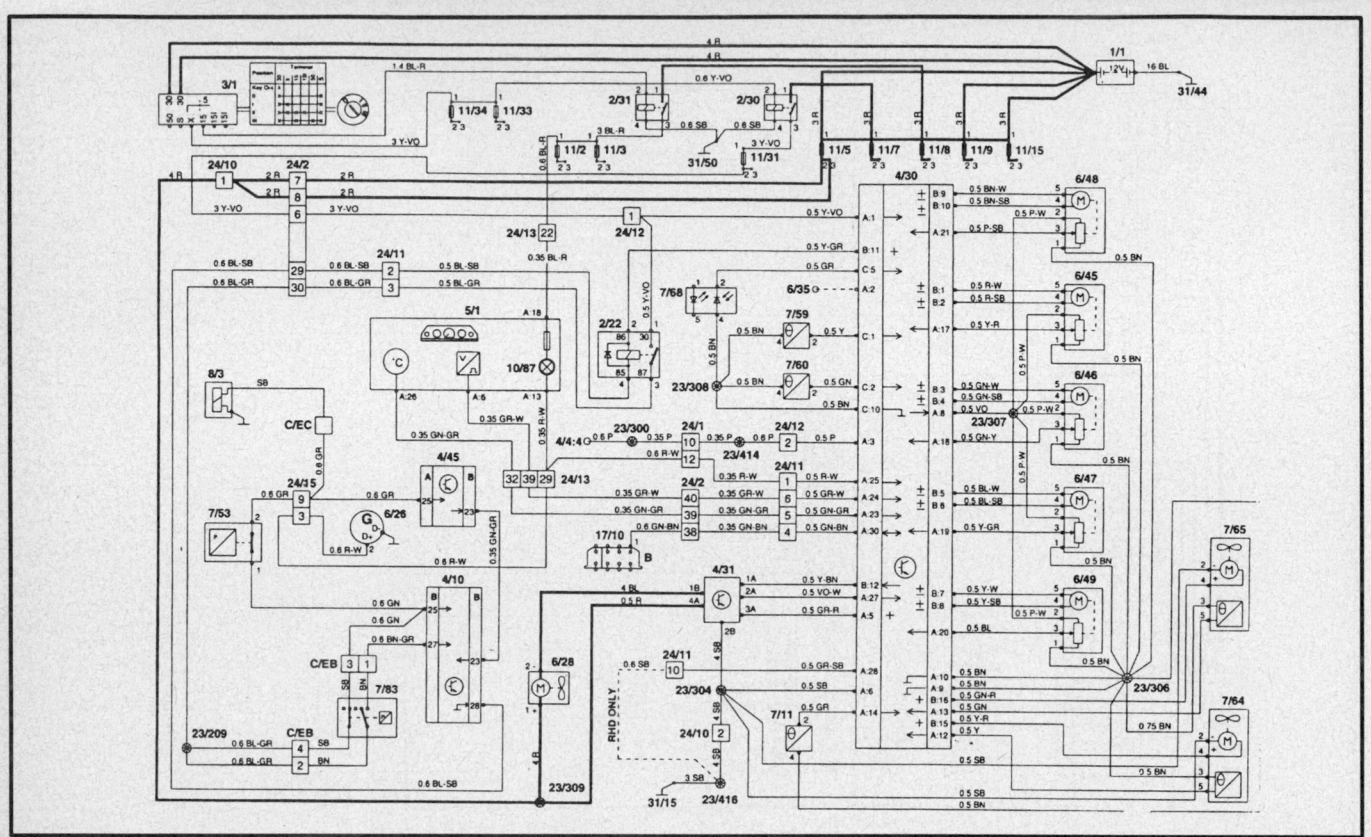

Electronic climate control system wiring schematic—1994–95 850 Series with Bosch LH 3.2

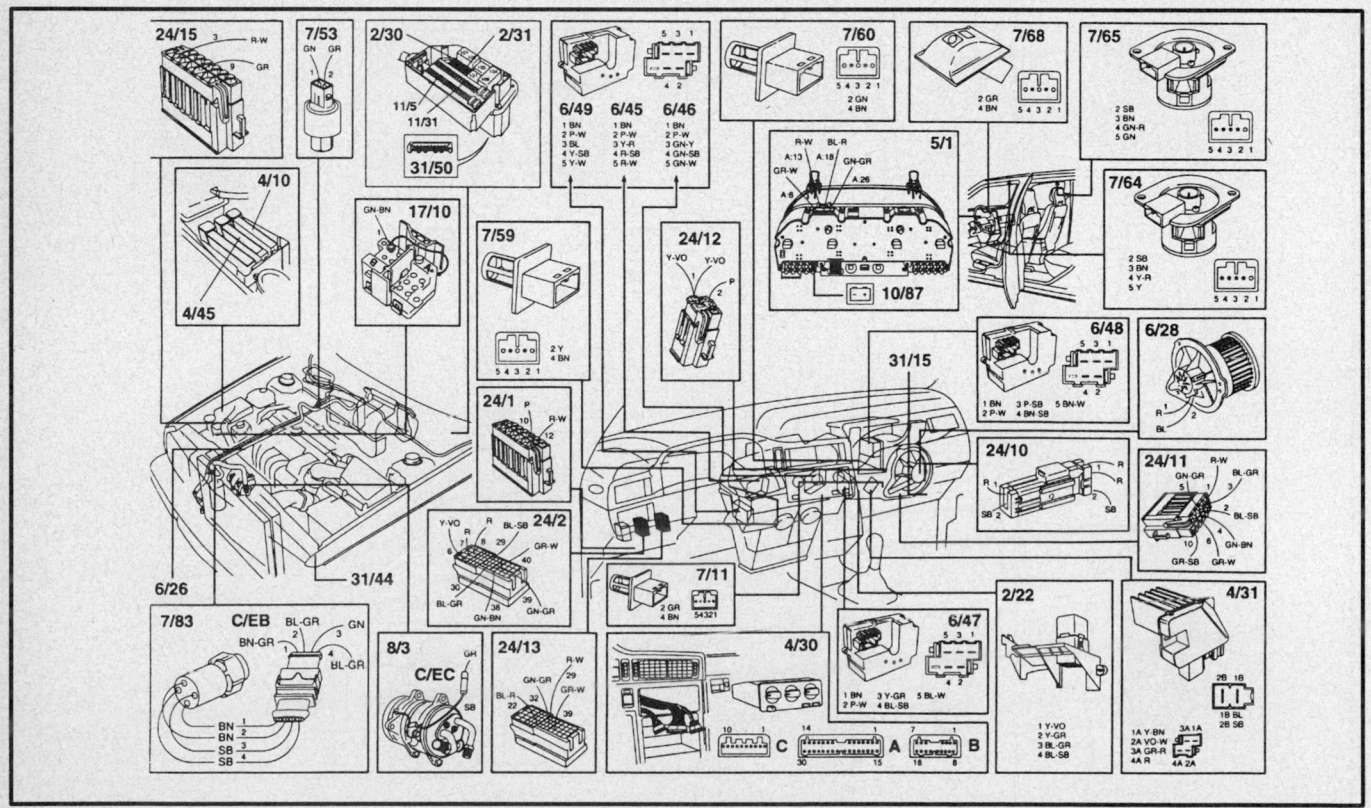

Electronic climate control system component locations—1994–95 850 Series with Bosch LH 3.2

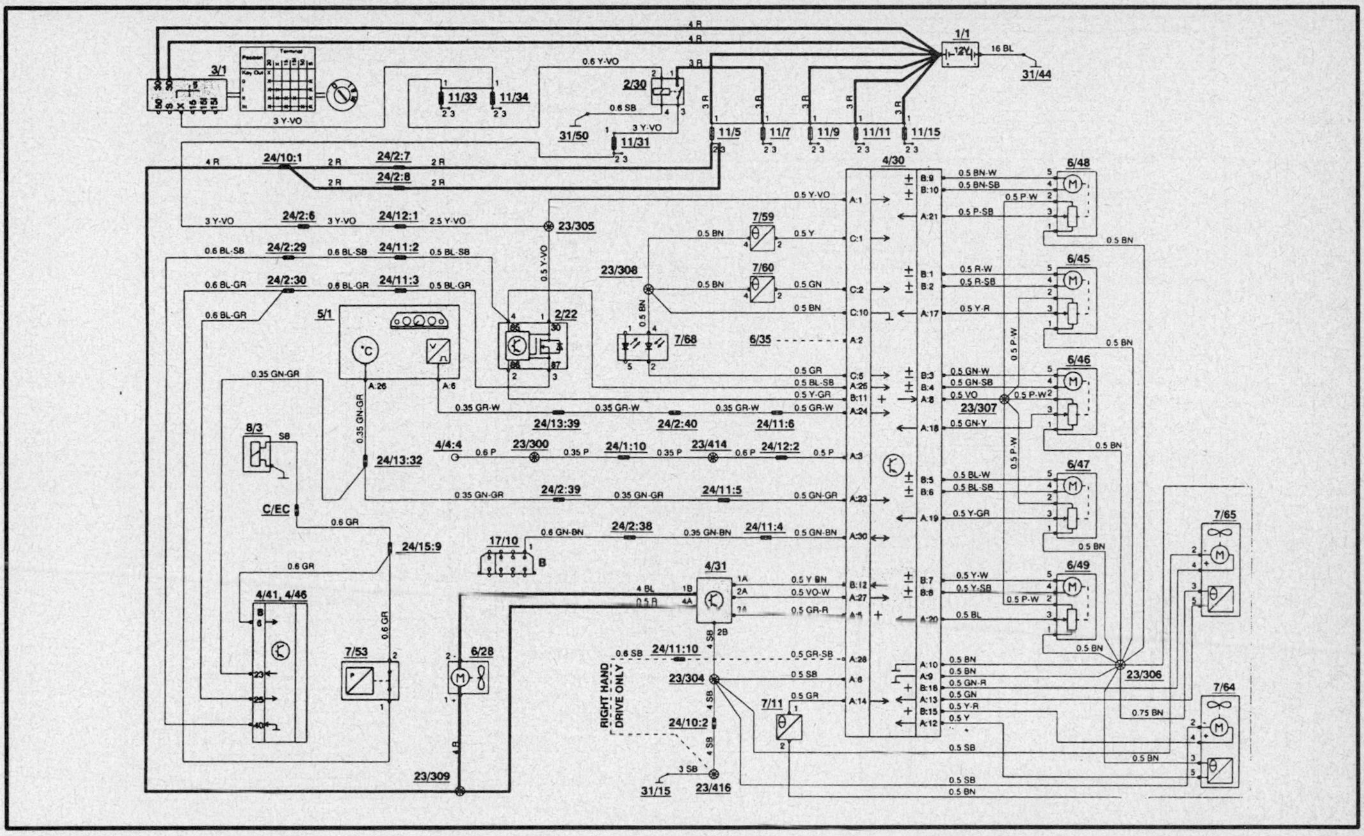

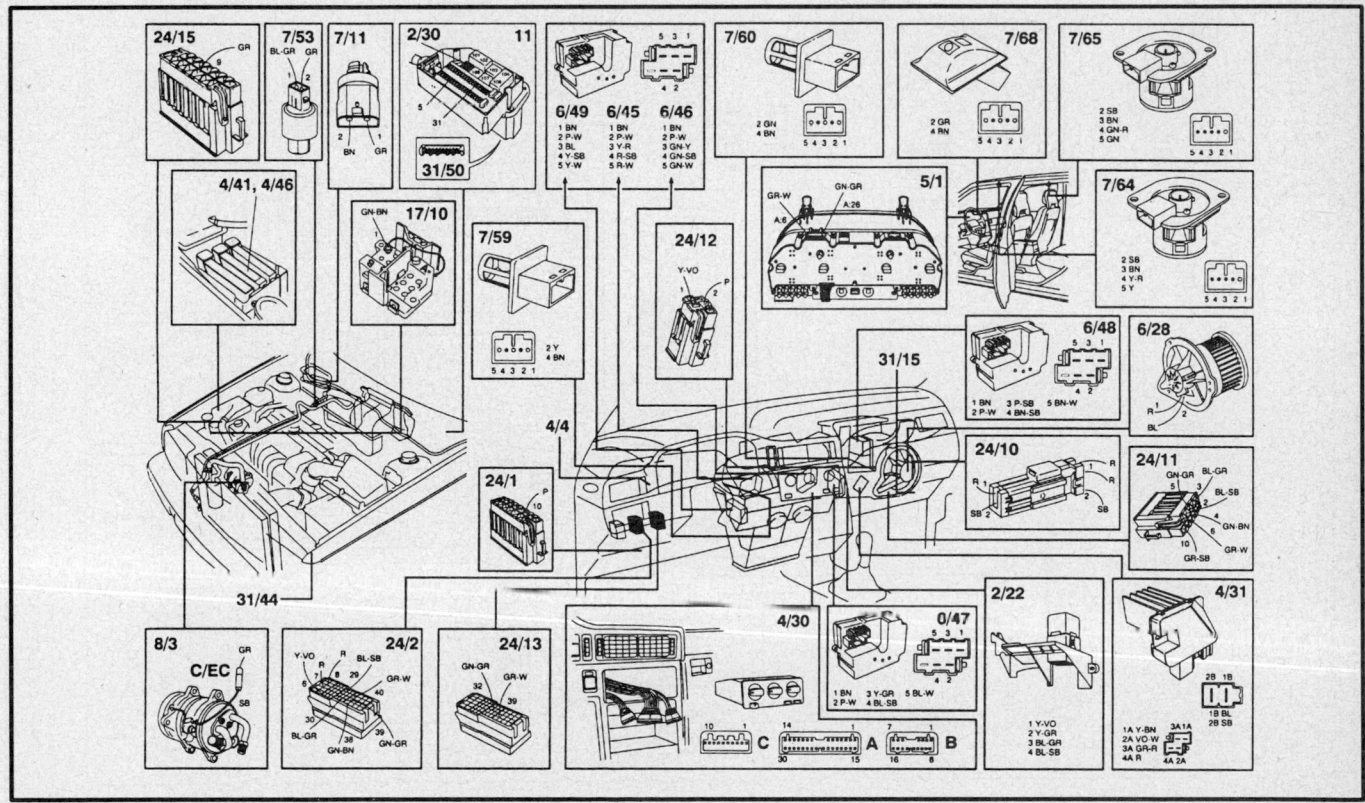

Electronic climate control system wiring schematic—1994 850 Series with Fenix 5.2 or Motronic 4.3

Electronic climate control system component locations—1994 850 Series with Fenix 5.2 or Motronic 4.3

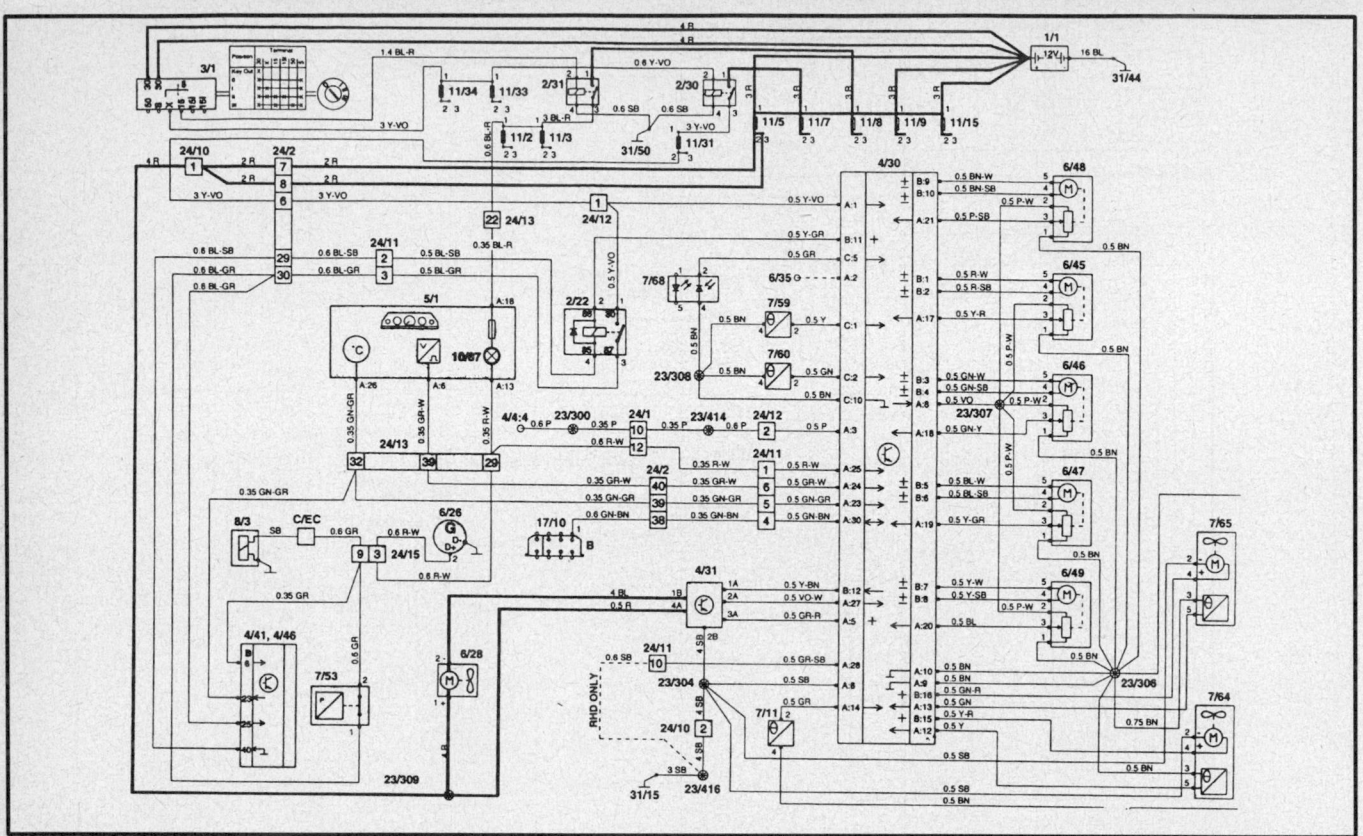

Electronic climate control system wiring schematic—1995 850 Series with Fenix 5.2 or Motronic 4.3

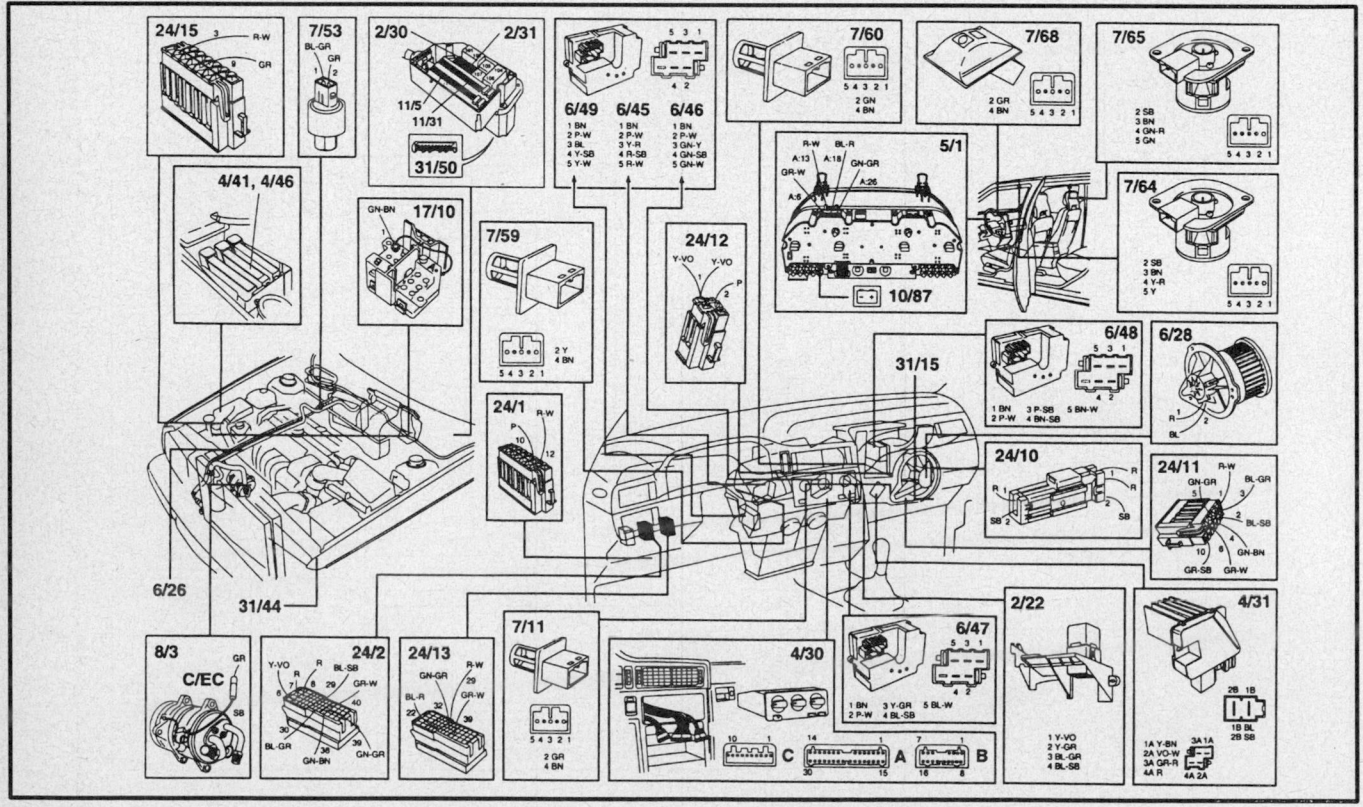

Electronic climate control system component locations—1995 850 Series with Fenix 5.2 or Motronic 4.3

ACURA
INTEGRA • LEGEND • VIGOR

LABOR
COOLING SYSTEM
LABOR

TESTING

(M) Pressure Test Cooling System

All models 3

SERVICE

(G) Belt, Drive, Renew

Alternator
1993-95 Integra 6
w/AC add .1
1993-95 Legend 4
1993-94 Vigor 6
Power Steering
1993 Integra 6
1994-95 Integra 4
1993-95 Legend 9
1993-94 Vigor 6
Air Conditioning
1993-95 Integra 4
1993-95 Legend 6
1993-94 Vigor 7

(G) Control Assy., Temperature, Renew

1993 Integra 1.9
1994-95 Integra 1.1

(G) Core, Heater, R&R or Renew

1993 Integra 7.2
1994-95 Integra 6.8
w/AC add 9
1993-95 Legend 6.2
1993-94 Vigor 6.2
Boil & Repair, add 1.2
Repair Core, add 9
Recore, add 1.2

(G) Expansion (Freeze) Plugs, Water Jacket, Renew

Add appropriate time to access plug.
All models, each 5

(G) Gauge, Temperature (Dash Unit), Renew

1993 Integra 1.7

Chilton Time

1994-95 Integra 7
1993-95 Legend 9
1993-94 Vigor 2.0

(G) Gauge, Temperature (Engine Unit), Renew

All models 6

(G) Hoses, By-Pass, Renew

All models, one 6

(G) Hoses, Heater, Renew

All models, each 7

(G) Hoses, Radiator, Renew

Includes: Drain and refill cooling system as required.
All models
upper .7
lower .7
both 1.1

(G) Motor, Heater Blower, Renew

1993 Integra 1.6
1994-95 Integra 3
w/AC add 9
1993-95 Legend 1.6
1993-94 Vigor 5.2

(G) Motor, Radiator Fan and/or Fan, Renew

1993-95 Integra 4
1993-95 Legend
one 1.4
both 2.1

(G) Pump and/or Gasket, Water, Renew

Includes: Drain and refill cooling system.
1993-95 Integra 4.2
w/AC add 2
1993-95 Legend 5.0
1993-94 Vigor 3.2

(G) Radiator Assy., R&R or Renew

1993-95 Integra 1.7
w/AT add 2

Chilton Time

w/AC add 2
1993-95 Legend 2.0
w/AT add 2
1993-94 Vigor 1.7
w/AT add 2
Boil & Repair, add 1.5
Rod Clean, add 1.9
Repair Core, add 1.3
Renew Tank, add 1.6
Renew Trans. Oil Cooler, add 1.9
Recore Radiator, add 1.7

(G) Relay, AC Condenser Cooling Fan, Renew

All models 3

(G) Resistor, Heater Blower Motor, Renew

1993 Integra 6
1994-95 Integra 3
1993-95 Legend 6
1993-94 Vigor 6

(G) Switch, Heater Blower Motor, Renew

1993-95 Integra 1.2
w/AC add 2
1993-95 Legend 8

(G) Switch, Radiator Fan Motor and/or O-Ring, Renew

1993-95 Integra 7
1993-95 Legend 7
1993-94 Vigor 4

(G) Thermostat, Coolant, Renew

1993-95 Integra 7
1993-95 Legend 1.1
1993-94 Vigor 4

(G) Winterize Cooling System

Includes: Run engine to check for leaks, tighten all hose connections. Test radiator and pressure cap, drain radiator and engine block. Add antifreeze and refill system.
All models 5

LABOR
AIR CONDITIONING
LABOR

Chilton Time

Note: If more than one item requires replacement where evacuation and discharging the system is already included in the operation, deduct 1.0 hour for each additional item from the time listed.

SERVICE AND TESTING

(G) Drain, Evacuate and Recharge System

All models 1.0

(G) Flush Refrigerant System, Complete

To be used in conjunction with component replacement which could contaminate system. Includes evacuate and recharge.
All models 1.3

Chilton Time

(G) Leak Check

Includes: Check all lines and connections.
All models 8

(G) Recover and/or Recycle AC Refrigerant

Add to evacuate and charge the AC system, as required.
All models 2

COMPONENTS

(G) Belt, Compressor Drive, Renew

1993-95 Integra 4
1993-95 Legend 6
1993-94 Vigor 7

Chilton Time

(G) Clutch Assy., Compressor, Renew

All models 2.8

(G) Coil, Evaporator, Renew

Includes: Evacuate and charge system.
1993 Integra 3.0
1994-95 Integra 2.4
1993-95 Legend 5.8

(G) Compressor Assy., Renew

Includes: Transfer parts as required. Evacuate and charge system.
All models 2.4

(G) Condenser Assy., Renew

Includes: Evacuate and charge system.
1993-95 Integra 2.0

LABOR

AIR CONDITIONING

LABOR

	Chilton Time
1993-95 Legend	2.2
1993-94 Vigor	3.1

(G) Control Assy., Temperature, Renew
| 1993 Integra | 1.9 |
| 1994-95 Integra | 1.1 |

(G) Hoses, AC, Renew
Includes: Evacuate and charge system.
1993-95 Integra suction or discharge	1.8
1993-95 Legend suction	3.2
discharge	2.9
1993-94 Vigor suction	2.7
discharge	.8

(G) Motor, Condenser Fan, Renew
1993-95 Integra	.4
1993-95 Legend	.8
1993-94 Vigor	.4

(G) Receiver/Drier Assy., Renew
Includes: Evacuate and charge system.
1993 Integra	1.9
1994-95 Integra	1.8
1993-95 Legend	2.3
1993-94 Vigor	1.6

(G) Relay, Condenser Fan Motor, Renew
| All models | .4 |

(G) Seal, Compressor Shaft, Renew
Includes: R&R compressor. Evacuate and charge system.
| All models | 2.8 |

(G) Switch, AC On/Off Control, Renew
| 1993-95 Integra | .5 |
| 1993-95 Legend | 1.2 |

(G) Valve, Expansion, Renew
Includes: Evacuate and charge system.
1993 Integra	2.6
1994-95 Integra	2.4
1993-95 Legend	3.8
1993-94 Vigor	6.2

(G) Thermostat, Renew
1993 Integra	2.8
1994-95 Integra	2.4
1993-95 Legend	1.9
1993-94 Vigor	1.6

AUDI
A6 • 80 • 90 • 100 • 200 • S4 • S6 • V8 • CABRIOLET

LABOR

COOLING SYSTEM

LABOR

TESTING
(M) Pressure Test Cooling System
| All models | .3 |

SERVICE
(G) Belt, Serpentine Drive, Adjust
| 1993-95 | .8 |

(G) Belt, Serpentine Drive, Renew
| 1993-95 | 1.2 |

(G) Core, Heater, R&R or Renew
1993-95 90/Quattro	5.8
1993-95 100/A6/Quattro	5.8
1993-95 S4/S6	5.8
1995 Cabriolet	5.8
Boil & Repair, add	1.2
Repair Core, add	.9
Recore, add	1.2

(G) Expansion (Freeze) Plugs, Water Jacket, Renew
Add appropriate time to access plug.
| All models, each | .5 |

(G) Fan, Viscous, Renew
| 1993-94 V8 Quattro | 1.1 |

(G) Gauge, Temperature (Dash Unit), Renew
1993-95 90/Quattro	2.2
1993-95 100/A6/Quattro	2.5
1993-94 V8 Quattro	2.5
1993-95 S4/S6	2.5
1995 Cabriolet	2.2

(G) Gauge, Temperature (Engine Unit), Renew
| 1993-95 | .6 |

(G) Hoses, Heater, Renew
| All models, one | .5 |

(G) Hoses, Radiator, Renew
Includes: Drain and refill cooling system as required.
1993-95 90/Quattro upper	.6
lower	.9
1993-95 100/A6/Quattro upper	.6
lower	.9
1993-94 V8 Quattro one	.5
all	2.0
1993-95 S4/S6 upper	.6
lower	.9
1995 Cabriolet upper	.6
lower	.9

(G) Motor, Electric Cooling Fan, Renew
| 1993-95 w/ABS | 2.0 |

(G) Motor, Heater Blower, Renew
1993-95 90/Quattro	1.5
1993-95 100/A6/Quattro	1.2
1993-94 V8 Quattro	4.5
1993-95 S4/S6	1.2
1995 Cabriolet	1.5

(G) Pump, Secondary Coolant, Renew
| 1993-95 Turbo | .6 |

(G) Pump and/or Gasket, Water, Renew
Includes: Drain and refill cooling system.
1993-95 100/A6/Quattro	3.0
1993-94 V8 Quattro	6.3
1993-95 S4/S6	4.0
1995 Cabriolet	3.0

(G) Radiator Assy., R&R or Renew
| 1993-95 90/Quattro | 2.7 |
| 1993-95 100/A6/Quattro | 3.0 |

1993-94 V8 Quattro	2.7
1993-95 S4/S6	2.7
1995 Cabriolet	3.0
Boil & Repair, add	1.5
Rod Clean, add	1.9
Repair Core, add	1.3
Renew Tank, add	1.6
Renew Trans. Oil Cooler, add	1.9
Recore Radiator, add	1.7

(G) Relay, Radiator Fan Motor, Renew
| 1993-95 | .4 |

(G) Resistor, Fan Motor, Renew
1993-95 5 cyl.	.6
V6	.6
V8	.8

(G) Resistor, Heater Blower Motor, Renew
1993-95 90/Quattro	1.0
1993-95 100/A6/Quattro	.8
1993-95 S4/S6	.8
1995 Cabriolet	1.0

(G) Switch, Electric Fan Thermo, Renew
| All models | .3 |

(G) Thermostat, Coolant, Renew
1993-95 90/Quattro	1.0
1993-95 100/A6/Quattro	1.0
1993-94 V8 Quattro	1.4
1993-95 S4/S6	1.0
1995 Cabriolet	1.0

(G) Winterize Cooling System
Includes: Run engine to check for leaks, tighten all hose connections. Test radiator and pressure cap, drain radiator and engine block. Add antifreeze and refill system.
| All models | .5 |

LABOR

AIR CONDITIONING

LABOR

Chilton Time

Note: If more than one item requires replacement where evacuation and discharging the system is already included in the operation, deduct 1.0 hour for each additional item from the time listed.

SERVICE AND TESTING

(G) Drain, Evacuate and Recharge System

All models **1.5**
Recover refrigerant, add . . . . **.2**

(G) Flush Refrigerant System, Complete

To be used in conjunction with component replacement which could contaminate system. Includes evacuate and recharge.

All models **1.3**
Recover refrigerant, add . . . . **.2**

(G) Leak Check

Includes: Check all lines and connections.

All models . . . . **.8**

(G) Recover and/or Recycle AC Refrigerant

Add to evacuate and charge the AC system, as required.

All models, add . . . . **.2**

COMPONENTS

(G) Accumulator Assy., Renew

Includes: Evacuate and charge system.

1993-95 . . . . **2.5**
Recover refrigerant, add . . . . **.2**

Chilton Time

(G) Belt, Compressor Drive, Renew

All models
Serpentine belt **1.2**

(G) Coil, Evaporator, Renew

Includes: Evacuate and charge system.

1993-95 90/Quattro **3.6**
1993-95 100/A6/Quattro **3.6**
1993-94 V8 Quattro **3.6**
1993-95 S4/S6 . . . . **3.6**
1995 Cabriolet **3.6**
Renew expansion valve, add . . . . **.2**
Recover refrigerant, add . . . . **.2**

(G) Compressor Assy., Renew

Includes: Transfer parts as required. Evacuate and charge system.

1993-95 90/Quattro **2.9**
1993-95 100/A6/Quattro **2.9**
1993-94 V8 Quattro **3.7**
1993-95 S4/S6 . . . . **3.1**
Renew clutch assy. add . . . . **.3**
Recover refrigerant, add . . . . **.2**

(G) Condenser Assy., Renew

Includes: Evacuate and charge system.

1993-95 90/Quattro **3.4**
1993-95 100/A6/Quattro **3.4**
1993-94 V8 Quattro **3.0**
1993-95 S4/S6 . . . . **3.4**
1995 Cabriolet **3.4**
Recover refrigerant, add . . . . **.2**

(G) Hoses, AC, Renew

Includes: Evacuate and charge system.

1993-95 90/Quattro, each **2.4**

Chilton Time

1993-95 100/A6/Quattro
each **2.4**
1993-94 V8 Quattro, each **2.4**
1993-95 S4/S6, each **2.4**
1995 Cabriolet, each **2.4**
Recover refrigerant, add . . . . **.2**

(G) Receiver/Drier Assy., Renew

Includes: Evacuate and charge system.

All models **1.6**
Recover refrigerant, add . . . . **.2**

(G) Seal, Compressor Shaft, Renew

Includes: R&R compressor. Evacuate and charge system.

1993-95 90/Quattro **3.4**
1993-95 100/A6/Quattro **3.4**
1993-94 V8 Quattro **4.0**
1993-95 S4/S6 . . . . **3.4**
1995 Cabriolet **3.4**
Recover refrigerant, add . . . . **.2**

(G) Servo Motor, Electronic, Renew

1993-95 100/A6/Quattro **1.8**
1993-95 S4/S6 . . . . **1.8**

(G) Switch, High Pressure Cut-Off, Renew

1993-95 . . . . **1.6**
Add time to evacuate & charge
AC system as needed
Recover refrigerant, add . . . . **.2**

(G) Switch, Thermostatic Control, Renew

1993-95 100/A6/Quattro . . . . **.6**
1993-94 V8 Quattro . . . . **.6**

BMW
3 SERIES • 5 SERIES • 7 SERIES • 8 SERIES

LABOR

COOLING SYSTEM

LABOR

Chilton Time

TESTING

(M) Pressure Test Cooling System

All models . . . . **.3**

SERVICE

(G) Belt, Drive, Renew

1994-95 540i
one **1.0**
each adtnl. **.5**
1994-95 740i, iL
one **1.0**
each adtnl. **.5**
1993-94 750iL
one **1.0**
each adtnl. **.5**
1994-95 840Ci
one **1.0**
each adtnl. **.5**

(G) Belt, Serpentine Drive, Renew

1993-94 750iL **1.0**

(G) Belt, Water Pump Drive, Renew

1993-95 850i, Ci, CSi **1.5**

Chilton Time

(G) Blades, Fan or Clutch Assy., Renew

All models . . . . **.5**

(G) Control Assy., Heater, Renew

1993-95 318i, is, iC **1.5**
1993-95 325i, 325is **1.5**
1993-95 525i . . . . **.7**
1993 535i, 535is **1.5**
1994-95 540i . . . . **.8**
1994-95 740i, iL **1.4**
1993-94 750iL **2.2**
1994-95 840Ci **1.1**
1993-95 850i, Ci, CSi **1.5**

(G) Core, Heater, R&R or Renew

1993-95 318i, is, iC
wo/AC **4.0**
w/AC **5.5**
1993-95 325i, 325is **5.0**
1993-95 525i **9.0**
1993 535i, 535is **6.5**
1994-95 540i **5.5**
1994-95 740i, iL **6.0**
1993-94 750iL **5.0**
1994-95 840Ci **8.0**

Chilton Time

1993-95 850i, Ci, CSi **7.0**
w/air bags add . . . . **.5**
Boil & Repair, add **1.2**
Repair Core, add . . . . **.9**
Recore, add **1.2**

(G) Coupling, Fan, Renew

1993-95 318i, is, iC . . . . **.5**
1993-95 325i, 325is . . . . **.5**
1993-95 525i . . . . **.5**
1993 535i, 535is . . . . **.5**
1994-95 540i . . . . **.5**
1994-95 740i, iL . . . . **.5**
1993-94 750iL . . . . **.5**
1994-95 840Ci . . . . **.5**
1993-95 850i, Ci, CSi . . . . **.5**
w/AT add . . . . **.3**

(G) Expansion (Freeze) Plugs, Water Jacket, Renew

Add appropriate time to access plug.

All models, each . . . . **.5**

(G) Fan, Auxiliary Cooling Assy., Renew

1993-95 318i, is, iC **2.0**

LABOR

COOLING SYSTEM

LABOR

	Chilton Time
1993-95 325i, 325is	2.0
1993-95 525i	2.0
1993 535i, 535is	2.0
1994-95 540i	1.1
1994-95 740i, iL	1.1
1993-94 750iL	2.0
1994-95 840Ci	1.1
1993-95 850i, Ci, CSi	

(G) Gauge, Temperature (Dash Unit), Renew

	Chilton Time
1993-95 318i, is, iC	1.0
1993-95 525i	1.0
1994-95 540i	1.4
1994-95 740i, iL	1.4
1993-94 750iL	1.0
1994-95 840Ci	1.4
1993-95 850i, Ci, CSi	1.5
w/air bags add	.5

(G) Gauge, Temperature (Engine Unit), Renew

	Chilton Time
1993-95 318i, is, iC	.5
1993-95 325i, 325is	.5
1993-95 525i	.5
1993 535i, 535is	.6
1994-95 540i	.6
1994-95 740i, iL	.5
1993-94 750iL	.6
1994-95 840Ci	1.0
1993-95 850i, Ci, CSi	1.0

(G) Hoses, Heater, Renew

	Chilton Time
All models	2.0

(G) Hoses, Radiator, Renew

Includes: Drain and refill cooling system as required.

	Chilton Time
Upper	
All models	.5
Lower	
1993-95 318i, is, iC	.7
1993-95 325i, 325is	.7
1993-95 525i	.7
1993 535i, 535is	.7

	Chilton Time
1994-95 540i	1.2
1994-95 740i, iL	1.2
1993-94 750iL	1.0
1994-95 840Ci	1.2
1993-95 850i, Ci, CSi	1.0

(G) Motor, Heater Blower, Renew

	Chilton Time
1993-95 318i, is, iC	1.0
1993-95 325i, 325is	3.5
1993-95 525i	2.0
1993 535i, 535is	
heater	.8
AC	4.5
1994-95 540i	2.0
1994-95 740i, iL	2.3
1993-94 750iL	2.5
1994-95 840Ci	1.3
1993-95 850i, Ci, CSi	4.0

(G) Pump, Auxiliary Water, Renew

	Chilton Time
1993-95 525i	1.0
1994-95 540i	1.1
1993-94 750iL	1.5
1994-95 840Ci	1.5

(G) Pump and/or Gasket, Water, Renew

Includes: Drain and refill cooling system.

	Chilton Time
1993-95 318i, is, iC	2.5
1993-95 325i, 325is	2.5
1993-95 525i	2.5
1993 535i, 535is	3.0
1994-95 540i	4.0
1994-95 740i, iL	3.9
1993-94 750iL	3.0
1994-95 840Ci	3.6
1993-95 850i, Ci, CSi	3.5

(G) Radiator Assy., R&R or Renew

	Chilton Time
1993-95 318i, is, iC	1.0
1993-95 325i, 325is	1.0
1993-95 525i	1.5
1993 535i, 535is	1.0
1994-95 540i	1.5
1994-95 740i, iL	1.5
1993-94 750iL	2.0

	Chilton Time
1994-95 840Ci	3.0
1993-95 850i, Ci, CSi	
MT	2.5
AT	3.0
Boil & Repair, add	1.5
Rod Clean, add	1.9
Repair Core, add	1.3
Renew Tank, add	1.6
Renew Trans. Oil Cooler, add	1.9
Recore Radiator, add	1.7

(G) Relay, Auxiliary Cooling Fan, Renew

	Chilton Time
All models	.2

(G) Tensioner, Drive Belt, Renew

	Chilton Time
1993-95 850i, Ci, CSi	1.5

(G) Thermostat, Coolant, Renew

	Chilton Time
1993-95 318i, is, iC	1.0
1993-95 325i, 325is	1.0
1993-95 525i	1.5
1993 535i, 535is	1.5
1994-95 540i	1.2
1994-95 740i, iL	1.4
1993-94 750iL	1.5
1994-95 840Ci	1.3
1993-95 850i, Ci, CSi	1.5

(G) Valve, Heater Water Shut-Off, Renew

	Chilton Time
1993-95 318i, is, iC	1.5
1993-95 325i, 325is	1.5
1993-94 525i	1.5
1993 535i, 535is	.4
1994-95 740i, iL	1.2
1993-94 750iL	1.5
1994-95 840Ci	1.6
1993-95 850i, Ci, CSi	2.0

(G) Winterize Cooling System

Includes: Run engine to check for leaks, tighten all hose connections. Test radiator and pressure cap, drain radiator and engine block. Add antifreeze and refill system.

	Chilton Time
All models	.5

LABOR

AIR CONDITIONING

LABOR

Note: If more than one item requires replacement where evacuation and discharging the system is already included in the operation, deduct 1.0 hour for each additional item from the time listed.

SERVICE AND TESTING

(G) Drain, Evacuate and Recharge System

	Chilton Time
All models	1.5

(G) Flush Refrigerant System, Complete

To be used in conjunction with component replacement which could contaminate system. Includes evacuate and recharge.

	Chilton Time
All models	1.3

(G) Recover and/or Recycle AC Refrigerant

Add to evacuate and charge the AC system, as required.

	Chilton Time
All models, add	.2

(G) Refrigerant, Add (Partial Charge)

	Chilton Time
All models	.6

COMPONENTS

(G) Belt, Compressor Drive, Adjust

	Chilton Time
1993-95 318i, is, iC	.4

(G) Belt, Compressor Drive, Renew

	Chilton Time
1993-95 318i, is, iC	.8
1993-95 325i, 325is	.8
1993-95 525i	.8
1993 535i, 535is	.8
1994-95 540i	1.0
1994-95 740i, iL	1.0
1993-94 750iL	1.0
1994-95 840Ci	.9
1993-95 850i, Ci, CSi	1.5

(G) Compressor Assy., Renew

Includes: Transfer parts as required. Evacuate and charge system.

	Chilton Time
1993-95 318i, is, iC	2.5

	Chilton Time
1993-95 325i, 325is	3.0
1993-95 525i	3.0
1993 535i, 535is	3.0
1994-95 540i	3.5
1994-95 740i, iL	3.5
1993-94 750iL	3.5
1994-95 840Ci	3.6
1993-95 850i, Ci, CSi	3.5

(G) Condenser Assy., Renew

Includes: Evacuate and charge system.

	Chilton Time
1993-95 318i, is, iC	0.0
1993-95 325i, 325is	4.3
1993-95 525i	3.5
1993 535i, 535is	3.0
1994-95 540i	4.3
1994-95 740i	3.9
1994-95 740i, iL	4.3
1993-94 750iL	3.5
1994-95 840Ci	4.7
1993-95 850i, Ci, CSi	5.0

LABOR — AIR CONDITIONING — LABOR

	Chilton Time
(G) Core, Evaporator, Renew	
Includes: Evacuate and charge system.	
1993-95 318i, is, iC	3.5
1993-95 325i, 325is	10.0
1993-95 525i	4.0
1993 535i, 535is	4.5
1994-95 540i	6.1
1994-95 740i, iL	6.2
1993-94 750iL	3.5
1994-94 840Ci	6.7
1993-95 850i, Ci, CSi	6.0
(G) Hoses, AC, Renew	
Includes: Evacuate and charge system.	
One	
1993-95 318i, is, iC	2.5
1993-95 325i, 325is	2.5

	Chilton Time
1993-95 525i	2.5
1993 535i, 535is	2.5
1994-95 540i	3.0
1994-95 740i	3.5
1994-95 740iL	4.0
1993-94 750iL	3.0
1994-95 840Ci	3.7
1993-95 850i, Ci, CSi	3.0
Renew each adtnl., add	.5
(G) Receiver/Drier Assy., Renew	
Includes: Evacuate and charge system.	
All models	2.5
(G) Switch, AC On/Off Control, Renew	
1993-95 318i, is, iC	.3
1993-95 525i	1.0
1994-95 740i, iL	.5

	Chilton Time
(G) Valve, Expansion, Renew	
Includes: Evacuate and charge system.	
1993-95 318i, is, iC	3.0
1993-95 325i, 325is	4.0
1993-95 525i	3.5
1993 535i, 535is	4.5
1994-95 540i	5.6
1994-95 740i, iL	5.8
1993-94 750iL	3.5
1994-95 840Ci	5.8
1993-95 850i, Ci, CSi	5.0
(G) Valve, Pressure Relief, Renew	
Includes: Evacuate and charge system.	
All models	2.5

CHRYSLER IMPORTS
COLT • VISTA

LABOR — COOLING SYSTEM — LABOR

SERVICE	Chilton Time
(G) Belt, Drive, Adjust	
All models	.2
(G) Blade, Fan, Renew	
All models	.5
w/AC add	.2
w/PS add	.1
(G) Control Assy., Heater, Renew	
All models	.9
(G) Cooler, Transaxle Auxiliary Oil, Renew	
All models	1.0
(G) Core, Heater, R&R or Renew	
1993 D-50	5.5
Boil & Repair, add	1.2
Repair Core, add	.9
Recore, add	1.2
(G) Expansion (Freeze) Plugs, Water Jacket, Renew	
Add appropriate time to access plug.	
All models, each	.5
(G) Fan & Alternator Belt, Renew	
All models	
one	.3
each adtnl.	.1

	Chilton Time
(G) Fluid Fan Drive or Fan Blade, Renew	
All models	.6
w/AC add	.2
w/PS add	.1
(G) Gauge, Temperature (Dash Unit), Renew	
All models	1.2
(G) Gauge, Temperature (Engine Unit), Renew	
All models	.4
(G) Hoses, Radiator, Renew	
Includes: Drain and refill cooling system as required.	
All models, upper or lower	
one	.4
both	.6
(G) Motor, Heater Blower, Renew	
All models	1.0
(G) Pump and/or Gasket, Water, Renew	
Includes: Drain and refill cooling system.	
1993 Four	
gas	
2.0L, 2.4L	2.0
w/PS add	.4

	Chilton Time
(G) Radiator Assy., R&R or Renew	
1993 Four	.7
w/AT add	.1
Boil & Repair, add	1.5
Rod Clean, add	1.9
Repair Core, add	1.3
Renew Tank, add	1.6
Renew Trans. Oil Cooler, add	1.9
Recore Radiator, add	1.7
(G) Resistor, Heater Blower Motor, Renew	
All models	.4
(G) Switch, Heater Blower Motor, Renew	
All models	.6
(G) Thermostat, Coolant, Renew	
All models	.5
(G) Valve, Heater Water Shut-Off, Renew	
1993	.7
w/AC add	.1
(G) Winterize Cooling System	
Includes: Run engine to check for leaks, tighten all hose connections. Test radiator and pressure cap, drain radiator and engine block. Add antifreeze and refill system.	
All models	.5

LABOR — AIR CONDITIONING — LABOR

Note: If more than one item requires replacement where evacuation and discharging the system is already included in the operation, deduct 1.0 hour for each additional item from the time listed.

SERVICE AND TESTING	Chilton Time
(G) Drain, Evacuate and Recharge System	
All models	1.0

	Chilton Time
(G) Flush Refrigerant System, Complete	
To be used in conjunction with component replacement which could contaminate system. Includes evacuate and recharge.	
All models	1.3

LABOR

AIR CONDITIONING

LABOR

Chilton Time

(G) Recover and/or Recycle AC Refrigerant
Add to evacuate and charge the AC system, as required.
All models, add 2

(G) Refrigerant, Add (Partial Charge)
All models 6

COMPONENTS

(G) Belt, Compressor Drive, Renew
All models 3

(G) Blower Motor, Renew
All models 1.6

(G) Clutch Assy., Compressor, Renew
All models 6

(G) Coil, Compressor Clutch Field, Renew
1993 .... 1.3

(G) Compressor Assy., Renew
Includes: Transfer parts as required.

Chilton Time

Evacuate and charge system.
All models 3.0
Renew receiver-drier add 2

(G) Condenser Assy., Renew
Includes: Evacuate and charge system.
All models 2.3
Renew receiver-drier add 2

(G) Control Assy., Temperature, Renew
All models 1.5

(G) Core, Evaporator, Renew
Includes: Evacuate and charge system.
All models 3.9

(G) Hoses, AC, Renew
Includes: Evacuate and charge system.
All models
one 1.7
each adtnl. 3
Renew receiver-drier add 2

(G) Receiver/Drier Assy., Renew
Includes: Evacuate and charge system.
All models 1.5

Chilton Time

(G) Resistor, Blower Motor, Renew
All models 1.1

(G) Switch, Blower Motor, Renew
All models 6

(G) Switch, High Pressure Cut-Off, Renew
All models 4

(G) Switch, Thermostatic Control Clutch Cycling, Renew
All models 1.0

(G) Valve, Expansion, Renew
Includes: Evacuate and charge system.
All models 3.1
Renew receiver-drier add 2

(G) Valve, Heater Water Control, Renew
All models 1.0

CHRYSLER IMPORT TRUCKS
D50

LABOR

COOLING SYSTEM

LABOR

Chilton Time

SERVICE

(G) Belt, Drive, Adjust
All models 2

(G) Blade, Fan, Renew
All models 5
w/AC add 2
w/PS add 1

(G) Control Assy., Heater, Renew
All models 9

(G) Cooler, Transaxle Auxiliary Oil, Renew
All models 1.0

(G) Core, Heater, R&R or Renew
1993 D-50 .... 5.5
Boil & Repair, add 1.2
Repair Core, add 9
Recore, add 1.2

(G) Expansion (Freeze) Plugs, Water Jacket, Renew
Add appropriate time to access plug.
All models, each 5

(G) Fan & Alternator Belt, Renew
All models
one 3
each adtnl. 1

Chilton Time

(G) Fluid Fan Drive or Fan Blade, Renew
All models 6
w/AC add 2
w/PS add 1

(G) Gauge, Temperature (Dash Unit), Renew
All models 1.2

(G) Gauge, Temperature (Engine Unit), Renew
All models 4

(G) Hoses, Radiator, Renew
Includes: Drain and refill cooling system as required.
All models, upper or lower
one 4
both 6

(G) Motor, Heater Blower, Renew
All models 1.0

(G) Pump and/or Gasket, Water, Renew
Includes: Drain and refill cooling system.
1993 Four
gas
2.0L, 2.4L 2.0
w/PS add 4

Chilton Time

(G) Radiator Assy., R&R or Renew
1993 Four 7
w/AT add 1
Boil & Repair, add 1.5
Rod Clean, add 1.9
Repair Core, add 1.3
Renew Tank, add 1.6
Renew Trans. Oil Cooler, add 1.9
Recore Radiator, add 1.7

(G) Resistor, Heater Blower Motor, Renew
All models 4

(G) Switch, Heater Blower Motor, Renew
All models 6

(G) Thermostat, Coolant, Renew
All models 5

(G) Valve, Heater Water Shut-Off, Renew
1993 7
w/AC add 1

(G) Winterize Cooling System
Includes: Run engine to check for leaks, tighten all hose connections. Test radiator and pressure cap, drain radiator and engine block. Add antifreeze and refill system.
All models 5

LABOR — AIR CONDITIONING — LABOR

	Chilton Time
Note: If more than one item requires replacement where evacuation and discharging the system is already included in the operation, deduct 1.0 hour for each additional item from the time listed.	

SERVICE AND TESTING

	Chilton Time
(G) Drain, Evacuate and Recharge System	
All models	1.0
(G) Flush Refrigerant System, Complete	
To be used in conjunction with component replacement which could contaminate system. Includes evacuate and recharge.	
All models	1.3
(G) Recover and/or Recycle AC Refrigerant	
Add to evacuate and charge the AC system, as required.	
All models, add	.2
(G) Refrigerant, Add (Partial Charge)	
All models	.6

COMPONENTS

	Chilton Time
(G) Belt, Compressor Drive, Renew	
All models	.3

	Chilton Time
(G) Blower Motor, Renew	
All models	1.6
(G) Clutch Assy., Compressor, Renew	
All models	.6
(G) Coil, Compressor Clutch Field, Renew	
1993	1.3
(G) Compressor Assy., Renew	
Includes: Transfer parts as required. Evacuate and charge system.	
All models	3.0
Renew receiver-drier add	.2
(G) Condenser Assy., Renew	
Includes: Evacuate and charge system.	
All models	2.3
Renew receiver-drier add	.2
(G) Control Assy., Temperature, Renew	
All models	1.5
(G) Core, Evaporator, Renew	
Includes: Evacuate and charge system.	
All models	3.9

	Chilton Time
(G) Hoses, AC, Renew	
Includes: Evacuate and charge system.	
All models	
one	1.7
each adtnl.	.3
Renew receiver-drier add	.2
(G) Receiver/Drier Assy., Renew	
Includes: Evacuate and charge system.	
All models	1.5
(G) Resistor, Blower Motor, Renew	
All models	1.1
(G) Switch, Blower Motor, Renew	
All models	.6
(G) Switch, High Pressure Cut-Off, Renew	
All models	.4
(G) Switch, Thermostatic Control Clutch Cycling, Renew	
All models	1.0
(G) Valve, Expansion, Renew	
Includes: Evacuate and charge system.	
All models	3.1
Renew receiver-drier add	.2
(G) Valve, Heater Water Control, Renew	
All models	1.0

HONDA

ACCORD • CIVIC • CRX • DEL SOL • PRELUDE

LABOR — COOLING SYSTEM — LABOR

TESTING

	Chilton Time
(M) Pressure Test Cooling System	
All models	.3

SERVICE

	Chilton Time
(G) Blade, Fan, Renew	
All models	.6
(G) Control Assy., Heater, Renew	
1993 Accord	2.0
1994-95 Accord	1.0
1993-95 del Sol	.5
1993-95 Civic	.5
1993-95 Prelude	.5
(G) Core, Heater, R&R or Renew	
1993 Accord	6.5
1994-95 Accord	3.0
1993-95 del Sol	3.0
1993-94 Civic	3.0
1993-95 Prelude	5.5
w/AC add	1.0
Boil & Repair, add	1.2
Repair Core, add	.9
Recore, add	1.2
(G) Expansion (Freeze) Plugs, Water Jacket, Renew	
Add appropriate time to access plug.	
All models, each	.5

	Chilton Time
(G) Gauge, Temperature (Dash Unit), Renew	
1993-95 Accord	2.5
1993-95 del Sol	1.5
1993-95 Civic	1.5
1993-95 Prelude	1.2
(G) Gauge, Temperature (Engine Unit), Renew	
All models	.6
(G) Hoses, Heater, Renew	
1993-95 each	.5
(G) Hoses, Radiator, Renew	
Includes: Drain and refill cooling system as required.	
All models	
upper	.5
lower	.6
by-pass	.6
(G) Motor, Heater Blower, Renew	
1993-95 Accord	1.4
1993-95 del Sol	1.2
1993-95 Civic	1.2
1993-95 Prelude	1.3
w/AC add	1.0

	Chilton Time
(G) Pump and/or Gasket, Water, Renew	
Includes: Drain and refill cooling system.	
1993-95 Accord	4.5
1993-95 del Sol	3.0
1993-94 Civic	3.0
1993-95 Prelude	3.0
w/AC add	.3
w/PS add	.2
(G) Radiator Assy., R&R or Renew	
All models	2.0
w/AC add	.3
w/AT add	.2
Boil & Repair, add	1.5
Rod Clean, add	1.9
Repair Core, add	1.3
Renew Tank, add	1.6
Renew Trans. Oil Cooler, add	1.9
Recore Radiator, add	1.7
(G) Relay, Radiator Fan Motor, Renew	
All models	.3
(G) Resistor, Heater Blower Motor, Renew	
1993-95 Accord	.8
1993-95 del Sol	.8
1993-95 Civic	.3
1993-95 Prelude	.3

LABOR | COOLING SYSTEM | LABOR

(G) Switch, Heater Blower Motor, Renew

	Chilton Time
1993-95 Accord	1.5
1993-95 del Sol	.8
1993-95 Civic	.8
1993-95 Prelude	.5

(G) Switch, Heater & AC Mode, Renew

1993-95 Accord	1.2
1993-95 del Sol	1.1
1993-95 Civic	1.1
1993-95 Prelude	.6

(G) Switch, Radiator Fan Motor (Coolant Temp.), Renew

	Chilton Time
1993-95	.7

(G) Thermostat, Coolant, Renew

1993-95 Accord	.8
1993-95 del Sol	.8
1993-95 Civic	.8
1993-95 Prelude	.8

(G) Timer, Cooling Fan, Renew

1993-95	.7

(G) Valve, Heater Water Shut-Off, Renew

	Chilton Time
All models	.8

(G) Winterize Cooling System

Includes: Run engine to check for leaks, tighten all hose connections. Test radiator and pressure cap, drain radiator and engine block. Add antifreeze and refill system.

All models	.5

LABOR | AIR CONDITIONING | LABOR

Note: If more than one item requires replacement where evacuation and discharging the system is already included in the operation, deduct 1.0 hour for each additional item from the time listed.

SERVICE AND TESTING

(G) Drain, Evacuate and Recharge System

All models	1.0

(G) Flush Refrigerant System, Complete

To be used in conjunction with component replacement which could contaminate system. Includes evacuate and recharge.

All models	1.3

(G) Leak Check

Includes: Check all lines and connections.

All models	.8

(G) Recover and/or Recycle AC Refrigerant

Add to evacuate and charge the AC system, as required.

All models, add	.2

COMPONENTS

(G) Belt, Compressor Drive, Renew

	Chilton Time
1993-95	.5
w/PS add	.4

(G) Clutch Assy., Compressor, Renew

1993-95 Accord	3.5
1993-95 del Sol	2.9
1993-95 Civic	2.9
1993-95 Prelude	3.5
w/PS add	.4

(G) Coil, Evaporator, Renew

Includes: Evacuate and charge system.

1993-95 Accord	2.0
1993-95 del Sol	2.0
1993-95 Civic	2.0
1993-95 Prelude	2.0

(G) Compressor Assy., Renew

Includes: Transfer parts as required. Evacuate and charge system.

1993-95 Accord	3.1
1993-95 del Sol	2.5
1993-95 Civic	2.5
1993-95 Prelude	3.1
w/transfer clutch assy. add	.4
w/PS add	.4

(G) Condenser Assy., Renew

Includes: Evacuate and charge system.

All models	2.5

(G) Hoses, AC, Renew

Includes: Evacuate and charge system.

	Chilton Time
1993-95	
one	2.2
each adtnl.	.5

(G) Receiver/Drier Assy., Renew

Includes: Evacuate and charge system.

All models	1.8

(G) Relay, Compressor or Fan, Renew

1993-95	.3

(G) Seal, Compressor Shaft, Renew

Includes: R&R compressor. Evacuate and charge system.

1993-95 Accord	3.8
1993-95 del Sol	2.7
1993-95 Civic	2.7
1993-95 Prelude	3.8
w/PS add	.4

(G) Valve, Expansion, Renew

Includes: Evacuate and charge system.

1993-95 Accord	2.0
1993-95 del Sol	2.0
1993-95 Civic	2.0
1993-95 Prelude	2.0

HONDA TRUCKS
PASSPORT

LABOR | COOLING SYSTEM | LABOR

TESTING

(M) Pressure Test Cooling System

	Chilton Time
All models	.3

SERVICE

(G) Control Assy., Heater, Renew

All models	.9

(G) Core, Heater, R&R or Renew

All models	5.5
Boil & Repair Core, add	1.2

	Chilton Time
Repair Core, add	.9
Recore, add	1.2

(G) Fan, Clutch and/or Pulley, Cooling, Renew

All models	
Four	.4
V6	.6
Renew fan clutch, add	.1

(G) Gauge, Temperature (Dash Unit), Renew

All models	.9

(G) Hoses, Heater, Renew

	Chilton Time
All models, one	.4

(G) Hoses, Radiator, Renew

Includes: Drain and refill cooling system as required.

All models	
upper or lower	.4
both	.8

(G) Motor, Heater Blower, Renew

All models	.8

LABOR — COOLING SYSTEM — LABOR

	Chilton Time
(G) Pump and/or Gasket, Water, Renew	
Includes: Drain and refill cooling system.	
All models	
Four	1.5
V6	2.5
w/AC add	.3
w/PS add	.3

	Chilton Time
(G) Radiator Assy., R&R or Renew	
All models	
Four	1.5
V6	.9
w/AT add	.2

	Chilton Time
(G) Switch, Heater Blower Motor, Renew	
All models	.9
(G) Thermostat, Coolant, Renew	
All models	.5

LABOR — AIR CONDITIONING — LABOR

Note: If more than one item requires replacement where evacuation and discharging the system is already included in the operation, deduct 1.0 hour for each additional item from the time listed.

SERVICE AND TESTING

	Chilton Time
(G) Drain, Evacuate and Recharge System	
All models	1.0
(G) Flush Refrigerant System, Complete	
To be used in conjunction with component replacement which could contaminate system. Includes evacuate and recharge.	
All models	1.3
(G) Leak Check	
Includes: Check all lines and connections.	
All models	.5
(G) Recover and/or Recycle AC Refrigerant	
Add to evacuate and charge the AC system, as required.	
All models	.2
(G) Refrigerant, Add (Partial Charge)	
All models	.6

COMPONENTS

	Chilton Time
(G) Belt, Compressor Drive, Renew	
All models	.4
(G) Coil, Evaporator, Renew	
Includes: Evacuate and charge system.	
All models	4.0
(G) Compressor Assy., Renew	
Includes: Transfer parts as required. Evacuate and charge system.	
All models	3.0
(G) Condenser Assy., Renew	
Includes: Evacuate and charge system.	
All models	
Four	3.3
V6	3.0
(G) Control Unit, Temperature, Renew	
All models	.6
(G) Hoses, AC, Renew	
Includes: Evacuate and charge system.	
All models	
high pressure	
Four	2.5
V6	2.4

	Chilton Time
suction	
Four	2.5
V6	2.3
discharge	
Four	2.4
V6	2.2
low pressure (liquid line)	4.0
(G) Receiver/Drier Assy., Renew	
Includes: Evacuate and charge system.	
All models	
Four	2.5
V6	2.6
(G) Seal, Compressor Shaft, Renew	
Includes: R&R compressor. Evacuate and charge system.	
All models	
Four	3.5
V6	3.9
(G) Thermostat, Renew	
Includes: Evacuate and charge system.	
All models	3.0
(G) Valve, Expansion, Renew	
Includes: Evacuate and charge system.	
All models	4.0

HYUNDAI
ACCENT • ELANTRA • EXCEL • SCOUPE • SONATA

LABOR — COOLING SYSTEM — LABOR

SERVICE

	Chilton Time
(G) Belt, Drive, Adjust	
All models	
one	.3
each adtnl.	.1
(G) Belt, Drive, Renew	
All models	.4
w/AC, add	.1
w/PS, add	.1
w/DOHC, add	.2
(G) Blade, Fan, Renew	
1993-94 Excel	.7
1995 Accent	.7
1993-95 Elantra	.7
1993-95 Sonata	.7
1993-95 Scoupe	.7

	Chilton Time
(G) Core, Heater, R&R or Renew	
1993-94 Excel	
wo/AC	4.6
w/AC	6.0
1995 Accent	
wo/AC	4.0
w/AC	4.8
1993-95 Elantra	
wo/AC	4.4
w/AC	6.0
1993-95 Sonata	
wo/AC	7.0
w/AC	8.7
1993-95 Scoupe	
wo/AC	4.0
w/AC	5.6
Boil & Repair, add	1.2

	Chilton Time
Repair Core, add	.9
Recore, add	1.2
(G) Expansion (Freeze) Plugs, Water Jacket, Renew	
Add appropriate time to access plug.	
All models, each	.5
(G) Fan Assy., Electric Cooling, Renew	
All models	.5
(G) Gauge, Temperature (Dash Unit), Renew	
1993-94 Excel	1.1
1995 Accent	1.1
1993-95 Elantra	1.3
1993-95 Sonata	1.0
1993-95 Scoupe	1.3

LABOR | COOLING SYSTEM | LABOR

(G) Hoses, Heater, Renew

	Chilton Time
1993-94 Excel	.6
1995 Accent	.6
1993-95 Elantra	.9
1993-95 Sonata	1.1
1993-95 Scoupe	.9

(G) Hoses, Radiator, Renew

Includes: Drain and refill cooling system as required.

All models	
upper or lower, each	.5

(G) Motor, Heater Blower, Renew

1993-94 Excel	.5
1995 Accent	.5
1993-95 Elantra	.5
1993-95 Sonata	.5
1993-95 Scoupe	.5

(G) Motor, Radiator Fan and/or Fan, Renew

All models	.8

(G) Pump and/or Gasket, Water, Renew

Includes: Drain and refill cooling system.

1993-94 Excel	3.5
1995 Accent	3.1
1993-95 Elantra	3.5
w/AC, add	.2
w/PS, add	.2
w/DOHC, add	.6
1993-95 Sonata	
4 cyl.	4.5
w/AC, add	.3
w/DOHC, add	.4
V6	5.3
w/AC, add	.1

1993-95 Scoupe	3.5
w/AC, add	.2
w/PS, add	.2

(G) Radiator Assy., R&R or Renew

1993-94 Excel	.9
1995 Accent	.9
1993-95 Elantra	.9
w/AC, add	.1
w/AT, add	.2
1993-95 Sonata	
4 cyl.	.9
w/AC, add	.1
w/AT, add	.2
V6	.9
w/AC, add	.1
1993-95 Scoupe	.9
w/AC, add	.1
w/AT, add	.2
Boil & Repair, add	1.5
Rod Clean, add	1.9
Repair Core, add	1.3
Renew Tank, add	1.6
Renew Trans. Oil Cooler, add	1.9
Recore Radiator, add	1.7

(G) Relay, Heater Blower Motor, Renew

All models	.3

(G) Relay, Radiator Fan Motor, Renew

1993-95 Sonata	.3

(G) Resistor, Fan Motor, Renew

All models	.4

(G) Resistor, Heater Blower Motor, Renew

1993-94 Excel	.5
1995 Accent	.5
1993-95 Elantra	.6

1993-95 Sonata	.5
1993-95 Scoupe	.6

(G) Sending Unit, Engine Coolant Temp., Renew

1993-94 Excel	.4
1995 Accent	.4
1993-95 Elantra	.4
1993-95 Sonata	.4
1993-95 Scoupe	.4

(G) Switch, Electric Fan Thermo, Renew

1993-94 Excel	.6
1995 Accent	.6
1993-95 Elantra	.6
1993-95 Sonata	
4 cyl.	.6
V6	.5
1993-95 Scoupe	.6

(G) Switch, Heater Blower Motor, Renew

1993-94 Excel	.7
1995 Accent	.7
1993-95 Elantra	.7
1993-95 Sonata	.9
1993-95 Scoupe	.7

(G) Thermostat, Coolant, Renew

1993-94 Excel	.6
1995 Accent	.6
1993-95 Elantra	.6
1993-95 Sonata	.6
1993-95 Scoupe	.6

(G) Winterize Cooling System

Includes: Run engine to check for leaks, tighten all hose connections. Test radiator and pressure cap, drain radiator and engine block. Add antifreeze and refill system.

All models	.5

LABOR | AIR CONDITIONING | LABOR

Note: If more than one item requires replacement where evacuation and discharging the system is already included in the operation, deduct 1.0 hour for each additional item from the time listed.

SERVICE AND TESTING

(G) Drain, Evacuate and Recharge System

All models	1.0
Recover refrigerant, add	.2

(G) Recover and/or Recycle AC Refrigerant

Add to evacuate and charge the AC system, as required.

All models, add	.2

(G) Refrigerant, Add (Partial Charge)

All models	.6

COMPONENTS

(G) Accumulator Assy., Renew

Includes: Evacuate and charge system.

All models	1.4
Recover refrigerant, add	.2

(G) Belt, Compressor Drive, Renew

All models	.3
w/DOHC, add	.3

(G) Blower Motor, Renew

1993-94 Excel	.4
1995 Accent	.7
1993-95 Elantra	.4
1993-95 Sonata	.4
1993-95 Scoupe	.4

(G) Clutch Assy., Compressor, Renew

1993-94 Excel	2.4
1995 Accent	1.5
1993-95 Elantra	2.3
1993-95 Sonata	
4 cyl.	2.4
V6	1.8
1993-95 Scoupe	2.0
Add time to evacuate & charge AC system as needed.	
Recover refrigerant, add	.2

(G) Compressor Assy., R&R and Recondition

Includes: Evacuate and charge system.

1993-94 Excel	3.0
1995 Accent	3.0

1993-95 Elantra	3.0
1993-95 Sonata	
4 cyl.	3.3
V6	3.0
1993-95 Scoupe	3.3
Recover refrigerant, add	.2

(G) Compressor Assy., Renew

Includes: Transfer parts as required. Evacuate and charge system.

1993-94 Excel	2.4
1995 Accent	1.8
1993-95 Elantra	2.5
1993-95 Sonata	
4 cyl.	2.9
V6	2.3
1993-95 Scoupe	2.9
Recover refrigerant, add	.2

(G) Condenser Assy., Renew

Includes: Evacuate and charge system.

1993-94 Excel	2.0
1995 Accent	1.9
1993-95 Elantra	2.0
1993-95 Sonata	2.8
1993-95 Scoupe	1.8
Recover refrigerant, add	.2

LABOR   AIR CONDITIONING   LABOR

Chilton Time

(G) Control Assy., Temperature, Renew

1993-95 Sonata 9

(G) Core, Evaporator, Renew

Includes: Evacuate and charge system.

1993-94 Excel	3.2
1995 Accent	2.9
1993-95 Elantra	3.3
1993-95 Sonata	
4 cyl.	6.8
V6	7.1
1993-95 Scoupe	3.2
Recover refrigerant, add	.2

(G) Hoses, AC, Renew

Includes: Evacuate and charge system.

Suction or Discharge
All models	2.0

Liquid Line
1993-94 Excel	2.7
1995 Accent	1.7
1993-95 Elantra	2.3

Chilton Time

1993-95 Sonata	1.7
1993-95 Scoupe	2.4
Recover refrigerant, add	.2

(G) Motor, Condenser Fan, Renew

1993-94 Excel	.5
1995 Accent	.7
1993-95 Elantra	.5
1993-95 Sonata	.5
1993-95 Scoupe	.5

(G) Receiver/Drier Assy., Renew

Includes: Evacuate and charge system.

1995 Accent	2.0
1993-95 Elantra	2.0
Recover refrigerant, add	.2

(G) Relay, Blower Motor, Renew

All models	.3

(G) Resistor, Blower Motor, Renew

1993-94 Excel	.5
1995 Accent	.6

Chilton Time

1993-95 Elantra	.6
1993-95 Sonata	.5
1993-95 Scoupe	.6

(G) Sensor, Ambient Temperature, Renew

1993-95 Sonata	.4

(G) Sensor, In-Vehicle, Renew

1993-95 Sonata	.9

(G) Switch, Blower Motor, Renew

1993-94 Excel	.7
1995 Accent	.7
1993-95 Elantra	.7
1993-95 Sonata	.9
1993-95 Scoupe	.7

(G) Valve, Expansion, Renew

Includes: Evacuate and charge system.

1995 Accent	3.7
1993-95 Elantra	3.9
Recover refrigerant, add	.2

INFINITI
G20 • J30 • M30 • Q45

LABOR   COOLING SYSTEM   LABOR

Chilton Time

SERVICE

(G) Belt, Drive, Adjust

All models
one	.4
each adtnl.	.1

(G) Belt, Drive, Renew

1993-95 G20
one	.6
two	1.0

1993-95 J30
one	.6
two	.7
three	1.0

1993-95 Q45
one	.6
two	.7
three	.8

(G) Blade, Fan, Renew

1993-95 G20
one	1.0
two	1.3
1993-95 Q45	1.1
1993-95 J30	.6

(G) Control Assy., Heater and AC, Renew

1993-95 Q45	.8
1993-95 G20	1.5
1993-95 J30	.8

(G) Core, Heater, R&R or Renew

1993-95 Q45	8.7
1993-95 G20	5.6
1993-95 J30	5.5
w/AC, add	.2

Chilton Time

Boil & Repair, add	1.2
Repair Core, add	.9
Recore, add	1.2

(G) Expansion (Freeze) Plugs, Water Jacket, Renew

Add appropriate time to access plug.
All models, each	.5

(G) Gauge, Temperature (Dash Unit), Renew

1993-95 Q45	1.7
1993-95 G20	1.3
1993-95 J30	1.1

(G) Gauge, Temperature (Engine Unit), Renew

1993-95 Q45	1.0
1993-95 G20	.5
1993-95 J30	.5

(G) Hoses, By-Pass, Renew

1993-95 Q45	5.4
1993-95 G20	.8
1993-95 J30	2.5

(G) Hoses, Heater, Renew

1993-95 Q45	2.1
1993-95 G20	1.0
1993-95 J30	1.1

(G) Hoses, Radiator, Renew

Includes: Drain and refill cooling system as required.

Upper
All models	.8

Chilton Time

Lower
1993-95 Q45	1.4
1993-95 G20	.8
1993-95 J30	.7

(G) Motor, Heater Blower, Renew

1993-95 Q45	1.3
1993-95 G20	.4
1993-95 J30	1.1

(G) Motor, Radiator Fan and/or Fan, Renew

1993-95 G20
one	1.1
two	1.5

(G) Pump and/or Gasket, Water, Renew

Includes: Drain and refill cooling system.

1993-95 Q45	2.5
1993-95 G20	2.8
1993-95 J30	4.1

(G) Radiator Assy., R&R or Renew

1993-95 Q45	1.7
1993-95 G20	1.3
1993-95 J30	1.7
w/AT, add	.2
Boil & Repair, add	1.5
Rod Clean, add	1.9
Repair Core, add	1.3
Renew Tank, add	1.6
Renew Trans. Oil Cooler, add	1.9
Recore Radiator, add	1.7

(G) Relay, Heater Blower Motor, Renew

1993-95 Q45	.4
1993-95 G20	.4
1993-95 J30	.4

LABOR

COOLING SYSTEM

LABOR

	Chilton Time
(G) Relay, Radiator Fan Motor, Renew	
1993-95 Q45	.4
1993-95 G20	.3
(G) Switch, Coolant Temperature Sensor, Renew	
1993-95 Q45	5.0

	Chilton Time
1993-95 G20	.4
1993-95 J30	.4
(G) Thermostat, Coolant, Renew	
1993-95 Q45	1.0
1993-95 G20	1.0
1993-95 J30	2.2

	Chilton Time
(G) Winterize Cooling System	
Includes: Run engine to check for leaks, tighten all hose connections. Test radiator and pressure cap, drain radiator and engine block. Add antifreeze and refill system.	
All models	.5

LABOR

AIR CONDITIONING

LABOR

	Chilton Time
Note: If more than one item requires replacement where evacuation and discharging the system is already included in the operation, deduct 1.0 hour for each additional item from the time listed.	

SERVICE AND TESTING

(G) Drain, Evacuate and Recharge System

All models	1.0
Recover refrigerant, add	.2

(G) Flush Refrigerant System, Complete

To be used in conjunction with component replacement which could contaminate system. Includes evacuate and recharge.

All models	1.3
Recover refrigerant, add	.2

(G) Recover and/or Recycle AC Refrigerant

Add to evacuate and charge the AC system, as required.

All models, add	.2

COMPONENTS

(G) Blower Motor, Renew

1993-95 Q45	1.3
1993-95 G20	.5
1993-95 J30	1.1

(G) Clutch Assy., Magnetic, Renew

1993-95 Q45	4.5
1993-95 G20	3.2
1993-95 J30	3.4

	Chilton Time
(G) Compressor Assy., Renew	
Includes: Transfer parts as required. Evacuate and charge system.	
1993-95 Q45	4.1
1993-95 G20	2.4
1993-95 J30	2.8
Recover refrigerant, add	.2
(G) Condenser Assy., Renew	
Includes: Evacuate and charge system.	
1993-95 Q45	3.8
1993-95 G20	2.9
1993-95 J30	2.0
Recover refrigerant, add	.2
(G) Core, Evaporator, Renew	
Includes: Evacuate and charge system.	
1993-95 Q45	2.7
1993-95 G20	2.1
1993-95 J30	2.1
Recover refrigerant, add	.2
(G) Hose, High Pressure, Renew	
1993-95 Q45	2.1
1993-95 G20	2.2
1993-95 J30	3.1
Recover refrigerant, add	.2
Add time to evacuate and charge A/C system as needed.	
(G) Hose, Low Pressure, Renew	
1993-95 Q45	1.7
1993-95 G20	3.1
1993-95 J30	2.2
Recover refrigerant, add	.2
Add time to evacuate and charge A/C system as needed.	
(G) Motor, Condenser Fan, Renew	
1993-95 Q45	2.0
1993-95 G20	1.2
1993-95 J30	1.2

	Chilton Time
(G) Receiver/Drier Assy., Renew	
Includes: Evacuate and charge system.	
1993-95 Q45	1.8
1993-95 G20	2.1
1993-95 J30	2.0
Recover refrigerant, add	.2
(G) Relay, Blower Motor, Renew	
1993-95 G20	.4
1993-95 Q45	.4
1993-95 J30	.4
(G) Relay, Condenser Fan Motor, Renew	
All models	.3
(G) Switch, Low Pressure and/or Cycling, Renew	
1993-95 Q45	1.8
1993-95 G20	1.7
1993-95 J30	1.8

AUTOMATIC TEMPERATURE CONTROL (ATC)

(G) Control Assy., Renew	
1993-95 Q45	.6
1993-95 J30	.6
(G) Sensor, Ambient, Renew	
1993-95 Q45	.6
1993-95 J30	.4
(G) Sensor, In-Take, Renew	
1993-95 Q45	.8
1993-95 J30	.8
(G) Sensor, In-Vehicle, Renew	
1993-95 Q45	1.0
(G) Switch, Coolant Temperature, Renew	
1993-95 Q45	.7

ISUZU
IMPULSE • STYLUS

LABOR

COOLING SYSTEM

LABOR

	Chilton Time
### SERVICE	
(G) Belt, Drive, Adjust	
All models	
one	.3
each adtnl.	.1

	Chilton Time
(G) Belt, Drive, Renew	
All models	
one	.4
each adtnl.	.1
(G) Core, Heater, R&R or Renew	
1993 Impulse, Stylus	
wo/AC	5.0
w/AC	6.0

	Chilton Time
Boil & Repair, add	1.2
Repair Core, add	.9
Recore, add	1.2
(G) Expansion (Freeze) Plugs, Water Jacket, Renew	
Add appropriate time to access plug.	
All models	.5

LABOR — COOLING SYSTEM — LABOR

(G) Gauge, Temperature (Dash Unit), Renew
1993 Impulse, Stylus 8

(G) Gauge, Temperature (Engine Unit), Renew
All models 5

(G) Hoses, Heater, Renew
All models, each 6

(G) Hoses, Radiator, Renew
Includes: Drain and refill cooling system as required.
Upper
All models 4
Lower
1993 I-Mark, Stylus
one 5
both 8

(G) Motor, Electric Cooling Fan, Renew
All models 9

(G) Motor, Heater Blower, Renew
1993 Impulse, Stylus 5

(G) Motor, Radiator Fan and/or Fan, Renew
1993 Impulse, Stylus 5

(G) Pump and/or Gasket, Water, Renew
Includes: Drain and refill cooling system.
1993 Impulse, Stylus
SOHC 1.4
DOHC
1.6L 2.0
1.8L 3.0
w/AC add 1
w/PS add 1

(G) Radiator Assy., R&R or Renew
1993 Impulse, Stylus 1.0
w/AT add 2
Boil & Repair, add 1.5
Rod Clean, add 1.9
Repair Core, add 1.3
Renew Tank, add 1.6
Renew Trans. Oil Cooler, add 1.9
Recore Radiator, add 1.7

(G) Relay, AC Condenser Cooling Fan, Renew
All models 3

(G) Relay, Heater/AC, Renew
1993 Impulse, Stylus 3

(G) Relay, Radiator Fan Motor, Renew
All models 3

(G) Resistor, Heater Blower Motor, Renew
1993 Impulse, Stylus 4

(G) Switch, Radiator Fan Motor (Coolant Temp.), Renew
All models 6

(G) Thermostat, Coolant, Renew
1993 Impulse, Stylus 5
w/1.8L DOHC add 2

(G) Valve, Water Control, Renew
1993 Impulse, Stylus 6

(G) Winterize Cooling System
Includes: Run engine to check for leaks, tighten all hose connections. Test radiator and pressure cap, drain radiator and engine block. Add antifreeze and refill system.
All models 5

LABOR — AIR CONDITIONING — LABOR

Note: If more than one item requires replacement where evacuation and discharging the system is already included in the operation, deduct 1.0 hour for each additional item from the time listed.

SERVICE AND TESTING

(G) Drain, Evacuate and Recharge System
All models 1.0

(G) Flush Refrigerant System, Complete
To be used in conjunction with component replacement which could contaminate system. Includes evacuate and recharge.
All models 1.3

(G) Leak Check
Includes: Check all lines and connections.
All models 5

(G) Recover and/or Recycle AC Refrigerant
Add to evacuate and charge the AC system, as required.
All models 2

COMPONENTS

(G) Belt, Compressor Drive, Renew
All models 4

(G) Blower Motor, Renew
1993 Impulse, Stylus 5

(G) Clutch Assy., Compressor, Renew
1993 Impulse, Stylus 1.7
w/PS add 2
Renew pulley bearing add 2

(G) Compressor Assy., R&R and Recondition
Includes: Evacuate and charge system.
1993 Impulse, Stylus 3.0
w/PS add 2

(G) Compressor Assy., Renew
1993 Impulse, Stylus 1.5
w/PS add 2

(G) Condenser Assy., Renew
Includes: Evacuate and charge system.
1993 Impulse, Stylus 1.5

(G) Core, Evaporator, Renew
Includes: Evacuate and charge system.
All models 3.0

(G) Fan, Condenser Cooling, Renew
1993 Impulse, Stylus 4
Renew fan motor add 2

(G) Hoses, AC, Renew
Includes: Evacuate and charge system.

1993
liquid line
high pressure 1.4
low pressure 2.5
suction hose 1.3

(G) Receiver/Drier Assy., Renew
Includes: Evacuate and charge system.
1993 Impulse, Stylus 1.5

(G) Relay, Condenser Fan Motor, Renew
1993 Impulse, Stylus 3

(G) Resistor, Blower Motor, Renew
1993 Impulse, Stylus 4

(G) Seal, Seat and O-Ring, Compressor Front, Renew
Includes: R&R clutch hub and drive plate assy. Evacuate and charge system.
1993 Impulse, Stylus 1.8
w/PS add 2

(G) Switch, Condenser Pressure, Renew
1993 Impulse, Stylus 1.1

(G) Switch, Evaporator Thermostatic, Renew
1993 Impulse, Stylus 2.0

(G) Valve, Expansion, Renew
Includes: Evacuate and charge system.
1993 . . . . 1.2

ISUZU TRUCKS
AMIGO • PICKUP • RODEO • TROOPER • TROOPER II

LABOR | COOLING SYSTEM | LABOR

Chilton Time

TESTING

(M) Pressure Test Cooling System
All models 3

SERVICE

(G) Belt, Drive, Adjust
All models
one 2
each adtnl. 1

(G) Belt, Drive, Renew
1993-95 Four
one 5
each adtnl. 1
1993-95 V6
one 3
each adtnl. 1

(G) Blade, Fan, Renew
1993-95 Four 5
1993-95 V6
2.8L, 3.1L 8
3.2L 6

(G) Clutch, Viscous (Fluid) Fan Assy., Renew
1993-95 Four 6
1993-95 V6
2.8L, 3.1L 9
3.2L 7

(G) Control Assy., Temperature, Renew
All models 9

(G) Core, Heater, R&R or Renew
All models 5.5
w/AC add 7
Boil & Repair, add 1.2
Repair Core, add 9
Recore, add 1.2

Chilton Time

(G) Expansion (Freeze) Plugs, Water Jacket, Renew
Add appropriate time to access plug.
All models, each 5

(G) Gauge, Temperature (Dash Unit), Renew
1993-95 Pickup 1.0
1993-95 Trooper 1.1
1993-95 Amigo 1.0
1993-95 Rodeo 1.0

(G) Gauge, Temperature (Engine Unit), Renew
All models 5

(G) Hoses, Heater, Renew
1993-95 Trooper 9
1993-95 Pickup 4
1993-95 Amigo 4
1993-95 Rodeo 4

(G) Hoses, Radiator, Renew
Includes: Drain and refill cooling system as required.
All models, each 4

(G) Motor, Heater Blower, Renew
1993-95 7

(G) Pump and/or Gasket, Water, Renew
Includes: Drain and refill cooling system.
1993-95 Four
2.3L 4.0
2.6L 2.9
1993-95 V6
2.8L, 3.1L 2.5
3.2L 3.5
w/AC add 3

Chilton Time

w/PS add 3
w/AT add 4

(G) Radiator Assy., R&R or Renew
1993-95 Four 1.3
1993-95 V6
2.8L, 3.1L 1.6
3.2L
Trooper 1.1
Rodeo 9
w/AC add 1
Boil & Repair, add 1.5
Rod Clean, add 1.9
Repair Core, add 1.3
Renew Tank, add 1.6
Renew Trans. Oil Cooler, add ...1.9
Recore Radiator, add 1.7

(G) Relay, Heater Blower Motor, Renew
All models 3

(G) Resistor, Heater Blower Motor, Renew
All models 4

(G) Tensioner, Drive Belt, Renew
1993-95 V6 5

(G) Thermostat, Coolant, Renew
1993-95 Four
gas 5
1993-95 V6
2.8L, 3.1L 7
3.2L 4

(G) Winterize Cooling System
Includes: Run engine to check for leaks, tighten all hose connections. Test radiator and pressure cap, drain radiator and engine block. Add antifreeze and refill system.
All models 5

LABOR | AIR CONDITIONING | LABOR

Chilton Time

Note: If more than one item requires replacement where evacuation and discharging the system is already included in the operation, deduct 1.0 hour for each additional item from the time listed.

SERVICE AND TESTING

(G) Drain, Evacuate and Recharge System
All models 1.0

(G) Flush Refrigerant System, Complete
To be used in conjunction with component replacement which could contaminate system. Includes evacuate and recharge.
All models 1.3

(G) Leak Check
Includes: Check all lines and connections.
All models 5

Chilton Time

(G) Recover and/or Recycle AC Refrigerant
Add to evacuate and charge the AC system, as required.
All models 2

(G) Refrigerant, Add (Partial Charge)
All models 6

COMPONENTS

(G) Belt, Compressor Drive, Renew
1993-95 Trooper 7
1993-95 Pickup 5
1993-95 Amigo 5
1993-95 Rodeo 5

(G) Blower Motor, Renew
1993-95 7

Chilton Time

(G) Clutch Plate & Hub Assy., Compressor, Renew
Includes: R&R hub and drive plate assy. Check air gap.
1993-95 ....2.0

(G) Compressor Assy., R&R and Recondition
Includes: Evacuate and charge system.
1993-95 Pickup 3.0
1993-95 Trooper
Four 3.5
V6 ....3.0
1993-95 Amigo 3.0
1993-95 Rodeo
Four 3.5
V6 ....3.0

(G) Compressor Assy., Renew
Includes: Transfer parts as required.

LABOR AIR CONDITIONING LABOR

	Chilton Time
Evacuate and charge system.	
1993-95 Pickup	1.5
1993-95 Trooper	
Four	2.0
V6	1.5
1993-95 Amigo	1.5
1993-95 Rodeo	
Four	2.0
V6	1.5

(G) Condenser Assy., Renew
Includes: Evacuate and charge system.

1993-95	2.0

(G) Control Unit, Temperature, Renew

All models	.9

(G) Core, Evaporator, Renew
Includes: Evacuate and charge system.

1993-95	3.0

(G) Hoses, AC, Renew
Includes: Evacuate and charge system.

	Chilton Time
1993-95 Trooper	
low pressure	1.2
high pressure	.9
evap. liquid line	1.4
1993-95 Pickup	
high & low pressure	1.7
evap. liquid line	3.0
1993-95 Amigo, Rodeo	
high & low pressure	1.7
evap. liquid line	3.0

(G) Pulley and/or Bearing, Compressor, Renew
Includes: R&R hub and drive plate.

1993-95	2.0

(G) Receiver/Drier Assy., Renew
Includes: Evacuate and charge system.

1993-95	1.4

(G) Resistor, Blower Motor, Renew

	Chilton Time
All models	.4

(G) Seal, Compressor Shaft, Renew
Includes: R&R compressor. Evacuate and charge system.

1993-95	2.1

(G) Switch, Condenser Pressure, Renew

1993-95 Trooper	1.4
1993-95 Rodeo	1.4

(G) Switch, Evaporator Thermostatic, Renew

All models	1.4

(G) Valve, Expansion, Renew
Includes: Evacuate and charge system.

1993-95	3.0

JAGUAR
XJ6 • XJ12 • XJS

LABOR COOLING SYSTEM LABOR

SERVICE

(G) Belt, Drive, Adjust

	Chilton Time
1994 XJ12	.3
1993-94 XJ6	.4
1993-94 XJS	.6

(G) Belt, Drive, Renew

1994 XJ12	.4
1993-94 XJ6	.5
1993-94 XJS, one	.7

(G) Belt, Water Pump Drive, Renew

1993-94 XJS	.5

(G) Blade, Fan, Renew

1993-94 XJ6	.9
1993-94 XJS	2.1

(G) Core, Heater, R&R or Renew

1994 XJ12	2.8
1993-94 XJ6	2.6
1993-94 XJS	
w/Mark III AC	3.5
Boil & Repair, add	1.2
Repair Core, add	.9
Recore, add	1.2

(G) Expansion (Freeze) Plugs, Water Jacket, Renew
Add appropriate time to access plug.

All models, each	.5

(G) Fan, Auxiliary Cooling Assy., Renew

1994 XJ12	1.8

(G) Gauge, Temperature (Dash Unit), Renew

1994 XJ12	2.0
1993-94 XJS	1.8

(G) Gauge, Temperature (Engine Unit), Renew

	Chilton Time
1993-94 XJ6	.4
1993-94 XJS	.6

(G) Hoses, Radiator, Renew
Includes: Drain and refill cooling system as required.

1994 XJ12, each	1.8
1993-94 XJ6	
upper	.9
lower	1.3
1993-94 XJS	
Six	
upper	.9
lower	1.4
V12	
upper	.5
lower	1.4

(G) Motor, Electric Cooling Fan, Renew

1994 XJ12	1.9
1993-94 XJ6, XJS	1.5

(G) Pump and/or Gasket, Water, Renew
Includes: Drain and refill cooling system.

1994 XJ12	4.2
1993-94 XJ6	3.0
1993-94 XJS	
Six	2.5
V12	6.1

(G) Radiator Assy., R&R or Renew

1994 XJ12	3.1
1993-94 XJ6	2.3
1993-94 XJS	
Six	3.2
V12	6.4

	Chilton Time
Boil & Repair, add	1.5
Rod Clean, add	1.9
Repair Core, add	1.3
Renew Tank, add	1.6
Renew Trans. Oil Cooler, add	1.9
Recore Radiator, add	1.7

(G) Relay, Radiator Fan Motor, Renew

1994 XJ12	1.1
1993-94 XJ6, XJS	.8

(G) Switch, Auxiliary Fan Temperature, Renew

1994 XJ12	2.2

(G) Switch, Thermostatic, Renew

1993-94 XJ6, XJS	1.4

(G) Thermostat, Coolant, Renew

1994 XJ12	1.4
1993-94 XJ6	.9
1993-94 XJS	
one	.9
both	1.2

(G) Valve, Water Control, Renew

1994 XJ12	3.1
1993-94 XJ6	1.0
1993-94 XJS	
Six	1.0
V12	1.4

(G) Winterize Cooling System
Includes: Run engine to check for leaks, tighten all hose connections. Test radiator and pressure cap, drain radiator and engine block. Add antifreeze and refill system.

1993-94 XJ6	1.5

LABOR

AIR CONDITIONING

LABOR

Chilton Time

Note: If more than one item requires replacement where evacuation and discharging the system is already included in the operation, deduct 1.0 hour for each additional item from the time listed.

SERVICE AND TESTING

(G) Drain, Evacuate and Recharge System
All models 1.0

(G) Flush Refrigerant System, Complete
To be used in conjunction with component replacement which could contaminate system. Includes evacuate and recharge.
All models 1.3

(G) Leak Check
Includes: Check all lines and connections.
All models .6

(G) Recover and/or Recycle AC Refrigerant
Add to evacuate and charge the AC system, as required.
All models, add 2

COMPONENTS

(G) Actuator, Center Ventilator Vacuum, Renew
1993-94 XJ6 . . . . 3.4

(G) Belt, Compressor Drive, Adjust
1993-94 XJ6 3
1993-94 XJS
Six 3
V12 2

(G) Belt, Compressor Drive, Renew
1994 XJ12 7
1993-94 XJ6 4
1993-94 XJS
Six 5
V12 . . . . 1.4

(G) Blower Motor, Renew
1994 XJ12
drivers side 2.2
passenger side 2.6
1993-94 XJ6
left side 1.3
right side 2.4
1993-94 XJS, each 2.7

(G) Compressor Assy., Renew
Includes: Transfer parts as required. Evacuate and charge system.
1994 XJ12 . . . . 3.6
1993-94 XJ6 . . . . 3.6
1993-94 XJS
Six 3.8
V12 . . . . 2.6

Chilton Time

(G) Condenser Assy., Renew
Includes: Evacuate and charge system.
1994 XJ12 . . . . 2.7
1993-94 XJ6 . . . . 2.6
1993-94 XJS
Six 2.8
V12 . . . . 3.1

(G) Core, Evaporator, Renew
Includes: Evacuate and charge system.
1994 XJ12 . . . . 10.4
1993-94 XJ6 . . . . 9.6
1993-94 XJS
Six 14.0
V12 . . . . 15.7

(G) Hoses, AC, Renew
Includes: Evacuate and charge system.
1994 XJ12
one 2.6
each adtnl. 5
1993-94 XJ6
compressor to evaporator 2.7
receiver-drier to evap. 2.3
compressor to condenser 2.3
muffler to condenser 2.3
1993-94 XJS
compressor to evaporator 2.4
compressor to condenser 2.5

(G) Module, AC Control, Renew
1993-94 XJ6 . . . . 1.2
1993-94 XJS 1.4

(G) Module, AC Electrical Control, Renew
1993-94 XJ6 . . . . 1.8
1993-94 XJS w/Mark III AC 1.4

(G) Module, AC Switch Control, Renew
1993-94 XJ6 . . . . 1.3

(G) Motor & Gearbox Assy., Flap, Renew
1993-94 XJ6 . . . . 1.8
1993-94 XJS
upper 13.1
lower 1.5

(G) Motor, Auxiliary Cooling Fan, Renew
1993-94 XJS 1.5

(G) Potentiometer, Lower Servo Feedback, Renew
1993-94 XJ6 9
1993-94 XJS 1.4

(G) Potentiometer, Upper Servo Feedback, Renew
1993-94 XJ6 9
1993-94 XJS 13.1

(G) Receiver/Drier Assy., Renew
Includes: Evacuate and charge system.
1994 XJ12 . . . . 2.5

Chilton Time

1993-94 XJ6 . . . . 2.2
1993-94 XJS
Six 2.5
V12 . . . . 2.0

(G) Relay, Blower Motor, Renew
1994 XJ12 . . . . 1.2
1993-94 XJ6 8
1993-94 XJS 1.7

(G) Relay, Compressor or Fan, Renew
1993-94 XJ6 7
1993-94 XJS 8

(G) Resistor, Blower Motor, Renew
1993-94 XJS 9

(G) Seal, Compressor Shaft, Renew
Includes: R&R compressor. Evacuate and charge system.
1993-94 XJ6 . . . . 3.2
1993-94 XJS
Six 3.6
V12 . . . . 4.5

(G) Sensor, Ambient Temperature, Renew
1993-94 XJ6 . . . . 2.6

(G) Sensor, Evaporator Temperature, Renew
1993-94 XJ6 9

(G) Sensor, In-Vehicle, Renew
1993-94 XJ6 . . . . 1.7

(G) Servo, Defroster Duct, Renew
1993-94 XJ6 . . . . 4.0

(G) Switch, Combination Temperature & Air Flow, Renew
1993-94 XJS 4

(G) Switch, Condenser Cooling Fan, Renew
1993-94 XJ6 . . . . 1.4
1993-94 XJS
Six 9
V12 . . . . 1.4

(G) Switch, Thermostatic Control, Renew
1993-94 XJS 2.3

(G) Valve, Expansion, Renew
Includes: Evacuate and charge system.
1994 XJ12 . . . . 2.5
1993-94 XJ6 . . . . 2.9
1993-94 XJS 3.9

LEXUS
ES250 • ES300 • GS300 • LS400 • SC300 • SC400

LABOR   COOLING SYSTEM   LABOR

	Chilton Time

TESTING

(M) Pressure Test Cooling System
All models 3

SERVICE

(G) Belt, Drive, Adjust
1993-95 ES250, ES300 3

(G) Belt, Fan Drive, Renew
1993-95 ES250, ES300 4

(G) Blade, Fan, Renew
1993-95 Six 6
1993-95 V8 8

(G) Core, Heater, R&R or Renew
1993-94 LS400 . . . . 12.5
1993-95 ES300 . . . . 2.4
1993-95 SC300, SC400 . . . . 19.0
1994-95 GS300 . . . . 10.0
Boil & Repair, add 1.2
Repair Core, add 9
Recore, add 1.2

(G) Expansion (Freeze) Plugs, Water Jacket, Renew
Add appropriate time to access plug.
All models, each 5

(G) Gauge, Temperature (Dash Unit), Renew
1993-94 LS400 . . . . 1.1
1993-95 ES300 . . . . 1.1
1993-95 SC300, SC400 . . . . 1.1
1994-95 GS300 7

(G) Gauge, Temperature (Engine Unit), Renew
1993-95 SC300, GS300 8
1993-95 ES250, ES300 8
1993-94 LS400 4
1993-95 SC400 8

	Chilton Time

(G) Hoses, By-Pass, Renew
1993-95 Six 1.2
1993-95 V6, V8 6

(G) Hoses, Heater, Renew
1993-94 LS400 8
1993-95 ES300 . . . . 1.1
1993-95 SC300, SC400 . . . . 1.1
1994-95 GS300 . . . . 1.1

(G) Hoses, Radiator, Renew
Includes: Drain and refill cooling system as required.
1993-95 SC300, GS300
upper 8
lower 1.2
1993-95 ES300
upper 8
lower 1.3
1993-94 LS400 9
1993-95 SC400 . . . . 1.2

(G) Module, Fan Motor, Renew
1993-95
ES300 6
SC300 . . . . 1.0

(G) Motor, Heater Blower, Renew
1993-94 LS400 . . . . 1.8
1993-95 ES300 5
1993-95 SC300, SC400 . . . . 1.1
1994-95 GS300 6

(G) Motor, Radiator Fan and/or Fan, Renew
1993-95 ES300 . . . . 2.2
1993-95 SC400 . . . . 1.8
hydraulic motor
V6 . . . . 2.3
V8 . . . . 1.8
hydraulic pump 2.3

	Chilton Time

(G) Pump and/or Gasket, Water, Renew
Includes: Drain and refill cooling system.
1993-95 SC300, GS300 . . . . 3.5
1993-95 ES300 . . . . 3.1
1993-94 LS400 . . . . 4.5
1993-95 SC400 . . . . 4.7

(G) Radiator Assy., R&R or Renew
1993-95 SC300, GS300 . . . . 1.8
1993-95 ES300 . . . . 1.9
1993-94 LS400 . . . . 1.6
1993-95 SC400 . . . . 1.7
Boil & Repair, add 1.5
Rod Clean, add 1.9
Repair Core, add 1.3
Renew Tank, add 1.6
Renew Trans. Oil Cooler, add 1.9
Recore Radiator, add 1.7

(G) Resistor, Heater Blower Motor, Renew
1993-94 LS400 . . . . 1.2
1993-95 ES300 6
1993-95 SC300, SC400 7

(G) Thermostat, Coolant, Renew
All models
Six 8
V6 . . . . 1.0
V8 9

(G) Valve, Water Control, Renew
1993-94 LS400 8
1993-95 ES300 . . . . 1.1
1993-95 SC300, SC400 . . . . 1.1
1994-95 GS300 . . . . 1.1

(G) Winterize Cooling System
Includes: Run engine to check for leaks, tighten all hose connections. Test radiator and pressure cap, drain radiator and engine block. Add antifreeze and refill system.
All models 5

LABOR   AIR CONDITIONING   LABOR

	Chilton Time

Note: If more than one item requires replacement where evacuation and discharging the system is already included in the operation, deduct 1.0 hour for each additional item from the time listed.

SERVICE AND TESTING

(G) Drain, Evacuate and Recharge System
All models 1.0

(G) Flush Refrigerant System, Complete
To be used in conjunction with component replacement which could contaminate system. Includes evacuate and recharge.
All models 1.3

	Chilton Time

(G) Recover and/or Recycle AC Refrigerant
Add to evacuate and charge the AC system, as required.
All models 2

(G) Refrigerant, Add (Partial Charge)
All models 6

COMPONENTS

(G) Blower Motor, Renew
1993-94 LS400 . . . . 1.9
1993-95 ES300 5
1993-95 SC300, SC400 . . . . 1.1
1994-95 GS300 6

(G) Clutch Assy., Compressor, Renew
1993-94 LS400 . . . . 2.1

	Chilton Time

1993-95 ES300 . . . . 3.0
1993-95 SC300 . . . . 2.3
1993-95 SC400 . . . . 1.9
1994-95 GS300 . . . . 2.7

(G) Compressor Assy., Renew
Includes: Transfer parts as required. Evacuate and charge system.
1993-94 LS400 . . . . 1.9
1993-95 SC300 . . . . 1.9
1993-95 ES300 . . . . 2.8
1993-95 SC400 . . . . 1.5
1994-95 GS300 . . . . 2.3

(G) Condenser Assy., Renew
Includes: Evacuate and charge system.
1993-94 LS400 . . . . 3.5
1993-95 ES300 . . . . 3.7
1993-95 SC300, SC400 . . . . 3.2

LABOR

AIR CONDITIONING

LABOR

	Chilton Time
1994-95 GS300	4.0

(G) Control Assy., AC, Renew

1993-94 LS400	.6
1993-95 ES300	.6
1993-95 SC300, SC400	.9
1994-95 GS300	.6

(G) Core, Evaporator, Renew

Includes: Evacuate and charge system.

1993-94 LS400	3.2
1993-95 ES300	2.2
1993-95 SC300, SC400	
wo/TRAC	3.5
w/TRAC	5.3
1994-95 GS300	2.3

(G) Hoses, AC, Renew

Includes: Evacuate and charge system.

1993-94 LS400	4.0

	Chilton Time
1993-95 ES300	1.7
1993-95 SC300, SC400	1.8
1994-95 GS300	1.8

(G) Receiver/Drier Assy., Renew

Includes: Evacuate and charge system.

1993-94 LS400	1.6
1993-95 ES300	1.6
1993-95 SC300, SC400	2.2
1994-95 GS300	1.6

(G) Regulator, Pressure, Renew

1993-94 LS400	1.5
1993-95 SC300, SC400	
wo/TRAC	2.4
w/TRAC	4.3
1994-95 GS300	1.5

(G) Resistor, Blower Motor, Renew

1993-94 LS400	1.3

	Chilton Time
1993-95 ES300	.6
1993-95 SC300, SC400	.7

(G) Switch, Low Pressure Cut-Off, Renew

Includes: Evacuate and charge system.

1993-94 LS400	1.5
1993-95 ES300	1.5
1993-95 SC300, SC400	1.5
1994-95 GS300	1.5

(G) Valve, Expansion, Renew

Includes: Evacuate and charge system.

1993-94 LS400	3.2
1993-95 ES300	2.2
1993-95 SC300, SC400	
wo/TRAC	3.5
w/TRAC	5.3
1994-95 GS300	2.3

MAZDA
323 • 626 • 929 • MX3 • MX6 • MIATA • MILLENIA • PROTEGE • RX7

LABOR

COOLING SYSTEM

LABOR

TESTING

(M) Pressure Test Cooling System

	Chilton Time
All models	.3

SERVICE

(G) Belt, Fan Drive, Renew

1993-95 929	.6
w/AC, add	.1

(G) Blade, Fan, Renew

1993-95	.5

(G) Control Assy., Heater, Renew

1993-95 MX-3	.6
1993-95 MX-5 Miata	.7
1995 Millenia	.6
1993-94 323, Protege	.9
1995 323, Protege	1.1
1993-95 626, MX-6	.6
1993-95 RX-7	.7

(G) Core, Heater, R&R or Renew

1993-95 MX-3	6.0
1993-95 MX-5 Miata	4.0
1995 Millenia	3.5
1993-94 323, Protege	3.2
1995 323, Protege	3.5
1993-95 626, MX-6	5.0
1993-95 929	6.5
1993-95 RX-7	4.5
Boil & Repair, add	1.2
Repair Core, add	.9
Recore, add	1.2

(G) Cover or Gasket, Water Pump, Renew

1993-95 RX-7	4.2

(G) Expansion (Freeze) Plugs, Water Jacket, Renew

Add appropriate time to access plug.

	Chilton Time
All models, each	.5

(G) Fluid Fan Drive or Fan Blade, Renew

1993-95 RX-7

MT	3.0
AT	3.2

(G) Gauge, Temperature (Dash Unit), Renew

1993-95 MX-3	1.4
1993-95 MX-5 Miata	1.0
1995 Millenia	1.0
1993-94 323, Protege	1.1
1995 323, Protege	1.2
1993-95 626, MX-6	.8
1993-95 929	1.5
1993-95 RX-7	1.0

(G) Gauge, Temperature (Engine Unit), Renew

Piston Engine

All models	.4

Rotary Engine

1993-95 RX-7	4.0

(G) Hoses, By-Pass, Renew

1993-95 MX-3	.9
1993 MX-5, Miata	.5
1994-95 MX-5 Miata	1.0
1995 Millenia	
2.3L	1.0
2.5L	.9
1993-94 323, Protege, each	.4
1995 323, Protege	1.0
1993-95 626, MX-6	.9
1993-95 929	.9

	Chilton Time
1993-95 RX-7	
main	1.1
return	1.6
both	1.8

(G) Hoses, Radiator, Renew

Includes: Drain and refill cooling system as required.

1993-95 MX-3	
upper	.6
lower	.9
1993-95 MX-5 Miata	
upper	.3
lower	.5
1995 Millenia	
upper	.9
lower	
2.3L	1.2
2.5L	1.0
1993-94 323, Protege	
upper	.3
lower	.5
1995 323, Protege	
upper	1.0
lower	1.2
1993-95 626, MX-6	
upper	.8
lower	1.0
1993-95 929, each	1.0
1993-95 RX-7	
upper	1.1
lower	1.0

(G) Motor, Condenser Fan, Renew

1993-95 MX-3	.7
1993-95 MX-5 Miata	.5
1995 Millenia	.7
1993-94 323, Protege	.4
1995 323, Protege	.6
1993-95 626, MX-6	.8

LABOR   COOLING SYSTEM   LABOR

	Chilton Time
(G) Motor, Heater Blower, Renew	
1993-95 MX-3	1.0
1993-95 MX-5 Miata	.9
1995 Millenia	1.0
1993-94 323, Protege	1.4
1995 323, Protege	.6
1993-95 626, MX-6	.7
1993-95 929	6.0
1993-95 RX-7	.5
(G) Motor, Radiator Fan and/or Fan, Renew	
1993-95 MX-3	.7
1993-95 MX-5 Miata	.6
1995 Millenia	.8
1993-94 323, Protege	.6
1995 323, Protege	
MT	1.4
AT	1.6
1993-95 626, MX-6	.8
1993-95 RX-7	
MT	3.1
AT	3.3
(G) Pump and/or Gasket, Water, Renew	
Includes: Drain and refill cooling system.	
1993-95 MX-3	
4 cyl.	3.0
V6	3.9
1993-95 MX-5 Miata	3.1
w/AC, add	.2
w/PS, add	.2
1995 Millenia	
2.3L	4.1
2.5L	3.3
1993-94 323, Protege	3.0
w/DOHC, add	.2
w/AC, add	.2
w/PS, add	.2
1995 323, Protege	3.5
1993-95 626, MX-6	
4 cyl.	3.0
V6	4.8
1993-95 929	4.2
1993-95 RX-7	4.0
(G) Radiator Assy., R&R or Renew	
1993-95 MX-3	
4 cyl.	1.2

	Chilton Time
V6	1.4
1993-95 MX-5 Miata	.8
1995 Millenia	
2.3L	1.5
2.5L	1.8
1993-94 323, Protege	.9
1995 323, Protege	1.5
1993-95 626, MX-6	
4 cyl.	1.2
V6	1.3
w/AT, add	.2
1993-95 929	1.6
1993-95 RX-7	2.8
w/AT, add	.2
Boil & Repair, add	1.5
Rod Clean, add	1.9
Repair Core, add	1.3
Renew Tank, add	1.6
Renew Trans. Oil Cooler, add	1.9
Recore Radiator, add	1.7
(G) Relay, Heater Blower Motor, Renew	
1995 Millenia	.3
1995 323, Protege	.3
1993-95 626, MX-6	.7
1993-95 929	.5
1993-95 RX-7	.4
(G) Relay, Radiator Fan Motor, Renew	
1993-95	.4
(G) Resistor, Heater Blower Motor, Renew	
1993-95 MX-3	.7
1993-95 MX-5 Miata	.6
1993-94 323, Protege	.4
1995 323, Protege	.5
1993-95 626, MX-6	.5
1993-95 929	.5
1993-95 RX-7	.4
(G) Switch, Heater Blower Motor, Renew	
1993-95 MX-3	1.0
1993-95 MX-5 Miata	.8
1993-95 626, MX-6	.6
(G) Switch, Radiator Fan Motor (Coolant Temp.), Renew	
1993-95 626, MX-6	.5

	Chilton Time
(G) Thermostat, Coolant, Renew	
1993-95 MX-3	1.3
1993-95 MX-5 Miata	.5
1995 Millenia	
2.3L	1.2
2.5L	1.0
1993-95 323, Protege	.6
1993-95 626, MX-6	
4 cyl.	1.5
w/AC, add	.3
V6	1.4
1993-95 929	1.8
1993-95 RX-7	2.5
(G) Transistor, Heater Blower Motor, Renew	
1995 Millenia	.5
(G) Valve, Heater Water Shut-Off, Renew	
Without AC	
1993-95 MX-3	.7
1993-95 MX-5 Miata	.7
1993-95 323, Protege	.7
1993-95 626, MX-6	.7
(G) Water Bypass Pipe and/or O Ring, Renew	
1993-95 MX-3	
4 cyl.	1.0
V6	2.0
1993 MX-5 Miata	.8
w/AC, add	.2
w/PS, add	.2
1994-95 MX-5, Miata	1.2
1995 Millenia	
2.3L	1.0
2.5L	2.4
1993-94 323, Protege	.8
1995 323, Protege	1.0
1993-95 626, MX-6	1.3
1993-95 929	1.4
(G) Winterize Cooling System	
Includes: Run engine to check for leaks, tighten all hose connections. Test radiator and pressure cap, drain radiator and engine block. Add antifreeze and refill system.	
All models	.5

LABOR   AIR CONDITIONING   LABOR

	Chilton Time
Note: If more than one item requires replacement where evacuation and discharging the system is already included in the operation, deduct 1.0 hour for each additional item from the time listed.	
SERVICE AND TESTING	
(G) Drain, Evacuate and Recharge System	
All models	1.0
Recover refrigerant, add	.2
(G) Flush Refrigerant System, Complete	
To be used in conjunction with component replacement which could contaminate system. Includes evacuate and recharge.	
All models	1.3
Recover refrigerant, add	.2

	Chilton Time
(G) Pressure Test System	
All models	.8
(G) Recover and/or Recycle AC Refrigerant	
Add to evacuate and charge the AC system, as required.	
All models, add	.2
COMPONENTS	
(G) Belt, Compressor Drive, Renew	
All models	.5
(G) Clutch Assy., Magnetic, Renew	
1993-95 MX-3	
4 cyl.	1.0
V6	1.5
1993-95 MX-5 Miata	1.0

	Chilton Time
1995 Millenia	1.2
1993-94 323, Protege	1.2
1995 323, Protege	1.3
1993-95 626, MX-6	1.0
1993-95 929	1.9
1993-95 RX-7	1.5
Note: Add time to evacuate & charge AC system as needed.	
Recover refrigerant, add	.2
(G) Coil, Evaporator, Renew	
Includes: Evacuate and charge system.	
1993-95 MX-3	2.7
1993-95 MX-5 Miata	1.8
1995 Millenia	2.2
1993-94 323, Protege	1.9
1995 323, Protege	2.1
1993-95 626, MX-6	2.0
1993-95 929	3.0

LABOR — AIR CONDITIONING — LABOR

	Chilton Time
1993-95 RX-7	2.0
Recover refrigerant, add	.2

(G) Compressor Assy., Renew
Includes: Transfer parts as required. Evacuate and charge system.

1993-95 MX-3	3.1
1993-95 MX-5 Miata	2.0
1995 Millenia	2.2
1993-94 323, Protege	2.2
1995 323, Protege	2.3
1993-95 626, MX-6	1.8
1993-95 929	3.5
1993-95 RX-7	2.1
Recover refrigerant, add	.2

(G) Condenser Assy., Renew
Includes: Evacuate and charge system.

1993-95 MX-3	2.2
1993-95 MX-5 Miata	1.6
1995 Millenia	2.6
1993-94 323, Protege	1.5
1995 323, Protege	1.6
1993-95 626, MX-6	1.5
1993-95 929	2.4
1993-95 RX-7	1.7
Recover refrigerant, add	.2

(G) Hoses, AC, Renew
Includes: Evacuate and charge system.

All models suction	1.7

	Chilton Time
discharge	2.0
Recover refrigerant, add	.2

(G) Receiver/Drier Assy., Renew
Includes: Evacuate and charge system.

1993-95 MX-3	2.1
1993-95 MX-5 Miata	1.5
1995 Millenia	2.6
1993-95 323, Protege	1.5
1993-95 626, MX-6	1.4
1993-95 929	2.1
1993-95 RX-7	1.5
Recover refrigerant, add	.2

(G) Seal, Compressor Shaft, Renew
Includes: R&R compressor. Evacuate and charge system.

1993-95 MX-3	
4 cyl.	2.2
V6	2.7
1993-95 MX-5 Miata	2.1
1995 Millenia	2.2
w/Turbo, add	.1
1993-95 626, MX-6	2.1
1993-95 929	4.0
1993-95 RX-7	2.2
Recover refrigerant, add	.2

(G) Sensor, Ambient Temperature, Renew

1995 Millenia	.3
1993-95 929	.4

	Chilton Time

(G) Sensor, In-Vehicle, Renew

1995 Millenia	.6
1993-95 929	.6

(G) Sensor, Sun/Photo, Renew

1995 Millenia	.5
1993-95 929	.5

(G) Switch, High or Low Pressure, Renew

1995 Millenia	1.3
1993-95 MX-3	2.0
1993-94 323, Protege	1.8
1995 323, Protege	1.3
1993-95 626, MX-6	1.3
1993-95 929	1.3
1993-95 RX-7	1.5
Note: Includes evacuate & charge AC system.	
Recover refrigerant, add	.2

(G) Valve, Expansion, Renew
Includes: Evacuate and charge system.

1993-95 MX-3	2.7
1993-95 MX-5 Miata	2.0
1995 Millenia	2.1
1993-94 323, Protege	1.9
1995 323, Protege	2.1
1993-95 626, MX-6	2.0
1993-95 929	3.1
1993-95 RX-7	2.0
Recover refrigerant, add	.2

MAZDA TRUCKS
MPV • NAVAJO • PICKUP

LABOR — COOLING SYSTEM — LABOR

TESTING

(M) Pressure Test Cooling System

	Chilton Time
All models	.3

SERVICE

(G) Belt, Fan Drive, Renew

All models	.3

(G) Belt, Serpentine Drive, Renew

1994-95 B Series	
4 cyl.	.6
V6	.8
1993-94 Navajo	.6

(G) Control Assy., Heater, Renew

1993 B2200, B2600	.7
1994-95 B Series	1.0
1993-95 MPV	.7
1993-94 Navajo	1.1

(G) Core, Heater, R&R or Renew

1993 B2200, B2600	4.5
1994 B Series	1.0
1995 B Series	3.5
1993-95 MPV	
front	3.0
rear	1.7
1993-94 Navajo	2.0

	Chilton Time
Boil & Repair, add	1.2
Repair Core, add	.9
Recore, add	1.2

(G) Expansion (Freeze) Plugs, Water Jacket, Renew
Add appropriate time to access plug.

All models, each	.5

(G) Fan Assy., Renew
Includes: R&R radiator shroud where required.

All models	.5

(G) Fan, Auxiliary Cooling Assy., Renew

1993-95 MPV	
one	.4
each adtnl.	.1

(G) Fan Assy., Electric Cooling, Renew

1993-95	.6

(G) Gauge, Temperature (Dash Unit), Renew

1993-95 All models	1.1

(G) Gauge, Temperature (Engine Unit), Renew

1993-95 All models	.5

	Chilton Time

(G) Hoses, By-Pass, Renew

1993-95 MPV	.6

(G) Hoses, Cooling System, Renew

All models, each	.4

(G) Hoses, Heater, Renew

All models	
one side	.6
both sides	1.0
rear, all	.8

(G) Hoses, Radiator, Renew
Includes: Drain and refill cooling system as required.

All models	
upper	.3
lower	.5

(G) Motor, Heater Blower, Renew

1993 B2200, B2600	1.0
1994-95 B Series	.8
1993-95 MPV	
front	.6
rear	1.0
1993-94 Navajo	.7

(G) Pump and/or Gasket, Water, Renew
Includes: Drain and refill cooling system.

LABOR — COOLING SYSTEM — LABOR

	Chilton Time
1993 B2200	2.5
1993 B2600	.8
1994-95 B Series	
4 cyl.	1.5
V6	2.0
w/AC, add	
4 cyl.	.5
V6	.2
1993-95 MPV	
4 cyl.	.8
V6	2.4
w/AC, add	.1
w/PS, add	.1
1993-94 Navajo	2.0
w/AC, add	.2

(G) Radiator Assy., R&R or Renew

	Chilton Time
1993-95 All models	1.2
w/AT, add	.2
Boil & Repair, add	1.5
Rod Clean, add	1.9
Repair Core, add	1.3
Renew Tank, add	1.6
Renew Trans. Oil Cooler, add	1.9
Recore Radiator, add	1.7

COOLING SYSTEM

(G) Relay, AC Condenser Cooling Fan, Renew

	Chilton Time
1993-95 MPV	.4

(G) Relay, Heater Blower Motor, Renew

1993-95 MPV	
front	.3
rear	1.0

(G) Resistor, Heater Blower Motor, Renew

1993 B2200, B2600	.5
1994-95 B Series	.4
1993-95 MPV	
front	.3
rear	1.0
1993-94 Navajo	.4

(G) Switch, Coolant Temperature Sensor, Renew

1993 B2200, B2600	.5

(G) Switch, Heater Blower Motor, Renew

1994-95 B Series	.8
1993-95 MPV	.8
1993-94 Navajo	.9

LABOR

	Chilton Time
(G) Tensioner, Drive Belt, Renew	
1994-95 B Series	.4
1993-94 Navajo	.5

(G) Thermostat, Coolant, Renew

1993 B2200, B2600	.7
1994-95 B Series	
4 cyl.	.8
V6	1.0
1993-95 MPV	.8
1993-94 Navajo	.9

(G) Valve, Heater Control, Renew

1993-95	.5

(G) Winterize Cooling System

Includes: Run engine to check for leaks, tighten all hose connections. Test radiator and pressure cap, drain radiator and engine block. Add antifreeze and refill system.

All models	.5

LABOR — AIR CONDITIONING — LABOR

Note: If more than one item requires replacement where evacuation and discharging the system is already included in the operation, deduct 1.0 hour for each additional item from the time listed.

SERVICE AND TESTING

(G) Drain, Evacuate and Recharge System

	Chilton Time
All models	1.0
Recover refrigerant, add	.2

(G) Flush Refrigerant System, Complete

To be used in conjunction with component replacement which could contaminate system. Includes evacuate and recharge.

All models	1.3
Recover refrigerant, add	.2

(G) Leak Check

Includes: Check all lines and connections.

All models	.5

(G) Recover and/or Recycle AC Refrigerant

Add to evacuate and charge the AC system, as required.

All models, add	.2

(G) Refrigerant, Add (Partial Charge)

All models	.6

COMPONENTS

(G) Belt, Compressor Drive, Renew

1993 B Series	.3
1994-95 B Series	
4 cyl.	.6
V6	.8
1993-95 MPV	.3
1993-94 Navajo	.6
w/PS, add	.1

AIR CONDITIONING

(G) Blower Motor, Renew

	Chilton Time
1993 B Series	1.0
1994-95 B Series	.8
1993-95 MPV	
front	.6
rear	1.0
1993-94 Navajo	.7

(G) Coil, Compressor Clutch, Renew

1993 B Series	2.2
1994-95 B Series	
4 cyl.	2.0
V6	1.5
1993-95 MPV	2.2
1993-94 Navajo	2.2

Note: Add time to evacuate & charge AC system as needed.

Recover refrigerant, add	.2

(G) Coil, Evaporator, Renew

Includes: Evacuate and charge system.

1993 B Series	2.0
1994-95 B Series	2.0
1993-95 MPV	
front	2.0
rear	2.0
1993-94 Navajo	2.9
Recover refrigerant, add	.2

(G) Compressor Assy., Renew

Includes: Transfer parts as required. Evacuate and charge system.

1993 B Series	2.0
1994-95 B Series	
4 cyl.	2.3
V6	1.9
1993-95 MPV	2.0
1993-94 Navajo	2.4
Recover refrigerant, add	.2

(G) Condenser Assy., Renew

Includes: Evacuate and charge system.

1993 B Series	1.5

LABOR

	Chilton Time
1994-95 B Series	1.5
1993-95 MPV	1.5
1993-94 Navajo	1.7
Recover refrigerant, add	.2

(G) Hoses, AC, Renew

Includes: Evacuate and charge system.

1993 B Series	
one	1.5
each adtnl.	.5
1994-95 B Series, each	1.4
1993-94 MPV	
one	1.5
each adtnl.	.5
1993-94 Navajo	
one	1.7
each adtnl.	.5
Recover refrigerant, add	.2

(G) Receiver/Drier Assy., Renew

Includes: Evacuate and charge system.

1993 B Series	1.1
1994-95 B Series	1.2
1993-95 MPV	1.4
1993-94 Navajo	1.4
Recover refrigerant, add	.2

(G) Relay, AC, Renew

1993-95 MPV	
front	.3
rear	.4

(G) Resistor, Blower Motor, Renew

1993-95, front or rear	.4

(G) Seal, Compressor Shaft, Renew

Includes: R&R compressor. Evacuate and charge system.

1993 B Series	2.3
1994-95 B Series	
4 cyl.	2.3
V6	1.8
1993-95 MPV	2.3

LABOR | AIR CONDITIONING | LABOR

	Chilton Time
1993-94 Navajo	2.5
Recover refrigerant, add	.2

(G) Switch, AC On/Off Control, Renew

1993-95 MPV	.4

(G) Switch, High or Low Pressure, Renew

	Chilton Time
1993 B Series	1.4
1993-94 Navajo	1.3

Note: Add time to evacuate & charge AC system as needed.

Recover refrigerant, add	.2

(G) Valve, Expansion, Renew

Includes: Evacuate and charge system.

	Chilton Time
1993 B Series	1.4
1993-95 MPV	
front	1.6
rear	1.7
Recover refrigerant, add	.2

MERCEDES-BENZ
190 • 220 • 280 • 380 • 400 • 420 • 500 • 560 • 600

LABOR | COOLING SYSTEM | LABOR

TESTING

(M) Pressure Test Cooling System

	Chilton Time
All models	.3\

SERVICE

(G) Belt, Alternator Drive, Renew

1993 190E 2.3	.3
1993 300SD	1.5
1993 300SD	.8
1993 300E	.8
1993 300CE, 300TE	1.0
1993 300SE	1.0
1993 300SL	1.0
1993 500SL	1.0

(G) Belt, Drive, Adjust

1993 190D, 190E	
one	.2
each adtnl.	.1
1993 300D	
one	.2
each adtnl.	.1
1993 300E	
one	.2
each adtnl.	.1
1993 300CE, 300TE, 300SE	
one	.2
each adtnl.	.1
1993 300SL	
one	.2
each adtnl.	.1
one	.2
each adtnl.	.1

(G) Belt, Power Steering Drive, Renew

1993 190E 2.3	.6
1993 300D	1.1
1993 300E	1.1
1993 300CE, 300TE	1.1
1993 300SE	1.1
1993 300SL	1.1
1993 500SL	1.1

(G) Belt, Serpentine Drive, Renew

1993 190D, 190E	.6
1994-95 C220	.5
1994-95 C280	.9
1993 300D	.6
1995 E300D	.9
1993 300SD	.6
1994-95 S350TD	.6
1993 300E	.9

	Chilton Time
1993 300CE, 300TE	.9
1993 300SE	.9
1993 300SL	.6
1994-95 E320	.9
1993 400E, 400SEL	.8
1994-95 E420	.8
1993-94 500E, E500	.6
1993 500SEC	.6
1993 500SEL	.6
1993 500SL	.8
1994-95 SL500	.6
1993 600SEC, 600SEL	1.5
1993 600SL	1.6
1994-95 S600	1.5
1994-95 SL600	1.6

(G) Core, Heater, R&R or Renew

1993 190D, 190E	9.0
1994-95 C220	16.0
1994-95 C280	16.0
1993 300D	15.4
1995 E300D	7.9
1993 300E	7.9
1993 300SD	22.5
1993 300CE, 300TE	7.9
1993 300SE	22.5
1993 300SL	15.0
1994-95 E320	7.9
1994-95 S350TD	22.5
1993 400E	7.9
1993 400SEL	22.5
1994-95 E420	7.9
1993-94 500E, E500	7.9
1993 500SL	16.5
1994-95 SL500	16.5
1993 500SEC	22.5
1993 500SEL	22.5
1993 600SEC, 600SEL	22.5
1993 600SL	16.5
1994-95 S600	22.5
1994-95 SL600	16.5
Boil & Repair, add	1.2
Repair Core, add	.9
Recore, add	1.2

(G) Fan Assy., Electric Cooling, Renew

1993 190E	
2.3	.6
2.6	2.5
1993 300D	1.2
1995 E300D	1.0
1993 300CE	1.1
1993 300E	1.1
1993 300SD	1.2

	Chilton Time
1993 300SE	1.2
1993 300SL	.9
1994-95 E320	1.1
1994-95 S350TD	1.2
1993 400E	2.0
1993 500SEC	1.2
1993 500SEL	1.2
1993 500SL	1.0
1994-95 SL500	1.0
1993 600SEC, 600SEL	1.2
1993 600SL	1.2
1994-95 S600	1.2
1994-95 SL600	1.2

(G) Hoses, Cooling System, Renew

1993 190D, 190E	1.2
1993 300E	1.4
1993 300D	1.1
1993 300SD	1.1
1993 300CE, 300TE	1.4
1993 300SE	.9
1994-95 E320	1.4
1994-95 S350TD	1.1
1993 400E, 400SEL	2.8
1994-95 E420	2.8
1993-94 500E, E500	2.8
1993 500SEC	2.4
1993 500SEL	2.4
1993 500SL	2.4
1994-95 SL500	2.4

(G) Hoses, Heater, Renew

1993 190D, 190E	2.0
1993 300D	2.8
1993 300E	2.8
1993 300CE, 300TE	2.8
1993 300SE	2.5
1993 300SL	8.7
1994-95 E320	2.8
1993 400E	2.2
1994-95 E420	2.2
1993-94 500E, E500	2.2
1993 500SL	8.7
1994-95 SL500	8.7

(G) Hoses, Radiator, Renew

Includes: Drain and refill cooling system as required.

Upper	
1993-95	.9
Lower	
1993 190D, 190E	1.1
1994-95 C220	.6
1994-95 C280	.6

LABOR   COOLING SYSTEM   LABOR

	Chilton Time
1993 300D	1.1
1993 300SD	.9
1993 300E	1.1
1993 300CE, 300TE	1.1
1993 300SE	1.1
1993 300SL	1.1
1993 400E, 400SEL	.9
1994-95 E420	.9
1993-94 500E	.9
1993 500SEC	.9
1993 500SEL	.9
1993 500SL	1.1
1993 600SEL	.9
1993 600SEC, 600SL	.9

(G) Motor, Heater Blower, Renew

	Chilton Time
1993 190D, 190E	2.7
1994-95 C220	.6
1994-95 C280	.6
1993 300D	.9
1995 E300D	3.1
1993 300SD	1.1
1993 300E	3.1
1993 300CE	3.1
1993 300SE	1.1
1993 300SL	3.1
1994-95 E320	3.1
1994-95 S350TD	1.1
1993 400E	3.1
1993 400SEL	1.1
1994-95 E420	3.1
1993-94 500E, E500	3.1
1993 500SEL	1.1
1993 500SEC	1.1
1993 500SL	3.1
1994-95 SL500	3.1
1993 600SEC, 600SEL	1.1
1993 600SL	3.1
1994-95 S600	1.1
1994-95 SL600	3.1

(G) Pump and/or Gasket, Water, Renew
Includes: Drain and refill cooling system.

	Chilton Time
1993 190E	3.7
1994-95 C220	3.3
1994-95 C280	4.9
1993 300D	4.5
1995 E300D	3.6
1993 300SD	2.1
1993 300E	5.7
1993 300SL	6.4
1993 300SE, 300SEL	5.8
1994-95 E320	6.4
1994-95 S350TD	2.1
1993 400E, 400SEL	6.4
1994-95 E420	6.4
1993-94 500E, E500	6.4
1993 500SEC	5.1
1993 500SEL	5.1
1993 500SL	5.5
1994-95 SL500	5.1
1993 600SEC, 600SEL	5.5

	Chilton Time
1993 600SL	4.2
1994-95 S600	5.5
1994-95 SL600	4.2

(G) Radiator Assy., R&R or Renew

	Chilton Time
1993 190E 2.6	3.3
1993 190E 2.3	1.7
1994-95 C220	1.9
1994-95 C280	2.2
1993 300SD	1.8
1993 300D	1.5
1995 E300D	1.5
1993 300E	1.5
1993 300CE, 300TE	1.5
1993 300SE	1.5
1993 300SL	2.2
1994-95 E320	1.5
1994-95 S350TD	1.8
1993 400E, 400SEL	2.5
1994-95 E420	2.5
1993-94 500E, E500	2.5
1993 500SEC	2.2
1993 500SEL	1.5
1993 500SL	2.7
1994-95 SL500	1.9
1993 600SEC, 600SEL	2.1
1993 600SL	1.8
1994-95 S600	2.1
1994-95 SL600	1.8
Boil & Repair, add	1.5
Rod Clean, add	1.9
Repair Core, add	1.3
Renew Tank, add	1.6
Renew Trans. Oil Cooler, add	1.9
Recore Radiator, add	1.7

(G) Sending Unit, Engine Coolant Temp., Renew

	Chilton Time
All models	.3

(G) Switch, Radiator Fan Motor (Coolant Temp.), Renew

	Chilton Time
1993 190E	.3

(G) Tensioner, Drive Belt, Renew

	Chilton Time
1993 190E 2.6	2.5
1994-95 C220	1.0
1994-95 C280	2.5
1993 300D	1.5
1995 E300D	1.5
1993 300E	2.5
1993 300SD	1.1
1993 300CE, 300TE	1.5
1993 300SE	2.8
1993 300SL	1.5
1994-95 E320	2.7

	Chilton Time
1994-95 S350TD	1.1
1993 400E, 400SEL	1.4
1994-95 E420	1.4
1993-94 500E, E500	1.4
1993 500SEC	1.1
1993 500SEL	1.1
1993 500SL	1.5
1994-95 SL500	1.5
1993 600SEC, 600SEL	2.5
1993 600SL	2.5
1994-95 S600	2.5
1994-95 SL600	2.5

(G) Thermostat, Coolant, Renew

	Chilton Time
1993 190D, 190E	.8
1994-95 C220	.6
1994-95 C280	.6
1993 300D	.8
1995 E300D	.8
1993 300E	.8
1993 300SD	.9
1993 300CE, 300TE	1.8
1993 300SE	.8
1993 300SL	.8
1994-95 E320	.8
1994-95 S350TD	.9
1993 400E, 400SEL	2.0
1994-95 E420	2.0
1993-94 500E, E500	2.0
1993 500SL	1.2
1994-95 SL500	1.2
1993 500SEC	1.4
1993 500SEL	1.4
1993 600SEC, 600SEL	1.8
1993 600SL	1.8
1994-95 S600	1.8
1994-95 SL600	1.8

(G) Valve, Heater Control, Renew

	Chilton Time
1993 190D, 190E	1.1
1994-95 C220	1.2
1994-95 C280	1.2
1993 300D	.9
1993 300CE	.8
1995 E300D	.8
1993 300E	.8
1993 300SD	1.1
1993 300SE	1.1
1993 300SL	.9
1993 300TE	.8
1994-95 E320	.8
1994-95 S350TD	1.1
1993 400E	.8
1994-95 E420	.8
1993-94 500E, E500	.8
1993 500SEC	1.1
1993 500SEL	1.1
1993 500SL	.9
1993 600SEC, 600SEL	1.1
1993 600SL	.9
1994-94 S600	1.1
1994-95 SL600	.9

LABOR AIR CONDITIONING LABOR

Note: If more than one item requires replacement where evacuation and discharging the system is already included in the operation, deduct 1.0 hour for each additional item from the time listed.

SERVICE AND TESTING

(G) Drain, Evacuate and Recharge System

	Chilton Time
All models	1.5

(G) Flush Refrigerant System, Complete

To be used in conjunction with component replacement which could contaminate system. Includes evacuate and recharge.

All models	1.3

(G) Leak Check

Includes: Check all lines and connections.

All models	.8

(G) Recover and/or Recycle AC Refrigerant

Add to evacuate and charge the AC system, as required.

All models, add	.2

(G) Refrigerant, Add (Partial Charge)

All models	.6

COMPONENTS

(G) Belt, Compressor Drive, Renew

1993 190E 2.3	.8
1993 300D	.6
1993 500SEC	.5

(G) Blower Motor, Renew

1993 190D, 190E	2.7
1994-95 C220	.6
1994-95 C280	.6
1993 300D	.9
1995 E300D	3.1
1993 300SD	1.1
1993 300E	3.1
1993 300CE	3.1
1993 300SE	1.1
1993 300SL	3.1
1994-95 E320	3.1
1994-95 S350TD	1.1
1993 400E	3.1
1993 400SEL	1.1
1994-95 E420	3.1
1993-94 500E, E500	3.1
1993 500SEL	1.1
1993 500SEC	1.1
1993 500SL	3.1
1994-95 SL500	3.1
1993 600SEC, 600SEL	1.1
1993 600SL	3.1
1994-95 S600	1.1
1994-95 SL600	3.1

(G) Coil, Evaporator, Renew

Includes: Evacuate and charge system.

1993 190D, 190E	5.1
1994-95 C220	18.3
1994-95 C280	18.3
1993 300SD	25.9
1995 E300D	17.4
1993 300E	16.5
1993 300CE, 300TE	16.5

	Chilton Time
1993 300SE	27.4
1993 300SL	16.9
1994-95 E320	16.5
1994-95 S350TD	25.9
1993 400E	16.5
1993 400SEL	24.3
1994-95 E420	24.3
1993-94 500E, E500	24.3
1993 500SEC	18.8
1993 500SEL	18.8
1993 500SL	16.9
1994-95 SL500	16.9
1993 600SEC, 600SEL	27.3
1993 600SL	18.3
1994-95 S600	27.3
1994-95 SL600	18.3

(G) Compressor Assy., Renew

1993 190D, 190E	2.7
1994-95 C220	3.6
1994-95 C280	3.6
1993 300D	2.7
1995 E300D	1.8
1993 300SD	1.8
1993 300E	2.2
1993 300CE, 300TE	2.2
1993 300SE	1.5
1993 300SL	2.2
1994-95 E320	2.2
1994-95 S350TD	1.8
1993 400E	2.2
1993 400SEL	1.5
1994-95 E420	2.2
1993-94 500E, E500	2.2
1993 500SEC	1.5
1993 500SEL	1.5
1993 500SL	2.1
1994-95 SL500	2.1
1993 600SEC, 600SEL	7.8
1993 600SL	2.1
1994-95 S600	7.8
1994-95 SL600	2.1

Add time to evacuate and charge system.

(G) Condenser Assy., Renew

Add time to evacuate and charge system.

1993 190E 2.6	1.1
1993 300D	2.5
1995 E300D	2.2
1993 300SD	1.5
1993 300E	2.2
1993 300CE, 300TE	2.2
1993 300SE	1.5
1993 300SL	3.7
1994-95 E320	2.2
1994-95 S350TD	1.5
1993 400E	3.3
1993 400SEL	1.5
1994-95 E420	3.3
1993-94 500E, E500	3.3
1993 500SEC	1.5
1993 500SEL	1.5
1993 500SL	3.7
1994-95 SL500	3.7
1993 600SEC, 600SEL	1.5
1993 600SL	3.7
1994-95 S600	1.5
1994-95 SL600	3.7

(G) Fan, Auxiliary, Renew

1993 190D, 190E	.8
1993 300D	1.1
1995 E300D	2.7

	Chilton Time
1993 300SD	1.2
1993 300E	2.7
1993 300CE, 300TE	2.7
1993 300SE	1.2
1993 300SL	3.7
1994-95 E320	2.7
1994-95 S350TD	1.2
1993 400E, 400SEL	2.7
1994-95 E420	2.7
1993-94 500E, E500	2.7
1993 500SEC	1.2
1993 500SEL	1.2
1993 500SL	3.7
1994-95 SL500	3.7
1993 600SEC, 600SEL	1.2
1993 600SL	3.7
1994-95 S600	1.2
1994-95 SL600	3.7

Add time to evacuate and charge system, where required.

(G) Module, AC Control, Renew

1993 190D, 190E	.6
1994-95 C220	.6
1994-95 C280	.6
1993 300D	.9
1995 E300D	.5
1993 300CE	.5
1993 300E	.5
1993 300SD	.9
1993 300SD	.9
1993 300TE	.5
1994-95 E320	.5
1994-95 S350TD	.9
1993 400E	.5
1993 400SEL	.9
1994-95 E420	.5
1993-94 500E, E500	.5
1993 500SEC	.9
1993 500SEL	.9
1993 500SL	.5
1994-95 SL500	.5
1993 600SEC, 600SEL	.9
1993 600SL	.5
1994-95 S600	.9
1994-95 SL600	.5

(G) Motor, Aspirator Blower, Renew

1993 190D, 190E	.8
1993 300D	.6
1995 E300D	.6
1993 300E	.6
1993 300CE, 300TE	.6
1994-95 E320	.6
1993 400E	.6
1994-95 E420	.6
1993-94 500E, E500	.6

(G) Receiver/Drier Assy., Renew

Includes: Evacuate and charge system.

1994-95 C220	1.8
1994-95 C280	1.8
1993 300D	2.0
1995 E300D	2.0
1993 300SD	2.0
1993 300E	2.0
1993 300CE, 300TE	2.0
1993 300SE	2.0
1993 300SL	2.7
1994-95 E320	2.0
1994-95 S350TD	2.0
1993 400E, 400SEL	2.0

LABOR

AIR CONDITIONING

LABOR

	Chilton Time
1994-95 E420	2.0
1993-94 500E, E500	2.5
1993 500SEC	2.0
1993 500SEL	2.0
1993 500SL	2.5
1994-95 SL500	2.5
1993 600SEC, 600SEL	2.1
1993 600SL	2.5
1994-95 S600	2.1
1994-95 SL600	2.5

(G) Relay, Auxiliary Fan, Renew

All models	.3

(G) Switch, Blower Motor, Renew

1993 190D, 190E	.6
1993 300D	1.1

(G) Switch, Compressor Cut-Off, Renew

All models	.3

(G) Valve, Expansion, Renew
Add time to evacuate and charge system.

1993 190D, 190E	1.2
1993 300SD	3.1
1993 300CE, 300TE	1.2
1993 300D	1.2
1995 E300D	1.5
1993 300SE	2.7

	Chilton Time
1993 300SL	3.6
1994-95 E320	1.5
1994-95 S350TD	3.1
1993 400E	2.0
1993 400SEL	2.7
1994-95 E420	2.0
1993-94 500E, E500	2.0
1993 500SEC	2.7
1993 500SEL	2.7
1993 500SL	3.6
1994-95 SL500	3.6
1993 600SEC, 600SEL	3.1
1993 600SL	3.6
1994-95 S600	3.1
1994-95 SL600	3.6

MITSUBISHI
DIAMANTE • ECLIPSE • GALANT • MIRAGE • PRECIS • 300GT

LABOR

COOLING SYSTEM

LABOR

TESTING

(M) Pressure Test Cooling System

All models	.3

SERVICE

(G) Belt, Drive, Adjust

All models
one	.3
each adtnl.	.2

(G) Belt, Drive, Renew

All models
V belt	.5
Serpentine belt	.7

(G) Combination Gauge Assy., Renew

1993-95 3000GT	3.0

(G) Cooler, Engine Oil, Renew

1993-94 Eclipse	1.5
1995 Eclipse	.8
1993-95 3000GT	1.2
1993-95 Diamante	1.6

(G) Core, Heater, R&R or Renew

1993 Galant	5.5
1994-95 Galant	6.3
w/AT add	.2
1993-95 Mirage	4.7
1993-95 Diamante	6.9
1993-95 3000GT	6.8
w/Turbo add	.3
1993-94 Eclipse	5.5
w/AC add	.7
1995 Eclipse	6.8
w/AC add	.3
w/AT add	.2
w/Turbo & cruise control add	.3
1993-94 Precis	
wo/AC	4.0
w/AC	5.0
Boil & Repair, add	1.2
Repair Core, add	.8
Recore, add	1.2

(G) Expansion (Freeze) Plugs, Water Jacket, Renew
Add appropriate time to access plug.

All models, each	.5

(G) Gauge, Temperature (Dash Unit), Renew

1993-94 Precis	.7
1993-95 Mirage	.7
1993 Galant	.9
1994-95 Galant	.7
1993-94 Eclipse	.7
1995 Eclipse	.9
1993-95 Diamante	.9
1993-95 3000GT	3.1

(G) Gauge, Temperature (Engine Unit), Renew

All models	.5

(G) Hoses, Heater, Renew

All models	.5

(G) Hoses, Radiator, Renew
Includes: Drain and refill cooling system as required.

Upper
1993-94 Precis	.4
1993-95 Mirage	.6
1993 Galant	.4
1994-95 Galant	.6
1993-94 Eclipse	.4
1995 Eclipse	.6
1993-95 Diamante	.6
1993-95 3000GT	.6
w/Turbo add	.3

Lower
1993-94 Precis	.5
1993-95 Mirage	1.3
1993 Galant	.6
1994-95 Galant	.8
1993-95 Eclipse	.8
1993-95 Diamante	.6
1993-95 3000GT	1.0
w/Turbo add	.3

(G) Motor, Heater or AC Blower, Renew

1993-94 Precis	.5
1993-95 Mirage	.4
1993 Galant	.7
1994-95 Galant	.8
1993-95 Diamante, 3000GT	.7
1993-94 Eclipse	.4
1995 Eclipse	.8

(G) Motor, Radiator Fan and/or Fan, Renew

1993-94 Precis	.7
1993-95 Mirage	.8
1993 Galant	.6
1994-95 Galant	.9
1993-94 Eclipse	.7
1995 Eclipse	.9
1993-95 Diamante	.8
1993-95 3000GT	.9

(G) Pump and/or Gasket, Water, Renew
Includes: Drain and refill cooling system.

1993-94 Precis	2.2
w/AC add	.2
w/PS add	.2
1993 Galant	3.5
w/AC add	.3
w/DOHC add	.7
1994-95 Galant	3.3
w/AC add	.3
w/DOHC add	.7
1993-95 Mirage	3.0
w/AC add	.3
w/PS add	.2
1993-95 Eclipse	3.3
w/AC add	.3
w/DOHC add	.7
1993-95 Diamante	4.5
1993-95 3000GT	4.1
w/AC add	.3

(G) Radiator Assy., R&R or Renew

1993-94 Precis	.9
w/AC add	.1
w/AT add	.2
1993-95 Mirage	1.2

LABOR COOLING SYSTEM LABOR

	Chilton Time
1993-95 Galant	1.0
1993-95 Diamante	1.2
1993-94 Eclipse	1.1
1995 Eclipse	1.0
1993-95 3000GT	1.5
w/AT add	.2
Boil & Repair, add	1.5
Rod Clean, add	1.9
Repair Core, add	1.3
Renew Tank, add	1.6
Renew Trans. Oil Cooler, add	1.9
Recore Radiator, add	1.7

(G) Relay, Heater Blower Motor, Renew

1993-95 Diamante	.6
1993-94 Eclipse	.4
1995 Eclipse	.3
1993-95 3000GT	.4
1993-95 Mirage	.4

(G) Relay, Radiator Fan Motor, Renew

All models	.4

(G) Resistor, Fan Motor, Renew

1993-94 Precis	.3

(G) Resistor, Heater Blower Motor, Renew

1993-94 Precis	.6
1993-95 Mirage	.6
1993 Galant	.3
1994-95 Galant	.4
1993-94 Eclipse	.6
1995 Eclipse	.4
1993-95 Diamante Wagon	.4
1993-95 3000GT	.7

(G) Switch, Heater Blower Motor, Renew

1993-95 Diamante	1.0
1993-95 3000GT	2.0
1993 Galant	.9
1994-95 Galant	1.1
1993-95 Mirage	1.0
1993-94 Eclipse	.6
1995 Eclipse	1.5

	Chilton Time
1993-94 Precis	.6

(G) Switch, Radiator Fan Motor (Coolant Temp.), Renew

1993-95 Mirage	.9
1993 Galant	.6
1993-95 Diamante	.6
1993-94 Eclipse	.8
1993-95 3000GT	1.0

(G) Thermostat, Coolant, Renew

1993-94 Precis	.4
1993-95 Eclipse	.6
1993-95 Mirage, Galant	.6
1993-95 Diamante, 3000GT	.6

(G) Winterize Cooling System

Includes: Run engine to check for leaks, tighten all hose connections. Test radiator and pressure cap, drain radiator and engine block. Add antifreeze and refill system.

All models	.5

LABOR AIR CONDITIONING LABOR

Note: If more than one item requires replacement where evacuation and discharging the system is already included in the operation, deduct 1.0 hour for each additional item from the time listed.

SERVICE AND TESTING

(G) Drain, Evacuate and Recharge System

	Chilton Time
All models	1.0

(G) Flush Refrigerant System, Complete

To be used in conjunction with component replacement which could contaminate system. Includes evacuate and recharge.

All models	1.3

(G) Recover and/or Recycle AC Refrigerant

Add to evacuate and charge the AC system, as required.

All models	.2

(G) Refrigerant, Add (Partial Charge)

All models	.6

COMPONENTS

(G) Accumulator Assy., Renew

Includes: Evacuate and charge system.

1993-94 Precis	1.4

(G) Belt, Compressor Drive, Renew

1993-95 V belt	.5
1993-95 serpentine belt	.7

(G) Blower Motor, Renew

1993-94 Precis	.5
1993-94 Mirage	.4
1993 Galant	.7
1994 Galant	.8
1993-94 Diamante, 3000GT	.7
1993-94 Eclipse	.4
1995 Eclipse	.8

(G) Clutch Assy., Compressor, Renew

	Chilton Time
1993-94 Precis	2.1
w/DOHC add	.2
1993-95 Mirage	2.2
1993 Galant	2.0
w/DOHC add	.2
1994-95 Galant	2.2
1993-94 Eclipse	1.7
w/DOHC add	.3
1995 Eclipse	2.0
w/Turbo add	.4
1993-95 Diamante	2.4
1993-95 3000GT	2.4
w/Turbo add	1.0

(G) Compressor Assy., Renew

Includes: Transfer parts as required. Evacuate and charge system.

1993-94 Precis	1.0
1993-95 Mirage	2.0
1993 Galant	1.8
w/DOHC add	.2
1994-95 Galant	2.2
1993-94 Eclipse	1.5
w/DOHC add	.3
1995 Eclipse	1.8
w/Turbo add	.4
1993-95 Diamante	2.1
1993-95 3000GT	2.1
w/Turbo add	1.0

(G) Condenser Assy., Renew

Includes: Evacuate and charge system.

1993-94 Precis	.8
1993-95 Mirage	1.7
1993 Galant	1.7
1994-95 Galant	2.1
1993-94 Eclipse	1.4
w/DOHC add	.2
1995 Eclipse	1.6
1993-95 Diamante	1.7
1993-95 3000GT	1.8
w/Turbo add	.7

(G) Core, Evaporator, Renew

Includes: Evacuate and charge system.

	Chilton Time
1993-94 Precis	2.5
1993-95 Mirage	2.2
1993 Galant	2.1
1994-95 Galant	2.2
1993-94 Eclipse	2.0
1995 Eclipse	3.9
1993-95 Diamante	2.1
1993-95 3000GT	2.2
w/auto AC add	.2

(G) Hoses, AC, Renew

Includes: Evacuate and charge system.

Discharge
1993-94 Precis	1.1
1993-95 Mirage	1.2
1993-95 Galant	1.2
1993-94 Eclipse	1.1
1995 Eclipse	1.4
1993-95 Diamante	1.1
1993-95 3000GT	1.1
w/Turbo add	.2

Suction
1993-94 Precis	1.1
1993-95 Mirage	1.2
1993 Galant	1.1
1994-95 Galant	1.2
1993-94 Eclipse	1.2
1995 Eclipse	1.1
1993-95 Diamante	1.1
1993-95 3000GT	1.1
w/Turbo add	.2

(G) Motor, Condenser Fan, Renew

1993-94 Precis	.4
1993-95 Mirage	.9
1993-95 Galant	.7
1993-94 Eclipse	.6
1995 Eclipse	.7
1993-95 Diamante	.6
1993-95 3000GT	.7

LABOR — AIR CONDITIONING — LABOR

(G) Receiver/Drier Assy., Renew
Includes: Evacuate and charge system.
	Chilton Time
All models	1.5
w/DOHC add	.1
w/Turbo add	.2
wo/Turbo add	.2

(G) Relay, Condenser Fan Motor, Renew
All models	.4

(G) Resistor, Blower Motor, Renew
All models	.7

(G) Switch, AC Low Pressure, Renew
	Chilton Time
1993-94 Precis	.9

(G) Switch, Blower Motor, Renew
1993-94 Precis	.6
1993-95 Mirage	1.0
1993 Galant	.9
1994-95 Galant	1.1
1993-94 Eclipse	.6
1995 Eclipse	1.5
1993-95 Diamante	1.0
1993-95 3000GT	2.0

(G) Valve, Expansion, Renew
Includes: Evacuate and charge system.
	Chilton Time
1993-94 Precis	2.2
1993-94 Mirage	2.1
1993-95 Galant	2.1
1993-94 Eclipse	2.0
1995 Eclipse	3.9
1993-95 Diamante	2.1
1993-95 3000GT	2.2
w/auto AC add	.2

MITSUBISHI TRUCKS
EXPO • LRV • MONTERO • PICKUP

LABOR — COOLING SYSTEM — LABOR

TESTING

(M) Pressure Test Cooling System
	Chilton Time
All models	.3

SERVICE

(G) Belt, Drive, Adjust
All models	.3

(G) Belt, Drive, Renew
1993-94 V belt	.4
1993-95 serpentine belt	.6

(G) Combination Gauge Assy., Renew
1993-95 Truck	.5
1993-95 Expo, LRV	.7
1993-95 Montero	.8
Renew speed sensor add	.3

(G) Cooler, Engine Oil, Renew
1993-95 Truck	.8
1993-95 Montero	.7

(G) Core, Front Heater, R&R or Renew
1993-95 Expo, LRV	4.5
1993-95 Truck	4.0
1993-95 Montero	5.2
Boil & Repair, add	1.2
Repair Core, add	.9
Recore, add	1.2

(G) Expansion (Freeze) Plugs, Water Jacket, Renew
Add appropriate time to access plug.
All models, each	.5

(G) Fluid Fan Drive or Fan Blade, Renew
1993-95 Truck	.5
1993-95 Montero	.5

(G) Gauge, Temperature (Dash Unit), Renew
1993-95 Montero	.9

	Chilton Time
1993-95 Truck	.6
1993-95 Expo, LRV	.6

(G) Hoses, Heater, Renew
All models	.8

(G) Hoses, Radiator, Renew
Includes: Drain and refill cooling system as required.
1993-95 Truck	
upper	.4
lower	.6
1993-95 Montero	
upper	.4
lower	.8
1993-95 Expo, LRV	
upper	.6
lower	1.0

(G) Motor, Electric Cooling Fan, Renew
1993-95 Expo, LRV	.5

(G) Motor, Front Heater Blower, Renew
1993-95 Expo, LRV	.6
1993-95 Truck	.5
1993-95 Montero	.5

(G) Pump and/or Gasket, Water, Renew
Includes: Drain and refill cooling system.
1993-95 Truck	
Four 2.0L, 2.4L	2.8
V6	3.6
w/AC add	.3
w/PS add	.2
1993-95 Montero	3.9
w/AC add	.3
1993-95 Expo, LRV	3.1
w/AC add	.3
w/PS add	.2

(G) Radiator Assy., R&R or Renew
1993-95 Truck	1.0
1993-95 Expo, LRV	1.3
1993-95 Montero	1.0

	Chilton Time
w/AT add	.2
Boil & Repair, add	1.5
Rod Clean, add	1.9
Repair Core, add	1.3
Renew Tank, add	1.6
Renew Trans. Oil Cooler, add	1.9
Recore Radiator, add	1.7

(G) Relay, Radiator Fan Motor, Renew
1993-95 Expo, LRV	.3

(G) Resistor, Front Heater Blower Motor, Renew
All models	.6

(G) Sending Unit, Engine Coolant Temp., Renew
All models	.4

(G) Switch, Front Heater Blower Motor, Renew
1993-95 Truck	.6
1993-95 Montero	.8
1993-95 Expo, LRV	1.1

(G) Switch, Radiator Fan Motor (Coolant Temp.), Renew
1993-95 Expo, LRV	.6

(G) Thermostat, Coolant, Renew
All models	.6

(G) Valve, Front Heater Water, Renew
1993-95 Truck	.7

(G) Winterize Cooling System
Includes: Run engine to check for leaks, tighten all hose connections. Test radiator and pressure cap, drain radiator and engine block. Add antifreeze and refill system.
All models	.5

LABOR | AIR CONDITIONING | LABOR

Chilton Time

Note: If more than one item requires replacement where evacuation and discharging the system is already included in the operation, deduct 1.0 hour for each additional item from the time listed.

SERVICE AND TESTING

(G) Drain, Evacuate and Recharge System
All models 1.0

(G) Flush Refrigerant System, Complete
To be used in conjunction with component replacement which could contaminate system. Includes evacuate and recharge.
All models 1.3

(G) Recover and/or Recycle AC Refrigerant
Add to evacuate and charge the AC system, as required.
All models 2

(G) Refrigerant, Add (Partial Charge)
All models 6

COMPONENTS

(G) Belt, Compressor Drive, Renew
All models 4

(G) Blower Motor, Renew
1993-95 Montero 5
1993-95 Truck 5
1993-95 Expo, LRV 6

(G) Clutch Assy., Compressor, Renew
1993-95 Montero 1.4
1993-95 Truck 1.4
1993-95 Expo 2.0
1993-94 LRV 1.6

(G) Compressor Assy., Renew
Includes: Transfer parts as required. Evacuate and charge system.
1993-95 Truck 1.3
1993-95 Montero 2.0
1993-95 Expo 1.8
1993-94 LRV 1.5

(G) Condenser Assy., Renew
Includes: Evacuate and charge system.
1993-95 Truck 1.0
1993-95 Montero 2.1
1993-95 Expo, LRV 2.0

(G) Core, Evaporator, Renew
Includes: Evacuate and charge system.
1993-95 Truck 1.5
1993-95 Montero 1.7
1993-95 Expo, LRV 1.5

(G) Hoses, AC, Renew
Includes: Evacuate and charge system.
All models
one 1.5
each adtnl. 5

(G) Receiver/Drier Assy., Renew
Includes: Evacuate and charge system.
1993-95 Truck 1.5
1993-95 Montero 1.7
1993-95 Expo, LRV 1.5

(G) Relay, Blower Motor, Renew
All models 5

(G) Resistor, Blower Motor, Renew
All models 6

(G) Switch, AC On/Off Control, Renew
1993-95 Truck 6
1993-95 Montero 4
1993-95 Expo, LRV 1.1

(G) Switch, Blower Motor, Renew
1993-95 Truck 6
1993-95 Montero 8
1993-95 Expo, LRV 1.1

(G) Valve, Expansion, Renew
Includes: Evacuate and charge system.
1993-95 Truck 1.7
1993-95 Montero 1.7
1993-95 Expo, LRV 1.5

NISSAN
ALTIMA • 240SX • 300ZX • MAXIMA • NX • SENTRA • STANZA

LABOR | COOLING SYSTEM | LABOR

Chilton Time

SERVICE

(G) Belt, Drive, Adjust
All models
one 4
each adtnl. 1

(G) Belt, Drive, Renew
All models 7
For each adtnl. belt, add 4

(G) Control Assy., Heater and AC, Renew
1993-95 Maxima 1.4
1993-95 Sentra, NX 1.4
1993-95 Altima 7
1993-95 240SX 1.9
1993-95 300ZX 8

(G) Core, Heater, R&R or Renew
1993-95 Maxima 4.0
1993-95 Sentra, NX 5.3
1993-95 Altima 4.3
1993-95 240SX 3.0
1993-95 300ZX 6.5
w/AC, add 5
Boil and Repair, add 1.2
Repair Core, add 9
Recore, add 1.2

(G) Expansion (Freeze) Plugs, Water Jacket, Renew
Add appropriate time to access plug.
All models, each 5

(G) Gauge, Temperature (Dash Unit), Renew
1993-95 Maxima 1.1
1993-95 Altima 1.1
1993-95 240SX 1.5
1993-95 300ZX 1.4

(G) Gauge, Temperature (Engine Unit), Renew
All models 4

(G) Hoses, Heater, Renew
1993-95 Maxima 6
1993-95 Sentra, NX 1.1
1993-95 Altima 1.0
1993-95 240SX 1.2
1993-95 300ZX 5

(G) Hoses, Radiator, Renew
Includes: Drain and refill cooling system as required.
All models, each 6

(G) Motor, Heater Blower, Renew
1993-95 Maxima 6
1993-95 Sentra, NX 5
1993-95 Altima 5
1993-95 240SX 6
1993-95 300ZX 5

(G) Motor, Radiator Fan and/or Fan, Renew
1993-95 Maxima
one 8
each adtnl. 5
1993-95 Sentra, NX
GA 5
SR 1.0
1993-95 Altima 1.0
1993-95 240SX 9
1993-95 300ZX 9

(G) Pump and/or Gasket, Water, Renew
Includes: Drain and refill cooling system.
1993-95 Maxima
SOHC 3.2
DOHC 3.7
1993-95 Sentra, NX
GA 3.1
SR 2.5
1993-95 Altima 2.3

LABOR | COOLING SYSTEM | LABOR

	Chilton Time
1993-95 240SX	1.7
1993-95 300ZX	3.6
w/AC, add	.4
w/PS, add	.3

(G) Radiator Assy., R&R or Renew

1993-95 Maxima	1.1
1993-95 Sentra, NX	
GA	.7
SR	1.1
1993-95 Altima	1.2
1993-95 240SX	2.3
1993-95 300ZX	1.8
w/AC, add	.2
w/AT, add	.1
Boil & Repair, add	1.5

	Chilton Time
Rod Clean, add	1.9
Repair Core, add	1.3
Renew Tank, add	1.6
Renew Trans. Oil Cooler, add	1.9
Recore Radiator, add	1.7

(G) Relay, Radiator Fan Motor, Renew

All models	.4

(G) Resistor, Heater Blower Motor, Renew

All models	.7

(G) Thermostat, Coolant, Renew

1993-95 Maxima	
SOHC	1.0

	Chilton Time
DOHC	1.8
1993-95 Sentra, NX	
GA	2.0
SR	.8
1993-95 Altima	.8
1993-95 240SX	1.2
1993-95 300ZX	2.2

(G) Winterize Cooling System

Includes: Run engine to check for leaks, tighten all hose connections. Test radiator and pressure cap, drain radiator and engine block. Add antifreeze and refill system.

All models	.5

LABOR | AIR CONDITIONING | LABOR

	Chilton Time

Note: If more than one item requires replacement where evacuation and discharging the system is already included in the operation, deduct 1.0 hour for each additional item from the time listed.

SERVICE AND TESTING

(G) Drain, Evacuate and Recharge System

All models	1.0
Recover refrigerant, add	.2

(G) Flush Refrigerant System, Complete

To be used in conjunction with component replacement which could contaminate system. Includes evacuate and recharge.

All models	1.3
Recover refrigerant, add	.2

(G) Recover and/or Recycle AC Refrigerant

Add to evacuate and charge the AC system, as required.

All models, add	.2

COMPONENTS

(G) Accumulator Assy., Renew

Includes: Evacuate and charge system.

All models	1.9
Recover refrigerant, add	.2

(G) Blower Motor, Renew

1993-95 Maxima	.5
1993-95 Sentra, NX	.4
1993-95 Altima	.4
1993-95 240SX	.5
1993-95 300ZX	.4

	Chilton Time

(G) Clutch Assy., Magnetic, Renew

1993-95 Maxima	2.3
1993-95 Sentra, NX	2.4
1993-95 Altima	2.4
1993-95 240SX	2.5
1993-95 300ZX	
wo/Turbo	2.8
w/Turbo	3.2

Add time to evacuate & charge A/C system as needed

Recover refrigerant, add	.2

(G) Compressor Assy., Renew

Includes: Transfer parts as required. Evacuate and charge system.

1993-95 Maxima	1.8
1993-95 Sentra, NX	1.9
1993-95 Altima	2.0
1993-95 240SX	2.0
1993-95 300ZX	
wo/Turbo	2.3
w/Turbo	2.6
Recover refrigerant, add	.2

(G) Condenser Assy., Renew

Includes: Evacuate and charge system.

1993-95 Maxima	2.8
1993-95 Sentra, NX	2.9
1993-95 Altima	1.6
1993-95 240SX	3.8
1993-95 300ZX	3.2
Recover refrigerant, add	.2

(G) Control Assy., Temperature, Renew

1993-95 Maxima	1.6
1993-95 Sentra, NX	2.1
1993-95 Altima	1.3
1993-95 240SX	1.9
1993-95 300ZX	1.3
Renew fan switch, add	.2

	Chilton Time

(G) Core, Evaporator, Renew

Includes: Evacuate and charge system.

1993-95 Maxima	3.0
1993-95 Sentra, NX	3.4
1993-95 Altima	3.0
1993-95 240SX	3.2
1993-95 300ZX	4.2
Recover refrigerant, add	.2

(G) Hoses, AC, Renew

Includes: Evacuate and charge system.

All models	
one	1.9
each adtnl.	.5
Recover refrigerant, add	.2

(G) Receiver/Drier Assy., Renew

Includes: Evacuate and charge system.

All models	1.9
Recover refrigerant, add	.2

(G) Relay, Blower Motor, Renew

All models	.4

(G) Relay, Compressor or Fan, Renew

All models	.5

(G) Switch, Low Pressure Cut-Off, Renew

Includes: Evacuate and charge system.

All models	1.5
Recover refrigerant, add	.2

(G) Valve, Expansion, Renew

Includes: Evacuate and charge system.

1993-95 Maxima	3.0
1993-95 Sentra, NX	3.7
1993-95 Altima	3.3
1993-95 240SX	3.7
1993-95 300ZX	3.7
Recover refrigerant, add	.2

NISSAN TRUCKS
PATHFINDER • PICKUP • QUEST

LABOR
COOLING SYSTEM
LABOR

	Chilton Time
SERVICE	
(G) Belt, Drive, Adjust	
All models	.4
(G) Belt, Drive, Renew	
1993-95 Pickup, Pathfinder	
Four	
KA	.4
V6	.7
1993-95 Quest	.6
Renew each adtnl. belt, add	.1
(G) Blade, Fan, Renew	
1993-95 Pickup, Pathfinder	.6
1993-95 Quest	1.0
(G) Control Assy., Rear Heater, Renew	
1993-95 Quest	.4
(G) Control Assy., Temperature, Renew	
1993-95 Pickup, Pathfinder	1.4
1993-95 Quest	.5
(G) Core, Heater, R&R or Renew	
1993-95 Pickup, Pathfinder	4.2
1993-95 Quest	4.4
w/AC, add	.2
Boil & Repair, add	1.2
Repair Core, add	.9
Recore, add	1.2
(G) Core, Rear Heater, R&R or Renew	
1993-95 Quest	4.6
(G) Coupling, Fan, Renew	
1993-95 Pickup, Pathfinder	.8
(G) Expansion (Freeze) Plugs, Water Jacket, Renew	
Add appropriate time to access plug.	
All models, each	.5
(G) Gauge, Temperature (Dash Unit), Renew	
1993-95 Pickup, Pathfinder	.8
1993-95 Quest	.8
(G) Gauge, Temperature (Engine Unit), Renew	
All models	.4

	Chilton Time
(G) Hoses, Auxiliary Heater, Renew	
1993-95 Quest	3.0
(G) Hoses, Heater, Renew	
1993-95 Pickup, Pathfinder	
Four	
KA	1.2
V6	.5
1993-95 Quest	1.3
(G) Hoses, Radiator, Renew	
Includes: Drain and refill cooling system as required.	
1993-95 Pickup, Pathfinder	
upper	.7
lower	
Four	
KA	1.0
1993-95 Quest	
upper	.5
lower	.4
(G) Motor, Front Heater Blower, Renew	
1993-95 Pickup, Pathfinder	.5
1993-95 Quest	.4
(G) Motor, Radiator Fan and/or Fan, Renew	
1993-95 Quest	1.0
(G) Motor, Rear Heater Blower, Renew	
1993-95 Quest	2.5
Renew blower motor resistor, add	.2
(G) Pump and/or Gasket, Water, Renew	
Includes: Drain and refill cooling system.	
1993-95 Pickup, Pathfinder	
Four	
KA	
4x2	2.0
4x4	2.3
V6	3.2
1993-95 Quest	3.5
(G) Radiator Assy., R&R or Renew	
1993-95 Pickup, Pathfinder	
Four	
KA	1.2

	Chilton Time
V6	1.2
w/AT, add	.1
1993-95 Quest	1.0
w/AT, add	.2
Boil & Repair, add	1.5
Rod Clean, add	1.9
Repair Core, add	1.3
Renew tank, add	1.6
Renew trans. oil cooler, add	1.9
Recore radiator, add	1.7
(G) Relay, Heater Blower Motor, Renew	
All models	.4
(G) Relay, Heater/AC, Renew	
1993-95 Pickup, Pathfinder	.3
1993-95 Quest	.3
(G) Relay, Radiator Fan Motor, Renew	
1993-95 Quest	.3
(G) Resistor, Heater Blower Motor, Renew	
All models	.4
(G) Switch, Coolant Temperature Sensor, Renew	
1993-95 Pickup, Pathfinder	
Four	.4
V6	.5
1993-95 Quest	.3
(G) Switch, Heater Blower Motor, Renew	
1993-95 Pickup, Pathfinder	1.4
1993-95 Quest	.5
(G) Thermostat, Coolant, Renew	
1993-95 Pickup, Pathfinder	
Four	
KA	1.4
V6	1.8
1993-95 Quest	1.3
(G) Winterize Cooling System	
Includes: Run engine to check for leaks, tighten all hose connections. Test radiator and pressure cap, drain radiator and engine block. Add antifreeze and refill system.	
All models	.5

LABOR
AIR CONDITIONING
LABOR

	Chilton Time
Note: If more than one item requires replacement where evacuation and discharging the system is already included in the operation, deduct 1.0 hour for each additional item from the time listed.	
SERVICE AND TESTING	
(G) Drain, Evacuate and Recharge System	
All models	1.0
Recover refrigerant, add	.2

	Chilton Time
(G) Flush Refrigerant System, Complete	
To be used in conjunction with component replacement which could contaminate system. Includes evacuate and recharge.	
All models	1.3
Recover refrigerant, add	.2
(G) Recover and/or Recycle AC Refrigerant	
Add to evacuate and charge the AC system, as required.	
All models	.2

	Chilton Time
COMPONENTS	
(G) Belt, Compressor Drive, Renew	
1993-95 Pickup, Pathfinder	.7
(G) Blower Motor, Renew	
1993-95 Pickup, Pathfinder	.5
1993-95 Quest	.4
(G) Blower Motor, Rear, Renew	
1993-95 Quest	3.7

LABOR — AIR CONDITIONING — LABOR

	Chilton Time
(G) Compressor Assy., Renew	
Includes: Transfer parts as required. Evacuate and charge system.	
1993-95 Pickup, Pathfinder	2.3
1993-95 Quest	2.2
Recover refrigerant, add	.2
(G) Condenser Assy., Renew	
Includes: Evacuate and charge system.	
1993-95 Pickup, Pathfinder	2.7
1993-95 Quest	2.6
Recover refrigerant, add	.2
(G) Control Assy., Temperature, Renew	
1993-95 Pickup, Pathfinder	1.4
w/auto air, add	.4
1993-95 Quest	
front	.6
rear	.5
Renew fan switch, add	.2
(G) Core, Evaporator, Renew	
Includes: Evacuate and charge system.	
1993-95 Pickup, Pathfinder	3.6

	Chilton Time
1993-95 Quest	2.2
Renew thermo switch, add	.3
Recover refrigerant, add	.2
(G) Evaporator Assy., Rear, Renew	
Includes: Evacuate and charge system.	
1993-95 Quest	4.9
Recover refrigerant, add	.2
(G) Hoses, AC, Renew	
Includes: Evacuate and charge system.	
1993-95 Pickup, Pathfinder	
Four	
KA	2.4
1993-95 Quest	2.5
Renew each adtnl., add	.5
Recover refrigerant, add	.2
(G) Motor, Condenser Fan, Renew	
1993-95 Quest	1.0
(G) Receiver/Drier Assy., Renew	
Includes: Evacuate and charge system.	
All models	1.8
Recover refrigerant, add	.2

	Chilton Time
(G) Relay, AC, Renew	
1993-95 Pickup, Pathfinder	.3
1993-95 Quest	.3
(G) Relay, Compressor or Fan, Renew	
All models	.5
(G) Seal, Compressor Shaft, Renew	
Includes: R&R compressor. Evacuate and charge system.	
All models	1.4
Recover refrigerant, add	.2
(G) Switch, Low Pressure and/or Cycling, Renew	
All models	.4
Add time to evacuate & charge AC system as needed.	
Recover refrigerant, add	.2
(G) Valve, Expansion, Renew	
Includes: Evacuate and charge system.	
1993-95 Pickup, Pathfinder	3.7
1993-95 Quest	2.3
Recover refrigerant, add	.2

PORSCHE
911

LABOR — COOLING SYSTEM — LABOR

	Chilton Time
SERVICE	
(G) Belt, Fan Drive, Renew	
1993-95 911	
wo/AC	.9
w/AC	1.2
(G) Exchanger, Heat, Renew	
1993-94 911 RS	
left	1.8
right	1.5
1993-94 911 Carrera 2/4	
left	1.8
right	1.5
1995 911 Carrera (993)	
one	1.4
both	2.0
(G) Fan Assy., Cooling, Renew	
1993-94 911 RS	1.0

	Chilton Time
1993-94 911 Carrera 2/4	1.0
1995 911 Carrera (993)	1.0
(G) Gauge, Temperature (Dash Unit), Renew	
All models	.3
(G) Motor, Heater Blower, Renew	
1993-94 911 RS	.9
1993-94 911 Carrera 2/4	.9
1995 911 Carrera (993)	
right	1.3
left	1.5
(G) Relay, Heater Blower Motor, Renew	
1993-94 911 RS	.3
1993-94 911 Carrera 2/4	.3
1995 911 Carrera (993)	.3

	Chilton Time
(G) Resistor, Heater Blower Motor, Renew	
1993-94 911 RS	.3
1993-94 911 Carrera 2/4	.3
(G) Sensor, Temperature, Renew	
All models	.3
(G) Silencers, Renew	
1993-94 911 RS	
one	4.3
both	7.8
1993-94 911 Carrera 2/4	
one	4.3
both	7.8
1995 911 Carrera (993)	
one	4.3
both	7.8

LABOR — AIR CONDITIONING — LABOR

	Chilton Time
Note: If more than one item requires replacement where evacuation and discharging the system is already included in the operation, deduct 1.0 hour for each additional item from the time listed.	
SERVICE AND TESTING	
(G) Drain, Evacuate and Recharge System	
All models	2.0
Recover refrigerant, add	.2

	Chilton Time
(G) Flush Refrigerant System, Complete	
To be used in conjunction with component replacement which could contaminate system. Includes evacuate and recharge.	
All models	1.3
Recover refrigerant, add	.2
(G) Leak Check	
Includes: Check all lines and connections.	
All models	.5

	Chilton Time
(G) Recover and/or Recycle AC Refrigerant	
Add to evacuate and charge the AC system, as required.	
All models, add	.2
COMPONENTS	
(G) Belt, Compressor Drive, Renew	
1993-94 911 RS	.8

LABOR | AIR CONDITIONING | LABOR

	Chilton Time
1993-94 911 Carrera 2/4	.8
1995 911 Carrera (993)	.8

(G) Coil, Evaporator, Renew
Includes: Evacuate and charge system.

1993-94 911 RS	7.8
1993-94 911 Carrera 2/4	7.8
Recover refrigerant, add	.2

(G) Compressor Assy., Renew
Includes: Transfer parts as required. Evacuate and charge system.

All models	2.7
Recover refrigerant, add	.2

(G) Condenser Assy., Renew
Includes: Evacuate and charge system.

1993-94 911 RS	4.5
1993-94 911 Carrera 2/4	4.5

	Chilton Time
1995 911 Carrera (993)	4.5
Recover refrigerant, add	.2

(G) Control Unit, Temperature, Renew

1993-94 911 RS	.3
1993-94 911 Carrera 2/4	.3
1995 911 Carrera (993)	.3

(G) Hoses, AC, Renew
Includes: Evacuate and charge system.

1993-94 911 RS	
condenser line	4.2
liquid line	3.3
1993-94 911 Carrera 2/4	
condenser line	4.2
liquid line	3.3
1995 911 Carrera (993)	
condenser line	4.2
liquid line	3.3
Recover refrigerant, add	.2

	Chilton Time

(G) Receiver/Drier Assy., Renew
Includes: Evacuate and charge system.

All models	3.0
Recover refrigerant, add	.2

(G) Switch, Low Pressure and/or Cycling, Renew

1993-94 911 RS	2.8
1993-94 911 Carrera 2/4	2.8
Add time to evacuate & charge AC system as needed	

(G) Valve, Expansion, Renew
Includes: Evacuate and charge system.

1993-94 911 RS	7.8
1993-94 911 Carrera 2/4	7.8
Recover refrigerant, add	.2

PORSCHE
928 • 944 • 968

LABOR | COOLING SYSTEM | LABOR

	Chilton Time
SERVICE	

(G) Belt, Drive, Renew

1993-94 928S4/GT	1.0

(G) Belt, Serpentine Drive, Renew

1993-95 968	1.0

(G) Blades, Fan or Clutch Assy., Renew

1993-95 968	.6

(G) Clutch, Magnetic Fan, Renew

1993-94 928	.8

(G) Control Assy., Heater, Renew

1993-94 928	3.5

(G) Core, Heater, R&R or Renew

w/AC, add	1.5
1993-94 928	10.5
1993-95 968	7.2
Boil & Repair, add	1.2
Repair Core, add	.9
Recore, add	1.2

(G) Fan Assy., Electric Cooling, Renew

1993-94 928	
2V	1.7
4V	2.5
1993-95 968	
one	1.3
both	1.5

(G) Gauge, Temperature (Dash Unit), Renew

1993-95 928, 968	1.4

(G) Gauge, Temperature (Engine Unit), Renew

1993-94 928	.7
1993-95 968	.5

	Chilton Time

(G) Hoses, Heater, Renew

1993-94 928, one	2.0
1993-95 968, one	1.5

(G) Hoses, Radiator, Renew
Includes: Drain and refill cooling system as required.

1993-95 928, 944, 968	
one	1.5

(G) Housing and/or Gasket, Thermostat, Renew
Includes: Partial removal of water pump and renew O-rings.

1993-94 928	.6
1993-95 968	1.4

(G) Motor, Heater Blower, Renew

1993-94 928	2.0
1993-95 968	1.4

(G) Pump and/or Gasket, Water, Renew
Includes: Drain and refill cooling system.

1993-94 928	
2V	7.2
4V	8.7
1993-95 968	6.7

(G) Radiator Assy., R&R or Renew

1993-94 928, 928S	1.8
1993-94 928S4/GT	3.1
w/AT, add	.5
1993-95 968	2.2
Boil and Repair, add	1.5
Rod Clean, add	1.9
Repair Core, add	1.3
Renew Tank, add	1.6
Renew Trans. Oil Cooler, add	1.9
Recore Radiator, add	1.7

	Chilton Time

(G) Relay, Heater Blower Motor, Renew

1993-95 928, 944, 968	.3

(G) Resistor, Fan Motor, Renew

1993-94 928	.8
1993-95 968	
one	.5
both	.6

(G) Resistor, Heater Blower Motor, Renew

1993-94 928GTS	1.8
1993-94 944	.3
1993-95 968	.3

(G) Sending Unit, Engine Coolant Temp., Renew

1993-94 928	.7
1993-95 968	.5

(G) Switch, Electric Fan Thermo, Renew

1993-95 968	1.2

(G) Switch, Heater Blower Motor, Renew

1993-94 944	.6

(G) Thermostat, Coolant, Renew

1993-94 928	.6
1993-95 968	1.4

(G) Valve, Heater Control, Renew

1993-94 928, 944	1.5
1993-95 968	1.4

(G) Winterize Cooling System
Includes: Run engine to check for leaks, tighten all hose connections. Test radiator and pressure cap, drain radiator and engine block. Add antifreeze and refill system.

All models	.5

LABOR — AIR CONDITIONING — LABOR

Chilton Time

Note: If more than one item requires replacement where evacuation and discharging the system is already included in the operation, deduct 1.0 hour for each additional item from the time listed.

SERVICE AND TESTING

(G) Drain, Evacuate and Recharge System

All models	2.0
Recover refrigerant, add	.2

(G) Leak Check

Includes: Check all lines and connections.

All models	.5

(G) Recover and/or Recycle AC Refrigerant

Add to evacuate and charge the AC system, as required.

All models, add	.2

COMPONENTS

(G) Belt, Compressor Drive, Adjust

1993-95 968	.6

(G) Belt, Compressor Drive, Renew

1993-94 928	1.4
1993-95 968	1.0

(G) Coil, Evaporator, Renew

Includes: Evacuate and charge system.

1993-94 928	12.5
1993-95 968	3.3
Recover refrigerant, add	.2

(G) Compressor Assy., Renew

Includes: Transfer parts as required. Evacuate and charge system.

1993-94 928	3.3
1993-95 968	3.3
Recover refrigerant, add	.2

(G) Condenser Assy., Renew

Includes: Evacuate and charge system.

1993-94 928	4.0
1993-95 968	3.0
Recover refrigerant, add	.2

(G) Hoses, AC, Renew

Includes: Evacuate and charge system.

1993-95 928, 944, 968	
suction	3.1

---

discharge	3.0
Recover refrigerant, add	.2

(G) Receiver/Drier Assy., Renew

Includes: Evacuate and charge system.

All models	3.0
Recover refrigerant, add	.2

(G) Seal, Compressor Shaft, Renew

Includes: R&R compressor. Evacuate and charge system.

1993-94 928	3.7
1993-95 968	3.4
Recover refrigerant, add	.2

(G) Switch, Compressor Pressure, Renew

1993-95 968	2.4
Recover refrigerant, add	.2

Add time to evacuate and charge AC system as needed.

(G) Valve, Expansion, Renew

Includes: Evacuate and charge system.

1993-94 928	3.9
1993-95 968	3.9
Recover refrigerant, add	.2

SAAB
900 • 9000

LABOR — COOLING SYSTEM — LABOR

Chilton Time

TESTING

(M) Pressure Test Cooling System

All models	.3

SERVICE

(G) Belt, Serpentine Drive, Renew

1993 900	.4
1994-95 900	
Four	.4
V6	.5
1993-95 9000	
2.0L	.5
2.3L	.7

(G) Blade, Fan, Renew

1993 900	.4

(G) Cooler, Engine Oil, Renew

1993 900	
16V	1.8
1994-95 900	
Four	.6
V6	3.5
1993-95 9000	
2.3L	
wo/Turbo	.9
w/Turbo	.5

(G) Core, Heater, R&R or Renew

1993 900	2.5
1993-95 9000	2.2
Boil & Repair, add	1.2

Repair Core, add	.9
Recore, add	1.2

(G) Expansion (Freeze) Plugs, Water Jacket, Renew

Add appropriate time to access plug.

All models, each	.5

(G) Gauge, Temperature (Dash Unit), Renew

1993 900	2.0
1994-95 900	.6
1993-95 9000	1.9

(G) Gauge, Temperature (Engine Unit), Renew

1993-95 900	.4
1993-95 9000	
2.3L	.4

(G) Hoses, Heater, Renew

1993 900	.5
1993-95 9000	.9

(G) Hoses, Radiator, Renew

Includes: Drain and refill cooling system as required.

1993 900	.5
1994-95 900	
upper	.3
lower	.5
1993-95 9000	
upper	.5
lower	.4

(G) Motor, Heater Blower, Renew

1993 900	2.2
1993-95 9000	2.2

(G) Motor, Radiator Fan and/or Fan, Renew

1993 900	
wo/Turbo	.5
w/Turbo	.7
1994-95 900	.5
1993-95 9000	.5

(G) Pump and/or Gasket, Water, Renew

Includes: Drain and refill cooling system.

1993 900	1.3
1994-95 900	1.2
1993-95 9000	
2.3L	1.5

(G) Radiator Assy., R&R or Renew

1993-95 900	1.3
1993-95 9000	
2.3L	1.7
w/Turbo	2.7
Boil & Repair, add	1.5
Rod Clean, add	1.9
Repair Core, add	1.3
Renew Tank, add	1.6
Renew Transmission oil cooler, add	1.9
Recore Radiator, add	1.7

LABOR

COOLING SYSTEM

LABOR

(G) Resistor, Heater Blower Motor, Renew

	Chilton Time
1993 900	.8
1994-95 900	.3
1993-95 9000	.4

(G) Switch, Heater Blower Motor, Renew

1993 900	1.1
1994-95 900	.4
1993-95 9000	.4

(G) Switch, Radiator Fan Motor (Coolant Temp.), Renew

	Chilton Time
1993 900	.4
1994-95 900	.3
1993-95 9000 2.3L	.5

(G) Thermostat, Coolant, Renew

1993 900	.6
1994-95 900	
Four	.9
V6	1.6

	Chilton Time
1993-95 9000 2.3L	.7

(G) Valve, Water Control, Renew

1993 900	1.8

(G) Winterize Cooling System

Includes: Run engine to check for leaks, tighten all hose connections. Test radiator and pressure cap, drain radiator and engine block. Add antifreeze and refill system.

All models	.5

LABOR

AIR CONDITIONING

LABOR

Note: If more than one item requires replacement where evacuation and discharging the system is already included in the operation, deduct 1.0 hour for each additional item from the time listed.

SERVICE AND TESTING

(G) Drain, Evacuate and Recharge System

	Chilton Time
All models	1.0

(G) Flush Refrigerant System, Complete

To be used in conjunction with component replacement which could contaminate system. Includes evacuate and recharge.

All models	1.3

(G) Recover and/or Recycle AC Refrigerant

Add to evacuate and charge the AC system, as required.

All models, add	.2

(G) Refrigerant, Add (Partial Charge)

All models	.6

COMPONENTS

(G) Belt, Compressor Drive, Renew

1993 900	.5
1994-95 900	
Four	.4
V6	.5
1993-95 9000 2.3L	.7

(G) Clutch & Pulley, Compressor, Renew

Includes: Evacuate and charge system.

	Chilton Time
1993 900	2.4
1994-95 900	
Four	.6
V6	.7

(G) Compressor Assy., Renew

Includes: Transfer parts as required. Evacuate and charge system.

1993 900	1.5
1994-95 900	
Four	2.0
w/Turbo add	.2
V6	2.1
1993-95 9000 2.3L	1.3

(G) Condenser Assy., Renew

Includes: Evacuate and charge system.

1993 900	1.5
1994-95 900	1.9
1993-95 9000	
wo/Turbo	1.1
w/Turbo	1.5

(G) Core, Evaporator, Renew

Includes: Evacuate and charge system.

1993 900	
16V	1.2
1994-95 900	
Four	2.5
V6	2.2
1993-95 9000	
front	1.6
rear	.9

(G) Hoses, AC, Renew

Includes: Evacuate and charge system.

1993 900	
compressor to condenser	1.3
each adtnl.	1.0

	Chilton Time
1993-95 9000	
compressor to condenser	.9
each adtnl.	.7

(G) Receiver/Drier Assy., Renew

Includes: Evacuate and charge system.

1993 900	1.3
1994-95 900	1.5
1993-95 9000	1.5

(G) Seal, Compressor Shaft, Renew

Includes: R&R compressor. Evacuate and charge system.

1993 900	2.6

(G) Switch, Low Pressure and/or Cycling, Renew

1994-95 900	.4
1993-94 9000	.4

(G) Valve, Expansion, Renew

Includes: Evacuate and charge system.

1993 900	1.1
1994-95 900	
Four	1.7
V6	1.8
1993-95 9000	
front	1.6
rear	.7

(G) Valve, Pressure Relief, Renew

Includes: Evacuate and charge system.

1993 900	.4
1993-95 9000	.4

SUBARU
IMPREZA • JUSTY • LEGACY • LOYALE • SVX • XT

LABOR | COOLING SYSTEM | LABOR

	Chilton Time
TESTING	
(M) Pressure Test Cooling System	
All models 3	
SERVICE	
(G) Belt, Drive, Adjust	
All models 3	
(G) Belt, Drive, Renew	
All models 4	
w/AC add 2	
w/PS add 2	
(G) Blade, Mechanical Cooling Fan, Renew	
All models 6	
(G) Core, Heater, R&R or Renew	
wo/AC	
1993-94 Justy 2.0	
1993-95 Legacy 3.5	
1993-95 Impreza 3.5	
1993-94 Loyale 5.0	
1993-95 SVX 6.3	
w/AC	
1993-94 Justy 2.2	
1993-95 Legacy 3.5	
1993-95 Impreza 3.5	
1993-94 Loyale 5.0	
1993-95 SVX 6.3	
Boil & Repair, add 1.2	
Repair Core, add 9	
Recore, add 1.2	
(G) Fan Assy., Electric Cooling, Renew	
1993-95 5	
w/6 cyl. add 1	
Renew motor add, each 1	
(G) Gauge, Temperature (Dash Unit), Renew	
1993-95 Impreza 9	
1993-94 Loyale 1.5	
1993-94 Justy 1.2	
1993-94 Legacy 1.2	
1995 Legacy 9	

	Chilton Time
(G) Gauge, Temperature (Engine Unit), Renew	
1993-95 . . . . 1.0	
w/6 cyl. add 1	
(G) Hoses, By-Pass, Renew	
All models .6	
w/AC add .3	
(G) Hoses, Heater, Renew	
1993-95 6	
(G) Hoses, Radiator, Renew	
Includes: Drain and refill cooling system as required.	
All models	
upper 3	
lower 4	
(G) Motor, Heater Blower, Renew	
1993-95 Legacy	
wo/AC 1.0	
w/AC 1.6	
1993-94 Justy 1.2	
1993-95 Impreza 1.0	
1993-94 Loyale 1.0	
1993-95 SVX 1.0	
(G) Pump and/or Gasket, Water, Renew	
Includes: Drain and refill cooling system.	
1993-95 4 cyl.	
OHC 2.9	
1993-95 6 cyl.	
3.3L 3.4	
(G) Radiator Assy., R&R or Renew	
All models 1.0	
w/AT add 2	
Boil & Repair, add 1.5	
Rod Clean, add 1.9	
Repair Core, add 1.3	
Renew Tank, add 1.6	
Renew Trans. Oil Cooler, add 1.9	
Recore Radiator, add 1.7	
(G) Relay, Heater Blower Motor, Renew	
1993-95 9	

	Chilton Time
(G) Resistor, Heater Blower Motor, Renew	
All models .8	
(G) Sensor, Coolant Fan Thermo, Renew	
1993-94 Justy 5	
(G) Switch, Heater Blower Motor, Renew	
1993-94 Justy 1.1	
1993-94 Legacy 1.8	
1995 Legacy 1.3	
1993-95 Impreza 1.3	
1993-94 Loyale 1.3	
1993-95 SVX 1.3	
(G) Switch, Heater & AC Mode, Renew	
1993-94 Justy 1.1	
1993-94 Legacy 1.7	
1995 Legacy 1.0	
1993-95 Impreza 1.0	
1993-94 Loyale 1.5	
1993-95 SVX 1.9	
(G) Switch, Radiator Fan Motor (Coolant Temp.), Renew	
1993-95 . . . . 1.1	
(G) Thermostat, Coolant, Renew	
All models .6	
w/MFI add 4	
(G) Water Pump, Cover or Gasket, Renew	
1993-94 Justy 1.0	
Renew impeller or seal, add 1	
w/AC add 1	
Renew water pump seal, add 4.5	
(G) Winterize Cooling System	
Includes: Run engine to check for leaks, tighten all hose connections. Test radiator and pressure cap, drain radiator and engine block. Add antifreeze and refill system.	
All models .5	

LABOR | AIR CONDITIONING | LABOR

	Chilton Time
Note: If more than one item requires replacement where evacuation and discharging the system is already included in the operation, deduct 1.0 hour for each additional item from the time listed.	
SERVICE AND TESTING	
(G) Drain, Evacuate and Recharge System	
All models 1.0	
(G) Flush Refrigerant System, Complete	
To be used in conjunction with component	

	Chilton Time
replacement which could contaminate system. Includes evacuate and recharge.	
All models 1.3	
(G) Recover and/or Recycle AC Refrigerant	
Add to evacuate and charge the AC system, as required.	
All models 2	
(G) Refrigerant, Add (Partial Charge)	
All models 6	

	Chilton Time
COMPONENTS	
(G) Belt, Compressor Drive, Renew	
All models .5	
(G) Blower Motor, Renew	
All models 1.0	
(G) Coil, Compressor Clutch, Renew	
All models 1.5	
(G) Coil, Evaporator, Renew	
Includes: Evacuate and charge system.	
All models 2.1	

LABOR   # AIR CONDITIONING   # LABOR

(G) Compressor Assy., Renew
Includes: Transfer parts as required. Evacuate and charge system.
All models 1.3
w/Turbo add 3

(G) Condenser Assy., Renew
Includes: Evacuate and charge system.
All models 2.0
w/Turbo add 1

(G) Hoses, AC, Renew
Includes: Evacuate and charge system.
All models
one 1.7
each adtnl. 3
w/PS add 2

(G) Pulley (w/Hub), Compressor Clutch, Renew
All models 2.2

(G) Receiver/Drier Assy., Renew
Includes: Evacuate and charge system.
All models 1.6

(G) Relay, Blower Motor, Renew
1993-95
wo/ATC 6
w/ATC
Legacy 4
SVX 5

(G) Seal, Compressor Shaft, Renew
Includes: R&R compressor. Evacuate and charge system.
All models 2.3
w/Turbo add 1

(G) Switch, Blower Motor, Renew
All models 1.0

(G) Valve, Expansion, Renew
Includes: Evacuate and charge system.
All models 2.5

AUTOMATIC TEMPERATURE CONTROL (ATC)

(G) Amplifier Control Unit and/or In-Vehicle Sensor, Renew
Does not include system test.
1993-94 Legacy 1.2
1993-95 SVX 8

(G) Amplifier, Fan Control, Renew
Does not include system test.
1993-94 Legacy 4
1993-95 SVX 6

(G) ATC System Diagnosis
1993-95 . . . . 1.0

(G) Compressor Clutch, Renew
Does not include system test.
1993-95 . . . . 1.9
Includes: Evacuate & recharge AC system.

(G) Motor, Air Mix Door, Renew
Does not include system test.
1993-95 7

(G) Motor, Intake Door, Renew
Does not include system test.
1993-94 Legacy 5
1993-95 SVX 3.6

(G) Motor, Mode Door, Renew
Does not include system test.
1993-95 7

(G) Relay, AC, Renew
Does not include system test.
1993-95 3

(G) Relay, AC Cut, Renew
Does not include system test.
1993-94 Legacy 4

(G) Sensor, Ambient, Renew
Does not include system test.
1993-95 5

(G) Sensor, Coolant Temperature, Renew
Does not include system test.
1993-94 Legacy 5
1993-95 SVX 7

(G) Sensor, In-Take, Renew
Does not include system test.
1993-94 Legacy 4
1993-95 SVX 2.5
w/dual air bags add 2
Includes: Evacuate & recharge AC system.

(G) Sensor, Sunload, Renew
Does not include system test.
1993-94 Legacy 3
1993-95 SVX 3.5

(G) Switch, Trinary, Renew
Does not include system test.
1993-94 Legacy 9
1993-95 SVX 1.5
Includes: Evacuate & recharge AC system.

SUZUKI
SAMURAI • SIDEKICK • SWIFT

LABOR   # COOLING SYSTEM   # LABOR

TESTING

(M) Pressure Test Cooling System
All models 3

SERVICE

(G) Belt, Water Pump Drive, Adjust
All models 3

(G) Belt, Water Pump Drive, Renew
1993-95 Samurai 8
1993-95 Swift, Sidekick 6

(G) Blades, Fan or Clutch Assy., Renew
1993-95 Samurai 1.0
1993-95 Swift 9
1993-95 Sidekick 1.4

(G) Control Assy., Temperature, Renew
1993-95 Samurai 2.2
1993-95 Sidekick 2.9
1993-95 Swift 1.9

(G) Core, Heater, R&R or Renew
1993-95 Samurai 4.5
1993-95 Sidekick
wo/AC 4.5
w/AC 6.0
1993-95 Swift 2.8
Boil & Repair, add 1.2
Repair Core, add 9
Recore, add 1.2

(G) Expansion (Freeze) Plugs, Water Jacket, Renew
Add appropriate time to access plug.
All models, each 5

(G) Gauge, Temperature (Dash Unit), Renew
1993-95 Samurai 1.1
1993-95 Sidekick 1.4
1993-95 Swift 1.1

(G) Gauge, Temperature (Engine Unit), Renew
1993-95 Samurai 5
1993-95 Swift 5
1993-95 Sidekick 4

(G) Hoses, By-Pass, Renew
1993-95 Samurai 5
1993-95 Sidekick 6

(G) Hoses, Heater, Renew
1993-95 Samurai, each 4
1993-95 Swift, each 6
1993-95 Sidekick, each 5

LABOR

COOLING SYSTEM

LABOR

(G) Hoses, Radiator, Renew
Includes: Drain and refill cooling system as required.
All models
upper 5
lower 7

(G) Motor, Heater Blower, Renew
1993-95 Samurai 4.3
1993-95 Sidekick 3.5
1993-95 Swift 6

(G) Motor, Radiator Fan and/or Fan, Renew
1993-95 Samurai 1.3
1993-95 Swift 1.0
1993-95 Sidekick 1.3

(G) Pump and/or Gasket, Water, Renew
Includes: Drain and refill cooling system.
1993-95 Samurai 3.2

	Chilton Time
1993-95 Swift	3.0
1993-95 Sidekick	3.6

(G) Radiator Assy., R&R or Renew
1993-95 Samurai 1.4
w/AC add 7
1993-94 Swift 1.2
w/AC add 7
1995 Swift 1.2
1993-95 Sidekick 1.3
Boil & Repair, add 1.5
Rod Clean, add 1.9
Repair Core, add 1.3
Renew Tank, add 1.6
Renew Trans. Oil Cooler, add 1.9
Recore Radiator, add 1.7

(G) Resistor, Heater Blower Motor, Renew
1993-95 Samurai 4.2
1993-95 Sidekick 5
1993-95 Swift 6

(G) Switch, Electric Fan Thermo, Renew
1993-94 Swift 5

(G) Switch, Heater Blower Motor, Renew
1993-95 Samurai 1.0
1993-95 Sidekick 6

(G) Thermostat, Coolant, Renew
1993-95 Samurai 4
1993-95 Swift 6
1993-95 Sidekick 5

(G) Valve, Water Control, Renew
1993-95 Samurai 8

(G) Winterize Cooling System
Includes: Run engine to check for leaks, tighten all hose connections. Test radiator and pressure cap, drain radiator and engine block. Add antifreeze and refill system.
All models 5

LABOR

AIR CONDITIONING

LABOR

Note: If more than one item requires replacement where evacuation and discharging the system is already included in the operation, deduct 1.0 hour for each additional item from the time listed.

SERVICE AND TESTING

(G) Drain, Evacuate and Recharge System
All models 1.0

(G) Flush Refrigerant System, Complete
To be used in conjunction with component replacement which could contaminate system. Includes evacuate and recharge.
All models 1.3

(G) Leak Check
Includes: Check all lines and connections.
All models 5

(G) Recover and/or Recycle AC Refrigerant
Add to evacuate and charge the AC system, as required.
All models, add 2

(G) Refrigerant, Add (Partial Charge)
All models 6

COMPONENTS

(G) Belt, Compressor Drive, Adjust
All models 3

(G) Belt, Compressor Drive, Renew
1993-95 Samurai 4
1993-95 Sidekick 4
1993-94 Swift 1.3
1995 Swift 4

(G) Clutch Assy., Compressor, Renew
1993-95 Samurai 2.3
1993-95 Sidekick 2.6
1993-95 Swift 3.2

(G) Compressor Assy., Renew
Includes: Transfer parts as required. Evacuate and charge system.
1993-95 Samurai 2.0
1993-95 Sidekick 2.3
1993-95 Swift 3.0

(G) Condenser Assy., Renew
Includes: Evacuate and charge system.
1993-95 Samurai 2.4
1993-95 Sidekick 2.5
1993-95 Swift 3.3

(G) Core, Evaporator, Renew
Includes: Evacuate and charge system.
1993-95 Samurai 2.4
1993-95 Sidekick 4.3
1993-95 Swift 3.5

(G) Fan, Condenser Cooling, Renew
1993-95 Sidekick 1.0
1993-95 Swift 2.8

(G) Hoses, AC, Renew
Includes: Evacuate and charge system.
1993-95 Samurai, one 1.7
1993-95 Sidekick, one 1.6

1993-95 Swift, one 1.6
For each adtnl., add 5

(G) Motor, Condenser Fan, Renew
1993-95 Samurai 9

(G) Receiver/Drier Assy., Renew
Includes: Evacuate and charge system.
1993-95 Samurai 1.4
1993-95 Sidekick 1.5
1993-95 Swift 3.0

(G) Resistor, Blower Motor, Renew
1993-95 Samurai 4.2
1993-95 Sidekick 5
1993-95 Swift 6

(G) Seal, Compressor Shaft, Renew
Includes: R&R compressor. Evacuate and charge system.
1993-95 Samurai 2.8
1993-95 Sidekick 3.1
1993-95 Swift 3.6

(G) Switch, Blower Motor, Renew
1993-95 Samurai 7
1993-95 Sidekick, Swift 5

(G) Valve, Expansion, Renew
Includes: Evacuate and charge system.
1993-95 Samurai 2.7
1993-95 Sidekick 4.5
1993-95 Swift 3.6

TOYOTA
AVALON • CAMRY • CELICA • COROLLA • CRESSIDA • MR2 • PASEO • SUPRA • TERCEL

LABOR	**COOLING SYSTEM**	**LABOR**

	Chilton Time
TESTING	
(M) Pressure Test Cooling System	
All models	.3
SERVICE	
(G) Belt, Drive, Adjust	
All models	
one	.3
each adtnl.	.1
(G) Belt, Drive, Renew	
1995 Avalon	.4
1993-95 Camry	.4
1993 Celica	.4
1994-95 Celica	.5
1993-05 Corolla	.4
1993-95 MR2	.7
1993-95 Paseo	.7
1994-95 Supra	
wo/Turbo	.3
w/Turbo	.6
1993-94 Tercel	.7
(G) Control Assy., Heater, Renew	
1995 Avalon	.4
1993-95 Camry	.6
1993 Celica	1.0
1994-95 Celica	.4
1993-95 Corolla	
2 WD	1.2
4 WD	1.9
1993-95 MR2	.8
1993-95 Paseo	1.1
1994-95 Supra	.6
1993-94 Tercel	1.1
(G) Core, Heater, R&R or Renew	
1995 Avalon	3.8
1993-95 Camry	2.5
1993 Celica	
wo/AC	4.5
w/AC	5.5
1994-95 Celica	
wo/AC	4.4
w/AC	5.4
1993-95 Corolla FWD	
2 WD	
wo/AC	5.8
w/AC	7.0
4 WD	
wo/AC	2.5
w/AC	4.0
1993-95 MR2	
wo/AC	6.5
w/AC	7.5
1993-95 Paseo	
wo/AC	5.5
w/AC	7.0
1993-95 Supra	
wo/AC	5.0
w/AC	6.0
1993-94 Tercel	
wo/AC	5.5
w/AC	7.0
Boil & Repair, add	1.2

	Chilton Time
Repair Core, add	.9
Recore, add	1.2
(G) Expansion (Freeze) Plugs, Water Jacket, Renew	
Add appropriate time to access plug.	
All models, each	.5
(G) Gauge, Temperature (Dash Unit), Renew	
1995 Avalon	1.0
1993-95 Camry	1.0
1993 Celica	1.5
1994-95 Celica	1.1
1993-95 Corolla FWD	
2 WD	.9
4 WD	1.1
1993-95 MR2	1.0
1993-95 Paseo	1.0
1994-95 Supra	.9
1993 Tercel	1.0
(G) Hoses, Heater, Renew	
One	
1995 Avalon	1.1
1993-95 Camry	1.1
1993-95 Celica	1.1
1993-95 Corolla FWD	1.1
1993-95 MR2	1.1
1993-95 Paseo	.8
1994-95 Supra	1.0
1993-94 Tercel	.8
(G) Hoses, Radiator, Renew	
Includes: Drain and refill cooling system as required.	
Upper	
1995 Avalon	.8
1993-95 Camry	.8
1993-95 Celica	.8
1993-95 Corolla FWD	.8
1993-95 Paseo	.9
1994-95 Supra	
wo/Turbo	.6
w/Turbo	.8
1993-94 Tercel	.8
Lower	
1995 Avalon	1.3
1993-95 Camry	
Four	1.0
V6	1.3
1993 Celica	1.0
1994-95 Celica	.8
1993-95 Corolla FWD	.9
1993-95 Paseo	1.0
1994-95 Supra	
wo/Turbo	.8
w/Turbo	1.0
1993-94 Tercel	1.0
(G) Motor, Heater Blower, Renew	
1995 Avalon	.5
1993-95 Camry	.5
1993 Celica	.4
1994-95 Celica	.6
1993-95 Corolla FWD	.5

	Chilton Time
1993-95 MR2	.4
1993-95 Paseo	.5
1994-95 Supra	.6
1993-94 Tercel	.5
(G) Motor, Radiator Fan and/or Fan, Renew	
1995 Avalon	.7
1993-94 Camry	
Four	.8
V6	2.2
1995 Camry	.8
1993 Celica	.8
1994-95 Celica	.5
1993-95 Corolla FWD	.8
1993-95 MR2	.8
1993-95 Paseo	1.1
1994-95 Supra	1.3
1993-94 Tercel	1.0
(G) Pump and/or Gasket, Water, Renew	
Includes: Drain and refill cooling system.	
1995 Avalon	2.8
1993-95 Camry	
Four	3.2
V6	3.1
1993 Celica	
wo/Turbo	3.4
w/Turbo	5.1
1994-95 Celica	
7AFE	3.0
5SFE	2.4
w/AC add	.3
1993-94 Corolla FWD	2.1
w/AC add	.2
1993-95 MR2	
wo/Turbo	3.8
w/Turbo	5.5
w/AC add	.5
1993-95 Paseo	1.8
1994-95 Supra	
wo/Turbo	2.2
w/Turbo	3.4
1993-94 Tercel	1.8
(G) Radiator Assy., R&R or Renew	
1995 Avalon	1.1
1993-95 Camry	
Four	1.5
V6	2.0
1993 Celica	1.4
1994-95 Celica	1.0
1993-95 Corolla FWD	1.5
1993-95 MR2	2.0
1993-95 Paseo	1.5
1994-95 Supra	
wo/Turbo	1.1
w/Turbo	1.7
1993-94 Tercel	1.3
Boil & Repair, add	1.5
Rod Clean, add	1.9
Repair Tank, add	1.3
Renew Tank, add	1.6
Renew Trans. Oil Cooler, add	1.9
Recore Radiator, add	1.7

LABOR | COOLING SYSTEM | LABOR

	Chilton Time
(G) Relay, Radiator Fan Motor, Renew	
1995 Avalon	.3
1993-95 Camry	.3
1993-95 Celica	.3
1993-95 Corolla	.3
1993-95 MR2	.3
1993-95 Paseo	.3
1994-95 Supra	.4
1993-94 Tercel	.3
(G) Resistor, Heater Blower Motor, Renew	
1995 Avalon	.6
1993-95 Camry	.6
1993 Celica	.4
1994-95 Celica	.6
1993-95 Corolla FWD	
2 WD	.4
4 WD	.5
1993-95 MR2	4.5
1993-95 Paseo	.4
1994-95 Supra	.7
1993-94 Tercel	.4
(G) Sending Unit, Engine Coolant Temp., Renew	
1995 Avalon	.8
1993-95 Camry	.8
1993-95 Celica	.8
1993-95 Corolla FWD	.8
1993-95 MR2	.9

	Chilton Time
1993-95 Paseo	.8
1993-95 Supra	.8
1993-94 Tercel	
Sedan	.8
(G) Switch, Heater Blower Motor, Renew	
1993 Celica	1.0
1993-95 Corolla FWD	
2 WD	1.2
4 WD	1.4
1993-95 MR2	.8
1993-95 Paseo	1.2
1993-94 Tercel	1.2
(G) Switch, Radiator Fan Motor (Coolant Temp.), Renew	
1995 Avalon	1.0
1993-95 Camry	
Four	1.1
V6	1.0
1993 Celica	.9
1994-95 Celica	1.0
1993-95 Corolla FWD	.9
1993-95 MR2	1.6
1993-95 Paseo	.9
1994-95 Supra	1.0
1993-94 Tercel	.9
(G) Thermostat, Coolant, Renew	
1995 Avalon	1.1
1993-95 Camry	
Four	1.1

	Chilton Time
V6	.9
1993 Celica	
wo/Turbo	1.1
w/Turbo	1.4
1994-95 Celica	.8
1993-95 Corolla FWD	1.0
1993-95 MR2	
wo/Turbo	1.1
w/Turbo	1.8
1993-95 Paseo	1.0
1994-95 Supra	
wo/Turbo	.9
w/Turbo	1.8
1993-94 Tercel	.9
(G) Valve, Heater Control, Renew	
1995 Avalon	1.1
1993-95 Camry	1.1
1993-95 Celica	1.1
1993-95 Corolla FWD	1.1
1993-95 MR2	1.1
1994-95 Supra	5.2
(G) Winterize Cooling System	

Includes: Run engine to check for leaks, tighten all hose connections. Test radiator and pressure cap, drain radiator and engine block. Add antifreeze and refill system.

All models	.5

LABOR | AIR CONDITIONING | LABOR

	Chilton Time

Note: If more than one item requires replacement where evacuation and discharging the system is already included in the operation, deduct 1.0 hour for each additional item from the time listed.

SERVICE AND TESTING

(G) Drain, Evacuate and Recharge System

All models	1.0

(G) Flush Refrigerant System, Complete

To be used in conjunction with component replacement which could contaminate system. Includes evacuate and recharge.

All models	1.3

(G) Leak Check

Includes: Check all lines and connections.

All models	.5

(G) Recover and/or Recycle AC Refrigerant

Add to evacuate and charge the AC system, as required.

All models	.2

(G) Refrigerant, Add (Partial Charge)

All models	.6

COMPONENTS

(G) Belt, Compressor Drive, Renew

1995 Avalon	.4
1993-95 Camry	.4

	Chilton Time
1993-95 Celica	.4
1993-95 Corolla FWD	.6
1993-95 MR2	.8
1993-95 Paseo	.4
1993-94 Tercel	.4
(G) Blower Motor, Renew	
1995 Avalon	.5
1993-95 Camry	.5
1993-95 Celica	.3
1993-95 Corolla FWD	.4
1993-95 MR2	.4
1993-95 Paseo	.4
1994-95 Supra	.6
1993-94 Tercel	.4
(G) Clutch Assy., Magnetic, Renew	
1995 Avalon	3.2
1993-95 Camry	
Four	1.8
V6	3.2
1993-95 Celica	1.7
1993-95 Corolla FWD	2.0
1993-95 MR2	2.1
1993-95 Paseo	1.9
1994-95 Supra	2.6
1993-94 Tercel	1.8
(G) Coil, Evaporator, Renew	
Includes: Evacuate and charge system.	
1995 Avalon	1.8
1993-95 Camry	2.1
1993 Celica	1.9
1994-95 Celica	1.5
1993-95 Corolla FWD	1.7
1993-95 MR2	1.9

	Chilton Time
1993-95 Paseo	2.0
1994-95 Supra	2.7
1993-94 Tercel	2.0
(G) Compressor Assy., Renew	
Includes: Transfer parts as required. Evacuate and charge system.	
1995 Avalon	3.0
1993-95 Camry	
Four	1.6
V6	3.0
1993-95 Celica	1.5
1993-95 Corolla FWD	2.0
1993-95 MR2	1.9
1993-95 Paseo	1.8
1994-95 Supra	2.6
1993-94 Tercel	1.7
(G) Condenser Assy., Renew	
Includes: Evacuate and charge system.	
1995 Avalon	1.8
1993-95 Camry	
Four	2.9
V6	3.9
1993 Celica	2.1
1994-95 Celica	1.5
1993-95 Corolla FWD	2.3
1993-95 MR2	2.0
1993-95 Paseo	2.0
1994-95 Supra	4.5
1993-94 Tercel	
Sedan	2.0
(G) Receiver/Drier Assy., Renew	
Includes: Evacuate and charge system.	
1995 Avalon	1.5

LABOR | AIR CONDITIONING | LABOR

	Chilton Time
1993-95 Camry	1.5
1993 Celica	1.7
1994-95 Celica	1.5
1993-95 Corolla	1.5
1993-95 MR2	1.7
1993-95 Paseo	1.5
1994-95 Supra	4.2
1993-94 Tercel	1.5

(G) Resistor, Blower Motor, Renew

1995 Avalon	.6
1993-95 Camry	.6
1993-95 Celica	.4
1993-95 Corolla FWD	.4
1993-95 MR2	4.5
1993-95 Paseo	.4
1994-95 Supra	.7
1993-94 Tercel	.4

(G) Switch, Blower Motor, Renew

1995 Avalon	.4
1993-95 Camry	.6
1993 Celica	1.0
1994-95 Celica	.6
1993-95 Corolla FWD	.3
1993-95 MR2	.8
1993-95 Paseo	.3
1994-95 Supra	.6
1993-94 Tercel	.3

(G) Switch, Low Pressure Cut-Off, Renew

Includes: Evacuate and charge system.

1995 Avalon	1.6
1993-95 Camry	1.6
1993-95 Celica	1.5
1993-95 Corolla FWD	1.5

1993-95 MR2	1.6
1993-95 Paseo	1.9
1994-95 Supra	1.3
1993-94 Tercel	1.9

(G) Valve, Expansion, Renew

Includes: Evacuate and charge system.

1995 Avalon	1.8
1993-95 Camry	2.1
1993 Celica	1.9
1994-95 Celica	1.5
1993-95 Corolla FWD	1.7
1993-95 MR2	1.9
1993-95 Paseo	1.8
1994-95 Supra	2.7
1993-94 Tercel	1.8

TOYOTA TRUCKS
LAND CRUISER • 4RUNNER • PICKUP • PREVIA • T100

LABOR | COOLING SYSTEM | LABOR

TESTING

(M) Pressure Test Cooling System

All models	.3

SERVICE

(G) Belt, Fan Drive, Adjust

1993-95 Previa	.5
1993-95 T100	.3
1993-95 Pickup	.3
1993-95 4Runner	.3
1993-95 Land Cruiser	.3

(G) Belt, Fan Drive, Renew

1993-95 Previa	.6
1993-95 T100	.4
1993-95 Pickup	.4
1993-95 4Runner	.4
1993-95 Land Cruiser	.4

(G) Control Assy., Heater, Renew

1993-95 Previa	2.7
1993-95 T100	1.5
1993-95 Pickup	1.0
1993-95 4Runner	1.0
1993-95 Land Cruiser	1.2

(G) Core, Heater, R&R or Renew

1993-95 Previa	5.5
1993-95 T100	
wo/AC	2.1
w/AC	4.5
1993-95 Pickup	
wo/AC	2.1
w/AC	4.5
1993-95 4Runner	
wo/AC	2.1
w/AC	4.5
1993-95 Land Cruiser	
wo/AC	4.0
w/AC	5.0

Boil & Repair, add	1.2
Repair Core, add	.9
Recore, add	1.2

(G) Expansion (Freeze) Plugs, Water Jacket, Renew

Add appropriate time to access plug.

All models, each	.5

(G) Gauge, Temperature (Dash Unit), Renew

1993-95 Previa	1.3
1993-95 T100	1.0
1993-95 Pickup	1.0
1993-95 4Runner	1.0
1993-95 Land Cruiser	1.0

(G) Gauge, Temperature (Engine Unit), Renew

1993-95 Previa	1.2
1993-94 T100	.6
1995 T100	
Four	.6
V6	2.1
1993-95 Pickup	.6
1993-95 4Runner	.6
1993-95 Land Cruiser	.8

(G) Hoses, By-Pass, Renew

Four	
1993-95 Previa	.4
1993-95 Pickup	.9
1993-95 4Runner	.9
Six	
1993-95 Land Cruiser	.7
V6	
1993-95 Pickup, 4Runner	.6
1993-95 T100	.6

(G) Hoses, Heater, Renew

1993-95 Previa	1.0
1993-95 T100	.6

1993-95 Pickup	.6
1993-95 4Runner	.6
1993-95 Land Cruiser	1.0

(G) Hoses, Radiator, Renew

Includes: Drain and refill cooling system as required.

All models	
upper	.8
lower	1.0

(G) Motor, Heater Blower, Renew

1993-95 Previa	1.3
1993-95 T100	
wo/AC	.5
w/AC	1.5
1993-95 Pickup	
wo/AC	.5
w/AC	1.5
1993-95 4Runner	
wo/AC	.5
w/AC	1.5
1993-95 Land Cruiser	
Wagon	.6

(G) Pump and/or Gasket, Water, Renew

Includes: Drain and refill cooling system.

Four	
1993-95 Previa	1.5
1995 T100	1.9
w/AC add	.1
1993-95 4Runner	1.4
w/AC add	.1
Six	
1993-95 Land Cruiser	1.8
V6	
1993-94 Pickup, 4Runner	4.5
w/AC add	.4
1993-94 T100	4.5
w/AC add	.4
1995 T100	2.7
w/AC add	.3

LABOR

COOLING SYSTEM

LABOR

Chilton Time

(G) Radiator Assy., R&R or Renew
Four
1993-95 Previa 1.5
1995 T100 .... 1.7
1993-95 Pickup 1.2
1993-95 4Runner 1.2
Six
1993-95 Land Cruiser 1.8
V6
1993-95 Pickup, 4Runner 1.1
1993-95 T100 .... 1.1
Boil & Repair, add 1.5
Rod Clean, add 1.9
Repair Core, add 1.3
Renew Tank, add 1.6
Renew Trans. Oil Cooler, add 1.9
Recore Radiator, add 1.7

Chilton Time

(G) Resistor, Heater Blower Motor, Renew
1993-95 Previa 1.3
1993-95 T100 4
1993-95 Pickup 4
1993-95 4Runner 4
1993-95 Land Cruiser 4

(G) Switch, Heater Blower Motor, Renew
1993-95 Pickup 8
1993-95 4Runner 8
1993-95 Land Cruiser 1.1
1993-95 Previa 2.8
1993-95 T100 .... 1.5

(G) Thermostat, Coolant, Renew
Four
1993-95 Previa 1.0
1995 T100 .... 1.0
1993-95 Pickup 9

Chilton Time

1993-95 4Runner 9
Six
1993-95 Land Cruiser 1.1
V6
1993-95 Pickup, 4Runner 1.0
1993-95 T100 .... 1.0

(G) Valve, Heater Control, Renew
1993-95 Previa 1.1
1993-95 T100 8
1993-95 Pickup, 4Runner 8
1993-95 Land Cruiser 1.1

(G) Winterize Cooling System
Includes: Run engine to check for leaks, tighten all hose connections. Test radiator and pressure cap, drain radiator and engine block. Add antifreeze and refill system.
All models 5

LABOR

AIR CONDITIONING

LABOR

Chilton Time

Note: If more than one item requires replacement where evacuation and discharging the system is already included in the operation, deduct 1.0 hour for each additional item from the time listed.

SERVICE AND TESTING

(G) Drain, Evacuate and Recharge System
All models 1.0

(G) Flush Refrigerant System, Complete
To be used in conjunction with component replacement which could contaminate system. Includes evacuate and recharge.
All models 1.3

(G) Recover and/or Recycle AC Refrigerant
Add to evacuate and charge the AC system, as required.
All models 2

(G) Refrigerant, Add (Partial Charge)
All models 6

COMPONENTS

(G) Belt, Compressor Drive, Renew
1993-95 Previa 1.4
1993-95 T100 5
1993-95 Pickup 5
1993-95 4Runner 5
1993-95 Land Cruiser
  factory installed 5

Chilton Time

(G) Blower Motor, Renew
1993-95 Previa 1.2
1993-95 Pickup, 4Runner 1.5
1993-95 Land Cruiser 6
1993-95 T100 .... 1.5

(G) Clutch Assy., Compressor, Renew
1993-95 Previa 2.7
1993-95 Pickup 1.8
1993-95 4Runner 1.8
1993-95 Land Cruiser
  factory installed 2.0
1993-95 T100 .... 1.8

(G) Coil, Evaporator, Renew
Includes: Evacuate and charge system.
1993-95 Previa 2.3
1993-95 T100 .... 1.8
1993-95 Pickup 1.8
1993-95 4Runner 1.8
1993-95 Land Cruiser
  factory installed 1.8

(G) Compressor Assy., Renew
Includes: Transfer parts as required. Evacuate and charge system.
1993-95 Previa 2.4
1993-95 T100 .... 1.5
1993-95 Pickup 1.5
1993-95 4Runner 1.5
1993-95 Land Cruiser
  factory installed 1.7

(G) Condenser Assy., Renew
Includes: Evacuate and charge system.
1993-95 Previa 1.7
1993-95 T100 .... 1.7
1993-95 Pickup 1.7

Chilton Time

1993-95 4Runner 1.7
1993-95 Land Cruiser
  factory installed 1.7

(G) Hoses, AC, Renew
Includes: Evacuate and charge system.
All models 1.6

(G) Receiver/Drier Assy., Renew
Includes: Evacuate and charge system.
1993-95 Previa 1.6
1993-95 T100 .... 1.4
1993-95 Pickup 1.4
1993-95 4Runner 1.4
1993-95 Land Cruiser
  factory installed 1.6

(G) Resistor, Blower Motor, Renew
1993-95 Previa 1.2
1993-95 T100 3
1993-95 Pickup 3
1993-95 4Runner 3
1993-95 Land Cruiser 3

(G) Switch, High or Low Pressure, Renew
1993-95 Previa 2.1
1993-95 T100 .... 1.8
1993-95 Pickup 1.8
1993-95 4Runner 1.8
1993-95 Land Cruiser 1.8

(G) Valve, Expansion, Renew
Includes: Evacuate and charge system.
1993-95 Previa 2.1
1993-95 T100 .... 1.7
1993-95 Pickup 1.7
1993-95 4Runner 1.7
1993-95 Land Cruiser 1.7

VOLKSWAGEN
CABRIOLET • CABRIO • CORRADO • FOX • GOLF • JETTA • PASSAT

LABOR   # COOLING SYSTEM   # LABOR

Chilton Time

SERVICE

(G) Belt, Drive, Renew or Adjust
1993-95 .... 1.0

(G) Belt, Serpentine Drive, Renew
1993-94 Corrado
  4 cyl. 1.1
  V6 .... 1.2
1993-95 Jetta, Golf
  4 cyl. 8
  V6 .... 1.0
1993-95 Passat 8

(G) Core, Heater, R&R or Renew
1993 Cabriolet
  wo/AC 1.7
  w/AC 5.9
1995 Cabrio 6.3
1993-94 Corrado 6.0
1993 Fox
  wo/AC 4.5
  w/AC 6.0
1993-95 Jetta, Golf 6.4
1993-95 Passat 6.0
Includes: Evacuate and charge
  AC system as needed
Boil & Repair, add 1.2
Repair Core, add 9
Recore, add 1.2

(G) Expansion (Freeze) Plugs, Water Jacket, Renew
Add appropriate time to access plug.
  All models, each 5

(G) Gauge, Temperature (Dash Unit), Renew
1993 Cabriolet 1.8
1995 Cabrio 1.8
1993-94 Corrado 1.1
1993 Fox 1.9
1993-95 Jetta, Golf 1.8
1993-95 Passat 1.1

(G) Gauge, Temperature (Engine Unit), Renew
1993-95 6

(G) Hoses, Heater, Renew
All models
  one 6
  both 9

Chilton Time

(G) Hoses, Radiator, Renew
Includes: Drain and refill cooling system as required.
1993-95
  one 6
  both 8

(G) Motor, Heater Blower, Renew
1993 Cabriolet 1.6
1995 Cabrio 1.6
1993-94 Corrado 5
1993 Fox 1.2
1993-95 Jetta, Golf 5
1993-95 Passat 1.2

(G) Motor, Radiator Fan and/or Fan, Renew
1993 Cabriolet 1.4
1995 Cabrio 1.6
1993-94 Corrado 1.6
1993 Fox 9
1993-95 Jetta, Golf 1.8
1993-95 Passat 1.4

(G) Pump and/or Gasket, Water, Renew
Includes: Drain and refill cooling system.
1993 Cabriolet 2.4
1995 Cabrio 2.0
1993-94 Corrado
  4 cyl. 3.6
  V6 .... 2.5
1993 Fox
  wo/AC 1.4
  w/AC 2.4
1993-95 Jetta, Golf
  gas
    wo/AC 2.1
    w/AC 2.4
  diesel
    wo/AC 2.9
    w/AC 3.6
1993-95 Passat 2.5
If necessary to evacuate and charge
  AC system, add 1.5

(G) Radiator Assy., R&R or Renew
1993 Cabriolet 1.1
1995 Cabrio 2.7
1993-94 Corrado
  4 cyl. 2.4
  V6 .... 3.0
1993 Fox 1.4
1993-95 Jetta, Golf 2.7
1993-95 Passat
  4 cyl. 1.8

Chilton Time

V6 .... 3.0
Boil & Repair, add 1.5
Rod Clean, add 1.9
Repair Core, add 1.3
Renew Tank, add 1.6
Renew Trans. Oil Cooler, add 1.9
Recore Radiator, add 1.7

(G) Relay, AC Condenser Cooling Fan, Renew
1993-95 9

(G) Resistor, Heater Blower Motor, Renew
1993 Cabriolet 1.6
1995 Cabrio 1.6
1993-94 Corrado 5
1993 Fox 1.4
1993-95 Jetta, Golf 5
1993-95 Passat 6

(G) Switch, Electric Fan Thermo, Renew
1993-95 .... 1.1

(G) Switch, Heater Blower Motor, Renew
1993-95 5

(G) Tensioner, Drive Belt, Renew
1993-94 Corrado 5

(G) Thermostat, Coolant, Renew
1993 Cabriolet
  wo/AC 8
  w/AC 1.2
1995 Cabrio 8
1993-94 Corrado
  wo/AC 1.2
  w/AC 1.6
1993 Fox
  wo/AC 1.2
  w/AC 2.5
1993-95 Jetta, Golf
  wo/AC 1.2
  w/AC 1.6
1993-95 Passat
  wo/AC 1.2
  w/AC 1.6

(G) Valve, Heater Control, Renew
1993-95 6

(G) Winterize Cooling System
Includes: Run engine to check for leaks, tighten all hose connections. Test radiator and pressure cap, drain radiator and engine block. Add antifreeze and refill system.
  All models 5

LABOR   # AIR CONDITIONING   # LABOR

Chilton Time

Note: If more than one item requires replacement where evacuation and discharging the system is already included in the operation, deduct 1.0 hour for each additional item from the time listed.

Chilton Time

SERVICE AND TESTING

(G) Drain, Evacuate and Recharge System
All models 1.0
Recover refrigerant, add 2

Chilton Time

(G) Flush Refrigerant System, Complete
To be used in conjunction with component replacement which could contaminate system. Includes evacuate and recharge.
All models 1.3
Recover refrigerant, add 2

LABOR AIR CONDITIONING LABOR

(G) Leak Check
Includes: Check all lines and connections.
All models 8

(G) Recover and/or Recycle AC Refrigerant
Add to evacuate and charge the AC system, as required.
All models, add 2

COMPONENTS

(G) Belt, Compressor Drive, Renew
1993-95 . . . . 1.0

(G) Clutch & Pulley, Compressor, Renew
Includes: Evacuate and charge system.
1993 Cabriolet 4.3
1995 Cabrio 4.3
1993-94 Corrado 5.4
1993 Fox 4.5
1993-95 Jetta, Golf
gas 4.0
diesel 3.1
1993-95 Passat 4.5
Recover refrigerant, add 2

(G) Coil, Evaporator, Renew
Includes: Evacuate and charge system.
1993 Cabriolet 4.0
1995 Cabrio 7.7
1993-94 Corrado 8.1
1993 Fox 5.8
1993-95 Jetta, Golf 8.7
1993-95 Passat 8.1
Recover refrigerant, add 2

(G) Compressor Assy., Renew
Includes: Transfer parts as required. Evacuate and charge system.
1993 Cabriolet 3.7
1995 Cabrio 3.1
1993-94 Corrado 4.8

1993 Fox 3.9
1993-95 Jetta, Golf
gas 3.4
diesel 2.5
Recover refrigerant, add 2

(G) Condenser Assy., Renew
Includes: Evacuate and charge system.
1993 Cabriolet 2.4
1995 Cabrio 3.0
1993-94 Corrado 3.7
1993 Fox 2.8
1993-95 Jetta, Golf 3.6
1993-95 Passat 3.3
Renew reciever/drier, add 2
Recover refrigerant, add 2

(G) Hoses, AC, Renew
Includes: Evacuate and charge system.
1993 Cabriolet
suction 1.7
discharge 1.8
1995 Cabrio
suction 1.7
discharge 1.8
1993-94 Corrado
suction 1.5
discharge 1.6
1993 Fox
suction 1.7
discharge 1.8
1993-95 Jetta, Golf
suction 1.5
discharge 1.6
1993-95 Passat
suction 1.5
discharge 1.6
Recover refrigerant, add 2

(G) Motor, Evaporator Fan, Renew
1993 Fox 1.4
1993-94 Corrado 1.5
1993-95 Jetta, Golf 8
1993-95 Passat 1.5

(G) Receiver/Drier Assy., Renew
Includes: Evacuate and charge system.
1993 Cabriolet 2.1
1995 Cabrio 1.5
1993-94 Corrado
4 cyl. 2.1
V6 . . . . 1.4
1993 Fox 2.5
1993-95 Jetta, Golf 1.4
1993-95 Passat 1.4
Recover refrigerant, add 2

(G) Relay, AC, Renew
1993-95 5

(G) Seal, Compressor Shaft, Renew
Includes: R&R compressor. Evacuate and charge system.
1993 Cabriolet 4.4
1993-94 Corrado 5.5
1993 Fox 4.6
1993-95 Jetta, Golf 4.1
1993-95 Passat 4.6
Recover refrigerant, add 2

(G) Switch, AC Low Pressure, Renew
1993-95 . . . . 1.2
Includes: Evacuate and charge system.
Recover refrigerant, add 2

(G) Switch, High Pressure Cut-Off, Renew
1993-95 . . . . 1.4
Includes: Evacuate and charge system.
Recover refrigerant, add 2

(G) Valve, Expansion, Renew
Includes: Evacuate and charge system.
1993 Cabriolet 2.2
1993-94 Corrado 1.8
1993 Fox 6.5
1993-95 Passat 1.8
Recover refrigerant, add 2

VOLKSWAGEN TRUCKS
EUROVAN

LABOR COOLING SYSTEM LABOR

TESTING

(M) Pressure Test Cooling System
All models .3

SERVICE

(G) Belt, Drive, Renew
1993-95 Eurovan 8

(G) Core, Heater, R&R or Renew
1993-95 Eurovan 5.1
Boil & Repair, add 1.2
Repair Core, add 9
Recore, add 1.2

(G) Core, Rear Heater, R&R or Renew
1993-95 Eurovan 1.5

(G) Electric Fan Relay, Renew
1993-95 Eurovan 9

(G) Fan Assy., Electric Cooling, Renew
1993-95 Eurovan 1.2

(G) Gauge, Temperature (Dash Unit), Renew
1993-95 Eurovan 9

(G) Gauge, Temperature (Engine Unit), Renew
1993-95 Eurovan 6

(G) Motor, Front Heater Blower, Renew
1993-95 Eurovan 5

(G) Motor, Rear Heater Blower, Renew
1993-95 Eurovan 5

(G) Pump and/or Gasket, Water, Renew
Includes: Drain and refill cooling system.
1993-95 Eurovan 3.6

(G) Radiator Assy., R&R or Renew
1993-95 Eurovan 2.2

(G) Switch, Rear Heater Blower Motor, Renew
1993-95 Eurovan 3

(G) Switch, Thermostatic, Renew
1993-95 Eurovan 1.1

(G) Thermostat, Coolant, Renew
1993-95 Eurovan 1.1

LABOR
AIR CONDITIONING
LABOR

Chilton Time

Note: If more than one item requires replacement where evacuation and discharging the system is already included in the operation, deduct 1.0 hour for each additional item from the time listed.

SERVICE AND TESTING

(G) Drain, Evacuate and Recharge System
All models **1.0**
Recover refrigerant, add . . . . **.2**

(G) Flush Refrigerant System, Complete
To be used in conjunction with component replacement which could contaminate system. Includes evacuate and recharge.
All models **1.3**
Recover refrigerant, add . . . . **.2**

(G) Leak Check
Includes: Check all lines and connections.
All models . . . . **.5**

(G) Recover and/or Recycle AC Refrigerant
Add to evacuate and charge the AC system, as required.
All models, add . . . . **.2**

Chilton Time

COMPONENTS

(G) Belt, Compressor Drive, Renew
1993-95 Eurovan **1.0**

(G) Clutch Assy., Compressor, Renew
1993-95 Eurovan **3.4**
Includes: Evacuate and charge system.
Recover refrigerant, add . . . . **.2**

(G) Coil, Evaporator, Renew
Includes: Evacuate and charge system.
1993-95 Eurovan
front **4.5**
rear **4.8**
Recover refrigerant, add . . . . **.2**

(G) Compressor Assy., Renew
Includes: Transfer parts as required. Evacuate and charge system.
1993-95 Eurovan **3.4**
Recover refrigerant, add . . . . **.2**

(G) Condenser Assy., Renew
Includes: Evacuate and charge system.
1993-95 Eurovan **3.1**
Recover refrigerant, add . . . . **.2**

(G) Control Assy., Temperature, Renew
1993-95 Eurovan **1.1**

Chilton Time

(G) Hoses, AC, Renew
Includes: Evacuate and charge system.
1993-95 Eurovan
suction **1.8**
discharge **1.8**
Recover refrigerant, add . . . . **.2**

(G) Motor, Evaporator Fan, Renew
1993-95 Eurovan . . . . **.6**

(G) Relay, AC, Renew
1993-95 Eurovan . . . . **.9**

(G) Seal, Compressor Shaft, Renew
Includes: R&R compressor. Evacuate and charge system.
1993-95 Eurovan **3.5**
Recover refrigerant, add . . . . **.2**

(G) Switch, AC Low Pressure, Renew
1993-95 Eurovan **1.2**
Includes: Evacuate and charge system.
Recover refrigerant, add . . . . **.2**

(G) Switch, High Pressure Cut-Off, Renew
1993-95 Eurovan **1.4**
Includes: Evacuate and charge system.
Recover refrigerant, add . . . . **.2**

VOLVO
240 • 740 • 780 • 850 • 940 • 960

LABOR
COOLING SYSTEM
LABOR

Chilton Time

TESTING

(M) Pressure Test Cooling System
All models . . . . **.3**

SERVICE

(G) Belt, Drive, Adjust
All models
one . . . . **.3**
each adtnl. . . . . **.1**

(G) Belt, Drive, Renew
All models
one . . . . **.7**
each adtnl. . . . . **.1**

(G) Belt, Serpentine Drive, Renew
1993-95 850 . . . . **.3**
1993-95 960 . . . . **.3**

(G) Blades, Fan or Clutch Assy., Renew
1993-94 240 . . . . **.6**
1993-95 940, 960 . . . . **.6**

(G) Control Assy., Temperature, Renew
1993-94 240 . . . . **1.0**

(G) Core, Heater, R&R or Renew
1993-94 240 . . . . **7.5**
1993-95 850 . . . . **2.6**

Chilton Time

1993-95 940, 960
wo/EEC **10.0**
w/EEC **12.0**
Boil & Repair, add **1.2**
Repair Core, add . . . . **.9**
Recore, add **1.2**

(G) Expansion (Freeze) Plugs, Water Jacket, Renew
Add appropriate time to access plug.
All models, each . . . . **.5**

(G) Fan Assy., Electric Cooling, Renew
1993-94 240 . . . . **.6**
1993-95 850 . . . . **.5**
1993-95 940, 960 . . . . **.5**

(G) Gauge, Temperature (Dash Unit), Renew
1993-94 240 . . . . **.9**
1993-95 850 . . . . **1.5**
1993-95 940, 960 . . . . **1.2**

(G) Gauge, Temperature (Engine Unit), Renew
All models . . . . **.6**

(G) Hoses, Heater, Renew
All models, each . . . . **.4**

Chilton Time

(G) Hoses, Radiator, Renew
Includes: Drain and refill cooling system as required.
All models
upper . . . . **.4**
lower . . . . **.5**

(G) Motor, Heater Blower, Renew
1993-94 240 . . . . **6.0**
1993-95 850 . . . . **.9**
1993-95 940, 960 . . . . **.9**

(G) Pump and/or Gasket, Water, Renew
Includes: Drain and refill cooling system.
1993-95 B230F/FT **2.1**
1993-95 B5254F **2.7**
1993-95 B6304F **2.4**
Renew thermostat, add . . . . **.3**

(G) Radiator Assy., R&R or Renew
All models
MT **1.2**
AT **1.4**
Boil & Repair, add **1.5**
Rod Clean, add **1.9**
Repair Core, add **1.3**
Renew Tank, add **1.6**
Renew Trans. Oil Cooler, add **1.9**
Recore Radiator, Renew **1.7**

LABOR — COOLING SYSTEM — LABOR

	Chilton Time
(G) Relay, Radiator Fan Motor, Renew	
All models	.4
(G) Sensor, Coolant Fan Thermo, Renew	
1993-95	.4
(G) Switch, Heater Blower Motor, Renew	
1993-94 240	.5
1993-95 850	.4
1993-95 940, 960	.4

	Chilton Time
(G) Switch, Radiator Fan Motor (Coolant Temp.), Renew	
All models	.4
(G) Tensioner, Drive Belt, Renew	
1993-95 850	.4
1993-95 960	.4
(G) Thermostat, Coolant, Renew	
All models	
4, 5 cyl.	.5
V6	.7

	Chilton Time
(G) Valve, Heater Control, Renew	
1993-94 240	1.4
1993-95 940, 960	.8
(G) Winterize Cooling System	
Includes: Run engine to check for leaks, tighten all hose connections. Test radiator and pressure cap, drain radiator and engine block. Add antifreeze and refill system.	
All models	.5

LABOR — AIR CONDITIONING — LABOR

Note: If more than one item requires replacement where evacuation and discharging the system is already included in the operation, deduct 1.0 hour for each additional item from the time listed.

SERVICE AND TESTING

	Chilton Time
(G) Drain, Evacuate and Recharge System	
All models	1.0
Recover refrigerant, add	.2
(G) Flush Refrigerant System, Complete	
To be used in conjunction with component replacement which could contaminate system. Includes evacuate and recharge.	
All models	1.3
Recover refrigerant, add	.2
(G) Recover and/or Recycle AC Refrigerant	
Add to evacuate and charge the AC system, as required.	
All models, add	.2

COMPONENTS

	Chilton Time
(G) Belt, Compressor Drive, Renew	
1993-94 240	.4
1993-95 940, 960	
4 cyl.	.4
V6	.3
(G) Clutch Assy., Compressor, Renew	
1993-94 240	1.0
1993-95 940, 960	
4 cyl.	1.0
V6	.9
Add time to evacuate & charge AC system as needed.	
Recover refrigerant, add	.2
(G) Compressor Assy., Renew	
Includes: Transfer parts as required.	

	Chilton Time
Evacuate and charge system.	
1993-94 240	3.3
w/PS, add	.5
1993-95 850	3.4
1993-95 940, 960	
4 cyl.	3.0
V6	2.3
Recover refrigerant, add	.2
(G) Condenser Assy., Renew	
Includes: Evacuate and charge system.	
1993-94 240	2.2
1993-95 850	3.0
1993-95 940, 960	2.2
Recover refrigerant, add	.2
(G) Core, Evaporator, Renew	
Includes: Evacuate and charge system.	
1993-94 240	4.5
1993-95 850	7.5
1993-95 940, 960	
w/ECC	3.9
w/ACC or MCC	5.0
Recover refrigerant, add	.2
(G) Hoses, AC, Renew	
Includes: Evacuate and charge system.	
All models	
one	1.7
each adtnl.	.3
Recover refrigerant, add	.2
(G) Receiver/Drier Assy., Renew	
Includes: Evacuate and charge system.	
1993-94 240	2.0
1993-95 850	2.8
1993-95 940, 960	2.0
Recover refrigerant, add	.2
(G) Relay, Compressor or Fan, Renew	
1993-95 850	.4
1993-95 940, 960	.4
(G) Switch, High Pressure Cut-Off, Renew	
1993-95 850	.4

	Chilton Time
1993-95 940, 960	.4
Add time to evacuate & charge AC system as needed.	
Recover refrigerant, add	.2
(G) Valve, Expansion, Renew	
Includes: Evacuate and charge system.	
1993-94 240	1.6
1993-95 850	1.6
1993-95 940, 960	1.6
Recover refrigerant, add	.2

AUTOMATIC TEMPERATURE CONTROL (ATC)

	Chilton Time
(G) Control Assy., Renew	
1993-95 940, 960	.6
(G) Motor, Air Mix Servo, Renew	
1993-95 850	.8
1993-95 940, 960	.8
(G) Power Servo Assy., R&R or Renew	
1993-95 940, 960	.8
(G) Programmer, Renew	
1993-95 940, 960	1.0
(G) Sensor, Ambient, Renew	
1993-95 850	.6
1993-95 940, 960	.4
(G) Sensor, Water Temperature, Renew	
1993-95 940, 960	.4
(G) Thermostat, Renew	
1993-94 240	1.7
(G) Vacuum Motor, Renew	
1993-95 940, 960	2.9
(G) Valve, Climate Control Solenoid, Renew	
1993-95 940, 960	.6

ENGLISH TO METRIC CONVERSION: TORQUE

Torque is now expressed as either foot-pounds (ft./lbs.) or inch-pounds (in./lbs.). The metric measurement unit for torque is the Newton-meter (Nm). This unit—the Nm—will be used for all SI metric torque references, both the present ft./lbs. and in./lbs.

ft lbs	N-m	ft lbs	N-m	ft lbs	N-m	ft lbs	N-m
0.1	0.1	33	44.7	74	100.3	115	155.9
0.2	0.3	34	46.1	75	101.7	116	157.3
0.3	0.4	35	47.4	76	103.0	117	158.6
0.4	0.5	36	48.8	77	104.4	118	160.0
0.5	0.7	37	50.7	78	105.8	119	161.3
0.6	0.8	38	51.5	79	107.1	120	162.7
0.7	1.0	39	52.9	80	108.5	121	164.0
0.8	1.1	40	54.2	81	109.8	122	165.4
0.9	1.2	41	55.6	82	111.2	123	166.8
1	1.3	42	56.9	83	112.5	124	168.1
2	2.7	43	58.3	84	113.9	125	169.5
3	4.1	44	59.7	85	115.2	126	170.8
4	5.4	45	61.0	86	116.6	127	172.2
5	6.8	46	62.4	87	118.0	128	173.5
6	8.1	47	63.7	88	119.3	129	174.9
7	9.5	48	65.1	89	120.7	130	176.2
8	10.8	49	66.4	90	122.0	131	177.6
9	12.2	50	67.8	91	123.4	132	179.0
10	13.6	51	69.2	92	124.7	133	180.3
11	14.9	52	70.5	93	126.1	134	181.7
12	16.3	53	71.9	94	127.4	135	183.0
13	17.6	54	73.2	95	128.8	136	184.4
14	18.9	55	74.6	96	130.2	137	185.7
15	20.3	56	75.9	97	131.5	138	187.1
16	21.7	57	77.3	98	132.9	139	188.5
17	23.0	58	78.6	99	134.2	140	189.8
18	24.4	59	80.0	100	135.6	141	191.2
19	25.8	60	81.4	101	136.9	142	192.5
20	27.1	61	82.7	102	138.3	143	193.9
21	28.5	62	84.1	103	139.6	144	195.2
22	29.8	63	85.4	104	141.0	145	196.6
23	31.2	64	86.8	105	142.4	146	198.0
24	32.5	65	88.1	106	143.7	147	199.3
25	33.9	66	89.5	107	145.1	148	200.7
26	35.2	67	90.8	108	146.4	149	202.0
27	36.6	68	92.2	109	147.8	150	203.4
28	38.0	69	93.6	110	149.1	151	204.7
29	39.3	70	94.9	111	150.5	152	206.1
30	40.7	71	96.3	112	151.8	153	207.4
31	42.0	72	97.6	113	153.2	154	208.8
32	43.4	73	99.0	114	154.6	155	210.2

MECHANIC'S DATA

ENGLISH TO METRIC CONVERSION: LENGTH

To convert inches (ins.) to millimeters (mm): multiply number of inches by 25.4

To convert millimeters (mm) to inches (ins.): multiply number of millimeters by .04

Inches	Decimals	Milli-meters	Inches to millimeters inches	mm	Inches	Decimals	Milli-meters	Inches to millimeters inches	mm
1/64	0.051625	0.3969	0.0001	0.00254	33/64	0.515625	13.0969	0.6	15.24
1/32	0.03125	0.7937	0.0002	0.00508	17/32	0.53125	13.4937	0.7	17.78
3/64	0.046875	1.1906	0.0003	0.00762	35/64	0.546875	13.8906	0.8	20.32
1/16	0.0625	1.5875	0.0004	0.01016	9/16	0.5625	14.2875	0.9	22.86
5/64	0.078125	1.9844	0.0005	0.01270	37/64	0.578125	14.6844	1	25.4
3/32	0.09375	2.3812	0.0006	0.01524	19/32	0.59375	15.0812	2	50.8
7/64	0.109375	2.7781	0.0007	0.01778	39/64	0.609375	15.4781	3	76.2
1/8	0.125	3.1750	0.0008	0.02032	5/8	0.625	15.8750	4	101.6
9/64	0.140625	3.5719	0.0009	0.02286	41/64	0.640625	16.2719	5	127.0
5/32	0.15625	3.9687	0.001	0.0254	21/32	0.65625	16.6687	6	152.4
11/64	0.171875	4.3656	0.002	0.0508	43/64	0.671875	17.0656	7	177.8
3/16	0.1875	4.7625	0.003	0.0762	11/16	0.6875	17.4625	8	203.2
13/64	0.203125	5.1594	0.004	0.1016	45/64	0.703125	17.8594	9	228.6
7/32	0.21875	5.5562	0.005	0.1270	23/32	0.71875	18.2562	10	254.0
15/64	0.234375	5.9531	0.006	0.1524	47/64	0.734375	18.6531	11	279.4
1/4	0.25	6.3500	0.007	0.1778	3/4	0.75	19.0500	12	304.8
17/64	0.265625	6.7469	0.008	0.2032	49/64	0.765625	19.4469	13	330.2
9/32	0.28125	7.1437	0.009	0.2286	25/32	0.78125	19.8437	14	355.6
19/64	0.296875	7.5406	0.01	0.254	51/64	0.796875	20.2406	15	381.0
5/16	0.3125	7.9375	0.02	0.508	13/16	0.8125	20.6375	16	406.4
21/64	0.328125	8.3344	0.03	0.762	53/64	0.828125	21.0344	17	431.8
11/32	0.34375	8.7312	0.04	1.016	27/32	0.84375	21.4312	18	457.2
23/64	0.359375	9.1281	0.05	1.270	55/64	0.859375	21.8281	19	482.6
3/8	0.375	9.5250	0.06	1.524	7/8	0.875	22.2250	20	508.0
25/64	0.390625	9.9219	0.07	1.778	57/64	0.890625	22.6219	21	533.4
13/32	0.40625	10.3187	0.08	2.032	29/32	0.90625	23.0187	22	558.8
27/64	0.421875	10.7156	0.09	2.286	59/64	0.921875	23.4156	23	584.2
7/16	0.4375	11.1125	0.1	2.54	15/16	0.9375	23.8125	24	609.6
29/64	0.453125	11.5094	0.2	5.08	61/64	0.953125	24.2094	25	635.0
15/32	0.46875	11.9062	0.3	7.62	31/32	0.96875	24.6062	26	660.4
31/64	0.484375	12.3031	0.4	10.16	63/64	0.984375	25.0031	27	690.6
1/2	0.5	12.7000	0.5	12.70					

ENGLISH TO METRIC CONVERSION: TORQUE

To convert foot-pounds (ft. lbs.) to Newton-meters: multiply the number of ft. lbs. by 1.3

To convert inch-pounds (in. lbs.) to Newton-meters: multiply the number of in. lbs. by .11

in lbs	N·m	in lbs	N·m	in lbs	N·m	in lbs	N·m	in lbs	N·m
0.1	0.01	1	0.11	10	1.13	19	2.15	28	3.16
0.2	0.02	2	0.23	11	1.24	20	2.26	29	3.28
0.3	0.03	3	0.34	12	1.36	21	2.37	30	3.39
0.4	0.04	4	0.45	13	1.47	22	2.49	31	3.50
0.5	0.06	5	0.56	14	1.58	23	2.60	32	3.62
0.6	0.07	6	0.68	15	1.70	24	2.71	33	3.73
0.7	0.08	7	0.78	16	1.81	25	2.82	34	3.84
0.8	0.09	8	0.90	17	1.92	26	2.94	35	3.95
0.9	0.10	9	1.02	18	2.03	27	3.05	36	4.0/

ENGLISH TO METRIC CONVERSION: MASS (WEIGHT)

Current mass measurement is expressed in pounds and ounces (lbs. & ozs.). The metric unit of mass (or weight) is the kilogram (kg). Even although this table does not show conversion of masses (weights) larger than 15 lbs, it is easy to calculate larger units by following the data immediately below.

To convert ounces (oz.) to grams (g): multiply th number of ozs. by 28
To convert grams (g) to ounces (oz.): multiply the number of grams by .035

To convert pounds (lbs.) to kilograms (kg): multiply the number of lbs. by .45
To convert kilograms (kg) to pounds (lbs.): multiply the number of kilograms by 2.2

lbs	kg	lbs	kg	oz	kg	oz	kg
0.1	0.04	0.9	0.41	0.1	0.003	0.9	0.024
0.2	0.09	1	0.4	0.2	0.005	1	0.03
0.3	0.14	2	0.9	0.3	0.008	2	0.06
0.4	0.18	3	1.4	0.4	0.011	3	0.08
0.5	0.23	4	1.8	0.5	0.014	4	0.11
0.6	0.27	5	2.3	0.6	0.017	5	0.14
0.7	0.32	10	4.5	0.7	0.020	10	0.28
0.8	0.36	15	6.8	0.8	0.023	15	0.42

ENGLISH TO METRIC CONVERSION: TEMPERATURE

To convert Fahrenheit (°F) to Celsius (°C): take number of °F and subtract 32; multiply result by 5; divide result by 9

To convert Celsius (°C) to Fahrenheit (°F): take number of °C and multiply by 9; divide result by 5; add 32 to total

Fahrenheit (F)		Celsius (C)		Fahrenheit (F)		Celsius (C)		Fahrenheit (F)		Celsius (C)	
°F	°C	°C	°F	°F	°C	°C	°F	°F	°C	°C	°F
−40	−40	−38	−36.4	80	26.7	18	64.4	215	101.7	80	176
−35	−37.2	−36	−32.8	85	29.4	20	68	220	104.4	85	185
−30	−34.4	−34	−29.2	90	32.2	22	71.6	225	107.2	90	194
−25	−31.7	−32	−25.6	95	35.0	24	75.2	230	110.0	95	202
−20	−28.9	−30	−22	100	37.8	26	78.8	235	112.8	100	212
−15	−26.1	−28	−18.4	105	40.6	28	82.4	240	115.6	105	221
−10	−23.3	−26	−14.8	110	43.3	30	86	245	118.3	110	230
−5	−20.6	−24	−11.2	115	46.1	32	89.6	250	121.1	115	239
0	−17.8	−22	−7.6	120	48.9	34	93.2	255	123.9	120	248
1	−17.2	−20	−4	125	51.7	36	96.8	260	126.6	125	257
2	−16.7	−18	−0.4	130	54.4	38	100.4	265	129.4	130	266
3	−16.1	−16	3.2	135	57.2	40	104	270	132.2	135	275
4	−15.6	−14	6.8	140	60.0	42	107.6	275	135.0	140	284
5	−15.0	−12	10.4	145	62.8	44	112.2	280	137.8	145	293
10	−12.2	−10	14	150	65.6	46	114.8	285	140.6	150	302
15	−9.4	−8	17.6	155	68.3	48	118.4	290	143.3	155	311
20	−6.7	−6	21.2	160	71.1	50	122	295	146.1	160	320
25	−3.9	−4	24.8	165	73.9	52	125.6	300	148.9	165	329
30	−1.1	−2	28.4	170	76.7	54	129.2	305	151.7	170	338
35	1.7	0	32	175	79.4	56	132.8	310	154.4	175	347
40	4.4	2	35.6	180	82.2	58	136.4	315	157.2	180	356
45	7.2	4	39.2	185	85.0	60	140	320	160.0	185	365
50	10.0	6	42.8	190	87.8	62	143.6	325	162.8	190	374
55	12.8	8	46.4	195	90.6	64	147.2	330	165.6	195	383
60	15.6	10	50	200	93.3	66	150.8	335	168.3	200	392
65	18.3	12	53.6	205	96.1	68	154.4	340	171.1	205	401
70	21.1	14	57.2	210	98.9	70	158	345	173.9	210	410
75	23.9	16	60.8	212	100.0	75	167	350	176.7	215	414

CHILTON *PROFESSIONAL AUTOMOTIVE*

CHILTON PROFESSIONAL AUTOMOTIVE
CUSTOMER COMMENT CARD

Dear Valued Customer:

*Please use this form
to advise us of any
questions, comments
and/or recommendations
that you may have
regarding this manual.*

*Your feedback is extremely
important to us so please
respond today.*

Thank you.

Complete Service Manual Title _____

Service Manual Part Number _____

Section No. _____ Page No. _____ Vehicle Model & Year _____

Comments _____

_____

_____

Name _____

Company _____

Address _____

City _____ State _____ Zip _____

Phone (____) _____ Date _____

CHILTON *PROFESSIONAL AUTOMOTIVE*

CHILTON PROFESSIONAL AUTOMOTIVE
CUSTOMER COMMENT CARD

Dear Valued Customer:

*Please use this form
to advise us of any
questions, comments
and/or recommendations
that you may have
regarding this manual.*

*Your feedback is extremely
important to us so please
respond today.*

Thank you.

Complete Service Manual Title _____

Service Manual Part Number _____

Section No. _____ Page No. _____ Vehicle Model & Year _____

Comments _____

_____

_____

Name _____

Company _____

Address _____

City _____ State _____ Zip _____

Phone (____) _____ Date _____

CHILTON *PROFESSIONAL AUTOMOTIVE*

CHILTON PROFESSIONAL AUTOMOTIVE
CUSTOMER COMMENT CARD

Dear Valued Customer:

*Please use this form
to advise us of any
questions, comments
and/or recommendations
that you may have
regarding this manual.*

*Your feedback is extremely
important to us so please
respond today.*

Thank you.

Complete Service Manual Title _____

Service Manual Part Number _____

Section No. _____ Page No. _____ Vehicle Model & Year _____

Comments _____

_____

_____

Name _____

Company _____

Address _____

City _____ State _____ Zip _____

Phone (____) _____ Date _____

BUSINESS REPLY MAIL
FIRST CLASS   PERMIT NO. 39   WAYNE, PA

POSTAGE WILL BE PAID BY ADDRESSEE

CHILTON BOOK COMPANY
Attn: Assistant Managing Editor—Professional
One Chilton Way
Radnor, PA   19080-9153

BUSINESS REPLY MAIL
FIRST CLASS   PERMIT NO. 39   WAYNE, PA

POSTAGE WILL BE PAID BY ADDRESSEE

CHILTON BOOK COMPANY
Attn: Assistant Managing Editor—Professional
One Chilton Way
Radnor, PA   19080-9153

BUSINESS REPLY MAIL
FIRST CLASS   PERMIT NO. 39   WAYNE, PA

POSTAGE WILL BE PAID BY ADDRESSEE

CHILTON BOOK COMPANY
Attn: Assistant Managing Editor—Professional
One Chilton Way
Radnor, PA   19080-9153